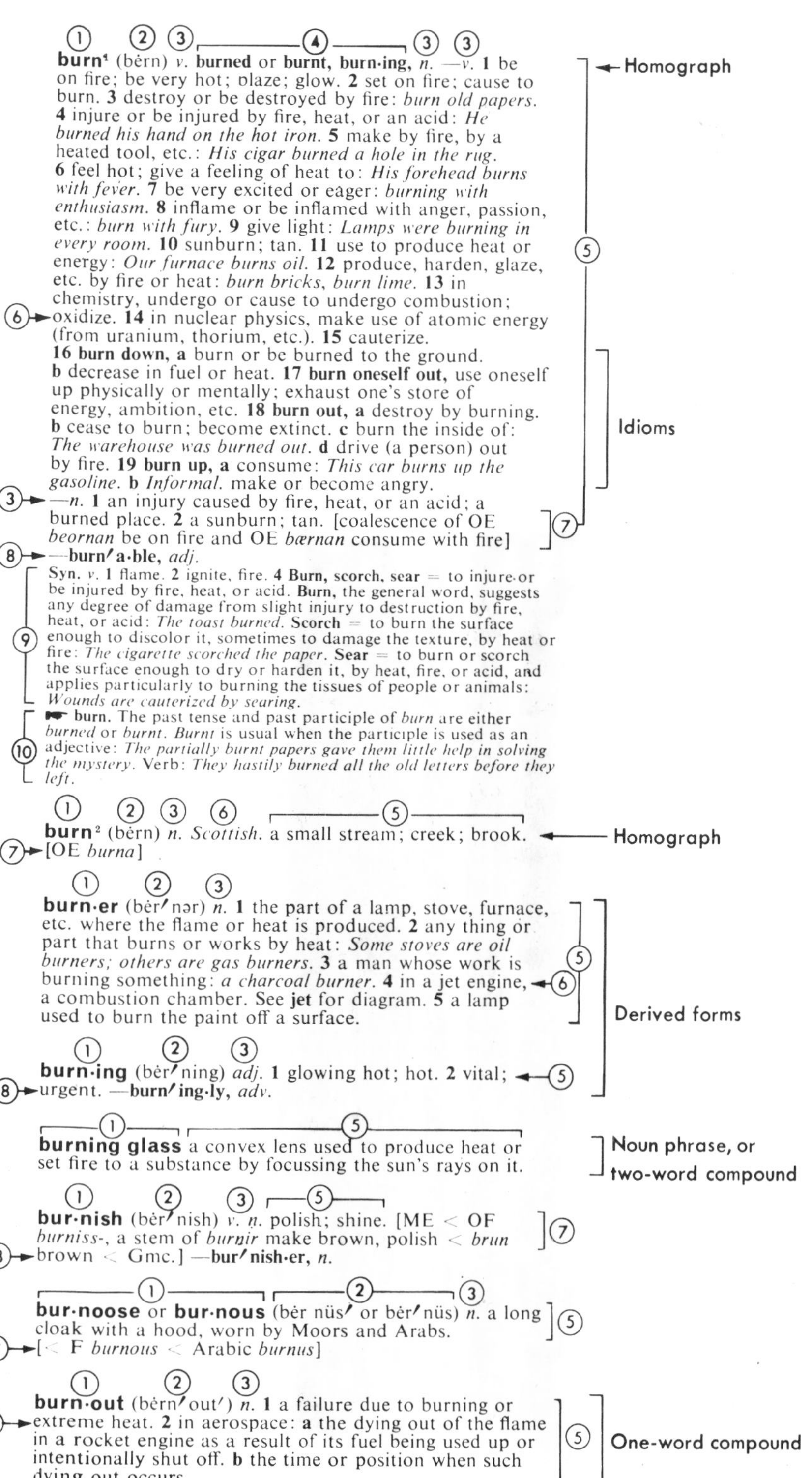

burn[1] (bėrn) *v.* **burned** or **burnt, burn·ing,** *n.* —*v.* **1** be on fire; be very hot; blaze; glow. **2** set on fire; cause to burn. **3** destroy or be destroyed by fire: *burn old papers.* **4** injure or be injured by fire, heat, or an acid: *He burned his hand on the hot iron.* **5** make by fire, by a heated tool, etc.: *His cigar burned a hole in the rug.* **6** feel hot; give a feeling of heat to: *His forehead burns with fever.* **7** be very excited or eager: *burning with enthusiasm.* **8** inflame or be inflamed with anger, passion, etc.: *burn with fury.* **9** give light: *Lamps were burning in every room.* **10** sunburn; tan. **11** use to produce heat or energy: *Our furnace burns oil.* **12** produce, harden, glaze, etc. by fire or heat: *burn bricks, burn lime.* **13** in chemistry, undergo or cause to undergo combustion; oxidize. **14** in nuclear physics, make use of atomic energy (from uranium, thorium, etc.). **15** cauterize.
16 burn down, a burn or be burned to the ground. **b** decrease in fuel or heat. **17 burn oneself out,** use oneself up physically or mentally; exhaust one's store of energy, ambition, etc. **18 burn out, a** destroy by burning. **b** cease to burn; become extinct. **c** burn the inside of: *The warehouse was burned out.* **d** drive (a person) out by fire. **19 burn up, a** consume: *This car burns up the gasoline.* **b** *Informal.* make or become angry.
—*n.* **1** an injury caused by fire, heat, or an acid; a burned place. **2** a sunburn; tan. [coalescence of OE *beornan* be on fire and OE *bærnan* consume with fire]
—**burn′a·ble,** *adj.*

Syn. *v.* **1** flame. **2** ignite, fire. **4 Burn, scorch, sear** = to injure or be injured by fire, heat, or acid. **Burn,** the general word, suggests any degree of damage from slight injury to destruction by fire, heat, or acid: *The toast burned.* **Scorch** = to burn the surface enough to discolor it, sometimes to damage the texture, by heat or fire: *The cigarette scorched the paper.* **Sear** = to burn or scorch the surface enough to dry or harden it, by heat, fire, or acid, and applies particularly to burning the tissues of people or animals: *Wounds are cauterized by searing.*

☛ **burn.** The past tense and past participle of *burn* are either *burned* or *burnt. Burnt* is usual when the participle is used as an adjective: *The partially burnt papers gave them little help in solving the mystery.* Verb: *They hastily burned all the old letters before they left.*

burn[2] (bėrn) *n. Scottish.* a small stream; creek; brook. [OE *burna*]

burn·er (bėr′nər) *n.* **1** the part of a lamp, stove, furnace, etc. where the flame or heat is produced. **2** any thing or part that burns or works by heat: *Some stoves are oil burners; others are gas burners.* **3** a man whose work is burning something: *a charcoal burner.* **4** in a jet engine, a combustion chamber. See **jet** for diagram. **5** a lamp used to burn the paint off a surface.

burn·ing (bėr′ning) *adj.* **1** glowing hot; hot. **2** vital; urgent. —**burn′ing·ly,** *adv.*

burning glass a convex lens used to produce heat or set fire to a substance by focussing the sun's rays on it.

bur·nish (bėr′nish) *v. n.* polish; shine. [ME < OF *burniss-*, a stem of *burnir* make brown, polish < *brun* brown < Gmc.] —**bur′nish·er,** *n.*

bur·noose or **bur·nous** (bėr nüs′ or bėr′nüs) *n.* a long cloak with a hood, worn by Moors and Arabs. [< F *burnous* < Arabic *burnus*]

burn·out (bėrn′out′) *n.* **1** a failure due to burning or extreme heat. **2** in aerospace: **a** the dying out of the flame in a rocket engine as a result of its fuel being used up or intentionally shut off. **b** the time or position when such dying out occurs.

Date Due

Canadian Senior Dictionary

A book in the

DICTIONARY OF

CANADIAN ENGLISH

series

Canadian Senior Dictionary

W. S. Avis, Royal Military College of Canada
P. D. Drysdale, Gage Educational Publishing Limited
R. J. Gregg, University of British Columbia
M. H. Scargill, University of Victoria

gage PUBLISHING LIMITED
TORONTO ONTARIO CANADA

Special illustrations drawn by Lionel R. Clarke, Graphic Artists, Dickinson Studios, Jean Galt, Mary Guest, Waltraud Markgraf, Aino Vesilind

Designed by Arnold Rockman
Cover design by Brant Cowie/Artplus

ISBN 0-7715-1977-X
2 3 4 5 [illegible] 82 81 80

Printed and bound in Canada

Contents

Introduction

The *Canadian Senior Dictionary* is designed for use by Canadians in the school, home, and office. Contemporary and comprehensive, it includes many words recently introduced into the language. Furthermore, special attention has been given to figurative meanings and idiomatic phrases, making the book particularly useful to those learning English as a second language.

This is the third volume in the *Dictionary of Canadian English* series. The first, the *Canadian Junior Dictionary*, is designed for children in Grades 4, 5, and 6 who are learning to use a dictionary and are beginning to acquire skill in the conscious use of language; the second, the *Canadian Intermediate Dictionary*, is a much larger volume and is tailored to the needs of students in senior elementary and junior high schools; the *Canadian Senior Dictionary* is intended for use in high school and beyond. Not only does it include nearly half as many entries again and many more meanings than the *Canadian Intermediate Dictionary*; it also pays much more attention to other types of linguistic information. Etymologies are given throughout; synonym lists are given in places where more extensive synonym studies are not required; and a wider range of usage notes is provided than in the other two dictionaries. All these features add to the usefulness of the dictionary as an aid to writing.

Each book in the series is based on the needs and understanding of a particular range of users, who are thus able to find the information they want in a form they can understand; they are not encumbered with a quantity of material that is irrelevant to their needs and meaningless to their minds. Moreover, all of these books, the *Canadian Senior Dictionary* no less than the others, adhere to certain basic principles. Foremost among these is clarity of definition, the general rule being that explanations should be simple and straightforward, without employing any language that is harder to understand than the word being defined. Another important characteristic of the series is the liberal use of illustrative phrases and sentences, which distinguish and reinforce the definitions by showing how the entry words are actually used in the living language.

But above all these are Canadian dictionaries, and the *Senior* is the first collegiate and desk dictionary of Canadian English. The editors are all established scholars in the field of Canadian English, and their special knowledge in this field is indicated by the many terms of everyday Canadian life, both past and present, that have been entered. Many entries have been based on material collected for *A Dictionary of Canadianisms on Historical Principles* (Gage, 1967), which shows even more vividly the richness and variety of the particularly Canadian element of our vocabulary. In addition, the editors of the *Canadian Senior Dictionary* have tried to ensure that each entry reflects the usage of educated Canadians, not only in style and vocabulary, but also in spelling and pronunciation. Since our linguistic habits have been influenced by both British and American usage, Canadians as a whole are by no means consistent in these areas. Moreover, many individual Canadians (and many Canadian newspapers and magazines) do not slavishly follow either a British or an American pattern; they are quite likely, for example, to spell *centre* in the British way and *program* in the American. The *Canadian Senior Dictionary*, therefore, gives a much greater range of alternative spellings and pronunciations than has hitherto been available in comparable British or American dictionaries. These alternatives have been selected on the basis of Canadian usage across the country.

For further information on these matters, the reader is directed to the relevant portions of the *Guide to the dictionary*, which follows on page *ix*. It is a great pity that such introductory matter in a dictionary is usually ignored. One cannot get the most out of a dictionary unless he knows the kind of information it contains and the ways in which this is arranged; moreover, a dictionary, like any other work, can be properly evaluated only if one knows what it aims to achieve. Particular care has been taken to make this *Guide* to the *Canadian Senior Dictionary* explicit and easy to read; it consists, for the most part, of simple, straightforward statements followed by extensive examples from the text of the dictionary. Attention is drawn also to the table of sample entries on the front endpapers, in which the reference numbers are keyed to the relevant section numbers in the *Guide*. Thus the number 7 on the table, identifying the etymology, refers also to section 7 of the second part of the *Guide*, on page *xxi*.

The *Guide*, then, is the key to the dictionary and its wealth of information about words—their spelling, pronunciation, meaning, and origin. But, however interesting such information may be in itself, a dictionary contains much more than this. For one thing, it bears testimony to the customs and interests of the people whose language it describes; it is an inventory of the things which the people live with and talk about. *Muskeg*, for example, is not just a Canadian word; it is also a fact of Canadian life. The *Canadian Senior Dictionary* is thus a catalogue of the things relevant to the lives of Canadians at a certain point in history. It contains, therefore, some clues to the true nature of our Canadian identity.

Canadian English

by

Walter S. Avis

Language in Canada, as in most countries, is taken for granted. Unfortunately, however, a great deal of nonsense is taken for granted by many Canadians. Some people, especially recent arrivals from the United Kingdom, refuse to accept the fact that the English spoken in Canada has any claim to recognition. Others, who themselves speak Canadian English, are satisfied with the view that British English is the only acceptable standard. To these people the argument that educated Canadians set their own standard of speech is either treasonable or ridiculous.

One Canadian I know had his eyes opened in a rather curious way. While shopping in a large Chicago department store, he asked where he might find chesterfields. Following directions to the letter, he was somewhat dismayed when he ended up at the cigar counter. He soon made other discoveries as well. Blinds were "shades" to his American neighbors; taps were "faucets," braces "suspenders," and serviettes "napkins."

Before long his American friends were pointing out differences between his speech and theirs. He said *been* to rhyme with "bean," whereas for them it rhymed with "bin"; and he said *shone* to rhyme with "gone," whereas for them it rhymed with "bone." In fact, their Canadian friend had quite a few curious ways of saying things: *ration* rhymed with "fashion" rather than with "nation"; *lever* with "beaver" rather than "sever"; *z* with "bed" rather than "bee." Moreover, he said certain vowels in a peculiar way, for *lout* seemed to have a different vowel sound from *loud*, and *rice* a different vowel from *rise*.

The Englishman is also quick to observe that Canadians talk differently from himself. For example, he doesn't say *dance, half, clerk, tomato, garage,* or *war* as Canadians do; and he always distinguishes *cot* from *caught*, a distinction that few Canadians make. He also finds that many of the words he used in England are not understood by people in Canada. Suppose he gets into a conversation about cars. Says he, "I think a car should have a roomy boot." No headway will be made till somebody rescues him by explaining that in Canada the boot is called a "trunk." Before the session is finished, he will probably learn that a bonnet is called a "hood" and the hood of a coupé is "the top of a convertible." Similarly, he must substitute *muffler* for *silencer, windshield* for *windscreen, truck* for *lorry*, and *gas* for *petrol.*

The examples I have mentioned suggest, quite correctly, that Canadian English, while different from both British and American English, is in large measure a blend of both varieties; and to this blend must be added many features which are typically Canadian. The explanation for this mixed character lies primarily in the settlement history of the country, for both Britain and the United States have exerted continuous influence on Canada during the past two hundred years.

As the several areas of Canada were opened to settlement, before, during, and after the Revolutionary War in the 1770's, Americans were prominent among the settlers in many, if not in most, communities. American influence has been great ever since: Canadians often learn from American textbooks, read American novels and periodicals, listen to American radio programs, and watch American T.V. and movies. Moreover, Canadians in large numbers are constantly moving back and forth across the border, as emigrants, as tourists, as students (especially on athletic scholarships), and as bargain hunters. Finally, Canada shares with the United States a large vocabulary denoting all manner of things indigenous to North America. One need only leaf through the full or concise *Dictionary of Canadianisms* or the *Dictionary of Americanisms* to appreciate this fact.

On the other hand, Britain has also made an enormous contribution to the settlement of English-speaking Canada. For more than a century and a half, Britishers in an almost continuous stream and speaking various dialects have immigrated to Canada. In most communities, especially those along the Canadian-American border (where most of Canada's population is still concentrated), these newcomers came into contact with already established Canadians; and, as might be expected, their children adopted the speech habits of the communities they moved into. Only in certain settlement areas where relatively homogeneous Old-Country groups established themselves did markedly British dialectal features survive through several generations. Such communities may be found in Newfoundland, the Ottawa Valley, the Red River Settlement in Manitoba, and on Vancouver Island. For the most part, however, the children of British immigrants, like those whose parents come from other European countries, adopt the kind of English spoken in Canada. Yet in the very process of being absorbed, linguistically speaking, they have made contributions to every department of the language.

That part of Canadian English which is neither British nor American is best illustrated by the vocabulary, for there are hundreds of words which are native to Canada or which have meanings peculiar to Canada. As might be expected, many of these words refer to topographical features, plants, trees, fish, animals, and birds; and many others to social, economic, and political institutions and activities. Few of these words, which may be called Canadianisms, find their way into British or American dictionaries, a fact which should occasion no surprise, for British and American dictionaries are based on British and American usage, being primarily intended for Britons and Americans, not for Canadians.

Prominent among Canadianisms are proper nouns, including names of regions: *Barren Grounds, French Shore, Lakehead*; names given to the natives of certain regions: *Bluenoses, Herringchokers*; names associated with political parties: *New Democratic Party,*

Union Nationale. In addition, there are a host of terms identified with places or persons: *Digby chicken, McIntosh apple, Quebec heater, Winnipeg couch*.

Languages other than English have contributed many Canadianisms to the lexicon: (from Canadian French) *brulé, fameuse, lacrosse, Métis, portage*; (from Amerindian) *babiche, kokanee, pemmican, shaganappi*; (from Eskimo) *komatik, kuletuk, ooloo, oomiak*. Sometimes the origin of such loan-words is obscured in the process of adoption; thus *carry-all, mush, Siwash, snye*, and *shanty* derive from Canadian French *cariole, marche, sauvage, chenail*, and *chantier*.

Other Canadianisms are more or less limited to certain regions—to Newfoundland: *jinker, nunny bag, tickle, tilt*; to the Maritimes: *aboideau, gaspereau, longliner*; to Ontario: *concession road, dew-worm, fire-reels*; to the Prairie Provinces: *bluff* (clump of trees), *grid road, local improvement district*; to British Columbia: *rancherie, skookum, steelhead*; to the Northland: *bush pilot, cat-swing, cheechako*.

Hundreds of Canadian words fall into the category of animal and plant names: *caribou, fool hen, inconnu, kinnikinnick, malemute, oolichan, saskatoon, sockeye, whisky-jack* or *Canada jay*. Many more fall into the class of topographical terms: *butte, coulee, dalles, sault*. Yet another extensive class includes hundreds of terms of historical significance: *Family Compact, Klondiker, North canoe, Red River cart, wintering partner, York boat*.

For many terms there are special Canadian significations: *Confederation, Grit, height of land, reeve, riding, warden*. From the sports field come a number of contributions, especially from hockey and a game we used to call rugby, a term now almost displaced by the American term football: *boarding, blueline, convert, cushion, flying wing, puck, rouge, snap*. And in the same area there are a number of slang terms that merit mention: *chippy, home-brew, import, rink rat*.

In pronunciation, as in vocabulary, Canadians are neither American nor British, though they have much in common with both. Although most Canadians pronounce *docile* and *textile* to rhyme with *mile*, as the British do, it is probable that most pronounce *fertile* and *missile* to rhyme with *hurtle* and *missal*, as the Americans do. And no doubt Canadians pronounce some words in a way that is typically Canadian. Most of us, for example, would describe the color of a soldier's uniform as *khaki*, pronounced (kär′kē). Yet no non-Canadian dictionary recognizes this Canadianism. Americans say (kak′ē), while the British say (kä′kē). In Canada, many people put flowers in a vase, pronounced (vāz); Americans use a (vās) and the British a (väz). To be sure, a number of Canadians say something like (väz), especially if the vase is Ming.

If we take imported dictionaries as our authority, such pronunciations as (kär′kē) and (vāz) are unacceptable. But surely the proper test of correctness for Canadians should be the usage of educated natives of Canada. Here are some other examples of pronunciations widely heard among educated Canadians; few of them are recorded in our imported dictionaries: *absolve* (ab zolv′), *arctic* (är′tik), *armada* (är mad′ə), *chassis* (chas′ē), *culinary* (kul′ə ner′ē), *evil* (ē′vəl), *finale* (fə nal′ē), *fungi* (fung′gī), *jackal* (jak′əl), *longitude* (long′gə tüd′), *official* (ō fish′əl), *opinion* (ō pin′yən), *placate* (plak′āt), *plenary* (plen′ə rē), *prestige* (pres tēj′), *resources* (ri zôr′səz), *senile* (sen′īl), *species* (spē′sēz), *Trafalgar* (trə fol′gər).

Of course, not everyone uses all of these forms; yet all are used regularly by educated Canadians in large numbers. Who can deny that (ri zôr′səz) and (spē′sēz) are more often heard at all levels of Canadian society than (ri sôrs′əz) and (spē′shēz), the pronunciations indicated in nearly all available dictionaries? Surely, when the evidence of usage justifies it, forms such as these should be entered as variants in any dictionary intended to reflect Canadian speech.

Another of the functions of a dictionary is to record the spellings used by the educated people of the community. In spelling, as in vocabulary and pronunciation, Canadian usage is influenced by the practice of both the Americans and the British. In areas where American and British practices differ, Canadian usage is far from uniform. Until recent years, British forms have predominated in most instances, for example, in *axe*, *catalogue*, *centre*, *colour*, *cheque*, *mediaeval*, *plough*, *skilful*, and *woollen* (and words of similar pattern), in spite of the obvious practical advantages of the American forms: *ax*, *catalog*, *center*, *check*, *color*, *medieval*, *plow*, *skillful*, and *woolen*. In some cases, however, American spellings have asserted themselves to the virtual exclusion of the corresponding British forms, as in *connection*, *curb*, *jail*, *net*, *recognize*, *tire*, and *wagon* for *connexion*, *kerb*, *gaol*, *nett*, *recognise*, *tyre*, and *waggon*.

In recent years there have been indications that American spellings are becoming more commonly used in Canada. Many have, for example, been adopted by Canadian newspapers, especially those in the larger centres, and by magazine and book publishers. Young people seem to use such spellings as *color*, *center*, *defense*, *medieval*, *program*, *skillful*, and *traveler* much more frequently than was formerly the case, the implication being that at least some American forms are accepted as proper in many Canadian schools. The fact is that usage is very much divided, varying from province to province and often from person to person. For the most part, however, Canadians respond to these variants with equal ease. Under such circumstances, a Canadian dictionary should include both forms, for here, as elsewhere, the lexicographer's obligation is to record usage, not to legislate it.

It has been argued in these pages that there is such a thing as a distinctive variety of Canadian English; yet it should be observed that this distinctive variety is referred to as "Canadian English" and not as "the Canadian language." The fact is that Canadians share one language with Britons, Americans, Australians, and a host of other people, both inside the Commonwealth and beyond it. To claim that there is a Canadian language, or, as many Americans do, an American language, is to distort the meaning of the word *language* for nationalistic purposes. On the other hand, it is a form of blindness to insist, as many do, that "English is English" and that only fools "dignify the slang and dialect" of Canada by giving it serious attention.

Guide to the dictionary

This guide is divided into two parts, "Locating an entry" and "Parts of an entry," which begins on page *xii*. Reference may also be made to the sample entries displayed on the front endpapers.

Locating an entry

All main entries—single words, two-word entries, contractions, combining forms, abbreviations—are to be found in the same alphabetical list. However, there is a system of priorities whereby, for example, prefixes come before abbreviations of the same spelling and abbreviations without periods come before the same forms with periods, as shown in the following sequence of entries from page 1:

ab-[1] *prefix.* from; away; away from; off, as in *abnormal*, *abduct*, *abjure*. Also: **a-** before *m*, *p*, *v*; **abs-** before *c*, *t*. [< L *ab-* < *ab*, prep.]
ab-[2] the form of **ad-** before *b*, as in *abbreviate*.
Ab alabamine.
AB one of the four main blood groups.
A.B. *U.S.* Bachelor of Arts; B.A. (for L *Artium Baccalaureus*)
A.B. or **a.b.** able-bodied (seaman); able seaman.
a·ba·cá or **a·ba·ca** (ä′bə kä′ or ä′bə ko′) *n.* **1** hemp made from the fibres of a Philippine banana plant; Manila hemp. **2** the plant itself. [< Malay]

For such entries it is advisable to be prepared to look a few lines above and below the place where one expects a particular item. Apart from such cases, there is only one place in the book to look for each entry.

Guide words

Guide words in a dictionary indicate the first and last entries commencing on each page. For example, on page 7 the guide words are *Acadian* and *accessible*, indicating that these two entries and all those that fall alphabetically between them are to be found on that page. Note that in this dictionary the guide words are placed at the outside top corner of each page so that they are easily seen when leafing through the book.

Homographs

Although homographs are spelled alike, they are different words because they have different meanings and origins. Homographs are entered separately and are distinguished from each other by means of small raised numerals called superscripts:

chuck[1] (chuk) *v.* **1** pat; tap, especially under the chin. **2** *Informal.* **a** toss someone out forcibly: *The intruder was chucked out of the hall.* **b** give up; finish with: *He has chucked his job.* —*n.* **1** a tap; slight blow under the chin. **2** a toss. [probably imitative]

chuck[2] (chuk) *n.* **1** a device for holding a tool or piece of work in a machine. **2** a cut of beef between the neck and the shoulder. See **beef** for diagram. [var. of *chock*]

chuck[3] (chuk) *n.* on the west coast, a large body of water, usually a river, but now sometimes the ocean. The sea is sometimes called the salt chuck. [< Chinook Jargon]

Note that homographs may be pronounced similarly, as above, or differently, as below:

slough[1] (slü *for 1*; *usually* slou *for 2-5*) *n.* **1** in the Prairie Provinces, a body of fresh water formed by rain or melted snow. **2** a soft, deep, muddy place; mud hole. **3** *Cdn.* in the Northwest, a side-channel of a stream; snye. **4** on the Pacific coast, a shallow inlet of the sea; lagoon. **5** a state of hopeless discouragement or degradation. Also, **slew, slue.** [OE *slōh*]

slough[2] (sluf) *n.* **1** the old skin shed or cast off by a snake. **2** a layer of dead skin or tissue that drops or falls off as a wound, sore, etc. heals. **3** anything that has been shed or cast off: *As savages become civilized, they cast off the slough of primitive ways, beliefs, etc.* —*v.* **1** drop off; throw off; shed. **2** be shed or cast; drop or fall: *A scab sloughs off when new skin takes its place.* **3** in card games, discard (a losing card). [ME *slugh(e)*, *slouh* < Gmc.; cf. G *Schlauch* skin bag]

Derivatives

Derivatives are words formed by adding prefixes or suffixes to other words or their roots. For example, the derivative *remake* is formed by adding the prefix *re-* to the verb *make*; the derivative *achievable* is formed by adding the suffix *-able* to the verb *achieve*, first dropping the final *e*.

Formed with suffixes

Derivatives formed with certain common suffixes are entered usually as "run-on" entries, that is they are printed in boldface type at the end of the entry for their root word. Thus *churlishly* and *churlishness* are shown at the end of the entry for churlish:

churl·ish (chėr′lish) *adj.* **1** rude; surly: *a churlish reply.* **2** niggardly; stingy; grudging; sordid. —**churl′ish·ly,** *adv.* —**churl′ish·ness,** *n.*

For further information on such words, see Section 8, "Run-on entries," on p. *xxiii.*

Derivatives formed with other suffixes are entered separately as main entries, as are all derivatives having meanings or pronunciations that cannot be inferred from those of their root words. Thus *absolutely* is an obvious derivative of *absolute*, but because it has a special meaning (and a special pronunciation) it has been entered separately:

ab·so·lute·ly (ab′sə lüt′lē *for 1, 2*; ab′sə lüt′lē *for 3*) *adv.* **1** completely. **2** positively. **3** *Informal.* yes: *"Are you going to the game?" "Absolutely!"*

Formed with prefixes

Derivatives formed with prefixes are listed in their alphabetical place in the dictionary, except for some words that are formed with *non-*, *over-*, *re-*, *ultra-*, and *un-* and have meanings that can be inferred from those of the prefix and the root word. These words are listed (without meanings or other information besides syllabication and stress marks) in columns following the entries for their respective prefixes. For example, *non-absorbent* is found in the list following *non-*, but *non-conformist* has special meanings and therefore appears as a main entry in its proper place in the alphabetical list.

Idioms and phrases

An idiom is a phrase or expression which cannot be fully understood from the meanings of the words that form it. Idioms are defined under the entry for their most important word, and they are printed in small boldface type.

For example, the idioms *have a care*, *take care*, and *take care of*, are explained under the noun meanings of *care*:

care (kãr) *n. v.* **cared, car·ing.** *—n.* **1** a burden of thought; worry: *Few people are free from care.* **2** serious attention; caution: *A good cook does her work with care.* **3** an object of concern or attention: *Keeping records is the care of the secretary of a club.* **4** watchful keeping; charge: *The child was left in her sister's care.* **5** food, shelter, and protection: *Your child will have the best of care.* **6 have a care,** be careful. **7 take care,** be careful. **8 take care of,** **a** attend to. **b** provide for. **c** be careful of. **d** *Informal.* deal with.

Verb phrases, such as *care for*, consisting of a verb and a preposition or adverb are entered under the meanings of the verb:

—v. **1** be concerned; feel an interest: *He cares about music.* **2** like; want; wish: *A cat does not care to be washed.* **3 care for, a** be fond of; like. **b** want; wish: *I don't care for any dessert tonight.* **c** attend to; provide for. [OE *caru*] **—car′er,** *n.*

Where there are more than five idioms for a particular entry (under one part of speech), they are not numbered but are set out in a separate list after the numbered definitions. See, for example, *boot*[1] on page 129.

Various other special uses of words, such as plural nouns, nouns or adjectives with articles, or capital-letter forms with special meanings, are treated in the same way as idioms:

ad·vance (ad vans′) *v.* **-vanced, -vanc·ing,** *n. adj.* . . . *—n.* **1** a movement forward: *The army's advance was very slow.* **2** the distance covered in such a movement. **3** a . . . **7** the money or goods furnished. **8 advances,** *pl.* personal approaches toward another or others to settle a difference, to make an acquaintance, etc. **9 in advance, a** in front; ahead. **b** ahead of time.

af·firm·a·tive (ə fėr′mə tiv) *adj.* stating that a fact is so; saying yes. *—n.* **1** a word or statement that gives assent or indicates agreement. **2 the affirmative,** the side arguing in favor of a question being debated. **—af·firm′a·tive·ly,** *adv.*

poor (pür) *adj.* **1** having few things or nothing . . . *—n.* **the poor,** persons who are needy. [ME < OF *povre* < L *pauper.* Doublet of PAUPER.] **—poor′ness,** *n.*

civil defence or **defense 1** the program for survival in the event of enemy attack on civilian centres, especially by aircraft, missiles, or nuclear weapons. The army and civil groups work together in planning civil defence. **2 Civil Defence,** the organization responsible for the planning and operation of the civil defence program . . . .

Many noun phrases of two or more words function almost as if they were one-word compounds. They are found as main entries if they have a meaning that is not obvious from the meanings of their separate elements. Examples are:

marked man a person watched as an object of suspicion, hatred, or vengeance.

mass number the whole number that most closely indicates the mass of an isotope, equal to the sum of the protons and neutrons in the nucleus.

master of ceremonies a person in charge of a ceremony or entertainment who announces the successive events and makes sure that they take place in the proper order. *Abbrev.*: M.C.

master stroke a very skilful act or achievement.

Some recognized phrases that do not merit separate entry are printed in small boldface type and explained within the entry for their main word. Such phrases are called "hidden entries":

ac·cel·er·a·tion (ak sel′ər ā′shən) *n.* **1** an accelerating. **2** a being accelerated. **3** a change in velocity. **Positive acceleration** is increase in velocity. **Negative acceleration** is decrease in velocity. **4** the rate of change in the velocity of a moving body.

ac·ces·so·ry (ak ses′ə rē) *n.* **-ries,** *adj.* *—n.* **1** an addition to help something of more importance; a subordinate part or detail: *All the accessories to her costume—gloves, stockings, handkerchief, and purse—were perfectly matched.* **2** in law, a person who helps an offender against the law; accomplice. An **accessory before the fact** helps an offender to break the law but is not present when he commits the offence. An **accessory after the fact** hides the offender or fails to report the offence.

Proper names

Biographical and gazetteer entries are not given in this dictionary, the space thus saved being given to enlarging the coverage of the contemporary general vocabulary and to increasing the number of illustrative phrases and sentences. However, entries are given for a number of proper names that have passed into the general language and to others that are frequently met with in literature.

Place names

Many mythical and legendary places are entered:

As·gard (as′gärd, az′gärd, or äs′gärd) *n.* the home of the Norse gods and heroes.

Shan·gri-La or **Shan·gri·la** (shang′gri lä′) *n.* an idyllic earthly paradise. [an inaccessible land in *Lost Horizon*, a novel by James Hilton (1900-1954), an English author]

In addition, some historical places and geographical areas are listed, often with maps:

A·ca·di·a (ə kā′dē ə) *n. Cdn.* **1** the areas of French settlement and culture in the Maritime Provinces. **2** the Maritime Provinces as a unit. **3** formerly, the French colony comprising the Maritime Provinces and adjacent parts of Quebec and New England. See map on the following page. [probably after *Arcadia*]
Bab·y·lon (bab′ə lən or bab′ə lon′) *n.* **1** the capital of ancient Babylonia, on the Euphrates River and, later, of the ancient Chaldean empire. Babylon was noted for its wealth, power, magnificence, and wickedness. **2** any great, rich, or wicked city.

Entries are also provided for some "places" of the modern world that have acquired general or figurative significance:

Bay Street *Cdn.* **1** in Toronto, a street on which is situated the Toronto Stock Exchange and many financial houses. **2** the financial or moneyed interests of Toronto.
Broad·way (brod′wā′ or brôd′-) *n.* **1** in New York City, a street famous for its bright lights, theatres, night clubs, etc. **2** the New York commercial theatre.

Personal names

People entered are mainly: prominent figures of myth, legend, or literature, especially those whose names have acquired a general significance, representing some particular quality or ideal; central figures of great religions; people who have given their names to specific things or qualities:

Bal·der (bol′dər or bôl′dər) *n.* in Norse mythology, the god of light, beauty, goodness, wisdom, and peace.
Bud·dha (bůd′ə, bü′də, or bud′ə) *n.* a title meaning "the Enlightened One," especially as applied to Gautama (563?-483? B.C.), a religious teacher and the founder of Buddhism. [< Skt.]
Pro·me·the·us (prə mē′thē əs or prə mē′thūs) *n.* in Greek mythology, one of the Titans. He stole fire from heaven and taught men its use. Zeus punished him by chaining him to a rock.
Xan·thip·pe (zan tip′ē) *n.* a scolding woman; shrew. [< *Xanthippe*, the wife of Socrates, famous as a scold]

In addition, information about many people is to be found in the etymologies of words derived from their names and under proper adjectives formed from their names:

Bae·de·ker (bā′də kər) *n.* a guidebook for travellers. [< Karl *Baedeker*, 1801-1859, German publisher of a series of guidebooks]
Ba·co·ni·an (bā kō′nē ən) *adj.* **1** of or having to do with Francis Bacon (1561-1626), an English essayist, statesman and philosopher. **2** of or suggestive of his writings or philosophy. **3** of or having to do with the theory that Bacon wrote the plays of Shakespeare. —*n.* **1** a person who supports or follows the philosophy of Francis Bacon. **2** a person who supports the theory that Bacon wrote the plays of Shakespeare.

Parts of an entry

Note. Abbreviations used in the text of the dictionary are listed and explained on the inside back endpaper.

1. Spelling

The first item in any dictionary entry is the entry word itself, which indicates the spelling of the basic form of the word:

a·rise (ə rīz′) *v.* **a·rose, a·ris·en, a·ris·ing. 1** rise up . . .
a·ris·to·crat (ə ris′tə krat′ or ar′is tə krat′) *n.* **1** a . . .

Note that syllabication, indicating where a word may be hyphenated, is shown by the placing of a midline dot between syllables. Syllabication is not shown in the case of entries made up of two or more words for each of which there is a main entry:

parliamentary secretary a member of the House of Commons appointed to assist a Cabinet Minister in his parliamentary work.

Variant spellings

Many words in Canadian English (and some words in all dialects of English) can be spelled in two or more ways. When both spellings are equally acceptable, they are shown as alternative entry words:

cen·tre or **cen·ter** (sen′tər) . . .
hon·or or **hon·our** (on′ər) . . .
pro·gram or **pro·gramme** (prō′gram or prō′grəm) . . .

In such cases, the form given first is generally that which is considered to be more frequently used by educated writers across Canada. It should be stressed, however, that though usage among individual writers and in particular regions may not be the same, any one writer will aim for consistency in his own work.
In cases where one form is much more frequently used in the country as a whole, the less common form is cross-referred to the other:

cat·a·log (kat′ə log′) *n. v.* **-loged, -log·ing.** catalogue.

If the two forms do not appear close together in the alphabetical list, a note of the alternative spelling is made toward the end of the main entry:

en·close (en klōz′) *v.* **-closed, -clos·ing. 1** shut in on all sides; surround. **2** put a wall or fence around. **3** put in an envelope along with something else: *A cheque was enclosed with the letter.* **4** contain. Also, **inclose.** [< *en-*[1] in + *close*, v., ME, after OF *enclos*, pp. of *enclore*]

In all cases where two variants are not very close together alphabetically, the less common variant is entered in its proper place as a cross-reference to the main entry:

cen·ter (sen′tər) *n. v.* centre.
in·close (in klōz′) *v.* **-closed, -clos·ing.** enclose.

Where there are differences in pronunciation, both spelling variants are entered separately even though the entries come very close together:

an·i·lin (an′ə lin) *n.* aniline.
an·i·line (an′ə lin, an′ə līn′, or an′ə lēn′) . . .

Spelling charts

It is often difficult to find the spelling of English words of which one knows only the pronunciation. The two charts that follow should help the reader to solve this difficulty. The first gives common spellings for sounds occurring at the beginning of words; the second gives common spellings for sounds occurring in all positions.

COMMON INITIAL SPELLINGS OF ENGLISH SOUNDS

SYMBOL	SPELLINGS (Rare spellings are in parentheses)
a	***a****t (****au****nt):* ***a (au)***
ā	***a****ge,* ***ai****d,* ***ei****ght (****é****clair):* ***a, ai, ei (é)***
ã	***a****rea,* ***ae****rial,* ***ai****r,* ***e****re:* ***a, ae, ai, e***
ä	***a****rgue,* ***ah****,* ***al****mond:* ***a, ah, al***
b	***b****ad:* ***b***
ch	cello, ***ch****ild:* ***c, ch***
d	***d****o:* ***d***
e	***a****ny,* ***ae****sthetic,* ***e****nd:* ***a, ae, e***
ē	***ae****gis,* ***e****qual,* ***ea****t,* ***ee****l,* ***ei****ther:* ***ae, e, ea, ee, ei***
ėr	***ear****th,* ***er****mine,* ***err****,* ***ir****k,* ***ur****ge:* ***ear, er, err, ir, ur***
f	***f****at,* ***ph****rase:* ***f, ph***
g	***g****o,* ***gh****ost,* ***gu****est:* ***g, gh, gu***
h	***h****e,* ***wh****o:* ***h, wh***
hw	***wh****eat:* ***wh***
i	***e****namel,* ***i****naction:* ***e, i***
ī	***ei****ther,* ***i****ce (****ai****sle,* ***ay****e,* ***ey****e):* ***ei, i (ai, ay, ey)***
j	***g****em,* ***j****am:* ***g, j***
k	***c****oat,* ***ch****emist,* ***k****ind,* ***q****uick (****qu****ay):* ***c, ch, k, q (qu)***
l	***l****and (****ll****ama):* ***l (ll)***
m	***m****e:* ***m***
n	***gn****aw,* ***kn****ife,* ***n****o,* ***pn****eumonia (****mn****emonic):* ***gn, kn, n, pn (mn)***
o	***a****ll,* ***al****mond,* ***au****to,* ***aw****ful,* ***e****ncore,* ***o****dd (****augh****t,* ***ough****t):* ***a, al, au, aw, e, o (augh, ough)***
ō	***o****pen,* ***oa****ts,* ***oh****,* ***ow****n:* ***o, oa, oh, ow***
ô	***a****ll,* ***au****to,* ***aw****ful,* ***o****rder,* ***oa****r (****augh****t,* ***ough****t):* ***a, au, aw, o, oa (augh, ough)***
oi	***oi****l:* ***oi***
ou	***ou****t,* ***ow****l:* ***ou, ow***
p	***p****ay:* ***p***
r	***r****un,* ***rh****ythm,* ***wr****ong:* ***r, rh, wr***
s	***c****ent,* ***ps****alm,* ***s****ay,* ***sc****ent (****sch****ism):* ***c, ps, s, sc (sch)***
sh	***ch****auffeur,* ***s****ure,* ***sch****wa,* ***sh****e (****psh****aw):* ***ch, s, sch, sh (psh)***
t	***pt****omaine,* ***t****ell (****Th****omas):* ***pt, t (th)***
th	***th****in:* ***th***
TH	***th****en:* ***th***
u	***o****ven,* ***u****p:* ***o, u***
ū	***eu****logy,* ***ew****er,* ***u****se,* ***you****,* ***Yu****le:* ***eu, ew, u, you, yu***
ü	***oo****ze (****ou****zel):* ***oo (ou)***
v	***v****ery:* ***v***
w	***w****ill,* ***wh****eat:* ***w, wh***
y	***y****es:* ***y***
z	***x****ylophone,* ***z****ero:* ***x, z***
zh	*(****j****abot:* ***j****)*
ə	***a****lone,* ***e****ssential,* ***o****blige,* ***u****pon:* ***a, e, o, u***

COMMON SPELLINGS OF ENGLISH SOUNDS

SYMBOL	SPELLINGS
a	h*a*t, pl*ai*d, h*al*f, l*au*gh
ā	*a*ge, *ai*d, g*ao*l, g*au*ge, s*ay*, br*ea*k, v*ei*n, w*eigh*, th*ey*
ã	c*a*re, *ai*r, pr*ay*er, wh*e*re, p*ea*r, th*ei*r
ä	d*a*rk, s*e*rgeant, h*ea*rt
b	*b*ad, ra*bb*it
ch	*ch*ild, wa*tch*, righ*te*ous, ques*ti*on, fu*tu*re
d	*d*id, a*dd*, fill*ed*
e	m*a*ny, *ae*sthetic, s*ai*d, s*ay*s, l*e*t, br*ea*d, h*ei*fer, l*eo*pard, fr*ie*nd, b*u*ry
ē	C*ae*sar, qu*ay*, *e*qual, t*ea*m, b*ee*, rec*ei*ve, p*eo*ple, k*ey*, mach*i*ne, rad*i*o, bel*ie*ve, ph*oe*nix, prett*y*
ėr	p*ear*l, st*er*n, f*ir*st, w*or*d, j*our*ney, t*ur*n, m*yr*tle
ər	li*ar*, moth*er*, elix*ir*, hon*or*, hon*our*, aug*ur*, zeph*yr*
f	*f*at, e*ff*ort, laug*h*, *ph*rase
g	*g*o, e*gg*, *gh*ost, *gu*est, catalo*gue*
h	*h*e, *wh*o
hw	*wh*eat
i	*E*ngland, b*ee*n, b*i*t, s*ie*ve, w*o*men, b*u*sy, b*ui*ld, h*y*mn
ī	*ai*sle, *aye*, h*ei*ght, *eye*, *i*ce, l*ie*, h*igh*, b*uy*, sk*y*, r*ye*
j	bri*dg*e, ver*d*ure, sol*di*er, tra*g*ic, exa*gg*erate, *j*am
k	*c*oat, a*cc*ount, *ch*emistry, ba*ck*, a*cq*uire, sa*cque*, *k*ind, fo*lk*, li*qu*or
l	*l*and, te*ll*
m	dra*chm*, paradi*gm*, ca*lm*, *m*e, cli*mb*, co*mm*on, sole*mn*
n	*gn*aw, *kn*ife, *mn*emonic, *n*o, ma*nn*er, *pn*eumonia
ng	i*n*k, lo*ng*, to*ngue*
o	w*a*tch, w*a*lk, t*au*ght, l*aw*, h*o*t, b*ou*ght
ō	b*eau*, *yeo*man, s*ew*, *o*pen, b*oa*t, t*oe*, *oh*, br*oo*ch, s*oul*, th*ough*, l*ow*
ô	*a*ll, w*a*lk, t*au*ght, l*aw*, *o*rder, b*oa*rd, b*ou*ght
oi	b*oi*l, b*oy*
ou	h*ou*se, b*ough*, n*ow*
p	cu*p*, ha*pp*y
r	*r*un, *rh*ythm, ca*rr*y, *wr*ong
s	*c*ent, ni*ce*, *ps*ychology, *s*ay, *sc*ent, *sch*ism, mi*ss*
sh	o*c*ean, ma*ch*ine, spe*ci*al, *ps*haw, *s*ure, *sch*ist, con*sci*ence, nau*se*ous, *sh*e, ten*si*on, i*ss*ue, mi*ssi*on, na*ti*on
t	stopp*ed*, bou*ght*, *pt*omaine, *t*ell, *Th*omas, bu*tt*on
th	*th*in
TH	*th*en, brea*the*
u	c*o*me, d*oe*s, fl*oo*d, tr*ou*ble, c*u*p
ū	b*eau*ty, f*eu*d, qu*eue*, f*ew*, ad*ieu*, *u*se, c*ue*, *you*, *yu*le
u̇	w*o*lf, g*oo*d, sh*ou*ld, f*u*ll
ü	thr*ew*, ad*ieu*, m*o*ve, sh*oe*, man*oeu*vre, f*oo*d, cr*ou*p, thr*ough*, r*u*le, bl*ue*, fr*ui*t
v	o*f*, Ste*ph*en, *v*ery, fli*vv*er
w	ch*o*ir, q*u*ick, *w*ill
y	opin*i*on, hallelu*j*ah, *y*es
z	ha*s*, di*sc*ern, sci*ss*ors, *X*erxes, *z*ero, bu*zz*
zh	gara*ge*, mea*s*ure, divi*si*on, a*z*ure, bra*zi*er
ə	*a*lone, fount*ai*n, mom*e*nt, penc*i*l, c*o*mplete, cauti*ous*, circ*u*s

2. Pronunciation

Pronunciation respellings are given in parentheses immediately after the entry words. The symbols used are those shown in the key on the inside of the back cover; a short key is given below the guide words at the top of the second column of each right-hand page:

but·tress (but′ris) *n.* 1 a support . . .
bu·ty·lene (bū′tə lēn′) *n.* a gaseous . . .
buzz (buz) *n.* 1 a humming sound made by flies . . .

In the case of entries of two or more words, no respelling is given for words that are entered separately:

squadron leader 1 the leader of a squadron . . .

Whenever one word of a phrase is entered separately and the other is not, only the word that does not have its own main entry is respelled:

bu·tyr·ic acid (bū tir′ik) a colorless liquid . . .
delirium tre·mens (trē′mənz) delirium characterized . . .

Syllabication

Syllabication in the respellings is shown by small spaces between the syllables. This phonetic syllabication is not necessarily the same as the spelling divisions shown by midline dots in the entry words.

Stress

Three degrees of stress are indicated in this dictionary: primary stress (′), secondary stress (′), and weak stress (unmarked). Stress is not indicated for words of one syllable, but primary stress is shown in all respellings of more than one syllable:

boy (boi) . . .
boy·hood (boi′hůd) . . .

Secondary stress is given in the case of compounds, whether they are hyphenated or not:

black·ber·ry (blak′ber′ē or blak′bər ē) . . .
bird·bath (bėrd′bath′) . . .
bell·flow·er (bel′flou′ər) . . .
flow·er·pot (flou′ər pot′) . . .
feath·er·bed·ding (feᴛʜ′ər bed′ing) *n.* the requiring of an employer to pay more employees than he considers are needed, or to pay full wages for unnecessary work or for restricted output.

In other cases, secondary stress is shown except when the syllable carrying it comes next to the primary stress:

an·o·dyne (an′ə dīn′) . . .
cal·cite (kal′sīt) . . .

Certain adjectival compounds, such as *hard-hearted*, are pronounced with two strong stresses in most sentence positions, but with primary-secondary stress when occurring before a noun. Compare *She is very hardhearted* with *She's a hardhearted woman.* Such words are shown in the respellings as having two primary stresses (härd′härt′id) but it must be remembered that (härd′härt′id) also occurs.

Variant pronunciations

The respellings show pronunciation variants that are generally acceptable in Canada, for example:

call (kol or kôl) . . .
fu·tile (fū′tīl or fū′təl) . . .
le·ver (lē′vər or lev′ər) . . .
khak·i (kär′kē, kä′kē, or kak′ē) . . .
al·ti·tude (al′tə tūd′ or al′tə tüd′, ol′tə tūd′ or ol′tə tüd′, ôl′tə tūd′ or ôl′tə tüd′) . . .

The first form given is generally the one considered to be most frequent in Canada as a whole, but, as with spelling, different forms are often preferred in different parts of the country or among different social groups. An individual's own usage is normally governed by that of the community to which he belongs, so that, unless otherwise indicated, all pronunciations given in this dictionary should be considered equally acceptable.

Variant pronunciations of compounds are abbreviated in respelling, the part that is pronounced the same in each variant not being repeated but being replaced by a hyphen:

white·fish (hwīt′fish′ or wīt′-) . . .
dead·fall (ded′fol′ or -fôl′) . . .

Words containing combining forms may be treated in the same way as true compounds if the abbreviation is easily recognizable and pronounceable by itself:

au·to·crat (o′tə krat′ or ô′tə-) . . .
breadth·wise (bredth′wīz′ or bretth′-) . . .

Labelled pronunciations

Some words are pronounced differently when they occur as different parts of speech. In such cases the respellings are labelled in the following manner:

ac·cent (*n.* ak′sent; *v.* ak′sent or ak sent′) . . .
mod·er·ate (*adj., n.* mod′ər it; *v.* mod′ər āt′) . . .

Some words have unusual pronunciations when used by members of a profession or in other specialized contexts. In such cases the restricted pronunciation, preceded by an appropriate label, is given after the respelling for the general pronunciation:

an·gi·na (an jī′nə; *in medicine, often* an′jə nə) *n.* **1** any inflammation of the throat, such as quinsy, croup, or mumps. **2** angina pectoris. **3** a sudden, acute pain. [< L *angina* quinsy < *angere* choke]

Pronunciation of foreign words

Where a foreign phrase is entered but has little currency in spoken English, the nearest possible approximation to the original pronunciation is given:

au jus (ō zhʏ′) *French.* in gravy or juice.

For words that have been anglicized but still sometimes have their original pronunciation when used in spoken English, the anglicized form is given first, followed by the labelled original form:

vo·ya·geur (voi′ə zhėr′; *French,* vwä yä zhœr′) *n.* **-geurs** (-zhėrz; *French,* -zhœr′). **1** a boatman, especially a French Canadian, in the service of the early fur-trading companies. **2** a boatman or woodsman of the Canadian forests, especially in the North. [< F *voyageur,* ult. < *voyage* voyage]

3. Parts of speech

The part of speech is given for all one-word and hyphenated entries, the label following immediately after the pronunciation respelling:

ant (ant) *n.* any of certain small insects . . .

If a word is used as more than one part of speech, and if no inflected forms are given (see Section 4 below), the most important part of speech and its meanings are normally given first, followed by a dash and the next part-of-speech label with its meanings:

an·er·oid (an′ər oid′) *adj.* using no liquid. —*n.* an aneroid barometer.

In the case of a long entry, such as *bar*[1], or one involving several parts of speech, such as *bang*[1], each part-of-speech label after the first normally begins a new line.
Where inflected forms are given, all parts of speech are listed after the respelling, their separate sets of meanings then being given in the normal way:

man (man) *n.* **men** (men), *v.* **manned, man·ning,** *interj.* . .

4. Inflected forms

Certain inflected forms—the plural of nouns, the past tense and past participle of verbs, and the comparative and superlative of adjectives and adverbs—are given whenever they are not regularly formed. They are set in boldface type and come immediately after the part of speech label; syllabication is indicated by midline dots, as in the entry words:

come (kum) *v.* **came, come, com·ing.** . . .
lib·er·ate (lib′ər āt′) *v.* **-at·ed, -at·ing.** . . .
clar·i·fy (klar′ə fī′) *v.* **-fied, -fy·ing.** . . .
da·tum (dā′təm or dat′əm) *n.* **da·ta.** . . .
goose (güs) *n.* **geese** *for 1-4,* **goos·es** *for 5.* . . .
ox (oks) *n.* **ox·en.** . . .
tes·ser·a (tes′ər ə) *n.* **tes·ser·ae** (tes′ər ē′ or tes′ər ī′). . . .
safe (sāf) *adj.* **saf·er, saf·est,** *n.* . . .
well[1] (wel) *adv. adj. interj.* **bet·ter, best.** . . .
wit·ty (wit′ē) *adj.* **-ti·er, -ti·est.** . . .

Note that the inflected forms are often abbreviated, the syllables shared with the entry word being omitted and replaced by a hyphen. Note also that the pronunciation of inflected forms is given wherever it is not obvious from that of the entry word (see *tessera* above), and when the inflected form is not itself an entry. Such respellings are abbreviated whenever this can be done without giving rise to confusion or ambiguity:

hyp·no·sis (hip nō′sis) *n.* **-ses** (-sēz). . . .

Inflected forms are given as main entries whenever they would not come immediately before or after their root word in alphabetical order. In such cases a form is cross-referred to the entry for its root word, where the full information is to be found:

came (kām) *v.* pt. of **come.**
nu·cle·i (nū′klē ī′ or nü′klē ī′) *n.* pl. of **nucleus.**
ox·en (ok′sən) *n.* pl. of **ox.**
slid (slid) *v.* pt. and pp. of **slide.**
taught (tot or tôt) *v.* pt. and pp. of **teach.**

Variant inflected forms are given whenever appropriate:

ap·pen·dix (ə pen′diks) *n.* **-dix·es** or **-di·ces. . . .**
car·i·bou (kar′ə bü′) *n.* **-bou** or **-bous. . . .**
crow[1] (krō) *n. v.* **crowed** (or **crew** *for 1*), **crowed, crow·ing. . . .**
dive (dīv) *v.* **dived** or **dove, dived, div·ing,** *n.* . . .
kid·nap (kid′nap) *v.* **-napped** or **-naped, -nap·ping** or **-nap·ing. . . .**
trav·el (trav′əl) *v.* **-elled** or **-eled, el·ling** or **-el·ing,** *n.*

5. Definitions

Definitions are intended to be as simple and straightforward as possible. Where there is more than one meaning for an entry, each meaning is introduced by a boldface numeral; within a single meaning, different glosses, or explanations, are separated by semicolons.

Order of definitions

(*a*) Definitions are grouped by parts of speech, all the noun meanings for an entry being together, all the verb meanings being together, and so on.
(*b*) Within one part of speech, meanings are grouped in the order likely to be most useful to the reader. Normally, this is the order of frequency, the most commonly used meanings being given first. It is usual, therefore, for general meanings to be at the beginning of an entry and for specific, technical senses to come later. Sometimes, however, it is easier to understand the different meanings of a word if they are arranged in a historical or a logical order. For instance, it is usually desirable for closely related senses to be kept together, as in the entry for *bar*[1]:

bar[1] (bär) *n. v.* **barred, bar·ring,** *prep.* —*n.* . . .
6 a counter over which drinks, usually alcoholic, are served. **7** the room or establishment containing such a counter. **8** a store-counter over which certain articles are sold: *a snack bar, a record bar, a hat bar.* **9** the profession of a lawyer: *After passing his law examinations, the young man was called to the bar.* **10** lawyers as a group: *Judges are chosen from the bar.* **11** the railing around the place where lawyers sit in a law court. **12** the place where an accused person stands in a law court. **13** a law court. **14** anything like a law court: *the bar of public opinion. . . .*

Here definitions 6 to 8 cover one group of meanings, while definitions 9 to 14 cover another group. This is the most convenient order in which to place these entries, but it does not mean, for example, that sense 10 is necessarily less common than sense 8.

Parentheses in definitions

Parentheses are used to enclose words that are not strictly part of the meaning of the word being defined but are necessary in order to understand that meaning or its use. For instance, in defining a transitive verb, it is often necessary to indicate the type of word that occurs as its object:

ab·duct (ab dukt′) *v.* **1** carry off (a person) unlawfully and by force; kidnap. **2** in physiology, draw (a part of the body) away from its normal position.

The meaning of sense 1 of *abduct* is not complete unless one understands that the action is something that is done to persons; similarly, in sense 2, the words in parentheses (the supplied object) are necessary to an understanding of the meaning. Other types of information are sometimes treated in the same way:

ac·cede (ak sēd′) *v.* **-ced·ed, -ced·ing. 1** give in; agree (*to*): *The king acceded to popular demand.* **2** come (*to*); attain (*to* an office or dignity): *When the king died, his oldest son acceded to the throne.* **3** become a party (*to*): *Our government acceded to the treaty.*

In addition, as also seen in the above example, parentheses are used to enclose prepositions that follow verbs in specific meanings:

a·gree (ə grē′) *v.* **a·greed, a·gree·ing. 1** have the same opinion or opinions: *I agree with you.* **2** be in harmony; correspond (*with*): *Your story agrees with mine.* **3** get along well together. **4** consent (*to*): *He agreed to accompany us.* **5** come to an understanding, especially in settling a dispute. **6 agree with,** have a good effect on; suit: *This food does not agree with me; it makes me sick.* **7** in grammar, have the same number, case, gender, person, etc. (*with*): *That verb agrees with its subject.*

In sense 1 of *agree, with* may be used but the verb may also occur without any preposition; in sense 2 the verb must be followed by *with,* and in sense 4, it must be followed by *to.* In such cases, the following preposition may be the only real clue as to which meaning of the verb is being used.

Expanded definitions

In many cases, especially with technical words, the normal style of gloss is not sufficient to explain a meaning, and a separate explanatory sentence is added, as in definition 4 of *aberration*:

ab·er·ra·tion (ab′ər ā′ shən) *n.* **1** a wandering from the right path or usual course of action. **2** a deviation from a standard or ordinary type; abnormal structure or development. **3** a temporary mental disorder. **4** in physics, the failure of a lens or mirror to bring to a single focus the rays of light coming from one point. Aberration causes a blurred image or an image with a colored rim.

Illustrations

Illustrative phrases and sentences, printed in italics, are widely used to support the definitions. Such verbal illustrations often show the type of context in which a word may be used in a particular meaning:

ac·tion (ak′ shən) *n.* **1** the doing of something; process of acting: *a machine in action.* **2** activity: *A soldier is a man of action.* **3** something done; act. . . .
de·mol·ish (di mol′ish) *v.* pull or tear down; destroy: *demolish a building. His reputation was demolished by slander.*

Illustrations are used also to highlight the contrast between related meanings of the same word:

a·bout . . . **3** somewhere near; not far from: *The dog was about the house.* **4** approximating; near: *He is about my size.*
beat (bēt) *v.* **beat, beat·en** or **beat, beat·ing,** *n. adj.* —*v.* . . . **10** move up and down; flap: *The bird beat its wings.* **11** make a sound by being struck: *The drums beat loudly.* **12** mark (time) with drumsticks or by tapping with hands or feet: *beat a tattoo.*
ob·scure (əb skūr′) *adj.* **-scur·er, -scur·est,** *v.* **-scured, -scur·ing.** —*adj.* **1** not clearly expressed: *an obscure passage in a book.* **2** not expressing meaning clearly: *an obscure style of writing.* **3** not well known; attracting no notice: *an obscure little village, an obscure poet, an obscure position in the government.* **4** not easily discovered; hidden: *an obscure path, an obscure meaning.* **5** not distinct; not clear: *an obscure form, obscure sounds, an obscure view.* **6** dark; dim: *an obscure corner.* **7** indefinite: *an obscure brown, an obscure vowel.*

Pictures, diagrams, and maps

The definitions are further supported and amplified by the various types of pictorial illustration that appear throughout the book. Some of these merely provide a picture or diagram of something hard to visualize from a verbal description:

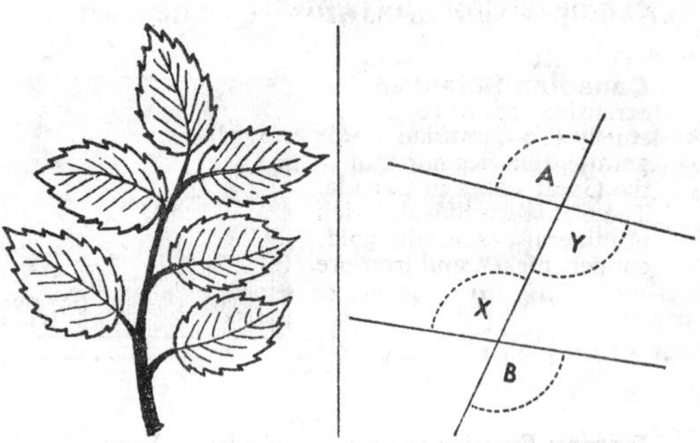

Alternate leaves   Alternate angles: A, B and X, Y

Others give a considerable amount of more-or-less technical information in diagram form, and these often label items that are entered elsewhere and are cross-referred to the same diagram:

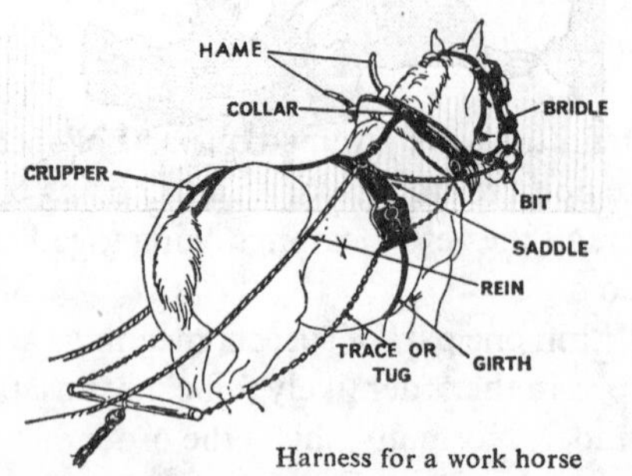

Harness for a work horse

Still others have captions which give information that, though not strictly part of a definition, is interesting and important for a full understanding of what the entry word represents:

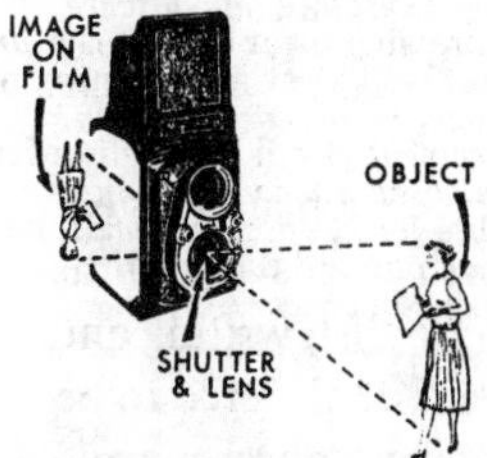

A camera. When the shutter is opened, light rays reflected from the object pass through the lens and are focussed by it on the film. Because the film is sensitive to light, it records the image.

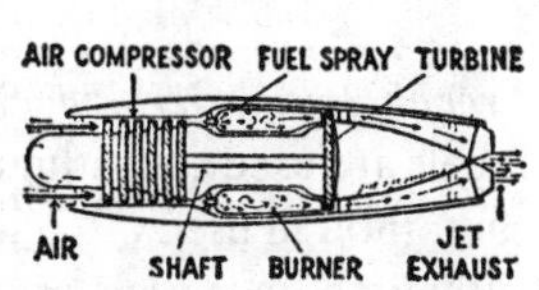

A diagram of a jet airplane engine. The air is sucked in through the front of the engine, compressed, and mixed with fuel. This mixture is burned in the burners, giving off gas which passes out through the rear of the engine, pushing the airplane forward.

Though few geographical names are entered in the dictionary, maps are used wherever possible to indicate the location and extent of items that can be territorially defined:

Canadian Shield an extensive area of rock, chiefly Pre-Cambrian granite, that lies north of the Great Lakes in Canada. The Canadian Shield is rich in minerals, especially gold, copper, nickel, and iron ore.

Roman Empire the empire of ancient Rome that lasted from 27 B.C. to A.D. 395, when it was divided into the **Eastern Roman Empire** and the **Western Roman Empire.**

Charts

Attention is drawn to the three full page charts, which give additional information to support the following entries: *geology, money, periodic table.*

6. Restrictions of use

Words and meanings that are appropriate only under certain conditions are indicated in two ways: by italicized labels, and by introductory phrases.

Restrictive labels

Labels are used mainly to indicate restrictions of usage in regard to level, style, currency, locality, etc. Those most commonly used are explained below, and further information may be had by looking up the entry word for each of these terms in the body of the dictionary.

Informal The word or meaning is quite acceptable in everyday use but would be out of place in formal speech or writing. Thus *Informal* simply means "not formal":

choos·y (chüz′ē) *adj.* **choos·i·er, choos·i·est.** *Informal.* particular or fussy in one's preferences; fastidious; selective.

Slang The word or meaning is not established in standard use but is used mainly in speech and only by certain groups, or by others in imitation or for special effects. When a word becomes generally known and acceptable, it ceases to be slang:

beef[1] (bēf) *n.* **beeves,** *v.* . . . —*v.* **beef up,** *Slang.* strengthen. [ME < OF *boef* < L *bos, bovis* ox]—**beef′less,** *n.*
beef[2] (bēf) *Slang.* —*v.* complain: *Some soldiers are always beefing.* —*n.* a complaint or grievance. [origin uncertain] —**beef′er,** *n.*
rink rat *Cdn. Slang.* a boy or young man who helps with the chores around a hockey rink, often in return for free skating, free admission to hockey games, etc.

Derogatory The word or meaning is not in polite use and is considered offensive by the person(s) to whom it refers:

Chi·na·man (chī′nə mən) *n.* **-men** (-mən). *Derogatory.* **1** a native or inhabitant of China. **2** a person of Chinese descent. ☛ See **Chinese** for usage note.

Many derogatory terms are also slang:

Po·lack (pō′lok *for 1;* pō′lak *for 2*) *n.* **1** *Derogatory slang.* a person of Polish descent. . . .
rube (rüb) *n. Derogatory slang.* a rustic; an unsophisticated person. [< *Reuben*, a traditional rural name]

Dialect The word or meaning is used only in the folk-speech of certain people or geographical areas:

cadge (kaj) *v.* **cadged, cadg·ing. 1** *Dialect.* peddle. **2** *Informal.* beg.
hun·ker (hung′kər) *v. Dialect.* squat on one's haunches.
hun·kers (hung′kərz) *n.pl. Dialect.* haunches.

Poetic The word or meaning is used only in poetry or in prose written in a poetic style:

a·wea·ry (ə wēr′ē) *adj. Poetic.* weary; tired.
e·ven[2] (ē′vən) *n. Poetic.* evening.

Archaic The word or meaning is out of place except in writings of earlier times and in modern literature that is written in the style of an earlier period:

a·vaunt (a vont′, ə vônt′ or ə vänt′) *interj. Archaic.* a command to get out, go away, etc.
glis·ter (glis′tər) *v. n. Archaic.* glisten; glitter; sparkle.
per·chance (pər chans′) *adv. Archaic or poetic.* perhaps.

Trademark The word or form is a proprietary name, owned by a particular company and valued by it as identifying its product. Trademarks have been labelled wherever possible, but the absence of such a label does not necessarily mean that a word is not a trademark:

Plex·i·glas (plek′sə glas′) *n. Trademark.* a light, transparent thermoplastic, often used in place of glass.
Or·lon (ôr′lon) *n. Trademark.* a light-weight synthetic fibre that resists sun, water, and chemicals, used for clothing, curtains, sails, awnings, etc.

Words that are trademarks are entered only when they are considered to be established as part of the general vocabulary. Some words that have passed into general use are shown as being derived from a trademark, even though the trademark is not entered separately:

ter·y·lene (ter′ə lēn′) *n.* a crease-resistant synthetic fibre, much used for shirts, dresses, suits, etc. and often mixed with wool or other yarns. [< *Terylene*, a trademark]
vas·e·line (vas′ə lēn′) *n.* a type of petroleum jelly, used as an ointment and as a lubricant. [< *Vaseline*, a trademark, coined from G *Wasser* water + Gk. *elaion* oil]

French, Latin, German, etc. Such language labels are used to distinguish words and phrases that, though used often in English writing and sometimes in speech, are still considered to be foreign. Such foreign words and phrases are usually italicized in print and underlined in writing or typing:

gar·çon (gär sôN′) *n.* **-çons** (-sôN′). *French.* **1** a young man; boy. **2** a servant. **3** a waiter.
Füh·rer (fū′rər; *German,* fY′rər) *n. German.* the title given to Adolf Hitler (1889-1945), the German dictator. Führer means leader.
per di·em (pər dē′əm or dī′əm) *Latin.* **1** per day; for each day. **2** an allowance of so much every day. [< L *per diem* per day]

Cdn. Indicates that a word or meaning originated in or is now peculiar to Canada:

reeve[1] (rēv) *n.* **1** *Cdn.* in Ontario and the western provinces, the elected head of a rural municipal council; in Ontario, also the elected head of a village or township council. **2** formerly, a bailiff; steward; overseer. [OE *(ge)rēfa*]
snye or **sny** (snī) *n.* **snyes** or **snies.** *Cdn.* a side channel of a stream. [< Cdn.F *chenail*; cf. F *chenal* channel]

Brit., Scottish, U.S., etc. Other national labels are used to distinguish words, meanings, or spellings that are used chiefly or solely in some particular part of the English-speaking world:

fen[1] (fen) *n. Brit.* a marsh; swamp; bog. [OE *fenn*]
boot[1] (büt) *n.* . . . **4** *Brit.* a car trunk. **5** a protecting apron or cover for the driver of an open carriage. **6** a kick. **7** *U.S. Slang.* a new recruit in training in the United States Navy or Marines.
Near East 1 *Canada and U.S.* the Balkans and the countries of S.W. Asia. **2** *Brit.* the Balkans.
road agent *Esp.U.S.* formerly, a highwayman.

Restrictive phrases

Phrases (such as "in the Maritimes," "in hockey," or "in architecture") are used at the beginning of definitions to show limitations of meaning. They may indicate that a word is used with reference to one particular region or country:

bank barn especially in Ontario, a two-storey barn built into a hill so as to permit entry to the bottom level from one side and to the top level from the other side.

They may also indicate that a word or meaning is used within or with reference to one particular field of activity, study, etc.:

can·ta·ta (kən tä′tə or kən tat′ə) *n.* in music, a story or play, usually with orchestral accompaniment, to be sung but not acted, by a chorus. [< Ital. < L *cantare* < *canere* sing]
celestial globe in astronomy, a globe indicating the position of the heavenly bodies, similar to a globe of the earth showing the geography of continents, oceans, etc.
cross-check (kros′chek′) *v.* **1** check again, or check against another source. **2** in hockey or lacrosse, give an illegal check by holding one's stick in both hands and thrusting it in front of an opponent's face or body. —*n.* **1** the act of cross-checking. **2** in hockey or lacrosse, an illegal check made by cross-checking.

Such phrases are often useful for contrasting different meanings of the same entry word, making it easier to find the particular meaning one is looking for.

The word "formerly" is used as if it were a restrictive phrase to indicate that the thing defined belongs to an earlier period of history, so that the word would now be used only in reference to that time:

Mont·re·al canoe (mont′rē ol′ or mun′trē ol′) *Cdn.* formerly, the largest canoe of the fur trade, used especially on the Great Lakes and the St. Lawrence River. It was up to 40 ft. long and could carry a cargo of four or five tons. Also, **canot du maître.**

Position

Note in the above examples that the position of both labels and phrases varies, depending on whether the restriction applies to a particular meaning (in which case it is placed after the numeral), to the meanings for one part of speech (placed after the part-of-speech label), or to the whole entry (placed before the part-of-speech label introducing the first group of meanings).

7. Etymologies

The etymology, or origin, of a word is given at the end of all the definitions and is enclosed in square brackets:

a·dult (ə dult′ or ad′ult) *adj.* **1** mature; grown-up. **2** of or for adults. —*n.* **1** a grown-up person. **2** a person who has reached an age of maturity as defined by law, usually the age of 21. **3** a full-grown plant or animal. [< L *adultus*, pp. of *adolescere.* See ADOLESCENT.]
an·thrax (an′thraks) *n.* an infectious, often fatal, disease of cattle, sheep, etc. that may be transmitted to human beings. [< LL < Gk. *anthrax* carbuncle, live coal]
ax·le (ak′səl) *n.* **1** a bar on which or with which a wheel turns. See **felloe** for diagram. **2** an axletree. [OE *eaxl* shoulder, crossbar; influenced by ON *öxul* axle]
bar·ri·cade (bar′ə kād′ or bar′ə kād′) *n. v.* **-cad·ed, -cad·ing.** —*n.* **1** a rough, hastily made barrier for defence. **2** any barrier or obstruction. **3** *Cdn.* large blocks of ice remaining frozen to a river or sea shore after the spring breakup. —*v.* block or obstruct with a barricade: *The road was barricaded with fallen trees.* [< F *barricade*, apparently < Provençal *barricada* < *barrica* cask; originally, made of casks. Related to BARREL.]
duc·at (duk′ət) *n.* **1** a gold or silver coin formerly used in some European countries. **2** *Slang.* a ticket. [ME < Ital. *ducato* < Med.L < L *dux, ducis* leader]
ki·osk (kē osk′ or kī′osk *for 1*; kē osk′ *for 2*) *n.* **1** a small building, usually with one or more sides open, used as a newsstand, bus shelter, telephone booth, etc. **2** in Turkey, Persia, etc., a light, open summerhouse. [< F < Turkish *kiushk* pavilion]
lem·on (lem′ən) *n.* **1** an acid-tasting, light-yellow citrus fruit growing in warm climates. **2** a thorny tree that bears this fruit. **3** a pale yellow. **4** *Slang.* a thing or person that is considered inferior or disagreeable: *The last car I bought was a lemon.* **5** a soft drink flavoured with lemon juice. —*adj.* pale-yellow. [ME < OF *limon* < Arabic *laimun* < Persian *limun*]
muk·luk (muk′luk) *n. Cdn.* **1** a high, waterproof boot, often made of sealskin, worn by Eskimos and others in the North. **2** *Informal.* any boot. [< Eskimo *muklok* bearded seal, a large seal]

The arrow sign (<), used to connect the earlier forms of a word given as a chain in the square brackets, means "from," "derived from," or "taken from." Thus *adult* is from L *adultus*; *anthrax* is taken from the Late Latin word of the same form, which in its turn is taken from the Greek *anthrax* meaning "carbuncle" or "live coal." The arrow sign that stands at the opening of a square bracket is dropped if the word is found in Old English or Middle English, as in the case of *axle*, which is a native English word found in Old English as *eaxl* meaning "shoulder."
Usually, etymological forms and their meanings are given only where they are distinctive in regard to sense, spelling, or pronunciation. Otherwise only the language symbol is given and not the form. Thus *ducat* is found in Middle English; it is derived from the Italian *ducato*,

which is from the Medieval Latin word of almost identical form (*ducatus*, not given), which is derived from the Latin *dux* meaning "leader." For Latin and Greek forms, the genitive case is also given when it sheds light on the form of spelling of the derived word, as in the case of *dux*, *ducis* for *ducat*.

Sometimes two parts of speech of the same word have followed different lines of development, in which case separate etymologies are given after the meanings for each part of speech:

de·sign (di zīn′) *n.* **1** a drawing, plan, or sketch made to serve as a pattern from which to work: *a design for a machine.* **2** in painting, weaving, building, etc., an arrangement of detail, form, and color: *a wallpaper design in tan and brown.* **3** the art of making designs: *a school of design.* **4** a piece of artistic work. **5** a plan in mind to be carried out. **6** a scheme of attack; evil plan: *The thief had designs upon the safe.* **7** a purpose; aim; intention: *Whether by accident or design, he overturned the lamp.* **8** the underlying plan or conception; organization of parts in relation to the whole and to its purpose: *the evidence of design in a communication satellite, unity of design in a novel.* **9 by design,** on purpose; by intention. [< MF *desseign* < Ital. *disegno* < *disegnare* < L *designare.* See verb.]
—*v.* **1** make a first sketch of; plan out; arrange the form and color of; draw in outline: *design a dress.* **2** make drawings, sketches, plans, etc.: *He designs for a firm of dressmakers.* **3** plan out; form in the mind; contrive: *The author of this detective story has designed a good plot.* **4** have in mind to do; purpose: *Did you design this, or did it just happen?* **5** set apart; intend: *His parents designed him for the ministry.* [< F *désigner* < L *designare* < *de-* (intensive) + *signum* mark] —**Syn.** *n.* **5** See **plan. 7** See **intention.**

No etymology is given for the following entries:
(*a*) abbreviations;
(*b*) words, including compounds, made up of elements separately entered in the dictionary as English forms;
(*c*) phrases of two or more words that are separately entered. However, etymologies are given for such entries when the origin would not be evident from the etymologies of the separate words:

dog-train (dog′trān′) *n. Cdn.* a sled pulled by a team of dogs.
dog days in the northern hemisphere, a period of very hot, humid, and uncomfortable weather during July and August. [with reference to the rising of Sirius, the Dog Star]

Related words

It is often desirable to show relationships between different entries, as in the case of two words that come from an identical source but have acquired different forms as a result of different linguistic histories; such words are called doublets:

frail (frāl) *adj.* **1** slender and not very strong; weak. **2** easily broken, damaged, or destroyed. **3** morally weak; liable to yield to temptation. [ME < OF *fraile* < L *fragilis* fragile. Doublet of FRAGILE.]
frag·ile (fraj′īl or fraj′əl) *adj.* easily broken, damaged, or destroyed; delicate; frail. [< L *fragilis* (related to *frangere* break). Doublet of FRAIL.]

In this case Latin *fragilis* became Old French *fraile*, resulting in the English form *frail*, while *fragile* was formed at a later date directly from the Latin.

Relationships that are slightly less close are shown by means of the phrase *related to*, or *akin to*:

ban·dit (ban′dit) *n.* **ban·dits** or **ban·dit·ti** (-ē). a highwayman; robber. [< Ital. *bandito*, pp. of *bandire* banish, proscribe, ult. < Gmc. Akin to BAN.]
beck·on (bek′ən) *v.* signal by a motion of the head or hand: *He beckoned me to follow him.* [OE *bēcnan*, var. of *biecnan.* Related to BEACON.]

Cross references are used to direct the reader to a related entry where the etymology he is studying is completed:

chap·el (chap′əl) *n.* **1** a building for worship, not so large as a church. **2** a small place for worship within a larger building. **3** a room or building for worship in a palace, school, etc. **4** a religious service in a chapel. **5** in Great Britain, a place for worship used by people who do not belong to the Established Church. **6** an association of journeymen printers for regulating conditions of work among themselves. [ME < OF *chapele* < LL *cappella*; originally a shrine in which was preserved the *cappa* or cape of St. Martin]
chap·lain (chap′lən) *n.* a clergyman officially authorized to perform religious functions for a family, court, society, public institution, or unit in the armed services. [ME < OF *chapelain* < LL *capellanus* < *cappella.* See CHAPEL.]

Referring the reader from *chaplain* to *chapel* avoids the necessity of repeating information about the origin of Latin *capella*, at the same time establishing the relationship between the two words. Further examples of this device are:

ab·bess (ab′is or ab′es) *n.* the woman in charge of an abbey of nuns. [ME < OF < LL *abbatissa* < *abbas, abbatis* abbot + *-issa*, Gk. fem. suffix. See ABBOT.]
ab·bot (ab′ət) *n.* the man in charge of an abbey of monks. [OE *abbad, abbod* < LL *abbas, -atis* < LGk. < Aramaic *abbā* father]
ben·e·fice (ben′ə fis) *n.* a permanent office or position created by ecclesiastical authority. [ME < OF < L *beneficium* benefit < *beneficus* beneficent < *benefacere.* See BENEFACTOR.]

ben·e·fac·tor (ben′ə fak′tər or ben′ə fak′tər) *n.* a person who has helped others, either by gifts of money or by some kind act. [ME < LL *benefactor* < *benefacere* < *bene* well + *facere* do]

Occasionally no extra information is to be found at the etymology for a related word but it is worthwhile to compare the two and to note the relationship, or similarity, between the two. In such cases the direction *Cf.* is used:

as[1] (ez; *stressed,* az) *adv.* **1** to the same degree or . . . [OE (unstressed) *ealswā* quite so. Cf. ALSO.]
al·so (ol′sō or ôl′sō) *adv.* in addition; besides; too. [OE *ealswā* all so, quite so]

8. Run-on entries

Run-ons are derived forms listed after the etymology position in many entries. See the first two paragraphs of the discussion of derivatives on page *x*.
Further examples of run-on entries are:

ab·jure (ab jür′) *v.* **-jured, -jur·ing.** renounce on oath; repudiate; swear to give up: *abjure one's religion.* [< L *abjurare* < *ab-* away + *jurare* swear] **—ab·jur′er,** *n.*
cool (kül) *adj.* **1** somewhat cold; more cold than hot . . . **—cool′ly,** *adv.* **—cool′ness,** *n.* **—Syn.** *adj.* **1 See cold.**
pat·ent (*n. adj. 1, v.* pat′ənt or pā′tənt; *adj. 2, 3* . . . —*v.* get a patent for. [< L *patens, -entis,* ppr. of *patere* lie open] **—pat′ent·a·ble,** *adj.*

Note that the part of speech is given for run-on entries, and that syllabication and stress marks are indicated; the rest of the pronunciation and the meaning are to be inferred from those of the root word and the suffix.

Run-on entries may be given for words formed with the following suffixes:

Suffixes forming adjectives

-able "able to be ——" or "capable of being ——"; added to verbs:
singable = able to be sung;
adaptable = capable of being adapted or capable of adapting.

-an
-ian
-n "of or having to do with ——"; added to nouns (names of places): *Albertan* = of or having to do with Alberta.

-less "having no ——"; added to nouns:
wingless = having no wings;
conscienceless = having no conscience.

-like "like a ——" or "like a ——'s"; added to nouns:
flowerlike = like a flower;
birdlike = like a bird or like a bird's.

Suffixes forming nouns

-an
-ian
-n "a native or inhabitant of ——"; added to nouns (names of places): *Albertan* = a native or inhabitant of Alberta.

-er
-or "one that ——s"; added to verbs:
deceiver = one that deceives,
extractor = one that extracts.

-ion
-ation
-tion "a ——ing or being ——ed"; added to verbs:
decontamination = a decontaminating or being decontaminated;
magnetization = a magnetizing or being magnetized.

-ment "a ——ing or being ——ed"; added to verbs:
encouragement = an encouraging or being encouraged, or something that encourages;
impalement = an impaling or being impaled.

-ness "the fact or quality of being ——"; added to adjectives:
exactness = the fact or quality of being exact;
timeliness = the fact or quality of being timely.

Suffixes forming adverbs

-ly "in a —— way or manner"; added to adjectives:
innocently = in an innocent manner;
plainly = in a plain way.

-ally "in a —— way or manner"; added to certain adjectives ending in *-ic*:
schematically = in a schematic manner.

9. Synonyms

Helpful synonyms that are not used in the definitions are listed at the end of an entry; longer notes (synonym studies) are used to distinguish words that have nearly but not quite the same meanings.

Synonym lists

These lists follow etymologies and derived forms, being introduced by the abbreviation *Syn.* The boldface numbers indicate the meaning of the entry word to which each synonym applies:

har·dy (här′dē) *adj.* **-di·er, -di·est. 1** able to bear hard treatment, fatigue, etc.; strong; robust. **2** able to withstand the cold of winter in the open air: *hardy plants.* **3** bold; daring. **4** too bold; rash. [ME < OF *hardi,* pp. of *hardir* harden < Gmc.] **—har′di·ly,** *adv.* **—Syn. 1** hale, hearty. **3** courageous, intrepid.

Thus *hale* and *hearty* are synonyms for definition 1 of *hardy* while *courageous* and *intrepid* are synonyms for definition 3.

Synonym studies

These notes are also introduced by the abbreviation *Syn.*, but they are in smaller type than the main text and start on a new line. Usually, the basic meaning common to the synonyms being discussed is given first, followed by the particular shades of meaning that distinguish each individual word:

dis·cov·er (dis kuv′ər) *v.* **1** see or learn of for the first time; find out. **2** *Archaic.* make known; reveal. [ME < OF *descovrir* < *des-* away + *covrir* cover < L *cooperire*] —**dis·cov′er·a·ble,** *adj.* —**dis·cov′er·er,** *n.*
Syn. 1 Discover, invent = find something not known before. **Discover** = find or find out something that already existed, but was not known about or had not been seen: *Pierre and Marie Curie discovered radium.* **Invent** = make or work out something that did not exist before: *Alexander Graham Bell invented the telephone.*

har·bor or **har·bour** (här′bər) *n.* **1** a naturally or artificially sheltered area of deep water where ships may dock or anchor. A harbor may have loading and unloading facilities for passengers and cargo. **2** any place of shelter. —*v.* **1** give shelter to; give a place to hide: *The dog's shaggy hair harbors fleas.* **2** take shelter or refuge. **3** keep or nourish in the mind: *Don't harbor unkind thoughts.* [OF *herebeorg* lodgings < *here* army + *beorg* shelter] —**har′bor·er** or **har′bour·er,** *n.* —**har′bor·less** or **har′bour·less,** *adj.*
Syn. *n.* **1 Harbor, port** = place of shelter for ships. **Harbor** emphasizes shelter, and applies to a protected part of the sea, or other large body of water, where land or breakwaters shield against wind and heavy waves: *Many yachts are lying at anchor in the harbor.* **Port** emphasizes the idea of a place to put in to land or unload at the end of a voyage, and applies particularly to a harbor where commercial ships dock for loading and unloading: *The ship arrived in port.* **2** refuge. –*v.* **3** See **cherish.**

A synonym study is given under the entry for the most common of the words discussed, cross-references to the study being given under the entries for the other words. These cross-references are given in the same style as synonym lists:

in·vent (in vent′) *v.* **1** make, create, or think out (something new): *Bell invented the telephone.* **2** make up; think up: *invent an excuse.* [< L *inventus,* pp. of *invenire* < *in-* in + *venire* come] —**Syn. 1** See **discover.**

port^1 (pôrt) *n.* **1** a harbor; a place where ships and boats can take shelter from storms. **2** a place where ships and boats can load and unload. **3** a city or town with a harbor. Halifax and Vancouver are important Canadian ports. **4** any place where one can find shelter. [OE < L *portus*] —**Syn. 1, 2** See **harbor.**

10. Usage notes

Usage notes, marked with the sign ☛, are found at the end of many entries. Like synonym studies, they are set in smaller type than the main text. Several examples are found on the very first page of the dictionary:

a^1 (ə; *stressed,* ā or a) *adj.* or *indefinite article.* **1** any: *a tree.* **2** one: *a pound of butter.* **3** each; every: *once a year, two at a time.* **4** a single: *not a one.* [var. of **an**^{1}]
☛ A is used before words pronounced with an initial consonant sound whether or not that consonant is shown by the spelling, as in *a* man, *a* year, *a* union, *a* hospital. Most people now write *a* hotel or *a* historian, but some use *an* in such cases.
☛ A regularly comes before other modifiers but follows *many, such, what,* and any adjective preceded by *as, how, so,* or *too,* as in *many a person, such a bore, so fine a picture.*

a^2 (ə; *stressed,* ā or a) *adj.* or *indefinite article.* to or for each: *He earned ten dollars a day. They asked for fifty cents a man.* [OE *on* on]

a-^{1} *prefix.* **1** in; on; to: *abed* = *in bed.* **2** in the act of —ing: *a-fishing* = *in the act of fishing.* [ME *a* < OE *an, on* in, on, at]
☛ **a-**^{1}. Adjectives originally formed with *a-* + noun (such as *alive, asleep*) are not used before a noun. We say *a man who is asleep* and *a man asleep,* but not *an asleep man.*

a-^{2} the form of **ab-**^{1} before *m, p, v,* as in *avert.*

a-^{3} the form of **ad-** before *sc, sp, st,* as in *ascribe, aspire, astringent.*

a-^{4} the form of **an-**^{1} before consonants except *h,* as in *atonal.*
☛ **A-** meaning *not* is of Greek origin and is used in words taken directly, or through Latin, from Greek, as in *apathy.* It is also used as a naturalized English prefix in new formations, as in *achromatic.* **A-**, called alpha privative, corresponds to English **un-** and Latin **in-**.

Many such notes deal with questions of conflicting usage or changing usage; others give information that, while not belonging in the main body of an entry, enables one to use the word appropriately and effectively. The main types of usage note are listed below.

Contrasts of meaning

Many usage notes distinguish between pairs of words, such as *council* and *counsel, accept* and *except,* that are frequently confused on account of their similarities in spelling or pronunciation:

con·temp·tu·ous (kən temp′chü əs) *adj.* showing contempt; scornful: *a contemptuous look.* —**con·temp′tu·ous·ly,** *adv.* —**con·temp′tu·ous·ness,** *n.*
☛ **Contemptuous** and **contemptible** are sometimes confused. The distinction will be clear if one observes that in *contemptible* the suffix *-ible* means deserving.

es·pe·cial·ly (es pesh′əl ē or es pesh′lē) *adv.* . . .
☛ **especially, specially. Especially** = pre-eminently or exceptionally. **Specially** = for that purpose and no other. You should say, *I came specially to see John*; but, *I came especially to see John* if you would see others after seeing John, or if you have other business in mind besides visiting. A parallel distinction exists between **especial** and **special,** although the latter word now replaces **especial** for most purposes.

Other words are sometimes confused because their meanings overlap, or because they stand for closely related (but still different) things:

rug·by (rug′bē) *n.* **1** in Canada, a game played by teams of twelve men who carry, pass, or kick an oval ball towards the opposing team's goal; football. **2** rugger. [< *Rugby*, a famous school for boys in Rugby, England]
☞ **rugby, rugger, soccer.** Though still heard in Canada, the term **rugby** (or **rugby football**) is gradually being displaced by the American term **football.** As such, it is distinct from **rugger,** played with 15 men a side, and **soccer,** played with 11 men a side, of whom only the goalie can play the ball with his hands.

In some cases a usage note shows that there is a choice between two words of virtually the same meaning:

o·ral (ô′rəl) *adj.* **1** spoken; using speech. **2** of the mouth. **3** taken by mouth: *oral medicine.* [< L *os, oris* mouth]
☞ **oral, verbal.** Strictly, *oral* means "spoken," and *verbal,* used as an adjective, means "in words"; but *verbal* has been used so long with the same sense as *oral* that there is no longer a distinction between the two: *He gave an oral report. They had only a verbal agreement.*

o·ri·en·tate (ô′rē en tāt′) *v.* **-tat·ed, -tat·ing. 1** put facing east. **2** place so that it faces in any indicated direction: *The building is orientated north and south.* **3** find the direction of. **4** place in the proper position. **5 orientate oneself,** get in the right relationship with one's surroundings; adjust oneself to a situation.
☞ **orientate, orient.** Though **orientate** has been considered the preferred form in British and Canadian use, **orient,** which is the common form in the United States, seems to be gaining in popularity among educated speakers of the language.

Cross references to usage notes under other entries are given in the following manner:

con·tempt·i·ble (kən temp′tə bəl) *adj.* deserving contempt or scorn; held in contempt; mean; low; worthless: *Cowards and cheats are contemptible.* **—con·tempt′i·ble·ness,** *n.* **—con·tempt′i·bly,** *adv.* ☞ See **contemptuous** for usage note.

Range of meaning

Some usage notes bring out shades of meaning, or connotations, that could not be so effectively indicated in the definitions of illustrative sentences:

fac·ile (fas′ĭl, fas′ēl, or fas′əl) *adj.* **1** easily done, used, etc.: *a facile task, facile methods.* **2** moving, acting, working, etc. with ease: *a facile hand, a facile tongue, a facile pen.* **3** having easy manners or temper; agreeable; yielding: *Her facile nature adapted itself to any company.* [< L *facilis* easy < *facere* do] **—fac′ile·ly,** *adv.* **—fac·ile′ness,** *n.*
☞ **Facile** often has a pejorative connotation so that it means "too easy" or "working too easily": *facile methods* could be naïve and superficial; *a facile tongue* could refer to a way of speaking that seemed too smooth and charming to be convincing or sincere.

gaf·fer (gaf′ər) *n. Informal.* an old man. [alteration of *godfather*]
☞ **gaffer** is now normally used in a humorous or unfavorable sense; it is the masculine counterpart of **gammer,** an old gossip.

Such notes may include a warning about the use of a word under certain conditions:

eth·nic (eth′nik) *adj.* **1** of or having to do with various cultural groups of people and the characteristics, language, and customs of each; of, having to do with, or peculiar to a people. **2** of or having to do with people of foreign birth or descent: *the ethnic groups of Toronto, ethnic newspapers.* **3** heathen; pagan; not Christian; not Jewish. [< L *ethnicus* < Gk. *ethnikos* < *ethnos* nation]
☞ **ethnic** (def. 2). The use of *ethnic* to mean *foreign* has become widespread in Canada though it is considered unacceptable usage by many and is resented as being condescending and inaccurate by others.

Etymology

Sometimes a significant point of etymology that cannot conveniently be given in the square brackets is included as a usage note:

Dutch (duch) *adj.* . . .
☞ The numerous derogatory expressions compounded of *Dutch,* such as **Dutch courage** and **Dutch uncle,** are a legacy from the Dutch-English commercial rivalry of the 17th and 18th centuries.

Level of usage

Distinctions between formal and informal usage, and between spoken and written usage, are often the subject of special notes, many of which indicate ways in which current usage is changing:

bunch (bunch) *n.* . . .
☞ **bunch.** Formal English limits the use of *bunch* to objects that grow together or can be fastened together: *a bunch of radishes, a bunch of flowers, a bunch of keys.* Informal English, however, clings to the older usage of *bunch,* applying it to a collection or group of any kind—including people: *A bunch of us meet at the Grill every night.*

hence (hens) *adv.* . . .
☞ **Hence** is a formal word for the less formal *consequently, therefore,* and the general *so that: He has not answered our last letter, hence it would seem he is not interested.* **Hence** is rare in current informal writing.

rise (rīz) *v.* **rose, ris·en, ris·ing,** *n.* **—***v.* **1** get up . . .
☞ In referring to people, **arise** is formal and poetic; **rise** is rather formal; **get up** is informal.

In this category, special attention is given to contemporary usage in such vexed areas as that of *can* and *may*, and other auxiliary verbs:

can[1] (kan; *unstressed,* kən) *v. pres. sing.* **1 can, 2 can** or (*Archaic*) **canst, 3 can;** *pt.* **could. 1** be able to: *He can read rapidly.* **2** know how to: *He can run that machine.* **3** have the right to: *Anyone can cross the street here.* **4** *Informal.* be allowed to: *You can go at four o'clock.* [OE *can(n)* know, know how, can (infinitive, *cunnan*)]
☞ **can, may.** In general informal usage *may* occurs rather rarely except in the sense of possibility: *It may be all right for her, but not for me.* *Can* is generally used for both permission and ability: *Can I go now? You can if you want to. I can go 80 miles an hour with my car.* This is in such general usage that it should be regarded as acceptable English in speaking and in informal writing. In formal English, however, some distinction is often made between the auxiliary *can,* implying ability, being able to, and *may,* implying permission: *You may go now. He can walk with crutches. You may if you can. May* also indicates possibility: *He may have been the one.*

Since much use is made of it, and since it is often misunderstood, the word *informal* has its own usage note:

in·for·mal (in fôr′məl) *adj.* **1** not formal; not in the regular or prescribed manner. **2** done without ceremony. **3** used in everyday, common speech, but not used in formal speaking or writing. Such an expression as *kids* for *children* is informal. —**in·for′mal·ly,** *adv.* —**Syn. 2** unconventional, easy. **3** colloquial.
☛ **Informal English** is the kind of English used by educated people in informal speaking or writing, as distinguished from formal English, which is used in lectures, speeches, learned articles legal documents, etc.

Plural nouns

Many nouns occur in the plural form but are often, if not always, singular in use; other nouns are always plural in form and use; and still others may be used as singular or plural. Usage notes indicate whether a singular or a plural verb should be used after such nouns:

da·ta (dā′tə or dat′ə) *n.* pl. of **datum.** the things known or granted; information from which conclusions can be drawn; facts.
☛ **Data** is the plural of the seldom-used singular *datum*. Since its meaning is often collective, referring to a group of facts as a unit, *data* is often used with a singular verb in informal English: *The data you have collected is not enough to convince me.* Formal English continues to regard *data* as a plural rather than as a collective noun: *We will analyse the data that have been obtained.*

sta·tis·tics (stə tis′tiks) *n.* **1** numerical facts about people, the weather, business conditions, etc. Statistics are collected and classified systematically. **2** the science of collecting and classifying such facts in order to show their significance. [ult. < G < NL *statisticus* political, ult. < L *status* state. See STATE.]
☛ **Statistics meaning** facts (def. 1) is plural in form and plural in use: *Statistics are classified systematically.* When the meaning is the science of collecting and classifying numerical facts (def. 2), *statistics* is plural in form and singular in use: *Statistics is taught in some colleges.*

bar·racks (bar′əks) *n.pl.* **1** a building or group of buildings for members of the armed services to live in. **2** a building housing local detachments of the Royal Canadian Mounted Police. **3** a large, plain building in which many people live. [See BARRACK[1].]
☛ **Barracks** appears with either a singular or plural verb: *John wrote that his barracks was a lively place. The barracks were inspected daily.*

Prepositional usage

Many usage notes indicate which prepositions should be used after certain words, or after contrasted meanings of the same word:

a·ble (ā′bəl) *adj.* **a·bler, a·blest. . . .**
☛ *Able* and *competent* may be followed by *to* plus an infinitive, but *capable* takes *of* plus a gerund: *able to think, competent to drive a car, capable of taking responsibility.*

ad·her·ent (ad hēr′ənt) *n.* a faithful supporter; follower. —*adj.* sticking fast; attached. —**ad·her′ent·ly,** *adv.* —**Syn.** *n.* See **follower.**
☛ **adherent.** The preposition used with the noun *adherent* is *of*: *He was an adherent of the Liberal Party.*

ad·mit (ad mit′) *v.* **-mit·ted, -mit·ting. . . .**
☛ **Admit** is followed by *to* or *into* when it means "give the right to enter or allow to enter": *Fifty cents will admit you to the game. The butler would not admit him into the house. Admit* is followed by *of* when it means "leave room for": *His conduct admits of no complaint.*

Spelling

Problems and variations of Canadian spelling are discussed in a number of usage notes:

ad·vis·er or **ad·vi·sor** (ad vīz′ər) *n.* **1** a person who gives advice. **2** a teacher appointed to advise students.
☛ **Adviser** has been the more common spelling, but the *-or* form, because of its similarity to *advisory*, is being increasingly used.

-or *Suffix.* **1** a person or thing that ——s, as in *actor, accelerator, orator, survivor, sailor.* **2** an act, state, condition, quality, characteristic, etc., especially in words from Latin, as in *error, horror, labor, terror.* [< L]
☛ **-or, -our.** In Canada usage varies, although most newspapers, magazines, etc. prefer *-or* in such words as *color, honor,* and *neighbor.* In the United States preference for *-or* is virtually universal. However, *Saviour* (referring to Jesus Christ) and *glamour* are considered exceptions, both in U.S. and Canadian usage. But even in British usage, which prefers *-our* spellings, derivatives ending in *-ation, -ary, -ific,* and *-ous* are spelled with *-or-*. Thus, *honorific, honorary, humorous, odoriferous* are so spelled on both sides of the Atlantic.

Hon·our·a·ble or **Hon·or·a·ble** (on′ər ə bəl) *adj.* **1** in Canada, a title given to members of the Privy Council (which includes the Federal Cabinet), to the Speakers of both the House of Commons and the provincial legislative assemblies, and to certain senior judges. **2** in Great Britain and elsewhere, a title of respect used under various conditions.
☛ **Honourable, Honorable.** The spelling *Honourable* is usually retained in Canada as an official title for Cabinet ministers, etc.

ren·ais·sance (ren′ə säns′, ren′ə säns′, or ri nā′səns) *n.* **1** a revival; new birth. **2 the Renaissance, a** the great revival of art, literature, and learning in Europe during the 14th, 15th, and 16th centuries. **b** the period of time when this revival occurred. **c** in art, architecture, etc., a style developed in this period and characterized by the simplicity, elegance, and proportion of classical Greek and Roman models. [< F *renaissance* < *renaitre* be born again, ult. < L *renasci.* See RENASCENT.]
☛ **renaissance.** The word is capitalized when it refers to the period of history: *art of the Renaissance.* It is not capitalized when it refers to a revival: *a renaissance of interest in old-time melodramas.*

Pronunciation

Variations in pronunciation are discussed in a similar way:

been (bin or bēn) *v.* pp. of **be.**
☛ **been.** The most common British pronunciation is (bēn), and the normal American pronunciation is (bin). In earlier English, (bēn) was the stressed form and (bin) the unstressed; many Canadian speakers still employ this distinction. Otherwise, Canadian usage varies between the two forms.

Grammatical and rhetorical terms

Detailed grammatical information is given at the end of the entries for such terms as: *adjective, adverb, gerund,* and *verbal noun*:

ad·verb (ad′ vėrb) *n.* a word that extends or limits the meaning of verbs but is also used to qualify adjectives or other adverbs, especially in place, time, manner, or degree: *Soon*, *here*, *very*, *gladly*, and *not* are adverbs. *Abbrev.*: adv. [< L *adverbium* < *ad-* to + *verbum* verb]

☛ **adverb. a. forms of adverbs.** Most adverbs are adjectives or participles plus the ending *-ly*: *He rowed badly. She was deservedly popular. Surely you hear that.* There are a number of adverbs with the same forms as adjectives. Some of these are: *cheap*, *close*, *deep*, *even*, *first*, *high*, *loud*, *much*, *near*, *right*, *slow*, *smooth*, *tight*, *well*, *wrong*. Most of these adverbs have forms in *-ly* as well so that we can write: *He sang loud. He sang loudly.* The *-ly* forms are more common in formal English and the shorter forms in informal and familiar writing. **b. comparison of adverbs.** Degrees of the condition or manner indicated by an adverb are shown by adding *-er*, *-est*, or by placing *more*, *most* before it: *hard*, *harder*, *hardest*; *slow*, *slower*, *slowest*; or *slowly*, *more slowly*, *most slowly*. *More* and *most* are used with most adverbs of more than one syllable.

restrictive clause in grammar, an adjectival clause that is an essential and inseparable part of the sentence in which it appears.

☛ A **restrictive clause** restricts the noun it modifies in that it identifies or defines the member of the class of things being referred to and is for this reason an inseparable part of the noun construction; such clauses are never set off by commas, nor is there any perceptible pause before or after them in speech. *Example*: The man *who came to dinner* stayed for a month.
A **non-restrictive clause** contains nothing more than descriptive detail and for this reason is merely a clause inserted in the main construction; such clauses must be set off from the main clause by commas and there is a perceptible pause, usually accompanied by a change in voice pitch, before and after them in speech. *Example*: The principal of the high school, *who is a most interesting man*, came to our house for dinner last evening.

Explanatory notes are provided also for such rhetorical entries as *epigram*, *irony*, and *metaphor*, care being taken to contrast and distinguish terms that are frequently confused:

ep·i·gram (ep′ ə gram′) *n.* **1** a short, pointed, witty saying. *Example*: "The only way to get rid of temptation is to yield to it." **2** a short poem ending in a witty or clever turn of thought. *Example*:

"Here lies our Sovereign Lord the King
Whose word no man relied on,
Who never said a foolish thing,
Nor ever did a wise one."

[< L < Gk. *epigramma* < *epigraphein* < *epi-* on + *graphein* write]

☛ **epigrams.** An *epigram* is a short, pointed, witty saying. A special type of epigram is the *paradox*, which makes a statement that, as it stands, contradicts fact or common sense or itself, and yet suggests a truth or at least a half truth: *All generalizations are false, including this one.* Closely related to epigrams are *aphorisms*—pithy statements but more likely to be abstract and not necessarily witty: *A living dog is better than a dead lion.* Proverbs are the often quoted, concrete expressions of popular wisdom. They are likely to make observations on character or conduct: *Still waters run deep.*

i·ro·ny (ī′ rə nē) *n.* **-nies. 1** a method of expression in which the intended meaning is the opposite of, or different from that expressed: *Calling their small bungalow a mansion is irony.* **2** an event contrary to what would naturally be expected: *It was the irony of fate that the great cancer doctor himself died of cancer.* **3** an ironical statement or expression; ironical quality. [< L *ironia* < Gk. *eirōneia* dissimulation < *eirōn* dissembler]

☛ **Irony, sarcasm, satire** are often confused. *Irony*, applying to a kind of humor or way of expressing wit, emphasizes deliberately saying the opposite of what one means, depending on tone of voice or writing to show the real meaning: *the thrill of sitting still for two hours at a time.* *Sarcasm* applies only to cruel, biting, contemptuous remarks that may be stated ironically or directly, but are always intended to hurt and ridicule: *When children call a boy "Four Eyes" because he wears glasses, they are using sarcasm.* *Satire* is the formal use of irony, sarcasm, and other kinds of humor to expose, criticize, or attack follies or vices.

Canadian Senior Dictionary

Full pronunciation key

The pronunciation of each word is shown just after the word, in this way: **a bom i na ble** (ə bom′ə nə bəl). The letters and signs used are pronounced as in the words below. The mark ′ is placed after a syllable with primary or heavy stress, as in the example above. The mark ′ after a syllable shows a secondary or lighter stress, as in **a bom i nate** (ə bom′ə nāt′) or **a bom i na tion** (ə bom′ə nā′shən).

Some words, taken from foreign languages, are spoken with sounds that otherwise do not occur in English. Symbols for these sounds are given at the bottom of the page as "Foreign Sounds."

a	hat, cap
ā	age, face
ã	care, air
ä	barn, far
b	bad, rob
ch	child, much
d	did, red
e	let, best
ē	equal, be, y in pretty
ėr	term, learn
f	fat, if
g	go, bag
h	he, how
i	it, pin
ī	ice, five
j	jam, enjoy
k	kind, seek
l	land, coal
m	me, am
n	no, in
ng	long, bring
o	hot, rock
ō	open, go
ô	order, door
oi	oil, voice
ou	out, loud
p	paper, cup
r	run, try
s	say, yes
sh	she, rush
t	tell, it
th	thin, both
TH	then, smooth
u	cup, butter
u̇	full, put
ü	rule, move
ū	use, music
v	very, save
w	will, woman
y	young, yet
z	zero, breeze
zh	measure, seizure

ə represents:
- a in above, pillar
- e in taken, under
- i in pencil, tapir
- o in lemon, favor
- u in circus, measure

foreign sounds

Y as in French *du*. Pronounce ē with the lips rounded as for English ü in rule.

œ as in French *peu*. Pronounce ā with the lips rounded as for ō.

N as in French *bon*. The N is not pronounced, but shows that the vowel before it is nasal.

H as in German *ach*. Pronounce k without closing the breath passage.

hat, āge, cãre, fär; let, ēqual, tėrm; it, īce
hot, ōpen, ôrder; oil, out; cup, pu̇t, rüle, ūse
əbove, takən, pencəl, lemən, circəs
ch, child; ng, long; sh, ship
th, thin; TH, then; zh, measure

A or **a** (ā) *n.* **A's** or **a's.** **1** the first letter of the English alphabet. **2** any speech sound represented by this letter, as in *cat, father, late,* etc. **3** any person or thing considered as the first in a series: *Company A in a battalion. A and B are friends.* **4** any person or thing considered as of the best group: *grade A eggs. He was awarded A in the examination.* **5** in music: **a** the sixth tone in the scale of C major. **b** a symbol representing this tone. **c** a key, string, etc. that produces this tone. **d** a scale or key that has A as its keynote: *a symphony in A.* **6** a known quantity, especially in equations, as in $ax + by + c = 0$. **7** anything shaped like A.

a[1] (ə; *stressed,* ā or a) *adj.* or *indefinite article.* **1** any: *a tree.* **2** one: *a pound of butter.* **3** each; every: *once a year, two at a time.* **4** a single: *not a one.* [var. of **an**[1]]

☛ A is used before words pronounced with an initial consonant sound whether or not that consonant is shown by the spelling, as in *a* man, *a* year, *a* union, *a* hospital. Most people now write *a* hotel or *a* historian, but some use *an* in such cases.

☛ A regularly comes before other modifiers but follows *many, such, what,* and any adjective preceded by *as, how, so,* or *too,* as in *many a person, such a bore, so fine a picture.*

a[2] (ə; *stressed,* ā or a) *adj.* or *indefinite article.* to or for each: *He earned ten dollars a day. They asked for fifty cents a man.* [OE *on* on]

a-[1] *prefix.* **1** in; on; to: *abed* = *in bed.* **2** in the act of —ing: *a-fishing* = *in the act of fishing.* [ME *a* < OE *an, on* in, on, at]

☛ **a-**[1]. Adjectives originally formed with *a-* + noun (such as *alive, asleep*) are not used before a noun. We say *a man who is asleep* and *a man asleep,* but not *an asleep man.*

a-[2] the form of **ab-**[1] before *m, p, v,* as in *avert.*

a-[3] the form of **ad-** before *sc, sp, st,* as in *ascribe, aspire, astringent.*

a-[4] the form of **an-**[1] before consonants except *h,* as in *atonal.*

☛ A- meaning *not* is of Greek origin and is used in words taken directly, or through Latin, from Greek, as in *apathy.* It is also used as a naturalized English prefix in new formations, as in *achromatic.* **A-**, called alpha privative, corresponds to English **un-** and Latin **in-**.

a **1** ampere; amperes. **2** anode. **3** are. (100 sq. metres) **4** before. (for L *ante*)

a. **1** about. **2** acre. **3** adjective. **4** acting. **5** active. **6** accepted. **7** afternoon. **8** amateur. **9** alto. **10** ampere; amperes. **11** in the year. (for L *anno*) **12** anode. **13** anonymous. **14** before. (for L *ante*) **15** are. (100 sq. metres) **16** in heraldry, argent. **17** in sports, assist; assists.

A **1** Angstrom; Angstrom unit. **2** argon. **3** one of the four main blood groups. **4** the air element of the Canadian Forces.

A. absolute temperature.

AI or **A-I** *Informal.* A-one; first-class.

AA or **A.A.** **1** in psychology, achievement age. **2** Alcoholics Anonymous. **3** anti-aircraft.

AAA or **A.A.A.** **1** Amateur Athletic Association. **2** American Automobile Association.

aard·vark (ärd′värk′) *n.* a burrowing African mammal that eats ants and termites. [< Afrikaans < Du. *aarde* earth + *vark* pig]

ab-[1] *prefix.* from; away; away from; off, as in *abnormal, abduct, abjure.* Also: **a-** before *m, p, v;* **abs-** before *c, t.* [< L *ab-* < *ab,* prep.]

ab-[2] the form of **ad-** before *b,* as in *abbreviate.*

Ab alabamine.

AB one of the four main blood groups.

A.B. *U.S.* Bachelor of Arts; B.A. (for L *Artium Baccalaureus*)

A.B. or **a.b.** able-bodied (seaman); able seaman.

a·ba·cá or **a·ba·ca** (ä′bə kä′ or ä′bə ko′) *n.* **1** hemp made from the fibres of a Philippine banana plant; Manila hemp. **2** the plant itself. [< Malay]

a·back (ə bak′) *adv.* **1** *Archaic.* toward the back; backward. **2** **taken aback,** suddenly surprised; upset or confused by something unexpected. [OE *on bæc*]

ab·a·cus (ab′ə kəs) *n.* **-cus·es** or **-ci** (-sī′ or -sē′). **1** a frame having rows of counters or beads that slide back and forth in grooves or on wires, used in calculating. See picture in the opposite column. **2** in architecture, a slab forming the top of the capital of a column. [< L < Gk. *abax, abacos*]

a·baft (ə baft′) *prep.* back of; behind. —*adv.* at the stern; toward the stern. [< *a-* on + ME *baft,* OE *beæftan* < *be* by + *æftan* behind]

ab·a·lo·ne (ab′ə lō′nē) *n.* an edible mollusc of the snail family, having a large, rather flat shell, found on the Pacific coast. The bright-colored lining of its shell is made into buttons and ornaments. [< Am.Sp. *abulón*]

a·ban·don[1] (ə ban′dən) *v.* **1** give up entirely: *abandon a career.* **2** leave without intending to return; desert: *abandon one's home.* **3** yield (oneself) completely (to a feeling, impulse, etc.): *abandon oneself to grief.* [ME < OF *abandoner,* earlier *a ban doner* give over to another's jurisdiction < *a* to (< L *ad*) + *ban* power (< Gmc.) + *doner* give < L *donare* grant < *donum* gift] —**a·ban′don·er,** *n.* —**Syn. 1** relinquish. **2** See **desert**[2].

a·ban·don[2] (ə ban′dən) *n.* freedom from restraint: *The students cheered with abandon, waving their arms and shouting.* [< F]

a·ban·doned (ə ban′dənd) *adj.* **1** deserted; forsaken. **2** shamelessly wicked; immoral: *an abandoned woman.*

a·ban·don·ment (ə ban′dən mənt) *n.* **1** an abandoning. **2** a being abandoned. **3** freedom from restraint; abandon.

a·base (ə bās′) *v.* **a·based, a·bas·ing.** make lower in rank, condition, or character; humiliate; degrade: *The prince abased himself by menial work.* [ME < OF *abaissier* bring low < LL *bassus* low]

a·base·ment (ə bās′mənt) *n.* humiliation; degradation.

a·bash (ə bash′) *v.* embarrass and confuse; make uneasy or shy and slightly ashamed: *The boys were abashed when the teacher pointed out all their mistakes.* [ME < OF *esbaïss-,* a stem of *esbaïr* be astonished < VL *batare* gape] —**a·bash′ment,** *n.* —**Syn.** chagrin.

a·bate (ə bāt′) *v.* **a·bat·ed, a·bat·ing.** **1** become less violent, intense, etc.: *The storm has abated.* **2** make less in amount, intensity, etc.: *The medicine abated his pain.* **3** put an end to (a nuisance, an action, or a writ). **4** deduct as part of a price. **5** omit. [ME < OF *abatre* beat down < *a-* to (< L *ad-*) + *batre* beat < VL *battere* < L *battuere*] —**a·bat′er,** *n.* —**Syn. 1, 2** decrease, diminish. **3** stop.

a·bate·ment (ə bāt′mənt) *n.* **1** a decrease; lessening. **2** a putting an end to. **3** the amount abated; reduction.

ab·a·tis (ab′ə tis) *n.* **ab·a·tis.** **1** a barricade of trees cut down and placed with their sharpened branches directed toward the enemy. **2** a barricade of barbed wire. [< F *abatis* mass of things thrown down]

ab·at·toir (ab′ə twär′ or ab′ə twär′) *n.* a slaughterhouse. [< F]

ab·ba·cy (ab′ə sē) *n.* **-cies.** **1** the position or power of an abbot. **2** the term of office of an abbot. **3** a district ruled by an abbot. [< LL *abbatia* < *abbas* abbot. See ABBOT.]

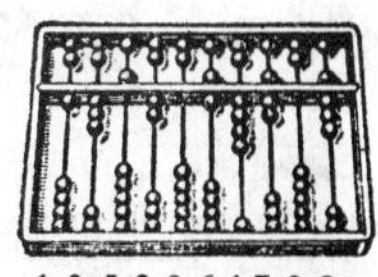

An abacus. The beads above the bar count 5 each when lowered. The beads below the bar count 1 each when raised. In the picture, the beads are set for 1,352,064,708.

Ab·bas·side (ə bas′īd or ab′ə sīd′) *n.* any of the caliphs of Baghdad belonging to the dynasty supposed to be descended from Abbas (A.D. 566-652), uncle and helper of Mohammed. This dynasty ruled the Moslem empire from A.D. 750 to 1258.

ab·bé (ab′ā or a bā′) *n. French.* **1** a priest. **2** an abbot. **3** in France, a title of respect given to any person entitled to wear clerical dress.

ab·bess (ab′is or ab′es) *n.* the woman in charge of an abbey of nuns. [ME < OF < LL *abbatissa* < *abbas, abbatis* abbot + *-issa* Gk. fem. suffix. See ABBOT.]

ab·bey (ab′ē) *n.* **-beys.** **1** the building or buildings where monks or nuns live a religious life ruled by an abbot or abbess; a monastery or convent. 2 the monks or nuns living there. 3 a church or residence that was once an abbey or a part of an abbey: *Westminster Abbey.* [ME < OF < LL *abbatia* < *abbas, -atis* abbot. See ABBOT.]

ab·bot (ab′ət) *n.* the man in charge of an abbey of monks. [OE *abbad, abbod* < LL *abbas, -atis* < LGk. < Aramaic *abbā* father]

abbrev. or **abbr.** 1 abbreviation. 2 abbreviated.

ab·bre·vi·ate (ə brē′vē āt′) *v.* **-at·ed, -at·ing.** 1 make (a word or phrase) shorter so that a part stands for the whole: *We can abbreviate "Alberta" to "Alta."* 2 make briefer: *Shortage of time forced us to abbreviate our shopping list.* [< L *abbreviare* < *ad-* to + *brevis* short. Doublet of ABRIDGE.] —**ab·bre′vi·a′tor,** *n.* —**Syn.** 2 condense. See **shorten.**

ab·bre·vi·a·tion (ə brē′vē ā′shən) *n.* 1 a shortened form of a word or phrase standing for the whole, such as *Ont.* for *Ontario* or *M.P.* for *Member of Parliament.* 2 a making shorter.

☛ **period with abbreviations.** As a general rule, a period is used after an abbreviation. There is a growing tendency today not to use a period after an abbreviation that ends with the last letter of the word abbreviated, that is, a form which really is a contraction: *Dr, Mr, Mrs, vs, Wm.* This practice is more common in British than in Canadian and American usage.

ABC American Broadcasting Company.

A B C (ā′bē′sē′) *n.* 1 the alphabet. 2 elementary principles; the part to be learned first.

A.B.C. book a primer.

A B C's (ā′bē′sēz′) *n.pl.* the alphabet.

ab·di·cate (ab′də kāt′) *v.* **-cat·ed, -cat·ing.** 1 give up or renounce formally; resign: *When the king abdicated his throne, his brother became king.* 2 renounce office or power: *Why did the king abdicate?* 3 withdraw oneself (*from*): *abdicate from pleasure or amusement.* [< L *abdicare* < *ab-* away + *dicare* proclaim] —**ab′di·ca′tor,** *n.*

ab·di·ca·tion (ab′də kā′shən) *n.* an abdicating; the giving up of an office, power, or authority; resigning.

ab·do·men (ab′də mən or ab dō′mən) *n.* 1 in anatomy, the part of the body containing the stomach, the intestines, and other digestive organs; belly. 2 the outer front surface of this. 3 of insects and crustaceans, the last of the three parts of the body. [< L]

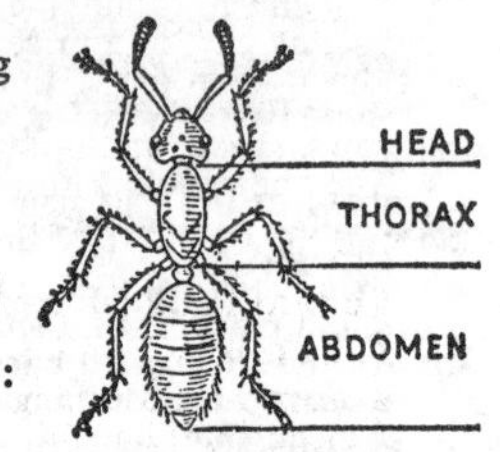

The three parts of an insect's body

ab·dom·i·nal (ab dom′ə nəl) *adj.* of, in, or for the abdomen: *the abdominal muscles.* —**ab·dom′i·nal·ly,** *adv.*

ab·dom·i·nous (ab dom′ə nəs) *adj.* potbellied.

ab·duct (ab dukt′) *v.* 1 carry off (a person) unlawfully and by force; kidnap. 2 in physiology, draw (a part of the body) away from its normal position. [< L *abductus,* pp. of *abducere* < *ab-* away + *ducere* lead] —**ab·duc′tion,** *n.*

ab·duc·tor (ab duk′tər) *n.* 1 a kidnapper; a person who abducts. 2 in physiology, a muscle that pulls a part of the body away from its normal position.

a·beam (ə bēm′) *adv.* 1 directly opposite to the middle part of a ship's side. 2 straight across a ship.

a·bed (ə bed′) *adv.* in bed.

A·bel (ā′bəl) *n.* in the Bible, the second son of Adam and Eve, killed in jealousy by his older brother Cain. Gen. 4:1-15.

Ab·e·na·ki (ab′ə nak′ē) *n.* **-ki** or **-kis.** 1 a loosely organized tribe of Indians formerly occupying northeastern Maine and southern Quebec. Some Abenaki are now living on reserves in Quebec. 2 a member of such a tribe. 3 an Algonquian language used by the Abenaki, Penobscot, etc. Also, **Abnaki.** [< Algonquin, literally, those living at the east, or easterners]

Aberdeen Angus (ab′ər dēn′ ang′gəs) 1 a breed of small, entirely black, hornless beef cattle. 2 an animal of this breed.

Ab·er·do·ni·an (ab′ər dō′nē ən) *adj.* of or having to do with Aberdeen or its people. —*n.* a native or inhabitant of Aberdeen.

ab·er·rance (ab er′əns) *n.* a wandering from what is regular, normal, or right.

ab·er·rant (ab er′ənt) *adj.* deviating from what is regular, normal, or right. —*n.* a person who deviates from normal behavior. [< L *aberrans, -antis,* ppr. of *aberrare* < *ab-* away + *errare* wander]

ab·er·ra·tion (ab′ər ā′shən) *n.* 1 a wandering from the right path or usual course of action. 2 a deviation from a standard or ordinary type; abnormal structure or development. 3 a temporary mental disorder. 4 in physics, the failure of a lens or mirror to bring to a single focus the rays of light coming from one point. Aberration causes a blurred image or an image with a colored rim. 5 in astronomy, a slight change in the apparent position of a heavenly body, caused by the combined effect of the earth's motion and of light.

a·bet (ə bet′) *v.* **a·bet·ted, a·bet·ting.** encourage or help, especially in doing something wrong: *One man did the actual stealing, but two others abetted him.* [ME < OF *abeter* arouse < *a-* to + *beter* to bait] —**a·bet′ment,** *n.* —**a·bet′tor, a·bet′ter,** *n.* —**Syn.** support.

a·bey·ance (ə bā′əns) *n.* 1 temporary inactivity; a state of suspended action: *The judge held the question in abeyance until he had the information necessary to make a decision.* 2 in law, a lapse in succession of title until ownership or possession is established: *The inheritance was in abeyance until the rightful owner came forward.* [< AF *abeiance* expectation < L *ad-* at + VL *batare* gape]

ab·hor (ab hôr′) *v.* **-horred, -hor·ring.** shrink from with horror; feel disgust or hate for; detest: *Some people abhor liquor.* [< L *abhorrere* < *ab-* from + *horrere* dread] —**ab·hor′rer,** *n.* —**Syn.** loathe, abominate. See **hate.**

ab·hor·rence (ab hôr′əns) *n.* a feeling of horror; disgust.

ab·hor·rent (ab hôr′ənt) *adj.* causing horror; disgusting; hateful. —**ab·hor′rent·ly,** *adv.*

a·bide (ə bīd′) *v.* **a·bode** or **a·bid·ed, a·bid·ing.** 1 stay; remain: *"Though much is taken, much abides."* 2 dwell; continue to live (in a place). 3 put up with; endure; tolerate: *A good housekeeper cannot abide dirt.* 4 stand firm. 5 wait for: *He shall abide my coming.* 6 **abide by, a** accept and follow out. **b** remain faithful to; fulfil: *You must abide by your promise.* [OE *ābīdan* stay on, and *onbidan* wait for] —**a·bid′er,** *n.* —**Syn.** 3 bear, stand.

a·bid·ing (ə bīd′ing) *adj.* permanent; continuing; lasting.

ab·i·gail (ab′ə gāl′) *n.* a lady's maid. [< *Abigail,* a character in Beaumont and Fletcher's play *The Scornful Lady*]

a·bil·i·ty (ə bil′ə tē) *n.* **-ties.** 1 the power to perform or accomplish: *He has the ability to hold an audience spellbound.* 2 skill: *He has great ability as a hockey player.* 3 the power to do some special thing; mental gift; talent: *Musical ability often shows itself early in life.* [< F *habilité* < L *habilitas* < *habilis* apt, fit, easily handled]

Syn. 3. **Ability, talent** = power to do or for doing something. **Ability** applies to a demonstrated physical or mental power, which may be either natural or acquired, to do a certain thing well: *He has unusual ability in science.* **Talent** applies to a capacity for doing a special thing, which is inborn in a person, never acquired, and which is or can be developed through training and use: *His Scout activities revealed a talent for leadership, which he is developing at school this year.*

☛ A verb following **ability** is in the infinitive form and is always preceded by *to*: *He has the ability to swim like a fish,* not: *He has the ability of swimming like a fish.*

ab in·i·tio (ab′ in ish′ē ō) *Latin.* from the beginning.

ab·ject (ab′jekt) *adj.* 1 wretched; miserable: *abject poverty.* 2 deserving contempt; degraded: *an abject flatterer.* 3 slavish: *abject submission.* [< L *abjectus,* pp. of *abjicere* < *ab-* down + *jacere* throw] —**ab·ject′ly,** *adv.* —**Syn.** 2 contemptible, despicable.

ab·ju·ra·tion (ab′jü rā′shən) *n.* an abjuring.

ab·jure (ab jür′) *v.* **-jured, -jur·ing.** renounce on oath;

repudiate; swear to give up: *abjure one's religion.* [< L *abjurare* < *ab-* away + *jurare* swear] —**ab·jur′er,** *n.*

abl. ablative.

ab·late (ab lāt′) *v.* **-lat·ed, -lat·ing. 1** remove by burning off; wear down; cut away. **2** in astronautics, **a** carry away (heat) by vaporizing or melting. **b** lose heat by being vaporized or melted. [< L *ablatus,* literally, having been carried away, pp. of *auferre* carry away]

ab·la·tion (ab lā′shən) *n.* **1** the removal of an organ by surgery. **2** in geology, the erosion of rocks or glaciers, especially by melting or evaporation. **3** in astronautics, the removal of heat by vaporizing or melting.

ab·la·tive (ab′lə tiv) *n.* in grammar: **1** the case that expresses place from which, place in which, source, agent, cause, association, or instrument. **2** a word or construction in this case. *Abbrev.*: abl. [< L *ablativus,* literally, of removal < *ablatus,* pp. of *auferre* < *ab-* away + *ferre* carry]

☛ **ablative case.** The work done in Latin by ablative case endings is done in English by the prepositions *at, by, from, in,* and *with* placed before the noun: *at the store, by the thief.*

ab·laut (ab′lout; *German,* äp′lout) *n.* the substitution of one root vowel sound for another, often accompanying a modification of use or meaning, as in *ring, rang, rung.* [< G *Ablaut* < *ab-* off + *Laut* sound]

a·blaze (ə blāz′) *adv. adj.* on fire; blazing; brightly lit.

a·ble (ā′bəl) *adj.* **a·bler, a·blest. 1** having power, skill, means, or talent; competent: *Little children are able to walk, but they are not able to earn a living.* **2** having the necessary qualifications; skilful; competent: *an able seaman.* **3** having more power or skill than most others have; clever: *She is an able teacher.* **4** competently done: *an able speech.* [ME < OF *hable, able* < L *habilis* fit, easily held or handled < *habere* hold]

Syn. 1 Able, capable, competent = having sufficient power to do or for doing something. **Able** (with *to*) emphasizes power to act or perform: *He is able to play the piano.* **Capable** emphasizes fitness for doing, capacity or ability to do something adequately, or, sometimes, general efficiency: *He has proved himself capable both as soldier and as administrator.* **Competent** emphasizes possession of sufficient skill or other requirements to do a certain kind of work satisfactorily: *A competent typist is not necessarily a competent secretary.* 3 expert, skilful. 4 effective.

☛ *Able* and *competent* may be followed by *to* plus an infinitive, but *capable* takes *of* plus a gerund: *able to think, competent to drive a car, capable of taking responsibility.*

-able *suffix.* **1** that can be —ed; able to be —ed: *obtainable = that can be obtained.* **2** likely to or suitable for: *comfortable = suitable for comfort.* **3** inclined to: *peaceable = inclined to peace.* **4** deserving to be —ed: *lovable = deserving to be loved.* See **-ible.** [< F < L *-abilis,* a suffix forming adjectives from verbs with infinitives in *-are,* being one form of the suffix *-bilis*]

☛ Instead of **-able**, a number of words have the spelling **-ible**, which originally belonged largely to words from Latin infinitives in *-ere* or *-ire* (as in *terrible*). *-able* is the living suffix and should be used in coining occasional words like *jumpable*. *-able* is attached to verbs (*actable*), nouns (*actionable*), and even verbal phrases (*get-at-able*) to form adjectives.

a·ble-bod·ied (ā′bəl bod′ēd) *adj.* physically fit; strong and healthy.

able-bodied seaman an experienced sailor who can perform all the ordinary duties of a sailor. *Abbrev.*: A.B. or a.b.

able seaman in the navy, a man senior to an ordinary seaman and junior to a leading seaman. *Abbrev.*: A.B. or a.b.

a·bloom (ə blüm′) *adv. adj.* in bloom; blossoming.

ab·lu·tion (ab lü′shən) *n.* **1** a washing of one's person. **2** a washing or cleansing as a religious ceremony of purification. **3** the water or other liquid used in washing. [< L *ablutio, -onis* < *abluere* < *ab-* away + *lavere* wash]

a·bly (ā′blē) *adv.* in an able manner; with skill.

Ab·na·ki (ab nak′ē) *n.* **-ki** or **-kis.** Abenaki.

ab·ne·gate (ab′nə gāt′) *v.* **-gat·ed, -gat·ing.** deny (anything) to oneself; renounce or give up (a privilege). [< L *abnegare* < *ab-* off, away + *negare* deny] —**ab′ne·ga′tion,** *n.*

ab·nor·mal (ab nôr′məl) *adj.* deviating from the normal, the standard, or a type; markedly irregular; unusual: *It is abnormal for a man to be seven feet tall.*

hat, āge, cãre, fär; let, ēqual, tėrm; it, īce
hot, ōpen, ôrder; oil, out; cup, pu̇t, rüle, ūse
əbove, takən, pencəl, lemən, circəs
ch, child; ng, long; sh, ship
th, thin; ᴛʜ, then; zh, measure

—**ab·nor′mal·ly,** *adv.* —**ab·nor′mal·ness,** *n.* —**Syn.** exceptional. See **irregular.**

ab·nor·mal·i·ty (ab′nôr mal′ə tē) *n.* **-ties. 1** an abnormal thing or happening. **2** an abnormal condition.

a·board (ə bôrd′) *adv.* **1** in or on a ship. **2** in or on a train, bus, airplane, etc. **3 all aboard,** everybody on (conductor's call directing passengers to enter a train, bus, etc. about to start). **4** alongside: *The yacht lay close aboard.* —*prep.* on board of; on, in, or into (a ship, train, etc.).

a·bode (ə bōd′) *n.* a place to live in; dwelling; residence. —*v.* a pt. and a pp. of **abide.** [OE *ābād*]

a·boi·deau (ab′ə dō′; *French,* ä bwä dō′) *n.* **-deaus** or **-deaux** (-dōz′; *French,* -dō′). *Cdn.* **1** in Nova Scotia and New Brunswick, a sluice-gate in the dikes along the Bay of Fundy. **2** the dike itself. [< Cdn.F]

a·boi·teau (ab′ə tō′; *French,* ä bwä tō′) *n.* **-teaus** or **-teaux** (-tōz′; *French,* tō′). *Cdn.* aboideau. [< Cdn.F]

a·bol·ish (ə bol′ish) *v.* do away with (a law, institution, or custom) completely; put an end to: *abolish slavery.* [< F *aboliss-,* stem of *abolir*; fusion of two verbs, L *abolere* destroy, and L *abolescere* die out] —**a·bol′ish·ment,** *n.*

Syn. Abolish, annihilate, extinguish = put an end to something. **Abolish** applies only to man-made things, usually long in existence, such as laws and customs: *Many countries have abolished hanging.* **Annihilate,** more general in application, suggests use of force and always retains its literal meaning of reducing to nothing, by wiping something out without a trace or by destroying its distinguishing qualities or form: *The enemy annihilated the regiment.* **Extinguish** applies to things or ideas which can be caused to die or be blotted out by overpowering force or circumstances: *You may extinguish a nation, but not the love of liberty.*

ab·o·li·tion (ab′ə lish′ən) *n.* **1** an abolishing or being abolished; complete destruction. **2** *U.S.* the suppression of Negro slavery. [< L *abolitio, -onis*]

ab·o·li·tion·ist (ab′ə lish′ən ist) *n.* a person who wishes to abolish something. The people who wished to put an end to slavery were called abolitionists.

ab·o·ma·sum (ab′ə mā′səm) *n.* the fourth stomach of cows, sheep, and other animals that chew the cud. The abomasum is the stomach that digests the food. [< NL < L *ab-* away from + *omasum* bullock's tripe]

ab·o·ma·sus (ab′ə mā′səs) *n.* abomasum.

A-bomb (ā′bom′) *n.* atomic bomb.

a·bom·i·na·ble (ə bom′ə nə bəl or ə bom′nə bəl) *adj.* **1** disgusting; hateful; causing hatred. **2** very unpleasant; distasteful: *an abominable error.* [< F < L *abominabilis* < *abominari.* See ABOMINATE.] —**a·bom′i·na·ble·ness,** *n.* —**a·bom′i·na·bly,** *adv.* —**Syn. 1** detestable, odious, revolting.

abominable snowman a manlike monster supposed to inhabit the higher parts of the Himalaya mountains, where huge footprints have been found in the snow. It is called "yeti" by the native Sherpa tribe.

a·bom·i·nate (ə bom′ə nāt′) *v.* **-nat·ed, -nat·ing. 1** feel disgust for; hate very much; abhor; detest. **2** dislike. [< L *abominari* deplore as an ill omen < *ab-* off + *ominari* prophesy < *omen, ominis* omen] —**a·bom′i·na′tor,** *n.* —**Syn. 1** loathe, despise.

a·bom·i·na·tion (ə bom′ə nā′shən) *n.* **1** a revolting thing: *Anything that degrades man is an abomination.* **2** a shamefully wicked action or custom. **3** a feeling of disgust; hate; loathing.

ab·o·rig·i·nal (ab′ə rij′ə nəl) *adj.* **1** existing from the beginning; first; original; native: *aboriginal inhabitants.* **2** of the earliest known inhabitants: *The use of horses was not aboriginal to the American Indians but was introduced by Europeans.* —*n.* an aborigine. —**ab′o·rig′i·nal·ly,** *adv.*

ab·o·rig·i·ne (ab′ə rij′ə nē′) *n.* **1** one of the earliest known inhabitants of a country. **2** in Australia, one of the native inhabitants. [< L *aborigines* < *ab origine* from the beginning]

☛ In the singular both **aborigine** and **aboriginal** are used, but in the plural **aborigines** is more common than **aboriginals.**

a·bort (ə bôrt′) *v.* **1** in medicine, give birth or cause to give birth to (offspring) prematurely, especially during the first twelve weeks of pregnancy. **2** in biology, fail to develop beyond the elementary stage. **3** end prematurely; fail to develop. [< L *abortus,* pp. of *aboriri* < *ab-* amiss + *oriri* be born]

a·bor·tion (ə bôr′shən) *n.* **1** in medicine, the act of delivering, or of causing to deliver, a human embryo before it is able to live, especially during the first twelve weeks of pregnancy. **2** in biology, a failure to develop; an imperfect development. **3** a plan, idea, etc. that fails to develop properly.

a·bor·tive (ə bôr′tiv) *adj.* **1** coming to nothing; unsuccessful; fruitless: *The early attempts to make airplanes were abortive.* **2** born before the right time; born prematurely. **3** not developed properly; rudimentary. **4** causing abortion. *—n.* a drug, etc. that causes abortion. **—a·bor′tive·ly,** *adv.* **—a·bor′tive·ness,** *n.*

a·bound (ə bound′) *v.* **1** be plentiful: *Fish abound in the ocean.* **2** be rich (*in*): *Alberta abounds in oil.* **3** be well supplied; be filled (*with*): *The ocean abounds with fish.* [ME < OF *abunder* < L *abundare* < *ab-* off + *undare* rise in waves < *unda* a wave]

a·bout (ə bout′) *prep.* **1** of; having to do with: *a book about bridges.* **2** in connection with: *something queer about him.* **3** somewhere near; not far from: *The dog was about the house.* **4** approximating; near: *He is about my size.* **5** on every side of; all around; around: *a fence about the garden.* **6** on (one's person); with: *She has no money about her.* **7** in many parts of; everywhere in: *scatter papers about the room.*
—adv. **1** nearly; almost: *The buckets and tubs are about full.* **2** somewhere near: *A tramp has been hanging about.* **3** all around; in every direction: *The boy looked about.* **4** in many places; here and there: *A rumor went about that he was ill.* **5** in the opposite direction: *Face about! After swimming a mile, the boys turned about and swam back to the shore.* **6** doing; working at: *An expert worker knows what he is about.* **7** one after another; by turns: *Turn about is fair play.* **8** stirring: *able to be up and about.* **9 about to,** on the point of; going, intending, or ready to: *The plane is about to take off.* [OE *onbūtan* on the outside of]

☛ **about (at about).** When we wish to approximate in a statement of time, we use either *about* or, in informal style, *at about,* meaning "somewhere near": *The game started about three o'clock. The play will be over at about eleven o'clock.* When we wish to be more precise, we use *at,* meaning "neither earlier nor later than": *I have an appointment to see the doctor at two o'clock.*

a·bout-face (*n.* ə bout′fās′; *v.* ə bout′fās′) *n. v.* **-faced, -fac·ing.** *—n.* a turning or going in the opposite direction. *—v.* turn or go in the opposite direction.

about turn a command to face in the opposite direction.

a·bove (ə buv′) *adv.* **1** overhead; in a higher place: *The sky is above.* **2** on the upper side or on top: *The leaves are dark above and light below.* **3** higher in rank or power: *the courts above.* **4** in or from a direction thought of as higher: *There's good fishing above.* **5** earlier, in a book or article: *as mentioned above.* **6** in heaven.
—prep. **1** in or to a higher place than: *Birds fly above the trees.* **2** higher than; over: *He kept his head above water. A captain is above a sergeant.* **3** too high in dignity or character for; superior to: *A great person should be above mean actions.* **4** more than: *The weight is above a ton.* **5** beyond: *Turn at the first corner above the school.*
—adj. **1** made or mentioned above: *the above remark.* **2** above zero: *The temperature is five above.*
—n. **the above,** something that is written above.
[OE *abufan*] **—Syn.** *prep.* **1, 2** See **over.**

a·bove·board (ə buv′bôrd′) *adv. adj.* in open sight; without tricks or concealment: *The official was aboveboard in his conduct.*

a·bove-men·tioned (ə buv′men′shənd) *adj.* previously referred to; mentioned earlier.

ab o·vo (ab′ō′vō) *Latin.* from the beginning. [< L *ab ovo* from the egg]

Abp. Archbishop.

abr. abridged.

ab·ra·ca·dab·ra (ab′rə kə dab′rə) *n.* **1** a word supposed to have magic power, used in incantations or as a charm to ward off disease. **2** meaningless talk; jargon. [< LL]

a·brade (ə brād′) *v.* **a·brad·ed, a·brad·ing.** wear away by rubbing; scrape off: *The skin on Tom's knees was abraded by his fall.* [< L *abradere* < *ab-* off + *radere* scrape]

A·bra·ham, Plains of (ā′brə ham′) a plain outside and just west of Quebec City, the site of the battle, in 1759, that gave the British supremacy in North America.

a·bra·sion (ə brā′zhən) *n.* **1** a place scraped or worn by rubbing: *Abrasions of the skin are painful.* **2** a scraping off; a wearing away by rubbing. [< L *abrasio, -onis* < *abradere.* See ABRADE.]

a·bra·sive (ə brā′siv or ə brā′ziv) *n.* a substance used for grinding, smoothing, or polishing. Sandpaper, pumice, and emery are abrasives. *—adj.* wearing away by rubbing; causing abrasion. **—a·bra′sive·ly,** *adv.* **—a·bra′sive·ness,** *n.*

a·breast (ə brest′) *adv. adj.* **1** side by side: *The soldiers marched three abreast.* **2 abreast of** or **abreast with,** up with; alongside of: *Keep abreast of what is going on.*

a·bri (ä brē′) *n.* **a·bris** (ä brē′) *French.* a shelter.

a·bridge (ə brij′) *v.* **a·bridged, a·bridg·ing. 1** make shorter, especially by using fewer words: *A long story can be abridged by leaving out unimportant parts.* **2** make less: *The rights of citizens must not be abridged without proper cause.* **3** deprive (*of*): *abridge citizens of their rights.* [ME < OF *abregier* < L *abbreviare* shorten. Doublet of ABBREVIATE.] **—a·bridg′a·ble** or **a·bridge′a·ble,** *adj.*

a·bridg·ment or **a·bridge·ment** (ə brij′mənt) *n.* **1** a shortened form, especially of a book or long article: *This book is an abridgment of a three-volume history.* **2** a making shorter; an abridging.

a·broad (ə brod′ or ə brôd′) *adv.* **1** outside one's country; to a foreign land; in foreign lands: *Go abroad.* **2** out in the open: *He walks abroad only at night.* **3** going around; current: *A rumor is abroad that school will close.* **4** far and wide; widely: *The news of his coming spread abroad.*

ab·ro·gate (ab′rə gāt′) *v.* **-gat·ed, -gat·ing. 1** abolish or annul (a law or custom) by legislation; repeal. **2** do away with. [< L *abrogare* < *ab-* away + *rogare* demand] **—ab′ro·ga′tion,** *n.* **—ab′ro·ga′tor,** *n.*

a·brupt (ə brupt′) *adj.* **1** sudden; hasty; unexpected: *an abrupt turn.* **2** very steep. **3** short or sudden in speech or manner; blunt. **4** disconnected: *an abrupt rhythm, an abrupt style.* **5** in botany, coming to an end suddenly; truncate: *the abrupt top of a tulip-tree leaf.* [< L *abruptus,* pp. of *abrumpere* < *ab-* off + *rumpere* break] **—a·brupt′ly,** *adv.* **—a·brupt′ness,** *n.*
—Syn. 2 See **steep. 3** brusque, curt.

abs- the form of **ab-**^{1} before *c* and *t* as in *abscond, abstain.*

abs. 1 absent. **2** absolute. **3** absolute temperature. **4** abstract.

Ab·sa·lom (ab′sə ləm) *n.* in the Bible, David's favorite son, who rebelled against his father. II Samuel 18.

ab·scess (ab′ses) *n.* a collection of pus in the tissues of some part of the body. An abscess results from an infection and usually makes a painful sore. [< L *abscessus* < *abscedere* < *ab-* away + *cedere* go]

ab·scessed (ab′sest) *adj.* having an abscess.

ab·scis·sa (ab sis′ə) *n.* **-scis·sas** or **-scis·sae** (-sis′ē or -sis′ī). in geometry, the line running from left to right on a graph that defines a point in a system of co-ordinates. In the diagram, the abscissa of the point P is the distance NP measured on the line X^1X. [< L (*linea*) *abscissa* (line) cut off < pp. stem (*ab*)*sciss-* of (*ab*)*scindere* cut]

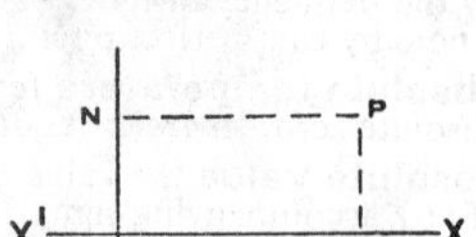

ab·scond (ab skond′) *v.* go away suddenly and secretly; go off and hide: *The dishonest cashier absconded with the bank's money.* [< L *abscondere* < *ab-* away + *condere* store] —**ab·scond′er,** *n.*

ab·sence (ab′səns) *n.* **1** a being away: *absence from work.* **2** the time of being away: *an absence of two weeks.* **3** a being without; lack: *Darkness is the absence of light.* **4** absent-mindedness.

absence of mind absent-mindedness.

ab·sent (*adj.* ab′sənt; *v.* ab sent′) *adj.* **1** not present; away: *John is absent from class today.* **2** not existing; lacking: *Snow is absent in some countries.* **3** absent-minded. —*v.* take or keep (oneself) away: *absent oneself from class.* [< L *absens, -entis*, ppr. of *abesse* < *ab-* away + *esse* to be]

ab·sen·tee (ab′sən tē′) *n.* a person who is absent or remains absent. —*adj.* of or for a voter or voters permitted to vote while absent from home.

ab·sen·tee·ism (ab′sən tē′iz əm) *n.* **1** the practice or habit of being an absentee. **2** an economic system under which a landowner controls the use of land in a country or place where he does not live.

absentee landlord a landowner who draws an income from his land but lives in another part of the country, or in another country.

ab·sent·ly (ab′sənt lē) *adv.* without paying attention to what is going on around one; inattentively.

ab·sent-mind·ed (ab′sənt mīn′did) *adj.* not paying attention to what is going on around one; inattentive. —**ab′sent-mind′ed·ly,** *adv.* —**ab′sent-mind′ed·ness,** *n.*

ab·sinthe or **ab·sinth** (ab′sinth) *n.* a bitter, green alcoholic drink flavored with wormwood and anise. [< F *absinthe* < L < Gk. *apsinthion* wormwood]

ab·sit o·men (ab′sit ō′mən) *Latin.* may there be no ill omen.

ab·so·lute (ab′sə lüt′) *adj.* **1** complete; whole; entire: *absolute ignorance.* **2** not mixed with anything else; pure. **3** free from imperfection; perfect: *absolute purity.* **4** with no limits or restrictions: *absolute liberty.* **5** not compared with anything else: *absolute velocity.* **6** real; actual. **7** certain; infallible: *absolute proof.* **8** in grammar: **a** forming a part of a sentence, but not connected with it grammatically. In "The train being late, we missed the boat," *the train being late* is an absolute phrase. **b** used without an expressed object. In "I will not ask again," *ask* is an absolute verb. **c** having its noun understood, but not expressed. In "The older pupils may help the younger," *younger* is an absolute adjective. In "Your house is larger than ours," *ours* is an absolute pronoun. **9** in physics, of or having to do with absolute temperature. 273° absolute is the same as 0° centigrade. •
—*n.* **the absolute,** that which is absolute; the fundamental, all-including reality, thought of as apart from all special relations or conditions. [< L *absolutus*, pp. of *absolvere.* See ABSOLVE.] —**ab′so·lute′ness,** *n.*

absolute alcohol ethyl alcohol that contains not more than one percent by weight of water.

ab·so·lute·ly (ab′sə lüt′lē *for 1, 2;* ab′sə lüt′lē *for 3*) *adv.* **1** completely. **2** positively. **3** *Informal.* yes: "*Are you going to the game?*" "*Absolutely!*"
☛ In speech **absolutely** has become generalized to mean "positively" or "quite": *He is absolutely the finest fellow I know.* As an answer to a question it usually means "yes." It is sometimes a useful word to put force into dialogue, but it would be out of place in most writing except in its original meaning of "completely."

absolute monarchy a monarchy in which the ruler has unlimited power.

absolute pitch **1** the pitch of a tone determined solely by the frequency of its vibrations. **2** the ability to identify a note by ear; perfect pitch.

absolute temperature temperature measured from absolute zero. *Abbrev.*: A. or abs.

absolute value the value of a real number regardless of any accompanying sign: *The absolute value of +5, or −5, is 5.*

absolute zero the temperature at which substances would have no heat whatever, and all molecules would stop moving. Theoretically, it is −273.15° centigrade or −459.67° Fahrenheit.

hat, āge, cãre, fär; let, ēqual, tėrm; it, īce
hot, ōpen, ôrder; oil, out; cup, pu̇t, rüle, ūse
əbove, takən, pencəl, lemən, circəs
ch, child; ng, long; sh, ship
th, thin; ᴛʜ, then; zh, measure

ab·so·lu·tion (ab′sə lü′shən) *n.* **1** in ecclesiastical use: **a** a freeing or freedom from guilt and punishment for sin; forgiveness. A person who confesses and is sorry for his sins and promises to do penance is granted absolution by a priest. **b** a promise or declaration that frees a person from guilt and punishment for sin. **2** a freeing or freedom from guilt or blame. **3** a release from a duty or promise.

ab·so·lut·ism (ab′sə lüt iz′əm) *n.* **1** a system or form of government in which the power of the ruler is not restricted; despotism. **2** the quality of being absolute; positiveness. **3** in philosophy, belief in absolute idealism, which holds that all things are manifestations of one universal spirit.

ab·so·lut·ist (ab′sə lüt′ist) *n.* a person in favor of despotism or absolutism. —*adj.* despotic.

ab·solve (ab solv′ or ab zolv′) *v.* **-solved, -solv·ing.** **1** declare (a person) free from sin, guilt, or blame. **2** set free (from a promise or duty). [< L *absolvere* < *ab-* from + *solvere* loosen. Doublet of ASSOIL.] —**Syn. 1** exonerate, acquit. **2** release.

ab·sorb (ab sôrb′ or ab zôrb′) *v.* **1** take in or suck up (liquids): *A blotter absorbs ink.* **2** take in and make a part of itself; assimilate: *Canada has absorbed millions of immigrants.* **3** take up all the attention of; interest very much: *The circus absorbed the boys.* **4** take in and hold: *Anything black absorbs most of the light rays that fall on it; that is, few of the light rays are reflected from it.* **5** in biology, take (digested food, oxygen, etc.) into the blood stream by osmosis. **6** grasp with the mind; understand. **7** in business: **a** pay (a cost, tax, etc.) without adding it to the price of an article, etc.: *The manufacturer absorbed the new tax, and the prices remained the same.* **b** take up: *The market absorbed the whole production.* **8** take up the impact of (bumps, shocks, sound, etc.): *The ceiling insulation absorbed the noise of the children's party.* [< L *absorbere* < *ab-* from + *sorbere* suck in]
Syn. 2 Absorb, assimilate = take something in, both literally and as used figuratively with reference to ideas. **Absorb** = swallow up a thing so that it loses its individual character or disappears: *Large companies sometimes absorb smaller ones.* **Assimilate** adds to *absorb* the idea of converting what is absorbed into an essential part of what has taken it in: *A person who reads intelligently assimilates what he reads by making it a part of his own thinking.*

ab·sorbed (ab sôrbd′ or ab zôrbd′) *adj.* very much interested; completely occupied. —**ab·sorb′ed·ly,** *adv.*

ab·sorb·en·cy (ab sôr′bən sē or ab zôr′bən sē) *n.* **1** the quality of being absorbent. **2** the degree to which anything is absorbent. **3** the ability to be assimilated.

ab·sorb·ent (ab sôr′bənt or ab zôr′bənt) *adj.* absorbing or taking in liquids, light, heat, etc.: *Absorbent paper is used to dry the hands.* —*n.* any thing or substance that absorbs liquids, light, heat, etc.

ab·sorb·ing (ab sôr′bing or ab zôr′bing) *adj.* extremely interesting. —**ab·sorb′ing·ly,** *adv.*

ab·sorp·tion (ab sôrp′shən or ab zôrp′shən) *n.* **1** an absorbing; a taking up and holding. In the absorption of light rays by black objects the light rays are changed to heat. **2** a great interest (in something). **3** in biology, the process of taking (digested food, oxygen, etc.) into the blood stream by osmosis. [< L *absorptio, -onis* <*absorbere.* See ABSORB.]

ab·sorp·tive (ab sôrp′tiv or ab zôrp′tiv) *adj.* able to absorb. —**ab·sorp′tive·ness,** *n.*

ab·stain (ab stān′) *v.* **1** do without something voluntarily; refrain (*from*): *Athletes usually abstain from smoking.* **2** refrain, especially from voting: *The Conservatives voted in favor of the motion, but the Liberals abstained.* [< F *abstenir* < L *abstinere* < *ab-* off + *tenere* hold] —**Syn.** forbear, desist. See **refrain**[1].

ab·stain·er (ab stān′ər) *n.* a person who abstains, especially from the use of alcoholic liquor.

ab·ste·mi·ous (ab stē′mē əs) *adj.* sparing in eating and drinking; moderate; temperate. [< L *abstemius* < *ab-* off + *tem-*, root of *temetum* potent liquor] **—ab·ste′mi·ous·ly,** *adv.* **—ab·ste′mi·ous·ness,** *n.*

ab·sten·tion (ab sten′shən) *n.* an abstaining: *His abstention from voting was severely criticized.* [< F < L *abstentio, -onis* < *abstinere.* See ABSTAIN.]

ab·sti·nence (ab′stə nəns) *n.* **1** an abstaining; partly or entirely giving up certain pleasures, food, drink, etc. **2** in ecclesiastical use, the avoiding of certain foods, such as meat on Friday. **3 total abstinence,** a refraining from drinking any alcoholic liquor. [< L *abstinentia* < *abstinere.* See ABSTAIN.]

abs·ti·nent (ab′stə nənt) *adj.* abstemious.

ab·stract (*adj. n.* ab′strakt; *v.* ab strakt′ *for 1, 3, 4,* ab′strakt *for 2*) *adj.* **1** thought of apart from any particular object or real thing; not concrete: *A lump of sugar is real; the idea of sweetness is abstract.* **2** expressing a quality that is thought of apart from any particular object or real thing. In "Honesty is the best policy," *honesty* is an abstract noun. **3** not practical; ideal; theoretical. **4** hard to understand; difficult: *abstract theories about the nature of the soul.* **5** in art, having little or no apparent resemblance to reality.
—*v.* **1** think of (a quality, such as redness, weight, or truth) apart from any object or real thing having that quality. **2** make an abstract of; summarize. **3** remove, especially stealthily: *In the crowd a thief abstracted my watch from my pocket.* **4** withdraw (the attention).
—*n.* **1** a short statement giving the main ideas of an article, book, case in court, etc.; summary. **2 in the abstract,** in theory rather than in practice. [< L *abstractus,* pp. of *abstrahere* < *ab-* away + *trahere* draw] **—ab·stract′er,** *n.* **—ab′stract·ly,** *adv.* **—ab′stract·ness,** *n.*

ab·stract·ed (ab strak′tid) *adj.* lost in thought; absent-minded. **—ab·stract′ed·ly,** *adv.* **—Syn.** preoccupied.

ab·strac·tion (ab strak′shən) *n.* **1** the idea of a quality thought of apart from any particular object or real thing having that quality; abstract idea or term: *Whiteness, bravery, and length are abstractions. A line that has no width is only an abstraction.* **2** the formation of such an idea. **3** a taking away; removal: *After the abstraction of the juice from an orange, only the pulp and peel are left.* **4** the state of being lost in thought; absence of mind. **5** a work of abstract art.

ab·strac·tion·ism (ab strak′shən iz′əm) *n.* the processes or principles of abstract art.

ab·struse (ab strüs′) *adj.* hard to understand. [< L *abstrusus,* pp. of *abstrudere* < *ab-* away + *trudere* thrust] **—ab·struse′ly,** *adv.* **—ab·struse′ness,** *n.*

ab·surd (ab sėrd′ or ab zėrd′) *adj.* plainly not true or sensible; so contrary to reason that it is laughable; foolish; ridiculous. [< L *absurdus* out of tune, senseless] **—ab·surd′ly,** *adv.* **—ab·surd′ness,** *n.* **—Syn.** See **ridiculous.**

ab·surd·i·ty (ab sėr′də tē or ab zėr′də tē) *n.* **-ties.** **1** something absurd. **2** an absurd quality or condition; folly.

a·bun·dance (ə bun′dəns) *n.* a quantity that is more than enough; great plenty; full supply. [ME < OF < L *abundantia* < *abundare.* See ABOUND.] **—Syn.** profusion.

a·bun·dant (ə bun′dənt) *adj.* more than enough; very plentiful. **—a·bun′dant·ly,** *adv.*

a·buse (*v.* ə būz′; *n.* ə būs′) *v.* **a·bused, a·bus·ing,** *n.*
—*v.* **1** use wrongly; make bad use of; misuse: *abuse a privilege.* **2** treat badly; mistreat. **3** use harsh and insulting language to.
—*n.* **1** a wrong or bad use. **2** a harsh or severe treatment of a person. **3** harsh and insulting language. **4** a bad practice or custom: *Abuses multiply when citizens are indifferent.* [ME < OF *abuser* < L *abusus,* pp. of *abuti* use up, misuse < *ab-* away + *uti* use] **—a·bus′er,** *n.* **—Syn.** *v.* **2** maltreat. **3** revile.

a·bu·sive (ə bū′siv or ə bū′ziv) *adj.* **1** using harsh and insulting language; reviling. **2** containing abuse: *an abusive letter.* **3** abusing; treating badly. **—a·bu′sive·ly,** *adv.*

a·but (ə but′) *v.* **a·but·ted, a·but·ting. 1** touch at one end or edge; end (*on* or *against*): *The sidewalk abuts on the street. The street abuts against the railway.* **2** join at a boundary; border (*on* or *upon*): *His land abuts upon mine.* [< OF *abouter* join end to end (< *a-* to + *bout* end) and OF *abuter* touch with an end (< *a-* to + *but* end)]

a·but·ment (ə but′mənt) *n.* **1** in architecture, a support for an arch or bridge. **2** the point or place where a support joins the thing supported. **3** an abutting.

ABUTMENTS

These abutments support the arches and also turn aside strong currents that might weaken the structure.

a·but·ting (ə but′ing) *adj.* adjacent.

a·bysm (ə biz′əm) *n.* abyss. [ME *abime* < OF *abisme* < L *abyssus.* See ABYSS.]

a·bys·mal (ə biz′məl) *adj.* too deep to be measured; bottomless. **—a·bys′mal·ly,** *adv.*

a·byss (ə bis′) *n.* **1** a bottomless or immeasurably deep space. **2** anything too deep to be measured; lowest depth. **3** in the Bible, the chaos before the Creation. [< L < Gk. *abyssos* < *a-* without + *byssos* bottom]

a·byss·al (ə bis′əl) *adj.* **1** of or having to do with the lowest depths of the ocean. **2** unfathomable.

Ab·ys·sin·i·an (ab′ə sin′ē ən) *adj.* of or having to do with Abyssinia (Ethiopia), a country in E. Africa.
—*n.* **1** a native or inhabitant of Abyssinia (Ethiopia). **2** a breed of medium-sized cat having short, fine, silky hair that is light brown in color. **3** a cat of this breed.

ac- the form of **ad-** before *c* and *q*, as in *accede, acquaint.*

Ac **1** actinium. **2** in meteorology, alto-cumulus.

A/C or **a/c** account.

A.C. **1** Air Commodore. **2** Aircraftman.

A.C., a.c., or **a-c** alternating current.

a·ca·cia (ə kā′shə) *n.* **1** a tree or shrub having finely divided leaves, found in tropical or warm regions. Several kinds yield gum arabic; other kinds are useful for timber, dye, etc. **2** a thorny North American tree having white flowers; the locust tree. [< L < Gk. *akakia,* a thorny Egyptian tree]

acad. academy.

ac·a·dem·ic (ak′ə dem′ik) *adj.* **1** of or having to do with schools, colleges, universities, and their studies. **2** concerned with general education rather than commercial, technical, or professional education. **3** scholarly. **4** theoretical; not practical: "*Which came first, the chicken or the egg?*" *is an academic question.* **5** formal; following rules and traditions. **—ac′a·dem′i·cal·ly,** *adv.*
—*n.* **1** a person engaged in scholarly pursuits. **2 academics,** *pl. Informal.* studies or courses concerned with formal general education, as opposed to technical, vocational, or professional studies.

ac·a·dem·i·cal (ak′ə dem′ə kəl) *adj.* academic.

academic freedom **1** the freedom of a teacher to investigate and discuss controversial issues and problems without fear of losing his position or standing. **2** the freedom of an educational institution to decide the subjects it will teach and how it will teach them.

a·cad·e·mi·cian (ə kad′ə mish′ən or ak′ə də mish′ən) *n.* **1** a member of a society for encouraging literature, science, or art. **2** an artist, writer, or composer who follows traditional or conventional rules.

academic year the part of the year during which a college or university is in regular session.

a·cad·e·my (ə kad′ə mē) *n.* **-mies. 1** a place for instruction. **2** a private high school. **3** a school where some special subject can be studied: *a military academy, a naval academy.* **4** a society of authors, scholars, scientists, artists, etc. for encouraging literature, science, or art. **5 Academy,** near ancient Athens, a park where Plato taught. [< L *academia* < Gk. *Akadēmeia,* the grove where Plato taught]

A·ca·di·a (ə kā′dē ə) *n. Cdn.* **1** the areas of French settlement and culture in the Maritime Provinces. **2** the Maritime Provinces as a unit. **3** formerly, the French colony comprising the Maritime Provinces and adjacent parts of Quebec and New England. See map on the following page. [probably after *Arcadia*]

hat, āge, cãre, fär; let, ēqual, tėrm; it, īce
hot, ōpen, ôrder; oil, out; cup, pu̇t, rüle, ūse
ə above, takən, pencəl, lemən, circəs
ch, child; ng, long; sh, ship
th, thin; ᴛʜ, then; zh, measure

A·ca·di·an (ə kād′ē ən) *adj.* of or relating to Acadia or, sometimes, Nova Scotia. —*n.* a native of Acadia or one of his descendants.

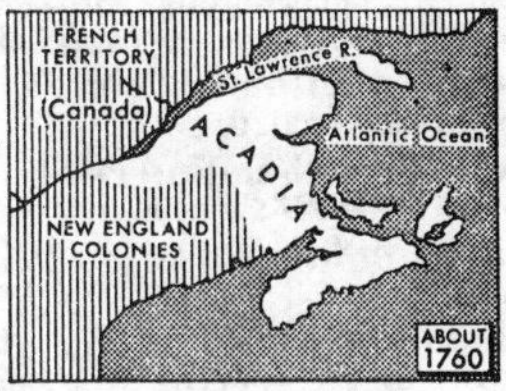

a·can·thus (ə kan′thəs) *n.* **-thus·es, -thi** (-thī or -thē). **1** a prickly plant having large, toothed leaves, found in Mediterranean regions. **2** in architecture, an ornament imitating these leaves. [< L < Gk. *akanthos* < *akē* thorn]

a cap·pel·la (ä'kə pel′ə) in music, without instrumental accompaniment. [< Ital. *a cappella* in the manner of chapel (music)]

acc. 1 accusative. **2** account.

ac·cede (ak sēd′) *v.* **-ced·ed, -ced·ing. 1** give in; agree (*to*): *The king acceded to popular demand.* **2** come (*to*); attain (*to* an office or dignity): *When the king died, his oldest son acceded to the throne.* **3** become a party (*to*): *Our government acceded to the treaty.* [< L *accedere* < *ad-* to + *cedere* come]

accel. accelerando.

ac·cel·er·an·do (ak sel'ər an′dō) *adv. adj.* in music, gradually increasing in speed. *Abbrev.*: accel. [< Ital.]

ac·cel·er·ate (ak sel′ər āt') *v.* **-at·ed, -at·ing. 1** go or cause to go faster; increase in speed; speed up. **2** cause to happen sooner; hasten: *Sunshine, fresh air, and rest often accelerate a person's recovery from sickness.* **3** change the speed or velocity of (a moving object). [< L *accelerare* < *ad-* to + *celer* swift]

ac·cel·er·a·tion (ak sel'ər ā′shən) *n.* **1** an accelerating. **2** a being accelerated. **3** a change in velocity. **Positive acceleration** is increase in velocity. **Negative acceleration** is decrease in velocity. **4** the rate of change in the velocity of a moving body.

ac·cel·er·a·tor (ak sel′ər ā'tər) *n.* **1** a means of increasing speed. **2** the pedal or lever that controls the flow of gasoline to an internal-combustion engine. **3** in nuclear physics, any device for greatly increasing the velocity of charged particles.

ac·cent (*n.* ak′sent; *v.* ak′sent or ak sent′) *n.* **1 a** the prominence given to words and syllables by higher musical pitch or by stress. **b** the degree of force or loudness with which words and syllables in words are uttered; stress. **2** a mark to indicate special force or emphasis. In this dictionary, we use (′) to show the main accent and (') to show a secondary or lesser accent. **3** a distinctive manner of pronunciation heard in different parts of the same country or in the speech of a person speaking a language not his own: *a foreign accent.* **4 accents,** *pl.* tone of voice: *She spoke in tender accents.* **5** a distinguishing mark, quality, etc.: *Many of Leacock's books have an accent of humor.* **6** *Informal.* approval; emphasis: *The manager placed considerable accent on good service to his customers.* **7** a mark used to indicate syllabic pitch, quality of vowel sound, etymological history, the fact of a letter's not being silent, etc. The acute (´), grave (`), and circumflex (^) accents are used in Greek, and in French words such as *blasé, à la carte,* and *tête-à-tête.* **8** in verse, the emphasis placed on certain syllables for rhythm. Thus, in "Tell me where is fancy bred," the accents fall on *tell, where, fan-,* and *bred.* **9** in music: **a** an emphasis on certain notes or chords. **b** a symbol indicating this.
—*v.* **1** pronounce or write with an accent. **2** emphasize; accentuate. [< L *accentus,* literally, song added to (speech) < *ad-* to + *cantus* singing < *canere* sing]
Syn. *v.* **2** accent, accentuate, both meaning "emphasize," are sometimes confused. In general use, **accent** = mark or say something with emphasis; **accentuate** = give emphasis to something by intensifying it or making it conspicuous: *Throughout his speech he accented the gravity of the situation. Her white dress accentuated her sunburn.*
☛ **accents.** French words in English sometimes keep their accent marks: *café, outré, attaché; crêpe, tête-à-tête, à la mode.* Words that are used frequently in English usually drop the accent marks after a time unless the marks are necessary to indicate pronunciation (as in *café, attaché*).

ac·cen·tu·al (ak sen′chü əl) *adj.* **1** of accent; formed by accent or stress. **2** having the same accent or stress as ordinary speech.

ac·cen·tu·ate (ak sen′chü āt') *v.* **-at·ed, -at·ing. 1** emphasize: *Her black hair accentuated the whiteness of her skin.* **2** pronounce with an accent. **3** mark with an accent. **4** make worse; increase in severity: *The problems of the pioneers were accentuated by the harsh climate.* — **ac·cen'tu·a′tion,** *n.* —**Syn. 1** See **accent.**

ac·cept (ak sept′) *v.* **1** take or receive (something offered or given); consent to take: *I accept the gift.* **2** agree to; consent to; say yes to: *accept a proposal.* **3** take as true or satisfactory; believe in: *accept an excuse.* **4** receive with favor; approve: *Einstein's new theory has been widely accepted.* **5** undertake as a responsibility: *accept the post of cashier.* **6** in business, sign and agree to pay: *accept a note.* **7** say yes to an invitation, offer, etc.: *I received an invitation to the mayor's banquet and I accepted.* [< L *acceptare,* frequentative of *accipere* < *ad-* to + *capere* take] —**ac·cept′er,** *n.* —**Syn. 1** See **receive. 2** accede to, assent to. **3** acknowledge. **5** assume.
☛ **Accept, except** are often misspelled because of similarity in sound. *Accept,* always a verb, has as its basic meaning "take to (oneself)" and is a synonym of *receive*: *He accepted the gift. Except,* sometimes a verb, sometimes a preposition, has the basic sense of taking *out*; the verb is a synonym of *omit, exclude,* the preposition, a synonym of *but*: *We can call his career brilliant if we except that one serious blunder. Everyone except John went home.*

ac·cept·a·bil·i·ty (ak sep'tə bil′ə tē) *n.* the quality of being acceptable or satisfactory.

ac·cept·a·ble (ak sep′tə bəl) *adj.* **1** worth accepting: *Flowers are an acceptable gift to a sick person.* **2** good enough but not outstanding; satisfactory: *an acceptable performance.* —**Syn. 1** agreeable, welcome.

ac·cept·a·bly (ak sep′tə blē) *adv.* in a way that pleases.

ac·cept·ance (ak sep′təns) *n.* **1** the taking of something offered or given. **2** a favorable reception; approval. **3** belief; a taking as true and satisfactory. **4** in business: **a** a promise or signed agreement to pay a draft or bill of exchange when it is due. **b** the draft or bill of exchange itself.

ac·cep·ta·tion (ak'sep tā′shən) *n.* **1** the usual meaning; generally accepted meaning: *It is more important to know the acceptation of a word than its derivation.* **2** a favorable reception; approval. **3** a belief; a taking as true and satisfactory.

ac·cept·ed (ak sep′tid) *adj.* generally approved; conventional: *the accepted behavior at formal dinners.*

ac·cep·tor (ak sep′tər) *n.* **1** a person who accepts. **2** a person who signs a draft or bill of exchange and agrees to pay it. **3** in chemistry, an atom sharing two electrons in bond with another atom but itself contributing neither electron. **4** in radio, a circuit that allows reception of a certain frequency and no other.

ac·cess (ak′ses) *n.* **1** the right to approach, enter, or use; admission: *All children have access to the library during the afternoon.* **2** the condition of being easy or hard to reach; approach: *Access to mountain towns is often difficult because of poor roads.* **3** a way or means of approach: *A ladder was the only access to the attic. He has access to men who can help him get work.* **4** of disease, an attack. **5** an outburst: *an access of pity and remorse.* [ME < L *accessus* < *accedere.* See ACCEDE.]

ac·ces·sa·ry (ak ses′ə rē) *n.* **-ries,** *adj.* accessory.

ac·ces·si·bil·i·ty (ak ses'ə bil′ə tē) *n.* **1** the condition of being easy to reach or get at. **2** the condition of being open to influence.

ac·ces·si·ble (ak ses′ə bəl) *adj.* **1** that can be entered or reached. **2** easy to get at; easy to reach or enter: *A telephone should be put where it will be accessible.* **3 accessible to,** capable of being reached or influenced by: *An open-minded person is accessible to reason.* **4** that can be obtained. —**Syn. 1** approachable. **3** susceptible to. **4** available.

ac·ces·si·bly (ak ses′ə blē) *adv.* so as to be accessible.

ac·ces·sion (ak sesh′ən) *n.* **1** the act of attaining to a right, office, etc.: *the prince's accession to the throne.* **2** an increase; addition: *The school was increased by the accession of forty new pupils.* **3** something added: *Each accession to the library means more expense.*
—*v.* in a library or museum, enter in a list, file, etc. details of a book, painting, etc. being added to a collection. [< L *accessio, -onis* < *accedere.* See ACCEDE.]
—**Syn. 1** attainment.

ac·ces·so·ry (ak ses′ə rē) *n.* **-ries,** *adj.* —*n.* **1** an addition to help something of more importance; a subordinate part or detail: *All the accessories to her costume—gloves, stockings, handkerchief, and purse—were perfectly matched.* **2** in law, a person who helps an offender against the law; accomplice. An **accessory before the fact** helps an offender to break the law but is not present when he commits the offence. An **accessory after the fact** hides the offender or fails to report the offence.
—*adj.* **1** helping something more important; added; additional; extra. **2** helping; helping as an accessory in an offence against the law. Also, **accessary.**
☛ This word is often mispronounced (a ses′ ə rē). The first syllable is (ak-), as in *accident.*

access road *Cdn.* **1** a road built to permit entry to a place or an area that is otherwise sealed off, as by dense brush, muskeg, etc. **2** a road permitting entry to an expressway.

ac·ci·dence (ak′sə dəns) *n.* the part of grammar dealing with those changes in words that show case, number, tense, etc.

ac·ci·dent (ak′sə dənt) *n.* **1** an unfortunate happening; something harmful or unlucky that happens: *an automobile accident.* **2** something that happens without being planned, intended, wanted, or known in advance: *Their meeting was an accident.* **3** a non-essential quality. **4** an irregularity in surface or structure. **5 by accident,** by chance; not on purpose: *I cut my foot by accident.* [ME < OF < L *accidens, -entis,* ppr. of *accidere* < *ad-* to + *cadere* fall] —**Syn. 1** misfortune.

ac·ci·den·tal (ak′sə den′təl) *adj.* **1** happening by chance; not planned or intended. **2** non-essential; not necessary; incidental. **3** in music, of or having to do with an accidental.
—*n.* in music, a sign to show a change of pitch; a flat (♭), a sharp (♯), or a natural (♮) inserted after the key signature and before the note to be changed.
Syn. *adj.* **1** fortuitous, unintentional, casual. **2 Accidental, incidental** = not essential or of primary importance. **Accidental** emphasizes that what it describes is not an essential or necessary part, result, etc. of some larger thing or scheme of things: *Songs are essential to musical comedy, but accidental to Shakespeare's plays.* **Incidental** emphasizes that what it describes, although perhaps necessary, is subordinate to something else in importance: *My father pays my tuition, board, and room at college, but not incidental expenses such as laundry and haircuts.*

ac·ci·den·tal·ly (ak′sə den′təl ē or ak′sə dent′lē) *adv.* in an accidental manner; by chance.

accident-prone (ak′sə dənt prōn′) *adj.* tending to have accidents.

ac·claim (ə klām′) *v.* show satisfaction and approval by words or sounds; shout welcome to; applaud: *The crowd acclaimed the fireman for rescuing two people from the burning house.* **2** announce with signs of approval; hail: *The newspapers acclaimed the fireman a hero.* **3** *Cdn.* elect to an office without opposition: *The voters acclaimed him mayor.*
—*n.* a shout or show of approval; applause; welcome. [< L *acclamare* < *ad-* to + *clamare* cry out]

ac·cla·ma·tion (ak′lə mā′shən) *n.* **1** a shout of welcome or show of approval by a crowd; applause. **2** an oral vote: *The club elected him president by acclamation.* **3 by acclamation,** *Cdn.* without opposition in an election: *Since no candidate opposed him, Mr. Smith was elected by acclamation.* **4** *Cdn.* an electing without opposition: *There were acclamations in five ridings.* [< L *acclamatio* a shouting. See ACCLAIM.]

ac·cli·mate (ak′lə māt′ or ə klī′mit) *v.* **-mat·ed, -mat·ing.** accustom or become accustomed to a new climate, surroundings, or conditions. [< F *acclimater* < à to (< L *ad-*) + *climat* climate]

ac·cli·ma·tion (ak′lə mā′shən) *n.* an acclimating or being acclimated.

ac·cli·ma·ti·za·tion (ə klī′mə tə zā′shən or ə klī′mə tī zā′shən) *n.* acclimation.

ac·cli·ma·tize (ə klī′mə tīz′) *v.* **-tized, -tiz·ing.** acclimate.

ac·cliv·i·ty (ə kliv′ə tē) *n.* **-ties.** an upward slope (of ground). [< L *acclivitas* < *acclivis, acclivus* ascending < *ad-* toward + *clivus* rising ground]

ac·co·lade (ak′ə lād′, ak′ə lād′ or ak′ə läd′) *n.* **1** a tap on the shoulder with the flat side of a sword, given in making a man a knight. Formerly an embrace or kiss was given instead. **2** praise; recognition; award. [< F < Ital. *accollata* an embrace about the neck < L *ad-* to + *collum* neck]

ac·com·mo·date (ə kom′ə dāt′) *v.* **-dat·ed, -dat·ing.** **1** have room for; hold comfortably: *This big bedroom will accommodate six beds.* **2** help out; oblige: *He wanted change for a quarter, but I could not accommodate him.* **3** furnish with lodging, sometimes with food as well. **4** supply; furnish. **5** provide (a person) with a loan of money. **6** make (oneself) fit or suitable: *The eye can accommodate to objects at different distances.* **7** reconcile; adjust: *accommodate arguers.* [< L *accommodare* < *ad-* to + *commodare* make fit < *com-* with + *modus* measure] —**ac·com′mo·dat′or,** *n.* —**Syn. 1** See **contain. 4** provide, equip. **7** See **adjust.**

ac·com·mo·dat·ing (ə kom′ə dāt′ing) *adj.* obliging; willing to help. —**ac·com′mo·dat′ing·ly,** *adv.*

ac·com·mo·da·tion (ə kom′ə dā′shən) *n.* **1** lodging, sometimes with food as well: *The hotel has accommodations for one hundred people.* **2** a help; favor; convenience: *It will be an accommodation to me if you will meet me tomorrow instead of today.* **3** a loan. **4** a willingness to help out. **5** a fitting or being fitted to a purpose or situation; adjustment; adaptation: *The accommodation of our desires to a smaller income took some time.* **6** settlement of differences; reconciliation; compromise: *The bankrupt and the men to whom he owed money arranged an accommodation.* **7** in physiology, the adjustment of the lens of the eye for seeing objects at various distances.

ac·com·pa·ni·ment (ə kum′pə nē mənt) *n.* **1** whatever goes along with something else: *Destruction and suffering are accompaniments of war.* **2** in music, a part added to help or enrich the main part.

ac·com·pa·nist (ə kum′pə nist) *n.* a person who plays a musical accompaniment.

ac·com·pa·ny (ə kum′pə nē) *v.* **-nied, -ny·ing.** **1** go along with: *accompany a friend on a walk.* **2** be or happen in connection with: *Fire is accompanied by heat.* **3** cause to be attended by; supplement (*with*): *accompany a speech with gestures.* **4** play or sing a musical accompaniment for or to. [ME < OF *acompagner* < *à* to + *compagne* companion. Related to COMPANION.] —**ac·com′pa·ni·er,** *n.*
Syn. 1 Accompany, attend, escort = go with someone or something. **Accompany** = go along as a companion or (of things) as a customary addition: *He accompanied the other boys to the game. Baked or fried potatoes often accompany steak.* **Attend** = go along as a subordinate: *The student attended the professor on a field trip.* **Escort** = go along as a protector: *He escorted a girl to the dance. Canadian destroyers escorted many Atlantic convoys during World War II.*

ac·com·plice (ə kom′plis) *n.* a person who aids another in committing a crime or other unlawful act. [earlier *a complice* a confederate < F *complice* < L *complex* < *com-* together with + *plectere* twist]
Syn. Accomplice, confederate in technical (legal) use mean "a partner in crime." **Accomplice** applies to a person who deliberately gives another help of any kind in connection with an unlawful act or crime, either before, during, or after the act itself: *Without an accomplice the thief could not have got into the house and stolen the jewels.* **Confederate** applies to a person who joins with others, or another, for the purpose of committing an unlawful act: *The head of the smuggling ring has not been found, but his confederates are in jail.*

ac·com·plish (ə kom′plish) *v.* **1** succeed in completing; carry out (a promise, plan, etc.): *accomplish a purpose.* **2** finish; complete: *accomplish nothing.* [ME < OF *acompliss-,* a stem of *acomplir* < LL *accomplere* < *ad-* + *complere* fill up] —**ac·com′plish·er,** *n.* —**Syn. 1, 2**

achieve, effect, complete, fulfil. See **do.**

ac·com·plished (ə kom′plisht) *adj.* **1** done; carried out; completed. **2** expert; skilled. **3** skilled in social arts and graces: *An accomplished woman has good manners.*

ac·com·plish·ment (ə kom′plish mənt) *n.* **1** an accomplishing or being accomplished; completion. **2** something accomplished; achievement; completed undertaking. **3** skill in some social art or grace. —**Syn. 2, 3** acquirement.

ac·compt (ə kount′) *n. v. Archaic.* account.

ac·cord (ə kôrd′) *v.* **1** be in harmony; agree (*with*): *His account of the accident accords with yours.* **2** grant (a favor, request, etc.): *We should accord Tom praise for good work.* **3** make agree; harmonize; reconcile. —*n.* **1** an agreement; harmony: *Their opinion of war was in accord with his.* **2** an informal agreement between nations. **3** harmony of color, pitch, or tone. **4 of one's own accord,** without being asked; without suggestion from another. **5 with one accord,** all agreeing. [ME < OF *acorder* < VL *acchordare* bring into harmony < L *ad-* to + *chorda* string] —**Syn.** *v.* **1** correspond, harmonize.

ac·cord·ance (ə kôr′dəns) *n.* agreement; harmony: *What he did was in accordance with what he said.*

ac·cord·ant (ə kôr′dənt) *adj.* agreeing; in harmony.

ac·cord·ing (ə kôr′ding) *adv.* **1 according to, a** in agreement with: *according to his promise.* **b** in proportion to: *Spend according to your income.* **c** on the authority of; as said by: *according to this book.* **2 according as,** in proportion as: *according as you have enriched your own mind, you will have influence upon other minds.* **3** accordingly. —*adj.* agreeing; in harmony.

ac·cord·ing·ly (ə kôr′ding lē) *adv.* **1** in agreement with something that has been stated. **2** for this reason; therefore.

☛ **Accordingly** is a conjunctive adverb most appropriately used in formal writing. A co-ordinate clause introduced by *accordingly* is preceded by a semicolon: *He was told to speak briefly; accordingly he cut short his remarks.*

ac·cor·di·on (ə kôr′dē ən) *n.* a portable musical wind instrument with a bellows, metallic reeds, and keys. An accordion is played by forcing air through the reeds by means of the bellows. —*adj.* with folds like the bellows of an accordion: *a skirt with accordion pleats.* [< Ital. *accordare* harmonize]

ac·cost (ə kost′) *v.* come up and speak to; address: *A ragged beggar accosted him, asking for money.* [< F *accoster* < Ital. < LL *accostare* < L *ad-* to + *costa* side, rib]

ac·couche·ment (ə küsh′mənt; *French,* ä küsh mäN′) *n.* a confinement for childbirth; delivery of a baby. [< F]

ac·count (ə kount′) *n.* **1** a statement telling in detail about an event or thing; explanation; story: *Please give an account of your trip.* **2** reason: *He was told not to lie on any account.* **3** sake: *Don't wait on my account.* **4** value; worth: *of little account.* **5** profit; advantage: *turn to account.* **6** a statement of money received and spent. **7** a record of business dealings between a bank and a depositor. **8** a periodic record of purchases for which a customer is billed. [ME < OF *acont* < *aconter* count up. See ACCOUNT, *v.*]
call to account, a demand an explanation of (someone). **b** scold; rebuke; reprimand.
on account, as part payment.
on account of, a because of. **b** for the sake of.
take account of, a make allowance for; consider. **b** make a note of; note.
take into account, make allowance for; reckon with; consider.
—*v.* **1** give a statement of money received or spent. **2 account for, a** give a reason for; explain. **b** tell what has been done with; answer for. **3** hold to be; consider. In law, a man is accounted innocent until he is proved guilty. [ME < OF *aconter* < VL *accomptare* < L *ad-* up + *computare* count < *com-* up + *putare* reckon] —**Syn.** *n.* **1** report, description, narrative.

ac·count·a·bil·i·ty (ə koun′tə bil′ə tē) *n.* the state of being accountable; responsibility.

ac·count·a·ble (ə koun′tə bəl) *adj.* **1** responsible; liable to be called to account: *Each person is accountable for his own work.* **2** explainable: *His bad temper is easily accountable; he has had a toothache all day.*

hat, āge, cãre, fär; let, ēqual, tėrm; it, īce
hot, ōpen, ôrder; oil, out; cup, pu̇t, rüle, ūse
əbove, takən, pencəl, lemən, circəs
ch, child; ng, long; sh, ship
th, thin; ᴛʜ, then; zh, measure

ac·count·a·bly (ə koun′tə blē) *adv.* in a manner that can be accounted for.

ac·count·an·cy (ə koun′tən sē) *n.* the work of an accountant; the examining or keeping of business accounts.

ac·count·ant (ə koun′tənt) *n.* a person who examines or manages business accounts.

account executive in advertising, an executive in charge of the work for a particular client or clients.

ac·count·ing (ə koun′ting) *n.* **1** the art or science of keeping, analysing, and interpreting business accounts. **2** a statement of accounts. **3** a reckoning up or balancing of accounts.

ac·cou·ter (ə kü′tər) *v.* accoutre.

ac·cou·ter·ments (ə kü′tər mənts) *n.pl.* accoutrements.

ac·cou·tre or **ac·cou·ter** (ə kü′tər) *v.* **-tred** or **-tered, -tring** or **-ter·ing.** equip; array: *Knights were accoutred in armor.* [< F *accoutrer*]

ac·cou·tre·ments or **ac·cou·ter·ments** (ə kü′tər mənts) *n.pl.* **1** a soldier's equipment with the exception of his weapons and clothing: *A soldier's accoutrements include a belt, blanket, and knapsack.* **2** personal equipment; outfit.

ac·cred·it (ə kred′it) *v.* **1** give (a person) credit for; regard (a person) as having: *accredit her with kindness.* **2** consider (a thing) as belonging or due (to a person): *We accredit the invention of the telephone to Bell.* **3** accept as true; believe; trust. **4** give authority to. **5** send or provide with credentials or a recommendation An ambassador is accredited as the representative of his own country in a foreign land. **6** recognize as coming up to an official standard. [< F *accréditer* < *à* to + *crédit* credit] —**Syn. 1, 2** attribute. See **credit. 4** authorize.

ac·cred·it·ed (ə kred′ə tid) *adj.* **1** worthy of acceptance, belief, or trust: *Einstein was an accredited authority in mathematics.* **2** recognized as coming up to an official standard.

ac·cre·tion (ə krē′shən) *n.* **1** a growth in size. **2** a growing together of separate things. **3** an increase in size by natural growth or gradual external addition. **4** a thing added; addition. **5** a whole that results from such growths or additions. [< L *accretio, -onis* < *accrescere.* See ACCRUE.]

ac·cru·al (ə krü′əl) *n.* **1** an accruing; progressive growth: *Money left in a savings bank increases by the accrual of interest.* **2** the amount accrued or accruing.

ac·crue (ə krü′) *v.* **-crued, -cru·ing.** come as a growth or result: *Interest on these accounts accrues at 4 per cent per annum.* [< F < L *accrescere* < *ad-* to + *crescere* grow] —**ac·crue′ment,** *n.*

acct. **1** account. **2** accountant.

ac·cul·tu·ra·tion (ə kul′chə rā′shən) *n.* **1** the modification of the culture of one group through the influence of the culture of another group. **2** the conditioning of a child to the ways of a particular society.

ac·cu·mu·late (ə kū′myu̇ lāt′) *v.* **-lat·ed, -lat·ing.** **1** collect or heap up little by little: *He accumulated a fortune by hard work.* **2** grow into a heap or mass: *Dust had accumulated during the weeks that she was gone.* [< L *ac-cumulare* < *ad-* up + *cumulus* heap]

Syn. 1 Accumulate, amass = collect a considerable or large amount. In figurative use, applied to resources, feelings, etc., **accumulate** emphasizes the idea, expressed in its literal meaning, of heaping up, little by little, pile on pile: *Through the years he accumulated sufficient money to buy a farm when he retired.* **Amass** emphasizes the idea of gathering to oneself all at once as in a mass, or in a short time in large amounts: *Before he was forty, he amassed a fortune.*

ac·cu·mu·la·tion (ə kū′myu̇ lā′shən) *n.* **1** a mass of material collected: *His accumulation of old papers filled three trunks.* **2** a collecting together: *The accumulation of knowledge is one result of reading.*

ac·cu·mu·la·tor (ə kū′myů lā′tər) *n.* **1** a person or thing that accumulates. **2** in nuclear physics, an apparatus that collects charged particles. **3** *Brit.* a storage battery.

ac·cu·ra·cy (ak′yů rə sē) *n.* the absence of errors or mistakes; correctness; exactness.

ac·cu·rate (ak′yů rit) *adj.* **1** making few or no errors: *an accurate observer.* **2** without errors or mistakes; exact; correct: *accurate measure.* [< L *accuratus* prepared with care, pp. of *accurare* take care of < *ad-* to + *cura* care] **—ac′cu·rate·ly,** *adv.* **—ac′cu·rate·ness,** *n.* **—Syn. 1** careful, precise. **2** See **correct.**

ac·curs·ed (ə kėr′sid or ə kėrst′) *adj.* **1** damnable; detestable; hateful. **2** under a curse.

ac·curst (ə kėrst′) *adj.* accursed.

accus. accusative.

ac·cu·sa·tion (ak′yů zā′shən) *n.* **1** a charge of having done something wrong, of being something bad, or of having broken the law. **2** the offence charged. **3** an accusing. **4** a being accused.

ac·cu·sa·tive (ə kū′zə tiv) *n.* **1** in grammar, a case form of nouns, pronouns, and adjectives, used to indicate the direct object and some other relations. **2** a word in the accusative case.
—adj. **1** having the accusative form. **2** in English, having the form used for object of a verb or preposition, such as *me, us, him, them.* The term **objective** is more commonly used in discussing English grammar, since the English noun has no special accusative form. *Abbrev.*: acc. or accus.

ac·cu·sa·to·ry (ə kū′zə tô′rē) *adj.* accusing.

ac·cuse (ə kūz′) *v.* **-cused, -cus·ing. 1** charge with having done something wrong, with being something bad, or with having broken the law. **2** find fault with; blame. [ME < OF < L *accusare* < *ad-* to + *causa* cause] **—ac·cus′er,** *n.* **—ac·cus′ing·ly,** *adv.* **—Syn. 1** denounce, arraign. See **charge.**

ac·cused (ə kūzd′) *adj.* charged with some offence.
—n. **the accused,** in law, the person or persons charged in a court of law.
☛ **accused, defendant.** The accused is the party charged in a criminal court; the **defendant** is the party sued in a civil suit.

ac·cus·tom (ə kus′təm) *v.* make familiar with by use or habit; get used (*to*); train: *accustom a hunting dog to the noise of a gun.* [ME < OF *acostumer* < *a-* to (< L *ad-*) + *costume* custom < L *consuescere* < *com-* + *suescere* accustom] **—Syn.** habituate, familiarize.

ac·cus·tomed (ə kus′təmd) *adj.* **1** usual; customary: *By Monday he was back in his accustomed place.* **2 accustomed to,** used to; in the habit of: *He was accustomed to hard work.*

ace (ās) *n.* **1** a playing card, domino, or side of a die having one spot. **2** a single spot or point. **3** in tennis and other games, a point won by a single stroke. **4** a person expert at anything. **5** a combat pilot who has shot down a large number of enemy planes. **6 ace in the hole, a** in the gambling game of stud poker, an ace dealt face downwards. **b** *Informal.* any decisive advantage held in reserve until needed. **7 within an ace of,** at the brink of; on the very point of.
—adj. of very high quality; expert.
—v. **1** in tennis, score against (an opponent) with a single stroke. **2** in golf and other games, make a hole in one stroke. **3** *Slang.* achieve high marks in.
[ME < OF *as* < L *as, assis* smallest unit]

a·cer·bi·ty (ə sėr′bə tē) *n.* **-ties. 1** acidity combined with astringency; sharpness of taste; sourness. **2** harshness of manner; severity. [< F *acerbité* < L *acerbitas* < *acerbus* bitter]

ac·e·tab·u·lum (as′ə tab′yů ləm) *n.* **-la** (-lə). in anatomy, a socket in the hipbone into which the top part of the thighbone fits. [< L *acetabulum* cup-shaped holder for vinegar < *acetum* vinegar]

ac·et·an·i·lid (as′ət an′ə lid) *n.* a white crystalline drug, used in medicines to relieve pain and lessen fever. *Formula*: $C_6H_5NH{\cdot}OC{\cdot}CH_3$ [< *acetic* + *aniline*]

ac·et·an·i·lide (as′ət an′ə līd′ or as′ət an′ə lid) *n.* acetanilid.

ac·e·tate (as′ə tāt′) *n.* a salt or ester of acetic acid. Cellulose acetate is used in making imitation leather, phonograph records, rayon, cellophane, etc.

a·ce·tic (ə sē′tik or ə set′ik) *adj.* of vinegar; producing vinegar. [< L *acetum* vinegar]

acetic acid a very sour, colorless acid, present in vinegar. *Formula*: CH_3COOH

a·cet·i·fy (ə set′ə fī′) *v.* **-fied, -fy·ing.** turn into vinegar or acetic acid.

ac·e·tone (as′ə tōn′) *n.* a colorless, volatile, inflammable liquid, used as a solvent for oils, fats, resins, cellulose, etc. and in making varnishes. *Formula*: C_3H_6O

a·cet·y·lene (ə set′ə lēn′ or ə set′ə lin) *n.* a colorless gas that burns with a bright light and very hot flame. It is used for lighting and, combined with oxygen, for welding metals. *Formula*: C_2H_2

ac·e·tyl·sal·i·cyl·ic acid (as′ə til sal′ə sil′ik or ə sē′təl sal′ə sil′ik) aspirin.

A·chae·an (ə kē′ən) *adj.* of Achaia, a country in the southern part of ancient Greece; Greek. *—n.* a native or inhabitant of Achaia; Greek.

A·chai·an (ə kā′ən) *adj. n.* Achaean.

A·cha·tes (ə kā′tēz) *n.* **1** in Roman legend, the faithful companion of Aeneas. **2** any faithful companion.

ache (āk) *v.* **ached, ach·ing,** *n. —v.* **1** be in continued pain. **2** *Informal.* be eager; wish very much. *—n.* a dull, steady pain. [OE *acan*] **—ach′ing·ly,** *adv.* **—Syn.** *v.* **1** hurt. **2** long, yearn. *—n.* See **pain.**

a·chene (ā kēn′) *n.* any small, dry, hard fruit consisting of one seed with a thin outer covering that does not burst open when ripe. Sunflower achenes are called seeds. Also, **akene.** [< NL *achaenium* < Gk. *a-* not + *chainein* gape; because it ripens without bursting]

Ach·er·on (ak′ər on′) *n.* in Greek and Roman mythology: **1** a river in Hades. **2** the lower world; Hades.

a·chieve (ə chēv′) *v.* **a·chieved, a·chiev·ing. 1** do; get done; carry out; accomplish: *achieve one's purpose.* **2** get by effort: *He achieved distinction in mathematics.* [ME < OF *achever* < (*venir*) *a chief* (come) to a head < LL *ad caput* (*venire*)] **—a·chiev′a·ble,** *adj.* **—a·chiev′er,** *n.* **—Syn. 1** finish, complete, effect. **2** gain, attain.

a·chieve·ment (ə chēv′mənt) *n.* **1** something achieved. **2** some plan or action carried out with courage or unusual ability. **3** an achieving; accomplishing. **—Syn. 1** an accomplishment, feat. **2** See **exploit.**

achievement age a measure of a student's learning, determined from his score on a special test. It is the average age of all students having that particular score.

achievement quotient the ratio of a person's achievement age to his actual age, usually multiplied by 100.

A·chil·les (ə kil′ēz) *n.* **1** in Greek legend, a great hero of Greece. When he was an infant, his mother plunged him into the Styx, making him invulnerable except at the heel by which she held him. At the siege of Troy he killed Hector, but he was himself killed when hit in the heel by a poisoned arrow. **2 Achilles heel,** any vulnerable area; a weak spot.

ach·ro·mat·ic (ak′rə mat′ik) *adj.* **1** that refracts white light without breaking it up into the colors of the spectrum. **2** colorless. **3** in biology, containing or consisting of material that resists ordinary stains: *achromatic cells.* **4** in music, having no accidentals or changes of key: *an achromatic scale.* **5** of soils, having a high concentration of hydrogen ions. [< Gk. *achrōmatos* < *a-* without + *chrōma* color] **—ach′ro·mat′i·cal·ly,** *adv.*

ach·tung (äʜ′tůng) *interj. German.* attention! pay attention! look out! be careful!

ac·id (as′id) *n.* **1** in chemistry, a compound that yields hydrogen ions when dissolved in water and usually reacts with a base to form a salt. The water solution of an acid turns blue litmus paper red. **2** a sour substance. **3** *Slang.* LSD (lysergic acid diethylamide), a hallucinogen.
—adj. **1** of acid; having the properties of an acid. **2** sour; sharp or biting to the taste. **3** ill-natured; sharp; biting: *acid humor.* [< L *acidus* sour] **—ac′id·ly,** *adv.* **—ac′id·ness,** *n.* **—Syn.** *adj.* **2** See **sour.**

a·cid·ic (ə sid′ik) *adj.* forming acid.

hat, āge, cãre, fär; let, ēqual, tėrm; it, īce
hot, ōpen, ôrder; oil, out; cup, pu̇t, rüle, ūse
ə above, takən, pencəl, lemən, circəs
ch, child; ng, long; sh, ship
th, thin; ᴛʜ, then; zh, measure

a·cid·i·fi·ca·tion (ə sid′ə fə kā′shən) *n.* an acidifying or being acidified.

a·cid·i·fy (ə sid′ə fī′) *v.* **-fied, -fy·ing. 1** make sour. **2** become sour. **3** change into an acid. **—a·cid′i·fi′er,** *n.*

a·cid·i·ty (ə sid′ə tē) *n.* **-ties.** an acid quality or condition; sourness: *the acidity of vinegar.*

ac·i·do·sis (as′ə dō′sis) *n.* in medicine, a harmful condition in which the blood and tissues are less alkaline than is normal. [< *acid* + *-osis* process (< Gk.)]

acid salt a salt formed from an acid of which only part of the hydrogen has been replaced by a metal or radical.

acid test 1 formerly, a test for gold using acid. **2** a decisive test of the real worth of some person or thing.

acid-tongued (as′id tungd′) *adj.* sarcastic; biting: *She resented their acid-tongued criticism of her behavior.*

a·cid·u·late (ə sij′u̇ lāt′) *v.* **-lat·ed, -lat·ing.** make slightly acid or sour. **—a·cid′u·la′tion,** *n.*

a·cid·u·lous (ə sij′u̇ ləs) *adj.* slightly acid or sour. **—a·cid′u·lous·ly,** *adv.* **—a·cid′u·lous·ness,** *n.*

ack-ack (ak′ak′) *n. Informal.* anti-aircraft fire. [British radio operator's code word for *A.A.* (anti-aircraft)]

ac·knowl·edge (ak nol′ij) *v.* **-edged, -edg·ing. 1** admit to be true: *He acknowledges his own faults.* **2** recognize the authority or claims of: *The boys acknowledged him to be the best player on the baseball team.* **3** express appreciation of (a gift, favor, etc.). **4** make known that one has received (a service, favor, gift, message, etc.). **5** in law, recognize or certify as genuine: *acknowledge a contract before a notary public.* [blend of ME *aknowen* admit (< OE *oncnāwan*) and *knowleche* knowledge] **—ac·knowl′edg·er,** *n.* **—Syn. 1** concede, confess. See **admit. 2** accept.

ac·knowl·edg·ment or **ac·knowl·edge·ment** (ak nol′ij mənt) *n.* **1** a verbal, written, or other recognition of a gift, service, favor, etc.: *He waved in acknowledgment of the crowd's cheers. A receipt is an acknowledgment that a bill has been paid.* **2** the act of admitting the existence or truth of anything. **3** the recognition of authority or claims. **4** an expression of thanks. **5** an official certificate in legal form. **—Syn. 2** admission. **3** acceptance.

A.C.M. Air Chief Marshal.

ac·me (ak′mē) *n.* the highest point. [< Gk. *akmē* point]

ac·ne (ak′nē) *n.* a skin disease in which the oil glands in the skin become clogged and inflamed, often causing pimples. [? < Gk. *akmē* point]

ac·o·lyte (ak′ə līt′) *n.* **1** a person who helps a priest during certain religious services; altar boy. **2** an attendant; assistant; follower. [ME < Med.L *acolitus* < Gk. *akolouthos* follower]

ac·o·nite (ak′ə nīt′) *n.* **1** a poisonous plant having blue, purple, or yellow flowers shaped like hoods. Wolf's-bane and monkshood are two kinds of aconite. **2** a drug used to relieve inflammation and pain, obtained from one of these plants. [< F *aconit* < L < Gk. *akoniton*]

a·corn (ā′kôrn) *n.* the nut, or fruit, of an oak tree. [OE *æcern*]

a·cous·tic (ə küs′tik) *adj.* **1** having to do with the sense of or the organs of hearing: *Earphones are acoustic aids for deaf people.* **2** having to do with sound. Acoustic tiles deaden sound. **3** exploded by sound: *an acoustic mine.* [< F *acoustique* < Gk. *akoustikos* having to do with hearing < *akouein* hear]

a·cous·ti·cal (ə küs′ti kəl) *adj.* having to do with the science of sound: *an acoustical engineer.*

a·cous·ti·cal·ly (ə küs′tik lē) *adv.* with regard to acoustics.

a·cous·tics (ə küs′tiks) *n.* **1** the qualities of a room, hall, auditorium, etc. that determine how well sounds can be heard in it; acoustic qualities. **2** the science of sound.
☛ **Acoustics** meaning "acoustic qualities" (def. 1) is plural in form and in use: *The acoustics were so good that people in the last row could hear the speaker well.* **Acoustics** meaning "the science of sound" is plural in form and singular in use: *Acoustics is taught in some colleges.*

ac·quaint (ə kwānt′) *v.* **1** inform (a person about a thing): *Acquaint him with your intention. He acquainted me of his plan.* **2** make familiar: *Let me acquaint you with the facts.* **3 be acquainted with,** have personal knowledge of: *He is acquainted with my father.* [ME *acointe* < OF *acointer* < LL *adcognitare* < L *adcognitus, accognitus* < *ad-* to + *cognitus,* pp. of *cognoscere* know < *com-* with + *gnoscere* come to know] **—Syn. 1** tell. See **inform. 2** familiarize.

ac·quaint·ance (ə kwān′təns) *n.* **1** a person known to one, but not a close friend. **2** a knowledge of persons or things gained from experience with them; personal knowledge. **—Syn. 2** familiarity.

ac·quaint·ance·ship (ə kwān′təns ship′) *n.* **1** personal knowledge; acquaintance. **2** the relation between acquaintances: *Their acquaintanceship lasted many years.*

ac·qui·esce (ak′wē es′) *v.* **-esced, esc·ing.** give consent by keeping silent; submit quietly: *We acquiesced in their plan because we could not suggest a better one.* [< F < L *acquiescere* < *ad-* to + *quiescere* to rest < *quies* rest]

ac·qui·es·cence (ak′wē es′əns) *n.* a consent without making objections; agreeing or submitting quietly: *He did not actually say we could go ahead with our plan but signified his acquiescence with a nod.*

ac·qui·es·cent (ak′wē es′ənt) *adj.* acquiescing; agreeing; quietly consenting.

ac·quire (ə kwīr′) *v.* **-quired, -quir·ing. 1** receive or get as one's own: *acquire land.* **2** get by one's own efforts or actions: *acquire an education.* [ME *acquere* < OF *acquerre* < L *acquirere* < *ad-* to + *quaerere* seek] **—ac·quir′a·ble,** *adj.* **— ac·quir′er,** *n.* **—Syn. 1** obtain. See **get. 2** gain, win.

ac·quire·ment (ə kwīr′mənt) *n.* **1** the act of acquiring. **2** something acquired; attainment: *Her musical acquirements are remarkable for a girl of her age.*

ac·qui·si·tion (ak′wə zish′ən) *n.* **1** an acquiring: *He spent hundreds of hours in the acquisition of skill with a rifle.* **2** something acquired. [< L *acquisitio, -onis* < *acquirere.* See ACQUIRE.]

ac·quis·i·tive (ə kwiz′ə tiv) *adj.* fond of acquiring; likely to get and keep: *A miser is acquisitive of money. A great scholar is acquisitive of ideas.* **—ac·quis′i·tive·ly,** *adv.* **—ac·quis′i·tive·ness,** *n.*

ac·quit (ə kwit′) *v.* **-quit·ted, -quit·ting. 1** declare (a person) not guilty (of an offence): *The jury acquitted the innocent man of the crime.* **2** set free or release (from a duty, obligation, etc.). **3** pay off or settle (a debt, claim, etc.). **4 acquit oneself,** do one's part; behave: *The soldiers acquitted themselves well in battle.* [ME < OF *aquiter* < *a-* to (< L *ad-*) + *quitte* free < L *quietus* quiet] **—ac·quit′ter,** *n.* **—Syn. 1** exonerate. **4** conduct.

ac·quit·tal (ə kwit′əl) *n.* **1** a setting free by declaring not guilty; discharge; release. **2** the performance (of a duty, obligation, etc.).

ac·quit·tance (ə kwit′əns) *n.* **1** a release from a debt or obligation. **2** a payment of a debt; settlement of a claim. **3** a written statement showing that a debt has been paid; receipt for the full amount.

a·cre (ā′kər) *n.* **1** a measure of land, 160 square rods or 43,560 square feet. **2 acres,** *pl.* lands; property. **3** a field (now used only in the phrase *God's acre,* a graveyard). [OE *æcer* field]

a·cre·age (ā′kər ij) *n.* **1** the number of acres: *The acreage of a square mile is 640.* **2** a piece of land sold by the acre.

ac·rid (ak′rid) *adj.* **1** sharp, bitter, or stinging to the nose, mouth, or skin. **2** sharp or irritating in manner or temper. [< L *acer, acris* sharp, after *acid*] **—ac′rid·ly,** *adv.* **—ac′rid·ness,** *n.*

a·crid·i·ty (ə krid′ə tē) *n.* bitterness; sharpness.

Ac·ri·lan (ak′rə lan′) *n. Trademark.* a synthetic acrylic fibre having a woolly texture, used for blankets, carpets, clothing, etc.

ac·ri·mo·ni·ous (ak′rə mō′nē əs) *adj.* sharp or bitter in temper, language, or manner. **—ac′ri·mo′ni·ous·ly,** *adv.* **—ac′ri·mo′ni·ous·ness,** *n.*

ac·ri·mo·ny (ak′rə mō′nē) *n.* **-nies.** sharpness or bitterness in temper, language, or manner. [< L *acrimonia* < *acer* sharp]

ac·ro·bat (ak′rə bat′) *n.* a person who can perform on a trapeze, turn handsprings, walk on a tightrope, etc. [< F *acrobate* < Gk. *akrobatēs* < *akros* tip (of the toes) + *-batos* going]

ac·ro·bat·ic (ak′rə bat′ik) *adj.* **1** of an acrobat. **2** like an acrobat's. **—ac′ro·bat′i·cal·ly,** *adv.*

ac·ro·bat·ics (ak′rə bat′iks) *n.pl.* **1** the skills or performance of an acrobat. **2** feats like those of an acrobat.

ac·ro·gen (ak′rə jən) *n.* in botany, a plant growing only at the apex, such as ferns and mosses. [< Gk. *akros* tip + E *-gen* growth < F < Gk. *-genēs* born]

a·cro·le·in (ə krō′lē in) *n.* a colorless, poisonous liquid that is used as a tear gas. *Formula*: C_3H_4O [< L *acer, acris* sharp + *olere* to smell + E *-in*]

ac·ro·me·gal·ic (ak′rō mə gal′ik) *adj.* **1** having to do with acromegaly. **2** affected with acromegaly.

ac·ro·meg·a·ly (ak′rō meg′ə lē) *n.* a disease caused by abnormal activity of the pituitary gland, in which the head, hands, and feet become permanently enlarged. [< F *acromégalie* < Gk. *akros* tip + *megas, -galou* big]

ac·ro·nym (ak′rə nim) *n.* a word formed from the first letters or syllables of other words, such as Unesco (United Nations Educational, Scientific, and Cultural Organization). [< Gk. *akros* tip + dial. *onyma* name]

a·crop·o·lis (ə krop′ə lis) *n.* in ancient Greece, the high, fortified part of a city. The Parthenon was built on **the Acropolis** of Athens. [< Gk. *akropolis* < *akros* topmost, outermost + *polis* city]

a·cross (ə kros′) *prep.* **1** from one side to the other of; to the other side of; over: *a bridge laid across a river.* **2** on the other side of; beyond: *across the sea.* **3** into contact with: *We come across unusual words in some books.* **4 across country,** by the shortest distance between two points, ignoring the usual roads, etc.
—adv. **1** from one side to the other: *What is the distance across?* **2** from side to side; crosswise: *with arms across.* **3** on or to the other side: *When are you going across?* **4 get** or **come across,** *Slang.* reach or be understood by the public or audience. **5 get** or **put across,** *Slang.* make something understood. [< *a-* on, in + *cross*]

a·cross-the-board (ə kros′ᴛʜə bôrd′) *adj.* benefiting all members of a group; all-embracing: *The contract called for across-the-board raises in pay.*

a·cros·tic (ə kros′tik) *n.* a composition in verse or an arrangement of words in which the first, last, or certain other letters in each line, taken in order, spell a word or phrase. [< L < Gk. *akrostichis* < *akros* tip + *stichos* row]

North
East
West
South

Acrostic of "news"

ac·ryl (ak′rəl) *n.* the radical of acrylic acid. *Formula*: C_3H_3O [< L *acr-* (< *acrolein*) + *-yl*]

ac·ryl·ate (ak′rəl āt′) *n.* a salt or ester of acrylic acid.

acrylate resin acrylic resin.

a·cryl·ic (ə kril′ik) *adj.* of, having to do with, or containing acryl or acrylic acid. *—n.* an acrylic resin.

acrylic acid a colorless liquid that is soluble in water and alcohol, used in various plastics. *Formula*: $C_3H_4O_2$

acrylic fibre or **fiber** any of various synthetic textile fibres, such as Orlon or Acrilan.

acrylic resin any of various tough, glasslike plastics used for instrument panels, dental plates, etc. Also, **acrylate resin.**

act (akt) *n.* **1** something done; a deed: *an act of kindness.* **2** the process of doing: *The thief was caught in the act of stealing.* **3** a main division of a play or opera. **4** one of several performances on a program: *the trained dog's act.* **5** a legislative decision; law. An Act of Parliament is a bill that has been passed by Parliament. **6** *Informal.* a display of affected or pretended behavior: *Her bad temper was just an act and failed to convince anyone.* **7 get into the act,** *Informal.* to take part in or join: *Now that coffee parties have become fashionable, everyone is getting into the act.* [ME < OF < L *actus* a doing, and *actum* (thing) done < *agere* do]
—v. **1** do something: *The firemen acted promptly and saved the burning house.* **2** behave: *act tired.* **3** behave like: *Most people act the fool now and then.* **4** have an effect or influence: *Yeast acts on dough and makes it rise.* **5** play a part; perform in a theatre. **6 act as** or **for,** take the place of; do the work of. **7 act on,** follow; obey: *I will act on your suggestion.* **8 act up,** *Informal.* **a** behave badly. **b** play tricks; make mischief. [< L *actus*, pp. of *agere* do; the development of the English verb *act* has been influenced by the noun *act*]

Syn. *n.* **1 Act, action** = a thing done. **Act** emphasizes singleness and completeness, and applies to something that is, or seems to be, a single thing done by a single effort in an instant: *Slapping his face was a childish act.* **Action** applies to something that consists of more than one act and therefore suggests continued or repeated effort over a period of time: *Covering the retreat of his platoon was the action for which he was decorated.* **5** decree, statute.

☛ **act.** In the sense "behave," *act* is a linking verb, so that its meaning can be completed by an adjective: *He acts old. He acts older than he is.*

ACTH a hormone obtained from the pituitary gland, used in treating arthritis, rheumatic fever, etc. [*a*dreno- *c*ortico- *t*rophic *h*ormone]

act·ing (ak′ting) *adj.* temporarily taking another's place and doing his duties: *While the principal was sick, one of the teachers was acting principal.*

ac·tin·ic (ak tin′ik) *adj.* **1** of actinism. **2** producing chemical changes by radiation. Actinic rays are important in photography. [< Gk. *aktis, -tinos* ray]

ac·tin·ide (ak′tin īd′) *n.* in chemistry, an element belonging to the series having the atomic numbers 90 through 103. All actinides are naturally radio-active.

ac·tin·ism (ak′tən iz′əm) *n.* in chemistry, the property in light that causes chemical changes.

ac·tin·i·um (ak tin′ē əm) *n.* a radio-active, metallic chemical element resembling radium, found in pitchblende after uranium has been extracted. *Symbol*: Ac; *at.no.* 89; *at.wt.* 227; *half-life*: 21.7 years.

ac·tin·on (ak′tə non′) *n.* a gaseous radio-active element formed by the decay of actinium. *Symbol*: An; *at.no.* 86; *at.wt.* 219; *half-life*: 3.9 seconds. [< *actinium*]

ac·ti·no·zo·an (ak′tə nə zō′ən) *n.* anthozoan. [< NL *Actinozoa* < Gk. *aktis, aktinos* ray + *zōia*, pl. of *zōion* animal]

ac·tion (ak′shən) *n.* **1** the doing of something; process of acting: *a machine in action.* **2** activity: *A soldier is a man of action.* **3** something done; act. **4 actions,** *pl.* conduct; behavior. **5** the effect or influence of one thing on another: *the action of the wind on a ship's sails.* **6** a way of moving or working; movement: *a motor with an easy action.* **7** the working parts of a machine, instrument, etc. The keys of a piano are part of its action. **8** a minor battle. **9** a combat between military forces. **10** a series of events in a story or play. **11** a legal proceeding by one party against another to enforce a right or punish a wrong; lawsuit. **12** in painting, sculpture, etc., an appearance of movement. **13 in action, a** active; taking part. **b** working. **14 take action, a** become active. **b** start working. **c** start a lawsuit; sue. [ME < OF < L *actio, -onis* < *agere* do] **—ac′tion·less,** *adj.*
—Syn. 3 See **act. 9** See **battle.**

ac·tion·a·ble (ak′shən ə bəl) *adj.* giving cause for a lawsuit; justifying a lawsuit.

ac·ti·vate (ak′tə vāt′) *v.* **-vat·ed, -vat·ing. 1** make active. **2** in physics, make radio-active. **3** in chemistry, make capable of reacting or of speeding up a reaction. **4** purify (sewage) by treating it with air and bacteria. **—ac′ti·va′tion,** *n.*

ac·ti·va·tor (ak′tə vā′tər) *n.* **1** something that activates. **2** in chemistry, a catalyst.

ac·tive (ak′tiv) *adj.* **1** acting; in action; working: *an active volcano.* **2** moving rather quickly; lively; brisk. **3** showing much or constant action: *an active market.* **4** real; effective; *take an active part.* **5** causing

action or change. **6** in grammar, of, in, or having to do with the active voice. In "He threw a stone and the window was broken," *threw* is active and *was broken* is passive.
—*n.* in grammar: **1** the active voice. **2** a verb form in the active voice. [ME < OF *actif* < L *activus* < *agere* act] —**ac′tive·ly,** *adv.* —**ac′tive·ness,** *n.* —**Syn.** *adj.* **2** nimble, quick. **3** vigorous, energetic.

active list a list of officers serving in the armed services or available for service.

active service or **duty** **1** military service with full pay and regular duties. **2** service in the armed services in time of war.

active voice in grammar, the form of the verb that shows the subject as acting rather than as being acted on. In "He broke the window," *broke* is in the active voice; in "The window was broken," *was broken* is in the passive voice.

ac·tiv·ism (ak′tə viz′əm) *n.* **1** the practice of doing things with vigor and decision. **2** a policy or doctrine advocating such action.

ac·tiv·ist (ak′tə vist) *n.* especially in politics, one who practises or believes in activism. —*adj.* **1** of or having to do with activism. **2** favoring activism.

ac·tiv·i·ty (ak tiv′ə tē) *n.* **-ties. 1** a being active; movement; use of power: *physical activity, mental activity.* **2** action; doing: *the activities of enemy spies.* **3** vigorous action; liveliness: *no activity in the market.* **4** a thing to do: *A student who has too many outside activities may find it hard to keep up with his studies.* **5** anything active; active force.

act of God something that could not be foreseen or prevented by human beings; a happening beyond a person's control. Floods, storms, and earthquakes are called acts of God.

Act of Union an act of the British Parliament, passed in 1840, to unite the provinces of Upper and Lower Canada.

ac·tor (ak′tər) *n.* **1** a person who acts on the stage, in motion pictures, on radio, or on television. **2** a person who does something. **3 bad actor,** *Informal.* a person, animal, or thing that is always misbehaving: *That horse is a bad actor.*

ac·tress (ak′tris) *n.* a woman actor.

ac·tu·al (ak′chü əl) *adj.* **1** existing as a fact; real: *What he told us was not a dream but an actual happening.* **2** now existing; present; current: *the actual state of affairs.* [ME < OF < LL *actualis* < L *actus* a doing. See ACT.] —**ac′tu·al·ness,** *n.* —**Syn. 1** true, genuine. See **real[1].**

ac·tu·al·i·ty (ak′chü al′ə tē) *n.* **-ties. 1** actual existence; reality. **2** an actual thing; fact.

ac·tu·al·ize (ak′chü əl īz′) *v.* **-ized, -iz·ing.** make actual; realize in action or as a fact. —**ac′tu·al·i·za′tion,** *n.*

ac·tu·al·ly (ak′chü əl ē) *adv.* really; in fact: *Are you actually going abroad this summer?*

ac·tu·ar·i·al (ak′chü ãr′ē əl) *adj.* **1** of actuaries or their work. **2** determined by actuaries.

ac·tu·ar·y (ak′chü er′ē) *n.* **-ar·ies.** a person whose work is figuring risks, rates, premiums, etc. for insurance companies. [< L *actuarius* account keeper < *actus* a doing. See ACT.]

ac·tu·ate (ak′chü āt′) *v.* **-at·ed, -at·ing. 1** put into action: *This pump is actuated by a belt driven by an electric motor.* **2** influence to act: *She was actuated by love for her mother.* [< LL *actuare* < L *actus* a doing. See ACT.] —**ac′tu·a′tion,** *n.* —**ac′tu·a′tor,** *n.*

a·cu·i·ty (ə kū′ə tē) *n.* sharpness; acuteness. [< Med.L *acuitas,* ult. < L *acus* needle]

a·cu·men (ə kū′mən or ak′yù mən) *n.* sharpness and quickness in seeing and understanding; keen insight. [< L *acumen* < *acuere* sharpen]

a·cu·mi·nate (ə kū′mə nit or ə kū′mə nāt′) *adj.* pointed: *a leaf with an acuminate tip.* [< L *acuminatus,* pp. of *acuminare* point < *acumen.* See ACUMEN.]

An acuminate leaf

hat, āge, cãre, fär; let, ēqual, tėrm; it, īce
hot, ōpen, ôrder; oil, out; cup, pùt, rüle, ūse
əbove, takən, pencəl, lemən, circəs
ch, child; ng, long; sh, ship
th, thin; ᴛʜ, then; zh, measure

a·cute (ə kūt′) *adj.* **1** having a sharp point. **2** sharp and severe: *A toothache can cause acute pain.* **3** brief and severe: *An acute disease like pneumonia reaches a crisis within a short time.* **4** keen: *Dogs have an acute sense of smell. An acute thinker is clever and shrewd.* **5** high in pitch; shrill: *Some sounds are so acute that we cannot hear them.* **6** critical; crucial: *Their situation became acute when their food supplies were exhausted.* **7** of a vowel, having the mark (′) over it. **8** less than a right angle. See **angle** for diagram. —*n.* an acute accent. [< L *acutus,* pp. of *acuere* sharpen] —**a·cute′ly,** *adv.* —**a·cute′ness,** *n.* —**Syn. 4** See **sharp.**

acute accent **1** a mark (′) placed over a vowel to show the quality of its sound, as in French *né,* or to show stress, as in Spanish *adiós.* **2** a mark (′) used to indicate emphasis in pronunciation. *Example:* So áll day lóng the nóise of báttle róll'd.

acute angle an angle less than a right angle. See **angle** for diagram.

A.C.W. Aircraftwoman.

ad (ad) *n. Informal.* advertisement.
☛ Ad is the clipped form of *advertisement,* has only one *d,* and should not be followed by a period.

ad- *prefix.* to; toward, as in *admit, administer, adverb, advert.* Also: **a-** before *sc, sp, st;* **ab-** before *b;* **ac-** before *c, q;* **af-** before *f;* **ag-** before *g;* **al-** before *l;* **an-** before *n;* **ap-** before *p;* **ar-** before *r;* **as-** before *s;* **at-** before *t.* [< L *ad-* < *ad,* prep.]

A.D. in the year of the Lord; since Christ was born. (for LL *anno Domini*)

ad·age (ad′ij) *n.* a wise saying that has been much used; well-known proverb. [< F < L *adagium*]

a·da·gi·o (ə dazh′ē ō, ə daj′ē ō, or ə dä′jō) *adv. adj. n.* **-gios.** —*adv.* in music, slowly. —*adj.* in music, slow. —*n.* **1** in music: **a** a slow part in a piece of music. **b** a composition to be played or sung at a slow tempo. **2** in ballet, a slow dance in which a man and woman do acrobatic feats. [< Ital. *ad agio* at ease]

Ad·am[1] (ad′əm) *n.* **1** in the Bible, the first man. With his wife Eve, he was driven from the Garden of Eden for eating the forbidden fruit. Gen. 1:5. **2 the old Adam,** human tendency to sin. **3 not to know someone from Adam,** *Informal.* be unable to recognize; be completely unacquainted with someone.

Adam[2] (ad′əm) *adj.* of, like, or having to do with a graceful ornamented style of furniture and architecture. —*n.* **1** this style of furniture or architecture. **2** a piece of furniture or architecture of this style. [after Robert and James Adam, 18th-century British designers]

ad·a·mant (ad′ə mənt) *n.* a substance too hard to be cut or broken. —*adj.* **1** too hard to be cut or broken. **2** unyielding; firm; immovable. [< OF *adamaunt* the hardest stone (= diamond) < L < Gk. *adamas, -antos* < *a-* not + *damaein* conquer, tame]

ad·a·man·tine (ad′ə man′tīn, ad′ə man′tēn, or ad′ə man′tin) *adj.* **1** too hard to be cut or broken. **2** unyielding; firm; immovable.

Adam's ale water.

Adam's apple the lump in the front of the throat formed by the thyroid cartilage. [< the story of the forbidden fruit getting stuck in Adam's throat]

a·dapt (ə dapt′) *v.* **1** make or become fit or suitable; adjust: *Can you adapt yourself to a new job? He has adapted well to the new school.* **2** modify or alter for a different use: *The farmer can adapt the barn for use as a garage.* [< L *adaptare* < *ad-* to + *aptare* fit] —**a·dapt′er,** *n.* —**Syn. 1** accommodate. See **adjust.**
☛ Adapt meaning "make suitable" is followed by the preposition *to: His style is not adapted to adults. Adapt* meaning "revise" is followed by *for* or *from: The story was adapted from the musical. It was adapted from a novel by Stephen Leacock.*

a·dapt·a·bil·i·ty (ə dap′tə bil′ə tē) *n.* the power to change easily to fit different conditions.

a·dapt·a·ble (ə dap′tə bəl) *adj.* 1 easily changed to fit different conditions. 2 changing easily to fit different conditions. **—a·dapt′a·ble·ness,** *n.*

ad·ap·ta·tion (ad′ap tā′shən) *n.* 1 an adapting. 2 a being adapted. 3 something made by adapting: *A motion picture is often an adaptation of a novel.* 4 in biology, a change in structure, form, or habits to fit different conditions: *Wings are adaptations of the upper limbs for flight.*

a·dapt·er (ə dap′tər) *n.* 1 a person or thing that adapts. 2 a device for fitting together parts that do not match: *An adapter can be used to fit this nozzle onto a larger hose.* 3 a device for changing the function of a machine, apparatus, etc. Also, **adaptor.**

a·dap·tive (ə dap′tiv) *adj.* 1 able to adapt. 2 showing adaptation. **—a·dap′tive·ly,** *adv.* **—a·dap′tive·ness,** *n.*

a·dap·tor (ə dap′tər) *n.* adapter.

A·dar (ə där′) *n.* in the Hebrew calendar, the twelfth month of the ecclesiastical year and the sixth month of the civil year.

ADC, A.D.C., or **a.d.c.** aide-de-camp.

add (ad) *v.* 1 join (one thing to another); put together; put with: *Add another stone to the pile. Add 8 and 2 and you have 10.* 2 make or form an addition; increase: *The fine weather added to our pleasure.* 3 say further; go on to say or write: *She said good-bye and added that she had had a pleasant visit.* 4 perform arithmetical addition: *The little boy is learning to add and subtract.* 5 **add in,** include. 6 **add up, a** find the sum of (a column, etc. of numbers). **b** *Informal.* make the correct total. **c** *Informal.* make sense; fit together: *There were many clues to the murder, but they just didn't add up.* 7 **add up to,** amount to. [ME < L *addere* < *ad-* to + *dare* put]

ad·dax (ad′aks) *n.* a large antelope of the Arabian peninsula and N. Africa [< L < an African word]

added line in music, a ledger line.

ad·dend (ad′end or ə dend′) *n.* a number or quantity to be added to another number or quantity.

ad·den·da (ə den′də) *n.* pl. of **addendum.**

ad·den·dum (ə den′dəm) *n.* **-da.** 1 a thing to be added. 2 the thing added; appendix. [< L]

ad·der (ad′ər) *n.* 1 a small poisonous snake of Europe. 2 a small harmless snake of North America. 3 a large poisonous snake of Africa; puff adder. [OE *nædre*; in ME *a nadder* was taken as *an adder*]

ad·der's-tongue (ad′ərz tung′) *n.* 1 a small fern having a spike that looks somewhat like a snake's tongue. 2 the dogtooth violet.

add·i·ble (ad′ə bəl) *adj.* that can be added.

ad·dict (*n.* ad′ikt; *v.* ə dikt′) *n.* a person who is a slave or devotee to a habit: *A drug addict finds it hard to stop using drugs.* —*v.* give (oneself) up to a habit. [< L *addictus,* pp. of *addicere* adjudge, devote < *ad-* to + *dicere* say]

ad·dict·ed (ə dik′tid) *adj.* slavishly following (a habit or practice); strongly inclined: *He was addicted to cigars.*

ad·dic·tion (ə dik′shən) *n.* the condition of being a slave to a habit; strong inclination.

ad·dic·tive (ə dik′tiv) *adj.* that causes or tends to cause addiction.

ad·di·tion (ə dish′ən) *n.* 1 the act or process of adding. 2 the result of adding; something added. 3 a part added to a building. 4 **in addition** or **in addition to,** besides; also. [ME < OF < L *additio, -onis* < *addere.* See ADD.]

ad·di·tion·al (ə dish′ən əl or ə dish′nəl) *adj.* added; extra; more.

ad·di·tion·al·ly (ə dish′ən əl ē or ə dish′nəl ē) *adv.* in addition.

ad·di·tive (ad′ə tiv) *n.* something added: *Vitamins and preservatives are frequently used as additives in foodstuffs.* —*adj.* to be added; involving addition.

ad·dle (ad′əl) *v.* **-dled, -dling,** *adj.* —*v.* 1 make or become muddled. 2 make or become rotten. —*adj.* 1 muddled; confused, as in **addlebrain, addleheaded,** etc. 2 of eggs, rotten. [OE *adela* liquid filth]

ad·dress (ə dres′; *also, for n. defs. 2 and 3,* ad′res) *n. v.* **-dressed** or **-drest, -dress·ing.** —*n.* 1 a speech, especially a formal one: *the Prime Minister's inaugural address.* 2 the place at which a person, business, etc. receives mail. 3 the writing on an envelope, package, etc. that shows where it is to be sent. 4 manner in conversation: *A salesman should be a man of pleasant address.* 5 skill: *A good manager shows much address in getting people to help him.* 6 a formal request to those in authority to do a particular thing: *an address from the colonists to the king, listing grievances.* 7 **addresses,** *pl.* attentions paid in courtship. [< F *adresse* (< *adresser,* v.) and E *address,* v.]

—*v.* 1 direct speech or writing to: *The Governor General addressed the nation over radio and television.* 2 use titles or other forms in speaking or writing to: *How do you address a mayor?* 3 direct to the attention: *address a warning to a friend.* 4 apply (oneself) in speech (to a person): *He addressed himself to the chairman.* 5 write on (a letter, package, etc.) the information that shows where it is to be sent. 6 apply or devote (oneself); direct one's energies: *He addressed himself to the task of doing his homework.* 7 in golf, prepare for a stroke by placing the head of a club behind (the ball). [ME < OF *adresser,* earlier *adrecier* < VL *addirectiare* < L *ad-* to + *directus* straight] **—ad·dress′er** or **ad·dres′sor,** *n.* **—Syn.** *n.* 1 See **speech.**

☛ **addresses.** When the various parts of a person's address are written on the same line, they are separated by commas: *Send the money to Miss Louise Finney, 48 Pine St., Kingston, Ontario. Mr. Davis was a native of Dundas County, Ontario, and a graduate of Queen's University.*

ad·dress·ee (ə dres ē′ or ad′res ē′) *n.* the person to whom a letter, package, etc. is addressed.

ad·duce (ə dūs′ or ə düs′) *v.* **-duced, -duc·ing.** offer as a reason; give as proof or evidence; bring up as an example. [< L *adducere* < *ad-* to + *ducere* lead]

ad·duct (ə dukt′) *v.* in physiology, pull (a part of the body) inward toward the main axis. [< L *adductus,* pp. of *adducere.* See ADDUCE.]

ad·duc·tion (ə duk′shən) *n.* 1 an adducing; the bringing forward of arguments. 2 in physiology, an adducting; pulling a part of the body inward.

ad·duc·tor (ə duk′tər) *n.* in physiology, a muscle that adducts.

ad·e·noid (ad′ə noid′) *adj.* 1 of the lymphatic glands. 2 like a gland; glandular.

ad·e·noi·dal (ad′ə noi′dəl) *adj.* adenoid.

ad·e·noids (ad′ə noidz′) *n.pl.* growths of glandular tissue in the upper part of the throat, just behind the nose. The adenoids sometimes swell up and hinder natural breathing and speaking. [< Gk. *adenoeidēs* < *adēn* gland, acorn]

ad·e·no·ma (ad′ə nō′mə) *n.* 1 in medicine, a tumor originating in a gland. 2 a tumor resembling a gland. [< Gk. *adēn* gland + *-oma*]

ad·ept (*n.* ad′ept or ə dept′; *adj.* ə dept′) *n.* a thoroughly skilled or expert person. —*adj.* thoroughly skilled; expert. [< L *adeptus,* pp. of *adipisci* attain < *ad-* to + *apisci* get] **—a·dept′ly,** *adv.* **—a·dept′ness,** *n.*

ad·e·qua·cy (ad′ə kwə sē) *n.* a being adequate; as much as is needed for a particular purpose; sufficiency.

ad·e·quate (ad′ə kwit) *adj.* 1 as much as is needed; fully sufficient: *His wages are adequate to support three people.* 2 suitable; competent: *an adequate person for the job.* [< L *adaequatus,* pp. of *adaequare* < *ad-* to + *aequus* equal] **—ad′e·quate·ly,** *adv.* **—ad′e·quate·ness,** *n.* **—Syn. 1** requisite, needful. See **enough.**

ad·here (ad hēr′) *v.* **-hered, -her·ing.** 1 stick fast; remain attached (*to*): *Mud adheres to your shoes.* 2 hold closely or firmly (*to*): *adhere to a plan.* 3 be devoted (*to*): *Most people adhere to the church of their parents.* [< L *adhaerere* < *ad-* to + *haerere* stick] **—ad·her′er,** *n.* **—Syn. 1** See **stick[2].**

ad·her·ence (ad hēr′əns) *n.* 1 an attachment or loyalty (to a person, group, belief, etc.); faithfulness. 2 a holding to and following closely: *rigid adherence to rules.*

ad·her·ent (ad hēr′ənt) *n.* a faithful supporter; follower. —*adj.* sticking fast; attached. **—ad·her′ent·ly,** *adv.* **—Syn.** *n.* See **follower.**

☛ **adherent.** The preposition used with the noun *adherent* is *of*: *He was an adherent of the Liberal Party.*

hat, āge, cãre, fär; let, ēqual, tėrm; it, īce
hot, ōpen, ôrder; oil, out; cup, pu̇t, rüle, ūse
əbove, takən, pencəl, lemən, circəs
ch, child; ng, long; sh, ship
th, thin; ᴛʜ, then; zh, measure

ad·he·sion (ad hē′zhən) *n.* **1** a sticking fast; attachment. **2** a following and supporting; faithfulness. **3** agreement; assent. **4** in physics, the attraction that holds unlike molecules together. **5** in medicine, the growing together of tissues that should be separate. If a wound heals incorrectly, there may be painful adhesions. [< L *adhaesio, -onis* < *adhaerere.* See ADHERE.]

ad·he·sive (ad hē′siv or ad hē′ziv) *adj.* **1** holding fast; adhering easily; sticky. **2** smeared with a sticky substance for holding (something) fast: *adhesive tape.* —*n.* **1** any substance, such as paste or gum, used to stick things together. **2** a gummed postage stamp. —**ad·he′sive·ly,** *adv.* —**ad·he′sive·ness,** *n.*

ad hoc (ad′hok′) *Latin.* for a certain purpose; special: *We appointed an ad hoc committee to discuss this new problem.*

ad ho·mi·nem (ad′ hom′ə nem) *Latin.* appealing to personal prejudices, interests, etc.

a·dieu (ə dū′ or ə dü′; *French,* ä dyœ′) *interj. n.* **a·dieus** or **a·dieux** (ə dūz′ or ə düz′). good-bye; farewell. [ME < OF *a dieu* to God]

ad in·fi·ni·tum (ad′ in′fə nī′təm) *Latin.* without limit.

ad in·te·rim (ad′ in′tə rim) *Latin.* **1** in the meantime. **2** temporary.

a·di·os (ä′dē ōs′ or ad′ē ōs′) —*interj.* good-bye. —*n.* a farewell. [< Sp. *a dios* to God]

ad·i·pose (ad′ə pōs′) *adj.* fatty. —*n.* animal fat. [< NL *adiposus* < L *adeps* fat] —**ad′i·pose·ness,** *n.*

ad·i·pos·i·ty (ad′ə pos′ə tē) *n.* **1** an adipose condition; fatness. **2** a tendency to become fat.

ad·it (ad′it) *n.* **1** an approach; entrance. **2** a nearly horizontal entrance to a mine. **3** admission; access. [< L *aditus* < *adire* approach < *ad-* to + *ire* go]

adj. 1 adjective. 2 adjunct. 3 adjustment. 4 adjacent.

Adj. Adjutant.

ad·ja·cen·cy (ə jā′sən sē) *n.* **-cies.** nearness.

ad·ja·cent (ə jā′sənt) *adj.* lying near or close; adjoining: *The house adjacent to ours has been sold.* [ME < L *adjacens, -entis,* ppr. of *adjacere* < *ad-* near + *jacere* to lie. Doublet of EASE.] —**ad·ja′cent·ly,** *adv.* —**Syn.** bordering, neighboring.

adjacent angles in mathematics, two angles that have the same vertex and the same line for one of their sides. In the diagram, ADB and BDC are adjacent angles.

ad·jec·ti·val (aj′ik tī′vəl or aj′ik tiv′əl) *adj.* **1** of an adjective. **2** used as an adjective. —*n.* a word or group of words used as an adjective.

ad·jec·ti·val·ly (aj′ik tī′vəl ē or aj′ik tiv′əl ē) *adv.* as an adjective.

ad·jec·tive (aj′ik tiv) *n.* a class of words that limit or add to the meaning of nouns. *Examples:* a *blue* shirt, a *powerful* car. —*adj.* **1** of an adjective. **2** used as an adjective. *Abbrev.:* adj. or a. [ME < LL *adjectivus* that which is added to < *adjicere, -jectum* put near < *ad-* to + *jacere* throw] —**ad′jec·tive·ly,** *adv.*

☛ **adjectives. a. forms of adjectives.** Many English adjectives are made by the addition of a suffix to a noun or verb. Some of these suffixes such as *-some* (as in *winsome*) are no longer active. Among those still in use are: *-able (-ible),* as in *eatable, dirigible,* and *-ed* as in *sugared,* and usually in adjectives that are compound words: *four-footed, well-lighted; -escent,* as in *florescent; -ese,* as in *Burmese, journalese; -ful,* as in *playful, soulful: -ish,* as in *babyish, cattish, womanish; -less,* as in *harmless, fearless; -like,* as in *birdlike; -y,* as in *cranky, dreamy, corny.* **b. position of adjectives.** According to its use in a sentence, an adjective is attributive, appositive, or predicative. In English, **attributive adjectives** ordinarily stand immediately before the word they modify, as in *the tiny brook, horseless carriages;* but in certain phrases attributive adjectives may come after the noun: *the day following, his lady fair,* etc. **Appositive adjectives** follow the word they describe, and they are placed between commas: *The boy, weary and discouraged, went to sleep.* **Predicative adjectives** are used with some form of the verb *be* or some other linking verb (*taste, feel, turn, . . .*): *The day is warm. The train was crowded. That pie smells good. For a while I felt bad. How tall you have grown! Blessed are the merciful.* **c. comparison of adjectives.** Degrees of the quality named by an adjective are shown by adding *-er* or *-est* to the adjective or by placing *more* or *most* before it: *learned, more learned, most learned; warm, warmer* or *more warm, warmest* or *most warm.*

ad·join (ə join′) *v.* **1** be next to; be in contact with: *Canada adjoins the United States.* **2** be next to or close to each other; be in contact: *These two countries adjoin.* [ME < OF *ajoindre* < L *adjungere* < *ad-* to + *jungere* join]

ad·join·ing (ə joi′ning) *adj.* being next to or in contact with; bordering: *adjoining rooms.*

ad·journ (ə jėrn′) *v.* **1** put off until a later time: *The members of the club voted to adjourn the meeting until 2 p.m.* **2** suspend the meeting of to a future time or to another place: *The judge adjourned the court for two hours.* **3** stop business or proceedings for a time: *The court adjourned from Friday until Monday.* **4** *Informal.* go to another place: *After the meeting we adjourned to the cafeteria.* [ME < OF *ajorner* < *a-* for (< L *ad-*) + *jorn* day < LL *diurnum* < L *diurnum* (neut.) daily < *dies* day]

ad·journ·ment (ə jėrn′mənt) *n.* **1** an adjourning or being adjourned. **2** the time during which a court, legislature, etc. is adjourned.

Adjt. Adjutant.

ad·judge (ə juj′) *v.* **-judged, -judg·ing. 1** decree or declare by law: *The accused man was adjudged guilty.* **2** condemn or sentence by law: *The thief was adjudged to prison for two years.* **3** decide or settle by law; judge: *The boy's case was adjudged in the juvenile court.* **4** award or assign by law: *The property was adjudged to the rightful owner.* [ME < OF *ajugier* < L *adjudicare* < *ad-* to + *judicare* judge. Doublet of ADJUDICATE.] —**ad·judg′ment** or **ad·judge′ment,** *n.*

ad·ju·di·cate (ə jü′də kāt′) *v.* **-cat·ed, -cat·ing. 1** decide or settle by law. **2** act as judge; pass judgment. **3** gauge; estimate. [< L *adjudicare.* Doublet of ADJUDGE.]

ad·ju·di·ca·tion (ə jü′də kā′shən) *n.* **1** an adjudicating. **2** a decision of a judge or court.

ad·ju·di·ca·tor (ə jü′də kā′tər) *n.* a judge.

ad·junct (aj′ungkt) *n.* **1** something added that is less important or not necessary, but helpful. **2** an assistant or associate of a more important person. **3** in grammar, a word or phrase that qualifies or modifies another word or phrase. Adjectives, adjectival phrases, adverbs, and adverbial phrases are adjuncts. [< L *adjunctus,* pp. of *adjungere* join to. See ADJOIN.]

ad·ju·ra·tion (aj′ů rā′shən) *n.* a solemn command; earnest appeal.

ad·jure (ə jür′) *v.* **-jured, -jur·ing. 1** command or charge (a person) on oath or under some penalty (to do something). **2** ask earnestly or solemnly: *I adjure you to speak the truth.* [ME < L *adjurare* < *ad-* to + *jurare* swear]

ad·just (ə just′) *v.* **1** fit or adapt (one thing to another): *adjust a seat to the right height for a child.* **2** regulate for use: *adjust a radio dial.* **3** arrange satisfactorily; set right; settle: *adjust a difference of opinion.* **4** accommodate oneself; get used (*to*): *He soon adjusted to army life.* **5** decide the amount to be paid in settling (a bill, insurance claim, etc.). [< F *ajuster* < *a-* for (< L *ad-*) + *juste* right < L *justus*] —**ad·just′a·ble,** *adj.*

Syn. 1 Adjust, adapt, accommodate = suit one thing (or person) to another. **Adjust** emphasizes the idea of matching one thing to another: *I have to adjust my expenditure to my income.* **Adapt** emphasizes the idea of making minor changes in a thing (or person) to make it fit, suit, or fit into something: *I adapted the pattern to the material.* **Accommodate** emphasizes that the things to be fitted together are so different that one must be subordinated to the other: *I have to accommodate my desires to my income.*

ad·just·er or **ad·jus·tor** (ə jus′tər) *n.* **1** a thing that adjusts something else. **2** a person who adjusts claims.

ad·just·ment (ə just′mənt) *n.* **1** the act or process of adjusting. **2** in psychology: **a** the process by which a person adapts himself to the conditions around him. **b** the orderly arrangement of parts or elements. **3** a means of adjusting: *There is a tone adjustment on our radio.* **4** a settlement of a dispute, a claim, etc.

ad·ju·tan·cy (aj′ ů tən sē or aj′ə tən sē) *n.* **-cies.** in the army, the rank or position of an adjutant.

ad·ju·tant (aj′ ů tənt or aj′ ə tənt) *n.* **1** in the army, an officer who assists a commanding officer by sending out orders, writing letters, giving messages, etc. *Abbrev.*: Adj. or Adjt. **2** a helper; assistant. **3** a very large species of stork of India and Africa.
—*adj.* helping. [< L *adjutans, -antis,* ppr. of *adjutare* assist, frequentative of *adjuvare* < *ad-* to + *juvare* help]

adjutant general *pl.* **adjutants general.** the adjutant of a division or a larger military unit. *Abbrev.*: A.G.

ad lib (ad′ lib′) *v.* **-libbed, -lib·bing.** *Informal.* make up as one goes along; extemporize. [shortened form of *ad libitum*]

ad lib. ad libitum.

ad lib·i·tum (ad′ lib′ə təm) **1** to any extent; without restriction. **2** in music, an instruction to change, omit, or expand a passage as the performer wishes. *Abbrev.*: ad lib. [< NL *ad libitum* at pleasure]

Adm. 1 Admiral. **2** Admiralty.

ad·min·is·ter (ad min′is tər) *v.* **1** manage the affairs of (a business, a city, etc.); control on behalf of others; direct: *The Minister of Defence administers a department of the government. A housekeeper administers a household.* **2** give (*to*); apply; dispense: *A doctor administers medicine to sick people. Judges administer justice and punishment.* **3** offer or tender (an oath). **4** in law, settle or take charge of (an estate). **5** act as administrator or executor. **6** be helpful; add something; contribute: *administer to a person's comfort or pleasure.* [ME < OF < L *administrare* < *ad-* to + *minister* servant]

ad·min·is·tra·tion (ad min′is trā′shən) *n.* **1** the managing of a business, office, etc.; management. **2** a group of persons in charge: *the administration of a university.* **3 a** the management of public affairs by government officials. **b** the officials as a group; the government. **c** the period of office of these officials or of a government. **4** the act or process of administering; a giving out, applying, or dispensing (of medicine, justice, etc.). **5** in law, the management, settling, etc. (of an estate).

ad·min·is·tra·tive (ad min′is trə tiv or ad min′ is trā′tiv) *adj.* having to do with administration; managing; executive. —**ad·min′is·tra·tive·ly,** *adv.*

ad·min·is·tra·tor (ad min′is trā′tər) *n.* **1** a person who administers. **2** in law, a person appointed by a court to take charge of or settle the estate of someone who has died without making a will or appointing an executor, or at the executor's death. [< L] —**Syn. 1** executive.

ad·min·is·tra·trix (ad min′is trā′triks) *n.* a woman administrator.

ad·mi·ra·ble (ad′mə rə bəl) *adj.* **1** worth admiring. **2** excellent; very good. [< L *admirabilis*]
—**ad′mi·ra·ble·ness,** *n.* —**ad′mi·ra·bly,** *adv.*

ad·mi·ral (ad′mə rəl) *n.* **1** the commander-in-chief of a fleet. **2** in the navy, a commissioned officer senior to a vice-admiral. **3** an admiral, vice-admiral, or rear-admiral. **4** the leader of a fishing fleet. *Abbrev.*: Adm. **5** a flagship. **6** any one of certain kinds of butterflies. [earlier *amiral* < OF < Arabic *amir* chief. Related to AMIR.]

admiral of the fleet in the navy, a commissioned officer of the highest rank, senior to an admiral.

ad·mi·ral·ty (ad′mə rəl tē) *n.* **-ties. 1** a law or court dealing with affairs of the sea and ships. **2** in Great Britain, until 1963, the government department in charge of naval affairs. **3 the Admiralty,** in London, the building that housed this department. **4** in the navy, the rank or position of an admiral.

ad·mi·ra·tion (ad′mə rā′shən) *n.* **1** a feeling of wonder, pleasure, and approval. **2** the act of regarding with delight (something fine or beautiful): *They paused in admiration of the beautiful view.* **3** a person or thing that is admired: *The well-dressed woman was the admiration of everyone at the party.* **4** *Archaic.* wonder.

ad·mire (ad mīr′) *v.* **-mired, -mir·ing. 1** regard with wonder, approval, and delight: *I admire your bravery.* **2** express admiration for: *He forgot to admire my dog.* [< L *admirari* < *ad-* at + *mirari* wonder < *mirus* wonderful]

ad·mir·er (ad mīr′ər) *n.* **1** a person who admires. **2** a person in love with or fond of another; suitor.

ad·mir·ing (ad mīr′ing) *adj.* full of admiration.
—**ad·mir′ing·ly,** *adv.*

ad·mis·si·bil·i·ty (ad mis′ə bil′ə tē) *n.* the quality or state of being admissible.

ad·mis·si·ble (ad mis′ə bəl) *adj.* **1** that can be permitted; allowable. **2** in law, that can be considered as evidence or proof. **3** having the right to enter or use (a position, occupation, group, place, etc.).
—**ad·mis′si·ble·ness,** *n.* —**ad·mis′si·bly,** *adv.*

ad·mis·sion (ad mish′ən) *n.* **1** the act of allowing (a person, animal, etc.) to enter; entrance: *admission of aliens into a country.* **2** the power or right to enter or use an office, place, etc. **3** the price paid for the right to enter. **4** acceptance into an office or position. **5** an acknowledging: *His admission that he was to blame kept the others from being punished.* **6** an accepting as true or valid. **7** the fact or point acknowledged; something accepted as true or valid. [< L *admissio, -onis* < *admittere.* See ADMIT.]

Syn. 2 Admission, admittance = right to enter. **Admission** is used of entrance both into places and into organizations, institutions, occupations, etc. and always emphasizes that certain purposes and privileges or duties are connected with the right to enter: *He has the requirements for admission into the university.* **Admittance** is used only of entrance to places and does not suggest purpose or additional rights: *With his ticket he gained admittance to the arena.*

ad·mit (ad mit′) *v.* **-mit·ted, -mit·ting. 1** say (something) is real or true; acknowledge: *admit a mistake.* **2** accept as true or valid. **3** allow to enter or use; let in. **4** give the right to enter to: *This ticket admits one person.* **5** make allowance for; leave room for; be capable (*of*): *His answer admits of no reply.* **6** allow; permit. **7** have room for: *The harbor admits three ships.* **8** let attain to a position, privilege, etc. [ME < L *admittere* < *ad-* to + *mittere* let go]

Syn. 1 Admit, acknowledge, confess = disclose or own that something is true. **Admit** = own or grant the existence or truth of something, usually after giving in to outside forces or the dictates of one's own conscience or judgment: *I admit that he is right.* **Acknowledge** = bring out into the open one's knowledge of the existence or truth of something, sometimes reluctantly: *They have now acknowledged defeat.* **Confess** = admit something unfavorable or criminal about oneself: *I confess I am a coward.*

☛ **Admit** is followed by *to* or *into* when it means "give the right to enter or allow to enter": *Fifty cents will admit you to the game. The butler would not admit him into the house.* **Admit** is followed by *of* when it means "leave room for": *His conduct admits of no complaint.*

ad·mit·tance (ad mit′əns) *n.* **1** a right to enter; permission to enter. **2** the act of admitting. **3** actual entrance. —**Syn. 1** See **admission.**

ad·mit·ted·ly (ad mit′id lē) *adv.* without denial; by general consent.

ad·mix (ad miks′) *v.* add in mixing; mix in.

ad·mix·ture (ad miks′chər) *n.* **1** the act of mixing; mixture. **2** anything added in mixing. [< L *admixtus,* pp. of *admiscere* < *ad-* in addition + *miscere* mix]

ad·mon·ish (ad mon′ish) *v.* **1** advise against something; warn: *The policeman admonished him for driving too fast.* **2** reprove gently: *The teacher admonished the student for his careless work.* **3** urge strongly; advise. **4** recall to a duty overlooked or forgotten; remind. [< *admonition*] —**ad·mon′ish·er,** *n.* —**ad·mon′ish·ment,** *n.*

☛ **admonish.** *Of,* not *against,* is used after this rather formal synonym for *warn*: *John admonished them of the impending peril.*

ad·mo·ni·tion (ad′mə nish′ən) *n.* an act of admonishing; warning; advice concerning the faults a person has shown or may show. [ME < OF < L *admonitio, -onis* < *ad-* to + *monere* warn]

ad·mon·i·to·ry (ad mon′ə tô′rē) *adj.* admonishing; warning.

ad nau·se·am (ad′ nos′ē am or ad′ nôs′ē am, ad′ noz′ē am or ad′nôz′ē am) *Latin.* to a disgusting extent.

a·do (ə dü′) *n.* stir; bustle. [ME *at do* to do]
—**Syn.** See **stir.**

a·do·be (ə dō′bē) *n.* **1** sun-dried clay or mud. **2** a brick or bricklike piece of such material, used in building. **3** a building made of such bricks or material. —*adj.* built or made of sun-dried bricks: *Many people in the southwestern United States and in Mexico live in adobe houses.* [< Sp. *adobe* < Arabic *at-tub* the brick]

ad·o·les·cence (ad′ə les′əns) *n.* **1** the stage of growth between childhood and manhood or womanhood. **2** the period or time of this growth; youth.

ad·o·les·cent (ad′ə les′ənt) *n.* a person from about 12 to 21 years of age. —*adj.* **1** growing up from childhood to manhood or womanhood. **2** of or characteristic of adolescents. [ME < OF < L *adolescens, -entis,* ppr. of *adolescere* < *ad-* to + *olescere* grow up. Related to ADULT.]

A·don·is (ə don′is or ə dō′nis) *n.* **1** in Roman and Greek mythology, a handsome young man who was loved by Venus. **2** any handsome young man.

a·dopt (ə dopt′) *v.* **1** take for one's own; take as one's own choice: *I liked your idea and adopted it.* **2** accept formally: *The club adopted the motion by a vote of 20 to 5.* **3** take (a child of other parents) and bring up as one's own. [< L *adoptare* < *ad-* to + *optare* choose] —**a·dopt′a·ble,** *adj.* —**a·dopt′er,** *n.*

a·dop·tion (ə dop′shən) *n.* **1** an adopting: *The teachers are talking about the adoption of a new course of study for the high school.* **2** a being adopted: *His adoption by the kind old man changed the boy's whole life.*

a·dop·tive (ə dop′tiv) *adj.* **1** tending to adopt. **2** related by adoption. —**a·dop′tive·ly,** *adv.*

a·dor·a·ble (ə dôr′ə bəl) *adj.* **1** worth adoring. **2** *Informal.* lovely; delightful. —**a·dor′a·bly,** *adv.*
☛ See **adore** for usage note.

ad·o·ra·tion (ad′ə rā′shən) *n.* **1** worship. **2** highest respect; devoted love.

a·dore (ə dôr′) *v.* **a·dored, a·dor·ing. 1** respect very highly; love deeply. **2** *Informal.* like very much. **3** worship. [ME < OF < L *adorare* < *ad-* to + *orare* pray] —**a·dor′ing·ly,** *adv.* —**Syn. 1** revere, idolize.
☛ **Adore, adorable** are often used in informal speech to express general and undiscriminating approval: *I adore hamburgers. What an adorable hat she is wearing!*

a·dor·er (ə dôr′ər) *n.* **1** a devoted admirer; lover. **2** a worshipper.

a·dorn (ə dôrn′) *v.* **1** add beauty to; make greater the splendor or honor of; add distinction to. **2** put ornaments on; decorate. [ME < OF < L *adornare* < *ad-* to + *ornare* fit out] —**a·dorn′er,** *n.* —**Syn. 2** See **decorate.**

a·dorn·ment (ə dôrn′mənt) *n.* **1** something that adds beauty; ornament; decoration. **2** an act of adorning.

a·down (ə doun′) *adv. prep. Poetic.* down.

ad·re·nal (ə drē′nəl) *adj.* **1** near or on the kidney. **2** of or from the adrenal glands. —*n.* an adrenal gland. [< L *ad-* near + *renes* kidneys]

adrenal gland one of the two ductless glands, one on the upper part of each kidney, that secrete adrenalin; suprarenal gland.

ad·ren·al·in (ə dren′əl in) *n.* **1** a hormone secreted by the adrenal glands. **2 Adrenalin,** *Trademark.* a white crystalline drug prepared from this hormone, used to stimulate the heart and stop bleeding. Adrenalin is obtained from the adrenal glands of animals.

ad·ren·al·ine (ə dren′əl in or ə dren′əl ēn′) *n.* adrenalin (def. 1).

a·drift (ə drift′) *adv. adj.* **1** drifting; floating without being guided. **2** confused through lack of guidance.

a·droit (ə droit′) *adj.* expert in the use of the hands or the mind; skilful: *A good teacher is adroit in asking questions.* [< F *adroit* < *à droit* rightly <L *ad* to, *directus* straight] —**a·droit′ly,** *adv.* —**a·droit′ness,** *n.* —**Syn.** clever, deft. See **dexterous.**

ad·sorb (ad sôrb′ or ad zôrb′) *v.* gather (a gas, liquid, or dissolved substance) on a surface in a condensed layer. [< L *ad-* to + *sorbere* suck in]

ad·sorp·tion (ad sôrp′shən or ad zôrp′shən) *n.* an adsorbing or being adsorbed.

ad·sorp·tive (ad sôrp′tiv or ad zôrp′tiv) *adj.* having to do with adsorption.

ADT, A.D.T., or **a.d.t.** Atlantic Daylight Time.

ad·u·late (aj′ů lāt′) *v.* **-lat·ed, -lat·ing.** praise too much; flatter slavishly. [< L *adulari*] —**ad′u·la′tor,** *n.*

hat, āge, cãre, fär; let, ēqual, tėrm; it, īce
hot, ōpen, ôrder; oil, out; cup, půt, rüle, ūse
əbove, takən, pencəl, lemən, circəs
ch, child; ng, long; sh, ship
th, thin; ᴛʜ, then; zh, measure

ad·u·la·tion (aj′ů lā′shən) *n.* too much praise; slavish flattery.

ad·u·la·to·ry (aj′ů lə tô′rē) *adj.* praising too much; slavishly flattering.

a·dult (ə dult′ or ad′ult) *adj.* **1** mature; grown-up. **2** of or for adults. —*n.* **1** a grown-up person. **2** a person who has reached an age of maturity as defined by law: *In some provinces, one is an adult at 19.* **3** a full-grown plant or animal. [< L *adultus,* pp. of *adolescere.* See ADOLESCENT.] —**a·dult′ness,** *n.*
☛ **adult.** Pronounced (ə dult′) or (ad′ult), the choice depending generally on which best fits the rhythm. When the adjective stands alone as a predicate complement, it is usually stressed on the second syllable: *He is adult′ in behavior.* When the adjective comes before the word it modifies, it is usually stressed on the first syllable: *His ad′ult behavior pleased them.*

a·dul·ter·ant (ə dul′tər ənt) *n.* a substance used in adulterating. —*adj.* adulterating.

a·dul·ter·ate (ə dul′tər āt′) *v.* **-at·ed, -at·ing.** make lower in quality by adding inferior or impure materials: *adulterate milk with water.* [< L *adulterare,* ult. < *ad-* to + *alter* other, different] —**Syn.** debase.

a·dul·ter·a·tion (ə dul′tər ā′shən) *n.* **1** an adulterating. **2** an adulterated substance; product that has been adulterated.

a·dul·ter·er (ə dul′tər ər) *n.* a person, especially a man, guilty of adultery.

a·dul·ter·ess (ə dul′tər is or ə dul′tris) *n.* a woman guilty of adultery.

a·dul·ter·ous (ə dul′tər əs or ə dul′trəs) *adj.* **1** guilty of adultery. **2** having to do with adultery. —**a·dul′ter·ous·ly,** *adv.*

a·dul·ter·y (ə dul′tər ē or ə dul′trē) *n.* **-ter·ies.** sexual unfaithfulness of a husband or wife. [< L *adulterium*]

a·dult·hood (ə dult′hůd or ad′ult hůd′) *n.* the state or condition of being an adult.

ad·umbrate (ad um′brāt′ or ad′əm brāt′) *v.* **-brat·ed, -brat·ing. 1** indicate faintly; outline. **2** foreshadow. **3** overshadow; obscure. [< L *adumbrare* overshadow < *ad-* + *umbra* shade] —**ad′um·bra′tion,** *n.*

adv. 1 adverb. **2** adverbial. **3** advertisement. **4** advocate.

ad val. ad valorem.

ad va·lo·rem (ad′ və lô′rəm) of merchandise, in proportion to the value: *an ad valorem tax. Abbrev.:* ad val. [< Med.L]

ad·vance (ad vans′) *v.* **-vanced, -vanc·ing,** *n. adj.* —*v.* **1** move forward; go forward: *The troops advanced.* **2** bring forward: *The troops were advanced.* **3** make progress; improve: *We advance in knowledge.* **4** help forward; further: *advance the cause of peace.* **5** put forward; suggest: *He advanced a new idea to help solve the city's transportation problems.* **6** raise to a higher rank; promote: *advance him from lieutenant to captain.* **7** rise in rank; be promoted: *advance in one's profession.* **8** raise (prices or value): *advance the price of milk.* **9** rise in price or value: *The stock advanced three points.* **10** make earlier; hasten: *advance the time of the meeting.* **11** move the hands (of a clock or watch) forward: *In summer, the clocks are advanced one hour.* **12** in internal-combustion engines, cause the sparking action to take place earlier in the cycle. **13** supply beforehand: *advance a salesman funds for expenses.* **14** lend (money), especially on security: *advance a loan.* **15** put forward; suggest: *advance an opinion.*
—*n.* **1** a movement forward: *The army's advance was very slow.* **2** the distance covered in such a movement. **3** a command, signal, etc. to move forward. **4** a step forward; progress. **5** a rise in price or value. **6** the furnishing of money or goods before they are due or as a loan. **7** the money or goods furnished. **8 advances,** *pl.* personal approaches toward another or others to settle

a difference, to make an acquaintance, etc. **9 in advance, a** in front; ahead. **b** ahead of time.
—adj. **1** going before: *the advance guard.* **2** ahead of time. **3** made available before the date of general publication, release, etc. [ME < OF *avancier* < VL *abantiare* < LL *abante* < *ab* from + *ante* before]
Syn. *v.* **1 advance, proceed, move on** = move forward.
Advance = move forward toward a definite end or destination: *In two plays the team advanced to the one-yard line.*
Proceed = move forward toward a goal from a definite point, often a point where one has stopped temporarily: *If we get the money to finish the hospital, we can proceed with construction.*
Move on, an informal expression, means "move forward from a place where one has stopped," but does not suggest a destination: *When the ambulance left, the crowd moved on.* **15** present, offer, propose.

ad·vanced (ad vanst′) *adj.* **1** in front of others; forward. **2** ahead of most others in progress, ideas, etc.: *The advanced class has studied history for three years.* **3** far along in life; very old: *the advanced age of ninety years.* **4** increased: *advanced prices.* **5** ahead of the times; progressive; unconventional: *advanced ideas on social welfare.*

ad·vance·ment (ad vans′mənt) *n.* **1** a movement forward; advance. **2** progress; improvement. **3** a promotion.

advance poll *Cdn.* in a general election, an arrangement whereby persons expecting to be absent from their home riding on election day may cast their votes on an earlier date.

ad·van·tage (ad van′tij) *n. v.* **-taged, -tag·ing.** *—n.* **1** a favorable condition, circumstance, or opportunity; a means helpful in getting something desired: *Good health is always a great advantage.* **2 take advantage of, a** use to help or benefit oneself. **b** impose upon. **3** a better or superior position: (FORMAL) *She is not wealthy, but has the advantage of Mrs. Allen, who has no money at all.* (INFORMAL) *Now Dick Tracy has the advantage over the racketeer.* **4 have the advantage of** (a person), know a person to whom one is not known. **5 to advantage,** to good effect; with a useful effect: *The decorator will arrange your furniture to advantage.* **6** in tennis, the first point scored after deuce.
—v. give an advantage to; help; benefit. [ME < OF *avantage* < *avant* before < LL *abante.* See ADVANCE.]
Syn. *n.* **3** superiority, ascendancy. **4 advantage, benefit, profit** = gain of some kind. **Advantage** applies to a gain resulting from a position of superiority, of any kind, over others: *The boy who can think for himself has an advantage when he begins work.* **Benefit** applies to gain in personal or social improvement: *His summer in Mexico was a benefit to him.* **Profit** applies especially to material gain, but also to gain in anything valuable, such as knowledge: *There is profit even in mistakes.*

ad·van·ta·geous (ad′vən tā′jəs) *adj.* giving advantage; favorable; helpful; profitable: *This advantageous position commands three roads.* **—ad′van·ta′geous·ly,** *adv.* **—ad′van·ta′geous·ness,** *n.*

ad·vec·tion (ad vek′shən) *n.* the transference of heat, cold, or other property of air by the horizontal movement of a mass of air. [< L *advectio, -onis* a conveying < *advehere* carry to < *ad-* to + *vehere* carry]
—ad·vec′tion·al, *adj.*

ad·vec·tive (ad vek′tiv) *adj.* of or having to do with advection.

ad·vent (ad′vent) *n.* **1** a coming; arrival. **2 Advent, a** the birth of Christ. **b** the season of devotion including the four Sundays before Christmas. **3 Second Advent,** the coming of Christ at the Last Judgment. [< L *adventus* < *advenire* arrive < *ad-* to + *venire* come]

Ad·vent·ist (ad′ven tist or ad ven′tist) *n.* a member of a Christian denomination that believes that the second coming of Christ is near at hand.

ad·ven·ti·tious (ad′ven tish′əs) *adj.* **1** coming from outside; additional; accidental: *The romantic life of the author gives his book an adventitious interest.* **2** in biology, appearing in an unusual position or place: *Adventitious roots sometimes grow from leaves.* [< L *adventicius*]
—ad′ven·ti′tious·ly, *adv.* **—ad′ven·ti′tious·ness,** *n.*

ad·ven·tive (ad ven′tiv) *adj.* in biology, introduced into a new environment; not native, though growing with cultivation.

Advent Sunday the first of the four Sundays in Advent.

ad·ven·ture (ad ven′chər) *n. v.* **-tured, -tur·ing.**
—n. **1** an exciting or unusual experience: *The trip to the West Indies was an adventure for her.* **2** a bold and difficult undertaking, usually exciting and somewhat dangerous: *Sailing across the Pacific on a raft was a daring adventure.* **3** a seeking of excitement or danger: *a spirit of adventure.* **4** a business undertaking; commercial speculation. **5** *Obs.* peril.
—v. venture. [ME < OF *aventure* < L *adventura* (*res*) (thing) about to happen < *advenire* arrive. See ADVENT.]

ad·ven·tur·er (ad ven′chər ər) *n.* **1** a person who seeks or has adventures. **2** a soldier ready to serve in any army that will hire him. **3** a person who lives by his wits; a person who schemes to get money, social position, etc. **4** a speculator.

ad·ven·ture·some (ad ven′chər səm) *adj.* bold and daring; adventurous.

ad·ven·tur·ess (ad ven′chər is) *n.* **1** a woman who schemes to get money, social position, etc. **2** a woman adventurer.

ad·ven·tur·ism (ad ven′chər iz′əm) *n.* the attempting of projects without sufficient forethought or preparation; imprudence.

ad·ven·tur·ist (ad ven′chər ist′) *n.* a person who attempts a project or undertakes a program without sufficient forethought. *—adj.* of or having to do with adventurists or adventurism.

ad·ven·tur·ous (ad ven′chər əs) *adj.* **1** fond of adventures; ready to take risks; daring: *a bold, adventurous explorer.* **2** full of risk; dangerous: *An expedition to the North Pole is an adventurous undertaking*
—ad·ven′tur·ous·ly, *adv.* **—ad·ven′tur·ous·ness,** *n.*

ad·verb (ad′vėrb) *n.* a word that extends or limits the meaning of verbs but is also used to qualify adjectives or other adverbs, especially in place, time, manner, or degree: *Soon, here, very, gladly,* and *not* are adverbs. *Abbrev.:* adv. [< L *adverbium* < *ad-* to + *verbum* verb]
☛ **adverb. a. forms of adverbs.** Most adverbs are adjectives or participles plus the ending *-ly*: *He rowed badly. She was deservedly popular. Surely you hear that.* There are a number of adverbs with the same forms as adjectives. Some of these are: *cheap, close, deep, even, first, high, loud, much, near, right, slow, smooth, tight, well, wrong.* Most of these adverbs have forms in *-ly* as well so that we can write: *He sang loud. He sang loudly.* The *-ly* forms are more common in formal English and the shorter forms in informal and familiar writing. **b. comparison of adverbs. Degrees** of the condition or manner indicated by an adverb are shown by adding *-er, -est,* or by placing *more, most* before it: *hard, harder, hardest; slow, slower, slowest;* or *slowly, more slowly, most slowly. More* and *most* are used with most adverbs of more than one syllable.

ad·ver·bi·al (ad vėr′bē əl) *adj.* **1** of an adverb. **2** used as an adverb. *—n.* a word or group of words used as an adverb.

ad·ver·bi·al·ly (ad vėr′bē əl ē) *adv.* as an adverb.

ad·ver·sar·y (ad′vər ser′ē) *n.* **-sar·ies. 1** a person opposing or resisting another person; enemy. **2** a person or group on the other side in a contest. [< L *adversarius*] **—Syn. 1** foe. **2** contestant, antagonist. See **opponent.**

ad·ver·sa·tive (ad vėr′sə tiv) *adj.* in grammar, expressing contrast or opposition. *But* and *yet* are adversative conjunctions. *—n.* in grammar, a word expressing contrast or opposition.

ad·verse (ad′vėrs or ad vėrs′) *adj.* **1** unfriendly in purpose; hostile: *adverse criticism.* **2** unfavorable; harmful: *adverse influences.* **3** acting in a contrary direction; opposing: *Adverse winds hinder ships.* **4** in botany, turned toward the stem. [< L *adversus* over against, pp. of *advertere.* See ADVERT.]
—ad·verse′ly, *adv.* **—ad·verse′ness,** *n.*
☛ **adverse.** The stress is correctly placed on either syllable: ad′vėrs or ad vėrs′. When *adverse* stands alone, the stress is usually on the second syllable: *The winds were ad verse′.* When *adverse* precedes its noun, the stress is usually on the first syllable: *Ad′verse criticism upsets him.*

ad·ver·si·ty (ad vėr′sə tē) *n.* **-ties. 1** a condition of unhappiness, misfortune, or distress. **2** a stroke of misfortune; an unfavorable or harmful thing or event. **—Syn. 1** See **misfortune.**

ad·vert[1] (ad vėrt′) *v.* direct attention; refer (*to*): *The* *speaker adverted to the need for more parks.* [ME *avert* < OF *avertir* < L *advertere* < *ad-* to + *vertere* turn] —**Syn.** allude.

ad·vert² (ad′vėrt) *n. Esp.Brit. Informal.* advertisement.

ad·ver·tise (ad′vər tīz′) *v.* **-tised, -tis·ing. 1** give public notice of in a newspaper, over the radio, etc.: *The meeting was well advertised in the newspaper.* **2** ask by public notice (*for*): *advertise for a job.* **3** make generally known. **4** inform: *We have advertised our correspondents in South America of our new process.* **5** praise the good qualities of (a product, etc.) in order to promote sales: *Manufacturers advertise things that they wish to sell.* **6** issue advertising: *It pays to advertise.* **7** call attention to (oneself). Also, **advertize.** [ME < OF *avertiss-*, a stem of *avertir* < *advertere.* See ADVERT.]

ad·ver·tise·ment (ad′vər tīz′ment, ad vėr′tis mənt, or ad vėr′tiz mənt) *n.* a public notice or announcement, as in a newspaper or magazine, over the radio, or on television. Also, **advertizement.**

ad·ver·tis·er (ad′vər tīz′ər) *n.* one who advertises. Also, **advertizer.**

ad·ver·tis·ing (ad′vər tīz′ing) *n.* **1** the business of preparing, publishing, or circulating advertisements. **2** advertisements. Also, **advertizing.**

ad·ver·tize (ad′vər tīz′) *v.* **-tized, -tiz·ing.** advertise. —**ad ver·tize′ment,** *n.* —**ad′ver tiz′er,** *n.* —**ad′ver·tiz′ ing,** *n.*

ad·vice (ad vīs′) *n.* **1** an opinion about what should be done: *Take the doctor's advice.* **2 advices,** *pl.* information; news: *advices from the battle front.* [ME < MF *advis*, var. of OF *avis* < L *ad-* + *visum* thing seen]
Syn. 1 Advice, counsel. Advice is the general word: *I asked her advice about buying a range.* Counsel is more formal, suggesting the giving of a professional or more carefully considered opinion: *He asked for counsel about his career.* **2** report, word.

ad·vis·a·bil·i·ty (ad vīz′ə bil′ə tē) *n.* the quality of being advisable; propriety; expediency.

ad·vis·a·ble (ad vīz′ə bəl) *adj.* to be recommended; wise; sensible. —**ad·vis′a·bly,** *adv.*

ad·vise (ad vīz′) *v.* **-vised, -vis·ing. 1** give advice to: *Advise him to be cautious.* **2** give advice: *I shall act as you advise.* **3** give notice; inform (often with *of*): *We were advised of the dangers before we began our trip.* [ME < OF *aviser* < *avis* opinion. See ADVICE.] —**Syn. 1** caution, admonish, warn. **2** recommend. **3** notify, acquaint, tell.

ad·vised (ad vīzd′) *adj.* planned; considered; thought-out.

ad·vis·ed·ly (ad vīz′id lē) *adv.* after careful consideration; deliberately.

ad·vise·ment (ad vīz′mənt) *n.* careful consideration: *The lawyer took our case under advisement and said he would give us an answer in two weeks.*

ad·vis·er or **ad·vi·sor** (ad vīz′ər) *n.* **1** a person who gives advice. **2** a teacher appointed to advise students.
☛ Adviser has been the more common spelling, but the *-or* form, because of its similarity to *advisory*, is being increasingly used.

ad·vi·so·ry (ad vīz′ə rē) *adj.* **1** having power to advise. **2** containing advice. —*n.* a bulletin or report containing advice or advance information: *a weather advisory.* —**ad·vi′so·ri·ly,** *adv.*

ad·vo·ca·cy (ad′və kə sē) *n.* a statement in favor; a public recommendation; support: *The Premier's advocacy got votes for the plan.*

ad·vo·cate (*v.* ad′və kāt′; *n.* ad′və kit or ad′və kāt′) *v.* **-cat·ed, -cat·ing,** *n.* —*v.* speak in favor of; recommend publicly: *He advocates building more schools.* —*n.* **1** a person who pleads or argues for: *an advocate of peace.* **2** a lawyer who pleads in a law court. [ME *avocat* < OF < L *advocare* < *ad-* to + *vocare* call] —**ad′vo·ca′tion,** *n.* —**ad′vo·c a′tor,** *n.* —**Syn.** *n.* **1** champion; supporter.

advt. advertisement.

adze or **adz** (adz) *n.* a tool resembling an axe but having a blade set across the end of the handle and curving inward. [OE *adesa*]

A man using an adze

AEA or **A.E.A.** *Brit.* Atomic Energy Authority.

AEC or **A.E.C.** *U.S.* Atomic Energy Commission.

hat, āge, cãre, fär; let, ēqual, tėrm; it, īce
hot, ōpen, ôrder; oil, out; cup, pu̇t, rüle, ūse
əbove, takən, pencəl, lemən, circəs
ch, child; ng, long; sh, ship
th, thin; ᴛʜ, then; zh, measure

ae·dile (ē′dīl) *n.* in ancient Rome, an official in charge of public buildings, games, streets, and markets. Also, **edile.** [< L *aedilis* < *aedes* building]

ae·gis (ē′jis) *n.* **1** in Greek mythology, a shield or breastplate used by the god Zeus or by his daughter Athena. **2** protection. **3 under the aegis of,** under the protection or patronage of. Also, **egis.** [< L < Gk. *aigis*]

ae·gro·tat (ī′grō tat′) *n.* **1** a certificate stating that a student is unable to write an examination because he is ill. **2** a pass degree awarded on the basis of such a certificate. [< L *aegrotat* he is sick]

Ae·ne·as (i nē′əs) *n.* in Greek and Roman legend, a Trojan hero, son of Anchises (a prince of Troy) and Venus. He escaped from burning Troy, carrying his father and leading his little son. After years of wandering he reached Italy, where, it is said, his descendants founded Rome.

Ae·ne·id (i nē′id) *n.* a Latin epic poem by Vergil, describing the wanderings of Aeneas.

Ae·o·li·an¹ (ē ō′lē ən) *adj.* **1** of Aeolus. **2 aeolian,** of, produced by, or carried by the winds. Also, **Eolian.**

Ae·o·li·an² (ē ō′lē ən) *adj.* belonging to a certain tribe of the ancient Greeks. The Aeolian Greeks lived in Boeotia, Thessaly, and Asia Minor. Also, **Eolian.**

aeolian harp a box with six or more tuned strings fitted across openings in the top, usually placed in a window. Air currents vibrate the strings, causing them to produce musical sounds.

Ae·o·lus (ē′ ə ləs) *n.* in Greek mythology, the god of the winds.

ae·on (ē′ən or ē′on) *n.* eon.

aer·ate (ãr′āt or ā′ər āt′) *v.* **-at·ed, -at·ing. 1** expose to air. **2** expose to and mix with air. Water in some reservoirs is aerated by being tossed high into the air in a fine spray. **3** charge with a gas. Soda water is water that has been aerated with carbon dioxide. **4** expose to chemical action with oxygen. Blood is aerated in the lungs. [< L < Gk. *aēr* air] —**aer·a′tion,** *n.* —**aer′a·tor,** *n.*

aer·i·al (*adj.* ãr′ē əl or ā ēr′ē əl; *n.* ãr′ē əl) *adj.* **1** in the air. **2** of or having to do with the air. **3** like air; thin and light as air. **4** ideal; imaginary. **5** relating to aircraft in any way.
—*n.* a wire or wires used in radio or television for sending out or receiving electric waves. [< L < Gk. *aerios* < *aēr* air] —**aer′i·al·ly,** *adv.*
☛ **aerial.** For the highly literary uses of the adjective (defs. 3 and 4), it is better to retain the pronunciation with four syllables, and in verse the four syllables are often useful to the metre. For the more common uses of the adjective and for the noun, the pronunciation with three syllables is established and natural: *aerial warfare, a radio aerial.*

aer·i·al·ist (ãr′ ē əl ist) *n.* an acrobat who performs feats on a trapeze, a high wire, etc.

aer·ie or **aer·y** (ēr′ē or ãr′ē) *n.* **-ies. 1** the lofty nest of an eagle or other bird of prey. **2** young eagles or the young of other birds of prey. **3** a house, castle, etc. built in a high place. Also, **eyrie, eyry.** [< Med.L *aeria* < OF < L *area* area or *atrium* atrium]

aer·o (ãr′ō) *adj.* having to do with aviation; of or for an airplane, dirigible, etc.

aero- *combining form.* **1** air; of the air. **2** gas; of gas or gases. **3** of or for aircraft. [< Gk. *aēr* air]

aer·o·bat·ic (ãr′ō bat′ik) *adj.* of or having to do with aerobatics.

aer·o·bat·ics (ãr′ō bat′iks) *n.* the performance of tricks, stunts, etc. with an aircraft in flight. [< *aero-* + (*acro*)*batics*]

aer·obe (ãr′ōb) *n.* a kind of bacteria that can live only in air containing oxygen.

aer·o·bic (ãr ō′bik or ā′ər ō′bik) *adj.* **1** living and growing only where there is oxygen. Some bacteria are aerobic. **2** having to do with or caused by aerobic bacteria. [ult. < Gk. *aēr* air + *bios* life]

aer·o·bi·ol·o·gist (ãr′ō bī ol′ə jist) *n.* an expert in aerobiology.

aer·o·bi·ol·o·gy (ãr′ō bī ol′ə jē) *n.* the branch of biology that studies how bacteria, viruses, etc. are borne through the air.

aer·o·drome (ãr′ə drōm′) *n. Esp.Brit.* airdrome.

aer·o·dy·nam·ic (ãr′ō dī nam′ik) *adj.* of or having to do with aerodynamics.

aer·o·dy·nam·ics (ãr′ō dī nam′iks) *n.* the branch of physics that deals with the motion of air and other gases, and with the forces that act on bodies moving through the air.

aer·o·em·bo·lism (ãr′ō em′bə liz′əm) *n.* in medicine, a blocking of blood vessels by nitrogen bubbles in the blood, caused by a sudden reduction of air pressure. It may affect airmen ascending quickly to high altitudes, skin-divers or tunnel workers rising too rapidly to the surface, etc.

aer·o·lite (ãr′ə līt′) *n.* meteorite. [< *aero-* + *-lite* < F < Gk. *lithos* stone]

aer·o·log·ic (ãr′ō loj′ik) *adj.* of or having to do with aerology.

aer·ol·o·gist (ãr ol′ə jist′) *n.* an expert in aerology.

aer·ol·o·gy (ãr ol′ə jē) *n.* the branch of meteorology that deals with the study of the upper atmosphere.

aer·o·me·chan·ic (ãr′ō mə kan′ik) *n.* **1** a mechanic who works on an aircraft. **2** an expert in aeromechanics.

aer·o·me·chan·ic·al (ãr′ō mə kan′ik əl) *adj.* of or having to do with aeromechanics.

aer·o·me·chan·ics (ãr′ō mə kan′iks) *n.* the branch of physics that deals with air and other gases, both in motion and at rest. It includes aerodynamics and aerostatics.

aer·o·naut (ãr′ə not′ or -nôt′) *n.* **1** a pilot of an airship or balloon; balloonist. **2** a person who travels in an airship or balloon. [< F *aéronaute* < Gk. *aēr* air + *nautēs* sailor]

aer·o·nau·tic (ãr′ə not′ik or -nô′tik) *adj.* of aeronautics or aeronauts.

aer·o·nau·ti·cal (ãr′ə not′ə kəl or -nô′tə kəl) *adj.* aeronautic. **—aer′o·nau′ti·cal·ly,** *adv.*

aer·o·nau·tics (ãr′ə not′iks or -nô′tiks) *n.* the science or art of the design, manufacture, and operation of aircraft.

aer·o·pause (ãr′ə poz′ or -pôz′) *n.* **1** level above the earth's surface beyond which the atmosphere has no effect on flight. **2** the upper limit of manned airborne flight.

aer·o·pho·bi·a (ãr′ō fō′bē ə) *n.* an abnormal fear of air or other gases, especially of drafts.

aer·o·plane (ãr′ə plān′) *n. Esp.Brit.* airplane. ☞ See **airplane** for usage note.

aer·o·quay (ãr′ə kē′) *n.* an airport building comprising ticket offices, shops, restaurants, etc. as well as docklike bays at which aircraft take on and let off passengers.

aer·o·sol (ãr′ə sol′ or ãr′ə sōl′) *n.* **1** a suspension of tiny liquid or solid particles in a gas, as in smoke, fog, foam, etc.: *Insecticide may be sprayed into the air as aerosol.* **2** an aerosol bomb, container, sprayer, etc. [< *aero-* + *sol,* short for *solution*]

aerosol bomb a small metal can charged with a liquefied gas under pressure and a substance to be expelled as a mist or foam. Shaving soap, paint, and insecticides are packaged in aerosol bombs.

aer·o·space (ãr′ə spās′) *n.* **1** the earth's atmosphere and space beyond it. **2** the space in which rockets, missiles, and other spacecraft operate. **3** the planning, building, and operating of rockets, missiles, and other spacecraft.

aer·o·stat (ãr′ə stat′) *n.* any lighter-than-air aircraft, such as a balloon or dirigible. [< *aero-* + Gk. *statos* standing]

aer·o·stat·ic (ãr′ō stat′ik) *adj.* **1** of or having to do with aerostatics. **2** of or having to do with an aerostat.

aer·o·stat·ics (ãr′ə stat′iks) *n.* the branch of physics that deals with the equilibrium of air and other gases, and with the equilibrium of solid objects floating in air and other gases.

aer·y (ēr′ē or ãr′ē) *n.* **aer·ies.** aerie.

Aes·cu·la·pi·us (es′kyu̇ lā′pē əs or ēs′kyu̇ lā′pē əs) *n.* in Roman mythology, the god of medicine and healing.

Ae·sir (ā′sər or ē′sər) *n.pl.* the chief Scandinavian gods, especially Odin, Thor, Balder, Loki, and Freya.

Ae·so·pi·an (ē sō′pē ən) *adj.* **1** of or having to do with Aesop (620?-560? B.C.), a Greek writer of fables. **2** of or suggestive of his writings.

aes·thete (ēs′thēt or es′thēt) *n.* **1** a person who is sensitive to beauty; lover of beauty. **2** a person who pretends to care a great deal about beauty; a person who gives too much attention to beauty. Also, **esthete.** [< Gk. *aisthētēs* one who perceives]

aes·thet·ic (ēs thet′ik or es thet′ik) *adj.* **1** having to do with the beautiful, as distinguished from the useful, scientific, etc. **2** (of persons) sensitive to beauty. **3** (of things) pleasing; artistic. Also, **esthetic.**

aes·thet·i·cal·ly (ēs thet′ik lē or es thet′ik lē) *adv.* **1** in an aesthetic manner. **2** according to aesthetics. Also, **esthetically.**

aes·thet·i·cism (ēs thet′ə siz′əm or es thet′ə siz′əm) *n.* **1** the belief in beauty as the basic standard of value in human life, underlying all moral and other considerations. **2** great love for and sensitivity to beauty and the arts. Also, **estheticism.**

aes·thet·ics (ēs thet′iks or es thet′iks) *n.* the study of beauty in art and nature; philosophy of beauty; theory of the fine arts. Also, **esthetics.**

aes·ti·val (es tī′vəl or es′tə vəl) *adj.* estival.

aes·ti·vate (es′tə vāt′) *v.* **-vat·ed, -vat·ing.** estivate.

aet. or **aetat.** of or at the age of. [for L *aetas, aetatis* age]

ae·ther (ē′thər) *n.* **1** the upper regions of space beyond the earth's atmosphere. **2** the invisible, elastic substance formerly supposed to be distributed through all space and to conduct light waves, electric waves, etc. Also, **ether.** [< L < Gk. *aithēr*]

ae·the·re·al (i thēr′ē əl) *adj.* ethereal.

ae·ti·ol·o·gy (ē′tē ol′ə jē) *n.* etiology.

af- the form of **ad-** before f, as in *affix.*

A.F. or **AF** Anglo-French.

A.F., a.f., or **a-f** audio frequency.

a·far (ə fär′) *adv.* far; far away; far off.

a·feard or **a·feared** (ə fērd′) *adj. Archaic* or *Dialect.* frightened; afraid.

af·fa·bil·i·ty (af′ə bil′ə tē) *n.* the state or quality of being affable; courteous and pleasant ways.

af·fa·ble (af′ə bəl) *adj.* easy to talk to; courteous and pleasant. [< F < L *affabilis* able to be spoken to < *affari* < *ad-* to + *fari* speak] **—af′fa·ble·ness,** *n.* **—af′fa·bly,** *adv.*

af·fair (ə fãr′) *n.* **1** anything done or to be done; matter; business: *a difficult affair.* **2 affairs,** *pl.* matters of interest, especially business matters: *government affairs, a man of affairs.* **3** in general terms, a particular action or event: *The party on Saturday was a lively affair.* **4** a private concern: *That's my affair.* **5** a thing: *This machine is a complicated affair.* **6** a romance. [ME < OF *afaire* < *a faire* to do < L *ad* to + *facere* do] **—Syn. 1** activity. **3** happening.

affair of honor or **honour** a duel.

af·fect[1] (ə fekt′) *v.* **1** have an effect on; act on; influence: *Disease affects the body.* **2** touch the heart of; stir the emotions of. [< L *affectus,* pp. of *afficere*; ult. < *ad-* to + *facere* do] **—Syn. 2** move.

af·fect[2] (ə fekt′) *v.* **1** pretend to have or feel: *He affected ignorance of the fight, but we knew that he had seen it.* **2** be fond of; like: *She affects old furniture.* **3** assume falsely or ostentatiously: *He affects a taste for abstract painting though he knows little about art.* [< MF < L *affectare* strive for; ult. < *ad-* to + *facere* do] **—Syn. 1** feign, simulate. See **pretend.**

☞ **affect, effect.** Since little or no distinction is made in pronouncing the first vowel of these words, the spelling is likely to be confused. Except in a few obsolete and technical uses, *affect* is always a verb: *The new rules affect the behavior of the entire student body. He affects a taste for imported clothes. Effect* is most commonly a noun, meaning "result": *The effect of the explosion was visible for miles around. Effect* is also a verb in formal English, meaning most commonly "bring about": *The School Spirit Club effected a marked change in the students' attitude toward sports.*

af·fec·ta·tion (af′ek tā′shən) *n.* **1** an artificial or unnatural way of behaving or talking: *His British accent is an affectation, for he has never lived outside Alberta.* **2** outward appearance; pretence: *an affectation of ignorance.*

af·fect·ed[1] (ə fek′tid) *adj.* **1** acted on; influenced. **2** influenced injuriously. **3** touched in the heart; moved in feeling.

af·fect·ed[2] (ə fek′tid) *adj.* **1** put on for effect; unnatural. **2** behaving, speaking, writing, etc. unnaturally for effect; artificial. —**af·fect′ed·ly,** *adv.* —**Syn. 1** pretended.

af·fect·ing (ə fek′ting) *adj.* causing emotion; touching the heart or moving the feelings. —**af·fect′ing·ly,** *adv.*

af·fec·tion (ə fek′shən) *n.* **1** friendly feeling; a warm liking; fondness. **2** a feeling; inclination. **3** a disease or unhealthy condition. **4** *Archaic.* a disposition; tendency. —**Syn. 1** See **love.**

af·fec·tion·ate (ə fek′shən it) *adj.* loving; fond; tender; having or showing affection. —**af·fec′tion·ate·ly,** *adv.*

af·fec·tive (ə fek′tiv) *adj.* of the feelings; emotional.

af·fer·ent (af′ər ənt) *adj.* in physiology, of nerves or blood vessels, carrying inward to a central organ or point (opposed to *efferent*). [< L *afferens, -entis,* ppr. of *afferre* < *ad-* to + *ferre* bring]

af·fi·ance (ə fī′əns or af′ē äns′) *v.* **-anced, -anc·ing,** *n.* —*v.* promise in marriage; betroth. [ME < OF *afiancer* to promise < *afiance,* n., trust] —*n.* **1** the pledging of faith; betrothal. **2** trust; confidence. [ME < OF *afiance* < *afier* to trust < VL *affidare* < *ad-* to + *fidare* trust < L *fidus* faithful]

af·fi·anced (ə fī′ənst or af′ē änst′) *adj.* promised in marriage; engaged or betrothed.

af·fi·da·vit (af′ə dā′vit) *n.* a statement written down and sworn to be true. An affidavit is usually made before a judge or notary public. [< Med.L *affidavit* he has stated on oath]

af·fil·i·ate (*v.* ə fil′ē āt′; *n.* ə fil′ ē it or ə fil′ē āt′) *v.* **-at·ed, -at·ing,** *n.* —*v.* **1** connect in close association: *The two clubs did not have the same members, but they were affiliated with each other.* **2** associate oneself (*with*): *affiliate with a political party.* **3** bring into relationship; adopt. —*n.* **1** an organization or group associated with other similar bodies. **2** a person or organization that is affiliated. [< LL *affiliare* adopt < L *ad-* to + *filius* son]

af·fil·i·a·tion (ə fil′ē ā′shən) *n.* association; relation.

af·fin·i·ty (ə fin′ə tē) *n.* **-ties. 1** a natural attraction to a person or a liking for a thing: *an affinity for dancing.* **2** a person to whom one is especially attracted. **3** a relationship by marriage. **4** a relation; connection. **5** a resemblance; likeness. **6** in chemistry, a force that attracts certain elements to others and keeps them combined. [ME < F *af(f)inite* < L *affinitas* < *ad-* on + *finis* boundary]

af·firm (ə fėrm′) *v.* **1** declare to be true; say firmly; assert. **2** confirm; ratify: *The higher court affirmed the lower court's decision.* **3** in law, declare solemnly, but without taking an oath. [ME < OF < L *affirmare* < *ad-* to + *firmus* strong]

af·fir·ma·tion (af′ər mā′shən) *n.* **1** in law, a solemn declaration made without taking an oath: *If a person's religion forbids him to take an oath, he can make an affirmation.* **2** an assertion; positive statement. **3** an affirming; confirmation; ratification.

af·firm·a·tive (ə fėr′mə tiv) *adj.* stating that a fact is so; saying yes. —*n.* **1** a word or statement that gives assent or indicates agreement. **2 the affirmative,** the side arguing in favor of a question being debated. —**af·firm′a·tive·ly,** *adv.*

af·fix (*v.* ə fiks′; *n.* af′iks) *v.* **1** make firm or fix (one thing to or on another). **2** add at the end. **3** make an impression

hat, āge, cãre, fär; let, ēqual, tėrm; it, īce
hot, ōpen, ôrder; oil, out; cup, pu̇t, rüle, ūse
əbove, takən, pencəl, lemən, circəs
ch, child; ng, long; sh, ship
th, thin; ᴛʜ, then; zh, measure

of (a seal, etc.). **4** connect with; attach: *affix blame.* —*n.* **1** something affixed, **2** a prefix or a suffix. *Un-* and *-ly* are affixes. [< Med.L *affixare,* ult. < L *ad-* to + *figere* fix] —**af·fixer,** *n.* —**Syn.** *v.* **1** See **attach.**

af·fla·tus (ə flā′təs) *n.* a divine inspiration. [< L *afflatus* < *afflare* < *ad-* on + *flare* blow]

af·flict (ə flikt′) *v.* cause pain to; trouble greatly; distress: *be afflicted with troubles.* [< L *afflictus,* pp. of *affligere* < *ad-* upon + *fligere* dash] —**Syn.** torment, harass.

af·flic·tion (ə flik′shən) *n.* **1** a state of pain or distress. **2** a cause of pain, trouble, or distress. —**Syn. 1** misery, wretchedness. **2** misfortune.

af·flic·tive (ə flik′tiv) *adj.* causing misery or pain; distressing.

af·flu·ence (af′lü əns) *n.* **1** wealth; riches. **2** abundant supply; great abundance. [< F < L *affluentia* < *affluere.* See AFFLUENT.]

af·flu·ent (af′lü ənt) *adj.* **1** very wealthy. **2** abundant; plentiful. —*n.* a stream flowing into a larger stream, lake, etc. [< L *affluens, -entis,* ppr. of *affluere* < *ad-* to + *fluere* flow] —**af′flu·ent·ly,** *adv.*

af·flux (af′luks) *n.* a flow toward a place. [< Med.L *affluxus* < *affluere.* See AFFLUENT.]

af·ford (ə fôrd′) *v.* **1** have or spare the money for: *We can't afford a new car.* **2** manage to give, spare, have, etc.: *A busy man cannot afford delay. Can you afford the time?* **3** be able without difficulty; have the means: *I can't afford to take the chance.* **4** furnish from natural resources; yield: *Some trees afford resin.* **5** yield or give as an effect or a result; provide: *Reading affords pleasure.* [OE *geforthian* further, accomplish]

af·for·est (ə fôr′ist) *v.* plant an area with trees.

af·for·est·a·tion (ə fôr′is tā′shən) *n.* the act or practice of afforesting.

af·fran·chise (ə fran′chīz′) *v.* **-chised, -chis·ing.** enfranchise.

af·fray (ə frā′) *n.* a noisy quarrel; a fight in public; a brawl. [ME < OF *affrei,* ult. < L *ex-* out of + Gmc. **fridhu* peace]

af·fri·cate (af′rə kit) *n.* in phonetics, a sound that begins with a stop and ends with a fricative. The *ch* in *chin* is an affricate because it starts with *t* and ends with *sh.* [< L *affricatus,* pp. of *affricare* < *ad-* against + *fricare* rub]

af·fright (ə frīt′) *Archaic. v.* frighten; terrify. —*n.* fright; terror.

af·front (ə frunt′) *n.* **1** a word or act that openly expresses disrespect. **2** a slight or injury to one's dignity. [< v.] —*v.* **1** insult openly; offend purposely: *The boy affronted the teacher by making a face at her.* **2** meet face to face; confront. [ME < OF *afronter* < *a front* against the forehead < L *ad frontem*] —**Syn.** *n.* **1** See **insult.**

Af·ghan (af′gan or af′gən) *n.* **1** a native of Afghanistan. **2 afghan,** a blanket or shawl made of knitted or crocheted wool, nylon, etc. —*adj.* of Afghanistan or its people.

Afghan hound 1 a breed of large, swift, hunting dog, having a narrow head, large and drooping ears, a heavy coat of silky hair, and a long lock of hair at the top of the head. **2** a dog of this breed.

af·ghan·i (af gan′ē) *n.* **1** a unit of money in Afghanistan. See table at **money. 2** a coin worth one afghani.

a·fi·cio·na·do (ə fē′syə nä′dō: *Spanish* ä fē′thyō nä′ᴛʜō) *n.* **-dos. 1** a person who takes a very great interest in bullfighting, but who is not himself a bullfighter. **2** a person who is very enthusiastic about something.

a·field (ə fēld′) *adv.* **1** away from home; away. **2** out of the way; astray.

a·fire (ə fīr′) *adj.* **1** on fire; burning. **2** enthusiastic.

a·flame (ə flām′) *adj.* **1** in flames; on fire. **2** in a glow; glowing. **3** eager; enthusiastic; excited.

AFL-CIO *U.S.* a labor organization made up of the American Federation of Labor and the Congress of Industrial Organizations.

a·float (ə flōt′) *adv. adj.* **1** floating. **2** on shipboard; at sea. **3** adrift. **4** flooded. **5** going around: *Rumors of a revolt were afloat.*

a·flut·ter (ə flut′ər) *adv. adj.* **1** fluttering; in a flutter. **2** excited; confused.

A.F.M. Air Force Medal.

a·foot (ə fůt′) *adv. adj.* **1** on foot; walking. **2** going on; in progress: *Preparations for dinner were afoot in the kitchen.*

a·fore (ə fôr′) *adv. prep. conj. Archaic and Dialect.* before. [OE *onforan* (< *on foran* in front) and *ætforan* (< *æt* at + *foran* in front)]

a·fore·men·tioned (ə fôr′men′shənd) *adj.* spoken of before; mentioned above.

a·fore·said (ə fôr′sed′) *adj.* spoken of before.

a·fore·thought (ə fôr′thot′ or -thôt′) *adj.* thought of beforehand; deliberately planned.

a·fore·time (ə fôr′tīm′) *adv.* in time past.

a for·ti·o·ri (ā′fôr′tē ôr′ī, ā′ fôr′tē ôr′ē, or a′fôr′tē ôr′ē) *Latin.* for a still stronger reason; all the more.

a·foul (ə foul′) *adv. adj.* **1** in a tangle; in a collision; entangled. **2 run afoul of,** get into difficulties with.

Afr. **1** Africa. **2** African.

a·fraid (ə frād′) *adj.* feeling fear; frightened: *afraid of the dark.* [originally pp. of archaic v. *affray* frighten]

Syn. Afraid, frightened, terrified = feeling fear. **Afraid,** which is never used before the noun, means being in a mental state ruled by fear which may have either a real or an imagined cause and may last a long or a short time: *I am afraid of snakes.* **Frightened,** commonly used instead of *afraid* before the noun, particularly means "made afraid suddenly, often only momentarily, by a real and present cause": *The frightened child ran home.* **Terrified** means "suddenly filled with a very great and paralysing fear": *The terrified mother watched the dog attack her child.*

☛ **afraid.** *Afraid* is used informally with a form of the verb *be,* usually with *am,* to soften a statement: *I am afraid you're wrong about that.*

af·reet (af′rēt or ə frēt′) *n.* in Arabic mythology, a powerful evil demon or giant. [< Arabic *ifrīt*]

a·fresh (ə fresh′) *adv.* once more; again.

Af·ric (af′rik) *adj.* African.

Af·ri·can (af′rə kən) *adj.* **1** of or having to do with Africa; from Africa. **2** Negro. —*n.* **1** a native of Africa. **2** a Negro.

Af·ri·can·ist (af′rə kən ist) *n.* **1** an expert in African art, history, culture, etc. **2** a person who supports African nationalism and African interests.

Af·ri·can·ize (af′rə kən īz′) *v.* **1** make African. **2** turn over (the government, civil service, etc. of a former colony) to Africans. —**af′ri·can·i·za′tion,** *n.*

African violet a perennial plant having violet, pink, or white flowers, originally tropical and now often grown as a house plant.

A·fri·di (ä′frē dē′) *n.* **-di** (-dē′) or **-dis** (dēz′) **1** a people originally from the Khyber Pass region but now living also in India and Pakistan, known for their fighting, feuding, etc. **2** a member of this people.

Af·ri·kaans (af′rə käns′ or af′rə känz′) *n.* a dialect of Dutch spoken in South Africa; South African Dutch. [< Afrikaans spelling of Du. *Afrikansch*]

Af·ri·kan·der (af′rə kän′der) *n.* **1** Afrikaner. **2** a breed of cattle found in southern Africa. [< Afrikaans *Afrikaander,* modelled after Du. *Hollander* Dutchman]

Af·ri·ka·ner (af′rə kä′nər) *n.* a person born in South Africa of European, especially Dutch, descent. [< Afrikaans *Afrikaander*]

Af·ro-A·mer·i·can (af′rō ə mer′ə kən) *adj.* of or having to do with American Negroes. —*n.* an American Negro.

Af·ro-A·sian (af′rō ā′zhən or af′rō a′shen) *adj.* of or having to do with Africa and Asia or their people. —*n.* a native of Africa or Asia.

Afro-Asian bloc a group of African and Asian countries considered together as a political force.

aft (aft) *adv.* at, near, or toward the stern; abaft. —*adj.* at, in, or near the stern. [OE *æftan* from behind]

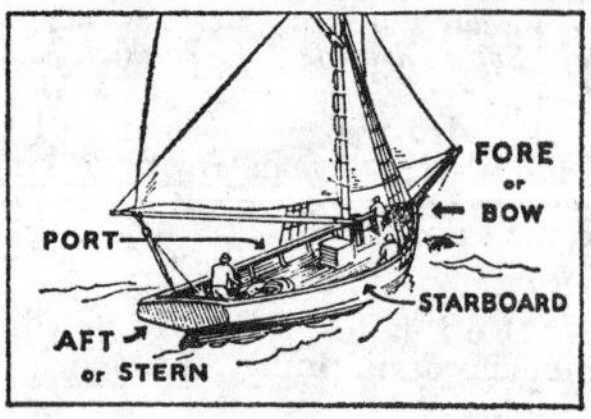

af·ter (af′tər) *prep.* **1** behind (in place): *in line one after another.* **2** next to; following: *day after day.* **3** in pursuit of; in search of: *Run after him. The spy was after a special set of documents.* **4** about; concerning: *Your aunt asked after you.* **5** later in time than: *after supper.* **6** considering; because of: *After the selfish way she acted, who could like her?* **7** in spite of: *After all her suffering, she is still cheerful.* **8** imitating; in imitation of: *He wrote a fable after the manner of Aesop.* **9** lower in rank or importance than: *A captain comes after a general.* **10** according to: *act after one's own ideas.* **11** for: *named after his cousin.*
—*adv.* **1** behind: *follow after.* **2** later: *three hours after.*
—*adj.* **1** later; subsequent: *In after years he regretted the mistakes of his boyhood.* **2** nearer or toward the stern: *after sails.*
—*conj.* later than the time that: *After he goes, we shall eat.* [OE *æfter* more to the rear, later] —**Syn.** *prep.* See **behind.**

af·ter·beat (af′tər bēt′) *n.* in music, a note (or notes), especially in accompaniment, that follows the beat.

af·ter·birth (af′tər bėrth′) *n.* the placenta and membranes forced out of the uterus after childbirth.

af·ter·burn·er (af′tər bėr′nər) *n.* in the engine of a jet plane, a device that supplies additional fuel to the exhaust and re-ignites it, thus increasing the thrust of the plane so that bursts of very high speed can be obtained.

af·ter·care (af′tər kâr′) *n.* **1** the care or treatment of convalescent patients. **2** the assistance given to people who have been discharged from prisons, mental hospitals, etc.

af·ter·damp (af′tər damp′) *n.* a dangerous mixture of gases left in coal mines after an explosion of firedamp.

af·ter·deck (af′tər dek′) *n.* the deck toward or at the stern of a ship.

af·ter-din·ner (af′tər din′ər) *adj.* following dinner: *an after-dinner speech.*

af·ter-ef·fect (af′tər i fekt′) *n.* a result or effect that follows something.

af·ter·glow (af′tər glō′) *n.* **1** the glow in the sky after sunset. **2** the glow after something exciting has passed.

af·ter·grass (af′tər gras′) *n.* a second growth of grass in a field that has been cut.

af·ter·growth (af′tər grōth′) *n.* a second stage of growth and development; a second growth.

af·ter·im·age (af′tər im′ij) *n.* a sensation that persists or recurs after the stimulus is withdrawn.

af·ter·life (af′tər līf′) *n.* life or existence after death.

af·ter·math (af′tər math′) *n.* **1** a result; consequence: *The aftermath of war is hunger and disease.* **2** a crop gathered after the first crop. [< *after* + *math* a mowing < OE *mæth*]

af·ter·most (af′tər mōst) *adj.* **1** nearest the stern of a ship. **2** hindmost; last.

af·ter·noon (*n.* af′tər nün′; *adj.* af′tər nün′) *n.* the part of the day between noon and evening. —*adj.* of, in, or suitable for the afternoon.

af·ter·taste (af′tər tāst′) *n.* a taste that remains after eating or drinking.

af·ter·thought (af′tər thot′ or -thôt′) *n.* **1** a thought that comes after the time when it could have been used. **2** a later thought or explanation.

af·ter·ward (af′tər wərd) *adv.* later. [OE *æfterweard*]

af·ter·wards (af′tər wərdz) *adv.* afterward; later.

ag- the form of **ad-** before *g,* as in *agglutinate.*

Ag silver. (for L *argentum*)

Ag. Agrégé.

A.G. 1 Attorney General. 2 Agent General. 3 sometimes **a.g.**, air gunner. 4 Adjutant General.

a·ga (ä′gə) *n.* in Moslem countries, a commander or chief officer: *The Aga Khan is the leader of a Moslem sect.* Also, **agha.** [< Turkish]

a·gain (ə gen′ or ə gān′) *adv.* **1** once more; another time: *try again.* **2** in return; in reply: *answer again.* **3** to the same place or person; back: *Bring us word again.* **4** moreover; besides: *Again, I must say that you are wrong.* **5** on the other hand: *It might rain, and again it might not.* **6 again and again,** often, frequently. **7 as much again,** twice as much; twice as many. [OE *ongean*]

a·gainst (ə genst′ or ə gānst′) *prep.* **1** in an opposite direction to, so as to meet; upon; toward: *sail against the wind.* **2** in opposition to: *against reason.* **3** directly opposite to; facing: *over against the wall.* **4** in contrast to or with: *The ship appeared against the sky.* **5** in contact with: *lean against a wall.* **6** in preparation for: *Squirrels store up nuts against the winter.* **7** from: *A fire is a protection against cold.* [ME *agenes* (< OE *ongean*) + *-t* as in *amidst, amongst.* See AGAIN.]

a·gape (ə gāp′) *adv. adj.* **1** gaping; with the mouth wide open in wonder or surprise. **2** wide open.

a·gar (ä′gər or ag′ər) *n.* **1** agar-agar. **2** a preparation containing agar-agar.

a·gar-a·gar (ä′gər ä′gər or ag′ər ag′ər) *n.* an extract, resembling gelatin, obtained from certain seaweeds and used in making cultures for bacteria, fungi, etc. and as a glue. [< Malay]

ag·a·ric (ag′ə rik or ə gar′ik) *n.* **1** a type of fungus, having blade-shaped gills on the under surface of the top. The group includes toadstools, edible mushrooms, and several shelflike fungi. **2** a corklike fungus that grows on trees. [< L *agaricum* < Gk. *agarikon* < *Agaria,* place name]

ag·ate (ag′it) *n.* **1** a stone with different-colored stripes, or clouded colors, or mosslike formations; a kind of quartz. **2** a piece of this stone, or a gem made from it. **3** a playing marble that resembles an agate. **4** in printing, a 5½ point size of type. This sentence is set in agate. [< F *agathe* < L *achates* < Gk.] **—ag′ate·like′,** *adj.*

ag·ate·ware (ag′it wãr′) *n.* steel or iron household ware covered with gray enamel.

a·ga·ve (ə gā′vē) *n.* any of several North American desert plants (the century plant, sisal, etc.). Soap, alcoholic drinks, and rope are made from certain kinds of agave. [< NL < Gk. *Agauē,* fem. proper name, noble]

Ag. de l'U. Agrégé de l'Université de Paris.

age (āj) *n. v.* **aged, age·ing** or **ag·ing.** *—n.* **1** time of life: *He died at the age of eighty.* **2** length of life; the time anything has existed: *Her actions belie her age. The age of these elms is greater than that of any other trees in the park.* **3** a period in life: *middle age.* **4** the latter part of life: *the wisdom of age.* **5 of age,** old enough to have full legal rights and responsibilities. **6** the full or average term of life: *The age of a horse is from 25 to 30 years.* **7** a period in history: *the golden age, the space age, the Ice Age.* **8** a generation: *ages yet unborn.* **9** *Informal.* a long, or apparently long, time: *We haven't been to the movies in ages.* **10** in psychology, the level of a person's attainment, mentally, educationally, emotionally, etc., determined by tests.
—v. **1** grow old: *He ages rapidly.* **2** make old: *Fear and worry aged him.* **3** improve by keeping for a time; mature: *to age wine.* [ME < OF *aage* < VL *aetaticum* < L *aetas, -tatis* age] **—Syn.** *n.* **7** era, epoch.

-age *suffix.* **1** the act of: *breakage = the act of breaking.* **2** a collection of; group of: *baggage = a group of bags.* **3** the condition of; status of: *peerage = status of peers.* **4** the cost of: *postage = the cost of posting.* **5** a home of or for: *orphanage = a home for orphans.* [<OF < L *-aticum* < Gk.]

a·ged (ā′jid *for adj.* 1, *n.* 3; ājd *for adj.* 2) *adj.* **1** having lived a long time; old: *The aged woman was wrinkled and bent.* **2** of the age of: *A child aged six.* **3** characteristic of old age. *—n.* **the aged,** elderly people.

age·less (āj′lis) *adj.* never growing old.

hat, āge, cãre, fär; let, ēqual, tėrm; it, īce
hot, ōpen, ôrder; oil, out; cup, pu̇t, rüle, ūse
əbove, takən, pencəl, lemən, circəs
ch, child; ng, long; sh, ship
th, thin; ᴛʜ, then; zh, measure

age·long (āj′long′) *adj.* lasting a long time.

a·gen·cy (ā′jən sē) *n.* **-cies. 1** a means; action: *Snow is drifted by the agency of the wind.* **2** the business of a person or company that has the authority to act for another: *An agency rented my house for me.* **3** the office of such a person or company.

a·gen·da (ə jen′də) *n.* **1** things to be done. **2** a list of things to be done: *The chairman's agenda gave the members of the club an opportunity to acquaint themselves in advance with matters to be discussed or acted upon.* [< L *agenda* things to be done, pl. of **agendum** < *agere* do]

☛ **Agenda** was originally a plural noun and is still so used in def. 1. In def. 2, however, it is commonly used as a singular noun and has the regular plural **agendas.**

a·gent (ā′jənt) *n.* **1** a person or company that has the authority to act for another. **2** a person who produces an effect: *The assassin was an agent of tragedy.* **3** an active power or cause that produces an effect: *Yeast is an important agent in the making of beer.* **4** a means; instrument. **5** a secret agent. **6** a travelling salesman. [< L *agens, -entis,* ppr. of *agere* do] **—Syn. 1** representative, intermediary.

agent general *pl.* **agents general** or **agent generals.** a representative in the United Kingdom of certain Canadian provinces. *Abbrev.*: A.G.

a·gent pro·vo·ca·teur (ä zhäɴ′ prô vô kä tœr′) *French.* a person hired to incite others to do something that will make them liable to punishment.

age of consent the minimum age, fixed by law, at which a person is considered competent to marry.

ag·er·a·tum (aj′ər ā′təm or ə jer′ə təm) *n.* any of several plants of the aster family having small, dense flower heads, usually blue, sometimes white. [<NL < Gk. *agēraton* < *a-* without + *gēras* old age]

ag·glom·er·ate (*v.* ə glom′ər āt′; *n. adj.* ə glom′ər it′ or ə glom′ər āt′) *v.* **-at·ed, -at·ing,** *n. adj. —v.* gather together in a mass; cluster together. *—n.* **1** a mass; collection; cluster. **2** in geology, a rock composed of volcanic fragments fused by heat. *—adj.* packed together in a mass. [< L *agglomerare* < *ad-* to + *glomus, glomeris* ball]

ag·glom·er·a·tion (ə glom′ər ā′shən) *n.* **1** the act of agglomerating. **2** an agglomerated condition. **3** a mass of things gathered or clustered together.

ag·glu·ti·nate (*v.* ə glü′tə nāt′; *adj.* ə glüt′tə nit or ə glü′tə nāt′) *v.* **-nat·ed, -nat·ing,** *adj. —v.* **1** stick together; join together. **2** of languages, form words by joining words, or words and affixes, together. **3** in bacteriology, cause (cells, etc.) to mass together.
—adj. stuck or joined together: "*Never-to-be-forgotten*" *is an agglutinate word.* [< L *agglutinare* < *ad-* to + *gluten, glutinis* glue]

ag·glu·ti·na·tion (ə glü′tə nā′shən) *n.* **1** the process of agglutinating. **2** an agglutinated condition. **3** a mass of parts sticking together. **4** in bacteriology, the massing together of cells, etc. **5** of languages, the forming of words by joining separate words, or words and affixes, together.

ag·glu·ti·na·tive (ə glü′tə nə tiv or ə glü′tə nā′tiv) *adj.* **1** tending to stick together. **2** of languages, forming words by joining words, or words and affixes, together.

ag·gran·dize (ə gran′dīz′ or ag′rən dīz′) *v.* **-dized, -diz·ing.** increase in power, wealth, rank, etc.; make greater: *The dictator sought to aggrandize himself at the expense of his people.* [< F *agrandiss-,* a stem of *agrandir,* ult. < L *ad-* + *grandis* large] **—ag·gran′diz·er,** *n.*

ag·gran·dize·ment (ə gran′diz mənt) *n.* an increase in power, wealth, rank, etc.; a making greater.

ag·gra·vate (ag′rə vāt′) *v.* **-vat·ed, -vat·ing. 1** make worse or more severe: *His bad temper was aggravated by* *his headache.* **2** *Informal.* annoy; irritate; provoke. [< L *aggravare* < *ad-* on, to + *gravis* heavy. Doublet of AGGRIEVE.] —**ag′gra·vat′ing·ly,** *adv.* —**ag′gra·va·tor,** *n.* —**Syn. 1** intensify, increase.

ag·gra·va·tion (ag′rə vā′shən) *n.* **1** a making worse or more severe. **2** a being made worse or more severe. **3** something that aggravates.

ag·gre·gate (*v.* ag′rə gāt′; *n. adj.* ag′rə git or ag′rə gāt′) *v.* **-gat·ed, -gat·ing,** *n. adj.* —*v.* **1** gather together in a mass or group; collect; unite. **2** amount to: *The money collected will aggregate $1,000.*
—*n.* **1** a mass of separate things joined together; collection. **2** a total: *The aggregate of all the gifts was $100.* **3** in geology, a rock composed of several kinds of mineral fragments. **4 in the aggregate,** together; as a whole.
—*adj.* **1** gathered together in one mass or group. **2** total. **3** in geology, composed of several kinds of mineral fragments. **4** in botany, consisting of a dense mass of many florets. [< L *aggregare* < *ad-* to + *grex, gregis* flock] —**ag′gre·gate·ly,** *adv.*

ag·gre·ga·tion (ag′rə gā′shən) *n.* a collection of separate things into one mass or whole.

ag·gres·sion (ə gresh′ən) *n.* **1** the first step in an attack or quarrel; an unprovoked attack. **2** the practice of making assaults or attacks on the rights or territory of others. **3** in psychology, an act or attitude of hostility, usually arising from feelings of inferiority or frustration. [< L *aggressio, -onis* < *aggredi* < *ad-* to + *gradi* to step]

ag·gres·sive (ə gres′iv) *adj.* **1** taking the first step in an attack or quarrel; attacking; quarrelsome: *An aggressive country is always ready to start a war.* **2** active; energetic: *The police are planning an aggressive campaign against crime.* —**ag·gres′sive·ly,** *adv.* —**ag·gres′sive·ness,** *n.*

ag·gres·sor (ə gres′ər) *n.* one who begins an attack or quarrel. —**Syn.** assailant, invader.

ag·grieve (ə grēv′) *v.* **-grieved, -griev·ing.** injure unjustly; cause grief or trouble to: *He was aggrieved at the insult from his friend.* [ME *agreve* < OF *agrever* < L *aggravare.* Doublet of AGGRAVATE.]

ag·grieved (ə grēvd′) *adj.* **1** injured or offended as to rights, position, etc.: *make amends to an aggrieved victim of injustice.* **2** feeling distressed or wronged, whether justly or not.

a·gha (ä′gə) *n.* aga.

a·ghast (ə gast′) *adj.* filled with horror; frightened; terrified. [ME pp. of obs. *agast* terrify < OE *on-* on + *gæstan* frighten. Related to GHOST.]

ag·ile (aj′īl or aj′əl) *adj.* moving quickly and easily; active; lively; nimble: *An acrobat has to be agile. You need an agile mind to solve puzzles.* [ME < OF < L *agilis* < *agere* move] —**ag′ile·ly,** *adv.* —**ag′ile·ness,** *n.* —**Syn.** sprightly, spry, brisk.

a·gil·i·ty (ə jil′ə tē) *n.* the ability to move quickly and easily; activeness; liveliness; nimbleness.

ag·i·tate (aj′ə tāt′) *v.* **-tat·ed, -tat·ing. 1** move or shake violently. **2** disturb; excite (the feelings or the thoughts): *She was much agitated by the news of her brother's illness.* **3** argue about; discuss vigorously. **4** keep arguing about and discussing a matter to arouse public interest: *agitate for a shorter working week.* [< L *agitare* move to and fro < *agere* drive, move] —**ag′i·tat′ed·ly,** *adv.*

ag·i·ta·tion (aj′ə tā′shən) *n.* **1** a violent moving or shaking. **2** a disturbed, upset, or troubled state. **3** an argument or discussion to arouse public interest.

a·gi·ta·to (ä′jē tä′tō) *adj.* in music, restless, agitated. —*adv.* in a restless or agitated manner. [< Ital.]

ag·i·ta·tor (aj′ə tā′tər) *n.* **1** a person who tries to make people discontented with things as they are. **2** a device for shaking or stirring.

a·gleam (ə glēm′) *adv. adj.* gleaming.

a·gley (ə glā′ or ə glē′; *Scottish,* ə glī′) *adv.* wrong; awry; askew; contrary to plan.

a·glit·ter (ə glit′ər) *adv. adj.* glittering.

a·glow (ə glō′) *adv. adj.* glowing; in a glow.

ag·nos·tic (ag nos′tik) *n.* a person who believes that nothing is known or can be known about the existence of God or about things outside human experience. —*adj.* of agnostics or their beliefs. [< Gk. *agnōstos* < *a-* not + *gnōstos* (to be) known] —**ag·nos′ti·cal·ly,** *adv.*

ag·nos·ti·cism (ag nos′tə siz′əm) *n.* the belief or intellectual attitude of agnostics.

Ag·nus De·i (ag′nəs dā′ē or dē′ī) **1** an image of a lamb as a symbol of Christ. **2** the part of the Mass beginning "Agnus Dei." **3** the music for it. **4** a blessed cake of wax bearing the image of a lamb. [< L *Agnus Dei* Lamb of God]

a·go (ə gō′) *adj.* gone by; past (always placed after the noun): *a year ago.* —*adv.* in the past: *He went long ago.* [OE *āgān* gone by]

a·gog (ə gog′) *adj.* eager; curious; excited. —*adv.* with eagerness, curiosity, or excitement. [? < F *en gogues* in happy mood]

ag·o·nize (ag′ə nīz′) *v.* **-nized, -niz·ing. 1** feel great anguish. **2** cause to suffer extreme pain; torture. **3** strive painfully; struggle. [< F *agoniser* < LL *agonizare* < Gk. *agōnizethai* struggle < *agōn* a contest] —**ag′o·niz′ing·ly,** *adv.*

ag·o·ny (ag′ə nē) *n.* **-nies. 1** great pain or suffering. **2** the struggle often preceding death. [ME < OF < LL < Gk. *agōnia* struggle] —**Syn. 1** anguish, torment.

☛ **agony.** Often used in informal English in a light vein in such expressions as: *My shoes hurt; I'm in agony. I have to do my Latin some time; I might as well get the agony over now.*

ag·o·ra[1] (ag′ə rə) *n.* **-rae** (-rē or -rī). the marketplace in an ancient Greek city. **The Agora** in Athens was used for public assemblies. [< Gk.]

ag·o·ra[2] (äg ə rä′) *n.* **ag·o·rot. 1** a unit of money in Israel, worth 1/100 of a pound. **2** a coin worth one agora. [< Hebrew *agora* a small coin]

ag·o·ra·phobe (ag′ə rə fōb′ or ag′rə fōb′) *n.* a person suffering from agoraphobia.

ag·o·ra·pho·bi·a (ag′ə rə fō′bē ə or ag′rə fō′bē ə) *n.* a morbid fear of open spaces.

ag·o·rot (ag′ə rōt′) *n.* pl. of **agora**[2].

a·gou·ti (ə gü′tē) *n.* **-tis** or **-ties.** a rodent related to the guinea pig but having longer legs, found in tropical America. [< F < Sp. *aguti* < native Indian name]

a·grar·i·an (ə grãr′ē ən) *adj.* **1** having to do with land, its use, or its ownership. **2** for the support and advancement of the interests of farmers. **3** agricultural. —*n.* a person who favors a new division of land. [< L *agrarius* < *ager* field]

a·grar·i·an·ism (ə grãr′ē ən iz′əm) *n.* **1** the principles, methods, or practices of agrarians. **2** an agitation for a redistribution of landed property.

a·gree (ə grē′) *v.* **a·greed, a·gree·ing. 1** have the same opinion or opinions: *I agree with you.* **2** be in harmony; correspond (*with*): *Your story agrees with mine.* **3** get along well together. **4** consent (*to*): *He agreed to accompany us.* **5** come to an understanding, especially in settling a dispute. **6 agree with,** have a good effect on; suit: *This food does not agree with me; it makes me sick.* **7** in grammar, have the same number, case, gender, person, etc. (*with*): *That verb agrees with its subject.* [ME < OF *agreer* < *a gre* to (one's) liking < L *ad* to, *gratum,* neut., pleasing]

Syn. 2 Agree, correspond, coincide = be in harmony. **Agree** = not only to be consistent or harmonious in all essentials, but also to be without inconsistencies or contradictions: *The views of the two leaders agree.* **Correspond** = to agree or to equal in essentials or as a whole, in spite of differences: *Dominion Day corresponds to the American Independence Day.* **Coincide** = agree so closely as to be identical: *His tastes coincide with mine.*

☛ **agree to, agree with.** One agrees *to* a plan and agrees *with* a person, but one thing agrees *with* another.

a·gree·a·bil·i·ty (ə grē′ə bil′ə tē) *n.* the quality of being agreeable.

a·gree·a·ble (ə grē′ə bəl) *adj.* **1** pleasant; pleasing: *agreeable manners.* **2** ready to agree; willing: *agreeable to a suggestion.* **3** in agreement; suitable (*to*): *music agreeable to the occasion.* —**a·gree′a·ble·ness,** *n.* —**a·gree′a·bly,** *adv.* —**Syn. 1** See **pleasant.**

a·greed (ə grēd′) *adj.* fixed by common consent.

a·gree·ment (ə grē′mənt) *n.* **1** an agreeing; an understanding reached by two or more nations, persons, or groups of persons among themselves. Nations make treaties and individuals make contracts; both are agreements. **2** sameness of opinion. **3** harmony; correspondence. **4** in grammar, correspondence of words with respect to number, case, gender, person.

a·gré·gé (ä′grā zhā′) *n. French.* a person who has passed a competitive examination conducted by the State for higher teaching appointments. *Abbrev.*: Ag.

Ag. Rep. or **ag. rep.** agricultural representative of a department having the function of advising farmers.

agric. agriculture.

ag·ri·cul·tur·al (ag′rə kul′chər əl) *adj.* **1** having to do with farming; of agriculture. **2** promoting the interests or the study of agriculture. **—ag′ri·cul′tur·al·ly,** *adv.*

ag·ri·cul·tur·al·ist (ag′rə kul′chər əl ist) *n.* an agriculturist.

ag·ri·cul·ture (ag′rə kul′chər) *n.* farming; the raising of crops and livestock; the science or art of cultivating the ground. [< L *agricultura* < *ager* field + *cultura* cultivation]

ag·ri·cul·tur·ist (ag′rə kul′chər ist) *n.* **1** a farmer. **2** an expert in farming.

ag·ri·mo·ny (ag′rə mō′nē) *n.* **-nies.** a plant having slender stalks of feathery leaves and small yellow flowers, whose roots are used as an astringent. [< L *agrimonia,* var. of *argemonia* < Gk. *argemōnē*]

ag·ro·bi·ol·o·gist (ag′rō bī ol′ə jist) *n.* an expert in agrobiology.

ag·ro·bi·ol·o·gy (ag′rō bī ol′ə jē) *n.* the study of plant nutrition and soil management.

a·grol·o·gist (ə grol′ə jist′) *n.* an expert in agrology.

a·grol·o·gy (ə grol′ə jē′) *n.* the branch of agriculture that deals with soils.

ag·ro·ma·ni·a (ag′rō mā′nē ə) *n.* an abnormal desire to live in the open country, away from people. [< Gk. *agros* field + *mania*]

ag·ro·nom·ic (ag′rə nom′ik) *adj.* of or having to do with agronomy.

a·gron·o·mist (ə gron′ə mist) *n.* a person skilled in agronomy.

a·gron·o·my (ə gron′ə mē) *n.* the science of managing farm land; the branch of agriculture dealing with crop production; husbandry. [< Gk. *agronomos* < *agros* land + *nemein* manage]

a·ground (ə ground′) *adv. adj.* on the shore; on the bottom in shallow water: *The ship ran aground.*

agt. agent.

a·gue (ā′gū) *n.* **1** a malarial fever with chills and sweating occurring at regular intervals. **2** a fit of shivering; chill. [ME < OF < L *acuta* (*febris*) severe (fever)]

a·gu·ish (ā′gū ish) *adj.* **1** of or like ague. **2** causing ague. **3** liable to have ague.

ah (ä) *interj.* an exclamation of pain, sorrow, regret, pity, admiration, surprise, joy, dislike, contempt, etc. The meaning of *ah* varies according to the way it is said.

a·ha (ä hä′) *interj.* an exclamation of triumph, satisfaction, surprise, etc.

a·head (ə hed′) *adv.* **1** in front; before: *Walk ahead of me.* **2** forward; onward: *Go ahead with this work.* **3** in advance: *Columbus was ahead of his times in his belief that the world was round.* **4 get ahead,** *Informal.* succeed. **5 get ahead of,** surpass; excel.

a·hem (ə hem′) *interj.* a sound made by coughing or clearing the throat, sometimes used to attract attention, express doubt, or gain time.

a·hoy (ə hoi′) *interj.* a call used by sailors to attract the attention of persons at a distance: *When sailors call to a ship, they shout, "Ship ahoy!"*

aid (ād) *v.* give support to; help: *The Red Cross aids flood victims.* **—*n.*** **1** help; support: *When my arm was broken, I could not dress without aid.* **2** a helper; assistant. [ME < OF *aidier* < L *adjutare,* frequentative of *adjuvare* < *ad-* to + *juvare* help] **—Syn.** *v.* assist. See **help.**

aide (ād) *n.* **1** an aide-de-camp. **2** an aid; helper. [< F]

aide-de-camp (ād′də kamp′; *French,* ād də käN′) *n.* **aides-de-camp.** in the armed services, an officer who acts as an assistant and secretary to a superior officer. *Abbrev.*: ADC, A.D.C., or a.d.c. [< F]

hat, āge, cãre, fär; let, ēqual, tėrm; it, īce
hot, ōpen, ôrder; oil, out; cup, pu̇t, rüle, ūse
əbove, takən, pencəl, lemən, circəs
ch, child; ng, long; sh, ship
th, thin; ᴛʜ, then; zh, measure

aide-mé·moire (ed me mwär′) *n. French.* **1** anything that reminds, such as a calendar note. **2** a written summary or outline of a communication or proposed agreement; memorandum.

ai·grette (ā′gret or ā gret′) *n.* **1** a tuft of feathers worn as an ornament on the head. **2** anything similar in shape or use. **3** an egret. [< F *aigrette* egret]

ai·guille (ā gwēl′) *n.* **1** in mountainous regions, a thin sharp-pointed peak of rock. **2** an instrument for boring holes, used in masonry or blasting. [< F *aiguille* needle < LL *acicula, acucula,* dim. of L *acus* needle]

ail (āl) *v.* **1** be the matter with; trouble: *What ails the man?* **2** be ill; feel sick: *He is ailing.* [OE *eglan*]

ai·lan·thus (ā lan′thəs) *n.* a tree having many leaflets and clusters of small, greenish flowers. The flowers of some ailanthus trees have a disagreeable odor. [< NL < Amboinan (language of Amboina in the Dutch East Indies) *aylanto* tree of heaven; form influenced by Gk. *anthos* flower]

ai·ler·on (ā′lər on′) *n.* a movable part of an airplane wing, that helps to keep the airplane balanced while in flight. See **airplane** for picture. [< F *aileron,* dim. of *aile* < L *ala* wing]

ail·ment (āl′mənt) *n.* a disorder of the body or mind; illness; sickness.

aim (ām) *v.* **1** point or direct (a gun, blow, etc.) in order to hit a target: *aim a gun.* **2** direct (words or acts): *The Prime Minister's speech was aimed at men in his own party.* **3** *Informal.* intend: *I aim to go.* **4** *Informal.* try; direct one's efforts: *He aims to be helpful.*
—*n.* **1** the act of aiming. **2** the direction aimed in; line of sighting. **3** purpose; intention. [ME < OF *esmer* < L *aestimare* appraise, and OF *aesmer* < VL *adaestimare*] **—Syn.** *n.* **3** intent, object.

aim·less (ām′lis) *adj.* without aim or purpose. **—aim′less·ly,** *adv.* **—aim′less·ness,** *n.*

ain't (ānt) *Substandard.* a contraction of the phrases: **a** am not. **b** are not; is not. **c** have not; has not.

Ai·nu (ī′nü) *n.* **1** a member of a very primitive, light-skinned people in N. Japan, now becoming extinct. **2** the language of this people. **—*adj.*** of this people or their language.

air (ãr) *n.* **1** the mixture of gases that surrounds the earth; atmosphere. Air consists of nitrogen, oxygen, argon, carbon dioxide, hydrogen, and small quantities of neon, helium, and other inert gases. **2** the space overhead; sky: *Birds fly in the air.* **3** a light wind; breeze. **4** a melody; tune. **5** public mention: *He gave air to his opinions.* **6** the general character or appearance of anything: *an air of mystery.* **7** bearing; manner: *The famous man had an air of importance.* **8 airs,** *pl.* unnatural or affected manners. **9** in music: **a** a composition to be played or sung as a solo: *Bach's Air on the G String.* **b** any tune or melody, especially a simple one. **c** the main melody in a harmonized composition, usually the soprano or treble part. **10** the medium through which radio waves travel. **11 get the air.** *Slang.* be dismissed or rejected. **12 give the air.** *Slang.* dismiss, especially scornfully. **13 in the air, a** going around: *Wild rumors were in the air.* **b** uncertain. **14 on the air,** broadcasting. **15 off the air, a** not broadcasting: *Our radio station is off the air from one till six a.m.* **b** not being broadcast: *That show is off the air now.* **16 take the air, a** go outdoors; take a walk or ride. **b** start broadcasting. **17 up in the air, a** *Informal.* uncertain; unsettled. **b** *Informal.* very angry or excited. **18 walk on air,** *Informal.* be very gay or pleased.
—*v.* **1** put out in the air; let air through: *air clothes.* **2** make known; mention publicly: *Do not air your troubles.* **3** take for a walk: *air the dog.* **4** *Informal.*

broadcast by radio or television: *The Olympic Games were aired to all of Canada.*
—*adj.* 1 conducting or supplying air: *air duct.* 2 compressing or confining air: *air valve.* 3 using or worked by compressed air: *air drill.* 4 relating to aviation; done by means of aircraft: *air photography.* [ME < OF < L *aer* < Gk. *aēr*]

air base *Esp.U.S.* headquarters and airport for military airplanes.

air bladder in most fish and various animals and plants, a sac that is filled with air. The air bladder of a fish is also called the swimming bladder.

air·borne (ãr′bôrn′) *adj.* 1 off the ground; aloft: *Our airplane will be air-borne in three minutes.* 2 carried in aircraft: *Air-borne troops may land by parachutes or remain in the plane until it lands.* 3 carried by air: *air-borne seeds.*

air brake a brake operated by a piston or pistons worked by compressed air.

air brush a device, operated by compressed air, that is used to spray paint on to a surface.

air·bus (ãr′bus′) *n.* a passenger aircraft, operating on a regular route and as part of a frequent service, which one may board without an advance reservation, simply by paying cash as on a bus or streetcar.

air castle a daydream; a castle in the air.

air chamber any compartment filled with air, especially one in a hydraulic engine.

air chief marshal in the air force, a commissioned officer senior to an air marshal. *Abbrev.*: A.C.M.

air coach *Esp.U.S.* an aircraft with low passenger rates.

air cock a small opening or valve for letting air in or out.

air commodore in the air force, a commissioned officer senior to a group captain and junior to an air vice-marshal. *Abbrev.*: A.C.

air-con·di·tion (ãr′kən dish′ən) *v.* 1 supply with the equipment for air conditioning. 2 treat (air) by means of air conditioning.

air-con·di·tioned (ãr′kən dish′ənd) *adj.* having air conditioning.

air conditioner an apparatus used to air-condition a room, building, train, etc.

air conditioning a means of treating air in buildings, rooms, trains, etc. to regulate its temperature and humidity and to free it from dust.

air-cool (ãr′kül′) *v.* 1 remove heat produced in motor cylinders by combustion, friction, etc. by blowing air. 2 remove heat in (a room) by blowing cool air in. —**air′cool′er**, *n.*

air·craft (ãr′kraft′) *n.* **-craft.** 1 a machine for air navigation that is supported in the air by buoyancy (such as a balloon) or by dynamic action (such as an airplane); an airplane, airship, or balloon. 2 such machines collectively or as a class; airplanes, airships, or balloons.

aircraft carrier a warship designed as a base for airplanes.

air·craft·man (ãr′kraft mən) *n.* **-men** (-mən). in the air force, a serviceman of the lowest rank. *Abbrev.*: A.C.

air·craft·wom·an (ãr′kraft wům′ən) *n.* **-wom·en.** in the air force, a servicewoman of the lowest rank. *Abbrev.*: A.C.W.

air curtain a mass of heated or cooled air circulated around the entrance of a building, in front of and around storage areas, etc., to hold in or keep out warm air and to serve in place of a door.

air cylinder a cylinder in which air is compressed by a piston, for checking the recoil of a gun.

air division a formation in the air element, made up of stations, commands, etc.

air·drome (ãr′drōm′) *n.* airport. Also, *esp.Brit.* **aerodrome.** [< *air* + Gk. *dromos* race course]

air drop a system of dropping food, supplies, etc. from aircraft, especially to allies who are caught behind enemy lines, living in occupied territory, etc.

air-drop (ãr′drop′) *v.* **-dropped** or **-dropt, -drop·ping.** deliver cargo, food, supplies, etc. from an aircraft in flight.

Aire·dale (ãr′dāl′) *n.* 1 a breed of large terrier having a wiry, brown or tan coat with dark markings. 2 a dog of this breed. [< *Airedale* in Yorkshire, England]

air element *Cdn.* the branch of the Canadian Armed Forces having to do with land-based aircraft, formerly known as the Royal Canadian Air Force.

air ex·press a quick or direct means of sending goods by aircraft.

air-ex·press (ãr′eks pres′) *v.* send by air express.

air·field (ãr′fēld′) *n.* the landing field of an airport.

air·flow (ãr′flō′) *n.* 1 the motion of air relative to the surface of an object, such as an automobile or airplane. 2 a natural movement of air or wind.
—*adj.* 1 streamlined: *airflow design.* 2 resulting from air currents: *The airflow pattern changes when an aircraft crosses the sound barrier.*

air·foil (ãr′ foil′) *n.* any surface, such as a wing, rudder, etc. designed to help lift or control an aircraft.

air force 1 the branch of the armed forces that uses airplanes. 2 in Canada, the air element. 3 a group of fliers for military aircraft.

air·frame (ãr′frām′) *n.* the structure or framework, excluding engines, of an airplane, rocket, etc.

air-freight (ãr′frāt′) *v.* send by air freight.

air freight 1 freight carried by aircraft. 2 the sending of freight carried by aircraft.

air·freight·er (ãr′frāt′ər) *n.* 1 an aircraft that carries freight. 2 a person or company operating such aircraft.

air gun a gun worked by compressed air.

air hole 1 a hole that air can pass through. 2 an open space in the ice on a river, pond, etc., often used as a breathing hole by seal, muskrat, etc. 3 an air pocket.

air·i·ly (ãr′ə lē) *adv.* in an airy manner.

air·i·ness (ãr′ē nis) *n.* an airy quality.

air·ing (ãr′ing) *n.* 1 exposure to air for drying, warming, etc.; putting out in the air; letting air through. 2 a walk, ride, or drive in the open air. 3 exposure to public discussion, criticism, etc.

air lane a regular route used by aircraft.

air·less (ãr′lis) *adj.* 1 without fresh air; stuffy. 2 without a breeze; still.

air·lift (ãr′lift′) *n.* 1 a system of using aircraft for passenger transportation and freight conveyance to a place when land approaches are closed: *the Berlin airlift.* 2 something transported by such a system. —*v.* transport by such a system.

air line or **airline** (ãr′līn′) *n.* 1 a company operating a system of transportation by means of aircraft. 2 the system itself. 3 a route for aircraft; airway.

air liner a large aircraft for carrying many passengers.

air lock a compartment holding air at a pressure different from that of the outside air.

air mail 1 mail sent by aircraft. 2 the system of sending mail by aircraft.

air-mail (ãr′māl′) *v.* send or transport letters or packages by air mail. —*adj.* 1 of mail, sent or to be sent by aircraft. 2 of or having to do with the system of sending mail by aircraft.

air·man (ãr′mən) *n.* **-men** (-mən). 1 the pilot of an airplane, airship, or balloon. 2 one of the crew of an aircraft. 3 a serviceman in the air force below the rank of corporal: *airmen, N.C.O.s, and officers.* 4 any man connected with flying.

air marshal in the air force, a commissioned officer senior to an air vice-marshal and junior to an air chief marshal. *Abbrev.*: A.M.

air mass a large area of the atmosphere that has nearly uniform temperature and humidity at any given level and moves horizontally over great distances without changing.

air mattress an inflatable mattress that can serve as a life raft, bed, etc.

air·plane (ãr′plān′) *n.* a mechanically driven, heavier-than-air aircraft supported in flight by the action of the air flowing past or thrusting upward on fixed wings.

☛ **airplane, aeroplane.** For several years these two words were both in general use, but in North America, at least, *airplane* is the usual form. *Aeroplane* is more commonly used in England. In Canada the pronunciation (ãr′ ə plān′) is used by many people who use the spelling *airplane.*

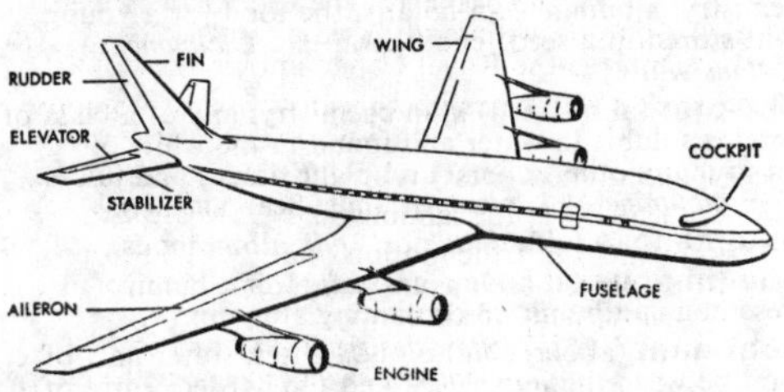

A jet airplane

air plant a plant that grows on other plants and draws nourishment from the air and the rain. Many orchids are air plants.

air pocket a downward air current formed by the sudden sinking of cooled air causing a sudden drop in the altitude of an aircraft.

air·port (ãr′pôrt′) *n.* a place where aircraft may land and take off to discharge and take on passengers or freight. It usually comprises several runways and a number of buildings housing staff and passenger facilities, as well as hangars for sheltering and maintaining aircraft.

air pump a machine for forcing air into or out of something.

air raid an attack by aircraft.

air-raid shelter (ãr′rād′) a place for protection during an air raid.

air rifle a gun that shoots a pellet or dart, worked by compressed air.

air rights the right to use the space above a building, road, railway, etc.: *A company has bought air rights over the freight yards in order to build a huge office block above the tracks.*

air sac an air-filled space in the body of a bird, connected with the lungs.

air shaft a passage for letting fresh air into a mine, tunnel, building, etc.

air·ship (ãr′ship′) *n.* a dirigible.

air·sick (ãr′sik′) *adj.* sick from travelling by air. **—air′sick′ness,** *n.*

air·space (ãr′spās′) *n.* **1** an enclosed area containing air. **2** space in the air, especially that belonging to a particular country: *a violation of our airspace.*

air speed the speed of an aircraft measured in relation to the movement of the air rather than to the ground.

air station a headquarters and airfield for air force operations and training.

air·strip (ãr′strip′) *n.* a paved or cleared strip on which planes can land and take off; a temporary airfield.

air·tight (ãr′tīt′) *adj.* **1** so tight that no air or gas can get in or out. **2** having no weak points open to attack: *an airtight explanation.*

air time 1 the time when a certain radio or television program begins to broadcast: *a few minutes to air time.* **2** an amount of broadcasting time: *The advertising program cost $75,000 in air time alone.*

air-to-air (ãr′tu̇ ãr′) *adj.* between two flying aircraft: *air-to-air refuelling, air-to-air missiles.*

air valve a valve for controlling the flow of air into or out of something.

air vice-marshal in the air force, a commissioned officer senior to an air commodore and junior to an air marshal. *Abbrev.:* A.V.M.

air·way (ãr′wā′) *n.* **1** a route for aircraft. **2** a passage for air. **3** a specified radio frequency for broadcasting. **4 airways, a** an airline. **b** channels for radio or television broadcasting.

air well air shaft.

air·wo·man (ãr′wu̇m′ən) *n.* **-wo·men. 1** a woman who pilots an aircraft; aviatrix. **2** a woman serving in an air force.

air·wor·thy (ãr′wėr′ᴛʜē) *adj.* fit or safe for service in the air. **—air′wor′thi·ness,** *n.*

air·y (ãr′ē) *adj.* **air·i·er, air·i·est. 1** like air; not solid or substantial. **2** light as air; graceful; delicate. **3** light-hearted; gay. **4** open to currents of air; breezy. **5** reaching high into the air; lofty. **6** of air; in the air. **7** unnatural; affected: *His airy manner made him seem very haughty.* **8** flippant.

aisle (īl) *n.* **1** a passage between rows of seats in a hall, theatre, school, church, etc. **2** the part of a church at the side of the nave, choir, or transept and set off by pillars. **3** any long or narrow passageway. See **apse** for diagram. [ME *ele* < OF < L *ala* wing; influenced in form by F *aile* and E *isle* and in meaning by *alley*]

a·jar[1] (ə jär′) *adv. adj.* of a door or gate, opened a little way. [ME *on char* on the turn; OE *cerr* turn]

☛ See **a-**[1] for usage note.

a·jar[2] (ə jär′) *adv.* not in harmony. [< *a-* in + *jar* discord]

A·ke·la (ə kā′lə or ə kē′lə) *n.* a cubmaster. [from *Akela,* the Lone Wolf, the leader of the wolf pack in Rudyard Kipling's *The Jungle Book*]

a·kene (ā kēn′) *n.* achene.

a·kim·bo (ə kim′bō) *adj. adv.* with the hands on the hips and the elbows bent outward. [ME *in kene bowe,* apparently, in keen bow, at a sharp angle]

a·kin (ə kin′) *adj.* **1** related by blood: *Your cousins are akin to you.* **2** in linguistics, descended from the same root: *"Guest" is akin to "host."* **3** alike; similar: *His opinions are akin to mine.* [for *of kin*]

al- the form of **ad-** before *l,* as in *ally.*

-al[1] *suffix.* of; like; having the nature of: *natural = of nature or like nature; ornamental = having the nature of ornament.* [< L *-alis* pertaining to]

-al[2] *suffix.* the act of —ing: *refusal = the act of refusing.* [< L *-ale,* neut. of *-alis*]

Al aluminum.

à la or a la (a′lə or ä′lə; *French,* ä lä) in the manner of; in the style of. [< F]

☛ **à la, a la.** Although originally French, **a la** is now regarded as an English preposition: *a la Hollywood, a la Winston Churchill.* In formal writing and some advertising (for cosmetics and fashionable clothes), the accent mark is usually kept: **à la.** In informal writing it is often dropped: **a la.**

Ala. Alabama.

al·a·bam·ine (al′ə bam′īn, al′ə bam′ēn, or al′ə bam′in) *n.* a rare, unisolated chemical element. *Symbol:* Ab [< *Alabama*]

al·a·bas·ter (al′ə bas′tər or al′ə bas′tər) *n.* **1** a smooth, white, translucent variety of gypsum. Alabaster is often carved into ornaments and vases. **2** a variety of calcite that is somewhat translucent and often banded like marble. *—adj.* smooth, white, and translucent like alabaster. [ME < OF < L < Gk. *alabast(r)os* alabaster]

à la carte (a′lə kärt′ or ä′ lə kärt′; *French,* ä lä kärt′) of food, menus, etc., with a stated price for each dish. [< F *à la carte* according to the bill of fare]

a·lack (ə lak′) *interj. Archaic.* an exclamation of sorrow or regret; alas.

a·lack·a·day (ə lak′ə dā′) *interj. Archaic.* alas! alack!

a·lac·ri·ty (ə lak′rə tē) *n.* **1** cheerful willingness: *The boy took to Latin with alacrity.* **2** liveliness. [< L *alacritas* < *alacer* brisk]

A·lad·din (ə lad′ən) *n.* in *The Arabian Nights*, a youth who found a magic lamp and a magic ring. By rubbing either one of them, he could call a powerful spirit, or genie, to do whatever he commanded.

Aladdin's lamp a means of making any dream come true.

à la king (a′ lə king′ or ä′ lə king′) creamed with mushrooms, pimento, and green pepper: *chicken à la king.*

à la mode, a la mode, or **a·la·mode** (a′ lə mōd′ or ä′ lə mōd′) *adv.* **1** according to the prevailing fashion; in style. **2** in a certain way. Desserts à la mode are served with ice cream. Beef à la mode is cooked with vegetables. [< F]

a·larm (ə lärm′) *n.* **1** sudden fear; fright; excitement caused by fear of danger. **2** a warning of approaching danger. **3** something that gives such a warning. **4** a call to arms or action. **5** a device that makes a noise to warn or awaken people.
—*v.* **1** fill with sudden fear; frighten: *He was alarmed because his friends were late in returning.* **2** warn (anyone) of approaching danger. **3** call to arms.
[ME < OF *alarme* < Ital. *allarme* < *all'arme!* to arms!]
—**Syn.** *n.* **1** See **fear.** —*v.* **1** See **frighten.**

alarm clock a clock that can be set to ring a bell, etc. at any desired time, especially to waken people from sleep.

a·larm·ing (ə lär′ming) *adj.* of a frightening nature.
—**a·larm′ing·ly,** *adv.*

a·larm·ist (ə lär′mist) *n.* one who raises alarms without good reason.

a·lar·um (ə lar′əm or ə lär′əm) *n. Archaic.* alarm.

a·la·ry (ā′lə rē or al′ə rē) *adj.* in zoology: **1** of or having to do with wings. **2** wing-shaped. [< L *alarius* < *ala* wing]

a·las (ə las′) *interj.* an exclamation of sorrow, grief, regret, pity, or dread. [ME < OF *a* ah + *las* miserable < L *lassus* weary]

Alas. Alaska.

Alaska Highway a highway that extends from Dawson Creek, British Columbia, to Fairbanks, Alaska.

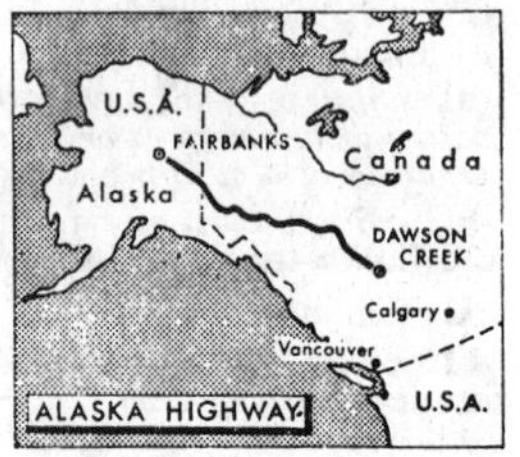

a·late (ā′lāt′) *adj.* having wings or winglike parts. [< L *alatus* < *ala* wing]

alb (alb) *n.* a white linen robe worn by Roman Catholic and some Anglican priests at certain church services. [< L (*vestis*) *alba* white (robe)]

al·ba·core (al′bə kôr′) *n.* **-core** or **-cores.** a long-finned, edible fish related to the tuna, found in the Atlantic. [< Pg. *albacor* < Arabic *al-bakūra*]

al·ba·tross (al′bə tros′) *n.* any of various large web-footed sea birds related to the petrel, that can fly long distances. [var. of obsolete *alcatras* frigate bird < Sp. < Pg. *alcatraz* < Arabic *al-qadus* the bucket < Gk. *kados* < Phoenician]

al·be·it (ol bē′it or ôl bē′it) *conj.* although; even though. [ME *al be it* although it be]

Al·ber·tan (al bėr′tən) *adj.* of or having to do with Alberta or its people. —*n.* a native or permanent resident of Alberta.

al·bert·ite (al′bər tīt′) *n.* a bituminous mineral resembling asphalt. [< *Albert* County, New Brunswick. + *-ite*]

al·bi·nism (al′bə niz′əm) *n.* the absence of color; the condition of being an albino.

al·bi·no (al bē′nō or al bī′nō) *n.* **-nos. 1** a person who from birth has a pale, milky skin, very light hair, and pink eyes. **2** any animal or plant that has pale, defective coloring. [< Pg. *albino* < *albo* < L *albus* white]

Al·bi·on (al′bē ən) *n. Poetic.* England. [< L]

al·bum (al′bəm) *n.* **1** a book with blank pages for pictures, stamps, autographs, etc. **2** a holder designed like a book for phonograph records. **3** a souvenir volume: *a school album.* [< L *album*, neut. of *albus* white]

al·bu·men (al bū′mən) *n.* **1** the white of an egg, consisting mostly of albumin dissolved in water. **2** in chemistry, albumin. **3** in botany, the food for a young plant stored in a seed; endosperm. [< L *albumen* < *albus* white]

al·bu·min (al bū′mən) *n.* in chemistry, any of a class of proteins soluble in water and found in the white of egg and in many other animal and plant tissues and juices. [< F *albumine* < L *albumen, -inis.* See ALBUMEN.]

al·bu·mi·nose (al bū′mə nōs′) *adj.* albuminous.

al·bu·mi·nous (al bū′mə nəs) *adj.* **1** of albumin. **2** resembling albumin. **3** containing albumin.

al·bur·num (al bėr′nəm) *n.* the lighter, softer part of wood between the inner bark and the harder centre of a tree; sapwood. [< L *alburnum* < *albus* white]

Al·can Highway (al′kan) Alaska Highway. [< *Al*aska + *Can*ada]

al·ca·zar or **al·cá·zar** (al′kə zär′ or al kaz′ər; *Spanish,* äl kä′thär) *n.* **1** a palace of the Spanish Moors. **2 Alcázar,** the palace of the Moorish kings at Seville, Spain, later occupied by the Spanish royal family. [< Sp. < Arabic *al-qasr* the castle < L *castrum* fort]

al·che·mist (al′kə mist) *n.* in the Middle Ages, a student of alchemy. Alchemists tried to turn base metals into gold and to find the elixir of life.

al·che·my (al′kə mē) *n.* **1** medieval chemistry, especially the search for a process by which base metals could be turned into gold. **2** any magic power or process for changing one thing into another: *the lovely alchemy of spring.* [ME < OF *alkemie* < Med.L *alchimia* < Arabic *al-kīmiyā* < LGk. *chēmeia* the extracting of medical juices < Gk. *chymeia* infusion < *chymos* juice of a plant]

al·co·hol (al′kə hol′ or al′kə hôl′) *n.* **1** the colorless liquid in wine, beer, whisky, gin, etc. that makes them intoxicating; grain alcohol; ethyl alcohol. Alcohol is used in medicine, in manufacturing, and as a fuel. *Formula*: C_2H_5OH **2** any intoxicating liquor containing this liquid. **3** in chemistry, any of a group of similar organic compounds. Alcohols contain a hydroxyl group and react with organic acids to form esters. Wood alcohol or methyl alcohol, CH OH, is very poisonous. [< Med.L *alcohol* (originally, "fine powder," then "essence") < Arabic *al-kuhl* powdered antimony]

al·co·hol·ic (al′kə hol′ik or al′kə hôl′ik) *adj.* **1** of alcohol. **2** containing alcohol. **3** suffering from the excessive use of alcoholic liquors. —*n.* a person suffering from alcoholism.

al·co·hol·ism (al′kə hol iz′əm or al′kə hôl iz′əm) *n.* **1** a disease which has as its chief symptom the inability to moderate the drinking of alcoholic liquors. **2** a diseased condition caused by drinking too much alcoholic liquor.

Al·co·ran (al′kô rän′ or al′kô ran′) *n.* the Koran.

al·cove (al′kōv) *n.* **1** a small room opening out of a larger room. **2** a large hollow space forming a recess in a wall. **3** a summerhouse. [< F < Sp. *alcoba* < Arabic *al-qubba* the vaulted chamber]

Ald. Alderman.

Al·deb·a·ran (al deb′ə rən) *n.* the brightest star in the constellation Taurus. [< Arabic *al-dabarān* the follower (i.e., of the Pleiades) < *dabar* follow]

al·de·hyde (al′də hīd′) *n.* **1** a transparent, colorless liquid, with a suffocating smell, produced by the partial oxidation of ordinary alcohol. *Formula*: CH_3CHO **2** any similar organic compound. [short for NL *al(cohol) dehyd(rogenatum)*, alcohol deprived of its hydrogen]

al·der (ol′dər or ôl′dər) *n.* any of several trees and shrubs, usually found in wet land, that have clusters of catkins which develop into small woody cones. [OE *alor*]

al·der·man (ol′dər mən or ôl′dər mən) *n.* **-men.** a person elected to represent the people of a ward on the governing council of a city. *Abbrev.*: Ald. or Aldm. [OE (*e*)*aldormann* < *ealdor* elder, chief + *mann* man]

hat, āge, cãre, fär; let, ēqual, tėrm; it, īce
hot, ōpen, ôrder; oil, out; cup, pu̇t, rüle, ūse
əbove, takən, pencəl, lemən, circəs
ch, child; ng, long; sh, ship
th, thin; ᴛʜ, then; zh, measure

al·der·man·ic (ol′dər man′ik or ôl′dər man′ik) *adj.* **1** of an alderman. **2** suitable for an alderman.

Al·der·ney (ol′dər nē or ôl′dər nē) *n.* **-neys. 1** either of the two breeds of dairy cattle that originated in the Channel Islands; Jersey or Guernsey. **2** an animal of either of these breeds.

Aldm. Alderman.

ale (āl) *n.* a heavy, bitter beer, fermented from hops and malt. [OE *alu*]

a·lee (ə lē′) *adv. adj.* on or toward the side of a ship that is away from the wind. [< a^1- + *lee*]

ale·house (āl′hous′) *n.* a place where ale or beer is sold.

a·lem·bic (ə lem′bik) *n.* **1** a glass or metal container formerly used in distilling. **2** something that transforms or refines: *Imagination is the alembic of the mind.* [ME < OF < Med.L *alembicus* < Arabic *al-anbiq* the still < Gk. *ambix* cup]

A·len·çon (ä läɴ sôɴ′; *often,* ə len′sən) *n.* a kind of fine lace. [< *Alençon,* a city in N.W. France where this lace is made]

a·lert (ə lėrt′) *adj.* **1** watchful; wide-awake: *A good hunting dog is alert to every sound and movement in the field.* **2** brisk; active; nimble: *A sparrow is very alert in its movements.*
—*n.* **1** a signal warning of an air attack or other impending danger. **2** the period of time in which this warning is in effect: *We stayed at home throughout a hurricane alert.* **3** a signal to troops, etc. to be ready for action. **4 on the alert,** on the lookout; watchful; wide-awake.
—*v.* call to arms; warn. [< F *alerte* < Ital. *all' erta* on the watch, ult. < L *erigere* raise up] —**a·lert′ly,** *adv.* —**a·lert′ness,** *n.* —**Syn.** *adj.* **1** attentive, vigilant. See **watchful.**

A·le·ut (al′ē üt′) *n.* **1** a native or inhabitant of the Aleutian Islands, southwest of Alaska. **2** the language of the Aleuts, which is distantly related to Eskimo. [< Russian]

al·e·vin (al′ə vin) *n.* a very young fish, usually a very young salmon. [< F < L *allevare* lift up, rear < *ad-* to + *levare* raise]

ale·wife[1] (āl′wīf′) *n.* **-wives.** a woman who keeps an alehouse.

ale·wife[2] (āl′wīf′) *n.* **-wife** or **-wives.** a sea fish found in great numbers along the Atlantic Coast, related to the herring and the shad but inferior as food. [origin uncertain]

Al·ex·an·dri·an (al′ig zan′drē ən) *adj.* **1** of Alexandria. **2** of Alexander the Great. **3** of Alexandrine verse.

al·ex·an·drine or **Al·ex·an·drine** (al′ig zan′drin) *n.* a line of poetry having six iambic feet, with a caesura (pause) after the third foot. *Example:*

He séeks | out míght | y chárms, | to tróu | ble sléep | y mínds.

[< F *alexandrin;* because this metre was used in OF poems on *Alexander* the Great]

al·fal·fa (al fal′fə) *n.* a plant, grown as food for horses and cattle, that has deep roots, cloverlike leaves, and bluish-purple flowers. Alfalfa can be cut several times a season and then dried as hay. [< Sp. < Arabic *al-fishfisha* the best kind of fodder]

al fi·ne (äl′fē′nā) *Italian.* to the end.

al·fres·co or **al fres·co** (al fres′kō) *adv. adj.* in the open air; outdoors. [< Ital.]

alg. algebra.

al·ga (al′gə) *n.* **-gae** (-jē or -jī). one of the algae.

al·gae (al′jē or al′jī) *n.pl.* a group of water plants that have chlorophyll but do not have true stems, roots, or leaves. Some algae are one-celled and form scum on rocks; others, such as the seaweeds, are very large. [< L *algae,* pl. of *alga* seaweed]

al·gal (al′gəl) *adj.* of or having to do with algae.

al·ge·bra (al′jə brə) *n.* **1** the branch of mathematics in which quantities are denoted by letters, in which negative numbers as well as ordinary numbers are used, and in which problems are solved in the form of equations. In algebra, $x + y = x^2$ is a way of stating that the sum of two numbers equals the square of one of them. **2** a textbook or handbook dealing with the subject. *Abbrev.:* alg. [< Med.L < Arabic *al-jabr* the bone setting; hence, reduction (i.e., of parts to a whole)]

al·ge·bra·ic (al′jə brā′ik) *adj.* of algebra; used in algebra: $(a + b)(a - b) = a^2 - b^2$ *is an algebraic statement.* —**al′ge·bra′i·cal·ly,** *adv.*

al·ge·bra·i·cal (al′jə brā′ə kəl) *adj.* algebraic.

al·ge·bra·ist (al′jə brā′ist) *n.* an expert in algebra.

Al·gon·ki·an (al gong′kē ən) *n. adj.* Algonquian.

Al·gon·kin (al gong′kin) *n.* Algonquin.

Al·gon·qui·an (al gong′kē ən or al gong′kwē ən) *n.* **1** the most widespread family of American Indian languages. **2** an Indian belonging to an Algonquian tribe. **3** in geology: **a** the late Proterozoic period, ending about 550 million years ago. **b** the rocks formed during this period.
—*adj.* **1** of or having to do with Algonquian languages. **2** of or having to do with the late Proterozoic period, or the rocks formed during it. [< *Algonquin*]

Al·gon·quin (al gong′kin or al gong′kwin) *n.* **1** a member of a family of tribes of the Algonquian linguistic stock. These tribes formerly lived in eastern Canada and E. United States, but they were pushed gradually westward. **2** the language of any of these tribes. **3** any Algonquian.

al·go·rism (al′gə riz′əm) *n.* **1** a form, method, or procedure for computing: *an algorism for long division.* **2** the system of Arabic numerals, using nine digits and zero; decimal system of counting. Also, **algorithm.** [ME < OF *algorisme* < Med.L *algorismus* < Arabic *al-khuwarizmi* < *al-Khowarizmi,* a famous Arab mathematician of the 9th century A.D.]

al·go·rithm (al′gə riᴛʜ′əm) *n.* algorism.

Al·ham·bra (al ham′brə) *n.* the palace of the Moorish kings near Granada, Spain. [< Sp. < Arabic *al-hamra'* the red (house)]

a·li·as (ā′lē əs) *n.* **a·li·as·es,** *adv.* —*n.* an assumed name; other name: *The spy's real name was Harrison, but he sometimes went by the alias of Johnson.* —*adv.* otherwise called; with the assumed name of. [< L *alias* at another time]

☛ In law, alias is still often written in italics (Harrison *alias* Johnson), in which case it stands for the Latin *alias dictus,* meaning "otherwise called."

al·i·bi (al′ə bī′) *n.* **-bis,** *v.,* **-bied, -bi·ing.** —*n.* **1** in law the plea that a person accused of a certain offence was somewhere else when the offence was committed. **2** *Informal.* an excuse. —*v. Informal.* make an excuse. [< L *alibi* elsewhere]

al·ien (ā′lē ən or āl′yən) *n.* **1** a person who is not a citizen of the country in which he lives. **2** a foreigner; stranger. —*adj.* **1** of another country; foreign. **2** unfamiliar; strange: *alien ideas.* **3 alien to,** not in agreement with; quite different from: *Unkindness is alien to her nature.* [ME < OF < L *alienus* < *alius* other]

al·ien·a·ble (ā′lē ən ə bəl or āl′yən ə bel) *adj.* capable of being transferred to another person: *alienable property.*

al·ien·ate (ā′lē ən āt′ or āl′yən āt′) *v.* **-at·ed, -at·ing. 1** turn away in feeling or affection; make unfriendly: *He was alienated from his sister by her foolish acts.* **2** transfer the ownership of (property) to another: *Enemy property was alienated during the war.* —**Syn. 1** estrange.

al·ien·a·tion (ā′lē ən ā′shən or āl′yən ā′shən) *n.* **1** a turning away in feeling or affection; making unfriendly. **2** a transfer of the ownership of property to another. **3** mental disease; insanity.

al·ien·ist (ā′lē ən ist or āl′yən ist) *n.* a psychiatrist, especially one who testifies in court. [< F *aliéniste* < L *alienus* insane]

al·i·form (al′i fôrm′) *adj.* of or having to do with wings;

wing-shaped. [< L *ala* wing + E *-form*]

a·light[1] (ə līt′) *v.* **a·light·ed** or (*Poetic*) **a·lit, a·light·ing.** **1** get down; get off: *alight from a horse.* **2** come down from the air and settle; come down from flight. **3** come by chance (*on* or *upon*). [OE *ālīhtan,* ult. < *līht* light (in weight); originally, with reference to taking one's weight off a horse or vehicle]

a·light[2] (ə līt′) *adv. adj.* on fire; lighted up: *Her face was alight with joy.* [OE *ālīht* illuminated]

a·lign (ə līn′) *v.* **1** bring into line; adjust to a line: *align the sights of a gun.* **2** form a line: *The troops aligned.* **3** form into a line. **4** join with others in a cause: *Germany was aligned with Japan in World War II.* Also, **aline.** [< F *aligner* < *a-* to (< L *ad-*) + *ligner* < L *lineare* < *linea* line]

a·lign·ment (ə līn′mənt) *n.* **1** an arrangement in a straight line; formation in a line; bringing into line. **2** the line or lines so formed. **3** a joining together (of persons, nations, etc.) for a common purpose. Also, **alinement.**

IN ALIGNMENT

OUT OF ALIGNMENT

a·like (ə līk′) *adv.* **1** in the same way: *Robert and his father walk alike.* **2** similarly; equally. *—adj.* like one another; similar: *These twins are very much alike.* [OE *gelīc, onlīc*]

al·i·ment (al′ə mənt) *n.* food; nourishment. [< L *alimentum* < *alere* nourish]

al·i·men·ta·ry (al′ə men′tə rē or al′ə men′trē) *adj.* **1** having to do with food and nutrition. **2** nourishing; nutritious. **3** providing support or sustenance.

alimentary canal the parts of the body through which food passes. The mouth, esophagus, stomach, intestines, and anus are parts of the alimentary canal.

al·i·men·ta·tion (al′ə men tā′shən) *n.* **1** nourishment; nutrition. **2** maintenance; support.

al·i·mo·ny (al′ə mō′nē) *n.* **1** the money paid under court order to a wife by her husband when separated, during divorce proceedings, or after divorce. **2** sustenance. [< L *alimonia* sustenance < *alere* nourish]

a·line (ə līn′) *v.* **a·lined, a·lin·ing.** align.

a·line·ment (ə līn′mənt) *n.* alignment

al·i·quant (al′ə kwənt) *adj.* not able to divide a number or quantity without leaving a remainder: *5 is an aliquant part of 14.* [< L *aliquantus* somewhat < *alius* some + *quantus* how much]

al·i·quot (al′ə kwət) *adj.* able to divide a number or quantity without leaving a remainder: *3 is an aliquot part of 12.* [< L *aliquot* some < *alius* some + *quot* how many]

a·lit (ə lit′) *v. Poetic.* a pt. and a pp. of **alight**[1].

a·live (ə līv′) *adj.* **1** living; not dead: *The man is alive.* **2** in continued activity or operation: *Keep the principles of liberty alive.* **3** of all living: *the happiest man alive.* **4** active; lively. **5** connected with a source of electricity; charged electrically. **6** of telephones, microphones, etc. not shut off; operating or functioning. **7 alive to,** noticing; awake to; sensitive to. **8 alive with,** full of; swarming with: *The streets were alive with people.* **9 look alive!** hurry up! be quick! [OE *on līfe*]

☛ *Alive* is not normally used before a noun, where *live* (līv) and *living* may appear: *a live animal, living people. Alive* occurs after its noun or in the predicate: *the oldest man alive. He is still alive.*

a·liz·a·rin (ə liz′ə rin) *n.* a red dye prepared from coal tar, formerly obtained from madder. *Formula:* $C_{14}H_8O_4$ Also, **alizarine.** [< F *alizarine* < *alizari* < Sp. < Arabic *al-ʿasara* the extract]

a·liz·a·rine (ə liz′ə rin or ə liz′ə rēn′) *n.* alizarin.

al·ka·li (al′kə lī′) *n.* **-lis** or **-lies** . **1** in chemistry, any base or hydroxide that is soluble in water, neutralizes acids and forms salts with them, and turns red litmus blue. Lye and ammonia are alkalis. **2** any salt or mixture of salts that neutralizes acids. Some desert soils contain much alkali. [< MF *alcali* < Arabic *al-qalī* the ashes of saltwort (a genus of plant)]

al·ka·line (al′kə līn′ or al′kə lin) *adj.* **1** of or like an alkali . **2** containing an alkali.

alkaline-earth metals calcium, strontium, and barium. Some authorities include beryllium, magnesium, and radium.

alkaline earths the oxides of the alkaline-earth metals.

al·ka·lin·i·ty (al′kə lin′ə tē) *n.* an alkaline quality or condition.

al·ka·lize (al′kə līz′) *v.* **-lized, -liz·ing.** make alkaline. **—al′ka·li·za′tion,** *n.*

al·ka·loid (al′kə loid′) *n.* an organic substance containing nitrogen; a substance that resembles an alkali and contains nitrogen. Many alkaloids obtained from plants are drugs, such as cocaine, strychnine, morphine, and quinine. Alkaloids are often very poisonous.

Al·ko·ran (al′kô rän′ or al′kô ran′) *n.* the Koran.

all (ol or ôl) *adj.* **1** the whole of: *all Europe.* **2** every one of: *all men.* **3** the greatest possible: *He made all haste to reach home in time.* **4** any; any whatever: *The prisoner denied all connection with the crime.* **5** nothing but; only: *all words and no thought.* **6 all in.** *Informal.* weary; worn out.
—pron. **1** the whole number; everyone: *All of us are going.* **2** the whole quantity; everything: *All that glitters is not gold.*
—n. everything one has: *He lost all in the fire.*
above all, before everything else.
after all, when everything has been considered; nevertheless.
all at once, suddenly.
all but, almost; nearly.
all in all, a everything. **b** completely.
at all, a under any conditions. **b** in any way.
for all (that), in spite of; notwithstanding.
in all, counting every person or thing; altogether: *There were 100 men in all.*
—adv. **1** wholly; entirely: *The cake is all gone.* **2** each; apiece: *The score was even at forty all.* **3 all of,** as much as; no less than. [OE *eall*]

al·la bre·ve (al′ə brā′vā) in music: **1** a measure having two or four beats in which a half note represents one beat. **2** the symbol indicating this. [< Ital.]

The symbol used to indicate alla breve

Al·lah (al′ə or ä′lə) *n.* the Moslem name of the one Supreme Being, or God.

al·lar·gan·do (ä′lär gän′dō) *adj.* in music, gradually becoming slower and louder. [< Ital.]

all-a·round (ol′ə round′ or ôl′-) *adj.* all-round.

al·lay (ə lā′) *v.* **-layed, -lay·ing.** **1** put at rest; quiet: *His fears were allayed by the news of the safety of his family.* **2** relieve; check: *Her fever was allayed by the medicine.* **3** make less; weaken. [OE *ālecgan*]
—Syn. 1 pacify, calm.

all clear a signal indicating the end of an air raid or other danger.

al·le·ga·tion (al′ə gā′shən) *n.* **1** an assertion without proof: *He makes so many wild allegations that no one will believe him.* **2** an assertion: *The lawyer's allegation was proved.* [ME < OF < L *allegatio, -onis* < *allegare* send a message, cite < *ad-* to + *legare* commission, ult. < *lex* law]

al·lege (ə lej′) *v.* **-leged, -leg·ing.** **1** assert without proof. **2** state positively; assert; declare: *This man alleges that his watch has been stolen.* **3** give or bring forward as a reason, argument, or excuse. [< AF *alegier* < L *ex-* out + *litigare* strive, sue; with sense of L *allegare* charge] **—al·leg′er,** *n.* **—Syn. 2** affirm. **3** cite.

al·leged (ə lejd′) *adj.* **1** asserted without proof: *The alleged theft never really happened.* **2** asserted; declared. **3** brought forward as a reason.

al·leg·ed·ly (ə lej′id lē) *adv.* according to what is or has been alleged.

al·le·giance (ə lē′jəns) *n.* **1** the loyalty owed by a citizen to his country or by a subject to his ruler. **2** loyalty; faithfulness to a person, cause, etc. that is entitled to obedience or honor. [ME *alegeaunce* < OF *ligeance* < *lige* liege]

al·le·gor·i·cal (al′ə gôr′ə kəl) *adj.* explaining or

teaching something by a story; using allegory. —al′le·gor′i·cal·ly, *adv.*

al·le·gor·ist (al′ə gôr′ist) *n.* a writer of allegories.

al·le·go·rize (al′ə gə rīz′) *v.* **-rized, -riz·ing. 1** make into an allegory. **2** treat or interpret as an allegory. **3** use allegory.

al·le·go·ry (al′ə gô′rē) *n.* **-ries.** a long and complicated story with an underlying moral meaning different from the surface meaning: *Bunyan's "The Pilgrim's Progress" is an allegory.* An allegory may be regarded as an extended metaphor. [ME < L < Gk. *allēgoria* < *allos* other + *agoreuein* speak]

☛ An **allegory,** a **fable,** or a **parable** is a story made up to present ideas in a concrete, vivid way. The incidents of an **allegory** may stand for political, spiritual, or romantic situations; its characters may be types (*Mr. Worldly Wiseman*) or personifications (*Courtesy, Jealousy*). A **fable** has as its characters animals or inanimate objects that by acting and talking like human beings call attention to human weaknesses and teach a common-sense lesson that is usually stated at the end: *Aesop's fables.* A **parable** is a short story of everyday life used to teach a moral by comparison or by implication: *Jesus often used parables.*

al·le·gret·to (al′ə gret′ō) *adj. adv. n.* **-tos.** in music: —*adj.* quick, but not as quick as allegro. —*adv.* in allegretto tempo. —*n.* such a part in a piece of music. [< Ital. *allegretto,* dim. of *allegro*]

al·le·gro (ə leg′rō or ə lā′grō) *adj. adv. n.* **-gros.** in music: —*adj.* quick; lively. —*adv.* in allegro time. —*n.* such a part in a piece of music. [< Ital. < L *alicer,* unrecorded popular variant of *alacer* brisk]

al·le·lu·ia (al′ə lü′yə) *interj.* a liturgical form of **hallelujah,** meaning "praise ye the Lord." —*n.* a hymn of praise to the Lord. [< L < Gk. < Hebrew *hallēlūjāh* praise ye Jehovah]

al·le·mande (a′lə mand′; *French.* äl mäNd′) *n.* **1** a German dance that became popular in France in the 1700's. **2** the music for such a dance. **3** in music, one of the movements of a classical suite.

al·ler·gen (al′ər jən) *n.* any substance that causes or reveals an allergy. [< *aller(gy)* + *-gen*]

al·ler·gen·ic (al′ər jen′ik) *adj.* of or having to do with allergens.

al·ler·gic (ə lėr′jik) *adj.* **1** of allergy. **2** having an allergy. **3** *Informal.* having a strong dislike: *I'm allergic to studying.*

al·ler·gist (al′ər jist′) *n.* in medicine, a doctor who specializes in the diagnosis and treatment of allergies.

al·ler·gy (al′ər jē) *n.* **-gies. 1** an unusual sensitiveness to a particular substance. Hay fever and asthma are often caused by allergies to certain pollens and dusts. **2** *Informal.* a strong dislike: *an allergy for work.* [< NL *allergia* < Gk. *allos* different, strange + *ergon* action]

al·le·vi·ate (ə lē′vē āt′) *v.* **-at·ed, -at·ing.** make easier to endure (suffering of the body or mind); relieve; lessen: *Heat often alleviates pain.* [< LL *alleviare* < L *ad-* up + *levis* light] —**al·le′vi·a′tor,** *n.* —**Syn.** allay, mitigate.

al·le·vi·a·tion (ə lē′vē ā′shən) *n.* **1** an alleviating. **2** a being alleviated. **3** something that alleviates.

al·le·vi·a·tive (ə lē′vē ə tiv or ə lē′vē ā′tiv) *adj.* alleviating. —*n.* anything that alleviates.

al·ley[1] (al′ē) *n.* **-leys. 1** a narrow back street in a city or town; alleyway. **2** a path in a park or garden, bordered by trees. **3** a long, narrow enclosed place for bowling. **4** a building having a number of alleys for bowling. [ME < OF *alee* a going < *aler* go]

al·ley[2] (al′ē) *n.* **-leys. 1** a large, white or colored glass marble used to shoot at the other marbles in a game. **2 alleys** any game played with such marbles. [shortened form of *alabaster*]

al·ley·way (al′ē wā′) *n.* **1** an alley in a city or town. **2** a narrow passageway.

All Fools' Day April 1, April Fools' Day.

all fours 1 all four legs of an animal. **2** the arms and legs of a person; hands and knees.

all hail an exclamation of greeting or welcome.

All·hal·lows (ol′hal′ōz or ôl′-) *n.* November 1, All Saints' Day.

Allhallows Eve October 31, Halloween.

hat, āge, cãre, fär; let, ēqual, tėrm; it, īce
hot, ōpen, ôrder; oil, out; cup, pu̇t, rüle, ūse
əbove, takən, pencəl, lemən, circəs
ch, child; ng, long; sh, ship
th, thin; ᴛʜ, then; zh, measure

al·li·ance (ə lī′əns) *n.* **1** a union formed by agreement; joining of interests. All alliance may be a joining of family interests by marriage, a joining of national interests by treaty, etc. **2** the nations, persons, etc. who belong to such a union. **3** an association; connection. **4** a similarity in structure or descent; relationship. [ME < OF *aliance* < *alier* unite < L *alligare* < *ad-* to + *ligare* bind]

al·lied (ə līd′ or al′īd) *adj.* **1** united by agreement or treaty; combined for some special purpose: *allied nations, allied armies.* **2** associated; connected: *allied banks.* **3** similar in structure or descent; related: *The dog and the wolf are allied animals.* **4 Allied,** of the Allies; by the Allies.

Al·lies (al′īz or ə līz′) *n.pl.* **1** the countries that fought against Germany and Austria in World War I. **2** the countries that fought against Germany, Italy, and Japan in World War II.

al·li·ga·tor (al′ə gā′tər) *n.* **1** a large reptile having a rather thick skin, similar to the crocodile but having a shorter and flatter head. Alligators live in the rivers and marshes of the warm parts of North and South America and China. **2** leather prepared from its skin. **3** *Cdn.* **a** a small boat used in handling floating logs, for hauling log booms, etc. **b** formerly, a sidewheel steamer especially designed for use in the small inland lakes and waterways of the northern bush country. **4** an amphibian vehicle for carrying troops ashore, etc. [< Sp. *el lagarto* the lizard < L *lacertus* lizard]

alligator pear avocado.

all-im·por·tant (ol′im pôr′tənt or ôl′-) *adj.* essential; extremely important.

al·lit·er·ate (ə lit′ər āt′) *v.* **-at·ed, at·ing. 1 a** have the same first sound. **b** loosely, have the same first letter. **2** use alliteration. [back-formation from ALLITERATION.]

al·lit·er·a·tion (ə lit′ər ā′shən) *n.* **1** repetition of the same first sound in a group of words or line of poetry. *Example*: "The *s*un *s*ank *s*lowly" shows alliteration of *s*. **2** less properly, repetition of the same first letter in a group of words or line of poetry. [< Med.L *alliteratio, -onis* < *ad-* to + L *litera* letter]

al·lit·er·a·tive (ə lit′ər ət iv or ə lit′ər ā′tiv) *adj.* **1** having words beginning with the same sound. **2** loosely, having words beginning with the same letter. —**al·lit′er·a′tive·ly,** *adv.* —**al·lit′er·a′tive·ness,** *n.*

al·lo·cate (al′ə kāt′) *v.* **-cat·ed, -cat·ing. 1** assign or allot. **2** locate. [< Med.L *allocare* < L *ad-* to, at + *locus* place] —**Syn. 1** distribute.

al·lo·ca·tion (al′ə kā′shən) *n.* an allotment, especially by government; distribution; assignment.

al·lo·morph (al′ə môrf′) *n.* **1** in chemistry, an allotrope. **2** in linguistics, one of the variant forms of a morpheme: *com-* in *compress, col-* in *collect, con-* in *connect,* and *cor-* in *correct* are allomorphs of the morpheme *com-*. [< Gk. *allos* other + *morphē* form]

al·lo·path (al′ə path′) *n.* **1** a doctor who uses allopathy. **2** a person who favors allopathy.

al·lo·path·ic (al′ə path′ik) *adj.* of allopathy; using allopathy. —**al′lo·path′i·cal·ly,** *adv.*

al·lop·a·thist (ə lop′ə thist) *n.* allopath.

al·lop·a·thy (ə lop′ə thē) *n.* a method of treating a disease by using remedies to produce effects different from those caused by the disease treated. Allopathy is the opposite of homeopathy. [< G *Allopathie* < Gk. *allos* other + *patheia* suffering]

al·lo·phone (al′ə fōn′) *n.* any one of a family of similar speech sounds that are heard as the same sound by speakers of a given language or dialect. In English, the *t* in *top* and the *t* in *stop,* although different in quality, are allophones of the phoneme *t.* [< Gk. *allos* other + E *-phone* sound (< Gk. *phōnē*)]

al·lo·saur (al′ə sôr′) *n.* a carnivorous dinosaur, remains of which have been found in North America. Some allosaurs were over 30 feet long and 15 feet high. [< Gk. *allos* other + *sauros* lizard]

al·lot (ə lot′) *v.* **-lot·ted, -lot·ting. 1** divide and distribute in parts or shares: *The profits have all been allotted.* **2** give as a share; assign: *The teacher allotted work to each student.* [< OF *aloter* < *a-* to (< L *ad-*) + *lot* lot < Gmc. Akin to LOT.]
Syn. 1 Allot, apportion = to give out in shares. **Allot** emphasizes giving set amounts for a definite purpose or to particular persons, and does not suggest the way in which the shares are set or distributed: *The Government is ready to allot homesteads in that area.* **Apportion** emphasizes division and distribution according to a fair plan, usually in proportions settled by some rule: *The reward money was apportioned among those who had helped in the rescue.* **2** See **assign.**

al·lot·ment (ə lot′mənt) *n.* **1** a division and distribution in parts or shares. **2** a share.

al·lo·trope (al′ə trōp′) *n.* an allotropic form.

al·lo·trop·ic (al′ə trop′ik) *adj.* in chemistry, occurring in two or more forms that differ in physical and chemical properties but not in the kind of atoms of which they are composed.

al·lot·ro·pism (ə lot′rə piz′əm) *n.* allotropy.

al·lot·ro·py (ə lot′rə pē) *n.* in chemistry, the property or fact of being allotropic. [< Gk. *allotropia* < *allos* other + *tropos* manner]

all-out (ol′out′ or ôl′-) *adj. Informal.* involving one's entire resources; total; complete. *—adv.* **1** completely. **2 go all-out,** employ all one's resources.

all·o·ver (ol′ō′vər or ôl′-) *adj.* **1** covering the whole surface. **2** having a pattern that is repeated over the whole surface.

al·low (ə lou′) *v.* **1** let; permit: *The class was not allowed to leave until the bell rang.* **2** let have; give: *His father allows him $2 a week as spending money.* **3** admit; acknowledge; recognize: *The judge allowed the claim of the man whose property was damaged.* **4** add or subtract to make up for something: *allow an extra hour for travelling time.* **5** permit to happen, especially through carelessness or neglect. **6** *Dialect.* say; think: *He allowed that he was going to the dance.* **7 allow for,** take into consideration; provide for: *She purposely made the dress large to allow for shrinking.* [ME < OF *alouer* < L *allaudare* (< *ad-* to + *laus* praise) and Med.L *allocare* (< L *ad-* to, at + *locus* place)] **—al·low′er,** *n.*
—Syn. 1 See **permit. 2** grant, yield, assign.

al·low·a·ble (ə lou′ə bəl) *adj.* allowed by law or by a person in authority; permitted by the rules of the game: not forbidden. **—al·low′a·ble·ness,** *n.* **—al·low′a·bly,** *adv.*

al·low·ance (ə lou′əns) *n.* **1** a limited share set apart; definite portion or amount given out: *His weekly allowance is $3.* **2** an amount added or subtracted to make up for something: *The salesman offered us an allowance of $700 on our old car; so we got a $2,800 car for $2,100.* **3** an allowing; conceding: *allowance of a claim.* **4** tolerance: *allowance of slavery.* **5** in machinery, the variation in dimension provided for in parts that fit together. **6** in coinage, the variation from the standard permitted by the mint. **7 make allowance** or **make allowance for,** take into consideration: allow for.

al·loy (*n.* al′oi; *v.* ə loi′) *n.* **1** an inferior metal mixed with a more valuable one: *This gold is not pure; there is some alloy in it.* **2** a metal made by mixing and fusing two or more metals, or a metal and a non-metal: *Brass is an alloy of copper and zinc.* **3** any injurious addition. [< F *aloi,* OF *alei* < *aleier,* v. See ALLOY, v.]
—v. **1** make into an alloy. **2** make less valuable by mixing with a cheaper metal. **3** make worse; debase. [< F *aloyer,* OF *aleier,* var. of *alier* unite, combine < L *alligare* < *ad-* to + *ligare* bind. Doublet of ALLY.]

all-pow·er·ful (ol′pou′ər fəl or ôl′-) *adj.* having power over all people, things, etc.; almighty; omnipotent.

all-pur·pose (ol′pėr′pəs or ôl′-) *adj.* suitable for all purposes for which a particular product, device, etc. is generally used: *All-purpose flour is as suitable for pastry and cakes as it is for bread.*

all right 1 all correct. **2** yes. **3** without doubt; certainly. **4** in good health. **5** satisfactory. ☛ See **alright** for usage note.

all-round (ol′round′ or ôl′-) *adj.* not limited or specialized; able to do many things; useful in many ways.

All Saints' Day November 1, a Christian church festival honoring all the saints; Allhallows.

All Souls' Day November 2, in the Roman Catholic Church, a day when services are held and prayers said for all the souls in purgatory.

all·spice (ol′spīs′ or ôl′-) *n.* **1** a spice supposed to have a flavor like that of a mixture of cinnamon, nutmeg, and cloves. **2** the berry of the West Indian pimento tree that this spice is made from.

all square *Informal.* **1** having paid what is due; having done what is needed. **2** having the same score; tied; even: *The teams were all square at the end of the second period.*

all-star (ol′stär′ or ôl′-) *adj.* made up of the best players or performers.

all-time (ol′tīm′ or ôl′-) *adj. Informal.* **1** for all time up to the present. **2** that sets a record: *an all-time high in wheat prices.*

al·lude (ə lüd′) *v.* **-lud·ed, -lud·ing.** refer indirectly (*to*); mention in passing: *Do not ask him about his failure; do not even allude to it.* [< L *alludere* < *ad-* with + *ludere* play] **—Syn.** See **refer.**

al·lure (ə lür′) *v.* **-lured, -lur·ing,** *n.* *—v.* **1** fascinate; charm. **2** tempt by the offer of some pleasure or reward. *—n.* attractiveness; fascination. [ME < OF *alurer* < *a-* to (< L *ad-*) + *leurre* lure < Gmc. Related to LURE.] **—al·lur′er,** *n.* **—Syn.** *v.* **2** See **lure.**

al·lure·ment (ə lür′mənt) *n.* **1** charm; fascination. **2** temptation; attraction.

al·lur·ing (ə lür′ing) *adj.* **1** tempting; attracting. **2** charming; fascinating. **—al·lur′ing·ly,** *adv.* **—al·lur′ing·ness,** *n.*

al·lu·sion (ə lü′zhən) *n.* an indirect or passing reference. [< L *allusio, -onis* < *alludere.* See ALLUDE.]
☛ See **illusion** for usage note.

al·lu·sive (ə lü′siv) *adj.* containing an allusion; full of allusions. **—al·lu′sive·ly,** *adv.* **—al·lu′sive·ness,** *n.*

al·lu·vi·al (ə lü′vē əl) *adj.* consisting of or formed by sand or mud left by flowing water. A delta is an alluvial deposit at the mouth of a river. *—n.* alluvial soil.

al·lu·vi·um (ə lü′vē əm) *n.* **-vi·ums** or **-vi·a** (-vē ə). the sand, mud, etc. left by flowing water. [< L *alluvium,* neut. of *alluvius* alluvial < *ad-* up + *luere* wash]

al·ly (*v.* ə lī′; *n.* al′ī or ə lī′) *v.* **-lied, -ly·ing,** *n.* **-lies.** *—v.* **1** combine for some special purpose; unite by formal agreement (*to* or *with*). One nation allies itself with another to protect its people and interests. **2** associate: connect: *This newspaper is allied with three others.* **3** be similar in structure, descent, etc.; relate: *Dogs are allied to wolves.*
—n. **1** a person or nation united with another for some special purpose. See also **Allies. 2** a related animal, plant, form, or thing. **3** a helper; supporter. [ME < OF *alier* < L *alligare* < *ad-* to + *ligare* bind. Doublet of ALLOY.]

al·ma ma·ter or **Al·ma Ma·ter** (al′mə mä′tər, äl′mə mä′tər, or al′mə mā′tər) a person's school, college, or university. [< L *alma mater* bounteous mother]

al·ma·nac (ol′mə nak′ or ôl′mə nak′) *n.* a calendar or table showing the days, weeks and months. Many almanacs give information about the weather, sun, moon, stars, tides, church days, and other facts. [ME < Med.L, probably < LGk. < Arabic *al-manākh*]

al·ma·nack (ol′mə nak′ or ôl′mə nak′) *n.* almanac.

Al·mey (al′mē) *n.* a Canadian variety of flowering crabapple having red wood, leaves, and flowers.

al·might·y (ol mīt′ē or ôl mīt′ē) *adj.* **1** having supreme power; all-powerful. **2** *Informal.* great; very. *—adv. Informal.* exceedingly. *—n.* **the Almighty,** God. **—al·might′i·ly,** *adv.* **—al·might′i·ness,** *n.* **—Syn.** *adj.* **1** omnipotent.

almighty dollar *Informal.* money thought of as all-powerful.

al·mond (o′mənd or ä′mənd) *n.* **1** the nut, or seed, of a peachlike fruit growing in warm regions. **2** the tree that it grows on. *—adj.* **1** shaped like an almond. **2** made from almonds: *almond paste.* [ME < OF *almande* < L < Gk. *amygdalē*] **—al′mond·like,** *adj.*

al·mond-eyed (o′mənd īd′ or ä′mənd-) *adj.* having eyes that appear to be oval-shaped and to have pointed ends. The Chinese and Japanese are almond-eyed.

al·mon·er (al′mən ər or ol′mə nər) *n.* a person who distributes alms for a king, monastery, etc. [ME < OF *almosnier* < LL *elemosynarius* < L *eleemosyna* alms. See ALMS.]

al·mon·ry (al′mən rē or ol′mən rē) *n.* **-ries.** a place where alms are distributed.

al·most (ol′mōst or ôl′mōst) *adv.* nearly: *Nine is almost ten.* [OE *eal māst* nearly] ☛ See **most** for usage note.

alms (omz or ämz) *n. sing. or pl.* money or gifts to help the poor. [OE *ælmysse* < VL *alimosina* < L *eleemosyna* < Gk. *eleēmosynē* compassion < *eleos* mercy]

alms·giv·er (omz′giv′ər or ämz′-) *n.* a person who helps the poor with money or other gifts.

alms·giv·ing (omz′giv′ing or ämz′-) *n. adj.* giving help to the poor.

alms·house (omz′hous′ or ämz′-) *n.* a home for persons too poor to support themselves.

al·ni·co (al′ni kō′ or al nē′ kō) *n.* an alloy containing aluminum, nickel, and cobalt, much used in making magnets. [< *al*uminum + *ni*ckel + *co*balt]

al·oe (al′ō) *n.* **-oes. 1** a plant having a long spike of flowers and thick, narrow leaves, found in South Africa and other warm, dry climates. **2** in North America, the century plant. **3 aloes,** *pl.* a bitter drug made from the dried juice of the leaves of certain aloes. [OE *aluwe* < L < Gk.]

☛ **Aloes,** the drug, is plural in form and singular in use: *Aloes is sometimes used as a tonic.*

a·loft (ə loft′) *adv. adj.* **1** far above the earth; high up. **2** high above the deck of a ship; up among the sails, rigging, or masts of a ship. [ME < ON *á lopt* in the air]

a·lo·ha (ə lō′ə or ä lō′hä) *n. interj.* **1** greetings; hello. **2** good-bye; farewell. [< Hawaiian]

a·lone (ə lōn′) *adj.* **1** apart from other persons or things; solitary: *He was alone.* **2** without anyone else; only: *He alone remained.* **3** without anything more: *Meat alone is not the best diet for children.* **4 leave alone,** not bother; not meddle with. **5 let alone, a** not bother; not meddle with. **b** not to mention: *It would have been a hot day for summer, let alone early spring.*
—adv. only; merely; exclusively. [ME *al one* all (completely) one] **—a·lone·ness,** *n.* **—Syn.** *adj.* **1** lone, isolated.

☛ As an adjective, *alone* is most frequently used predicatively: *The little girl was alone.* Otherwise, it is usually used after the noun it modifies, rarely before the noun: *The dessert alone would have been enough for a whole meal.*

a·long (ə long′) *prep.* from one end to the other of: *walk along a river.*
—adv. **1** further; forward: *Let us walk along.* **2 along with, a** in company with: *I'll go along with you.* **b** together with: *Take some pop along with the food.* **3 along by,** alongside of: *Cars were parked along by the stadium.* **4** together with someone or something: *You should take a tent along if you are going camping. He took his dog along.* **5** *Informal.* of time, somewhere: *along about four o'clock.* **6 all along,** all the time. **7 get along, a** *Informal.* manage with at least some success. **b** agree. **c** go away. **d** advance. **e** succeed; prosper. [OE *andlang*]

a·long·shore (ə long′shôr′) *adv.* near or along the shore.

a·long·side (*adv.* ə long′sīd′; *prep.* ə long′sīd′) *adv.* **1** at the side; close to the side; side by side. **2 alongside of,** beside; next to. *—prep.* by the side of; beside.

a·loof (ə lüf′) *adv.* at a distance; withdrawn; apart: *One boy stood aloof from all the others.*
—adj. unsympathetic; not interested; reserved. [< *a-* on + *loof* windward, probably < Du. *loef*] **—a·loof′ly,** *adv.* **—a·loof′ness,** *n.*

a·loud (ə loud′) *adv.* **1** loud enough to be heard; not in a whisper. **2** in a loud voice; loudly.

alp (alp) *n.* a high mountain. [< L *Alpes* the Alps]

hat, āge, cãre, fär; let, ēqual, tėrm; it, īce
hot, ōpen, ôrder; oil, out; cup, pu̇t, rüle, ūse
əbove, takən, pencəl, lemən, circəs
ch, child; ng, long; sh, ship
th, thin; TH, then; zh, measure

al·pac·a (al pak′ə) *n.* **1** a South American animal, a kind of llama, having long, soft, silky hair or wool. **2** its wool. **3** cloth made from this wool. **4** glossy, wiry cloth made of wool and cotton, usually black. **5** a rayon and alpaca crepe. [< Sp. < Arabic *al* the + Peruvian *paco* alpaca]

al·pen·horn (al′pən hôrn′) *n.* a long, powerful horn used in Switzerland for military signals and for calling cattle. [< G *Alpen* Alps + *Horn* horn]

al·pen·stock (al′pən stok′) *n.* a strong staff with an iron point, used in climbing mountains. [< G *Alpen* Alps + *Stock* stick]

al·pha (al′fə) *n.* **1** the first letter of the Greek alphabet (A, α). **2** a beginning; first in a series.

alpha and omega the first and the last; the beginning and the end.

al·pha·bet (al′fə bet′) *n.* **1** a set of letters or characters representing sounds, used in writing a language. **2** the letters of a language, arranged in their conventional order. **3** the parts to be learned first; elementary principles. *Abbrev.*: ABC or ABC's. [< LL *alphabetum* < LGk. *alphabetos* < *alpha* + *beta*]

al·pha·bet·ic (al′fə bet′ik) *adj.* alphabetical.

al·pha·bet·i·cal (al′fə bet′ə kəl) *adj.* **1** arranged with the initial letters in the order of the alphabet. **2** of the alphabet.

al·pha·bet·ize (al′fə bə tīz′) *v.* **-ized, -iz·ing. 1** arrange in alphabetical order. **2** express by the letters of an alphabet.

Al·pha Cru·cis (krü′sis) the brightest star in the Southern Cross, and one of the brightest in the heavens. Its surface temperature is about 45,000 degrees Fahrenheit, making it one of the hottest stars known. [< L *alpha* alpha + *crux, crucis* cross]

Al·pha Her·cu·lis (hėr′kyə lis′) the largest star in our galaxy, over 2,400,000,000 miles in diameter (almost 2,800 times the diameter of the sun). [< *alpha* alpha + *Hercules, -is* Hercules]

alpha particle in physics, a positively charged particle consisting of two protons and two neutrons, released in the disintegration of radium and similar radio-active substances.

alpha rays in physics, a stream of alpha particles.

Al·pine (al′pīn) *adj.* **1** of or like the Alps. **2 alpine, a** of or like high mountains. **b** very high.

alpine fir 1 a fir tree of western North America, growing especially in mountainous regions. **2** the pale-yellow or white wood of this tree, used for lumber and for pulpwood.

alpine larch a larch tree of western North America. It grows at high altitudes and is found at the timber line on the mountains of southern Alberta and British Columbia.

al·read·y (ol red′ē or ôl red′ē) *adv.* **1** before this time; by this time; even now: *The house is already full.* **2** so soon: *Must you go already?* [for *all ready*]

☛ **All ready,** as distinguished from the adverb **already,** is used as an adjective phrase meaning quite or completely ready: *He was all ready for his next job.*

al·right (ol rīt′ or ôl rīt′) *adv. Informal.* all right.

☛ **All right** is the correct spelling of both the adjective phrase (*He is all right*) and the sentence adverb meaning "yes, certainly" (*All right, I'll come*). The spelling **alright** is not used in formal nor in most informal writing. Occasionally it is found in advertising and in comic strips, but it is not as yet generally acceptable.

Al·sa·tian (al sā′shən) *adj.* of or having to do with Alsace or its people. *—n.* **1** a native or inhabitant of Alsace. **2** a German shepherd dog.

al·so (ol′sō or ôl′sō) *adv.* in addition; besides; too. [OE *ealswā* all so, quite so] **—Syn.** likewise, furthermore.

☛ **Also** is a weak connective; ordinarily, *and* is to be preferred: *He came with tents, cooking things, and* (better than *also*) *about fifty pounds of photographic equipment.*

al·so-ran (ol′sō ran′ or ôl′sō-) *n.* a loser; unsuccessful contestant; nonentity.

alt. 1 alternate; alternating. 2 altitude. 3 alto.

Alta. Alberta.

Al·ta·ic (al tā′ik) *adj.* 1 of or having to do with a family of languages that includes Turkish, Mongolian, and Manchu. 2 of or having to do with the Altai Mountains in Central Asia.

Al·ta·ir (al tä′ir) *n.* a first magnitude star in the constellation Aquila. It is about ten times as bright as the sun. [< Arabic *al-ta'ir* bird, literally, flyer.]

al·tar (ol′tər or ôl′tər) *n.* 1 a table or stand in the most sacred part of a church, synagogue, or temple. In Christian churches the Communion service or Mass is held at the altar. 2 a raised place built of earth or stone on which to make sacrifices or burn offerings to a god. 3 **lead to the altar,** marry. [OE < LL *altare* < L *altus* high]

altar boy a person who helps a priest during certain religious services, especially Mass; acolyte.

al·tar·piece (ol′tər pēs′ or ôl′tər-) *n.* a decorated panel or wall behind and above an altar in a church; reredos.

al·ta·zi·muth (al taz′i məth) *n.* an instrument equipped with a telescope for measuring angles vertically and horizontally, used in astronomy to determine the position of stars, planets, etc. and in surveying. A theodolite is a portable altazimuth. [< *alt*itude + *azimuth*]

al·ter (ol′tər or ôl′tər) *v.* 1 make different; change; vary: *If this coat is too large, a tailor can alter it to fit you.* 2 become different: *Since her trip to Europe, her whole outlook has altered.* [ME < OF < LL *alterare* < L *alter* other] —**al′ter·a·ble,** *adj.* —**al′ter·a·bly,** *adv.* —**Syn. 1** See **change.**

al·ter·a·tion (ol′tər ā′shən or ôl′tər ā′shən) *n.* 1 a change in the appearance, form, or condition of anything: *have alterations made in a dress.* 2 the act or process of making a change.

al·ter·a·tive (ol′tər ā′tiv or ôl′tər ā′tiv) *adj.* 1 causing change; having the power to cause change. 2 in medicine, gradually restoring the healthy bodily functions. —*n.* in medicine, a remedy that gradually restores health.

al·ter·cate (ol′tər kāt′ or ôl′tər kāt′) *v.* **-cat·ed, -cat·ing.** dispute angrily; quarrel. [< L *altercari* < *alter* other]

al·ter·ca·tion (ol′tər kā′shən or ôl′tər kā′shən) *n.* an angry dispute; quarrel: *The two teams had an altercation over the umpire's decision.*

al·ter e·go 1 another aspect of one's nature. 2 a very intimate friend. [< L *alter ego,* translation of Gk. *heteros egō*]

al·ter·nate (*v.* ol′tər nāt′ or ôl′tər nāt′; *adj.* ol tėr′nit or ôl tėr′nit, ol′tər nit or ôl′tər nit; *n.* ol′tər nit or ôl′tər nit) *v.* **-nat·ed, -nat·ing,** *adj. n.*
—*v.* 1 occur by turns, first one and then the other; happen or be arranged by turns. *Squares and circles alternate in this row:* □ ○ □ ○ □ ○ □ ○. 2 arrange by turns; do by turns: *We try to alternate work and pleasure.* 3 take turns: *Lucy and her sister will alternate in setting the table.* 4 interchange regularly: 5 in electricity: a reverse direction at regular intervals: *Some electric currents alternate 120 times a second.* b produce or be operated by such a current.
—*adj.* 1 placed or occurring by turns; first one and then the other: *The row has alternate squares and circles.* 2 every other: *alternate days.* 3 reciprocal. 4 in botany, placed singly at different heights along a stem; not opposite. See picture in the opposite column.
—*n.* 1 a person appointed to take the place of another if necessary; substitute. 2 a player who relieves another during a game. [< L *alternare* < *alternus* every second < *alter* other]

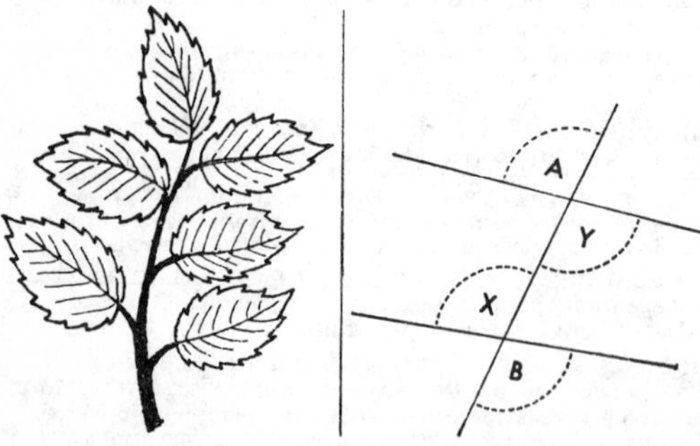

Alternate leaves

Alternate angles: A, B and X, Y

alternate angles two angles, both interior or both exterior but not adjacent, formed when two lines are crossed by a third and being on opposite sides of the third line. If the two lines are parallel, the alternate angles are equal. See picture in the opposite column.

al·ter·nate·ly (ol′tər nit lē or ôl′tər nit lē) *adv.* by turns, first one and then the other.

alternating current an electric current that reverses its direction at regular intervals. *Abbrev.*: A.C., a.c., or a-c.

al·ter·na·tion (ol′tər nā′shən or ôl′tər nā′shən) *n.* an alternating; occurring by turns, first one and then the other: *There is an alternation of red and white stripes on the sign outside a barber shop.*

al·ter·na·tive (ol tėr′nə tiv or ôl tėr′nə tiv) *adj.* 1 giving or requiring a choice between only two things. 2 giving a choice from among more than two things: *There are several alternative routes from Ottawa to Toronto.*
—*n.* 1 a choice between two things: *His father gave John the alternative of staying in high school or going to work.* 2 a choice from among more than two things. 3 one of the things to be chosen: *John chose the former alternative and stayed in school.* —**al·ter′na·tive·ly,** *adv.*
—**Syn.** *n.* **1, 2** selection. See **choice.**

☛ Alternative comes from the Latin *alter,* meaning the second of two. Some writers, in deference to the word's origin, confine its meaning to one of two possibilities, but it is commonly used to mean one of several possibilities.

alternative conjunction a conjunction connecting terms that are alternative. *Examples*: either . . . or, neither . . . nor, whether . . . or.

al·ter·na·tor (ol′tər nā′tər or ôl′tər nā′tər) *n.* a dynamo or generator for producing an alternating electric current.

al·the·a or **al·thae·a** (al thē′ə) *n.* the rose of Sharon, a flowering garden shrub. [< L *althaea* < Gk. *althaia* wild mallow, ? < *althainein* heal]

alt·horn (alt′hôrn′) *n.* a brass musical instrument similar to the French horn. Also, **alto horn.** [< G]

al·though (ol ᴛʜō′ or ôl ᴛʜō′) *conj.* even if; in spite of the fact that; though. [ME *al thogh* even though]

☛ **although, though.** There is no difference in meaning between the subordinate conjunctions *although* and *though.* Either may be used to connect an adverbial clause with the main clause of a sentence. *Although* is more likely to introduce a clause that precedes a main clause, and *though* one that follows: *Although it rained all morning, they went on the hike. They went on the hike, though it rained all morning.*

al·tim·e·ter (al tim′ə tər or al′tə mē′tər) *n.* any instrument for measuring altitude. Altimeters are used in aircraft to indicate height above the earth's surface. [< L *altus* high + E *-meter*]

al·ti·tude (al′tə tūd′ or al′tə tüd′, ol′tə tūd′ or ol′tə tüd′, ôl′tə tūd′ or ôl′tə tüd′) *n.* 1 the height above the earth's surface: *The airplane was flying at an altitude of 10,000 feet.* 2 the height above sea level: *The altitude of Banff, Alberta, is 4,534 feet.* 3 a high place: *At these altitudes snow never melts.* 4 a position of high rank or great power. 5 in geometry, the vertical distance from the base of a figure to its highest point. 6 in astronomy, the angular distance of a star, planet, etc. above the horizon. *Abbrev.*: alt. [ME < L *altitudo* < *altus* high]

al·to (al′tō, ol′tō or ôl′tō) *n.* **-tos,** *adj.* —*n.* 1 a the lowest, or deepest, female voice; contralto. b the highest adult male voice. 2 in music: a a singer with such a voice. b a part for such a voice or for a corresponding instrument. c an instrument playing such a part.
—*adj.* 1 of or for an alto. 2 that can sing or play an

alto part. *Abbrev.*: a. or alt. [< Ital. < L *altus* high]

al·to-cu·mu·lus (al′tō kū′myu̇ ləs) *n.* **-li** (-lī). a fleecy cloud formation having rounded heaps of white or grayish clouds, often partly shaded, at heights of between 8,000 and 20,000 feet. *Abbrev.*: Ac

al·to·geth·er (*adv.* ol′tə geᴛʜ′ər or ôl′tə geᴛʜ′ər; *n.* ol′tə geᴛʜ′ər or ôl′tə geᴛʜ′ər) *adv. n.* —*adv.* **1** completely; entirely: *altogether wicked.* **2** on the whole; considering everything: *Altogether, I'm sorry it happened.* **3** all included: *Altogether there were ten books.* —*n. Informal.* **in the altogether,** naked: *We went swimming in the altogether.* [ME *altogedere*]

☛ **All together** as distinguished from the adverb **altogether** is used as an adjective phrase meaning everyone in a group: *We found the boys all together in the kitchen.*

alto horn althorn.

al·to-re·lie·vo (al′tō ri lē′vō) *n.* **-vos.** sculpture in high relief, in which the figures stand out at least half their thickness from the background. [< Ital.]

al·to-stra·tus (al′tō strā′təs or -strat′əs) *n.* **-ti** (-tī or -tē). a bluish-gray sheetlike cloud formation, ill-defined at the base, occurring at heights between 6,500 and 20,000 feet. *Abbrev.*: As [< L *altus* high + E *stratus*]

al·tru·ism (al′trü iz′əm) *n.* unselfishness; unselfish devotion to the interests and welfare of others. [< F *altruisme* < Ital. *altrui* of or for others < L *alter* other]

al·tru·ist (al′trü ist) *n.* an unselfish person; a person who works for the welfare of others.

al·tru·is·tic (al′trü is′tik) *adj.* thoughtful of the welfare of others; unselfish. —**al′tru·is′ti·cal·ly,** *adv.*

al·um (al′əm) *n.* **1** a white mineral salt used in medicine and in dyeing. Alum is sometimes used to stop the bleeding of a small cut. *Formula*: $KAl(SO_4)_2 \cdot 12H_2O$ **2** a colorless, crystalline salt containing ammonia, used in baking powder, in medicine, etc. *Formula*: $NH_4Al(SO_4)_2 \cdot 12H_2O$ [ME < OF < L *alumen*]

a·lu·mi·na (ə lü′mə nə) *n.* aluminum oxide, Al_2O_3. Clay is mostly alumina; emery, rubies, and sapphires are crystalline forms of alumina colored by various impurities. [< NL < L *alumen, -minis* alum]

al·u·min·i·um (al′ū min′ē əm) *n. Esp.Brit.* aluminum.

a·lu·mi·nous (ə lü′mə nəs) *adj.* **1** of or containing alum. **2** of or containing aluminum.

a·lu·mi·num (ə lü′mə nəm) *n.* a silver-white, very light, ductile, metallic chemical element that occurs in nature only in combination. It resists tarnish and is used for making utensils, instruments, etc. *Symbol*: Al; *at.no.* 13; *at.wt.* 26.9815. [< *alumina*]

a·lu·mi·num hy·drox·ide a white, tasteless, odorless powder used in medicine and for dyeing, waterproofing, and ceramic glazing. *Formula*: $Al(OH_3)$

aluminum oxide alumina.

al·u·mi·num phos·phate a white powder, or colorless crystals, used in making dental cements and, in ceramics, as a flux. *Formula*: $AlPO_4$

a·lu·mi·num sul·phate or **sul·fate** a white crystalline salt, available in powder or crystals, used in medicine and in the paper and leather industries, also in dyeing and waterproofing. *Formula*: $Al_2(SO_4)_3$

a·lum·na (ə lum′nə) *n.* **-nae.** a woman graduate or former student of a school, college, or university. [< L]

a·lum·nae (ə lum′nē) *n.* pl. of **alumna.** See **alumni** for usage note.

a·lum·ni (ə lum′nī) *n.* pl. of **alumnus.**

☛ Generally, two pronunciations are given in this dictionary for Latin-derived words ending in "-ae" and "-i". However, because of the distinction in meaning between **alumnae** and **alumni,** the two words should be kept separate, one pronunciation being given for each.

a·lum·nus (ə lum′nəs) *n.* **-ni.** a graduate or former student of a school, college, or university. [< L *alumnus* foster child < *alere* nourish]

al·ve·o·lar (al vē′ə lər or al′vē ōl′ər) *adj.* **1** in anatomy and zoology: **a** of the part of the jaws where the sockets of the teeth are. **b** of, like, or having to do with an alveolus or alveoli. **2** in phonetics, formed by touching the tip of the tongue to or bringing it near the upper alveoli. English *t* and *d* are alveolar sounds. —*n.* in phonetics, a speech sound formed in this manner.

al·ve·o·lus (al vē′ə ləs or al vē ō′ləs) *n.* **-li** (-lī′ or lē′). **1** in anatomy and zoology: **a** a small vacuity, pit, or cell. The air cells of the lungs are alveoli. **b** the socket of a tooth. **2** *often pl.,* in phonetics, the ridge behind and above the upper teeth. [< L *alveolus,* dim. of *alveus* cavity]

hat, āge, cãre, fär; let, ēqual, tėrm; it, īce
hot, ōpen, ôrder; oil, out; cup, pu̇t, rüle, ūse
əbove, takən, pencəl, lemən, circəs
ch, child; ng, long; sh, ship
th, thin; ᴛʜ, then; zh, measure

al·way (ol′wā or ôl′wā) *adv. Archaic* or *Poetic.* always.

al·ways (ol′wiz, ol′wāz, ôl′wiz, or ôl′wāz) *adv.* **1** every time; at all times: *Water always has some air in it.* **2** all the time; continually: *Mother is always cheerful.* **3** forever; for all time to come: *I'll love you always.* [< *all* + *way*] —**Syn. 2** forever, unceasingly, perpetually.

a·lys·sum (ə lis′əm) *n.* **1** a plant of the same family as the mustard, having small white or yellow flowers. **2** sweet alyssum. [< NL < Gk. *alysson,* name of a plant thought to cure rabies]

am (am; *unstressed,* əm) *v.* the first person singular, present indicative of **be.** I *am,* you *are,* and he *is* are forms of the verb *be.* [OE *eom*]

am- *word element.* the form of **ambi-** before *p,* as in *amputate.*

a.m. or **A.M. 1** before noon. **2** the time from midnight to noon. [for L *ante meridiem*]

☛ A.m. and p.m. are usually written in small letters except in headlines and tables. In consecutive writing they are used only with figures for specific hours: *from 2 to 4 a.m.*

Am americium.

Am. 1 America. **2** American.

AM or **A.M.** amplitude modulation.

A.M. 1 Air Marshal. **2** Albert Medal. **3** *U.S.* Master of Arts; M.A. (for L *Artium Magister*)

AMA or **A.M.A.** American Medical Association.

a·ma·bi·lis fir (ə mä′bə lis) **1** a fir tree of the western coast of North America, found especially on Vancouver Island and along the coast of the British Columbia mainland. **2** the light, soft wood of this tree, used for pulpwood and lumber.

a·mah (ä′mə or am′ə) *n.* in India, China, etc., a nurse or maid. [< Anglo-Indian < Pg. *ama*]

a·main (ə mān′) *adv. Archaic.* **1** at full speed. **2** in haste. **3** with full force; violently. [< *a-*[1] in + *main* force]

a·mal·gam (ə mal′gəm) *n.* **1** an alloy of mercury with some other metal or metals. Tin amalgam is used in silvering mirrors. Silver amalgam is used as fillings for teeth. **2** a mixture; blend. [< Med.L *amalgama* < Arabic < Gk. *malagma* emollient < *malassein* soften]

a·mal·gam·ate (ə mal′gə māt′) *v.* **-at·ed, -at·ing.** unite together; combine; mix; blend: *The two companies amalgamated to form one big company. Many different ethnic groups are being amalgamated in Canada.*

a·mal·gam·a·tion (ə mal′gə mā′shən) *n.* a union; combination; mixture; blend: *Our nation is an amalgamation of many races.*

a·man·u·en·sis (ə man′yu̇ en′sis) *n.* **-ses** (-sēz). a person who writes down what another says; a person who copies what another has written. [< L *amanuensis* < (*servus*) *a manu* literally, hand servant + *-ensis* belonging to]

am·a·ranth (am′ə ranth′) *n.* **1** *Poetic.* a flower that never fades. **2** a plant having showy purple or crimson flowers. Love-lies-bleeding is a variety of amaranth. **3** purple; purplish red. [< L < Gk. *amarantos* everlasting < *a-* not + *marainein* wither; influenced by Gk. *anthos* flower]

am·a·ran·thine (am′ə ran′thīn, am′ə ran′thēn, or am′ə ran′thin) *adj.* **1** never-fading; undying. **2** purple; purplish-red.

am·a·ryl·lis (am′ə ril′is) *n.* a lily-like plant having clusters of large red, white, or pink flowers. [< L < Gk. *Amaryllis,* typical name for a country girl]

a·mass (ə mas′) *v.* heap together; pile up; accumulate:

The miser amassed a fortune for himself. [< F *amasser* < *a-* to (< L *ad-*) + *masse* mass < L *massa* kneaded dough. Related to MASS[1].] —**Syn.** See **accumulate.**

am·a·teur (am′ə chər, am′ə chür′, am′ə tūr′, or am′ə tėr′) *n.* **1** a person who undertakes some activity for pleasure, not for money or as a profession. **2** a person who does something without showing the proper skills. **3** an athlete who is not a professional. —*adj.* **1** of amateurs; made or done by amateurs. **2** being an amateur: *an amateur pianist.* [< F < L *amator* lover < *amare* love]

am·a·teur·ish (am′ə chür′ish, am′ə tūr′ish, or am′ə tėr′ish) *adj.* done as an amateur might do it; not expert; not very skilful. —**am′a·teur′ish·ly,** *adv.*

am·a·teur·ism (am′ə chər iz′əm, am′ə chür iz′əm, am′ə tūr iz′əm, or am′ə tėr′iz əm) *n.* **1** an amateurish way of doing things. **2** the position or rank of an amateur.

am·a·tol (am′ə tol′) *n.* an explosive substance composed of ammonium and trinitrotoluene. [< *am*monium + trinitro*tol*uene]

am·a·to·ry (am′ə tô′rē) *adj.* of love; causing love; having to do with making love or with lovers. [< L *amatorius* < *amare* love]

a·maze (ə māz′) *v.* **a·mazed, a·maz·ing,** *n.* —*v.* surprise greatly; strike with sudden wonder. —*n. Poetic.* amazement. [OE *āmasian*] —**Syn.** *v.* astonish, astound. See **surprise.**

a·mazed (ə māzd′) *adj.* greatly surprised.

a·maz·ed·ly (ə māz′id lē) *adv.* lost in wonder or astonishment.

a·maze·ment (ə māz′mənt) *n.* great surprise; sudden wonder; astonishment.

a·maz·ing (ə māz′ing) *adj.* very surprising; wonderful; astonishing. —**a·maz′ing·ly,** *adv.*

Am·a·zon (am′ə zon′ or am′ə zən) *n.* **1** in Greek legend, one of a race of women warriors supposed to live near the Black Sea. **2** Also, **amazon.** a tall, strong, aggressive woman. [ME < L < Gk.; origin uncertain]

Am·a·zo·ni·an (am′ə zō′nē ən) *adj.* **1** of the Amazon River or the region it drains. **2** of the Amazons. **3** Also, **amazonian.** of women or girls, like an Amazon or the Amazons; aggressive; warlike.

am·a·zon·ite (am′ə zə nīt′) *n.* **1** a bright, bluish-green, semiprecious stone, a variety of feldspar. **2** a piece of this stone or a gem made from it. [< *Amazon* (River) + *-ite*[1]]

am·bas·sa·dor (am bas′ə dər or am bas′ə dôr′) *n.* **1** the highest-ranking diplomatic representative sent by one government or ruler to another. **2** an official representative of a government or a ruler at the meetings of an international organization, on a special mission, etc.: *the Canadian ambassador to N.A.T.O.* **3** any representative of a group who reflects its typical qualities: *Visiting scouts can be ambassadors of good will for their country.* Also, **embassador.** [ME < MF *ambassadeur* < Ital. *ambasciatore*]

ambassador-at-large (am bas′ə dər ət lärj′) *n.* a minister or representative appointed for a special occasion, but not accredited to any government.

am·bas·sa·do·ri·al (am bas′ə dô′rē əl) *adj.* of an ambassador or ambassadors.

am·bas·sa·dor·ship (am bas′ə dər ship′) *n.* **1** the position or rank of an ambassador. **2** the term of office of an ambassador.

am·ber (am′bər) *n.* **1** a hard, translucent, fossilized resin, yellow or yellowish-brown in color, used for jewellery. **2** the color of amber; yellow; yellowish brown. —*adj.* **1** made of amber. **2** yellow; yellowish-brown. [ME < OF *ambre* < Arabic *ʿanbar* ambergris]

am·ber·gris (am′bər grēs′ or am′bər gris) *n.* a waxlike, grayish substance secreted by sperm whales. Ambergris is used in making perfumes. [< F *ambre gris* gray amber]

ambi- *combining form.* on both sides; in both ways; both: *ambidextrous* = *dextrous with both hands.* Also: **am-** before *p*; **amb-** before vowels. [< L *ambi-* around or *ambo* both]

am·bi·dex·ter·i·ty (am′bə deks ter′ə tē) *n.* **1** the ability to use both hands equally well. **2** unusual skilfulness. **3** deceitfulness.

am·bi·dex·trous (am′bə dek′strəs) *adj.* **1** able to use both hands equally well. **2** very skilful. **3** deceitful. [< LL *ambidexter* < L *ambi-* both + *dexter* right] —**am′bi·dex′trous·ly,** *adv.* —**am′bi·dex′trous·ness,** *n.*

am·bi·ent (am′bē ənt) *adj.* surrounding. [< L *ambiens, -entis,* ppr. of *ambire* < *ambi-* around + *ire* go]

am·bi·gu·i·ty (am′bə gū′ə tē) *n.* **-ties. 1** a possibility of two or more meanings: *The ambiguity of the speaker's reply made it impossible to know which side he was on.* **2** a word or expression that can have more than one meaning. **3** lack of clarity; vagueness; uncertainty: *On his first day as a clerk in the office, the president's son was embarrassed by the ambiguity of his position.*

am·big·u·ous (am big′ū əs) *adj.* **1** having more than one possible meaning: *"After John hit Dick, he ran away," is ambiguous because one cannot tell which boy ran away.* **2** doubtful; not clear; uncertain: *He was left in an ambiguous position by his friend's failure to appear and help him.* [< L *ambiguus* < *ambigere* < *ambi-* in two ways + *agere* drive] —**am·big′u·ous·ly,** *adv.* —**am·big′u·ous·ness,** *n.* —**Syn. 1** equivocal. See **obscure. 2** vague.

am·bi·tion (am bish′ən) *n.* **1** a strong desire for fame or honor; seeking after a high position or great power. **2** something strongly desired or sought after: *Her ambition was to be a great actress.* [ME < OF < L *ambitio, -onis* a canvassing for votes < *ambire* < *ambi-* around + *ire* go] —**am·bi′tion·less,** *adj.* —**Syn. 1** aspiration.

am·bi·tious (am bish′əs) *adj.* **1** having or guided by ambition. **2** arising from or showing ambition: *an ambitious plan.* **3** desiring strongly; eager: *ambitious of power. John is ambitious to get through high school in three more years.* **4** showy; pretentious. —**am·bi′tious·ly,** *adv.* —**am·bi′tious·ness,** *n.*

am·biv·a·lence (am biv′ə lens′) *n.* the state or condition of having simultaneously conflicting feelings or attitudes, such as love and hate, towards persons, places, or things. [< *ambi-* + L *valentia* value < *valere* be worth]

am·biv·a·lent (am biv′ə lənt) *adj.* acting in opposite ways; having conflicting feelings or attitudes, such as love and hate, at the same time: *The politician was spurred on by the ambivalent mixture of a ruthless ambition and an earnest desire to serve his country.*

am·ble (am′bəl) *n. v.* **-bled, -bling.** —*n.* **1** the gait of a horse when it lifts first the two legs on one side and then the two on the other. **2** an easy, slow pace in walking. —*v.* **1** walk at an easy, slow pace. **2** (of a horse) move at an amble. [ME < OF *ambler* < L *ambulare* walk]

am·bler (am′blər) *n.* **1** a horse or mule that ambles. **2** a person who ambles.

am·bro·sia (am brō′zhə or am brō′zē ə) *n.* **1** in Greek and Roman mythology, the food of the gods. **2** something especially pleasing to taste or smell. [< L < Gk. *ambrosia* < *ambrotos* < *a-* not + *brotos* mortal]

am·bro·sial (am brō′zhəl or am brō′zē əl) *adj.* **1** like ambrosia; especially pleasing to taste or smell. **2** divine; worthy of the gods.

Am·bro·sian chant (am brō′zhən) a style of plain song introduced by St. Ambrose in the cathedral of Milan about A.D. 384. The melody had more ornamentation than the later Gregorian chant.

am·bu·lance (am′byů ləns) *n.* a vehicle, boat, or airplane equipped to carry sick or wounded persons. [< F *ambulance* < (*hôpital*) *ambulant* walking (hospital) < L *ambulare* walk]

am·bu·lant (am′byů lənt) *adj.* walking.

am·bu·late (am′byů lāt′) *v.* **-lat·ed, -lat·ing.** walk; move about. [< L *ambulare*] —**am′bu·la′tion,** *n.*

am·bu·la·to·ry (am′byů lə tô′rē) *adj. n.* **-ries.** —*adj.* **1** having to do with walking; fitted for walking. **2** capable of walking; not bedridden. **3** moving from place to place. **4** not permanent; changeable. —*n.* a covered place for walking; cloister.

am·bus·cade (am′bəs kād′) *n. v.* **-cad·ed, -cad·ing.**

ambush. [< F *embuscade* < Ital. *imboscata* < *imboscare* ambush] —**am′bus·cad′er,** *n.*

am·bush (am′bu̇sh) *n.* **1** soldiers, etc. hidden to make a surprise attack on an approaching enemy. **2** the place where they are hidden. **3** the act of lying in wait: *Indians often trapped their enemies by ambush instead of meeting them in open battle.* [ME < OF *embusche* < *embuscher.* See AMBUSH, *v.*]
—*v.* **1** attack from an ambush. **2** wait in hiding to make a surprise attack. **3** put (soldiers) in hiding for a surprise attack: *The general ambushed his troops in the woods on either side of the road.* [ME < OF *embuscher* < *en* -in (< L *in-*) + *busche* wood, bush < VL *busca* < Gmc.]

a·me·ba (ə mē′bə) *n.* **-bas** or **-bae** (-bē or -bī). amoeba.

a·me·bic (ə mē′bik) *adj.* amoebic.

a·me·boid (ə mē′boid) *adj.* amoeboid.

a·meer (ə mēr′) *n.* amir.

a·mel·io·ra·ble (ə mēl′yə rə bəl or ə mē′lē ə rə bəl) *adj.* that can be improved.

a·mel·io·rate (ə mēl′yə rāt′ or ə mē′lē ə rāt′) *v.* **-rat·ed, -rat·ing.** make better; become better; improve: *New housing ameliorated living conditions in the slums.* [< F *améliorer,* ult. < LL *meliorare* < L *melior* better]

a·mel·io·ra·tion (ə mēl′yə rā′shən or ə mē′lē ə rā′shən) *n.* improvement.

a·mel·io·ra·tive (ə mēl′yə rə tiv or ə mēl′yə rā′tiv, ə mē lē ə rə tiv or ə mē′lē ə rā′tiv) *adj.* improving.

a·men (ā′men′ or ä′men′) *interj.* **1** be it so; may it become true. *Amen* is said after a prayer or wish. **2** *Informal.* an expression of approval. —*n.* the word *amen.* [< L < Gk. < Hebrew *amen* truth, certainty < *aman* strengthen]

a·me·na·bil·i·ty (ə mē′nə bil′ə tē or ə men′ə bil′ə tē) *n.* the fact, quality, state, or condition of being amenable.

a·me·na·ble (ə mē′nə bəl or ə men′ə bəl) *adj.* **1** open to suggestion or advice; responsive; submissive: *A reasonable person is amenable to persuasion.* **2** accountable; answerable: *People living in a country are amenable to its laws.* [< AF *amener* < *a-* to (< L *ad-*) + *mener* lead < L *minare* drive (with shouts) < *minae* threats] —**a·me′na·ble·ness,** *n.* —**a·me′na·bly,** *adv.*

a·mend (ə mend′) *v.* **1** change the form of (a law, bill, motion, etc.) by addition, omission, etc. **2** change for the better; improve. **3** free from faults; make right; correct. [ME < OF *amender* < L *emendare* < *ex-* out of + *mendum, menda* fault. Doublet of EMEND.] —**a·mend′a·ble,** *adj.* —**a·mend′er,** *n.* —**Syn. 3** emend.

a·mende (ə mend′; *French,* ä mäɴd′) *n.* **1** recompense or satisfaction for an injury done. **2** a fine or penalty. [< F]

a·mend·ment (ə mend′mənt) *n.* **1** a change made in a law, bill, motion, etc. **2** a change for the better; improvement. **3** a change made to remove an error; correction.

a·mends (ə mendz′) *n.sing. or pl.* a payment for loss; satisfaction for an injury; compensation.

a·men·i·ty (ə mē′nə tē or ə men′ə tē) *n.* **-ties. 1** a pleasant way; polite act: *Saying "Thank you" and holding the door open for a person to pass through are amenities.* **2** a pleasant feature; something which makes life easier and more pleasant. **3** a pleasantness; agreeableness: *the amenity of a warm climate.* [ME < OF < L *amoenitas* < *amoenus* pleasant]

a·men·or·rhe·a (ā men′ə rē′ə) *n.* failure to menstruate; the absence of menstruation. [< NL *amenorrhea* < Gk. *a-* not + *men* month + *rhoia* flux, flow]

A·men-Ra (ä′men rä′) *n.* the principal god of ancient Egypt.

am·ent (am′ənt or ā′mənt) *n.* a long, slender, scaly flower spike that grows on willows, birches, etc.; catkin. [< L *amentum* thong]

Amer. 1 America. **2** American.

a·merce (ə mėrs′) *v.* **a·merced, a·merc·ing. 1** punish by a fine. **2** punish. [ME < AF *amercier* < *a merci* at the mercy (of)] —**a·merce′ment,** *n.* —**a·merc′er,** *n.*

A·mer·i·can (ə mer′ə kən) *adj.* **1** of or having to do with the United States; in the United States: *an American citizen.* **2** of or in the Western Hemisphere: *the Amazon and other American rivers.*
—*n.* **1** a citizen of the United States, or of the earlier British colonies, not belonging to one of the aboriginal races. **2** a native or inhabitant of the Western Hemisphere. *Abbrev.:* Am. or Amer.

hat, āge, cãre, fär; let, ēqual, tėrm; it, īce
hot, ōpen, ôrder; oil, out; cup, pu̇t, rüle, ūse
əbove, takən, pencəl, lemən, circəs
ch, child; ng, long; sh, ship
th, thin; ᴛʜ, then; zh, measure

A·mer·i·ca·na (ə mer′ə ka′nə, ə mer′ə kän′ə, or ə mer′ə kā′nə) *n.pl.* a collection of objects, documents, books, facts, etc. about America, especially its history.

American aloe the century plant.

American Beauty a variety of red rose.

American eagle the bald eagle. The coat of arms of the United States has a representation of the American eagle on it.

A·mer·i·can·ism (ə mer′ə kən iz′əm) *n.* **1** devotion or loyalty to the United States, its customs, traditions, etc. **2** a word, phrase, or meaning originating in the United States. **3** a custom or trait peculiar to the United States.

A·mer·i·can·i·za·tion (ə mer′ə kən ə zā′shən or ə mer′ə kən ī zā′shən) *n.* the act or process of making or becoming American in habits, customs, or character.

A·mer·i·can·ize (ə mer′ə kən īz′) *v.* **-ized, -iz·ing.** make or become American in habits, customs, or character.

American organ a kind of small reed organ; melodeon.

American plan a system used in hotels where one price covers room, board, and service. See also **European plan.**

am·er·i·ci·um (am′ər ish′ē əm) *n.* an artificial, radio-active metallic chemical element. *Symbol:* Am; *at.no.* 95; *at.wt.* 243. *Abbrev.:* Am. [< NL < *America*]

Am·er·in·di·an (am′ər in′dē ən) *n.* **1** an American Indian. **2** an Eskimo. —*adj.* of or having to do with Amerindians.

am·e·thyst (am′ə thist) *n.* **1** a purple or violet variety of quartz, used for jewellery. **2** a piece of this stone, or a gem made from it. **3** a violet-colored corundum, used for jewellery. **4** purple; violet. [ME < OF < L < Gk. *amethystos* < *a-* not + *methy* wine; thought to prevent intoxication] —**am′e·thyst·like′,** *adj.*

Am·har·ic (am har′ik) *n.* the official and literary language of Ethiopia since the twelfth century, a Semitic language of the Ethiopic group. —*adj.* of or having to do with this language.

a·mi·a·bil·i·ty (ā′mē ə bil′ə tē) *n.* good nature; friendliness; pleasantness; agreeableness.

a·mi·a·ble (ā′mē ə bəl) *adj.* good-natured and friendly; pleasant and agreeable. [ME < OF *amiable* < LL *amicabilis* < L *amicus* friend. Doublet of AMICABLE.] —**a′mi·a·bly,** *adv.*

am·i·ca·bil·i·ty (am′ə kə bil′ə tē) *n.* friendliness.

am·i·ca·ble (am′ə kə bəl) *adj.* peaceable; friendly: *Instead of fighting, the two nations settled their quarrel in an amicable way.* [< LL *amicabilis* < L *amicus* friend. Doublet of AMIABLE.] —**am′i·ca·bly,** *adv.*

am·ice (am′is) *n.* an oblong piece of white linen worn by priests at Mass. It is placed around the neck and over the shoulders. [ME < OF *amis* < L *amictus* cloak]

a·mi·cus cu·ri·ae (ə mē′kəs kūr′ē ī or ə mī′kəs kūr′ē ē) in law, a person with no interest in a case who is called in to advise the judge. [< NL *amicus curiae* friend of the court]

a·mid (ə mid′) *prep.* in the middle of; among. [OE *amiddan* < *on middan* in the middle]

a·mid·ship (ə mid′ship) *adv.* amidships.

a·mid·ships (ə mid′ships) *adv.* in or toward the middle of a ship; halfway between the bow and stern.

a·midst (ə midst′) *prep.* amid.

a·mi·go (ə mē′gō) *n.* a friend. [< Sp. < L *amicus*]

a·mine (ə mēn′ or am′in) *n.* in chemistry, any of a group of organic compounds formed from ammonia by replacement of one or more of its three hydrogen atoms by univalent hydrocarbon radicals. [< *ammonia* + *-ine*[2]]

a·mi·no acids (ə mē′nō or am′ə nō) in chemistry, certain complex organic compounds of nitrogen that combine in various ways to form proteins.

a·mir (ə mēr′) *n.* in Moslem countries, a commander, ruler, or prince. Also, **ameer.** [< Arabic *amir* commander. Related to ADMIRAL.]

Am·ish (am′ish or ä′mish) *n.* **Am·ish,** *adj.* —*n.* a member of a strict Mennonite sect, founded in the 17th century.
—*adj.* of this sect or its members. [after Jacob *Amen,* 17th cent. Mennonite preacher]

am·isk (am′isk) *n.* a beaver. [< Cree]

a·miss (ə mis′) *adv.* **1** not the way it should be; out of order; at fault. **2 take amiss,** be offended at.
—*adj.* improper; wrong. [ME *a mis* by (way of) fault. Related to MISS[1].]

am·i·to·sis (am′ə tō′sis) *n.* in biology, a simple or direct method of cell division; reproduction without mitosis. In amitosis the cell separates into new cells without an exact division of the chromosomes. [< *a-*[4] not + *mitosis*]

am·i·ty (am′ə tē) *n.* **-ties.** peace and friendship; friendly relations: *If there were amity between nations, there would be no wars.* [ME < OF *amitie,* ult. < L *amicus* friend]

am·me·ter (am′mē′tər or am′ē′tər) *n.* an instrument for measuring in amperes the strength of an electric current. [< *am*pere + *meter*]

am·mo·nia (ə mōn′yə or ə mō′nē ə) *n.* **1** a strong-smelling, colorless gas, consisting of nitrogen and hydrogen. *Formula*: NH_3 **2** this gas dissolved in water. Ammonia is very useful for cleaning. *Formula*: NH_3OH [< NL; so named because obtained from sal *ammoniac*]

am·mo·ni·ac (ə mō′nē ak′) *n.* a gum resin used for medicines and as a cement for porcelain; gum ammoniac.
—*adj.* ammoniacal. [< L *ammoniacum* < Gk. *ammōniakon*; applied to a salt obtained near the shrine of Ammon in Libya]

am·mo·ni·a·cal (am′ə nī′ə kəl) *adj.* of or like ammonia.

ammonia water ammonia gas dissolved in water.

am·mon·i·fy (ə mon′ə fī′) *v.* combine or be combined with ammonia or an ammonium compound.
—**am·mon′i·fi·ca′tion,** *n.*

am·mo·nite (am′ə nīt′) *n.* the fossil shell of a mollusc extinct in the Cretaceous period, coiled in a flat spiral and up to 6 ft. in diameter. [< NL *ammonites* < Med.L *cornu Ammonis* horn of Ammon]

am·mo·ni·um (ə mō′nē əm) *n.* a group of atoms consisting of nitrogen and hydrogen. *Formula*: NH_4 Ammonium never appears in a free state by itself, but acts as a unit in chemical reactions.

ammonium chloride colorless crystals or a white powder used in medicine, in printing on cloth, etc.; sal ammoniac. *Formula*: NH_4Cl

ammonium hydroxide an alkali formed when ammonia gas dissolves in water. *Formula*: NH_4OH

am·mu·ni·tion (am′yů nish′ən) *n.* **1** bullets, shells, gunpowder, etc. for guns or other weapons; military supplies that can be used against an enemy. **2** anything that can be shot, hurled, or thrown. **3** a means of attack or defence. [< obsolete F *amunition,* used for *munition*]

am·ne·sia (am nē′zhə or am nē′zē ə) *n.* loss of memory caused by injury to the brain, or by disease or shock. [< NL < Gk. *amnēsia* < *a-* not + *mnasthai* remember]

am·nes·ty (am′nis tē) *n.* **-ties,** *v.* **-tied, -ty·ing.**
—*n.* a general pardon for past offences against a government: *After order was restored, the king granted amnesty to those who had plotted against him.* —*v.* give amnesty to; pardon. [< L < Gk. *amnēstia* < *a-* not + *mnasthai* remember]

am·ni·on (am′nē ən) *n.* **-ni·ons** or **-ni·a** (-nē ə). a membrane lining the sac that encloses the embryos of reptiles, birds, and mammals. [< Gk. *amnion,* dim. of *amnos* lamb]

am·ni·ote (am′nē ōt′) *n.* in zoology, any of the group of vertebrates, including reptiles, birds, and mammals, that develop amnions in their embryonic stages.

am·ni·ot·ic (am′nē ot′ik) *adj.* **1** of or contained in the amnion. **2** having an amnion.

a·moe·ba or **a·me·ba** (ə mē′bə) *n.* **-bas** or **-bae** (-bē or -bī). a microscopic one-celled animal that moves by forming temporary projections that are constantly changing. Many amoebas live in water; others live as parasites in other animals. [< Gk. *amoibē* change]

a·moe·bic or **a·me·bic** (ə mē′bik) *adj.* **1** of or like an amoeba or amoebas. **2** caused by amoebas.

a·moe·boid or **a·me·boid** (ə mē′boid) *adj.* of or like an amoeba; like that of an amoeba; related or having to do with amoebas.

a·mok (ə muk′ or ə mok′) *adv. adj.* amuck. —*n.* a violent nervous disorder, occurring chiefly among the Malays; a murderous frenzy. [< Malay]

a·mong (ə mung′) *prep.* **1** surrounded by: *a house among the trees.* **2** in with: *He fell among thieves.* **3** one of: *Canada is among the largest countries in the world.* **4** in the number or class of: *That book is the best among modern novels.* **5** in comparison with: *one among many.* **6** to each of; by or for distribution to: *Divide the money among them.* **7** by the combined action of: *Among them they have spoiled the child.* **8 among ourselves, yourselves,** or **themselves, a** some with others: *They fought among themselves.* **b** each with all the others: *They agreed among themselves to have a party.* **9** by, with, or through the whole of: *political unrest among the people.* [OE *amang* < *on gemang* in a crowd]

☛ **among, between.** *Among* implies more than two objects: *They distributed the provisions among the survivors. Between* is always used when only two are concerned: *They divided the prize between Tom and Joseph.* But *between* is also often used of several. It then tends to suggest the individuals involved more than the situation: *The family of seven hadn't a pair of shoes between them.*

a·mongst (ə mungst′) *prep.* among.

a·mon·til·la·do (ə mon′tə lä′dō; *Spanish,* ä mōn′tē lyä′ᴛʜō) *n.* **-dos** (-dōz; *Spanish,* -ᴛʜōs). a pale, moderately dry sherry. [< Sp. *Montilla,* a district in Spain where this wine is made]

a·mor·al (ā môr′əl or a môr′əl) *adj.* not involving any question of morality; non-moral. [< *a-*[4] not + *moral*]
—**a·mor′al·ly,** *adv.*

a·morce (ə môrs′) *n.* **1** an explosive to set off the main charge; priming charge. **2** a percussion cap for a toy pistol. [< F < OF *amordre* bite]

am·o·ro·so (am′ə rō′sō) *adj.* in music, tender; loving.
—*n.* a lover [< Ital. *amoroso* loving < LL *amorosus* < L *amor* love]

am·o·rous (am′ə rəs) *adj.* **1** inclined to love. **2** in love. **3** showing love; loving. **4** having to do with love or courtship. [ME < OF *amorous* < *amour* love < L *amor*] — **am′o·rous·ly,** *adv.* —**am′o·rous·ness,** *n.*
—**Syn. 2** enamored. **3** fond, devoted.

a·mor pa·tri·ae (ä′môr pa′trē ī′ or ā′môr pā′trē ē′) *Latin.* love of one's own country; patriotism.

a·mor·phous (ə môr′fəs) *adj.* **1** not consisting of crystals: *Glass is amorphous; sugar is crystalline.* **2** of no particular kind or type. **3** having no definite form; shapeless; formless; not organized. **4** in geology, lacking stratification or other division. **5** in biology, having no definite shape or structure. [< Gk. *amorphos* < *a-* without + *morphē* shape] —**a·mor′phous·ly,** *adv.*

am·or·tise (am′ər tīz′ or ə môr′tīz) *v.* **-tised, -tis·ing.** *Esp.Brit.* amortize.

am·or·ti·za·tion (am′ər tə zā′shən or ə môr′tə zā′shən) *n.* **1** an amortizing or being amortized. **2** the money regularly set aside for this purpose.

am·or·tize (am′ər tīz′ or ə môr′tīz) *v.* **-tized, -tiz·ing.** **1** set money aside regularly in a special fund for future wiping out of (a debt, etc.). **2** in accounting, write off (expenditures, debts, etc.) proportionately over a fixed period. [ME < OF *amortiss-*, a stem of *amortir* deaden < *a-* to (< L *ad-*) + *mort* death < L *mors, mortis*]

a·mor·tize·ment (ə môr′tiz mənt) *n.* amortization.

a·mount (ə mount′) *n.* **1** a sum; total: *What is the amount of the day's sales?* **2** the full effect, value, or extent: *The amount of evidence against him is great.* **3** a quantity viewed as a whole: *a great amount of intelligence.* [< v.]
—*v.* **1** be equal; add up (*to*): *The loss from the flood amounts to ten million dollars.* **2** be equivalent in quantity, value, force, effect, etc. (*to*): *Keeping what belongs to another amounts to stealing.* [ME < OF *amonter* < *a mont* up, literally, to the mountain < L *ad* to, *mons, montis* mountain]
☛ **amount, number.** *Amount* is used of things viewed in the bulk, weight, or sum; *number* is used of persons or things that can be counted: *an amount of milk, a number of cans of milk.*

a·mour (ə mür′) *n.* **1** a love affair. **2** a secret or illicit love affair. [< F *amour*, probably < Provençal < L *amor* love]

a·mour-pro·pre (ä mür′prô′prə) *n. French.* conceit; self-esteem.

amp. 1 ampere; amperes. **2** amperage.

am·per·age (am′pər ij or am pēr′ij) *n.* the strength of an electric current measured in amperes. *Abbrev.*: a., a, or amp.

am·pere (am′pēr or am pēr′, am per′ or am′pər) *n.* a unit for measuring the strength of an electric current; the amount of current one volt can send through a resistance of one ohm. Ordinary light bulbs take from ¼ to ½ ampere. *Abbrev.*: a., a, or amp. [after André-Marie Ampère (1775-1836), a French physicist]

am·per·sand (am′pər sand′) *n.* the sign &, meaning "and." [alteration of *and per se = and*, & by itself = and]
☛ An ampersand is used chiefly in business correspondence and reference works.

am·phet·a·mine (am fet′ə mēn′ or am fet′ə min) *n.* a drug used as an inhalant or, in solution, as a spray for the relief of colds, hay fever, etc., also used, in tablet form, as a stimulant to combat fatigue or reduce appetite; Benzedrine. *Formula*: $C_9H_{13}N$ [*a*lpha-*m*ethyl-beta-*ph*enyl-*et*hyl-*amine*]

amphi- *combining form.* **1** around; on both sides, as in *amphitheatre.* **2** in two ways; of two kinds, as in *amphibious.* [< Gk. *amphi-* < *amphi*, prep., adv.]

Am·phib·i·a (am fib′ē ə) *n.pl.* in zoology, a class of cold-blooded vertebrates that includes frogs, toads, newts, salamanders, etc. They have moist, scale-less skin, and their young usually develop as tadpoles that have gills and live in water. [< NL *Amphibia*, neut. pl. of *amphibius* < Gk. *amphibios*. See AMPHIBIOUS.]

am·phib·i·an (am fib′ē ən) *n.* **1** an animal that lives on land and in water. **2** one of the Amphibia. **3** a plant that grows on land or in water. **4** an aircraft that can take off from and alight on either land or water. **5** a vehicle that travels across land or water.
—*adj.* **1** of both land and water; able to live both on land and in water. **2** that can travel on, start from, and alight on either land or water.

am·phi·bi·ol·o·gy (am fib′ē ol′ə jē) *n.* the branch of zoology that deals with amphibians.

am·phib·i·ous (am fib′ē əs) *adj.* **1** able to live both on land and in water. **2** suited for use on land or water: *an amphibious tank.* **3** having two qualities, kinds, natures, or parts. **4** by the combined action of land, water, and air forces: *an amphibious attack.* [< Gk. *amphibios* living a double life < *amphi-* both + *bios* life]
—**am·phib′i·ous·ly,** *adv.* —**am·phib′i·ous·ness,** *n.*

am·phi·bole (am′fə bōl′) *n.* any of a group of silicate minerals, including hornblende and asbestos. [< F < L *amphibolus* < Gk. *amphibolos* ambiguous < *amphi-* on both sides + *-bolos* struck]

am·phi·brach (am′fə brak′) *n.* in poetry, a measure or foot consisting of one strongly stressed syllable between two weakly stressed syllables, or one long syllable between two short syllables. *Example*:

Behínd shut | the póstern, | the líghts sank | to rest,
And ínto | the mídnight | we gálloped | abreast.

[< L *amphibrachus* < Gk. *amphibrachys* short at both ends < *amphi-* both + *brachys* short]

hat, āge, cãre, fär; let, ēqual, tėrm; it, īce
hot, ōpen, ôrder; oil, out; cup, pu̇t, rüle, ūse
əbove, takən, pencəl, lemən, circəs
ch, child; ng, long; sh, ship
th, thin; ᴛʜ, then; zh, measure

am·phi·the·a·tre or **am·phi·the·a·ter** (am′fə thē′ə tər) *n.* **1** a circular or oval building with tiers of seats around a central open space. **2** something resembling an amphitheatre in shape. [< L < Gk. *amphitheatron* < *amphi-* on all sides + *theatron* theatre]

A Roman amphitheatre

am·pho·ra (am′fə rə) *n.* **-rae** (-rē′ or -rī′). a tall two-handled jar, used by the ancient Greeks and Romans. [< L < Gk. *amphoreus*, short for *amphiphoreus* < *amphi-* on both sides + *phoreus* bearer; with reference to the two handles]

am·ple (am′pəl) *adj.* **-pler, -plest. 1** large; big; extensive; roomy. **2** more than enough; abundant: *Take an ample supply of food for a day's journey.* **3** enough: *My allowance is ample for carfare and lunches.* [< F < L *amplus*] —**Syn. 2** plentiful, copious, liberal.

am·pli·fi·ca·tion (am′plə fə kā′shən) *n.* **1** the act of amplifying; expansion. **2** a detail or example that amplifies a statement, narrative, etc. **3** an expanded statement, narrative, etc. **4** an increase in the strength of electric current.

am·pli·fi·er (am′plə fī′ər) *n.* **1** a person or thing that amplifies. **2** a radio vacuum tube or other device for strengthening electrical impulses. **3** a loudspeaker.

am·pli·fy (am′plə fī′) *v.* **-fied, -fy·ing. 1** make greater; make stronger. **2** make fuller and more extensive; expand; enlarge. **3** write or talk at length. **4** increase the strength of (a sound or an electrical impulse). [ME < OF *amplifier* < L *amplificare* < *amplus* ample + *facere* make]

am·pli·tude (am′plə tūd′ or am′plə tüd′) *n.* **1** width; breadth; size. **2** abundance; fullness. **3** in physics, one half the range of regular vibrations: *A pendulum swinging through 10° has an amplitude of 5°.* **4** in electricity, the peak strength of an alternating current in a given cycle. [< L *amplitudo* < *amplus* ample]

amplitude modulation the purposeful alteration of the amplitude of radio waves. Ordinary broadcasting uses amplitude modulation. See also **frequency modulation.** *Abbrev.*: AM, A.M., or a-m

am·ply (am′plē) *adv.* in an ample manner; to an ample degree; liberally; sufficiently.

am·poule (am′pül or am pül′) *n.* a small, sealed glass container, usually holding one dose of a drug, medicine, etc. [< F < L *ampulla* small bottle]

am·pul·la (am pül′ə) *n.* **1** a two-handled jar or bottle used in ancient Rome to hold oil, perfume, wine, etc. It was smaller than an amphora. **2** a vessel used in churches to hold consecrated oil. **3** in anatomy and zoology, the dilated portion of a canal or duct. **4** in botany, a flask-shaped organ or bladder on an aquatic plant. [< L]

am·pu·tate (am′pyu̇ tāt′) *v.* **-tat·ed, -tat·ing.** cut off: *The doctor amputated the soldier's wounded leg.* [< L *amputare* < *ambi-* about + *putare* prune]
—**am′pu·ta′tor,** *n.*

am·pu·ta·tion (am′pyu̇ tā′shən) *n.* the act of cutting off a leg, arm, finger, etc.; a cutting off.

am·pu·tee (am′pyu̇ tē′) *n.* a person who has had an arm, leg, etc. amputated.

amt. amount.

a·muck (ə muk′) *adv. adj.* **1** in a murderous frenzy; with a crazy desire to attack. **2 run amuck**, run about in a murderous frenzy. Also, amok. [< Malay *amok* engaging furiously in battle]

am·u·let (am′yů lit) *n.* some object worn as a magic charm against evil. [< L *amuletum*]

a·muse (ə mūz′) *v.* **a·mused, a·mus·ing. 1** cause to laugh or smile. **2** keep pleasantly interested; cause to feel cheerful or happy; entertain: *The new toys amused the children.* [ME < OF *amuser* divert < *a-* + *muser* stare] —**a·mus′er,** *n.*

Syn. 2 amuse, entertain = to keep pleasantly interested. **Amuse** emphasizes the idea of passing time by keeping one's attention occupied with something interesting and pleasing: *While waiting, she amused herself by counting the cars that passed.* **Entertain** emphasizes greater effort, usually by others but sometimes by one's own mind, or more elaborate means to hold attention: *Some people entertain themselves by reading; others have to be entertained by the radio or television.*

a·mused (ə mūzd′) *adj.* pleasantly entertained. —**a·mus′ed·ly,** *adv.*

a·muse·ment (ə mūz′mənt) *n.* **1** the condition of being amused. **2** something that amuses; entertainment; sport.

a·mus·ing (ə mūz′ing) *adj.* **1** entertaining. **2** causing laughter, smiles, etc. —**a·mus′ing·ly,** *adv.*

am·yl (am′əl) *n.* a group of carbon and hydrogen atoms that acts as a unit in forming compounds. *Formula:* C_5H_{11} [< L < Gk. *amylon,* starch, originally, unground < *a-* not + *mylē* mill]

am·yl·ase (am′ə lās′) *n.* an enzyme in saliva, the pancreatic juice, etc., or in parts of plants, that helps to change starch into sugar. [< *amyl*]

am·y·lop·sin (am′ə lop′sin) *n.* an enzyme in the pancreatic juice that changes starch into simpler compounds such as glucose. [< *amyl* + *trypsin*]

an[1] (ən; *stressed,* an) *adj.* or *indefinite article.* used in place of *a* before a vowel or silent *h*: *an apple, an heir.* **1** any: *Have you an answer to this accusation?* **2** one: *Take an orange.* **3** each; every: *twice an hour.* [OE (unstressed) *ān* (before vowels)] ☛ See **a**[1] for usage note.

an[2] (ən; *stressed,* an) *adj.* or *indefinite article.* to or for each: *It cost fifty cents an ounce. The contest organizers wanted two dollars an entry.* [OE *ān* one]

an[3] (ən; *stressed,* an) *conj.* **1** *Dialect* or *Informal.* and. **2** *Archaic.* if. [var. of *and*]

an-[1] *prefix.* not; without, as in *anhydrous.* Also, **a-,** before consonants except *h.* [< Gk.]

an-[2] the form of **ad-** before *n,* as in *annex.*

-an *suffix.* **1** of or having to do with ——: *Mohammedan = of or having to do with Mohammed.* **2** of or having to do with —— or its people: *Asian = of or having to do with Asia or its people.* **3** a native or inhabitant of ——: *American = native or inhabitant of America.* [< L *-anus*]

ana- *prefix.* back; again; thoroughly; up, as in *anachronism, analysis.* [< Gk. *ana-* < *ana,* prep.]

-ana *suffix.* sayings, writings, or articles by, belonging to or associated with ——: *Shakespeariana = things written by or associated with Shakespeare. Canadiana = things associated with Canada.* [< L *-ana,* neuter pl. of *-anus,* -an]

an·a·bap·tism (an′ə bap′tiz əm) *n.* **1** a second baptism. **2** the doctrines, principles, and practices of the Anabaptists.

An·a·bap·tist (an′ə bap′tist) *n.* a member of a Protestant sect opposing infant baptism and requiring adult baptism.

an·a·bol·ic (an′ə bol′ik) *adj.* of anabolism.

a·nab·o·lism (ə nab′ə liz′əm) *n.* in biology, the process by which food substances are changed into the tissues of a living animal or plant. [coined from *metabolism* by substitution of Gk. *ana-* up]

a·nach·ro·nism (ə nak′rə niz′əm) *n.* **1** the putting of a person, thing, or event in some time where he or it does not belong: *It would be an anachronism to speak of John Milton riding in an automobile.* **2** something placed or occurring out of its proper time. [< F < Gk. *anachronismos* < *ana-* backwards + *chronos* time]

a·nach·ro·nis·tic (ə nak′rə nis′tik) *adj.* having or involving an anachronism. —**a·nach′ro·nis′ti·cal·ly,** *adv.*

a·nach·ro·nous (ə nak′rə nəs) *adj.* placed or occurring out of the proper time. —**a·nach′ro·nous·ly,** *adv.*

an·a·co·lu·thon (an′ə kə lü′thon) *n.* **-tha** (-thə). a change from one grammatical construction to another in the same sentence. [< LL < Gk. *anakolouthos* < *an-* not + *akolouthos* following]

an·a·con·da (an′ə kon′də) *n.* **1** a large snake, found in tropical South America, that crushes its prey in its coils; water boa. **2** any large snake that crushes its prey in its coils, such as the python, or boa. **3** originally, a large python native to Ceylon. [? < Singhalese *henakandayā,* a kind of thin, green snake]

a·nad·ro·mous (ə nad′rə məs) *adj.* going up rivers from the sea to spawn. Salmon are anadromous. [< LGk. *anadromos* < *ana-* up + *dromos* a running]

a·nae·mi·a (ə nē′mē ə) *n.* anemia.

a·nae·mic (ə nē′mik) *adj.* anemic.

an·aer·obe (an ãr′ōb or an ā′ər ōb′) *n.* **1** an organism that cannot live in the presence of free oxygen. **2** an organism that can live without free oxygen. [< NL *anaerobium* < Gk. *an-* without + *aēr* air + *bios* life]

an·aer·o·bic (an′ãr ō′bik or an ā′ər ō′bik) *adj.* living or growing where there is no free oxygen. Anaerobic bacteria get their oxygen by decomposing compounds containing oxygen.

an·aes·the·sia (an′is thē′zhə or an′is thē′zē ə) *n.* anesthesia.

an·aes·thet·ic (an′is thet′ik) *adj. n.* anesthetic.

an·aes·the·tist (ə nēs′thə tist or ə nes′thə tist) *n.* anesthetist.

an·aes·the·tize (ə nēs′thə tīz′ or ə nes′thə tīz′) *v.* **-tized, -tiz·ing.** anesthetize. —**an·aes′the·ti·za′tion,** *n.*

an·a·gram (an′ə gram′) *n.* **1** a word or phrase formed from another by transposing the letters. *Example:* table—bleat. **2 anagrams,** *pl.* a game in which the players make words by changing and adding letters. [< NL *anagramma* < Gk. *anagrammatizein* transpose letters < *ana-* up or back + *gramma* letter]

a·nal (ā′nəl) *adj.* **1** of the anus. **2** near the anus.

an·al·ge·si·a (an′əl jē′zē ə or an′əl jē′sē ə) *n.* the deadening or absence of sense of pain. [< NL < Gk. *analgēsia* < *an-* not + *algeein* feel pain]

an·al·ge·sic (an′əl jē′zik or an′əl jē′sik) *adj.* of or causing analgesia. —*n.* a medicine or other agent that causes analgesia.

an·a·log (an′ə log′) *n.* analogue.

an·a·log·i·cal (an′ə loj′ə kəl) *adj.* based on analogy; using analogy; having to do with analogy.

analogical change in linguistics, the alteration of a form to make it conform to a dominant pattern. *Examples:* the form *climbed* in place of earlier *clomb, crowed* in place of earlier *crew, horses* in place of earlier *hors.*

a·nal·o·gous (ə nal′ə gəs) *adj.* **1** alike in some way; similar; comparable. **2** in biology, corresponding in function, but not in structure and origin. —**a·nal′o·gous·ly,** *adv.*

an·a·logue (an′ə log′) *n.* something analogous.

analogue computer an electronic calculating machine or automatic control that deals directly with physical quantities (weights, voltages, etc.) rather than with a numerical code. See **digital computer.**

a·nal·o·gy (ə nal′ə jē) *n.* **-gies. 1** a likeness in some ways between things that are otherwise unlike; similarity: *the analogy between words like "man" and "pan."* **2** a comparison of such things: *It is easy to draw analogies between the past and the present.* **3** in biology, correspondence in function but not in structure and origin. **4** in logic, the inference that things alike in some respects will be alike in others: *It is risky to argue by analogy.* [< L < Gk. *analogia* equality of ratios, proportion]

☛ One says **analogy** *between* **things, and that one thing has analogy** *to* **or** *with* **another.**

an·a·lyse or **an·a·lyze** (an′ə līz′) *v.* **-lysed** or **-lyzed, -lys·ing** or **-lyz·ing. 1** separate into its parts. **2** examine critically the parts or elements of; find out the essential features of: *analyse a sentence.* **3** examine carefully and in detail. **4** in chemistry, subject to analysis. **5** in mathematics, solve a problem by means of algebra especially by calculus. **6** examine minutely a mind or personality; psychoanalyse. **—an′a·lys′er** or **—an′a·lyz′er,** *n.*

a·nal·y·sis (ə nal′ə sis) *n.* **-ses** (-sēz′). **1** the separation of a thing into its parts; examination of a thing's parts to find out their essential features. An analysis can be made of a book, a person's character, a medicine, soil, etc. **2** in chemistry, **a** the intentional separation of a substance into its ingredients or elements to determine their amount or nature. **b** the determination of the kind or amount of one or more of the constituents of a substance, whether actually obtained in separate form or not. **3** a statement giving the results of an analysis. **4** in physics, the resolution of light into its color constituents. **5** in mathematics, **a** the method of solving problems by reducing them to equations. **b** the branch of the subject that uses differential or integral calculus. [< Med.L < Gk. *analysis* a breaking up < *analyein* unloose < *ana-* up + *lyein* loose]

an·a·lyst (an′ə list) *n.* **1** a person who analyses. **2** a person who practises psycho-analysis.

an·a·lyt·ic (an′ə lit′ik) *adj.* analytical.

an·a·lyt·i·cal (an′ə lit′ə kəl) *adj.* of analysis; using analysis. **—an′a·lyt′i·cal·ly,** *adv.*

analytic geometry in mathematics, the use of algebra and co-ordinates (or the calculus) to solve problems in geometry.

an·a·lyt·ics (an′ə lit′iks) *n.* mathematical or algebraic analysis.

an·a·lyze (an′ə līz′) *v.* **-lyzed, -lyz·ing.** analyse.

An·a·ni·as (an′ə nī′əs) *n.* **1** in the Bible, a member of the church at Jerusalem. He and his wife were struck dead for lying (Acts 5: 1-10). **2** *Informal.* any liar.

an·a·paest or **an·a·pest** (an′ə pēst′ or an′ə pest′) *n.* in verse, a measure or foot consisting of two weakly stressed syllables followed by a strongly stressed syllable, or two short syllables followed by one long syllable. *Example*:

From the cén | tre all róund | to the séa
I am lórd | of the fówl | and the brúte.

[< L *anapaestus* < Gk. *anapaistos* < *ana-* back + *paiein* strike]

an·a·paes·tic or **an·a·pes·tic** (an′ə pēs′tik or an′ə pes′tik) *adj.* having to do with or consisting of anapests.

an·arch (an′ärk) *n.* an anarchic leader.

an·ar·chic (an är′kik) *adj.* lawless; favoring anarchy.

an·ar·chi·cal (an är′kə kəl) *adj.* anarchic.

an·ar·chism (an′ər kiz′əm) *n.* **1** the political theory that all systems of government and law are a restraint on the individual and therefore harmful. **2** the practice or support of this belief. **3** lawlessness.

an·ar·chist (an′ər kist) *n.* **1** a person who favors and supports anarchism as a political idea. **2** one who supports and encourages the violent overthrow of organized government. **3** one who promotes disorder or rebels against established laws or customs.

an·ar·chis·tic (an′ər kis′tik) *adj.* of anarchism; like that of anarchists.

an·ar·chy (an′ər kē) *n.* **1** the absence of a system of government and law. **2** disorder; confusion; lawlessness. [< Gk. *anarchia* < *an-* without + *archos* ruler]

an·a·tase (an′ə tās′) *n.* a variety of native titanium oxide; octahedrite. [< F *anatase* < Gk. *anatasis* extension < *ana-* up + *teinein* stretch, so named because of elongated crystals]

a·nath·e·ma (ə nath′ə mə) *n.* **-mas. 1** a solemn curse by church authorities excommunicating a person. **2** the act of denouncing and condemning a person or thing as evil; curse. **3** a person or thing accursed. **4** a person or thing that is detested and condemned. [< L < Gk. *anathema* thing devoted, esp. to evil < *ana-* up + *tithenai* set]

a·nath·e·ma·tize (ə nath′ə mə tīz′) *v.* **-tized, -tiz·ing.** pronounce an anathema against; denounce; curse. **—a·nath′e·ma·ti·za′tion,** *n.* **—a·nath′e·ma·tiz′er,** *n.*

An·a·to·li·an (an′ə tō′lē ən) *adj.* of or having to do with Anatolia (Asia Minor) or its people. *—n.* a native or inhabitant of Anatolia.

an·a·tom·ic (an′ə tom′ik) *adj.* anatomical.

hat, āge, cãre, fär; let, ēqual, tėrm; it, īce
hot, ōpen, ôrder; oil, out; cup, pu̇t, rüle, ūse
əbove, takən, pencəl, lemən, circəs
ch, child; ng, long; sh, ship
th, thin; ᴛʜ, then; zh, measure

an·a·tom·i·cal (an′ə tom′ə kəl) *adj.* of anatomy; having to do with anatomy. **—an′a·tom′i·cal·ly,** *adv.*

a·nat·o·mist (ə nat′ə mist) *n.* **1** an expert in anatomy. **2** a person who dissects or analyses.

a·nat·o·mize (ə nat′ə mīz′) *v.* **-mized, -miz·ing. 1** divide (a plant or a body) into parts to study the structure; dissect. **2** examine the parts of; analyse. **—a·nat′o·mi·za′tion** .*n.*

a·nat·o·my (ə nat′ə mē) *n.* **-mies. 1** the structure of an anima lor plant: *The anatomy of an earthworm is much simpler than that of a man.* **2** the science of the structure of animals and plants. **3** a textbook or handbook dealing with this subject. **4** the dissecting of animals or plants to study their structure. **5** an examination of the parts or elements of a thing; analysis. **6** a skeleton. [<LL *anatomia* < Gk. *anatomē* dissection < *ana-* up + *temnein* cut]

anc. ancient.

-ance *suffix.* **1** the act or fact of ——ing: *avoidance = the act or fact of avoiding.* **2** the quality or state of being ——ed: *annoyance = the quality or state of being annoyed.* **3** the quality or state of being ——ant: *importance = the quality or state of being important.* **4** something that ——s: *conveyance = something that conveys.* **5** what is ——ed: *contrivance = what is contrived.* [< F < L *-antia, -entia*]

an·ces·tor (an′ses tər) *n.* **1** a person from whom one is descended, such as one's father, mother, grandfather, or grandmother. **2** that from which anything is descended; forerunner. [ME < OF *ancestre* < L *antecessor* <*antecedere* < *ante* before + *cedere* go]
—Syn. forefather.

an·ces·tral (an ses′trəl) *adj.* **1** of or having to do with ancestors: *The ancestral home of the Acadians was France.* **2** inherited from ancestors: *Black hair is an ancestral trait in that family.* **—an·ces′tral·ly,** *adv.*

an·ces·tress (an′ses tris) *n.* a woman from whom one is descended.

an·ces·try (an′ses trē) *n.* **-tries. 1** one's parents, grandparents, and other ancestors: *Many of the early settlers in North America had English ancestry.* **2** a line of descent from ancestors; lineage. **3** honorable descent.

an·chor (ang′kər) *n.* **1** a heavy piece of shaped iron having at one end a ring to which a cable is attached, used for keeping a ship fast to the sea bottom. **2** a thing for holding something else in place. **3** something that makes a person feel safe and secure. **4 at anchor,** held by an anchor. **5 cast anchor,** drop the anchor. **6 ride at anchor,** be kept at some place by being anchored. **7 weigh anchor,** take up the anchor.

An anchor (def. 1)

—v. **1** hold in place with an anchor: *anchor a ship.* **2** drop anchor; stop or stay in place by using an anchor. **3** hold in place; fix firmly: *anchor a tent to the ground.* [OE *ancor* <L *ancora, anchora* < Gk. *ankyra*]

an·chor·age (ang′kər ij) *n.* **1** a place to anchor. **2** money paid for the right to anchor. **3** an anchoring; a being anchored. **4** something to hold on to or depend on.

an·cho·ret (ang′kə rit or ang′kə ret′) *n.* an anchorite.

anchor ice ice formed below the surface; ground ice.

an·cho·rite (ang′kə rīt′) *n.* **1** a person who lives alone in a solitary place for religious meditation. **2** a hermit. [< Med.L *anachorita* < LL < Gk. *anachōrētēs* <*anachōreein* < *ana-* back + *chōreein* withdraw]

anchor man 1 in sports: **a** the last man to swim or run on a relay team. **b** the last player of a team to bowl in each frame. **c** the end man of a tug-of-war team. **2** in radio or television, the co-ordinator of a broadcast consisting of direct reports from several different cities or locations.

an·cho·vy (an′chō vē, an′chə vē, or an chō′vē) *n.* **-vies.** a very small fish that resembles a herring. Anchovies are pickled or made into a paste that is used as an appetizer. [< Sp., Pg. *anchova* < VL *apiuva*, probably < Gk. *aphyē*]

an·cienne no·blesse (äɴ syen′nôbles′) *French.* **1** in France, the nobles before the Revolution in 1789. **2** the old nobility.

an·cien ré·gime (äɴ syaɴ′ rā zhēm′) *French.* **1** the social and political structure of France before the Revolution of 1789. **2** the old order of things. **3** the former management or administration: *The energy of the new government was a welcome change from the apathy of the ancien régime.*

an·cient (ān′shənt) *adj.* **1** of or belonging to times long past: *ancient history, ancient records.* **2** of great age; very old: *an ancient city.* **3** old-fashioned.
—*n.* **1** a very old person. **2 the ancients,** people who lived long ago, such as the Greeks and Romans, the Egyptians, Hebrews, etc. [ME < OF *ancien* < LL *antianus* former < L *ante* before] **—an′cient·ness,** *n.*
—Syn. *adj.* **2** See **old.**

ancient history **1** history from the earliest times to the fall of the western part of the Roman Empire in A.D. 476. **2** *Informal.* a well-known fact or event of the recent past.

an·cient·ly (ān′shənt lē) *adv.* in ancient times.

an·cil·lar·y (an sil′ə rē or an′sə ler′ē) *adj.* **1** subordinate; dependent. **2** assisting; auxiliary.
—*n.* something subordinate or auxiliary. [< L *ancillaris* < *ancilla* handmaid]

an·con (ang′kon) *n.* **an·co·nes** (ang kō′nēz). in architecture, a projection like a bracket, used to support a cornice. [< L < Gk. *ankōn* bend]

-ancy *suffix.* a variant of **-ance,** as in *infancy.*

and (ənd or ən; *stressed,* and) *conj.* **1** as well as: *nice and cold.* **2** added to; with: *4 and 2 make 6. He likes ham and eggs.* **3** as a result: *The sun came out and the grass dried.* **4** *Informal.* to: *try and do better.* [OE]

and. andante.

an·dan·te (an dan′tē or än dän′tā) *adv. adj.* in music, moderately slow. —*n.* in music, a moderately slow movement or passage; a composition to be played or sung in this tempo. *Abbrev.*: and. [< Ital. *andante* < *andare* walk]

an·dan·ti·no (an′dan tē′nō or än′dän tē′nō) *adv. adj. n.* **-nos.** in music: *adv. adj.* slightly faster than andante. —*n.* a composition or part of one that is played or sung andantino. [< Ital. *andantino*, dim. of *andante*]

and·i·ron (and′ī′ərn) *n.* one of a pair of metal supports for wood burned in a fireplace; a firedog. [ME < OF *andier*; *-iron* by association with *iron*]

and/or both or either.
☛ And/or is used primarily in business and legal writing. It is useful when three choices exist (both items mentioned or either one of the two).

an·drog·y·nous (an droj′ə nəs) *adj.* **1** in botany, having flowers with stamens and flowers with pistils in the same cluster. **2** being both male and female. [< L < Gk. *androgynos* < *anēr, andros* man + *gynē* woman]

An·drom·e·da (an drom′ə də) *n.* **1** in Greek legend, an Ethiopian princess, who, to save her country, was to be sacrificed to a sea monster. Perseus killed the monster and married Andromeda. **2** in astronomy, a northern constellation.

an·ec·do·tal (an′ik dō′təl or an′ik dō′təl) *adj.* of anecdotes; containing anecdotes.

an·ec·dote (an′ik dōt′) *n.* a short account of some interesting incident or event: *Many anecdotes are told about Sir John A. Macdonald.* [< Med.L *anecdota* < Gk. *anekdota* (things) unpublished < *an-* not + *ek-* out + *didonai* give] **—Syn.** See **story**[1].

a·ne·mi·a (ə nē′mē ə) *n.* an insufficiency of hemoglobin or of red corpuscles in the blood. Also, **anaemia.** [< NL < Gk. *anaimia* lack of blood < *an-* not + *haima* blood]

a·ne·mic (ə nē′mik) *adj.* of anemia; having anemia. Also, **anaemic.**

an·e·mom·e·ter (an′ə mom′ə tər) *n.* an instrument for measuring the velocity or pressure of the wind. [< Gk. *anemos* wind + E *-meter*]

a·nem·o·ne (ə nem′ə nē) *n.* **1** a plant having slender stems and small, white flowers. It blossoms early in the spring. **2** the sea anemone. [< L < Gk. *anemōnē* wind flower < *anemos* wind]

a·nent (ə nent′) *prep. Archaic.* concerning; about. [OE *on emn, on efn* on even (ground with)]

an·er·oid (an′ər oid′) *adj.* using no liquid. —*n.* an aneroid barometer. [< F *anéroïde* < Gk. *a-* without + LGk. *nēros* wet]

aneroid barometer a barometer that works by the pressure of the atmosphere on the elastic lid of a box containing no air.

an·es·the·sia (an′əs thē′zhə or an′əs thē′zē ə) *n.* entire **(general)** or partial **(local)** loss of the feeling of pain, touch, cold, etc., produced by anesthetics, hypnotism, etc., or as the result of hysteria, paralysis, or disease. Also, **anaesthesia.** [< NL < Gk. *anaisthēsia* insensibility < *an-* without + *aisthēsis* sensation]

an·es·thet·ic (an′əs thet′ik) *n.* a substance that causes anesthesia. Ether, pentothal, and scopolamine are anesthetics. —*adj.* **1** causing anesthesia. **2** of or with anesthesia. Also, **anaesthetic. —an′es·thet′i·cal·ly,** *adv.*

an·es·the·tist (ə nēs′thə tist or ə nes′thə tist) *n.* a person whose work is giving anesthetics during surgical operations, etc. Also, **anaesthetist.**

an·es·the·ti·za·tion (ə nēs′thə tə zā′shən or ə nes′thə tə zā′shən, ə nēs′thə tī zā′shən or ə nes′thə tī-zā′shən) *n.* **1** the act or process of anesthetizing. **2** the state of being anesthetized. Also, **anaesthetization.**

an·es·the·tize (ə nēs′thə tīz′ or ə nes′thə tīz′) *v.* **-tized, -tiz·ing. 1** make unable to feel pain, touch, cold, etc.; make insensible. **2** reduce (a person's) emotional or critical responses. Also, **anaesthetize. —an·es′the·tiz′er,** *n.*

an·eu·rysm or **an·eu·rism** (an′yů riz′əm) *n.* a permanent swelling of an artery, caused by pressure of the blood on a part weakened by disease or injury. [< Gk. *aneurysma* dilation < *ana-* up + *eurys* wide]

a·new (ə nū′ or ə nü′) *adv.* **1** once more; again: *He made so many mistakes he had to begin his work anew.* **2** in a new form or way: *plan a building anew.* [OE *of niowe*]

an·ge·kok (an′gə kok′) *n. Cdn.* an Eskimo medicine man; shaman. [< Eskimo]

an·gel (ān′jəl) *n.* **1** one of an order of spiritual beings thought of as attendants and messengers of God. **2** a conventional representation of such a being. **3** a person as good or lovely as an angel. **4** any supernatural (but not divine) spirit, either good or bad. **5** *Slang.* a person who pays, or helps to pay for the production of a play. **6** an old English gold coin in use between 1465 and 1634. [OE *engel*, OF *angele* < L < Gk. *angelos* messenger]

angel cake angel food cake.

an·gel·fish (ān′jəl fish′) *n.* **-fish** or **-fish·es. 1** a shark having large fins that spread out like wings. **2** any of several tropical fish having spiny fins and brilliant colors.

angel food cake a light, springy sponge cake containing whites of eggs but no shortening or egg yolks.

an·gel·ic (an jel′ik) *adj.* **1** of angels; heavenly. **2** like an angel; pure; innocent; good and lovely.
—an·gel′i·cal·ly, *adv.*

an·gel·i·ca (an jel′ə kə) *n.* a perennial plant of the same family as the carrot, used in cooking, in medicine, and in making perfume. Candied angelica is cut into shapes to decorate cakes, etc. [< Med.L; named from its use as an antidote]

an·gel·i·cal (an jel′ə kəl) *adj.* angelic.

An·ge·lus (an′jə ləs) *n.* in the Roman Catholic Church: **1** a prayer said in memory of Christ's assuming human form. **2** the bell, **Angelus bell,** rung at morning, noon, and night as a signal for the saying of this prayer. [from the first word in the prayer]

an·ger (ang′gər) *n.* the feeling one has toward something that hurts, opposes, offends, or annoys; wrath; strong displeasure. —*v.* **1** make angry: *The boy's disobedience angered his father.* **2** become angry: *He angers easily.* [ME < ON *angr* trouble]

Syn. *n.* **Anger, indignation, wrath** = the feeling of strong displeasure against anyone or anything that has hurt or wronged us or others. **Anger** is the general word for the emotion: *He never speaks in anger.* **Indignation,** more formal, means intense anger mixed with scorn, caused by something mean, base, or unjust, and therefore often justified: *The atrocity caused widespread indignation.* **Wrath,** a formal word, means great anger or indignation accompanied by a desire to punish: *By their sins they provoked the wrath of God.*

An·ge·vin (an′jə vin) *adj.* **1** of or from Anjou. The Plantagenet family of the kings of England was Angevin. **2** of or belonging to the Plantagenet family. *—n.* **1** a member of the Plantagenet family. **2** a native or inhabitant of Anjou.

an·gi·na (an jī′nə; *in medicine, often* an′jə nə) *n.* **1** any inflammation of the throat, such as quinsy, croup, or mumps. **2** angina pectoris. **3** a sudden, acute pain. [< L *angina* quinsy < *angere* choke]

angina pec·to·ris (pek′tə ris or pek tôr′is) a serious disease of the heart characterized by sharp chest pains and a feeling of suffocation. [< NL *angina pectoris* angina of the chest]

an·gi·o·sperm (an′jē ō spėrm′) *n.* any plant having its seeds enclosed in an ovary or fruit; a flowering plant. [< NL *angiospermus* < Gk. *angeion* vessel + *sperma* seed]

an·gle[1] (ang′gəl) *n. v.* **-gled, -gling.** *—n.* **1** the space between two lines or surfaces that meet. **2** the figure formed by two such lines or surfaces. **3** the difference in direction between two such lines or surfaces: *The roads lie at an angle of about 45 degrees.* **4** a corner. **5** *Informal.* point of view. **6** one aspect of something; phase. *—v.* **1** move at an angle. **2** turn or bend at an angle. **3** present with bias or prejudice. [ME < OF < L *angulus*]

ACUTE RIGHT OBTUSE
Angles

an·gle[2] (ang′gəl) *v.* **-gled, -gling.** **1** fish with a hook and line. **2** try to get something by using tricks or schemes: *She angled for an invitation to his party by flattering him.* [OE *angel* fish-hook]

An·gle (ang′gəl) *n.* a member of a Germanic tribe that settled in England in the fifth century A.D.

angle iron a strip of iron or steel in the shape of an angle, used for joining two other pieces at an angle.

angle of attack the acute angle between the chord of an airplane wing or other airfoil and the direction of flight. See **chord** for picture.

angle of deviation the angle made between a beam of light as it enters a prism or other optical medium and the beam, or any one ray, that emerges.

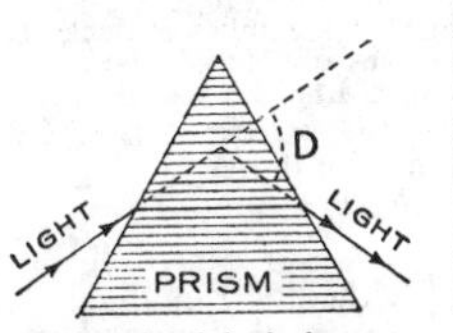

D, angle of deviation

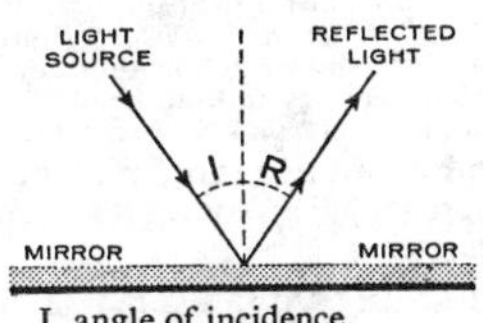

I, angle of incidence
R, angle of reflection

angle of incidence the angle made by a ray of light falling upon a surface with a line perpendicular to that surface.

angle of reflection the angle that a ray of light makes on reflection from a surface with a line perpendicular to that surface.

angle of refraction the angle made between a ray of light refracted at a surface separating two media and a line perpendicular to the surface.

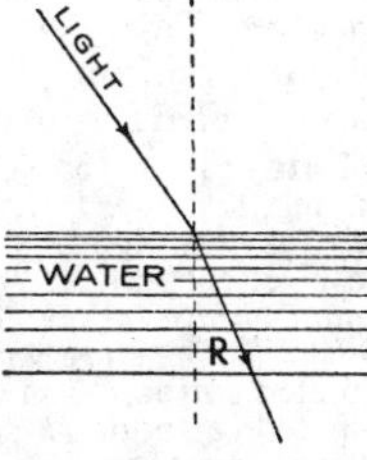

R, angle of refraction

an·gler (ang′glər) *n.* **1** a person who fishes with a hook and line. **2** a person who tries to get something by using tricks and schemes. **3** a kind of seafish, found on the coasts of Europe and North America, that attracts and eats smaller fish.

an·gle·worm (ang′gəl wėrm′) *n.* earthworm.

hat, āge, cãre, fär; let, ēqual, tėrm; it, īce
hot, ōpen, ôrder; oil, out; cup, pu̇t, rüle, ūse
əbove, takən, pencəl, lemən, circəs
ch, child; ng, long; sh, ship
th, thin; ᴛʜ, then; zh, measure

An·gli·an (ang′glē ən) *adj.* of or having to do with the Angles, their dialect, or customs. *—n.* **1** an Angle. **2** the dialect of the Angles.

An·gli·can (ang′glə kən) *adj.* of or associated with the Church of England or other churches of the same faith elsewhere: *The first Anglican church in Canada was built in Halifax in 1750.* *—n.* a member of the Church of England or of a church associated with it.

Anglican Church of Canada a Christian church associated with the Church of England, until 1955 known as the Church of England in Canada.

An·gli·can·ism (ang′glə kən iz′əm) *n.* the principles and beliefs of the Church of England or of other churches associated with it.

An·gli·cism (ang′glə siz′əm) *n.* **1** a word, phrase, or meaning used in England, but not in widespread use in other English-speaking countries; a Briticism. **2** a custom or trait peculiar to the English.

An·gli·cize or **an·gli·cize** (ang′glə sīz′) *v.* **-cized, -ciz·ing.** make or become English in form, pronunciation, habits, customs, or character. *Cajole, lace,* and *cousin* are French words that have been Anglicized. **—An′gli·ci·za′tion, an′gli·ci·za′tion,** *n.*

Anglo- *combining form.* **1** English, as in *Anglo-Catholic church.* **2** English and, as in *the Anglo-American alliance.* [< LL *Angli* the English]

An·glo-A·mer·i·can (ang′glō ə mer′ə kən) *adj.* **1** British and American. **2** of Americans, especially those of English descent. *—n.* an American, especially a United States citizen of English descent.

An·glo-Ca·na·di·an (ang′glō kə nā′dē ən) *adj.* **1** British and Canadian. **2** of or having to do with English-speaking Canadians. *—n.* an English-speaking Canadian; a Canadian whose native language is English.

An·glo-Cath·o·lic (ang′glō kath′ə lik or -kath′lik) *n.* a member of the Church of England who believes that it is and always has been a Catholic church. *—adj.* **1** of or having to do with Anglo-Catholics. **2** of or having to do with the Church of England as a Catholic church, as distinct from the Roman Catholic and Greek churches.

An·glo-Ca·thol·i·cism (ang′glō kə thol′ə siz′əm) *n.* the beliefs and practices of Anglo-Catholics.

An·glo-French (ang′glō french′) *adj.* of or having to do with Great Britain and France together. *—n.* the dialect of French introduced into England mainly by the Norman conquerors after 1066, and used to some extent even through the fourteenth century; Anglo-Norman; Norman-French.

An·glo-In·di·an (ang′glō in′dē ən) *adj.* **1** English and Indian. **2** of or having to do with Anglo-Indians. *—n.* **1** a person of British birth living in India. **2** the dialect of English spoken by Anglo-Indians. **3** officially in India, an Indian citizen of mixed European, especially British, and Indian descent; Eurasian.

An·glo·ma·ni·a (ang′glō mā′nē ə) *n.* an excessive admiration for and imitation of English institutions and customs.

An·glo·ma·ni·ac (ang′glō mā′nē ak′) *n.* a person who likes and imitates the English to an extreme degree.

An·glo-Nor·man (ang′glō nôr′mən) *n.* **1** any of the Normans who settled in England following the Norman Conquest. **2** a descendant of an English Norman. **3** Anglo-French. *—adj.* English and Norman.

An·glo·phile (ang′glō fīl′) *n.* **1** a person who greatly admires England, its people, and its culture. **2** in Canada, a French Canadian who shows particular sympathy with the policies and culture of English-speaking Canada.

An·glo·phil·i·a (ang′glō fil′ēə) *n.* **1** a strong admiration for or devotion to England, its people, and its culture. **2** in Canada, a particular sympathy among French Canadians for the policies and culture of English-speaking Canada.

An·glo·phobe (ang′glō fōb′) *n.* **1** a person who hates or fears England and its people. **2** in Canada, a French Canadian who hates or especially fears the policies and culture of English-speaking Canadians.

An·glo·pho·bi·a (ang′glō fō′bē ə) *n.* **1** a hatred or very great fear of England and anything English. **2** in Canada, a hatred or especial fear of the policies and culture of English-speaking Canadians.

An·glo·phone (ang′glō fōn′) *n. Cdn.* an English-speaking inhabitant of a bilingual or multilingual country.

An·glo-Sax·on (ang′glō sak′sən) *n.* **1** a member of the English-speaking world; a person who in any period of history has spoken English as his native language. **2** a person of English descent. **3** plain English, without Latin or other foreign words. **4** the English language as spoken or written in any part of the world at any date; English. **5** a member of the Germanic tribes, including the Angles and Saxons, who conquered and inhabited Britain between A.D. 449 and 1066. **6** his speech; Old English. —*adj.* **1** of the Anglo-Saxons. **2** of Anglo-Saxon. *Abbrev.*: AS or A.S.

An·go·ra (ang gô′rə) *n.* **1** an Angora cat. **2** an Angora goat. **3** an Angora rabbit. **4** mohair. **5** Ankara, the capital of Turkey.

Angora cat **1** a breed of cat having long, silky hair that is usually white. **2** a cat of this breed.

Angora goat **1** a breed of goat having long, silky hair that is used for wool. **2** a goat of this breed.

Angora rabbit **1** a breed of rabbit having long, soft hair that is used for wool. **2** a rabbit of this breed.

an·gos·tu·ra (ang′gəs tür′ə or ang′gəs tür′ə) *n.* **1** the bitter bark of a South American tree. **2 Angostura,** *Trademark.* Angostura Bitters. [after *Angostura,* a town in Venezuela]

Angostura Bitters *Trademark.* a bitter tonic derived from angostura bark and various other roots, barks, etc. It is sometimes used as a flavoring in food.

an·gry (ang′grē) *adj.* **-gri·er, -gri·est. 1** feeling or showing anger: *an angry reply.* **2** raging or stormy: *an angry sky.* **3** moved by anger: *angry words.* **4** inflamed and sore: *An infected cut looks angry.* [< *anger*] **—an′gri·ly,** *adv.* **—an′gri·ness,** *n.* **—Syn. 1** irate, enraged, furious.

☛ **angry.** In reference to a thing, *angry at* and *angry about* are used: *I was angry at his slipshod work. Do you ever get angry about the cheating you see?* In reference to a person, *angry with* is general: *He was angry with his son.* Formal English uses *angry at* or *angry with,* making the following distinctions: when the angry feeling is being stressed, *at* is used; when the stress is on the directing of that anger upon a person, *with* is used: *We were angry at the boys for their tardiness. I was so angry with John that he drew back in fear.*

ang·strom (ang′strəm) one ten-millionth of a millimetre, a unit of measurement of the wave length of light. *Symbol*: λ *Abbrev.*: A [after Anders John *Angstrom,* 1814-1874, a Swedish physicist]

angstrom unit angstrom.

an·guish (ang′gwish) *n.* very great pain or grief; great suffering or distress. —*v.* cause or feel anguish: *News of the flood anguished the nation. The boy anguished over the loss of his pet.* [ME < OF *anguisse* < L *angustia* tightness < *angustus* narrow] —**Syn.** agony, torment, woe.

an·guished (ang′gwisht) *adj.* **1** suffering anguish. **2** full of anguish; showing anguish.

an·gu·lar (ang′gyů lər) *adj.* **1** having angles; sharp-cornered. **2** measured by an angle. In the diagram, the angular distance of P from Q, when measured from O, is the angle X. **3** not plump; bony. **4** stiff and awkward. [< L *angularis* < *angulus* angle] **—an′gu·lar·ly,** *adv.*

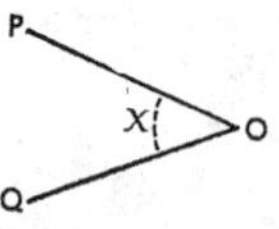

an·gu·lar·i·ty (ang′gyů lar′ə tē) *n.* **-ties. 1** the condition of having sharp or prominent corners. **2 angularities,** *pl.* sharp corners.

an·hy·drid (an hī′drid) *n.* anhydride.

an·hy·dride (an hī′drīd or an hī′drid) *n.* **1** any oxide that unites with water to form an acid or base. Sulphur trioxide, SO_3, is the anhydride of sulphuric acid. **2** any compound formed by the removal of water.

an·hy·drite (an hī′drīt) *n.* a white to bluish-gray mineral consisting of anhydrous sulphate of calcium. *Formula*: $CaSO_4$

an·hy·drous (an hī′drəs) *adj.* **1** without water. **2** in chemistry, containing no water of crystallization. [< Gk. *anydros* < *an-* without + *hydōr* water]

an·il (an′il) *n.* **1** a West Indian leguminous shrub from whose leaves and stalks indigo is made. **2** indigo. [< F < Pg. < Arabic *al-nil* < *al* the + *nil* indigo < Skt. *nili* indigo < *nila* dark blue]

an·ile (an′īl or ā′nīl) *adj.* old-womanish; suitable for a weak or doting old woman. [< L *anilis* < *anus* old woman]

an·i·lin (an′ə lin) *n.* aniline.

an·i·line (an′ə lin, an′ə līn′, or an′ə lēn′) *n.* a poisonous, oily liquid, obtained from coal tar and especially from nitrobenzene, used in making dyes, plastics, etc. Aniline is a compound of carbon, nitrogen, and oxygen. *Formula*: $C_6H_5NH_2$ —*adj.* made from aniline. [< *anil*]

aniline dye **1** a dye made from aniline. **2** any artificial dye.

a·nil·i·ty (ə nil′ə tē) *n.* **-ties. 1** an anile condition. **2** an anile act or notion.

an·i·ma (an′ə mə) *n. Latin.* life; soul.

an·i·mad·ver·sion (an′ə mad vėr′zhən) *n.* criticism; blame; unfavorable comment. [< L *animadversio, -onis* < *animadvertere.* See ANIMADVERT.]

an·i·mad·vert (an′ə mad vėrt′) *v.* make criticisms; express blame; comment unfavorably. [< L *animadvertere* < *animus* mind + *ad-* to + *vertere* turn]

an·i·mal (an′ə məl) *n.* **1** any living thing that is not a plant. Most animals can move about, whereas most plants cannot; most animals are unable to make their own food from carbon dioxide, water, nitrogen, etc., but most plants can. **2** an inferior living being, as distinguished from man; brute; beast. **3** any four-footed creature. **4** a person like a brute or beast. —*adj.* **1** of animals. **2** like an animal. [< L *animal* < *anima* life, breath]

Syn. *n.* **2 Animal, beast, brute** = a living creature of a lower order than man. **Animal,** the general word, suggests nothing more: *He likes animals.* **Beast** applies to four-legged animals, as distinct from birds, insects, etc.: *The horse is a noble beast.* **Brute,** used chiefly in formal or special styles, emphasizes lack of the power to reason which sets man above animals: *With the instinct of the brute, the deer found safety.* **4** Used figuratively, applied to man, **animal, beast,** and **brute** express attitudes of the speaker toward the persons named. **Animal,** objective, emphasizes the body: *Those boys are healthy young animals.* **Beast,** emotional, emphasizes giving up control over physical desires: *Living only for self-indulgence, he is a beast.* **Brute,** emotional, emphasizes lack of reason as shown by mental dullness or lack of control over violent feelings and inhuman treatment of others: *The brute guarding him beat him to a pulp.*

an·i·mal·cule (an′ə mal′kūl) *n.* a minute or microscopic animal. [< NL *animalculum,* dim. of L *animal*]

an·i·mal·ism (an′ə məl iz′əm) *n.* **1** the doctrine that men are mere animals without spirit or soul. **2** animal existence, nature, or enjoyment. **3** sensuality.

an·i·mal·ist (an′ə mə list′) *n.* **1** one who believes in animalism. **2** a sensualist. **3** an artist whose main subject is animal life.

an·i·mal·i·ty (an′ə mal′ə tē) *n.* **1** animal nature or character in man. **2** animal life.

an·i·mal·ize (an′ə mə līz′) *v.* **-ized, -iz·ing. 1** change into animal matter: *Food assimilated into the body is animalized.* **2** make bestial; dehumanize. **3** make sensual.

animal kingdom all animals.

animal spirits natural liveliness; healthy cheerfulness.

an·i·mate (*v.* an′ə māt′; *adj.* an′ə mit) *v.* **-mat·ed, -mat·ing,** *adj.* —*v.* **1** give life to; make alive. **2** make lively, gay, or vigorous. **3** move to action; stir up; incite. **4** inspire; encourage: *The soldiers were animated by their captain's brave speech.* **5** put into motion; cause to act or work: *Windmills are animated by the wind.* **6** produce an animated cartoon. **7** make the drawings, etc. for an animated cartoon: *The television commercial was animated by a group of artists.*
—*adj.* **1** living; having life: *Animate nature means all*

living plants and animals. **2** lively; gay; vigorous. [< L *animare* < *anima* life, breath]

an·i·mat·ed (an′ə māt′id) *adj.* **1** lively; vigorous: *an animated discussion.* **2** gay, joyful: *an animated smile.* **3** simulating life: *animated dolls.* **4** living, alive, animate. **—an′i·mat′ed·ly,** *adv.*

animated cartoon a series of drawings arranged to be photographed and shown in rapid succession as a motion picture. Each drawing shows a slight change from the one before it so that, when the film is projected, the figures in the drawings seem to move.

an·i·ma·tion (an′ə mā′shən) *n.* **1** an animating or being animated. **2** life. **3** liveliness; spirit. **4** the production or preparation of an animated cartoon.

a·ni·ma·to (ä′ni mä′tō) *adj.* in music, lively; gay; vigorous. [< Ital.]

an·i·ma·tor (an′ə mā′tər) *n.* **1** a person or thing that animates. **2** a person who makes drawings for animated cartoons.

an·i·mism (an′ə miz′əm) *n.* **1** a belief in the existence of soul as distinct from matter; belief in spiritual beings, such as souls, angels, and devils. **2** a belief that there are living souls in trees, stones, stars, etc. [< L *anima* life, breath]

an·i·mist (an′ə mist) *n.* a person who believes in some form of animism.

an·i·mis·tic (an′ə mis′tik) *adj.* of or associated with animism.

an·i·mos·i·ty (an′ə mos′ə tē) *n.* **-ties.** violent hatred; ill will; active dislike or enmity. [< L *animositas* < *animosus* spirited]

an·i·mus (an′ə məs) *n.* **1** violent hatred; ill will; active dislike or enmity. **2** moving spirit; intention. [< L *animus* spirit, feeling]

an·i·on (an′ī ən) *n.* **1** a negatively charged ion that moves toward the positive pole in electrolysis. See **cathode** for diagram. **2** an atom or group of atoms having a negative charge. [< Gk. *anion* (thing) going up, ppr. neut. of *anienai* < *ana-* up + *ienai* go]

an·ise (an′is) *n.* **1** a plant of the same family as the carrot, grown for its fragrant seeds. **2** the seed of this plant. [ME < OF *anis* < L < Gk. *anison*]

an·i·seed (an′ə sēd′ or an′is sēd′) *n.* the seed of anise, used as a flavoring or in medicine.

an·kle (ang′kəl) *n.* **1** the joint that connects the foot and the leg. **2** the part of the leg between this joint and the calf. See SHIN for diagram. [ME < Scand.; cf. Danish *ankel*]

an·kle·bone (ang′kəl bōn′) *n.* the bone of the ankle; talus.

an·klet (ang′klit) *n.* **1** a short sock. **2** a band worn around the ankle. An anklet may be an ornament, a brace, or a fetter.

an·ky·lose (ang′kə lōs′) *v.* **-losed, -los·ing. 1** make or become stiff, by or as if by ankylosis. **2** of bones, grow together; unite. [< Gk. *ankylosis* < *ankylos* crooked]

an·ky·lo·sis (ang′kə lō′sis) *n.* in medicine: **1** a growing together of bones as a result of disease or injury. **2** stiffness of a joint caused by this. [< NL < Gk. *ankylosis* < *ankyloein* stiffen < *ankylos* crooked]

an·na (an′ə) *n.* **1** a unit of money in Ceylon and, formerly, in India and Pakistan, worth 1/16 of a rupee. **2** a coin worth one anna. [< Hind. *ana*]

an·nal·ist (an′əl ist) *n.* a writer of annals.

an·nals (an′əlz) *n.pl.* **1** a written account of events year by year. **2** historical records; history. [< L *annales* (*libri* books) annual record < *annus* year]

An·na·mese (an′ə mēz′) *adj. n.* **-mese.** *—adj.* of or associated with Annam or its people. *—n.* **1** a native or inhabitant of Annam. **2** the language spoken by the Annamese.

an·neal (ə nēl′) *v.* toughen (glass, metals, etc.) by heating and then cooling; temper. [OE *anǣlan* < *an-* on + *ǣlan* burn]

an·ne·lid (an′ə lid) *n.* a worm having a body composed of a series of similar segments. Earthworms, leeches, and various sea worms are annelids. [< F *annélide* < OF *annel* ring < L *anellus,* double dim. of *anus* ring]

hat, āge, cãre, fär; let, ēqual, tėrm; it, īce
hot, ōpen, ôrder; oil, out; cup, pu̇t, rüle, ūse
əbove, takən, pencəl, lemən, circəs
ch, child; ng, long; sh, ship
th, thin; ᴛʜ, then; zh, measure

an·nex (*v.* ə neks′; *n.* an′eks) *v.* **1** join or add to a larger thing: *Britain annexed Acadia in 1713.* **2** *Informal.* take as one's own; appropriate, especially without permission. *—n.* **1** something added or attached; an added part: *Our hotel has an annex.* **2** *Slang.* a backhouse; outhouse. [ME < Med.L *annexare* < L *annexus,* pp. of *annectere* < *ad-* to + *nectere* bind] **—Syn.** *v.* **1** See **attach.**

an·nex·a·tion (an′ək sā′shən) *n.* **1** an annexing or being annexed: *the annexation of several suburbs to the metropolitan area.* **2** something annexed.

Annexation Movement the name given to groups in Canada that have advocated political union with the United States.

An·nie Oak·ley (an′ē ōk′lē) *Slang.* a free pass to a play, etc. Also, **Oakley.** [after *Annie Oakley,* 1860-1926, a noted woman marksman; in allusion to the resemblance between a punched pass and a small target used by her]

an·ni·hi·late (ə nī′ə lāt′) *v.* **-lat·ed, -lat·ing. 1** destroy completely; wipe out of existence. **2** bring to ruin or confusion. [< LL *annihilare* < L *ad-* + *nihil* nothing] **—an·ni′hi·la′tor,** *n.* **—Syn. 1** See **abolish.**

an·ni·hi·la·tion (ə nī′ə lā′shən) *n.* **1** complete destruction. **2** in nuclear physics: **a** the destruction of a positron (positive electron) and an electron, the energy turning into one or more protons of radiation. **b** the uniting of an electron and a positron to produce a gamma ray.

an·ni·hi·la·tive (ə nī′ə lə tiv or ə nī′ə lā′tiv) *adj.* able or likely to annihilate.

an·ni·ver·sa·ry (an′ə vėr′sə rē or an′ə vėrs′rē) *n.* **-ries,** *adj. —n.* **1** the yearly return of a date: *Tomorrow is the anniversary of her wedding.* **2** the celebration of the yearly return of a date.
—adj. **1** celebrated each year on the same date. **2** having to do with an anniversary: *an anniversary dinner.*
[ME < L *anniversarius* returning annually < *annus* year + *vertere* turn]

an·no Dom·i·ni (an′ō dom′ə nī or an′ō dom′ə nē) *Latin.* in the year of our Lord; any year since the birth of Christ. *Abbrev.:* A.D.

an·no·tate (an′ō tāt′) *v.* **-tat·ed, -tat·ing. 1** provide with explanatory notes or comments: *Shakespeare's plays are often annotated to make them easier to understand.* **2** make explanatory notes or comments. [< L *annotare* < *ad-* to + *nota* note] **—an′no·ta′tor,** *n.*

an·no·ta·tion (an′ō tā′shən) *n.* **1** the act of providing with notes; being provided with notes: *The book's annotation required hundreds of hours.* **2** a note added to explain or criticize: *The editor's annotations were printed in small type.*

an·nounce (ə nouns′) *v.* **-nounced, -nounc·ing. 1** give formal or public notice of: *announce a wedding in the papers.* **2** make known the presence or arrival of: *The butler announced each guest in a loud voice.* **3** give or be evidence of: *Black clouds announced the coming thunderstorm.* **4** in radio or television, act as an announcer; be an announcer for. [ME < OF *anoncier* < L *annuntiare* < *ad-* to + *nuntius* messenger. Doublet of ANNUNCIATE.]

Syn. 1 Announce, proclaim, declare = make known formally or publicly. **Announce** = give formal notice of something of interest to the public or a particular group: *They announced the birth of their first baby.* **Proclaim** = announce publicly and with authority something of importance to the general public: *The Prime Minister proclaimed an emergency.* **Declare** = make known clearly and plainly, often formally or officially: *An armistice was declared.*

an·nounce·ment (ə nouns′mənt) *n.* **1** the act of announcing. **2** a public or formal notice: *Announcements of marriages appear in the newspapers.*

an·nounc·er (ə noun′sər) *n.* **1** a person or thing that announces. **2** in radio or television, a person who announces programs, delivers commercials, reads news, etc.

an·noy (ə noi′) *v.* **1** make angry; disturb; trouble: *annoy by teasing.* **2** hurt; harm; molest: *annoy the enemy by raids.* [ME < OF *anuier* < LL *inodiare* < L *in odio* in hatred] —**Syn. 1** irritate, bother, vex, irk, tease. See **worry.**

an·noy·ance (ə noi′əns) *n.* **1** an annoying. **2** a being annoyed; vexation; feeling of dislike or irritation. **3** a thing that annoys. —**Syn. 3** bother, pest.

an·noyed (ə noid′) *adj.* **1** disturbed; troubled. **2** molested; hurt.

☛ **annoyed.** With reference to a thing, *annoyed at* is used: *I was annoyed at the interruption.* With reference to a person, *annoyed with* is used: *I was annoyed with Mary again.* When it means molested (def. 2), *annoyed by* is used: *I was annoyed by hecklers during the latter half of my speech.*

an·noy·ing (ə noi′ing) *adj.* disturbing; troublesome. —**an·noy′ing·ly,** *adv.* —**an·noy′ing·ness,** *n.*

an·nu·al (an′yů əl) *adj.* **1** coming once a year: *Your birthday is an annual event.* **2** in a year; for a year: *an annual salary of $6,000.* **3** accomplished during a year: *the earth's annual course around the sun.* **4** of a plant, living only one year or season.
—*n.* **1** a book, journal, etc. published once a year. **2** a plant that lives only one year or season. [ME < OF *annuel* < LL *annualis* < L *annus* year.]

an·nu·al·ly (an′yū əl ē) *adv.* yearly; each year; year by year.

an·nu·i·tant (ə nū′ə tənt or ə nü′ə tənt) *n.* a person who receives an annuity.

an·nu·i·ty (ə nū′ə tē or ə nü′ə tē) *n.* **-ties. 1** a sum of money paid every year. **2** the right to receive or duty to pay such a yearly sum. **3** an investment that provides a fixed yearly income during one's lifetime. [ME < OF *annuite* < Med.L *annuitas* < L *annus* year]

an·nul (ə nul′) *v.* **-nulled, -nul·ling.** do away with; destroy the force of; make void: *The judge annulled the contract because one of the signers was too young.* [ME < OF *anuller* < LL *annullare* < L *ad-* + *nullus* none] —**Syn.** abolish, cancel.

an·nu·lar (an′yů lər) *adj.* ringlike; ring-shaped; ringed. [< L *anularis* (sometimes misspelled *annularis* in late and poor MSS) < *anulus* ring. See ANNULUS.]

an·nu·let (an′yů lit) *n.* **1** a little ring. **2** in architecture, a narrow, ringlike moulding of wood, stone, etc. [< L *anulus* ring. See ANNULUS.]

an·nul·ment (ə nul′mənt) *n.* an annulling or being annulled; cancellation.

☛ The annulment of a marriage is not the same as a **divorce.** An annulment is a declaration that a marriage was illegal and therefore not valid from the beginning, so that the partners never were legally married. A **divorce** is the dissolution of a marriage that was legal and officially valid.

an·nu·lus (an′yů ləs) *n.* **-li** (-lī′ or -lē′) or **-lus·es.** a ringlike part, band, or space. [< L *anulus* (sometimes misspelled *annulus* in late and poor MSS), dim. of *anus* ring]

an·num (an′əm) *n. Latin.* year (acc. of *annus*).

an·nun·ci·ate (ə nun′sē āt′ or ə nun′shē āt′) *v.* **-at·ed, -at·ing.** make known; announce. [< Med.L *annunciare* < L *annuntiare* < *ad-* to + *nuntius* messenger. Doublet of ANNOUNCE.]

an·nun·ci·a·tion (ə nun′sē ā′shən or ə nun′shē ā′shən) *n.* **1** an announcement. **2 the Annunciation, a** the angel Gabriel's announcement to the Virgin Mary that she was to be the mother of Christ. Luke 1:26-33. **b** a painting, sculpture, etc. of this. **c** Lady Day.

an·nun·ci·a·tor (ə nun′sē ā′tər or ə nun′shē ā′tər) *n.* **1** an indicator for showing where a signal comes from. **2** a person or thing that announces.

an·ode (an′ōd) *n.* a positive electrode. The carbon of a dry cell and the plate of a radio tube are anodes. See **cathode** and **electrode** for diagram. *Abbrev.*: a [< Gk. *anodos* < *ana-* up + *hodos* way]

an·o·dyne (an′ə dīn′) *n.* anything that lessens pain. [< L < Gk. *anōdynos* < *an-* without + *odynē* pain]

a·noint (ə noint′) *v.* **1** put oil on; rub with ointment; smear: *Anoint sunburned skin with cold cream.* **2** put oil on in a ceremony as a sign of consecration to office; make sacred with oil: *The archbishop anointed the new king.* [< OF *enoint*, pp. of *enoindre* < L *inunguere* < *in-* on + *unguere* smear] —**a·noint′ment,** *n.*

a·nom·a·lous (ə nom′ə ləs) *adj.* departing from the common rule; irregular; abnormal: *A position as head of a department, but with no real authority, is anomalous.* [< LL < Gk. *anōmalos* < *an-* not + *homalos* even]

a·nom·a·ly (ə nom′ə lē) *n.* **-lies. 1** a departure from a general rule; irregularity. **2** something abnormal: *A dog that cannot bark would be an anomaly.*

a·non (ə non′) *adv. Archaic.* **1** in a little while; soon. **2** at another time; again. **3 ever and anon,** now and then. [OE *on ān* into one, *on āne* in one, at once]

anon. anonymous.

an·o·nym·i·ty (an′ə nim′ə tē) *n.* **1** a failure to declare one's name. **2** the condition of being without a name.

a·non·y·mous (ə non′ə məs) *adj.* **1** by or from a person whose name is not known or given: *An anonymous book is one published without the name of the author.* **2** having no name; nameless. *Abbrev.*: a. or anon. [< Gk. *anōnymos* < *an-* without + (dialectal) *onyma* name] —**a·non′y·mous·ly,** *adv.*

a·noph·e·les (ə nof′ə lēz′) *n.* **-les.** a mosquito that can transmit malaria. [< NL < Gk. *anōphelēs* harmful]

an·oth·er (ə nuᴛʜ′ər) *adj.* **1** one more: *Have another glass of milk.* **2** different; not the same: *That is another matter entirely.*
—*pron.* **1** one more: *He ate a bar of candy and then asked for another.* **2** a different one: *I don't like this book; give me another.* **3** one of the same kind: *His father is a scholar, and he is another.* [for *an other*]

ans. 1 answer. **2** answered.

An·schluss (än′shlůs) *n. German.* a union, especially that of Germany and Austria in 1938.

an·ser·ine (an′sər īn′, an′sər ēn′, or an′sər in) *adj.* **1** of, like, or having to do with a goose or geese. **2** stupid; foolish. [< L *anserinus* < *anser* goose]

an·swer (an′sər) *n.* **1** the words spoken or written in reply to a question: *The boy gave a quick answer.* **2** a gesture or act done in return: *A nod was her only answer.* **3** a solution to a problem: *What is the correct answer to this algebra problem?* **4 know all the answers,** *Informal.* **a** be extremely well-informed. **b** make a boastful and annoying display of one's knowledge.
—*v.* **1** reply to: *He answered my question.* **2** make answer; reply: *I asked him a question, but he would not answer.* **3** reply or respond by act: *He knocked on the door, but no one answered.* **4** act or move in response to: *She answered the doorbell.* **5** serve: *This will answer your purpose. Such a poor excuse will not answer.* **6** reply to (a charge): *answer a summons.* **7** bear the consequences of; be responsible (*for*): *answer for a crime, answer for his safety.* **8** correspond (*to*): *This house answers to his description.* **9 answer back,** *Informal.* reply in a rude, saucy way. [OE *andswaru* < *and-* against + *swerian* swear] —**an′swer·less′,** *adj.*

Syn. *n.* **1** rejoinder, retort, return. *-v.* **2 Answer, reply, respond** = say something in return to something said, asked, or demanded. **Answer** is the general word, meaning "speak or write in return": *I called, but no one answered.* **Reply** is used in more formal style or to suggest more formal answering, as with thought and care: *I sent in my application, and the university replied immediately.* **Respond,** formal in this sense, suggests giving the answer hoped for or counted on: *When we requested information and instructions, the chairman responded.*

an·swer·a·ble (an′sər ə bəl) *adj.* **1** responsible: *The club treasurer is held answerable to the club for the money that is given to him.* **2** that can be answered. **3** *Archaic.* corresponding.

answering service a business organization that takes the telephone calls of a subscriber in his absence and, when he returns, reports to him on the calls received.

ant (ant) *n.* any of certain small insects that live with others in colonies of from dozens of individuals to half a million or more. Ants are black, brown, reddish, or yellowish and live in tunnels in the ground or in wood. Ants, bees, and wasps belong to the same group of insects. [OE *ǣmete*] —**ant′like′,** *adj.*

ant- the form of **anti-** before vowels and *h*, as in *antacid.*

-ant *suffix.* **1** ——ing: *buoyant* = *buoying, compliant* = *complying, triumphant* = *triumphing.* **2** one that ——s: *assistant* = *one that assists.* See also **-ent.** [< F < L *-ans, -antis*; *-ens, -entis*]

hat, āge, cãre, fär; let, ēqual, tėrm; it, īce
hot, ōpen, ôrder; oil, out; cup, pu̇t, rüle, ūse
əbove, takən, pencəl, lemən, circəs
ch, child; ng, long; sh, ship
th, thin; ᴛʜ, then; zh, measure

ant. 1 antonym. 2 antiquary.

ant·ac·id (ant as′id) *n.* a substance, such as baking soda or magnesia, that neutralizes acids. —*adj.* tending to neutralize acids; counteracting acidity.

an·tag·o·nism (an tag′ə niz′əm) *n.* active opposition; conflict; hostility.

an·tag·o·nist (an tag′ə nist) *n.* one who fights, struggles, or contends with another: *The knight defeated each antagonist.* —**Syn.** adversary, foe. See **opponent.**

an·tag·o·nis·tic (an tag′ə nis′tik) *adj.* acting against each other: *Cats and dogs are antagonistic.* —**an·tag′o·nis′ti·cal·ly,** *adv.* —**Syn.** opposing, conflicting, hostile.

an·tag·o·nize (an tag′ə nīz′) *v.* **-nized, -niz·ing. 1** make an enemy of; arouse dislike in: *Her unkind remarks antagonized people who had been her friends.* **2** oppose. **3** neutralize; counteract. [< Gk. *antagōnizesthai* < *anti-* against + *agōn* contest] —**an·tag′o·niz·er,** *n.*

ant·arc·tic (ant ärk′tik or ant är′tik) *adj.* around or near the South Pole; of the south polar region. [ME < OF < L *antarcticus* < Gk. *antarktikos* opposite the north < *anti-* opposite + *arktikos* of the north. See ARCTIC.]

Antarctic (ant ärk′tik or ant är′tik) *n.* the south polar region.

Antarctic Circle the imaginary boundary of the south polar region, running parallel to the equator at 23 degrees 30 minutes (23 30′) north of the South Pole.

An·tar·es (an tãr′ēz) *n.* a first magnitude star in the constellation Scorpio.

ant·ar·thrit·ic (ant′är thrit′ik) *adj.* relieving or preventing arthritis. —*n.* a remedy for arthritis.

ant·asth·ma·tic (ant′az mat′ik or ant′as mat′ik) *adj.* relieving or preventing asthma. —*n.* a remedy for asthma.

ant bear 1 a large, shaggy, gray anteater of South America. **2** an aardvark.

an·te (an′tē) *n. v.* **-ted** or **-teed, -te·ing.** —*n.* in the game of poker, a stake that every player must put up before receiving a hand or drawing new cards.
—*v. Informal.* **1** in poker, put (one's stake) into the pool. **2** pay (one's share). **3 ante up, a** in poker, put in one's stake. **b** pay one's share. [See ANTE-.]

ante- *prefix.* **1** before; earlier: *antenatal.* **2** in front of: *anteroom.* [< L *ante-* < *ante,* adv., prep.]

ant·eat·er (ant′ēt′ər) *n.* **1** any of various toothless mammals, having a long, slender, sticky tongue, that feed on ants and termites. **2** a pangolin, or scaly anteater. **3** an echidna, or spiny anteater. **4** an aardvark.

an·te·bel·lum (an′tē bel′əm) *adj.* **1** before the war. **2** *U.S.* before the American Civil War. [< L *ante bellum* before the war]

an·te·ced·ence (an′tə sēd′əns) *n.* **1** a going before; precedence; priority. **2** in astronomy, the apparent motion of a planet from east to west.

an·te·ced·ent (an′tə sēd′ənt) *n.* **1** a previous thing or event; something happening before an event and leading up to another. **2** in grammar, a word, phrase, or clause that is referred to by a pronoun or relative adverb. In "This is the house that Jack built," *house* is the antecedent of *that.* In "I remember the house where I was born," *house* is the antecedent of *where.* **3** in mathematics, the first term of a ratio; the first or third term in a proportion. **4** in logic, a condition upon which a theoretical conclusion depends. **5 antecedents,** *pl.* **a** past life or history: *No one knew the antecedents of the mysterious stranger.* **b** ancestors. [< *adj.*]
—*adj.* coming or happening before; preceding; previous. [< L *antecedens, -entis,* ppr. of *antecedere* < *ante-* before + *cedere* go] —**Syn.** *adj.* prior, earlier.

an·te·cham·ber (an′tē chām′bər) *n.* anteroom.

an·te·date (an′tē dāt′) *n. v.* **-dat·ed, -dat·ing.**
—*v.* **1** be or happen before. **2** give too early a date to.
—*n.* a date, set on a document or assigned to an event, earlier than the actual date.

an·te·di·lu·vi·an (an′tē də lü′vē ən) *adj.* **1** before the Flood. **2** very old; old-fashioned. —*n.* **1** a person who lived before the Flood. **2** a very old person; an old-fashioned person. [< *ante-* + L *diluvium* deluge]

an·te·lope (an′tə lōp′) *n.* **-lope** or **-lopes. 1** a cud-chewing, hoofed mammal that belongs to the same family as the goat but looks like a deer. **2** the pronghorn of the sagebrush area of Alberta and Saskatchewan and of the western plains of the United States. [ME < OF *antelop* < Med.L < LGk. *antholops*]

an·te me·rid·i·em (an′tē mə rid′ē əm) *Latin.* before noon. *Abbrev.*: a.m. or A.M.

an·te·na·tal (an′tē nā′təl) *adj.* before birth.

an·ten·na (an ten′ə) *n.* **-ten·nae** *for 1*; **-ten·nas** *for 2.* **1** one of two feelers on the head of an insect, lobster, etc. **2** in radio and television, a long wire or set of wires for sending out or receiving electromagnetic waves; aerial. [< L *antenna,* originally, sailyard]

an·ten·nae (an ten′ē or an ten′ī) *n.* pl. of **antenna** (def. 1).

an·te·nup·tial (an′tē nup′shəl) *adj.* before marriage.

an·te·pe·nult (an′tē pə nult′ or -pē′nult) *n.* the third syllable from the end of a word. In *anthropology* the syllable *pol* is the antepenult.

an·te·pe·nul·ti·mate (an′tē pə nul′tə mit) *adj.* third from the end; last but two. —*n.* antepenult.

an·te·ri·or (an tēr′ē ər) *adj.* **1** toward the front; fore: *The anterior part of a fish's body contains the head and gills.* **2** going before; earlier; previous. [< L *anterior,* comparative of *ante* before]

an·te·room (an′tē rüm′ or -rům′) *n.* a small room leading to a larger one; a waiting room.

an·them (an′thəm) *n.* **1** a song of praise, devotion, or patriotism. Most countries have a **national anthem. 2** a piece of sacred music, usually with words from some passage in the Bible. [OE *antefne* < LL < Gk. *antiphōna* antiphon. Doublet of ANTIPHON.]

an·ther (an′thər) *n.* of a flower, the part of the stamen that bears the pollen. See STAMEN for diagram. [< NL < Gk. *anthēra,* fem. of *anthēros* flowery < *anthos* flower]

an·ther·id·i·um (an′thər id′ē əm) *n.* **-id·i·a** (-id′ē ə). the part of a fern, moss, etc. that produces male reproductive cells. [< NL *antheridium,* dim. of Gk. *anthēra* anther. See ANTHER.]

ant hill a heap of dirt piled up by ants around the entrance to their underground nest.

an·thol·o·gist (an thol′ə jist) *n.* a person who makes an anthology.

an·thol·o·gy (an thol′ə jē) *n.* **-gies.** a collection of poems or prose selections from various authors [< L < Gk. *anthologia* < *anthos* flower + *legein* gather]

an·tho·zo·an (an′thə zō′ən) *n.* any sea anemone, coral, or other polyp having radial segments. [< Gk. *anthos* flower + *zōa* animals]

an·thra·cene (an′thrə sēn′) *n.* a colorless, crystalline, complex compound of hydrogen and carbon. It is obtained by distilling coal tar and is used in making alizarin dyes. *Formula*: $C_{14}H_{10}$ [< Gk. *anthrax* live coal]

an·thra·cite (an′thrə sīt′) *n.* a coal of almost pure carbon that burns with very little smoke or flame; hard coal. [< L < Gk. *anthrakitēs* coal-like < *anthrax* charcoal]

an·thrac·nose (an thrak′nōs) *n.* any of various fungus diseases of plants that form spores which break through the surface as blackish spots, chiefly on fruit and leaves, sometimes destroying whole crops. [< Gk. *anthrax* carbuncle, charcoal + *nosos* disease]

an·thrax (an′thraks) *n.* an infectious, often fatal, disease of cattle, sheep, etc. that may be transmitted to human beings. [< LL < Gk. *anthrax* carbuncle, live coal]

anthropo- *combining form.* of human beings, as in *anthropology, anthropometry.* [< Gk. *anthrōpos* man]

an·thro·poid (an′thrə poid′) *adj.* of certain apes, manlike; resembling man. —*n.* a manlike ape, such as a chimpanzee or a gorilla. [< Gk. *anthrōpoeidēs* <*anthrōpos* man]

an·thro·poi·de·a (an′thrə poi′dē ə) *n.* in zoology, a suborder of mammals, including monkeys, baboons, apes, and man.

an·thro·po·log·i·cal (an′thrə pə loj′ə kəl) *adj.* of or having to do with anthropology.

an·thro·pol·o·gist (an′thrə pol′ə jist) *n.* an expert in anthropology.

an·thro·pol·o·gy (an′thrə pol′ə jē) *n.* the science that deals with the origin, development, and customs of mankind. **Physical anthropology** deals with the physiological and anatomical evolution and the racial classifications of man; **cultural anthropology** deals with the social development, practices, and beliefs of man.

an·thro·po·met·ric (an′thrə pə met′rik) *adj.* of or having to do with anthropometry.

an·thro·po·met·ri·cal (an′thrə pə met′rə kəl) *adj.* anthropometric.

an·thro·pom·e·try (an′thrə pom′ə trē) *n.* the branch of anthropology that deals with measurement of the human body.

an·thro·po·mor·phic (an′thrə pə môr′fik) *adj.* attributing human form or qualities to gods, animals, etc. The religion of ancient Greece was anthropomorphic. [< Gk. *anthrōpomorphos* < *anthrōpos* man + *morphē* form]

an·thro·po·mor·phism (an′ thrə pə môr′fiz əm) *n.* an attributing of human form or qualities to gods or things.

anti (an′ tē) *n.* **-tis,** *adj. prep. Informal.* —*n.* a person opposed to some plan, idea, political party, etc. —*adj.* opposed: *He is anti by nature.* —*prep.* against: *anti everything new.* [see ANTI-]

anti- *prefix.* **1** against; opposed to ——: *anti-aircraft = against aircraft*; *anti-administration = opposed to the administration.* **2** not; the opposite of ——: *antisocial = the opposite of social*; *antiwarlike = not warlike.* **3** rival ——: *antipope = rival pope.* **4** preventing or counteracting ——: *antirust = preventing or counteracting rust.* **5** preventing, curing, or alleviating ——: *antiscorbutic = preventing, curing, or alleviating scurvy.* Also, **ant-** before vowels and *h.* [< Gk. *anti-* < *anti,* prep.]

☛ **Anti-,** in this dictionary, is hyphenated only before root words beginning with a vowel and before proper nouns and proper adjectives: *anti-intellectual, anti-Confederation, anti-American, Anti-* is generally pronounced (an′ tē) in Canada; the pronunciation (an′ tī) is frequent in the U.S.

an·ti·air·craft (an′tē ãr′kraft′) *adj.* used in defence against enemy airplanes, dirigibles, etc. *Abbrev.*: AA or A.A.

an·ti·at·om (an′tē at′əm) *n.* an atom of antimatter.

an·ti·bac·te·ri·al (an′tē bak tēr′ē əl) *adj.* counteracting or destroying viruses.

an·ti·bi·ot·ic (an′tē bī ot′ik) *n.* a product of an organism that destroys or weakens harmful micro-organisms. Penicillin is an antibiotic.

an·ti·bod·y (an′tē bod′ē) *n.* **-bod·ies.** a substance, produced in the blood of animals or man, that destroys or weakens bacteria or neutralizes poisons of organic origin.

an·tic (an′tik) *n.* **1** Often, **antics,** *pl.* a grotesque gesture or action; a silly trick: *The clown amused us by his antics.* **2** *Archaic.* a clown. [< Ital. *antico* old (with sense of *grottesco* grotesque) < *antiquus* ancient]

An·ti·christ (an′tē krīst′) *n.* **1** the great enemy of Christ, expected to spread evil in the world until overcome by Christ in the final battle between good and evil. I John 2:18. **2** one who denies or opposes Christ. **3** one who sets himself up as Christ.

an·tic·i·pate (an tis′ə pāt′) *v.* **-pat·ed, -pat·ing.** **1** look forward to; expect: *He had anticipated a good vacation in the mountains; but when the time came, he was sick.* **2** do, make, or use in advance: *The Chinese anticipated some modern discoveries.* **3** take care of ahead of time: *The nurse anticipated all the patient's wishes.* **4** be before (another) in thinking, acting, etc. **5** consider or mention before the proper time. **6** cause to happen sooner; hasten. [< L *anticipare* < *ante-* before + *capere* take]

an·tic·i·pa·tion (an tis′ə pā′shən) *n.* the act of anticipating; looking forward to; expectation: *He cut more wood than usual, in anticipation of a long winter.*

an·tic·i·pa·tive (an tis′ə pā′tiv) *adj.* involving anticipation; having a tendency to anticipate.

an·tic·i·pa·to·ry (an tis′ə pə tô′rē) *adj.* anticipating.

an·ti·cler·i·cal (an′tē kler′ə kəl) *adj.* opposed to the influence of the church and clergy, especially in public affairs.

an·ti·cler·i·cal·ism (an′tē kler′ə kəl iz′əm) *n.* opposition to the influence of the church and clergy, especially in public affairs.

an·ti·cler·i·cal·ist (an′tē kler′ə kə list) *n.* a person who is opposed to the influence of the church or the clergy, especially in public affairs.

an·ti·cli·mac·tic (an′tē klī mak′tik) *adj.* of or like an anticlimax.

an·ti·cli·max (an′tē klī′maks) *n.* **1** an abrupt descent from the important to the trivial. *Example*: "Alas! Alas! what shall I do? I've lost my wife and best hat, too!" **2** a descent (in importance, interest, etc.) contrasting with a previous rise.

an·ti·cli·nal (an′tē klī′nəl) *adj.* of or like an anticline.

an·ti·cline (an′tē klīn′) *n.* in geology, a fold of rock strata that bends downward on both sides from its centre. See **stratum** for picture. [< *anti-* + Gk. *klinein* lean; modelled on *incline*]

an·ti·co·ag·u·lant (an′tē kō ag′yů lənt) *n.* a substance or agent that prevents or slows up the clotting of blood, used in the treatment of certain heart diseases, etc. —*adj.* preventing or delaying coagulation.

an·ti·co·lo·ni·al·ism (an′tē kə lō′nē əl iz′əm) *n.* opposition to the system of one country ruling another as a colony.

an·ti·com·mun·ist or **an·ti-Com·mun·ist** (an′tē kom′yů nist) *n.* a person who is opposed to the principles and practices of communism. —*adj.* opposed to communism.

an·ti·con·vul·sant (an′tē kən vul′sənt) *n.* a substance or agent that prevents, or alleviates the effects of, convulsions. —*adj.* preventing, or alleviating the effects of, convulsions.

an·ti·cy·clone (an′tē sī′klōn) *n.* **1** an area in which winds rotate around and away from a centre of high pressure, which also moves. **2** an atmospheric disturbance at the fringes of such an area.

an·ti·cy·clon·ic (an′tē sī klon′ik) *adj.* of or having to do with an anticyclone.

an·ti·do·tal (an′tē dō′təl) *adj.* like an antidote; serving as an antidote.

an·ti·dote (an′tə dōt′ or an′tē dōt′) *n.* **1** a medicine or remedy that counteracts a poison: *Milk is an antidote for some poisons.* **2** a remedy for any evil: *Prosperity is a good antidote for crime.* [< L < Gk. *antidoton* (thing) given against < *anti-* against + *didonai* give]

an·ti·freeze (an′tē frēz′) *n.* a substance added to a liquid to prevent it from freezing. Alcohol is much used as an antifreeze in automobile radiators.

an·ti·fric·tion (an′tē frik′shən) *n.* a substance that prevents or reduces friction.

an·ti·gen (an′tə jən) *n.* any substance that can stimulate the production of antibodies. [< *anti*body + *gen* something that produces (< F < Gk. *-genēs* born, produced)]

An·tig·o·ne (an tig′ə nē′) *n.* in Greek legend, a daughter of Oedipus. She gave her dead brother a proper burial against the orders of her uncle; when he condemned her to be buried alive, she took her own life.

an·ti·he·ro (an′tē hē′rō) *n.* a person in a novel, play, etc. who, though the central character, has none of the qualities normally expected of a hero.

an·ti·he·ro·ic (an′tē hi rō′ik) *adj.* **1** opposed to the traditional or conventional idea of heroism; unlike a conventional hero. **2** opposed to the use of heroic couplets. *—n.* **1** an imitation, satire, burlesque, etc. composed to ridicule conventional or traditional heroism. **2** a mock-heroic poem, verse, etc. **3 antiheroics,** writings or actions that ridicule the traditional or conventional idea of heroism.

an·ti·his·ta·mine (an′tē his′tə mēn′ or -his′tə min) *n.* a medicine used in the treatment of colds and allergies.

an·ti·knock (an′tē nok′) *n.* a substance added to the fuel of an internal-combustion engine to reduce noise caused by too rapid combustion. *—adj.* serving to reduce such noise.

an·ti·log·a·rithm (an′tē log′ə riᴛʜ′əm) *n.* a number corresponding to a given logarithm: *The antilogarithms of the logarithms 1, 2, and 3 are 10, 100, and 1,000.*

an·ti·ma·cas·sar (an′tē mə kas′ər) *n.* a small covering to protect the back or arms of a chair, chesterfield, etc. [< *anti-* against + *macassar,* a hair oil from Macassar]

an·ti·mat·ter (an′tē mat′ər) *n.* physical matter identical in appearance with ordinary matter but having the electric charges of its particles reversed.

an·ti·mis·sile (an′tē mis′īl or -mis′əl) *adj.* for use in defence against ballistic missiles, rockets, etc.

an·ti·mo·ny (an′tə mō′nē) *n.* a crystalline, metallic chemical element, having a bluish-white lustre that occurs chiefly in combination with other elements. It is used mainly in alloys to make them harder and in medicinal compounds. *Symbol:* Sb; *at.no.* 51; *at.wt.* 121.75 [< Med.L *antimonium*]

an·ti·nu·cle·ar (an′tē nū′klē ər or -nü′klē ər) *adj.* **1** opposed to the military use of nuclear energy. **2** of or having to do with the nuclei of an anti-atom: *antinuclear particles.*

an·ti·pas·to (an′tē pas′tō; *Italian,* än′tē päs′tō) *n.* **-tos.** an Italian dish consisting of fish, meats, etc., served as an appetizer; hors d'oeuvres. [< Ital.]

an·tip·a·thet·ic (an tip′ə thet′ik or an′tē pə thet′ik) *adj.* having antipathy; contrary or opposed in nature or disposition: *Dogs and cats are antipathetic.*

an·tip·a·thet·i·cal (an tip′ə thet′ə kəl or an′tē pə thet′ə kəl) *adj.* antipathetic.

an·tip·a·thy (an tip′ə thē) *n.* **-thies.** a strong or fixed dislike; a feeling against. [< L < Gk. *antipatheia* < *anti-* against + *-patheia* < *pathos* feeling]

an·ti·per·son·nel (an′tē pėr′sə nel′) *adj.* in military use, directed against persons rather than against mechanized equipment, supplies, etc.

an·ti·phon (an′tə fon′) *n.* **1** a psalm, hymn, or prayer sung or chanted in alternate parts. **2** verses sung or chanted in response in a church service. [< LL < Gk. *antiphōna* sounding in response < *anti-* opposed to + *phōnē* sound. Doublet of ANTHEM.]

hat, āge, cãre, fär; let, ēqual, tėrm; it, īce
hot, ōpen, ôrder; oil, out; cup, pu̇t, rüle, ūse
əbove, takən, pencəl, lemən, circəs
ch, child; ng, long; sh, ship
th, thin; ᴛʜ, then; zh, measure

an·tiph·o·nal (an tif′ə nəl) *adj.* like an antiphon; sung or chanted alternately. *—n.* a book of antiphons.

an·tip·o·dal (an tip′ə dəl) *adj.* **1** on the opposite side of the earth. **2** directly opposite; exactly contrary.

an·ti·pode (an′tə pōd′) *n.* anything exactly opposite; direct opposite.

an·tip·o·de·an (an tip′ə dē′ən) *adj.* antipodal.

an·tip·o·des (an tip′ə dēz′) *n.pl.* **1** two places on directly opposite sides of the earth: *The North Pole and the South Pole are antipodes.* **2** a place on the opposite side of the earth. **3** two opposites or contraries: *Forgiveness and revenge are antipodes.* **4** the direct opposite. [< L < Gk. *antipodes,* pl. of *antipous* < *anti-* opposite to + *pous* foot]

☛ **Antipodes is plural in form and plural or singular in use for defs. 2 and 4.**

an·ti·pope (an′tē pōp′) *n.* a pope set up by a rival group in opposition to the true pope.

an·ti·pro·ton (an′tē prō′ton) *n.* in physics, a tiny particle of the same mass as a proton, but negatively charged, created when a proton hits a neutron.

an·ti·py·ret·ic (an′tē pī ret′ik) *adj.* checking or preventing fever. *—n.* any medicine or remedy for checking or preventing fever.

an·ti·quar·i·an (an′tə kwãr′ē ən) *adj.* having to do with antiques or antiquaries: *The antiquarian section of the museum was full of old furniture and pottery.* *—n.* an antiquary.

an·ti·quar·y (an′tə kwer′ē) *n.* **-quar·ies.** a student or collector of relics from ancient times. [< L *antiquarius*]

an·ti·quate (an′tə kwāt′) *v.* **-quat·ed, -quat·ing.** make old-fashioned; make out-of-date. [< L *antiquare* < *antiquus* ancient] **—an′ti·qua′tion,** *n.*

an·ti·quat·ed (an′tə kwāt′id) *adj.* **1** old-fashioned; out-of-date. **2** too old for work, service, etc.

an·tique (an tēk′) *adj.* **1** old-fashioned; out-of-date: *She wore an antique gown to the costume party.* **2** of or belonging to ancient Greece or Rome. **3** of times long ago; from times long ago; ancient: *This antique chair was made in 1750.* **4** in the style of times long ago: *An antique gold finish is dull and slightly greenish.* *—n.* **1** something made long ago. **2** an antique style, usually of Greek or Roman art: *a statue imitating the antique.* **3** in printing, a style of type. **This sentence is in antique.** [< L *antiquus* < *ante* before]

an·tiq·ui·ty (an tik′wə tē) *n.* **-ties. 1** oldness; great age. **2** times long ago; early ages of history. Antiquity usually refers to the period from 5000 B.C. to A.D. 476. **3** people of long ago. **4 antiquities,** *pl.* **a** things from times long ago. **b** the customs and life of olden times.

an·ti·ra·chit·ic (an′tē rə kit′ik) *adj.* preventing or curing rickets.

an·ti·scor·bu·tic (an′tē skôr bū′tik) *adj.* preventing or curing scurvy. *—n.* a remedy for scurvy.

an·ti-Se·mit·ic (an′tē sə mit′ik) *adj.* having or showing dislike or hatred for Jews; prejudiced against Jews.

☛ **anti-Semitic.** This and the following word are based on a misunderstanding, since Jews form only one group of Semites. Other Semitic peoples include the Arabs, Syrians, etc.

an·ti-Sem·i·tism (an′tē sem′ə tiz′əm) *n.* a dislike or hatred for Jews; prejudice against Jews.

an·ti·sep·sis (an′tə sep′sis) *n.* **1** the prevention of infection. **2** a method or medicine that prevents infection.

an·ti·sep·tic (an′tə sep′tik) *adj.* preventing infection. *—n.* a substance that prevents infection. Iodine, peroxide, mercurochrome, alcohol, and boric acid are antiseptics.

an·ti·sep·ti·cal·ly (an′tə sep′tik lē) *adv.* by the use of antiseptics.

an·ti·slav·er·y (an′tē slāv′ər ē or -slāv′rē) *adj.* opposed to slavery; against slavery.

an·ti·so·cial (an′tē sō′shəl) *adj.* **1** opposed to the principles upon which society is based: *Murder, stealing, and the spreading of diseases are antisocial acts.* **2** averse to the society or companionship of others; not sociable.

an·ti·spas·mod·ic (an′tē spaz mod′ik) *adj.* preventing or curing spasms. —*n.* a drug to prevent or cure spasms.

an·tis·tro·phe (an tis′trə fē) *n.* **1** a part of an ancient Greek ode sung by the chorus when moving from left to right. **2** a stanza following a strophe and usually in the same metre. [< LL < Gk. *antistrophē* a turning about < *anti-* against + *strephein* turn]

an·ti·tank (an′tē tangk′) *adj.* in military use, designed for use against armored vehicles, especially tanks. *Abbrev.*: AT

an·tith·e·sis (an tith′ə sis) *n.* **-ses** (-sēz′). **1** the direct opposite: *Hate is the antithesis of love.* **2** contrast of ideas. *Example*: "To err is human; to forgive, divine." **3** opposition; contrast (*of* or *between*): *antithesis of theory and fact.* [< L < Gk. *antithesis* < *anti-* against + *tithenai* set]

an·ti·thet·ic (an′tə thet′ik) *adj.* **1** of or using antithesis. **2** contrasted; opposite.

an·ti·thet·i·cal (an′tə thet′ə kəl) *adj.* antithetic.

an·ti·tox·ic (an′tē tok′sik) *adj.* **1** counteracting diseases or poisonings caused by toxins. **2** having to do with or like an antitoxin.

an·ti·tox·in (an′tē tok′sin) *n.* **1** a substance formed in the body to counteract a disease or poison. **2** a serum containing antitoxin. Diphtheria antitoxin, obtained from the blood of horses infected with diphtheria, is injected into a person to make him immune to diphtheria, or to treat him if already infected.

an·ti·trades (an′tē trādz′) *n.* the winds that blow in the opposite direction to that of the trade winds, on a level above them in the tropic zone and at the earth's surface in the temperate zones.

an·ti·trust (an′tē trust′) *adj.* opposed to large corporations that control the trade practices of certain kinds of business.

an·ti·vi·ral (an′tē vī′rəl) *adj.* counteracting or destroying viruses.

an·ti·vi·ta·min (an′tē vī′tə min) *n.* **1** any substance that prevents or inhibits the absorption of a vitamin. **2** an enzyme that destroys vitamins.

an·ti·viv·i·sec·tion (an′tē viv′ə sek′shən) *n.* opposition to the practice of cutting into or experimenting on living animals for scientific study.

an·ti·viv·i·sec·tion·ist (an′tē viv′ə sek′shən ist) *n.* a person opposed to the practice of vivisection.

ant·ler (ant′lər) *n.* **1** a branched horn of a deer or similar animal. **2** a branch of such a horn. [ME < OF *antoillier* < L *ante* before + *oculus* eye]

ant·lered (ant′lərd) *adj.* having antlers.

ant lion **1** an insect whose larva digs a pit, where it lies in wait to catch ants, etc. **2** the larva; doodlebug.

an·to·nym (an′tə nim′) *n.* a word that means the opposite of another word: "*Right*" *is the antonym of* "*wrong.*" *Abbrev.*: ant. [< Gk. *antonymia* < *anti-* opposite to + (dialectal) *onyma* word]

A number l *Informal.* A-one; first-class.

a·nus (ā′ nəs) *n.* the opening at the lower end of the alimentary canal. [< L *anus*, originally, ring]

an·vil (an′vəl) *n.* **1** an iron or steel block on which metals are hammered and shaped. **2** in anatomy, the incus. See the diagram of ear[1]. [OE *anfilt*]

anvil chorus in opera, a stage device to create an atmosphere of tension and crisis by means of striking small steel bars, as in Verdi's *Il Trovatore.*

anx·i·e·ty (ang zī′ə tē) *n.* **-ties. 1** uneasy thoughts or fears about what may happen; a troubled, worried, or uneasy feeling: *We all felt anxiety when the airplane was caught in a hurricane.* **2** eager desire: *anxiety to succeed.* **3** in psychiatry, a state of abnormal fear or mental tension. [< L *anxietas* < *anxius* troubled. See ANXIOUS.] —**Syn. 1** concern, apprehension, dread, misgiving.

anx·ious (angk′shəs or ang′shəs) *adj.* **1** uneasy because of thoughts or fears of what may happen; troubled; worried. **2** causing uneasy feelings or troubled thoughts. **3** eagerly desiring; wishing very much: *The boy was anxious for a new bicycle.* [< L *anxius* troubled < *angere* choke, cause distress] —**anx′ious·ly,** *adv.*—**anx′ious·ness,** *n.* —**Syn. 1** concerned, apprehensive. **3** See **eager.**

☛ **anxious.** The idiom is *anxious for* when eagerly desiring is meant: *He is anxious for news of her.* When worried is meant, the idioms are *anxious about*, referring to persons, and *anxious at*, referring to things: *Her mother was anxious about her. They became anxious at her delay.*

anxious seat or **bench** *U.S.* **1** a seat near the pulpit at a revival meeting for those who are troubled about their religious life and want to strengthen their faith. **2 on the anxious seat,** in an uneasy or troubled condition.

an·y (en′ē) *adj.* **1** one (no matter which) out of many: *Any book will do.* **2** some: *Have you any fresh fruit?* **3** every: *Any child knows that.* **4** even one; even one or two: *He was forbidden to go into any house.* **5** in no matter what quantity or number: *Have you any sugar?* **6** enough to be noticed: *He had hardly any money.* —*pron.* **1** any person or thing; any part: *Keep the cake; I don't want any.* **2** some: *I need more ink; have you any?* —*adv.* **1** to some extent or degree; at all: *Has the sick child improved any?* **2** even a little: *Do not go any closer.* [OE *ǣnig*]

☛ **any.** In comparisons of things of the same class, idiom calls for *any other*: *This book is better than any other on the subject.* But: *I think a movie is more entertaining than any book* (not the same class of things). See also **anyone** and **anyway.**

an·y·bod·y (en′ē bud′ē or -bod′ē) *pron. n.* **-bod·ies. 1** any person; anyone: *Has anybody been here?* **2** an important person: *Is he anybody?*

an·y·how (en′ē hou′) *adv.* **1** in any way whatever: *The answer is wrong anyhow you look at it.* **2** in any case; at least: *I can see as well as you, anyhow.* **3** carelessly; in ways that are not right and proper: *He does his work anyhow.*

an·y·one (en′ē wun′ or en′ē wən) *pron.* any person; anybody.

an·y·place (en′ē plās′) *adv. Informal.* anywhere.

an·y·thing (en′ē thing′) *pron.* any thing. —*n.* a thing of any kind whatever. —*adv.* at all.

an·y·way (en′ē wā′) *adv.* **1** in any way whatever. **2** in any case; at least: *I am coming anyway, no matter what you say.* **3** carelessly; in ways not right and proper.

☛ The form *anyways* is usually regarded as sub-standard and should be avoided.

an·y·where (en′ē hwār′ or -wār′) *adv.* in, at, or to any place.

an·y·wise (en′ē wīz′) *adv.* in any way; to any degree; at all.

An·zac (an′zak) *n.* a member of the armed services of Australia or New Zealand. [an acronym for *A*ustralia and *N*ew *Z*ealand *A*rmy *C*orps]

ANZUS (an′zəs) an acronym for *Australia, New Zealand,* and the *United States* acting collectively for mutual defence in the Pacific.

A-one (ā′ wun′) *adj. Informal.* first-rate; first-class; excellent. Also, **A 1.**

a·o·rist (ā′ə rist) *n.* **1** one of the past tenses of Greek verbs, showing that an action took place at some time in the past without indicating whether the act was completed, repeated, or continued. **2** a tense having a similar form or purpose in other languages. **3** a verb form in the aorist. [< Gk. *aoristos* < *a-* not + *horos* boundary]

a·or·ta (ā ôr′tə) *n.* **-tas** or **-tae** (-tē or -tī). the main artery that carries the blood from the left side of the heart and, with its branches, distributes it to all parts of the body except the lungs. See **heart** for diagram. [< NL or Med.L < Gk. *aortē* that which is hung]

a·or·tic (ā ôr′tik) *adj.* having to do with the aorta.

a·ou·dad (ä′ ů dad′) *n.* a wild sheep of northern Africa. [< F < Berber *audad*]

ap-[1] the form of **ad-** before *p*, as in *apprehend.*

ap-[2] the form of **apo-** before vowels and *h*, as in *aphelion.*

Ap. April.

AP Associated Press.

a·pace (ə pās′) *adv.* swiftly; quickly; fast.

hat, āge, cãre, fär; let, ēqual, tėrm; it, īce
hot, ōpen, ôrder; oil, out; cup, pu̇t, rüle, ūse
əbove, takən, pencəl, lemən, circəs
ch, child; ng, long; sh, ship
th, thin; ᴛʜ, then; zh, measure

A·pach·e (ə pach′ē) *n.* **A·pach·e** or **A·pach·es.** **1** a tribe of warlike, nomadic Indians living in the S.W. United States. **2** a member of this tribe. **3** their language. [apparently < Am.Sp. *ápachu* enemy]

a·pache (ə päsh′ or ə pash′) *n.* one of a band of gangsters of Paris, Brussels, etc. *—adj.* of or having to do with a very lively dance in which the partners dress like an apache and his girl. [< F; special use of *Apache*]

ap·a·nage (ap′ə nij) *n.* appanage.

a·part (ə pärt′) *adv.* **1** to pieces; in pieces; in separate parts: *Take the watch apart.* **2** away from each other: *Keep the dogs apart.* **3** to one side; aside: *He stood apart from the others.* **4** away from others; independently: *View each idea apart.* [ME < OF *à part* aside]

a·part·heid (ə pärt′hāt or ə pärt′hīt) *n.* in South Africa, the policy of economic and political segregation of the native people as a principle of society upheld by law; racial segregation. [< Afrikaans]

a·part·ment (ə pärt′mənt) *n.* a room or rooms to live in. [< F < Ital. *appartamento*, ult. < *a parte* apart]

apartment block a building containing a number of apartments.

apartment house apartment block.

ap·a·thet·ic (ap′ə thet′ik) *adj.* **1** with little interest in or desire for action; indifferent. **2** lacking in feeling. **—ap′a·thet′i·cal·ly,** *adv.*

ap·a·thy (ap′ə thē) *n.* **-thies. 1** a lack of interest in or desire for activity; indifference: *The miser heard the old beggar's story with apathy.* **2** a lack of feeling. [< L < Gk. *apatheia* < *a-* without + *pathos* feeling]
—Syn. 1 See **indifference.**

ap·a·tite (ap′ə tīt′) *n.* a mineral containing a high proportion of calcium. It occurs in the form of either crystals or masses, and is used as a fertilizer. [< Gk. *apatē* deceit + E *-ite*, so called because its various forms were often wrongly identified]

ape (āp) *n. v.* **aped, ap·ing.** *—n.* **1** any large, tail-less monkey that can stand almost erect and walk on two feet. Chimpanzees, gorillas, orang-utans, and gibbons are apes. **2** any monkey. **3** a person who imitates or mimics. **4** a rough, clumsy person. **5** a fool.
—v. imitate; mimic. [OE *apa*] **—ape′like′,** *adj.*

APEC or **A.P.E.C.** Atlantic Provinces Economic Council.

a·pep·si·a (ə pep′sē ə) *n.* faulty digestion; dyspepsia. [< NL < Gk. *apepsia* < *a-* not + *peptein* to digest]

a·pe·ri·ent (ə pēr′ē ənt) *adj. n.* laxative. [< L *aperiens, -entis*, ppr. of *aperire* open]

a·pe·ri·od·ic (ā′pēr ē od′ik) *adj.* **1** not periodic; irregular. **2** in physics, having irregular vibrations.

a·per·i·tif (ə per′ə tēf′; *French*, ä pā rē tēf′) *n.* an alcoholic drink taken before a meal to stimulate the appetite. [< F *apéritif*]

ap·er·ture (ap′ər chər or ap′ər chür′) *n.* **1** an opening; gap; hole. **2** in a camera, telescope, etc. **a** the opening through which light passes. **b** the diameter of such an opening. [< L *aperture* < *aperire* open. Doublet of OVERTURE.]

a·pet·al·ous (ā pet′əl əs) *adj.* having no petals.

a·pex (ā′peks) *n.* **a·pex·es** or **ap·i·ces. 1** the highest point; tip: *the apex of a triangle.* **2** the climax. [< L]

a·pha·sia (ə fā′zhə or ə fā′zē ə) *n.* a total or partial loss of the ability to use or understand words, usually caused by injury or disease that affects the brain. [< NL < Gk. *aphasia* < *a-* not + *phanai* speak]

a·phe·li·on (ə fē′lē ən) *n.* **-lions** or **-li·a** (-lē ə). in astronomy, the point most distant from the sun, in the orbit of a planet or comet. [< NL *aphelium* < Gk. *apo-* away from + *hēlios* sun]

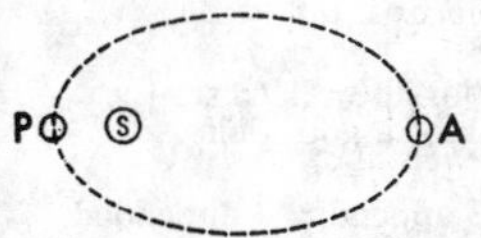

An orbit of a planet around the sun. A, aphelion; P, perihelion.

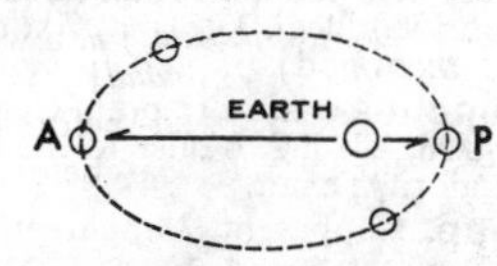

An orbit of the moon around the earth. A, apogee; P, perigee.

a·phid (ā′fid or af′id) *n.* a very small insect that lives by sucking juices from plants; plant louse. [< NL *aphis, aphidis*]

a·phis (ā′fis or af′is) *n.* **aph·i·des** (ā′fə dēz′ or af′ə dēz′) aphid.

aph·o·rism (af′ə riz′əm) *n.* **1** a terse sentence expressing a general thought; maxim; proverb. *Example*: "A living dog is better than a dead lion." **2** a concise statement of a principle. [< LL < Gk. *aphorismos* definition < *apo-* off + *horos* boundary] ☛ See **epigram** for usage note.

aph·o·rist (af′ər ist) *n.* a person who composes or uses aphorisms.

aph·o·ris·tic (af′ə ris′tik) *adj.* of aphorisms; containing aphorisms; like aphorisms.

aph·o·rize (af′ər īz′) *v.* **-rized, -riz·ing.** compose aphorisms; write or speak in aphorisms.

aph·ro·dis·i·ac (af′rō diz′ē ak′) *adj.* arousing or increasing sexual desire. *—n.* any drug, food, etc. that arouses or increases sexual desire. [< Gk. *aphrodisiakos* < *aphrodisios* of Aphrodite, the goddess of love]

Aph·ro·di·te (af′rə dī′tē) *n.* **1** in Greek mythology, the goddess of love and beauty, identified by the Romans with Venus. **2** a North American butterfly that is brown and has black spots.

a·pi·an (ā′pē ən) *adj.* of or having to do with bees.

a·pi·a·rist (ā′pē ə rist) *n.* a person who keeps bees.

a·pi·ar·y (ā′pē er′ē) *n.* **-ar·ies.** a place where bees are kept; group of beehives. [< L *apiarium* < *apis* bee]

a·pi·cal (ā′pə kəl or ap′ə kəl) *adj.* of the apex; at the apex; forming the apex.

ap·i·ces (ā′pə sēz′ or ap′ə sēz′) *n.* a pl. of **apex.**

a·pic·u·late (ə pik′yu̇ lāt′) *adj.* of leaves, ending abruptly, in a short, distinct point. [< NL *apiculatus* < *apiculus* tip, dim. of L *apex, apicis* apex]

a·pi·cul·ture (ā′pə kul′chər) *n.* the raising and care of bees; beekeeping. [< L *apis* bee + E *culture*]

a·piece (ə pēs′) *adv.* for each one; each: *These apples are five cents apiece.*

à pied (ä pyā′) *French.* on foot.

A·pis (ā′pis) *n.* the sacred bull worshipped by the ancient Egyptians.

ap·ish (āp′ish) *adj.* **1** like an ape. **2** senselessly imitative. **3** rough; clumsy. **4** foolish; silly. **—ap′ish·ly,** *adv.*

A-plane (ā′plān′) *n.* an aircraft driven by atomic energy.

a·plen·ty (ə plen′tē) *adv. Informal.* in plenty.

a·plomb (ə plom′) *n.* self-possession; assurance; poise. [< F *aplomb* < *à plomb* according to the plummet]

apo- *prefix.* from; away; quite, as in *apostasy*. Also, **ap-,** before vowels and *h*. [< Gk.]

Apoc. 1 Apocalypse. **2** Apocrypha. **3** Apocryphal.

a·poc·a·lypse (ə pok′ə lips′) *n.* **1** a revelation. **2 the Apocalypse,** the last book of the New Testament; book of Revelation. *Abbrev.*: Apoc. [< L *apocalypsis* < Gk. *apokalypsis* < *apo-* off, un- + *kalyptein* cover]

a·poc·a·lyp·tic (ə pok′ə lip′tik) *adj.* **1** of the Apocalypse. **2** like a revelation; giving a revelation.

a·poc·a·lyp·ti·cal (ə pok′ə lip′tə kəl) *adj.* apocalyptic.

a·poc·o·pe (ə pok′ə pē) *n.* the dropping out of the last sound, syllable, or letter in a word. *Th'* for *the* and *i'* for *in* are examples of apocope. [< L < Gk. *apokopē* < *apo-* off + *koptein* cut]

A·poc·ry·pha (ə pok′rə fə) *n.pl.* **1** fourteen books found in a Greek Bible of the 3rd century B.C. Eleven of them are included in the Roman Catholic Bible though none are included in the Jewish or, usually, the Protestant Bibles. **2 apocrypha,** any writings or statements of doubtful authorship or authority. [ME < LL *apocrypha*, neut. pl. of *apocryphus* < Gk. *apokryphos* hidden < *apo-* from + *kryptein* hide]

a·poc·ry·phal (ə pok′rə fəl) *adj.* **1** of doubtful authorship or authority. **2** false; counterfeit. **3 Apocryphal,** of the Apocrypha. *Abbrev.*: Apoc.

ap·o·gee (ap′ə jē′) *n.* **1** the point farthest from the earth in the orbit of a planet, comet, etc. See **aphelion** for diagram. **2** the furthermost point; highest point. [< F *apogée* < Gk. *apogaion* < *apo-* away from + *gē* or *gaia* earth]

à point (ä pwaN′) *French.* just right; just enough. A good chef cooks each dish *à point.*

a·po·lit·i·cal (ā′pə lit′ə kəl) *adj.* not concerned with politics or political issues: *an apolitical decision.*

A·pol·lo (ə pol′ō) *n.* **-los. 1** in Greek and Roman mythology, the god of the sun, poetry, music, prophecy, and healing. The Greeks and Romans considered Apollo the highest type of youthful, manly beauty. He was the first Greek god accepted by the Romans. **2** any extremely handsome young man.

A·poll·yon (ə pol′yən) *n.* the Devil. Rev. 9:11.

a·pol·o·get·ic (ə pol′ ə jet′ik) *adj.* **1** making an apology; expressing regret; acknowledging a fault; excusing failure. **2** defending by speech or writing. —*n.* **1** an apology; defence. **2 Apologetics,** the branch of theology that deals with the rational defence of a religious faith. —**a·pol′o·get′i·cal·ly,** *adv.*

ap·o·lo·gi·a (ap′ə lō′jē ə) *n.* a statement in defence or justification; apology. [< L < Gk.]

a·pol·o·gist (ə pol′ə jist) *n.* a person who defends an idea, belief, religion, etc. in speech or writing.

a·pol·o·gize (ə pol′ə jīz′) *v.* **-gized, -giz·ing. 1** make an apology; express regret; acknowledge a fault; offer an excuse. **2** make a defence in speech or writing. —**a·pol′o·giz′er,** *n.*

ap·o·logue (ap′ə log′) *n.* a fable with a moral: *Aesop's fables are apologues.* [< F < L < Gk. *apologos* story, tale]

a·pol·o·gy (ə pol′ə jē) *n.* **-gies. 1** words of regret for an offence or accident; statement that one is sorry; request for pardon: *Make an apology to the lady for hitting her.* **2** a defence in speech or writing; explanation of the truth or justice of something: *an apology for the Christian religion.* **3** a poor substitute; makeshift: *a skimpy apology for a breakfast.* [< LL < Gk. *apologia* a speech in defence, ult. < *apo-* off + *legein* speak] —**Syn. 1** See **excuse. 2** justification.

ap·o·phthegm (ap′ə them′) *n.* apothegm.

ap·o·plec·tic (ap′ə plek′tik) *adj.* **1** of or causing apoplexy. **2** suffering from apoplexy. **3** showing symptoms of a tendency to apoplexy. —*n.* a person who has apoplexy; person likely to have apoplexy.

ap·o·plex·y (ap′ə plek′sē) *n.* a sudden loss of the power to feel or think or move; stroke. Apoplexy is caused by injury to the brain when a blood vessel breaks or the blood supply becomes obstructed. [< LL < Gk. *apoplēxia* < *apo-* off, from + *plēssein* strike]

a·port (ə pôrt′) *adv.* to the port side; to the left.

a·pos·ta·sy (ə pos′tə sē) *n.* **-sies.** a complete forsaking of one's religion, faith, political party, or principles. [ME < LL < Gk. *apostasia* < *apo-* away from + *stenai* stand]

a·pos·tate (ə pos′tāt′ or ə pos′tit) *n.* a person who completely forsakes his religion, faith, political party, or principles. —*adj.* guilty of apostasy.

a·pos·ta·tize (ə pos′tə tīz′) *v.* **-tized, -tiz·ing.** forsake completely one's religion, faith, party, or principles.

a pos·te·ri·o·ri (ā′ pos tēr′ē ô′rī or a′ pos tēr′ē ô′rē) from effect to cause; from particular cases to a general rule; based on actual observation or experience. [< Med.L *a posteriori* from what comes after]

a·pos·tle (ə pos′əl) *n.* **1 Apostle,** one of the twelve disciples, **the Apostles,** chosen by Christ to go forth and preach the gospel to all the world. **2** any early Christian leader or missionary: *Paul was frequently called the "Apostle to the Gentiles."* **3** the first Christian missionary to any country or region. **4** a leader of any reform movement or belief. **5** in the Mormon Church, one of the council of twelve administrative officials. [OE < LL < Gk. *apostolos* messenger < *apo-* off + *stellein* send]

Apostles' Creed the statement of belief that contains the fundamental doctrines of Christianity, beginning "I believe in God, the Father . . ." In its present form it dates back to about A.D. 600 and was formerly supposed to have been composed by the Apostles.

ap·os·tol·ic (ap′əs tol′ik) *adj.* **1** of the Apostles; having to do with the Apostles. **2** according to the beliefs and teachings of the Apostles. **3** of or having to do with the Pope; papal.

ap·os·tol·i·cal (ap′əs tol′ə kəl) *adj.* apostolic.

Apostolic Fathers 1 a group of early Christian authors who lived very soon after the Apostles. **2** the writings attributed to these authors, written probably between A.D. 95 and 150.

Apostolic See the bishopric of the Pope.

apostolic succession especially in Roman Catholic, Greek Orthodox, and Anglican churches, the unbroken line of succession from the Apostles down to the present-day bishops and priests, by which it is held that religious authority has been transmitted.

a·pos·tro·phe[1] (ə pos′trə fē) *n.* a sign (') used: **a** to show the omission of one or more letters in contractions, as in *o'er* for *over, thro'* for *through.* **b** to show the possessive forms of nouns or indefinite pronouns, as in *John's book, the lions' den, everybody's business.* **c** to form certain plurals, as in *2 o's, four 9's in 9,999.* **d** to show that certain sounds represented in the usual spelling have not been spoken: *'lectric.* [< F < LL < Gk. *apostrophos* a turning away, omission (mark) < *apostrephein* avert, get rid of. See APOSTROPHE[2].]

a·pos·tro·phe[2] (ə pos′trə fē) *n.* words addressed to an absent person as if he were present or to a thing or idea as if it could appreciate them. [< LL < Gk. *apostrophē* < *apostrephein* < *apo-* away from + *strephein* turn]

a·pos·tro·phize (ə pos′trə fīz′) *v.* **-phized, -phiz·ing.** in a speech, poem, etc., address some thing or absent person, usually with emotion: *The poet apostrophizes judgment in these words: "Oh, judgment! thou art fled to brutish beasts."*

apothecaries' measure a system of units used in compounding and dispensing liquid drugs:

60 minims (♏) = 1 fluid dram (ʒ)
8 fluid drams = 1 fluid ounce (℥)
20 fluid ounces = 1 pint
8 pints = 1 gallon (277.274 cubic inches)

In the United States the pint (being the eighth part of a gallon of 231 cubic inches) is divided into 16 fluid ounces, with subdivisions corresponding to the table above.

apothecaries' weight a system of weights used in mixing drugs and filling prescriptions:

20 grains = 1 scruple
3 scruples = 1 dram
8 drams = 1 ounce
16 ounces = 1 pound

a·poth·e·car·y (ə poth′ə ker′ē) *n.* **-car·ies. 1** a person who prepares and sells drugs and medicines; druggist. **2** formerly, a person who prescribed medicines and sold them. [ME < LL *apothecarius* warehouseman < L *apotheca* storehouse < Gk. *apothēkē* < *apo-* away + *tithenai* put]

ap·o·thegm (ap′ə them′) *n.* a short, forceful saying; maxim. *Example*: "Beauty is only skin-deep." Also, **apophthegm.** [< Gk. *apophthegma* < *apo-* forth + *phthengesthai* utter]

a·poth·e·o·sis (ə poth′ē ō′sis or ap′ə thē′ə sis) *n.* **-ses** (-sēz). **1** the raising of a human being to the rank of a god; deification: *The apotheosis of the emperor became a Roman custom.* **2** glorification; exaltation. **3** a glorified ideal. [< L < Gk. *apotheosis,* ult. < *apo-* + *theos* god]

a·poth·e·o·size (ə poth′ē ə sīz′ or ap′ə thē′ə sīz′) *v.* **-sized, -siz·ing. 1** raise to the rank of a god; deify. **2** glorify; exalt.

app. 1 apparent. **2** apparently. **3** appendix. **4** appended. **5** apprentice.

ap·pal or **ap·pall** (ə pol′ or ə pôl′) *v.* **-palled, -pall·ing.** fill with horror; dismay; terrify: *We were appalled* *at the thought of another war. She was appalled when she saw the river had risen to the doorstep.* [ME < OF *apallir* become or make pale < *a-* to (< L *ad-*) + *pale* < L *pallidus.* Related to PALE¹.]

ap·pall (ə pol′ or ə pôl′) *v.* appal.

ap·pall·ing (ə pol′ ing or ə pôl′ ing) *adj.* dismaying; terrifying; horrifying. **—ap·pall′ing·ly,** *adv.*

ap·pa·loo·sa (ap′ə lü′ sə) *n.* **1** a breed of horse having mottled skin, spots or blotches of color on the rump, and a skimpy tail. **2** a horse of this breed. [< *a Palouse* horse, named after the Palouse River country in Washington, where the breed is said to have been developed by the Nez Percé Indians]

ap·pa·nage (ap′ə nij) *n.* **1** land, property, or money set aside to support the younger children of kings, princes, etc. **2** a person's assigned portion; rightful property. **3** something that accompanies; an adjunct: *The millionaire had three houses, a yacht, and all the other appanages of wealth.* **4** a territory controlled by another country. Also, **apanage.** [< F *apanage* < *apaner* give bread to, ult. < L *ad-* to + *panis* bread]

ap·pa·ra·tus (ap′ə rā′ təs or ap′ə rat′əs) *n.* **-tus** or **-tus·es.** the things necessary to carry out a purpose or for a particular use: *apparatus for an experiment in chemistry, gardening apparatus, our digestive apparatus.* [< L *apparatus* preparation < *ad-* + *parare* make ready]

ap·par·el (ə par′əl) *n. v.* **-elled** or **-eled, -el·ling** or **-el·ing.** *—n.* clothing; dress. *—v.* clothe; dress up. [ME < OF *apareil* < *apareiller* clothe, ult. < L *ad-* + *par* equal] **—Syn.** *n.* raiment, garb, attire.

ap·par·ent (ə par′ənt or ə per′ənt) *adj.* **1** plain to see; so plain that one cannot help seeing it; easily understood. **2** according to appearances; seeming: *The apparent truth was really a lie.* [ME < OF *aparant,* ppr. of *apareir* < L *apparere.* See APPEAR.] **—Syn. 1** evident, clear, perceptible. See **obvious.**

ap·par·ent·ly (ə par′ənt lē or ə per′ənt lē) *adv.* **1** seemingly; as far as one can judge by appearances. **2** clearly; plainly; obviously.

ap·pa·ri·tion (ap′ə rish′ən) *n.* **1** a ghost; phantom. **2** something strange, remarkable, or unexpected that comes into view. **3** the act of appearing; appearance. [< LL *apparitio, -onis* < L *apparere.* See APPEAR.] **—Syn. 1** see **ghost.**

ap·peal (ə pēl′) *v.* **1** make an earnest request (*to* or *for*); apply for help, sympathy, etc.: *The children appealed to their mother to know what to do on a rainy day.* **2** in law: **a** ask that a case be taken to a higher court to be reviewed or heard again. **b** apply for a retrial of (a case) before a higher court. **3** call on some person to decide some matter in one's favor. **4** be attractive, interesting, or enjoyable: *Blue and red appeal to me, but I don't like gray or yellow.*
—n. **1** an earnest request; call for help, sympathy, etc. **2** in law: **a** a request to have a case heard again before a higher court or judge. **b** the right to have a case heard again. **3** a call on some person for proof, decision, etc. **4** an attraction, interest. [ME < OF < L *appellare* accost, alteration of *appellere* < *ad-* up to + *pellere* drive] **—ap·peal′ing·ly,** *adv.* **—Syn.** *n.* **1** plea, entreaty, petition, solicitation.

ap·pear (ə pēr′) *v.* **1** be seen; come in sight: *One by one the stars appear.* **2** seem; look: *The apple appeared sound on the outside, but it was rotten inside.* **3** be published: *The book appeared in the autumn.* **4** present oneself publicly or formally: *appear on the stage.* **5** become known to the mind: *It appears that we must go.* **6** stand before an authority: *appear in court.* [ME < OF *apareir* < L *apparere* < *ad-* + *parere* come in sight] **—Syn. 2** See **seem.**

ap·pear·ance (ə pēr′əns) *n.* **1** the act of appearing: *John's appearance in the doorway, a singer's first appearance in a city.* **2** outward look; aspect: *The appearance of the house made us think that it was empty.* **3** outward show: *keep up appearances.* **4** a thing that appears in sight; object seen. **5** the coming into court of a party to a lawsuit. **6** apparition.
Syn. 2 Appearance, aspect = the look or looks of a person or thing. **Appearance** is the general word applying to what one sees when he looks at someone or something: *The appearance of the city is pleasing.* **Aspect** applies to the appearance at certain times or under certain conditions: *I love the bay in all its aspects, even its stormy, frightening aspect in winter.* **3** semblance, guise.

hat, āge, cãre, fär; let, ēqual, tėrm; it, īce
hot, ōpen, ôrder; oil, out; cup, pu̇t, rüle, ūse
əbove, takən, pencəl, lemən, circəs
ch, child; ng, long; sh, ship
th, thin; ᴛʜ, then; zh, measure

ap·pease (ə pēz′) *v.* **-peased, -peas·ing. 1** satisfy (an appetite or desire): *A good dinner will appease your hunger.* **2** make calm; quiet. **3** give in to the demands of (especially those of a potential enemy): *Hitler was appeased at Munich.* [ME < OF *apaisier* < *a-* to (< L *ad-*) + *pais* peace < L *pax*] **—ap·peas′er,** *n.* **—ap·peas′ing·ly,** *adv.*
Syn. 2 Appease, pacify = make calm. **Appease** = calm or quiet a person who is excited or upset, and usually making demands, by pleasing and contenting: *When he left school to go to work, he had to appease his father.* **Pacify** = quiet people or things that are quarrelling or fighting among themselves or against some condition, by making peace though not necessarily by eliminating the cause of the disturbance: *He pacified the angry mob.*

ap·pease·ment (ə pēz′mənt) *n.* an appeasing or being appeased; pacification; satisfaction.

ap·pel·lant (ə pel′ənt) *n.* a person who appeals. *—adj.* **1** having to do with appeals. **2** in the process of appealing.

ap·pel·late (ə pel′it) *adj.* having to do with appeals. [< L *appellatus,* pp. of *appellare.* See APPEAL.]

appellate court a court having the power to re-examine and reverse the decisions of a lower court.

ap·pel·la·tion (ap′ə lā′shən) *n.* **1** a name or title. In "John the Baptist," John's appellation is *the Baptist.* **2** the act of calling by a name.

ap·pel·la·tive (ə pel′ə tiv) *n.* **1** a descriptive name. **2** a common noun; one that can be applied to any member of a class. *—adj.* that names; naming.

ap·pend (ə pend′) *v.* add to a larger thing; attach as a supplement: *The amendments to the association's constitution are appended to it.* [< L *appendere* < *ad-* on + *pendere* hang] **—Syn.** annex.

ap·pend·age (ə pen′dij) *n.* **1** something attached; addition. **2** in biology, any of various external or subordinate parts. Arms, tails, fins, legs, etc. are appendages.

ap·pend·ant (ə pen′dənt) *adj.* added; attached. *—n.* an appendage.

ap·pen·dec·to·my (ap′ən dek′tə mē) *n.* **-mies.** the surgical removal of the vermiform appendix. [< *appendix* + *ectomy* (< Gk. *ek* out of + *-tomia* a cutting <*temnein* cut)]

ap·pen·di·ces (ə pen′də sēz′) *n.* a pl. of **appendix.**

ap·pen·di·ci·tis (ə pen′də sī′tis) *n.* an inflammation of the vermiform appendix, the small saclike growth on the large intestine. [< L *appendix, -icis* + E *-itis*]

ap·pen·dix (ə pen′diks) *n.* **-dix·es** or **-di·ces. 1** an addition at the end of a book or document. **2** in anatomy, an outgrowth of an organ, etc. The small saclike growth attached to the large intestine is the **vermiform appendix.** See **intestine** for diagram. [< L *appendix* < *appendere.* See APPEND.] **—Syn. 1** See **supplement.**
☛ The English plural **appendixes** is rapidly overtaking the Latin **appendices** and occurs more frequently except in quite formal usage.

ap·per·cep·tion (ap′ər sep′shən) *n.* **1** the assimilation of a new perception by means of a mass of ideas already in the mind. **2** a clear perception; full understanding. [< F *aperception* < NL. Related to PERCEPTION.]

ap·per·cep·tive (ap′ər sep′tiv) *adj.* of or having to do with apperception.

ap·per·tain (ap′ər tān′) *v.* belong as a part; pertain; relate: *The control of traffic appertains to the police. Forestry appertains to geography, to botany, and to agriculture.* [ME < OF *apartenir* < LL *appertinere* < L *ad-* to + *pertinere* pertain]

ap·pe·tite (ap′ə tīt′) *n.* **1** a desire for food. **2** a desire: *an appetite for amusement.* [ME < OF < L *appetitus* < *ad-* + *petere* seek] **—Syn. 1** hunger, craving, longing.

ap·pe·tiz·er (ap′ə tīz′ər) *n.* food or drink served, especially before a meal, to stimulate the appetite.

ap·pe·tiz·ing (ap′ə tīz'ing) *adj.* arousing or exciting the appetite: *appetizing food.* —**ap′pe·tiz'ing·ly,** *adv.*

ap·plaud (ə plod′ or ə plôd′) *v.* **1** express approval by clapping hands, shouting, etc.: *The crowd applauded lustily.* **2** express approval of (a person, speech, performance, etc.) in this way: *We applauded the speaker.* **3** approve; praise. [< L *applaudere* < *ad-* to + *plaudere* clap]

ap·plause (ə ploz′ or ə plôz′) *n.* **1** approval expressed by clapping the hands, shouting, etc. **2** approval; praise. [< L *applausus,* pp. of *applaudere.* See APPLAUD.]

ap·ple (ap′əl) *n.* **1** the firm, fleshy, roundish fruit of a tree widely grown in temperate regions. Apples belong to the same family as the quince, pear, and hawthorn. **2** the tree. **3** any of various other fruits or fruitlike products, such as the oak apple and love apple. [OE *æppel*]

apple butter a smooth spread made by stewing apples, usually with spices and cider.

apple cart **1** a cart for carrying apples. **2 upset the apple cart,** *Informal.* spoil or disrupt a plan or program: *The delegates hoped that no one would upset the apple cart before the agreement was signed.*

ap·ple·jack (ap′əl jak') *n.* an intoxicating liquor made from apple cider.

apple of discord **1** in Greek legend, a golden apple inscribed "For the fairest" and claimed by Aphrodite, Athena, and Hera. Paris awarded it to Aphrodite. **2** any cause of jealousy and trouble.

apple of the eye something very precious.

apple-pie order perfect order or condition.

ap·ple-pol·ish (ap′əl pol'ish) *v. Informal.* **1** curry favor with; flatter. **2** use flattery. —**ap′ple-pol'ish·er,** *n.*

ap·ple·sauce (ap′əl sos' or ap′əl sôs') *n.* **1** apples cut in pieces and cooked with sugar and water until soft. **2** *Slang.* nonsense.

apple slump brown betty.

ap·ple·wood (ap′əl wud') *n.* the wood of the apple tree, used for cabinetmaking, firewood, etc.

ap·pli·ance (ə plī′əns) *n.* **1** a tool, small machine, or some other device used in doing something: *Can openers, vacuum cleaners, washing machines, refrigerators, etc. are household appliances.* **2** an applying; the act of putting into use.

ap·pli·ca·bil·i·ty (ap'lə kə bil′ə tē) *n.* the quality of being applicable.

ap·pli·ca·ble (ap′lə kə bəl or ə plik′ə bəl) *adj.* capable of being put to practical use; appropriate; suitable; fitting: *The rule "Look before you leap" is almost always applicable.*

ap·pli·cant (ap′lə kənt) *n.* a person who applies (for money, position, help, office, etc.).

ap·pli·ca·tion (ap'lə kā′shən) *n.* **1** the act of using; the use: *The application of what you know will help you solve new problems.* **2** the act of applying; a putting on: *the application of paint to a house.* **3** ways of using: *Freedom is a word of wide application.* **4** something applied: *This application is made of cold cream and ointment.* **5** a request (for employment, an award, tickets, etc.): *He made an application for the position of clerk.* **6** continued effort; close attention: *By application to his work he won promotion.* [ME < MF < L *applicatio, -onis* a joining to < *applicare.* See APPLY.] —**Syn. 6** See **effort.**

ap·pli·ca·tor (ap′lə kā'tər) *n.* any device for applying medicine, polish, paints, cosmetics, etc.

ap·plied (ə plīd′) *adj.* put to practical use; used to solve actual problems: *Engineers study applied mathematics.*

applied science science that uses facts, laws, and theories to solve practical problems such as building a bridge, designing a radio, testing intelligence, etc.

ap·pli·qué (ap'lə kā′) *n. v.* **-quéd, -qué·ing,** *adj.* —*n.* ornaments made of one material sewn or otherwise fastened on another. —*v.* trim or ornament with appliqué. —*adj.* trimmed in this way. [< F *appliqué* < *appliquer* apply]

ap·ply (ə plī′) *v.* **-plied, -ply·ing. 1** put: *apply paint to a house.* **2** put to practical use; put into effect: *He knows the rule but does not know how to apply it.* **3** be useful or suitable; fit: *When does this rule apply?* **4** use for a special purpose: *apply a sum of money to charity.* **5** make a request: *apply for a job.* **6** use (a word or words) appropriately with reference to a person or thing: *apply a nickname. Don't apply that adjective to me.* **7** set to work and stick to it: *He applied himself to learning French.* [ME < OF *aplier* < L *applicare* < *ad-* on + *plicare* fold, lay]

ap·pog·gia·tu·ra (ə poj'ə tūr′ə or ə poj'ə tūr′ə) *n.* in music, a grace note. [< Ital. *appoggiatura* < *appoggiare* lean, ult. < L *ad-* on + *podium* podium]

WRITTEN PLAYED

An appoggiatura

ap·point (ə point′) *v.* **1** name to an office or position; choose: *This man was appointed postmaster.* **2** decide on; set: *appoint a time for the meeting.* **3** fix; prescribe. **4** furnish; equip: *a well-appointed office.* [ME < OF *apointer* < LL *appunctare* < L *ad-* to + *punctum* point. Related to POINT.] —**ap·point′er,** *n.* —**Syn. 1** designate. **4** supply.

ap·point·ee (ə poin'tē′) *n.* a person appointed.

ap·poin·tive (ə poin′tiv) *adj.* filled by appointment: *Positions in the Senate are appointive.*

ap·point·ment (ə point′mənt) *n.* **1** the act of naming to an office or position; choosing: *The appointment of Ann as secretary pleased her friends.* **2** an office or position. **3** an engagement to be somewhere or to meet someone. **4 appointments,** *pl.* furniture; equipment. —**Syn. 2** post.

ap·por·tion (ə pôr′shən) *v.* divide and give out in fair shares; distribute according to some rule: *The father's property was apportioned among his children after his death.* [< obsolete F *apportionner,* ult. < L *ad-* to + *portio, -onis* portion] —**Syn.** See **allot.**

ap·por·tion·ment (ə pôr′shən mənt) *n.* the act of dividing and giving out in fair shares.

ap·pose (a pōz′) *v.* **-posed, -pos·ing. 1** put next; place side by side. In the phrase "Columbus, the discoverer of America," the word *discoverer* is apposed to *Columbus.* **2** put (one thing to another); apply: *An official seal was apposed to the document.* [< F *apposer* < a- to (< L *ad-*) + *poser* put (see POSE[1])]

ap·po·site (ap′ə zit) *adj.* appropriate; suitable; apt. [< L *appositus,* pp. of *apponere* < *ad-* near + *ponere* place] —**ap′po·site·ly,** *adv.* —**ap′po·site·ness,** *n.*

ap·po·si·tion (ap'ə zish′ən) *n.* **1** the act of putting side by side. **2** a position side by side. **3** in grammar: **a** a placing together in the same relation. **b** the relation of two parts of a sentence when the one is added as an explanation to the other. In "Mr. Brown, our neighbor, has a new car," *Mr. Brown* and *neighbor* are in apposition.

ap·pos·i·tive (ə poz′ə tiv) *n.* a noun added to another noun as an explanation; word, phrase, or clause in apposition. —*adj.* placed beside another noun as an explanation.

ap·prais·al (ə prāz′əl) *n.* **1** an estimate of the value, amount, etc. **2** an appraising; valuation.

ap·praise (ə prāz′) *v.* **-praised, -prais·ing. 1** estimate the value, amount, quality, etc. of: *An employer should be able to appraise ability and character.* **2** set a price on; fix the value of: *Property is appraised for taxation.* [< *praise,* ? after *prize*[3], *apprize*[1]] —**ap·prais′ing·ly,** *adv.* —**Syn. 1** See **estimate.**

ap·praise·ment (ə prāz′mənt) *n.* appraisal.

ap·prais·er (ə prāz′ər) *n.* **1** a person authorized to fix the value of property, imported goods, etc. **2** a person who appraises.

ap·pre·ci·a·ble (ə prē′shē ə bəl or ə prē′shə bəl) *adj.* enough to be felt or estimated: *The difference between the two prices is appreciable.* —**ap·pre′ci·a·bly,** *adv.*

ap·pre·ci·ate (ə prē′shē āt') *v.* **-at·ed, -at·ing. 1** think highly of; recognize the worth or quality of; value; enjoy: *Almost everybody appreciates good food.* **2** have an opinion of the value, worth, or quality of; estimate: *appreciate knowledge.* **3** be sensitive to; be aware of: *A musician can appreciate small differences in sounds.*

4 estimate correctly. 5 raise in value: *New buildings appreciate the value of land.* 6 rise in value: *This land will appreciate as soon as good roads are built.* [< L *appretiare* appraise < *ad-* + *pretium* price. Doublet of APPRIZE[1].] —**Syn. 1** esteem, prize. See **value.** 2 appraise.

ap·pre·ci·a·tion (ə prē′shē ā′shən) *n.* **1** an appreciating; a valuing. **2** a valuing highly; sympathetic understanding: *She has an appreciation of art and music.* **3** favorable criticism. **4** a rise in value.

ap·pre·ci·a·tive (ə prē′shē ə tiv, ə prē′shē ā′tiv or ə prē′shə tiv) *adj.* having appreciation; showing appreciation; recognizing the value: *appreciative of the smallest kindness.* —**ap·pre′ci·a′tive·ly,** *adv.*

ap·pre·hend (ap′ri hend′) *v.* **1** look forward to with fear; fear; dread: *A guilty man apprehends danger in every sound.* **2** arrest: *The thief was apprehended and put in jail.* **3** understand; grasp with the mind. [< L *apprehendere* < *ad-* upon + *prehendere* seize]
☛ See **comprehend** for usage note.

ap·pre·hen·sion (ap′ri hen′shən) *n.* **1** expectation of evil; fear; dread. **2** a seizing; being seized; arrest. **3** understanding; grasp by the mind. [< L *apprehensio, -onis* < *apprehendere.* See APPREHEND.]

ap·pre·hen·sive (ap′ri hen′siv) *adj.* **1** afraid; anxious; worried. **2** quick to understand; able to learn. —**ap′pre·hen′sive·ness,** *n.*

ap·pren·tice (ə pren′tis) *n. v.* **-ticed, -tic·ing.** —*n.* **1** a person learning a trade or art. In return for instruction the apprentice agrees to work for his employer a certain length of time with little or no pay. **2** a beginner; learner. —*v.* bind or take as an apprentice. [ME < OF *aprentis* < *apprendre* learn < L *apprehendere.* See APPREHEND.]

ap·pren·tice·ship (ə pren′tis ship′) *n.* **1** the condition of being an apprentice. **2** the time during which one is an apprentice.

ap·prise[1] (ə prīz′) *v.* **-prised, -pris·ing.** apprize[2].

ap·prise[2] (ə prīz′) *v.* **-prised, -pris·ing.** apprize[1].

ap·prize[1] (ə prīz′) *v.* **-prized, -priz·ing.** appraise. Also, **apprise.** [ME < OF *apriser* < L *appretiare.* Doublet of APPRECIATE.]

ap·prize[2] (ə prīz′) *v.* **-prized, -priz·ing.** inform; notify; advise. Also, **apprise.** [< F *appris,* pp. of *apprendre* learn < L *apprehendere.* See APPREHEND.]

ap·proach (ə prōch′) *v.* **1** come near or nearer to: *We're approaching the town.* **2** come near or nearer to (in character, quality, amount): *The wind was approaching gale force.* **3** come near or nearer (in space, time, character, condition, or amount): *Winter approaches.* **4** bring near (to something): *Approach the magnet to this heap of filings.* **5** make advances or overtures to: *Will you approach your father with our plan for a party?* —*n.* **1** the act of coming near: *the approach of night.* **2** a way by which a place or a person can be reached; access. **3** a nearness in quality, likeness, or character: *In mathematics there must be more than an approach to accuracy.* **4** Also, **approaches,** *pl.* an advance; overture: *Our approaches to the manager were met with disdain.* **5** a way of dealing with or accomplishing something: *a new approach to mathematics.* **6** in golf, a stroke by which a player tries to get his ball onto the putting green. [ME < OF *aprochier* < LL *appropiare* < L *ad-* to + *prope* near]

ap·proach·a·bil·i·ty (ə prōch′ə bil′ə tē) *n.* an approachable quality or condition.

ap·proach·a·ble (ə prōch′ə bəl) *adj.* **1** that can be approached. **2** easy to approach.

ap·pro·ba·tion (ap′rə bā′shən) *n.* **1** approval; favorable opinion. **2** sanction. [ME < OF < L *approbatio, -onis* < *approbare* approve. See APPROVE.]

ap·pro·pri·a·ble (ə prō′prē ə bəl) *adj.* capable of being appropriated.

ap·pro·pri·ate (*adj.* ə prō′prē it; *v.* ə prō′prē āt′) *adj. v.* **-at·ed, -at·ing.** —*adj.* suitable; proper: *Plain, simple clothes are appropriate for school wear.* —*v.* **1** set apart for some special use: *The government appropriated money for roads.* **2** take for oneself: *You should not appropriate other people's belongings without their permission.* [< LL *appropriatus,* pp. of *appropriare* < L *ad-* to + *proprius* one's own]

hat, āge, cãre, fär; let, ēqual, tėrm; it, īce
hot, ōpen, ôrder; oil, out; cup, pu̇t, rüle, ūse
əbove, takən, pencəl, lemən, circəs
ch, child; ng, long; sh, ship
th, thin; ᴛʜ, then; zh, measure

—**ap·pro′pri·ate·ly,** *adv.* —**ap·pro′pri·ate·ness,** *n.* —**ap·pro′pri·a′tor,** *n.* —**Syn.** *adj.* fitting, meet. See **fit**[1].

ap·pro·pri·a·tion (ə prō′prē ā′shən) *n.* **1** a sum of money or other thing appropriated. **2** the act of appropriating: *His appropriation of their money was not right.* **3** a being appropriated: *The appropriation of the land made it possible to have a park.*

ap·prov·al (ə prüv′əl) *n.* **1** an approving; favorable opinion: *This plan has the teacher's approval.* **2** consent: sanction: *The principal gave his approval to plans for the holiday.* **3 on approval,** so that the customer can decide whether to buy or not. **4 approvals,** *pl.* items sent to a customer on approval. —**Syn. 1** commendation.

ap·prove (ə prüv′) *v.* **-proved, -prov·ing.** **1** think or speak well of; be pleased with: *The teacher looked at John's work and approved it.* **2** give approval (*of*). **3** sanction; consent to: *Parliament approved the bill.* **4** prove to be; show. [ME < OF *aprover* < L *approbare* < *ad-* to + *probus* good] —**ap·prov′er,** *n.* —**ap·prov′ing·ly,** *adv.*
Syn. 1 laud, like. See **praise. 3 Approve, sanction, ratify** mean to give formal consent or support. **Approve,** the general word, means to consent to something one thinks favorably of : *The school board approved the budget.* **Sanction,** more formal, means to give official consent or support: *Society does not sanction child labor.* **Ratify** is more formal still, expressing approval or confirmation: *The club council ratified the by-laws.*

approx. **1** approximate. **2** approximately.

ap·prox·i·mate (*adj.* ə prok′sə mit; *v.* ə prok′sə māt′) *adj. v.* **-mat·ed, -mat·ing.** —*adj.* **1** nearly correct: *The approximate length of a metre is 40 inches; the exact length is 39.37 inches.* **2** very near. **3** very like. —*v.* **1** come near to; approach: *Your account of what happened approximated the truth, but there were several small errors. The crowd approximated a thousand people.* **2** bring near. *Abbrev.:* approx. [< L *approximatus,* pp. of *approximare* < *ad-* to + *proximus* nearest < *prope* near]

ap·prox·i·mate·ly (ə prok′sə mit lē) *adv.* nearly; about. *Abbrev.:* approx.

ap·prox·i·ma·tion (ə prok′sə mā′shən) *n.* **1** an approximating; approach: *an approximation to the truth.* **2** a nearly correct amount; close estimate: *Twenty-five thousand miles is an approximation of the circumference of the earth.*

ap·pur·te·nance (ə pėr′tə nəns) *n.* **1** an addition to something more important; added thing; accessory. **2** a right or privilege that is subordinate to another. [< AF *apurtenance.* Related to APPERTAIN.]

ap·pur·te·nant (ə pėr′tə nənt) *adj.* pertaining; belonging: appertaining (*to*).

Apr. April.

ap·ri·cot (ap′rə kot′ or ā′prə kot′) *n.* **1** a roundish, pale, orange-colored fruit that tastes something like both a peach and a plum. **2** the tree that it grows on. **3** a pale orange yellow. —*adj.* pale orange-yellow. [earlier *apricock* (< Pg. *albricoque*), later influenced by F *abricot* < Pg. < Sp. < Arabic *al-burquq* < Gk., ult. < L *praecox* or *praecoquis* early-ripe < *prae* before + *coquere* cook, ripen]

A·pril (ā′prəl) *n.* the fourth month of the year. It has 30 days. *Abbrev.:* Ap. or Apr. [< L *Aprilis*]

April fool any person who gets fooled on April Fools' Day.

April Fools' Day April 1, a day observed by fooling people with tricks and jokes.

a pri·o·ri (a′ prē ô′rē or ā′ prī ô′rī) **1** from cause to effect; from a general rule to a particular case. **2** based on opinion or theory rather than on actual observation or experience. [< Med.L *a priori* from (something) previous]

a·pron (ā′prən) *n.* **1** a garment worn over the front

part of the body to cover or protect clothes: *a kitchen apron, a carpenter's apron.* **2** something resembling an apron in use or shape. **3** a protective shield or structure to prevent the washing away of a surface, such as a sea wall, river bank, etc. **4** a platform at the bottom of a sluice to intercept the fall of water. **5** *Lumbering.* a platform at the bottom of a log chute used to break the fall of the logs as they enter the water. **6** at an airport, an area, usually paved, next to the hangars or terminal. **7** in a theatre, the part of the stage in front of the curtain. **8** in geology, a sheet of sand or gravel in front of a moraine. **9** a thick formation of skin on the chest of a ram.
—*v.* put an apron on; provide with an apron. [ME *a napron* taken as *an apron* < OF *naperon*, dim. of *nape* < L *mappa* napkin] —**a′pron·like′**, *adj.*

apron strings **1** the ties used to fasten an apron. **2 tied to one's mother's apron strings,** dependent on, or dominated by, one's mother.

ap·ro·pos (ap′rə pō′) *adv.* **1** fittingly; opportunely. **2 apropos of,** with regard to. —*adj.* fitting; suitable; to the point: *an apropos remark.* [< F *à propos* to the purpose]

apse (aps) *n.* a semicircular or many-sided recess in a church, usually at the east end, having an arched or vaulted roof. [< L *apsis* < Gk. *hapsis* loop, arch < *haptein* fasten]

A plan of a church showing an apse

apt (apt) *adj.* **1** fitted by nature; likely: *A careless person is apt to make mistakes.* **2** suitable; fitting: *an apt reply.* **3** quick to learn: *an apt pupil.* [ME < L *aptus* joined, fitted] —**apt′ly**, *adv.* —**apt′ness**, *n.*
—**Syn. 1** prone, inclined, liable. **2** apposite, appropriate. **3** prompt, ready, clever, bright, intelligent.
☛ See **likely** for usage note.

apt. *pl.* **apts.** apartment.

ap·ter·ous (ap′tər əs) *adj.* in biology, wingless. Lice are apterous insects. [< Gk. *apteros* < *a-* without + *pteron* wing]

ap·ter·yx (ap′tər iks′) *n.* **-yx·es** (-ik′siz). any of several nearly extinct birds such as the kiwi, found in New Zealand. They are wingless, have hairlike feathers, and are about the size of a chicken. [< NL *apteryx* < *a-* without + Gk. *pteryx* wing]

ap·ti·tude (ap′tə tūd′ or ap′tə tüd′) *n.* **1** a natural tendency; ability; capacity: *Edison had a great aptitude for inventing new things.* **2** readiness in learning; quickness to understand. **3** a special fitness. [< LL *aptitudo* < L *aptus* joined, fitted. Doublet of ATTITUDE.]

aptitude test a test given to a person to find out the sort of work, studies, etc. for which he is specially suited.

AQ achievement quotient.

aq. aqua.

aq·ua (ak′wə) *n.* **1** water. **2** in pharmacy and chemistry, a liquid solution: *aqua fortis.* **3** aquamarine. —*adj.* light bluish-green. *Abbrev.:* aq. [< L]

aq·ua·cade (ak′wə kād′) *n.* a water entertainment consisting of swimming, diving, water skiing, group formations, etc., usually performed to the accompaniment of music. [< *aqua* + (*caval*)*cade*]

aq·ua for·tis (ak′wə fôr′tis) nitric acid. [< L *aqua fortis* strong water]

aq·ua·lung (ak′wə lung′) *n.* **1** a diving apparatus consisting of cylinders of compressed air strapped to the diver's back and a watertight mask placed over the eyes and nose. The supply of air to the diver is regulated automatically by a valve. **2 Aqua-Lung,** a trademark for such an apparatus.

aq·ua·ma·rine (ak′wə mə rēn′) *n.* **1** a transparent, bluish-green precious stone; a variety of beryl. **2** a piece of this stone, or a gem made from it. **3** a color ranging from pale to light greenish blue.
—*adj.* light bluish-green. [< L *aqua marina* sea water]

aq·ua·naut (ak′wə not′ or ak′wə nôt′) *n.* an underwater explorer. [< *aqua* + (*astro*)*naut*]

aq·ua·plane (ak′wə plān′) *n. v.* **-planed, -plan·ing.** —*n.* a wide board on which a person stands as it is towed by a speeding motorboat. —*v.* ride on an aquaplane. [< L *aqua* water + E *plane*[1]]

aq·ua re·gi·a (ak′wə rē′jē ə) a mixture of nitric acid and hydrochloric acid that will dissolve gold and platinum. [< NL *aqua regia* royal water, because it dissolves gold]

aq·ua·relle (ak′wə rel′) *n.* **1** a painting done with ink and transparent water colors. **2** the method of painting in this way.

a·quar·i·um (ə kwãr′ē əm) *n.* **a·quar·i·ums** or **a·quar·i·a** (ə kwãr′ē ə). **1** a pond, tank, or glass bowl in which living fish, water animals, and water plants are kept. **2** a building used for showing collections of living fish, water animals, and water plants. [< L *aquarium*, neut. of *aquarius* of water < *aqua* water]

A·quar·i·us (ə kwãr′ē əs) *n.* **1** in astronomy, a northern constellation supposed to represent a man standing with his left hand extended upward, and with his right pouring a stream of water out of a vase. **2** in astrology, the 11th sign of the zodiac; the Water Carrier. The sun enters Aquarius about January 12. See **zodiac** for diagram.

a·quat·ic (ə kwat′ik or ə kwot′ik) *adj.* **1** growing or living in water: *Water lilies are aquatic plants.* **2** taking place in or on water: *Swimming and sailing are aquatic sports.*
—*n.* **1** a plant or animal that lives in water. **2 aquatics,** *pl.* sports that take place in or on water.

aq·ua·tint (ak′wə tint′) *n.* **1** a process in which spaces, not lines, are etched by acid. **2** an etching made by this process. [< F *aquatinte* < Ital. *acqua tinta* < L *aqua* water, and *tincta* (fem.) dipped]

aq·ua·tone (ak′wə tōn′) *n.* **1** a process of photo-engraving in which the design is transferred to a sensitized aluminum plate coated with a mixture of gelatin and celluloid. **2** a print made by this process.

aq·ua vi·tae (ak′wə vī′tē or ak′wə vē′tī) **1** alcohol. **2** brandy; whisky, etc. [< NL *aqua vitae* water of life]

aq·ue·duct (ak′wə dukt′) *n.* **1** an artificial channel or large pipe for bringing water from a distance. **2** a structure that supports such a channel or pipe. **3** in anatomy, a canal or passage. [< L *aquaeductus* < *aqua* water + *ductus*, pp. of *ducere* lead, convey]

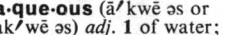

An aqueduct

a·que·ous (ā′kwē əs or ak′wē əs) *adj.* **1** of water; like water; watery. **2** containing water; made with water. **3** produced by the action of water: *Aqueous rocks are formed of the sediment carried and deposited by water.*

aqueous humor or **humour** the watery liquid that fills the space in the eye between the cornea and the lens. See **eye** for diagram.

Aq·ui·la (ak′wə lə) *n.* a northern constellation thought to resemble the outline of an eagle. It contains the star Altair. [< L *aquila* eagle]

aq·ui·line (ak′wə līn′ or ak′wə lin) *adj.* **1** of or like an eagle. **2** curved like an eagle's beak; hooked: *an aquiline nose.* [< L *aquilinus* < *aquila* eagle]

a·quiv·er (ə kwiv′ər) *adj.* trembling.

Ar argon.

Ar. **1** Arabia. **2** Arabic. **3** Aramaic. **4** silver. (for L *argentum*)

ar- the form of **ad-** before *r*, as in *arrive.*

Ar·ab (ar′əb) *n.* **1** a native or inhabitant of Arabia; member of a Semitic people now widely scattered over S.W. and S. Asia and N., E., and central Africa. **2** a member of an Arabic-speaking people. **3** a breed of swift, graceful horses that originally came from the Arabian peninsula. **4** a horse of this breed. **5** a

homeless little waif; street Arab.
—adj. of the Arabs; of the Arabian peninsula.
☛ **Arab, Arabian, Arabic should not be used interchangeably. Arab applies most commonly to the people or their culture:** ***Arab customs, the Arab world.*** **Arabian usually applies more to the territory traditionally recognized as the home of these people, specifically to the Arabian peninsula:** ***Arabian sands.*** **Arabic applies to the language of the Arabs and to their literature, art, etc.:** ***Arabic poetry.***

ar·a·besque (ar′ə besk′) *n.* **1** an elaborate and fanciful design of flowers, leaves, geometrical figures, etc. **2** in ballet, a pose in which the dancer stands on one leg with the other leg extended horizontally behind him. Traditionally, one arm is extended in front and the other arm behind. **3** in music: **a** an ornamentation, often elaborate, of a melody. **b** a short, graceful composition, often highly ornamented, resembling a rondo: *Debussy's piano arabesques.* *—adj.* **1** carved or painted in arabesque. **2** like arabesque; elaborate; fanciful.
—v. **1** decorate with arabesques. **2** in ballet, execute an arabesque. [< F < Ital. *arabesco* < *Arabo* Arab]

A·ra·bi·an (ə rā′bē ən) *adj.* of Arabia; of the Arabs.
—n. an Arab; a native or inhabitant of Arabia.
☛ See **Arab** for usage note.

Arabian Nights *The Thousand and One Nights,* a collection of old tales from Arabia, Persia, and India, dating from the tenth century A.D.

Ar·a·bic (ar′ə bik) *adj.* of the Arabs or their language; belonging to Arabia; coming from the Arabs: *Arabic figures.* *—n.* the language of the Arabs. ☛ See **Arab** for usage note.

Arabic numerals or **figures** the figures 1, 2, 3, 4, 5, 6, 7, 8, 9, 0. The Arabic numerals are so called because they were introduced into western Europe by Arabian scholars, but most probably they were derived from India. A more accurate name for the Arabic figures is Hindu-Arabic.

ar·a·ble (ar′ə bəl) *adj.* fit for ploughing: *There is little arable land on the side of a mountain.* [< L *arabilis* < *arare* plough]

Ar·a·by (ar′ə bē) *n. Poetic.* Arabia.

A·rach·ne (ə rak′nē) *n.* in Greek legend, a maiden who dared to challenge Athena to a contest in weaving, and was changed by her into a spider.

a·rach·nid (ə rak′nid) *n.* any of a large group of small arthropods including spiders, scorpions, mites, etc. An arachnid breathes air, has four pairs of walking legs and no antennae; its body is usually divided into only two segments. [< NL *Arachnidae* < Gk. *arachnē* spider, web]

A·rach·ni·dae (ə rak′ni dē′ or ə rak′ni dī′) *n.* in zoology, the class of arthropods comprising the arachnids. [< NL, pl. of *Arachnida* < Gk. *arachnē* spider, web]

a·rach·ni·dan (ə rak′nə dən) *adj.* of or having to do with arachnids. *—n.* an arachnid.

a·rach·noid (ə rak′noid) *adj.* **1** like a cobweb. **2** of or resembling an arachnid. **3** in physiology, of or having to do with the thin serous membrane that envelops the brain and spinal cord. **4** in botany, formed of, or covered with, fine hairs or fibres resembling cobwebs.
—n. **1** an arachnid. **2** the arachnoid membrane. [< NL < Gk. *arachnoeidēs* cobweblike < *arachnē* spider, web]

Ar·a·ma·ic (ar′ə mā′ik) *n.* a Semitic language or group of dialects, including Syriac and the language spoken in Palestine at the time of Christ. *—adj.* of or in Aramaic.

A·ra·wak (ä′rä wäk′) *n.* an American Indian belonging to an Arawakan-speaking tribe. Of short stature and peaceful disposition, the Arawaks now live mostly in Brazil.

A·ra·wak·an (ä′rä wä′kən) *n.* **1** a family of South American Indian languages, spoken by a group of tribes now found chiefly in northern South America, formerly found in the West Indies and Florida. **2** a member of one of these tribes; an Arawak. *—adj.* of or having to do with the Arawaks or their language.

ar·ba·lest or **ar·ba·list** (är′bə list) *n.* a powerful crossbow having a steel bow. [< OF *arbaleste* < LL *arcu-ballista* < *arcus* bow + *ballista* military engine, ult. < Gk. *ballein* throw]

ar·bi·ter (är′bə tər) *n.* **1** a person chosen to decide a dispute. **2** a person with full power to decide. [< L *arbiter*] **—Syn. 1** judge, umpire, arbitrator.

hat, āge, cãre, fär; let, ēqual, tėrm; it, īce
hot, ōpen, ôrder; oil, out; cup, pu̇t, rüle, ūse
əbove, takən, pencəl, lemən, circəs
ch, child; ng, long; sh, ship
th, thin; ᴛʜ, then; zh, measure

ar·bi·tra·ble (är′bə trə bəl) *adj.* capable of being decided by arbitration.

ar·bi·trage (är′bə trij) *n.* in commerce: **1** the calculation of the prices of certain stocks, bonds, etc. in different places at the same time, allowing for exchange rates. **2** the buying and selling of stocks, bonds, etc. in several markets simultaneously, to take advantage of price differences between markets. [< F < *arbitrer* arbitrate < L *arbitrare* < *arbiter* arbiter]

ar·bi·tral (är′bə trəl) *adj.* of arbiters; of arbitration.

ar·bit·ra·ment (är bit′rə mənt) *n.* **1** a decision by an arbitrator or arbiter. **2** the power to judge and decide.

ar·bi·trar·y (är′bə trer′ē) *adj.* **1** based on one's own wishes, notions, or will; not going by rule or law: *A good judge tries to be fair and does not make arbitrary decisions.* **2** capricious. **3** tyrannical: *an arbitrary general.* **—ar′bi·trar′i·ly,** *adv.* **—ar′bi·trar′i·ness,** *n.*
—Syn. 3 despotic.

ar·bi·trate (är′bə trāt′) *v.* **-trat·ed, -trat·ing. 1** give a decision in a dispute; act as arbiter: *arbitrate between two persons in a quarrel.* **2** settle by arbitration; submit to arbitration: *The two nations finally agreed to arbitrate their dispute.* [< L *arbitrari* < *arbiter.* See ARBITER.]

ar·bi·tra·tion (är′bə trā′shən) *n.* the settlement of a dispute by the decision of a judge, umpire, or arbiter.

ar·bi·tra·tor (är′bə trā′tər) *n.* **1** a person chosen to decide a dispute. **2** a person with full power to judge and decide. **—Syn. 1** judge, umpire.

ar·bi·tress (är′bə tris) *n.* a woman arbiter.

ar·bor[1] or **ar·bour** (är′bər) *n.* a shady place formed by trees or shrubs or often by vines growing on latticework. [ME < AF *erber* < LL *herbarium* < *herba* herb. Doublet of HERBARIUM.]

ar·bor[2] (är′bər) *n.* the main shaft or axle of a machine. [< F *arbre*]

Arbor Day or **Arbour Day** a day observed in certain Canadian provinces and in some other countries by planting trees. The date varies in different places.

ar·bo·re·al (är bô′rē əl) *adj.* **1** of trees; like trees. **2** living in or among trees: *A squirrel is an arboreal animal.*

ar·bo·re·tum (är′bə rē′təm) *n.* a place where trees and shrubs are grown for educational, scientific, and other purposes. [< L *arboretum* < *arbor* tree]

ar·bor·vi·tae (är′bər vī′tē or -vē′tī) *n.* **1** any of several evergreen trees of the pine family, having scale leaves and light, soft wood that is highly resistant to decay, often referred to as cedars. The white cedar and the western red cedar are arborvitae. **2** the wood of any of these trees, used especially for making posts, shingles boats, etc. Also, **arbor vitae.** [< L *abor vitae* tree of life]

ar·bour (är′bər) *n.* arbor[1].

ar·bu·tus (är būt′təs) *n.* **1** a trailing plant of E. North America, that has clusters of fragrant, pink or white flowers very early in the spring; Mayflower; trailing arbutus. **2** a shrub or tree of the same family as the heath, having large clusters of white or pinkish flowers and scarlet or orange-red berries. [< L]

arc (ärk) *n. v.* **arced** (ärkt) **arc·ing** (är′king) *—n.* **1** any part of a circle. **2** in geometry, a part of a curved line. **3** in electricity, a curved stream of brilliant light or sparks formed as the current jumps from one conductor to another. **4** in astronomy: **a** the part of a circle through which a heavenly body appears to pass above the horizon, called the **diurnal arc. b** the part of the same circle below the horizon, called the **nocturnal arc.**
—v. form an arc. [< L *arcus* bow]

Arcs of circles

ar·cade (är kād′) *n.* **1** a passageway with an arched roof. **2** any covered passageway: *Some buildings have arcades with small stores along either side.* **3** in architecture, a row of arches supported by columns. [< F < Provençal *arcado*, ult. < VL *arca*. See ARCH¹.]

An arcade (def. 1)

Ar·ca·di·a (är kā′dē ə) *n.* **1** a mountain district in the southern part of ancient Greece, famous for the simple, contented life of its people. **2** any region of simple, quiet contentment. [< L < Gk.] —**Ar·ca′di·an,** *adj., n.*

Ar·ca·dy (är′kə dē) *n. Poetic.* Arcadia.

ar·cane (är kān′) *adj.* hidden. [< L. See ARCANUM.]

ar·ca·num (är kā′nəm) *n.* **-nums** or **-na** (-nə). a secret; mystery. [< L *arcanum* (thing) hidden < *arca* chest]

arch¹ (ärch) *n.* **1** in architecture, a curved structure used in bridges, gateways, etc. as a support for the weight above it. **2** a structure containing an arch or arches, built as an ornament or gateway: *a triumphal arch.* **3** any curve in the shape of an arch. **4** in anatomy, the instep. Fallen arches cause flat feet. **5** something like an arch: *the great blue arch of the sky.* —*v.* **1** bend into an arch; curve. **2** furnish with an arch: *The rainbow arches the sky.* **3** form an arch over; span. [ME < OF < *arche* < VL *arca*, pl. < L *arcus* bow]

arch² (ärch) *adj.* **1** chief: *The arch rebel was Satan.* **2** playfully mischievous: *The little girl gave her mother an arch look.* [< *arch-*] —**arch′ly,** *adv.* —**arch′ness,** *n.*

arch- *prefix.* chief; principal: *archbishop = principal bishop; archduke = principal duke.* Also, **archi-.** [ME *arche-* < OE *arce-* < L *archi-* < Gk. *arche-*, combining form of *archos* chief]

arch. **1** archaic. **2** archaism. **3** architecture. **4** architect. **5** archipelago.

Arch. **1** Archbishop. **2** Archdeacon. **3** Archduke.

archaeo- *combining form.* ancient; primitive, as in *archaeology.* [< Gk. *archaios* ancient < *archē* beginning]

ar·chae·o·log·i·cal (är′kē ə loj′ə kəl) *adj.* of or having to do with archaeology. Also, **archeological.**

ar·chae·ol·o·gist (är′kē ol′ə jist) *n.* an expert in archaeology. Also, **archeologist.**

ar·chae·ol·o·gy (är′kē ol′ə jē) *n.* the study of the people, customs, and life of ancient times. Students of archaeology excavate, classify, and study the remains of ancient cities, tools, monuments, etc. Also, **archeology.** [< Gk. < *archaios* ancient + *-logos* treating of]

ar·chae·op·ter·yx (är′kē op′tər iks) *n.* the oldest-known fossil bird of the European Upper Jurassic period, about the size of a crow, having teeth, a lizardlike tail, and well-developed wings. Also, **ar·che·op·ter·yx.** [< *archaeo-* + Gk. *pteryx* wing]

ar·cha·ic (är kā′ik) *adj.* **1** no longer in general use. **2** old-fashioned; out-of-date. **3** ancient. [< Gk. *archaikos*, ult. < *archē* beginning]

ar·cha·ism (är′kē iz′əm or är′kā iz′əm) *n.* **1** a word or expression no longer in general use. *In sooth* and *methinks* are archaisms meaning *in truth* and *it seems to me.* **2** the use of something out of date in language or art.

arch·an·gel (ärk′ān′jəl) *n.* an angel of a very high rank. [ME < LL < Gk. *archangelos* < *arch-* chief + *angelos* angel]

arch·bish·op (ärch′bish′əp) *n.* a bishop of the highest rank. He presides over a church district called an archbishopric or archdiocese.

arch·bish·op·ric (ärch′bish′əp rik) *n.* **1** a church district governed by an archbishop. **2** the position, rank, or dignity of an archbishop.

arch·dea·con (ärch′dē′kən) *n.* an assistant to a bishop. In the Anglican Church, he superintends the work of other members of the clergy.

arch·dea·con·ate (ärch′dē′kən it) *n.* the office of an archdeacon.

arch·dea·con·ry (ärch′dē′kən rē) *n.* **-ries.** **1** a district under the supervision of an archdeacon. **2** the position or rank of an archdeacon. **3** the residence of an archdeacon.

arch·di·oc·e·san (ärch′dī os′ə sən) *adj.* of or having to do with an archdiocese.

arch·di·o·cese (ärch′dī′ə sis or ärch′dī′ə sēs′) *n.* the church district governed by an archbishop.

arch·du·cal (ärch′dū′kəl or ärch′dü′kəl) *adj.* of an archduke; of an archduchy.

arch·duch·ess (ärch′duch′is) *n.* **1** the wife or widow of an archduke. **2** a princess of the former ruling house of Austria-Hungary.

arch·duch·y (ärch′duch′ē) *n.* **-duch·ies.** the territory under the rule of an archduke or archduchess.

arch·duke (ärch′dūk′ or ärch′dük′) *n.* a prince of the former ruling house of Austria-Hungary.

arched (ärcht) *adj.* having an arch or arches.

ar·che·go·ni·um (är′kə gō′nē əm) *n.* **-ni·a** (-nē ə). in botany, the female reproductive organ in ferns, mosses, etc. [< NL *archegonium*, ult. < Gk. *archē* beginning + *genos* race]

arch·en·e·my (ärch′en′ə mē) *n.* **-mies.** **1** the chief enemy. **2** Satan.

ar·che·o·log·i·cal (är′kē ə loj′ə kəl) *adj.* archaeological.

ar·che·ol·o·gist (är′kē ol′ə jist) *n.* archaeologist.

ar·che·ol·o·gy (är′kē ol′ə jē) *n.* archaeology.

Ar·che·o·zo·ic (är′kē ə zō′ik) *n.* in geology: **1** the oldest era. During this era, commencing about 2 billion years ago, living things first appeared. See the chart under **geology. 2** the rocks formed during this era. —*adj.* of or having to do with this era or the rocks formed during it. [< *archeo-* (var. of *archaeo-*) + Gk. *zōē* life]

arch·er (är′chər) *n.* **1** a person who shoots with a bow and arrows. **2 Archer,** in astrology, the ninth sign of the zodiac; Sagittarius. [< AF < L *arcarius* < *arcus* bow]

arch·er·y (är′chər ē) *n.* **1** the practice or art of shooting with bows and arrows. **2** a troop of archers. **3** the weapons of an archer; bows, arrows, etc.

ar·che·type (är′kə tīp′) *n.* an original model or pattern from which copies are made, or out of which later forms develop: *That little engine is the archetype of huge modern locomotives.* [< L < Gk. *archetypon*, neut. of *archetypos* original]

arch·fiend (ärch′fēnd′) *n.* **1** the chief fiend. **2** Satan.

archi- *prefix.* a variant of **arch-,** as in *archi-episcopal.*

ar·chi·e·pis·co·pal (är′kē i pis′kə pəl) *adj.* of or having to do with an archbishop.

Ar·chi·me·de·an (är′kə mē′dē ən) *adj.* of, having to do with, or invented by Archimedes.

Ar·chi·me·des principle (är′kə mē′dēz) in physics, the principle that the apparent loss of weight of a body when partly or totally immersed in a liquid is equal to the weight of the liquid displaced. [after *Archimedes*, 287?-212 B.C., a Greek mathematician, physicist, and inventor, who discovered this principle]

ar·chi·pel·a·go (är′kə pel′ə gō′) *n.* **-gos** or **-goes.** **1** a sea having many islands in it. **2** a group of many islands: *The islands in the Arctic Ocean north of Canada are called the Canadian Archipelago. Abbrev.:* arch. [< Ital. *arcipelago* < *arci-* chief (ult. < Gk. *archi-*) + *pelago* sea (ult. < Gk. *pelagos*); originally, the Aegean]

ar·chi·tect (är′kə tekt′) *n.* **1** a person skilled in architecture. **2** a person who designs buildings and sees that his plans are followed by the contractors and workers who actually put up the buildings. **3** a designer; maker; creator. [< L *architectus* < Gk. *architekton* < *archi-* chief + *tekton* builder]

ar·chi·tec·ton·ic (är′kə tek ton′ik) *adj.* **1** having to do with architecture, construction, or design. **2** showing skill in construction or design. **3** directive; controlling.

ar·chi·tec·ton·ics (är′kə tek ton′iks) *n.* **1** the science of architecture. **2** skill in architecture. **3** any skill in the construction or design of a work of art. **4** the product of such skill; the design or structure of a work of art.

ar·chi·tec·tur·al (är′kə′tek′chər əl) *adj.* of architecture; having to do with architecture. —**ar′chi·tec′tur·al·ly,** *adv.*

ar·chi·tec·ture (är′kə tek′chər) *n.* **1** the science or art of building; the planning and designing of buildings. **2** a style or special manner of building: *Greek architecture made much use of columns.* **3** construction: *the flimsy architecture of some buildings.* **4** a building; structure.

ar·chi·trave (är′kə trāv′) *n.* in architecture: **1** the main beam resting on the top of a column. See **entablature** for diagram. **2** the moulding around a door, window, or arch. [< Ital. *architrave* < *archi-* chief (ult. < Gk.) + *trave* beam < L *trabs, trabis*]

ar·chives (är′kīvz) *n.pl.* **1** a place where public records or historical documents are kept: *The Dominion Archives are in Ottawa.* **2** the records and documents kept in such a place. [< F < L *archivum* < Gk. *archeia* < *archē* government]

ar·chon (är′kon) *n.* **1** in ancient Athens, a chief magistrate. **2** a ruler. [< Gk. *archōn*, ppr. of *archein* rule]

arch·way (ärch′wā′) *n.* **1** an entrance or passageway with an arch above it. **2** an arch covering a passageway.

arc lamp a lamp in which the light comes from an electric arc.

arc light 1 the brilliant light given by an arc lamp. **2** an arc lamp.

arc·tic (ärk′tik or är′tik) *adj.* **1** near the North Pole; of the north polar region: *the arctic fox.* **2** extremely cold; frigid. *—n.pl.* **arctics**, warm, waterproof overshoes. [ME < OF < L *arcticus* < Gk. *arktikos* of the Bear (constellation) < *arktos* bear]

Arc·tic (ärk′tik or är′tik) *n.* **1** the north polar region. **2** the Arctic Ocean.

arctic char a kind of trout found in the far north.

Arctic Circle or **arctic circle 1** an imaginary boundary of the north polar region running parallel to the equator at 23 degrees 30 minutes (23°30′) south of the North Pole. **2** the polar region surrounded by this parallel.

arctic fox a fox of the arctic regions, valued for its fur. Its coat is bluish- or brownish-gray in summer and white in winter.

Arc·tu·rus (ärk tūr′əs or ärk tür′əs) *n.* a first magnitude star in the constellation Boötes.

Ar·den (är′dən) *n.* **1** a district or forest in the central and formerly also the eastern part of England. **2** a land of the imagination or of romance.

ar·den·cy (är′dən sē) *n.* the condition of being ardent.

ar·dent (är′dənt) *adj.* **1** full of zeal; very enthusiastic; eager. **2** burning; fiery; hot. **3** glowing. [ME < OF < L *ardens, -entis*, ppr. of *ardere* burn] —**ar′dent·ly,** *adv.*
—**Syn. 1** fervent, keen.

ardent spirits strong alcoholic liquor.

ar·dor or **ar·dour** (är′dər) *n.* **1** eagerness; warmth of emotion; great enthusiasm: *patriotic ardor.* **2** burning heat. [ME < OF < L *ardor* < *ardere* burn]

ar·du·ous (är′jü əs) *adj.* **1** hard to do; requiring much effort; difficult: *an arduous lesson.* **2** using up much energy; strenuous: *an arduous effort to learn the lesson.* **3** hard to climb; steep: *an arduous hill.* [< L *arduus* steep] —**ar′du·ous·ly,** *adv.* —**ar′du·ous·ness,** *n.*

are[1] (är; *unstressed,* ər) *v.* the plural and the second person singular, present indicative of **be**: *we are, you are, they are.* [OE (Northumbrian) *aron*]

are[2] (ãr or är) *n.* in the metric system, a unit of surface measure equal to 100 square metres, or 119.6 square yards. *Abbrev.*: a [< F < L *area* area]

ar·e·a (ãr′ē ə) *n.* **1** the amount of surface; extent of surface: *The area of this floor is 600 square feet.* **2** a region: *The Rocky Mountain area is the most mountainous in Canada.* **3** range; scope: *The provincial governments often try to limit the area of federal responsibility.* **4** a field of study or activity: *He is working in the area of foreign policy.* **5** a level space. **6** a yard or court of a building. **7** in the Canadian Army, an administrative subdivision commanded by a brigadier and responsible to Command Headquarters. [< L *area* piece of level ground]
—**Syn. 3** tract.

hat, āge, cãre, fär; let, ēqual, tėrm; it, īce
hot, ōpen, ôrder; oil, out; cup, pu̇t, rüle, ūse
əbove, takən, pencəl, lemən, circəs
ch, child; ng, long; sh, ship
th, thin; ᴛʜ, then; zh, measure

ar·e·a·way (ãr′ē ə wā′) *n.* **1** a sunken area or court at the entrance to a cellar or basement. **2** an area serving as a passageway between buildings.

ar·e·ca (ar′i kə or ə rē′kə) *n.* a kind of tropical palm. [< Port. < Tamil *adaikay*]

ar·e·ca-nut (ar′ik ə nut′ or ə rē′kə-) *n.* the nut of the areca palm, often called the betel nut.

a·re·na (ə rē′nə) *n.* **1** a space where contests or shows take place. **2** any place of conflict and trial. **3** a building in which certain sports are played. [< later var. of L *harena* sand; because the floors of Roman arenas were covered with sand]

ar·e·na·ceous (ar′ə nā′shəs) *adj.* sandy.

arena rat *Slang.* rink rat.

aren't (ärnt) are not.

a·re·o·la (ə rē′ə lə) *n.* **-lae** (-lē′ or -lī′) or **-las. 1** a little area. **2** in anatomy, the small, often colored, ring around something, as around a nipple, pimple, etc. **3** in biology, an interstice. The spaces between the veins of a leaf are areolae. Also, **ar·e·ole** (är′ē ōl′). [< L *areola* dim. of *area* area]

Ar·e·op·a·gus (ar′ē op′ə gəs) *n.* **1** the hill of Ares in Athens. **2** the highest judicial court of ancient Athens, which met there.

Ar·es (ãr′ēz) *n.* in Greek mythology, the god of war, identified with the Roman god Mars.

a·rête (ə rāt′) *n.* a sharp, rocky ridge on a mountain, usually above the winter snow line. [< F]

ar·e·thu·sa (ar′ə thü′zə or ar′ə thü′sə) *n.* any of a genus of plants of the orchid family having a single, fragrant, pink or purple flower. [< *Arethusa*, a nymph in Greek mythology]

ar·gent (är′jənt) *n.* **1** *Archaic or Poetic.* silver. **2** in heraldry, the silver or white coloring in a coat of arms. *—adj.* silvery. *Abbrev.*: a. [< F < L *argentum*]

Ar·gen·tine (är′jən tēn′ or är′jən tīn′) *adj.* of Argentina or its people. *—n.* **1** a native or inhabitant of Argentina. **2 the Argentine,** Argentina.

ar·gen·tite (är′jen tīt′) *n.* a native silver sulphide, found in veins in granite and other rock strata. This dark-gray substance is an important ore of silver. *Formula*: Ag_2S [< L *argentum* silver + E *-ite*[1]]

ar·gil (är′jil) *n.* clay; especially, clay used for pottery. [< F *argille* < L < Gk. *argilla* < *argos* shining]

ar·gil·lite (är′jə līt′) *n.* a slate or schist derived from clay. [< L *argilla* white clay + E *-ite*[1]]

Ar·give (är′jīv or är′gīv) *adj.* **1** of Argos. **2** Greek. *—n.* **1** a native or inhabitant of Argos. **2** Greek.

Ar·go (är′gō) *n.* in Greek legend, the ship in which Jason and his companions sailed in search of the Golden Fleece.

ar·gon (är′gon) *n.* a chemical element that is a colorless, odorless, inert gas forming a very small part of the air. Argon is used in electric light bulbs and radio tubes. *Symbol*: A or Ar; *at.no.* 18; *at.wt.* 39.948. [< NL< Gk. *argos* idle < *a-* without + *ergon* work]

Ar·go·naut (är′gə not′ or är′gə nôt′) *n.* **1** in Greek legend, one of the men who sailed with Jason in search of the Golden Fleece. **2** a person who went to California to search for gold in 1849. **3** a person who went from E. Canada in 1862 to search for gold in the Cariboo in British Columbia. [< L *Argonauta* < Gk. *Argonautēs* < *Argō*, the name of the ship used by Jason, + *nautēs* sailor]

ar·go·sy (är′gə sē) *n.* **-sies. 1** a large merchant ship. **2** a fleet of such ships. [< Ital. *Ragusea* ship of Ragusa, Italian port formerly trading extensively with England]

ar·got (är′gō or är′gət) *n.* the jargon or slang used by a particular class of persons: *the argot of thieves.* [< F]

ar·gue (är′gū) *v.* **-gued, -gu·ing. 1** discuss with someone who disagrees. **2** give reasons for or against something: *argue a question. He argued against the passage of the bill.* **3** persuade by giving reasons: *He argued me into going.* **4** try to prove by reasoning; maintain: *Columbus argued that the world was round.* **5** indicate; show; prove: *Her rich clothes argue her wealth.* **6** raise objections; dispute. [ME < OF *arguer* < L *argutare*, frequentative of *arguere* make clear] —**ar′gu·er,** *n.* —**Syn. 1** debate. See **discuss. 5** demonstrate, denote, imply.

ar·gu·ment (är′gyů mənt) *n.* **1** a discussion by persons who disagree. **2** the act of giving reasons for or against something. **3** the reason or reasons given for or against something. **4** a short statement of what is in a book, poem, etc.

Syn. 1 Argument, controversy, dispute = a discussion by persons who disagree. **Argument** applies to a discussion in which each of two persons uses facts and reasons to try to win the other over: *He won the argument by producing figures.* **Controversy** applies chiefly to a formal argument between groups, often carried on in writing or speeches: *The Canadian school controversy still continues.* **Dispute** suggests contradicting rather than reasoning, and applies to an argument marked by feeling: *The dispute over the property was settled in court.*

ar·gu·men·ta·tion (är′gyů men tā′shən) *n.* **1** the process of arguing; reasoning. **2** discussion; debate.

ar·gu·men·ta·tive (är′gyů men′tə tiv) *adj.* **1** fond of arguing. **2** containing argument. —**ar′gu·men′ta·tive·ly,** *adv.*

Ar·gus (är′gəs) *n.* **1** in Greek legend, a giant with a hundred eyes. He was killed by Hermes, and his eyes were put in the peacock's tail. **2** any watchful guardian.

Ar·gus-eyed (är′gəs īd′) *adj.* watchful; observant.

ar·gyle or **Ar·gyle** (är gīl′) *adj.* of or having to do with a diamond-shaped pattern of various colors, often knitted into articles such as socks, neckties, etc. [< *Argyll*, a county in Scotland]

Ar·gy·rol (är′jə rōl′ or är′jə rol′) *n. Trademark.* a compound of silver and a protein, used in the treatment of inflamed mucous membranes. [< Gk. *argyros* silver]

a·ri·a (ä′rē ə or ãr′ē ə) *n.* an air or melody; a melody for a single voice with instrumental or vocal accompaniment. [< Ital. < L *aer* air < Gk.]

Ar·i·ad·ne (ar′ē ad′nē) *n.* in Greek legend, the daughter of Minos, king of Crete. She fell in love with Theseus and gave him a ball of thread to help him find his way out of the Labyrinth of the Minotaur.

Ar·i·an (ãr′ē ən) *adj.* of or having to do with the doctrine of Arius of Alexandria (4th c.) who taught that Jesus Christ is not of the same substance as God the Father. —*n.* a believer in this doctrine.

ar·id (ar′id) *adj.* **1** dry; barren: *Desert lands are arid.* **2** dull; uninteresting: *an arid, tiresome speech.* [< L *aridus* < *arere* be dry] —**ar′id·ly,** *adv.* —**ar′id·ness,** *n.* —**Syn. 1** See **dry. 2** lifeless.

a·rid·i·ty (ə rid′ə tē) *n.* **1** dryness; barrenness. **2** dullness; lack of interest, life, or spirit.

Ar·ies (ãr′ēz or ãr′ē ēz′) *n.* **1** in astronomy, a northern constellation named from its fancied arrangement in the shape of a ram. **2** in astrology, the first sign of the zodiac; the Ram. The sun enters Aries about March 21. See the diagram of **zodiac.**

a·right (ə rīt′) *adv.* correctly; rightly.

ar·il (ar′il) *n.* in botany, an outside covering of certain seeds. The pulpy inner pod of the bittersweet is an aril. [< NL *arillus* < Med.L *arilli* raisins]

ar·il·late (ar′ə lāt′) *adj.* in botany, having an aril.

a·ri·o·so (ä′rē ō′sō) *adj. adv. n.* **-sos.**—*adj. adv.* in music, as or like an aria or song. —*n.* a passage or piece of music to be sung as an aria or song. [< Ital. *arioso* songlike < *aria* aria]

a·rise (ə rīz′) *v.* **a·rose, a·ris·en, a·ris·ing. 1** rise up; get up: *The children arose from their seats to greet the teacher.* **2** move upward: *Smoke arises from the chimney.* **3** come into being or action; come about; appear; begin: *A great wind arose.* **4** result (*from*); be caused: *Accidents arise from carelessness.* [OE *ārīsan*] —**Syn. 2** ascend, mount. ☛ See **rise** for usage note.

a·ris·en (ə riz′ən) *v.* pp. of **arise.**

ar·is·toc·ra·cy (ar′is tok′rə sē) *n.* **-cies. 1** people of noble rank, title, or birth; a ruling body of nobles; nobility. **2** any class that is considered superior because of birth, intelligence, culture, or wealth; upper class. **3** a government in which a privileged upper class rules. **4** a country or state having such a government; oligarchy. **5** government by the best citizens. [< LL *aristocratia* < Gk. *aristokratia* < *aristos* best + *kratein* rule]

a·ris·to·crat (ə ris′tə krat′ or ar′is tə krat′) *n.* **1** a person who belongs to the aristocracy; noble. **2** a person who has the tastes, opinions, manners, etc. of the upper classes. **3** a person who favors government by an aristocracy.

a·ris·to·crat·ic (ə ris′tə krat′ik or ar′is tə krat′ik) *adj.* **1** belonging to the upper classes; superior in birth, intelligence, culture, or wealth. **2** like an aristocrat in manners, tastes, etc.; proud. **3** having to do with an aristocracy. —**a·ris′to·crat′i·cal·ly,** *adv.*

Ar·is·to·te·li·an (ar′is tə tē′lē ən or ar′is tə tēl′yən) *adj.* having to do with the Greek philosopher Aristotle (384-322 B.C.) or his philosophy. —*n.* a follower of Aristotle.

arith. 1 arithmetic. **2** arithmetical.

a·rith·me·tic (ə rith′mə tik′) *n.* **1** the science of positive real numbers; art of computing by figures. **2** a textbook or handbook dealing with this subject. [ME < OF < L *arithmetica* < Gk. *arithmētikē* < *arithmos* number]

ar·ith·met·i·cal (ar′ith met′ə kəl) *adj.* of arithmetic; having to do with arithmetic.

ar·ith·met·i·cal·ly (ar′ith met′ik lē) *adv.* according to arithmetic; by the use of arithmetic.

arithmetical progression a series in which there is always the same difference between a number and the one next after it. 2, 4, 6, 8, 10 are in arithmetical progression; so are 8, 5, 2, –1.

a·rith·me·ti·cian (ə rith′mə tish′ən or ar′ith mə tish′ən) *n.* an expert in arithmetic.

Ariz. Arizona.

Ar·i·zo·nan (ar′ə zō′nən) *adj.* of or having to do with Arizona. —*n.* a native or inhabitant of Arizona.

Ar·i·zo·ni·an (ar′ə zō′nē ən) *adj. n.* Arizonan.

ark (ärk) *n.* **1** in the Bible, the large boat in which Noah saved himself, his family, and a pair of each kind of animal from the Flood. **2** *Informal.* any large, clumsy boat. **3** the Ark of the Covenant. [OE *arc* < L *arca* chest]

Ark. Arkansas.

Ark of the Covenant 1 the wooden chest or box in which the ancient Hebrews kept the two tablets of stone containing the Ten Commandments. **2** the wooden chest in a synagogue that symbolizes this.

arm[1] (ärm) *n.* **1** the upper limb of the human body between the shoulder and the hand. **2** a forelimb of an animal. The front legs of a bear are sometimes called arms. **3** anything resembling an arm in shape or use: *the arm of a chair, an arm of the sea.* **4** the part of a garment covering the arm. **5** power; authority: *the strong arm of the law.* **6 arm in arm,** with arms linked: *She walked arm in arm with her sister.* **7 with open arms,** in a warm, friendly way; cordially. [OE *earm*] —**arm′less,** *adj.*

arm[2] (ärm) *n.* **1** a weapon: *A gun, a sword, an axe, a stick—any of these might be arms for defence or attack.* See **arms. 2** a branch of the armed services: *the air arm. The navy is the most vital arm of Britain's forces.* **3** a branch of one of the armed services, such as the infantry, the artillery, or the Fleet Air Arm.
—*v.* **1** supply with weapons; equip with armament. **2** take up weapons; prepare for war. **3** provide with a protective covering. **4** provide with a means of defence or attack: *Armed with additional statistics, he convinced the committee that more parks were necessary.* [sing. of *arms*, ME *armes* < OF < L *arma*, pl.]

Arm. Armenian.

ar·ma·da (är mad′ə or är mä′də) *n.* **1** a fleet of warships.

2 a fleet of airplanes. 3 **the Armada,** the Spanish fleet that was sent to attack England in 1588. [< Sp. < L *armata* armed force, originally pp. neut. pl. of *armare* to arm. Doublet of ARMY.]

ar·ma·dil·lo (är′mə dil′ō) *n.* **-los.** any of several small burrowing mammals of South America and some parts of southern North America, having an armorlike shell of bony plates. Some armadillos can roll up into a ball when attacked. [< Sp. *armadillo* dim. of *armado* armed (one) < L *armatus,* pp. of *armare* arm]

Ar·ma·ged·don (är′mə ged′ən) *n.* 1 in the Bible, the scene of a great and final conflict between the forces of good and evil. Rev. 16:16. 2 any great and final conflict. [< LL < Gk., probably < Hebrew]

ar·ma·ment (är′mə mənt) *n.* 1 war equipment and supplies. 2 all the armed services of a nation. 3 preparation for war. 4 the guns on a naval vessel, tank, airplane, etc.

ar·ma·ture (är′mə chər) *n.* 1 armor. 2 a part of an animal or plant serving for offence (teeth, claws) or defence (shells, thorns): *A turtle's shell is an armature.* 3 wire wound round and round a cable. 4 a piece of soft iron placed in contact with the poles of a magnet. 5 a revolving part of an electric motor or dynamo. 6 a movable part of an electric relay or buzzer. 7 in sculpture, a framework over which a figure is modelled. [< L *armatura* < *armare* arm. Doublet of ARMOR.]

arm·band (ärm′band′) *n.* a circlet of cloth, worn around the sleeve as a sign of rank, office, etc. Black armbands are usually a sign of mourning.

arm·chair (ärm′chãr′) *n.* a chair with side pieces to support a person's arms or elbows.
—*adj.* 1 of or having to do with an armchair. 2 of or having to do with actions, opinions, etc. based on theory rather than on practical experience or knowledge: *Armchair politicians have no idea of the real difficulties of government.* 3 sharing by reading, etc. in another's experiences: *an armchair explorer.* 4 of or having to do with work done by the intellect rather than by physical effort: *an armchair detective.*

armed forces the combined military strength of a nation, including sea, land, and air elements, or navy, army, and air force. Also, **armed services.**

arm·ful (ärm′fu̇l′) *n.* **-fuls.** as much as one arm or both arms can hold.

arm·hole (ärm′hōl′) *n.* a hole for the arm in a garment.

Ar·min·i·an (är min′ē ən) *adj.* of Arminius, an early Dutch theologian (1560-1609), or his doctrines. —*n.* a believer in Arminian doctrines.

ar·mi·stice (är′mə stis) *n.* a temporary stop in fighting by agreement on all sides; truce. [< NL *armistitium* < L *arma* arms + *sistere* stop, stand]

Armistice Day 1 November 11, the date of the cessation of fighting (1918) in World War I, now called **Remembrance Day.** 2 the anniversary of this date, celebrating also the cessation of fighting in World War II.

arm·let (ärm′lit) *n.* 1 an ornamental band for the upper arm. 2 a small inlet of the sea.

ar·moire (är′mwär′) *n.* a large, usually ornate, wardrobe, closet, or cupboard. [< F *armoire* < OF *armarie* < L *armarium* cabinet, ult. < *arma* weapons]

ar·mor or **ar·mour** (är′mər) *n.* 1 a covering worn to protect the body in fighting. 2 any kind of protective covering. A diver's suit and the scales of a fish are armor. 3 the steel or iron plates or other protective covering of a warship, airplane, or fortification. 4 anything that protects or defends: *An informed public opinion is the best armor against propaganda.*
—*v.* cover or protect with armor. [ME < OF *armeüre* < L *armatura* < *armare* arm. Doublet of ARMATURE.]

HELMET
GORGET
BRASSARD
BREAST-PLATE
GAUNTLET
CUISSE
JAMB

Armor (def. 1)

ar·mor·bear·er or **ar·mour·bear·er** (är′mər bãr′ər) *n.* formerly, an attendant who carried the armor or weapons of a warrior.

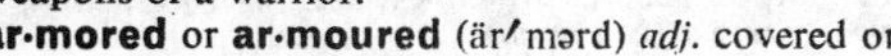

ar·mored or **ar·moured** (är′mərd) *adj.* covered or protected with armor.

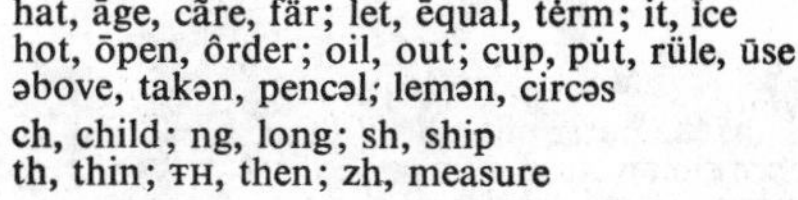

armored car or **armoured car** 1 a car or truck for transporting large sums of money, etc., shielded from small-arms fire by armor plate. 2 a similarly protected military vehicle, used especially for reconnaissance.

ar·mored corps or **ar·moured corps** the part of the army equipped with tanks and other armored vehicles.

ar·mor·er or **ar·mour·er** (är′mər ər) *n.* 1 a maker or repairer of armor. 2 a manufacturer of firearms. 3 a man in charge of firearms. The armorer of a warship takes care of the revolvers, pistols, and rifles on the ship.

ar·mo·ri·al (är mô′rē əl) *adj.* having to do with coats of arms or heraldry.

armorial bearings a coat of arms.

ar·mor·ies or **ar·mour·ies** (är′mər ēz′) *n.pl.* an armory (def. 3).

armor plate or **armour plate** steel or iron plating to protect warships, forts, etc.

ar·mor·y or **ar·mour·y** (är′mər ē) *n.* **-ies.** 1 a place where weapons are kept; arsenal. 2 a building where militia or reserve units of the armed services do their training. 3 *U.S.* a place where weapons are made.

ar·mour (är′mər) *n. v.* armor.

arm·pit (ärm′pit′) *n.* the hollow under the arm at the shoulder.

arms (ärmz) *n.pl.* 1 weapons. 2 fighting; war. 3 symbols and designs used in heraldry or, as emblems of official dignity, by governments, cities, corporations, etc. 4 **bear arms, a** serve as a soldier. **b** possess and display a coat of arms. 5 **carry arms,** have weapons. 6 **to arms!** a command to prepare for battle. 7 **under arms,** having weapons; equipped for fighting. 8 **up in arms, a** preparing for battle. **b** in rebellion. **c** angry; indignant.

ar·my (är′mē) *n.* **-mies.** 1 a large, organized group of soldiers trained and armed for war. 2 Often, **Army.** a nation's army. 3 in Canada, the land element. 4 a body organized on military lines: *the Salvation Army.* 5 a very large number; multitude: *an army of ants.* [ME < OF *armee* < L *armata.* Doublet of ARMADA.]
—**Syn. 1** troops. 4 throng, host.

army of occupation an army sent into a defeated country to enforce a treaty, keep order, etc.

army worm the larva of any of various moths that travel in large numbers and destroy grass and grain crops.

ar·ni·ca (är′nə kə) *n.* 1 a healing liquid used on bruises, sprains, etc., prepared from the dried flowers, leaves, or roots of a plant of the aster family. 2 the plant itself, which has showy yellow flowers. [< NL]

a·ro·ma (ə rō′mə) *n.* 1 a fragrance; spicy odor. 2 a distinctive fragrance or flavor; subtle quality. [ME < OF < L < Gk. *arōma* spice]

ar·o·mat·ic (ar′ə mat′ik) *adj.* sweet-smelling; fragrant; spicy. —*n.* a fragrant plant or substance.

a·rose (ə rōz′) *v.* pt. of **arise**: *She arose from her chair.*

a·round (ə round′) *prep.* 1 in a circle about: *travel around the world.* 2 closely surrounding: *She had a coat around her shoulders.* 3 on all sides of: *Woods lay around the house.* 4 *Informal.* here and there in: *He leaves his books around the house.* 5 *Informal.* somewhere near: *play around the house.* 6 *Informal.* approximately; near in amount, number, etc. to: *That hat cost around five dollars.* 7 on the far side of: *just around the corner.*
—*adv.* 1 in a circle. 2 in circumference: *The tree measures four feet around.* 3 on all sides: *A dense fog lay around.* 4 here and there: *We walked around to see the town.* 5 *Informal.* somewhere near: *Wait around awhile.* 6 in the opposite direction: *Turn around! You are going the wrong way.* ☞ See **round** for usage note.

a·rouse (ə rouz′) *v.* **a·roused, a·rous·ing.** 1 awaken. 2 stir to action; excite. —**a·rous′er,** *n.* —**Syn. 2** stimulate, kindle.

ar·peg·gi·o (är pej′ē ō or är pej′ō) *n.* **-gi·os.** in music: **1** the sounding of the notes of a chord in rapid succession instead of together. **2** a chord sounded in this way. [< Ital. *arpeggio* < *arpa* harp < Gmc.]

An arpeggio

ar·pent (är′pənt; *French,* är päN′) *n.* **1** a unit of length equal to about 63 yards. **2** an ancient French measure of land, used in Quebec, equal almost to an acre. [< F]

ar·que·bus (är′kwə bəs) *n.* harquebus.

arr. **1** arrange. **2** arranged. **3** arrangements. **4** arrival. **5** arrive. **6** arrived.

ar·raign (ə rān′) *v.* **1** in law, bring before a court for trial: *The tramp was arraigned on a charge of stealing.* **2** call in question; find fault with. [ME < AF *arainer* < VL < L *ad-* to + *ratio, -onis* account] **—ar·raign′er,** *n.* —**Syn. 2** accuse.

ar·raign·ment (ə rān′mənt) *n.* **1** in law, the act of bringing before a court to answer a charge; indictment. **2** unfavorable criticism.

ar·range (ə rānj′) *v.* **-ranged, -rang·ing. 1** put in the proper order: *The army is arranged for battle.* **2** settle (a dispute). **3** come to an agreement. **4** plan; prepare: *Can you arrange to meet me this evening?* **5** in music, adapt (a composition) to voices or instruments for which it was not written. [ME < OF *arangier* < *a-* to + *rang* rank[1] < Gmc.] **—ar·rang′er,** *n.* —**Syn. 1** group, sort, classify, organize. **2** adjust. **4** contrive.

ar·range·ment (ə rānj′mənt) *n.* **1** a putting or being put in proper order. **2** a way or order in which things or persons are put: *You can make six arrangements of the letters A, B, and C.* **3** an adjustment; settlement. **4** Usually, **arrangements,** *pl.* a plan; preparation: *make arrangements for a journey.* **5** something arranged in a particular way. **6** in music: **a** an adaptation of a composition to voices or instruments for which it was not written. **b** a composition so adapted.

ar·rant (ar′ənt) *adj.* thoroughgoing; downright: *He was such an arrant liar that nobody believed him.* [var. of *errant*]

ar·ras (ar′əs) *n.* **1** a kind of tapestry. **2** a curtain or hangings of tapestry. [from *Arras,* a city in France]

ar·ray (ə rā′) *n.* **1** order: *The troops were formed in battle array.* **2** a display of persons or things: *The array of good players on the other team made our side lose confidence.* **3** military force; soldiers. **4** clothes; dress: *bridal array.* **5** in law, the list of jurors summoned for a trial.
—*v.* **1** arrange in order: *The general arrayed his troops for the battle.* **2** dress in fine clothes; adorn. [ME < OF *a* to (< L *ad*) + *rei* order < Gmc.] —**Syn.** *n.* **1** formation. **3** troops. **4** attire. —*v.* **1** marshal.

ar·rear·age (ə rēr′ij) *n.* debts; arrears.

ar·rears (ə rērz′) *n.pl.* **1** money due but not paid; debts. **2** unfinished work; things not done on time. **3 in arrears,** behind in payments, work, etc. [ME < OF *arere* < LL *ad retro* to the rear]

ar·rest (ə rest′) *v.* **1** seize a person or persons by legal authority; take to jail or court. **2** stop; check: *Filling a tooth arrests decay.* **3** catch and hold.
—*n.* **1** the seizing of a person or persons by legal authority; a taking to jail or court. **2** a stopping; checking. **3 under arrest,** held by the police. [ME < OF *arester* < VL *adrestare* < L *ad-* + *re-* back + *stare* stand] **—ar·rest′er,** *n.* —**Syn.** *v.* **1** apprehend. **2** halt. See **stop. 3** capture.

ar·rest·ing (ə rest′ing) *adj.* catching the attention; striking: *She is not beautiful, but she has arresting eyes.*

ar·ris (ar′is) *n.* in architecture: **1** a sharp edge formed by two straight or curved surfaces meeting at an angle. **2** a sharp ridge. A Doric column has arrises. [< OF *areste* < L *arista* ear of corn, fishbone]

ar·riv·al (ə rīv′əl) *n.* **1** the act of arriving; a coming. **2** a person or thing that arrives.

ar·rive (ə rīv′) *v.* **-rived, -riv·ing. 1 arrive at,** come to; reach: *You should arrive at school before nine o'clock. You must arrive at a decision soon.* **2** reach the end of a journey; come to a place. **3** come; occur: *The time has arrived for you to study.* **4** be successful. [ME < OF *ar(r)iver* < VL < L *ad ripam* to the shore] — **Syn. 2** See **come.**

☛ Arrive is generally followed by *at,* especially when the place reached is only a temporary stopping point: *We arrived at the bridge, the stadium, the seashore, at Winnipeg* (when the city is just a stage in a journey). *He has not yet arrived at a decision.* When a city or town is thought of as the end of a journey, *arrive in* is used: *We arrived in Kingston a week ago.*

ar·ro·gance (ar′ə gəns) *n.* too great pride; haughtiness.

ar·ro·gant (ar′ə gənt) *adj.* too proud; haughty. [ME < OF < L *arrogans, -antis,* ppr. of *arrogare* < *ad-* to + *rogare* ask] **—ar′ro·gant·ly,** *adv.* —**Syn.** overbearing, presumptuous. See **haughty.**

ar·ro·gate (ar′ə gāt′) *v.* **-gat·ed, -gat·ing. 1** claim or take without right: *The despotic king arrogated to himself the power that belonged to the nobles.* **2** claim for another without good reasons: *People are only too ready to arrogate dishonesty to a politician.* [< L *arrogare* < *ad-* to + *rogare* ask]

ar·ro·ga·tion (ar′ə gā′shən) *n.* the act of arrogating.

ar·ron·disse·ment (ä rôN dēs mäN′) *n.* **-ments** (-mäN′). *French.* in France, the largest administrative subdivision of a department.

ar·row (ar′ō) *n.* **1** a slender, pointed shaft or stick for shooting from a bow. **2** anything resembling an arrow in shape or speed. **3** a sign (→) used to show direction or position in maps, on road signs, and in writing.
—*v.* **1** indicate with an arrow: *The main points are arrowed in the margin.* **2** move swiftly like an arrow: *Jet planes arrowed through the sky.* [OE *arwe*] **—ar′row-like′,** *adj.*

ar·row·head (ar′ō hed′) *n.* **1** the head or tip of an arrow. **2** a marsh or water plant, many varieties of which have leaves shaped like arrowheads.

An Indian arrowhead attached to the shaft of an arrow

ar·row·root (ar′ō rüt′) *n.* **1** an easily digested starch made from the roots of a tropical American plant. **2** the plant itself.

ar·row-wood (ar′ō wu̇d′) *n.* viburnum or other shrub having a tough, straight stem, formerly used by the Indians for making arrows.

ar·row·y (ar′ō ē) *adj.* **1** of arrows. **2** like an arrow in shape or speed.

ar·roy·o (ə roi′ō) *n.* **-roy·os. 1** the dry bed of a stream; gully. **2** a small river. [< Sp.]

ar·se·nal (är′sə nəl) *n.* a building for storing or manufacturing weapons and ammunition for the armed services. [< Ital. *arsenale* < Arabic *dar accina'ah* house (of) the manufacturing]

ar·se·nate (är′sə nāt′ or är′sə nit) *n.* a salt of arsenic acid. **Arsenate of lead** is a poison that is used to kill insects.

ar·se·nic (*n.* är′sə nik′; *adj.* är′sə nik′ or är sen′ik) *n. adj.* —*n.* **1** a grayish-white chemical element, having a metallic lustre and volatilizing when heated. *Symbol:* As; *at.no.* 33; *at.wt.* 74.9216. **2** a violently poisonous, tasteless, white compound of arsenic, used in industry and in medicine. *Formula:* As_2O_3 or As_4O_6
—*adj.* of or containing arsenic. [< L *arsenicum* < Gk. *arsenikon* < Hebrew < Old Persian **zarnika-* golden]

arsenic acid a colorless crystalline compound. *Formula:* H_3AsO_4

ar·sen·i·cal (är sen′ə kəl) *adj.* arsenious.

ar·se·ni·ous (är sē′nē əs) *adj.* **1** of arsenic. **2** containing arsenic.

ar·son (är′sən) *n.* the crime of intentionally setting fire to a building or other property. [< OF < LL *arsio, -onis* a burning < L *ardere* burn]

art[1] (ärt) *n.* **1** any form of human activity that is the product of and appeals primarily to the imagination, especially drawing, painting, and sculpture, also architecture, poetry, music, dancing, etc. **2** these types of activity taken together: *"Art is long and time is fleeting."* **3** a branch of learning that depends more on special practice than on general principles: *Writing composition is an art; grammar is a science.* **4** a branch or division of learning: *Literature is one of the liberal arts.* **5** *Archaic.* learning in general. **6** skill: *This furniture was made with art.* **7** human skill: *This well-kept garden owes more to art than to nature.* **8** some kind of skill or practical application of skill: *Cooking, sewing, and housekeeping are household arts.* **9** working principles; methods: *the art of making friends, the art of war.* **10** a skilful act. **11** a trick. [ME < OF < L *ars, artis*]

art² (ärt) *v. Archaic or Poetic.* are. "Thou art" means "You are" (sing.). [OE *eart*]

art. **1** article. **2** artillery. **3** artist. **4** artificial.

ARTC or **A.R.T.C.** Air Route Traffic Control.

ar·te·fact (är′tə fakt′) *n.* artifact.

Ar·te·mis (ar′tə mis) *n.* in Greek mythology, the goddess of the hunt, the forest, wild animals, and the moon. She was identified by the Romans with Diana.

ar·te·ri·al (är tēr′ē əl) *adj.* **1** in anatomy, having to do with or resembling the arteries. **2** in physiology, having to do with the bright-red blood of the arteries. **3** serving as a major route of transportation, supply, etc.: *an arterial highway.* **4** having a main channel with many branches.

ar·te·ri·o·scle·ro·sis (är tēr′ē ō sklə rō′sis) *n.* in medicine, a hardening and thickening of the walls of the arteries. It makes circulation of the blood difficult.

ar·te·ri·o·scle·rot·ic (är tēr′ē ō sklə rot′ik) *adj.* of, having to do with, or afflicted with arteriosclerosis. —*n.* a person afflicted with arteriosclerosis.

ar·ter·y (är′tər ē) *n.* **-ter·ies.** **1** in anatomy, any of the blood vessels or tubes that carry blood from the heart to all parts of the body. **2** a main road; an important channel: *Yonge Street is one of the main arteries of Toronto.* [ME < L *arteria* < Gk.]

ar·te·sian well (är tē′zhən) a deep-drilled well. In most artesian wells, the pressure is such that the water gushes up to the surface. [< F *artésien* of Artois, an old French province where such wells were first made]

art·ful (ärt′fəl) *adj.* **1** crafty; deceitful: *A swindler uses artful tricks to get money out of people.* **2** skilful; clever. **3** artificial. **—art′ful·ly,** *adv.* **—art′ful·ness,** *n.*

ar·thrit·ic (är thrit′ik) *adj.* of arthritis; caused by arthritis.

ar·thri·tis (är thrī′tis) *n.* in medicine, an inflammation of a joint or joints. [< L < Gk. *arthritis* < *arthron* joint]

ar·thro·plas·ty (är′thrə plas′tē) *n.* **1** the making of an artificial joint to replace a natural one. **2** surgery performed on a joint. [< Gk. *arthron* joint + *plastos* moulded]

ar·thro·pod (är′thrə pod′) *n.* one of a large group of invertebrate animals having segmented (jointed) bodies and legs. Insects, arachnids, and crustaceans are arthropods. [< *arthro-* joint (< Gk. *arthron*) + Gk. *pous, podos* foot]

Ar·thur (är′thər) *n.* in medieval legend, a king of ancient Britain who gathered about him a company of famous knights, who sat at a Round Table so that all would have equal rank. The real Arthur was a British chieftain or general of the 5th or 6th century A.D.

Ar·thu·ri·an (är thür′ē ən or är thūr′ē ən) *adj.* of or having to do with King Arthur and his knights.

ar·ti·choke (är′tə chōk′) *n.* **1** a thistle-like plant whose flowering head is cooked and eaten. **2** the flowering head. **3** a kind of sunflower having an edible root; Jerusalem artichoke. **4** the root of the Jerusalem artichoke. [< Ital. *articiocco* < Provençal < Arabic *alkharshuf*]

ar·ti·cle (är′tə kəl) *n. v.* **-cled, -cling.** —*n.* **1** a literary composition, complete in itself, but forming part of a magazine, newspaper, or book: *an article on gardening in a newspaper.* **2** a clause in a contract, treaty, statute, etc.: *the third article of the club's constitution deals with fees.* **3** a particular thing; item: *Bread is a main article of food.* **4** one of the words *a, an,* or *the* or the corresponding words in certain other languages. *A(n)* is the **indefinite article**; *the* is the **definite article.** —*v.* **1** bind by a contract: *The apprentice was articled to serve the master craftsman for seven years.* **2** bring charges; accuse. [ME < OF < L *articulus,* dim. of *artus* joint]

hat, āge, cãre, fär; let, ēqual, tėrm; it, īce
hot, ōpen, ôrder; oil, out; cup, pu̇t, rüle, ūse
əbove, takən, pencəl, lemən, circəs
ch, child; ng, long; sh, ship
th, thin; ᴛʜ, then; zh, measure

Articles of Confederation *U.S.* the constitution adopted by the thirteen original states of the United States in 1781. It was replaced by the present Constitution in 1789.

ar·tic·u·lar (är tik′yu̇ lər) *adj.* of the joints: *Arthritis is an articular disease.*

ar·tic·u·late (*adj.* är tik′yu̇ lit; *v.* är tik′yu̇ lāt′) *adj. v.* **-lat·ed, -lat·ing.** —*adj.* **1** uttered in distinct syllables of words: *A baby cries and gurgles, but does not use articulate speech.* **2** able to put one's thoughts into words: *Julia is the most articulate of the sisters.* **3** made up of distinct parts; distinct. **4** jointed; segmented. —*v.* **1** speak distinctly: *Be careful to articulate your words so that everyone in the room can understand you.* **2** unite by joints. **3** fit together in a joint: *After his knee was injured, he was lame because the bones did not articulate well.* **4** form or join together in a system, sequence, etc.: *An articulated English program is being introduced in all schools.* [< L *articulatus,* pp. of *articulare* divide into single joints < *articulus.* See ARTICLE.] **—ar·tic′u·late·ly,** *adv.* **—ar·tic′u·la·tor,** *n.*

ar·tic·u·la·tion (är tik′yu̇ lā′shən) *n.* **1** a way of speaking; enunciation. **2** a joint. **3** in anatomy and zoology, the act or manner of connecting by a joint or joints: *the articulation of the bones.* **4** the act or process of forming or joining together in a system, sequence, etc.: *the articulation of all manufacturing processes in the plant.*

ar·ti·fact or **ar·te·fact** (är′tə fakt′) *n.* anything made by human skill or work; an artificial product. [< L *ars, artis* art + *factus* made]

ar·ti·fice (är′tə fis) *n.* **1** a clever device; trick: *She will use any artifice to get her way.* **2** trickery; craft. [< F < L *artificium* < *ars, artis* art+ *facere* make] **—Syn. 1** See **stratagem.**

ar·tif·i·cer (är tif′ə sər) *n.* **1** a skilled workman; craftsman. **2** a maker; inventor.

ar·ti·fi·cial (är′tə fish′əl) *adj.* **1** made by human skill or labor; not natural: *When you read at night, you read by artificial light.* **2** made as a substitute for or in imitation of; not real: *artificial flowers, artificial silk.* **3** assumed; false; affected: *an artificial tone of voice, an artificial manner.* **4** of plants, not native or growing naturally in a place; cultivated. [< L *artificialis*] **—ar′ti·fi′cial·ly,** *adv.* **—ar′ti·fi′cial·ness,** *n.*

Syn. 1 Artificial, synthetic = not natural. **Artificial** describes things which are made by human skill and labor, in contrast to those produced in nature, but which often correspond to natural things: *You can get burned by the artificial light of a sun lamp.* **Synthetic** describes things that are put together in a laboratory by chemical combination or treatment of natural substances, and that often serve as substitutes for natural products: *Nylon is a synthetic fabric.*

ar·ti·fi·ci·al·i·ty (är′tə fish′ē al′ə tē) *n.* **-ties.** **1** an artificial quality or condition. **2** something unnatural or unreal.

artificial respiration the process of restoring or starting the breathing of another person, accomplished by forcing air into or out of the lungs, often by breathing directly into the mouth.

ar·ti·gi or **ar·tig·gi** (är′tə gē or är tē′gē) *n. Cdn.* atigi.

ar·til·ler·y (är til′ər ē) *n.* **1** mounted guns; cannon. **2** the part of an army that uses and manages big guns. **3** the science of firing, and co-ordinating the firing of, guns of larger calibre than machine guns. [ME < OF *artillerie* < *artiller* equip]

ar·til·ler·y·man (är til′ər ē mən) *n.* **-men** (-mən). a soldier who belongs to the artillery; gunner.

ar·ti·san (är′tə zən or är′tə zan′) *n.* a workman skilled in some industry or trade; craftsman. [< F < Ital. *artigiano* < L *ars, artis* art] **—Syn.** mechanic. See **artist.**

art·ist (är′tist) *n.* **1** a person who paints pictures. **2** a person skilled in any of the fine arts, such as sculpture, music, or literature. **3** a person who does work with skill

and good taste. **4** an actor, singer, musician, etc.; artiste. [< F < Ital. *artista* < VL < L *ars, artis* art]
Syn. 3 Artist, artisan = a person who does work with skill. **Artist** emphasizes use of taste, imagination, and creative ability in addition to skill, and usually applies to a person working in the fine arts: *Her creative interpretation makes that dancer an artist.* **Artisan** emphasizes skill, and applies to a person working in the manual or mechanic arts: *Factories want artisans in all departments.*

ar·tiste (är tēst′) *n.* a very skilful performer or worker. An artiste may be a singer, a dancer, or a cook. [<F]

ar·tis·tic (är tis′tik) *adj.* **1** of art or artists: *artistic knowledge.* **2** done with the skill and good taste proper to a work of art: *an artistic design.* **3** showing skill in art or an appreciation of art.

ar·tis·ti·cal·ly (är tis′tik lē) *adv.* **1** with skill and good taste. **2** from an artistic point of view.

art·ist·ry (är′tis trē) *n.* **-ries.** artistic work; workmanship of an artist.

art·less (ärt′lis) *adj.* **1** without awareness of conventions; simple: *Small children ask many artless questions.* **2** natural; not artificial: *artless eloquence.* **3** without art; unskilled; ignorant. **4** without guile or deceit. **—art′less·ly,** *adv.* **—art′less·ness,** *n.*

art·y (är′tē) *adj.* **art·i·er, art·i·est.** *Informal.* making a pretence or show of being artistic. **—art′i·ness,** *n.*

ar·um (ãr′əm) *n.* **1** a plant having a club-shaped spike of small flowers that is partly surrounded by a hooded sheath, such as the jack-in-the-pulpit. **2** a plant resembling the arum; calla lily. [< L < Gk. *aron*]

-ary *suffix.* **1** a place for ——, as in *infirmary, library.* **2** a collection of ——, as in *dictionary, statuary.* **3** a person or thing that is, does, belongs to, etc. ——, as in *adversary, boundary, commentary.* **4** of or having to do with ——, as in *legendary, missionary.* **5** being; having the nature of ——, as in *secondary, supplementary.* **6** characterized by ——, as in *customary, honorary.* [< L *-arius* or (neut.) *-arium*]

Ar·y·an (ar′ē ən or er′ē ən, ar′yən or er′yən) *adj.* of or having to do with a family of languages from which the Indo-Iranian and most European languages are descended; Indo-European. *—n.* **1** the assumed prehistoric language from which these languages are derived. **2** a person belonging to a prehistoric group of people who spoke this language. **3** a person supposed to be descended from this prehistoric group of people. **4** in Nazi use, a non-Jew of Indo-European descent. Also, **Arian.** [< Skt. *arya* noble]

as[1] (ez; *stressed,* az) *adv.* **1** to the same degree or extent; equally: *as black as coal.* **2** for example: *Some animals, as dogs and cats, eat meat.*
—conj. **1** to the same degree or extent that: *She worked just so much as she was told to.* **2** in the same way that: *run as I do.* **3** during the time that; when; while: *She sang as she worked.* **4** because: *As he was a skilled worker, he received good wages.* **5** though: *Brave as they were, the danger made them afraid.* **6** that the result was: *The child so marked the picture as to spoil it.*
as for, about; concerning; referring to: *As for the children, they are impatient for Christmas.*
as from, beginning; considered as dating from: *The school bus will leave five minutes later as from tomorrow.*
as good as, practically; almost: *He looks as good as dead.*
as if, as it would be if.
as is, *Informal.* in the present condition: *If you buy the car as is, you will have to put it in running order yourself.*
as it were, so to speak.
as well, also; besides.
as well as, in addition to.
as though, as it would be if.
as to, a about; concerning; referring to. **b** in order to.
as yet, up to this time; so far: *Nothing has been done as yet.*
—prep. in the character of; doing the work of: *Who will act as teacher?*
—pron. **1** a condition or fact that: *She is very careful, as her work shows.* **2** that: *Do the same thing as I do.* [OE (unstressed) *ealswā* quite so. Cf. ALSO.]
—Syn. *conj.* **4** See **because.**
☛ **As to** is often a clumsy substitute for a single preposition, usually *about* or *of*: *Practice usually proves the best teacher as to (in, for, of) the use of organ stops.* ☛ See **like**[1] for another usage note.

as[2] (as) *n.* **as·ses** (as′iz). in ancient Rome: **1** a pound (weight), equal to twelve ounces. **2** a coin worth a few cents. [< L]

As 1 arsenic. **2** altostratus.

AS or **A.S.** Anglo-Saxon.

as- the form of **ad-** before *s,* as in *assist.*

as·a·fet·i·da or **as·a·foet·i·da** (as′ə fet′ə də or as′ə fē′tə də) *n.* a gum resin with a garliclike odor, used in medicine and cooking. Also, **assafetida, assafoetida.** [< Med.L *asafetida* < *asa* mastic (< Persian *azā*) + L *fetidus* stinking]

as·bes·tos (as bes′təs or az bes′təs) *n.* **1** a mineral, a silicate of calcium and magnesium, that does not burn or conduct heat, usually occurring in fibres. **2** a fireproof fabric made of these fibres. [ME < OF < L < Gk. *asbestos* unquenchable (originally, of quicklime) < *a-* not + *sbennunai* quench]

as·cend (ə send′) *v.* **1** go up; rise; move upward: *He watched the airplane ascend higher and higher.* **2** climb; go to or toward the top of: *Another expedition is planning to ascend Mt. Everest.* **3** in music, rise in pitch. **4 ascend the throne,** become king, queen, etc. [ME < L *ascendere* < *ad-* up + *scandere* climb]
—Syn. 2 scale. See **climb.**

as·cend·ance (ə sen′dəns) *n.* ascendancy.

as·cend·an·cy (ə sen′dən sē) *n.* a controlling influence; domination; rule.

as·cend·ant (ə sen′dənt) *adj.* **1** ascending; rising. **2** superior; dominant; ruling; controlling.
—n. **1** a position of power; controlling influence. **2** in astrology: **a** the sign of the zodiac rising above the horizon at a certain time. **b** a horoscope. **3 in the ascendant, a** supreme; dominant. **b** increasing in influence.

as·cend·ency (ə sen′dən sē) *n.* ascendancy.

as·cend·ent (ə sen′dənt) *adj.* ascendant.

as·cend·er (ə sen′dər) *n.* **1** a person or thing that ascends. **2** in printing: **a** the upper part of a lower-case letter, such as b, d, h, or k. **b** any such letter.

ascend·ing (ə sen′ding) *adj.* **1** rising or sloping upwards; mounting. **2** in botany, rising or gradually curving upwards to a vertical position.

as·cen·sion (ə sen′shən) *n.* **1** the act of ascending; ascent. **2 Ascension, a** the bodily passing of Christ from earth to heaven. **b** Also, **Ascension Day.** a Christian church festival in honor of this on the fortieth day after Easter. [< L *ascensio, -onis* < *ascendere.* See ASCEND.]

as·cent (ə sent′) *n.* **1** the act of going up; a rising. **2** the act of climbing. **3** a place or way that slopes up. [< *ascend*; modelled after *descent*]

as·cer·tain (as′ər tān′) *v.* find out; determine. [ME < OF *acertener* < *a-* to + *certain* certain < L *certus* sure] **—as′cer·tain′a·ble,** *adj.* **—as′cer·tain′a·bly,** *adv.*

as·cer·tain·ment (as′ər tān′mənt) *n.* an ascertaining.

as·cet·ic (ə set′ik) *n.* **1** a person who practises unusual self-denial and devotion, or severe discipline of self for religious reasons. **2** a person who refrains from pleasures and comforts. *—adj.* refraining from pleasures and comforts; self-denying. [< Gk. *askētikos* < *askeein* exercise; hence, discipline] **—as·cet′i·cal·ly,** *adv.*

as·cet·i·cism (ə set′ə siz′əm) *n.* **1** the life or habits of an ascetic. **2** the doctrine that by abstinence and self-denial a person can train himself to be in conformity with God's will.

as·cid·i·an (ə sid′ē ən) *n.* a sea animal having a tough saclike covering.

as·cid·i·um (ə sid′ē əm) *n.* **-cid·i·a** (-sid′ē ə). in botany, a baglike or pitcherlike part of a plant. [< NL < Gk. *askidion,* dim. of *askos* bag]

as·co·my·cete (as′kō mī sēt′) *n.* in botany, any of a large group of fungi, including yeasts, moulds, mildews, etc. [< Gk. *askos* bag + *mykēs, mykētos* fungus]

a·scor·bic acid (ə skôr′bik or ā skôr′bik) vitamin C. *Formula*: $C_6H_8O_6$ [< *a-*[4] + *scorbutic*]

as·cot (as′kət or as′kot) *n.* a necktie with broad ends, tied so that the ends may be laid flat, one across the other. [from *Ascot*, famous English race track]

as·cribe (əs krīb′) *v.* **-cribed, -crib·ing. 1** assign; attribute: *The police ascribed the automobile accident to fast driving.* **2** consider as belonging: *Men have ascribed their own characteristics to their gods.* [ME < OF < L *ascribere* < *ad-* to + *scribere* write] **—Syn. 1** See **attribute.**

as·crip·tion (əs krip′shən) *n.* **1** the act of ascribing: *the ascription of selfishness to a miser.* **2** a statement or words ascribing something. [< L *ascriptio, -onis* < *ascribere.* See ASCRIBE.]

a·sep·sis (ə sep′sis or ā sep′sis) *n.* **1** an aseptic condition. **2** aseptic methods or treatment.

a·sep·tic (ə sep′tik or ā sep′tik) *adj.* free from germs causing infection. **—a·sep′ti·cally,** *adv.*

a·sex·u·al (ā sek′shü əl) *adj.* in biology: **1** having no sex. **2** independent of sexual processes. In the liverworts and mosses, and in some of the lower animals, sexual and asexual reproduction alternate. **—a·sex′u·al·ly,** *adv.*

As·gard (as′gärd, az′gärd, or äs′gärd) *n.* the home of the Norse gods and heroes.

ash[1] (ash) *n.* **1** what remains of a thing after it has been thoroughly burned. **2** fine particles of lava. **3** the color of wood ash; silvery gray. *—adj.* silvery-gray. [OE *æsce*]

ash[2] (ash) *n.* **1** a kind of shade tree having grayish twigs and straight-grained wood. **2** its tough, springy wood. [OE *æsc*]

a·shamed (ə shāmd′) *adj.* **1** feeling shame; disturbed or uncomfortable because one has done something wrong, improper, or silly. **2** unwilling because of shame.

Syn. 1 Ashamed, humiliated, mortified = feeling embarrassed and disgraced. **Ashamed** emphasizes a feeling of having disgraced oneself by doing something wrong, improper, or foolish: *I was ashamed when I cried at the movies.* **Humiliated** emphasizes a painful feeling of being lowered and shamed in the eyes of others: *Parents are humiliated if their children behave badly when guests are present.* **Mortified** = feeling greatly embarrassed and humiliated, sometimes ashamed: *He was mortified when he forgot his speech.*

A·shan·ti (ə shan′tē or ə shän′tē) *n.* **-ti** or **-tis. 1** the native people of the Ashanti region of Ghana. **2** a native of this region. **3** the language of its people. *—adj.* of or having to do with the Ashanti region or its people.

ash·can (ash′kan′) *n.* any receptacle, such as a barrel, drum, or large can, for holding rubbish, garbage, ashes, etc.

ash·en[1] (ash′ən) *adj.* **1** like ashes; pale as ashes. **2** of ashes.

ash·en[2] (ash′ən) *adj.* **1** of the ash tree. **2** made from the wood of the ash tree.

ash·es (ash′iz) *n.pl.* **1** what remains of a thing after it has been burned. **2** remains; dead body. **3** fine particles of lava.

Ash·ke·naz·ic (ash′kə naz′ik or äsh′kə nä′zik) *adj.* of, having to do with, or descended from the Ashkenazim.

Ash·ke·naz·im (ash′kə naz′im or äsh′kə nä′zim) *n.pl.* the Jews of central and eastern Europe, distinguished from the Spanish and Portuguese Jews, who are called the Sephardim. The Yiddish language developed among the Ashkenazim.

ash·lar or **ash·ler** (ash′lər) *n.* **1** a square stone used in building. **2** masonry composed of ashlars. [ME < OF *aisselier* < VL *axillarium* < *axis* plank]

a·shore (ə shôr′) *adv. adj.* **1** to the shore; to land. **2** on the shore; on land.

Ash·to·reth (ash′tə reth′) *n.* Astarte. Also, **Ashtaroth.**

ash tray a small receptacle to put tobacco ashes in.

Ash Wednesday the first day of Lent; the seventh Wednesday before Easter.

ash·y (ash′ē) *adj.* **ash·i·er, ash·i·est. 1** like ashes; pale as ashes. **2** of ashes. **3** covered with ashes.

A·sian (ā′zhən or ā′shən) *n.* a native of Asia. *—adj.* Asiatic.

Asian flu a kind of influenza, first identified in Hong Kong in 1957.

A·si·at·ic (ā′zhē at′ik or ā′shē at′ik) *adj.* of or having to do with Asia or its people. *—n.* Asian.

Asiatic cholera an infectious disease, usually fatal, marked by diarrhea, vomiting, cramps, etc.

hat, āge, cãre, fär; let, ēqual, tėrm; it, īce
hot, ōpen, ôrder; oil, out; cup, pu̇t, rüle, ūse
əbove, takən, pencəl, lemən, circəs
ch, child; ng, long; sh, ship
th, thin; ᴛʜ, then; zh, measure

a·side (ə sīd′) *adv.* **1** on one side; to one side; away: *Move the table aside.* **2** out of one's thoughts, consideration, etc.: *Put your troubles aside.* **3 aside from, a** apart from. **b** *Informal.* except for.
—n. in a play, a remark or speech that other actors are supposed not to hear.

as·i·nine (as′ə nīn′) *adj.* **1** of asses. **2** like an ass. **3** stupid; silly. [< L *asininus* < *asinus* ass] **—as′i·nine·ly,** *adv.*

as·i·nin·ity (as′ə nin′ə tē) *n.* **-ties.** silliness.

ask (ask) *v.* **1** try to find out by words; inquire: *Why don't you ask? She asked about our health. Ask the way.* **2** seek the answer to: *Ask any questions you wish.* **3** put a question to; inquire of: *Ask him how old he is.* **4** try to get by words; request: *Ask Kate to sing.* **5** claim; demand: *ask too high a price for a house.* **6** invite: *She asked ten guests to the party.* **7** need; require: *This job asks hard work.* **8 ask for it,** *Informal.* ask for trouble. [OE *āscian*]

Syn. 1 Ask, inquire = try to find out by a question. **Ask** is the general word meaning to seek information from someone: *Joe asked about you. Ask someone where that street is.* **Inquire** is more formal, but suggests more strongly going into a subject, asking in an effort to get definite information: *He inquired about you, wanted to know when you are leaving. You had better inquire how to get there.* **3** query, interrogate.
4 Ask, request, solicit = try to get by words. **Ask** is the general word: *I asked permission to do it.* **Request,** a more formal word, means to ask in a polite and more formal way: *We request contributions to the library.* **Solicit,** a formal word, means to request respectfully or earnestly: *They are soliciting funds for a new hospital.*

a·skance (ə skans′) *adv.* **1** with suspicion or disapproval: *The students looked askance at the suggestion of classes on Saturday.* **2** sideways; to one side. [origin uncertain]

a·skant (ə skant′) *adv.* askance.

a·skew (ə skū′) *adv. adj.* to one side; out of the proper position; turned or twisted the wrong way: *Her hat is on askew.*

a·slant (ə slant′) *adv.* in a slanting direction. *—prep.* slantingly across. *—adj.* slanting.

a·sleep (ə slēp′) *adj.* **1** sleeping: *The cat is asleep.* **2** in a condition of sleep. **3** dull; inactive. **4** numb: *My foot is asleep.* **5** dead.
—adv. into a condition of sleep: *The tired boy fell asleep.*

a·slope (ə slōp′) *adv. adj.* at a slant.

a·so·cial (ā sō′shəl) *adj.* **1** paying no attention to social customs or laws; not social. **2** avoiding association with others; not sociable.

asp[1] (asp) *n.* **1** any of several small, poisonous snakes of Africa, especially the Egyptian cobra. **2** a small, poisonous snake of Europe; adder. [< L *aspis* < Gk.]

asp[2] (asp) *n. Poetic.* aspen. [OE *æspe*]

as·par·a·gus (əs par′ə gəs) *n.* **1** a perennial plant of the lily family, but having pulpy fruit and no bulb. The stems have many branches covered with threadlike branchlets, the true leaves being reduced to scales. **2** the shoots of one kind of this plant, used as a vegetable. [< L < Gk. *asparagos*]

a·spar·kle (ə spär′kəl) *adj.* sparkling.

as·pect (as′pekt) *n.* **1** one side or part or view (of a subject): *various aspects of a plan.* **2** look; appearance: *aspect of the countryside.* **3** countenance; expression: *the solemn aspect of a judge.* **4** direction in which anything faces; exposure: *This house has a western aspect.* **5** a side fronting in a given direction: *the southern aspect of a house.* **6** in astrology, the relative position of planets as determining their supposed influence upon human affairs. **7** in grammar: **a** the nature of the action of a verb, regarded as beginning, continuing, ending, being repeated, etc. **b** a verb form that expresses action as beginning, continuing, ending, being repeated, etc.: *Aspects indicate a quality of the action; tenses indicate time.* **c** in English, a verb phrase performing a similar function. *He is walking* is, properly speaking, an aspect. **d** a set of such forms or phrases for the various persons: *The Russian verb has many aspects.* **8** in physics, the position of a plane surface relative to a fluid or gas through which it moves. [< L *aspectus* < *aspicere* < *ad-* at + *specere* look] —**Syn. 2** See **appearance.**

as·pec·tu·al (as pek′chü əl) *adj.* in grammar, of or having to do with aspect (def. 7). —*n.* in grammar, a verb form indicating aspect.

as·pen (as′pən) *n.* **1** any of several poplar trees, especially the *trembling aspen,* whose leaves tremble and rustle in the slightest breeze. **2** the wood of any aspen tree.
—*adj.* **1** of this tree. **2** quivering; trembling. [earlier meaning "of the asp[2]"]

as·per·i·ty (as per′ə tē) *n.* **-ties.** roughness; harshness; severity. [ME *asprete* < OF < L *asperitas* < *asper* rough]

as·perse (əs pėrs′) *v.* **-persed, -pers·ing. 1** spread damaging or false reports about; slander. **2** sprinkle. [< L *aspersus,* pp. of *aspergere* < *ad-* on + *spargere* sprinkle] —**as·pers′er,** *n.*

as·per·sion (əs pėr′zhən or əs pėr′shən) *n.* **1** a damaging or false report; slander. **2** a sprinkling with water.

as·phalt (as′folt or as′fôlt) *n.* **1** a dark-colored substance, much like tar, that occurs in many parts of the world. **2** a similar artificial substance, obtained by evaporating petroleum. **3** a mixture of this substance with crushed rock, used for pavements, roofs, etc. —*v.* surface or seal with asphalt. [< LL < Gk. *asphaltos*]

asphalt jungle *Informal.* a densely populated city area in which crime and violence are common.

as·phal·tum (as fal′təm) *n.* asphalt.

as·pho·del (as′fə del′) *n.* **1** a plant of the lily family, having spikes of white or yellow flowers. **2** *Poetic.* a daffodil. [< L < Gk. *asphodelos*]

as·phyx·i·a (as fik′sē ə) *n.* in medicine, suffocation or an unconscious condition caused by lack of oxygen and excess of carbon dioxide in the blood. [< NL < Gk. *asphyxia* < *a-* without + *sphyxis* pulse < *sphyzein* throb]

as·phyx·i·ant (as fik′sē ənt′) *n.* a cause of asphyxiation. —*adj.* causing or producing asphyxiation.

as·phyx·i·ate (as fik′sē āt′) *v.* **-at·ed, -at·ing.** suffocate because of lack of oxygen and excess of carbon dioxide in the blood. —**as·phyx′·i·a′·tion,** *n.* —**as·phyx′i·a·tor,** *n.*

as·pic[1] (as′pik) *n.* a kind of jelly made from meat, tomato juice, etc. [< F]

as·pic[2] (as′pik) *n. Poetic.* the asp. [< F *aspic,* var. (by influence of *piquer* to sting) of L *aspis.* See ASP[1].]

as·pi·dis·tra (as′pə dis′trə) *n.* a plant having large, green leaves and very small flowers, much used as a house plant. [< NL < Gk. *aspis, aspidos* shield + *astra* stars]

as·pir·ant (əs pīr′ənt or as′pə rənt) *n.* a person who aspires; a person who seeks a position of honor, advancement, etc. —*adj.* aspiring.

as·pi·rate (*v.* as′pə rāt′; *adj., n.* as′pə rit) *v.* **-rat·ed, -rat·ing,** *adj., n.* —*v.* in phonetics: **1** begin a word or syllable with an *h*-sound, as in *hoot* (hüt). **2** pronounce (a stop) with a following or accompanying puff of air. *P* is aspirated in *pin* but not in *spin* or *nip.*
—*adj.* pronounced with a breathing or *h*-sound. The *h* in *here* is aspirate.
—*n.* an aspirated sound. English *p* is an aspirate in *pat,* but not in *tap.* [< L *aspirare.* See ASPIRE.]

as·pi·ra·tion (as′pə rā′shən) *n.* **1** an earnest desire; longing. **2** the drawing of air into the lungs; breathing. **3 a** an aspirating (of sounds). **b** an aspirated sound.

as·pi·ra·tor (as′pə rā′tər) *n.* an apparatus or device employing suction: *A vacuum cleaner is an aspirator.*

as·pire (əs pīr′) *v.* **-pired, -pir·ing. 1** have an ambition for something; desire earnestly: *Scholars aspire after knowledge. Tom aspired to be captain of the team.* **2** rise high. [< L *aspirare* < *ad-* toward + *spirare* breathe] —**as·pir′ing·ly,** *adv.* —**Syn. 1** aim, long, crave.

as·pi·rin (as′pə rin) *n.* a white, crystalline drug, the acetate of salicylic acid, used to relieve headaches, colds, etc. *Formula:* $C_9H_8O_4$ [< trademark]

a·squint (ə skwint′) *adv. adj.* with a squint; sideways. [origin uncertain]

ass (as) *n.* **1** a long-eared mammal of the horse family; donkey. When domesticated, the ass is a patient, sure-footed beast of burden. **2** a stupid fool; silly person. [OE *assa* < Celtic < L *asinus*]

as·sa·fet·i·da or **as·sa·foet·i·da** (as′ə fet′ə də or as′ə fē′tə də) *n.* asafetida.

as·sa·gai (as′ə gī′) *n.* **-gais.** a slender spear or javelin of hard wood, used by some African tribes. Also, **assegai.** [< Sp. *azagaya* < Arabic *azzaghayah* < Berber]

as·sail (ə sāl′) *v.* **1** set upon with violence; attack: *assail a fortress.* **2** set upon vigorously with arguments, abuse, etc. **3** come over (a person); trouble: *He was assailed with feelings of panic.* [ME < OF *asalir* < VL *adsalire* < L *ad-* at + *salire* leap] —**as·sail′a·ble,** *adj.* —**Syn. 1** See **attack.**

as·sail·ant (ə sāl′ənt) *n.* a person who attacks: *The injured man did not know his assailant.*

as·sas·sin (ə sas′ən) *n.* **1** a murderer, especially one hired to murder. **2** any person who destroys or does serious damage: *a character assassin.* [< F < Ital. < Arabic *ḥashshāshīn* hashish eaters; with reference to murderers under the influence of hashish]

as·sas·si·nate (ə sas′ə nāt′) *v.* **-nat·ed, -nat·ing. 1** kill by a sudden or secret attack; murder. **2** destroy or do serious damage, especially by slander, treachery, etc. —**as·sas′si·na′tor,** *n.*

as·sas·si·na·tion (ə sas′ə nā′shən) *n.* a killing by a sudden or secret attack; murder, usually of an important public figure: *the assassination of President Kennedy.*

as·sault (ə solt′ or ə sôlt′) *n.* **1** an attack, especially a sudden, vigorous attack. **2** the final phase of a military attack; closing with the enemy in hand-to-hand fighting. **3** in law, a threat or an attempt to do physical harm to another person.
—*v.* make an assault on. [ME < OF *asauter* < L *ad-* at + *saltare* leap] —**as·sault′er,** *n.* —**Syn.** *n.* **1** onslaught, charge. —*v.* See **attack.**

assault and battery in law, the striking of a person; intentionally doing physical harm to a person.

as·say (ə sā′ or as′ā) *v.* **1** analyse (an ore, alloy, etc.) to find out the quantity of gold, silver, or other metal in it. **2** try; test; examine. **3** (of ore) contain, as shown by analysis, a certain proportion of metal. **4** *Archaic.* attempt.
—*n.* **1** an analysis of an ore, alloy, etc. to find out the amount of metal in it. **2** a trial; test; examination. **3** the substance analysed or tested. **4** a list of the results of assaying an ore, drug, etc. [ME < OF *a(s)sayer,* ult. < LL < VL *exagere* weigh] —**as·say′er,** *n.*

as·se·gai (as′ə gī′) *n.* assagai.

as·sem·blage (ə sem′blij) *n.* **1** a group of persons gathered together; assembly. **2** a collection; group. **3** a bringing together; coming together; meeting. **4** a putting together: *the assemblage of the parts of a machine.*

as·sem·ble (ə sem′bəl) *v.* **-bled, -bling. 1** gather together; bring together. **2** come together; meet. **3** put together; fit together. [ME < OF *as(s)embler* < VL *assimulare* bring together < L *assimulare* compare, ult. < *ad-* to + *similis* like, or *simul* together] —**as·sem′bler,** *n.* —**Syn. 1** See **gather. 2** congregate.

as·sem·bly (ə sem′blē) *n.* **-blies. 1** a group of people gathered together for some purpose; meeting. A reception or a ball may be called an assembly. **2** a lawmaking group. **3** a putting together; fitting together: *the assembly of the parts of an automobile.* **4** the set of parts fitted or required to be fitted together: *the wing assembly of a model plane.* **5** a signal on a bugle or drum for troops to form in ranks. **6** the act of gathering or coming together: *unlawful assembly.* **7 Assembly,** in some states of the United States, the lower branch of the state legislature. —**Syn. 1** convention, congregation. See **meeting. 2** legislature.

assembly line a row of workers and machines along which work is passed until the final product is made: *Automobiles are produced on an assembly line.*

as·sem·bly·man (ə sem′blē mən) *n.* **-men** (-mən). **1** in Prince Edward Island, one of fifteen members of the Legislative Assembly elected by both property-holders and non-property-holders; a member of the Legislative Assembly who is not a councillor. **2** in the United States, a member of a lawmaking group.

as·sent (ə sent′) *v.* express agreement; agree. —*n.* an acceptance of a proposal, statement, etc.: agreement. [ME < OF < L *assentari* < *ad-* along with + *sentire* feel, think] —**as·sent′er,** *n.* —**as·sent′ing·ly,** *adv.* —**Syn.** *v.* See **consent.**

as·sert (ə sėrt′) *v.* **1** state positively; declare. **2** insist on (a right, a claim, etc.); defend. **3 assert oneself, a** put oneself forward; make demands. **b** insist on one's rights. [< L *assertus,* pp. of *asserere* < *ad-* to + *serere* join] —**as·sert′er** or **as·ser′tor,** *n.* —**Syn. 1** affirm, aver, maintain. See **declare.**

as·ser·tion (ə sėr′shən) *n.* **1** a positive statement; declaration. **2** an insisting on one's right, a claim, etc.

as·ser·tive (ə sėr′tiv) *adj.* **1** too confident and certain; positive: *John is an assertive boy, always insisting on his rights and opinions.* **2** declarative: *an assertive sentence.* —**as·ser′tive·ly,** *adv.* —**as·ser′tive·ness,** *n.*

as·sess (ə ses′) *v.* **1** estimate the value of (property or income) for taxation. **2** fix the amount of (a tax, fine, damages, etc.). **3** put a tax on or call for a contribution from (a person, property, etc.): *Each member of the club will be assessed one dollar to pay for the trip.* **4** portion out as a tax; apportion. **5** examine critically and estimate the merit, significance, value, etc. of: *The committee met to assess the idea of establishing a new university.* [ME < OF < VL *assessare* fix a tax < L *assidere* < *ad-* by + *sedere* sit] —**as·sess′a·ble,** *adj.*

as·sess·ment (ə ses′mənt) *n.* **1** the act of assessing. **2** the amount assessed. **3** an evaluation; critical appraisal.

as·ses·sor (ə ses′ər) *n.* a person who estimates the value of property or income for taxation.

as·set (as′et) *n.* something having value: *Ability to sway a crowd is a necessary asset for a politician.*

as·sets (as′ets) *n.pl.* **1** things of value; property. **2** property that can be used to pay debts. **3** in accounting, the entries on a balance sheet showing total resources. [< OF *asez* enough < L *ad-* + *satis* enough]

as·sev·er·ate (ə sev′ər āt′) *v.* **-at·ed, -at·ing.** declare solemnly; state positively. [< L *asseverare* < *ad-* + *severus* serious] —**as·sev′er·a·tive,** *adj.*

as·sev·er·a·tion (ə sev′ər ā′shən) *n.* a solemn declaration; emphatic assertion.

as·si·du·i·ty (as′ə dū′ə tē or as′ə dü′ə tē) *n.* **-ties.** careful and steady attention; diligence.

as·sid·u·ous (ə sij′ü əs) *adj.* careful and attentive; diligent. [< L *assiduus* < *assidere* sit at. See ASSESS.] —**as·sid′u·ous·ly,** *adv.* —**as·sid′u·ous·ness,** *n.*

as·sign (ə sīn′) *v.* **1** give as a share, task, duty, etc.: *The teacher has assigned ten problems for tonight's homework.* **2** appoint (to a post or duty): *The captain assigned two soldiers to guard the gate.* **3** name definitely; fix; set: *The judge assigned a day for the trial.* **4** refer; ascribe; attribute: *A student should be able to assign events to their places in history.* **5** in law, transfer or hand over (property, rights, etc.): *Mr. Jones assigned his home and farm to his creditors.* —*n.* a person to whom property, rights, etc. are legally transferred. [ME < OF *assigner* < L *assignare* < *ad-* to, for + *signare* to mark < *signum* mark] —**as·sign′a·ble,** *adj.* —**as·sign′er,** *n.*

Syn. *v.* **1 assign, allot** = give something to a particular person or purpose as a share or responsibility. **Assign** emphasizes giving something that has been established as due by some plan or principle: *The teacher assigned me a seat near the window.* **Allot** suggests giving an amount or part that is set more or less by chance: *Each student was allotted two tickets.*

as·sig·nat (as′ig nat′; *French,* ä sē nyä′) *n.* a piece of paper money issued from 1789 to 1796 in France by a revolutionary government. Assignats were based on the value of confiscated lands. [< F < L *assignatum* < *assignare.* See ASSIGN.]

as·sig·na·tion (as′ig nā′shən) *n.* **1** an appointment for a meeting, often an illicit meeting of lovers. **2** in law, a transfer of property, a right, etc. **3** an allotting.

hat, āge, cãre, fär; let, ēqual, tėrm; it, īce
hot, ōpen, ôrder; oil, out; cup, pu̇t, rüle, ūse
əbove, takən, pencəl, lemən, circəs
ch, child; ng, long; sh, ship
th, thin; ᴛʜ, then; zh, measure

as·sign·ee (ə sī nē′ or as′ə nē′) *n.* in law, a person to whom some property, right, etc. is transferred.

as·sign·ment (ə sīn′mənt) *n.* **1** something assigned, especially a piece of work to be done. **2** an assigning. **3** in law, a transfer of some property, right, etc.

as·sign·or (ə sī nôr′ or as′ə nôr′) *n.* in law, a person who transfers to another some property, right, etc.

as·sim·i·la·ble (ə sim′ə lə bel) *adj.* that can be assimilated.

as·sim·i·late (ə sim′ə lāt′) *v.* **-lat·ed, -lat·ing. 1** absorb; digest: *Mary reads too fast to assimilate everything. The human body will not assimilate sawdust.* **2** make or become like (people of a nation, etc.) in customs and viewpoint: *Canada has assimilated people from many lands. Hungarians have assimilated readily in this country.* **3** in phonetics, make like. A consonant is frequently assimilated to the consonant it precedes; *ads-* becomes *ass-*; *comr-*, *corr-*; *disf-*, *diff-*; etc. **4** become like. [< L *assimilare* < *ad-* to + *similis* like] —**as·sim′i·la′tor,** *n.* —**Syn. 1** See **absorb.**

as·sim·i·la·tion (ə sim′ə lā′shən) *n.* **1** an assimilating: *Nutrition depends on the assimilation of food.* **2** a being assimilated.

as·sim·i·la·tive (ə sim′ə lə tiv or ə sim′ə lā′tiv) *adj.* assimilating.

As·sin·i·boine (ə sin′ə boin′) *n.* **1** a tribe of North American Indians now living in Alberta, Saskatchewan, and Montana; Stoney. **2** a member of this tribe. **3** the language of this tribe. —*adj.* of or having to do with the Assiniboines.

as·sist (ə sist′) *v.* **1** help; give aid to. **2** take part or have a hand (*in*): *He assisted in the scoring of the goal.* —*n.* **1** an instance of giving help. **2** in hockey, the credit given to a player who helps score a goal. **3** in baseball, the credit given to a player who helps to put an opposing player out. *Abbrev.* for 2, 3: a. [< F < L *assistere* < *ad-* by + *sistere* take a stand] —**Syn.** *v.* **1** See **help.**

as·sist·ance (ə sis′təns) *n.* help; aid.

as·sist·ant (ə sis′tənt) *n.* **1** a helper; aid. **2** an assistant professor. —*adj.* helping; assisting.

assistant professor a college or university teacher ranking below an associate professor but above a lecturer.

as·size (ə sīz′) *n.* **1** a session of a law court. **2** the time or place of such a session. [ME < OF *as(s)ise* < *aseeir* < VL *assedere* sit at < L *assidere.* See ASSESS.]

as·siz·es (ə sīz′iz) *n.pl.* periodical sessions of a law court.

assn. or **Assn.** association.

assoc. or **Assoc. 1** associate. **2** association.

as·so·ci·ate (*v.* ə sō′shē āt′; *n., adj.* ə sō′shē it or ə sō′shē āt′) *v.* **-at·ed, -at·ing,** *n. adj.* —*v.* **1** connect in thought: *We associate giving presents with Christmas.* **2** join as a companion, partner, or friend: *He has always associated with large enterprises.* **3** join; combine; unite. **4** combine for a common purpose. **5** keep company (*with*): *Do not associate with bad companions.* —*n.* **1** anything usually connected with something else. **2** a companion; partner; friend. **3** a member without full rights and privileges. **4** an associate professor. —*adj.* **1** joined in companionship, interest, action, etc. **2** admitted to some, but not all, rights and privileges, etc.: *an associate member.* [< L *associare* < *ad-* to + *socius* companion] —**as·so′ci·a′tor,** *n.* —**Syn.** *n.* **2** ally, colleague, comrade. —*adj.* **1** allied.

☛ **associate.** Referring to a person, *with* is used after *associate*: *He is associated with Frisby in a law firm partnership.* Referring to a thing, *in* is used: *They were associated in several clothing companies.*

associate professor a college or university teacher ranking below a professor but above an assistant professor.

as·so·ci·a·tion (ə sō′sē ā′shən or ə sō′shē ā′shən) *n.* 1 an associating or being associated. 2 a group of people joined together for some purpose; society. 3 companionship; partnership; friendship. 4 the connection of ideas in thought. —**Syn.** 1 alliance. 2 club. *Abbrev.*: assn. or Assn., assoc. or Assoc.

association area the part of the brain that is believed to bring together impulses from the sensory nerves, sort them, and send them to the motor area.

association football soccer.

as·so·ci·a·tive (ə sō′shē ə tiv or ə sō′shē ā′tiv) *adj.* 1 tending to associate. 2 having to do with association.

as·soil (ə soil′) *v. Archaic.* 1 absolve. 2 atone for. [ME < OF *assoil*, pres. indicative of *as(s)oldre* < L *absolvere*. Doublet of ABSOLVE.]

as·so·nance (as′ə nəns) *n.* 1 a kind of rhyme in which the vowels are alike but the consonants are different. *Examples*: *brave—vain, lone—show.* 2 *Informal.* a resemblance in sound. *Example*: "So all day long the noise of battle rolled." [< F < L *assonans*, ppr. of *assonare* < *ad-* to + *sonare* sound]

as·sort (ə sôrt′) *v.* 1 sort out; classify; arrange in sorts. 2 furnish with an assortment of goods. 3 group (*with*). 4 agree in sort or kind; fall into a class. 5 associate (*with*). [< F *assortir* < *à-* to (< L *ad-*) + *sorte* sort < L *sors, sortis,* originally, lot] —**as·sort′er,** *n.*

as·sort·ed (ə sôr′tid) *adj.* 1 selected so as to be of different kinds; various. 2 arranged by kinds; classified. 3 matched; suited, one to another.

as·sort·ment (ə sôrt′mənt) *n.* 1 an assorting. 2 a collection of various sorts. 3 a group; class.

ASSR or **A.S.S.R.** Autonomous Soviet Socialist Republic.

asst. or **Asst.** assistant.

as·suage (ə swāj′) *v.* **-suaged, -suag·ing.** 1 make easier or milder: *assuage pain.* 2 satisfy; appease; quench: *assuage thirst.* [ME < OF *assuagier*, ult. < L *ad-* + *suavis* sweet] —**as·suag′er,** *n.*

as·suage·ment (ə swāj′mənt) *n.* 1 an assuaging or being assuaged. 2 something that assuages.

as·sume (ə süm′ or ə sūm′) *v.* **-sumed, -sum·ing.** 1 take for granted; suppose: *He assumed that the train would be on time.* 2 take upon oneself; undertake. 3 take on; put on. 4 appropriate; usurp. 5 pretend: *assume ignorance.* [ME < L *assumere* < *ad-* to + *sumere* take] —**Syn.** 1 presume. 5 feign, simulate. See **pretend.**

as·sumed (ə sümd′ or ə sūmd′) *adj.* 1 pretended; not real. 2 supposed.

as·sum·ing (ə süm′ing or ə sūm′ing) *adj.* taking too much on oneself; presumptuous.

as·sump·tion (ə sump′shən or ə sum′shən) *n.* 1 the act of assuming: *She bustled about with an assumption of authority.* 2 the thing assumed: *John's assumption that he would win the prize proved incorrect.* 3 presumption; arrogance; unpleasant boldness. 4 **the Assumption,** a the bodily taking of the Virgin Mary from earth to heaven after her death. b a Christian church festival in honor of this, held on August 15. [ME < L *assumptio, -onis* < *assumere.* See ASSUME.]

as·sur·ance (ə shür′əns) *n.* 1 a making sure or certain. 2 a positive declaration inspiring confidence. 3 a security; certainty; confidence. 4 self-confidence. 5 impudence; too much boldness. 6 insurance. —**Syn.** 2 guarantee. 4 See **confidence.** 5 audacity, presumption.

as·sure (ə shür′) *v.* **-sured, -sur·ing.** 1 make sure or certain: *The man assured himself that the bridge was safe before crossing it.* 2 tell confidently or positively: *The captain of the ship assured the passengers that there was no danger.* 3 make safe; secure. 4 make safe against loss; insure. 5 give or restore confidence to; reassure. [ME < OF *aseürer* < VL < L *ad-* + *securus* safe] —**as·sur′er,** *n.*

as·sured (ə shürd′) *adj.* 1 sure; certain. 2 confident; bold. 3 insured against loss. —*n.* 1 a person whose life or property is insured. 2 a person who is the beneficiary of an insurance policy. —**as·sur′ed·ness,** *n.*

as·sur·ed·ly (ə shür′id lē) *adv.* 1 surely; certainly. 2 confidently; boldly.

As·syr·i·an (ə sir′ē ən) *adj.* of or having to do with Assyria, an ancient country and empire in S.W. Asia. —*n.* a native or inhabitant of Assyria.

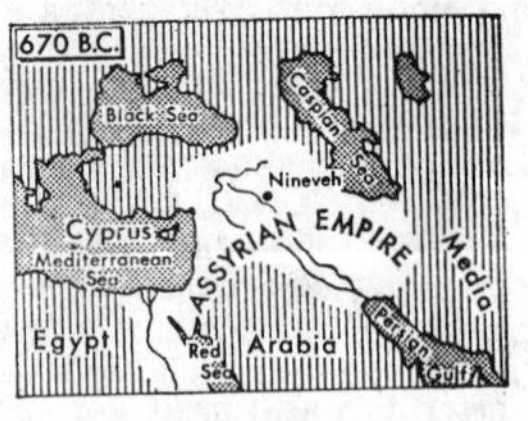

AST, A.S.T., or **a.s.t.** Atlantic Standard Time.

As·tar·te (as tär′tē) *n.* in Phoenician mythology, the goddess of love and fertility, known to the Hebrews as Ashtoreth.

a·stat·ic (ā stat′ik) *adj.* 1 in physics, not tending to take a fixed or definite position: *A magnetic needle may be made astatic by neutralizing it.* 2 not stationary; unstable.

as·ta·tine (as′tə tēn′ or as′tə tin) *n.* a radio-active chemical element. It is produced artificially, and various isotopes have been discovered. *Symbol*: At; *at.no.* 85; *at.wt.* 210 (most stable isotope). [< Gk. *astatos* unstable + E *-ine*[2]]

as·ter (as′tər) *n.* 1 a plant having daisy-like flowers with yellow centres. 2 any plant like this: *China asters look much like small chrysanthemums.* 3 **aster family,** a group of plants whose blossoms are really compact heads of florets surrounded by small leaves or bracts. The daisy belongs to the aster family. [< L < Gk. *astēr* star]

as·ter·isk (as′tər isk′) *n.* in printing and writing, a star-shaped mark (*) to call attention to a footnote, indicate an omission, etc. —*v.* mark with an asterisk. [< LL < Gk. *asteriskos*, dim. of *astēr* star]

as·ter·ism (as′tər iz′əm) *n.* 1 in astronomy: a a group of stars. b a constellation. 2 in geology, a starlike figure produced in some crystallized minerals by reflected or transmitted light.

a·stern (ə stėrn′) *adv.* 1 at or toward the rear of a ship. 2 backward. 3 behind.

as·ter·oid (as′tər oid′) *n.* 1 in astronomy, any of the many very small planets revolving about the sun between the orbit of Mars and the orbit of Jupiter. 2 any starfish. —*adj.* 1 starlike. 2 resembling a starfish. [< Gk. *asteroeidēs* starlike < *astēr* star]

as·the·ni·a (as thē′nē ə) *n.* lack or loss of strength; debility. [< NL *asthenia* < Gk. *astheneia* < *asthenēs* weak < *a-* without + *sthenos* strength]

as·then·ic (as then′ik) *adj.* 1 of or having to do with asthenia; weak. 2 characterized by a tall, lean physique.

asth·ma (az′mə or as′mə) *n.* a chronic disease that causes difficulty in breathing, a feeling of suffocation, and coughing. [ME *asma* < Med.L < Gk. *asthma* panting < *azein* breathe hard]

asth·mat·ic (az mat′ik or as mat′ik) *adj.* 1 of or having to do with asthma. 2 suffering from asthma. —*n.* a person suffering from asthma.

as·tig·mat·ic (as′tig mat′ik) *adj.* 1 having astigmatism. 2 having to do with astigmatism. 3 correcting astigmatism

a·stig·ma·tism (ə stig′mə tiz′əm) *n.* 1 a defect of an eye or of a lens that makes objects look indistinct or gives imperfect images. With perfect focus, all the rays of light from any one point of an object converge at one point on the retina of the eye or other receiving surface; with astigmatism they do not. 2 the state of being unable or of refusing to accept or believe what is true or right. [< *a-*[4] without + Gk. *stigma* point]

a·stir (ə stėr′) *adv. adj.* in motion; up and about: *Although it was past midnight, the whole town was astir.*

as·ton·ish (əs ton′ish) *v.* surprise greatly; amaze: *The gift of ten dollars astonished the beggar.* [var. of *astoun* < OF *estoner* < VL **extonare;* cf. L *tonare* thunder] —**Syn.** astound. See **surprise.**

as·ton·ish·ing (əs ton′ish ing) *adj.* very surprising; amazing. —**as·ton′ish·ing·ly,** *adv.*

as·ton·ish·ment (əs ton′ish mənt) *n.* 1 great surprise; amazement; sudden wonder. 2 anything that causes great surprise.

as·tound (əs tound′) *v.* shock with alarm or surprise; surprise very greatly; amaze. [earlier *astoun.* See ASTONISH.] —**as·tound′ing·ly,** *adv.*

astr. 1 astronomer. 2 astronomy.

a·strad·dle (ə strad′əl) *adv. adj.* astride.

as·tra·gal (as′trə gəl) *n.* in architecture: 1 a small, convex moulding cut into the form of a string of beads. 2 plain, convex moulding.

as·trag·a·lus (as trag′ə ləs) *n.* **-li** (-lī′ or -lē′). in anatomy, the uppermost bone of the tarsus; anklebone; talus. [< L < Gk. *astragalos*]

as·tra·khan or **as·tra·chan** (as′trə kən) *n.* 1 the curly furlike wool of young lambs from Astrakhan, a district in the southern Soviet Union. 2 a woollen cloth that looks like this. 3 a variety of apple having a reddish skin and crisp, white flesh.

as·tral (as′trəl) *adj.* of the stars; starry. [< LL *astralis* < L *astrum* star < Gk. *astron*]

astral body 1 a ghostlike double of the human body supposed to be able to leave it at will. 2 a star or planet.

astral lamp an oil lamp so made that it casts no shadow on the table below.

a·stray (ə strā′) *adj. adv.* out of the right way.

a·stride (ə strīd′) *adj. adv.* 1 with one leg on each side. 2 with legs far apart. —*prep.* with one leg on each side of (something).

as·trin·gen·cy (əs trin′jən sē) *n.* the property of being astringent.

as·trin·gent (əs trin′jənt) *adj.* 1 having the property of shrinking or contracting bodily tissue. 2 severe. —*n.* a substance that shrinks tissues and checks the flow of blood by contracting blood vessels. Alum is an astringent. [< L *astringens, -entis,* ppr. of *astringere* < *ad-* to + *stringere* bind] —**as·trin′gent·ly,** *adv.*

astro- *combining form.* 1 a star, planet, or other heavenly body as in *astrophysics.* 2 space; outer space as in *astronaut.*

as·tro·bi·ol·o·gist (as′trō bī ol′ə jist) *n.* an expert in astrobiology.

as·tro·bi·ol·o·gy (as′trō bī ol′ə jē) *n.* the branch of biology that deals with the discovery and study of life on other planets, etc.

as·tro·bot·a·ny (as′trō bot′ə nē) *n.* the branch of botany that deals with the discovery and study of plant life on other planets, etc.

as·tro·chem·is·try (as′trō kem′is trē) *n.* the branch of chemistry that deals with the chemical properties of heavenly bodies.

astro compass an instrument used to determine direction by sighting on a heavenly body.

as·tro·dy·nam·ics (as′trō dī nam′iks) *n.* the branch of dynamics that deals with the motion of bodies in outer space and the forces acting upon them.

as·tro·labe (as′trə lāb′ or as′trə lab′) *n.* an astronomical instrument formerly used for measuring the altitude of the sun or stars. [ME < OF *astrelabe* < Med.L < Gk. *astrolabon,* originally, star-taking < *astron* star + *lambanein* take]

as·trol·o·ger (əs trol′ə jər) *n.* a person who claims to interpret the influence of the stars and planets on persons, events, etc.

as·tro·log·i·cal (as′trə loj′ə kəl) *adj.* having to do with astrology.

as·trol·o·gy (əs trol′ə jē) *n.* 1 a pseudo-science that interprets the supposed influence of the stars and planets on persons, events, etc.; the study of the stars to foretell what will happen. 2 *Archaic.* practical astronomy. [ME < L < Gk. *astrologia* < *astron* star + *-logos* treating of]

astron. 1 astronomer. 2 astronomical. 3 astronomy.

as·tro·naut (as′trə not′ or as′trə nôt′) *n.* 1 a pilot or crew member of a space ship. 2 a person interested in astronautics. [< *astro* + (*Argo*)*naut*]

as·tro·nau·tics (as′trə no′tiks or as′trə nô′tiks) *n.* 1 the designing, manufacturing, and operating of space vehicles. 2 space travel.

as·tron·o·mer (əs tron′ə mər) *n.* an expert in astronomy.

hat, āge, cãre, fär; let, ēqual, tėrm; it, īce
hot, ōpen, ôrder; oil, out; cup, pu̇t, rüle, ūse
əbove, takən, pencəl, lemən, circəs
ch, child; ng, long; sh, ship
th, thin; ᴛʜ, then; zh, measure

as·tro·nom·ic (as′trə nom′ik) *adj.* astronomical.

as·tro·nom·i·cal (as′trə nom′ə kəl) *adj.* 1 of astronomy; having to do with astronomy. 2 enormous; like the numbers reported in astronomy.

as·tro·nom·i·cal·ly (as′trə nom′ik lē) *adv.* according to astronomy.

astronomical unit the mean distance of the earth from the sun, used as a yardstick for many astronomical units.

astronomical year the period of the earth's revolution around the sun; solar year. It lasts 365 days, 5 hours, 48 minutes, and 45.51 seconds.

as·tron·o·my (əs tron′ə mē) *n.* 1 the science that treats of the sun, moon, and other heavenly bodies. It deals with their composition, motions, positions, distances, sizes, etc. 2 a textbook or handbook dealing with this science. *Abbrev.*: astr. [ME < L < Gk. *astronomia* < *astron* star + *nomos* distribution]

as·tro·phys·i·cal (as′trō fiz′ə kəl) *adj.* of or having to do with astrophysics.

as·tro·phys·ics (as′trō fiz′iks) *n.* the branch of astronomy that deals with the physical and chemical characteristics of heavenly bodies.

as·tute (əs tūt′ or əs tüt′) *adj.* shrewd; discerning; sagacious: *Many lawyers are astute.* [< L *astutus* < *astus* sagacity] —**as·tute′ly,** *adv.* —**as·tute′ness,** *n.* —**Syn.** See **shrewd.**

a·sun·der (ə sun′dər) *adv.* in pieces; into separate parts. —*adj.* apart; separate. [OE *on sundran*]

ASW antisubmarine warfare.

a·swarm (ə swôrm′) *adv. adj.* in a crowded, swarming state: *The bleachers were aswarm with baseball fans.*

a·sy·lum (ə sī′ləm) *n.* 1 an institution for the support and care of the insane, the blind, orphans, etc. 2 a refuge; shelter. In olden times a church was an asylum for a debtor or a criminal since no one was allowed to drag a person from the altar. [ME < L < Gk. *asylon* refuge < *a-* without + *sylē* right of seizure] —**Syn. 2** sanctuary.

a·sym·met·ric (ā′sə met′rik or as′ə met′rik) *adj.* not symmetrical; lacking symmetry.

a·sym·met·ri·cal (ā′sə met′rə kəl or as′ə met′rə kəl) *adj.* asymmetric.

a·sym·me·try (ā sim′ə trē or a sim′ə trē) *n.* lack of symmetry.

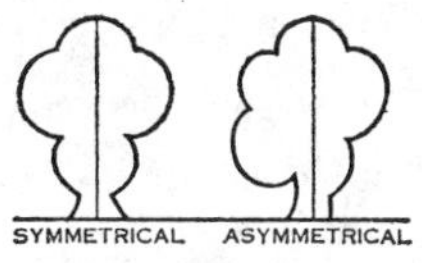

Asymmetry

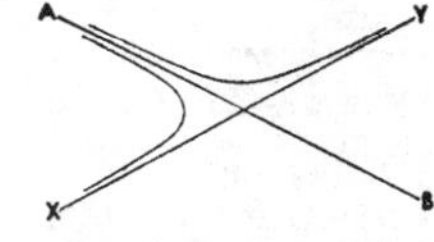

The lines AB and XY are asymptotes

as·ymp·tote (as′im tōt′) *n.* in mathematics, a straight line that continually approaches a curve, but does not meet it within a finite distance. [< Gk. *asymptōtos* < *a-* not + *syn-* together + *ptōtos* apt to fall]

at[1] (ət; *stressed,* at) *prep.* 1 in; on; near: *at school, at the front door.* 2 toward; in the direction of: *aim at the mark. Look at me.* 3 in a place or condition of: *at right angles, at war.* 4 on or near the time of: *at midnight.* 5 through; by way of: *Smoke came out at the chimney.* 6 engaged in; trying to do: *at work.* 7 because of; as a result of: *The shipwrecked sailors were happy at the arrival of the rescue ship.* 8 for: *two books at a dollar each.* 9 according to: *at will.* 10 from: *The sick man got good treatment at the hands of his doctor.* [OE *æt*]

☞ **At,** in are used to connect to a sentence a word stating a place or a time. **At** is used when the place or time is thought of as a point, as on a map or a clock. **In** is used when the place or time is thought of as having boundaries and the idea to be expressed is that of being *inside* or *within* the boundaries: *On our trip we stopped at Toronto and stayed two days in Montreal. We left Montreal at noon and in the afternoon drove to Quebec.*

at² (ät) *n.* **1** a unit of money in Laos, worth 1/100 of a kip. **2** a coin worth one at. [< Thai]

At astatine.

AT antitank.

AT, A.T., or **a.t.** Atlantic Time.

at- the form of **ad-** before *t*, as in *attain.*

at. 1 atmosphere; atmospheres. **2** atomic.

At·a·lan·ta (at′ə lan′tə) *n.* in Greek legend, a maiden famous for her beauty and for her speed in running. She required each of her suitors to run a race with her; those who lost the race were killed.

at·a·vism (at′ə viz′əm) *n.* **1** resemblance to a remote ancestor. If a child of very quiet, home-loving parents and grandparents should display the love of travel and adventure that had characterized a sea-captain ancestor, it would be called a case of atavism. **2** reversion to a primitive type. [< L *atavus* ancestor]

at·a·vis·tic (at′ə vis′tik] *adj.* **1** having to do with atavism. **2** having a tendency to atavism.

a·tax·i·a (ə tak′sē ə) *n.* in medicine, an inability to co-ordinate voluntary movements. [< NL < Gk. *ataxia* < *a-* without + *taxis* order]

ATC or **A.T.C. 1** air traffic control. **2** Air Transport Command.

ate (āt) *v.* pt. of **eat.**

A·te (ā′tē) *n.* in Greek mythology, the goddess of recklessness and mischief, later regarded as the goddess of revenge.

-ate¹ *suffix.* **1** of or having to do with: *novitiate* = *having to do with novices.*
2 having; containing: *compassionate* = *having compassion.*
3 having the form of; like: *stellate* = *having the form of a star.*
4 become: *maturate* = *become mature.*
5 cause to be: *alienate* = *cause to be alien.*
6 produce: *ulcerate* = *produce ulcers.*
7 supply or treat with: *aerate* = *treat with air.*
8 combine with: *oxygenate* = *combine with oxygen.* [< L *-atus, atum,* pp. endings]

-ate² *suffix.* a salt made from ——ic acid: *nitrate* = *salt made from nitric acid.* [special use of *-ate¹*]

-ate³ *suffix.* the office, rule, or condition of: *caliphate* = *rule of a caliph.* [< L *-atus,* from 4th declension nouns]

at·el·ier (at′əl yā′) *n.* a workshop, especially an artist's studio. [< F *atelier* originally, pile of chips < OF *astele* chip < L *astula*]

a tem·po (ä tem′pō) in music, in time; returning to the former speed. [< Ital.]

Ath·a·na·sian Creed (ath′ə nā′zhən or ath′ə nā′shən) one of the three main Christian creeds or professions of faith, the other two being the Apostles' Creed and the Nicene Creed. Its authorship is unknown, but it was probably composed around A.D. 430. [< St. *Athanasius* (296 ?-373), bishop of Alexandria, formerly supposed to be the author of the creed]

Ath·a·pas·can (ath′ə pas′kən) *n.* **1** a family of American Indian languages spoken in Canada, Alaska, and the S.W. United States. **2** an Indian who speaks one of these languages.

a·the·ism (ā′thē iz′əm) *n.* the belief that there is no God. [< F *athéisme* < Gk. *atheos* denying the gods < *a-* without + *theos* a god]

a·the·ist (ā′thē ist) *n.* a person who believes that there is no God.

a·the·is·tic (ā′thē is′tik) *adj.* of atheism or atheists. —**a′the·is′ti·cal·ly,** *adv.*

a·the·is·ti·cal (ā′thē is′tə kəl) *adj.* atheistic.

ath·el·ing (ath′ə ling′) *n.* an Anglo-Saxon prince or noble, especially a crown prince. [OE *ætheling* < *æthelu* noble family + *-ling* belonging to]

A·the·na (ə thē′nə) *n.* in Greek mythology, the goddess of wisdom, arts, industries, and prudent warfare, identified with the Roman goddess Minerva. Also, **Pallas, Pallas Athena.**

ath·e·nae·um or **ath·e·ne·um** (ath′ə nē′əm) *n.* **1** a scientific or literary club. **2** a reading room; library. [< L < Gk. *Athēnaion* temple of Athena]

Ath·e·nae·um (ath′ə nē′əm) *n.* in Athens, the temple of Athena. Poets and learned men gathered there.

A·the·ne (ə thē′nē) *n.* Athena.

A·the·ni·an (ə thē′nē ən or ə thēn′yən) *adj.* of Athens or its people. —*n.* **1** a person having the right of citizenship in ancient Athens. **2** a native or inhabitant of Athens.

ath·er·o·ma (ath′ə rō′mə) *n.* **1** a fatty degeneration of the lining of the arteries. **2** a sebaceous cyst. [< L < Gk. *athērē* mush + *-ōma* tumor]

a·thirst (ə thėrst′) *adj.* **1** thirsty. **2** eager.

ath·lete (ath′lēt) *n.* a person trained in exercises of physical strength, speed, and skill. Ballplayers, runners, boxers, and swimmers are athletes. [< L *athleta* < Gk. *athlētēs* < *athlēo* contend for a prize (*athlon*)]

athlete's foot a contagious skin disease of the feet, caused by a fungus; ringworm of the feet.

ath·let·ic (ath let′ik) *adj.* **1** active and strong. **2** of, like, or suited to an athlete. **3** having to do with active games and sports. —**ath·let′i·cal·ly,** *adv.*

ath·let·ics (ath let′iks) *n.* **1** (*usually pl. in use*) exercises of strength, speed and skill; active games and sports: *Athletics include baseball and basketball.*
2 (*usually sing. in use*) the practice and principles of athletic training: *Athletics is recommended for every student.*

at-home (ət hōm′) *n.* an informal reception, usually in the afternoon.

a·thwart (ə thwôrt′) *adv.* crosswise; across from side to side. —*prep.* **1** across. **2** across the line or course of. **3** in opposition to; against. [< *a-* on + *thwart,* adv.]

at·i·gi (at′ə gē or ə tē′gē) *n. Cdn.* **1** a hooded, knee-length inner shirt made of summer skins with the hair inward against the body, used mainly by Eskimos, often for indoor wear. **2** a hooded outer garment of fur or other material; parka. Also, **artigi, artiggi.** [< Eskimo]

a·tilt (ə tilt′) *adj. adv.* **1** at a tilt; tilted. **2** in a tilting encounter.

a·tin·gle (ə ting′gəl) *adj.* tingling; in a tingling or excited condition.

-ation *suffix.* **1** the act or state of ——ing: *admiration* = *act or state of admiring.* **2** the condition or state of being ——ed: *cancellation* = *condition or state of being cancelled.* **3** the result of ——ing: *civilization* = *result of civilizing.* [< L *-atio, -onis* < *-at-* of pp. stem (cf. *-ate¹*) + *-io* (cf. *-ion*)]

-ative *suffix.* **1** tending to ——: *talkative* = *tending to talk.* **2** having to do with ——: *qualitative* = *having to do with quality.* [< F *-ative* (fem. of *-atif* < L *-ativus*) or directly < L *-ativus* < *-at-* of pp. stem (cf. *-ate¹*) + *-ivus* (cf. *-ive*)]

At·lan·te·an (at′lan tē′ən) *adj.* **1** resembling Atlas; strong. **2** having to do with the legendary island of Atlantis. [< L *Atlanteus*]

At·lan·tic (at lan′tik) *n.* the Atlantic Ocean. —*adj.* **1** of the Atlantic Ocean. **2** on or near the Atlantic Ocean. **3** of or having to do with NATO: *the Atlantic nations.* [< L < Gk. *Atlantikos* pertaining to Atlas]

Atlantic Charter the joint declaration of President Roosevelt and Prime Minister Churchill on August 14, 1941, asserting the need for guaranteed freedom of all nations.

Atlantic Provinces Newfoundland, Prince Edward Island, Nova Scotia, and New Brunswick.

At·lan·tis (at lan′tis) *n.* a legendary island in the Atlantic, said to have sunk beneath the sea. [< L < Gk.]

at·las (at′ləs) *n.* **1** a book of maps. **2** a book of plates or tables illustrating any subject. [< L < Gk.]

At·las (at′ləs) *n.* **1** in Greek mythology, one of the Titans. He rebelled against Zeus and was punished by being made to support the heavens with his head and hands. **2** a person or thing that bears the main burden of anything. **3** any person who is exceptionally strong.

atm. 1 atmosphere; atmospheres. **2** atmospheric.

at·mom·e·ter (at mom′ə tər) *n.* an instrument for measuring rate of evaporation. [< Gk. *atmos* vapor + E *-meter*]

at·mos·phere (at′məs fēr′) *n.* **1** air that surrounds the earth for about 200 miles upwards; the air. **2** mental and moral environment; surrounding influence. **3** in astronomy, a mass of gases that surrounds any heavenly body. **4** air in any given place: *a damp atmosphere.* **5** in physics, a unit of pressure equal to 14.69 pounds per square inch. **6** a coloring or feeling that pervades a work of art: *music steeped in the atmosphere of old Vienna, the sombre atmosphere of "The Scarlet Letter." Abbrev.*: at. or atm. [< NL *atmosphaera* < Gk. *atmos* vapor + *sphaira* sphere]

at·mos·pher·ic (at′məs fer′ik) *adj.* **1** of or having to do with the atmosphere. **2** in the atmosphere: *Atmospheric conditions often prevent observations of the stars.* **3** caused, produced, or worked by the atmosphere. —*n.* **atmospherics,** *pl.* static; interference in a radio or television set, caused by electrical disturbance of the atmosphere.

at·mos·pher·i·cal (at′məs fer′ə kəl) *adj.* atmospheric.

at·mos·pher·i·cal·ly (at′məs fer′ik lē) *adv.* as regards the atmosphere; by atmospheric force or influence.

atmospheric pressure the pressure caused by the weight of the air. The atmospheric pressure at sea level is 14.69 pounds to the square inch. See **atmosphere** (def. 5).

at. no. atomic number.

at·oll (at′ol or ə tol′) *n.* a ring-shaped coral island enclosing or partly enclosing a lagoon. [< Maldive (lang. of the Maldive Islands in the Indian Ocean), ? < Malayalam *adal* uniting]

at·om (at′əm) *n.* **1** the smallest particle of a chemical element that can take part in a chemical reaction without being permanently changed. A molecule of water is made by the combination of two atoms of hydrogen with one atom of oxygen. **2** a very small particle; tiny bit. [< L < Gk. *atomos* indivisible < *a-* not + *tomos* a cutting]

atom bomb atomic bomb.

a·tom·ic (ə tom′ik) *adj.* **1** of atoms; having to do with atoms. **2** extremely small; minute. *Abbrev.*: at.

atomic age the era that began with the first use of atomic energy.

atomic bomb a bomb that uses the energy from the splitting of atoms to cause an explosion of tremendous force. Also, **A-bomb.**

atomic clock a highly accurate clock that is run by controlled radio waves.

atomic energy the energy that exists in atoms. Some atoms can be made to release this atomic energy, either slowly (in a reactor) or very suddenly (in a bomb); it is generated through alteration of an atomic nucleus, chiefly by fission.

atomic furnace a reactor that provides heat for the generation of steam by which turbines or other engines may be run: *Scientists believe that atomic furnaces may some day provide a great part of our electricity.*

atomic hypothesis atomic theory.

at·o·mic·i·ty (at′ə mis′ə tē) *n.* **1** in chemistry: **a** the number of atoms in one molecule of an element. **b** valence. **c** the number of atoms or groups that can be replaced in the molecule of a compound. **2** the state or condition of being composed of atoms.

atomic number in chemistry and physics, a number used in describing a chemical element and giving its relation to other elements. It is the number of positive charges on the nucleus of one of its atoms. *Abbrev.*: at. no.

atomic pile See **reactor.**

atomic submarine a submarine powered by a reactor.

atomic theory in chemistry and physics, the theory that all matter is composed of atoms; especially, the modern theory that an atom is made of a positive nucleus around which electrons speed.

atomic warfare warfare using atomic weapons.

atomic weight the relative weight of an atom of a chemical element, using oxygen or hydrogen as a standard of comparison. *Abbrev.*: at. wt.

hat, āge, cãre, fär; let, ēqual, tėrm; it, īce
hot, ōpen, ôrder; oil, out; cup, pu̇t, rüle, ūse
əbove, takən, pencəl, lemən, circəs
ch, child; ng, long; sh, ship
th, thin; ᴛʜ, then; zh, measure

at·om·ize (at′əm īz′) *v.* **-ized, -iz·ing. 1** reduce to atoms. **2** change (a liquid) into a fine spray. —**at′om·i·za′tion,** *n.*

at·om·iz·er (at′əm īz′ər) *n.* an apparatus used to blow a liquid in a spray of very small drops.

atom smasher cyclotron.

at·o·my[1] (at′ə mē) *n.* **-mies. 1** a very small thing; atom. **2** a tiny being; pygmy. [< L *atomi,* pl. of *atomus.* See ATOM.]

at·o·my[2] (at′ə mē) *n.* **-mies.** *Archaic.* a skeleton. [for *anatomy* taken as *an atomy*]

a·ton·al (ā tōn′əl) *adj.* in music, using a system of tones in which each tone is equal in relation to the others, no one tone being central; having no key. —**a·ton′al·ly,** *adv.*

a·to·nal·i·ty (ā′tō nal′ə tē) *n.* in music, the state or condition of being atonal; absence of tonality.

a·tone (ə tōn′) *v.* **a·toned, a·ton·ing.** make up; make amends (*for*): *Tom atoned for his unkindness to Joyce by taking her to the movies.* [< *atonement*]

a·tone·ment (ə tōn′mənt) *n.* **1** a making up for something; giving satisfaction for a wrong, loss, or injury; amends. **2 the Atonement,** the reconciliation of God with sinners through the sufferings and death of Christ. **3** Yom Kippur; Day of Atonement. [< *at onement* a being at one, i.e., in accord; *onement* < ME *onen* unite, ult. < OE *ān* one]

a·top (ə top′) *adv.* on or at the top. —*prep.* on the top of.

at·ra·bil·ious (at′rə bil′yəs) *adj.* **1** melancholy; hypochondriac. **2** bad-tempered. [< L *atra bilis* black bile]

a·tri·um (ā′trē əm or at′rē əm) *n.* **a·tri·a** (ā′trē ə or at′rē ə) **1** the main room of an ancient Roman house. **2** a hall; court. **3** in anatomy, an auricle (def. 1). **4** any of various other cavities in animals. [< L *atrium* (def. 1) < Etruscan]

a·tro·cious (ə trō′shəs) *adj.* **1** very wicked or cruel; very savage or brutal: *The behavior of the barbarians was atrocious.* **2** *Informal.* very bad; abominable: *atrocious weather.* —**a·tro′cious·ly,** *adv.* —**a·tro′cious·ness,** *n.*

a·troc·i·ty (ə tros′ə tē) *n.* **-ties. 1** very great wickedness or cruelty. **2** a very cruel or brutal act. **3** *Informal.* a very bad blunder. [< L *atrocitas* < *atrox, -ocis* fierce < *ater* dark]

at·ro·phy (at′rə fē) *n. v.* **-phied, -phy·ing.** —*n.* **1** a wasting away; wasting away of a part or parts of the body: *atrophy of a civilization, muscular atrophy.* **2** a failure to develop: *atrophy of the intellect.* —*v.* **1** waste away. **2** undergo atrophy. [< LL < Gk. *atrophia* < *a-* without + *trophē* nourishment]

at·ro·pin (at′rə pin) *n.* atropine.

at·ro·pine (at′rə pēn′ or at′rə pin) *n.* a poisonous drug obtained from belladonna and similar plants. Atropine relaxes muscles and dilates the pupil of the eye. *Formula*: $C_{17}H_{23}NO_3$ [< NL *Atropa* belladonna < Gk. *Atropos* one of the Fates]

At·ro·pos (at′rə pos′) *n.* in Greek mythology, one of the three Fates. Atropos cuts the thread of life.

at·tach (ə tach′) *v.* **1** fasten (*to*): *The boy attached a rope to his wagon.* **2** connect with for duty, etc.: *He was attached as mate to the ship "Clio."* **3** affix: *The signers attached their names to the petition.* **4** attribute: *The world at first attached little importance to the policies of Hitler.* **5** fasten itself; belong: *The blame attaches to you.* **6** bind by affection: *May is much attached to her cousin.* **7** in law, take (person or property) by legal authority: *If you owe money to a man, he can attach a part of your salary.* [ME < OF *atachier* < L *ad-* to + Gmc. source of OF *tache* a fastening, a nail. Related to TACK.] —**at·tach′a·ble,** *adj.*

Syn. 4 Attach, affix, annex = to add one thing to another. **Attach,** the general word, used literally and figuratively, suggests only joining or fastening one thing to another by some means: *He attached a trailer to his car.* **Affix** suggests putting one thing, usually something smaller or less important, on another firmly and permanently: *He affixed his seal to the document.* **Annex** = add to and make a part of (usually something larger): *The Board annexed the new suburb to the school district.*

at·ta·ché (ə tash′ā or at′ə shā′) *n.* a person belonging to the official staff of an ambassador or minister to a foreign country. [< F]

attaché case a small, rectangular, leather or plastic case for carrying documents, books, etc.

at·tach·ment (ə tach′mənt) *n.* **1** an attaching. **2** a being attached. **3** something that is or can be attached: *A sewing machine has various attachments, such as a hemmer and a darner.* **4** a means of attaching; fastening. **5** affection. **6** in law: **a** the legal seizure of property. **b** the arrest of a person. **c** the writ authorizing an attachment.

at·tack (ə tak′) *v.* **1** use force or weapons on to hurt; go against as an enemy; begin fighting against: *The dog attacked the cat.* **2** talk or write against. **3** begin to work vigorously on: *The hungry boy attacked his dinner as soon as it was served.* **4** act harmfully on: *Fever attacked the man who had been bitten by insects.* **5** make an attack: *The enemy attacked at dawn.*
—*n.* **1** a sudden occurrence of illness, discomfort, etc.: *an attack of malaria.* **2** an attacking; assault: *The attack of the enemy took us by surprise.* [< F < Ital. *attaccare* (from the same source as OF *atachier*). See ATTACH.] —**at·tack′er,** *n.*
Syn. *v.* **1 Attack, assail, assault** = set upon with force. **Attack,** the general word, emphasizes the idea of falling upon a person or enemy without warning, sometimes without cause, or of starting the fighting: *Germany attacked Belgium in 1914.* **Assail** = attack with violence and repeated blows: *The enemy assailed our defence positions.* **Assault** = attack suddenly with furious or brutal force, and always suggests actual contact as in hand-to-hand fighting: *In a rage he assaulted his neighbor with a knife.* **2** criticize, blame.

at·tain (ə tān′) *v.* **1** arrive at; reach: *attain years of discretion.* **2** gain; accomplish. **3 attain to,** succeed in coming to or getting: *attain to a position of great influence.* [ME < OF *ataindre* < VL *attangere* < L *ad-* to + *tangere* touch] —**Syn. 2** achieve.

at·tain·a·bil·i·ty (ə tān′ə bil′ə tē) *n.* the quality of being attainable.

at·tain·a·ble (ə tān′ə bəl) *adj.* that can be attained: *The office of Prime Minister is one of the highest attainable in Canada.*

at·tain·der (ə tān′dər) *n.* formerly, the loss of property and civil rights as the result of being sentenced to death or being outlawed. [ME < OF *ataindre* attain; influenced by E *taindre* taint]

at·tain·ment (ə tān′mənt) *n.* **1** an attaining. **2** something attained. **3** an accomplishment: *Leonardo da Vinci was a man of varied attainments; he was a painter, engineer, and inventor.*

at·taint (ə tānt′) *v.* **1** in law, condemn to the loss of property and civil rights. **2** disgrace. —*n.* a disgrace. [< OF *ataint,* pp. of *ataindre.* See ATTAIN.] —**at·taint′ment,** *n.* —**Syn.** *v.* **2** stain, taint.

at·tar (at′ər) *n.* a perfume made from the petals of roses or other flowers. [< Persian *'aṭar* < Arabic *'uṭur* aroma]

attar of roses a fragrant oil made from rose petals.

at·tempt (ə tempt′) *v.* **1** make an effort at; try. **2** try to take or destroy (life, etc.). —*n.* **1** a putting forth of effort to accomplish something, especially something difficult. **2** an attack. [< OF < L *attemptare* < *ad-* to + *temptare* try] —**Syn.** *v.* **1** essay, endeavor. See **try.**

at·tend (ə tend′) *v.* **1** be present at: *Children must attend school.* **2** give care and thought; pay attention: *Attend to the laboratory instructions.* **3** apply oneself: *Attend to your music if you want to play well.* **4** go with; accompany: *Noble ladies attend the queen.* **5** go with as a result: *Danger attends delay. Success often attends hard work.* **6** wait on; care for; tend: *Nurses attend the sick.* **7** be ready; wait. [ME < OF < *atendre* < L *attendere* < *ad-* toward + *tendere* stretch] —**Syn. 4 See accompany. 6 serve.**

at·tend·ance (ə ten′dəns) *n.* **1** a being present; an attending: *Attendance at all classes is compulsory.* **2** the people present; the number attending: *The attendance at church was over 200 last Sunday.* **3 dance attendance on,** wait on with excessive attentions: *The ambitious courtier danced attendance on any noble he thought might help him.* **4 in attendance,** waiting (*on*); on duty.

at·tend·ant (ə ten′dənt) *adj.* **1** waiting on another to help or serve: *an attendant nurse.* **2** going with as a result; accompanying: *weakness attendant on illness, attendant circumstances.* **3** present: *attendant hearers.* —*n.* **1** a person who waits on another, such as a servant or a follower. **2** an accompanying thing or event. **3** a person who is present.

at·ten·tion (ə ten′shən) *n.* **1** the act or fact of attending: *The children paid attention to the teacher.* **2** the faculty of noticing: *James called my attention to the cat trying to catch the mouse.* **3** care and thought; consideration: *The boy shows his mother much attention.* **4** courtesy. **5 attentions,** *pl.* acts of courtesy or devotion, especially of a suitor. **6** a military attitude of readiness. **7 come to attention,** take a straight and motionless position. **8 stand at attention,** stand straight and still.
—*interj.* a command to come to attention. [ME < L *attentio, -onis* < *attendere.* See ATTEND.] —**Syn.** *n.* **4** deference, civility.

at·ten·tive (ə ten′tiv) *adj.* **1** paying attention; observant. **2** courteous; showing consideration for or interest in. —**at·ten′tive·ly,** *adv.* —**at·ten′tive·ness,** *n.*

at·ten·u·ate (ə ten′ū āt′) *v.* **-at·ed, -at·ing. 1** make or become thin or slender. **2** weaken; reduce. **3** make less dense; dilute. **4** in bacteriology, make (micro-organisms, etc.) less harmful. [< L *attenuare* < *ad-* + *tenuis* thin]

at·ten·u·a·tion (ə ten′ū ā′shən) *n.* an attenuating or being attenuated.

at·ten·u·a·tor (ə ten′ū ā′tər) *n.* **1** a person or thing that attenuates. **2** in radio, a device used to reduce amplitude.

at·test (ə test′) *v.* **1** give proof or evidence of: *The child's good health attests his mother's care.* **2** declare to be true or genuine; certify. **3** bear witness; testify: *The handwriting expert attested to the genuineness of the signature.* **4** put on oath. [< L *attestari* < *ad-* to + *testis* witness]

at·tes·ta·tion (at′es tā′shən) *n.* **1** the act of attesting. **2** proof; evidence. **3** testimony.

at·tic (at′ik) *n.* a space in a house just below the roof and above the other rooms. [< F *attique* < L *Atticus* Attic < Gk.]

At·tic (at′ik) *adj.* **1** of Attica; of Athens; Athenian. **2** simple; elegant; refined. —*n.* **1** a native of Attica. **2** the speech of Attica, the language of Plato, Sophocles, Euripides, and Pericles. [< L *Atticus* < Gk. *Attikos*]

at·tire (ə tīr′) *v.* **-tired, -tir·ing,** *n.* dress; array: *The queen wears rich attire. She is attired in purple.* [ME < OF *atirer* arrange < *a-* to (< L *ad-*) + *tire* row < Gmc.]

at·ti·tude (at′ə tūd′ or at′ə tüd′) *n.* **1** a way of thinking, acting, or feeling: *His attitude toward school changed from dislike to great enthusiasm.* **2** a position of the body appropriate to an action, purpose, emotion, etc. **3** the position of an aircraft, space capsule, etc. in relation to some line or plane, such as the horizon or the horizontal. **4 strike an attitude,** pose for effect. [< F < Ital. *attitudine* < LL *aptitudo.* Doublet of APTITUDE.] —**Syn. 2** posture, pose.

attn. attention.

at·tor·ney (ə tėr′nē) *n.* **-neys. 1** a person who has power to act for another. **2** a lawyer. *Abbrev.:* atty. [ME < OF *atourne,* pp. of *atourner* assign, appoint < *a-* to (< L *ad-*) + *tourner* turn < L *tornare* turn on a lathe < *tornus* lathe < Gk.] —**Syn. 1** agent.

attorney at law a lawyer.

attorney general or **Attorney General** *pl.* **attorneys general** or **attorney generals. 1** a chief law officer. **2 a** the chief law officer of Canada. **b** the chief law officer of a province. *Abbrev.:* A.G.

at·tract (ə trakt′) *v.* **1** draw to oneself: *A magnet attracts iron.* **2** be pleasing to; win the attention and liking of: *Bright colors attract children.* [< L *attractus,* pp. of *attrahere* < *ad-* to + *trahere* draw] —**Syn. 2 allure,** fascinate.

at·trac·tion (ə trak′shən) *n.* **1** the act or power of attracting. **2** anything that delights or attracts people: *The elephants were the chief attraction at the circus.* **3** charm; fascination. **4** in physics, the force exerted by molecules on one another, tending to draw or hold them together.

at·trac·tive (ə trak′tiv) *adj.* **1** pleasing; winning attention and approval: *She wore an attractive hat.* **2** attracting. —**at·trac′tive·ly,** *adv.* —**at·trac′tive·ness,** *n.* —**Syn. 1** alluring.

attrib. 1 attribute. 2 attributive.

at·trib·ut·a·ble (ə trib′yủ tə bəl) *adj.* that can be attributed: *Some diseases are attributable to lack of cleanliness.*

at·trib·ute (*v.* ə trib′yủt; *n.* at′rə būt′) *v.* **-ut·ed, -ut·ing,** *n.* —*v.* consider (something) as belonging or appropriate (to a person or thing); regard as an effect of; think of as caused by: *We attribute his success to intelligence and hard work.*
—*n.* **1** a quality considered as belonging to a person or thing; a characteristic: *Prudence is an attribute of a judge.* **2** an object considered appropriate to a person, rank, or office; symbol: *The eagle was the attribute of Jupiter.* **3** an adjective; a word or phrase used as an adjective. [ME < L *attributus,* pp. of *attribuere* < *ad-* to + *tribuere* assign, originally, divide among the tribes < *tribus* tribe]
Syn. *v.* **Attribute, ascribe** = consider something as belonging or due to someone or something, and are often interchangeable. But **attribute** suggests believing something appropriate to a person or thing or belonging to it by nature or right: *We attribute importance to the words of great men.* **Ascribe** suggests guessing or basing a conclusion on evidence and reasoning: *I ascribe his failure to his careless habits.* —*n.* 1 trait, property.

at·tri·bu·tion (at′rə bū′shən) *n.* **1** the act of attributing. **2** the thing attributed; attribute.

at·trib·u·tive (ə trib′yủ tiv) *adj.* **1** expressing a quality or attribute. An adjective used before or after a noun is an attributive adjective. **2** that attributes. **3** of or like an attribute.
—*n.* an attributive word. In the phrase "big brown dog," *big* and *brown* are attributives; in "morning star," *morning* is an attributive. —**at·trib′u·tive·ly,** *adv.*
☛ **attributive.** An adjective that stands next to its noun is attributive (a *blue* shirt; the church *militant*), as contrasted with a predicate adjective that is related to its noun by a linking verb (The shirt is *blue*).

at·tri·tion (ə trish′ən) *n.* **1** a wearing away by rubbing: *Pebbles become smooth by attrition.* **2** any gradual process of wearing down: *a war of attrition.* **3** sorrow for one's sins, less perfect than contrition. [ME < LL *attritio, -onis* < *atterere* < *ad-* against + *terere* rub]

at·tune (ə tūn′ or ə tün′) *v.* **-tuned, -tun·ing.** tune; put or be in tune or harmony. —**at·tune′ment,** *n.*

atty. attorney.

at. wt. atomic weight.

a·typ·i·cal (ā tip′ə kəl or a tip′ə kəl) *adj.* not typical; irregular; abnormal. —**a·typ′i·cal·ly,** *adv.*

Au gold. (for L *aurum*)

au·berge (ō berzh′) *n.* an inn. [< F]

au·burn (o′bərn or ô′bərn) *n. adj.* reddish brown. [ME < OF *auborne* < L *alburnus* whitish < *albus* white; apparently confused with ME *brun* brown]

Au·bus·son (ō bʏ sôɴ′) *n. French.* **1** a rich tapestry of scenes or figures used for wall hangings, upholstery, etc. **2** a rug woven like an Aubusson tapestry. [< *Aubusson,* France, where these tapestries were first made in the 16th century]

A.U.C. from the founding of the city (of Rome). (for L *ab urbe condita*)

au cou·rant (ō kü räɴ′) *French.* in the current of events; well informed; up-to-date on the topics of the day.

auc·tion (ok′shən or ôk′shən) *n.* **1** a public sale in which each thing is sold to the person who offers the most money for it. **2** auction bridge. —*v.* sell at an auction. [< L *auctio, -onis* < *augere* increase]

auction bridge a card game for four people playing in two opposing pairs. Tricks made by the highest-bidding team in excess of their bid may be counted toward a game. Compare **contract bridge.**

auc·tion·eer (ok′shən ēr′ or ôk′shən ēr′) *n.* a man

hat, āge, cãre, fär; let, ēqual, tėrm; it, īce
hot, ōpen, ôrder; oil, out; cup, pủt, rüle, ūse
əbove, takən, pencəl, lemən, circəs
ch, child; ng, long; sh, ship
th, thin; ᴛʜ, then; zh, measure

whose business is conducting auctions. —*v.* sell at an auction.

aud. auditor.

au·da·cious (o dā′shəs or ô dā′shəs) *adj.* **1** bold; daring. **2** too bold; impudent. —**au·da′cious·ly,** *adv.* —**au·da′cious·ness,** *n.*

au·dac·i·ty (o das′ə tē or ô das′ə tē) *n.* **-ties. 1** boldness; reckless daring. **2** rudeness; impudence. [< L *audacia* < *audax* bold < *audere* dare] —**Syn. 2** presumption.

au·di·bil·i·ty (o′də bil′ə tē or ô′də bil′ə tē) *n.* **1** a being audible. **2** the relative loudness of a sound, usually measured in decibels.

au·di·ble (o′də bəl or ô′də bəl) *adj.* capable of being heard; loud enough to be heard. [< LL *audibilis* < L *audire* hear] —**au′di·bly,** *adv.*

au·di·ence (o′dē əns or ô′dē əns) *n.* **1** people gathered in a place to hear or see. **2** any persons within hearing: *People who listen to a program over the radio may be called the audience.* **3** a chance to be heard; hearing: *The committee will give you an audience to hear your plan.* **4** a formal interview with a person of high rank: *The king granted an audience to the reporter.* **5** the act or fact of hearing. **6** the readers of a book or journal. [ME < OF < L *audientia* hearing < *audire* hear]

au·di·o (o′dē ō or ô′dē ō) *adj.* **1** of or having to do with sound. **2** in television, having to do with the broadcasting or receiving of sound: *An audio problem is a sound problem; a video problem involves the image that appears on the screen.* —*n.* in television and motion pictures, sound reproduction.

audio frequency in physics, a frequency corresponding to audible sound vibrations, from about 15 to about 20,000 cycles per second. *Abbrev.:* A.F., a.f., or a-f.

au·di·om·e·ter (o dē om′ə tər or ô dē om′ə tər) *n.* an instrument for measuring the power of hearing.

au·di·o-vid·e·o (o′dē ō vid′ē ō or ô′dē ō-) *adj.* of or having to do with the transmission or reception of both sounds and pictures.

au·di·o-vis·u·al (o′dē ō vizh′ü əl or ô′dē ō-) *adj.* of or having to do with both hearing and sight. Moving pictures, slides, and records are used as audio-visual aids.

au·dit (o′dit or ô′dit) *v.* **1** examine and check (business accounts) officially. **2** at a college or university, attend a class as a listener without being allowed to take the examinations or get credit for the course. [< n.] —*n.* **1** an official examination and check of business accounts. **2** a statement of an account that has been examined and checked authoritatively. [< L *auditus* a hearing < *audire* hear]

au·di·tion (o dish′ən or ô dish′ən) *n.* **1** a trial performance by an actor, musician, etc. to demonstrate his skill, suitability for a part, etc. **2** a hearing. **3** the power or sense of hearing. —*v.* **1** hold an audition: *The producer auditioned six singers for the lead in the musical.* **2** give an audition; perform at an audition: *She auditioned for the role of the maid.* [< L *auditio, -onis* a hearing < *audire* hear]

au·di·tor (o′də tər or ô′də tər) *n.* **1** a hearer; listener. **2** a person who audits business accounts. **3** at a college or university, a person permitted to attend a class as a listener without being allowed to take the examinations or get credit for the course.

auditor general *pl.* **auditors general** or **auditor generals.** in Canada, an official who audits government accounts.

au·di·to·ri·um (o′də tô′rē əm or ô′də tô′rē əm) *n.* **-to·ri·ums** or **-to·ri·a** (-tô′rē ə) **1** a large room for an audience in a church, theatre, school, etc.; a large hall. **2** a building especially designed for lectures, concerts, etc. [< L]

au·di·to·ry (o′də tô′rē or ô′də tô′rē) *adj. n.* **-ries.** —*adj.* of or having to do with hearing, the sense of hearing, or the organs of hearing: *the auditory nerve.* —*n.* 1 an assembly of hearers; audience. 2 an auditorium.

au fait (ō fā′) *French.* 1 well-informed; familiar (*with*). 2 expert; very skilled.

auf Wie·der·seh·en (ouf vē′dər zā′ən) *German.* good-bye; till we see each other again.

Aug. August.

Au·ge·an stables (o jē′ən or ô jē′ən) in Greek legend, the stables, sheltering 3,000 oxen, that remained uncleaned for 30 years, until Hercules turned two rivers through them.

au·gend (o′jend or ô′jend) *n.* in mathematics, a number or quantity to which another, the addend, is to be added. [< L *augendum,* gerund of *augere* to increase]

au·ger (o′gər or ô′gər) *n.* 1 a tool for boring holes in wood. 2 a tool for boring holes in the earth. 3 a similar device for propelling some substance into or through a pipe, conduit, etc.: *A snowblower takes in snow by means of a horizontal auger at the front.* [OE *nafugār,* originally, a nave borer < *nafu* nave of a wheel + *gār* spear; ME *a nauger* taken as *an auger*]

An auger (def. 1). Each turn of the handle makes the spiral cutting edge bite farther into the wood.

aught[1] (ot or ôt) *n.* anything: *You may resign your job for aught I care.* —*adv.* in any way; to any degree; at all: *Help came too late to avail aught.* [OE *āwiht* < *ā-* ever + *wiht* a thing]

aught[2] (ot or ôt) *n.* zero; cipher; nothing. [< *naught; a naught* taken as *an aught; naught,* OE *nāwiht* < *nā* no + *wiht* a thing]

au·gite (o′jīt or ô′jīt) *n.* a pure black, bluish, or greenish mineral, found mostly in volcanic rocks. [< L *augites* < Gk. *augitēs,* ult. < *augē* lustre]

aug·ment (og ment′ or ôg ment′) *v.* increase; enlarge: *He had to augment his income by working in the evenings.* —**aug·men′ta·ble,** *adj.* [ME < LL *augmentare* < *augmentum* < *augere* increase] —**Syn.** See **increase.**

aug·men·ta·tion (og′men tā′shən or ôg′men tā′shən) *n.* 1 enlargement; increase. 2 in music, the transformation of a melody by increasing the time values of the notes.

aug·ment·ed (og men′tid or ôg men′tid) *adj.* in music, of or having to do with an interval that is one half step higher than the corresponding normal interval.

au grat·in (ō grat′ən or ô grä′tən; *French,* ō grä taN′) *French.* with crumbs; cooked with crumbs and cheese; cooked with cheese.

au·gur (o′gər or ô′gər) *n.* 1 in ancient Rome, a priest who made predictions and gave advice. 2 a prophet; fortuneteller.
—*v.* 1 predict; foretell. 2 be a sign or promise. 3 **augur ill,** be a bad sign. 4 **augur well,** be a good sign. [< L *augur,* apparently, Increase, Growth (of crops), personified in ritual service < *augere* increase]

au·gu·ry (o′gyu̇ rē or ô′gyu̇ rē) *n.* **-ries.** 1 the art or practice of foretelling the future by the flight of birds, the appearance of the internal organs of sacrificed animals, thunder and lightning, etc. 2 a prediction; indication; sign; omen. 3 a rite or ceremony performed by an augur.

Au·gust (o′gəst or ô′gəst) *n.* the eighth month of the year. It has 31 days. *Abbrev.:* Aug. [after *Augustus* Cæsar, 63 B.C.–A.D. 14, first emperor of Rome]

au·gust (o′gəst or ô′gəst, o gust′ or ô gust′) *adj.* inspiring reverence and admiration; majestic; venerable. [< L *augustus* < unrecorded *augus* increase, power < *augere* to increase] —**au·gust′ly,** *adv.* —**au·gust′ness,** *n.*

Au·gus·tan (o gus′tən or ô gus′tən) *adj.* of the Roman emperor Augustus or his reign. —*n.* any writer during the Augustan age of Latin or English literature.

Augustan age 1 the period of Latin literature covering the reign of Emperor Augustus, from 27 B.C. to A.D. 14. 2 the period of English literature from about 1700 to 1750, noted for classicism and elegance of style.

Au·gus·tin·i·an (o′gəs tin′ē ən or ô′gəs tin′ē ən) *adj.* of or having to do with Saint Augustine, A.D. 354-430, his teachings, or the religious orders named for him. —*n.* 1 a person who follows the teachings of Saint Augustine. 2 a member of any of the religious orders named for Saint Augustine.

au jus (ō zhY′) *French.* in gravy or juice.

auk (ok or ôk) *n.* a diving sea bird of the arctic regions, having short wings that are used only as paddles. [< ON *álka*]

auk·let (ok′lit or ôk′lit) *n.* a small kind of auk.

auld lang syne (old′ lang sīn′ or ôld′ lang sīn′, old′ lang zīn′ or ôld′lang zīn′) *Scottish.* old times; long ago in one's life.

au na·tu·rel (ō nä tY rel′) *French.* 1 in the plainest or simplest manner. 2 natural; like life; nude.

aunt (ant) *n.* 1 a sister of one's father or mother. 2 one's uncle's wife. [ME < OF *ante* < L *amita* father's sister]

au·ra (ô′rə) *n.* **au·ras** or **au·rae** (ô′rē or ô′rī). something supposed to come from a person or thing and surround him or it as an atmosphere: *An aura of holiness surrounded the saint.* [< L < Gk.]

au·ral[1] (ô′rəl) *adj.* of the ear; having to do with hearing. [< L *auris* ear]

au·ral[2] (ô′rəl) *adj.* of or like an aura.

au·re·ate (ô′rē it or ô′rē āt′) *adj.* golden; gilded. [< L *aureatus* < *aurum* gold]

au·re·o·la (ô rē′ə lə) *n.* aureole.

au·re·ole (ô′rē ōl′) *n.* 1 an encircling radiance; halo. 2 in astronomy, a ring of light surrounding the sun. [< L *aureola* (*corona*) golden (crown) < *aurum* gold]

au·re·o·my·cin (ô′rē ō mī′sin) *n.* an antibiotic, similar to penicillin. [< L *aureus* golden + Gk. *mykēs* fungus]

au re·voir (ō rə vwär′) *French.* good-bye; till we see each other again.

au·ric (ôr′ik) *adj.* 1 of or having to do with gold. 2 containing gold, especially gold with a valence of 3.

au·ri·cle (ô′rə kəl) *n.* 1 in anatomy and zoology: **a** a chamber of the heart that receives the blood from the veins. The heart of a bird or mammal has two auricles and two ventricles. See diagram of **heart.** **b** the outer part of the ear. 2 in botany and zoology, an earlike part. [< L *auricula,* dim. of *auris* ear]

au·ric·u·lar (ô rik′yu̇ lər) *adj.* 1 of the ear; near the ear. 2 heard by or addressed to the ear. 3 shaped like an ear. 4 having to do with an auricle of the heart.

au·rif·er·ous (ô rif′ər əs) *adj.* yielding gold. [< L *aurifer* < *aurum* gold + *ferre* bear]

Au·ri·ga (ô rī′gə) *n.* a large northern constellation supposed to represent a charioteer kneeling in his chariot. [< L *Auriga* charioteer]

au·rist (ô′rist) *n.* a doctor who treats diseases of the ear. [< L *auris* ear]

au·rochs (ô′roks) *n.* **-rochs.** 1 the European bison, now almost extinct. 2 an extinct wild ox. [< G *Auerochs* < OHG *ūr-ohso* < *ūr* wild bull + *ohso* ox]

au·ro·ra (ô rô′rə) *n.* 1 dawn. 2 streamers or bands of light appearing in the sky at night. [< L]

Au·ro·ra (ə rô′rə) *n.* in Roman mythology, the goddess of the dawn, identified with the Greek goddess Eos.

aurora aus·tra·lis (os trā′lis or ôs trā′lis) streamers or bands of light appearing in the southern sky at night. [< NL]

aurora bo·re·al·is (bô′rē al′is or bô′rē ā′lis) streamers or bands of light appearing in the northern sky at night; northern lights. [< NL]

au·ro·ral (ô rô′rəl) *adj.* 1 of or like the dawn; first; rosy. 2 of the aurora borealis or the aurora australis. 3 shining; bright.

au·rous (ôr′əs) *adj.* 1 of or having to do with gold. 2 containing gold, especially gold with a valence of 1.

aus·cul·tate (os′kəl tāt′) *v.* **-tat·ed, -tat·ing.** in medicine, listen to; examine by auscultation.

aus·cul·ta·tion (os′kəl tā′shən or ôs′kəl tā′shən) *n.*

1 the act of listening. 2 in medicine, the act of listening, usually with a stethoscope, to sounds within the human body to determine the condition of the heart or lungs. [< L *auscultatio, -onis* < *auscultare* listen]

aus·pice (os′pis or ôs′pis) *n.* **aus·pic·es** (os′pə siz or ôs′pə siz). 1 **under the auspices of,** under the patronage of: *The school fair was held under the auspices of the Home and School Association.* 2 a favorable circumstance; indication of success. 3 an omen; sign. 4 a divination or prophecy, especially one made from the flight of birds. [< F < L *auspicium* < *avis* bird + *specere* look at. See def. 4]

aus·pi·cious (os pish′əs or ôs pish′əs) *adj.* 1 with signs of success; favorable. 2 fortunate. —**aus·pi′cious·ly,** *adv.* —**Syn.** 1 See **favorable.**

Aust. 1 Austria. 2 Austrian.

aus·tere (os tēr′ or ôs tēr′) *adj.* 1 harsh; stern: *Frank's father was a silent, austere man, very strict with his children.* 2 strict in morals: *The Puritans were austere.* 3 severely simple: *The tall, plain columns stood against the sky in austere beauty.* 4 sour-tasting. [ME < OF < L < Gk. *austēros* < *auein* dry] —**aus·tere′ness,** *n.* —**aus·tere′ly,** *adv.*

aus·ter·i·ty (os ter′ə tē or ôs ter′ə tē) *n.* **-ties.** 1 sternness; strictness; severity. 2 severe simplicity. 3 economic stringency or restriction. 4 **austerities,** severe practices, such as going without food or sitting up all night to pray.

Austl. 1 Australia. 2 Australasia.

aus·tral (os′trəl or ôs′trəl) *adj.* southern. [< L *australis* < *auster* the south wind]

Aus·tral·a·sian (os′trəl ā′zhən or ôs′trəl ā′zhen, os′trəl ā′shən or ôs′trəl ā′shən) *adj.* of or having to do with Australasia or its people. —*n.* a native or inhabitant of Australasia.

Aus·tral·ian (os trāl′yən or ôs trāl′yən) *adj.* of Australia or its people. —*n.* a native or inhabitant of Australia.

Australian ballot a ballot with the names of all candidates for election to public office on it. The ballot is marked by the voter in a private booth to guarantee secrecy.

aut- the form of **auto-** before vowels and *h,* as in *authentic.*

au·tar·chic (o tär′kik or ô tär′kik) *adj.* of, having to do with, or resembling autarchy.

au·tar·chy (o′tär kē or ô′tär kē) *n.* **-chies.** absolute or autocratic rule; despotism. [< Gk. *autarchos* absolute ruler < *autos* self + *archein* rule]

au·tar·ky (o′tär kē or ô′tär kē) *n.* **-kies.** the state of being self-sufficient, especially of being independent of imports from other nations. [< Gk. *autarkeia* < *auto-* self + *arkeein* suffice]

au·then·tic (o then′tik or ô then′tik) *adj.* 1 reliable: *an authentic account.* 2 genuine: *A comparison of signatures showed that the letter was authentic.* [ME < OF *autentique* < LL < Gk. *authentikos* < *auto-* by oneself + *hentēs* one who acts] —**Syn.** 2 See **genuine.**

au·then·ti·cal·ly (o then′tik lē or ô then′tik lē) *adv.* 1 reliably. 2 genuinely.

au·then·ti·cate (o then′tə kāt′ or ô then′tə kāt′) *v.* **-cat·ed, -cat·ing.** 1 establish the truth of; show to be valid or genuine. 2 establish the authorship of. —**Syn.** 1 See **confirm.**

au·then·ti·ca·tion (o then′tə kā′shən or ô then′tə kā′shən) *n.* an authenticating or being authenticated.

au·then·tic·i·ty (o′then tis′ə tē or ô′then tis′ə tē) *n.* 1 reliability. 2 genuineness: *to question the authenticity of a signature.*

au·thor (o′thər or ô′thər) *n.* 1 a person who writes books, stories, or articles. 2 an author's publications: *Do read this author.* 3 a person who creates or begins anything. [ME < OF *autor* < L *auctor* < *augere* increase] —**Syn.** 1 writer. 3 creator.

au·thor·ess (o′thər is or ô′thər is) *n.* a female author.

au·thor·i·tar·i·an (ə thôr′ə tãr′ē ən) *adj.* favoring obedience to authority instead of individual freedom. —*n.* a person who favors obedience to authority instead of individual freedom.

hat, āge, cãre, fär; let, ēqual, tėrm; it, īce
hot, ōpen, ôrder; oil, out; cup, pu̇t, rüle, ūse
əbove, takən, pencəl, lemən, circəs
ch, child; ng, long; sh, ship
th, thin; ᴛʜ, then; zh, measure

au·thor·i·tar·i·an·ism (ə thôr′ə tãr′ē en iz′əm) *n.* the principle of obeying the authority of one person or of a small group of persons.

au·thor·i·ta·tive (ə thôr′ə tā′tiv) *adj.* 1 having authority; officially ordered: *Authoritative orders came from the general.* 2 commanding: *In authoritative tones the policeman shouted, "Keep back!"* 3 that ought to be believed or obeyed; having the authority of expert knowledge. —**au·thor′i·ta′tive·ly,** *adv.*

au·thor·i·ty (ə thôr′ə tē) *n.* **-ties.** 1 the power to enforce obedience; right to command or act: *A father has authority over his children.* 2 a person who has such power or right. 3 **the authorities, a** officials of the government. **b** persons in control. 4 a government body that runs some activity or business on behalf of the public: *the St. Lawrence Seaway Authority.* 5 an influence that creates respect and confidence. 6 a source of correct information or wise advice: *A good dictionary is an authority on the meanings of words.* 7 an expert on some subject. [ME < OF *authorite* < L *auctoritas*]
Syn. 1 **Authority, control, influence** = power to direct or act on others. **Authority** applies to legal power, given by a person's position or office, to give commands and enforce obedience: *Teachers have authority over pupils.* **Control** applies to power, given by a person's position, to direct people and things: *Parents have control over their children.* **Influence** applies to personal power, coming from a person's character, personality, or position, to shape the actions of others: *Some teachers have great influence over young people.* 5 prestige.

au·thor·i·za·tion (o′thər ə zā′shən or ô′thər ə zā′shən, o′thər ī zā′shən or ô′thər ī zā′shən) *n.* 1 an authorizing: *the general's authorization of the attack.* 2 a legal right; sanction; warrant.

au·thor·ize (o′thər īz′ or ô′thər īz′) *v.* **-ized, -iz·ing.** 1 give power or right to: *The Prime Minister authorized him to attend the conference.* 2 make legal; sanction: *Parliament authorized the spending of money for rearmament.* 3 give authority for; justify: *The dictionary authorizes the two spellings "traveller" and "traveler."* —**Syn.** 1 empower.

au·thor·ized (o′thər īzd′ or ô′thər īzd′) *adj.* 1 having authority. 2 supported or sanctioned by authority.

Authorized Version the English translation of the Bible published in 1611; the King James Version. *Abbrev.:* A.V.

au·thor·ship (o′thər ship′ or ô′thər ship′) *n.* 1 the occupation of an author; writing. 2 the origin as to author: *What is the authorship of that novel?* 3 the origin or source of anything.

au·to (o′tō or ô′tō) *n.* **au·tos.** automobile.

auto- *combining form.* 1 self, as in *autobiography, autointoxication.* 2 automobile, as in *autobus.* Also, **aut-** before vowels and *h.* [< Gk.]

Au·to·bahn (ou′tō bän′) *n.* **Au·to·bah·nen** (ou′tō bä′nən). in Germany, a four-lane express highway. [< G *Auto* motorcar + *Bahn* road]

au·to·bi·og·ra·pher (o′tə bī og′rə fər or ô′tə-) *n.* a person who writes the story of his own life.

au·to·bi·o·graph·ic (o′tə bī ə graf′ik or ô′tə-) *adj.* 1 having to do with the story of one's own life. 2 telling or writing the story of one's own life.

au·to·bi·o·graph·i·cal (o′tə bī ə graf′ə kəl or ô′tə-) *adj.* autobiographic. —**au′to·bi′o·graph′i·cal·ly,** *adv.*

au·to·bi·og·ra·phy (o′tə bī og′rə fē or ô′tə-) *n.* **-phies.** the story of a person's life written by himself.

au·toch·tho·nous (o tok′thə nəs or ô tok′thə nəs) *adj.* originating where found; aboriginal; indigenous. [< Gk. *autochthon* sprung from the land itself < *auto-* self + *chthōn* earth, soil]

au·to·clave (o′tə klāv′ or ô′tə-) *n.* 1 a strong, closed vessel that develops superheated steam under pressure, used for sterilizing, cooking, etc. 2 a strong vessel for effecting chemical reactions under high pressure. —*v.* cook or sterilize in an autoclave. [< F *autoclave* < *auto-* self + L *clavis* key]

auto court a group of cabins providing shelter for automobile travellers; motel.

au·toc·ra·cy (o tok′rə sē or ô tok′rə sē) *n.* **-cies. 1** a government having absolute power over its citizens. **2** a country having such a government. **3** absolute authority; unlimited power over a group.

au·to·crat (o′tə krat′ or ô′tə-) *n.* **1** a ruler having absolute power over his subjects. **2** a person who uses his power in a harsh way: *Most children think their parents are autocrats.* [< Gk. *autokratēs* < *auto-* self + *kratos* strength]

au·to·crat·ic (o′tə krat′ik or ô′tə-) *adj.* of or like an autocrat; absolute in authority; ruling without checks or limitations. **—au′to·crat′i·cal·ly,** *adv.*

au·to-da-fé (o′tō də fā′, ô′tō- or ou′tō-) *n.* **au·tos-da-fé. 1** a public ceremony accompanying the passing of sentence by the Spanish Inquisition. **2** the carrying out of such a sentence. **3** the burning of a heretic. [< Pg. *auto-da-fé* act of the faith < L *actus* act and *fides* faith]

au·to·gi·ro or **au·to·gy·ro** (o′tə jī′rō or ô′tə-) *n.* **-ros. 1** an aircraft powered by a single ordinary propeller but deriving its lift mainly from a set of free-wheeling rotors that turn as the aircraft moves forward. **2 Autogiro,** *Trademark.* an autogiro. [< Sp. *autogiro* < Gk. *auto-* self + *gyros* circle]

An autogiro

au·to·graph (o′tə graf′ or ô′tə-) *n.* **1** a person's signature. **2** something written in a person's own handwriting. —*v.* **1** write one's signature in or on. **2** write with one's own hand.

au·to·graph·ic (o′tə graf′ik or ô′tə-) *adj.* **1** of or for an autograph. **2** in one's own handwriting.

au·to·graph·i·cal (o′tə graf′ə kəl or ô′tə-) *adj.* autographic.

au·to-in·tox·i·ca·tion (o′tō in tok′sə kā′shən or ô′tō-) *n.* in medicine, a poisoning by substances formed within the body.

au·to·mat (o′tə mat′ or ô′tə-) *n.* a restaurant in which food is obtained from compartments that open when coins are inserted in slots. [short for *automatic*]

au·to·mate (o′tə māt′ or ô′tə-) *v.* **-mat·ed, mat·ing. 1** convert to automatic operation or automation: *Fewer people are employed in a plant when it is automated.* **2** make use of automation: *Many industries now face the problem of whether to automate or not.* [back formation from *automation*]

au·to·mat·ic (o′tə mat′ik or ô′tə-) *adj.* **1** moving or acting by itself: *an automatic pump.* **2** done without thought or attention: *Breathing and swallowing are usually automatic.* **3** of an automatic firearm, pistol, etc. —*n.* a gun that throws out the used shell, puts in a new one, and continues to fire until the pressure on the trigger is released. [< Gk. *automatos* self-acting]

Syn. 2 Automatic, involuntary = not controlled by the will. **Automatic** = done unconsciously, always reacting in exactly the same way to the same stimulus: *A boy who has good manners stands up in an automatic movement when a lady enters the room.* **Involuntary** = done without conscious intention: *She reached toward it with an involuntary movement of her hand.*

au·to·mat·i·cal·ly (o′tə mat′ik lē or ô′tə-) *adv.* in an automatic manner.

automatic pilot a gyroscopic mechanism designed to keep an aircraft, missile, etc. on a given course and at a given altitude without human assistance.

automatic transmission in a motor vehicle, any of various mechanisms for automatically altering the speed of the driving wheels in relation to engine speed.

au·to·ma·tion (o′tə mā′shən or ô′tə-) *n.* a method of making a manufacturing process, a production line, etc. operate more efficiently by the use of built-in or supplementary controls in a machine or number of machines. [< *automatic* + oper*ation*]

au·tom·a·tism (o tom′ə tiz′əm or ô tom′ə tiz′əm) *n.* **1** an action not controlled by the will; involuntary action; automatic action. **2** the quality or condition of being automatic or of acting mechanically.

au·tom·a·ton (o tom′ə ton′ or ô tom′ə ton′) *n.* **-tons** or **-ta** (-tə). **1** a person or animal whose actions are purely mechanical. **2** a machine that has its motive power concealed. [< Gk. *automaton,* neut., self-acting]

au·to·mo·bile (*n.,* o′tə mə bēl′ or ô′tə- ; *adj.* o′tə mō′bēl or ô′tə-) *n. adj. v.* **-biled, -bil·ing.** —*n.* a passenger vehicle that carries its own engine and is driven on roads and streets. —*adj.* self-moving: *an automobile torpedo.* —*v.* travel by automobile. [< F]

au·to·mo·bil·ist (o′tə mə bēl′ist or ô′tə-) *n.* a person who uses an automobile.

au·to·mo·tive (o′tə mō′tiv or ô′tə-) *adj.* **1** of automobiles. Automotive engineering deals with the design and construction of automobiles. **2** self-moving; self-propelling; furnishing its own power.

au·to·nom·ic (o′tə nom′ik or ô′tə-) *adj.* autonomous.

autonomic system in physiology, the ganglia and nerves of the nervous system of vertebrates, which control digestive, reproductive, and other involuntary reactions.

au·ton·o·mous (o ton′ə məs or ô ton′ə məs) *adj.* self-governing; independent. **—au·ton′o·mous·ly,** *adv.*

au·ton·o·my (o ton′ə mē or ô ton′ə mē) *n.* **-mies. 1** self-government; independence. **2** a self-governing community. [< Gk. *autonomia* < *auto-* of oneself + *nomos* law]

au·top·sy (o′top sē or ô′top sē, o′təp sē or ô′təp sē) *n.* **-sies.** a dissection and examination of a dead body to find the cause of death. [< NL < Gk. *autopsia* < *auto-* for oneself + *opsis* a seeing]

au·to·sug·ges·tion (o′tō sə jes′chən or ô′tō-, o′tō səg jes′chən or ô′tō-) *n.* a suggestion to oneself of ideas that produce mental or physiological effects.

au·to·ther·a·py (o′tō ther′ə pē or ô′tō-) *n.* in medicine: **1** self-treatment. **2** a spontaneous cure.

au·to·truck (o′tō truk′ or ô′tō-) *n.* a truck.

au·tumn (o′təm or ô′təm) *n.* **1** the season of the year between summer and winter; fall. **2** a time of maturity and the beginning of decay. —*adj.* of autumn; coming in autumn; in autumn: *autumn flowers, autumn rains.* [ME < OF < L *autumnus*]

au·tum·nal (o tum′nəl or ô tum′nəl) *adj.* of or coming in autumn.

autumnal equinox the equinox occurring about September 22.

aux·il·ia·ry (og zil′yə rē or ôg zil′yə rē, og zil′ə rē or ôg zil′ə rē) *adj. n.* **-ries.** —*adj.* **1** helping; assisting. **2** additional. **3** of a boat, having an engine as well as sails. —*n.* **1** a helper; aid. **2** an assisting or subsidiary group or organization: *Our scout troop has a ladies' auxiliary.* **3** a naval vessel designed for duties other than fighting. **4** an auxiliary verb. **5 auxiliaries,** *pl.* foreign or allied troops that help the army of a nation at war. [< L *auxiliarius* < *auxilium* aid]

auxiliary verb a verb used to form the tenses, moods, aspects, or voices of other verbs, such as *be, can, do, have, may, must, shall,* and *will*: I *am* going; he *will* go; they *are* lost; they *were* lost.

Av (av) in the Hebrew calendar, the fifth month of the ecclesiastical year, and the eleventh month of the civil year.

av. 1 avenue. 2 average. 3 avoirdupois.

Av. Avenue.

AV audio-visual.

A.V. 1 Authorized Version. 2 audio-visual.

a·vail (ə vāl′) *v.* 1 be of use or value to: *Money will not avail you after you are dead.* 2 help: *Talk will not avail without work.* 3 **avail oneself of,** take advantage of; profit by; make use of. —*n.* use; help; benefit: *Crying is of no avail now.* [apparently < *a-* to (< L *ad-*) + *vail* < F < L *valere* be worth]

a·vail·a·bil·i·ty (ə vāl′ə bil′ə tē) *n.* a being available; being at hand; being ready: *availability of water power.*

a·vail·a·ble (ə vāl′ə bəl) *adj.* 1 that can be secured: *That man is not available for the job: he has other work.* 2 that can be had: *All available tickets were sold.* 3 in law, valid. —**a·vail′a·bly,** *adv.*

av·a·lanche (av′ə lanch′) *n. v.* **-lanched, -lanch·ing.** —*n.* 1 a large mass of snow and ice, or of dirt and rocks, sliding or falling down a mountainside. 2 anything like an avalanche: *an avalanche of questions.*
—*v.* move like an avalanche. [< F < Swiss F *lavenche* (< a pre-Latin Alpine language), influenced by F *avaler* go down < *à val* < L *ad vallem* to the valley]

avalanche lily the dogtooth violet of the Rocky Mountains.

Av·a·lon (av′ə lon′) *n.* in Celtic legend, an earthly paradise in the western seas, to which King Arthur and other heroes were carried at death.

a·vant-garde (ä′vän gärd′) *n.* especially in the arts, an advanced group or movement, characterized by experiment and innovation. [< F *avant-garde* literally, advance guard]

av·a·rice (av′ə ris) *n.* a greedy desire for money or property. [ME < OF < L *avaritia* < *avarus* greedy] —**Syn.** greed.

av·a·ri·cious (av′ə rish′əs) *adj.* greedy for wealth. —**av′a·ri′cious·ly,** *adv.* —**av′a·ri′cious·ness,** *n.*

a·vast (ə vast′) *interj.* in nautical use, a command to stop: "*Avast there!*" *shouted the sailor.* [probably < Du. *houd vast* hold fast]

av·a·tar (av′ə tär′) *n.* 1 in Hindu mythology, the descent of a god to earth in bodily form; incarnation. 2 a manifestation in bodily form. [< Skt. *avatāra* descent < *ava* down + *tar-* pass over]

a·vaunt (a vont′, ə vônt′ or ə vänt′) *interj. Archaic.* a command to get out, go away, etc. [ME < OF *avant* < L *ab ante* forward, in front]

avdp. avoirdupois.

a·ve (ā′vā or ā′vē) *interj. Latin.* hail! farewell! —*n.* **Ave,** the prayer Ave Maria.

Ave. or **ave.** avenue.

A·ve Ma·ri·a (ā′vā mə rē′ə or ā′vē mə rē′ə) in the Roman Catholic Church: 1 "Hail Mary!", the first words of the Latin form of a prayer. 2 the prayer.

A·ve Mar·y (ā′vē mãr′ē) Ave Maria.

a·venge (ə venj′) *v.* **a·venged, a·veng·ing.** 1 get retribution for: *The Indian will avenge the death of his brother by killing the murderer.* 2 take vengeance on behalf of: *The clan avenged their slain chief.* 3 get revenge. [ME < OF *avengier* < *a-* to (< L *ad-*) + *vengier* < L *vindicare* punish < *vindex* champion] —**a·veng′er,** *n.* —**Syn. 1** See **revenge.**

av·ens (av′inz) *n.* any of several perennials of the rose family, native to temperate and cold regions. [ME < OF *avence;* origin unknown]

a·ven·tu·rine (ə ven′chə rēn′ or ə ven′chə rin) *n.* a kind of quartz containing bright specks of mica or some other mineral. [< F < Ital. *avventurino* < *avventura* chance < L *adventura;* because discovered accidentally. See ADVENTURE.]

av·e·nue (av′ə nū′; *Esp.U.S.,* av′ə nü′) *n.* 1 a wide or main street. 2 a road or walk bordered by trees. 3 a way of approach or departure; passage: *avenues to fame.* 4 in some cities, a thoroughfare running at right angles to others, which are properly called "streets." [< F *avenue,* fem. pp. of *avenir* < L *advenire* < *ad-* to + *venire* come] —**Syn. 1** thoroughfare, boulevard.

hat, āge, cãre, fär; let, ēqual, tėrm; it, īce
hot, ōpen, ôrder; oil, out; cup, pu̇t, rüle, ūse
əbove, takən, pencəl, lemən, circəs
ch, child; ng, long; sh, ship
th, thin; ᴛʜ, then; zh, measure

a·ver (ə vėr′) *v.* **a·verred, a·ver·ring.** state to be true; assert. [ME < OF *averer,* ult. < L *ad-* + *verus* true]

av·er·age (av′rij or av′ər ij) *n. adj. v.* **-aged, -ag·ing.** —*n.* 1 an arithmetical mean; the quantity found by dividing the sum of several quantities by the number of those quantities: *The average of 3, 5, and 10 is 6.* 2 a usual kind or quality; ordinary amount or rate: *His mind is about like the average.* 3 in commerce: **a** a small charge payable by the master of a ship, covering the cost of pilotage, towing, etc. **b** a loss or expense arising as a result of damage at sea to ship or cargo. **c** the fair, proportionate distribution of such loss or expense among all the parties involved.
—*adj.* 1 obtained by averaging; being an average: *an average price, the average temperature.* 2 usual; ordinary: *average intelligence.* 3 in commerce, estimated or assessed according to the rules of average.
—*v.* 1 find the average of. 2 amount on an average to; come close to: *The cost of our lunches at school averaged one dollar a week.* 3 do, get, yield, etc. on an average: *He averages six hours work a day. The wheat averaged forty bushels to the acre.* 4 divide among several proportionately: *We averaged our gains according to what each had put in. Abbrev.:* av. [< F *avarie* damage to ship or cargo < Arabic *'awārīya* damage from sea water. In English, extended to "equal distribution" (at first, "of loss")]

a·ver·ment (ə vėr′mənt) *n.* a statement that something is true; assertion.

A·ver·nus (ə vėr′nəs) *n.* 1 in Roman mythology, the lower world; Hades. 2 a small lake in the crater of an extinct volcano near Naples, Italy. In ancient times the entrance to Hades was supposed to be at the side of this lake.

a·verse (ə vėrs′) *adj.* 1 opposed; unwilling: *She was averse to fighting.* 2 in botany, turned away from the stem. [< L *aversus,* pp. of *avertere.* See AVERT.] —**a·verse′ness,** *n.*

a·ver·sion (ə vėr′zhən or ə vėr′shən) *n.* 1 a strong or fixed dislike; antipathy. 2 a thing or person disliked. 3 an unwillingness.

☛ **aversion.** Either *to* or *for* follows aversion: *He has an aversion to moving fast and working hard. We'll eat alone; they have an aversion for fried shrimp.*

a·vert (ə vėrt′) *v.* 1 prevent; avoid: *He averted the accident by a quick turn of his steering wheel.* 2 turn away; turn aside: *She averted her eyes from the wreck.* [ME < OF < L *avertere* < *ab-* from + *vertere* turn]

A·ves (ā′vēz) n.pl. in zoology, a class of vertebrates comprising the birds. [< L]

A·ves·ta (ə ves′tə) *n.* the sacred writings of the ancient Zoroastrian religion, still in use by the Parsees.

av·gas (av′gas′) *n.* aviation gasoline.

a·vi·an (ā′vē ən) *adj.* of or having to do with birds.

a·vi·ar·y (ā′vē er ē) *n.* **-ar·ies.** an enclosure or large cage in which to keep birds. [< L *aviarium* < *avis* bird]

a·vi·a·tion (ā′vē ā′shən or av′ē ā′shən) *n.* 1 designing, manufacturing, and operating of aircraft, especially airplanes. 2 airplanes, their personnel, and their equipment. [< F *aviation* < L *avis* bird]

aviation gasoline a high-octane gasoline prepared especially for use in piston-engined aircraft.

a·vi·a·tor (ā′vē ā′tər or av′ē ā′tər) *n.* a person who flies an airplane; an airplane pilot.

a·vi·a·trix (ā′vē ā′triks or av′ē ā′triks) *n.* a female aviator.

a·vi·cul·ture (ā′və kul′chər) *n.* the rearing or keeping of birds.

a·vi·cul·tur·ist (ā′və kul′chər ist) *n.* a bird expert or fancier.

av·id (av′id) *adj.* eager; greedy: *The miser was avid for gold.* [< L *avidus* < *avere* crave] —**av′id·ly,** *adv.*

a·vid·i·ty (ə vid′ə tē) *n.* **1** eagerness; greediness. **2** in chemistry, the relative strength of an acid or base.

A.V.M. Air Vice-Marshal.

av·o·ca·do (av′ə kä′dō) *n.* **-dos. 1** a pear-shaped tropical fruit having a dark-green skin and a very large stone; alligator pear. **2** the tree that it grows on. [< Sp. *avocado,* var. of *aguacate* < Mexican *ahuacatl*]

av·o·ca·tion (av′ə kā′shən) *n.* **1** something that a person does besides his regular business; a minor occupation; hobby: *Mr. Brown is a lawyer, but writing stories is his avocation.* **2** *Informal.* one's regular business; occupation. [< L *avocatio, -onis* < *avocare* < *ab-* away + *vocare* to call] ☛ See **vocation** for usage note.

av·o·cet (av′ə set′) *n.* a web-footed wading bird with long legs and a long, slender beak that curves upward. Also, **avoset.** [< F *avocette* < Ital. *avosetta*]

A·vo·gad·ro's law (ä′vō gäd′rōz) in physics, the law stating that equal volumes of different gases, under like conditions of pressure and temperature, contain the same number of molecules. [after Count Amedeo *Avogadro* (1776-1856), an Italian physicist, who stated it]

a·void (ə void′) *v.* **1** keep away from; keep out of the way of: *We avoided driving through large cities on our trip.* **2** make void; annul. [< AF var. of OF *esvuidier* empty, quit < *es-* out (< L *ex-*) + *vuidier* < VL *vocitare* empty]

a·void·a·ble (ə voi′də bəl) *adj.* **1** that can be escaped or avoided. **2** in law, voidable.

a·void·ance (ə void′əns) *n.* **1** an avoiding; a keeping away from. **2** the fact of being or becoming vacant: *the avoidance of the office of vice-president.* **3** in law, the act of making void; an invalidating; annulment.

av·oir·du·pois (av′ər də poiz′) *n.* **1** avoirdupois weight. **2** *Informal.* a person's weight. *Abbrev.*: av. or avdp. [ME < OF *aveir de peis* goods of weight < L *habere* have, *de* of, and *pensum* weight < *pendere* weight]

avoirdupois weight a system of weighing in which a pound containing sixteen ounces is used:
16 drams = 1 ounce
16 ounces = 1 pound
2,000 pounds = 1 ton

av·o·set (av′ə set′) *n.* an avocet.

a·vouch (ə vouch′) *v.* **1** declare to be true. **2** guarantee. **3** acknowledge; affirm. [ME < OF *avochier* < *a-* to (< L *ad-*) + *vochier* call < L *vocare*]

a·vow (ə vou′) *v.* declare frankly or openly; confess; admit; acknowledge: *He avowed that he could not sing.* [ME < OF *avouer* < *a-* to (< L *ad-*) + *vouer* vow < VL *votare*]

a·vow·al (ə vou′əl) *n.* a frank or open declaration; confession; admission; acknowledgment.

a·vowed (ə voud′) *adj.* openly declared; admitted.

a·vow·ed·ly (ə vou′id lē) *adv.* admittedly; openly.

a·vun·cu·lar (ə vung′kyů lər) *adj.* **1** of an uncle. **2** like an uncle. [< L *avunculus* mother's brother, dim. of *avus* grandfather]

a·wait (ə wāt′) *v.* **1** wait for; look forward to: *He has awaited your coming for a week.* **2** be ready for; be in store for: *Many pleasures await you.* [ME < OF *awaitier* < *a-* for (< L *ad-*) + *waitier* wait < Gmc.] —**Syn. 1** expect. ☛ See **wait** for usage note.

a·wake (ə wāk′) *v.* **a·woke** or **a·waked, a·wak·ing,** *adj.* —*v.* wake up; arouse. —*adj.* not asleep; aware of one's surroundings; alert. [OE *āwacian* + OE *onwæcnan*]

a·wak·en (ə wāk′ən) *v.* wake up; arouse.

a·ward (ə wôrd′) *v.* **1** give after careful consideration; grant: *A medal was awarded to the best speller in the class.* **2** decide or settle by law; adjudge: *The court awarded damages of $5,000.*
—*n.* **1** something given after careful consideration; a prize: *Frank's dog won the highest award.* **2** in law, a decision by a judge. [< AF var. of OF *esguarder* observe, decide < VL *ex-* from + *wardare* guard < Gmc.]

a·ware (ə wãr′) *adj.* knowing; realizing; conscious: *I was too sleepy to be aware how cold it was.* [OE *gewær*] —**a·ware′ness,** *n.* —**Syn.** See **conscious.**

a·wash (ə wosh′) *adv. adj.* **1** level with the surface of the water; just covered with water. **2** carried about by water; floating.

a·way (ə wā′) *adv.* **1** from a place; to a distance: *Get away from the fire.* **2** at a distance; far: *The sailor was far away from home.* **3** in another direction; aside: *turn away.* **4** out of one's possession, notice, or use: *He gave his boat away.* **5** out of existence: *The sounds died away.* **6** without stopping; continuously: *She worked away at her job.* **7** without waiting; at once. **8 away back,** *Informal.* far back in space or time. **9 away with** (used only in commands) take someone or something away: **Away with you,** go away. **10 do away with, a** put an end to; get rid of. **b** kill.
—*adj.* **1** at a distance; far. **2** absent; gone. [OE *onweg*]

awe (o or ô) *n. v.* **awed, aw·ing.** —*n.* great fear and wonder; fear and reverence. —*v.* **1** cause to feel awe; fill with awe: *The majesty of the mountains awed us.* **2** influence or restrain by awe. [ME *age* < ON *agi*]

a·wea·ry (ə wēr′ē) *adj. Poetic.* weary; tired.

a·weath·er (ə weᴛʜ′ər) *adj. adv.* on or toward the windward, or weather, side.

a·weigh (ə wā′) *adj.* raised off the bottom: *The ship sailed off as soon as its anchor was aweigh.*

awe·some (o′səm or ô′-) *adj.* **1** causing awe: *A great fire is an awesome sight.* **2** showing awe; awed.

awe-strick·en (o′strik′ən or ô′-) *adj.* filled with awe.

awe-struck (o′struk′ or ô′-) *adj.* filled with awe.

aw·ful (o′fəl or ô′fəl) *adj.* **1** dreadful; terrible: *an awful storm.* **2** *Informal.* very bad, great, ugly, etc. **3** deserving great respect and reverence: *the awful power of God.* **4** filling with awe; impressive.
—*adv. Informal.* very: *He was awful mad.* [< *awe* + *-ful*] —**aw′ful·ness,** *n.* —**Syn.** *adj.* **1** fearful. **3** sublime. **4** imposing.

☛ In formal English **awful** = filling with awe. In familiar and informal English it is a general utility word of disapproval: *awful manners, an awful cold, an awful mistake.* As a result, the word is seldom used in careful writing; *awe-inspiring* has taken its place.

aw·ful·ly (o′flē or ô′flē, o′fə lē or ô′fəl ē) *adv.* **1** dreadfully; terribly. **2** *Informal.* very: *I'm awfully sorry that I hurt your feelings.*

a·while (ə hwīl′ or ə wīl′) *adv.* for a short time.

awk·ward (ok′wərd or ôk′wərd) *adj.* **1** clumsy; not graceful or skilful: *The seal is very awkward on land, but quite at home in the water.* **2** not well suited to use: *The handle of this pitcher has an awkward shape.* **3** not easily managed: *This is an awkward corner to turn.* **4** embarrassing: *He asked me an awkward question.* [< obs. *awk* perversely, in the wrong way (ME < ON *afug* turned the wrong way) + *-ward*] —**awk′ward·ly,** *adv.* —**awk′ward·ness** *n.*

Syn. 1 Awkward, clumsy, ungainly = not graceful. **Awkward** = lacking grace, ease, quickness, and skill: *An awkward girl is no help in the kitchen.* **Clumsy** suggests moving heavily and stiffly: *The clumsy boy bumped into the furniture.* **Ungainly** = awkward in moving one's body: *He is as ungainly as a newborn calf.* **4** trying, disconcerting. —**Ant. 2** handy.

A.W.L. a military abbreviation for absent without leave. Also, **A.W.O.L.**

awl (ol or ôl) *n.* a tool used for making small holes in leather or wood. [OE *al*]

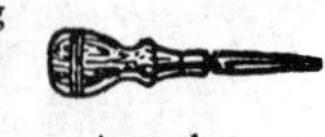
An awl

awn (on or ôn) *n.* one of the bristly hairs forming the beard on a head of barley, oats, etc. [ME < ON *ögn* chaff]

awn·ing (on′ing or ôn′ing) *n.* a piece of material, usually canvas, plastic, or metal, spread on a frame and hung above a window, door, or porch as a protection from the sun and rain. [origin uncertain]

a·woke (ə wōk′) *v.* pt. and pp. of **awake.**

A.W.O.L. or **a.w.o.l.** absent without leave.

a·wry (ə rī′) *adv. adj.* **1** with a twist or a turn to one side: *Her hat was blown awry by the wind.* **2** wrong: *Our plans have gone awry.* [< *a-* in + *wry*]

axe or **ax** (aks) *n.* **ax·es. 1** a tool with a bladed head on a handle, used for chopping wood. **2** a weapon like this; battle-axe. **3 get the axe,** be dismissed or discharged. **4 have an axe to grind,** have a special purpose or reason for taking action or being interested. [OE *æx*] —**axe′like′**, *adj.*

axe·man or **ax·man** (aks′mən) *n.* **-men** (-mən). a man who uses an axe in chopping or fighting.

ax·es[1] (ak′sēz) *n.* pl. of **axis.**

ax·es[2] (ak′siz) *n.* pl. of **axe** or **ax.**

ax·i·al (ak′sē əl) *adj.* **1** of an axis; forming an axis. **2** on or around an axis.

ax·il (ak′sil) *n.* in botany, the angle between the upper side of a leaf or stem and the supporting stem or branch. [< L *axilla* armpit]

ax·il·la (ak sil′ə) *n.* **ax·il·lae** (-ē or -ī). **1** in anatomy, an armpit. **2** in botany, an axil. [< L]

ax·il·lar·y (ak′sə ler′ē) *adj.* **1** of or near the armpit. **2** in or growing from an axil.

ax·i·om (ak′sē əm) *n.* **1** a statement seen to be true without proof; a self-evident truth: *It is an axiom that if equals are added to equals the results will be equal.* **2** an established principle. [< L < Gk. *axiōma* < *axios* worthy]

ax·i·o·mat·ic (ak′sē ə mat′ik) *adj.* **1** self-evident: *That a whole is greater than any of its parts is axiomatic.* **2** full of axioms or maxims.

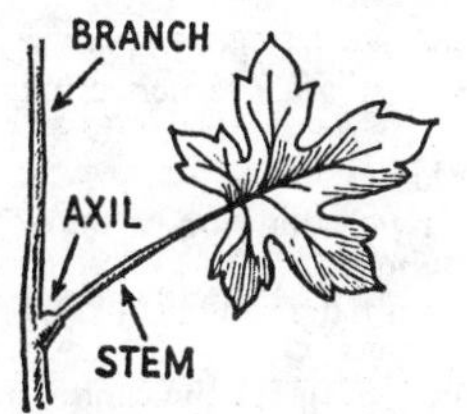

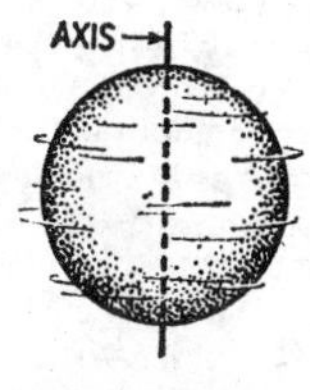

An axis (def. 1)

ax·is (ak′sis) *n.* **ax·es** (-sēz). **1** an imaginary or real line that passes through an object and about which an object turns or seems to turn. The earth's axis passes through the North and South Poles. **2** a central or principal line around which parts are arranged regularly. The axis of a cone is the straight line joining its apex and the centre of its base. **3** a central or principal structure extending lengthwise. The axis of a plant is the stem. The axis of the skeleton is the spinal column. **4** an important line of relation: *the Berlin-Rome axis.* **5 the Axis,** in World War II, Germany, Italy, Japan, and their allies. [< L]

ax·le (ak′səl) *n.* **1** a bar on which or with which a wheel turns. See **felloe** for diagram. **2** an axletree. [OE *eaxl* shoulder, crossbar; influenced by ON *öxul* axle]

ax·le·tree (ak′səl trē′) *n.* a crossbar that connects two opposite wheels.

ax·man (aks′mən) *n.* **-men** (-mən). axeman.

Ax·min·ster (aks′min stər) *n.* a kind of carpet with a finely tufted velvetlike pile. [< *Axminster,* a town in England where such carpets were first made]

ax·o·lotl (ak′sə lot′əl) *n.* any of several salamanders that usually retain their gills and tadpole form through life. [< Sp. < a Nahuatl word meaning "water doll"; literally, servant of water]

ax·on (ak′son) *n.* in anatomy, the part of a nerve cell that carries impulses away from the body of the cell. [< Gk. *axōn* axis]

ax·one (ak′sōn′) *n.* axon.

ay[1] (ā) *adv.* aye.

ay[2] (ī) *adv. n.* aye.

a·yah (ä′yə) *n.* a native maid or nurse in India. [< Hind. *āya* < Pg. *aia* governess]

aye[1] or **ay** (ā) *adv.* always; ever. [ME < ON *ei*]

aye[2] or **ay** (ī) *adv. n.* yes: *Aye, aye, sir. The ayes were in the majority when the vote was taken.* [origin uncertain]

aye-aye (ī′ī′) *n.* a squirrel-like lemur of Malagasy. [< F < Malagasy *aiay*]

Ayr·shire (ãr′shēr or ãr′shər) *n.* **1** a breed of dairy cattle that are red and white or brown and white. **2** an animal of this breed. [< *Ayrshire,* a county in S.W. Scotland]

az. **1** azimuth. **2** azure.

hat, āge, cãre, fär; let, ēqual, tėrm; it, īce
hot, ōpen, ôrder; oil, out; cup, pu̇t, rüle, ūse
əbove, takən, pencəl, lemən, circəs
ch, child; ng, long; sh, ship
th, thin; ᴛʜ, then; zh, measure

a·zal·ea (ə zāl′yə) *n.* **1** a shrub having many showy flowers. Azaleas resemble rhododendrons, but usually are not evergreen. **2** the flower. [< NL < Gk. *azaleos* dry < *azein* parch]

a·zan (ä zän′ or ə zan′) *n.* the Moslem call to public prayer, proclaimed five times a day by the muezzin, or crier, from the minaret of a mosque. [< Arabic *adhān* invitation]

az·i·muth (az′ə məth) *n.* in astronomy, the angular distance east or west from the north point: *The azimuth of the North Star is 0 degrees. A star due northeast from the observer has an azimuth of 45 degrees E. Abbrev.*: az. [ME < OF *azimut* < Arabic *as-sumūt* the ways < *samt* way]

az·o (az′ō or ā′zō) *adj.* containing nitrogen. [< F *azote* nitrogen < Gk. *a-* not + *zōē* life, because nitrogen does not support life]

a·zo·ic (ə zō′ik) *adj.* **1** in geology, having no trace of life or organic remains. **2** of or having to do with geological time previous to the existence of living things. [< Gk. *azōos* without life + E *-ic*]

Az·tec (az′tek) *n.* **1** a member of a highly civilized people who ruled Mexico before its conquest by the Spaniards in 1519. **2** their language. —*adj.* of the Aztecs or their language.

az·ure (azh′ər or ā′zhər) *n.* **1** blue; sky blue. **2** the clear blue of the unclouded sky. —*adj.* blue; sky-blue. [ME < OF *l'azur* the azure < Arabic < Persian *lajward* lapis lazuli]

az·u·rite (azh′ů rīt′) *n.* a blue copper ore; a basic carbonate of copper. *Formula*: $2CuCO_3{\cdot}Cu(OH)_2$

B or **b** (bē) *n.* **B's** or **b's.** **1** the second letter of the English alphabet. **2** any speech sound represented by this letter. **3** any person or thing considered as the second in a series. *Company B in a battalion. B is A's friend.* **4** any person or thing considered as the second best in a group: *grade B oranges. He received a B in the English course.* **5** in music: **a** the seventh tone in the scale of C major. **b** a symbol standing for this tone. **c** a key or string that produces this tone. **d** a scale or key that has B as its keynote. **6** a known quantity, especially in equations, as in $ax + by + c = D$.

B **1** boron. **2** one of the four main blood groups.

B. **1** Bay. **2** Bible. **3** British. **4** bacillus.

B. or **b.** **1** born. **2** book. **3** base. **4** baseman. **5** bat. **6** bass. **7** basso. **8** bachelor.

Ba barium.

B.A. Bachelor of Arts. (for L *Baccalaureus Artium*)

baa (bä or ba) *n. v.* **baaed, baa·ing.** bleat.

Ba·al (bā′əl or bāl) *n.* **Ba·al·im** (bā′əl im). **1** any of a number of local deities among the ancient Semitic peoples. **2** the chief god of the Canaanites and Phoenicians. In some places he was the god of fertility; in others, he was the sun god. **3** a false god. [< Hebrew]

ba·ba (bä′ba; *French* bä bä′) *n.* a small, light cake, made with yeast and flavored with rum, kirsch, etc. [< F < Polish *baba,* originally, old woman]

bab·bitt (bab′it) *n.* a whitish alloy of tin, antimony, and copper, or a similar alloy, used in bearings, etc. to lessen friction. —*v.* furnish (a bearing) with babbitt. [after Isaac *Babbitt,* 1799-1862, an American inventor]

Bab·bitt (bab′it) *n.* a self-satisfied businessman who readily conforms to middle-class ideas of respectability and business success. [after the hero of the novel *Babbitt* by Sinclair Lewis]

Babbitt metal babbitt.

bab·bitt·ry or **Bab·bitt·ry** (bab′it rē) *n.* conformity to middle-class ideas of respectability and business success. [< *Babbitt*]

bab·ble (bab′əl) *v.* **-bled, -bling.** *n.* —*v.* **1** make indistinct sounds like a baby. **2** talk or speak foolishly. **3** talk too much; tell secrets. **4** reveal foolishly: *babble a secret.* **5** murmur.
—*n.* **1** talk that cannot be understood. **2** foolish talk. **3** a murmur: *the babble of the brook.* [ME *babel;* imitative] —**bab′bler,** *n.*

babe (bāb) *n.* **1** a baby. **2** an innocent or inexperienced person; a person who is like a child. **3** *Slang.* a girl or young woman, especially an attractive one. [ME]

babe in the wood or **woods** a naïve, gullible, or childlike person; one who is so innocent or inexperienced as to be a likely victim of an unscrupulous person or plan.

Ba·bel (bā′bəl or bab′əl) *n.* **1** Babylon. **2 Tower of Babel,** in the Bible, a high tower built to reach heaven. God punished the builders by changing their language into several new languages. When they could not understand one another, they had to leave the tower unfinished. Gen. 11:1-9. **3** Also, **babel.** **a** a confusion of many different sounds; noise. **b** a place of noise and confusion. [< Hebrew]

ba·biche (bä bēsh′) *n. Cdn.* rawhide thongs or lacings: *In the far north babiche is often used in making snowshoes.* [< Cdn.F < Algonquian]

ba·bies'-breath (bā′bēz breth′) *n.* a tall plant bearing numerous small, fragrant, white or pink flowers.

bab·i·ru·sa, bab·i·rous·sa, or **bab·i·rus·sa** (bab′ə rü′sə or bä′bə rü′sə) *n.* a wild hog found in the East Indies. The boar has long, curved tusks. [< Malay *bābi* hog + *rūsa* deer]

ba·boo (bä′bü) *n.* **-boos.** In India: **1** a Hindu title meaning "sir," "Mr.," "gentleman." **2** an Indian with a smattering of English education. **3** an Indian clerk who writes English. [< Hind. *babu*]

ba·boon (ba bün′) *n.* **1** any of various large, fierce monkeys of Africa and the Arabian peninsula having a doglike face and a short tail. **2** a clumsy, uncouth person; lout. [ME < OF *babouin* stupid person]

ba·bu (bä′bü) *n.* **-bus.** baboo.

ba·bush·ka or **ba·boush·ka** (bə büsh′kə; *Russian,* bä′bůsh kə) *n.* a woman's scarf or kerchief worn on the head and knotted under the chin. [< Russian *babushka* grandmother, dim. of *baba* old woman]

ba·by (bā′bē) *n.* **-bies,** *adj. v.* **-bied, -by·ing.** —*n.* **1** a very young child. **2** the youngest of a family or group. **3** a person who acts like a baby; childish person. **4** *Slang.* a plan, idea, project, etc. that a person, group, etc. creates or is responsible for: *The society's baby for next year is the building of a new theatre.* **5** *Slang.* a term of praise or approval applied to a person or thing.
—*adj.* **1** of or for a baby. **2** young. **3** small for its kind; small. **4** childish.
—*v.* treat as a baby; pamper. [ME *babe*] —**ba′by-like′,** *adj.*

baby beef **1** the prime beef of a calf that has been fattened for one to two years before slaughtering. **2** a calf thus fattened.

baby bonus *Cdn. Informal.* the Family Allowance.

baby buggy *Informal.* a baby carriage.

baby carriage a light carriage used for wheeling a baby about.

ba·by-faced (bā′bē fāst′) *adj.* **1** appearing to have extreme youth and innocence. **2** having a rather round, chubby, smooth face.

baby grand a small grand piano.

ba·by·hood (bā′bē hůd′) *n.* **1** the condition or time of being a baby. **2** babies as a group.

ba·by·ish (bā′bē ish) *adj.* like a baby; childish; silly. —**ba′by·ish·ly,** *adv.* —**ba′by·ish·ness,** *n.*

Bab·y·lon (bab′ə lən or bab′ə lon′) *n.* **1** the capital of ancient Babylonia, on the Euphrates River and, later, of the ancient Chaldean empire. Babylon was noted for its wealth, power, magnificence, and wickedness. **2** any great, rich, or wicked city.

Bab·y·lo·ni·an (bab′ə lō′nē ən) *adj.* of or having to do with Babylon or Babylonia.
—*n.* **1** an inhabitant of Babylonia. **2** the language of Babylonia.

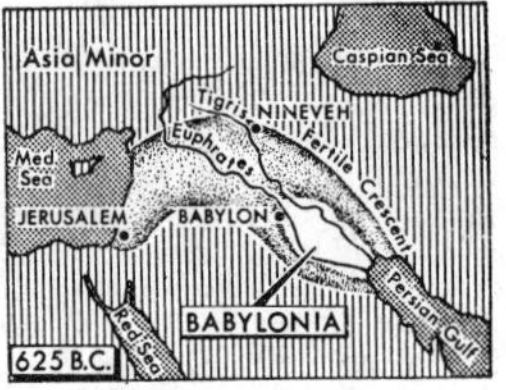

ba·by-sit (bā′bē sit′) *v.* **-sat, -sit·ting.** take care of a child during the temporary absence of its parents.

ba·by-sit·ter (bā′bē sit′ər) *n.* a person who baby-sits.

bac·ca·lau·re·ate (bak′ə lô′rē it) *n.* **1** a degree of bachelor given by a college or university. **2** a speech delivered to a graduating class at commencement. [< Med.L *baccalaureatus* < *baccalaureus* bachelor, var. of *baccalarius,* because of a supposed derivation from L *bacca* berry + *laurus* laurel]

bac·ca·rat or **bac·ca·ra** (bak′ə rä′ or bak′ə rä′) *n.* a kind of card game played for money. [< F]

Bac·chae (bak′ē or bak′ī) *n.pl.* **1** woman companions or worshippers of Bacchus. **2** priestesses of Bacchus.

bac·cha·nal (bak′ə nəl or bak′ə nal′) *adj.* having to do with Bacchus or his worship.
—*n.* **1** a worshipper of Bacchus. **2** a drunken reveller. **3** a wild, noisy party; drunken revelry; orgy. **4 Bacchanals,** *pl.* the Bacchanalia. [< L *bacchanalis* < *Bacchus* god of wine < Gk. *Bakchos*]

Bac·cha·na·li·a (bak′ə nāl′lē ə or bak′ə nāl′yə) *n.pl.* **1** in ancient Rome, a wild, noisy festival in honor of Bacchus. **2 bacchanalia,** a wild, noisy party; drunken revelry; orgy.

bac·cha·na·li·an (bak′ə nā′lē ən or bak′ə nāl′yən) *adj.* **1** having to do with the Bacchanalia. **2** drunken and riotous.— *n.* a drunken reveller.

bac·chant (bak′ənt) *n.* **bac·chants** or **bac·chan·tes** (bə kan′tēz). **1** a priest or worshipper of Bacchus. **2** a drunken reveller. [< L *bacchans, -antis,* ppr. of *bacchari* celebrate the festival of Bacchus]

bac·chan·te (bə kan′tē, bə kant′, or bak′ənt) *n.* a priestess or woman worshipper of Bacchus. [< F]

Bac·chic (bak′ik) *adj.* 1 of Bacchus or his worship. 2 Also, **bacchic.** drunken; riotous.

Bac·chus (bak′əs) *n.* in Greek and Roman mythology, the god of wine. The Greeks also called him Dionysus.

bach (bach) *Informal. v.* Sometimes, **bach it.** live alone and keep house for oneself. —*n.* a bachelor. Also, **batch.** [< *bachelor*]

bach·e·lor (bach′ə lər or bach′lər) *n.* 1 a man who has not married. 2 a person who has taken the primary degree of a college or university. 3 formerly, a young knight who served under the banner of another. [ME < OF *bacheler* squire < Med.L *baccalarius* the holder of a small farm, a young man]

bach·e·lor-at-arms (bach′ə lər ət ärmz′ or bach′lər-) *n.* **bachelors-at-arms.** bachelor (def. 3).

bach·e·lor·hood (bach′ə lər hůd′ or bach′lər-) *n.* the condition of being a bachelor.

bachelor of arts a degree awarded by a college or university and involving at least three or four years' study beyond high school, the emphasis being generally on the liberal arts. *Abbrev.*: B.A.

bach·e·lor's-but·ton (bach′ə lərz but′ən or bach′lərz-) *n.* 1 a plant having a flower resembling a button; cornflower. 2 the flower. 3 any similar flower.

Bach·i·an (bäʜ′ē ən or bäk′ē ən) *adj.* 1 of or having to do with Johann Sebastian Bach (1685-1750), a German composer of music. 2 in the style of his music. —*n.* an interpreter or admirer of Bach's music.

ba·cil·lar (be sil′ər or bas′ə lər) *adj.* 1 of or like a bacillus. 2 characterized by bacilli. 3 rod-shaped.

ba·cil·li (bə sil′ī or bə sil′ē) *n.* pl. of **bacillus.**

ba·cil·li·form (ba sil′ə fôrm′) *adj.* rod-shaped. [< LL *bacillus* + E *-form*]

ba·cil·lus (bə sil′əs) *n.* **-cil·li.** 1 any of the rod-shaped bacteria. 2 any of the bacteria. [< LL *bacillus*, dim. of *baculus* rod]

back[1] (bak) *n.* 1 the rear part of a person's body, from the neck to the end of the backbone. 2 the upper part of an animal's body from the neck to the end of the backbone. 3 the backbone. 4 the rear, upper, or farther part: *the back of the head, the back of the hand, the back of a hill, the back of the room.* 5 the reverse, under, or wrong side: *the back of a rug, the back of a medal.* 6 the part of an object serving to support or protect: *the back of a chair, the back of a book.* 7 the part of a garment covering the back. 8 in football, etc., a player whose position is behind the front line.
behind one's back, without one's knowing it; in one's absence; secretly.
get off a person's back, *Slang.* stop criticizing a person; stop ordering a person around.
get one's back up, a make one angry. **b** become angry. **c** be stubborn.
on a person's back, *Slang.* continually criticizing a person or ordering him around.
on one's back, a helpless. **b** sick.
put one's back up, a make one angry. **b** be stubborn.
turn one's back on, abandon; forsake.
with one's back to the wall, hard pressed; unable to escape without fighting.
—*v.* 1 support; help: *Many of his friends backed his plan.* 2 give financial support to. 3 move in reverse or backward: *He backed away from the gun.* 4 cause to move in reverse or backward: *He backed his car slowly.* 5 endorse: *back a cheque.* 6 bet on: *back a football team in the Grey Cup.* 7 make or be a back for: *A forest backed our little farm.* 8 provide with a back: *back satin with crepe.*
back and fill, a trim sails so as to keep a boat in a channel and floating with the current. **b** of cars and trucks, go forward and backward alternately in order to get out of mud or snow, or to make a difficult turn. **c** *Informal.* be undecided; keep changing one's mind.
back down, give up an attempt or claim; withdraw.
back into, *Informal.* gain (something) mainly by accident: *He backed into a place on the hockey team when our star defenceman fell ill.*
back out or **out of,** *Informal.* **a** withdraw from an undertaking. **b** break a promise.

hat, āge, cãre, fär; let, ēqual, tėrm; it, īce
hot, ōpen, ôrder; oil, out; cup, půt, rüle, ūse
əbove, takən, pencəl, lemən, circəs
ch, child; ng, long; sh, ship
th, thin; ᴛʜ, then; zh, measure

back up, a move backward. **b** support; help. **c** endorse: *They backed up his claim to the throne.*
back water, 1 stop or slow down a boat or ship by reversing the action of the oars or propeller. 2 retreat; withdraw.
—*adj.* 1 opposite the front; behind the front: *the back seat of a car.* 2 belonging to the past: *the back numbers of a newspaper.* 3 due but not yet paid; overdue. 4 in phonetics, pronounced at the back of the mouth. the *o* in *go* is a back vowel. 5 in distant or frontier regions: *back country.* [OE *bæc*] —**Syn.** *v.* 1 uphold, second. —*adj.* 1 rear, hinder.

back[2] (bak) *adv.* 1 to or toward the rear; backward; behind: *Please step back.* 2 in or toward the past: *some years back.* 3 in return: *Pay back what you borrow.* 4 in the place from which something or somebody came: *Put the books back.* 5 **back and forth,** first one way and then the other. 6 in reserve: *Keep back enough sugar to do the icing.* 7 in check: *Hold back your temper.* 8 **back of,** *Informal.* **a** in the rear of; behind. **b** supporting; helping. 9 **in back of,** *Esp.U.S.* behind; back of. 10 **go back on, a** withdraw from (a plan, etc.). **b** *Informal.* break a promise to. [var. of *aback*]

back·ache (bak′āk′) *n.* a continuous pain in the back.

back·bench·er (bak′bench′ər) *n.* an ordinary member of Parliament or of a legislative assembly.

back·bite (bak′bīt′) *v.* **-bit, -bit·ten** or (*Informal*) **-bit, -bit·ing.** say malicious things; slander (an absent person). —**back′bit′er,** *n.*

back·bone (bak′bōn′) *n.* 1 in vertebrates, the main bone along the middle of the back; spine. The backbone consists of many separate bones, called vertebrae, held together by muscles and tendons. See **skeleton** for diagram. 2 anything like a backbone. 3 the chief strength or support. 4 strength of character.

back·break·ing (bak′brāk′ing) *adj.* physically very exhausting or tiring. —**back′break′ing·ly,** *adv.*

back·chat (bak′chat′) *n. Informal.* impudent or insolent retorts; talking back.

back-check[1] (bak′chek′) *n.* the examination of completed work to verify its accuracy. —*v.* examine completed work to verify its accuracy.

back-check[2] (bak′chek′) *v.* in hockey, skate back toward one's own goal to cover an opponent's rush, used especially of forwards who have themselves been attacking.

back concessions *Cdn.* mainly in Ontario and Quebec, rural or bush districts, as opposed to urban centres: *He has a small farm on the back concessions.*

back country a region away from any centre of population; rural or undeveloped areas; backwoods.

back-country (bak′kun′trē) *adj.* of or having to do with the back country.

back·date (bak′dāt′) *v.* **-dat·ed, -dat·ing.** 1 put a date on (something) earlier than the actual date. 2 count as from a date earlier than the actual one.

back·door (bak′dôr′) *adj.* secret; underhand; sly.

back·drop (bak′drop′) *n.* 1 the curtain at the back of a stage. 2 a background.

back East *Cdn.* in or to eastern Canada: *People in western Canada speak of Ontario as being back East.*

back·er (bak′ər) *n.* a person who backs or supports another person, some plan or idea, a theatrical production, etc.

back·field (bak′fēld′) *n.* 1 in football, the players behind the front line: the quarterback, two halfbacks, flying wing, and fullback. In American football there is no flying wing. 2 in baseball, the outfield.

back·fill (bak′fil′) *v.* refill (an excavation) with soil or other material. —*n.* the soil or other material used.

back·fire (bak′fīr′) *n. v.* **-fired, -fir·ing.** —*n.* **1** in gasoline engines, etc., an explosion of gas occurring too soon or in the wrong place: *The backfire from the car sounded like a shot.* **2** a fire set to check a forest fire or prairie fire by burning off the area in front of it. —*v.* **1** explode too soon. **2** use a backfire. **3** *Informal.* have unfavorable results, not turn out as planned: *The thief's plan to steal the ring backfired.*

back formation a word formed from another word o which it appears to be the root. *Examples: burgle* from *burglar*; *edit* from *editor*; *pea* from *pease* taken as plural.

back·gam·mon (bak′gam′ən or bak′gam′ən) *n.* a game for two played on a special board with pieces moved according to the throw of dice. [< *back*[1], adj. + *gammon* game; because the men are sometimes set back]

back·ground (bak′ground′) *n.* **1** the part of a picture or scene toward the back: *In this photograph, the cottage stands in the foreground with the mountains in the background.* **2** a surface against which things are seen; surface upon which things are made or placed: *Her dress had pink flowers on a white background.* **3** earlier conditions or events that help to explain some later condition or event: *the background of the two-party system.* **4** one's past experience, knowledge, and training. **5** the accompanying music or sound effects in a play, motion picture, etc. **6 in the background,** out of sight; not in clear view.

back·hand (bak′hand′) *n.* **1** a stroke made with the back of the hand turned outward. **2** handwriting in which the letters slope to the left. —*adj.* backhanded.

back·hand·ed (bak′han′did) *adj.* **1** done or made with the back of the hand turned outward. **2** slanting to the left. **3** awkward; clumsy. **4** indirect; insincere: *A backhanded compliment is really a criticism.* —**back′hand′ed·ly,** *adv.* —**back′hand′ed·ness,** *n.*

back·hoe (bak′hō′) *n. v.* **-hoed, -hoe·ing.** —*n.* a machine for digging trenches for water mains, etc. —*v.* use such a machine.

back·house (bak′hous′) *n.* **1** a small outside toilet; a privy. **2** a small building at the back of a main one.

back·ing (bak′ing) *n.* **1** support; help. **2** financial support. **3** supporters; helpers. **4** something placed at the back of anything to support or strengthen it.

back·lash (bak′lash′) *n.* **1** the jarring reaction of a machine or mechanical device. **2** the movement or play between worn or loosely fitting parts. **3** a tangle in the part of a fishing line still on the reel after a cast. **4** a sudden, adverse reaction: *a backlash of anger.*

back·less (bak′lis) *adj.* **1** having no back. **2** of women's dresses, swim suits, etc., having the back of the bodice cut low.

back·log (bak′log′) *n.* **1** a large log at the back of a wood fire. **2** something serving as a basis or support. **3** a reserve of orders, commitments, etc. that have not yet been filled.

back number 1 an old issue of a magazine or newspaper. **2** *Informal.* an old-fashioned person; out-of-date thing.

back order an order for goods not currently in stock, received and acknowledged for filling at a later date.

back-order (bak′ôr′dər) *v.* hold an order (for out-of-stock goods) for filling at a later date.

back·ped·al (bak′ped′əl) *v.* **-alled** or **aled, -al·ling** or **-al·ing. 1** move the pedals of a bicycle backward, often to give a braking action. **2** in boxing, move backwards to keep away from an advancing opponent. **3** modify or retreat from (an opinion, promise, policy, etc.).

back·rest (bak′rest′) *n.* **1** anything that supports the back. **2** a support at the back, as on a lathe.

back road any little-used road, especially one in the country; side road.

back·room (bak′rüm′ or -rům′) *adj.* *Informal.* done or decided without public knowledge: *backroom politics.*

back·scratch·er (bak′skrach′ər) *n.* **1** any device for scratching the back. **2** *Informal.* a person who tries to gain advancement or maintain a position by flattering a superior; a toady.

back·scratch·ing (bak′skrach′ing) *n.* *Informal.* the giving and taking of favors for reciprocal advantage.

back seat 1 a seat at or in the back. **2** *Informal.* a place of inferiority or insignificance.

back-seat driver 1 a passenger in an automobile who criticizes and advises the driver. **2** a person who offers criticism and advice without himself assuming any responsibility.

back·set (bak′set′) *n.* a check to progress; setback.

back·sheesh or **back·shish** (bak′shēsh) *n.* baksheesh.

back·side (bak′sīd′) *n.* **1** the back. **2** the rump; buttocks.

back·slap·per (bak′slap′ər) *n.* *Informal.* **1** a person whose habit it is to slap others on the back. **2** any person whose friendly manner is so hearty and effusive as to seem insincere.

back·slide (bak′slīd′) *v.* **-slid, -slid** or **-slid·den, -slid·ing.** slide back into wrongdoing; lose one's enthusiasm, especially for religion. —**back′slid′er,** *n.*

back·space (bak′spās′) *v.* **-spaced, -spac·ing.** move the carriage of a typewriter backward a space or a set number of spaces.

back·stab·ber (bak′stab′ər) *n.* *Informal.* a person who tries to harm another in secret, usually by slander or betrayal.

back·stage (bak′stāj′) *adv.* **1** in the dressing rooms of a theatre. **2** toward the rear of a stage. —*adj.* **1** located backstage. **2** of or having to do with people and activities backstage. **3** not known to the general public; confidential: *backstage negotiations.*

back stairs 1 stairs in the back part of a house, used mainly by servants. **2** a secret or underhand method or course: *Some people never do anything in the open but approach every deal by the back stairs.*

back·stairs (bak′stãrz′) *adj.* secret or underhand: *backstairs political bargaining.*

back·stay (bak′stā′) *n.* **1** a rope extending from the top of the mast to a ship's side and helping to support the mast. See the picture under **shroud. 2** a spring, rod, strap, etc. used for support at the back of something.

back·stitch (bak′stich′) *n.* a stitching or stitch in which the thread doubles back each time on the preceding stitch. —*v.* sew with such stitches.

back·stop (bak′stop′) *n. v.* **-ped, -ping.** —*n.* in various games: **1** a fence or screen used to keep the ball from going too far away. **2** a player who stops balls that get past another player. —*v.* *Informal.* **1** serve as a backstop. **2** support; reinforce.

back·stroke (bak′strōk′) *n.* **1** in swimming, a stroke made with the swimmer lying on his back. **2** a backhanded stroke.

back talk *Informal.* a talking back; impudent answers.

back·track (bak′trak′) *v.* **1** go back over a course or path. **2** withdraw from an undertaking, position, etc.: *Tom backtracked on the claim he made last week.*

back·ward (bak′wərd) *adv.* **1** toward the back: *walk backward.* **2** with the back first: *tumble over backward.* **3** toward the starting point: *look backward.* **4** opposite to the usual way; in the reverse way: *read backward.* **5** from better to worse: *Educational conditions in the town went backward.* **6** toward the past. Also, **backwards.** —*adj.* **1** directed toward the back: *a backward look.* **2** with the back first. **3** directed to or toward the starting point; returning: *a backward movement.* **4** done in the reverse way or order: *backward process.* **5** reaching back into the past. **6** slow in development; dull: *Backward children need a special kind of schooling.* **7** behind time; late: *a backward season.* **8** shy; bashful. [ME *bakward* < *bak* back + *-ward*] —**back′ward·ness,** *n.*

☛ **Backward** and **backwards** are used interchangeably as adverbs: *Try doing the work backward. Try doing the work backwards.* Only *backward* is used as an adjective: *He hurried off without a backward glance.*

back·wards (bak′wərdz) *adv.* **1** backward. **2 fall, lean,** or **bend over backwards,** try extremely hard; be especially accommodating. ☛ See **backward** for usage note.

back·wash (bak′wosh′) *n.* **1** the water thrown back by oars, paddle wheels, the passing of a ship, etc. **2** a backward current.

back·wa·ter (bak′wo′tər or -wô′tər) *n.* **1** a stretch of still water close to the bank of a river or stream: *Because they are not moved by the current, backwaters are often stagnant.* **2** a stretch of water that is held or pushed back, as by a dam. **3** a condition or place that is thought of as backward, stagnant, etc.: *The small, provincial town was often referred to as a cultural backwater.* **4** a backward current; backwash.

back·woods (bak′wu̇dz′) *n.pl.* uncleared forests or wild regions far away from towns. *—adj.* **1** of the backwoods. **2** crude; rough.

back·woods·man (bak′wu̇dz′mən) *n.* **-men** (-mən). a man who lives or works in the backwoods.

ba·con (bā′kən) *n.* **1** salted and smoked meat from the back and sides of a pig. See **pork** for diagram. **2 bring home the bacon,** *Informal.* be successful; win the prize. [ME < OF < Gmc.]

Ba·co·ni·an (bā kō′nē ən) *adj.* **1** of or having to do with Francis Bacon (1561-1626), an English essayist, statesman and philosopher. **2** of or suggestive of his writings or philosophy. **3** of or having to do with the theory that Bacon wrote the plays of Shakespeare. *—n.* **1** a person who supports or follows the philosophy of Francis Bacon. **2** a person who supports the theory that Bacon wrote the plays of Shakespeare.

bac·te·ri·a (bak tēr′ē ə) *n.* pl. of **bacterium**. microscopically tiny and simple plants. Bacteria consist of single cells, have no chlorophyl, and multiply by fission. Certain bacteria cause diseases such as pneumonia, typhoid fever, etc.; others perform useful functions such as turning cider into vinegar.

SPHERE ROD SPIRAL

Bacteria of three main types. Their technical names are (from left to right) coccus, bacillus, and spirillum.

bac·te·ri·al (bak tēr′ē əl) *adj.* of bacteria; caused by bacteria: *bacterial life, bacterial diseases.*

bac·te·ri·cid·al (bak tēr′ə sīd′əl) *adj.* destructive to bacteria.

bac·te·ri·cide (bak tēr′ə sīd′) *n.* a substance that destroys bacteria. [< *bacterium* + *-cide*[2]]

bac·te·ri·o·log·i·cal (bak tēr′ē ə loj′ə kəl) *adj.* having to do with bacteriology. **—bac·te′ri·o·log′i·cal·ly,** *adv.*

bac·te·ri·ol·o·gist (bak tēr′ē ol′ə jist) *n.* an expert in bacteriology.

bac·te·ri·ol·o·gy (bak tēr′ē ol′ə jē) *n.* the science that deals with bacteria.

bac·te·ri·um (bak tēr′ē əm) *n.* **-te·ri·a.** one of the bacteria. [< NL < Gk. *baktērion,* dim. of *baktron* stick, staff]

Bac·tri·an camel (bak′trē ən) a camel having two humps on its back. [< *Bactria,* an ancient country in Asia]

bad[1] (bad) *adj.* **worse, worst,** *n., adv. —adj.* **1** not good; not as it ought to be: *Students often used to work in bad light.* **2** unfavorable: *He came at a bad time.* **3** distressing; severe: *She has a bad cold.* **4** evil; wicked: *Only a thoroughly bad man would hurt a helpless person.* **5** disagreeable; churlish; sullen: *a bad temper.* **6** harmful: *It is bad for your eyes to read in dim light.* **7** sick; suffering. **8** worthless: *a bad cheque.* **9** incorrect; faulty: *a bad guess.* **10** rotten; spoiled: *a bad egg.* **11** sorry; regretful; disturbed: *I feel bad about missing your visit.* **12** in law, not valid: *a bad debt.* **13 not bad,** *Informal.* fairly good. **14 not half bad,** *Informal.* rather good. **15 not so bad,** *Informal.* rather good.
—n. **1** that which is bad; a bad condition, quality, etc.; bad thing or things: *to take the good with the bad.* **2 be in bad,** *Slang.* be in disfavor (with a person over something). **3 to the bad, a** toward ruin. **b** to the bad side of an account.
—adv. Slang. badly. [ME *badde*; ? < OE *bæddel* hermaphrodite] **—bad′ness,** *n.*

Syn. *adj.* **1** inferior, poor. **3 Bad, evil, wicked** = morally wrong. **Bad,** the common word, is very general, applying to behavior ranging from naughtiness to being very corrupt, immoral, vile, etc.: *Drinking is a bad habit.* **Evil** = very bad and sometimes suggests threatening great harm: *It is evil for judges to accept bribes.* **Wicked** emphasizes willfully defying and breaking moral laws: *Deliberately leading an evil life is wicked.*

☛ **bad, badly.** Following a linking verb, formal English prefers the predicate adjective *bad,* not the adverb *badly*: *He feels bad about the news.* Informal speech sometimes uses *badly*: *He feels badly about the news.* In both formal and informal writing, the adverb *badly* is used to modify verbs: *She sings badly.*

hat, āge, cãre, fär; let, ēqual, tėrm; it, īce
hot, ōpen, ôrder; oil, out; cup, pu̇t, rüle, ūse
əbove, takən, pencəl, lemən, circəs
ch, child; ng, long; sh, ship
th, thin; ŦH, then; zh, measure

bad[2] (bad) *v.* a pt. of **bid** (defs. 1, 2).

bad blood an unfriendly feeling; hate: *The bad blood between the two men grew to a full-scale feud.*

bade (bad or bād) *v.* pt. of **bid** (defs. 3-10).

☛ **Bade** is used chiefly in formal and literary English: *The king bade her remain.*

badge (baj) *n.* **1** something worn to show that a person belongs to a certain occupation, school, class, club, society, etc.: *The Red Cross badge is a red cross on a white background.* **2** a symbol; sign: *A mayor's chain is his badge of office.* [ME *bagè*; origin unknown]

badg·er (baj′ər) *n.* **1** a hairy, gray animal found in Europe and America, related to the weasel. **2** its fur. *—v.* keep on teasing or annoying; torment by nagging and bullying: *The lawyer badgered the witnesses with questions.* [? < *badge*; with reference to the white spot on its head]

bad·i·nage (bad′ə näzh′ or bad′ə nij) *n.* good-natured joking; banter. [< F *badinage* < *badiner* banter < *badin* silly < VL *batare* gape]

bad·lands (bad′landz′) *n.* a barren region marked by ridges, gullies, and weird rock formations caused by erosion, as found in parts of southern Saskatchewan and Alberta.

bad·ly (bad′lē) *adv.* **1** in a bad manner. **2** greatly; very much: *Rain is badly needed.* ☛ See **bad** for usage note.

bad·min·ton (bad′min tən) *n.* a game like tennis, but played with a shuttlecock instead of a ball. [< *Badminton,* the Duke of Beaufort's estate in Gloucestershire, England]

bad-tem·pered (bad′tem′pərd) *adj.* **1** having a bad temper or disposition; angry or cross: *a bad-tempered horse.* **2** displaying irritation: *a bad-tempered remark.*

Bae·de·ker (bā′də kər) *n.* a guidebook for travellers. [< Karl *Baedeker,* 1801-1859, German publisher of a series of guidebooks]

baff (baf) *v.* **1** in golf, strike the ground with the sole of the club in making a stroke. **2** *Scottish.* strike a blow. *—n.* **1** in golf, the act of baffing. **2** *Scottish.* a blow. [probably < OF *baffe* a blow]

baf·fle (baf′əl) *v.* **-fled, -fling,** *n. —v.* **1** be too hard for (a person) to understand or solve: *This puzzle baffles me.* **2** hinder or thwart. **3** struggle without success: *The ship baffled bravely with the storm.* *—n.* a wall, screen, or similar device controlling the flow of air, water, sound, etc. by hindering its movement or changing its course. [? < Scots *bauchle* ridicule] **—baf′fler,** *n.* **—Syn.** *v.* **2** See **frustrate.**

baf·fle·ment (baf′əl mənt) *n.* **1** the act of baffling. **2** the state of being baffled.

baf·fling (baf′ling) *adj.* **1** puzzling. **2** hindering; thwarting.

bag (bag) *n. v.* **bagged, bag·ging.** *—n.* **1** a container made of paper, cloth, leather, etc. that can be closed at the top. **2** the amount that a bag can hold. **3** a bag and its contents. **4** a sac in an animal's body: *the honey bag of a bee.* **5** something suggesting a bag by its use or shape. **6** the game or fish killed or caught by a hunter. **7** in baseball, a base. **8** *Slang.* a woman. **9 bag and baggage,** with all one's belongings; entirely. **10 hold the bag,** *Informal.* **a** be left empty-handed. **b** be left to take the blame, responsibility, etc. **11 in the bag,** *Informal.* sure; certain to succeed.
—v. **1** put in a bag. **2** swell; bulge. **3** hang loosely. **4** in hunting, kill or catch. **5** *Slang.* catch; take; steal. **6** *Slang.* claim the right to: *Bags I go first.* [ME < ON *baggi* pack] **—bag′ger,** *n.*

Syn. *n.* **1 Bag, sack** = a container made of paper, cloth, etc. that can be closed at the top. **Bag** is the general word, applying to any such container of suitable size and material: *Fresh vegetables are sometimes sold in cellophane bags.* **Sack** applies particularly to a large bag made of coarse cloth: *a sack of grain or potatoes.*

ba·gasse (bə gas′) *n.* the pulp of sugar cane after the juice has been extracted. [< F < Provençal *bagasso* husks]

bag·a·telle (bag′ə tel′) *n.* **1** a mere trifle; thing of no importance. **2** a game resembling billiards. **3** in music, a short, light composition. [< F < Ital. *bagatella*, dim. of *baga* berry]

ba·gel (bā′ gəl) *n.* a doughnut-shaped roll of yeast dough that is simmered in water and then baked. [< Yiddish < *beigen* twist; related to OE *bēag* ring]

bag·gage (bag′ij) *n.* **1** the trunks, bags, suitcases, etc. that a person takes with him when he travels. **2** the equipment that an army takes with it, such as tents, blankets, ammunition, etc. [ME < OF *bagage* < *bagues* bundles]
Syn. baggage (def. 1) and **luggage** are synonymous; however, the former term is usual in the United States, the latter in Great Britain. In Canada, both terms are used, but *luggage* often has special reference to suitcases, overnight bags, and other bags carried by hand; *baggage* is the more general term for heavier and more bulky items such as trunks, boxes, and crates.

baggage car a railway car used to carry passengers' baggage, mail bags, etc.

bag·gage·man (bag′ij man′) *n.* **-men** (-men′). a man whose job it is to carry, check, or handle baggage.

bag·gage·mas·ter (bag′ij mas′tər) *n.* a person in charge of receiving and dispatching baggage, especially at a railway station.

bag·gat·a·way (bə gat′ə wā′) *n. Cdn.* formerly, an Indian game from which lacrosse developed. It was sometimes played between tribes, with as many as 200 men to a team. Also, **baggatiway.** [< Algonquian]

bag·ging (bag′ing) *n.* cloth for making bags.

bag·gy (bag′ē) *adj.* **-gi·er, -gi·est. 1** swelling; bulging. **2** hanging loosely: *baggy trousers.*

bag·man (bag′mən) *n.* **-men** (-mən). *Brit.* a travelling salesman.

bagn·io (ban′yō or bän′yō) *n.* **bagn·ios. 1** a house of prostitution; brothel. **2** a bathhouse. **3** a prison. [< Ital. *bagno* bath or bathhouse < L < Gk. *balaneion* bath]

bag·pipe (bag′pīp′) *n.* Often, **bagpipes,** *pl.* a shrill-toned musical instrument consisting of a windbag and pipes, associated chiefly with Scotland.

bag·pip·er (bag′pīp′ər) *n.* a person who plays the bagpipe.

bah (bä) *interj.* an exclamation of scorn or contempt.

Ba·ha·i (bə hä′ē) *n.* **1** a person who believes in Bahaism. **2** Bahaism. —*adj.* of or having to do with Bahaism. [< Persian]

Ba·ha·ism (bə hä′iz əm) *n.* a religious system founded in 1863 by Mussein Ali, a Persian religious leader who taught the basic unity of all religions.

baht (bät) *n.* **1** a unit of money in Thailand. See table at **money. 2** a coin worth one baht. [< Thai *bāt*]

bail[1] (bāl) *n.* **1** a security necessary to set a person free from arrest until he is due to appear for trial. **2** the amount guaranteed. **3 go bail for, a** supply bail for. **b** speak for; guarantee: *I'll go bail for his good behavior on the trip.*
—*v.* **1** obtain the freedom of (a person under arrest) by guaranteeing to pay bail. **2** deliver goods in trust without change of ownership. **3 bail out,** supply bail for.
[ME < OF *bail* custody < *baillier* deliver < L *bajulare* carry]

bail[2] (bāl) *n.* **1** the arched handle of a kettle or pail. **2** a hooplike support. The bails of a covered wagon hold up the canvas. [ME < ON *beygla* sword guard]

bail[3] (bāl) *n.* a scoop or pail used to throw water out of a boat. —*v.* **1** throw (water) out of a boat with a pail, a dipper, or any other container. **2 bail out, a** drop from an aircraft in a parachute. **b** throw accumulated water out of (something) with a pail, a dipper, or any other container. [< F *baille* < L *bajulus* carrier]

bail[4] (bāl) *n.* **1** in cricket, either of two small bars that form the top of a wicket. **2** a partition separating horses in a stable. [ME < OF *bail* barrier]

bail·a·ble (bāl′ə bəl) *adj.* **1** capable of being bailed. **2** permitting bail to be paid: *a bailable offence.*

bail·ee (bāl′ē′) *n.* one to whom goods are committed in bailment.

bail·ey (bāl′ē) *n.* **-eys.** the outer wall or court of a medieval castle. [var. of *bail*[4]]

Bail·ey bridge (bāl′ē) a portable bridge made from prefabricated steel sections in a lattice design. [after Sir Donald C. *Bailey*, a British engineer]

bail·ie (bāl′ē) *n.* in Scotland, an official of a town or city corresponding to an alderman. [ME < OF *baillis*, variant of *baillif.* See BAILIFF.]

bail·iff (bāl′if) *n.* **1** an official in charge of writs, processes, arrests, etc.; an assistant to a sheriff. **2** the officer of a court who has charge of prisoners while they are in the courtroom. **3** the overseer or steward of an estate. The bailiff collects rents, directs the work of employees, etc. for the owner. **4** in England, the chief magistrate in certain towns. [ME < OF *baillif* < *baillir* govern < *bail* guardian, manager < L *bajulus* carrier]

bail·i·wick (bāl′ə wik′) *n.* **1** the district over which a sheriff or bailiff has authority. **2** the place or locality that a person is identified with: *He is a big man in his own bailiwick.* **3** a person's field of knowledge, work, or authority. [< *bailie* + *wick* office < OE *wīce*]

bail·ment (bāl′mənt) *n.* **1** in law, the delivery of goods by one person to another in trust. **2** the act of bailing an accused person.

bails·man (bālz′mən) *n.* **-men** (-mən). a person who gives bail.

Bai·ram (bī räm′) *n.* either of two Moslem festivals, the lesser Bairam, following immediately after Ramadan, and the greater Bairam, occurring 70 days later.

bairn (bãrn) *n. Scottish.* a child. [OE *bearn* < pp. of *beran* to bear, influenced by ON *barn* child]

bait (bāt) *n.* **1** anything, especially food, used to attract fish, birds, or animals to catch them. **2** anything used to tempt or attract. [partly < ON *beita* food, and *beit* pasture; partly < E *bait*, v.]
—*v.* **1** put bait on (a hook) or in (a trap). **2** tempt; attract. **3** set dogs to attack: *Men used to bait bulls and bears for sport.* **4** attack; torment: *The dogs baited the bear.* **5** torment or worry by unkind or annoying remarks. **6** stop and feed: *The coachman baited his horses.* [ME *beyten* < ON *beita* cause to bite] —**bait′er,** *n.*

baize (bāz) *n.* a thick woollen cloth used for curtains, table covers, etc. [< F *baies*, pl. of *bai* chestnut-colored < L *badius*]

bake (bāk) *v.* **baked, bak·ing,** *n.* —*v.* **1** cook (food) by dry heat without exposing it directly to the fire: *bake bread and cake in the oven.* **2** dry or harden by heat: *bake bricks or china.* **3** become baked: *Cookies bake quickly.* **4** make or become very warm: *I'm just going to lie in the sun and bake.* —*n.* a baking. [OE *bacan*]

bake apple the fruit of the cloudberry bush.

Ba·ke·lite (bā′kə līt′) *n. Trademark.* a plastic used to make beads, stems of pipes, umbrella handles, fountain pens, electric insulators, etc. [after L. H. *Baekeland*, 1863-1944, who invented it]

bak·er (bāk′ər) *n.* **1** a person who makes or sells bread, pies, cakes, etc. **2** a dish or utensil in which to bake something. **3** a small portable oven.

baker's dozen thirteen.

bak·er·y (bāk′ər ē or bāk′rē) *n.* **-er·ies.** a baker's shop; a place where bread, pies, cakes, etc. are made or sold.

bak·ing (bāk′ing) *n.* **1** the process of cooking in dry heat. **2** the process of drying or hardening by heat. **3** the amount baked at one time; a batch.

baking powder a mixture of soda and cream of tartar, or of other substances, used instead of yeast to raise biscuits, cakes, etc.

baking soda sodium bicarbonate. *Formula*: $NaHCO_3$

bak·sheesh or **bak·shish** (bak′shēsh) *n.* in Egypt, Turkey, India, etc., money given as a tip. Also,

hat, āge, cãre, fär; let, ēqual, tėrm; it, īce
hot, ōpen, ôrder; oil, out; cup, pu̇t, rüle, ūse
əbove, takən, pencəl, lemən, circəs
ch, child; ng, long; sh, ship
th, thin; ᴛʜ, then; zh, measure

backsheesh, backshish. [< Persian < *bakhshidan* give]

bal. balance.

bal·a·clav·a (bal′ə klav′ə or bal′ə klä′və) *n.* a type of knitted woollen headgear that covers all of the head and neck except the upper part of the face: *Balaclavas were issued to Canadian soldiers during World War II.* [< *Balaklava,* site of a battle in the Crimean War]

bal·a·lai·ka (bal′ə lī′kə) *n.* a Russian musical instrument resembling a guitar. [< Russian]

A balance or scale for weighing. The thing to be weighed is put in one pan and metal weights in the other. When the bar is straight across, the contents of the two pans weigh the same.

A balcony (def. 1)

bal·ance (bal′əns) *n. v.* **-anced, -anc·ing.** —*n.* **1** an instrument for weighing. **2** equality in weight, amount, force, effect, etc. **3** a comparison of weight, value, importance, etc.; estimate. **4** harmony; proportion in design: *the balance of space in a Japanese print.* **5** a steady condition or position; steadiness: *He lost his balance and fell off the ladder.* **6** mental steadiness; poise: *His balance is never disturbed by the tantrums of others.* **7** anything that counteracts the effect, weight, etc. of something else. **8** the difference between the credit and debit sides of an account. **9** the part that is left over; remainder: *He was dismissed from school for the balance of the term.* **10** a wheel that regulates the rate of movement of a clock or watch. **11** the greatest weight, amount, or power. **12** in dancing, a balancing movement. **13 in the balance,** undecided. **14 Balance,** in astrology, the seventh sign of the zodiac; Libra.
—*v.* **1** weigh in a balance. **2** make or be equal to in weight, amount, force, effect, etc. **3** compare the value, importance, etc. of. **4** make or be proportionate to. **5** bring into or keep in a steady condition or position: *Can you balance a coin on its edge?* **6** counteract the effect, influence, etc. of; make up for. **7** make the credit and debit sides of (an account) equal. **8** be equal in the credit and debit sides of an account. **9** hesitate; waver. [ME < OF < LL *bilanx, bilancis* two-scaled < *bi-* two + *lanx* scale[2]] —**bal′anc·er,** *n.* —**Syn.** *n.* **1** scale, scales. **5** poise. **9** rest, surplus. —*v.* **5** steady. **6** offset.

balanced diet a diet having the correct amounts of all the kinds of food necessary for health.

balance of power **1** an even distribution of military and economic power among nations or groups of nations. **2** any even distribution of power. **3** the power of a small group to give control to a large group by joining forces with it.

balance of trade the difference between the value of all the imports and that of all the exports of a country.

balance sheet a written statement showing the profits and losses, the assets and liabilities, and the net worth of a business.

balance wheel a wheel for regulating motion: *A clock or watch has a balance wheel that controls the movement of the hands.*

bal·a·ta (bal′ə tə) *n.* **1** a tropical tree whose dried gumlike juice is used in making chewing gum, golf balls, insulation for wires, etc. **2** the dried gumlike juice. [< Sp.]

bal·bo·a (bal bō′ə) *n.* **1** a unit of money in Panama. See table at **money.** **2** a coin worth one balboa. [< Vasco de *Balboa* (1475-1517), a Spanish explorer]

bal·brig·gan (bal brig′ən) *n.* **1** a type of knitted cotton cloth, used for stockings, underwear, etc. **2** a similar type of knitted woollen cloth. **3 balbriggans,** knitted cotton stockings or pyjamas. [originally made at *Balbriggan,* Ireland]

bal·co·ny (bal′kə nē) *n.* **-nies. 1** a projecting platform with an entrance from an upper floor of a building. See picture in the opposite column. **2** a projecting upper floor in a theatre or hall with seats for an audience. [< Ital. *balcone* < *balco* scaffold < OHG *balcho* beam]

bald (bold or bôld) *adj.* **1** wholly or partly without hair on the head. **2** without its natural covering: *A mountain top with no trees or grass on it is bald.* **3** bare; plain; unadorned. **4** undisguised: *The bald truth is that he is a thief.* **5** of tires, having little or no tread remaining. **6** in zoology, having white on the head: *the bald eagle.* [ME *balled,* apparently < obsolete *ball* white spot] —**bald′ly,** *adv.* —**bald′ness,** *n.*

bal·da·chin or **bal·da·quin** (bal′də kin or bôl′də kin) *n.* **1** a canopy of stone, metal, or other material over an altar, throne, etc. **2** a canopy of silk brocade or other fabric carried in solemn procession. **3** a similar canopy above a dais, etc. **4** a heavy brocade, formerly made of silk and gold. [< F *baldaquin* < Ital. *baldacchine* < *Baldacco,* Italian name of Bagdad, where the silk was made]

bald eagle a large, powerful, North American eagle having white feathers on its head, neck, and tail.

Bal·der (bol′dər or bôl′dər) *n.* in Norse mythology, the god of light, beauty, goodness, wisdom, and peace.

bal·der·dash (bol′dər dash′ or bôl′dər-) *n.* nonsense. [< 16th cent. slang, meaning a senseless mixture of drinks such as milk and beer]

bald-faced (bold′fāst′ or bôld′-) *adj.* **1** of animals, having a white face or white markings on the face. **2** open and without shame or embarrassment: *a bald-faced lie.*

bald·head (bold′hed′ or bôld′-) *n.* **1** a person who has a bald head. **2** a breed of pigeons. **3** any of various birds with a whitish spot on the head.

bald·head·ed (bold′hed′id or bôld′-) *adj.* **1** denoting a person having little or no hair on his head. **2** *Cdn.* devoid of trees or brush: *baldheaded prairie.*

bald·ing (bol′ding or bôl′ding) *adj.* becoming bald.

Bal·dor (bol′dər or bôl′dər) *n.* Balder.

bald·pate (bold′pāt′ or bôld′-) *n.* **1** a person who has a bald head. **2** a kind of duck; widgeon.

bald prairie that part of the western prairie which is virtually without trees.

bal·dric (bol′drik or bôl′drik) *n.* a belt for a sword, horn, etc., hung from one shoulder to the opposite side of the body. [ME *baudry* < OF *baudrei,* of obscure origin; akin to MHG *balderich* girdle]

Baldur (bol′dər or bôl′dər) *n.* Balder.

bale[1] (bāl) *n. v.* **baled, bal·ing.** —*n.* a large bundle of merchandise or material securely wrapped or bound for shipping or storage: *a bale of cotton.* —*v.* make into bales; tie in large bundles. [ME, probably < Flemish < OF < OHG *balla* ball[1]]

bale[2] (bāl) *n. Poetic* or *Archaic.* **1** evil; harm. **2** sorrow; pain. [OE *bealu*]

ba·leen (bə lēn′) *n.* whalebone. [ME < OF *baleine* < L *ballena,* var. of *ballaena* < Gk. *phallaina* whale]

bale·ful (bāl′fəl) *adj.* evil; harmful. —**bale′ful·ly,** *adv.* —**bale′ful·ness,** *n.*

bal·er (bāl′ər) *n.* **1** a person who bales. **2** a machine that compresses and ties up into bundles such things as hay, straw, paper, and scrap metal.

Ba·li·nese (bä′lə nēz′) *n.* **-nese,** *adj.* —*n.* **1** a native or inhabitant of Bali. **2** the people of Bali. **3** the language of Bali. —*adj.* of Bali, its people, or their language.

balk (bok or bôk) *v.* **1** stop short and stubbornly; refuse to go on. **2** thwart; hinder; check: *The police balked the robber's plans.* **3** fail to use; let slip; miss. **4** in baseball, make a balk. [< n.]
—*n.* **1** a hindrance; check; defeat. **2** a blunder or mistake. **3** a ridge between furrows; strip left unploughed. **4** a large beam or timber. **5** in baseball, the failure of a pitcher to complete a pitch he has started. Also, **baulk.** [OE *balca* ridge]

Bal·kan (bol′kən or bôl′kən) *adj.* **1** of the Balkan peninsula; having to do with the countries there. **2** of the people living in these countries. **3** of the Balkan Mountains. —*n.* **the Balkans,** the Balkan States.

balk·y (bok′ē or bôk′ē) *adj.* **balk·i·er, balk·i·est.** stopping short and stubbornly refusing to go on; likely to balk. —**balk′i·ness,** *n.*

ball[1] (bol or bôl) *n.* **1** anything round or roundish. **2** a game in which some kind of ball is thrown, hit, or kicked. **3** a ball in motion: *a fast ball.* **4** the game of baseball. **5** a baseball pitched too high, too low, or not over the plate and not struck at by the batter. **6** a bullet. **7** something that resembles a ball. **8** a globe or sphere; the earth. **9 play ball, a** begin a game or start it again after stopping. **b** work together; co-operate: *The boss asked us to play ball with the management.* **10 keep the ball rolling,** do one's part.
—*v.* **1** make or form into a ball. **2 ball up,** *Slang.* confuse. [ME < ON *böllr*]
Syn. 1 Ball, globe = something round. **Ball** is the general word for any round or roundish object: *Mother put melon balls in the salad.* **Globe** applies to anything shaped like a ball, solid or hollow, which is perfectly round or thought of as being perfectly round: *The principal uses a glass globe as a paperweight.*

ball[2] (bol or bôl) *n.* **1** a large, formal party for dancing. **2** *Slang.* a very good time; a lot of fun: *We had a ball at the party.* [< F *bal* < *baler* to dance < LL *ballare*]

bal·lad (bal′əd) *n.* **1** a simple song. **2** a poem that tells a story in a simple verse form, especially one that tells a popular legend and is passed orally from one generation to another. **3** the music for such a poem. [ME < OF *balade* < Provençal *balada* dancing song]

bal·lade (bə läd′) *n.* **1** a poem having three stanzas of eight or ten lines each, followed by an envoy of four or five lines. The last line of each stanza and of the envoy are the same, and the same rhyme sounds recur throughout. **2** in music, an instrumental composition, usually rather simple and romantic: *Chopin's Ballades.* [< F < OF *balade.* See BALLAD.]

bal·lad·eer (bal′ə dēr′) *n.* **1** a singer of ballads. **2** *Informal.* a singer of popular songs.

ball and chain 1 a heavy metal ball attached by a short chain to the leg of a prisoner to prevent his escaping. **2** *Informal.* anything that restricts one's freedom of action. **3** *Slang.* a wife.

ball-and-socket joint a flexible joint formed by a ball or knob fitting in a socket, such as the shoulder or hip joint, and permitting some motion in every direction. See **socket** for diagram.

bal·last (bal′əst) *n.* **1** something heavy carried in a ship to steady it. **2** the weight carried in a balloon or dirigible to control it. **3** anything that steadies a person or thing. **4** the gravel or crushed rock used in making the bed for a road or railway track.
—*v.* **1** put ballast in (ships, balloons, etc.). **2** put gravel or crushed rock on. [apparently < Scand.; cf. ODanish *barlast* < *bar* bare + *last* load] —**bal′ last·er,** *n.*

ballast tube in fluorescent lighting, etc., a device to keep the electric current constant, usually consisting of an iron wire in a vacuum tube filled with hydrogen. Its varying resistance counteracts changes of voltage.

ball bearing 1 a bearing in which the shaft turns upon a number of loose metal balls to lessen friction. **2** any of the metal balls so used.

ball cock a valve for regulating the supply of water in a tank, cistern, etc., opened or closed by the fall or rise of a hollow, floating ball.

bal·le·ri·na (bal′ə rē′nə) *n.* **-nas.** a female ballet dancer. [< Ital.]

bal·let (bal′ā or ba lā′) *n.* **1** an artistic dance that usually tells a story or expresses a mood, performed by either a soloist or a group of dancers in a theatre, concert hall, etc. **2** the art of creating or performing ballets. **3** a performance of a ballet. **4** the music for a ballet. **5** a company of dancers that performs ballets. [< F *ballet,* dim. of *bal* dance. See BALL[2].]

bal·let·ic (ba let′ik) *adj.* of or having to do with ballet. —**bal·let′i·cal·ly,** *adv.*

bal·let·o·mane (ba let′ə mān′) *n.* a person who is enthusiastic about ballet. [< F *balletomane* < *ballet* + *-mane* < *manie* < Gk. *mania* enthusiasm]

bal·lis·ta (bə lis′tə) *n.* **-tae** (-tē or -tī). in ancient times, a machine used in wars to throw stones and other heavy missiles. [< L *ballista,* ult. < Gk. *ballein* throw]

bal·lis·tic (bə lis′tik) *adj.* **1** having to do with the motion or throwing of projectiles. **2** having to do with the science of ballistics. —**bal·lis′ti·cal·ly,** *adv.*

ballistic missile a projectile powered by a rocket engine or engines but reaching its target as a result of aim at the time of launching, used especially as a long-range weapon of offence.

bal·lis·tics (bə lis′tiks) *n.* the science that deals with the motion of projectiles such as bullets, shells, and bombs.

bal·lo·net (bal′ə net′) *n.* a small bag inside a balloon or airship that holds air or gas to regulate ascent or descent. [< F *ballonnet,* dim. of *ballon* balloon]

bal·loon (bə lün′) *n.* **1** an airtight bag filled with air or a gas lighter than air, so that it will rise and float. Small balloons are used as toys and decorations; larger balloons can be used as signals, advertisements, etc. **2** a large airtight bag from which is suspended either a gondola to carry two or more persons or a container to carry instruments. **Observation balloons** are used to observe and record data on weather, atmospheric radiation, etc. **3** in cartoons, a boxed space in which the words of a speaker are written.
—*v.* **1** ride in a balloon. **2** swell out like a balloon.
—*adj.* puffed out like a balloon. [< Ital. *ballone* < *balla* ball] —**bal·loon′like′,** *adj.*

balloon barrage an anti-aircraft screen of barrage balloons.

bal·loon·ist (bə lün′ist) *n.* **1** a person who goes up in balloons. **2** a pilot of a dirigible balloon.

balloon tire a large tire containing air under low pressure.

bal·lot (bal′ət) *n. v.* **-lot·ed, -lot·ing.** —*n.* **1** a piece of paper or other object used in voting. **2** the total number of votes cast. **3** vote; voting: *The ballot went in favor of the new party.* **4** a method of voting by paper slips, voting machines, etc.
—*v.* vote or decide by using ballots. [< Ital. *ballotta,* dim. of *balla* ball]

ballot box the box into which voters put their ballots.

ball·play·er (bol′plā′ər or bôl′-) *n.* **1** a baseball player. **2** a person who plays ball.

ball-point or **ball·point** (bol′point′ or bôl′-) *n.* a pen having a small metal ball in place of a nib. The movement and pressure of writing make the ball turn against a cartridge of semisolid ink, transferring some of the ink to the paper.

ball·room (bol′rüm′ or bôl′-, bol′rům′ or bôl′-) *n.* a large room for dancing.

bal·ly·hoo (*n.* bal′ē hü′; *v.* bal′ē hü′ or bal′ē hü′) *n.* **-hoos,** *v.,* **-hooed, -hoo·ing.** *Slang.* —*n.* **1** noisy advertising; a sensational way of attracting attention. **2** an uproar or outcry. —*v.* advertise noisily; make exaggerated or false statements about. [origin uncertain] —**bal′ly·hoo′ er,** *n.*

balm (bom or bäm) *n.* **1** a fragrant, oily, sticky substance obtained from certain kinds of trees, used to heal or relieve pain. **2** anything that heals or soothes: *Mother's praise was balm to Jane's wounded feelings.* **3** a fragrant ointment or oil used in anointing. **4** a fragrance; sweet odor. **5** a fragrant plant of the same family as mint. [ME < OF *basme* < L < Gk. *balsamon* balsam. Doublet of BALSAM.]

balm of Gilead 1 a fragrant ointment prepared from the resin of a small evergreen tree of Asia and Africa.

2 the tree itself. 3 a North American poplar, the balsam poplar. 4 the balsam fir.

Bal·mung (bäl′mu̇ng) *n.* Siegfried's sword.

balm·y[1] (bom′ē or bäm′ē) *adj.* **balm·i·er, balm·i·est.** 1 mild; gentle; soothing: *a balmy breeze.* 2 fragrant. [< *balm*] —**balm′i·ly,** *adv.* —**balm′i·ness,** *n.*

balm·y[2] (bom′ē or bäm′ē) *adj.* **balm·i·er, balm·i·est.** *Slang.* silly; crazy. [var. of *barmy*]

ba·lo·ney (bə lō′nē) *n.* 1 *Slang.* nonsense. 2 *Informal.* bologna. Also, **boloney.** [< *bologna*]

bal·sa (bol′sə or bôl′sə) *n.* 1 a tropical American tree with very light, strong wood. 2 its wood. 3 a raft, especially one consisting of two or more floats fastened to a framework. [< Sp. *balsa* raft]

bal·sam (bol′səm or bôlsəm) *n.* 1 any of several resins that contain benzoic acid. 2 a balsam-yielding tree, such as the balsam fir. 3 an ointment or preparation for healing or soothing. 4 any of several resin-and-oil compounds that are insoluble in water. 5 any of various transparent, liquid turpentines. 6 a garden plant having seed vessels that burst open when ripe. [< L < Gk. *balsamon.* Doublet of BALM.]

balsam fir 1 an evergreen tree of North America of the same family as the pine. Its resin is used in making varnish. 2 its wood.

balsam poplar 1 a North American poplar having oval or heart-shaped leaves and large buds covered with resin; balm of Gilead; tacamahac. 2 the wood of this tree, used for lumber, veneer, etc.

Bal·tic (bol′tik or bôl′tik) *adj.* 1 having to do with the Baltic Sea. 2 having to do with the Baltic States. —*n.* a group of languages belonging to this region.

Baltimore oriole (bol′tə môr′ or bôl′tə môr′) a North American bird the male of which has orange and black feathers, and the female greenish or yellowish feathers.

Ba·lu·chi (bə lü′chē) *n.* **-chi.** 1 a native or inhabitant of Baluchistan, a province of West Pakistan. 2 the language of Baluchistan.

bal·us·ter (bal′əs tər) *n.* 1 a support for a railing. 2 **balusters,** a balustrade. [< F *balustre* < Ital. < L < Gk. *balaustion* pomegranate blossom; from the shape]

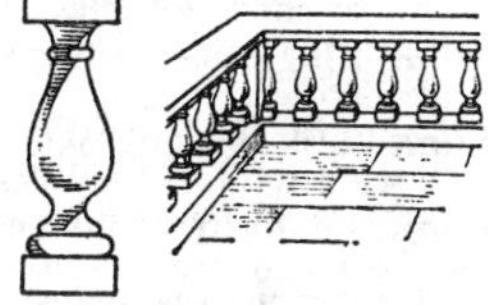
A baluster and balustrade

bal·us·trade (bal′əs trād′ or bal′əs trād′) *n.* a row of balusters and the railing on them. [< F *balustrade* < *balustre.* See BALUSTER.]

bam·bi·no (bam bē′nō) *n.* **-nos** or **-ni** (-nē). *Italian.* 1 a baby; little child. 2 an image or picture of the baby Jesus. [< Ital. *bambino,* dim. of *bambo* silly]

bam·boo (bam bü′) *n.* **-boos,** *adj.* —*n.* any of various woody or tree-like tropical or semitropical grasses that have stiff, hollow stems and hard, thick joints: *He bought a fishing-rod made of bamboo.* —*adj.* of bamboo; made of the stems of this plant. [< Du. *bamboes,* probably < Malay]

Bamboo Curtain an imaginary wall or dividing line between China and non-communist nations.

bam·boo·zle (bam bü′zəl) *v.* **-zled, -zling.** *Informal.* 1 impose upon; cheat; trick. 2 puzzle; perplex. [origin uncertain] —**bam·boo′zler,** *n.*

ban[1] (ban) *v.* **banned, ban·ning,** *n.* —*v.* 1 prohibit; forbid: *Swimming is banned in this lake.* 2 place a ban on; pronounce a curse on.
—*n.* 1 the forbidding of an act or speech by authority of the law, the church, or public opinion. 2 a solemn curse by the church. 3 a sentence of outlawry. [OE *bannan* summon] —**Syn.** *v.* 2 curse. —*n.* 1 prohibition, taboo. 2 excommunication.

ban[2] (ban) *n.* 1 a public proclamation or edict. 2 in medieval times: **a** the summoning of the king's vassals for war. **b** the whole body of these vassals. [fusion of OE *gebann* summons and Old North French *ban* proclamation, jurisdiction < Gmc.]

ban[3] (bän) *n.* **ba·ni** (bä′nē). 1 a unit of money in Romania, worth 1/100 of a leu. 2 a coin worth one ban. [< Romanian]

hat, āge, cãre, fär; let, ēqual, tėrm; it, īce
hot, ōpen, ôrder; oil, out; cup, pu̇t, rüle, ūse
əbove, takən, pencəl, lemən, circəs
ch, child; ng, long; sh, ship
th, thin; ᴛʜ, then; zh, measure

ba·nal (bā′nəl or bə nal′) *adj.* commonplace; trite; trivial. [< F *banal* < *ban* proclamation < Gmc.; original sense "of feudal service"; later, "open to the community"] —**ba′nal·ly,** *adv.* —**Syn.** hackneyed.

ba·nal·i·ty (bə nal′ə tē) *n.* **-ties.** commonplaceness; triteness; triviality.

ba·nan·a (bə nan′ə) *n.* 1 a slightly curved, yellow or red tropical fruit having firm, creamy flesh. 2 a tree-like tropical plant on which bananas grow. 3 the flavor of this fruit. [< Pg. or Sp.]

banana oil 1 a colorless liquid having a smell resembling that of bananas, used in flavorings and as a solvent. 2 *Slang.* pretentious but insincere talk; excessive flattery.

band[1] (band) *n.* 1 a number of persons or animals joined or acting together: *a band of robbers, a band of wild dogs.* 2 a group of musicians playing various instruments together, especially one that plays only wind and percussion instruments: *a military band.* 3 an orchestra that plays popular music, jazz, etc.: *a dance band.* 4 *Cdn.* a group of reservation Indians recognized by the federal government as an administrative unit. 5 a drove or flock of animals; herd. [< MF *bande* < ult. Gmc. Related to BANNER.]
—*v.* unite or cause to unite in a group. —**Syn.** *n.* 1 party, gang, group, crew.

band[2] (band) *n.* 1 a thin, flat strip of material for binding, trimming, etc. 2 a stripe: *a white cup with a gold band.* 3 a collar with two strips hanging in front, worn with certain clerical, legal, and academic robes. 4 in radio broadcasting, a particular range of wave lengths.
—*v.* 1 put a band on. 2 mark with stripes. [ME < MF *bande* < Gmc. Related to BAND[1], BEND[2].]

band[3] (band) *n.* anything that ties, binds, or unites. [ME < ON *band*]

band·age (ban′dij) *n. v.* **-aged, -ag·ing.** —*n.* a strip of cloth or other material used in binding up and dressing a wound, injured leg or arm, etc. —*v.* bind, tie up, or dress with a bandage. [< F *bandage* < *bande.* See BAND[1].] —**band′ag·er,** *n.*

Band-Aid (band′ād′) *n. Trademark.* a bandage made of a piece of cotton gauze attached to a strip of adhesive tape.

ban·dan·a or **ban·dan·na** (ban dan′ə) *n.* a large, colored handkerchief. [probably < Hind. *bandhnu* tying cloth to produce a design when dyed]

band·box (band′boks′) *n.* a light cardboard box for holding hats, collars, etc.

ban·deau (ban dō′ or ban′dō) *n.* **-deaux** (-dōz′ or -dōz). 1 a band worn around the head. 2 a narrow band. 3 a narrow brassiere. [< F *bandeau,* dim. of *bande* band[1], ult. < Gmc.]

ban·de·role or **ban·de·rol** (ban′də rōl′) *n.* a small flag or streamer on a lance, mast, etc. [< F < Ital. *banderuola* < *bandiera* banner < LL *bandum* < Gmc.]

ban·di·coot (ban′də küt′) *n.* 1 a very large rat of India that is about two feet long. 2 a small ratlike animal of Australia that carries its young in a pouch. [< Telegu *pandikokku* pig-rat]

ban·dit (ban′dit) *n.* **ban·dits** or **ban·dit·ti** (-ē). a highwayman; robber. [< Ital. *bandito,* pp. of *bandire* banish, proscribe, ult. < Gmc. Akin to BAN.]
—**Syn.** outlaw, brigand, desperado.

ban·dit·ry (ban′dit rē) *n.* 1 the work of bandits. 2 bandits.

ban·dit·ti (ban dit′ē) *n.* a pl. of **bandit.**

band·mas·ter (band′mas′tər) *n.* the leader or conductor of a band (def. 3).

ban·do·lier or **ban·do·leer** (ban′də lēr′) *n.* 1 a broad belt worn over the shoulder and across the breast. Some bandoliers have loops for carrying cartridges; others have small cases for bullets, gunpowder, etc. 2 one of these cases. [< F *bandoulière* < Sp. *bandolera* < *banda* band[1], ult. < Gmc.]

band saw a saw in the form of an endless steel belt.

band shell an outdoor platform for musical concerts that has a shell-shaped, resonant covering open on one side.

bands·man (bandz′mən) *n.* **-men** (-mən). a member of a band of musicians.

band·stand (band′stand′) *n.* an outdoor platform, usually roofed, for band concerts.

band·wag·on (band′wag′ən) *n.* **1** a wagon that carries a musical band in a parade. **2 climb on the bandwagon,** *Informal.* join what appears to be the winning side in a political campaign, contest, etc.

ban·dy (ban′dē) *v.* **-died, -dy·ing,** *adj.* —*v.* **1** throw back and forth; toss about. **2** give and take; exchange: *To bandy words with a foolish person is a waste of time.*
—*adj.* bent or curved outward: *bandy legs.* [cf. F *bander* bandy, *se bander* band together < Gmc.]

ban·dy-leg·ged (ban′dē leg′id or -legd′) *adj.* having legs that curve outward; bowlegged.

bane (bān) *n.* **1** a cause of death, ruin, or harm: *Wild animals were the bane of the mountain village.*
2 destruction of any kind. [OE *bana* murderer]

bane·ber·ry (bān′ber′ē or bān′bər ē) *n.* **-ries. 1** any of several plants that have spikes of small, white flowers and clusters of white or red, poisonous berries. **2** one of these berries.

bane·ful (bān′fəl) *adj.* deadly; harmful. —**bane′ful·ly,** *adv.*

bang[1] (bang) *n.* **1** a sudden, loud noise: *the bang of a gun.* **2** a violent, noisy blow. **3** vigor, impetus. **4** *Slang.* a thrill. [< v.]
—*v.* **1** make a sudden loud noise. **2** hit with violent and noisy blows; strike noisily. **3** shut with a noise; slam: *bang a door.* **4** handle roughly.
—*adv.* **1** suddenly and loudly: *The windows fell bang.*
2 violently and noisily: *The boy on the bicycle went bang into a telephone pole.*
—*interj.* an imitation of gunfire: "*Bang! Bang!*" *shouted the boys.* [? < ON *banga* to hammer]

bang[2] (bang) *n.* **1** a fringe of short hair over the forehead. **2 bangs,** *pl.,* hair cut straight across the forehead. —*v.* cut hair in this way: *She wears her hair banged.* [< short for *bangtail* docked tail (of a horse)]

ban·gle (bang′gəl) *n.* **1** a ring worn around the wrist, arm, or ankle. **2** a small ornament suspended from a bracelet. [< Hind. *bangri, bangli* glass bracelet]

Bang's disease (bangz) an infectious disease in cattle that often results in abortion. [< Bernhard *Bang,* 1848-1932, a Danish physician who described it]

ban·ian (ban′yən or ban′yan) *n.* **1** a banyan. **2** a Hindu merchant of a caste that eats no meat. [< Pg. *banian,* probably < Arabic *banyan* < Gujarati (a lang. of western India), ult. < Skt.]

ban·ish (ban′ish) *v.* **1** condemn to leave a country; exile. **2** force to go away; send away; drive away. [ME < OF *baniss-,* a stem of *banir* < LL *bannire* ban < Gmc.] —**ban′ish·er,** *n.*
Syn. 1 Banish, exile, deport = force to leave a country. **Banish** = to force a person, by order of authority, to leave his own or a foreign country, permanently or for a stated time: *Napoleon was banished to Elba.* Exile also means to compel a person to leave his own country or home, but the authority may be the force of circumstances or his own will: *The Kaiser was exiled from Germany after World War I.* **Deport** = to banish a person from a country of which he is not a citizen: *We deport aliens who slip across our borders.*

ban·ish·ment (ban′ish mənt) *n.* **1** the act of banishing. **2** the state of being banished; exile.

ban·is·ter (ban′is tər) *n.* **1** a baluster. **2 banisters,** *pl.,* the balustrade of a staircase. [var. of *baluster*]

ban·jo (ban′jō) *n.* **-jos** or **-joes.** a stringed musical instrument played with the fingers or a plectrum. [< alteration of *bandore* < Sp. < LL < Gk. *pandoura,* a three-stringed instrument]

ban·jo·ist (ban′jō ist) *n.* a person who plays a banjo.

bank[1] (bangk) *n.* **1** a long pile or heap: *a bank of snow.* **2** the ground bordering a river, lake, etc. **3** a shallow place in an ocean, sea, etc.; shoal: *the fishing banks of Newfoundland.* **4** a slope: *the bank of a corner on a race track.* **5** the sloping of an airplane to one side when making a turn. **6** in mining, **a** the top of a shaft. **b** the face being worked in a coal mine.
—*v.* **1** raise a ridge or mound about; border with a bank or ridge. **2** form into a bank; pile up; heap up: *The wind had banked snow against the wall.* **3** form banks: *Clouds are banking along the horizon.* **4** slope: *The pavement of a curve on an expressway should be well banked, upward and outward from the centre.* **5** make (an airplane) slope to one side when making a turn. **6** of an airplane, slope to one side when turning. **7** cover (a fire) with ashes or fresh fuel so that it will burn slowly. [ME < ON; cf. OIcelandic *bakki*] —**Syn.** *n.* **1** ridge, mound, embankment. **3** bar, reef.

bank[2] (bangk) *n.* **1** an institution for keeping, lending, exchanging, and issuing money. **2** a container used for saving small sums at home: *a plastic piggy bank.* **3** in gambling games, the fund of money out of which the dealer or manager pays his losses. **4** in games, a stock of pieces from which players draw. **5** any place where reserve supplies are kept. The place where blood plasma is kept for transfusions is called a bank.
—*v.* **1** keep a bank; act as a banker. **2** keep money in a bank. **3** put (money) in a bank. **4 bank on,** *Informal.* depend on; be sure of. [< F *banque* < Ital. *banca,* originally, bench, later applied to the table used by money changers < Gmc.] —**bank′a·ble,** *adj.*

bank[3] (bangk) *n.* **1** in a galley: **a** a bench for rowers. **b** the rowers on a bench. **c** a row or tier of oars. **2** a row of keys on an organ, typewriter, etc. **3** a row or close arrangement of things: *a bank of switches, a bank of machines.* —*v.* arrange in rows. [ME < OF *banc* < LL *bancus* < Gmc. Akin to BENCH.]

bank account 1 an account with a bank: *We have two bank accounts, a chequing account and a savings account.* **2** the money that a depositor has in such an account.

bank barn especially in Ontario, a two-storey barn built into a hill so as to permit entry to the bottom level from one side and to the top level from the other side.

bank bill 1 a cheque drawn by one bank on another. **2** a bank note.

bank·book (bangk′bůk′) *n.* a book in which a record of a person's account at a bank is kept.

bank discount an amount of money deducted from a loan by a bank at the time the loan is made, equal to the interest chargeable from the date the loan is made until the date when the final payment is due.

bank·er[1] (bangk′ər) *n.* **1** a person or company that keeps a bank. **2** a dealer or manager in a gambling game.

bank·er[2] (bangk′ər) *n.* **1** a fisherman who fishes off the Grand Banks. **2** a fishing vessel that operates off the Grand Banks.

bank holiday any day (from Monday to Friday inclusive) on which banks are legally closed: a legal holiday.

bank·ing (bangk′ing) *n.* the business of a bank or banker.

bank note a note that is issued by a bank and must be paid in cash on demand. Bank notes are used as money.

bank rate the standard rate of discount for a specified type of note, security, etc., set by a central bank, such as the Bank of Canada, or by a chartered bank.

bank·roll (bangk′rōl′) *n.* *Informal.* the amount of money a person has in his possession or easily available.
—*v.* *Slang.* provide or put up the money for: *A group of businessmen bankrolled the opera company's tour.*

bank·rupt (bangk′rupt) *n.* **1** a person declared by a law court to be unable to pay his debts and whose property is distributed among or administered on behalf of his creditors. **2** a person who is unable to pay his debts.
3 a person who is completely lacking in something: *a moral bankrupt.*
—*adj.* **1** unable to pay one's debts; declared legally unable to pay debts. **2** at the end of one's resources; destitute. **3** completely lacking in something: *The story was entirely bankrupt of any new ideas.*
—*v.* make bankrupt. [< F *banqueroute* < Ital.

bancarotta bankruptcy < *banca* bank + *rotta*, fem. pp. of *rompere* break < L *rumpere*]

bank·rupt·cy (bangk′rəp sē or bangk′rupt sē) *n.* **-cies.** the condition of being bankrupt.

ban·ner (ban′ər) *n.* **1** a flag. **2** a piece of cloth with some design or words on it, attached by its upper edge to a pole or staff. **3** in newspapers, a headline in large type, usually extending across the entire width of the page. *—adj.* leading or outstanding; foremost: *Ours is the banner class.* [ME < OF *baniere* < LL *bandum* < Gmc.] —**Syn.** *n.* **1, 2** ensign or standard.

ban·ner·et (ban′ər it) *n.* **1** formerly, a knight entitled to lead his vassals into battle under his own banner. **2** a former rank of knighthood, senior to that of knight bachelor. [ME < OF *baneret* < *banere* banner + *-et* -ate[1]]

ban·ner·ette or **ban·ner·et** (ban′ər et′) *n.* a small banner.

ban·nock (ban′ək) *n.* **1** a flat cake, usually unleavened, made of oatmeal or barley flour. **2** *Cdn.* a flat, round cake, made of unleavened flour, salt, and water. Baking powder is sometimes added. [OE *bannuc* bit, piece]

banns (banz) *n.pl.* a public notice, given three times in church, that a man and a woman are to be married. [pl. of *bann*, var. of *ban* proclamation, OE *gebann*]

ban·quet (bang′kwit) *n. v.* **-quet·ed, -quet·ing.** *—n.* **1** a feast. **2** a formal dinner with speeches. *—v.* **1** give a banquet to. **2** enjoy a banquet. [< F < Ital. *banchetto*, dim. of *banco* bench < Gmc.] —**Syn.** *n.* **1** See **feast.**

ban·quette (bang ket′) *n.* **1** a platform along the inside of a parapet or trench for soldiers to stand on when firing. **2** an upholstered bench, especially one along a wall in restaurants, etc. [< F]

ban·shee (ban′shē or ban shē′) *n.* a spirit whose wails are supposed to mean that there will soon be a death in the family. [< Irish *bean sidhe* woman of the fairies]

ban·tam (ban′təm) *n.* **1** Often, **Bantam.** a small-sized kind of fowl. **2** a very small person, usually one fond of fighting. **3** in sports: **a** a class for players under 15 years. **b** a player in such a class. **c** a bantamweight. *—adj.* **1** light in weight; small. **2** of or having to do with players under 15 years: *a bantam hockey league.* [probably from *Bantam*, a city in Java]

ban·tam·weight (ban′təm wāt′) *n.* a boxer who weighs 112-118 pounds. *—adj.* very small or light of its kind; miniature: *a bantamweight camera.*

ban·ter (ban′tər) *n.* playful teasing; joking. *—v.* **1** tease playfully; make fun of. **2** talk in a joking way. [origin unknown] —**ban′ter·er,** *n.* —**ban′ter·ing·ly,** *adv.*

bant·ling (bant′ling) *n.* a young child; brat. [? alteration of G *Bänkling* bastard < *Bank* bench]

Ban·tu (ban′tü) *n.* **-tu** or **-tus,** *adj.* *—n.* **1** a large group of Negroid tribes living in central and southern Africa. **2** a member of any of these tribes. **3** any of the languages of these tribes. *—adj.* of these tribes or their languages.

ban·yan (ban′yən or ban′yan) *n.* a fig tree of India whose branches have hanging roots that grow down to the ground and start new trunks. One tree may cover several acres. Also, **banian.** [var. of *banian*; originally a specific tree under which stood a banian pagoda]

ban·zai (bän′zī′) *interj.* **1** a Japanese greeting or patriotic cheer meaning: "May you live ten thousand years!" **2** the battle cry of Japanese soldiers in a banzai attack.

banzai attack a suicidal assault by Japanese soldiers, usually on an entrenched position.

ba·o·bab (bā′ō bab′ or bä′ō bab′) *n.* a tall, tropical tree having a very thick trunk. The fibres of its bark are used for making rope, cloth, etc. [? < native African]

Bap. or **Bapt.** Baptist.

bap·tism (bap′tiz əm) *n.* **1** a baptizing or being baptized. **2** the rite or sacrament of baptizing or being baptized. **3** an experience that cleanses a person or introduces him into a new kind of life.

bap·tis·mal (bap tiz′məl) *adj.* having to do with baptism; used in baptism: *baptismal vows.* —**bap·tis′mal·ly,** *adv.*

baptism of fire **1** the first time that a soldier is under fire. **2** a severe trial or test; ordeal.

hat, āge, cãre, fär; let, ēqual, tėrm; it, īce
hot, ōpen, ôrder; oil, out; cup, put, rüle, ūse
əbove, takən, pencəl, lemən, circəs
ch, child; ng, long; sh, ship
th, thin; ᴛʜ, then; zh, measure

Bap·tist (bap′tist) *n.* **1** a member of a Christian church that believes that baptism should be given to adults only and should be administered by immersing the whole person under water. **2** **baptist,** a person who baptizes. *—adj.* of or having to do with the Baptists.

bap·tis·ter·y (bap′tis trē or bap′tis tər ē) *n.* **-ter·ies.** a place where baptism is performed. A baptistery may be a section of a church or a separate building.

bap·tist·ry (bap′tis trē) *n.* **-ries.** baptistery.

bap·tize (bap tīz′ or bap′tīz) *v.* **-tized, -tiz·ing.** **1** dip into water or wash with water as a sign of purification from sin and of admission into a Christian church. **2** purify; cleanse. **3** give a first name to (a person) at baptism; christen. **4** give a name to. [ME < OF *baptiser* < LL < Gk. *baptizein* < *baptein* dip] —**bap·tiz′er,** *n.*

bar[1] (bär) *n. v.* **barred, bar·ring,** *prep.* *—n.* **1** an evenly shaped piece of some solid, longer than it is wide or thick: *a bar of iron, a bar of soap, a bar of chocolate.* **2** a pole or rod put across a door, gate, window, etc. to fasten or shut off something. **3** anything that blocks the way or prevents progress: *A bar of sand kept boats out of the harbor. A bad temper is a bar to making friends.* **4** a band of color; stripe. **5** in music: **a** a unit of rhythm. **b** a line between two such units on a staff. **6** a counter over which drinks, usually alcoholic, are served. **7** the room or establishment containing such a counter. **8** a store-counter over which certain articles are sold: *a snack bar, a record bar, a hat bar.* **9** the profession of a lawyer: *After passing his law examinations, the young man was called to the bar.* **10** lawyers as a group: *Judges are chosen from the bar.* **11** the railing around the place where lawyers sit in a law court. **12** the place where an accused person stands in a law court. **13** a law court. **14** anything like a law court: *the bar of public opinion.*
—v. **1** put bars across; fasten or shut off with a bar: *He bars the doors every night.* **2** block; obstruct: *The exits were barred by chairs.* **3** exclude; forbid: *All talking is barred during a study period.* **4** mark with stripes or bands of color.
—prep. except; excluding: *He is the best student, bar none.* [ME *barre* < OF < VL *barra* thick ends of bushes (collectively) < Celtic] —**Syn.** *n.* **3** barrier, obstacle, obstruction.

BAR BAR DOUBLE BAR
BAR BAR BAR

Bar (def. 5)

bar[2] (bär) *n.* a unit of pressure equal to one million dynes per square centimetre, or a pressure of 29.531 inches of mercury at 32° F. [< Gk. *baros* weight]

bar. **1** barometer. **2** barometric. **3** barrel.

barb[1] (bärb) *n.* **1** a point projecting backward from the main point. **2** in zoology, one of the hairlike branches on the shaft of a bird's feather. **3** a long, thin growth hanging from the mouth; barbel: *the barbs of a catfish.* **4** something sharp and wounding: *the stinging barbs of unfair criticism.*
—v. equip with a barb; furnish with barbs. [ME < OF *barbe* < L *barba* beard]

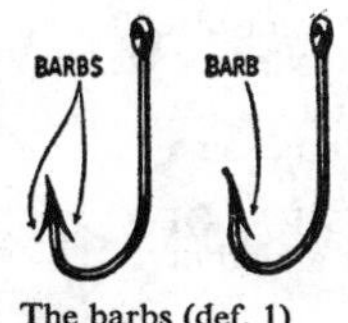

The barbs (def. 1) on fish-hooks

Barbs (def. 2)

barb[2] (bärb) *n.* **1** a kind of horse that has great speed, endurance, and gentleness. **2** a kind of domestic pigeon, related to the carrier pigeon, having a short, stout beak. [< F *barbe* < *Barbarie* Barbary]

Bar·ba·di·an (bär bā′dē ən) *adj.* of or having to do with the island of Barbados in the West Indies. *—n.* a native or inhabitant of Barbados.

bar·bar·i·an (bär bãr′ē ən) *n.* **1** a person who is not civilized. **2** a foreigner differing from the speaker or writer in language and customs. In ancient times a barbarian was a person who was not a Greek, a person outside of the Roman Empire, or a person who was not a Christian. **3** a person without sympathy for literary culture or art.
—adj. **1** not civilized; cruel and coarse. **2** differing from the speaker or writer in language and customs. [< F *barbarien* ult. < Gk. *barbaros* foreign. See BARBAROUS.]
Syn. *adj.* **1 Barbarian, barbaric, barbarous** = not civilized. **Barbarian** suggests nothing more: *The Roman Empire was conquered by barbarian peoples.* **Barbaric** emphasizes the lack of refinement and gentleness and the love of show that distinguish less highly civilized peoples: *The dress of gypsies is barbaric.* **Barbarous** emphasizes the harshness and cruelty of uncivilized peoples: *Torture of prisoners is a barbarous custom.*

bar·bar·i·an·ism (bär bãr′ē ə niz′əm) *n.* the state or condition of being a barbarian.

bar·bar·ic (bär bar′ik or bär ber′ik) *adj.* **1** resembling barbarians; rough and rude. **2** crudely rich or splendid. [ME < L < Gk. *barbarikos* < *barbaros* foreign. See BARBAROUS.] **—bar·bar′i·cal·ly,** *adv.* **—Syn. 1** See **barbarian.**

bar·ba·rism (bär′bə riz′əm) *n.* **1** the condition of uncivilized people. **2** a barbarous act, custom, or trait. **3** the use of a word or expression not in accepted use. **4** a word or expression not in accepted use. *Example*: "his'n" instead of "his."

bar·bar·i·ty (bär bar′ə tē or bär ber′ə tē) *n.* **-ties.** **1** brutal cruelty. **2** an act of cruelty. **3** a barbaric manner, taste, or style.

bar·ba·rize (bär′bə rīz′) *v.* **-rized, -riz·ing.** make barbarous; become barbarous. **—bar′ba·ri·za′tion,** *n.*

bar·ba·rous (bär′bə rəs) *adj.* **1** not civilized; savage. **2** rough and rude; coarse; unrefined. **3** cruelly harsh; brutal. [< L *barbarus* < Gk. *barbaros* foreign, apparently originally, stammering < the reduplication of the syllable *bar* suggesting unintelligible speech]
—bar′ba·rous·ly, *adv.* **—bar′ba·rous·ness,** *n.*
—Syn. 1 See **barbarian.**

Bar·ba·ry (bär′bə rē) *n.* the Moslem countries west of Egypt on the northern coast of Africa.

Barbary ape a tail-less monkey that lives in N. Africa and on the Rock of Gibraltar.

Barbary States a former name for Morocco, Algeria, Tunisia, and Tripoli, once noted as pirate strongholds.

bar·be·cue (bär′bə kū′) *n. v.* **-cued, -cu·ing.** *—n.* **1 a** a feast at which animals are roasted whole. **b** an outdoor meal at which meat or fish is roasted over a grill or open fire. **c** the food at such a feast or meal. **d** a party for such a feast or meal. **2** a grill or open fireplace for cooking meat, usually over charcoal. **3** an animal roasted whole. **4** meat roasted before an open fire. **5** a party meal prepared on a barbecue.
—v. **1** roast (an animal) whole. **2** roast (meat) on a grill or before an open fire. **3** cook (meat or fish) in a highly flavored sauce. [< Sp. *barbacoa* < Haitian *barboka* framework of sticks]

barbed (bärbd) *adj.* **1** having a barb or barbs. **2** sharp and wounding: *barbed sarcasm.*

barbed wire wire with sharp points fixed to it at intervals of a few inches, used for fences, etc.

bar·bel (bär′bəl) *n.* **1** a long, thin growth hanging from the mouth of some fishes. **2** a large fresh-water fish of Europe having such growths. [ME < OF < LL *barbellus,* dim. of *barbus* a kind of fish < L *barba* beard]

BARBELS

bar·bell (bär′bel′) *n.* a device for performing lifting exercises, similar to a dumbbell but having a longer bar and provision for weights at each end.

bar·ber (bär′bər) *n.* a person whose business is cutting, shaving, or dressing hair. *—v.* cut the hair of; shave; trim the beard of. [ME < AF *barbour* < L *barba* beard]

bar·ber·ry (bär′ber′ē or bär′bər ē) *n.* **-ries.** **1** a shrub having yellow flowers and sour red berries. **2** the berry. [ME *barbere* < Med.L *barbaris, berberis*]

bar·ber·shop (bär′bər shop′) *n.* a barber's place of business. *—adj.* of, having to do with, or suggesting a barbershop quartet: *barbershop harmony.*

barbershop quartet or **quartette** a male quartet that sings and improvises on popular sentimental ballads, usually in close harmony.

bar·bette (bär bet′) *n.* **1** a platform in a fort from which guns may be fired over the side. **2** an armored cylinder protecting a gun turret on a warship. [< F *barbette,* dim. of *barbe* beard < L *barba*]

bar·bi·can (bär′bə kan′ or bär′bə kən) *n.* a tower for defence built over a gate or bridge leading into a city or castle. [ME < OF *barbacane* < Med.L *barbacana*]

bar·bi·tal (bär′bə tol′, bär′bə tôl′, or bär′bə tal′) *n.* a drug containing barbituric acid, used as a sedative or hypnotic.

bar·bi·tu·rate (bär bich′ə rāt′, bär bich′ə rit, bär′bə tūr′āt, or bär′bə tür′āt) *n.* a salt or ester of barbituric acid.

bar·bi·tu·ric acid (bär′bə tūr′ik or bär′bə tür′ik) an acid much used as the basis of sedatives and hypnotics. *Formula*: $C_4H_4O_3N_2$ [*barbituric* < NL (*Usnea*) *barbata,* a kind of lichen (< L *barba* beard) + E *uric*]

barb·wire (bärb′wīr′) *n.* barbed wire.

bar·ca·role or **bar·ca·rolle** (bär′kə rōl′) *n* **1** a Venetian boating song. **2** music imitating such a song. [< F *barcarolle* < Ital. *barcarola* boatman's song < *barca* bark. See BARK[3].]

B.Arch. Bachelor of Architecture.

bard (bärd) *n.* **1** a poet and singer of long ago. Bards sang their own poems to the music of their harps. **2** a poet. [< Irish and Scots Gaelic *bárd* poet]

Bard of Avon Shakespeare.

bare[1] (bãr) *adj.* **bar·er, bar·est,** *v.* **bared, bar·ing.**
—adj. **1** without covering; not clothed; naked: *bare hands.* **2** without a hat or other head-dress. **3** not concealed; not disguised; open. **4** not furnished; empty: *The room was bare of furniture.* **5** plain; unadorned: *He lived in a bare little house.* **6** much worn; threadbare. **7** just enough and no more; mere: *He earns a bare living by his work.* **8 lay bare,** uncover; expose; reveal.
—v. make bare; uncover; reveal: *The knight bared his sword.* [OE *bær*]
Syn. 1 Bare, naked, nude = without covering. **Bare** emphasizes the idea of being without the usual covering and therefore lying open to view: *The sun burned her bare shoulders.* **Naked** emphasizes the idea of being stripped of all covering, especially customary protective covering, and laid open to view: *The little boy wandered naked through the streets.* **Nude** = unclothed, but expresses an objective attitude toward the body: *Many famous artists have painted nude models.*

bare[2] (bãr) *v. Archaic.* a pt. of **bear**[1].

bare·back (bãr′bak′) *adv. adj.* without a saddle; on the bare back of a horse, etc.

bare·bones (bãr′bōnz′) *n.* a very skinny person. *—adj.* meagre: *His barebones generosity will not make us rich.*

bare·faced (bãr′fāst′) *adj.* **1** with the face bare. **2** not disguised. **3** shameless; impudent: *a barefaced lie.* **—bare′faced′ly,** *adv.*

bare·fist·ed (bãr′fist′əd) *adj.* **1** without boxing gloves. **2** ruthless; unprincipled: *The industrialist was notorious for his barefisted treatment of competitors.*

bare·foot (bãr′fu̇t′) *adj. adv.* without shoes and stockings.

bare·foot·ed (bãr′fu̇t′id) *adj.* barefoot.

bare·hand·ed (bãr′han′did) *adj.* **1** without any covering on the hands. **2** with empty hands.

bare·head·ed (bãr′hed′id) *adj. adv.* wearing nothing on the head.

bare-knuck·le (bãr′nuk′əl) *adj.* **1** without boxing gloves. **2** in which quarter is neither asked nor given: *a bare-knuckle argument.*

bare·leg·ged (bãr′leg′id or bãr′legd′) *adj.* without stockings.

hat, āge, cãre, fär; let, ēqual, tėrm; it, īce
hot, ōpen, ôrder; oil, out; cup, pu̇t, rüle, ūse
ǝbove, takǝn, pencǝl, lemǝn, circǝs
ch, child; ng, long; sh, ship
th, thin; ᴛʜ, then; zh, measure

bare·ly (bãr′lē) *adv.* **1** only just; scarcely: *He has barely enough money to live on.* **2** openly; plainly: *He presented the facts barely without comment or explanation.* **3** poorly or scantily: *The room was furnished barely but neatly.* —**Syn. 1 See hardly.**

bare·ness (bãr′nis) *n.* the state or condition of being bare; a lack of covering; lack of furnishings and contents.

bar·fly (bär′flī′) *n.* **-flies.** *Slang.* a frequenter of bar-rooms, especially one who drinks to excess.

bar·gain (bär′gǝn) *n.* **1** an agreement to trade or exchange. **2** something offered for sale cheap, or bought cheap. **3** a good trade or exchange; price below the real value. **4 into the bargain,** besides; also. **5 strike a bargain,** make a bargain; reach an agreement.
—*v.* **1** try to get good terms. **2** make a bargain; come to terms. **3** trade. **4 bargain for,** be ready for; expect: *It is raining, and that is more than I bargained for.* [ME < OF *bargaigne*] —**bar′gain·er,** *n.*
—**Syn.** *n.* **1** contract. **2** deal.

barge (bärj) *n. v.* **barged, barg·ing.** —*n.* **1** a large flat-bottomed boat for carrying freight. **2** a large boat used for excursions, pageants, and special occasions. **3** a large motorboat or rowboat used by the commanding officer of a flagship. **4** a houseboat.
—*v.* **1** carry by barge. **2** move clumsily like a barge. **3** *Informal.* push oneself rudely: *Don't barge in where you're not wanted.* [ME < OF < L < Gk. *baris* boat used on the Nile]

barge·man (bärj′mǝn) *n.* **-men** (-mǝn). a man who works on a barge.

bar·ite (bãr′īt or bar′īt) *n.* a rock that consists mostly of barium sulphate.

bar·i·tone (bar′ǝ tōn′) *n.* **1** a male voice between tenor and bass. **2** in music: **a** a singer with such a voice. **b** a part for such a voice or for a corresponding instrument. **c** an instrument playing such a part.
—*adj.* **1** of or for a baritone. **2** that can sing or play a baritone part. [Gk. *barytonos* < *barys* deep + *tonos* pitch]

bar·i·um (bar′ē ǝm or ber′ē ǝm) *n.* a soft, silvery-white metallic element. *Symbol:* Ba; *at.no.* 56; *at.wt.* 137.34. [< NL < Gk. *barytēs* weight]

bark[1] (bärk) *n.* the tough outside covering of the trunk, branches, and roots of trees and woody plants.
—*v.* **1** strip the bark from (a tree, etc.). **2** cut out a circle of bark from (a tree) in order to kill it. **3** cover with bark. **4** tan (hides, etc.). **5** scrape the skin from (shins, knuckles, etc.). [ME < ON *börkr*]

bark[2] (bärk) *n.* **1** the short, sharp sound that a dog makes. **2** a sound like this: *the bark of a fox, a squirrel, a gun, or a cough.* [< v.]
—*v.* **1** make this sound or one like it. **2** shout sharply; speak gruffly: *Some officers bark out their orders.* **3** *Informal.* cough. **4** *Informal.* call or shout to attract people into a circus tent, sideshow at a fair, store, etc. **5 bark at the moon,** make a noise or fuss to no effect. **6 bark up the wrong tree,** go after something by mistake or use wrong means to get at something. [OE *beorcan*]
—**Syn.** *n.* **1** yelp, bay.

bark[3] (bärk) *n.* barque.

bark beetle any of a family of beetles that damage trees by burrowing through the bark to lay eggs: *Dutch elm disease is transmitted by bark beetles.*

bar·keep (bär′kēp′) *n. Esp.U.S.* barkeeper.

bar·keep·er (bär′kēp′ǝr) *n.* a man who tends a bar where alcoholic drinks are sold.

bar·ken·tine (bär′kǝn tēn′) *n.* a three-masted ship with the foremast square-rigged and the other masts fore-and-aft-rigged. Also, **barquentine.** [< *bark*[3]; modelled on *brigantine*]

bark·er (bär′kǝr) *n.* **1** one that barks. **2** a person who stands in front of a circus tent, sideshow at a fair, store, etc. urging people to go in. [< *bark*[2]]

bar·ley (bär′lē) *n.* **1** the seed or grain of a cereal grass that has compact spikes of flowers. Barley is used for food and for making malt. **2** the plant yielding this grain. [OE *bærlic*]

Bar·ley·corn (bär′lē kôrn′) *n.* **John,** a name for intoxicating liquor, especially whisky.

barley sugar a clear, brittle candy, originally made by boiling sugar with an extract of barley.

barley water water in which barley has been boiled, formerly much used as a drink for invalids and babies.

barm (bärm) *n.* a foamy yeast that forms on malt liquors while they are fermenting. [OE *beorma*]

bar·maid (bär′mād′) *n.* a woman who works in a bar, serving alcoholic drinks to customers.

bar·man (bär′mǝn) *n.* **-men** (-mǝn). barkeeper.

Bar·me·cide feast (bär′mǝ sīd′) **1** a pretended feast with empty dishes. **2** the empty pretence of hospitality, generosity, etc. [from *Barmecide,* a wealthy man in the *Arabian Nights* who gave a beggar a pretended feast on empty dishes]

bar mitz·vah (bär mits′vǝ) **1** a ceremony marking the initiation of a boy into the Jewish religious community, usually held when the boy is thirteen years old. **2** a boy who has reached the age of thirteen, the age of religious responsibility. [< Hebrew *bar miswah* son of the commandment]

barm·y (bär′mē) *adj.* **barm·i·er, barm·i·est. 1** full of barm; fermenting. **2** *Informal.* silly; crazy; flighty.

barn (bärn) *n.* **1** a building for storing hay, grain, farm machinery, etc. and often for sheltering livestock. **2** any place that resembles a barn in use or appearance. [OE *bern* < *bere* barley + *ærn* storing place]
—**barn′like′,** *adj.*

bar·na·cle (bär′nǝ kǝl) *n.* **1** an animal having a shell that attaches itself to rocks, the bottoms of ships, the timbers of wharves, etc. **2** *Informal.* a person or thing that clings persistently. [ME *bernacle* < OF (cf. F *barnacle, bernicle*); earlier ME *bernake* < OF *bernaque*]

bar·na·cled (bär′nǝ kǝld) *adj.* covered with barnacles.

barn dance 1 a dance held in a barn. **2** a lively dance resembling a polka.

barn raising a gathering of neighbors to build a barn. In colonial days, such gatherings were usually social affairs, the day's work being followed by dancing, eating, and drinking.

barn·storm (bärn′stôrm′) *v. Informal.* **1** act plays, make speeches, etc. in small towns and country districts. **2** tour country districts giving short airplane rides, exhibitions of stunt flying, etc. —**barn′storm′er,** *n.*

barn swallow a swallow that usually nests in barns.

barn·yard (bärn′yärd′) *n.* the yard around a barn for livestock, etc.

baro- *combining form.* weight; atmospheric pressure: *Barometer = something that measures (a meter of) atmospheric pressure.* [< Gk. *baros* weight]

bar·o·gram (bar′ǝ gram′) *n.* a record made by a barograph or similar instrument.

bar·o·graph (bar′ǝ graf′) *n.* an instrument that automatically records changes in air pressure.

ba·rom·e·ter (bǝ rom′ǝ tǝr) *n.* **1** an instrument for measuring the pressure of the atmosphere, thus determining height above sea level, or probable changes in the weather. **2** something that indicates changes: *Newspapers are often barometers of public opinion.*

A barometer

bar·o·met·ric (bar′ǝ met′rik) *adj.* **1** of a barometer. **2** indicated by a barometer.

bar·o·met·ri·cal (bar′ǝ met′rǝ kǝl) *adj.* barometric.

bar·on (bar′ǝn or ber′ǝn) *n.* **1** in the United Kingdom, a nobleman of the lowest rank, below a viscount. **2** in some other countries, a nobleman having a similar rank. **3** in England during the Middle Ages, a nobleman who held his lands directly from the king. **4** the title of a baron. **5** a powerful merchant or financier: *a railway baron.* [ME < OF < OHG *baro* man, fighter]

☛ **baron.** In the United Kingdom, a baron is referred to as Lord M —, rather than as Baron M — as is the case in other European countries.

bar·on·age (bar′ən ij or ber′ən ij) *n.* **1** all the barons. **2** the nobility. **3** the rank or title of a baron.

bar·on·ess (bar′ən is or ber′ən is) *n.* **1** the wife or widow of a baron. **2** a woman whose rank is equal to that of a baron.

bar·on·et (bar′ən it or ber′ən it, bar′ən et′ or ber′ən et′) *n.* **1** in the United Kingdom, a man below a baron in rank, but above a knight. **2** the title of a baronet. *Abbrev.*: Bart. or Bt.

☛ **baronet.** A baronet is normally spoken of as if he were a knight: *Sir John is here. Sir John Browne.* In formal usage he has "Sir" before his name and "Bart." after it: *Sir John Browne, Bart.*

bar·on·et·cy (bar′ən it sē or ber′ən it sē) *n.* **-cies.** **1** the rank or position of a baronet. **2** a document that makes a person a baronet.

ba·ro·ni·al (bə rō′nē əl) *adj.* **1** of a baron; of barons. **2** suitable for a baron; splendid; stately; magnificent.

bar·o·ny (bar′ə nē or ber′ə nē) *n.* **-nies.** **1** the lands of a baron. **2** the rank or title of a baron. **3** a vast region or undertaking under private ownership or control.

ba·roque (bə rōk′ or bə rok′) *n.* **1** in art and architecture, a style that prevailed in Europe from about 1550 to the late 18th century, characterized by the use of curved forms and lavish ornamentation. **2** in music, a style that prevailed between about 1600 and 1750, characterized by much melodic and harmonic variety and ornamentation.
—*adj.* **1** of or having to do with baroque art or architecture. **2** of or having to do with baroque music. **3** tastelessly odd; fantastic; grotesque. **4** irregular in shape: *baroque pearls.* [< F < Pg. *barroco* irregular]

bar·o·scope (bar′ə skōp′) *n.* an instrument for showing changes in the pressure or density of the air. [< Gk. *baros* weight + E *-scope* instrument for viewing < Gk. *skopein* look at]

ba·rouche (bə rüsh′) *n.* a four-wheeled carriage with two seats facing each other, and a folding top. [< dial. G *Barutsche* < Ital. < L *birotus* two-wheeled < *bi-* two + *rota* wheel]

barque (bärk) *n.* **1** *Poetic.* any boat or ship. **2** a sailing ship with three masts, square-rigged on the first two masts and fore-and-aft rigged on the other. Also, **bark.** [< F *barque* < Ital. *barca* < LL]

A barque (def. 2)

bar·quen·tine (bär′kən tēn′) *n.* barkentine.

bar·rack[2] (bar′ək) *n.* barracks. [< F *baraque* < Ital. *baracca*]

bar·rack[1] (bar′ək) *v. Brit.* express opinions noisily; applaud or, especially, jeer. [< Australian slang *barracking* banter]

bar·racks (bar′əks) *n.pl.* **1** a building or group of buildings for members of the armed services to live in. **2** a building housing local detachments of the Royal Canadian Mounted Police. **3** a large, plain building in which many people live. [See BARRACK[1].]

☛ **Barracks** appears with either a singular or plural verb: *John wrote that his barracks was a lively place. The barracks were inspected daily.*

bar·ra·cu·da (bar′ə kü′də) *n.* **-da** or **-das.** a large, fierce fish found in the seas off the S.E. and S.W. coasts of North America. [< Sp. < West Indian name]

bar·rage (bə räzh′ *for n. 1, 3 and v.*; bär′ij *for n. 2*) *n. v.* **-raged, -rag·ing.** —*n.* **1** a barrier of artillery fire to check the enemy or to protect one's own soldiers in advancing or retreating. **2** an artificial barrier in a river; dam. **3** any heavy onslaught or attack: *a barrage of words.* —*v.* fire with artillery at; subject to a barrage. [< F *barrage* < *barrer* to bar]

barrage balloon a large balloon intended to force enemy aircraft out of bombing range. It floats from a cable and is equipped with a self-sealing, bulletproof fabric.

bar·ra·try (bar′ə trē) *n.* **1** fraud or gross negligence of a ship's officer or seaman against owners, insurers, etc. **2** the act of stirring up lawsuits or quarrels. [ME < OF *baraterie* < *barater* to exchange, cheat. Related to BARTER.]

barre (bär) *n.* the supporting rail that ballet dancers use when practising. [< F]

barred (bärd) *adj.* **1** having bars: *a barred window.* **2** marked with stripes: *a chicken with barred feathers.* **3** not permitted; forbidden: *Smoking is barred in the library.*

bar·rel (bar′əl) *n. v.* **-relled** or **-reled, -rel·ling** or **-rel·ing.** —*n.* **1** a container with round, flat ends and slightly curved sides, usually made of thick boards held together by hoops. **2** the amount that a barrel can hold. **3** any container, case, or part shaped like a barrel: *the barrel of a drum.* **4** the metal tube of a gun, rifle, or pistol. **5** *Informal.* a considerable number or quantity. —*v.* put in barrels. [ME < OF *baril,* probably < VL *barra* bar, stave] —**Syn.** *n.* **1** cask.

barrel chair an upholstered chair with a high, curved back, resembling a barrel that has been partly cut away.

bar·rel·ful (bar′əl fu̇l′) *n.* the amount that a barrel can hold.

barrel organ a hand organ.

bar·ren (bar′ən or ber′ən) *adj.* **1** not producing anything: *A sandy desert is barren.* **2** not able to bear offspring. **3** without interest; not attractive; dull. **4** fruitless; unprofitable. —*n.* **1** Usually, **barrens,** *pl.* a barren stretch of land; a wasteland. **2 Barrens,** the Barren Ground. [ME < OF *baraine*] —**bar′ren·ness,** *n.*
—**Syn.** *adj.* **1, 2** unproductive, sterile.

Barren Ground the treeless, thinly populated region in northern Canada, lying between Hudson Bay on the east and Great Slave Lake and Great Bear Lake on the west: *Much of the Barren Ground is covered, in season, with short grass, moss, and small flowering plants.*

Barren Lands the Barren Ground.

bar·rette (bə ret′) *n.* a pin with a clasp, used by women and girls for holding the hair in place. [< F *barrette,* dim. of *barre* bar]

bar·ri·cade (bar′ə kād′ or bar′ə kād′) *n. v.* **-cad·ed, -cad·ing.** —*n.* **1** a rough, hastily made barrier for defence. **2** any barrier or obstruction. **3** *Cdn.* large blocks of ice remaining frozen to a river or sea shore after the spring breakup. —*v.* block or obstruct with a barricade: *The road was barricaded with fallen trees.* [< F *barricade,* apparently < Provençal *barricada* < *barrica* cask; originally, made of casks. Related to BARREL.]

bar·ri·ca·do (bar′ə kā′dō) *n.* **-does.** barricade.

bar·ri·er (bar′ē ər) *n.* **1** something that stands in the way; something stopping progress or preventing approach. **2** something that separates or keeps apart. **3** in horse racing, a movable starting gate. [ME < AF *barrere* < LL *barraria* < *barra* bar < Celtic]

barrier reef a long line of rocks or coral reef not far from the mainland.

bar·ring (bär′ing) *prep.* except; not including: *Barring accidents, we shall reach Vancouver at twelve o'clock.*

bar·ris·ter (bar′is tər) *n.* **1** a lawyer who pleads in court. **2** in the United Kingdom, a lawyer entitled to plead in any court, as opposed to a solicitor. [< *bar* + *-ster*]

bar·room (bär′rüm′ or -ru̇m′) *n.* a room with a bar for the sale of alcoholic drinks.

bar·row[1] (bar′ō) *n.* **1** a frame with two short shafts for handles at each end, used for carrying a load. 2 a wheelbarrow. 3 a handcart. [OE *bearwe.* Related to BEAR[1].]

bar·row[2] (bar′ō) *n.* a mound of earth or stones over an ancient or prehistoric grave. [OE *beorg*]

barrow pit especially in the West, a borrow pit.

bar sinister a sign of illegitimacy on a coat of arms. See also def. 4 of **baton,** for the term regularly used in heraldry.

Bart. Baronet.

bar·tend·er (bär′tən′dər) *n.* a man who mixes or serves alcoholic drinks.

bar·ter (bär′tər) *v.* 1 trade goods for other goods without using money. 2 exchange. 3 give (away) without an equal return. —*n.* 1 the act of bartering. 2 an exchange. 3 something bartered. [< OF *barater* to exchange. Related to BARRATRY.]

☛ When **barter** means "exchange," it is followed by *for*: *The colonists bartered calico for Indian land.* When it means "surrender without an equal return" it is followed by *away*: *He pretended to be happy about his new contract although he realized that he had bartered away his chance of fame.*

bar·ti·zan (bär′tə zən or bär′tə zan′) *n.* in architecture, a small overhanging turret on a wall or tower. [alteration of *bratticing* < *brattice* parapet < OF *bretesche,* probably < OE *brittisc* British (type of fortification)]

A bartizan

Bart·lett pear (bärt′lit) a large, juicy kind of pear. [after E. *Bartlett,* who introduced it into America]

bar·y·sphere (bar′əs fēr′) *n.* the heavy inside part of the earth within the outer crust. [< Gk. *barys* heavy + E *sphere*]

bas·al (bās′əl) *adj.* 1 of the base; at the base; forming the base. 2 fundamental; basic.

basal metabolism the amount of energy used by an animal or plant at rest, measured in terms of the rate at which oxygen is taken in. The basal metabolism for an average man 30 years old is between 1,400 and 1,500 calories per day.

ba·salt (bə solt′ or bə sôlt′, bā′solt or bā′sôlt, bas′olt or bas′ôlt) *n.* 1 a hard, dark-colored rock of volcanic origin. 2 basalt ware. [< LL *basaltes,* a manuscript corruption of L *basanites* < Gk. *basanos* touchstone]

ba·sal·tic (bə sol′tik or bə sôl′tik) *adj.* 1 of or having to do with basalt. 2 like basalt.

basalt ware a black, unglazed pottery having a dull gloss, developed by Josiah Wedgwood (1730-1795).

bas·cule (bas′kūl) *n.* a device that works like a seesaw. In a **bascule bridge** the rising part is counterbalanced by a weight. [< F *bascule* seesaw, ult. < *battre* beat (influenced by *bas* low) + *cul* posterior]

A bascule bridge, opened to let a tall ship pass through

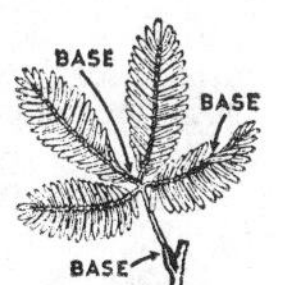

Base (def. 5)

base[1] (bās) *n. v.* **based, bas·ing.** —*n.* 1 an underlying support: *The machine rests on a wide base of steel.* 2 a fundamental principle; basis; foundation. 3 the most important element of anything; essential part. 4 in architecture: a the part of a column on which the shaft rests. See **column** for diagram. b the part at the bottom of a wall or monument. 5 in biology: a the part of an organ nearest its point of attachment. b the point of attachment. 6 in chemistry, a compound that reacts with an acid to form a salt. Calcium hydroxide is a base. 7 in certain games, such as baseball, a station or goal: *The player slid into third base.* 8 a starting place. 9 the place from which a navy, army, or air force operates and from which supplies are obtained; headquarters. 10 the number that is a starting point for a system of numeration or logarithms. In arithmetic, 10 is the base of the decimal system. 11 a line or surface forming that part of a geometrical figure on which it is supposed to stand: *Any side of a triangle can be its base.* 12 in surveying, a line used as the starting point. 13 in linguistics, the form of a word to which prefixes and suffixes are attached; root. 14 **get to first base,** make the first step successfully. —*v.* 1 make or form a base or foundation for. 2 establish; found (*on* or *upon*): *His large business was based on good service.* [ME < MF < L < Gk. *basis* base; literally, a step. Doublet of BASIS.]

hat, āge, cãre, fär; let, ēqual, têrm; it, īce
hot, ōpen, ôrder; oil, out; cup, pu̇t, rüle, ūse
əbove, takən, pencəl, lemən, circəs
ch, child; ng, long; sh, ship
th, thin; ᴛʜ, then; zh, measure

Syn. *n.* **1, 2 Base, basis, foundation** = the part of anything on which the rest stands for support. **Base,** chiefly used literally, applies to the bottom and supporting part of objects: *The Christmas tree must have a base.* **Basis,** chiefly used figuratively, applies to the part that supports beliefs, arguments, etc.: *The basis of his opinion is something he read in the paper.* **Foundation,** used literally and figuratively, emphasizes the firmness and solidness of the base or basis: *His honesty and willingness to work are the foundation of his success.*

☛ **base.** The plural of this word is regular: **bases** (bā′siz). The plural of **basis** is spelled **bases** but pronounced (bā′sēz).

base[2] (bās) *adj.* **bas·er, bas·est,** *n.* —*adj.* 1 morally low; mean; selfish; cowardly: *To betray a friend is a base action.* 2 fit for an inferior person or thing; menial; unworthy: *No needful service is to be looked on as base.* 3 *Archaic.* of humble birth or origin. 4 having little comparative value; inferior: *Iron and lead are base metals; gold and silver are precious metals.* 5 debased; counterfeit: *base coin.* 6 deep or grave in sound. —*n.* the lowest male voice; bass. [ME < MF *bas* < LL *bassus* low. Doublet of BASSO.]

Syn. *adj.* **1 Base, vile, low** = morally inferior and contemptible. **Base** = reduced to a low moral state, without honor or without moral standards, usually by selfishness or cowardliness: *To betray a friend for a reward is base.* **Vile** = without moral standards or sense of decency; evil; disgustingly dirty: *In the slums of some cities even small children learn vile language.* **Low** = without a sense of decency or of what is honorable: *To steal from the collection plate in church is low.*

base·ball (bās′bol′ or -bôl′) *n.* 1 a game played with bat and ball by two teams of nine players each, on a field with four bases. 2 the ball used in this game.

base·board (bās′bôrd′) *n.* 1 a line of boards around the walls of a room, next to the floor. 2 a board forming the base of anything.

base·born (bās′bôrn′) *adj.* 1 born of slaves, peasants, or other humble parents. 2 born of a mother who was not married; illegitimate.

base·burn·er (bās′bėr′nər) *n.* a stove or furnace fed automatically as the fuel below is burned.

base hit in baseball, a successful hitting of the ball by a batter so that he gets at least to first base without the help of an error.

base·less (bās′lis) *adj.* groundless; without foundation: *A rumor is baseless if it is not supported by facts.* —**base′less·ness,** *n.*

base line 1 a line used as a base for measuring or calculating, especially in land surveys, etc. 2 a line between bases.

base·ly (bās′lē) *adv.* in a low, mean, or unworthy manner: *The prince acted basely towards the captives.*

base·man (bās′mən) *n.* **-men** (-mən). in baseball, a player guarding one of the bases.

base·ment (bās′mənt) *n.* 1 the lowest storey of a building, partly or wholly below ground; cellar. 2 the lowest division of the wall of a building.

base metal 1 any of the non-precious metals, such as lead, zinc, iron, etc. 2 the chief metallic element in an alloy.

base·ness (bās′nis) *n.* low, mean, or unworthy character or conduct.

ba·sen·ji (bə sen′jē) *n.* **1** a breed of terrierlike hunting dog native to Africa. **2** a dog of this breed. A basenji rarely barks. [< Afrikaans]

base runner in baseball, a member of the team at bat who is on a base or trying to reach a base.

ba·ses[1] (bā′sēz) *n.* pl. of **basis.**

bas·es[2] (bās′iz) *n.* pl. of **base**[1].

bash (bash) *Informal.* —*v.* strike with a smashing blow. —*n.* **1** a smashing blow. **2** *Esp.Brit. Slang.* **a** a try: *We all had a bash at the games on the midway.* **b** an entertaining or exciting time; a party; spree. [? imitative]

ba·shaw (bə sho′ or bə shô′) *n.* **1** a pasha, a Turkish official. **2** an important person. [< Turkish *basha*]

bash·ful (bash′fəl) *adj.* uneasy and awkward in the presence of strangers; shy. [< *bash,* v. (var. of *abash*) + *-ful*] —**bash′ful·ly,** *adv.* —**bash′ful·ness,** *n.* —**Syn.** See **shy**[1].

ba·sic (bā′sik) *adj.* **1** of the base; at the base; forming the base; fundamental: *Addition, subtraction, multiplication, and division are the basic processes of arithmetic.* **2** in chemistry: **a** containing a base. **b** alkaline.

ba·si·cal·ly (bā′sik lē) *adv.* as a basic principle; fundamentally.

Basic English a simplified system of English, consisting of 850 essential words and a further 150 scientific words. It was invented by C. K. Ogden (1889-1957). [*Basic,* considered as an acronym for *B*ritish, *A*merican, *S*cientific, *I*nternational, *C*ommercial]

ba·sic·i·ty (bā sis′ə tē) *n.* in chemistry: **1** the state or quality of being a base. **2** the ability of an acid to combine with bases, dependent on the number of replaceable hydrogen atoms contained in a molecule of the acid.

bas·il (baz′əl) *n.* a tropical, sweet-smelling plant of the same family as mint, used in cooking. [ME < OF *basile* < L < Gk. *basilikon* royal < *basileus* king]

bas·i·lar (bas′ə lər) *adj.* of the base; at the base.

ba·sil·i·ca (bə sil′ə kə) *n.* **1** an oblong hall with a row of columns at each side and a semicircular structure at one end. The Romans used such buildings for law courts and public meetings. **2** an early Christian church built in this form. **3** in the Roman Catholic Church, a title of honor given to some churches, conferring certain rights and privileges. [< L < Gk. *basilikē* (*oikia*) royal (house) < *basileus* king]

bas·i·lisk (bas′ə lisk′ or baz′ə lisk′) *n.* **1** in Greek and Roman legend, a fabled reptile whose breath and look were thought to be fatal. It was supposed to resemble a lizard and to have a black-and-yellow skin and fiery, red eyes. **2** a tropical American lizard having along its back a crest that it can raise or lower. [< L *basiliscus* < Gk. *basiliskos,* dim. of *basileus* king]

ba·sin (bā′sən) *n.* **1** a wide, shallow bowl; bowl. **2** the amount that a basin can hold. **3** a hollow or cavity holding water: *The deep part of a harbor is often called a basin.* **4** all the land drained by a river and the streams that flow into it: *the St. Lawrence basin.* [ME < OF *bacin* < LL *baccinum* < *bacca* water vessel < Celtic]

bas·i·net (bas′ə net′) *n.* a round steel helmet. [ME < OF *bacinet,* dim. of *bacin.* See BASIN.]

ba·sis (bā′sis) *n.* **-ses** (-sēz). **1** the main part; base. **2** a fundamental principle or set of principles; foundation. **3** the principal ingredient: *The basis of this medicine is an oil.* **4** a starting point. **5** *Rare.* a military base. [< L < Gk. *basis.* Doublet of BASE[1].] —**Syn. 1, 2** See **base**[1].

bask (bask) *v.* warm oneself pleasantly: *The cat is basking before the fire.* [ME < ON *bathask* bathe oneself]

bas·ket (bas′kit) *n.* **1** a container made of twigs, grasses, fibres, strips of wood, etc. woven together. **2** the amount that a basket holds: *She bought a basket of peaches.* **3** anything that looks like or is shaped like a basket. **4** the structure beneath a balloon for carrying passengers or ballast. **5** in basketball: **a** a net shaped like a basket, used as a goal. **b** a score made by tossing the ball into the basket. [ME; origin unknown] —**bas′ket·like′,** *adj.*

bas·ket·ball (bas′kit bol′ or bas′kit bôl′) *n.* **1** a game played with a large, round leather ball between two teams, usually of five players each. **2** the ball used in this game.

bas·ket·ry (bas′kit rē) *n.* **1** basketwork; baskets. **2** the art or occupation of making baskets.

basket weave a weave in cloth that looks like the weave in a basket.

bas·ket·work (bas′kit wėrk′) *n.* **1** work woven as a basket is; wickerwork. **2** the art or occupation of making baskets.

ba·son (bā′sən) *n.* in ecclesiastical use, a basin.

Basque (bask) *n.* **1** a people living in the Pyrenees in S. France and in N. Spain. **2** a member of this people. **3** the language of this people. **4 basque,** a woman's garment consisting of a close-fitting bodice extending over the hips.
—*adj.* having to do with the Basques or their language.

bas-re·lief (bä′ri lēf′ or bas′ri lēf′) *n.* a type of carving or sculpture in which the figures project only slightly from the background. See **relief** for picture. [< F < Ital. *basso-rilievo* low relief]

bass[1] (bās) *adj. n.* **bass·es.** —*adj.* **1** low or deep in sound. **2** in music: **a** of or for a bass. **b** that can sing or play a bass part.
—*n.* **1** the lowest male voice. **2** in music: **a** a singer with such a voice. **b** a part in music for such a voice or for a corresponding instrument. **c** an instrument playing such a part, especially a bass viol. [var. of *base*[2]; after Ital. *basso*]

bass[2] (bas) *n.* **bass** or **bass·es.** any of various spinyfinned, edible North American fishes, found in both fresh and salt water. [var. of *barse* perch, OE *bears*]

bass[3] (bas) *n.* **1** basswood. **2** bast. [alteration of *bast*]

bass-bar·i·tone (bās′bar′ə tōn′) *n.* in music: **1** a male voice nearer to a bass than to a baritone but not including in its range the lowest bass tones. **2** a singer with such a voice. **3** a part for such a voice. —*adj.* **1** of or for a bass-baritone. **2** that can sing a bass-baritone part.

bass clef (bās′ klef′) in music, a symbol (𝄢) showing that the pitch of the notes on a staff is below middle C.

bass drum (bās) a large drum that makes a deep, low sound when struck.

bas·set[1] (bas′it) *n.* **1** a breed of hunting dog having short legs and a long body, similar to a dachshund, but bigger. **2** a dog of this breed. [< F *basset,* dim. of *bas* low]

bas·set[2] (bas′it) *n.* in geology, the edge of a rock stratum, etc. appearing at ground surface; outcropping. —*v.* appear or crop out at the surface.

basset hound basset.

bass horn (bās) tuba.

bas·si·net (bas′ə net′ or bas′ə net′) *n.* **1** a baby's basketlike cradle. **2** a baby carriage of similar shape. [< F *bassinet,* dim. of *bassin* basin]

bas·so (bas′ō; *Italian,* bäs′sō) *n.* **bas·sos;** *Italian,* **bas·si** (bäs′sē). a singer with a bass voice. [< Ital. < LL *bassus* low. Doublet of BASE[2].]

bas·soon (bə sün′ or bə zün′) *n.* a deep-toned wind instrument with a doubled wooden tube and a curved metal mouthpiece. [< F < Ital. *bassone* < *basso* basso]

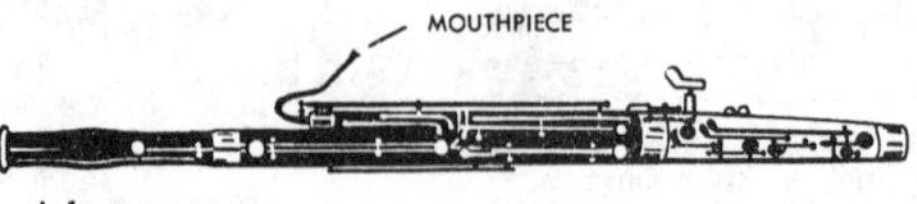

A bassoon

basso pro·fon·do (prə fon′dō; *Italian* prō fōn′dō) **1** the lowest bass voice. **2** a singer with such a voice. **3** a part for such a voice. [< Ital. *profondo* < L *profundus* deep]

basso pro·fun·do (prə fun′dō) basso profondo.

bass viol (bās′ vī′əl) a deep-toned stringed instrument resembling, but larger than, a violin.

bass·wood (bas′wu̇d′) *n.* **1** a linden tree. **2** its wood.

bast (bast) *n.* **1** the inner layer of the bark of trees that contains cells for carrying sap. **2** the tough fibres in this inner layer of certain trees, used in making rope, matting, etc. [OE *bæst*]

bas·tard (bas′tərd) *n.* **1** a child born of parents not legally married; illegitimate child. **2** anything inferior or not genuine. **3** *Slang.* a worthless, cruel, or unpleasant person.
—*adj.* **1** born of parents not legally married; illegitimate. **2** inferior; not genuine. **3** irregular or unusual in shape, size, style, etc. [ME < OF *bastard*, originally, mule < *bast* packsaddle + *-ard* (< Gmc.)]

bas·tard·y (bas′tər dē) *n.* illegitimacy.

baste[1] (bāst) *v.* **bast·ed, bast·ing.** drip or pour melted fat or butter on (meat, etc) while roasting: *Meat is basted to keep it from drying out and to improve its flavor.* —**bast′er,** *n.* [originally pp. of a verb < OF *basser* moisten. Related to BASIN.]

baste[2] (bāst) *v.* **bast·ed, bast·ing.** sew with long, loose stitches to hold the cloth until the final sewing. [ME < OF *bastir* < Gmc.; cf. OHG *bestan* tie up, sew with bast] —**bast′er,** *n.*

baste[3] (bāst) *v.* **bast·ed, bast·ing.** beat; thrash. [< ON *beysta*]

Bas·tille (bas tēl′; *French,* bäs tēy′) *n.* **1** in Paris, an old fort used as a prison, especially for political offenders. It was captured and destroyed by a mob on July 14, 1789. **2 bastille** or **bastile,** a prison, especially one considered oppressive. [< F < LL *bastilia* < *bastire* build]

bas·ti·na·do (bas′tə nā′dō or bas′tə nā′dō) *n.* **-does,** *v.,* **-doed, -do·ing.** —*n.* **1** a beating with a stick, especially on the soles of the feet. **2** a stick; cudgel. —*v.* beat or flog with a stick, especially on the soles of the feet. [< Sp. *bastonada* < *baston* cudgel, ult. < Gmc.]

bast·ings (bās′tingz) *n.pl.* long, loose stitches to hold cloth in place until the final sewing.

bas·tion (bas′chən or bas′tē ən) *n.* **1** a projecting part of a fortification made so that the defenders can fire at attackers from as many angles as possible. **2** any fortification or fortified area. **3** something that provides or acts as a stronghold: *a bastion of freedom.* [< F < Ital. *bastione* < *bastire* build < LL]

A bastion

bas·tioned (bas′chənd or bas′tē ənd) *adj.* provided with or defended by bastions.

bat[1] (bat) *n. v.* **bat·ted, bat·ting.** —*n.* in baseball, cricket, etc., **1** a specially shaped wooden stick or club, used for hitting the ball. **2** the act of batting. **3** a turn at batting. **4** *Informal.* a stroke or blow. **5** *Slang.* a wild, gay time; spree. **6** batting. **7 at bat,** in the batter's position; taking one's turn as a batter. **8 go to bat for,** *Informal.* support the cause of. **9 right off the bat,** *Informal.* immediately; without hesitation: *He bought the car right off the bat.*
—*v.* **1** hit with a bat; hit. **2 bat around, a** in baseball, go right through the batting order in one inning. **b** *Slang.* go here and there with no definite purpose: *He is always batting around town in his new car.* **c** *Slang.* discuss (a topic) freely and informally. [ME < OF *batte* club < *battre* strike] —**bat′ter,** *n.*

bat[2] (bat) *n.* **1** a flying mammal having a mouselike body and membranous wings supported on the highly developed bones of the forelimbs. There are over 600 species; most of them are insect-eating, but some live on fruit and a few suck the blood of other mammals. **2** *Informal.* **bats in the belfry,** the state of being, or appearing, odd, peculiar, or insane. **3 blind as a bat,** completely blind. [alteration of ME *bakke* < Scand.] —**bat′like′,** *adj.*

bat[3] (bat) *v.* **bat·ted, bat·ting.** *Informal.* flutter; wink: *He didn't bat an eye.* [variant of obsolete *bate* flutter]

bat. **1** battalion. **2** battery.

batch[1] (bach) *n.* **1** a quantity of bread made at one baking. **2** a quantity of anything made as one lot or set: *a batch of candy.* **3** a number of persons or things taken together: *a batch of essays.* [ME *bacche* < OE *bacan* bake]

batch[2] (bach) *n. v. Informal.* bach (shortened form of *bachelor*).

bate (bāt) *v.* **bat·ed, bat·ing. 1** abate; lessen; hold back. **2 with bated breath,** holding the breath in great fear, awe, interest, etc.: *The boys listened with bated breath to the sailor's stories of his adventures.* [var. of *abate*]

hat, āge, cãre, fär; let, ēqual, tėrm; it, īce
hot, ōpen, ôrder; oil, out; cup, pu̇t, rüle, ūse
əbove, takən, pencəl, lemən, circəs
ch, child; ng, long; sh, ship
th, thin; ᴛʜ, then; zh, measure

ba·teau or **bat·teau** (ba tō′) *n.* **-teaux** (-tōz′) *Cdn.* formerly: **1** a flat-bottomed river boat about 30 feet long, having tapered ends, and propelled by oars, poles, or sails. Bateaux were used to carry both freight and passengers, especially on the upper St. Lawrence River. **2** any of several similar, usually smaller, light river boats. [< Cdn.F < F *bâteau* boat, ult. < OE *bāt* boat]

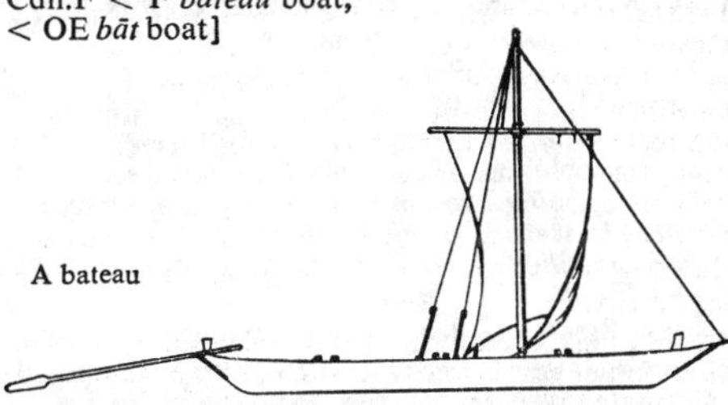

A bateau

bath (bath) *n.* **baths** (baᴛʜz). **1** a washing of the body. **2** the water, etc. for a bath: *Your bath is ready.* **3** a tub, room, or other place for bathing: *In ancient Rome, baths were often elaborate public buildings which were used also as clubs.* **4** a resort having baths for medical treatment. **5** a liquid, such as a solution for fixing photographic prints or film, in which something is washed or dipped. **6** the container holding the liquid.
—*v.* **1** give a bath to. **2** take a bath. [OE *bæth*]

bathe (bāᴛʜ) *v.* **bathed, bath·ing. 1** take a bath. **2** give a bath to. **3** apply water to; wash or moisten with any liquid: *The doctor told her to bathe her eyes with the lotion.* **4** go swimming; go into a river, lake, ocean, etc. for pleasure or to get cool. **5** cover; surround: *The valley was bathed in sunlight.* [OE *bathian*] —**bath′er,** *n.*

ba·thet·ic (bə thet′ik) *adj.* showing bathos; characterized by bathos.

bath·house (bath′hous′) *n.* **1** a house or building fitted up for bathing. **2** a building containing one or more dressing rooms for swimmers.

bathing suit (bāᴛʜ′ing) a garment worn for swimming.

bath·o·lith (bath′ə lith′) *n.* in geology, a great mass of intruded igneous rock, often forming the base of a mountain range and uncovered only by erosion. [< Gk. *bathos* depth + *lithos* stone]

ba·thos (bā′thos) *n.* **1** dullness or commonplaceness in speech or writing, especially when immediately following more elevated expression. *Example*: The exile came back to his home, crippled, unfriended, and hatless. **2** strained or insincere pathos. [< Gk. *bathos* depth]

bath·robe (bath′rōb′) *n.* a long, loose garment worn when going to and from a bath and when resting or lounging; a dressing gown.

bath·room (bath′rüm′ or -ru̇m′) *n.* **1** a room fitted up for taking baths, usually equipped with a washbasin, a toilet, and a bathtub. **2** a toilet.

bath·tub (bath′tub′) *n.* a tub to bath in.

bath·y·sphere (bath′ə sfēr′) *n.* a watertight chamber having glass windows, in which men can go deep down in the sea to study animal and plant life. [< Gk. *bathys* deep + E *sphere*]

ba·tik (bə tēk′ or bat′ik) *n.* **1** the art and method of making designs on cloth by dyeing only part at a time, the rest being protected by a removable coating of wax. **2** cloth dyed in this way. **3** a design formed in this way. —*adj.* **1** made by batik; made of batik. **2** like batik; brightly or gaily colored. —*v.* dye by batik. [< Malay]

ba·tiste (bə tēst′) *n.* a fine, thin cotton cloth. [< F *Baptiste,* probably the name of the maker]

bat·man (bat′mən) *n.* **-men.** a private soldier assigned to act as an officer's servant. [< OF *bast* packsaddle + *man*]

ba·ton (ba ton′) *n.* **1** a staff or stick used as a symbol of office or authority. **2** the stick used by the leader of an orchestra, band, etc. for directing and beating time to the music. **3** a stick passed from runner to runner in a relay race. **4** in heraldry, a sign (in Great Britain) of illegitimacy. It is a short, narrow stripe placed diagonally on a coat of arms, its upper end on the bearer's left. [< F *baton* stick]

ba·tra·chi·an (bə trā′kē ən) *adj.* **1** in zoology, of or belonging to the division of vertebrates that consists of tail-less amphibians. **2** like frogs and toads. **3** of frogs and toads. —*n.* a tail-less amphibian. Frogs and toads are batrachians. [< Gk. *batrachos* frog]

bats·man (bats′mən) *n.* **-men** (-mən). *Esp.Brit.* in cricket, a player who is batting.

batt. **1** battalion. **2** battery.

bat·tal·ion (bə tal′yən) *n.* **1** a formation of four companies within a regiment of infantry, usually commanded by a lieutenant-colonel. **2** any large number of soldiers organized to act together. **3** an organized group. **4** **battalions,** *pl.* armies; military forces. *Abbrev.*: Bn. [< F *bataillon* < Ital. *bataglione,* dim. of *battaglia* battle < LL *battalia.* See BATTLE.]

bat·teau (ba tō′) *n.* **-teaux** (-tōz′). bateau.

bat·ten[1] (bat′ən) *v.* **1** grow fat. **2** fatten. **3** feed greedily. [< ON *batna* < *bati* improvement]

bat·ten[2] (bat′ən) *n.* **1** a board used for flooring, usually 6 or more feet long, 7 inches wide, and 2½ inches thick. **2** a strip of wood. Battens are nailed across parallel boards to strengthen them. They are also used to nail down the canvas over a ship's hatchway and to cover cracks between boards. **3** in the theatre: **a** a wooden or metal bar from which to hang lights, scenery, etc. **b** the lights hung from such a bar.
—*v.* fasten down or strengthen with strips of wood. [var. of *baton*]

bat·ter[1] (bat′ər) *v.* **1** beat with repeated blows; beat so as to bruise, break, or knock out of shape; pound: *Violent storms battered the coast for days.* **2** damage by hard use. [< *bat*[1]]

bat·ter[2] (bat′ər) *n.* a mixture of flour, milk, eggs, etc. that becomes solid when cooked. Cakes, pancakes, etc. are made from batter. [ME *batour,* probably < OF *bature* beating < *batre.* See BAT[3].]

bat·ter[3] (bat′ər) *n.* in baseball, cricket, etc., a player who is batting. [< *bat*[1]]

battering ram **1** in ancient times, a military machine for battering down walls, gates, etc. **2** any heavy object used to break down a door, wall, etc.

bat·ter·y (bat′ər ē or bat′rē) *n.* **-ter·ies.** **1** any set of similar or connected things. **2** a set of one or more electric cells that produce electric current. **3** a set of guns or other weapons such as mortars, machine guns, and artillery pieces for combined action in attack or defence. **4** a formation of several troops in an artillery regiment. **5** a platform or fortification equipped with big guns. **6** the armament, or one part of it, of a warship. **7** in baseball, the pitcher and catcher together. **8** in law, the unlawful striking of another person; any threatening touch to the clothes or body of another. [< F *batterie* < *battre* beat < L *battuere.* Related to BAT[3], BATTLE.]

bat·ting (bat′ing) *n.* **1** the act of hitting a ball: *I have a good average in batting.* **2** cotton or wool pressed into thin layers.

bat·tle (bat′əl) *n. v.* **-tled, -tling.** —*n.* **1** a fight between opposing armed forces. **2** fighting or war: *wounds received in battle.* **3** a fight; contest: *a battle of words.*
—*v.* **1** take part in a battle. **2** fight; struggle; contend. [ME *batayle* < OF *bataille* < LL *battalia* < L *battuere* beat. Related to BAT[3], BATTERY.] —**bat′tler,** *n.*

Syn. 1 Battle, action, engagement = a fight between armed forces. **Battle** applies to a fight between large forces, such as armies, navies or air forces, lasting some time: *The battle for Caen lasted many weeks.* **Action** applies to a lively offensive or defensive part of a battle or campaign: *The Normandy landing during World War II was a decisive action.* **Engagement** emphasizes the meeting of forces, large or small, in combat: *The engagement at Dieppe cost the attacking Canadians many casualties.*

battle array **1** the order of troops, ships, etc. ready for battle. **2** armor and equipment for battle.

bat·tle-axe or **bat·tle-ax** (bat′əl aks′) *n.* **1** a kind of axe used as a weapon of war. **2** *Slang.* a formidable, disagreeable, and obstinate person, especially a woman.

battle cruiser a large, fast warship, not as heavily armored as a battleship.

battle cry **1** the shout of soldiers in battle. **2** a motto or slogan in any contest.

bat·tle·dore (bat′əl dôr′) *n.* in **battledore and shuttlecock,** a small racket used to hit a shuttlecock back and forth. [ME *batyldore,* apparently < Pg. *batedor* beater < *bater* beat < L *battuere*]

battledore and shuttlecock, an old-fashioned game resembling badminton, played by two persons.

battle dress a two-piece uniform consisting of a blouse and trousers and worn by the armed forces for field training and combat.

battle fatigue a neurosis caused by prolonged anxiety and emotional tension during combat.

bat·tle·field (bat′əl fēld′) *n.* the place where a battle is fought or has been fought.

bat·tle·front (bat′əl frunt′) *n.* the place where actual fighting between two armies is taking place.

bat·tle·ground (bat′əl ground′) *n.* battlefield.

bat·tle·ment (bat′əl mənt) *n.* **1** a wall for defence at the top of a tower or wall, with indentations through which soldiers could shoot. **2** a wall built like this for ornament. [ME *batelment* < OF *bateillier* fortify + E *-ment*]

bat·tle·ment·ed (bat′əl men′tid) *adj.* furnished with battlements.

battle royal **1** a fight in which several people take part; riot. **2** a long, hard fight.

bat·tle-scarred (bat′əl skärd′) *adj.* **1** injured or damaged during a battle. **2** showing the effects of many battles.

bat·tle·ship (bat′əl ship′) *n.* the largest and most heavily armored type of warship.

bat·tue (ba tū′ or ba tü′) *n.* **1** the driving of game from cover toward the hunters. **2** a hunt where this is done. **3** a general slaughter. [< F *battue,* fem. pp. of *battre* beat < L *battuere*]

bat·ty (bat′ē) *adj.* **-ti·er, -ti·est.** *Slang.* crazy; queer. [< *bat*[2]]

bau·ble (bo′bəl or bô′bəl) *n.* **1** a showy trifle having no real value. Useless toys and trinkets are baubles. **2** a jester's staff. [ME *babel, babulle* < OF *babel, baubel* toy, of uncertain origin]

baulk (bok or bôk) *v. n.* balk.

baux·ite (bok′sīt or bôk′sīt) *n.* a clay-like mineral from which aluminum is obtained. It is also used in making alum and fire bricks. *Formula*: $Al_2O_3{\cdot}2H_2O$ [from Les *Baux,* France]

Ba·var·i·an (bə văr′ē ən) *adj.* of or having to do with Bavaria, its people, or the dialect of German spoken there. —*n.* **1** a native or inhabitant of Bavaria. **2** the High German dialect spoken in Bavaria and in neighboring parts of Austria and southern Germany.

baw·bee (bo bē′ or bô bē′, bo′bē or bô′bē) *n.* *Scottish.* a halfpenny.

bawd (bod or bôd) *n.* a person who keeps a brothel. [ME < OF *bald* bold < Gmc.]

bawd·ry (bod′rē or bôd′rē) *n.* obscenity; lewdness.

bawd·y (bod′ē or bôd′ē) *adj.* **bawd·i·er, bawd·i·est,** *n.* —*adj.* lewd; obscene. —*n.* lewd writing or language. —**bawd′i·ly,** *adv.* —**bawd′i·ness,** *n.*

bawdy-house (bo′dē hous′ or bô′dē-) *n.* a brothel.

bawl (bol or bôl) *v.* **1** shout or cry out in a noisy way: *The peddler bawled his wares in the street.* **2** weep loudly: *The small boy bawled whenever he hurt himself.* **3** **bawl out,** **a** cry out. **b** *Slang.* reprimand; scold.
—*n.* **1** a noisy shout at the top of one's voice. **2** a loud crying. [probably < Med.L *baulare* bark]

bay[1] (bā) *n.* a part of a sea or lake that extends into the land. [ME < OF *baie* < LL *baia*]

bay[2] (bā) *n.* **1** a space or division of a wall or building between columns, pillars, buttresses, etc. **2** a space with a window or set of windows in it, projecting out from a wall. **3** a place in a barn for storing hay or grain; mow. **4** a compartment in an airplane, especially one for carrying bombs. **5** a recess, platform, etc. for a specified purpose: *an unloading bay.* [ME < OF *baee* opening < VL *batare* gape]

bay[3] (bā) *n.* **1** the long, deep howl of a hound: *The hunters heard the distant bay of the hounds.* **2** the stand made by a hunted animal to face pursuers when escape is impossible: *The stag stood at bay on the edge of the cliff.* **3** a similar stand made by a person against persecution, etc. **4** the position of the pursuers or enemies who are being kept off: *The stag held the hounds at bay.* **5 bring to bay,** put in a position from which escape is impossible. [ME *bay, abay* < OF *abai* a barking]
—*v.* **1** howl; bark: *Dogs sometimes bay at the moon. They bay defiance.* **2** bark at; attack or pursue with barking. **3** bring to bay. [ME *bayen* (< OF *bayer* bark) and ME *abayen* (< OF *abayer* bark)]

bay[4] (bā) *n.* **1** a small evergreen tree having smooth, shiny leaves; laurel tree. Bay leaves are used for flavoring food. **2 bays,** *pl.* **a** a laurel wreath worn by poets or victors. **b** honor; renown; fame. [< OF *baie* < L *baca* berry]

bay[5] (bā) *n.* **1** a reddish brown. **2** a reddish-brown horse. —*adj.* reddish-brown: *a bay horse.* [< OF *bai* < L *badius*]

bay·ard (bā′ərd) *n. Archaic.* **1** a bay horse. **2** a mock-heroic name for any horse. —*adj.* of a horse, bay-colored; bay. [< OF *baiard* a red-brown horse < *bai* bay[5]]

Bay·ard (bā′ərd; French bä yär′) *n.* a man of heroic nature. [< Pierre du Terrail, Chevalier de *Bayard* (1473?-1524), a heroic French knight]

bay·ber·ry (bā′ber′ē or bā′bər ē) *n.* **-ries. 1** a North American shrub having clusters of grayish-white berries coated with wax. The leaves of the shrub are aromatic, and candles made from the wax of the berries burn with a pleasant fragrance. **2** one of the berries. **3** a West Indian tree whose leaves contain an oil used in bay rum.

Ba·yeux Tapestry (bā ü′; *French,* bä yœ′) a famous tapestry of the 11th century that pictures events leading to the Norman Conquest of England. [from *Bayeux,* a town in northern France, where it is preserved]

bay·o·net (bā′ə nit or bā′ə net′) *n. v.* **-net·ed, -net·ing.** —*n.* a blade for piercing or stabbing, attached to a rifle. —*v.* pierce or stab with a bayonet. [< F *baïonnette*; from *Bayonne,* France]

bay·ou (bī′ü) *n.* **-ous.** *Esp.U.S.* a marshy inlet or outlet of a lake, river, or gulf. [< Louisiana F < Choctaw *bayuk* small stream]

bay rum a fragrant liquid originally made from the leaves of a tree growing in the West Indies, used in medicine and cosmetics.

Bay Street *Cdn.* **1** in Toronto, a street on which is situated the Toronto Stock Exchange and many financial houses. **2** the financial or moneyed interests of Toronto.

bay window **1** a window or set of windows projecting out from a wall, thereby providing extra space in a room. **2** a large abdomen: *He was a short, fat man, whose expensive watch chain called attention to his bay window.*

A bay window

ba·zaar (bə zär′) *n.* **1** in Oriental countries, a street or streets full of shops. **2** a place for the sale of many kinds of goods. **3** a sale held for some charity or other special purpose. [< F < Arabic < Persian *bazar*]

ba·zoo·ka (bə zü′kə) *n.* a rocket gun used against tanks. [from its resemblance to a trombonelike instrument created and named by Bob Burns, an American humorist]

BB (bē′bē) *n.* **1** a standard size of shot, approximately 0.13 inch. **2** a shot of this size, especially for use in an air rifle.

BBC or **B.B.C.** British Broadcasting Corporation.

BBG or **B.B.G.** Board of Broadcast Governors.

hat, āge, cãre, fär; let, ēqual, tėrm; it, īce
hot, ōpen, ôrder; oil, out; cup, pu̇t, rüle, ūse
əbove, takən, pencəl, lemən, circəs
ch, child; ng, long; sh, ship
th, thin; ᴛʜ, then; zh, measure

BB gun an air rifle. Also, **bee-bee gun.**

bbl. barrel; barrels.

bbls. barrels.

B.C. **1** before Christ; before the birth of Christ. **2** British Columbia.

bch. *pl.* **bchs.** bunch.

B.C.L. Bachelor of Civil Law.

bd. **1** board. **2** bond. **3** bound.

B.D. Bachelor of Divinity.

bd. ft. board foot; board feet.

bdl. bundle.

Bdr or **Bdr.** Bombardier.

B.D.S. Bachelor of Dental Surgery.

be (bē) *v. pres. indic. sing.* **am, are, is,** *pl.* **are;** *pt. indic.* **was, were, was,** *pl.* **were;** *pp.* **been;** *ppr.* **be·ing.** **1** have reality; live: *To be is to exist. Wolfe and Montcalm are no more.* **2** take place; happen: *The circus was last month.* **3** remain; continue: *He will be here all year.* **4** equal; represent: *Let "x" be the unknown quantity.* **5** *Be* is used as a linking verb between a subject and a predicate: *Jerome was the secretary* (predicate noun). *She is sick* (predicate adjective). **6** *Be* is used as an auxiliary verb with: **a** the present participle of another verb to form the progressive tense: *I am asking. He was asking. You will be asking.* **b** the past participle of another verb to form the passive voice: *I am asked. He was asked. You will be asked.* **7** *Be* is used to express future time, duty, intention, and possibility: *He is to arrive here at nine. No shelter was to be seen.* **8** *Be* is used with the past participles of some verbs to form the perfect tense: *Christ is risen.* [OE *bēon*]

be- *prefix.* **1** thoroughly; all around, as in *bespatter.* **2** at; on; to; for; about; against, as in *bewail.* **3** make; cause to seem, as in *belittle.* **4** provide with, as in *bespangle.* [OE *be-*, unstressed form of *bī* by]

Be beryllium.

beach (bēch) *n.* the almost flat shore of sand or small stones over which the water washes when high or at high tide. —*v.* run (a boat) ashore; draw up on the shore. [origin uncertain] —**beach′less,** *adj.* —**Syn.** *n.* strand, coast, seashore.

beach·comb (bēch′kōm′) *v.* live as a beachcomber.

beach·comb·er (bēch′kōm′ər) *n.* **1** a vagrant or loafer on the islands of the Pacific Ocean or elsewhere. **2** a long wave rolling in from the ocean.

beach·head (bēch′hed′) *n.* the first position established by an invading army on an enemy shore.

beach·wear (bēch′wãr′) *n.* articles of clothing, such as bathing suits, shorts, or robes, for wearing at a beach.

bea·con (bē′kən) *n.* **1** a fire or light used as a signal to guide or warn. **2** a radio signal for guiding aircraft or ships through fogs, storms, etc. **3** a tall tower from which to signal. **4** a lighthouse. **5** any thing or person that guides or warns.
—*v.* **1** give light to; guide; warn. **2** shine brightly. **3** supply with beacons. [OE *bēacn*]

bead (bēd) *n.* **1** a small ball or bit of glass, metal, etc. with a hole through it, so that it can be strung on a thread with others like it. **2 beads,** *pl.,* **a** a string of beads. **b** a rosary; string of beads for keeping count in saying prayers. **3 say, tell,** or **count one's beads,** say prayers, using a rosary. **4** any small, round object like a drop or bubble: *beads of sweat.* **5** the metal aiming piece found at the front of a rifle or pistol barrel. **6 draw a bead on,** aim at. **7** a narrow, semicircular moulding.
—*v.* **1** put beads on; ornament with beads. **2** form beads. [OE *bedu* prayer. See def. 2b.] —**bead′like′,** *adj.*

bead·ed (bēd′id) *adj.* **1** trimmed with beads; having beads; covered with beads: *His brow was beaded with sweat.* **2** formed into beads; like beads.

bead·ing (bēd′ing) *n.* 1 a trimming made of beads threaded into patterns. 2 a narrow lace or openwork trimming through which ribbon may be run. 3 on woodwork, silver, etc., a pattern or edge made of small beads. 4 a narrow, rounded moulding.

bea·dle (bē′dəl) *n.* in the Church of England, a minor officer. Formerly, if a person slept in church, the beadle would wake him up. [OE *bydel*]

bea·dle·dom (bē′dəl dəm) *n.* stupid officiousness.

bead-ru·by (bēd′ rü′bē) *n.* **-bies.** a low-growing plant of the lily family, found in Canada and the northern United States, having small white flowers and red berries that grow in a beadlike arrangement.

beads·man (bēdz′mən) *n.* **-men** (-mən). a person who says prayers for others, especially one hired to do so.

beads·wom·an (bēdz′wům′ən) *n.* **-wom·en.** a woman who says prayers for others, especially one hired to do so.

bead·work (bēd′wėrk′) *n.* beading.

bead·y (bēd′ē) *adj.* **bead·i·er, bead·i·est.** 1 small, round, and shiny. 2 trimmed with beads. 3 covered with drops or bubbles.

bea·gle (bē′gəl) *n.* 1 a breed of small hunting dog having smooth hair, short legs, and drooping ears. 2 a dog of this breed. [ME *begle* < ? OF *begueule* wide throat]

beak[1] (bēk) *n.* 1 a bird's bill, especially one that is strong and hooked and useful in striking or tearing. Eagles, hawks, and parrots have beaks. 2 a similar part in other animals. A hooked nose is sometimes called a beak. 3 the projecting bow of an ancient warship. 4 a spout. [ME < OF *bec* < L *beccus* < Celtic]

beak[2] (bēk) *n. Brit. Slang.* 1 a magistrate. 2 a schoolmaster, especially a headmaster.

beaked (bēkt) *adj.* 1 having a beak. 2 shaped like a beak; hooked.

beak·er (bēk′ər) *n.* 1 a large cup or drinking glass. 2 the contents of a beaker. 3 a thin glass or metal cup with a small lip for pouring and no handle, used in laboratories. [ME < ON *bikarr* < LL *becarium*, var. of *bacarium*. Related to BASIN.]

beak·y (bēk′ē) *adj.* 1 having a beaklike nose; beaklike. 2 prying; meddlesome.

be-all and end-all 1 the main purpose or reason of anything. 2 *Informal.* the most important person or thing: *She thinks she is the be-all and end-all.*

beam (bēm) *n.* 1 a large, long piece of timber, ready for use in building. 2 a similar piece of metal, stone, reinforced concrete, etc. 3 any of the main horizontal supports of a building or ship. 4 the part of a plough by which it is pulled. 5 the crossbar of a balance, from the ends of which the scales or pans are suspended. 6 the balance itself. 7 a ray or rays of light or heat. 8 a bright look or smile. 9 a radio signal directed in a straight line, used to guide aircraft, ships, etc. 10 the side of a ship, or the direction at right angles to the keel, with reference to wind, sea, etc. 11 the greatest width of a ship. 12 **off the beam, a** of an aircraft, off the course indicated by directing signals. **b** *Informal.* on the wrong track; mistaken. 13 **on the beam, a** of a ship, at right angles to the keel. **b** of an aircraft, in the right path as indicated by directing signals. **c** *Informal.* just right; on the right track.
—*v.* 1 send out rays of light; shine. 2 smile radiantly. 3 direct (a broadcast): *beam programs at the Yukon.* [OE *bēam* tree, piece of wood, ray of light]
Syn. 7 Beam, ray = a line of light. **Beam** applies to a shaft, long and with some width, coming from something that gives out light: *The beam from the flashlight showed a kneeling man.* **Ray** applies to a thin line of light, usually thought of as radiating, or coming out like the spokes of a wheel, from something bright: *There was not a ray of moonlight in the forest.*

beamed (bēmd) *adj.* furnished with beams.

beam-ends (bēm′endz′) *n.pl.* 1 the ends of a ship's beams. 2 **on her beam-ends,** of a ship, almost capsizing. 3 **on one's beam-ends,** seriously short of money; impoverished.

beam·ing (bēm′ing) *adj.* 1 shining; bright. 2 smiling brightly; cheerful. **—beam′ing·ly,** *adv.*

beam-on (bēm′on′) *adv.* of a ship, with the beam ahead; against the beam.

bean (bēn) *n.* 1 a smooth, kidney-shaped seed used as a vegetable. 2 the long pod containing such seeds. The young pods of some varieties are also used as a vegetable. 3 the plant that beans grow on. 4 any seed shaped like a bean. Coffee beans are the seeds of the coffee plant. 5 *Slang.* the head. 6 **full of beans,** *Slang.* in high spirits; lively. 7 **old bean,** *Esp.Brit. Slang.* old man; old fellow: *How are you, old bean?*
—*v. Slang.* hit (someone) on the head, especially with a baseball or other thrown object: *The pitcher beaned one batter twice.* [OE *bēan*] **—bean′like′,** *adj.*

beanie (bē′nē) *n.* a small cap, often having no peak, worn especially by schoolboys but often by students of both sexes.

bean·pole (bēn′pōl′) *n.* 1 a pole stuck in the ground for bean vines to climb on as they grow. 2 *Slang.* a tall, thin person.

bean·stalk (bēn′stok′ or -stôk′) *n.* the stem of a bean plant.

bear[1] (bãr) *v.* **bore** or (*Archaic*) **bare, borne** (or, for 6, **born**), **bear·ing.** 1 carry: *A voice was borne upon the wind.* 2 support: *The ice is too thin to bear your weight.* 3 put up with; abide: *She can't bear the noise.* 4 undergo; experience: *He cannot bear any more pain.* 5 produce; yield: *This tree bears fine apples.* 6 give birth to; have (off-spring): *That woman has borne four boys. He was born on June 4.* 7 produce; create; cause to come into existence: *On the opening night of the play a star was born: The idea of the plot was born at a secret meeting.* 8 have a connection or effect; relate: *His answer did not bear on the question.* 9 behave; conduct: *He bore himself with great dignity.* 10 bring forward; give: *bear company, bear a hand. A person who has seen an accident can bear witness to what happened.* 11 hold; hold in mind: *bear a grudge, affection, etc.* 12 have as an identification or characteristic: *He bears the name of John, the title of earl, and a reputation for learning.* 13 have as a duty, right, privilege, etc.: *The king bears sway over the empire.* 14 take on oneself as a duty: *bear the cost, responsibility, etc.* 15 press; push: *Don't bear so hard on the lever.* 16 move; go: *The ship bore north.* 17 lie; be situated: *The land bore due north of the ship.* 18 allow; permit: *The accident bears two explanations.* 19 **bear down** or **bear down on, a** put pressure on; press or push: *Don't bear down so hard on him.* **b** move toward; approach. **c** try hard; work seriously: *You'll have to bear down if you expect to pass the examination.* 20 **bear out,** support; prove. 21 **bear up,** keep one's courage; not lose hope or faith. 22 **bear with,** put up with; be patient with. [OE *beran*]
Syn. 1 transport, convey, bring. **2** sustain. **3** tolerate, brook. **4 Bear, endure, stand** = to undergo something hard to take. **Bear,** the general word, suggests only being able to hold up: *He is bearing his grief very well.* **Endure** = to bear hardship or misfortune for a long time without giving in: *The pioneers endured many hardships in settling the West.* **Stand** is the informal word used interchangeably with *bear*, but it suggests bearing stubbornly and bravely: *He can stand more pain than anyone else I know.* **11** cherish, harbor. **15** thrust, drive. ☞ See **borne** for usage note.

bear[2] (bãr) *n.* 1 any of a family of large, heavy mammals having coarse hair, flat feet, and a very short tail. Bears feed on fruit, insects, and, in the case of some varieties, flesh. 2 a gruff or surly person. 3 a person who tries to lower prices in the stock market, etc. —*adj.* having to do with lowering prices in the stock market, etc. [OE *bera*]

Bear (bãr) *n.* one of two northern constellations; the Little Bear or the Great Bear.

bear·a·ble (bãr′ə bəl) *adj.* that can be borne; endurable. **—bear′a·ble·ness,** *n.* **—bear′a·bly,** *adv.*

bear·bait·ing (bãr′bāt′ing) *n.* the sport of setting dogs to fight a chained bear, now illegal.

bear·ber·ry (bãr′ber′ē or bãr′bər ē) *n.* **-ries.** 1 a trailing evergreen shrub having small bright-red berries and astringent leaves. 2 a similar shrub having black berries.

beard (bērd) *n.* 1 the hair growing on a man's face. 2 something resembling or suggesting this. The chin tuft of a goat is a beard; so are the stiff hairs around the beak of a bird. 3 the hairs on the heads of plants like oats, barley, and wheat; awns. 4 a plushlike growth on parts of certain flowers: *This variety of iris has a beard.*
—*v.* 1 face boldly; defy. 2 grasp by the beard. [OE] **—beard′like′,** *adj.*

beard·ed (bēr′did) *adj.* having a beard.

bearded seal *Cdn.* a large seal having beardlike bristles about its mouth. Also, **square-flipper seal.**

bear·er (bãr′ər) *n.* **1** a person or thing that carries. **2** a person who holds or presents a cheque, draft, or note for payment. **3** a tree or plant that produces fruit or flowers: *This apple tree is a good bearer.* **4** the holder of a rank or office. **5** a pallbearer.

bear·ing (bãr′ing) *n.* **1** a way of standing, sitting, walking, etc.; manner: *A soldier should have a military bearing.* **2** reference; relation: *His foolish question has no bearing on the problem.* **3** a part of a machine on which another part turns or slides. **4** a supporting part. **5** in heraldry, a single device in a coat of arms. **6** the act of a person or thing that bears. **7 bearings,** a direction; position in relation to other things: *Having no compass, he got his bearings from the sun.*

Syn. **1 Bearing, carriage** = manner of carrying oneself. **Bearing** applies to a person's manner of managing his whole body, including his gestures, mannerisms, posture, the way he holds his head, and the way he walks and sits: *His manly bearing won the confidence of his employers.* **Carriage** applies only to a person's way of holding his head and body when he stands and walks: *Her awkward carriage prevented the pretty girl from becoming a model.*

bear·ish (bãr′ish) *adj.* **1** like a bear; rough; surly. **2** aiming at or tending to lower prices in the stock market, etc. **—bear′ish·ly,** *adv.* **—bear′ish·ness,** *n.*

bear·skin (bãr′skin′) *n.* **1** the fur of a bear. **2** a tall, black, fur cap worn by the members of certain regiments.

A bearskin (def. 2)

beast (bēst) *n.* **1** any animal except man, especially a four-footed animal. **2** a coarse, dirty, or brutal person. [ME < OF *beste* < LL *besta*] **—beast′like′,** *adj.* **—Syn. 1, 2** See **animal.**

beast·ly (bēst′lē) *adj.* **-li·er, -li·est,** *adv.* *—adj.* **1** like a beast; brutal; coarse; vile. **2** *Informal.* very unpleasant; disagreeable: *a beastly headache.* *—adv. Informal.* very; unpleasantly: *He is beastly ill-mannered.* **—beast′li·ness,** *n.*

beast of burden an animal used for carrying loads.

beast of prey an animal that kills other animals.

beat (bēt) *v.* **beat, beat·en** or **beat, beat·ing,** *n. adj.* *—v.* **1** strike again and again; strike; whip; thrash: *The cruel man beats his horse.* **2** throb: *Her heart beats fast with joy.* **3** drive by blows; force by blows: *He beat the savage dog away from him.* **4** defeat or overcome: *Their team beat ours by a huge score.* **5** *Informal.* baffle: *This problem beats me.* **6** *Informal.* cheat; swindle. **7** make flat; shape with a hammer: *beat gold into thin strips.* **8** make flat by much walking; tread (a path). **9** mix by stirring; mix by striking with a fork, spoon, or other utensil: *beat eggs.* **10** move up and down; flap: *The bird beat its wings.* **11** make a sound by being struck: *The drums beat loudly.* **12** mark (time) with drumsticks or by tapping with hands or feet: *beat a tattoo.* **13** in music, show (a unit of time or accent) by a stroke of the hand, etc. **14** go through in a hunt or search: *The men beat the woods in search of the lost child.* **15** move against the wind by a zigzag course: *The sailboat beat along the coast.* **16** outdo; surpass: *Nothing can beat yachting as a sport.* **17 beat about,** search around; try to discover. **18 beat a retreat, a** run away; retreat. **b** sound a retreat on a drum. **19 beat down,** *Informal.* force to set a lower price. **20 beat off, a** drive off or away by blows: *He beat off the two men who attacked him.* **b** drive away; repel: *Our unit beat off the enemy attack.* **21 beat up,** *Slang.* thrash soundly.
—n. **1** a stroke or blow made again and again: *the beat of a drum, the beat of waves on a beach.* **2** in music, **a** a unit of time or accent: *three beats to a measure.* **b** a stroke of the hand, baton, etc. showing a beat. **3** a regular round made by a policeman or watchman. **4 off one's beat,** not at one's regular work. **5** *Slang.* in journalism, the securing and publishing of news ahead of one's competitors. **6** *Slang.* a beatnik.
—adj. Informal. **1** worn out; exhausted: *He was beat after a hard day at the factory.* **2** overcome by astonishment; taken aback. **3** *Slang.* of or characteristic of beatniks: *beat attitudes.* [OE *bēatan*]

Syn. *v.* **1 Beat, hit, pound** = to strike. **Beat** = to strike again and again, but does not suggest how hard nor with what: *The cruel driver beat his horse.* **Hit** = to strike a single blow with force and aim: *The batter hit the ball.* **Pound** = to hit hard again and again with the fist or something heavy: *The child pounded the floor with a hammer.* **4** vanquish, conquer.

beat·en (bēt′ən) *v.* a pp. of **beat.** *—adj.* **1** whipped; struck: *a beaten dog.* **2** shaped by blows of a hammer: *beaten silver.* **3** much walked on or travelled: *a beaten path.* **4** defeated; overcome: *a beaten army.* **5** exhausted.

beat·er (bēt′ər) *n.* **1** a person or thing that beats. **2** a man hired to rouse game during a hunt. **3** a device or utensil for beating eggs, cream, etc.

be·a·tif·ic (bē′ə tif′ik) *adj.* making blessed; blissful: *The saint had a beatific smile.*

be·at·i·fi·ca·tion (bē at′ə fə kā′shən) *n.* **1** the act of making blessed. **2** the state of being made blessed. **3** in the Roman Catholic Church, an official declaration by the Pope that a dead person is among the blessed in heaven.

be·at·i·fy (bē at′ə fī′) *v.* **-fied, -fy·ing. 1** make supremely happy; bless. **2** in the Roman Catholic Church, declare (a dead person) by a papal decree to be among the blessed in heaven. [< L *beatificare* < *beatus* happy + *facere* make]

beat·ing (bēt′ing) *n.* **1** the act of one that beats. **2** a whipping or a thrashing. **3** a defeat. **4** a throbbing.

be·at·i·tude (bē at′ə tūd′ or bē at′ə tüd′) *n.* **1** supreme happiness; bliss. **2** a blessing. **3 the Beatitudes,** in the Bible, the verses beginning "Blessed are the poor in spirit." Matt. 5:3-12. [< L *beatitudo* < *beatus* blessed]

beat·nik (bēt′nik) *n.* a person who adopts a mode of life calculated to show contempt for conventions and accepted standards in dress, speech, art expression, etc. [< *beat* + Yiddish *-nik*]

beat-up (bēt′up′) *adj. Slang.* in very bad condition; worn out.

beau (bō) *n.* **beaus** or **beaux** (bōz). **1** a young man courting a young woman; suitor; lover. **2** a man who pays much attention to the way he dresses and to the fashionableness or stylishness of his clothes. [< F *beau* handsome < L *bellus* fine] **—Syn. 1** swain. **2** dude.

☛ **Beaux** is the more formal plural form; ordinarily, use **beaus.**

Beau Brum·mell (bō′ brum′əl) **1** the nickname of George Bryan Brummell (1778-1840), an English leader in men's fashions. **2** any dandy.

Beau·fort scale (bō′fərt) an internationally used scale of wind velocities, having code numbers ranging from 0 for speeds below one mile an hour (calm) to 12 or higher for speeds above 72 m.p.h. (hurricane).

beau geste (bō′zhest′) *pl.* **beaux gestes** (bō′zhest′). *French.* **1** a graceful or kindly act. **2** a pretence of kindness or unselfishness merely for effect.

beau i·de·al (bō′ ī dē′əl; *French,* bō′ē dā äl′) *pl.* **beau ideals** or **beaus ideal.** a perfect type of excellence or beauty; the highest ideal or model. [< F]

beau monde (bō′ mond′) fashionable society. [< F]

beau·te·ous (bū′tē əs) *adj. Esp.Poetic.* beautiful. **—beau′te·ous·ly,** *adv.* **—beau′te·ous·ness,** *n.*

beau·ti·cian (bū tish′ən) *n.* a specialist in the use of cosmetics, especially a person who works in a beauty parlor.

beau·ti·ful (bū′tə fəl) *adj.* very pleasing to see or hear; delighting the mind or senses: *a beautiful picture, beautiful music.* **—beau′ti·ful·ly,** *adv.* **—beau′ti·ful·ness,** *n.*

Syn. **Beautiful, lovely, handsome** = pleasing the senses or mind. **Beautiful** suggests delighting the senses by excellence and harmony, and often also giving great pleasure to the mind by an inner goodness: *Looking at a beautiful painting always gives one satisfaction.* **Lovely** suggests appealing to the emotions and giving delight to the heart as well as to the senses and mind: *Her lovely* *smile shows a sweet disposition.* Handsome = pleasing to look at because well formed, well proportioned, etc.: *That is a handsome chest of drawers. Handsome* may be applied to men but *beautiful* and *lovely* are not so applied, except in contempt or sarcasm.

beau·ti·fy (bū′tə fī′) *v.* **-fied, -fy·ing. 1** make beautiful; make more beautiful: *Flowers beautify a garden.* **2** become beautiful. [< *beauty* + *-fy*] —**beau′ti·fi′er,** *n.* —**Syn. 1** ornament, adorn.

beau·ty (bū′tē) *n.* **-ties. 1** good looks. **2** the quality that pleases in flowers, pictures, music, etc. **3** something beautiful. **4** a beautiful woman. [ME < OF *beaute* < *beau* beautiful < L *bellus* fine] —**Syn. 2** loveliness.

beauty parlor or **parlour** a place where women go for hairdressing, skin care, manicures, etc.

beauty shop beauty parlor.

beauty sleep *Informal.* **1** any short nap. **2** the hours of sleep taken before midnight, supposed to be those that are most beneficial.

beauty spot 1 a small, black patch worn on the face to show off by contrast the whiteness of the skin. **2** a mole or small spot or mark on the skin. **3** any place or natural feature of especial beauty.

beaux (bōz) *n.* a pl. of **beau.**

beaux-arts (bō zär′) *n.pl. French.* fine arts; painting, sculpture, music, etc.

bea·ver[1] (bē′vər) *n.* **1** a large, amphibious rodent having soft fur, a broad, flat tail, and feet adapted to swimming and walking. The beaver has been a Canadian emblem for over two hundred years. **2** its soft brown fur. **3** a coat or other garment made of this fur. **4** a man's high silk hat, formerly made of beaver fur. **5** a heavy woollen cloth. **6** *Informal.* an especially hard-working person; eager beaver. **7** *Cdn.* a coin formerly issued by the Hudson's Bay Company, widely used in the North-west for trade. [OE *beofor*]

bea·ver[2] (bē′vər) *n.* **1** the movable lower part of a helmet, protecting the chin and mouth. **2** the movable front part of a helmet; a visor. **3** *Informal.* **a** a full beard. **b** a man wearing such a beard. [ME < OF *bavière*, originally, bib < *bave* saliva]

B

B, beaver[2] (def. 1)

Beaver (bē′vər) *n., pl.* **-ver** or **-vers. 1** a group of Athapaskan Indians of the Peace River valley in Alberta. **2** a member of this group. **3** the language of this group. [translation of native name meaning "dwellers among beavers"]

bea·ver·board (bē′vər bôrd′) *n.* **1** a lightweight material resembling very thick, strong cardboard, used for making ceilings, partitions, etc. **2 Beaverboard,** a trademark for such material.

be·bop (bē′bop′) *n.* in music, a form of jazz characterized by much improvisation of melody, by dissonance, and, frequently, by the singing of meaningless syllables. [imitative]

be·calm (bi kom′ or bi käm′) *v.* **1** prevent (a ship, boat, etc.) from moving by lack of wind. **2** make (sea, waves, etc.) calm.

be·calmed (bi komd′ or bi kämd′) *adj.* **1** of the sea, waves, etc., calm. **2** of a ship boat, etc., kept from moving because there is no wind.

be·came (bi kām′) *v.* pt. of **become.**

be·cause (bi koz′, bi kôz′, or bi kuz′) *conj.* for the reason that; since: *Boys play ball because they enjoy the game.* —*adv.* **because of,** by reason of; on account of: *We did not go because of the rain.* [ME *bicause* by cause]

☛ **Because** introduces a subordinate clause that gives the reason for the main clause: *Because we were late, we hurried.* As can be used in such clauses, but is less definite and more characteristic of informal speech than of writing. **Since** has a similar function but may be ambiguous: *Since she went away, he has taken to drink. For,* which introduces co-ordinate clauses of reason, is a more formal word.

be·chance (bi chans′) *v.* **-chanced, -chanc·ing.** happen; happen to; befall.

beck (bek) *n.* **1** a motion of the head or hand meant as a call or command. **2 at one's beck and call, a** ready whenever wanted. **b** under one's complete control. —*v.* beckon to. [< *beck*, v., short for *beckon*]

beck·on (bek′ən) *v.* signal by a motion of the head or hand: *He beckoned me to follow him.* [OE *bēcnan*, var. of *bīecnan.* Related to BEACON.]

☛ **beckon.** The idiom is *beckon to*, not *beckon at*: *The tall man beckoned to her. Beckon* is used also without a preposition: *The guard beckoned us forward.*

be·cloud (bi kloud′) *v.* **1** hide by a cloud or clouds. **2** make obscure: *Too many big words becloud the meaning.*

be·come (bi kum′) *v.* **be·came, be·come, be·com·ing. 1** come to be; grow to be: *He became wiser as he grew older.* **2** be suitable for; suit: *It does not become me to question your decision.* **3** look well on: *A white dress becomes her.* **4 become of,** happen to: *What will become of her? What has become of the box of candy?* [OE *becuman*]

☛ **Become** is one of the common linking verbs: *At his words she became more angry. Become* differs from the linking verb *be* in that it adds a meaning of its own to its linking function, suggesting change or development rather than identity.

be·com·ing (bi kum′ing) *adj.* **1** suitable; appropriate: *becoming conduct for a gentleman.* **2** that looks well on the person wearing it: *a becoming dress.* —**be·com′ing·ly,** *adv.* —**Syn. 1** proper, meet, seemly. See **fitting.**

Becque·rel rays (bek′rel) invisible rays given off by radium, uranium, and other radio-active substances. [after A. H. *Becquerel* (1852-1908), a French physicist]

B.Ed. Bachelor of Education.

bed (bed) *n. v.* **bed·ded, bed·ding.** —*n.* **1** anything to sleep or rest on. A bed usually consists of a mattress raised upon a support and covered with sheets and blankets. **2** any place where people or animals rest or sleep. **3** a flat base on which anything rests; foundation: *They set the lathe in a bed of concrete.* **4** the ground under a body of water: *the bed of a river.* **5** the piece of ground in a garden in which plants are grown. **6** in geology, a layer or stratum: *a bed of coal.* **7 bed and board,** sleeping accommodation and meals. **8 get up on the wrong side of the bed,** become irritable or bad-tempered. **9 take to one's bed,** stay in bed because of sickness or weakness.
—*v.* **1** provide with a bed; put to bed: *The man bedded down his horse with straw.* **2** fix or set in a permanent position; embed. **3** plant in a garden bed: *These roses should be bedded in rich soil.* **4** form a compact layer. **5** lay flat or in order. **6 bed down, a** make or arrange a bed or sleeping place for. **b** go to bed; lie down to sleep. [OE *bedd*] —**Syn.** *n.* **1** couch, berth.

be·dab·ble (bi dab′əl) *v.* **-bled, -bling.** spatter over with dirt.

be·daub (bi dob′ or -dôb′) *v.* **1** smear with something dirty or sticky. **2** ornament in a gaudy or showy way.

be·daze (bi dāz′) *v.* **-dazed, -daz·ing.** daze completely; stupefy; bewilder.

be·daz·zle (bi daz′əl) *v.* **-zled, -zling.** dazzle completely; confuse.

bed·bug (bed′bug′) *n.* a small, reddish-brown, flat blood-sucking insect found especially in beds.

bed·cham·ber (bed′chām′bər) *n.* bedroom.

bed chesterfield a chesterfield that opens out into a bed.

bed·clothes (bed′klōz′ or bed′klōTHz′) *n.pl.* sheets, blankets, quilts, etc.

bed·cov·er (bed′kuv′ər) *n.* a bedspread; coverlet.

bed·ding (bed′ing) *n.* **1** sheets, blankets, quilts, etc.; bedclothes. **2** material for beds: *Straw is used as bedding for cows and horses.* **3** a foundation; bottom layer.

be·deck (bi dek′) *v.* adorn; decorate.

be·dev·il (bi dev′əl) *v.* **-illed** or **-iled, -il·ling** or **-il·ing. 1** trouble greatly; torment. **2** confuse completely; muddle. **3** put under spell; bewitch.

be·dev·il·ment (bi dev′əl mənt) *n.* **1** great trouble; torment. **2** complete confusion; muddle. **3** the state of being under a spell; being bewitched.

be·dew (bi dū′ or bi dü′) *v.* make wet with dew or with drops like dew: *Tears bedewed her cheeks.*

bed·fast (bed′fast′) *adj.* confined to bed; bedridden.

hat, āge, cãre, fär; let, ēqual, tėrm; it, īce
hot, ōpen, ôrder; oil, out; cup, pu̇t, rüle, ūse
əbove, takən, pencəl, lemən, circəs
ch, child; ng, long; sh, ship
th, thin; ᴛʜ, then; zh, measure

bed·fel·low (bed′fel′ō) *n.* **1** the sharer of one's bed. **2** an associate: *A businessman finds himself working with a variety of bedfellows.*

Bed·ford cord (bed′fərd) a heavy cloth ribbed like corduroy. [< *Bedford,* a town in S. England]

be·dight (bi dīt′) *v.* **-dight, -dight** or **dight·ed, -dight·ing,** *adj. Archaic.* —*v.* adorn; array. —*adj.* adorned; arrayed. [< *be-* + *dight*]

be·dim (bi dim′) *v.* **-dimmed, -dim·ming.** make dim; darken; obscure. —**Syn.** overcast.

be·di·zen (bi dī′zən or bi diz′ən) *v.* dress in gaudy clothes; ornament with showy finery. [< *be-* + *dizen*]

bed·lam (bed′ləm) *n.* **1** an uproar; confusion: *When the home team won, there was bedlam in the arena.* **2** an insane asylum; madhouse. **3 Bedlam,** in London, an insane asylum. [alteration of *Bethlehem* (for the Hospital of St. Mary of Bethlehem)]

bed·lam·ite (bed′ləm īt′) *n. Archaic.* an insane person; lunatic.

bed linen sheets and pillowcases for a bed.

Bed·ling·ton (bed′ling tən) *n.* **1** a breed of medium-sized terrier having rough, woolly fur, usually bluish- or grayish-brown, noted for its speed and pluck. **2** a dog of this breed. [< *Bedlington,* a town in England]

Bed·ou·in (bed′ü in) *n.* **1** a member of certain tribes of wandering Arabs who live in the deserts of the Arabian peninsula, Syria, and northern Africa. **2** a wanderer; nomad. —*adj.* of the Bedouins. [ME < OF < Arabic *badawin,* pl. of *badawiy* desert dweller]

bed·pan (bed′pan′) *n.* **1** a pan used as a toilet by sick people in bed. **2** a pan filled with hot coals for warming a bed.

bed·post (bed′pōst′) *n.* an upright support at a corner of a bed.

be·drag·gle (bi drag′əl) *v.* **-gled, -gling.** make limp and soiled.

be·drag·gled (bi drag′əld) *adj.* **1** wet and hanging limp. **2** dragged in the dirt.

bed·rid (bed′rid′) *adj.* bedridden. [OE *bedreda, bedrida,* literally, bed rider]

bed·rid·den (bed′rid′ən) *adj.* confined to bed for a long time because of sickness or weakness. [var. (by confusion with *ridden*) of *bedrid*]

bed·rock (bed′rok′) *n.* **1** the solid rock beneath the soil and looser rocks. **2** a firm foundation. **3** the lowest level; bottom.

bed·room (bed′rüm′ or -ru̇m′) *n.* a room to sleep in.

bed·side (bed′sīd′) *n.* the side of a bed. —*adj.* with the sick; attending the sick: *Young doctors need bedside practice.*

bed·sore (bed′sôr′) *n.* a sore caused by lying too long in the same position.

bed·spread (bed′spred′) *n.* a cover that is spread over the blankets to make a bed look neat.

bed·spring (bed′spring′) *n.* **1** a set of springs forming the part of the bed that supports the mattress. **2** one of these springs.

bed·stead (bed′sted′) *n.* the wooden or metal framework of a bed.

bed·straw (bed′stro′ or -strô′) *n.* a small plant having clusters of white flowers, formerly dried and used as straw for beds.

bed·tick (bed′tick′) *n.* the cloth covering of a mattress or a box spring.

bed·tick·ing (bed′tick′ing) *n.* the strong cotton cloth from which bedticks are made.

bed·time (bed′tīm′) *n.* the usual time for going to bed.

bee (bē) *n.* **1** any of various insects, especially the common honeybee, that make honey and wax. Honeybees live in highly organized communities, each including a queen (developed female), workers (undeveloped females), and drones (males). Only workers and queens have stings. Wild bees show various gradations from elaborately organized colonies to solitary nests. **2** a gathering for work or amusement: *a husking bee, a spelling bee.* **3 have a bee in one's bonnet** or **one's head,** *Informal.* **a** be preoccupied or overenthusiastic about one thing. **b** be slightly crazy. [OE *bēo*]

bee-bee gun a BB gun; air rifle.

bee·bread (bē′bred′) *n.* a brownish, bitter substance consisting of pollen, or pollen mixed with honey, used by bees as food.

beech (bēch) *n.* **1** a tree having a smooth, gray bark and glossy leaves. It bears a sweet, edible nut. **2** the wood of this tree. —*adj.* of the tree or its wood. [OE *bēce*]

beech·en (bēch′ən) *adj.* made of beechwood.

beech·nut (bēch′nut′) *n.* the small, triangular nut of the beech tree.

beech·wood (bēch′wu̇d′) *n.* the wood of a beech tree.

beef[1] (bēf) *n.* **beeves,** *v.* —*n.* **1** the meat from a steer, cow, or bull. **2** a steer, cow, or bull when full-grown and fattened for food. **3** *Informal.* strength; muscle. **4** *Informal.* weight or heaviness. —*v.* **beef up,** *Slang.* strengthen. [ME < OF *boef* < L *bos, bovis* ox] —**beef′less,** *n.*

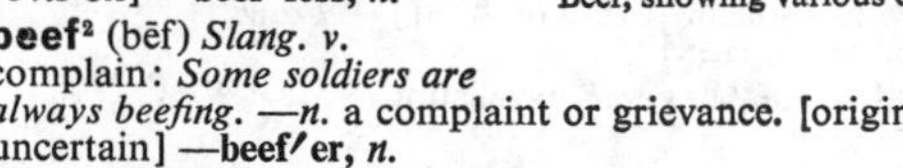

Beef, showing various cuts

beef[2] (bēf) *Slang.* *v.* complain: *Some soldiers are always beefing.* —*n.* a complaint or grievance. [origin uncertain] —**beef′er,** *n.*

beef cattle cattle raised for meat.

beef·eat·er (bēf′ēt′ər) *n.* in England: **1** a yeoman of the royal guard. **2** a warder of the Tower of London.

beef extract an extract of beef or beef juices, for use in making broth, gravy, sauce, etc.

beef·steak (bēf′stāk′) *n.* a slice of beef for broiling or frying.

beef tea a strong beef broth.

beef·y (bēf′ē) *adj.* **beef·i·er, beef·i·est. 1** like beef: *a beefy taste.* **2** strong; muscular. **3** heavy; solid. —**beef′i·ness,** *n.*

bee·hive (bē′hīv′) *n.* **1** a hive or house for bees. See **hive** for picture. **2** a busy, swarming place.

bee·keep·er (bē′kēp′ər) *n.* a person who raises bees for their honey.

bee·line (bē′līn′) *n.* the straightest way or line between two places.

Be·el·ze·bub (bē el′zə bub′) *n.* **1** the Devil. **2** a devil. **3** in Milton's poem *Paradise Lost,* the fallen angel next to Satan in power.

been (bin or bēn) *v.* pp. of **be.**

☛ **been.** The most common British pronunciation is (bēn), and the normal American pronunciation is (bin). In earlier English, (bēn) was the stressed form and (bin) the unstressed; many Canadian speakers still employ this distinction. Otherwise, Canadian usage varies between the two forms.

beep (bēp) *n.* **1** in radio, a short, sharp sound occurring as a signal. **2** any short, sharp sound: *the beep of a car horn.* —*v.* cause something to emit short, sharp sounds. [imitative]

beer (bēr) *n.* **1** an alcoholic drink made from malt and, usually, hops. **2** a drink made from roots or plants: *root beer, ginger beer.* **3 beer and skittles,** *Informal.* enjoyment; material comforts: *Life is not all beer and skittles.* [OE *bēor*]

beer parlor or **parlour** *Cdn.* a room in a hotel or tavern where beer is sold; beverage room.

Beer·she·ba (bēr shē′bə or bēr′shi bə) *n.* **1** a city in central Israel, formerly near the southern boundary of Palestine. **2 from Dan to Beersheba,** from one end of a place to the other.

beer·y (bēr′ē) *adj.* **beer·i·er, beer·i·est. 1** of beer. **2** like beer. **3** caused by beer. —**beer′i·ly,** *adv.*

beest·ings (bēs′tingz) *n.pl.* the first milk from a cow after it has given birth to a calf. [OE *bȳsting* < *bēost* beestings]

bees·wax (bēz′waks′) *n.* the wax given out by bees, from which they make their honeycomb. —*v.* rub, polish, or treat with beeswax.

bees·wing (bēz′wing′) *n.* **1** a thin film that forms in some old wines. **2** an old wine that has such a film.

beet (bēt) *n.* **1** the thick, fleshy root of a biennial plant. Red beets are eaten as vegetables. Sugar is made from white beets. **2** the plant, the leaves of which are sometimes eaten as greens. [< L *beta*] —**beet′like′**, *adj.*

bee·tle[1] (bē′təl) *n.* **1** any insect having the forward pair of wings modified as hard sheaths that, when at rest, cover the hinder membranous pair. **2** *Informal.* any similar insect. —*v. Informal.* move quickly; scurry. [OE *bitela* < *bītan* bite]

bee·tle[2] (bē′təl) *n. v.* **-tled, -tling.** —*n.* **1** a heavy wooden mallet for ramming, crushing, or smoothing. **2** a wooden household utensil for beating or mashing. —*v.* pound with a beetle. [OE *bīetel* < *bēatan* beat]

A beetle[2] (def. 1)

bee·tle[3] (bē′təl) *v.* **-tled, -tling,** *adj.* —*v.* project; overhang: *Great cliffs beetled above the narrow path.* —*adj.* projecting; overhanging. [< *beetle-browed*]

bee·tle-browed (bē′təl broud′) *adj.* **1** having projecting or overhanging eyebrows. **2** scowling; sullen. [ME *bitel* biting + *brow.* Related to BEETLE[1].]

bee·tling (bēt′ling) *adj.* projecting; overhanging.

beet root the root of a beet plant.

beet sugar the sugar obtained from white beets.

beeves (bēvz) *n.* pl. of **beef**[1] (def. 2).

be·fall (bi fol′ or bi fôl′) *v.* **-fell, -fall·en, -fall·ing.** **1** happen to: *Be careful that no harm befalls you.* **2** happen. [OE *befeallan*] —**Syn. 2** occur.

be·fall·en (bi fol′ən or bi fôl′ən) *v.* pp. of **befall.**

be·fell (bi fel′) *v.* pt. of **befall.**

be·fit (bi fit′) *v.* **-fit·ted, -fit·ting.** be suitable for; be proper for; be suited to.

be·fit·ting (bi fit′ing) *adj.* suitable; proper. —**be·fit′ting·ly,** *adv.*

be·fog (bi fog′) *v.* **-fogged, -fog·ging. 1** surround with fog; make foggy. **2** obscure; confuse.

be·fool (bi fül′) *v.* fool; deceive; dupe.

be·fore (bi fôr′) *prep.* **1** in front of; in advance of; ahead of: *Walk before me.* **2** earlier than: *Come before five o'clock.* **3** rather than; sooner than: *I would choose death before dishonor.* **4** in the presence of or in sight of: *stand before the king.*
—*adv.* **1** in front; in advance; ahead: *He went before to see if the road was safe.* **2** earlier: *Come at five o'clock, not before.* **3** until now; in the past: *I didn't know that before.*
—*conj.* **1** previously to the time when: *Before she goes, I would like to talk to her.* **2** rather than; sooner than: *I will die before I give in.* [OE *beforan*]

be·fore·hand (bi fôr′hand′) *adv. adj.* ahead of time; in advance: *I am going to get everything ready beforehand.*

be·fore·time (bi fôr′tīm′) *adv. Archaic.* formerly.

be·foul (bi foul′) *v.* **1** make dirty; cover with filth. **2** entangle: *The rope was befouled by weeds and sticks.* —**be·foul′ment,** *n.*

be·friend (bi frend′) *v.* act as a friend to; help.

be·fud·dle (bi fud′əl) *v.* **-dled, -dling. 1** stupefy; confuse. **2** make stupid with alcoholic drink. —**be·fud′dle·ment,** *n.*

beg (beg) *v.* **begged, beg·ging. 1** ask help or charity: *Must I beg for a living?* **2** ask for (food, money, clothes, etc.) as a charity: *The tramp begged his meals.* **3** ask as a favor; ask earnestly or humbly: *He begged his mother to forgive him.* **4** ask formally and courteously: *I beg your pardon.* **5 beg off,** get free by pleading. **6 beg the question,** take for granted the very thing argued about. **7 go begging,** find no acceptance: *The architect's suggestion went begging.* [ME *beggen* < AF *begger* < MF *begard,* of uncertain origin]

Syn. 3 Beg, implore, beseech = to ask earnestly. **Beg** = to ask earnestly or humbly: *He begged me to think about his offer.* **Implore,** more formal, adds to *beg* the idea of pleading with warm feeling or great humility: *We implored him not to ruin his life by doing anything so foolish.* **Beseech,** formal, suggests greater earnestness of humility than *beg*: *The mother besought the prince to pardon her son.*

be·gan (bi gan′) *v.* pt. of **begin.**

be·gat (bi gat′) *v. Archaic.* a pt. of **beget.**

be·get (bi get′) *v.* **be·got** or (*Archaic*) **be·gat, be·got·ten** or **be·got, be·get·ting. 1** become the father of. **2** cause to be; produce: *Hate begets hate.* [ME *begete(n), begite(n),* alteration of earlier unrecorded *beyiten* (OE *begitan*) under the influence of *gete(n)* get (< ON *geta*)] —**be·get′ter,** *n.*

beg·gar (beg′ər) *n.* **1** a person who makes his living by begging. **2** a very poor person. **3** a fellow: *That dog's a friendly little beggar.* —*v.* **1** bring to poverty: *Your reckless spending will beggar your father.* **2** make to seem poor or useless: *The grandeur of Niagara Falls beggars description.*

beg·gar-lice (beg′ər līs′) *n.sing. or pl.* beggar's-lice.

beg·gar·ly (beg′ər lē) *adj.* fit for a beggar; poor. —**beg′gar·li·ness,** *n.*

beg·gar's-lice (beg′ərz līs′) *n.* **1** (*pl. in use*) burrs or seeds of various plants that stick to clothes. **2** (*pl. or sing. in use*) the weed on which such burrs or seeds grow.

beg·gar's-ticks (beg′ərz tiks′) *n.sing. or pl.* beggar's-lice.

beg·gar-ticks (beg′ər tiks′) *n.sing. or pl.* beggar's-lice.

beg·gar·y (beg′ər ē) *n.* a condition of great poverty.

be·gin (bi gin′) *v.* **be·gan, begun, be·gin·ning. 1** do the first part; start: *Let's begin. She began to speak.* **2** do the first part of: *I began reading the book yesterday.* **3** come into being: *The club began two years ago.* **4** bring into being: *Two brothers began the club ten years ago.* **5** be near; come near: *That suit doesn't even begin to fit you.* [OE *beginnan*]

Syn. 1 Begin, commence, start = to get something going. **Begin** is the general word: *We will begin work soon.* **Commence** is formal and applies particularly to beginning a formal action: *The dedication ceremonies will commence at two o'clock.* **Start** emphasizes taking the first step in doing something, setting about doing it: *At last they have started building that hotel.* **3** arise, originate.

☛ **Begin** is followed by *at* when the meaning is "start from": *Let us begin at the third chapter.* It is followed by *on* or *upon* when the meaning is "set to work at": *We must begin on the government survey tomorrow.* When the meaning is "take first in an order of succession," the idiom is *begin with*: *We always begin with the hardest problems.*

be·gin·ner (bi gin′ər) *n.* **1** a person who is doing something for the first time; a person who lacks skill and experience. **2** a person who begins anything. —**Syn. 1** amateur.

be·gin·ning (bi gin′ing) *n.* **1** a start: *make a good beginning.* **2** the time when anything begins: *"In the beginning God created the heaven and the earth."* **3** the first part. **4** a first cause; source; origin.
—*adj.* **1** that begins; first in order: *a beginning course.* **2** for beginners: *a beginning dictionary.* **3** who is just starting: *a beginning student.* —**Syn.** *n.* **1** initiation.

be·girt (bi gėrt′) *adj.* surrounded; encircled.

be·gone (bi gon′) *interj. v.* be gone; go away; depart: *"Begone!" the old lady cried out to the tramp in her garden.*

be·go·ni·a (bi gō′nē ə or bi gōn′yə) *n.* a tropical plant having handsome leaves and waxy flowers. [after Michel *Bégon* (1638-1710), a French colonial governor]

be·got (bi got′) *v.* a pt. and a pp. of **beget.**

be·got·ten (bi got′ən) *v.* a pp. of **beget.**

be·grimed (bi grīmd′) *adj.* made grimy; soiled and dirty.

be·grudge (bi gruj′) *v.* **-grudged, -grudg·ing. 1** be reluctant to give (something); grudge: *She is so stingy that she begrudges her dog a square meal.* **2** envy (someone) the possession of: *They begrudge us our new house.* —**be·grudg′ing·ly,** *adv.*

be·guile (bi gīl′) *v.* **-guiled, -guil·ing. 1** deceive; cheat: *His pleasant ways beguiled me into thinking that he was my friend.* **2** take away from deceitfully or cunningly. **3** entertain; amuse. **4** pass or while away (time) pleasantly. —**be·guil′er,** *n.* —**Syn. 1** delude. **4** See **while.**

be·guil·ing (bi gīl′ing) *adj.* **1** deceiving. **2** entertaining; amusing. —**be·guil′ing·ly,** *adv.*

be·gum (bē′gəm) *n.* in India, a Moslem queen, princess, or lady of high rank. [< Hind. *begam*]

be·gun (bi gun′) *v.* pp. of **begin.**

be·half (bi haf′) *n.* **1** side; interest; favor: *His friends will act in his behalf.* **2 in behalf of,** in the interest of; for: *He worked for weeks in behalf of the Community Chest.* **3 on behalf of, a** as a representative of: *The lawyer spoke convincingly on behalf of his client.* **b** in behalf of. [ME *behalve* beside, on the side of]

be·have (bi hāv′) *v.* **-haved, -hav·ing. 1** conduct (oneself): *The little boy behaves himself badly in school. The ship behaves well.* **2** act well; do what is right: *Did you behave today?* **3** act: *Water behaves in different ways when it is heated and when it is frozen.* [< *be-* + *have*]

☞ **behave.** In speaking to or of children, *behave* = behave properly or use good manners: *Did you behave at the party, Mary?* Otherwise, *behave,* meaning act or conduct oneself in a certain way, is ordinarily modified by a qualifying word: *He behaved well in spite of his boredom.*

be·hav·ior or **be·hav·iour** (bi hāv′yər) *n.* **1** a way of acting; actions; acts: *His sullen behavior showed that he was angry.* **2** manners; deportment. —**Syn. 1** See **conduct.**

be·hav·ior·al or **be·hav·iour·al** (bē hāv′yər əl) *adj.* of or having to do with behavior: *Sociology and psychology are behavioral sciences.*

be·hav·ior·ism or **be·hav·iour·ism** (bi hāv′yər iz′əm) *n.* the theory that the objectively observed acts of persons and animals are the chief or only subject matter of scientific psychology.

be·hav·ior·ist or **be·hav·iour·ist** (bi hāv′yər ist) *n.* a person who believes in behaviorism.

be·hav·ior·is·tic or **be·hav·iour·is·tic** (bi hāv′yər is′tik) *adj.* having to do with behaviorists or behaviorism.

be·hav·iour (bi hāv′yər) *n.* behavior.

be·head (bi hed′) *v.* cut off the head of.

be·held (bi held′) *v.* pt. and pp. of **behold.**

be·he·moth (bi hē′məth or bē′ə məth) *n.* **1** in the Bible, a huge and powerful animal, possibly the hippopotamus. Job 40:15-24. **2** any large and powerful person or animal. **3** something that is especially large and powerful. [< Hebrew *b'hēmōth,* pl. of *b'hēmah* beast]

be·hest (bi hest′) *n.* a command or order. [OE *behǣs* promise]

be·hind (bi hīnd′) *prep.* **1** at the back of; in the rear of: *The child hid behind the door.* **2** at or on the far side of: *A beautiful valley lies behind the hill.* **3** concealed by: *Treachery lurked behind the spy's smooth manner.* **4** inferior to; less advanced than: *He is behind other boys in his class.* **5** later than; after: *The milkman is behind his usual time today.* **6** remaining after: *The dead man left a family behind him.* **7** in support of; supporting: *His friends are behind him.*
—*adv.* **1** at or toward the back; in the rear: *The dog's tail hung down behind.* **2** farther back in place or time: *The rest of the hikers are still far behind.* **3** in reserve: *More supplies are behind.* **4** not on time; slow; late: *The train is behind today.*
—*n.* the part of the body used in sitting; the rear end; seat. [OE *behindan* < *be-* by + *hindan* from behind]
Syn. *prep.* **1, 2 Behind, after** express a relation in which one thing is thought of as following another. **Behind** always suggests standing at the back of, and is used chiefly to express position in space, but sometimes to express time when one thing is thought of as being and staying in the rear: *The workmen are far behind schedule in erecting the new school.* **After** suggests moving in succession or being in a definite order, in either place or time: *His dog ran after him. He came after school.*

be·hind·hand (bi hīnd′hand′) *adv. adj.* **1** behind time; late. **2** behind others in progress; backward; slow. **3** in debt; in arrears.

be·hold (bi hōld′) *v.* **be·held, be·hold·ing,** *interj.* **1** see; look at. **2** look; take notice. [OE *behealdan*] —**be·hold′er,** *n.* —**Syn.** *v.* **1** observe.

hat, āge, cãre, fär; let, ēqual, tėrm; it, īce
hot, ōpen, ôrder; oil, out; cup, pu̇t, rüle, ūse
əbove, takən, pencəl, lemən, circəs
ch, child; ng, long; sh, ship
th, thin; ᴛʜ, then; zh, measure

be·hold·en (bi hōl′dən) *adj.* under an obligation or in debt to somebody: *I am much beholden to you for your help.*

be·hoof (bi hüf′) *n. Archaic.* use; advantage; benefit: *The father toiled for his children's behoof.* [OE *behōf* need]

be·hoove (bi hüv′) *v.* **-hooved, -hoov·ing. 1** be necessary for: *It behooves you to work hard if you want to keep this job.* **2** be proper for: *It behooves a child to obey his parents.* [OE *behōfian* to need]

be·hove (bi hōv′) *v.* **-hoved, -hov·ing.** behoove.

beige (bāzh) *n. adj.* pale brown; brownish gray. [< F]

be·ing (bē′ing) *n.* **1** a person; living creature: *human beings.* **2** life; existence: *A new era came into being.* **3** nature; constitution: *Her whole being thrilled to the beauty of the music.* —*adj.* existing; present: *All is well for the time being.*

be·jew·el (bi jü′əl) *v.* **-elled** or **-eled, -el·ling** or **-el·ing.** adorn with jewels, or as if with jewels: *The sky is bejewelled with stars.*

be·la·bor or **be·la·bour** (bi lāb′ər) *v.* **1** beat vigorously: *The man belabored his poor donkey.* **2** abuse; ridicule.

be·lat·ed (bi lāt′id) *adj.* **1** delayed; too late: *The belated letter has arrived at last.* **2** overtaken by darkness: *The belated travellers lost their way in the mountains.* —**be·lat′ed·ly,** *adv.* —**be·lat′ed·ness,** *n.*

be·lay (bi lā′) *v.* **be·layed, be·lay·ing. 1** fasten (a rope) by winding it around a pin or cleat. **2** *Informal.* stop. [OE *belecgan*]

belaying pin a pin around which ropes can be wound and fastened.

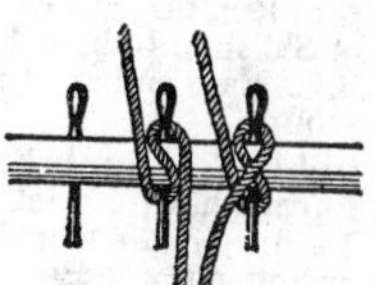

Belaying pins with ropes on them

bel canto (bel kän′tō) in music, a style of singing marked by fullness and breadth of tone and the display of great technical skill. It originated in Italy in the 17th century. [< Ital. *bel canto,* literally, fine singing]

belch (belch) *v.* **1** expel gas from the stomach through the mouth. **2** throw out with force: *The volcano belched fire and smoke.* —*n.* the act of belching. [cf. OE *bealcian*] —**belch′er,** *n.*

bel·dam or **bel·dame** (bel′dəm) *n.* **1** an old woman. **2** an ugly old woman; hag. [< *bel-* grand- (< OF *bel, belle* fair) + *dam* dame < OF *dame*]

be·lea·guer (bi lē′gər) *v.* **1** besiege. **2** surround: *He was so beleaguered with debts that he was forced into bankruptcy.* [< Du. *belegeren* < *leger* camp]

bel·fry (bel′frē) *n.pl.* **-fries. 1** a tower for a bell or bells. **2** a room, cupola, or turret in which a bell or bells may be hung. [ME *berfrey* < OF *berfrei* < Gmc.]

Belg. 1 Belgium. **2** Belgian.

Bel·gian (bel′jən) *adj.* of or having to do with Belgium or its people. —*n.* a native or inhabitant of Belgium.

Belgian hare a large, reddish-brown rabbit.

Be·li·al (bē′lē əl or bēl′yəl) *n.* **1** the Devil. **2** in Milton's poem *Paradise Lost,* a fallen angel.

be·lie (bi lī′) *v.* **-lied, -ly·ing. 1** give a false idea of; misrepresent: *Her frown belied her usual good nature.* **2** show to be false; prove to be mistaken. **3** fail to come up to; disappoint: *He stole again, and so belied our hopes.* [OE *belēogan*]

be·lief (bi lēf′) *n.* **1** what is held to be true; something believed; opinion: *the beliefs of one's church.* **2** an acceptance as true or real: *a belief in ghosts.* **3** faith; trust: *He expressed his belief in the boy's honesty.* **4** a particular religious faith: *What is your belief?* [ME *bileafe* < OE]
Syn. 1 Belief, faith, conviction = what is held true. **Belief** is the

general word: *His belief in superstition gets him into trouble.* **Faith** applies to a belief without proof, based on one's trust in a person or thing: *I have faith in his ability to succeed.* **Conviction** applies to a firm belief based on one's own certainty after one has been convinced by someone or something. *It is my conviction that he will succeed.*

be·lieve (bi lēv′) *v.* **-lieved, -liev·ing. 1** accept as true or real: *We all believe that the earth revolves.* **2** have faith (in a person or thing); trust. **3** think somebody tells the truth: *His friends believe him.* **4** have religious belief. **5** think; suppose. [ME *bileve(n)* < OE] —**be·liev′a·ble,** *adj.* —**be·liev′a·ble·ness,** *n.*

be·liev·er (bi lēv′ər) *n.* **1** a person who believes. **2** a follower of some religion.

be·like (bi līk′) *adv. Archaic.* very likely; probably; perhaps.

be·lit·tle (bi lit′əl) *v.* **-tled, -tling. 1** cause to seem little, unimportant, or less important; speak slightingly of: *Jealous people belittled the explorer's great discoveries.* **2** make small. —**be·lit′tler,** *n.* —**be·lit′tling·ly,** *adv.* —**Syn. 1** depreciate, disparage.

bell[1] (bel) *n.* **1** a hollow metal cup that makes a musical sound when struck by a clapper or a hammer. **2** the sound of a bell. **3** on shipboard, the stroke of a bell every half hour to tell time. 1 bell = 12:30, 4:30, or 8:30; 2 bells = 1:00, 5:00, or 9:00; and so on up to 8 bells = 4:00, 8:00, or 12:00. **4** anything shaped like a bell. **5 ring a bell,** evoke a response.
—*v.* **1** put a bell on. **2** swell out like a bell. **3 bell the cat,** take on oneself a dangerous role for the common good. [OE *belle*] —**bell′-like′,** *adj.*

bell[2] (bel) *v. n.* bellow; roar; cry. [OE *bellan*]

Bel·la Bel·la (bel′ə bel′ə) *n., pl.* **-la** or **-las. 1** a group of Wakashan Indians living on the southern part of the British Columbia coast. **2** a member of this group. **3** the language of this group.

Bel·la Coo·la (bel′ə kü′lə) *n., pl.* **-la** or **-las. 1** a group of Salishan Indians living near Queen Charlotte Sound, B.C. **2** a member of this group. **3** the language of this group.

bel·la·don·na (bel′ə don′ə) *n.* **1** a poisonous plant of Europe having black berries and red, bell-shaped flowers. **2** a drug made from this plant and used as an anodyne or antispasmodic; atropine. [< Ital. *belladonna,* literally, fair lady]

belladonna lily amaryllis.

bell-bot·tom (bel′bot′əm) *adj.* of trousers, having the bottoms of the legs flared like a bell.

bell-bot·tomed (bel′bot′əmd) *adj.* bell-bottom.

bell·boy (bel′boi′) *n.* a man or boy whose work is carrying hand baggage and doing errands for the guests of a hotel or club.

bell buoy a buoy with a bell that is rung by the movement of the waves.

belle (bel) *n.* **1** a beautiful woman or girl. **2** the prettiest or most admired woman or girl: *the belle of the ball.* [< F *belle,* fem. of *beau.* See BEAU.]

Bel·leek (bə lēk′) *n.* a kind of thin, delicate porcelain having a multicolored glaze. [< *Belleek,* a town in Northern Ireland, where this porcelain is made]

Bel·ler·o·phon (bə ler′ə fon′) *n.* in Greek legend, a hero who killed a dreadful monster, the chimera, with the help of the winged horse Pegasus.

belles-let·tres (bel′let′rə) *n.pl.* the finer forms of literature; literature as a fine art. [< F]

bell·flow·er (bel′flou′ər) *n.* a plant having bell-shaped flowers; campanula.

bell glass a bell-shaped container or cover made of glass.

bell·hop (bel′hop′) *n. Slang.* bellboy.

bel·li·cose (bel′ə kōs′) *adj.* warlike; fond of fighting. [< L *bellicosus* < *bellum* war] —**bel′li·cose′ly,** *adv.*

bel·li·cos·i·ty (bel′ə kos′ə tē) *n.* a bellicose quality or attitude.

bel·lig·er·ence (bə lij′ər əns) *n.* **1** a warlike attitude; fondness for fighting. **2** fighting; war.

bel·lig·er·en·cy (bə lij′ər ən sē) *n.* **1** the state of being a belligerent. **2** belligerence.

bel·lig·er·ent (bə lij′ər ənt) *adj.* **1** fond of fighting; warlike. **2** at war; engaged in war; fighting. **3** having to do with nations or persons at war. —*n.* a nation or person at war. [< L *belligerans, -antis,* ppr. of *belligerare* < *bellum* war + *gerere* wage] —**bel·lig′er·ent·ly,** *adv.* —**Syn.** *adj.* **1** hostile, pugnacious, quarrelsome.

bell jar a bell-shaped container or cover made of glass.

bell·man (bel′mən) *n.* **-men** (-mən). a town crier.

Bel·lo·na (bə lō′nə) *n.* in Roman mythology, the goddess of war; the sister, wife, or, in some cases, daughter of Mars.

bel·low (bel′ō) *v.* **1** roar as a bull does. **2** shout loudly, angrily, or from pain. **3** make a loud, deep noise; roar. —*n.* **1** a roar like a bull's. **2** any noise made by bellowing; deep, roaring noise. [ME *belwe,* akin to OE *bellan* roar and *bylgan* bellow] —**bel′low·er,** *n.*

bel·lows (bel′ōz or bel′əs) *n.pl. or sing.* **1** an instrument for producing a strong current of air, used for blowing fires or sounding an organ. **2** in certain cameras, the folding part behind the lens. [OE *belgas,* pl. of *belg* bag, belly]

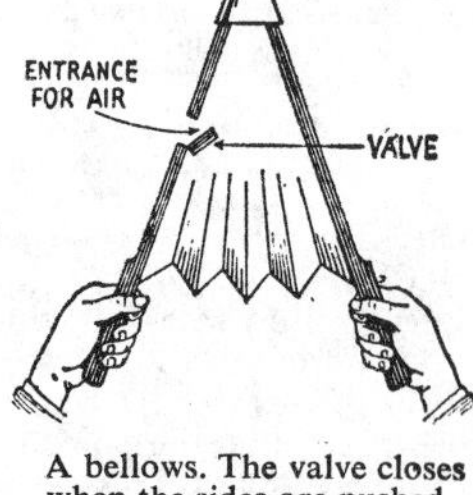

A bellows. The valve closes when the sides are pushed together.

bell·weth·er (bel′weᴛʜ′ər) *n.* **1** a male sheep that wears a bell and leads the flock. **2** any leader, especially of a group thought to resemble sheep in lack of foresight, intelligence, etc.: *a bellwether of the mob.* **3** any person, group, or thing thought of as setting a standard or pattern: *Our riding is considered the political bellwether for the rest of the province.*

bel·ly (bel′ē) *n.* **-lies,** *v.* **-lied, -ly·ing.** —*n.* **1** the lower part of the human body that contains the stomach and bowels; abdomen. **2** the under part of an animal's body. **3** the stomach. **4** the bulging part of anything. —*v.* swell out; bulge: *The ship's sails bellied in the wind.* [ME *bely* < OE *belg, belig* bag]

bel·ly·ache (bel′ē āk′) *n. v.* **-ached, -ach·ing.** *Informal.* —*n.* **1** a pain in the abdomen. **2** an excuse for complaining; grievance. —*v.* complain or grumble, especially over trifles. —**bel′ly·ach′er,** *n.*

bel·ly·band (bel′ē band′) *n.* a strap around the middle of an animal's body to keep a saddle, harness, etc. in place.

bel·ly·flop (bel′ē flop′) *v. n.* **-flopped, -flop·ping.** *Slang.* —*v.* **1** ride prone on a sleigh, with the stomach downward. **2** in diving, strike the water with the chest, or with the chest and abdomen. —*n.* a dive or sleigh-ride executed in this manner.

be·long (bi long′) *v.* **1** have a proper place: *That book belongs on this shelf.* **2 belong to, a** be the property of. **b** be a part of; be connected with. **c** be a member of. **d** be the duty or concern of: *This responsibility belongs to the club secretary.* [ME *bilonge(n)* < *bi-* by + *longen* belong, ult. < OE *gelang* belonging to]

be·long·ings (bi long′ingz) *n.pl.* the things that belong to a person; possessions.

be·lov·ed (bi luv′id or bi luvd′) *adj.* dearly loved; dear. —*n.* a person who is loved; darling.

be·low (bi lō′) *adv.* **1** in a lower place; to a lower place: *From the airplane we could see the fields below.* **2** on or to a lower floor or deck; downstairs: *The sailor went below.* **3** on earth. **4** in hell. **5** in a book or article, after: *See the note below.*
—*prep.* **1** lower than; under: *below the third floor.* **2** less than; lower in rank or degree than: *four degrees below zero.* **3** unworthy of: *below contempt.* —*adj.* below zero: *It was ten below last night.* [ME *bilogh*e by low] —**Syn.** *prep.* **1** See **under.**

belt (belt) *n.* **1** a strip of leather, cloth, etc. fastened around the body to hold in or support clothes or weapons.

2 any broad strip or band: *a belt of trees.* 3 a region having distinctive characteristics: *The wheat belt is the region where wheat is grown.* 4 a an endless band that moves the wheels and pulleys it passes over. b a similar band used as a conveyor. 5 *Slang.* a blow. 6 **below the belt, a** foul; unfair. b foully; unfairly. 7 **tighten one's belt, a** in time of famine, poverty, etc., go without food. b be thrifty. —*v.* 1 put a belt around. 2 fasten on with a belt. 3 beat with a belt. 4 hit. 5 strike without let-up: *The boxer belted his opponent across the ring.* [OE *belt*, apparently ult. < L *balteus* girdle] —**Syn.** *n.* 3 zone.

Bel·tane (bel′tān) *n.* 1 in Scotland, May 1 (Old Style Calendar). 2 an ancient Celtic May-day celebration. [< Scots Gaelic *bealltainn* May Day, the May festival]

belt·ed (bel′tid) *adj.* 1 having a belt: *a belted jacket.* 2 wearing a special belt as a sign of honor: *a belted earl.* 3 marked by a belt or band of color: *a belted kingfisher.*

belt·ing (bel′ting) *n.* 1 a material for making belts or lining waistbands. 2 belts. 3 a beating.

belt line a railway, bus line, etc. that takes a more-or-less circular route around a city or other special area.

be·lu·ga (bə lü′gə) *n.* 1 a large, white sturgeon of the Black Sea and the Caspian Sea. 2 a large, white dolphin that lives in arctic seas. [def. 1 < Russian *beluga*, def. 2 < Russian *belukha*; both from *bielo-* white]

bel·ve·dere (bel′və dēr′) *n.* a structure, sometimes set high on a building, designed to be open on several sides to afford a wide view. [< Ital. *belvedere* fine view]

B.E.M. British Empire Medal.

be·mire (bi mīr′) *v.* **-mired, -mir·ing.** 1 make dirty with mud. 2 sink in mud.

be·moan (bi mōn′) *v.* 1 moan about; bewail. 2 mourn.

be·mock (bi mok′) *v. Archaic.* mock; mock at.

be·muse (bi mūz′) *v.* **-mused, -mus·ing.** bewilder; confuse; stupefy. —**be·mused,** *adj.* —**be·mus′ed·ly,** *adv.* —**be·muse′ment,** *n.*

bench (bench) *n.* 1 a long seat, usually of wood or stone. 2 the worktable of a carpenter, or of any worker with tools and materials. 3 the seat where judges sit in a law court. 4 a judge or group of judges sitting in a law court. 5 the position of a judge. 6 a law court. 7 in hockey and certain other games: a the place where players sit while not actually taking part in the game. b these players collectively. 8 **on the bench, a** sitting in a law court as a judge. b sitting among the substitute players. 9 a narrow stretch of high, flat land: *Apples are grown on the benches of the Okanagan Valley in British Columbia.* 10 a platform on which dogs are placed for judging at a show. 11 a dog show. —*v.* 1 furnish with benches. 2 assign a seat on a bench. 3 take (a player) out of a game. [OE *benc*]

bench dog a dog exhibited at dog shows.

ben·cher (ben′chər) *n.* 1 a person who sits on a bench, especially a judge, magistrate, etc. 2 in Canada, one of the elected officials of a provincial law society, who, through committees, govern the affairs of the society. 3 in England, one of the senior members governing a society of lawyers and law students called an Inn of Court.

bench mark in surveying, a mark made on a rock, post, etc. as a starting point or guide in a line of levels for determining altitudes.

bench penalty or **bench minor** *Cdn.* in hockey, a minor (two-minute) penalty imposed against a team and served by a player designated by the team's coach or manager.

bench warrant a written order from a judge or law court to arrest a person.

bend[1] (bend) *v.* **bent** or (*Archaic*) **bend·ed, bend·ing,** *n.* —*v.* 1 make, be, or become curved or crooked: *The branch began to bend as I climbed along it.* 2 stoop; bow: *She bent to the ground and picked up a stone.* 3 force to submit. 4 submit: *I bent to his will.* 5 turn in a certain direction; direct (mind or effort): *She bent her mind to the new work.* 6 fasten (a sail, rope, etc.). —*n.* 1 a part that is not straight; curve or turn: *There is a sharp bend in the road here.* 2 a stoop; bow. 3 a knot for tying two ropes together or tying a rope to something else. 4 **the bends,** *Informal.* cramps caused by changing too suddenly from high air pressure to ordinary air pressure. [OE *bendan* bind, band] —**Syn.** *v.* 1 turn, twist, warp. 2 incline. 5 apply. —*n.* 1 crook, angle, twist.

hat, āge, cãre, fär; let, ēqual, tėrm; it, īce
hot, ōpen, ôrder; oil, out; cup, pu̇t, rüle, ūse
əbove, takən, pencəl, lemən, circəs
ch, child; ng, long; sh, ship
th, thin; ᴛʜ, then; zh, measure

bend[2] (bend) *n.* in heraldry, a bar consisting of two parallel lines drawn from the upper right to the lower left of a shield. See **bend sinister.** [OE *bend* strap, influenced by OF *bende* band]

bend·ed (ben′did) —*adj.* bent: *on bended knees.* —*v. Archaic.* a pt. and a pp. of **bend.**

bend·er (ben′dər) *n.* 1 a person or thing that bends. 2 *Slang.* a drinking spree.

bend sinister in heraldry, a bar drawn from the upper left to the lower right of a shield, used as a sign of illegitimacy; baton.

be·neath (bi nēth′) *adv.* below, underneath: *Whatever you drop will fall upon the spot beneath.* —*prep.* 1 below; under; lower than: *The dog sat beneath the tree.* 2 unworthy of; worthy not even of: *A traitor is so low that he is beneath contempt.* [OE *beneothan* < *be-* by + *neothan* below] —**Syn.** *prep.* 1 See **under.**

ben·e·dic·i·te (ben′ə dis′ə tē) *n.* 1 a blessing. 2 **Benedicite, a** a hymn of praise to God. b a musical setting for such a hymn. —*interj.* bless (you, them, etc.). [< L *benedicite*, 2nd person pl. imperative of *benedicere* bless < *bene* well + *dicere* say]

ben·e·dict (ben′ə dikt′) *n.* 1 a recently married man, especially one who was a bachelor for a long time. 2 a married man. Also, **Benedick.** [< *Benedick*, character in Shakespeare's *Much Ado About Nothing*]

Ben·e·dic·tine (ben′ə dik′tēn or ben′ə dik′tin) *adj.* of Saint Benedict (480?-543?), the founder of the first order of monks, or of a religious order following his rule. —*n.* 1 in the Roman Catholic Church, a monk or nun following the rule of Saint Benedict or of the order founded by him. 2 a kind of liqueur. [< F *bénédictin*]

Benedictine rule the set of rules for a plan of life, used in monasteries and convents established by Saint Benedict.

ben·e·dic·tion (ben′ə dik′shən) *n.* 1 the asking of God's blessings at the end of a religious service. 2 a blessing. 3 mercy. [< L *benedictio, -onis* < *benedicere* bless. See BENEDICITE. Doublet of BENISON.]

Ben·e·dic·tus (ben′ə dik′təs) *n.* 1 a short hymn or canticle beginning in English "Blessed is He that cometh in the name of the Lord," taken from Psalm 118:26 and Matt. 21:9. 2 a canticle or hymn beginning in English "Blessed be the Lord God of Israel," Luke 1:68. 3 a musical setting of either of these canticles. [< L *benedictus*, pp. of *benedicere.* See BENEDICITE.]

ben·e·fac·tion (ben′ə fak′shən) *n.* 1 a doing good; kind act. 2 a benefit conferred; gift for charity; help given for any good purpose.

ben·e·fac·tor (ben′ə fak′tər or ben′ə fak′tər) *n.* a person who has helped others, either by gifts of money or by some kind act. [ME < LL *benefactor* < *benefacere* < *bene* well + *facere* do]

ben·e·fac·tress (ben′ə fak′tris or ben′ə fak′tris) *n.* a woman who has helped others, either by gifts of money or by some kind act.

ben·e·fice (ben′ə fis) *n.* a permanent office or position created by ecclesiastical authority. [ME < OF < L *beneficium* benefit < *beneficus* beneficent < *benefacere.* See BENEFACTOR.]

be·nef·i·cence (bə nef′ə səns) *n.* 1 the performance of good deeds. 2 a kindly act; gift. [< L *beneficentia* < *beneficus.* See BENEFICE.]

be·nef·i·cent (bə nef′ə sənt) *adj.* 1 kindly; doing good. 2 having good results: *beneficent acts.*

ben·e·fi·cial (ben′ə fish′əl) *adj.* favorable; helpful; good for; productive of good: *Sunshine and moisture are beneficial to plants.* —**ben′e·fi′cial·ly,** *adv.*

ben·e·fi·ci·ar·y (ben′ə fish′ər ē or ben′ə fish′ē er′ē) *n.* **-ar·ies.** 1 a person who receives benefit: *All the children are beneficiaries of the new playground.* 2 a person who receives or is to receive money or property from an insurance policy, a will, etc.

ben·e·fit (ben′ə fit) *n. v.* **-fit·ed, -fit·ing.** *—n.* **1** anything for the good of a person or thing; an advantage: *Universal peace would be of great benefit to the world.* **2** an act of kindness; a favor. **3** money paid to the sick, disabled, etc. **4** a performance at the theatre, a game, etc. to raise money that goes to a special person or persons or to a worthy cause.
—v. **1** give benefit to; be good for: *Rest will benefit a sick person.* **2** receive good; profit: *He benefited by the medicine. He will benefit from the new way of doing business.* [ME < AF *benfet* < L *benefactum* < *bene-* well + *factum*, pp. of *facere* do] **—Syn.** *n.* **1** profit, help. See **advantage.**

benefit of clergy **1** formerly, the privilege of being tried in church courts instead of regular courts. **2** the services and rites or approval of the church.

Ben·e·lux (ben′ə luks′) *n.* the economic association of Belgium, the Netherlands, and Luxemburg, first organized in 1948 and now part of the European Common Market. [< *Be*lgium, *Ne*therlands, *Lux*emburg]

be·nev·o·lence (bə nev′ə ləns) *n.* **1** good will; kindly feeling. **2** an act of kindness; something good that is done; a generous gift. **3** formerly, a forced loan to an English king. [ME < OF < L *benevolentia* < *bene* well + *velle* wish]

be·nev·o·lent (bə nev′ə lənt) *adj.* kindly; charitable. **—be·nev′o·lent·ly,** *adv.* **—Syn.** generous, bountiful, philanthropic.

Ben·ga·lese (beng′gə lēz′) *n.* **-lese,** *adj.* *—n.* a native of Bengal. *—adj.* of Bengal, its people, or their language.

Ben·ga·li (beng go′lē or beng gô′lē) *adj.* of Bengal, its people, or their language. *—n.* **1** a native of Bengal. **2** the language of Bengal.

ben·ga·line (beng′gə lēn′ or beng′gə lēn′) *n.* a corded silk or rayon cloth with wool or cotton in it. [< F]

be·night·ed (bi nīt′id) *adj.* **1** not knowing right from wrong; ignorant. **2** overtaken by night; being in darkness. [< obsolete verb *benight* < *be-* + *night*]

be·nign (bi nīn′) *adj.* **1** gentle; kindly: *a benign old lady.* **2** favorable; mild: *a benign climate.* **3** in medicine: **a** mild; doing no permanent harm: *benign leukemia.* **b** of tumors, not likely to recur after removal or to spread; not malignant. [ME *benigne* < OF < L *benignus* < *bene* well + *-gnus* born] **—be·nign′ly,** *adv.*
—Syn. 1 gracious. **2** salutary.

be·nig·nan·cy (bi nig′nən sē) *n.* a benignant quality.

be·nig·nant (bi nig′nənt) *adj.* **1** kindly; gracious: *a benignant ruler.* **2** favorable; beneficial.
—be·nig′nant·ly, *adv.*

be·nig·ni·ty (bi nig′nə tē) *n.* **-ties. 1** the quality of kindliness or graciousness. **2** a kind act; favor.

ben·i·son (ben′ə zen or ben′ə sən) *n.* a blessing. [ME < OF *beneison* < L *benedictio, -onis.* Doublet of BENEDICTION.]

Ben·ja·min (ben′jə mən) *n.* **1** in the Bible, the youngest and favorite son of Jacob. **2** one of the twelve tribes of Israel.

bent[1] (bent) *v.* pt. and pp. of **bend.** *—adj.* **1** not straight; curved; crooked. **2** strongly inclined; determined: *He was bent on going home.* *—n.* an inclination; a tendency: *a bent for drawing.* **—Syn.** *adj.* **2** resolved, bound, set. *–n.* penchant, bias.

bent[2] (bent) *n.* **1** any of several fine, very resistant grasses used for lawns and pasture. **2** a stiff, wiry grass that grows on sandy or waste land. **3** *Archaic.* a heath; moor. [OE *beonet-*]

bent grass bent[2] (def. 1).

be·numb (bi num′) *v.* **1** make numb. **2** stupefy; deaden. [OE *benumen*, pp. of *beniman* deprive < *be-* + *niman* take] **—be·numb′ing·ly,** *adv.*

Ben·ze·drine (ben′zə drēn′ or ben′zə drin) *n.* *Trademark.* a drug that causes wakefulness; amphetamine. *Formula:* $C_9H_{13}N$

ben·zene (ben′zēn or ben zēn′) *n.* a colorless, volatile, inflammable liquid that is obtained chiefly from coal tar and is used for removing grease and in making dyes. *Formula:* C_6H_6 [< *benzoin*]

ben·zine (ben′zēn or ben zēn′) *n.* a colorless, volatile, inflammable liquid consisting of a mixture of hydrocarbons obtained in distilling petroleum. It is used in cleaning and dyeing and as a motor fuel. [< *benzoin*]

ben·zo·ate (ben′zō āt′ or ben′zō it) *n.* a salt or ester of benzoic acid. **Benzoate of soda** is used as a food preservative.

ben·zo·ic acid (ben zō′ik) an acid occurring in benzoin, cranberries, etc. that is used as an antiseptic or as a food preservative. *Formula:* C_6H_5COOH

ben·zo·in (ben′zō in) *n.* **1** a fragrant resin obtained from certain species of trees of Java, Sumatra, etc. and used in perfume and medicine. **2** a substance resembling camphor made from this resin. [< F *benjoin* < Sp. or Pg. < Arabic *luban jawi* incense of Java]

ben·zol (ben′zol or ben′zōl) *n.* **1** benzene. **2** a liquid containing about 70 per cent of benzene and 20 to 30 per cent of toluene. It is obtained from coal tar and is used in making dyes.

Be·o·thic (bē oth′ik or bē ot′ik) *n.* **-thic** or **-thics.** Beothuk.

Be·o·thuk (bē oth′ək or bē ot′ək) *n.* **-thuk** or **-thuks. 1** an extinct tribe of North American Indians, the aboriginal inhabitants of Newfoundland. **2** a member of this tribe. The last Beothuk died in 1829. **3** the language of this tribe. Also, **Beothic.**

Be·o·wulf (bā′ə wůlf′) *n.* **1** an Old English epic poem in alliterative verse, probably composed in England about A.D. 700. **2** the hero of this poem.

be·praise (bi prāz′) *v.* **-praised, -prais·ing.** praise greatly; praise too much.

be·queath (bi kwēᴛʜ′ or bi kwēth′) *v.* **1** give or leave (property, etc.) by a will: *The father bequeathed the farm to his son.* **2** hand down to posterity: *One age bequeaths its civilization to the next.* [OE *becwethan* < *be-* to, for + *cwethan* say] **—be·queath′er,** *n.*

be·queath·al (bi kwēᴛʜ′əl) *n.* the act of bequeathing.

be·quest (bi kwest′) *n.* **1** something bequeathed; legacy: *Mr. Quail died and left a bequest of ten thousand dollars to the university.* **2** the act of bequeathing. [ME *biqueste*]

be·rate (bi rāt′) *v.* **-rat·ed, -rat·ing.** scold sharply.
—Syn. upbraid, reprimand.

Ber·ber (bėr′bər) *n.* **1** a people living in N. Africa, west of Egypt. **2** a member of this people. **3** the Hamitic language of this people.

ber·ceuse (bãr sœz′) *n.* *French.* **1** a lullaby. **2** in music, a vocal or instrumental composition.

be·reave (bi rēv′) *v.* **be·reaved** or **be·reft, be·reav·ing. 1** deprive (*of*) ruthlessly; rob: *bereave of hope.* **2** leave desolate. [OE *berēafian* < *be-* away + *rēafian* rob]

be·reaved (bi rēvd′) *adj.* deprived (*of*) by death: *Bereaved of their mother at an early age, the children learned to take care of themselves.*

be·reave·ment (bi rēv′mənt) *n.* **1** the act of bereaving. **2** a bereaved condition: *Everyone sympathized with her in her bereavement.* **3** the loss (of a relative or friend) by death.

be·reft (bi reft′) *adj.* **1** bereaved; deprived: *bereft of hope.* **2** left desolate. *—v.* a pt. and a pp. of **bereave.**

be·ret (bə rā′ or ber′ā) *n.* a soft, round cap of wool, felt, etc. [< F *béret* < Provençal *birret* < LL *birretum.* See BIRETTA.]

berg (bėrg) *n.* iceberg.

ber·ga·mot[1] (bėr′gə mot′) *n.* **1** a pear-shaped variety of orange grown in S. Italy. **2** the tree on which it grows. **3** an oil obtained from its rind, used in perfume. **4** any of various plants of the mint family. [from *Bergamo*, a town in Italy]

ber·ga·mot[2] (bėr′gə mot′) *n.* a kind of pear with a fine flavor. [< F *bergamote* < Ital. *bergamotta* < Turkish *beg-armudi* prince's pear < *beg* prince + *armudi* pear]

Berg·so·ni·an (berg sō′nē ən) *adj.* of or having to do with Henri Bergson (1859-1941), a French philosopher who thought of the universe as being in a continual process of creative evolution. *—n.* a person who supports or believes in the philosophy of Bergson.

be·rib·boned (bi rib′ənd) *adj.* **1** trimmed with many ribbons. **2** decorated with ribbons: *a beribboned general.*

ber·i·ber·i (ber′ē ber′ē) *n.* a tropical disease affecting the nerves, accompanied by weakness, loss of weight, and wasting away. It is probably caused by lack of vitamin B in the diet. [< Singhalese (the lang. of Ceylon) *beriberi,* reduplication of *beri* weakness]

ber·ke·li·um (bėr kē′lē əm) *n.* an artificial, radio-active, metallic element produced by bombarding americium with alpha particles. *Symbol*: Bk; *at.no.* 97; *at.wt.* 249 (most stable isotope). [< *Berkeley,* California (site of the University of California campus where berkelium was first produced)]

Berk·shire (bėrk′shər) *n.* **1** a breed of black-and-white pig. **2** a pig of this breed. [< *Berkshire,* a county in S. England]

ber·lin (bėr lin′ or bėr′lin) *n.* **1** a four-wheeled carriage with two hooded seats and a platform in the rear for footmen. **2** a soft woollen yarn. [from *Berlin,* Germany]

Ber·mu·da onion (ber mū′də) a large, mild onion grown in Bermuda, Texas, California, etc.

Bermuda shorts short trousers that end just above the knee.

ber·ry (ber′ē) *n.* **-ries,** *v.* **-ried, -ry·ing.** —*n.* **1** a small, juicy fruit having many seeds. **2** a dry seed or kernel. Coffee is made from the berries of the coffee plant. **3** a simple fruit with the seeds in the pulp and a skin or rind. Botanists classify grapes, tomatoes, currants, and bananas as berries.
—*v.* **1** gather or pick berries. **2** produce berries. [OE *berie*]

ber·serk (bėr′zėrk or bėr′sėrk, bėr zėrk′ or bėr sėrk′) *adj. adv.* in a frenzy. [< Icelandic *berserkr* (accus. sing. *berserk*) wild warrior < *ber-* bear + *serkr* shirt]

ber·serk·er (bėr′zėr kər or bėr′sėr kər) *n.* a fierce Norse warrior. [< Icelandic *berserkr*]

berth (bėrth) *n.* **1** a place to sleep on a ship, train, or airplane. **2** a ship's place at a wharf. **3** a place for a ship to anchor conveniently or safely. **4** an appointment or position; job. **5** a stand of timber. **6 give a wide berth to,** keep well away from.
—*v.* **1** put in a berth; provide with a berth. **2** have or occupy a berth. [? < *bear*[1]]

ber·tha (bėr′thə) *n.* a woman's wide collar that often extends over the shoulders. [after *Berthe,* mother of Charlemagne]

berth·ing (bėr′thing) *n.* a space to berth a ship, motorboat, etc. in a harbor or beside a pier.

Ber·til·lon system (bėr′tə lon′) a system of identifying persons, especially criminals, by a record of individual measurements and physical peculiarities. Fingerprinting is now the most important part of the system.
[after A. *Bertillon* (1853-1914), the French police officer who introduced the system]

ber·yl (ber′əl) *n.* **1** a very hard clear or cloudy mineral, usually green or greenish-blue, a silicate of beryllium and aluminum. **2** a piece of this stone, or a gem made from it. Emeralds and aquamarines are beryls.
[ME < OF < L < Gk. *bēryllos,* cognate with Skt. *vaidurya* cat's-eye]

be·ryl·li·um (bə ril′ē əm) *n.* a rare metallic element; glucinum. *Symbol*: Be; *at.no.* 4; *at.wt.* 9.0122. [< *beryl*]

B. ès A. Bachelier ès Arts; Bachelor of Arts.

be·seech (bi sēch′) *v.* **-sought** or **-seeched, -seech·ing.** ask earnestly; beg. [ME *biseche(n)* < *be-* thoroughly + *seche(n)* seek] —**be·seech′er,** *n.* —**Syn.** entreat; implore. See **beg.**

be·seech·ing (bi sēch′ing) *adj.* that beseeches.
—**be·seech′ing·ly,** *adv.*

be·seem (bi sēm′) *v.* be proper for; be fitting to: *It does not beseem you to leave your friend without help.*

be·set (bi set′) *v.* **-set, -set·ting. 1** attack on all sides; attack: *In the swamp we were beset by mosquitoes.* **2** surround; hem in: *beset by enemies.* **3** set; stud: *Her bracelet was beset with gems.* [OE *besettan* < *be-* around + *settan* set] —**Syn. 1** besiege. **2** encompass.

be·set·ting (bi set′ing) *adj.* habitually attacking; constantly harassing: *Laziness is a loafer's besetting sin.*

be·shrew (bi shrü′) *v. Archaic.* call down evil upon; curse mildly. [ME *beshrewe(n)*]

hat, āge, cãre, fär; let, ēqual, tėrm; it, īce
hot, ōpen, ôrder; oil, out; cup, pu̇t, rüle, ūse
əbove, takən, pencəl, lemən, circəs
ch, child; ng, long; sh, ship
th, thin; ᴛʜ, then; zh, measure

be·side (bi sīd′) *prep.* **1** by the side of; near; close to: *Grass grows beside the brook.* **2** in addition to: *Other men beside ourselves were helping.* **3** compared with: *Nell seems dull beside her sister.* **4** away from; aside from; not related to: *That question is beside the point.* **5 beside oneself,** out of one's mind; crazy; upset. —*adv.* besides. [OE *be sīdan* by side]

be·sides (bi sīdz′) *adv.* **1** also; moreover; further: *He didn't want to quarrel; besides, he had come to enjoy himself.* **2** in addition: *We tried two other ways besides.* **3** otherwise; else: *He is ignorant of politics, whatever he may know besides.*
—*prep.* **1** in addition to; over and above: *The picnic was attended by others besides our own club members.* **2** except; other than: *We spoke of no one besides you.*

be·siege (bi sēj′) *v.* **-sieged, -sieg·ing. 1** make a long-continued attempt to get possession of (a place) by armed force; surround and try to capture: *For ten years the Greeks besieged the city of Troy.* **2** crowd around: *Hundreds of admirers besieged the famous aviator.* **3** overwhelm with requests, questions, etc.: *During the flood the Red Cross was besieged with calls for help.*
—**be·sieg′er,** *n.*

B. ès L. Bachelier ès Lettres; Bachelor of Letters.

B.E.S.L. British Empire Service League.

be·smear (bi smēr′) *v.* **1** smear over. **2** sully; dishonor: *The lies and half-truths in the newspaper article besmeared the diplomat's reputation.*

be·smirch (bi smėrch′) *v.* **1** make dirty; soil. **2** dim the lustre or purity of; sully: *The greed of a few besmirches the whole group.* —**be·smirch′er,** *n.*

be·som (bē′zəm) *n.* a broom made of twigs. [OE *besma*]

be·sot (bi sot′) *v.* **-sot·ted, -sot·ting. 1** make foolish. **2** stupefy. **3** intoxicate.

be·sot·ted (bi sot′id) *adj.* **1** foolish; infatuated. **2** stupefied. **3** intoxicated.

be·sought (bi sot′ or bi sôt′) *v.* a pt. and a pp. of **beseech.**

be·spake (bi spāk′) *v. Archaic.* a pt. of **bespeak.**

be·span·gle (bi spang′gəl) *v.* **-gled, -gling.** adorn with spangles or anything like them.

be·spat·ter (bi spat′ər) *v.* **1** spatter all over; soil by spattering. **2** slander. —**be·spat′ter·er,** *n.*

be·speak (bi spēk′) *v.* **-spoke** or (*Archaic*) **-spake, -spo·ken** or **-spoke, -speak·ing. 1** engage in advance; order; reserve: *We have bespoken two tickets for the new play.* **2** show; indicate: *A neat appearance bespeaks care.* **3** *Poetic* or *Archaic.* speak to; address.

be·spec·ta·cled (bi spek′tə kəld) *adj.* wearing glasses.

be·spoke (bi spōk′) *v.* a pt. and a pp. of **bespeak.**
—*adj. Esp.Brit.* made-to-order: *bespoke tailoring; a bespoke overcoat.*

be·spread (bi spred′) *v.* **-spread, -spread·ing.** spread over.

be·sprent (bi sprent′) *adj. Poetic.* sprinkled; strewed; scattered. [OE *besprenged,* pp. of *besprengan*]

be·sprin·kle (bi spring′kəl) *v.* **-kled, -kling.** sprinkle all over.

B. ès Sc. Bachelier ès Science; Bachelor of Science.

Bes·se·mer converter (bes′ə mər) a large container for making molten iron into steel by the Bessemer process.

Bessemer process a method of making steel by burning out carbon and impurities in molten iron with a blast of air. [after Sir Henry *Bessemer* (1813-1898), the English engineer who invented the process]

Bessemer steel steel made by the Bessemer process.

best (best) *adj. superlative of* **good. 1** the most desirable, valuable, superior, etc.: *The best food to eat.* **2** of the

greatest advantage, usefulness, etc.: *the best thing to do.* **3** largest: *the best part of a day.* **4** chief: *a best seller.*
—*adv. superlative of* **well**[1]. **1** in the most excellent way; most thoroughly: *Who reads best?* **2** in the highest degree: *I like this book best.* **3 had best,** should; ought to; will be wise to.
—*n.* **1** the best thing or state: *We want the best.* **2** utmost: *I did my best to finish the work on time.*
all for the best, not so bad as it seems.
at best, under the most favorable circumstances.
get the best of, defeat.
have the best of, be superior to; defeat.
make the best of, do as well as possible with.
with the best, as well as anyone.
—*v. Informal.* outdo; defeat: *Our team was bested in the final game.* [OE *betst*]

be·stead (bi sted′) *v.* **-stead·ed, -stead·ed** or **-stead, -stead·ing,** *adj. Archaic.* —*v.* help; assist; serve. —*adj.* placed; situated. [< *be-* + *stead,* v., help]

bes·tial (bes′chəl or best′ē əl) *adj.* **1** beastly; brutal; vile. **2** of beasts. [ME < OF < L *bestialis* < *bestia* beast] —**bes′tial·ly,** *adv.*

bes·ti·al·i·ty (bes′chē al′ə tē or bes′tē al′ə tē) *n.* bestial character or conduct.

be·stir (bi stėr′) *v.* **-stirred, -stir·ring.** stir up; rouse to action: *Please bestir yourselves and put some zest into your work.*

best man the chief attendant of the bridegroom at a wedding.

be·stow (bi stō′) *v.* **1** give (something) as a gift; give; confer: *The king bestowed many benefits on his favorite courtiers.* **2** make use of; apply. **3** *Archaic.* put safely; put; place. **4** *Archaic.* find quarters for; lodge. [ME *bistowe(n)*]

be·stow·al (bi stō′əl) *n.* the act of bestowing.

be·strad·dle (bi strad′əl) *v.* **-dled, -dling.** bestride; straddle.

be·strew (bi strü′) *v.* **-strewed, -strewed** or **-strewn, -strew·ing.** **1** strew; scatter; sprinkle: *The children bestrewed the path with flowers.* **2** strew (things) around; scatter about. **3** lie scattered over. [OE *bestrēowian*]

be·strewn (bi strün′) *adj.* scattered about. —*v.* a pp. of **bestrew.**

be·strid (bi strid′) *v.* a pt. and a pp. of **bestride.**

be·strid·den (bi strid′ən) *v.* a pp. of **bestride.**

be·stride (bi strīd′) *v.* **-strode** or **-strid, -strid·den** or **-strid, -strid·ing.** **1** get on or sit on (something) with one leg on either side: *One can bestride a horse, a chair, or a fence.* **2** stand over something with one leg on each side. **3** stride across; step over. [OE *bestrīdan*]

be·strode (bi strōd′) *v.* a pt. of **bestride.**

best seller **1** anything, especially a book, that has a very large sale. **2** the author of such a book.

bet (bet) *v.* **bet** or **bet·ted, bet·ting,** *n.* —*v.* **1** agree to risk one's money (or anything else) against that of another on the outcome of a doubtful issue: *I bet you a dollar it will snow today.* **2** make a bet. **3 I bet (you), you bet,** *Informal.* certainly; definitely: *"Are you going to the game?" "You bet!"* —*n.* **1** a pledge or promise to give some money or something else to someone if he proves to be right and you wrong. **2** the money or thing promised. **3** a thing to bet on: *That horse is a good bet.* [origin uncertain]

be·ta (bā′tə or bē′tə) *n.* **1** the second letter of the Greek alphabet (Β, β). **2** the second of a series.

be·take (bi tāk′) *v.* **-took, -tak·en, -tak·ing.** **betake oneself, a** go: *betake oneself to the mountains.* **b** try doing; apply (oneself): *He betook himself to hard work.*

be·tak·en (bi tāk′ən) *v.* pp. of **betake.**

beta particle an electron in a stream of electrons.

beta rays a stream of electrons from radium and other radio-active substances.

be·ta·tron (bā′tə tron′ or bē′tə-) *n.* an apparatus in which electrons are accelerated to high speeds by magnetic induction. [< *beta* ray + elec*tron*]

be·tel (bē′təl) *n.* a vine whose leaves are chewed in Asian countries with areca-nut and lime. The areca-nut is often called **betel nut.** [< Port. < Malayalam *vettila*]

Be·tel·geuse (bē′təl jüz′) *n.* a very large reddish star in the constellation Orion. [< F ? < Arabic *bīt-al-jāuza* house of the twins]

bête noire (bet nwär′) a thing or person especially dreaded or detested. [< F *bête noire* black beast]

beth·el (beth′əl) *n.* **1** a holy place. **2** a church or chapel for seamen. [< Hebrew *beth-el* house of God]

be·think (bi thingk′) *v.* **-thought, -think·ing.** **1 bethink oneself, a** consider; reflect. **b** remember. **2** think about; call to mind. [OE *bethencan*]

be·thought (bi thot′ or bi thôt′) *v.* pt. and pp. of **bethink.**

be·tide (bi tīd′) *v.* **-tid·ed, -tid·ing.** **1** happen to: *Woe betide you if you betray us.* **2** happen: *No matter what betides, the family will hold together.* [ME *betiden* < *be-* + *tiden* happen]

be·times (bi tīmz′) *adv. Archaic.* **1** early: *He rose betimes in the morning.* **2** soon; before it is too late. [ME *bitime* by time]

be·to·ken (bi tō′kən) *v.* be a sign or token of; indicate; show: *His smile betokens satisfaction.*

be·took (bi tůk′) *v.* pt. of **betake.**

be·tray (bi trā′) *v.* **1** deliver into the enemy's hands by treachery: *The traitor betrayed his country.* **2** be unfaithful to: *She betrayed her friends.* **3** mislead; deceive. **4** give away (a secret); disclose unintentionally. **5** reveal; show: *His mistakes betrayed his lack of education.* [ME *bitraie(n)* < *be-* (intensive) + *traie(n)* betray < OF < L *tradere* hand over] —**be·tray′er,** *n.*

be·tray·al (bi trā′əl) *n.* a betraying or being betrayed.

be·troth (bi trōᴛʜ′ or bi troth′) *v.* promise in marriage; engage: *He betrothed his daughter to a rich man.* [ME *betrouthe(n),* var. of *betreuthien* < *be-* + *treuthe* < OE *trēowth* pledge]

be·troth·al (bi trōᴛʜ′əl or bi troth′əl) *n.* a promise of marriage; engagement.

be·trothed (bi trōᴛʜd′ or bi trotht′) *n.* a person engaged to be married.

bet·ter[1] (bet′ər) *adj. comparative of* **good. 1** more desirable, useful, etc. than another: *a better plan.* **2** of superior quality: *better bread.* **3** less sick: *The sick child is better today.* **4** larger: *Four days is the better part of a week.*
—*adv. comparative of* **well**[1]. **1** more desirably, usefully, etc.; in a more excellent way: *Do better another time.* **2** in a higher degree; more: *I know her better than anyone else.* **3 better off,** in a better condition: *The theatre was full, and we would have been better off if we had stayed at home watching television.* **4 had better,** should; ought to; would be wise to: *You had better be there on time.* **5 think better of,** think over and change one's mind.
—*n.* **1** a person, thing, or state that is better: *the better of two roads.* **2** Usually, **betters,** *pl.* one's superiors: *Listen to the advice of your betters.* **3 get** or **have the better of,** be superior to; defeat.
—*v.* **1** make or become better: *We can better that work by being more careful.* **2** do better than; surpass: *The other class cannot better our grades.* [OE *betera*]
—**Syn.** *v.* **1** improve. **2** outdo, excel.

bet·ter[2] or **bet·tor** (bet′ər) *n.* a person who bets.

better half *Informal.* wife.

bet·ter·ment (bet′ər mənt) *n.* **1** improvement: *Most men work for the betterment of their position in life.* **2** Usually, **betterments** (*pl. in form and use*). an improvement of real estate property.

bet·ty (bet′ē) *n.* a pudding made of diced bread or toast, fruit, and sweetening: *apple brown betty.*

be·tween (bi twēn′) *prep.* **1** in the space or time separating: *Many cities lie between Halifax and Toronto.* **2** in the range or part separating: *shades between pink and red.* **3** from one to the other of; joining; connecting: *a link between two parts.* **4** involving; concerning; having to do with: *war between two countries.* **5** by the combined action of: *They caught twelve fish between them.* **6** in the combined possession of: *They own the property between them.* **7 between you and me,** as a secret; confidentially.
—*adv.* **1** in the intervening space or time; in an

intermediate position or relation: *We could not see the moon, for a cloud came between.* **2 in between, a** in the middle. **b** in the middle of. [OE *betwēonum* < *be-* by + *twā* two]

☛ **between, among.** Among implies more than two objects: *The money was divided among the four of us.* Properly used, **between** implies only two objects: *The money was divided between my brother and me.*

☛ **between you and me.** Since the object of a preposition is grammatically in the objective case, good English uses the objective case pronouns: *between you and me* (or *between you and her, between you and him, between you and us, between you and them*). ☛ See **among** for another usage note.

be·tween·times (bi twēn′tīmz′) *adv.* at intervals.

be·twixt (bi twikst′) *prep. adv.* **1** between. **2 betwixt and between,** in the middle; neither one nor the other. [OE *betweox*]

Bev or **bev** (bev) *n.* a billion electron volts, used as a measure of energy in nuclear physics. [an acronym for *b*illion *e*lectron *v*olts.]

bev·a·tron (bev′ə tron′) *n.* a high-energy cyclotron. [< *bev* + cyclo*tron*]

bev·el (bev′əl) *n. v.* **-elled** or **-eled, -el·ling** or **-el·ing,** *adj.* —*n.* **1** a sloping edge: *There is often a bevel on a picture frame, on a piece of plate glass, etc.* **2** an instrument for drawing angles or for adjusting the surfaces of work to a particular angle.
—*v.* cut a square edge to make a sloping edge; cause to slope
—*adj.* slanting; oblique. [? < OF]

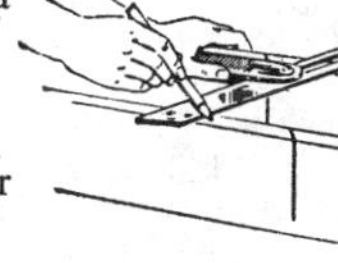

A bevel (def. 2)

bev·er·age (bev′ər ij or bev′rij) *n.* a liquid used or prepared for drinking. *Examples*: milk, tea, coffee, beer, and wine. [ME < OF *bevrage* < *bevre* drink < L *bibere*]

beverage room *Cdn.* beer parlor.

bev·y (bev′ē) *n.* **bev·ies.** a small group: *a bevy of quail, a bevy of girls.* [ME *bevey* ? < AF *bevee* a drinking group]

be·wail (bi wāl′) *v.* mourn; weep; weep for; complain of.

be·ware (bi wãr′) *v.* be on one's guard against; be careful. [< *be* + *ware*]

☛ **Beware** is a formal word for "be careful." It is followed by *of* or by *lest, how,* or *that . . . not* introducing a subordinate clause: *Beware of the sharpers at the fair. They were told to beware lest they wake him. We must beware how we approach him. Beware that you do not anger him. Beware* is sometimes followed directly by its object: *Beware the dog.*

be·wil·der (bi wil′dər) *v.* confuse completely; perplex: *The little girl was bewildered by the crowds. Difficult problems in arithmetic bewilder me.* [< *be-* + OE *wilder* lead astray] —**Syn.** See **puzzle.**

be·wil·der·ing (bi wil′dər ing) *adj.* perplexing; puzzling; confusing. —**be·wil′der·ing·ly,** *adv.*

be·wil·der·ment (bi wil′dər mənt) *n.* a bewildered condition; complete confusion; perplexity.

be·witch (bi wich′) *v.* **1** put under a spell; use magic on; *The wicked magician bewitched the princess, and she fell into a long sleep.* **2** charm; delight; fascinate: *We were all bewitched by our pretty little cousin.* —**be·witch′er,** *n.*
—**Syn. 2** enchant, captivate.

be·witched (bi wicht′) *adj.* **1** under the influence of magic. **2** charmed; delighted; fascinated.

be·witch·ing (bi wich′ing) *adj.* fascinating; delightful; charming. —**be·witch′ing·ly,** *adv.*

be·wray (bi rā′) *v. Archaic.* reveal; make known. [ME *bewreie(n)* < *be-* + *wreie(n)* < OE *wrēgan* accuse]

bey (bā) *n.* **beys. 1** in Turkey, the governor of a province. **2** a Turkish title of respect for a person of rank. **3** formerly, a ruler of Tunisia. [< Turkish *beg*]

be·yond (bi yond′) *prep.* **1** on or to the farther side of: *He lives beyond the sea.* **2** farther on than: *The school is beyond the last house on this street.* **3** later than: *They stayed beyond the time set.* **4** out of the reach, range, or understanding of: *The dying man was beyond help.* **5** more than; exceeding: *The price of the suit was beyond what he could pay.* **6** in addition to; besides: *I will do nothing beyond the job given me.*
—*adv.* farther away: *Beyond were the hills.*
—*n.* **the beyond** or **the great beyond,** life after death. [OE *begeondan* < *be-* at, near + *geondan* beyond]

hat, āge, cãre, fär; let, ēqual, tėrm; it, īce
hot, ōpen, ôrder; oil, out; cup, pu̇t, rüle, ūse
əbove, takən, pencəl, lemən, circəs
ch, child; ng, long; sh, ship
th, thin; ᴛʜ, then; zh, measure

bez·el (bez′əl) *n.* **1** a slope or sloping edge. **2** the sloping sides or faces of a cut jewel. **3** a grooved ring that holds a jewel in its setting. [< OF form of F *biseau*]

be·zique (bə zēk′) *n.* a card game resembling pinochle. [< F *bésigue,* origin uncertain]

B.F. Bachelor of Forestry.

bf. boldface (type).

B.F.A. Bachelor of Fine Arts.

bg. *pl.* **bgs.** bag.

Bha·ga·vad Gi·ta (bag′ə vəd gē′tə) a philosophical dialogue embodied in the *Mahabharata,* an ancient Sanskrit epic. [< Skt. *Song of the Blessed One*]

bhang (bang) *n.* **1** a variety of hemp growing in India. **2** a preparation of dried hemp leaves and seed cases smoked or eaten as a narcotic and intoxicant. [< Hind. < Skt. *bhanga* hemp]

bi- *prefix.* **1** twice, as in *biannual, bimonthly.* **2** doubly, as in *bipolar, biconcave.* **3** two, as in *bicuspid, bilateral.* **4** having two, as in *bicarbonate, bichloride.* [< L]

Bi bismuth.

bi·an·nu·al (bī an′ū əl) *adj.* occurring twice a year.

☛ **biannual, biennial. Biannual** = occurring twice a year; *biennial* = occurring once in two years: *Our doctor recommends a biannual visit to the dentist. The senior students are taking the biennial intelligence test this afternoon.*

bi·an·nu·al·ly (bī an′ū əl ē) *adv.* twice a year.

bi·as (bī′əs) *n. adj. adv. v.* **bi·assed** or **bi·ased, bi·as·sing** or **bi·as·ing.** —*n.* **1** a slanting or oblique line. Cloth is cut on the bias when it is cut diagonally across the weave. **2** an opinion formed without adequate reason; a leaning of the mind. **3** in bowling: **a** the lopsided shape of a ball that makes it swerve when rolled. **b** the weight or force that makes it swerve.
—*adj.* slanting across the threads of cloth; oblique; diagonal.
—*adv.* obliquely.
—*v.* influence, usually unfairly; prejudice. [< F *biais* slant < VL *biaxius* having a double axis]
—**Syn.** *n.* **2** inclination, bent, partiality. See **prejudice.**

bi·assed or **bi·ased** (bī′əst) *adj.* favoring one side too much; warped or prejudiced.

bi·ax·i·al (bī ak′sē əl) *adj.* having two axes (ak′sēz): *a biaxial crystal.* —**bi·ax′i·al·ly,** *adv.*

bib (bib) *n. v.* **bibbed, bib·bing.** —*n.* **1** a cloth worn under the chin, especially by babies and small children to protect their clothing. **2** the part of an apron above the waist. **3** anything similar to a bib in purpose or design.
—*v.* drink; tipple. [ME < *bib* drink, ? < L *bibere*]

Bib. 1 Bible. **2** Biblical.

bib and tucker *Informal.* clothes.

bib·cock (bib′kok′) *n.* a tap having a nozzle bent downward.

bi·be·lot (bib′lō; *French,* bē blō′) *n.* a small object valued for its beauty, rarity, or interest. [< F]

Bi·ble (bī′bəl) *n.* **1** the collection of sacred writings belonging to the Christian religion and comprising the Old and New Testaments. **2** the Old Testament in the form used by the Jews. **3 bible,** any book accepted as an authority. [ME < OF < Med.L < Gk. *biblia,* pl. dim. of *biblos* book]

☛ **Bible,** referring to the Christian scriptures, is capitalized: *You will find it in the Bible.* Bible in the sense of an authoritative book is not capitalized: *"Smith's Manual," the botanist's bible, was most useful to the medical students.*

Bib·li·cal or **bib·li·cal** (bib′lə kəl) *adj.* **1** of the Bible. **2** according to the Bible. —**Bib′li·cal·ly** or **bib′li·cal·ly,** *adv.*

biblio- *combining form.* book; books: *bibliophile = a lover of books.* [< Gk. *biblion* book]

bib·li·og·ra·pher (bib′lē og′rə fər) *n.* an expert in bibliography.

bib·li·o·graph·ic (bib′lē ə graf′ik) *adj.* bibliographical.

bib·li·o·graph·i·cal (bib′lē ə graf′ə kəl) *adj.* of bibliography. —**bib′li·o·graph′i·cal·ly,** *adv.*

bib·li·og·ra·phy (bib′lē og′rə fē) *n.* **-phies. 1** a list of books, articles, etc. about a subject or person. **2** a list of books, articles, etc. by a certain author. **3** a study of the authorship, editions, dates, etc. of books, articles, etc.

bib·li·o·ma·ni·a (bib′lē ō mā′nē ə) *n.* a craze for collecting books.

bib·li·o·ma·ni·ac (bib′lē ō mā′nē ak′) *n.* a person who has a craze for collecting books.

bib·li·o·phil (bib′lē ə fil′) *n.* bibliophile.

bib·li·o·phile (bib′lē ə fīl′) *n.* a lover of books, especially one who likes to collect books.

bib·u·lous (bib′yu̇ ləs) *adj.* **1** fond of drinking alcoholic liquor. **2** absorbent. —**bib′u·lous·ly,** *adv.* —**bib′u·lous·ness,** *n.* [< L *bibulus* < *bibere* drink]

bi·cam·er·al (bī kam′ər əl) *adj.* having or consisting of two legislative assemblies: *The Canadian Parliament is bicameral; it has both a Senate and a House of Commons.* [< *bi-* two + L *camera* chamber < Gk. *kamara*]

bi·car·bo·nate (bī kär′bə nit or bī kär′bə nāt′) *n.* a salt of carbonic acid that contains a base and hydrogen.

bicarbonate of soda sodium bicarbonate.

bice (bīs) *n.* **1** a kind of green paint. **2** a kind of blue paint. [< F *bis*]

bi·cen·ten·ar·y (bī′sen ten′ər ē or bī′sen tē′nə rē) *adj. n.* **-nar·ies.** —*adj.* having to do with a period of 200 years. —*n.* **1** a period of 200 years. **2** a 200th anniversary. **3** its celebration.

bi·cen·ten·ni·al (bī′sen ten′ē əl or bī′sen tē′nē əl) *adj.* **1** having to do with a period of 200 years. **2** recurring every 200 years. —*n.* **1** a 200th anniversary. **2** its celebration.

bi·ceps (bī′seps) *n.* **1** any muscle having two heads or origins: **a** the large muscle in the front part of the upper arm. **b** the large muscle in the back of the thigh: *His biceps are well developed.* **2** *Informal.* muscular strength, especially in the upper arm. [< L *biceps* two-headed < *bi-* two + *caput* head]

☛ **Biceps** is singular in its strict technical use, but is popularly thought of and used as both a plural and a collective noun.

bi·chlo·rid (bī klô′rid) *n.* bichloride.

bi·chlo·ride (bī klô′rīd or bī klô′rid) *n.* **1** a compound containing two atoms of chlorine combined with another element or radical. **2** bichloride of mercury.

bichloride of mercury an extremely poisonous, white substance, used in solution as an antiseptic, in medicine, and in dyeing. *Formula*: $HgCl_2$

bi·chro·mate (bī krō′māt) *n.* a salt containing two atoms of chromium combined with another element or radical.

bick·er (bik′ər) *v.* **1** quarrel. **2** babble; patter. **3** flash; flicker. —*n.* **1** a quarrel. **2** a babble; patter. [ME *biker(en)*]

bi·col·ored or **bi·col·oured** (bī′kul′ərd) *adj.* having two colors: *bicolored roses.*

bi·con·cave (bī′kon′kāv or bī′kon kāv′) *adj.* concave on both sides.

bi·con·vex (bī′kon′veks or bī′kon veks′) *adj.* convex on both sides.

bi·cul·tur·al (bī kul′chər əl) *adj.* **1** having two distinct cultures existing side by side in the same country, province, etc. **2** in Canada, having to do with the coexistence of English and French cultures.

bi·cul·tur·al·ism (bī kul′chər əl iz′əm) *n.* **1** the fact or condition of being bicultural. **2** a policy that favors a country, province, etc. being bicultural. **3** the practice or support of such a policy.

bi·cus·pid (bī′kus′pid) *n.* a double-pointed tooth. A human adult has eight bicuspids. See **tooth** for picture. —*adj.* having two points. [< *bi-* two + L *cuspis, -pidis* point]

bi·cy·cle (bī′sə kəl) *n., v.* **-cled, -cling.** —*n.* a vehicle consisting of a metal frame with two wheels, handles for steering, and a seat for the rider. An ordinary bicycle has pedals; a motor bicycle has an engine. —*v.* ride a bicycle. [< F *bicycle* < *bi-* two (< L *bis*) + Gk. *kyklos* circle, wheel] —**bi′cy·cler,** *n.*

☛ **bicycle, bike.** Informal speech generally uses the shortened form *bike.*

bi·cy·clist (bī′sə klist) *n.* a bicycle rider; cyclist.

b.i.d. of medicine, (take) twice a day. [for L *bis in die*]

bid (bid) *v.* **bade, bad,** or **bid, bid·den** or **bid, bid·ding** (*for 1, 2, 5, 6, 10*), **bid, bid·ding.** (*for 3, 4, 7, 8, 9*). *n.* —*v.* **1** command: *Do as I bid you.* **2** say or tell: *His friends came to bid him good-bye.* **3** offer: *She bid five dollars for the table.* **4** offer a price; state a price: *Several companies will bid for the contract.* **5 bid fair,** seem likely; have a good chance: *The plan bids fair to succeed.* **6** proclaim; declare: *He bade defiance to them all.* **7** in some card games, state as what one proposes to make or to win. **8 bid in,** at an auction, overbid on behalf of the owner with the intention of keeping the article unsold. **9 bid up,** raise the price of something by bidding more. **10** invite. —*n.* **1** a bidding. **2** an offer. **3** the amount offered: *My bid was $7.* **4** the amount bid in a card game. **5** an attempt to secure, achieve, etc.: *He made a bid for our sympathy.* **6** *Informal.* an invitation. [OE *biddan* ask; meaning influenced by OE *bēodan* offer] —**Syn.** *v.* **1** order, direct. **3** proffer, tender.

☛ In the sense "command," now somewhat archaic, **bid** in the active voice is usually followed by an infinitive without *to*: *You bade me forget what is unforgettable.* With the passive *to* is used: *They were bidden to assemble.*

bid·da·ble (bid′ə bəl) *adj.* **1** obedient; docile. **2** that is suitable to bid on in card games.

bid·den (bid′ən) *v.* a pp. of **bid.** —*adj.* invited.

bid·der (bid′ər) *n.* **1** a person who bids. **2** a person who offers to pay a certain price at an auction.

bid·ding (bid′ing) *n.* **1** a command. **2** an invitation. **3** the offers at an auction. **4** in card games, the bids collectively. **5 do someone's bidding,** obey someone.

bid·dy[1] (bid′ē) *n.* a hen. [? imitative]

biddy[2] (bid′ē) *n.* a talkative old woman. [Anglo-Irish *Biddy,* dim. of *Bridget*]

bide (bīd) *v.* **bode** or **bid·ed, bid·ed, bid·ing.** *Archaic* except in def. 5. **1** dwell; abide. **2** continue; wait. **3** wait for. **4** bear; endure; suffer. **5 bide one's time,** wait for a good chance. [OE *bīdan*]

bi·den·tate (bī den′tāt) *adj.* having two teeth.

bi·en·ni·al (bī en′ē əl) *adj.* **1** of plants, lasting two years. **2** occurring every two years. —*n.* **1** any plant that lives two years. Carrots and onions are biennials. **2** an event that occurs every two years. [< L *biennium* < *bi-* two + *annus* year] —**bi·en·ni·al·ly,** *adv.* ☛ See **biannual** for usage note.

bier (bēr) *n.* a movable stand on which a coffin or dead body is placed. [OE *bēr* < *beran* bear[1]]

biff (bif) *n. v. Slang.* hit; slap. [probably imitative]

bif·fy (bif′ē) *n. Slang. Esp.Cdn.* **1** a toilet. **2** a bathroom. [origin uncertain]

bi·fid (bī′fid) *adj.* divided into two parts by a cleft. [< L *bifidus* < *bi-* two + *fid-* base of *findere* cleave]

bi·fo·cal (bī fō′kəl) *adj.* having two focuses: *Bifocal glasses have two parts: the upper part for far vision, the lower for near vision.* —*n.* **1** Usually, **bifocals,** *pl.* a pair of glasses having bifocal lenses. **2** a bifocal lens.

Bif·rost (bēf′rost) *n.* in Norse mythology, the rainbow bridge between heaven and earth.

bi·fur·cate (*v.* bī′fər kāt′ or bī fėr′kāt; *adj.* bī′fər kāt′ or bī fėr′kit) *v.* **-cat·ed, -cat·ing,** *adj.* —*v.* divide into two branches. —*adj.* divided into two branches; forked. [< Med.L *bifurcatus* < L *bifurcus* < *bi-* two + *furca* fork]

bi·fur·ca·tion (bī′fər kā′shən) *n.* **1** a splitting into two parts. **2** the place where the split occurs.

big (big) *adj.* **big·ger, big·gest,** *adv.* —*adj.* **1** great in extent, amount, size, etc.; large: *a big room, a big book, big business.* **2** grown up: *a big girl.* **3** *Informal.* important; great: *This is big news.* **4** full; loud: *a big voice.* **5** boastful: *big talk.* **6 big with child,** pregnant. —*adv. Informal.* boastfully: *He talks big.* [ME] —**big′ness,** *n.* —**Syn.** *adj.* **1** huge, extensive, immense. See **great.**

big·a·mist (big′ə mist) *n.* a person guilty of bigamy.

big·a·mous (big′ə məs) *adj.* **1** guilty of bigamy. **2** involving bigamy. —**big′a·mous·ly,** *adv.*

big·a·my (big′ə mē) *n.* the fact or state of having two wives or two husbands at the same time. [ME < OF *bigamie* < *bigame* < Med.L *bigamus* < *bi-* twice + Gk. *gamos* married]

Big Ben (ben) in London, England, a huge bell in the clock tower of the Houses of Parliament.

Big Bertha *Informal.* **1** in World War I, a long-range gun used by the Germans to fire on Paris. **2** any powerful artillery gun. **3** anything large or of great range for its kind.

Big Brother a tyrannical dictator or government whose subjects are kept constantly under secret observation. [after the dictator, who is frequently mentioned, but never appears, in George Orwell's novel *1984*]

Big Dipper a group of stars in the constellation of Ursa Major.

Big Four the United States, the United Kingdom, France, and the Soviet Union.

big game **1** large animals sought by hunters. Elephants, tigers, and lions are big game. **2** a very important thing that is sought.

big·head (big′hed′) *n.* **1** any of several diseases of animals, especially sheep, characterized by swelling about the head. **2** infectious sinusitis in turkeys. **3** also **big head,** *Informal.* **a** a swelled head; conceit. **b** a conceited or arrogant person.

big-heart·ed (big′här′tid) *adj.* kindly; generous.

big·horn (big′hôrn′) *n.* the wild sheep of the Rocky Mountains, having thick, gracefully curved horns.

bight (bīt) *n.* **1** a long curve in a coastline, mountain range, etc. **2** a bay[1]. **3** a bend; angle; corner. **4** a loop of rope; the slack of rope between the fastened ends. **5** the width of sewing-machine stitch selected for making a buttonhole. [OE *byht*]

big·no·ni·a (big nō′nē ə) *n.* a vine having showy, trumpet-shaped orange flowers; trumpet vine. [< NL, named after Abbé *Bignon*, librarian to Louis XIV]

big·ot (big′ət) *n.* a bigoted person; an intolerant, prejudiced person. [< F]

big·ot·ed (big′ət id) *adj.* sticking to an opinion, belief, party, etc. unreasonably and without tolerating other views; intolerant. —**big′ot·ed·ly,** *adv.*

big·ot·ry (big′ət rē) *n.* **-ries.** bigoted conduct or attitude; intolerance. —**Syn.** prejudice.

big shot *Slang. n.* an important person; a big wheel. —**big′shot′,** *adj.*

big time *Slang.* in public affairs, the arts, sports, etc., the top level of advancement or achievement. —**big′time′,** *adj.*

big wheel *Informal.* an influential or otherwise important person, especially in a particular activity, industry, etc.: *a big wheel in hockey, in automobile manufacturing, etc.*

big·wig (big′wig′) *n. Informal.* an important person.

bi·jou (bē′zhü) *n.* **-joux** (-zhüz). **1** a jewel. **2** something small and fine. [< F]

bi·ju·gate (bī′jù gāt′ or bī jü′gāt) *adj.* in botany, having two pairs of leaflets. [< *bi-* two + L *jugatus* yoked]

bike (bīk) *n. v.* **biked, bik·ing.** *Informal.* bicycle. [< *bicycle*]

bi·ki·ni (bi kē′nē) a scanty two-piece swim suit for women. [< *Bikini*, an atoll in the Marshall Islands in the W. Pacific Ocean, site of a series of U.S. atomic bomb tests]

bi·la·bi·al (bī lā′bē əl) *adj.* **1** having two lips. **2** formed by both lips. —*n.* a sound formed by both lips: *The bilabials in English are* b, p, *and* m.

bi·la·bi·ate (bī lā′bē āt′ or bī lā′bē it) *adj.* in botany, having an upper and lower lip.

bi·lat·er·al (bī lat′ər əl) *adj.* **1** having two sides. **2** on two sides. **3** affecting or influencing two sides. —**bi·lat′er·al·ly,** *adv.*

bil·ber·ry (bil′ber′ē or bil′bər ē) *n.* **-ries.** **1** an edible berry much like a blueberry. **2** the shrub that it grows on. [apparently Scand.; cf. Danish *böllebær*]

hat, āge, cãre, fär; let, ēqual, tėrm; it, īce
hot, ōpen, ôrder; oil, out; cup, pùt, rüle, ūse
əbove, takən, pencəl, lemən, circəs
ch, child; ng, long; sh, ship
th, thin; ᴛʜ, then; zh, measure

bil·bo (bil′bō) *n.* **-boes.** *Archaic.* **1** Usually, **bilboes,** *pl.* a long iron bar with sliding shackles and a lock, formerly used to confine the feet of prisoners. **2** a sword. [apparently short for *Bilboa*, English name for Bilbao, a Spanish town, famous for its ironworks and steel]

bile (bīl) *n.* **1** a bitter, yellow or greenish liquid secreted by the liver and stored in the gall bladder. It aids digestion in the small intestine by neutralizing acids and emulsifying fats. **2** ill humor; anger. [< F < L *bilis*]

bilge (bilj) *n. v.* **bilged, bilg·ing.** —*n.* **1** the lowest part of a ship's hold; bottom of a ship's hull. **2** bilge water. **3** the bulging part of a barrel. **4** *Informal.* nonsense. —*v.* **1** break in (the bottom of a ship). **2** spring a leak in the bilge. **3** come to rest or settle on the bilge. **4** bulge; swell out. [origin uncertain]

bilge water the dirty water that collects by seeping or leaking in the bottom of a ship or boat.

bil·i·ar·y (bil′ē er′ē) *adj.* **1** of bile. **2** carrying bile. **3** caused by trouble with the bile; bilious.

bi·lin·e·ar (bī lin′ē ər) *adj.* of, having to do with, or involving two lines.

bi·lin·gual (bī ling′gwəl) *adj.* **1** able to speak one's own language and another equally or almost equally well. **2** containing or written in two languages. **3** in Canada, **a** speaking both French and English. **b** written in both French and English: *The Government plans to introduce bilingual cheques.* —*n.* a bilingual person. [< L *bilinguis* speaking two languages < *bi-* two + *lingua* language] —**bi·lin′gual·ly,** *adv.*

bi·lin·gual·ism (bī ling′gwə liz′əm) *n.* **1** the ability to speak one's own language and another equally or almost equally well. **2** in Canada, the ability to speak both French and English. **3** the principle that two languages should enjoy equal status in a country, province, etc.

bil·ious (bil′yəs) *adj.* **1** having to do with bile. **2** suffering from or caused by some trouble with the bile or the liver: *a bilious person, a bilious attack.* **3** peevish; cross; bad-tempered. [< L *biliosus* < *bilis* bile] —**bil′ious·ly,** *adv.* —**bil′ious·ness,** *n.*

bilk (bilk) *v.* **1** avoid payment of. **2** defraud; cheat; deceive. —*n.* **1** a fraud; deception. **2** a person who avoids paying his bills; petty swindler. [origin uncertain] —**bilk′er,** *n.*

bill[1] (bil) *n.* **1** an amount of money owed for work done or things supplied; an account: *Pay your bills promptly.* **2** a piece of paper money: *a dollar bill.* **3** a written or printed public notice; advertisement; poster; handbill. **4** a written or printed statement; list of items. **5** a theatre program. **6** the entertainment in a theatre. **7** a proposed law presented to a lawmaking body. In Canada, a bill becomes an act after it has received a majority vote in Parliament and been given royal assent. **8** a bill of exchange. **9** a written request or complaint presented to a court. **10** **fill the bill,** *Informal.* satisfy requirements. **11** **foot the bill,** *Informal.* pay; settle the bill. —*v.* **1** send a bill to. **2** enter in a bill; charge in a bill. **3** announce by bills or public notice. **4** post bills in or on. **5** list on a theatrical program. [ME *bille*, Anglo-L *billa*, alteration of Med.L *bulla* document, seal, bull[2]. See BULL[2].] —**bill′er,** *n.* —**Syn.** *n.* **1** invoice. **3** placard, circular, bulletin.

bill[2] (bil) *n.* **1** the horny mouth of a bird; beak. **2** anything shaped like a bird's bill: *the bill of a turtle.* —*v.* **1** join beaks; touch bills. **2** show affection. **3** **bill and coo,** kiss, caress, and talk as lovers do. [OE *bile*]

bill[3] (bil) *n.* **1** a spear with a hook-shaped blade. **2** a billhook; tool for pruning or cutting. [OE *bil*]

bil·la·bong (bil′ə bong′) *n.* in Australia: **1** a branch of a river flowing away from the main stream. **2** a backwater; stagnant pool. [native Australian name < *billa* river + *bung* dual]

bill·board (bil′bôrd′) *n.* a board for posting advertisements or notices on.

billed (bild) *adj.* having a bill or beak.

bil·let[1] (bil′it) *n. v.* **-let·ed, -let·ing.** —*n.* **1** a written order to provide board and lodgings, especially for a soldier. **2** a place where someone, especially a soldier, is assigned to be lodged. **3** a job; position.
—*v.* assign to quarters by billet: *Soldiers were billeted in all the houses in the village.* [ME *billette,* dim. of *bille* bill[1]]

bil·let[2] (bil′it) *n.* **1** a thick stick of wood. **2** a bar of iron or steel. [< F *billette,* dim. of *bille* log, tree trunk]

bil·let-doux (bil′ē dü′; *French,* bē′ye dü′) *n.* **bil·lets-doux** (bil′ē düz′; *French,* bē′ye dü′) a love letter. [< F]

bill·fold (bil′fōld′) *n.* a folding pocketbook for money, papers, etc.; wallet.

bill·head (bil′hed′) *n.* **1** a sheet of paper with the name and the address of a business firm printed at the top, used in making out bills. **2** the name and address of a business firm printed at the top of a sheet of paper.

bill·hook (bil′hůk′) *n.* a tool for pruning or cutting.

bil·liard (bil′yərd) *adj.* of or for billiards. —*n.* in billiards, a score made by striking one ball so that it hits the other two; carom.

bil·liards (bil′yərdz) *n.* a game played with two white balls and a red one on a special table. A long stick called a cue is used to hit the balls. [< F *billard(s),* dim. of *bille* log, tree trunk]

bill·ing (bil′ing) *n.* **1** on a playbill or similar advertisement: **a** the order in which the names of the performers, acts, etc. are listed. **b** the position in such a listing: *Some actresses always demand top billing.* **2** a listing of the total amount of goods and services owed by a client or customer.

bil·lings·gate (bil′ingz gāt′) *n.* vulgar, abusive language. [< *Billingsgate,* a fish market in London, England]

bil·lion (bil′yən) *n. adj.* **1** in Canada, the United States, and France, a thousand million; 1,000,000,000. **2** in Great Britain and Germany, a million million; 1,000,000,000,000. [< F *billion* < *bi-* two (i.e., to the second power) + mil*lion* million]

bil·lion·aire (bil′yən ãr′) *n.* **1** a person who has a billion dollars, francs, marks, etc. **2** an extremely wealthy person.

bil·lionth (bil′yənth) *adj.* the last in a series of a billion. —*n.* one of a billion equal parts.

bill of attainder formerly, an act of a lawmaking body that deprives a person of property and civil rights because of a sentence of death or outlawry.

bill of exchange a written instruction to pay a certain sum of money to a specified person or to his order.

bill of fare a list of the articles of food served at a meal or of those that can be ordered; menu.

bill of goods **1** a shipment of merchandise. **2 sell a bill of goods,** *Slang.* mislead or seek to mislead.

bill of health **1** a certificate stating whether or not there are infectious diseases on a ship or in a port. It is given to a captain when his ship sails. **2 clean bill of health, a** a bill of health showing absence of infectious diseases. **b** *Informal.* a clean record; a favorable report.

bill of lading a receipt given by a shipping or express company, etc. showing a list of goods delivered to it for transportation.

bill of rights **1** a statement of the fundamental rights of the people of a nation. **2 Bill of Rights, a** in Canada, a statement of human rights and fundamental freedoms enacted by Parliament in 1960. **b** in the United Kingdom, a declaration of rights and liberties, which also established the succession to the throne, enacted under William III in 1689. **c** in the United States, the first ten amendments to the Constitution.

bill of sale a written statement transferring ownership of something from the seller to the buyer.

bil·low (bil′ō) *n.* **1** a great wave or surge of the sea. **2** any great wave: *billows of smoke.* —*v.* **1** rise or roll, as big waves. **2** swell out; bulge. [< ON *bylgja*]

bil·low·y (bil′ō ē) *adj.* **-low·i·er, -low·i·est. 1** rising or rolling in big waves. **2** swelling out; bulging.

bill·post·er (bil′pōs′tər) *n.* a workman who puts up advertisements or notices in public places.

bil·ly[1] (bil′ē) *n.* **-lies.** a club; stick: *Policemen carry billies.* [< *billet*[2]]

bil·ly[2] (bil′ē) *n.* **-lies.** billycan.

bil·ly·can (bil′ē kan′) *n.* a can for boiling water or for holding hot liquids. [< native Australian *billa-* water + E *can*]

billy goat *Informal.* a male goat.

bil·tong (bil′tong) *n.* in South Africa, strips of dried lean meat of antelope, buffalo, etc. [< Afrikaans *biltong* < *bil* buttock + *tong* tongue]

bi·me·tal·lic (bī′mə tal′ik) *adj.* **1** using two metals. **2** of bimetallism; based on bimetallism.

bi·met·al·lism (bī met′əl iz′əm) *n.* the use of both gold and silver as the basis of the money system of a nation. The amount in weight of each metal necessary to make coins having the same money value is fixed by law.

bi·mo·lec·u·lar (bī mə lek′yə lər) *adj.* having to do with, or formed from, two molecules.

bi·month·ly (bī munth′lē) *adj. n.* **-lies,** *adv.*
—*adj.* **1** happening once every two months. **2** happening twice a month. —*n.* a magazine published bimonthly. —*adv.* **1** once every two months. **2** twice a month.

bin (bin) *n.* a box or enclosed place for holding grain, coal, etc. —*v.* put or store in a bin. [OE *binn*]

bi·na·ry (bī′nə rē) *adj.* consisting of two; involving two; dual. [< L *binarius* < *bini* two at a time]

binary digit the basic unit of information in a digital computing system, specifying a choice between two possibilities; bit.

binary scale a numerical system having a base of 2 rather than 10, so that 1 of the ordinary scale is expressed as 1, 2 as 10, 3 as 11, 4 as 100, and so on. It is used especially in digital computers.

binary star a pair of stars that revolve around a common centre of gravity.

bi·nate (bī′nāt) *adj.* in botany, growing in pairs; double. [< NL *binatus* < L *bini* two at a time]

bin·aur·al (bin ôr′əl or bīn ôr′əl) *adj.* **1** of, for, or having to do with both ears: *a binaural stethoscope.* **2** of or having to do with two speakers, etc.; stereophonic: *binaural broadcasting.* **3** having two ears.

bind (bīnd) *v.* **bound, bind·ing,** *n.* —*v.* **1** tie together; hold together; fasten: *She bound the package with a bright ribbon.* **2** stick together. **3** hold by some force; restrain. **4** hold by a promise, love, duty, etc.; oblige: *in duty bound to help.* **5** put under legal obligation: *bound over to keep the peace.* **6** put under legal obligation to serve as an apprentice: *bound out to be a carpenter.* **7** put a bandage on: *bind up a wound.* **8** put a band or wreath around. **9** put a border or edge on to strengthen. **10** tie up for the sake of appearance or convenience: *She bound her hair with red ribbons.* **11** fasten (sheets of paper) into a cover; put a cover on (a book): *The pages were bound into a small book.* **12** constipate. **13 bind hand and foot, a** tie up thoroughly. **b** restrict or constrain without choice or freedom: *The strict contract bound us hand and foot.*
—*n.* **1** anything that binds or ties. **2** in music, a slur; tie. **3** *Informal.* something annoying; a nuisance. [OE *bindan*] —**Syn.** *v.* **1** connect, attach. **4** obligate, constrain.

bind·er (bīn′dər) *n.* **1** a person who binds. **2** anything that ties or holds together. **3** a cover for holding loose sheets of paper together. **4** a machine that cuts grain and ties it in bundles.

binder twine a strong, coarse string used especially for binding up grain into sheaves.

bind·er·y (bīn′dər ē or bīn′drē) *n.* **-er·ies.** a place where books are bound.

bind·ing (bīn′ding) *n.* **1** the covering of a book. **2** a strip protecting or ornamenting an edge: *Binding is used on the seams of dresses.* **3** the foot fastenings on a ski.

—*adj.* **1** that binds, fastens, or connects. **2** having force or power to hold to some agreement, pledge, etc. obligatory. **—bind′ing·ly,** *adv.*

binding energy the energy necessary to break a particular atomic nucleus into its smaller component parts.

bin·dle (bin′dəl) *n. Slang.* a bundle of clothing, toilet articles, etc., usually tied to a stick carried by a hobo over his shoulder. [? < *bundle*]

bin·dle·stiff (bin′dəl stif′) *n. Slang.* a hobo.

bind·weed (bīnd′wēd′) *n.* a plant having long runners that twine around the stems of other plants.

binge (binj) *n. Slang.* **1** a heavy drinking session. **2** a bout or spree of indulgence in anything. [< dial. E *binge* to soak]

bin·go (bing′gō) *n.* **1** a game in which each player covers the numbers on his card as they are read out by a caller. **2** a public affair where large numbers of people play bingo for prizes. [origin uncertain]

bin·na·cle (bin′ə kəl) *n.* a box or stand that contains a ship's compass, placed near the man who is steering. [alteration of *bittacle* < Sp. *bitácula* or Pg. *bitácola* < L *habitaculum* dwelling place < *habitare* dwell]

bin·o·cle (bin′ə kəl) *n.* a telescope or field glass for both eyes.

bi·noc·u·lar (bə nok′yů lər or bī nok′yů lər) *adj.* **1** using both eyes. **2** for both eyes. —*n.* **binoculars,** *pl.* field glasses or opera glasses. See **field glasses** for picture. [< L *bini* two at a time + *oculi* eyes].

bi·no·mi·al (bī nō′mē əl) *adj.* consisting of two terms. —*n.* an expression or name consisting of two terms: *8a + 2b is a binomial. "Homo sapiens" is a binomial.* [< LL *binomius* having two names + *bi-* two + *nomen* name] **—bi·no′mi·al·ly,** *adv.*

binomial theorem in mathematics, an algebraic system, invented by Sir Isaac Newton, for raising a binomial to any power. *Example*:

$$(a + b)^2 = a^2 + 2ab + b^2$$

bi·nom·i·nal (bī nom′ə nəl) *adj.* having or using two names. Scientific classification by genus and species uses a binominal system.

bio- *combining form.* **1** life; living things: *biology = the science of life.* **2** biological: *biochemistry = biological chemistry.*

bi·o·chem·i·cal (bī′ō kem′ə kəl) *adj.* having to do with biochemistry. **—bi·o·chem′i·cal·ly,** *adv.*

bi·o·chem·ist (bī′ō kem′ist) *n.* an expert in biochemistry.

bi·o·chem·is·try (bī′ō kem′is trē) *n.* the chemistry of living animals and plants; biological chemistry.

bi·o·de·grad·a·ble (bī′ō di grā′də bəl) *adj.* that is able to be decomposed by bacterial action: *biodegradable detergents. Plastics are not biodegradable.*

bi·o·dyne (bī′ə dīn′) *n.* a substance, produced by an injured cell, that aids recovery by promoting growth, reproduction, etc. It is similar in effect to a hormone. [< *bio-* + *-dyne* < Gk. *dynamis* power]

biog. 1 biographical. **2** biography.

bi·o·gen·e·sis (bī′ō jen′ə sis) *n.* **1** the theory that living things can be produced only by other living things. **2** the production of living things from other living things.

bi·o·ge·net·ic (bī′ō jə net′ik) *adj.* of or having to do with biogenesis.

bi·og·ra·pher (bī og′rə fər) *n.* a person who writes a biography.

bi·o·graph·ic (bī′ə graf′ik) *adj.* biographical.

bi·o·graph·i·cal (bī′ə graf′ə kəl) *adj.* **1** of a person's life. **2** having to do with biography. **—bi′o·graph′i·cal·ly,** *adv.*

bi·og·ra·phy (bī og′rə fē) *n.* **-phies. 1** the written story of a person's life. **2** the part of literature that consists of biographies.

bi·o·log·ic (bī′ə loj′ik) *adj.* biological.

bi·o·log·i·cal (bī′ə loj′ə kəl) *adj.* **1** of plant and animal life. **2** having to do with biology. —*n.* a drug prepared from animal tissue or some other living source. **—bi′o·log′i·cal·ly,** *adv.*

hat, āge, cãre, fär; let, ēqual, tėrm; it, īce
hot, ōpen, ôrder; oil, out; cup, pu̇t, rüle, ūse
əbove, takən, pencəl, lemən, circəs
ch, child; ng, long; sh, ship
th, thin; ᴛʜ, then; zh, measure

biological warfare the waging of war by using disease germs, bacteria, etc. against the enemy.

bi·ol·o·gist (bī ol′ə jist) *n.* an expert in biology.

bi·ol·o·gy (bī ol′ə jē) *n.* **1** the science of life or living matter in all its forms and phenomena; the study of the origin, reproduction, structure, etc. of plant and animal life. **2** the plant and animal life of a particular area or region. **3** the biological facts about a particular plant or animal. **4** a textbook or handbook dealing with biology.

bi·o·me·chan·ics (bī′ō mə kan′iks) *n.* the science that deals with the effects of forces on a living organism, especially the effects of gravity.

bi·o·met·rics (bī′ə met′riks) *n.* biometry (def. 2).

bi·om·e·try (bī om′ə trē) *n.* **1** the calculation of the probable duration of human life. **2** the branch of biology that deals with living things by measurements and statistics. [< Gk. *bios* life + E *-metry*]

bi·o·phys·i·cal (bī′ō fiz′ə kəl) *adj.* of or having to do with biophysics.

bi·o·phys·i·cist (bī′ō fiz′ə sist) *n.* an expert in biophysics.

bi·o·phys·ics (bī′ō fiz′iks) *n.* the study of biology in relation to the laws of physics.

bi·op·sy (bī′op sē) *n.* **-sies.** the surgical removal of a sample of tissue from a living body for examination and diagnosis. [< *bio-* + Gk. *opsis* a viewing]

bi·o·sphere (bī′əs fēr′) *n.* the region round the earth that can support life.

bi·ot·ic (bī ot′ik) *adj.* of or having to do with life or living things. [< Gk. *biōtikos* < *bios* life]

bi·o·tin (bī′ə tin) *n.* in food chemistry, a crystalline acid of the vitamin B family. It promotes growth and is found in liver, eggs, and yeast. *Formula*: $C_{10}H_{16}N_2O_3S$ [< Gk. *biotos* life + E *-in*]

bi·o·tite (bī′ə tīt′) *n.* black or dark-colored mica. [after J. B. *Biot*, French mineralogist]

bip·a·rous (bip′ər əs) *adj.* **1** of animals, bringing forth two at a birth. **2** of flower clusters, having two axes or branches. [< *bi-* two + L *parere* to produce + E *-ous*]

bi·par·ti·san (bī pär′tə zən or bī pär′tə zan′) *adj.* of or representing two political parties: *a bipartisan foreign policy.*

bi·par·tite (bī pär′tīt) *adj.* **1** having two parts. **2** in botany, divided into two parts nearly to the base: *a bipartite leaf.* [< L *bipartitus*, pp. of *bipartire* < *bi-* two + *partire* divide]

bi·par·ty (bī′pär′tē) *adj.* combining two different political groups, religious groups, etc.

bi·ped (bī′ped) *n.* an animal having two feet. Birds are bipeds. —*adj.* having two feet. [< L *bipes* < *bi-* two + *pes, pedis* foot]

bi·pet·al·ous (bī pet′əl əs) *adj.* in botany, having two petals.

bi·pin·nate (bī pin′āt) *adj.* in botany, doubly pinnate. A leaf with leaflets on each side of a stalk is pinnate; a pinnate leaf with pinnate leaflets is bipinnate.

bi·plane (bī′plān′) *n.* an airplane having two wings, one above the other

bi·po·lar (bī pō′lər) *adj.* **1** having two poles. **2** of or at both poles.

bi·ra·cial (bī rā′shəl) *adj.* of or having to do with two races: *a biracial community.*

birch (bėrch) *n.* **1** a slender tree whose smooth bark peels off in thin layers. The Indians used a type of birch bark to cover the framework of their canoes. **2** its close-grained wood, often used in making furniture. **3** a bundle of birch twigs or a birch stick, used for flogging. —*v.* whip with a birch; flog. [OE *bierce*]

bird (bėrd) *n.* **1** any of a group of warm-blooded vertebrates having a body covered with feathers and the forelimbs modified to form wings by means of which most kinds fly. **2** a bird hunted for sport; game bird. **3** *Informal.* a person. **4** *Slang.* a ballistic missile. **5** a shuttlecock. **6** a clay pigeon. **7 bird in the hand,** something certain because one already has it. **8 birds of a feather,** people of the same kind. **9 kill two birds with one stone,** get two things done by one action. **10 the bird,** a jeering or ridiculing. [OE *bridd,* bird] —**bird′like′,** *adj.*

bird·bath (bėrd′bath′) *n.* a shallow basin raised off the ground and filled with water for birds to bathe in or drink.

bird·brain (bėrd′brān′) *n. Slang.* a shallow, foolish person.

bird call 1 the sound that a bird makes. **2** an imitation of it. **3** an instrument for imitating the sound that a bird makes.

bird dog a dog trained to find or bring back birds that a hunter has shot.

bird·ie (bėr′dē) *n.* **1** a little bird. **2** in golf, a score of one stroke less than par for any hole on a golf course.

bird·lime (bėrd′līm′) *n. v.* **-limed, -lim·ing.** —*n.* a sticky substance smeared on trees to catch small birds. It is often made from the inner bark of holly or mistletoe. —*v.* **1** smear with birdlime; lime. **2** catch (birds) with birdlime.

bird·man (bėrd′man′) *n.* **-men** (-men′). *Informal.* **1** an aviator. **2** a person who catches or sells birds; fowler. **3** one who studies birds; ornithologist.

bird of ill omen 1 a person who is always bringing bad luck. **2** an unlucky person.

bird of paradise a bird of New Guinea noted for its magnificent plumage.

bird of passage 1 a bird that flies from one region to another as the seasons change. **2** *Informal.* a person who roams from place to place.

bird of peace a dove.

bird of prey any of a group of birds that eat flesh, including eagles, hawks, owls, and vultures.

bird·seed (bėrd′sēd′) *n.* **1** a mixture of small seeds fed to caged birds. **2** seed put outside for wild birds.

bird's-eye (bėrdz′ī′) *adj.* **1** seen from above or from a distance; general: *You can get a bird's-eye view of the city from an airplane.* **2** having markings somewhat like bird's eyes. **Bird's-eye maple** is a wood used in making furniture.
—*n.* **1** a cotton cloth having markings that resemble bird's eyes. **2** any of various plants having small, round, bright-colored flowers. A primrose is a bird's-eye.

bird shot a small size of lead shot, used in shooting birds.

bird-watch (bėrd′woch′) *v.* observe and study wild birds in their natural surroundings. [back formation < *bird watcher*]

bird watcher a person who observes and studies wild birds in their natural surroundings.

bird watching the observation and study of wild birds in their natural surroundings.

bi·reme (bī′rēm) *n.* in ancient times, a ship with two rows of oars on each side, one above the other. [< L *biremis* < *bi-* two + *remus* oar]

bi·ret·ta (bə ret′ə) *n.* a stiff, square cap with three upright projecting pieces, worn by Roman Catholic priests on certain occasions. [< Ital. *berretta* < LL *birretum* cap, dim. of L *birrus* cloak]

A biretta

birl (bėrl) *v.* **1** rotate a log in the water by moving the feet while standing on it. **2** spin rapidly. —**birl·er,** *n.* [< *birr,* influenced by *whirl*]

birr (bėr) *n. v.* **birred, birr·ing.** —*n.* *Esp.Scottish.* **1** the force of the wind or of something moving; momentum. **2** vigor. **3** a whirring sound. —*v.* make or move with a whirring sound. [< ON *byrr* favoring wind]

birth (bėrth) *n.* **1** a coming into life; a being born: *the birth of a child.* **2** a beginning or origin: *the birth of a nation.* **3** a bringing forth: *the birth of a plan.* **4** natural inheritance: *a musician by birth.* **5** descent; family: *He was a man of humble birth.* **6** noble family or descent: *He is a man of birth and breeding.* **7** that which is born; something produced. **8 give birth to, a** bear; bring forth. **b** be the origin or cause of. [ME *birthe,* probably < ON *burthr*] —**Syn. 5** parentage, extraction.

birth control 1 the control of the birthrate by artificial means. **2** the use of contraceptive methods or devices.

birth·day (bėrth′dā′) *n.* **1** the day on which a person is born. **2** the day on which something began: *July 1, 1867, was the birthday of Canada.* **3** the anniversary of the day on which a person was born, or on which something began.

birthday honors or **honours** in the United Kingdom, the titles and decorations awarded annually by the sovereign on his or her official birthday.

birth·mark (bėrth′märk′) *n.* a congenital spot or mark on the skin.

birth·place (bėrth′plās′) *n.* **1** the place where a person was born. **2** the place of origin.

birth rate the proportion of the number of births per year to the total population or to some other stated number.

birth·right (bėrth′rīt′) *n.* the rights belonging to a person because he is the eldest son, or because he was born in a certain country, or because of any other circumstance about his birth.

birth·stone (bėrth′stōn′) *n.* a jewel associated with a certain month of the year. It is supposed to bring good luck when worn by a person born in that month.

bis (bis) *adv.* **1** twice; again; encore. **2** in music, a direction to repeat a passage. [< L *bis*]

bis·cuit (bis′kit) *n.* **-cuits** or, rarely, **-cuit,** *adj.* —*n.* **1** a kind of bread baked in small, soft cakes, made with baking powder, soda, or yeast. **2** a cracker. **3** pottery or china that has been fired (baked) once but not yet glazed. **4** a pale brown. —*adj.* pale-brown. [< OF *bescuit* < *bes* twice (< L *bis*) + *cuit,* pp. of *cuire* cook < L *coquere*]

bi·sect (bī sekt′) *v.* **1** divide into two parts. **2** divide into two equal parts. [< *bi-* two + L *sectus,* pp. of *secare* cut]

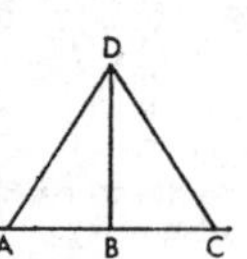

The line DB bisects the angle ADC.

bi·sec·tion (bī sek′shən) *n.* **1** the act of bisecting. **2** the place of bisecting. **3** one of two equal parts.

bi·sec·tor (bī sek′tər) *n.* a line that bisects something.

bi·sex·u·al (bī sek′shü əl) *adj.* **1** of or having to do with both sexes. **2** combining both male and female organs or characteristics in one individual plant or animal. —*n.* a plant or animal that is bisexual.

bi·sex·u·al·ism (bī sek′shü ə liz′əm) *n.* a bisexual condition or quality.

bish·op (bish′əp) *n.* **1** in certain Christian churches, a clergyman of high rank who has certain spiritual duties and who administers the religious affairs of a district called a diocese. **2** in chess, one of two pieces held by each player. [OE *bisc(e)op* < VL *(e)biscopus,* var. of L *episcopus* < Gk. *episkopos* overseer < *epi-* on, over + *skopos* watcher]

bish·op·ric (bish′əp rik) *n.* **1** the position, office, or rank of bishop. **2** a church district under the charge of a bishop; diocese. [OE *bisceoprīce* < *bisceop* bishop + *rīce* dominion. See BISHOP.]

bis·muth (biz′məth) *n.* a brittle, reddish-white, metallic chemical element. Some compounds are used in medicine and in alloys. *Symbol:* Bi; *at.no.* 83; *at.wt.* 208.980. [< G]

bi·son (bī′sən or bī′zən) *n.* **-son. 1** the North American buffalo; a wild ox having a big, shaggy head and strong front legs. **2** the European buffalo, slightly larger than the American buffalo, and now almost extinct. [< L < Gmc.]

bisque (bisk) *n.* **1** a thick soup made of crawfish, lobsters, birds, rabbits, etc. **2** a smooth, creamy soup made of strained tomatoes, asparagus, etc. **3** ice cream containing powdered macaroons or crushed nuts. [< F]

bis·sex·tile (bī seks′ tĭl or bī seks′ təl) *n.* leap year. *—adj.* containing the extra day of leap year. February is the bissextile month. [< L *bissextilis* (*annus*) leap (year) < *bis* twice + *sextus* sixth. The Julian calendar added an extra day after the *sixth* day before the calends of March.]

bis·tre or **bis·ter** (bis′ tər) *n.* **1** a dark-brown coloring matter made from soot. **2** a dark brown. [< F *bistre*]

bi·sul·phate or **bi·sul·fate** (bī sul′ fāt) *n.* a salt of sulphuric acid in which half of the hydrogen is replaced by a metal; acid sulphate.

bi·sul·phid or **bi·sul·fid** (bī sul′ fid) *n.* bisulphide.

bi·sul·phide or **bi·sul·fide** (bī sul′fīd or bī sul′ fid) *n.* disulphide.

bit[1] (bit) *n. v.* **bit·ted, bit·ting.** *—n.* **1** the part of a bridle that goes in a horse's mouth. See **harness** for picture. **2** anything that curbs or restrains. **3** the biting or cutting part of a tool. **4** a tool for boring or drilling, usually fitted into a handle called a brace. See **brace and bit** for picture. **5** the part of a key that goes into a lock and makes it turn. **6 take the bit in one's teeth, a** of a horse, bite on the bit so that it cannot be pulled against the soft part of the mouth. **b** take control and act on one's own, especially in an irresponsible or wilful manner: *The young soldier took the bit in his teeth and charged the enemy, despite the order to wait for the lieutenant's signal.*
—v. **1** put a bit in the mouth of; bridle. **2** curb; restrain. [OE *bite* a bite < *bītan* bite]

bit[2] (bit) *n.* **1** a small piece; small amount. **2** *Informal.* a short time. **3 two bits,** *Informal.* 25 cents. **4 do one's bit,** do one's share. [OE *bita* < *bītan* bite]
—Syn. 1 particle, speck.

bit[3] (bit) *v.* pt. and a pp. of **bite.**

bit[4] (bit) *n.* the basic unit of information in an electronic computer; binary digit. [< *bi*nary digi*t*]

bitch (bich) *n.* **1** a female dog, wolf, fox, etc. **2** *Slang. Derogatory.* a lewd or spiteful woman. *—v. Slang.* **1** complain. **2** botch; bungle. [OE *bicce*]

bitch·y (bich′ ē) *adj. Slang.* malicious; ill-tempered.

bite (bīt) *v.* **bit, bit·ten** or **bit, bit·ing,** *n.* *—v.* **1** seize, cut into, or cut off with the teeth: *She bit the apple. The nervous boy bites his fingernails.* **2** cut; pierce: *The sword bit the knight's helmet.* **3** wound with teeth, fangs, etc.; sting: *My dog never bites. A mosquito bit me.* **4** nip; snap: *a dog biting at fleas.* **5** cause a sharp, smarting pain to: *His fingers were bitten by frost.* **6** take a tight hold on; grip: *The wheels bite the rails.* **7** take a bait; be caught: *The fish are biting well today.* **8** eat into: *Acid bites metal.* **9 bite back,** hold back (words, temper, etc.) by biting the lips. **10 bite off more than one can chew,** attempt more than one is able to accomplish. **11 bite the dust,** *Informal.* **a** fall dead. **b** be defeated.
—n. **1** a piece bitten off; bit of food; mouthful: *Have the whole apple, not just a bite.* **2** a snack: *We usually have a bite before going to bed.* **3** the act of biting: *The dog gave a bite or two at the bone.* **4** the result of a bite, wound, sting, etc.: *The man soon recovered from the snake's bite.* **5** a sharp, smarting pain: *the bite of a cold wind.* **6** a cutting or wounding quality: *the bite of his sarcasm. There was a sharp bite to his humor.* **7** a tight hold: *the bite of the wheels on the rails.* **8** action of acid in eating into a metal, etc. [OE *bītan*] **—bit′ er,** *n.*
—Syn. *v.* **1** chew, gnaw, nibble.

bit·ing (bīt′ ing) *adj.* **1** sharp; cutting: *a biting wind.* **2** sarcastic; sneering: *a biting remark.* **—bit′ ing·ly,** *adv.*

bitt (bit) *n.* a strong post on a ship's deck to which ropes, cables, etc. are fastened. *—v.* put (ropes, cables, etc.) around the bitts. [var. of BIT[1]]

bit·ten (bit′ ən) *v.* a pp. of **bite.**

bit·ter (bit′ ər) *adj.* **1** having a sharp, harsh, unpleasant taste: *bitter medicine.* **2** unpleasant to the mind or feeling; hard to admit or bear: *a bitter defeat. Failure is bitter.* **3** harsh or cutting: *bitter words.* **4** causing pain; sharp; severe: *a bitter wound, a bitter fight.* **5** of weather, very cold: *a bitter winter.* **6** expressing grief, pain, misery, etc.: *a bitter cry.* **7 to the bitter end, a** until the very last. **b** to death.
—n. that which is bitter; bitterness: *You must take the bitter with the sweet.* [OE *biter.* Related to BITE.]
—bit′ ter·ly, *adv.* **—bit′ ter·ness,** *n.* **—Syn.** *adj.* **1** acrid. **2** painful, distressing. **3** caustic.

hat, āge, cãre, fär; let, ēqual, tėrm; it, īce
hot, ōpen, ôrder; oil, out; cup, pu̇t, rüle, ūse
əbove, takən, pencəl, lemən, circəs
ch, child; ng, long; sh, ship
th, thin; ᴛʜ, then; zh, measure

bitter end[1] *Informal.* the very end or last extremity, such as defeat or death.

bitter end[2] the inboard end of a ship's anchoring rope or cable.

bit·tern (bit′ ərn) *n.* a small kind of heron that lives in marshes and has a peculiar booming cry. [ME < OF *butor*]

bit·ter·root (bit′ ər rüt′) *n.* a small plant having fleshy roots and pink flowers, found in the northern Rocky Mountains.

bit·ters (bit′ ərz) *n.pl.* a liquid, usually alcoholic, flavored with some bitter plant. It is sometimes used as medicine.

bit·ter·sweet (bit′ ər swēt′) *n.* **1** a climbing plant having purple flowers and poisonous, scarlet berries. **2** a climbing shrub of North America, having greenish flowers, and orange seed cases that open and show red seeds. **3** sweetness and bitterness mixed. *—adj.* sweet and bitter mixed.

bi·tu·men (bə tū′ mən, bə tü′ mən, or bich′ u̇ mən) *n.* any of a number of minerals that will burn, such as asphalt, petroleum, naphtha, etc. [< L]

bi·tu·mi·nous (bə tū′ mə nəs or bə tü′ mə nəs) *adj.* **1** containing or made with bitumen. **2** like bitumen.

bituminous coal a coal that burns with much smoke and a yellow flame; soft coal.

bi·va·lence (bī vā′ ləns or biv′ ə ləns) *n.* a bivalent quality or condition.

bi·va·lent (bī vā′ lənt or biv′ ə lənt) *adj.* in chemistry: **1** having a valence of two. **2** having two valences. [< *bi-* two + L *valens, -entis,* ppr. of *valere* be worth]

bi·valve (bī′ valv′) *n.* **1** any mollusc whose shell consists of two parts hinged together. Oysters and clams are bivalves. **2** any seed, such as the pod of a pea, that splits into two halves. *—adj.* having two parts hinged together.

biv·ou·ac (biv′ ü ak′) *n. v.* **-acked, -ack·ing.** camp outdoors without tents: *The soldiers made a bivouac for the night in a field. They bivouacked there until morning.* [< F, probably < G *Beiwacht* additional night guards]

bi·week·ly (bī wēk′ lē) *adj. n.* **-lies,** *adv.* *—adj.* **1** happening once every two weeks. **2** happening twice a week; semiweekly.
—n. a newspaper or magazine published biweekly.
—adv. **1** once every two weeks. **2** twice a week; semiweekly.

bi·year·ly (bī yēr′ lē) *adj. adv.* twice a year.

bi·zarre (bə zär′) *adj.* odd; queer; fantastic; grotesque. [< F < Sp. *bizarro* brave < Basque *bezar* beard] **—bi·zarre′ ly,** *adv.* **—bi·zarre′ ness,** *n.*

B.J. Bachelor of Journalism.

bk. **1** bank. **2** book. **3** block. **4** bark.

Bk berkelium.

bkg. banking.

bks. **1** books. **2** barracks.

bkt. *pl.* **bkts. 1** basket. **2** bracket.

bl. **1** bale. **2** barrel. **3** blue.

b.l. or **B/L** bill of lading.

blab (blab) *v.* **blabbed, blab·bing,** *n.* *—v.* tell (secrets); talk too much. *—n.* **1** blabbing talk; chatter. **2** a person who blabs. [ME *blabbe*] **—blab′ ber,** *n.*

black (blak) *adj.* **1** opposite of white: *This print is black.* **2** without any light; very dark: *The room was black as night.* **3** having a dark skin. **4** Negro. **5** dirty; filthy: *black hands.* **6** dismal; gloomy: *a black day.* **7** sullen; angry: *a black look.* **8** evil; wicked: *black magic.*
—n. **1** the opposite of white. **2** black coloring matter. **3** black clothes; mourning. **4** a person who has dark skin. **5** a Negro. **6** in chess, checkers, or backgammon: **a** the black or dark-colored squares or other shapes on the board. **b** the black or dark-colored pieces. **c** the player

holding these pieces. **7 in the black,** showing a profit, or at least no loss; thriving.
—*v.* **1** make or become black. **2** put blacking on boots, shoes, etc. **3 black out, a** become temporarily blind or unconscious. **b** put out or screen all lights; darken completely. [OE *blæc*] —**black′er,** *n.* —**Syn.** *adj.* **3** swarthy, dusky. **7** lowering.

black·a·moor (blak′ə mür′) *n.* **1** a Negro. **2** a dark-skinned person. [var. of *black Moor*]

black-and-blue (blak′ənd blü′) *adj.* bruised.

Black and Tan a member of the constabulary force sent to Ireland in 1919-1921 by the British government to put down the rebellion there, so called because members of the force wore a black and tan uniform.

black and white 1 writing; print: *I asked him to put his promise down in black and white.* **2** a picture or sketch using only black and white.

black art evil magic.

black·ball (blak′bol′ or -bôl′) *v.* **1** vote against. **2** ostracize. —*n.* a vote against a person or thing. [from the practice of voting against a candidate by placing a black ball in the ballot box] —**black′ball′er,** *n.*

black bass an eastern North American game fish that lives in fresh water.

black bear a large North American bear that has dense black fur.

black·ber·ry (blak′ber′ē or blak′bər ē) *n.* **-ries,** *v.* **-ried, -ry·ing.** —*n.* **1** a small, black or dark-purple, edible fruit of certain bushes and vines that belong to the same family as the rose. **2** the thorny bush or vine that it grows on. —*v.* gather blackberries.

black·bird (blak′bėrd′) *n.* **1** any North American bird so named because the male is mainly black. The cowbird, purple grackle, and red-winged blackbird are blackbirds. **2** the European thrush; merle.

black blizzard on the prairies, a dust storm.

black·board (blak′bôrd′) *n.* a dark, smooth surface for writing or drawing on with chalk or crayon.

black book a book containing the names of people to be criticized or punished.

black box *Informal.* any self-contained electronic or automatic device for recording data, controlling a mechanical process, etc. One type is used to detect earthquakes and nuclear explosions.

black bread heavy, coarse, dark rye bread.

black·cap (blak′kap′) *n.* **1** a black raspberry. **2** a bird whose head has a black top, such as the chickadee.

Black Death a violent outbreak of bubonic plague that spread through Asia and Europe in the 14th century. It was at its worst in 1348.

black diamond 1 an opaque, dark type of diamond found chiefly in Brazil. **2 black diamonds,** *pl.* coal.

black·en (blak′ən) *v.* **-ened, -en·ing. 1** make black. **2** become black. **3** speak evil of. —**black′en·er,** *n.* —**Syn. 1, 2** darken. **3** slander, defame.

black eye 1 a bruise around an eye. **2** *Informal.* **a** a severe blow: *The insult gave his pride a black eye.* **b** a cause of disgrace or discredit. **c** disgrace or discredit: *The substandard housing in that section is a black eye to the whole community.*

black-eyed Su·san (blak′īd sü′zən) a yellow daisy having a black centre.

black·face (blak′fās′) *n.* **1** a Negro minstrel; an actor made up as a Negro. **2** the make-up for Negro parts in a show, etc. **3** in printing, a type with thick, heavy lines: *The entry words in this dictionary are printed in blackface.*

Black·feet (blak′fēt′) *n.pl.* a union of three North American Indian tribes, originally, the Blackfoot proper, the Bloods, and the Piegan, now living in Alberta, Saskatchewan, and Montana.

black·fish (blak′fish′) *n.* **1** any of various dark-colored fishes, such as the sea bass, tautog, etc. **2** a small, black whale. **3** a small fresh-water fish of Alaska and Siberia.

black flag the pirates' flag: *The black flag or Jolly Roger usually had a white skull and crossbones on it.*

black-fly (blak′flī′) *n.* **-flies.** a small black fly whose bite is very painful.

Black·foot (blak′füt′) *n.* **-feet** or **-foot. 1 a** one of the three tribes that make up the Blackfeet union or confederacy. **b.** the confederacy itself. **2** a member of the Blackfoot tribe. **3** the Algonquian language spoken by the members of the confederacy. [a translation of the tribal name *Siksika*, believed to refer to their moccasins]

Black Friar a Dominican friar.

Black Friday any Friday on which some calamity happens.

black grouse a large grouse of Europe and Asia.

black·guard (blag′ärd or blag′ərd) *n.* a scoundrel. —*v.* **1** abuse with vile language. **2** behave like a blackguard. [< *black* + *guard*] —**black′guard·ly,** *adj., adv.*

Black Hand a secret society organized to commit blackmail and crimes of violence.

black·head (blak′hed′) *n.* **1** a small, black-tipped, fatty mass in a pore of the skin. **2** any of various birds that have a black head. **3** a disease that attacks turkeys, chickens, etc.

black·heart (blak′härt′) *n.* **1** a variety of dark-skinned cherry. **2** a plant disease, especially of potatoes, in which the internal tissues turn black.

black hole a cell or dungeon; a place of punishment. [< the *Black Hole of Calcutta*, a small cell in which many English prisoners were supposedly confined in 1756]

black·ing (blak′ing) *n.* a black polish used on shoes, stoves, etc.

black·ish (blak′ish) *adj.* somewhat black.

black·jack (blak′jak′) *n.* **1** a club with a flexible handle, used as a weapon. **2** a large drinking cup or jug, formerly made of leather. **3** the black flag of a pirate. **4** a small oak tree of the southern United States, having a bark that is almost black. **5 a** a card game in which the players try to get a count of twenty-one. **b** a count of twenty-one with only two cards, namely an ace and a ten or any face card. —*v.* **1** hit (a person) with a blackjack. **2** coerce.

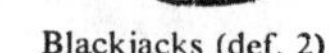
Blackjacks (def. 2)

black lead graphite.

black·leg (blak′leg′) *n.* **1** *Informal.* a swindler. **2** *Brit.* a worker who takes a striker's job. **3** an infectious, usually fatal disease of cattle and sheep.

black letter in printing, a type with thick, heavy lines.

black list a list of persons who are believed to deserve punishment, blame, suspicion, etc.

black-list (blak′list′) *v.* put on a black list.

black·ly (blak′lē) *adv.* **1** dismally; gloomily. **2** sullenly; angrily. **3** evilly; wickedly.

black magic evil magic.

black·mail (blak′māl′) *n.* **1** the extortion of money, etc. by threats, especially threats of disgracing a person by revealing his secrets. **2** the money or other advantage obtained in this way. —*v.* get or try to get blackmail from. [< *black* + *mail* rent, tribute, coin < OF *maille* < *mail, medaille* coin, medal] —**black′mail′er,** *n.*

Black Ma·ri·a (mə rī′ə) *Informal.* a police patrol wagon, used to carry prisoners to and from jail.

black mark a mark of criticism or punishment.

black market the selling of goods at illegal prices or in illegal quantities.

black mar·ket·eer (mär′kə tēr′) one who deals on the black market.

Black Mass 1 a Mass for the dead at which black vestments are worn by the priest. **2** a ceremony in which the Mass of Christian worship is caricatured by so-called devil-worshippers.

black measles a severe type of measles.

black·ness (blak′nis) *n.* **1** the state of being black. **2** wickedness.

black nightshade a plant having white flowers, black berries, and leaves that have a poisonous juice.

black oak 1 any of various large North American oaks, having dark bark and foliage. 2 the wood of any of these trees.

black·out (blak′out′) *n.* 1 a turning out or concealing of all the lights of a city, district, etc. as a protection against an air raid. 2 a temporary blindness or unconsciousness resulting from lack of circulation of blood in the brain. It may occur after too much exertion or be experienced by a pilot during rapid changes in the velocity or direction of his airplane. 3 a temporary failure of memory. 4 a turning off of all the lights on the stage of a theatre. 5 a failure in radio reception. 6 the withholding of news or other information.

black pepper 1 a seasoning with a hot taste, made by grinding the dried berries of a woody vine grown in the East Indies. 2 the vine itself.

black race the Negro race.

Black Rod 1 the chief usher in the British House of Lords, whose symbol of authority is a black rod. 2 in Canada, the chief usher of the Senate. 3 the chief usher in various other legislatures of the British Commonwealth.

black rot 1 any of several diseases of cultivated plants including apples and grapes, characterized by dark-brown spots. 2 the fungus that causes any of these diseases.

black sheep a person considered by his group or family to be a disgrace.

Black Shirt 1 formerly, a member of the Italian Fascists, who wore a black shirt as part of their uniform. 2 a member of any similar fascist organization.

black·smith (blak′smith′) *n.* a man who works with iron. Blacksmiths mend tools and also make and fit horseshoes. [with ref. to black metals, e.g., iron]

black·snake (blak′snāk′) *n.* 1 a harmless, dark-colored snake of North America. 2 a heavy whip made of braided leather.

black spruce 1 a North American evergreen tree having cones and dark-green foliage. 2 its light, soft wood.

black tea tea which has been allowed to wither and ferment in the air for some time, before being subjected to a heating process.

black·thorn (blak′thôrn′) *n.* 1 a thorny European shrub of the same family as the peach, that has white flowers and dark-purple, plumlike fruit called sloes. 2 a walking stick or club made from the stem of this shrub.

black tie 1 a black tie, especially a black bow tie, for wear with a dinner jacket or tuxedo. 2 a dinner jacket or tuxedo, as opposed to full evening dress, or tails: *The men will wear black ties for the dinner.*

black·top (blak′top′) *n. v.* **-topped, -top·ping.** —*n.* 1 asphalt mixed with crushed rock, used as a surface for roads, highways, runways, etc. 2 any surface so paved, such as a highway, driveway, etc. —*v.* pave or surface a road with blacktop.

black walnut 1 an oily, round, edible nut with a rough shell. 2 the tall tree that it grows on. 3 its dark-brown wood, often used for furniture.

black widow a poisonous female spider having a glossy, bulbous black body about the size of a small button, with reddish marks on the under side. It gets its name from its color and its habit of eating its mate.

black·work (blak′wėrk′) *n.* iron wrought or forged by blacksmiths, not brightened by burnishing, filing, etc.

blad·der (blad′ər) *n.* 1 a soft, thin bag in the body that receives and, for a time, retains urine from the kidneys. 2 any similar bag in animals or plants. 3 a strong bag, often made of rubber, that will hold liquids or air: *The rubber bag inside a football is a bladder.* [OE *blǣdre*]

blad·der·wort (blad′ər wėrt′) *n.* any of various plants having yellow or purple flowers. Some varieties float on the water by means of small bladders on the leaves; others take root in mud.

blade (blād) *n.* 1 the cutting part of anything like a knife or sword. 2 a sword. 3 a swordsman. 4 a smart or dashing fellow. 5 a leaf of grass. 6 the flat, wide part of a leaf; a leaf. 7 a flat, wide part of anything. An oar or a paddle has a blade at one end of the shaft. 8 the wide flat part of a bone: *the shoulder blade.* 9 the front, flat part of the tongue. [OE *blæd*] —**blade′like′,** *adj.*

hat, āge, cãre, fär; let, ēqual, tėrm; it, īce
hot, ōpen, ôrder; oil, out; cup, pu̇t, rüle, ūse
əbove, takən, pencəl, lemən, circəs
ch, child; ng, long; sh, ship
th, thin; ᴛʜ, then; zh, measure

blad·ed (blād′id) *adj.* having a blade or blades.

blain (blān) *n.* an inflamed swelling or sore; blister; pustule. [OE *blegen*]

blam·a·ble (blām′ə bəl) *adj.* deserving blame.

blame (blām) *v.* **blamed, blam·ing,** *n.* —*v.* 1 hold responsible (for something bad or wrong): *We blamed the fog for our accident.* 2 find fault with: *The teacher will not blame us if we do our best.* 3 **be to blame,** deserve blame. 4 **blame on,** attribute to: *The accident was blamed on the icy road.*
—*n.* 1 the responsibility for something bad or wrong: *Lack of care deserves the blame for many mistakes.* 2 a finding fault. [ME < OF *blasmer* < L *blasphemare* < Gk. *blasphēmeein,* ult. < *blas-* false, slanderous + *phēmē* word. Doublet of BLASPHEME.] —**blam′er,** *n.*
Syn. *v.* 1 accuse. 2 **Blame, censure, reproach** = find fault with. **Blame,** the least formal word, means find fault with a person for doing something wrong or that the person passing judgment thinks is wrong: *We blame people for doing what they know is wrong.* **Censure** adds to *blame* the idea of expressing disapproval, often publicly: *People often censure the Government.* **Reproach** adds to *censure* the idea of expressing one's personal feelings of displeasure or resentment, sometimes unjustly: *She reproached him for being late.* —*n.* 1 guilt. 2 censure, condemnation, reproach.
☛ **Blame** is followed directly by its object: *He blamed me for the accident.* In informal speech the idiom *blame on* is often used: *He blamed the accident on me.*

blame·less (blām′lis) *adj.* free from blame. —**blame′less·ly,** *adv.* —**blame′less·ness,** *n.*
—**Syn.** See **innocent.**

blame·wor·thy (blām′wėr′ᴛʜē) *adj.* deserving blame.

blanch (blanch) *v.* 1 make white; bleach: *Almonds are blanched by removing their skins.* 2 turn white or pale: *blanch with fear.* 3 whiten or prevent from becoming green by excluding the light, as the stems or leaves of plants such as celery or lettuce. 4 in cookery, boil briefly and then chill (vegetables, etc.). —*adj.* in heraldry, white; argent. [ME < OF *blanchir* < *blanc* white < Gmc.]

blanc·mange (blə mänzh′) *n.* a sweet dessert made of milk thickened with gelatin, cornstarch, etc. [ME < OF *blancmanger* white food]

bland (bland) *adj.* 1 smooth; mild; gentle; soothing: *a bland diet. A warm spring breeze is bland.* 2 agreeable; polite, especially in an ingratiating manner. [< L *blandus* soft] —**bland′ly,** *adv.* —**bland′ness,** *n.* —**Syn.** 1 soft, balmy. 2 suave, urbane.

blan·dish (blan′dish) *v.* coax; flatter. [ME < OF *blandiss-,* a stem of *blandir* < L *blandiri* flatter]

blan·dish·ment (blan′dish mənt) *n.* 1 a coaxing; flattery. 2 an expression or action that coaxes or flatters.

blank (blangk) *n.* 1 a space left empty or to be filled in: *Leave a blank after each word.* 2 a paper with spaces to be filled in: *an application blank.* 3 an empty or vacant place: *When he saw the difficult test, his mind became a complete blank.* 4 a lottery ticket that does not win a prize. 5 a piece of metal prepared to be stamped or filed into a coin, key, etc. 6 a white spot in the centre of a target. 7 anything aimed at. 8 a blank cartridge. 9 **draw a blank,** end an attempt without success; be unsuccessful: *He tried to get support for his nomination, but he drew a blank with us.*
—*adj.* 1 not written or printed on: *blank paper.* 2 with spaces to be filled in: *a blank cheque.* 3 empty; vacant: *a blank stare.* 4 without interest or meaning; dull: *a blank look.* 5 complete; entire: *blank stupidity.* 6 lacking some usual feature: *a blank cartridge.*
—*v.* 1 in games, keep from scoring. 2 hide; obscure. [F *blanc* white, shining < Gmc.] —**blank′ly,** *adv.* —**blank′ness,** *n.* —**Syn.** *adj.* 3 void, bare.

blank cartridge a cartridge with no bullet or shot.

blank cheque or **check** 1 a signed cheque that allows the bearer to fill in the amount. 2 *Informal.* freedom or permission to do as one pleases; carte blanche.

blan·ket (blang′kit) *n.* **1** a soft, heavy covering woven from wool, cotton, etc., used to keep people or animals warm. **2** anything like a blanket: *A blanket of snow covered the ground.*
—*v.* **1** cover with a blanket. **2** cover; hinder; obscure: *Snow blanketed the ground.*
—*adj.* covering several or all: *A blanket insurance policy insures a car against all kinds of accidents.* [ME < OF *blankete* < *blanc* white < Gmc. Related to BLANK.]

blank verse unrhymed verse having five iambic feet in each line: *Shakespeare's plays are written mainly in blank verse.*

blare (blãr) *v.* **blared, blar·ing,** *n.* —*v.* **1** make a loud, harsh sound: *The trumpets blared, announcing the king's arrival.* **2** utter harshly or loudly. —*n.* **1** a loud, harsh sound: *The blare of the horn was startling.* **2** brilliance of color; glare. [ME < MDu. *blaren*]

blar·ney (blär′nē) *n. v.* **-neyed, -ney·ing.** —*n.* flattering, coaxing talk. —*v.* flatter; coax. [< *Blarney Stone*]

Blarney Stone a stone built into a castle near Cork, Ireland. Anyone who kisses it is supposed to acquire skill in flattering and coaxing people.

bla·sé (blä zā′ or blä′zā) *adj.* tired of pleasures; bored. [< F *blasé,* pp. of *blaser* exhaust with pleasure]

blas·pheme (blas fēm′) *v.* **-phemed, -phem·ing.** speak about God or sacred things with abuse or contempt; utter blasphemy. [ME *blasfemen* < OF *blasfemer* < L *blasphemare* < Gk. *blasphēmeein.* Doublet of BLAME.] —**blas·phem·er,** *n.*

blas·phe·mous (blas′fə məs) *adj.* **1** speaking about God or sacred things with abuse or contempt. **2** of thoughts, actions, etc., characterized by contempt for God or sacred things. —**blas′phe·mous·ly,** *adv.* —**blas′phe·mous·ness,** *n.*

blas·phe·my (blas′fə mē) *n.* **-mies.** abuse of or contempt for God or sacred things. —**Syn.** profanity.

blast (blast) *n.* **1** a strong, sudden rush of wind or air: *the icy blasts of winter.* **2 a** the blowing of a trumpet, horn, etc. **b** the sound so made. **3** a current of air used in smelting, etc. A furnace is **in blast** when in operation; it is **out of blast** when stopped. **4** a charge of dynamite or some other explosive that blows up rocks, earth, etc. **5** a blasting; explosion. **6** a cause of withering, blight, or ruin. **7** *Slang.* an outburst of anger, severe criticism, etc. **8 in full blast,** in full operation.
—*v.* **1** blow up (rocks, earth, etc.) with dynamite, or some other explosive. **2** wither; blight; ruin: *The intense heat blasted the vines. His conviction for fraud blasted his reputation.* **3** blow (a trumpet, horn, whistle, etc.). **4** criticize angrily and severely. **5 blast off, a** of rockets, missiles, etc., fire; take off: *Make ready to blast off.* **b** *Slang.* get out; go away. [OE *blǣst*] —**blast′er,** *n.* —**Syn.** *v.* **2** destroy.

blast·ed (blas′tid) *adj.* **1** withered; blighted; ruined. **2** damned; cursed.

blast furnace a furnace in which ores are smelted by blowing a strong current of air from the bottom to produce intense heat.

blas·to·derm (blas′tə dėrm′) *n.* in biology, a layer of cells formed by the growth of a fertilized egg. It later divides into three layers, from which all parts of the animal are formed. [< Gk. *blastos* germ + E *-derm* (< Gk. *derma* skin)]

blast-off or **blast·off** (blast′of′) *n.* of rockets, missiles, etc., the moment or process of taking off; launching: *All communication circuits must be carefully checked before blast-off.*

blas·tu·la (blas′chů lə) *n.* **-lae** (-lē′ or -lī′). in zoology, the embryo of an animal. It usually consists of a sac or hollow sphere formed by a single layer of cells. [< NL *blastula,* dim. of Gk. *blastos* sprout, germ]

blas·tu·lar (blas′chə lər) *adj.* having to do with, or resembling, a blastula.

blat (blat) *v.* **blat·ted, blat·ting. 1** cry like a calf or sheep; bleat. **2** *Informal.* say loudly and foolishly; blurt out. [imitative]

bla·tan·cy (blā′tən sē) *n.* a blatant quality.

bla·tant (blā′tənt) *adj.* **1** noisy; loud-mouthed. **2** showy in dress, manner, etc. **3** obvious; easily recognized: *blatant hypocrisy, blatant lies.* [coined by Spenser < L *blatire* babble] —**bla′tant·ly,** *adv.* —**Syn. 1** clamorous.

blath·er (blaŧʜ′ər) *n.* foolish talk. —*v.* talk foolishly. Also, **blether.** [ME < ON *blathr*]

blath·er·skite (blaŧʜ′ər skīt′) *n. Informal.* a person who talks much and says little.

blaze[1] (blāz) *n. v.* **blazed, blaz·ing.** —*n.* **1** a bright flame or fire. **2** an intense light; glare. **3** a bright display. **4** a violent outburst: *a blaze of temper.*
—*v.* **1** burn with a bright flame; be on fire: *A fire was blazing in the fireplace.* **2** show bright colors or lights: *On Christmas Eve the big house blazed with lights.* **3** make a bright display. **4** burst out in anger or excitement. **5 blaze away,** fire a gun, etc. [OE *blæse*] —**Syn.** *n.* **1** conflagration. See **flame. 2** brilliance.

blaze[2] (blāz) *n. v.* **blazed, blaz·ing.** —*n.* **1** a mark made on a tree by chipping off a piece of bark. **2** a white mark on an animal's forehead. —*v.* mark (a tree, trail, etc.) by chipping off a piece of the bark. [< LG *bläse*]

blaze[3] (blāz) *v.* **blazed, blaz·ing.** make known; proclaim. [< MDu. *blasen*]

blaz·er (blāz′ər) *n.* **1** a jacket for recreational wear. **2** a navy-blue jacket cut like a suit coat, often worn with grey flannels by men as dressy but informal wear.

bla·zon (blā′zən) *v.* **1** make known; proclaim: *Big posters blazoned the wonders of the coming circus.* **2** decorate; adorn. **3** describe or paint (a coat of arms). **4** display; show. [< n., or < F *blasonner* (< OF *blason* shield)]
—*n.* **1** a coat of arms; shield with a coat of arms on it. **2** a description or painting of a coat of arms. **3** a display; a show. [ME < OF *blason* shield]

bla·zon·ry (blā′zən rē) *n.* **1** a bright decoration or display. **2** a coat of arms. **3** a description or painting of a coat of arms.

bldg. *pl.* **bldgs.** building.

bleach (blēch) *v.* **1** whiten by exposing to sunlight or by using chemicals. **2** turn white or pale. —*n.* **1** a chemical used in bleaching. **2** the act of bleaching. [OE *blǣcean* < *blāc, blǣce* pale. Related to BLEAK.] —**Syn.** *v.* **1** See **whiten.**

bleach·er (blēch′ər) *n.* **1** a person who bleaches. **2** a thing that bleaches or is used in bleaching. **3 bleachers,** *pl.* the roofless stands of low-priced seats at outdoor games such as baseball and football.

bleaching powder 1 any powder used in bleaching. **2** chloride of lime.

bleak (blēk) *adj.* **1** swept by winds; bare: *bleak and rocky mountain peaks.* **2** chilly; cold: *a bleak wind.* **3** dreary; dismal: *Life in jail is bleak for prisoners.* [ME *bleke* pale < Scand., related to OE *blāc, blǣce.* See BLEACH.] —**bleak′ly,** *adv.* —**bleak′ness,** *n.* —**Syn. 1** desolate. **2** raw.

blear (blēr) *adj.* dim; blurred. —*v.* make dim or blurred. [ME *blere(n)*]

blear-eyed (blēr′īd′) *adj.* having inflamed or watery eyes.

blear·y (blēr′ē) *adj.* **blear·i·er, blear·i·est.** dim; blurred. —**blear′i·ly,** *adv.* —**blear′i·ness,** *n.*

bleat (blēt) *n.* **1** the cry made by a sheep, goat, or calf. **2** a sound like a bleat. [< v.] —*v.* **1** make the cry of a sheep, goat, or calf, or a sound like it. **2** complain, especially feebly or with a whine. **3** blather; babble. [OE *blǣtan*] —**bleat′er,** *n.*

bleb (bleb) *n.* **1** a blister. **2** a bubble. [probably imitative]

bled (bled) *v.* pt. and pp. of **bleed.**

bleed (blēd) *v.* **bled, bleed·ing.** *n.* —*v.* **1** lose blood: *This cut is bleeding.* **2** shed one's blood; suffer wounds or death: *He bled to death. He fought and bled for his country.* **3** take blood from: *Doctors used to bleed sick people.* **4** lose sap, juice, etc.: *The injured elm is bleeding.* **5** take sap, juice, etc. from. **6** feel pity, sorrow, or grief. **7** *Informal.* get money from by extortion. **8** in printing: **a** extend to the edge of a page, leaving no margin: *This photograph will look best on the page if it bleeds both*

sides. **b** print (an illustration) or trim (a page) so that there is no margin. **9 bleed white,** take all the power, strength, money, etc. of: *Blackmailers and gamblers have bled him white.*
—*n.* **1** in printing: **a** an illustration or page that bleeds. **b** the paper trimmed off such a page. **2** a valve or tap. [OE *blēdan* < *blōd* blood]

bleed·er (blēd′ər) *n.* a person who bleeds very easily because his blood fails to clot.

bleeding heart a common garden plant that has drooping clusters of red or pink, heart-shaped flowers.

blem·ish (blem′ish) *n.* **1** a stain; spot; scar: *A mole is a blemish on a person's skin.* **2** an imperfection; fault: *A quick temper was the only blemish in his character.* [< v.] —*v.* **1** stain; spot; scar. **2** injure; mar: *One bad deed can blemish a good reputation.* [ME < OF *blemiss-*, a stem of *ble(s)mir* make livid] —**blem′ish·er,** *n.*
—**Syn.** *v.* **1** deface, disfigure. **2** tarnish, sully.

blench[1] (blench) *v.* draw back; shrink away. [apparently OE *blencan* deceive]

blench[2] (blench) *v.* **1** turn pale. **2** make white. [var. of *blanch*]

blend (blend) *v.* **blend·ed** or **blent, blend·ing,** *n.*
—*v.* **1** mix together thoroughly so that the things mixed cannot be distinguished or separated: *Oil and water will not blend. Blend these ingredients to make a cake.* **2** make by mixing several kinds together: *blend tea.* **3** shade into each other, little by little; merge: *The colors of the rainbow blend into one another.* **4** go well together; harmonize: *Purple and dark blue do not blend.*
—*n.* **1** a thorough mixture. **2** a mixture of several kinds: *a blend of coffee.* **3** a word made by fusing two words, often with a syllable in common. *Blotch* is a blend of *blot* and *botch.* **4** a gradual shading or merging. [ME < ON *blanda* mix] —**blend′er,** *n.* —**Syn.** *v.* **1** combine. See **mix.**

blende (blend) *n.* **1** the chief ore of zinc; zinc sulphide. **2** any of certain other sulphides. [< G *Blende* < *blenden* blind, deceive; because the yield from the ore is disappointing]

blend·er (blen′dər) *n.* **1** a person or thing that blends. **2** a mechanical device for mixing things uniformly.

blen·ny (blen′ē) *n.* **-ny** or **-nies.** a small, salt-water fish having a slender, tapering body. [< L *blennius*, var. of *blendius* < Gk. *blennos* < *blenna* slime]

blent (blent) *v. Poetic.* a pt. and a pp. of **blend.**

bless (bles) *v.* **blessed** or **blest, bless·ing. 1** make holy or sacred: *bless a church.* **2** ask God's favor for: *Bless these little children.* **3** wish good to; feel grateful to: *I bless him for his kindness.* **4** make happy or successful: *May this country always be blessed with prosperity.* **5** praise or glorify: *Bless the Lord, O my soul.* **6** guard; protect: *Heaven bless this house.* **7** make the sign of the cross over. **8** *Informal.* curse. [OE *blētsian* consecrate (i.e., with blood) < *blōd* blood]

bless·ed (bles′id or blest) *adj.* **1** holy; sacred. **2** in heaven; beatified. **3** fortunate; happy; successful. **4** bringing joy; joyful: *The birth of a baby is often called a blessed event.* **5** *Informal.* annoying; cursed.
—**bless′ed·ly,** *adv.* —**bless′ed·ness,** *n.*

Blessed Virgin the Virgin Mary.

bless·ing (bles′ing) *n.* **1** a prayer asking God to show His favor; benediction: *At the end of the church service, the bishop gave the blessing.* **2** a giving of God's favor. **3** a wish for happiness or success: *When he left home, he received his father's blessing.* **4** approval or consent: *The marriage had the blessing of all four parents.* **5** anything that makes one happy or contented: *A good temper is a great blessing.* —**Syn. 1** invocation. **4** favor, gift, boon, benefit.

blest (blest) *v.* a pt. and a pp. of **bless.** —*adj.* blessed.

bleth·er (bleᴛʜ′ər) *n. v.* blather.

blew (blü) *v.* pt. of **blow**[2] and **blow**[3].

blight (blīt) *n.* **1** any disease that causes plants, trees, or fruit to wither or decay: *The apple crop was wiped out by a blight.* **2** an insect or fungus that causes such a disease. **3** anything that causes destruction or ruin. **4** decay; deterioration: *The closing of the mines cast a blight on the whole community.*
—*v.* **1** cause to wither or decay. **2** destroy; ruin. [origin uncertain]

hat, āge, cãre, fär; let, ēqual, tėrm; it, īce
hot, ōpen, ôrder; oil, out; cup, pu̇t, rüle, ūse
əbove, takən, pencəl, lemən, circəs
ch, child; ng, long; sh, ship
th, thin; ᴛʜ, then; zh, measure

blimp (blimp) *n. Informal.* **1** a small, non-rigid dirigible airship. **2** any dirigible. [apparently from Type *B limp*, designation for "limp dirigible"]

Blimp or **blimp** (blimp) *n.* an ultra-conservative, stupidly short-sighted person. [< *Colonel Blimp*, an English newspaper cartoon character created by David Low]

blind (blīnd) *adj.* **1** not able to see: *a blind man.* **2** without thought, judgment, or good sense: *blind fury, a blind guess.* **3** hard to see; hidden: *a blind curve on a highway.* **4** without an opening: *a blind wall.* **5** with only one opening: *a blind canyon.* **6** of or for blind persons. **7** made without previous knowledge: *a blind purchase.* **8** arranged for one by someone else: *a blind date.* **9** of sewing or stitches, not showing through on the right side of the work. **10** not producing buds, etc.: *a blind shoot.* **11** of a boil etc., not having come to a head. **12 blind to,** unable to understand, perceive, or appreciate: *She is blind to the beauties of abstract art.*
—*v.* **1** make unable to see: *The bright lights blinded me for a moment.* **2** darken; dim; cover; conceal: *Clouds blind the stars from my view.* **3** rob of power to understand or judge: *His prejudices blinded him.*
—*n.* **1** something that keeps out light or hinders sight; a shutter: *Venetian blinds. A window shade is a blind.* **2** anything that conceals an action or purpose. **3** a hiding place for a hunter. [OE] —**blind′ly,** *adv.* —**blind′ness,** *n.* —**Syn.** *adj.* **1** sightless.

blind alley 1 a passageway closed at one end. **2** anything that gives no chance for progress or improvement.

blind date 1 a social date arranged by a third person. **2** either of the two persons thus dated.

blind·er (blīn′dər) *n.* a leather flap designed to keep a horse from seeing to the side.

blind flying the act of piloting an airplane by instruments only.

blind·fold (blīnd′fōld′) *v.* cover the eyes to prevent seeing: *The robbers blindfolded, gagged, and bound their victim.*
—*adj.* **1** with the eyes covered: *He said he could walk the line blindfold.* **2** reckless.
—*n.* something covering the eyes to prevent seeing: *Putting a blindfold on the horse, the man led him from the burning barn.* [OE *blindfellian*, ult. < *blind* blind + *fell*, var. of *fiell* a fall; influenced by *fold*]

Blinders

blind·man's buff (blīnd′manz buf′) a game in which a blindfolded person tries to catch and identify one of the other players.

blind spot 1 a round spot on the retina of the eye that is not sensitive to light: *The optic nerve enters the eye at the blind spot.* See **eye** for diagram. **2** a matter on which a person does not know that he is prejudiced or poorly informed. **3** in radio, an area of poor reception. **4** an area of poor visibility: *There is a blind spot where the road dips on that steep curve.*

blind·stitch (blīnd′stich′) *v.* sew with stitches not visible on the right side of the work. —*n.* Also, **blind stitch,** a stitch or stitching of this kind.

blind·worm (blīnd′wėrm′) *n.* a small lizard having a snakelike body and very tiny eyes.

blink (blingk) *v.* **1** look with the eyes opening and shutting: *Mary blinked at the sudden light.* **2** move the eyelids; wink: *He blinked his eyes.* **3** shine with an unsteady light: *A little lantern blinked in the night.* **4** look with indifference at; ignore: *Don't blink the fact that there is a risk of war. She blinks at all his faults.*
—*n.* **1** a blinking. **2** a glimpse. **3 on the blink,** *Slang.* not working properly: *Our television set is on the blink again.* [ME *blenken*]

blink·er (blingk′ər) *n.* **1** a blinder. **2** a warning signal with flashing lights.

blintz or **blintze** (blints) *n.* a thin, rolled pancake filled with cheese, fruit, jam, etc. [< Yiddish *blintz* < Ukrainian *blynci*]

blip (blip) *n.* an image on a radar screen, showing that radar waves are being reflected from an object.

bliss (blis) *n.* **1** great happiness; perfect joy. **2** the joy of heaven; blessedness. [OE *blīths* < *blīthe* blithe]
—**Syn. 1** ecstasy, rapture. See **happiness.**

bliss·ful (blis′fəl) *adj.* very happy; joyful.
—**bliss′ful·ly,** *adv.* —**bliss′ful·ness,** *n.*

blis·ter (blis′tər) *n.* **1** a little baglike swelling under the skin filled with watery matter. Blisters are often caused by burns or rubbing. **2** a swelling on the surface of a plant, on metal, or on painted wood, etc. **3** a bulge below the waterline in the hull of a ship, for protection against torpedoes. **4** a bulgelike, often transparent, projection on the fuselage of an aircraft, for an observer, navigator, or air gunner.
—*v.* **1** raise a blister on. **2** become covered with blisters; have blisters. **3** attack with sharp words. [ME < OF *blestre* tumor, lump < ON *blastr* swelling]

blister rust a fungus disease of white pine trees.

blithe (blīTH or blīth) *adj.* gay; happy; cheerful. [OE *blīthe*] —**blithe′ly,** *adv.* —**blithe′ness,** *n.*

blith·er·ing (blith′ər ing′) *adj.* talking nonsense; jabbering; blathering: *a blithering idiot.* [var. of *blathering*]

blithe·some (blīTH′səm or blīth′səm) *adj.* gay; cheerful; happy. —**blithe′some·ly,** *adv.*
—**blithe′some·ness,** *n.*

B.Litt. or **B.Lit.** Bachelor of Letters (or Literature). (for L *Baccalaureus Lit(t)erarum*)

blitz (blits) *n.* **1** a blitzkrieg. **2** a sudden, violent attack using many airplanes and tanks. **3** any sudden violent attack. —*v.* attack by blitz. [< G *Blitz* lightning]

blitz·krieg (blits′krēg′) *n.* a type of offensive action designed by its speed and violence to crush the enemy quickly. [< G *Blitzkrieg* lightning war]

bliz·zard (bliz′ərd) *n.* **1** a violent, blinding snowstorm with a strong wind and severe cold. **2** a similar storm of wind-blown sand, dust, etc. [var. of *blizzer* blow, shot; originally, flash; cf. OE *blysian* burn] —**bliz′zard·y,** *adj.*

blk. **1** black. **2** block. **3** bulk.

bloat (blōt) *v.* **1** swell up; puff up: *His face was bruised and bloated after the fight.* **2** preserve (herring) by salting and smoking. —*n.* **1** a swelling of the stomach of cattle, sheep, etc. caused by an accumulation of gases brought on by eating moist feed that ferments. **2** *Informal.* needless or wasteful expansion of staff, budget, etc. [ME *blout* soft with moisture < ON *blautr* soft, pulpy]

bloat·ed (blō′tid′) *adj.* **1** puffy and swollen. **2** pampered; glutted. **3** inflated. **4** cured as a bloater: *a bloated herring.*

bloat·er (blōt′ər) *n.* a herring preserved by salting and smoking.

blob (blob) *n. v.* **blobbed, blob·bing.** —*n.* **1** a small lump; drop: *Blobs of wax covered the candlestick.* **2** a splash or daub of color. —*v.* mark or put on with blobs. [probably imitative]

bloc (blok) *n.* a group of persons, companies, or nations, etc. united for a purpose: *The communist bloc includes those nations that accept and follow the leadership of Russia.* [< F < OF *bloc.* See BLOCK.]

block (blok) *n.* **1** a solid piece of wood, stone, metal, etc. **2** an obstruction; hindrance. **3** a part of a city enclosed by streets on each side. **4** the length of one side of a city block. **5** a number of townships, usually surrounded by land that has not been surveyed: *the Peace River Block.* **6** a group of things of the same kind: *a block of seats in a theatre.* **7** a building containing a number of apartments: *an apartment block.* **8** a number of buildings close together. **9** a building containing offices, often an annex to another building. **10** a short section of railway track with signals for spacing trains. **11** a piece of wood placed under the neck of a person being beheaded. **12** a platform where things are put up for sale at an auction. **13** a pulley on a hook. **14** a mould on which things are shaped. **15** in printing, a piece of engraved metal, wood, or other substance; cut. **16** *Slang.* a person's head. **17** in sports, the hindering of an opponent's play. **18 go to the block, a** have one's head cut off. **b** be for sale at an auction. **19 on the block,** for sale, especially at an auction.
—*v.* **1** fill so as to prevent passage or progress: *The country roads were blocked with snow.* **2** put things in the way of; obstruct; hinder: *Her sickness blocks my plans for the party.* **3** mount on a block. **4** shape with a mould: *Felt hats are blocked.* **5** in sports, hinder an opponent's play. **6** prevent (a nerve) from transmitting impulses. **7 block in** or **out,** plan roughly; outline. **8 block off,** close off: *The police will have to block off the street to all traffic.* **9 block up, a** fill up so as to prevent passage or progress. **b** raise on blocks. [ME < OF *bloc* < Gmc.] —**Syn.** *v.* **2** bar, blockade.

B, a block (def. 13)

block·ade (blok ād′) *n. v.* **-ad·ed, -ad·ing.** —*n.* **1** the control of who or what goes into or out of a place by the use of an army or navy: *A complete blockade of all the harbors and ports of North America would take hundreds of enemy warships.* **2** an army or navy used to blockade a place. **3** anything that blocks up or obstructs. **4 run the blockade,** sneak into or out of a port that is being blockaded.
—*v.* **1** put under blockade. **2** block up; obstruct.
—**block·ad′er,** *n.* —**Syn.** *n.* **1** See **siege.**

blockade runner a ship that tries to sneak into or out of a port that is being blockaded.

block and tackle an arrangement of pulleys and ropes used in lifting heavy weights. See **block** for picture.

block booking the renting or selling of motion pictures, comic books, etc. in groups without permitting the exhibitor or retail seller to make a selection.

block·bust·er (block′bus′tər) *n. Informal.* a destructive aerial bomb that weighs two or more tons.

block·head (blok′hed′) *n.* a stupid person; fool.

block·house (blok′hous′) *n.* **1** a fort or building having loopholes to shoot from. **2** a structure for protection against blast, heat, radiation, etc.: *There is an observation blockhouse near the missile launching pad.*

block·ish (blok′ish) *adj.* stupid. —**block′ish·ly,** *adv.*
—**block′ish·ness,** *n.*

block plane a small plane used to smooth the ends of boards across the grain.

block printing printing from engraved blocks of wood, etc.

block signal a signal to show whether a short section of railway track ahead has a train on it or not.

block system the system of dividing a railway track into short sections with signals to warn a train when the section ahead is not clear.

block·y (blok′ē) *adj.* **block·i·er, block·i·est. 1** like a block; chunky. **2** having patches of light and shade.
—**block′i·ly,** *adv.* —**block′i·ness,** *n.*

blond (blond) *adj.* **1** light-colored: *blond hair, blond furniture.* **2** having yellow or light-brown hair, usually blue or gray eyes, and light skin: *blond people.*
—*n.* a blond man or boy. [< F < Gmc.]
—**Syn.** *adj.* **2** fair.

☛ **blond, blonde.** As a noun, *blond* is used for men and boys, while *blonde* is used for women and girls; in ambiguous or doubtful cases, *blond* is used: *Mary and her brother are both blonds.* The normal form of the adjective is *blond* for all cases, but some people prefer to use *blonde* as an adjective when referring to women or girls: *a blond young man, a blond actress* or *a blonde actress.* Those who make such distinctions are following a French grammatical pattern.

blonde (blond) *n.* a woman or girl having fair hair.
—*adj.* blond. [< F *blonde,* feminine form of *blond*]
☛ See **blond** for usage note.

blood (blud) *n.* **1** in vertebrates, the red liquid in the veins and arteries. Blood is circulated by the heart,

hat, āge, cãre, fär; let, ēqual, tėrm; it, īce
hot, ōpen, ôrder; oil, out; cup, půt, rüle, ūse
əbove, takən, pencəl, lemən, circəs
ch, child; ng, long; sh, ship
th, thin; ᴛʜ, then; zh, measure

carrying oxygen and digested food to all parts of the body and taking away waste materials. **2** the corresponding liquid in lower animals. **3** bloodshed; slaughter. **4** family; birth; relationship; parentage; descent: *Love of the sea runs in his blood.* **5** high lineage, especially royal lineage: *a prince of the blood.* **6** temper; state of mind: *There was bad blood between them.* **7** a man of dash and spirit. **8** of animals, pure breeding; thoroughbred stock. **9 Blood is thicker than water.** The ties that bind families are stronger than those that link friends. **10 draw first blood,** hit or score first. **11 in cold blood, a** cruelly; without emotion. **b** on purpose.
—*v.* give the first taste or experience of blood to: *Our raw troops were blooded in that battle.* [OE *blōd*]

Blood (blud) *n.* **1** Usually, **Bloods.** one of the three tribes that make up the Blackfeet union or confederacy. The Bloods now live on reserves near Calgary. **2** a member of this tribe.

blood bank 1 a place for storing blood. **2** the blood kept in storage.

blood brother 1 a brother by birth; real brother. **2** a person who goes through a ceremony of mixing some of his blood with another person's.

blood count a count of the number of red and white corpuscles in a sample of a person's blood.

blood·cur·dling (blud′kėr′dling) *adj.* terrifying; horrible: *a bloodcurdling story.*

blood donor a person who gives his blood to a blood bank.

blood·ed (blud′id) *adj.* **1** coming from good stock; of good breed: *blooded horses.* **2 -blooded,** *combining form.* having a —— kind of blood: *red-blooded = having red blood. Snakes are called cold-blooded; lions are warm-blooded.*

blood group any of the main types into which blood is classified.

blood·guilty (blud′gil′tē) *adj.* guilty of murder or bloodshed. —**blood′guilt′i·ness,** *n.*

blood heat the normal temperature of human blood; 98.6 degrees Fahrenheit.

blood·hound (blud′hound′) *n.* **1** a breed of large, powerful dog having a keen sense of smell. **2** a dog of this breed. Bloodhounds are best known for use in tracking fugitives, etc. **3** *Slang.* a detective.

blood·less (blud′lis) *adj.* **1** without blood; pale. **2** without bloodshed. **3** without energy; spiritless. **4** cold-hearted or cruel. —**blood′less·ly,** *adv.* —**blood′less·ness,** *n.*

blood·let·ting (blud′let′ing) *n.* **1** the act of opening a vein to take out blood. **2** bloodshed; wholesale slaughter.

blood·mo·bile (blud′mə bēl′) *n.* a small bus or other vehicle usually staffed with a doctor and a nurse, in which people can give donations of blood without going to a hospital or clinic.

blood money 1 the money paid to have somebody killed. **2** the money paid to make up for killing somebody. **3** *Informal.* money gained at the cost of another person's life, freedom, welfare, etc.

blood poisoning a diseased condition of the blood, caused by poisonous matter or germs.

blood pressure the pressure of the blood against the inner walls of the blood vessels, varying with exertion, excitement, health, age, etc.

blood relation or **relative** a person related by birth.

blood·root (blud′rüt′) *n.* a common wild plant of the poppy family that has a red root, red sap, and a white flower that blooms in early spring.

blood royal the royal family.

blood·shed (blud′shed′) *n.* the shedding of blood; slaughter.

blood·shot (blud′shot′) *adj.* red and sore from inflamed blood vessels; tinged with blood: *Your eyes become bloodshot if you get dirt in them.*

blood·stained (blud′stānd′) *adj.* **1** stained with blood. **2** guilty of murder or bloodshed.

blood·stone (blud′stōn′) *n.* **1** a semiprecious green stone with specks of red jasper scattered through it; heliotrope. **2** a piece of this stone, or a gem made from it.

blood·suck·er (blud′suk′ər) *n.* **1** an animal that sucks blood; leech. **2** a person who gets all he can from others.

blood test an examination of a sample of a person's blood to determine the type of blood, to diagnose illness, etc.

blood·thirst·y (blud′thėrs′tē) *adj.* eager for bloodshed; cruel; murderous. —**blood′thirst′i·ly,** *adv.* —**blood′thirst′i·ness,** *n.*

blood transfusion an injection of blood from one person or animal into another.

blood type blood group.

blood vessel a tube in the body through which the blood circulates: *An artery, vein, or capillary is a blood vessel.*

blood·y (blud′ē) *adj.* **blood·i·er, blood·i·est,** *adv. v.* **blood·ied, blood·y·ing.** —*adj.* **1** bleeding: *a bloody nose.* **2** stained with blood. **3** with much bloodshed: *a bloody battle.* **4** eager for bloodshed; cruel. **5** *Slang.* cursed; confounded; terrible.
—*adv. Slang.* confoundedly, terribly.
—*v.* **1** cause to bleed. **2** stain with blood. —**blood′i·ly,** *adv.* —**blood′i·ness,** *n.* —**Syn.** *adj.* **4** bloodthirsty, murderous.

☛ **bloody,** in its slang usages, is a general intensifier. It is sometimes considered vulgar.

bloom[1] (blüm) *n.* **1** a flower; blossom. **2** the condition or time of flowering. **3** the condition or time of greatest health, vigor, or beauty: *in the bloom of youth.* **4** a glow of health and beauty. **5** the powdery or downy coating on some fruits and leaves. There is a bloom on peaches and plums.
—*v.* **1** have flowers; open into flowers; blossom: *Many plants bloom in the spring.* **2** be in the condition or time of greatest health, vigor, or beauty. **3** glow with health and beauty. [ME < ON *blóm*] —**Syn.** *n.* **3** freshness, prime.

bloom[2] (blüm) *n.* **1** an unmelted, spongy mass of wrought iron. **2** a bar of iron or steel. [OE *blōma* lump]

bloom·er[1] (blüm′ər) *n.* something that blooms.

bloom·er[2] *n. Brit. Slang.* a blunder or mistake.

bloom·ers (blüm′ərz) *n.pl.* **1** loose trousers, gathered at the knee, formerly worn by women and girls for physical training. **2** underwear made like these. [first referred to in a magazine published by Amelia J. *Bloomer* 1851]

bloom·ing (blüm′ing) *adj.* **1** having flowers; blossoming. **2** flourishing. **3** *Brit. Slang.* terrible; confounded: *It's a blooming shame.*

☛ **blooming,** in this slang usage, is a general intensifier and is a euphemism for **bloody** (def. 5).—**bloom′ing·ly,** *adv.*

bloop·er (blüp′ər) *n. Slang.* **1** a mistake; boner. **2** in baseball: **a** a slow-moving, looping, pitched ball. **b** a weakly hit ball.

blos·som (blos′əm) *n.* **1** a flower, especially of a plant that produces fruit: *apple blossoms.* **2** the condition or time of flowering: *a cherry tree in blossom.* —*v.* **1** have flowers; open into flowers. **2** open out; develop. [OE *blōstma*]

blos·som·y (blos′əm ē) *adj.* full of blossoms.

blot (blot) *v.* **blot·ted, blot·ting,** *n.* —*v.* **1** spot with ink; stain; make blots. **2** dry (ink, etc.) with paper that soaks up liquids. **3** blemish; disgrace. **4 blot one's copybook,** spoil one's record or reputation: *He failed to get his promotion after blotting his copybook at the staff party.* **5 blot out, a** hide; cover up. **b** make dim; obscure. **c** wipe out; destroy. [< n.]
—*n.* **1** a spot of ink; stain of any kind. **2** a blemish; disgrace. [ME; origin uncertain] —**Syn.** *v.* **1** blotch, smear. **3** sully, dishonor.

blotch (bloch) *n.* **1** a large, irregular spot or stain. **2** a place where the skin is red or broken out.
—*v.* cover or mark with blotches. [blend of *blot* and *botch*]

blotch·y (bloch′ē) *adj.* **blotch·i·er, blotch·i·est.** having blotches.

blot·ter (blot′ər) *n.* **1** a piece of blotting paper. **2** a book for writing down happenings or transactions: *A police station blotter is a record of arrests.* **3** anything that soaks up or absorbs: *He has a blotter of a mind; he remembers everything.* **4** *Slang.* a drunkard.

blotting paper a soft paper used to dry writing by soaking up the ink.

blouse (blouz or blous) *n.* **1** a loose or fitted garment for the upper part of the body, worn by women and children. **2** any loosely fitted garment for the upper part of the body. Sailors wear blouses. **3** the upper part of a battle dress. **4** a kind of smock reaching to the knees, worn by European peasants and workmen to protect their clothes. [< F < Provençal (*lano*) *blouso* short (wool)]—**blouse′like′**, *adj.*

blow[1] (blō) *n.* **1** a hard hit; knock; stroke. **2** a sudden happening that causes misfortune or loss; severe shock; misfortune: *His mother's death was a great blow to him.* **3** a sudden attack or assault: *The army struck a swift blow at the enemy.* **4 at one blow,** by one act or effort. **5 come to blows,** start fighting. **6 without striking a blow,** with no effort; without even trying. [ME *blaw*]
Syn. **1 Blow, stroke** = a sudden hard hit. **Blow,** both figuratively and literally, emphasizes the force, roughness, and heaviness of a hard knock against something or a hit with the fist or something heavy: *He got a blow on the head.* **Stroke** emphasizes the sharpness and precision of a hit with the hand or something long and narrow, but is most often used in specific senses, as in tennis or art, and figuratively: *His scar was made by a sword stroke across the face.* **2** calamity, disaster.

blow[2] (blō) *v.* **blew, blown, blow·ing,** *n.* —*v.* **1** send forth a strong current of air. **2** move in a current; move rapidly or with power: *The wind blows.* **3** drive or carry by a current of air: *The wind blew the curtains.* **4** force a current of air into, through, or against. **5** clear or empty by forcing air through. **6** form or shape by air: *blow glass.* **7** make or cause to make a sound by a current of air or steam: *The whistle blows at noon.* **8** puff up; swell with air: *blow bubbles.* **9** break by an explosion; blow up; open, etc. **10** be out of breath. **11** put out of breath. **12** *Informal.* boast; brag. **13** of whales, spout water and air. **14** of insects, lay eggs in. Some flies blow fruit. **15** *Slang.* **a** spend (money) recklessly. **b** treat; entertain. **16** melt: *A short circuit will blow a fuse.* **17** publish or spread (news). **18** *Slang.* botch; make a mess of: *The golfer blew his putt.* **19** *Slang.* leave; get out of: *He blew town.*
blow hot and cold, change from a favorable opinion to an unfavorable one; view with fluctuating enthusiasm.
blow in, a *Informal.* appear unexpectedly; drop in. **b** of an oil well, start production; come into production.
blow off, get rid of noisily.
blow out, a extinguish or be extinguished by a puff of breath or other current of air: *Please blow out the candle. The candle has blown out.* **b** have or cause to have a blowout.
blow over, a pass by. **b** be forgotten.
blow up, a explode. **b** fill with air. **c** *Informal.* become very angry. **d** *Informal.* scold; abuse. **e** arise; become stronger: *A storm suddenly blew up.* **f** enlarge (a photograph).
—*n.* **1** the act or fact of forcing air into, through, or against something; blast. **2** a blowing. **3** a gale of wind. [OE *blāwan*]

blow[3] (blō) *v.* **blew, blown, blow·ing,** *n.* blossom; bloom (now used mostly as a past participle: *a full-blown rose*). [OE *blōwan*]

blow·er (blō′ər) *n.* **1** a person or thing that blows: *a glass blower.* **2** a machine for forcing air into a building, furnace, mine, etc.; a fan. **3** a whale. **4** *Informal.* a telephone.

blow·fly (blō′flī′) *n.* **-flies.** any of various two-winged flies that deposit their eggs on meat or in wounds.

blow·gun (blō′gun′) *n.* a tube through which a person blows arrows, darts, dried beans, etc.

blow·hole (blō′hōl′) *n.* **1** a hole where air or gas can escape. **2** a hole for breathing, in the top of the head of whales and some other animals. **3** a hole in the ice where whales, seals, etc. come to breathe. **4** a defect in a piece of metal due to a bubble of air or gas. **5** a defect; flaw.

blown (blōn) *adj.* **1** out of breath; exhausted: *He was blown after climbing the steep hill.* **2** tainted by flies; flyblown; tainted. **3** shaped by blowing. **4** of cattle, having the stomach distended by eating too much green food; bloated.
—*v.* pp. of **blow**[2] and **blow**[3].

blow·out (blō′out′) *n.* **1** the bursting of the inner tube and casing of an automobile tire. **2** a sudden or violent escape of air, steam, etc. **3** the melting of an electric fuse caused by too much current. **4** *Slang.* a big party or meal.

blow·pipe (blō′pīp′) *n.* **1** a tube for blowing air or gas into a flame to increase the heat. **2** a blowgun. **3** a long metal tube used for blowing molten glass into the required shape. **4** in medicine, an instrument for blowing air into a body cavity for cleaning or examination.

blow·torch (blō′tôrch′) *n.* a small torch that shoots out a hot flame. It is used to melt metal and burn off paint.

A blowtorch

blow·up (blō′up′) *n.* **1** an explosion. **2** *Informal.* **a** an outburst of anger. **b** a quarrel. **3** *Informal.* an enlargement (of a photograph).

blow·y (blō′ē) *adj.* **blow·i·er, blow·i·est.** windy.

blowz·y (blouz′ē) *adj.* **blowz·i·er, blowz·i·est. 1** untidy; frowzy. **2** red-faced and coarse-looking. [< *blowze* wench, slattern] —**blowz′i·ly,** *adv.* —**blowz′i·ness,** *n.*

B.L.S. Bachelor of Library Science.

bls. 1 barrels. **2** bales.

blub·ber (blub′ər) *n.* **1** the fat of whales and some other sea animals. **2** a noisy weeping. —*v.* **1** weep noisily. **2** disfigure or swell with crying: *a face all blubbered.* [probably imitative]

blu·cher (blü′chər or blü′kər) *n.* a shoe whose tongue and front part are made from one piece of leather. [after Field Marshal von *Blücher* (1742-1819), a Prussian general]

bludg·eon (bluj′ən) *n.* a short club with a heavy end. —*v.* **1** strike with a club. **2** bully; threaten. [origin unknown] —**bludg′eon·er,** *n.*

blue (blü) *n. adj.* **blu·er, blu·est,** *v.* **blued, blu·ing** or **blue·ing.** —*n.* **1** the color of the clear sky in daylight. **2** a variation of this color. **3** something having this color; blue coloring matter, dye, or pigment. **4 into the blue,** into the far distance; out of sight and knowledge: *disappear into the blue.* **5 out of the blue,** from an unforeseen source; from an unknown place; completely unexpected. **6 the blue, a** the sky. **b** the sea. **7 the blues, a** *Informal.* low spirits. **b** a melancholy popular song with jazz rhythm. **8 Blue,** a Conservative.
—*adj.* **1** having the color of the clear sky in daylight or any tone of this color. **2** livid: *blue from cold or a bruise.* **3** sad; gloomy; discouraged: *She is always feeling blue.* **4** dismal; dispiriting: *The weather is blue.* **5** *Informal.* indecent; obscene: *a blue joke.* **6** of or having to do with Conservatives.
—*v.* **1** make blue. **2** use bluing on. [ME < OF *bleu* < Gmc.] —**blue′ness,** *n.* —**Syn.** *adj.* **3** depressed, despondent, dejected.

Blue·beard (blü′bērd′) *n.* **1** in legend, a man who murdered six of his wives and hid their bodies in a room which he forbade anyone to enter. **2** any man who marries women with the intention of killing them.

Bluebeard's chamber any place where mysteries or terrible secrets are hidden.

blue·bell (blü′bel′) *n.* any of various plants having blue flowers shaped like bells, such as the bluebell of Scotland and the wild hyacinth.

blue·ber·ry (blü′ber′ē or blü′bər ē) *n.* **-ries. 1** a small, sweet, edible, blue berry that has smaller seeds than the huckleberry. **2** the shrub that this berry grows on.

blue·bird (blü′bėrd′) *n.* a small songbird of North America that is related to the robin. The male usually is a bright blue on the back and wings and has an orange breast.

blue-black (blü′blak′) *adj.* bluish-black; very dark blue.

blue blood 1 aristocratic descent. 2 an aristocrat.

blue-blood·ed (blü′blud′id) *adj.* aristocratic.

blue·bon·net (blü′bon′it) *n.* 1 a plant having blue flowers resembling sweet peas. 2 a wide, flat cap made of blue woollen cloth. 3 a person wearing such a cap. 4 a Scotsman.

blue book 1 a book that lists socially prominent people. 2 a booklet with a blue paper cover, used for writing answers to examinations. 3 an official statement of public accounts, published annually by the Government of Canada. 4 a parliamentary or other official publication.

blue·bot·tle (blü′bot′əl) *n.* 1 a large blowfly that has a blue abdomen and a hairy body. 2 any similar fly. 3 a cornflower.

blue·coat (blü′kōt′) *n.* policeman.

blue devils 1 the blues; low spirits. 2 delirium tremens; horrible things seen during delirium tremens.

blue·fin (blü′fin′) *n.* a type of tuna.

blue·fish (blü′fish′) *n.* **-fish** or **-fish·es.** a blue-and-silver salt-water fish of the Atlantic Coast, much esteemed as food.

blue flag an iris that has blue flowers.

blue·grass (blü′gras′) *n.* any of various North American grasses with bluish-green stems, especially **Kentucky bluegrass.**

blue gum eucalyptus.

blue·ing (blü′ing) *n.* bluing.

blue·jacket (blü′jak′it) *n.* a sailor in the navy.

blue·jay (blü′jā′) *n.* a noisy, chattering North American bird having a crest and having blue feathers on its back.

blue laws any very strict and puritanical laws.

blue·line (blü′līn′) *n.* either of the two blue lines drawn midway between the centre of a hockey rink and each goal: *The blueline plays an important part in the rules of hockey.*

Blue·nose (blü′nōz′) *n. Informal.* 1 a Nova Scotian; less often, a New Brunswicker. 2 a ship built in Nova Scotia and manned by Nova Scotians. 3 **bluenose,** a prudish or puritanical person.

blue-pen·cil (blü′pen′səl) *v.* **-cilled** or **-ciled, -cil·ling** or **-cil·ing.** 1 change, cut down, or cross out with a pencil that makes a blue mark. 2 edit; censor.

blue·point (blü′point′) *n.* a kind of small oyster. [< *Blue Point* on Long Island, N.Y., where such oysters are found]

blue·print (blü′print′) *n.* 1 a building plan or map copied photographically on sensitized paper, that shows white outlines on a blue background. 2 a detailed plan for any enterprise. —*v.* 1 make a blueprint of. 2 make or explain a plan in detail.

blue racer a dark-blue, harmless variety of the American black snake.

blue ribbon first prize; highest honor.

blues (blüz) *n.pl.* 1 *Informal.* low spirits. 2 in music, a slow, melancholy song written and composed in a jazz rhythm.

blue·stock·ing (blü′stok′ing) *n. Informal.* a woman who displays great interest in intellectual or literary subjects. [< nickname "*Blue Stocking* Society" given to a group of English women who met (about 1750) to discuss literature]

blue·stone (blü′stōn′) *n.* 1 bluish sandstone. 2 blue vitriol.

blu·et (blü′it) *n.* a small plant of N. America having pale bluish flowers. [< F *bluet,* dim. of *bleu* blue < Gmc.]

blue vitriol copper sulphate. *Formula*: $CuSO_4.5H_2O$

bluff[1] (bluf) *n.* 1 a high, steep bank or cliff. 2 *Cdn.* a clump of trees standing on the flat prairie; copse: *The farmhouse was screened from the wind and the sun by a bluff of poplars.* —*adj.* 1 rising with a straight, broad front. 2 frank and hearty in manner. [probably < Du. *blaf* broad flat face] —**bluff′ly,** *adv.* —**bluff′ness,** *n.* —**Syn.** *adj.* 1 steep. 2 plain-spoken. See **blunt.**

bluff[2] (bluf) *n.* 1 a show of pretended confidence, used to deceive or mislead. 2 an act of bluffing. 3 a threat that cannot be carried out. 4 a person who bluffs. 5 **call a person's bluff,** recognize and refuse to be misled by another's pretence.
—*v.* 1 deceive by a show of pretended confidence. 2 frighten with a threat that cannot be carried out. [? < Du. *bluffen,* baffle; mislead; brag] —**bluff′er,** *n.*

hat, āge, cãre, fär; let, ēqual, tėrm; it, īce
hot, ōpen, ôrder; oil, out; cup, pu̇t, rüle, ūse
əbove, takən, pencəl, lemən, circəs
ch, child; ng, long; sh, ship
th, thin; ᴛʜ, then; zh, measure

blu·ing or **blue·ing** (blü′ing) *n.* a blue liquid or powder put in water when rinsing white clothes, in order to prevent them from turning yellow.

blu·ish (blü′ish) *adj.* somewhat blue.

blun·der (blun′dər) *n.* a stupid mistake. —*v.* 1 make a stupid mistake. 2 do clumsily or wrongly; bungle. 3 move clumsily or blindly; stumble. 4 blurt out; say clumsily or foolishly. [ME *blondre(n)*; origin uncertain] —**blun′der·er,** *n.* —**Syn.** *n.* bungle.

blun·der·buss (blun′dər bus′) *n.* 1 formerly, a short gun with a wide muzzle. 2 a person who blunders. [alteration of Du. *donderbus* thunder box]

blunt (blunt) *adj.* 1 without a sharp edge or point. 2 plain-spoken; outspoken; frank. 3 slow in perceiving or understanding.
—*v.* 1 make blunt. 2 become blunt. [ME; origin uncertain] —**blunt′ly,** *adv.* —**blunt′ness,** *n.*
Syn. *adj.* 1 See **dull.** 2 **Blunt, bluff, curt** = abrupt in speaking or manner. **Blunt** emphasizes speaking plainly and frankly in open disregard of the feelings of others and simple good manners: *He thinks that blunt speech proves he is honest.* **Bluff** suggests a frank and rough manner of speaking and acting combined with heartiness and genuineness: *Everyone likes the bluff policeman on the beat.* **Curt** = rudely abrupt and brief: *A curt nod was the only notice he gave that he knew she was there.*

blur (blėr) *v.* **blurred, blur·ring,** *n.* —*v.* 1 make confused in form or outline: *Mist blurred the hills.* 2 make dim: *Tears blurred my eyes.* 3 become dim or indistinct: *Her eyes blurred with tears.* 4 smear; blot; stain: *He blurred the writing by touching the ink before it was dry.*
—*n.* 1 a blurred condition; dimness. 2 something seen dimly or indistinctly. 3 a smear; blot; stain. [? var. of *blear*]

blurb (blėrb) *n. Informal.* an advertisement or announcement, especially of a book, full of extremely high praise. [supposedly coined in 1907 by Gelett Burgess (1866-1951), an American humorist]

blur·ry (blėr′ē) *adj.* 1 dim; indistinct. 2 smeary; full of blots and stains. —**blur′ri·ness,** *n.*

blurt (blėrt) *v.* say suddenly or without thinking: *In his anger he blurted out the secret.* [imitative]

blush (blush) *n.* 1 a reddening of the skin caused by shame, confusion, or excitement. 2 a rosy color. 3 **at first blush,** on first glance; on first consideration. [< v.]
—*v.* 1 make or become red because of shame, confusion, or excitement: *She was so shy that she blushed every time she was spoken to.* 2 be ashamed: *I blush to observe the errors in my manuscript.* 3 be or become rosy. [ME *blusche* < OE *blyscan* redden]

blus·ter (blus′tər) *v.* 1 storm or blow noisily and violently: *The wind blustered around the house.* 2 talk noisily and violently: *He blusters to cover up his ignorance.* 3 make loud, empty threats: *A cowardly bully often blusters.* 4 do or say noisily and violently. 5 make or get by blustering.
—*n.* 1 stormy noise and violence. 2 noisy and violent talk. [apparently < LG *blüstern* blow violently]

blus·ter·y (blus′tər ē) *adj.* blustering.

blvd. boulevard.

Bn. battalion.

BNA Act or **B.N.A. Act** British North America Act.

B'nai B'rith (bə nā′ brith′ or bə rēth′) a Jewish fraternal society.

BO body odor.

bo·a (bō′ə) *n.* **bo·as.** 1 any of various large tropical snakes, including anacondas, pythons, and boa constrictors. Boas are not poisonous, but kill their prey by coiling around it and squeezing it to death. **2** a long scarf made of fur or feathers, worn around a woman's neck. [< L *boa*, a type of serpent]

BOAC or **B.O.A.C.** British Overseas Aircraft Corporation.

boa constrictor a large tropical American boa.

boar (bôr) *n.* **1** an uncastrated male pig or hog. **2** a wild pig or hog. [OE *bār*]

board (bôrd) *n.* **1** a broad, thin piece of wood ready for use in building, etc. **2** a flat piece of wood used for some special purpose: *an ironing board.* **3** pasteboard: *a book with covers of board.* **4** a flat, specially marked piece of wood, cardboard, etc. on which to play a game: *a chessboard.* **5** a table to serve food on; table. **6** the food served on a table. **7** meals provided for pay. **8** a group of persons managing something; council: *a board of health.* **9** the side of a ship. **10** a border; edge. **11 go by the board, a** fall over the side of a ship. **b** be given up, neglected, or ignored. **12 on board,** on a ship, train, etc. **13 the boards, a** the stage of a theatre. **b** the wooden guard fence surrounding the ice of a hockey rink. **14 tread the boards,** act in a play.
—*v.* **1** cover with boards. **2** provide with regular meals, or room and meals, for pay. **3** get meals, or room and meals, for pay: *Mr. Jones boards at our house.* **4** get on (a ship, train, etc.). **5** come alongside of or against (a ship). **6** sail in a zigzag course against the wind; tack. **7** in hockey, body-check an opposing player into the boards of the rink. [OE *bord*]

board check in hockey, a check made by body-checking an opposing player into the boards of a rink, the checker being subject to a penalty if the referee judges the act to have been violent; boarding.

board-check (bôrd′chek′) *v.* give a board check to (an opposing player).

board·er (bôr′dər) *n.* **1** a person who pays for meals, or for room and meals, at another's house. **2** one of the men assigned to go on board an enemy ship. **3** a resident pupil at a boarding school.

board foot a unit of measure equal to a board one foot square and one inch thick; 144 cubic inches, used for measuring logs and lumber. *Abbrev.*: bd.ft.

board·ing (bôr′ding) *n.* **1** in hockey, the act of checking an an opposing player into the boards of the rink in a rough and illegal manner; board-check. **2** boards. **3** a structure made of boards.

boarding house a house where meals, or room and meals, are provided for pay.

boarding school a school where pupils are lodged and fed.

board measure a system for measuring logs and lumber. The unit is the board foot.

board of control the executive branch of the governing council of certain large cities, consisting of the mayor and two or more controllers.

board of education a group of people, usually elected, who manage the schools in a certain area; school board.

board of health the department of a local government in charge of public health.

board of trade 1 an association of businessmen to protect and advance their interests. **2 Board of Trade,** in Great Britain, the governmental department in charge of commerce and industry.

board·walk (bôrd′wok′ or -wôk′) *n.* a sidewalk or promenade made of boards.

boar·hound (bôr′hound′) *n.* a large dog such as a Great Dane, used for hunting boars.

boast (bōst) *v.* **1** praise oneself; brag. **2** brag about. **3** be proud of. **4** have and be proud of: *Our town boasts many fine parks.* —*n.* **1** a praising of oneself; bragging. **2** something to be proud of. [ME *boste(n)*; origin uncertain] —**boast′er,** *n.* —**boast′ing·ly,** *adv.*
Syn. *v.* **1. Boast, brag** = to praise oneself. **Boast** = talk too much about something one has done or about one's possessions, family, etc., even though there may be some reason to be proud: *He boasts about his new convertible.* **Brag** is informal, and always suggests showing off and exaggerating: *He is always bragging about what he can do with a car.*

boast·ful (bōst′fəl) *adj.* **1** boasting; speaking too well about oneself. **2** fond of boasting. —**boast′ful·ly,** *adv.* —**boast′ful·ness,** *n.*

boat (bōt) *n.* **1** a small, open vessel for travelling on water. **2** a ship. **3** a boat-shaped dish for gravy, sauce, etc. **4 burn one's boats,** cut off all chances of retreat. **5 in the same boat,** in the same position or condition; taking the same chances.
—*v.* **1** go in a boat. **2** put or carry in a boat. [OE *bāt*]

boat hook a pole having a metal hook at one end, used for pulling or pushing a boat, raft, etc.

boat·house (bōt′hous′) *n.* a house or shed for sheltering a boat or boats.

boat livery a boathouse where boats are hired out.

boat·load (bōt′lōd′) *n.* **1** as much or as many as a boat can hold or carry. **2** the load that a boat is carrying.

boat·man (bōt′mən) *n.* **-men** (-mən). **1** a man who rents out boats or takes care of them. **2** a man who rows or sails boats for pay. **3** a man who works on a boat.

boat·swain (bō′sən; *less often,* bōt′swān′) *n.* a ship's officer in charge of the deck crew, the anchors, ropes, rigging, etc. Also **bo's'n, bosun.**

bob[1] (bob) *v.* **bobbed, bob·bing,** *n.* —*v.* **1** move up and down, or to and fro, with short, quick motions: *bob a curtsy. The bird bobbed its head up and down.* **2** try to catch with the teeth something floating or hanging: *One game at the party was to bob for apples in a bowl of water.* **3 bob up,** appear suddenly or unexpectedly.
—*n.* a short, quick motion up and down, or to and fro. [ME; origin uncertain]

bob[2] (bob) *n. v.* **bobbed, bob·bing.** —*n.* **1** a short haircut. **2** a horse's docked tail. **3** a weight on the end of a pendulum or plumb line. **4** a float for a fishing line. **5** a bobsled.
—*v.* **1** cut (hair) short. **2** fish with a bob. [ME *bobbe* bunch; origin uncertain]

bob[3] (bob) *n. v.* **bobbed, bob·bing.** —*n.* a light rap; tap. —*v.* rap lightly; tap. [ME; origin uncertain]

bob[4] (bob) *n.* **bob.** *Brit. Slang.* a shilling. [origin uncertain]

bob·bin (bob′ən) *n.* a reel or spool for holding thread, yarn, etc. Bobbins are used in spinning, weaving, machine sewing, and lacemaking. Wire is also wound on bobbins. [< F *bobine*]

bob·bi·net (bob′ə net′) *n.* a cotton netting or lace made by machines. [< *bobbin* + *net*[1]]

bob·by (bob′ē) *n.* **-bies.** *Brit. Slang.* a policeman. [after Sir *Robert* Peel (1788-1850), who improved the London police system]

bobby pin a metal hairpin whose prongs close on and hold tightly to the hair.

bob·by·socks (bob′ē soks′) *n.pl. Informal.* ankle-length socks, worn by young girls.

bob·by·sox·er (bob′ē sok′sər) *n. Informal.* an adolescent girl, especially one who enthusiastically follows every new fad.

bob·cat (bob′kat′) *n.* a wildcat; lynx.

bob·o·link (bob′ə lingk′) *n.* a North American songbird that lives in fields and meadows. [imitative]

bob·skate (bob′skāt′) *n.* a child's skate that consists of two sections of double runners and is adjustable to the size of the wearer's foot.

bob·sled (bob′sled′) *n. v.* **-sled·ded, -sled·ding.** —*n.* **1** two short sleds fastened together by a plank, or a long sled with two sets of runners and a continuous seat. **2** either of the short sleds. —*v.* ride or coast on a bobsled.

bob·sleigh (bob′slā′) *n. v.* **-sleighed, -sleigh·ing.** bobsled.

bob·stay (bob′stā′) *n.* on a ship, a rope or chain to hold a bowsprit down. See picture under **bowsprit.**

bob·tail (bob′tāl′) *n.* **1** a short tail; tail cut short. **2** a horse or dog having a bobtail. —*adj.* having a bobtail.

bob·white (bob′hwīt′ or -wīt′) *n.* a North American quail that has a grayish body with brown and white markings. Its call sounds like its name. [imitative]

bob·wire (bob′wīr′) *n.* barbed wire.

Boche or **boche** (bosh or bōsh) *n. Derogatory.* a German. [< F *boche* < *tête de boche* blockhead, earlier *tête de caboche* < *caboche* skull, ult. < L *caput* head]

bock (bok) *n.* bock beer.

bock beer a strong, dark beer, usually sold in the spring. [< G *Bockbier* for *Eimbocker Bier* beer of *Eimbock*, variant of Einbeck, a city in Germany]

bode[1] (bōd) *v.* **bod·ed, bod·ing.** **1** be a sign of; indicate beforehand: *Dark clouds boded rain.* **2 bode ill,** be a bad sign. **3 bode well,** be a good sign. [OE *bodian* < *boda* messenger] —**Syn. 1** portend, foreshadow.

bode[2] (bōd) *v.* pt. of **bide.**

bod·ice (bod′is) *n.* **1** the waist of a woman's dress. **2** a close-fitting, sometimes sleeveless, waist worn over a dress or blouse, laced up the front. In some districts of Europe, it forms part of a peasant woman's costume. [var. of pl. of *body*, part of a dress]

-bodied *combining form.* having a certain kind of body: *lean-bodied = having a lean body.*

bod·i·less (bod′ē lis) *adj.* without a body.

bod·i·ly (bod′ə lē) *adj.* of the body; in the body: *bodily pain.* —*adv.* **1** in person: *The man we thought dead walked bodily into the room.* **2** all together; as one group: *The audience rose bodily.* —**Syn.** *adj.* corporeal, physical.

bod·kin (bod′kin) *n.* **1** a large, blunt needle. **2** a long hairpin. **3** a pointed tool for making holes. [ME *boydekyn* dagger; origin unknown]

bod·y (bod′ē) *n.* **bod·ies,** *v.* **bod·ied, bod·y·ing.** —*n.* **1** the whole material part of a man, animal, or plant. **2** the main part or trunk of an animal, apart from the head or limbs. **3** the main part; larger part, such as the nave of a church, the hull of a ship. **4** the part of a vehicle that holds the passengers or the load. **5** the fuselage of an airplane. **6** the main part of a speech or document, excluding the introduction, etc. **7** a group of persons considered together; collection of persons or things: *a body of troops.* **8** *Informal.* a person: *He is a good-natured body.* **9** a dead person; corpse. **10** a mass; portion of matter: *A lake is a body of water.* **11** matter; substance; density; substantial quality: *Thick soup has more body than thin soup.* **12** that part of a garment that covers the trunk above the waist. **13 keep body and soul together,** keep alive.
—*v.* **1** provide with a body; give substance to; embody. **2 body forth, a** give a real form to. **b** be a sign of. [OE *bodig*]

bod·y·check (bod′ē chek′) *n.* in hockey, lacrosse, etc., a defensive play by which a player impedes an opponent's progress by body contact. Also, **body check.** —*v.* employ a bodycheck.

bod·y·guard (bod′ē gärd′) *n.* **1** a man or men who guard a person. **2** a retinue; escort.

body politic the people forming a political group with an organized government.

body snatcher a person who steals bodies from graves.

Boe·o·tian (bē ō′shən) *adj.* **1** of Boeotia, a district in ancient Greece, or its people. **2** stupid. —*n.* **1** a native of Boeotia. The Boeotians were considered stupid. **2** a stupid person.

Boer (bür or bôr) *n.* a person of Dutch descent living in South Africa. [< Du. *boer* farmer]

Boer War the war between Great Britain and the Boers of South Africa, which lasted from 1899 to 1902.

bog (bog) *n. v.* **bogged, bog·ging.** —*n.* soft, wet, spongy ground; a marsh or swamp. —*v.* **1** sink or get stuck in a bog. **2 bog down,** get stuck as if in mud. [< Irish or Scots Gaelic *bog* soft]

bo·gan (bō′gən) *n. Esp.Cdn.* in the Maritimes, a backwater or quiet tributary stream of a river. [< Algonquian *pokelogan.* Doublet of LOGAN.]

bo·gey[1] (bō′gē) *n.* **-geys,** *v.* —*n.* in golf: **1** one stroke over par: *He shot a bogey on the seventh hole.* **2** the score that players try to equal; par.

hat, āge, cãre, fär; let, ēqual, tėrm; it, īce
hot, ōpen, ôrder; oil, out; cup, pu̇t, rüle, ūse
əbove, takən, pencəl, lemən, circəs
ch, child; ng, long; sh, ship
th, thin; ᴛʜ, then; zh, measure

—*v.* play a hole in one stroke over par. [< Colonel *Bogey*, imaginary partner]

bo·gey[2] or **bo·gy** (bō′gē) *n.* **-geys** or **-gies.** **1** an evil spirit or goblin. **2** a person or thing that is feared; bugbear. **3** *Slang.* an unidentified aircraft. Also, **bogie.** [< obsolete *bog* bugbear]

bog·gle (bog′əl) *v.* **-gled, -gling,** *n.* —*v.* **1** blunder; bungle; botch. **2** hold back; hesitate. **3** jump with fright; shy. —*n.* a blunder; bungle; botch. [? < *bogle*] —**bog′gler,** *n.* —**bog′gling·ly,** *adv.*

bog·gy (bog′ē) *adj.* **-gi·er, -gi·est.** soft and wet like a bog; marshy; swampy.

bo·gie (bō′gē) *n.* bogey[2].

bo·gle (bō′gəl) *n.* bogey[2]. [See BOGEY[2].]

bo·gus (bō′gəs) *adj.* counterfeit; sham: *a bogus ten-dollar bill.*

bo·gy (bō′gē) *n.* **-gies.** bogey[2].

Bo·he·mi·a (bō hē′mē ə or bō hēm′yə) *n.* **1** a former country in central Europe, now a region of Czechoslovakia. **2** a free and easy, unconventional sort of life; a place where artists, writers, etc. live such a life.

Bo·he·mi·an (bō hē′mē ən or bō hēm′yən) *adj.* **1** of Bohemia, its people, or their language. **2** Often, **bohemian.** free and easy; unconventional.
—*n.* **1** a native or inhabitant of Bohemia. **2** the language of Bohemia; Czech. **3** Often, **bohemian.** an artist, writer, etc. who lives in a free and easy, unconventional way. **4** a gypsy.

Bo·he·mi·an·ism (bō hē′mē ən iz′əm or bō hēm′yən iz′əm) *n.* a free and easy way of living; unconventional habits.

Bo·hunk (bō′hungk) *n. Slang. Derogatory.* a central-European immigrant; hunky[2]. [< *Bo*hemian + *Hung*arian]

boil[1] (boil) *v.* **1** of liquids, bubble up and give off vapor. **2** cause to boil. **3** cook by boiling: *boil eggs.* **4** of a container, have its contents boil. **5** clean or sterilize by boiling. **6** be very excited or angry: *He boiled with anger.* **7** move violently. **8 boil down, a** reduce by boiling. **b** reduce by getting rid of unimportant parts. **9 boil over, a** come to the boiling point and overflow. **b** show excitement or anger.
—*n.* **1** a boiling. **2** a boiling condition. [ME *boille* < OF *boillir* < L *bullire* form bubbles]

Syn. *v.* **6 Boil, simmer, seethe,** figuratively used, mean "to be emotionally excited." **Boil** suggests being so stirred up by emotion, usually anger, that one's feelings and, often, blood are thought of as heated to boiling point: *My blood boils at the suggestion.* **Simmer** suggests less intense emotion or greater control, so that one's feelings are just below the boiling point: *I was simmering with laughter.* **Seethe** suggests being violently stirred up, so that a person's mind or feelings or a group of people are thought of as boiling and foaming: *The people seethed with discontent.*

boil[2] (boil) *n.* **1** a painful, red swelling on the skin, formed by pus around a hard core. Boils are often caused by infection. **2 blind boil,** a boil that has no visible pus sac. [OE *bȳl(e)*]

boil·er (boil′ər) *n.* **1** a container for heating liquids. **2** a tank for making steam to heat buildings or drive engines. **3** a tank for holding hot water.

boiling point the temperature at which a liquid boils. The boiling point of water at sea level is 212 degrees Fahrenheit or 100 degrees centigrade.

bois-brû·lé (bwä′brü lā′; *French,* bwä bʀʏ lā′) *Cdn.* formerly, a half-breed Indian, especially one that is half French; Métis. [< Cdn.F *bois brûlé* charred wood, referring to the complexion of half-breeds]

bois·ter·ous (bois′tər əs or bois′trəs) *adj.* **1** noisily cheerful: *a boisterous game.* **2** violent; rough: *a boisterous wind, a boisterous child.* [ME *boistrous,* earlier *boistous*; origin unknown] —**bois′ter·ous·ly,** *adv.* —**bois′ter·ous·ness,** *n.*

bo·la (bō′lə) *n.* a weapon consisting of stone or metal balls tied to cords. South American cowboys throw the bola so that it winds around the animal at which it is aimed. [< Sp. and Pg. *bola* ball < L *bulla* bubble]

bo·las (bō′ ləs) *n.* bola.

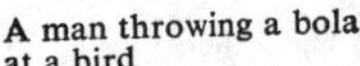
A man throwing a bola at a bird

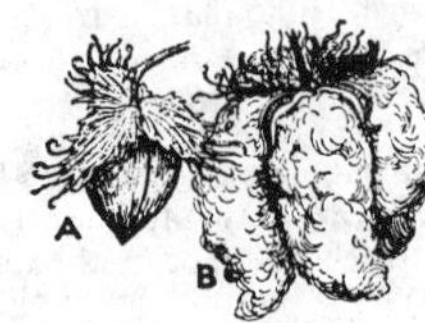

Cotton bolls: A, unopened; B, opened.

bold (bōld) *adj.* **1** without fear; daring: *a bold knight, a bold explorer.* **2** showing or requiring courage: *a bold act.* **3** too free in manner; impudent: *The bold little boy made faces at us as we passed.* **4** striking; vigorous; free; clear: *The mountains stood in bold outline against the sky.* **5** steep; abrupt: *Bold cliffs overlooked the sea.* **6 make bold,** take the liberty; dare. [OE *bald*] —**bold′ly,** *adv.* —**bold′ness,** *n.*
Syn. 1 fearless, courageous, brave. **3 Bold, brazen, forward** = too free in manner. **Bold** suggests lacking proper shame and modesty and pushing oneself forward too rudely: *He swaggered into school late with a bold look on his face.* **Brazen** = defiantly and insolently shameless: *He is brazen about being expelled.* **Forward** suggests being too sure of oneself, too disrespectful of others, too pert in pushing oneself forward: *With her forward ways, that girl will make no friends.*

bold·face (bōld′fās′) *n.* a heavy type that stands out clearly. **This sentence is in boldface.** *Abbrev.*: bf.

bole (bōl) *n.* the trunk of a tree. [ME < ON *bolr*]

bo·le·ro (bə lãr′ ō) *n.* **-ros. 1** a lively Spanish dance in 3/4 time. **2** the music for it. **3** a short, loose jacket. [< Sp.]

bol·i·var (bol′ ə vər; *Spanish,* bō lē′vär) *n.* **1** a unit of money in Venezuela. See table at **money. 2** a coin worth one bolivar. [< Simon *Bolivar* (1783-1830), Venezuelan general and statesman]

bo·liv·i·a (bə liv′ ē ə) *n.* a soft, woollen cloth resembling plush. [< *Bolivia,* a country in South America]

boll (bōl) *n.* a rounded seed pod or capsule of cotton or flax. See the picture above. [var. of *bowl*]

boll weevil a long-billed beetle whose larva damages young cotton bolls.

boll·worm (bōl′wėrm′) *n.* **1** a moth larva that eats the seeds of cotton and cotton bolls. **2** a moth larva that eats the ears of corn, cotton bolls, and parts of other plants.

bo·lo (bō′ lō) *n.* **-los.** a long, heavy knife, used in the Philippine Islands. [< Sp. < Philippine dial.]

bo·lo·gna (bə lō′ nē or bə lō′ nə) *n.* a large sausage made of beef, veal, and pork. [< *Bologna,* a city in Italy]

bo·lom·e·ter (bō lom′ə tər) *n.* an instrument used to measure the intensity of radiant energy, especially in small amounts. [< Gk. *bolē* ray + E *-meter*]

bo·lo·ney (bə lō′ nē) *n. Esp.Brit.* baloney.

Bol·she·vik or **bol·she·vik** (bol′ shə vik′ or bōl′ shə vik′) *n.* **Bol·she·viks** or **bol·she·viks, Bol·she·vi·ki** or **bol·she·vi·ki** (bol′ shə vē′ kē or bōl′ shə vē′ kē), *adj.* —*n.* **1** in Russia, a member of the radical wing of the Social Democratic Party, which seized power in November, 1917. The Bolsheviks formed the Communist party in 1918. **2** an extreme radical. —*adj.* **1** of the Bolsheviks or Bolshevism. **2** extremely radical. [< Russian *bolshevik* < *bolshe* greater; because it was at one time the majority wing. Opposed to MENSHEVIK.]

Bol·she·vism or **bol·she·vism** (bol′ shə viz′əm or bōl′ shə viz′əm) *n.* **1** the doctrines and methods of the Bolsheviks. **2** extreme radicalism.

Bol·she·vist or **bol·she·vist** (bol′ shə vist or bōl′ shə vist) *n. adj.* Bolshevik.

Bol·she·vis·tic or **bol·she·vis·tic** (bol′ shə vis′ tik or bōl′ shə vis′ tik) *adj.* of or like the Bolsheviks.

Bol·she·vize or **bol·she·vize** (bol′ shə vīz′ or bōl′ shə vīz′) *v.* **-vized, -viz·ing.** make Bolshevistic.

bol·ster (bōl′ stər) *n.* **1** a long pillow for a bed. **2** a pad or cushion, often ornamental. —*v.* **1** support with a bolster; support. **2 bolster up,** support; keep from falling; prop. [OE]

bolt[1] (bōlt) *n.* **1** a rod with a head on one end and a screw thread for a nut on the other. Bolts are used to fasten things together or hold them in place. See **nut** for diagram. **2** a sliding fastener for a door. **3** the part of a lock moved by a key. **4** a sliding bar that opens and closes the breech of a rifle, etc. The opening and closing of the bolt after firing ejects the used cartridge case and places a new one in position for firing. **5** a short arrow with a thick head. Bolts were shot from crossbows. **6** a discharge of lightning. **7** a sudden start; a running away. **8** a roll of cloth or wallpaper. **9** refusal to support one's political party or its candidates. **10 bolt from the blue,** a sudden, unexpected happening; surprise. **11 shoot one's bolt,** do as much or as well as one can; do all one can so that further effort is either useless or impossible: *He would like to have tried again for the championship, but he was over age and had shot his bolt.*
—*v.* **1** fasten with a bolt. **2** dash away; run away: *The horse bolted.* **3** break away from or refuse to support one's political party or its candidates. **4** move suddenly; rush. **5** swallow (food) without chewing. **6** go to seed very quickly; become too tall, tough, etc. for use as food: Some kinds of lettuce often bolt in hot weather. —*adv.* **bolt upright,** stiff and straight. [OE *bolt* arrow]

bolt[2] (bōlt) *v.* **1** sift through a cloth or sieve: *Flour is bolted to remove the bran.* **2** examine carefully; separate. [ME *bulte* < OF *bulter*]

bolt·er[1] (bōl′ tər) *n.* **1** a horse that runs away. **2** a person who breaks away from or refuses to support his political party or its candidates. [< *bolt*[1]]

bolt·er[2] (bōl′ tər) *n.* a cloth or sieve used for sifting flour, meal, etc. [< *bolt*[2]]

bo·lus (bō′ ləs) *n.* **1** a small, rounded mass, especially of medicine. **2** a lump of masticated food, ready to swallow. **3** any small, rounded mass. [< L < Gk. *bōlos* lump]

bomb (bom) *n.* **1** a container filled with an explosive charge or a chemical substance and exploded by a fuse, a time mechanism, or the force with which it hits something. **2** a container filled with liquid under pressure, such as paint, insect poison, etc.: *We used a bomb to rid the house of moths.* **3** a sudden, unexpected happening; disturbing surprise.
—*v.* attack with bombs; hurl bombs at; drop bombs on. [< MF *bombe* < Ital. < L *bombus* < Gk. *bombos* boom[1]]

bom·bard (bom bärd′) *v.* **1** attack with heavy fire of shot and shell from big guns: *The artillery bombarded the enemy all day.* **2** drop bombs on: *Aircraft bombarded the hydro-electric plant and destroyed it.* **3** keep attacking vigorously: *The lawyer bombarded the witness with question after question.* **4** subject (atomic nuclei) to a stream of fast-moving particles, thus changing the structure of the nuclei. [< F *bombarder* < *bombarde* cannon < Med.L *bombarda* < L *bombus.* See BOMB.]

bom·bar·dier[1] (bom′ bə dēr′ or bom′ə dēr′) *n.* **1** a corporal in the artillery. **2** the man in a bomber who aims and releases the bombs. *Abbrev.*: Bdr. [< MF *bombardier* < *bombarde* cannon. See BOMBARD.]

bom·bar·dier[2] (bom′ bə dēr′) *n. Cdn.* **1** a vehicle used for travelling over snow and ice, sometimes equipped with tracked wheels at the rear and a set of skis at the front. **2 Bombardier,** a trademark for such a machine. [< Armand *Bombardier* (1908-1964), inventor and manufacturer of the machine]

bom·bard·ment (bom bärd′ mənt) *n.* **1** an attack with heavy fire of shot and shell or with bombs. **2** the subjection of atomic nuclei to a stream of fast-moving particles. **3** any vigorous attack, especially one that is prolonged.

bom·ba·sine (bom′ bə zēn′ or bom′ bə zēn′) *n.* bombazine.

bom·bast (bom′ bast) *n.* high-sounding, pompous language. [earlier *bombace* < OF *bombace, bambace*

< Med.L < Med.Gk. *bambax* cotton < Gk. *bombyx* silkworm, silk]

bom·bas·tic (bom bas′tik) *adj.* using bombast. —**bom·bas′ti·cal·ly,** *adv.*

bom·ba·zine (bom′bə zēn′ or bom′bə zēn′) *n.* a twilled cloth made of silk and wool or cotton and wool. Also, **bombasine.** [< early modern F *bombasin* < Ital. *bambagino* made of cotton, ult. < Med.Gk. *bambax* cotton. See BOMBAST.]

bomb bay in an airplane, the space in which bombs are carried and from which they are dropped.

bomb·er (bom′ər) *n.* **1** a combat airplane used for dropping bombs on the enemy. **2** a person who throws or drops bombs.

bomb·proof (bom′prüf′) *adj.* strong enough to be safe from bombs and shells. —*n.* a bombproof shelter.

bomb·shell (bom′shel′) *n.* **1** a bomb. **2** a sudden, unexpected happening; disturbing surprise.

bomb·sight (bom′sīt′) *n.* an instrument used to find that point in the flight of an airplane where dropping a bomb will cause the bomb to fall exactly on the target.

bo·na fi·de (bō′nə fīd′, bō′nə fī′dē, or bō′nə fē′dā) in good faith; genuine; without make-believe or fraud. [< L]

bo·nan·za (bə nan′zə) *n.* **1** a rich mass of ore in a mine. **2** *Informal.* any rich source of profit. [< Sp. *bonanza* fair weather, prosperity < L *bonus* good]

Bo·na·part·ist (bō′nə pär′tist) *n.* a follower or supporter of Napoleon Bonaparte (1769-1821) and his family.

bon·bon (bon′bon′) *n.* a piece of candy. Bonbons often have fancy shapes. [< F]

bond[1] (bond) *n.* **1** anything that ties, binds, or unites: *a bond of affection between sisters.* **2** a certificate issued by a government or company promising to pay back with interest the money borrowed. **3** a written agreement by which a person says he will pay a certain sum of money if he does not perform certain duties properly. **4** any agreement or binding engagement. **5** a person who acts as surety for another. **6** the condition of goods placed in a warehouse until taxes are paid: *Imported jewellery is held in bond until customs duty has been paid.* **7** a way of arranging bricks, stones, or boards to bind them together. **8** a brick, stone, or board that binds together. **9** a substance that binds together the other ingredients of a mixture: *Cement is the bond in concrete.* **10** a kind of paper having a high rag content and treated so that it absorbs very little ink or moisture. **11 bonds,** *pl.* **a** chains; shackles. **b** imprisonment.
—*v.* **1** issue bonds on; mortgage. **2** provide surety against financial loss for: *bond an employee.* **3** put (goods) under bond. **4** bind or join firmly together. [var. of *band*[2]] —**bond′a·ble,** *adj.* —**bond′er,** *n.*

Syn. *n.* **1 Bond, tie,** used figuratively, mean something that joins people. **Bond** applies particularly to a connection that brings two people or a group so closely together that they may be considered as one: *The members of the club are joined by bonds of fellowship.* **Tie** may be used interchangeably with bond, but applies particularly to connections of a more involved and less voluntary nature: *When he went away, he severed all ties with his old life.* **4** compact. **5** security.

bond[2] (bond) *adj.* in slavery; captive; not free. [ME < ON *bóndi* peasant, originally, dweller]

bond·age (bon′dij) *n.* **1** the lack of freedom; slavery. **2** the condition of being under some power or influence.

bond·ed (bon′did) *adj.* **1** secured by bonds. **2** put in a warehouse until taxes are paid.

bond·hold·er (bond′hōl′dər) *n.* a person who owns bonds issued by a government or company.

bond·maid (bond′mād′) *n.* a girl or woman slave.

bond·man (bond′mən) *n.* **-men** (-mən). **1** a slave. **2** in the Middle Ages, a serf.

bond paper bond (def. 10).

bond servant 1 a servant bound, sometimes for a specified time only, to work without pay. **2** a slave.

bonds·man (bondz′mən) *n.* **-men** (-mən). **1** a person who becomes responsible for another by giving a bond. **2** a slave. **3** in the Middle Ages, a serf.

bond·wom·an (bond′wům′ən) *n.* **-wom·en.** a woman slave.

bone (bōn) *n. v.* **boned, bon·ing.** —*n.* **1** in vertebrates,

hat, āge, câre, fär; let, ēqual, tėrm; it, īce
hot, ōpen, ôrder; oil, out; cup, půt, rüle, ūse
əbove, takən, pencəl, lemən, circəs
ch, child; ng, long; sh, ship
th, thin; ᴛʜ, then; zh, measure

one of the pieces of the skeleton. **2** the hard substance of which bones are made. **3** anything like bone. Ivory is sometimes called bone. **4 bones,** *pl.* **a** *Slang.* dice. **b** wooden clappers used in keeping time to music. **c** an end man in a minstrel show. **d** a skeleton. **5 feel in one's bones,** be sure without knowing why. **6 have a bone to pick,** have cause for argument or complaint. **7 make no bones,** *Informal.* have no scruples; show no hesitation. **8 near the bone, a** very exacting; mean: *A harsh employer comes near the bone.* **b** nearly indecent or obscene: *The speaker's jokes were very near the bone.*
—*v.* **1** take bones out of: *bone fish.* **2** stiffen by putting whalebone or steel strips in. **3** *Slang.* **a** study hard. **b bone up on,** study, especially for an examination: *I must bone up on algebra before tomorrow.* [OE *bān*]
—**bone′less,** *adj.* —**bone′like′,** *adj.*

bone·black (bōn′blak′) *n.* a black powder made by roasting bones in closed containers, used to remove color from liquids and as a coloring matter.

bone china a particularly white and translucent type of china made by mixing bone ash or calcium phosphate with clay.

bone-dry (bōn′drī) *adj.* very dry.

bone meal crushed or ground bones, used as fertilizer and as food for animals.

bon·er (bōn′ər) *n. Slang.* a foolish mistake; stupid error; blunder.

bon·fire (bon′fīr′) *n.* a fire built outdoors. [ME *bonefire* bone fire]

bon·go (bong′gō) *n.* a small, tuned drum played in pairs with the hands. [< Am. Sp.]

bon·ho·mie (bon′ə mē′) *n.* good nature; courteous and pleasant ways. [< F *bonhomie* < *bonhomme* good fellow]

bo·ni·to (bə nē′tō) *n.* **-tos** or **toes.** a type of saltwater fish having red, edible flesh. Bonitos are related to the mackerel and the tuna. [< Sp. *bonito* pretty < L *bonus* good]

bon jour (bôɴ zhür′) *French.* good morning; good day.

bonk (bongk) *n. v. Slang.* hit, especially on the head.

bon mot (bôɴ mō′) **bons mots** (bôɴ mōz′; *French,* bôɴ mō′). *French.* a clever saying; witty remark.

bon·net (bon′it) *n.* **1** a head covering usually tied under the chin with strings or ribbons, worn by women and children. **2** especially in Scotland, a cap worn by men and boys. **3** a head-dress of feathers worn by North American Indians. **4** a covering that protects a machine or chimney. **5** *Esp.Brit.* the hood covering the engine of a car, truck, etc.
—*v.* put a bonnet on. [ME < OF *bonet, bonnet,* originally, fabric for hats]

bon·nie or **bon·ny** (bon′ē) *adj.* **-ni·er, -ni·est. 1** pretty; handsome. **2** fine; excellent. **3** healthy-looking. [ME *bonie,* apparently < OF *bon, bonne* good < L *bonus*] —**bon′ni·ly,** *adv.* —**bon′ni·ness,** *n.*

bon soir (bôɴ swär′) *French.* good evening.

bon·spiel (bon′spēl′) *n.* in curling, a tournament among different clubs or among teams of the same club. [? < Du. *bond* contract, league + *spel* game]

bon ton (bôɴ tôɴ′) *French.* **1** good style; fashion. **2** fashionable society. **3** good breeding.

bo·nus (bō′nəs) *n.* something extra; something given in addition to what is due: *The company gave all its employees a Christmas bonus.* —*v. Cdn.* offer a bonus for (work to be done, as for the construction of a railway line); subsidize. [< L *bonus* good]

bon vi·vant (bôɴ vē väɴ′) **bons vi·vants** (bôɴ vē väɴ′). *French.* a person who is fond of good food and luxury.

bon vo·yage (bôɴ vwä yäzh′) *French.* good-bye; good luck; pleasant trip.

bon·y (bōn′ē) *adj.* **bon·i·er, bon·i·est. 1** of bone. **2** like bone. **3** full of bones. **4** having big bones that stick out. **5** thin. **—bon′i·ness,** *n.*

boo (bü) *n.* **boos,** *interj., v.* **booed, boo·ing.** *—n., interj.* a sound made to show dislike or contempt or to frighten. *—v.* **1** make such a sound. **2** cry "boo" at.

boob (büb) *n. Slang.* **1** a stupid person; fool; dunce. **2** a foolish mistake. *—v. Slang.* make a foolish mistake. [< *booby.* See BOOBY.]

boo·by (bü′bē) *n.* **-bies. 1** a stupid person; fool; dunce. **2** a kind of large sea bird of the tropics. **3** the person who does worst in a game or contest. [probably < Sp. *bobo* (defs. 1, 2) < L *balbus* stammering]

booby hatch 1 the covering over a hatchway on a boat. **2** *Slang.* an asylum for the insane.

booby prize a prize given to the person who does worst in a game or contest.

booby trap 1 a trick arranged to annoy some unsuspecting person. **2** a bomb arranged to explode when an object is grasped, pushed, etc. by an unsuspecting person.

boo·dle (bü′dəl) *n. Slang.* **1** graft; money from bribes. **2** the lot; pack; crowd (used especially in the phrase, *the whole kit and boodle*). [Du. *boedel* goods]

boog·ie-woog·ie (bůg′ē wůg′ē) *n.* in music, a form of jazz marked by a repeating bass figure under the melody.

boo·hoo (bü′hü′) *v.* **-hooed, -hoo·ing,** *n.* **-hoos.** *—v.* cry loudly. *—n.* loud crying.

book (bůk) *n.* **1** a written or printed work of considerable length, especially on sheets of paper bound together. **2** blank sheets bound together. **3** a division of a literary work: *the books of the Bible.* **4** the words of an opera, operetta, etc.; libretto. **5** a record of bets. **6** something fastened together like a book: *a book of tickets.* **7** in certain card games, a trick or a specified number of tricks forming a set.
books, the complete records of a business.
bring to book, a demand an explanation from. **b** rebuke.
by the book, authoritatively; with careful attention to accuracy and detail: *He speaks by the book. He never risks an opinion but always works by the book.*
close the books, stop entering items in an account book.
in one's book, *Informal.* in one's opinion or judgment: *In my book, swearing is always unnecessary.*
keep a book, run a betting system.
keep books, keep a record or business accounts.
in one's good (or **bad**) **books,** in favor (or disfavor) with one: *He may be wild, but he is still in my good books.*
on the books, on the official list (of members of a club, university, etc.).
the Book, the Bible.
throw the book at, *Slang.* **a** punish to the full limit of the law. **b** reprimand severely.
—v. **1** enter in a book or list. **2** engage (a place, passage, etc.): *They booked two staterooms on the steamship.* **3** engage; make engagements for: *The lecturer is booked for every night of the week.* [OE *bōc*] **—book′er,** *n.* **—book′less,** *adj.*

book agent a book salesman.

book·bind·er (bůk′bīn′dər) *n.* a person whose work or business is binding books.

book·bind·er·y (bůk′bīn′dər ē or -bīn′drē) *n.* **-er·ies.** an establishment for binding books.

book·binding (bůk′bīnd′ing) *n.* **1** the binding of a book. **2** the art or business of binding books.

book·case (bůk′kās′) *n.* a piece of furniture with shelves for holding books.

book club a business organization that regularly supplies selected books to subscribers.

book end something placed at the end of a row of books to hold them upright.

book·ie (bůk′ē) *n. Informal.* bookmaker (def. 2).

book·ing (bůk′ing) *n.* **1** an engagement to perform, lecture, etc.: *The pianist has bookings for a six-week tour.* **2** a reservation: *He made a booking for his flight to Yellowknife. We have a booking at the hotel.*

book·ish (bůk′ish) *adj.* **1** fond of reading or studying. **2** knowing books better than real life. **3** having to do with books. **4** learned; pedantic. **—book·ish·ly,** *adv.* **—book′ish·ness,** *n.*

book·keep·er (bůk′kēp′ər) *n.* a person who keeps a record of business accounts.

book·keep·ing (bůk′kēp′ing) *n.* the work or art of keeping a record of business accounts.

book learning knowledge learned from books, not from real life.

book·let (bůk′lit) *n.* a little book; a thin book or pamphlet. It usually has paper covers.

book·lore (bůk′lôr′) *n.* book learning.

book·mak·er (bůk′māk′ər) *n.* **1** a maker of books. **2** a person who makes a business of accepting bets on horse races.

book·mak·ing (bůk′māk′ing) *n.* **1** the business of taking bets on horse races, etc. at odds fixed by the takers. **2** the compiling and manufacture of books.

book·man (bůk′mən) *n.* **1** a scholar or literary man. **2** a publisher, editor, or other person engaged in the book business.

book·mark (bůk′märk′) *n.* **1** something put between the pages of a book to mark the place. **2** a bookplate.

book matches a strip of paper matches enclosed in a cardboard folder.

book·mo·bile (bůk′mə bēl′) *n.* a large van that serves as a travelling branch of a library.

Book of Common Prayer the book containing the prayers and services of the Church of England or the Anglican Church of Canada.

Book of Mormon the sacred book of the Mormon Church.

Book of the Dead a collection of ancient Egyptian religious maxims that were intended to guide the soul on its way out of this world.

book·plate (bůk′plāt′) *n.* a label for pasting in books, having the owner's name or emblem printed on it.

book·rack (bůk′rak′) *n.* **1** a rack for holding an open book. **2** a rack for holding a row of books.

book review an article written about a book, discussing its merits, faults, etc.

book·sell·er (bůk′sel′ər) *n.* a person whose business is selling books.

book·shelf (bůk′shelf′) *n.* a shelf for holding books.

book·shop (bůk′shop′) *n.* bookstore.

book·stall (bůk′stol′ or -stôl′) *n.* a place where books, usually second-hand, are sold, often outdoors.

book·stand (bůk′stand′) *n.* **1** a stand for holding an open book. **2** a stand or counter for showing books for sale. **3** a place where books are sold.

book·store (bůk′stôr′) *n.* a store where books are sold.

book value the value of anything as it appears on the account books of the owner. It may be higher or lower than the real or present value.

book·work (bůk′wėrk′) *n.* **1** the keeping of records, ledgers, etc. for a business. **2** the study or use of books: *He always did far better in the laboratory than in his bookwork.*

book·worm (bůk′wėrm′) *n.* **1** any insect larva that gnaws the binding or leaves of books. **2** a person who is excessively fond of reading and studying.

boom[1] (büm) *n.* **1** a deep, hollow sound like the roar of cannon or of big waves. **2** a sudden activity and increase in business, prices, or values of property; rapid growth: *Our town is having such a boom that it is likely to double its size in two years.* **3** a vigorous pushing or urging. *—v.* **1** make a deep, hollow sound: *The big man's voice boomed out above the rest.* **2** utter with such a sound: *The big guns boomed their message.* **3** increase suddenly in activity; grow rapidly: *Business is booming.* **4** push or urge vigorously: *The alderman's friends are booming him for mayor.* *—adj.* produced by a boom: *boom prices.* [imitative]

boom[2] (büm) *n.* **1** a long pole or beam, used to extend the bottom of a sail or as the lifting pole of a derrick. See picture on the opposite page. **2** a chain, cable, or line of timbers used to keep logs from floating away. **3** a large raft of logs being floated to a mill. [< Du. *boom* tree, pole]

hat, āge, cãre, fär; let, ēqual, tėrm; it, īce
hot, ōpen, ôrder; oil, out; cup, pu̇t, rüle, ūse
 əbove, takən, pencəl, lemən, circəs
ch, child; ng, long; sh, ship
th, thin; ᴛʜ, then; zh, measure

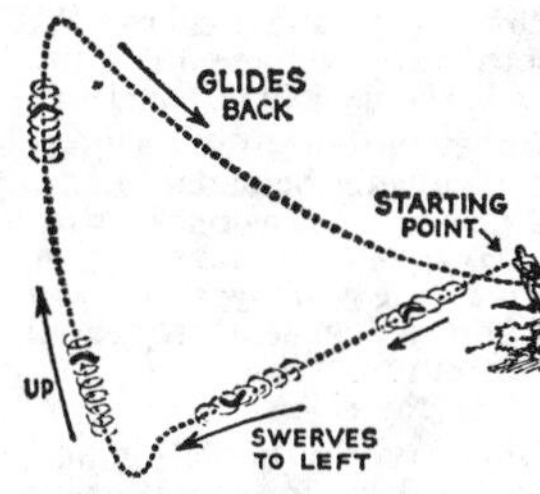

The path of a boomerang

boom·er·ang (büm′ər ang′) *n.* **1** a curved piece of wood, used as a weapon by Australian aborigines. It can be thrown so that it returns to the thrower. **2** anything that recoils or reacts to harm the doer or user. —*v.* act as a boomerang. [< native dial. of New South Wales]

boom town a town that has grown up suddenly, usually as a result of an increase in economic activity. Boom towns are often found near newly discovered oil fields, gold strikes, etc.

boon[1] (bün) *n.* **1** a blessing; great benefit: *Those warm stockings were a boon to me in the cold weather.* **2** *Archaic.* something asked or granted as a favor. [ME < ON *bón* petition] —**Syn. 1** favor, gift.

boon[2] (bün) *adj.* **1** jolly; gay; merry: *a boon companion.* **2** *Poetic.* kindly; pleasant. [ME < OF *bon* good < L *bonus*]

boon·docks (bün′doks) *n.pl. Slang.* rough backwoods; bush country. [< Tagalog *bundók* mountain]

boon·dog·gle (bün′dog′əl) *v.* **-gled, -gling,** *n. U.S. Informal.* —*v.* do useless work. —*n.* a worthless work or product. [origin uncertain] —**boon′dog′gler,** *n.*

boor (bür) *n.* **1** a rude, bad-mannered, or clumsy person. **2** a farm laborer; peasant. [< LG *bur* or Du. *boer* farmer]

boor·ish (bür′ish) *adj.* rude; having bad manners; clumsy. —**boor′ish·ly,** *adv.* —**boor′ish·ness,** *n.*

boost (büst) *Informal.* —*n.* **1** a push or shove that helps a person in rising or advancing. **2** an increase.
—*v.* **1** lift or push from below or behind. **2** speak favorably of. **3** raise; cause to be raised; improve; increase: *boost a person's spirits; boost prices.*
[blend of *boom* and *hoist*]

boost·er (büst′ər) *n.* **1** a person or thing that boosts. **2** the first stage of a multistage rocket. **3** the device used to orbit an artificial satellite. **4** any auxiliary device for increasing force, power, etc. **5** *Informal.* a booster shot.

booster shot a supplementary injection of vaccine or serum, given to reinforce an earlier inoculation.

booster station a television or radio installation that picks up, amplifies, and relays signals from the main transmitting station.

boot[1] (büt) *n.* **1** a leather or rubber covering for the foot and lower part of the leg. **2** formerly, an instrument of torture used to crush a person's leg. **3** the place for baggage in a coach. **4** *Brit.* a car trunk. **5** a protecting apron or cover for the driver of an open carriage. **6** a kick. **7** *U.S. Slang.* a new recruit in training in the United States Navy or Marines.
bet your boots, depend on it; be sure: *You can bet your boots that our team will win.*
die with one's boots on, a die in battle; die fighting.
b die working, especially for a cause.
have one's heart in one's boots, be dejected or discouraged.
lick the boots of, flatter; follow or obey slavishly.
the boot, *Slang.* dismissal.
the boot is on the other leg, the situation is reversed; the responsibility is on the other party.
too big for one's boots, *Informal.* having an excessively high opinion of oneself; conceited: *When he won the athlete-of-the-year award, he became much too big for his boots.*
wipe one's boots on, treat in an insulting way.
—*v.* **1** put boots on. **2** kick. **3** *Informal.* get rid of; dismiss. [ME < OF *bote* < Gmc.]

boot[2] (büt) *n.* **1** *Archaic.* profit; benefit. **2 to boot,** in addition; besides: *He gave me his knife for my book and a dime to boot.* —*v.* profit; benefit. [OE *bōt* advantage]

boot·black (büt′blak′) *n.* a person whose work is shining shoes and boots.

boot·ee (bü tē′) *n.* **1** a baby's soft shoe. **2** a woman's short boot.

Bo·ö·tes (bō ō′tēz) *n.* in astronomy, a northern constellation that includes the star Arcturus. [< L < Gk. *boōtēs* ox-driver < *bous* ox]

booth (büth) *n.* **booths** (büᴛʜz or büths). **1** a place where goods are displayed for sale at a fair, market, etc. **2** a small, closed place for a telephone, motion-picture projector, etc. **3** a small, closed place for voting at elections. **4** a partly enclosed space in a restaurant, cafe, etc., containing a table and seats for a few persons. [ME < Scand.; cf. ODanish **bóth*]

boot·jack (büt′jak′) *n.* a device to help in pulling off boots.

boot·leg (büt′leg′) *v.* **-legged, -leg·ging,** *adj. n.* —*v.* sell, transport, or make unlawfully.
—*adj.* made, transported, or sold unlawfully.
—*n. Informal.* alcoholic liquor made, sold, or transported unlawfully. [modern use from the practice of smuggling liquor in boot legs]

boot·leg·ger (büt′leg′ər) *n. Informal.* a person who bootlegs.

boot·less[1] (büt′lis) *adj.* without shoes or boots.

boot·less[2] (büt′lis) *adj.* of no avail; useless. [< *boot*[2]] —**boot′less·ly,** *adv.*

boot·lick·er (büt′lik′ər) *n. Slang.* a flatterer; person who follows or obeys another slavishly.

boots (büts) *n. Brit.* a servant who shines shoes and boots and does other menial tasks.

boots and saddles a bugle call to mount horses.

boot tree a wooden or metal device shaped like a foot and put into a boot to keep it in shape.

boo·ty (bü′tē) *n.* **-ties. 1** things taken from the enemy in war. **2** plunder. **3** any valuable thing or things obtained; prize. [Related to BOOT[2].] —**Syn. 1, 2** pillage, loot, spoils. See **plunder.**

booze (büz) *n. v.* **boozed, booz·ing.** *Informal.* —*n.* **1** any intoxicating liquor. **2** a spree. —*v.* drink heavily. [probably < MDu. *busen* drink to excess]
—**booz′er,** *n.*

booz·y (büz′ē) *adj.* **booz·i·er, booz·i·est.** *Informal.* **1** rather drunk. **2** habitually drunken. —**booz′i·ly,** *adv.* —**booz′i·ness,** *n.*

bop[1] (bop) *n. v.* **bopped, bop·ping.** *Slang.* —*n.* a blow with the hand, a club, etc. —*v.* hit; strike.

bop[2] (bop) *n. Slang.* bebop.

bor. borough.

bo·rac·ic (bə ras′ik) *adj.* boric.

bor·age (bėr′ij or bôr′ij) *n.* a plant having hairy leaves and blue or purplish flowers, native to S. Europe. It is used in salads, in flavoring beverages, and in medicine. [< OF *bourrache* < Med.L *borrago* < *burra* rough hair]

bo·rate (bô′rāt or bô′rit) *n.* a salt or ester of boric acid.

bo·rat·ed (bô′rāt id) *adj.* mixed or treated with boric acid or borax.

bo·rax (bô′raks) *n.* white crystalline powder, used as an antiseptic, in washing clothes, in fusing metals, and in preserving foods; sodium borate. *Formula*: $Na_2B_4O_7$ [ME *boras* < Med.L < Arabic *buwraq* < Persian *bōrah*]

bor·a·zon (bôr′ə zon′) *n.* in chemistry, a crystalline compound of boron and nitrogen, harder than diamond and having a higher melting point. [< *boron* + *azo* + *nitrogen*]

Bor·deaux (bôr dō′) *n.* a red or white wine made in the Bordeaux region of S.W. France.

Bordeaux mixture a liquid mixture of copper sulphate, lime, and water, used as a spray on trees and plants to kill insects, fungi, etc.

bor·del·lo (bôr del′ō) *n.* a brothel. [< Ital. < Med.L *bordellus,* dim. of *borda* cottage]

bor·der (bôr′dər) *n.* **1** a side, edge, or boundary of anything, or the neighboring area. **2** a boundary separating two provinces, states, countries, etc.; a frontier: *We reached Detroit by crossing the border at Windsor.* **3** a strip on the edge of anything for strength or ornament.
—*v.* **1** form a boundary to; bound. **2** put a border on; edge. **3 border on** or **upon, a** touch at the border; be next to; adjoin. **b** be close to; resemble. [ME < OF *bordure* < *border* to border < *bord* side < Gmc.]
—**Syn.** *n.* **1** margin, rim.

bor·der·er (bôr′dər ər) *n.* a person who lives on the border of a country or region.

bor·der·land (bôr′dər land′) *n.* **1** the land forming, or next to, a border. **2** an uncertain district, space, or condition: *the borderland between sleeping and waking.*

bor·der·line (bôr′dər līn′) *n.* a boundary; dividing line. —*adj.* **1** on a border or boundary. **2** uncertain; in between.

bor·dure (bôr′jər) *n.* in heraldry, a border around a shield, covering one fifth of its surface. [earlier form of *border*]

bore[1] (bôr) *v.* **bored, bor·ing,** *n.* —*v.* **1** make a hole by means of a tool that keeps turning, or by penetrating as a worm does in fruit. **2** make (a hole, passage, entrance, etc.) by pushing through or digging out: *A mole has bored its way under the hedge.* **3** bore a hole in; hollow out evenly. **4** be bored; admit of being bored: *This wood bores easily.*
—*n.* **1** a hole made by a revolving tool. **2** the hollow space inside a pipe, tube, or gun barrel: *He cleaned the bore of his gun.* **3** the distance across the inside of a hole or tube. [OE *borian*] —**Syn.** *v.* **1** pierce, perforate, drill.

bore[2] (bôr) *v.* **bored, bor·ing,** *n.* —*v.* make weary by dull or tiresome behavior or conversation. —*n.* a dull, tiresome person or thing. [origin unknown] —**Syn.** *v.* tire, fatigue.

bore[3] (bôr) *v.* pt. of **bear**[1].

bore[4] (bôr) *n.* a sudden, high tidal wave that rushes up a channel with great force. [< ON *bára* wave]

bo·re·al (bô′rē əl) *adj.* **1** northern. **2** of or having to do with Boreas.

Bo·re·as (bô′rē əs) *n.* the north wind. [< Gk.]

bore·dom (bôr′dəm) *n.* a bored condition; weariness caused by dull, tiresome people or events.

bor·er (bôr′ər) *n.* **1** a tool for boring holes. **2** an insect or worm that bores into wood, fruit, etc.

bore·some (bôr′səm) *adj.* boring; dull; tiresome.

bo·ric (bô′rik) *adj.* of or containing boron. Also, **boracic.**

boric acid a white crystalline substance used as a mild antiseptic, as a food preservative, etc. *Formula*: $B(OH)_3$

born (bôrn) *adj.* **1** brought into life; brought forth. **2** thought up; conceived. **3** by birth; by nature: *a born athlete.* —*v.* a pp. of **bear**[1]. [pp. of *bear*[1]]
☛ See **borne** for usage note.

borne (bôrn) *v.* a pp. of **bear**[1].
☛ **borne. a. Borne** is the past participle of *bear* in most of its meanings: *The ship was borne along by the breeze. The men had borne these burdens without complaint. He had borne himself with great dignity.* **b.** In the sense "give birth to," the past participle of *bear* is *borne* except in the very commonly used passive voice form when not followed by *by*: *She had borne five children. He was born in 1900.*

bo·ron (bô′ron) *n.* a non-metallic, chemical element found in borax. *Symbol*: B; *at.no.* 5; *at.wt.* 10.811. [blend of *borax* and *carbon*]

bor·ough (bėr′ō) *n.* **1** in some countries, an area of local government, often with a charter guaranteeing certain rights. **2** in England: **a** a town with a municipal corporation and a charter that guarantees the right of local self-government. **b** a town that sends representatives to Parliament. [OE *burg*]

bor·row (bôr′ō) *v.* **1** get (something) from another person with the understanding that it is to be returned. **2** take and use as one's own; take: *Rome borrowed many ideas from Greece.* **3** take from another language: *The word "wigwam" was borrowed from the Indians.*
4 borrow trouble, worry about something before there is reason to. [OE *borgian* < *borg* pledge, surety]
—**bor′row·er,** *n.*

bor·row·ing (bôr′ō ing) *n.* **1** something borrowed. **2** a word taken direct from one language into another; loan words. The English word *voyageur* is a borrowing from Canadian French.

borrow pit a pit or ditch from which earth has been dug for use as fill, especially in road or railway construction.

borsch (bôrsh) *n.* a Russian soup containing meat stock, beets, etc. [< Russian *borshch*]

bor·zoi (bôr′zoi) *n.* **1** a breed of tall, slender, swift dog having long, silky hair; Russian wolfhound. **2** a dog of this breed. [< Russian *borzoy* swift]

bos·cage (bos′kij) *n.* a small woods; thicket; shrubbery. [ME < OF *boscage* < *bosc* < Gmc.; cf. Frankish *busk* woods. Related to BUSH.]

bosh[1] (bosh) *n. interj. Informal.* nonsense; foolish talk or ideas. [< Turkish *boş* empty, worthless]

bosh[2] (bosh) *n.* **1** a trough for cooling ingots, etc. **2 boshes,** the lower part of a blast furnace. [< G *Böschung* slope]

bosk (bosk) *n.* a grove; small woods; thicket. [var. of *busk,* dial. for *bush*]

bosk·y (bos′kē) *adj.* **1** wooded. **2** shady.

bo's'n (bō′sən) *n.* boatswain.

bos·om (bůz′əm or bü′zəm) *n.* **1** the upper, front part of the human body; breast. **2** the part of a garment covering the bosom. **3** the centre or inmost part: *He did not mention it even in the bosom of his family.* **4** the heart, thoughts, affections, desires, etc. **5** the surface (of a sea, lake, river, the ground, etc.).
—*adj.* close; trusted: *a bosom friend.*
—*v.* cherish. [OE *bōsm*]

boss[1] (bos) *Informal. n.* **1** a person who hires workers or watches over or directs them; foreman; manager. **2** a person who controls a political organization.
—*v.* be the boss of; direct; control.
—*adj.* chief: *He is boss man.* [< Du. *baas*]

boss[2] (bos) *n.* **1** an ornamentation of silver, ivory, or other material rising above a flat surface. **2** in machinery, the enlarged part of a shaft. **3** in geology, a domelike body of igneous rock protruding above the surface or into a stratum of other rock. —*v.* decorate with bosses. [ME *boce* < OF]

boss·y[1] (bos′ē) *adj.* **boss·i·er, boss·i·est.** *Informal.* fond of telling others what to do and how to do it; domineering. [< *boss*[1]]

boss·y[2] (bos′ē) *adj.* decorated with bosses. [< *boss*[2]]

bos·sy[3] or **bos·sie** (bos′ē′) *n.* a familiar name for a calf or cow. [< dial. E *borse, boss* young calf]

Boston bull (bos′tən) Boston terrier.

Boston fern a variety of sword fern having long, drooping fronds, popular as a house plant.

Boston Tea Party a raid on some British ships in Boston harbor in 1773. Disguised as Indians, colonists threw chests of tea overboard as a protest against taxation by the British Parliament.

Boston terrier 1 a breed of small, dark-brown or black dog having white markings and smooth, short hair. **2** a dog of this breed.

bo·sun (bō′sən) *n.* boatswain.

Bos·well (boz′wel or boz′wəl) *n.* an author of a biography of a close friend. [< James Boswell (1740-1795), the Scottish author of a famous biography of Samuel Johnson]

bot (bot) *n.* the larva of a botfly. It is a parasite of horses, cattle, and sheep. Also, **bott.** [origin uncertain]

bo·tan·ic (bə tan′ik) *adj.* botanical. [< Med.L

botanicus < Gk. *botanikos* < *botanē* plant]

bo·tan·i·cal (bə tan′i kəl) *adj.* 1 having to do with plants and plant life. 2 having to do with botany.

bo·tan·i·cal·ly (bə tan′ik lē) *adv.* in a botanical manner; according to the principles of botany.

bot·a·nist (bot′ə nist) *n.* an expert in botany.

bot·a·nize (bot′ə nīz′) *v.* **-nized, -niz·ing.** 1 study plants in their natural environment. 2 collect plants for study. 3 explore the plant life of. **—bot′a·niz′er,** *n.*

bot·a·ny (bot′ə nē) *n.* **-nies.** 1 the science of plants; the branch of biology that deals with the structure, growth, classification, diseases, etc. of plants. 2 a scientific book about plants. 3 the plant life of a particular area: *the botany of the Canadian Shield.* 4 the botanical facts and characteristics concerning a particular type or group of plants: *the botany of roses.* [< *botanic*]

Botany Bay (bot′ə nē) a bay on the southeastern coast of Australia, near Sydney. A penal colony was formerly located there.

Botany wool a fine merino wool used in high quality fabrics. [< *Botany* Bay, Australia, near which it was originally grown]

botch (boch) *v.* 1 spoil by poor workmanship; bungle. 2 patch or mend clumsily. *—n.* 1 a poor piece of workmanship. 2 a clumsy patch. [ME *bocchen*; origin uncertain] **—botch′er,** *n.*

botch·y (boch′ē) *adj.* **botch·i·er, botch·i·est.** botched; poorly made or done.

bot·fly (bot′flī) *n.* **-flies.** a two-winged fly whose larvae are parasites of horses, cattle, and sheep.

both (bōth) *adj.* the two; the one and the other: *Both houses are white.*
—pron. the two together: *Both belong to him.*
—adv. together; alike; equally: *He can both sing and dance.*
—conj. together; alike; equally: *He is both strong and healthy.* [ME, apparently < ON *báthar*]
☛ **Both** is used in informal English to emphasize the fact that two persons or places or things are involved in a situation: *The twins were both there.* Strictly speaking, the *both* is redundant, but it gives emphasis.

both·er (boTH′ər) *n.* 1 worry; fuss; trouble. 2 a person or thing that causes worry, fuss, or trouble. *—v.* worry; fuss; trouble: *Don't bother about my breakfast; I'll eat what is here.* [apparently an Anglo-Irish modification of *pother*] **—Syn.** *v.* annoy, vex.

both·er·a·tion (boTH′ər ā′shən) *n. interj. Informal.* bother.

both·er·some (boTH′ər səm) *adj.* causing worry or fuss; troublesome. **—Syn.** annoying.

bots (bots) *n.* a disease of cattle caused by botfly larvae infesting the stomach and intestines. Also, **botts.**

bott (bot) *n.* bot.

bot·tle (bot′əl) *n. v.* **-tled, -tling.** *—n.* 1 a container for holding liquids, usually made of glass, and without handles. Usually, though not always, bottles have narrow necks which can be closed with stoppers or caps. 2 the amount that a bottle can hold. 3 a bottle and its contents. 4 **the bottle,** alcoholic liquor. 5 *Slang.* **hit the bottle,** drink alcoholic liquor to excess.
—v. 1 put into bottles: *bottle milk.* 2 hold in; keep back; control. 3 **bottle up,** hold in; keep back; control: *bottle up one's anger.* [ME *botel* < OF *bouteille* < VL *butticula,* dim. of LL *buttis* butt[4]] **—bot′tle-like′,** *adj.* **—bot′tler,** *n.*

bottle green a very dark green.

bot·tle·neck (bot′əl nek′) *n.* 1 the neck of a bottle. 2 a narrow passageway or street. 3 a person or thing that hinders progress. 4 a situation in which progress is hindered.

bot·tle·nose (bot′əl nōz′) *n.* a kind of dolphin having a bottle-shaped nose; porpoise.

bot·tom (bot′əm) *n.* 1 the lowest part: *The berries at the bottom of the basket were small.* 2 the part on which anything rests: *The bottom of that cup is wet.* 3 the ground under water: *the bottom of the sea.* 4 the low land along a river. 5 the seat: *This chair needs a new bottom.* 6 a basis; foundation; origin: *He is at the bottom of this mischief.* 7 **the buttocks.** 8 the keel or hull of a ship;

hat, āge, cãre, fär; let, ēqual, tėrm; it, īce
hot, ōpen, ôrder; oil, out; cup, pu̇t, rüle, ūse
əbove, takən, pencəl, lemən, circəs
ch, child; ng, long; sh, ship
th, thin; TH, then; zh, measure

ship. 9 **at bottom,** fundamentally. 10 **be at the bottom of,** be the cause or source of. 11 **bottoms up!** *Informal.* drink up! empty your glass! 12 **get to the bottom of,** discover the underlying source, cause, or meaning of.
—v. 1 put a seat on. 2 get to the bottom of; understand fully. 3 set upon a foundation; base; rest.
—adj. 1 lowest; last: *bottom prices. I bet my bottom dollar.* 2 underlying; fundamental. [OE *botm*] **—Syn.** *n.* 6 groundwork, base.

bottom land the low land along a river.

bot·tom·less (bot′əm lis) *adj.* 1 without a bottom. 2 so deep that the bottom cannot be reached; extremely deep.

bot·tom·most (bot′əm mōst′) *adj.* deepest; lowest.

bot·tom·ry (bot′əm rē) *n.* **-ries.** in law, a contract by which a shipowner mortgages his ship in order to get money to make a voyage. If the ship is lost, the lender loses the money. [< *bottom* ship, after Du. *bodemerij*]

botts (bots) *n.* bots.

bot·u·lism (boch′u̇ liz′əm) *n.* a kind of poisoning caused by eating food that has been spoiled by the action of certain bacteria; food poisoning. [< L *botulus* sausage; originally attributed especially to sausages]

bou·clé (bü klā′) *n.* 1 a knitted cloth having a surface with tiny loops and curls. 2 the yarn used in making such a surface. *—adj.* of cloth, having such a surface. [< F *bouclé* buckled]

bou·doir (bü′dwär or bü dwär′) *n.* a lady's private dressing room or sitting room. [< F *boudoir* < *bouder* sulk]

bouf·fant (bü fänt′, *French,* bü fäN′) *adj.* puffed out: *bouffant sleeves, a bouffant skirt.* [< F]

bou·gain·vil·le·a (bü′gən vil′ē ə) *n.* any of several tropical climbing shrubs having large, brilliant, deep-red leaves surrounding tiny flowers. [after L. A. de *Bougainville,* 1729-1811, a French navigator and explorer]

bough (bou) *n.* 1 one of the main branches of a tree. 2 a branch cut from a tree. [OE *bōg* bough, shoulder] **—Syn. 1, 2.** See **branch.**

bought (bot or bôt) *v.* pt. and pp. of **buy.**

bought·en (bot′ən or bôt′ən) *adj. Dialect.* bought; not homemade.
☛ **Boughten** is a nonstandard expression used only in certain North American dialects: *Is that a boughten dress?*

bouil·la·baisse (bül′yə bās′) *n.* a fish chowder highly seasoned with wine, herbs, etc. [< F *bouillabaisse* < Provençal *bouiabaisso* < *boui* boil + *abaisso* go down (from its being brought quickly to boil and then simmered down)]

bouil·lon (bu̇l′yon; *French,* bü yôN′) *n.* 1 a clear, thin soup or broth. 2 a liquid, nutritive medium used for growing cultures of bacteria. [< F *bouillon* < *bouillir* boil < L *bullire*]

boul·der (bōl′dər) *n.* a large rock rounded or worn by the action of water or weather. Also, rarely, **bowlder.** [for *boulderstone,* ME < Scand.; cf. Swedish *bullersten* < *bullra* roar + *sten* stone]

boul·e·vard (bu̇l′ə värd′) *n.* 1 a broad street. 2 the strip of grass between a sidewalk and a curb. 3 the centre strip dividing any road into two lanes for traffic going in opposite directions. *Abbrev.:* blvd. [< F *boulevard,* originally, the passageway along a rampart < MLG < MDu. *bolwerc.* Akin to BULWARK.]

bounce (bouns) *v.* **bounced, bounc·ing,** *n. —v.* 1 bound like a ball: *The baby likes to bounce on his bed.* 2 cause to bounce. 3 burst noisily, angrily, etc.: *She bounced out of the room.* 4 *Slang.* throw out. 5 *Slang.* discharge from work or employment. 6 *Slang.* of a cheque, be returned by a bank as a result of the person who signed the cheque having insufficient funds in his account to meet it. *—n.* 1 a bound; a spring; a bouncing. 2 a boasting; a bragging. 3 *Informal.* energy; spirit: *He was in hospital for a week, but he is as full of bounce as ever.* 4 a heavy blow or thump. 5 *Slang.* discharge from work or employment. [ME *bunse(n)*; cf. Du. *bonzen* thump] —**boun′cy,** *adj.* —**boun′ci·ness,** *n.*

bounc·er (boun′sər) *n.* 1 anything very big. 2 *Informal.* a person who boasts or brags. 3 *Slang.* a strong man hired by a cabaret, hotel, etc. to remove people who do not behave properly.

bounc·ing (boun′sing) *adj.* 1 that bounces. 2 big; strong. 3 vigorous; healthy.

bouncing Bet or **Bess** a plant of the pink family, that grows wild by roadsides, etc. and has white or pink, often double, flowers; soapwort.

bound[1] (bound) *v.* pt. and pp. of **bind.**
—*adj.* 1 put in covers: *a bound book.* 2 under some obligation; obliged. 3 certain; sure: *It is bound to get dark soon.* 4 *Informal.* determined; resolved. 5 **bound up in** or **with, a** closely connected with. **b** very devoted to. [pp. of *bind*]

bound[2] (bound) *v.* 1 leap; spring lightly along; jump: *The deer bounds through the woods.* 2 leap or spring upward or onward. 3 spring back; bounce: *The ball bounded from the wall.*
—*n.* 1 a leap or spring upward or onward. 2 a spring back; a bounce. [< F *bondir* leap, originally, resound, ? < L *bombus.* See BOMB.]

bound[3] (bound) *n.* 1 Usually, **bounds,** *pl.* boundary; limiting line; limit: *Keep your hopes within bounds.* 2 **bounds,** *pl.* **a** land on or near a boundary. **b** an area included within boundaries: *The taverns near the camp were declared out of bounds.*
—*v.* 1 form the boundary of; limit. 2 name the boundaries of: *Bound the Yukon.* 3 have its boundary (*on*): *Canada bounds on the United States.* [ME *bunne* < AF *bounde* < OF *bodne* < LL *butina*] —**Syn.** *n.* 1 border, confine.

bound[4] (bound) *adj.* going; on the way: *I am bound for home.* [ME *boun* < ON *búinn,* pp. of *búa* get ready]

bound·a·ry (boun′drē or boun′də rē) *n.* **-ries.** 1 a limiting line; limit; border: *the boundary between Canada and the United States.* 2 in cricket: **a** the limit of the field. **b** a hit to or beyond this limit.

bound·en (boun′dən) *adj.* 1 required; obligatory. 2 under obligation; obliged. [pp. of *bind*]

bound·er (boun′dər) *n. Esp.Brit. Informal.* a rude, vulgar person; upstart; cad.

bound·less (bound′lis) *adj.* not limited; infinite; vast: *the boundless ocean.* —**bound′less·ly,** *adv.* —**bound′less·ness,** *n.*

boun·te·ous (boun′tē əs) *adj.* 1 generous; given freely. 2 plentiful; abundant. —**boun′te·ous·ly,** *adv.* —**boun′te·ous·ness,** *n.* —**Syn.** 1 liberal. 2 copious, ample.

boun·ti·ful (boun′tə fəl) *adj.* 1 generous; giving freely. 2 plentiful; abundant. —**boun′ti·ful·ly,** *adv.* —**boun′ti·ful·ness,** *n.*

boun·ty (boun′tē) *n.* **-ties.** 1 generosity. 2 a generous gift. 3 a reward; premium for capturing or killing: *a bounty on wolves.* [ME < OF *bonte* < L *bonitas* < *bonus* good] —**Syn.** 1 munificence, liberality.

bou·quet (bō kā′ or bü kā′ *for 1;* bü kā′ *for 2*) *n.* 1 a bunch of flowers. 2 a fragrance; aroma. [< F *bouquet* little wood, dim. of OF *bosc* wood < Gmc. **busk.* See BOSCAGE.]

bour·bon (bėr′bən) *n.* a kind of whisky, distilled from a grain mash containing at least 51% corn. [< *Bourbon* County, Kentucky, where this whisky was originally made]

Bour·bon (bür′bən, *occasionally* bėr′bən) *n.* a person who clings to old ideas and opposes any change; an extreme conservative. [< *Bourbon,* the name of a former royal family of France, Spain, Naples, and Sicily]

Bour·bon·ism (bür′bən iz′ əm; *occasionally,* bėr′bən iz′ əm) *n.* 1 support of the Bourbons. 2 extreme conservatism in politics, etc.

bour·geois[1] (bür zhwä′ or bür′zhwä) *n.* **-geois,** *adj.* —*n.* 1 a person of the middle class. 2 a property owner or business man, as contrasted with a member of the working class. 3 formerly, a partner in a fur-trading company, in charge of a trading post or expedition; wintering partner. 4 *Cdn.* formerly, an employer; boss. —*adj.* 1 of the middle class. 2 like the middle class; ordinary. 3 influenced chiefly by the interests of property ownership and business. [< F *bourgeois* < LL *burgensis* < *burgus* fort < Gmc. Doublet of BURGESS.]

bour·geois[2] (bėr jois′) *n.* a size of type; 9 point. This sentence is in bourgeois. [from the name of a French printer]

bour·geoi·sie (bür′zhwä zē′) *n.* 1 the people of the middle class. 2 property owners and businessmen as a class, as contrasted with the proletariat. 3 the middle class. [< F]

bourn[1] or **bourne**[1] (bôrn) *n.* a small stream; brook. [OE *burna*]

bourn[2] or **bourne**[2] (bôrn) *n.* 1 *Archaic.* a boundary; limit. 2 a goal. [< F *borne.* Akin to BOUND[3].]

bourse (bürs) *n.* in Paris, and in certain other European cities, the stock exchange; an exchange where merchants transact business. [< F *bourse,* originally, purse < LL *bursa* < Gk. *byrsa* hide, wineskin. Doublet of BURSA, PURSE.]

bout (bout) *n.* 1 a trial of strength; contest. 2 a spell; period spent in some particular way: *a long bout of flu.* [var. of *bought* a bending, turn. Related to BOW[1].]

bou·tique (bü tēk′) *n.* a small shop or department in a store that specializes in fashionable clothes, accessories, and gifts. [< F]

bou·ton·niere or **bou·ton·nière** (bü′tə nyãr′; *French,* bü tô nyãr′) *n.* a flower or flowers worn in a buttonhole. [< F *boutonnière* buttonhole]

bo·vine (bō′vīn) *adj.* 1 of an ox or cow; like an ox or cow. 2 slow; stupid. 3 without emotion; stolid. —*n.* an ox, cow, etc. [< LL *bovinus* < L *bos, bovis* ox, cow]

bow[1] (bou) *v.* 1 bend the head or body in greeting, respect, worship, or submission. 2 show by bowing: *bow one's thanks.* 3 cause to stoop: *The man was bowed by old age.* 4 submit; yield: *We must bow to necessity.* 5 **bow and scrape,** be too polite or slavish. 6 **bow down, a** weigh down: *bowed down with care.* **b** to worship. 7 **bow out, a** withdraw (from): *He sprained his wrist and had to bow out of the tennis tournament.* **b** usher out.
—*n.* 1 a bending of the head or body in greeting, respect, worship, or submission. 2 **make one's bow, a** make an entrance. **b** make an initial appearance before the public as a performer. **c** retire from public notice. 3 **take a bow,** accept praise, applause, etc. for something done. [OE *būgan*] —**Syn.** *n.* nod, curtsy.

bow[2] (bō) *n.* 1 a weapon for shooting arrows, consisting of a strip of springy wood bent by a string. 2 a curve; bend. 3 a looped knot: *a bow of ribbon.* 4 a slender rod with horsehairs stretched on it, for playing a violin, etc. See **violin** for picture. 5 something curved; a curved part: *A rainbow is a bow.*
—*v.* 1 curve; bend. 2 play (a violin, etc.) with a bow. [OE *boga*] —**bow′less,** *adj.* —**bow′-like′,** *adj.*

bow[3] (bou) *n.* 1 the forward part of a ship, boat, or airship. See **aft** for picture. 2 the person who rows with the oar nearest the bow of a boat. [probably of LG or Scand. origin. Akin to BOUGH.]

bowd·ler·ize (boud′lər īz′) *v.* **-ized, -iz·ing.** remove words and passages thought to be improper. [< Dr. T. *Bowdler* (1754-1825), who published an expurgated edition of Shakespeare in 1818]

bow·el (bou′əl) *n.* 1 a part of the bowels; intestine. 2 Usually, **bowels,** *pl.* a tube in the body into which digested food passes from the stomach; intestines. 3 **bowels,** *pl.* **a** the inner part; depths: *Miners dig for coal in the bowels of the earth.* **b** *Archaic.* pity; tender feelings. [ME < OF *boel* < L *botellus,* dim. of *botulus* sausage]

bow·er[1] (bou′ər) *n.* 1 a shelter of leafy branches. 2 a summerhouse or arbor. 3 *Archaic.* a bedroom. [OE *būr* dwelling] —**bow′er·like′,** *adj.*

bow·er[2] (bou′ər) *n.* an anchor carried at the bow of a ship. [< *bow*[3]]

bow·er[3] (bou′ər) *n.* the high card in certain games. The **right bower** is a jack of the suit that is trump;

hat, āge, cãre, fär; let, ēqual, tėrm; it, īce
hot, ōpen, ôrder; oil, out; cup, pu̇t, rüle, ūse
əbove, takən, pencəl, lemən, circəs
ch, child; ng, long; sh, ship
th, thin; ᴛʜ, then; zh, measure

the **left bower,** the jack of the suit of the same color as trump; the **best bower,** the joker. [< G *Bauer* jack (in cards), peasant]

bow·er[4] (bou′ər) *n.* one who bows or stoops.

bow·er·y (bou′ər ē) *adj.* like a bower; leafy; shady.

bow·fin (bō′fin′) *n.* a small fish found chiefly in the rivers of eastern North America; mudfish.

bow·ie knife (bō′ē or bü′ē) a long, single-edged hunting knife carried in a sheath. [after Col. James *Bowie,* American pioneer]

bow·knot (bō′not′) *n.* a slipknot such as is made in tying shoelaces. It may be tied as a single bow or as a double bow.

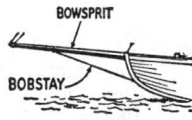

A single bowknot

bowl[1] (bōl) *n.* **1** a hollow, rounded dish. **2** the amount that a bowl can hold. **3** a hollow, rounded part: *the bowl of a spoon or a pipe.* **4** a large drinking cup. **5** a drink. **6** a formation or structure shaped like a bowl: *The Malkin Bowl in Vancouver is used for outdoor entertainment in the summer.* [ME *bolle* < OE *bolla*] —**bowl′-like′,** *adj.*

bowl[2] (bōl) *n.* **1** a fairly large, heavy ball used in certain games. **2** in the game of bowls or in bowling, a throw or casting.
—*v.* **1** play the game of bowls. **2** roll or move along rapidly and smoothly: *Our car bowled along on the good road.* **3** in cricket: **a** throw (the ball) to the batsman. **b** dismiss (a batsman), especially by knocking off the bails or knocking down a wicket. **4 bowl down,** knock down. **5 bowl over, a** knock over. **b** *Informal.* make helpless and confused. [ME *boule* < L *bulla* ball, bubble]

bowl·der (bōl′dər) *n.* boulder.

bow·leg (bō′leg′) *n.* **1** a leg that curves outward. **2** an outward curve of the legs.

bow·leg·ged (bō′leg′id or -legd′) *adj.* having the legs curved outward.

bowl·er[1] (bōl′ər) *n.* **1** a person who bowls. **2** in cricket, the player who throws the ball at the wicket. [< *bowl*[2], v.]

bowl·er[2] (bōl′ər) *n.* a man's hat having a small brim and a hard, round crown; derby. [< *bowl*[2], n.]

bow·line (bō′lən or bō′līn′) *n.* **1** a knot used in making a loop. **2** the rope tied to the edge of a square sail nearest the wind. It holds the sail steady when sailing into the wind. [ME; *bow*[3] + *line*[1]]

A bowline (def. 1)

bowline knot bowline (def. 1).

bowl·ing (bōl′ing) *n.* **1** a game played indoors, in which balls are rolled down an alley at bottle-shaped wooden pins: *Fivepins, ninepins, and tenpins are forms of bowling.* **2** playing the game of bowls.

bowling alley **1** in the game of bowling, the lane or alley down which balls are rolled. **2** an establishment having a number of lanes for bowling: *There is a snack bar at the bowling alley.*

bowling green a smooth, flat stretch of grass for playing bowls.

bowls (bōlz) *n.* **1** a game played by rolling a lopsided or unsymmetrically weighted wooden ball toward a small, white ball that is stationary. **2** bowling (def. 1). [pl. of *bowl*[2]]

bow·man (bō′ mən) *n.* **-men** (-mən). a soldier armed with bow and arrows; archer.

bow net (bō) a wickerwork trap for catching lobsters and other shellfish. [< *bow*[2] + *net*]

bow·shot (bō′shot′) *n.* **1** a shot from a bow. **2** the distance that a bow will shoot an arrow.

bow·sprit (bou′sprit′ or bō′sprit′) *n.* a pole or spar projecting forward from the bow of a ship: *Ropes from the bowsprit help to steady sails and masts.* [probably < LG or Du.]

BOWSPRIT
BOBSTAY

bow·string (bō′string′) *n.* **1** a strong cord stretched from the ends of a bow, pulled back by the archer and then released in order to send the arrow forward. **2** a cord like this. —*v.* strangle with a bowstring; garrote.

bow tie (bō) a necktie worn in a small bowknot.

bow window (bō) a curved bay window.

bow-wow (bou′wou′) *n. v.* —*n.* **1** the bark of a dog, or an imitation of this sound. **2** a child's word for a dog. —*v.* bark like a dog. [imitative]

box[1] (boks) *n.* **1** a container made of wood, metal, cardboard, paper, etc. to pack or put things in. **2** the amount that a box can hold. **3** in theatres, etc. a small boxlike space with chairs. **4** in courts of law, etc. an enclosed space for a jury, witnesses, etc. **5** a small shelter: *a sentry box.* **6** anything shaped or used like a box. **7** a hollow part that encloses or protects some piece of machinery. **8** the driver's seat on a coach, carriage, etc. **9** in baseball: **a** the place where a pitcher stands to throw the ball. **b** the place where the batter stands to hit the ball. **10** a compartment for a horse in a stable or car: *The horse's box was so large that the horse could walk around in it.* **11** in newspapers, magazines, etc., a space set off by enclosing lines. **12** a receptacle in a post office for a subscriber's mail.
—*v.* **1** pack in a box; put into a box. **2 box the compass, a** name the points of a compass in order. **b** go all the way around and end up where one started. **3 box up,** shut in; keep from getting out. **4** put playing cards face to face when shuffling. [specialization of meaning of *box*[3]]
—**box′like′,** *adj.* —**Syn.** *n.* **1** receptacle, chest, carton.

box[2] (boks) *n.* a blow with the open hand or the fist, especially on the ear. —*v.* **1** strike such a blow. **2** fight (as a sport) with the fists, which are usually covered with padded gloves. [origin uncertain]

box[3] (boks) *n.* **1** a shrub or small, bushy tree that stays green all winter, much used for hedges, borders, etc. **2** the hard, durable wood of this tree. [< L *buxus* < Gk. *pyxos*]

box camera a simple camera in the form of a box which does not fold up and which has a fixed focus.

box·car (boks′kär′) *n.* a railway freight car enclosed on all sides.

box elder a North American maple tree having compound leaves, often grown for shade or ornament; Manitoba maple.

box·er[1] (bok′sər) *n.* a person or machine whose work is to pack things in boxes. [< *box*[1] + *er*]

box·er[2] (bok′sər) *n.* **1** a man who fights with his fists in padded gloves according to special rules. **2** a breed of dog having a smooth, brown coat, related to the bulldog and terrier. **3** a dog of this breed. **4 Boxer,** in China, a member of a society opposed to foreigners and Christianity. The Boxers rose in armed rebellion in 1900, but were defeated by foreign soldiers.

box·ing[1] (bok′sing) *n.* the sport of fighting with the fists. [< *box*[2]]

box·ing[2] (bok′sing) *n.* **1** the material used for boxes. **2** the sides of a window; casing. [< *box*[1]]

Boxing Day December 26, a legal holiday in England and certain parts of Canada. Formerly, "boxes" or presents were given on this day to employees, postmen, etc.

boxing gloves the padded gloves worn for boxing.

box kite a kite consisting of two rectangular boxes with open ends, joined together one above the other.

box lacrosse *Cdn.* a form of lacrosse played by teams of seven players on an enclosed playing area about the size of a hockey rink.

box office **1** the place where tickets are sold in a theatre, hall, etc. **2** the money taken in at the box office.

box pleat or **box plait** a double pleat with the cloth folded under at each side.

box score in baseball, a complete record of the plays of a game arranged in a table by the names of the players.

box seat a chair or seat in a box of a theatre, hall, auditorium, stadium, etc.

box set in a theatre, a stage set with back and side walls.

box spring a cloth-covered frame containing rows of coil springs and used as a spring for a bed.

box·wood (boks′wůd′) *n.* **1** the hard, fine-grained wood of the box. **2** the shrub or tree itself.

boy (boi) *n.* **1** a male child from birth to about eighteen. **2** a male servant. **3** a familiar term for a man. —*interj. Informal.* an exclamation of surprise, dismay, etc.: "*Boy! Isn't it hot!*" [ME *boy, boi*; origin uncertain] —**Syn. 1** lad, youngster, youth.

boy·cott (boi′kot) *v.* **1** combine against and have nothing to do with (a person, business, nation, etc.). If people are boycotting someone, they do not associate with him, or buy from or sell to him, and they try to keep others from doing so. **2** refuse to buy or use (a product, etc.).
—*n.* a boycotting. [< Captain *Boycott* (1832-1897), an English land agent in Ireland who was so treated]

boy·hood (boi′hůd) *n.* **1** the time or condition of being a boy. **2** boys as a group: *The boyhood of the nation produces the leaders of the future.*

boy·ish (boi′ish) *adj.* **1** of a boy. **2** like a boy. **3** like a boy's. **4** fit for a boy. —**boy′ish·ly,** *adv.* —**boy′ish·ness,** *n.*

Boyle's law (boilz) in physics, the statement that at a constant temperature the volume of a gas varies inversely as the pressure to which it is subjected. [< Robert *Boyle*, 1627-1691, an Irish scientist and philosopher who formulated this law]

Boy Scout a member of the Boy Scouts.

Boy Scouts an organization for boys which develops manly qualities and usefulness to others.

boy·sen·ber·ry (boi′zən ber′ē) *n.* **-ries. 1** a purple berry like a blackberry in size and shape, and like a raspberry in flavor. **2** the plant it grows on. [after R. *Boysen* of California, who developed it]

bp. birthplace.

Bp. Bishop.

B/P or **b/p** bills payable.

B.Paed. Bachelor of Pedagogy. (for L *Baccalaureus Paedagogiae*)

B.Péd. Bachelier de Pédagogie; Bachelor of Pedagogy.

B.Ph. Bachelor of Philosophy. (for L *Baccalaureus Philosophiae*)

B.Pharm. Bachelor of Pharmacy. (for L *Baccalaureus Pharmaciae*)

Br bromine.

Br. **1** Britain. **2** British.

br. **1** branch. **2** brand. **3** brother. **4** bronze.

bra (brä) *n. Informal.* brassiere.

brac·cate (brak′āt) *adj.* of certain birds, having the shanks and feet covered with feathers. [< L *braccatus* wearing breeches < *braccae* breeches]

brace (brās) *n. v.* **braced, brac·ing.** —*n.* **1** something that holds parts together or in place; a support: *An iron rod or a piece of timber used to support a roof or a wall is called a brace.* **2** a pair; couple: *a brace of ducks.* **3** a handle for a tool or drill used for boring. See **brace and bit** for picture. **4** in music, etc., either of these signs { } used to enclose words, figures, staves. **5 braces,** *pl.* a pair of crossed straps, usually elasticized, that pass over the shoulders and are attached to the trousers at the back and front. **6** Often, **braces,** *pl.* a metal wire used to straighten crooked teeth. **7** a leather thong that slides up and down the cord of a drum, used to regulate the tension of the skins and thus the pitch. [< v., but partly < OF *brace* the two arms]
—*v.* **1** give strength or firmness to; support. **2** plant firmly; set down rigidly: *He braced his feet and stood ready for the attack.* **3 brace oneself** or **brace up,** *Informal.* summon one's strength or courage. [ME < OF *bracier* embrace < *brace* the two arms < L *bracchia*, pl. of *bracchium* < Gk. *brachion* upper arm]

brace and bit a tool for boring, consisting of a drill fitted into a handle.

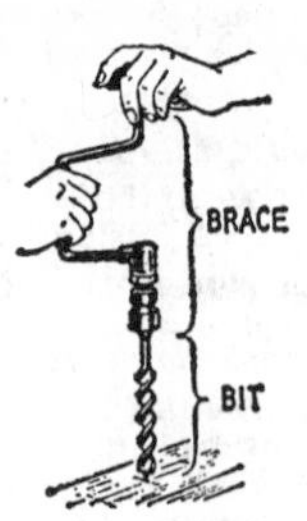

A brace (def. 3) and bit. The user bears down with the upper hand and turns with the lower. A bit cuts in much the same way as an auger.

brace·let (brās′lit) *n.* **1** a band or chain worn for ornament around the wrist or arm. **2** *Informal.* a handcuff. [ME < OF *bracelet*, dim. of *bracel*, ult. < L *bracchium* arm < Gk. *brachion*]

brac·er (brās′ər) *n.* **1** a person or thing that braces. **2** *Slang.* a stimulating drink.

brachi·a (brak′ē ə or brā′kē ə) *n.* pl. of **brachium.**

bra·chi·al (brak′ē əl or brā′kē əl) *adj.* **1 a** of or belonging to the arm: *the brachial artery.* **b** of or belonging to the forelimb of a vertebrate. **2** armlike: *the brachial appendages of a starfish.* [< L *bracchialis* of the arm < *bracchium* arm < Gk. *brachion* upper arm]

brach·i·o·pod (brak′ē ə pod′ or brā′kē ə pod′) *n.* in zoology, one of a group of sea animals characterized by a shell with upper and lower valves and a pair of cilia-covered "arms" coiled within the shell. [< NL *brachiopoda*, pl. < Gk. *brachion* arm + *pous* foot]

bra·chi·um (brak′ē əm or brā′kē əm) *n.* **-chi·a. 1** the part of the arm from the elbow to the shoulder; upper arm. **2** in biology, a similar part in any animal. **3** in zoology, any armlike appendage. [< L *bracchium* arm < Gk. *brachion* upper arm]

brach·y·ce·phal·ic (brak′ə sə fal′ik) *adj.* having a short, broad skull; having a skull whose breadth is 80 per cent or more of its length; broad-headed, opposed to *dolichocephalic.* [< Gk. *brachys* short + *kephalē* head]

brac·ing (brās′ing) *adj.* giving strength and energy; refreshing. —*n.* a brace or braces. —**brac′ing·ly,** *adv.*

brack·en (brak′ən) *n.* **1** a large fern. **2** a field of ferns. [ME *braken*, apparently < Scand.]

brack·et (brak′it) *n.* **1** a flat piece of stone, wood, or metal projecting from a wall as a support for a shelf, a statue, etc. **2** a support in the shape of a right triangle. **3** a shelf supported by brackets. **4** a gas or electric fixture projecting from a wall. **5** either of these signs [ ], used to enclose words, symbols, or figures. **6** either of these signs ( ); parenthesis. **7** in mathematics, a straight line placed over an expression and meaning the same as parentheses around the expression; vinculum. **8** the (specified) distance between a pair of shots fired, one beyond the target and one short of it, in order to find the range for artillery. **9** a group considered or mentioned collectively: *in the low-income bracket.*
—*v.* **1** support with brackets. **2** enclose within brackets. **3** think of together; mention together; group. **4** fire two shots, one beyond and one short of (a target). [< F *braguette* < Sp. *bragueta*, dim. of *braga* < L *bracae* breeches; by confusion with *brachia* arms]

brack·ish (brak′ish) *adj.* **1** rather salty. **2** distasteful; unpleasant. [< *brack* brackish < Du. *brak*] —**brack′ish·ness,** *n.*

bract (brakt) *n.* in botany, a small leaf at the base of a flower or flower stalk. [< L *bractea* thin metal plate]

BRACTS
BRACT

brad (brad) *n.* a small, thin nail with a small head. [var. of *brod* < ON *broddr* spike]

brad·awl (brad′ol′ or brad′ôl′) *n.* an awl with a cutting edge for making small holes for brads, etc.

brae (brā) *n. Scottish.* a slope; hillside. [ME *bra* < ON *brá-* (first member of a compound) brow; intermediate sense being "brow of a hill"]

brag (brag) *n. v.* **bragged, brag·ging.** —*n.* **1** a boast. **2** boastful talk. **3** a person who boasts. —*v.* boast. [ME; origin uncertain] —**brag′ger,** *n.*
—**Syn.** *v.* See **boast.**

brag·ga·do·ci·o (brag′ə dō′shē ō or brag′ə dō′chē ō) *n.* **-ci·os. 1** a boasting or bragging. **2** a boaster; braggart. [coined by Spenser as the name of a character in his *Faerie Queene*]

brag·gart (brag′ərt) *n.* a boaster. —*adj.* boastful. [< F *bragard* < *braguer* brag]

brah·ma (brä′mə or brā′mə) *n.* **1** one of a breed of large chicken with feathered legs and small wings and tail. **2 a** a breed of cattle usually having a large hump on the back, originally imported from India; zebu. **b** an animal of this breed. [< *Brahmaputra*, a river in E. India]

Brah·ma (brä′mə) *n.* in Hindu theology: **1** the Supreme God of creation, thought of as a trinity (Brahma the Creator, Vishnu the Preserver, Siva the Destroyer). **2** one of the gods of this trinity; the Creator. [< Skt.]

Brah·man (brä′mən) *n.* **-mans. 1** in India, a member of the priestly caste, the highest Hindu caste. **2** a kind of cattle; brahma. Also, **Brahmin.**

Brah·man·ism (brä′mən iz′əm) *n.* the religious and social system of the Brahmans.

Brah·min (brä′mən) *n.* **-min. 1** a Brahman. **2** any highbrow intellectual, especially one belonging to an upper-class family.

braid (brād) *n.* **1** a band formed by weaving together three or more strands of hair, ribbon, straw, etc. **2** a narrow band of fabric used to trim or bind clothing. **3** a band for confining the hair. [< v.]
—*v.* **1** weave together strips or strands. **2** form by weaving together three or more strands of hair, ribbon, straw, etc. **3** trim or bind with braid. **4** confine (hair) with a band. [OE *bregdan*] —**braid′er,** *n.*

braid·ed (brād′id) *adj.* **1** formed by weaving together three or more strands of hair, ribbon, straw, etc. **2** trimmed or bound with braid.

brail (brāl) *n.* a rope fastened to a sail, used in drawing the sail up or in. —*v.* gather or haul in with brails. [ME < OF < VL *bracale* belt < *bracae* breeches. See BRACKET.]

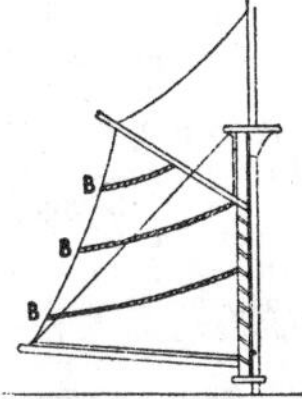

B, brails on a sail

braille or **Braille** (brāl) *n.* **1** a system of writing and printing for blind people. The letters in Braille are made of raised points which the reader touches and learns to recognize with his finger tips. **2** the letters themselves. [named after Louis *Braille* (1809-1852), a French teacher of the blind]

brain (brān) *n.* **1** in vertebrates, the mass of nerve tissue enclosed in the skull or head. The brain is used in feeling and thinking. **2** in invertebrates, the part of the nervous system corresponding to the brain of vertebrates. **3** Often, **brains,** *pl.* mind; intelligence. **4** *Informal.* an electronic computer. **5 beat one's brains,** try hard to think of something. **6** *Slang.* a clever person. **7 have something on the brain,** *Informal.* to be extremely interested in or eager about something: *She has ballet on the brain.* **8 pick the brains of,** to extract useful information or material from (someone). **9 turn the brains of,** to make conceited or foolish.
—*v.* dash the brains out of: *The Indian brained the wolf with a large stone.* [OE *brægen*]

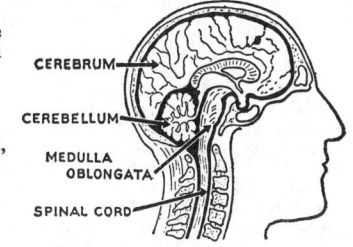

CEREBRUM
CEREBELLUM
MEDULLA OBLONGATA
SPINAL CORD

Parts of the human brain

brain cell a nerve cell in the brain.

brain·child (brān′chīld′) *n.* **chil·dren.** *Informal.* an invention or discovery, thought of as the child of a person's intelligence.

brain·less (brān′lis) *adj.* **1** without a brain. **2** stupid; foolish. —**brain′less·ly,** *adv.* —**brain′less·ness,** *n.*

brain·pan (brān′pan′) *n.* the part of the skull enclosing the brain; cranium.

hat, āge, cãre, fär; let, ēqual, tėrm; it, īce
hot, ōpen, ôrder; oil, out; cup, pu̇t, rüle, ūse
əbove, takən, pencəl, lemən, circəs
ch, child; ng, long; sh, ship
th, thin; ᴛʜ, then; zh, measure

brain·power (brān′pow′ər) *n.* **1** the power of the mind; brains. **2** intellect thought of as a force or as an instrument to be used.

brain·sick (brān′sik′) *adj.* crazy; insane.

brain storm 1 *Informal.* a sudden inspired idea. **2** a sudden and violent, but temporary, mental disturbance.

brain·storm (brān′stôrm′) *v.* attempt to solve a problem in a group, committee, etc. by having the members suggest every possible solution they can think of. Discussion is postponed until suggestions are exhausted. —**brain′storm·er,** *n.*

brain trust or **brains trust 1** a group of experts acting as advisers to an administrator, a political leader, or an executive. **2** a group of experts in various fields who discuss on the radio or television problems sent in for their attention.

brain·wash (brān′wosh′) *v.* subject to brainwashing.

brain·wash·ing (brān′wosh′ing) *n.* a process of systematic and intensive indoctrination by which a person's mind is purged of his political, economic, and social ideas, enabling other ideas to be imposed in their place.

brain wave 1 in physiology, rhythmic differences in electric potential in the brain as shown on an electro-encephalograph. **2** a telepathic vibration. **3** *Informal.* a sudden bright idea; inspiration.

brain·work (brān′wėrk′) *n.* work requiring the use of the mind, as distinguished from manual or mechanical work.

brain·y (brān′ē) *adj.* **brain·i·er, brain·i·est.** *Informal.* intelligent; clever. —**brain′i·ness,** *n.*

braise (brāz) *v.* **braised, brais·ing.** brown (meat) quickly and then cook it long and slowly in a covered pan with very little water. [< F *braiser* < *braise* hot charcoal < Gmc.]

brake[1] (brāk) *n. v.* **braked, brak·ing.** —*n.* **1** anything used to check the motion of a wheel or vehicle by pressing or scraping. **2** a tool or machine for breaking up flax or hemp into fibres. **3** a machine for kneading or rolling. **4** a large, high, four-wheeled carriage; break. —*v.* **1** slow up or stop by using a brake: *brake an automobile.* **2** use a brake on. **3** break up (flax or hemp) into fibres. [< MLG or MDu. *braeke*. Akin to BREAK.]

brake[2] (brāk) *n.* a thicket. [cf. MLG *brake*]

brake[3] (brāk) *n.* a large, coarse fern. [probably var. of *bracken*]

brake[4] (brāk) *v. Archaic.* a pt. of **break.**

brake band a band acting as a brake or controlling a brake.

brake drum on the wheel, axle, or transmission shaft of a vehicle, a metal cylinder against which a shoe or brake band is pressed in braking.

brake·man (brāk′mən) *n.* **-men** (-mən). a man who works the brakes or helps the conductor of a railway train.

bram·ble (bram′bəl) *n.* **1** any of a large group of the rose family, of which many varieties, such as the blackberry and raspberry, are prickly. **2** any rough, prickly shrub. [OE *bræmbel*, var. of *brēmel* < *brōm* broom]

bram·bly (bram′blē) *adj.* **-bli·er, -bli·est. 1** full of brambles. **2** like brambles; prickly.

bran (bran) *n.* the broken coat of the grains of wheat, rye, etc. separated from the flour. [ME < OF]

branch (branch) *n.* **1** a part of a tree, shrub, etc. growing out from the trunk; any woody part of a tree above the ground except the trunk: *A bough is a main branch. A twig is a very small branch.* **2** any division that resembles a branch of a tree: *a branch of a river, a*

branch of a family. **3** a division or part: *History is a branch of learning.* **4** a local office: *a branch of a bank.*
—*v.* **1** put out branches; spread in branches. **2** divide into branches: *The road branches at the bottom of the hill.* **3 branch off,** divide into branches. **4 branch out, a** put out branches. **b** extend business, interests, activities, etc. [ME < OF *branche* < LL *branca* paw] —**branch′less,** *adj.* —**branch′like′,** *adj.*

Syn. 1 Branch, bough, limb = a part of a tree growing out from the trunk or from another similar part. **Branch** is the general word, and applies to any of the woody outgrowths, large or small, of a tree or shrub: *The branches waved in the breeze.* **Bough** applies particularly to a main branch, but often is used to suggest any branch covered with blossoms, fruit, etc., especially when it has been cut from the tree: *Those boughs of flowering plum are beautiful on the table.* **Limb** applies to a main or large branch: *The wind broke a whole limb from the tree.*

bran·chi·o·pod (brang′kē ə pod′) *n.* any of a group of mainly fresh-water crustaceans having an elongated body and numerous pairs of leaflike appendages that serve as gills. [< NL < Gk. *branchia* gills + *pous, podos* foot]

branch·let (branch′lit) *n.* a small branch.

brand (brand) *n.* **1** a certain kind, grade, or make: *a brand of coffee.* **2** a trademark. **3** a mark made by burning the skin with a hot iron: *Cattle and horses on big ranches are marked with brands to show who owns them.* **4** an iron stamp for burning a mark. **5** a mark of disgrace. **6** a piece of wood that is burning or partly burned. **7** in botany: **a** a fungus disease in which the leaves and stems of plants appear as if burned. **b** any fungus producing such a disease. **8** *Archaic and Poetic.* a sword.
—*v.* **1** mark by burning the skin with a hot iron: *In former times criminals were often branded.* **2** put a mark of disgrace on: *He has been branded as a traitor.* [OE] —**brand′er,** *n.*

bran·died (bran′dēd) *adj.* prepared, mixed, or flavored with brandy.

bran·dish (bran′dish) *v.* wave or shake threateningly; flourish: *The knight drew his sword and brandished it at his enemy.* —*n.* a threatening shake; flourish. [< OF *brandiss-*, stem of *brandir* < *brand* sword < Gmc.]

brand name 1 a distinctive name or symbol identifying a product; trade name. **2** a product with a well-known trade name.

brand-new (bran′nū′ or -nü′) *adj.* quite new.

bran·dy (bran′dē) *n.* **-dies,** *v.* **-died, -dy·ing.** —*n.* **1** a strong alcoholic liquor distilled from wine. **2** an alcoholic liquor distilled from fruit juice. —*v.* mix, flavor, or preserve with brandy. [< Du. *brandewijn* burnt (i.e., distilled) wine]

brant (brant) *n.* **brants** or (*esp. collectively*) **brant.** a small, dark, wild goose that breeds in Arctic regions and migrates south in the autumn. [origin uncertain]

brash[1] (brash) *adj.* **1** hasty; rash. **2** impudent; saucy. [origin uncertain] —**brash′ly,** *adv.* —**brash′ness,** *n.*

brash[2] (brash) *n.* small fragments of ice broken off from an ice pack or floe. [? < MF *breche* breach]

bra·sier (brā′zhər) *n.* brazier.

brass (bras) *n.* **1** a yellow metal, an alloy of copper and zinc. **2** anything made of brass, such as ornaments, dishes, etc. **3** in music: **a** a wind instrument, usually made of brass, such as the trumpet, trombone, and French horn. **b** often, **brasses,** *pl.* the section of an orchestra or band composed of brass instruments. **4** *Informal.* money. **5** *Informal.* shamelessness; impudence. **6** *Slang.* high-ranking military officers; any high-ranking person or persons. **7** a memorial plate of brass marked with an effigy, coat of arms, inscription, etc.
—*adj.* made of brass. [OE *bræs*]

bras·sard (bras′ärd or brə särd′) *n.* **1** a band worn above the elbow as a badge. **2** armor for the upper part of the arm. See **armor** for picture. [< F *brassard* < *bras* arm]

bras·sart (bras′ərt) *n.* brassard (def. 2).

brass band a group of musicians playing brass wind instruments.

brass·bound (bras′bound′) *adj.* **1** *Informal.* keeping strictly to rule. **2** bound with brass: *a brassbound box.*

brass hat *Slang.* a high-ranking military officer, such as a general or staff officer.

brass·ie (bras′ē) *n.* **brass·ies.** a golf club with a wooden head on the bottom of which is a metal plate. Also, **brassy.**

bras·siere or **bras·sière** (brə zēr′) *n.* a woman's undergarment worn to support the breasts. [< F *brassière* bodice < *bras* arm]

brass knuckles a metal bar that fits across the knuckles, used in fighting.

brass tacks *Informal.* the actual facts or details: *Let's get down to brass tacks.*

brass·ware (bras′wãr′) *n.* things made of brass.

brass-wind (bras′wind′) *adj.* of or having to do with the brass winds.

brass winds the metal musical instruments that are played by blowing, such as trumpets and trombones.

brass·y (bras′ē) *adj.* **brass·i·er, brass·i·est,** *n.* **brass·ies.** —*adj.* **1** of brass. **2** like brass. **3** loud and harsh. **4** *Informal.* shameless; impudent.
—*n.* brassie. —**brass′i·ly,** *adv.* —**brass′i·ness,** *n.*

brat (brat) *n. Derogatory.* a child. [? special use of ME *brat* coarse garment, OE *bratt* cloak, covering, probably < Celtic; with reference to a bib]

bra·va·do (brə vä′dō) *n.* a great show of boldness without much real courage; boastful defiance without much real desire to fight. [< Sp. *bravada* < *bravo.* See BRAVE.]

brave (brāv) *adj.* **brav·er, brav·est,** *n. v.* **braved, brav·ing.** —*adj.* **1** without fear; having courage: *brave knights.* **2** making a fine appearance; showy: *The fair had brave displays.* **3** *Archaic.* fine; excellent.
—*n.* **1** a courageous person. **2** a North American Indian warrior.
—*v.* **1** meet without fear: *Soldiers brave much danger.* **2** dare; defy: *He braved the king's anger.* [< F < Ital. *bravo* brave, bold < Sp. *bravo* vicious (as applied to bulls), ? < L *pravus*] —**brave′ly,** *adv.* —**brave′ness,** *n.*

Syn. *adj.* **1 Brave, courageous** = showing no fear. **Brave** suggests being able to face danger or trouble boldly and with determination without giving in to fear: *The brave girl went into the burning house to save a baby.* **Courageous** suggests being fearless in the face of danger, having a strength and firmness of character that makes one able to endure any trial or even to welcome it: *The courageous pioneers were not stopped by the dangers of the journey westward.*

brav·er·y (brāv′ər ē or brāv′rē) *n.* **-er·ies. 1** fearlessness. **2** fine appearance; showy dress; finery. —**Syn. 1** boldness, daring, pluck, intrepidity. See **courage.**

bra·vo[1] (brä′vō) *interj. n.* **-vos.** —*interj.* well done! fine! excellent! —*n.* the cry of "Bravo!" [< Ital. See BRAVE.]

bra·vo[2] (brä′vō) *n.* **-voes** or **-vos.** a hired fighter or murderer. [< Ital. See BRAVE.]

bra·vu·ra (brə vūr′ə) *n.* **1** a piece of music requiring skill and spirit in the performer. **2** a display of daring; attempt at brilliant performance; dash; spirit. [< Ital. *bravura* bravery]

braw (bro or brô) *adj. Scottish.* **1** making a fine appearance. **2** excellent; fine. [var. of *brave*]

brawl[1] (brol or brôl) *n.* **1** a noisy quarrel: *The hockey game turned into a brawl when the players began fighting.* **2** a babble. [< v.] —*v.* **1** quarrel noisily. **2** babble. [ME *brallen*] —**brawl′er,** *n.* —**Syn.** *n.* **1** fracas, fray.

brawl[2] (brol or brôl) *n.* **1** an old French folk dance similar to the cotillion. **2** the music for this dance. **3** *Slang.* a dance or party. [< *brawl*[1] influenced by MF *branle* dance]

brawn (bron or brôn) *n.* **1** muscle; firm, strong muscles. **2** muscular strength: *Football requires brain as well as brawn.* **3** boiled and pickled meat from a boar or pig. [ME < OF *braon* < Gmc.]

brawn·y (bron′ē or brôn′ē) *adj.* **brawn·i·er, brawn·i·est.** strong; muscular. —**brawn′i·ness,** *n.* —**Syn.** sinewy, powerful.

bray[1] (brā) *n.* **1** the loud, harsh sound made by a donkey **2** any noise like it. [< v.] —*v.* **1** make a loud, harsh sound: *The man brayed with laughter.* **2** utter in a loud, harsh voice. [ME < OF *braire*]

hat, āge, cãre, fär; let, ēqual, tėrm; it, īce
hot, ōpen, ôrder; oil, out; cup, pu̇t, rüle, ūse
əbove, takən, pencəl, lemən, circəs
ch, child; ng, long; sh, ship
th, thin; ᴛʜ, then; zh, measure

bray[2] (brā) *v.* pound or crush into fine bits; grind into a powder. [ME < OF *breier*]

Braz. 1 Brazil. 2 Brazilian.

braze[1] (brāz) *v.* **brazed, braz·ing. 1** cover or decorate with brass. **2** make like brass. [OE *brasian* < *bræs* brass]

braze[2] (brāz) *v.* **brazed, braz·ing.** solder with brass or other hard solder that has a high melting point. [? < F *braser* < OF *braise* embers]

bra·zen (brā′zən) *adj.* **1** made of brass. **2** like brass in color or strength. **3** loud and harsh. **4** shameless; impudent.
—*v.* **1** make shameless or impudent. **2 brazen a thing out** or **through,** act as if unashamed of it. [OE *bræsen* < *bræs* brass] —**bra′zen·ly,** *adv.* —**bra′zen·ness,** *n.*
—**Syn.** *adj.* **4** See **bold.**

bra·zier[1] (brā′zhər or brā′zē ər) *n.* a metal container to hold burning charcoal or coal: *Braziers are used in some countries for heating rooms.* Also, **brasier.** [< F *brasier* < *braise* hot coals]

bra·zier[2] (brā′zhər) *n.* a person who works with brass. Also, **brasier.** [< *braze*[1]]

Bra·zil·ian (brə zil′yən) *adj.* of Brazil or its people.
—*n.* a native or inhabitant of Brazil.

Brazil nut a large, triangular, edible nut of a tree growing in South America.

bra·zil·wood (brə zil′wu̇d′) *n.* a large tropical tree whose wood is used for making dyes.

breach (brēch) *n.* **1** an opening made by breaking down something solid; gap. **2** a breaking (of a law, promise, duty, etc.); neglect: *For me to go away today would be a breach of duty.* **3** a breaking of friendly relations; quarrel. **4** a whale's leap clear of the sea.
—*v.* **1** break through; make an opening in: *The enemy's fierce attack finally breached the wall.* **2** of whales, rise or leap clear of the sea. [ME *breche* < OF < Gmc.]
—**Syn.** *n.* **1** fracture, crack, rent. **3** estrangement, alienation.

breach of faith a breaking of a promise.

breach of promise a breaking of a promise to marry.

breach of the peace a public disturbance; riot.

bread (bred) *n.* **1** a food made of flour or meal mixed with milk or water and baked. **2** food; livelihood. **3 break bread, a** share a meal. **b** administer or take Communion. **4 cast one's bread upon the waters,** do good with little or no prospect of reward. **5 know which side one's bread is buttered on,** know what is to one's advantage. **6 take the bread out of one's mouth, a** to take away a person's livelihood. **b** to take from a person what he is on the point of enjoying.
—*v.* cover with bread crumbs before cooking.
[OE *brēad*] —**bread′less,** *adj.*

bread and butter 1 bread spread with butter. **2** *Informal.* necessities; a living.

bread-and-but·ter (bred′ən but′ər) *adj.* **1** *Informal.* prosaic; commonplace. **2** expressing thanks for hospitality: *a bread-and-butter letter.* **3** *Informal.* adolescent: *a bread-and-butter girl.*

bread·bas·ket (bred′bas kit) *n.* **1** a basket or tray for bread. **2** a region that is a chief source of grain: *The Prairies are the breadbasket of Canada.* **3** *Slang.* the stomach.

bread·board (bred′bôrd′) *n.* **1** a board on which dough is kneaded, pastry is rolled, etc. **2** a board on which bread is cut.

bread·crumb or **bread-crumb** (bred′krum′) *n.* **1** a crumb of bread. **2** the soft part of bread as distinguished from the crust. —*v.* cover with breadcrumbs.

bread·fruit (bred′früt′) *n.* **1** a large, round, starchy, tropical fruit of the Pacific islands, much used for food. When baked, it tastes somewhat like bread. **2** the tree that it grows on.

bread line a line of people waiting to get food issued as charity or relief.

bread·stuff (bred′stuf′) *n.* **1** grain, flour, or meal for making bread. **2** bread.

breadth (bredth or bretth) *n.* **1** how broad a thing is; the distance across; width: *The breadth of his shoulders showed his great strength.* **2** a piece of a certain width: *a breadth of cloth.* **3** freedom from narrowness: *A tolerant person usually has breadth of mind.* **4** spaciousness; extent. [ME *bredethe* < *brede* breadth, OE *brædu* < *brād* broad] —**Syn. 3** latitude, liberality. **4** amplitude.

breadth·ways (bredth′wāz′ or bretth′-) *adv. adj.* in the direction of the breadth.

breadth·wise (bredth′wīz′ or bretth′-) *adv. adj.* breadthways.

bread·win·ner (bred′win′ər) *n.* a person who earns a living for those dependent on him.

break (brāk) *v.* **broke** or (*Archaic*) **brake, bro·ken** or (*Archaic*) **broke, break·ing,** *n.* —*v.* **1** cause to come to pieces by a blow or pull: *How did you break my glasses?* **2** come apart; crack; burst: *The plate broke into pieces when it fell on the floor.* **3** destroy evenness, wholeness, etc.: *break a five-dollar bill.* **4** injure; damage; ruin; destroy: *She broke her watch by winding it too tightly.* **5** fracture the bone of; dislocate: *break one's arm, one's neck.* **6** fail to keep; act against: *break a law, break a promise.* **7 a** escape or become free from: *to break jail. The boat broke its moorings in the storm.* **b** force open: *to break the enemy's ranks.* **8** force one's way: *break loose from prison, break into a house.* **9** come suddenly: *The storm broke within ten minutes.* **10** change suddenly: *The spell of rainy weather has broken.* **11** lessen the force of: *The trees break the wind.* **12** be crushed; give way: *The dog's heart broke when his master died.* **13** dawn; appear: *The day is breaking.* **14** of plants: **a** to bud. **b** to flower too soon. **15** stop; put an end to: *break one's fast.* **16** reduce in rank: *The captain was broken for neglect of duty.* **17** train to obey; tame: *break a colt.* **18** ruin financially; make bankrupt. **19** go beyond; exceed: *The speed of the new train has broken all records.* **20** dig or plough land, especially for the first time: *In the forests of Upper Canada the pioneers had to work hard to break the ground.* **21** of boxers, come out of a clinch. **22** make known; reveal: *break the bad news gently.* **23** train (someone) away from a habit. **24** open an electric circuit.
break away, a start before the signal. **b** go suddenly. **c** change suddenly.
break down, a have an accident; fail to function. **b** collapse; become weak; lose one's health. **c** begin to cry. **d** analyse: *These figures on living expenses must be broken down into food, shelter, education, medical bills, etc.*
break even, *Informal.* finish with the same amount one started with; neither win nor lose in a game of chance.
break in, a prepare for work or use; train. **b** enter by force. **c** interrupt.
break off, a stop suddenly. **b** stop being friends.
break out, a start suddenly (especially of something harmful, such as a fire, an epidemic, or a war). **b** have pimples, rashes, etc.
break up, *Informal.* **a** scatter. **b** stop; put an end to. **c** upset; disturb greatly. **d** break into pieces.
break with, stop being friends with.
—*n.* **1** a broken place; gap; crack. **2** a breaking or shattering; fracture; rupture. **3** a forcing of one's way out. **4** an abrupt or marked change. **5** a short interruption in work, athletic practice, etc. **6** *Slang.* an awkward remark; mistake in manners. **7** *Slang.* a chance or opportunity. **8** the act or fact of making an electric circuit incomplete. **9** a large four-wheeled carriage or wagon; brake. **10 get a break** or **the breaks,** *Informal.* have things come easily; have lots of luck. [OE *brecan*]
Syn. *v.* **1 Break, shatter, smash** = to make something come or go to pieces. **Break,** the general word = to divide something into two or more pieces by pulling, hitting, or striking it: *I broke the handle off a cup.* **Shatter** = to break suddenly into a number of pieces that fly in all directions. *I shattered the cup when I dropped it on the floor.* **Smash** = to break to pieces with sudden violence and noise: *He smashed the headlights when he hit the wall.* **2** split, splinter. **6** violate, disobey.

break·a·ble (brāk′ə bəl) *adj.* that can be broken.

break·age (brāk′ij) *n.* **1** a breaking; break. **2** damage or loss caused by breaking. **3** an allowance made for such damage or loss.

break·a·way (brāk′ə wā′) *n.* **1** the act or fact of separating sharply from a group or pattern. **2** the separation of the shock wave from the fireball of an atomic explosion as it moves ahead. **3** *Slang.* in the theatre, a stage property made so that it breaks easily and harmlessly when struck by or against something. **4** a start: *Three of the horses in the race got well ahead of the others at the breakaway.* **5** in hockey and lacrosse, a situation in which a player of one team launches an attack on goal, the defensive players being caught out of position in their opponents' zone.

break·down (brāk′doun′) *n.* **1** a failure to work. **2** a loss of health; weakness; collapse: *a mental breakdown.* **3** a noisy, lively dance. **4** the division of a process into steps or stages; an analysis. **5** chemical decomposition or analysis.
—*adj.* especially on railways, used in repairing a breakdown: *a breakdown crew, breakdown train.*

break·er[1] (brāk′ər) *n.* **1** a wave that breaks into foam on the shore, rocks, etc. **2** a machine for breaking things into smaller pieces. **3** a person or thing that breaks. [< *break*] —**Syn. 1** See **wave.**

break·er[2] (brāk′ər) *n.* a small water cask for use in a boat. [alteration of Sp. *barrica*]

break·fast (brek′fəst) *n.* the first meal of the day.
—*v.* eat breakfast. [< *break* + *fast*[2]]

breakfast food a cereal eaten at breakfast.

break-in (brāk′in′) *n.* a burglary.

breaking and entering in law, the entry by force or guile into private or business premises with the object of committing a crime.

break·neck (brāk′nek′) *adj.* likely to cause a broken neck; very dangerous: *breakneck speed, a breakneck slope.*

break of day the dawn.

break·out (brāk′out′) *n.* **1** the act or condition of escaping from a prison, etc. **2** a breakthrough (def. 1).

break·through (brāk′thrü′) *n.* **1** an offensive military operation that gets all the way through a defensive system into the unorganized area in the rear. **2** a solving of the major problem or problems hindering an undertaking, as in science.

break-up (brāk′up′) *n.* **1** the time when the ice breaks up on the rivers of the North; spring: *They planned to start work on the new road after break-up.* **2** a scattering; separation. **3** a stopping; end. **4** a collapse; decay.

break·wa·ter (brāk′wot′ər or -wô′tər) *n.* a wall or barrier built to break the force of waves.

bream[1] (brēm) *n.* **bream** or **breams. 1** a carp of inland European waters. **2** any of various related fishes that have rather deep bodies. **3** the common fresh-water sunfish. [ME *breme* < OF *bre(s)me* < Gmc.]

bream[2] (brēm) *v. Archaic.* clean (a ship's bottom). [cf. MDu. *brem* broom]

breast (brest) *n.* **1** either of the milk-producing organs on the chest of the human female. **2** the upper, front part of the human body; chest. **3** the upper, front part of a coat, dress, etc. **4** anything suggesting the female breast in shape or position. **5** the heart; feelings. **6 make a clean breast of,** confess completely.
—*v.* struggle with; advance against; oppose; face: *He breasted every trouble as it came.* [OE *brēost*]

breast·bone (brest′bōn′) *n.* the thin, flat bone in the front of the chest to which the ribs are attached; sternum. See SKELETON for picture.

breast-feed (brest′fēd′) *n.* **-fed, -feed·ing.** feed at the mother's breast rather than from a bottle; nurse.

breast·pin (brest′pin′) *n.* an ornamental pin worn on the breast; brooch.

breast·plate (brest′plāt′) *n.* **1** a piece of armor for the chest. See **armor** for picture. **2** in ancient times, a vestment set with jewels, worn by Jewish high priests.

breast stroke in swimming, a stroke in which both arms at once are brought from in front of the head to the sides.

breast·work (brest′wėrk′) *n.* a low, hastily built wall for defence.

breath (breth) *n.* **1** air drawn into and forced out of the lungs. **2** the act of breathing. **3** moisture from breathing: *You can see your breath on a very cold day.* **4** the ability to breathe easily: *Running makes a person lose his breath.* **5 a** a single drawing in and forcing out of air from the body. **b** the air drawn in. **c** the time required for one breath; a moment. **6** time to breathe freely; respite. **7** a slight movement in the air; light breeze. **8** a whisper. **9** life. **10** in phonetics, an expulsion of air without vibration of the vocal cords, as in pronouncing *s, f, p, t, k.* **11** the fragrance given off by flowers, etc. **12** a stain, film, or taint, as from the breath: *the breath of suspicion.* [OE *brǣth* odor, steam]
below one's breath, in a whisper.
catch one's breath, a gasp; pant. **b** stop for breath; rest.
hold one's breath, check exhalation.
in the same breath, at the same time.
save one's breath, keep silent.
under one's breath, in a whisper.

breath·a·lyz·er (breth′ə līz′ər) *n.* a device for measuring the alcoholic content in a person's blood by a test of the breath. Also, **breathalyser.**

breathe (brēᴛʜ) *v.* **breathed, breath·ing. 1** draw (air) into the lungs and force it out. **2** stop for breath; rest; allow to rest and breathe. **3** put out of breath. **4** blow lightly. **5** say softly; whisper; utter. **6** be alive; live. **7** in phonetics, utter with breath and not with voice. **8** draw into the lungs; inhale. **9** send out from the lungs; exhale. **10** inspire; impart: *The captain breathed new life into his tired soldiers.* **11 breathe again** or **freely,** be relieved; feel easy. [ME *brethen* < *breth* breath]

breath·er (brēᴛʜ′ər) *n.* **1** a short stop for breath; rest. **2** *Informal.* something that puts a person out of breath.

breath·ing (brēᴛʜ′ing) *n.* **1** respiration. **2** a single breath. **3** the time needed for a single breath. **4** a remark; utterance. **5** a slight breeze. **6** the sound of the letter *h.*

breathing space room or time enough to breathe easily; an opportunity to rest.

breathing spell a pause to catch one's breath.

breath·less (breth′lis) *adj.* **1** out of breath: *Running very fast makes you breathless.* **2** unable to breathe freely because of excitement. **3** without breath; lifeless. **4** without a breeze. —**breath′less·ly,** *adv.* —**breath′less·ness,** *n.*

breath-tak·ing (breth′tāk′ing) *adj.* thrilling; exciting.

breath·y (breth′ē) *adj.* characterized by audible sounds of breathing. —**breath′i·ly,** *adv.* —**breath′i·ness,** *n.*

brec·ci·a (brech′ē ə or bresh′ē ə) *n.* a rock consisting of angular fragments of older rocks cemented together in a matrix. [< Ital. < Gmc. Akin to BREAK.]

bred (bred) *v.* pt. and pp. of **breed.**

breech (brēch) *n.* **1** the lower part; back part. **2** in a rifle or gun, the opening directly behind the barrel, where the shells are inserted. **3** the rump; buttocks.
—*v.* **1** clothe with breeches. **2** provide (a gun) with a breech. [back formation from *breeches*]

breech·cloth (brēch′kloth′) *n.* a cloth worn around the buttocks, especially by North American Indians; loincloth.

breech·clout (brēch′klout′) *n.* breechcloth.

breech·es (brich′iz) *n.pl.* **1** short trousers reaching from the waist to the knees. **2** *Informal.* trousers; pants. [OE *brēc*, pl. of *brōc* breech]

breeches buoy a pair of short canvas trousers fastened to a belt or life preserver. A breeches buoy slides along a rope on a pulley and is used to rescue people from sinking ships.

A breeches buoy

breech·ing (brich′ing or brēch′ing) *n.* the part of a harness that passes around a horse's rump.

breech·load·er (brēch′lōd′ər) *n.* a gun that is loaded from behind the barrel, instead of at the mouth.

breech·load·ing (brēch′lōd′ing) *adj.* of guns, loading from behind the barrel instead of at the mouth.

breed (brēd) *v.* **bred, breed·ing,** *n.* —*v.* **1** produce (young): *Rabbits breed rapidly.* **2** raise (livestock, etc.): *This farmer breeds cattle and pigs for market.* **3** produce; cause: *Careless driving breeds accidents.* **4** be produced or caused. **5** bring up; train: *He was bred a sailor.* **6** convert (non-fissionable material) into fissionable material.
—*n.* **1** a race; stock: *Jerseys and Guernseys are breeds of cattle.* **2** a kind; sort. [OE *brēdan*] —**Syn.** *v.* **3** occasion. **5** educate, school.

breed·er (brēd′ər) *n.* **1** a person who breeds animals: *a cattle breeder, a dog breeder.* **2** an animal that produces offspring. **3** a source; cause: *Great inequalities are breeders of revolutions.* **4** a breeder reactor.

breeder pile breeder reactor.

breeder reactor in nuclear physics, a reactor that produces at least as much fissionable material as it uses. One type of reactor consumes uranium and produces plutonium.

breed·ing (brēd′ing) *n.* **1** the producing of offspring. **2** the producing of animals, especially to get improved strains. **3** upbringing or training; behavior; manners: *Politeness is a sign of good breeding.* **4** in nuclear physics, the producing in a reactor of at least as much fissionable material as is used.

breeding ground **1** a place where animals, insects, etc. breed, or to which they return to breed. **2** a place where anything easily grows or flourishes: *Colonialism made Africa a breeding ground of nationalism.*

breeks (brēks) *n. Informal.* breeches.

breeze (brēz) *n. v.* **breezed, breez·ing.** —*n.* **1** a light wind. **2** *Informal.* a disturbance; quarrel. **3** *Informal.* something easy: *The quiz was a breeze.* **4 shoot the breeze,** *Slang.* engage in small talk; gossip.
—*v. Informal.* proceed easily or briskly. [< OSp. and Pg. *briza* northeast wind] —**Syn.** *n.* **1** See **wind**[1].

breez·y (brēz′ē) *adj.* **breez·i·er, breez·i·est. 1** that has a breeze; with light winds blowing. **2** brisk; lively; jolly: *We like his breezy joking manner.* —**breez′i·ly,** *adv.* —**breez′i·ness,** *n.*

Bren gun or **Bren** (bren) a fast, accurate, gas-operated machine gun used by the Allies in World War II. [< *Br*no, Czechoslovakia + *En*field, England, towns where these guns were manufactured]

br'er (brėr) *n. Dialect.* brother.

breth·ren (breᴛʜ′rən) *n.pl.* **1** *Archaic.* brothers. **2** the fellow members of a church or society. ☛ See **brother** for usage note.

bret·on (bret′ən) *n.* a hat having a shallow crown and a slightly rolled brim. [< *Breton*]

Bret·on (bret′ən) *n.* **1** a native or inhabitant of Brittany. **2** the Celtic language of Brittany. —*adj.* having to do with Brittany, its people, or their language. [< F < L *Bretto, -onis*]

breve (brēv) *n.* **1** the curved mark (˘) put over a vowel or syllable to show that it is short. **2** in music, a note equal to two whole notes. [< Ital. < L *brevis* short]

bre·vet (brə vet′; *esp.Brit.,* brev′it) *n. adj. v.* **-vet·ted** or **-vet·ed, -vet·ting** or **-vet·ing.** —*n.* a commission promoting an army officer to a higher rank without an increase in pay. —*adj.* having or giving rank by a brevet. —*v.* give rank by a brevet. [ME < OF *brevet,* diminutive of *bref* letter < OF *bref* short. See BRIEF.]

bre·vi·ar·y (brē′vē er′ē or brev′ē er′ē) *n.* **-ar·ies.** in the Roman Catholic Church, a book of prescribed prayers to be said daily by certain clergymen and religious. [< L *breviarium* summary < *brevis* short]

bre·vier (brə vēr′) *n.* a size of type; 8 point. This sentence is in brevier. [< G or OF < L *breviarium,* from its use in printing breviaries. See BREVIARY.]

brev·i·ty (brev′ə tē) *n.* **-ties.** the quality of shortness or briefness. [< L *brevitas* < *brevis* short] —**Syn.** conciseness, terseness.

brew (brü) *v.* **1** make (beer, ale, etc.) from malt, etc. by soaking, boiling, and fermenting. **2** make (a drink) by soaking, boiling, or mixing: *Tea is brewed in boiling water.* **3** bring about; plan; plot: *Those boys are brewing some mischief.* **4** begin to form; gather: *Dark clouds show that a storm is brewing.*
—*n.* **1** a drink that is brewed. **2** the quantity brewed at one time. [OE *brēowan*]

brew·er (brü′ər) *n.* a person who brews beer, ale, et[c.]

brew·er·y (brü′ər ē) *n.* **-er·ies.** a place where beer, al[e,] etc. are brewed.

brew·ing (brü′ing) *n.* **1** the preparing of a brew. **2** the amount brewed at one time.

brewis (brüz) *n.* in Newfoundland, a kind of stew prepare[d] by boiling hardtack with codfish, pork fat, and vegetables.

bri·ar[1] or **bri·er** (brī′ər) *n.* **1** a thorny or prickly bush, especially the wild rose. **2** a thorn or thorny twig. **3** a tangled growth of briars. [OE *brēr*]

bri·ar[2] or **bri·er** (brī′ər) *n.* **1** a white heath tree. The root of the briar is much used in making tobacco pipes. **2** a tobacco pipe made of this wood. [< F *bruyère* heath < Celtic]

bri·ar·wood or **bri·er·wood** (brī′ər wu̇d′) *n.* **1** the wood of briar tree roots. **2** any of various woods of which tobacco pipes are made. **3** a pipe made from such wood.

bri·ar·y or **bri·er·y** (brī′ər ē) *adj.* full of thorns or briars.

bribe (brīb) *n. v.* **bribed, brib·ing.** —*n.* **1** an inducement offered to a person to act dishonestly or against the law for the benefit of the giver. **2** a reward for doing something that one does not want to do: *A child should not need a bribe to obey his parents.* —*v.* influence by giving a bribe. [ME < OF *bribe* bit of bread given to a beggar] —**brib′a·ble,** *adj.* —**brib′er,** *n.*

brib·er·y (brīb′ər ē or brīb′rē) *n.* **-er·ies. 1** the giving or offering of a bribe. **2** the taking of a bribe.

bric-a-brac or **bric-à-brac** (brik′ə brak′) *n.* interesting or curious knick-knacks used as decorations; small ornaments, such as vases, old china, or small statues. [< F]
☛ **Bric-a-brac** is a collective noun; it never adds *s* to form the plural, nor is it ever modified by *a*: *The bric-a-brac showed evidence of her good taste.*

brick (brik) *n.* **bricks** or (*esp. collectively*), **brick,** *adj. v.* —*n.* **1** a block of clay baked by sun or fire, used in building and paving. **2** bricks collectively. **3** anything shaped like a brick: *Ice cream is often sold in bricks.* **4** Usually, **Brick.** a light-colored cheese made from whole milk, similar to a mild Cheddar. A whole cheese is shaped like a brick. **5** *Informal.* a good fellow; a person who is generous and dependable.
—*adj.* **1** made of bricks. **2** resembling brick.
—*v.* build or pave with bricks; wall in with bricks. [< F *brique* < MDu. *bricke*] —**brick′like′,** *adj.*

brick·bat (brik′bat′) *n.* **1** a piece of broken brick, especially one used as a missile. **2** *Informal.* an insult.

brick·lay·er (brik′lā′ər) *n.* a man whose work is building with bricks.

brick·lay·ing (brik′lā′ing) *n.* the act or work of building with bricks.

brick-red (brik′red′) *adj.* yellowish-red or brownish-red.

brick·work (brik′wėrk′) *n.* **1** anything made of bricks. **2** the act or process of building with bricks; bricklaying.

brick·yard (brik′yärd′) *n.* a place where bricks are made or sold.

brid·al (brīd′əl) *adj.* of a bride or a wedding. —*n.* a wedding. [OE *brȳdealo* bride ale] —**Syn.** *adj.* nuptial.

bridal wreath a shrub having long sprays of small white flowers that bloom in the spring; a kind of spiraea.

bride (brīd) *n.* a woman just married or about to be married. [OE *brȳd*]

bride·groom (brīd′grüm′) *n.* a man just married or about to be married. [OE *brȳdguma* < *brȳd* bride + *guma* man; influenced by *groom*]

brides·maid (brīdz′mād′) *n.* a young woman, usually unmarried, who attends the bride at a wedding.

bride·well (brīd′wel′) *n.* a house of correction for

…n. [from a former …on]

…g·ing. —*n.* **1** a structure … that people, trains, etc. … above the deck of a ship … **3** the upper, bony part of the … se teeth fastened to the adjacent … ole piece of wood over which the … are stretched. **6** in music, a passage …nnecting one theme, movement, etc. … urved central part of a pair of … sts on the nose. **8** an apparatus for … lectrical resistance of a conductor. … pool, etc., a player's hand arched to steady … ng shots, or a notched wooden or metal … end of a long rod used for the same purpose. … her thing like a bridge in form or use. … **one's bridges,** cut off all chances of retreat. … build a bridge over: *The engineers bridged the* … **2** extend over; span: *A log bridged the creek.* … make a way over: *Politeness will bridge many difficulties.* [OE *brycg*]

bridge[2] (brij) *n.* a card game for four players in two teams, played with 52 cards. Auction bridge and contract bridge are two varieties of this game. [origin uncertain]

bridge·head (brij′hed′) *n.* **1** a position obtained and held by advance troops within enemy territory, used as a starting point for further attack. **2** a fortification protecting the end of a bridge nearer to the enemy. **3** either end of a bridge.

Bridge of Sighs **1** in Venice, the bridge through which prisoners were led for trial. **2** in New York City, the bridge leading to the Tombs prison.

bridge table a small table, about 2½ feet square, having legs that fold in under the table top, used for playing cards and for many other purposes.

bridge·work (brij′wėrk′) *n.* a number of false teeth in a mounting fastened to the adjacent natural teeth.

bridg·ing (brij′ing) *n.* the braces placed between two beams to strengthen them and to keep them apart.

bri·dle (brī′dəl) *n. v.* **-dled, -dling.** —*n.* **1** the head part of a horse's harness, used to guide or control a horse. See **harness** for diagram. **2** anything that holds back or controls. —*v.* **1** put a bridle on. **2** hold back; check; control: *Bridle your temper.* **3** hold the head up high with the chin drawn back to express pride, vanity, scorn or anger. [OE *brīdel, brigdels* < *bregdan* to braid] —**bri′dler,** *n.* —**Syn.** *v.* **2** curb, restrain.

bridle path a path for people riding horses.

Brie (brē) *n.* a variety of soft, white cheese. [< F]

brief (brēf) *adj.* **1** lasting only a short time: *a brief meeting.* **2** using few words: *a brief announcement.* —*n.* **1** a short statement; summary. **2** a statement of the facts and the points of law concerning a case to be pleaded in court. **3 hold a brief for,** argue for; support; defend. **4 hold no brief for,** have no commitment or desire to argue for or support: *He is my friend, but I hold no brief for his political opinions.* **5** *Informal.* a client; a case at law to plead. **6** a briefing. **7** in the Roman Catholic Church, a papal letter, less formal than a bull. **8 briefs,** short, close-fitting underpants. **9 in brief,** in a few words.
—*v.* **1** make a brief of; summarize. **2** furnish with a brief. **3** retain as a lawyer or counsel. **4** give a briefing to. [ME *bref* < OF < L *brevis* short] —**brief′ly,** *adv.* —**brief′ness,** *n.* —**Syn.** *adj.* **1** fleeting, transitory. See **short. 2** concise, succinct, terse.

brief case a flat leather container for carrying loose papers, books, drawings, etc.

brief·ing (brēf′ing) *n.* **1** a short summary of the details about a flight mission, given to the crew of a combat airplane just before it takes off. **2** any similar short outline of plans, etc.

bri·er (brī′ər) *n.* briar[1] and briar[2].

Bri·er (brī′ər) *n. Cdn.* the competition or bonspiel that determines the curling champions of Canada. [< name of the trophy, the Macdonald *Brier* Tankard]

bri·er·wood (brī′ər wůd′) *n.* briarwood.

bri·er·y (brī′ər ē) *adj.* briary.

brig (brig) *n.* **1** a square-rigged ship with two masts. **2** the prison on a warship. [short for *brigantine*]

A brig

Brig. **1** Brigadier. **2** brigade.

bri·gade (bri gād′) *n.* **1** a part of an army, usually made up of two or more regiments. **2** any group of people organized for a particular purpose: *A fire brigade puts out fires.* **3** a fur brigade.
—*v.* **1** form into a brigade. **2** form (people) as if into a brigade; combine; associate. [< F *brigade* < Ital. *brigata* < *brigare* strive, fight < *briga* strife < Celtic]

brig·a·dier (brig′ə dēr′) *n.* in the army, a commissioned officer senior to a colonel and junior to a major-general, commanding usually a brigade, a military college, etc. *Abbrev.*: Brig. [< F *brigadier* < *brigade.* See BRIGADE.]

brigadier general *pl.* **brigadier generals.** brigadier.

brig·and (brig′ənd) *n.* a man who robs travellers on the road; a robber; bandit. [ME < OF < Ital. *brigante* fighter < *brigare* to brawl. See BRIGADE.]

brig·and·age (brig′ən dij) *n.* robbery; plundering.

brig·an·dine (brig′ən dēn′ or brig′ən dīn′) *n.* a coat of armor made of linen, leather, etc. strengthened with metal rings or thin metal pieces. [< MF *brigandine* armor for a brigand < *brigant* < Ital. *brigante* fighter. See BRIGAND.]

brig·an·tine (brig′ən tēn′ or brig′ən tīn′) *n.* a ship with two masts: *The foremast of a brigantine is square-rigged; the mainmast is fore-and-aft-rigged.* [< F < Ital. *brigantino* < *brigare.* See BRIGAND, BRIGADE.]

bright (brīt) *adj.* **1** giving much light; shining: *bright stars.* **2** very light or clear: *a bright day.* **3** quickwitted; clever: *A bright girl learns quickly.* **4** vivid; glowing: *a bright fire.* **5** lively; gay; cheerful: *a bright smile.* **6** favorable: *a bright outlook for the future.* **7** famous; glorious: *The knight was a bright example of courage in battle.*
—*adv.* in a bright manner: *The fire shines bright.* [OE *briht, beorht*] —**bright′ly,** *adv.* —**bright′ness,** *n.*
Syn. *adj.* **1 Bright, radiant, brilliant** = shining. **Bright** is the general word, and applies to anything thought of as giving out or reflecting light: *Her silver earrings are bright.* **Radiant** suggests giving out light in rays as the sun does, shining with a light that comes from deep within the thing or person described: *Her radiant face told us of her happiness.* **Brilliant** = very bright or excessively bright and often suggests sparkling or flashing: *The surface of the water is brilliant in the sunlight.* **3** smart, intelligent. **5** vivacious, animated. **6** promising.

bright·en (brīt′ən) *v.* **1** become bright or brighter: *The sky brightened.* **2** make bright or brighter. **3** make happy or cheerful. **4** become happy or cheerful: *Her face brightened.*

Bright's disease a kidney disease characterized by albumin in the urine. [after R. *Bright* (1789-1858), a British physician]

brill (bril) *n.* **brill** or **brills.** a European flatfish related to the turbot. [origin uncertain]

bril·liance (bril′yəns) *n.* **1** great brightness; radiance; sparkle. **2** splendor; magnificence. **3** great ability: *brilliance as a pianist.* **4** in music, clarity and vividness of sound: *the brilliance of modern high-frequency recordings.*

bril·lian·cy (bril′yən sē) *n.* brilliance.

bril·liant (bril′yənt) *adj.* **1** shining brightly; sparkling: *brilliant jewels, brilliant sunshine.* **2** splendid; magnificent: *a brilliant performance.* **3** having great ability: *a brilliant musician.*
—*n.* **1** a diamond or other gem cut to sparkle brightly. **2** the smallest size of type; 3½ point: This sentence is set in brilliant. [< F *brillant,* ppr. of *briller* shine, ? < L *beryllus* beryl] —**bril′liant·ly,** *adv.* —**Syn.** *adj.* **1** See **bright.**

bril·lian·tine (bril′yən tēn′) *n.* **1** an oily liquid used to make the hair glossy. **2** a glossy cloth of cotton and wool. [< F *brillantine*]

hat, āge, cãre, fär; let, ēqual, tėrm; it, īce
hot, ōpen, ôrder; oil, out; cup, pu̇t, rule, ūse
əbove, takən, pencəl, lemən, circəs
ch, child; ng, long; sh, ship
th, thin; ᴛʜ, then; zh, measure

brim (brim) *n. v.* **brimmed, brim·ming.** —*n.* **1** the edge of a cup, bowl, etc.; rim. **2** the projecting edge of a hat. **3** any water's edge: *He drank at the fountain's brim.* —*v.* fill to the brim; be full to the brim. [ME *brimme*] —**brim′less,** *adj.*

brim·ful (brim′fu̇l′) *adj.* full to the brim; full to the very top.

brim·mer (brim′ər) *n.* a cup, bowl, etc. full to the brim.

brim·stone (brim′stōn′) *n.* sulphur. [ME *brinston* < *brinnen* burn + *ston* stone]

brin·dle (brin′dəl) *adj.* brindled. —*n.* **1** a brindled color. **2** a brindled animal. [< *brindled*]

brin·dled (brin′dəld) *adj.* gray, tan, or tawny with darker streaks and spots. [earlier *brinded*, ME *brended.* Probably related to BRAND.]

brine (brīn) *n.* **1** very salty water: *Pickles are often kept in brine.* **2** a salt lake or sea; ocean. [OE *brȳne*]

bring (bring) *v.* **brought, bring·ing. 1** carry (some thing or person) with the hands or by some other means from another place; take along to a place or person: *The waiter brought me a clean plate and took the dirty one away.* **2** cause to come: *What brings you into town today?* **3** influence; lead: *He was brought to agree by our arguments.* **4** present before a law court: *He brought a charge against me.* **5** sell for: *Meat is bringing a high price this week.*
bring about, cause; cause to happen.
bring around or **bring round, a** restore to consciousness. **b** convince; persuade.
bring forth, a give birth to; bear. **b** reveal; show.
bring forward, a reveal; show. **b** in accounting or bookkeeping, carry over from one page to another.
bring home to, a prove beyond doubt. **b** make realize.
bring in, a introduce or try out. **b** report or announce officially; return: *bring in a verdict.* **c** cause to flow by drilling: *bring in an oil well.*
bring off, cause to happen; carry to a successful conclusion.
bring on, cause; cause to happen.
bring out, a reveal; show. **b** offer to the public.
bring over, convince; persuade.
bring to, a restore to consciousness. **b** stop; check.
bring up, a care for in childhood. **b** educate; train. **c** suggest for action or discussion. **d** stop suddenly. **e** advance to the scene of action: *bring up reinforcements.* **f** vomit. [OE *bringan*] —**bring′er,** *n.*
Syn. 1 Bring, fetch = to come to a person or place with something. **Bring** = to come with someone or something from another place to the place where the speaker is: *I brought some cake home with me.* **Fetch** = to go and get something and bring it back: *Please take the car and fetch him.*

bring·ing-up (bring′ing up′) *n.* **1** care in childhood. **2** education; training.

brink (bringk) *n.* **1** the edge at the top of a steep place. **2** an edge. **3 on the brink of,** very near. [ME; probably < Scand.]

brink·man·ship (bringk′mən ship′) *n.* **1** the maintaining or urging of a foreign policy to the brink of war before giving ground. **2** the fact or process of manoeuvering any dangerous situation to the very limits of safety before giving ground.

brin·y (brīn′ē) *adj.* **brin′i·er, brin′i·est.** of or like brine; salty. —**brin′i·ness,** *n.*

bri·oche (brē osh′ or brē′osh) *n.* a roll or bun rich in butter and eggs. [< F]

bri·quette or **bri·quet** (bri ket′) *n.* **1** a moulded block of coal dust used for fuel. **2** a similar block of some other material. [< F *briquette*, dim. of *brique* brick]

brisk (brisk) *adj.* **1** quick and active; lively: *He took brisk steps.* **2** keen; sharp: *brisk weather.* [? akin to *brusque*] —**brisk′ly,** *adv.* —**brisk′ness,** *n.* —**Syn. 1** nimble, spry.

bris·ket (bris′kit) *n.* **1** the meat from the breast of an animal. See **beef** for diagram. **2** the breast of an animal. [ME < OF *bruschet* < Gmc.]

bris·tle (bris′əl) *n. v.* **-tled, -tling.** —*n.* **1** one of the short, stiff hairs of a pig: *Bristles are used to make brushes.* **2** something similar on a brush: *My toothbrush has nylon bristles.* **3** any short, stiff hair of an animal or plant. **4** a synthetic substitute for a pig's bristle. —*v.* **1** provide with bristles. **2** stand up straight: *The angry dog's hair bristled.* **3** cause (hair) to stand up straight. **4** have one's hair stand up straight: *The dog bristled.* **5** show that one is aroused and ready to fight. **6** be thickly set: *Our path bristled with difficulties.* [ME *bristel* < OE *byrst* bristle]

bris·tle·tail (bris′əl tāl′) *n.* a wingless insect having long appendages like bristles.

bris·tly (bris′lē) *adj.* **-tli·er, -tli·est. 1** rough with bristles. **2** resembling bristles; short and stiff; prickly.

Bristol board a fine, smooth cardboard or pasteboard.

Brit (brit) *n. Slang.* a Britisher; Englishman.

Brit. 1 Britain. **2** British. **3** Briticism.

Bri·tan·ni·a (bri tan′yə) *n.* **1** Great Britain. **2** *Poetic.* the British Empire. **3** a woman symbolizing Britain, shown (as on coins) with helmet, shield, and trident.

Britannia metal a white alloy of tin, copper, and antimony, used in making tableware.

Bri·tan·nic (bri tan′ik) *adj.* of Britain; British.

Brit·i·cism (brit′ə siz′əm) *n.* a word or phrase used especially by the British. "*Wings*" meaning "*fenders* of a car" is a Briticism.

Brit·ish (brit′ish) *adj.* of Great Britain, the British Commonwealth, or its people.—*n.* the people of Great Britain or the British Commonwealth. [OE *brittisc* < *Brittas* Britons < Celtic]

Brit·ish Co·lum·bi·an (kə lum′bē ən) *adj.* of or having to do with British Columbia or its people. —*n.* a native or permanent resident of British Columbia.

Brit·ish·er (brit′ish ər) *n.* an Englishman; a British subject.

British North America Act the Act of Parliament that in 1867 created the Government of Canada for the union of Ontario, Quebec, Nova Scotia, and New Brunswick. The other six provinces joined the federation as follows: Manitoba, 1870; British Columbia, 1871; Prince Edward Island, 1873; Alberta, 1905; Saskatchewan, 1905; and Newfoundland, 1949. *Abbrev.*: BNA Act or B.N.A. Act.

British thermal unit a unit for measuring heat; the amount of heat necessary to raise a pound of water one degree Fahrenheit at its maximum density. *Abbrev.*: B.T.U.

Brit·on (brit′ən) *n.* **1** a native or inhabitant of Great Britain. **2** a member of a Celtic people that lived in ancient Britain. [< Med.L *Brito, -onis* < Celtic]

brit·tle (brit′əl) *adj.* very easily broken; breaking with a snap; apt to break: *Glass and ice are brittle.* [ME *britel* < OE *brēotan* break] —**brit′tle·ness,** *n.*

bro. or **Bro.** brother.

broach (brōch) *n.* **1** a pointed tool for making and shaping holes. **2** a sharp-pointed, slender rod on which meat is roasted. —*v.* **1** open by making a hole: *broach a barrel of cider.* **2** begin to talk about: *broach a subject.* [ME < OF < L *broccus* projecting] —**broach′er,** *n.*

broad (brod or brôd) *adj.* **1** large across; wide: *Many cars can go on that broad road.* **2** extensive: *a broad experience.* **3** not limited; liberal; tolerant: *broad ideas.* **4** main; general: *Give the broad outlines of what the speaker had to say.* **5** clear; full: *broad daylight.* **6** plain; plain-spoken. **7** coarse; not refined: *broad jokes.* **8** in phonetics: **a** pronounced with the vocal passage open wide. The *a* in *father* is broad. **b** indicating pronunciation in general terms: *a broad phonetic transcription.* —*n. Derog. Slang.* **1** a woman, especially an immoral or promiscuous one. **2** a prostitute. [OE *brād*] —**broad′ly,** *adv.* —**Syn.** *adj.* **1** See **wide. 2** vast, ample. **7** gross, indecent.

broad·axe or **broad·ax** (brod′aks′ or brôd′-) *n.* **-ax·es.** an axe with a broad blade.

broad·brim (brod′brim′ or brôd′-) *n.* **1** a hat with a very wide brim. **2** *Informal.* a person who wears such a hat.

broad·cast (brod′kast′ or brôd′-) *v.* **-cast** or **-cast·ed, -cast·ing,** *n. adj. adv.* —*v.* **1** send out by radio or television. **2** scatter widely: *broadcast seed.*
—*n.* **1** a sending out by radio or television. **2** speech, music, etc. sent out by radio or television. **3** a radio or television program. **4** a scattering far and wide.
—*adj.* **1** sent out by radio or television. **2** scattered widely.
—*adv.* over a wide surface. —**broad′cast′er,** *n.*

broad·cloth (brod′kloth′ or brôd′-) *n.* **1** a smooth, cotton or silk cloth, used in making shirts and dresses. **2** a smooth, closely woven woollen cloth, used in making suits, coats, etc. [originally two yards "broad"]

broad·en (brod′ən or brôd′ən) *v.* **1** make broad or broader. **2** become broad or broader: *The river broadens at its mouth.*

broad-gauge (brod′gāj′ or brôd′-) *adj.* having rails more than 56½ inches apart.

broad-gauged (brod′gājd′ or brôd′-) *adj.* broad-gauge.

broad jump a jump to cover as much ground as possible.

broad·loom (brod′lüm′ or brôd′-) *adj.* woven on a wide loom in one color: *a broadloom carpet.*
—*n.* material woven in this way: *gray broadloom.*

broad-mind·ed (brod′mīnd′id or brôd′-) *adj.* liberal; tolerant; not prejudiced or bigoted.
—**broad′-mind′ed·ly,** *adv.* —**broad′-mind′ed·ness,** *n.*

broad·sheet (brod′shēt′ or brôd′-) *n.* a large sheet of paper printed on one side as a newsletter, advertisement, etc.

broad·side (brod′sīd′ or brôd′-) *n.* **1** the whole side of a ship above the water line. **2** all the guns that can be fired from one side of a ship. **3** the firing of all these guns at the same time. **4** *Informal.* a violent attack; storm of abuse. **5** a broad surface or side, as of a house. **6** a large sheet of paper printed on one side only: *broadsides announcing a big sale.* —*adv.* with the side turned: *The ship drifted broadside to the pier.*

broad·sword (brod′sôrd′ or brôd′-) *n.* a sword with a broad, flat blade.

broad·tail (brod′tāl′ or brôd′-) *n.* **1** Also, **broadtail sheep.** a kind of Asiatic sheep having a broad tail. **2** the skin of a prematurely born broadtail lamb, having dark, flat, wide curls. **3** a coat or other garment made from such skins.

Broad·way (brod′wā′ or brôd′-) *n.* **1** in New York City, a street famous for its bright lights, theatres, night clubs, etc. **2** the New York commercial theatre.

Brob·ding·nag (brob′ding nag′) *n.* the land of giants in Jonathan Swift's book *Gulliver's Travels.*

Brob·ding·nag·i·an (brob′ding nag′ē ən) *adj.* **1** of or like Brobdingnag. **2** gigantic; huge; enormous. —*n.* a giant.

bro·cade (brō kād′) *n. v.* **-cad·ed, -cad·ing.** —*n.* a cloth woven with elaborate raised designs on it: *silk brocade, velvet brocade.* —*v.* weave or decorate with raised designs. [< Sp., Pg. *brocado,* pp. of *brocar* embroider]

bro·cad·ed (brō kād′id) *adj.* woven or wrought into a brocade.

broc·co·li (brok′ə lē) *n.* a variety of cauliflower whose green branching stems and flower heads are used as a vegetable. [< Ital. *broccoli,* pl., sprouts < L *broccus* projecting]

bro·chure (brō shür′) *n.* a pamphlet. [< F *brochure* < *brocher* stitch]

bro·gan (brō′gən) *n.* a coarse, strong shoe. [< Irish, Scots Gaelic *brōgan,* dim. of *brōg* shoe]

brogue[1] (brōg) *n.* **1** any coarse, strong shoe. **2** more recently, a shoe made for comfort and long wear. [< Irish, Scots Gaelic *brōg* shoe]

brogue[2] (brōg) *n.* **1** an Irish accent in the speaking of English. **2** the accent or pronunciation peculiar to any dialect. [probably < Irish *barrōg* defect of speech]

broi·der (broi′dər) *v. Archaic.* embroider. [ME < OF *broder;* influenced by archaic E *broid* braid]

broi·der·y (broi′dər ē) *n. Archaic* embroidery.

broil[1] (broil) *v.* **1** cook something by putting or holding it near the fire. **2** make very hot. **3** be very hot.
—*n.* broiled meat, etc. [ME *brule; bruyle* < OF *bruler; bruillir* burn]

broil[2] (broil) *n.* an angry quarrel or struggle; brawl. [< v.] —*v.* quarrel; fight. [< OF *brouiller* to disorder]

broil·er (broil′ər) *n.* **1** a person or thing that broils. **2** a pan or rack for broiling. **3** a young chicken suitable for broiling.

broke (brōk) *v.* **1** a pt. of **break. 2** *Archaic.* a pp. of **break.** broken. —*adj. Slang.* without money.

bro·ken (brō′kən) *v.* a pp. of **break.** —*adj.* **1** crushed; in pieces: *a broken cup.* **2** weakened in strength, spirit, etc.; tamed: *His courage was broken by his failure.* **3** rough; uneven: *broken ground.* **4** acted against; not kept: *a broken promise.* **5** imperfectly spoken: *The French boy speaks broken English.* **6** interrupted: *broken sleep.* **7** bankrupt; ruined: *a broken man.* —**bro′ken·ly,** *adv.* —**bro′ken·ness,** *n.*

bro·ken-down (brō′kən doun′) *adj.* **1** shattered; ruined: *broken-down health.* **2** unfit for use.

bro·ken-heart·ed (brō′kən här′tid) *adj.* crushed by sorrow or grief; heartbroken.

bro·ken-wind·ed (brō′kən win′did) *adj.* of a horse, breathing with sudden, short efforts; suffering from heaves.

bro·ker (brō′kər) *n.* a person who buys and sells stocks, bonds, grain, cotton, etc. for other people; agent. [ME < AF *brocour* tapster, retailer of wine. Akin to BROACH.]

bro·ker·age (brō′kər ij) *n.* **1** the business of a broker. **2** the money charged by a broker for his services.

bro·mid (brō′mid) *n.* bromide (def. 1).

bro·mide (brō′mīd or brō′mid) *n.* **1** a compound of bromine with another element or radical. **2** potassium bromide, a drug used to induce sleep, as a tranquillizer, sedative, etc. *Formula:* KBr **3** *Slang.* a commonplace idea; trite remark. [def. 3 has reference to the effect of the drug]

bro·mid·ic (brō mid′ik) *adj. Informal.* like a bromide; commonplace; trite.

bro·min (brō′min) *n.* bromine.

bro·mine (brō′mēn or brō′mīn) *n.* a non-metallic, chemical element resembling chlorine and iodine. Bromine is a dark-brown liquid that gives off an irritating vapor. It is used in drugs and dyes and in developing photographs. *Symbol:* Br; *at.no.* 35; *at.wt.* 79.909. [< Gk. *bromos* stench]

bron·chi (brong′kī or brong′kē) *n.* pl. of **bronchus.** in anatomy: **1** the two main branches of the windpipe. **2** the smaller, branching tubes in the lungs. See **lungs** for picture.

bron·chi·a (brong′kē ə) *n.pl.* the bronchial tubes, especially the smaller tubes.

bron·chi·al (brong′kē əl) *adj.* of the bronchi or their branching tubes.

bronchial tubes the bronchi and their branching tubes.

bron·chit·ic (brong kit′ik) *adj.* **1** of or having to do with bronchitis. **2** having bronchitis.

bron·chi·tis (brong kī′tis) *n.* inflammation of the lining of the bronchial tubes. [< NL < *bronchus* + *-itis*]

bron·cho (brong′kō) *n.* **-chos.** bronco.

bron·cho·scope (brong′kə skōp′) *n.* in medicine, an instrument for examining and treating the bronchi.

bron·chus (brong′kəs) *n.* **-chi** (-kī or -kē). one of the bronchi. [< NL < Gk. *bronchos*]

bron·co or **bron·cho** (brong′kō) *n.* **-cos** or **-chos.** a western pony, often wild or only half tamed. [< Sp. *bronco* rough, rude]

bron·co·bust·er or **bron·cho·bust·er** (brong′kō bus′tər) *n. Slang.* in the West, one who breaks broncos to the saddle.

bron·to·sau·rus (bron′tə sô′rəs) *n.* a huge, extinct dinosaur. Some kinds were up to sixty feet long and up to fourteen feet tall. [< NL < Gk. *brontē* thunder + *sauros* lizard]

hat, āge, cãre, fär; let, ēqual, tėrm; it, īce
hot, ōpen, ôrder; oil, out; cup, pu̇t, rüle, ūse
əbove, takən, pencəl, lemən, circəs
ch, child; ng, long; sh, ship
th, thin; ᴛʜ, then; zh, measure

bronze (bronz) *n. adj. v.* **-bronzed, bronz·ing.** —*n.* **1** a brown metal, an alloy of copper and tin. **2** a similar alloy of copper with zinc or other metals. **3** a statue, medal, etc. made of bronze. **4** a yellowish brown; reddish brown.
—*adj.* **1** made of bronze. **2** yellowish-brown; reddish-brown.
—*v.* make or become bronze in color: *The sailor was bronzed from the sun.* [< F < Ital. *bronzo* bell metal]

Bronze Age the period in man's history after the Stone Age, when bronze tools, weapons, etc. were used, lasting in different parts of Europe from about 3500 B.C. to about 1000 B.C. It was followed by the Iron Age.

bronze·smith (bronz′smith′) *n.* a man who works with bronze.

brooch (brōch) *n.* an ornamental pin having the point secured by a catch. [var. of *broach,* n.]

brood (brüd) *n.* **1** the young birds hatched at one time in the nest or cared for together. **2** young animals or humans who are cared for by the same mother. **3** a breed; kind.
—*v.* **1** sit on in order to hatch. **2** think a long time about some one thing. **3** dwell on in thought: *For years he brooded vengeance.* **4 brood on** or **over, a** keep thinking about. **b** hover over; hang close over. [OE *brōd*]

brood·er (brüd′ər) *n.* **1** a closed place that can be heated, used in raising chicks, etc. **2** somebody or something that broods. **3** a hen hatching or ready to hatch eggs.

brood·ing (brüd′ing) *adj.* **1** hovering around, as a mother bird hovers over her nest. **2** pondering or thinking moodily on a subject.

brood·mare (brüd′mãr′) *n.* a mare kept for breeding.

brood·y (brüd′ē) *adj.* **1** brooding. **2** ready to brood: *A broody hen will sit on duck eggs as well as on her own.*

brook[1] (bru̇k) *n.* a small, natural stream of water. [OE *brōc*] —**Syn.** creek, rivulet.

brook[2] (bru̇k) *v.* put up with; endure; tolerate: *Her pride would not brook such insults.* [OE *brūcan* use]

brook trout a fresh-water game fish; speckled trout.

broom (brüm or bru̇m) *n.* **1** a long-handled brush for sweeping. **2** a shrub of the same family as the pea, having slender branches, small leaves, and yellow flowers. **3 a new broom,** a new person or management that starts actively and tries to put everything right at once, from the saying "A new broom sweeps clean." [OE *brōm*]

broom·ball (brüm′bol′ or -bôl′, bru̇m′bol′ or -bôl′) *n. Cdn.* a game similar to hockey but using cornbrooms and a volleyball, usually played on a hockey rink.

broom·corn (brüm′kôrn′ or bru̇m′-) *n.* a tall plant resembling corn, having flower clusters with long, stiff stems used for making brooms.

broom·stick (brüm′stik′ or bru̇m′-) *n.* the long handle of a broom.

bros. or **Bros.** brothers.

broth (broth) *n.* **1** water in which meat has been boiled; thin soup. **2** a medium in which cultures of bacteria are grown [OE]

broth·el (broth′əl) *n.* a house of prostitution. [ME < OE *brēothan* go to ruin]

broth·er (bruᴛʜ′ər) *n.* **broth·ers** or (*Archaic*) **breth·ren. 1** a son of the same parents; sometimes, a son only of the same mother or father (a half brother). **2** a close friend; companion, countryman. **3** a fellow member of a church, union, association, fraternal order, society, etc. **4** a member of a religious order who is not a priest.
—*adj.* being in or of the same profession or calling: *brother officers.* [OE *brōther*] —**broth′er·less,** *adj.* —**broth′er·like,** *adj.*

☛ **Brothers** is the normal plural The older form, **brethren,** is now used only of fellow members of a church or society, and in the names of certain religious groups, such as the Plymouth Brethren.

broth·er·hood (bruᴛʜ′ər hu̇d′) *n.* **1** the bond between brothers; feeling of brother for brother. **2** persons joined as brothers; an association of men with some common aim, characteristic, belief, profession, etc.

broth·er-in-law (bruᴛʜ′ər in lo′ or -lô′) *n.* **broth·ers-in-law 1** the brother of one's husband or wife. **2** the husband of one's sister. **3** the husband of the sister of one's wife or husband.

Brother Jonathan *Archaic.* **1** The United States or its people. **2** an inhabitant of the United States.

broth·er·ly (bruᴛʜ′ər lē) *adj.* **1** of a brother. **2** like a brother. **3** friendly; kindly; affectionate. —*adv.* like a brother. —**broth′er·li·ness,** *n.*

brougham (brō′əm, brüm, or brü′əm) *n.* a closed carriage or automobile having an outside seat for the driver. [after Lord *Brougham* (1778-1868), a British statesman]

brought (brot or brôt) *v.* pt. and pp. of **bring.**

brow (brou) *n.* **1** the forehead. **2** the arch of hair over the eye; eyebrow. **3** the ridge or prominence above the eye, on which the eyebrow grows. **4** the edge of a steep place; top of a slope: *the brow of a hill.* [OE *brū*]

brow·beat (brou′bēt′) *v.* **-beat, -beat·en, -beat·ing.** frighten into doing something by overbearing looks or words; bully. —**brow′beat′er,** *n.* —**Syn.** intimidate, domineer.

brown (broun) *n.* **1** a color like that of toast, potato skins, and coffee. **2** a paint or dye having this color. **3** something brown.
—*adj.* **1** having a color like that of toast, potato skins, or coffee. **2** dark-skinned; tanned.
—*v.* **1** make or become brown. **2 browned off,** *Slang.* fed up; exasperated. [OE *brūn*] —**brown′ness,** *n.*

brown bear a North American or northern European bear that has brown fur.

brown betty a baked pudding made of apples, sugar, and bread crumbs.

brown bread 1 dark, steamed bread containing molasses. **2** bread made of dark flour, such as graham bread.

brown coal dark-brown coal, often having a woody texture; lignite.

Brown·i·an motion (broun′ē ən) in physics, Brownian movement.

Brownian movement in physics, a rapid oscillatory motion often observed in very minute particles suspended in water or other liquids. [after Dr. Robert *Brown* (1773-1858), a Scottish botanist]

brown·ie (broun′ē) *n.* **1** a good-natured, helpful elf or fairy. **2** a flat, sweet, chocolate cake containing nuts.

Brown·ie (broun′ē) *n.* a member of the junior division of the Girl Guides.

brown·ish (broun′ish) *adj.* rather brown.

brown race the Malay people living mainly in Malaya and Polynesia.

brown rice rice that is not polished, having the grain and the bran layer more or less intact.

brown shirt a member of the group of German storm troopers that was organized by Adolf Hitler in 1923 and discontinued in 1934.

brown·stone (broun′stōn′) *n.* **1** a reddish-brown sandstone, used as a building material. **2** a building, especially a house, built of this sandstone.

brown study the condition of being absorbed in thought; a serious reverie.

brown sugar sugar that is not refined or only partly refined.

brown thrasher a brown-and-white bird resembling a thrush.

browse (brouz) *v.* **browsed, brows·ing,** *n.* —*v.* **1** feed; graze. **2** read here and there in a book or in books; pass the time looking at books in a library, bookstore, etc. **3** look casually at goods in a store. [< n., or < F *brouster* feed on buds and shoots]
—*n.* the tender shoots of shrubs; green food for cattle, etc. [apparently < MF *broust* bud, shoot < Gmc.] —**brows′er,** *n.*

bru·in (brü′ən) *n.* bear. [< MDu. *bruin* brown]

bruise (brüz) *n. v.* **bruised, bruis·ing.** —*n.* 1 an injury to the body, caused by a fall or a blow, that changes the color of the skin without breaking it: *The bruise on my arm turned black and blue.* 2 an injury to the outside of a fruit, vegetable, plant, etc. 3 a hurt or injury: *His insult was a bruise to her pride.* [< v.]
—*v.* 1 injure the outside of. 2 injure; hurt: *Harsh words bruised her feelings.* 3 become bruised: *Her flesh bruises easily.* 4 pound or crush (drugs or food). [fusion of ME *bruse* < OE *brȳsan* crush and AF *bruser,* OF *bruisier* break, shatter]

bruis·er (brüz′ər) *n. Informal.* 1 a prize fighter. 2 a bully. 3 a very muscular person.

bruit (brüt) *v.* spread (a report or rumor): *Rumors of the princess's engagement were bruited about.* [< n.]
—*n. Archaic.* a report or rumor. [< OF *bruit* noise, rumor < *bruire* roar]

bru·lé or **bru·le** (brü lā′ or brü′lē) *n. Cdn.* 1 a forest area that has been destroyed by fire. 2 rocky, untillable land. 3 **Brulé,** a half-breed; a Métis. [< F *brûlé* burnt]

brum·ma·gem (brum′ə jəm) *Informal.* —*adj.* cheap and showy.—*n.* anything cheap and showy. [alteration of *Birmingham,* England]

brunch (brunch) *n.* a meal, taken in the late morning, that combines breakfast and lunch. [< *b*reakfast + l*unch*]

bru·net (brü net′) *adj.* 1 dark-colored; having an olive color. 2 having dark-brown or black hair, usually brown or black eyes, and a dark skin. —*n.* a man or boy having dark hair. [< F *brunette,* fem., dim. of *brun* brown < Gmc.]

bru·nette (brü net′) *n.* a woman or girl having dark hair. [< F]

Brun·hild (brün′hild) *n.* in Germanic legend (especially in the *Nibelungenlied*), a queen of Iceland who, won by Siegfried's magic, becomes the wife of the King of Burgundy. In Norse legend, she is a Valkyrie and the daughter of Odin. Also, **Brynhild.**

Brünn·hil·de (bryn hil′də) *n.* in Wagner's opera *Die Walküre,* a Valkyrie cast into a magic sleep, from which Siegfried wakens her.

brunt (brunt) *n.* the main force or violence; hardest part: *bear the brunt.* [ME *brunt* a blow; origin uncertain]

brush[1] (brush) *n.* 1 a tool for cleaning, rubbing, painting, etc. A brush is made of bristles, hair, or wires set in a stiff back or fastened to a handle. 2 a brushing; a rub with a brush. 3 a light touch in passing. 4 a short, brisk fight or quarrel. 5 the bushy tail of an animal, especially of a fox. 6 a piece of carbon, copper, etc. used to conduct the electricity from the revolving part of a motor or generator to the outside circuit. 7 the art or skill of an artist.
—*v.* 1 clean, rub, paint, etc. with a brush; use a brush on. 2 wipe away; remove: *The child brushed the tears from his eyes.* 3 touch lightly in passing. 4 move quickly. 5 **brush aside or away,** put aside; refuse to consider. 6 **brush off,** *Informal.* refuse or dismiss a request, person, etc. 7 **brush up** or **brush up on,** refresh the memory by study; review: *He brushed up on his algebra before writing the examination.* [ME *brusshe* < OF *broisse* < Gmc.]
—**brush′er,** *n.* —**brush′like′,** *adj.*

brush[2] (brush) *n.* 1 branches broken or cut off. 2 a thick growth of shrubs, bushes, small trees, etc. 3 thinly settled country; backwoods. [ME *brusche* < OF *broche*]

brush·off (brush′of′) *n. Informal.* a refusal or dismissal of a request, person, etc.: *When I asked her for a date I got a polite brushoff.*

brush·up (brush′up′) *n.* 1 a refreshing of memory or a reviewing of knowledge, skill, etc. 2 a smartening or freshening of one's appearance.

brush·wood (brush′wu̇d′) *n.* brush[2] (defs. 1 and 2).

brush·work (brush′wėrk′) *n.* an artist's characteristic technique in applying paint with a brush.

brush·y[1] (brush′ē) *adj.* **brush·i·er, brush·i·est.** like a brush; rough and shaggy. [< *brush*[1]]

brush·y[2] (brush′ē) *adj.* **brush·i·er, brush·i·est.** covered with bushes, shrubs, etc. [< *brush*[2]]

brusque (brusk) *adj.* abrupt in manner or speech; blunt. [< F < Ital. *brusco* coarse < LL *bruscus,* blend of *ruscum* broom and Gaulish *brucus* broom]
—**brusque′ly,** *adv.* —**brusque′ness,** *n.*

Brus·sels carpet (brus′əlz) a carpet with a pattern made of small loops of yarn having various colors.

Brussels lace a type of heavy lace with a very elaborate design.

Brussels sprouts 1 a variety of cabbage that has many small heads growing along a stalk. 2 the heads of this plant, used as a vegetable.

bru·tal (brü′təl) *adj.* coarse and savage; like a brute.
—**brut′al·ly,** *adv.* —**Syn.** See **cruel.**

bru·tal·i·ty (brü tal′ə tē) *n.* **-ties.** 1 cruelty; savageness; coarseness. 2 a cruel, savage, or coarse act.
—**Syn.** 1 inhumanity, barbarity.

bru·tal·ize (brü′təl īz′) *v.* **-ized, -iz·ing.** 1 make brutal: *War brutalizes many men.* 2 become brutal.
—**bru′tal·i·za′tion,** *n.*

brute (brüt) *n.* 1 an animal without power to reason. 2 a stupid, cruel, coarse, or sensual person. 3 man's animal nature.
—*adj.* 1 without power to reason. 2 stupid; cruel; coarse; sensual. 3 unconscious; without feeling: *Man has struggled long against the brute forces of nature.* [< F *brut* < L *brutus* heavy, dull] —**Syn.** *n.* **1, 2** See **animal.**

brut·ish (brüt′ish) *adj.* stupid; coarse; savage.
—**brut′ish·ly,** *adv.* —**brut′ish·ness,** *n.*

Bryn·hild (brin′hild or bryn′hild) *n.* Brunhild.

bry·ol·o·gy (brī ol′ə jē) *n.* a branch of botany that deals with mosses and liverworts. [< Gk. *bryon* moss + E *-logy*]

bry·o·ny (brī′ə nē) *n.* **-nies.** a climbing plant of the same family as the gourd, having small, greenish flowers. The roots of some kinds are used in medicine. [< L < Gk. *bryonia* < *bryein* swell]

bry·o·phyte (brī′ə fīt′) *n.* any of a division of non-flowering plants comprising the moss and liverwort families. [< NL *bryophia* < Gk. *bryon* tree moss + *phyton* plant < *phyein* grow]

Bryth·on (brith′ən) *n.* 1 any member of a large Celtic group once living in South Britain but later driven into Wales, Cornwall, and ancient Cumbria. 2 a Briton of Wales, Cornwall, or ancient Cumbria. [< Welsh *Brython* < Old Celtic *Britton* a Briton]

Bry·thon·ic (bri′thon′ik) *adj.* 1 of or having to do with the Brythons. 2 of, having to do with, or denoting the Celtic language group to which Breton, Cornish, and Welsh belong.
—*n.* one of the two main divisions of the Celtic language (the other being Goidelic), including Breton, Cornish, and Welsh; Cymric.

b.s. 1 bill of sale. 2 balance sheet.

B.S. or **B.Sc.** Bachelor of Science. (for L *Baccalaureus Scientiae*)

B.Sc.Eng. Bachelor of Science in Engineering.

B.Sc.F. Bachelor of Science in Forestry.

B.Sc.M. Bachelor of Science in Medicine.

B.Sc.N. Bachelor of Science in Nursing.

B.Sc.S.S. Bachelor of Science in Social Science.

B.S.M. Battery Sergeant-Major.

B.S.W. Bachelor of Social Work.

Bt. Baronet.

B.T. or **B.Th.** Bachelor of Theology. (for L *Baccalaureus Theologiae*)

Btn. or **btn.** battalion.

BTU, B.T.U., or **b.t.u.** British thermal unit or units.

bu. 1 bushel; bushels. 2 bureau.

bub·ble (bub′əl) *n. v.* **-bled, -bling.** —*n.* 1 a pocket of air or gas in a solid or liquid. 2 a thin film of liquid enclosing air or gas: *soap bubbles.* 3 the act or process of bubbling; sound of bubbling. 4 a plan or idea that looks good, but soon goes to pieces. 5 *Archaic.* a swindle.

—*v.* **1** have bubbles; make bubbles; look like water boiling. **2** make sounds like water boiling; gurgle. **3 bubble over, a** overflow. **b** be very enthusiastic. [ME *bobel*] —**bub′bling·ly,** *adv.*

bubble chamber a small vessel filled with a superheated liquid, especially pentane or hydrogen under pressure, through which sub-atomic particles make a bubbly track by means of which they may be isolated and identified.

bubble gum a type of chewing gum that can be inflated so as to form a large bubble.

bub·bly (bub′lē) *adj.* full of bubbles. —*n. Informal.* champagne.

bu·bo (bū′bō) *n.* **bu·boes.** an inflammatory swelling of a lymphatic gland, especially in the groin or armpits. [< LL *bubo* < Gk. *boubon* groin]

bu·bon·ic (bū bon′ik) *adj.* having or characterized by inflammatory swelling of the lymphatic glands.

bubonic plague a dangerous disease, accompanied by fever, chills, and swelling of the lymphatic glands, carried to human beings by fleas from rats or squirrels.

buc·cal (buk′əl) *adj.* in anatomy: **1** of the cheek. **2** of the mouth or of the sides of the mouth. [< L *bucca* cheek, mouth]

buc·ca·neer (buk′ə nēr′) *n.* a pirate or freebooter. [< F *boucanier* < Tupi *boucan* frame for curing meat, as done by the French in Haiti]

Bu·ceph·a·lus (bū sef′ə ləs) *n.* the war horse of Alexander the Great.

Buch·man·ism (buk′mə niz′əm) *n.* a twentieth-century religious movement; Moral Rearmament. [< Frank *Buchman* (1878-1961), U.S. evangelist and founder of the movement]

buck[1] (buk) *n.* **1** a male deer, goat, hare, rabbit, antelope, or sheep. **2** a young male Indian. **3** a dandy. **4** *Informal.* a man. [a fusion of OE *buc* male deer, and OE *bucca* male goat]

buck[2] (buk) *v.* **1** *Informal.* **a** fight against; resist stubbornly. **b** push or hit with the head; butt. **c** rush at; charge against; work against: *The swimmer bucked the current with strong strokes.* **2** in football, charge into (the opposing line) with the ball. **3** of horses, jump into the air with back curved and come down with the front legs stiff. **4** throw or attempt to throw (a rider) in this way. **5** *Informal.* of an automobile, motor, etc., run unevenly; jerk, as when the fuel supply is low or the motor cold. **6 buck up,** *Informal.* cheer up; be brave, energetic, or enterprising.
—*n.* a throw or an attempt to throw by bucking. [special use of *buck*[1]] —**buck′er,** *n.*

buck[3] (buk) *n.* **1** a sawhorse; sawbuck. **2** in gymnastics, a padded, adjustable frame used for vaulting, etc. [short for *sawbuck*]

buck[4] (buk) *n.* **pass the buck,** *Informal.* shift the responsibility, blame, work, etc. to someone else. [origin uncertain]

buck[5] (buk) *n. Slang.* a dollar.

buck·a·roo (buk′ə rü′ or buk′ə rü′) *n.* **-roos.** cowboy [< alteration of Sp. *vaquero* < *vaca* cow < L *vacca*]

buck·board (buk′bôrd′) *n.* an open four-wheeled carriage having a seat fastened to a platform of long, springy boards instead of having a body and springs.

buck·et (buk′it) *n. v.* **-et·ed, -et·ing.** —*n.* **1** a wood or metal pail used for carrying water, milk, coal, etc. **2** the amount that a bucket can hold. **3** the scoop of a dredging machine. **4** *Slang.* a ship, car, etc., especially one that is old and slow. **5 kick the bucket,** *Slang.* die.
—*v.* **1** lift or carry in a bucket or buckets. **2** ride (a horse) hard. **3** *Informal.* **a** move fast. **b** move jerkily and irregularly. **4** swing forward too hurriedly before taking the stroke in rowing. **5** conduct a bucket shop. [ME < AF *buket* washtub, milk pail, perhaps < OE *būc* vessel, pitcher]

buck·et·ful (buk′it fůl′) *n.* **-fuls.** the amount that a bucket can hold.

bucket seat a single, low-slung seat with a curved back, used especially in sports cars, small airplanes, etc.

bucket shop a fraudulent establishment conducted ostensibly for buying and selling stocks or commodities, but really for making bets on the rise and fall of their prices, with no actual buying and selling.

hat, āge, cãre, fär; let, ēqual, tėrm; it, īce
hot, ōpen, ôrder; oil, out; cup, pů t, rüle, ūse
əbove, takən, pencəl, lemən, circəs
ch, child; ng, long; sh, ship
th, thin; ᴛʜ, then; zh, measure

buck·eye (buk′ ī′) *n.* a tree or shrub closely related to the horse chestnut, having showy clusters of small flowers, large divided leaves, and large brown seeds. [< *buck*[1] + *eye*; with reference to mark on the seed]

Buckingham Palace the official London residence of all British sovereigns since 1837.

buck·le[1] (buk′əl) *n. v.* **-led, -ling.** —*n.* **1** a catch or clasp for fastening together the ends of a belt, strap, etc. **2** a metal ornament for a shoe.
—*v.* **1** fasten together with a buckle. **2 buckle down to,** begin to work hard at. [ME *bocle* < OF *boucle* < L *buccula* cheek strap on helmet, dim. of *bucca* cheek]

buck·le[2] (buk′əl) *v.* **-led, -ling,** *n.* —*v.* bend; bulge; give way under a heavy weight or strain: *The heavy snowfall caused the roof of the arena to buckle.* —*n.* a bend; bulge; kink; wrinkle. [< F *boucler* bulge]

buck·ler (buk′lər) *n.* **1** a small, round shield. **2** a protection; defence. [ME < OF *boucler* shield, originally, one with a boss < *boucle* boss < L *buccula.* See BUCKLE.]

buck private *Slang.* a common soldier below the rank of lance corporal.

buck·ram (buk′rəm) *n.* **1** a coarse cloth made stiff with glue or some similar substance. **2** stiffness of manner.
—*v.* pad or stiffen with buckram.
—*adj.* **1** made of buckram. **2 a** like buckram. **b** stiff; formal; haughty. [ME < AF ? ult. < *Bukhara,* var. of *Bokhara*]

buck·saw (buk′so′ or -sô′) *n.* a saw set in a light frame and held with both hands.

A man using a bucksaw

buck scraper an earth-digging device having a scoop that is drawn along the ground and two runners to lift it when filled.

buck·shee (buk′shē) *adj. Slang.* free: *We were given two buckshee tickets for the dance.* [< *baksheesh*]

buck·shot (buk′shot′) *n.* a large lead shot used for shooting large game such as deer.

buck·skin (buk′skin′) *n.* **1** a kind of strong, soft, yellowish or grayish leather made from the skins of deer or sheep. **2 buckskins,** *pl.* breeches made of buckskin.

buck·thorn (buk′thôrn′) *n.* **1** a small, sometimes thorny tree or shrub having clusters of black berries, each containing several nutlets. **2** a low, thorny tree having black, cherrylike fruit.

buck·tooth (buk′tüth′) *n.* **-teeth.** a tooth that sticks out.

buck·toothed (buk′tütht′ or -tüᴛʜd′) *adj.* having protruding upper-front teeth.

buck·wheat (buk′hwēt′ or -wēt′) *n.* **1** a plant having brown, triangular seeds and fragrant white flowers. **2** the seeds, used as food for animals or ground into flour. **3** meal, flour, or batter made from buckwheat. [< *buck* (< OE *bōc* beech) + *wheat*; from its beechnut-shaped seeds]

buckwheat cake a pancake made of buckwheat flour.

bu·col·ic (bū kol′ik) *adj.* **1** of shepherds; pastoral: *Bucolic poetry is seldom written by shepherds themselves.* **2** rustic; rural. —*n.* a poem about shepherds. [< L *bucolicus* < Gk. *boukolikos* rustic < *boukolos* shepherd] —**bu·col′i·cal·ly,** *adv.*

bud (bud) *n. v.* **bud·ded, bud·ding.** —*n.* **1** on a plant, a small swelling that will develop into a flower, leaf, or branch. **2** the time or state of budding: *The pear tree is in bud.* **3** a partly opened flower. **4** anything in its beginning stage. **5** a child; young girl. **6** in certain

animals of simple organic structure, a small swelling that develops into a new individual of the same species. 7 a minute, bud-shaped part or organ: *a taste bud.* **8 nip in the bud,** stop at the very beginning.
—*v.* **1** put forth buds: *The rosebush has budded.* **2** graft (a bud) from one kind of plant into the stem of a different kind. See **graft** for picture. **3** begin to grow or develop. [ME *budde*] —**bud′der,** *n.*

Bud·dha (bůd′ə, bü′də, or bud′ə) *n.* a title meaning "the Enlightened One," especially as applied to Gautama (563?-483? B.C.), a religious teacher and the founder of Buddhism. [< Skt.]

Bud·dhism (bůd′iz əm, bü′diz əm, or bud′iz əm) *n.* one of the world's great religions. It originated in the sixth century B.C. in N. India and spread widely over central, S.E. and E. Asia. Buddhism teaches that right living will enable people to attain Nirvana, the condition of absolute happiness.

Bud·dhist (bůd′ist, bü′dist, or bud′ist) *adj.* having to do with Buddha or Buddhism. —*n.* a believer in Buddhism.

bud·dy (bud′ē) *n.* **-dies.** *Informal.* **1** a brother. **2** comrade; pal. **3** a little boy.

budge (buj) *v.* **budged, budg·ing.** move or cause to move: *He wouldn't budge from his chair.* [< F *bouger* stir < VL *bullicare* boil furiously < L *bullire* boil]

budg·er·i·gar (buj′ər i gär′) *n.* a small, brightly-colored parakeet, native to Australia. [< native Australian *budgereegah* < *budgeri* good + *gar* cockatoo]

budg·et (buj′it) *n. v.* **-et·ed, -et·ing.** —*n.* **1** an estimate of the amount of money that can be spent, and the amounts to be spent for various purposes, in a given time. Governments, schools, and companies often draw up budgets. **2** a stock or collection: *a budget of news.*
—*v.* **1** make a plan for spending: *budget your time.* **2** put in a budget. [ME < OF *bougette*, dim. of *bouge* bag < L *bulga* < Celtic]

budg·et·ar·y (buj′ə ter′ē) *adj.* of a budget.

budg·ie (buj′ē) *n. Informal.* budgerigar.

buff[1] (buf) *n.* **1** a strong, soft, dull-yellow leather having a fuzzy surface, made from buffalo skin or oxhide **2** a soldier's coat made of this leather. **3** a dull yellow. **4** a polishing wheel or stick covered with leather. **5** *Informal.* bare skin.
—*adj.* **1** made of buff leather. **2** dull-yellow.
—*v.* **1** polish with a buff. **2** stain or dye a dull yellow. [earlier *buffle* < F *buffle* < Ital. *bufalo.* See BUFFALO.]

buff[2] (buf) *n. Informal.* a self-styled expert; fan; enthusiast: *a hockey buff, a hot-rod buff, a theatre buff.* [origin uncertain]

buf·fa·lo (buf′ə lō′) *n.* **-loes, -los,** or (*esp. collectively*) **-lo,** *v.* **-loed, -lo·ing.** —*n.* **1** the North American bison, the male of which has a big, shaggy head and strong front legs. **2** any of several kinds of oxen. The tame **water buffalo** of India and the wild **Cape buffalo** of Africa are two different kinds.
—*v. Slang.* **1** intimidate or overawe. **2** puzzle; mystify. [< Ital. *bufalo* < L *bubalus* < Gk. *boubalos* wild ox]

buffalo berry 1 the edible fruit of a western shrub. **2** the shrub itself.

buffalo fish any of several large suckers having a humplike back, found from Southern Canada to Guatemala.

buffalo grass a short type of grass that grows in central and western North America, often used for pasture.

buffalo jump a place where the Plains Indians slaughtered buffalo by stampeding them over a precipice.

buff·er[1] (buf′ər) *n.* **1** an apparatus that softens the shock of a blow. **2** anything helping to soften or sustain a shock or to neutralize opposing forces: *Mother was a buffer between my father's anger and me.* [< *buff* deaden force, (earlier meaning) strike; cf. OF *buffe* a blow]

buff·er[2] (buf′ər) *n.* **1** a person who polishes. **2** something for polishing, covered with leather. [< *buff*]

buf·fer[3] (buf′ər) *n. Slang.* a fellow, often used humorously or contemptuously of an older person. [origin uncertain]

buffer state a small country lying between two larger countries that are enemies or competitors.

buf·fet[1] (buf′it) *n. v.* **-fet·ed, -fet·ing.** —*n.* **1** a blow of the hand or fist. **2** a knock; stroke; hurt.
—*v.* **1** strike with the hand or fist. **2** knock about; strike; hurt: *The waves buffeted him.* **3** fight or struggle against: *He reached home exhausted from buffeting the storm.* [ME < OF *buffet*, dim. of *buffe* blow]

buf·fet[2] (bů fā′ or bu fā′) *n.* **1** a piece of dining-room furniture for holding dishes, silver, and table linen; sideboard. **2** a counter where food and drinks are served. **3** a restaurant with such a counter. **4** a meal at which guests serve themselves from a table on which the food is laid out. [< F]

buffet car a railway car having a small area where light meals may be obtained.

buffet lunch a buffet (def. 4).

buffet supper a buffet (def. 4), served at night.

buf·fle·head (buf′əl hed′) *n.* **1** a small North American diving duck having black feathers on top and white underneath. The male has very full head feathers. **2** a foolish or stupid person; blockhead. [< obs. *buffle* buffalo + *head*]

buf·fo (bü′fō; *Ital.*, büf′fō) *n.* in opera, a male singer of comic roles, usually a basso. —*adj.* comic. [< Ital. *buffo*]

buf·foon (bu fün′) *n.* **1** a person who amuses people with tricks, pranks, and jokes; clown. **2** a person given to coarse or undignified jesting. —*v.* behave like a buffoon. [< F *bouffon* < Ital. *buffone* < *buffa* jest]

buf·foon·er·y (bu fün′ər ē) *n.* **-er·ies. 1** the tricks, pranks, and jokes of a clown. **2** undignified or rude joking.

bug (bug) *n. v.* **bugged, bug·ging.** —*n.* **1** an insect, such as the chinch bug, that is wingless or has a front pair of wings thickened at the base, and has a sucking beak. **2** any insect or insectlike animal. Ants, spiders, beetles, and flies are often called bugs. **3** a bedbug. **4** *Informal.* a disease germ or microbe: *the flu bug.* **5** *Informal.* a mechanical defect; any structural fault or difficulty: *smooth out the bugs in the automatic fire-prevention system.* **6** *Slang.* a very small concealed microphone.
—*v. Slang.* **1** annoy; irritate: *His constant grumbling bugs me.* **2** fit (a room, telephone, etc.) with a very small concealed microphone. [? < obsolete Welsh *bwg* ghost]

bug·a·boo (bug′ə bü′) *n.* **-boos.** an imaginary thing that is feared: *The child was frightened by tales of witches, ghosts, and other bugaboos.* [< *bug* bogy + *boo*, interjection]

bug·bear (bug′bãr′) *n.* **1** something feared or disliked without reason; bugaboo. **2** the chief snag: *Out-of-date machinery is the bugbear in this plant.* [< *bug* bogy + *bear*[2]]

bug-eyed (bug′īd′) *adj. Slang.* having eyes wide open and bulging, especially from wonder or excitement.

bug·gy[1] (bug′ē) *n.* **-gies. 1** a light carriage drawn by one horse and having a seat for two people. **2** a wheeled cart used for shopping in a grocery store, etc. **3** a baby carriage. [origin uncertain]

bug·gy[2] (bug′ē) *adj.* **-gi·er, -gi·est.** swarming with bugs.

bu·gle[1] (bū′gəl) *n. v.* **-gled, -gling.** —*n.* a musical wind instrument like a small trumpet, made of brass or copper. Bugles are used in the army and navy for sounding calls and orders. —*v.* **1** blow a bugle. **2** direct or summon by blowing on a bugle. [ME < OF < L *buculus*, dim. of *bos* ox; with reference to early hunting horns]

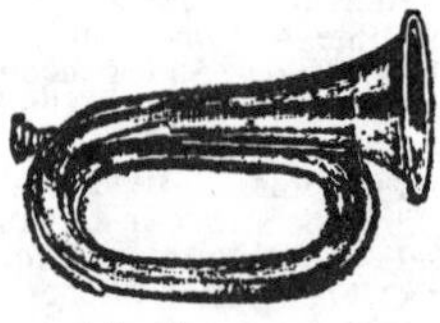
A bugle

bu·gle[2] (bū′gəl) *n.* a long glass bead used for trimming on dresses, blouses, etc. [origin uncertain]

bu·gler (bū′glər) *n.* a person who blows a bugle.

bu·gloss (bū′glos) *n.* a European plant having bristly leaves and stems and blue flowers. [< F < L *buglossa*

< Gk. *bouglōssos* ox tongue < *bous* ox + *glōssa* tongue]

buhl (bül) *n.* wood inlaid in elaborate patterns with metal, tortoise shell, ivory, etc. and used for furniture. [< G spelling of F *boule* or *boulle*, after A.C. *Boule* or *Boulle* (1642-1732), a French cabinetmaker]

build (bild) *v.* **built** or (*Archaic*) **build·ed, build·ing,** *n.* —*v.* **1** make by putting materials together; construct: *Men build houses, dams, bridges.* **2** form gradually; develop: *build a business, an empire, etc.* **3** establish; base: *build a case on facts.* **4** rely; depend: *We can build on that man's honesty.* **5** make a structure: *He builds for a living.* **6 build up, a** form gradually; develop: *The firm has built up a wide reputation for fair dealing.* **b** fill; block up. **c** fill with houses, etc. **d** accumulate, causing congestion: *The traffic always builds up at the toll bridge at rush hours.*
—*n.* a form, style, or manner of construction; structure; physique: *An elephant has a heavy build.* [OE *byldan* < *bold* dwelling]

build·ed (bil′did) *v. Archaic.* a pt. and a pp. of **build.** built.

build·er (bil′dər) *n.* **1** a person or animal that builds. **2** a person whose business is building.

build·ing (bil′ding) *n.* **1** something built, such as a house, factory, barn, store, etc. **2** the business, art, or process of making houses, stores, bridges, ships, etc.
Syn. 1 Building, edifice, structure = something constructed. **Building** is the general word and has a wide range of uses because it does not suggest purpose, size, materials, etc.: *From the hill we could see the buildings in the city.* **Edifice** is a formal word, applying to a large and imposing building: *The cathedral is a handsome edifice.* **Structure** emphasizes the type of construction: *The new library is a fireproof structure.*

build-up (bild′up′) *n.* **1** an increasing of strength, especially of military strength. **2** a campaign to bring someone or something to public attention. **3** a congestion: *a traffic build-up.*

built (bilt) *v.* a pt. and a pp. of **build.**

built-in (bilt′in′) *adj.* **1** built as part of the building: *The room has a built-in bookcase.* **2** having as a part of one's nature, or as an integral part: *a built-in sense of humor.*

bulb (bulb) *n.* **1** a round underground bud from which certain plants grow. Onions, tulips, and lilies grow from bulbs. **2** any plant that has a bulb or grows from a bulb, as a narcissus. **3** the thick part of an underground stem resembling a bulb; tuber: *a crocus bulb.* **4** any rounded, swelling object or part: *an electric-light bulb, the bulb of a thermometer.* [< L *bulbus* < Gk. *bolbos* onion]
—**bulb′less,** *adj.* —**bulb′like′,** *adj.*

bulb·ar (bul′bər) *adj.* having to do with a bulb-shaped organ, especially the bulb of the spinal cord: *bulbar poliomyelitis.*

bulb·let (bulb′lit′) *n.* a small flower or vegetable bulb.

bulb·ous (bul′bəs) *adj.* **1** having bulbs; growing from bulbs: *Daffodils are bulbous plants.* **2** shaped like a bulb; rounded and swelling: *a bulbous nose.*

bul·bul (bůl′bůl) *n.* a songbird living in S. Asia, often mentioned in Persian poetry. [< Arabic or Persian]

Bul·gar (bul′gär or bůl′gär) *adj. n.* Bulgarian.

Bul·gar·i·an (bul gãr′ē ən) *adj.* of or having to do with Bulgaria, its people, or their language. —*n.* **1** a native or inhabitant of Bulgaria. **2** the language of Bulgaria.

bulge (bulj) *v.* **bulged, bulg·ing,** *n.* —*v.* **1** swell outward: *His pockets bulged with apples and candy.* **2** cause to swell outward: *The apples bulged his pockets.* [< n.]
—*n.* **1** an outward swelling. **2** of a ship: **a** the bottom of the hull; bilge. **b** a structure attached outside the hull to protect it from mines, torpedoes, etc.; a blister. **3** a temporary increase: *The graph shows a bulge in the birth rate.* [ME < OF *boulge* < L *bulga* bag]
—**Syn.** *v.* **1** protrude. —*n.* protuberance, prominence, bump.

bulg·y (bul′jē) *adj.* having a bulge or bulges.
—**bul′gi·ness,** *n.*

bulk (bulk) *n.* **1** size, especially large size: *an elephant of great bulk.* **2** the largest part; main mass: *The ocean forms the bulk of the earth's surface.* **3** of a ship: **a** the hold. **b** the cargo. **4 in bulk, a** loose, not in packages. **b** in large quantities.
—*v.* **1** have size; be of importance. **2** grow large; swell.

hat, āge, cãre, fär; let, ēqual, tėrm; it, īce
hot, ōpen, ôrder; oil, out; cup, pu̇t, rüle, ūse
əbove, takən, pencəl, lemən, circəs
ch, child; ng, long; sh, ship
th, thin; ᴛʜ, then; zh, measure

[< Scand.; cf. OIcelandic *bulki* heap] —**Syn.** *n.* **1** volume, magnitude. See **size.**

bulk carrier a lake freighter designed to carry bulk commodities such as ore and grain.

bulk·er (bul′kər) *n.* bulk carrier.

bulk·head (bulk′hed′) *n.* **1** one of the upright partitions dividing a ship into watertight compartments to prevent sinking. **2** a wall or partition built to hold back water, earth, rocks, air, etc. **3** a boxlike structure covering the top of a staircase or other opening.

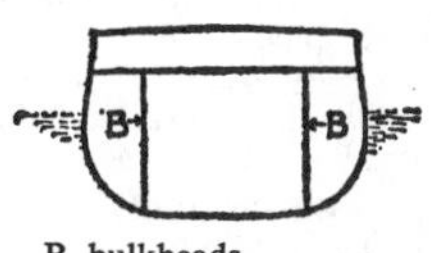

B, bulkheads

bulk·y (bul′kē) *adj.* **bulk·i·er, bulk·i·est. 1** taking up much space; large: *a bulky package.* **2** hard to handle; clumsy. —**bulk′i·ly,** *adv.* —**bulk′i·ness,** *n.* —**Syn. 1** massive, ponderous. **2** unwieldy.

bull[1] (bůl) *n.* **1** the male of cattle, buffalo, etc. **2** the uncastrated adult male of the whale, elephant, seal, walrus, and other large animals. **3** a person whose size or loudness resembles that of a bull. **4** a person who tries to raise prices in the stock market, etc. **5** *Slang.* foolish talk. **6** a bulldog. **7** a bull's eye. **8 Bull,** in astrology, the second sign of the zodiac; Taurus. **9 shoot the bull,** *Slang.* talk idly; speculate or boast. **10 take the bull by the horns,** deal bravely and directly with a dangerous or difficult situation.
—*adj.* **1** like a bull; large; strong; roaring. **2** having to do with rising prices in the stock market, etc. —*v.* push or force one's way. [ME *bole* < ON *boli.* Related to BULLOCK.]

bull[2] (bůl) *n.* in the Roman Catholic Church, a formal announcement or official order from the Pope.
[< Med.L *bulla* document, seal < L *bulla* amulet, bubble]

bull[3] (bůl) *n.* an absurd and amusing mistake in language, especially one that is self-contradictory. *Example:* If you don't receive this letter, write and let me know. [origin uncertain]

Bull (bůl) *n.* **John,** a name symbolizing England or its people.

bull. bulletin.

bull-baiting (bůl′bā′ting) *n.* formerly, a popular sport in which dogs were set to attack a chained bull.

bull·cook (bůl′kůk′) *n.* in a lumber camp, a janitor or handyman. In some camps it used to be his duty to prepare mash for the oxen used in hauling logs.

bull·dog[1] (bůl′dog′) *n. adj. v.* **-dogged, -dog·ging.**
—*n.* **1** a breed of heavily built dog having a large head, stubby nose, jutting underjaw, and short hair. **2** a dog of this breed.
—*adj.* like that of a bulldog: *bulldog courage.*
—*v.* in the western parts of Canada and the United States, throw (a steer, etc.) by grasping its horns and twisting its neck.

bull·dog[2] (bůl′dog′) *n. Cdn.* a kind of horsefly about the size of a bumblebee, having a vicious bite and a great appetite for blood. Also, **bulldog fly** or **bull fly.**

bull·doze (bůl′dōz′) *v.* **-dozed, -doz·ing. 1** *Informal.* frighten by violence or threats; bully. **2** move, clear, dig, or level with a bulldozer. [back formation < *bulldozer*]

bull·doz·er (bůl′dōz′ər) *n.* **1** a powerful tractor that moves dirt, etc. for grading, road building, etc. by means of a wide steel blade attached to the front. **2** *Informal.* one who bulldozes.

bul·let (bůl′it) *n.* a streamlined piece of lead or steel, designed to be shot from a rifle, pistol, machine gun, etc. [< F *boulette,* dim. of *boule* ball]

bul·let·head (bůl′it hed′) *n.* **1** a short, round head. **2** a person with such a head. **3** *Informal.* a stubborn, pig-headed person.

bul·let-head·ed (bu̇l′it hed′id) *adj.* having a round head.

bul·le·tin (bu̇l′ə tən) *n.* **1** a short statement of news: *In times of crisis newspapers publish bulletins about the latest happenings. Doctors issue bulletins about the condition of a sick person.* **2** a magazine or newspaper appearing regularly, especially one published by a club or society for its members. —*v.* make known by a bulletin. [< F < Ital. *bullettino*, double dim. of *bulla* bull[2]]

bulletin board a board on which notices are posted.

bul·let·proof (bu̇l′it prüf′) *adj.* made so that a bullet cannot pass through: *a bulletproof jacket.*

bull·fight (bu̇l′fīt′) *n.* a fight between men and a bull in an enclosed arena: *Bullfights are popular among the Spanish-speaking peoples.*

bull·fight·er (bu̇l′fīt′ər) *n.* a man who fights a bull in an enclosed arena.

bull·fight·ing (bu̇l′fīt′ing) *n.* the act of fighting a bull in an enclosed arena.

bull·finch (bu̇l′finch′) *n.* a European songbird having handsome, colorful plumage and a short, stout bill.

bull fly (bu̇l′flī′) *n.* bulldog[2].

bull·frog (bu̇l′frog′) *n.* a large frog of North America that makes a loud croaking noise.

bull·head (bu̇l′hed′) *n.* **1** any of several North American fishes having a large, broad head, such as the catfish. **2** a stupid fellow; a blockhead.

bull·head·ed (bu̇l′hed′id) *adj.* stupidly stubborn; obstinate. —**bull′head′ed·ness,** *n.*

bul·lion (bu̇l′yən) *n.* lumps, bars, etc. of gold or silver. [< AF *bullion* < *bouillir* boil; influenced by OF *billon* debased metal]

bull·ish (bu̇l′ish) *adj.* **1** like a bull. **2** trying or tending to raise prices in the stock market, etc. —**bull′ish·ly,** *adv.* —**bull′ish·ness,** *n.*

bull-market a rising investment market.

bull-mastiff (bu̇l′mas′tif) *n.* **1** a breed of thick-coated, powerful dog, a cross between a bulldog and a mastiff. **2** a dog of this breed.

bull·necked (bu̇l′nekt′) *adj.* having a thick neck.

bull·ock (bu̇l′ək) *n.* a young bull; an ox or steer. [OE *bulluc* bull calf]

bull pen *Esp.U.S.* **1** *Slang.* **a** a temporary prison. **b** a jail of any kind. **2** in baseball, a place outside the playing limits in which pitchers warm up during a game.

bull ring an enclosed arena for bullfights.

bull·roar·er (bu̇l′rôr′ər) *n.* **1** a flat piece of wood tied to a string so as to produce a roaring sound when whirled in the air, used in religious rites by certain North American Indian tribes, Australian aborigines, etc. **2** a similar device used as a toy.

bull session *Informal.* **1** a frank discussion about any vitally interesting topic. **2** any rambling discussion.

bull's-eye (bu̇lz′ī′) *n.* **1** the centre of a target. **2** a shot that hits the centre. **3** a thick disk or hemispherical piece of glass in the deck or side of a ship to let in light. **4** a lens shaped like a half-sphere to concentrate light. **5** a lantern with such a lens. **6** a small, round opening or window.

bull terrier 1 a breed of strong, active dog, a cross between a bulldog and a terrier. **2** a dog of this breed.

bull trout 1 salmon trout. **2** Dolly Varden trout.

bull·whip (bu̇l′hwip′ or -wip′) *n. v.* **-whipped, -whip·ping.** —*n.* a long, heavy leather whip. —*v.* strike with a bullwhip.

bull work rough chores; manual labor: *He did the bull work around the camp.*

bul·ly (bu̇l′ē) *n.* **-lies,** *v.* **-lied, -ly·ing,** *adj. interj.*
—*n.* a person who teases, frightens, or hurts smaller or weaker people.
—*v.* **1** be a bully. **2** frighten into doing something by noisy talk or threats.
—*adj.* **1** *Informal.* first-rate; excellent. **2** jovial; gallant; spirited.
—*interj. Informal.* bravo! well done! [origin uncertain]

bully beef canned or pickled beef. [? < F *bouilli* boiled beef < *bouillir* boil]

bul·ly·rag (bu̇l′ē rag′) *v.* **-ragged, -rag·ging.** *Informal.* bully; tease; abuse.

bul·rush (bu̇l′rush′) *n.* **1** a tall, slender plant that grows in or near water; cat-tail. **2** in the Bible, the papyrus of Egypt. [ME *bulrysche* < *bule* (see BULL[1], adj. def. 1) + *rysche*, OE *rysc* rush]

bul·wark (bu̇l′wərk) *n.* **1** a defence; protection. **2** an earthwork or other wall for defence against an enemy. **3** a breakwater for protection against the force of the waves. **4** Usually, **bulwarks,** *pl.* a ship's side above the level of the deck.
—*v.* **1** defend; protect. **2** provide with a bulwark or bulwarks. [ME *bulwerk*, apparently < *bole* + *work*, a work made of tree trunks. Akin to BOULEVARD.]

The bulwark of a ship

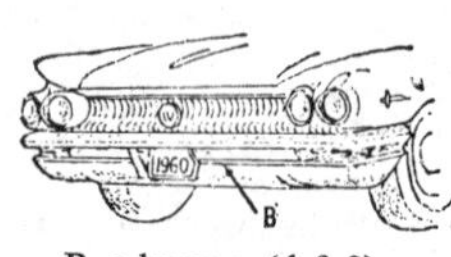

B, a bumper (def. 2)

bum[1] (bum) *n. v.* **bummed, bum·ming,** *adj.* **bum·mer, bum·mest.** *Slang.* —*n.* **1** an idle or good-for-nothing person; loafer; tramp. **2** a drunken loafer. **3** a spree. **4 on the bum, a** living as a bum: *He spent two years on the bum.* **b** not functioning; in disrepair: *Our toaster is on the bum.* **5 the bum's rush,** a forcible ejection (of a person from a place).
—*v.* **1** loaf around; idle about. **2** drink heavily. **3** sponge on others; beg. **4** get (a ride, food, money, etc.) by sponging on others.
—*adj.* **1** of poor quality. **2** physically depressed. [partly Scottish dial. *bum* a lazy, dirty person (a special use of *bum*[2]); partly a shortening of earlier American *bummer* loafer < G *Bummler*] —**bum′mer,** *n.*

bum[2] (bum) *n.* a person's seat or behind; rump; buttocks. [ME, probably < *botem* bottom]

bum·bail·iff (bum bā′lif) *n.* a bailiff or sheriff's officer, especially one employed in serving attachments and making arrests. [< *bum*[2] + *bailiff*]

bum·ble (bum′bəl) *n. v.* **-bled, -bling.** —*n.* an awkward mistake. —*v.* act in a bungling or awkward way; blunder; botch. [origin uncertain]

bum·ble·bee (bum′bəl bē′) *n.* a large bee having a thick, hairy body, usually banded with yellow. Bumblebees live in colonies, usually small, in underground nests, where they store honey. [< *bumble* buzz + *bee*]

bum·ble·dom (bum′bəl dəm) *n.* an incompetent, officious group of people. [< *Bumble*, the pompous beadle in Dickens' *Oliver Twist* + *-dom*]

bum·boat (bum′bōt′) *n.* a boat used for peddling small wares and provisions to ships in port or off-shore. [? < LG *Bumboot* a broad-beamed boat]

bump (bump) *v.* **1** push, throw, or strike (against something fairly large or solid). **2** move (along) in a bumpy fashion: *Our car bumped along the rough road.* **3** hit or come against with heavy blows: *That truck bumped our car.* **4 bump off,** *Slang.* kill.
—*n.* **1** a heavy blow or knock. **2** a swelling caused by a bump. **3** any swelling or lump. **4** of an airplane a jolt or upward thrust due to a rising current of air. **5** an earthquake-like shock or concussion caused by rock subsidence in and around mines. [imitative]

bump·er (bump′ər) *n.* **1** a person or thing that bumps. **2** the bar or bars of metal that protect the main part of a car or truck from being damaged if the vehicle is bumped. See the picture above. **3** a cup or glass filled to the brim. **4** *Informal.* something unusually large of its kind.—*adj.* unusually large: *The farmer raised a bumper crop of wheat last year.*

bump·kin (bump′kin) *n.* an awkward person from the country. [< MDu. *bommekyn* little barrel]

bump·tious (bump′shəs) *adj.* unpleasantly assertive or conceited. [< *bump*] —**bump′tious·ly,** *adv.* —**bump′tious·ness,** *n.*

bump·y (bump′ē) *adj.* **bump·i·er, bump·i·est.** having bumps; causing bumps; rough: *a bumpy road.* —**bump′i·ly,** *adv.* —**bump′i·ness,** *n.*

bun (bun) *n.* **1** a slightly sweet roll, often containing spice, raisins, or fruit. **2** hair coiled at the back of the head in a knot suggesting a bun. [ME *bunne*; origin uncertain]

bu·na (bü′nə or bū′nə) *n.* an artificial rubber made from butadiene. [< *bu*tadiene + *Na*, symbol for sodium]

bunch (bunch) *n.* **1** a group of things of the same kind growing or fastened together, placed together, or thought of together: *a bunch of grapes, a bunch of flowers.* **2** *Informal.* a group: *a bunch of thieves.* **3** *Informal.* a large quantity: *There is a whole bunch of paint in the basement.*
—*v.* **1** come together in one place. **2** bring together and make into a bunch. [ME *bunche*; origin uncertain]
—**Syn.** *n.* **1** See **bundle.** —**bunch′er,** *n.*
☛ **bunch.** Formal English limits the use of *bunch* to objects that grow together or can be fastened together: *a bunch of radishes, a bunch of flowers, a bunch of keys.* Informal English, however, clings to the older usage of *bunch*, applying it to a collection or group of any kind—including people: *A bunch of us meet at the Grill every night.*

bunch·ber·ry (bunch′ber′ē) *n.* **-ries.** a shrub having clusters of bright-red berries.

bunch grass any of various grasses, found in the western parts of Canada and the United States, that grow in bunches or tufts.

bunch·y (bun′chē) *adj.* **bunch·i·er, bunch·i·est. 1** having bunches. **2** growing in bunches. —**bunch′i·ness,** *n.*

bun·co (bung′kō) *n.* **-cos,** *v.* **-coed, -co·ing.** bunko.

bun·combe (bung′kəm) *n. Informal.* bunkum.

Bund (bůnd; *German,* bůnt) *n.* **Bün·de** (byn′də). *German.* an association; society; league.

Bun·des·rat (bun′dəs rät′) *n.* **1** in West Germany, the upper house of the federal legislature. **2** in Switzerland or the former German Empire, the federal council or chief executive authority. [< G *Bund* league, federation + *Rat* council]

bun·dle (bun′dəl) *n. v.* **-dled, -dling.** —*n.* **1** a number of things tied or wrapped together. **2** a parcel or package. **3** a group; bunch. **4 a bundle of nerves,** a person in a state of nervous tension.
—*v.* **1** wrap or tie together; make into a bundle. **2** send or go in a hurry; hustle: *They bundled me off to the hospital against my will.* **3** collect; gather together in a mass. **4** conduct a courtship, fully dressed, in bed. **5 bundle up,** dress warmly. [cf. MDu. *bondel.* Akin to BIND.] —**bun′dler,** *n.*
Syn. *n.* **1, 2 Bundle, bunch, parcel** = something fastened or wrapped together. **Bundle** suggests a number of things of the same or different sizes and shapes bound or wrapped together, often clumsily: *We gave away several bundles of old newspapers and magazines.* **Bunch** suggests a number of things of the same kind bound or fastened together, usually closely and neatly: *I bought a bunch of flowers.* **Parcel** suggests one or more things wrapped and tied neatly for carrying: *I had too many parcels to carry on the bus.*

bung (bung) *n.* **1** a stopper for closing the hole in the side or end of a barrel, keg, or cask. **2** a bunghole.
—*v.* **bung up, a** close (a bunghole) with a stopper. **b** stop up; choke up. **c** *Slang.* bruise. [probably < MDu. *bonghe*]

bun·ga·low (bung′gə lō′) *n.* a one-storey house, often small; a house having no living space above the main floor. [< Hind. *bangla* of Bengal]

bung·hole (bung′hōl′) *n.* a hole in the side or end of a barrel, keg, or cask through which it is filled and emptied.

bun·gle (bung′gəl) *v.* **-gled, -gling,** *n.* —*v.* **1** do or make (something) in a clumsy, unskilful way. **2** spoil by unskilful workmanship. —*n.* a clumsy, unskilful performance. [origin uncertain] —**bun′gler,** *n.* —**bun′gling·ly,** *adv.*

bun·ion (bun′yən) *n.* a painful, inflamed swelling on the foot, especially on the first joint of the big toe. [origin uncertain]

bunk[1] (bungk) *n.* **1** a narrow bed set against or fixed to a wall. **2** *Informal.* any place to sleep. —*v.* **1** *Informal.* sleep (*at*); spend the night (*at*): *Tom bunked at our house last night.* **2** sleep in or occupy a bunk. **3** sleep in rough quarters. [? < *bunker*]

hat, āge, cãre, fär; let, ēqual, tėrm; it, īce
hot, ōpen, ôrder; oil, out; cup, pút, rüle, ūse
əbove, takən, pencəl, lemən, circəs
ch, child; ng, long; sh, ship
th, thin; ᴛʜ, then; zh, measure

bunk[2] (bungk) *n. Slang.* insincere talk; humbug; bunkum. [short for *buncombe*]

bunk beds two single beds made in such a way that they may be fitted one above the other.

bunk·er (bungk′ər) *n.* **1** a place or bin for coal on a ship. **2** a sandy hollow or mound of earth on a golf course, used as an obstacle. **3** a steel-and-concrete fortification, usually part of a defence system and built partly or entirely below ground. —*v.* **1** hit (a golf ball) into a bunker. **2** supply (a ship) with coal or other fuel. [origin uncertain]

bunk·house (bungk′hous′) *n.* a building equipped with bunks for sleeping.

bun·ko (bung′kō) *n.* **-kos,** *v.* **-koed, -ko·ing.** *Slang.* —*n.* **1** a kind of card game. **2** *Slang.* a swindle. —*v.* swindle. Also, **bunco.** [short for *buncombe*]

bun·kum (bung′kəm) *n. Informal.* insincere talk; humbug. Also, **buncum.** [after *Buncombe* Co., N.C., whose congressman kept making pointless speeches "for Buncombe"]

bun·ny (bun′ē) *n.* **-nies.** *Informal.* a rabbit. [origin uncertain]

Bun·sen burner (bun′sən) a gas burner with a very hot, blue flame, used in laboratories. Air is let in at the base of the burner and mixed with gas. [after Robert *Bunsen* (1811-1899), a German chemist who invented it]

AIR
GAS
A Bunsen burner

bunt[1] (bunt) *v.* **1** strike with the head or horns, as a goat does. **2** push; shove. **3** in baseball, hit a ball lightly so that it goes to the ground and rolls only a short distance. —*n.* **1** push; shove. **2** in baseball: **a** a hit made by hitting the ball lightly so that it goes to the ground and rolls only a short distance. **b** a baseball that is bunted. [cf. *butt*[3]] —**bunt′er,** *n.*

bunt[2] (bunt) *n.* **1** the central, bellying part of a square sail. **2** the bagging part of a fishing net.
—*v.* **1** swell out; belly: *sails bunting before the wind.* **2 bunt up,** haul (a sail) up to a yard. [origin uncertain]

bunt[3] (bunt) *n.* **1** a disease of wheat in which a parasitic fungus turns the centre kernels into a foul-smelling black powder. **2** the fungus itself. [origin uncertain]

bun·ting[1] (bun′ting) *n.* **1** a thin cloth used for flags. **2** long pieces of cloth in flag colors and designs, used to decorate buildings and streets on holidays, etc.; flags. [? < ME *bonten* sift, since the cloth was used for sifting]

bun·ting[2] (bun′ting) *n.* a small bird, having a stout bill and resembling a sparrow. [origin uncertain]

bunt·line (bunt′lin or bunt′līn′) *n.* a rope fastened to a sail, used to haul it up to the yard for furling. [< *bunt* middle part of a sail (origin uncertain) + *line*[1]]

Bun·yan (bun′yən) *n.* **Paul,** a legendary hero of the lumber camps. He is thought of as a giant lumberjack who does marvellous deeds.

buoy (boi or bü′ē) *n.* **1** a floating object anchored in a certain place on the water to warn or guide: *Buoys mark hidden rocks or shallows, indicate the safe part of the channel, etc.* **2** a cork belt, ring, or jacket used to keep a person from sinking; a life buoy or life preserver.
—*v.* **1** furnish with buoys; mark with a buoy. **2** keep from sinking. **3** hold up; sustain; encourage. [< OF *boie* (< Gmc.; akin to E *beacon*) and MDu. *boeie* (< OF *boie*)]

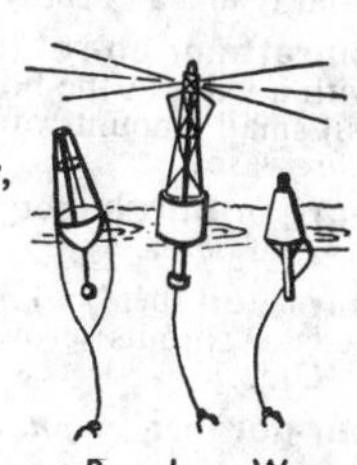

Buoys: B, a bell buoy; L, a light buoy; W, a whistle buoy.

buoy·an·cy (boi′ən sē) *n.* **1** the power to float: *Wood has more buoyancy than iron.* **2** the power to keep things afloat: *Salt water has more buoyancy than fresh water.* **3** a tendency to rise. **4** the ability to rise above or recover quickly from low spirits; light-heartedness; cheerfulness; hopefulness. **5** a body's loss in weight when immersed in a liquid.

buoy·ant (boi′ənt) *adj.* **1** able to float: *Wood and cork are buoyant; iron and lead are not.* **2** able to keep things afloat: *Air is buoyant; balloons float in it.* **3** tending to rise. **4** light-hearted; cheerful; hopeful: *Children are usually more buoyant than old people.* —**buoy′ant·ly,** *adv.*

BUP British United Press.

bur (bėr) *n. v.* **burred, bur·ring.** burr.

Bur·ber·ry (bėr′bər ē) *n. Trademark.* **1** a kind of waterproof material for clothing. **2** a coat made of this material.

bur·ble (bėr′bəl) *v.* **-bled, -bling. 1** make a bubbling noise. **2** speak in a confused, excited manner. [probably imitative]

bur·bot (bėr′bət) *n.* **-bot** or **-bots.** a fresh-water fish having a slender body, related to the cod. [< F *bourbotte* < L *barba* beard; influenced by F *bourbe* mud]

bur·den[1] (bėr′dən) *n.* **1** what is carried; a load. **2** anything difficult to carry or bear; a heavy load. **3** the quantity of freight that a ship can carry; weight of a ship's cargo.
—*v.* **1** put a burden on; load. **2** load too heavily; oppress: *She was burdened with work.* [OE *byrthen.* Related to BEAR[1].] —**Syn.** *n.* **1** See **load. 2** weight, encumbrance.

bur·den[2] (bėr′dən) *n.* **1** the main idea or message: *The value of peace was the burden of the Prime Minister's speech.* **2** a repeated verse in a song; chorus; refrain. [< MF *bourdon* humming, drone of bagpipe < LL *burda* pipe]

burden of proof the obligation of proving that something said is true.

bur·den·some (bėr′dən səm) *adj.* hard to bear; very heavy; oppressive: *The Principal's many duties are burdensome.* —**bur′den·some·ly,** *adv.* —**bur′den·some·ness,** *n.* —**Syn.** oppressing, onerous. See **heavy.**

bur·dock (bėr′dok′) *n.* a coarse weed having prickly burrs and broad leaves. [< *bur* + *dock*[4]]

bu·reau (būr′ō) *n.* **bu·reaus** or **bu·reaux** (būr′ōz). **1** a chest of drawers for clothes: *Bureaus are often equipped with mirrors.* **2** a desk or writing table with drawers. **3** an office: *a travel bureau.* **4** a government department: *The Weather Bureau makes daily reports on weather conditions.* [< F *bureau* desk (originally cloth-covered) < OF *burel,* dim. of *bure* coarse woollen cloth < LL *burra*]

bu·reauc·ra·cy (byů rok′rə sē) *n.* **-cies. 1** government by groups of officials. **2** the officials administering the government. **3** a concentration of power in administrative bureaus. **4** excessive insistence on rigid routine; red tape.

bu·reau·crat (būr′ə krat′) *n.* **1** an official in a bureaucracy. **2** a formal, pretentious government official. [blend of *bureau* + *autocrat*]

bu·reau·crat·ic (būr′ə krat′ik) *adj.* **1** having to do with a bureaucracy or a bureaucrat. **2** arbitrary. —**bu′reau·crat′i·cal·ly,** *adv.*

bu·rette or **bu·ret** (byů ret′) *n.* a graduated glass tube with a valve at the bottom, used for accurately measuring out small amounts of a liquid or gas. [< F *burette,* dim. *buire* vase]

burg or **burgh** (bėrg) *n. Informal.* a town or city. [var. of *borough*]

bur·geon (bėr′jən) *n.* a bud or sprout. —*v.* put forth buds or sprouts; grow. [ME < OF *burjon,* apparently < Gmc.]

bur·ger (bėr′gər) *n. Informal.* a hamburger.

bur·gess (bėr′jis) *n.* **1** the citizen of a borough. **2** in Saskatchewan, a property owner who has the right to vote on money by-laws in a municipality. [ME < OF *burgeis* < LL *burgensis* citizen. Doublet of BOURGEOIS[1].]

burgh (bėrg) *n.* **1** a burg. **2** in some countries, a chartered town. [var. of *borough*]

burgh·er (bėr′gər) *n.* a citizen of a burgh or town; citizen.

bur·glar (bėr′glər) *n.* **1** a person who breaks into a house, building, etc. at night to steal or commit some other crime. **2** sometimes, anyone who breaks into a building to steal. See **burglary** (def. 2). [< Anglo-L *burglator,* ? partly < OE *burgbryce*]

bur·glar·i·ous (bėr glãr′ē əs) *adj.* having to do with burglary. —**bur·glar′i·ous·ly,** *adv.*

bur·glar·ize (bėr′glər īz′) *v.* **-ized, -iz·ing.** *Informal.* break into (a building) to steal.

bur·glar·proof (bėr′glər prüf′) *adj.* so strong or safe that burglars cannot break in.

bur·glar·y (bėr′glər ē) *n.* **-glar·ies. 1** the act of breaking into a dwelling at night to steal or commit some other crime. **2** under the laws of certain places, breaking into any of various buildings, by night or day.

bur·gle (bėr′gəl) *v.* **-gled, -gling.** *Informal.* break into (a building) to steal; burglarize. [< *burglar*]

bur·go·mas·ter (bėr′gə mas′tər) *n.* in the Netherlands, Flanders, and Germany, the mayor of a town. [< Du. *burgemeester* < *burg* borough + *meester* master]

Bur·gun·di·an (bėr gun′dē ən) *adj.* of Burgundy, a region in E. France, or its people. —*n.* a native or inhabitant of Burgundy.

Bur·gun·dy (bėr′gən dē) *n.* **-dies.** a red or white wine made in Burgundy, a region in E. France.

bur·i·al (ber′ē əl) *n.* a burying. —*adj.* having to do with burying: *a burial service.*

burial ground a graveyard or cemetery.

burke (bėrk) *v.* **burked, burk·ing. 1** murder by suffocation so as to leave no marks on the body. **2** suppress; hush up. [< William *Burke,* 1792-1829, hanged for murder; he suffocated his victims so that he could sell their unmarked bodies for dissection]

burl (bėrl) *n.* a knot in wool, cloth, or wood. —*v.* remove knots from. [< MF *bourle* < LL *burra* flock of wool]

bur·lap (bėr′lap) *n.* a coarse fabric made from jute or hemp, often used to make bags. A superior grade of burlap is used for curtains, wall coverings, and upholstery. [origin uncertain]

bur·lesque (bėr lesk′) *n. v.* **-lesqued, -les·quing,** *adj.* —*n.* **1** a literary or dramatic composition in which a serious subject is treated ridiculously, or with mock seriousness: *Mark Twain's story, "A Connecticut Yankee in King Arthur's Court," is a burlesque of some old legends.* **2** vaudeville that features strip tease. **3** a debasing representation of anything elevated or dignified; mockery: *He made a burlesque of his high office.*
—*v.* imitate so as to ridicule.
—*adj.* comical; making people laugh. [< F < Ital. *burlesco* < *burla* jest] —**bur·les′quer,** *n.*
—**Syn.** *n.* **1** parody, take-off.

bur·ley or **Bur·ley** (bėr′lē) *n.* **-leys.** a kind of thin-leaved tobacco.

bur·ly (bėr′lē) *adj.* **-li·er, -li·est. 1** strong; sturdy; big. **2** bluff; rough. [OE *borlīce* excellently) —**bur′li·ness,** *n.* —**bur′li·ly,** *adv.*

Bur·man (bėr′mən) *n. adj.* Burmese.

Bur·mese (bėr mēz′) *n.* **-mese,** *adj.* —*n.* **1** a native of Burma. **2** the language of Burma. **3** a breed of medium-sized cat having a compact, muscular body and short, glossy, brown hair. **4** a cat of this breed. —*adj.* of Burma, its people, or their language.

burn[1] (bėrn) *v.* **burned** or **burnt, burn·ing,** *n.* —*v.* **1** be on fire; be very hot; blaze; glow. **2** set on fire; cause to burn. **3** destroy or be destroyed by fire: *burn old papers.* **4** injure or be injured by fire, heat, or an acid: *He burned his hand on the hot iron.* **5** make by fire, by a heated tool, etc.: *His cigar burned a hole in the rug.* **6** feel hot; give a feeling of heat to: *His forehead burns with fever.* **7** be very excited or eager: *burning with enthusiasm.* **8** inflame or be inflamed with anger, passion, etc.: *burn with fury.* **9** give light: *Lamps were burning in every room.* **10** sunburn; tan. **11** use to produce heat or energy: *Our furnace burns oil.* **12** produce, harden, glaze, etc. by fire or heat: *burn bricks, burn lime.* **13** in

chemistry, undergo or cause to undergo combustion; oxidize. **14** in nuclear physics, make use of atomic energy (from uranium, thorium, etc.). **15** cauterize. **16 burn down, a** burn or be burned to the ground. **b** decrease in fuel or heat. **17 burn oneself out,** use oneself up physically or mentally; exhaust one's store of energy, ambition, etc. **18 burn out, a** destroy by burning. **b** cease to burn; become extinct. **c** burn the inside of: *The warehouse was burned out.* **d** drive (a person) out by fire. **19 burn up, a** consume: *This car burns up the gasoline.* **b** *Informal.* make or become angry.
—*n.* **1** an injury caused by fire, heat, or an acid; a burned place. **2** a sunburn; tan. [coalescence of OE *beornan* be on fire and OE *bærnan* consume with fire]
—**burn′a·ble,** *adj.*

Syn. *v.* **1** flame. **2** ignite, fire. **4 Burn, scorch, sear** = to injure or be injured by fire, heat, or acid. **Burn,** the general word, suggests any degree of damage from slight injury to destruction by fire, heat, or acid: *The toast burned.* **Scorch** = to burn the surface enough to discolor it, sometimes to damage the texture, by heat or fire: *The cigarette scorched the paper.* **Sear** = to burn or scorch the surface enough to dry or harden it, by heat, fire, or acid, and applies particularly to burning the tissues of people or animals: *Wounds are cauterized by searing.*

☛ **burn.** The past tense and past participle of *burn* are either *burned* or *burnt*. *Burnt* is usual when the participle is used as an adjective: *The partially burnt papers gave them little help in solving the mystery.* Verb: *They hastily burned all the old letters before they left.*

burn² (bėrn) *n. Scottish.* a small stream; creek; brook. [OE *burna*]

burn·er (bėr′nər) *n.* **1** the part of a lamp, stove, furnace, etc. where the flame or heat is produced. **2** any thing or part that burns or works by heat: *Some stoves are oil burners; others are gas burners.* **3** a man whose work is burning something: *a charcoal burner.* **4** in a jet engine, a combustion chamber. See **jet** for diagram. **5** a lamp used to burn the paint off a surface.

burn·ing (bėr′ning) *adj.* **1** glowing hot; hot. **2** vital; urgent.—**burn′ing·ly,** *adv.*

burning glass a convex lens used to produce heat or set fire to a substance by focussing the sun's rays on it.

bur·nish (bėr′nish) *v. n.* polish; shine. [ME < OF *burniss-*, a stem of *burnir* make brown, polish < *brun* brown < Gmc.] —**bur′nish·er,** *n.*

bur·noose or **bur·nous** (bėr nüs′ or bėr′nüs) *n.* a long cloak with a hood, worn by Moors and Arabs. [< F *burnous* < Arabic *burnus*]

burn·out (bėrn′out′) *n.* **1** a failure due to burning or extreme heat. **2** in aerospace: **a** the dying out of the flame in a rocket engine as a result of its fuel being used up or intentionally shut off. **b** the time or position when such dying out occurs.

burn·sides or **Burn·sides** (bėrn′sīdz) *n.pl.* a growth of hair on the cheeks but not on the chin. Also, **sideburns.** [after Gen. A. E. *Burnside*]

burnt (bėrnt) *v.* a pt. and a pp. of **burn¹.**
☛ See **burn¹** for usage note.

burnt offering 1 the burning of an animal, harvest, fruits, etc. on an altar as a religious sacrifice. **2** anything offered as a sacrifice.

burnt sienna 1 a dark-brown color. **2** a pigment of this color, especially when made by burning raw sienna to powder. —**burnt′sien′na,** *adj.*

burnt umber 1 a reddish-brown paint. **2** a reddish-brown color.

bur oak 1 an American oak tree whose acorns have large cups covered with scales. **2** its tough, close-grained wood.

burp (bėrp) *Informal. n.* a belch. —*v.* **1** belch. **2** cause to belch. [imitative]

burr¹ or **bur** (bėr) *n.* **1** a prickly, clinging seedcase or flower. **2** a plant or weed bearing burrs. **3** a person or thing that clings like a burr. **4** a rough ridge or edge left by a tool on metal, wood, etc. after cutting or drilling it. **5** a tool that resembles a burr: *Dentists use tiny burrs.*
—*v.* remove burrs from. [ME, probably < Scand.; cf. Danish *borre* burdock] —**bur′ry,** *adj.*

burr² (bėr) *n.* **1** a prominent pronunciation of *r*. **2** a pronunciation in which *r* sounds are prominent: *a Scottish burr.* **3** a whirring sound.
—*v.* **1** pronounce *r* prominently. **2** make a whirring sound. [probably imitative] —**bur′ry,** *adj.*

hat, āge, cãre, fär; let, ēqual, tėrm; it, īce
hot, ōpen, ôrder; oil, out; cup, pu̇t, rüle, ūse
əbove, takən, pencəl, lemən, circəs
ch, child; ng, long; sh, ship
th, thin; ᴛʜ, then; zh, measure

burr³ (bėr) *n.* **1** a washer placed on the end of a rivet before swaging it. **2** a disc or blank punched out of a sheet of metal. [ME *burwe* circle < Scand.; cf. Icelandic *borg* wall]

bur·ro (bėr′o) *n.* **-ros.** a kind of small, agile donkey. [< Sp. *burro* < *burrico* small horse < LL *burricus*]

bur·row (bėr′ō) *n.* **1** a hole dug in the ground by an animal for refuge or shelter: *Rabbits live in burrows.* **2** a similar passage for dwelling, shelter, or refuge.
—*v.* **1** dig a hole in the ground: *The mole soon burrowed out of sight.* **2** live in burrows. **3** hide. **4** dig. **5** search. [cf. OE *beorg* burial place, *byrgen* grave]

bur·row·er (bėr′ō ər) *n.* one who burrows.

bur·sa (bėr′sə) *n.* **-sae** (-sē or -sī) or **-sas.** in anatomy, a sac, especially one containing a lubricating fluid; a pouch or cavity. [< LL *bursa* < Gk. *byrsa* hide, wineskin. Doublet of BOURSE, PURSE.]

bur·sar (bėr′sər or bėr′sär) *n.* a treasurer, especially of a college or university. [< Med.L *bursarius* < LL *bursa* purse]

bur·sa·ry (bėr′sə rē) *n.* **-ries. 1** a grant of money to a student at a college or university. **2** a treasury, especially of a college or university.

bur·si·tis (bər sī′tis) *n.* inflammation of a bursa, usually in the shoulder or the hip. [*bursa* + *-itis*]

burst (bėrst) *v.* **burst, burst·ing,** *n.* —*v.* **1** break open; break out; fly apart suddenly with force; explode: *The bomb burst.* **2** be very full: *The barns were bursting with grain.* **3** go, come, do, etc. by force or suddenly: *He burst into the room.* **4** open or be opened suddenly or violently: *The trees burst into bloom.* **5** act or change suddenly in a way suggesting a break or explosion: *She burst into loud laughter.* **6** cause to break open or into pieces; shatter: *burst a blood vessel. The prisoner burst his chains.*
—*n.* **1** an outbreak: *a burst of feeling.* **2** a sudden and violent issuing forth; sudden opening to view or sight. **3** a bursting; split; explosion. **4** a sudden display of activity or energy: *a burst of speed.* **5** a series of shots fired by one pressure of the trigger of an automatic weapon. [OE *berstan*]

bur·then (bėr′ᴛʜən) *n. v. Archaic.* burden¹.

bur·weed (bėr′wēd′) *n.* any of a group of plants having burry fruit, such as cocklebur and burdock.

bur·y (ber′ē) *v.* **bur·ied, bur·y·ing. 1** put (a dead body) in the earth, a tomb, etc. **2** perform a funeral service for. **3** cover up; hide: *Many nuts were buried under the dead leaves.* **4** plunge; sink: *He buried himself in a book.* **5** forget. **6** withdraw or cause to move to obscurity or retirement: *bury oneself in the country.* [OE *byrgan*]
—**bur′i·er,** *n.* —**Syn. 1** inter, entomb. **3** conceal, secrete.

bus (bus) *n.* **bus·es** or **bus·ses. 1** a large automobile used to carry passengers along a certain route; omnibus. **2** *Informal.* an automobile or airplane. **3 miss the bus,** *Slang.* lose an opportunity. [short for *omnibus*]

bus. business.

bus boy a waiter's assistant. He brings bread and butter, fills glasses, carries off dishes, etc.

bus·by (buz′bē) *n.* **-bies.** a tall fur hat with a bag hanging from the top over the right side, worn by hussars.

A busby

bush (bu̇sh) *n.* **1** a woody plant smaller than a tree, often having many separate branches starting from or near the ground. **2** open forest. **3** the tree-covered part of a farm; a bush lot or wood lot: *They went to the bush to get firewood.* **4 beat around the bush,** approach a matter in a roundabout way; not come straight to the point.
—*v.* **1** spread out like a bush; grow thickly. **2** set (ground) with bushes; cover with bushes. **3** *Informal.* exhaust

completely. **4 bush out, a** spread out like a bush. **b** set out small evergreen trees to mark (a route) across a frozen river, lake, etc. [ME *busch,* var. of *busk* < ON *buskr* < Gmc. **busk-*]

bush·craft (bu̇sh′kraft′) *n.* knowledge of how to keep alive and find one's way in the bush.

bushed (bu̇sht) *adj.* **1** lost in the bush. **2** *Informal.* **a** acting strangely as a result of being isolated from other people. **b** exhausted.

bush·el[1] (bu̇sh′əl) *n.* **1** a measure for grain, fruit, vegetables, and other dry things, equal to 4 pecks or 32 quarts. **2** a container that holds a bushel. [ME < OF *boissiel,* dim. of *boisse* a measure]

bush·el[2] (bu̇sh′əl) *v.* **-elled** or **-eled, -el·ling** or **-el·ing.** repair or alter (clothing). [origin uncertain] —**bush′el·ler** or **bush′el·er,** *n.*

Bu·shi·do or **bu·shi·do** (bü′shē dō′) *n.* in Japan, the moral code of the feudal knights and warriors; chivalry. In its fully developed form, Bushido lasted from the 12th to the 19th centuries. [< Japanese *bushi* warrior + *do* way]

bush·ing (bu̇sh′ing) *n.* **1** a removable metal lining used to protect parts of machinery from wear. **2** a metal lining inserted in a hole, pipe, etc. to reduce its size. **3** a lining for a hole, to insulate one or more wires or other electrical conductors passing through. [< *bush* bushing < MDu. *busse* box]

bush league *Slang.* **1** in baseball, a minor league. **2** any insignificant or inexpert person, group, organization, etc.: *His poor advice puts him in the bush league of lawyers.* —**bush leaguer.**

bush line *Cdn.* an airline that transports freight and passengers over the northern bush country.

bush lot *Cdn.* that part of a farm where the trees have been left standing to provide firewood, fence posts, etc.; a wood lot.

bush·man (bu̇sh′mən) *n.* **-men** (-mən). **1** in Australia, a settler in the bush. **2** a person who knows much about life in the bush. **3 Bushman, a** a member of a South African tribe of roving hunters. **b** the language of this tribe.

bush partridge *Cdn.* a bird found in Canada and the Northern United States; spruce grouse.

bush pilot *Cdn.* an aviator who does most of his flying in the bush country of the far north.

bush·rang·er (bu̇sh′rān′jər) *n.* **1** a person who lives in the bush. **2** in Australia, a criminal who hides in the bush and lives by robbery.

bush telegraph 1 any of various means of communication between natives in wild country: *The call to arms seemed to have spread instantly over the whole area by the amazing bush telegraph.* **2** a grapevine (def. 2): *I heard on the bush telegraph that you were being nominated for president of our club.*

bush·whack (bu̇sh hwak′ or -wak′) *v.* **1** work in the bush or backwoods. **2** ambush or raid.

bush·whack·er (bu̇sh′hwak′ər or -wak′ər) *n.* **1** a person who lives or works in the bush or backwoods. **2** a scythe for cutting bushes. **3** a guerrilla fighter.

bush·whack·ing (bu̇sh′hwak′ing or -wak′ing) *n.* **1** the act or fact of living or working in the bush. **2** the act of ambushing or of fighting from behind bushes, rocks, etc.; guerrilla warfare.

bush·work·er (bu̇sh′wėrk′ər) *n.* *Cdn.* a person who works in the bush, especially a lumberjack.

bush·y (bu̇sh′ē) *adj.* **bush·i·er, bush·i·est. 1** spreading out like a bush; growing thickly. **2** overgrown with bushes. —**bush′i·ness,** *n.*

bus·ied (biz′ēd′) *v.* pt. and pp. of **busy.**

bus·i·ly (biz′ə lē) *adv.* in a busy manner; actively.

busi·ness (biz′nis) *n.* **1** whatever one is busy at; one's work or occupation: *Business comes before pleasure.* **2** a matter or affair: *His dismissal was a sad business.* **3** activities of buying and selling; trade; commercial dealings: *This store does a big business.* **4** a commercial enterprise; an industrial establishment: *a bakery business. They sold their business for ten million dollars.* **5** the right to interfere; concern: *That's not your business.* **6** an action in a play; something done to make a play seem like real life. **7 have no business,** have no right. **8 mean business,** *Informal.* be in earnest; be serious. **9 mind your own business,** avoid interfering in the affairs of others. [< *busy* + *-ness*] —**Syn. 1** profession, vocation, job. See **occupation.**

business card a calling card for use in business, printed with the owner's name, position, business address and telephone number, etc.

business college a school that gives training in shorthand, typewriting, bookkeeping, and other commercial subjects.

business end *Informal.* the area or part of something that does the important or essential work: *The nib is the business end of a pen.*

busi·ness·like (biz′nis līk′) *adj.* having system and method; well-managed; practical: *He ran his store in a businesslike manner.*

busi·ness·man (biz′nis man′ or biz′nis mən) *n.* **-men** (-men′ or -mən). **1** a man in business. **2** a man who runs a business.

business school business college.

busi·ness·wom·an (biz′nis wu̇m′ən) *n.* **-wom·en. 1** a woman in business. **2** a woman who runs a business.

busk·er (bus′kər) *n.* *Brit. Slang.* a strolling entertainer of passers-by, theatre queues, etc. [< dial. *busk* peddle, provide entertainment, etc.]

bus·kin (bus′kin) *n.* **1** formerly, a boot reaching to the calf or knee. **2** a high shoe with a very thick sole, worn by Greek and Roman actors of tragedies. **3** tragedy; tragic drama. [probably < OF *brousequin* < MDu. *brosekin*]

Ancient buskins (def. 2)

bus·man (bus′mən) *n.* a conductor or driver of a bus.

bus·man's holiday a holiday spent in doing what one normally does at one's daily work.

buss (bus) *v. n.* *Archaic* or *Dialect.* kiss.

bus·ses (bus′iz) *n.* a pl. of **bus.**

bust[1] (bust) *n.* **1** a statue of a person's head, shoulders, and chest. **2** the upper, front part of the body. **3** a woman's bosom. [< F < Ital. < L *bustum* funeral monument]

bust[2] (bust) *v.* **1** *Substandard.* burst. **2** *Slang.* make bankrupt; ruin financially. **3** *Slang.* fail financially; become bankrupt. **4** *Informal.* punch; hit. **5** train to obey; tame. **6** break up (a trust) into smaller companies. —*n.* **1** *Substandard.* burst. **2** *Slang.* a total failure; bankruptcy. **3** *Informal.* a spree. [var. of *burst*]

☛ **Bust** is the substandard form of *burst* in the sense of "explode or break out." It is slang in the sense of "fail financially," but is good English in *busting a bronco* or *busting a trust.*

bus·tard (bus′tərd) *n.* a large game bird having long legs and a heavy body, found on the deserts and plains of Africa, Europe, and Asia. [blend of OF *bistarde* and *oustarde,* both < L *avis tarda* slow bird]

-busted *combining form.* having a certain kind of bust: *small-busted = having a small bust.*

bust·er (bus′tər) *n.* *Slang.* **1** as a form of address: **a** a little boy. **b** a fellow. **2** something remarkable or outstanding. **3** a dashing fellow. **4** a wild frolic; spree. **5** in Australia, a terrific gale.

bus·tle[1] (bus′əl) *v.* **-tled, -tling,** *n.* —*v.* **1** be noisily busy and in a hurry. **2** make (others) hurry or work hard. —*n.* noisy or excited activity: *There was a great bustle as the party broke up.* [? imitative] —**bus′tler,** *n.* —**Syn.** *n.* commotion, ado. See **stir**[1].

bus·tle[2] (bus′əl) *n.* **1** formerly, a pad or framework used to puff out the upper back part of a woman's skirts. **2** a fullness at the back of a woman's skirt just below the waist, made by a bow or gathering of material. [? special use of *bustle*[1]]

bust-up (bust′up′) *n.* *Slang.* **1** a quarrel. **2** a fight.

bus·y (biz′ē) *adj.* **bus·i·er, bus·i·est,** *v.* **bus·ied, bus·y·ing.** —*adj.* **1** working; active: *a busy person.* **2** of a telephone

hat, āge, cãre, fär, let; ēqual, tėrm; it, īce
hot, ōpen, ôrder; oil, out; cup, pu̇t, rüle, ūse
əbove, takən, pencəl, lemən, circəs
ch, child; ng, long; sh, ship
th, thin; ᴛʜ, then; zh, measure

line, in use. **3** full of work or activity: *a busy day, a busy street.* **4** prying into other people's affairs; meddling: *That inquisitive woman is always busy.* **5** *Informal.* having too much design, ornament, etc.: *a busy drawing, busy decoration.*
—*v.* make busy; keep busy: *The bees busied themselves at making honey.* [OE *bisig*] —**bus′y·ness,** *n.*
Syn. *adj.* **1 Busy, industrious, diligent** = actively or attentively occupied. **Busy** = habitually active or working steadily or at the moment: *He is a busy man, and it is hard to get an appointment with him.* **Industrious** = hard-working by nature or habit: *He is an industrious worker.* **Diligent** = hard-working at a particular thing, usually something one likes or especially wants to do: *She is a diligent mother, but a poor housekeeper.*

bus·y·bod·y (biz′ē bod′ē) *n.* **-bod·ies.** a person who pries into other people's affairs; meddler.

but (but; *unstressed,* bət) *conj.* **1** on the other hand; yet: *It rained, but I went anyway.* **2** if not; unless; except that: *It never rains but it pours.* **3** other than; otherwise than: *We cannot choose but hear.* **4** that: *I don't doubt but he will come.* **5** that not: *He is not so sick but he can eat.*
—*prep.* **1** except; save: *He works every day but Sunday.* **2** other than: *No one replied but me.*
—*adv.* **1** only; merely: *He is but a boy.* **2 all but,** nearly; almost. **3 but for,** were it not for; excepting; save: *He was right but for one thing.* **4 but that,** were it not that: *I would have come but that I felt too ill.*
—*n.* an objection: *Not so many buts, please.* [OE *būtan* without, unless < *be-* + *ūtan* outside < *ūt* out]
Syn. *conj.* **1 But, however** express a relationship in which two things or ideas are thought of as standing in opposition or contrast to each other. **But** expresses the contrast or contradiction clearly and sharply by placing the two things or ideas side by side in perfect balance: *He is sick, but he can eat.* **However** is more formal, and suggests that the second idea should be compared and contrasted with the first: *We have not yet reached a decision; however, our opinion of your plan is favorable.* —*prep.* **1** See **except.**
☛ **But** is the natural co-ordinating conjunction to connect two contrasted expressions that are equal grammatically. It is more natural than the heavy and formal *however* or *yet*: *He worked fast, but he seldom made mistakes.* Two clauses connected by *but* should ordinarily be separated by a comma. The contrast in idea suggests the use of punctuation even when the clauses are relatively short: *I couldn't get the licence number, but it was a Saskatchewan plate.*

bu·ta·di·ene (bū′tə dī′ēn) *n.* a colorless gas made from oil, used in making synthetic rubber and as an anaesthetic. *Formula*: C_4H_6 [< *but*ane + *di-* + *-ene,* chemical suffix (< L *-enus*)]

bu·tane (bū′tān or bū tān′) *n.* a gaseous hydrocarbon, used as a fuel and as an anaesthetic. *Formula*: C_4H_{10} [< L *butyrum* butter < Gk. *boutyron*]

butch·er (bu̇ch′ər) *n.* **1** a man whose work is the killing and cutting up of animals for food. **2** a man who sells meat. **3** a brutal killer; murderer. **4** *Informal.* a person who botches or bungles.
—*v.* **1** kill (animals) for food. **2** kill (people, wild animals, or birds) wholesale, needlessly, or cruelly. **3** kill brutally; murder. **4** spoil by poor work: *The tailor has butchered this suit.* [ME < OF *bocher* < *boc* he-goat, buck[1] < Gmc.] —**butch′er·er,** *n.*

butcher bird any of several kinds of shrike that impale their prey on thorns.

butch·er·y (bu̇ch′ər ē) *n.* **-er·ies. 1** brutal killing; wholesale murder. **2** a slaughter house; butcher shop. **3** a butcher's work; the act or business of killing animals for food.

but·ler (but′lər) *n.* **1** a manservant in charge of the pantry and table service in a household. **2** a male servant in charge of wines and liquors; wine steward. [ME < AF var. of OF *bouteillier* < *bouteille* bottle. See BOTTLE.]

butler's pantry a small room between the kitchen and dining room, for use by a butler, serving maid, etc.

butt[1] (but) *n.* **1** the thicker end of a tool, weapon, ham, etc. **2** the end that is left; a stub or stump: *a cigar butt.* **3** *Informal.* the buttocks; rump. [fusion of ME *but, bott* (related to *buttocks*) and OF *bout* end < Gmc.]

butt[2] (but) *n.* **1** a target. **2** an object of ridicule or scorn: *That queer-looking boy was the butt of many jokes.* **3 a** on a rifle, archery, or artillery range, a mound of earth or sawdust behind the target to stop shots. **b** a mound on which an archery target is set. **4** a joint where two boards or timbers meet end to end. **5** a hinge that fits between two surfaces, as between the door and the jamb. **6** a small, open shelter for grouse shooting. **7 the butts,** a place to practise shooting in.
—*v.* **1** join end to end. **2** attach with a butt hinge. [< F *bout* end < Gmc.]

butt[3] (but) *v.* **1** push or hit with the head: *a goat butts.* **2** place (a timber, etc.) with its end against something; put (planks, etc.) end to end. **3** cut off the rough ends of (boards, logs, etc.). **4** project; run out; jut (out or into): *One wing of the house butted out as far as the roadway.* **5 butt in,** *Slang.* meddle; interfere.
—*n.* a push or hit with the head. [ME < OF *bouter* thrust < Gmc.]

butt[4] (but) *n.* **1** a large barrel for wine or beer. **2** a liquid measure equal to 126 gallons. [ME < OF *botte* < LL *butta*]

butte (būt) *n.* a steep, flat-topped hill standing alone. [< F]

butt-end·ing (but′end′ing) *n.* in hockey, the jabbing or thrusting of the handle end of the stick into an opponent's body.

but·ter (but′ər) *n.* **1** the solid, yellowish fat obtained from cream by churning. **2** something like butter: *Apple butter is made by boiling apples to a thick jam.* **3** a substance with a thick consistency at ordinary temperature, as certain vegetable oils or prepared medicines: *peanut butter.*
—*v.* **1** put butter on. **2** *Informal.* flatter. **3 butter up,** flatter. [OE *butere* < L *butyrum* < Gk. *boutyron*] —**but′ter·less,** *adj.*

but·ter·ball (but′ər bol′ or -bôl′) *n.* **1** bufflehead. **2** *Informal.* a plump person.

but·ter·cup (but′ər kup′) *n.* a plant having bright-yellow flowers shaped like cups.

but·ter·fat (but′ər fat′) *n.* the fat in milk, which can be made into butter.

but·ter·fin·gered (but′ər fing′gərd) *adj.* always letting things drop or slip through one's fingers.

but·ter·fin·gers (but′ər fing′gərz) *n. Informal.* **1** a person who drops something that he ought to hold. **2** a careless or clumsy person.

but·ter·fish (but′ər fish′) *n.* **-fish** or **-fish·es.** a small, silvery fish of the Atlantic coast, used for food.

but·ter·fly (but′ər flī′) *n.* **-flies. 1** any of various insects having slender bodies and four large, usually bright-colored, wings: *Butterflies fly mostly in the daytime.* **2** a person who suggests a butterfly by delicate beauty, bright clothes, fickleness, etc. [OE *buterflēoge*]

butterfly valve a valve consisting of a disk turning on an axis. A damper on a furnace and a throttle valve in a carburetor are examples.

butterfly weed a milkweed having orange-colored flowers.

but·ter·milk (but′ər milk′) *n.* the liquid left after butter has been separated from milk. Milk can also be changed to buttermilk artificially.

but·ter·nut (but′ər nut′) *n.* **1** an oily kind of edible walnut grown in North America. **2** the tree that bears butternuts. **3** a brown dye made from butternut husks and bark.

but·ter·scotch (but′ər skoch′) *n.* a candy made from brown sugar and butter. —*adj.* flavored with brown sugar and butter.

but·ter·wort (but′ər wėrt′) *n.* any of several small herbs of the bladderwort family, whose stemless greenish-yellow leaves secrete a sticky substance to catch insects.

but·ter·y[1] (but′ər ē) *adj.* **1** like butter. **2** containing butter; spread with butter. [< *butter*]

but·ter·y[2] (but′ər ē or but′rē) *n.* **-ter·ies.** a pantry. [ME < OF *boterie* < *botte* butt[4] < LL *butta*]

but·tocks (but′əks) *n.pl.* the rump. [OE *buttuc* end, small piece of land]

but·ton (but′ən) *n.* **1** a knob or round piece sewn or otherwise fixed to clothing and other things to fasten them, decorate them, etc. **2** a knob used as a handle or a catch to take hold of, or push, or to turn so that it holds or closes something. **3** anything that resembles or suggests a button. The knob or disk pressed to ring an electric bell is called a button. **4** a young or undeveloped mushroom. **5** a small knob on the end of a fencing foil. **6** *Slang.* especially in boxing, the centre of the chin. **7** a badge. **8 buttons,** *pl., Brit. Informal.* a bellboy or page in a hotel, etc.
—*v.* **1** fasten with buttons; close with buttons. **2** *Informal.* close (anything) tightly: *I buttoned my mouth and did not reply to the question.* **3 button up,** *Informal.* complete satisfactorily: *button up the details of a contract.* [ME < OF *boton* < *bouter* thrust. See BUTT³.] —**but′ton·less,** *adj.* —**but′ton·like′,** *adj.*

but·ton·hole (but′ən hōl′) *n. v.* **-holed, -hol·ing.** —*n.* **1** a slit or loop through which a button is passed. **2** a flower or flowers worn in a buttonhole. —*v.* **1** make buttonholes in. **2** sew with the stitch used in making buttonholes. **3** hold in conversation; force to listen.

but·ton·hook (but′ən hůk′) *n.* a hook for pulling the buttons of shoes, gloves, etc. through the buttonholes.

but·ton·wood (but′ən wůd′) *n.* **1** a tall tree having button-shaped fruit; sycamore; plane tree. **2** the wood of one of these trees.

but·tress (but′ris) *n.* **1** a support built against a wall or building to strengthen it. **2** a support or prop. **3** a projecting portion of a hill or mountain resembling the buttresses of a building.
—*v.* **1** strengthen with a buttress. **2** support; prop. [ME < OF *bouterez* (pl.) < *bouter* thrust against. See BUTT³.]

Buttresses: B, ordinary; F, flying.

bu·tyl (bū′təl) *n.* one of the three univalent radicals obtained from butane. Butyl is used in making inner tubes, insulation for electrical appliances, etc. *Formula*: C_4H_9

bu·ty·lene (bū′tə lēn′) *n.* a gaseous hydrocarbon of the ethylene series, often used in making synthetic rubber. *Formula*: C_4H_8

bu·tyr·ic acid (bū tir′ik) a colorless liquid that has an unpleasant odor and is formed by fermentation in rancid butter, cheese, etc. *Formula*: $C_4H_8O_2$ [*butyric* < L *butyrum* butter < Gk. *boutyron*]

bux·om (buk′səm) *adj.* plump and good to look at; healthy and cheerful. [ME *buhsum* < OE *būgan* bend]

buy (bī) *v.* **bought, buy·ing,** *n.* —*v.* **1** get by paying a price: *You can buy a pencil for five cents.* **2** buy things. **3** bribe: *It was charged that two members of the jury had been bought.* **4** *Informal.* accept as valid, feasible, etc.: *If you say it's true, I'll buy it.* **5 buy into,** obtain an interest or footing in by purchase: *He bought into the new aluminum company, obtaining 500 shares.* **6 buy off,** get rid of by paying money to. **7 buy out,** buy all the shares, rights, etc. of. **8 buy up,** buy all that one can of; buy.
—*n.* **1** *Informal.* something bought; a purchase. **2** *Informal.* a bargain. [OE *bycgan*]
Syn. *v.* **1 Buy, purchase** = to get something by paying a price. **Buy** is the general and informal word: *A person can buy anything in that store if he has the money.* **Purchase** is used in more formal style and suggests buying after careful planning or by business dealings or on a large scale: *The bank has purchased some property on which to construct a new building.*
☛ **Buy** is used with *from*, but, informally, also with *off*: *He bought it from a stranger he met on the street.*

buy·er (bī′ər) *n.* **1** a person who buys. **2** a person whose work is buying goods for a department store or other business.

buyer's market an economic condition that arises when more goods are offered for sale than people are immediately willing to buy. Prices tend to be low in a buyer's market.

buyers' strike a combined refusal of consumers to buy in protest against existing high prices, etc.

buzz (buz) *n.* **1** a humming sound made by flies, mosquitoes, or bees. **2** the low, confused sound heard at some distance when many people are talking quietly. **3** a whisper; rumor. **4** *Informal.* a call on the telephone. **5 a** busy movement; stir; state of activity or excitement. **b** the sound of such activity.
—*v.* **1** hum loudly. **2** sound in a low, confused way. **3** talk excitedly. **4** of places, be filled with the noise of conversation, etc. **5** move busily or fussily about. **6** utter or express by buzzing. **7** whisper; rumor. **8** *Informal.* call (a person) by telephone. **9** approach quickly and closely with an airplane or a small boat. **10 buzz about,** move about busily. **11 buzz off,** *Slang.* go away. [imitative]

buz·zard (buz′ərd) *n.* **1** any of various heavy birds of prey of the same family as the hawk. **2** a kind of vulture; turkey buzzard. [ME < OF *busart*, ult. < L *buteo* hawk]

buzz bomb an aerial projectile that can be guided to a target where it explodes; robot bomb.

buzz·er (buz′ər) *n.* **1** a thing that buzzes. **2** an electrical device that makes a buzzing sound as a signal.

buzz saw a circular saw.

B.V.M. Blessed Virgin Mary. (for L *Beata Virgo Maria*)

B.W.I. British West Indies.

bx. *pl.* **bxs.** box.

by (bī) *prep.* **1** near; beside: *The garden is by the house.* **2** along; over; through: *go by the bridge.* **3** through the act of; through the means or use of: *travel by airplane.* **4** combined with in multiplication or relative dimensions: *a room ten by twenty feet.* **5** in the measure of: *eggs by the dozen.* **6** to the extent of: *larger by half.* **7** according to: *work by rule.* **8** in relation to: *She did well by her children.* **9** taken separately as units or groups in a series: *two by two. Algebra must be mastered step by step.* **10** during: *by day.* **11** not later than: *by six o'clock.* **12** toward: *The island lies south by east from here.* **13 by oneself, a** having no company; alone. **b** single-handed; unaided. **14 by the way, a** aside from the main point: *By the way, what time is it?* **b** at the roadside: *We stopped by the way to eat.*
—*adv.* **1** at hand: *near by.* **2** past: *days gone by. A car dashed by.* **3** aside or away: *to put something by.* **4** *Informal.* at, in, or into another's house when passing: *Please come by and eat with me.* **5 by and by,** after a while. **6 by and large,** in every way or aspect; on the whole.
—*adj.* **1** situated at the side; out of the way. **2** away from the main purpose; secondary; private.
—*n.* **1** bye. **2 by the by,** incidentally. [OE *bī*]
Syn. *prep.* **3 By, through, with** are used to connect to a sentence a word naming the agent that has performed an action or the means or instrument used to perform it. **By** is used to connect the word naming the agent when it has not been named in the subject of the sentence, and sometimes to name the means: *The meat was taken by the dog. I travel by airplane.* **Through** is used to connect the word naming the means or the reason: *They ran through fear. We found out through him.* **With** is used to connect the word naming the instrument: *We cut meat with a knife.*

by- *prefix.* **1** secondary; minor; less important: *by-product* = *less important product.* **2** near by: *bystander* = *person standing near by.*

by-and-by (bī′ənd bī′) *n.* the future.

bye (bī) *n.* **1** in sports: **a** the condition of being the odd man or team not required to play one round of a contest in which players or teams are grouped in pairs: *Our team had a bye to the semifinal.* **b** the player or team not required to play a round. **2** in cricket, a run made on a missed ball. **3** in golf, the holes not played after one player has won. **4 by the bye,** incidentally. [var. of *by*, prep.]

bye-bye (bī′bī′) *interj. Informal.* good-bye.

by-e·lec·tion (bī′i lek′shən) *n.* an election held in one riding because of the death or resignation of its Member of Parliament or of the Legislative Assembly.

by·gone (bī′gon′) *adj.* past; former; departed: *The Romans lived in bygone days.* —*n.* **1** something in the past. **2** the past. **3 let bygones be bygones,** let the past be forgotten.

by-law (bī′lo′ or bī′lô′) *n.* **1** a local law; a law made by a city, company, club, etc. for the control of its own affairs: *Our city has by-laws to control parking, traffic,* *and building practices.* **2** a secondary law or rule; not one of the main rules. [ME, probably < earlier *byrlaw* < ON *býr* town + *lög* law; meaning influenced by *by-*]

by-line (bī′līn′) *n.* a line at the beginning of a newspaper or magazine article giving the name of the writer.

by-name (bī′nām′) *n.* **1** a second name; surname. **2** a nickname.

by-pass (bī′pas′) *n.* **1** a road, channel, pipe, etc. providing a secondary passage to be used instead of the main passage. **2** an express road going around a city or other congested area to take through traffic. **3** in electricity, a shunt.
—*v.* **1** provide a secondary passage for. **2** make a detour around: *by-pass a city.* **3** pass over the head of (a superior, etc.) to a higher authority. **4** set aside or ignore (regulations, etc.) in order to reach a desired objective. **5** get away from; avoid; escape: *by-pass a question.* **6** in military use, flank.

by-path (bī′path′) *n.* a side path; byway.

by-play (bī′plā′) *n.* especially on the stage, an action that is not part of the main action.

by-prod·uct (bī′prod′əkt) *n.* something produced in making or doing something else; not the main product.

byre (bīr) *n.* a cowhouse or cow shed. [OE *byre*]

by-road (bī′rōd′) *n.* a side road.

By·ron·ic (bī ron′ik) *adj.* **1** of or having to do with George Gordon, Lord Byron (1788-1824), an English poet. **2** like Byron; arrogant; cynical; unconventional: romantic. **3** of or like his poetry.

by·stand·er (bī′stan′dər) *n.* a person who stands near or looks on but does not take part.

by-street (bī′strēt′) *n.* a side street.

by·way or **by-way** (bī′wā′) *n.* a side path or road; a way that is little used.

by·word (bī′wėrd′) *n.* **1** a common saying; proverb. **2** a person or thing commonly or proverbially taken as typifying a certain characteristic, especially an unfavorable one: *His name has become a byword for meanness.* **3** an object of contempt; something scorned: *His cowardice made him a byword to all who knew him.* [OE *bīword*]

Byz·an·tine (biz′ən tēn′, bi zan′tin, or biz′ən tīn′) *adj.* **1** of or having to do with Byzantium, an ancient city on the Bosporus. **2** of or having to do with Byzantine art or architecture.
—*n.* **1** a native or inhabitant of Byzantium. **2** in architecture, a style developed in Byzantium in the 5th and 6th centuries, characterized by rounded arches, domes, and a lavish use of mosaics and murals. **3** in art, a style developed in Byzantium in the 6th century, characterized by brilliant colors, formal designs, and distorted proportions. [< L *Byzantinus*]

Byzantine Empire the eastern part of the Roman Empire after the division in A.D. 395. It ceased to exist after the fall of its capital Constantinople in 1453.

Bz. benzene.

hat, āge, cãre, fär; let, ēqual, tėrm; it, īce
hot, ōpen, ôrder; oil, out; cup, pu̇t, rüle, ūse
əbove, takən, pencəl, lemən, circəs
ch, child; ng, long; sh, ship
th, thin; ᴛʜ, then; zh, measure

C or **c** (sē) *n.* **C's** or **c's. 1** the third letter of the English alphabet. **2** any speech sound represented by this letter. **3** a person or thing designated as the third in a series. **4** a person or thing considered as belonging to the third best group: *grade C eggs; C grade in Latin.* **5** in music: **a** the first tone in the scale of C major; the third tone of A minor. **b** a symbol representing this tone. **c** a key, string, etc. that produces this tone. **d** the scale or key that has C as its keynote. **6** a known quantity, especially in equations, as in $ax + by + c = O$.

c. 1 cent, cents. **2** about; approximately. (for L *circa*) **3** in sports, catcher. **4** centre. **5** centimeter. **6** copyright. **7** cubic. **8** century. **9** in physics, capacity. **10** cathode. **11** chapter. **12** current. **13** hundredweight. **14** city.

C 1 carbon. **2** central. **3** the Roman numeral for 100. **4** in mathematics, constant.

C. 1 centigrade. **2** Cape. **3** Catholic. **4** Conservative. **5** Celtic. **6** Church. **7** Celsius.

C_{14} carbon 14.

ca. about; approximately. (for L *circa*) Also, **c.**

Ca calcium.

CA in psychology, chronological age.

C.A. 1 Central America. **2** Consular Agent. **3** Catholic Action. **4** Court of Appeal. **5** Chartered Accountant.

C/A or **c/a 1** capital account. **2** credit account. **3** current account.

CAA or **C.A.A.** Canadian Automobile Association.

Caa·ba (kä′bə) *n.* Kaaba.

C.A.A.P. Certified Advertising Agency Practitioner.

CAAT or **C.A.A.T.** College of Applied Arts and Technology.

cab (kab) *n. v.* **cab·bed, cab·bing.** —*n.* **1** an automobile that can be hired; taxi. **2** a one-horse carriage that can be hired. **3** the enclosed part of a locomotive, truck, etc. where the operator or driver stands or sits. —*v.* go by cab. [a shortened form of *cabriolet*]

CAB or **C.A.B. 1** Canadian Association of Broadcasters. **2** in the United States, Civil Aeronautics Board.

ca·bal (kə bal′) *n. v.* **-balled, -bal·ling.** —*n.* **1** a small group of people working or plotting in secret. **2** a secret scheme of such a group; plot. —*v.* form such a group; conspire. [< F < Med.L *cabbala.* See CABALA.]
—**Syn.** *n.* **1** faction, junto, conspiracy.

cab·a·la (kab′ə lə or kə bä′lə) *n.* **1** a secret religious philosophy of the Jewish rabbis, based on a mystical interpretation of the Scriptures. **2** a mystical belief; secret doctrine. [< Med.L *cabbala* < Hebrew *qabbalah* tradition]

cab·a·lis·tic (kab′ə lis′tik) *adj.* **1** of or suitable for the Jewish cabala. **2** having a mystical meaning; secret.

cab·al·le·ro (kab′ə lãr′ō or kab′əl yãr′ō; *Spanish,* kä′bä lyā′rō) *n.* **-ros.** *Spanish.* **1** a gentleman. **2** a knight. [< Sp. < LL *caballarius* horseman < L *caballus* horse]

ca·ba·ña (kə ban′ə, kə bän′yə or kə bä′nə) *n.* **1** a cabin (def. 1). **2** a bathhouse. [< Sp. < LL *capanna.* Doublet of CABIN.]

cab·a·ret (kab′ə rā′ or kab′ə rā′) *n.* **1** a restaurant where singing and dancing are provided as entertainment. **2** the entertainment provided there. [< F *cabaret* tavern]

cab·bage (kab′ij) *n.* a vegetable whose leaves are closely folded into a round head growing from a short stem. [< F *caboche* < Provençal, ult. < L *caput* head]

cab·bage·town (kab′ij toun′) *n. Cdn.* a run-down urban area; slum. [< *Cabbagetown,* a depressed area on the east side of the older part of downtown Toronto, so-called from the supposed diet of the area's English population]

cab·by (kab′ē) *n.* **-bies.** *Informal.* cabman.

ca·ber (kā′bər) *n.* a long, heavy pole or beam tossed as a trial of strength in Scottish Highland games. [< Scots Gaelic *cabar*]

cab·in (kab′ən) *n.* **1** a small, often roughly built house; hut: *a tourist cabin.* **2** a room in a ship. **3** a place for passengers in an airplane or airship. —*v.* **1** live in a cabin. **2** *Archaic.* confine; cramp. [< F *cabane* < LL *capanna.* Doublet of CABAÑA.] —**Syn.** *n.* **1** a shanty, shack. See **cottage.**

cabin boy a boy whose work is to wait on the officers and passengers on a ship.

cabin cruiser a motorboat having a cabin and equipped with facilities for living on board.

cab·i·net (kab′ə nit or kab′nit) *n.* **1** a piece of furniture having shelves or drawers to hold things, such as jewels, dishes, or letters. A kitchen cabinet is used for storing food supplies and dishes. **2** the advisers of a prime minister or premier: *The cabinet of a provincial government is called the Executive Council.* **3** the federal cabinet, an executive committee of ministers of the Crown chosen by the Prime Minister from the majority party in the House of Commons: *The Minister of Defence is a member of the cabinet.* **4** a group of advisers chosen by the head of a nation to help him with the administration of the government: *the U.S. President's Cabinet.* **5** a small private room.
—*adj.* **1** of or having to do with a political cabinet. **2** private. **3** of a kind suited for a private room or for displaying in a cabinet. [dim. of *cabin*]

cab·i·net·mak·er (kab′ə nit māk′ər or kab′nit-) *n.* a man whose work is making fine furniture and woodwork.

cab·i·net·mak·ing (kab′ə nit māk′ing or kab′nit-) *n.* the business, work, or art of a cabinetmaker.

cabinet minister the head of a department of the government of certain countries, including Canada, or of a province; a member of the cabinet.

cab·i·net·work (kab′ə nit wėrk′ or kab′nit-) *n.* **1** any beautifully made furniture or woodwork. **2** the making of such furniture and woodwork.

cabin ship a ship carrying only one class of passengers.

ca·ble (kā′bəl) *n. v.* **-bled, -bling.** —*n.* **1** a strong, thick rope, usually made of wires twisted together. **2** the rope or chain by which an anchor is raised and lowered. **3** a cable's length. **4** an insulated bundle of wires made to carry an electric current. Telegraph messages are sent under the ground or under the ocean by cable. **5** a message sent by cable; cablegram. **6** an ornament with a design like that of a cable. **7** cable television.
—*v.* **1** tie or fasten with a cable. **2** send (a message) by cable. [ME < OF < Provençal < L *capulum* halter]

cable car a car pulled by a moving cable that is operated by an engine.

ca·ble·gram (kā′bəl gram′) *n.* a message sent by cable.

cable's length a unit of measurement at sea. A cable's length is accepted as 607.56 feet in the Canadian and British navies and 720 feet in the United States navy.

cable stitch in knitting, a combination of stitches that produces a pattern resembling a twisted cable.

cable television a system for the delivery of television signals by cable direct to an individual house, apartment, etc. Also, **cable vision.**

cab·man (kab′mən) *n.* **-men** (-mən). a man who drives a cab.

ca·boo·dle (kə bü′dəl) *n. Slang.* a group of people or things: *the whole caboodle.*

ca·boose (kə büs′) *n.* **1** a small car on a freight train in which the trainmen can rest and sleep. It is usually the last car. **2** a kitchen on the deck of a ship. **3** *Cdn.* **a** a mobile bunkhouse used by lumberjacks, threshing crews, etc. **b** a small cabin built on a sleigh and equipped with benches and a stove. **c** in the North, a bunkhouse or cook-house on runners for the crew of a cat train, etc. **4** *Cdn.* in the North, a portable house. [< Du. *kabuis* wretched hut, cabin < MLG *kabūse*; cf. CAMBOOSE]

cab·o·tage (kab′ə täzh′ or kab′ə tij; *French,* kä bô täzh′) *n.* **1** navigation or trade between ports along a coast. **2** transportation or trade between points within one country. [< F *cabotage* coastal trade < *caboter* sail along a coast]

cab·o·teur (kab′ə tėr′; *French,* kä bô tœr′) *n. Cdn.* **1** a ship engaged in coastal trade, especially along the St. Lawrence River and in the Gulf of St. Lawrence. **2** a captain or a member of the crew of such a ship. [< Cdn.F < F. See CABOTAGE.]

cab·ri·ole (kab′rē ōl′) *n.* in furniture, a curved tapering leg with a decorated foot, characteristic of Queen Anne and Chippendale furniture. The foot was usually carved as a claw grasping a ball. —*adj.* **1** in this style. **2** having such legs. [< F *cabriole*, var. of *capriole* a leap, because it resembled the foreleg of an animal making a capriole]

cab·ri·o·let (kab′rē ə lā′) *n.* **1** an automobile resembling a coupé but having a folding top. **2** a light one-horse carriage with one or two seats, two wheels, and, often, a folding top. [< F *cabriolet* < *cabrioler* caper < Ital. < L *caper* goat; from bouncing motion]

ca·ca·o (kə kā′ō or kə kä′ō) *n.* **-ca·os. 1** the seeds from which cocoa and chocolate are made. They are washed or fermented to remove a sticky coating and then dried. **2** the tropical American tree that they grow on. [< Sp. < Mexican *caca-uatl*]

cach·a·lot (kash′ə lot′ or kash′ə lō′) *n.* a large square-headed whale; sperm whale. [< F < Pg. *cachalote*]

cache (kash) *n. v.* **cached, cach·ing.** —*n.* **1** a hiding place. **2** *Cdn.* a place for storing supplies, furs, equipment, etc. away from foraging animals and the weather. **3** the things hidden or stored in a cache. **4** *Cdn.* a supply of goods stockpiled for future use. —*v.* **1** hide or conceal. **2** *Cdn.* deposit in a cache. [< F *cache* < *cacher* conceal]

ca·chet (ka shā′ or kash′ā) *n.* **1** a private seal or stamp: *The letter was sealed with the king's cachet.* **2** a distinguishing mark of quality or genuineness. **3** a capsule for enclosing a medicine with an unpleasant taste. **4** a slogan, design, etc. stamped or printed on mail. [< F *cachet* < *cacher* hide]

cach·in·nate (kak′ə nāt′) *v.* **-nat·ed, -nat·ing.** laugh loudly. [< L *cachinnare*]

cach·in·na·tion (kak′ə nā′shən) *n.* loud laughter.

ca·chou (kə shü′ or ka shü′) *n.* a pill or lozenge, usually silvered, composed of cashew nut and other ingredients and used to perfume the breath, thus cloaking the odor of tobacco smoke, alcohol, etc. Also **cashew.** [< F *cachou*]

ca·cique (kə sēk′) *n.* in the West Indies, Mexico, etc., a native chief. [< Sp. < Haitian]

cack·le (kak′əl) *v.* **-led, -ling,** *n.* —*v.* **1** of a hen, make a shrill, intermittent cry after laying an egg. **2** laugh shrilly, harshly, and intermittently: *The old man cackled after each joke.* **3** chatter.
—*n.* **1** the shrill, intermittent cry that a hen makes after laying an egg. **2** shrill, harsh, intermittent laughter. **3** noisy chatter; silly talk. [ME *cakelen*; imitative]

ca·coph·o·nous (kə kof′ə nəs) *adj.* harsh and clashing; dissonant; discordant. —**ca·coph′o·nous·ly,** *adv.*

ca·coph·o·ny (kə kof′ə nē) *n.* **-nies.** a harsh, clashing sound; dissonance; discord. [< NL *cacophonia* < Gk. *kakophōnia* < *kakos* bad + *phōnē* sound]

cac·tus (kak′təs) *n.* **-tus·es** or **-ti** (-tī or -tē). a plant whose thick, fleshy stems have spines or scales but usually have no leaves. Cactuses are found in hot, dry regions and often have brightly colored flowers. [< L < Gk. *kaktos*]

cad (kad) *n.* a person who does not act like a gentleman; an ill-bred person. [< *caddie*]

ca·das·tral (kə das′trəl) *adj.* of or having to do with a cadastre; according to a cadastre: *cadastral survey.*

ca·das·tre or **ca·das·ter** (kə das′tər) *n.* a public register of the ownership, value, and extent of land as a basis of taxation. [< LL *capitastrum* register of poll tax < L *caput, -itis* head]

ca·dav·er (kə dav′ər) *n.* a dead body; corpse. [< L]

ca·dav·er·ous (kə dav′ər əs) *adj.* **1** of or like a cadaver. **2** pale and ghastly. **3** thin and worn. —**ca·dav′er·ous·ly,** *adv.* —**ca·dav′er·ous·ness,** *n.*

cad·die or **cad·dy** (kad′ē) *n. v.* **-died, -dy·ing.** —*n.* in golf, a person who helps a player by carrying clubs, finding the ball, etc. —*v.* help a golf player in this way. [< F *cadet* younger brother. See CADET.]

cad·dis fly (kad′is) an insect resembling a moth, whose larva lives under water and forms itself a case from sand, bits of leaves, etc. [origin uncertain]

cad·dish (kad′ish) *adj.* like a cad; ungentlemanly. —**cad′dish·ly,** *adv.* —**cad′dish·ness,** *n.*

caddis worm the larva of a caddis fly, sometimes used as bait in fishing.

cad·dy[1] (kad′ē) *n.* **-dies.** a small box, can, or chest, often used to hold tea. [< Malay *kati* a small weight]

hat, āge, cãre, fär; let, ēqual, tėrm; it, īce
hot, ōpen, ôrder; oil, out; cup, pu̇t, rüle, ūse
əbove, takən, pencəl, lemən, circəs
ch, child; ng, long; sh, ship
th, thin; ᴛʜ, then; zh, measure

cad·dy[2] (kad′ē) *n.* **-dies,** *v.* **-died, -dy·ing.** caddie.

ca·dence (kā′dəns) *n.* **1** rhythm. **2** the measure or beat of any rhythmical movement. **3** a fall of the voice. **4** a rising and falling sound; modulation. **5** in music, a series of chords, a trill, etc. that brings part of a composition to an end. [< F < Ital. *cadenza* < L *cadentia.* Doublet of CADENZA and CHANCE.]

ca·den·za (kə den′zə) *n.* in music, an elaborate flourish or showy passage for an unaccompanied voice or solo instrument in an aria, concerto, etc. [< Ital. < L *cadentia* < *cadere* fall. Doublet of CADENCE and CHANCE.]

ca·det (kə det′) *n.* **1** a young man who is training to be an officer in one of the armed services: *The cadets at the Royal Military College wear smart scarlet tunics.* **2** *Archaic.* a younger son or brother. [< F < Gascon *capdel* < L *capitellum,* dim. of *caput* head]

ca·det·ship (kə det′ship) *n.* the rank or position of a cadet.

cadge (kaj) *v.* **cadged, cadg·ing. 1** *Dialect.* peddle. **2** *Informal.* beg. [origin uncertain] —**cadg′er,** *n.*

ca·di (kä′dē or kā′dē) *n.* **-dis.** a minor Moslem judge, usually of a town or village. [< Arabic *qadi* judge]

Cad·me·an (kad′mē ən or kad mē′ən) *adj.* having to do with Cadmus: *The Cadmean alphabet was the earliest form of writing used by the ancient Greeks.*

cad·mi·um (kad′mē əm) *n.* a bluish-white, ductile metallic chemical element, resembling tin, used in making certain alloys. *Symbol:* Cd; *at.no.* 48; *at.wt.* 112.40. [< NL < L *cadmia* zinc ore < Gk. *kadmeia*]

Cad·mus (kad′məs) *n.* in Greek legend, a Phoenician prince who killed a dragon and sowed its teeth, from which armed men sprang up and fought until only five were left. Cadmus and these men founded the Greek city of Thebes. Cadmus is also supposed to have introduced alphabetic writing to Greece from Phoenician sources.

ca·dre (kä′dər; *in military use,* kad′rē) *n.* **1** a framework. **2** the staff of officers and enlisted men of a military unit necessary to establish and train a new unit. **3** a similar group of people working closely together or as the nucleus of an organization. [< F < Ital. < L *quadrum* square]

ca·du·ce·us (kə dū′sē əs or kə dü′sē əs) *n.* **-ce·i** (-sē ī′ or -sē ē′). a staff with two snakes twined around it and a pair of wings on top. Mercury, or Hermes, the messenger of the gods, is usually shown carrying a caduceus. The caduceus is often used as an emblem of the medical profession. [< L < dial. Gk. *karykeion* herald's staff]

A caduceus

cae·cum (sē′kəm) *n.* **-ca** (-kə). in anatomy and zoology, the first part of the large intestine. It is closed at one end. [< L *caecum* blind (thing)]

Cae·sar (sē′zər) *n.* **1** a title of the Roman emperors from Augustus to Hadrian, and later of the heir to the throne. **2** an emperor. **3** a dictator; tyrant. [< Gaius Julius *Caesar* (100?-44 B.C.), a Roman general, statesman, and historian, conqueror of Gaul]

Cae·sar·e·an (si zãr′ē ən) *adj.* **1** of Julius Caesar. **2** of the Caesars. **3** by Caesarean operation: *a Caesarean birth.* —*n.* a Caesarean operation. Also (for *n.* and *adj.,* def. 3) **Cesarean, Cesarian.**

Caesarean operation or **section** an operation by which a baby is removed from the uterus by cutting through the abdominal wall. [from the belief that Julius Caesar was born in this way]

Cae·sar·i·an (si zãr′ē ən) *adj.* Caesarean.

cae·sar·ism (sē′zər iz′ əm) *n.* imperialism; autocracy.

cae·si·um (sē′zē əm) *n.* cesium.

cae·su·ra (si zūr′ə or si zhür′ə) *n.* **-sur·as.** a pause in a line of verse, generally agreeing with a pause required by the sense. The caesura is the chief pause if there is more than one. In Greek and Latin poetry the caesura falls within a foot, not far from the middle of a line. Whenever it occurs in English poetry, it usually comes near the middle of a line, either within or after a metrical foot. *Example*: "To err is human, | to forgive, divine." Also, **cesura.** [< L *caesura* cutting < *caedere* cut]

CAF Canadian Armed Forces.

C.A.F. or **c.a.f.** **1** cost and freight. **2** cost, assurance, and freight.

ca·fé (ka fā′ or kə fā′) *n.* **1** a restaurant. **2** a coffee shop. **3** *French.* coffee. [< F]

ca·fé au lait (kä fā′ ō lā′ or kaf′ē-; *French,* kä fā ō le′) *French.* **1** coffee with milk or cream. **2** brownish yellow.

ca·fé noir (kä fā nwär′) *French.* coffee without milk or cream; black coffee.

caf·e·te·ri·a (kaf′ə tēr′ē ə) *n.* a restaurant where customers serve themselves. [< Mexican Sp. *cafeteria* coffee shop]

caf·fè es·pres·so (kaf fā′ es pres′sō) *Italian.* espresso coffee.

caf·feine or **caf·fein** (kaf′ēn or kaf′ē in) *n.* a stimulating drug found in coffee and tea. *Formula*: $C_8H_{10}N_4O_2$ [< F *caféine* < *café* coffee]

caf·tan (kaf′tən or käf tän′) *n.* in Turkey, Egypt, etc., a long tunic with a girdle, worn under the coat. Also, **kaftan.** [< Turkish *qaftan*]

cage (kāj) *n. v.* **caged, cag·ing.** —*n.* **1** a frame or box closed in with wires, bars, etc. Birds and wild animals are kept in cages. **2** anything shaped or used like a cage: *The bank teller worked in a cage.* **3** especially in a mine shaft, the car or closed platform of an elevator. **4** a prison. **5** in ice hockey, etc., the network and frame forming the goal. **6** a steel framework for supporting guns. **7** in baseball: **a** a place enclosed by a net, for batting practice. **b** a catcher's mask.
—*v.* put or keep in a cage. [ME < OF < L *cavea* cell < *cavus* hollow]

cage·ling (kāj′ling) *n.* a bird kept in a cage.

cage·y (kāj′ē) *adj.* **cag·i·er, cag·i·est.** *Informal.* shrewd; sharp; cautious. —**cag′i·ly,** *adv.* —**cag′i·ness,** *n.*

CAHA or **C.A.H.A.** Canadian Amateur Hockey Association.

ca·hoot (kə hüt′) *n. Slang.* **1 in cahoots** or **cahoot,** in partnership. **2 go cahoots,** go into partnership. [origin uncertain]

ca·hot (kə hō′) *n. Cdn.* **1** a ridge of snow on a road: *The cahots made the ride a very bumpy one.* **2** a ridge or bump in an unpaved road. [< F]

cai·man (kā′mən) *n.* **-mans.** cayman.

Cain (kān) *n.* **1** in the Bible, the oldest son of Adam and Eve and the murderer of his brother Abel. Genesis 4: 1-17. **2** any murderer. **3 raise Cain,** *Slang.* make a great disturbance.

ca·ïque (kä ēk′) *n.* **1** a long, narrow Turkish rowboat, much used on the Bosporus. **2** a Mediterranean sailing ship. [< F < Ital. *caicco* < Turkish *qāyik*]

cairn[1] (kărn) *n.* a pile of stones heaped up as a memorial, tomb, or landmark. [< Scots Gaelic *carn* heap of stones]

cairn[2] (kărn) *n.* cairn terrier.

cairn·gorm (kărn′gôrm′) *n.* **1** a yellow or smoky-brown variety of quartz. **2** a gem made of this stone. Cairngorms are often used for brooches and other ornaments, especially by the Scots. [< *Cairngorm,* a peak in the Grampians, Scotland]

cairn terrier **1** a breed of small, long-haired, working terrier, having a soft undercoat and a hard, wiry topcoat. **2** a dog of this breed.

cais·son (kā′sən or kā′son) *n.* **1** a box for ammunition. **2** a wagon to carry ammunition. **3** a watertight box or chamber in which men can work under water. See picture on the opposite page. **4** a watertight float used in raising sunken ships. [< F *caisson* < *caisse* chest < L *capsa* box]

caisson disease an illness caused by moving too suddenly from high air pressure to ordinary air pressure; the bends.

cai·tiff (kā′tif) *n. Archaic.* a mean, contemptible person; coward. —*adj.* vile; cowardly; contemptible. [ME < OF *caitif* < L *captivus* captive. Doublet of CAPTIVE.]

ca·jole (kə jōl′) *v.* **-joled, -jol·ing.** persuade by pleasant words, flattery, or false promises; coax. [< F *cajoler*] —**ca·jol′er,** *n.* —**ca·jol′ing·ly,** *adv.* —**Syn.** beguile, wheedle.

ca·jol·er·y (kə jōl′ər ē or kə jōl′rē) *n.* **-er·ies.** persuasion by smooth, deceitful words; flattery; coaxing.

cake (kāk) *n. v.* **caked, cak·ing.** —*n.* **1** a baked mixture of flour, sugar, eggs, flavoring, and other things: *a sponge cake, a fruit cake.* **2** a flat, thin mass of dough baked or fried. **3** any small, flat mass of food fried on both sides: *a fish cake.* **4** a shaped mass: *a cake of soap, a cake of ice.* **5 take the cake,** *Slang.* **a** win first prize. **b** excel. **c** used ironically, be the last straw.
—*v.* form into a solid mass; harden: *Mud cakes as it dries.* [ME, probably < ON *kaka*]

cake flour a fine wheat flour having a low gluten content, used for baking cakes, cookies, etc.

cakes and ale good things; the pleasures of life.

cake·walk (kāk′wok′ or -wôk′) *n.* a march or dance done to music. Negroes used to compete to see who could do the best or most original steps. The winner got a cake. —*v.* do a cakewalk. —**cake′walk′er,** *n.*

cal. **1** calendar. **2** calibre. **3** calorie; calories.

Cal. California.

cal·a·bash (kal′ə bash′) *n.* **1** a gourd whose dried shell is used to make bottles, bowls, drums, rattles, etc. **2** the tropical plant or tree that it grows on. **3** a bottle, bowl, etc. made from such a dried shell. [< F *calebasse* < Sp. *calabaza,* probably < Persian *kharbuz* melon]

cal·a·boose (kal′ə büs′ or kal′ə büs′) *n. Informal.* a jail or prison. [< Sp. *calabozo* dungeon]

ca·la·di·um (kə lā′dē əm) *n.* a tropical plant having large leaves. [< Malay *kelady*]

cal·a·man·co (kal′ə mang′kō) *n.* a glossy woollen cloth, checked or brocaded in the warp so that the pattern shows on one side only. [origin uncertain]

cal·a·mine (kal′ə mīn′ or kal′ə min) *n.* **1** a pink powder made of zinc oxide and ferric oxide. **2** a kind of zinc ore; hydrous zinc silicate. *Formula*: $(ZnOH)_2SiO_3$ [< F < Med.L *calamina* < L *cadmia.* See CADMIUM.]

ca·lam·i·tous (kə lam′ə təs) *adj.* causing a calamity; accompanied by a calamity; disastrous. —**ca·lam′i·tous·ly,** *adv.* —**ca·lam′i·tous·ness,** *n.* —**Syn.** dire, grievous.

ca·lam·i·ty (kə lam′ə tē) *n.* **-ties.** **1** a great misfortune, such as a flood, a fire, or loss of one's sight or hearing. **2** serious trouble; misery: *Calamity may come to anyone.* [< F *calamité* < L *calamitas*] —**Syn. 1** catastrophe. See **disaster.**

cal·a·mus (kal′ə məs) *n.* **-mi** (-mī′ or -mē′). **1** a plant having long, sword-shaped leaves; sweet flag. **2** its fragrant root. **3** in ancient times, a reed pen used in the Orient. [< L < Gk. *kalamos* reed]

ca·lash (kə lash′) *n.* **1** formerly, calèche. **2** a folding top or hood. **3** a woman's silk hood or bonnet, worn in the 18th and 19th centuries. [< F *calèche*]

cal·car·e·ous (kal kăr′ē əs) *adj.* **1** of or containing lime or limestone. **2** of or containing calcium. [< L < *calx* lime]

cal·ces (kal′sēz) *n.* a pl. of **calx.**

cal·cif·er·ous (kal sif′ər əs) *adj.* containing calcite. [< L *calx, calcis* lime + E *-ferous* containing (< L *ferre* bear)]

cal·ci·fi·ca·tion (kal′sə fə kā′shən) *n.* **1** the process of calcifying. **2** a calcified part. **3** the accumulation of calcium in certain soils.

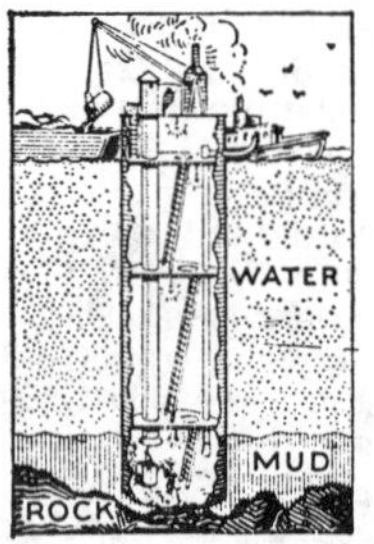

A caisson (def. 3). The weight of the masonry on the bottom of the caisson forces it into the sand and mud at the bottom of the water. Air under pressure is then forced into the caisson, driving out the water and permitting workmen to enter through air locks.

hat, āge, cãre, fär; let, ēqual, tėrm; it, īce
hot, ōpen, ôrder; oil, out; cup, pu̇t, rüle, ūse
əbove, takən, pencəl, lemən, circəs
ch, child; ng, long; sh, ship
th, thin; ᴛʜ, then; zh, measure

cal·ci·fy (kal′sə fī′) *v.* **-fied, -fy·ing.** become hard by the deposit of lime. An injured cartilage sometimes calcifies.

cal·ci·mine (kal′sə mīn′ or kal′sə min) *n. v.* **-mined, -min·ing.** —*n.* a white or colored liquid consisting of a mixture of water, coloring matter, glue, etc., used on ceilings and walls. —*v.* cover with calcimine. Also, **kalsomine.**

cal·ci·na·tion (kal′sə nā′shən) *n.* **1** the act or operation of calcining. **2** anything formed by calcining.

cal·ci·na·tor (kal′sə nā′tər) *n.* a furnace or incinerator that reduces radio-active waste to ashes, so that it can be transported and dumped with greater care and safety.

cal·cine (kal′sīn or kal′sin) *v.* **-cined, -cin·ing. 1** change to lime by heating. **2** burn to ashes or powder: *calcined bones.* **3** oxidize. [ME < OF *calciner* < L *calx* lime]

cal·cite (kal′sīt) *n.* a mineral composed of calcium carbonate. It occurs as limestone, chalk, marble, etc. *Formula*: $CaCO_3$

cal·ci·um (kal′sē əm) *n.* a soft, silvery-white, metallic, chemical element. It is a part of limestone, chalk, milk, bones, etc. *Symbol*: Ca; *at.no.* 20; *at.wt.* 40.08. [< L *calx, calcis* lime]

calcium carbide a heavy, gray substance that reacts with water to form acetylene gas. *Formula*: CaC_2

calcium carbonate a mineral occurring in rocks as marble and limestone, in animals as bones, shells, teeth, etc. and to some extent in plants; calcite. *Formula*: $CaCO_3$

calcium chloride a compound of calcium and chlorine, used in making ice and chlorine. *Formula*: $CaCl_2$

calcium hydroxide slaked lime. *Formula*: $Ca(OH)_2$

calcium light a strong, white light produced by making lime incandescent with a very hot flame; limelight.

calcium oxide quicklime. *Formula*: CaO.

calcium phosphate a compound of calcium and phosphoric acid, used in medicine, in making enamels, etc. It is found in bones and as rock. *Formula*: $Ca_3(PO_4)_2$

cal·cu·la·ble (kal′kyu̇ lə bəl) *adj.* **1** that can be calculated. **2** reliable; dependable. —**cal′cu·la·bly,** *adv.*

cal·cu·late (kal′kyu̇ lāt′) *v.* **-lat·ed, -lat·ing. 1** find out by adding, subtracting, multiplying, or dividing; figure: *calculate the cost of furnishing a house.* **2** find out beforehand by any process of reasoning; estimate: *Calculate the day of the week on which Christmas will fall.* **3** rely; depend; count: *You can calculate on earning $55 a week if you take the job.* **4** *Informal.* plan; intend: *That remark was calculated to hurt my feelings.* **5** *Informal.* think; believe; suppose. [< L *calculare* < *calculus* pebble used in counting, dim. of *calx* stone]

cal·cu·lat·ing (kal′kyu̇ lāt′ing) *adj.* **1** that calculates: *calculating machines.* **2** shrewd; careful. **3** scheming; selfish. —**cal′cu·lat′ing·ly,** *adv.* —**Syn. 2** crafty, astute.

cal·cu·la·tion (kal′kyu̇ lā′shən) *n.* **1** the act of calculating. **2** a result found by calculating. **3** careful thinking; deliberate planning. —**Syn. 3** forethought, caution.

cal·cu·la·tive (kal′kyu̇ lə tiv or kal′kyu̇ lā′tiv) *adj.* **1** having to do with calculation. **2** tending to be calculating.

cal·cu·la·tor (kal′kyu̇ lā′tər) *n.* a person or machine that calculates.

cal·cu·lus (kal′kyu̇ ləs) *n.* **-lus·es** or **-li** (-lī′ or -lē′). **1** in higher mathematics, a method of calculation. **2** in symbolic logic, a method of argument using algebraic symbols and operations. **3** a stone or hard mass of mineral salts that has formed in the body because of a diseased condition. Gallstones are calculuses. [< L *calculus.* See CALCULATE.]

cal·dron (kol′drən or kôl′drən) *n.* cauldron.

ca·lèche (kə lesh′) *n. Cdn.* a light, two-wheeled, one-horse carriage for two passengers, having a seat in front for the driver and, usually, a folding top. Also, **calash.** [< F]

A calèche

☛ The alternative form *calash* was once more common than it is today. Since the vehicle is now little used except as a conveyance for sightseers in Quebec City and Montreal, *calèche*, the French form of the word, is generally used.

Cal·e·do·ni·a (kal′ə dō′nē ə) *n. Poetic.* Scotland. —**Cal′e·do′ni·an,** *adj. n.*

cal·en·dar (kal′ən dər) *n.* **1** a table showing the months and weeks of the year and the day of the week on which each day of the month comes. **2** a system by which the beginning, length, and divisions of the year are fixed. **3** list; record; register: *The judge proceeded to hear the next case on the calendar.* **4** a volume or booklet issued by a college or university listing regulations, courses to be given, etc.
—*v.* enter in a calendar or list; register. [ME < AF *calender* < L *calendarium* account book < *calendae* calends (day bills were due)]

calendar day the 24 hours from one midnight to the next midnight.

calendar month one of the 12 parts into which a year is divided; month.

calendar year a period of 365 days (or in leap year, 366 days) that begins on January 1 and ends on December 31.

cal·en·der (kal′ən dər) *n.* a machine in which cloth, paper, etc. is smoothed and glazed by pressing between rollers. —*v.* make smooth and glossy by pressing in a calender. [< F *calandre* < L < Gk. *kylindros* cylinder]

cal·ends (kal′endz or kal′əndz) *n.pl.* in the ancient Roman calendar, the first day of the month. Also, **kalends.** [ME < L *calendae*]

ca·len·du·la (kə len′ju̇ lə) *n.* a kind of marigold having yellow or orange flowers. [< NL *calendula*, dim. of *calendae* the calends]

cal·en·ture (kal′ən chər) *n.* a tropical fever accompanied by delirium. [< F < Sp. *calentura* < L *calere* be hot]

calf[1] (kaf) *n.* **calves. 1** a young cow or bull. **2** a young elephant, whale, seal, etc. **3** leather made from the skin of a calf. **4** *Informal.* a clumsy, silly boy or young man. **5** a small mass of ice that has become detached from a glacier, iceberg, etc. **6 kill the fatted calf,** prepare a feast to celebrate something or to welcome someone. [OE]

calf[2] (kaf) *n.* **calves.** the thick, fleshy part of the back of the human leg below the knee. See **shin** for diagram. [< ON *kálfi*]

calf love puppy love.

calf·skin (kaf′skin′) *n.* **1** the skin of a calf. **2** leather made from it.

Cal·i·ban (kal′ə ban′) *n.* **1** in Shakespeare's play *The Tempest*, a beastlike slave. **2** any bestial or degraded man.

cal·i·ber (kal′ə bər) *n.* calibre.

cal·i·brate (kal′ə brāt′) *v.* **-brat·ed, -brat·ing. 1** determine, check, or adjust the scale of (a thermometer, gauge, or other measuring instrument). This is usually done by comparison with a standard instrument. **2** find the calibre of. —**cal′i·bra′tor,** *n.*

cal·i·bra·tion (kal′ə brā′shən) *n.* **1** a calibrating. **2** a being calibrated.

cal·i·bre or **cal·i·ber** (kal′ə bər) *n.* **1** diameter, especially inside diameter. A .45 calibre revolver has a barrel with an inside diameter of 45/100 of an inch. **2** ability; quality: *The president of a railway or a big factory should be a man of high calibre.* [< F *calibre* < Arabic *qalib* mould]

cal·i·co (kal′ə kō′) *n.* **-coes** or **-cos,** *adj.* —*n.* a cotton cloth that usually has colored patterns printed on one side. —*adj.* **1** made of calico. **2** spotted in colors. [< *Calicut*, India]

cal·i·co·back (kal′ə kō bak′) *n.* a red-and-black bug that feeds on cabbages and other garden plants.

calico salmon the chum salmon.

ca·lif (kā′lif or kal′if) *n.* caliph.

Calif. California.

cal·if·ate (kal′ə fāt′ or kā′lə fāt′) *n.* caliphate.

Cal·i·for·nia poppy (kal′ə fôrn′yə or kal′ə fôr′nē ə) **1** a small poppy having finely divided leaves and orange, yellow, or cream-colored flowers. **2** its flower.

cal·i·for·ni·um (kal′ə fôr′nē əm) *n.* a highly radio-active chemical element, produced artificially in 1950 by nuclear physicists at the University of California. *Symbol*: Cf; *at.no.* 98; *at.wt.* 251. [< *California*]

cal·i·pers (kal′ə pərz) *n.* callipers. [var. of *caliber*]

ca·liph (kā′lif or kal′if) *n.* the head of a Moslem state. Also, **calif, khalif.** [< OF *calife* < Med.L < Arabic *khalifah* successor, vicar]

cal·iph·ate (kal′ə fāt′ or kā′l ə fāt′) *n.* the rank, reign, government, or territory of a caliph. Also, **califate.**

cal·is·then·ic (kal′is then′ik) *adj.* callisthenic.

cal·is·then·ics (kal′is then′iks) *n.* callisthenics.

calk[1] (kok or kôk) *v.* caulk.

calk[2] (kok or kôk) *n.* **1** a projecting piece on a horseshoe that catches in the ground or ice and prevents slipping. **2** a sharp, projecting piece of metal on the bottom of a shoe to prevent slipping. **3** a calked shoe or boot. —*v.* put calks on: *Loggers use calked boots.* [< L *calx* heel or *calcar* spur]

calk·er (kok ər′ or kôk′ər) *n.* caulker.

call (kol or kôl) *v.* **1** speak loudly; cry; shout: *He called from downstairs.* **2** of a bird or animal, utter its characteristic sound. **3** give a signal (*to*): *The bugle called the men to assemble.* **4** rouse; waken: *Call me at seven o'clock.* **5** invite; command; summon: *Obey when duty calls. He called on us to help him.* **6** ask to come; cause to come: *Call back the postman. Call off your dog. The assembly was called to order. His case will be called in court tomorrow.* **7** get; bring: *call forth a reply, call out the best in a person.* **8** give a name to; term: *They called the baby John.* **9** consider; estimate: *All called the party a success.* **10** make a short visit or stop: *They called on us last night. We must call on our new neighbor.* **11** read over aloud: *The teacher called the roll of the class.* **12** end; stop: *The ball game was called on account of rain.* **13** ring up on the telephone; telephone: *Call me tomorrow morning.* **14** demand payment of: *The bank called my loan.* **15** demand for payment: *The company will call its bonds on April first.* **16** in poker, demand a show of hands.
call back, a ask (a person) to return; recall. **b** take back; retract. **c** telephone to someone who has called earlier.
call down, *Informal.* scold.
call for, a go and get; stop and get. **b** need; require.
call in, a summon for advice or consultation: *call in a lawyer, doctor, etc.* **b** withdraw from free action, circulation, or publicity: *call in a book.* **c** collect as debts: *call in a mortgage.*
call off, a order back; order away. **b** cancel.
call on, a visit. **b** appeal to.
call out, a make utterance in a loud voice; shout. **b** summon into service. **c** in the armed services, commission an officer temporarily for some special assignment or duty. **d** elicit; bring into play; evoke.
call up, a bring to mind; bring back. **b** telephone. **c** summon to the service of the country.
—*n.* **1** a shout; a cry. **2** the characteristic sound of a bird or other animal. **3** a signal given by sound: *Army calls are played on the bugle.* **4** an invitation; request; command; summons. **5** a claim or demand: *A busy person has many calls on his time.* **6** a need, occasion: *You have no call to meddle in other people's business.* **7** a short visit or stop. **8** a demand for payment. **9** a notice requiring actors and stagehands to attend a rehearsal. **10** the act of calling. **11** a calling by telephone: *I want to make a call to Montreal.* **12** in poker, the demand that all hands still active be shown after their players have matched the current bet. **13** in square dancing, an instruction that is chanted or shouted. **14** a calling, vocation. **15 on call, a** subject to payment on demand. **b** ready. **16 within call,** near enough to hear a call. [OE **callian*, dial. var. of *ceallian*]
Syn. *v.* **1** yell, shriek, scream. **5 Call, summon, invite** = ask or order someone to come. **Call** is the general and informal word: *The principal called the student leaders together for a talk.* **Summon** = call with authority, and is used especially of a formal calling up to duty or to some formal meeting: *The principal summoned the student leaders to his office.* **Invite** = ask politely, and suggests giving a person a chance to do something he would like to do: *The principal invited the student leaders to come in and talk things over.*

cal·la (kal′ə) *n.* **1** a plant having a large, petal-like, white leaf around a thick spike of yellow florets. **2** a marsh plant having heart-shaped leaves. [< NL]

calla lily 1 a calla (def. 1). **2** its blossom, formed of a white leaf around a yellow spike.

call·back (kol′bak′ or kôl′-) *n. Informal.* **1** a recalling of workers who were previously laid off. **2** an additional visit to a client or customer: *The salesman made no new calls, but spent the whole day on callbacks.*

call·boy (kol′boi′ or kôl′-) *n.* **1** a bellboy in a hotel, ship, etc. **2** a boy who calls actors from their dressing rooms when they are due to appear on the stage.

call·er (kol′ər or kôl′ər) *n.* **1** a person who makes a short visit. **2** a person who calls. **3** a person who calls out dance steps, etc. in square dancing.

call girl a prostitute with whom appointments may be made by telephone.

cal·lig·ra·pher (kə lig′rə fər) *n.* **1** a person having good handwriting, especially one practising the art of elegant penmanship. **2** a professional transcriber of manuscripts; penman.

cal·li·graph·ic (kal′ə graf′ik) *adj.* having to do with calligraphy.

cal·lig·ra·phy (kə lig′rə fē) *n.* **1** handwriting. **2** beautiful handwriting. [< Gk. *kalligraphia* < *kallos* beauty + *graphein* write]

call·ing (kol′ing or kôl′ing) *n.* **1** a business; occupation; profession; trade. **2** an invitation; command; summons. **3** a spiritual or divine summons to a special service or office; call.

calling card a small card with a person's name on it. It is used when visiting someone, in acknowledging gifts, etc.

cal·li·o·pe (kə lī′ə pē′ or kal′ē ōp′) *n.* a musical instrument having a series of steam whistles played by pushing keys. [< L < Gk. *Kalliopē* beautiful-voiced < *kallos* beauty + *ops* voice]

Cal·li·o·pe (kə lī′ ə pē′) *n.* in Greek mythology, the Muse of eloquence and heroic poetry.

cal·li·op·sis (kal′ē op′sis) *n.* coreopsis.

cal·li·per or **cal·i·per** (kal′ə pər) *n.* Usually, **callipers,** *pl.* an instrument used to measure the diameter or thickness of something.

Callipers for measuring inside and outside diameters

cal·lis·then·ic or **cal·is·then·ic** (kal′is then′ik) *adj.* of callisthenics; developing a strong and graceful body.

cal·lis·then·ics or **cal·is·then·ics** (kal′is then′iks) *n.* **1** (*sing. in use*) the practice or art of callisthenic exercises. **2** (*pl. in use*) exercises to develop a strong and graceful body. [< Gk. *kallos* beauty + *sthenos* strength]

call loan a loan that must be paid back on demand.

call money a sum of money borrowed that must be paid back on demand.

cal·los·i·ty (kə los′ə tē) *n.* **-ties. 1** a callus (def. 1). **2** lack of feeling; hardness of heart.

cal·lous (kal′əs) *adj.* **1** hard; hardened. Parts of the skin that are subjected to friction often become callous. **2** unfeeling; insensitive: *Only a callous person can see suffering without trying to relieve it.* [< L *callosus* < *callus* hard skin] **—cal′lous·ly,** *adv.* **—cal′lous·ness,** *n.* **—Syn. 2** insensible.

call-out (kol′out′ or kôl′-) *n.* in the armed services, an officer temporarily commissioned for a special assignment or duty.

cal·low (kal′ō) *adj.* **1** young and inexperienced. **2** not fully developed. **3** of birds, without feathers sufficiently developed for flight. [OE *calu* bald] **—cal′low·ness,** *n.* **—Syn. 1** green. **2** immature.

call-up (kol′up′ or kôl′-) *n.* a summoning to training or duty, especially military training or duty.

cal·lus (kal′əs) *n.* **-lus·es. 1** a hard, thickened place on the skin. **2** a new growth that unites the ends of a broken bone. **3** a substance that grows over the wounds of plants. [< L. Related to CALLOUS.]

calm (kom or käm) *adj.* **1** not stormy or windy; quiet; still; not moving: *a calm sea.* **2** peaceful; not excited: *Although she was frightened, she answered with a calm voice.* **3** in meteorology, a condition in which the wind has a velocity of less than one mile per hour (on the Beaufort scale, force 0).
—*n.* **1** the absence of motion or wind; quietness; stillness. **2** the absence of excitement; peacefulness.
—*v.* **1** become calm: *The crying baby soon calmed down.* **2** make calm: *She soon calmed the baby.* [ME < OF *calme* < Ital. < VL < Gk. *kauma* heat of the day; hence, time for rest, stillness] —**calm′ly,** *adv.* —**calm′ness,** *n.*
Syn. *adj.* **1** motionless, smooth, placid. **2 Calm, composed, collected** = not disturbed or excited. **Calm** = being or seeming to be completely undisturbed, showing no sign of being confused or excited: *Mother's calm behavior quieted the frightened boy.* **Composed** = calm as the result of having or having got command over one's thoughts and feelings and, sometimes, an inner peace: *She looked composed at the funeral.* **Collected** emphasizes having control over one's actions, thoughts, and feelings, especially at times of danger or disturbance: *He looked collected as he led the rescuers.*

cal·o·mel (kal′ə mel′) *n.* mercurous chloride, a white, tasteless, crystalline powder, used in medicine as a cathartic. *Formula*: Hg_2Cl_2 [< Gk. *kalos* beautiful + *melas* black]

ca·lor·ic (kə lôr′ik) *n.* heat. —*adj.* **1** having to do with heat. **2** of or having to do with calories.

cal·o·rie or **cal·o·ry** (kal′ə rē) *n.* **-ries. 1** a unit of heat. The quantity of heat necessary to raise the temperature of a gram of water one degree centigrade is a **small calorie.** The quantity of heat necessary to raise the temperature of a kilogram of water one degree centigrade is a **large calorie. 2** a unit of the energy supplied by food, corresponding to a large calorie. An ounce of sugar will produce about a hundred such calories. **3** a quantity of food capable of producing such an amount of energy. [< F < L *calor* heat]

cal·o·rif·ic (kal′ə rif′ik) *adj.* producing heat.

cal·o·rim·e·ter (kal′ə rim′ə tər) *n.* an apparatus for measuring the quantity of heat, the specific heat of different substances, the heat of chemical combination, etc.

cal·u·met (kal′yů met′) *n.* a long, ornamented tobacco pipe smoked by North American Indians on special occasions, especially at peace councils. [< F < L *calamus* < Gk. *kalamos* reed]

ca·lum·ni·ate (kə lum′nē āt′) *v.* **-at·ed, -at·ing.** say false and injurious things about; slander. [< L *calumniari* < *calumnia* false accusation. Doublet of CHALLENGE, v.]

ca·lum·ni·a·tion (kə lum′nē ā′shən) *n.* a slander; calumny.

ca·lum·ni·a·tor (kə lum′nē ā′tər) *n.* a slanderer.

ca·lum·ni·ous (kə lum′nē əs) *adj.* slanderous. —**ca·lum′ni·ous·ly,** *adv.*

cal·um·ny (kal′əm nē) *n.* **-nies.** a false statement made to injure someone's reputation; slander. [< L *calumnia.* Doublet of CHALLENGE, n.] —**Syn.** defamation.

Cal·va·dos or **cal·va·dos** (kal′və dōs′) *n.* a kind of brandy distilled from hard cider and originating in Normandy, France. [< *Calvados,* a department of N.W. France]

calve (kav) *v.* **calved, calv·ing. 1** give birth to a calf. **2** of ice, break up into icebergs. [OE *calfian* < *calf* calf[1]]

calves (kavz) *n.* pl. of **calf**[1] and **calf**[2].

Cal·vin·ism (kal′vən iz′əm) *n.* the religious teachings of John Calvin (1509-1564), a French leader of the Protestant Reformation at Geneva, and his followers. Calvinism taught that only certain persons, the elect, were chosen by God to be saved and these could be saved only by God's grace.

Cal·vin·ist (kal′vən ist) *n.* a follower of the teachings of Calvin.

Cal·vin·is·tic (kal′vən is′tik) *adj.* of Calvinism.

calx (kalks) *n.* **calx·es** or **cal·ces** (kal′sēz). an ashy substance left after a metal or a mineral has been thoroughly roasted, burned, etc. [< L *calx* lime]

hat, āge, cãre, fär; let, ēqual, tėrm; it, īce
hot, ōpen, ôrder; oil, out; cup, pu̇t, rüle, ūse
əbove, takən, pencəl, lemən, circəs
ch, child; ng, long; sh, ship
th, thin; ᴛʜ, then; zh, measure

cal·y·ces (kal′ə sēz′ or kā′lə sēz′) *n.* a pl. of **calyx.**

Cal·y·do·ni·an (kal′ə dō′nē ən) *adj.* of Calydon, a city in ancient Greece. The **Calydonian boar** was a wild boar sent by Artemis to attack Calydon. Meleager finally killed it.

ca·lyp·so (kə lip′sō) *n.* a type of improvised song that originated in the West Indies. [? < Calypso]

Ca·lyp·so (kə lip′sō) *n.* in Greek legend, a sea nymph who detained Odysseus on her island for seven years.

ca·lyx (kā′liks or kal′iks) *n.* **ca·lyx·es** or **cal·y·ces. 1** in botany, the outer part of a flower that is a holder for the petals. The calyx is made up of sepals. See **sepal** for picture. **2** in anatomy and zoology, any cuplike structure or organ. [< L < Gk. *kalyx* covering]

cam (kam) *n.* a projection on a wheel or shaft that changes a regular circular motion into an irregular circular motion or into a back-and-forth motion. [< Du. *kam* cog, comb]

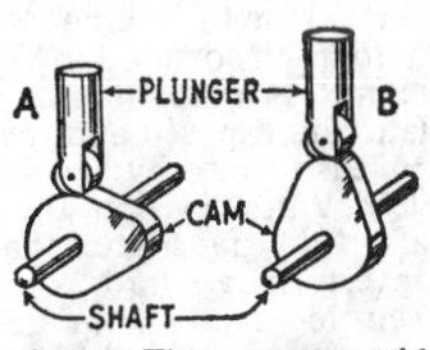

A cam. The cam turns with the shaft. The wheel of the plunger follows the edge of the cam. Thus the downward movement (figure A) and upward movement (figure B) of the plunger are caused by the two different curves of the cam.

ca·ma·ra·de·rie (kä′mə rä′də rē) *n.* comradeship; friendliness and loyalty among comrades. [< F]

cam·a·ril·la (kam′ə ril′ə; *Spanish,* kä′mä rē′lyä) *n.* a group of private advisers, cabal; clique. [< Sp. *camarilla,* dim. of *cámara* chamber]

cam·as or **cam·ass** (kam′əs) *n.* a plant of the lily family. North American Indians eat its sweet, nourishing bulbs. [< Chinook *quamash* bulb]

cam·ber (kam′bər) *v.* arch slightly; bend or curve upward in the middle. —*n.* **1** a slight arch; an upward bend or curve in the middle. **2** a slightly arching piece of timber. **3** the rise and fall in the curve of an airplane airfoil. [< F *cambre* bent < L *camur* crooked]

cam·bi·um (kam′bē əm) *n.* the layer of soft, growing tissue between the bark and the wood of trees and shrubs, from which new bark and new wood grow. [< LL *cambium* exchange]

cam·boose (kam′büs′) *n. Cdn.* formerly: **1** the living quarters of a gang of loggers or shantymen; shanty (def. 2). **2** an open fireplace in such a building. [< Cdn.F < F *cambuse* store, hut < Du. *kambuis* < MLG; cf. CABOOSE]

Cam·bri·a (kam′brē ə) *n.* an old name for Wales.

Cam·bri·an (kam′brē ən) *adj.* **1** Welsh. **2** having to do with an early geological period or group of rocks. —*n.* **1** a Welshman. **2** in geology: **a** an early period, beginning approximately 550 million years ago. **b** a group of rocks formed during this period. See the chart under **geology.**

cam·bric (kām′brik) *n.* a fine, thin linen or cotton cloth. [< *Cambrai,* France]

cambric tea a drink made of hot water, milk, and sugar, flavored with a little tea.

came (kām) *v.* pt. of **come.**

cam·el (kam′əl) *n.* a large, cud-chewing mammal having one or two humps on its back, used as a beast of burden. The **Arabian camel,** or dromedary, has one hump; the **Bactrian camel** of southern Asia has two humps. Camels are used in the deserts of Africa and Asia because they can go for a long time without drinking water. [< L *camelus* < Gk. *kamēlos*; of Semitic origin]

ca·mel·lia (kə mēl′yə or kə mē′lē ə) *n.* **1** a shrub or tree having glossy leaves and waxy, white or red flowers shaped like roses. **2** the flower. [after G. J. *Kamel* or *Camellus* (1661-1706), missionary in Luzon]

ca·mel·o·pard (kə mel′ə pärd′) *n.* **1** a giraffe. **2** in astronomy, a constellation in the northern sky between Cassiopeia and Ursa Major. [< LL < L < Gk. *kamēlopardalis* < *kamēlos* camel + *pardalis* leopard]

Cam·e·lot (kam′ə lot′) *n.* a legendary place in England where King Arthur had his palace and court.

camel's hair 1 the hair of a camel, used in making cloth, paintbrushes, etc. 2 cloth made of this hair or something like this hair.

Cam·em·bert (kam′əm bãr′) *n.* a rich, soft cheese. [after *Camembert*, France]

cam·e·o (kam′ē ō′) *n.* **-e·os. 1** a precious or semi-precious stone carved so that there is a part raised above the background. Agates and other stones having a layered structure are much used for cameos. **2** a piece of engraving or sculpture carved in this way. **3** a brief composition, dramatic performance, etc. that highlights a certain character or event. [< Ital.]

cam·er·a (kam′ər ə or kam′rə) *n.* **-er·as** *for 1 and 2,* **-er·ae** (-ər ē′ or -ər ī′) *for 3.* **1** a machine for taking photographs or motion pictures, in which film or plates are exposed and the image is formed by means of a lens. **2** in television, the part of the transmitter that converts images into electronic impulses for transmitting. **3** a judge's private office. **4 in camera, a** in a judge's private office. **b** of a trial, parliamentary session, or other meeting, with the press and public excluded. **c** privately. [< L *camera* arched chamber, arch < Gk. *kamara.* Doublet of CHAMBER.]

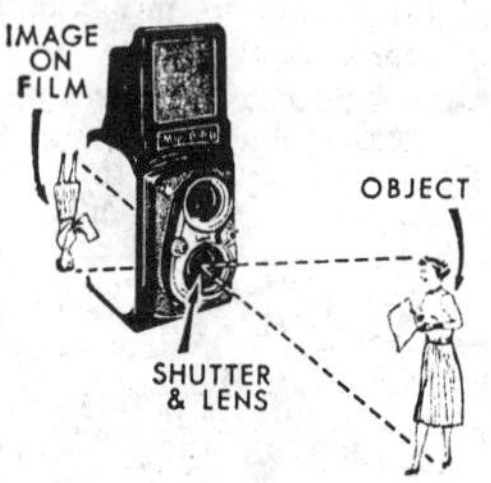

A camera. When the shutter is opened, light rays reflected from the object pass through the lens and are focussed by it on the film. Because the film is sensitive to light, it records the image.

camera lu·ci·da (lü′ sə də) an instrument by which the image of an object is made to appear on a sheet of paper, etc. upon which it may be traced.

cam·er·a·man (kam′ər ə man′ or kam′rə-) *n.* **-men** (-men′). a man who operates a motion-picture camera.

camera ob·scu·ra (ob skūr′ə) a camera in which images of external objects, received through an aperture, are exhibited in their natural colors on a surface arranged to receive them. The camera obscura is used for sketching, exhibition purposes, etc. [< NL]

cam·i·on (kam′ē ən) *n.* **1** a strongly built cart. **2** a truck for carrying cannon. [< F]

cam·i·sole (kam′ə sōl′) *n.* **1** a woman's under-bodice. **2** a woman's short, loose dressing gown. [< F < Sp. *camisola,* dim. of *camisa* shirt. Akin to CHEMISE.]

cam·let (kam′lit) *n.* **1** a cloth of silk and wool made in the Orient. **2** a strong, waterproof cloth. [< F *camelot* < Arabic *khamlat* wool plush < *khaml* nap²]

cam·o·mile (kam′ə mīl′) *n.* a plant of the same family as the aster, having daisy-like flowers. Its flowers and leaves are sometimes dried and used in medicine. [ME < OF < LL *camomilla,* var. of L *chamaemelon* < Gk. *chamaimēlon* earth apple]

Ca·mor·ra (kə môr′ə) *n.* **1** a secret society formed in Naples, Italy, about 1820, which developed into a powerful political organization. Later it was associated with blackmail, robbery, etc. **2 camorra,** a secret society like the Camorra.

cam·ou·flage (kam′ə fläzh′) *n. v.* **-flaged, -flag·ing.** —*n.* **1** a disguise; deception. The white fur of a polar bear is a natural camouflage; it prevents the bear from being easily seen against the snow. **2** in warfare, the practice of giving things a false appearance to help conceal them from the enemy. —*v.* give a false appearance to (something) in order to conceal it; disguise. [< F *camouflage* < *camoufler* disguise] **—cam′ou·flag′er,** *n.*

camp (kamp) *n.* **1** a group of tents, huts, or other shelters where people live temporarily rather than permanently: *A marching army usually makes camp every night.* **2** a place where a camp is. **3** the people living in a camp. **4** any tent, hut, or other shelter to live in temporarily: *Many people live in a camp near a lake or in the woods during the summer.* **5** the act of living an outdoor life with very simple shelter; camping. **6** a group of people who agree or work together. **7** military life. **8** a place where athletes train together. **9** *Slang.* affectation considered amusing in a sophisticated way. **10 break camp,** pack up tents and equipment. **11 in the same camp,** in agreement; working together.
—*v.* **1** make a camp; put up tents, huts, or other shelters. **2** live in a camp for a time. **3** live simply without comforts for a time. **4 camp out, a** spend the night outdoors. **b** live in the open in a tent or camp. [< F < Ital. < L *campus* field. Doublet of CAMPUS.] **—camp′er,** *n.*

cam·paign (kam pān′) *n.* **1** a series of related military operations that have some special purpose in view: *The general's staff planned a campaign to capture the enemy's most important city.* **2** a series of connected activities planned to achieve some goal or to acquire something; a planned course of action for some special purpose: *a campaign to raise money for a college, a campaign to advertise some article, a campaign to elect someone to political office.*
—*v.* take part in or serve in a campaign; go on a campaign. [< F *campagne* open country < Ital. *campagna* < LL *campanea, campania* level country < L *campus* field. Doublet of CHAMPAIGN.] **—cam·paign′er,** *n.*

cam·pa·ni·le (kam′pə nē′lē) *n.* **-ni·les** or **-ni·li** (-nē′lē). a bell tower. [< Ital. < LL *campana* bell]

cam·pan·u·la (kam pan′yů lə) *n.* a bluebell, Canterbury bell, or other similar plant having bell-shaped flowers. [< LL *campanula,* dim. of *campana* bell]

camp bed a light folding cot or bed.

camp chair a lightweight folding chair.

cam·per (kamp′ər) *n.* **1** a person who camps or goes camping. **2** camper truck.

camper truck a truck carrying a small living unit.

camp·fire (kamp′fīr′) *n.* **1** a fire in a camp, for warmth or cooking. **2** a social gathering for soldiers, scouts, etc.

Camp Fire Girls *U.S.* an organization for promoting the health and welfare of young girls by training them in co-operation, outdoor activities, etc.

camp follower 1 a civilian hanger-on in an army camp, especially a prostitute or a seller of small wares. **2** *Informal.* any person who attaches himself for his own profit to a more important person, a group, a cause, etc.

camp·ground (kamp′ground′) *n.* **1** a place where a camp is. **2** the place where a camp meeting is held.

cam·phor (kam′fər) *n.* a white, crystalline substance with a strong odor and a bitter taste. Camphor is used in medicine, to protect clothes from moths, in the manufacture of celluloid, etc. *Formula:* $C_{10}H_{16}O$ [< Med.L *camphora* < Arabic, ult. < Malay *kāpūr*]

cam·phor·at·ed (kam′fər āt′id) *adj.* containing camphor: *camphorated oil.*

camphor ball a small ball made of camphor, naphthalene, etc. used to keep moths out of clothes, furniture, etc.

cam·pi·on (kam′pē ən) *n.* any of certain plants of the same family as the pink, having red or white flowers. [< L *campus* field]

camp meeting a religious gathering held outdoors or in a tent, usually lasting several days.

cam·po·ree (kam′pə rē′) *n.* **1** a gathering of scouts or guides for competitions in campcraft, etc. **2** a kind of bivouac outing for a troop. [*camp* + jamb*oree*]

camp robber *Cdn. Informal.* Canada jay.

camp·site (kamp′sīt′) *n.* **1** a place where people may camp: *Many provincial parks contain well-managed campsites.* **2** any place where someone camps or has camped: *We made our campsite in the bush.* **3** the site of an ancient or prehistoric camp: *The archaeologists found a Stone-Age campsite.*

camp·stool (kamp′stül′) *n.* a lightweight folding seat.

cam·pus (kam′pəs) *n.* the grounds and buildings of a college, university, or school. [< L *campus* field, plain. Doublet of CAMP.]

cam·shaft (kam′shaft′) *n.* a rod or shaft on which a

cam is fastened, or of which a cam forms an essential part. See **cam** for picture.

can[1] (kan; *unstressed*, kən) *v. pres. sing.* 1 **can,** 2 **can** or (*Archaic*) **canst,** 3 **can;** *pt.* **could.** 1 be able to: *He can read rapidly.* 2 know how to: *He can run that machine.* 3 have the right to: *Anyone can cross the street here.* 4 *Informal.* be allowed to: *You can go at four o'clock.* [OE *can(n)* know, know how, can (infinitive, *cunnan*)]

☛ **can, may.** In general informal usage *may* occurs rather rarely except in the sense of possibility: *It may be all right for her, but not for me. Can* is generally used for both permission and ability: *Can I go now? You can if you want to. I can go 80 miles an hour with my car.* This is in such general usage that it should be regarded as acceptable English in speaking and in informal writing. In formal English, however, some distinction is often made between the auxiliary *can,* implying ability, being able to, and *may,* implying permission: *You may go now. He can walk with crutches. You may if you can. May* also indicates possibility: *He may have been the one.*

can[2] (kan) *n. v.* **canned, can·ning.** —*n.* 1 a metal container: *an oil can, a milk can.* 2 the contents of a can. 3 a can and its contents. 4 a drinking cup. 5 *Slang.* **a** a depth charge. **b** a destroyer. 6 **in the can,** *Slang.* of motion picture film, ready to show; completed. —*v.* 1 put in a can; preserve by putting in airtight cans or jars: *can fruit.* 2 *Slang.* dismiss from a job; get rid of. 3 *Slang.* do away with or cease doing (something): *Can the chatter.* 4 *Slang.* make intoxicated. [OE *canne*]

can. 1 canon. 2 canto.

Can. 1 Canada. 2 Canadian.

Ca·naan (kā′nən) *n.* 1 a region in Palestine between the Jordan River and the Mediterranean. God promised Canaan to Abraham and his descendants. 2 a land of promise.

Ca·naan·ite (kā′nən īt′) *n.* an inhabitant of Canaan before its conquest by the Hebrews.

Can·a·da Act (kan′ə də) the Act of 1791 that divided the province of Quebec into Upper and Lower Canada.

Canada anemone a species of anemone having large, white flowers, found from Quebec to British Columbia.

Canada balsam a sticky, yellow resin obtained from the balsam fir tree. It is used in medicine and for mounting on glass slides objects to be examined under a microscope.

Canada Council a body founded by Parliament in 1957 to administer funds for the encouragement of writing, music, painting, and other cultural and scholarly activities. *Abbrev.*: C.C.

Canada goose a large wild goose of North America having a black head and neck, a white throat, and a brownish-gray body.

Canada jay a North American bird having black and gray feathers and lacking a crest. The Canada jay is also known as lumberjack, whisky-jack, venison hawk, and moosebird.

Ca·na·di·an (kə nā′dē ən) *adj.* of Canada or its people. —*n.* a native or inhabitant of Canada; a citizen of Canada. [< *Canada* < Cdn F < Iroquoian *kanata* village, community]

Ca·na·di·a·na (kə nā′dē an′ə or kə nā′dē ä′nə) *n.* things relating to Canada and its history, especially early Canadian furniture, textiles, books, etc.

Canadian bacon boneless loin of cured, smoked pork, having the flavor of ham.

Canadian English the kind of English spoken by English-speaking Canadians.

Canadian French the kind of French spoken by French-speaking Canadians.

Ca·na·di·an·ism (kə nā′dē ən iz′əm) *n.* 1 a word or expression originating in or peculiar to Canada. The words "muskeg" and "caribou" are Canadianisms. 2 a custom peculiar to Canada. 3 devotion and loyalty to Canada, its customs, traditions, and laws. 4 the state of being Canadian; the fact of Canada's existence as a separate entity.

Ca·na·di·an·ize (kə nā′dē ə nīz′) *v.* **-ized, -iz·ing.** 1 make or become Canadian in habits, customs, or character. 2 make suitable for Canadian use. 3 bring under Canadian ownership or control: *Steps should be taken to Canadianize more of our industries.*

Canadian Legion Royal Canadian Legion.

hat, āge, cãre, fär; let, ēqual, tėrm; it, īce
hot, ōpen, ôrder; oil, out; cup, pu̇t, rüle, ūse
əbove, takən, pencəl, lemən, circəs
ch, child; ng, long; sh, ship
th, thin; ᴛʜ, then; zh, measure

Canadian Shield an extensive area of rock, chiefly Pre-Cambrian granite, that lies north of the Great Lakes in Canada. The Canadian Shield is rich in minerals, especially gold, copper, nickel, and iron ore.

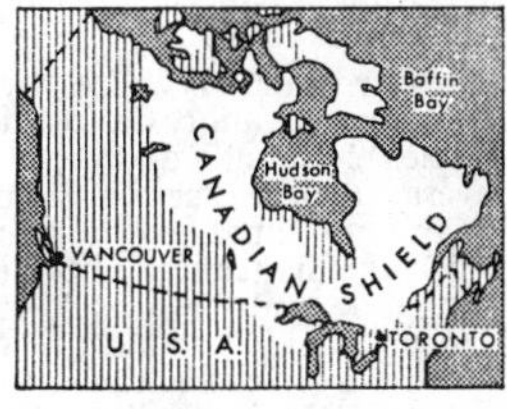

Canadian whisky or **whiskey** a blended whisky containing a high proportion of rye whisky. It is often referred to as "rye."

Ca·na·di·en (kə nā′dē en′; *French,* kä nä dyeɴ′) *n.* a French Canadian.

Ca·na·di·enne (kə nā′dē en′; *French,* kä nä dyen′) *n.* a French-Canadian girl or woman.

ca·naille (kə nāl′; *French,* kä nī′) *n. French.* the lowest class of people; rabble; riffraff. [< F < Ital. *canaglia* < *cane* dog < L *canis*]

ca·nal (kə nal′) *n. v.* **-nalled** or **-naled, -nal·ling** or **nal·ing.** —*n.* 1 a waterway dug across land. Some canals are for boats and ships; others are for carrying water to places that need it. 2 a tube in the body or in a plant for carrying food, liquid, or air: *the alimentary canal.* 3 a long arm of a large body of water. 4 any of the long, narrow markings on the planet Mars. —*v.* 1 dig or cut a canal through or across. 2 furnish with canals. [< L *canalis* trench, pipe. Doublet of CHANNEL.]

canal boat a long, narrow boat used on canals. Canal boats are sometimes pulled along by horses.

ca·nal·i·za·tion (kə nal′ə zā′shən, kan′ə lə zā′shən or kan′ə lī zā′shən) *n.* 1 the act of canalizing. 2 a system of canals. 3 the draining of wounds by surgical means rather than by the use of tubes.

ca·nal·ize (kə nal′īz or kan′ə līz′) *v.* **-ized, -iz·ing.** 1 make a canal or canals through. 2 make into or like a canal. 3 lead in a desired direction so as to control or regulate; channel: *an attempt to canalize the energies of children into worth-while activities.*

can·a·pé (kan′ə pā′ or kan′ə pē) *n.* a cracker, a thin piece of toasted or fried bread, etc. spread with a seasoned mixture of fish, cheese, etc. [< F *canapé,* originally, a couch with curtains of mosquito netting. See CANOPY.]

ca·nard (kə närd′) *n.* a false rumor; an exaggerated report; hoax. [< F *canard,* literally, duck]

ca·nar·y (kə nãr′ē) *n.* **-nar·ies.** 1 a small, yellow songbird. Canaries are often kept in cages. 2 a light yellow. 3 a wine from the Canary Islands. —*adj.* light-yellow. [after the *Canary Islands*]

canary yellow light yellow.

ca·nas·ta (kə nas′tə) *n.* a card game similar to rummy in which the players try to earn as many points as possible by making sets of seven or more cards.

can·can (kan′kan′) *n.* a kind of dance marked by extravagant kicking and leaping; a form of quadrille. [< F]

can·cel (kan′səl) *v.* **-celled** or **-celed, -cel·ling** or **-cel·ing,** *n.*—*v.* 1 cross out; mark (something) so that it cannot be used or used again: *cancel a stamp.* 2 in mathematics: **a** reduce a fraction by dividing both the numerator and the denominator by the same quantity. **b** reduce an equation by dividing both members by a common factor. 3 do away with; abolish: *He cancelled his order for the books.* 4 make up for; balance; compensate; neutralize: *The little boy's sweet smile cancelled his earlier crossness.* 5 in music, nullify the power of a sharp or a flat by inserting the sign ♮. —*n.* 1 a cancelling. 2 a cancelled part. [< L *cancellare* cross out with latticed lines < *cancelli* crossbars, dim.

of *cancri*, altered from *carcer*, originally, network, grating] —**can′cel·ler** or **can′cel·er,** *n.* —**Syn.** *v.* 3 annul, nullify, revoke.

can·cel·la·tion (kan′sə lā′shən) *n.* **1** a cancelling or being cancelled; striking out. **2** the marks made when something is cancelled or crossed out. **3** something that has been cancelled.

can·cer (kan′sər) *n.* **1** a harmful growth in the body; a malignant tumor. Cancer tends to spread and destroy the healthy tissues and organs of the body. **2** any of several fatal diseases characterized by such a growth or by any abnormal growth of cells, as carcinoma, sarcoma, and leukemia (cancer of the blood). **3** an evil or harmful thing that tends to spread. **4 Cancer, a** the tropic of Cancer, a circle around the world 23.45 degrees north of the equator. See **Capricorn** for diagram. **b** in astronomy, a northern constellation that was thought of as having the shape of a crab. **c** in astrology, the fourth sign of the zodiac; the Crab. The sun enters Cancer about June 21. See **zodiac** for diagram. [< L *cancer* crab, tumor. Doublet of CANKER, CHANCRE.]

can·cer·o·gen·ic (kan′sər ə jen′ik) *adj.* carcinogenic.

can·cer·ous (kan′sər əs) *adj.* **1** like cancer. **2** having cancer.

can·de·la (kan dē′lə) *n.* a unit for measuring the strength or intensity of light, replacing the international candle. [< L *candela* candle]

can·de·la·bra (kan′də lä′brə) *n.* **-bras** (-brəz). candelabrum.

☛ Though **candelabrum** is the original form, its plural **candelabra** is now often treated as singular, with its own plural **candelabras.**

can·de·la·brum (kan′də lä′brəm) *n.* **-bra** (-brə) or **-brums.** an ornamental candlestick with several branches for holding candles. [< L *candelabrum* < *candela* candle]

A candelabrum

can·des·cent (kan des′ənt) *adj.* glowing with heat; incandescent. [< L *candescens, -entis,* ppr. of *candescere* begin to glow] —**can·des′cent·ly,** *adv.*

can·did (kan′did) *adj.* **1** frank; sincere: *a candid reply.* **2** fair; impartial: *a candid decision.* [< L *candidus* white] —**can′did·ly,** *adv.* —**Syn. 1** truthful, straightforward. See **frank.**

can·di·da·cy (kan′də də sē) *n.* the state of being a candidate: *Please support my candidacy for treasurer.*

can·di·date (kan′də dāt′ or kan′də dit) *n.* **1** a person who seeks, or is proposed for, some office or honor: *There are three candidates for president of the club.* **2** a person studying for a degree: *a doctoral candidate.* **3** a person applying for a position. [< L *candidatus* clothed in a white toga]

can·di·da·ture (kan′də də chür′ or kan′də dā′chər) *n.* candidacy.

candid camera 1 a small camera with a fast lens for photographing persons unposed, and often unaware that their picture is being taken. **2** any very small camera.

can·died (kan′dēd) *adj.* **1** turned into sugar: *candied honey.* **2** cooked in sugar; covered with sugar: *candied sweet potatoes.* **3** sweet or agreeable: *candied words.*

can·dle (kan′dəl) *n. v.* **-dled, -dling.** —*n.* **1** a stick of wax or tallow containing a wick that may be burned to give light. **2** anything shaped or used like a candle. Sulphur candles are burned to disinfect rooms. **3** a unit for measuring the strength of a light. The **international candle** is the light from 5 square millimetres of platinum at the temperature at which it solidifies. **4 burn the candle at both ends,** use up one's strength and resources rapidly. **5 not hold a candle to,** not compare with: *She cannot hold a candle to her sister in piano playing.*
—*v.* test (eggs) for freshness by holding them in front of a light. [OE *candel* < L *candela* < *candere* shine]

can·dle·fish (kan′dəl fish′) *n.* oolichan.

can·dle·hold·er (kan′dəl hōl′dər) *n.* a candlestick.

candle hour a unit of light equivalent to the energy derived in one hour from a source of light equal to one candle power.

candle ice or **candled ice** *Cdn.* ice on a river, lake, etc. that has deteriorated into candle-like shapes, usually occurring shortly before break-up.

can·dle·light (kan′dəl līt′) *n.* **1** the light from a candle or candles. **2** the time when candles are lighted; dusk; twilight; nightfall.

Can·dle·mas (kan′dəl məs) *n.* February 2, a Christian church festival in honor of the purification of the Virgin Mary and the presentation of the infant Jesus in the Temple. It is celebrated with lighted candles. [OE *candelmæsse*]

candle power the intensity of light given by a standard candle, used as a unit for measuring light. A light having 30 candle power gives 30 times as much light as one standard candle does.

can·dle·stick (kan′dəl stik′) *n.* a holder for a candle, to make it stand upright.

can·dle·wick (kan′dəl wik′) *n.* **1** the wick of a candle. **2** a soft, loosely twisted cotton thread similar to that used for candlewicks. —*adj.* having a pattern made with tufts of such threads: *a candlewick bedspread.*

can·dor or **can·dour** (kan′dər) *n.* **1** frankness; open-heartedness in giving one's view or opinion. **2** fairness, impartiality. [< L *candor* whiteness, purity < *candere* shine] —**Syn. 1** sincerity.

can·dy (kan′dē) *n.* **-dies,** *v.* **-died, -dy·ing.** —*n.* **1** sugar or syrup, cooked and flavored, then cooled and divided into small pieces for eating. **2** a piece of this confection. —*v.* **1** turn into sugar. **2** cook in sugar; preserve by boiling in sugar. **3** make sweet or agreeable. [< F (*sucre*) *candi* (sugar) candy < Persian *qand* sugar] —**Syn.** *n.* **1** confection. **2** bonbon.

candy cane a stick of brittle, white peppermint candy having a spiralling red stripe and shaped like a walking stick with a curved handle.

candy floss spun sugar candy; cotton candy.

can·dy-pull (kan′dē pu̇l′) *n.* **1** a social gathering where candy, while it is still soft enough to handle, is pulled and twisted to the color and consistency of taffy. **2** a turn at doing this.

candy stripe a narrow stripe of two alternating colors, generally red and white. —**can′dy-striped′,** *adj.*

can·dy·strip·er (kan′dē strīp′ər) *n.* a young girl who does volunteer work in a hospital. [from the uniform of a jumper with vertical red and white stripes, worn over a white blouse]

can·dy·tuft (kan′dē tuft′) *n.* a plant of the same family as mustard, having clusters of white, purple, or pink flowers. [< *Candia,* former name of Crete + *tuft*]

cane (kān) *n. v.* **caned, can·ing.** —*n.* **1** a stick to help a person in walking; a walking stick. **2** a stick used for inflicting punishment. **3** a long, jointed stem, such as that of the bamboo. **4** a plant having such stems. Sugar cane and bamboo are canes. **5** the material made of such stems. Cane is sometimes used for furniture, chair seats, etc. **6** a slender stalk or stem.
—*v.* **1** beat with a cane. **2** make or provide with material made of long, jointed stems. [< F < L *canna* < Gk. *kanna* reed. Doublet of CANNA.] —**can′er,** *n.*

cane·brake (kān′brāk′) *n.* a thicket of cane plants.

cane sugar sugar made from sugar cane.

ca·nine (kā′nīn) *adj.* **1** of a dog; like a dog. **2** belonging to a group of meat-eating animals including dogs, foxes, and wolves. —*n.* **1** a dog. **2** a canine tooth. [< L *caninus* < *canis* dog]

canine tooth one of the four pointed teeth next to the incisors; cuspid. See **tooth** for diagram.

Ca·nis Ma·jor (kā′nis mā′jər) in astronomy, a group of stars southeast of Orion that contains Sirius, the brightest of the stars. [< L *canis major* greater dog]

Ca·nis Mi·nor (kā′nis mī′nər) in astronomy, a group of stars east of Orion, separated from Canis Major by the Milky Way. [< L *canis minor* lesser dog]

can·is·ter (kan′is tər) *n.* **1** a small box or can, especially for tea. **2** a bullet-filled case that is shot from a cannon. [< L *canistrum* < Gk. *kanastron* basket]

can·ker (kang′kər) *n.* **1** a spreading sore, especially one in the mouth. **2** a disease of plants that causes slow decay. **3** anything that causes decay, rotting, or gradual eating away. **4** a cankerworm.

—*v.* infect or be infected with canker; decay; rot. [OE *cancer* < L *cancer* crab, tumor, gangrene. Doublet of CANCER, CHANCRE.]

can·ker·ous (kang′kər əs) *adj.* 1 of or like canker. 2 causing canker.

can·ker·worm (kang′kər wėrm′) *n.* a caterpillar that eats away the leaves of trees and plants.

can·na (kan′ə) *n.* 1 a plant having large, pointed leaves and large, red, pink, or yellow flowers. 2 the flower. [< L *canna* reed. Doublet of CANE.]

can·na·bis (kan′ə bis) *n.* 1 hemp. 2 a narcotic made from its dried leaves and flowers; hashish; marijuana. [< L *cannabis* hemp < Gk. *kánnabis*]

canned (kand) *adj.* 1 put in a can; preserved by being put in airtight cans or jars. 2 *Slang.* preserved on a record; recorded: *canned music.* 3 *Informal.* drunk; intoxicated.

can·nel (kan′əl) *n.* cannel coal.

cannel coal a type of soft coal in large lumps that burns with a bright flame. [apparently var. of *candle*]

can·ner (kan′ər) *n.* a person who cans food.

can·ner·y (kan′ər ē) *n.* **-ner·ies.** a factory where meat, fish, fruit, vegetables, etc. are canned.

can·ni·bal (kan′ə bəl) *n.* 1 any person who eats human flesh. 2 an animal or fish that eats others of its own kind. —*adj.* of or like cannibals. [< Sp. *Canibal* < *Caribe* Carib]

can·ni·bal·ism (kan′ə bəl iz′əm) *n.* 1 the practice of eating the flesh of one's own kind. 2 barbarity; extreme cruelty.

can·ni·bal·is·tic (kan′ə bəl is′tik) *adj.* of cannibals; characteristic of cannibals.

can·ni·bal·ize (kan′ə bəl īz′) *v.* **-ized, -iz·ing.** 1 assemble or repair (a vehicle, piece of machinery, etc.) by using parts from others that are useless as a whole: *My brother cannibalized a radio set from two old ones that would not work.* 2 take usable parts from (a vehicle, piece of machinery, etc.) to assemble or repair another: *The soldiers cannibalized the wrecked jeep for tires.*

can·ni·kin (kan′ə kin) *n.* a small can; cup. [< *can*[2] + *-kin*]

can·non (kan′ən) *n.* **-non** or **-nons,** *v.* —*n.* 1 a big gun that is fixed to the ground or mounted on a carriage, especially the old-fashioned type of gun that fired cannon balls. 2 the cannon bone. 3 in mechanics, a hollow, cylindrical piece that revolves or is capable of revolving on and independently of a shaft. 4 the metal loop by which a bell is suspended; ear. 5 in billiards, a carom. —*v.* 1 fire a cannon. 2 attack with cannon. 3 in billiards, carom. 4 come into collision: *cannon against a tree.* [< F *canon* < Ital. < L *canna* reed, tube < Gk. *kanna*]

can·nonade (kan′ən ād′) *n. v.* **-ad·ed, -ad·ing.** —*n.* 1 a continued firing of cannon. 2 *Informal.* a verbal assault: *a furious political cannonade.* —*v.* attack with cannon. [< F *canonnade*]

cannon ball a large iron or steel ball, formerly fired from cannons.

cannon bone in horses, etc., the bone between the hock and the fetlock. See **fetlock** for diagram.

cannon cracker a large firecracker.

can·non·eer (kan′ən ēr′) *n.* an artilleryman; gunner.

can·non·ry (kan′ən rē) *n.* **-ries.** 1 a continuous firing of cannons. 2 artillery.

cannon shot 1 cannon balls or other shot for a cannon. 2 the range of a cannon.

can·not (kan′ot, ka not′, or kə not′) *v.* can not.
☛ **cannot, can not.** Written usage is divided, but *cannot* is the more common. *Can not* is perhaps slightly more formal; it should be used if the negative is to be emphasized.

can·ny (kan′ē) *adj.* **-ni·er, -ni·est.** *Scottish.* 1 shrewd; cautious. 2 thrifty. 3 knowing; wise: *a canny lad.* 4 safe to meddle with; lucky: *Ghosts are not canny.* 5 quiet; gentle: *a canny little kitten.* 6 snug; comfortable; pleasant; cosy: *a canny kitchen.* 7 *Archaic.* skilful; clever. [< *can*[1]] —**can′ni·ly,** *adv.* —**can′ni·ness,** *n.*

ca·noe (kə nü′) *n. v.* **ca·noed, ca·noe·ing.** —*n.* a light boat moved with paddles. See picture in the next column. —*v.* paddle a canoe; go in a canoe. [< Sp. < Haitian *canoa* < Arawakan]

hat, āge, cãre, fär; let, ēqual, tėrm; it, īce
hot, ōpen, ôrder; oil, out; cup, pu̇t, rüle, ūse
əbove, takən, pencəl, lemən, circəs
ch, child; ng, long; sh, ship
th, thin; ᴛʜ, then; zh, measure

ca·noe·ist (kə nü′ist) *n.* 1 a person who paddles a canoe. 2 an expert in paddling a canoe.

ca·noe·man (kə nü′mən) *n.* **-men** (-mən). a man whose business is handling a canoe; voyageur: *The fur company employed some skilled canoemen.*

can·on[1] (kan′ən) *n.* 1 a law of a church; a body of church law. 2 a rule by which a thing is judged; standard: *the canons of good taste.* 3 the official list of the books contained in the Bible; the books of the Bible accepted by the Christian church as being inspired by God. 4 the list of saints. 5 an official list. 6 the part of the Mass coming after the offertory. 7 in music, a kind of composition in the style of a fugue, the different voice parts repeating the same subject one after another either at the same or at a different pitch. 8 a large size of type; 48 point. [OE < L < Gk. *kanōn*] —**Syn. 2** criterion.

can·on[2] (kan′ən) *n.* 1 a member of a group of clergymen belonging to a cathedral or to certain churches. 2 in the Roman Catholic Church, a member of a group of clergymen living according to a certain rule. [ME < OF < L *canonicus* canonical < *canon* canon[1]]

ca·ñon (kan′yən) *n.* canyon.

ca·non·i·cal (kə non′ə kəl) *adj.* 1 according to or prescribed by the laws of a church. 2 in the canon of the Bible. 3 authorized; accepted. —*n.* **canonicals,** *pl.* clothes worn by a clergyman at a church service. —**ca·non′i·cal·ly,** *adv.*

canonical hours the periods of the day fixed by canon law for prayer and worship.

can·on·i·za·tion (kan′ən ə zā′shən or kan′ən ī zā′shən) *n.* a canonizing or being canonized.

can·on·ize (kan′ən īz′) *v.* **-ized, -iz·ing.** 1 declare (a dead person) to be a saint; place in the official list of saints: *Joan of Arc was canonized by the Roman Catholic Church in 1920.* 2 treat as a saint; glorify. 3 make or recognize as canonical. 4 authorize.

canon law the laws of a church that govern ecclesiastical affairs.

Can·o·pus (kə nō′pəs) *n.* a first magnitude star in the southern constellation Argo. It is the second brightest star in the sky; only Sirius is brighter.

can·o·py (kan′ə pē) *n.* **-pies,** *v.* **-pied, -py·ing.** —*n.* 1 a covering fixed over a bed, throne, entrance, etc.; covering carried on poles over a person. 2 a rooflike covering; a shelter; shade. 3 the sky. 4 of a parachute, the umbrella-like supporting area.
—*v.* cover with a canopy. [< F *canapé* < Med.L < L *conopeum* < Gk. *kōnōpeion* a couch with curtains of mosquito netting < *kōnōps* gnat]

ca·not du maître (kä nō′ dô me′trə) *Cdn.French.* Montreal canoe. [literally, master's canoe]

ca·not du nord (kä nō dʏ nôr′) *Cdn.French.* North canoe.

canst (kanst) *v. Archaic.* 2nd pers. sing. present tense of **can**[1]. "Thou canst" means "you can" (sing.).

cant[1] (kant) *n.* 1 insincere talk; moral and religious statements that many people make, but few really believe or follow. 2 the peculiar language of a special group, including many words incomprehensible to outsiders: *thieves' cant.* 3 a whining manner of speaking, especially as adopted by beggars; whine.

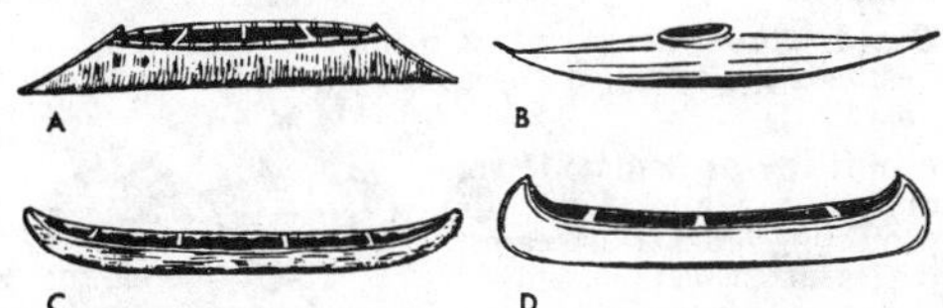

Canoes: A, Kootenay; B, Eskimo Kayak; C, dugout; D, birch bark.

—*adj.* **1** peculiar to a special group: *cant words of thieves.* **2** used for the sake of fashion; affected: *borrow a cant phrase.* **3** marked by affected piety; insincere.
—*v.* use cant; talk in cant. [< L *cantus* song]

cant[2] (kant) *n. v.* **1** slant; slope; bevel. **2** tip; tilt. **3** throw with a sudden jerk; pitch; toss. [probably < MDu., MLG < OF < *cant* < L *cantus* corner, side < Celtic]

can't (kant) cannot or can not.
☛ **can't, mayn't.** *Can't* almost universally takes the place of *mayn't: Can't I go now?*
☛ **can't help.** See **help** for usage note.

Cantab. of Cambridge. (for L *Cantabrigiensis*)

can·ta·bi·le (kän tä′bē lā′) *adj.* in music, in a smooth and flowing style; songlike. [< Ital. < L *cantare* < *canere* sing]

Can·ta·brig·i·an (kan′tə brij′ē ən) *adj.* of Cambridge, England, or Cambridge University. —*n.* **1** a native or inhabitant of Cambridge, England. **2** a student or graduate of Cambridge University. [< *Cantabrigia,* Latin form of *Cambridge*]

can·ta·loupe or **can·ta·loup** (kan′tə lōp′) *n.* a sweet, juicy melon with a hard, rough rind; muskmelon. [< F *cantaloup* < Ital. *Cantalupo,* place where first cultivated]

can·tan·ker·ous (kan tang′kər əs) *adj.* hard to get along with because ready to make trouble and oppose anything suggested; ill-natured: *The old man had a cantankerous way of speaking.* [alteration, influenced by *rancorous,* of earlier **conteckerous* < ME *contecker* contentious person < *conteck* strife, quarrelling] —**can·tan′ker·ous·ly,** *adv.*
—**can·tan′ker·ous·ness,** *n.*

can·ta·ta (kən tä′tə or kən tat′ə) *n.* in music, a story or play, usually with orchestral accompaniment, to be sung but not acted, by a chorus. [< Ital. < L *cantare* < *canere* sing]

can·teen (kan tēn′) *n.* **1** a small container for carrying water or other drinks. **2** a place where food and drink are sold to servicemen. **3** a place in a factory, school, camp, etc. where refreshments and sundries are sold. **4** a box of cooking utensils for use in camp. **5** a set of cutlery in a box or case. [< F < Ital. *cantina* cellar < LL *canthus* side]

can·ter (kan′tər) *v.* gallop gently. —*n.* a gentle gallop. [for *Canterbury gallop,* the supposed easy pace of pilgrims riding to Canterbury]

Can·ter·bur·y bell (kan′tər ber′ē) a plant having tall stalks of bell-shaped flowers, usually purplish-blue, pink, or white.

cant hook or **cant-hook** (kant′hu̇k′) *n.* a pole with a movable hook at one end, used to grip and turn over logs; peavey. [< *cant* a slabbed log < *cant*[2] + *hook*]

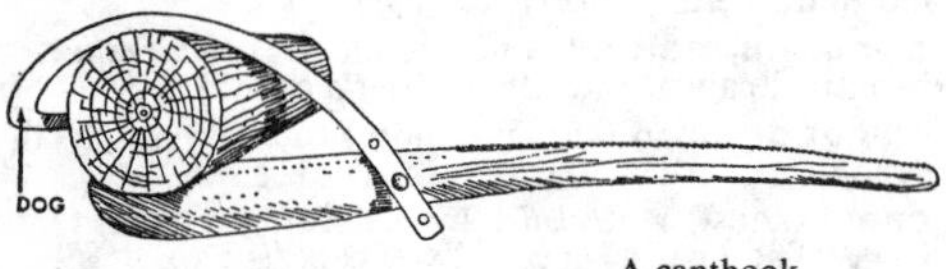

A canthook

can·ti·cle (kan′tə kəl) *n.* a short song, hymn, or chant used in religious services. [< L *canticulum* little song < *cantus* song]

Canticle of Canticles in the Douay Bible, the Song of Solomon.

Can·ti·cles (kan′tə kəlz) *n.* a book of the Old Testament, also called *The Song of Solomon* or *Song of Songs.*

can·ti·lev·er (kan′tə lē′vər or -lev′ər) *n.* a large, projecting bracket or beam that is fastened at one end only. —*v.* **1** build (something) with cantilevers or a cantilever. **2** extend outward on or as a cantilever: *The artist's studio cantilevers out over a sheer cliff.* [origin uncertain]

A cantilever bridge

cantilever bridge a bridge made of two cantilevers whose projecting ends meet but do not support each other. See the picture in the previous column.

can·tle (kan′təl) *n.* the part of a saddle that sticks up at the back. See **saddle** for diagram. [< OF < Med.L *cantellus* little corner]

can·to (kan′tō) *n.* **-tos. 1** one of the main divisions of a long poem. A canto of a poem corresponds to a chapter of a novel. **2** in music, the soprano part; melody. [< Ital. < L *cantus* song]

can·ton (kan′ton or kan ton′; *French,* kän tôn′) *n.* **1** a small part or political division of a country: *Switzerland is made up of 22 cantons.* **2** a township. **3** in Quebec, a municipal unit roughly equal to a township.
—*v.* **1** divide into parts; subdivide. **2** allot quarters to or provide quarters for (soldiers, etc.). [< F *canton* corner, portion < OF *cant.* See CANT[2].]

can·ton·al (kan′tən əl) *adj.* of a canton.

Can·ton crepe (kan′tən) a soft silk cloth with a crinkled surface.

Can·ton·ese (kan′tən ēz′) *n.* **-ese. 1** a native or inhabitant of Canton. **2** the dialect spoken in or near Canton. —*adj.* of Canton, its people, or their dialect.

Can·ton flannel (kan′tən) a strong cotton cloth that is soft and fleecy on one side.

can·ton·ment (kan ton′mənt or kan tōn′mənt) *n.* a place where soldiers live; quarters. [< F]

can·tor (kan′tər or kan′tôr) *n.* **1** a man who leads the singing of a choir or congregation. **2** a soloist in a synagogue. [< L *cantor* singer < *canere* sing]

Ca·nuck (kə nuk′) *n. adj. Cdn. Informal.* **1** a Canadian. **2** a French Canadian. [origin uncertain]

can·vas (kan′vəs) *n.* **1** a strong cloth made of cotton, flax, or hemp, used to make tents and sails. **2** something made of canvas. **3** a sail or sails. **4** a piece of canvas on which to paint a picture, especially in oils. **5** an oil painting. **6** any coarse, stiffened fabric of wide weave used for working tapestry, as a basis for embroidery, etc. **7** of a racing boat: **a** the covered end. **b** the length of this: *The college eight won the race by a canvas.* **8 under canvas, a** in tents. **b** with sails spread.
—*adj.* made of canvas.
—*v.* cover, line, or furnish with canvas. [ME < OF *canevas* < L *cannabis* hemp]

can·vas·back (kan′vəs bak′) *n.* a wild duck of North America, having grayish feathers on its back.

can·vass (kan′vəs) *v.* **1** examine carefully; examine: *John canvassed the papers, hunting for notices of jobs.* **2** discuss: *The city council canvassed the mayor's plan thoroughly.* **3** go about asking for subscriptions, votes, orders, etc.: *Each student canvassed his own block for contributions to the Community Chest.* **4** ask for votes, orders, etc. **5** examine and count the votes cast in an election.
—*n.* **1** the act, fact, or process of canvassing. **2** a personal visiting of homes or stores in a district to sell something. [< *canvas,* originally, toss (someone) in a sheet, later, shake out, discuss] —**can′vass·er,** *n.*

can·yon (kan′yən) *n.* a narrow valley with high, steep sides, usually with a stream at the bottom. Also, **cañon.** [< Sp. *cañón* tube < L *canna* cane]

can·zo·net (kan′zə net′) *n.* a short, light song. [< Ital. *canzonetta,* ult. < L *cantare* sing]

caou·tchouc (kou chük′ or kü′chu̇k) *n.* the gummy, coagulated juice of various tropical plants; rubber. [< F < Sp. < South Am.Ind.]

cap (kap) *n. v.* **capped, cap·ping.** —*n.* **1** a close-fitting covering for the head with little or no brim. **2** a special head covering worn to show rank, occupation, etc.: *a nurse's cap.* **3** anything like a cap. The top of a mushroom is called a cap. **4** the highest part; top. **5** a small quantity of explosive in a wrapper or covering. **6** a capital letter. **7** especially of writing and wrapping papers, any of various sizes: *legal cap, bag cap.* **8 cap in hand,** in humble fashion. **9 set one's cap for,** *Informal.* try to get as a husband.
—*v.* **1** put a cap on. **2** put a top on; cover the top of: *Whipped cream capped the dessert.* **3** do or follow with

something as good or better; surpass: *Each clown capped the last joke of the other.* **4** form or serve as a cap, covering or crown to; lie on top of. **5** take off the cap as a mark of respect to another. **6** *Scottish.* confer an academic degree on. **7** place the white cap of a nurse upon (a nursing school graduate). **8** *Brit.* award a place on a team to. **9 cap the climax,** go to the extreme limit; go beyond expectation or belief. [OE *cæppe* < LL *cappa.* Doublet of CAPE[1]. Cf. L *caput* head.] —**cap′per,** *n.* —**cap′less,** *adj.* —**cap′like′,** *adj.*

cap. **1** *pl.* **caps.** capital letter. **2** capitalize. **3** capacity. **4** capital. **5** chapter. (for L *caput*)

ca·pa·bil·i·ty (kā′pə bil′ə tē) *n.* **-ties. 1** ability; power; fitness; capacity. **2** legal or moral qualifications: *A contract has the capability of binding people to a common purpose.*

ca·pa·ble (kā′pə bəl) *adj.* **1** having fitness or ability; able; efficient; competent: *a capable teacher.* **2 capable of, a** having ability, power, or fitness for: *capable of criticizing music.* **b** open to; ready for: *a statement capable of many interpretations.* [< LL *capabilis* < L *capere* take] —**ca′pa·ble·ness,** *n.* —**ca′pa·bly,** *adv.* —**Syn. 1** proficient, qualified, fitted. ☛ See **able** for usage note.

ca·pa·cious (kə pā′shəs) *adj.* able to hold much; roomy; large: *a capacious closet.* —**ca·pa′cious·ly,** *adv.* —**ca·pa′cious·ness,** *n.* —**Syn.** spacious.

ca·pac·i·tor (kə pas′ə tər) *n.* a condenser (def. 2).

ca·pac·i·ty (kə pas′ə tē) *n.* **-ties. 1** the amount of room or space inside; the largest amount that can be held by a container: *This can has a capacity of four quarts.* **2** the power of receiving and holding: *the capacity of a metal for retaining heat. The theatre has a capacity of 400.* **3** ability; power; fitness: *a great capacity for learning.* **4** a position; relation: *A person may act in the capacity of guardian, trustee, voter, friend, etc.* [< L *capacitas* < *capere* take] —**Syn. 1** volume. **3** competency. **4** character.

cap and bells a cap trimmed with bells, worn by a jester.

cap and gown a flat cap, or mortarboard, and loose gown, worn by university professors and students on certain occasions.

cap-a-pie or **cap-à-pie** (kap′ ə pē′) *adv.* from head to foot; completely. [< F]

ca·par·i·son (kə par′ə sən or kə per′ə sən) *n.* **1** an ornamental covering for a horse. **2** any rich dress; equipment; outfit. —*v.* dress richly; fit out. [< F *caparasson* < Provençal *capa* cape]

A caparison (def. 1)

cape[1] (kāp) *n.* an outer garment, or part of one, without sleeves, that falls loosely from the shoulders. [< F < *cape* < Sp. < LL *cappa.* Doublet of CAP.]

cape[2] (kāp) *n.* **1** a point of land extending into the water. **2 the Cape,** the Cape of Good Hope. [< F *cap* < Provençal < L *caput* head]

Cape buffalo a large, savage buffalo of southern Africa.

cap·e·lin (kāp′lin or kap′lin) *n.* caplin. [< F < Provençal *capelan* chaplain]

Ca·pel·la (kə pel′ə) *n.* the brightest star in the constellation Auriga, one of the six brightest stars in the sky. [< L *capella,* dim. of *caper* goat]

ca·per[1] (kā′pər) *v.* leap or jump about playfully. —*n.* **1** a playful leap or jump. **2** a prank; trick. **3 cut a caper** or **capers,** dance in a frolicsome way. [< L *caper* he-goat] —**Syn.** *v.* skip, spring, gambol.

ca·per[2] (kā′pər) *n.* **1** a prickly shrub of the Mediterranean region. **2 capers,** *pl.* the green flower buds of this shrub, pickled and used for seasoning. [< L *capparis* < Gk. *kapparis*]

cap·er·cail·lie (kap′ər kāl′yē) *n.* a large, black grouse of northern Europe. Also, **capercailzie.** [< Scots Gaelic *capullcoille*]

cape·skin (kāp′skin′) *n.* a soft, durable leather made of lambskin or sheepskin, used for gloves, jackets, etc.

hat, āge, cãre, fär; let, ēqual, tėrm; it, īce
hot, ōpen, ôrder; oil, out; cup, pu̇t, rüle, ūse
əbove, takən, pencəl, lemən, circəs
ch, child; ng, long; sh, ship
th, thin; ᴛʜ, then; zh, measure

[< *Cape* of Good Hope, where the strong leather from its goats was first made]

Ca·pe·tian (kə pē′shən) *adj.* of or having to do with Hugh Capet (A.D. 938?-996), King of France from 987 to 996, or the kings named Capet who reigned over France till 1328. —*n.* one of these rulers.

ca·pi·as (kā′pē əs or kap′ē əs) *n.* in law, a writ ordering an officer to arrest a certain person. [< L *capias* you may take]

cap·il·lar·i·ty (kap′ə lar′ə tē) *n.* **1** capillary attraction or repulsion. **2** the quality of having or causing capillary attraction or repulsion.

cap·il·lar·y (kap′ə ler′ē or ka pil′ə rē) *adj. n.* **-lar·ies.** —*adj.* **1** hairlike; very slender. **2** of or in capillary tubes. —*n.* a tube with a very slender, hairlike opening or bore. Capillaries join the end of an artery to the beginning of a vein. [< L *capillaris* of hair, hairlike < *capillus* hair]

capillary action the raising or lowering of the surface of a liquid in a slender cylinder or other narrow space. The action is caused by surface tension.

capillary attraction **1** the force that raises the part of the surface of a liquid that is in contact with a solid. **2** the ability of a porous substance to soak up a liquid. A blotter absorbs ink by means of capillary attraction.

capillary tube a tube with a very slender, hairlike opening or bore.

cap·i·tal[1] (kap′ə təl) *n.* **1** the city where the government of a country, province, or state is located. **2** a capital letter, as distinct from a, b, c, etc. **3** the amount of money or property that a company or a person uses in carrying on a business: *The Smith Company has a capital of $30,000.* **4** a source of power or advantage; resources. **5** national or individual wealth as produced by industry and available for reinvestment in the production of goods. **6** in accounting: **a** the net worth of a business after the deduction of taxes and other liabilities. **b** the total investment of owners in a business often expressed as capital stock. **7** capitalists as a group. **8 make capital of,** take advantage of; use to one's own advantage: *He made capital of his father's reputation.*
—*adj.* **1** of capital; having to do with capital. **2** important; leading. **3** main; chief. **4** of the best kind; excellent: *A maple tree gives capital shade.* **5** involving death; punishable by death: *Murder is a capital crime in most countries.* [ME < OF < L *capitalis* chief, pertaining to the head < *caput* head. Doublet of CATTLE and CHATTEL.] —**Syn.** *adj.* **2** foremost. **3** principal.
☛ **Capital, capitol** are often confused because they sound and look alike. **Capital** is the common word, sometimes a noun, sometimes an adjective, but always with the basic meaning of chief, head, first in its class or in importance. The noun applies particularly to the head city of a country or province, and to money, property, goods, and other wealth. **Capitol** is always a noun and applies only to a building, particularly in the United States to the building in which Congress or a state legislature meets: *There is a dome on the capitol in Sacramento, the capital of California.*

cap·i·tal[2] (kap′ə təl) *n.* the top part of a column or pillar. See the diagram under **column.** [ME < OF *capitel* < L *capitellum,* dim. of *caput* head]

capital goods any goods, such as machinery, equipment, etc. that can be used to produce other goods.

cap·i·tal·ism (kap′ə təl iz′əm) *n.* **1** an economic system based on the ownership of land, factories, and other means of production by private individuals who compete with one another, using the hired labor of other persons, to produce goods and services that are offered on a free market for whatever profit may be obtainable. **2** the concentration of wealth in the hands of a few.

cap·i·tal·ist (kap′ə təl ist) *n.* **1** a person whose money and property are used in carrying on business. **2** *Informal.* a wealthy person. **3** a person who supports capitalism.

cap·i·tal·is·tic (kap′ə təl is′tik) *adj.* **1** of or having to do with capitalism or capitalists. **2** favoring or supporting capitalism. —**cap′i·tal·is′ti·cal·ly,** *adv.*

cap·i·tal·i·za·tion (kap′ə təl ə zā′shən or kap′ə təl ī zā′shən) *n.* **1** a capitalizing or being capitalized. **2** the amount at which a company is capitalized; capital stock of a business.

cap·i·tal·ize (kap′ə təl īz′) *v.* **-ized, -iz·ing. 1** write or print with a capital letter. **2** set the capital of (a company) at a certain amount. **3** turn into capital; use as capital. **4** take advantage (of); use to one's own advantage: *capitalize on another's mistake.*

capital letter A, B, C, D, etc. or any similar large letter, as distinct from a, b, c, d, etc.

cap·i·tal·ly (kap′ə təl ē) *adv.* very well; excellently.

capital murder in Canada, murder that carries the death penalty. Persons 18 years and over charged with premeditated murder or the killing of a policeman may be convicted of capital murder.

capital punishment the death penalty for a crime.

capital ship a large warship; battleship.

capital stock capital used in carrying on a business. It is divided into shares.

cap·i·ta·tion (kap′ə tā′shən) *n.* a tax, fee, or charge of the same amount for every person. [< LL *capitatio, -onis* < L *caput* head]

Cap·i·tol (kap′ə təl) *n.* **1** in Washington, D.C., the building in which the United States Congress meets. **2** *U.S.* Often, **capitol.** the building in which a state legislature meets. **3** in Rome: **a** the ancient temple of Jupiter on the Capitoline hill. **b** the Capitoline hill. [ME < ONF *capitolie* < L *Capitolium* chief temple (of Jupiter) < *caput* head] ☛ See **capital**[1] for usage note.

Cap·i·to·line (kap′ə tə līn′ or kə pit′ə līn′) *n.* in Rome, one of the seven hills on which ancient Rome was built. *—adj.* having to do with this hill or the Capitol.

ca·pit·u·late (kə pich′ů lāt′) *v.* **-lat·ed, -lat·ing.** surrender on certain terms or conditions: *The men in the fort capitulated on condition that they be allowed to go away unharmed.* [< Med.L *capitulare* draw up under separate heads, arrange in chapters < L *caput* head] **—ca·pit′u·la′tor,** *n.*

ca·pit·u·la·tion (kə pich′ů lā′shən) *n.* **1** a surrender on certain terms or conditions. **2** an agreement; condition. **3** statement of the main facts of a subject; summary.

cap·lin or **cape·lin** (kāp′lin or kap′lin) *n.* a small fish of the N. Atlantic Ocean, used for food and as bait for cod; a kind of smelt.

Cap'n Captain.

ca·pon (kā′pon or kā′pən) *n.* a rooster specially raised to be eaten. It is castrated and fattened. *—v.* make a capon of; caponize. [OE *capūn* < OF < L *capo, caponis*]

ca·pon·ize (kā′pə nīz′) *v.* **-ized, -iz·ing.** make (a young male chicken) into a capon.

ca·pote (kə pōt′) *n.* **1** a long cloaklike outer garment, often having a hood. **2** a close-fitting bonnet with strings. [< F]

ca·pric·ci·o (kə prē′chē ō) *n.* **-ci·os. 1** a caper; prank; caprice. **2** in music, a lively composition in a free, irregular style. [< Ital. *capriccio* < *capro* he-goat < L *caper.* Doublet of CAPRICE.]

ca·pric·ci·o·so (kə prē′chē ō′sō; *Ital.* kä′prēt chō′sō) *adj.* in music, to be played in a light, fanciful style.

ca·price (kə prēs′) *n.* **1** a sudden change of mind without any reason; unreasonable notion or desire: *Her decision to wear only blue clothes was pure caprice.* **2** a tendency to change suddenly and without reason. **3** a capriccio (def. 2). [< F < Ital. *capriccio.* Doublet of CAPRICCIO.] **—Syn. 1** whimsy, whim, humor, fancy.

ca·pri·cious (kə prish′əs or kə prē′shəs) *adj.* guided by one's fancy; full of unreasonable notions; changeable; fickle: *A spoiled child is often capricious.* **—ca·pri′cious·ly,** *adv.* **—ca·pri′cious·ness,** *n.*

Cap·ri·corn (kap′rə kôrn′) *n.* **1** the tropic of Capricorn, an imaginary circle around the world, 23.45 degrees south of the equator. See picture in the next column. **2** in astronomy, a southern constellation that was thought by ancient astronomers to be in the shape of a goat. **3** in astrology, the tenth sign of the zodiac; the Goat. The sun enters Capricorn about December 22. See **zodiac** for diagram. [< L *capricornus* < *caper* goat + *cornu* horn]

cap·ri·ole (kap′rē ōl′) *n. v.* **-oled, -ol·ing.** *—n.* **1** a high leap made by a horse without moving forward. **2** a leap; caper. *—v.* **1** of a horse, make a high leap without moving forward. **2** leap; caper. [< F < Ital. *capriola,* ult. < *capro* goat. See CAPRICCIO.]

caps. 1 capital letters. **2** capitalize.

cap screw a bolt that screws into an opening, used to secure a cover, etc.

cap·si·cum (kap′sə kəm) *n.* **1** any of several plants having red or green pods containing seeds that usually have a hot, peppery taste. Green peppers, chilies, and pimientos are pods of different kinds of capsicum. **2** such pods prepared for seasoning or medicine. [< NL < L *capsa* box]

cap·size (kap sīz′ or kap′sīz) *v.* **-sized, -siz·ing.** of a ship, boat, etc., turn bottom side up; upset; overturn. [origin unknown]

cap·stan (kap′stən) *n.* a machine for lifting or pulling that revolves on a vertical shaft or spindle: *Sailors hoist the anchor on some boats by turning the capstan.* [< Provençal *cabestan* < L *capistrum* halter < *capere* take]

Sailors turning a capstan. As it revolves, it winds up the rope that hoists the anchor.

capstan bar a pole used to turn a capstan.

cap·stone (kap′stōn′) *n.* the top stone of a wall or other structure.

cap·su·lar (kap′sə lər or kap′syů lər) *adj.* **1** of or having to do with a capsule. **2** in a capsule. **3** shaped like a capsule.

cap·sule (kap′səl or kap′sūl) *n.* **1** a small case or covering; a gelatin case for enclosing a dose of medicine. **2** the part of a spaceship rocket containing instruments, astronaut, etc., separated in flight from the rocket proper, so that it may go into orbit or be directed back to earth. **3** in botany, a dry seedcase that opens when ripe. **4** in anatomy, a membrane enclosing an organ; a membranous bag or sac. **5** a concise summary. *—adj.* in condensed or abridged form: *a capsule history of Quebec.* *—v.* furnish with or enclose within a capsule: *It will be capsuled in a cylinder.* [< L *capsula,* dim. of *capsa* box]

Capt. Captain.

cap·tain (kap′tən) *n.* **1** a leader; chief. **2** in the navy, a commissioned officer senior to a commander and junior to a commodore. **3** in the army, a commissioned officer senior to a lieutenant and junior to a major. **4** the commander of a ship. **5** in sports, the leader of a team. *Abbrev.:* Capt. *—v.* lead or command as captain: *Tom will captain the team.* [ME < OF *capitain(e)* < LL *capitaneus* chief < L *caput* head. Doublet of CHIEFTAIN.]

cap·tain·cy (kap′tən sē) *n.* **-cies.** the rank, commission, or authority of a captain.

cap·tain·ship (kap′tən ship′) *n.* **1** the rank, position, or authority of a captain. **2** ability as a captain; leadership.

cap·tion (kap′shən) *n.* **1** the title or heading at the top of a page, article, chapter, etc. or under a picture explaining it. **2** in motion pictures, a subtitle. **3** of a legal document, the part that gives the time, place, or authority for the document. *—v.* put a caption on. [< L *captio, -onis* a taking < *caper* take]

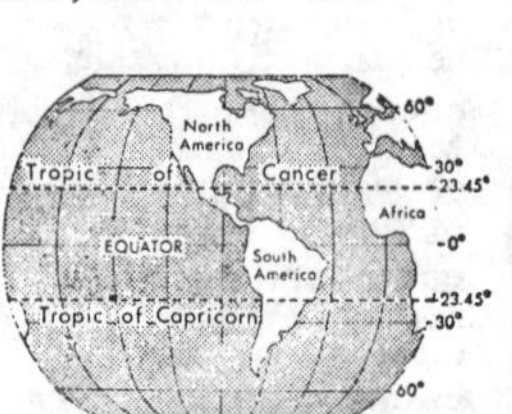

cap·tious (kap′shəs) *adj.* **1** hard to please; faultfinding. **2** apt or designed to entrap or entangle by subtlety: *captious arguments.* [< L *captiosus* < *capere* take]

—**cap′tious·ly,** *adv.* —**cap′tious·ness,** *n.* —**Syn.** carping, contentious.

cap·ti·vate (kap′tə vāt′) *v.* **-vat·ed, -vat·ing. 1** hold captive by beauty or interest; charm; fascinate: *The children were captivated by the animal story.* **2** *Obsolete.* capture. —**cap′ti·vat′ing·ly,** *adv.* —**cap′ti·va′tor,** *n.* —**Syn. 1** enchant, entrance.

cap·ti·va·tion (kap′tə vā′shən) *n.* **1** a captivating or being captivated. **2** charm; fascination.

cap·tive (kap′tiv) *n.* a prisoner: *The army brought back a thousand captives.* —*adj.* **1** held as a prisoner; made a prisoner. **2** captivated. **3** of or having to do with a captive or captivity: *captive bonds.* [ME < OF *captif* < L *captivus* < *capere* take. Doublet of CAITIFF.]

cap·tiv·i·ty (kap tiv′ə tē) *n.* **-ties. 1** the state or condition of being in prison. **2** the state of being held or detained anywhere against one's will: *Some animals that cannot bear captivity die after a few weeks in a cage.*
—**Syn. 1** imprisonment. **2** bondage, servitude, slavery.

cap·tor (kap′tər) *n.* a person who takes or holds a prisoner.

cap·ture (kap′chər) *v.* **-tured, -tur·ing,** *n.* —*v.* make a prisoner of; take by force, skill, or trick; seize: *Three enemy soldiers were captured during the raid.* [< n.]
—*n.* **1** anything taken in this way. **2** the act of capturing; the fact of capturing or being captured. [< F < L *captura* taking < *capere* take] —**cap′tur·er,** *n.*
—**Syn.** *v.* apprehend. See **catch.** –*n.* **2** seizure, arrest, apprehension.

cap·u·chin (kap′ū chin′ or kap′ū shin′) *n.* **1** a South American monkey having on its head black hair that looks like a hood. **2** a woman's cloak with a hood. **3 Capuchin,** a friar belonging to a branch of the Franciscan order. Capuchins are distinguished by their long, pointed hood or cowl. [< F < Ital. *cappuccio* hood]

ca·put (kap′ət or kā′pət) *n.* **cap·i·ta** (kap′ə tə). *Latin.* head.

cap·y·ba·ra (kap′ə bär′ə) *n.* a large tailless South American water rat. The largest rodent extant, it grows up to two feet high and four feet long. [< Pg. *capybara* < the Brazilian native name]

car (kär) *n.* **1** a vehicle that moves on wheels. **2** an automobile. **3** a railway vehicle for freight or passengers. **4** a vehicle that runs on rails: *A streetcar is often called a car.* **5** the closed platform of an elevator, balloon, etc. for carrying passengers or cargo. **6** *Poetic.* a chariot. [ME < ONF *carre* < Med.L *carra* < L *carrus* two-wheeled cart]
☛ **Car** now commonly replaces *automobile, auto, motorcar,* and other terms for four-wheeled vehicles powered by a gasoline engine. But it is not used in referring to trucks, buses, and other specifically commercial vehicles.

ca·ra·ba·o (kä′rə bä′ō) *n.* **-ba·os.** the water buffalo of the Philippine Islands. [< Sp. < Malay *karbau*]

car·a·bi·neer or **car·a·bi·nier** (kar′ə bə nēr′) *n.* in former times, a cavalry soldier armed with a carbine. Also, **carbineer.** [< F]

car·a·cole (kar′ə kōl′) *n. v.* **-coled, -col·ing.** —*n.* a half turn to the right or left, made by a horse and rider. —*v.* make such half turns; prance from side to side. [< F < Ital. < Sp. *caracol* spiral shell]

car·a·cul (kar′ə kəl) *n.* a type of flat, loose, curly fur made from the skin of newborn lambs. Also, **karakul.** [< *Kara Kul,* a lake in Turkestan]

ca·rafe (kə raf′) *n.* a glass bottle for holding water, wine, etc. [< F < Ital. *caraffa* < Sp. < Arabic *gharrâf* drinking vessel]

car·a·ga·na (kar′ə gan′ə) *n.* **1** any of a group of trees or shrubs of the pulse family native to China and Siberia, having feathery pale-green foliage and yellow flowers appearing in early spring. **2** a shrub of this group, much used on the prairies for hedges, windbreaks, etc. [< NL < Tartar]

caragana break a hedge of caragana serving as a windbreak.

car·a·mel (kar′ə məl or kär′məl) *n.* **1** burnt sugar used for coloring and flavoring food, etc. **2** a small block of chewy candy. [< F < Sp. *caramelo*]

car·a·pace (kar′ə pās′) *n.* the shell on the back of a turtle, lobster, crab, etc. [< F < Sp. *carapacho*]

hat, āge, cãre, fär; let, ēqual, tėrm; it, īce
hot, ōpen, ôrder; oil, out; cup, pu̇t, rüle, ūse
əbove, takən, pencəl, lemən, circəs
ch, child; ng, long; sh, ship
th, thin; ᴛʜ, then; zh, measure

car·at (kar′ət) *n.* **1** a unit of weight for precious stones, equal to ⅕ gram. **2** one 24th part. A gold ring of 18 carats is 18 parts pure gold and 6 parts alloy. [< F < Ital. < Arabic < Gk. *keration,* a small horn-shaped bean used as a weight, dim. of *keras* horn]

car·a·van (kar′ə van′) *n.* **1** a group of merchants, pilgrims, tourists, etc. travelling together, especially for safety. **2** any similar group of travellers. **3** the vehicles or beasts of burden used by such a group. **4** *Esp.Brit.* a mobile home, especially one pulled by a car; trailer. **5** camper. **6** in military use, a mobile headquarters for a senior officer. [< F *caravane* < Persian *karwan*]

car·a·van·sa·ry (kar′ə van′sə rē) *n.* **-ries. 1** an inn or hotel where caravans stop to rest in the Orient: *There used to be many caravansaries on the trade routes from China to Arabia.* **2** a large inn or hotel. [< Persian *karwansarai* < *karwan* caravan + *sarai* inn]

car·a·van·se·rai (kar′ə van′sə rī′ or -sə rā′) *n.* caravansary.

car·a·vel (kar′ə vel′) *n.* any of various small sailing ships of former times. One type was used by Columbus and other navigators of the same period. [< OF *caravelle* < Ital. < LL *carabus* < Gk. *karabos* kind of light ship < ancient Macedonian]

A caravel

car·a·way (kar′ə wā′) *n.* **1** a plant of the same family as the parsley, that yields fragrant, spicy seeds used to flavor food. **2** its seeds. [< Med.L *carui* < Arabic *karawya*]

car·bide (kär′bīd) *n.* **1** a compound of carbon with another element, usually a metal. **2** calcium carbide.

car·bine (kär′bīn) *n.* a short rifle or musket. [< F *carabine*]

car·bi·neer (kär′bə nēr′) *n.* carabineer.

car·bo·hy·drate (kar′bō hī′drāt′) *n.* a substance composed of carbon, hydrogen, and oxygen. Sugar and starch are carbohydrates. Carbohydrates are made from carbon dioxide and water by green plants in sunlight. [< *carbo(n)* + *hydrate*]

car·bo·lat·ed (kär′bə lāt′id) *adj.* containing carbolic acid.

car·bol·ic (kär bol′ik) *adj.* made from carbon or coal tar. [< L *carbo* coal + *oleum* oil]

carbolic acid a poisonous, corrosive, white, crystalline substance, used in solution as a disinfectant and antiseptic; phenol. *Formula*: C_6H_5OH

car·bo·lize (kär′bə līz′) *v.* **-lized, -liz·ing.** add carbolic acid to; treat with carbolic acid.

car·bon (kär′bən) *n.* **1** a very common non-metallic chemical element, forming organic compounds in combination with hydrogen, oxygen, etc. Diamond and graphite are pure carbon; coal and charcoal are impure carbon. *Symbol*: C; *at.no.* 6; *at.wt.* 12.01115. **2** a piece of carbon used in batteries, arc lamps, etc. **3** a piece of carbon paper. **4** a copy made with carbon paper. [< F *carbone* < L *carbo, -onis* coal]

carbon 13 a heavy, stable isotope of carbon having a mass number of 13, used as a tracer in physiological studies, especially in cancer research.

carbon 14 a heavy radio-active isotope of carbon, produced by the bombardment of nitrogen atoms. It is used as a tracer in biological research and in carbon dating.

car·bo·na·ceous (kär′bə nā′shəs) *adj.* **1** of or containing carbon. **2** like or containing coal.

car·bo·na·do[1] (kär′bə nā′dō) *n.* a piece of meat, fish, etc. scored and then broiled. —*v.* **1** score and broil. **2** *Archaic.* slash; hack. [< Sp. *carbonada* something cooked in coals < *carbon* charcoal < L *carbo, -onis*]

car·bo·na·do[2] (kär′bə nā′dō) *n.* a bulky dark-colored type of diamond, used for drills and found mostly in Brazil; black diamond. [< Pg. *carbonado* carbonized (from its color)]

carbon arc **1** a curved stream of light or sparks formed when a strong electric current jumps from one carbon electrode or conductor to another. **2** an arc lamp having carbon electrodes emitting such a stream of light or sparks.

car·bon·ate (*n.* kär′bən āt′ or kär′bən it; *v.* kär′bən āt′) *n. v.* **-at·ed, -at·ing.** —*n.* a salt or ester of carbonic acid. —*v.* **1** change into a carbonate. **2** charge with carbon dioxide. Soda water is carbonated to make it bubble and fizz. **3** burn to carbon; char; carbonize. —**car′bon·a′tion,** *n.*

carbon black a smooth, black pigment of pure carbon formed by deposits from burning gas, oil, etc.; a black soot, finer than lampblack.

carbon copy **1** a copy made by using carbon paper. **2** anything that appears to be a duplicate of something else: *His ideas are a carbon copy of his father's.*

carbon cycle **1** in physics, the process whereby nuclear changes in the interior of stars bring about the liberation of atomic energy that gradually transforms hydrogen to helium. **2** in biology, the circulation of carbon in nature.

carbon dating a method of determining the age of a once-organic archaeological or geological specimen by examining the extent to which the carbon 14 in it has disintegrated.

carbon dioxide a heavy, colorless, odorless gas, present in the atmosphere. Plants absorb it from the air to make plant tissue. The air that comes from an animal's lungs contains carbon dioxide. *Formula*: CO_2

car·bon·ic (kär bon′ik) *adj.* of or containing carbon.

carbonic acid the acid made when carbon dioxide is dissolved in water. *Formula*: H_2CO_3

Car·bon·if·er·ous (kär′bən if′ər əs) *n.* in geology: **1** the period, beginning approximately 315 million years ago, when the warm, moist climate produced a rank growth of tree ferns, horsetail rushes, and conifers, whose remains form the great coal beds. See the chart under **geology. 2** the rocks and coal beds formed during this period.
—*adj.* **carboniferous,** containing coal. [< *carbon* + *-ferous* containing (< L *ferre* to bear)]

car·bon·i·za·tion (kär′bən ə zā′shən or kär′bən ī zā′shən) *n.* a carbonizing or being carbonized.

car·bon·ize (kär′bən īz′) *v.* **-ized, -iz·ing. 1** change into carbon by burning. **2** cover or combine with carbon.

carbon monoxide a colorless, odorless, poisonous gas, formed when carbon burns with an insufficient supply of air. It is part of the exhaust gases of automobile engines. *Formula*: CO

carbon paper a thin paper having a preparation of carbon or other inky substance on one surface, used for making copies when writing, typing, etc.

carbon tet·ra·chlo·ride (tet′rə klô′rīd or -klô′rid) a poisonous, colorless, non-flammable liquid, often used in fire extinguishers and in cleaning fluids. *Formula*: CCl_4

car·bo·run·dum (kär′bə run′dəm) *n.* **1** an extremely hard compound of carbon and silicon, used for grinding, polishing, etc. *Formula*: SiC **2 Carborundum,** the trademark for this compound. [< *carbon* + *corundum*]

car·boy (kär′boi) *n.* a very large glass bottle, usually enclosed in basketwork or in a wooden box or crate to keep it from being broken. [< Persian *qarabah* large flagon]

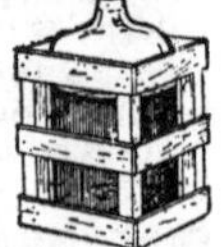

A carboy

car·bun·cle (kär′bung kəl) *n.* **1** a painful, inflamed swelling under the skin. **2** a pimple. **3** a smooth, round garnet or other deep-red jewel. [ME < OF < L *carbunculus* < *carbo* coal]

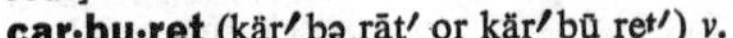

car·bu·ret (kär′bə rāt′ or kär′bū ret′) *v.* **-ret·ted** or **-ret·ed, -ret·ting** or **-ret·ing. 1** mix (air or gas) with carbon compounds, such as gasoline, benzine, etc. **2** combine with carbon. [< *carbon*]

car·bu·re·tion (kär′bə rā′shən or kär′bū resh′ən) *n.* **1** a carburetting. **2** a being carburetted.

car·bu·re·tor or **car·bu·ret·tor** (kär′bə rā′tər or kär′bə ret′ər) *n.* a device for sending air through or over a liquid fuel, so as to produce an explosive mixture.

car·ca·jou (kär′kə zhü′) *n.* wolverine. [< Cdn.F < Algonquian]

car·ca·net (kär′kə net′) *n. Archaic.* an ornamental necklace or band of gold or jewels. [< F *carcan* + E *-et*]

car·case (kär′kəs) *n.* carcass.

car·cass (kär′kəs) *n.* **1** the dead body of an animal. A human body or corpse is sometimes contemptuously called a carcass. **2** the whole trunk of a butchered animal, after removal of the head, limbs, and offal. **3** the lifeless shell or husk of anything: *the carcass of his disappointed hopes.* **4** the shell or framework of a structure, as of a building, ship, or piece of furniture. **5** of a pneumatic tire, the inner, corded wall of the casing. [< F < Ital. *carcassa*]

car·cin·o·gen (kär sin′ə jən) *n.* any substance or agent that produces cancer.

car·cin·o·gen·ic (kär sin′ə jen′ik) *adj.* **1** tending to cause cancer. **2** caused by cancer. Also, **cancerogenic.**

car·ci·no·ma (kär′sə nō′mə) *n.* **-mas, -ma·ta** (-mə tə). a type of cancer. [< L < Gk. *karkinōma* ulcer]

car coat a short topcoat for casual wear, cut for ease and comfort when driving.

card[1] (kärd) *n.* **1** a piece of stiff paper or thin cardboard, usually small and rectangular: *a filing card.* **2** a similar piece of stiff paper, usually folded and decoratively designed: *a get-well card, Christmas cards.* **3** one of a deck of cards used in playing games. **4 cards,** *pl.* **a** a game or games played with such a deck. **b** the playing of such games: *Many of the guests were busy at cards.* **5** a round piece of paper, etc. on which the 32 points of the compass are marked. **6** *Informal.* an amusing person.
a card up one's sleeve, a plan in reserve; extra help kept back until needed.
hold all the cards, have complete control (over).
in or **on the cards,** likely to happen; possible.
play one's cards, deal or act in a calculating manner to gain an end.
put one's cards on the table, show what one has or what one can do; be perfectly frank about plans, resources, etc.
show one's cards, reveal one's plans.
throw up one's cards, give up.
—*v.* **1** provide with a card. **2** put on a card. [< F *carte* < L *charta* < Gk. *chartēs* a leaf of papyrus. Doublet of CHART.]

card[2] (kärd) *n.* a toothed tool or wire brush. —*v.* clean or comb with such a tool. [ME < OF *carde* < Provençal < L *carere* to card; influenced by L *carduus* thistle]

Card. Cardinal.

car·da·mom or **car·da·mum** (kär′də məm) *n.* **1** a spicy seed used as seasoning and in medicine. **2** the Asiatic plant that it grows on. [< L < Gk. *kardamōmon*]

car·da·mon (kär′də mən) *n.* cardamom.

card·board (kärd′bôrd′) *n.* a stiff material made of paper, used to make cards and boxes.

card catalogue a reference catalogue of cards individually listing books and other items in a library or collection; card index.

card·er (kär′dər) *n.* a person or machine that cards wool, cotton, flax, etc.

card file a set of cards arranged systematically and containing data or information.

car·di·ac (kär′dē ak′) *adj.* **1** of or having to do with the heart: *cardiac symptoms.* **2** having to do with the upper part of the stomach.
—*n.* a medicine that stimulates the heart. [< L *cardiacus* < Gk. *kardiakos* < *kardia* heart]

car·di·gan (kär′də gən) *n.* a knitted woollen jacket that buttons up the front; a kind of sweater. [after the Earl of *Cardigan* (1797-1868)]

car·di·nal (kär′də nəl) *adj.* **1** of first importance; main:

His idea has cardinal importance to the plan. **2** bright-red. —*n.* **1** a bright red. **2** in the Roman Catholic Church, one of the princes, or high officials, appointed by the Pope. **3** a cardinal bird. **4** a cardinal number. [ME < OF < L *cardinalis* chief, having to do with a hinge < *cardo* hinge] —**Syn.** *adj.* **1** chief, principal.

car·di·nal·ate (kär′də nəl āt′) *n.* the position or rank of cardinal.

cardinal bird a North American songbird of the finch family, having bright-red feathers marked with black.

cardinal flower **1** the bright-red flower of a North American plant. **2** the plant it grows on.

cardinal grosbeak a cardinal bird.

cardinal number a number that shows how many are meant.

☛ **Cardinal numbers,** like three, ten, 246, and 9,371, are numbers used in counting and to show quantity. They are contrasted with **ordinal numbers,** like first, second, and 24th, which are used to indicate order or position in a series.

cardinal points the four main directions of the compass; north, south, east, and west.

cardinal virtues prudence, fortitude, temperance, and justice. They were considered by the ancient philosophers to be the basic qualities of a good character.

card index a file of cards each referring to a separate item in a collection, list, research study, etc., so arranged as to aid in finding items desired; card catalogue.

card·ing (kär′ding) *n.* the preparation of the fibres of wool, cotton, flax, etc. for spinning by combing them.

cardio- *combining form.* **1** the heart: *Cardiology = the science of the heart.* **2** the heart and —: *Cardiovascular = relating to the heart and blood vessels.*

car·di·o·gram (kär′dē ə gram′) *n.* a graphic record of the action of the heart, made by a cardiograph.

car·di·o·graph (kär′dē ə graf′) *n.* an instrument that records the strength and nature of movements of the heart. [< Gk. *kardia* heart + E *-graph*]

car·di·og·ra·phy (kär′dē og′rə fē) *n.* **-phies.** an examination of the action of the heart by means of a cardiograph.

car·di·ol·o·gist (kär′dē ol′ə jist) *n.* one who studies the heart and its functions, or who specializes in the treatment of heart diseases.

car·di·ol·o·gy (kär′dē ol′ə jē) *n.* the study of the heart and its functions, and the diagnosis and treatment of heart diseases.

car·di·o·vas·cu·lar (kär′dē ō vas′kyů lər) *adj.* of or having to do with both the heart and the blood vessels: *Hardening of the arteries is a cardiovascular disease.*

car·di·tis (kär dī′tis) *n.* inflammation of the heart. [< NL < Gk. *kardia* heart + *-itis*]

card·sharp (kärd′shärp′) *n.* a person who cheats at cards, especially one who does so for a livelihood.

card·sharp·er (kärd′shärp′ər) *n.* a cardsharp.

care (kãr) *n. v.* **cared, car·ing.** —*n.* **1** a burden of thought; worry: *Few people are free from care.* **2** serious attention; caution: *A good cook does her work with care.* **3** an object of concern or attention: *Keeping records is the care of the secretary of a club.* **4** watchful keeping; charge: *The child was left in her sister's care.* **5** food, shelter, and protection: *Your child will have the best of care.* **6 have a care,** be careful. **7 take care,** be careful. **8 take care of, a** attend to. **b** provide for. **c** be careful of. **d** *Informal.* deal with.
—*v.* **1** be concerned; feel an interest: *He cares about music.* **2** like; want; wish: *A cat does not care to be washed.* **3 care for, a** be fond of; like. **b** want; wish: *I don't care for any dessert tonight.* **c** attend to; provide for. [OE *caru*] —**car′er,** *n.*

Syn. *n.* **1 Care, concern, solicitude** = a troubled, worried, or anxious state of mind. **Care** emphasizes the idea of a burden which weighs a person down with responsibilities or worries and fears: *It is care that has made her sick.* **Concern** suggests uneasiness over someone or something one likes or is interested in: *He expressed concern over her health.* **Solicitude** suggests great concern, often together with loving care: *Her friends wait on her with solicitude.*

CARE (kãr) Co-operative for American Remittances to Everywhere, Inc.

ca·reen (kə rēn′) *v.* **1** lean to one side; tilt; tip: *The ship careened in the strong wind.* **2** cause to lean to one side: *The strong wind careened the ship.* **3** lay (a ship) over on one side for cleaning, painting, repairing, etc. **4** rush along with a bobbing, leaning movement: *The waitress careened among the tables, balancing a heavy tray on one hand.* [< F < L *carina* keel]

hat, āge, cãre, fär; let, ēqual, tėrm; it, īce
hot, ōpen, ôrder; oil, out; cup, pùt, rüle, ūse
əbove, takən, pencəl, lemən, circəs
ch, child; ng, long; sh, ship
th, thin; ᴛʜ, then; zh, measure

ca·reer (kə rēr′) *n.* **1** a way of living; occupation; profession: *The boy planned to make law his career.* **2** a general course of action or progress through life: *It is interesting to read of the careers of great men and women.* **3** speed; full speed: *We were in full career when we struck the post.*
—*v.* rush along wildly; dash: *The runaway horse careered through the streets.*
—*adj.* having to do with someone who has seriously followed a profession: *a career diplomat.* [< F *carrière* race course < L *carrus* wagon]

ca·reer·ist (kə rēr′ist) *n.* a person interested only in advancing in his profession, often at the expense of other people.

care·free (kãr′frē′) *adj.* without worry; gay; happy.

care·ful (kãr′fəl) *adj.* **1** thinking what one says; watching what one does; taking pains; watchful; cautious. **2** done with thought or pains; exact; thorough. **3** *Archaic.* anxious; worried. —**care′ful·ly,** *adv.* —**care′ful·ness,** *n.*

Syn. **1 Careful, cautious, wary** = watchful in speaking and acting. **Careful** = being observant and giving serious attention and thought to what one is doing, especially to details: *He is careful to tell the truth at all times.* **Cautious** = very careful, looking ahead for possible risks or dangers, and guarding against them by taking no chances: *He is cautious about making promises.* **Wary** emphasizes the idea of being suspicious and on the alert for danger or trouble: *He is wary of people who suddenly become very friendly.* **2** painstaking, particular.

care·less (kãr′lis) *adj.* **1** not thinking what one says; not watching what one does; not taking enough pains; not watchful or cautious: *One careless step may cost a life.* **2** done without enough thought or pains; not exact or thorough: *careless work.* **3** not troubling oneself. **4** without worry; happy; gay. —**care′less·ly,** *adv.* —**care′less·ness,** *n.* —**Syn. 1** inattentive, thoughtless. **2** inaccurate, negligent. **3** indifferent, unconcerned.

ca·ress (kə res′) *n. v.* touch or stroke to show affection; embrace; kiss. [< F *caresse* < Ital. *carezza* < L *carus* dear]

car·et (kar′ət) *n.* a mark (∧) to show where something should be put in, used in writing and in correcting proof. [< L *caret* is lacking]

care·tak·er (kãr′tāk′ər) *n.* a person, especially a janitor, who takes care of another person, a place, or a thing.
—*adj.* of a government or management, carrying on the functions of an office on a temporary basis pending an election or the accession of a new administration.

care·worn (kãr′wôrn′) *adj.* showing signs of worry; tired; weary.

car·fare (kär′fãr′) *n.* the money that has to be paid for riding on a streetcar, bus, etc.: *He had just enough money for the carfare home.*

car·ful (kär′fůl) *n.* **-fuls.** as much as a car will hold; enough to fill a car: *a carful of children.*

car·go (kär′gō) *n.* **-goes** or **-gos.** the load of goods carried on a ship or airplane. [< Sp. *cargo* < *cargar* load, ult. < L *carrus* wagon]

Car·ib (kar′ib) *n.* **1** a member of an Indian tribe of N.E. South America. **2** a family of languages found primarily in N.E. South America, and to a lesser extent in Central America and the West Indies.

Car·ib·be·an (kar′ə bē′ən or kə rib′ē ən) *adj.* **1** of or having to do with the Caribbean Sea or the islands in it. **2** of or having to do with the Caribs (def. 1).

car·i·boo (kar′ə bü′) *n.* caribou.

Car·i·boo (kar′ə bü′) *n.* **1** a mountain range in British Columbia at the northernmost part of the Fraser River Valley and west of the Rocky Mountains. **2** the area covered by these mountains: *The Gold Rush to the Cariboo began in 1860.*

car·i·bou (kar′ə bü′) *n.* **-bou** or **-bous.** **1** any of several kinds of North American reindeer. The caribou is a provincial emblem of Newfoundland. **2** caribou hide: *caribou parkas*; *caribou mocassins.* [< Cdn.F < Algonquian *xalibu* pawer, from its habit of pawing snow in search of grass]

Caribou Eskimo any of a group of Eskimos living in the Barren Ground of N. Canada. [with reference to their living on caribou]

car·i·ca·ture (kar′ə kə chür′ or kar′ə kə chər) *n. v.* **-tured, -tur·ing.** —*n.* **1** a picture, cartoon, description, etc. that ridiculously exaggerates the peculiarities or defects of a person or thing. **2** the art of making such pictures or descriptions. **3** a very poor imitation.
—*v.* make a caricature of. [< F < Ital. *caricatura* < *caricare* overload, exaggerate] —**Syn.** *n.* **1** burlesque.

car·i·ca·tur·ist (kar′ə kə chür′ist or kar′ə kə chər ist) *n.* a person who makes caricatures.

car·ies (kãr′ēz or kãr′ē ēz′) *n.* the decay of teeth, bones, or tissues. [< L]

car·il·lon (kar′ə lon′, kar′ə lən, or kə ril′yən) *n.* **1** a set of bells arranged for playing melodies: *There is a carillon in the Peace Tower in Ottawa.* **2** a melody played on such bells. **3** a part of an organ that imitates the sound of bells. [< F, ult. < L *quattuor* four; originally consisted of four bells]

car·il·lon·neur (kar′ə lə nėr′) *n.* a person who plays a carillon.

car·i·o·ca (kar′ē ō′kə) *n.* **1** a dance of South America. **2 Carioca,** a native or inhabitant of Rio de Janeiro. [< Brazilian Portuguese *carioca*]

car·i·ole[1] or **car·ri·ole**[1] (kar′ē ōl′) *n.* **1** a small, one-horse carriage. **2** a covered cart. [< F < Ital. *carriuola* < L *carrus* wagon]

car·i·ole[2] or **car·ri·ole**[2] (kar′ ē ōl′) *n. v.* **-oled, -ol·ing.** *Cdn.* —*n.* **1** a light, open sleigh having a single seat for the driver, drawn by one or two horses or, sometimes, by dogs. **2** a light sleigh usually drawn by two horses and having seats for a driver and two passengers. **3** a dogsled, often ornately decorated, for carrying freight or equipped to carry one person lying down: *The sick trapper was brought to the post on a cariole.* —*v.* ride in a cariole. [< Cdn.F]

car·i·ous (kãr′ē əs) *adj.* having caries; decayed. [< L *cariosus* < *caries* decay]

car jockey *Informal.* **1** a person employed by a hotel, restaurant, etc. to park customers' cars and return them to the customer when needed. **2** a person employed by a car rental agency to deliver cars to customers and to collect cars returned by customers.

cark·ing (kär′king) *adj.* troublesome; worrying. [< obs. *cark* burden, worry < AF *karke,* ult. < LL *carricare* load]

carl or **carle** (kärl) *n.* **1** *Archaic.* a peasant; rustic. **2** *Scottish.* a boor; churl. [< ON *karl* man]

car·lin or **car·line** (kär′lin or ker′lin) *n. Scottish.* **1** *Often derogatory.* a woman, especially an old woman. **2** a witch, or a woman charged with being a witch. [ME < Scand.; cf. ON *kerling* < *karl* man + *-ing,* a feminine suffix]

car·load (kär′lōd′) *n.* as much as a car can hold or carry.

Car·lo·vin·gi·an (kar′lə vin′jē ən) *adj. n.* Carolingian.

Car·ma·gnole (kär′mən yōl′) *n.* a dance and song popular during the French Revolution. [< F < *Carmagnola,* a town in Piedmont taken by the revolutionaries]

car·man (kär′mən) *n.* **-men** (-mən). **1** a motorman or conductor of a streetcar. **2** a person who drives a cart.

Car·mel·ite (kär′məl īt′) *n.* a mendicant friar or nun of a religious order founded in the 12th century or earlier.

car·min·a·tive (kär min′ə tiv, kär′mə nə tiv, or kär′mə nā′tiv) *adj.* expelling gas from the stomach and intestines. —*n.* a medicine that does this. [< L *carminatus* carded; cleansed]

car·mine (kär′mən or kär′mīn) *n.* **1** a deep red with a tinge of purple. **2** a light crimson. **3** a crimson coloring matter found in cochineal, used to stain microscopic slides and formerly as a dye.
—*adj.* **1** deep-red with a tinge of purple. **2** light-crimson. [< Med.L *carminium* < Arabic *qirmiz* the kermes insect, and L *minium* red lead. See CRIMSON.]

car·nage (kär′nij) *n.* the slaughter of a great number: *The carnage caused by the atomic bomb was shocking.* [< F < Ital. *carnaggio* < L *caro, carnis* flesh]

car·nal (kär′nəl) *adj.* **1** worldly; not spiritual. **2** bodily; sensual: *Gluttony and drunkenness have been called carnal vices.* [< L *carnalis* < *caro, carnis* flesh. Doublet of CHARNEL.] —**car′nal·ly,** *adv.*

car·nal·i·ty (kär nal′ə tē) *n.* **-ties. 1** worldliness. **2** sensuality.

car·na·tion (kär nā′shən) *n.* **1** a red, white, or pink flower having a sweet, spicy fragrance. **2** the plant that it grows on. **3** a rosy pink.
—*adj.* rosy-pink. [< F < Ital. *carnagione* flesh color < *carnaggio.* See CARNAGE.]

car·nel·ian (kär nēl′yən or kär nēl′ē ən) *n.* **1** a red or reddish-brown stone used in jewellery; a kind of quartz. **2** a piece of this stone, or a gem made from it. Also, **cornelian.** [alteration of *cornelian*; influenced by L *caro* flesh]

car·nie (kär′nē) *n.* **-nies.** *Slang.* **1** a carnival. **2** a person who works or performs in a carnival. Also, **carny.**

car·ni·val (kär′nə vəl) *n.* **1** a place of amusement or a travelling show having merry-go-rounds, side shows, etc. **2** an organized program of events involving a particular sport, institution, etc.: *a water carnival.* **3** feasting and merrymaking; noisy and unrestrained revels; celebration. **4** a time of feasting and merrymaking just before Lent. [< Ital. *carnevale* < Med.L < L *carnem levare* the putting away of meat (before Lent)]

Car·niv·o·ra (kär niv′ə rə) *n.pl.* in zoology, a large group or order of flesh-eating animals. Cats, dogs, lions, tigers, and bears belong to the Carnivora. [< NL]

car·ni·vore (kär′nə vôr′) *n.* **1** in zoology, a flesh-eating animal, one of the Carnivora. **2** in botany, a plant that eats insects. [< F]

car·niv·o·rous (kär niv′ə rəs) *adj.* **1** flesh-eating: *Wolves and bears are carnivorous animals.* **2** of or having to do with the Carnivora. [< L *carnivorus* < *caro, carnis* flesh + *vorare* devour]

car·no·tite (kär′nə tīt′) *n.* a yellowish, radio-active mineral found in the W. and S.W. United States. It is a source of radium. [after Adolphe *Carnot* (1839-1920), a French inspector-general of mines]

car·ny (kär′nē) *n.* carnie.

car·ol (kar′əl) *n. v.* **-olled** or **oled, -ol·ling** or **-ol·ing.** —*n.* **1** a song of joy. **2** a hymn: *Christmas carols.*
—*v.* **1** sing; sing joyously: *The birds were carolling in the trees.* **2** praise with carols. [ME < OF *carole,* probably < L < Gk. *choraulēs* flute player accompanying a choral dance < *choros* dance + *aulos* flute] —**car′ol·ler** or —**car′ol·er,** *n.*

Car·o·line (kar′ə līn′ or kar′ə lin) *adj.* of or having to do with Charles, especially Charles I or Charles II of England.

Car·o·lin·gi·an (kar′ə lin′jē ən) *adj.* of or having to do with the second Frankish dynasty. It ruled in France from A.D. 751 to 987, in Germany from A.D. 751 to 911, and in Italy from A.D. 751 to 887. —*n.* a ruler during the Carolingian dynasty: *Charlemagne was a Carolingian.* Also, **Carlovingian.**

Car·o·lin·i·an (kar′ə lin′ē ən) *adj.* of North Carolina and South Carolina, or of either of them. —*n.* a native or inhabitant of North Carolina or South Carolina.

car·om (kar′əm) *n.* **1** in billiards, a kind of shot in which the ball struck with the cue hits two balls, one after the other. **2** a similar shot in other games. **3** a hitting and bouncing off.
—*v.* **1** make a carom. **2** hit and bounce off. [< F < Sp. *carambola,* ? < Malay *carambil,* name of fruit]

car·oms (kar′əmz) *n.pl.* a game played on a square board by two or four players, who try to shoot 24 round counters into pockets at the corners.

ca·rot·id (kə rot′id) *n.* in anatomy, either of two large arteries, one on each side of the neck, that carry blood to the head. —*adj.* having to do with these arteries. [< F < Gk. *karōtides* < *karos* stupor (state produced by compression of carotids)]

ca·rous·al (kə rouz′əl) *n.* a noisy revel; a drinking party.

ca·rouse (kə rouz′) *n. v.* **-roused, -rous·ing.** —*n.* a noisy feast; a drinking party. —*v.* drink heavily; take part in noisy feasts or revels. [< obs. adv. < G *gar aus(trinken)* (drink) all up] —**ca·rous′er,** *n.*

car·ou·sel (kar′ə zel′ or kar′ə sel′) *n.* carrousel.

carp[1] (kärp) *v.* find fault; complain. [< ON *karpa* wrangle] —**carp′er,** *n.* —**carp′ing·ly,** *adv.* —**Syn.** cavil.

carp[2] (kärp) *n.* **carp** or **carps. 1** a fresh-water fish that has many bones. It feeds mostly on plants. **2** any of a group of similar fishes, including goldfish, minnows, chub, and dace. [ME < OF *carpe* < Provençal < LL *carpa* < Gmc.]

car·pal (kär′pəl) *adj.* of the carpus. —*n.* in anatomy, a bone of the carpus. [< NL *carpalis* < Gk. *karpos* wrist]

car·pe di·em (kär′pē dē′em or dī′em) *Latin.* enjoy today; make the most of the present.

car·pel (kär′pəl) *n.* in botany, a pistil of a flower, either simple, or one member of a compound pistil. It is regarded as a modified leaf. [< Gk. *karpos* fruit]

car·pen·ter (kär′pən tər) *n.* a man whose work is building with wood. —*v.* do such work. [ME < ONF *carpentier* < L *carpentarius* < *carpentum* wagon]

car·pen·try (kär′pən trē) *n.* the work of a carpenter.

car·pet (kär′pit) *n.* **1** a heavy, woven fabric for covering floors and stairs. **2** a covering made of this fabric. **3** anything like a carpet: *He walked on a carpet of grass.* **4 on the carpet, a** in the condition of being considered or discussed. **b** *Informal.* in the state of being scolded or rebuked.
—*v.* cover with a carpet: *In the spring, the ground was carpeted with violets.* [ME < OF < Med.L *carpeta* thick cloth < L *carpere* card (wool)]

car·pet·bag (kär′pit bag′) *n.* a travelling bag made of carpet.

car·pet·bag·ger (kär′pit bag′ər) *n. Derogatory.* in the United States, a Northerner who went to the South to get political or other advantages during the time of disorganization that followed the Civil War.

carpet beetle or **bug** a small beetle whose larva destroys carpets and other woollen fabrics.

car·pet·ing (kär′pit ing) *n.* **1** a fabric for carpets. **2** carpets.

carpet sweeper a device for cleaning carpets and rugs.

car pool an arrangement by which members of a group take turns at providing transportation in their own cars, especially to and from work.

car·port (kär′pôrt′) *n.* a roofed shelter for one or more automobiles. It is usually attached to a house and open on at least one side.

carp·suck·er (kärp′suk′ər) *n.* any of several large carplike fresh-water fishes of North America; buffalo fish.

car·pus (kär′pəs) *n.* **-pi** (-pī or -pē). in anatomy: **1** wrist. **2** bones of the wrist. [< NL < Gk. *karpos* wrist]

car·rack (kar′ək) *n.* in former times, a large sailing ship; galleon. [ME < OF *carraque* < Sp. < Arabic *qaraqir*, pl.]

car·ra·geen or **car·ra·gheen** (kar′ə gēn′) *n.* a purplish edible seaweed common on North Atlantic coasts, used in medicine and in processing certain foods. [< *Carragheen*, near Waterford, Ireland, where it is abundant]

car·rel (kar′əl) *n.* an enclosed space for individual study in a library, usually containing a desk and bookshelves. [alteration of ME *carole* ring. See CAROL.]

car·riage (kar′ij; *for 6, also* kar′ē ij) *n.* **1** a vehicle that moves on wheels. Carriages are usually pulled by horses and are used to carry people. **2** a frame on wheels that supports a gun. **3** a moving part of a machine that supports some other part: *the carriage of a typewriter.* **4** the manner of holding the head and body; bearing: *She has a queenly carriage.* **5** the act of taking persons or goods from one place to another; carrying; transporting: *carriage charges.* **6** the cost or price of carrying. **7** management; a way of handling: *I congratulate you on your carriage of this enterprise.* [ME < ONF *cariage* < *carier.* See CARRY.] —**Syn. 4** See **bearing.**

hat, āge, cãre, fär; let, ēqual, tėrm; it, īce
hot, ōpen, ôrder; oil, out; cup, pu̇t, rüle, ūse
əbove, takən, pencəl, lemən, circəs
ch, child; ng, long; sh, ship
th, thin; ᴛʜ, then; zh, measure

carriage bolt a bolt having a round shaft but for a square part just under the head, formerly used chiefly to fasten together parts of a carriage.

carriage trade the wealthy patrons, or customers, of a theatre, restaurant, store, etc. so called because such persons formerly drove in private carriages.

car·ri·er (kar′ē ər) *n.* **1** a person or thing that carries something: *A postman is a mail carrier. Trains, buses, and ships are carriers.* **2** anything designed to carry something in or on. **3** a person or thing that carries or transmits a disease. Carriers are often healthy persons who are immune to a disease but carry its germs: *a typhoid carrier.* **4** carrier wave. **5** a company that transports goods, people, etc., usually over certain routes and according to fixed schedules: *Bus systems, railways, airlines, and truck companies are carriers.* **6** an aircraft carrier. **7** a carrier pigeon.

Car·ri·er (kar′ē ər) *n.* **1** a group of Athapascan Indians living over a large area in the interior of British Columbia. **2** a member of this group. **3** the Athapascan language of this group. [from the custom of a Carrier widow carrying the charred bones of her dead husband in a net bag]

carrier pigeon 1 *Informal.* a homing pigeon. **2** in technical use: **a** a breed of large domestic pigeon. **b** a bird of this breed.

carrier wave a radio wave whose intensity and frequency are varied in order to transmit a signal.

car·ri·ole (kar′ē ōl′) *n.* cariole.

car·ri·on (kar′ē ən) *n.* **1** dead and decaying flesh. **2** rottenness; filth. —*adj.* **1** dead and decaying. **2** feeding on dead and decaying flesh. **3** rotten; filthy. [ME < OF *carogne*, ult. < L *caro* flesh. Doublet of CRONE.]

carrion crow 1 the common European crow. **2** a black vulture of the southern United States.

car·ro·nade (kar′ə nād′) *n.* formerly, a short cannon with a large bore. [< *Carron*, Scotland]

car·rot (kar′ət) *n.* **1** a plant having a long, tapering, orange-red root that is eaten as a vegetable. **2** its root. [< F *carotte* < L < Gk. *karōton*]

car·rot·y (kar′ət ē) *adj.* **1** like a carrot in color; orange-red. **2** red-haired.

car·rou·sel or **car·ou·sel** (kar′ə zel′ or kar′ə sel′) *n.* **1** a merry-go-round. **2** at an airport, a revolving circular platform onto which the baggage of arriving passengers is delivered from a central chute. [< F < Ital. *carosello* < L *carrus* cart]

car·ry (kar′ē) *v.* **-ried, -ry·ing,** *n.* **-ries.** —*v.* **1** take from one place or time to another: *Buses carry passengers. Railways carry coal from the mines to the town.* **2** bear the weight of; hold up; support; sustain: *Those columns carry the roof.* **3** hold (one's body and head) in a certain way; have a certain kind of posture: *This boy carries himself well.* **4** capture; win: *Our troops carried the enemy's fort.* **5** get (a motion or bill) passed or adopted: *The motion to adjourn the meeting was carried.* **6** continue; extend: *carry a road into the mountains.* **7** cover the distance; have the power of throwing or driving: *His voice will carry to the back of the room. This gun will carry a half mile.* **8** keep in stock: *This store carries clothing for men.* **9** of a newspaper, magazine, etc., print an article in its pages: *The evening newspapers carried a review of the new play.* **10** sing with correct or nearly correct pitch: *He can carry a tune.* **11** sing or play (a

melody, part, etc.): *She will carry the soprano solos. The first violins carry the melody.* **12** influence greatly; lead: *His acting carried the audience.* **13** have as a result; have as an attribute, property, etc.; involve: *His judgment carries great weight.* **14** keep on the account books of a business. **15** in adding, take over to the column of the next denomination.
carry away, arouse strong feeling in; influence beyond reason.
carry everything before one, meet with uninterrupted success; be very successful in spite of opposition.
carry forward, a go ahead with; make progress with. **b** in bookkeeping, re-enter (an item or items already entered) on the next or a later page or column of an accounting record.
carry off, a win (a prize, honor, etc.). **b** succeed with.
carry on, a do; manage; conduct. **b** go ahead with; go on with after being stopped. **c** keep going; continue. **d** *Informal.* behave wildly or foolishly.
carry out, do; get done; accomplish; complete.
carry over, a have left over; be left over. **b** keep until later; continue; extend.
carry the ball, *Informal.* take the chief part in promoting or carrying through a plan or activity.
carry the day, a be victorious in battle. **b** be successful against opposition.
carry through, a do; get done; accomplish; complete. **b** bring through trouble; keep from being discouraged.
—*n.* **1** the distance covered; distance that something goes. **2** the act of carrying boats and supplies from one body of water to another; portage. **3** a place where this is done. **4** in golf, the distance a ball travels in the air before hitting the ground. [< ONF *carier* < LL *carricare* < L *carrus* wagon, cart. Doublet of CHARGE.]
Syn. *v.* **1 Carry, convey, transport** = to take or bring from one place to another. **Carry,** the general word, emphasizes the idea of holding and moving a person or thing in or with something, such as a vehicle, container, hands, or paws: *John was carrying a heavy box.* **Convey** emphasizes getting a person or thing to a place by some means or through some channel, and therefore is used figuratively in the sense of communicate: *Escalators convey people. Language conveys ideas.* **Transport** = to carry or convey people and goods in a ship, plane, or vehicle: *Trucks transport freight.*

car·ry·all[1] (kar′ē ol′ or -ôl′) *n.* **1** a light, covered one-horse carriage. **2** a cariole. [alteration of *cariole*]

car·ry·all[2] (kar′ē ol′ or -ôl′) *n.* **1** any of several vehicles so named because of their large capacity. **2** a kind of spacious shopping bag.

carry cot a collapsible, boxlike cradle equipped with handles and used for carrying a baby: *Mother always uses the carry cot when she takes the baby out in the car.*

carrying charge the interest charged on money owing for goods or services bought on credit.

car·ry·ing-on (kar′ē ing on′) *n.* **carry·ings-on.** *Informal.* **1** a loud disturbance; fuss. **2** conspicuous, uninhibited, or indiscreet behavior.

carrying place *Cdn.* a portage.

car·ry-o·ver (kar′ē ō′vər) *n.* the part left over.

car seat 1 the seat of an automobile. **2** a small, light seat for a child, designed to hook over a standard automobile seat.

car-sick (kär′sik′) *adj.* nauseated by travelling in a car, train, etc. —**car′sick′ness,** *n.*

cart (kärt) *n.* **1** a strong, wheeled vehicle. **2** a light wagon, used to deliver goods, etc. **3** a small, wheeled vehicle, moved by hand. **4 put the cart before the horse,** reverse the proper or natural order of things.
—*v.* carry in a cart. [ME < ON *kartr*]

cart·age (kär′tij) *n.* **1** the act of carting. **2** the cost or price of carting.

carte[1] (kärt) *n.* **1** a card. **2** a bill of fare. **3** a map; chart. [< F. See CARD[1].]

carte[2] (kärt) *n.* in fencing, a thrust or parry. [< F *quarte* < Ital. *quarta* fourth]

carte blanche (kärt′ bläNsh′) *French.* **1** full authority; freedom to use one's discretion. **2** freedom to do whatever one pleases.

car·tel (kär tel′ or kär′təl) *n.* **1** a large group of business companies that agree to regulate prices and production, generally with the aim of obtaining maximum profits. **2** a written agreement between countries at war for the exchange of prisoners or for some other purpose. **3** a ship used for the exchange of prisoners or for carrying proposals between opposing forces. **4** formerly, a written challenge to a duel. [< F < Ital. *cartello* little card[1]]

car·tel·ize (kär tel′īz or kär′təl īz′) *v.* **-ized, -iz·ing.** **1** combine in a cartel. **2** join with other businesses to form a cartel.

cart·er (kär′tər) *n.* **1** a man whose work is driving a cart or truck. **2** a person who runs a trucking business.

Car·te·sian (kär tē′zhən) *adj.* **1** of or having to do with René Descartes (1596-1650), a French philosopher and mathematician. **2** of or suggestive of his doctrines or methods. [< NL *Cartesianus* < *Cartesius,* Latinized form of *Descartes*]

Cartesian set in mathematics and logic, the set of all ordered pairs that can be formed by matching each member of one set in turn with each member of a second set.

Car·tha·gin·i·an (kär′thə jin′ē ən) *adj.* of Carthage. —*n.* a native or inhabitant of Carthage.

Car·thu·sian (kär thü′zhən) *n.* in the Roman Catholic Church, a monk or nun of an order founded by St. Bruno in 1086. —*adj.* of this order. [< *Cartusia,* now *Chartreuse,* the village in the French Alps where the first monastery of the order was founded]

car·ti·lage (kär′tə lij) *n.* in vertebrates: **1** the firm, tough, elastic, flexible substance forming parts of the skeleton; gristle. **2** a part formed of this substance. The nose consists partly of cartilage. [< F < L *cartilago*]

car·ti·lag·i·nous (kär′tə laj′ə nəs) *adj.* **1** of or like cartilage; gristly. **2** having the skeleton formed mostly of cartilage.

cart·load (kärt′lōd′) *n.* as much as a cart can hold or carry.

car·to·gram (kär′tə gram′) *n.* a map that gives information by means of dots, lines, etc.

car·tog·ra·pher (kär tog′rə fər) *n.* a maker of maps or charts.

car·to·graph·ic (kär′tə graf′ik) *adj.* having to do with cartography or cartographers.

car·tog·ra·phy (kär tog′rə fē) *n.* the making of maps or charts. [< Med.L *carta* chart, map + E *-graphy*]

car·ton (kär′tən) *n.* **1** a box made of cardboard, etc. **2** the amount that a carton can hold. **3** a carton and its contents. [< F *carton* cardboard < Ital. *cartone* < *carta* < L *charta.* Related to CARD[1].]

car·toon (kär tün′) *n.* **1** a sketch or drawing that interests or amuses by showing persons, things, political events, etc. in an exaggerated way. **2** a full-size drawing of a design or painting, used as model for a fresco, mosaic, tapestry, etc. **3** a comic strip. **4** a movie made up of a series of drawings; animated cartoon: *Cartoons often show animals engaging in human activities.*
—*v.* make a cartoon of. [var. of *carton;* because drawn on paper]

car·toon·ist (kär tün′ist) *n.* a person who draws cartoons.

car·tridge (kär′trij) *n.* **1** a case made of metal or cardboard for holding gunpowder. **2** a small container holding a refill, or refills, of ink, film, razor blades, etc.: *I need a cartridge for my pen.* **3** a container holding an endless loop of pre-recorded sound tape, videotape, or film. **4** a unit containing the stylus (needle) in the pick-up of a phonograph. [alteration of F *cartouche* roll of paper]

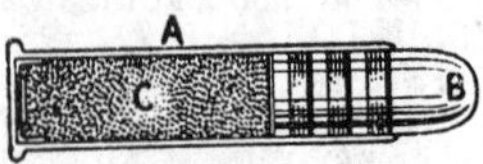

Cartridge; A, metal case; B, bullet; C, powder.

cartridge paper 1 a thick paper formerly used to make cartridges, later as drawing paper. **2** a kind of wallpaper.

cart·wheel (kärt′hwēl′ or -wēl′) *n.* **1** the wheel of a cart. **2** a sideways handspring or somersault. **3** *Informal.*

hat, āge, cãre, fär; let, ēqual, tėrm; it, īce
hot, ōpen, ôrder; oil, out; cup, pu̇t, rüle, ūse
əbove, takən, pencəl, lemən, circəs
ch, child; ng, long; sh, ship
th, thin; ᴛʜ, then; zh, measure

a woman's hat with a very wide brim. **4** *Slang.* a large coin; silver dollar. —*v.* **1** make a sideways handspring or somersault. **2** move like a rotating wheel.

carve (kärv) *v.* **carved, carv·ing. 1** cut into slices or pieces: *carve the meat at the table.* **2** cut; make by cutting: *Statues are carved from marble, stone, or wood.* **3** decorate with figures or designs cut on the surface: *carve a wooden tray.* **4** cut (a design, etc.) on or into a surface: *They carved their initials on the tree.* **5** make as if by cutting: *He ruthlessly carved himself a financial empire.* [OE *ceorfan*]

car·vel (kär′vəl) *n.* caravel.

carv·en (kär′vən) *adj.* carved; decorated by carving; sculptured.

carv·er (kär′vər) *n.* **1** a person who carves. **2** a large knife for carving meat.

carv·ing (kär′ving) *n.* **1** the act or art of one that carves. **2** a piece of carved work; a carved decoration: *a wood carving.*

car·y·at·id (kar′ē at′id) *n.* **-ids, -i·des** (-ə dēz′). in architecture, a statue of a woman used as a column. [< L *Caryatides* < Gk. *Karyatides* women of Caryae]

ca·sa·ba or **cas·sa·ba** (kə sä′bə) *n.* a kind of winter muskmelon with a yellow rind. [< *Kasaba*, a town near Izmir (formerly Smyrna), Turkey]

Cas·a·no·va (kas′ ə nō′ və or kaz′ ə nō′və) *n.* a man who has many affairs with women, especially an immoral adventurer with women. [< Giovanni Giacomo *Casanova* (1725-1798), an Italian adventurer, known for his *Memoirs*]

Cas·bah (käz′bä) *n.* **1** the native section of Algiers. **2 casbah,** the Arab section of any city with a large Arab population. [< Arabic *qasaba* fortress, citadel]

cas·cade (kas kād′) *n. v.* **-cad·ed, -cad·ing.** —*n.* **1** a small waterfall. **2** anything like a waterfall. —*v.* fall, or cause to fall, in a cascade. [< F < Ital. *cascata* < L *cadere* fall]

cas·car·a (kas kãr′ə) *n.* **1** a kind of buckthorn yielding cascara sagrada. **2** cascara sagrada. [< Sp. *cáscara* bark]

cas·car·a sa·gra·da (sə grä′də or sə grā′də) the dried bark of cascara, used as a laxative. [< Sp. *cascara sagrada* sacred bark]

cas·ca·ril·la (kas′kə ril′ə) *n.* **1** Also, **cascarilla bark,** the aromatic bark of a West Indian shrub of the spurge family used as flavoring for tobacco or as a tonic. **2** the shrub itself. [< Sp. *cascarilla*, dim. of *cáscara*. See CASCARA.]

case[1] (kās) *n.* **1** an instance; example: *a case of poor work.* **2** a condition; situation; state: *a case of poverty.* **3** the actual condition; real situation; true state: *He said he had done the work, but that was not the case.* **4** an instance of a disease or injury: *a case of measles.* **5** a person who has a disease or injury; patient. **6** a matter for a law court to decide. **7** a statement of facts raising a point of view for a court to consider. **8** a convincing argument. **9** in grammar: **a** the various forms of a noun or pronoun and, in some languages, of an adjective used to show a relation to other words. *I* is the nominative case; *me* is the objective case. **b** the relation shown by such a form. *I* is in the nominative case. **10** *Informal.* a queer or unusual person. **11 in any case,** under any circumstances; no matter what happens; in any event; anyhow. **12 in case,** if it should happen that; if; supposing. **13 in case of,** if there should be; in the event of: *In case of fire, walk to the nearest door.* **14 in no case,** under no circumstances. [ME < OF *cas* < L *casus* a falling, chance < *cadere* fall]

Syn. 1 Case, instance = example. **Case** applies to a fact, actual happening, situation, etc. that is typical of a general kind or class: *His accident is a case of reckless driving.* **Instance** applies to an individual case used to illustrate a general idea or conclusion: *Going through a stop signal is an instance of his recklessness.*

☛ **case.** Writers often make unnecessary and ineffective use of expressions containing the word *case*: *Although I read many stories, in not one case was I satisfied with the ending. She used the same plot before in the case of a short story about pioneer days. In many cases students did extensive research on their projects.* In the first sentence, *case* is entirely unnecessary. The second can be improved by dropping *the case of.* The third can be made less wordy and more emphatic by substituting *Many students* for *In many cases students.*

case[2] (kās) *n. v.* **cased, cas·ing.** —*n.* **1** anything to hold or cover something. **2** a covering; sheath: *Put the knife back in the case.* **3** a box: *There is a big case full of books in the hall.* **4** the quantity in a box, etc.: *My mother bought a case of ginger ale.* **5** a frame: *A window fits in a case.* **6** in printing, a tray for type, with a space for each letter. **7 lower case,** small letters. **8 upper case,** capital letters.
—*v.* **1** put in a case; cover with a case. **2** *Slang.* look over carefully; inspect; examine: *The thieves cased the bank.* [ME < ONF *casse* < L *capsa* box < *capere* hold. Doublet of CASH[1], CHASE[3].]

ca·se·fy (kā′sə fī′) *v.* **-fied, -fy·ing.** make or become like cheese. [< L *caseus* cheese + E *-fy*]

case·hard·en (kās′här′dən) *v.* **1** harden (iron or steel) on the surface. **2** render callous; make unfeeling.

case history all the facts about a person or group that may be useful in deciding what medical or psychiatric treatment, social services, etc. are needed.

ca·sein (kā′sēn or kā′sē in) *n.* the protein present in milk, the chief ingredient of cheese. It is used in making plastics, synthetic fibres, and various paints. [< L *caseus* cheese]

case knife 1 a knife carried in a case. **2** a table knife.

case law law based on previous judicial decisions rather than on statutes.

case·mate (kās′māt) *n.* **1** a bombproof chamber in a fort or rampart, with openings through which cannon may be fired. **2** an armored enclosure protecting guns on a warship. [< F < Ital. *casamatta* (influenced by *casa* house), earlier *camata*, apparently < Gk. *chasmata* openings]

case·ment (kās′mənt) *n.* **1** a window opening on vertical hinges. **2** *Poetic.* any window. **3** a casing; covering; frame.

ca·se·ous (kā′sē əs) *adj.* of or like cheese. [< L *caseus* cheese]

ca·serns or **ca·sernes** (kə zėrnz′) *n. pl.* formerly, places for soldiers to live in a fortified town; barracks. [< F < Sp. *caserna* < L *casa* house]

case·work (kās′wėrk′) *n.* a thorough study of the character and present and past circumstances of a maladjusted person, family, or group, carried out by a social worker to serve as a basis for guidance or treatment. —**case′work′er,** *n.*

cash[1] (kash) *n.* **1** ready money; coins and bills. **2** money, or something recognized as the equivalent of money, such as a cheque, paid at the time of buying something.
—*v.* **1** get cash for: *cash a cheque.* **2** give cash for: *The bank will cash your five-dollar cheque.* **3 cash in, a** *Informal.* change (poker chips, etc.) into cash. **b** *Slang.* die. **4 cash in on,** *Informal.* **a** make a profit from. **b** take advantage of; use to advantage. [< F *caisse* < Provençal < L *capsa* box, coffer. Doublet of CASE[2], CHASE[3].]
—**cash′a·ble,** *adj.*

cash[2] (kash) *n.* **cash. 1** in China, India, etc., a coin of small value. **2** in China, a copper coin with a square hole in it. [< Tamil *kasu*]

cash-and-carry (kash′ən kar′ē) *adj.* **1** with immediate payment for goods and without delivery service. **2** operated on this basis: *a cash-and-carry store.*

cash·book (kash′bu̇k′) *n.* a book in which a record is kept of money received and paid out.

cash crop a crop grown for sale, rather than for consumption on the farm.

cash·ew (kash′ü or kə shü′) *n.* **1** a small, edible, kidney-shaped nut. **2** the tropical American tree that this nut grows on. [< F *acajou* < Brazilian Pg. *acajú* < Tupi-Guarani]

cash·ier[1] (kash ēr′) *n.* a person who has charge of money in a bank or business. [< F *caissier* treasurer < *caisse.* See CASH[1].]

cash·ier[2] (kash ēr′) *v.* dismiss from the armed services for some dishonorable act; discharge in disgrace: *The dishonest officer was deprived of his rank and cashiered.* [< Du. *casseren* < F < L *quassare* shatter and LL *cassare* annul]

cashier's cheque a cheque drawn by a bank on its own funds and signed by its cashier.

cash·mere (kash'mēr) *n.* **1** a fine, soft wool from a breed of goats found in Kashmir and Tibet. **2** an expensive kind of shawl made of this wool. **3** a fine, soft wool from sheep. **4** a fine, soft woollen cloth. [< *Kashmir*, north of India]

cash on delivery payment when goods are delivered. *Abbrev.*: C.O.D. or c.o.d.

cash register a machine that records and shows the amount of a sale. It usually has a drawer to hold money.

cas·ing (kās'ing) *n.* **1** a covering; case. **2** the part of a tire that encloses the inner tube. **3** a frame: *A window fits in a casing.*

ca·si·no (kə sē'nō) *n.* **-nos. 1** a building or room for public shows, dancing, gambling, etc. **2** cassino. [< Ital. *casino*, dim. of *casa* house < L *casa*]

cask (kask) *n.* **1** a barrel. A cask, which may be large or small, is usually made to hold liquids. **2** the amount that a cask holds. **3** a cask and its contents. [< Sp. *casco* skull, cask of wine, ult. < L *quassare* break]

cas·ket (kas'kit) *n.* **1** a small box to hold jewels, letters, etc. **2** a coffin. [origin uncertain]

casque (kask) *n.* a helmet. [< F < Sp. *casco*. See CASK.]

cas·sa·ba (kə sä'bə) *n.* casaba.

Cas·san·dra (kə san'drə) *n.* **1** in Greek legend, a daughter of King Priam of Troy. Apollo gave her the gift of prophecy, but later in anger decreed that no one should believe her. **2** any person who prophesies misfortune but is not believed.

cas·sa·tion (ka sā'shən) *n.* an annulment; reversal. [< LL *cassatio, -onis* < *cassare* annul]

cas·sa·va (kə sa'və) *n.* **1** a tropical plant having starchy roots. **2** a nutritious starch from its roots. Tapioca is made from cassava. [< F *cassave* < Sp. < Haitian *cacábi* < Arawakan]

cas·se·role (kas'ə rōl') *n.* **1** a covered baking dish in which food can be both cooked and served. **2** a mould, often of boiled rice, mashed potatoes, etc., filled with meat or vegetables. **3** the food prepared in a casserole. **4** a small, deep dish with a handle, used in chemical laboratories. [< F *casserole* < *casse* pan < VL *cattia* < Gk. *kyathion*, dim. of *kyathos* cup]

cas·sette (ka set') *n.* **1** a cartridge for roll film. **2** a sealed container holding a built-in reel of sound tape, videotape, or film, and a pick-up reel. **3** a case of baked clay in which china and other delicate ware are enclosed while baking. **4** *Cdn.* formerly, a specially made box or trunk used by the fur traders for transporting personal effects on journeys inland. [< F *cassette* small case < OF *casse* case[2]]

cas·sia (kas'ē ə or kash'ə) *n.* **1** an inferior kind of cinnamon. **2** the tree of southern China that produces it. **3** the plant from whose leaves and pods the drug senna is obtained. **4** the pods or their pulp. [OE < L < Gk. < Hebrew *q'tsi'ah*]

cas·si·no or **ca·si·no** (kə sē'nō) *n.* a card game in which the ten of diamonds and the two of spades have special counting value. [var. of *casino*]

Cas·si·o·pe·ia (kas'ē ə pē'ə) *n.* **1** in Greek legend, the wife of an Ethiopian king and mother of Andromeda. **2** in astronomy, a northern constellation thought to resemble Cassiopeia sitting in a chair.

cas·sock (kas'ək) *n.* a long outer garment, usually black, worn by a clergyman. See picture in the next column. [< F *casaque* < Ital. *casacca*]

cas·socked (kas'əkt) *adj.* wearing a cassock.

cas·so·war·y (kas'ə wer'ē) *n.* **-war·ies.** a large bird of Australia and New Guinea, like an ostrich, but smaller. Cassowaries run swiftly, but cannot fly. [< Malay *kasuari*]

cast (kast) *v.* **cast, cast·ing,** *n. adj.* **—*v.* 1** throw. **2** throw one end of a fishing line out into the water. **3** throw off; discard; let fall: *The snake cast its skin.* **4** direct or turn: *He cast me a look.* **5** shape by pouring or squeezing into a mould to harden. Metal is first melted and then cast. **6** arrange: *He cast his plans into final form.* **7** in the theatre: **a** assign the various parts of (a play). **b** appoint (actors) for the parts. **c** fill (a part) by assigning an actor to it. **8** add; calculate.
cast a ballot, vote.
cast about, search or seek; look around.
cast away, a abandon. **b** shipwreck.
cast down, a turn downward; lower. **b** make sad or discouraged.
cast off, a let loose; set free; untie from moorings: *cast off a boat.* **b** in knitting, make the last row of stitches.
cast on, in knitting, make the first row of stitches.
cast out, drive away; banish or expel.
cast up, a turn upward; raise. **b** add up; find the sum of.
—*n.* 1 a throw; the distance a thing is thrown. **2** the act of throwing a fishing line: *He made a skilful cast from the river bank.* **3** something made by casting; something that is moulded. **4** a mould used in casting. **5** a plaster cast used to support a broken bone while it is mending: *He had his arm in a cast for more than a month.* **6** the actors in a play. **7** the form; look or appearance. **8** a kind or sort. **9** a slight amount of color; tinge: *a white dress with a pink cast.* **10** a slight squint.
—*adj.* made by casting. [ME < ON *kasta* throw]
—Syn. *v.* **1** see **throw.**

cas·ta·net (kas'tə net') *n.* a pair, or one of a pair, of instruments like little cymbals, made of hard wood or ivory. Castanets are held in the hand and clicked together to beat time for dancing or music. [< Sp. *castaneta* < L *castanea.* See CHESTNUT.]

cast·a·way (kast'ə wā') *adj.* **1** thrown away; cast adrift. **2** outcast. **—*n.* 1** a shipwrecked person. **2** an outcast.

Castanets

caste (kast) *n.* **1** a Hindu social class. By tradition, a Hindu is born into the caste of his father and cannot rise from it. **2** the system or basis of this division. **3** an exclusive social group; distinct class. **4** a social system having class distinctions based on birth, rank, wealth, position, etc. **5 lose caste,** lose social rank or position. [< Sp., Pg. *casta* race < L *castus* pure. Doublet of CHASTE.]

cas·tel·lan (kas'tə lən) *n.* the governor of a castle. [< L *castellanus* occupant of a stronghold < *castellum.* See CASTLE.]

cas·tel·lat·ed (kas'tə lāt'id) *adj.* **1** like a castle; having turrets and battlements. **2** having many castles.

cast·er[1] (kas'tər) *n.* a person or thing that casts.

cast·er[2] or **cast·or** (kas'tər) *n.* **1** a small wheel beneath a leg of a piece of furniture. **2** a bottle containing salt, mustard, vinegar, or other seasoning for table use. **3** a stand or rack for such bottles.

cas·ti·gate (kas'tə gāt') *v.* **-gat·ed, -gat·ing.** criticize severely; punish. [< L *castigare*, ult. < *castus* pure] **—cas'ti·ga'tor,** *n.*

cas·ti·ga·tion (kas'tə gā'shən) *n.* severe criticism; punishment.

A clergyman wearing a cassock

Cas·tile soap or **cas·tile soap** (kas'tēl or kas tēl') a pure, hard soap made from olive oil and soda. [< *Castile*, a region in north and central Spain]

Cas·til·ian (kas til'yən or kas til'ē ən) *adj.* of Castile, its people, or their language. In Spain, **Castilian Spanish** is the accepted or standard form of the language. **—*n.* 1** Castilian Spanish. **2** a native or inhabitant of Castile.

cast·ing (kas'ting) *n.* **1** something shaped by being poured into a mould to harden. **2** the process of making casts in a mould. **3** the assignment of the parts in a play, film, etc.

casting vote a vote by the presiding officer to decide a question when the votes of an assembly, council, board, or committee are evenly divided.

cast iron a hard, brittle form of iron made by casting.

cast-i·ron (kast′ī′ərn) *adj.* 1 made of cast iron. 2 hard; not yielding. 3 hardy; strong. 4 **cast-iron alibi,** an alibi that cannot be disproved.

cas·tle (kas′əl) *n. v.* **-tled, -tling.** —*n.* 1 a building or group of buildings with thick walls, towers, and other defences against attack. 2 a palace that once had defences against attack. 3 a large and imposing residence. 4 in chess, a piece shaped like a tower; rook.
—*v.* 1 place in or as if in a castle. 2 in chess: **a** move (the king) beyond the castle or rook. **b** (of the king) be moved in this way. [< L *castellum,* dim. of *castrum* fort. Doublet of CHÂTEAU.] —**Syn. 1** fortress, citadel, stronghold. 3 mansion, château.

castle in Spain a daydream; castle in the air.

castle in the air something imagined but not likely to come true; a daydream.

cast·off (kast′of′) *adj.* thrown away; abandoned.
—*n.* a person or thing that has been cast off.

cas·tor[1] (kas′tər) *n.* caster[2].

cas·tor[2] (kas′tər) *n.* 1 a hat made of beaver fur. 2 an oily substance with a strong odor, secreted by beavers. It is used in making perfume and in medicines. 3 a beaver. [< L < Gk. *kastōr* beaver]

Cas·tor (kas′tər) *n.* 1 in Greek and Roman legend, the mortal twin brother of Pollux. 2 the fainter of the two bright stars, of which Pollux is the other, in the constellation Gemini.

castor bean the seed of the castor-oil plant.

castor oil a yellow oil obtained from castor beans, used as a strong cathartic, a lubricant, etc.

cas·tor-oil plant (kas′tər oil′) a tall tropical plant from whose seeds castor oil is obtained.

cas·trate (kas′trāt) *v.* **-trat·ed, -trat·ing.** 1 remove the male glands of. 2 mutilate; expurgate. [< L *castrare*]

cas·tra·tion (kas trā′shən) *n.* the act of castrating.

cast steel steel that has undergone fusion.

cas·u·al (kazh′ü əl) *adj.* 1 happening by chance; not planned or expected; accidental: *a casual meeting.* 2 without plan or method; careless: *a casual answer, a casual glance.* 3 uncertain; indefinite; indifferent; vague. 4 informal; easy-going: *casual manners; casual living.* 5 occasional; irregular. A **casual laborer** has no regular job. 6 designed for informal wear: *casual clothes.*
—*n.* 1 a casual laborer. 2 a person occasionally receiving charity. 3 a member of the armed services awaiting orders, transportation, etc. at a post or station to which he is not attached or assigned. [< L *casualis* < *casus* chance] —**cas′u·al·ly,** *adv.* —**cas′u·al·ness,** *n.* —**Syn.** *adj.* 1 chance, fortuitous, unexpected.

cas·u·al·ty (kazh′ü əl tē or kazh′əl tē) *n.* **-ties.** 1 an accident. 2 an unfortunate accident; mishap. 3 a member of the armed services who has been wounded, killed, or captured as a result of enemy action. 4 a person injured or killed in an accident or disaster, or as a result of enemy action: *The earthquake caused many casualties.*

cas·u·ist (kazh′ü ist) *n.* 1 a person who decides questions of conduct, duty, etc. 2 a person who reasons cleverly but falsely, especially in regard to right and wrong. [< F *casuiste* < L *casus* case]

cas·u·is·tic (kazh′ü is′tik) *adj.* 1 of or like casuistry. 2 too subtle; sophistical. —**cas′u·is′ti·cal·ly,** *adv.*

cas·u·is·ti·cal (kazh′ü is′tə kəl) *adj.* casuistic.

cas·u·ist·ry (kazh′ü is trē) *n.* **-ries.** 1 the act or process of deciding questions of right and wrong in regard to conduct, duty, etc. 2 clever but false reasoning.

ca·sus bel·li (kā′səs bel′ī or kä′sůs bel′ē) *Latin.* a cause for war.

cat[1] (kat) *n. v.* **cat·ted, cat·ting.** —*n.* 1 a small, four-footed, flesh-eating mammal often kept as a pet or for catching mice. 2 any animal of the family including cats, lions, tigers, leopards, etc. 3 an animal resembling a cat. 4 a mean, spiteful woman. 5 a catfish. 6 the cat-o'-nine-tails. 7 the tackle for hoisting an anchor. 8 *Slang.* a man or fellow, especially a hepcat. 9 **let the cat out of the bag,** tell a secret.

hat, āge, cãre, fär; let, ēqual, tėrm; it, īce
hot, ōpen, ôrder; oil, out; cup, půt, rüle, ūse
əbove, takən, pencəl, lemən, circəs
ch, child; ng, long; sh, ship
th, thin; ᴛʜ, then; zh, measure

—*v.* hoist (an anchor) and fasten it to a beam on the ship's side. [OE *catt(e),* probably < LL *catta*]

cat[2] (kat) *n.* caterpillar tractor.

cat. 1 catalogue. 2 catechism.

cata- *prefix.* down; against; entirely, as in *cataract.* Also, **cat-** before vowels and *h,* as in *category, cathode.* [< Gk. *kata-* < *kata,* prep.]

ca·tab·o·lism (kə tab′ə liz′əm) *n.* in biology, the process of breaking down living tissues into simpler substances or waste matter, thereby producing energy. Also, **katabolism.** [probably < *metabolism,* by substitution of *cata-* down]

cat·a·chre·sis (kat′ə krē′sis) *n.* **-ses** (-sēz). the misuse of words. [< L < Gk. *katachrēsis* misuse < *kata-* amiss + *chrēsthai* use]

cat·a·clysm (kat′ə kliz′əm) *n.* 1 a flood, earthquake, or any sudden, violent change in the earth. 2 any violent change: *World War II was a cataclysm for all of Europe.* [< L *cataclysmos* < Gk. *kataklysmos* flood < *kata-* down + *klyzein* wash]

cat·a·clys·mal (kat′ə kliz′məl) *adj.* cataclysmic.

cat·a·clys·mic (kat′ə kliz′mik) *adj.* of or like a cataclysm; extremely sudden and violent.

cat·a·comb (kat′ə kōm′) *n.* Usually, **catacombs,** *pl.* an underground gallery forming a burial place. [< LL *catacumbae,* pl. < *cata* (< Gk. *kata*) *tumbas* (< Gk. *tymbos*) among the tombs]

cat·a·falque (kat′ə falk′) *n.* a stand or frame to support the coffin in which a dead person lies. [< F < Ital. *catafalco,* of uncertain origin]

Cat·a·lan (kat′ə lan′ or kat′ə lən) *adj.* of Catalonia, a region in N.E. Spain, its people, or their language.
—*n.* 1 a native or inhabitant of Catalonia. 2 the traditional language of Catalonia.

cat·a·lep·sis (kat′ə lep′sis) *n.* catalepsy.

cat·a·lep·sy (kat′ə lep′sē) *n.* a kind of fit during which a person loses consciousness and the power to feel, and his muscles become rigid. [< LL *catalepsis* < Gk. *katalēpsis* seizure < *kata-* down + *lambanein* seize]

cat·a·lep·tic (kat′ə lep′tik) *adj.* 1 of catalepsy. 2 having catalepsy. —*n.* a person who has catalepsy.

cat·a·log (kat′ə log′) *n. v.* **-loged, -log·ing.** catalogue. —**cat′a·log′er,** *n.*

cat·a·logue (kat′ə log′) *n. v.* **-logued, -logu·ing.** —*n.* 1 a list of items in a collection, identifying each item very briefly and sometimes describing it. A library has a catalogue of its books, arranged in alphabetical order. A company sometimes prints a catalogue with pictures and prices of the things that it sells. 2 a volume or booklet issued by a college or university listing rules, courses to be given, etc.; calendar. 3 a list; series: *a catalogue of lies, tricks, and deceits.*
—*v.* make a catalogue of; put in a catalogue: *He catalogued all the insects in his collection.* [< F < LL < Gk. *katalogos* list < *kata-* down + *legein* count] —**cat′a·logu′er,** *n.* —**Syn.** *n.* 1 See **list.**

☞ **catalogue, catalog.** Although *catalogue* is the preferred spelling in Canada, the shorter, American form is occasionally seen in Canadian newspapers.

ca·tal·pa (kə tal′pə) *n.* a tree of North America and Asia having large, heart-shaped leaves, clusters of bell-shaped flowers, and long pods. [< NL < Creek Indian *kutuhlpa*]

ca·tal·y·sis (kə tal′ə sis) *n.* **-ses** (-sēz′). in chemistry, the causing or speeding up of a chemical reaction by the presence of a substance that itself undergoes no permanent change. [< NL < Gk. *katalysis* dissolution < *kata-* down + *lyein* to loose]

cat·a·lyst (kat′ə list) *n.* 1 a substance that causes catalysis. 2 anything that brings about some change or changes, without being directly affected itself: *The* *catalyst that caused the sudden modernization of this government department was the new minister himself.*

cat·a·lyt·ic (kat′ə lit′ik) *adj.* **1** of catalysis. **2** causing catalysis.

cat·a·lyz·er (kat′ə līz′ər) *n.* catalyst.

cat·a·ma·ran (kat′ə mə ran′) *n.* **1** a boat with two hulls side by side. **2** a raft made of pieces of wood lashed together. **3** *Cdn.* a type of platform on two runners, used for hauling lumber, etc. [< Tamil *kattamaram* tied tree]

A catamaran (def. 1)

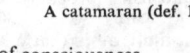

cat·a·mount (kat′ə mount′) *n.* a wildcat, such as a puma or lynx. [short for *catamountain* cat of (the) mountain]

cat·a·plex·y (kat′ə plek′sē) *n.* a momentary loss of muscular power and control, without loss of consciousness.

cat·a·pult (kat′ə pult′) *n.* **1** in ancient times, a weapon for shooting stones, arrows, etc. **2** a slingshot. **3** a device for launching an airplane from the deck of a ship. —*v.* shoot from a catapult; throw; hurl. [< L *catapulta* < Gk. *katapeltēs*, probably < *kata-* down + *pallein* hurl]

cat·a·ract (kat′ə rakt′) *n.* **1** a large, steep waterfall. **2** a violent rush or downpour of water; flood. **3** an opaque condition in the lens of the eye, or its capsule, that causes partial or total blindness. [< L *cataracta* < Gk. *katarrhaktēs* < *kata-* down + *arassein* dash]

ca·tarrh (kə tär′) *n.* an inflamed condition of a mucous membrane, usually that of the nose or throat, causing a discharge of mucus or phlegm. [< F *catarrhe* < L < Gk. *katarrhous* < *kata-* down + *rheein* flow]

ca·tarrh·al (kə tär′əl) *adj.* **1** like catarrh. **2** caused by catarrh.

ca·tas·tro·phe (kə tas′trə fē) *n.* **1** a sudden, widespread, or extraordinary disaster; great calamity or misfortune. A big earthquake or flood is a catastrophe. **2** the outcome; unhappy ending: *The catastrophe of a tragedy usually brings death or ruin to the leading character.* **3** a disastrous end; ruin. [< Gk. *katastrophē* overturning < *kata-* down + *strephein* turn] —**Syn. 1** See **disaster.**

cat·a·stroph·ic (kat′ə strof′ik) *adj.* of or caused by disaster; calamitous.

Ca·taw·ba (kə tob′ə or kə tô′bə) *n.* **-bas. 1** a light-red grape of North America. **2** a light wine made from it. [< river in South Carolina along which the vine was first raised]

cat·bird (kat′bėrd′) *n.* a slate-gray North American songbird, having black on its head, wings, and tail. The catbird can make a sound like a cat mewing.

cat·boat (kat′bōt′) *n.* a sailboat with one mast set far forward. It has no bowsprit or jib.

A catboat

cat·call (kat′kol′ or -kôl′) *n.* a shrill cry or whistle to express disapproval: *The politician's speech was interrupted by catcalls from the audience.* —*v.* **1** make catcalls. **2** attack with catcalls.

catch (kach) *v.* **caught, catch·ing,** *n. adj.* —*v.* **1** take and hold something moving; seize; capture: *The policeman caught the thief. Catch the ball with both hands.* **2** attract and hold the attention of: *Bright colors catch the eye.* **3** take; get: *Paper catches fire easily.* **4** become caught: *My dress caught in the door.* **5** reach or get to in time: *catch a train before it leaves the station.* **6** become lighted; burn: *Tinder catches easily.* **7** take notice of; discover: *He thought I wouldn't catch his error.* **8** come on suddenly; surprise: *Mother caught me just as I was hiding her present.* **9** check one's breath suddenly: *She caught her breath.* **10** catch up; overtake. **11** apprehend by the senses or intellect; hear, see, understand, etc. by an effort: *She tried hard to catch what the man across the room was saying.* **12** act as catcher in baseball.
catch as catch can, grab or wrestle in any way.
catch at, a try to catch. **b** seize eagerly.
catch it, *Informal.* be scolded or punished.
catch on, *Informal.* **a** understand; get the idea. **b** become popular; be widely used or accepted.
catch up, a come up even with a person or thing; overtake: *The dog ran as fast as he could to catch up with the car.* **b** pick up suddenly; snatch; grab. **c** interrupt and annoy with critical comments or questions; heckle. **d** hold up in loops.
—*n.* **1** the act of catching: *Dick made a fine catch with one hand.* **2** anything that catches. A fastener for a door or window is a catch. **3** the thing caught: *A dozen fish is a good catch.* **4** *Informal.* a desirable person to marry because of his or her wealth, position, etc. **5** in music, a short song sung by several persons or groups who begin to sing at regular intervals one after another. **6** a scrap or fragment of anything: *He sang catches of songs.* **7** a choking or stoppage of the breath: *He had a catch in his voice.* **8** a game that consists of throwing and catching a ball. **9** *Informal.* a hidden or tricky condition or meaning; some difficulty that does not appear on the surface: *There's a catch to that question.*
—*adj.* **1** getting one's attention; arousing one's interest: *Advertisements often contain catch phrases.* **2** tricky; deceptive: *a catch question.* [ME < OF *cachier* < LL *captiare* < L *capere* take. Doublet of CHASE[1].]
Syn. *v.* **1 Catch, capture** = to take and hold someone or something. **Catch,** the general word, suggests overtaking or taking something fleeing or hidden, by force, surprise, or cleverness, and often is used figuratively to suggest overtaking and seizing with the senses or mind: *We caught the thief. We caught sight of him. I didn't catch his words.* **Capture** suggests greater difficulty or obstacles to overcome and therefore taking by greater force, skill, or trickery: *We captured the criminal. He captured her heart.*

catch·all (kach′ol′ or -ôl′) *n.* a container for odds and ends.

catch-as-catch-can (kach′əz kach′kan′) *n.* a style of wrestling in which one may use the legs and feet, or hold one's opponent's legs and feet, to gain advantage. —*adj.* **1** unrestrained; free-for-all. **2** haphazard; random.

catch basin 1 a sievelike receptacle at the entrance of a sewer to retain matter that might block the flow of sewage. **2** a reservoir for catching and holding surface drainage over large areas.

catch·er (kach′ər) *n.* **1** a person or thing that catches. **2** in baseball, a player who stands behind the batter to catch the ball thrown by the pitcher.

catch·ing (kach′ing) *adj.* **1** liable to spread from one to another; contagious; infectious: *Colds are catching.* **2** attractive; fascinating.

catch·ment (kach′mənt) *n.* **1** the act or fact of catching. **2** a reservoir for catching drainage. **3** the water collected in such a reservoir.

catchment basin or **area** a land area where the rainfall is drained by one river system.

catch·pen·ny (kach′pen′ē) *adj. n.* **-nies.** —*adj.* showy but worthless or useless; made to sell quickly. —*n.* a showy but worthless article.

catch·pole or **catch·poll** (kach′pōl′) *n.* formerly, a deputy sheriff or bailiff whose duties included arresting debtors for nonpayment.

catch stitch a stitch that makes parallel rows of lines as in a herringbone design.

catch·up (kach′əp) *n.* ketchup.

catch·word (kach′wėrd′) *n.* **1** a word or phrase used again and again for effect; slogan: *"No taxation without representation" was a political catchword.* **2** a word placed so as to catch attention.

catch·y (kach′ē) *adj.* **catch·i·er, catch·i·est. 1** easy to remember; attractive: *The new musical play has several catchy tunes.* **2** tricky; misleading; deceptive: *The third question on the test was catchy; nearly everyone in the class gave the wrong answer.* —**catch′i·ly,** *adv.* —**catch′i·ness,** *n.*

cate (kāt) *n. Archaic.* Usually, **cates,** *pl.* a delicacy; choice food. [var. of ME *acate* < ONF *acat* a purchase < *acater* buy < VL *accaptare* acquire < L *ad-* to + *capere* take]

cat·e·chet·i·cal (kat′ə ket′ə kəl) *adj.* **1** teaching by questions and answers. **2** like or according to a catechism.

cat·e·chise (kat′ə kīz′) *v.* **-chised, -chis·ing.** catechize. **—cat′e·chis′er,** *n.*

cat·e·chism (kat′ə kiz′əm) *n.* **1** a book of questions and answers about religion, used for teaching religious doctrine. **2** a set of questions and answers about any subject. **3** a long or formal set of questions.

cat·e·chist (kat′ə kist) *n.* a person who catechizes.

cat·e·chize (kat′ə kīz′) *v.* **-chized, -chiz·ing. 1** teach by questions and answers. **2** question closely. [< L *catechizare* < Gk. *katēchizein* teach orally < *katēcheein* < *kata-* thoroughly + *ēcheein* sound] **—cat′e·chiz′er,** *n.* **—cat′e·chi·za′tion,** *n.*

cat·e·chu (kat′ə chü′ or kat′ə kü′) *n.* a hard, brown, brittle substance obtained from certain acacia trees of Asia and Africa. It is an astringent used in medicine, in dyeing, and in tanning. [< NL < Malay *kachu*]

cat·e·chu·men (kat′ə kū′mən) *n.* **1** a person who is being taught the elementary facts of Christianity. **2** a person who is being taught the fundamentals of any field of study. [< LL *catechumenus* < Gk. *katēchoumenos* one being instructed, ppr. passive of *katēcheein.* See CATECHIZE.]

cat·e·gor·i·cal (kat′ə gôr′ə kəl) *adj.* **1** without conditions or qualifications; positive. **2** of or in a category. **—cat′e·gor′i·cal·ly,** *adv.*

cat·e·gor·i·za·tion (kat′ə gər ə zā′shən or kat′ə gər ī zā′shən) *n.* the act or fact or process of categorizing.

cat·e·gor·ize (kat′ə gə rīz′) *v.* **-ized, -iz·ing.** place in a category; classify.

cat·e·gor·iz·er (kat′ə gə rī′zər) *n.* a person who categorizes.

cat·e·go·ry (kat′ə gô′rē) *n.* **-ries.** a group or division in a general system of classification; class: *She groups all people into two categories: those she likes and those she dislikes.* [< L *categoria* < Gk. *katēgoria* assertion < *kata-* down + *agoreuein* speak]

cat·e·nar·y (kat′ə ner′ē or kə tē′nər ē) *n.* **-nar·ies.** *adj.* in mathematics: *—n.* the curve formed by a heavy flexible cord hanging freely from two points not in a vertical line. *—adj.* of or having to do with a catenary. [< L *catenarius* relating to a chain < *catena* chain]

cat·e·nate (kat′ə nāt′) *v.* **-nat·ed, -nat·ing.** link together like a chain; connect in a series. [< L *catenare* < *catena* chain] **—cat′e·na′tion,** *n.*

ca·ter (kā′tər) *v.* **1** provide food or supplies: *He has a small hotel and also caters for weddings and parties.* **2** supply means of instruction and enjoyment (*to*): *The new magazine caters to boys by publishing stories about aviation, athletics, and camping.* [verbal use of *cater,* n., ME *acatour* buyer of provisions < OF *acateor* < *acater* buy. See CATE.]

cat·er-cor·nered (kat′ər kôr′nərd) *adj.* diagonal; kitty-corner. *—adv.* diagonally. Also, **cater-corner, catty-cornered.** [< E dial. *cater* diagonally (< F *quatre* four) + *cornered*]

ca·ter·er (kā′tər ər) *n.* a person who provides food or supplies for entertainments, parties, etc.

cat·er·pil·lar (kat′ər pil′ər) *n.* the wormlike form or larva of a butterfly or moth. [cf. OF *chatepelose* hairy cat]

caterpillar tractor 1 a tractor that can travel over rough land on wheels that run inside two endless belts of linked, steel plates. **2 Caterpillar,** a trademark for this tractor.

A caterpillar tractor

cat·er·waul (kat′ər wol′ or kat′ər wôl′) *v.* **1** howl like a cat; screech. **2** quarrel noisily. *—n.* such a howl or screech. [ME *caterwrawe* < *cater,* apparently, cat + *wrawe* wail, howl]

cat·fish (kat′fish′) *n.* **-fish** or **-fish·es.** any of several scaleless fish having around the mouth long, slender feelers that resemble a cat's whiskers.

cat·gut (kat′gut′) *n.* a tough string made from the dried and twisted intestines of sheep or other animals, used for violin strings and tennis rackets, and by surgeons for stitching wounds. [origin uncertain]

hat, āge, cãre, fär; let, ēqual, tėrm; it, īce
hot, ōpen, ôrder; oil, out; cup, pu̇t, rüle, ūse
əbove, takən, pencəl, lemən, circəs
ch, child; ng, long; sh, ship
th, thin; ᴛʜ, then; zh, measure

Cath. Catholic.

ca·thar·sis (kə thär′sis) *n.* **1** a purging. **2** an emotional purification or relief. [< NL < Gk. *katharsis,* ult. < *katharos* clean]

ca·thar·tic (kə thär′tik) *n.* a strong laxative. Epsom salts and castor oil are cathartics. *—adj.* strongly laxative.

Ca·thay (ka thā′) *n. Poetic* or *Archaic.* China.

cat·head (kat′hed′) *n.* a beam on a ship's side near the bow to which the anchor is hoisted and fastened.

ca·the·dra (kə thē′drə or kath′ə drə) *n.* **1** a bishop's throne in a cathedral. **2** a seat of authority. **3 ex cathedra,** from authority; with authority. [< L < Gk. *kathedra* seat < *kata-* down + *hedra* seat. Doublet of CHAIR.]

ca·the·dral (kə thē′drəl) *n.* **1** the official church of a bishop. **2** a large or important church. *—adj.* **1** having a bishop's throne. **2** of, like, or having to do with a cathedral. [< Med.L *cathedralis* of the (bishop's) seat < L < Gk. *kathedra* seat. See CATHEDRA.]

Cath·e·rine wheel (kath′ə rin or kath′rin) **1** in heraldry, a figure of a wheel with projecting spikes. **2** a firework that revolves while burning; pinwheel. [< St. *Catherine* of Alexandria, condemned to torture on the wheel]

cath·e·ter (kath′ə tər) *n.* a slender tube to be inserted into a passage or cavity of the body. A catheter is used to distend a passage, remove urine from the bladder, etc. [< LL < Gk. *katheter* < *kata-* down + *hienai* send]

cath·ode (kath′ōd) *n.* a negative electrode. The zinc case of a dry cell and the filament of a radio tube are cathodes. [< Gk. *kathodos* a way down < *kata-* down + *hodos* way]

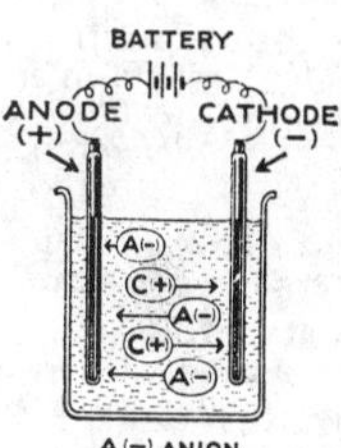

cathode rays the invisible streams of electrons from the cathode in a vacuum tube. When cathode rays strike a solid substance, they produce X rays.

cath·o·lic (kath′ə lik′ or kath′lik) *adj.* **1** of interest or use to all people; including all; universal. **2** having sympathies with all; broad-minded; liberal. **3** of the whole Christian church. [< L *catholicus* < Gk. *katholikos* < *kata-* in respect to + *holos* whole] **—Syn. 1** all-embracing, general. **2** tolerant.

Cath·o·lic (kath′ə lik′ or kath′lik) *adj.* **1** of the Christian church governed by the Pope; Roman Catholic. **2** of the ancient undivided Christian church, or of its present representatives including the Anglican, Orthodox, and Roman Catholic churches. *—n.* a member of a Catholic church, especially a Roman Catholic.

ca·thol·i·cism (kə thol′ə siz′əm) *n.* catholicity.

Ca·thol·i·cism (kə thol′ə siz′əm) *n.* the faith, doctrine, organization, and methods of the Roman Catholic Church.

cath·o·lic·i·ty (kath′ə lis′ə tē) *n.* **1** universality; wide prevalence. **2** broad-mindedness; liberalness.

Cath·o·lic·i·ty (kath′ə lis′ə tē) *n.* Catholicism.

ca·thol·i·cize (kə thol′ə sīz′) *v.* **-cized, -ciz·ing.** make or become catholic or universal.

cat·i·on (kat′ī′ən) *n.* a positive ion. During electrolysis, cations move toward the cathode. See **cathode** for diagram. [< Gk. *kation* going down < *kata-* down + *ienai* go]

cat·kin (kat′kin) *n.* the downy or scaly spike of the flowers of willows, poplars, birches, etc.; ament. [< Du. *katteken* little cat]

cat·like (kat′līk′) *adj.* **1** like a cat. **2** noiseless; stealthy. **3** active; nimble.

cat·lin·ite (kat′lə nīt′) *n.* a smooth, hard, bright-red clay, used by Prairie Indians for tobacco pipes. [< George *Catlin* (1796-1872), an American artist + *ite*]

cat·mint (kat′mint′) *n. Esp.Brit.* catnip.

cat nap a short nap or doze.

cat·nip (kat′nip) *n.* a kind of mint having strongly scented leaves that cats are fond of. Also, *Esp.Brit.*, **catmint.** [< *cat* + *nip*, var. of *nep* catnip < L *nepeta*]

cat-o'-nine-tails (kat′ə nīn′ tālz′) *n.* **-tails.** a whip of nine pieces of knotted cord fastened to a handle.

cat power *Cdn. Slang.* tracked work-vehicles, such as bulldozers, caterpillar tractors, etc.

cat-rigged (kat′rigd′) *adj.* rigged like a catboat.

cat's cradle a child's game played with a string looped over the fingers of both hands.

cat's-eye (kats′ī′) *n.* **1** a gem showing beautiful changes of color suggesting a cat's eye. **2** one of a row of small reflectors set on a road or curb to act as guides by catching the headlights of approaching vehicles.

cat·skin·ner (kat′skin′ər) *n.* a person who operates a caterpillar tractor: *Catskinners worked on the highway through the bush.* [< *cat*[2] + *skinner*, after *mule-skinner*]

cat's-paw or **cats·paw** (kats′po′ or -pô′) *n.* **1** a person used by another to do something unpleasant or dangerous. **2** a light breeze that ruffles a small stretch of water. **3** a type of hitch or knot, used for attaching a tackle to a hook.

cat·sup (kat′səp or kech′əp) *n.* ketchup.

cat-swing (kat′swing′) *n. Cdn.* cat-train. [< *cat*[2] + *swing*]

cat·tail (kat′tāl′) *n.* a tall marsh plant having flowers in long, round, furry, brown spikes; bulrush.

cat·tish (kat′ish) *adj.* **1** catlike. **2** catty.

cat·tle (kat′əl) *n.* **1** cows, bulls, and steers; oxen. **2** formerly, farm animals; livestock. **3** *Derogatory.* people; any low, worthless people. [ME < OF *catel* < L *capitale* property, neut. of *capitalis.* Doublet of CAPITAL[1] and CHATTEL.]

cat·tle·man (kat′əl mən) *n.* **-men** (-mən). a man who raises or takes care of cattle.

cat-train (kat′trān′) *n. Cdn.* a series of large sleds pulled by a caterpillar tractor. Cat-trains are used in the North for hauling goods over the frozen muskeg in wintertime.

cat·ty (kat′ē) *adj.* **-ti·er, -ti·est. 1** mean; spiteful. **2** catlike. **3** of cats. **—cat′ti·ly,** *adv.* **—cat′ti·ness,** *n.*

cat·ty-cor·nered (kat′ē kôr′nərd) *adj. adv.* cater-cornered.

cat·walk (kat′wok′ or -wôk′) *n.* a narrow place to walk, especially on a bridge or in an airship.

Cau·ca·sian (ko kā′zhən or ko kā′shən, kô kā′zhən or kô kā′shən) *n.* **1** a member of the so-called white race, including the chief peoples of Europe, S.W. Asia, N. Africa, the Western Hemisphere, Australia, and New Zealand. **2** a native of the Caucasus, a region in the S. Soviet Union. —*adj.* **1** of or having to do with the so-called white race. **2** of or having to do with the Caucasus or its inhabitants.

cau·cus (ko′kəs or kô′kəs) *n.* **1** in Canada and the United Kingdom, a meeting of the members of Parliament of one party to discuss policy, plan strategy, etc. **2** in the United States, a meeting of members or leaders of a political party to make plans, choose candidates, decide how to vote, etc. **3** any similar meeting for the private discussion of policy.
—*v.* hold a caucus. [perhaps < LL *caucus*, var. of *caucum* drinking vessel; cf. LGk. *kaukos*; "in allusion to the convivial feature" of the Caucus Club, a political club of the 18th century in Boston, Massachusetts.]

cau·dal (ko′dəl or kô′dəl) *adj.* **1** of, at, or near the tail. **2** tail-like. [< NL *caudalis* < L *cauda* tail] **—cau′dal·ly,** *adv.*

cau·date (ko′dāt or kô′dāt) *adj.* having a tail.

cau·dil·lo (ko dēl′yō or kô dēl′yō: *Spanish*, kou ᴛʜē′lyō) *n.* a leader or head of state, especially a military one. [< Sp. < L *capitellum* little head]

cau·dle (ko′dəl or kô′dəl) *n.* a warm drink for sick people; gruel sweetened and flavored with wine, ale, spices, etc. [< ONF *caudel* < L *calidus* warm]

Caugh·na·waugh·a (kok′nə wo′gə) *n.* **-waugh·a** or **-waugh·as. 1** a band of Iroquoian-speaking Indians (Mohawks) living on the Caughnawaugha Reserve on the south shore of the St. Lawrence opposite Montreal. **2** a member of this group.

caught (kot or kôt) *v.* pt. and pp. of **catch.**

caul (kol or kôl) *n.* a portion of the membrane enclosing a child in the womb that is sometimes found clinging to the head at birth. It was supposed to be a good omen, especially against drowning. [ME *calle*, perhaps < OF *cale* a little cap]

caul·dron or **cal·dron** (kol′drən or kôl′drən) *n.* **1** a large kettle or boiler. **2** anything thought to resemble a boiling cauldron or its bubbling contents: *a cauldron of political intrigue and unrest.* [ME *caudron* < ONF < LL *caldaria* pot for boiling (L *calidus* warm)]

cau·li·flow·er (kol′ē flou′ər or kôl′ē flou′ər) *n.* **1** a vegetable of the cabbage family, having a flower cluster that forms a solid, white head (the edible part) with a few leaves around it. **2** the head itself. [half-translation of NL *cauliflora* < *caulis* cabbage + *flos, floris* flower]

cauliflower ear an ear that has been misshapen by injuries received in boxing, etc.

caulk or **calk** (kok or kôk) *v.* fill up a seam, crack, or joint so that it will not leak. [< OF *cauquer* < L *calcare* tread, press in]

caulk·er or **calk·er** (kok′ər or kôk′ər) *n.* **1** a person who caulks. **2** a tool for caulking.

caus·a·ble (koz′ə bəl or kôz′ə bəl) *adj.* capable of being caused.

caus·al (koz′əl or kôz′əl) *adj.* **1** of a cause; being a cause. **2** having to do with cause and effect. **3** showing a cause or reason. *Because* is a causal conjunction. **—caus′al·ly,** *adv.*

cau·sal·i·ty (ko zal′ə tē or kô zal′ə tē) *n.* **-ties. 1** the relation of cause and effect; principle that nothing can happen or exist without a cause. **2** a causal quality or agency.

cau·sa·tion (ko zā′shən or kô zā′shən) *n.* **1** a causing or being caused. **2** whatever produces an effect: cause or causes. **3** the relation of cause and effect; the principle that nothing can happen or exist without a cause.

caus·a·tive (koz′ə tiv or kôz′ə tiv) *adj.* **1** being a cause; productive. **2** expressing causation. In *enrich*, *en-* is a causative prefix. **—caus′a·tive·ly,** *adv.* **—caus′a·tive·ness,** *n.*

cause (koz or kôz) *n. v.* **caused, caus·ing.** —*n.* **1** whatever produces an effect; a person or thing that makes something happen: *The flood was the cause of much damage.* **2** an occasion for action; reason; ground; motive: *cause for celebration.* **3** a good reason; reason enough: *He was angry without cause.* **4** a subject or movement in which many people are interested and to which they give their support: *World peace is the cause she works for.* **5** a matter for a law court to decide; lawsuit. **6 make common cause with,** join efforts with; side with; help and support. —*v.* produce as an effect; make happen; make do; bring about: *The fire caused much damage.* [< L *causa*] **—caus′er,** *n.* **—Syn.** *n.* **2** See **reason.**

cause cé·lè·bre (kōz sā leb′rə) *French.* **1** in law, a famous case. **2** a notorious case or incident.

cause·less (koz′lis or kôz′lis) *adj.* **1** without any known cause; happening by chance. **2** without good reason; not having reason enough. **—cause′less·ly,** *adv.*

cau·se·rie (kō′zə rē′) *n.* **1** an informal talk or discussion; chat. **2** a short written article. [< F *causerie* < *causer* chat]

cause·way (koz′wā′ or kôz′-) *n.* **1** a raised road or path, usually built across wet ground, shallow water, etc. **2** a paved road; highway. —*v.* **1** provide with a causeway. **2** pave with cobbles or pebbles. [var. of *causey* (influenced by *way*) < ME *cauci* < ONF *caucie* < LL *calciata* paved way < L *calx* limestone]

caus·tic (kos′tik or kôs′tik) *n.* a substance that burns or destroys flesh; corrosive substance. —*adj.* **1** that burns or destroys flesh; corrosive. Lye is sometimes known as caustic soda or caustic potash. **2** sarcastic; stinging; biting: *The director's caustic remarks made the actors very angry.* [< L *causticus* < Gk. *kaustikos*] —**Syn.** *adj.* **2** satirical, cutting.

caus·ti·cal·ly (kos′tik lē or kôs′tik lē) *adv.* sarcastically; stingingly; bitingly.

caustic soda a brittle, white substance used in medicine, manufacturing, etc.; sodium hydroxide. *Formula*: NaOH

cau·ter·i·za·tion (ko′tər ə zā′shən or kô′tər ə zā′shən, ko′tər ī zā′shən or kô′tər ī zā′shən) *n.* the act of cauterizing; state of being cauterized.

cau·ter·ize (ko′tər īz′ or kô′tər īz′) *v.* **-ized, -iz·ing.** burn with a hot iron or a caustic substance: *Doctors sometimes cauterize wounds to prevent bleeding or infection.*

cau·ter·y (ko′tər ē or kô′tər ē) *n.* **-ter·ies. 1** a cauterizing. **2** an instrument or substance used in cauterizing. [< L *cauterium* < Gk. *kautērion*, dim. of *kautēr* branding iron]

cau·tion (ko′shən or kô′shən) *n.* **1** the state or practice of being very careful; the practice of taking care to be safe or of never taking chances: *Use caution in crossing streets.* **2** a warning: *A sign with "Danger" on it is a caution.* **3** in law, a warning to an accused person that anything he says may be used as evidence against him. **4** *Informal.* a very unusual person or thing. —*v.* **1** warn; urge to be careful. **2** in law, warn an accused person that anything he says may be used as evidence against him. [ME < OF < L *cautio, -onis* < *cavere* beware] —**cau′tion·er,** *n.* —**Syn.** *n.* **1** prudence, wariness. **2** admonition, advice, counsel. –*v.* See **warn.**

cau·tion·ar·y (ko′shən er′ē or kô′shən er′ē) *adj.* warning; urging care.

cau·tious (ko′shəs or kô′shəs) *adj.* very careful; taking care to be safe; never taking chances: *a cautious driver.* —**cau′tious·ly,** *adv.* —**cau′tious·ness,** *n.* —**Syn.** prudent, wary. See **careful.**

Cav. Cavalry.

cav·al·cade (kav′əl kād′ or kav′əl kād′) *n.* **1** a procession of persons riding on horses or in carriages. **2** a series of shows; a display or exhibition: *a cavalcade of sports.* [< F < Ital. *cavalcata* < *cavalcare* ride horseback < LL *caballicare* < L *caballus* horse]

cav·a·lier (kav′ə lēr′) *n.* **1** a horseman; mounted soldier; knight. **2** a courteous gentleman. **3** a courteous escort for a lady. **4 Cavalier,** in England, a person who supported Charles I in his struggle with Parliament from 1641 to 1649. —*adj.* **1** free and easy; offhand. **2** proud and scornful; haughty; arrogant: *People were often irritated by his cavalier attitude towards them.* **3 Cavalier,** of the Cavaliers. [< F < Ital. *cavalliere* < *cavallo* horse < L *caballus* horse] —**cav′a·lier′ly,** *adv.*

cav·al·ry (kav′əl rē) *n.* **-ries. 1** soldiers who fight on horseback. **2** the branch of an army made up of such soldiers. **3** an armored corps. [< F *cavalerie* < Ital. *cavalleria* knighthood < *cavalliere.* See CAVALIER.]

cav·al·ry·man (kav′əl rē mən) *n.* **-men** (-mən). a soldier who fights on horseback.

cav·a·ti·na (kav′ə tē′nə) *n.* in music, a short, simple song; melody; air. [< Ital.]

cave (kāv) *n. v.* **caved, cav·ing.** —*n.* a hollow space underground. —*v.* **cave in, a** fall in; sink: *The roof caved in.* **b** cause to fall in; smash. **c** *Informal.* give in; yield; submit. [ME < OF < L *cava* hollow (places)] —**cave′like′,** *adj.* —**Syn.** *n.* cavern, grotto.

ca·ve·at (kā′vē at′) *n.* **1** a warning. **2** in law, a notice given to a law officer or some legal authority not to do something until the person giving notice can be heard. [< L *caveat* let him beware]

caveat emp·tor (emp′tôr) *Latin.* let the buyer beware; you buy at your own risk.

cave dweller 1 a person who lived in a cave in prehistoric times. **2** any person who lives in a cave.

cave-in (kāv′in′) *n.* **1** a falling-in, or collapse, of a mine, tunnel, etc. **2** the site of such a collapse.

cave man 1 a man who lived in a cave in prehistoric times. **2** *Informal.* a rough, crude man.

hat, āge, cãre, fär; let, ēqual, tėrm; it, īce
hot, ōpen, ôrder; oil, out; cup, pu̇t, rüle, ūse
əbove, takən, pencəl, lemən, circəs
ch, child; ng, long; sh, ship
th, thin; ᴛʜ, then; zh, measure

cav·ern (kav′ərn) *n.* a large cave. [ME < MF *caverne* < L *caverna* < *cavus* hollow]

cav·ern·ous (kav′ər nəs) *adj.* **1** like a cavern; large and hollow. **2** full of caverns. **3** deepset: *cavernous eyes.* **4** hollow-sounding; resonant: *a cavernous voice.* —**cav′ern·ous·ly,** *adv.*

cav·i·ar or **cav·i·are** (kav′ē är′ or kä′vē är′) *n.* **1** a salty relish made from the eggs of sturgeon or other large fish. **2 caviar to the general,** too good a thing to be appreciated by ordinary people. [< F < Ital. < Turkish *khaviar*]

cav·il (kav′əl) *v.* **-illed** or **-iled, -il·ling** or **-il·ing,** *n.* —*v.* find fault unnecessarily; raise trivial objections. —*n.* a petty objection; trivial criticism. [< F < L *cavillari* jeer] —**cav′il·ler** or **cav′il·er,** *n.* —**Syn.** *v.* carp, criticize.

cav·i·ty (kav′ə tē) *n.* **-ties. 1** a hole; hollow place: *a cavity in a tooth.* **2** an enclosed space inside the body: *the abdominal cavity, the four cavities of the heart.* [< F *cavité* < LL *cavitas* < L *cavus* hollow] —**Syn. 1** See **hole.**

ca·vort (kə vôrt′) *v. Informal.* prance about; jump around: *The horses cavorted with excitement.* [origin uncertain]

ca·vy (kā′vē) *n.* **-vies.** any of a group of South American rodents, the best known being the guinea pig. [< NL *Cavia*]

caw (ko or kô) *n.* the harsh cry made by a crow or raven. —*v.* make this cry. [imitative]

cay (kā or kē) *n.* a low island; reef; key. [< Sp. *cayo* shoal, rock]

cay·enne (kī en′ or kā en′) *n.* a very hot, biting powder made from the seeds or fruit of a pepper plant; red pepper. [< *Cayenne*, French Guiana]

cay·man (kā′mən) *n.* **-mans.** a large alligator of tropical America. Also, **caiman.** [< Sp. *caiman* < Carib]

Ca·yu·ga (kā ū′ gə or kī ū′gə) *n.* **1** a tribe of North American Indians belonging to the Five Nations confederacy, living mainly in W. New York State and, later, in Ontario. **2** a member of this tribe. **3** the Iroquoian language of this tribe.

cay·use (kī ūs′) *n.* in western Canada and the United States, an Indian pony. [after the *Cayuse* Indians]

Cb columbium.

C.B. 1 Cape Breton. **2** Companion of (the Order of) the Bath. **3** Confined to Barracks.

CBC the Canadian Broadcasting Corporation.

C.B.E. Commander of (the Order of) the British Empire.

CBS or **C.B.S.** Columbia Broadcasting System.

cc. or **c.c.** cubic centimetre; cubic centimetres.

C.C. 1 Canada Council. **2** Companion of the Order of Canada.

C.C.F. the Co-operative Commonwealth Federation.

CCG Canadian Coast Guard.

C clef in music, a symbol that means that the line on which it is placed represents middle C.

Cd cadmium.

cd. cord; cords.

C.D. or **CD 1** Civil Defence. **2** Canadian (Forces) Decoration.

cd. ft. cord foot; cord feet.

Cdn. Canadian.

Cdn. Fr. Canadian French.

CDT, C.D.T., or **c.d.t.** Central Daylight Time.

Ce cerium.

C.E. 1 Civil Engineer. **2** Church of England.

cease (sēs) *v.* **ceased, ceas·ing. 1** come to an end: *The music ceased suddenly.* **2** put an end or stop to: *Cease trying to do more than you can.* [ME < OF < L *cessare*] —**Syn. 1** discontinue, quit, pause, desist. See **stop.**

cease·fire (sēs′fīr′) *n.* a halt in military operations, especially for the purpose of discussing peace.

cease·less (sēs′lis) *adj.* never stopping; going on all the time. —**cease′less·ly,** *adv.* —**cease′less·ness,** *n.*

Ce·cro·pi·a moth (sə krō′pē ə) a large silkworm moth of E. North America whose larvae feed on trees. [< NL *Cecropia,* a type of mulberry]

ce·dar (sē′dər) *n.* **1** any of several Old-World evergreen trees of the pine family, such as the deodar and the cedar of Lebanon, having spreading branches and fragrant, durable wood. **2** any of several North American evergreen trees of the pine family having similar wood, especially the arborvitae, the red cedar (red juniper), and yellow cedar (Nootka cypress). **3** the wood of any of these trees. [ME < OF *cedre* < L < Gk. *kedros*]

ce·dar·bird (sē′dər bėrd′) *n.* cedar waxwing.

cedar waxwing a small North American bird having a crest and small red markings on its wings; waxwing.

cede (sēd) *v.* **ced·ed, ced·ing. 1** surrender; hand over to another: *In 1763, France ceded Canada to Britain.* **2** give up; yield: *His argument was so convincing that I ceded my point.* [< L *cedere* yield] —**Syn.** yield, relinquish, deliver.

ce·di (sā dē′) *n.* **1** a unit of money in Ghana. See table at **money. 2** a coin worth one cedi.

ce·dil·la (sə dil′ə) *n.* a mark resembling a comma put under *c* (ç) before *a, o,* or *u* in certain words to show that it has the sound of *s. Example*: façade. [< Sp. *cedilla,* dim. of *ceda* < L *zeta,* the letter *z* < Gk.]

CEGEP Collège d'Enseignement Général et Professionel (General and Vocational College).

ceil (sēl) *v.* **1** put a ceiling in. **2** cover the ceiling of. [? < F *ciel* canopy, sky < L *caelum* heaven]

ceil·ing (sēl′ing) *n.* **1** the inside, top covering of a room; the surface opposite to the floor. **2** the greatest height to which an aircraft can go under certain conditions. **3** the distance between the earth and the lowest clouds. **4** an upper limit set for prices, wages, rents, etc. [< *ceil*]

cel·an·dine (sel′ən dīn′) *n.* **1** a plant having yellow flowers, belonging to the same family as the poppy. **2** the **lesser celandine,** a plant closely related to the buttercup, having yellow flowers and heart-shaped leaves. [ME < OF *celidoine* < L < Gk. *chelidonion* < *chelidōn* swallow²]

Cel·a·nese (sel′ə nēz′ or sel′ə nēz′) *n. Trademark.* an acetate rayon material.

cel·e·brant (sel′ə brənt) *n.* **1** a person who performs a ceremony or rite. **2** a priest who performs Mass. **3** anyone who celebrates.

cel·e·brate (sel′ə brāt′) *v.* **-brat·ed, -brat·ing. 1** observe with the proper ceremonies or festivities: *We celebrated Christmas with trees and presents.* **2** perform publicly with the proper ceremonies and rites: *The priest celebrates Mass in church.* **3** make known publicly; proclaim. **4** praise; honor. **5** observe a festival or event with ceremonies or festivities: *On her birthday she was too sick to celebrate.* **6** have a gay time. [< L *celebrare*] —**Syn. 1, 2** solemnize. **4** laud.

cel·e·brat·ed (sel′ə brāt′id) *adj.* famous; well-known; much talked about: *a celebrated author.* —**Syn.** noted, renowned, eminent.

cel·e·bra·tion (sel′ə brā′shən) *n.* **1** the act of celebrating. **2** whatever is done to celebrate something: *A Dominion Day celebration often includes a display of fireworks.*

cel·e·bra·tor (sel′ə brā′tər) *n.* a person who celebrates.

ce·leb·ri·ty (sə leb′rə tē) *n.* **-ties. 1** a famous person; a person who is well known or much talked about. **2** fame; the state of being well known or much talked about.

ce·ler·i·ac (sə ler′ē ak′) *n.* **1** a variety of celery grown for its edible, bulblike root. **2** the root itself.

ce·ler·i·ty (sə ler′ə tē) *n.* swiftness; speed. [ME < OF < L *celeritas* < *celer* swift]

cel·er·y (sel′ər ē or sel′rē) *n.* a vegetable whose long green stalks can be whitened by keeping them covered. Celery is usually eaten raw. [< F *céleri* < dial. Ital. < L < Gk. *selinon* parsley]

ce·les·ta (sə les′tə) *n.* a musical instrument with a keyboard, the tones being made by hammers hitting steel plates. [< F < L *caelestis* heavenly < *caelum* heaven]

ce·les·tial (sə les′chəl) *adj.* **1** of the sky; having to do with the heavens: *The sun, moon, planets, and stars are celestial bodies.* **2** heavenly; divine; very good or beautiful: *celestial music.* **3 Celestial,** of the Chinese people or the former Chinese Empire. —*n.* **1** a heavenly being **2 Celestial,** humorously, a Chinese. [ME < OF *celestiel* < L *caelestis* heavenly < *caelum* heaven] —**ce·les′tial·ly,** *adv.*

celestial equator in astronomy, the imaginary great circle that represents the intersection of the plane of the earth's equator with the celestial sphere.

celestial globe in astronomy, a globe indicating the position of the heavenly bodies, similar to a globe of the earth showing the geography of continents, oceans, etc.

celestial navigation in astronomy, a method of navigation in which the position of a ship or an aircraft is calculated from the position of heavenly bodies.

celestial sphere in astronomy, the imaginary sphere that apparently encloses the universe, of a size approaching infinity.

ce·li·ac (sē′lē ak′) *adj.* **1** of or having to do with the abdominal cavity. **2** of or suffering from celiac disease. [< L *coeliacus* < Gk. *koiliakos* < *koilia* bowels, belly < *koilos* hollow]

celiac disease a chronic intestinal disorder of childhood, resulting in diarrhea, swelling of the abdomen, etc.

cel·i·ba·cy (sel′ə bə sē) *n.* **-cies.** unmarried state; the single life.

cel·i·bate (sel′ə bit or sel′ə bāt′) *n.* an unmarried person; a person who takes a vow to lead a single life. —*adj.* unmarried; single. [< L *caelibatus* < *caelebs* unmarried]

cell (sel) *n.* **1** a small room in a prison, convent, or monastery. **2** a small, hollow place: *Bees store honey in the cells of a honeycomb.* **3** in biology, a unit of living matter. Most cells contain a central nucleus, which contains the chromosomes and is surrounded by cytoplasm, and are enclosed by a **cell wall** or **membrane.** Plants and animals are made of cells. **4** a container holding materials for producing electricity by chemical action; a small battery. **5** a small group that acts as a political, social, or religious unit for a larger, sometimes revolutionary, organization. **6** any enclosed space in an organism or tissue. [< L *cella* small room]

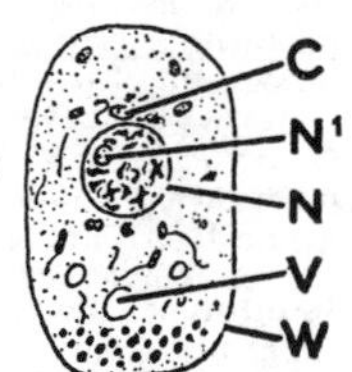

A diagram of a cell (def. 3). C, centrosomes; N¹, nucleolus; N, nucleus; V, vacuole; W, cell wall.

cel·lar (sel′ər) *n.* **1** an underground room or rooms, usually under a building and often used for storing food or fuel; basement. **2** such a room for wines. **3** a supply of wines. —*v.* put into a cellar; store as if in a cellar. [ME *celer* < OF *celier* < L *cellarium* < *cella* small room]

cel·lar·age (sel′ər ij) *n.* **1** the space in a cellar. **2** cellars. **3** a charge for storage in a cellar.

cel·lar·er (sel′ər ər) *n.* a person who takes care of a cellar and the food or wines in it.

cel·lar·et (sel′ə ret′) *n.* a cabinet to hold wine bottles, glasses, etc.

cel·lar·man (sel′ər mən) *n.* **-men** (-mən). **1** a man in charge of or employed in a cellar, especially a wine cellar. **2** a wine merchant.

cell block an individual building of cells in a prison.

cel·list or **'cel·list** (chel′ist) *n.* a person who plays the cello. Also, **violoncellist.**

cel·lo or **'cel·lo** (chel′ō) *n.* **-los.** a musical instrument resembling a violin, but much larger; bass violin. It is held between the knees while being played. See picture on the opposite page. Also, **violoncello.**

hat, āge, cãre, fär; let, ēqual, tėrm; it, īce
hot, ōpen, ôrder; oil, out; cup, pu̇t, rüle, ūse
əbove, takən, pencəl, lemən, circəs
ch, child; ng, long; sh, ship
th, thin; ᴛʜ, then; zh, measure

cel·lo·phane (sel′ə fān′) *n.* a transparent substance made from cellulose, used as a wrapping to keep food, candy, tobacco, etc. fresh and clean. [< *cell(ul)o(se)* + Gk. *phanein* appear]

cel·lu·lar (sel′yu̇ lər) *adj.* **1** having to do with cells. **2** consisting of cells: *All animal and plant tissue is cellular.*

cel·lule (sel′ūl) *n.* a tiny cell. [< L *cellula*, dim. of *cella* small room]

cel·lu·loid (sel′yu̇ loid′) *n.* **1** a hard, transparent, combustible substance made from cellulose and camphor: *Combs, toilet articles, camera films, etc. are often made of white or colored celluloid.* **2 Celluloid,** the trademark for this substance.
—*adj.* **1** of celluloid. **2** having to do with motion pictures. [< *cellul(ose)* + *-oid*]

cel·lu·lose (sel′yu̇ lōs′) *n.* the substance that forms the walls of plant cells; the woody part of trees and plants. Wood, cotton, flax, and hemp are largely cellulose. Cellulose is used to make paper, rayon, plastics, explosives, etc. [< L *cellula* small cell]

cel·lu·lous (sel′yu̇ ləs) *ad* . **1** full of cells. **2** made of cells.

Celsius scale (sel′sē əs) the official name of the scale used in a centigrade thermometer, based on a freezing point of 0 degrees and a boiling point of 100 degrees. [< Anders *Celsius*, 1701-1744, a Swedish astronomer, who invented it]

Celsius thermometer a centigrade thermometer.

Celt (selt or kelt) *n.* a member of a people to which the Irish, Highland Scots, Welsh, Manx, and Bretons belong. The ancient Gauls and Britons were also Celts. Also, **Kelt.** [< L *Celtae*, pl. < Gk. *Keltoi*]

Celt·ic (sel′tik or kel′tik) *adj.* of the Celts or their language. —*n.* the group of languages spoken by the Celts, including Irish and Scots Gaelic, Manx, Welsh, Cornish, and Breton. Also, **Keltic.**

Celtic cross a cross having a circle or circles intersecting the four arms. The design is of Celtic origin.

A Celtic cross

cel·tuce (sel′təs) *n.* a crisp, leafy vegetable that combines the flavors of celery and lettuce. [< *cel*ery + let*tuce*]

ce·ment (sə ment′) *n.* **1** a substance made by burning clay and limestone. **2** this substance mixed with sand and water to make sidewalks, streets, cellar floors, and walls. Cement becomes hard like stone. **3** any soft substance that hardens and holds things together: **rubber cement. 4** a substance used to fill cavities in teeth or to fasten fillings into them. **5** anything that joins together or unites.
—*v.* **1** fasten together with cement. **2** cover with cement: *The workmen were cementing the sidewalk.* **3** join firmly; unite. [ME < OF *ciment* < L *caementum* chippings of stone < *caedere* cut] **—ce·ment′er,** *n.*

cem·e·ter·y (sem′ə ter′ē) *n.* **-ter·ies.** a place for burying the dead; graveyard. [< LL *coemeterium* < Gk. *koimētērion* < *koimaein* lull to sleep]

cen. central.

ce·no·bite (sē′nə bīt′ or sen′ə bīt′) *n.* a member of a religious group living in a monastery or convent. Also, **coenobite.** [< LL *coenobita* < *coenobium* < Gk. *koinobion* convent < *koinos* common + *bios* life]

ce·no·bit·ic (sē′nə bit′ik or sen′ə bit′ik) *adj.* **1** of or having to do with a cenobite. **2** living in community: *Monks in a monastery are cenobitic.*

cen·o·taph (sen′ə taf) *n.* **1** a monument in memory of a dead person whose body is elsewhere. **2** a monument in memory of many dead persons, such as all those from one country, city, etc. killed in a war. [< L *cenotaphium* < Gk. *kenotaphion* < *kenos* empty + *taphos* tomb]

A cello

Ce·no·zo·ic (sē′nə zō′ik or sen′ə zō′ik) *n.* in geology: **1** the most recent era; age of mammals. The Cenozoic began about 60 or 70 million years ago, when mammals began to dominate the animal kingdom, and includes the present time. See the chart under **geology. 2** the rocks formed in this era.
—*adj.* of this era or its rocks. [< Gk. *kainos* recent + *zoē* life]

cen·ser (sen′sər) *n.* a container in which incense is burned. [ME < OF (*en*)*censier*, ult. < L *incensum* incense]

cens et rentes (säɴ zä räɴt′) *Cdn.French.* formerly, in New France and Lower Canada, a payment in cash and kind to a seignior in recognition of his rights.

cen·sor (sen′sər) *n.* **1** a person who examines and, if necessary, changes books, plays, motion pictures, etc. to see that they contain nothing wrong, immoral, or offensive. **2** an official who, especially in wartime, examines letters, messages, newspapers, etc. to see that they do not contain any information the government wishes kept secret. **3** in ancient Rome, a magistrate who took the census and supervised the conduct of citizens. **4** a person who exercises supervision over the morals or behavior of others. **5** a person who likes to find fault.
—*v.* **1** act as censor; examine. **2** remove, cut out, or change anything thought to be unsuitable by a censor. [< L *censor* < *censere* appraise]

cen·so·ri·al (sen sô′rē əl) *adj.* of or suitable for a censor.

cen·so·ri·ous (sen sô′rē əs) *adj.* too ready to find fault; severely critical. **—cen·so′ri·ous·ly,** *adv.*
—cen·so′ri·ous·ness, *n.* **—Syn.** hypercritical, carping.

cen·sor·ship (sen′sər ship′) *n.* **1** the act or system of censoring: *the censorship of motion pictures.* **2** the position or work of a censor.

cen·sur·a·ble (sen′shər ə bəl) *adj.* worthy of censure. **—cen′sur·a·bil′i·ty,** *n.* **—cen′sur·a·bly,** *adv.*

cen·sure (sen′shər) *n. v.* **-sured, -sur·ing.** —*n.* the act of blaming; expression of disapproval; criticism.
—*v.* express disapproval of; find fault with; blame; criticize. [ME < OF < L *censura* < *censere* appraise] **—cen′sur·er,** *n.* **—Syn.** *n.* faultfinding, reproof, rebuke. -*v.* reprove. See **blame.**

cen·sus (sen′səs) *n.* an official count of the people of an area. It is taken to find out the number of people, their ages, occupations, etc. [< L < *censere* appraise]

cent (sent) *n.* **1** a unit of money in Canada and the United States, worth 1/100 of a dollar. **2** a unit of money equalling 1/100 of the standard unit of currency in certain other countries. See table at **money. 3** a coin worth one cent. [< F < L *centum* hundred]

cent. 1 central. **2** century. **3** centigrade.

cen·taur (sen′tôr) *n.* in Greek legend, a creature that had the head, arms, and chest of a man, and the body and legs of a horse. [< L *centaurus* < Gk. *kentauros*]

cen·ta·vo (sen tä′vō) *n.* **1** a unit of money in Portugal, Cuba, Mexico, and many Central and South American countries, worth 1/100 of a peso. **2** a coin worth one centavo. [< Sp. < L *centum* hundred]

cen·te·nar·i·an (sen′tə nãr′ē ən) *n.* a person who is 100 years old or more. —*adj.* **1** 100 years old or more. **2** of 100 years.

cen·ten·ar·y (sen ten′ə rē, sen tē′nə rē, or sen′tə ner′ē) *n.* **-ar·ies,** *adj.* —*n.* **1** a period of 100 years. **2** a 100th anniversary. **3** the celebration of the 100th anniversary.
—*adj.* having to do with a period of 100 years. [< L *centenarius* relating to a hundred < *centum* hundred]

cen·ten·ni·al (sen ten′ē əl, sen ten′yəl, or sen tēn′yəl) *adj.* **1** of or having to do with 100 years or the 100th anniversary: *a centennial exhibition.* **2** 100 years old.
—*n.* **1** a 100th anniversary: *The town is celebrating its centennial.* **2** the celebration of the 100th anniversary. [< L *cent(um)* hundred + E (*bi*)*ennial*]

cen·ten·ni·al·ly (sen ten′ē əl ē or sen ten′yəl ē) *adv.* once in every hundred years.

cen·ter (sen′tər) *n. v.* centre.

cen·ter·board (sen′tər bôrd′) *n.* centreboard.

cen·ter·piece (sen′tər pēs′) *n.* centrepiece.

cen·tes·i·mal (sen tes′ə məl) *adj.* **1** 100th. **2** divided into 100ths. [< L *centesimus* hundredth]

cen·tes·i·mo (sen tes′ ə mō′) *n.* **1** a unit of money in Italy. **2** a unit of money equalling 1/100 of the standard unit of currency in Chile, Panama, and Uruguay. **3** a coin worth one centesimo. [< Sp. < L *centesimus* hundredth]

centi- *combining form.* **1** 100. **2** 100th part of. [< L *centum* hundred]

cen·ti·are (sen′tē ãr′) *n.* 1/100 of an are; one square metre. [< F]

cen·ti·grade (sen′tə grād′) *adj.* **1** divided into 100 degrees. **2** of or according to a centigrade thermometer. *Abbrev.*: C. [< F < L *centum* hundred + *gradus* degree]

centigrade thermometer a thermometer having 0 for the temperature at which water freezes and 100 for the temperature at which water boils. See **thermometer** for diagram.

cen·ti·gram (sen′tə gram′) *n.* 1/100 of a gram. *Abbrev.*: cg. or cgm. [< F]

cen·ti·gramme (sen′tə gram′) *n.* centigram.

cen·ti·li·ter (sen′tə lē′tər) *n.* centilitre. *Abbrev.*: cl.

cen·ti·li·tre (sen′tə lē′tər) *n.* 1/100 of a litre. [< F]

cen·time (sän tēm′) *n.* **1** a unit of money in France, Belgium, Luxemburg, and Switzerland, worth 1/100 of a franc. **2** a unit of money equalling 1/100 of the standard unit of currency in certain countries of the French Community. **3** a coin worth one centime. [< F < L *centum* hundred]

cen·ti·me·ter (sen′tə mē′tər) *n.* centimetre.

cen·ti·me·tre (sen′tə mē′tər) *n.* 1/100 of a metre. *Abbrev.*: cm. [< F]

centimetre-gram-second (sen′tə mē′tər gram′sek′ənd) *adj.* having to do with a system of measurement in which the centimetre is the unit of length, the gram is the unit of mass, and the second is the unit of time. *Abbrev.*: C.G.S. or c.g.s.

cen·ti·mo (sen′ tə mō′) *n.* **1** a unit of money in Spain, worth 1/100 of a peseta. **2** a unit of money equalling 1/100 of the standard unit of currency in Costa Rica, Paraguay, and Venezuela. **3** a coin worth one centimo. [< Sp. < F *centime*]

cen·ti·pede (sen′tə pēd′) *n.* a small, wormlike animal having many pairs of legs. In some centipedes the front pair of legs is connected with a poison gland. [< L *centipeda* < *centum* hundred + *pes, pedis* foot]

CENTO (sen′tō′) Central Treaty Organization.

cen·tral (sen′trəl) *adj.* **1** of the centre; being the centre. **2** at the centre; near the centre. **3** from the centre. **4** equally distant from all points; easy to get to or from. **5** main; chief: *What is the central idea in the story?* **6** in anatomy and physiology: **a** of or designating the brain and spinal cord as a major division of the nervous system of vertebrates. **b** arising from or affecting these parts of the nervous system: *central anesthesia.*
—*n.* **1** a telephone exchange. **2** a telephone operator. [< L *centralis* < *centrum.* See CENTRE.]
—**cen′tral·ness,** *n.* —**Syn.** *adj.* **5** leading, principal.

Central American 1 having to do with Central America or its people. **2** a native or inhabitant of Central America.

cen·tral·ism (sen′trə liz′əm) *n.* a theory or system of concentrating control in a central agency, especially a government.

cen·tral·ist (sen′trəl ist) *n.* a person who promotes or favors centralism.

cen·tral·i·za·tion (sen′trəl ə zā′shən or sen′trəl ī zā′shən) *n.* **1** the coming or bringing to a centre. **2** concentration at a centre: *Centralization of relief agencies may prevent waste of effort.* **3** the concentration of administrative power in a central government.

cen·tral·ize (sen′trəl īz′) *v.* **-ized, -iz·ing. 1** collect at a centre; gather together. **2** bring or come under one control. —**cen′tra·liz′er,** *n.*

cen·tral·ly (sen′trəl ē) *adv.* at or near the centre.

Central Powers during World War I, Germany and Austria-Hungary, sometimes also their allies Turkey and Bulgaria.

cen·tre or **cen·ter** (sen′tər) *n. v.* **-tred** or **-tered, -tring** or **-ter·ing.** —*n.* **1** a point within a circle or sphere equally distant from all parts of the circumference or surface. **2** the middle point, place, or part: *the centre of a room.* **3** the person, thing, or group in a middle position. **4** a point toward which people or things go, or from which they come; main point: *Toronto is a centre of trade.* **5** in football, basketball, hockey, etc., a player who has the centre position of a forward line. **6** the part of a lawmaking body that sits in front of the presiding officer. It is made up of the political groups having moderate opinions. **7** all the people and parties having moderate views. **8** a mass of nerve cells closely connected and acting together; nerve centre: *the respiratory centre, the centre of balance.*
—*v.* **1** place in or at the centre. **2** collect or gather together at a centre. **3** be at a centre. **4** rest on; be concentrated in: *All his hopes centred on his promised promotion.* **5** mark or provide with a centre: *a smooth lawn centred by a pool.* [ME < OF *centre* < L *centrum* < Gk. *kentron* sharp point] —**Syn.** *n.* **1, 2** See **middle.**
☛ **Centre around** (or **about**) is an informal idiom: *The story centres around a robbery.* The formal idiom is *centre on* or *upon.*

cen·tre·board or **cen·ter·board** (sen′tər bôrd′) *n.* a movable keel of a sailboat. It is lowered through a slot in the bottom of a boat to prevent drifting to leeward.

centre field or **center field** in baseball, the section of the outfield behind second base.

centre ice or **center ice** in hockey: **1** the centre of the ice surface from which play begins at the start of each period. **2** the area of ice surface between the blue lines.

centre line or **center line** in hockey, a red line passing through centre ice at an equal distance from each of the blue lines.

centre of gravity or **center of gravity** the point in something around which its weight is evenly balanced.

cen·tre·piece or **cen·ter·piece** (sen′tər pēs′) *n.* an ornamental piece of glass, lace, etc. for the centre of a dining table.

cen·tric (sen′trik) *adj.* central. —**cen′tri·cal·ly,** *adv.*

cen·trif·u·gal (sen trif′ə gəl or sen trif′yů gəl) *adj.* **1** moving away from the centre. **2** making use of or acted upon by centrifugal force. [< NL *centrifugus* < L *centrum* centre + *fugere* flee] —**cen·trif′u·gal·ly,** *adv.*

centrifugal force the inertia of a body revolved around a centre, tending to move it away from the centre.

cen·tri·fuge (sen′trə fūj′) *n.* a machine for separating cream from milk, bacteria from a fluid, etc. by means of centrifugal force. [< F]

cen·trip·e·tal (sen trip′ə təl) *adj.* **1** moving toward the centre. **2** making use of or acted upon by centripetal force. [< NL *centripetus* < L *centrum* centre + *petere* seek] —**cen·trip′e·tal·ly,** *adv.*

centripetal force a force that tends to move things toward the centre around which they are turning. Gravitation is a centripetal force.

cen·trist (sen′trist) *n.* in several countries of continental Europe, a member of moderate political parties whose political views are neither radical nor conservative.

cen·tro·some (sen′trə sōm′) *n.* in biology, a tiny body in a cell that separates into two parts and attracts the divided chromosomes, one group to each part. [< *centro-* centre (< L *centrum* and Gk. *kentron*) + *-some* body (< Gk. *sōma*)]

cen·tro·sphere (sen′trə sfēr′) *n.* **1** in biology, a mass of protoplasm around a centrosome. **2** in geology, the central core of the earth. [< *centro-* centre (< L *centrum* and Gk. *kentron*) + *sphere*]

cen·tu·ple (sen tü′pəl or sen′tə pəl) *adj. v.* **-pled, -pling.** —*adj.* 100 times as much or as many; a hundredfold. —*v.* make 100 times as much or as many; increase a hundredfold. [< F < LL *centuplus* hundredfold]

cen·tu·ri·on (sen tūr′ē ən or sen tür′ē ən) *n.* in the ancient Roman army, a commander of a group of about 100 soldiers. [< L *centurio, -onis* < *centuria.* See CENTURY.]

cen·tu·ry (sen′chə rē) *n.* **-ries.** **1** each 100 years, counting from some special time, such as the birth of Christ. **2** a period of 100 years. **3** a group of 100 people or things. **4** in the ancient Roman army, a body of soldiers, originally probably consisting of 100 soldiers. **5** in ancient Rome, a division of the people for voting. Each century had one vote. **6** in cricket, a score of 100 runs. [< L *centuria* a division of a hundred units < *centum* hundred]

☛ **centuries.** Remember that the fifth century A.D. ran from the beginning of the year 401 to the end of the year 500, the nineteenth century from January 1, 1801, through December 31, 1900. That is, to name the century correctly, add one to the number of its hundred. Dates before Christ are figured like those after. The first century B.C. runs back from the birth of Christ through 100, the second century from 101 through 200, the fifth century from 401 through 500, and so on.

century plant a large, thick-leaved plant growing in Mexico and the southwestern United States, wrongly supposed to bloom only once every 100 years.

ce·phal·ic (sə fal′ik) *adj.* **1** of the head. **2** near, on, or in the head. **3** toward the head. [< L *cephalicus* < Gk. *kephalikos* < *kephalē* head]

cephalic index the ratio of the breadth of the human skull to its length, multiplied by 100. Also, **cranial index.**

ceph·a·lo·pod (sef′ə lə pod′) *n.* any of the most highly organized class of molluscs, characterized by long, armlike tentacles around the mouth, a pair of large eyes, and a sharp, birdlike beak. Cuttlefish and squids are cephalopods. [< NL *cephalopoda,* pl. < Gk. *kephalē* head + *pous, podos* foot]

ceph·a·lo·tho·rax (sef′ə lō thô′raks) *n.* the combined head and thorax of some animals, such as crabs, spiders, etc. [< *cephalo-* the head (< Gk. *kephalē*) + *thorax*]

Ce·phe·us (sē′fē əs or sē′fūs) *n.* **1** in Greek legend, the father of Andromeda. **2** in astronomy, a northern constellation near Cassiopeia.

ce·ram·ic (sə ram′ik) *adj.* having to do with pottery, earthenware, porcelain, etc., or with their production. [< Gk. *keramikos* < *keramos* potter's clay]

ce·ram·ics (sə ram′iks) *n.* **1** the art of making pottery, earthenware, porcelain, etc. **2** articles made of pottery, earthenware, porcelain, etc.

☛ **Ceramics** is singular in use when it means the art of making pottery, earthenware, etc.: *Ceramics is taught in some colleges.* It is plural in use when it means articles made of pottery, earthenware, etc.: *Those ceramics are beautiful.*

cer·a·mist (ser′ə mist) *n.* **1** an expert in ceramics. **2** a manufacturer of ceramics.

ce·rate (sēr′āt) *n.* a firm ointment made of lard or oil mixed with wax, resin, etc. [< L *ceratum,* pp. neut. of *cerare* to wax < *cera* wax]

Cer·ber·us (sėr′bər əs) *n.* **1** in Greek and Roman mythology, a three-headed dog that guarded the entrance to Hades. **2** a surly, watchful guard.

cere (sēr) *n.* a waxy-looking membrane near the beak of certain birds, especially birds of prey and parrots, in which the nostrils open. [< L *cera* wax < Gk. *kēros*]

ce·re·al (sēr′ē əl) *n.* **1** any grass that produces a grain used as food. Wheat, rice, corn, oats, and barley are cereals. **2** the grain. **3** food, especially breakfast food, made from the grain. Oatmeal and corn flakes are cereals. —*adj.* of or having to do with grain or the grasses producing it. [< L *Cerealis* of or having to do with Ceres]

cer·e·bel·lum (ser′ə bel′əm) *n.* **-bel·lums, -bel·la** (-bel′ə). in anatomy and zoology, the part of the brain that controls the co-ordination of the muscles. See **brain** for diagram. [< L *cerebellum,* dim. of *cerebrum* brain]

cer·e·bral (ser′ə brəl or sə rē′brəl) *adj.* **1** of the brain: *Paralysis may be caused by a cerebral hemorrhage.* **2** of the cerebrum. **3** involving thought and reason; intellectual: *Chess is a cerebral game.* [< L *cerebrum* brain]

cerebral palsy paralysis due to a lesion of the brain.

cer·e·brate (ser′ə brāt′) *v.* **-brat·ed, -brat·ing.** use the brain; think.

cer·e·bra·tion (ser′ə brā′shən) *n.* **1** the action of the brain. **2** the act of thinking.

hat, āge, cãre, fär; let, ēqual, tėrm; it, īce
hot, ōpen, ôrder; oil, out; cup, pút, rüle, ūse
əbove, takən, pencəl, lemən, circəs
ch, child; ng, long; sh, ship
th, thin; ᴛʜ, then; zh, measure

cer·e·bro·spi·nal (ser′ə brō spī′nəl) *adj.* of or affecting both the brain and spinal cord.

cer·e·brum (ser′ə brəm or sə rē′brəm) *n.* **-brums, -bra** (-brə). **1** the part of the human brain that controls thought and voluntary muscular movements. See **brain** for diagram. **2** the corresponding part of the brain of any vertebrate except man. [< L]

cere·cloth (sēr′kloth′) *n.* **1** waxed cloth. **2** the waxed cloth in which a dead person is wrapped for burial. [originally *cered cloth; cere* wax < L *cerare* < *cera* wax. See CERE.]

cere·ment (sēr′mənt) *n.* Usually, **cerements,** *pl.* the cloth or garment in which a dead person is wrapped for burial. [< obs. *cere* wrap for burial, wax < L *cerare.* See CERECLOTH.]

cer·e·mo·ni·al (ser′ə mō′nē əl) *adj.* **1** formal: *She welcomed her guests in a ceremonial way.* **2** of or having to do with ceremony: *The ceremonial costumes were beautiful.* —*n.* **1** formal action proper to an occasion. Bowing the head and kneeling are ceremonials of religion. **2** a rite or ceremony. **3** a formality of courtesy or manners. **4** the observance of these in social life. —**cer′e·mo′ni·al·ly,** *adv.*

☛ **Ceremonial, ceremonious** differ in meaning and use. **Ceremonial** = having to do with ceremony, and applies to things involving or belonging to the ceremonies and formalities of the church, law, polite conduct, fraternities, etc.: *Shriners wear ceremonial costumes.* **Ceremonious** = full of ceremony, and applies to things done with ceremony or showy formality or to people who pay very strict attention to the details of polite conduct: *The banquet was a ceremonious affair.*

cer·e·mo·ni·ous (ser′ə mō′nē əs) *adj.* **1** full of ceremony. **2** very formal; extremely polite. —**cer′e·mo′ni·ous·ly,** *adv.* —**cer′e·mo′ni·ous·ness,** *n.* —**Syn. 2** stiff.

☛ See **ceremonial** for usage note.

cer·e·mo·ny (ser′ə mō′nē) *n.* **-nies.** **1** a special form or set of acts to be done on special occasions such as weddings, funerals, graduations, Christmas, or Easter: *The marriage ceremony was performed in the church.* **2** very polite conduct; a way of conducting oneself that follows all the rules of polite social behavior: *The old gentleman showed us to the door with a great deal of ceremony.* **3** an empty form; meaningless formality. **4** formality; formalities: *The democratic prince disliked the traditional ceremony of court life.* **5 stand on ceremony,** be too polite; be very formal. [< L *caerimonia* rite]

Syn. 1 Ceremony, rite = a form followed on special occasions. **Ceremony** applies to a special form or procedure used on religious, public, or other solemn occasions: *The graduation ceremony was inspiring.* **Rite** applies to a ceremonial procedure that is laid down to be followed in a religious service or other solemn ceremony and in which both the acts to be done and the words to be said are prescribed: *A priest went to administer the last rites to the dying victims of the explosion.*

Ce·res (sēr′ēz) *n.* in Roman mythology, the goddess of agriculture and the harvest, identified with the Greek goddess Demeter.

ce·re·us (sēr′ē əs) *n.* any of several kinds of American cactus. The **night-blooming cereus** has fragrant flowers that open at night. [< L *cereus* wax candle < *cera* wax]

ce·rise (sə rēz′ or sə rēs′) *n. adj.* bright pinkish-red. [< F *cerise* cherry < VL < LGk. *kerasia* cherry tree < Gk. *kerasos* cherry. Doublet of CHERRY.]

ce·ri·um (sēr′ē əm) *n.* a grayish, metallic chemical element. *Symbol:* Ce; *at.no.* 58; *at.wt.* 140.12. [< NL *cerium,* from the asteroid *Ceres*]

cer·tain (sėr′tən) *adj.* **1** sure: *It is certain that 2 and 3 do not make 6.* **2** settled; fixed: *at a certain hour.* **3** reliable; dependable: *I have certain information that school will end a day earlier this year.* **4** definite but not named; some; one: *A certain person left the room.* **5** sure to happen; inevitable. **6 for certain,** surely; without a doubt. [ME < OF < L *certus* sure] —**cer′tain·ness,** *n.* —**Syn.** *adj.* **1** See **sure. 3** trustworthy, unfailing. **4** particular.

cer·tain·ly (sėr′tən lē) *adv.* surely; without doubt.

☛ **certainly.** In informal speech *certainly* is often used as an intensive or as an affirmative answer to questions: *I'm certainly pleased that you came. Are you going to the football game Friday? Certainly.*

cer·tain·ty (sėr′tən tē) *n.* **-ties. 1** a being certain; freedom from doubt: *The man's certainty was amusing, for we could all see that he was wrong.* **2** something certain; a fact: *The annual recurrence of the seasons is a certainty.*

cer·tes (sėr′tēz) *adv. Archaic.* certainly; in truth. [ME < OF < VL *certas* surely]

cer·ti·fi·a·ble (sėr′tə fī′ə bəl) *adj.* that can be certified. —**cer′ti·fi′a·bly,** *adv.*

cer·tif·i·cate (*n.* sər tif′ə kit; *v.* sər tif′ə kāt′) *n. v.* **-cat·ed, -cat·ing.** —*n.* a written or printed statement that declares something to be a fact. A person's birth certificate gives the date and place of his birth and the names of his parents. —*v.* **1** give a certificate to. **2** authorize by a certificate. [< Med.L *certificatum,* neut. pp. of *certificare.* See CERTIFY.]

cer·ti·fi·ca·tion (sėr′tə fə kā′shən) *n.* **1** the act of certifying. **2** the state of being certified. **3** a certified statement. **4** the writing on the face of a cheque which certifies it. **5** the process of providing with a certificate of training, qualifications, etc.; authorization. **6** the process of legally certifying an insane person as such.

cer·ti·fied (sėr′tə fīd′) *adj.* **1** guaranteed. **2** having a certificate.

certified cheque or **check** a cheque whose value is guaranteed by a bank.

certified milk raw or pasteurized milk guaranteed to meet certain official standards.

cer·ti·fi·er (sėr′tə fī′ər) *n.* one that certifies.

cer·ti·fy (sėr′tə fī′) *v.* **-fied, -fy·ing. 1** guarantee as certain; attest the reliability of. **2** declare (something) true or correct by means of a spoken, written, or printed statement. **3** guarantee the quality or value of. **4** assure; make certain. **5** of a bank, guarantee in writing on the face of (a cheque) that the drawer has sufficient funds in the bank to meet it. **6** declare (a person) legally insane. [ME < OF < Med.L *certificare* < L *certus* sure + *facere* make]

cer·ti·o·rar·i (sėr′shē ə rãr′ē or sėr′shē ə rãr′ī) *n.* in law, an order from a higher court to a lower one, calling for the record of a case for review. [< LL *certiorari* be informed]

cer·ti·tude (sėr′tə tūd′ or sėr′tə tüd′) *n.* certainty; sureness. [< LL *certitudo* < L *certus* sure]

ce·ru·le·an (sə rü′lē ən) *adj. n.* sky blue. [< L *caeruleus* dark blue]

ce·ru·men (sə rü′mən) *n.* a waxlike substance in the ears; earwax. [< NL < L *cera* wax]

cer·vi·cal (sėr′və kəl or sėr vī′kəl) *adj.* **1** of the neck. **2** of a cervix.

cer·vi·ces (sər vī′sēz) *n.* a pl. of **cervix.**

cer·vine (sėr′vīn or sėr′vin) *adj.* of or like a deer. [< L *cervinus* < *cervus* deer]

cer·vix (sėr′viks) *n.* **cer·vix·es** or **cer·vi·ces. 1** the neck, especially the back of the neck. **2** a necklike part. [< L]

Ce·sar·e·an or **Ce·sar·i·an** (si zãr′ē ən) *adj. n.* Caesarean.

ce·si·um or **cae·si·um** (sē′zē əm) *n.* a silvery metallic chemical element. *Symbol:* Cs; *at.no.* 55; *at.wt.* 132.905. [< NL *caesium* < L *caesius* bluish-gray]

ces·sa·tion (se sā′shən) *n.* a ceasing or stopping: *During the summer there is a cessation of schoolwork.* [< L *cessatio, -onis* < *cessare* cease] —**Syn.** pause.

ces·sion (sesh′ən) *n.* a handing over to another; ceding; giving up; surrendering. [< L *cessio, -onis* < *cedere* yield]

cess·pool (ses′pül′) *n.* **1** a pool or pit for house drains to empty into. **2** any filthy place. [origin uncertain]

ces·tode (ses′tōd) *n.* a tapeworm; type of parasitic worm that may infest the intestine of various animals. [< Gk. *kestos* girdle]

ces·tus (ses′təs) *n.* in ancient times, a boxer's hand covering made of strips of leather, often loaded with metal. [< L *caestus,* ? var. of *cestus* girdle < Gk. *kestos*]

A cestus

ce·su·ra (sə zhür′ə or si zūr′ə) *n.* **-su·ras, -su·rae** (-zhür′ē, -zhür′ī, -zūr′ē or -zūr′ī). caesura.

Ce·ta·cea (sə tā′shə) *n.pl.* a group of mammals that live in the water, including whales, dolphins, and porpoises. [< NL < L *cetus* whale < Gk. *kētos*]

ce·ta·cean (sə tā′shən) *adj.* of or belonging to the Cetacea. —*n.* an animal that belongs to the Cetacea.

ce·ta·ceous (sə tā′shəs) *adj.* cetacean.

Ce·tus (sē′təs) *n.* a constellation near the celestial equator. [< L *Cetus* < Gk. *Kētos* the Whale]

Cey·lo·nese (sē′lə nēz′) *adj. n.* **-nese.** —*adj.* of Ceylon or its people. —*n.* a native or inhabitant of Ceylon.

cf. compare. (for L *confer*)

c/f in bookkeeping, carried forward.

Cf californium.

CF Canadian Forces.

CFB Canadian Forces Base.

C.F.I. or **c.f.i.** cost, freight, and insurance.

CFL or **C.F.L.** Canadian Football League.

cg. or **cgm.** centigram; centigrams.

C.G.I.T. or **CGIT** Canadian Girls in Training.

C.G.M. Conspicuous Gallantry Medal.

C.G.S. or **c.g.s.** centimetre-gram-second.

CGSB Canadian Government Standards Board.

ch. or **Ch. 1** chapter. **2** church. **3** chaplain. **4** child; children. **5** chain.

C.H. Companion of Honor.

cha·bouk or **cha·buk** (chä′bůk) *n.* in the Orient, a long whip used to punish people. [< Persian or Hind. *chabuk*]

cha-cha (chä′chä′) *n.* cha-cha-cha.

cha-cha-cha (chä′ chä′ chä′) *n.* **1** a ballroom dance with a fast, strongly-marked rhythm, originally Latin American. **2** the music for such a dance. —*v.* dance the cha-cha-cha. Also, **cha-cha.** [imitative]

chafe (chāf) *v.* **chafed, chaf·ing,** *n.* —*v.* **1** rub to make warm: *She chafed her cold hands.* **2** wear or be worn away by rubbing. **3** make or become sore by rubbing: *The stiff collar chafed the man's neck.* **4** make angry; irritate: *His big brother's teasing chafed him.* **5** become angry or irritated: *He chafed under his big brother's teasing.* **6** formerly, heat; make warm. —*n.* **1** a chafing; irritation. **2** an annoyance; temper. **3** an impatience at restraints, etc; sense of frustration. [ME < OF *chaufer* < L *calefacere* < *calere* be warm + *facere* make] —**Syn.** *v.* **4** gall, annoy, vex, exasperate.

chaf·er (chāf′ər) *n. Esp.Brit.* any of a group of beetles including the June bugs, scarabs, etc. that usually feed on plants. [OE *ceafor*]

chaff[1] (chaf) *n.* **1** the husks of wheat, oats, rye, etc. separated from the grain by threshing. **2** hay or straw cut fine for feeding cattle. **3** worthless stuff. **4** strips of aluminum foil dropped by aircraft to confuse enemy radar systems. [OE *ceaf*]

chaff[2] (chaf) *v.* make fun of (someone) in a good-natured way: *The girls chaffed the French boy about his English.* —*n.* good-natured joking about a person in front of him. [origin uncertain] —**Syn.** *v.* banter, tease.

chaf·fer[1] (chaf′ər) *v.* dispute about a price; bargain. [< n.] —*n.* a disputing about price; bargaining. [ME *chaffare* < OE *cēap* bargain + *faru* journey]

chaf·finch (chaf′inch) *n.* a European songbird having a pleasant, short song, often kept as a cage bird. [OE *ceaffinc* < *ceaf* chaff[1] + *finc* finch]

chaff·y (chaf′ē) *adj.* **1** full of chaff. **2** worthless.

chafing dish a pan with a heater under it, used to cook food at the table or to keep it warm.

cha·grin (shə grin′) *n.* a feeling of disappointment, failure, or humiliation. —*v.* cause to feel chagrin. [< F < MF *chagrin* sad, gloomy] —**Syn.** *n.* mortification, vexation.

hat, āge, cãre, fär; let, ēqual, tėrm; it, īce
hot, ōpen, ôrder; oil, out; cup, pu̇t, rüle, ūse
əbove, takən, pencəl, lemən, circəs
ch, child; ng, long; sh, ship
th, thin; ᴛʜ, then; zh, measure

chain (chān) *n.* **1** a series of metal or other links joined together. **2** a series of things joined or linked together: *a mountain chain, a chain of events, a chain of thoughts.* **3** anything that binds or restrains. **4** a measuring instrument like a chain. A surveyor's chain is 66 feet long; an engineer's chain is 100 feet long. **5** a number of restaurants, stores, theatres, etc. owned and operated by one person or company. **6 chains,** *pl.* **a** bonds; fetters. **b** imprisonment; bondage. **7** a number of atoms of the same element linked together like a chain. **8** in biology, a group of organisms, as bacteria, connected end to end. —*v.* **1** join together with a chain; fasten with a chain. **2** bind; restrain. **3** keep in prison; make a slave of. **4** restrain with chains; fetter. [ME < OF *chaeine* < L *catena*]

chain gang in S. United States, a gang of convicts, etc. chained together while at work outdoors or on their way to work.

chain letter a letter that each receiver is asked to copy and send to several other people in order to get some supposed benefit.

chain mail a kind of flexible armor made of metal rings linked together.

chain·man (chān′mən) *n.* **-men.** in surveying, a man who carries the measuring chain.

chain measure a system of measurement used by surveyors:

7.92 inches	=	1 link
100 links or 66 ft.	=	1 chain
10 chains	=	1 furlong
80 chains	=	1 mile

chain reaction 1 in nuclear physics, a process that goes on automatically when it has once been started and is marked by an explosive release of atomic energy. A reactor is designed to produce a controlled chain reaction; the explosion of an atomic bomb is an uncontrolled chain reaction. **2** any rapid succession of events, each of which is caused by the preceding one or ones.

chain-smoke (chān′smōk′) *v.* **-smoked, -smok·ing.** smoke cigarettes one after another.

chain stitch in sewing or crocheting, a kind of stitch in which each stitch makes a loop through which the next stitch is taken.

chain-stitch (chān′stich′) *v.* sew or crochet using a chain stitch.

chain store one of a group of retail stores owned and operated by a single company.

chair (chãr) *n.* **1** a single seat that has a back and, sometimes, arms. **2** a seat of position, dignity, or authority. **3** the position or authority of a person who has such a seat: *Professor Smith occupies the chair of philosophy at this college.* **4** the chairman of a meeting. **5** a covered chair carried on poles by two men; a sedan chair. **6** the electric chair. **7 take the chair, a** begin a meeting. **b** be in charge of or preside at a meeting. **8 get the chair,** *Informal.* die or be sentenced to die in the electric chair.
—*v.* **1** put or carry in a chair. **2** carry high up, as if in a chair: *The winning team chaired their captain.* **3** put in a position of authority. **4** act as chairman of: *My brother chaired the meeting.* [ME < OF *chaiere* < L < Gk. *kathedra* seat. Doublet of CATHEDRA.]

chair lift an apparatus for conveying people, especially skiers, up a slope or between two points, consisting of a number of chairs suspended from an endless cable.

chair·man (chãr′mən) *n.* **-men** (-mən). **1** a person who presides at or is in charge of a meeting. **2** the head of a committee. **3** in New Brunswick, the elected head of a village council. **4** a man whose work is carrying or wheeling people in a chair. ☛ See **chairwoman** for usage note.

chair·man·ship (chãr′mən ship′) *n.* **1** the position of chairman. **2** the length of time one is a chairman.

chair·wom·an (chãr′wu̇m′ən) *n.* **-wom·en. 1** a woman who presides at or is in charge of a meeting. **2** a woman at the head of a committee.

☛ **chairman, chairwoman.** The word *chairman* may quite properly be used for either a man or a woman in charge of a meeting or committee. The forms of address are: *Mr. Chairman, Madam Chairman.*

chaise (shāz) *n.* a lightweight carriage, usually with a folding top. [< F *chaise* chair, var. of *chaire,* OF *chaiere.* See CHAIR.]

chaise longue (shāz′ long′) a chair with a long seat and a back support at one end, resembling a couch. [< F *chaise longue* long chair]

chal·ced·o·ny (kal sed′ə nē or kal′sə dō′nē) *n.* **-nies. 1** a variety of quartz having a waxy lustre that occurs in various colors and forms. Agate, onyx, carnelian, jasper, etc. are chalcedony. **2** a piece of this stone, or a gem made from it. [< L *chalcedonius* < Gk. *chalkēdōn*]

chal·cid (kal′sid) *n.* a small four-winged insect whose larvae live as parasites on other insects. [< Gk. *chalkos* copper; in reference to their color]

chal·co·py·rite (kal′kə pī′rīt or -pir′īt) *n.* a rich copper ore consisting of a sulphide of copper and iron; copper pyrites. *Formula:* $CuFeS_2$ [< Gk. *chalkos* copper + E *pyrite*]

Chal·da·ic (kal dā′ik) *adj. n.* Chaldean.

Chal·de·a (kal dē′ə) *n.* in ancient times, a region in S.W. Asia, on either side of the lower part of the Euphrates River.

Chal·de·an (kal dē′ən) *adj.* **1** of or having to do with Chaldea, its people, or their language. **2** of or having to do with astrology or magic. —*n.* **1** a native or inhabitant of Chaldea. The Chaldeans were a Semitic tribe closely related to the Babylonians. **2** the language of Chaldea. **3** an astrologer; magician. [< L *Chaldaeus* < Gk. *Chaldaios*]

Chal·dee (kal dē′ or kal′dē) *adj. n.* Chaldean.

cha·let (shal′ā or sha lā′) *n.* **1** a herdsman's hut or cabin in the Alps. **2** a Swiss house with wide, overhanging eaves. **3** any house of similar design. [< Swiss F]

chal·ice (chal′is) *n.* **1** a cup. **2** the cup that holds the wine used in the Communion service. **3** a flower shaped like a cup. [ME < OF < L *calix* cup]

chal·iced (chal′ist) *adj.* **1** having a flower shaped like a cup. **2** contained in a chalice.

chalk (chok or chôk) *n.* **1** a soft limestone, made up mostly of tiny fossil sea shells. Chalk is white, gray, or yellow and is used for making lime and for writing or drawing. **2** a substance like chalk, used for writing or drawing on a blackboard. **3** a piece of this substance. **4** a record of credit given; tally.
—*v.* **1** mark, write, or draw with chalk. **2** mix or rub with chalk; whiten with chalk. **3** score; record. **4 chalk up, a** write down; record. **b** score. [OE *cealc* < L *calx, calcis* lime] —**chalk′like′,** *adj.*

chalk·board (chok′bôrd′ or chôk′-) *n.* a smooth, light-yellow or green board of plastic, wallboard, metal, etc., used instead of a blackboard for writing or drawing on with chalk or crayon.

chalk talk a lecture illustrated by drawings and diagrams in chalk on a blackboard.

chalk·y (chok′ē or chôk′ē) *adj.* **chalk·i·er, chalk·i·est. 1** of chalk; containing chalk. **2** like chalk; white as chalk: *The clown's face was chalky.* —**chalk′i·ness,** *n.*

chal·lenge (chal′ənj) *v.* **-lenged, -leng·ing,** *n.* —*v.* **1** call to fight, especially in a duel. **2** call to a game or contest. **3** call on to answer and explain: *A sentry challenges all people who come near the fort, asking them who they are and what they are doing.* **4** question; doubt; dispute: *I challenge your statement: you must prove it before I believe it.* **5** object to (a juror, vote, etc.): *The counsel for the defence challenged the juror.* **6** claim; demand: *Preventing disease is a problem that challenges everyone's attention.* [ME < OF *chalenger* < L *calumniari* slander < *calumnia* false accusation. Doublet of CALUMNIATE.]
—*n.* **1** a call to fight; especially, a call to fight in a duel. **2** a call to a game or contest. **3** a call to answer and

explain: *"Who goes there?" is the sentry's challenge.* **4** an objection made to a juror, vote, etc.: *The judge sustained the challenge and dismissed the juror from duty.* [ME < OF *chalenge*, earlier *chalonge* < L *calumnia* false accusation. Doublet of CALUMNY.]
—**chal′lenge·a·ble,** *adj.* —**chal′leng·er,** *n.*

chal·lis or **chal·lie** (shal′ē) *n.* a lightweight woollen, cotton and woollen, or rayon cloth, used for dresses, blouses, etc. [origin uncertain]

cha·lyb·e·ate (kə lib′ē it or kə lib′ē āt′) *adj.* containing salts of iron. —*n.* water, medicine, etc. containing salts of iron. [< NL **chalybeatus* < L < Gk. *chalyps* steel]

cham (kam) *n. Archaic.* khan[1].

cham·ber (chām′bər) *n.* **1** a room (in a house). **2** a bedroom. **3** a hall where a legislature or a governing body meets. **4** a group of lawmakers: *Parliament has two chambers, the Senate and the House of Commons.* **5** a group of people organized for some business purpose: *Chamber of Commerce.* **6** any enclosed space in the body of an animal or plant, or in some kinds of machinery. The part of a gun that holds the charge is called the chamber. The heart has four chambers. **7** chamber pot. **8 chambers,** *pl.* **a** a set of rooms in a building to live in or use as offices. **b** the office of a lawyer or judge.
—*v.* provide with a chamber.
—*adj.* **1** designed for use in a chamber; suitable for performance in a chamber: *chamber music.* **2** of, having to do with, or performing chamber music. [ME < OF *chambre* < L *camera* < Gk. *kamara* vaulted place. Doublet of CAMERA.]

cham·bered (chām′bərd) *adj.* having a chamber or chambers; divided into compartments.

cham·ber·lain (chām′bər lin) *n.* **1** the person who manages the household of a sovereign or a lord; steward. **2** a high official of a royal court. [ME < OF *chamberlenc* < L *camera* vault + Gmc. *-ling*]

cham·ber·maid (chām′bər mād′) *n.* a maid who makes beds, cleans bedrooms, etc.

chamber music music suited to a room or small hall; music for a trio, quartet, etc.

Chamber of Commerce an organization of businessmen whose aim is to increase business opportunities by improving the community in which they live.

chamber pot a receptacle for urine, etc., used in the bedroom.

cham·bray (sham′brā) *n.* a cotton cloth woven from white and colored threads, used for dresses and men's shirts. It is a kind of gingham. [var. of *cambric*]

cha·me·le·on (kə mē′lē ən or kə mēl′yən) *n.* **1** a type of lizard that can change the color of its skin according to its surroundings. **2** a changeable or fickle person. [< L *chamaeleon* < Gk. *chamaileōn*, literally, ground lion < *chamai* on the ground, dwarf + *leōn* lion]

cham·fer (cham′fər) *n.* a slanting surface made by cutting off an edge or corner. —*v.* **1** cut off at an edge or corner to make a slanting surface. **2** make a groove or furrow in. [< F *chamfrain*, apparently < *chant fraindre* (< L *cantum frangere*) break the side]

cham·ois (sham′ē or sham wä′ *for 1*) *n.* **-ois. 1** a small, goatlike antelope that lives in the high mountains of Europe and S.W. Asia. **2** a soft leather made from the skin of sheep, goats, deer, etc. [< F < LL *camox*]

champ[1] (champ) *v.* **1** bite and chew noisily. **2** bite on impatiently: *The race horse champed its bit.* **3 champ (at) the bit,** be restless or impatient: *After months with his leg in plaster, the boy was champing at the bit to go skiing again.* Also, **chomp.** [? related to CHAP[3]]

champ[2] (champ) *n. Informal.* champion.

cham·pagne (sham pān′) *n.* **1** a sparkling, bubbling wine, first made in Champagne, France. **2** a pale brownish-yellow. —*adj.* pale brownish-yellow.

cham·paign (sham pān′) *n.* a wide plain; level, open country. —*adj.* level and open. [ME < OF *champaigne* < LL *campania* < L *campus* field. Doublet of CAMPAIGN.]

cham·pi·gnon (sham pin′yən or cham pin′yən; *French,* shäN pē nyôN′) *n.* any edible mushroom, especially the common field mushroom. [< MF]

cham·pi·on (cham′pē ən) *n.* **1** a person, animal, or thing that wins first place in a game or contest: *the swimming champion of the world.* **2** a person who fights or speaks for another; defender; supporter: *a great champion of peace.*
—*adj.* having won first place; ahead of all others: *a champion boxer.*
—*v.* fight or speak in behalf of; defend; support: *John championed his friends.* [ME < OF < LL *campio, -onis* < L *campus* field (i.e., of battle)]
—**cham′pi·on·less,** *adj.* —**Syn.** *n.* **2** protector.

cham·pi·on·ship (cham′pē ən ship′) *n.* **1** the position of a champion; first place. **2** defence; support.

chance (chans) *n. v.* **chanced, chanc·ing,** *adj.* —*n.* **1** an opportunity: *a chance to make some money.* **2** a possibility; probability: *There's a chance that the sick child will get well.* **3** fate; luck. **4** a happening: *Chance led to the finding of the diamond mine.* **5** a risk: *He took a chance when he swam the channel.* **6** in baseball, any handling of the ball which results in a put-out, an assist, or an error by a defensive player. **7** in cricket, a possible catch. **8** in gambling, lotteries, etc., a number, lot, etc. on which a bet is risked. **9 by chance,** accidentally. **10 on the chance,** depending on the possibility. **11 on the off chance,** depending on luck: *He went to the theatre on the off chance of getting a returned ticket.* **12 stand a chance,** have favorable prospects: *Our team still stands a chance of winning the cup.*
—*v.* **1** happen. **2** *Informal.* risk. **3 chance upon** or **on,** happen to find or meet. —*adj.* not expected or planned; accidental; casual: *a chance visit.* [ME < OF *cheance* < L *cadentia* a falling < *cadere* fall. Doublet of CADENCE, CADENZA.] —**Syn.** *n.* **2** likelihood. *-adj.* fortuitous, unexpected.
☛ **Chance** is followed by *on* or *upon* when it means "happen to find or meet": *There they chanced on a real treasure—a first edition.*

chan·cel (chan′səl) *n.* the space around the altar of a church, used by the clergy and the choir. It is often separated from the rest of the church by a railing, lattice, or screen. See **apse** for diagram. [ME < OF < L *cancelli* a grating]

chan·cel·ler·y (chan′sə lər ē or chan′slər ē) *n.* **-ler·ies. 1** the position of a chancellor. **2** the office of a chancellor. **3** the office of an ambassador in a foreign country.

chan·cel·lor (chan′sə lər or chan′slər) *n.* **1** a very high official who is the secretary of a nobleman, king, or embassy. **2** in West Germany and in Austria, the prime minister. **3** any of various high British government officials, especially: **a** the Chancellor of the Exchequer. **b** the Lord Chancellor. **4** in certain universities, the highest official. [ME < AF *canceler, chanceler* < LL *cancellarius* officer stationed at a tribunal < *cancelli* a grating, bars (which enclosed the chancel)]

Chancellor of the Exchequer in Great Britain, the highest official of the treasury.

chan·cel·lor·ship (chan′sə lər ship′ or chan′slər-) *n.* **1** the position of a chancellor. **2** the term of office of a chancellor.

chan·cer·y (chan′sər ē) *n.* **-cer·ies. 1** a court of equity. **2** equity. **3** the office where public records are kept. **4** the office of a chancellor. **5** in wrestling, a grip on the head. **6 in chancery, a** in a court of equity. **b** in a helpless position. [var. of CHANCELLERY]

chan·cre (shang′kər) *n.* an ulcer or sore with a hard base. [< F < L *cancer*. Doublet of CANCER, CANKER.]

chanc·y (chan′sē) *adj. Informal.* **1** subject to chance; risky; uncertain. **2** *Scottish.* lucky; favorable.

chan·de·lier (shan′də lēr′) *n.* a fixture with branches for lights, usually hanging from the ceiling. [ME < OF < VL *candelarius* < L *candela* candle < *candere* shine. Doublet of CHANDLER.]

A chandelier

chan·dler (chan′dlər) *n.* **1** a maker or seller of candles. **2** a dealer in groceries and supplies: *a ship chandler.* [ME < AF *chandeler* < VL *candelarius.* Doublet of CHANDELIER.]

chan·dler·y (chan′dlər ē) *n.* **-dler·ies. 1** a storeroom for candles. **2** the warehouse, goods, or business of a chandler.

hat, āge, cãre, fär; let, ēqual, tėrm; it, īce
hot, ōpen, ôrder; oil, out; cup, pu̇t, rüle, ūse
əbove, takən, pencəl, lemən, circəs
ch, child; ng, long; sh, ship
th, thin; ᴛʜ, then; zh, measure

change (chānj) *v.* **changed, chang·ing,** *n.* —*v.* **1** become different: *The wind changed from east to west.* **2** make different: *She changed the room by painting the walls green.* **3** put (one thing) in place of another; substitute: *change dirty clothes for clean ones.* **4** take in place of: *change a dollar bill for ten dimes.* **5** give and take; exchange: *I changed seats with my brother.*
—*n.* **1** a changing. **2** a changed condition. **3** a lack of sameness; variety. **4** something to be used in place of another thing of the same kind. **5** the money returned to a person when he has given an amount larger than the price of what he buys. **6** smaller pieces of money given in place of a large piece of money: *Can you give me change for a quarter?* **7** small coins: *I have a dollar bill and some change.* **8 changes,** *pl.* the different ways in which a set of bells can be rung. **9 ring the changes, a** ring a set of bells in all its different ways. **b** do a thing in many different ways; say the same thing in different ways. [ME < OF *changer* < LL *cambiare*]
—**chang′er,** *n.*
Syn. *v.* **1, 2 Change, alter** = make or become different. **Change** is the general word, but emphasizes the idea of a fundamental difference in the make-up of the person or thing, of making or becoming completely different: *She used to be shy, but has changed since she went to college.* **Alter** = change in one particular way, without changing the person or thing as a whole: *We can alter the kitchen enough to put in a freezer if we rehang the door.* -*n.* **1** alteration. **2** transformation. **3** diversity. **4** substitute.

'change (chānj) *n.* an exchange; a place where people trade.

change·a·bil·i·ty (chān′jə bil′ə tē) *n.* a changeable quality or condition.

change·a·ble (chān′jə bəl) *adj.* **1** that can change; likely to change. **2** that can be changed; likely to be changed. **3** having a color or appearance that changes: *Silk is called changeable when it looks different in different lights.* —**change′a·ble·ness,** *n.* —**change′a·bly,** *adv.* —**Syn. 1** inconstant, unstable. **2** alterable, variable.

change·ful (chānj′fəl) *adj.* full of changes; likely to change; changing. —**change′ful·ly,** *adv.* —**change′ful·ness,** *n.*

change·less (chānj′lis) *adj.* not changing; not likely to change; constant; steadfast. —**change′less·ly,** *adv.* —**change′less·ness,** *n.* —**Syn.** unalterable, unvarying.

change·ling (chānj′ling) *n.* **1** a child secretly substituted for another. **2** a strange, stupid, or ugly child, supposed to have been left by fairies in place of a child carried off by them.

change of heart a change of feeling; conversion.

change of venue 1 a change of the place of a trial. **2** a change in place for any activity.

change-o·ver (chānj′ō′vər) *n.* **1** in industry, a shifting to the manufacture of a new model. **2** a transfer of ownership or control.

chan·nel (chan′əl) *n. v.* **-nelled** or **-neled -nel·ling** or **-nel·ing.** —*n.* **1** the bed of a stream, river, etc. **2** a body of water joining two larger bodies of water: *the English Channel.* **3** the deeper part of a waterway: *There is shallow water on both sides of the channel in this river.* **4** a passage for liquids; groove. **5** the means by which something is carried: *The information came through secret channels.* **6** a course of action; field of activity: *He sought to find a suitable channel for his enthusiasm.* **7** a narrow band of radio or television frequencies, sufficient for one-way transmission.
—*v.* **1** form a channel in; cut out as a channel: *The river had channelled its way through the rocks.* **2** convey through or as if through a channel. **3** to direct into a particular course; concentrate. [ME < OF *chanel* < L *canalis.* Doublet of CANAL.]

chan·son (shäɴ sôɴ′) *n. French.* a song.

chant (chant) *n.* **1** a song. **2** a short, simple song in which several syllables or words are sung in one tone. Chants are used in church services. **3** a psalm, prayer, or other song for chanting. **4** a singsong way of talking. [probably < v.]
—*v.* **1** sing. **2** sing to a chant, or in the manner of a chant. A choir chants psalms or prayers. **3** keep talking about; say over and over again. [ME < OF *chanter* < L *cantare* < *canere* sing]

chan·ter (chan′tər) *n.* **1** a person who sings or chants. **2 a** one who sings in a choir; chorister. **b** the chief singer in a choir; cantor. **3** a priest who sings Mass in a chantry. **4** in a bagpipe, the pipe on which the melody, or chant, is played.

chan·teuse (shäɴ tœz′) *n. French.* a female singer.

chant·ey (shan′tē or chan′tē) *n.* **chant·eys.** a song sung by sailors in rhythm with the motions made during their work. Also, **shanty, chanty.** [alteration of F *chanter* sing]

chan·ti·cleer (chant′tə klēr′) *n.* a rooster. [ME < OF *chantecler* < *chanter* sing + *cler* clear; from the name of the cock in the medieval tale of *Reynard the Fox*]

Chan·til·ly (shan til′ē; *French,* shäɴ tē yē′) *n.* a type of fine lace, having a netlike pattern of six-pointed stars. [< *Chantilly,* a town in N.France, formerly famous for lace manufacturing]

chan·try (chan′trē) *n.* **-tries. 1** a chapel attached to a church, used for the less important services. **2** an endowment to pay for the singing or saying of Masses for a person's soul. **3** a chapel, altar, or part of a church similarly endowed. **4** the priests thus endowed. [ME < OF *chanterie* singing < *chanter* sing]

chant·y (shan′tē or chan′tē) *n.* **chant·ies.** chantey.

cha·os (kā′os) *n.* **1** great confusion; complete disorder: *The whirlwind left chaos behind it.* **2** the infinite space or formless matter thought to have existed before the universe came into being. [< L < Gk.]

cha·ot·ic (kā ot′ik) *adj.* in great confusion; very confused; completely disordered.

cha·ot·i·cal·ly (kā ot′ik lē) *adv.* in a chaotic manner; in great confusion or disorder.

chap[1] (chap) *v.* **chapped, chap·ping,** *n.* —*v.* crack open; make or become rough: *A person's lips or skin often chap in cold weather.* —*n.* a place where the skin is chapped. [ME *chappe(n)* cut]

chap[2] (chap) *n. Informal.* a fellow; man; boy. [a shortened form of *chapman*]

chap[3] (chap) *n.* chop[2]. [? < *chap*[1]]

chap. 1 chapter. **2** chaplain. **3** chapel.

cha·pa·ra·jos (chä′pə rä′hōs) *n.pl.* in the southwestern United States, strong leather trousers worn by cowboys; chaps. [< Mexican Sp.]

chap·ar·ral (chap′ə ral′) *n.* in the southwestern United States, a thicket of low shrubs, thorny bushes, etc. [< Sp. *chaparral* < *chaparro* evergreen oak]

chap·book (chap′bu̇k′) *n.* a small book or pamphlet of popular tales, ballads, etc., formerly sold on the streets. [because sold by *chapmen*]

cha·peau (sha pō′; *French,* shä pō′) *n.* **-peaux** (-pō′) or **-peaus** (-pōz′). a hat. [< F < OF *chapel* hat < VL *cappellum* < LL *cappa* cape. Related to CAP, CAPE.]

chap·el (chap′əl) *n.* **1** a building for worship, not so large as a church. **2** a small place for worship within a larger building. **3** a room or building for worship in a palace, school, etc. **4** a religious service in a chapel. **5** in Great Britain, a place for worship used by people who do not belong to the Established Church. **6** an association of journeymen printers for regulating conditions of work among themselves. [ME < OF *chapele* < LL *cappella;* originally a shrine in which was preserved the *cappa* or cape of St. Martin]

chap·er·on·age (shap′ər ōn′ij) *n.* the activities of a chaperone; protection of a chaperone.

chap·er·one or **chap·er·on** (shap′ər ōn′) *n. v.* **-oned, -on·ing.** —*n.* **1** a married woman or an older woman who accompanies a young unmarried woman in public for the sake of convention and protection. **2** an older person who attends young people's parties, student dances, etc. to ensure proper behavior.
—*v.* act as a chaperone to. [< F *chaperon* hood, protector < *chape* cape < LL *cappa.* Related to CAP, CAPE.]

chap·fall·en (chop′fol′ən or -fôl′ən, chap′fol′ən or

-fôl′ən) *adj.* dejected; discouraged; humiliated. Also, **chopfallen.**

chap·lain (chap′lən) *n.* a clergyman officially authorized to perform religious functions for a family, court, society, public institution, or unit in the armed services. [ME < OF *chapelain* < LL *capellanus* < *cappella.* See CHAPEL.]

chap·lain·cy (chap′lən sē) *n.* the position of a chaplain.

chap·lain·ship (chap′lən ship′) *n.* chaplaincy.

chap·let (chap′lit) *n.* **1** a wreath worn on the head. **2** a string of beads. **3** in the Roman Catholic Church: **a** a string of beads, one third as long as a rosary used for keeping count in saying prayers. **b** the prayers said with such beads. [ME *chapelet* < OF, dim. of *chapel* headdress. See CHAPEAU.]

chap·let·ed (chap′lit id) *adj.* wearing a wreath on the head.

chap·man (chap′mən) *n.* **-men** (-mən). *Archaic.* **1** a peddler. **2** a man whose business is buying and selling; merchant, trader; dealer. [OE *cēapman* < *cēap* trade + *man* man]

chaps (shaps or chaps) *n.pl.* strong leather trousers without a back, worn over other trousers by cowboys. [short for *chaparajos*]

chap·ter (chap′tər) *n.* **1** a main division of a book or other writing, dealing with a certain part of the story or subject. **2** anything like a chapter; part; section: *The development of television is an interesting chapter in modern science.* **3** a local division of an organization; branch of a club, society, etc. **4** a group of clergymen, usually attached to a cathedral. **5** a meeting of such a group.
—*v.* divide into chapters; arrange in chapters. [ME < OF *chapitre* < L *capitulum,* dim. of *caput* head]

chapter and verse 1 the exact reference for a passage of Scripture. **2** precise authority (*for*): *He cited chapter and verse for his opinions.* **3** exact information and complete detail.

chapter house 1 the building where the chapter of a cathedral holds its meetings. **2** the house of a college fraternity or sorority.

char[1] (chär) *v.* **charred, char·ring. 1** burn to charcoal. **2** burn slightly; scorch. [? < *charcoal*]

char[2] (chär) *n. v.* **charred, char·ring.** *Esp.Brit.*
—*n.* **1** charwoman. **2** an odd job; chore. —*v.* **1** do housework by the day or hour. **2** do odd jobs. [OE *cerr* turn, occasion]

char[3] (chär) *n.* **char.** a fish of the trout family, having a red underside and small scales.

char-à-banc (shar′ə bang′ or -bangk′; *French,* shä rä bäɴ′) *n.* **char-à-bancs** (shar′ə bangz′ or shar′ə bangks′; *French,* shä rä bäɴ′) a large motorbus, used for excursions. [< F *char à bancs* car with benches]

char·ac·ter (kar′ik tər) *n.* **1** all the qualities or features possessed; kind; sort; nature: *He dislikes people of that character. The soil on the prairies is of a different character from that in the mountains.* **2** moral strength or weakness; the special way in which any person feels, thinks, and acts: *a shallow, changeable character.* **3** moral firmness, self-control, integrity: *It takes character to endure calumny. The boy has no character whatever.* **4** reputation. **5** a good reputation. **6** in biology, a trait or characteristic. The size and form of a given breed of dog and the fragrance of a sweet pea are characters. **7** position; condition: *The treasurer of the club also serves in the character of a secretary.* **8** a person in a play, book, etc. **9** *Informal.* a person who attracts attention because he is strange or eccentric. **10** in writing or printing, a letter, mark, or sign. A, a, %, +, –, 1, 2, and 3 are characters. **11** a description of a person's qualities. **12** a written testimonial, especially from a former employer, describing the qualities and capacities of an employee. **13 in character, a** in the theatre, true to character: *The actor remained in character throughout the play.* **b** fitting; appropriate. **14 out of character, a** in the theatre, not true to character. **b** not appropriate. [ME < OF *caractere* < L < Gk. *charaktēr* stamped mark < *charassein* engrave]

Syn. *n.* **2 Character, personality, individuality** = the qualities that make a person what he is. **Character** applies to the moral qualities that determine the way a person thinks, feels, and acts in the important matters of life, especially in relation to the principles of right and wrong. **Personality** applies to the personal qualities that make one person different from another and determine the way he acts in his social and personal relations. **Individuality** applies to the particular qualities that make a person himself, an individual: *He has a weak character, but a winning personality and great individuality.*

char·ac·ter·is·tic (kar′ik tər is′tik) *adj.* distinguishing (a person or thing) from others; special: *Bananas have a characteristic smell.*
—*n.* **1** a special quality or feature; whatever distinguishes one person or thing from others: *Cheerfulness is a characteristic that we admire in people. An elephant's trunk is its most noticeable characteristic.* **2** in mathematics, the integral part of a logarithm. In the logarithm 2.95424, the characteristic is 2 and the mantissa is .95424. —**Syn.** *n.* **1** attribute, trait. See **feature.**

char·ac·ter·is·ti·cal·ly (kar′ik tər is′tik lē) *adv.* in a way that shows characteristics; specially; typically.

char·ac·ter·i·za·tion (kar′ik tər ə zā′shən or kar′ik tər ī zā′shən) *n.* **1** the act of characterizing; description of characteristics. **2** the creation of characters in a play, book, etc.

char·ac·ter·ize (kar′ik tər īz′) *v.* **-ized, -iz·ing. 1** describe the special qualities or features of a person or thing; describe. **2** be a characteristic of; distinguish: *A camel is characterized by the humps on its back and the ability to do without water for several days.* **3** give character to: *The author characterized his heroine in a few short paragraphs.*

char·ac·ter·less (kar′ik tər lis) *adj.* **1** without character. **2** without distinction; uninteresting.

char·ac·ter·y (kar′ik tər ē) *n.* the signs or symbols used to express ideas.

cha·rade (shə rād′ or shə räd′) *n.* a game of guessing a word, title, proverb, etc. from the descriptive or dramatic representation of each syllable or part in succession, and, finally, of the whole. [< F < Provençal *charrada* < *charra* chatter]

char·coal (chär′kōl′) *n.* **1** a form of carbon; a black substance made by partly burning wood or bones in a place from which the air is shut out. Charcoal is used as fuel and in filters. **2** a pencil made of charcoal for drawing. **3** a drawing made with such a pencil.
—*v.* mark, write, or blacken with charcoal. [ME *charcole*]

charcoal burner 1 anything in which charcoal is burned, such as a stove. **2** a person whose work is making charcoal.

chard (chärd) *n.* a kind of beet whose large leaves are eaten as a vegetable. [< F *charde* < L *carduus* thistle, artichoke]

charge (chärj) *v.* **charged, charg·ing,** *n.* —*v.* **1** load; fill. A gun is charged with powder and shot. A battery is charged with electricity. **2** give a task, duty, or responsibility to: *The law charges policemen with keeping order.* **3** give an order or command to; direct: *He charged us to keep the plan secret. The judge charged the jury.* **4** accuse: *The driver was charged with speeding.* **5** ask as a price; put on a price of: *He charged us $5 for repairing the radio.* **6** put down as an obligation or debt: *This store will charge things that you buy. Library books are charged at the exit.* **7** put down against: *Please charge my account.* **8** attack; rush with force: *The soldiers charged the enemy.* **9** attribute (a fault, etc.) to a person. **10** in heraldry: **a** place (a bearing or charge) on an escutcheon, shield, etc.: *charge crosses on a field.* **b** bear upon (an escutcheon, shield, etc.) with a bearing or charge: *charge a field with crosses.* **11 charge off, a** subtract as a loss. **b** put down as belonging: *A bad mistake must be charged off to experience.* **c** *Informal.* dash away. **12 charge up,** charge off.
—*n.* **1** the quantity needed to load or fill something. A gun is fired by exploding the charge of powder and shot. **2** a task; duty; responsibility: *Arresting criminals is the charge of the police.* **3** care; management: *Doctors and nurses have charge of sick people.* **4** a person, persons, or thing under the care or management of someone: *Sick people are the charges of doctors and nurses.* **5** an order; command; direction: *a judge's charge to the jury.* **6** an accusation: *He admitted the charge and paid the fine.* **7** a price asked for or put on something. **8** a debt to be

paid: *Taxes are a charge on property.* **9** an attack; forceful rush: *The charge drove the enemy back.* **10** an accumulation of electricity in a storage battery, condenser, etc., which may be again discharged. **11** in heraldry, a device borne on an escutcheon; bearing. **12 in charge,** having the care or management. **13 in charge of, a** having the care or management of: *Dr. Brown is in charge of the case.* **b** under the care or management of. **c** in command of: *The corporal was in charge of the patrol.* [ME < OF *charger* < LL *carricare* load < L *carrus* wagon. Doublet of CARRY.]
Syn. *v.* **4 Charge, accuse** = put the blame on a person. **Charge** may suggest the blame for some minor wrongdoing, such as breaking a rule, but it commonly suggests a serious offence, such as breaking a law, and making a formal statement before the proper authority: *He was charged with leaving the grounds without permission.* **Accuse** suggests making the charge directly to the person blamed and expressing disapproval, but not necessarily taking him before authority: *He accused me of lying.* **8** assault. -*n.* **3** custody. **6** indictment, complaint. **7** See **price. 9** assault, onset.

charge·a·ble (chär′jə bəl) *adj.* **1** that can be charged; likely to be charged: *If you take anything that belongs to someone else, you are chargeable with theft. Taxes are chargeable against the owners of property.* **2** liable to become a public charge.

charged (chärjd) *adj.* that has been loaded; filled.

char·gé d'af·faires (shär zhā′ də fãr′) *pl.* **char·gés d'af·faires** (shär zhāz′ də fãr′; *French,* shär zhā′dä fãr′). an official who takes the place of an ambassador, minister, or other diplomat. [< F]

charge plate a stencil that identifies a customer and is used to print his name and account number on bills.

charg·er[1] (chär′jər) *n.* **1** a war horse. **2** a person or thing that charges. [< *charge*]

charg·er[2] (chär′jər) *n. Archaic.* a large, flat dish; platter. [< OF **chargeour* or *chargeoir* < *charger* load. See CHARGE.]

charg·ing (chär′jing) *n.* the act of loading; filling. —*adj.* that charges.

char·i·ly (chãr′ə lē) *adv.* carefully; warily.

char·i·ness (chãr′ē nis) *n.* caution; sparingness.

char·i·ot (char′ē ət) *n.* **1** in ancient times, a two-wheeled car pulled by horses, used in fighting, racing, and for driving in processions. **2** a four-wheeled carriage or coach. [ME < OF *chariot* < *char* < L *carrus* four-wheeled cart]

char·i·ot·eer (char′ē ə tēr′) *n.* a person who drives a chariot.

char·ism (kar′iz əm) *n.* charisma.

charisma (kə riz′mə) *n.* **-ma·ta** (-mə tə). **1** in theology, a spiritual gift or grace giving a person the gift of prophesying, healing, etc. **2** an extraordinary personal power thought of as belonging to a few great and popular leaders. [< Gk. *charisma, -atos*]

char·is·mat·ic (kar′iz mat′ik) *adj.* **1** of or having to do with a charisma. **2** having charisma; capable of inspiring popular allegiance.

char·i·ta·ble (char′ə tə bəl) *adj.* **1** of charity; for charity. **2** generous in giving help to poor or suffering people. **3** kindly in judging people and their actions. **—char′i·ta·ble·ness,** *n.* **—char′i·ta·bly,** *adv.* —**Syn. 2** liberal, bountiful.

char·i·ty (char′ə tē) *n.* **-ties. 1** help given to the poor or suffering. **2** an act or work of charity. **3** a fund, institution, or organization for helping the poor or suffering. **4** Christian love of one's fellow men. **5** kindness in judging the faults of other people. [ME < OF *charite* < L *caritas* dearness < *carus* dear] **—Syn. 1** philanthropy, beneficence.

cha·riv·a·ri (shiv′ə rē′, shə riv′ə rē′, or shä′rē vä′rē) *n.* **-ris.** shivaree. [< F]

char·la·tan (shär′lə tən) *n.* a person who pretends to have more knowledge or skill than he really has; quack. [< F < Ital. *ciarlatano,* ult. < Mongolian *dzar* proclaim, tell lies] **—Syn.** impostor, cheat.

char·la·tan·ism (shär′lə tən iz′əm) *n.* the practices or methods of a charlatan; quackery.

char·la·tan·ry (shär′lə tən rē) *n.* charlatanism.

Charles's Wain (chärl′zíz wān′) the Big Dipper. [OE *Carles Wægn* Carl's (Charlemagne's) wagon]

hat, āge, cãre, fär; let, ēqual, tėrm; it, īce
hot, ōpen, ôrder; oil, out; cup, pu̇t, rüle, ūse
əbove, takən, pencəl, lemən, circəs
ch, child; ng, long; sh, ship
th, thin; ᴛʜ, then; zh, measure

Charles·ton (chärlz′tən) *n.* a kind of dance popular during the 1920's. —*v.* dance the Charleston. [< *Charleston,* the early capital of South Carolina]

char·ley horse (chär′lē) *Informal.* **1** a severe stiffness caused by straining a muscle, especially in an arm or leg. **2** a cramp in a muscle.

char·lock (chär′lək) *n.* a weed having yellow flowers; wild mustard. [OE *cerlic*]

char·lotte russe (shär′lət rüs′) a dessert made of sponge cake filled with whipped cream or custard. [< F *charlotte russe* Russian charlotte (a type of dessert)]

charm (chärm) *n.* **1** the power of delighting or fascinating; attractiveness: *We were much impressed with the grace and charm of our hostess.* **2** a very pleasing quality or feature. **3** a small ornament or trinket worn on a watch chain, bracelet, etc. **4** a word, verse, act, or thing supposed to have magic power to help or harm people. —*v.* **1** please greatly; delight; fascinate; attract: *The old sailor's stories of his adventures charmed the boys.* **2** act on as if by magic: *Laughter charmed away his troubles.* **3** give magic power to; protect as by a charm: *Sir Galahad seemed to bear a charmed life.* [ME < OF *charme* < L *carmen* song, enchantment < *canere* sing] **—charm′less,** *adj.*
Syn. *n.* **1** allurement. -*v.* **1 Charm, attract, allure** = win a person by pleasing. **Charm** emphasizes winning and holding a person's attention and admiration by giving delight: *Her beautiful voice charms everyone.* **Attract** emphasizes drawing attention and good will by being pleasing: *She attracts everyone she meets.* **Allure** emphasizes attracting a person by appealing to the senses and feelings: *Mountain scenery allures many tourists to the Rockies.*

charmed (chärmd) *adj.* **1** delighted; fascinated. **2** enchanted. **3** protected as by a charm: *He bears a charmed life.*

charm·er (chär′mər) *n.* one who charms, delights, or fascinates.

charm·ing (chär′ming) *adj.* very pleasing; delightful; fascinating; attractive. **—charm′ing·ly,** *adv.*

char·nel (chär′nəl) *n.* a charnel house. —*adj.* **1** of or used for a charnel. **2** like a charnel; deathlike; ghastly. [ME < OF < LL *carnale,* originally neut. of L *carnalis.* Doublet of CARNAL.]

charnel house *Archaic.* a place where dead bodies or bones are laid.

char·o·lais (shär′ə lā′) *n.* a breed of large, white beef cattle. [< F < *Charolles,* a province in France where the breed originated]

Char·on (kãr′ən) *n.* in Greek mythology, the boatman who ferried the spirits of the dead across the river Styx to Hades.

chart (chärt) *n.* **1** a map. A sailor's chart shows the coasts, rocks, and shallow places of a sea. The course of a ship is marked on a chart. **2** an outline map showing special conditions or facts: *a weather chart.* **3** a sheet giving information in lists, pictures, tables, or diagrams. **4** such a list, table, picture, or diagram. **5** a graphic representation of any variable, such as temperature, pressure, production, or sales. —*v.* **1** make a chart of; show on a chart: *chart a course.* **2** plan in detail: *He is now charting the course of his campaign.* [< F *charte* < L *charta* < Gk. *chartēs* leaf of paper. Doublet of CARD[1].] **—chart′less,** *adj.* **—Syn. 1** See **map.**

char·ter (chär′tər) *n.* **1** a written grant by a government to a colony, a group of citizens, a commercial company, or other institution bestowing the right of organization, with other privileges, and specifying the form of organization. **2** a written order from the authorities of a society, giving to a group of persons the right to organize a new chapter, branch, or lodge. **3** a document setting forth aims and purposes of a group of nations, organizations, or individuals in a common undertaking: *the Charter of the United Nations.* **4** in transportation:

a the renting of a ship, aircraft, bus, etc. for private use. b a contract or deal arranging such transportation. c a ship, bus, or aircraft so rented. 5 a special right, privilege, or immunity.
—*v.* 1 give a charter to. 2 in transportation: a rent a ship, aircraft, bus, etc. for private use: *He chartered a plane and flew to Montreal.* b arrange a flight, voyage, trip, etc. by exclusive means of transportation: *a chartered flight.* [ME < OF *chartre* < L *chartula*, dim. of *charta.* See CHART.] —**char′ter·er,** *n.* —**char′ter·less,** *adj.*

chartered accountant a member of an accountants' institute that is chartered by the Crown. *Abbrev.*: C.A.

chartered bank in Canada, any of the privately owned banks chartered by Parliament and working under the provisions of the Bank Act with an extensive network of branches.

charter member one of the original members of a club, society, or company.

Chart·ism (chär′tiz əm) *n.* 1 in England, a reform movement organized by workingmen who drew up the People's Charter. The movement was active between 1838 and 1848. 2 the principles of this movement.

Chart·ist (chär′tist) *n.* an adherent of Chartism. —*adj.* of or having to do with Chartism.

char·treuse (shär trœz′; *also, for n. 2 and adj.*, shär trüz′) *n.* 1 a green, yellow, or white liqueur first made by Carthusian monks. 2 a light, yellowish-green. —*adj.* light yellowish-green. [< F *chartreuse* Carthusian]

char·wom·an (chär′wům′ən) *n.* **-wom·en.** a woman whose work is doing odd jobs by the day. She cleans and scrubs homes, offices, and public buildings. [< OE *cerr* turn, occasion + *woman*]

char·y (chãr′ē) *adj.* **char·i·er, char·i·est.** 1 careful: *A cat is chary of wetting its paws.* 2 shy: *A bashful person is chary of strangers.* 3 sparing; stingy: *A jealous person is chary of praising others.* [OE *cearig* < *caru* care] —**Syn.** 1 wary, cautious. 3 frugal.

Cha·ryb·dis (kə rib′dis) *n.* 1 a dangerous whirlpool off the northeastern coast of Sicily. See **Scylla.** 2 **between Scylla and Charybdis,** between two dangers, one of which must be met.

chase[1] (chās) *v.* **chased, chas·ing,** *n.* —*v.* 1 run after to catch or kill. 2 drive; drive away. 3 hunt. 4 follow; pursue: *The catcher chased the ball.* 5 *Informal.* rush; hurry: *He is always chasing about.*
—*n.* 1 a chasing: *We watched the chase.* 2 hunting as a sport. 3 a hunted animal: *The chase escaped the hunter.* 4 an open piece of privately owned ground or other place reserved for hunting animals. 5 **give chase,** run after; chase. [ME < OF *chacier* < LL *captiare.* Doublet of CATCH.]

chase[2] (chās) *v.* **chased, chas·ing.** engrave. [var. of *enchase*]

chase[3] (chās) *n.* 1 a groove; furrow; trench. 2 in printing, an iron frame to hold type that is ready to print or make plates from. [< F *châsse* < L *capsa* box. Doublet of CASE[2], CASH[1].]

chas·er[1] (chās′ər) *n.* 1 a person or thing that chases. 2 a hunter. 3 a small, speedy airplane or ship for pursuing the enemy. 4 a gun on the bow or stern of a ship, used when chasing, or being chased by, another ship. 5 *Informal.* a drink of water or something mild after a drink of strong liquor. [< *chase*[1]]

chas·er[2] (chās′ər) *n.* 1 an engraver. 2 a tool for engraving. [< *chase*[2]]

chasm (kaz′əm) *n.* 1 a deep opening or crack in the earth; gap. 2 a wide difference of feelings or interests between people or groups: *The chasm between England and the American colonies grew wider and wider until it finally resulted in the American Revolution.* 3 a break in continuity. [< L *chasma* < Gk.] —**Syn.** 1 fissure, gorge, cleft, breach, abyss.

chas·seur (sha sœr′) *n.* 1 a soldier of a group of cavalry or infantry equipped and trained to move rapidly. 2 a hunter. 3 an attendant or servant in uniform. [< F]

chas·sis (shas′ē or chas′ē) *n.* **chas·sis** (shas′ēz or chas′ēz) 1 the frame, wheels, and machinery of a motor vehicle that support the body. 2 the main landing gear that supports the body of an aircraft. 3 the frame on which a gun carriage moves backward and forward. 4 the base or frame for the parts of a radio, television set, etc. 5 *Slang.* the body. [< F < OF *châsse* frame or sash]

chaste (chāst) *adj.* 1 pure; virtuous. 2 decent; modest. 3 simple in taste or style; not excessively ornamented. [ME < OF < L *castus* pure. Doublet of CASTE.] —**chaste′ly,** *adv.* —**chaste′ness,** *n.* —**Syn.** 1 innocent. 3 classic.

chas·ten (chās′ən) *v.* 1 punish with the intention of improving. 2 restrain from excess; subdue: *The father found it necessary to chasten his boisterous son.* [obs. v. *chaste* < F < L *castigare* make pure < *castus* pure] —**chas′ten·er,** *n.* —**Syn.** 1 discipline.

chas·tise (chas tīz′) *v.* **-tised, -tis·ing.** punish; beat. [< obs. *chaste.* See CHASTEN.] —**chas·tis′er,** *n.* —**Syn.** See **punish.**

chas·tise·ment (chas′tiz mənt or chas tīz′mənt) *n.* a punishment; beating.

chas·ti·ty (chas′tə tē) *n.* 1 purity; virtue. 2 decency; modesty. 3 simplicity of style or taste; absence of excessive decoration.

chas·u·ble (chaz′yů bəl or chas′yů bəl) *n.* in certain churches, a sleeveless outer vestment worn over other vestments by a priest when celebrating Mass, or Eucharist. [ME *chesible* < OF < LL *casubula* < L *casa* cottage. Akin to CASSOCK.]

C, chasuble

chat (chat) *n. v.* **chat·ted, chat·ting.** —*n.* 1 easy, familiar talk. 2 any of several birds having a chattering cry. —*v.* talk in an easy, familiar way. [short for *chatter*]

châ·teau (sha tō′ or shə tō′; *French,* shä tō′) *n.* **-teaux** (-tōz′; *French,* -tō′). 1 in France, a castle. 2 in French Canada, the residence of a governor or a seignior. 3 **Château.** formerly, the Château St. Louis in Quebec City, the residence of the Governor of Quebec. 4 a large country house. [< F *château* < L *castellum* castle. Doublet of CASTLE.]

chat·e·laine (shat′ə lān′) *n.* 1 the mistress or lady of a castle. 2 a clasp worn at a woman's waist. Keys, a purse, etc. are fastened to it by a chain. [< F *chatelaine,* fem. to *chatelain* keeper of a castle < L *castellanus.* See CASTELLAN.]

chat·tel (chat′əl) *n.* a movable possession; a piece of property that is not real estate. Furniture, automobiles, slaves, and animals are chattels. [ME < OF *chatel* < L *capitale,* neut. of *capitalis.* Doublet of CAPITAL[1] and CATTLE.]

chat·ter (chat′ər) *v.* 1 talk constantly, rapidly, and foolishly. 2 make sharp, rapid sounds: *Monkeys chatter.* 3 rattle together: *Fear or cold sometimes make a person's teeth chatter.*
—*n.* 1 rapid, foolish talk. 2 sharp, rapid sounds: *The chatter of sparrows annoyed her.* [imitative] —**chat′ter·er,** *n.*

chat·ter·box (chat′ər boks′) *n.* a person who is given to chattering.

chat·ty (chat′ē) *adj.* **-ti·er, -ti·est.** fond of friendly, familiar talk. —**chat′ti·ly,** *adv.* —**chat′ti·ness,** *n.*

Chau·ce·ri·an (cho sēr′ē ən or chô sēr′ē ən) *adj.* 1 of or having to do with Geoffrey Chaucer, 1340?-1400, an English poet and author of *The Canterbury Tales.* 2 of or suggestive of his writings. —*n.* a student of Chaucer, or a specialist in his writings.

chauf·feur (shō′fər or shō fėr′) *n.* a man whose work is driving an automobile, usually as the employee of a private person or company: *The president of our bank has a chauffeur.* —*v.* act as a chauffeur to; drive around. [< F *chauffeur* stoker < *chauffer* heat; from the days of steam automobiles]

chaunt (chont or chônt) *n. v. Archaic.* chant.

chau·tau·qua or **Chau·tau·qua** (shə to′kwə or shə tô′kwə) *n.* an assembly for education and entertainment of adults by lectures, concerts, etc. held for several days. [with reference to meetings of a religious and educational nature, the first of which were held at *Chautauqua*, New York]

chau·vin·ism (shō′vən iz′əm) *n.* unreasoning enthusiasm for the military glory of one's country; boastful, warlike patriotism. [< F *chauvinisme*; from Nicolas *Chauvin*, an over-enthusiastic French patriot and supporter of Napoleon I]

chau·vin·ist (shō′vən ist) *n.* an unreasoning patriot; a boastful, warlike person. *—adj.* chauvinistic.

chau·vin·is·tic (shō′vən is′tik) *adj.* of chauvinism or chauvinists. **—chau′vin·is′ti·cal·ly,** *adv.*

Ch.B. Bachelor of Surgery. (for L *Chirurgiae Baccalaureus*)

Ch.E. or **Che.E.** Chemical Engineer.

cheap (chēp) *adj.* **1** costing little. **2** costing less than it is worth. **3** charging low prices: *a cheap market.* **4** easily obtained. **5** of low value; common: *cheap entertainment.* **6** of little account; not esteemed. **7** of money, obtainable at a low rate of interest. **8** reduced in value or purchasing power, as money depreciated by inflation: *cheap silver.* **9** reduced in price for a special occasion or in prescribed circumstances: *cheap rates.* **10** stingy; mean. **11 feel cheap,** feel inferior and ashamed.
—adv. at a low price; at small cost. [short for *good cheap* a good bargain; OE *cēap* price, bargain < Gmc. (cf. OHG *kouf*) < L *caupō* small tradesman] **—cheap′ness,** *n.*
Syn. *adj.* **1 Cheap, inexpensive** = costing little. **Cheap** = low in price, but often is used to express an attitude toward the thing, suggesting low quality worth no more or even less than the price: *Eggs are cheap now. I won't wear cheap shoes.* **Inexpensive** = not expensive, worth the price or even more, and usually expresses a more impersonal attitude: *An inexpensive car gives good mileage.* **5** poor, mean, inferior, paltry, worthless.

cheap·en (chēp′ən) *v.* make or become cheap. **—cheap′en·er,** *n.*

cheap·ly (chēp′lē) *adv.* at a low price; at small cost.

Cheap·side (chēp′sīd′) *n.* in London, a famous street that was a busy market place in medieval times.

cheap·skate (chēp′skāt′) *n. Slang.* a stingy, miserly person.

cheat (chēt) *v.* deceive or trick; play or do business in a way that is not honest: *The peddler cheated the woman of ten cents in change.* *—n.* **1** a person who is not honest and does things to deceive and trick others. **2** a fraud; trick. [var. of *escheat*] **—cheat′a·ble,** *adj.* **—cheat′er,** *n.*
Syn. *v.* **Cheat, deceive, trick** = use underhand means for a purpose. **Cheat** = do something dishonest in an underhand way to get something one wants: *He cheated to pass the test.* **Deceive** means to lead others to believe what is not true in order to hide the truth or get what one wants: *He deceived the teacher by lying.* **Trick** emphasizes using a sly scheme or device to deceive and indirectly get what one wants: *The R.C.M.P. used fake plans to trick the spy.* *–n.* **1** swindler, impostor, deceiver. **2** swindle, deception, hoax.

check (chek) *v.* **1** stop suddenly: *They checked their steps.* **2** hold back; control; restrain: *check one's anger.* **3** rebuff; repulse; reverse: *check an enemy attack.* **4** in hockey, impede the progress of (the puck-carrier), using either the stick or the body: *check a person into the boards.* **5** correspond accurately when compared, usually with a duplicate or the original: *The two copies check.* **6** examine or compare to prove true or right: *Check your answers with mine.* **7** mark to show that something has been checked and found true or right. **8** get a check for; put a check on: *check one's hat.* **9** mark in a pattern of squares. **10** of wood, steel, paintwork, etc., crack or split. **11** cause to crack. **12** send (baggage) to a particular place: *I shall check my bag through to Halifax.* **13** in chess, have (an opponent's king) in a position of danger so that it must be moved or the danger avoided in some other way. **14 check in, a** arrive and register at a hotel, etc. **b** *Slang.* die. **15 check off,** mark as checked and found true or right. **16 check out, a** settle accounts at a hotel, store, etc. on leaving. **b** *Slang.* die. **17 check up,** examine or compare to prove true or correct. [ME *cheke* < OF *eschequier* < *eschec.* See CHECK, n.]
—n. **1** a sudden stop: *The message gave a check to our plans.* **2** a holding back; control; restraint. **3** any person, thing, or event that controls or holds back action. A rein used to prevent a horse from lowering his head is a check. **4** in hockey, **a** an impeding of the progress of the puck-carrier, by means of either the body or the stick. **b** a forward who is covered by an opposing forward: *The coach told him to keep better watch on his check.* **5** a rebuff; repulse; reverse. **6** an examination or comparison to prove something true or right: *My work will be a check on yours.* **7** a mark to show that something has been checked and found true or right. **8** a ticket or metal piece given in return for a coat, hat, baggage, package, etc. to show ownership. **9** a bill for a meal, etc. **10** a cheque. **11** a pattern of squares: *Do you want a check or a stripe for your new dress?* **12** one of these squares: *The checks are small in this pattern.* **13** a crack; split. **14** in chess: **a** a call warning that an opponent's king is in danger. **b** the position of an opponent's king when it is in danger and must be moved or the threatening piece blocked off or removed. **15 in check,** held back; controlled.
—adj. **1** used in checking. **2** marked in a pattern of squares.
—interj. in chess, a call warning that an opponent's king is in danger and must be moved. [ME < OF *eschec* a check at chess, ult. < Persian *shah* king, king at chess] **—check′a·ble,** *adj.* **—check′er,** *n.*
Syn. *v.* **1** halt, block. See **stop. 2 Check, restrain, curb** = hold someone or something back. **Check** suggests use of some means that slows up or stands in the way of action or progress: *The awning checked his fall.* **Restrain** suggests use of some force to keep down or within limits or to prevent completely: *A bystander restrained him from jumping off the bridge.* **Curb** suggests use of a control that pulls back suddenly or keeps from acting freely: *His good sense curbed his impulse to hit the man.* *–n.* **1** stoppage. **3** restriction, curb, bridle, obstruction, obstacle, hindrance. **7** tag, token, coupon.

check·book (chek′bu̇k′) *n.* cheque book.

checked (chekt) *adj.* marked in a pattern of squares.

check·er (chek′ər) *v.* **1** mark in a pattern of squares of different colors. **2** mark off with patches different from one another: *The ground under the trees was checkered with sunlight and shade.* **3** have ups and downs; change. [< n.]
—n. **1** a pattern of squares of different colors. **2** one of these squares. **3** in checkers, one of the flat, round pieces. **4** the checker tree. **5** *Obsolete.* a checkerboard. Also, **chequer.** [ME < AF *escheker* < Med.L *scaccarium* chessboard]

check·er·ber·ry (chek′ər ber′ē) *n.* **-ries. 1** the bright-red berry of the North American wintergreen plant. **2** the plant. **3** partridgeberry.

check·er·board (chek′ər bôrd′) *n.* a board marked in a pattern of 64 squares of two alternating colors and used in playing checkers or chess. Also, **chequerboard.**

check·ered (chek′ərd) *adj.* **1** marked in a pattern of squares of different colors. **2** marked in patches. **3** often changing; varied; irregular: *a checkered career.* Also, **chequered.**

check·ers (chek′ərz) *n.* a game played on a checkerboard by two people, each having 12 round, flat pieces to move. Also, **chequers,** *Brit.* **draughts.**

check·mate (chek′māt′) *v.* **-mat·ed, -mat·ing,** *n. interj.*
—v. **1** in chess, put (an opponent's king) in check and so win the game. **2** defeat completely. **3** counteract a scheme or action of (an opponent), making it useless or ineffective: *The spy checkmated his pursuers at every turn.*
—n. **1** in chess, a move that ends the game by putting the opponent's king in check. **2** a complete defeat.
—interj. in chess, a declaration that the opposing king is in check. [ME < OF *eschec et mat* < Persian *shāh māt* king is dead]

check·off (chek′of′) *n.* **1** a system of collecting union dues through wage deductions made by the employer on the union's behalf. **2** the amount deducted under such a system.

check-out (chek′out′) *n.* **1** in a supermarket or other self-service store: **a** the process of checking and charging for a customer's purchases. **b** the counter where this is done: *The new store will have ten check-outs.* **2** in a hotel: **a** the process of vacating and paying for a room. **b** the time by which this must be done: *Check-out is at 4:00* *p.m. and persons leaving later will be charged for an extra day.* **3** the sequence of checks by which a machine or device is tested for proper functioning or performance.

check·rein (chek′rān′) *n.* **1** a short rein to keep a horse from lowering its head. **2** a short rein connecting the bit of one of a team of horses to the driving rein of the other.

check·room (chek′rüm′ or -rům′) *n.* a place where coats, hats, baggage, packages, etc. can be left until required again.

check·up (chek′up′) *n.* **1** a careful examination. **2** a thorough physical examination.

ched·dar (ched′ər) *v.* pile and turn (strips of curd) so as to remove any whey left after draining, as in making cheddar cheese. [< *Cheddar*]

Ched·dar (ched′ər) *n.* a kind of hard, white or yellow cheese. [< *Cheddar,* in Somerset, England]

chee·cha·ko (chē cho′kō) *n.* a newcomer; tenderfoot; greenhorn: *It took the cheechako many months to learn the ways of the Yukon.* [< Chinook jargon < Chinook *t'shi* new + *chakho* come]

cheek (chēk) *n.* **1** the side of the face below either eye. **2** something suggesting the human cheek in form or position. **3** *Informal.* saucy talk or behavior; impudence: *The boy's cheek annoyed the neighbors.* **4 cheek by jowl, a** side by side; close together. **b** close; intimate; familiar. **5 tongue in cheek,** insincere; saying one thing and meaning another. [OE *cēce*]

cheek·bone (chēk′bōn′) *n.* a bone just below either eye.

-cheeked *combining form.* having a —— cheek or cheeks: *red-cheeked = having red cheeks.*

cheek pouch a pouch in the cheek. Squirrels have cheek pouches.

cheek strap one of the two side straps of a bridle. They connect the band around the head with the bit.

cheek·y (chēk′ē) *adj.* **cheek·i·er, cheek·i·est.** *Informal.* saucy; impudent. —**cheek′i·ly,** *adv.* —**cheek′i·ness,** *n.*

cheep (chēp) *v.* make a short, sharp sound like a young bird; chirp; peep. —*n.* a short, sharp sound like that of a young bird; chirp; peep. [imitative] —**cheep′er,** *n.*

cheer (chēr) *n.* **1** joy; gladness; comfort; encouragement: *The warmth of the fire and a good meal brought cheer to our hearts again.* **2** a shout of encouragement, approval, praise, etc. **3** food: *We enjoyed our Christmas cheer.* **4** a state of mind; condition of feeling: *Christmas is a season of good cheer.* **5 What cheer?** How are you?
—*v.* **1** fill with cheer; give joy to; gladden; comfort; encourage: *Our visit cheered the old lady.* **2** shout encouragement, approval, praise, etc. **3** urge on with cheers: *Everyone cheered our team.* **4** greet or welcome with cheers. **5 cheer up,** make or become happier; be glad.
—*interj.* **cheers,** a word used in drinking a person's health. [ME *chere* < OF < LL *cara* face < Gk. *kara* head, face] —**cheer′er,** *n.*
Syn. *n.* **2** acclamation, shouting, applause. –*v.* **1 Cheer, gladden** = raise a person's spirits. **Cheer** suggests either making a person feel less downhearted by giving comfort and encouragement (often *cheer up*) or putting him in high spirits by giving pleasure or joy: *The news cheered everyone.* **Gladden** suggests putting a person in good spirits by giving delight and making him feel happy: *The sight of the countryside gladdened the crippled children.* **2** applaud, acclaim.

cheer·ful (chēr′fəl) *adj.* **1** full of cheer; joyful; glad: *a smiling, cheerful person.* **2** filling with cheer; pleasant; bright: *a cheerful, sunny room.* **3** willing: *a cheerful giver.* —**cheer′ful·ly,** *adv.* —**cheer′ful·ness,** *n.* —**Syn. 1** gay, cheery, joyous.

cheer·i·o (chēr′ē ō′) *interj. n.* **-i·os.** *Informal.* **1** good-bye! **2** hello! **3** hurrah!

cheer leader a person who leads the organized cheering of a crowd, usually at high-school or college athletic events: *The cheer leaders spent weeks practising the school yells.* See the picture under **megaphone.**

cheer·less (chēr′lis) *adj.* without joy or comfort; gloomy; dreary. —**cheer′less·ness,** *n.* —**Syn.** dismal.

cheer·y (chēr′ē) *adj.* **cheer·i·er, cheer·i·est.** cheerful; pleasant; bright; gay. —**cheer′i·ly,** *adv.* —**cheer′i·ness,** *n.*

cheese (chēz) *n.* **1** a solid food made from the curds of milk. **2** a mass of this substance pressed into a shape. [OE *cēse* < L *caseus*] —**cheese′like′,** *adj.*

cheese·burg·er (chēz′bėrg′ər) *n.* a hamburger with a slice of cheese melted on top of the meat.

cheese cake or **cheese·cake** (chēz′kāk′) *n.* **1** a dessert made of cheese, eggs, sugar, etc. baked together. **2** *Slang.* photographs or photography of girls, emphasizing their physical charms.

cheese·cloth (chēz′kloth′) *n.* a thin, loosely woven cotton cloth, originally used for wrapping cheese.

cheese·mon·ger (chēz′mung′gər or -mong′gər) *n.* a person who sells cheese.

chees·y (chēz′ē) *adj.* **chees·i·er, chees·i·est. 1** of or like cheese. **2** *Slang.* not well made; inferior.

chee·tah (chē′tə) *n.* a flesh-eating mammal resembling a leopard, found in S. Asia and Africa. Cheetahs can be trained to hunt deer and antelope. Also, **chetah.** [< Hind. *chita*]

chef (shef) *n.* **1** a head cook. **2** a cook [< F *chef (de cuisine)* < L *caput* head. Doublet of CHIEF.]

chef-d'oeu·vre (she dœ′vrə) *n.* **chefs-d'oeuvre** (she dœ′vrə). a masterpiece. [< F]

Che·khov·i·an (che kō′vē ən) *adj.* **1** of or having to do with Anton Chekhov (1860-1904), a Russian dramatist and writer of short stories. **2** of or suggestive of his writings.

che·la (kē′lə) *n.* **-lae** (-lē or -lī). a claw of a lobster, crab, scorpion, etc. It is like pincers. [< L < Gk. *chēlē* claw]

A chela of a lobster

che·lo·ni·an (ki lō′nē ən) *adj.* of turtles and tortoises. —*n.* a turtle; tortoise. [< NL *Chelonia* < Gk. *chelōnē* tortoise]

chem. **1** chemistry. **2** chemical. **3** chemist.

chem·ic (kem′ik) *adj.* *Archaic.* **1** chemical. **2** of alchemy.

chem·i·cal (kem′ə kəl) *adj.* **1** of chemistry. **2** made by or used in chemistry. **3** working or achieved by the use of chemicals: *a chemical rocket.* —*n.* a substance obtained by or used in a chemical process. Sulphuric acid, bicarbonate of soda, and borax are chemicals.

chemical engineering the science or profession of using chemistry for industrial purposes.

chem·i·cal·ly (kem′ik lē) *adv.* **1** according to chemistry. **2** by chemical processes.

chemical warfare the technique or use of gases, flames, smoke, or any chemicals other than explosives as weapons.

che·mise (shə mēz′) *n.* **1** a loose, shirtlike undergarment worn by women and girls. **2** a loose, straight-cut dress. [< F < LL *camisia* shirt < Celtic]

chem·ist (kem′ist) *n.* **1** an expert in chemistry. **2** *Esp.Brit.* a druggist. [var. of *alchemist*]

chem·is·try (kem′is trē) *n.* **-tries. 1** the science that deals with the characteristics of elements or simple substances, the changes that take place when they combine to form other substances, and the laws of their combination and behavior under various conditions. **2** the application of this science to a certain subject. **3** a textbook or handbook dealing with chemistry.

chem·o·sphere (kem′ə sfēr′) *n.* in meteorology, a region of the atmosphere from 26 to 70 miles above the earth, where the sun's radiation produces predominant photochemical activity.

chem·ur·gist (kem′ėr jist) *n.* an expert in chemurgy.

chem·ur·gy (kem′ėr jē) *n.* the branch of chemistry that deals with the use of farm products, such as casein and cornstalks, for purposes other than food and clothing. [< *chemistry* + *-urgy* < Gk. *ergon* work + *ia*]

che·nille (shə nēl′) *n.* **1** a soft, velvety cord of cotton, silk, etc. used in embroidery, fringes, etc. **2** a fabric, usually cotton, woven with threads from this cord. **3** a cotton fabric having ornamental designs or an overall pattern of tufts of this cord, used in drapes, housecoats, etc. [< F *chenille* caterpillar < L *canicula* little dog; from its furry look]

cheque or **check** (chek) *n.* a written order directing a bank to pay money to the person or company named on it: *Father pays most of his bills by cheque.*

cheque book or **check·book** (chek′bůk′) *n.* a book of blank cheques.

cheq·uer (chek′ər) *v. n.* checker.

cheq·uer·board (chek′ər bôrd′) *n.* checkerboard.

cheq·uered (chek′ərd) *adj.* checkered.

cheq·uers (chek′ərz) *n.* checkers.

Cheq·uers (chek′ərz) *n.* the official country residence of the British prime minister, in Buckinghamshire, northwest of London.

chequing or **checking account** a bank account against which cheques may be drawn.

cher·ish (cher′ish) *v.* **1** hold dear; treat with affection; care for tenderly: *A mother cherishes her baby.* **2** keep in mind; cling to: *For many years the old woman cherished the hope that her wandering son would come home.* [ME < OF *cheriss-*, a stem of *cherir* < *cher* dear < L *carus*]
Syn. 2 Cherish, foster, harbor, used figuratively, mean "keep and care for in the mind." **Cherish,** literally, means "hold dear," emphasizes treasuring an idea or feeling and watching over it with loving care: *He cherishes friendship.* **Foster** suggests nourishing an idea or feeling, and helping it to grow: *He tries to foster tolerance.* **Harbor,** literally, means "give shelter to something hunted or bad," suggests letting in a bad idea or feeling and brooding over it: *He harbors a grudge.*

cher·no·zem (chėr′nə zem′) *n.* a fertile soil typical of wet grasslands, consisting of a rich, black layer with a high organic content, overlying a layer of accumulated lime. [< Russian *chernozem* < *chernyi* black + *zemlja* land, soil]

Cher·o·kee (cher′ə kē or cher′ə kē′) *n.* **-kee** or **-kees.** **1** a tribe of North American Indians, now living mostly in Oklahoma. **2** a member of this tribe. **3** their language. [alteration of native *Tsalagi* or *Tsaragi*]

che·root (shə rüt′) *n.* a cigar cut off square at both ends. [< F *chéroute* < Tamil *shuruttu* roll]

cher·ry (cher′ē) *n.* **-ries,** *adj.* —*n.* **1** a small, round, juicy fruit with a stone or pit in it. **2** the tree it grows on. **3** its wood. **4** a bright red.
—*adj.* **1** made of the wood of the cherry tree. **2** bright-red. [ME *chery*, back formation from *cherys* < ONF *cherise* < VL < LGk. *kerasia* cherry tree < Gk. *kerasos* cherry. Doublet of CERISE.]

cherry stone **1** the stone of a cherry. **2** a kind of clam that is small and round; quahog.

chert (chėrt) *n.* a dark, impure mineral resembling flint and containing quartz and hydrated silica.

cher·ub (cher′əb) *n.* **cher·u·bim** *for 1 and 2,* **cher·ubs** *for 3 and 4.* **1** one of the second highest order of angels. **2** a picture or statue of a child with wings, or of a child's head with wings but no body. **3** a beautiful, innocent, or good child. **4** a person with a chubby, innocent face. [< Hebrew *kerūb*]

che·ru·bic (chə rü′bik) *adj.* **1** of or like a cherub; angelic. **2** innocent; good. **3** chubby. —**che·ru′bi·cal·ly,** *adv.*

cher·u·bim (cher′ə bim′ or cher′yů bim′) *n.* **1** pl. of **cherub. 2** (*pl., formerly used as sing.*) a cherub.

cher·vil (chėr′vəl) *n.* a plant of the same family as the parsley. The leaves are used to flavor soups, salads, etc. [OE *cerfille* < L < Gk. *chairephyllon* < *chairein* rejoice + *phyllon* leaf]

cher·vo·nets (cher vô′nets) *n.* **-von·tsi** (-vôn′tsē). **1** a former monetary unit of the Soviet Union. **2** a gold coin worth one chervonets. [< Russian]

Chesh·ire (chesh′ər) *n.* a crumbly cheese, similar to Cheddar, either white or colored red. Some red Cheshire develops a blue veining as it ripens. [< *Cheshire*, a county in W. England]

Cheshire cat **1** anybody with a fixed grin. **2** the grinning cat in *Alice in Wonderland* by Lewis Carroll.

chess (ches) *n.* a game played on a chessboard by two people. Each has 16 pieces that have to be moved in various ways. [ME < OF *esches*, pl. of *eschec*. See CHECK.]

chess·board (ches′bôrd′) *n.* a board marked in a pattern of 64 squares of two alternating colors, used in playing chess.

chess·man (ches′man′ or -mən) *n.* **-men** (-men′ or -mən). one of the pieces used in playing chess.

hat, āge, cãre, fär; let, ēqual, tėrm; it, īce
hot, ōpen, ôrder; oil, out; cup, půt, rüle, ūse
əbove, takən, pencəl, lemən, circəs
ch, child; ng, long; sh, ship
th, thin; ᴛʜ, then; zh, measure

chest (chest) *n.* **1** in vertebrates, the part of the body enclosed by the ribs. **2** a large box with a lid, in which various things may be kept: *a linen chest, a tool chest.* **3** a piece of furniture with drawers. **4** a tight container for gas, steam, etc. **5** a place where money is kept; treasury. **6** the money itself; money for a special purpose. [OE *cest, cist* < L *cista* < Gk. *kistē* box]

-chested *combining form.* having a ——chest: *broadchested = having a broad chest.*

ches·ter·bed (ches′tər bed′) *n.* a chesterfield that can be opened out to form a bed.

ches·ter·field (ches′tər fēld′) *n.* **1** a long, upholstered seat or couch having a back and arms; sofa. **2** a single-breasted overcoat with the buttons hidden by a flap down the front. [after a 19th-century Earl of *Chesterfield*]

Chester White **1** a breed of large, white pig. **2** an animal of this breed.

chest·nut (ches′nut or -nət) *n.* **1** a large tree belonging to the same family as the beech, that bears sweet edible nuts with prickly outer shells. **2** the nut of this tree. **3** the wood of this tree. **4** a reddish brown. **5** a reddish-brown horse. **6** *Informal.* a stale joke or story.
—*adj.* reddish-brown. [< obs. *chesten* chestnut (< OF *chastaigne* < L *castanea* < Gk. *kastanea* or *kastaneia* < *kastanon*) + *nut*]

che·tah (chē′tə) *n.* cheetah.

chet·nik (chet′nik) *n.* **chet·ni·ci** (chet nē′tsē) or **-niks.** in Yugoslavia, one of a guerrilla force that was active against the Nazis during World War II. [< Serbian *chetnik* < *cheta* band]

che·val glass (shə val′) a tall mirror mounted in a frame so that it swings between its supports. [*cheval* < F *cheval* horse, support < L *caballus* horse]

chev·a·lier (shev′ə lēr′; *French,* she vä lyā′) *n.* **1** *Archaic.* a knight. **2** in France, a member of the lowest rank in the Legion of Honor. [< F *chevalier* < *cheval* horse < L *caballus*]

Chev·i·ot (chev′ē ət or chē′vē ət *for 1 and 2;* shev′ē ət *for 3*) *n.* **1** a breed of sheep that originated in the Cheviot Hills on the boundary between England and Scotland. **2** an animal of this breed. **3 cheviot, a** a rough woollen cloth. **b** a cotton cloth like it.

chev·ron (shev′rən) *n.* **1** a V-shaped bar, usually of cloth, worn on the sleeve or sleeves by a serviceman, policeman, etc. to show his rank: *A sergeant wears three chevrons.* **2** a V-shaped bar worn on the lower sleeve of a uniform to show years of service. **3** any V-shaped design. [ME < OF *chevron* rafter < *chevre* goat < L *caper*]

chev·y (chev′ē) *n.* **chev·ies,** *v.* **chev·ied, chev·y·ing.** *Brit.* —*n.* **1** a hunting cry. **2** a hunt; chase. —*v.* **1** hunt; chase. **2** scamper; race. **3** worry. [shortened form of *Chevy Chase*, from the ballad of that name]

chew (chü) *v.* **1** crush or grind with the teeth. **2** *Informal.* think over; consider. **3** grind, cut, or mark as if by chewing: *The tracks and wheels of the heavy vehicles chewed up the ground.* —*n.* **1** a chewing. **2** the thing chewed; something to chew. [OE *cēowan*]
—**chew′a·ble,** *adj.* —**chew′er,** *n.*

chewing gum gum for chewing. It is usually made of chicle that has been sweetened and flavored.

che·wink (chi wingk′) *n.* a bird of eastern and central North America, whose cry sounds rather like its name. The chewink is a kind of finch. [imitative]

chew·y (chü′ē) *adj.* requiring chewing; becoming sticky and pliable when chewed.

Chey·enne (shī en′) *n.* **-enne** or **-ennes. 1** an Algonquian tribe of North American Indians, now living in Montana and Oklahoma. **2** a member of this tribe. **3** their language. [< the Sioux name *Shahi'yena, Shai-ena* people of alien speech]

chg. *pl.* **chgs.** charge.

chgd. charged.

chi (kī) *n.* the 22nd letter of the Greek alphabet (Χ, χ), appearing as *ch*, but usually sounded as *k*, in English words of Greek origin.

Chi·an·ti (kē än′tē or kē an′tē) *n.* **1** a dry, red Italian wine. **2** any similar wine. [< the *Chianti* Mountains in Italy]

chi·a·o (tyä′ü) *n.* **1** a unit of money in China, worth 1/10 of a yuan. **2** a coin worth one chiao. [< Chinese]

chi·a·ro·scu·ro (kē ä′rə skūr′ō; *Italian,* kyä′rō skü′rō) *n.* **-ros. 1** the treatment of light and shade in a picture. **2** the effect of light and shade in a picture. **3** a style of painting, drawing, etc. that uses only light and shade. **4** a picture, especially a painting, in which chiaroscuro is used. **5** stylistic effects of variation, relief, contrast, etc. used in any of the arts. [< Ital. < *chiaro* clear (< L *clarus*) + *oscuro* dim (< L *obscurus*)]

chic (shēk or shik) *n.* style. *—adj.* stylish. [< F]

chi·cane (shi kān′) *n. v.* **-caned, -can·ing.** *—n.* chicanery. *—v.* **1** use chicanery. **2** get by chicanery. [< F *chicane* < *chicaner* quibble]

chi·can·er·y (shi kān′ər ē) *n.* **-er·ies.** low trickery; unfair practice; quibbling: *Only a dishonest lawyer would use chicanery to win a lawsuit.* —**Syn.** deception.

chick (chik) *n.* **1** a young chicken. **2** a young bird. **3** a child. **4** *Slang.* an attractive girl. [ME *chicke,* var. of *chicken*]

chick·a·dee (chik′ə dē′) *n.* a small bird having black, white, and gray feathers. [imitative of its cry]

chick·a·ree (chik′ə rē′) *n.* the red squirrel of North America. [imitative of its cry]

chick·en (chik′ən) *n.* **1** a young hen or rooster. **2** any hen or rooster. **3** the flesh of a chicken used for food. **4** a young bird of certain other kinds. **5** *Slang.* a young person, especially a girl.
—adj. **1** young; small: *a chicken lobster.* **2** *Slang.* afraid or scared; cowardly.
—v. **chicken out,** *Slang.* behave in a cowardly manner, especially, refuse a dare. [OE *cicen*]

chick·en·burg·er (chik′ən bėrg′ər) *n.* a hamburger made with slices of cooked chicken instead of ground beef.

chicken feed *Slang.* **1** small change such as pennies, nickels, dimes; any small amount of money. **2** a small undertaking or project.

chick·en-heart·ed (chik′ən här′tid) *adj.* cowardly; timid.

chick·en-liv·ered (chik′ən liv′ərd) *adj. Informal.* cowardly.

chicken pox a mild contagious disease, chiefly affecting children, accompanied by a rash on the skin.

chick·weed (chik′wēd′) *n.* a common weed having small white flowers whose leaves and seeds are eaten by birds.

chic·le (chik′əl) *n.* a tasteless, gumlike substance used in making chewing gum. It is the dried, milky juice of the sapodilla tree of tropical America. [< Am.Sp. < Mexican *jiktli*]

chic·o·ry (chik′ə rē) *n.* **-ries. 1** a plant having bright-blue flowers, whose leaves are used for salad. **2** its root, roasted and used either as a substitute for coffee or with coffee. [< F *chicorée* < L < Gk. *kichōrion*]

chid (chid) *v.* a pt. and a pp. of **chide.**

chid·den (chid′ən) *v.* a pp. of **chide.**

chide (chīd) *v.* **chid·ed** or **chid, chid·ed, chid,** or **chid·den, chid·ing.** reproach; blame; scold: *She chided the little girl for soiling her dress.* [OE *cīdan*]
—**chid′er,** *n.* —**chid′ing·ly,** *adv.* —**Syn.** rebuke, reprove, reprimand. See **scold.**

chief (chēf) *n.* **1** the person highest in rank or authority; head of a group; leader. **2** the head of a tribe or clan. **3** in heraldry, the upper third of an escutcheon. **4 in chief,** at the head; of the highest rank or authority.
—adj. **1** highest in rank or authority; at the head; leading. **2** most important; main: *the chief thing to do.* [ME < OF < L *caput* head. Doublet of CHEF.]
—**chief′less,** *adj.* —**Syn.** *adj.* **2** prime, essential, cardinal.

chief·dom (chēf′dəm) *n.* the position or authority of a chief, or the territory ruled by him.

chief justice a judge who acts as chairman of a group of judges in a court.

chief·ly (chēf′lē) *adv.* **1** mainly; mostly: *We visited Ottawa chiefly to see the Parliament Buildings.* **2** first of all; above all.

chief of staff in the armed services, an officer at the head of a group of senior officers.

chief petty officer in the navy, the highest non-commissioned rank.

chief·tain (chēf′tən) *n.* **1** the chief of a tribe or clan. **2** a leader; the head of a group. [ME *chevetaine* < OF < LL *capitaneus.* Doublet of CAPTAIN.]

chief·tain·cy (chēf′tən sē) *n.* the position or rank of a chieftain.

chief·tain·ship (chēf′tən ship′) *n.* chieftaincy.

chif·fon (shi fon′ or shif′on) *n.* **1** a thin cloth made of silk, rayon, etc. and used for dresses, blouses, etc. **2 chiffons,** *pl.* laces, ribbons, finery. [< F *chiffon* < *chiffe* rag]

chif·fo·nier (shif′ə nēr′) *n.* a high bureau or chest of drawers, often having a mirror. [< F *chiffonnier* < *chiffon.* See CHIFFON.]

chig·ger (chig′ər) *n.* **1** a mite whose larvae stick to the skin and cause severe itching. **2** a kind of flea; chigoe. [alteration of *chigoe*]

chi·gnon (shēn′yon; *French,* shē nyôɴ′) *n.* a knot or roll of hair worn at the back of the head by women. [< F *chignon* nape of the neck < VL *catenio* < L *catena* chain; referring to the vertebrae]

chig·oe (chig′ō) *n.* **1** a flea of the West Indies and South America. The female burrows under the skin of people and animals, where it causes severe itching and sores. **2** a kind of mite; chigger. [< W. Indian]

chi·hua·hua (chē wä′wä) *n.* **1** an ancient Mexican breed of the smallest known dog. **2** a dog of this breed. [< *Chihuahua,* a state and city in N. Mexico]

chil·blain (chil′blān′) *n.* Usually, **chilblains,** *pl.* an itching sore or redness on the hands or feet, caused by cold. [< *chill* + *blain*]

Chil·cot·in (chil′kō′tin) *n.* **1** a tribe of Athapascan Indians living in the valley of the Chilcotin River, British Columbia. **2** a member of this tribe. **3** the Athapascan language of the tribe.

child (chīld) *n.* **chil·dren. 1** a baby; infant. **2** a boy or girl. **3** a son or daughter. **4** a descendant. **5** a person like one's child in nearness, affection, interest, etc. **6** an immature person; childish person. **7** a result; product: *Invention is the child of necessity.* **8 with child,** pregnant. [OE *cild*]

child·bear·ing (chīld′bãr′ing) *n.* the act or process of giving birth to children. *—adj.* of or having to do with this act or process.

child·bed (chīld′bed′) *n.* the condition of a woman giving birth to a child.

child·birth (chīld′bėrth′) *n.* the act or process of giving birth to a child.

child·hood (chīld′hůd′) *n.* the condition or time of being a child.

child·ish (chīl′dish) *adj.* **1** of a child. **2** like a child. **3** not suitable for a grown person; weak; silly; foolish: *Crying for things you can't have is childish.*
—**child′ish·ly,** *adv.* —**Syn. 2** immature, infantile, babyish.
☛ **Childish, childlike** differ widely. **Childish** = resembling or having the characteristics of a child, emphasizes the physical helplessness, lack of control over feelings, and undeveloped mind of a child, and therefore expresses an unfavorable opinion of an adult described as childish: *Pouting when scolded is childish.* **Childlike** = characteristic of and suitable to a child, emphasizes the innocence, simplicity, and frankness of children and suggests a favorable opinion: *She has a childlike love for her parents.*

child·ish·ness (chīl′dish nis) *n.* **1** the fact or condition of being like a child. **2** weakness, silliness.

child labor or **labour** work done by children in factories, business, etc.

child·less (chīld′lis) *adj.* having no child. **—child′less·ness,** *n.*

child·like (chīld′līk′) *adj.* **1** like a child; innocent; frank; simple: *The charming old lady had a childlike honest manner.* **2** suitable for a child. **—child′like′ness,** *n.*
☛ See **childish** for usage note.

chil·dren (chil′drən) *n.* pl. of **child.**

children of Israel Israelites; Hebrews; Jews.

Children's Crusade an unsuccessful expedition to recover the Holy Sepulchre, undertaken by thousands of French and German children in 1212.

child's play something very easy to do.

chil·e (chil′ē) *n.* chili.

Chil·e·an (chil′ē ən) *adj.* of or having to do with Chile or its people. *—n.* a native or inhabitant of Chile.

chil·e con car·ne or **chil·i con car·ne** (chil′ē kon kär′nē) meat cooked with red peppers and, usually, beans. [< Sp. *chile con carne* chili with meat]

Chile saltpetre sodium nitrate.

chil·i (chil′ē) *n.* **chil·ies. 1** a hot-tasting pod of red pepper, used for seasoning. **2** the tropical shrub that it grows on. **3** chile con carne. Also, **chilli.** [< Sp. *chile* < Mexican *chilli*]

chili sauce a sauce made of red peppers, tomatoes, and spices. Also, **chilli sauce.**

Chil·kat (chil′kat) *n.* **1** a Tlingit Indian people formerly living mainly in S.E. Alaska, noted for their making of brightly-colored blankets of mountain-goat wool and cedar bark. **2** a member of this people.

chill (chil) *n.* **1** unpleasant coldness. **2** a sudden coldness of the body accompanied by shivering. **3** the state or condition of feeling cold; shivering. **4** unfriendliness; lack of heartiness. **5** a depressing influence; discouraging feeling. **6** a metal mould, or a piece of iron in a sand mould, for making chilled castings.
—adj. **1** unpleasantly cold. **2** cold in manner; unfriendly. **3** depressing; discouraging.
—v. **1** make cold. **2** become cold; feel cold. **3** of metals (especially cast iron), harden or become hard on the surface by sudden cooling. **4** depress; dispirit. [OE *ciele*] **—chill′ness,** *n.*

chilled (child) *adj.* made cold.

chill·er (chil′ər) *n.* **1** a person or thing that chills. **2** *Informal.* a horror story or film.

chil·li (chil′ē) *n.* **chil·lies.** chili.

chill·i·ness (chil′ē nis) *n.* a chilly quality.

chill·ing (chil′ing) *n.* a making rather cold. *—adj.* that chills. **—chill′ing·ly,** *adv.*

chilli sauce chili sauce.

chill·y (chil′ē) *adj.* **chill·i·er, chill·i·est. 1** unpleasantly cool; rather cold: *a chilly day.* **2** cold in manner; unfriendly: *a chilly greeting.* **—Syn. 1** chill, raw. See **cold.**

Chil·tern Hundreds (chil′tərn) *Brit.* an office under the Crown that members of the House of Commons are said to apply for when they wish to resign.

chime (chīm) *n. v.* **chimed, chim·ing.** *—n.* **1** a set of tuned bells to make musical sounds. **2** the musical sound made by a set of tuned bells. **3** agreement; harmony. **4** a carillon. **5** a set of metal tubes hung vertically from a frame, played by striking with a hammer held in the hand, used in orchestras. **6** an apparatus or arrangement for striking a bell or set of bells so as to produce a musical sound.
—v. **1** make musical sounds on (a set of tuned bells). **2** ring out musically: *The bells chimed at midnight.* **3** speak or sing in cadence or singsong. **4** produce a musical sound from a bell (or the like) by striking it or using means other than ringing. **5** agree; be in harmony. **6** say or utter in cadence or singsong. **7 chime in, a** be in harmony; agree: *His ideas chimed in with mine.* **b** *Informal.* break into or join in a conversation. [ME *chymbe,* ult. < L < Gk. *kymbalon.* See CYMBAL.] **—chim′er,** *n.*

chi·me·ra or **chi·mae·ra** (kə mēr′ə or kī mēr′ə) *n.* **-ras. 1** Often, **Chimera.** in Greek legend, a monster with a lion's head, a goat's body, and a serpent's tail, supposed to breathe out fire. **2** a horrible creature of the imagination. **3** an absurd or impossible idea; wild fancy: *The idea of changing lead to gold was a chimera.* [ME < OF < L < Gk. *chimaira* she-goat]

hat, āge, cãre, fär; let, ēqual, tėrm; it, īce
hot, ōpen, ôrder; oil, out; cup, pu̇t, rüle, ūse
əbove, takən, pencəl, lemən, circəs
ch, child; ng, long; sh, ship
th, thin; ŦH, then; zh, measure

chi·mer·ic (kə mer′ik or kī mer′ik) *adj.* chimerical.

chi·mer·i·cal (kə mer′ə kəl or kī mer′ə kəl) *adj.* **1** unreal; imaginary. **2** absurd; impossible: *chimerical schemes for getting rich.* **3** wildly fanciful; visionary. **—chi·mer′i·cal·ly,** *adv.*

chim·ney (chim′nē) *n.* **-neys. 1** an upright structure used to make a draft and carry away smoke. **2** the part of this structure that rises above a roof. **3** a glass tube put around the flame of a lamp. **4** a crack or opening in a rock, mountain, volcano, etc. [ME *chimenee* < OF *cheminee* < LL *caminata* < L *caminus* oven < Gk. *kaminos*] **—chim′ney·less,** *adj.*

chimney corner the corner or side of a fireplace; a place near the fire.

chimney piece mantelpiece.

chimney pot a pipe of earthenware or metal fitted on top of a chimney to increase the draft.

chimney swallow 1 the chimney swift of North America. **2** the European barn swallow.

chimney sweep a person whose work is cleaning out chimneys.

chimney swift a bird of North America that often builds its nest in unused chimneys.

chim·o (chē′mō or chī′mō) *interj. Cdn.* an Eskimo greeting. [< Eskimo]

chim·pan·zee (chim′pan zē′ or chim pan′zē) *n.* an African manlike ape, smaller than a gorilla. It is probably the most intelligent of the apes. [< a native West African (Bantu) name]

chin (chin) *n. v.* **chinned, chin·ning.** *—n.* **1** the front of the lower jaw below the mouth. **2** the whole lower surface of the face, below the mouth. **3** *Informal.* a chat; gossip. **4 keep one's chin up,** bear adversity without flinching or complaining.
—v. **1 chin oneself,** hang by the hands from an overhead bar and pull oneself up until one's chin is even with or above the bar. **2** *Informal.* chat; gossip. **3** *Informal.* place (a violin) under the chin, in order to play it. [OE *cinn*] **—chin′less,** *adj.*

chi·na (chī′nə) *n.* **1** a fine, white ware made of clay baked by a special process that was first used in China. Colored designs can be baked into china and made permanent by glazing. **2** dishes, vases, ornaments, etc. made of this clay. **3** earthen dishes of any kind. [short for earlier *china-ware* ware from China]

Chi·na·man (chī′nə mən) *n.* **-men** (-mən). *Derogatory.* **1** a native or inhabitant of China. **2** a person of Chinese descent. ☛ See **Chinese** for usage note.

Chi·na·town (chī′nə toun′) *n.* the section of a city where the Chinese live.

chi·na·ware (chī′nə wãr′) *n.* **1** dishes, vases, ornaments, etc. made of china. **2** earthen dishes of any kind.

chinch (chinch) *n. Esp.U.S.* **1** a bedbug. **2** a chinch bug. [< Sp. *chinche* < L *cimex, -micis* bedbug]

chinch bug *Esp.U.S.* a small, black-and-white bug that does much damage to wheat, corn, and other cereal plants in dry weather.

chin·chil·la (chin chil′ə) *n.* **1** a South American rodent that resembles a squirrel. **2** its very valuable soft, whitish-gray fur. **3** a coat or other garment made of this fur. **4** a thick woollen fabric woven in small, closely set tufts, used for overcoats. **5** a breed of cat, having a large body and long, soft, pure-white hair. It is a variety of Persian cat. **6** a cat of this breed. [< Sp. *chinchilla,* dim. of *chinche.* See CHINCH.]

chine (chīn) *n.* **1** the backbone; spine. **2** a piece of an animal's backbone with the meat on it, suitable for cooking. **3** a ridge; crest. [ME < OF *eschine* < Gmc.]

Chi·nee (chī′nē) *n. Derogatory slang.* a Chinese. [back formation < Chinese]

Chi·nese (chī nēz′) *n.* **-nese,** *adj.* —*n.* **1** a native or inhabitant of China. **2** a person of Chinese descent. **3** the language of China. —*adj.* of China, its people, or their language.
☛ Chinese is preferred by natives of China (and others) to *Chinaman, Chinamen,* because of the derogatory suggestions of those words.

Chinese calendar the ancient lunar calendar formerly used in China, having cycles of 60 years, 12 months in a year, 29 or 30 days in a month, with an extra month added after each half cycle. The Chinese adopted the Gregorian calendar in 1912, the first year of the Republic, and years are now counted from that date.

Chinese checkers a game played by two to six persons using small marbles on a board patterned as a six-pointed star. The object of the game is to be the first player to move all one's marbles into the corresponding positions on the opposite side of the board. Also, **Chinese chequers.**

Chinese Empire China before it became a republic in 1912, including Manchuria, Mongolia, Tibet, and Sinkiang.

Chinese lantern a lantern of thin, colored paper that can be folded up.

Chinese puzzle something that is very complicated and hard to solve. [from the wood and metal puzzles which the Chinese invented and produced first]

chink[1] (chingk) *n.* a narrow opening; crack; slit: *The chinks between the logs of the cabin let in the wind and snow.* —*v.* **1** fill up the chinks in: *The cracks in the walls of the cabin were chinked with mud.* **2** make chinks in. [? < ME *chine* fissure < OE *cinu*]

chink[2] (chingk) *n.* a short, sharp, ringing sound like coins or glasses hitting together. —*v.* **1** make a short, sharp, ringing sound. **2** cause to make such a sound: *He chinked the coins in his pocket.* [imitative]

Chink (chink) *n. Derogatory slang.* a Chinese.

Chi·nook (chə nük′ or shi nůk′) *n.* **-nook** or **-nooks.** **1** a group of North American Indian tribes living along the Columbia River in the northwestern United States. **2** a member of this group of tribes. **3** the language of these Indians.

chi·nook (shi nůk′) *n.* **1** a warm winter wind that blows from the Pacific Ocean across the Rocky Mountains. It primarily affects the foothills east of the Rockies from the Peace River to Colorado, but sometimes blows across Alberta and into Saskatchewan. **2** the most important and largest species of Pacific salmon; spring salmon. **3** a Siberian husky. —*v.* blow a chinook.

chinook arch a phenomenon that often accompanies a chinook wind, appearing as an archlike strip of blue sky between the peaks of the Rockies and the cloud cover above.

Chinook jargon or **Jargon** a language used in trading on the Pacific coast, based on Chinook and Nootka, with additional French and English elements.

chintz (chints) *n.* a cotton cloth printed in patterns of various colors and often glazed. [originally pl., < Hind. *chint* < Skt. *citra* variegated]

chip (chip) *n. v.* **chipped, chip·ping.** —*n.* **1** a small, thin piece cut or broken off. **2** a place where a small, thin piece has been cut or broken off. **3** a small, thin piece of food or candy. Potato chips are thin fried slices of potatoes. **4** in games, a round, flat piece used for counting. **5** a strip of wood, palm leaf, or straw used in making baskets or hats. **6** a piece of dried dung, used for fuel in some regions: *buffalo chips.* **7** in golf, a chip shot.
cash in one's chips, a change (poker chips) into cash. **b** *Slang.* close or sell a business; retire. **c** *Slang.* die.
chip off the old block, a child that is like its father.
chip on one's shoulder, *Informal.* **a** a readiness to quarrel or fight. **b** a permanent sense of grievance.
in the chips, *Slang.* wealthy; affluent.
when the chips are down, when the moment of decision or definite action arrives: in a crisis. [< v.]
—*v.* **1** cut or break off in small, thin pieces: *chip off old paint. This china chips easily.* **2** shape by cutting at the surface or edge with an axe or chisel. **3 chip in,** *Informal.* **a** join with others in giving (money or help). **b** put in (a remark) when others are talking. [OE (*for*)*cippian*]

Chip·e·wy·an (chip′ə wī′ən) *n.* **-an** or **ans. 1** a small tribe of Athapascan Indians, scattered throughout the northern parts of Manitoba and Saskatchewan, and the Northwest Territories. **2** a member of this tribe. **3** the Athapascan language of this tribe.

chip·munk (chip′mungk) *n.* a small, striped North American squirrel. [< obs. Cdn. dial. *chitmunk* < Algonquian; cf. Ojibwa *atchitamon* one who descends trees head first]

chipped (chipt) *adj.* of meat, smoked and cut in very thin slices: *chipped beef.*

A Chippendale chair

Chip·pen·dale (chip′ən dāl′) *adj.* of, like, or having to do with a graceful, often richly ornamented style of furniture. —*n.* **1** this style of furniture. **Chinese Chippendale** reflects an Oriental influence. **2** a piece of furniture in this style. [after Thomas *Chippendale* (1718-1779), an English cabinetmaker]

chip·per (chip′ər) *adj. Informal.* lively; cheerful. [origin uncertain; cf. Northern E. dial. *kipper* frisky]

Chip·pe·wa (chip′ə wä′ or chip′ə wā′) *n.* **-wa** or **-was.** Ojibwa.

chipping sparrow a small sparrow of eastern and central North America. [< *chip,* imitative of its cry]

chip·py (chip′ē) *n.* **-pies. 1** the chipping sparrow. **2** the chipmunk. **3** *Slang.* **a** a frivolous young girl. **b** a woman of loose morals. —*adj. Cdn. Slang.* **1** short-tempered; quarrelsome; aggressive: *He was known as a chippy player.* **2** having much rough and short-tempered play: *a chippy hockey game.*

chi·rog·ra·pher (kī rog′rə fər) *n.* a person who writes by hand.

chi·ro·graph·ic (kī′rə graf′ik) *adj.* of chirography.

chi·rog·ra·phy (kī rog′rə fē) *n.* handwriting. [< Gk. *cheir* hand + E *-graphy* writing < Gk. *graphein* write]

chi·rop·o·dist (kə rop′ə dist or kī rop′ə dist) *n.* a person who removes corns and treats other troubles of the feet.

chi·rop·o·dy (kə rop′ə dē or kī rop′ə dē) *n.* the work of a chiropodist. [< Gk. *cheir* hand + *pous, podos* foot; originally, treatment of hands and feet]

chi·ro·prac·tic (kī′rə prak′tik) *n.* **1** the treatment of diseases by manipulating the spine. **2** a chiropractor. —*adj.* having to do with the treatment of diseases by manipulating the spine. [< Gk. *cheir* hand + *praktikos* referring to practice (< *prassein* do)]

chi·ro·prac·tor (kī′rə prak′tər) *n.* a person who treats diseases by manipulating the spine.

Chi·rop·te·ra (kī rop′tə rə) *n.pl.* in zoology, an order of mammals (the bats) having the forelimbs modified as wings. [< NL < Gk. *cheir* hand + *pteron* wing]

chirp (chėrp) *v.* **1** make a short, sharp sound such as certain small birds and insects make: *The sparrows and crickets chirped outside the house.* **2** utter with a chirp. **3** greet or urge on by chirping: *He chirped his horses on.* **4** make any similar sound.
—*n.* a short, sharp sound such as certain small birds and insects make. [? var. of *chirk* be cheerful, OE *circian* roar] —**chirp′er,** *n.*

chirp·y (chėr′pē) *adj.* **-i·er, -i·est.** *Informal.* **1** disposed to chirp. **2** lively and cheerful; enthusiastic. **chirp′i·ly,** *adv.* —**chirp′i·ness,** *n.*

chirr (chėr) *v.* make a shrill, trilling sound: *The grasshoppers chirred in the fields.* —*n.* a shrill, trilling sound. Also, **churr.** [imitative]

chir·rup (chėr′əp or chir′əp) *v.* **-rupped** or **-ruped, -rup·ping** or **-rup·ing,** *n.* —*v.* chirp again and again: *He chirrupped to his horse to make it go faster.* —*n.* the sound of chirruping. [< *chirp*]

chi·rur·geon (kī rėr′jən) *n. Archaic.* surgeon. [ME < OF *cirurgien* < *cirurgie* surgery. See SURGERY.]

chi·rur·ger·y (kī rėr′jər ē) *n. Archaic.* surgery.

chis·el (chiz′əl) *n. v.* **-elled** or **-eled, -el·ling** or **-el·ing.** —*n.* a cutting tool with a sharp edge at the end of a strong blade, used to cut or shape wood, stone, or metal.

—*v.* **1** cut or shape with a chisel. **2** *Slang.* use unfair practices; cheat; swindle. [ME < OF < VL *cisellum,* var. of *caesellum* < L *caedere* cut]

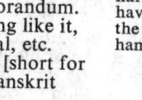

A chisel in use. It is made to cut very hard materials by having the end of the handle hit with a hammer or mallet.

chis·el·ler or **chis·el·er** (chiz′əl ər) *n.* **1** a person or thing that chisels. **2** *Slang.* a cheat.

chi-square test or **chi-square** (kī′skwãr′) *n.* in statistics, a test of the validity of a specific frequency distribution, made by matching the results obtained from the actual data with the results expected in theory.

chit[1] (chit) *n.* **1** a child. **2** a saucy, forward girl. [related to KITTEN. Cf. dial. *chit* kitten.]

chit[2] (chit) **1** a note; memorandum. **2** a signed note or something like it, given for a purchase, a meal, etc. that is to be paid for later. [short for *chitty* < Hind. *chitthi* < Sanskrit *chitra* a spot, mark]

chit-chat (chit′chat′) *n.* **1** friendly, informal talk; chat. **2** gossip. [< *chat*]

chi·tin (kī′tin) *n.* a horny substance forming the hard outer covering of beetles, lobsters, crabs, etc. [< F *chitine* < Gk. *chiton* tunic]

chi·tin·ous (kī′tə nəs) *adj.* of or like chitin.

chi·ton (kī′tən or kī′ton) *n.* in ancient Greece, a long, loose garment worn next to the skin by both men and women. [< Gk.]

chit·ter·lings (chit′ər lingz) *n.pl.* the small intestines of pigs, cooked as food. [ME; origin uncertain]

chiv·al·ric (shiv′əl rik or shə val′rik) *adj.* **1** having to do with chivalry. **2** chivalrous.

chiv·al·rous (shiv′əl rəs) *adj.* **1** having the qualities of an ideal knight; gallant, courteous, considerate, helpful, and honorable. **2** devoted to the service of the female sex. **3** having to do with chivalry. **—chiv′al·rous·ly,** *adv.* **—chiv′al·rous·ness,** *n.*

chiv·al·ry (shiv′əl rē) *n.* **1** the qualities of an ideal knight. Chivalry includes bravery, honor, courtesy, respect for women, protection of the weak, generosity, and fairness to enemies. **2** in the Middle Ages, the rules and customs of knights; system of knighthood. **3** knights as a group. **4** gallant warriors or gentlemen. [ME *chivalrie* < OF *chevalerie* horsemanship, knighthood < Med.L *caballerius* horseman < L *caballus* horse]

chive (chīv) *n.* Usually, **chives,** *pl.* a plant of the same family as the onion, having a very small bulb. Its long, slender leaves are used as seasoning. [ME < OF < L *caepa* onion]

Ch.J. Chief Justice.

chla·mys (klā′mis or klam′is) *n.* in ancient Greece, a short cloak worn by men. [< L < Gk.]

chlo·ral (klô′rəl) *n.* **1** a colorless liquid, made from chlorine and alcohol. *Formula*: CCl_3CHO **2** chloral hydrate. [< *chlor*ine + *al*cohol]

chloral hydrate a white, crystalline drug used to quiet nervousness and induce sleep. *Formula*: $CCl_3CH(OH)_2$

chlo·rate (klô′rāt or klô′rit) *n.* a salt of chloric acid.

chlo·ric (klô′rik) *adj.* of or containing chlorine. **Chloric acid,** $HClO_3$, occurs as a colorless solution or in the form of chlorates.

chlo·rid (klô′rid) *n.* chloride.

chlo·ride (klô′rīd or klô′rid) *n.* **1** a compound of chlorine with another element or radical. **2** salt of hydrochloric acid. **3** chloride of lime.

chloride of lime a white powder used for bleaching and disinfecting, made by treating slaked lime with chlorine. *Formula*: $CaOCl_2$

chlo·rin (klô′rin) *n.* chlorine.

chlo·rin·ate (klô′rə nāt′) *v.* **-at·ed, -at·ing. 1** combine or treat with chlorine. **2** disinfect with chlorine.

chlo·rin·a·tion (klô′rə nā′shən) *n.* a chlorinating or being chlorinated.

chlo·rine (klô′rēn or klô rēn′) *n.* a poisonous, greenish-yellow, gaseous chemical element, used in bleaching and disinfecting. It is very irritating to the nose, throat, and lungs. *Symbol*: Cl; *at.no.* 17; *at.wt.* 35.453. [< Gk. *chlōros* green]

hat, āge, cãre, fär; let, ēqual, tėrm; it, īce
hot, ōpen, ôrder; oil, out; cup, pu̇t, rüle, ūse
əbove, takən, pencəl, lemən, circəs
ch, child; ng, long; sh, ship
th, thin; ᴛʜ, then; zh, measure

chlo·rite (klô′rīt) *n.* a salt of chlorous acid.

chlo·ro·form (klô′rə fôrm′) *n.* a colorless liquid with a sweetish smell, used as an anesthetic and to dissolve rubber, resin, wax, and many other substances. *Formula*: $CHCl_3$ —*v.* **1** make (a person or animal) unable to feel pain by giving chloroform. **2** kill with chloroform. [< *chloro-* (< *chlorine*) + *formyl*]

chlo·ro·my·ce·tin (klô′rə mī′sə tin) *n. Trademark.* an antibiotic drug, used in treating bacterial and viral diseases, including typhoid fever and certain types of pneumonia. [< *chloro-* green (< Gk. *chlōros*) + Gk. *mykēs, -ētos* fungus]

chlo·ro·phyl or **chlo·ro·phyll** (klô′rə fil′) *n.* **1** in botany, the green coloring matter of plants produced only in the presence of sunlight and where iron is available in the plant cell. It converts carbon dioxide and water into carbohydrates, such as starch and sugar. **2** a dark-green, waxy plant extract, containing chlorophyl, that is used as a dye and for its supposed deodorizing qualities. [< F *chlorophylle* < Gk. *chlōros* pale green + *phyllon* leaf]

chlo·ro·plast (klô′rə plast′) *n.* in botany, the part of a plant cell that contains chlorophyl. [< Gk. *chlōros* pale green + *plastos* formed]

chlo·ro·prene (klôr′ə prēn′) *n.* a colorless liquid used in making synthetic rubber. *Formula*: C_4H_5Cl [< Gk. *chlōros* green + iso*prene*]

chlo·ro·quine (klô′rə kwīn′) *n.* a medicine used against malaria.

chlo·ro·sis (klə rō′sis) *n.* **1** in botany, a blanching or yellowing of plants, usually resulting from a lack of iron and other minerals in the soil. **2** in medicine, a form of anemia affecting young girls and characterized by pallor, hysteria, etc. [< NL *chlorosis* < Gk. *chlōros* pale green + *-osis*]

chlo·rous (klô′rəs) *adj.* of or containing trivalent chlorine.

Ch.M. Master of Surgery. (for L *Chirurgiae Magister*)

chm. or **chmn.** chairman.

chock (chok) *n.* **1** a block; wedge. A chock can be put under a barrel or wheel to keep it from rolling. A boat on a ship's deck is put on chocks. **2** a block with two arms curving inward for a rope to pass through. —*v.* **1** provide or fasten with chocks. **2** put (a boat) on chocks. —*adv.* as close or as tight as can be; quite. [apparently < ONF *choque* log]

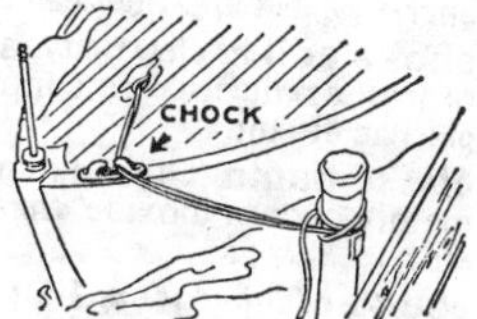

A chock (def. 2)

chock-a-block (chok′ə blok′) *adj.* **1** with the blocks drawn close together. **2** jammed together; crowded; packed.

chock-full (chok′fu̇l′) *adj.* as full as can be. Also, **chuck-full.**

choc·o·late (chok′lit or chok′ə lit) *n.* **1** a preparation made by roasting and grinding cacao seeds. **2** a drink made of chocolate with hot milk or water and sugar. **3** a type of candy made of chocolate. **4** a dark brown. —*adj.* **1** made of chocolate. **2** dark-brown. [< Sp. < Mexican *chocolatl*]

choice (chois) *n. adj.* **choic·er, choic·est.** —*n.* **1** the act of choosing: *She made a careful choice in buying dress goods.* **2** the power or opportunity to choose: *You have no other choice but to leave now.* **3** the person or thing chosen: *This hat is my choice.* **4** an alternative. **5** a

quantity and variety to choose from: *There is a wide choice of vegetables in the market.* **6** the best: *These flowers are the choice of my garden.*
—*adj.* **1** of fine quality; excellent; superior: *a choice steak.* **2** carefully chosen: *choice arguments.* [ME *chois* < OF *choisir* < Gmc.] —**choice′ly,** *adv.* —**choice′ness,** *n.*
Syn. *n.* **1** selection. **2 Choice, alternative, preference** = the opportunity to choose or the thing to be chosen. **Choice,** the general and most informal word, emphasizes freedom in choosing, both in the way one chooses and in the number of possibilities from which to choose: *Take your choice of the puppies.* **Alternative** emphasizes limitation of the possibilities, usually to two, but sometimes several, between which one must choose: *You have the alternative of sheltering from the rain or getting drenched.* **Preference** emphasizes choosing according to one's own liking: *Which is your preference?* –*adj.* **1** select, exquisite. See **fine.**

choir (kwīr) *n.* **1** the group of singers used in a church service. **2** the part of a church set apart for such a group. **3** any group of singers. **4** in music: **a** instruments of the same class in an orchestra: *the string choir, the brass choir.* **b** the musicians playing such a class of instruments. **5** any of the nine orders of angels.
—*v.* sing all together at the same time. [ME *quer* < OF *cuer* < L *chorus.* Doublet of CHORUS.]

choir boy (kwīr′boi′) a boy who sings in a choir.

choir·mas·ter (kwīr′mas′tər) *n.* the director or conductor of a choir.

choke (chōk) *v.* **choked, chok·ing,** *n.* —*v.* **1** keep from breathing by squeezing or blocking up the throat. **2** be unable to breathe. **3** check or extinguish by cutting off the supply of air: *to choke a fire.* **4** control; hold; suppress: *She choked back her tears.* **5** block; fill; clog: *Sand is choking the river.* **6** in an internal-combustion engine, reduce or close the air intake in order to make a richer fuel mixture, especially in starting. **7** kill or injure (a plant) by depriving it of air and light or of room to grow. **8 choke off,** put an end to; get rid of; stop. **9 choke up, a** block up; fill up; clog up. **b** of actors, athletes, etc., perform badly as a result of nervous tension.
—*n.* **1** the act or sound of choking. **2** in internal-combustion engines, a valve that cuts off the supply of air. **3** a narrow or constricted part of a tube, etc. as in a chokebore. [OE **cēocian,* var. of *ācēocian*] —**Syn.** *v.* **1, 2** suffocate, stifle, smother.

choke·bore (chōk′bôr′) *n.* **1** the bore of a shotgun that narrows toward the muzzle in order to keep the shot from scattering too widely. **2** a shotgun with such a bore.

choke·cher·ry (chōk′cher′ē) *n.* **-ries. 1** a bitter wild cherry of North America. **2** the tree that it grows on.

choke coil in electricity, a coil of wire around a core of iron or air, used to control alternating currents in an electric circuit.

choke·damp (chōk′damp′) *n.* a heavy, suffocating gas, mainly carbon dioxide, that gathers in mines, old wells, etc.

chok·er (chōk′ər) *n.* **1** a person or thing that chokes. **2** *Informal.* **a** a high collar. **b** a necklace that fits closely around the neck. **3** in lumbering, a cable and hook used in hauling and loading logs.

chol·er (kol′ər) *n.* **1** an irritable disposition; anger. **2** yellow bile, the one of the four humors of ancient physiology believed to cause irritability. **3** bilious disorder. [ME *colre* < OF < L < Gk. *cholera* cholera, apparently < *cholē* bile]

chol·er·a (kol′ər ə) *n.* **1** an acute, infectious, often fatal disease of the stomach and intestines, characterized by vomiting, cramps, and diarrhea; Asiatic cholera. **2** any of several diseases occurring chiefly in hot weather and causing acute diarrhea. [< L < Gk. See CHOLER.]

cholera mor·bus (môr′bəs) an old term applied to any inflammation of the intestines accompanied by diarrhea, fever, and pain. [< L *cholera morbus* cholera disease]

chol·er·ic (kol′ər ik) *adj.* easily made angry; irritable.

cho·les·ter·ol (kə les′tər ol′ or kə les′tər ōl′) *n.* a white crystalline substance, contained in all animal fats, bile, gallstones, egg yolk, etc. It is important in metabolism. *Formula*: $C_{27}H_{45}OH$ [< Gk. *cholē* bile + *stereos* solid]

chomp (chomp) *v.* champ[1].

chon (chon) *n.* **1** a unit of money in Korea, worth 1/100 of a won. **2** a coin worth one chon. [< Korean]

choose (chüz) *v.* **chose, cho·sen** or (*obsolete*) **chose, choos·ing. 1** pick out; select from a number: *He chose a book from the library.* **2** prefer and decide; think fit: *He did not choose to go.* **3** make a choice: *You must choose.* [OE *cēosan*] —**choos′er,** *n.*

choos·y (chüz′ē) *adj.* **choos·i·er, choos·i·est.** *Informal.* particular or fussy in one's preferences; fastidious; selective. —**choos′i·ness,** *n.*

chop[1] (chop) *v.* **chopped, chop·ping,** *n.* —*v.* **1** cut by hitting with something sharp: *chop wood with an axe.* **2** cut into small pieces: *chop up cabbage.* **3** make quick, sharp movements; jerk. **4** make by cutting: *The explorer chopped his way through the bushes.* **5** in tennis, cricket, etc., slice or cut at (a ball); hit with a chop stroke.
—*n.* **1** a cutting stroke or blow. **2** a slice of lamb, pork, veal, etc.: *There are rib, loin, and shoulder chops.* **3** a short, irregular, broken motion of waves. **4** an area of rough or choppy water. [ME *choppe(n)*] —**Syn.** *v.* **1** hew, hack. See **cut. 2** mince.

chop[2] (chop) *n.* **1** the jaw. **2** the cheek. Also, **chap. 3** the mouth. **4 lick one's chops,** *Slang.* relish the prospect of something good to come: *The children licked their chops over the coming holiday.* [< *chop*[1]]

chop[3] (chop) *v.* **chopped, chop·ping. 1** change suddenly; shift quickly: *The wind chopped around from west to north.* **2 chop and change,** change one's tactics or ways; make frequent changes; change about. [var. of obs. *chap* buy and sell, exchange. Related to CHEAP.]

chop·fall·en (chop′fol′ən or -fôl′ən) *adj.* chapfallen.

chop·house (chop′hous′) *n.* a restaurant that makes a specialty of serving chops, steaks, etc.

cho·pine (chō pēn′ or chop′in) *n.* formerly, a woman's shoe with a very thick sole. [< Sp. *chapín* < *chapa* piece of leather]

chop·per (chop′ər) *n.* **1** a person who chops. **2** a tool or machine for chopping: *A short axe or a heavy knife are kinds of choppers.* **3** *Slang.* a helicopter. **4 choppers,** *pl. Slang.* teeth.

chop·py[1] (chop′ē) *adj.* **-pi·er, -pi·est. 1** making quick, sharp movements; jerky. **2** moving in short, irregular, broken waves: *The lake is choppy today.* [< *chop*[1]] —**chop′pi·ness,** *n.*

chop·py[2] (chop′ē) *adj.* **-pi·er, -pi·est.** changing suddenly; shifting quickly. [< *chop*[3]]

chop·sticks (chop′stiks′) *n.pl.* the small sticks used in pairs by some Orientals, especially Chinese, to raise food to the mouth. [< Chinese Pidgin English *chop* quick + E *stick*[1]]

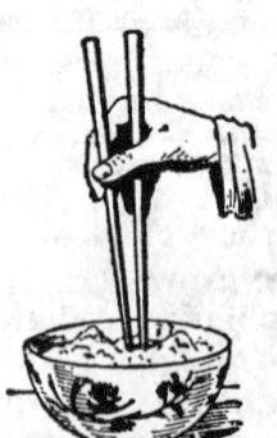

Chopsticks. They are held in one hand and used, much like pliers, to pick up food.

chop su·ey (chop′sü′ē) fried or stewed meat and vegetables cut up and cooked together in a sauce. It is often served with rice. [alteration of Chinese *tsa-sui* odds and ends]

cho·ral (*adj.* kô′rəl; *n.* kə ral′, kə räl′, or kô′rəl) *adj.* **1** of a choir or chorus. **2** sung by a choir or chorus. —*n.* chorale.

cho·rale (kə ral′, kə räl′, or kô′rəl) *n.* hymn tune, especially a simple one sung in unison. [< G *Choral*gesang]

chord[1] (kôrd) *n.* in music, a combination of three or more notes sounded together in harmony. [var. of *cord,* var. of *accord,* n.]

chord[2] (kôrd) *n.* **1** in geometry, a straight line connecting two points on a circumference. See diagram on the opposite page. **2** a structure in an animal's body that looks like a string; cord. **3** the string of a harp or other musical instrument. **4** a feeling; emotion: *touch a sympathetic chord.* **5** in engineering, a main horizontal part of a bridge truss. **6** in aeronautics: **a** a straight line drawn across an airfoil from the leading to the trailing edge. **b** the length of such a line. See diagram on the opposite page. [< L < Gk. *chordē* string made of gut; string of a lyre. Doublet of CORD.]

chord·al (kôr′dəl) *adj.* in music: **1** of or having to do with the strings of an instrument. **2** of or having to do with chords.

chor·date (kôr′dāt) *n.* any of the large group of animals whose members have an internal skeleton (a notochord in primitive forms) and a dorsally placed nervous system. The group includes man and all other vertebrates. *—adj.* of or having to do with this group. [< NL *chordata* < L *chorda* chord. See CHORD[2].]

chore (chôr) *n.* **1** an odd job; minor task, especially one that must be done daily: *Feeding the chickens was John's chore on the farm.* **2** a task that is disagreeable or irritating: *He found the work quite a chore.* [OE *cyrr*, var. of *cierr*, *cerr* turn, business. Cf. CHAR[2].]

cho·re·a (kô rē′ə) *n.* a nervous disorder characterized by involuntary twitching of the muscles; St. Vitus's dance. [< NL < Gk. *choreia* dance]

chore·boy (chôr′boi′) *n.* a person who does odd jobs or routine tasks around a farm, ranch, tourist resort, lumber camp, etc.

cho·re·o·graph (kôr′ē ə graf′) *v.* arrange or compose choreography for (a ballet, etc.).

cho·re·og·ra·pher (kôr′ē og′rə fər) *n.* a creator or designer of ballets and other stage dances.

cho·re·o·graph·ic (kôr′ē ə graf′ik) *adj.* **1** of or having to do with the art of dancing. **2** of or having to do with choreography.

cho·re·o·graph·i·cal·ly (kôr′ē ə graf′ə klē) *adv.* **1** in a choreographic manner. **2** in terms of choreography.

cho·re·og·ra·phy (kôr′ē og′rə fē) *n.* **1** the art of creating, designing, and arranging dances; dance composition. **2** the art of stage dancing. **3** dance composition as an art. **4** a dance composition arranged for the stage or motion picture. **5** formerly, any written notation of dancing. [< Gk. *choreia* dance + E *-graphy* writing < Gk. *graphein* write]

cho·ric (kô′rik) *adj.* of, having to do with, or for a chorus, especially one in an ancient Greek play.

chor·is·ter (kôr′əs tər) *n.* **1** a singer in a choir. **2** a boy who sings in a choir. **3** the leader of a choir. [< Med.L *chorista* chorister < L *chorus*. See CHORUS.]

cho·roid (kô′roid) in anatomy: *—adj.* having to do with a delicate coat or membrane between the sclerotic coat and the retina of the eyeball. *—n.* the choroid coat or membrane. See **eye** for diagram. [< Gk. *choroeidēs* < *chorion* membrane + *eidos* resemblance]

chor·tle (chôr′təl) *v.* **-tled, -tling,** *n.* *—v.* chuckle and snort with glee simultaneously. *—n.* a simultaneous gleeful chuckle and snort. [blend of *chuckle* and *snort*; coined by Lewis Carroll] **—chor′tler,** *n.*

cho·rus (kô′rəs) *n.* **-rus·es,** *v.* **-rused, -rus·ing.** *—n.* **1** in music: **a** a group of singers who sing together. **b** a song sung by many singers together. **c** a composition to be sung by a whole group of singers, usually in four parts. **d** the part of a song that is repeated after each stanza. **2** a similar or identical utterance by many at the same time: *My question was answered by a chorus of No's.* **3** a group of singers and dancers. **4 in chorus,** all together at the same time.
—v. sing or speak all at the same time: *The birds were chorusing around me.* [< L < Gk. *choros* dance, band of dancers. Doublet of CHOIR.]

chose (chōz) *v.* **1** pt. of **choose. 2** *Obsolete.* a pp. of **choose.**

cho·sen (chō′zən) *v.* a pp. of **choose.** *—adj.* picked out; selected from a group: *the chosen book.*

Chosen People, The in the Bible, the Israelites.

chough (chuf) *n.* a type of European crow having red feet and a red beak. [ME *choughe*]

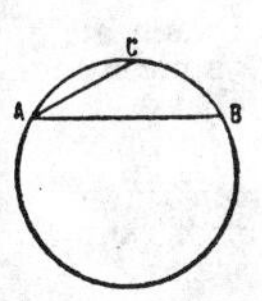

AB and AC are chords (def. 1).

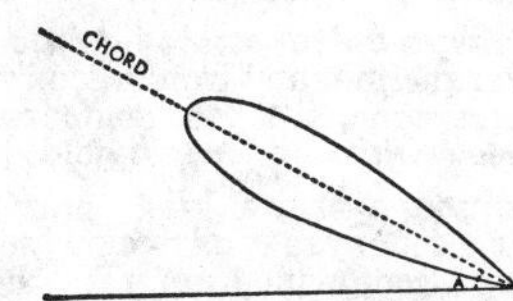

The chord of an aircraft wing: A, angle of attack.

hat, āge, cãre, fär; let, ēqual, tėrm; it, īce
hot, ōpen, ôrder; oil, out; cup, pu̇t, rüle, ūse
əbove, takən, pencəl, lemən, circəs
ch, child; ng, long; sh, ship
th, thin; TH, then; zh, measure

chow (chou) *n.* **1** chow-chow. **2** *Slang.* **a** food. **b** the time when food is served. [short for *chow-chow*]

chow chow or **Chow Chow 1** a medium-sized Chinese breed of dog having a short, compact body, a large head, and a thick coat of uniform color, usually brown or black. **2** a dog of this breed. [< Chinese dial.]

chow-chow (chou′chou′) *n.* **1** a Chinese mixed preserve. **2** any mixed pickles chopped up. [< Chinese Pidgin English]

chow·der (chou′dər) *n.* a thick soup or stew, often made of clams or fish with potatoes, onions, etc. [apparently < F *chaudière* pot, ult. < L *calidus* hot]

chow mein (chou′ mān′) fried noodles served with a thickened stew of onions, celery, bean sprouts, egg, meat, etc. [< Chinese *ch'ao mien* fried flour]

Chr. 1 Christ. **2** Christian.

chres·tom·a·thy (kres tom′ə thē) *n.* **-thies. 1** a collection of literary passages chosen to help in the learning of a language. **2** a selection of passages from the works of one author. [< Gk. *chrēstomatheia* < *chrēstos* useful + *-matheia* learning]

chrism (kriz′əm) *n.* **1** the consecrated oil, used by some churches in baptism and other sacred rites.
2 a sacramental anointing; the ceremony of confirmation, especially as practised in the Greek church. [OE *crisma* < L *chrisma* < Gk. *chrisma* < *chriein* anoint]

chris·mal (kriz′məl) *adj.* having to do with chrism.

Christ (krīst) *n.* a title meaning the Messiah, the Lord's Anointed, used as a proper name when applied to Jesus of Nazareth, the founder of the Christian religion.

Chris·ta·del·phi·an (kris′tə del′fē ən) *n.* a member of a religious sect founded in the United States about 1850 by Dr. John Thomas. This sect rejects the doctrine of the Trinity and holds that only the righteous attain immortality. [< L < Gk. *Christadelphos* brother of Christ < Gk. *Christos* Christ + *adelphos* brother + E *-ian*]

chris·ten (kris′ən) *v.* **1** admit to a Christian church by baptism; baptize. **2** give a name to (someone) at baptism. **3** give a name to: *The new ship was christened before it was launched.* **4** *Informal.* make the first use of.
[OE *cristnian* make Christian < *cristen* Christian < LL < LGk. *christianos* Christian; belonging to Christ]

Chris·ten·dom (kris′ən dəm) *n.* **1** Christian countries; the Christian part of the world. **2** all Christians. [OE *cristendōm* < *cristen* Christian + *-dōm* state < *dōm* statute]

chris·ten·ing (kris′ən ing or kris′ning) *n.* the act or ceremony of baptizing and naming; baptism.

Chris·tian (kris′chən) *adj.* **1** of Christ, His teachings, or the religion that bears His name. **2** believing in Christ; following His example or teachings; belonging to the religion founded by Him. **3** of Christians or Christianity. **4** showing a gentle, humble, helpful spirit: *Christian charity.* **5** human; not animal. **6** *Informal.* decent; respectable.
—n. **1** a believer in Christ; follower of His example or teachings; member of the religion founded by Him. **2** *Informal.* a decent person. **3** a member of the Christian Church. **—Chris′tian·like′,** *adj.* **—Chris′tian·ly,** *adj. adv.*

Christian Church the Disciples of Christ.

Christian Era the time since the birth of Christ. A.D. means in the Christian Era; B.C. means before it.

Chris·ti·an·i·ty (kris′chē an′ə tē) *n.* **-ties. 1** the religion taught by Christ and His followers, one of the world's great religions. **2** the Christian beliefs or faith; Christian spirit or character. **3** all Christians; Christendom.

Chris·tian·ize (kris′chən īz′) *v.* **-ized, -iz·ing.** make Christian; convert to Christianity. **—Chris′tian·i·za′tion,** *n.* **—Chris′tian·iz′er,** *n.*

Christian name in Christian countries, a person's first name; a name given at baptism: *John is the Christian name of my young brother.*

Christian Science a religion and system of healing founded by Mary Baker Eddy in 1866, based on the belief that a full understanding of Jesus' healing and teaching will result in eliminating sin, sickness, and death. It treats disease by mental and spiritual means.

Christian Scientist a believer in Christian Science.

Christ·like (krīst′līk′) *adj.* like Christ; like that of Christ; showing the spirit of Christ. **—Christ′like′ness,** *n.*

Christ·ly (krīst′lē) *adj.* of Christ; Christlike. **—Christ′li·ness,** *n.*

Christ·mas (kris′məs) *n.* **1** the yearly Christian celebration commemorating the birth of Christ; in most Christian churches, December 25. **2** the season of Christmas. [OE *Cristes mæsse* Christ's Mass]

Christmas Day in most Christian churches, December 25.

Christ·mas·tide (kris′məs tīd′) *n.* the Christmas season, especially from the midnight of December 24-25 to New Year's Day, or, as in England, to Epiphany. [< *Christmas* + *tide* time]

Christ·mas·time (kris′məs tīm′) *n.* Christmastide.

Christmas tree **1** an evergreen tree hung with decorations at Christmas time. **2** a party held at Christmas time for entertaining children and presenting gifts to them, usually sponsored by a church, school, or other organization.

chro·mate (krō′māt) *n.* a salt of chromic acid.

chro·mat·ic (krō mat′ik) *adj.* **1** of or having to do with color or colors. **2** in music: **a** involving the use of tones not belonging to any particular scale. **b** of tones that are marked with accidentals, are not normal to the scale in which they occur, but do not cause modulation. **c** having to do with progression and harmony built upon the free use of a scale of 12 half tones. [< L *chromaticus* < Gk. *chrōmatikos* < *chrōma, -atos* color] **—chro·mat′i·cal·ly,** *adv.*

chro·mat·ics (krō mat′iks) *n.* the branch of science that deals with colors.

chromatic scale in music, a scale in which each octave is divided equally into twelve half tones.

chro·ma·tid (krō′mə tid) *n.* in biology, either of the two identical halves into which a chromosome splits during cell division.

chro·ma·tin (krō′mə tin) *n.* in biology, that part of the nucleus of an animal or plant cell that absorbs stains readily and comprises the chromosomes. [< Gk. *chrōma, chrōmatos* color]

chrome (krōm) *n.* **1** chromium. **2 a** the name given to several different paint pigments, as chrome yellow. **b** in dyeing, potassium or sodium dichromate. **3** chrome steel. —*v.* cover or plate with chrome. [< F < Gk. *chrōma* color]

chrome steel an extremely hard, strong steel containing chromium.

chrome yellow a yellow coloring matter made from lead chromate.

chro·mic (krō′mik) *adj.* of or containing chromium.

chro·mite (krō′mīt) *n.* **1** a mineral containing iron and chromium. *Formula*: $FeCr_2O_4$ **2** a salt of chromium.

chro·mi·um (krō′mē əm) *n.* a shiny, hard, brittle metallic chemical element that does not rust or easily become dull when exposed to air. *Symbol*: Cr; *at.no.* 24; *at.wt.* 51.996. [< Gk. *chrōma* color]

chromium steel chrome steel.

chro·mo (krō′mō) *n.* **-mos.** a colored picture printed from a series of stones or plates. [< *chromo*lithograph < Gk. *chrōma* color + E *lithograph*]

chro·mo·some (krō′mə sōm′) *n.* in biology, any of the microscopic filaments composed of chromatin that appear in a fertilized animal or plant cell during mitosis or division. Chromosomes are derived from the parents and carry the genes that determine heredity. [< G *Chromosom* < Gk. *chrōma* color + *sōma* body]

chro·mo·sphere (krō′mə sfēr′) *n.* in astronomy: **1** a scarlet layer of gas around the sun. **2** a similar layer around a star. [< Gk. *chrōma* color + E *sphere*]

chron- *combining form.* the form of *chrono-* before vowels, as in *chronic.*

chron. **1** chronological. **2** chronology.

Chron. Chronicles.

chron·ic (kron′ik) *adj.* **1** of a disease, lasting a long time: *The doctor told him rheumatism was a chronic disease.* **2** constant; habitual: *a chronic liar, a chronic smoker.* [< L *chronicus* < Gk. *chronikos* < *chronos* time] **—Syn.** inveterate, confirmed.

chron·i·cal·ly (kron′ik lē) *adv.* in a chronic manner; always.

chron·i·cle (kron′ə kəl) *n. v.* **-cled, -cling.** —*n.* **1** a record of happenings in the order in which they happened. **2** a narrative; account. —*v.* record in a chronicle; write the history of; tell the story of. [ME < AF var. of OF *cronique* < L < Gk. *chronika* annals, neut. pl. of *chronikos.* See CHRONIC.] **—Syn.** *n.* history, story.

chron·i·cler (kron′ə klər) *n.* the writer of a chronicle; a recorder of events; historian.

chrono- *combining form.* time: *chronometer* = *an instrument that measures time.* Also, before vowels, *chron-.* [< Gk. *chronos* time]

chron·o·graph (kron′ə graf′) *n.* an instrument that measures very short intervals of time accurately; stop watch. [< Gk. *chronos* time + E *-graph*]

chro·nol·o·ger (krə nol′ə jər) *n.* chronologist.

chron·o·log·ic (kron′ə loj′ik) *adj.* chronological.

chron·o·log·i·cal (kron′ə loj′ə kəl) *adj.* arranged in the order in which the events happened: *In telling a story, a person usually arranges the events in chronological order.* **—chron′o·log′i·cal·ly,** *adv.*

chro·nol·o·gist (krə nol′ə jist) *n.* an expert in chronology.

chro·nol·o·gy (krə nol′ə jē) *n.* **-gies. 1** an arrangement of time in periods; giving the exact dates of events arranged in the order in which they happened. **2** a table or list giving the exact dates of events arranged in the order in which they happened. [< Gk. *chronos* time + E *-logy*]

chro·nom·e·ter (krə nom′ə tər) *n.* a clock or watch that keeps very accurate time: *A ship's chronometer is used in determining longitude.* [< Gk. *chronos* time + E *-meter*]

chron·o·scope (kron′ə skōp′) *n.* an instrument for measuring very small intervals of time. [< Gk. *chronos* time + E *-scope* instrument of viewing (< Gk. *skopein* look at)]

chrys·a·lid (kris′ə lid) *n.* chrysalis. —*adj.* of a chrysalis.

chrys·a·lis (kris′ə lis) *n.* **chrys·a·lis·es, chry·sal·i·des** (krə sal′ə dēz′). **1** the inactive form of an insect when it is in a case; pupa. A butterfly has this form after it has been a caterpillar or larva and before it becomes a winged adult. **2** the case; cocoon. **3** a stage of development or change. [< L < Gk. *chrysallis* golden sheath < *chrysos* gold]

chry·san·the·mum (krə san′thə məm) *n.* **1** any of several cultivated plants of the aster family, which bloom in the autumn. **2** one of these flowers. Most chrysanthemums are white, yellow, rose-colored, or bronze. [< L < Gk. *chrysanthemon* < *chrysos* gold + *anthemon* flower]

chrys·o·ber·yl (kris′ə ber′əl) *n.* **1** a yellow or pale-green semiprecious stone. **2** a piece of this stone, or a gem made from it. [< L < Gk. *chrysoberyllos* < *chrysos* gold + *beryllos* beryl]

chrys·o·lite (kris′ə līt′) *n.* **1** a green or yellow silicate of magnesium and iron, a semiprecious stone. **2** a piece of this stone, or a gem made from it. [< L < Gk. *chrysolithos* < *chrysos* gold + *lithos* stone]

chrys·o·prase (kris′ə prāz′) *n.* **1** a light-green kind of chalcedony, a semiprecious stone. **2** a piece of this stone, or a gem made from it. [< L < Gk. *chrysoprasos* < *chrysos* gold + *prason* leek]

chub (chub) *n.* **chub** or **chubs. 1** a thick fresh-water fish, related to the carp. **2** any of various North American fishes, such as the tautog, black bass, etc. [ME *chubbe*; origin unknown]

chub·by (chub′ē) *adj.* **-bi·er, -bi·est.** round and plump: *chubby cheeks.* —**chub′bi·ness,** *n.*

chuck[1] (chuk) *v.* **1** pat; tap, especially under the chin. **2** *Informal.* **a** toss someone out forcibly: *The intruder was chucked out of the hall.* **b** give up; finish with: *He has chucked his job.* —*n.* **1** a tap; slight blow under the chin. **2** a toss. [probably imitative]

chuck[2] (chuk) *n.* **1** a device for holding a tool or piece of work in a machine. **2** a cut of beef between the neck and the shoulder. See **beef** for diagram. [var. of *chock*]

chuck[3] (chuk) *n.* on the west coast, a large body of water, usually a river, but now sometimes the ocean. The sea is sometimes called the salt chuck. [< Chinook jargon]

chuck-full (chuk′fůl′) *adj.* chock-full.

chuck·le (chuk′əl) *v.* **chuck·led, chuck·ling,** *n.* —*v.* laugh to oneself. —*n.* a soft, quiet laugh. [< *chuck* cluck, laugh; imitative] —**chuck′ler,** *n.*

chuck·le·head (chuk′əl hed′) *n. Informal.* **1** a thick or large head. **2** a stupid person. —**chuck′le·head′ed,** *adj.* —**chuck′le·head′ed·ness,** *n.*

chuck race a chuckwagon race.

chuck·wag·on (chuk′wag′ən) *n.* in the western parts of Canada and the United States: **1** a wagon that carries food and cooking equipment for cowboys, harvest hands, etc. **2** a truck used for the same purpose.

chuckwagon race *Cdn.* a race between horse-drawn chuckwagons, a thrilling and highly popular event at rodeos and stampedes.

chug (chug) *n. v.* **chugged, chug·ging.** —*n.* a short, loud, explosive sound: *the chug of an engine.* —*v.* **1** make short, loud, explosive sounds. **2** *Informal.* go or move with short, loud, explosive sounds: *The engine chugged along.* [imitative]

chu·kar or **chuk·kar** (chə kär′) *n.* a rock partridge having gray feathers with black and white bars on the sides and a red bill and red legs, imported from India. It is valued as a game bird. [< Hind. *chakor* < Skt. *chakora*]

chuk·ker or **chuk·kar** (chuk′ər) *n.* in polo, one of the periods of play, lasting about eight minutes. [< Hind. *chakar*]

chum[1] (chum) *n. v.* **chummed, chum·ming.** *Informal.* —*n.* a close friend. —*v.* be close friends: *Tom and Bill have chummed for years.* [? shortened form of *chamber mate, chamber fellow*]

chum[2] (chum) *n.* bait for fish. —*v.* scatter bait to attract fish. [origin unknown]

chum[3] (chum) *n.* a species of Pacific salmon. [origin unknown]

chum·my (chum′ē) *adj.* **-mi·er, -mi·est.** *Informal.* like a chum; very friendly; intimate. —**chum′mi·ly,** *adv.* —**chum′mi·ness,** *n.*

chump (chump) *n.* **1** *Informal.* a foolish or stupid person; blockhead. **2** a short, thick block of wood. **3** a thick, blunt end. **4** *Slang.* the head. **5 off one's chump,** *Slang.* off one's head; out of one's senses. [origin uncertain]

chunk (chungk) *n. Informal.* **1** a thick piece or lump: *a chunk of wood.* **2** a stocky person or animal: *His horse was a strong, sturdy chunk.* [var. of *chuck*[2]]

chunk·y (chungk′ē) *adj.* **chunk·i·er, chunk·i·est.** *Informal.* **1** like a chunk; short and thick. **2** stocky. —**chunk′i·ly,** *adv.* —**chunk′i·ness,** *n.*

church (chėrch) *n.* **1** a building for public, especially Christian, worship or religious services. **2** public worship or religious service in a church. **3** Christians as a whole. **4** a group of Christians with the same beliefs and under the same authority; a denomination: *the United Church, the Presbyterian Church.* **5** a locally organized unit of a group of Christians for religious services: *We go to the Baptist Church.* **6** the organization of a church; ecclesiastical authority or power. **7** the profession of a clergyman: *John is going into the church as a career.* **8 a** any religious body other than Christian; a non-Christian creed or congregation: *the Jewish church.*

hat, āge, cãre, fär; let, ēqual, tėrm; it, īce
hot, ōpen, ôrder; oil, out; cup, půt, rüle, ūse
əbove, takən, pencəl, lemən, circəs
ch, child; ng, long; sh, ship
th, thin; ᴛʜ, then; zh, measure

b a building for public worship or religious services of such a body.
—*adj.* of a church. [OE *circe* < Gk. *kyriakon* (*doma*) (house) of the Lord < *kyrios* lord] —**church′less,** *adj.* —**church′like′,** *adj.* —**Syn.** *n.* **1** cathedral, temple, chapel. **4** denomination, sect.

church day a day on which a festival of the Christian church is celebrated: *Ascension Day is a church day.*

church·go·er (chėrch′gō′ər) *n.* a person who goes to church regularly.

Church·il·li·an (chėr chil′ē ən) *adj.* **1** of, having to do with, or resembling Sir Winston Churchill (1874-1965). **2** of or suggestive of his writings, speeches, etc.

church·ly (chėrch′lē) *adj.* **1** of a church. **2** suitable for a church. —**church′li·ness,** *n.*

church·man (chėrch′mən) *n.* **-men** (-mən). **1** a clergyman. **2** a member of a church.

Church of Christ, Scientist the official name of the Christian Science Church.

Church of England 1 the Christian church that is recognized in England as the established church of the country. **2** in Canada, the Anglican Church of Canada.

Church of Jesus Christ of Latter-day Saints the official name of the Mormon Church.

Church of the Brethren a Protestant sect practising adult baptism by immersion and opposed to oaths and military service. Its members are known as Dunkards.

church·ward·en (chėrch′wôr′dən) *n.* **1** in Anglican churches, a lay official who manages the business matters of a church. **2** a clay tobacco pipe with a very long stem.

church·wom·an (chėrch′wům′ən) *n.* **-wom·en.** a woman member of a church.

church·yard (chėrch′yärd′) *n.* the ground around a church. Part of a churchyard is sometimes used as a burial ground.

churl (chėrl) *n.* **1** a rude, surly person. **2** a person of low birth; peasant. **3** a person who is stingy in money matters; niggard; miser. [OE *ceorl* freeman (of low rank)]

churl·ish (chėr′lish) *adj.* **1** rude; surly: *a churlish reply.* **2** niggardly; stingy; grudging; sordid. —**churl′ish·ly,** *adv.* —**churl′ish·ness,** *n.*

churn (chėrn) *n.* **1** a container or machine in which butter is made from cream or milk by beating and shaking. **2** a violent stirring.
—*v.* **1** stir or shake (cream or milk) in a churn. **2** make (butter) by using a churn. **3** stir violently; make or become foamy: *The propeller of the steamboat churned the waves.* **4** move as if beaten and shaken: *The crowd churned about the speaker's platform.* [OE *cyrn*] —**churn′er,** *n.*

churr (chėr) *v. n.* chirr.

chute[1] (shüt) *n.* **1** an inclined trough, tube, etc. down which things are dropped or slid to a lower level. **2** rapids in a river; a waterfall. **3** a steep slope.
—*v.* send or go down a chute. [apparently blend of F *chute* fall (of water) and E *shoot*]

chute[2] (shüt) *n. v.* **chut·ed, chut·ing.** parachute.

chut·ney (chut′nē) *n.* **-neys.** a spicy sauce or relish made of fruits, herbs, pepper, etc. [< Hind. *chatni*]

chutz·pah (hůts′pə) *n. Slang.* effrontery; impudence; gall. [< Yiddish *khutspe*]

chyle (kīl) *n.* in physiology, a milky liquid composed of digested fat and lymph, formed from the chyme in the small intestine and carried from there into the veins. [< Med.L < Gk. *chylos* < *cheein* pour]

chyme (kīm) *n.* in physiology, a pulpy, semiliquid mass into which food is changed by the action of the stomach. Chyme passes from the stomach into the small intestine. [< Med.L < Gk. *chymos* < *cheein* pour]

CIA or **C.I.A.** Central Intelligence Agency.

ci·bo·ri·um (sə bô′rē əm) *n.* **-ri·a** (-rē ə). **1** a covered container used to hold the sacred bread of the Eucharist. **2** a dome-shaped canopy over an altar. [< Med.L *ciborium* canopy over an altar < L *ciborium* drinking cup < Gk. *kiborion* cuplike seed vessel]

ci·ca·da (sə kā′də or sə kā′də) *n.* **-das, -dae** (-dē or -dī). a large insect having two pairs of transparent wings. The male makes a loud, shrill sound in hot, dry weather. [< L]

cic·a·trice (sik′ə tris) *n.* cicatrix.

cic·a·trix (sik′ə triks′) *n.* **cic·a·tri·ces** (sik′ə trī′sēz). **1** in medicine, the scar left by a healed wound. **2** in botany: **a** the scar left on a tree or plant by a fallen leaf, branch, etc. **b** the scar on a seed where it was attached to the pod or seed container. [< L]

cic·a·trize (sik′ə trīz′) *v.* **-trized, -triz·ing.** heal by forming a scar.

cic·e·ro·ne (sis′ə rō′nē) *n.* **-nes.** a guide for sightseers who explains curiosities, antiquities, etc. [< Ital. < L *Cicero,-onis* Cicero]

Cic·e·ro·ni·an (sis′ə rō′nē ən) *adj.* **1** resembling the literary style of M. T. Cicero (106-43 B.C.), a Roman orator, writer, and statesman. **2** eloquent.

C.I.D. Criminal Investigation Department.

CIDA Canadian International Development Agency.

-cide[1] *combining form.* killing of: *regicide*[1] = *killing of a king.* [< L *-cidium* a killing < *caedere* kill]

-cide[2] *combining form.* killer of: *regicide*[2] = *killer of a king.* [< L *-cida* killer < *caedere* kill]

ci·der (sī′dər) *n.* **1** the juice pressed out of apples, used as a drink and in making vinegar. **Sweet cider** is the unfermented juice; **hard cider,** the fermented juice. **2** the juice pressed from other fruits. [ME *sidre* < OF < LL *sicera* < Gk. < Hebrew *shēkār* liquor]

cider press a machine for pressing the juice out of apples.

ci-de·vant (sē də väɴ′) *adj. French.* former; late: *The ci-devant general led the revolt against his government.*

CIE. or **cie.** company. (for F *compagnie*)

C.I.F. or **c.i.f.** cost, insurance, and freight.

ci·gar (sə gär′) *n.* dried tobacco leaves made into a tight roll for smoking. [< Sp. *cigarro*]

cig·a·rette (sig′ə ret′ or sig′ə ret′) *n.* a small roll of finely shredded tobacco enclosed in a thin sheet of paper. Also, **cigaret.** [< F *cigarette,* dim. of *cigare* cigar]

cil·i·a (sil′ē ə) *n.* pl. of **cil·i·um** (sil′ē əm). **1 eyelashes. 2** in zoology, very small hairlike projections: *Some microscopic animals use cilia to move themselves or to set up currents in the surrounding water.* **3** in botany, delicate hairs resembling eyelashes, especially those that form a fringe on the margins of leaves. [< L]

cil·i·ar·y (sil′ē er′ē) *adj.* **1** of cilia; resembling cilia. **2** having to do with certain delicate structures of the eyeball.

cil·i·ate (sil′ē āt′ or sil′ē it) *adj.* provided with cilia.

Ci·li·cian (sə lish′ən) *adj.* of or having to do with Cilicia, an ancient country in S.E. Asia Minor. —*n.* a native or inhabitant of Cilicia.

Cim·me·ri·an (sə mēr′ē ən) *n.* one of a mythical people said to live in perpetual mists and darkness. —*adj.* very dark and gloomy.

C. in C. Commander-in-Chief.

cinch (sinch) —*n.* **1** a strong girth for fastening a saddle or pack on a horse. **2** *Informal.* a firm hold or grip. **3** *Informal.* something sure and easy: *We were a cinch to win the game.*
—*v.* **1** fasten on with a cinch; bind firmly. **2** *Informal.* get a firm hold on. [< Sp. *cincha* < L *cincta* girdle < *cingere* bind]

cin·cho·na (sin kō′nə) *n.* **1** a tree having light green leaves that is native to South America and is grown in the East Indies and India, valuable for its bark. **2** its bitter bark, from which quinine and other drugs are obtained; Peruvian bark. [< NL; after Francesca de Ribera, Countess *Chinchón* (?-1641?), the wife of a Spanish viceroy of Peru]

cinc·ture (singk′chər) *n. v.* **-tured, -tur·ing.** —*n.* **1** a belt; girdle. **2** a border; enclosure. —*v.* encircle; surround. [< L *cinctura* < *cingere* bind, gird]

cin·der (sin′dər) *n.* **1** a piece of burned-up wood or coal. **2 cinders,** *pl.* **a** wood or coal partly burned but no longer flaming. **b** ashes. [OE *sinder*]

Cin·der·el·la (sin′dər el′ ə) *n.* **1** in the fairy tale, a girl who is cruelly treated by her stepmother and ugly stepsisters. Her fairy godmother makes it possible for her to go to a ball, where she meets a prince who later marries her. **2** any person whose real worth or beauty is not recognized.

cin·e·ma (sin′ə mə) *n.* **1** a motion picture. **2** a motion-picture theatre. **3 the cinema,** motion pictures. [short for *cinematograph*]

Cin·e·ma·Scope (sin′ə mə skōp′) *n. Trademark.* a motion-picture medium in which the use of a special lens on both a standard camera and projector gives the images greater depth when projected on a large curved screen. [< *cinema* + *-scope*]

cin·e·mat·o·graph (sin′ə mat′ə graf′) *n.* **1** *Brit.* a machine for projecting motion pictures on a screen. **2** a camera for taking motion pictures. Also, **kinematograph.** [< Gk. *kinema, -atos* motion + E *-graph*]

cin·e·ma·tog·ra·phy (sin′ə mə tog′rə fē) *n.* the art and science of making motion pictures. Also, **kinematography.**

ci·né·ma vé·ri·té (si nā mä′ vā ri tā′) *French.* a motion-picture style that aims to reflect reality by filming spontaneous action.

Cin·er·am·a (sin′ər am′ə or sin′ər äm′ə) *n. Trademark.* a motion-picture medium that uses three projectors, a large, three-panelled, curved screen, and a stereophonic sound system to produce the illusion of three dimensions. [< *cine*ma + pano*rama*]

cin·e·rar·i·a (sin′ə rãr′ē ə) *n.* **1** (*sing.*) a small plant having large, heart-shaped leaves and clusters of white, red, or blue flowers. **2** pl. of **cinerarium.** [< NL < L *cinerarius* of ashes; with reference to down on leaves]

cin·e·rar·i·um (sin′ə rãr′ē əm) *n.* **-rar·i·a.** a place for keeping the ashes of cremated bodies. [< L]

cin·e·rar·y (sin′ə rer′ē) *adj.* **1** used to hold the ashes of a cremated body. **2** of or for ashes.

cin·na·bar (sin′ə bär′) *n.* **1** a reddish or brownish mineral that is the chief source of mercury; native mercuric sulphide. *Formula*: HgS **2** artificial mercuric sulphide, used as a red pigment in making paints, dyes, etc. **3** a bright red; vermilion. [< L < Gk. *kinnabari*; ult. < Persian *Zanjifrah*]

cin·na·mon (sin′ə mən) *n.* **1** a spice made from the dried, reddish-brown inner bark of a tropical laurel tree or shrub. **2** this bark. **3** the tree or shrub yielding this bark. **4** a light, reddish brown.
—*adj.* **1** flavored with cinnamon. **2** light reddish-brown: *a cinnamon bear.* [ME < OF *cinnamome* < LL < Gk. *kinnamon*; of Semitic origin]

cinnamon bear the reddish-brown variety of the North American black bear.

cin·que·cen·to (ching′kwə chen′tō) *n.* the 16th century, especially with regard to the art and architecture of Italy at that time. —*adj.* of or having to do with the 16th century. [< Ital. *cinquecento* short for *mil cinque cento* one thousand five hundred]
☛ Note that *cinquecento* refers to the 1500's, and so to the sixteenth rather than the fifteenth century.

cinque·foil (singk′foil′) *n.* **1** a plant having small, yellow flowers and leaves divided into five parts. **2** in architecture, an ornament made of five connected semicircles or part circles. **3** in heraldry, an ornamental design resembling the leaf of the cinquefoil. [ME *synkefoile* < OF (unrecorded) < L *quinquefolium* < *quinque* five + *folium* leaf]

A cinquefoil (def. 2)

ci·on (sī′ən) *n.* scion (def. 2).

ci·pher (sī′fər) *n.* **1** a person or thing of no importance. **2** a zero; 0. **3** a method of secret writing that transposes the letters of a message according to a set pattern, or replaces the proper letters with the

substitutes called for in the system used, or combines both methods; code: *All important plans were sent to the police in cipher.* **4** something in secret writing or code. **5** the key to a method of secret writing or code. **6** interlaced initials; a monogram.
—*v.* **1** do arithmetic. **2** work by arithmetic. **3** *Informal.* figure out; calculate; think. **4** express by characters of any kind, especially in code or secret writing. Also, **cypher.** [ME < Med.L *ciphra* < Arabic *sifr* empty. Doublet of ZERO.]

cir·ca (sėr′kə) *prep. adv.* about: *Mohammed was born circa A.D. 570.* [< L]

Cir·cas·sian (sər kash′ən or sər kash′ē ən) *n.* **1** a native or inhabitant of Circassia, a region in southern Russia on the Black Sea. **2** a language of the northern Caucasus. —*adj.* of or having to do with Circassia, its people, or their language.

Circe (sėr′sē) *n.* **1** in Greek legend, an enchantress who changed men to beasts. **2** any enchantress.

cir·ci·nate (sėr′sə nāt′) *adj.* **1** rolled up into a coil. **2** in botany, coiled from tip toward the base: *The new leaves of a fern are circinate.* [< L *circinatus* made round, pp. of *circinare* < *circinus* pair of compasses < Gk. *kirkinos*]

cir·cle (sėr′kəl) *n. v.* **-cled, -cling.** —*n.* **1** a continuously curving line, every point of which is equally distant from a fixed point called the centre. **2** a plane figure bounded by such a line. See **conic section** for diagram. **3** a halo, crown, or anything shaped like a circle or part of one. **4** a ring. **5** a set of seats in the balcony of a theatre. **6** a complete series or course; period; cycle: *A year is a circle of 12 months.* **7** in astronomy: **a** the orbit of a heavenly body. **b** the period of revolution of a heavenly body. **8** a group of people held together by the same interests: *the family circle; a circle of friends.* **9** a sphere of influence, action, etc. **10** a set of parts that form a connected whole: *the circle of the sciences.*
—*v.* **1** go around in a circle; revolve around: *The moon circles the earth. An airplane circles before it lands.* **2** form a circle around; surround; encircle.
[ME < OF *cercle* < L *circulus*, dim. of *circus* ring]
—**cir′cler,** *n.*
Syn. *n.* **8 Circle, clique** = a group of people held together by a common tie. **Circle** applies to a group held together around a person or a common interest, cause, occupation, etc.: *The book is praised in literary circles.* **Clique** applies to a small, exclusive, sometimes snobbish, group, and often expresses an attitude of disapproval on the part of the speaker toward the group: *Every school has its cliques.*

cir·clet (sėr′klit) *n.* **1** a small circle. **2** a round ornament worn on the head, neck, arm, or finger.

cir·cuit (sėr′kit) *n.* **1** a going around; a trip around: *It takes a year for the earth to make its circuit of the sun.* **2** the route along which a person or group makes repeated journeys at certain times: *Some theatre companies travel over regular circuits. Some judges make a circuit, stopping at certain places along the way to conduct trials.* **3** the persons making such a circuit. **4** the part of the country through which such circuits are made. **5** the district under the jurisdiction of a circuit court. **6** a number of theatres under the same management, presenting the same shows, often with the same companies, or otherwise associated. **7** the distance around any space. **8** a line enclosing any space. **9** the space enclosed. **10** in electricity: **a** the complete path or a part of it over which a current flows. **b** an arrangement of conductors, tubes, etc. for studying or making use of electrical energy. **c** a diagram showing the connections of such an arrangement; hook up.
—*v.* make a circuit of; go in a circuit. [ME < L *circuitus* a going around < *circum* around + *ire* go] —**Syn.** *n.* **2** route, course.

circuit breaker a switch that automatically opens or interrupts an electric circuit when the current gets too strong.

circuit court a court whose judges regularly conduct trials at certain places in a district.

cir·cu·i·tous (sər kū′ə təs) *adj.* roundabout; not direct: *We took a circuitous route home to avoid poor roads.* —**cir·cu′i·tous·ly,** *adv.* —**cir·cu′i·tous·ness,** *n.* —**Syn.** indirect, devious.

circuit rider formerly, a Methodist minister who rode from place to place over a circuit to preach.

hat, āge, cãre, fär; let, ēqual, tėrm; it, īce
hot, ōpen, ôrder; oil, out; cup, pu̇t, rüle, ūse
əbove, takən, pencəl, lemən, circəs
ch, child; ng, long; sh, ship
th, thin; ᴛʜ, then; zh, measure

cir·cuit·ry (sėr′kə trē) *n.* **-ries. 1** the science of electrical or electronic circuits. **2** the component parts of a circuit.

cir·cu·lar (sėr′kyu̇ lər) *adj.* **1** round like a circle. **2** moving in a circle; going around a circle. **3** having to do with a circle. **4** sent to each of a number of people: *a circular letter.* **5** roundabout; indirect. **6** moving or occurring in a round or cycle of repetition: *a circular sequence of events.*
—*n.* a letter, notice, or advertisement sent to each of a number of people. [ME < AF < LL *circularis* < *circulus.* See CIRCLE.] —**cir′cu·lar·ly,** *adv.*

cir·cu·lar·i·ty (sėr′kyu̇ lar′ə tē) *n.* **-ties.** circular shape.

cir·cu·lar·ize (sėr′kyu̇ lər īz′) *v.* **-ized, -iz·ing. 1** send circulars to. **2** make circular. —**cir′cu·lar·i·za′tion,** *n.* —**cir′cu·lar·iz′er,** *n.*

circular measure a system used for measuring circles:

60 seconds	= 1 minute
60 minutes	= 1 degree
90 degrees	= 1 quadrant
4 quadrants or 360 degrees	= 1 circle

circular saw a thin steel disk with saw-teeth round its edge, turned at high speed by machinery.

cir·cu·late (sėr′kyu̇ lāt′) *v.* **-lat·ed, -lat·ing. 1** go around, pass from place to place or person to person: *Water circulates in the pipes of a building. Money circulates as it changes hands.* **2** be distributed: *A newspaper circulates among the people who read it.* **3** send around from person to person or place to place: *He circulated the news of the holiday. This book has been widely circulated among boys.* **4** of the blood, flow from the heart through the arteries and veins, and back to the heart again. [< L *circulare* < *circulus.* See CIRCLE.]

circulating library a library whose books can be rented or borrowed.

circulating medium the coins, notes, bills, etc. that are in use as money; currency.

cir·cu·la·tion (sėr′kyu̇ lā′shən) *n.* **1** a going around; a circulating: *Open windows increase the circulation of air in a room.* **2** the movement of blood from the heart through the body and back to the heart. **3** a sending around of books, papers, news, etc. from person to person or place to place. **4** the number of copies of a book, newspaper, magazine, etc. that are sent out during a certain time.

cir·cu·la·tor (sėr′kyu̇ lā′tər) *n.* a person or thing that circulates news, money, gossip, etc.

cir·cu·la·to·ry (sėr′kyu̇ lə tô′rē) *adj.* having to do with circulation: *Arteries and veins are parts of the human body's circulatory system.*

circum- *prefix.* in a circle; around: *circumnavigate= navigate around; circumpolar = around the North or South Pole.* [< L]

cir·cum·am·bi·ent (sėr′kəm am′bē ənt) *adj.* surrounding; encircling.

cir·cum·cise (sėr′kəm sīz′) *v.* **-cised, -cis·ing.** cut off the foreskin of. [ME < L *circumcisus*, pp. of *circumcidere* < *circum* around + *caedere* cut] —**cir′cum·cis′er,** *n.*

cir·cum·ci·sion (sėr′kəm sizh′ən) *n.* a circumcising.

cir·cum·fer·ence (sər kum′fər əns) *n.* **1** the boundary line of a circle or of certain other surfaces. Every point on the circumference of a circle is at the same distance from the centre. **2** the distance around: *The circumference of the earth at the equator is almost 25,000 miles.* [< L *circumferentia* < *circum* around + *ferre* bear]

cir·cum·fer·en·tial (sər kum′fər en′shəl) *adj.* of a circumference; located at or near the circumference. —**cir·cum′fer·en′tial·ly,** *adv.*

cir·cum·flex (sėr′kəm fleks′) *n.* a circumflex accent. —*adj.* **1** of or having a circumflex accent. **2** bending or winding around. [< L *circumflexus* bent around < *circum* around + *flectere* bend]

circumflex accent a mark (∧ or ⌒ or ~) placed over a vowel to indicate some feature of the pronunciation. The circumflex in the French word *fête* (in Old French, *feste*) indicates that the vowel over which it is written is long and at the same time marks the loss of the letter *s*.

cir·cum·flu·ent (sər kum′flü ənt) *adj.* flowing around; surrounding. [< L *circumfluens, -entis,* ppr. of *circumfluere* < *circum* around + *fluere* flow]

cir·cum·fuse (sėr′kəm fūz′) *v.* **-fused, -fus·ing. 1** pour or spread around. **2** surround; suffuse. [< L *circumfusus,* pp. of *circumfundere* < *circum* around + *fundere* pour] **—cir′cum·fu′sion,** *n.*

cir·cum·lo·cu·tion (sėr′kəm lō kū′shən or -lə kū′shən) *n.* a roundabout way of speaking. "The wife of your father's brother" is a circumlocution for "Your aunt." [< L *circumlocutio, -onis* < *circum* around + *loqui* speak]

cir·cum·nav·i·gate (sėr′kəm nav′ə gāt′) *v.* **-gat·ed, -gat·ing.** sail around: *Magellan's ship circumnavigated the earth.* **—cir′cum·nav′i·ga′tor,** *n.*

cir·cum·nav·i·ga·tion (sėr′kəm nav′ə gā′shən) *n.* the act of sailing around.

cir·cum·po·lar (sėr′kəm pō′lər) *adj.* **1** around the North or South Pole. **2** around either pole of the heavens.

cir·cum·scribe (sėr′kəm skrīb′ or sėr′kəm skrīb′) *v.* **-scribed, -scrib·ing. 1** draw a line around; mark the boundaries of. **2** surround. **3** limit; restrict: *A prisoner's activities are circumscribed.* **4** in geometry: **a** draw (a figure) around another figure so as to touch as many points as possible: *A circle that is circumscribed around a square touches it at four points.* **b** be so drawn around: *A circle can circumscribe a hexagon.* [< L *circumscribere* < *circum* around + *scribere* write, draw] **—cir′cum·scrib′er,** *n.* **—Syn. 3** confine.

cir·cum·scrip·tion (sėr′kəm skrip′shən) *n.* **1** the act of circumscribing. **2** the state of being circumscribed. **3** the thing that circumscribes. **4** an inscription around a coin, medal, etc. **5** an outline; boundary. **6** a space circumscribed. **7** a limitation; restriction. [< L *circumscriptio, -onis* < *circumscribere.* See CIRCUMSCRIBE.]

cir·cum·spect (sėr′kəm spekt′) *adj.* careful; cautious; prudent. [< L *circumspectus,* pp. of *circumspicere* < *circum* around + *specere* look] **—cir′cum·spect′ly,** *adv.* **—cir′cum·spect′ness,** *n.* **—Syn.** watchful, wary, discreet.

cir·cum·spec·tion (sėr′kəm spek′shən) *n.* care; caution; prudence.

cir·cum·stance (sėr′kəm stans′) *n.* **1** a condition that contributes to or modifies an act or event: *The place, the weather, and other circumstances made the picnic a great success.* **2** a particular or detail connected with an event. **3** an incident or occurrence: *His arrival was a fortunate circumstance.* **4 under no circumstances,** never; no matter what the conditions are. **5 under the circumstances,** because of conditions; things being as they are or were. **6** a fact or event: *If you give all the details in telling a story, you are telling every circumstance of it.* **7 circumstances,** *pl.* financial position: *A rich person is in easy circumstances. A poor person is in bad or reduced circumstances.* **8** full detail: *The explorer told of his adventure with great circumstance.* **9** ceremony, display: *The royal procession advanced with pomp and circumstance.* [< L *circumstantia* surrounding condition < *circumstans, -antis,* ppr. of *circumstare* < *circum* around + *stare* stand]

cir·cum·stan·tial (sėr′kəm stan′shəl) *adj.* **1** depending on or based on circumstances: *circumstantial evidence.* **2** incidental; not essential; not important: *Minor details are circumstantial compared with the main facts.* **3** giving full and exact details; complete: *a circumstantial report of an accident.* **—cir′cum·stan′tial·ly,** *adv.*

circumstantial evidence events or facts that make certain conclusions apparent. If stolen jewels are found in a man's possession, it is circumstantial evidence that he stole them; if somebody saw him steal them, that would be direct evidence.

cir·cum·stan·ti·ate (sėr′kəm stan′shē āt′) *v.* **-at·ed, -at·ing.** give the circumstances of; support or prove with details. **—cir′cum·stan′ti·a′tion,** *n.*

cir·cum·vent (sėr′kəm vent′) *v.* **1** get the better of; defeat by trickery: *circumvent the law.* **2** go around. **3** catch in a trap. [< L *circumventus,* pp. of *circumvenire* < *circum* around + *venire* come] **—cir′cum·ven′tor,** *n.*

cir·cum·ven·tion (sėr′kəm ven′shən) *n.* the act of circumventing.

cir·cus (sėr′kəs) *n.* **1** a company of acrobats, clowns, horses, riders, and wild animals. **2** the show that such a company gives. **3** *Informal.* **a** an amusing person or thing. **b** a lively time. **4** in ancient Rome, a round or oval space with rows of seats around it, each row higher than the one in front of it. [< L *circus* ring. Doublet of CIRQUE.]

Circus Max·i·mus (mak′sə məs) in ancient Rome, a huge amphitheatre.

cirque (sėrk) *n.* **1** a circular space. **2** *Poetic.* a circlet; ring. **3** in geology, a hollow formed in a valley by erosion at the head of a glacier. [< F *cirque* < L *circus.* Doublet of CIRCUS.]

cir·rho·sis (sə rō′sis) *n.* in medicine, a disease of the liver marked by degeneration of the liver cells and excessive formation of connective tissue. [< NL < Gk. *kirrhos* orange-yellow]

cir·ri·ped (sir′ə ped′) *n.* any of a group of crustaceans having threadlike appendages instead of legs. A barnacle is a kind of cirriped. [< NL *Cirripeda* < L *cirrus* curl + *pes, pedis* foot]

cir·ro·cu·mu·lus (sir′ō kū′myů ləs) *n.* a cloud made up of rows or groups of small, fleecy clouds. [< *cirrus* + *cumulus*]

cir·ro·stra·tus (sir′ō strā′təs or -strat′əs) *n.* a thin, veil-like cloud high in the air. [< *cirrus* + *stratus*]

cir·rus (sir′əs) *n.* **cir·ri** (sir′ī or sir′ē). a thin, fleecy cloud very high in the air. [< L *cirrus* curl]

cis·al·pine (sis al′pīn or sis al′pin) *adj.* on the southern side of the Alps. [< L *cisalpinus* < *cis* on this (i.e., the Roman) side of + *alpinus* < *Alpes* the Alps]

cis·co (sis′kō) *n.* **-coes** or **-cos.** a kind of whitefish found in the Great Lakes and in some other large lakes. [< Cdn.F *ciscoette* < ? Algonquian]

Cis·ter·cian (sis tėr′shən) *n.* in the Roman Catholic Church, a monk or nun of a very strict order founded in France in 1098 as an offshoot of the Benedictines. *—adj.* of or having to do with this order. [< Med.L *Cistercium* Citeaux, where the order was founded]

cis·tern (sis′tərn) *n.* a reservoir or tank for storing water or other liquids. [< L *cisterna* < *cista* box]

cit. 1 citation. **2** cited. **3** citizen.

cit·a·del (sit′ə dəl or sit′ə del′) *n.* **1** a fortress commanding a city. **2** a strongly fortified place; stronghold. **3** a strong, safe place; refuge. [< F *citadelle* < Ital. *cittadella,* dim. of *città* city]

ci·ta·tion (sī tā′shən) *n.* **1** a quotation or reference given as an authority for facts, opinions, etc. **2** a specific mention in an official dispatch. **3** an honorable mention for bravery in war. **4** the commendation of a civilian for public service by some official or institution. **5** a summons to appear before a law court.

cite (sīt) *v.* **cit·ed, cit·ing. 1** quote (a passage, book, or author), especially as an authority: *He cited the Bible and Shakespeare to prove his statement.* **2** refer to; mention as an example: *The lawyer cited another case similar to the one being tried.* **3** mention for bravery in war. **4** commend publicly for service to the community. **5** summon to appear before a law court. **6** arouse to action; summon. [< F *citer* < L *citare* summon < *ciere* set in motion] **—cite′a·ble,** *adj.* **—Syn. 1** See **quote.**

cith·a·ra (sith′ə rə) *n.* an ancient musical instrument resembling a lyre. [< L < Gk. *kithara.* Doublet of GUITAR and ZITHER.]

cith·er (sith′ər) *n.* **1** cithern. **2** cithara.

cith·ern (sith′ərn) *n.* cittern.

cit·i·fied (sit′i fīd′) *adj.* *Informal.* having city ways or fashions.

cit·i·zen (sit′ə zən) *n.* **1** a person who by birth or by choice is a member of a state or nation that gives him certain rights and claims his loyalty: *Many immigrants have become citizens of Canada.* **2** a person who is not a soldier, policeman, etc.; civilian. **3** an inhabitant of a city or town. [ME < AF *citisein* < OF *cite.* See CITY.] —**Syn. 1** national, subject. **3** resident.

cit·i·zen·ess (sit′ə zən is) *n.* a woman citizen.

citizen of the world a person who is interested in the affairs of the whole world; cosmopolitan.

cit·i·zen·ry (sit′ə zən rē) *n.* **-ries.** citizens as a group.

cit·i·zen·ship (sit′ə zən ship′) *n.* **1** the condition of being a citizen. **2** the duties, rights, and privileges of a citizen.

cit·rate (sit′rāt) *n.* a salt or ester of citric acid.

cit·ric (sit′rik) *adj.* of or from fruits such as lemons, limes, oranges, etc.

citric acid a white, odorless, sour-tasting acid that occurs in such fruits as lemons, limes, etc. It is used as a flavoring, as a medicine, and in making dyes. *Formula*: $C_6H_8O_7$

cit·rine (sit′rin) *n. adj.* pale yellow. [< F *citrin* < L *citrus* citrus tree]

cit·ron (sit′rən) *n.* **1** a pale-yellow fruit resembling a lemon but larger, less acid, and having a thicker rind. **2** the candied rind of this fruit, used in fruit cakes, plum pudding, candies, etc. **3** the shrub or small tree that this fruit grows on. **4** a citron melon. [< F < Ital. *citrone* < L *citrus* citrus tree]

cit·ron·el·la (sit′rən el′ə) *n.* **1** an oil used in making perfume, soap, liniment, etc. and for keeping mosquitoes away. **2** a fragrant grass of S. Asia from which this oil is made. [< NL; from its citronlike smell]

citron melon a kind of small watermelon having white flesh.

cit·rous (sit′rəs) *adj.* having to do with fruits such as lemons, limes, oranges, etc.

cit·rus (sit′rəs) *n.* **1** any tree bearing lemons, limes, oranges, or similar fruit. **2** Also, **citrus fruit.** the fruit of such a tree. —*adj.* of such trees. [< L]

cit·tern (sit′ərn) *n.* a musical instrument resembling a guitar, popular in the 16th and 17th centuries. [blend of L *cithara* cithara and E *gittern*]

cit·y (sit′ē) *n.* **cit·ies,** *adj.* —*n.* **1** a large and important town. **2** in Canada, a municipality, varying in size from province to province, that manages its own affairs: *In Ontario a city must have at least 15,000 persons. Montreal and Toronto are the largest cities in Canada.* **3** in the United States, a similar division of local government. **4** in the United Kingdom, a borough, usually the seat of a bishop, which has been granted the rank of "city" by royal authority. **5** a city-state. **6 the City,** in London, the business and financial district. —*adj.* **1** of a city. **2** in a city. [ME < OF < L *civitas* citizenship, state, city < *civis* citizen]

city editor 1 the newspaper editor in charge of collecting and editing local news. **2** *Brit.* financial editor.

city fathers the councilmen, aldermen, magistrates, or other leading men of a city.

city hall 1 the headquarters of the local government in a city: *The mayor's office is in the city hall.* **2** a building housing a local government. **3** the officials of a municipal government, considered collectively.

city manager a person appointed by a city council or commission to manage the government of a city.

city of David 1 Jerusalem. **2** Bethlehem.

City of God heaven.

City of Seven Hills Rome.

city slicker *Slang.* a glib, worldly-wise person; one who is smooth and sophisticated.

cit·y-state (sit′ē stāt′) *n.* an independent state consisting of a city and the territories depending on it, as in ancient Greece and Renaissance Italy.

civ·et (siv′it) *n.* **1** a yellowish secretion of certain glands of the civet cat. This secretion has a musky smell and is used in making perfume. **2** the civet cat. [< F *civette* < Ital. < Arabic *zabad*]

civet cat 1 a small, spotted mammal of Africa, Europe,

hat, āge, cãre, fär; let, ēqual, tėrm; it, īce
hot, ōpen, ôrder; oil, out; cup, pu̇t, rüle, ūse
əbove, takən, pencəl, lemən, circəs
ch, child; ng, long; sh, ship
th, thin; ᴛʜ, then; zh, measure

and Asia, having glands that secrete a yellowish substance with a musky smell. **2** any of certain similar animals.

civ·ic (siv′ik) *adj.* **1** of a city. **2** of or having to do with citizenship: *Every person has some civic duties, such as obeying the law, voting, or paying taxes.* **3** of citizens. [< L *civicus* < *civis* citizen]

civic centre or **center 1** the departmental headquarters of the government of a city. **2** buildings housing the city hall, courts, etc., usually in the centre of the city. **3** a building serving as a centre for community activities, concerts, games, etc.

civ·ics (siv′iks) *n.* the study of the duties, rights, and privileges of citizens.

civ·ies (siv′ēz) *n.pl.* civvies.

civ·il (siv′əl) *adj.* **1** of a citizen or citizens; having to do with citizens. **2** of or having to do with the government, state, or nation: *civil servants.* **3** not connected with the armed services or the church. **4** polite; courteous: *The stranger spoke to us in a very civil way.* **5** having to do with the private rights of individuals or with legal proceedings connected with these rights: *civil law.* **6** such as occurs among citizens of one community, state, or nation: *civil war, civil strife.* **7** of, belonging to, or in accordance with Roman civil law, or civil law derived from it. [< L *civilis* < *civis* citizen] —**Syn. 4** respectful, gracious, affable. See **polite.**

civil defence or **defense 1** the program for survival in the event of enemy attack on civilian centres, especially by aircraft, missiles, or nuclear weapons. The army and civil groups work together in planning civil defence. **2 Civil Defence,** the organization responsible for the planning and operation of the civil defence program: *The Civil Defence will be responsible for helping the wounded, fighting fires, distributing food, etc.*

civil disobedience refusal because of one's principles to obey the laws, especially by not paying taxes.

civil engineer a person whose profession is civil engineering.

civil engineering the planning and directing of the construction of bridges, roads, harbors, etc.

ci·vil·ian (sə vil′yən) *n.* a person who is not in the armed services. —*adj.* of civilians; not of the armed services: *Soldiers often wear civilian clothes when on leave.*

ci·vil·i·ty (sə vil′ə tē) *n.* **-ties. 1** politeness; courtesy. **2** an act of politeness or courtesy.

civ·i·li·za·tion (siv′ə lə zā′shən or siv′ə lī zā′shən) *n.* **1** the act of civilizing. **2** the process of becoming civilized; improvement in culture. **3** a civilized condition; advanced stage in social development. **4** nations and peoples that have reached advanced stages in social development: *All civilization should be aroused against war.* **5** the culture and ways of living of a people, nation, etc.: *Chinese civilization differs from ours.*

civ·i·lize (siv′ə līz′) *v.* **-lized, -liz·ing. 1** bring out of a savage or barbarian condition; train in culture, science, and art: *The church did much to civilize the Anglo-Saxons.* **2** improve in culture and good manners; refine. [< Med.L *civilizare* < L *civilis.* See CIVIL.] —**civ′i·liz′er,** *n.*

civ·i·lized (siv′ə līzd′) *adj.* **1** advanced in social customs, art, and science: *a civilized people.* **2** of nations or persons so advanced: *civilized entertainments.* **3** showing culture and good manners; refined.

civ·i·liz·ing (siv′ə līz′ing) *adj.* that civilizes; promoting civilization.

civil law 1 the body of law that regulates and protects private rights and is controlled and used by civil (not military) courts, opposed to *criminal law* and *military law.* **2** Roman law or a system of law based on Roman law.

civil liberty the right of a person to do, think, and say what he pleases as long as he does not harm anyone else or break established laws.

civil list 1 a list of sums appropriated to pay the members of the civil government and civil servants (obsolete in Canada). 2 in the United Kingdom, a list of sums appropriated by Parliament as allowances for the sovereign and members of the royal family.

civ·il·ly (siv′ə lē) *adv.* 1 politely; courteously. 2 according to the civil law.

civil marriage a marriage performed by a government official, rather than by a clergyman.

civil rights the rights of a citizen.

civil servant a member of the civil service.

civil service the federal or provincial body that administers public service and conducts the day-to-day work of government departments.

civil war 1 a war between two groups of citizens of one nation. 2 **Civil War, a** in England, the war between the king and Parliament, 1642-1646 and 1648-1652. **b** in the United States, the war between the northern and southern states, 1861-1865.

civil year the calendar year.

civ·vies (siv′ēz) *n.pl. Informal.* civilian clothes, as distinguished from military uniform. Also, **civies.**

ck. *pl.* **cks.** cask.

Cl chlorine.

cl. 1 centilitre. 2 class. 3 clause. 4 clerk. 5 clergyman.

clab·ber (klab′ər) *n.* thick sour milk. —*v.* become thick in souring; curdle. [< Irish *clabar* curds, short for *bainne clabair* bonnyclabber (curdled milk)]

clack (klak) *v.* 1 make or cause to make a short, sharp sound: *Her needles clacked as she knitted.* 2 chatter. —*n.* 1 a short, sharp sound: *We heard the clack of her heels on the sidewalk.* 2 chatter. [imitative] —**clack′er,** *n.*

clad (klad) *v.* a pt. and a pp. of **clothe.**

claim (klām) *v.* 1 say that one has and demand that others recognize (a right, title, possession, etc.); assert one's right to: *claim a tract of land.* 2 demand as one's own or one's right: *Does anyone claim this pencil?* 3 declare as a fact; say strongly; maintain: *She claimed that her answer was correct.* 4 require; call for; deserve: *Business claims his attention.* [ME < OF *clamer* < L *clamare* call, proclaim]
—*n.* 1 a demand for something due; assertion of a right. 2 a right or title to something. 3 something that is claimed. 4 a piece of public land that a settler or prospector marks out for himself. When the government offers the land for sale, the settler must buy his claim or forfeit it. 5 the assertion of something as a fact. [ME < OF *claim(e).* See v.] —**claim′a·ble,** *adj.* —**claim′er,** *n.* —**Syn.** *v.* 2 exact. See **demand.**

claim·ant (klām′ənt) *n.* one who makes a claim.

clair·voy·ance (klãr voi′əns) *n.* 1 the supposed power of knowing about things that are out of sight. 2 exceptional insight. [< F]

clair·voy·ant (klãr voi′ənt) *adj.* 1 supposedly having the power of seeing things that are out of sight. 2 exceptionally keen. —*n.* a person who has, or claims to have, the power of seeing things that are out of sight: *The clairvoyant claimed to be able to locate lost articles, and to give news of faraway people.* [< F *clairvoyant* clear-sighted < *clair* clear + *voyant,* ppr. of *voir* see]

clam (klam) *n. v.* **clammed, clam·ming.** —*n.* 1 a mollusc resembling an oyster, having a shell in two halves. Clams live in sand along the seashore or at the edges of rivers, lakes, etc. Some clams are edible. 2 *Informal.* a person who speaks very little. —*v.* 1 go out after clams; dig for clams. 2 **clam up,** *Slang.* refuse to speak or give information. [apparently special use of *clam* pair of pincers; OE *clamm* fetter] —**clam′like′,** *adj.*

clam·bake (klam′bāk′) *n.* 1 a picnic where clams are baked or steamed. A clambake may be an elaborate meal, with much to eat besides clams. 2 *Informal.* a large, noisy entertainment or social gathering.

clam·ber (klam′bər) *v.* 1 climb, using both hands and feet; climb awkwardly or with difficulty; scramble. 2 of plants, climb by means of tendrils, etc. 3 climb or struggle into a position of eminence; attain with effort. —*n.* an awkward or difficult climb. [ME *clambre(n).* Related to CLIMB.] —**clam′ber·er,** *n.*

clam·my (klam′ē) *adj.* **-mi·er, -mi·est.** cold and damp. [ME; probably < *clammen* smear < OE *clǣman*; cf. OE *clām* clay] —**clam′mi·ness,** *n.*

clam·or or **clam·our** (klam′ər) *n.* 1 a loud noise, continual uproar; shouting. 2 a noisy demand or complaint. 3 any loud, sustained noise. —*v.* 1 make a loud noise or continual uproar; shout. 2 demand or complain noisily. [ME < OF < L *clamor* < *clamare* cry out] —**clam′or·er** or **clam′our·er,** *n.*

clam·or·ous (klam′ər əs) *adj.* 1 noisy; shouting. 2 making noisy demands or complaints. —**clam′or·ous·ly,** *adv.* —**clam′or·ous·ness,** *n.*

clam·our (klam′ər) *n. v.* clamor.

clamp (klamp) *n.* a brace, band, wedge, or other device for holding things tightly together: *He used a clamp to hold the arm on the chair until the glue dried.* —*v.* 1 fasten together with a clamp; put in a clamp; strengthen with a clamp. 2 **clamp down on,** *Informal.* put pressure on; take strict measures against: *The police clamped down on careless driving.* [< MDu. *klampe*]

A clamp

clan (klan) *n.* 1 a group of related families that have the same surname and claim to be descended from a common ancestor. 2 a group of people closely joined together by some common interest. [< Scots Gaelic *clann* family] —**clan′like′,** *adj.*

clan·des·tine (klan des′tən) *adj.* secret; concealed; underhand: *a clandestine plan.* [< L *clandestinus* < *clam* secretly] —**clan·des′tine·ly,** *adv.* —**Syn.** hidden, furtive, covert. See **secret.**

clang (klang) *n.* a loud, harsh, ringing sound, as of metal being hit: *The clang of the fire bell aroused the town.* —*v.* 1 make or cause to make a clang. 2 strike together with a clang. [imitative]

clan·gor or **clang·our** (klang′gər or klang′ər) *n.* 1 continued clanging. 2 clang. [< L *clangor* < *clangere* clang]

clan·gor·ous (klang′gər əs or klang′ər əs) *adj.* clanging.

clan·gour (klang′gər or klang′ər) *n.* clangor.

clank (klangk) *n.* a sharp, harsh sound like the rattle of a heavy chain. —*v.* 1 make a sharp, harsh sound: *The swords clashed and clanked as the men fought one another.* 2 cause to clank. [imitative; probably < Du. *klank*]

clan·nish (klan′ish) *adj.* 1 of or having to do with a clan. 2 closely united; not liking outsiders. —**clan′nish·ly,** *adv.* —**clan′nish·ness,** *n.*

clans·man (klanz′mən) *n.* **-men** (-mən). a member of a clan.

clans·wom·an (klanz′wům′ən) *n.* **-wom·en.** a female member of a clan.

clap (klap) *n. v.* **clapped, clap·ping.** —*n.* 1 a sudden noise, such as a single burst of thunder, the sound of the hands struck together, or the sound of a loud slap. 2 the act of clapping: *They gave the speaker a polite clap.* 3 a hit or blow; slap: *a clap on the shoulder.*
—*v.* 1 strike together loudly: *clap one's hands.* 2 applaud by striking the hands together. 3 strike with a quick blow: *He clapped his friend on the back.* 4 put or place quickly and effectively: *The police clapped the thief into jail.* 5 of a bird, flap (the wings). 6 **clap eyes on,** *Informal.* look at; see. [OE *clæppan*]

clap·board (klap′bôrd or klab′ərd) *n.* a thin board, thicker along one edge than along the other, used to cover the outer walls of wooden buildings. —*v.* cover with clapboards.

clap·per (klap′ər) *n.* 1 a person or thing that claps. 2 the movable part inside a bell that strikes and rings the outer part. 3 a device for making noise: *We had horns and clappers at the party.*

clap·trap (klap′trap′) *n.* empty talk aimed at merely getting attention or applause. —*adj.* cheap and showy.

claque (klak) *n.* 1 a group of persons hired to applaud in a theatre. 2 a group that applauds or follows another person for selfish reasons. [< F *claque* < *claquer* clap]

clar·et (klar′ət) *n.* 1 a kind of red wine. 2 a dark,

purplish red. —*adj.* dark purplish-red. [ME < OF *claret* light-colored, dim. of *cler*. See CLEAR.]

clar·i·fi·ca·tion (klar′ə fə kā′shən) *n.* **1** the act or process of clarifying. **2** the state of being clarified.

clar·i·fi·er (klar′ə fī′ər) *n.* **1** a substance used to clarify liquids. **2** a large metal pan used in clarifying sugar.

clar·i·fy (klar′ə fī′) *v.* **-fied, -fy·ing. 1** make or become clear; purify: *The cook clarified the fat by heating it with a little water and straining it through cloth.* **2** make clear; explain: *The explanation in the footnote clarified the difficult sentence.* [ME < OF *clarifier* < LL *clarificare* < L *clarus* clear + *facere* make]

clar·i·net (klar′ə net′) *n.* a wooden wind musical instrument with a single reed, played by means of holes and keys. [< L *clarinette,* dim. of *clarine* bell < L *clarus* clear]

A clarinet

clar·i·net·tist or **clar·i·net·ist** (klar′ə net′ist) *n.* a person who plays a clarinet.

clar·i·on (klar′ē ən) *adj.* clear and shrill. —*n.* **1** a trumpet with clear, shrill tones. **2** *Poetic.* the sound made by this trumpet. **3** *Poetic.* a clear, shrill sound like it. [< Med.L *clario, -onis* < L *clarus* clear]

clar·i·o·net (klar′ē ə net′) *n.* clarinet.

clar·i·ty (klar′ə tē) *n.* clearness. [< L *claritas*]

clar·sach (klär′saH) *n.* **clar·saich** (klär′siH). the ancient festival harp of Ireland and Scotland, having from 29 to 58 strings. [< Gaelic]

clash (klash) *n.* **1** a loud, harsh sound like that of two things running into each other, or striking metal, or of bells rung together but not in tune. **2** a strong disagreement; conflict: *a clash of opinion.*
—*v.* **1** strike with a clash. **2** throw, shut, etc. with a clash. **3** disagree strongly; conflict: *Your feelings and your judgment sometimes clash. These two colors clash badly.* [imitative] —**clash′er,** *n.* —**clash′ing·ly,** *adv.*
—**Syn.** *n.* **2** discord, collision.

clasp (klasp) *n.* **1** something to fasten two parts or pieces together. A buckle on a belt is one kind of clasp. **2** a close hold with the arms or hands. **3** a firm grip with the hand: *He gave my hand a warm clasp.* **4** a small bar of metal placed across the ribbon of a medal, indicating the battle area, etc. in which the medal was won.
—*v.* **1** fasten together with a clasp. **2** hold closely with the arms or hands: *The mother clasped her baby to her breast.* **3** grip firmly with the hand. [ME *claspe(n)*] —**clasp′er,** *n.* —**Syn.** *v.* **1** hook. **2** embrace, hug. **3** grasp, clutch.

clasp knife a knife with a blade or blades folding into the handle; especially, one with a clasp to hold each blade open.

class (klas) *n.* **1** a group of persons or things alike in some way; kind; sort. **2** a group of students taught together. **3** a meeting of such a group: *The class was at 9:00 a.m.* **4** a group of pupils entering a school together and graduating in the same year: *The class of 1970 is to graduate in 1970.* **5** a rank or division of society: *the middle class.* **6** a system of ranks or divisions in society. **7** *U.S.* a group of military draftees of the same age. **8** high rank in society. **9** grade; quality: *First class is the best and most costly way to travel.* **10** *Slang.* excellence; style. **11** in biology, a group of animals or plants ranking below a phylum or sub-kingdom and above an order: *Crustaceans and insects are two classes in the phylum of arthropods.*
—*v.* put or be in a class or group. [< L *classis* class, fleet < dial. Gk. *klasis* a calling, summoning]

class. 1 classical. **2** classified.

class·book (klas′bu̇k′) *n.* **1** a book in which a teacher records the absences and keeps the grades of students. **2** an annual book usually published by the graduating class of a high school or college. It contains pictures of the students, teachers, school buildings, etc.

class day *Esp.U.S.* the day on which the members of a class celebrate their graduation with special ceremonies.

hat, āge, cãre, fär; let, ēqual, tėrm; it, īce
hot, ōpen, ôrder; oil, out; cup, pu̇t, rüle, ūse
əbove, takən, pencəl, lemən, circəs
ch, child; ng, long; sh, ship
th, thin; ᴛʜ, then; zh, measure

clas·sic (klas′ik) *adj.* **1** of the highest grade or quality; excellent; first-class. **2** of or having to do with the literature, art, and life of ancient Greece and Rome. **3** in literature, music, art, etc.: **a** resembling or modelled on the literature, art, etc. of ancient Greece or Rome. **b** conforming to set principles of simplicity, regularity, and restraint. **4** famous in literature or history.
—*n.* **1** a literary or artistic work of the highest quality: "*Robinson Crusoe*" *is a classic.* **2** an author or artist of acknowledged excellence: *Shakespeare is a classic.* **3** a person who follows the principles of classicism. **4** in sports, a race, match, etc. of particular importance, involving participants of proved excellence. **5 the classics,** the literature of ancient Greece and Rome. [< L *classicus* < *classis.* See CLASS.]

clas·si·cal (klas′ə kəl) *adj.* **1** classic (defs. 1, 2, and 3). **2** acquainted with or having to do with the classics: *classical studies, classical students.* **3** based on the classics. Tennyson's "Ulysses" is a classical poem. **4** orthodox and sound, but not quite up to date: *classical physics.* **5** in music: **a** of high artistic quality, especially as contrasted with popular or folk music. **b** conforming to certain recognized forms, such as the fugue, sonata, etc. **c** of or having to do with classicism (def. 5). Haydn and Mozart were classical composers.

classical college *Cdn.* in French Canada, an educational establishment at the secondary-school and college levels that offers an eight-year course, mainly in the classics and liberal arts, leading to the B.A. degree, which is conferred by the university to which the college is affiliated.

clas·si·cal·ly (klas′ik lē) *adv.* in a classical style; according to the manner of classic authors.

clas·si·cism (klas′ə siz′əm) *n.* **1** the principles of the literature and art of ancient Greece and Rome. They include simplicity, regularity, and restraint. **2** the following of these principles. **3** knowledge of the literature of ancient Greece and Rome; classical scholarship. **4** an idiom or form from Greek or Latin introduced into another language. **5** in music, a style developed in Europe during the latter half of the 18th century, characterized by simplicity, dignity, proportion, and elegance.

clas·si·cist (klas′ə sist) *n.* **1** a follower of the principles of classicism in literature and art. **2** an expert in the literature of ancient Greece and Rome. **3** a person who urges the study of Greek and Latin.

clas·si·fi·ca·tion (klas′ə fə kā′shən) *n.* **1** the act or process of arranging in classes or groups; a grouping according to some system. **2** the result of classifying; a systematic arrangement in groups or classes. **3** in biology, the grouping of plants and animals on the basis of ancestral relationship or structure. The categories now used are (in descending order): phylum (also, in botany, division), class, order, family, genus, and species.

clas·si·fied (klas′ə fīd′) *adj.* **1** of government documents, having a classification as secret, confidential, or restricted. **2** *Informal.* secret.

classified advertisement an advertisement inserted in a special part of a newspaper, magazine, etc. under one of a set of special headings.

clas·si·fy (klas′ə fī′) *v.* **-fied, -fy·ing.** arrange in classes or groups; group according to some system: *Men in the post office classify mail according to the places where it is to go.* [< L *classis* class + E *-fy*] —**clas′si·fi′a·ble,** *adj.* —**clas′si·fi′er,** *n.*

class·less (klas′lis) *adj.* not divided into classes, especially social and economic classes: *a classless society.* —**class′less·ness,** *n.*

classmate (klas′māt′) *n.* a member of the same class in school.

class·room (klas′rüm′ or -ru̇m′) *n.* a room where classes meet in school; schoolroom.

class struggle any conflict between divisions of society, especially between capital and labor.

class·y (klas′ē) *adj.* **-i·er, -i·est.** *Informal.* of, or appearing to be of, high social or economic standing; stylish; elegant.

clat·ter (klat′ər) *n.* **1** a confused noise like that of many plates being struck together: *There was such a clatter in the big dining room that we could hardly hear one another talk.* **2** noisy talk. [< v.]
—*v.* **1** move or fall with confused noise; make a confused noise: *The horses clattered over the stones.* **2** talk fast and noisily. **3** cause to clatter. [OE *clatrian*] —**clat′ter·er,** *n.*

clause (kloz or klôz) *n.* **1** that part of a sentence having a subject and predicate. In "He came before we left," "He came" is a **main clause,** and "before we left" is a **subordinate clause.** A subordinate caluse functions as a noun, adjective, or adverb. **2** a single provision of a law, treaty, or any other written agreement: *There is a clause in our contract that says we may not keep a dog in this building.* [< Med.L *clausa* for L *clausula* close of a period < *claudere* close]
☞ A clause (def. 1) may be either of two kinds—main or subordinate. Main clauses are grammatically independent; that is, they can stand alone as sentences. A compound sentence is made up of two or more main clauses, of equal grammatical value, that are joined by *and, but, for, nor,* or some other co-ordinating conjunction: *Tim enjoys trigonometry, and Kathy likes solid geometry. Tim enjoys studying, but Kathy prefers dancing.* **Subordinate** clauses cannot stand alone as sentences. Their complete meaning is generally dependent upon the rest of the sentence: *If he comes, you can go home.* Without the main clause, the subordinate clause "If he comes" does not make complete sense—there is no explanation of the "If." A complex sentence has at least one main clause to which one or more subordinate clauses are connected by *as, because, since, when,* or some other subordinating conjunction, or by a relative pronoun, *who, that,* or *which*: *Because he is ill, he will not be able to attend class. Do the work when you have time.*

claus·tro·pho·bi·a (klos′trə fō′bē ə or klôs′trə fō′bē ə) *n.* a morbid fear of enclosed spaces. [< NL < L *claustrum* closed place + E *-phobia* fear]

claus·tro·pho·bic (klos′trə fō′bik or klôs′trə fō′bik) *adj.* of or having to do with claustrophobia.

claus·tro·pho·bi·cal·ly (klos′trə fō′bə klē or klôs′trə fō′bə klē) *adv.* in a claustrophobic manner; in a way that is or feels confined or stifled.

cla·vate (klā′vāt) *adj.* club-shaped. [< L *clavatus* < *clava* club]

clave (klāv) *v. Archaic.* a pt. of **cleave**[2].

clav·i·chord (klav′ə kôrd′) *n.* a stringed musical instrument with a keyboard. The piano evolved from it. [< Med.L *clavichordium* < L *clavis* key + *chorda* string]

clav·i·cle (klav′ə kəl) *n.* the collarbone. [< L *clavicula* bolt, dim. of *clavis* key]

clav·i·er[1] (klav′ē ər or klə vēr′) *n.* **1** the keyboard of a piano, organ, etc. **2** a soundless keyboard used for practice. [< F *clavier,* orig. key bearer < *clef* key < L *clavis*]

clav·i·er[2] (klə vēr′) *n.* any musical instrument having a keyboard, such as the harpsichord and the clavichord. [< G *Klavier* < F *clavier* keyboard, clavier[1]]

claw (klo or klô) *n.* **1** a sharp, hooked nail on a bird's or animal's foot. **2** a foot with such sharp, hooked nails. **3** one of the pincers of a lobster, crab, etc. **4** anything like a claw. The part of a hammer used for pulling nails is the claw.
—*v.* scratch, tear, seize, or pull with claws or hands. [OE *clawu*] —**claw′-like′,** *adj.*

The claws of a bird

claw hammer 1 a hammer with one end of the head curved like a claw and forked for pulling nails. **2** *Informal.* a dress coat; swallowtail coat.

clay (klā) *n.* **1** a stiff, sticky kind of earth, that can be easily shaped when wet and hardens after drying or baking. Bricks, dishes, and vases may be made from clay. **2** earth. **3** in the Bible, the human body. [OE *clæg*]

clay·ey (klā′ē) *adj.* **clay·i·er, clay·i·est. 1** of, like, or containing clay. **2** covered or smeared with clay.

clay·more (klā′môr) *n.* a heavy, two-edged sword, formerly used by Scottish Highlanders. [< Scots Gaelic *claidheamh mor* great sword]

clay pigeon 1 a saucerlike clay target thrown in the air. **2** any person in an especially vulnerable position.

CLC Canadian Labor Congress.

-cle *suffix.* **1** little, as in *corpuscle, particle.* **2** other meanings, as in *receptacle, vehicle.* [< L *-culus, -cula, -culum* (dim.) or < F *-cle* (< L)]

clean (klēn) *adj.* **1** free from dirt or filth; not soiled or stained: *clean clothes.* **2** pure; innocent: *a clean heart.* **3** having clean habits: *Cats are clean animals.* **4** of atomic weapons, causing little or no radio-active fall-out. **5** fit for food: *Moslems and Jews do not consider pork a clean meat.* **6** clear; even; regular: *a clean cut.* **7** well-shaped; trim: *a clean figure.* **8** clever; skilful: *a clean performance.* **9** complete; entire; total: *make a clean sweep.* **10** free from foreign matter; pure; unmixed. **11** of printer's proofs, relatively free from corrections or alterations. **12** of written or typed copy, free from errors or corrections; final; fair.
—*adv.* **1** completely; entirely; totally: *The horse jumped clean over the brook.* **2** in a clean manner.
—*v.* **1** make clean: *clean a room.* **2** undergo cleaning: *This room cleans easily because it doesn't have much furniture in it.* **3** do cleaning: *I'm going to clean this morning.* **4 clean out, a** make clean by emptying. **b** empty; use up. **c** *Slang.* deprive of money, especially cash. **5 clean up, a** make clean by removing dirt, rubbish, etc. **b** put in order. **c** *Informal.* finish; complete. **d** *Slang.* make money; profit. [OE *clǣne*]
Syn. *adj.* **1** unstained, unsoiled. **2** chaste, virtuous. –*v.* **1 Clean, cleanse** = make free from dirt or filth. **Clean** is the general word meaning "to remove dirt, impurities, or stains," especially from objects: *The men cleaned the streets.* **Cleanse,** formal or archaic in the sense of "make clean," is used commonly in the sense of "make pure," applying particularly to removing impurities by chemical or other technical processes: *Health experts are trying to cleanse the air in cities. We cleanse wounds.*

clean-cut (klēn′kut′) *adj.* **1** having clear, sharp outlines. **2** well-shaped. **3** clear; definite; distinct. **4** having a clear, definite character or a distinct personality.

clean·er (klēn′ər) *n.* **1** a person whose work is keeping buildings, windows, or other objects clean. **2** a tool or machine for cleaning. **3** anything that removes dirt, grease, or stains.

clean-limbed (klēn′limd′) *adj.* having well-shaped limbs.

clean·li·ness (klen′lē nis) *n.* cleanness; habitual cleanness.

clean·ly[1] (klen′lē) *adj.* **-li·er, -li·est.** clean; habitually clean: *A cat is a cleanly animal.* [OE *clǣnlīc*]

clean·ly[2] (klēn′lē) *adv.* in a clean manner: *The butcher's knife cut cleanly through the meat.* [OE *clǣnlīce*]

clean·ness (klēn′nis) *n.* a clean condition or quality.

cleanse (klenz) *v.* **cleansed, cleans·ing. 1** make clean. **2** make pure. [OE *clǣnsian* < *clǣne* clean]
—**cleans′a·ble,** *adj.* —**cleans′er,** *n.* —**Syn. 1** See **clean. 2** purify.

cleans·er (klenz′ər) *n.* a substance that cleans: *The housewife can choose from many cleansers.*

clean-shav·en (klēn′shāv′ən) *adj.* with the face shaved.

cleans·ing (klenz′ing) *n.* the act or process of making clean. —*adj.* that cleanses.

clean-up (klēn′up′) *n.* **1** a cleaning up. **2** *Slang.* an exceptional amount of money made on a transaction; profit.

clear (klēr) *adj.* **1** not cloudy; bright; light: *a clear day.* **2** transparent: *clear glass.* **3** having a pure, even color: *a clear blue.* **4** not confused; easily seen, heard, or understood; plain; distinct: *a clear idea, a clear voice.* **5** sure; certain: *It is clear that it is going to rain.* **6** not blocked or obstructed; open: *a clear view.* **7** without touching; without being caught: *The ship was clear of the iceberg.* **8** free from blame or guilt; innocent: *The police thought the man was a thief, but they learned that he was clear.* **9** free from debts or charges: *clear profit.* **10** without limitation; complete: *the clear contrary.* **11** of lumber, free from knots or other imperfections.

—*v.* **1** make clear; get clear: *He cleared the field of trees.* **2** become clear: *It rained and then it cleared.* **3** remove to leave a space clear: *She cleared the dishes from the table.* **4** get by or over without touching or being caught: *The horse cleared the fence.* **5** make free from blame or guilt; prove to be innocent: *The jury's verdict cleared the accused man.* **6** make as profit free from debts or charges. **7** get (a ship or cargo) free by meeting requirements on entering or leaving a port. **8** leave a port after doing this. **9** give authority to or for: *The control tower cleared the airplane for landing.* **10** exchange (cheques and bills) and settle accounts between different banks. **11** settle a business account or certify a cheque as valid. **12 clear away** or **off, a** remove to leave a space clear. **b** *Informal.* disappear; go away. **c** clear dishes, etc. from a table. **13 clear out, a** make clear by throwing out or emptying. **b** *Informal.* go away; leave. **14 clear up, a** make or become clear. **b** put in order by clearing. **c** explain: *John cleared up the question of why he had not been there by saying that he had been ill.* **d** become clear after a storm.
—*adv.* **1** in a clear manner. **2** completely; entirely: *The bullet went clear through the door.*
—*n.* **in the clear, a** between the outside parts; in interior measurement: *The house was 40 feet wide, in the clear.* **b** free of guilt, blame, or suspicion. **c** free from limitations or encumbrances: *Having paid all his debts, he was finally in the clear again.* **d** in plain text; not in cipher or code. [ME *cler* < OF < L *clarus*]
—**clear′ly,** *adv.* —**clear′ness,** *n.* —**Syn.** *adj.* **5** evident, obvious, manifest, apparent, patent. -*v.* **5** absolve, acquit.

clear·ance (klēr′ən s) *n.* **1** the act of making clear. **2** a clear space; the distance between things that pass by each other without touching. **3** the meeting of requirements to get a ship or cargo free on entering or leaving a port. **4** a certificate showing this. **5** authority; permission to proceed: *Before taking off the pilot got clearance from the central tower.* **6** the exchanging of cheques and bills and settling of accounts between different banks.

clear-cut (klēr′kut′) *adj.* **1** having clear, sharp outlines. **2** clear; definite; distinct: *He had clear-cut ideas about his work.*

clear-eyed (klēr′īd′) *adj.* **1** having bright, clear eyes. **2** having acute and undistorted perception.

clear-head·ed (klēr′hed′id) *adj.* having or showing a clear understanding. —**clear′-head′ed·ly,** *adv.* —**clear′-head′ed·ness,** *n.*

clear·ing (klēr′ing) *n.* **1** an open space of cleared land in a forest. **2** exchanging of cheques and bills and settling of accounts between different banks.

clearing house a place where banks exchange cheques and bills and settle their accounts.

clear-sight·ed (klēr′sīt′id) *adj.* **1** able to see clearly. **2** able to understand or think clearly. —**clear′-sight′ed·ly,** *adv.* —**clear′-sight′ed·ness,** *n.*

clear·sto·ry (klēr′stô′rē) *n.* **-ries.** clerestory.

cleat (klēt) *n.* **1** a strip of wood or iron fastened across anything for support or for sure footing. A gangway has cleats to keep people from slipping. **2** a small, wedge-shaped block fastened to a mast, spar, etc. as a support, check, etc. **3** a piece of wood or iron used for securing ropes or lines. **4** a piece of metal, wood, or stiff leather attached to the sole or heel of a shoe to prevent slipping.
—*v.* fasten to or with a cleat.
[ME *cleete*]

A cleat (def. 3)

cleav·age (klēv′ij) *n.* **1** a split; division. **2** the way in which something splits or divides. **3** in biology, any of the series of divisions by which a fertilized egg develops into an embryo. **4** in chemistry, the splitting of a compound into simpler compounds. **5** in mineralogy, a tendency in some rocks and crystals to break in definite layers.

cleave[1] (klēv) *v.* **cleft** or **cleaved** or **clove, cleft** or **cleaved** or **clo·ven, cleav·ing. 1** split; divide. **2** pass through; pierce; penetrate: *The airplane cleaved the clouds.* **3** make by cutting: *They cleft a path through the wilderness.* [OE *clēofan*] —**cleav′a·ble,** *adj.*

hat, āge, cãre, fär; let, ēqual, tėrm; it, īce
hot, ōpen, ôrder; oil, out; cup, pu̇t, rüle, ūse
əbove, takən, pencəl, lemən, circəs
ch, child; ng, long; sh, ship
th, thin; ᴛʜ, then; zh, measure

cleave[2] (klēv) *v.* **cleaved** or (*Archaic*) **clave, cleaved, cleav·ing.** hold fast (*to*); cling; be faithful (*to*): *cleave to an idea.* [OE *cleofian*]

cleav·er (klēv′ər) *n.* **1** one that cleaves. **2** a cutting tool with a heavy blade and a short handle. A butcher uses a cleaver to chop through meat or bone.

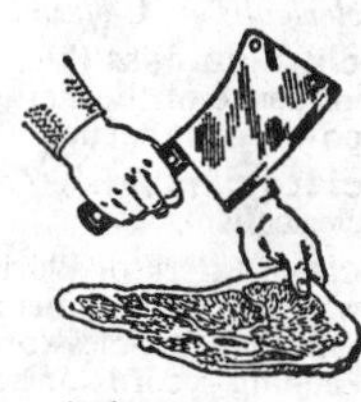
A cleaver

cleek (klēk) *n.* a golf club with a narrow head and less slope than a midiron. [related to CLUTCH]

clef (klef) *n.* in music, a symbol indicating the pitch of the notes on a staff. [< F < L *clavis* key]

cleft (kleft) *v.* a pt. and a pp. of **cleave**[1]. —*adj.* split; divided.
—*n.* a space or opening made by splitting; crack. [OE (*ge*)*clyft*] —**Syn.** *n.* fissure, crevice, chink.

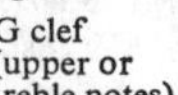
G clef (upper or treble notes) F clef (lower or bass notes)

cleft palate a narrow opening running lengthwise in the roof of the mouth, caused by failure of the two parts of the palate to join.

clem·a·tis (klem′ə tis or klə mā′tis) *n.* a vine having clusters of fragrant white, red, or purple flowers. [< L < Gk. *klēmatis* < *klēma* vine branch]

clem·en·cy (klem′ən sē) *n.* **-cies. 1** mercy: *The judge showed clemency to the prisoner.* **2** mildness: *the clemency of the weather.* —**Syn. 1** See **mercy.**

clem·ent (klem′ənt) *adj.* **1** merciful. **2** mild. [< L *clemens, -entis*] —**clem′ent·ly,** *adv.*

clench (klench) *v.* **1** close tightly together: *clench one's fists, clench one's teeth.* **2** grasp firmly; grip tightly: *The policeman clenched his prisoner's arm.* **3** clinch (a nail, etc.).
—*n.* a firm grasp; tight grip: *I felt the clench of his hand on my arm.* [OE (*be*)*clencan* hold fast] —**clench′er,** *n.*
Syn. *v.* **1, 2 Clench, clinch** agree in their basic meaning of holding fast or making hold fast, but differ in emphasis and application. **Clench** emphasizes the idea of holding fast by clamping together and is used in the senses of close tightly (fist, teeth, lips, etc.) and grasp firmly (a hammer, etc.). **Clinch** emphasizes the idea of fastening firmly and securely, and applies chiefly to fastening nails and bolts, etc., or fastening things together.

clep·sy·dra (klep′sə drə) *n.* **-dras, -drae** (-drē′ or -drī′). in ancient times, a device for measuring time by the flow of water, mercury, etc. through a small opening. [< L < Gk. *klepsydra* < *kleptein* steal + *hydōr* water]

clere·sto·ry (klēr′stô′rē) *n.* **-ries. 1** in architecture, the upper part of the wall of a church, having windows in it above the roofs of the aisles. **2** any similar structure. Also, **clearstory.** [apparently < *clere* clear + *story*[2]]

cler·gy (klėr′jē) *n.* **-gies.** persons ordained for religious work; ministers, pastors, rabbis, etc. [ME < OF *clergie,* ult. < L *clericus.* See CLERIC.]

cler·gy·man (klėr′jē mən) *n.* **-men** (-mən). a member of the clergy; minister; pastor; priest; rabbi.

Clergy Reserves the lands set aside in Lower and Upper Canada in 1791 for the support of a Protestant clergy. In practice, this was interpreted to mean the Church of England clergy.

cler·ic (kler′ik) *n.* a clergyman. —*adj.* of a clergyman or the clergy. [< L *clericus* < Gk. *klērikos* < *klēros* clergy; originally, lot, allotment; first applied (in the Septuagint) to the Levites, the service of God being the priest's lot. Doublet of CLERK.]

cler·i·cal (kler′ə kəl) *adj.* **1** of a clerk or clerks; for clerks: *Keeping records or accounts and copying letters are clerical jobs in an office.* **2** of a clergyman or the clergy. **3** supporting the power or influence of the clergy in politics.
—*n.* **1** a clergyman. **2** a supporter of the power or influence of the clergy in politics. **3 clericals,** *pl.* the distinctive clothes worn by certain clergymen. [< LL *clericalis* < L *clericus.* See CLERIC.] —**cler′i·cal·ly,** *adv.*

cler·i·cal·ism (kler′ə kəl iz′əm) *n.* **1** the power or influence of the clergy in politics. **2** the support of such power or influence.

cler·i·cal·ist (kler′ə kəl ist) *n.* a person who favors clericalism.

clerk (klėrk or klärk) *n.* **1** a person whose work is waiting on customers and selling goods in a store; salesman or saleswoman. **2** a person whose work is keeping records or accounts, copying letters, etc. in an office. **3** an official who keeps records and takes care of regular business in a law court, legislature, etc. **4** a layman who has minor church duties. **5** *Archaic.* a clergyman. **6** *Archaic.* a person who can read and write; scholar.
—*v.* work as a clerk. [partly OE *clerc, cleric,* partly < OF *clerc* < L *clericus.* Doublet of CLERIC.]

clerk·ly (klėrk′lē or klärk′lē) *adj.* **1** of or like a clerk. **2** of the clergy. **3** *Archaic.* scholarly.

clerk·ship (klėrk′ship or klärk′-) *n.* the position or work of a clerk.

clev·er (klev′ər) *adj.* **1** having a quick mind; bright; intelligent. **2** skilful or expert in doing some particular thing: *a clever carpenter.* **3** showing skill or intelligence: *a clever trick, a clever answer.* **4** *Informal.* good-natured; obliging. [ME *cliver;* origin uncertain] —**clev′er·ly,** *adv.* —**clev′er·ness,** *n.*
Syn. 1 Clever, ingenious = having a quick mind. **Clever** is the general word, and suggests a natural quickness in learning things and skill in using the mind: *He had no training, but was clever enough to become a good salesman.* **Ingenious** = quick to see ways of doing things, skilful in inventing and clever at making things: *Some ingenious person designed the first electric can opener.* **2** adroit.

clev·is (klev′is) *n.* a U-shaped piece of metal with a bolt or pin through the ends. A clevis may be used to fasten a whippletree to a wagon or plough. [related to CLEAVE[1]]

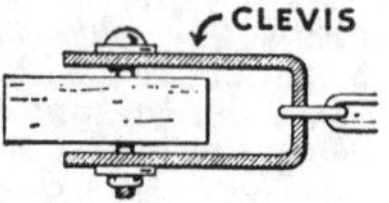

clew (klü) *n.* **1** a clue. **2** a ball of thread or yarn. **3** a lower corner of a sail. **4** a metal ring fastened there.
—*v.* raise or lower a sail by the clews. [OE *cleowen*]

cli·ché (klē shā′) *n.* a timeworn expression or idea. [< F *cliché,* pp. of *clicher* stereotype]

click (klik) *n.* **1** a light, sharp sound: *We heard the click as he turned his key in the lock.* **2** a pawl.
—*v.* **1** make a light, sharp sound. **2** cause to make such a sound: *The soldier clicked his heels together and saluted.* **3** *Slang.* **a** go well; be effective or successful: *This scene will click.* **b** come to an understanding; agree. [imitative]

cli·ent (klī′ənt) *n.* **1** a person for whom a lawyer or other professional person acts. **2** a customer. **3** in ancient Rome, a poor or humble person depending on a noble or wealthy man for assistance. **4** a personal follower; dependant. [< L *cliens, -entis* (related to *clinare* lean)] —**cli′ent·less,** *adj.*

cli·en·tele (klī′ən tel′) *n.* **1** clients; customers. **2** personal followers. **3** a number of clients. [< F < L *clientela*]

cliff (klif) *n.* a very steep slope of rock, clay, etc. [OE *clif*] —**cliff′like′,** *adj.*

cliff dweller 1 a person living in a cave or house built in a cliff. **2** *Slang.* a person living in a large apartment house.

cliff dwelling a cave or house built in a cliff.

cliff hanger *Slang.* **1** a person living in a large, tall apartment block. **2** a story, motion picture, etc. that is full of suspense, especially a serial in which each episode ends with the hero or heroine in an extremely dangerous situation. **3** a race, election, or other contest in which the result is in doubt until the very end.

cliff swallow a North American swallow that builds a bottle-shaped nest of mud, straw, and feathers, and usually fastens it to a cliff.

cli·mac·ter·ic (klī mak′tər ik or klī′mak ter′ik) *n.* **1** the time when some important event occurs, changing the course of things; crucial period. **2** menopause. **3** any of various stages of life when the body becomes fundamentally changed. —*adj.* of or like a period when some important event occurs; crucial. [< L < Gk. *klimaktērikos* of a critical period < *klimaktēr* rung of a ladder < *klimax* ladder]

cli·mac·tic (klī mak′tik) *adj.* of or forming a climax. —**cli·mac′ti·cal·ly,** *adv.*

cli·mate (klī′mit) *n.* **1** the kind of weather a place has over a period of years. Climate includes conditions of heat and cold, moisture and dryness, clearness and cloudiness, wind and calm. **2** any geographical region, with reference to its conditions of heat and cold, rainfall, wind, sunlight, etc: *The doctor ordered him to go to a drier climate.* **3** the prevailing state or trend: *the climate of public opinion.* [< L *clima, -atis* < Gk. *klima* slope (of the earth) < *klinein* incline]

cli·mat·ic (klī mat′ik) *adj.* of or having to do with climate.

cli·mat·i·cal·ly (klī mat′ik lē) *adv.* with reference to climate.

cli·ma·tol·o·gist (klī′mə tol′ə jist) *n.* an expert in climatology.

cli·ma·tol·o·gy (klī′mə tol′ə jē) *n.* the science that deals with climate.

cli·max (klī′maks) *n.* **1** the highest point; point of greatest interest; most exciting part. **2** the arrangement of ideas in a rising scale of force and interest. —*v.* bring or come to a climax. [< LL < Gk. *klimax* ladder]
—**Syn.** *n.* **1** peak, zenith, culmination.

climb (klīm) *v.* **climbed** or (*Archaic*) **clomb, climb·ing,** *n.*
—*v.* **1** go up, especially by using the hands or feet, or both; ascend: *The painter climbed the ladder. We had been climbing for hours but we had not reached the top of the mountain.* **2** rise slowly or with steady effort: *It takes a poor person many years to climb from poverty to wealth.* **3** grow upward by holding on or twining around: *Some vines climb.* **4** increase: *The price of coffee has climbed during the past year.* **5 climb down, a** go down by using the hands and feet. **b** *Informal.* give in; back down; withdraw from an impossible position or unreasonable attitude.
—*n.* **1** a climbing; ascent: *Our climb took two hours.* **2** a place to be climbed. **3** increase: *a climb in price.* [OE *climban*]
Syn. *v.* **1 Climb, ascend, mount** = go to or toward the top. **Climb** suggests a need for effort, or support of some kind: *This car will never climb that hill.* **Ascend** is more formal, but suggests going straight up, high up, or (in contrast to *climb*) up with ease: *She ascended the steps like a great lady.* **Mount** is close to *ascend,* but in contrast to it can also mean to get on top of: *He mounted the stepladder.*

climb·er (klīm′ər) *n.* **1** a person or thing that climbs. **2** *Informal.* a person who is always trying to get ahead socially. **3** a spike attached to a shoe to help in climbing. **4** a climbing plant; vine.

climbing iron one of a pair of frames having metal spikes, attached to boots to help in climbing.

clime (klīm) *n.* *Poetic.* **1** a country; region. **2** the climate. [< L *clima.* See CLIMATE.]

clinch (klinch) *v.* **1** fasten (a driven nail, a bolt, etc.) firmly by bending over the part that projects. **2** fasten (things) together in this way. **3** fix firmly; settle decisively: *A deposit of five dollars clinched the bargain.* **4** in boxing or wrestling, grasp one another tightly; grapple: *When the boxers clinched, the crowd hissed.* **5** clench.
—*n.* **1** in boxing or wrestling, a tight grasp; close grip: *The referee broke the boxers' clinch.* **2** a kind of sailor's knot in which the end of the rope is lashed back. [var. of *clench*] —**Syn.** *v.* **1** See **clench.**

clinch·er (klin′chər) *n.* **1** a tool for clinching nails, bolts, etc. **2** *Informal.* an argument, statement, etc. that is decisive.

cling (kling) *v.* **clung, cling·ing. 1** stick; hold fast: *A vine* *clings to its support. We cling to the beliefs of our fathers.* **2** keep near. **3** grasp; embrace. [OE *clingan*]

cling·ing (kling′ing) *adj.* that clings or holds fast.

cling·stone (kling′stōn′) *n.* a peach whose stone clings to the fleshy part. —*adj.* having such a stone.

clin·ic (klin′ik) *n.* **1** a place where poor people can receive medical treatment free or at low cost. A clinic is usually connected with a hospital or medical school. **2** a place for the medical treatment of certain people or diseases: *The children's clinic was open during school hours.* **3** the practical instruction of medical students by examining or treating patients in the presence of the students. **4** a class of students receiving such instruction. **5** a brief course of practical instruction in some non-medical field. [< L < Gk. *klinikos* of a bed < *klinē* bed]

clin·i·cal (klin′ə kəl) *adj.* **1** of or having to do with a clinic. **2** used or performed in a sickroom. **3** having to do with the study of disease by observation of the patient.

clin·i·cal·ly (klin′ik lē) *adv.* by clinical methods.

clinical thermometer a thermometer for measuring the temperature of the body.

clink[1] (klingk) *n.* a light, sharp, ringing sound like that of glasses hitting together. —*v.* **1** make a clink. **2** cause to clink. [ME, ? < Du. *klinken*]

clink[2] (klingk) *n. Informal.* a prison. [origin uncertain; possibly from the sound of fetters]

clink·er (klingk′ər) *n.* **1** a piece of the rough, hard mass left in a furnace or stove after coal has been burned; large, rough cinder. **2** a very hard brick. **3** a mass of bricks fused together. **4** slag. **5** *Informal.* a bad or stupid mistake, or its result. [< Du. *klinker* brick < *klinken* ring]

clink·er-built (klingk′ər bilt′) *adj.* made of boards or metal plates that overlap one another: *The lifeboat was clinker-built.* [*clinker*, dial. var. of *clincher*]

cli·nom·e·ter (klī nom′ə tər or klə nom′ə tər) *n.* an instrument for measuring deviation from the horizontal. [< L *clinare* incline + E *-meter*]

Clio (klī′ō) *n.* in Greek mythology, the Muse of history.

clip[1] (klip) *v.* **clipped, clip·ping,** *n.* —*v.* **1** trim with shears or scissors; cut; cut short: *A sheep's fleece is clipped to get wool.* **2** cut the hair or fleece of: *Our dog is clipped every summer.* **3** damage (a coin) by cutting off the edge. **4** omit sounds in pronouncing. **5** *Informal.* move fast. **6** *Informal.* hit or punch sharply. **7** cut pieces from a magazine, newspaper, etc. **8** *Informal.* swindle or rob, especially by overcharging: *clip a customer.* —*n.* **1** the act of clipping. **2** the amount of wool clipped from sheep at one time. **3** *Informal.* a fast motion. **4** *Informal.* a sharp blow or punch. **5** *Informal.* one time; single occasion: *at one clip.* [ME *clippe(n)* < ON *klippa*]

clip[2] (klip) *v.* **clipped, clip·ping,** *n.* —*v.* hold tight; fasten: *clip papers together.* —*n.* **1** something used for clipping (things) together: *a paper clip.* **2** of certain firearms: **a** a metal holder for cartridges. **b** the rounds it holds. [OE *clyppan* embrace]

clip·board (klip′ bôrd′) *n.* a board with a heavy spring clip at one end for holding papers.

clip·per (klip′ər) *n.* **1** a person who clips or cuts. **2** Often, **clippers,** *pl.* a tool for cutting. **3** a sailing ship built and rigged for speed. **4** a large, fast aircraft.

clip·ping (klip′ing) *n.* **1** a piece cut out of a newspaper, magazine, etc. **2** a piece cut out of or from something.

clique (klēk or klik) *n.* a small, exclusive set or a snobbish group of people. —*v. Informal.* form or associate in a clique. [< F *clique* < *cliquer* click] —**Syn.** See **circle.**

cli·quish (klē′kish or klik′ish) *adj.* **1** like a clique. **2** tending to form a clique. —**cli′quish·ly,** *adv.* —**cli′quish·ness,** *n.*

clo·a·ca (klō ā′kə) *n.* **-cae** (-sē or -sī). **1** a sewer. **2** a privy. **3** in zoology, a cavity in the body of birds, reptiles, amphibians, etc. into which the intestinal, urinary, and generative canals open. [< L *cloaca*, probably < *cluere* purge]

cloak (klōk) *n.* **1** an outer garment, usually loose, with or without sleeves. **2** anything that hides or conceals.

hat, āge, cãre, fär; let, ēqual, tėrm; it, īce
hot, ōpen, ôrder; oil, out; cup, pu̇t, rüle, ūse
əbove, takən, pencəl, lemən, circəs
ch, child; ng, long; sh, ship
th, thin; ᴛʜ, then; zh, measure

—*v.* **1** cover with a cloak. **2** hide; conceal: *cloak evil purposes under friendly words.* [ME < OF *cloque* < LL *clocca*, originally, bell < OIrish *cloc*. Doublet of CLOCHE, CLOCK[1].] —**Syn.** *n.* **1** mantle. **2** mask, disguise.

cloak-and-dagger (klōk′ən dag′ər) *adj.* of or having to do with spies and espionage, secret intrigue and adventure. —*adv.* in a manner suggestive of spies, secrecy, intrigue and adventure.

cloak·room (klōk′rüm′ or -ru̇m′) *n.* a room where coats, hats, etc. can be left for a time.

clob·ber (klob′ər) *v. Slang.* **1** attack violently. **2** defeat severely.

cloche (klōsh) *n.* **1** a bell-shaped glass cover to protect tender plants. **2** a woman's close-fitting hat. [< F *cloche* bell, ult. < LL *clocca.* Doublet of CLOAK, CLOCK[1].]

clock[1] (klok) *n.* **1** an instrument for measuring and showing time, specifically one that is not carried around like a watch. **2 around the clock,** all day and all night. —*v.* **1** measure the time of. **2** record (time, distance, number, etc.) mechanically: *The racing car clocked over 150 m.p.h. On his long drive Smith clocked up 400 miles by lunch time.* **3 clock in** or **out,** register on a time card the beginning or end of a day's work. [ME < MDu. *clocke* < OF *cloque* or LL *clocca.* Doublet of CLOAK, CLOCHE.] —**clock′er,** *n.* —**clock′like′,** *adj.*

clock[2] (klok) *n.* an ornamental pattern sewn or woven on the side of a stocking, extending up from the ankle. [origin uncertain]

clock·mak·er (klok′māk′ər) *n.* a man whose business is making or repairing clocks.

clock radio a radio with a built-in clock that can be set to turn the radio on or off at any desired time, used as or instead of an alarm clock.

clock·wise (klok′wīz′) *adv. adj.* in the direction in which the hands of a clock rotate.

clock·work (klok′wėrk′) *n.* **1** machinery used to run a clock, consisting of gears, wheels, and springs. **2** any mechanism like this. Many mechanical toys are run by clockwork. **3 like clockwork,** with great regularity.

clod (klod) *n.* **1** a lump of earth; lump. **2** earth; soil. **3** a stupid person; blockhead. [OE *clod*]

clod·hop·per (klod′hop′ər) *n.* **1** a clumsy boor. **2** a large, heavy shoe.

clog (klog) *v.* **clogged, clog·ging,** *n.* —*v.* **1** fill up; choke up: *Greasy water clogged the drain.* **2** become filled or choked up. **3** hinder; interfere with; hold back: *Heavy clothes clogged the swimmer.* **4** dance by beating a heavy rhythm on the floor with wooden-soled shoes. [< n.] —*n.* **1** something that hinders or interferes. **2** any weight, such as a block of wood, fastened to the leg of an animal to hinder motion. **3** a heavy shoe with a wooden sole. **4** a lighter shoe with a wooden sole, used in clog dancing. **5** a dance in which wooden-soled shoes are worn. [ME *clogge* block; origin uncertain]

clog dance 1 a dance in which the dancer wears clogs (def. 4) to beat time. **2** perform such a dance.

cloi·son·né (kloi′zə nā′; *French,* klwä zô nā′) *n.* a type of enamel ornamentation in which the patterns of the design are separated by thin metal strips fastened on the surface. —*adj.* enamelled in this way. [< F *cloisonné* partitioned < *cloison* partition, ult. < L *clausus*, pp. of *claudere* close]

clois·ter (klois′tər) *n.* **1** a covered walk along the wall of a building, with a row of pillars on the open side. A cloister is often built around the courtyard of a monastery, church, or college building. **2** a place of religious retirement; convent or monastery. **3** a quiet place shut

A cloister (def. 1)

away from the world. —*v.* shut away in a quiet place. [ME < OF < L *claustrum* closed place, lock < *claudere* close]

clois·tral (klois′trəl) *adj.* **1** like a cloister. **2** of or suitable for a convent, monastery, etc.

clomb (klōm) *v. Archaic.* a pt. and a pp. of **climb.**

clone (klōn) *n. v.* **cloned, clon·ing.** —*n.* a group of organisms derived from a single individual by asexual reproduction. —*v.* reproduce asexually.

clo·nus (klō′nəs) *n.* a series of muscular spasms. [< NL < Gk. *klonos* turmoil]

clop (klop) *n. v.* **clopped, clop·ping.** —*n.* a sharp, hard sound such as is made by a horse's hoof on a paved road. —*v.* make such a sound. [imitative]

close[1] (klōz) *v.* **closed, clos·ing,** *n.* —*v.* **1** shut: *Close the door. The sleepy child's eyes are closing.* **2** stop up; fill; block: *close a gap.* **3** bring together; come together: *close the ranks of troops.* **4** end; finish: *close a debate. The meeting closed with a speech by the president.* **5** come to terms; agree: *The labor union closed with the company.* **6** grapple. **7** in electricity, unite the parts of (a circuit) so as to make it complete. **8 close down,** shut completely; stop. **9 close in,** come near and shut in on all sides. **10 close out,** sell to get rid of. **11 close up, a** shut completely; stop up; block. **b** bring or come nearer together. **c** of a wound, heal.
—*n.* the end; finish. [ME < OF *clos-*, stem of *clore* < L *claudere* close] —**clos′a·ble,** *adj.* —**clos′er,** *n.*
Syn. *v.* **1 Close, shut** = put something in a position where it is not open. Although sometimes used interchangeably, **close** is more general in application because both literally and figuratively it emphasizes the idea of placing something in a position where it is not open, without suggesting the means or way: *Please close the window a little.* **Shut** means to close by pushing or pulling a door, lid, some part, etc. into place across the opening, and therefore puts the emphasis on keeping out or in, literally and figuratively: *Please shut the door. Shut your ears to gossip.*

close[2] (klōs) *adj.* **clos·er, clos·est,** *adv. n.* —*adj.* **1** with very little in between; near together; near: *close teeth.* **2** fitting tightly; tight; narrow: *close quarters.* **3** having its parts near together; compact: *a close texture.* **4** intimate; dear: *a close friend.* **5** careful; exact: *a close translation.* **6** thorough; strict: *close attention.* **7** having little fresh air: *a close room.* **8** hard to breathe. **9** not fond of talking; keeping quiet about oneself. **10** secret; hidden. **11** strictly guarded; confined: *keep a man close at home.* **12** restricted; limited. **13** stingy. **14** hard to get; scarce. **15** nearly equal; almost even: *a close contest.* **16** closed; shut; not open. **17** in phonetics, of a vowel, pronounced with some part of the tongue raised to a point near the palate, as the vowels in *leap* and *loop.*
—*adv.* **1** in a close manner. **2 close to the wind, a** with the ship pointed as nearly as possible in the direction from which the wind is blowing. **b** *Informal.* just barely following rules or laws.
—*n.* **1** an enclosed place. **2** the grounds around a cathedral or abbey. [ME < OF < L *clausum* closed place < *claudere* close] —**close′ness,** *n.* —**Syn.** *adj.* **3** dense, condensed.

close call *Informal.* a narrow escape from danger.

closed-cir·cuit (klōzd′sėr′kit) *adj.* denoting or having to do with television broadcasting that is limited to a certain audience, as in a chain of theatres, a school, etc.

closed season any part of the year when hunting or fishing is restricted.

closed shop a factory or business that employs only members of labor unions.

closed syllable a syllable that ends in a consonant sound. *Example: can-* in *candy.*

close-fist·ed (klōs′fis′tid) *adj.* stingy.

close-fit·ting (klōs′fit′ing) *adj.* fitting tightly; tight.

close-grained (klōs′grānd′) *adj.* having a fine, close grain. Mahogany is a close-grained wood.

close-hauled (klōs′hold′ or -hôld′) *adj.* having sails set for sailing as nearly as possible in the direction from which the wind is blowing.

close-knit (klōs′nit′) *adj.* firmly united by affection or common interests: *a close-knit family.*

close-lipped (klōs′lipt′) *adj.* close-mouthed.

close·ly (klōs′lē) *adv.* in a close manner; to a close degree or extent.

close-mouthed (klōs′mouᴛʜd′ or -moutht′) *adj.* tending to be silent; taciturn; secretive.

close quarters 1 at close quarters, very close together. **2** a place or position with little space: *We are living in close quarters here.*

close shave *Informal.* a narrow escape from danger.

clos·et (kloz′it) *n.* **1** a small room used for storing clothes or household supplies, such as canned food, china, or linen. **2** a cupboard for holding china, linen, etc. **3** a small, private room for prayer, study, or interviews. **4** a toilet; water closet.
—*v.* shut up in a private room for a secret talk: *The president was closeted with his personal advisers for several hours.* [ME < OF, dim. of *clos.* See CLOSE[2].]

close-up (klōs′up′) *n.* **1** a picture taken at close range. **2** a close view.

close-wo·ven (klōs′wō′vən) *adj.* woven so that the threads are close together.

clo·sure (klō′zhər) *n.* **1** a closing. **2** a closed condition. **3** a thing that closes. **4** the end; finish; conclusion. **5** in a legislative body, a means of ending a debate and getting an immediate vote on the question being discussed. In Canada, closure may be moved after due notice by a cabinet minister. [ME < OF < LL *clausura* < L *clausus*, pp. of *claudere* close]

clot (klot) *n. v.* **clot·ted, clot·ting.** —*n.* **1** a half-solid lump; thickened mass: *A clot of blood formed in the cut and stopped the bleeding.* **2** a clod. —*v.* form into clots: *Milk clots when it turns sour.* [OE *clott*]

cloth (kloth) *n.* **cloths** (kloᴛʜz or kloths) *adj.* —*n.* **1** a material made from wool, cotton, silk, linen, hair, etc. by weaving, knitting, or rolling and pressing. **2** a piece of this material intended for some specific purpose: *a dishcloth, a tablecloth.* **3** the customary clothing worn by the clergy. **4** the profession of a clergyman. **5 the cloth,** clergymen; the clergy.
—*adj.* made of cloth. [OE *clāth*]

clothe (klōᴛʜ) *v.* **clothed** or **clad, cloth·ing. 1** put clothes on; cover with clothes; dress. **2** provide with clothes. **3** cover: *The sun clothes the earth with light.* **4** provide; furnish; equip: *A judge is clothed with the authority of the state.* **5** express: *The moral of a fable is usually clothed in simple words.* [OE *clāthian* < *clāth* cloth]
Syn. 1 Clothe, dress = put clothes on. **Clothe,** always followed by a word naming the thing or person, means to cover with clothes. It nearly always needs a modifying word or phrase telling how or with what: *He clothed himself in an old tweed suit.* **Dress** emphasizes the idea of arranging or getting ready, and suggests putting clothes on oneself or another with care, or suitable for the occasion, etc.: *I can't go because I haven't time to dress,* that is, dress properly.

clothes (klōz or klōᴛʜz) *n.pl.* **1** the covering for a person's body. **2** the coverings for a bed.—**Syn. 1** apparel, clothing, attire, garb.

clothes horse 1 a frame to hang clothes on in order to dry or air them. **2** *Slang.* a person who places great value on being well dressed, especially one who slavishly follows the latest styles and fashions.

clothes line a rope or wire to hang clothes on in order to dry or air them.

clothes peg 1 a peg for hanging clothes on. **2** a clothes pin.

clothes pin a clip, generally wooden, to hold clothes on a clothes line.

clothes pole 1 a stick to support a clothes line. **2** a pole supporting a frame and ropes for drying clothes.

clothes press a chest, cupboard, or closet in which to keep clothes.

clothes tree an upright pole with branches on which to hang coats and hats.

cloth·ier (klōᴛʜ′yər or klōᴛʜ′ē ər) *n.* **1** a seller or maker of clothing. **2** a seller of cloth.

cloth·ing (klōᴛʜ′ing) *n.* **1** clothes. **2** covering.

Clo·tho (klō′thō) *n.* in Greek mythology, one of the three Fates. Clotho spins the thread of life.

cloth of gold cloth made of gold threads woven with silk or wool threads.

cloth yard one yard; three feet.

clo·ture (klō′chər) *n. Esp.U.S.* closure (def. 5).

cloud (kloud) *n.* **1** a white, gray, or almost black mass in the sky, made up of tiny drops of water. **2** a mass of smoke or dust. **3** a great number of things moving close together: *a cloud of birds, a cloud of arrows.* **4** a streak; spot. **5** anything that darkens or dims. **6** a cause of gloom, trouble, suspicion, or disgrace. **7** in architecture, a lozenge-shaped form hung from the ceiling of a theatre, auditorium, etc. It usually contains a light or lights and acts as a reflector of sound. **8 in the clouds, a** far above the earth. **b** unreal; imaginary; fanciful; theoretical; not practical. **c** daydreaming; absent-minded. **9 under a cloud, a** under suspicion; in disgrace. **b** in gloom or trouble.
—*v.* **1** cover with a cloud or clouds. **2** grow cloudy: *The sky clouded.* **3** streak; spot. **4** make or become gloomy or troubled; darken; dim. **5** make or become suspected or disgraced. [OE *clūd* a mass of rock, hence, a mass of vapor] —**cloud′like′,** *adj.*

cloud·ber·ry (kloud′ber′ē) *n.* **-ries. 1** *Cdn.* a berry that grows in northern latitudes and resembles a small raspberry; bake apple. **2** the bush it grows on.

cloud·burst (kloud′bėrst′) *n.* a sudden, violent rainfall.

cloud chamber a large vessel filled with a vapor, especially a vapor of hydrogen and methyl alcohol, through which subatomic particles may be caused to move leaving a trail by which they may be identified.

cloud·less (kloud′lis) *adj.* without clouds; clear; bright; sunny. —**cloud′less·ly,** *adv.* —**cloud′less·ness,** *n.*

cloud·let (kloud′lit) *n.* a little cloud.

cloud rack a group of broken clouds.

cloud seeding the scattering, usually from aircraft, of particles of carbon dioxide or certain other chemicals in clouds to produce rain.

cloud·y (kloud′ē) *adj.* **cloud·i·er, cloud·i·est. 1** covered with clouds; having clouds in it: *a cloudy sky.* **2** of or like clouds. **3** not clear: *a cloudy liquid.* **4** streaked; spotted: *cloudy marble.* **5** dark; dim; confused; indistinct: *a cloudy notion.* **6** gloomy; frowning.
—**cloud′i·ly,** *adv.* —**cloud′i·ness,** *n.*

clough (kluf or klou) *n.* a narrow valley; glen. [OE *clōh*]

clout (klout) *n.* **1** *Informal.* a hit with the hand; rap; knock; cuff. **2** in archery: **a** a white cloth target. **b** a shot that hits this. **3** *Archaic.* **a** a cloth; rag. **b** a garment.
—*v. Informal.* hit with the hand; rap; knock; cuff.
[OE *clūt* small piece of cloth or metal]

clove[1] (klōv) *n.* **1** a strong, fragrant spice obtained from the dried flower buds of a tropical evergreen tree. **2** the dried flower bud. **3** the tree. [ME *cloue* (apparently misread as *clove*) < OF *clou* < L *clavus* nail]

clove[2] (klōv) *n.* a small, separate section of a bulb: *a clove of garlic.* [OE *clufu*]

clove[3] (klōv) *v.* a pt. of **cleave**[1].

clove hitch a knot used in tying a rope around a pole, spar, etc.

A clove hitch

clo·ven (klō′vən) *v.* a pp. of **cleave**[1].
—*adj.* split; divided.

cloven foot cloven hoof.

clo·ven-foot·ed (klō′vən fu̇t′id) *adj.* **1** having cloven feet. **2** devilish.

cloven hoof a hoof divided into two parts. Cows have cloven hoofs. The Devil is traditionally pictured with cloven hoofs.

clo·ven-hoofed (klō′vən hu̇ft′ or -hüft′) *adj.* **1** having cloven hoofs. **2** devilish.

clo·ver (klō′vər) *n.* **1** a low plant of the same family as the pea, having three leaflets to each leaf and rounded heads of small red, white, yellow, or crimson flowers. It is grown as food for horses and cattle **2** any similar plant, such as sweet clover. **3 in clover,** *Informal.* enjoying a life of pleasure and luxury without work or worry. [OE *clāfre*]

clo·ver·leaf (klō′vər lēf′) *n.* a series of roads at the intersection of two highways, so arranged that traffic may move from one highway to the other without having to cross in front of other traffic.

clown (kloun) *n.* **1** a man whose business is to amuse others by tricks and jokes. **2** a bad-mannered, awkward, or uneducated person. —*v.* act like a clown; play tricks; act in a silly way. [origin uncertain; cf. Icelandic *klunni* clumsy person, boor]

hat, āge, cãre, fär; let, ēqual, tėrm; it, īce
hot, ōpen, ôrder; oil, out; cup, pu̇t, rüle, ūse
əbove, takən, pencəl, lemən, circəs
ch, child; ng, long; sh, ship
th, thin; ᴛʜ, then; zh, measure

clown·er·y (kloun′ər ē) *n.* **-er·ies.** the tricks and jokes of a clown; clownish act.

clown·ish (kloun′ish) *adj.* like a clown; like a clown's. —**clown′ish·ly,** *adv.* —**clown′ish·ness,** *n.*

cloy (kloi) *v.* **1** weary by too much, too sweet, or too rich food. **2** weary by too much of anything pleasant. [ME *acloy, ancloy* drive a nail into, stop up, fill full < OF *encloyer* < *en-* in (< L *in-*) + *clou* nail (< L *clavus*)] —**cloy′ing·ly,** *adv.* —**cloy′ing·ness,** *n.*
—**Syn. 2** surfeit, pall.

club (klub) *n. v.* **clubbed club·bing.** —*n.* **1** a heavy stick of wood, thicker at one end, used as a weapon. **2** in games, a stick or bat used to hit a ball. **3** a group of people joined together for some special purpose: *a tennis club.* **4** a building or rooms used by a club. **5 a** a playing card with one or more black designs on it shaped like this: ♣ **b clubs,** *pl.* a suit of cards marked with this design.
—*v.* **1** beat or hit with a club. **2** join or combine for some special purpose: *The children clubbed together to buy their mother some flowers for her birthday.*
[ME < ON *klubba*] —**Syn.** *n.* **1** cudgel, **3** association, society.

club·foot (klub′fu̇t′) *n.* **-feet. 1** a deformed foot, short and distorted. **2** a deformity of the foot caused by faulty development before birth.

club·foot·ed (klub′fu̇t′id) *adj.* having a clubfoot.

club·house (klub′hous′) *n.* a building used by a club.

club·man (klub′mən) *n.* **-men.** a man who is a member of a fashionable club or clubs, especially one who makes frequent use of them.

club moss a flowerless plant that grows along the ground and looks much like a vine covered with pine needles.

club·room (klub′rüm′ or -ru̇m′) *n.* a room used for club meetings and activities.

club sandwich a sandwich consisting of toast and at least two layers of meats (especially chicken), lettuce, tomato, etc.

club steak a small piece of beef cut from the loin.

club·wom·an (klub′wu̇m′ən) *n.* **-wom·en.** a woman who belongs to a club or clubs, especially one who makes frequent use of them.

cluck (kluk) *n.* **1** the sound made by a hen calling her chickens. **2** a sound like this. **3** *Slang.* a stupid person; blockhead; fool. —*v.* **1** of a hen, make a cluck when calling chickens. **2** make a sound like this. [imitative]

clue (klü) *n.* **1** a guide to the solving of a mystery or problem: *The police could find no clues to help them in solving the crime.* **2** clew. —*v.* **1** indicate something by means of a clue. **2** *Informal.* give a clue to. **3 clue up,** *Informal.* provide (someone) with the essential details or information: *The new minister is not yet clued up about the working of his department.* [var. of *clew*]

clum·ber (klum′bər) *n.* **1** a breed of hunting dog having short legs, a long, heavy body, and white with orange or yellow markings. **2** a dog of this breed.
[< *Clumber,* an estate of the Duke of Newcastle, England]

clump (klump) *n.* **1** a cluster: *a clump of trees.* **2** a lump: *a clump of earth.* **3** the sound of heavy, clumsy walking.
—*v.* **1** form a clump; plant in clusters. **2** walk heavily and clumsily. [earlier *clumper,* OE *clympre* lump of metal]

clump·y (klump′ē) *adj.* **1** full of clumps. **2** like clumps. **3** heavy and clumsy.

clum·si·ness (klum′zē nis) *n.* the state or condition of being clumsy; awkwardness.

clum·sy (klum′zē) *adj.* **-si·er, -si·est. 1** not graceful or skilful; awkward. **2** awkwardly done; poorly contrived: *a clumsy apology.* **3** not well-shaped or well-made. [< *clumse* be numb with cold, probably < Scand.] —**clum′si·ly,** *adv.* —**Syn. 1** ungraceful, ungainly. See **awkward.**

clung (klung) *v.* pt. and pp. of **cling.**

Cluny lace a kind of lace made of heavy linen or cotton thread. [< *Cluny,* town in E. France]

clus·ter (klus′tər) *n.* **1** a number of things of the same kind growing or grouped together: *a cluster of grapes, a cluster of curls, a little cluster of houses.* **2** a group of persons or things. **3** in phonetics, a sequence of two or more vowel or, especially, consonant sounds. *Str-* in *string* is a consonant cluster. **4** in astronomy, a group of stars relatively close to each other and often found to have a common motion in space. **5** *U.S.* a small metal device placed on the ribbon standing for a military medal, to show that the same medal has been awarded again.
—*v.* form into a cluster; gather in clusters; group together closely: *The girls clustered around their teacher.* [OE]

clutch[1] (kluch) *n.* **1** a tight grasp. **2** a grasping claw, paw, hand, etc.: *Quick shooting saved the hunter from the bear's clutches.* **3** Usually, **clutches,** *pl.* control; power: *in the clutches of the police.* **4** a device in a machine for connecting or disconnecting the engine or motor that drives it. **5** the lever or pedal operating this device. [< v.]
—*v.* **1** grasp tightly: *The girl clutched her doll to her breast.* **2** seize eagerly; snatch: *A drowning man will clutch at a straw.* [OE *clyccan* bend, clench] —**Syn.** *v.* **1** See **seize.**

clutch[2] (kluch) *n.* **1** a nest of eggs. **2** a brood of chickens. **3** a group of people or things: *There was a clutch of journalists covering the story.* [var. of *cletch* < *cleck* hatch < ON *klekja*]

clutch bag a woman's handbag that is carried under the arm; a purse without handles.

clut·ter (klut′ər) *n.* **1** a litter; confusion; disorder. **2** confused noise; loud clatter. —*v.* **1** litter (with things): *Her desk was all cluttered with old papers, strings, and trash.* **2** make a confused noise; clatter loudly. [< *clot*]

Clydes·dale (klīdz′dāl′) *n.* **1** a breed of strong draft horses. **2** a horse of this breed. [< *Clydesdale,* Scotland, where they were raised originally]

Cm curium.

cm. or **cm** centimetre; centimetres.

C.M. Canada Medal.

CMA Canadian Medical Association.

Cmdr. Commander.

Cmdre. Commodore.

C.M.G. Companion of (the Order of) St. Michael and St. George.

CMHC or **C.M.H.C.** Central Mortgage and Housing Corporation.

cml. commercial.

CNIB Canadian National Institute for the Blind.

CNR Canadian National Railways.

co- *prefix.* **1** with; together: *co-operate = act with or together.* **2** joint; fellow: *co-author = joint or fellow author.* **3** equally: *co-extensive = equally extensive.* [< L *co-,* var. of *com-*]

Co cobalt.

Co. or **co.** *pl.* **cos. 1** company. **2** county.

c.o. or **c/o 1** in care of. **2** carried over.

C.O. 1 Commanding Officer. **2** *Informal.* conscientious objector.

coach (kōch) *n.* **1** formerly, a large, closed carriage with seats inside and often on top. It carried passengers along a regular route, stopping for meals and for fresh horses. **2** a passenger car of a railway train. **3** a closed automobile having two doors. **4** a bus. **5** a person who teaches or trains athletic teams, etc.: *a football coach.* **6** in baseball, a person stationed near first or third base to direct base runners and the batter. **7** a private teacher who helps a student prepare for a special test. **8** an instructor who supervises the training of actors, singers, etc.: *a drama coach, a music coach.*
—*v.* **1** carry or ride in a coach. **2** teach; train; instruct: *He coached a winning team that fall. He coaches baseball. She coaches the young singer.* **3** act as a coach: *He is coaching this winter.* **4** help to prepare for a special test. [ME < MF *coche* prob. < Magyar *kocsi,* after *Kocs,* a Hungarian village where coaches were supposedly made first]

☛ The senses of *instructor, teacher, trainer,* and the related verb meanings appear to derive from the idea of a university tutor being a means for carrying, or driving, the student through his examinations.

A coach

coach-and-four (kōch′ənd fôr′) *n.* a coach pulled by four horses.

coach dog Dalmatian.

coach·man (kōch′mən) *n.* **-men** (-mən). a man whose work is driving a coach or carriage.

co·ad·ju·tor (kō aj′ů tər or kō′ə jü′tər) *n.* **1** an assistant; helper. **2** a bishop appointed to assist another bishop. [ME < LL < L *co-* with + *adjutor* helper < *adjuvare* < *ad-* + *juvare* help]

co·ag·u·lant (kō ag′yů lənt) *n.* a substance that produces coagulation.

co·ag·u·late (kō ag′yů lāt′) *v.* **-lat·ed, -lat·ing.** change from liquid form into a thickened mass; thicken: *Cooking coagulates the white of egg.* [< L *coagulare* < *coagulum* means of curdling < *co-* together + *agere* drive] —**co·ag′u·la′tor,** *n.*

co·ag·u·la·tion (kō ag′yů lā′shən) *n.* **1** the act of coagulating. **2** a coagulated mass.

co·ag·u·la·tive (kō ag′yů lə tiv or kō ag′yů lā′tiv) *adj.* tending to coagulate or cause coagulation.

coal (kōl) *n.* **1** a black mineral, composed mostly of carbon, that burns and gives off heat. It was formed many millions of years ago from partly decayed vegetable matter under great pressure in the earth. Hard coal and soft coal are two kinds. **2** a piece of this mineral. **3** a piece of wood, coal, etc., burning, partly burned, or all burned. **4** charcoal. **5 call over the coals,** scold; blame. **6 haul over the coals,** scold; blame. **7 heap coals of fire on one's head,** make a person sorry by returning good for evil.
—*v.* **1** supply with coal. **2** take in a supply of coal. [OE *col* (def. 3)]

coal·er (kōl′ər) *n.* **1** a ship, railway, freight car, etc. used for carrying or supplying coal. **2** a worker or merchant who supplies coal.

co·a·lesce (kō′ə les′) *v.* **-lesced, -lesc·ing. 1** grow together. **2** unite into one body, mass, party, etc.; combine: *Two political groups coalesced to form a new party.* [< L *coalescere* < *co-* together + *alescere* grow]

co·a·les·cence (kō′ə les′əns) *n.* **1** a growing together. **2** a union; combination.

co·a·les·cent (kō′ə les′ənt) *adj.* coalescing.

coal field a region where beds of coal are found.

coal gas 1 the gas made from coal, used for heating and lighting. **2** the gas given off by burning coal.

coal hod coal scuttle.

coaling station a place where ships, trains, etc. are supplied with coal.

co·a·li·tion (kō′ə lish′ən) *n.* **1** a union; combination. **2** a temporary alliance of statesmen, political parties, etc. for some special purpose. [< Med.L *coalitio, -onis* < L *coalescere.* See COALESCE.]

coal measures beds of coal; strata containing coal.

coal mine a mine or pit where coal is dug from the earth.

hat, āge, cãre, fär; let, ēqual, tėrm; it, īce
hot, ōpen, ôrder; oil, out; cup, pu̇t, rüle, ūse
əbove, takən, pencəl, lemən, circəs
ch, child; ng, long; sh, ship
th, thin; ᴛʜ, then; zh, measure

coal oil 1 kerosene: *coal-oil lamps.* 2 petroleum.

coal pit 1 a coal mine. 2 a place where charcoal is made.

coal scuttle a bucket for holding or carrying coal.

coal tar a black, sticky residue left after soft coal has been distilled to make coal gas, used as a basis for aniline dyes, flavorings, perfumes, benzene, etc.

coam·ing (kōm′ing) *n.* 1 a raised edge around a hatch or opening in the deck of a ship to prevent water from running down below. 2 any similar raised edge around an opening. [origin uncertain]

coarse (kôrs) *adj.* **coars·er, coars·est.** 1 made up of fairly large parts; not fine: *coarse sand.* 2 rough: *coarse cloth.* 3 common; poor; inferior: *coarse food.* 4 not delicate or refined; crude; vulgar: *coarse manners.* [adjectival use of *course,* n., meaning "ordinary"] —**coarse′ly,** *adv.* —**coarse′ness,** *n.*

Syn. 4 Coarse, vulgar = not refined in feelings, manners, language, taste. Coarse emphasizes roughness and crudeness, and means "not refined, delicate, polished, or polite": *The soldier's coarse language was fit only for the barracks.* **Vulgar,** which usually suggests an attitude of distaste on the part of the speaker toward the person described, means "unrefined, indelicate, rude": *He is so vulgar that no one at school likes him.*

coarse-grained (kôrs′grānd′) *adj.* 1 having a coarse texture; made up of large, coarse fibres. 2 not delicate or refined; crude.

coars·en (kôr′sən) *v.* make or become coarse.

coast (kōst) *n.* 1 the land along the edge of the sea; seashore. 2 a region near a coast. 3 **the Coast,** in Canada and the United States, the region along the Pacific Ocean. 4 a ride or slide down a hill without the use of power. 5 a slope for sliding downhill on a sleigh, etc. 6 **The coast is clear.** No one is in the way. The danger is past.
—*v.* 1 go along or near the coast of. 2 sail from port to port of a coast. 3 ride or slide down a hill without using power. [ME < OF < L *costa* side]
—**Syn.** *n.* 1 seaboard, strand. See **shore.**

coast·al (kōs′təl) *adj.* of, near, or along a coast.

coastal plain a flat stretch of land along a coast.

coast·er (kōs′tər) *n.* 1 a person or thing that coasts. 2 a ship trading along a coast. 3 a sleigh to coast on. 4 an amusement railway whose track dips and curves abruptly; roller coaster. 5 a little tray or mat on which a glass or bottle may be placed.

coaster brake a brake on the rear wheel of a bicycle, worked by pushing back on the pedals.

coast guard 1 an organization whose work is saving lives and preventing smuggling along the coasts of a country. 2 a member of any such group.

coasting trade 1 the trade carried on by ships between the ports of one country. 2 the trade carried on by ships along the coasts of several countries.

coast·land (kōst′land′) *n.* the land along a coast.

coast·line (kōst′līn′) *n.* the outline of a coast.

Coast Salish 1 a North American Indian people living in southern British Columbia, including the southeastern part of Vancouver Island, famous for their skill in basketry. 2 a member of this people.

coast·ward (kōst′wərd) *adv. adj.* toward the coast.

coast·ways (kōst′wāz′) *adv.* coastwise.

coast·wise (kōst′wīz′) *adv. adj.* along the coast.

coat (kōt) *n.* 1 an outer garment of cloth, fur, etc. with sleeves. 2 an outer covering: *a dog's coat of hair, a coat of bark on a tree.* 3 a layer covering a surface: *a coat of paint.* —*v.* 1 provide with a coat. 2 cover with a layer: *The old books were coated with dust.* [ME < OF *cote* < Gmc.] —**coat′er,** *n.* —**coat′less,** *adj.*

coated paper paper that has been coated with clay or sizing to give a glossy, smooth surface especially suitable for reproducing half-tone illustrations.

co·a·ti (kō ä′tē) *n.* **-tis.** a small mammal resembling a raccoon, living in Central and South America. It has a long body and tail and a flexible snout. [< Tupi-Guarani, an Indian language family of central South America]

coat·ing (kōt′ing) *n.* 1 a layer covering a surface: *a coating of paint.* 2 cloth for making coats.

coat of arms 1 a shield, or drawing of a shield, bearing designs symbolic of a family's history, used especially by noble families in Europe. 2 a similar device adopted as an emblem of authority by a government, a city, or even a corporation. [translation of F *cotte d'armes,* a light coat decorated with heraldic designs worn over armor by knights in the Middle Ages]

A coat of arms

coat of mail a garment made of metal rings or plates, worn as armor.

coat·tail (kōt′tāl′) *n.* 1 the back part of a coat below the waist; one of a pair of tails or flaps on such a part of a coat. 2 **coattails,** *pl.* the skirts of a formal coat. 3 **ride on someone's coattails,** advance in career or popularity by associating with a more successful or more popular person.

co-au·thor (kō o′thər or -ô′thər) *n.* a joint author. —*v. Informal.* write with the help of another.

coax (kōks) *v.* 1 persuade by soft words; influence by pleasant ways: *She coaxed her father to let her go to the dance.* 2 get by coaxing: *The nurse coaxed a smile from the baby.* [< obs. *cokes* a fool] —**coax′er,** *n.*
—**Syn.** 1 wheedle, cajole, inveigle.

co·ax·i·al (kō ak′sē əl) *adj.* 1 having a common axis. 2 of or having to do with a coaxial cable.

coaxial cable 1 a cable enclosing two or more concentric insulated conductors capable of operating singly or in combination to carry radio, television, telegraph, and telephone signals. 2 a large cable containing a system of many coaxial cables to carry several video circuits and a large number of telephone circuits.

cob (kob) *n.* 1 the centre part of an ear of corn, on which the kernels grow. 2 a sturdy horse having short legs. [ME *cob, cobbe* < Scand. and LG, a word suggesting something round or plump]

co·balt (kō′bolt or kō′bôlt) *n.* 1 a silver-white metallic chemical element with a pinkish tint, used in making steel, paints, etc. *Symbol:* Co; *at.no.* 27; *at.wt.* 58.9332. 2 a dark-blue coloring matter made from cobalt. [< G *kobalt,* var. of *kobold* goblin]

cobalt bomb 1 a hydrogen bomb encased in a shell of cobalt instead of steel. 2 **cobalt-60 bomb,** radio-active cobalt **(cobalt-60)** enclosed in a lead case, used in the treatment of cancer and in nuclear research.

cob·ble[1] (kob′əl) *v.* **-bled, -bling.** 1 mend (shoes, etc.); repair; patch. 2 put together clumsily. [probably akin to COB]

cob·ble[2] (kob′əl) *n. v.* **-bled, -bling.** —*n.* 1 a cobblestone. 2 a round lump of coal about the size of a cobblestone. —*v.* pave with cobblestones. [apparently dim. of ME *cob, cobbe.* See COB.]

cob·bler (kob′lər) *n.* 1 a man whose work is mending or making shoes; shoemaker. 2 a clumsy workman. 3 a fruit pie baked in a deep dish, usually with a crust only on top. 4 an iced drink made of wine, fruit juice, etc.

cob·ble·stone (kob′əl stōn′) *n.* a rounded stone formerly much used in paving streets, sidewalks, etc.

co-bel·lig·er·ent (kō′bə lij′ər ənt) *n.* a nation that helps another nation carry on a war.

co·bra (kō′brə) *n.* a very poisonous snake of S. Asia and Africa. It can dilate its head and neck so that they assume a hoodlike form. [short for Pg. *cobra de capello* snake with a hood]

cob·web (kob′web′) *n.* 1 a spider's web or the stuff it is made of. 2 anything thin and slight or entangling like a spider's web. [OE (*ātor*)*coppe* spider + *web*]

cob·web·by (kob′web′ē) *adj.* 1 of or like a cobweb. 2 covered with cobwebs.

co·ca (kō′kə) *n.* 1 a small tropical shrub growing in South America. Its dried leaves are used to make cocaine and other alkaloids. 2 its dried leaves. [< Peruvian *cuca*]

co·caine or **co·cain** (kō kān′ or kō′kān) *n.* a white, bitter, crystalline drug used to deaden pain and as a stimulant. [< *coca*]

coc·cus (kok′əs) *n.* **coc·ci** (kok′sī or kok′sē). **1** a bacterium shaped like a sphere. See **bacteria** for picture. **2** in botany, a part of a compound pistil; carpel. [< NL < Gk. *kokkos* seed]

coc·cyx (kok′siks) *n.* **coc·cy·ges** (kok sī′jēz) **1** in anatomy, a small triangular bone at the lower end of the spinal column. **2** in zoology, a similar part in certain animals and birds. [< L < Gk. *kokkyx*, originally, cuckoo; because shaped like cuckoo's bill]

Co·chin or **co·chin** (kō′chin or koch′in) *n.* **1** a large breed of domestic fowl that have many feathers on their legs. **2** a chicken of this breed. [after *Cochin China*, a former French colony in S. Indo-China, now part of South Vietnam]

coch·i·neal (koch′ə nēl′ or koch′ə nēl′) *n.* a bright-red dye made from the dried bodies of the females of a scale insect that lives on cactus plants of tropical America. [< F < Sp. *cochinilla*, ult. < L *coccinus* scarlet < Gk. *kokkos* berry (gall) of a kind of oak]

coch·le·a (kok′lē ə) *n.* **-le·ae** (-lē ē′ or -lē ī′). in anatomy, a spiral-shaped cavity of the inner ear, containing the sensory ends of the auditory nerve. See **ear** for diagram. [< L < Gk. *kochlias* snail]

coch·le·ar (kok′lē ər) *adj.* of the cochlea.

cock[1] (kok) *n.* **1** a male chicken; rooster. **2** the male of other birds. **3** a tap used to turn the flow of a liquid or gas on or off. **4** the hammer of a gun. **5** the position of the hammer of a gun when it is pulled back ready to fire. **6** a weathercock. **7** *Informal.* a leader; head; main person. **8** in curling, the mark aimed at.
—*v.* pull back the hammer of (a gun), ready to fire.
[OE *cocc*]

cock[2] (kok) *v.* **1** turn up jauntily; stick up defiantly or inquiringly: *The little bird cocked his eye at me.* **2** set (one's hat) at a jaunty angle on the head. **3** turn up the brim of (one's hat). —*n.* **1** an upward turn or bend of the nose, eye, or ear. **2** the turn of a brim of a hat. [apparently < *cock*[1]]

cock[3] (kok) *n.* a small, cone-shaped pile of hay in a field. —*v.* pile in cocks. [ME]

cock·ade (kok ād′) *n.* a knot of ribbon or a rosette worn on the hat as a badge. [alteration of *cockard* < F *cocarde* < *coq* cock]

cock-a-hoop (kok′ə hüp′) *adj. Esp.Brit.* elated; triumphant and boastful.

Cock·aigne (kok ān′) *n.* an imaginary land of luxury and idleness. [ME < OF *cokaigne* < MLG *kokenje* little sugar cake, ult. < L *coquere* cook]

cock-and-bull story an absurd, incredible story.

cock·a·too (kok′ə tü′ or kok′ə tü′) *n.* **-toos.** a large, brightly colored parrot of Australia, the East Indies, etc. [< Du. *kaketoe* < Malay *kakatua*]

cock·a·trice (kok′ə tris) *n.* a fabled serpent whose look was supposed to cause death. [ME < OF *cocatris* (influenced by *coq* cock), ult. < L *calcare* tread]

cock·boat (kok′bōt′) *n.* a small rowboat.

cock·chaf·er (kok′chāf′ər) *n.* a large European beetle that destroys plants.

cock·crow (kok′krō′) *n.* **1** the crowing of a rooster. **2** the time when roosters begin to crow; dawn.

cocked hat **1** a hat with the brim turned up. **2** a hat pointed in front and at the back. See picture in the opposite column. **3 knock into a cocked hat,** *Slang.* defeat; destroy completely; ruin.

cocker (kok′ər) *n.* cocker spaniel.

cock·er·el (kok′ər əl or kok′rəl) *n.* a young rooster, not more than one year old.

cocker spaniel **1** a breed of small dog having long, silky hair and drooping ears. **2** a dog of this breed.

cock-eyed (kok′īd′) *adj.* **1** cross-eyed. **2** *Slang.* tilted or twisted to one side. **3** *Slang.* foolish; silly.

cock·fight (kok′fīt′) *n.* a fight between roosters or between gamecocks armed with steel spurs.

cock·fight·ing (kok′fīt′ing) *n.* fighting by roosters or gamecocks for the entertainment of spectators.

cock·horse (kok′hôrs′) *n.* a child's hobbyhorse; rocking horse.

cock·le[1] (kok′əl) *n. v.* **-led, -ling.** —*n.* **1** an edible salt-water mollusc having two ridged, heart-shaped shells. **2** one of these shells. **3** a small, light, shallow boat. **4** a wrinkle; pucker; bulge on the surface. **5 cockles of one's heart,** the inmost part of one's heart or feelings. —*v.* wrinkle; pucker: *Paper sometimes cockles when you paste it.* [ME < MF *cokille* < VL < L *conchylia*, pl. of *conchylium* < Gk. *konchylion*, ult. < *konchē* conch]

cock·le[2] (kok′əl) *n.* a weed that grows in grain fields, such as the corn cockle, darnel, etc. [OE *coccel*, ? < L < Gk. *kokkos* berry]

cock·le·boat (kok′əl bōt′) *n.* a small, light, shallow boat.

cock·le·bur (kok′əl bėr′) *n.* any of several weeds having spiny burrs.

cock·le·shell (kok′əl shel′) *n.* **1** the shell of the cockle. **2** a small, light, shallow boat.

cock·loft (kok′loft′) *n.* a small attic; garret.

Cock·ney or **cock·ney** (kok′nē) *n.* **-neys,** *adj.*
—*n.* **1** a native or inhabitant of London, England, especially a native of its East End or the City of London proper who speaks a particular dialect. **2** this dialect.
—*adj.* **1** of or like this dialect. **2** of or like Cockneys.
[ME *cokeney* cock's egg, pampered child, city fellow < *cocken* of cocks (OE *cocc*) + *ey* egg (OE *ǣg*)]

cock·pit (kok′pit′) *n.* **1** a small, open place in an airplane, boat, etc., where the pilot or passengers sit. See **airplane** for diagram. **2** an enclosed place for cockfights. **3** a scene of many fights or battles: *Belgium is often called the cockpit of Europe.* **4** in former times, rooms below the deck of warships, used as quarters for junior officers, or as a hospital during battle.

cock·roach (kok′rōch′) *n.* a small brownish or yellowish insect often found in kitchens, around water pipes, etc. [alteration of Sp. *cucaracha*]

cocks·comb (koks′kōm′) *n.* **1** the fleshy, red crest on the head of a rooster. **2** a pointed cap somewhat like this, worn by a jester or clown. **3** a plant having crested or feathery clusters of red or yellow flowers. **4** *Obsolete.* a coxcomb.

A cockscomb

cock·spur (kok′spėr′) *n.* **1** the spur of a cock. **2** a North American hawthorn having long thorns.

cock·sure (kok′shür′) *adj.* **1** perfectly sure; absolutely certain. **2** too sure.
—**cock′sure′ness,** *n.*

cock·swain (kok′sən or -swān′) *n.* coxswain.

cock·tail (kok′tāl′) *n.* **1** an iced drink, often composed of gin or whisky mixed with bitters, vermouth, fruit juices, etc. **2** an appetizer: *a tomato-juice cocktail.* **3** shellfish served in a small glass with a highly seasoned sauce: *a sea-food cocktail.* **4** mixed fruits, diced and usually served in a glass.

cock·y (kok′ē) *adj.* **cock·i·er, cock·i·est.** *Informal.* conceited; swaggering. —**cock′i·ly,** *adv.* —**cock′i·ness,** *n.*

co·co (kō′kō) *n.* **co·cos.** **1** a tall palm tree on which coconuts grow. **2** its fruit or seed. Also, **cocoa.** [< Pg. *coco* grinning face]

co·coa[1] (kō′kō) *n.* **1** a powder made by roasting and grinding cacao seeds. **2** a drink made of this powder with milk or water and sugar. **3** a dull brown.
—*adj.* of or having to do with cocoa. [var. of *cacao*]

co·coa[2] (kō′kō) *n.* coco.

cocoa butter a yellowish-white fat obtained from cacao

A cocked hat

seeds, used in making soap, cosmetics, etc.

co·co·nut or **co·coa·nut** (kō′kə nut′ or kō′kə nət) *n.* the large, round, brown, hard-shelled fruit of the coco palm. Coconuts have an edible white lining and contain a white liquid called **coconut milk.**

coconut oil the oil obtained from coconuts, used for making soap, candles, etc.

coconut palm a tall palm tree on which coconuts grow.

co·coon (kə kün′) *n.* **1** the silky case spun by the larvae of many insects to live in while in the pupa stage. **2** any similar protective covering. —*v.* wrap or enclose in or as if in a cocoon; encase. [< F *cocon* < *coque* shell]

cod (kod) *n.* **cod** or **cods.** an important food fish found in the cold parts of the N. Atlantic Ocean. It is usually about three feet long when fully grown. [ME; origin uncertain]

C.O.D. or **c.o.d.** cash on delivery; collect on delivery.

co·da (kō′də) *n.* in music, an addition to a composition, usually designed to give a spectacular ending. [< Ital. < L *cauda* tail]

cod·der (kod′ər) *n. Cdn.* in the Maritimes: **1** a boat used for cod fishing. **2** a cod fisherman.

cod·dle (kod′əl) *v.* **-dled, -dling. 1** treat tenderly; pamper: *coddle sick children.* **2** cook in hot water without boiling: *coddle an egg.* [var. of n. *caudle* gruel < OF < L *calidus* hot] —**cod′dler,** *n.* —**Syn. 1** humor, indulge.

code (kōd) *n. v.* **cod·ed, cod·ing.** —*n.* **1** a collection of the laws of a country. **2** any set of rules: *A moral code is made up of the notions of right and wrong conduct held by a person, a group of persons, or a society.* **3** a system of signals for sending messages by telegraph, flags, etc. The Morse code is used in telegraphy. **4** a system of symbols for representing information in a computer. **5** a secret writing; arrangement of words, figures, etc. to keep a message short or secret.
—*v.* change or translate into a code. [< F < L *codex* codex. Doublet of CODEX.]

co·de·in (kō′dēn or kō′dē in) *n.* codeine.

co·deine (kō′dēn or kō′dē in) *n.* a white crystalline drug obtained from opium, used to relieve pain and cause sleep. [< Gk. *kōdeia* poppy head]

co·dex (kō′deks) *n.* **co·di·ces.** a manuscript; a volume of manuscripts. [< L *codex*, var. of *caudex* tree trunk, block, book. Doublet of CODE.]

cod·fish (kod′fish′) *n.* **-fish** or **-fish·es. 1** cod. **2 codfish cakes,** any fried cakes made of cod, or cod and mashed potato.

codg·er (koj′ər) *n. Informal.* a peculiar person. [origin uncertain]

cod-haul·er (kod′hol′ər or -hôl′ər) *n. Cdn. Slang.* a Newfoundlander.

co·di·ces (kō′də sēz′ or kod′ə sēz′) *n.* pl. of **codex.**

cod·i·cil (kod′ə səl) *n.* **1** in law, something added to a will to change it, add to it, or explain it. **2** something added. [< L *codicillus*, dim. of *codex*. See CODEX.]

cod·i·cil·la·ry (kod′ə sil′ə rē) *adj.* of the nature of a codicil.

cod·i·fi·ca·tion (kō′də fə kā′shən or kod′ə fə kā′shən) *n.* **1** the act or process of arranging according to a system. **2** the state or fact of being so arranged.

cod·i·fy (kōd′ə fī′ or ko′də fī′) *v.* **-fied, -fy·ing.** arrange (laws, etc.) according to a system: *The laws of France were codified between 1804 and 1810 by order of Napoleon I.* [< *code* + *-fy*] —**cod′i·fi′er,** *n.*

cod·lin (kod′lin) *n.* codling[1].

cod·ling[1] (kod′ling) *n.* **1** a small, unripe apple. **2** a kind of long, tapering apple. [ME *querd(e)lyng(e)* apple with a hard core, apparently < AF *quer de lion* heart of lion]

cod·ling[2] (kod′ling) *n.* **1** a young or small cod. **2** a hake.

codling moth a small moth whose larvae destroy apples, pears, etc.

cod-liver oil (kod′liv′ər) the oil extracted from the liver of cod or of related species, used as a medicine. It is rich in vitamins A and D.

co-ed or **co·ed** (kō′ed′) *n. Informal.* a female student at a co-educational school, college, or university.

hat, āge, cãre, fär; let, ēqual, tėrm; it, īce
hot, ōpen, ôrder; oil, out; cup, pu̇t, rüle, ūse
əbove, takən, pencəl, lemən, circəs
ch, child; ng, long; sh, ship
th, thin; ᴛʜ, then; zh, measure

co-ed·u·ca·tion (kō′ej u̇ kā′shən) *n.* the education of boys and girls or men and women together in the same school or classes.

co-ed·u·ca·tion·al (kō′ej u̇ kā′shən əl) *adj.* **1** educating boys and girls or men and women together in the same school or classes. **2** having to do with co-education. —**co′-ed·u·ca′tion·al·ly,** *adv.*

co·ef·fi·cient (kō′ə fish′ənt) *n.* **1** in mathematics, a number or symbol put before and multiplying another. In *3x*, *3* is the coefficient of *x*; in *axy*, *a* is the coefficient of *xy*. **2** in physics, a ratio used as a multiplier to calculate the behavior of a substance under different conditions of heat, light, etc.: *coefficient of expansion.* —*adj.* co-operating.

coe·la·canth (sē′lə kanth′) *n.* any of a group of fishes having rounded scales and lobed fins, formerly considered extinct. A coelacanth is similar to the primitive sea vertebrates that gave rise to all land vertebrates. [< NL *coelacanthus* < Gk. *koilos* hollow + *akantha* thorn, spine]

coe·len·ter·ate (si len′tər āt′ or si len′tər it) *n.* one of a group of salt-water invertebrates with saclike bodies: *Hydras, jellyfish, corals, etc. are coelenterates.* —*adj.* belonging to this group. [< NL *coelenterata*, pl. < Gk. *koilos* hollow + *enteron* intestine]

coe·li·ac (sē′lē ak′) *adj.* in anatomy, of or in the abdominal cavity. [< L < Gk. *koiliakos* < *koilia* belly, bowels < *koilos* hollow]

coe·no·bite (sē′nə bīt′ or sen′ə bīt′) *n.* cenobite.

co-e·qual (kō ē′kwəl) *adj.* equal in rank, degree, etc. —*n.* one that is co-equal. —**co-e′qual·ly,** *adv.*

co·erce (kō ėrs′) *v.* **co·erced, co·erc·ing. 1** compel; force: *The prisoner was coerced into confessing to the crime.* **2** control or restrain by force. [< L *coercere* < *co-* together + *arcere* restrain] —**co·erc′er,** *n.*

co·er·cion (kō ėr′shən) *n.* **1** the use of force; compulsion; constraint. **2** government by force.

co·er·cive (kō ėr′siv) *adj.* **1** compelling; forcing. **2** restraining. —**co·er′cive·ly,** *adv.* —**co·er′cive·ness,** *n.*

co·e·val (kō ē′vəl) *adj.* **1** of the same age, date, or duration. **2** contemporary. —*n.* a contemporary. [< LL *coaevus* < *co-* equal + *aevum* age] —**co·e′val·ly,** *adv.*

co-ex·ec·u·tor (kō′eg zek′yů tər) *n.* a person who, along with another, is an executor of a will.

co-ex·ist (kō′eg zist′) *v.* exist together or at the same time: *Orange trees have co-existing fruit and flowers.*

co-ex·ist·ence (kō′eg zis′təns) *n.* existence together or at the same time.

co-ex·ist·ent (kō′eg zis′tənt) *adj.* co-existing.

co-ex·tend (kō′eks tend′) *v.* extend equally or to the same limits.

co-ex·ten·sion (kō′eks ten′shən) *n.* **1** extension over an equal amount of space. **2** extension over exactly the same time.

co-ex·ten·sive (kō′eks ten′siv) *adj.* extending equally; extending over the same space or time. —**co-ex·ten′sive·ly,** *adv.*

C. of E. Church of England.

cof·fee (kof′ē) *n.* **1** a dark-brown drink, served hot or cold, made with boiling water and the ground seeds of a certain shrub. Coffee became known in Europe about 1600. **2** coffee beans, especially when roasted and ground. **3** the tall, tropical shrub on which coffee beans grow. **4** the color of coffee. **5** a social gathering at which coffee is served. [< Turkish *qahveh* < Arabic *qahwa*]

coffee bean the seed of the coffee shrub. Coffee beans are roasted and ground to make coffee.

coffee house a place where coffee and other refreshments are served.

coffee klatsch or **klatch** (kläch) *n.* a get-together at which coffee is served. [*coffee* + G *Klatsch* chitchat]

coffee mill a machine for grinding coffee.

coffee pot a container for making or serving coffee.

coffee shop especially in a hotel, a place where coffee, light refreshments, and inexpensive meals are served.

coffee table a low table, usually placed in front of a chesterfield and used for serving coffee and other refreshments, etc.

cof·fer (kof′ər) *n.* **1** a box, chest, or trunk, especially one used to hold money or other valuable things. **2** an ornamental panel in a ceiling, etc. **3** a cofferdam. **4 coffers,** *pl.* treasury; funds. —*v.* **1** deposit or enclose in or as if in a coffer. **2** build or ornament with coffers: *a coffered ceiling.* [ME < OF *cofre* < L < Gk. *kophinos* basket. See COFFIN.]

Coffers (def. 2)

cof·fer·dam (kof′ər dam′) *n.* a watertight enclosure built in a shallow river, lake, etc. It is pumped dry so that the foundations of a bridge, etc. may be built.

cof·fin (kof′ən) *n.* a box into which a dead person is put to be buried; a casket. —*v.* **1** put into a coffin. **2** shut up tightly. [ME < OF *cofin* < L *cophinus* < Gk. *kophinos* basket]

cog (kog) *n.* **1** one of a series of teeth on the edge of a wheel that transfer motion by locking into the teeth of a similar wheel. **2** a wheel with such a row of teeth on it. **3** a person who plays a small but necessary part in an action, process, system, etc. **4** a projection on one piece of wood that fits into a notch on another piece to make a joint. **5** *Informal.* **slip a cog,** make a mistake. [ME *cogge* < Scand.; cf. Swedish *kugge*]

co·gen·cy (kō′jən sē) *n.* a forcible quality; power of convincing.

co·gent (kō′jənt) *adj.* forcible; convincing: *The lawyer's cogent arguments convinced the jury.* [< L *cogens, -entis,* ppr. of *cogere* < *co-* together + *agere* drive] —**co′gent·ly,** *adv.* —**Syn.** potent, compelling. See **valid.**

cogged (kogd) *adj.* having cogs.

cog·i·tate (koj′ə tāt′) *v.* **-tat·ed, -tat·ing.** think over; consider with care; meditate; ponder. [< L *cogitare* < *co-* (intensive) + *agitare* consider < *agere* discuss] —**cog′i·ta·tor,** *n.*

cog·i·ta·tion (koj′ə tā′shən) *n.* deep thought; careful consideration; pondering; meditation.

cog·i·ta·tive (koj′ə tā′tiv) *adj.* thoughtful; meditative. —**cog′i·ta′tive·ly,** *adv.*

co·gnac (kōn′yak or kon′yak; *French,* kô nyäk′) *n.* a kind of French brandy. [< F < *Cognac,* a town and region in France]

cog·nate (kog′nāt) *adj.* **1** related by family or origin. English, Dutch, and German are cognate languages. **2** having a similar nature or quality. —*n.* a person, word, or thing related to another by having a common source. German *Wasser* and English *water* are cognates. [< L *cognatus* < *co-* together + *gnatus* born]

cog·ni·tion (kog nish′ən) *n.* **1** the act of knowing; perception; awareness. **2** the thing known, perceived, or recognized. [< L *cognitio, -onis* < *cognoscere* < *co-* (intensive) + *gnoscere* know]

cog·ni·za·ble (kog′nə zə bəl) *adj.* **1** that can be known or perceived; recognizable. **2** within the jurisdiction of a law court.

cog·ni·zance (kog′nə zəns or kon′ə zəns) *n.* **1** knowledge; perception; awareness: *The dictator had cognizance of plots against him.* **2** in law: **a** knowledge upon which a judge is bound to act without having it proved in evidence. **b** the right or power to deal with (something) judicially. **3** jurisdiction; responsibility; charge. [ME *conisance* < OF *conoissance* < *conoistre* know < L *cognoscere.* See COGNITION.]

cog·ni·zant (kog′nə zənt or kon′ə zənt) *adj.* aware: *The general was cognizant of the enemy's movements.*

cog·no·men (kog nō′mən) *n.* **1** a surname; family name; last name. **2** any name. **3** a nickname. **4** in ancient Rome, the third or family name of a person, as *Cicero* in *Marcus Tullius Cicero.* [< L *cognomen* < *co-* with + *nomen* name; form influenced by *cognoscere* recognize]

cog·wheel (kog′hwēl′ or -wēl′) *n.* a wheel with teeth projecting from the rim for transmitting or receiving motion.

Cogwheels. As one wheel turns, its teeth push against the teeth of the other wheel, causing it to turn.

co·hab·it (kō hab′it) *v.* **1** live together as husband and wife. **2** *Archaic.* live together. [< LL *cohabitare* < L *co-* with + *habitare* dwell]

co·hab·i·ta·tion (kō hab′ə tā′shən) *n.* the act or state of living together as husband and wife.

co·heir (kō är′) *n.* an heir with another or others.

co·heir·ess (kō är′is) *n.* an heiress with another or others.

co·here (kō hēr′) *v.* **-hered, -her·ing.** **1** stick or hold together as parts of the same mass or substance: *The particles making up a brick cohere.* **2** be connected logically; be consistent. [< L *cohaerere* < *co-* together + *haerere* stick]

co·her·ence (kō hēr′əns) *n.* **1** a logical connection; consistency. **2** a sticking together; cohesion. —**Syn. 1** congruity.

co·her·en·cy (kō hēr′ən sē) *n.* coherence.

co·her·ent (kō hēr′ənt) *adj.* **1** logically connected; consistent in structure and thought: *A sentence that is not coherent is hard to understand.* **2** sticking together; holding together. —**co·her′ent·ly,** *adv.*

co·her·er (kō hēr′ər) *n.* a device for detecting radio waves, formerly used instead of vacuum tubes in radio sets.

co·he·sion (kō hē′zhən) *n.* **1 a** a sticking together. **b** tendency to hold together: *Wet sand has more cohesion than dry sand.* **2** in physics, the attraction between molecules of the same kind: *The forming of water into drops is a result of cohesion.* **3** in botany, the union of one part with another. [< stem of L *cohaesus* pressed together, pp. of *cohaerere.* See COHERE.]

co·he·sive (kō hē′siv) *adj.* sticking together; tending to hold together. —**co·he′sive·ly,** *adv.* —**co·he′sive·ness,** *n.*

co·ho or **co·hoe** (kō′hō) *n.* **-hoes.** a Pacific salmon that ranges from northern California to northwestern Alaska. [origin uncertain]

co·hort (kō′hôrt) *n.* **1** in ancient Rome, a part of a legion. There were from 300 to 600 soldiers in each cohort, and ten cohorts in each legion. **2** a group of soldiers. **3** a group; band; company. [< L *cohors, -ortis* court, enclosure. Doublet of COURT.]

coif (koif) *n.* **1** a cap or hood that fits closely around the head. **2** a cap worn under a veil by a nun. **3** any of various caps worn by European women. —*v.* provide or cover with a coif or something like a coif. [ME < OF *coife* < LL *cofia* < Gmc.]

coif·feur (kwä fėr′; *French,* kwä fœr′) *n.* a hairdresser. [< F *coiffeur* < *coiffer* coif]

coif·fure (kwä fūr′; *French,* kwä fYr′) *n.* **1** a style of arranging the hair. **2** a covering for the hair; headdress. [< F *coiffure* < *coiffer* coif]

coign (koin) *n.* a projecting corner. [var. of *coin*]

coign of vantage a good location for watching or doing something.

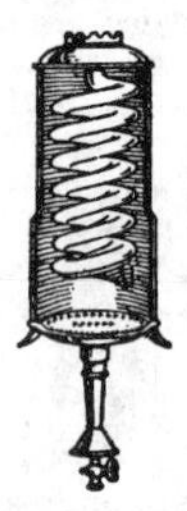
A coil of pipe in a heater

coil[1] (koil) *v.* **1** wind around and around in circular or spiral shape: *A snake is able to coil itself up or coil around a branch.* **2** move in a winding course. —*n.* **1** anything wound around and around in circular or spiral shape: *a coil of rope.* **2** one wind or turn of a coil. **3** a series of connected pipes arranged in a coil or row, as in a radiator. **4** a spiral of wire for conducting electricity. **5** a twist of hair. **6** a small, round pile of hay. [< OF *coillir* < L *colligere*. See COLLECT.] **—coil′er,** *n.*

coil[2] (koil) *n. Archaic.* disturbance; trouble. [origin uncertain]

coin (koin) *n.* **1** a piece of metal stamped by a government for use as money. Nickels, dimes, and quarters are coins. **2** metal money: *The Mint makes coin by stamping metal.* **3 pay someone back in his own coin,** treat someone as he treated oneself or others.
—*v.* **1** make (money) by stamping metal.
2 make (metal) into money. **3** make up; invent: *The word "blurb" was coined by Gelett Burgess.* **4 coin money,** *Informal.* become rich; have a prospering business.
[ME < OF *coin* corner < L *cuneus* wedge]

coin·age (koin′ij) *n.* **1** the making of coins. **2** coins; metal money. **3** a system of coins: *Canada has a decimal coinage.* **4** the right to coin money. **5** the act or process of making up; inventing: *the coinage of new words.* **6** the word, phrase, etc. invented.

co·in·cide (kō′in sīd′) *v.* **-cid·ed, -cid·ing. 1** occupy the same place in space: *If these triangles △ △ were placed one over the other, they would coincide.* **2** occupy the same time: *The working hours of my two friends coincide.*
3 correspond exactly; agree: *Her opinion coincides with mine.* [< Med.L *coincidere* < L *co-* together + *in* upon + *cadere* fall] —**Syn. 3** concur, harmonize, tally. See **agree.**

co·in·ci·dence (kō in′sə dəns) *n.* **1** the chance occurrence of two things at such a time as to seem remarkable, fitting, etc. **2** an exact correspondence; agreement. **3** a coinciding; occupying of the same time or place.

co·in·ci·dent (kō in′sə dənt) *adj.* **1** coinciding; happening at the same time. **2** occupying the same place or position. **3** in exact agreement. **—co·in′ci·dent·ly,** *adv.*

co·in·ci·den·tal (kō in′sə den′təl) *adj.* **1** coincident. **2** showing coincidence. **—co·in′ci·den′tal·ly,** *adv.*

coin·er (koin′ər) *n.* **1** a person who makes coins. **2** a maker of counterfeit coins. **3** a maker; inventor.

coin-op·er·at·ed (koin′op′ə rā′tid) *adj.* worked by the insertion of a coin or coins: *Machines that sell candy, cigarettes, etc. are coin-operated.*

co·in·sur·ance (kō′in shür′əns) *n.* insurance jointly with another or others.

Coin·treau (kwän′trō; *French,* kwaN trō′) *n.* a clear, orange-flavored liqueur, a French brand of curaçao.

coir (koir) *n.* a fibre obtained from the outer husks of coconuts, used to make rope, mats, etc. [< Malayalam *kayar* cord]

coke[1] (kōk) *n. v.* **coked, cok·ing.** —*n.* a fuel made from coal by heating it in a closed oven until the gases have been removed. Coke burns with much heat and little smoke; it is used in furnaces, for melting metal, etc.
—*v.* change into coke. [? var. of *colk* core]

coke[2] (kōk) *n. Slang.* cocaine.

col- form of **com-** before l, as in *collect.*

col. *pl.* **cols. 1** column. **2** colony.

Col. 1 Colonel. **2** Columbia. **3** Colossians.

col·an·der (kul′ən dər or kol′ən dər) *n.* a vessel or dish full of small holes for draining off liquids. [< VL *colator* or Med.L *colatorium* < L *colare* strain]

Col·by (kōl′bē) *n.* a soft cheese, made by stirring curd as the whey drains off instead of allowing it to settle.

col·chi·cum (kol′chə kəm) *n.* **1** a plant having purple or white flowers that resemble crocuses. **2** a medicine for gout, obtained from this plant. [< L < Gk. *kolchikon* < *Colchis*]

Col·chis (kol′kis) *n.* an ancient country on the eastern shore of the Black Sea. In Greek legend it is the country where the Golden Fleece was found by Jason and the Argonauts.

cold (kōld) *adj.* **1** much less warm than the body: *Snow and ice are cold.* **2** having a relatively low temperature: *This coffee is cold.* **3** lacking in feeling; unfriendly: *a cold greeting.* **4** lacking in feeling, passion, sympathy, or enthusiasm; indifferent: *a cold nature.* **5** faint; weak: *a cold scent.* **6** of colors, blue, green, or gray; not red or yellow.
—*n.* **1** the lack of heat or warmth; low temperature.
2 a sickness that causes running at the nose, sore throat,

hat, āge, cãre, fär; let, ēqual, tėrm; it, īce
hot, ōpen, ôrder; oil, out; cup, pu̇t, rüle, ūse
əbove, takən, pencəl, lemən, circəs
ch, child; ng, long; sh, ship
th, thin; ᴛʜ, then; zh, measure

sneezing, etc. **3 catch cold,** become sick with a cold. **4 (out) in the cold,** all alone; neglected; not taking part. **5 take cold,** become sick with a cold. [OE *cald*]
Syn. *adj.* **1, 2 Cold, chilly, cool** = having a low temperature, especially in comparison with body heat. **Cold** = having a low temperature, judged by the standard of normal body heat: *A cold wind is blowing.* **Chilly** = cold enough to be uncomfortable and make a person shiver a little: *Without my coat I feel chilly.* **Cool** = neither hot nor cold, but closer to cold: *After the hot day the evening seems cool.* **4** unresponsive, apathetic.

cold-blood·ed (kōld′blud′id) *adj.* **1** having blood whose temperature varies with that of the surroundings. Snakes and turtles are called cold-blooded, but their blood is actually very close to the temperature of the air or water in which they live. **2** feeling the cold because of poor circulation. **3** lacking in feeling; cruel. **4** without emotion or interest; unimpassioned: *He gave a cold-blooded account of the accident.* **—cold′-blood′ed·ly,** *adv.* **—cold′-blood′ed·ness,** *n.*

cold chisel a strong, steel chisel for cutting cold metal.

cold comfort something without consolation, cheer, or encouragement.

cold cream a creamy, soothing salve for the skin.

cold cuts cooked or prepared meats or fowl, such as beef, chicken, salami, ham, etc., sliced and served cold.

cold feet *Informal.* fear or timidity; a reluctance to continue with some enterprise because of fear or timidity.

cold frame a wooden frame with a glass top used out of doors to protect young or delicate plants from the cold.

cold front in meteorology, the advancing edge of a cold air mass as it overtakes and passes beneath a warmer one.

cold-heart·ed (kōld′här′tid) *adj.* lacking in feeling; unsympathetic; unkind. **—cold′-heart′ed·ly,** *adv.* **—cold′-heart′ed·ness,** *n.*

cold light light without heat. Phosphorescence and fluorescence are kinds of cold light.

cold·ly (kōld′lē) *adv.* in a cold manner; without friendliness, warmth, or enthusiasm.

cold·ness (kōld′nis) *n.* **1** the state or quality of being cold. **2** a lack of warmth of feeling or friendliness; indifference.

cold pack 1 something cold put on the body for medical purposes. **2** a method of canning fruits or vegetables.

cold-pack (kōld′pak′) *v.* **1** put a cold pack on. **2** can (food) by cold pack.

cold rubber a tough synthetic rubber formed at a low temperature.

cold shoulder *Informal.* deliberately unfriendly or indifferent treatment; neglect.

cold-shoul·der (kōld′shōl′dər) *v. Informal.* treat in an unfriendly or indifferent way.

cold snap a sudden spell of cold weather.

cold sore a blister near or on the mouth, often accompanying a cold or a fever.

cold steel a steel weapon, such as a knife or sword.

cold storage storage in a very cold place. Perishable foods are put in cold storage to preserve them.

cold sweat perspiration accompanied by a chilly feeling.

cold war a prolonged contest for national advantage, conducted by diplomatic, economic, and psychological rather than military means.

cold wave[1] a period of very cold weather.

cold wave[2] a permanent wave applied to the hair by means of chemicals rather than heat.

cole (kōl) *n.* any of various plants belonging to the same family as the cabbage, especially rape. [OE *cāl,* var. of *cāw(e)l* < L *caulis* cabbage]

co·le·op·ter (kō′lē op′tər or kol′ē op′tər) *n.* **1** a coleopterous insect. 2 an experimental jet aircraft designed to take off and land vertically.

co·le·op·ter·ous (kō′lē op′tər əs or kol′ē op′tər əs) *adj.* belonging to a group of insects including beetles and weevils. In this group the front pair of wings is horny, serving to sheathe the second and membranous pair. [< Gk. *koleopteros* < *koleos* sheath + *pteron* wing]

cole·slaw (kōl′slo′ or -slô′) *n.* a salad made of shredded raw cabbage. [< Du. *kool sla* cabbage salad]

co·le·us (kō′lē əs) *n.* a plant often grown for its showy, colorful leaves. [< NL < Gk. *koleos* sheath; from the union of the filaments]

cole·wort (kōl′wėrt′) *n.* **1** a cole. **2** a kind of cabbage having a loosely packed head of curly leaves.

col·ic (kol′ik) *n.* severe pains in the abdomen. [< LL < Gk. *kolikos* of the colon]

col·ick·y (kol′ik ē) *adj.* **1** of colic. **2** having colic.

col·i·se·um (kol′ə sē′əm) *n.* **1** a large building or stadium for games, contests, etc. **2** **Coliseum,** Colosseum. [< Med.L var. of LL *colosseum.* See COLOSSEUM.]

co·li·tis (kō lī′tis or kə lī′tis) *n.* in medicine, inflammation of the colon, often causing severe pain in the abdomen. [< NL *colitis* < Gk. *kolon* colon + *-itis*]

coll. **1** college. **2** collection. **3** collector. **4** colleague. **5** colloquial. **6** collegiate.

col·lab·o·rate (kə lab′ə rāt′) *v.* **-rat·ed, -rat·ing.** **1** work together: *Two authors collaborated on that book.* **2** aid or co-operate with someone traitorously. [< L *collaborare* < *com-* with + *laborare* work]

col·lab·o·ra·tion (kə lab′ə rā′shən) *n.* **1** the act of working together. **2** the act of aiding or co-operating with someone traitorously.

col·lab·o·ra·tive (kə lab′ə rə tiv or kə lab′ə rā′tiv) *adj.* of or resulting from collaboration.

col·lab·o·ra·tor (kə lab′ə rā′tər) *n.* **1** a person who works with another, usually in literary work. **2** a person who aids or co-operates with someone traitorously.

col·lage (kə läzh′) *n.* a picture made by pasting on a background such items as portions of photographs, newspapers, fabrics, string, etc. [< MF *collage* a gluing < OF *colle* < VL *colla* < Gk. *kolla* glue]

col·lapse (kə laps′) *v.* **-lapsed, -laps·ing,** *n.* —*v.* **1** fall in; shrink together suddenly: *Sticking a pin into the balloon caused it to collapse.* **2** break down; fail suddenly: *Both his health and his business collapsed within a year.* **3** fold or push together: *collapse a telescope.* **4** of lungs, become deflated.
—*n.* **1** a falling in; sudden shrinking together: *A heavy flood caused the collapse of the bridge.* **2** a breakdown; failure: *She is suffering from a nervous collapse.* [< L *collapsus,* pp. of *collabi* < *com-* (intensive) + *labi* fall]

col·laps·i·ble (kə lap′sə bəl) *adj.* made so that it can be folded or pushed into a smaller space.

col·lar (kol′ər) *n.* **1** a straight or turned-over neckband of a coat, a dress, or a shirt. **2** a separate band of linen, lace, or other material worn around the neck. **3** a leather or metal band for the neck of a dog or other pet animal. **4** a leather roll for a horse's neck to bear the weight of the loads he pulls. See the picture of **harness.** **5** a colored stripe or other mark around an animal's neck. **6** a ring, disk, or flange on a rod, shaft, etc. that keeps a part from moving to the side. **7** a short pipe connecting two other pipes.
—*v.* **1** put a collar on. **2** seize by the collar; capture. **3** *Informal.* lay hold of; take. [ME < AF < L *collare* < *collum* neck] —**col′lar·less,** *adj.* —**col′lar·like′,** *adj.*

col·lar·bone (kol′ər bōn′) *n.* the bone connecting the breastbone and the shoulder blade; clavicle. See **skeleton** for diagram.

col·late (kə lāt′ or kol′āt) *v.* **-lat·ed, -lat·ing.** **1** compare carefully. **2** arrange in order; put together. [< L *collatus,* pp. to *conferre* < *com-* together + *ferre* bring]

col·lat·er·al (kə lat′ər əl) *adj.* **1** parallel; side by side. **2** related but less important; secondary; indirect. **3** in a parallel line of descent; descended from the same ancestors, but in a different line: *Cousins are collateral relatives.* **4** additional. **5** secured by stocks, bonds, etc.
—*n.* **1** a collateral relative. **2** stocks, bonds, etc. pledged as security for a loan. [< Med.L *collateralis* < *com-* together + L *lateralis* lateral] —**col·lat′er·al·ly,** *adv.*

col·la·tion (kə lā′shən) *n.* **1** a collating; a careful comparison. **2** a light meal. Originally, in Benedictine monasteries, a light meal following readings of the Lives of the Fathers (*collationes patrum*). [ME < OF < L *collatio, -onis* a putting together]

col·la·tor (kə lā′tər or kol′āt ər) *n.* a person who collates.

col·league (kol′ēg) *n.* an associate; a fellow worker: *The doctor invited a colleague to examine the patient.* [< F *collègue* < L *collega* < *com-* together + *legare* send or choose as deputy]

col·lect[1] (kə lekt′) *v.* **1** bring or come together; gather together: *Dust collects on the furniture. A crowd collects at the scene of an accident.* **2** gather together for a set: *collect stamps.* **3** ask and receive pay for (bills, debts, dues, taxes, etc.). **4** regain control of: *After a shock a person must collect himself.*
—*adj. adv.* to be paid for at the place of delivery: *a collect telegram, telephone collect.* [< L *collectus,* pp. of *colligere* < *com-* together + *legere* gather]
—**Syn.** *v.* **1** See **gather.**

col·lect[2] (kol′ekt) *n.* a short prayer used in certain church services. [ME < OF *collecte* < Med.L, short for *oratio ad collectam* prayer on assembly < L *collecta* a gathering in or gathering together < *colligere.* See COLLECT[1].]

col·lect·a·ble (kə lek′tə bəl) *adj.* that can be collected.

col·lect·ed (kə lek′tid) *adj.* **1** brought together; gathered together. **2** under control; not confused or disturbed; calm. —**col·lect′ed·ly,** *adv.* —**col·lect′ed·ness,** *n.* —**Syn. 2** See **calm.**

col·lect·i·ble (kə lek′tə bəl) *adj.* collectable.

col·lec·tion (kə lek′shən) *n.* **1** the act or practice of collecting: *The collection of these stamps took ten years.* **2** a group of things gathered from many places and belonging together: *The library has a large collection of books.* **3** money collected: *A church takes up a collection during services.* **4** a mass; heap: *There is a collection of dust in an unused room.*

col·lec·tive (kə lek′tiv) *adj.* **1** of a group; as a group; taken all together. **2** in grammar, singular in form, but plural in meaning. *Crowd, people, troop,* and *herd* are collective nouns. **3** formed by collecting. **4** owned, worked, or conducted on a co-operative basis: *a collective farm, collective farming.*
—*n.* **1** in grammar, a noun whose singular form names a group of objects or persons. **2** a farm, factory, or other organization with collectivistic management.

☛ **collective nouns.** Whether to use the singular or the plural form of verbs and pronouns with collective nouns depends on the meaning intended. When the collective noun means the group as a whole, it takes a singular form of the verb or pronoun: *The committee is planning its work carefully.* When it means the individuals of the group, it takes a plural verb or pronoun: *After the plans are completed, the committee are going to their homes.*

collective bargaining negotiation about wages, hours, and other working conditions between workers organized as a group and their employer or employers.

col·lec·tive·ly (kə lek′tiv lē) *adv.* **1** as a group; all together. **2** in a singular form, but with a plural meaning.

col·lec·tiv·ism (kə lek′tiv iz′əm) *n.* the control of the production of goods and services and the distribution of wealth by people as a group or by a government.

col·lec·tiv·ist (kə lek′tiv ist) *n.* a person who favors or supports collectivism. —*adj.* collectivistic.

col·lec·tiv·is·tic (kə lek′tiv is′tik) *adj.* of collectivism or collectivists.

col·lec·ti·vize (kə lek′tə vīz′) *v.* **-vized, -viz·ing.** make (a state, economy, agricultural community, etc.) collective; transfer ownership of, from an individual or individuals to the state or all the people collectively. —**col·lec′ti·vi·za′tion,** *n.*

col·lec·tor (kə lek′tər) *n.* **1** a person or thing that collects. **2** a person hired to collect money owed.

col·lec·tor·ship (kə lek′tər ship′) *n.* **1** the office of a collector. **2** the district covered by a collector.

col·leen (kol′ēn or kə lēn′) *n. Irish.* a girl. [< Ir. *cailín,* dim. of *caile* girl]

col·lege (kol′ij) *n.* **1** an institution of higher learning that gives degrees or diplomas. **2** a university. **3** the academic department of a university for general instruction, as distinguished from the special, professional, or graduate schools. **4** a school for special or professional instruction, as in medicine, pharmacy, agriculture, or music. **5** an organized association of persons having certain powers, rights, duties, and purposes: *the electoral college.* **6** a building or buildings used by a college. *—adj.* of or associated with college or university. [ME < OF *colege* < L *collegium* < *collega.* See COLLEAGUE.]

collège classique (kô lezh klä sēk′) *Cdn. French.* classical college.

College of Cardinals the cardinals of the Roman Catholic Church collectively. The College of Cardinals elects and advises the Pope.

col·le·gian (kə lē′jən or kə lē′jē ən) *n.* a college student.

col·le·giate (kə lē′jit or kə lē′jē it) *adj.* **1** of or like a college. **2** of or like college students. *—n. Cdn.* **1** a collegiate institute. **2** *Informal.* any high school or secondary school.

collegiate church **1** a church that has a chapter or college but no bishop's see. **2** *U.S.* an association of churches administered by several pastors jointly. **3** a church belonging to such an association. **4** in Scotland, a church served by two or more ministers of equal rank.

collegiate institute *Cdn.* in some provinces, a secondary school providing specified facilities, or having a set minimum number of specialist teachers, over and above those required in a high school.

col·lide (kə līd′) *v.* **-lid·ed, -lid·ing. 1** come violently into contact; come together with force; crash: *Two large ships collided in the harbor.* **2** clash; conflict. [< L *collidere* < *com-* together + *laedere,* originally, strike]

col·lie (kol′ē) *n.* **1** a breed of large, intelligent, thick-haired dog, used for tending sheep or kept as a pet. **2** a dog of this breed. [origin uncertain]

col·lier (kol′yər) *n.* **1** a ship for carrying coal. **2** a coal miner. [ME *colier* < *col* coal]

col·lier·y (kol′yər ē) *n.* **-lier·ies.** a coal mine and its buildings and equipment.

col·li·mate (kol′ə māt′) *v.* **-mat·ed, -mat·ing. 1** bring into line; make parallel. **2** adjust accurately the line of sight of (a surveying instrument, telescope, etc.). [< L *collimare,* misreading for *collineare,* ult. < *com-* together + *linea* line] **—col′li·ma′tion,** *n.*

col·li·ma·tor (kol′ə mā′tər) *n.* in optics: **1** a small fixed telescope used for adjusting the line of sight of other instruments. **2** in a spectroscope, a tube used to throw parallel rays of light on the prism. **3** the lens of this tube.

col·lin·e·ar (kə lin′ē ər) *adj.* in geometry, lying in the same straight line: *collinear points.*—**col·lin′e·ar·ly,** *adv.*

col·li·sion (kə lizh′ən) *n.* **1** a violent rushing against; hitting or striking violently together. **2** a clash; conflict. [< LL *collisio, -onis* < L *collidere.* See COLLIDE.]

col·lo·cate (kol′ō kāt′) *v.* **-cat·ed, -cat·ing. 1** place together. **2** arrange. [< L *collocare* < *com-* together + *locare* place]

col·lo·ca·tion (kol′ō kā′shən) *n.* an arrangement: *the collocation of words in a sentence.*

col·lo·di·on (kə lō′dē ən) *n.* a glue-like liquid solution of guncotton in ether or in ether and alcohol. It dries very rapidly and leaves a tough, waterproof, transparent film. [< Gk. *kollōdēs* gluey < *kolla* glue]

col·loid (kol′oid) *n.* in chemistry, a substance composed of particles that are extremely small but larger than most molecules. Colloids do not actually dissolve, but remain suspended in a suitable gas, liquid, or solid. *—adj.* colloidal. [< Gk. *kolla* glue]

col·loi·dal (kə loi′dəl) *adj.* being a colloid; containing a colloid; like a colloid.

col·lop (kol′əp) *n.* **1** a small slice of meat. **2** a small slice or piece of anything. **3** a fold of flesh or skin on the body. [ME *colope;* origin uncertain]

hat, āge, cãre, fär; let, ēqual, tėrm; it, īce
hot, ōpen, ôrder; oil, out; cup, pu̇t, rüle, ūse
əbove, takən, pencəl, lemən, circəs
ch, child; ng, long; sh, ship
th, thin; ᴛʜ, then; zh, measure

colloq. **1** colloquial. **2** colloquialism.

col·lo·qui·al (kə lō′kwē əl) *adj.* used in everyday informal talk, but not in formal speech or writing. *They've had it* and *It's a cinch* are colloquial expressions. **—col·lo′qui·al·ly,** *adv.* **—Syn.** conversational.

☛ **Colloquial** = conversational, used in speaking. Since the speech of people varies with their education, work, and social status, there are obviously many different types of colloquial English. Since the bulk of conversation is informal, *colloquial* suggests informal rather than formal English. It need not, however, mean the speech of uneducated people. As used in many dictionaries, *colloquial* refers to informal cultivated English; the equivalent label in this dictionary is *Informal.* See usage note at **informal.**

col·lo·qui·al·ism (kə lō′kwē əl iz′əm) *n.* **1** a colloquial word or phrase. **2** colloquial style or usage.

col·lo·qui·um (kə lō′kwē əm) *n.* **-qui·ums** or **-qui·a. 1** a meeting or conference, especially of scholars, scientists, etc. on a particular subject. **2** a seminar. [< L *colloquium* conversation]

col·lo·quy (kol′ə kwē) *n.* **-quies. 1** a talking together; conversation; conference. **2** a written dialogue: *Erasmus' Colloquies.* [< L *colloquium* < *colloqui* < *com-* with + *loqui* speak]

col·lude (kə lüd′) *v.* **-lud·ed, -lud·ing.** act together through a secret understanding; conspire in a fraud. [< L *colludere* < *com-* with + *ludere* play]

col·lu·sion (kə lü′zhən) *n.* a secret agreement for some wrong purpose. [< L *collusio, -onis* < *colludere.* See COLLUDE.]

col·lu·sive (kə lü′siv) *adj.* involving collusion; fraudulent. **—col·lu′sive·ly,** *adv.*

Colo. Colorado.

co·logne (kə lōn′) *n.* a fragrant liquid, not so strong as perfume. [< F *eau de Cologne,* meaning water of Cologne < *Cologne,* West Germany, where it was first made]

Co·lom·bi·an (kə lum′bē ən) *n.* a native or inhabitant of the South American republic of Colombia. *—adj.* of or having to do with Colombia.

Colombo Plan (kə lum′bō) a co-operative effort to help countries of southern and southeastern Asia to attain a higher standard of living. [< *Colombo,* the capital of Ceylon]

co·lon[1] (kō′lən) *n.* a mark (:) of punctuation used before a series of items, explanations, illustrations, long quotations, etc. to set them off from the rest of the sentence. [< L < Gk. *kōlon* limb, clause]

co·lon[2] (kō′lən) *n.* **co·lons** or **co·la** (kō′lə). in anatomy, the lower part of the large intestine. [ME < L < Gk. *kolon*]

co·lon[3] (kō lōn′) *n.* **co·lons** or **co·lo·nes** (kō lō′nās). **1** a unit of money in Costa Rica and El Salvador. See able at **money. 2** a coin worth one colon. [< Sp. *colón* < Christóbal *Colón* Christopher Columbus]

co·lon[4] (kô lôn′) *n. French.* a French settler or the descendant of a French settler; a colonial.

colo·nel (kėr′nəl) *n.* in the army, a commissioned officer senior to a lieutenant-colonel and junior to a brigadier. He usually commands a regiment. *Abbrev.:* Col. [earlier also *coronel,* < F *coronel,* var. of *colonel* < Ital. *colonnello* commander of a regiment, ult. < *colonna* column < L *columna*]

☛ **Colonel** is a spelling that has survived a change of pronunciation. The word, from the French, had two parallel forms, *colonel, coronel,* each pronounced in three syllables. For 150 years the word has been pronounced (kėr′nəl), from the *coronel* form, but the spelling has survived as *colonel.*

colo·nel·cy (kėr′nəl sē) *n.* **-cies.** the rank, commission, or authority of a colonel.

co·lo·ni·al (kə lō′nē əl) *adj.* **1** of a colony; having to do with colonies. **2** of the time when a nation was a colony: *colonial furniture.* **—n. 1** a person living in a colony. **2** a style of furniture, architecture, etc. that prevailed at the time when a nation was a colony. —**co·lo′ni·al·ly,** *adv.*

co·lo·ni·al·ism (kə lō′nē ə liz′əm) *n.* **1** the practice or policy of a nation that rules or seeks to rule over other countries as colonies. **2** the state of being a colony.

co·lo·ni·al·ist (kə lō′nē ə list) *n.* a person who supports or practises colonialism. *—adj.* **1** of or having to do with colonialism or colonialists. **2** supporting or practising colonialism.

col·o·nist (kol′ə nist) *n.* **1** a person who helps to found a colony; settler. **2** a person living in a colony.

col·o·ni·za·tion (kol′ə nə zā′shən or kol′ə nī zā′shən) *n.* the establishment of a colony or colonies: *the colonization of North America.*

col·o·nize (kol′ə nīz′) *v.* **-nized, -niz·ing. 1** establish a colony or colonies in: *The English colonized Newfoundland.* **2** establish (persons) in a colony; settle in a colony. **3** form a colony. —**col′o·niz′er,** *n.*

col·on·nade (kol′ə nād′) *n.* in architecture, a series of columns set the same distance apart. [< F < Ital. *colonnata* < *colonna* column < L *columna*]

A colonnade

col·on·nad·ed (kol′ə nād′id) *adj.* having a colonnade.

col·o·ny (kol′ə nē) *n.* **-nies. 1** a group of people who leave their own country and go to settle in another land, but who still remain citizens of their original country. **2** the settlement made by such a group of people. **3** a territory distant from the country that governs it. **4** a group of people of one country, faith, or occupation living as a group: *There is a large Chinese colony in Vancouver. There are several Doukhobor colonies in British Columbia. There is an artists' colony in Paris.* **5** in biology, a group of animals or plants of the same kind, living or growing together: *a colony of ants. A coral island is a colony.* **6** in bacteriology, a mass of bacteria arising from a single cell, living on or in a solid or partially solid medium. **7 the Colonies, a** the thirteen British colonies that became the United States of America: New Hampshire, Massachusetts, Rhode Island, Connecticut, New York, New Jersey, Pennsylvania, Delaware, Maryland, Virginia, North Carolina, South Carolina, and Georgia. **b** formerly, the colonies, as opposed to self-governing dominions, within the British Empire. [< L *colonia* < *colonus* cultivator, settler < *colere* cultivate] —**Syn. 3** possession.

col·o·phon (kol′ə fon′ or kol′ə fən) *n.* **1** the words or inscription formerly placed at the end of a book, telling the name of the publisher, the date of publication, etc. **2** a small design or device of a publisher placed on the last page or on the title page of a book. [< LL < Gk. *kolophōn* summit, final touch]

col·or or **col·our** (kul′ər) *n.* **1** the sensation produced by the different effects of waves of light striking the retina of the eye. Different colors are produced by rays of light having different wave lengths. **2** red, yellow, green, blue, purple, etc., or any combination of these: *She never wears colors, but always dresses in black, white, or gray.* **3** a paint; dye; pigment. **4** redness of the face; a ruddy complexion. **5** a flush caused by blushing. **6** the skin color of any people or race that is not white. **7** an outward appearance; show: *His lies had some color of truth.* **8** a distinguishing quality; vividness: *His gift for description adds color to his stories.* **9** character; tone: *a horse of a different color.* **10** in music: **a** a quality of tone by which any musical instrument or combination of instruments can be recognized, used especially in orchestration; tone color; timbre. **b** the quality of expression in a musical performance or style of musical interpretation which may produce an emotional reaction in the listener or audience: *His playing has color and vigor.* **11 colors** or **colours,** *pl.* a badge, ribbon, dress, etc. worn to show allegiance. **12 the colors** or **colours, a** the flag of a nation, regiment, etc.: *He carried the colors in the parade.* **b** the ceremony of raising the flag in the morning and lowering it in the evening. **c** the army, navy, or air force: *Soldiers, sailors, and airmen serve the colors.* **13 change color** or **colour, a** turn pale. **b** blush. **14 give** or **lend color** or **colour to,** cause to seem true or likely. **15 lose color** or **colour,** turn pale. **16 show one's colors** or **colours, a** show oneself as one really is. **b** declare one's opinions or plans.
—v. **1** give color to; put color on; change the color of. **2** become red in the face; blush. **3** present so as to give a wrong idea; put in a false light: *The general colored his report of the battle to make his own mistakes seem the fault of his officers.* **4** give a distinguishing quality to: *Love of nature colored all of Wordsworth's writing.* [ME < OF < L] —**col′or·er** or **col′our·er,** *n.*
Syn. *n.* **1 Color, hue, shade** = a sensation produced by the effect of waves of light striking the retina of the eye. **Color** is the general word: *Her dress is the color of grass.* **Hue** is poetic in the general meaning of color. Technically, *hue* = the quality of a color that gives the name: red, blue, etc. It is also used to suggest partial alteration of a color: *This pottery is blue with a greenish hue.* **Shade** applies to a degree of intensity of color: *I like a blue car, but of a lighter shade than navy.* -*v.* **1** paint, dye, stain, tint, tinge. **2** flush.

col·or·a·ble or **col·our·a·ble** (kul′ər ə bəl) *adj.* **1** plausible. **2** pretended; deceptive.

col·or·ant (kul′ər ənt) *n.* a coloring agent, such as a pigment or dye. [< F *colorant,* ppr. of *colorer* to color < L *colorare*]

col·or·a·tion or **col·our·a·tion** (kul′ər ā′shən) *n.* a coloring; way in which something is colored: *The coloration of some animals is like that of their surroundings.*

col·o·ra·tu·ra (kul′ə rə tūr′ə or kul′ə rə tür′ə) in music: *—n.* **1** ornamental passages such as trills, runs, etc. **2** a vocal composition containing such passages. **3** a soprano who sings such passages.
—adj. **1** suited for singing ornamental passages: *a coloratura soprano.* **2** having ornamental passages. [< Ital. < L *color* color]

color bar or **colour bar 1** the denial, especially to Negroes, of rights, privileges, and opportunities enjoyed by white people. **2** the denial of rights, privileges, and opportunities on the grounds of skin color.

col·or·bear·er or **col·our·bear·er** (kul′ər bãr′ər) *n.* a person who carries the flag or colors; standardbearer.

col·or-blind or **col·our-blind** (kul′ər blīnd′) *adj.* unable to tell certain colors apart, especially red and green; unable to perceive certain colors or any colors. —**col′or-blind′ness** or **col′our-blind′ness,** *n.*

col·or·cast or **col·our·cast** (kul′ər kast′) *n.* a television program broadcast in color. *—v.* broadcast (over television) in color.

col·ored or **col·oured** (kul′ərd) *adj.* **1** having color; not colorless. **2** not black or white. **3** having a certain kind of color. **4** of the Negro race or any other race than the white. **5** tinged by prejudice, emotion, desire for effect, etc.

col·or·fast or **col·our·fast** (kul′ər fast′) *adj.* resistant to loss or change of color by fading or washing.

color film or **colour film 1** a film for making photographs in color. **2** a motion picture made with such film.

col·or·ful or **col·our·ful** (kul′ər fəl) *adj.* **1** abounding in color. **2** picturesque; vivid. —**col′or·ful·ly** or **col′our·ful·ly,** *adv.* —**col′or·ful·ness** or **col′our·ful·ness,** *n.*

col·or·ing or **col·our·ing** (kul′ər ing) *n.* **1** the way in which a person or thing is colored. **2** a substance used to color; pigment. **3** a false appearance: *His lies have a coloring of truth.*

coloring matter or **colouring matter** a substance used to color; pigment.

col·or·ist or **col·our·ist** (kul′ər ist) *n.* **1** an artist who is skilful in painting with colors. **2** a user of color.

col·or·less or **col·our·less** (kul′ər lis) *adj.* **1** without color. **2** without excitement or variety; uninteresting: *a colorless person.* —**col′or·less·ly** or **col′our·less·ly,** *adv.* —**col′or·less·ness** or **col′our·less·ness,** *n.*

hat, āge, cãre, fär; let, ēqual, tėrm; it, īce
hot, ōpen, ôrder; oil, out; cup, pu̇t, rüle, ūse
əbove, takən, pencəl, lemən, circəs
ch, child; ng, long; sh, ship
th, thin; ᴛʜ, then; zh, measure

color line or **colour line** a distinction in social, economic, or political privileges between members of different races.

color photography or **colour photography** photography that uses color film.

co·los·sal (kə los′əl) *adj.* huge; gigantic; vast. [< *colossus*] —**co·los′sal·ly,** *adv.*

Col·os·se·um (kol′ə sē′əm) *n.* in Rome, a large, outdoor theatre, completed in A.D. 80. The Colosseum was used for games and contests. Also, **Coliseum.** [< LL *colosseum,* neut. of L *colosseus* gigantic < *colossus* < Gk. *kolossos* gigantic statue]

Co·los·sians (kə losh′ənz) *n.* a book of the New Testament, written by the apostle Paul to the Christian people of Colossae, an ancient city of Asia Minor.

co·los·sus (kə los′əs) *n.* **-los·sus·es** or **-los·si** (-los′ī or -los′ē). **1** a huge statue. **2** anything huge; gigantic person or thing. [< L < Gk. *kolossos*]

Colossus of Rhodes a huge statue of Apollo made on the island of Rhodes about 280 B.C. It was one of the seven wonders of the ancient world.

co·los·to·my (kə los′tə mē) *n.* **-mies.** in medicine, the making of an artificial opening in the colon. [< *colon*[2] + Gk. *stoma* opening]

co·lot·o·my (kə lot′ə mē) *n.* **-mies.** in medicine, a surgical incision into the colon. [< *colon*[2] + Gk. *-tomia* -cutting]

col·our (kul′ər) *n. v.* color.

col·por·teur (kol′pôr′tər) *n.* **1** a person who travels about and distributes Bibles, tracts, etc. **2** a hawker of books, broadsides, newspapers, etc. [< F *colporteur* < *colporter* hawk, carry for sale (on the neck) < *col* neck (< L *collum*) + *porter* carry (< L *portare*)]

colt (kōlt) *n.* **1** a young horse, donkey, etc. A male horse under four or five years old is a colt. **2** a young or inexperienced person. [OE]

Colt a famous type of revolver. [< Samuel *Colt* (1814-1862), the inventor]

col·ter (kōl′tər) *n.* coulter.

colt·ish (kōl′tish) *adj.* like a colt; lively and frisky. —**colt′ish·ly,** *adv.*

colts·foot (kōlts′fu̇t′) *n.* a plant of the aster family having yellow flowers and large, heart-shaped leaves that were formerly much used in medicine.

Co·lum·bi·a (kə lum′bē ə) *n.* a name for the United States of America. Columbia is often represented as a woman dressed in red, white, and blue. [after Christopher *Columbus*]

col·um·bine (kol′əm bīn′) *n.* a plant whose flowers have petals shaped like hollow spurs. Wild columbines have red-and-yellow or blue-and-white flowers. [ME < OF < LL *columbina* < L *columbina,* fem., dovelike < *columba* dove]

Col·um·bine (kol′ əm bīn′) *n.* in traditional Italian comedy and in pantomime, a girl who is the sweetheart of Harlequin.

co·lum·bi·um (kə lum′bē əm) *n.* a rare, steel-gray, metallic chemical element that resembles tantalum in its chemical properties; niobium. *Symbol:* Cb; *at.no.* 41; *at.wt.* 92.91. [< NL < *Columbia,* the United States]

col·umn (kol′əm) *n.* **1** in architecture, a slender, upright structure; pillar. Columns are usually made of stone, wood, or metal, and may be used as supports or ornaments to a building. Sometimes a column stands alone as a monument. **2** anything that seems slender and upright like a column: *a column of smoke, a long column of figures, the spinal column.* **3** in the armed services, an arrangement of persons in rows one behind another. **4** a line of ships or aircraft, one behind another. **5** any similar line of persons, things, etc.: *A long column of cars followed the procession down the street.* **6** a narrow division of a page reading from top to bottom, kept separate by lines or by blank spaces. A newspaper often has eight columns on a page. **7** a part of a newspaper or periodical used for a special subject or written by a special writer. **8** a line or series of letters, figures, etc. arranged vertically. [< L *columna*]

CAPITAL
SHAFT
BASE
A column (def.1)

☛ **column.** In sense 6, *column* is occasionally pronounced (kol′ yəm) although considered by most to be substandard. This pronunciation is also used humorously.

co·lum·nar (kə lum′nər) *adj.* **1** like a column. **2** made of columns. **3** written or printed in columns.

col·umned (kol′əmd) *adj.* **1** having columns. **2** formed into columns.

co·lum·ni·a·tion (kə lum′nē ā′shən) *n.* the use or arrangement of columns in a building.

col·um·nist (kol′əm ist or kol′əm nist) *n.* a person who writes or selects and edits the material for a special column in a newspaper.

☛ **Columnist is sometimes pronounced (kol′ yəm ist). See note under column.**

col·za (kol′zə) *n.* **1** cole seed. **2** an oil made from these seeds, used as a fuel in lamps, as a lubricant, etc. [< Du. *koolsaad,* literally, cabbage seed]

com- *prefix.* **1** with; together: *commingle = mingle with one another. Compress = press together.* **2** altogether (intensive): *collapse* = break down. [< *com-* + L *labi* fall]. Also: **col-,** before *l;* **con-,** before *n* and before consonants except *b, h, l, m, p, r, w;* **cor-,** before *r.* [< L *com-* < *cum,* prep.]

com. 1 comedy. **2** commerce. **3** common. **4** commonly. **5** communication.

Com. 1 Commander. **2** Commodore. **3** Commissioner. **4** Committee. **5** Communist.

co·ma[1] (kō′mə) *n.* **co·mas.** a prolonged unconsciousness caused by disease, injury, or poison; stupor. [< Gk. *kōma*]

co·ma[2] (kō′mə) *n.* **co·mae** (-mē or -mī). **1** a cloudlike mass around the nucleus of a comet. **2** in botany, a tuft of hairs at the end of a seed. [< L < Gk. *komē* hair]

Co·man·che (kə man′chē) *n.* **-che** or **-ches. 1** a tribe of North American Indians that formerly roamed from Wyoming to N. Mexico, now living in Oklahoma. **2** a member of this tribe. **3** the language of this tribe. [<Mexican Sp. *Comanche* < Shoshonean *Komanchi*]

co·mat·ik (kō′mə tik′) *n.* komatik.

com·a·tose (kom′ə tōs′ or kō′mə tōs′) *adj.* **1** in a stupor or coma; unconscious. **2** drowsy; lethargic. [< F < Gk. *kōma, -atos* sleep]

comb[1] (kōm) *n.* **1** a narrow, short piece of metal, rubber, celluloid, etc. with teeth, used to arrange or clean the hair or to hold it in place. **2** anything shaped or used like a comb. One kind of comb cleans and takes out the tangles in wool or flax. **3** a currycomb. **4** the thick, red, fleshy crest on the top of the head in some fowls. **5** a honeycomb. **6** the top of a wave rolling over or breaking. —*v.* **1** arrange, clean, or take out tangles in, with a comb. **2** search through; look everywhere in: *We had to comb the whole city before we found our lost dog.* **3** of waves, roll over or break at the top. [OE] —**comb′like′,** *adj.*

comb[2] (küm or kōm) *n.* combe.

com·bat (*v. n.* kom′bat; *v.,* also, kəm bat′) *v.* **-bat·ted** or **-bat·ed, -bat·ting** or **-bat·ing,** *n.* —*v.* **1** fight; struggle; battle. **2** fight against. —*n.* **1** a fight, especially between two. **2** a struggle; conflict; battle. [< F *combattre* < LL < L *com-* (intensive) + *battuere* beat] —**Syn.** *n.* **1** duel, engagement. See **fight.**

com·bat·ant (kəm bat′ənt or kom′bə tənt) *n.* a fighter. —*adj.* **1** fighting. **2** ready to fight; fond of fighting.

combat fatigue a state of mental exhaustion that sometimes occurs among soldiers as a result of warfare in the front lines.

com·bat·ive (kəm bat′iv or kom′bə tiv) *adj.* ready to fight or oppose; fond of fighting. —**com·bat′ive·ly,** *adv.* —**com·bat′ive·ness,** *n.*

combat team two or more units of different military branches acting together in battle.

combe or **comb** (küm or kōm) *n.* a narrow valley; deep hollow surrounded on three sides by hills. [OE *cumb,* probably < Celtic]

comb·er (kōm′ər) *n.* **1** a person or thing that combs. **2** a wave that rolls over or breaks at the top.

com·bi·na·tion (kom′bə nā′shən) *n.* **1** the act of combining. **2** the state of being combined. **3** one whole made by combining two or more different things. **4** a group of persons or parties joined together for some common purpose. **5** a combination lock. **6** a series of numbers or letters used in opening or closing such a lock: *the combination of a safe.* **7** a suit or underwear having the shirt and drawers in one piece. **8** in mathematics, the arrangement of individual items in groups so that each group has a certain number of items; the groups thus formed. Possible combinations of *a, b,* and *c* are *ab, ac,* and *bc.* **9** in chemistry, the union of substances to form a compound. —**Syn. 4** league, combine.

combination lock a lock having a movable dial with numbers or letters on it. The lock will not open until the dial has been turned through a certain sequence of numbers or letters.

com·bine (*v.* 1, 2 kəm bīn′; *v.* 3 kom′bīn or kəm bīn′; *n.* kom′bīn) *v.* **-bined, -bin·ing,** *n.* —*v.* **1** join together; unite. **2** in chemistry, unite to form a compound. Two atoms of hydrogen combine with one of oxygen to form water. **3** use a combine: *We combined the wheat last week.* —*n.* **1** *Informal.* a group of people joined together for business or political purposes; combination: *The companies formed a combine to keep prices up.* **2** a machine for harvesting and threshing grain. It separates the seeds from the stalks as it moves across a field. [< LL *combinare* < *com-* together + *bini* two by two]
—**com·bin′a·ble,** *adj.* —**Syn.** *v.* **1** associate, mix. See **join.**
☛ Combine is primarily a verb, although a noun form has come into good informal use to mean a group of people joined together for business or political purposes.

com·bined (kəm bīnd′) *adj.* **1** joined together; united. **2** done by groups, persons, etc. acting together.

combined operations **1** military operations carried on by two or more allies acting together. **2** military operations in which land, sea, and air forces co-operate; amphibious operations.

comb·ings (kōm′ingz) *n.pl.* the hairs removed by a comb.

combining form a word element used in forming derivatives. The element *tele-* in the word *television* is a combining form.

com·bo (kom′bō) *n.* **-bos.** *Informal.* a small group of jazz musicians playing together regularly. [shortened form of *combination*]

com·bus·ti·bil·i·ty (kəm bus′tə bil′ə tē) *n.* a combustible quality or condition; inflammability.

com·bus·ti·ble (kəm bus′tə bəl) *adj.* **1** capable of taking fire and burning; easily burned: *Gasoline is highly combustible.* **2** easily excited; fiery. —*n.* a combustible substance.

com·bus·tion (kəm bus′chən) *n.* **1** the act or process of burning: *The explosion in the coal mine was caused by the combustion of gases.* **2** in chemistry, a rapid oxidation accompanied by high temperature and, usually, by light. **3** a slow oxidation not accompanied by high temperature and light. Food is transformed into energy by this type of combustion. **4** violent excitement; tumult. [< LL *combustio, -onis* < L *comburere,* a blend of *co-urere* burn together or simultaneously and *amburere* burn on both sides]

Comdr. Commander.

Comdt. Commandant.

come (kum) *v.* **came, come, com·ing.** **1** move toward the speaker or the place where he is or will be; approach: *Come this way.* **2** arrive: *The girls will come home tomorrow.* **3** appear: *Light comes and goes.* **4** reach; extend: *The dress comes to her knees.* **5** happen; take place; occur: *Come what may.* **6** be caused; result: *You see what comes of meddling.* **7** be derived; issue: *Many English words came originally from Latin.* **8** be born: *That boy comes of a poor family.* **9** get to be; turn out to be; become: *His dream came true.* **10** be brought; pass; enter: *come into use.* **11** occur to the mind: *The solution of the problem has just come to me.* **12** be available: *This soup comes in a can.* **13** be equal; amount: *The total comes to $100.* **14** here! look! stop! behave!
come about, a happen; take place; occur. **b** turn around; change direction.
come across, a meet by chance; happen to meet; find. **b** *Slang.* hand over; pay.
come around or **come round, a** return to consciousness or health; recover. **b** give in; yield; agree. **c** turn around; change direction.
come at, a reach; get. **b** rush toward; attack.
come back, a return. **b** *Informal.* return to a former condition or position: *Old fighters rarely try to come back.*
come between, divide; separate; intervene.
come by, get; obtain; acquire.
come down, a lose position, rank, money, etc. **b** be handed down or passed along. **c** *Informal.* become ill (*with*).
come down on, a *Informal.* scold; blame. **b** attack suddenly.
come forward, offer oneself for work or duty; volunteer.
come in, a begin; be brought into use. **b** enter.
come in for, get; receive.
come into, a get; receive. **b** inherit.
come off, a happen; take place; occur. **b** turn out to be. **c** reach the end of (a course, contest, etc.) in a certain manner: *come off with flying colors.*
come on, a improve; develop; progress. **b** meet by chance; find. **c** make an entrance onto the stage.
come out, a be revealed or shown. **b** be offered to the public. **c** put in an appearance: *How many boys came out for football this year?* **d** be introduced to society; make a debut. **e** finish an activity in a certain way: *How did the ball game come out?* **f** volunteer; offer one's services.
come out with, a reveal; show. **b** offer to the public. **c** say; speak.
come over, happen to; take hold of.
come through, a be successful; win. **b** last through successfully. **c** *Slang.* hand over; pay.
come to, a return to consciousness. **b** anchor; stop.
come up, arise; develop.
[OE *cuman*]
Syn. 2 Come, arrive = get to a place or point. **Come** emphasizes the movement or progress involved in getting to a place or point: *We came to a conclusion.* **Arrive** emphasizes the idea of reaching an end or goal: *A letter arrived today. We arrived at the airport.*

come-all-ye (kum′ol yē′ or -ôl yē′) *n.* a folk song or ballad of England, Ireland, or Canada. [< *Come all ye,* a frequent first line in such ballads]

come·back (kum′bak′) *n.* **1** *Informal.* a return to a former condition or position. **2** *Slang.* a clever answer; sharp reply. **3** *Slang.* a cause for complaining.

co·me·di·an (kə mē′dē ən) *n.* **1** an actor in comedies; an actor of comic parts. **2** a writer of comedies. **3** a person who amuses others with his funny talk and actions. [< F *comédien*]

co·me·di·enne (kə mē′dē en′) *n.* an actress in comedies; an actress of comic parts. [< F *comédienne,* fem. of *comédien*]

come·down (kum′doun′) *n. Informal.* a loss of position, rank, money, etc.

com·e·dy (kom′ə dē) *n.* **-dies.** **1** an amusing play or show having a happy ending. **2** such plays or shows as a class; the branch of drama concerned with such plays. **3** an amusing happening; funny incident. **4** the comic element of drama or literature, or of life in general: *the human comedy.* **5** any literary work having a theme suited to comedy or using the methods of comedy. [ME < OF < L *comœdia* < Gk. *kōmōidia* + *kōmōidos* comedian < *kōmos* merrymaking + *aoidos* singer]

come·li·ness (kum′lē nis) *n.* **1** pleasant appearance. **2** fitness; suitableness; propriety.

come·ly (kum′lē) *adj.* **-li·er, -li·est.** **1** having a pleasant appearance; attractive. **2** fitting; suitable; proper. [OE *cȳmlic*]

come-on (kum′on′) *n. Informal.* something that lures or entices; an inducement: *The grocer cut the price of milk as a come-on to customers.*

com·er (kum′ər) *n.* **1** a person who comes. **2** a person who has recently come. **3** *Informal.* a person who shows promise or seems likely to succeed.

hat, āge, cãre, fär; let, ēqual, tėrm; it, īce
hot, ōpen, ôrder; oil, out; cup, pu̇t, rüle, ūse
əbove, takən, pencəl, lemən, circəs
ch, child; ng, long; sh, ship
th, thin; ᴛʜ, then; zh, measure

co·mes·ti·ble (kə mes′ tə bəl) *n.* something to eat; an article of food. *—adj.* eatable. [< LL *comestibilis* < L *comestus*, var. of *comesus*, pp. of *comedere* < *com-* with + *edere* eat]

com·et (kom′ it) *n.* in astronomy, a bright heavenly body having a starlike centre and, often, a cloudlike tail of light that is always directed away from the sun. Comets move around the sun in an elliptical or, sometimes, a parabolic or hyperbolic course. [ME *comete* < OF < L *cometa* < Gk. *komētēs* wearing long hair < *komē* hair]

come-up·pance (kum′ up′ əns) *n. Informal.* whatever penalty, change of luck, etc. one deserves; one's just deserts.

com·fit (kum′ fit or kom′ fit) *n.* a piece of candy; sweetmeat. [ME < OF *confit* < L *confectus* prepared, pp. of *conficere* < *com-* together + *facere* make]

com·fort (kum′ fərt) *v.* **1** ease the grief or sorrow of (someone); cheer. **2** give ease to. **3** *Archaic or legal.* help; support.
—n. **1** anything that makes trouble or sorrow easier to bear. **2** freedom from pain or hardship; ease. **3** a person or thing that makes life easier or takes away hardship. **4** a comforter for a bed. **5** *Archaic or legal.* help; support. [ME < OF *confort* < LL *confortare* strengthen < *com-* together + *fortis* strong]
—com′ fort·ing·ly, *adv.*
Syn. *v.* **1 Comfort, console** = ease sorrow, trouble, or pain. **Comfort** = ease the grief or sorrow of a person by making him more cheerful and giving him hope or strength: *Neighbors comforted the mother of the burned child.* **Console** = make grief or trouble easier to bear by doing something to lighten it or make the person forget it temporarily: *Her music consoled the widow.* *-n.* **2** See **ease.**

com·fort·a·ble (kum′ fər tə bəl) *adj.* **1** giving comfort: *A soft, warm bed is comfortable.* **2** in comfort; at ease; free from pain or hardship. **3** easy; tranquil; undisturbed: *a comfortable sleep.* **4** *Informal.* enough for one's needs: *He has a comfortable income.*
—n. a comforter for a bed. **—com′ fort·a·ble·ness,** *n.* **—com′ fort·a·bly,** *adv.*

com·fort·er (kum′ fər tər) *n.* **1** a person or thing that gives comfort. **2** a padded or quilted covering for a bed. **3** a long woollen scarf. **4 the Comforter,** the Holy Spirit.

com·fort·less (kum′ fərt lis) *adj.* **1** bringing no comfort or ease of mind: *comfortless words.* **2** without the comforts of life: *a comfortless room.*

comfort station a public lavatory.

com·ic (kom′ ik) *adj.* **1** of comedy. **2** amusing, funny. *—n.* **1** the amusing or funny side of literature, life, etc. **2** *Informal.* a comic book. **3 comics,** *pl. Informal.* comic strips. **4** a comedian. [< L *comicus* < Gk. *kōmikos* < *kōmos* merrymaking] ☛ See **comical** for usage note.

com·i·cal (kom′ ə kəl) *adj.* **1** amusing; funny. **2** *Informal.* queer; strange; odd. **—com′ i·cal·ly,** *adv.* **—com′ i·cal·ness,** *n.*
☛ **comical, comic. Comical** emphasizes the merry, gleeful, or hilarious laughter, produced by something funny, foolishly out of place, ridiculous, or very humorous: *The clown's actions were comical.* **Comic,** used of a person or thing, describes a quality that makes people smile in amusement or laugh: *Bob Hope is a comic actor.*

comic book a magazine containing comic strips.

comic opera an amusing opera having a happy ending.

comic strip a series of drawings, sometimes amusing, often presenting an adventure or a series of incidents.

Com·in·form (kom′ in fôrm′) *n.* an international Communist organization intended to co-ordinate the propaganda of Communist parties throughout the world, formed in 1947 by the signatories of the Warsaw Pact and dissolved in 1956. [< *Com*munist *Inform*ation Bureau]

com·ing (kum′ ing) *n.* the approach; arrival. *—adj.* **1** approaching; next: *this coming spring.* **2** *Informal.* on the way to importance or fame.

Com·in·tern (kom′ in tėrn′) *n.* the Third Communist International, an organization to spread communism, founded at Moscow in 1919 and dissolved in 1943. [< *Com*munist *Intern*ational]

co·mi·ti·a (kə mish′ ē ə) *n.pl.* in ancient Rome, a meeting of citizens to pass laws, elect officials, etc. [< L *comitia*, pl. of *comitium* meeting place]

com·i·ty (kom′ ə tē) *n.* **-ties.** courtesy; civility. [< L *comitas* < *comis* friendly]

com·ma (kom′ ə) *n.* a mark of punctuation (,) used to set off such parts of a sentence as appositional and non-restrictive phrases and clauses and to separate co-ordinate adjectives, items in a series, etc. It usually corresponds with the slight pause and change of pitch occurring when the same sentence is uttered under normal speaking conditions. [< L < Gk. *komma* piece cut off < *koptein* to cut]

comma bacillus the bacterium that causes Asiatic cholera.

com·mand (kə mand′) *v.* **1** give an order to; direct: *The captain commanded the men to fire.* **2** give orders. **3** have authority or power over; be in control of: *The captain commands his ship.* **4** be commander. **5** have a position of control over; overlook: *A hilltop commands the plain around it.* **6** be able to have and use: *He cannot command so large a sum of money.* **7** deserve and get; force to be given: *Scarce goods command higher prices.*
—n. **1** an order; direction: *They obeyed the captain's command.* **2** authority; power; control: *The general is in command of the army.* **3** the position of a person who has the right to command. **4** the soldiers, ships, district, etc. under a person who has the right to command them. **5** one of the administrative divisions of the Canadian armed forces. **6** mastery or control by position: *The hill fort had command of the plain below.* **7** outlook (over); range of vision. **8** the ability to use or control effectively; mastery: *A good writer must have a command of words.* **9** a royal invitation. **10 at one's command,** at one's disposal; available: *He always seems to have the right words at his command.* [ME < OF *comander* < LL *commandare* < L *com-* with + *mandare* commit, command]
Syn. *v.* **1 Command, order, direct** = tell someone to do something. **Command** = give an order with authority in a formal way: *The sentry commanded him to halt.* **Order,** a more general word, also means "tell with authority," but suggests either a less official and more personal way of giving the order or a domineering way: *Her father ordered him to leave.* **Direct** suggests giving instructions rather than a formal order, but also emphasizes expecting to be obeyed: *The policeman directed the motorists to stop.* **3** govern, rule. **7** exact. *-n.* **1** charge, injunction, mandate.

com·man·dant (kom′ ən dant′) *n.* **1** the commander of a navy, army, or air-force station. **2** the officer in charge of a military college or training school. *Abbrev.:* Comdt. [< F, originally ppr. of *commander* command]

com·man·deer (kom′ ən dēr′) *v.* **1** seize (private property) for military or public use: *All the automobiles in the town were commandeered by the army.* **2** force (men) into military service. **3** *Informal.* take by force. [< Afrikaans *commandeeren* < F *commander*]

com·mand·er (kə man′ dər) *n.* **1** a person who commands. **2** an officer in charge of an army or a part of an army. **3** in the navy, a commissioned officer senior to a lieutenant commander and junior to a captain. **4** a member of a high rank in an order of knighthood or a society. *Abbrev.:* Comdr., Cmdr., Cdr., or Com.

commander-in-chief (kə man′ dər in chēf′) *n.* **commanders-in-chief. 1** a person who has complete command of the armed services of a country in a theatre of war, a garrison, etc. **2** an officer in command of part of the armed services of a country. *Abbrev.:* C. in C.

com·mand·ing (kə man′ ding) *adj.* **1** in command: *a commanding officer.* **2** controlling; powerful: *commanding influences.* **3** authoritative; impressive: *a commanding voice.* **4** having a position of control. **—com·mand′ ing·ly,** *adv.*

com·mand·ment (kə mand′ mənt) *n.* **1** an order; law. **2** in the Bible, one of the ten laws that God gave to Moses.

command module the main section of a spacecraft, from which a smaller section may be detached for independent flight, a lunar landing, etc.

com·man·do or **Com·mando** (kə man′ dō) *n.* **-dos** or **-does. 1** a soldier who makes brief, daring raids upon enemy territory and does close-range fighting. **2** a group of such soldiers. **3** in South Africa: **a** an armed force raised by Portuguese or Dutch settlers against bandits and marauders, or by the Boers against the British. **b** a raid by such a force. [< Afrikaans < Pg.]

command performance a stage performance, etc. given before royalty by request or order.

com·me·dia dell'ar·te (kôm mā′ dyä del lär′tā) *Italian.* a form of comedy originating in the sixteenth century in Italy, in which a company of professional actors play stock characters in conventional situations but improvise their speeches and comic actions.

comme il faut (kô mēl fō′) *French.* as it should be; proper; in accordance with etiquette.

com·mem·o·rate (kə mem′ə rāt′) *v.* **-rat·ed, -rat·ing.** **1** preserve the memory of: *Roman emperors built arches to commemorate their victories.* **2** honor the memory of: *Christmas commemorates Christ's birth.* [< L *commemorare* < *com-* together + *memorare* remind]

com·mem·o·ra·tion (kə mem′ə rā′shən) *n.* **1** the act of commemorating. **2** a service, celebration, etc. in memory of some person or event. **3 in commemoration of,** in honor of the memory of.

com·mem·o·ra·tive (kə mem′ə rə tiv or kə mem′ə rā′tiv) *adj.* calling to remembrance; honoring the memory of.
—*n.* a postage stamp issued to commemorate some person, event, etc. —**com·mem′o·ra′tive·ly,** *adv.*

com·mence (kə mens′) *v.* **-menced, -menc·ing.** begin; start. [ME < OF *comencer* < VL < L *com-* together + *initiare* begin (ult. < *inire* begin < *in-* in + *ire* go)] —**com·menc′er,** *n.* —**Syn.** See **begin.**

com·mence·ment (kə mens′mənt) *n.* **1** a beginning; start. **2** the day when a school or college gives diplomas or degrees to students who have completed the required course of study; graduation day. **3** the ceremonies on this day; exercises of graduation.

com·mend (kə mend′) *v.* **1** praise. **2** mention favorably; recommend. **3** hand over for safekeeping: *She commended the child to her aunt's care.* [ME < L *commendare* < *com-* (intensive) + *mandare* commit, command. Cf. COMMAND.] —**Syn. 1** See **praise.**

com·mend·a·ble (kə men′də bəl) *adj.* worthy of praise; deserving approval. —**com·mend′a·bly,** *adv.*

com·men·da·tion (kom′ən dā′shən) *n.* **1** praise; approval. **2** favorable mention; recommendation. **3** a handing over to another for safekeeping; an entrusting.

com·mend·a·to·ry (kə men′də tô rē) *adj.* **1** praising; expressing approval. **2** mentioning favorably; recommending.

com·men·su·ra·ble (kə men′sə rə bəl or kə men′shə rə bəl) *adj.* **1** measurable by the same set of units: *Greenness and weight are not commensurable.* **2** corresponding in size, amount, or degree; proportionate: *He was a big man, very tall and of commensurable weight.* —**com·men′su·ra·ble·ness,** *n.* —**com·men′su·ra·bly,** *adv.*

com·men·su·rate (kə men′sə rit or kə men′shə rit) *adj.* **1** in the proper proportion; proportionate: *The pay should be commensurate with the work.* **2** of the same size, extent, etc.; equal. **3** measurable by the same set of units; commensurable. [< LL *commensuratus,* pp. of *commensurare* < L *com-* together + *mensurare* measure < *mensura* a measure]
—**com·men′su·rate·ly,** *adv.* —**com·men′su·rate·ness,** *n.*

com·ment (kom′ənt) *n.* **1** a short statement, note, or remark that explains, praises, or finds fault with something that has been written, said, or done. **2** a remark. **3** talk; gossip.
—*v.* **1** make a comment or comments: *Everyone commented on her new hat.* **2** talk; gossip. [ME < LL *commentum* < *commentus,* pp. of L *comminisci* < *com-* with + *minisci* think]

com·men·tar·y (kom′ən ter′ē) *n.* **-tar·ies. 1** a series of notes for explaining the text of a book; explanation: *Bibles are often provided with commentaries.* **2** a comment. **3** an explanatory essay or treatise. **4** a description of a sporting event, ceremony, etc., especially one given on radio or television.

com·men·ta·tor (kom′ən tā′tər) *n.* **1** a person who makes comments explaining or criticizing books, concerts, recent events, etc. **2** a person who describes sporting or other events on radio or television while they are in progress. [< L]

com·merce (kom′ėrs) *n.* buying and selling in large amounts between different places; business. [< F < L *commercium,* ult. < *com-* with + *merx, mercis* wares] —**Syn.** dealings, traffic. See **trade.**

com·mer·cial (kə mėr′shəl) *adj.* **1** of or having to do with commerce. **2** made to be sold. **3** supported or subsidized by an advertiser: *a commercial radio program.* **4** for business purposes, especially in advertising: *commercial art.*
—*n.* a radio or television program, or the part of a program, that advertises something. —**com·mer′cial·ly,** *adv.*

com·mer·cial·ism (kə mėr′shəl iz′əm) *n.* **1** the methods and spirit of commerce: *Making money is often the only object of commercialism.* **2** a business custom. **3** an expression used in business.

com·mer·cial·ize (kə mėr′shəl īz′) *v.* **-ized, -iz·ing.** apply the methods and spirit of commerce to (something); make (something) a matter of business or trade. —**com·mer′cial·i·za′tion,** *n.*

commercial traveller or **traveler** a travelling salesman.

com·mi·na·tion (kom′ə nā′shən) *n.* **1** in Anglican churches, a recital of divine threats against sinners. **2** a threat; denunciation. [< L *comminatio, -onis* < *comminari* < *com-* with + *minari* threaten]

com·min·gle (kə ming′gəl) *v.* **-gled, -gling.** mingle together; blend.

com·mi·nute (kom′ə nūt′ or kom′ə nüt′) *v.* **-nut·ed, -nut·ing.** reduce to a powder or to small fragments; pulverize. [< L *comminutus,* pp. of *comminuere* < *com-* intensive + *minuere* make smaller < *minus* less] —**com′mi·nu′tion,** *n.*

com·mis·er·ate (kə miz′ər āt′) *v.* **-at·ed, -at·ing.** feel or express sorrow for; sympathize with; pity. [< L *com-* with *miserari* < *com-* + *miser* wretched]

com·mis·er·a·tion (kə miz′ər ā′shən) *n.* pity; sympathy.

com·mis·sar (kom′ə sär′) *n.* in the Soviet Union, the head of a government department; minister. [< Russian *kommisar* < F *commissaire*]

com·mis·sar·i·at (kom′ə sãr′ē ət) *n.* **1** a food supply. **2** formerly, a department of the Soviet government. [< F < Med.L *commissarius.* See COMMISSARY.]

com·mis·sar·y (kom′ə ser′ē) *n.* **-sar·ies. 1** a store handling food and supplies in a mining camp, lumber camp, etc. **2** a deputy; representative. [< Med.L *commissarius* < L *commissus* entrusted, pp. of *committere.* See COMMIT.]

com·mis·sion (kə mish′ən) *n.* **1** a written paper giving certain powers, privileges, and duties. **2** a written order giving rank and authority as an officer in the armed services: *My brother has received his commission as a lieutenant in the Royal Canadian Navy.* **3** the rank and authority given by such an order. **4** a giving of authority. **5** the authority, power, or right given. **6** the thing for which authority is given; task entrusted to a person. **7** a group of people appointed or elected with authority to do certain things. **8** a doing or committing; performance: *People are punished for the commission of crimes.* **9** pay based on a percentage of the amount of business done: *She gets a commission of 10 per cent on all the sales she makes.* **10 in commission, a** in service; in use. **b** ready for service or use; in working order. **11 out of commission, a** not in service or use. **b** not ready for use; not in working order.
—*v.* **1** give a commission to. **2** give authority to; give (a person) the right or power (to do something): *Some businessmen commission others to buy or sell property for them.* **3** put in service or use; make ready for service or use. A new warship is commissioned when it has the officers, sailors, and supplies needed for a voyage. [ME < OF < L *commissio, -onis* < *committere.* See COMMIT.] —**Syn.** *n.* **1** warrant, licence. *-v.* **2** license, authorize, empower.

hat, āge, cãre, fär; let, ēqual, tėrm; it, īce
hot, ōpen, ôrder; oil, out; cup, pu̇t, rüle, ūse
 əbove, takən, pencəl, lemən, circəs
ch, child; ng, long; sh, ship
th, thin; ᴛʜ, then; zh, measure

com·mis·sion·aire (kə mish′ən ãr′) *n.* **1** a person whose job is to open doors, carry bags, etc. at the entrance of a hotel or a club. **2** a member of the Corps of Commissionaires: *Some Canadian cities employ commissionaires to check parking meters and to issue parking tickets to persons whose cars are parked overtime.* [< F]

com·mis·sioned (kə mish′ənd) *adj.* having a commission: *a commissioned officer.*

com·mis·sion·er (kə mish′ən ər or kə mish′nər) *n.* **1** a member of a commission. **2** an official in charge of some department of a government: *a police commissioner.* **3** one of a group of persons elected or appointed to govern a city or a county. **4 Commissioner, a** the highest ranking officer of the Royal Canadian Mounted Police. **b** the chief executive officer of the Yukon Territory or the Northwest Territories.

commission merchant a person who buys or sells goods for others who pay him a commission.

com·mit (kə mit′) *v.* **-mit·ted, -mit·ting. 1** hand over for safekeeping; deliver: *He committed himself to the doctor's care.* **2** put officially in the care of an institution, such as a mental hospital or prison. **3** refer to a committee for consideration. **4** do or perform (usually something wrong): *Criminals commit crimes.* **5** reveal one's opinion. **6** involve; pledge: *He would not commit himself in any way.* **7 commit to memory,** learn by heart. **8 commit to paper** or **writing,** write down. [ME < L *committere* < *com-* with + *mittere* send, put] **—com·mit′ta·ble,** *adj.*

Syn. 1 Commit, consign, entrust = hand over a person or thing. **Commit** = hand over to be kept safe or taken care of: *The court committed the financial affairs of the orphan to a guardian.* **Consign** suggests formally handing over control: *He consigned his share of the bonds to his sister.* **Entrust** = commit with trust and confidence in the receiver: *I entrusted my door key to my neighbor.*

com·mit·ment (kə mit′mənt) *n.* **1** a committing. **2** a being committed. **3** a sending to prison or to a mental hospital. **4** an order sending a person to prison or to a mental hospital. **5** a pledge; promise. **6** an agreement to buy or sell stocks, securities, etc. **7** a sale or purchase made by such an agreement.

com·mit·tal (kə mit′əl) *n.* commitment.

com·mit·tee (kə mit′ē) *n.* **1** a group of persons appointed or elected to do certain things. **2 standing committee,** a permanent committee, as of a legislative body or club, selected or elected to deal with all matters in a particular sphere. [< AF *committee* committed]

☛ **Committee** is a collective noun, to be construed as singular or plural according as the group or the individuals are meant. The singular would usually be the form desired: *The committee meets today at four. The committee get together with difficulty.*

com·mit·tee·man (kə mit′ē mən) *n.* **-men** (-mən). a member of a committee.

committee of the whole a committee made up of all the members present of a legislature, club, etc.

com·mix (kə miks′) *v.* mix together.

com·mix·ture (kə miks′chər) *n.* mixture.

com·mode (kə mōd′) *n.* **1** a chest of drawers. **2** a stand in a bedroom, to hold a washbasin, pitcher of water, etc.; washstand. [< F < L *commodus* convenient < *com-* with + *modus* measure]

com·mo·di·ous (kə mō′dē əs) *adj.* **1** roomy. **2** convenient; handy. [< Med.L *commodiosus* < L *commodus.* See COMMODE.] **—com·mo′di·ous·ly,** *adv.* **—com·mo′di·ous·ness,** *n.*

com·mod·i·ty (kə mod′ə tē) *n.* **-ties. 1** anything that is bought and sold. **2** a useful thing.

com·mo·dore (kom′ə dôr′) *n.* **1** in the navy, a commissioned officer senior to a captain and junior to a rear admiral. **2** the officer in charge of a convoy of ships. **3** a title of honor given to the president or head of a yacht club, power squadron, etc. **4** a commodore's ship. *Abbrev.:* Cmdre., Com. [earlier *commandore,* ? < Du. *kommandeur* < F *commandeur* < *commander* to command]

com·mon (kom′ən) *adj.* **1** belonging equally to each or all of a group: *The house was the common property of the three brothers.* **2** of all; from all; by all; to all; general: *common knowledge, a common nuisance.* **3** joint; united: *Science and medicine form a common front against ignorance and disease.* **4** generally or publicly known; notorious: *a common pickpocket, a common liar.* **5** belonging to the community at large; public: *a common council.* **6** often met with; usual; familiar: *Snow is common in cold countries.* **7** of the ordinary type or quality; everyday; ordinary: *the business of common life, the common run of mankind.* **8** without rank: *the common people. A common soldier is a private.* **9** below ordinary; inferior; coarse; vulgar. **10** in grammar: **a** (of gender) that can be either masculine or feminine: *The words "parent" and "child" are common, whereas "father" and "son" are masculine.* **b** (of nouns) that can be applied to any member of a class: *"City" is a common noun; "Edmonton" is a proper noun.* **11** belonging equally to two or more quantities: *a common factor, a common multiple.*
—n. **1** Also, **commons.** land owned or used by all the people of a town, village, etc. **2** in law, the right to use the land of another, which a man shares with the owner or others, as the right to fish, pasture animals, take wood for domestic use, etc. **3 commons, a** the common people; people who are not noblemen. **b** land used by all the people of a community; common. **4 Commons,** the House of Commons. **5 in common,** equally with another or others; owned, used, done, etc. by both or all. [ME < OF *comun* < L *communis*] **—com′mon·ness,** *n.*

Syn. *adj.* **1** joint. **2** popular, universal. See **general. 4 Common, ordinary** = usual. **Common** = often met with or usual because shared by many people or things: *Colds are common in winter.* **Ordinary** = usual because in agreement with the normal standards and order of things: *I use ordinary gasoline.*

☛ **common.** Formal English distinguishes between *common* = belonging equally to each or all, and *mutual* = each to the other: *The estate is the common property of the five brothers. Bud and Mary felt a mutual dislike.*

com·mon·age (kom′ən ij) *n.* **1** the right to pasture animals on land owned by the town, village, etc. **2** the ownership of land in common. **3** land owned in common. **4** the common people.

com·mon·al·ty (kom′ən əl tē) *n.* **-ties. 1** the common people; persons without rank or title; the middle and lower classes of society. **2** people as a group. **3** the members of a corporation.

common carrier a person or company whose business is conveying goods or people for pay. A railway company is a common carrier.

common council the lawmaking group of a city, town, etc.

common denominator 1 in mathematics, a common multiple of the denominators of a group of fractions. A common denominator of $\frac{1}{2}$, $\frac{2}{3}$, and $\frac{3}{4}$ is 12. **2** a quality, attribute, opinion, etc. shared by all the persons or things in a group.

common divisor a number that will divide two or more other numbers without a remainder. A common divisor of 4, 6, 8, and 10 is 2.

com·mon·er (kom′ən ər) *n.* **1** one of the common people; a person who is not a nobleman. **2** a member of the House of Commons.

common fraction a fraction with a numerator and the denominator separated by a horizontal or diagonal line. *Examples:* $\frac{1}{2}$, 7/8.

common gender the gender of words that are not definitely either masculine or feminine. *Examples:* child, writer.

common law 1 the law based on custom and usage and confirmed by the decisions of judges, as distinct from statute law. **2** the law of all countries whose legal systems derive from English law, as distinct from *civil* or *canon law.* **3** law based on the decisions of judges in actual cases; case law.

com·mon-law (kom′ən lo′ or -lô′) *adj.* of or having to do with a marital relationship that is not initiated by a civil or religious ceremony: *a common-law wife.*

com·mon·ly (kom′ən lē) *adv.* usually; as a rule; generally: *Arithmetic is commonly taught in elementary schools.*

common market 1 an association of countries to promote mutual free trade. **2 Common Market,** the European Economic Community.

common noun in grammar, the name for any one of a class. *Boy, city,* and *dog* are common nouns. *John, Boston,* and *Rover* are proper nouns.

com·mon-or-garden (kom′ən ər gär′dən) *adj. Informal.* ordinary; familiar; everyday: *common-or-garden pencils.*

com·mon·place (kom′ən plās′) *n.* **1** a common or everyday thing: *Forty years ago broadcasting was a rare novelty; today it is a commonplace.* **2** an ordinary or obvious remark. **3** one of a collection of notable passages written down for reference. *—adj.* not new or interesting; everyday; ordinary: *We thought the speech rather commonplace.* **—com′mon·place′ness,** *n.*

common pleas lawsuits between private individuals that do not involve criminal cases.

com·mons (kom′ənz) *n.pl.* **1** the common people; people who are not noblemen. **2** a dining hall or building where food is served to a large group at common tables. **3** the food served. **4** food: *The poor orphans were kept on short commons.* **5 the Commons, a** House of Commons. **b** the members of the House of Commons.

common school in the United States and formerly in Canada, an elementary public school.

common sense good sense in everyday affairs; practical intelligence.

com·mon-sense (kom′ən sens′) *adj.* having or showing ordinary good sense; sensible; practical.

common stock ordinary stock in a company. Common stock has no guaranteed rate of dividend and does not carry the privileges of preferred stock.

com·mon·weal (kom′ən wēl′) *n.* **1** the general welfare; public good. **2** *Archaic.* a commonwealth.

com·mon·wealth (kom′ən welth′) *n.* **1 Commonwealth, a** in England, the government under Oliver Cromwell and later under his son. It lasted from 1649 to 1660. **b** the British Commonwealth of Nations. **2** a group of people who make up a nation; the citizens of a state. **3** a democratic state; republic. **4** a group of persons, nations, etc. united by some common interest.

Commonwealth Day Victoria Day.

com·mo·tion (kə mō′shən) *n.* **1** confusion; agitation; violent movement. **2** public disturbance; tumult. [< L *commotio, -onis* < *commovere* < *com-* with + *movere* move]

com·mu·nal (kom′yů nəl or kə mū′nəl) *adj.* **1** of a community; public. **2** owned jointly by all; used or participated in by all members of a group or community. **3** of a commune. **—com′mu·nal·ly,** *adv.*

com·mu·nal·ism (kom′yů nəl iz′əm or kə mū′nəl iz′əm) *n.* a theory or system of government according to which each commune is virtually an independent state and the nation is merely a federation of communes.

com·mune[1] (*v.* kə mūn′; *n.* kom′ūn) *v.* **-muned, -mun·ing,** *n.* —*v.* talk intimately. —*n.* intimate talk. [< OF *communer* < *comun.* See COMMON.]

com·mune[2] (kom′ūn) *n.* **1** in France, Belgium, Italy, and several other European countries, the smallest division for local government. **2** the people or government of a commune. **3** a unit of local government in Communist China, comprising a group of collective farms organized to carry out planned communal work that includes industrial, administrative, and educational projects. **4** a community of people living together. **5** in Imperial Russia, a mir. **6 Commune,** in France: **a** a revolutionary group that governed Paris 1792-1794. **b** a similar group that governed Paris from March 18 to May 28, 1871. [< F *commune,* alteration of OF *comugne* < VL *communia,* originally neut. pl. of L *communis.* See COMMON.]

com·mu·ni·ca·ble (kə mū′nə kə bəl) *adj.* that can be communicated: *Ideas are communicable by words. Scarlet fever is a communicable disease.*—**com·mu′ni·ca·bly,** *adv.*

com·mu·ni·cant (kə mū′nə kənt) *n.* **1** a person who receives Holy Communion. **2** a regular attender at a church. **3** a person who gives information by talking, writing, etc. *—adj.* communicating.

com·mu·ni·cate (kə mū′nə kāt′) *v.* **-cat·ed, -cat·ing. 1** pass along; transfer: *A stove communicates heat to a room.* **2** give (information) by talking, writing, etc.; talk, write, telephone, telegraph, etc.; send and receive messages. **3** be connected: *The dining room communicates with the kitchen.* **4** receive Holy Communion. [< L *communicare* < *communis.* See COMMON.]
—com·mu′ni·ca′tor, *n.*

Syn. 1 Communicate, impart = pass knowledge, ideas, or information along. **Communicate,** the general word, emphasizes the idea of passing something along from one person or thing to another, so that it becomes the common property of giver and receiver: *He has not communicated his wishes to me.* **Impart** emphasizes the idea of giving to another a share of what one has: *A teacher imparts knowledge to his students.*

com·mu·ni·ca·tion (kə mū′nə kā′shən) *n.* **1** the act or fact of passing along; transfer. **2** exchange of information by talking, writing, etc.: *Communication with people who are deaf is difficult.* **3** the information given in this way. **4** a letter, message, etc. that gives information: *Your communication came in time to change all my plans.* **5** a means of going from one place to the other; connection; passage: *There is no communication between these two rooms.* **6 communications,** *pl.* a system of communicating by telephone, radio, etc.

com·mu·ni·ca·tive (kə mū′nə kə tiv or kə mū′nə kā′tiv) *adj.* **1** ready to give information; talkative. **2** of or having to do with communication. **—com·mu′ni·ca′tive·ly,** *adv.* **—com·mu′ni·ca′tive·ness,** *n.*

com·mun·ion (kə mūn′yən) *n.* **1** the act of sharing; a having in common. **2** an exchange of thoughts and feelings; intimate talk; fellowship. **3** a close spiritual relationship. **4** a group of people having the same religious beliefs. **5 Communion,** in the Christian church: **a** the act of sharing in the Lord's Supper. **b** the celebration of the Lord's Supper. [ME < L *communio, -onis* < *communis.* See COMMON.]

Communion service 1 the celebration of the Lord's Supper. **2** the proper order or service for this ceremony.

com·mu·ni·qué (kə mū′nə kā′ or kə mū′nə kā′) *n.* an official bulletin, statement, or other communication. [< F]

com·mu·nism (kom′yů niz′əm) *n.* **1** a philosophy or system derived from Marxism, advocating state ownership of land and property and seeking the overthrow of non-communist societies in behalf of the proletariat. **2** a political, social, and economic system in which the state, governed by an elite party, controls production, labor, distribution, and, largely, the social and cultural life and thought of the people. **3** a social order in which property is held in common by the community or the state. [< F *communisme* < *commun,* OF *comun.* See COMMON.]

☛ **communism, socialism.** Communism and socialism are systems of social organization under which the means of production and distribution of goods are transferred from private hands to the government. The basic difference between the two systems may be said to lie today in the different means they take to establish themselves: communism emphasizes the impossibility of setting up their new social order by any means other than armed force; socialism seeks to establish itself by peaceful means, through legislation rather than armed force.

com·mu·nist (kom′yů nist) *n.* **1** a person who favors and supports communism. **2 Communist,** a member of the Communist Party. *—adj.* having to do with communism or with the Communist Party.

com·mu·nis·tic (kom′yů nis′tik) *adj.* **1** of or having to do with communists or communism. **2** favoring communism. **—com′mu·nis′ti·cal·ly,** *adv.*

Communist Party a political party that supports communism.

com·mu·ni·ty (kə mū′nə tē) *n.* **-ties. 1** a number of people having common ties or interests and living in the same place and subject to the same laws; people of any district or town. **2** a group of people living together: *a community of monks.* **3** the public: *the approval of the community.* **4** ownership together; sharing together: *community of food supplies, community of ideas.* **5** a group of animals or plants living together. **6** likeness; similarity;

identity: *Community of interests causes people to work together.* [ME *com(m)unete* < OF < L *communitas* <*communis.* See COMMON.]

community centre or **center** 1 a hall used for recreation, entertainment, public meetings, etc. in a community. 2 *Cdn.* an arena run by the community as a centre for sporting events, skating, dancing, and other forms of entertainment.

Community Chest a fund of money contributed voluntarily by people to support welfare work in their community.

community college a college for post-secondary and adult education, offering a range of courses for job preparation and general interest.

com·mu·nize (kom′yů nīz′) *v.* **-nized, -niz·ing.** 1 subject all property to state ownership. 2 enforce the practice or adoption of communism. **—com′mu·ni·za′tion.**

com·mu·tate (kom′yů tāt′) *v.* **-tat·ed, -tat·ing.** in electricity, reverse the direction of (current). [back formation from *commutation*]

com·mu·ta·tion (kom′yů tā′shən) *n.* 1 an exchange; substitution. 2 the reduction (of an obligation, penalty, etc.) to a less severe one: *The prisoner obtained a commutation of his sentence from death to life imprisonment.* 3 in electricity, a reversal of the direction of a current by a commutator. 4 regular, daily travel back and forth to work by train, bus, automobile, etc.

com·mu·ta·tive (kom′yů tā′tiv) *adj.* 1 in electricity, having to do with reversal of the direction of a current. 2 having to do with exchange or mutual dealings: *commutative justice.* 3 in mathematics, of or governed by the commutative law.

commutative law or **principle** in mathematics, a law stating that the order in which certain operations are performed will not affect the result.

com·mu·ta·tor (kom′yů tā′tər) *n.* 1 a device for reversing the direction of an electric current. 2 a revolving part in a dynamo or motor that carries the current to or from the brushes. See **dynamo** for diagram.

com·mute (kə mūt′) *v.* **-mut·ed, -mut·ing.** 1 exchange; substitute. 2 change (an obligation, penalty, etc.) to an easier one: *The prisoner's sentence of death was commuted to one of life imprisonment.* 3 in electricity, reverse the direction of (a current) by a commutator. 4 travel regularly back and forth to work by train, bus, automobile, etc. [< L *commutare* < *com-* (intensive) + *mutare* change]

com·mut·er (kə mūt′ər) *n.* a person who regularly travels to and from his work by car, bus, train, etc.

comp. 1 compound. 2 compare. 3 comparative. 4 composition. 5 compositor. 6 composer.

com·pact[1] (*adj.* kəm pakt′ or kom′pakt; *v.* kəm pakt′; *n.* kom′pakt) *adj.* 1 firmly packed together; closely joined: *The leaves of the cabbage were folded into a compact head.* 2 *Poetic.* composed or made (*of*): *It was a tale compact of moonstruck fancy.* 3 using few words; brief and well organized.
—v. 1 pack firmly together; join closely. 2 make by putting together firmly. 3 condense.
—n. 1 a small case containing face powder and often rouge. 2 a compact car. [< L *compactus,* pp. of *compingere* < *com-* together + *pangere* fasten]
—com·pact′ly, *adv.* **—com·pact′ness,** *n.*

com·pact[2] (kom′pakt) *n.* an agreement: *We made a compact not to tell anyone our secret.* [< L *compactum* < *compacisci* < *com-* (intensive) + *pacisci* contract]

compact car an automobile that is smaller and more economical than the standard models.

com·pan·ion[1] (kəm pan′yən) *n.* 1 a person who goes along with another; person who shares in what another is doing. 2 anything that matches or goes with another in kind, size, color, etc. 3 a person paid to live or travel with another as a friend and helper. 4 in orders of knighthood, a member of the lowest rank.
—v. be a companion to; go along with. [ME < OF *compaignon* < LL *companio, -onis* < L *com-* together + *panis* bread] **—com·pan′ion·less,** *adj.*
—Syn. *n.* 1 comrade, associate.

com·pan·ion[2] (kəm pan′yən) *n.* 1 a covering over the top of a companionway. 2 a companionway. [< Du. *kompanje* quarterdeck < OF *compagne* steward's room in a galley < VL *compania* < L *com-* together + *panis* bread]

hat, āge, cãre, fär; let, ēqual, tėrm; it, īce
hot, ōpen, ôrder; oil, out; cup, půt, rüle, ūse
əbove, takən, pencəl, lemən, circəs
ch, child; ng, long; sh, ship
th, thin; ᴛʜ, then; zh, measure

com·pan·ion·a·ble (kəm pan′yən ə bəl) *adj.* fitted to be a companion; pleasant; agreeable; sociable.
—com·pan′ion·a·ble·ness, *n.* **—com·pan′ion·a·bly,** *adv.*

com·pan·ion·ate (kəm pan′yən it) *adj.* of or like companions.

com·pan·ion·ship (kəm pan′yən ship′) *n.* an association as companions; fellowship.

com·pan·ion·way (kəm pan′yən wā′) *n.* on a ship: 1 a stairway leading from the deck to the rooms below. 2 the space where such a stairway is.

A companionway

com·pa·ny (kum′pə nē or kump′nē) *n.* **-nies.** 1 a group of people. 2 a group of people joined together for some purpose: *a business company, a company of actors.* 3 a gathering of persons for social purposes: *She behaves well in company.* 4 a companion or companions: *You are known by the company you keep.* 5 companionship; fellowship. 6 *Informal.* one or more guests or visitors: *We often have company in the evening.* 7 a ship's crew; the officers and sailors of a ship. 8 a part of an army commanded by a captain. 9 a troop of Girl Guides. 10 partners not named in the title of a firm. 11 **bear company,** go with. 12 **keep company, a** go (with). **b** go together. 13 **part company, a** go separate ways. **b** end companionship. [ME < OF *compagnie* < *compagne* companion < LL *companio.* See COMPANION[1].]

Company of New France a company founded in 1627 in Paris by Cardinal Richelieu to foster immigration to New France and to maintain loyalty to the French Crown and the Catholic Church. The company, which was granted the monopoly of all French commerce in North America and sovereignty over the territories of the New World, ceased to function in 1657.

company town a town built by a company for its workers, to whom it rents houses, provides services, etc.

company union 1 a union of workers in one factory, store, etc. that is not part of a larger union. 2 a union of workers dominated by the employers.

compar. comparative.

com·pa·ra·ble (kom′pə rə bel, kom′prə bəl, or kəm pãr′ə bəl) *adj.* 1 able to be compared: *A fire is comparable with the sun; both give light and heat.* 2 fit to be compared: *A cave is not comparable to a house as a comfortable place. to live in.* **—com′pa·ra·ble·ness,** *n.*
—com′pa·ra·bly, *adv.*

☛ Although many people avoid the pronunciation (kəm pãr′ə bəl), the form has wide currency among educated Canadians.

com·par·a·tive (kəm par′ə tiv or kəm per′ə tiv) *adj.* 1 that compares; of or having to do with comparison: *the comparative method of studying.* 2 measured by comparison with something else: *Screens give us comparative freedom from flies.* 3 in grammar, showing the comparative form.
—n. 1 the second degree of comparison of an adjective or adverb. 2 a form or combination of words that shows this degree. *Fairer, better,* and *more slowly* are the comparatives of *fair, good,* and *slowly.*

com·par·a·tive·ly (kəm par′ə tiv lē or kəm per′ə tiv lē) *adv.* 1 by comparison; relatively. 2 rather; somewhat. 3 in a comparative manner.

com·pare (kəm pãr′) *v.* **-pared, -par·ing,** *n.* *—v.* 1 find out or point out how persons or things are alike and how they differ: *He compared the two books to see which one had the better bibliography.* 2 consider as similar; liken: *A fish's fins can be compared to a bird's wings; both are used in moving.* 3 be compared; be considered like or

equal to: *Artificial light cannot compare with daylight for general use.* **4** in grammar, change the form of (an adjective or adverb) to show the comparative and superlative degrees; name the positive, comparative, and superlative degrees of. **5 not to be compared with, a** very different from. **b** not nearly so good as.
—*n.* **beyond compare,** without an equal; most excellent. [< F < L *comparare* < *com-* with + *par* equal]

☛ **compare, contrast.** *Compare* is commonly used in two senses: **a** to point out likenesses (used with *to*): *She compared his poetry to a meandering stream.* **b** to examine two or more objects to find both likenesses and differences (used with *with*): *The teacher compared his poem with one of Robert Frost's. Contrast* means to point out differences: *I contrasted John's report card with Mary's to show him how poorly he was doing.*

com·par·i·son (kəm par′ə sən or kəm per′ə sən) *n.* **1** the act or process of comparing; finding the likenesses and differences: *The teacher's comparison of the heart to a pump helped the student to understand its action.* **2** a likeness; similarity. **3** in grammar, a change in an adjective or adverb to show degrees. The three degrees of comparison are positive, comparative, and superlative. *Examples*: good, better, best; cold, colder, coldest; helpful, more helpful, most helpful. **4 in comparison with,** compared with. **5 There is no comparison between them.** One is very much better than the other. [ME < OF *comparaison* < L *comparatio* < *comparare.* See COMPARE.] ☛ See **adjective** and **adverb** for usage notes.

com·part·ment (kəm pärt′mənt) *n.* **1** a separate division or section; part of an enclosed space set off by walls or partitions. A ship's hold is often built in watertight compartments, so that a leak will fill up only one and not the whole ship. **2** on a train, a private room with sleeping accommodations. **3** any part or division: *the less imaginative compartments of her mind.* [< F *compartiment* < Ital. *compartimento* < *compartire* divide < LL < L *com-* with + *partiri* share]

com·part·men·tal·ize (kom′pärt men′tə līz′) *v.* **-ized, -iz·ing. 1** divide into sections or compartments. **2** separate mentally into categories: *compartmentalize information.* —**com·part·men′tal·i·za′tion,** *n.*

com·pass (kum′pəs) *n.* **1** an instrument for showing directions, consisting of a needle that points to the North Magnetic Pole, which is near the North Pole. **2** the boundary; circumference: *A prison lies within the compass of those massive walls.* **3** the space within limits; extent; range: *The old sailor had had many adventures within the compass of his lifetime.* **4** the range of a voice or musical instrument. **5** a circuit; going around. **6** Also, **compasses,** *pl.* an instrument for drawing circles and measuring distances.

A compass (def. 1)

—*v.* **1** make a circuit of; go around. **2** form a circle around; surround. **3** do; accomplish; get. **4** plot; scheme. **5** grasp with the mind; understand completely. [ME <OF *compas* < *compasser* divide equally < VL *compassare* measure off < *compassus* equal step < L *com-* with + *passus* step]
—**Syn.** *n.* **3** reach, scope. See **range.**

compass card a circular card set beneath the needle of a compass showing the 32 points of direction and the degrees of the circle.

A compass (def. 6)

com·pas·sion (kəm pash′ən) *n.* feeling for another's sorrow or hardship that leads one to help the sufferer; sympathy; pity. [ME < OF < L *compassio, -onis* < *compati* < *com-* with + *pati* suffer]
—**Syn.** See **pity.**

com·pas·sion·ate (kəm pash′ən it) *adj.* **1** desiring to relieve another's suffering; deeply sympathetic; pitying. **2** given by superiors or sought for the comfort or convenience of a person and not necessarily in the military interest: *compassionate leave.*
—**com·pas′sion·ate·ly,** *adv.*

compass saw a handsaw with a very narrow, straight blade for cutting curves.

com·pat·i·bil·i·ty (kəm pat′ə bil′ə tē) *n.* the ability to exist together; ability to get on well together; agreement; harmony.

com·pat·i·ble (kəm pat′ə bəl) *adj.* **1** able to exist together; that can get on well together; agreeing; in harmony: *Health and hard work are compatible.* **2** in television, of or having to do with the type of broadcasting that permits reception either in color on special sets or in black and white on ordinary sets. [< Med.L *compatibilis* < L *compati* suffer with. See COMPASSION.]
—**com·pat′i·bly,** *adv.*

com·pa·tri·ot (kəm pā′trē ət or kəm pat′rē ət) *n.* a fellow countryman. —*adj.* of the same country. [< LL *compatriota* < *com-* with + *patriota* fellow countryman < Gk. *patriōtēs* < *patria* clan < *patēr* father]

com·peer (kəm pēr′ or kom′pēr) *n.* **1** an equal; peer. **2** a comrade; companion. [ME < OF *comper* < L *compar* < *com-* with + *par* equal]

com·pel (kəm pel′) *v.* **-pelled, -pel·ling. 1** force: *Rain compelled them to stop.* **2** cause or get by force: *A policeman can compel obedience.* **3** drive or gather by force. [< L *compellere* < *com-* (intensive) + *pellere* drive] —**com·pell′er,** *n.*
Syn. 1 Compel, impel = force. **Compel** = force a person to do something one wants or to give in to something: *It is impossible to compel a person to love his fellow men.* **Impel** = force to move forward, but is most often used figuratively to mean "drive forward by strong desire": *Hunger impelled him to beg.*

com·pel·ling (kəm pel′ing) *adj.* **1** forcing, commanding, or constraining. **2** forcing attention or interest: *She has compelling beauty.* **3** strongly persuasive or convincing: *a compelling argument.* —**com·pel′ling·ly,** *adv.*

com·pend (kom′pend) *n.* compendium.

com·pen·di·ous (kəm pen′dē əs) *adj.* brief but comprehensive; concise. [ME < LL *compendiosus* < *compendium.* See COMPENDIUM.] —**com·pen′di·ous·ly,** *adv.*

com·pen·di·um (kəm pen′dē əm) *n.* **-di·ums, -di·a** (-dē ə). a summary that gives much information in a little space; concise treatise. [< L *compendium* a saving, shortening < *compendere* < *com-* together + *pendere* weigh]

com·pen·sate (kom′pən sāt′) *v.* **-sat·ed, -sat·ing. 1** make an equal return to; give an equivalent to: *The hunters compensated the farmer for killing his cow.* **2** balance by equal weight, power, etc.; make up (*for*): *Hard work often compensates for lack of ability.* **3** pay: *The company compensated her for extra work.* **4** in mechanics, adjust so as to offset variations or produce equilibrium; counter-balance: *Watches and clocks are compensated in order to keep the wheels and springs properly balanced.* **5** stabilize the buying power of (money) to meet varying price levels by changing the amount of gold in coins or the quantity of gold held in reserve to back up the currency. [< L *compensare* < *com-* with + *pensare* weigh < *pendere*] —**com′pen·sa′tor,** *n.*
—**Syn. 1** recompense. See **pay. 2** offset.

com·pen·sa·tion (kom′pən sā′shən) *n.* **1** a compensating or a being compensated. **2** something given as an equivalent; something given to make up for a loss, injury, etc. **3** a balancing by equal power, weight, etc. **4** the means for doing this. **5** pay: *He said that equal compensation should be given to men and women for equal work.* **6** in biology, an increased activity of one part to make up for loss or weakness of another: *The blind man developed especially sharp hearing as a compensation for his loss of sight.* **7** in psychology: **a** behavior which emphasizes some desirable personal trait, feeling, etc. in order to conceal an undesirable one: *His hearty manner was a compensation for his feeling of insecurity.* **b** the cancellation of one sensation by another.

com·pen·sa·tive (kom′pən sā′tiv or kəm pen′sə tiv) *adj.* compensating.

com·pen·sa·to·ry (kəm pen′sə tô′rē) *adj.* compensating.

com·pete (kəm pēt′) *v.* **-pet·ed, -pet·ing. 1** try hard to obtain something wanted by others; be rivals; contend. **2** take part (in a contest): *An injury kept him from competing in the final race.* [< L *competere* < *com-* together + *petere* seek] —**Syn. 1** See **contend.**

com·pe·tence (kom′pə təns) *n.* **1** ability; fitness: *No one doubted the guide's competence.* **2** enough money or property to provide a comfortable living. **3** in law, legal power, capacity, or authority.

com·pe·ten·cy (kom′pə tən sē) *n.* competence.

com·pe·tent (kom′pə tənt) *adj.* **1** able; fit: *a competent cook.* **2** in law, legally qualified: *Two competent witnesses testified.* **3** rightfully belonging; permissible (*to*): *It is not competent to the jury to pronounce the sentence.* [< L *competens, -entis* being fit, ppr. of *competere* meet. See COMPETE.] **—com′pe·tent·ly,** *adv.* **—Syn. 1** capable. See **able.**

com·pe·ti·tion (kom′pə tish′ən) *n.* **1** an effort to obtain something wanted by others; rivalry: *There is competition among business firms for trade.* **2** a contest.

com·pet·i·tive (kəm pet′ə tiv) *adj.* of competition; having competition; based on competition; decided by competition: *a competitive examination for a job.* **—com·pet′i·tive·ly,** *adv.* **—com·pet′i·tive·ness,** *n.*

com·pet·i·tor (kəm pet′ə tər) *n.* a person who competes.

com·pi·la·tion (kom′pə lā′shən) *n.* **1** the act of compiling. **2** a book, list, etc. that has been compiled.

com·pile (kəm pīl′) *v.* **-piled, -pil·ing. 1** collect and bring together in one list or account. **2** make (a book, report, etc.) out of various materials. [ME < OF *compiler* < L *compilare* steal, originally, pile up < *com-* together + *pilare* press] **—com·pil′er,** *n.*

com·pla·cence (kəm plā′səns) *n.* complacency.

com·pla·cen·cy (kəm plā′sən sē) *n.* **-cies. 1** the state or condition of being pleased with oneself; self-satisfaction: *The defendant's complacency during the trial angered the jury.* **2** contentment.

com·pla·cent (kəm plā′sənt) *adj.* pleased with oneself; self-satisfied: *The winner's complacent smile annoyed some people.* [< L *complacens, -entis,* ppr. of *complacere* < *com-* with + *placere* please] **—com·pla′cent·ly,** *adv.*

com·plain (kəm plān′) *v.* **1** say that something is unsatisfactory; find fault. **2** talk about one's pains, troubles, etc. **3** make an accusation or charge: *She complained to the police about her neighbor's dog.* [ME < OF *complaindre* < VL *complangere* < L *com-* (intensive) + *plangere* lament] **—com·plain′er,** *n.* **—com·plain′ing·ly,** *adv.*

Syn. 1 Complain, grumble = express discontent. **Complain** = say one is discontented with some situation: *He is always complaining about the weather.* **Grumble** = mutter complaint in a bad-tempered way: *He is grumbling about the food.*

com·plain·ant (kəm plān′ənt) *n.* **1** a person who complains. **2** a person who brings a lawsuit against another; plaintiff: *The complainant accused the defendant of cheating him.*

com·plaint (kəm plānt′) *n.* **1** a complaining; a voicing of dissatisfaction; a finding fault. **2** a cause for complaining. **3** an accusation; charge. **4** a sickness; ailment: *A cold is a very common complaint.*

com·plai·sance (kəm plā′zəns or kəm plā′səns, kom′plə zans or kom′plə sans) *n.* **1** obligingness; agreeableness; courtesy. **2** compliance. [< F]

com·plai·sant (kəm plā′zənt or kəm plā′sənt, kom′plə zant or kom′plə sant) *adj.* **1** obliging; gracious; courteous. **2** compliant. [< F *complaisant,* ppr. of *complaire* acquiesce < L *complacere* < *com-* (intensive) + *placere* please] **—com·plai′sant·ly,** *adv.*

com·ple·ment (*n.* kom′plə mənt; *v.* kom′plə ment′) *n.* **1** something that completes or makes perfect. **2** the number required to fill (something): *The ship now had its full complement of men, and no more could be taken on.* **3** in grammar, a word or group of words completing a predicate. In "The man is good", *good* is a complement. **4** in mathematics, the amount needed to make an angle or an arc equal to 90 degrees. **5** in music, the interval which, added to a given interval, completes an octave. **6** either of two parts that complete each other. **—***v.* supply a lack of any kind; complete: *My furniture just complemented my sister's, so that together we had what we needed.* [ME < L *complementum* < *complere.* See COMPLETE.]

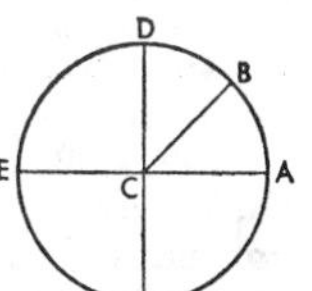

A complement (def. 4). The arc BD is the complement of the arc AB and the angle BCD is the complement of the angle ACB.

Syn. *v.* **Complement, supplement** = complete. **Complement** = complete by supplying something that is missing but necessary to make a perfect whole: *The information from the encyclopedia complemented what he already had and he was ready to write his essay.* **Supplement** = add something to make better or bigger or richer in some way: *School activities supplement one's education.*
☛ **complement, compliment. Complement** = something that completes or makes perfect, or a number required to fill something (related to *complete*): *She has her full complement of good looks.* **Compliment** has to do with politeness and praise: *He paid her a nice compliment.*

com·ple·men·tal (kom′plə men′təl) *adj.* complementary.

com·ple·men·ta·ry (kom′plə men′tə rē or kom′plə men′trē) *adj.* forming a complement; completing: *Two complementary colors mixed make white.*

complementary angle an angle needed to make another angle equal to 90 degrees, or right angle. A 30-degree angle is the complementary angle of a 60-degree angle.

complementary colors or **colours** two colors that combine to produce white or gray light. Red and green are complementary colors.

com·plete (kəm plēt′) *adj. v.* **-plet·ed, -plet·ing.** **—***adj.* **1** with all the parts; whole; entire: *a complete set of Dickens' novels.* **2** perfect; thorough: *a complete surprise.* **3** ended; finished; done: *My homework is complete.* **—***v.* **1** make up all the parts of; make whole or entire: *She completed her set of dishes by buying a sugar bowl.* **2** make perfect or thorough: *The good news completed my happiness.* **3** get done; end; finish: *She completed her homework early in the evening.* [ME < OF *complet* < L *completus,* pp. of *complere* < *com-* (intensive) + *plere* fill] **—com·plete′ness,** *n.*

Syn. *adj.* **1 Complete, entire** = with all the parts. **Complete** = with all the parts needed to make something whole or full: *I have the complete story now.* **Entire** = with no parts taken away: *He gave the entire day to his work, not even taking time for lunch.*

com·plete·ly (kəm plēt′lē) *adv.* in a complete manner; entirely; thoroughly.

com·ple·tion (kəm plē′shən) *n.* **1** the act of completing; finishing. **2** the condition of being completed: *The work is near completion.*

com·plex (*adj.* kəm pleks′ or kom′pleks; *n.* kom′pleks) *adj.* **1** made up of a number of parts: *A complex sentence has one or more clauses besides the main clause.* **2** complicated: *The instructions for building the radio were too complex for us to follow.* **—***n.* **1** a complicated whole: *A new industrial complex is planned in this suburb.* **2** in psychology, an idea or group of ideas giving rise to an emotional disturbance that influences a person's behavior to an abnormal degree. **3** *Informal.* an unreasonable prejudice; strong dislike. [< L *complexus,* pp. of *complecti* embrace < *com-* together + *plectere* twine] **—com·plex′ly,** *adv.* **—com·plex′ness,** *n.* **—Syn.** *adj.* **1** composite, compound. **2** intricate, involved.

complex fraction a fraction having a fraction in the numerator, in the denominator, or in both. *Examples:* $\frac{1\frac{1}{4}}{3}, \frac{1}{3\frac{1}{3}}, \frac{\frac{3}{4}}{1\frac{7}{8}}$

com·plex·ion (kəm plek′shən) *n.* **1** the color, quality, and general appearance of the skin, particularly of the face. **2** general appearance; nature; character. **3** in medieval physiology, the combination of the four humors (cold, heat, dryness, and moisture) in certain proportions, believed to determine the nature of an animal, plant, or human body. [ME < LL *complexio, -onis* constitution < L *complexio* combination < *complexus.* See COMPLEX.]

com·plex·ioned (kəm plek′shənd) *adj.* having a certain kind of complexion: *dark-complexioned.*

com·plex·i·ty (kəm plek′sə tē) *n.* **-ties. 1** a complex quality, condition, or structure: *The complexity of the road map puzzled him.* **2** something complex; complication.

complex sentence a sentence having one main clause and one or more subordinate clauses. *Example:* When the engineer pulls the cord, the whistle blows. ☛ See **clause** for usage note.

com·pli·ance (kəm plī′əns) *n.* **1** the act of complying or doing as another wishes; act of yielding to a request or command. **2** a tendency to yield to others. **3 in compliance with,** complying with; according to. —**Syn. 1** consent, submission.

com·pli·an·cy (kəm plī′ən sē) *n.* compliance.

com·pli·ant (kəm plī′ənt) *adj.* complying; yielding; obliging: *A compliant person gives in to other people.* —**com·pli′ant·ly,** *adv.* —**Syn.** See **obedient.**

com·pli·cate (*v.* kom′plə kāt′; *adj.* kom′plə kit) *v.* **-cat·ed, -cat·ing. 1** make hard to understand, settle, cure, etc.; mix up; confuse. **2** make worse or more mixed up: *a headache complicated by eye trouble.* **3** twist together. —*adj.* **1** in botany, folded upon itself. **2** of insect's wings, folded lengthwise one or more times. [< L *complicare* < *com-* together + *plicare* fold]

com·pli·cat·ed (kom′plə kāt′id) *adj.* made up of many parts; involved; intricate.

com·pli·ca·tion (kom′plə kā′shən) *n.* **1** a complex or confused state of affairs that is hard to understand, settle, cure, etc. **2** a difficulty or problem added to one or more already existing: *Pneumonia was the complication we most feared.* **3** the act or process of complicating. **4** an element in a story or play which complicates the plot.

com·plic·i·ty (kəm plis′ə tē) *n.* **-ties.** partnership in wrongdoing: *Knowingly receiving stolen goods is complicity in theft.* [< F *complice* a confederate < LL *complex, -plicis* interwoven < L *complicare* < *com-* together + *plicare* fold]

com·pli·ment (*n.* kom′plə mənt; *v.* kom′plə ment′) *n.* **1** something good said about one; something said in praise of one's work. **2** a polite greeting: "*With the compliments of a friend.*"
—*v.* **1** praise; pay a compliment to; congratulate: *The principal complimented the boy on his good grades.* **2** give something to (a person) as a polite attention. [< F < Ital. < Sp. *cumplimiento* fulfilment of courtesy < *cumplir* fulfil < L *complere* fill up] —**com′pli·ment·er,** *n.* —**Syn.** *n.* **1** commendation, tribute. ☛ See **complement** for usage note.

com·pli·men·ta·ry (kom′plə men′tə rē or kom′plə men′trē) *adj.* **1** like or containing a compliment; praising. **2** given free: *a complimentary ticket to a concert.*

com·plin (kom′plin) *n.* **1** the last of the seven canonical hours. **2** the service for it, now usually following vespers. [ME < OF *complie* < L *completa* (*hora*) completed hour]

com·pline (kom′plin or kom′plīn) *n.* complin.

com·ply (kəm plī′) *v.* **-plied, -ply·ing.** act in agreement (with a request or a command): *We should comply with the doctor's orders.* [< Ital. *complire* < Sp. *cumplir* < L *complere* complete; influenced by *ply*[1]] —**com·pli′er,** *n.*

com·po·nent (kəm pō′nənt) *adj.* constituent; that composes: *Blade and handle are the component parts of a knife.* —*n.* a part, especially an essential part: *A chemist can separate a medicine into its components.* [< L *componens, -entis,* ppr. of *componere* < *com-* together + *ponere* put] —**Syn.** *n.* See **element.**

com·port[1] (kom′pôrt) *n.* a compote.

com·port[2] (kəm pôrt′) *v.* **1** behave: *A judge should comport himself with dignity.* **2** agree; suit: *Silliness does not comport with a position of authority.* [< F *comporter* < L *comportare* < *com-* together + *portare* carry]

com·port·ment (kəm pôrt′mənt) *n.* behavior.

com·pose (kəm pōz′) *v.* **-posed, -pos·ing. 1** make up: *The ocean is composed of salt water.* **2** invent or write music. **3** put together, arrange into a system: *compose a poem.* **4** get oneself ready, put in proper state: *compose oneself to read a book.* **5** make calm (oneself or one's features): *Compose yourself.* **6** set up type in a printing office. **7** settle; arrange: *compose a dispute.* [ME < OF *composer* < *com-* together + *poser* place (see POSE[1])]

com·posed (kəm pōzd′) *adj.* calm; quiet; self-controlled; tranquil. —**Syn.** See **calm.**

com·pos·ed·ly (kəm pōz′id lē) *adv.* in a composed manner.

com·pos·er (kəm pōz′ər) *n.* **1** a person who composes. **2** a writer of music. **3** an author.

com·pos·ite (kom′pə zit or kəm poz′it) *adj.* **1** made up of various parts; compound: *The photographer made a composite picture by putting together parts of several others.* **2** in botany, belonging to a group of plants in which the florets are borne in dense heads. Daisies and dandelions are composite flowers. —*n.* **1** a composite plant. **2** any composite thing. **3** a composite number. [< L *compositus,* pp. of *componere* < *com-* together + *ponere* put. Doublet of COMPOST.] —**com′pos·ite·ly,** *adv.*

composite number a number that can be exactly divided by some number other than itself or 1; a number that has more than 2 factors. Thus 8 is a composite number, because its factors are 1, 2, 4, and 8; 5 is not, because its only factors are 5 and 1.

composite school (kom′pə zit) *Cdn.* a secondary school in which a student may receive academic, commercial, or industrial training.

com·po·si·tion (kom′pə zish′ən) *n.* **1** the make-up of anything: *What is the composition of this candy? It is made of sugar, chocolate, and milk.* **2** a putting together of a whole: *Writing sentences, painting pictures, and setting type in printing are all forms of composition.* **3** the thing composed, such as a piece of music, writing, etc. **4** a short essay written as a school exercise. **5** a mixture of substances; amalgam: *The dentist filled my tooth with a composition that has silver in it.* **6** an agreement; settlement.

com·pos·i·tor (kəm poz′ə tər) *n.* typesetter.

com·post (kom′pōst) *n.* **1** a mixture. **2** a mixture of leaves, manure, etc. for fertilizing soil. —*v.* **1** make compost of (something). **2** fertilize using compost. [ME < OF < L *compositus,* pp. of *componere.* See COMPOSITE.]

com·po·sure (kəm pō′zhər) *n.* calmness; quietness; self-control.

com·pote (kom′pōt) *n.* **1** a dish with a supporting stem, used for fruit, candy, etc. **2** stewed fruit. [< F < OF *composte* < L *compos(i)ta,* fem. of *compositus.* See COMPOSITE.]

A compote (def. 1)

com·pound[1] (*adj.* kom′pound or kom pound′; *n.* kom′pound; *v.* kom pound′) *adj.* having more than one part: *A clover leaf is a compound leaf.* "*Steamship*" *is a compound word.* "*John bought a hat, Philip bought a coat*" *is a compound sentence.* [< v.]
—*n.* **1** something made by combining parts; a mixture: *A medicine is usually a compound.* **2** a word made by joining together two or more separate words: *Highway is a compound.* **3** in chemistry, a substance formed by a combination of two or more substances: *Water is a compound of hydrogen and oxygen.* [< adj.]
—*v.* **1** mix; combine: *The druggist compounds medicines.* **2** settle (a quarrel or a debt) by a compromise. **3 compound a felony,** accept money or other payment not to prosecute a person who has committed an indictable offence. **4** charge, pay, or increase by compound interest. [ME *compoune* < OF *compondre* < L *componere* < *com-* together + *ponere* put] —**com·pound′a·ble,** *adj.* **com·pound′er,** *n.*

com·pound[2] (kom′pound) *n.* an enclosed yard with buildings in it. [probably < Malay *kampong*]

Compound E cortisone.

compound fraction a complex fraction.

compound fracture a fracture in which a broken bone cuts through the flesh and sticks out.

compound interest the interest paid on both the original sum of money borrowed and on all the unpaid interest added to it.

compound number a quantity expressed in two or more kinds of units. *Examples:* 3 ft., 5 in.; 2 hr., 18 min., 40 sec.

compound sentence a sentence made up of co-ordinate independent clauses. *Examples:* He ran away from home, but he soon came back. The winds blew, the rains fell, and the water covered the earth. ☛ See **clause** for usage note.

hat, āge, cãre, fär; let, ēqual, tėrm; it, īce
hot, ōpen, ôrder; oil, out; cup, pu̇t, rüle, ūse
əbove, takən, pencəl, lemən, circəs
ch, child; ng, long; sh, ship
th, thin; ᴛʜ, then; zh, measure

com·pre·hend (kom′pri hend′) *v.* **1** understand fully with the mind: *He comprehends geometry and advanced algebra.* **2** include; contain: *His report comprehended all the facts.* [ME < L *comprehendere* < *com-* (intensive) + *prehendere* seize) **—com′pre·hend′er,** *n.* **—com′pre·hend′ing·ly,** *adv.* **—Syn. 1** grasp, perceive. **2** comprise. See **include.**

☛ **Comprehend, apprehend** = take hold of something mentally, but should not be confused. **Comprehend** = take complete hold of the meaning of something and understand it fully and perfectly: *He comprehends atomic energy.* **Apprehend** = take hold of a fact or idea and see something of its meaning, but not to see its relationships or implications, and therefore to understand it only partly: *He dimly apprehended what the foreign sailors were talking about.*

com·pre·hen·si·bil·i·ty (kom′pri hen′sə bil′ə tē) *n.* intelligibility; a comprehensible quality.

com·pre·hen·si·ble (kom′pri hen′sə bəl) *adj.* understandable. **—com′pre·hen′si·bly,** *adv.*

com·pre·hen·sion (kom′pri hen′shən) *n.* **1** the act or power of understanding; ability to get the meaning: *Calculus is beyond his comprehension.* **2** the act or fact of including. **3** comprehensiveness. [< L *comprehensio, -onis* < *comprehendere.* See COMPREHEND.]

com·pre·hen·sive (kom′pri hen′siv) *adj.* **1** including; including much: *The term's work ended with a comprehensive review.* **2** comprehending much: *The philosopher had a comprehensive mind.* **—com′pre·hen′sive·ly,** *adv.* **—com′pre·hen′sive·ness,** *n.* **—Syn. 1** inclusive. **2** understanding.

comprehensive school *Cdn.* a composite school.

com·press (*v.* kəm pres′; *n.* kom′pres) *v.* squeeze together; make smaller by pressure. [ME < LL *compressare,* frequentative of L *comprimere* < *com-* together + *premere* press] *—n.* **1** a pad of wet cloth applied to some part of the body to create pressure or to reduce inflammation. **2** a machine for pressing cotton into bales. [< F *compresse,* ult. < L *comprimere.* See verb.]

com·pressed (kəm prest′) *adj.* **1** squeezed together; made smaller by pressure. **2** flattened.

compressed air air that has been put under extra pressure so that it has a great deal of force when released. The air in an automobile tire is compressed. Compressed air is used to operate certain kinds of brakes, guns, and atomizers.

com·press·i·bil·i·ty (kəm pres′ə bil′ə tē) *n.* a compressible quality.

com·press·i·ble (kəm pres′ə bəl) *adj.* that can be compressed.

com·pres·sion (kəm presh′ən) *n.* **1** the act or process of compressing. **2** a compressed condition. **3** the reduction in volume of a gas by the application of pressure: *A car with worn piston rings will have poor compression.*

com·pres·sive (kəm pres′iv) *adj.* compressing; tending to compress.

com·pres·sor (kəm pres′ər) *n.* **1** one that compresses. **2** in anatomy, a muscle that compresses a part of the body. **3** in surgery, an instrument for compressing a part of the body. **4** a machine for compressing air, gas, etc. See **jet** for diagram. [< L]

com·prise (kəm prīz′) *v.* **-prised, -pris·ing.** consist of; include: *Canada comprises ten provinces and two territories.* [ME < OF *compris,* pp. of *comprendre* < L *comprehendere.* See COMPREHEND.] **—Syn.** embrace. See **include.**

com·prize (kəm prīz′) *v.* **-prized, -priz·ing.** comprise.

com·pro·mise (kom′prə mīz′) *v.* **-mised, -mis·ing,** *n.* *—v.* **1** settle (a dispute) by agreeing that each contestant will give up a part of what he demands. **2** put under suspicion; put in danger: *You will compromise your good name if you go around with thieves and liars.* [< n.] *—n.* **1** a settlement of a dispute by a partial yielding on both sides. **2** the result of such a settlement. **3** anything halfway between two different things. **4** an exposing to danger, suspicion, etc.; an endangering: *Such a compromise of his reputation was most unwise.* [ME < OF *compromis* < L *compromissum* < *compromittere* < *com-* together + *promittere* promise] **—com′pro·mis′er,** *n.*

Comp·tom·e·ter (komp tom′ə tər) *n. Trademark.* a machine that adds, subtracts, divides, and multiplies.

comp·trol·ler (kən trōl′ər) *n.* controller (def. 1). [var. spelling of *controller*]

comp·trol·ler·ship (kən trōl′ər ship′) *n.* the position or rank of a comptroller.

com·pul·sion (kəm pul′shən) *n.* **1** the act of compelling; use of force; force: *People must obey the law, either willingly or under compulsion.* **2** in psychology: **a** an irresistible impulse to perform some irrational act: *Wealthy people sometimes feel a compulsion to steal things they can easily afford to buy.* **b** the act itself. [ME < LL *compulsio, -onis* < L *compellere.* See COMPEL.] **—Syn. 1** constraint, coercion.

com·pul·sive (kəm pul′siv) *adj.* **1** compelling. **2** using compulsion. **3** in psychology, of or having to do with compulsion: *She had a compulsive desire to keep her house perfectly neat.* **—com·pul′sive·ly,** *adv.*

com·pul·so·ry (kəm pul′sə rē) *adj.* **1** compelled; required: *Attendance at school is compulsory.* **2** compelling; using force. **—com·pul′so·ri·ly,** *adv.*

com·punc·tion (kəm pungk′shən) *n.* **1** the pricking of conscience; remorse: *The murderer did his work cruelly and without compunction.* **2** a slight or passing regret: *He had no compunction about declining the offer.* [ME < LL *compunctio, -onis* pricking, remorse < L *compungere* < *com-* (intensive) + *pungere* prick]

com·pu·ta·tion (kom′pyu̇ tā′shən) *n.* a reckoning; calculation. Addition and subtraction are forms of computation.

com·pute (kəm pūt′) *v.* **-put·ed, -put·ing.** find out by mathematical work; reckon; calculate. [< L *computare* < *com-* up + *putare* reckon. Doublet of COUNT[1].] **—com·put′a·ble,** *adj.*

com·put·er (kəm pūt′ər) *n.* **1** a person skilled or trained in computing. **2** a calculating machine, especially an electronic one, that performs mathematical and logical operations at high speed and processes masses of coded data. See **analogue computer, digital computer.**

com·rade (kom′rad or kom′rid) *n.* **1** a companion and friend; partner. **2** a person who shares in what another is doing; partner; fellow worker. **3** a fellow member of a union, political party, etc. [< F < Sp. *camarada* roommate < L *camera.* See CHAMBER.] **—Syn. 1** chum, pal.

comrade in arms a fellow soldier.

com·rade·ship (kom′rad ship′ or kom′rid ship′) *n.* **1** the condition of being a comrade. **2** the relation of comrades; friendship; fellowship.

comte (kôɴt) *n. French.* a count or earl.

com·tesse (kôɴ tes′) *n. French.* a countess.

con[1] (kon) *adv.* against: *The two debating teams argued the question pro and con.* *—n.* a reason against. The pros and cons of a question are the arguments for and against it. [short for L *contra* against]

con[2] (kon) *v.* **conned, con·ning. 1** learn well enough to remember; study. **2** examine carefully; pore over. [var. of *can*[1]]

con[3] (kon) *v.* **conned, con·ning,** *n.* *—v.* direct the steering of: *He conned the ship between the rocks.* *—n.* **1** the act or process of conning. **2** the post or station from which this is done. [var. of *cond* < OF *conduire* lead, guide < L *conducere* conduct]

con[4] (kon) *adj. v.* **conned, con·ning.** *n. Slang.* *—adj.* swindling: *a con man, a con game.* *—v.* dupe; swindle: *He was conned into buying an overpriced used car.* *—n.* a confidence trick or swindle. [< *con*fidence game, man, etc.]

con[5] (kon) *n. Slang.* a convict.

con- a form of **com-** before *n,* as in *connote,* and before consonants except *b, h, l, m, p, r, w,* as in *concern, conduct.*

con. 1 conclusion. **2** contra. **3** concession road. **4** in music, concerto. **5** continued.

Con. 1 Consul. **2** Conservative.

con a·mo·re (kôn ä mō′rā) *Italian.* **1** with love; with tenderness. **2** heartily; with enthusiasm. **3** in music, with sentiment.

con brio (kôn brē′ō) *Italian.* in music, to be played spiritedly.

con·cat·e·nate (kon kat′ə nāt′) *v.* **-nat·ed, -nat·ing,** *adj.* —*v.* link together. —*adj.* linked together. [< L *concatenare* < *com-* together + *catena* chain]

con·cat·e·na·tion (kon kat′ə nā′shən) *n.* **1** the act of linking together. **2** the state of being linked together. **3** a connected series.

con·cave (*adj.* kon kāv′, kon′kāv, or kong′kāv; *n.* kon′kāv or kong′kāv) *adj.* hollow and curved like the inside of a circle or sphere. —*n.* a concave surface or thing. [< L *concavus* < *com-* (intensive) + *cavus* hollow] —**con·cave′ly,** *adv.*

Concave lenses seen from the side

con·cav·i·ty (kon kav′ə tē) *n.* **-ties. 1** a concave condition or quality. **2** a concave surface or thing.

con·ca·vo-con·vex (kon kā′vō kon veks′) *adj.* concave on one side and convex on the other.

con·ceal (kən sēl′) *v.* **1** hide. **2** keep secret. [ME < OF *conceler* < L *concelare* < *com-* (intensive) + *celare* hide] —**con·ceal′er,** *n.* —**Syn. 1** shroud, veil, cloak, mask. See **hide**[1].

con·ceal·ment (kən sēl′mənt) *n.* **1** the act of hiding or keeping secret. **2** the state of being hidden or kept secret. **3** a means or place for hiding.

con·cede (kən sēd′) *v.* **-ced·ed, -ced·ing. 1** admit as true; admit: *Everyone concedes that 2 and 2 make 4.* **2** give (what is asked or claimed); grant; yield: *He conceded us the right to walk through his land.* [< L *concedere* < *com-* together + *cedere* yield]

con·ceit (kən sēt′) *n.* **1** too high an opinion of oneself or of one's ability, importance, etc.: *What we call conceit in others, we usually call self-confidence in ourselves.* **2** a fanciful notion; witty thought or expression, often a far-fetched one. [< *conceive,* on analogy with *deceit*] —**Syn. 1** See **pride.**

con·ceit·ed (kən sēt′id) *adj.* having too high an opinion of oneself or one's ability, importance, etc.; vain. —**con·ceit′ed·ly,** *adv.* —**con·ceit′ed·ness,** *n.* —**Syn.** egotistical, proud, self-satisfied.

con·ceiv·a·ble (kən sēv′ə bəl) *adj.* that can be conceived or thought of; imaginable: *We should take every conceivable precaution against fire.* —**con·ceiv′a·ble·ness,** *n.* —**con·ceiv′a·bly,** *adv.*

con·ceive (kən sēv′) *v.* **-ceived, -ceiv·ing. 1** form in the mind; think up: *The architect has conceived a design for a completely new kind of house.* **2** have an idea or feeling: *He conceived a violent dislike for his aunt.* **3** think; imagine: *It is hard to conceive of life apart from time. We cannot conceive that such a thing will happen.* **4** put in words; express: *The warning was conceived in the plainest language.* **5** become pregnant. **6** become pregnant with: *She conceived a child.* [ME < OF *conceveir* < L *concipere* take in < *com-* (intensive) + *capere* take] —**con·ceiv′er,** *n.* —**Syn. 1** See **imagine.**

con·cen·trate (kon′sən trāt′) *v.* **-trat·ed, -trat·ing,** *n.* —*v.* **1** bring or come together to one place: *A convex lens is used to concentrate rays of light.* **2** pay close attention; focus the mind: *He concentrated upon the problem.* **3** make stronger: *An acid solution is concentrated when it has a high proportion of acid in it.* **4** (in mining) remove rock, sand, etc. from (metal or ore). —*n.* something that has been concentrated. [< *con-* together + L *centrum* centre] —**con′cen·tra′tor,** *n.* —**Syn.** *v.* **1** gather, collect, assemble, focus. **3** intensify.

☛ The verb concentrate is followed by *on* or *upon*: *I cannot concentrate on this problem because of the noise. You will have to concentrate upon your work if you want to finish today.*

con·cen·trat·ed (kon′sən trāt′id) *adj.* **1** brought together in one place. **2** of liquids and solutions, made stronger. —**con′cen·trat′ed·ly,** *adv.*

con·cen·tra·tion (kon′sən trā′shən) *n.* **1** a concentrating or being concentrated. **2** close attention: *He gave the problem his full concentration.* **3** the strength of a solution. —**Syn. 1** collection, gathering.

concentration camp a camp where political enemies, prisoners of war, and interned foreigners are held.

con·cen·tric (kən sen′trik) *adj.* having the same centre. —**con·cen′tri·cal·ly,** *adv.*

con·cen·tri·cal (kən sen′trə kəl) *adj.* concentric.

Concentric circles

con·cept (kon′sept) *n.* a general notion; an idea of a class of objects; idea: *the concept of equality, basic concepts of chivalry.* [< L *conceptus,* pp. of *concipere.* See CONCEIVE.]

con·cep·tion (kən sep′shən) *n.* **1** the act or power of conceiving. **2** the state of being conceived. **3** a thought; idea; impression: *His conception of the problem is different from mine.* **4** a becoming pregnant. **5** a design; plan.

con·cep·tu·al (kən sep′chü əl) *adj.* having to do with concepts or general ideas. —**con·cep′tu·al·ly,** *adv.*

con·cern (kən sėrn′) *v.* **1** have to do with; have an interest for; be the business or affair of: *The message is private; it concerns nobody but me.* **2** trouble; make anxious: *We didn't want to concern Mother with the details of the accident.* **3 as concerns,** about; with reference to. **4 concern oneself, a** take an interest; be busy. **b** be troubled or worried; be anxious or uneasy. —*n.* **1** whatever has to do with a person or thing; interest; important matter; business affair: *Keeping the house clean is my wife's concern.* **2** a troubled state of mind; worry; anxiety; uneasiness: *The mother's concern over her sick child kept her awake all night.* **3** a business company; firm. **4** relation; reference: *Children have little concern with politics.* **5 of concern,** of vital interest. [< Med.L *concernere* relate to < LL *concernere* mingle with, mix < L *concretus,* pp. of *concrescere* < *com-* together + *crescere* grow] —**Syn.** *v.* **1** affect, touch. -*n.* **2** See **care.**

☛ Concern used with *in* or *with* means "take part in or have to do with": *He is concerned in the real estate business. They could not prove he was concerned with the crime.* Concern used with *for* or *about* means "be worried": *Are you concerned about his escape? Naturally we were concerned for him when we heard of the accident.*

con·cerned (kən sėrnd′) *adj.* **1** interested; affected; involved. **2** busy; occupied. **3** troubled; worried; anxious. —**con·cern′ed·ly,** *adv.*

con·cern·ing (kən sėr′ning) *prep.* having to do with; with regard to; regarding; relation to; about: *The policeman asked many questions concerning the accident.*

con·cern·ment (kən sėrn′mənt) *n.* **1** importance; interest. **2** worry; anxiety. **3** affair.

con·cert (*n. adj.* kon′sərt; *v.* kən sėrt′) *n.* **1** a musical performance in which several musicians or singers take part. **2** agreement; harmony; union. **3 in concert,** all together; in harmony or agreement. —*adj.* **1** used in concerts; for concerts. **2** performing in a concert or concerts: *a concert pianist.* —*v.* arrange by agreement; plan or make together. [< F < Ital. *concerto,* probably < *concertare* < L *com-* with + *certare* strive. Doublet of CONCERTO.]

con·cert·ed (kən sėr′tid) *adj.* **1** arranged by agreement; planned or made together; combined: *a concerted attack.* **2** in music, arranged in parts for several voices or instruments. —**con·cert′ed·ly,** *adv.*

concert grand a grand piano having the volume and brilliancy of tone required for use in a large hall or with an orchestra.

con·cer·ti·na (kon′sər tē′nə) *n.* a small musical instrument resembling an accordion. [< *concert*]

con·cert·mas·ter (kon′sərt mas′tər) *n.* the leader, usually the first violinist, of an orchestra, ranking next to the conductor.

con·cert·meis·ter (kon′ sərt mīs′tər) *n.* concertmaster. [< G]

con·cer·to (kən cher′tō) *n.* **-tos,** *Italian,* **-ti** (tē). a musical composition, usually in three movements and usually written for one or more solo instruments, such as a violin, piano, etc., accompanied by an orchestra. [< Ital. Doublet of CONCERT.]

concerto grosso (kən cher′tō grō′sō) a concerto for a group of solo instruments and a full orchestra, usually played in four movements. [< Ital.]

concert pitch 1 in music, a slightly heightened pitch, often used for tuning instruments for concert use. 2 the height of fitness, readiness, co-ordination, etc.: *Our Olympic runners were at concert pitch.*

con·ces·sion[1] (kən sesh′ən) *n.* 1 the act of conceding; granting; yielding: *Concession to popular demands was the monarch's weakness.* 2 anything yielded or conceded; admission; acknowledgement: *As a concession, Mother let me stay up an hour longer.* 3 something conceded or granted by a government or controlling authority; grant. Land, privileges, etc. given by a government to a business company are called concessions. A circus leases space for booths as concessions. 4 a privilege or space granted or leased for a particular use within specified premises: *There is a soft-drink concession at the ball park.* [< L *concessio, -onis* < *concedere.* See CONCEDE.] —**Syn.** 3 franchise.

con·ces·sion[2] (kən sesh′ən) *n. Cdn.* 1 mainly in Ontario and Quebec, a subdivision of land in township surveys, formerly one of the rows of thirty-two 200-acre lots into which each new township was divided. 2 a concession road. 3 **concessions,** *pl.* rural or bush districts: *He relies on the concessions for his political support.*

con·ces·sion·aire (kən sesh′ən ãr′) *n.* a person, business company, etc. to whom a concession has been granted. [< F *concessionnaire*]

concession road *Cdn.* especially in Ontario, a rural road following the road allowance between concessions, running as a rule east and west and connected to other concession roads by north-south side roads. Concession roads are usually 1¼ miles apart.

con·ces·sive (kən ses′iv) *adj.* 1 yielding; making or implying concession. 2 in grammar, expressing concession. *Though* and *although* introduce concessive clauses.

conch (konch or kongk) *n.* **conch·es** (kon′chiz) or **conchs** (kongks). 1 any of several molluscs of tropical waters having large spiral shells. 2 its shell. 3 in architecture: **a** the concave surface of a dome. **b** an apse. Also, **concha.** [< L *concha* < Gk. *konchē*]

con·cha (kong′kə) *n.* 1 in medicine: **a** the large, open hollow of the outer ear. **b** the outer ear. 2 in architecture, a conch. [< L *concha* conch]

con·chi·lite (kong′kə līt′) *n.* a bowl-shaped rock composed chiefly of limonite and goethite, having a smooth or irregularly scalloped outline resembling an oyster shell and varying in diameter from 1 in. to 1 yd., discovered in 1943 on the bedrock floor of Finlayson Lake (Ont.).

con·cho·log·i·cal (kong′kə loj′ə kəl) *adj.* of or having to do with conchology.

con·chol·o·gist (kong kol′ə jist) *n.* an expert in conchology.

con·chol·o·gy (kong kol′ə jē) *n.* the branch of zoology that deals with shells and shellfish. [< Gk. *konchē* shell + E *-logy*]

con·ci·erge (kon′sē ėrzh′; *French,* kôɴ syerzh′) *n.* 1 a doorkeeper. 2 a janitor. [< F]

con·cil·i·ar (kən sil′ē ər) *adj.* of or having to do with a council or councils.

con·cil·i·ate (kən sil′ē āt′) *v.* **-at·ed, -at·ing.** 1 win over; soothe: *Mrs. Lee conciliated her disgruntled cook with a present.* 2 gain (good will, regard, favor, etc.) by friendly acts. 3 reconcile; bring into harmony. [< L *conciliare* < *concilium.* See COUNCIL.] —**con·cil′i·at′ing·ly,** *adv.*

con·cil·i·a·tion (kən sil′ē ā′shən) *n.* a conciliating or being conciliated.

con·cil·i·a·tive (kən sil′ē ə tiv or kən sil′ē ā′tiv) *adj.* conciliatory.

con·cil·i·a·tor (kən sil′ē ā′tər) *n.* a person who conciliates; arbitrator; peacemaker.

con·cil·i·a·to·ry (kən sil′ē ə tô′rē) *adj.* tending to win over, soothe, or reconcile.

con·cise (kən sīs′) *adj.* expressing much in a few words; brief but full of meaning. [< L *concisus,* pp. of *concidere* < *com-* (intensive) + *caedere* cut] —**con·cise′ly,** *adv.* —**con·cise′ness,** *n.* —**Syn.** terse, succinct.

hat, āge, cãre, fär; let, ēqual, tėrm; it, īce
hot, ōpen, ôrder; oil, out; cup, pu̇t, rüle, ūse
əbove, takən, pencəl, lemən, circəs
ch, child; ng, long; sh, ship
th, thin; ᴛʜ, then; zh, measure

con·clave (kon′klāv or kong′klāv) *n.* 1 a private meeting. 2 in the Roman Catholic Church: **a** a meeting of the cardinals for the election of a pope. **b** the rooms where the cardinals meet in private for this purpose. [ME < OF < L *conclave* a room that can be locked < *com-* with + *clavis* key]

con·clude (kən klüd′) *v.* **-clud·ed, -clud·ing.** 1 end; finish: *The book concluded happily.* 2 arrange; settle: *The two countries concluded an agreement on trade.* 3 find out by thinking; reach or arrive at (a decision, judgment, or opinion) by reasoning; infer: *From the tracks we saw, we concluded that the animal must have been a deer.* 4 decide; resolve: *I concluded not to go.* [< L *concludere* < *com-* (intensive) + *claudere* close] —**con·clud′er,** *n.* —**Syn.** 1 terminate. See **end.**

☛ **Conclude** is used: **a** with *by* before the *-ing* form of the verb: *He concluded his remarks by quoting a passage from Chaucer.* **b** with *with* before a noun: *I will conclude my remarks with a plea addressed to your president.* **c** with *from* when it means "infer": *I must conclude from what you say that you are dissatisfied.*

con·clu·sion (kən klü′zhən) *n.* 1 an end. 2 the last main division of a speech, essay, etc. 3 a final result; outcome. 4 an arrangement; settlement: *the conclusion of a peace treaty between enemies.* 5 a decision, judgment, or opinion reached by reasoning. 6 **in conclusion,** finally; lastly; to conclude. 7 **try conclusions,** engage in a struggle (*with*). [ME < L *conclusio, -onis* < *concludere.* See CONCLUDE.] —**Syn.** 1 termination. 5 inference.

con·clu·sive (kən klü′siv) *adj.* decisive; convincing; final: *conclusive evidence.* —**con·clu′sive·ly,** *adv.* —**con·clu′sive·ness,** *n.*

con·coct (kən kokt′ or kon kokt′) *v.* prepare; make up: *The children concocted some queer messes in the kitchen.* [< L *concoctus,* pp. of *concoquere* < *com-* together + *coquere* cook] —**con·coct′er,** *n.*

con·coc·tion (kən kok′shən or kon kok′shən) *n.* 1 the act of concocting. 2 the thing concocted.

con·com·i·tance (kən kom′ə təns or kon kom′ə təns) *n.* accompaniment.

con·com·i·tant (kən kom′ə tənt or kon kom′ə tənt) *adj.* accompanying; attending: *a concomitant result.* —*n.* an accompanying thing, quality, or circumstance; accompaniment. [< L *concomitans, -antis,* ppr. of *concomitari* < *com-* (intensive) + *comitari* accompany] —**con·com′i·tant·ly,** *adv.*

con·cord (kon′kôrd or kong′kôrd) *n.* 1 agreement; harmony. 2 in music, a harmonious combination of tones sounded together. 3 a treaty. [ME < OF < L *concordia,* ult. < *com-* together + *cor, cordis* heart]

Concord (kong′kərd or kon′kôrd) *n.* a large, sweet, bluish-black grape. [after *Concord,* a town in Massachusetts]

con·cord·ance (kən kôr′dəns or kon kôr′dəns) *n.* 1 an agreement; harmony. 2 an alphabetical list of the principal words of a book with references to the passages in which they occur.

con·cord·ant (kən kôr′dənt or kon kôr′dənt) *adj.* agreeing; harmonious. —**con·cord′ant·ly,** *adv.*

con·cor·dat (kon kôr′dat) *n.* 1 an agreement; compact. 2 a formal agreement between the Pope and a government about church affairs. 3 a similar agreement between any religious body and a government. [< F < LL *concordatum,* pp. neut. of *concordare* make harmonious]

con·course (kon′kôrs or kong′kôrs) *n.* 1 a running, flowing, or coming together; confluence: *The fort was built at the concourse of two rivers.* 2 a crowd. 3 a place where crowds gather. 4 an open space in a railway station: *We met in the concourse of Union Station.* 5 a driveway; boulevard. [ME < OF *concours* < L *concursus* < *concurrere* < *com-* together + *currere* run]

con·cres·cence (kon kres′əns) *n.* 1 a growing together

of parts. **2** an increase by the adding of particles. [< L *concrescentia* < *concrescere.* See CONCRETE.]

con·crete (*adj. n. and v.1* kon′krēt or kon krēt′; *v. 2* kon krēt′) *adj. n. v.* **-cret·ed, -cret·ing.** —*adj.* **1** existing of itself in the material world, not merely as an idea or as a quality; real: *All actual objects are concrete. A painting is concrete; its beauty is abstract.* **2** not abstract or general; specific; particular: *The lawyer gave concrete examples of the prisoner's cruelty.* **3** naming a thing, especially something perceived by the senses. *Sugar* and *people* are concrete nouns; *sweetness* and *humanity* are *abstract nouns.* **4** made of concrete: *a concrete sidewalk.* **5** formed into a mass; solid; hardened.
—*n.* a mixture of crushed stone or gravel, sand, cement, and water that hardens as it dries.
—*v.* **1** cover with concrete. **2** form or mix into a mass; harden into a mass. [< L *concretus,* pp. of *concrescere* < *com-* together + *crescere* grow] —**con·crete′ly,** *adv.* —**con·crete′ness,** *n.*

con·cre·tion (kon krē′shən) *n.* **1** a forming into a mass; a solidifying. **2** a solidified mass; hard formation. Gallstones are concretions.

con·cu·bi·nage (kon kū′bə nij) *n.* **1** the living together of a man and a concubine. **2** the condition of a concubine.

con·cu·bine (kong′kyů′ bīn or kon′kyů bīn′) *n.* **1** a woman who lives with a man without being legally married to him. **2** in certain polygamous societies, a wife having inferior rank, rights, etc.; secondary wife. [< L *concubina* < *com-* with + *cubare* lie]

con·cu·pis·cence (kon kū′pə səns) *n.* sensual desire; lust.

con·cu·pis·cent (kon kū′pə sənt) *adj.* **1** eagerly desirous. **2** lustful; sensual. [< L *concupiscens, -entis,* ppr. of *concupiscere* < *com-* (intensive) + *cupere* desire]

con·cur (kən kėr′) *v.* **-curred, -cur·ring. 1** be of the same opinion; agree: *The judges all concurred in giving John the prize.* **2** work together: *The events of the boy's life concurred to make him what he is.* **3** come together; happen at the same time. [< L *concurrere* < *com-* together + *currere* run] —**con·cur′rer,** *n.* —**Syn. 1** See **consent.**

con·cur·rence (kən kėr′əns) *n.* **1** the holding of the same opinion; agreement. **2** a working together. **3** a happening at the same time. **4** in geometry, a coming together; a meeting at a point.

con·cur·rent (kən kėr′ənt) *adj.* **1** existing side by side; happening at the same time. **2** co-operating. **3** having equal authority or jurisdiction; co-ordinate. **4** agreeing; consistent; harmonious. **5** coming together; meeting in a point.
—*n.* a concurrent thing or event. —**con·cur′rent·ly,** *adv.*

con·cuss (kən kus′) *v.* **1** agitate or shake violently by or as if by a blow. **2** in medicine, injure (the brain) by concussion. [< L *concussus* < *concutere.* See CONCUSSION.]

con·cus·sion (kən kush′ən) *n.* **1** a sudden, violent shaking; shock: *The concussion caused by the explosion broke many windows.* **2** an injury to the brain, spine, etc. caused by a blow, fall, or other shock. [< L *concussio, -onis* < *concutere* shake violently < *com-* (intensive) + *quatere* shake]

con·cus·sive (kən kus′iv) *adj.* **1** of or having to do with concussion. **2** tending to cause concussion.

con·demn (kən dem′) *v.* **1** express strong disapproval of: *We should condemn cruelty wherever we find it.* **2** pronounce guilty of crime or wrong: *The prisoner is sure to be condemned.* **3** sentence; doom: *He was condemned to death.* **4** assign to an unhappy or unpleasant fate or condition: *His poverty condemned him to a life of continual frustration.* **5** declare not sound or suitable for use: *This bridge has been condemned because it is no longer safe for traffic.* **6** take for public use under special provision of the law: *These four blocks have been condemned; the area will be made into a park.* [ME < OF *condem(p)ner* < L *condemnare* < *com-* (intensive) + *damnare* cause loss to, condemn < *damnum* loss] —**con·demn′er,** *n.*
—**Syn. 1** denounce, damn. **2** convict.

con·dem·na·ble (kən dem′nə bəl) *adj.* that should be condemned; blamable.

con·dem·na·tion (kon′dem nā′shən) *n.* **1** the act of condemning: *the condemnation of a prisoner by a judge, the condemnation of an unsafe bridge.* **2** the condition of being condemned: *His condemnation made him an outcast.* **3** a cause or reason for condemning.

con·dem·na·to·ry (kən dem′nə tô′rē) *adj.* condemning; expressing condemnation.

con·demned (kən demd′) *adj.* pronounced guilty of a crime or wrong.

con·den·sa·ble (kən den′sə bəl) *adj.* capable of being condensed.

con·den·sa·tion (kon′dən sā′shən) *n.* **1** a condensing. **2** a being condensed. **3** something condensed; a condensed mass: *A cloud is a condensation of water vapor in the atmosphere.* **4** the act of changing a gas or vapor to a liquid: *the condensation of steam into water.* **5** in chemistry, a reaction in which two or more molecules unite to form a larger, more dense, and more complex molecule, often with the separation of water or some other simple substance.

con·dense (kən dens′) *v.* **-densed, -dens·ing. 1** make or become denser or more compact. **2** make stronger; concentrate: *Light is condensed by means of lenses.* **3** change from a gas or vapor to a liquid. If steam comes in contact with cold surfaces, it condenses or is condensed into water. **4** put into fewer words; express briefly: *He condensed the paragraph into one line.* [< L *condensare* < *com-* together + *densus* thick] —**Syn. 1** compress, contract. **4** reduce, shorten.

con·densed (kən denst′) *adj.* **1** expressed briefly. **2** changed from a gas or vapor to a liquid. **3** made denser: *condensed milk.* —**con·dens′ed·ly,** *adv.*

condensed milk a thick milk prepared by evaporating some of the water from sweetened cow's milk.

con·dens·er (kən den′sər) *n.* **1** whatever condenses something. **2** a device for receiving and holding a charge of electricity. **3** an apparatus for changing gas or vapor into a liquid. **4** a strong lens or lenses for concentrating light upon a small area.

con·de·scend (kon′di send′) *v.* **1** come down willingly or graciously to the level of one's inferiors in rank: *The king condescended to eat with the beggars.* **2** grant a favor with a patronizing attitude. **3** stoop or lower oneself: *He would not condescend to taking a bribe.* [ME < OF *condescendre* < LL *condescendere* < L *com-* together + *descendere* descend] —**Syn.** deign, stoop.

con·de·scend·ing (kon′di sen′ding) *adj.* **1** stooping to the level of one's inferiors. **2** patronizing; acting in a way that shows scorn for others: *The women were annoyed by the condescending manner of the colonel's wife.* —**con′de·scend′ing·ly,** *adv.*

con·de·scen·sion (kon′di sen′shən) *n.* **1** pleasantness to inferiors. **2** a patronizing attitude. [< LL *condescensio, -onis* < *condescendere.* See CONDESCEND.]

con·dign (kən dīn′) *adj.* deserved; adequate; fitting: *a condign punishment.* [ME < OF *condigne* < L *condignus* very worthy < *com-* (intensive) + *dignus* worthy]

☛ Because **condign** is so often coupled with *punishment,* it is sometimes misunderstood and used incorrectly as a synonym for *severe.*

con·di·ment (kon′də mənt) *n.* something, such as pepper and spices, used to give flavor and relish to food. [< L *condimentum* spice < *condire* to spice, preserve]

con·di·tion (kən dish′ən) *n.* **1** the state in which a person or thing is: *The victim of the accident was in poor condition.* **2** physical fitness; good health: *People who take part in sports must keep in condition.* **3** rank; social position: *The Premier's parents were people of humble condition.* **4** anything on which something else depends; that without which something else cannot exist: *Ability and effort are conditions of success.* **5** something demanded as an essential part of an agreement. **6** in grammar, a clause that expresses or contains a condition. **7** a grade calling for re-examination or special work; report of such a grade. **8 on condition that,** if; provided that: *I'll go on condition that you will too.*
—*v.* **1** put in good condition: *Exercise conditions your muscles.* **2** be a condition of: *Ability and effort condition success.* **3** make depend on (a condition); subject to (a condition): *The gift to the boy was conditioned on his good behavior.* **4** make conditions; make it a condition.

5 require re-examination or special work of: *He was conditioned in Latin.* 6 shape behavior of (a person or animal) by repeated exposure to particular conditions, with which responses become associated: *This dog has been conditioned to expect food when he hears a bell.* [< L *condicio, -onis* agreement < *condicere* < *com-* together + *dicere* say] —**con·di′tion·er,** *n.* —**Syn.** *n.* **1** situation. See **state. 3** circumstances, station. **4** requirement, prerequisite.

con·di·tion·al (kən dish′ən əl or kən dish′nəl) *adj.* **1** depending on something else; not absolute; limited. "You may go if the sun shines" is a conditional promise. **2** expressing or containing a condition. "If the sun shines" is a conditional clause. —*n.* in grammar, a word, phrase, clause, mood, or tense that expresses a condition. — **con·di′tion·al·ly,** *adv.*

con·di·tioned (kən dish′ənd) *adj.* **1** put under a condition; subject to certain conditions. **2** in or having a certain kind of condition. **3** produced by conditioning: *a conditioned reflex.*

conditioned response or **reflex** in psychology, a learned response which is predictable as a result of the subject having been repeatedly subjected to a certain stimulus or set of stimuli.

con·dole (kən dōl′) *v.* **-doled, -dol·ing.** express sympathy; sympathize: *The widow's friends condoled with her at the funeral.* [< L *condolere* < *com-* with + *dolere* grieve, suffer]

con·do·lence (kən dō′ləns) *n.* an expression of sympathy: *Her friends sent her their condolences.*

con·do·min·i·um (kon′də min′ē əm) *n.* **1** a joint control, especially of two or more countries over the government of another country. **2** a country whose government is controlled jointly by two or more others: *The Anglo-Egyptian Sudan was a condominium.* **3 a** a residential building in which apartments or town houses are purchased as pieces of real estate. **b** an apartment in such a building. [< NL < L *com-* with + *dominium* lordship]

con·do·na·tion (kon′dō nā′shən) *n.* the forgiving of an offence, especially by ignoring or overlooking it.

con·done (kən dōn′) *v.* **-doned, -don·ing.** forgive; overlook. [< L *condonare* < *com-* (intensive) + *donare* give]

con·dor (kon′dər) *n.* a large vulture having a neck and head bare of feathers. Condors live on high mountains in South America and California. [< Sp. *cóndor* < Peruvian *cuntur*]

con·duce (kən dūs′ or kən düs′) *v.* **-duced, -duc·ing.** lead; contribute; be favorable (*to*): *Darkness and quiet conduce to sleep.* [< L *conducere* < *com-* together + *ducere* lead]

con·du·cive (kən dū′siv or kən dü′siv) *adj.* helpful; favorable: *Exercise is conducive to health.* —**con·du′cive·ly,** *adv.*

con·duct (*n.* kon′dukt; *v.* kən dukt′) *n.* **1** behavior; way of acting: *Her conduct was inexcusable. He won a medal for good conduct.* **2** direction; management: *the conduct of an office.* **3** a leading; guidance: *Give the messenger safe conduct to the king.* [< v.]
—*v.* **1** act in a certain way; behave: *She always conducts herself like a lady.* **2** direct; manage. **3** direct (an orchestra, etc.) as leader. **4** lead; guide. **5** transmit (heat, electricity, etc.); be a channel to. [< L *conductus,* pp. of *conducere* < *com-* together + *ducere* lead]
Syn. *n.* **1 Conduct, behavior** = way of acting. **Conduct** applies to a person's general manner of acting, especially in relation to others and to the principles of right and wrong set up by society: *His conduct is always admirable.* **Behavior,** used of people and animals, applies to the way of acting toward and in front of others, especially in certain situations: *His behavior shows his lack of consideration for others.* –*v.* **2** See **manage. 4** See **guide.**

con·duct·ance (kən duk′təns) *n.* **1** the power of conducting electricity as affected by the shape, length, etc. of the conductor. **2** the ease with which a substance or a solution of it permits the passage of an electrical current. Its unit of measurement is the mho, or reciprocal ohm.

con·duct·i·bil·i·ty (kən duk′tə bil′ə tē) *n.* the power of conducting heat, electricity, etc.

con·duct·i·ble (kən duk′tə bəl) *adj.* **1** capable of conducting heat, electricity, etc. **2** capable of being conducted.

hat, āge, cãre, fär; let, ēqual, tėrm; it, īce
hot, ōpen, ôrder; oil, out; cup, pu̇t, rüle, ūse
əbove, takən, pencəl, lemən, circəs
ch, child; ng, long; sh, ship
th, thin; ᴛʜ, then; zh, measure

con·duc·tion (kən duk′shən) *n.* **1** in physics, the transmission of heat, electricity, etc. by the transferring of energy from one particle to another. **2** a conveying.

con·duc·tive (kən duk′tiv) *adj.* **1** having conductivity. **2** of conduction.

con·duc·tiv·i·ty (kon′duk tiv′ə tē) *n.* **1** the power of conducting heat; electricity; etc. **2** the ability of a given substance to conduct electricity between opposite faces of a one-centimetre cube of the material, measured in mhos, or reciprocal ohms, per centimetre cube. **3** the rate of transfer of heat by conduction between opposite faces of a one-centimetre cube of a substance, having unit temperature difference between opposite faces.

con·duc·tor (kən duk′tər) *n.* **1** a person who conducts; director; manager; leader; guide. **2** the director of an orchestra, chorus, etc. The conductor of an orchestra or chorus selects the music to be used, rehearses the performers, and directs them at performances. **3** the person in charge of a streetcar, bus, railway train, etc. The conductor usually collects the tickets or fares from the passengers. **4** anything that transmits heat, electricity, light, sound, etc. Copper is a good conductor of heat and electricity. —**con′duc·tor′i·al,** *adj.*

con·duit (kon′dū it, kon′dü it, or kon′dit) *n.* **1** a channel or pipe for carrying liquids over long distances. **2** a tube or underground passage for electric wires. [ME < OF *conduit* < Med.L *conductus* a leading, a pipe < L *conductus* contraction < *conducere* < *com-* together + *ducere* draw]

cone (kōn) *n.* **1** in geometry, a solid with a flat, circular base that tapers evenly to a point at the top. **2** a surface traced by a moving straight line, one end of which is fixed and the opposite end constantly touching a fixed curve. **3** anything shaped like a cone: *an ice-cream cone, the cone of a volcano.* **4** in botany, the part that bears the seeds on pine, cedar, fir, and similar evergreen trees. [ME < L *conus* < Gk. *kōnos* pine cone, cone] —**cone′less,** *adj.*

A cone (def. 1)

cone·flow·er (kōn′flou′ər) *n.* **1** any of a group of plants having orange or yellow flowers with dark cone-shaped centres, such as the black-eyed susan. **2** any of various related plants of western North America.

Con·el·rad (kon′əl rad′) *n.* *U.S.* a system for broadcasting instructions, etc. over radio stations while shifting frequencies, going on and off the air irregularly, etc. to keep enemy airplanes from utilizing the beams of the station for navigation. [short for *Con*trol of *El*ectromagnetic *Rad*iation]

Con·es·to·ga wagon (kon′is tō′gə) a covered wagon with broad wheels, formerly used for travelling on soft ground or on the prairie. [< *Conestoga,* Pa., where such wagons were first built]

co·ney[1] (kō′nē) *n.* **co·neys. 1** rabbit fur, often used to trim coats. **2** a rabbit. **3** a small rabbitlike rodent; pika. **4** in the Bible, a small, rodentlike animal having hoofs; hyrax. Also, **cony.** [ME *coni* < OF *conil* < L *cuniculus* rabbit < Iberian]

co·ney[2] (kō′nē) *n.* inconnu. Also, **cony.**

con·fab·u·late (kən fab′yu̇ lāt′) *v.* **-lat·ed, -lat·ing.** talk together informally and intimately; chat. [< L *confabulari* < *com-* together + *fabula* fable]

con·fab·u·la·tion (kən fab′yu̇ lā′shən) *n.* an informal, intimate talking together; chat.

con·fec·tion (kən fek′shən) *n.* **1** a piece of candy, candied fruit, jam, etc. **2** an elaborate hat or dress. [< L *confectio, -onis* < *conficere* < *com-* with + *facere* make]

con·fec·tion·er (kən fek′shən ər) *n.* a person whose business is making or selling candies, ice cream, etc.

con·fec·tion·er·y (kən fek′shən er′ē) *n.* **-er·ies.**

1 candies, sweets, etc.; confections. 2 the business of making or selling confections. 3 a place where confections, ice cream, etc. are made or sold; candy shop.

con·fed·er·a·cy (kən fed′ər ə sē or kən fed′rə sē) *n.* **-cies.** 1 a union of countries or states; group of people joined together for a special purpose. 2 a league; alliance. 3 a conspiracy. 4 **Confederacy,** Confederate States of America. —**Syn.** 1 confederation, federation.

con·fed·er·ate (*adj. n.* kən fed′ər it or kən fed′rit; *v.* kən fed′ər āt′) *adj., n., v.,* **-at·ed, -at·ing.** —*adj.* 1 joined together for a special purpose; allied. 2 **Confederate,** of or belonging to the Confederate States of America: *the Confederate uniform.*
—*n.* 1 a country, person, etc. joined with another for a special purpose; ally; companion. 2 an accomplice; partner in crime: *The thief was arrested, but his confederate escaped.* 3 **Confederate,** a person who lived in and supported the Confederate States of America.
—*v.* join together for a special purpose; ally. [< L *confoederatus,* pp. of *confoederare* unite in a league < *com-* together + *foedus, -deris* league] —**Syn.** *n.* 2 accessory. See **accomplice.**

Confederate States of America the group of eleven southern states that seceded from the United States in 1860 and 1861. Their secession lasted until 1865.

con·fed·er·a·tion (kən fed′ər ā′shən) *n.* 1 a federation; the act of joining together in a league; state of being united in a league or alliance: *The conference devised a scheme for the confederation of the foreign colonies.* 2 a group of countries, states, etc. joined together for a special purpose; league. 3 **Confederation,** the name given to the federation of Ontario, Quebec, Nova Scotia, and New Brunswick in 1867. Six other provinces have joined Confederation since 1867. 4 **the Confederation, a** the ten provinces of Canada. **b** in the United States, the confederation of the American states, 1781-1789.

con·fer (kən fėr′) *v.* **-ferred, -fer·ring.** 1 consult together; exchange ideas; talk things over: *The Prime Minister often confers with his advisers.* 2 give; award; bestow (*on*): *The general conferred a medal on the brave soldier.* [< L *conferre* < *com-* together + *ferre* bring] —**Syn.** 1 See **consult.** 2 See **give.**

con·fer·ee (kon′fər ē′) *n.* 1 a person who takes part in a conference. 2 a person on whom something is conferred.

con·fer·ence (kon′fər əns or kon′frəns) *n.* 1 a meeting of interested persons to discuss a particular subject: *A conference was called to discuss getting a playground for the school.* 2 the act of taking counsel; the act of talking something over; consultation with a person or a group of persons: *You cannot see Mr. Smith just now; he is in conference.* 3 an association of schools, churches, etc. joined together for some special purpose.

con·fer·ment (kən fėr′mənt) *n.* a giving; bestowal.

con·fess (kən fes′) *v.* 1 acknowledge; admit; own up. 2 concede; grant: *I confess you are right on one point.* 3 admit one's guilt. 4 tell (one's sins) to a priest in order to obtain forgiveness. 5 hear (a person) tell his sins in order to obtain forgiveness; act as a confessor. [ME < OF *confesser* < LL *confessare* < L *confiteri* < *com-* (intensive) + *fateri* confess] —**Syn.** 1 See **admit.**

con·fessed (kən fest′) *adj.* acknowledged; admitted.

con·fess·ed·ly (kən fes′id lē) *adv.* by acknowledgment; admittedly.

con·fes·sion (kən fesh′ən) *n.* 1 acknowledgment; admission; owning up. 2 admission of guilt. 3 the telling of one's sins to a priest in order to obtain forgiveness. 4 the thing confessed. 5 an acknowledgment of belief; profession of faith. 6 the belief acknowledged; creed.

con·fes·sion·al (kən fesh′ən əl or kən fesh′nəl) *n.* 1 a small booth where a priest hears confessions. 2 the practice of confessing sins to a priest. —*adj.* of or having to do with confession.

confession of faith 1 an acknowledgment of belief. 2 the belief acknowledged; creed.

con·fes·sor (kən fes′ər) *n.* 1 a person who confesses. 2 a priest who has the authority to hear confessions. 3 a person who acknowledges belief.

con·fet·ti (kən fet′ē) *n.* bits of colored paper thrown about at carnivals, weddings, etc. [< Ital. *confetti,* pl., sweetmeats]

con·fi·dant (kon′fə dant′ or kon′fə dant′) *n.* a person entrusted with one's secrets, private affairs, etc.; a close friend.

con·fi·dante (kon′fə dant′ or kon′fə dant′) *n.* a woman entrusted with one's secrets, etc.; a close woman friend.

con·fide (kən fīd′) *v.* **-fid·ed, -fid·ing.** 1 tell as a secret: *He confided his troubles to his brother.* 2 express trust (*in*) by imparting secrets, private affairs, etc.: *The girl always confided in her mother.* 3 hand over (a task, person, etc.) in trust; give to another for safekeeping: *The collection of dues is confided to the treasurer.* 4 put trust or have faith (*in*): *You can confide in his good intentions.* [< L *confidere* < *com-* (intensive) + *fidere* trust] —**con·fid′er,** *n.*

con·fi·dence (kon′fə dəns) *n.* 1 a firm belief; trust. 2 a firm belief in oneself and one's abilities. 3 boldness; too much boldness: *Although he could not swim, he dived into the water with confidence.* 4 a feeling of trust; assurance that a person will not tell others what is said: *The story was told to me in strict confidence.* 5 something told as a secret. 6 in politics, trust, as expressed by the majority vote of a legislature, in the actions and policy of the cabinet: *A government that loses a vote of confidence must resign.*
Syn. *n.* 1 conviction. 2 **Confidence, assurance** = a firm belief in oneself. **Confidence** emphasizes its basic meaning of faith or trust, and means "a strong belief in oneself and one's abilities": *He tackles his work with confidence.* **Assurance** emphasizes its basic meaning of certainty, and means "sureness of oneself and lack of fears or doubts about one's abilities": *He went into the contest with the assurance of a born fighter.* 3 presumption.

confidence game a type of fraud in which a swindler works on his victim after gaining his confidence.

confidence man a swindler who uses the confidence game.

con·fi·dent (kon′fə dənt) *adj.* 1 firmly believing; certain: sure. 2 sure of oneself and one's abilities. 3 too bold; too sure. —*n.* a close, trusted friend; confidant.
—**con′fi·dent·ly,** *adv.* —**Syn.** *adj.* 1 See **sure.** 2 assured, sanguine. 3 presumptuous.

con·fi·den·tial (kon′fə den′shəl) *adj.* 1 told or written as a secret: *a confidential report.* 2 showing confidence. 3 trusted with secrets, private affairs, etc.: *a confidential secretary.* —**con′fi·den′tial·ness,** *n.* —**Syn.** 3 See **familiar.**

con·fi·den·tial·ly (kon′fə den′shəl ē) *adv.* in a confidential manner.

con·fid·ing (kən fīd′ing) *adj.* trustful; trusting.
—**con·fid′ing·ly,** *adv.*

con·fig·u·ra·tion (kən fig′yů rā′shən or kən fig′ər ā′shən) *n.* 1 the relative position of parts; manner of arrangement; form; shape; outline: *Geographers study the configuration of the earth's surface.* 2 in astronomy: **a** the relative position of heavenly bodies, especially of the sun, moon, and planets. **b** any grouping of stars. 3 the relative spatial positions of atoms in a molecule. [< L *configuratio, -onis* < *configurare* form after some pattern < *com-* with + *figura* a form]

con·fig·u·ra·tive (kən fig′yůr ə tiv or kən fig′ər ə tiv) *adj.* of or having to do with configuration.

con·fine (*v.* kən fīn′; *n.* kon′fīn) *v.* **-fined, -fin·ing,** *n.* —*v.* 1 keep within limits; restrict. 2 keep indoors; shut in. 3 imprison. 4 **be confined,** give birth to a child.
—*n.* Usually, **confines,** *pl.* a boundary; border; limit: *These people have never been beyond the confines of their own valley.* [< F *confiner* < *confins,* pl., bounds < L *confinium* < *com-* together + *finis* end, border]
—**con·fin′er,** *n.* —**Syn.** *v.* 1 restrain. 3 jail.

con·fined (kən fīnd′) *adj.* 1 restricted. 2 imprisoned.

con·fine·ment (kən fīn′mənt) *n.* 1 the act of confining. 2 the fact or state of being confined. 3 imprisonment. 4 the period for which a mother is confined to bed during and after childbirth. [< F *confinement* < *confiner.* See CONFINE.]

con·firm (kən fėrm′) *v.* 1 prove to be true or correct; make certain: *confirm a rumor.* 2 approve by formal consent; approve; consent to: *Parliament confirmed the treaty.* 3 strengthen; make firmer: *A sudden storm confirmed my decision not to leave.* 4 admit to full membership in a church, synagogue, etc. after completing the required study and preparation. [ME < OF confermer < L confirmare < com- (intensive) + firmus firm] —**con·firm′a·ble,** *adj.* —**con·firm′er,** *n.*

Syn. 1 Confirm, corroborate, authenticate = prove to be true or genuine. **Confirm** = make certain that something is true or correct, by facts or a statement that cannot be doubted: *The Mayor confirmed the report that he had resigned.* **Corroborate** = make more certain that something suspected is true, by a statement or new evidence: *Finding the weapon corroborates the police theory.* **Authenticate** = prove something is genuine or reliable, by the evidence of someone who knows: *Handwriting experts authenticated the will.* **2** ratify, sanction.

con·fir·ma·tion (kon′fər mā′shən) *n.* **1** a confirming. **2** something that confirms; proof. **3** the ceremony of admitting a person to full membership in a church, synagogue, etc. after the completion of required study and preparation.

con·firm·a·tive (kən fėr′mə tiv) *adj.* confirmatory.

con·firm·a·to·ry (kən fėr′mə tô′rē) *adj.* confirming.

con·firmed (kən fėrmd′) *adj.* **1** firmly established; proved. **2** habitual; constant; permanent: *a confirmed bachelor.*

con·fis·cate (kon′fis kāt′) *v.* **-cat·ed, -cat·ing. 1** seize for the public treasury: *The government confiscated the property of all traitors.* **2** seize by authority; take and keep: *The customs officer confiscated the smuggled cigarettes.* [< L *confiscare,* originally, lay away in a chest < *com-* (intensive) + *fiscus* chest, public treasury] —**con′fis·ca′tor,** *n.* —**Syn. 1, 2** appropriate.

con·fis·ca·tion (kon′fis kā′shən) *n.* a confiscating or being confiscated: *the confiscation of wealth.*

con·fis·ca·to·ry (kən fis′kə tô′rē) *adj.* **1** of or like confiscation; tending to confiscate. **2** confiscating.

con·fla·gra·tion (kon′flə grā′shən) *n.* a great, destructive fire: *A conflagration destroyed most of the city.* [< L *conflagratio, -onis* < *conflagrare* < *com-* (intensive) + *flagrare* burn]

con·flict (*n.* kon′flikt; *v.* kən flikt′) *n.* **1** a fight; struggle. **2** direct opposition; a disagreement; clash: *A conflict of opinions divided the members into two groups.* —*v.* **1** fight; struggle. **2** be directly opposed; disagree; clash. [< L *conflictus,* pp. of *confligere* < *com-* together + *fligere* strike) —**Syn.** *n.* **1** strife. See **fight. 2** discord, contention.

con·flict·ing (kən flik′ting) *adj.* that conflicts; disagreeing; clashing.

con·flu·ence (kon′flü əns) *n.* **1** a flowing together: *the confluence of two rivers.* **2** the place where two or more rivers, streams, etc. come together: *They pitched camp at the confluence of the two streams.* **3** a coming together of people or things; throng.

con·flu·ent (kon′flü ənt) *adj.* **1** flowing or running together; blending into one: *confluent rivers.* **2** in medicine: **a** tending to join or run together: *confluent eruptions of the skin.* **b** characterized by such eruptions. —*n.* **1** a stream which unites and flows with another of nearly equal size. **2** a smaller stream flowing into a larger one. [< L *confluens, -entis,* ppr. of *confluere* < *com-* together + *fluere* flow]

con·flux (kon′fluks) *n.* confluence.

con·form (kən fôrm′) *v.* **1** act according to law or rule; be in agreement with generally accepted standards of business, law, conduct, or worship. **2** become the same in form; correspond in form or character. **3** make similar. **4** adapt: *The stranger conformed his ways to ours.* **5** in the British Isles, comply with the usages of the Church of England. [ME < OF *conformer* < L *conformare* < *com-* with + *forma* a shape] —**con·form′er,** *n.* —**Syn. 4** adjust, accommodate, reconcile.

con·form·a·ble (kən fôr′mə bəl) *adj.* **1** similar. **2** adapted; suited. **3** in agreement; agreeable; harmonious. **4** obedient; submissive: *The boy was conformable to his father's wishes.* —**con·form′a·bly,** *adv.* —**con·form′a·ble·ness,** *n.*

con·form·ance (kən fôr′məns) *n.* the act of conforming; conformity.

con·for·ma·tion (kon′fôr mā′shən) *n.* **1** a structure; shape; the form of a thing resulting from the arrangement of its parts. **2** a symmetrical arrangement of the parts of a thing. **3** a conforming; adaptation.

con·form·ist (kən fôr′mist) *n.* **1** a person who conforms. **2** in the British Isles, a person who complies with the usages of the Church of England. —*adj.* of or having to do with conformity or conformism.

hat, āge, cãre, fär; let, ēqual, tėrm; it, īce
hot, ōpen, ôrder; oil, out; cup, pu̇t, rüle, ūse
əbove, takən, pencəl, lemən, circəs
ch, child; ng, long; sh, ship
th, thin; ᴛʜ, then; zh, measure

con·form·i·ty (kən fôr′mə tē) *n.* **-ties. 1** a similarity; correspondence; agreement. **2** behavior in agreement with generally accepted standards of business, law, conduct, or worship; fitting oneself and one's thoughts or actions to the ideas of others; compliance. **3** obedience; submission. **4** in the British Isles, compliance with the usages of the Church of England.

con·found (kən found′ or kon found′ *for 1-5;* kon′found′ *for 6*) *v.* **1** confuse; mix up: *The shock confounded her.* **2** be unable to tell apart: *He confounds "deprecate" and "depreciate."* **3** surprise and puzzle. **4** *Archaic.* make uneasy and ashamed. **5** *Archaic.* defeat; overthrow. **6** damn. *Confound* is used as a mild oath. [ME < OF *confondre* < L *confundere* < *com-* together + *fundere* pour] —**con·found′er,** *n.*

con·found·ed (kən foun′did or kon foun′did) *adj.* **1** damned. *Confounded* is used as a mild oath. **2** hateful; detestable. —**con·found′ed·ly,** *adv.*

con·fra·ter·ni·ty (kon′frə tėr′nə tē) *n.* **-ties. 1** brotherhood. **2** a group of men united for some purpose or in a profession. [ME *confraternite* < Med.L *confraternitas* < *confrater.* See CONFRERE.]

con·frere (kon′frãr) *n.* a fellow member; colleague. [< F *confrère* < OF < Med.L *confrater* < L *com-* together + *frater* brother]

con·front (kən frunt′) *v.* **1** meet face to face; stand facing. **2** face boldly; oppose. **3** bring face to face; place before: *The lawyer confronted the prisoner with the forged cheque.* **4** compare. [< F *confronter* < Med.L *confrontare* < L *com-* together + *frons, frontis* forehead —**con′fron·ta′tion,** *n.*

Con·fu·cian (kən fū′shən) *adj.* of or having to do with Confucius, his teachings, or his followers. —*n.* a follower of Confucius or his teachings.

Con·fu·cian·ism (kən fū′shən iz′əm) *n.* the moral teachings of Confucius and his followers.

Con·fu·cian·ist (kən fū′shə nist) *n.* a supporter or follower of Confucianism. —*adj.* of or having to do with Confucianism.

Con·fu·cius (kən fū′shəs) *n.* 551?-478 B.C., a Chinese philosopher and teacher of morals. He taught that the chief virtues are respect for parents and ancestors, kindliness, faithfulness, intelligence, and proper behavior. [latinized form of *Kung Fu-tse* Kung the master]

con·fuse (kən fūz′) *v.* **-fused, -fus·ing. 1** mix up; throw into disorder. **2** bewilder: *So many people talking to me at once confused me.* **3** be unable to tell apart; mistake (one thing for another): *Even their own mother sometimes confused the twins.* **4** make uneasy and ashamed; embarrass: *Confused by her blunder, she could not say anything for a moment.* [< *confused* < F *confus* < L *confusus,* pp. of *confundere.* See CONFOUND.] —**con·fus′ing·ly,** *adv.*

Syn. 2 puzzle, perplex. **3** confound. **4 Confuse, embarrass, disconcert** = disturb a person. **Confuse** = make a person so uneasy and bewildered that he cannot think clearly or act sensibly: *Honking at a driver who has stalled his car often confuses him.* **Embarrass** = make one so uneasy and self-conscious that he cannot talk or act naturally: *Meeting strangers embarrasses her.* **Disconcert** = disturb someone so suddenly or badly that for a moment he loses his poise and ability to handle the situation: *Forgetting the words disconcerted the singer.*

con·fused (kən fūzd′) *adj.* **1** mixed up; disordered. **2** bewildered.

con·fus·ed·ly (kən fūz′id lē or kən fūzd′lē) *adv.* in a confused manner.

con·fu·sion (kən fū′zhən) *n.* **1** the act or fact of confusing. **2** a confused condition; disorder: *There was confusion in the busy street after the accident.* **3** a failure to distinguish clearly: *confusion between red and orange.* **4** bewilderment; inability to think clearly: *In her confusion she quite forgot her appointment.* **5** uneasiness and shame. —**Syn. 4** perplexity. **5** embarrassment.

con·fu·ta·tion (kon′fyů tā′shən) *n.* **1** the act of confuting. **2** the thing that confutes.

con·fute (kən fūt′) *v.* **-fut·ed, -fut·ing. 1** prove (an argument, testimony, etc.) to be false or incorrect: *The lawyer confuted the testimony of the witness by showing actual photographs of the accident.* **2** prove (a person) to be wrong; overcome by argument: *The speaker confuted his opponents by facts and logic.* [< L *confutare*] —**con·fut′er,** *n.*

☛ **confute, refute** = prove an adversary to be wrong. But *confute* is more intensive and has the force of "silencing or overcoming" a person by refutation.

con·ga (kong′gə) *n.* **1** a Cuban dance in 4/4 time, with a kick on every fourth beat. **2** the music for such a dance. [< Sp.]

con·gé (kon′zhā; *French,* kôɴ zhā′) *n.* **1** dismissal; permission to leave. **2** formal leave-taking or departure. [< F < L *commeatus* going to and fro < *com-* (intensive) + *meare* wander]

con·geal (kən jēl′) *v.* **1** freeze. **2** thicken; stiffen. [ME < OF *congeler* < L *congelare* < *com-* (intensive) + *gelare* freeze] —**con·geal′er,** *n.* —**con·geal′ment,** *n.*

con·ge·ner (kon′jə nər) *n.* a person or thing of the same kind or class. [< L *congener* of the same kind < *com-* (intensive) + *genus, -neris* kind]

con·ge·ni·al (kən jē′nē əl or kən jēn′yəl) *adj.* **1** having similar tastes and interests; getting on well together: *congenial companions.* **2** agreeable; suitable: *congenial work.* [< NL **congenialis* < L *com-* together + *genialis* < *genius* spirit. —**con·gen′ial·ly,** *adv.*

con·ge·ni·al·i·ty (kən jē′nē al′ə tē or kən jēn yal′ə tē) *n.* a congenial quality.

con·gen·i·tal (kən jen′ə təl) *adj.* inborn; present at birth. [< L *congenitus* born with < *com-* with + *genitus* born]

con·gen·i·tal·ly (kən jen′ə təl ē) *adv.* from the time of birth.

con·ger (kong′gər) *n.* a large ocean eel that is caught for food along the coasts of Europe. [ME < OF *congre* < L < Gk. *gongros*]

conger eel conger.

con·ge·ries (kon jēr′ēz or kon jēr′ē ēz′) *n.sing. and pl.* a collection; heap; mass. [< L *congeries* < *congerere.* See CONGEST.]

con·gest (kən jest′) *v.* **1** fill too full; overcrowd: *The city centre is often congested with traffic.* **2** cause too much blood to gather in (one part of the body). **3** become too full of blood. [< L *congestus,* pp. of *congerere* < *com-* together + *gerere* carry]

con·ges·tion (kən jes′chən) *n.* **1** an overcrowded or congested condition: *congestion of traffic.* **2** too much blood in one part of the body: *An ice bag will relieve congestion.*

con·ges·tive (kən jes′tiv) *adj.* accompanied by congestion; produced by congestion; causing congestion.

con·glom·er·ate (*v.* kən glom′ər āt′; *adj. n.* kən glom′ər it) *v.* **-at·ed, -at·ing,** *adj. n.* —*v.* gather in a rounded mass; collect together.
—*adj.* **1** gathered into a rounded mass; clustered. **2** made up of miscellaneous materials gathered from various sources. **3** in geology, of or forming a conglomerate.
—*n.* **1** a mass formed of fragments. **2** in geology, a rock consisting of pebbles, gravel, etc. held together by a cementing material. [< L *conglomerare* < *com-* together + *glomus, -meris* ball]

con·glom·er·a·tion (kən glom′ər ā′shən) *n.* **1** a mixed-up mass of various things or persons; mixture. **2** a conglomerating or being conglomerated.

Con·go·lese (kong′gə lēz′) *n.* a native or inhabitant of the Congo region, the former French Congo, the former Belgian Congo, or either of the Congo republics. —*adj.* of or having to do with any of these regions.

congo snake or **eel** a snakelike amphibian that has very small, weak legs. Congo snakes live in swampy regions in the southeastern United States.

con·grat·u·late (kən grach′ů lāt′) *v.* **-lat·ed, -lat·ing.** express one's pleasure to someone at his happiness or good fortune. [< L *congratulari* < *com-* with + *gratulari* show joy] —**con·grat′u·la′tor,** *n.*

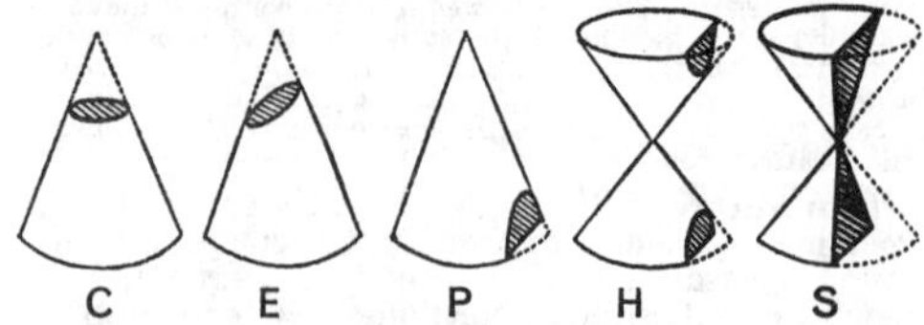

Conic sections: C, circle; E, ellipse; P, parabola; H, hyperbola; S, straight line.

con·grat·u·la·tion (kən grach′ů lā′shən) *n.* **1** the act of congratulating or wishing a person joy. **2** Usually, **congratulations,** *pl.* an expression of pleasure at another's happiness or good fortune.

con·grat·u·la·to·ry (kən grach′ů lə tô′rē) *adj.* expressing pleasure at another's happiness or good fortune.

con·gre·gate (kong′grə gāt′) *v.* **-gat·ed, -gat·ing.** come together into a crowd or mass; assemble. [< L *congregare* < *com-* together + *grex, gregis* flock]

con·gre·ga·tion (kong′grə gā′shən) *n.* **1** the act of coming together into a crowd or mass; the act of assembling. **2** a gathering of people or things; assembly. **3** at some universities, a ceremony at which degrees are conferred. **4** a group of people gathered together for religious worship or instruction. **5** in the Roman Catholic Church: **a** a committee of cardinals or other clergymen. **b** a religious community or order having a common rule and with or without solemn vows.

con·gre·ga·tion·al (kong′grə gā′shən əl or kong′grə gāsh′nəl) *adj.* **1** of a congregation; done by a congregation. **2 Congregational,** of or belonging to Congregationalism or Congregationalists.

con·gre·ga·tion·al·ism (kong′grə gā′shən əl iz′əm or kong′grə gāsh′nəl iz′əm) *n.* **1** a system of church government in which each individual church governs itself. **2 Congregationalism,** the principles and system of organization of a Protestant denomination in which each individual church governs itself.

Con·gre·ga·tion·al·ist (kong′grə gā′shən əl ist or kong′grə gāsh′nəl ist) *n.* **1** a member of a Congregational church. **2** a believer in Congregationalism.

con·gress (kong′gris) *n.* **1** the lawmaking body of a nation, especially of a republic. **2 Congress,** in the United States: **a** the national lawmaking body, consisting of the Senate and House of Representatives, with members from each state. **b** its session. **3** a formal meeting of representatives of interested groups to discuss some subject. **4** a coming together; meeting. [< L *congressus* < *congredi* < *com-* together + *gradi* go]

congress boot a high shoe with a wide strip of elastic in each side.

con·gres·sion·al (kən gresh′ən əl or kən gresh′nəl) *adj.* **1** of a congress; having to do with a congress. **2 Congressional,** of Congress; having to do with Congress.

con·gress·man (kong′gris mən) *n.* **-men** (-mən). Often, **Congressman.** in the United States: **1** a member of Congress. **2** a member of the House of Representatives.

con·gress·wom·an (kong′gris wům′ən) *n.* **-wom·en.** in the United States: **1** a woman member of Congress. **2** a woman member of the House of Representatives.

con·gru·ence (kong′grü əns) *n.* agreement; harmony.

con·gru·en·cy (kong′grü ən sē) *n.* congruence.

con·gru·ent (kong′grü ənt) *adj.* **1** agreeing; harmonious. **2** in geometry, exactly coinciding: *congruent triangles.* **3** in mathematics, producing the same remainder when divided by a given number. [< L *congruens, -entis,* ppr. of *congruere* agree] —**con′gru·ent·ly,** *adv.*

con·gru·i·ty (kən grü′ə tē) *n.* **-ties. 1** agreement; harmony. **2** in geometry, the exact coincidence of lines, angles, figures, etc. **3** a point of agreement.

con·gru·ous (kong′grü əs) *adj.* **1** agreeing; harmonious. **2** fitting; appropriate. **3** in geometry, exactly coinciding. [< L *congruus* < *congruere* agree] —**con′gru·ous·ly,** *adv.* —**con′gru·ous·ness,** *n.*

con·ic (kon′ik) *adj.* conical.

con·i·cal (kon′ə kəl) *adj.* 1 cone-shaped; like a cone: *a conical hat.* 2 of a cone. —**con′i·cal·ly,** *adv.*

con·ics (kon′iks) *n.* the part of geometry dealing with ellipses, parabolas, and hyperbolas.

conic section in geometry, a curve formed by the intersection of a plane with a right circular cone. Circles, ellipses, parabolas, and hyperbolas are conic sections. See picture on the opposite page.

conic sections the part of geometry dealing with circles, ellipses, parabolas, and hyperbolas.

co·ni·fer (kō′nə fər or kon′ə fər) *n.* any of a large group of trees and shrubs, most of which are evergreen and bear cones: *The pine, fir, spruce, larch, and yew are conifers.* [< L *conifer* cone-bearing < *conus* cone (< Gk. *kōnos*) + *ferre* to bear]

co·nif·er·ous (kō nif′ər əs) *adj.* 1 bearing cones. 2 belonging to or having to do with the conifers.

conj. 1 conjunction. 2 conjugation.

con·jec·tur·al (kən jek′chər əl) *adj.* 1 involving conjecture. 2 inclined to conjecture. —**con·jec′tur·al·ly,** *adv.*

con·jec·ture (kən jek′chər) *n. v.* **-tured, -tur·ing.** —*n.* 1 the formation of an opinion admittedly without sufficient evidence for proof; guessing. 2 a guess. —*v.* guess. [ME < L *conjectura* < *conjicere* < *com-* together + *jacere* throw] —**con·jec′tur·a·ble,** *adj.* —**con·jec′tur·a·bly,** *adv.* —**con·jec′tur·er,** *n.* —**Syn.** *n.* 2 supposition. -*v.* suppose. See **guess.**

con·join (kən join′) *v.* join together; unite; combine. [ME *conjoignen* < OF *conjoindre* < L *conjungere* < *com-* together + *jungere* join] —**con·join′er,** *n.*

con·joint (kən joint′ or kon′joint) *adj.* 1 joined together; united; combined. 2 formed by two or more in combination; joint. [< F *conjoint*, pp. of *conjoindre.* See CONJOIN.] —**con·joint′ly,** *adv.*

con·ju·gal (kon′jù gəl) *adj.* 1 of marriage; having to do with marriage. 2 of husband or wife. [< L *conjugalis* < *com-* with + *jugum* yoke] —**con′ju·gal·ly,** *adv.*

con·ju·gate (*v.* kon′jù gāt′; *adj. n.* kon′jù git or kon′jù gāt′) *v.* **-gat·ed, -gat·ing,** *adj. n.* —*v.* 1 in grammar, give the forms of (a verb) according to a systematic arrangement. 2 join together; couple. —*adj.* 1 joined together; coupled. 2 in grammar, derived from the same root. —*n.* in grammar, a word derived from the same root as another. [< L *conjugare* < *com-* with + *jugum* yoke]

con·ju·ga·tion (kon′jù gā′shən) *n.* 1 in grammar: **a** a systematic arrangement of the forms of a verb. **b** a group of verbs having similar forms in such an arrangement. **c** the act of giving the forms of a verb according to such an arrangement. 2 a joining together; coupling.

con·junct (kən jungkt′ or kon′jungkt) *adj.* joined together; joint; associated; combined. [< L *conjunctus*, pp. of *conjungere.* See CONJOIN.]

con·junc·tion (kən jungk′shən) *n.* 1 a joining or being joined together. 2 union; combination: *A severe illness in conjunction with hot weather has left the baby very weak.* 3 in grammar, a word that connects words, phrases, clauses, or sentences. 4 in astronomy, the apparent nearness of two or more heavenly bodies.

☛ **Conjunctions** are used to connect words, phrases, clauses, or sentences. Some conjunctions also serve the double purpose of introducing a clause and connecting it with the rest of the sentence. Conjunctions are classified as follows: **a Co-ordinating:** those that connect words, phrases, clauses, or sentences of equal rank: *and, but, for, nor, or, so, yet.* **b Correlative:** co-ordinating conjunctions that are used in pairs: *both . . . and, either . . . or, neither . . . nor, not only . . . but also, whether . . . or.* **c Subordinating:** those that serve to introduce and to connect subordinate clauses with the main clauses of sentences: *after, although, as, because, before, if, since, when, whenever, where, while,* and so on. **d** See also **conjunctive adverbs,** under **conjunctive.**

con·junc·ti·va (kon′jungk tī′və) *n.* **-vas, -vae** (-vē or -vī). in anatomy, the mucous membrane that covers the front of the eyeball and the inner surface of the eyelids. [< NL (*membrana*) *conjunctiva* connecting membrane]

con·junc·tive (kən jungk′tiv) *adj.* 1 joining together; connecting; uniting; combining. 2 joined together; joint; united; combined. 3 in grammar: **a** like a conjunction; like that of a conjunction. *Then* is a conjunctive adverb. **b** connecting words, phrases, or clauses in both meaning and construction. *And, also,* and *moreover* are conjunctive conjunctions.

hat, āge, cãre, fär; let, ēqual, tėrm; it, īce
hot, ōpen, ôrder; oil, out; cup, pùt, rüle, ūse
əbove, takən, pencəl, lemən, circəs
ch, child; ng, long; sh, ship
th, thin; ᴛʜ, then; zh, measure

—*n.* a conjunctive word; conjunction. —**con·junc′tive·ly,** *adv.*

☛ **conjunctive adverbs.** A number of words that are ordinarily used as adverbs are sometimes used also to connect main clauses, thus forming compound sentences. They are called *conjunctive adverbs.* Even though they serve as connectives, their adverbial meaning remains important. The most common are: *accordingly, also, anyhow, anyway* (informal), *besides, consequently, furthermore, hence, however, indeed, likewise, moreover, namely, nevertheless, then, therefore.* Both formal and informal writing generally use a semicolon before a clause introduced by a conjunctive adverb: *He is extremely conceited; however, he is so charming that people overlook it.*

con·junc·ti·vi·tis (kən jungk′tə vī′tis) *n.* in medicine, an inflammation of the conjunctiva. [< NL *conjunctivitis* < *conjunctiva* + *-itis* (< Gk.)]

con·junc·ture (kən jungk′chər) *n.* 1 a combination of events or circumstances. 2 a critical state of affairs; crisis.

con·ju·ra·tion (kon′jù rā′shən) *n.* 1 the act of invoking by a sacred name. 2 a magic form of words used in conjuring; magic spell. 3 the practice of magic: *In the fairy tale, the princess was changed into a toad by conjuration.* 4 *Archaic.* a solemn appeal.

con·jure (kun′jər or kon′jər *for 1-6*; kən jür′ *for 7*) *v.* **-jured, -jur·ing.** 1 **conjure up, a** cause to appear in a magic way. **b** cause to appear in the mind. 2 compel (a spirit, devil, etc.) to appeal or disappear by magic words. 3 summon a devil, spirit, etc. 4 cause to be or to happen by magic or as if by magic. 5 practise magic. 6 perform tricks by skill and nimbleness in moving the hands. 7 make a solemn appeal to; request earnestly; entreat: *I conjure you not to betray your country.* [ME < OF < L *conjurare* make a compact < *com-* together + *jurare* swear]

con·jur·er (kun′jər ər or kon′jər ər) *n.* 1 a magician. 2 a person who performs tricks with quick, deceiving movements of the hands; juggler.

con·jur·or (kun′jər ər or kon′jər ər) *n.* conjurer.

conk[1] (kongk) *Slang.* —*n.* 1 the head. 2 a hit on the head. —*v.* hit on the head. [origin uncertain]

conk[2] (kongk) *v.* **conk out,** 1 break down; stall: *The engine conked out after we had driven only a few miles.* 2 be overcome with weakness; collapse: *The runner conked out before the end of the race.* [origin uncertain]

con mo·to (kôn mō′tō) *Italian.* in music, with spirited movement (used as a direction).

Conn. Connecticut.

con·nect (kə nekt′) *v.* 1 join (one thing to another); link (two things together); fasten together; unite. 2 join in some business or interest; bring into some relation. 3 think of (one thing) with (another); associate in the mind. 4 be connected; become connected. 5 join or link together in an electrical circuit. 6 of trains, ships, airplanes, etc., be scheduled so that passengers can change from one to another without delay. 7 in sports, hit, throw, or pass successfully. 8 *Informal.* achieve one's aim; be successful. [< L *connectere* < *com-* together + *nectere* tie] —**con·nect′er** or **con·nec′tor,** *n.*

☛ **Connect** is used with *to, with,* or *by*: *Now let's connect this wire to that. Be sure this piece connects with that. The two towns are connected by a railway. Up* is unnecessary after *connect*: *He should connect this wire* (*up*) *with that.*

con·nect·ed (kə nek′tid) *adj.* 1 joined together; fastened together. 2 joined in orderly sequence: *connected ideas.* 3 having ties and associates: *She is well connected socially.* —**con·nect′ed·ly,** *adv.*

☛ **Connected with** and **in connection with** are wordy expressions, usually for *in* or *with*: *The social life in connection with a fraternity* (in a fraternity) *will be something you have never experienced before.*

connecting rod a bar connecting two or more moving parts in a machine. See **dead centre** for diagram.

con·nec·tion (kə nek′shən) *n.* 1 the act of connecting. 2 the condition of being joined together or connected; union. 3 something that connects; a connecting part. 4 a contact between two circuits or electrical wires. **5** any kind of practical relation with another thing: *I have no connection with my brother's firm.* **6** a group of people associated together. **7** a considering of persons or things together; linking together of words or ideas in proper order. **8** the scheduled meeting of trains, ships, airplanes, etc. so that passengers can change from one to the other without delay. **9** a related person; relative: *She is a connection of ours by marriage.* **10** a religious denomination. **11 in connection with,** together with; in regard to. Also, *esp.Brit.* **connexion.** —**Syn. 2** junction. **3** bond, tie, link. **9** kin, kinsman. ☛ See **connected** for usage note.

con·nec·tive (kə nek′tiv) *adj.* that connects. —*n.* **1** something that connects. **2** in grammar, a word used to connect words, phrases, and clauses: *Conjunctions and relative pronouns are connectives.*

connective tissue in anatomy, tissue that connects, supports, or encloses other tissues and organs in the body.

con·nex·ion (kə nek′shən) *n. Esp.Brit.* connection.

con·nie (kon′ē) *n.* inconnu.

conn·ing tower (kon′ing) **1** on a submarine, a small tower on the deck, used as an entrance and as a place for observation. **2** an armored control station on the deck of a warship, occupied by the captain during battle. **3** any similar observation tower from which supervision can be carried out. [*conning,* ppr. of *con* direct the steering of (a ship), var. of earlier *cond,* shortened from ME *condue, condye* guide < OF *conduire* < L *conducere.* See CONDUCT.]

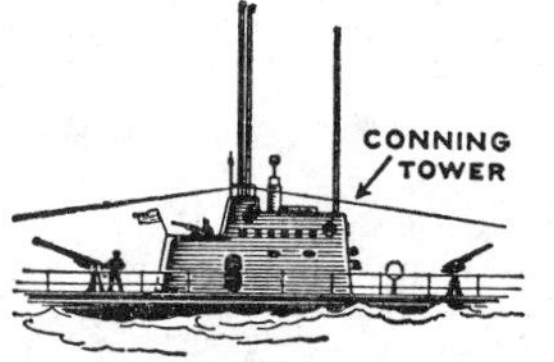

con·niv·ance (kə nīv′əns) *n.* **1** the act of conniving; pretended ignorance or secret encouragement of wrongdoing. **2** in law, guilty assent to, or knowledge or encouragement of, wrongdoing, without participation in it.

con·nive (kə nīv′) *v.* **-nived, -niv·ing. 1** shut one's eyes to something wrong; give aid to wrongdoing by not telling of it, or by helping it secretly: *Some policemen connive at gambling.* **2** co-operate secretly: *The treacherous general connived with the enemies of his country.* [< L *connivere* shut the eyes, wink < *com-* together + *niv-* press (related to *nictere* wink)] —**con·niv′er,** *n.*

con·nois·seur (kon′ə sėr′) *n.* an expert; critical judge: *He is a connoisseur of antique furniture.* [< F *connoisseur* (now *connaisseur*), ult. < L *cognoscere* < *co-* (intensive) + *gnoscere* recognize]

con·no·ta·tion (kon′ə tā′shən) *n.* **1** a connoting. **2** what is suggested in addition to the simple meaning. ☛ See **denotation** for usage note.

con·no·ta·tive (kon′ə tā′tiv or kə nōt′ə tiv) *adj.* **1** connoting; having connotation. **2** having to do with connotation.

con·note (kə nōt′) *v.* **-not·ed, -not·ing.** suggest in addition to the literal meaning; imply. *Portly, corpulent,* and *obese* all mean fleshy; but *portly* connotes dignity; *corpulent,* bulk; and *obese,* an unpleasant excess of fat. [< Med.L *connotare* < L *com-* with + *notare* to note]

con·nu·bi·al (kə nū′bē əl or kə nü′bē əl) *adj.* of or having to do with marriage. [< L *connubialis* < *connubium* marriage < *com-* (intensive) + *nubere* marry] —**con·nu′bi·al·ly,** *adv.*

co·noid (kō′noid) *adj.* shaped like a cone. —*n.* **1** in geometry, a surface formed by the revolution of a conic section about its axis. **2** something shaped like a cone, such as a bullet. [< Gk. *kōnoeidēs* < *kōnos* cone + *eidos* form]

co·noi·dal (kə noi′dəl) *adj.* conoid.

con·quer (kong′kər) *v.* **1** get by fighting; win in war: *conquer a country.* **2** overcome by force; defeat; get the better of: *conquer an enemy, conquer a bad habit.* **3** be victorious; be the conqueror: *The general said he would conquer or die.* [ME < OF *conquerre* < L *conquaerere* < *com-* (intensive) + *quaerere* seek] —**con′quer·a·ble,** *adj.* —**Syn. 2** vanquish, subdue. See **defeat.**

con·quer·or (kong′kər ər) *n.* **1** a person who conquers. **2 the Conqueror,** King William I of England. As Duke of Normandy, he conquered England in 1066, and reigned as king till his death in 1087.

con·quest (kon′kwest or kong′kwest) *n.* **1** the act of conquering. **2** the thing conquered; land, people, etc. conquered. **3** a person whose love or favor has been won. **4 the Conquest,** the conquering of England in 1066 by William the Conqueror. [ME < OF *conqueste* < *conquest,* pp. of *conquerre.* See CONQUER.] —**Syn. 1** triumph. See **victory.**

con·quis·ta·dor (kon kwis′tə dôr′ or kon kis′tə dôr′) *n.* **-dors** or **-dores. 1** a Spanish conqueror in North or South America during the 16th century. **2** a conqueror. [< Sp. *conquistador* < *conquistar* conquer]

con·san·guin·e·ous (kon′sang gwin′ē əs) *adj.* descended from the same parent or ancestor; related by blood. [< L *consanguineus* < *com-* together + *sanguis, -guinis* blood] —**con′san·guin′e·ous·ly,** *adv.*

con·san·guin·i·ty (kon′sang gwin′ə tē) *n.* **1** relationship by descent from the same parent or ancestor; relationship by blood: *Brothers and cousins are united by ties of consanguinity.* **2** any close relationship or connection.

con·science (kon′shəns) *n.* **1** the sense of right and wrong; ideas and feelings within a person that warn him of what is wrong: *The boy's conscience forced him to return the book he had stolen.* **2 in all conscience,** **a** reasonably; fairly. **b** surely; certainly. [ME < OF < L *conscientia* < *conscire* < *com-* with + *scire* know] —**con′science·less,** *adj.*

conscience money money paid by a person whose conscience bothers him because of some payment owed by him.

con·science-strick·en (kon′shəns strik′ən) *adj.* suffering from a feeling of having done wrong.

con·sci·en·tious (kon′shē en′shəs) *adj.* **1** careful to do what one knows is right; controlled by conscience. **2** done with care to make it right: *Conscientious work is careful and exact.* —**con′sci·en′tious·ly,** *adv.* —**con′sci·en′tious·ness,** *n.* —**Syn. 1** upright, honorable. **2** particular, painstaking.

conscientious objector a person whose beliefs do not let him act as a combatant in time of war.

con·scion·a·ble (kon′shən ə bəl) *adj.* according to conscience; just. —**con′scion·a·bly,** *adv.*

con·scious (kon′shəs) *adj.* **1** aware; knowing: *conscious of a sharp pain.* **2** able to feel: *He was knocked out by the blow but soon became conscious again.* **3** known to oneself; felt: *conscious guilt.* **4** meant; intended: *a conscious lie.* **5** self-conscious; shy; embarrassed. [< L *conscius* < *conscire* < *com-* (intensive) + *scire* know] —**con′scious·ly,** *adv.*

Syn. 1 Conscious, aware = knowing that something exists. **Conscious** emphasizes the idea of realizing or knowing in one's mind that one sees, feels, hears, etc. something either physically or emotionally: *He was conscious of a great uneasiness.* **Aware** emphasizes the idea of noticing something one sees, smells, hears, tastes, feels, or is told: *I was aware that someone was talking, but not conscious of what was being said.* **4** deliberate.

con·scious·ness (kon′shəs nis) *n.* **1** the state of being conscious; awareness. People and animals have consciousness; plants and stones do not. **2** all the thoughts and feelings of a person or group of people: *the moral consciousness of our generation.* **3** awareness of what is going on about one: *A severe shock often makes a person lose consciousness for a time.* **4** in philosophy, the power of the mind, whether rational or not, to be aware of acts, sensations, emotions, etc. **5** in psychology, the mental activity of which the individual is aware, in contrast to unconscious mental activity.

con·script (*v.* kən skript′; *adj. n.* kon′skript) *v.* **1** compel by law to enlist in the armed services; draft. **2** take for government use: *The dictator proposed to conscript both capital and labor.* —*adj.* conscripted; drafted. —*n.* a conscripted soldier, sailor, or airman. [< L *conscriptus,* pp. of *conscribere* < *com-* (intensive) + *scribere* write]

conscript fathers (kon′skript) **1** in ancient Rome, the senators. **2** the senators or legislators of any nation.

hat, āge, cãre, fär; let, ēqual, tėrm; it, īce
hot, ōpen, ôrder; oil, out; cup, pu̇t, rüle, ūse
əbove, takən, pencəl, lemən, circəs
ch, child; ng, long; sh, ship
th, thin; ᴛʜ, then; zh, measure

con·scrip·tion (kən skrip′shən) *n.* **1** the compulsory enlistment of men in the armed services; draft. **2** the act or system of forcing contributions of money, labor, or other service to the government or as the government directs.

con·se·crate (kon′sə krāt′) *v.* **-crat·ed, -crat·ing,** *adj.* —*v.* **1** set apart as sacred; make holy: *A church is consecrated to God.* **2** make an object of veneration or cherished regard; hallow: *Time has consecrated these customs.* **3** devote to a purpose: *A doctor's life is consecrated to curing sick people.* —*adj. Archaic.* consecrated. [< L *consecrare* < *com-* (intensive) + *sacer* sacred] —**con′se·cra′tor,** *n.* —**Syn.** *v.* **1** sanctify. **3** dedicate. See **devote.**

con·se·crat·ed (kon′sə krāt′id) *adj.* set apart as sacred; made holy.

con·se·cra·tion (kon′sə krā′shən) *n.* **1** the act of consecrating. **2** the condition of being consecrated. **3** an ordination to a sacred office, especially to that of bishop.

con·sec·u·tive (kən sek′yu̇ tiv) *adj.* **1** following without interruption; successive: *Monday, Tuesday, and Wednesday are consecutive days.* **2** made up of parts that follow each other in logical order: *From all the reports, he put together a consecutive account of the accident.* **3** in grammar, expressing consequence or result: *a consecutive clause.* **4** in music, having to do with the immediate succession of intervals of the same kind: *consecutive thirds, fifths, octaves, etc.* [< F *consécutif* < L *consecutivus* < *consecutus* following closely, pp. of *consequi* < *com-* (intensive) + *sequi* follow] —**con·sec′u·tive·ly,** *adv.* —**con·sec′u·tive·ness,** *n.* —**Syn. 1** See **successive.**

con·sen·sus (kən sen′səs) *n.* general agreement. The consensus of opinion means the opinion of all or most of the people consulted. [< L *consensus* < *consentire.* See CONSENT.]

con·sent (kən sent′) *v.* agree; give approval or permission: *My father would not consent to my leaving school.* —*n.* agreement; approval; permission. [ME < OF *consentir* < L *consentire* < *com-* together + *sentire* feel, think]

Syn. *v.* **Consent, assent, concur** = agree. **Consent** = agree *to* something asked for, by giving approval willingly or by giving in to the wishes of others: *He consented to run for president.* **Assent** = agree *with,* think along with, something stated or put forward for consideration, by accepting it or expressing agreement: *He assented to the suggested change in plans.* **Concur** = agree *with* others, by having the same opinion: *The majority concurred in the decision to raise the dues.* -*n.* assent.

con·se·quence (kon′sə kwens′ or kon′sə kwəns) *n.* **1** a result of some previous action or occurrence; effect: *The consequence of breaking his leg was the loss of his job.* **2** a logical result; deduction; inference. **3** importance: *This matter is of little consequence.* **4** importance in rank or position: *a man of little consequence.* **5 in consequence,** as a result; therefore. **6 in consquence of,** as a result of; because of. **7 take the consequences,** accept what happens because of one's action. —**Syn. 1** outcome, issue. See **effect. 3** See **importance.**

con·se·quent (kon′sə kwent′ or kon′sə kwənt) *adj.* **1** following as an effect; resulting: *His long illness and consequent absence put him far behind in his work.* **2** following as a logical conclusion. **3** logically consistent. —*n.* **1** anything that follows something else; result; effect. **2** in mathematics, the second term of a ratio: *In the ratio 1:4, 4 is the consequent, and 1 the antecedent.* [< L *consequens, -entis,* ppr. of *consequi.* See CONSECUTIVE.]

con·se·quen·tial (kon′sə kwen′shəl) *adj.* **1** following as an effect; resulting. **2** self-important; pompous. —**con′se·quen′tial·ly,** *adv.* —**con′se·quen′tial·ness,** *n.*

con·se·quent·ly (kon′sə kwent′lē or kon′sə kwənt lē) *adv.* as a result; therefore. —**Syn.** See **therefore.**

con·ser·va·tion (kon′sər vā′shən) *n.* **1** a preserving from harm or decay; protecting from loss or from being used up: *the conservation of natural resources.* **2** the official protection and care of forests, rivers, etc. **3** a forest, etc. or a part of it, under official protection and care.

con·ser·va·tion·ist (kon′sər vā′shən ist) *n.* a person who believes in and advocates conservation of the forests, rivers, etc. of a country.

conservation of energy in physics, the principle that the total amount of energy in the universe does not vary, although energy can be changed from one form into another.

con·serv·a·tism (kən sėr′və tiz′əm) *n.* **1** an inclination to keep things as they are; opposition to change. **2** Often, **Conservatism.** the principles and practices of a conservative political party.

con·serv·a·tive (kən sėr′və tiv) *adj.* **1** inclined to keep things as they are; opposed to change. **2** Often, **Conservative. a** of or belonging to a political party that opposes changes in national institutions. **b** of Conservatives or their party. **3** cautious; moderate: *conservative business methods.* **4** free from novelties and fads: *It is economical to choose suits of a conservative style.* **5** having the power to preserve from harm or decay; conserving; preserving.
—*n.* **1** a conservative person. **2** Often, **Conservative. a** a member of a conservative political party. **b** in Canada, a member of the Progressive-Conservative Party, one of the principal political groups; a person who supports the views and principles of this party. **c** in Great Britain, a member of the Conservative Party. **3** a means of preserving. —**con·serv′a·tive·ly,** *adv.* —**con·serv′a·tive·ness,** *n.*

Conservative Party 1 in Great Britain, a political party that favors existing national institutions or a return to some of those recently existing. **2** in Canada, the Progressive-Conservative Party.

con·ser·va·toire (kən sėr′və twär′) *n.* a school for instruction in music; conservatory. [< F]

con·ser·va·tor (kən sėr′və tər or kon′sər vā′tər) *n.* a preserver; guardian.

con·serv·a·to·ry (kən sėr′və tô′rē) *n.* **-ries. 1** a greenhouse or glass-enclosed room for growing and displaying plants and flowers. **2** a school for instruction in music.

con·serve (*v.* kən sėrv′; *n.* kon′sėrv or kən sėrv′) *v.* **-served, -serv·ing,** *n.* —*v.* **1** keep from harm or decay; protect from loss or from being used up. **2** preserve (fruit) with sugar. [ME < L *conservare* < *com-* (intensive) + *servare* preserve]
—*n.* Often, **conserves,** *pl.* fruit preserved in sugar; jam. [< MF *conserve* < *conserver* < L *conservare.* See v.] —**con·serv′a·ble,** *adj.* —**con·serv′er,** *n.*

con·sid·er (kən sid′ər) *v.* **1** think about in order to decide: *Take time to consider the problem.* **2** think to be; think of as: *We consider Shakespeare a great poet.* **3** allow for; take into account: *This watch runs very well, if you consider how old it is.* **4** be thoughtful of (others and their feelings). **5** think carefully; reflect: *He considered fully before accepting the offer.* **6** *Archaic.* look at carefully. [< L *considerare,* originally, examine the stars < *com-* (intensive) + *sidus* star; with reference to augury]

Syn. 1 Consider, study, weigh = think about something in order to decide. **Consider** = think something over, to give it some careful thought before making a decision about it: *He considered going to college.* **Study** = think out, to consider with serious attention to details: *He studied ways to support himself.* **Weigh** = balance in the mind, to consider carefully both or all sides of an idea or action: *He weighed the idea of going to the local junior college.* **2** deem, judge. **4** respect, regard. **5** deliberate, ponder.

con·sid·er·a·ble (kən sid′ər ə bəl or kən sid′rə bəl) *adj.* **1** worth thinking about; important: *a considerable sum of money.* **2** not a little; much. —*n. Informal.* not a little; much.

☛ **considerable, considerably.** In speech there is a tendency not to distinguish between the adverb *considerably* and the adjective *considerable.* In formal and informal writing the distinction is observed: *The teacher's explanation helped them considerably* (modifies verb *helped*). *The teacher's explanation was of considerable help to them* (modifies noun *help*).

con·sid·er·a·bly (kən sid′ər ə blē or kən sid′rə blē) *adv.* a good deal; much. ☛ See **considerable** for usage note.

con·sid·er·ate (kən sid′ər it or kən sid′rit) *adj.* thoughtful of others and their feelings. —**con·sid′er·ate·ly,**

adv. —**con·sid′er·ate·ness,** *n.* —**Syn.** See **thoughtful.**

con·sid·er·a·tion (kən sid′ər ā′shən) *n.* **1** careful thought about something before making a decision: *Please give careful consideration to this question.* **2** something thought of as a reason; something to be considered: *Price and quality are two important considerations in buying anything.* **3** money or other payment: *Dishonest people will do almost anything for a consideration.* **4** thoughtfulness for others and their feelings. **5** importance. **6 in consideration of, a** because of. **b** in return for. **7 on no consideration,** not at all; never. **8 take into consideration,** allow for; take into account. **9 under consideration,** being thought about. —**Syn. 1** attention, deliberation. **3** compensation, recompense.

con·sid·ered (kən sid′ərd) *adj.* **1** carefully thought out: *in my considered opinion.* **2** honored; respected: *He is highly considered as a poet.*

con·sid·er·ing (kən sid′ər ing or kən sid′ring) *prep.* taking into account; making allowance for: *Considering her age, she reads well.* —*adv.* taking everything into account: *He does very well, considering.*

con·sign (kən sīn′) *v.* **1** hand over; deliver: *The man was consigned to prison. The father consigned the child to his sister's care.* **2** transmit; send: *They consigned the goods to him by express.* **3** set apart; assign. [< F *consigner* < L *consignare* furnish with a seal < *com-* with + *signum* seal] —**con·sign′a·ble,** *adj.* —**Syn. 1** See **commit.**

con·sign·ee (kon′sī nē′) *n.* the person or company to whom goods are consigned.

con·sign·er (kən sīn′ər) *n.* consignor.

con·sign·ment (kən sīn′mənt) *n.* **1** the act of consigning. **2** a shipment sent to a person or company for safekeeping or sale. **3 on consignment,** consigned to a person or company with the understanding that the goods will not be paid for until sold.

con·sign·or (kən sīn′ər or kon′sī nôr′) *n.* a person or company who consigns goods to another.

con·sist (kən sist′) *v.* **1** be made up; be formed: *A week consists of seven days.* **2** agree; be in harmony. **3 consist in, a** be contained in. **b** be made up of: *True success consists in what a man makes of himself, not how much money he makes.* [< L *consistere* come to a stand, exist, consist < *com-* together + *sistere* stand]

con·sist·ence (kən sis′təns) *n.* consistency.

con·sist·en·cy (kən sis′tən sē) *n.* **-cies. 1** firmness; stiffness. **2** degree of firmness or stiffness: *Frosting for a cake must be of the right consistency to spread easily without dripping.* **3** a keeping to the same principles, course of action, etc.: *He was much admired for his consistency of purpose.* **4** harmony; agreement; accordance.

con·sist·ent (kən sis′tənt) *adj.* **1** keeping or inclined to keep to the same principles, course of action, etc.: *What a consistent person says or does today agrees with what he said or did yesterday.* **2** in agreement; in accord; compatible: *Driving an automobile at very high speed is not consistent with safety. So much noise is not consistent with comfort.* —**con·sist′ent·ly,** *adv.*

con·sis·to·ry (kən sis′tə rē) *n.* **-ries. 1** a church council or court, especially one composed of the Pope and cardinals; the College of Cardinals. **2** a meeting of such a council or court. **3** the place where it meets. [< ONF *consistorie* < L *consistorium* place of assembly < *consistere.* See CONSIST.]

con·so·la·tion (kon′sə lā′shən) *n.* **1** comfort. **2** a comforting person, thing, or event.

consolation prize a prize given to a person or team that has not won but has done well.

con·sol·a·to·ry (kən sol′ə tô′rē) *adj.* consoling; comforting.

con·sole[1] (kən sōl′) *v.* **-soled, -sol·ing.** comfort. [< L *consolari* < *com-* (intensive) + *solari* soothe] —**con·sol′a·ble,** *adj.* —**con·sol′er,** *n.* —**Syn.** See **comfort.**

con·sole[2] (kon′sōl) *n.* **1** the desklike part of an organ, containing the keyboard, stops, and pedals. **2** a radio, phonograph, television cabinet, etc. made to stand on the floor. **3** a panel of buttons, switches, dials, etc. used to control electrical or electronic equipment in a computer, automobile, missile, etc. **4** in architecture, a heavy, ornamental bracket. **5** a console table. [< F]

con·sole table (kon′sōl) a narrow table, usually placed against a wall, under a mirror, etc.

con·sol·i·date (kən sol′ə dāt′) *v.* **-dat·ed, -dat·ing. 1** unite; combine; merge: *The three banks consolidated and formed a single, large bank.* **2** make secure; strengthen: *The army spent a day in consolidating its gains by digging trenches.* **3** make or become solid. [< L *consolidare* < *com-* (intensive) + *solidus* solid]

con·sol·i·dat·ed (kən sol′ə dāt′id) *adj.* united; combined.

Consolidated Revenue Fund *Cdn.* the pooled income of the Federal Government.

consolidated school a school for pupils from several school districts; a school built to replace two or more smaller ones so as to provide improved facilities.

con·sol·i·da·tion (kən sol′ə dā′shən) *n.* the act of consolidating; state of being consolidated; strengthening; combination.

con·sol·ing (kən sōl′ing) *adj.* that consoles. —**con·sol′ing·ly,** *adv.*

con·sols (kon′solz or kən solz′) *n.pl.* bonds of the government of Great Britain. [short for *consolidated annuities*]

con·som·mé (kon′sə mā′) *n.* a clear soup made by boiling meat with seasoning and, sometimes, vegetables in water. [< F *consommé,* pp. of *consommer* < L *consummare* finish. See CONSUMMATE.]

con·so·nance (kon′sə nəns) *n.* **1** harmony; agreement; accordance. **2** in music, harmony of sounds, a simultaneous combination of tones that is agreeable to the ear.

con·so·nan·cy (kon′sə nən sē) *n.* consonance.

con·so·nant (kon′sə nənt) *n.* **1** a speech sound formed by completely or partially stopping the breath. Languages are systems of consonants and vowels. There are two consonants in *tab.* **2** any letter of the alphabet that is not a vowel. —*adj.* **1** harmonious; in agreement; in accord. **2** agreeing in sound. **3** consonantal. [< L *consonans, -antis,* ppr. of *consonare* < *com-* together + *sonare* sound] —**con′so·nant·ly,** *adv.*

con·so·nan·tal (kon′sə nan′təl) *adj.* having to do with a consonant or its sound.

con·sort (*n.* kon′sôrt; *v.* kən sôrt′) *n.* **1** a husband or wife, especially of a monarch. **2** an associate. **3** a ship accompanying another; an escort vessel. —*v.* **1** associate: *Do not consort with thieves.* **2** agree; accord. [< MF < L *consors, -ortis* sharer < *com-* with + *sors* lot]

con·sor·ti·um (kən sôr′shē əm or kən sôr′tē əm) *n.* **-ti·a** (-shē ə). **1** a partnership; association. **2** an agreement among bankers of several nations to give financial aid to another nation. **3** a group, association, etc. formed by such an agreement. [< L *consortium* partnership]

con·spec·tus (kən spek′təs) *n.* **1** a general or comprehensive view. **2** a short summary or outline of a subject; digest; résumé. [< L *conspectus* < *com-* + *specere* look at]

con·spic·u·ous (kən spik′yů əs) *adj.* **1** easily seen: *A traffic sign should be conspicuous.* **2** readily attracting attention; striking: *an actress of conspicuous charm.* **3** worthy of notice; remarkable: *Canada has played a conspicuous part in the work of the United Nations.* [< L *conspicuus* visible < *conspicere* < *com-* (intensive) + *specere* look at] —**con·spic′u·ous·ly,** *adv.* —**con·spic′u·ous·ness,** *n.* —**Syn. 1** noticeable. See **prominent. 3** notable, noteworthy.

con·spir·a·cy (kən spir′ə sē) *n.* **-cies. 1** a secret planning with others to do something wrong, especially a wrong against a government, public personage, etc. **2** a plot made by such planning. **3** in law, an agreement by two or more persons to act unlawfully. —**Syn. 1** intrigue.

con·spir·a·tor (kən spir′ə tər) *n.* a person who conspires; plotter: *A group of conspirators planned to kill the dictator.*

con·spir·a·to·ri·al (kən spir′ə tô′rē əl) *adj.* having to do with conspiracy or conspirators.

con·spire (kən spīr′) *v.* **-spired, -spir·ing. 1** plan secretly with others to do something wrong; plot. **2** act together; have as a combined effect: *All things conspired to make her birthday a happy one.* [ME < OF *conspirer* < L *conspirare* < *com-* together + *spirare* breathe] **—con·spir′er,** *n.* **—Syn. 1** See **plot.**

const. in mathematics, constant.

Const. Constable.

con·sta·ble (kon′stə bəl) *n.* **1** a police officer; policeman. **2** especially in the Middle Ages, a chief officer of a household, court, army, etc. **3** the keeper of a royal fortress or castle. [ME < OF *conestable* < LL *comes stabuli* count of the stable; later, chief household officer]

con·stab·u·lar·y (kən stab′yu̇ ler′ē) *n.* **-lar·ies,** *adj.* *—n.* **1** the constables of a district. **2** a police force organized like an army; provincial police. *—adj.* of the constables of a district; of police officers, or a police force.

con·stan·cy (kon′stən sē) *n.* **1** the condition of being always the same; absence of change. **2** firmness in belief or feeling; faithfulness; loyalty.

con·stant (kon′stənt) *adj.* **1** always the same; not changing: *If you walk due north, your direction is constant.* **2** never stopping; continuous: *Three days of constant rain soaked everything.* **3** happening often or again and again; repeated: *A clock makes a constant ticking sound.* **4** habitual: *a constant smoker.* **5** faithful; loyal; steadfast: *A constant friend helps you when you are in trouble.* **6** in mathematics and physics, retaining the same value; remaining the same in quantity, size, etc.: *a constant force.* *—n.* **1** something that is always the same; a number or quantity that does not change. **2** in mathematics, a quantity assumed to be invariable throughout a given calculation or discussion. **3** in physics, a numerical quantity expressing a relation or value, as of a physical property of a substance, that remains unchanged under certain conditions. **4** in some provinces of Canada, any compulsory subject in high school; core subject; opposed to *elective.* [ME < OF < L *constans, -antis,* ppr. of *constare* stand firm < *com-* (intensive) + *stare* stand] **—Syn.** *adj.* **1** unchangeable, steady. **2** ceaseless, continuous. **5** true, staunch. See **faithful.**

con·stant·ly (kon′stənt lē) *adv.* **1** without change. **2** without stopping. **3** often; again and again.

con·stel·la·tion (kon′stə lā′shən) *n.* **1** in astronomy: **a** a set or group of stars: *The Big Dipper is the easiest constellation to locate.* **b** a division of the heavens occupied by such a group. **2** a brilliant gathering: *There was a constellation of ministers and ambassadors at the reception.* [< LL *constellatio, -onis* < L *com-* together + *stella* star]

con·ster·na·tion (kon′stər nā′shən) *n.* great dismay; paralysing terror: *To our consternation the train rushed on toward the burning bridge.* [< L *consternatio, -onis* < *consternare* terrify, var. of *consternere* lay low < *com-* (intensive) + *sternere* strew] **—Syn.** See **dismay.**

con·sti·pate (kon′stə pāt′) *v.* **-pat·ed, -pat·ing.** cause constipation in. [< L *constipare* < *com-* together + *stipare* press. Doublet of COSTIVE.]

con·sti·pat·ed (kon′stə pāt′id) *adj.* suffering from constipation.

con·sti·pa·tion (kon′stə pā′shən) *n.* a condition in which bowel movements are difficult or infrequent.

con·stit·u·en·cy (kən stich′ü ən sē) *n.* **-cies. 1** in Canada, a district, or riding, represented by a Member of Parliament or a Member of the Legislative Assembly. **2** a similar district in other countries. **3** the voters in such a district.

con·stit·u·ent (kən stich′ü ənt) *adj.* **1** forming a necessary part; necessary in the composition; composing: *Flour, liquid, salt, and yeast are constituent parts of bread.* **2** appointing; electing. **3** having the power to make or change a political constitution: *a constituent assembly.* *—n.* **1** a necessary part of a whole; ingredients; component. **2** a person who votes or appoints; voter: *The Member of Parliament received many letters from his constituents.* [< L *constituens, -entis,* ppr. of *constituere.* See CONSTITUTE.] **—Syn.** *n.* **1** See **element.**

con·sti·tute (kon′stə tūt′ or kon′stə tüt′) *v.* **-tut·ed, -tut·ing. 1** make up; form: *Seven days constitute a week.* **2** establish or enact. **3** appoint; elect: *The group constituted one member its leader.* **4** set up; establish: *Courts are constituted by law to dispense justice.* **5** give legal form to. [< L *constitutus,* pp. of *constituere* < *com-* (intensive) + *statuere* set up] **—con′sti·tu·tor,** *n.*

con·sti·tu·tion (kon′stə tū′shən or kon′stə tü′shən) *n.* **1** a person's physical or mental nature or make-up: *A person with a good constitution is strong and healthy.* **2** the way in which anything is organized; structure: *The constitution of the world is the arrangement of all the things in it.* **3** the system of fundamental principles according to which a nation, state, or group is governed: *Our club has a written constitution.* **4** a document stating these principles. **5** an appointing; making. **6** a setting up; establishment. **7** a law; decree.

con·sti·tu·tion·al (kon′stə tū′shən əl or kon′stə tü′shən əl) *adj.* **1** of or in the constitution of a person or thing: *A constitutional weakness makes him subject to colds.* **2** of, in, or according to the constitution of a nation, state, or group: *Some lawyers are experts in constitutional law.* **3** for one's health. *—n. Informal.* a walk or other exercise taken for one's health. **—con·sti·tu′tion·al·ly,** *adv.* **—Syn.** *adj.* **1** inherent.

con·sti·tu·tion·al·i·ty (kon′stə tū′shən al′ə tē or kon′stə tü′shən al′ə tē) *n.* accordance with the constitution of a nation, state, or group: *The constitutionality of the new law was disputed.*

constitutional monarchy a monarchy in which the ruler has only the powers given to him by the constitution and laws of the nation.

con·sti·tu·tive (kon′stə tū′tiv or kon′stə tü′tiv) *adj.* having power to establish or enact; making a thing what it is; formative; constituent; essential. **—con′sti·tu′tive·ly,** *adv.*

con·strain (kən strān′) *v.* **1** force; compel. **2** confine; imprison. **3** repress; restrain. [ME < OF *constreindre* < L *constringere* < *com-* together + *stringere* pull tightly] **—con·strain′er,** *n.*

con·strained (kən strānd′) *adj.* **1** forced. **2** compelled by pity, love, gratitude, etc.: *He felt constrained to help the wounded man.* **3** restrained; stiff; unnatural: *a constrained smile.*

con·straint (kən strānt′) *n.* **1** confinement. **2** restraint. **3** a holding back of natural feelings; forced or unnatural manner; embarrassed awkwardness. **4** force; compulsion. [ME < OF *constreinte,* fem. pp. of *constreindre.* See CONSTRAIN.]

con·strict (kən strikt′) *v.* draw together; contract; compress: *A rubber band constricts what it encircles.* [< L *constrictus,* pp. of *constringere.* See CONSTRAIN.]

con·stric·tion (kən strik′shən) *n.* **1** the act of drawing together; contraction; compression. **2** a feeling of tightness: *He coughed and complained of a constriction in his chest.* **3** a constricted part. **4** something that constricts.

con·stric·tive (kən strik′tiv) *adj.* drawing together; contracting; compressing. **—con·stric′tive·ly,** *adv.*

con·stric·tor (kən strik′tər) *n.* **1** any snake that kills its prey by squeezing it with its coils. **2** in anatomy, a muscle that constricts some part of the body.

con·struct (*v.* kən strukt′; *n.* kon′strukt) *v.* **1** put together; build. **2** draw (a geometrical figure) so as to fulfil given conditions. *—n.* something systematically put together or constructed. [< L *constructus,* pp. of *construere* < *com-* together + *struere* pile] **—Syn. 1** See **make.**

con·struc·tion (kən struk′shən) *n.* **1** the act of constructing, building, or putting together. **2** the way in which a thing is constructed. **3** the thing constructed; building. **4** a meaning; explanation; interpretation: *He put an unfair construction on what she said.* **5** in grammar: **a** the arrangement, connection, or relation of words in a sentence, clause, phrase, etc. **b** any meaningful sequence or grouping.

con·struc·tion·al (kən struk′shən əl) *adj.* having to do with construction; structural.

con·struc·tion·ist (kən struk′shən ist) *n.* a person who gives a certain interpretation to laws, a constitution, etc.: *a strict constructionist.*

con·struc·tive (kən struk′tiv) *adj.* **1** tending to build or improve; building up; helpful: *People appreciate constructive suggestions, not destructive criticisms.* **2** having to do with construction; structural. **3** not directly expressed; inferred. **—con·struc′tive·ly,** *adv.* **—con·struc′tive·ness,** *n.*

con·struc·tor (kən struk′tər) *n.* a person who constructs; builder.

con·strue (kən strü′) *v.* **-strued, -stru·ing. 1** show the meaning of; explain; interpret: *Different lawyers may construe the same law differently.* **2** put a particular interpretation on: *His inability to hold a job can only be construed as indifference.* **3** translate. **4** in grammar, analyse the arrangement and connection of words in (a sentence, clause, phrase, etc.). [< L *construere.* See CONSTRUCT.] **—con·stru′a·ble,** *adj.*

con·sul (kon′səl) *n.* **1** an official appointed to represent a government in some foreign city: *A consul looks after the business interests of his country and his countrymen in the place to which he is appointed.* **2** in ancient Rome, either of the two chief magistrates of the republic. **3** in France, one of the three chief magistrates of the Consulate, 1799-1804. [< L *consul,* probably originally, one who consults the senate]

con·su·lar (kon′sə lər or kon′syů lər) *adj.* **1** of or belonging to a consul. **2** serving as a consul; having the duties of a consul.

con·su·late (kon′sə lit or kon′syů lit) *n.* **1** the duties, authority, and position of a consul. **2** a consul's term of office. **3** the official residence or offices of a consul. **4** government by consuls: *France was governed by a consulate from 1799 to 1804.*

consul general *pl.* **consuls general.** a consul of the highest rank. He is stationed at an important place or has authority over several other consuls.

con·sul·ship (kon′səl ship′) *n.* **1** the duties, authority, and position of a consul. **2** a consul's term of office.

con·sult (kən sult′) *v.* **1** seek information or advice from; refer to: *Consult a dictionary for the meaning of a word.* **2** exchange ideas; talk things over: *He is consulting with his lawyer.* **3** take into consideration; have regard for: *A good ruler consults the interests and feelings of his people.* [< L *consultare* < *consulere* take counsel, consult]
Syn. 2 Consult, confer = talk something over with someone in order to make a decision. **Consult** = talk over something of importance with another or others who are in a position to give wise advice: *He decided to consult with his attorney before buying the property.* **Confer** = exchange ideas, opinions, or information with another, usually as equals: *The manager conferred with the committee of employees.*

con·sult·ant (kən sul′tənt) *n.* **1** a person who consults another. **2** a person who gives professional or technical advice: *a medical consultant.*

con·sul·ta·tion (kon′səl tā′shən) *n.* **1** the act of consulting; act of seeking information or advice. **2** a meeting to exchange ideas or talk things over.

con·sult·a·tive (kən sul′tə tiv) *adj.* having to do with consultation; advisory.

con·sult·ing (kən sul′ting) *adj.* **1** that consults or asks advice. **2** employed in giving professional advice.

con·sume (kən süm′ or kən sūm′) *v.* **-sumed, -sum·ing. 1** use up: *A student consumes much of his time in studying.* **2** eat or drink up. **3** destroy; burn up. **4** waste away; be destroyed. **5** spend; waste (time, money, etc.). **6 consumed with,** absorbed by curiosity, envy, etc. [ME < L *consumere* < *com-* (intensive) + *sumere* take up] **—con·sum′a·ble,** *adj.* **—Syn. 1** expend, exhaust. **5** squander.

con·sum·ed·ly (kən süm′id lē or kən sūm′id lē) *adv.* very much; too much.

con·sum·er (kən süm′ər or kən sūm′ər) *n.* **1** a person or thing that uses up, makes away with, or destroys. **2** a person who uses food, clothing, or anything grown or made by producers.

con·sum·mate (*v.* kon′sə māt′; *adj.* kən sum′it or kon′sů mit) *v.* **-mat·ed, -mat·ing,** *adj.* **—***v.* **1** complete; fulfil: *His ambition was consummated when he won the first prize.* **2** complete (marriage) by sexual intercourse. **—***adj.* **1** complete; perfect; in the highest degree: *The paintings of great artists show consummate skill.* **2** accomplished; supremely qualified: *a consummate artist.* [< L *consummare* bring to a peak < *com-* (intensive) + *summa* highest degree] **—con·sum′mate·ly,** *adv.*

con·sum·ma·tion (kon′sə mā′shən) *n.* a completion; fulfilment.

con·sump·tion (kən sump′shən) *n.* **1** the act of using or using up: *We took along some food for consumption on our trip. The science of economics deals with the production, distribution, and consumption of wealth.* **2** the amount used up: *The consumption of fuel oil is much greater in winter than in summer.* **3** destruction. **4** a wasting disease of the lungs or of some other part of the body; tuberculosis of the lungs. [< L *consumptio, -onis* < *consumere.* See CONSUME.]

con·sump·tive (kən sump′tiv) *adj.* **1** having or likely to have tuberculosis of the lungs. **2** of tuberculosis of the lungs. **3** tending to consume; destructive; wasteful. **—***n.* a person who has tuberculosis of the lungs. **—con·sump′tive·ly,** *adv.* **—con·sump′tive·ness,** *n.*

cont. 1 continue. **2** continued. **3** continent. **4** continental. **5** contents. **6** containing.

Cont. Continental.

con·tact (kon′takt) *n.* **1** the condition of touching; a touching together: *When two balls are in contact, one can be moved by touching the other.* **2** connection: *The insurance salesman tried to make contacts with wealthy people. The control tower lost contact with the pilot.* **3** a person one is acquainted with: *He has a useful contact in an advertising agency.* **4** in electricity: **a** the connection between two conductors of electricity through which a current passes. **b** a device or component for producing such a connection: *The electric light went out when the wire broke off at the contact.* **5** in medicine: **a** exposure to a contagious disease. **b** a person who has been exposed to a contagious disease. **6** in geology, the surface of the boundary between adjacent rocks. **—***adj.* in aeronautics, within sight of the ground: *contact flying.* **—***v. Informal.* get in touch with; make a connection with. [< L *contactus* a touching < *contingere* < *com-* with + *tangere* touch]

contact lens a thin, curved lens of glass or plastic to correct defects in vision, that fits under the eyelids and covers the eyeball.

con·ta·gion (kən tā′jən) *n.* **1** the spreading of disease by contact. **2** a disease spread in this way; contagious disease. **3** a means by which disease is spread. **4** the spreading of any influence from one person to another: *A contagion of fear swept through the audience and caused a panic.* **5** an evil influence; moral corruption. [< L *contagio, -onis* a touching < *contingere.* See CONTACT.]

con·ta·gious (kən tā′jəs) *adj.* **1** spread by contact: *Scarlet fever is a contagious disease.* **2** causing contagious diseases. **3** easily spread from one person to another: *Yawning is often contagious.* **—con·ta′gious·ly,** *adv.* **—con·ta′gious·ness,** *n.*

con·tain (kən tān′) *v.* **1** have within itself; hold as contents; include: *This purse contains plenty of money.* **2** be capable of holding: *That pitcher will contain a quart of milk.* **3** be equal to: *A pound contains 16 ounces.* **4** control; hold back; restrain: *He contained his anger.* **5** in warfare, control or restrain (enemy forces) by stopping, holding, or surrounding: *The British fleet under Admiral Nelson contained Napoleon's ships at Trafalgar.* **6** in mathematics, be divisible by; be divisible by without a remainder: *12 contains 2, 3, 4, and 6.* [ME < OF *contenir* < L *continere* < *com-* together + *tenere* hold] **—con·tain′a·ble,** *adj.*
Syn. 1, 2 Contain, hold, accommodate = have within itself or be capable of having and keeping. **Contain** emphasizes the idea of actually having something within itself as contents or parts: *The house contains five rooms.* **Hold** emphasizes the idea of being capable of taking in and keeping or of having room, but is often used interchangeably with *contain*: *A paper bag won't hold water. My car holds six people.* **Accommodate** = hold comfortably:

Most hotel rooms accommodate two people. 3 comprise.

con·tain·er (kən tān′ər) *n.* 1 a person or thing that contains. 2 a box, can, jar, etc. used to hold or contain something.

con·tain·er·ize (kən tā′nə rīz′) *v.* **-ized, -iz·ing.** pack (cargo) in very large standardized containers. —**con·tain′er·iz·a′tion,** *n.*

con·tain·ment (kən tān′mənt) *n.* the confinement of a hostile or potentially hostile political or military force within its existing geographical boundaries.

con·tam·i·nant (kən tam′ə nənt) *n.* something that contaminates.

con·tam·i·nate (kən tam′ə nāt′) *v.* **-nat·ed, -nat·ing.** make impure by contact; defile; pollute: *Flies contaminate milk.* [< L *contaminare* < *contamen* contamination < *com-* with + *tag-*, root of *tangere* touch] —**con·tam′i·na′tor,** *n.*

con·tam·i·na·tion (kən tam′ə nā′shən) *n.* 1 a contaminating or being contaminated; pollution: *Milk should be kept in a clean place to avoid contamination.* 2 anything that contaminates; an impurity.

contd. continued.

con·temn (kən tem′) *v.* treat with contempt; despise; scorn. [< L *contemnere* < *com-* (intensive) + *temnere* disdain, originally, cut]

con·tem·plate (kon′təm plāt′) *v.* **-plat·ed, -plat·ing.** 1 look at for a long time; gaze at. 2 think about for a long time; study carefully. 3 meditate: *All day he did nothing but contemplate.* 4 have in mind; consider; intend: *She contemplated going to Europe after graduation. She is contemplating a change of work.* [< L *contemplari* survey < *com-* with + *templum* restricted area marked off for the taking of auguries] —**Syn. 1** survey, regard.

con·tem·pla·tion (kon′təm plā′shən) *n.* 1 the act of looking at or thinking about something for a long time. 2 deep thought; meditation: *sunk in contemplation.* 3 expectation; intention.

con·tem·pla·tive (kən tem′plə tiv or kon′təm plā′tiv) *adj.* 1 thoughtful; meditative. 2 devoted to religious meditation and prayer. —*n.* a person who leads a contemplative life, especially a monk or a nun. —**con′tem·pla′tive·ly,** *adv.*

con·tem·po·ra·ne·ous (kən tem′pə rā′nē əs) *adj.* belonging to the same period of time. [< L *contemporaneus* < *com-* with + *tempus, -poris* time]

con·tem·po·ra·ne·ous·ly (kən tem′pə rā′nē əs lē) *adv.* at the same time; during the same period of time.

con·tem·po·rar·y (kən tem′pə rer′ē) *adj. n.* **-rar·ies.** —*adj.* 1 belonging to or living in the same period of time. 2 of the same age or date. 3 of or having to do with the present time: *a course in contemporary literature.* —*n.* 1 a person who belongs to the same period of time as another or others. 2 a person, magazine, etc. of the same age or date: *We all tend to seek the society of our contemporaries.* [< *com-* together + L *temporarius* belonging to time < *tempus, -poris* time]

con·tempt (kən tempt′) *n.* 1 the feeling that a person, act, or thing is mean, low, or worthless; scorn; a despising: *We feel contempt for a liar.* 2 the condition of being scorned or despised; disgrace: *A traitor is held in contempt.* 3 in law, disobedience to or open disrespect for the rules or decisions of a court, a lawmaking body, etc. A person can be put in jail for **contempt of court.** [< L *contemptus* < *contemnere.* See CONTEMN.] —**Syn. 1** disdain. See **scorn.**

con·tempt·i·ble (kən temp′tə bəl) *adj.* deserving contempt or scorn; held in contempt; mean; low; worthless. —**con·tempt′i·ble·ness,** *n.* —**con·tempt′i·bly,** *adv.* ☛ See **contemptuous** for usage note.

con·temp·tu·ous (kən temp′chü əs) *adj.* showing contempt; scornful: *a contemptuous look.* —**con·temp′tu·ous·ly,** *adv.* —**con·temp′tu·ous·ness,** *n.*

☛ **Contemptuous** and **contemptible** are sometimes confused. The distinction will be clear if one observes that in *contemptible* the suffix *-ible* means deserving.

con·tend (kən tend′) *v.* 1 fight; struggle: *The first settlers in America had to contend with the Indians, sickness, and lack of food.* 2 take part in a contest; compete: *Five runners were contending in the first race.* 3 argue; dispute. 4 declare to be a fact; maintain as true: *Columbus contended that the earth was round.* [< L *contendere* < *com-* (intensive) + *tendere* stretch] —**con·tend′er,** *n.*

Syn. 1 cope, wrestle, battle. 2 **Contend, compete** = take part in a contest for something. **Contend** emphasizes the idea of trying hard and struggling against opposition: *Our football team is contending with one from the next town for the championship.* **Compete** emphasizes the idea of rivalry and trying hard to win, as well as contending with another: *Only two boys are competing for the cup.* 3 wrangle. 4 affirm, assert.

hat, āge, cãre, fär; let, ēqual, tėrm; it, īce
hot, ōpen, ôrder; oil, out; cup, pu̇t, rüle, ūse
əbove, takən, pencəl, lemən, circəs
ch, child; ng, long; sh, ship
th, thin; TH, then; zh, measure

con·tent[1] (kon′tent) *n.* 1 Usually, **contents,** *pl.* what is contained in anything; all things inside. 2 the facts and ideas stated: *The content of his speech was good, but the form was not.* 3 the power of containing; capacity. 4 the amount contained; volume. 5 the amount of a certain substance contained in anything: *Cottage cheese has a high protein content.* 6 the subject matter or range of any field of study: *the content of our mathematics course.* [< L *contentum,* pp. neut. of *continere.* See CONTAIN.] —**Syn. 2** substance, matter.

☛ **content, contents.** *Content* is used largely as an abstract term: *the content of the course;* it is used in specifying the amount of an ingredient: *the moisture content. Contents* is rather more concrete: *the contents of the box.*

con·tent[2] (kən tent′) *v.* 1 satisfy; please; make easy in mind: *Nothing contents her; she is always complaining.* 2 **content oneself,** be contented. —*adj.* 1 satisfied; pleased; easy in mind: *Will you be content to wait until tomorrow?* 2 willing; ready. —*n.* 1 contentment; satisfaction; ease of mind. 2 **to one's heart's content,** to whatever extent one desires: *On your birthday you may eat cake to your heart's content.* [< Med.L *contentare* < L *contentus* satisfied, pp. of *continere.* See CONTAIN.] —**Syn.** *v.* 1 gratify, appease. See **satisfy.** *-n.* gratification.

con·tent·ed (kən ten′tid) *adj.* satisfied; pleased; easy in mind: *A contented person is happy with what he has.* —**con·tent′ed·ly,** *adv.* —**con·tent′ed·ness,** *n.*

con·ten·tion (kən ten′shən) *n.* 1 an argument; dispute; quarrel. 2 a statement or point that one has argued for; statement maintained as true: *Columbus' contention that the earth was round turned out to be correct.* 3 an arguing; disputing; quarrelling: *Contention has no place in a church.* 4 a struggle; contest. [< L *contentio, -onis* < *contendere.* See CONTEND.]

con·ten·tious (kən ten′shəs) *adj.* 1 quarrelsome; fond of arguing; given to disputing: *A contentious person argues and disputes about trifles.* 2 characterized by contention: *a contentious campaign.* —**con·ten′tious·ly,** *adv.* —**con·ten′tious·ness,** *n.*

con·tent·ment (kən tent′mənt) *n.* satisfaction; being pleased; ease of mind.

con·tents (kon′tents) *n.pl.* 1 what is contained in anything; all the things inside. 2 what is written in a book; what is said in a speech. ☛ See **content**[1] for usage note.

con·ter·mi·nous (kən tėr′mə nəs) *adj.* coterminous.

con·test (*n.* kon′test; *v.* kən test′) *n.* 1 a trial to see which can win. A game or a race is a contest. 2 a fight; struggle. 3 an argument; dispute. [< v.] —*v.* 1 try to win. 2 fight for; struggle for: *The soldiers contested every inch of ground.* 3 argue against; dispute about: *The lawyer contested the claim and tried to prove that it was false.* 4 take part in a contest. [< F *contester* < L *contestari* call to witness < *com-* (intensive) + *testis* witness] —**con·test′a·ble,** *adj.*

con·test·ant (kən tes′tənt) *n.* 1 a person who contests; person who takes part in a contest. 2 a person who contests election returns, a will, a judgment, etc.

con·text (kon′tekst) *n.* 1 the parts directly before and after a word, sentence, etc. that influence its meaning: *You can often tell the meaning of an unfamiliar word from its context.* 2 the immediate environment; attendant circumstances or conditions; background: *the political context of his speech.* [< L *contextus* < *contexere* *com-* together + *texere* weave]

con·tex·tu·al (kən teks′chü əl) *adj.* having to do with the context; depending on the context.

con·ti·gu·i·ty (kon′tə gū′ə tē) *n.* **-ties.** 1 nearness: *The contiguity of the house and garage was a convenience in bad weather.* 2 contact. 3 a continuous mass; unbroken stretch.

con·tig·u·ous (kən tig′ū əs) *adj.* 1 in actual contact; touching: *A fence showed where the two farms were contiguous.* 2 adjoining; near. [< L *contiguus* < *com-* with + *tag-*, root of *tangere* touch. Related to CONTACT.] **—con·tig′u·ous·ly,** *adv.* **—con·tig′u·ous·ness,** *n.*

con·ti·nence (kon′tə nəns) *n.* 1 self-control; self-restraint; moderation. 2 chastity.

con·ti·nen·cy (kon′tə nən sē) *n.* **-cies.** continence.

con·ti·nent[1] (kon′tə nənt) *n.* 1 one of the seven great masses of land on the earth. The continents are Asia, Africa, North America, South America, Europe, Australia, and Antarctica. 2 the mainland. 3 **the Continent,** the mainland of Europe. It does not include the British Isles. [< L *continens,* short for *terra continens* land held together. See CONTINENT[2].]

con·ti·nent[2] (kon′tə nənt) *adj.* 1 showing restraint with regard to the desires or passions; using self-control; temperate. 2 chaste. [< L *continens, -entis,* ppr. of *continere.* See CONTAIN.]

con·ti·nen·tal (kon′tə nen′təl) *adj.* 1 of a continent; characteristic of a continent; like that of a continent. 2 Usually, **Continental.** belonging to or characteristic of the mainland of Europe; of or like that of the Continent: *Continental customs differ from those of England.* 3 **Continental,** in the United States, of or having to do with the thirteen colonies at the time of the American Revolution.
—*n.* 1 **Continental,** in the United States: **a** a soldier of the American army during the American Revolution. **b** a piece of paper money issued during the American Revolution. It was considered almost worthless by the time the war was over. 2 Usually, **Continental.** a person living on the Continent. 3 **not worth a continental.** *Informal.* worthless.

continental bed a bed that has no headboard or footboard, being made up of a spring mattress set on top of a box-spring base that has short legs.

continental drift in geology, the supposed slow movement of the earth's land masses, thought to be caused by the shifting of underlying molten material.

con·ti·nen·tal·ist (kon′tə nen′tə list) *n.* an advocate of economic co-operation, mutual aid, or union, between nations of the same continent, especially in North America.

continental shelf the submerged shelf of land that borders most continents and ends in a steep slope (the **continental slope**) to deep water.

con·tin·gen·cy (kən tin′jən sē) *n.* **-cies.** 1 uncertainty of occurrence; dependence on change. 2 an accidental happening; unexpected event; chance. 3 a happening or event depending on something that is uncertain; possibility: *The explorer carried supplies for every contingency.*

con·tin·gent (kən tin′jənt) *adj.* 1 conditional; depending on something not certain: *Our plans for a picnic tomorrow are contingent upon pleasant weather.* 2 likely to happen or not to happen; possible; uncertain: *The traveller set aside five dollars a day for contingent expenses.* 3 happening by chance; accidental; unexpected. 4 in law, dependent on events or circumstances that may or may not occur.
—*n.* 1 a share of soldiers, workers, etc. furnished to a force from other sources: *Canada sent a large contingent of troops to France in World War I.* 2 a group that is part of a larger group: *The Kingston contingent had seats together at the convention.* 3 an accidental or unexpected event. [< L *contingens, -entis* touching, ppr. of *contingere.* See CONTACT.] **—con·tin′gent·ly,** *adv.*

con·tin·u·al (kən tin′ū əl) *adj.* 1 never stopping: *the continual flow of the river.* 2 repeated many times; very frequent.
☛ **continual, continuous.** *Continual* in most instances means repeated frequently or at close intervals: *Dancing requires continual practice.* It may, however, also mean uninterruptedly, with reference to an action regarded as never coming to an end, whereas *continuous* means without interruption in the case of actions whose end can be envisaged: *a continuous procession of cars.*

con·tin·u·al·ly (kən tin′ū əl ē) *adv.* 1 always; without stopping. 2 again and again; very frequently.

con·tin·u·ance (kən tin′ū əns) *n.* 1 the time during which anything lasts; duration. 2 a staying; the act of remaining: *A public official is paid during his continuance in office.* 3 a continuing: *We admired his continuance of work in spite of illness.* 4 a continuation; sequel: *the continuance of a story.* 5 in law, formerly, an adjournment or postponement.

con·tin·u·a·tion (kən tin′ū ā′shən) *n.* 1 the act of going on with a thing after stopping; a beginning again: *Continuation of my work was hard after I had been ill for a month.* 2 anything by which a thing is continued; an added part: *The continuation of the story will appear in next month's magazine.* 3 the act or fact of not stopping.

continuation school 1 a school that provides training in the evening for adults wishing to take courses in academic, commercial, or industrial subjects. 2 in Ontario, a small secondary school administered by an elementary-school board.

con·tin·ue (kən tin′ū) *v.* **-tin·ued, -tin·u·ing.** 1 keep up; keep on; go on; go on with: *The road continues for miles. We continued our efforts to raise money for the hospital.* 2 go on, or go on with (something), after stopping; begin again: *He ate lunch and then continued his work.* 3 last; endure: *The king's reign continued for 20 years.* 4 cause to last. 5 extend in space: *The farmer continued his fence from the pasture to the highway.* 6 stay: *The children must continue in school till the end of June.* 7 cause to stay: *The club continued the president in office for another term.* 8 put off until a later time; postpone; adjourn: *The judge continued the case until next month.* [ME < OF *continuer* < L *continuare* < *continere* hold together. See CONTAIN.] **—con·tin′u·a·ble,** *adj.*
Syn. 1 prolong, extend. 2 resume. 3 **Continue, last** = go on for a long time. **Continue** emphasizes the idea of going on and on without an end, usually without a break: *The heavy snow continued all winter.* **Last** emphasizes the idea of holding out, either in good condition or full strength or for an unusually long time: *Those flowers lasted for two weeks.*

con·ti·nu·i·ty (kon′tə nū′ə tē or kon′tə nü′ə tē) *n.* **-ties.** 1 the state or quality of being continuous. 2 a continuous or connected whole; an uninterrupted succession; unbroken series: *The continuity of the movie was broken when the power failed.* 3 a detailed plan of the sequence of scenes in a motion picture. 4 in radio or television: **a** any connecting comments or announcements between the parts of a program. **b** a script for such comments or announcements.

con·tin·u·ous (kən tin′ū əs) *adj.* without a stop or break; connected; unbroken: *a continuous line, a continuous sound, continuous work, a continuous line of cars.* **—con·tin′u·ous·ly,** *adv.* **—con·tin′u·ous·ness,** *n.*
—Syn. ceaseless, incessant, perpetual. ☛ See **continual** for usage note.

con·tin·u·um (kən tin′ū əm) *n.* **-tin·u·a.** a continuous quantity; an unbroken series, etc. [< L]

con·tort (kən tôrt′) *v.* twist or bend out of shape; distort: *The clown contorted his face.* [< L *contortus,* pp. of *contorquere* < *com-* (intensive) + *torquere* twist]

con·tor·tion (kən tôr′shən) *n.* 1 a twisting or bending out of shape; a distorting. 2 a contorted condition; distorted form or shape.

con·tor·tion·ist (kən tôr′shən ist) *n.* a person who can twist or bend his body into odd and unnatural positions.

con·tour (kon′tür) *n.* 1 the outline of a figure: *The contour of the Atlantic coast of Canada is very irregular.* 2 the line that defines or bounds anything.
—*adj.* 1 showing the outlines of hills, valleys, etc. at regular intervals above sea level: *a contour map.* 2 following natural ridges and furrows to avoid erosion: *contour planting, contour ploughing.* 3 shaped to fit the contour of a particular object: *a contour chair.*
—*v.* 1 build (a road, etc.) according to a contour. 2 make an outline or contour of. [< F < Ital. *contorno* < *contornare* encircle < L *com-* with + *tornus* turning lathe < Gk. *tornos*] **—Syn.** *n.* See **outline.**

contour line a line on a map, showing height above sea

level. All points on a contour line have the same elevation.

contour map a map showing heights at regular intervals above sea level by means of contour lines.

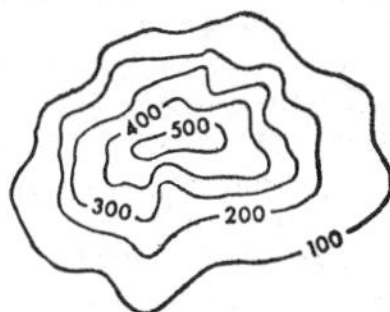

A contour map of a hill. Lines join points the same number of feet above sea level.

contr. 1 contract. 2 contracted. 3 contraction.

contra- *prefix.* in opposition; against: *contradistinction* = *distinction by opposition or contrast.* [< L *contra-* < *contra* against, adv., prep.]

con·tra·band (kon′trə band′) *adj.* against the law; prohibited: *contraband trade.*
—*n.* **1** goods imported or exported contrary to law; smuggled goods. **2** trading contrary to law; the act of smuggling. **3** contraband of war. **4** *U.S.* a Negro slave who escaped to or was brought within the Union lines during the Civil War. [< Sp. < Ital. *contrabando* < *contra-* against (< L) + *bando* < LL *bandum* ban < Gmc.]

contraband of war any materials supplied to warring nations by neutral countries and subject to seizure by the opposite side according to international law: *Ammunition is always contraband of war.*

con·tra·bass (kon′trə bās′) *n.* **1** the lowest bass voice or musical instrument. **2** a large, stringed musical instrument shaped like a cello and having a very low bass tone; double bass.
—*adj.* in music, sounding an octave lower than the normal bass.

con·tra·cep·tion (kon′trə sep′shən) *n.* the prevention of conception. [< *contra-* + *conception*]

con·tra·cep·tive (kon′trə sep′tiv) *adj.* of or for contraception. —*n.* a means or device for preventing conception.

con·tract (*v.* kən trakt′ *for 1-3,* kon′trakt or kən trakt′ *for 4*; *n.* kon′trakt) *v.* **1** draw together; make or become narrow; shorten; make or become smaller; shrink: *Wrinkling your forehead contracts your brow. Rubber stretches and contracts.* **2** in grammar, shorten (a word, etc.) by omitting some of the letters or sounds: *In talking we contract "do not" to "don't."* **3** get; form; enter upon; bring on oneself: *Bad habits are easy to contract and hard to get rid of. He contracted a cold by not keeping warm and dry.* **4** make a contract; agree by contract: *The builder contracted to build the new library.* **5** in anatomy, draw together and thicken muscle fibre to move a part of the body.
—*n.* **1** an agreement, especially a written agreement that can be enforced by law: *All professional hockey players sign contracts each year, agreeing to play for a certain salary.* **2** a formal agreement of marriage. **3** contract bridge. **4** in contract bridge, the tricks that the declarer undertakes to win. [< L *contractus,* pp. of *contrahere* < *com-* together + *trahere* draw] —**Syn.** *n.* **1** pact, compact.

contract bridge a card game played by four people divided into two opposing pairs. The highest bidder can score toward a game only as many points as he promises to make in his bid.

con·tract·ed (kən trak′tid) *adj.* **1** draw together; made narrow; shortened; made smaller, shrunken. **2** narrow-minded. —**con·tract′ed·ly,** *adv.*

con·tract·i·ble (kən trak′tə bəl) *adj.* capable of being contracted.

con·trac·tile (kən trak′tīl or kən trak′təl) *adj.* **1** capable of contracting: *Muscle is contractile tissue.* **2** producing contraction: *Cooling is a contractile force.*

con·trac·til·i·ty (kon′trak til′ə tē) *n.* the ability to contract.

con·trac·tion (kən trak′shən) *n.* **1** the process of contracting: *Cold causes the contraction of liquids, gases, and metals, whereas heat causes expansion.* **2** the state of being contracted: *A fall in temperature leads to the contraction of the mercury in a thermometer.* **3** something contracted; shortened form: *"Can't" is a contraction of "cannot."* **4** in anatomy, the drawing together and thickening of muscle fibre.

con·trac·tive (kən trak′tiv) *adj.* **1** capable of contracting. **2** producing contraction. **3** of contraction.

hat, āge, cãre, fär; let, ēqual, tėrm; it, īce
hot, ōpen, ôrder; oil, out; cup, pu̇t, rüle, ūse
əbove, takən, pencəl, lemən, circəs
ch, child; ng, long; sh, ship
th, thin; ᴛʜ, then; zh, measure

con·trac·tor (kon′trak tər or kən trak′tər *for 1*; kən trak′tər *for 2*) *n.* **1** a person who agrees to furnish materials or to do a piece of work for a certain price; person who makes a contract. **2** in anatomy, a muscle that draws together some part or parts of the body.

con·trac·tu·al (kən trak′chü əl) *adj.* **1** of or having to do with a contract. **2** having the nature of a contract.

con·tra·dict (kon′trə dikt′) *v.* **1** deny (a statement, rumor, etc.). **2** deny the words of (another person); say the opposite of what (another person) has said: *To contradict a guest is rude.* **3** be contrary to; disagree with: *His quick anger contradicted his previous statement that he never lost his temper.* [< L *contradictus,* pp. of *contradicere,* earlier *contra dicere* say in opposition]
—**Syn. 1, 2** See **deny.**

con·tra·dic·tion (kon′trə dik′shən) *n.* **1** the act of denying what has been said. **2** a statement that contradicts another; denial. **3** a contrary condition; disagreement; opposition: *a contradiction in terms.* **4** inconsistency.

con·tra·dic·to·ry (kon′trə dik′tə rē or kon′trə dik′trē) *adj.* **1** contradicting; contrary; in disagreement: *Reports of the result of the battle were so contradictory that we did not know which side had won.* **2** inclined to contradict.

con·tra·dis·tinc·tion (kon′trə dis tingk′shən) *n.* a distinction made by opposition or contrast: *Beasts, in contradistinction to man, do not speak.*

con·trail (kon′trāl) *n.* the trail of vapor left by a plane flying at a high altitude. [< *con*densation + *trail*]

con·tral·to (kən tral′tō) *n.* **-tos,** *adj.* —*n.* **1 a** the lowest, or deepest, female voice. **b** the highest adult male voice. **2** in music: **a** a singer with such a voice. **b** a part for such a voice or for a corresponding instrument. **c** an instrument playing such a part. —*adj.* of or for a contralto; that can sing or play a contralto part. [< Ital. *contralto* < *contra-* counter to (< L) + *alto* high < L *altus*]

con·tra·po·si·tion (kon′trə pə zish′ən) *n.* a placing over against; opposite position; contrast.

con·trap·tion (kən trap′shən) *n. Informal.* a contrivance; device; gadget. [? < *contrive*]

con·tra·pun·tal (kon′trə pun′təl) *adj.* in music: **1** of or having to do with counterpoint. **2** according to the rules of counterpoint. [< Ital. *contrapunto* (now *contrappunto*) counterpoint] —**con′tra·pun′tal·ly,** *adv.*

con·tra·pun·tist (kon′trə pun′tist) *n.* a person skilled in the rules and practice of counterpoint.

con·tra·ri·e·ty (kon′trə rī′ə tē) *n.* **-ties. 1** the state or quality of being contrary. **2** something contrary; a contrary fact or statement.

con·tra·ri·wise (kon′trer ē wīz′ *for 1 and 2*; kon′trer ē wīz′ or kən trãr′ē wīz′ *for 3*) *adv.* **1** in the opposite way or direction. **2** on the contrary. **3** perversely.

con·tra·ry (kon′trer ē *for adj. 1, 2, 3, n., and adv.*; kon′trer ē or kən trãr′ē *for adj. 4*) *adj. n.* **-ries,** *adv.*
—*adj.* **1** opposed; opposite; completely different. **2** opposite in direction, position, etc. **3** unfavorable: *a contrary wind.* **4** opposing others; stubborn; perverse.
—*n.* **1** a fact or quality that is the opposite of something else; the opposite. **2 on the contrary,** exactly opposite to what has been said. **3 to the contrary,** with the opposite effect.
—*adv.* in opposition. [ME < AF *contrarie* < L *contrarius* < *contra* against] —**con′tra·ri·ly,** *adv.* —**con′tra·ri·ness,** *n.* —**Syn.** *adj.* **1** See **opposite. 2** counter.

con·trast (*n.* kon′trast; *v.* kən trast′) *n.* **1** a great difference; difference; striking difference: *the contrast between black and white.* **2** a person, thing, event, etc. that shows differences when put side by side with another: *Her black hair is a sharp contrast to her white skin.* **3** in the arts, the use of varied colors, shapes, sounds, etc. to heighten the effect of a composition.

—*v.* **1** compare (two things) so as to show their differences: *Contrast birds with reptiles.* **2** show differences when compared or put side by side: *Blue and yellow contrast prettily in a design.* **3** form a contrast to; set off: *The strained language of his speeches contrasts oddly with the ease and naturalness of his letters.* **4** put close together to heighten an effect by emphasizing differences. [< F < Ital. *contrasto* < *contrastare* < VL *contrastare* < L *contra-* against + *stare* stand] —**con·trast′a·ble,** *adj.* —**con·trast′ing·ly,** *adv.* —**Syn.** *n.* **1** distinction. ☛ See **compare** for usage note.

con·tra·vene (kon′trə vēn′) *v.* **-vened, -ven·ing.** **1** conflict with; oppose: *A dictatorship contravenes the liberty of individuals.* **2** contradict. **3** violate; infringe. [< LL *contravenire* < L *contra-* against + *venire* come] —**con′tra·ven′er,** *n.*

con·tra·ven·tion (kon′trə ven′shən) *n.* **1** a conflict; opposition. **2** a contradiction. **3** a violation; infringement.

con·tre·danse (kôN trə däNs′) *n. French.* **1** a dance in which the partners stand in two lines facing each other. **2** the music written for such a dance. [< E *country-dance*]

con·tre·temps (kôN′trə täN′) *n.* **-temps** (-täNz′). *French.* an unfortunate accident; embarrassing or awkward happening. [< OF *contrestant,* ppr. of *contrester* oppose < VL *contrastare* (see CONTRAST); influenced by F *temps* time < L *tempus*]

con·trib·ut·a·ble (kən trib′yů tə bəl) *adj.* **1** capable of being contributed; payable as a contribution. **2** of persons, subject to contribution.

con·trib·ute (kən trib′ūt) *v.* **-ut·ed, -ut·ing.** **1** give (money, help, etc.) along with others; furnish as a share: *We should all contribute to the Red Cross. Everyone was asked to contribute suggestions for the party.* **2** write (articles, stories, etc.) for a newspaper or magazine. **3** contribute to, help bring about: *Poor food contributed to the child's illness.* [< L *contributus,* pp. of *contribuere* bring together, collect < *com-* together + *tribuere* bestow, assign, originally, divide among the tribes < *tribus* tribe]

con·tri·bu·tion (kon′trə bū′shən) *n.* **1** the act of giving money, help, etc. along with others. **2** the money, help, etc. given; gift. **3** an article, story, etc. written for a newspaper or magazine. **4** a tax; levy.

con·trib·u·tive (kən trib′yů tiv) *adj.* contributing; helping to bring about. —**con·trib′u·tive·ly,** *adv.* —**con·trib′u·tive·ness,** *n.*

con·trib·u·tor (kən trib′yů tər) *n.* **1** a person or thing that contributes. **2** a person who writes articles, stories, etc. for a newspaper or magazine.

con·trib·u·to·ry (kən trib′yů tô′rē) *adj.* contributing; helping to bring about: *The workman's carelessness was a contributory cause of the accident.* —*n.* a person or thing that contributes.

con·trite (kon′trīt or kən trīt′) *adj.* **1** broken in spirit by a sense of guilt; penitent. **2** showing deep regret and sorrow: *He wrote an apology in contrite words.* [< L *contritus* crushed, pp. of *conterere* < *com-* (intensive) + *terere* rub, grind] —**con·trite′ly,** *adv.* —**con·trite′ness,** *n.*

con·tri·tion (kən trish′ən) *n.* **1** sorrow for one's sins or guilt; being contrite; sincere penitence. **2** deep regret.

con·triv·ance (kən trīv′əns) *n.* **1** something invented; a mechanical device. **2** the act or manner of contriving. **3** the power or ability of contriving. **4** a plan; scheme.

con·trive (kən trīv′) *v.* **-trived, -triv·ing.** **1** invent; design: *contrive a new kind of engine.* **2** plan; scheme; plot: *contrive a robbery.* **3** manage; arrange to have something happen: *I will contrive to be there by ten o'clock.* **4** bring about. [ME < OF *controver* < *con-* (< L *com-*) (intensive) + *trover* find < L *turbare* stir up < *turba* commotion] —**con·triv′er,** *n.* —**Syn. 1** devise.

con·trol (kən trōl′) *n. v.* **-trolled, -trol·ling.** —*n.* **1** power; authority; direction: *A child is under its parents' control.* **2** the power or ability to restrain, check, or keep down: *He lost control of his temper.* **3** a means of restraint; check: *The R.C.M.P. is our chief control against the drug traffic.* **4** a device that controls a machine. **5** a standard of comparison for testing the results of scientific experiments. **6** a spirit that directs a medium in a spiritualistic séance. **7** **controls,** the instruments and devices by which a car, an airplane, a locomotive, etc. is operated: *After the crash, the pilot was found dead at the controls.* **8** regulation; prevention: *birth control.* [probably < v.]
—*v.* **1** have power or authority over; direct: *A captain controls his ship and its crew.* **2** hold back; keep down; restrain. **3** regulate: *control prices and wages.* **4** check or verify (an experiment, the effects of a drug, testimony, etc.) by some standard of comparison or by independent investigation. **5** in accounting, check, verify, or regulate (expenditures, accounts, etc.) [< F *contrôler* < OF *contreroller* < *contrerolle* register < *contre* against (< L *contra*) + *rolle* roll < L *rotulus,* dim. of *rota* wheel] —**con·trol′ling·ly,** *adv.* —**Syn.** *n.* **1** regulation, management. See **authority.**

con·trol·la·ble (kən trōl′ə bəl) *adj.* that can be controlled; capable of being checked or restrained.

con·trol·ler (kən trōl′ər) *n.* **1** a person employed to supervise expenditures or to manage financial affairs; comptroller. **2** a person who controls, directs, or restrains. **3** a device that controls or regulates the speed of a machine. **4** in certain city councils, a member of the board of control.

con·trol·ler·ship (kən trōl′ər ship′) *n.* the position or office of a controller.

control panel a panel containing all the instruments necessary for the control and operation of a complex mechanism such as an electronic computer or an aircraft.

control rod **1** in a nuclear reactor, a mechanism, containing fuel or other matter, used to control the rate of a chain reaction. **2** in an aircraft, a rod for transmitting movements from the controls in the cockpit to the rudder, ailerons, etc.

control room **1** in a radio or television studio, a soundproof room from which the transmission of a broadcast can be controlled. **2** a room containing all the instruments necessary to control a complex operation, such as the launching of a rocket.

control stick the lever that controls the direction of an airplane's movement.

control tower at an airfield, a structure from which aircraft traffic, and the movement of ground vehicles near runways, can be controlled.

con·tro·ver·sial (kon′trə vėr′shəl) *adj.* **1** of controversy; having to do with controversy. **2** open to controversy; debatable; disputed: *a controversial question.* **3** fond of controversy. —**con′tro·ver′sial·ly,** *adv.*

con·tro·ver·sial·ist (kon′trə vėr′shəl ist) *n.* a person who takes part in or is skilled in controversy.

con·tro·ver·sy (kon′trə vėr′sē) *n.* **-sies.** **1** the act of arguing a question about which differences of opinion exist; debate; dispute: *The controversy between the company and the union ended in a strike.* **2** a quarrel; wrangle. [< L *controversia* < *controversus* < *contro-* against + *versus,* pp. of *vertere* turn] —**Syn. 1** See **argument.**

con·tro·vert (kon′trə vėrt′ or kon′trə vėrt′) *v.* **1** dispute; deny; oppose: *The statement of the last witness controverts the evidence of the first two.* **2** dispute about; discuss; debate. [< L *contro-* against + *vertere* turn] —**con′tro·vert′er,** *n.*

con·tro·vert·i·ble (kon′trə vėr′tə bəl) *adj.* that can be controverted; debatable. —**con·tro·vert′i·bly,** *adv.*

con·tu·ma·cious (kon′tyů mā′shəs or kon′tů mā′shəs) *adj.* stubbornly rebellious; obstinately disobedient. —**con′tu·ma′cious·ly,** *adv.* —**con′tu·ma′cious·ness,** *n.*

con·tu·ma·cy (kon′tyů mə sē or kon′tů mə sē) *n.* **-cies.** stubborn resistance to authority; obstinate disobedience. [< L *contumacia* < *contumax* insolent < *tumere* swell up]

con·tu·me·li·ous (kon′tyů mē′lē əs or kon′tů mē′lē əs) *adj.* contemptuously insolent; insulting. —**con′tu·me′li·ous·ly,** *adv.* —**con′tu·me′li·ous·ness,** *n.*

con·tu·me·ly (kon′tū mə lē, kon′tū mə lē, kən tū′mə lē or kən tū′mə lē) *n.* **-lies.** **1** insolent contempt; insulting words or actions; humiliating treatment. **2** a humiliating insult. [< L *contumelia,* originally, insolent action < *tumere* swell up]

con·tuse (kən tūz′ or kən tüz′) *v.* **-tused, -tus·ing.** injure without breaking the skin, bruise. [< L *contusus,*

hat, āge, cãre, fär; let, ēqual, tėrm; it, īce
hot, ōpen, ôrder; oil, out; cup, pu̇t, rüle, ūse
əbove, takən, pencəl, lemən, circəs

ch, child; ng, long; sh, ship
th, thin; ᴛʜ, then; zh, measure

pp. of *contundere* < *com-* (intensive) + *tundere* pound]

con·tu·sion (kən tū′zhən or kən tü′zhən) *n.* a bruise.

co·nun·drum (kə nun′drəm) *n.* **1** a riddle whose answer involves a pun or play on words. "When is a door not a door?" is a conundrum. (*Answer*: "When it's ajar.") **2** any puzzling problem. [origin unknown]

con·ur·ba·tion (kon′ėr bā′shən) *n.* a number of urban communities that have expanded and thus grown so close together that they can be considered as one large community.

con·va·lesce (kon′və les′) *v.* **-lesced, -lesc·ing.** regain strength after illness; make progress toward health. [< L *convalescere* < *com-* (intensive) + *valescere* grow strong < *valere* be strong]

con·va·les·cence (kon′və les′əns) *n.* **1** a gradual recovery of health and strength after illness. **2** the time during which one is convalescing.

con·va·les·cent (kon′və les′ənt) *adj.* recovering health and strength after illness. —*n.* a person recovering after illness.

con·vec·tion (kən vek′shən) *n.* **1** the act of conveying. **2** in physics, the transfer of heat from one place to another by the circulation of heated particles of a gas or liquid. [< L *convectio, -onis* < *convehere* < *com-* together + *vehere* carry]

con·vec·tion·al (kən vek′shə nəl) *adj.* of or characterized by convection.

con·vec·tive (kən vek′tiv) *adj.* **1** capable of conveying; transporting. **2** having to do with or resulting from convection.

con·vec·tive·ly (kən vek′tiv lē) *adv.* by means of convection.

con·vec·tor (kən vek′tər) *n.* a convective agent.

con·vene (kən vēn′) *v.* **-vened, -ven·ing. 1** meet for some purpose; gather together; assemble: *Parliament convenes in Ottawa at least once a year.* **2** call together (members of an organization, etc.) [< L *convenire* < *com-* together + *venire* come]

con·ven·er (kən vē′nər) *n.* convenor.

con·ven·ience (kən vēn′yəns or kən vēn′ē əns) *n.* **1** the fact or quality of being convenient: *The convenience of packaged goods increases their sale.* **2** comfort; advantage: *Many provincial parks have camping places for the convenience of tourists.* **3** anything handy or easy to use; something that saves trouble or work: *A folding table is a convenience in a small room.* **4 at one's convenience,** under conditions or at a time one finds convenient or advantageous: *Write at your convenience.*

con·ven·ien·cy (kən vēn′yən sē or kən vēn′ē ən sē) *n.* **-cies.** convenience.

con·ven·ient (kən vēn′yənt or kən vēn′ē ənt) *adj.* **1** saving trouble; well arranged; easy to reach or use; handy; suitable: *use a convenient tool, take a convenient bus, live in a convenient house, meet at a convenient place.* **2** easily done; not troublesome. **3 convenient to,** *Informal.* near. [< L *conveniens, -entis,* ppr. of *convenire* meet, agree, be suitable. See CONVENE.]—**con·ven′ient·ly,** *adv.*

con·ven·or or **con·ven·er** (kən vē′nər) *n.* a person who is responsible for calling together the members of a committee, etc. and who often acts as their chairman.

con·vent (kon′vent) *n.* **1** a community of persons dedicated to a religious life; in modern usage, a community of nuns. **2** the building or buildings in which they live. [ME < AF *covent* < L *conventus* assembly < *convenire.* See CONVENE.] —**Syn. 2** cloister, abbey.

con·ven·ti·cle (kən ven′tə kəl) *n.* **1** a secret or unauthorized meeting, especially for religious worship. **2** a secret religious meeting or assembly of certain Protestants who dissented from the doctrines and forms of the Church of England during the 16th and 17th centuries. **3** the place of such a meeting. [< L *conventiculum,* dim. of *conventus* assembly. See CONVENT.]

con·ven·tion (kən ven′shən) *n.* **1** a meeting for some purpose; gathering; assembly. A political party holds a convention to choose candidates for public offices. **2** the delegates to a meeting or assembly. **3** an agreement. A convention signed by two or more countries is usually about less important matters than those in a treaty. **4** general agreement; common consent; custom. **5** a custom approved by general agreement; rule based on common consent: *Using the right hand to shake hands is a convention.* **6** in the arts, a procedure or detail not taken literally, but accepted by the beholder, reader, etc. as fitting: *It is a convention of the theatre that asides are not heard by persons on the stage with the speaker.* [< L *conventio, -onis* < *convenire.* See CONVENE.] —**Syn. 1** conference. **3** compact. **5** usage, etiquette.

con·ven·tion·al (kən ven′shən əl) *adj.* **1** depending on conventions; customary: *"Good morning" is a conventional greeting.* **2** formal; not natural; not original. **3** in art, following custom rather than nature. Flowers and leaves are often drawn in a conventional design without any idea of making them look real. **4** of weapons, warfare, etc., not nuclear or biological. —**con·ven′tion·al·ly,** *adv.* —**Syn. 1** See **formal.**

con·ven·tion·al·ism (kən ven′shən əl iz′əm) *n.* **1** a tendency to follow conventional usages; adherence to custom. **2** something conventional; formal usage, word, phrase, etc.

con·ven·tion·al·i·ty (kən ven′shən al′ə tē) *n.* **-ties. 1** a conventional quality or character: *the conventionality of modern life.* **2** conventional behavior; adherence to custom. **3** a conventional custom or rule: *The girls at boarding school were required to observe the conventionalities very strictly.*

con·ven·tion·al·ize (kən ven′shən əl īz′) *v.* **-ized, -iz·ing. 1** make conventional. **2** in art, design, draw, etc. according to customary patterns rather than nature. —**con·ven′tion·al·i·za′tion,** *n.*

con·ven·tu·al (kən ven′chü əl) *adj.* of or like a convent. —*n.* a member of a convent.

con·verge (kən vėrj′) *v.* **-verged, -verg·ing. 1** tend to meet in a point. **2** turn toward each other: *If you look at the end of your nose, your eyes converge.* **3** come together; centre: *The interest of all the students converged upon the celebration.* **4** cause to converge. [< LL *convergere* < L *com-* together + *vergere* incline]

C

These lines converge at C

con·ver·gence (kən vėr′jəns) *n.* **1** the act, process, or fact of converging; tendency to meet in a point. **2** the point of meeting. **3** in biology, the tendency in animals or plants not closely related to develop similar characteristics when living under the same conditions.

con·ver·gen·cy (kən vėr′jən sē) *n.* **-cies.** convergence.

con·ver·gent (kən vėr′jənt) *adj.* converging.

con·vers·a·ble (kən vėr′sə bəl) *adj.* **1** easy or pleasant to talk to. **2** fond of talking. **3** having to do with or proper for social intercourse. —**con·vers′a·bly,** *adv.*

con·ver·sant (kən vėr′sənt or kon′vər sənt) *adj.* familiar by use or study; acquainted: *He is not conversant with the history of philosophical thought.* —**con·ver′sant·ly,** *adv.*

con·ver·sa·tion (kon′vər sā′shən) *n.* **1** informal or friendly talk; the exchange of thoughts by talking informally: *There is much pleasure in good conversation.* **2** a talk; a meeting for the purpose of informal talk: *The professor invited his students to his home for a conversation.*

con·ver·sa·tion·al (kon′vər sā′shən əl or kon′vər sāsh′nəl) *adj.* **1** of or having to do with conversation. **2** fond of conversation; good at conversation. **3** characteristic of conversation.

con·ver·sa·tion·al·ist (kon′vər sā′shən əl ist or kon′vər sāsh′nəl ist) *n.* a person who is fond of or good at conversation; one who cultivates the art of conversation.

con·ver·sa·tion·al·ly (kon′vər sā′shən əl ē or kon′vər sāsh′nəl ē) *adv.* **1** in a conversational manner. **2** in conversation.

con·verse[1] (*v.* kən vėrs′; *n.* kon′vėrs) *v.* **-versed,**

-vers·ing, *n.* —*v.* talk informally together: *The two old veterans liked conversing about their experiences during the war.* —*n.* conversation. [ME < OF *converser* < L *conversari* live with < *com-* with + *versari* live, be busy < *verti* turn] —**con·vers′er,** *n.* —**Syn.** *v.* chat.

con·verse[2] (*adj.* kən vėrs′ or kon′vėrs; *n.* kon′vėrs) *adj.* **1** opposite; contrary. **2** reversed in order; turned about. —*n.* **1** something that is opposite or contrary. **2** something that is turned around: "*Honest but poor*" *is the converse of* "*Poor but honest.*" [< L *conversus* turned around, pp. of *convertere.* See CONVERT.]

con·verse·ly (kən vėrs′lē or kon′vėrs lē) *adv.* if or when turned the other way around: *Six is more than five; conversely, five is less than six.*

con·ver·sion (kən vėr′zhən or kən vėr′shən) *n.* **1** the act of converting; a changing; a turning; change: *Heat causes the conversion of water into steam.* **2** a change from unbelief to faith; change from one religion, party, etc. to another. **3** an exchange into an equivalent. **4** in rugby football, the act or fact of kicking a point after a touchdown. **5** the act of taking and using unlawfully: *He was arrested for the conversion of public money to his own use.* **6** the exchanging of an issue of public securities, bonds, stocks, etc. for another, usually carrying a lower rate of interest.

con·vert (*v.* kən vėrt′; *n.* kon′vėrt) *v.* **1** change; turn: *These machines convert cotton into cloth.* **2** change from unbelief to faith; change from one religion, political party, etc. to another: *The missionaries converted many people to the Christian religion.* **3** take and use unlawfully: *The dishonest treasurer converted the club's money to his own use.* **4** turn the other way around; invert; transpose. **5** exchange for an equivalent: *He converted his bank notes into gold.* **6** in rugby football, kick a goal after a touchdown. **7** exchange (a bond or other security) for another type of security, as common stock.
—*n.* **1** a person who has been converted. **2** in rugby football: **a** a goal kicked after a touchdown. **b** the point made by successfully kicking such a goal. [< L *convertere* < *com-* (intensive) + *vertere* turn] —**Syn.** *v.* **1** See **transform.**

con·vert·er (kən vėr′tər) *n.* **1** a person or thing that converts. **2** a machine for changing the form of an electric current. **3** a furnace in which pig iron is changed into steel by the Bessemer process.

con·vert·i·bil·i·ty (kən vėr'tə bil′ə tē) *n.* the quality of being convertible.

con·vert·i·ble (kən vėr′tə bəl) *adj.* **1** capable of being converted: *Wood is convertible into paper. A dollar bill is convertible into coins.* **2** of an automobile, having a top that may be folded down. **3** of securities, that can be exchanged for others of the same value.
—*n.* an automobile with a folding top. —**con·vert′i·bly,** *adv.*

con·vert·i·plane (kən vėr′tə plān') *n.* an aircraft that operates like a conventional airplane in level flight, but that takes off and lands like a helicopter. [< *convert*ible + air*plane*]

con·vex (kon veks′ or kon′veks) *adj.* curved out, like the outside of a circle or sphere: *The crystal of a watch is slightly convex.* —*n.* a convex surface or thing. [< L *convexus* vaulted, probably < *com-* around + *vac-* bend (related to *vacillare* totter, sway)] —**con·vex′ly,** *adv.*

Convex lenses seen from the side

con·vex·i·ty (kon vek′sə tē) *n.* **-ties. 1** a convex condition or quality. **2** a convex surface or thing.

con·vey (kən vā′) *v.* **1** carry; transport: *A bus conveys passengers.* **2** transmit; conduct: *A wire conveys an electric circuit.* **3** express; make known; communicate: *His words convey no meaning to me.* **4** in law, transfer the ownership of (property) from one person to another: *The old farmer conveyed his farm to his son.* [ME < OF *conveier* < VL < L *com-* with + *via* road. Doublet of CONVOY.] —**con·vey′a·ble,** *adj.* —**Syn. 1** See **carry.**

con·vey·ance (kən vā′əns) *n.* **1** the act of carrying; transportation; transmission. **2** anything that carries people and goods; vehicle. **3** communication. **4 in law:** a transfer of the ownership of property from one person to another. **b** a written statement that shows such a transfer; deed.

con·vey·anc·er (kən vā′ən sər) *n.* a lawyer who investigates the ownership of property and prepares contracts, deeds, etc., for its transfer from one person to another.

con·vey·anc·ing (kən vā′ən sing) *n.* the preparation of deeds, etc. for the transfer of the ownership of property from one person to another.

con·vey·or or **con·vey·er** (kən vā′ər) *n.* **1** a person or thing that conveys. **2** a mechanical device that carries things from one place to another: *Grain is carried from one floor of an elevator to another by means of a conveyor.*

con·vict (*v.* kən vikt′; *n.* kon′vikt) *v.* **1** prove guilty. **2** declare guilty: *The jury convicted the prisoner of murder.* **3** impress with a sense of guilt: *a person convicted of sin.* —*n.* **1** a person convicted by a court. **2** a person serving a prison sentence for some crime. [< L *convictus,* pp. of *convincere.* See CONVINCE.]

con·vic·tion (kən vik′shən) *n.* **1** the act of proving or declaring guilty. **2** the state of being proved or declared guilty. **3** the act of convincing (a person). **4** a being convinced. **5** a firm belief. —**Syn. 5** certainty, assurance. See **belief.**

con·vince (kən vins′) *v.* **-vinced, -vinc·ing.** make (a person) feel sure; cause to believe; persuade by argument or proof: *The mistakes she made convinced me that she had not studied her lesson.* [< L *convincere* < *com-* (intensive) + *vincere* overcome] —**Syn.** See **persuade.**
☛ **Convince** is followed by *of* plus a noun or by a *that*-clause: *I can easily convince you of his innocence. You will soon be convinced that I am right.*

con·vin·ci·ble (kən vin′sə bəl) *adj.* capable of being convinced.

con·vinc·ing (kən vin′sing) *adj.* that convinces: *a convincing argument.* —**con·vinc′ing·ly,** *adv.* —**con·vinc′ing·ness,** *n.* —**Syn.** persuasive, cogent.

con·viv·i·al (kən viv′ē əl) *adj.* **1** fond of eating and drinking with friends; jovial; sociable. **2** of or suitable for a feast or banquet; festive. [< LL *convivialis* < L *convivium* feast < *com-* with + *vivere* live] —**con·viv′i·al·ly,** *adv.*

con·viv·i·al·i·ty (kən viv'ē al′ə tē) *n.* **-ties. 1** a fondness for eating and drinking with friends; good-fellowship. **2** eating and drinking with friends; festivity.

con·vo·ca·tion (kon'və kā′shən) *n.* **1** a calling together; an assembling by a summons. **2** an assembly; a number of persons gathered in answer to a summons: *The convocation of clergymen passed a resolution condemning war.* **3** at certain universities: **a** the officials and graduates as a legislative, advisory, or electoral body. **b** a meeting of this body. **4** at other universities: **a** an assembly of the members of a university for a specific purpose. **b** a ceremony at which degrees are conferred.

con·voke (kən vōk′) *v.* **-voked, -vok·ing.** call together; summon to assemble. [< L *convocare* < *com-* together + *vocare* call] —**con·vok′er,** *n.*

con·vo·lute (kon′və lüt') *adj. v.* **-lut·ed, -lut·ing.** —*adj.* coiled; rolled up into a spiral shape with one part over another. —*v.* coil. [< L *convolutus,* pp. of *convolvere* < *com-* together + *volvere* roll]

con·vo·lut·ed (kon′və lüt'id) *adj.* having convolutions; coiled; twisted.

con·vo·lu·tion (kon'və lü′shən) *n.* **1** a coiling, winding, or twisting together. **2** a coil; winding; twist. **3** in anatomy, an irregular fold or ridge on the surface of the brain.

con·vol·vu·lus (kən vol′vyů ləs) *n.* **-lus·es, -li** (-lī' or -lē'). any of a group of plants, usually vines, having flowers shaped like trumpets. The morning glory is a convolvulus. [< L *convolvulus* bindweed < *convolvere* roll around; with reference to its twining stems. See CONVOLUTE.]

con·voy (*v.* kən voi′ or kon′voi; *n.* kon′voi) *v.* accompany in order to protect; escort: *Warships convoy merchant ships in wartime.* —*n.* **1** an escort; protection: *The gold was moved from the ship to the bank's vault under convoy of soldiers.* **2** warships, soldiers, etc. that convoy; a protecting escort. **3** the ship, fleet, supplies, etc.

accompanied by a protecting escort. [ME < OF *convoier, conveier*. Doublet of CONVEY.]

con·vul·sant (kən vul′sənt) *adj.* that causes convulsions. —*n.* a drug or other agent that causes convulsions.

con·vulse (kən vuls′) *v.* **-vulsed, -vuls·ing. 1** shake violently: *An earthquake convulsed the island.* **2** cause violent disturbance in; disturb violently: *His face was convulsed with rage.* **3** throw into convulsions; shake with spasms of pain: *The sick child was convulsed before the doctor came.* **4** throw into a fit of laughter; cause to shake with laughter: *The clown convulsed the audience with his funny acts.* [< L *convulsus*, pp. of *convellere* tear away < *com-* (intensive) + *vellere* tear]

con·vul·sion (kən vul′shən) *n.* **1** a violent, involuntary contracting and relaxing of the muscles; spasm: *The sick child's convulsions frightened its mother.* **2** a fit of laughter. **3** a violent disturbance: *The country was undergoing a political convulsion.*

con·vul·sive (kən vul′siv) *adj.* **1** violently disturbing. **2** having convulsions. **3** producing convulsions. —**con·vul′sive·ly,** *adv.*

co·ny (kō′nē) *n.* **-nies.** coney.

coo (kü) *n. v.* **cooed, coo·ing.** —*n.* a soft, murmuring sound made by doves or pigeons. —*v.* **1** make a soft, murmuring sound. **2** murmur softly; speak in a soft, loving manner. [imitative] —**coo′er,** *n.*

coo·ee (kü′ē) *n.* **-ees,** *interj.* in Australia, a long, shrill signal call of the aborigines, adopted by the colonists. —*v.* make this call.

coo·ey (kü′ē) *n.* **-eys,** *interj.* cooee.

cook (ku̇k) *v.* **1** prepare (food, etc.) by using heat. **2** undergo cooking; be cooked. **3** act as cook; work as cook. **4** apply heat or fire to. **5** *Informal.* subject to atomic radiation, especially by means of a nuclear reactor. **6** *Informal.* tamper with: *He cooked the accounts.* **7 cook up,** *Informal.* **a** make up; prepare. **b** prepare falsely. [< n.] —*n.* a person who cooks. [OE *cōc* < LL *cocus* < L *coquus*]

cook·book (ku̇k′bu̇k′) *n.* a book containing directions for cooking various kinds of food; book of recipes.

cook·er (ku̇k′ər) *n.* an apparatus or container to cook things in.

cook·er·y (ku̇k′ər ē) *n.* **-er·ies. 1** the art or occupation of cooking. **2** a cookhouse at a lumber camp or mine. **3** a place for cooking.

cook·house (ku̇k′hous′) *n.* a room or place for cooking.

cook·ie or **cook·y** (ku̇k′ē) *n.* a small, flattish, sweet cake. [< Du. *koekje* little cake]

cook-out (ku̇k′out′) *n.* the cooking and eating of a meal out-of-doors; a picnic, etc. where the food is cooked outdoors.

cook·shop (ku̇k′shop′) *n.* a place where food is cooked and sold; small restaurant.

cook·stove (ku̇k′stōv′) *n.* a stove for cooking.

cook·y (ku̇k′ē) *n.* **cook·ies.** cookie.

cool (kül) *adj.* **1** somewhat cold; more cold than hot: *a cool day.* **2** allowing or giving a cool feeling: *cool clothes.* **3** not excited; calm. **4** having little enthusiasm or interest; not cordial: *a cool greeting.* **5** bold; impudent. **6** *Informal.* without exaggeration or qualification: *a cool million dollars.* **7** of colors, blue, green, or gray. **8** not contaminated by radioactivity. **9** *Slang.* admirable; excellent. **10** *Slang.* of jazz music and musicians, characterized by a sophisticated, unemotional, and relaxed style, rendition, technique, etc.: *Cool jazz shows a marked influence of classical music.*
—*n.* **1** something cool; a cool part, place, or time: *the cool of the evening.* **2** *Slang.* control of one's actions, feelings, etc.; self-control: *Maintain your cool.*
—*v.* **1** become cool. **2** make cool. **3 cool one's heels,** *Informal.* be kept waiting for a long time. [OE *cōl*] —**cool′ly,** *adv.* —**cool′ness,** *n.* —**Syn.** *adj.* **1** See **cold. 4** indifferent.

cool·ant (kül′ənt) *n.* a cooling agent, used for machinery, etc.

cool·er (kül′ər) *n.* **1** an apparatus or container that cools foods or drinks, or keeps them cool. **2** anything that cools. **3** *Slang.* a jail: *He got drunk and landed in the cooler.*

hat, āge, cãre, fär; let, ēqual, tėrm; it, īce
hot, ōpen, ôrder; oil, out; cup, pu̇t, rüle, ūse
əbove, takən, pencəl, lemən, circəs
ch, child; ng, long; sh, ship
th, thin; ᴛʜ, then; zh, measure

cool-head·ed (kül′hed′id) *adj.* calm; not easily excited. —**cool′-head′ed·ly,** *adv.* —**cool′-head′ed·ness,** *n.*

coo·lie (kü′lē) *n.* **1** in China, India, etc., an unskilled laborer. **2** a laborer who does hard work for very little pay. [probably < Tamil *kuli* hire, hired servant]

coo·ly (kü′lē) *n.* **-lies.** coolie.

coomb (küm or kōm) *n.* combe.

coon (kün) *n.* **1** *Informal.* a raccoon. **2** *Derogatory.* a Negro.

coon·skin (kün′skin′) *n.* the skin of a raccoon, used in making caps, coats, etc. —*adj.* made of coonskin.

coop (küp) *n.* **1** a small cage or pen for chickens, rabbits, etc. **2** *Slang.* a jail. —*v.* **1** keep or put in a coop. **2** confine in a very small space: *The children were cooped up indoors by the rain.* [ME *cupe* basket < L *cupa* cask]

co-op or **co·öp** (kō′op or kō op′) *n. Informal.* a co-operative.

coop·er (küp′ər) *n.* a man who makes or repairs barrels, casks, etc. —*v.* make or repair (barrels, casks, etc.). [? < MDu., MLG *kuper* < L *cuparius* < *cupa* cask]

coop·er·age (küp′ər ij) *n.* **1** the work done by a cooper. **2** the price paid for such work. **3** the shop where such work is done.

co-op·er·ate (kō op′ər āt′) *v.* **-at·ed, -at·ing.** work together; unite in producing a result. Also, **co·öp·er·ate, co·op·er·ate.** [< LL *cooperari* < *co-* together + *operari* to work < L *opera* effort, work] —**co-op′er·a′tor,** *n.*

co-op·er·a·tion (kō op′ər ā′shən) *n.* **1** the act of working together; united effort or labor. **2** a combination of persons for purposes of production, purchase, or distribution for their joint benefit. Also, **co·öp·er·a·tion, co·op·er·a·tion.**

co-op·er·a·tive (kō op′ər ə tiv or kō op′ər ā′tiv) *adj.* **1** wanting or willing to work together with others. **2** of, having to do with, or being a co-operative.
—*n.* a union, usually of farmers, for selling and buying to the best advantage; an organization in which the profits and losses are shared by all members: *Co-operatives may take the form of wheat-marketing agencies, general stores, gas stations, etc.* Also, **co·öp·er·a·tive, co·op·er·a·tive.** —**co-op′er·a′tive·ly,** *adv.* —**co-op′er·a′tive·ness,** *n.*

Co-operative Commonwealth Federation a Canadian political party, commonly spoken of as the C.C.F., established in 1932. In 1961, at the federal level and in most provinces, it was absorbed into the New Democratic Party. *Abbrev.*: CCF or C.C.F.

co-operative store a store where merchandise is sold to members who share in the profits and losses according to the amount they buy.

co-opt (kō opt′) *v.* of a committee, etc., add or elect a new member. Also, **co·öpt, co·opt.**

co-or·di·nate (*adj. n.* kō ôr′də nit or kō ôr′də nāt′; *v.* kō ôr′də nāt′) *adj. n. v.* **-nat·ed, -nat·ing.** —*adj.* **1** equal in importance; of equal rank. **2** made up of co-ordinate parts. **3** joining words, phrases, or clauses that are grammatically equivalent. *And* and *but* are co-ordinate conjunctions. **4** in mathematics, having to do with or involving the use of co-ordinates. **5** in chemistry, in which one atom shares two electrons with another atom: *a co-ordinate bond.*
—*n.* **1** a co-ordinate person or thing. **2** in mathematics, any of two or more magnitudes that define the position of a point, line, or plane by reference to a fixed figure, system of lines, etc.
—*v.* **1** make co-ordinate; make equal in importance. **2** arrange in proper order or relation; harmonize; adjust: *A swimmer should co-ordinate the movements of his arms and legs.* Also, **co·ör·di·nate, co·or·di·nate.** [< *co-* with + L *ordinatus*, pp. of *ordinare* regulate < *ordo, -inis* rank, order] —**co-or′di·nate·ly,** *adv.* —**co-or′di·nate·ness,** —*n.* **co-or′di·na′tor,** *n.*

co·or·di·na·tion (kō ôr′də nā′shən) *n.* **1** the proper order or proper relation. **2** a harmonious adjustment or working together (often used with reference to muscles). **3** a putting or being put into the same order or rank. Also, **co·ör·di·na·tion, co·or·di·na·tion.**

co·or·di·na·tive (kō ôr′də nə tiv or kō ôr′də nā′tiv) *adj.* co-ordinating. Also, **co·ör·di·na·tive, co·or·di·na·tive.**

coot (küt) *n.* **1** a wading and swimming bird having short wings and toes broadened by lobes of skin. **2** a large, black duck of northern regions and seas. **3** *Informal.* a fool; simpleton. [? < Du. *koet*]

coot·ie (küt′ē) *n. Slang.* a louse.

cop[1] (kop) *n. Informal.* a policeman. [short for *copper* policeman < *cop*[2]]

cop[2] (kop) *v.* **copped, cop·ping. 1** *Slang.* steal. **2 cop a plea,** plead guilty to one charge in order to avoid being tried for a more serious one. **3** capture; catch; nab. [OE *coppian*]

cop. 1 copper. **2** copyright. **3** copyrighted.

co·pal (kō′pəl) *n.* a hard, lustrous resin from various tropical trees, used chiefly in making varnish. [< Sp. < Mexican *kopalli*]

co-part·ner (kō pärt′nər) *n.* a fellow partner; associate.

co-part·ner·ship (kō pärt′nər ship′) *n.* partnership.

cope[1] (kōp) *v.* **coped, cop·ing.** struggle with some degree of success; struggle on even terms; deal successfully (*with*). [ME < OF *coper* strike < *coup*. See COUP.]

cope[2] (kōp) *n. v.* **coped, cop·ing.** —*n.* **1** a long cape worn by clergymen during certain religious rites. **2** anything like a cope; a cloaklike covering, such as a canopy, a high, arched roof, or the sky. **3** in architecture, a coping.
—*v.* **1** cover with a cope or something like a cope. **2** provide with a coping or something like a coping. [OE **cāpe* < Med.L *capa* cloak, var. of LL *cappa* hood, apparently < L *caput* head]

C, a cope

co·peck (kō′pek) *n.* kopeck.

Co·per·ni·can (kə pėr′nə kən) *adj.* of or having to do with Nikolaus Copernicus (1473-1543), a Polish astronomer, or the Copernican system.

Copernican system in astronomy, the theory developed by Nicolaus Copernicus (1473-1543) that the earth revolves on its axis and the planets move around the sun.

cope·stone (kōp′stōn′) *n.* **1** the top stone of a wall; a stone used for or in a coping. **2** a finishing touch; climax. [< *cope*[2] + *stone*]

cop·i·er (kop′ē ər) *n.* **1** a person who copies; imitator. **2** a person who makes written copies; copyist. **3** a machine that makes copies; duplicator.

co-pi·lot (kō′pī′lət) *n.* the assistant or second pilot in an aircraft.

cop·ing (kōp′ing) *n.* the top layer of a brick or stone wall. It is usually built with a slope to shed water. [< *cope*[2]]

COPING

coping saw a narrow saw in a U-shaped frame, used to cut curves.

co·pi·ous (kō′pē əs) *adj.* **1** plentiful; abundant: *copious rainfall*; *a copious harvest.* **2** containing much matter. **3** containing many words: *a copious argument.* [< L *copiosus* < *copia* plenty < *copis* well supplied < *co-* with + *ops* resources] —**co′pi·ous·ly,** *adv.* —**co′pi·ous·ness,** *n.* —**Syn.** ample.

co·pla·nar (kō plā′nər) *adj.* in mathematics, (of points, lines, figures) lying in the same plane. A circle is a set of coplanar points.

cop·per (kop′ər) *n.* **1** a tough, reddish-brown metallic chemical element that is easily shaped into thin sheets or fine wire and resists rust. Copper is an excellent conductor of heat and electricity. *Symbol*: Cu; *at.no.* 29; *at.wt.* 63.54. **2** anything made of copper. **3** a coin made of copper or bronze; penny. **4** a large boiler or cauldron. **5** a reddish brown.
—*v.* cover with copper.
—*adj.* **1** made of copper. **2** reddish-brown. [OE *coper* < L *cuprum*, for earlier *aes Cyprium* metal of Cyprus]

cop·per·as (kop′ər əs) *n.* a green sulphate of iron, used in dyeing, in making ink, in medicine as a disinfectant, and in photography. *Formula*: $FeSO_4 \cdot 7H_2O$ [ME < OF *couperose* < Med.L (*aqua*) *cuprosa* (water) of copper < L *cuprum*. See COPPER.]

Copper Eskimo any of a group of Eskimos living along the coast of the Arctic near the Coppermine River. [with reference to their use of copper tools]

cop·per·head (kop′ər hed′) *n.* **1** a poisonous North American snake having a copper-colored head, related to the water moccasin and the rattlesnake. **2 Copperhead,** in the United States, a person in the North who sympathized with the South during the Civil War 1861-1865.

cop·per·plate (kop′ər plāt′) *n.* **1** a thin, flat piece of copper on which a design, writing, etc. is engraved or etched. **2** an engraving, picture, or print made from a copperplate. **3** copperplate printing or engraving. **4** a type of elegant handwriting.

cop·per·smith (kop′ər smith′) *n.* a man who makes things out of copper.

copper sulphate blue vitriol.

cop·per·y (kop′ər ē) *adj.* **1** of or containing copper. **2** like copper. **3** copper-colored.

cop·pice (kop′is) *n.* copse.

cop·ra (kop′rə) *n.* the dried meat of coconuts: *Coconut oil is obtained from copra.* [< Pg. < Malayalam *koppara*]

copse (kops) *n.* a thicket of small trees, bushes, shrubs, etc. [< OF *copeiz* a cut-over forest < *couper* cut, ult. < L < Gk. *kolaphos* a blow]

Copt (kopt) *n.* **1** a native of Egypt descended from the ancient Egyptians. **2** a member of the Coptic Church. [< NL *Coptus* < Arabic *Quft, Qubt* the Copts]

cop·ter (kop′tər) *n. Informal.* helicopter.

Cop·tic (kop′tik) *adj.* of or having to do with the Copts. —*n.* the language formerly spoken by the Copts. Coptic is now used only in the rituals of the Coptic Church.

Coptic Church the national Christian church of Egypt and of Ethiopia.

cop·u·la (kop′yů lə) *n.* **-las, lae** (-lē′ or -lī′). **1** linking verb. **2** in anatomy, a connecting bone, cartilage, etc. [< L *copula* bond. Doublet of COUPLE.]

cop·u·late (kop′yů lāt′) *v.* **-lat·ed, -lat·ing.** unite in sexual intercourse. [< L *copulare* < *copula*. See COPULA.]

cop·u·la·tion (kop′yů lā′shən) *n.* **1** a joining together. **2** the act of sexual union.

cop·u·la·tive (kop′yů lə tiv or kop′yů lā′tiv) *adj.* **1** serving to couple or connect. **2** in grammar: **a** serving to connect words or clauses of equal rank: "*And*" *is a copulative conjunction.* **b** of the nature of a copula: "*Be*" *is a copulative verb.* —*n.* a copulative word. In "He became captain," *became* is a copulative. —**cop′u·la′tive·ly,** *adv.*

cop·y (kop′ē) *n.* **cop·ies,** *v.* **cop·ied, cop·y·ing.** —*n.* **1** anything made to be just like another; anything made on the pattern or model of another. **2** something to be followed as a pattern or model. **3** one of a number of books, newspapers, magazines, pictures, etc. made at the same printing. **4** the material to be set up in type for a book, newspaper, or magazine.
—*v.* **1** make a copy; make a copy of. **2** be like; follow as a pattern or model; imitate. [ME < OF *copier* < Med.L *copia* transcript < L *copia* plenty. See COPIOUS.]
Syn. *n.* **1** duplicate, transcript, reproduction, imitation. –*v.* **1 Copy, imitate** = try to make a thing like something else by following a pattern or model. **Copy** = follow a model as closely and exactly as possible: *He copied all the pictures in his book.* **Imitate** = try to make or do something like a pattern or model: *Sometimes a teacher asks a class to imitate something written by a great author.*

cop·y·book (kop′ē bůk′) *n.* a book with models of handwriting to be copied in learning to write. —*adj.* commonplace; conventional; ordinary: *a copybook speech.*

copy cat *Slang.* one who imitates another's behavior,

appearance, etc. (used derogatorily by children).

copy desk in a newspaper office, the desk where news stories and articles are edited and prepared for publication.

copy editor a person who edits written material and prepares it for publication.

cop·y·hold (kop′ē hōld′) *n.* formerly: **1** in law: ownership of land proved by a copy of the roll of a manorial court. **2** the land held in this way.

cop·y·hold·er (kop′ē hōl′dər) *n.* **1** a person who reads manuscripts aloud to a proofreader. **2** in law, a person who owns land by copyhold.

cop·y·ist (kop′ē ist) *n.* **1** a person who makes written copies. **2** a person who copies; imitator.

cop·y·right (kop′ē rīt′) *n.* the exclusive right granted by law for a definite number of years to an author, composer, artist, etc. or to his delegate, to sell, print, publish, or reproduce his work in any way. —*v.* get a copyright for.

co·quet (kō ket′) *v.* **-quet·ted, -quet·ting. 1** flirt. **2** trifle. [< F *coqueter* < *coquet,* dim. of *coq* cock]

co·quet·ry (kō′kə trē or kō ket′rē) *n.* **-ries. 1** flirting. **2** trifling.

co·quette (kō ket′) *n.* a woman who tries to attract men merely to please her vanity; flirt. [< F *coquette,* fem. of *coquet.* See COQUET.]

co·quet·tish (kō ket′ish) *adj.* **1** of a coquette. **2** like a coquette; like a coquette's. **—co·quet′tish·ly,** *adv.*

co·qui·na (kō kē′nə) *n.* a soft, whitish rock composed of fragments of sea shells and corals. [< Sp. *coquina* shellfish. Akin to CONCH.]

cor. 1 corner. **2** coroner. **3** correction. **4** corrected. **5** corresponding.

Cor. 1 Corinthians. **2** Coroner.

cor- the form of **com-** before *r,* as in *correct.*

cor·a·cle (kôr′ə kəl) *n.* a small, light boat made by covering a wooden frame with waterproof material. [< Welsh *corwgl* < *corwg* round body or vessel, torso, carcass]

cor·a·coid (kôr′ə koid′) *n.* **1** in birds and reptiles, the bone between the shoulder blade and the breastbone. **2** in mammals, a bony process extending from the shoulder blade to or toward the breastbone. —*adj.* of this bone or bony process. [< NL < Gk. *korakoeidēs* < *korax, -akos* crow + *eidos* form]

cor·al (kôr′əl) *n.* **1** a stony substance consisting of the skeletons of certain kinds of very small sea animals called polyps. Reefs and small islands consisting of coral are common in the South Seas. Red and pink coral are often used in making jewellery. **2** any of the skeletons forming this substance. **3** a polyp that secretes a skeleton of coral and forms large branching colonies by budding. **4** a piece of coral, especially red or pink coral, made into jewellery. **5** a deep pink; red.
—*adj.* **1** made of coral. **2** deep-pink; red. [ME < OF < L *corallum* < Gk. *koral(l)ion*]

coral reef a reef consisting mainly of coral.

coral snake a small, poisonous American snake whose body is often banded with alternating rings of red, yellow, and black.

cor·bel (kôr′bəl) *n. v.* **-belled** or **-beled, -bel·ling** or **-bel·ing.** —*n.* in architecture, a bracket of stone, wood, etc. on the side of a wall. It helps support a projecting ledge above. —*v.* furnish with corbels; support by corbels. [ME < OF *corbel,* dim. of *corp* raven < L *corvus*]

cor·bie (kôr′bē) *n. Scottish,* a raven; crow. [alteration of ME *corbin* < OF < L *corvinus* of a raven < *corvus* raven]

cord (kôrd) *n.* **1** a thick string; very thin rope. **2** a small, flexible, insulated cable with fittings, used to connect an electrical appliance, as an iron or a lamp, to a socket. **3** anything resembling a cord. **4** a structure in an animal body that resembles a cord; chord. The spinal cord is in the backbone. The vocal cords are in the larynx. **5** a ridge on cloth. **6** cloth with ridges on it; corduroy. **7 cords,** *pl.* corduroy trousers. **8** a measure of cut wood; 128 cubic feet. A pile of wood 4 feet wide, 4 feet high, and 8 feet long is a cord.
—*v.* **1** fasten or tie with a cord; provide with a cord. **2** pile (wood) in cords. [ME < OF *corde* < L < Gk. *chordē* gut. Doublet of CHORD[2].] **—cord·less,** *adj.*

hat, āge, cãre, fär; let, ēqual, tėrm; it, īce
hot, ōpen, ôrder; oil, out; cup, pu̇t, rüle, ūse
əbove, takən, pencəl, lemən, circəs
ch, child; ng, long; sh, ship
th, thin; ᴛʜ, then; zh, measure

cord·age (kôr′dij) *n.* **1** cords; ropes. The cordage of a ship is also called its rigging. **2** a quantity of wood measured in cords.

cor·date (kôr′dāt) *adj.* heart-shaped. [< NL *cordatus* < L *cor, cordis* heart]

cord·ed (kôr′did) *adj.* **1** having ridges on it; ribbed. **2** fastened with a cord; bound with cords. **3** made of cords; furnished with cords. **4** of wood, piled in cords.

cor·delle (kôr del′ or kôr′dəl) *n. v.* **-elled, -el·ling.** *Cdn.* —*n.* a towline. —*v.* tow a canoe, etc. with a cordelle. [< Cdn.F < F *córdelle,* dim. of OF *corde.* See CORD.]

cor·dial (kôr′jəl or kôr′dē əl) *adj.* **1** sincere; hearty; warm; friendly: *a cordial welcome.* **2** strengthening; stimulating. —*n.* **1** a food, drink, or medicine that strengthens or stimulates. **2** a liqueur. [ME < Med.L *cordialis* < L *cor, cordis* heart] **—cor′dial·ly,** *adv.* **—cor′dial·ness,** *n.*

cor·dial·i·ty (kôr jal′ə tē or kôr′dē al′ə tē) *n.* **-ties.** a cordial quality or feeling; sincerity; heartiness; warmth.

cor·dil·le·ra (kôr′dəl yãr′ə or kôr dil′ər ə) *n.* a long mountain range; chain of mountains. [< Sp., ult. < L *chorda* rope, cord. See CORD.]

Cor·dil·le·ran (kôr′dil yãr′ən or kôr dil′ər ən) *adj.* **1** of the Cordilleras, a mountain system in western North America and South America. **2** in the Cordilleras.

cord·ite (kôr′dīt) *n.* a smokeless gunpowder composed chiefly of nitroglycerin and guncotton. [< *cord,* n.]

cor·do·ba (kôr′də bə) *n.* **1** a unit of money in Nicaragua. See table at **money. 2** a coin worth one cordoba. [< Francisco de *Córdoba* (1475-1526), a Spanish explorer]

cor·don (kôr′dən) *n.* **1** a line or circle of soldiers, policemen, forts, etc. placed at intervals to guard a place. **2** a cord, braid, or ribbon worn as an ornament or badge of honor. [< F *cordon* < *corde* cord]

Cor·do·van (kôr′də vən or kôr dō′vən) *adj.* **1** of or having to do with Cordova. **2** of or having to do with a kind of soft leather. —*n.* a kind of soft, fine-grained leather. [< Sp. *cordobán* < *Córdoba,* a city in S. Spain]

cor·du·roy (kôr′də roi′ or kôr′də roi′) *n.* **1** a thick cotton cloth having close, velvetlike ridges. **2** a corduroy road or bridge. **3** the logs comprising a corduroy road or bridge. **4 corduroys,** *pl.* **a** trousers made of corduroy. **b** a corduroy suit.
—*adj.* **1** made of corduroy. **2** having ridges like corduroy.
—*v.* surface or bridge with logs laid crosswise: *They corduroyed the muddy portage road.* [< *cord* + obs. *duroy,* a kind of woollen cloth produced formerly]

corduroy bridge 1 a corduroy road. **2** a bridge built over a stream or river and having a surface of logs laid crosswise.

corduroy road a road or stretch of road surfaced with logs laid crosswise, usually across low-lying, swampy or muddy land.

cord·wain (kôrd′wān) *n. Archaic.* Cordovan leather. [ME < AF *cordewan,* OF *cordouan* < Sp. *cordobán.* See CORDOVAN.]

cord·wain·er (kôrd′wān ər) *n. Obsolete.* a shoemaker. [< AF *cordewaner* < *cordewan* Cordovan < Sp. *cordobán* < *Córdoba*]

cord·wood (kôrd′wu̇d′) *n.* **1** wood sold by the cord; firewood piled in cords. **2** wood cut in 4-foot lengths.

core (kôr) *n. v.* **cored, cor·ing.** —*n.* **1** the hard, central part, containing the seeds, of fruits like apples

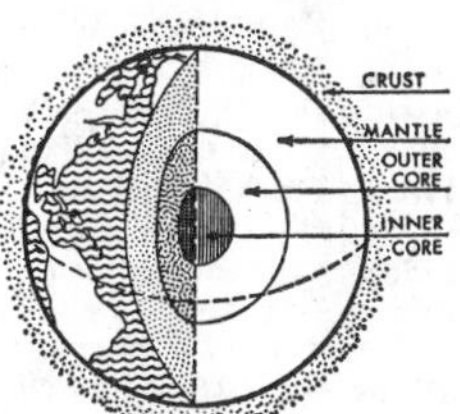

The earth, showing the two divisions of the core (def. 3)

and pears. 2 the central or most important part: *the core of a boil, the core of a hurricane, the core of an argument.* 3 the central part of the earth, probably composed largely of molten iron and having a radius of about 2,100 miles. See picture on the previous page. 4 in electricity: **a** the conducting wire and its insulation in a subterranean or submarine cable. **b** a bar of soft iron, bundle of iron wires, etc. forming the centre of an electromagnet, induction coil, etc., and serving to increase and concentrate the induced magnetic field. 5 in metallurgy, an inner mould made of sand and other ingredients filling the space intended to be left hollow in a hollow casting. 6 **a** the heartwood of a tree. **b** the lumber from this wood, usually soft and inexpensive, used as a base for veneers. 7 the central strand of a rope around which other strands are woven. 8 a cylindrical portion of rock or other material extracted from the centre of a mass by cutting or drilling.
—*v.* take out the core of: *The cook cored the apples.* [ME; origin uncertain] —**cor′er,** *n.* —**Syn.** *n.* 2 heart, essence.

co·re·op·sis (kô′rē op′sis) *n.* 1 a plant of the same family as the aster having yellow, red-and-yellow, or reddish flowers shaped like daisies. 2 the flower. [< NL < Gk. *koris* bedbug + *opsis* appearance; from the shape of the seed]

co-re·spond·ent (kō′rə spon′dənt or kôr′ə spon′dənt) *n.* in law, a person accused of adultery with one (husband or wife) who is being sued for divorce.

cor·gi (kôr′gē) *n.* Welsh corgi.

co·ri·an·der (kô′rē an′dər) *n.* 1 a plant having a disagreeable odor. 2 its seedlike fruit. The oil from the seeds is used as a flavoring and in medicine. [< F *coriandre* < L < Gk. *koriandron,* var. of *koriannon,* the name of this plant]

Co·rin·thi·an (kə rin′thē ən) *adj.* 1 of or having to do with Corinth (a city in S. Greece) or its people. 2 in architecture: **a** of or having to do with the latest of the three orders of ancient Greek architecture, characterized by lightness, grace, and elegant ornamentation. **b** of or having to do with the type of column characteristic of Corinthian architecture. The Corinthian column consists of a tall, slender, deeply fluted, circular shaft, with an ornate bell-shaped capital covered with acanthus leaves and shoots. See **order** for picture.
—*n.* 1 a native or inhabitant of Corinth. 2 **Corinthians,** *pl.* either of two books of the New Testament, written by the Apostle Paul to the Christian people of Corinth.

cork (kôrk) *n.* 1 the light, thick, outer bark of the cork oak, used for bottle stoppers, floats for fishing lines, inner soles of shoes, fillings for some kinds of life preservers, etc. 2 a shaped piece of cork: *the cork of a bottle.* 3 any stopper made of other materials such as glass, rubber, etc. 4 in botany, an outer bark of woody plants, serving as a protective covering.
—*v.* 1 stop up with a cork. 2 confine; restrain; check. 3 blacken with burnt cork.
—*adj.* made of or with cork. [< Sp. *alcorque* < Arabic < L *quercus* oak]

cork·age (kôr′kij) *n.* a charge made by a hotel or restaurant for uncorking and serving wine supplied by a client.

cork oak an oak tree of the Mediterranean area from which cork is obtained.

cork·screw (kôrk′skrü′) *n.* an instrument for pulling out the corks of bottles. —*adj.* shaped like a corkscrew; spiral. —*v.* move or advance in a spiral or zigzag course.

cork tree cork oak.

cork·y (kôr′kē) *adj.* **cork·i·er, cork·i·est.** *Informal.* 1 of cork. 2 like a cork: *a corky flavor.* —**cork′i·ness,** *n.*

corm (kôrm) *n.* in botany, a fleshy, bulblike underground stem that has leaves and buds on the upper surface and roots usually on the lower. [< NL *cormus* < Gk. *kormos* stripped tree trunk < *keirein* shear]

The corm of a crocus

cor·mo·rant (kôr′mə rənt) *n.* 1 a very large, greedy sea bird that has a pouch under its beak for holding captured fish. 2 a greedy person. [ME < OF *cormaran* < *corp* raven (< L *corvus*) + *marenc* of the sea < L *mare*]

corn[1] (kôrn) *n.* 1 a kind of grain that grows on large ears; maize; Indian corn. 2 the plant that it grows on. 3 any small, hard seed or grain, especially of cereal plants. 4 in England, grain in general, especially wheat. 5 in Scotland and Ireland, oats. 6 any small, hard particle, as of sand or salt. 7 in skiing, snow having the consistency of grain or granules. 8 *Slang.* anything trite, sentimental, or old-fashioned.
—*v.* 1 preserve (meat) with strong salt water or by dry salt. 2 form into grains, as gunpowder; granulate. [OE]

corn[2] (kôrn) *n.* a hardening of the skin, usually on a toe. Corns are caused by pressure or rubbing and are often very painful. [ME < OF *corn* horn < L *cornu*]

corn boil corn roast.

corn borer a moth larva that destroys corn and other plants.

corn bread a type of bread made of corn meal instead of flour.

corn·cob (kôrn′kob′) *n.* 1 the central, woody part of an ear of corn, on which the kernels grow. 2 a tobacco pipe with a bowl hollowed out of a piece of dried corncob.

corn cockle a weed having red or white flowers and poisonous seeds that grows in grainfields.

corn crake a bird common in the grainfields of Europe.

corn·crib (kôrn′krib′) *n.* a bin or small, ventilated building for storing unshelled corn.

cor·ne·a (kôr′nē ə) *n.* the transparent part of the outer coat of the eyeball. The cornea covers the iris and the pupil. See **eye** for diagram. [< Med.L *cornea* (*tela*) horny (web) < L *cornu* horn]

cor·ne·al (kôr′nē əl) *adj.* of or having to do with the cornea.

corned (kôrnd) *adj.* 1 preserved with strong salt water or dry salt: *corned beef.* 2 *Slang.* drunk.

cor·nel (kôr′nəl) *n.* 1 in North America, the flowering dogwood. 2 in Europe, a shrub or small tree with yellow flowers. [< G < Med.L *cornolius,* ult. < L *cornus*]

cor·nel·ian (kôr nēl′yən) *n.* carnelian.

cor·ne·ous (kôr′nē əs) *adj.* horny; like horn. [< L *corneus* < *cornu* horn]

cor·ner (kôr′nər) *n.* 1 the point or place where lines or surfaces meet. 2 the space between two lines or surfaces near where they meet; an angle. 3 the place where two streets meet. 4 something that protects or decorates a corner. 5 a secret place; a place away from crowds. 6 a place that is far away; region; part: *People have searched in all corners of the earth for gold.* 7 an awkward or difficult position; a place from which escape is impossible: *a tight corner.* 8 in business, a buying up of the available supply of some stock or article to raise its price: *a corner in cotton.* 9 **cut corners, a** shorten the way by going across corners. **b** save money, effort, time, etc. by cutting down. 10 **turn the corner,** pass the worst or most dangerous point.
—*adj.* 1 at a corner. 2 for a corner.
—*v.* 1 put in a corner; drive into a corner. 2 force into an awkward or difficult position; drive into a place from which escape is impossible. 3 in business, buy up all or nearly all that can be had of (something) to raise its price: *Some speculators have tried to corner wheat.* 4 drive a car around a sharp corner. 5 of an automobile, round sharp corners at relatively high speeds without sway. [ME < AF var. of OF *cornere* < L *cornu* horn, tip]

cor·ner·stone (kôr′nər stōn′) *n.* 1 a stone at the corner of two walls which it holds together. 2 such a stone built into the corner of a building as its formal beginning. The laying of a cornerstone is often accompanied with ceremonies. 3 a main part on which something else rests; foundation; basis: *Clear thinking is the cornerstone of good writing.*

cor·ner·ways (kôr′nər wāz′) *adj.* cornerwise.

cor·ner·wise (kôr′nər wīz′) *adv.* 1 with the corner in front; so as to form a corner. 2 from corner to corner; diagonally.

cor·net[1] (kôr net′ *for 1*; kôr′nit or kôr net′ *for 2*) *n.* 1 a musical wind instrument resembling a trumpet, usually made of brass. It has three pistons that control the notes. 2 a piece of paper rolled into a cone and twisted at one

hat, āge, cãre, fär; let, ēqual, tėrm; it, īce
hot, ōpen, ôrder; oil, out; cup, pu̇t, rüle, ūse
əbove, takən, pencəl, lemən, circəs
ch, child; ng, long; sh, ship
th, thin; ᴛʜ, then; zh, measure

end, used to hold candy, nuts, etc. [ME < OF, ult. < L *cornu* horn]

cor·net[2] (kôr′nit or kôr net′) *n.* **1** a large, spreading, white cap worn by Sisters of Charity. **2** formerly: **a** an officer in a British cavalry troop who carried the flag. **b** a troop of British cavalry. **3** in nautical use, a pennant used as a signal. [< F *cornette*, dim. of *corne*, ult. < L *cornua* horns]

cor·net·tist or **cor·net·ist** (kôr net′ist) *n.* a musician who plays a cornet.

corn·field (kôrn′fēld′) *n.* a field in which corn is grown.

corn·flow·er (kôrn′flou′ər) *n.* a plant having blue, pink, white, or purple flowers; bachelor's-button.

corn·husk (kôrn′husk′) *n.* the husk of an ear of corn.

cor·nice (kôr′nis) *n. v.* **-niced, -nic·ing.** —*n.* **1** in architecture, an ornamental moulding that projects along the top of a wall, pillar, building, etc. See **entablature** for diagram. **2** a moulding, usually of wood or plaster, around the walls of a room just below the ceiling. **3** any of various other ornamental mouldings, as for concealing a curtain rod or otherwise decorating the top of a window. —*v.* furnish or finish with a cornice. [< F < Ital. < Med.Gk. *korōnis* copestone < Gk. *korōnis* something bent]

Cor·nish (kôr′nish) *adj.* of or having to do with Cornwall (a county in England), its people, or the language formerly spoken by them. —*n.* the ancient Celtic language of Cornwall.

Cor·nish·man (kôr′nish mən) *n.* **-men** (-mən). a native or inhabitant of Cornwall.

corn meal meal made from Indian corn; corn ground up.

corn pone in the southern United States, a flat loaf of corn meal shaped by hand; a simple kind of corn bread.

corn roast *Cdn.* a picnic held usually in the fall, at which corn is roasted or boiled for eating off the cob.

corn silk the glossy threads at the end of an ear of corn.

corn·stalk (kôrn′stok′ or -stôk′) *n.* a stalk of Indian corn.

corn·starch (kôrn′stärch′) *n.* a starchy flour made from Indian corn, used to thicken puddings, etc.

corn stook a stack of cornstalks cut and set up on end together in a field.

corn sugar sugar made from cornstarch.

corn syrup syrup made from corn.

cor·nu·co·pi·a (kôr′nyü kō′pē ə) *n.* **1** a horn-shaped container or ornament. **2** the horn of plenty, represented overflowing with fruits and flowers. **3** an overflowing supply; abundance. [< LL *cornucopia*, for L *cornu copiae* horn of plenty]

A cornucopia, or horn of plenty

corn·y (kôr′nē) *adj.* **corn·i·er, corn·i·est.** *Slang.* **1** sentimental or unsophisticated, as certain types of music. **2** trite; of poor quality.

co·rol·la (kə rol′ə) *n.* in botany, the internal envelope or floral leaves of a flower, usually of some color other than green; the petals. [< L *corolla* garland, dim. of *corona* crown]

cor·ol·lar·y (kə rol′ə rē, kə rôl′ə rē, or kôr′ə ler′ē) *n.* **-lar·ies. 1** something proved incidentally in proving something else. **2** an inference; deduction. **3** a natural consequence or result: *Good health is a corollary of having good habits.* [< LL *corollarium* < L *corollarium* gift < *corolla* garland. See COROLLA.]

co·ro·na (kə rō′nə) *n.* **-nas, -nae** (-nē). **1** in astronomy: **a** the ring of light seen around the sun or moon, or some other luminous body. **b** a halo of light around the sun, visible to the naked eye only during an eclipse. **2** a crownlike part; crown. **3** a kind of cigar. [< L *corona* crown. Doublet of CROWN.]

A corona (def. 1)

Corona Aus·tral·is (o strā′lis or ô strā′lis) a southern constellation near Sagittarius; the Southern Crown; Wreath. [< L *Corona australis* the Southern Crown]

Corona Bo·re·al·is (bôr′ē al′is or bôr′ē ā′lis) a northern constellation, the Northern Crown. [< L *Corona borealis* the Northern Crown]

cor·o·nach (kôr′ə nəᴋʜ) *n. Scottish* and *Irish.* a dirge.

cor·o·nal (*n.* kôr′ə nəl; *adj.* kə rō′nəl or kôr′ə nəl) *n.* **1** a crown or coronet. **2** a garland. —*adj.* of or having to do with a crown or a corona.

cor·o·nar·y (kôr′ə ner′ē) *adj.* **1** in anatomy, of or designating either or both of the two arteries that supply blood to the muscular tissue of the heart. **2** having to do with or resembling a crown. —*n. Informal.* a coronary thrombosis. [< L *coronarius* encircling < *corona* crown]

coronary thrombosis the stopping up of a branch of a coronary artery by a blood clot.

cor·o·na·tion (kôr′ə nā′shən) *n.* the ceremony of crowning a king, queen, emperor, etc.

cor·o·ner (kôr′ə nər) *n.* an official of a local government who investigates in the presence of a jury any death not clearly due to natural causes. [ME < AF *corouner* officer of the crown < *coroune.* See CROWN.]

coroner's inquest an inquiry by a coroner, usually with a jury, into the cause of a death that is not clearly due to natural causes.

coroner's jury a group of persons chosen to witness a coroner's investigation and to determine the cause of any death not clearly due to natural causes.

cor·o·net (kôr′ə net′) *n.* **1** a small crown worn as a mark of high rank. A king wears a crown; princes and nobles wear coronets. **2** a circle of gold, jewels, or flowers worn around the head as an ornament. [< MF *coronete,* dim. of OF *corone* crown < L *corona*]

Corp. **1** Corporation. **2** Corporal.

cor·po·ral[1] (kôr′pə rəl or kôr′prəl) *adj.* of or having to do with the body: *corporal punishment.* [< L *corporalis* < *corpus* body]

cor·po·ral[2] (kôr′pə rəl or kôr′prəl) *n.* **1** in the army, a non-commissioned officer senior to a private and junior to a sergeant. **2** in the air force, a non-commissioned officer senior to a leading aircraftman and junior to a sergeant. **3** in the Royal Canadian Mounted Police, a non-commissioned officer senior to a first constable and junior to a staff sergeant. *Abbrev.*: Cpl., Corp. [< F *corporal,* former var. of *caporal* < Ital. *caporale* < *capo* head < L *caput*]

cor·po·ral·cy (kôr′pə rəl sē or kôr′prəl sē) *n.* the rank or position of a corporal.

cor·po·ral·ly (kôr′pə rəl ē or kôr′prəl ē) *adv.* bodily; in or with the body.

corporal punishment punishment inflicted on the body, such as flogging. In law, corporal punishment includes imprisonment and death.

cor·po·rate (kôr′pə rit or kôr′prit) *adj.* **1** forming a corporation; incorporated. **2** belonging to a corporation; having to do with a corporation. **3** united; combined. [< L *corporatus,* pp. of *corporare* form into a body < *corpus* body]

cor·po·rate·ly (kôr′pə rit lē or kôr′prit lē) *adv.* **1** in a corporate capacity. **2** bodily; in the body.

cor·po·ra·tion (kôr′pə rā′shən) *n.* **1** a group of persons having a charter that gives them as a group certain legal rights and privileges distinct from those of the individual members of the group. A corporation can buy and sell, own property, etc. as if it were a single person. **2** a group of persons with authority to act as a single person. The mayor and aldermen of a city are a corporation. **3** *Informal.* a prominent abdomen.

cor·po·re·al (kôr pô′rē əl) *adj.* **1** of or for the body; bodily: *Food and water are corporeal nourishment.*

2 material; tangible: *Land, trees, and money are corporeal things.* [< L *corporeus* < *corpus* body] —**cor·po′re·al·ly,** *adv.*

corps (kôr) *n.* **corps** (kôrz) **1** in the armed services: **a** a formation made up of more than one division. **b** one of the branches that provides special services: *the Signal Corps.* **2** a group of people with special training, organized for working together: *a corps of nurses.* **3** corps de ballet. [< F < OF *corps* < L *corpus* body. Doublet of CORPSE, CORPUS, CORSE.]

corps de bal·let (kôr′də ba lā′; *French,* kôr də bä lā′) a group of ballet dancers, especially the members of a company as distinct from the soloists. [< F]

corpse (kôrps) *n.* a dead body, usually that of a human being. [ME < OF *cors* < L *corpus* body. Doublet of CORPS, CORPUS, CORSE.]

Corps of Commissionaires an organization of ex-servicemen who can be hired as gatekeepers, guards, night watchmen, etc. Members of the Corps of Commissionaires, who wear dark-blue uniforms, are often employed to protect property.

cor·pu·lence (kôr′pyů ləns) *n.* fatness.

cor·pu·len·cy (kôr′pyů lən sē) *n.* corpulence.

cor·pu·lent (kôr′pyů lənt) *adj.* fat. [< L *corpulentus* < *corpus* body] —**cor′pu·lent·ly,** *adv.*

cor·pus (kôr′pəs) *n.* **-po·ra** (-pə rə). **1** a body, especially the dead body of a person or animal. **2** a complete collection of writings on some subject, or of some period, or of laws, etc. **3** any body of material, data, etc., especially as the object of study or research. [< L *corpus* body. Doublet of CORPS, CORPSE, CORSE.]

Cor·pus Chris·ti (kôr′pəs kris′tē) in the Roman Catholic Church and some other Christian churches, the feast in honor of the Eucharist, celebrated on the first Thursday after Trinity Sunday. [< L *corpus Christi* body of Christ]

cor·pus·cle (kôr′pəs əl or kôr′pus əl) *n.* **1** any of the cells that float in the blood, lymph, etc. Red corpuscles carry oxygen and carbon dioxide; some white corpuscles destroy disease germs. **2** a very small particle. [< L *corpusculum,* dim. of *corpus* body]

cor·pus·cu·lar (kôr pus′kyů lər) *adj.* of corpuscles; consisting of corpuscles; like that of corpuscles.

cor·pus de·lic·ti (kôr′pəs di lik′tī or di lik′tē) **1** in law, the actual facts that prove a crime or offence against the law has been committed. **2** *Informal.* the body of a murdered person. [< L *corpus delicti* body of the crime]

cor·pus ju·ris (kôr′pəs jür′is) a complete collection of laws. [< L]

corr. 1 correspondent. **2** corresponding. **3** correspondence. **4** correct. **5** corrected.

cor·ral (kə ral′) *n. v.* **-ralled, -ral·ling.** —*n.* **1** an enclosed space where horses, cattle, etc. are captured or kept. **2** a circular camp formed by wagons, carts, etc. for defence against attack. **3** a trap for game, fish, etc.
—*v.* **1** drive into or keep in a corral. **2** hem in; surround; capture. **3** form (wagons) into a circular camp. **4** *Slang.* catch; get; collect: *Our club has corralled several new members.* [< Sp. *corral* < *corro* ring. Doublet of CRAWL².]

cor·rect (kə rekt′) *adj.* **1** agreeing with fact or reason; free from mistakes or faults; right: *the correct answer.* **2** agreeing with a recognized standard; proper: *correct manners.*
—*v.* **1** change to what is right; remove mistakes or faults from: *Correct any wrong spellings that you find.* **2** alter or adjust to agree with some standard: *correct the reading of a barometer.* **3** point out or mark the errors of: *The teacher corrects the test papers and returns them to the students.* **4** set right by punishing; find fault with in order to improve; punish: *The mother corrected the child.* **5** counteract (something hurtful); cure; overcome: *Medicine can sometimes correct stomach trouble.* [< L *correctus,* pp. of *corrigere* make straight < *com-* + *regere* direct] —**cor·rect′a·ble,** *adj.* —**cor·rect′ly,** *adv.* —**cor·rect′ness,** *n.* —**cor·rec′tor,** *n.*

Syn. *adj.* **1 Correct, accurate, exact** = without error or mistake. **Correct,** the most general word, suggests only the absence of mistakes or errors: *He gave correct answers to the questions.* **Accurate** emphasizes the suggestion of careful effort to make something agree with facts or a model: *He gave an accurate account of the accident.* **Exact** emphasizes the suggestion of complete agreement in every detail with the facts or model: *His painting is an exact copy of the original.* –*v.* **1** amend. **4** discipline. **5** remedy.

cor·rect·ed (kə rek′tid) *adj.* made free from mistakes or faults.

cor·rec·tion (kə rek′shən) *n.* **1** the act of correcting. **2** something put in place of an error or mistake. **3** a punishment; rebuke; scolding. **4** an amount added or subtracted to correct a result. **5** the counteracting or neutralizing of harmful or unpleasant effects, as of a medicine.

cor·rec·tion·al (kə rek′shən əl) *adj.* of or having to do with correction; corrective.

cor·rec·tive (kə rek′tiv) *adj.* tending to correct; setting right; making better: *Corrective exercises will make weak muscles strong.* —*n.* something that tends to correct or set right anything that is wrong or hurtful. —**cor·rec′tive·ly,** *adv.*

cor·re·late (kôr′ə lāt′) *v.* **-lat·ed, -lat·ing. 1** be related one to the other; have a mutual relation: *Robert's teacher explained that the diameter and the circumference of a circle correlate.* **2** place in or bring into proper relation with one another; show the connection or relation between: *Try to correlate your conclusions with the facts.* —*n.* either of two related things, especially when one implies the other. [< *cor-* together + *relate*]

cor·re·lat·ed (kôr′ə lāt′id) *adj.* related one to another.

cor·re·la·tion (kôr′ə lā′shən) *n.* **1** the mutual relation of two or more things: *There is a close correlation between climate and vegetation.* **2** a correlating or being correlated.

cor·rel·a·tive (kə rel′ə tiv) *adj.* **1** mutually dependent; so related that each implies the other. **2** in grammar, having a mutual relation and commonly used together. Conjunctions used in pairs, such as *either . . . or* and *both . . . and,* are correlative words.
—*n.* **1** either of two closely related things. **2** in grammar, a correlative word. —**cor·rel′a·tive·ly,** *adv.*

cor·re·spond (kôr′ə spond′) *v.* **1** be in harmony; agree: *Her white hat and shoes correspond with her white dress.* **2** be similar: *The arms of a man correspond to the wings of a bird.* **3** agree in amount or position. **4** exchange letters; write letters to each other. [< Med.L *correspondere* < L *com-* together, with + *respondere* answer] —**Syn. 1** harmonize, match. See **agree. 2** parallel.

cor·re·spond·ence (kôr′ə spon′dəns) *n.* **1** an agreement; harmony. **2** a similarity; resemblance in structure or function. **3** an exchange of letters; letter writing. **4** letters: *answer your correspondence.* **5** in mathematics, a matching of the members of one set of objects with the members of a second set of objects.

correspondence course a set of lessons on a certain subject given by a correspondence school.

correspondence school a school that gives lessons by mail. Instructions, explanations, and questions are sent to the student, and he returns his written answers for correction or approval.

cor·re·spond·ent (kôr′ə spon′dənt) *n.* **1** a person who exchanges letters with another. **2** a person employed by a newspaper, a radio or television network, etc. to send news from a distant place. A foreign correspondent is a reporter who gathers news in another country. **3** a person or company that has regular business with another in a distant place: *This important bank has correspondents in all the large cities of the world.* **4** anything that corresponds to something else.
—*adj.* corresponding; in agreement.

cor·re·spond·ing (kôr′ə spon′ding) *adj.* **1** agreeing; in harmony. **2** similar; matching. **3** exchanging letters; writing letters to each other.

cor·re·spond·ing·ly (kôr′ə spon′ding lē) *adv.* in a corresponding manner; so as to correspond.

cor·ri·dor (kôr′ə dər or kôr′ə dôr′) *n.* **1** a long hallway; passage in a large building from which doors lead into separate rooms. **2** a narrow strip of land connecting two parts of a country or an inland country with a seaport. [< F < Provençal *corredor* < *correr* run < L *currere*] —**Syn. 1** passageway, hall.

hat, āge, cãre, fär; let, ēqual, tėrm; it, īce
hot, ōpen, ôrder; oil, out; cup, pu̇t, rüle, ūse
əbove, takən, pencəl, lemən, circəs
ch, child; ng, long; sh, ship
th, thin; ᴛʜ, then; zh, measure

cor·rie (kôr′ē) *n. Scottish.* a circular hollow on a mountainside; cirque. [< Scots Gaelic *coire*, literally, cauldron]

cor·ri·gen·dum (kôr′ə jen′dəm) *n.* **-da** (-də). an error in a book, manuscript, etc. to be corrected. [< L *corrigendum* (thing) to be corrected < *corrigere.* See CORRECT.]

cor·ri·gi·ble (kôr′ə jə bəl) *adj.* **1** that can be corrected. **2** yielding to correction; willing to be corrected. **—cor′ri·gi·bil′i·ty,** *n.* **—cor′ri·gi·bly,** *adv.* [Med.L *corrigibilis* < L *corrigere.* See CORRECT.]

cor·rob·o·rate (kə rob′ə rāt′) *v.* **-rat·ed, -rat·ing.** make more certain; confirm: *Witnesses corroborated the policeman's statement.* [< L *corroborare* strengthen < *com-* + *robur* oak] **—cor·rob′o·ra′tor,** *n.* **—Syn.** See **confirm.**

cor·rob·o·ra·tion (kə rob′ə rā′shən) *n.* **1** confirmation by additional proof. **2** something that corroborates; additional proof.

cor·rob·o·ra·tive (kə rob′ər ə tiv or kə rob′ə rā′tiv) *adj.* corroborating; confirming. **—cor·rob′o·ra′tive·ly,** *adv.*

cor·rob·o·ra·to·ry (kə rob′ə rə tô′rē) *adj.* corroborative.

cor·rob·o·ree (kə rob′ər ē) *n.* **1** a tribal dance of Australian aborigines, held at night. **2** *Esp.Australian.* a noisy gathering or celebration. [< Australian native name]

cor·rode (kə rōd′) *v.* **-rod·ed, -rod·ing.** **1** eat away gradually, especially by or as if by chemical action: *Rust had corroded the steel rails. Ambition had corroded his natural generosity.* **2** become corroded. [< L *corrodere* < *com-* + *rodere* gnaw]

cor·rod·ed (kə rōd′id) *adj.* eaten away.

cor·ro·sion (kə rō′zhən) *n.* **1** the act or process of corroding. **2** a corroded condition. **3** a product of corroding, such as rust. [< LL *corrosio, -onis* < *corrodere.* See CORRODE.]

cor·ro·sive (kə rō′siv) *adj.* producing corrosion; corroding; eating away. —*n.* a substance that corrodes: *Most acids are corrosives.* **—cor·ro′sive·ly,** *adv.*

corrosive sublimate bichloride of mercury.

cor·ru·gate (kôr′ə gāt′) *v.* **-gat·ed, -gat·ing.** bend or shape (a surface or a thin sheet of material) into wavelike folds; wrinkle; furrow. [< L *corrugare* < *com-* (intensive) + *ruga* wrinkle]

cor·ru·gat·ed (kôr′ə gāt′id) *adj.* bent or shaped into a row of wavelike ridges: *corrugated iron, corrugated paper.*

corrugated iron sheet iron or steel, usually galvanized, that is shaped into curved ridges. It is sometimes used for roofs, walls, etc.

corrugated paper paper or cardboard that is bent into a row of wavelike ridges, used in wrapping packages, etc.

cor·ru·ga·tion (kôr′ə gā′shən) *n.* **1** a corrugating. **2** a being corrugated. **3** one of a series of wavelike ridges; a wrinkle; furrow.

cor·rupt (kə rupt′) *adj.* **1** evil; wicked. **2** influenced by bribes; dishonest: *a corrupt judge.* **3 a** of a text, manuscript, etc., damaged by inaccurate copying, insertions, alterations, etc.: *The manuscript is so corrupt that parts of it make no sense at all.* **b** of a language, dialect, form, etc., considered inferior by some because of change in meaning or form, or deviation from standard usage: *Some people use corrupt English.* **4** rotten; decayed. —*v.* **1** make evil or wicked. **2** bribe. **3 a** make worse by changing; make impure or incorrect. **b** cause (a form, meaning, dialect, etc.) to differ from standard usage. **4** rot; decay. **5** become corrupt. [< L *corruptus,* pp. of *corrumpere* < *com-* + *rumpere* break] **—cor·rupt′er,** *n.* **—cor·rupt′ly,** *adv.* **—cor·rupt′ness,** *n.*

Syn. *adj.* **1 Corrupt, depraved** = made morally bad. **Corrupt** emphasizes the idea that the person or thing was good, pure, honorable and has been made bad by evil influences: *The Medical Association took away the licence of the doctor because of his corrupt practices.* **Depraved** emphasizes the idea that a person's morals have become worse and worse until his character, desires, pleasures, etc. are evil: *This murder was committed by a depraved criminal.*

cor·rupt·i·bil·i·ty (kə rup′tə bil′ə tē) *n.* a corruptible quality; willingness to be bribed.

cor·rupt·i·ble (kə rup′tə bəl) *adj.* **1** that can be corrupted; that can be bribed. **2** liable to be corrupted; perishable. **—cor·rupt′i·ble·ness,** *n.* **—cor·rupt′i·bly,** *adv.*

cor·rup·tion (kə rup′shən) *n.* **1** a making or being made evil or wicked. **2** evil conduct; wickedness. **3** bribery; dishonesty: *The police force must be kept free of corruption.* **4 a** a changing for the worse; making impure or incorrect. **b** the causing of (a form, meaning, dialect, etc.) to differ from standard usage: *the corruption of a language.* **5** rot; decay. **6** the matter that comes out of pimples and boils; pus. **7** a corrupting influence; thing that causes corruption.

cor·rup·tive (kə rup′tiv) *adj.* tending to corrupt; causing corruption.

cor·sage (kôr säzh′) *n.* **1** a bouquet to be worn at a woman's waist, on her shoulder, etc. **2** the upper part of a woman's dress. [< F < OF < *cors* body < L *corpus*]

cor·sair (kôr′sãr) *n.* **1** a privateer, especially a Saracen or Turkish privateer of the Barbary Coast. **2** a pirate. **3** the ship of a pirate or a privateer. [< F *corsaire* < Ital. < VL *cursarius* runner < L *cursus* a run. Doublet of HUSSAR.]

corse (kôrs) *n. Archaic and poetic.* corpse. [ME < OF *cors* < L *corpus* body. Doublet of CORPS, CORPSE, CORPUS.]

corse·let (kôrs′lit *for 1*; kôr′sə let′ *for 2*) *n.* **1** a piece of armor for the body. Also, **corslet. 2** a woman's undergarment that combines a brassiere and a girdle. [< F *corselet,* double of dim. of OF *cors* body. See CORPSE.]

cor·set (kôr′sit) *n.* Sometimes, **corsets,** *pl.* **1** a close-fitting undergarment, made of a firm woven material and usually boned, laced, and hooked, that extends from the waist or above the waist to below the hips. **2** a corselet. **3** a close-fitting undergarment of firm woven material, often laced and hooked, that may be worn for support or correction of injured or deformed muscles or bones. [< F *corset,* dim. of OF *cors* body. See CORPSE.]

Cor·si·can (kôr′sə kən) *adj.* of or having to do with Corsica (a French island in the Mediterranean Sea), its people, or their dialect. —*n.* **1** a native or inhabitant of Corsica. **2** an Italian dialect spoken in Corsica. **3 the Corsican,** Napoleon Bonaparte.

cors·let (kôrs′lit) *n.* corselet (def. 1).

cor·tege or **cor·tège** (kôr tāzh′ or kôr tezh′) *n.* **1** a procession: *The funeral cortege was a mile long.* **2** a group of followers, attendants, etc.; retinue. [< F < Ital. *corteggio* < *corte* court]

Cor·tes (kôr′tez or kôr′tes) *n.* in Spain, the national legislature.

cor·tex (kôr′teks) *n.* **-ti·ces** (-tə sēz′). **1** in botany, bark or rind. **2** in anatomy and zoology, the outer layers of an internal organ: *the cortex of the kidney.* **3** in anatomy, the layer of gray matter that covers most of the surface of the brain: *the cerebral cortex.* [< L *cortex* bark]

cor·ti·cal (kôr′tə kəl) *adj.* **1** of or having to do with a cortex. **2** consisting of cortex. **—cor′ti·cal·ly,** *adv.*

cor·ti·cate (kôr′tə kāt′) *adj.* having a cortex; covered with bark. [< L *corticatus* < *cortex* bark]

cor·ti·cat·ed (kôr′tə kāt′id) *adj.* corticate.

cor·ti·sone (kôr′tə zōn′) *n.* a hormone obtained from the cortex of the adrenal gland, used in the treatment of rheumatoid arthritis, certain skin diseases, etc. Also, **Compound E.**

co·run·dum (kə run′dəm) *n.* an extremely hard mineral consisting of aluminum oxide. The dark-colored variety is used for polishing and grinding. Sapphires and rubies are transparent varieties of corundum. *Formula:* Al_2O_3 [< Tamil *kurundam*; cf. Skt. *kuruvinda* ruby]

cor·us·cate (kôr′əs kāt′) *v.* **-cat·ed, -cat·ing.** give off flashes of light; sparkle; glitter. [< L *coruscare* < *coruscus* darting, flashing]

cor·us·ca·tion (kôr′əs kā′shən) *n.* **1** a flash of light; sparkle. **2** a flashing; sparkling.

cor·vée (kôr vā′) *n.* **1** unpaid work done by a peasant for his feudal lord. **2** unpaid or partly unpaid labor imposed by authorities on the residents of a district. [< F < Med.L *corrogata* (*opera*) (work) requisitioned

< L *corrogare* < *com-* together + *rogare* ask]

cor·vette or **cor·vet** (kôr vet′) *n.* **1** formerly, a warship equipped with sails and only one tier of guns. **2** a small warship for use in antisubmarine and convoy work. [? < MDu. *korf,* a kind of ship < L *corbis* basket]

cor·vine (kôr′vīn or kôr′vin) *adj.* of or like a crow. [< L *corvinus* < *corvus* crow]

Cor·y·bant (kôr′ə bant′) *n.* **Cor·y·ban·tes** (kôr′ə ban′tēz) or **Cor·y·bants. 1** one of the attendants of Cybele, an ancient nature goddess of Asia Minor. The Corybantes followed her over the mountains by torchlight with wild music and dancing. **2** a priest of Cybele.

Cor·y·ban·tic (kôr′ə ban′tik) *adj.* **1** of the Corybantes. **2** resembling the Corybantes or their rites.

cor·ymb (kôr′imb or kôr′im) *n.* in botany, a flat cluster of flowers in which the outer flowers blossom first. Small flowers on short stems grow from a longer, central stem to form a round, rather flat cluster. Cherry blossoms are corymbs. [< L *corymbus* < Gk. *korymbos* top, cluster]

co·rym·bose (kə rim′bōs) *adj.* **1** growing in corymbs. **2** of or like a corymb.

cor·y·phée (kôr′ə fā′) *n.* **1** the leader of a dance. **2** in some ballet companies, a dancer ranking below a soloist but above the corps de ballet. **3** any ballet dancer. [< F < L < Gk. *koryphaios* leader < *koryphē* head]

co·ry·za (kə rī′zə) *n.* a cold in the head. [< LL < Gk. *koryza* catarrh]

cos[1] (kos) *n.* a kind of lettuce. [< the island of *Cos* in the Aegean Sea]

cos[2] cosine.

cos. 1 companies. **2** countries.

Cosa Nostra a secret criminal society; the Mafia. [< Ital.; literally, "our affair"]

cosec cosecant.

co·se·cant (kō sē′kənt or -sē′kant) *n.* in trigonometry, the ratio of the length of the hypotenuse to the length of the opposite side; the secant of the complement of a given angle or arc. See **cosine** for diagram.

co·sig·na·to·ry (kō sig′nə tô′ rē) *adj. n.* **-ries.** —*adj.* signing along with another or others. —*n.* a person who signs something along with another or others.

co·sine (kō′sīn′) *n.* in trigonometry, the ratio of the length of the adjacent side to the length of the hypotenuse; the sine of the complement of a given angle or arc.

BC being the hypotenuse in the right triangle ABC, the cosine of angle ACB is AC/BC; the cosecant of angle ACB is BC/AB; and the cotangent of angle ACB is AC/AB.

cos·met·ic (koz met′ik) *n.* a preparation for beautifying the skin, hair, nails, etc. Powder, lipstick, and face creams are cosmetics. —*adj.* **1** beautifying to the skin, hair, nails, etc. **2** of or having to do with cosmetics. —**cos·met′i·cal·ly,** *adv.* [< Gk. *kosmētikos* of order, adornment < *kosmos* order]

cos·mic (koz′mik) *adj.* **1** of or belonging to the cosmos; having to do with the whole universe: *Cosmic forces produce stars and meteors.* **2** vast. [< Gk. *kosmikos* < *kosmos* order, world]

cos·mi·cal·ly (koz′mik lē) *adv.* according to cosmic laws; on a vast or cosmic scale.

cosmic dust fine particles of matter falling upon the earth from outer space.

cosmic noise radio-frequency radiation from the Milky Way that may be detected by radio receivers.

cosmic rays rays of very short wave lengths and very great penetration that come to the earth from beyond the earth's atmosphere.

cos·mo·gon·ic (koz′mə gon′ik) *adj.* of or having to do with cosmogony.

cos·mog·o·nist (koz mog′ə nist) *n.* an expert in cosmogony.

cos·mog·o·ny (koz mog′ə nē) *n.* **-nies. 1** the origin of the universe. **2** a theory of its origin. [< Gk. *kosmogonia* < *kosmos* world + *gonos* birth]

cos·mog·ra·pher (koz mog′rə fər) *n.* an expert in cosmography.

cos·mo·graph·ic (koz′mə graf′ik) *adj.* of or about cosmography.

cos·mog·ra·phy (koz mog′rə fē) *n.* **1** the science that deals with the general appearance and structure of the universe. Cosmography includes astronomy, geography, and geology. **2** a description of the general features of the earth or the universe. [< Gk. *kosmographia* < *kosmos* world + *graphein* write]

cos·mo·log·i·cal (koz′mə loj′ə kəl) *adj.* of or having to do with cosmology.

cos·mol·o·gist (koz mol′ə jist) *n.* an expert in cosmology.

cos·mol·o·gy (koz mol′ə jē) *n.* the science or theory of the universe, its parts, and its laws. [< Gk. *kosmos* world + E *-logy*]

cos·mo·naut (koz′mə not′ or koz′mə nôt′) *n.* astronaut.

cos·mo·pol·i·tan (koz′mə pol′ə tən) *adj.* **1** belonging to all parts of the world; not limited to any one country or its inhabitants; widely spread: *Music is one of the most cosmopolitan of the arts.* **2** free from national or local prejudices; feeling at home in any part of the world. **3** having to do with or characteristic of a cosmopolitan person. **4** of animals and plants, widely distributed over the earth.
—*n.* a cosmopolitan person or thing; a person who feels at home in all parts of the world.

cos·mop·o·lite (koz mop′ə līt′) *n.* **1** a cosmopolitan person. **2** an animal or plant found in all or many parts of the world. [< Gk. *kosmopolitēs* < *kosmos* world + *politēs* citizen < *polis* city]

cos·mos (koz′məs or koz′mos) *n.* **1** the universe thought of as an orderly, harmonious system; the opposite of chaos. **2** any complete system that is orderly and harmonious. **3** a tall garden plant of the aster family, having much-divided leaves and white, pink, purple, or orange flowers that bloom in the fall. [< NL < Gk. *kosmos* order, world]

cos·mo·tron (koz′mə tron′) *n.* a nuclear accelerator designed to produce particles with energy of over two billion electron volts. [apparently < *cosmic* + *cyclotron*]

Cos·sack (kos′ak) *n.* **1** a people living in S. Soviet Union, noted as horsemen. **2** a member of this people. [< Russian *kozak, kazak*]

cos·set (kos′it) *n.* a pet lamb; a pet. [< v.] —*v.* treat as a pet; pamper. [OE **cossettan* kiss < *coss* a kiss]

cost (kost) *n. v.* **cost, cost·ing.** —*n.* **1** the price paid: *The cost of this hat was $10.* **2** a loss; sacrifice: *The poor fox escaped from the trap at the cost of a leg.* **3** outlay or expenditure of time, labor, trouble, effort, etc. **4 at all costs** or **at any cost,** by all means; no matter what must be done. **5 costs,** *pl.* the expenses of a lawsuit or case in court.
—*v.* **1** be obtained at the price of: *This hat costs $10.* **2** require: *The production of the school play cost much time and effort.* **3** estimate the expenditure required for the production or completion of: *The company is costing a new project.* [ME < OF *cost* < *coster* < L *constare* < *com-* with + *stare* stand] —**Syn.** *n.* **1** See **price.**

cost accountant an accountant who specializes in cost accounting.

cost accounting 1 a system of accounting that records all expenses, including overhead, incurred in making and distributing a product. **2** the keeping of such accounts.

cos·tal (kos′təl) *adj.* in anatomy, having to do with a rib or the ribs. [< LL *costalis* < L *costa* rib]

co-star (*n.* kō′stär′; *v.* kō′stär′) *n. v.* **-starred, -star·ring.** —*n.* an actor or actress of equal prominence with another (or others) playing a leading role in a motion picture, play, etc. —*v.* be or cause to be a co-star.

cos·tard (kos′tərd) *n.* a variety of large English apple. [earlier meaning, "a ribbed apple"; probably < OF *coste* rib < L *costa*]

Cos·ta Ri·can (kos′tə rē′kən) **1** of or having to do with Costa Rica (a country in Central America) or its people. **2** a native or inhabitant of Costa Rica.

cos·ter (kos′tər) *n.* costermonger.

cos·ter·mon·ger (kos′tər mung′gər or -mong′gər) *n. Brit.* a person who sells fruit, vegetables, fish, etc. from a handcart or stand in the street. [earlier *costardmonger* < *costard* + *monger* dealer, trader]

cos·tive (kos′tiv) *adj.* **1** constipated. **2** producing constipation. [ME < OF *costive* < L *constipatus*, pp. of *constipare*. Doublet of CONSTIPATE.] —**cos′tive·ly,** *adv.* —**cos′tive·ness,** *n.*

cost·li·ness (kost′lē nis) *n.* great cost; expensiveness.

cost·ly (kost′lē) *adj.* **-li·er, -li·est. 1** of great value: *costly jewels.* **2** costing much: *costly mistakes.* **3** costing too much. —**Syn. 1** precious, valuable, sumptuous, rich. **2** dear. See **expensive.**

cost of living the average price paid by a person, family, etc. for food, rent, clothing, transportation, etc. within a given period.

cost of living index a comparative study of the cost of living in a country or area; in Canada, especially that made monthly by the Dominion Bureau of Statistics.

cost plus an arrangement or contract under which the selling price is based on the cost of production plus an agreed profit.

cos·tume (*n.* kos′tūm; *v.* kos tūm′) *n. v.* **-tumed, -tum·ing.** —*n.* **1** a style of dress, outer clothing, etc., including the way the hair is worn, kind of jewellery worn, etc. **2** dress belonging to another time or place, worn on the stage, at masquerades, etc.: *The actors wore Spanish costumes.* **3** a complete set of outer garments: *a street costume, a hunting costume.*
—*v.* provide a costume or costumes for; dress. [< F < Ital. < VL *consuetumen* custom. Doublet of CUSTOM.]

cos·tum·er (kos tūm′ər) *n.* a person who makes, sells, or rents costumes or dresses.

cos·tum·i·er (kos tūm′ē ər; *French,* kôs tʏ myā′) *n.* costumer.

co·sy (kō′zē) *adj.* **co·si·er, co·si·est,** *n.* **co·sies.** —*adj.* warm and comfortable; snug: *She liked to read in a cosy corner by the fire.* —*n.* a padded cloth cover used to keep a teapot warm. Also, **cozy.** [< Scand., origin uncertain] —**co′si·ly,** *adv.* —**co′si·ness,** *n.* —**Syn.** *adj.* See **snug.**

cot[1] (kot) *n.* **1** a narrow bed, sometimes made of canvas stretched on a frame that folds together. **2** *Brit.* a child's crib. [< Anglo-Indian < Hind. *khāt*; cf. Skt. *khatvā*]

cot[2] (kot) *n.* **1** a cottage; small house. **2** something small built for shelter or protection. **3** a protective covering; sheath: *a cot for an injured finger.* [OE]

cot[3] cotangent.

co·tan·gent (kō tan′ jənt) *n.* in trigonometry, the ratio of the length of the adjacent side (not the hypotenuse) to the length of the opposite side; the tangent of the complement of a given angle or arc. See **cosine** for diagram.

COTC or **C.O.T.C.** Canadian Officers Training Corps.

cote (kōt) *n.* a shelter or shed for small animals, birds, etc.: *a dovecote.* [OE. Related to COT[2].]

co·teau (kə tō′; *French,* kō tō′) *n.* **1** a small hill; hillock. **2** a line of hills or ridges, often functioning as a watershed. [< Cdn.F]

co·ten·ant (kō ten′ənt) *n.* one of a group of tenants of the same place; joint tenant.

co·te·rie (kō′tə rē) *n.* a set or circle of acquaintances; group of people who often meet socially. [< F *coterie*, originally, an association for tenants of the same farm owner < OF *cotier* cotter < *cote* hut < MDu. *kote*] —**Syn.** clique, ring.

co·ter·mi·nous (kō tėr′mə nəs) *adj.* **1** having a common boundary; bordering; meeting at their ends. **2** having the same boundaries or limits; co-extensive. Also, **conterminous.** [< L *conterminus* < *com-* with + *terminus* boundary]

co·til·lion (kə til′yən) *n.* **1** a dance with complicated steps and much changing of partners, led by one couple. **2** a quadrille. **3** a piece of music for a cotillion. [< F *cotillon*, originally, petticoat, dim. of *cotte* coat]

Cots·wold (kots′wōld or kots′wəld) *n.* **1** a breed of large sheep having long wool. **2** an animal of this breed. [< *Cotswolds,* hills in S.W. England]

hat, āge, cãre, fär; let, ēqual, tėrm; it, īce
hot, ōpen, ôrder; oil, out; cup, pu̇t, rüle, ūse
əbove, takən, pencəl, lemən, circəs
ch, child; ng, long; sh, ship
th, thin; ᴛʜ, then; zh, measure

cot·tage (kot′ij) *n.* **1** a small house, especially in the suburbs or the country. **2** a house at a summer resort. [< *cot*[2]]
Syn. 1 Cottage, cabin = a small house. **Cottage,** the general word, once applied only to a small, simple house lived in by poor people, but now applies to any small and simple house: *He has an apartment in town and a cottage in the country.* **Cabin** applies to a small, roughly built or rough-looking house: *He has a hunting cabin in the hills.*

cottage cheese a soft, white cheese made from the curds of sour milk.

cottage pudding cake covered with a sweet sauce.

cot·tag·er (kot′ij er) *n.* **1** a person who lives in a cottage. **2** a person who has a summer cottage in a municipality and is thus only a part-time resident there.

cot·ter[1] (kot′ər) *n.* **1** a pin or wedge that is inserted through a slot to hold small parts of machinery, etc. together. **2** a cotter pin. [origin uncertain]

cot·ter[2] or **cot·tar** (kot′ər) *n.* in Scotland, a man who works for a farmer and is allowed to use a small cottage and a plot of land. [< Med.L *cotarius* < *cota* < OE *cot* cot[2]]

cotter pin a split pin used as a cotter. The ends are bent outwards to keep it in its slot.

A cotter pin

cot·to·lene (kot′ə lēn′) *n.* a preparation of cottonseed oil, used as a shortening in cooking.

cot·ton (kot′ən) *n.* **1** soft, white fibres in a fluffy mass around the seeds of a plant of the mallow family, used in making fabrics, thread, guncotton, etc. **2** the plant that produces these fibres. **3** the crop of such plants. **4** a thread made of cotton fibres. **5** cloth made of cotton thread. **6** any downy substance resembling cotton fibres, growing on other plants.
—*adj.* made of cotton.
—*v. Slang.* **1** agree; get along. **2** take a liking. **3 cotton on,** understand. [ME < OF *coton* < Ital. *cotone* < Arabic *qutn*]

cotton batting soft, fluffy cotton pressed into thin layers.

cotton candy a light, fluffy candy made by spinning melted sugar.

cotton gin a machine for separating the fibres of cotton from the seeds.

cotton grass any of a group of plants of the sedge family having cottonlike spikes.

cot·ton·seed (kot′ən sēd′) *n.* **-seed** or **-seeds.** the seed of cotton, used for making cottonseed oil, fertilizer, cattle food, etc.

cottonseed oil oil pressed from cottonseed, used for cooking, for making soap, etc.

cot·ton·tail (kot′ən tāl′) *n.* a common North American wild rabbit having a fluffy, white tail.

cot·ton·wood (kot′ən wu̇d′) *n.* **1** any of several varieties of North American poplar. All poplars have cottonlike tufts of white hair on the tiny seeds. **2** the wood of any of these trees.

cotton wool raw cotton, before or after picking.

cot·ton·y (kot′ən ē) *adj.* **1** of cotton. **2** like cotton; soft; fluffy; downy.

cot·y·le·don (kot′ə lē′dən) *n.* in botany, an embryo leaf in the seed of a plant; the first leaf, or one of the first pair of leaves, growing from a seed. [< L < Gk. *kotylēdōn* cup-shaped hollow < *kotylē* small vessel]

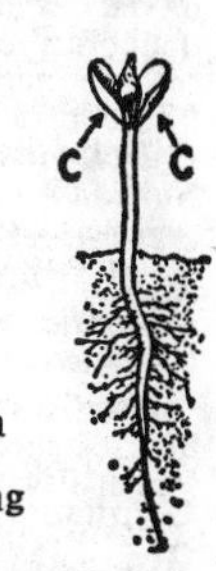

C, a cotyledon

cot·y·le·don·ous (kot′ə lē′dən əs) *adj.* having cotyledons.

couch (kouch) *n.* **1** a piece of furniture on which to sleep or rest, usually wide enough for one person to lie down on. A chesterfield is a couch. **2** any place to sleep or rest: *The deer sprang up from its grassy couch.* **3** *Poetic.* a bed. **4** the burrow of an otter. **5** the frame on which barley is spread to be malted. **6** a coat of paint, varnish, or other material.
—*v.* **1** put on a couch. **2** lie down on a couch. **3** put in words; express: *Some poets couch their ideas in beautiful language.* **4** lower; bring down; put in a level position ready to attack: *The knights couched their lances and prepared to charge.* **5** lie hidden ready to attack. [ME < OF *couche* < *coucher* lay in place < L *collocare* < *com-* (intensive) + *locus* a place] —**couch′like′**, *adj.*

couch·ant (kouch′ənt) *adj.* in heraldry, lying down, but with the head raised. [< F *couchant*, ppr. of *coucher* lie]

couch grass a coarse, weedlike grass whose stems creep underground and spread very rapidly in all directions.

cou·gar (kü′gər) *n.* a large, tawny American wildcat; puma; mountain lion. [< F *couguar* < NL < Tupi-Guarani *guaçu ara*]

cough (kof) *v.* **1** force air from the lungs with sudden effort and noise. **2 cough up, a** expel from the throat by coughing. **b** *Slang.* give; bring out; produce; pay what is due.
—*n.* **1** the act of coughing. **2** the sound or a sound of coughing. **3** repeated acts of coughing. **4** the condition or symptom of coughing at short intervals: *She has a bad cough.* [ME *coghen*, related to OE *cohhetan*]

cough drop a small tablet containing medicine to relieve coughs, hoarseness, etc.

cough·ing (kof′ing) *n.* the forcing of air from the lungs with a harsh sound.

could (kůd; unstressed, kəd) *v.* pt. of **can.** [OE *cūthe*; the *l* was inserted on analogy with *should, would.*]
☛ **could, might.** *Could*, the past of *can*, and *might*, originally the past of *may*, are now used chiefly to convey a shade of doubt, or a slight degree of possibility: *It might be all right for her, but it isn't for me. Perhaps I could write a poem, but I doubt it.*

could·n't (kůd′ənt) could not.

couldst (kůdst) *v. Archaic or poetic.* could. "Thou couldst" means "You could" (sing.).

cou·lee (kü′lē) *n.* **1** in the western parts of Canada and the United States, a deep ravine or gulch that is usually dry in summer. **2** a stream of lava. [< F *coulée*, fem. pp. of *couler* flow < L *colare* strain]

cou·loir (kü lwär′) *n.* a deep gorge or gully on the side of a mountain. [< F < OF *couloir* passage, literally, a slide, glide < *couler* flow. See COULEE.]

cou·lomb (kü lom′) *n.* the quantity of electricity furnished by a current of one ampere in one second. [after Charles A. de *Coulomb* (1736-1806), a French physicist]

coul·ter or **col·ter** (kōl′tər) *n.* a sharp blade or disk on a plough to cut the earth ahead of the ploughshare.

coun·cil (koun′səl) *n.* **1** a group of people called together to give advice, talk things over, or settle questions. **2** a small group of people elected by citizens to make laws for and govern a city, town, village, municipal district, or township. **3** a group of people appointed to advise a monarch, governor, etc.: *the Privy Council.* **4** the deliberation or consultation that takes place at the meeting of a council. **5 in council, a** at a meeting of a council. **b** in consultation; deliberating together: *The family is in council planning a vacation.* [ME < OF *concile* < L *concilium* < *com-* together + *calare* call]—**Syn. 1** assembly.
☛ **council, counsel.** *Council* is a noun: *They called together a council* (group) *of the town's industrial leaders. Counsel* may be a noun or a verb: *Mrs. Smith could always be counted on for good counsel* (advice). *Each side tried to get Mr. Avery as its counsel* (adviser). *I do not like to counsel* (advise) *you on that point.*

coun·cil·lor or **coun·cil·or** (koun′sə lər or koun′slər) *n.* **1** an elected member of a council of a town, village, etc. **2** in Prince Edward Island, a member of the Legislative Assembly elected by the property owners.

Council of the Northwest Territories in Canada, a body consisting of 12 members, seven elected and five appointed, and responsible for local government in the Northwest Territories.

Council of Trent the council of the Roman Catholic Church held at Trent, Italy, from time to time between 1545 and 1563. It formulated many of the present Catholic doctrines, corrected certain abuses within the church, and organized the Catholic opposition to the Protestant movement.

council of war 1 a conference of high officers of the armed services to give advice and talk over matters of special importance. **2** an important conference to decide on a plan of action.

coun·ci·lor (koun′sə lər or koun′slər) *n.* councillor.

coun·sel (koun′səl) *n. v.* **-selled** or **-seled, -sel·ling** or **-sel·ing.** —*n.* **1** the act of exchanging ideas; act of talking things over. **2** advice: *A wise person gives good counsel.* **3** a lawyer or group of lawyers. Each side of a case in court has its own counsel. **4** *Archaic.* wisdom; prudence. **5 keep one's own counsel,** keep quiet about one's ideas and plans; not tell one's secrets. **6 take counsel,** exchange ideas; talk things over; consult together.
—*v.* **1** give advice to; advise. **2** recommend: *He counselled acting at once.* **3** exchange ideas; consult together; deliberate. [ME < OF *conseil* < L *consilium* < *consulere* consult, originally, convoke < *com-* together + *sel-* take] —**Syn.** *n.* **1** consultation, deliberation. **2** recommendation. See **advice. 3** counsellor. –*v.* **1** admonish. ☛ See **council** for usage note.

coun·sel·lor or **coun·sel·or** (koun′sə lər or koun′slər) *n.* **1** a person who gives advice; adviser. **2** a lawyer.

count[1] (kount) *v.* **1** name numbers in order: *Wait till I count ten.* **2** add; find how many: *He counted the books and found there were fifty.* **3** include in counting; take into account: *Let's not count that game.* **4** be included in counting; be taken into account: *Your first race is only for practice; it won't count.* **5** have an influence; be of value: *Every little bit counts.* **6** consider; think of as: *He counts himself fortunate in having good health.* **7** depend; rely: *We count on your help.* **8 count for,** be worth. **9 count off,** divide into equal groups by counting. **10 count out, a** fail to consider or include. **b** in boxing, declare (a fallen fighter) the loser when he fails to rise after ten seconds have been counted.
—*n.* **1** an adding up; a finding out how many: *The count showed that 5,000 votes had been cast.* **2** the total number; amount. **3** in law, each charge in a formal accusation: *The thief was found guilty on all four counts.* **4** in boxing, the ten seconds counted to give a fallen fighter time to get up before he is declared the loser. **5 a** a standard of fineness of yarn for many textile fibres, based on the length of the yarn in relation to a fixed weight, usually the number of hanks to a pound. **b** a standard of the fineness of a fabric, usually the number of cross threads to the inch. [ME < OF *conter* < L *computare* < *com-* up + *putare* reckon. Doublet of COMPUTE.]

count[2] (kount) *n.* a European nobleman having a rank about the same as that of a British earl. [< OF *conte* < L *comes, -itis* companion < *com-* with + *ire* go]

count·a·ble (koun′tə bəl) *adj.* capable of being counted.

count down or **count-down** (kount′doun′) *n.* **1** the period of time immediately preceding the firing of a missile, rocket, etc. **2** the calling out of the minutes (and seconds, in the last stage) of this period as they pass.

coun·te·nance (koun′tə nəns) *n. v.* **-nanced, -nanc·ing.** —*n.* **1** an expression of the face: *His angry countenance frightened us all.* **2** face; features: *The king had a noble countenance.* **3** approval; encouragement: *He gave countenance to our plan, but no active help.* **4** calmness; composure. **5 keep one's countenance, a** be calm; not show feeling. **b** keep from smiling or laughing. **6 lose countenance,** get excited. **7 put out of countenance,** embarrass and confuse; make uneasy and ashamed.
—*v.* tolerate; sanction: *A dictator will not countenance opposition.* [ME < OF *contenance* < Med.L *continentia* demeanor < L *continentia* self-control < *continere.* See CONTAIN.] —**coun′te·nanc·er,** *n.* —**Syn.** *n.* **1, 2** visage. See **face. 3** support.

count·er[1] (koun′tər) *n.* **1** something used for counting. **2** an imitation coin. **3** in a store, restaurant, etc., a long table on which money is counted out, and across which goods, etc. are given to customers. **4** a wall table in a kitchen, bathroom, etc. [< AF *counteour* < *conter.* See COUNT[1].]

count·er[2] (koun′tər) *n.* a person or thing that counts. [< *count*[1]]

coun·ter³ (koun′tər) *adv.* in the opposite direction; opposed; contrary: *His wild idea runs counter to common sense.*
—*adj.* opposite; contrary.
—*v.* **1** go or act counter to; oppose: *She did not like our plan; so she countered it with one of her own.* **2** meet or answer (a move, blow, etc.) by another in return.
—*n.* **1** that which is opposite or contrary to something else. **2** in boxing, a blow given in return for another. **3** a stiff piece inside the back of a shoe around the heel. **4** the part of a ship's stern from the water line up to the end of the curved part. **5** the depressed part of the face of a type, coin, medal, etc. [< F < L *contra* against]

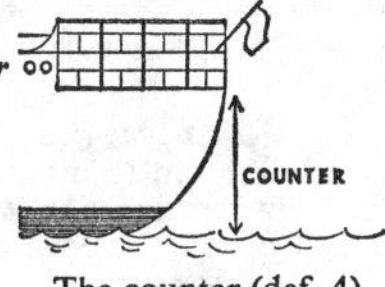

The counter (def. 4) of a ship

counter- *combining form.* **1** against; in opposition to: *counteract = act against.* **2** in return: *counterattack = attack in return.* **3** so as to correspond: *counterpart = part that corresponds.* [see COUNTER³]

☞ **counter-.** As with many such combining forms, usage is divided as to whether or not *counter* should be followed by a hyphen when used in combinations. In this dictionary a hyphen is used before a following "r" and in nouns, adjectives, and adverbs in which the primary stress falls on the second element of the compound: *counter-revolution, counter-clockwise, counter-offensive;* but *counterattack, counterpane,* etc.

coun·ter·act (koun′tər akt′) *v* act against; neutralize the action or effect of; hinder.

coun·ter·ac·tion (koun′tər ak′shən) *n.* an action opposed to another action; hindrance.

coun·ter·ac·tive (koun′tər ak′tiv) *adj.* tending to counteract. —*n.* something that counteracts.

coun·ter·at·tack (koun′tər ə tak′) *n.* an attack made to counteract an attack. —*v.* attack in return.

coun·ter·bal·ance (*n.* koun′tər bal′əns; *v.* koun′tər bal′əns) *n. v.* **-anced, -anc·ing.** —*n.* **1** a weight balancing another weight. **2** influence, power, etc. balancing or offsetting another. —*v.* act as a counterbalance to; offset: *Studying hard often counterbalances slowness at learning.*

coun·ter·charge (*n.* koun′tər chärj′; *v.* koun′tər chärj′) *n. v.* **-charged, -charg·ing.** —*n.* a charge or accusation made to oppose one made by an accuser. —*v.* charge or accuse (someone) after being oneself charged or accused.

coun·ter·check (koun′tər chek′) *n.* **1** something that restrains or opposes; an obstacle. **2** a check made upon a check; double check for verification. —*v.* **1** restrain or oppose by some obstacle. **2** make a second check of; check again.

counter cheque or **check** a blank cheque obtainable for use in a bank or at a store.

coun·ter·claim (koun′tər klām′) *n.* an opposing claim; claim made by a person to offset a claim made against him. —*v.* ask for or make a counterclaim.

coun·ter-clock·wise (koun′tər klok′wīz′) *adv. adj.* in the direction opposite to that in which the hands of a clock move.

coun·ter·cur·rent (koun′tər kėr′ənt) *n.* a current running in the opposite direction; an opposing current. —*adv.* in an opposite manner or direction; contrary.

coun·ter-es·pi·o·nage (koun′tər es′pē ə nij or koun′tər es′pē ə näzh′) *n.* the taking of measures to prevent or confuse enemy espionage.

coun·ter·feit (koun′tər fit) *v.* **1** copy (money, handwriting, pictures, etc.) in order to deceive or defraud: *He was sent to prison for counterfeiting five-dollar bills.* **2** resemble closely. **3** pretend; dissemble: *She counterfeited a grief she did not feel.* [< adj.]
—*n.* a copy made to deceive or defraud and passed as genuine: *This portrait is a counterfeit.* [< adj.]
—*adj.* **1** not genuine; sham. **2** pretended; dissembled. [ME < OF *contrefait* imitated, pp. of *contrefaire* < *contre-* against (< L *contra-*) + *faire* make < L *facere*] —**coun′ter·feit′er,** *n.* —**Syn.** *adj.* **1** forged, fraudulent. See **false.**

coun·ter·foil (koun′tər foil′) *n.* the part of a cheque, receipt, etc. kept as a record. [< *counter-* + *foil* leaf]

coun·ter-in·tel·li·gence (koun′tər in tel′ə jəns) *n.* **1** a government or military department whose work is to track down and prevent espionage, sabotage, etc. **2** the system or methods used by such a department.

hat, āge, cãre, fär; let, ēqual, tėrm; it, īce
hot, ōpen, ôrder; oil, out; cup, pu̇t, rüle, ūse
əbove, takən, pencəl, lemən, circəs
ch, child; ng, long; sh, ship
th, thin; ᴛʜ, then; zh, measure

coun·ter·ir·ri·tant (koun′tər ir′ə tənt) *n.* something used to produce irritation in one place in order to relieve disease or pain elsewhere.

coun·ter·mand (koun′tər mand′) *v.* **1** withdraw or cancel (an order, command, etc.). **2** recall or stop by a contrary order; order back. [ME < OF *contremander* < L *contra-* against + *mandare* order]

coun·ter·march (koun′tər märch′) *v. n.* march in the opposite direction; march back.

coun·ter·meas·ure (koun′tər mezh′ər) *n.* a measure or move taken to offset another.

coun·ter·mine (koun′tər mīn′) *n. v.* **-mined, -min·ing.** —*n.* a submarine mine intended to set off enemy mines prematurely. —*v.* place countermines (against).

coun·ter·mis·sile (koun′tər mis′īl or -mis′əl) *n.* a missile designed to intercept and destroy another missile.

coun·ter-of·fen·sive (koun′tər ə fen′siv) *n.* an aggressive action on a large scale undertaken by a defending force to regain the initiative from the attacking force.

coun·ter·pane (koun′tər pān′) *n.* an outer covering for a bed; bedspread. [alteration of *counterpoint* quilt < OF]

coun·ter·part (koun′tər pärt′) *n.* **1** a copy; duplicate. **2** a person or thing closely resembling another: *This twin is her sister's counterpart.* **3** a person or thing that complements another: *Night is the counterpart of day.*

coun·ter·plot (koun′tər plot′) *n. v.* **-plot·ted, -plot·ting.** plot to defeat another plot.

coun·ter·point (koun′tər point′) *n.* in music: **1** a melody added to another as an accompaniment. **2** the art of combining two or more melodies to give a satisfying musical texture and produce good harmony by the interaction of parts. **3** the style of composition resulting from the way in which more or less individual melodies are combined according to fixed rules. [< F *contrepoint*]

coun·ter·poise (koun′tər poiz′) *n. v.* **-poised, -pois·ing.** —*n.* **1** a weight balancing another weight. **2** an influence; equilibrium. —*v.* act as a counterpoise to; offset. [ME < OF *countrepeis* < *contre-* against + *peis* weight, later, *pois* < L *pensum* < *pendere* weigh]

coun·ter-ref·or·ma·tion (koun′tər ref′ər mā′shən) *n.* a reform movement opposed to a previous reform movement.

Counter Reformation in the Roman Catholic Church, the movement during the 16th and 17th centuries to correct certain abuses within the church, formulate many doctrines of the church, and organize Catholic opposition to Protestantism.

coun·ter-rev·o·lu·tion (koun′tər rev′ə lü′shən) *n.* a revolution against a government established by a previous revolution.

coun·ter·scarp (koun′tər skärp′) *n.* the outer slope or wall of a moat, ditch, etc. in a fortification. [< F *contrescarpe*]

coun·ter·shaft (koun′tər shaft′) *n.* a shaft that transmits motion from the main shaft to the working parts of a machine.

coun·ter·sign (koun′tər sīn′) *n.* **1** a password given in answer to the challenge of a sentinel: *The soldier had to give the countersign before he could pass the sentry.* **2** a signature added to another signature to confirm it. —*v.* sign (something already signed by another) to confirm it. [< F *contresigne*]

coun·ter·sink (koun′tər singk′) *v.* **-sunk, -sink·ing,** *n.* —*v.* **1** enlarge the upper part of (a hole) to make room for the head of screw, bolt, etc. **2** sink the head of (a screw, bolt, etc.) into such a hole so that it is even with or below the surface. —*n.* **1** a countersunk hole. **2** a tool for countersinking holes.

coun·ter·ten·or (koun′tər ten′ər) *n.* **1** an adult male voice, often falsetto, that is higher than the tenor. **2** in music: **a** a singer with such a voice. **b** a part for such a voice.

coun·ter·vail (koun′tər vāl′ or koun′tər vāl′) *v.* **1** counteract; avail against. **2** compensate; offset; make up for. **3** *Obsolete.* be of equal force in opposition. [ME < AF *countrevaloir* < L *contra valere* be of worth against]

coun·ter·weight (koun′tər wāt′) *n.* a weight that balances another weight.

count·ess (koun′tis) *n.* **1** the wife or widow of an earl or count. **2** a woman whose rank is equal to that of an earl or count. [ME < OF *contesse* < Med.L *comitissa*, fem. of L *comes.* See COUNT².]

counting house a building or office used for keeping accounts and doing business.

counting room an office used for keeping accounts and doing business.

count·less (kount′lis) *adj.* too many to count; very many; innumerable: *the countless sands of the seashore, the countless stars.*

coun·tri·fied (kun′tri fīd′) *adj.* **1** looking or acting like a person from the country; rustic. **2** like the country; rural. **3** suitable for the country or rural living; rustic.

coun·try (kun′trē) *n.* **-tries,** *adj.* —*n.* **1** the land; a region; district: *The country around the mining town was mountainous.* **2** all the land of a nation. **3** the people of a nation. **4** one's native or adopted land; the land where a person was born or is a citizen. **5** land without many houses; a rural district. **6** a tract of land having more or less definite boundaries, especially natural boundaries, and inhabited by people of the same race, blood, or speech. —*adj.* **1** of the country; in the country. **2** like the country. [ME < OF *contree* < VL *contrata* region lying opposite < L *contra* against]

country club a club in the country near a city, having a clubhouse and facilities for outdoor sports.

country cousin a relation of countrified appearance and manners.

coun·try-dance (kun′trē dans′) *n.* a dance in which partners face each other in two long lines. The Virginia reel is a country-dance.

coun·try·folk (kun′trē fōk′) *n.* the people who live in the country.

country gentleman a gentleman who lives on his estate in the country.

country house a home in the country.

coun·try·man (kun′trē mən) *n.* **-men** (-mən). **1** a man of one's own country. **2** a man who lives in the country.

coun·try·seat (kun′trē sēt′) *n.* a residence or estate in the country, especially a fine one.

coun·try·side (kun′trē sīd′) *n.* **1** a rural district; country. **2** a certain section of the country. **3** its people.

coun·try-wide (kun′trē wīd′) *adj.* nation-wide.

coun·try·wom·an (kun′trē wům′ən) *n.* **-wom·en. 1** a woman of one's own country. **2** a woman living in the country.

count·ship (kount′ship) *n.* **1** the title or rank of a count. **2** the territory owned by or under the control of a count.

coun·ty (koun′tē) *n.* **-ties. 1** an administrative district of a country, province, state, etc. The county form of municipal government is used in Nova Scotia, New Brunswick, Quebec, Ontario, and Alberta. **2** in Great Britain and Ireland, one of the districts into which the country is divided for administrative, judicial, and political purposes. **3** the people of a county. [ME < AF *counte* < *counte*, var. of OF *conte.* See COUNT².]

county court a court having limited jurisdiction in the county or district where it is held.

county farm formerly, a farm supported by a county, on which poor people were allowed to live and work.

county seat a town or city where the county government is located and where assizes are held.

coup (kü) *n.* **coups** (küz). **1** a sudden, brilliant action; an unexpected, clever move; master stroke. **2** a stroke or blow. **3** a cleverly organized crime. **4** a coup d'état. [< F < L < Gk. *kolaphos*]

coup de grâce (kü′ də gräs′) **1** an action that gives a merciful death to a suffering animal or person. **2** a finishing stroke: *The runner's final sprint gave the coup de grâce to his opponents.* [< F *coup de grâce*, literally, stroke of grace]

coup d'é·tat (kü′ dā tä′) in politics, a sudden and decisive measure, especially one effecting a change of government illegally or by force. [< F *coup d'état,* literally, stroke of state]

coup d'oeil (kü dœ′ē) *French.* a view taken in at a glance.

cou·pé (kü pā′ or küp *for 1*; kü pā′ *for 2*) *n.* **1** a closed two-door automobile seating two to five people. **2** a closed carriage with a seat for two people inside and a seat for the driver outside. [< F *coupé*, pp. of *couper* cut]

cou·ple (kup′əl) *n. v.* **-pled, -pling.** —*n.* **1** two things of the same kind that go together; a pair. **2** a man and woman who are married, engaged, or paired together for a dance, party, game, etc.
—*v.* **1** join together; join together in pairs. **2** in electricity, connect by a coupler. [ME < OF *cople* < L *copula* bond. Doublet of COPULA.] —**Syn.** *n.* **1** mates. See **pair.** –*v.* unite.

☛ **Couple** = strictly two persons or things associated in some way: *a married couple.* In everyday speech *couple* is equivalent to the numeral two: *He borrowed a couple of pencils.*

cou·pler (kup′lər) *n.* **1** a person or thing that couples. **2** in an organ, a device for coupling keys or keyboards so they can be played together. **3** a device used to join together two railway cars. **4** a device used to connect electric circuits, as a transformer that joins parts of a radio apparatus together by means of induction.

cou·plet (kup′lit) *n.* **1** two successive lines of verse that rhyme and have the same number of metrical feet. *Example*:

"Be not the first by whom the new are tried,
Nor yet the last to lay the old aside."

2 a couple; pair. [< F *couplet*, dim. of *couple* couple]

cou·pling (kup′ling) *n.* **1** the act or process of joining. **2** a device for joining parts of machinery. **3** a device used to join two railway cars. **4** a device or arrangement for transferring electrical energy from one circuit to another.

cou·pon (kü′pon or kū′pon) *n.* **1** a printed statement of interest due on a bond, which can be cut from the bond and presented for payment. **2** a part of a ticket, advertisement, package, etc. that gives the person who holds it certain rights: *She saved the coupons that came with each box of soap.* [< F *coupon* < *couper* cut]

cour·age (kėr′ij) *n.* **1** bravery; fearlessness; the meeting of danger without fear. **2 have the courage of one's convictions,** act as one believes one should. [ME < OF *corage, curage* < *cuer* heart < L *cor*]

Syn. 1 Courage, bravery = fearlessness. **Courage** applies to moral strength that makes a person face any danger, trouble, or pain steadily and without fear: *Although blinded by the explosion, he faced the future with courage.* **Bravery** applies to a kind of courage that is shown by bold, fearless, daring action in the presence of danger: *The Commandos are famous for their bravery.*

cou·ra·geous (kə rā′jəs) *adj.* full of courage; brave; fearless. —**cou·ra′geous·ly,** *adv.* —**cou·ra′geous·ness,** *n.* —**Syn.** See **brave.**

cou·reur de bois (kü rėr′ də bwo′; *French,* kü rœr də bwä′) *pl.* **coureurs de bois.** in the North and Northwest, a French or half-breed woodsman, trapper, canoeman, etc. The coureurs de bois played an important part in the fur trade. [< Cdn. F]

cour·i·er (kėr′ē ər or kür′ē ər) *n.* **1** a messenger sent in haste: *Government dispatches were sent by couriers.* **2** a secret agent who transfers information to and from other agents. **3** a person who goes with a group of travellers and takes care of hotel reservations, tickets, etc. [< F *courrier* < Ital. < L *currere* run]

course (kôrs) *n. v.* **coursed, cours·ing.** —*n.* **1** an onward movement: *the course of events.* **2** a direction taken: *The ship's course was east.* **3** a line of action; way of doing: *You must take the course that leads to success.* **4** a way; path; track; channel: *the course of a stream.* **5** a group of similar things arranged in some regular order. **6** the regular order: *the course of nature.* **7** in a school, college,

or university: **a** a series of studies. A student must complete a certain course in order to graduate. **b** one of the studies: *Each course in geography lasts two terms.* **8** a part of a meal served at one time: *Soup was the first course.* **9** a place for races or games: *a golf course.* **10** a layer of bricks, stones, shingles, etc.; row. **11** the lowest square sail on any mast of a square-rigged ship. **12 in due course,** at the proper or usual time; after a while. **13 in the course of,** during; in the process of. **14 of course, a** surely; certainly. **b** naturally; as should be expected.
—*v.* **1** race; run: *The blood courses through the arteries.* **2** hunt with hounds. **3** cause (hounds) to hunt for game. [< F *cours* < L *cursus* a running, and < F *course* < Ital. *corsa* a running < L *currere* run] —**Syn.** *n.* **1** progress. **3** process, method, manner, mode, procedure. **4** road, passage. **5** sequence, succession.

cours·er (kôr′sər) *n. Poetic.* a swift horse. [ME < OF *coursier* < *cours* a running < L *cursus*]

court (kôrt) *n.* **1** a space partly or wholly enclosed by walls or buildings. **2** a short street. **3** a place marked off for a game: *a tennis court.* **4** the residence of a king, queen, or other sovereign; a royal palace. **5** the family, household, or followers of a sovereign. **6** a sovereign and his advisers as a ruling power. **7** a formal assembly held by a sovereign. **8** in law: **a** a place where justice is administered. **b** the persons who are chosen to administer justice; a judge or judges. **c** an assembly of such persons to administer justice. **d** a session of a judicial body. **9** attention paid to get favor; effort to please. **10** the act of making love; act of wooing. **11 hold court, a** of a sovereign, hold a formal assembly. **b** receive or entertain (people) in a lordly way. **12 out of court,** not to be considered. **13 pay court to, a** pay attention to (a person) to get his favor; try to please. **b** make love to; woo.
—*v.* **1** pay attention to (a person) to get his favor; try to please. **2** make love to; woo. **3** try to get; act so as to get; seek: *It is foolish to court danger.* [ME < OF *cort* < L *cohors* enclosure, retinue. Doublet of COHORT.]
—**Syn.** *n.* **1** yard. –*v.* **3** invite, solicit.

court card the king, queen, or jack, of any suit of playing cards.

cour·te·ous (kėr′tē əs) *adj.* polite; thoughtful of others: *It is a courteous act to help an old lady cross the street.* [ME < OF *corteis* < *cort.* See COURT.] —**cour′te·ous·ly,** *adv.* —**cour′te·ous·ness,** *n.* —**Syn.** civil. See **polite.**

cour·te·san (kôr′tə zən or kôr′tə zan′) *n.* a prostitute. [< F *courtisane* < Ital. *cortigiana* woman of the court < *corte* < L *cohors.* Related to COURT.]

cour·te·sy (kėr′tə sē) *n.* **-sies. 1** polite behavior; thoughtfulness for others. **2** a polite act; a thoughtful act; favor. **3 by courtesy,** as a favor, rather than as something rightfully owing. **4 by courtesy of, through the courtesy of,** with the consent of; with the permission of or approval of. [ME < OF *cortesie* < *corteis.* See COURTEOUS.] —**Syn. 1** politeness, civility.

cour·te·zan (kôr′tə zən or kôr′tə zan′) *n.* courtesan.

court·house (kôrt′hous′) *n.* a building where law courts are held.

cour·ti·er (kôr′tē ər) *n.* **1** a person often present at the court of a king, prince, etc.; court attendant. **2** a person who tries to win the favor of another by flattering and pleasing him.

court·li·ness (kôrt′lē nis) *n.* politeness; elegance; polish.

court·ly (kôrt′lē) *adj.* **-li·er, -li·est. 1** suitable for a king's court; polite; elegant. **2** trying hard to please one's superior; flattering.

court-mar·tial (kôrt′mär′shəl) *n.* **courts-mar·tial,** *v.* **-tialled** or **-tialed, -tial·ling** or **-tial·ing.** —*n.* **1** a court made up of officers of one of the armed services for the purpose of trying offenders against the laws of that service. **2** a trial by such a court: *The captain's court-martial will be held next week.*
—*v.* try by such a court.

Court of St. James's the official name for the court of the British sovereign, which gets its name from St. James's Palace in London, where royal receptions were formerly held.

court plaster cloth with a sticky substance on one side, used for covering and protecting slight cuts.

court·room (kôrt′rüm′ or -rům′) *n.* a room where a law court is held.

hat, āge, cãre, fär; let, ēqual, tėrm; it, īce
hot, ōpen, ôrder; oil, out; cup, půt, rüle, ūse
əbove, takən, pencəl, lemən, circəs
ch, child; ng, long; sh, ship
th, thin; ᴛʜ, then; zh, measure

court·ship (kôrt′ship) *n.* **1** the act or process of paying court to a woman with the intention of marrying her; a wooing. **2** the period of time that this process lasts: *Their courtship was very short, for they were soon married.*

court tennis a game in which a ball is hit back and forth over a low net. It is played on an enclosed court, as distinguished from lawn tennis which is played outdoors.

court·yard (kôrt′yärd′) *n.* a space enclosed by walls in or near a large building.

cous·in (kuz′ən) *n.* **1** a son or daughter of one's uncle or aunt. First cousins have the same grandparents; second cousins have the same great-grandparents; and so on for third and fourth cousins, etc. Your father's or mother's first cousin is your first cousin once removed. **2** a distant relative. **3** the citizen of a related nation: *The British, Canadians, and Americans might be called cousins.* **4** any person or thing thought of as related to another: *A good swimmer is first cousin to a beaver.* **5** a term used by one sovereign in speaking to another sovereign or to a great nobleman. [ME < OF *cosin, cusin* < L *consobrinus* mother's sister's child ⋖ *com-* together + *soror* sister]

cous·in-ger·man (kuz′ən jėr′mən) *n.* **cous·ins-ger·man.** a son or daughter of one's uncle or aunt; first cousin. [< F *cousin-germain; germain* < L *germanus*]

cous·in·ly (kuz′ən lē) *adj.* **1** like a cousin or a cousin's. **2** suitable for a cousin. —*adv.* in the manner of a cousin.

cous·in·ship (kuz′ən ship′) *n.* the relationship of a cousin or cousins.

cou·tu·ri·er (kü tür′ē ər; *French,* kü ᴛʏ ryā′) *n.* a male dressmaker or dress designer. [< F *couturier* tailor < *couture* sewing < VL < L *consuere* < *com-* together + *suere* sew]

cou·tu·ri·ère (kü tür′ē ãr′; *French,* kü ᴛʏ ryãr′) *n.* a woman dressmaker or dress designer. [< F. See COUTURIER.]

co·va·lence (kō vā′ləns) *n.* in chemistry: **1** a bond in which two atoms share a pair of electrons. **2** the ability to form such a bond. **3** the total of the pairs of electrons which one atom can share with surrounding atoms.
—**co·va′len·cy,** *n.*

co·va·lent (kō vā′lənt) *adj.* of or having to do with covalence.

cove (kōv) *n.* **1** a small, sheltered bay; an inlet on the shore; the mouth of a creek. **2** a sheltered nook. [OE *cofa* chamber]

cov·e·nant (kuv′ə nənt) *n.* **1** a solemn agreement between two or more persons or groups to do or not to do a certain thing; compact. **2 Covenant, a** the agreement signed by Scottish Presbyterians and members of the English Parliament in 1643. It set up the Presbyterian Church in England. **b** an earlier agreement signed by Scottish Presbyterians in 1638, for the defence of the Presbyterian faith. **c** the Covenant of the League of Nations. **3** in the Bible, the solemn promises of God to man; compact between God and man. **4** a legal contract; a formal agreement binding at law.
—*v.* **1** solemnly agree (to do certain things). **2** enter into a covenant or formal agreement. [ME < OF *covenant* < *covenir* < L *convenire.* See CONVENE.]

cov·e·nant·er (kuv′ə nən tər; *also* kuv′ə nan′tər *for 2*) *n.* **1** a person who makes a solemn agreement. **2 Covenanter,** a person who signed and supported either of the Covenants of the Scottish Presbyterians in the 17th century.

Covenant of the League of Nations the constitution of the League of Nations. It comprises the first part of the Treaty of Versailles that was signed in 1919.

cov·e·nan·tor (kuv′ə nən tər) *n.* in law, a person who makes a covenant and assumes its obligations.

Cov·ent Garden (kuv′ənt or kov′ənt) in London: **1** a great market district, formerly the garden of a convent. **2** a famous theatre in this district.

Cov·en·try (kuv′ən trē or kov′ən trē) *n.* **send to Coventry,** refuse to associate with; ostracize. [< *Coventry,* city in central England]

cov·er (kuv′ər) *v.* **1** put something over: *Cover this box with a wide board. The book was covered with a leather binding.* **2** be or extend over; occupy the surface of: *Snow covered the ground.* **3** clothe; wrap up: *People in the Arctic cover themselves with furs.* **4** be thick over: *Dust covered his shoes.* **5** invest (oneself or one's reputation): *He covered himself with glory.* **6** hide; conceal: *cover a mistake.* **7** protect; shelter: *The cave covered him from the snow.* **8** go or travel over: *We covered more than 200 miles on the first day of our trip.* **9** include; take in: *The review covered everything we learned last term.* **10** be enough for; provide for: *Thirty cents a day covers his carfare.* **11** aim straight at: *cover a person with a pistol.* **12** have within range: *The guns of the fort on the hill covered the territory around it.* **13** put one's hat or cap on: *Cover your head when you are in the sun.* **14** act as a reporter or photographer of an event or subject: *He covered the police court news.* **15** in sports, watch over and try to thwart an opposing player. **16** deposit the equivalent of (money deposited in betting); accept the conditions of (a bet). **17** in business, buy (commodities, securities, etc.) for future delivery as a protection against loss. **18** (of a male animal) copulate with (the female). **19** brood or sit on (eggs or chicks). **20** stand behind; support: *The shortstop covered the second baseman in case the ball got by him.* **21 cover up, a** cover completely. **b** hide; conceal; refuse to tell or show. **c** seek to protect oneself: *The boxer covered up under the onslaught of blows.*
—*n.* **1** anything that covers: *She always puts covers on her school books.* **2** protection; shelter: *The wounded fox sought cover in a cave.* **3** in hunting, a covert (def. 2). **4** in sports, a player who watches over and tries to thwart an opposing player. **5** a place for one person at a table, set with a plate, knife, fork, spoon, napkin, etc. **6** funds adequate to cover or meet a liability or secure against possible loss. **7** in philately: **a** an envelope or wrapper with stamp and any postal markings affixed. **b** a letter addressed on the reverse side after folding to form an envelope. **8 break cover,** come out in the open. **9 under cover, a** hidden; secret; disguised. **b** secretly. [ME < OF *covrir* < L *cooperire* < *co-* up + *operire* cover]
—**cov′er·er,** *n.* —**cov′er·less,** *adj.* —**Syn.** *v.* **3** envelop. **6** screen, cloak, shroud. -*n.* **1** lid, top, case, envelope, wrapping. **2** refuge, retreat.

cov·er·age (kuv′ər ij) *n.* **1** the section of the potential buying public presumably reached by a given advertising campaign, medium, etc. **2** the scope and manner of presenting information by a reporter, newspaper, etc. **3** an amount held to meet liabilities: *a 60% gold coverage of paper money.* **4** in insurance, the risks covered by a policy.

cov·er·alls (kuv′ər ols′ or -ôls′) *n.pl.* a work garment of heavy cloth that includes shirt and trousers in a single unit. Mechanics wear coveralls.

cover charge a charge made in some restaurants for service, entertainment, etc. in addition to the charge for food.

cover crop a crop sown in a field or orchard to protect the soil, especially in winter.

cov·ered (kuv′ərd) *adj.* **1** having a cover or covering. **2** wearing one's hat or cap.

covered wagon a wagon having a removable canvas cover.

cover girl an attractive girl or woman whose picture is used on the cover of a magazine.

cov·er·ing (kuv′ər ing or kuv′ring) *n.* anything that covers.

cov·er·let (kuv′ər lit) *n.* **1** an outer covering for a bed; bedspread. **2** any covering. [ME *coverlite,* apparently < OF *covrir* (see COVER) + *lit* bed < L *lectus*]

cov·er·lid (kuv′ər lid) *n.* coverlet.

cov·ert (kuv′ərt) *adj.* secret; hidden; disguised: *covert glances.* —*n.* **1** a shelter; hiding place. **2** a thicket in which animals hide. [ME < OF *covert,* pp. of *covrir.* See COVER.] —**cov′ert·ly,** *adv.* —**cov′ert·ness,** *n.* —**Syn.** *adj.* See **secret.**

co·vert cloth (kō′vərt or kuv′ərt) cloth of wool, silk and wool, or rayon, usually brownish, used for coats.

cov·er·ture (kuv′ər chür′ or kuv′ər chər) *n.* **1** a cover; a covering. **2** a shelter; hiding place.

cov·et (kuv′it) *v.* desire eagerly (something that belongs to another). [ME < OF *coveitier,* ult. < L *cupere* desire] —**cov′et·er,** *n.* ☛ See **envy** for usage note.

cov·et·ous (kuv′ə təs) *adj.* desiring things that belong to others. —**cov′et·ous·ly,** *adv.* —**cov′et·ous·ness,** *n.* —**Syn.** greedy, avaricious.

cov·ey (kuv′ē) *n.* **-eys. 1** a brood of partridges, quail, etc. **2** a small flock, especially of partridges, quail, etc.; group. [ME < OF *covee* < *cover* incubate < L *cubare* lie]

cow[1] (kou) *n.* **cows** or (*Archaic or dialect*) **kine. 1** a female of the bovine family, especially the common dairy animal that furnishes milk. **2** the female of various other large vertebrates: *an elephant cow, a buffalo cow, a cow moose.* **3** *Informal.* a clumsy, awkward, or stupid person. [OE *cū*] —**cow′-like′,** *adj.*

cow[2] (kou) *v.* make afraid; frighten. [? < ON *kúga*] —**Syn.** scare, bully.

cow·ard (kou′ərd) *n.* a person who lacks courage or is afraid; person who runs from danger, trouble, etc. —*adj.* lacking courage; cowardly. [ME < OF *coart* < *coe* tail < L *coda,* dial. var. of *cauda*; with reference to an animal with its tail between its legs]

cow·ard·ice (kou′ər dis) *n.* lack of courage; the state of being easily made afraid.

cow·ard·li·ness (kou′ərd lē nis) *n.* the state or quality of being cowardly.

cow·ard·ly (kou′ərd lē) *adj.* **1** lacking courage. **2** of a coward; suitable for a coward. —*adv.* in a cowardly manner. —**Syn. 1** See **timid.**

cow·bane (kou′bān′) *n.* any of various plants of the carrot family, supposedly poisonous to cattle.

cow·bell (kou′bel′) *n.* a bell hung around a cow's neck to indicate her whereabouts.

cow·bird (kou′bėrd′) *n.* a small North American blackbird that is often found with cattle. Most cowbirds lay their eggs in the nests of other birds.

cow·boy (kou′boi′) *n.* a man who looks after cattle on a ranch and on the range.

cow·catch·er (kou′kach′ər) *n.* a metal frame on the front of a locomotive, streetcar, etc. intended to clear the tracks of anything in the way.

COWCATCHER

cow·er (kou′ər) *v.* **1** crouch in fear or shame. **2** draw back tremblingly from another's threats, blows, etc. [ME *couren* < Scand.]

cow·fish (kou′fish′) *n.* **-fish** or **-fish·es. 1** a fish having hornlike projections above its eyes. **2** any of certain small animals related to the whales.

cow·girl (kou′gėrl′) *n.* a girl who helps to look after cattle, especially one who appears as a performer at rodeos, etc.

cow hand a person who works on a cattle ranch.

cow·herd (kou′hėrd′) *n.* a person whose work is looking after cattle while they are at pasture.

cow·hide (kou′hīd′) *n.* **1** the hide of a cow. **2** leather made from it.

Cow·i·chan (kou′i chən) *n.* **1** a group of Coast Salish Indians living mainly on Vancouver Island, noted for their knitting of distinctively patterned sweaters. **2** a member of this group.

cowl (koul) *n.* **1** a monk's cloak with a hood. **2** the hood itself. **3** anything shaped like a cowl. **4** the part of an automobile body that includes the windshield and the dashboard. **5** a cowling. **6** a covering for the top of a chimney, designed to increase the draft.

A cowl (def. 2)

—*v.* **1** put a monk's cowl on. **2** cover with a cowl or something resembling a cowl. [OE *cūle, cug(e)le* < LL *cucullа*, var. of L *cucullus* hood]

cow·lick (kou′lik′) *n. Informal.* a small tuft of hair that will not lie flat, usually just above the forehead.

cowl·ing (koul′ing) *n.* a metal covering over an airplane engine.

cow·man (kou′mən) *n.* **-men** (-mən). an owner of cattle; ranchman.

co-work·er (kō wėr′kər) *n.* a person who works with another.

cow·poke (kou′pōk′) *n. Informal.* cowboy.

cow·pox (kou′poks′) *n.* a disease of cows causing small pustules on their udders. The vaccine for smallpox is obtained from cows that have cowpox.

cow·punch·er (kou′pun′chər) *n. Informal.* a cowboy.

cow·rie or **cow·ry** (kou′rē) *n.* **1** a glossy, yellow sea shell, used as money in some parts of Africa and Asia. **2** the mollusc that forms this shell. [< Hind. *kauri*]

cow·skin (kou′skin′) *n.* cowhide.

cow·slip (kou′slip) *n.* **1** a wild plant having yellow flowers. **2** the marsh marigold. [OE *cūslyppe* < *cū* cow + *slyppe* slime]

cox (koks) *n. Informal.* coxswain.

cox·comb (koks′kōm′) *n.* **1** a vain, empty-headed man; a conceited dandy. **2** a cockscomb. [var. of *cock's comb*]

cox·comb·ry (koks′kōm′rē) *n.* **-ries. 1** silly vanity; empty-headed conceit. **2** an example of this.

cox·swain (kok′sən or -swān′) *n.* a person who steers a boat, racing shell, etc. and is in charge of the crew. Also, **cockswain.** [< *cock* cockboat + *swain*]

coy (koi) *adj.* **1** shy; modest; bashful. **2** pretending to be shy: *The actress wore a coy smile.* [ME < OF *coi* < L *quietus* at rest. Doublet of QUIET and QUIT, adj.] —**coy′ly,** *adv.* —**coy′ness,** *n.*

coy·o·te (kī ō′tē or kī′ōt) *n.* **-tes** or (*esp. collectively*) **-te.** a small wolf living on the prairies of western North America. It is noted for its loud howling at night. [< Mexican Sp. < Nahuatl *koyotl*]

coy·pu (koi′pü) *n.* **-pus** or (*esp. collectively*) **-pu.** a large water rodent of South America, whose fur, called nutria, resembles beaver. [< Sp. *coipu* < Araucanian (S. Am.Ind. linguistic stock) *koypu*]

coz (kuz) *n. Informal.* cousin.

coz·en (kuz′ən) *v.* cheat; deceive; beguile. [origin unknown] —**coz′en·er,** *n.*

coz·en·age (kuz′ən ij) *n.* a cozening; fraud; deception.

co·zi·ly (kō′zə lē) *adv.* cosily.

co·zi·ness (kō′zē nis) *n.* cosiness.

co·zy (kō′zē) *adj.* **co·zi·er, co·zi·est,** *n.* **co·zies.** cosy.

CP or **C.P.** **1** Command Post. **2** Canadian Press.

cp. **1** compare. **2** *pl.* **cps.** coupon.

c.p. **1** candle power. **2** chemically pure.

C.P. **1** Common Prayer. **2** Court of Probate. **3** Common Pleas. **4** Chemically Pure. **5** Communist Party. **6** Chief Patriarch.

C.P.A. Certified Public Accountant.

cpd. *pl.* **cpds.** compound.

Cpl. Corporal.

cpm or **c.p.m.** cycles per minute.

C.P.O. Chief Petty Officer.

CPR Canadian Pacific Railway.

Cr chromium.

cr. **1** credit. **2** creditor. **3** crown.

Cr. **1** Crescent. **2** Creek.

crab[1] (krab) *n. v.* **crabbed, crab·bing.** —*n.* **1** a crustacean that has a short, broad body with the abdomen or tail folded under, four pairs of legs, and one pair of pincers. **2** any of various similar animals, such as a horseshoe crab. **3** a machine for raising heavy weights. **4 Crab,** in astrology, the fourth sign of the zodiac; Cancer. **5 catch a crab,** make a faulty stroke in rowing.
—*v.* **1** catch crabs for eating. **2** *Informal.* spoil. [OE *crabba*] —**crab′ber,** *n.*

hat, āge, cãre, fär; let, ēqual, tėrm; it, īce
hot, ōpen, ôrder; oil, out; cup, pu̇t, rüle, ūse
əbove, takən, pencəl, lemən, circəs
ch, child; ng, long; sh, ship
th, thin; ᴛʜ, then; zh, measure

crab[2] (krab) *n. v.* **crabbed, crab·bing.** —*n.* **1** a crab apple. **2** a cross, sour, ill-natured person; one who is always complaining or finding fault. —*v.* be always complaining or finding fault; criticize: *Some people crab too much.* [origin uncertain]

crab apple **1** any of various small, sour apples, used for making jelly. **2** a small, sour wild apple. **3** a tree that bears crab apples.

crab·bed (krab′id or krabd) *adj.* **1** peevish: ill-natured; cross. **2** hard to understand; perplexing. **3** hard to read or decipher because irregular: *The teacher objected to crabbed handwriting.* [< *crab*[1]] —**crab′bed·ly,** *adv.* —**crab′bed·ness,** *n.*

crab grass a coarse grass that spreads rapidly and spoils lawns, etc.

crab louse a type of body louse.

crab tree a crab-apple tree.

crack (krak) *n.* **1** a place, line, surface, or opening made by breaking without separating into parts: *a crack in a cup.* **2** a sudden, sharp noise: *the crack of a whip.* **3** *Informal.* a blow that makes a sudden, sharp noise. **4** a narrow opening: *There are cracks between the boards in this old floor.* **5** *Informal.* an instant; moment. **6** *Slang.* a try; attempt. **7** *Slang.* a joke. **8** *Slang.* a nasty or sharp remark. **9** *Informal.* a superior person or thing: *She is a crack at skiing.* [ME *crak,* OE **crac.* Related to CRACK, v.]
—*v.* **1** break without separating into parts: *crack a window.* **2** break with a sudden, sharp noise: *crack nuts.* **3** make or cause to make a sudden, sharp noise. **4** *Informal.* hit with a sudden, sharp noise. **5** make or become harsh and shrill: *His voice cracked.* **6** *Slang.* give way; break down. **7** *Slang.* break into: *crack a safe.* **8** in chemistry, separate (petroleum, coal tar, etc.) into various substances. **9** solve; decipher: *crack a code.* **10 crack a bottle,** *Informal.* open a bottle and drink what is in it. **11 crack a joke,** tell a joke; say something funny. **12 crack down,** *Informal.* take stern measures. **13 crack up,** **a** *Informal.* praise. **b** crash; go to pieces: *The airplane cracked up.* **c** suffer a breakdown in mental or physical health.
—*adj. Informal.* very good; excellent, first-rate. [OE *cracian*] —**Syn.** *n.* **1** cleft, fissure, crevice. **2** clap, report. **4** chink. –*v.* **1** split, fracture. **3** snap.

crack-brained (krak′brānd′) *adj. Informal.* crazy; insane.

crack·down (krak′doun′) *n. Informal.* swift disciplinary action: *The police intensified their crackdown on drunken drivers.*

cracked (krakt) *adj.* **1** broken without separating into parts. **2** of the voice, lacking evenness; broken; having harsh notes. **3** *Informal.* crazy; insane.

crack·er (krak′ər) *n.* **1** a thin, crisp biscuit or wafer: *a soda cracker, a graham cracker.* **2** a firecracker. **3** a small paper roll used as a party favor, containing candy, a motto, a paper cap, etc. It explodes when pulled at both ends. **4** *U.S.* a poor white person living in the hills and backwoods regions of Georgia, Florida, etc. **5** a person or instrument that cracks.

cracker barrel an open barrel for salted crackers, formerly common in grocery and country stores.

cracker-barrel (krak′ər bar′əl) *adj.* of or having the informality and simplicity of country people; down-to-earth: *cracker-barrel humor.*

crack·er·jack (krak′ər jak′) *Slang.* —*n.* **1** a person or thing especially fine of its kind. **2** candied popcorn. —*adj.* of superior ability or quality.

crack·ing (krak′ing) *n.* the process of changing certain hydrocarbons in petroleum and other oils into lighter hydrocarbons by heat and pressure. Gasoline may be produced by cracking.

crack·le (krak′əl) *v.* **-led, -ling,** *n.* —*v.* **1** make slight, sharp sounds: *A fire crackled on the hearth.* **2** of china, glass, etc., become minutely cracked. —*n.* **1** a slight, sharp sound, such as paper makes when it is crushed. **2** a glazed surface containing very small cracks on some kinds of china, glass, etc. **3** china, glass, etc. made with such a surface; crackleware. [< *crack*]

crack·ling (krak′ling) *n.* **1** the crisp, browned skin of roasted pork. **2** Usually, **cracklings,** *pl. Dialect.* the crisp part left after lard has been fried out of pig's fat.

crack·nel (krak′nəl) *n.* **1** a hard, brittle biscuit. **2 cracknels,** *pl.* **a** small pieces of fat pork fried crisp. **b** cracklings. [< F *craquelin* < MDu. *crakelinc*]

crack of doom **1** the signal for the Last Judgment. **2** a signal for the end of everything.

crack·pot (krak′pot′) *Slang. n.* a very eccentric or crack-brained person. —*adj.* eccentric; crack-brained; impractical.

cracks·man (kraks′mən) *n.* **-men** (-mən). *Slang.* a burglar.

crack-up (krak′up′) *n.* **1** a smash-up; crash: *That pilot has been in more than one crack-up.* **2** *Informal.* a mental or physical collapse.

cra·dle (krā′dəl) *n. v.* **-dled, -dling.** —*n.* **1** a baby's small bed, usually on rockers. **2** the place where a thing begins its growth: *The authorities seem to disagree on where we should look for the cradle of civilization.* **3** a frame to support a ship, aircraft, or other large object while it is being built, repaired, lifted, etc. **4** a box on rockers designed to wash gold from the earth. **5** a frame attached to a scythe for laying grain evenly as it is cut. **6** a cradle scythe. **7 rob the cradle,** *Informal.* choose as a companion, or marry, a person much younger than oneself.
—*v.* **1** put or rock in a cradle; hold as in a cradle. **2** shelter or train in early life. **3** support (a ship, etc.) in a cradle. **4** wash (gold from earth) in a cradle. **5** cut with a cradle scythe. [OE *cradol*] —**cra′dle-like′,** *adj.*

cra·dle-board (krā′dəl bôrd′) *n.* a board and framework used by Indian mothers for carrying their babies. When it is tied to the mother's back, she is free to do work with her hands.

A cradle-board in use

cradle hill *Cdn.* especially in the Maritimes, a small mound such as might have originally been formed at the base of an uprooted tree.

cradle scythe a scythe with a frame attached to it for laying grain evenly as it is cut.

cradle song or **cra·dle·song** (krā′dəl song′) *n.* a lullaby.

craft (kraft) *n.* **1** a special skill: *These totem poles are an excellent example of the Haida Indians' craft.* **2** a trade, an art, or work requiring special skill. **3** the members of a trade requiring special skill: *Carpenters compose a craft.* **4** skill in deceiving others; slyness; trickiness: *By craft he got all their money from them.* **5** boats, ships, or aircraft. **6** a boat, ship, or aircraft. [OE *cræft*]
—**Syn. 4** guile, wile. See **cunning.**

craft·i·ness (kraf′tē nis) *n.* skill in deceiving others; being crafty; cunning.

crafts·man (krafts′mən) *n.* **-men** (-mən). **1** a skilled workman. **2** an artist.

crafts·man·ship (krafts′mən ship′) *n.* the work or skill of a craftsman; craft.

craft union a labor union made up of persons in the same craft. Unions of carpenters, plumbers, or bricklayers are craft unions.

craft·y (kraf′tē) *adj.* **craft·i·er, craft·i·est.** skilful in deceiving others; sly; tricky: *a crafty fox, a crafty villain.* —**craft′i·ly,** *adv.*

crag (krag) *n.* a steep, rugged rock or cliff; a projecting rock. [< Celtic (compare Welsh *craig*)]

crag·ged (krag′id) *adj.* craggy.

crag·gy (krag′ē) *adj.* **-gi·er, -gi·est. 1** with many crags; rocky: *a craggy hillside.* **2** rugged; rough; uneven: *a craggy face.* —**crag′gi·ly,** *adv.* —**crag′gi·ness,** *n.*

crake (krāk) *n.* any of various short-billed birds of the rail family. [ME < ON *kráka* crow]

cram (kram) *v.* **crammed, cram·ming. 1** force; stuff: *He crammed all his clothes quickly into the bag.* **2** fill too full: *The hall was crammed with people.* **3** eat too fast or too much. **4** *Informal.* stuff with knowledge or information. **5** *Informal.* learn hurriedly: *He is cramming facts and dates for his history examination.*
—*n.* **1** a crammed or crowded condition; crush. **2** the act of cramming a subject, especially in preparation for an examination. **3** information acquired by cramming. **4** a person who crams. [OE *crammian* < *crimman* insert] —**cram′mer,** *n.*

cram·bo (kram′bō) *n.* a game in which a player must think up a rhyme for a word or line given by another. [< earlier *crambe* < L *crambe* (*repetita*) cabbage (served up again)]

cramp[1] (kramp) *n.* **1** a metal bar bent at both ends, used for holding together blocks of stone, timbers, etc. **2** a clamp. **3** something that confines or hinders; limitation; restriction.
—*v.* **1** fasten together with a cramp. **2** confine in a small space; limit; restrict. **3 cramp one's style,** *Slang.* keep one from showing one's skill, ability, etc.
—*adj.* **1** confined; limited; restricted. **2** hard to read; difficult to understand. [< MDu.; cf. MLG *krampe*]

cramp[2] (kramp) *n.* **1** a sudden, painful contracting of muscles as a result of chill, strain, etc. **2** a paralysis of particular muscles as a result of using them too much. **3 cramps,** *pl.* very sharp pains in the abdomen.
—*v.* cause to have a cramp. [ME < OF *crampe* < MDu. *kramp.* Akin to CRAMP[1].]

cram·pon (kram′pən) *n.* **1** a strong iron bar with hooks at one end, used to lift heavy things; grappling iron. **2** a spiked, iron plate on a shoe, used to prevent slipping when climbing. [< F < Frankish **crampo* crampon (def. 1). Akin to CRAMP[1].]

cran·ber·ry (kran′ber′ē or kran′bər ē) *n.* **-ries. 1** a firm, sour, dark-red berry, used for jelly, sauce, etc. **2** any of various shrubs that the berries grow on. It grows in marshes or bogs. [< LG *kraanbere*]

cranberry bog a marsh where cranberries grow.

crane (krān) *n. v.* **craned, cran·ing.** —*n.* **1** a machine with a long, swinging arm, for lifting and moving heavy weights. **2** a swinging metal arm in a fireplace, from which a kettle or pot may be hung over the fire. **3** a large wading bird having very long legs and a long neck. **4** any of various herons, especially the great blue heron.
—*v.* **1** move by, or as if by, a crane. **2** stretch (the neck) as a crane does, in order to see better. [OE *cran*]

crane's-bill or **cranes·bill** (krānz′bil′) *n.* **1** any wild geranium, so called from the long, slender beak of the fruit. **2** any variety of geranium.

cran·i·al (krā′nē əl) *adj.* of or having to do with the skull; from the skull.

cranial index the cephalic index.

cra·ni·ol·o·gist (krā′nē ol′ə jist) *n.* an expert in craniology.

cra·ni·ol·o·gy (krā′nē ol′ə jē) *n.* the science that deals with the size, shape, and other characteristics of skulls. [< Gk. *kranion* skull + E *-logy*]

cra·ni·om·e·try (krā′nē om′ə trē) *n.* the science of measuring skulls; measurement of skulls. [< Gk. *kranion* skull + E *-metry*]

cra·ni·ot·o·my (krā′nē ot′ə mē) *n.* a surgical operation that involves the opening of the skull. [< Gk. *kranion* skull + *-tomia* a cutting]

cra·ni·um (krā′nē əm) *n.* **-ni·ums, -ni·a** (-nē ə). **1** the skull of a vertebrate. **2** the part of the skull enclosing the brain. [< LL < Gk. *kranion*]

crank (krangk) *n.* **1** a part or handle of a machine connected at right angles to a shaft to transmit motion. See **dead centre** for diagram. **2** a turn of speech or thought. **3** a queer notion or act. **4** *Informal.* a person with queer notions or habits; person possessed by some idea, hobby, etc. **5** *Informal.* a cross or ill-tempered person.
—*v.* **1** work or start by means of a crank: *crank an engine.* **2** bend into the shape of a crank.
—*adj.* loose; shaky; unsteady. [OE *cranc*]

crank·case (krangk′kās′) *n.* a heavy, metal case

forming the bottom part of an internal-combustion engine. The crankcase of a gasoline engine encloses the crankshaft, connecting rods, etc.

crank·shaft (krangk′shaft′) *n.* a shaft turning or turned by a crank.

crank·y (krangk′ē) *adj.* **crank·i·er, crank·i·est. 1** cross; irritable; ill-natured. **2** odd; queer. **3** liable to capsize; loose; shaky. **—crank′i·ly,** *adv.* **—crank′i·ness,** *n.*

cran·nied (kran′ēd) *adj.* full of crannies.

cran·ny (kran′ē) *n.* **-nies.** a small, narrow opening; crack; crevice. [< F *cran* fissure, ult. < Med.L *crena* notch]

crape (krāp) *n.* **1** a thin silk, cotton, rayon, or woollen cloth with a crinkled surface. **2** a piece of black crape used as a sign of mourning: *The officers all wore crape armbands to the funeral.* Also, **crepe** or **crêpe.**

crap·pie (krap′ē) *n.* a small fresh-water fish sometimes used for food. [< Cdn.F *crapet*]

craps (kraps) *n.* a gambling game played with two dice. [< Louisiana F *craps* the game of hazard < F *craps, crabs* < E *crabs* the lowest throw in hazard]

crap·shoot·er (krap′shüt′ər) *n.* a person who plays craps.

crash[1] (krash) *n.* **1** a sudden, loud noise: *The dishes fell with a crash.* **2** a falling, hitting, or breaking with force and a loud noise. **3** sudden ruin; a severe failure in business. **4** a fall to the earth or a bad landing of an aircraft. **5** a collision, especially between motor vehicles.
—*v.* **1** make a sudden, loud noise. **2** fall, hit, or break with force and a loud noise. **3** move or go with force and a loud noise. **4** be suddenly ruined; fail in business. **5** land in such a way as to damage or wreck an aircraft; make a very bad landing. **6** collide: *The two cars crashed into each other at the intersection.* **7** *Slang.* go to (a party, etc.) although not invited. **8 crash the gate,** *Slang.* attend a game, entertainment, etc. without paying the admission fee or having a ticket.
—*adj.* to be carried out with all possible speed, at whatever cost: *a crash program.* [blend of *craze* shatter and *mash*] **—crash′er,** *n.* **—Syn.** *n.* **2** smash. **3** bankruptcy. -*v.* **2** smash.

crash[2] (krash) *n.* a coarse linen cloth, used for towels, curtains, upholstering, etc. [probably < Russian; cf. Russian *krashenina* colored linen]

crash dive 1 of submarines, a fast descent made in an emergency. **2** of aircraft, a downward plunge ending in a crash.

crash-dive *v.* **-dived, -div·ing. 1** of submarines, make a fast descent in an emergency. **2** of aircraft, make a downward plunge in crashing.

crash helmet a heavily padded head covering worn by automobile racers, etc.

crash-land (krash′land′) *v.* of aircraft, make a forced landing in an emergency.

crash landing a forced landing made by an aircraft in an emergency.

crass (kras) *adj.* **1** gross; stupid. **2** thick; coarse. [< L *crassus* thick] **—crass′ly,** *adv.* **—crass′ness,** *n.*

crate (krāt) *n. v.* **crat·ed, crat·ing.** —*n.* a large frame, box, basket, etc. used to pack furniture, glass, fruit, etc. for shipping or storage. —*v.* pack in a crate. [< L *cratis* wickerwork]

cra·ter[1] (krā′tər) *n.* **1** a depression around the opening at the top of a volcano. **2** a bowl-shaped hole: *The battlefield was full of craters made by exploding shells.* **3** a round, ringlike elevation on the surface of the moon, resembling the crater of a volcano. [< L < Gk. *kratēr* bowl < *kra-* mix]

crat·er[2] (krāt′ər) *n.* a person or thing that packs or stores goods in a crate.

cra·vat (krə vat′) *n.* **1** a necktie. **2** a neckcloth; scarf. [< F *cravate,* special use of *Cravate* Croat]

crave (krāv) *v.* **craved, crav·ing. 1** long for; yearn for; desire strongly: *The thirsty man craved water.* **2** ask earnestly; beg: *crave a favor.* [OE *crafian* demand]

cra·ven (krā′vən) *adj.* cowardly. —*n.* **1** a coward. **2 cry craven,** surrender; admit defeat. [ME *cravant;* origin uncertain] **—cra′ven·ly,** *adv.* **—cra′ven·ness,** *n.*

hat, āge, cãre, fär; let, ēqual, tėrm; it, īce
hot, ōpen, ôrder; oil, out; cup, pu̇t, rüle, ūse
əbove, takən, pencəl, lemən, circəs
ch, child; ng, long; sh, ship
th, thin; ᴛʜ, then; zh, measure

Crav·en·ette (krā′vən et′ or krav′ən et′) *n. Trademark.* a waterproofed cloth used for raincoats, topcoats, etc. [< *Craven* Street, in London, England]

crav·ing (krāv′ing) *n.* a longing or yearning; strong desire. **—Syn.** See **desire.**

craw (kro or krô) *n.* **1** the crop of a bird or insect. **2** the stomach of any animal. [ME *crawe* < OE **craga* neck]

craw·fish (kro′fish′ or krô′-) *n.* **-fish** or **-fish·es.** *v.* —*n.* a crayfish. —*v. Informal.* move backwards; back out of something; retreat. [var. of *crayfish*]

crawl[1] (krol or krôl) *v.* **1** move slowly, pulling the body along the ground: *Worms and snakes crawl.* **2** move slowly on hands and knees: *crawl through a hole.* **3** move slowly. **4** swarm with crawling things: *The ground was crawling with ants.* **5** feel creepy: *My flesh crawled when I saw a big snake.* **6** move stealthily. **7** act slavishly. **8** swim with overarm strokes.
—*n.* **1** a crawling; slow movement. **2** a fast way of swimming with overarm strokes. [ME ? < ON *krafla*] **—crawl′er,** *n.*

Syn. *v.* **1, 3 Crawl, creep,** literally and figuratively mean "move slowly," and are frequently interchangeable. However, **crawl** has come to mean a more prostrate movement, implying the dragging of the body along the ground; it is suggestive of loathsome creatures, and has a servile connotation: *He tried to crawl back into favor.* **Creep** has a more sinister connotation and is suggestive of lurking danger: "*Louder yelled and nearer crept the Indian tiger.*"

crawl[2] (krol or krôl) *n.* an enclosure made with stakes in shallow water, used to hold turtles, fish, etc. [< Du. *kraal* < Sp. *corral.* Doublet of CORRAL.]

crawl·y (krol′ē or krôl′ē) *adj.* **crawl·i·er, crawl·i·est.** feeling as if things are crawling over one's skin; creepy.

cray·fish (krā′fish′) *n.* **-fish** or **-fish·es.** any of numerous crustaceans resembling small lobsters: *Crayfish often propel themselves backwards.* [ME *crevice,* influenced by E *fish* < OF < Gmc. Akin to CRAB[1].]

cray·on (krā′on or krā′ən) *n. v.* **-oned, -on·ing.** —*n.* **1** a stick of chalk, of charcoal, or of a waxlike, colored substance, used for drawing or writing. **2** a drawing made with crayons.
—*v.* draw with a crayon or crayons. [< F *crayon* < *craie* chalk < L *creta*]

craze (krāz) *n. v.* **crazed, craz·ing.** —*n.* something everybody is very much interested in for a short time; a fad. [< v.]
—*v.* **1** make or become crazy: *She was nearly crazed with pain.* **2** of earthenware, pottery, etc.: **a** make tiny cracks all over the surface. **b** become minutely cracked. [ME *crase(n)* break; ? < ON **krasa*]

cra·zy (krā′zē) *adj.* **-zi·er, -zi·est. 1** having a diseased mind; insane. **2** of or suitable for a crazy person; showing insanity. **3** *Informal.* unreasonably eager or enthusiastic. **4** not strong or sound; shaky; frail. **—cra′zi·ly,** *adv.* **—cra′zi·ness,** *n.*

Syn. **1, 2 Crazy, mad, insane** = showing characteristics of someone mentally ill. **Crazy** suggests being greatly distressed or disturbed by worry or strong emotion: *She is nearly crazy with fear.* **Mad** emphasizes wildness, and suggests being completely out of control or beyond reason, wildly foolish or reckless: *Crossing the Pacific on a raft seems a mad enterprise.* **Insane,** the legal term describing someone seriously ill mentally, suggests being utterly irrational or senseless: *He planned an insane revenge.*

crazy bone the funny bone.

crazy quilt a quilt made of pieces of cloth of various shapes, colors, and sizes, sewed together with no definite pattern.

creak (krēk) *v.* squeak loudly: *The hinges on our doors creak because they need oiling.* —*n.* a creaking noise. [ME *creke(n)*; apparently imitative]

creak·y (krēk′ē) *adj.* **creak·i·er, creak·i·est.** likely to creak; creaking. **—creak′i·ly,** *adv.* **—creak′i·ness,** *n.*

cream (krēm) *n.* **1** the oily, yellowish part of milk. Cream rises to the top when milk is allowed to stand.

Butter is made from cream. **2** food made of cream; food like cream: *ice cream, chocolate creams.* **3** an oily preparation put on the skin to make it smooth and soft. **4** a yellowish white. **5** the best part: *The cream of this class should make good university students.* **6** a thick, sweet liqueur; crème.
—*v.* **1** put cream in. **2** take or skim cream from. **3** form like cream on the top; foam; froth. **4** allow (milk) to form cream. **5** cook with cream, milk, or a sauce made of cream or milk with butter and flour. **6** make into a smooth mixture like cream.
—*adj.* **1** containing cream or milk; resembling cream: *cream sauce, cream soup.* **2** yellowish-white. [ME *creme* < OF *cresme* < LL *crama* cream < Gaulish, and < Ecclesiastical L *chrisma* ointment < Gk. *chrisma* < *chriein* anoint]

cream cheese a soft, white cheese made from cream or milk and cream.

cream·er (krēm′ər) *n.* **1** a small pitcher for holding cream. **2** a machine for separating cream from milk; separator. **3** a refrigerator in which milk is placed while the cream is rising.

cream·er·y (krēm′ər ē) *n.* **-er·ies. 1** a place where butter and cheese are made. **2** a place where cream, milk, and butter are sold or bought. **3** a place where milk is set for cream to rise.

cream of tartar a very sour, white powder used in cooking and in medicine; potassium bitartrate. Cream of tartar is obtained from the deposit in wine casks. *Formula*: $KHC_4H_4O_6$

cream sauce a sauce made of cream or milk with flour and butter.

cream·y (krēm′ē) *adj.* **cream·i·er, cream·i·est. 1** like cream; smooth and soft. **2** having much cream in it. **3** having the color of cream; yellowish-white. **—cream′i·ly,** *adv.* **—cream′i·ness,** *n.*

crease[1] (krēs) *n. v.* **creased, creas·ing.** —*n.* **1** a line or mark made by folding cloth, paper, etc.; fold; wrinkle. **2** in certain games, a small area marked off in front of a goal: *In hockey, a goal scored when the shooter is inside the crease is not counted.* **3** in cricket: **a** either of two lines at each end of the pitch that define the positions of the bowler and the batsman. **b** the space enclosed by these two lines.
—*v.* **1** make a crease or creases in. **2** become creased or wrinkled. **3** graze with a bullet. [origin unknown] **—creas′er,** *n.* **—crease′less,** *adj.*

crease[2] (krēs) *n.* kris.

cre·ate (krē āt′) *v.* **-at·ed, -at·ing. 1** cause to be; bring into being; make: *She created this garden in a patch of waste ground.* **2** make by giving a new character, function, or status to: *create a man a knight.* **3** give rise to; cause: *create a disturbance.* **4** be the first to represent (a part or role): *Maude Adams created the part of Barrie's Peter Pan.* [< L *creare*] **—Syn. 1** originate, produce, invent. **3** occasion.

cre·a·tion (krē ā′shən) *n.* **1** the act of creating or the state of being created. **2** all things created; the world and everything in it; the universe. **3** anything created: *That painting is a magnificent creation.* **4 the Creation,** the creating of the universe by God.

cre·a·tive (krē ā′tiv) *adj.* **1** having the power to create; inventive; productive: *Sculptors are creative artists.* **2** showing originality or imagination; artistic: *creative engineering, creative writing.* **—cre·a′tive·ly,** *adv.* **—cre·a′tive·ness,** *n.*

cre·a·tiv·i·ty (krē′ā tiv′ə tē) *n.* creative ability; the quality of being creative.

cre·a·tor (krē ā′tər) *n.* **1** a person who creates. **2 the Creator,** God.

crea·ture (krē′chər) *n.* **1** anything created. **2** a living being; an animal or person. **3** a person who is completely under the influence of another; a person who is ready to do anything that another asks. [< L *creatura* < *creare* create]

creature comforts the things that give bodily comfort. Food, clothing, and shelter are creature comforts.

crèche (kresh or krāsh) *n.* **1** a place where children are taken care of while their mothers are at work; day nursery. **2** a model of the Christ child in the manger, with attendant figures, that is often displayed in homes, churches, etc. at Christmas. [< F < Gmc. Akin to CRIB.]

cre·dence (krē′dəns) *n.* **1** belief: *Never give credence to gossip.* **2** an introduction or recommendation in confidence; credential: *a letter of credence.* [< Med.L *credentia* < L *credere* believe]

cre·den·tial (kri den′shəl) *n.* **1** something that gives or recommends credit or confidence. **2 credentials,** letters of introduction, entitling the bearer to credit or confidence; references: *After showing his credentials, the new inspector was allowed to see the bank's records.*

cred·i·bil·i·ty (kred′ə bil′ə tē) *n.* the fact or quality of being credible.

cred·i·ble (kred′ə bəl) *adj.* believable; reliable; trustworthy: *It seems hardly credible that Bill has grown so tall in one year.* [ME < L *credibilis* < *credere* believe] **—cred′i·ble·ness,** *n.* **—cred′i·bly,** *adv.*

☛ **Credible, creditable,** and **credulous** are sometimes confused. *Credible* = believable: *His story is hardly credible; how could all that happen to one person? Creditable* = bringing honor or praise: *He turned in a creditable performance, though his heart was no longer in his acting. Credulous* = too ready to believe: *He was credulous enough to think he would really be given the job.*

cred·it (kred′it) *n.* **1** belief; faith; trust. **2** trust in a person's ability and intention to pay. **3** the money in a person's bank account, etc. **4** in accounting: **a** an entry of money paid on account. **b** the right-hand side of an account where such entries are made. **c** the amount entered or shown on this side. **5** a delayed payment; the time allowed for delayed payment. **6** reputation in money matters: *If you pay your bills your credit will be good.* **7** good reputation: *a man of credit.* **8** honor; praise: *The person who does the work should get the credit.* **9** a person or thing that brings honor or praise: *A bright child is a credit to its parents.* **10** entry on a student's record showing that he has passed a course of study. **11** a point credited to a student who passes a course: *She needs five more credits to complete her university entrance requirements.* **12** an acknowledgment of the authorship, source, etc. of material used in a publication, work done on a dramatic show, radio or television program, etc. **13** Usually, **credits,** *pl.* a listing of the producers, directors, actors, technicians, and others who have contributed their skills to a motion picture, radio or television show, or a play. **14 do credit to,** bring honor or praise to. **15 give a person credit for,** think that he has. **16 give credit to,** believe; have faith in; trust. **17 on credit,** on a promise to pay later. When you buy something and promise to pay for it later, you are getting it on credit.
—*v.* **1** believe; have faith in; trust. **2** give credit in a bank account, etc. **3** enter on the credit side of an account. **4** assign to as a credit. **5** put an entry on the record of (a student) showing that he has passed a course of study. **6** ascribe or attribute (to); give credit for: *He credited me with the original idea.* **7 credit to a person,** think that he has. [< F < Ital. < L *creditum* a loan < *credere* trust, entrust]

Syn. *n.* **7** repute, standing. **8** commendation, esteem, appreciation. *-v.* **1 Credit, accredit** = believe someone or something responsible for saying, doing, feeling, or causing something. **Credit** emphasizes the idea of believing, not always with enough reason or evidence: *He credits me with doing things I never thought of.* **Accredit** emphasizes the idea of accepting because of some proof: *We accredit Peary with having discovered the North Pole.*

cred·it·a·ble (kred′ə tə bəl) *adj.* bringing honor or praise: *Her record of perfect attendance is very creditable.* **—cred′it·a·ble·ness,** *n.* **—cred′it·a·bly,** *adv.* ☛ See **credible** for usage note.

credit agency a business that collects information regarding the credit ratings of individuals or companies and offers this information as a service to subscribers.

credit card an identification card entitling its holder to charge the cost of goods or services.

Cred·i·tiste (kred′i tēst′) *Cdn.* —*adj.* of or having to do with the Social Credit Rally. —*n.* a member of this party. [< Cdn.F *Créditiste*]

Creditiste Party Social Credit Rally.

cred·i·tor (kred′ə tər) *n.* a person to whom money or goods are due; one to whom a debt is owed.

credit rating the financial standing and reputation of a company or individual, used to set the amount of money or credit that one may borrow or obtain.

credit union a co-operative association that makes loans to its members at low rates of interest.

cre·do (krē′dō or krā′dō) *n.* **-dos. 1** a creed: *His credo in art was purity of form.* **2** Also, **Credo. a** the Apostles' Creed or the Nicene Creed. **b** the music that accompanies either of these Creeds. [< L *credo* I believe. Doublet of CREED.]

cre·du·li·ty (krə dū′lə tē or krə dü′lə tē) *n.* an excessive readiness to believe.

cred·u·lous (krej′ů ləs) *adj.* too ready to believe; easily deceived. [< L *credulus* < *credere* believe]
—**cred′u·lous·ly,** *adv.* —**cred′u·lous·ness,** *n.* ☛ See **credible** for usage note.

Cree (krē) *n.* **Cree** or **Crees. 1** a tribe of Indians living in central Canada. The Cree were divided into two main groups, the Plains Cree and the Swampy Cree. **2** a member of this tribe. **3** the Algonquian language of this tribe.

creed (krēd) *n.* **1** a brief statement of the essential points of religious belief as approved by some church. **2** any statement of faith, principles, opinions, etc. **3** Also, **Creed.** the Apostles' Creed or the Nicene Creed. [OE *crēda* < L *credo* I believe. Doublet of CREDO.]

creek (krēk or krik) *n.* **1** a small stream. **2** a narrow bay, running inland for some distance. [ME *creke*; cf. MDu. *creke*]

Creek (krēk) *n.* **Creek** or **Creeks. 1** a group of Indian tribes formerly living in Alabama, Georgia, and N. Florida, now living in Oklahoma. **2** a member of this group of tribes. **3** their language.

creel (krēl) *n.* **1** a basket for holding fish. **2** a basketlike trap for fish, lobsters, etc. [ME *crele* ? < OF *creil*, ult. < L *cratis* wickerwork]

creep (krēp) *v.* **crept, creep·ing,** *n.* —*v.* **1** move with the body close to the ground or floor: *The cat crept toward the mouse.* **2** move slowly. **3** grow along the ground or over a wall by means of clinging stems: *a creeping plant. Ivy had crept up the wall of the old house.* **4** move or behave in a timid, stealthy, or servile manner: *The robbers crept toward their victims.* **5** slip slightly out of place. **6** feel as if things were creeping over the skin; shiver; shudder: *I could feel my flesh creep, and my hair stood on end.*
—*n.* **1** a creeping; slow movement. **2** in geology, slow movement of soil or disintegrated rock down a slope, due to gravity, frost, or ground water: *tangential creep, continental creep.* **3** in physics, the process of softening, flexing, or melting of material with accompanying changes in shape and dimension that result from increased stress or temperature. **4** *Slang.* a person who gives one the creeps; an undesirable or unlikable person. **5 the creeps,** *Informal.* a feeling as if things were creeping over one's skin. [OE *crēopan*] —**Syn.** *v.* **1, 2** See **crawl.**

creep·er (krēp′ər) *n.* **1** a person or thing that creeps. **2** any plant that grows along a surface, sending out rootlets from the stem, such as the Virginia creeper and ivy. **3** a small bird that creeps around on trees and bushes looking for food. **4** a piece of canvas attached to a ski for better gripping in climbing uphill. **5 creepers,** *pl.* **a** a garment combining waist and pants, worn by babies. **b** spiked, iron plates worn on shoes to prevent slipping.

creep·y (krēp′ē) *adj.* **creep·i·er, creep·i·est. 1** having a feeling as if things were creeping over one's skin; frightened. **2** causing such a feeling. **3** creeping; moving slowly. —**creep′i·ly,** *adv.* —**creep′i·ness,** *n.*

creese (krēs) *n.* kris.

cre·mate (kri māt′ or krē′māt) *v.* **-mat·ed, -mat·ing. 1** burn (a dead body) to ashes. **2** burn. [< L *cremare* burn]

cre·ma·tion (kri mā′shən) *n.* the burning of a dead body to ashes instead of burying it.

cre·ma·tor (kri mā′tər or krē′mā tər) *n.* **1** a person who cremates. **2** a furnace for cremating. [< LL]

cre·ma·to·ry (krē′mə tô′rē or krem′ə tô′rē) *n.* **-ries,** *adj.* —*n.* **1** a furnace for cremating. **2** a building that has a furnace for cremating. —*adj.* of or having to do with cremating.

hat, āge, cãre, fär; let, ēqual, tėrm; it, īce
hot, ōpen, ôrder; oil, out; cup, pu̇t, rüle, ūse
əbove, takən, pencəl, lemən, circəs
ch, child; ng, long; sh, ship
th, thin; ᴛʜ, then; zh, measure

crème (krem) *n. French.* **1** cream. **2** a thick, sweet liqueur.

crème de ca·ca·o (krem′də kə kā′ō or -kə kä′ō) chocolate-flavored liqueur. [< F]

crème de la crème (krem′də lä krem′) *French.* the very best; most select. [literally, cream of the cream]

crème de menthe (krem də mäɴt′) *French.* a liqueur flavored with mint.

Cre·mo·na (kri mō′nə) *n.* any of the fine violins made in Cremona, Italy, by the Amati family, Antonio Stradivari, etc. during the 16th, 17th, and 18th centuries.

cre·nate (krē′nāt) *adj.* with a scalloped edge. [< NL *crenatus* < Med.L *crena* notch]

cre·na·tion (kri nā′shən) *n.* a crenate formation.

cren·el·ate (kren′əl āt′) *v.* **-at·ed, -at·ing.** crenellate.

cren·el·late (kren′əl āt′) *v.* **-lat·ed, -lat·ing.** furnish with battlements. [< F *créneler* < *crenel* notch, ult. < Med.L *crena*] —**cren′el·la′tion,** *n.*

Cre·ole or **cre·ole** (krē′ōl) *n.* **1** a white person who is a descendant of the original French settlers of Louisiana. **2** the modified form of the French language as spoken in Louisiana. **3** a French or Spanish person born in Spanish America or the West Indies. **4 creole,** a person who is part Negro and part Creole.
—*adj.* of or having to do with the Creoles. [< F *créole* < Sp. < Pg. *crioulo* < *criar* bring up < L *creare* create]

cre·o·lized language (krē′ə līzd′) a mixed language resulting from continual contact between peoples speaking two mutually unintelligible languages. [< *Creole*]

cre·o·sol (krē′ə sōl′ or krē′ə sol′) *n.* a colorless, oily liquid obtained from wood tar and a resin of the guaiacum tree, used as an antiseptic. *Formula*: $C_8H_{10}O_2$ [< *creosote*]

cre·o·sote (krē′ə sōt′) *n. v.* **-sot·ed, -sot·ing.** —*n.* **1** an oily liquid with a penetrating odor, obtained by distilling wood tar. It is used to preserve wood and in cough medicine. **2** a similar substance obtained from coal tar.
—*v.* treat with creosote. [originally, a meat preservative; < Gk. *kreo-* (for *kreas* flesh) + *sōtēr* savior < *sōzein* save]

crepe or **crêpe** (krāp) *n.* **1** a thin silk, cotton, rayon, or woollen cloth with a crinkled surface; crape. **2** crepe paper. **3** crepe rubber. **4** *Rare.* crape (def. 2). **5** a light, thin pancake. [< F *crêpe* < L *crispa* curled]

crepe de Chine (krāp′ də shēn′) a soft, thin, medium-weight, silk crepe. [< F *crêpe de Chine* China crepe]

crepe paper or **crêpe paper** very thin crinkled paper used for making Christmas decorations, etc.

crepe rubber or **crêpe rubber** crude or synthetic rubber, made with a crinkled surface and used especially for the soles of shoes.

crep·i·tant (krep′ə tənt) *adj.* crackling; rattling.

crep·i·tate (krep′ə tāt′) *v.* **-tat·ed, -tat·ing.** crackle; rattle. [< L *crepitare* crackle < *crepare* crack]

crep·i·ta·tion (krep′ə tā′shən) *n.* a crepitating.

crept (krept) *v.* pt. and pp. of **creep.**

cre·pus·cu·lar (kri pus′kyů lər) *adj.* **1** of twilight; resembling twilight; dim; indistinct. **2** of certain birds, insects, etc., appearing or flying by twilight. [< L *crepusculum* twilight]

cres. or **cresc.** crescendo.

Cres. Crescent.

cre·scen·do (krə shen′dō) *adj. adv. n.* **-dos,** *v.* in music: —*adj. adv.* gradually increasing in force or loudness.
—*n.* **1** a gradual increase in force or loudness. The sign for a crescendo is <. **2** a passage to be played or sung with a crescendo.

—*v.* increase gradually in force or loudness. *Abbrev.*: cres. or cresc. [< Ital. *crescendo*, ppr. of *crescere* increase < L]

cres·cent (kres′ənt) *n.* **1** the shape of the moon in its first or last quarter. **2** anything having this or a similar shape. A curved street or a curved row of houses is sometimes called a crescent. **3** the emblem of the former Turkish Empire and of the present republic of Turkey. **4** the Turkish or Moslem power. **5** a light roll, made of yeast dough, shaped like a crescent moon.
—*adj.* **1** shaped like the moon in its first or last quarter. **2** growing; increasing. [< L *crescens*, *-entis*, ppr. of *crescere* grow] —**cres′cent·like′**, *adj.*

A crescent moon

cre·sol (krē′sōl or krē′sol) *n.* an oily liquid obtained from tar, used as a disinfectant. *Formula*: C_7H_8O [var. of *creosol*]

cress (kres) *n.* a plant whose leaves have a peppery taste, used as a garnish or in salads. [OE *cresse*]

cres·set (kres′it) *n.* a metal container for burning oil, wood, etc. to give light. Cressets are mounted on poles or hung from above. [ME < OF *cresset*, earlier *craisset* < *crois* cross < L *crux* (with reference to light from the Cross of Christ); influenced by *craisse* grease]

crest (krest) *n.* **1** a comb, tuft, etc. on the head of a bird or animal. **2** a decoration, plumes, etc. on the top of a helmet. **3** a decoration at the top of a coat of arms. A family crest is sometimes put on silverware, dishes, stationery, etc. **4** an emblem, usually of felt cloth, worn by members of various organizations, athletic teams, championship teams, etc.: *He was proud of his hockey crest. The soldier wore his regimental crest on the pocket of his blue blazer.* **5** a similar emblem awarded as a sign of merit in studies, athletics, etc. **6** the top part; top of a hill, wave, etc.; ridge; peak; summit.
—*v.* **1** furnish with a crest. **2** of waves, form or rise into a crest. **3** serve as a crest to; top; crown. **4** reach the crest or summit of (a hill, wave, etc.) [ME < OF *creste* < L *crista* tuft] —**crest′like′**, *adj.*

A crest on a coat of arms

crest·ed (kres′tid) *adj.* having a crest.

crest·fall·en (krest′fol′ən or -fôl′ən) *adj.* with bowed head; dejected; discouraged. —**crest′fall′en·ly**, *adv.*

cre·ta·ceous (kri tā′shəs) *adj.* **1** like chalk; containing chalk. **2 Cretaceous,** of or having to do with the geological period when most of the chalk deposits were made; of or having to do with rocks formed in this period.
—*n.* **Cretaceous,** in geology: **a** the period, beginning approximately 130 million years ago, when most of the chalk deposits were made. **b** the group of rocks formed in this period. See the chart under **geology**. [< L *cretaceus* < *creta* chalk < *Creta*, the island of Crete]

Cre·tan (krē′tən) *adj.* of or having to do with Crete (a Greek island in the Mediterranean Sea, S.E. of Greece) or its people. —*n.* a native or inhabitant of Crete.

cre·tin (krē′tən or kre′tən) *n.* a person afflicted with cretinism. [< F *crétin* < Swiss dial. < OF *chrestien* < L *Christianus* Christian; came to mean "man," then "fellow," then "poor fellow"]

cre·tin·ism (krē′tən iz′əm or kre′tən iz′əm) *n.* an inborn deformity, usually accompanied with idiocy, caused by a deficiency in the thyroid gland.

cre·tonne (kri ton′ or krē ton′) *n.* a strong cotton cloth with designs printed in colors on one or both sides, used for curtains, furniture covers, etc. [< F *cretonne*, probably < *Creton*, a village in Normandy, France]

cre·vasse (krə vas′) *n.* a deep crack or crevice in the ice of a glacier. —*v.* make crevasses in. [< F *crevasse* < OF *crevace*. Doublet of CREVICE.]

A crevasse

crev·ice (krev′is) *n.* a narrow split or crack. [ME *crevace* < OF < VL *crepacia* < L *crepare* crack. Doublet of CREVASSE.]

crew[1] (krü) *n.* **1** the men needed to do the work on a ship, or to row a boat. **2** a group of people working or acting together: *A train crew runs a railway train.* **3** a group; crowd; gang; mob. —*v.* **1** staff (a ship) with a crew. **2** act as a crew or as a member of a crew. [ME *crue* < MF *creüe* increase, reinforcement < *creistre* grow < L *crescere*]

crew[2] (krü) *v.* a pt. of **crow**[1].

crew cut a close-cropped haircut for men.

crew·el (krü′əl) *n.* a loosely twisted, woollen yarn, used for embroidery. [origin uncertain]

crew neck a neckline resembling a shoulder-to-shoulder slit, adapted from the pull-overs usually worn by oarsmen.

crib (krib) *n. v.* **cribbed, crib·bing.** —*n.* **1** a small bed with high sides to keep a baby from falling out. **2** a rack or manger for horses and cows to eat from. **3** a building or box for storing grain, salt, etc.: *a corn crib.* **4** a framework of logs or timbers used in building. The wooden lining inside a mine shaft is a crib. **5** *Informal.* the use of another's words or ideas as one's own. **6** *Informal.* notes or helps that are not supposed to be used in doing schoolwork or in examinations. **7** a small room or house. **8** in cribbage, a set of cards made up of discards from each hand and scored by the dealer after the deal has been played. **9** a raft of logs lashed together for floating downstream.
—*v.* **1** provide with a crib. **2** *Informal.* use (another's words or ideas) as one's own. **3** *Informal.* use notes or helps unfairly in doing schoolwork or in examinations. **4** shut up in a small space. [OE *cribb*]

crib·bage (krib′ij) *n.* a card game for two, three, or four people. The players keep score with a narrow board having holes into which movable pegs fit.

crib·bing (krib′ing) *n.* in mining: **1** the lining of timber in a shaft; crib. **2** the pieces of timber used in a crib.

crick[1] (krik) *n.* a sudden muscular cramp; painful stiffness of muscles. [origin uncertain]

crick[2] (krit) *n. Dialect.* a creek (def. 1).

crick·et[1] (krik′it) *n.* a small, black insect related to the grasshopper. Male crickets make a chirping noise by friction of the front wings. [ME < OF *criquet*; imitative]

crick·et[2] (krik′it) *n.* **1** an outdoor game played by two teams of eleven players each, with ball, bats, and wickets. **2** *Informal.* fair play; good sportsmanship.
—*adj. Informal.* fair; according to good sportsmanship.
—*v.* play the game of cricket. [< OF *criquet* goal post, stick, probably < MDu. *cricke* stick to lean on]

crick·et[3] (krik′it) *n.* a small, low, wooden stool. [origin uncertain]

crick·et·er (krik′ə tər) *n.* a person who plays cricket.

cried (krīd) *v.* pt. and pp. of **cry**.

cri·er (krī′ər) *n.* **1** an official who shouts out public announcements. **2** a person who shouts out announcements of goods for sale. **3** a person who cries.

cries (krīz) *n.* pl. of **cry**.

crime (krīm) *n.* **1** an act that is against the law. **2** the activity of criminals; violation of law. **3** a wrong act; sin. [ME < OF < L *crimen* accusation, offence]
Syn. 1 Crime, offence = an act that breaks a law. **Crime** applies particularly to an act that breaks a law that has been made by men for the public good. Crimes are punishable by public law: *Murder and swindling are crimes.* But what constitutes a crime varies to some extent with place and period. It is no longer a crime in Great Britain for a man to marry his deceased wife's sister. Certain conduct on the Sabbath may be a crime in one country and be entirely overlooked by the law in another country. (Contrast **sin.**) **Offence** is more general, and applies to any act, not always serious, that breaks any moral, public, or social law: *Lying and cruelty are offences.*

Cri·me·an (krī mē′ən) *adj.* of or having to do with the Crimea, a peninsula in S.W. Russia, extending into the Black Sea.

crim·i·nal (krim′ə nəl or krim′nəl) *n.* a person guilty of a crime. —*adj.* **1** guilty of crime. **2** having to do with crime: *criminal court, criminal law.* **3** like crime; wrong; sinful. [< L *criminalis* < *crimen.* See CRIME.]

crim·i·nal·i·ty (krim′ə nal′ə tē) *n.* **-ties. 1** the fact or quality of being a criminal; guilt. **2** a criminal act.

crim·i·nal·ly (krim′ə nəl ē or krim′nəl ē) *adv.* **1** in a criminal manner. **2** according to criminal law.

crim·i·nate (krim′ə nāt′) *v.* **-nat·ed, -nat·ing. 1** accuse of a crime. **2** furnish evidence as to the guilt of (someone). [< L *criminare* < *crimen.* See CRIME.]

crim·i·na·to·ry (krim′ə nə tô′rē) *adj.* criminating.

crim·i·no·log·i·cal (krim′ə nə loj′ə kəl) *adj.* of or having to do with criminology. **—crim′i·no·log′i·cal·ly,** *adv.*

crim·i·nol·o·gist (krim′ə nol′ə jist) *n.* an expert in criminology.

crim·i·nol·o·gy (krim′ə nol′ə jē) *n.* the study of crimes and criminals. [< L *crimen, -minis* crime + E *-logy*]

crimp[1] (krimp) *v.* **1** press into small, narrow folds; make wavy: *The girl crimped her hair before going to the party.* **2** pinch, fold, or bend into shape.
—*n.* 1 a crimping. **2** something crimped; fold; wave. **3** a waved or curled lock of hair. **4** the natural curl or wave in wool fibre. **5 put a crimp in,** *Slang.* interfere with; hinder. [OE *(ge)crympan*] **—crimp′er,** *n.*

crimp[2] (krimp) *n.* formerly, a person who makes a business of forcing or tricking men into becoming sailors, soldiers, etc. **—*v.*** formerly, force or trick (men) into becoming sailors, soldiers, etc. [origin uncertain]

crim·ple (krim′pəl) *v.* **-pled, -pling.** wrinkle; crumple; curl. [< *crimp*[1]]

crimp·y (krimp′ē) *adj.* **crimp·i·er, crimp·i·est.** having small, narrow folds; wavy.

crim·son (krim′zən) *n.* a deep red. **—*adj.*** deep-red.
—*v.* turn deep red: *His face crimsoned with shame.* [< Ital. *cremesino* < *cremisi, chermisi* the color crimson < Arabic *qirmazi* < *qirmiz* the kermes insect (from which a red dye was derived) < Skt. *krmis* worm, insect]

cringe (krinj) *v.* **cringed, cring·ing,** *n.* **—*v.* 1** shrink from danger or pain; crouch in fear. **2** bow down timidly; try to get favor or attention by servile behavior: *The beggar cringed as he put out his hand for money.*
—*n.* a cringing. [ME *crengen* < OE *cringan* give way] **—cring′er,** *n.* **—cring′ing·ly,** *adv.*

crin·gle (kring′gəl) *n.* a small loop or ring of rope on the edge of a sail. The sail can be fastened by putting a rope through the cringle. [apparently < LG *kringel,* dim. of *kring* ring]

crin·kle (kring′kəl) *v.* **-kled, -kling,** *n.* **—*v.* 1** become or cause to be wrinkled: *His suit was crinkled from lying on the floor.* **2** rustle: *Paper crinkles when it is crushed.*
—*n.* 1 a wrinkle; ripple. **2** a rustle. [ME *crenkle(n)* < OE *crincan* bend]

crin·kly (kring′klē) *adj.* **-kli·er, -kli·est.** full of crinkles.

cri·noid (krī′noid or krin′oid) *n.* any of a group of flower-shaped sea animals, usually anchored by a stalk. **—*adj.*** of or like a crinoid. [< Gk. *krinoeidēs* < *krinon* lily]

crin·o·line (krin′ə lin or krin′ə lēn′) *n.* **1** a stiff cloth used as a lining to hold a skirt out, make a coat collar stand up, etc. **2** a petticoat of crinoline to hold a skirt out. **3** a hoop skirt. [< F < Ital. *crinolino* < *crino* horsehair (< L *crinis* hair) + *lino* thread < L *linum*]

crip·ple (krip′əl) *n. v.* **-pled, -pling. —*n.*** a lame person or animal; one that cannot use his legs, arms, or body properly because of injury or deformity.
—*v.* 1 make a cripple of. **2** damage; disable; weaken: *The ship was crippled by the storm.* [OE *crypel.* Related to CREEP.] **—crip′pler,** *n.*
Syn. *v.* **1 Cripple, disable** = deprive of the ability or power to carry on normal activities. **Cripple** = deprive a person or animal of the use of a leg, foot, or arm: *He was crippled when he broke his hip.* **Disable** = deprive of the ability to work or act normally: *The man is disabled by a heart condition.* **2** impair.

cri·sis (krī′sis) *n.* **-ses** (-sēz). **1** the turning point in a disease, toward life or death. **2** a deciding event in history. **3** a time of danger or anxious waiting: *England faced a serious crisis during the Battle of Britain.* [< L < Gk. *krisis* < *krinein* decide] **—Syn. 3** See **emergency.**

crisp (krisp) *adj.* **1** hard and thin; breaking easily with a snap: *Dry toast and fresh celery are crisp.* **2** fresh; sharp and clear; bracing: *The air was cool and crisp.* **3** clear-cut; decisive: *"Don't talk; fight" is a crisp sentence.* **4** curly and wiry: *crisp hair.*
—*v.* make or become crisp.
—*n.* 1 something crisp. **2** *Esp.Brit.* a potato chip. **3** *Slang.* a bank note. [< L *crispus* curled] **—crisp′er,** *n.* **—crisp′ness,** *n.* **—Syn.** *adj.* **1** brittle. **2** brisk.

hat, āge, cãre, fär; let, ēqual, tėrm; it, īce
hot, ōpen, ôrder; oil, out; cup, pu̇t, rüle, ūse
əbove, takən, pencəl, lemən, circəs
ch, child; ng, long; sh, ship
th, thin; ᴛʜ, then; zh, measure

crisp·ly (krisp′lē) *adv.* in a crisp manner.

crisp·y (kris′pē) *adj.* **crisp·i·er, crisp·i·est.** crisp.

criss·cross (kris′kros′) *adj.* marked or made with crossed lines; crossed; crossing. **—*adv.*** crosswise.
—*v.* mark or cover with crossed lines. **—*n.*** a mark or pattern made of crossed lines. [alteration of *Christ's cross*]

cri·te·ri·a (krī tēr′ē ə) *n.* a pl. of **criterion.**

cri·te·ri·on (krī tēr′ē ən) *n.* **-te·ri·a** or **-te·ri·ons.** a rule or standard for making a judgment; test: *Wealth is only one criterion of success.* [< Gk. *kritērion* < *krinein* judge] **—Syn.** See **standard.**

crit·ic (krit′ik) *n.* **1** a person who makes judgments of the merits and faults of books, music, pictures, plays, acting, etc. **2** a person whose profession is preparing such judgments for a newspaper, magazine, radio, television program, etc. **3** a person who disapproves or finds fault; faultfinder. [< L *criticus* < Gk. *kritikos* critical < *krinein* to judge]

crit·i·cal (krit′ə kəl) *adj.* **1** inclined to find fault or disapprove: *a critical disposition.* **2** skilled as a critic. **3** coming from one who is skilled as a critic: *a critical judgment.* **4** belonging to the work of a critic: *critical essays.* **5** of a crisis; important at a time of danger and difficulty: *the critical moment.* **6** full of danger or difficulty: *His delay was critical.* **7** of supplies, labor, or resources, necessary for some work or project but existing in inadequate supply. **8** in physics and mathematics, of or having to do with a point at which some action, property, or condition undergoes a change. **9** in nuclear physics, having to do with, or capable of producing, a chain reaction: *critical mass.* **10** of or involving the operation of an atomic reactor: *a critical experiment.* **—crit′i·cal·ly,** *adv.* **—crit′i·cal·ness,** *n.*

critical angle 1 in optics, the smallest possible angle of incidence that gives total reflection. **2** in aeronautics, the angle of attack of a wing at which maximum lift is momentarily reached and above which turbulence occurs, drag is greatly increased, lift is destroyed, and the airfoil tends to stall.

critical mass in nuclear physics, the minimum quantity of fissionable material required in a reactor to produce or maintain a chain reaction.

crit·i·cise (krit′ə sīz′) *v.* **-cised, -cis·ing.** criticize. **—crit′i·cis′er,** *n.*

crit·i·cism (krit′ə siz′əm) *n.* **1** disapproval; faultfinding. **2** the making of judgments; the act of approving or disapproving; an analysis of merits and faults. **3** the rules and principles used in making careful judgments of the merits and faults of books, music, pictures, plays, acting, etc. **4** a critical comment, essay, review, etc. **—Syn. 4** See **review.**

crit·i·cize (krit′ə sīz′) *v.* **-cized, -ciz·ing. 1** disapprove; find fault with: *Do not criticize him until you know all the facts.* **2** judge as a critic; discuss the merits and faults of. **3** act or speak as a critic. **—crit′i·ciz′er,** *n.*

cri·tique (kri tēk′) *n.* **1** a critical essay or review. Some newspapers regularly publish critiques of new books. **2** the art of criticism; criticism. [< F < Gk. *kritikē* *(technē)* the critical art, fem. of *kritikos.* See CRITIC.]

crit·ter (krit′ər) *Dialect.* **1** any living creature. **2** an animal, especially a cow, raised as livestock.

croak (krōk) *n.* a deep, hoarse sound, made by a frog, crow, raven, etc. [< v.]
—*v.* 1 make a deep, hoarse sound. **2** utter in a deep, hoarse voice. **3** be always prophesying misfortune; be dissatisfied; grumble. **4** *Slang.* die. [OE **crācian*; related to *crācettan* of the same meaning] **—croak′er,** *n.*

croak·y (krōk′ē) *adj.* **croak·i·er, croak·i·est. 1** deep and hoarse; making a croaking sound. **2** having a tendency to croak. **—croak′i·ly,** *adv.* **—croak·i·ness,** *n.*

Croat (krō′at) *n.* a native or inhabitant of Croatia, a district in N.W. Yugoslavia.

Cro·a·tian (krō ā′shən) *adj.* of or having to do with Croatia or the Croats. —*n.* **1** a Croat. **2** the Slavic dialect of Croatia.

cro·chet (krō shā′) *v.* **-cheted** (-shād′), **-chet·ing** (-shā′ing) *n.* —*v.* knit (sweaters, lace, etc.) with a single needle having a hook at one end. [< n.]
—*n.* knitting done in this way. [< F *crochet*, dim. of *croc* hook < Gmc. Doublet of CROCKET, CROTCHET.]
—**cro·chet′er** (-shā′ər), *n.*

crock (krok) *n.* **1** a pot or jar made of baked clay. **2** *Slang.* a bottle of liquor. **3** *Slang.* a worthless, old, or decrepit person, horse, car, etc. [OE *crocc(a)*]

crocked (krokt) *adj. Slang.* drunk.

crock·er·y (krok′ər ē or krok′rē) *n.* dishes, jars, etc. made of baked clay; earthenware.

crock·et (krok′it) *n.* in architecture, an ornament, usually made to resemble foliage, along the edges of a spire, pinnacle, gable, etc. [< AF *croket*, var. of OF *crochet*, dim. of *croc* hook < Gmc. Doublet of CROCHET, CROQUET, CROTCHET.]

croc·o·dile (krok′ə dīl′) *n.* a large, lizardlike reptile having a thick skin, a long, narrow head, and webbed feet. Crocodiles live in rivers and marshes in warm climates. [ME < OF < LL *crocodilus* < Gk. *krokodilos*, earlier, lizard < *krokē* pebble + *drilos* worm]

crocodile tears pretended or insincere grief.

croc·o·dil·i·an (krok′ə dil′ē ən) *adj.* of or like a crocodile. —*n.* any of a group of reptiles that includes crocodiles, alligators, etc.

cro·cus (krō′kəs) *n.* **cro·cus·es** or **cro·ci** (-sī or -sē). **1** a small plant that grows from a bulblike stem, having white, yellow, or purple flowers that bloom very early in the spring. **2** the flower of this plant. **3** a prairie wild flower, having large, purple, or violet blossoms in early spring: *The prairie crocus is the floral emblem of Manitoba.* **4** a deep-yellow color; saffron. **5** a polishing powder consisting of iron oxide: *jeweller's crocus.* [< L < Gk. *krokos* < Semitic]

Croe·sus (krē′səs) *n.* **1** King of Lydia from 560 to 546 B.C., famous for his great wealth. **2** any very rich person.

croft (kroft) *n. Brit.* **1** a small enclosed field. **2** a very small rented farm. [OE]

croft·er (krof′tər) *n. Brit.* a person who cultivates a small farm.

crois·sant (krwä′sän; *French*, krwä säN′) *n.* a small roll of bread shaped like a crescent. [< F *croissant* ppr. of *croître* grow < L *crēscere*. See CRESCENT.]

croix de guerre (krwä′də gär′) in France, a medal given to servicemen for bravery under fire. [< F *croix de guerre* war cross]

Cro-Mag·non (krō mag′non) *adj.* of or having to do with the Cro-Magnons. —*n.* **1** a group of prehistoric people who lived in southwestern Europe. They used stone and bone implements. **2** a member of this group. [< *Cro-Magnon* cave, near Dordogne, S.W. France, where their remains have been found]

crom·lech (krom′lək) *n.* **1** a circle of upright stones erected in prehistoric times. **2** upright stones with a large, flat stone laid horizontally on them. [< Welsh *cromlech* < *crom* bent + *llech* flat stone]

crone (krōn) *n.* a shrivelled, wrinkled, old woman. [< MDu. *croonje* < OF *carogne* carcass, hag. Doublet of CARRION.]

Cro·nus (krō′nəs) *n.* in Greek mythology, a Titan who was ruler of the universe until overthrown by his son Zeus. He was identified with the Roman god Saturn.

cro·ny (krō′nē) *n.* **-nies.** a very close friend; chum. [origin uncertain]

crook (krůk) *v.* **crooked** (krůkt), **crook·ing**, *n.* —*v.* hook; bend; curve: *The soldier crooked his finger around the trigger of his gun.* [< n.]
—*n.* **1** a hook; bend; curve: *a crook in a stream.* **2** a hooked, curved, or bent part. **3** a shepherd's staff. Its upper end is curved or bent into a hook. **4** *Informal.* a dishonest person; thief; swindler. [ME *crōc* < ON *krókr*]

crooked (krůk′id) *adj.* **1** not straight; bent; curved; twisted. **2** dishonest. —**crook′ed·ly**, *adv.* —**crook′ed·ness**, *n.*

crooked knife (krůk′id) *Cdn.* a wood-working knife having a blade that ends in a hook, used widely in the North, especially by the Indians, in making snowshoe frames, pelt stretchers, canoes, etc. [translation of Cdn.F *couteau croché*]

crook·neck (krůk′nek′) *n.* a kind of squash having a long, curved neck.

crook·necked (krůk′nekt′) *adj.* having a hooked or curved neck.

croon (krün) *v.* **1** murmur; hum; sing in a low tone: *The mother was crooning to her baby.* **2** sing in a low voice with exaggerated emotion. —*n.* a low singing; a humming or murmuring. [ME < MDu. *kronen* murmur] —**croon′er**, *n.*

crop (krop) *n. v.* **cropped, crop·ping.** —*n.* **1** a product grown or gathered for use, especially for use as food: *Wheat is the main crop of the Prairie Provinces.* **2** the whole amount (of wheat, corn, or the produce of any plant or tree) that is yielded in one season: *The potato crop was very small this year.* **3** anything like a crop; a group; collection: *a crop of lies.* **4** the act or result of cropping. A short haircut is a crop. **5** a mark produced by clipping the ears. **6 a** the baglike swelling in a bird's food passage where food is prepared for digestion. **b** a similar organ in other animals or in insects. **7** a short whip having a loop at the end away from the handle. **8** the handle of a whip. **9** in mining, an outcrop of a vein or seam.
—*v.* **1** plant and cultivate a crop. **2** cut or bite off the top of: *Sheep crop grass very short.* **3** clip; cut short (the tail, ear, hair, edge of a book, etc.). **4** in mining, come to the surface of the ground, as a vein of ore. **5 crop out** or **up, a** appear; come to the surface: *Great ridges of rock cropped out all over the hillside.* **b** appear, occur, or be shown unexpectedly: *All sorts of difficulties cropped up.* [OE *cropp* sprout, craw]

Syn. *n.* **1 Crop, yield, harvest** = a product of the land, grown or gathered for use. **Crop** is the general word, applying to the product while growing and when gathered: *The tomato crop was damaged by frost.* **Yield** applies to the quantity or amount of a crop produced: *The yield from those trees was poor this year.* **Harvest**, more formal, emphasizes the idea of gathering and applies to the process or time of gathering or to the amount gathered in one season: *The wheat is ready for harvest.*

crop·land (krop′land′) *n.* land under cultivation for crops. Also, **croplands.**

crop·per (krop′ər) *n.* **1** a person or thing that crops. **2** a person who raises a crop or crops, especially on land owned by another, receiving a share of the produce; sharecropper. **3** a plant that furnishes a crop: *The soybean is a hardy cropper.* **4** *Informal.* a heavy fall. **5** *Informal.* a failure; collapse. **6 come a cropper,** *Informal.* **a** fall heavily. **b** fail; collapse.

crop rotation in agriculture, a way of conserving the fertility of soil by successively planting on the same ground different crops with varying food requirements.

cro·quet (krō kā′) *n. v.* **-quet·ted** or **-quet·ed** (-kād′), **-quet·ting** or **quet·ing** (-kā′ing). —*n.* **1** an outdoor game played by driving wooden balls through small wire arches by means of mallets. **2** a driving away of an opponent's ball by striking one's own when the two are in contact. —*v.* drive away (an opponent's ball) by striking one's own ball when the two are in contact. [< F *croquet*, dial. var. of *crochet*. See CROCHET.]

cro·quette (krō ket′) *n.* a small cake of chopped, cooked meat, fish, vegetables, etc. coated with crumbs and fried. [< F *croquette* < *croquer* crunch]

cro·sier or **cro·zier** (krō′zhər) *n.* **1** an ornamental staff carried by or before bishops or certain abbots. **2** in botany, the curled top of a young fern. [ME < OF *crossier* crook bearer < VL *croccia* crook < Gmc.]

cross (kros) *n.* **1** a stick or post with another across it making a shape like a T or an X. **2** any thing, design, or mark shaped like a cross. A cross is the symbol of the Christian religion. A person who cannot write his name makes a cross instead. A soldier is sometimes given a medal in the form of a cross for bravery in war. **3** a

crossing; lying or going across. **4** a burden of duty; suffering; trouble. **5** a mixing of kinds, breeds, or races. **6** the result of such mixing: *A mule is a cross between a horse and a donkey.* **7** in boxing, a countering blow crossing over the opponent's lead. **8 take the cross,** join a crusade. **9 the Cross, a** the cross on which Christ died. **b** the sufferings and death of Christ; the Atonement. **c** the Christian religion.
—*v.* **1** mark with a cross. **2** draw a line across: *cross a "t".* **3** cancel by drawing a line or lines across: *cross off a name on a list. He crossed out the wrong word.* **4** put or lay across. **5** lie across; be in the form of a cross. **6** go across; move across: *cross a bridge. Our street crosses the highway.* **7** meet and pass: *My letter to her and hers to me crossed.* **8** make the sign of the cross on or over: *The priest crossed himself.* **9** oppose; hinder: *If anyone crosses him, he gets very angry.* **10** mix kinds, breeds, or races of: *A new plant is sometimes made by crossing two others.* **11 cross a person's path,** meet a person. **12 cross one's fingers,** put one finger over another in a superstitious gesture intended to keep trouble away, or when saying something but keeping back part of one's thoughts. **13 cross one's heart,** make the sign of the cross over one's heart when swearing that something is true. **14 cross one's mind,** occur to one. **15 cross the t's.** See **dot the i's and cross the t's. 16 cross swords, a** fight with swords in single combat. **b** engage in controversy. **17 cross the floor,** of a member of a legislature, leave one's party by moving from one's assigned seat with that party to a seat in another section of the chamber.
—*adj.* **1** crossing; laying or going across. **2** in a bad temper. **3** mixed in kind, breed, or race. [OE *cros* < OIrish *cros* < L *crux.* Doublet of CRUX.] —**cross′ly,** *adv.* —**cross′ness,** *n.* —**Syn.** *n.* **4** trial, affliction. **6** hybrid.

GREEK MALTESE ST. ANDREW'S
LATIN PATRIARCHAL PAPAL

Crosses (def. 2)

cross- *combining form.* **1** cross-shaped: *cross-stitch = a stitch crossed over another.* **2** moving across: *crossfire = lines of fire crossing one another.* **3** counter: *cross-purpose = a purpose counter to another.* **4** across regular lines of affinity: *cross-fertilization = fertilization of one plant by pollen from another.*

cross·bar (kros′bär′) *n.* a bar, line, or stripe going crosswise.

cross·beam (kros′bēm′) *n.* a large beam that crosses another or extends from wall to wall.

cross·bill (kros′bil′) *n.* a small bird whose powerful bill has points that cross.

cross·bones (kros′bōnz′) *n.pl.* two large bones placed crosswise. A pirate flag has crossbones below a skull as a symbol of death. Poisonous medicines are sometimes marked with a skull and crossbones.

cross·bow (kros′bō′) *n.* a medieval weapon with a bow and a grooved stock in the middle to direct the arrows, stones, etc.

cross·bow·man (kros′bō′mən) *n.* **-men** (-mən). formerly, a soldier who used a crossbow.

cross·bred (kros′bred′) *adj.* produced by crossbreeding. —*n.* an animal or plant produced by crossbreeding.

cross·breed (kros′brēd′) *v.* **-bred, -breed·ing,** *n.* —*v.* breed by mixing kinds, breeds, or races. —*n.* an individual or breed produced by crossbreeding. A loganberry is a crossbreed, developed by crossing the blackberry and the raspberry.

cross bun a bun marked with a cross on the top. Hot cross buns are traditionally eaten on Good Friday.

cross-check (kros′chek′) *v.* **1** check again, or check against another source. **2** in hockey or lacrosse, give an illegal check by holding one's stick in both hands and thrusting it in front of an opponent's face or body. —*n.* **1** the act of cross-checking. **2** in hockey or lacrosse, an illegal check made by cross-checking.

cross-coun·try (kros′kun′trē) *adj.* across fields or open country instead of by road: *a cross-country race.*

cross·cur·rent (kros′kėr′ənt) *n.* **1** a current of air blowing across another. **2** a contradictory tendency or trend: *the crosscurrents of political thought.*

hat, āge, cãre, fär; let, ēqual, tėrm; it, īce
hot, ōpen, ôrder; oil, out; cup, pu̇t, rüle, ūse
əbove, takən, pencəl, lemən, circəs
ch, child; ng, long; sh, ship
th, thin; ᴛʜ, then; zh, measure

cross·cut (kros′kut′) *adj. n. v.* **-cut, -cut·ting.** —*adj.* **1** used or made for cutting across. **2** cut across. —*n.* **1** a crosscut saw. See **saw** for picture. **2** a cut across. **3** a short cut. —*v.* cut across.

crosscut saw a saw used or made for cutting across the grain of wood.

crosse (kros) *n.* a lacrosse stick. [< Cdn.F < F *crosse* a hooked stick]

cross-ex·am·i·na·tion (kros′eg zam′ə nā′shən) *n.* **1** in law, examination to check a previous examination, especially the questioning of a witness by the lawyer for the opposing side to test the truth of his evidence. **2** a close or severe questioning.

cross-ex·am·ine (kros′eg zam′ən) *v.* **-ined, -in·ing. 1** in law, question (a witness for the opposing side) closely to test the truth of his evidence. **2** question closely or severely. —**cross′-ex·am′in·er,** *n.*

cross-eye (kros′ī′) *n.* a strabismus, especially the form in which both eyes are turned toward the nose.

cross-eyed (kros′īd′) *adj.* having both eyes turned toward the nose.

cross-fer·ti·li·za·tion (kros′fėr′tə lə zā′shən or kros′fėr tə lī zā′shən) *n.* in botany, the fertilization of one flower by pollen from another.

cross-fer·ti·lize (kros′fėr′tə līz′) *v.* **-lized, -liz·ing. 1** cause the cross-fertilization of. **2** be subjected to cross-fertilization.

cross·fire (kros′fīr′) *n.* **1** gun-fire coming from two or more opposite directions so as to cross. **2** a verbal attack from two or more sources or directions.

cross-grained (kros′grānd′) *adj.* **1** of wood, having the grain running across the regular grain; having an irregular or gnarled grain. **2** hard to get along with; contrary.

cross·hatch (kros′hach′) *v.* mark or shade with two sets of parallel lines crossing each other. —*n.* any one of these lines.

Cross-hatching

cross·hatch·ing (kros′hach′ing) *n.* **1** the making of crosshatches. **2** the marking or shading made.

cross·ing (kros′ing) *n.* **1** a place where things cross each other. **2** a place at which a street, river, etc. may be crossed. **3** the act of crossing, especially a voyage across water.

crossing guard a member of a school patrol, or other individual, who escorts children across busy streets.

cross·jack (kros′jak′) *n.* a square sail on the lower yard of a mizzenmast.

cross-leg·ged (kros′leg′id or kros′legd′) *adj.* **1** with one leg over the other and the knees together. **2** with the ankles crossed and the knees apart.

cross·let (kros′lit) *n.* a small cross.

cross·o·ver (kros′ō′vər) *n.* **1** a place at which a crossing is made. **2** anything that crosses over or connects, as a bridge over a highway.

cross·patch (kros′pach′) *n. Informal.* a cross, bad-tempered person.

cross·piece (kros′pēs′) *n.* a piece that is placed across something.

cross-pol·li·nate (kros′pol′ə nāt′) *v.* **-nat·ed, -nat·ing. 1** cause cross-pollination in. **2** be subjected to cross-pollination.

cross-pol·li·na·tion (kros′pol′ə nā′shən) *n.* the transfer of pollen from the anther of one flower to the stigma of another. Insects and wind are agents of cross-pollination.

cross-pur·pose (kros′pėr′pəs) *n.* **1** an opposing or contrary purpose. **2 at cross-purposes, a** misunderstanding each other's purpose. **b** acting under such a misunderstanding.

cross-ques·tion (kros′kwes′chən) *v.* question closely or severely; cross-examine. —*n.* a question asked in cross-examining.

cross·rail (kros′rāl′) *n.* a piece of wood, metal, etc. that lies across something.

cross-re·fer (kros′ri fėr′) *v.* **-ferred, -fer·ring. 1** refer from one part to another. **2** make a cross reference.

cross reference a reference from one part of a book, index, etc. to another. Under **crupper,** the instruction "See **harness** for diagram" is a cross reference.

cross·road (kros′rōd′) *n.* **1** a road that crosses another. **2** a road connecting main roads. **3** Often, **crossroads,** *pl.* a place where roads cross. **4 at the crossroads,** in a situation where a choice must be made.

cross·ruff (kros′ruf′) *n.* in card games, a play in which each of two partners leads a card that the other can trump.

cross section 1 the act of cutting anything across: *John's mother was slicing tomatoes for a salad by making a series of cross sections.* **2** a piece cut in this way. **3** a drawing showing levels and profiles, as in surveying. **4** a representative sample; small selection of people, things, etc. with the same qualities as the entire group.

CROSS SECTION

A cross section of a tree trunk

cross-staff (kros′stäf′) *n.* a surveying instrument for measuring distances at right angles to the main line.

cross-stitch (kros′stich′) *n.* **1** one stitch crossed over another, forming an X. **2** embroidery made with this stitch. —*v.* embroider or sew with one stitch crossed over another.

cross street 1 a street that crosses another. **2** a street connecting main streets.

cross·trees (kros′trēz′) *n.pl.* on a ship, two horizontal bars of wood near the top of a mast.

C, crosstrees

cross·walk (kros′wok′ or -wôk′) *n.* a street crossing marked with white lines: *In some cities approaching vehicles must stop when pedestrians are using a crosswalk.*

cross·way (kros′wā′) *n.* crossroad.

cross·ways (kros′wāz′) *adv.* crosswise.

cross·wise (kros′wīz′) *adv.* **1** so as to cross; across. **2** in the form of a cross. **3** opposite to what is required; wrongly.

cross·word puzzle (kros′wėrd′) a puzzle with sets of squares to be filled in with words, one letter to each square. Synonyms or definitions of the words are given with numbers corresponding to numbers in the squares.

cross·yard (kros′yärd′) *n.* on a ship, a pole or spar fastened crosswise.

crotch (kroch) *n.* **1** a forked piece or part; place where a tree, bough, etc. divides into two limbs or branches. **2** the place where the human body divides into its legs. [var. of *crutch*]

crotched (krocht) *adj.* having a crotch; forked.

crotch·et (kroch′it) *n.* **1** an odd notion; unreasonable whim. **2** a small hook or hooklike part. **3** in music, a quarter note. [ME < OF *crochet,* dim. of *croc* hook < Gmc. Doublet of CROCHET, CROCKET.]

crotch·et·y (kroch′ə tē) *adj.* full of odd notions or unreasonable whims. —**crotch′et·i·ness,** *n.*

crot·on (krō′tən) *n.* a tropical shrub or tree of Asia with a strong odor. The seeds of a croton tree yield an oil used in medicine. [< NL < Gk. *krotōn* tick[2]]

croton bug a small cockroach.

croton oil a thick, bitter oil obtained from croton seeds, used in medicine as a cathartic and as a counter-irritant.

crouch (krouch) *v.* **1** stoop low with legs bent like an animal ready to spring, or in hiding, or shrinking in fear. **2** bow down in a timid or slavish manner; cower. **3** bend low. —*n.* **1** the act or state of crouching. **2** a crouching position. A baseball catcher's squatting stance is called a crouch. [ME < OF *crochir* < *croc* hook < Gmc.]

croup[1] (krüp) *n.* an inflammation or diseased condition of the throat and windpipe characterized by a hoarse cough and difficult breathing. [< *croup,* v., ? blend of *croak* and *whoop*]

croup[2] (krüp) *n.* the rump of a horse, etc. [ME < OF *croupe* < Gmc.]

crou·pi·er (krü′pē ər) *n.* the attendant at a gambling table who rakes in the money and pays the winners. [< F *croupier* < *croupe;* see CROUP[2]; originally, one who rides behind]

croup·y (krüp′ē) *adj.* **1** sick with croup. **2** hoarse and having difficulty in breathing. **3** of croup; resembling croup.

crou·ton (krü′ton) *n.* a small piece of toasted or fried bread, often served in soup. [< F *croûton* < *croûte* crust < L *crusta*]

crow[1] (krō) *n. v.* **crowed (or crew** *for 1***), crowed, crow·ing.** —*n.* **1** a loud cry made by a rooster. **2** a happy sound made by a baby. [< v.]
—*v.* **1** make the cry of a rooster. **2** make the happy sound of a baby. **3** show happiness and pride; boast: *The winning team crowed over its victory.* [OE *crāwan;* imitative]

crow[2] (krō) *n.* **1** a large, glossy-black bird that has a harsh cry or caw. **2** any similar bird, such as a raven, magpie, jay, etc. **3** a crowbar. **4 as the crow flies,** in a straight line; in or by the shortest way. **5 eat crow,** *Informal.* be forced to do something very disagreeable and humiliating. **6 have a crow to pick with,** *Informal.* have a complaint or criticism against; have something unpleasant to talk over with. [OE *crāwe*]

Crow (krō) *n.* **Crow or Crows. 1** a tribe of Indians living in Montana and Wyoming. **2** a member of this tribe. **3** the Siouan language of this tribe.

crow·bar (krō′bär′) *n.* a strong iron or steel bar, used as a lever.

crow·ber·ry (krō′ber′ē) *n.* **-ries. 1** a tasteless blackberry, the fruit of a heathlike evergreen shrub of North America and northern Europe. **2** the shrub itself. **3** a large cranberry.

crow-boot (krō′büt′) *n. Cdn.* a mukluk, usually made of muskrat fur and having a thick moosehide sole.

crowd (kroud) *n.* **1** a large number of people together: *A crowd gathered to hear the speaker.* **2** the common people; people in general; the masses: *Many newspapers appeal to the crowd.* **3** *Informal.* a group; set: *The boy went out with his crowd to the dance.* **4** a large number of things together. [< v.]
—*v.* **1** collect in large numbers. **2** fill; fill too full: *crowd a bus.* **3** push; shove. **4** press forward; force one's way: *crowd into a building.* **5 crowd on sail,** raise more sails to make a ship go faster. [OE *crūdan* press]

Syn. *n.* **1 Crowd, throng, swarm** = a large number of people together. **Crowd** applies to a large number of people pressed closely together without much order: *A crowd was waiting in the lobby.* **Throng** suggests still larger numbers and more movement of pressing together and pushing forward: *At Christmas there are throngs in the streets.* **Swarm** emphasizes the idea of a large, confused, moving mass: *A swarm of students gathered.*
-*v.* **1** throng, swarm. **2** cram, pack.

crowd·ed (kroud′id) *adj.* **1** filled with a crowd. **2** filled; filled too full; packed. **3** close together; too close together. —**crowd′ed·ly,** *adv.* —**crowd′ed·ness,** *n.*

crow·foot (krō′fu̇t′) *n.* **-foots** *for 1,* **-feet** *for 2, 3, 4.* **1** a buttercup or other plant having leaves shaped like a crow's foot. **2** on a ship, an arrangement of small ropes used to suspend awnings, etc. **3** a piece of zinc used as one of the poles or electrodes in some kinds of batteries. **4** formerly, an iron ball having four spikes, thrown on the ground to hinder the advance of enemy cavalry.

crown (kroun) *n.* **1** a head covering of precious metal and jewels, worn by a monarch. **2** the power and authority of a monarch; royal power. **3** a monarch; a king, queen, etc. **4** a design or thing shaped like a crown. **5** a wreath for the head: *The winner of the race received a crown.* **6** an honor; reward. **7** the head. **8** the highest part; top: *the crown of the head.* **9** the top

The Crown of England

part of a hat, cap, etc. **10** the highest state or quality of anything. **11 a** the part of a tooth above the gum. **b** the chewing surface of a tooth. **c** an artificial substitute for either of these. **12** a former British silver coin, worth 5 shillings. **13** the end of an anchor between the arms. **14** in botany: **a** the corona of a flower or seed. **b** the top of a root of a plant, from which the stem arises. **c** the leaves and branches of a tree or shrub. **15** the crest of a bird. **16** the tip of a deer's horn. **17** crown glass. **18** a size of printing paper, usually 15 × 20 inches. **19 the Crown, a** the power and authority of a monarch, or of the officials who exercise that authority; royal power. **b** a monarch acting in his official capacity. —*v.* **1** put a crown on; make king, queen, etc. **2** honor; reward. **3** be on top of; cover the highest part of: *A fort crowns the hill.* **4** make perfect or complete; add the finishing touch to: *Success crowned his efforts.* **5** supply (a tooth) with a crown. **6** in checkers, make a king of (a piece that has been moved across the checkerboard). **7** *Informal.* hit on the head. **8** of forest fires, spread rapidly from treetop to treetop.
—*adj.* of a crown; having to do with a crown: *the crown jewels.* [ME < AF *coroune* < L *corona* garland, wreath, crown. Doublet of CORONA.] —**Syn.** *n.* **8, 10.** See **top.**

Crown attorney a lawyer who represents the Crown, or state, in a trial.

crown colony a colony under the power and authority of the British government.

Crown corporation a legal agency or company through which the Government of Canada or one of the provincial governments carries on certain activities. Air Canada and the St. Lawrence Seaway Authority are Crown corporations.

crown fire a forest fire that spreads from treetop to treetop.

crown glass 1 a very clear glass used in optical instruments. **2** an old kind of window glass that is in round sheets with a thick part in the middle.

crown jewels jewels that are a traditional part of the regalia of a royal family: *The British crown jewels are kept in the Tower of London.*

crown land 1 public land; land belonging to a government. **2** land that is the personal property of a monarch.

crown prince the oldest living son of a king, queen, etc.; the heir apparent to a kingdom.

crown princess 1 the wife of a crown prince. **2** a girl or woman who is heir apparent to a kingdom.

crow's-foot (krōz′fu̇t′) *n.* **-feet. 1** Usually, **crow's-feet,** *pl.* a wrinkle at the outer corner of the eye. **2** in tailoring, a three-pointed embroidered design used to finish the ends of seams, openings, etc. **3** crowfoot (def. 4).

crow's-nest or **crows-nest** (krōz′nest′) *n.* **1** on a ship, a small, enclosed platform near the top of a mast, used by the lookout. **2** any similar platform ashore.

cro·zier (krō′zhər) *n.* crosier.

CRTC Canadian Radio-Television Commission.

cru·cial (krü′shəl) *adj.* **1** very important; critical; decisive. **2** very trying; severe. **3** having the form of a cross; cross-shaped. [< NL (medical) *crucialis* < L *crux, crucis* cross; with reference to the fork of a road] —**cru′cial·ly,** *adv.*

cru·ci·ble (krü′sə bəl) *n.* **1** a container in which metals, ores, etc. can be melted. **2** a severe test or trial. [< Med.L *crucibulum* originally, night lamp]

cru·ci·fix (krü′sə fiks′) *n.* **1** a cross with the figure of Christ crucified on it. **2** a cross. [< LL *crucifixus,* alteration of L *cruci fixus* fixed to a cross < *crux* cross and *fixus,* pp. of *figere* fasten]

cru·ci·fix·ion (krü′sə fik′shən) *n.* **1** the act of crucifying. **2** the fact or state of being crucified. **3 Crucifixion, a** the putting to death of Christ on the cross. **b** a picture, statue, etc. of this death.

cru·ci·form (krü′sə fôrm′) *adj.* shaped like a cross. [< L *crux, crucis* cross + E *-form* shaped (< L *-formis*)]

cru·ci·fy (krü′sə fī′) *v.* **-fied, -fy·ing. 1** put to death by nailing or binding the hands and feet to a cross. **2** treat severely; persecute; torture. **3** blame and punish for the errors and crimes of someone else: *The newspapers crucified the mayor for a mistake made by his secretary.*

hat, āge, cãre, fär; let, ēqual, tėrm; it, īce
hot, ōpen, ôrder; oil, out; cup, pu̇t, rüle, ūse
əbove, takən, pencəl, lemən, circəs
ch, child; ng, long; sh, ship
th, thin; ᴛʜ, then; zh, measure

[ME < OF *crucifier* < LL *crucifigere* (alteration of L *cruci figere;* see CRUCIFIX); influenced by OF verbs ending in *-fier* (< L *-ficare*)] —**cru′ci·fi′er,** *n.*

crude (krüd) *adj.* **crud·er, crud·est. 1** in a natural or raw state; unrefined. Oil, ore, sugar, etc. before being refined and prepared for use are crude. **2** not mature; unripe. **3** rough; coarse: *a crude log cabin.* **4** lacking finish, grace, taste, or refinement: *crude manners.*
—*n.* crude oil. [< L *crudus* raw] —**crude′ly,** *adv.* —**crude′ness,** *n.* —**Syn. 1** unfinished. See **raw. 2** green. **4** rude.

cru·di·ty (krü′də tē) *n.* **-ties. 1** a crude quality or condition; roughness; lack of finish. **2** a crude action, thing, etc.

cru·el (krü′əl) *adj.* **1** fond of causing pain to others and delighting in their suffering; not caring about the pain and suffering of others: *a cruel master.* **2** showing a cruel nature: *cruel acts.* **3** causing pain and suffering: *a cruel war.* [ME < OF < L *crudelis* rough. Related to CRUDE.] —**cru′el·ly,** *adv.* —**cru′el·ness,** *n.*

Syn. 1 Cruel, brutal, pitiless = unfeeling in treatment of people and animals. **Cruel** emphasizes the idea of being completely untouched by the suffering of others and suggests taking pleasure in watching it or causing pain: *Most people abhor cruel behavior.* **Brutal** suggests the cruelty of a wild animal, shown by unrestrained force and fury: *The brutal captors beat their prisoners.* **Pitiless** means completely without pity or willingness to show mercy to those who are suffering: *The pitiless woman refused to help the poor sick girl.*

cru·el·ty (krü′əl·tē) *n.* **-ties. 1** the state or condition of being cruel; readiness to give pain to others or to delight in their suffering. **2** a cruel act.

cru·et (krü′it) *n.* **1** a glass bottle to hold vinegar, oil, etc. for the table. **2** a set of such bottles on a stand. [ME < OF *cruet,* dim. of *cruie* pot < Gmc.]

cruise (krüz) *v.* **cruised, cruis·ing,** *n.* —*v.* **1** sail about from place to place on pleasure or business; sail over or about: *He bought a yacht so that he could cruise along the coast.* **2** journey or travel from place to place. **3** move about without a special destination: *The taxi cruised about in search of passengers. Many police cars are cruising the streets.* **4** travel in an airplane or automobile at the speed of maximum mechanical efficiency.
—*n.* the act of sailing about from place to place on pleasure or business; a voyage in search of something whose position is not known exactly. [< Du. *kruisen* move, especially, sail crosswise < *kruis* cross < L *crux*]

cruis·er (krüz′ər) *n.* **1** a warship with less armor and more speed than a battleship. **2** an airplane, taxi, power boat, etc. that cruises. **3** a police car connected with headquarters by radio; a patrol car or squad car used for patrolling streets and highways. **4** a man who marks trees to be cut down by lumberjacks. **5** a person who goes on a cruise. **6** a cabin cruiser.

crul·ler (krul′ər) *n.* a kind of doughnut made by twisting together pieces of rich, sweet dough and frying them in fat. [apparently < Du. *kruller* < *krullen* curl]

crumb (krum) *n.* **1** a very small piece of bread, cake, etc. broken from a larger piece. **2** the soft, inside part of bread. **3** a little bit: *a crumb of comfort.* **4** *Informal.* a worthless person; a person of no importance.
—*v.* **1** break into crumbs. **2** cover with crumbs for frying or baking. **3** *Informal.* brush or wipe the crumbs from (a tablecloth, etc.). [OE *cruma*]

crum·ble (krum′bəl) *v.* **-bled, -bling. 1** break into very small pieces or crumbs. **2** fall to pieces; decay: *The old wall was crumbling away at the edges.* [earlier *crimble* < OE *(ge)crymman* < *cruma* crumb]

crum·bly (krum′blē) *adj.* **-bli·er, -bli·est.** tending to crumble; easily crumbled. —**crum′bli·ness,** *n.*

crumb·y (krum′ē) *adj.* **crumb·i·er, crumb·i·est. 1** full of crumbs. **2** soft like the inside part of bread. **3** *Slang.* crummy.

crum·my (krum′ē) *adj.* **-mi·er, -mi·est.** *Slang.* cheap; shoddy; inferior. Also, **crumby.**

crump (krump) *v. n.* crunch.

crum·pet (krum′pit) *n.* a round, flat cake, thicker than a pancake, baked on a griddle. Crumpets are usually toasted and eaten while hot. [OE *crompeht* full of crumples]

crum·ple (krum′pəl) *v.* **-pled, -pling,** *n.* —*v.* **1** crush together; wrinkle: *He crumpled the letter into a ball.* **2** fall down; collapse: *The boxer crumpled to the floor.* —*n.* a wrinkle made by crushing something together. [OE *crump* bent]

crunch (krunch) *v.* **1** crush noisily with the teeth. **2** produce a crunching noise: *The hard snow crunched under our feet.* **3** proceed with a crunching noise: *The children crunched through the snow.* —*n.* **1** the act or sound of crunching. **2** *Slang.* a crucial stage or turning point; crisis. [earlier *cra(u)nch*; apparently influenced by *crush, munch*]

crup·per (krup′ər) *n.* **1** a strap attached to the back of a harness and passing under a horse's tail. See **harness** for diagram. **2** the rump of a horse. [ME < OF *cropier* < *crope* croup² < Gmc.]

cru·ral (krür′əl) *adj.* of the leg. [< L *cruralis* < *crus, cruris* leg]

cru·sade (krü sād′) *n. v.* **-sad·ed, -sad·ing.** —*n.* **1** Often, **Crusade.** any one of the Christian military expeditions between the years 1096 and 1272 whose aim was to recover the Holy Land from the Moslems. **2** a war having a religious purpose and approved by religious authorities. **3** an evangelistic campaign; a revival. **4** a vigorous campaign against a public evil or in favour of some new idea: *the crusade against tuberculosis.* —*v.* take part in a crusade. [anglicization of earlier *crusada* < Sp. *cruzada,* ult. < L *crux* cross]

cru·sad·er (krü sād′ər) *n.* a person who takes part in a crusade. The crusaders of the Middle Ages fought to win the Holy Land from the Moslems.

cruse (krüz or krüs) *n. Archaic.* a jug, pot, or bottle made of earthenware. [< MDu. *croes*]

crush (krush) *v.* **1** squeeze together so violently as to break or bruise. **2** wrinkle or crease by wear or rough handling: *His hat was crushed when the girl sat on it.* **3** break into fine pieces by grinding, pounding, or pressing. **4** flatten by heavy pressure. **5** subdue; conquer. —*n.* **1** a crushing or being crushed. **2** a violent pressure like grinding or pounding. **3** a mass of people crowded close together. **4** *Slang.* **a** a sudden, strong liking for a person. **b** the object of a sudden, strong liking. [ME *crusch(en),* apparently < OF *croissir* < Gmc.] —**crush′a·ble,** *adj.* —**crush′er,** *n.*

crust (krust) *n.* **1** the hard, outside part of bread, rolls, etc. **2** a piece of this; any hard, dry piece of bread, etc. **3** the baked outside covering of a pie. **4** any hard outside covering: *The crust on the snow was thick enough for us to walk on it.* **5** in geology, the outer layer of the earth, consisting of a shell of rock varying in thickness between as little as 3 miles below oceans and as much as 24 miles below continents. See **core** for diagram. **6** *Slang.* nerve; impudence. —*v.* **1** cover or become covered with a crust. **2** form or collect into a crust. [< L *crusta* rind] —**crust′like′,** *adj.*

Crus·ta·cea (krus tā′shə) *n.pl.* a class of arthropods, mainly aquatic, having hard shells and, usually, gills for breathing. Crabs, lobsters, shrimps, etc. belong to the Crustacea. [< NL < L *crusta* shell, rind]

crus·ta·cean (krus tā′shən) *n.* any of a group of water animals belonging to the Crustacea. —*adj.* of or belonging to this group.

crus·ta·ceous (krus tā′shəs) *adj.* **1** crustacean. **2** having a shell or crust. **3** of or like a crust.

crust·y (krus′tē) *adj.* **crust·i·er, crust·i·est. 1** having a crust; crustlike: *crusty bread.* **2** bad-tempered or harsh in manner, speech, etc. —**crust′i·ly,** *adv.* —**crust′i·ness,** *n.*

crutch (kruch) *n.* **1** a support to help a lame person walk. A crutch is a stick having a padded piece at the top to fit under the arm and, often, a handgrip lower down. With its help the user can move along without having to use both feet. **2** anything like a crutch in shape or use; support; prop. [OE *crycc*]

crux (kruks) *n.* **crux·es** or **cru·ces** (krü′sēz). **1** the essential or crucial part; the most important point. **2** a puzzling or perplexing question; difficult point to explain. [< L *crux* cross. Doublet of CROSS.]

cru·zei·ro (krü zãr′ ō) *n.* **1** a unit of money in Brazil. See table at **money. 2** a coin worth one cruzeiro. [< Pg.]

cry (krī) *v.* **cried, cry·ing,** *n.* **cries.** —*v.* **1** make a sound that shows pain, fear, sorrow, etc. **2** shed tears; weep. **3** of an animal, make its usual noise or call. **4** call loudly; shout. **5** announce in public: *Peddlers cried their wares in the street. The king ordered the news cried in the streets.*
cry down, make little of; speak of as unimportant or of little value; deprecate.
cry for, a ask earnestly for; beg for. **b** need very much.
cry off, break an agreement; refuse to do something.
cry one's eyes or **heart out,** shed many tears.
cry out, a call loudly; shout. **b** scream; yell. **c** complain.
cry up, praise; speak of as important or valuable.
—*n.* **1** a sound made by a person or animal that shows some strong feeling, such as pain, fear, anger, or sorrow; noise that shows grief, pain, etc. **2** a spell of shedding tears; fit of weeping. **3** the noise or call of an animal: *a gull's cry, the cry of the wolf.* **4** a loud call; shout: *a cry for help.* **5** a call to action; slogan: *"Forward" was the army's cry as it attacked.* **6** a public announcement; proclamation: *a peddler's cry.* **7** an opinion generally expressed; public voice. **8** an appeal; entreaty. **9 a** the yelping of hounds in the chase. **b** a pack of hounds. **10 a far cry, a** a long way. **b** a great difference. **11 in full cry,** in close pursuit. [ME < OF *crier* < L *quiritare,* originally, implore the aid of the *Quirites* or Roman citizens]

cry·ba·by (krī′bā′bē) *n.* **-bies.** a person who cries easily or pretends to be hurt.

cry·ing (krī′ing) *adj.* **1** that cries. **2** demanding attention; very bad: *a crying evil.*

cry·o·gen (krī′ə jən) *n.* a substance for producing low temperatures. [< Gk. *kryos* frost + *-gen*]

cry·o·gen·ics (krī′ə jen′iks) *n.* the study of the behavior of matter at extremely low temperatures.

cry·o·lite (krī′ə līt′) *n.* a fluoride of sodium and aluminum found in Greenland. It is used in making soda, aluminum, etc. *Formula:* Na_3AlF_6 [< Gk. *kryos* frost + E *-lite* (< F < Gk. *lithos* stone)]

crypt (kript) *n.* an underground room or vault. The crypt beneath the main floor of a church was formerly often used as a burial place. [< L *crypta* < Gk. *kryptē* vault < *kryptos* hidden. Doublet of GROTTO.]

cryp·tic (krip′tik) *adj.* having a hidden meaning; secret; mysterious: *a cryptic message, a cryptic reply.* [< LL *crypticus* < Gk. *kryptikos* < *kryptos* hidden] —**cryp′ti·cal·ly,** *adv.*

cryp·ti·cal (krip′tə kəl) *adj.* cryptic.

cryp·to·gam (krip′tə gam′) *n.* in botany, one of a group of plants having no seeds, including ferns, mosses, and others. [< NL *cryptogamia* < Gk. *kryptos* hidden + *gamos* marriage]

cryp·to·gram (krip′tə gram′) *n.* something written in secret code or cipher. [< Gk. *kryptos* hidden + E *-gram* something written (< Gk. *-gramma*)]

cryp·to·graph (krip′tə graf′) *n.* cryptogram. [< Gk. *kryptos* hidden + E *-graph*]

crys·tal (kris′təl) *n.* **1** a clear, transparent mineral, a kind of quartz, that looks like ice. **2** a piece of crystal cut to a special shape for use or ornament. Crystals are used as beads, and hung around lights. **3 a** glass of great brilliance and transparency, used especially in making drinking glasses, serving dishes, etc.: *The wine glasses were made of crystal.* **b** glasses, dishes, etc. made of crystal: *Crystal glistened on the dinner table.* **4** the glass over the face of a watch. **5** a regularly shaped mass with angles and flat surfaces, into which a substance solidifies: *Crystals of sugar can be distinguished from crystals of snow by their difference in form.* **6** a piece of quartz used to control the frequency of a radio-frequency oscillator or filter.
—*adj.* **1** made of crystal: *crystal ornaments.* **2** clear and transparent like crystal. [ME < OF < L *crystallus* < Gk. *krystallos* clear ice, ult. < *kryos* frost]

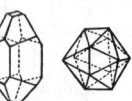

Crystal shapes (def. 5)

hat, āge, cãre, fär; let, ēqual, tėrm; it, īce
hot, ōpen, ôrder; oil, out; cup, pu̇t, rüle, ūse
əbove, takən, pencəl, lemən, circəs
ch, child; ng, long; sh, ship
th, thin; ᴛʜ, then; zh, measure

crystal ball a ball of crystal or glass, used in crystal gazing.

crys·tal-clear (kris′ təl klēr′) *adj.* **1** as clear as crystal; extremely clear and transparent. **2** very easy to understand; simple and lucid.

crystal detector in a radio, a device for rectifying alternating currents, consisting of a crystal embedded in soft metal.

crystal gazing 1 the act or practice of staring into a crystal ball, supposedly to induce a vision of remote events, future happenings, etc. **2** *Informal.* speculation about the future.

crys·tal·line (kris′ tə līn′ or kris′ təl in) *adj.* **1** consisting of crystals; solidified in the form of crystals: *Sugar and salt are crystalline.* **2** of rocks, composed of crystals. **3** of or having to do with crystals and their formation. **4** made of crystal. **5** clear and transparent like crystal.

crystalline lens the lens of the eye.

crys·tal·li·za·tion (kris′ təl ə zā′ shən or kris′ təl ī zā′ shən) *n.* **1** a crystallizing or being crystallized. **2** a crystallized substance or formation. **3** the taking on of a real, concrete, or permanent form: *The meeting resulted in the crystallization of our plans.*

crys·tal·lize (kris′ təl īz′) *v.* **-lized, -liz·ing. 1** form into crystals; solidify into crystals: *Water crystallizes to form snow.* **2** form into definite shape: *His vague ideas crystallized into a clear plan.* **3** coat with sugar.
—**crys′ tal·liz′ er,** *n.*

crys·tal·lized (kris′ təl īzd′) *adj.* formed into crystals.

crys·tal·log·ra·pher (kris′ tə log′ rə fər) *n.* an expert in crystallography.

crys·tal·log·ra·phy (kris′ tə log′ rə fē) *n.* the science that deals with the form, structure, and properties of crystals. [< Gk. *krystallos* crystal + E *-graphy*]

crys·tal·loid (kris′ təl oid′) *adj.* like crystal.
—*n.* in chemistry, a substance (usually capable of crystallization) that, when dissolved in a liquid, will diffuse readily through vegetable or animal membranes. [< Gk. *krystalloeidēs* < *krystallos* crystal + *eidos* form]

crystal set a radio that uses a crystal detector instead of vacuum tubes.

Cs 1 cesium. **2** cirro-stratus.

C.S. 1 Civil Service. **2** Christian Science.

CSC 1 Civil Service Commission. **2** Canadian Services College.

CST, C.S.T., or **c.s.t.** Central Standard Time.

CT, C.T., or **c.t.** Central Time.

ct. 1 cent. **2** county. **3** court. **4** one hundred. (for L *centum*)

Ct. Connecticut. (official abbrev. **Conn.**)

cten·o·phore (ten′ ə fôr′ or tē′ nə-) *n.* **1** any of a large group of invertebrate sea animals having an oval jelly-like body with eight pairs of comblike plates that aid in swimming. **2** one of these plates. [< NL *ctenophora* the class name < Gk. *kteis, ktenos* comb + *phorein* to bear]

ctn cotangent.

ctn. *pl.* **ctns.** carton.

cts. cents.

CTV Canadian Television (Canadian Television Network, Ltd.).

Cu 1 copper. **2** cumulus.

cu. cubic.

cub (kub) *n.* **1** a young bear, fox, lion, etc. **2** a boy who belongs to the Wolf Cubs. **3** an inexperienced or awkward boy. **4** a boy who behaves badly. [origin uncertain]

Cu·ban (kū′ bən) *adj.* of or having to do with Cuba or its people. —*n.* a native or inhabitant of Cuba.

cub·by·hole (kub′ ē hōl′) *n.* a small, enclosed space. [<*cubby* (dim. of Brit. dial. word *cub* shed, coop) + *hole*]

cube (kūb) *n. v.* **cubed, cub·ing.** —*n.* **1** a solid with six equal, square sides. **2** in mathematics, the product obtained when a number is cubed: *The cube of 4 is 64.* **3** an ice cube.
—*v.* **1** make or form into the shape of a cube: *The beets we had for supper were cubed instead of sliced.* **2** in mathematics, use (a number) three times as a factor: *5 cubed is 125, for 5 × 5 × 5 = 125.* [< L *cubus* < Gk. *kybos* cube, die]

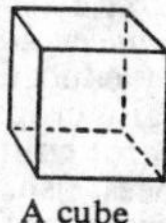
A cube

cu·beb (kū′ beb) *n.* **1** a dried, unripe berry of a tropical shrub of the pepper family, used as a spice and in medicine. Cubebs were formerly crushed and smoked in pipes or cigarettes for the treatment of catarrh. **2** a cigarette containing the crushed berries. [< F *cubèbe* < Arabic *kabāba*]

cube root in mathematics, a number used as the factor of a cube: *The cube root of 125 is 5.*

cu·bic (kū′ bik) *adj.* **1** shaped like a cube. **2** having length, breadth, and thickness. A cubic inch is the volume of a cube whose edges are one inch long. The cubic content of a room is the number of cubic feet it contains. **3** in mathematics, having to do with or involving the cubes of numbers. *Abbrev.:* cu.

cu·bi·cal (kū′ bə kəl) *adj.* shaped like a cube.

cu·bi·cle (kū′ bə kəl) *n.* a small room or compartment, especially one of the divisions of a large dormitory. [< L *cubiculum* bedroom < *cubare* lie]

cubic measure a system of measurement of volume in cubic units:
1,728 cubic inches = 1 cubic foot
27 cubic feet = 1 cubic yard
1,000 cubic millimetres = 1 cubic centimetre
1,000 cubic centimetres = 1 cubic decimetre
1,000 cubic decimetres = 1 cubic metre

cub·ism (kū′ biz əm) *n.* in art, a style (developed in the early part of the 20th century) in which people, objects, etc. are represented by means of geometric forms, including squares, triangles, etc. as well as cubes.

cub·ist (kūb′ ist) *n.* an artist or sculptor whose art is based on the theories of cubism. —*adj.* of or having to do with cubism or cubists.

cu·bit (kū′ bit) *n.* an ancient measure of length, about 18 to 22 inches. [< L *cubitum* elbow, cubit]

cub·mas·ter (kub′ mas′ tər) *n.* a man in charge of a pack of Wolf Cubs.

cu·boid (kū′ boid) *adj.* shaped like a cube. —*n.* something shaped like a cube.

cub reporter a young, inexperienced newspaper reporter.

cuck·old (kuk′ əld) *n.* the husband of an unfaithful wife.
—*v.* make a cuckold of. [ME *cukeweld* < OF *cucuault* < *coucou* cuckoo; from the cuckoo's habit of laying its eggs in another bird's nest]

cuck·old·ry (kuk′ əl drē) *n.* making a cuckold of a husband.

cuck·oo (ku̇k′ ü or *esp. for adj.* kü′ kü) *n.* **-oos,** *adj. v.*
—*n.* **1** a bird whose call sounds much like its name. The common European cuckoo lays its eggs in the nests of other birds instead of hatching them itself. The American cuckoo builds its own nest and has a call less like its name. **2** a bird call that sounds like the word *cuckoo.*
—*adj. Slang.* crazy; silly.
—*v.* make the sound of the cuckoo, or an imitation of it. [imitative]

cuckoo clock a clock with a toy bird that pops suddenly out of a little door and makes a sound like that of the European cuckoo to mark intervals of time.

cu. cm. cubic centimetre; cubic centimetres.

cu·cul·late (kū′ kə lāt′ or kyu̇ kul′ āt) *adj.* in biology, having a hood; shaped like a hood. [< LL *cucullatus* < L *cucullus* cap]

cu·cum·ber (kū′ kum bər) *n.* **1** a vegetable that has a green skin with firm flesh inside, used in salads and for pickles. **2** the vine that it grows on. **3 cool as a cucumber, a** very cool. **b** calm and unruffled; not excited. [ME < OF *cocombre* < L *cucumis*]

cud (kud) *n.* **1** a mouthful of food that cattle and similar animals bring back into the mouth from the first stomach for a slow second chewing. **2** *Dialect.* a quid of tobacco. [OE *cudu,* var. of *cwidu*]

cud·dle (kud′əl) *v.* **-dled, -dling,** *n.* —*v.* **1** hold closely and lovingly in one's arms or lap: *The mother cuddled her baby.* **2** lie close and snug; curl up: *The two puppies cuddled together in front of the fire.* **3** hug. —*n.* a hug. [origin uncertain]

cud·dy (kud′ē) *n.* **-dies. 1** a small cabin on a boat. **2** a small room or cupboard. [origin uncertain]

cudg·el (kuj′əl) *n. v.* **-elled** or **-eled, -el·ling** or **-el·ing.** —*n.* **1** a short, thick stick used as a weapon; club. **2 take up the cudgels for,** defend strongly.
—*v.* **1** beat with a cudgel. **2 cudgel one's brains,** try very hard to think. [OE *cycgel*]

cue[1] (kū) *n. v.* **cued, cu·ing** or **cue·ing.** —*n.* **1** a hint or suggestion as to what to do or when to act: *Being a stranger, he took his cue from the actions of the natives.* **2** an action or speech on or behind the stage, which gives the signal for an actor, singer, musician, etc. to enter or to begin. In a play the last word or words of one actor's speech is the cue for another to come on the stage, begin speaking, etc. **3** the part one is to play; course of action. **4** a frame of mind; mood.
—*v.* give a signal to an actor, singer, etc. [probably < F *queue* tail, end < L *coda,* dial. var. of *cauda*; with reference to the end of a preceding actor's speech]

cue[2] (kū) *n.* **1** a queue; pigtail. **2** in billiards, pool, etc., a long, tapering stick used for striking the ball. [var. of *queue*]

cues·ta (kwes′tə) *n.* a ridge or hill that has a steep face on one side and a gentle slope on the other. [< Sp. < L *costa* side, rib]

cuff[1] (kuf) *n.* **1** a band around the wrist, either attached to a sleeve or separate. **2** a turned-up fold around the bottom of a trouser leg. **3** the part of a long glove or gauntlet that covers the wrist or part of the arm. **4** a handcuff. **5 off the cuff,** without preparation; impromptu; offhand: *He had no notes but spoke off the cuff.* **6 on the cuff,** on credit: *Some people buy all their furniture on the cuff.* [ME *cuffe* glove; origin uncertain] —**cuff′less,** *adj.*

cuff[2] (kuf) *v. n.* hit with the hand; slap. [origin uncertain]

cuff button a button for the cuff of a shirt.

cuff link a device for linking together the open ends of a shirt cuff.

cu. ft. cubic foot; cubic feet.

cui bo·no (kwē′ bō′nō or kī′ bō′nō) *Latin.* **1** for whose benefit? **2** of what good? for what use?

cu. in. cubic inch; cubic inches.

cui·rass (kwi ras′) *n.* **1** a piece of armor for the body, that is made of a breastplate and fastened to a plate protecting the back. **2** the breastplate alone. **3** the armor plate of a warship. [ME < OF *cuirasse* < Ital. *corazza* < VL < LL *coriacea* (*vestis*) (garment) of leather < L *corium* leather; form influenced by F *cuir* leather < L *corium*]

A soldier wearing a cuirass

cui·ras·sier (kwē′rə sēr′) *n.* a cavalry soldier wearing a cuirass.

cui·sine (kwi zēn′) *n.* **1** a style of cooking or preparing food. **2** food. **3** a kitchen. [< F < L *cocina,* var. of *coquina* < *coquus* a cook]

cuisse (kwis) *n.* a piece of armor to protect the thigh. See **armor** for picture. [< F *cuisse* thigh < L *coxa* hip]

cul-de-sac (kul′də sak′ or ku̇l′də sak′; *French,* kʏd säk′) *n.* a street or passage open at only one end; blind alley. [< F *cul-de-sac* bottom of the sack]

cu·lex (kū′leks) *n.* **-li·ces** (-lə sēz′). the most common mosquito of North America and Europe. [< L *culex* gnat]

cu·li·nar·y (kul′ə ner′ē or kū′lə ner′ē) *adj.* **1** having to do with cooking or the kitchen: *Mother is often praised for her culinary skill.* **2** used in cooking. [< L *culinarius* < *culina* kitchen]

cull (kul) *v.* **1** pick out; select: *The lawyer culled a few important facts from the mass of evidence.* **2** pick over; make selections from. —*n.* something picked out as being inferior or worthless. Poor fruit, stale vegetables, and lumber and animals not up to standard are called culls. [ME < OF *cuillir* < L *colligere.* See COLLECT.] —**cull′er,** *n.*

culm[1] (kulm) *n.* **1** coal dust. **2** hard coal of poor quality. [? related to COAL]

culm[2] (kulm) *n.* in botany, the jointed stem characteristic of grasses, usually hollow. [< L *culmus* stalk]

cul·mi·nate (kul′mə nāt′) *v.* **-nat·ed, -nat·ing.** reach its highest point; reach a climax; result (*in*): *The Christmas party at school culminated in the distribution of the presents.* [< LL *culminare* < L *culmen* top]

cul·mi·na·tion (kul′mə nā′shən) *n.* **1** the highest point; climax. **2** a reaching of the highest point. —**Syn. 1** acme, zenith, peak.

cu·lottes (kū lots′) *n.pl.* a divided skirt. [< F]

cul·pa·bil·i·ty (kul′pə bil′ə tē) *n.* the fact or condition of being culpable.

cul·pa·ble (kul′pə bəl) *adj.* deserving blame. [ME < OF < L *culpabilis* < *culpa* fault] —**cul′pa·ble·ness,** *n.* —**cul′pa·bly,** *adv.*

cul·prit (kul′prit) *n.* **1** a person guilty of a fault or a crime; offender. **2** a prisoner in court who has been accused of a crime. [apparently < AF *cul. prit.* earlier *cul. prist,* short for *culpable,* deserving punishment < L *culpabilis* and *prist,* var. of OF *prest* ready (for trial), ult. < L *praesto* on hand]

cult (kult) *n.* **1** a system of religious worship: *Buddhism includes many cults.* **2** great admiration for a person, thing, idea, etc.; worship: *In the Soviet Union, the cult of Stalin was discouraged after his death.* **3** a group showing such admiration; worshippers. [< L *cultus* worship < *colere* worship]

cul·ti·va·ble (kul′tə və bəl) *adj.* that can be cultivated.

cul·ti·vat·a·ble (kul′tə vāt′ə bəl) *adj.* cultivable.

cul·ti·vate (kul′tə vāt′) *v.* **-vat·ed, -vat·ing. 1** prepare and use (land) to raise crops by ploughing it, planting seeds, and taking care of the growing plants. **2** help (plants) grow by labor and care. **3** loosen the ground around (growing plants) to kill weeds, etc. **4** improve; develop by education or training: *It takes time, thought, and effort to cultivate your mind.* **5** give time, thought, and effort to; practise: *An artist cultivates art.* **6** promote the growth or development of (an art, science, etc.). **7** establish or strengthen: *Friendships cultivated in school often last a lifetime.* **8** seek better acquaintance with; seek the friendship of. [< Med.L *cultivare* < *cultivus* under cultivation < L *cultus,* pp. of *colere* till]

cul·ti·vat·ed (kul′tə vāt′id) *adj.* **1** prepared and used to raise crops: *A field of wheat is cultivated land; a pasture is not.* **2** produced by cultivation; not wild: *All hybrid tea roses are cultivated flowers.* **3** improved; developed. **4** cultured; refined.

cul·ti·va·tion (kul′tə vā′shən) *n.* **1** the act of preparing land and growing crops by ploughing, planting, and the necessary care. **2** improvement; development. **3** the act of giving time and thought to improving and developing (the body, mind, or manners). **4** the result of improvement or growth through education and experience; culture. **5 under cultivation,** of land, planted with crops or prepared for planting. —**Syn. 4** refinement.

cul·ti·va·tor (kul′tə vā′tər) *n.* **1** a person or thing that cultivates. **2** a tool or machine used to loosen the ground and destroy weeds.

cul·tur·al (kul′chər əl) *adj.* of or having to do with culture: *Music and art are cultural studies.* —**cul′tur·al·ly,** *adv.*

cultural lag or **culture lag** in sociology, delay in the adaptation of one aspect of a culture to accommodate changes in another aspect; especially delay in the adaptation of social institutions to technological advances.

cul·ture (kul′chər) *n. v.* **-tured, -tur·ing.** —*n.* **1** fineness of feelings, thoughts, tastes, manners, etc. **2** the civilization of a given people or nation at a given time; its customs, arts, conveniences, etc.: *She spoke on the cultures of the Cree Indians, of the Pygmies, of the ancient Incas, and of modern Denmark.* **3** the development of the mind or body by education, training, etc. **4** the preparation of land to raise crops by ploughing, planting, and the necessary care; cultivation. **5** proper care given to the raising of bees, fish, silk, grapes, etc. **6** in biology, a colony or growth of viruses or germs of a given kind that has

been carefully made for a special purpose.
—*v.* **1** cultivate. **2** in biology, grow viruses or germs for a special purpose. [< F < L *cultura* a tending < *colere* cultivate] —**Syn.** *n.* **1** breeding, refinement. See **education.**

cul·tured (kul′chərd) *adj.* **1** having or showing culture; refined. **2** produced or raised by culture.

cultured pearl a natural pearl artificially cultivated by introducing a foreign body into an oyster, so causing the oyster to secrete a protective substance that hardens round the irritant.

culture lag cultural lag.

cul·tus[1] (kul′təs) *n.* a religious cult. [< L. See CULT.]

cul·tus[2] (kul′təs) *adj.* worthless; unimportant; bad. —*n.* cultus cod. [< Chinook jargon < Chinook *cultus* worthless]

cultus cod ling cod.

cul·ver·in (kul′vər in) *n.* **1** a musket used in the Middle Ages. **2** a long, heavy cannon, used in the 16th and 17th centuries. [ME < OF *coulevrine* < *couleuvre* < L *colubra* serpent]

cul·vert (kul′vərt) *n.* a small channel or drain that allows water to run under a road, railway, canal, etc. [origin uncertain]

cum·ber (kum′bər) *v.* **1** burden; trouble: *Household cares cumber a busy mother.* **2** hinder; hamper: *The lumberman's heavy boots cumbered him in walking.* —*n.* a hindrance. [ME, probably < OF *combrer* impede < *combre* barrier < Celtic] —**cum′ber·er,** *n.*

cum·ber·some (kum′bər səm) *adj.* clumsy; unwieldy; burdensome: *The armor worn by medieval knights seems cumbersome to us today. Long, badly constructed sentences are cumbersome.* —**cum′ber·some·ly,** *adv.* —**cum′ber·some·ness,** *n.*

cum·brous (kum′brəs) *adj.* cumbersome.—**cum′brous·ly,** *adv.* —**cum′brous·ness,** *n.*

cum·in or **cum·min** (kum′ən) *n.* a small plant whose seedlike fruits are used in cookery and medicine. [OE *cymen* < L *cuminum* < Gk. *kyminon*]

cum lau·de (kům lou′dā or kum lô′dā) *Latin.* **1** with praise or honor. To graduate *cum laude* is to graduate with high rank. **2** a person who has graduated from a high school or university with high honors.

cum·mer·bund (kum′ər bund′) *n.* a broad sash worn around the waist. Also, **kummerbund.** [< Hind. *kamarband* < Persian *kamar* waist, loins (< Arabic) + *band* band, bandage]

cum·quat (kum′kwot) *n.* kumquat.

cu·mu·late (kū′myů lāt′) *v.* **-lat·ed, -lat·ing,** *adj.* —*v.* heap up; accumulate. —*adj.* heaped up. [< L *cumulare* < *cumulus* heap]

cu·mu·la·tion (kū′myů lā′shən) *n.* **1** a heaping up; accumulating. **2** a heap; accumulation.

cu·mu·la·tive (kū′myů lə tiv or kū′myů lā′tiv) *adj.* heaped up; accumulated; increasing or growing in amount, force, etc., by additions: *a cumulative argument.* A cumulative dividend is one that must be added to future dividends if not paid when due. —**cu′mu·la′tive·ly,** *adv.* —**cu′mu·la′tive·ness,** *n.*

cu·mu·lo-cir·rus (kū′myů lō sir′əs) *n.* **-cir·ri** (-sir′ī or -sir′ē). a cloud that is part cumulus, part cirrus.

cu·mu·lo-nim·bus (kū′myů lō nim′bəs) *n.* **-bus·es** or **-bi** (-bī or -bē). a massive cloud formation having peaks that resemble mountains.

cu·mu·lo-stra·tus (kū′myů lō strā′təs or -strat′əs) *n.* a cumulus cloud with its base spread out horizontally like a stratus cloud.

cu·mu·lous (kū′myů ləs) *adj.* of or like cumulus clouds.

cu·mu·lus (kū′myů ləs) *n.* **-li** (-lī′ or -lē′) **1** a cloud formation of rounded heaps having a flat base. **2** a heap. [< L *cumulus* heap]

cu·ne·ate (kū′nē it or kū′nē āt′) *adj.* tapering to a point at the base; wedge-shaped. [< L *cuneatus* < *cuneus* wedge]

NUMERAL 1
10
TAP
BE
ME
Cuneiform characters

cu·ne·i·form (kū′nē ə fôrm′ or kū nē′ə-) *n.* **1** the wedge-shaped characters used in the writing of ancient Babylonia, Assyria, Persia, etc. **2** in anatomy, a wedge-shaped bone, especially one of the three bones of the human ankle. —*adj.* **1** wedge-shaped. **2** of or having to do with cuneiform characters. **3** in anatomy, of or denoting any wedge-shaped bone. [< L *cuneus* wedge + E *-form* shaped (< L *formis*)]

hat, āge, cãre, fär; let, ēqual, tėrm; it, īce
hot, ōpen, ôrder; oil, out; cup, půt, rüle, ūse
əbove, takən, pencəl, lemən, circəs
ch, child; ng, long; sh, ship
th, thin; ᴛʜ, then; zh, measure

cun·ner (kun′ər) *n.* **1** a small, edible fish of the wrasse family, found off the Atlantic coast, from the Maritimes to New England, especially in rocky waters. **2** a small wrasse found off the coast of England. [origin unknown]

cun·ning (kun′ing) *adj.* **1** clever in deceiving; sly: *a cunning villain.* **2** made, showing, or done with skill, knowledge, or cleverness: *cunning workmanship.* **3** *Archaic.* skilful; expert; clever. **4** *Informal.* pretty and dear; attractive: *a cunning baby.*
—*n.* **1** slyness in getting what one wants; cleverness in deceiving one's enemies: *a fox's cunning.* **2** *Archaic.* skill; cleverness. [OE *cunnung* < *cunnan* know (how). Related to CAN[1].] —**cun′ning·ly,** *adv.* —**cun′ning·ness,** *n.*
Syn. *adj.* 1 See **sly.** –*n.* 1 **Cunning, craft** = skill in getting what one wants. **Cunning** suggests slyness and the use of clever tricks or false appearances to hide one's real purpose and get the better of others: *He has the cunning of a cat chasing a mouse.* **Craft** suggests skill in deceiving others by clever and artful plans, devices, and underhand methods: *He has the craft of a successful swindler.*

cup (kup) *n. v.* **cupped, cup·ping.** —*n.* **1** a small but rather deep dish to drink from. **2** as much as a cup holds; a cupful. In cooking, a cup is eight ounces. **3** anything shaped like a cup. The petals of some flowers form a cup. **4** an ornamental cup, vase, etc. given to the winner of a contest; a trophy. **5** a drink or mixture: *a claret cup.* **6** in the Christian Communion: **a** a cup. **b** the wine, etc. used in Communion. **7** something to be endured or experienced; fate: *His was a bitter cup.* **8 in one's cups,** drunk.
—*v.* **1** shape like a cup: *She cupped her hands to catch the ball. The old man cupped a hand behind one ear.* **2** take or put in a cup. **3** take blood from (a person) by using a cup. **4** become cup-shaped. [OE *cuppe* < LL *cuppa*; cf. L *cupa* tub] —**cup′like′,** *adj.*

CUP **1** Canadian University Press. **2** Cambridge University Press.

cup·bear·er (kup′bãr′ər) *n.* **1** a person who fills and passes around the cups in which drinks are served. **2** formerly, in royal households, a noble who tasted the wine before handing it to his master.

cup·board (kub′ərd) *n.* **1** a closet or cabinet with shelves for dishes, food, etc. **2** a closet for storing clothing, linens, etc.

cupboard love insincere expressions of love for selfish reasons; affection offered for the sake of something, such as food and care to be received in return.

cup·cake (kup′kāk′) *n.* a small cake baked in a cup-shaped tin.

cup·ful (kup′fůl) *n.* **-fuls.** as much as a cup can hold. In cooking, a cupful is eight ounces.

Cu·pid (kū′pid) *n.* **1** in Roman mythology, the god of love, son of Mercury and Venus, identified with the Greek god Eros. Cupid is usually represented as a winged boy with bow and arrows. **2 cupid,** a figure of a winged baby used as a symbol of love: *the cupids on a valentine.*

cu·pid·i·ty (kū pid′ə tē) *n.* eager desire, especially to possess something; greed. [< L *cupiditas* < *cupidus* desirous < *cupere* long for, desire] —**Syn.** avarice.

cu·po·la (kū′pə lə) *n.* **1** a rounded roof; dome. **2** a small dome or tower on a roof. **3** a

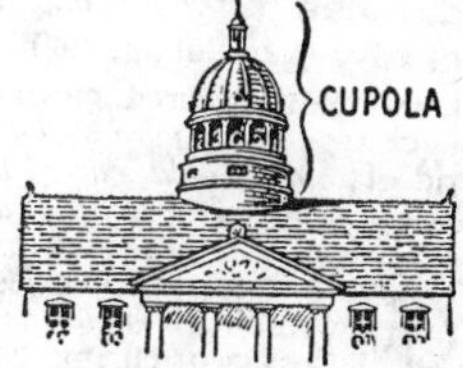

A cupola (def. 2)

domelike thing or part. [< Ital. < LL *cupula*, dim. of L *cupa* tub]

cup·ping (kup′ing) *n.* the use of a glass cup to create a partial vacuum for drawing blood up to or through the skin.

cu·pre·ous (kū′prē əs) *adj.* **1** of or containing copper. **2** copper-colored. [< L *cupreus* < *cuprum* copper]

cu·pric (kū′prik) *adj.* in chemistry, of or containing divalent copper.

cu·prous (kū′prəs) *adj.* in chemistry, of or containing monovalent copper.

cu·prum (kū′prəm) *n.* copper. [< L. See COPPER.]

cur (kėr) *n.* **1** a worthless dog; mongrel. **2** an ill-bred, worthless person. [ME *curre*]

cur·a·bil·i·ty (kūr′ə bil′ə tē) *n.* a being curable.

cur·a·ble (kūr′ə bəl) *adj.* that can be cured. **—cur′a·ble·ness,** *n.* **—cur′a·bly,** *adv.*

cu·ra·çao (kūr′ə sō′) *n.* a liqueur or cordial flavored with orange peel. [< *Curaçao*, a Dutch island in the West Indies]

cu·ra·cy (kūr′ə sē) *n.* **-cies.** the position, rank, or work of a curate.

cu·ra·re (kyů rä′rē) *n.* **1** a poisonous, blackish, resinlike extract of certain tropical plants used by some South American Indians as an arrow poison. Curare is used in medicine to relax muscles and in general anaesthesia. **2** a plant from which it is extracted. Also, *curara, curari.* [< Sp. *curaré* or Portuguese *curare* < Tupi]

cu·rate (kūr′it) *n.* a clergyman who is an assistant to a pastor, rector, or vicar. [< Med.L *curatus* < *cura* cure (def. 5) < L *cura* care. Doublet of CURÉ.]

cur·a·tive (kūr′ə tiv) *adj.* having the power to cure; curing; tending to cure. *—n.* a means of curing. **—cur′a·tive·ly,** *adv.* **—cur′a·tive·ness,** *n.*

cu·ra·tor (kyů rā′tər) *n.* a person in charge of all or part of a museum, library, etc. [< L *curator* < *curare* care for < *cura* care]

curb (kėrb) *n.* **1** a raised border of concrete or stone along the edge of a street, driveway, etc. **2** an enclosing framework or border supporting the base or outer edge of a dome, shaft, etc. **3** a chain or strap fastened to a horse's bit and passing under its lower jaw. When the reins are pulled tight, the curb checks the horse. **4** any check or restraint. **5** a market that deals in stocks and bonds not listed on the regular stock exchange.
—v. **1** hold in check; restrain. **2** provide with a curb. [ME < OF *courbe* < L *curvus* bent] **—Syn.** *v.* **1** See **check.**

curb bit a horse's bit having a curb.

curb·ing (kėr′bing) *n.* **1** material for making a curb. **2** a raised border of concrete, etc.; curb.

curb roof a roof having two slopes on each side.

curb·stone (kėrb′stōn′) *n.* a stone or stones forming a curb; a raised border of concrete, etc. along the sides of a street, driveway, etc.

cur·cu·li·o (kėr kū′lē ō′) *n.* **-li·os.** a snout beetle, some kinds of which destroy fruit. [< L]

curd (kėrd) *n.* Often, **curds,** *pl.* the thick part of milk that separates from the watery part when milk sours. *—v.* form into curds; curdle. [ME *curd, crud*]

cur·dle (kėr′dəl) *v.* **-dled, -dling. 1** form into curds. Milk curdles when it is kept toq long. **2** thicken. **3 curdle the blood,** horrify; terrify. [< *curd*]

cur·dled (kėr′dəld) *adj.* formed into curds.

curd·y (kėr′dē) *adj.* **1** full of curds. **2** like curdled milk.

cure (kūr) *v.* **cured, cur·ing,** *n. —v.* **1** make well; bring back to health: *cure a child of a cold or of a fever.* **2** get rid of: *cure a cold, cure a bad habit.* **3** prepare for keeping; preserve: *They dried and salted the meat to cure it.* **4** become cured. **5** treat (a substance) chemically in order to give it special properties or fit it for a particular purpose: *To cure rubber is to vulcanize it.*
—n. **1** the act of curing. **2** a means of curing; treatment intended to bring one back to health: *a rest cure.* **3** a successful medical treatment; restoration to health. **4** a medicine that is a means of curing; remedy. **5** spiritual charge; religious care. **6** a method or process of curing meat, fish, etc. **7** a quantity of meat, fish, etc. cured at one time or in one place. [ME < OF *curer* < L *curare* care for < *cura* care] **—cure′less,** *adj.* **—cur′er,** *n.*

Syn. *v.* **1 Cure, heal, remedy** = make well or right. **Cure** applies particularly to bringing back to health after sickness and disease: *The new treatment cured his skin disease.* **Heal** = make whole, and is used particularly of wounds, burns, etc.: *This medicine will heal that cut.* **Remedy** = put right, and applies to curing or relieving any unhealthy physical or mental condition: *The operation remedied his twisted foot.*

cu·ré (kū rā′; *French,* kʏ rā′) *n.* a parish priest. [< F < Med.L *curatus.* Doublet of CURATE.]

cure-all (kūr′ol′ or -ôl′) *n.* a remedy supposed to cure all diseases or evils.

cur·few (kėr′fū) *n.* **1** the giving of a signal, such as a bell ringing, at a fixed time every evening. In the Middle Ages, it announced the time to put out lights and cover fires. More recently it has been used as a direction for persons, usually children, to leave streets and public places. **2** the signal given: "*The curfew tolls the knell of parting day.*" **3** the time when it is given. **4** a regulation forbidding persons to be on the streets after a certain hour. [ME < AF *coeverfu* < *covrir* cover (< L *cooperire*) + *feu* fire < L *focus* hearth]

cu·ri·a (kūr′ē ə) *n.* **cu·ri·ae** (kūr′ē ē′ or kūr′ē ī′). **1** in ancient Rome: **a** the meeting place of the senate. **b** one of the ten divisions of each of the three tribes into which all Roman citizens were divided. **c** the meeting place of one of these divisions. **2** in the Middle Ages, a council or law court. **3 Curia,** in the Roman Catholic Church, a group of high officials who assist the Pope in the government and administration of the Church; the papal court. [< L]

cu·rie (kūr′ē or kū rē′) *n.* a unit of radio-activity. [after Mme. Marie *Curie* (1867-1934), a French physicist and chemist]

cu·ri·o (kūr′ē ō′) *n.* **cu·ri·os.** an object valued as a curiosity: *The traveller brought back many curios from foreign lands.* [short for *curiosity*]

cu·ri·os·i·ty (kūr′ē os′ə tē) *n.* **-ties. 1** an eager desire to know: *Her curiosity made her open the forbidden door.* **2** the condition of being too eager to know; inquisitiveness: *Curiosity killed the cat.* **3** a strange, rare, or novel object. **4** an odd, unusual, or interesting quality: *He was intrigued with the curiosity of the place.*

cu·ri·ous (kūr′ē əs) *adj.* **1** eager to know: *a curious student.* **2** too eager to know; prying: *That old woman is curious about other people's business.* **3** strange; odd; unusual: *a curious old book.* **4** *Archaic.* very careful; exact: *a curious inquiry into the customs of the Blackfoot.* **5** *Informal.* very odd; eccentric: *curious notions.* [ME < OF *curios* < L *curiosus* inquisitive, full of care, ult. < *cura* care]
—cu′ri·ous·ly, *adv.* **—cu′ri·ous·ness,** *n.*

Syn. 1, 2 Curious, inquisitive, prying = eager to find out about things. **Curious** = eager to learn things, but sometimes suggests being too eager to know about other people's business: *A normal child is curious about how things work.* **Inquisitive** suggests constantly asking questions to find out what one wants to know, especially about personal matters: *She is too inquisitive about my dates.* **Prying** adds to *inquisitive* the idea of peeping and of busying oneself about other people's business: *I had a prying landlady.*

cu·ri·um (kūr′ē əm) *n.* a radio-active chemical element produced by the bombardment of plutonium and uranium by helium ions. *Symbol:* Cm; *at.no.* 96; *at.wt.* 247 (most stable isotope). [after Mme. Marie *Curie* (1867-1934), a French physicist and chemist]

curl (kėrl) *v.* **1** twist into rings; roll into coils: *Her hair curls naturally. The smoke curled slowly from the chimney.* **2** twist out of shape; bend into a curve: *Paper curls when it burns.* **3** in the game of curling: **a** slide a curling stone down the ice. **b** engage in the game of curling. **4 curl up, a** roll up. **b** draw up one's legs: *The child curled up on the sofa.* **c** *Informal.* break down; give up.
—n. **1** a curled lock of hair. **2** anything like it. **3** a curling or being curled. **4 in curl,** curled. [ME *curle(n), crulle(n)* < *crul* curly]

curl·er (kėr′lər) *n.* **1** a person or thing that curls. **2** a device on which hair is twisted to make it curl.

cur·lew (kėr′lü) *n.* **-lew** or **-lews.** a wading bird having a long, thin bill. [ME < OF *courlieu;* imitative]

curl·i·cue (kėr′lə kū′) *n.* a fancy twist, curl, flourish, etc.: *curlicues in handwriting* [< *curly* + *cue*[2]]

hat, āge, cãre, fär; let, ēqual, tėrm; it, ice
hot, ōpen, ôrder; oil, out; cup, pu̇t, rüle, ūse
əbove, takən, pencəl, lemən, circəs
ch, child; ng, long; sh, ship
th, thin; ᴛʜ, then; zh, measure

curl·ing (kėr′ling) *n.* a game played on ice, in which large, smooth stones are slid toward a target at the end of the rink.

curling iron an instrument for curling or waving hair.

curling stone or **rock** the object, usually granite, slid down the ice in the game of curling.

A curling stone

curl·pa·per (kėrl′pā′pər) *n.* a piece of folded paper over which a lock of hair is rolled up tightly to curl it.

curl·y (kėr′lē) *adj.* **curl·i·er, curl·i·est. 1** curling; having a tendency to curl; wavy. **2** having curls. **—curl′i·ness,** *n.*

cur·mudg·eon (kər muj′ən) *n.* a rude, stingy, bad-tempered person; miser. [origin unknown]

cur·rant (kėr′ənt) *n.* **1** a small, seedless raisin, used in cakes, etc. **2** a small, sour, edible berry that grows in bunches. Currants are red, white, or black and are used for making jelly. **3** a bush that bears currants. [ME (*raysons of*) *Coraunte* < AF (*raisins de*) *Corauntz* raisins of Corinth]

cur·ren·cy (kėr′ən sē) *n.* **-cies. 1** the money in actual use in a country: *Coins and paper money are currency in Canada.* **2** a passing from person to person; circulation: *The town gossips gave the rumor currency.* **3** general use or acceptance; common occurrence: *Old words which have passed out of general currency are occasionally used to give an archaic effect.*

cur·rent (kėr′ənt) *n.* **1** a flow; stream. Running water or moving air makes a current. **2** a flow of electricity along a wire, etc. **3** the rate or amount of such a flow, usually expressed in amperes: *Heating requires much more current than lighting does.* **4** a course; movement; general direction: *the current of public opinion.*
—adj. **1** of the present time. The current issue of a magazine is the one most recently published. **2** generally used or accepted; commonly occurring: *Long ago it was the current belief that the earth was flat.* **3** going around; passing from person to person: *A rumor is current that prices will go up.* [ME < OF < L *currens, -entis,* ppr. of *currere* run]
Syn. *n.* **1** See **stream.** *-adj.* **2 Current, present, prevailing** = generally used or occurring at a certain time. **Current** emphasizes the notion of continuity in circulation or use at a given time: *English usage current in the 17th century.* **Present** means here and now: *This apartment meets my present needs.* **Prevailing** emphasizes relative predominance or vogue: *This bathing suit agrees with the prevailing fashion.*

cur·rent·ly (kėr′ənt lē) *adv.* **1** at the present time; now. **2** generally; commonly.

cur·ri·cle (kėr′ə kəl) *n.* a two-wheeled carriage drawn by two horses. [< L *curriculum.* See CURRICULUM.]

cur·ric·u·lar (kə rik′yu̇ lər) *adj.* having to do with a curriculum.

cur·ric·u·lum (kə rik′yu̇ ləm) *n.* **-lums** or **-la** (-lə). **1** the whole range of studies offered in a school, college, etc. or in a type of school: *the university curriculum. Our high-school curriculum includes English, mathematics, science, history, and foreign languages.* **2** a program of studies leading to a particular degree, certificate, etc.: *the curriculum of the Law School.* [< L *curriculum* race course, chariot, dim. of *currus* chariot < *currere* run]

cur·ri·er (kėr′ē ər) *n.* **1** a person who curries tanned leather. **2** a person who curries horses, etc. [ME < OF *corier* < L *coriarius* tanner < *corium* leather]

cur·rish (kėr′ish) *adj.* of or like a cur; snarling; ill-bred; worthless. **—cur′rish·ly,** *adv.* **—cur′rish·ness,** *n.*

cur·ry[1] (kėr′ē) *v.* **-ried, -ry·ing. 1** rub and clean (a horse, etc.) with a brush or currycomb. **2** prepare (tanned leather) for use by soaking, scraping, beating, coloring, etc. **3 curry favor,** seek a person's favor by flattery, constant attentions, etc. [ME < OF *correiier* put in order < *con-* (intensive) + *reiier* arrange < Gmc.]

cur·ry[2] (kėr′ē) *n.* **-ries,** *v.* **-ried, -ry·ing.** *—n.* **1** a peppery sauce or powder containing a mixture of spices, seeds, vegetables, etc: *curried lamb.* **2** a stew flavored with curry. *—v.* prepare or flavor with curry. [< Tamil *kari*]

cur·ry·comb (kėr′ē kōm′) *n.* a brush with metal teeth for rubbing and cleaning a horse. *—v.* use a currycomb on; brush with a currycomb.

curse (kėrs) *v.* **cursed** or **curst, curs·ing,** *n.* *—v.* **1** ask God, or a god, to bring evil or harm on. **2** bring evil or harm on. **3** swear; swear at; blaspheme. **4** excommunicate. **5 be cursed with,** have and suffer from: *Job was cursed with boils.* [OE *cūrsian*]
—n. **1** the words that a person says when he asks God, or a god, to curse someone or something. **2** something that is cursed. **3** harm or evil that comes as if in answer to a curse; a source of trouble or friction. **4** a cause of evil or harm. **5** the word or words used in swearing. [OE *cūrs*] **—curs′er,** *n.*
Syn. *v.* **3 Curse, swear** = use profane or foul language. **Curse** emphasizes anger or hatred, and suggests calling down harm or evil on a person by calling on God to condemn him to eternal punishment, etc.: *He cursed the poor waitress who had spilled soup on him.* **Swear** suggests using the names of holy persons or things or similar words to punctuate one's speech or express feelings: *He swore horrible oaths when he hurt himself.* Both words mean "to use foul language." *-n.* **5** oath.

curs·ed (kėr′sid or kėrst) *adj.* **1** under a curse. **2** deserving a curse; evil; hateful. **—curs′ed·ly,** *adv.* **—cur′sed·ness,** *n.*

cur·sive (kėr′siv) *adj.* written with the letters joined together. Ordinary handwriting is cursive. *—n.* **1** a letter made to join other letters. **2** a style of printing type imitating handwriting. **3** cursive script. [< Med.L *cursivus* < *cursus,* pp. of L *currere* run] **—cur′sive·ly,** *adv.*

cur·so·ri·al (kėr sô′rē əl) *adj.* **1** for running. **2** having legs fitted for running: *The ostrich is a cursorial bird.*

cur·so·ry (kėr′sə rē) *adj.* hasty; superficial; without attention to details: *Even a cursory reading of the letter showed many errors.* [< LL *cursorius* of a race < *currere* run] **—cur′so·ri·ly,** *adv.* **—cur′so·ri·ness,** *n.* **—Syn.** rapid, hurried.

curst (kėrst) *adj.* cursed. *—v.* a pt. and a pp. of **curse.**

curt (kėrt) *adj.* short; rudely brief; abrupt: *a curt way of talking.* [< L *curtus* cut short] **—curt′ly,** *adv.* **—curt′ness,** *n.* **—Syn.** See **blunt.**

cur·tail (kėr tāl′) *v.* cut short; cut off part of; reduce; lessen. [< *curtal,* adj., cut short (especially of tails) < OF *cortald* < L *curtus*; influenced by *tail*] **—Syn.** See **shorten.**

cur·tail·ment (kėr tāl′mənt) *n.* a curtailing; diminution.

cur·tain (kėr′tən) *n.* **1** a piece of cloth hung at windows or in doorways for protection or ornament. **2** in the theatre: **a** a hanging screen that separates the stage of a theatre from the auditorium. **b** the fall or closing of the curtain at the end of an act or scene. **3** anything that covers or hides: *a curtain of artillery fire.* **4** the part of a wall between two bastions, towers, or the like.
bring down the curtain on, terminate; end: *The merger brought down the curtain on the independent company.*
curtain off, separate or divide by means of a curtain or curtains.
draw the curtain over or **on,** conceal.
raise the curtain on, disclose; reveal.
—v. **1** provide with a curtain; shut off with a curtain; decorate with a curtain. **2** cover; hide.
[ME < OF *curtine* < LL *cortina*] **—cur′tain·less,** *adj.*
—Syn. *n.* **1** hanging, drapery.

curtain call a call for an actor, musician, etc. to return to the stage and acknowledge the applause of the audience.

curtain lecture a scolding given by a wife to her husband. [originally with reference to the old-fashioned curtained bed]

curtain raiser 1 in a theatre, a short play given before the main play. **2** a little thing used to introduce something bigger: *The walkout of a few workers was the curtain raiser to a major strike.*

curtain wall a wall between columns or piers of a frame or skeleton of a building which supports no load other than its own weight, and is not supported by girders or beams.

cur·te·sy (kėr′tə sē) *n.* **-sies.** in law, the right a husband has, under certain conditions, in the land left by his dead wife. [var. of *courtesy*]

curt·sey (kėrt′sē) *n.* **-seys,** *v.* **-seyed, -sey·ing.** curtsy.

curt·sy (kėrt′sē) *n.* **-sies,** *v.* **-sied, -sy·ing.** —*n.* a bow of respect or greeting by women, made by bending the knees and lowering the body slightly. —*v.* make a curtsy. [var. of *courtesy*]

cu·rule chair (kūr′ül) in ancient Rome, a special seat that only certain of the highest magistrates or officials were permitted to use. [< L *curulis* < *currus* chariot]

cur·va·ceous (kėr vā′shəs) *adj. Informal.* of a girl or woman, having a full figure; attractively well-developed.

cur·va·ture (kėr′və chər or kėr′və chür′) *n.* **1** a curving or bending. **2** a curved condition, especially an abnormal one: *a curvature of the spine.* **3** a curved piece or part; curve. **4** the degree of curving; curve: *the curvature of the earth's surface.*

curve (kėrv) *n. v.* **curved, curv·ing,** *adj.* —*n.* **1** a line that has no straight part. **2** something having the shape of a curve; bend: *The automobile had to slow down for the curves in the road.* **3** in baseball, a ball thrown so as to curve just before it reaches the batter. **4** the degree or manner to or in which something curves. **5** in mathematics, a line whose course can be defined by an equation.
—*v.* **1** bend so as to form a curve. **2** move in the course of a curve.
—*adj.* curved. [< L *curvus* bending]

curved (kėrvd) *adj.* bent so as to form a curve.

cur·vet (*n.* kėr′vit; *v.* kėr vet′ or kėr′vit) *n.v.* **-vet·ted** or **-vet·ed, -vet·ting** or **-vet·ing.** —*n.* a leap in the air made by a horse. The forelegs are first raised and then the hind legs, so that all legs are off the ground for a second.
—*v.* **1** of a horse, make a leap in the air. **2** make (a horse) leap in the air. [< Ital. *corvetta,* dim. of *corvo* curve < L *curvus* bending. Doublet of CAVORT.]

cur·vi·lin·e·al (kėr′və lin′ē əl) *adj.* curvilinear.

cur·vi·lin·e·ar (kėr′və lin′ē ər) *adj.* consisting of a curved line or lines; enclosed by curved lines.

cush·ion (kůsh′ən) *n.* **1** a soft pillow or pad used to sit, lie, or kneel on. **2** anything used or shaped like a cushion. Air or steam forms a cushion in some machines to protect them from sudden shocks or jars. **3** anything that lessens the effects of distress or adversity, relieves a burden, or makes for greater comfort or ease: *a cushion of savings against sickness or retirement.* **4** *Cdn.* an enclosed ice surface on which hockey is played. **5** the elastic lining of the sides of a billiard table. **6** the layer of soft rubber in the casing of a pneumatic tire.
—*v.* **1** put or seat on a cushion; support with cushions. **2** supply with a cushion. **3** protect from sudden shocks or jars with a cushion of steam. **4** ease the effects of; protect: *His family's wealth had always cushioned him against failure.* [ME < OF *coussin,* probably < VL *coxinum* < L *coxa* hip] —**cush′ion·like′,** *adj.*

cusk (kusk) *n.* **cusk** or **cusks. 1** a species of codfish. **2** the burbot. [origin unknown]

CUSO or **C.U.S.O.** Canadian Universities Service Overseas.

cusp (kusp) *n.* **1** a pointed end; point: *A crescent has two cusps.* **2** a blunt or pointed protuberance of the crown of a tooth. [< L *cuspis, -pidis*]

cus·pid (kus′pid) *n.* a tooth having one cusp; a canine tooth. [see CUSP]

cus·pi·dal (kus′pə dəl) *adj.* **1** of or having to do with a cusp. **2** having a pointed end.

cus·pi·date (kus′pə dāt′) *adj.* having a sharp, pointed end.

cus·pi·dor (kus′pə dôr′) *n.* a container to spit into; spittoon. [< Pg. *cuspidor* spitter < *cuspir* spit < L *conspuere* spit on < *com-* + *spuere* spit]

cuss (kus) *Informal.* —*n.* **1** a curse. **2** an odd or troublesome person or animal. —*v.* curse. [var. of *curse*]

cuss·ed (kus′id) *adj. Informal.* **1** cursed. **2** stubborn. —**cuss·ed·ly,** *adv.* —**cuss′ed·ness,** *n.*

cus·tard (kus′tərd) *n.* a baked or boiled pudding made of eggs, sugar, milk, etc. [var. of *crustade* < F < Provençal *croustado* pasty[2] < L *crustare* encrust < *crusta* crust]

custard apple 1 a heart-shaped tropical fruit with sweet, yellowish flesh. **2** the tree that it grows on. **3** any tree or shrub of the same family, such as the North American papaw, sweetsop, or soursop. In Canada, the custard apple grows on the Niagara peninsula.

cus·to·di·al (kus tō′dē əl) *adj.* having to do with custody or custodians.

cus·to·di·an (kus tō′dē ən) *n.* the person in charge; a guardian; keeper; caretaker: *the custodian of a museum.*

cus·to·di·an·ship (kus tō′dē ən ship′) *n.* the position or duties of a custodian.

cus·to·dy (kus′tə dē) *n.* **-dies. 1** the keeping; care: *Parents have the custody of their young children.* **2** a being confined or detained; imprisonment. **3 in custody,** in the care of the police; in prison. **4 take into custody,** arrest. [< L *custodia* < *custos, -odis* guardian]

cus·tom (kus′təm) *n.* **1** a usual action; habit: *It was his custom to rise early.* **2** a habit maintained for so long that it has almost the force of law. **3** the regular business given by a customer to a storekeeper. **4 customs,** *pl.* **a** taxes paid to the government on things imported, or brought in, from a foreign country. **b** the office at a seaport, international airport, or border-crossing point where imported goods are checked. **c** the department of the government that collects taxes on imported goods. **5** in feudal times, a tax or service regularly due from tenants to their lord.
—*adj.* **1** made specially for individuals; made to order; not ready-made: *custom clothes.* **2** making things to order; not selling ready-made goods: *a custom tailor.* [ME < OF *custume* < VL *consuetumen* < L *consuescere.* Doublet of COSTUME.]
Syn. *n.* **1 Custom, habit, practice** = a usual action or way of acting. **Custom** applies to a usage adopted and practised by an individual or group over a period of time: *Eating fish on Friday is a custom among some people.* **Habit** refers to a settled tendency or practice that an individual has acquired and is second nature to him: *Winding one's watch becomes a habit.* **Practice** applies to a habitual mode of activity or procedure: *He makes a practice of cheating.*

cus·tom·ar·i·ly (kus′təm ãr′ə lē or kus′təm er′ə lē) *adv.* in a customary manner; usually.

cus·tom·ar·y (kus′təm er′ē) *adj.* according to custom; as a habit; usual. —**Syn.** habitual. See **usual.**

cus·tom-built (kus′təm bilt′) *adj.* built to order; not ready-made.

cus·tom·er (kus′təm ər) *n.* **1** a person who buys, especially a regular patron of a particular store. **2** *Informal.* a person; fellow: *An ugly customer is a person hard to deal with.*

custom house a government building or office where taxes on things brought into a country are collected.

cus·tom-made (kus′təm mād′) *adj.* made to order; made specially for individuals; not ready-made.

customs officer a government official who examines goods being brought into a country and charges any taxes that may be payable.

cut (kut) *v.* **cut, cut·ting,** *adj. n.* —*v.* **1** open, remove, or separate with something sharp: *cut meat, timber, grass, one's nails, etc.* **2** make or prepare by cutting: *He cut a hole through the wall with an axe.* **3** make a cut, opening, channel, etc.: *This knife cuts well. The river has cut deep through the rock.* **4** be cut; admit of being cut: *Stale bread cuts better than fresh bread.* **5** wound with a knife, saw, etc.: *She cut her finger.* **6** reduce; decrease: *cut expenses.* **7** prepare (a stencil) for mimeographing or the like: *cut a stencil.* **8** go by a short, direct way: *cut through the woods to get home.* **9** go across; divide by crossing: *A brook cuts that field.* **10** make a recording on: *cut a record, tape, etc.* **11** hit or strike sharply: *The cold wind cut me to the bone.* **12** in tennis, baseball, etc., hit with a slicing stroke: *He cut the ball so that it bounded almost backward.* **13** hurt the feelings of: *His mean remarks cut me.* **14** *Informal.* refuse to recognize socially: *Everyone in the class cut the boy who came first in the test by cheating.* **15** *Informal.* be absent from (a class, lecture, etc.): *He wanted to cut history when he heard there was going to be a test.* **16** make less sticky or stiff; dissolve: *Gasoline cuts grease and tar.* **17** draw (a card) at random from a pack. **18** divide (a pack of cards) at random. **19** *Informal.* do; perform; make: *cut a caper.* **20** shorten by omitting some

part or parts: *Your speech will be more effective if you cut it in several places.* **21** come to an end; conclude; stop (especially as an order to stop cameras filming a motion picture or television scene).
cut across, go straight across or through.
cut back, a go back suddenly. **b** shorten (a plant) by cutting off the end. **c** reduce output, expenditure, etc.
cut down, a cause to fall by cutting. **b** reduce; decrease.
cut in, a go in suddenly. **b** break in; interrupt. **c** interrupt a dancing couple to take the place of one of them. **d** move a vehicle suddenly into a line of moving traffic. **e** connect, join, etc., especially to a machine or working part.
cut off, a remove by cutting: *cut off a branch.* **b** shut off: *cut off the gas.* **c** stop suddenly: *cut off all hope of success.* **d** break; interrupt: *cut off a retreat.* **e** disinherit: *He cut his nephew off without a cent.* **f** isolate: *Rural homes were cut off by the storm.*
cut out, a remove by cutting. **b** take out; leave out: *cut out a part of a novel.* **c** take the place of; get the better of: *cut out a rival.* **d** make by cutting; make; form. **e** *Slang.* stop doing or using: *cut out candy.* **f** move out of an assigned or expected position: *The reckless driver suddenly cut out from his own lane.* **g** suit as if by nature: *She was cut out to be a teacher.*
cut short, interrupt.
cut teeth, have teeth grow through the gums.
cut up, a cut to pieces. **b** *Informal.* hurt. **c** *Slang.* show off; play tricks.
cut up rough, a become physically violent. **b** make difficulties. **c** misbehave badly.
—*adj.* **1** that has been cut: *a cut pie.* **2** shaped or formed by cutting. **3** reduced: *at cut prices.* **4 cut and dried, a** ready for use; arranged in advance. **b** dead; dull; uninteresting.
—*n.* **1** a wound or opening made by cutting. **2** a passage, channel, etc. made by cutting or digging. **3** a piece cut off or cut out. **4** the way in which a thing is cut; style; fashion. **5** a decrease; reduction. **6** a way straight across or through; short cut. **7** a sharp blow or stroke. **8** in tennis, baseball, etc., a slicing stroke. **9** an action or speech that hurts feelings. **10** *Informal.* refusal to recognize socially. **11** *Informal.* an absence from a class, lecture, etc. **12** in lumbering, the amount of wood cut: *Nearly half the cut is pulpwood.* **13** in printing: **a** a block or plate with a picture engraved on it. **b** a picture made from such a block or plate. **14** *Informal.* a share of booty, loot, etc. **15 a** a random division of a pack of playing cards. **b** the random selection of one card. [ME *cutte(n)*; origin uncertain]
Syn. *v.* **1 Cut, chop, hack** = separate or remove with something sharp. **Cut** is the general word: *He cut some branches for kindling.* **Chop** = cut by hitting: *A guillotine was used to chop off heads during the French Revolution.* **Hack** = cut or chop roughly and unevenly: *The body of the murder victim was found hacked to pieces.* –*n.* **9** slight.

cut-and-dried (kut′ ən drīd′) *adj.* **1** ready for use; prepared in advance: *a cut-and-dried scheme.* **2** dull; routine; lacking suspense or vitality: *a cut-and-dried lecture.*

cut and fill a system by which material excavated to make a road, canal, etc. is used to form an adjacent embankment.

cut and thrust 1 hand to hand fighting, especially with swords. **2** in swordplay, the action of cutting and thrusting. **3** vigorous and lively interchange: *the cut and thrust of debate.*

cu·ta·ne·ous (kū tā′ nē əs or kū tā′ nyəs) *adj.* of the skin; having to do with the skin; on the skin. [< Med.L *cutaneus* < L *cutis* skin]

cut·a·way (kut′ ə wā′) *n.* a coat having the lower part cut back in a curve or slope from the waist in front to the tails in back. Cutaways are used by men for formal wear in the daytime.

cut·back (kut′ bak′) *n.* a reduction in output, expenditure, etc.: *Many factories made cutbacks when their orders were cancelled.*

cut·bank (kut′ bangk′) *n.* the outer side of a stream or river where the force of the current has cut away the earth, leaving an overhanging bank.

cute (kūt) *adj.* **cut·er, cut·est.** *Informal.* **1** pleasing or attractive because pretty, lovable, dainty, etc. **2** clever; shrewd; cunning. **3** consciously stylish or mannered: *cute dialogue.* [var. of *acute*] **—cute′ly,** *adv.* **—cute′ness,** *n.*

hat, āge, cãre, fär; let, ēqual, tėrm; it, īce
hot, ōpen, ôrder; oil, out; cup, pu̇t, rüle, ūse
əbove, takən, pencəl, lemən, circəs
ch, child; ng, long; sh, ship
th, thin; ᴛʜ, then; zh, measure

cut·ey (kū′ tē) *n. Informal.* cutie.

cut glass glass shaped or decorated by grinding and polishing.

cu·ti·cle (kū′ tə kəl) *n.* **1** the outer skin of vertebrates. **2** the hard skin around a fingernail or toenail. **3** in botany, a very thin film covering the surface of a plant. [< L *cuticula*, dim. of *cutis* skin]

cut·ie (kū′ tē) *n. Informal.* a cute person. Also, **cutey.**

cu·tin (kū′ tən) *n.* in botany, a waxy substance that is the chief ingredient of the outer skin of many plants. [< L *cutis* skin]

cu·tis (kū′ tis) *n.* the skin beneath the epidermis; derma. [< L]

cut·lass or **cut·las** (kut′ ləs) *n.* a short, heavy, slightly curved sword. [< F *coutelas* < L *culter* knife]

cut·ler (kut′ lər) *n.* a person who makes, sells, or repairs knives, scissors, and other cutting instruments. [ME < OF *coutelier* < *coutel* small knife < L *cultellus*, dim. of *culter* knife]

cut·ler·y (kut′ lər ē) *n.* **1** knives, scissors, and other cutting instruments. **2** knives, forks, and spoons for table use. **3** the business of a cutler.

cut·let (kut′ lit) *n.* **1** a slice of meat from the leg or ribs for broiling or frying: *a veal cutlet.* **2** a flat, fried cake of chopped meat or fish; croquette. [< F *côtelette*, dim. of *côte* < L *costa* rib]

cut·off (kut′ of′) *n.* **1** a short way across or through; a road or passage shorter than the one normally used. **2 a** a new passage cut by a river across a bend. **b** the water in the old channel, thus cut off. **3** a stopping of the passage of steam or working fluid to the cylinder of an engine. **4** the mechanism or device that does this. **5** the act or an instance of cutting off; cessation; end. **6** the point in an electrical circuit at which a mechanism prevents the flow of current of certain frequencies to or from the circuit. **7** in baseball, the interception of a ball thrown to a base from the outfield.

cut·out (kut′ out′) *n.* **1** a shape or design to be cut out: *Some books for children have cutouts.* **2** a device for disconnecting an internal-combustion engine from its muffler. Automobiles have cutouts to let the exhaust from the engine directly out into the air. **3** a device for breaking an electric current.

cut·o·ver (kut′ ō′ vər) *adj.* from which the trees have been cut: *cutover land.*

cut·purse (kut′ pėrs′) *n.* a thief; pickpocket. [from the former practice of stealing purses by cutting them from belts, where they used to be hung]

cut·ter (kut′ ər) *n.* **1** a person who cuts: *A garment cutter cuts out clothes.* **2** a tool or machine for cutting: *a meat cutter.* **3** a small, light sleigh, usually pulled by one horse. **4** a small sailboat with one mast. **5** a boat belonging to a warship, used to carry people and supplies to and from the ship. **6** a small, armed ship used for patrolling coastal waters.

A cutter (def. 3)

cut·throat (kut′ thrōt′) *n.* **1** a murderer. **2** cutthroat trout. —*adj.* **1** murderous. **2** relentless; merciless; severe: *cutthroat competition.*

cutthroat trout a kind of large trout distinguished by a red mark under the lower jaw, found mainly in the Rocky Mountain region and highly valued as a game fish.

cut·ting (kut′ ing) *n.* **1** something cut off or cut out. **2** a small shoot cut from a plant to grow a new plant. **3** a newspaper or magazine clipping. **4** a place or way cut through high ground for a road, track, etc. **5** the act of one that cuts.
—*adj.* **1** that cuts; sharp. **2** that hurts the feelings; sarcastic: *a cutting remark.* **—cut′ting·ly,** *adv.*

cut·tle (kut′əl) *n.* cuttlefish.

cut·tle·bone (kut′əl bōn′) *n.* the hard internal shell of cuttlefish, used for making polishing powder, as food for canaries, etc.

cut·tle·fish (kut′əl fish′) *n.* **-fish** or **-fish·es.** a salt-water mollusc having ten sucker-bearing arms and a hard internal shell. One kind of cuttlefish squirts out an inky fluid when frightened. [*cuttle*, OE *cudele* cuttlefish]

cut·up (kut′up′) *n. Slang.* a person who shows off or plays tricks.

cut·wa·ter (kut′wot′ər or -wô′tər) *n.* the front part of a ship's prow.

cut·work (kut′wėrk′) *n.* openwork embroidery in which part of the cloth is cut away.

cut·worm (kut′wėrm′) *n.* a caterpillar that cuts off the stalks of young plants near or below the ground when feeding on them at night.

cu. yd. cubic yard; cubic yards.

C.V.O. Commander (of the Royal) Victorian Order.

C.V.S.M. Canadian Volunteer Service Medal.

C.W.A.C. or **CWAC** Canadian Women's Army Corps.

cwt. hundredweight.

-cy *suffix.* **1** the office, position, or rank of, as in *captaincy.* **2** the quality, state, condition, or fact of being, as in *bankruptcy.* [(directly or < F *-cie*) < L *-cia*, Gk. *-keia*; (directly or < F *-cie* or *-tie*) < L *-tia*, Gk. *-tia*, *-teia*]

cy·an·a·mide (sī an′ə mīd′ or sī an′ə mid) *n.* **1** a white crystalline chemical compound prepared by the action of ammonia on cyanogen chloride and in other ways. **2** a salt of this compound. *Formula*: CH_2N_2

cy·a·nate (sī′ə nāt′) *n.* a salt of cyanic acid.

cy·an·ic (sī an′ik) *adj.* **1** of cyanogen; containing cyanogen. **2** blue. [< Gk. *kyanos* dark blue]

cyanic acid a colorless, poisonous liquid. *Formula*: HOCN

cy·a·nide (sī′ə nīd′ or sī′ə nid) *n.* a salt of hydrocyanic acid, especially potassium cyanide (a powerful poison).

cy·a·nite (sī′ ə nīt′) *n.* a silicate of aluminum usually occurring in blue, blade-shaped crystals. *Formula*: Al_2SiO_5 Also, **kyanite.** [< Gk. *kyanos* blue substance + E- *ite*[1]]

cy·an·o·gen (sī an′ə jən) *n.* **1** a colorless, poisonous, inflammable gas having the odor of bitter almonds. *Formula*: C_2N_2 **2** a univalent radical (-CN) consisting of one atom of carbon and one of nitrogen. [< F *cyanogène* < Gk. *kyanos* dark-blue substance + *-genēs* born, produced]

cy·a·no·sis (sī′ə nō′sis) *n.* blueness or lividness of the skin, caused by lack of oxygen in the blood. [< NL < Gk. *kyanōsis* dark-blue color < *kyanos* dark blue]

cy·a·not·ic (sī′ ə not′ik) *adj.* of, having to do with, or affected with cyanosis.

cy·ber·net·ic (sī′ bər net′ik) *adj.* of or having to do with cybernetics.

cy·ber·net·ics (sī′bər net′iks) *n.* the comparative study of complex calculating machines and the human nervous system in order to understand better the functioning of the human brain. [< Gk. *kybernētikos* of a pilot < *kybernētēs* pilot < *kybernaein* steer]

cy·cad (sī′kad) *n.* a large, tropical, palmlike plant having a cluster of long, fernlike leaves either rising from an underground stem or borne at the top of a thick trunk that resembles a column. [< NL *cycas*, *-adis* < Gk. *kykas*, scribal mistake for *koïkas*, pl. of *koïx* palm]

cyc·la·men (sik′lə mən) *n.* a plant of the same family as the primrose, having heart-shaped leaves and showy white, purple, pink, or crimson flowers, whose five petals bend backwards. [< NL < L < Gk. *kyklaminos*]

cy·cle (sī′kəl) *n. v.* **-cled, -cling.** —*n.* **1** a period of time or complete process of growth or action that repeats itself in the same order: *The seasons of the year—spring, summer, autumn, and winter—make a cycle.* **2** a complete set or series. **3** all the stories, poems, legends, etc. about a great hero or event: *There is a cycle of stories about the adventures of King Arthur and his knights.* **4** a very long period of time; age. **5** a bicycle, tricycle, etc. **6** in electricity, a complete or double alternation or reversal of an alternating current. The number of cycles per second is the measure of frequency. **7** in biology, a recurring series of changes. **8** in botany, a closed circle or whorl of leaves. **9** in astronomy, an orbit or circle in the heavens: *the cycle of a planet.* **10** in physics, a series of operations by which a substance or operation is finally brought back to the initial state. **11** the series of strokes of a piston in the cylinder of an engine.
—*v.* **1** pass through a cycle; occur over and over again in the same order. **2** ride a bicycle, tricycle, etc. [< LL *cyclus* < Gk. *kyklos* wheel]

cy·clic (sī′klik or sik′lik) *adj.* **1** of a cycle. **2** moving or occurring in cycles. **3** in chemistry: **a** containing a ring of atoms. **b** of or having to do with an arrangement of atoms in a ring or closed chain.

cy·cli·cal (sī′klə kəl or sik′lə kəl) *adj.* cyclic.

cy·clist (sī′klist) *n.* the rider of a bicycle, tricycle, etc.

cyclo- *combining form.* **1** circle; of a circle: cycloid = shaped somewhat like a circle. **2** cyclic, as in *cyclopropane.* [< Gk. *kyklos* wheel]

cy·cloid (sī′kloid) *adj.* like a circle.
—*n.* in geometry, a curve traced by a point on the circumference, on a radius, or on a prolonged radius of a circle when the circle is rolled along a straight line and kept in the same plane.

C, a cycloid

cy·clom·e·ter (sī klom′ə tər) *n.* an instrument that measures the distance that a wheel travels by recording the revolutions that it makes.

cy·clone (sī′klōn) *n.* **1** a very violent windstorm; tornado. **2** a storm moving around and towards a calm centre of low pressure, which also moves. [< Gk. *kyklōn*, ppr. of *kykloein* move around in a circle]
☛ A cyclonic storm is called **typhoon** in the western Pacific regions and **hurricane** in the western Atlantic. A **tornado** is a violent seasonal whirlwind that strikes W. Africa and N. America, and is accompanied by a funnel-shaped cloud.

cy·clon·ic (sī klon′ik) *adj.* **1** of a cyclone. **2** like a cyclone.

cy·clon·i·cal (sī klon′ə kəl) *adj.* cyclonic.
—**cy·clon′i·cal·ly,** *adv.*

cy·clo·pae·di·a (sī′klə pē′dē ə) *n.* cyclopedia.

cy·clo·pae·dic (sī klə pē′dik) *adj.* cyclopedic.

Cy·clo·pe·an (sī′klə pē′ən) *adj.* **1** of or having to do with the Cyclopes. **2** Also, **cyclopean.** huge; gigantic.

cy·clo·pe·di·a or **cy·clo·pae·di·a** (sī′klə pē′dē ə) *n.* a book giving information on all branches of one subject. A cyclopedia is different from an encyclopedia in that it usually does not go beyond one field or classification of knowledge. [shortened form of *encyclopedia*]

cy·clo·pe·dic or **cy·clo·pae·dic** (sī′klə pē′dik) *adj.* **1** wide and varied. **2** having to do with a cyclopedia.

cy·clo·pro·pane (sī′ klə prō′pān) *n.* a colorless, inflammable gas used as an anaesthetic. *Formula*: C_3H_6

Cy·clops (sī′klops) *n.* **Cy·clo·pes** (sī klō′pēz). in Greek mythology, one of a group of one-eyed giants. [< L < Gk. *Kyklōps* < *kyklos* circle + *ōps* eye]

cy·clo·ram·a (sī′klə ram′ə) *n.* **1** a large picture of a landscape, battle, etc. on the wall of a circular room. **2** in the theatre, a curved screen crossing the width of a stage and used as a background for the scenery. [< *cyclo-* + Gk. *horama* spectacle]

cy·clo·tron (sī′klə tron′) *n.* a powerful apparatus for giving very high speeds to electrically charged particles. The accelerated particles may be used to bombard, and to effect changes in, atomic nuclei. [< *cyclo-* + *-tron* (as in *electron*)]

cyg·net (sig′nit) *n.* a young swan. [ME < OF *cygne* < L *cygnus*, earlier *cycnus* < Gk. *kyknos*]

Cyg·nus (sig′nəs) *n.* in astronomy, a northern constellation in the Milky Way, thought of by the ancients as being arranged in the shape of a swan. [< L *cygnus* swan]

hat, āge, cãre, fär; let, ēqual, tėrm; it, īce
hot, ōpen, ôrder; oil, out; cup, pu̇t, rüle, ūse
əbove, takən, pencəl, lemən, circəs
ch, child; ng, long; sh, ship
th, thin; ᴛʜ, then; zh, measure

cyl. 1 cylinder. 2 cylindrical.

cyl·in·der (sil′ən dər) *n.* 1 a solid bounded by two equal, parallel circles and a curved surface, formed by moving a straight line of fixed length so that its ends always lie on the two parallel circles. 2 the volume of such a solid. 3 any long, round object, solid or hollow, with flat ends: *a cylinder of cardboard.* 4 the part of a revolver that contains chambers for cartridges. 5 the piston chamber of an engine. 6 **a** a vessel or container having the form of a cylinder. **b** its contents. [< L *cylindrus* < Gk. *kylindros* < *kylindein* to roll]

A cylinder

cy·lin·dric (sə lin′drik) *adj.* cylindrical.

cy·lin·dri·cal (sə lin′drə kəl) *adj.* shaped like a cylinder; having the form of a cylinder. —**cy·lin′dri·cal·ly,** *adv.*

cym·bal (sim′bəl) *n.* one of a pair of brass or bronze plates, used as a musical instrument. Cymbals are struck together to make a loud, ringing sound; a cymbal can be hit with a drumstick, hammer, or wire brush. [OE < L *cymbalum* < Gk. *kymbalon* < *kymbē* hollow of a vessel]

Cymbals

cyme (sīm) *n.* in botany, a flower cluster in which there is a flower at the top of the main stem and of each branch of the cluster. The flower in the centre opens first. The sweet william has cymes. [< F < L *cyma* < Gk. *kyma* something swollen, sprout < *kyein* be pregnant]

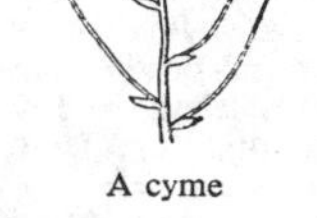

A cyme

cy·mose (sī′mōs or sī mōs′) *adj.* in botany: 1 having a cyme or cymes. 2 like a cyme.

Cym·ric (kim′rik) *adj.* 1 Welsh. 2 of or having to do with the group of Celts that includes the Welsh, Cornish, and Bretons, or their languages; Brythonic. —*n.* Welsh.

Cym·ry (kim′rē) *n.* 1 the Welsh people. 2 the branch of the Celts that includes the Welsh, Cornish, and Bretons.

cyn·ic (sin′ik) *n.* 1 a person inclined to believe that the motives for people's actions are insincere and selfish. 2 a sneering, sarcastic person. 3 **Cynic,** in ancient Greece, a member of a group of philosophers who taught that self-control is the essential part of virtue. They despised pleasure, money, and personal comfort.
—*adv.* 1 cynical. 2 **Cynic,** of or having to do with the Cynics or their doctrines. [< L *cynicus* < Gk. *kynikos* doglike < *kyōn* dog]

cyn·i·cal (sin′ə kəl) *adj.* 1 doubting the sincerity and goodness of others. 2 sneering; sarcastic. —**cyn′i·cal·ly,** *adv.* —**cyn′i·cal·ness,** *n.*

Syn. 1 Cynical, pessimistic = doubting and mistrustful. **Cynical** emphasizes the idea of doubting the honesty, sincerity, and disinterestedness of people and their motives for doing things: *People cannot make friends with a person who is cynical about friendship.* **Pessimistic** emphasizes the idea of always looking on the dark side of things and expecting the most unpleasant or worst things to happen: *He has a very pessimistic attitude toward the value of this work.*

cyn·i·cism (sin′ə siz′əm) *n.* 1 a cynical quality or disposition. 2 a cynical remark. 3 **Cynicism,** the doctrines of the Cynics.

cy·no·sure (sī′nə shür′ or sin′ə shür′) *n.* 1 the centre of attraction, interest, or attention. 2 something used for guidance or direction. 3 **Cynosure,** in astronomy: **a** a constellation containing the North Star. **b** the North Star. [< L *Cynosura* (def. 3) < Gk. *kynosoura* dog's tail + *kyōn* dog + *oura* tail]

Cyn·thi·a (sin′thē ə) *n.* 1 Artemis or Diana, regarded as the goddess of the moon. 2 the moon.

cy·pher (sī′fər) *n. v.* cipher.

cy·press (sī′prəs) *n.* 1 any of several evergreen trees having hard wood and dark leaves. 2 in Canada: **a** jack pine. **b** yellow cedar, or Nootka cypress. 3 the wood of any of these trees. [ME < OF < L *cupressus* < Gk. *kyparissos*]

Cyp·ri·an (sip′rē ən) *adj.* of or having to do with Cyprus (an island in the E. Mediterranean Sea, south of Turkey). —*n.* a native or inhabitant of Cyprus.

cyp·ri·noid (sip′rə noid′) *n.* any of a large group of fresh-water fish, including the carp, sucker, goldfish, bream, most minnows, etc. —*adj.* of or belonging to this group of fish. [< L *cyprinus* carp (< Gk.) + E *-oid* resembling (< Gk. *eidos* form)]

Cyp·ri·ot (sip′rē ət) *adj.* of or having to do with Cyprus (an island in the E. Mediterranean Sea, south of Turkey). —*n.* a native or inhabitant of Cyprus.

cyp·ri·pe·di·um (sip′rə pē′dē əm) *n.* **-di·a** (-dē ə). any of several orchids that have drooping flowers with a protruding saclike lip, including the lady's-slipper, moccasin flower, etc. [< NL *cypripedium*, apparently, alteration of *cypripodium* < Gk. *Kypris* Aphrodite + *podion*, dim. of *pous, podos* foot]

Cy·ril·lic (si ril′ik) *adj.* of or having to do with an ancient Slavic alphabet from which the Russian, Bulgarian, and Serbian alphabets have developed. [< St. *Cyril*, an apostle to the Slavs in the 9th century, who is traditionally supposed to have invented it]

cyst (sist) *n.* 1 an abnormal, saclike growth in animals or plants. Cysts usually contain liquid and diseased matter. 2 a saclike structure in animals or plants. [< NL *cystis* < Gk. *kystis* pouch, bladder]

cyst·ic (sis′tik) *adj.* 1 of or like a cyst. 2 having a cyst or cysts.

-cyte *combining form.* a cell: *leucocyte* = *a white (blood) cell.* [< Gk. *kytos* anything hollow]

Cyth·er·e·a (sith′ər ē′ə) *n.* in Greek mythology, Aphrodite, the goddess of love and beauty.

cyto- *combining form.* cell; cells: *cytology* = *the study of cells.* Also, **cyt-** before vowels. [< Gk. *kytos* anything hollow]

cy·to·ge·net·ics (sī′tō jə net′iks) *n.* in biology, the study of the relation of cells to the phenomena of heredity and variation.

cy·tol·o·gist (sī tol′ə jist) *n.* an expert in cytology.

cy·tol·o·gy (sī tol′ə jē) *n.* the branch of biology that deals with the formation, structure, and function of the cells of animals and plants. [< Gk. *kytos* receptacle, cell + E *-logy*]

cy·to·plasm (sī′tə plaz′əm) *n.* in biology, the living substance or protoplasm of a cell, exclusive of the nucleus. [< Gk. *kytos* receptacle, cell + E *-plasm* something moulded (< Gk. *plasma*)]

cy·to·plas·mic (sī′tə plaz′mik) *adj.* having to do with cytoplasm.

C.Z. Canal Zone.

czar or **tsar** (zär) *n.* 1 an emperor. It was the title of the former emperors of Russia. 2 an autocrat; a person with absolute power: *Al Capone was a czar of crime.* Also, **tzar.** [< Russian *tsar* < Old Church Slavic < Gothic < L *Caesar* Caesar]

czar·das (chär′däsh) *n.* a complicated Hungarian dance consisting of a slow, sad part followed by a fast, lively one. Also, **csardas.** [< Hungarian *csárdás*]

czardom or **tsar·dom** (zär′dəm) *n.* 1 the position or power of a czar. 2 the territory ruled by a czar.

czar·e·vitch or **tsar·e·vitch** (zär′ə vich′) *n.* 1 the eldest son of a Russian czar. 2 the son of a Russian czar. Also, **tzarevitch.** [< Russian *tsarevich*]

cza·rev·na or **tsa·rev·na** (zä rev′nə) *n.* 1 the daughter of a Russian czar. 2 the wife of a czarevitch. Also, **tzarevna.** [< Russian *tsarevna*]

cza·ri·na or **tsa·ri·na** (zä rē′nə) *n.* the wife of a czar; a Russian empress. Also, **tzarina.** [< G *Zarin* (earlier *Czarin*), fem. of *Zar* < Russian *tsar.* See CZAR.]

Czech (chek) *n.* 1 a member of the most westerly branch of the Slavs. Bohemians and Moravians are Czechs. 2 their language; Bohemian. —*adj.* of or having to do with Czechoslovakia, its language, or its people.

Czech·ish (chek′ish) *adj.* Czech.

Czech·o·slo·vak or **Czech·o-Slo·vak** (chek′ə slō′vak) *adj.* of or having to do with Czechoslovakia, its people, or their language. —*n.* **1** a native or inhabitant of Czechoslovakia. **2** their language.

Czech·o·slo·va·ki·an or **Czech·o-Slo·va·ki·an** (chek′ə slō vak′ē ən) *adj. n.* Czechoslovak.

D or **d** (dē) *n.* **D's** or **d's. 1** the fourth letter of the English alphabet. **2** any speech sound represented by this letter. **3** the fourth in a series or group designated alphabetically **4** in music: **a** the second tone in the scale of C major. **b** a symbol representing this tone. **c** a key or string that produces this tone. **d** the scale or key that has D as its keynote. **5** anything shaped like D.

D 1 the Roman numeral for 500. **2** deuterium. **3** diameter. **4** didymium. **5** in physics, density.

d. 1 died. **2** dead. **3** English penny; pence: *6d. = about 7 cents.* **4** dime. **5** dollar. **6** diameter. **7** day. **8** date. **9** delete. **10** daughter. **11** degree. **12** dyne.

D. 1 December. **2** Democrat. **3** Dutch. **4** *U.S.* Department. **5** Duke. **6** Duchess.

D.A. *U.S.* District Attorney.

dab[1] (dab) *v.* **dabbed, dab·bing,** *n.* —*v.* **1** touch lightly; pat with something soft or moist; tap; peck: *The girl dabbed her face with a powder puff.* **2** put on (paint, etc.) with light strokes. —*n.* **1** a quick, light touch or blow; pat; tap; peck. **2** a small, soft or moist mass: *a dab of butter.* **3** a little bit. [ME] —**dab′ber,** *n.*

dab[2] (dab) *n.* **1** any of various flat fishes related to the flounder. **2** any flat fish. [origin uncertain]

dab[3] (dab) *n. Informal.* an expert. [origin uncertain]

dab·ble (dab′əl) *v.* **-bled, -bling. 1** dip (hands, feet, etc.) in and out of water; splash. **2** do superficially; work a little: *dabble at painting, dabble in stocks.* [≤ Flemish *dabbelen*] —**dab′bler,** *n.*

da capo (dä kä′pō) *Italian.* in music: **1** from the beginning (a direction to repeat a passage). **2** the passage to be repeated. *Abbrev.*: d.c. [literally, from the head]

dace (dās) *n.* **dace** or **daces.** any of several small fresh-water fish. [ME *darse* < OF *dars* dart < Med.L *darsus*]

dachs·hund (dash′hůnd′ or daks′hůnd′; *German,* däks′hůnt′) *n.* **1** a German breed of small, hardy, hunting dog, having a long body, short legs, and large, drooping ears. **2** a dog of this breed. [< G *Dachshund* < *Dachs* badger + *Hund* dog]

Da·cia (dā′shə) *n.* an ancient Roman province in S. Europe. See **Roman Empire** for map.

da·coit (də koit′) *n.* in India or Burma, a member of a gang of robbers. [< Hind. *dakait* < *daka* gang-robbery]

Da·cron (dak′ron or dā′kron) *n.* a trademark for a synthetic wrinkle- and abrasion-resistant fibre used for shirts, suits, etc.; terylene.

dac·tyl (dak′təl) *n.* in verse, a foot consisting of one strongly stressed syllable followed by two weakly stressed syllables or one long syllable followed by two short syllables. *Example*: "Táke her up ténderly." [< L < Gk. *daktylos* finger. Doublet of DATE[2].]

dac·tyl·ic (dak til′ik) *adj.* **1** of dactyls. **2** consisting of dactyls. —**dac′tyl·i·cal·ly,** *adv.*

dac·ty·lol·o·gy (dak′tə lol′ə jē) *n.* the language of signs made with fingers, such as used by the deaf. [< Gk. *daktylos* finger + E *-logy*]

dad (dad) *n. Informal.* father.

Da·da·ism or **da·da·ism** (dä′də iz′əm) *n.* in art and literature, a style developed during World War I, characterized by the use of unconventional materials and techniques, by witty satire of all previous art forms and methods, and by an attitude of revolt against existing standards. [< F *dada* horse, hobbyhorse (a child's word) + E *-ism*]

Da·da·ist or **da·da·ist** (dä′də ist) *n.* a follower of Dadaism. —*adj.* of or having to do with Dadaism. —**Dadaistic** or **dadaistic,** *adj.*

dad·dy (dad′ē) *n.* **-dies.** *Informal.* father.

dad·dy-long·legs (dad′ē long′legz′) *n.sing. or pl.* an animal that looks much like a spider but does not bite.

da·do (dā′dō) *n.* **-does** or **-dos. 1** in architecture, the part of a pedestal between the base and the cap. **2** the lower part of an inside wall when covered with a special finish of wood, wall-paper, etc. [< Ital. *dado* die[2] < L *datus* given]

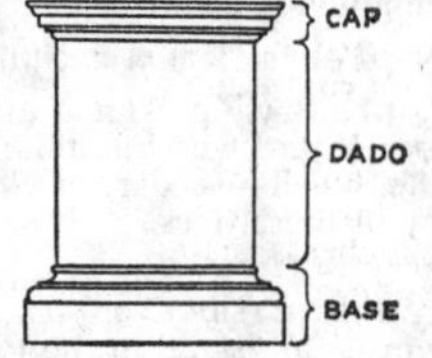

dae·dal (dē′dəl) *adj. Poetic.* **1** ingenious; skilful: *the sculptor's* *daedal hand.* **2** intricately made; with complex ornamentation. **3** like a maze; complex. [< L < Gk. *daidalos* skilful; skilfully wrought < *daidallein* work cunningly]

Dae·da·li·an or **Dae·da·le·an** (di dā′lē ən or di dal′yən) *adj.* **1** skilful; ingenious. **2** intricate; mazelike.

Daed·al·us (ded′ə ləs or dē′də ləs) *n.* in Greek legend, a skilful inventor who built the labyrinth in Crete. He and his son Icarus were imprisoned there by King Minos, but they escaped by means of wings made by Daedalus.

dae·mon (dē′mən) *n.* demon. [< L < Gk. *daimon*]

daf·fo·dil (daf′ə dil′) *n.* **1** a narcissus with yellow, white, or partly white flowers and long, slender leaves. Its flower has a long, trumpet-shaped corona growing out from the centre of the petals. **2** the flower. **3** a bright yellow. —*adj.* bright yellow. [var. of *affodill* < VL *affodillus* < L < Gk. *asphodelos*]

daff·y (daf′ē) *adj.* **daff·i·er, daff·i·est.** *Informal.* **1** foolish; silly. **2** crazy; insane. **3 daffy on,** crazy about: *The girl was daffy on the young soldier.*

daft (daft) *adj.* **1** silly; foolish. **2** crazy; insane. [OE (*ge*)*dæfte* gentle] **—daft′ly,** *adv.* **—daft′ness,** *n.*

dag (dag) *n. Cdn.* a heavy, flat, double-edged triangular blade, used by the Indians as a weapon and tool. [< Cdn.F < F *dague* dagger]

D.A.G. Deputy Adjutant General.

dag·ger (dag′ər) *n.* **1** a small weapon with a short pointed blade, used for stabbing. **2** in printing, a sign (†) to refer the reader to a footnote, a note at the back of the book, etc. **3 look daggers at,** look at (someone or something) with hatred or anger.
—*v.* **1** stab with a dagger. **2** mark with a dagger sign. [probably < obs. *dag* stab]

da·go or **Da·go** (dā′gō) *n.* **-gos** or **-goes.** *Slang. Derogatory.* a person of Spanish, Portuguese, or, nowadays especially, Italian origin. [supposedly < *Diego* James, a common Spanish name]

da·guerre·o·type (də ger′ə tīp′ or də ger′ē ə tīp′) *n.* **1** an early method of photography, in which the pictures were made on silvered metal plates. **2** a picture made in this way. [after L. *Daguerre*, 1789-1851, its inventor]

dahl·ia (dāl′yə or dal′yə) *n.* **1** a tall plant of the aster family, which has large, showy flowers in the autumn. **2** the flower of this plant. [< NL; after A. *Dahl*, Swedish botanist]

Dail Eir·eann (dol âr′ən, dôl, or doil) the lower house of parliament of the Republic of Ireland. [< Irish *dáil* assembly, and *Éireann*, gen. of *Éire* Ireland]

dai·ly (dā′lē) *adj. n.* **-lies,** *adv.* —*adj.* done, happening, or appearing every day, or every day but Sunday: *a daily paper, a daily visit.*
—*n.* a newspaper appearing every day, or every day but Sunday.
—*adv.* every day; day by day.

daily double a system of betting on two horses at once in two separate races, usually the first two races of the day.

dai·mio (dī′myō) *n.* **-mio** or **-mios.** in Japan, one of the great feudal nobles who, from the 14th to the 19th century, were vassals of the emperor. [< Japanese < Chinese *dai* great + *mio* name]

dain·ti·ness (dān′tē nis) *n.* **1** the state or quality of being fresh, delicate, and pretty. **2** fineness of taste.

dain·ty (dān′tē) *adj.* **-ti·er, -ti·est,** *n.* **-ties.** —*adj.* **1** having delicate beauty; fresh and pretty: *a dainty flower.* **2** having or showing delicate tastes and feelings; particular: *She is dainty about her eating.* **3** good to eat; delicious. [< n.] —*n.* something very good to eat; a delicious bit of food. [< OF *deinte* < L *dignitas* worthiness. Doublet of DIGNITY.] **—dain′ti·ly,** *adv.*
—Syn. *adj.* **1** See **delicate.**

dai·qui·ri (dak′ər ē or dī′kər ē) *n.* a cocktail made from rum, lime juice, and sugar. [< *Daiquiri* Cuba]

dair·y (dãr′ē) *n.* **dair·ies. 1** a room or building where milk and cream are kept and made into butter and cheese. **2** a farm where milk and cream are produced and butter and cheese made. **3** a store or company that sells milk, cream, butter, and cheese. **4** the business of producing milk and cream and making butter and cheese. [ME *deierie* < *deie* maid (OE *dǣge* breadmaker)]

hat, āge, cãre, fär; let, ēqual, tėrm; it, īce
hot, ōpen, ôrder; oil, out; cup, pu̇t, rüle, ūse
əbove, takən, pencəl, lemən, circəs
ch, child; ng, long; sh, ship
th, thin; ᴛʜ, then; zh, measure

dairy cattle cows kept to give milk for human consumption.

dair·y·ing (dãr′ē ing) *n.* the business of raising cows to produce milk and cream, or of making butter and cheese.

dair·y·maid (dãr′ē mād′) *n.* a girl or woman who works in a dairy.

dair·y·man (dãr′ē mən) *n.* **-men** (-mən). **1** a man who works in a dairy. **2** a man who owns or manages a dairy. **3** a man who sells milk, cream, butter, and cheese.

da·is (dā′is) *n.* a raised platform at one end of a hall or a large room. A throne, seats of honour, a lecture desk, etc. are set on a dais. [ME < OF *deis* < L *discus* quoit, dish < Gk. *diskos.* Doublet of DESK, DISCUS, DISH, and DISK.]

dai·sy (dā′zē) *n.* **-sies,** *adj.* —*n.* **1** a plant of the aster family whose flowers or petals are usually white or pink around a yellow centre. **2** a tall plant of the same family whose flower heads have a yellow disk and white rays; the common "white daisy" of North America. **3** the flower of either of these plants. **4** *Slang.* something fine or first-rate.
—*adj. Slang.* first-rate. [OE *dæges ēage* day's eye]

Da·ko·ta (də kō′tə) *n.* **-ta** or **-tas. 1** a tribe of Indians living on the plains of southern Canada and the northern United States. **2** a member of this tribe. **3** the Siouan language of this tribe.

dale (dāl) *n.* a valley. [OE *dæl*]

dalle (dal) *n.* **dalles** (dal′əs or dalz) *Cdn.* **1** a natural slide or chute in a river; rapids. **2** Usually, **dalles,** *pl.* a narrow stretch of river between high rock walls, characterized by whirlpools, rapids, and treacherous currents. [< Cdn.F < F *dalle* gutter]

dal·li·ance (dal′ē əns) *n.* **1** flirtation; dallying. **2** a playing; trifling.

dal·ly (dal′ē) *v.* **-lied, -ly·ing. 1** act in a playful manner: *The spring breeze dallies with the flowers.* **2** flirt (with danger, temptation, etc.); trifle: *He dallied with the offer for days, but finally refused it.* **3** flirt with or make love to a person in a playful manner. **4.** linger idly; loiter. **5** waste (time): *James dallied away the afternoon.* [< OF *dalier* chat] **—dal′ly·ing·ly,** *adv.* **—Syn. 2** See **trifle.**

Dal·ma·tian (dal mā′shən) *adj.* of, or having to do with Dalmatia, a region in Yugoslavia, or its people. —*n.* **1** a native or inhabitant of Dalmatia. **2** a breed of large, short-haired dog, usually white with black spots; coach dog. **3** a dog of this breed.

Dal·to·ni·an (dol tō′nē ən or dôl tō′nē ən) *adj.* **1** of or having to do with John Dalton (1766-1844), an English chemist and physicist who described color-blindness and was himself color-blind. **2** of or suggestive of his writings and theories. **3** of or having to do with color-blindness. —*n.* a person who is color-blind.

Dal·ton·ism or **dal·ton·ism** (dol′tə niz′əm or dôl′tə niz′əm) *n.* color-blindness, especially the inability to distinguish red from green. [< F *daltonisme* < John *Dalton* + *-isme* -ism. See DALTONIAN.]

dam[1] (dam) *n. v.* **dammed, dam·ming.** —*n.* **1** a wall built to hold back flowing water. **2** the water held back by a dam. **3** anything resembling a dam. **4** on the Prairies, a reservoir of water collected from the spring thaw and from rainfall, used for watering cattle, etc.; dugout; pothole.
—*v.* **1** provide with a dam; hold back by means of a dam: *They tried to dam the river.* **2** hold back; block up: *dam one's efforts.* [ME] **—dam′like′,** *adj.* **—Syn.** *n.* **1** dike.

dam[2] (dam) *n.* **1** the female parent of four-footed animals. **2** a mother. [var. of *dame*]

dam·age (dam′ij) *n. v.* **-aged, -ag·ing.** —*n.* **1** injury or harm that lessens value or usefulness. **2** *Slang.* cost; price: *What's the damage?* **3 damages,** *pl.* money claimed by

law or paid to make up for some harm done to a person or his property. —*v.* injure or harm so as to lessen value or usefulness; harm; hurt: *I damaged my sweater in football practice.* [ME < OF < *dam* < L *damnum* loss, hurt] —**dam′age·a·ble,** *adj.* —**dam′ag·ing·ly,** *adv.*
—**Syn.** *n.* **1** detriment, impairment. –*v.* impair, disfigure. See **harm.**

dam·a·scene (dam′ə sēn′ or dam′ə sēn′) *v.* **-scened, -scen·ing,** *n. adj.* —*v.* ornament (metal) with inlaid gold or silver or with a wavy design. —*n.* ornamentation of this kind. —*adj.* of, having, or resembling such ornament. [< L *Damascenus* < Gk. *Damaskēnos* of Damascus]

Dam·a·scene (dam′ə sēn′ or dam′ə sēn′) *adj.* of or having to do with the city of Damascus. —*n.* a native or inhabitant of Damascus.

Damascus steel a kind of ornamented steel, used in making swords, etc.

dam·ask (dam′əsk) *n.* **1** reversible linen, silk, or cotton fabric with woven designs. **2** a linen material of this type, used especially for tablecloths and serviettes. **3** damascened metal. **4** a rose color; pink.
—*adj.* **1** made of damask. **2** pink; rose-colored: *damask cheeks.* **3** of or named after the city of Damascus.
—*v.* **1** damascene. **2** weave with the design of damask fabric. [< L *Damascus* < Gk. *Damaskos* Damascus]

dame (dām) *n.* **1 Dame,** in the United Kingdom: **a** a title given to a woman with an honorable rank corresponding to that of a knight. **b** the legal title of the wife or widow of a knight or baronet. **2** an elderly woman **3** *Slang.* any woman, especially a young one. **4** in former times: **a** a lady. **b** in former times, a title given to a woman having authority in a household. [ME < OF < L *domina* mistress]

damn (dam) *v.* **1** declare to be bad or inferior; condemn. **2** cause to fail; ruin. **3** doom to eternal punishment; condemn to hell. **4** swear or swear at by saying "damn"; curse. **5 damn with faint praise,** praise with so little enthusiasm as to condemn.
—*n.* **1** an utterance of "damn." **2** a contemptible amount: *not worth a damn.* [ME < OF *damner* < L *damnare* condemn < *damnum* loss] —**Syn.** *v.* **1** denounce, proscribe, execrate.

dam·na·ble (dam′nə bəl) *adj.* **1** abominable; outrageous; detestable. **2** deserving damnation. —**dam′na·ble·ness,** *n.* —**dam′na·bly,** *adv.*

dam·na·tion (dam nā′shən) *n.* **1** a damning or being damned; condemnation. **2** a condemnation to eternal punishment. **3** a curse.

dam·na·to·ry (dam′nə tô′rē) *adj.* damning; assigning to damnation; condemnatory.

damned (damd) *adj.* **1** condemned as bad or inferior. **2** doomed to eternal punishment. **3** cursed; abominable. —*adv. Informal.* very. —*n.* **the damned,** the souls in hell.

Dam·o·cles (dam′ə klēz′) *n.* **1** a flatterer and courtier of Dionysius, King of Syracuse. Damocles thought Dionysius must be the happiest of men, but Dionysius asked him to share the happiness of a king. He gave a banquet for Damocles, seating his guest beneath a naked sword that hung above his head by a single hair. By this means Damocles was made aware of the dangers surrounding kings. **2 sword of Damocles,** any imminent danger.

dam·oi·selle (dam′ə zel′) *n. Archaic.* damsel.

Da·mon (dā′mən) *n.* **1** in classical legend, a man who pledged his life for his friend Pythias (or Phintias), who had been sentenced to death. **2 Damon and Pythias,** any loyal and devoted friends.

dam·o·sel or **dam·o·zel** (dam′ə zel′ or dam′ə zel′) *n. Archaic.* damsel.

damp (damp) *adj.* slightly wet; moist.
—*n.* **1** moisture. **2** something that checks or deadens. **3** any harmful gas that collects in mines, such as choke-damp or firedamp: *The mine disaster was caused by exploding damp.*
—*v.* **1** make moist or slightly wet. **2** check; deaden; discourage. **3** in music, stop the vibrations of (a string, etc.). [< MDu. or MLG *damp* vapor] —**damp′ly,** *adv.* —**damp′ness,** *n.*

Syn. *adj.* **Damp, moist, humid** = rather wet. **Damp** means more wet than dry, although not completely covered or soaked with liquid, and often suggests the idea that the wetness is unpleasant or unwanted: *This house is damp in rainy weather.* **Moist** suggests less wetness than *damp,* and often simply means not dry, usually implying a pleasant or desirable degree of wetness: *Use a moist, not a damp, cloth.* **Humid** is literary or scientific, but is used commonly to describe a high degree of moisture in the air: *In the East the air is humid in summer.*

damp·en (dam′pən) *v.* **1** make or become damp; moisten. **2** deaden; depress; discourage. —**damp′en·er,** *n.*

damp·er (dam′pər) *n.* **1** a person or thing that discourages or depresses. **2** a movable plate to control the draft in a stove or furnace. **3** in music: **a** a device for checking vibration and reducing the volume of sound, especially of piano strings. **b** a mute for muffling the sound of a horn, etc. **4** in electricity: **a** a device for checking the vibration of a magnetic needle. **b** a piece of copper in or near the poles of a synchronous machine to decrease hunting. **5 put a damper on,** suppress; curb; curtail; squelch: *The chairman put a damper on every suggestion the committee made.*

damp·ing-off (damp′ing of′) *n.* the decaying of newly planted seedlings, cuttings, etc. at the surface of the ground.

dam·sel (dam′zəl) *n.* a maiden or a young girl. [ME *dameisele* < OF, ult. < L *domina* lady, mistress. Doublet of DEMOISELLE.]

damsel fly a small, delicate insect similar to a dragonfly but having four wings that when at rest fold together vertically over the back.

dam·son (dam′zən) *n.* **1** a small, dark-purple plum. **2** the tree that it grows on. [< L (*prunum*) *damascenum* (plum) of Damascus]

dan (dan) *n. Cdn.* in the North: **1** a sealskin used as a container for oil. **2** a buoy made of inflated sealskin or sheepskin sewn airtight, used as a mark in deep-sea fishing. [origin uncertain]

Dan (dan) *n.* **1** in the Bible: **a** one of the sons of Jacob. **b** one of the tribes of Israel. **c** a city in the extreme north of Canaan. **2 from Dan to Beersheba,** from one end of the country to the other.

Dan. **1** Daniel. **2** Danish.

Da·na·id or **Da·na·ïd** (dan′ē id) *n.* one of the Danaides.

Da·na·i·des or **Da·na·ï·des** (də nā′ə dēz′) *n.pl.* in Greek legend, the fifty daughters of Danaus, King of Argus. All but one killed their husbands on their wedding night, and were condemned to draw water with a sieve forever in Hades.

dance (dans) *v.* **danced, danc·ing,** *n. adj.* —*v.* **1** move in rhythm, usually in time with music. **2** do or take part in (a dance). **3** jump up and down; move in a lively way. **4** bob up and down. **5 dance attendance on,** wait on often and attentively; be excessively polite and obedient to.
—*n.* **1** a movement in rhythm, usually in time with music. **2** some special groups of steps, etc.: *The waltz and fox trot were the dances she knew best.* **3** the art of dancing. **4** one round of dancing. **5** a piece of music for dancing or in a dance rhythm. **6** a party where people dance. **7** a movement up and down; lively movement. **8 lead someone a dance,** cause a person trouble, especially by luring him into a vain pursuit. **9 the dance,** the art of dancing; ballet.
—*adj.* of dancing; for dancing. [ME < OF *danser,* probably < Gmc.] —**danc′ing·ly,** *adv.*

dance hall a public hall or room for dancing.

dance of death a representation of a dance in which a skeleton, symbolizing Death, dances with people to remind them of human mortality.

danc·er (dan′sər) *n.* **1** a person who dances. **2** a person whose occupation is dancing.

dan·de·li·on (dan′də lī′ən) *n.* a weed with deeply notched leaves and bright-yellow flowers. [< F *dent de lion* lion's tooth; from its toothed leaves]

dan·der (dan′dər) *n. Informal.* **1** temper; anger. **2 get one's dander up,** get angry; lose one's temper. [origin uncertain]

Dan·die Din·mont (dan′dē din′mont) **1** a breed of small terrier, having a long body, long ears, short legs, and a rough coat. **2** a dog of this breed. [< *Dandie Dinmont*

hat, āge, cãre, fär; let, ēqual, tėrm; it, īce
hot, ōpen, ôrder; oil, out; cup, pu̇t, rule, ūse
əbove, takən, pencəl, lemən, circəs
ch, child; ng, long; sh, ship
th, thin; ᴛʜ, then; zh, measure

a character in Sir W. Scott's *Guy Mannering*), who owned such terriers]

dan·dle (dan′dəl) *v.* **-dled, -dling. 1** move (a child, etc.) up and down on one's knee or in one's arms. **2** pet; pamper. [? < earlier Ital. *dandolare*, var. of *dondolare* swing] **—dan′dler,** *n.*

dan·druff (dan′drəf) *n.* small, whitish scales that form on the scalp. [origin uncertain]

dan·dy (dan′dē) *n.* **-dies,** *adj.* **-di·er, -di·est. —***n.* **1** a man who is too careful of his dress and appearance. **2** *Slang.* anything that is excellent and pleasing. —*adj.* **1** of a dandy; too carefully dressed. **2** *Slang.* excellent; first-rate: *Everything is just dandy.* [originally Scottish, ? < *Dandy*, a Scottish var. of *Andrew*]
—Syn. *n.* **1** fop. *-adj.* **1** foppish.

Dane (dān) *n.* **1** a native or inhabitant of Denmark. **2** a person of Danish descent.

Dane·geld or **dane·geld** (dān′geld′) *n.* from the 10th to 12th centuries, an annual tax levied in Britain to buy off the Danish invaders, later continued as a land tax. [ME *Dane* Dane (< ON) + ON *gjeld* payment]

Dane·law (dān′lo′ or -lô′) *n.* **1** a set of laws enforced by the Danes when they held N.E. England in the ninth and tenth centuries A.D. **2** the part of England under these laws.

dan·ger (dān′jər) *n.* **1** a situation in which there is a chance of harm: *The signs warned us of danger.* **2** nearness to harm; risk; peril: *A soldier's life is full of danger.* **3** anything that may cause harm: *Hidden rocks are a danger to ships.* **4 in danger of,** liable to (with the accompanying threat of injury, harm, or death): *The old bridge is in danger of collapsing. The sick man is in danger of dying.* [ME < OF *dangier* < L *dominium* sovereignty < *dominus* master]
Syn. 1 Danger, peril = threat of harm. **Danger** is the general word, always suggesting there is a definite chance of harm, but the harm is not always near or certain: *Miners at work are always in danger.* **Peril** suggests great harm is very near at hand and probable: *When a mine caves in, the miners are in peril.* **2** menace, threat.

dan·ger·ous (dān′jər əs) *adj.* likely to cause harm; not safe; risky. **—dan′ger·ous·ly,** *adv.* **—dan′ger·ous·ness,** *n.*
—Syn. perilous, precarious, unsafe.

dan·gle (dang′gəl) *v.* **gled, -gling. 1** hang and swing loosely: *The curtain cord dangles.* **2** hold or carry (something) so that it swings loosely: *The nurse dangled the toys in front of the baby.* **3** hang about; follow. **4** cause to dangle. [< Scand.; cf. Danish *dangle*] **—dan′gler,** *n.*

dangling participle a participle, past or present, that is not logically or grammatically attached to the noun or pronoun it is intended to modify. Also called **unattached participle.**
☛ The dangling participle can have ambiguous and often ludicrous effects. Thus, in *Swimming in the pond, the car was out of sight*, the participle *swimming* seems to refer to the car, which is logically ludicrous. Such a faulty sentence can be improved in several ways. The dangling participle can be attached to a noun or pronoun capable of modification: *Swimming in the pond, I could not see the car.* The participial phrase can be replaced by a clause: *When I was swimming in the pond, I could not see the car.* Do not confuse a phrase containing a dangling or unattached participle with an **absolute phrase** (see **absolute,** def. 8).

Dan·iel (dan′yəl) *n.* **1** in the Bible, a Hebrew prophet whose great faith in God kept him unharmed in the lions' den. Dan. 6:16-27. **2** any upright judge.

Dan·ish (dān′ish) *adj.* of or having to do with the Danes, their language, or Denmark. —*n.* **1** the language of the Danes. **2** *Informal.* a Danish pastry. [OE *Denisc*]

Danish pastry 1 a rich, flaky pastry made with yeast. **2** a piece of such pastry.

dank (dangk) *adj.* unpleasantly damp; moist; wet: *The cave was dark, dank, and chilly.* [ME; cf. Swedish *dank* marshy spot] **—dank′ly,** *adv.* **—dank′ness,** *n.*

danse ma·ca·bre (däns mä kä′brə) *French.* dance of death.

dan·seur (däɴ sœr′) *French.* a male dancer, especially one in a ballet company. [< OF *danser.* See DANCE.]

dan·seuse (däɴ sœz′) *n.* **-seuses** (-sœz′). a female dancer, especially in a ballet. [< F]

Dan·u·bi·an (dan ū′bē ən) *adj.* of or having to do with the Danube River or the people living near it.

Daph·ne (daf′nē) *n.* in Greek legend, a nymph who was pursued by Apollo and was saved by being changed into a laurel tree.

dap·per (dap′ər) *adj.* **1** neat; trim; spruce. **2** small and active. [ME < MDu. *dapper* agile, strong] **—dap′perly,** *adv.* **—dap′per·ness,** *n.*

dap·ple (dap′əl) *adj. n. v.* **-pled, -pling.** —*adj.* spotted: *a dapple horse.* —*n.* **1** a spotted appearance or condition. **2** an animal with a spotted or mottled skin. —*v.* mark or become marked with spots. [cf. ON *depill* spot]

dap·pled (dap′əld) *adj.* spotted.

dap·ple-gray or **dap·ple-grey** (dap′əl grā′) *adj.* gray with spots of darker gray.

darb (därb) *n. Cdn. Slang.* any thing or person thought to be especially large, good, etc. [origin uncertain]

Dar·by and Joan (där′bē ən jōn′) any old and devoted married couple. [from characters in an English ballad of the eighteenth century]

dare (dãr) *v.* **dared** or **durst, dared, dar·ing,** *n.* —*v.* **1** have courage; be bold; be bold enough to: *He doesn't dare dive from the bridge.* **2** have courage for; not be afraid of; be bold enough for: *The explorer dared the dangers of the barren ground.* **3** meet and resist; face and defy. **4** challenge: *I dare you to jump.* **5 I dare say,** probably; maybe; perhaps. —*n.* a challenge. [OE *dearr* infinitive, *durran*)] **—dar′er,** *n.*
Syn. *v.* **1 Dare, venture** = be courageous or bold enough to do something. **Dare** emphasizes the idea of meeting fearlessly any danger or trouble, especially in doing something that is or seems important: *Only one man dared to enter the burning building.* **Venture** emphasizes the idea of being willing to take chances: *He decided to venture into a new business.* **3** brave.

dare·dev·il (dãr′dev′əl) *n.* a reckless person. —*adj.* reckless.

dar·ing (dãr′ing) *n.* the courage to take risks; boldness. —*adj.* courageous; bold. **—dar′ing·ly,** *adv.* **—dar′ing·ness,** *n.*

dark (därk) *adj.* **1** without light; with very little light: *a dark night.* **2** not light-colored: *a dark complexion.* **3** nearly black: *a dark green.* **4** hard to understand or explain: *a dark chapter in a book.* **5** secret; hidden: *a dark plan.* **6** without knowledge or enlightenment; ignorant: *The Dark Ages in Europe lasted from the fifth to the eleventh century.* **7** evil; wicked: *a dark deed.* **8** gloomy; dull; dismal: *a dark day.* **9** sad; sullen; frowning: *a dark face.* **10** of radio or television stations, not broadcasting. **11 keep dark,** keep silent; not tell about.
—*n.* **1** the absence of light. **2** night; nightfall. **3 after dark,** after night has fallen. **4** a dark color. **5** obscurity. **6** secrecy. **7** ignorance. **8 in the dark,** without knowledge or information. [OE *deorc*] **—dark′ly,** *adv.* **—dark′ness,** *n.*
Syn. *adj.* **1 Dark, dim** = without light. **Dark** = without any light or with very little light: *The house is dark, not a light is on.* **Dim** = without enough light to see clearly or distinctly: *With only the fire burning, the room was dim.*

Dark Ages 1 the early part of the Middle Ages, from the fifth to the eleventh century. **2** the period between ancient and modern times, from about A.D. 500 to about A.D. 1450; the Middle Ages.

Dark Continent a term applied to Africa.

dark·en (där′kən) *v.* make or become dark or darker. **—dark′en·er,** *n.*

dark·ey (där′kē) *n.* **-eys.** darky.

dark horse *Informal.* **1** an unexpected winner about which little is known. **2** a person who is unexpectedly nominated for a political or other office.

dark·ish (där′kish) *adj.* rather dark. **—dark′ish·ness,** *n.*

dark lantern a lantern whose light can be hidden by a cover or dark glass.

dark·ling (därk′ling) *adv. Poetic.* in the dark. —*adj.* dark; dim; obscure. [< *dark* + OE *-ling*, an adverbial suffix indicating state or manner]

dark·room (därk′rüm′ or -ru̇m′) *n.* a room arranged for developing photographs. It usually has a very dim, colored light.

dark·some (därk′səm) *adj. Poetic.* 1 dark. 2 gloomy.

dark·y (där′kē) *n.* **dark·ies.** *Informal and often derogatory.* Negro. Also, **darkey.**

dar·ling (där′ling) *n.* 1 a person very dear to another; a person much loved. 2 a favorite. —*adj.* 1 very dear; much loved. 2 favorite. [OE *dēorling* < *dēore* dear] —**dar′ling·ly,** *adv.* —**dar′ling·ness,** *n.*

darn[1] (därn) *v.* mend by making rows of stitches back and forth across a hole, torn place, etc. —*n.* 1 the act of darning. 2 a place mended by darning. [< dial. F *darner* mend < *darne* piece < Breton *darn*]

darn[2] (därn) *v. n. Informal.* damn; curse. [< *damn*; influenced by *tarnal* (informal for *eternal*)]
☛ **Darn** is used to express mild annoyance or irritation.

darned (därnd) *adj. Informal.* damned.

dar·nel (där′nəl) *n.* a weed that resembles rye and often grows in grain fields. [ME; cf. F dial. *darnelle*]

darn·er (där′nər) *n.* 1 a person who darns. 2 a darning needle.

darn·ing (där′ning) *n.* 1 the act of mending with stitches. 2 the articles darned or to be darned.

darning needle 1 a long needle with an eye large enough to take the heavy thread used for darning. 2 *Informal.* a dragonfly.

dart (därt) *n.* 1 a slender, pointed weapon to be thrown or shot. 2 a sudden, swift movement. 3 the stinger of an insect. 4 a seam to make a garment fit better. 5 a sharp look, word, etc. 6 **darts,** a game in which small darts are thrown at a circular target.
—*v.* 1 throw or shoot suddenly and quickly. 2 move suddenly and swiftly. 3 send suddenly: *She darted an angry glance at her sister.* 4 sew darts in a garment. [ME < OF < Gmc.] —**Syn.** *n.* 2 dash. -*v.* 1 hurl, launch. 2 dash, bolt.

dart·er (där′tər) *n.* 1 an animal or person that moves suddenly and swiftly. 2 a small fresh-water fish resembling a perch. 3 a snakebird.

Dar·win·i·an (där win′ē ən) *adj.* 1 of or having to do with Charles Darwin (1809-1882), an English scientist. 2 of or having to do with his theory of evolution. —*n.* a person who believes in Darwinism.

Dar·win·ism (där′wən iz′əm) *n.* Charles Darwin's theory of evolution, that in successive generations all plants and animals tend to develop slightly varying forms. The forms that survive are those which through natural selection have adapted themselves to their environment better than the forms that become extinct.

dash (dash) *v.* 1 throw: *We dashed water over him.* 2 splash: *She dashed some paint on the canvas.* 3 rush: *They dashed by in a car.* 4 strike violently against something. 5 smash: *He dashed the bowl to bits on a rock.* 6 ruin: *Our hopes were dashed.* 7 depress; discourage. 8 mix with a small amount of something else. 9 abash; confound: *He was dashed by the sudden questioning of the teacher.* 10 **dash off,** do, make, write, etc. in a hurry.
—*n.* 1 a splash. 2 a rush. 3 a smash. 4 anything that depresses or discourages; a check. 5 a small amount. 6 a short race: *the hundred-yard dash.* 7 a blow; a stroke. 8 a mark (—) used in writing or printing to show a break in thought, parenthetical material, the omission of letters or words, etc. 9 a long sound used in sending messages by telegraph or radiotelegraphy; opposed to *dot.* 10 energy; spirit; liveliness. 11 showy appearance or behavior. 12 a dashboard. [ME *dasche(n)*; cf. Danish *daske* slap] —**Syn.** *n.* 5 touch, tinge, smack, trace.

dash·board (dash′bôrd′) *n.* 1 the panel with instruments and gauges in front of the driver in an automobile, airplane, etc. 2 a protection on the front of a wagon, boat, etc. that prevents mud or water from being splashed into it.

dash·er (dash′ər) *n.* 1 one that dashes. 2 a device for stirring the cream in a churn or ice-cream freezer.

dash·ing (dash′ing) *adj.* 1 full of energy and spirit; lively. 2 having or showing a sense of style; showy. —**dash′ing·ly,** *adv.*

das·tard (das′tərd) *n.* a mean coward; sneak. —*adj.* mean and cowardly; sneaking. [ME, originally, a dullard, apparently < *dazed,* pp. of *daze*] —**das′tard·ly,** *adj.* —**das′tard·li·ness,** *n.*

dat. dative.

da·ta (dā′tə or dat′ə) *n.* pl. of **datum.** the things known or granted; information from which conclusions can be drawn; facts.
☛ **Data** is the plural of the seldom-used singular *datum.* Since its meaning is often collective, referring to a group of facts as a unit, *data* is often used with a singular verb in informal English: *The data you have collected is not enough to convince me.* Formal English continues to regard *data* as a plural rather than as a collective noun: *We will analyse the data that have been obtained.*

data bank a body of information stored and available for processing in a computer.

date[1] (dāt) *n. v.* **dat·ed, dat·ing.** —*n.* 1 the time when something happens. 2 a statement of time: *There is a date stamped on every piece of Canadian money.* 3 a period of time. 4 *Informal.* an appointment for a certain time. 5 *Informal.* a person of the opposite sex with whom an appointment is made. 6 **out of date,** old-fashioned; not in present use. 7 **to date,** till now; yet. 8 **up to date, a** to the present time. **b** modern; according to the latest style.
—*v.* 1 mark with a date; put a date on. 2 find out the date of; give a date to: *The scientist was unable to date the fossil.* 3 belong to a certain period of time; have its origin: *That house dates from the 18th century.* 4 *Informal.* have or make a social appointment with (a person of the opposite sex). 5 be or become out of date. [ME < MF < Med.L *data,* pp. fem. of L *dare* give]
☛ **dates.** The usual Canadian method of writing dates is: *July 1, 1867*; *November 23, 1966.* However, in military use, and increasingly among scientists, the day of the month is placed first: *23 Nov. 1966.* Names of months having more than four letters are often abbreviated. In informal writing, figures are often used, Canadian and British practice being to indicate the day, month, and year in that order: 23/11/66. American practice is to put the month before the day: 11/23/66. Good usage now usually omits the *-st, -nd, -th* from the days of the month: *June 1* rather than *June 1st.* In formal style the day of the month is often written out when the year is not given (*September fifteen* or *September fifteenth*), but the year is never written out except in formal social announcements, invitations, etc.

date[2] (dāt) *n.* 1 the oblong, fleshy, sweet fruit of a kind of palm tree. 2 a date palm. [ME < OF < L *dactylus* < Gk. *daktylos* date, finger. Doublet of DACTYL.]

dat·ed (dāt′id) *adj.* 1 marked with a date; showing a date. 2 out-of-date. —**dat′ed·ly,** *adv.* —**dat′ed·ness,** *n.*

date·less (dāt′lis) *adj.* 1 without a date; not dated. 2 endless; unlimited. 3 so old that it cannot be given a date. 4 old but still admirable, in good style, etc.

date line 1 an imaginary line agreed upon as the place where each calendar day first begins. It runs north and south through the Pacific, mostly along the 180th meridian. When it is Sunday just east of the date line, it is Monday just west of it. 2 a line in a letter, newspaper, etc. giving the date and place of writing.

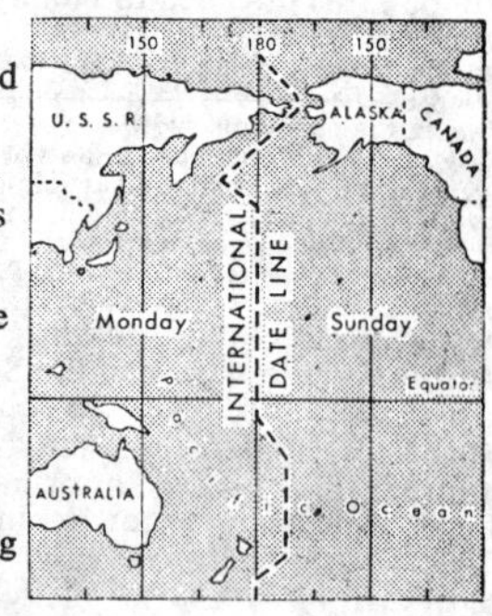

date palm a palm tree on which dates grow.

da·tive (dā′tiv) *adj.* in grammar, of languages that are inflected for case, denoting or having to do with the special form or function of nouns, pronouns, and adjectives proper to the indirect object. In English, the dative function is expressed by word order or by a prepositional phrase: "Give *him* the book." "Give the book *to him.*" —*n.* 1 the dative case. 2 a word in this case. *Abbrev.*: dat. [< L *dativus* of giving < *datus,* pp. of *dare* give]
☛ **dative case.** Most English grammars now describe the dative and the accusative cases under the general term *objective case.*

da·tum (dā′təm or dat′əm) *n.* **da·ta.** a fact from which conclusions can be drawn. [< L *datum* (thing) given, pp. neut. of *dare.* Doublet of DIE[2].] ☛ See **data** for usage note.

daub (dob or dôb) *v.* 1 coat or cover with plaster, clay, mud, etc. 2 apply (greasy or sticky stuff). 3 make dirty; soil; stain. 4 paint unskilfully.

—*n.* **1** something used to daub. **2** a mark made by a daub; smear. **3** a crudely painted picture. [ME < OF *dauber* < L *dealbare* < *de-* + *albus* white] —**daub′er,** *n.*

daugh·ter (do′tər or dô′tər) *n.* **1** a female child (immediate descendant of her parents). **2** a female descendant. **3** a girl or woman thought of as related to something in the same way that a child is related to its parents: *a daughter of France.* **4** anything thought of as a daughter in relation to its origin: *Skill is the daughter of hard work.* [OE *dohtor*]

daughter element in physics, an element produced by the decay of a radio-active element.

daugh·ter-in-law (do′tər in lo′ or dô′tər in lô′) *n.* **daugh·ters-in-law.** the wife of one's son.

daugh·ter·ly (do′tər lē or dô′tər lē) *adj.* **1** of a daughter. **2** like that of a daughter. **3** proper for a daughter.

daunt (dont or dônt) *v.* **1** frighten. **2** discourage. [ME < OF *danter* < L *domitare* < *domare* tame] —**Syn. 1** intimidate. **2** dismay, dishearten.

daunt·less (dont′lis or dônt′lis) *adj.* not to be frightened or discouraged; brave. —**daunt′less·ly,** *adv.* —**daunt′less·ness,** *n.*

dau·phin (do′fən or dô′fən; *French,* dō faN′) *n.* the title given to the oldest son of the king of France, from 1349 to 1830. [< F *dauphin,* originally a family name]

dau·phine (do′fēn or dô′fēn; *French,* dō fēn′) *n.* the wife of a dauphin. [< F. See DAUPHIN.]

dau·phin·ess (do′fən is or dô′fən is) *n.* dauphine.

dav·en·port (dav′ən pôrt′) *n.* **1** a long couch having a back and arms; sofa; chesterfield. Some davenports can be opened up to make a bed. **2** a writing desk with drawers and a hinged shelf to write on. [origin uncertain]

Da·vid (dā′vid) *n.* **1** in the Bible, the second king of Israel, who organized the Jewish tribes into a national state. **2 David and Jonathan,** any pair of devoted friends.

dav·it (dav′it or dā′vit) *n.* **1** one of a pair of curved arms at the side of a ship, used to hold or lower a small boat. **2** a crane for raising or lowering the anchor of a ship. [ME < AF *daviot*]

Davits (def. 1)

Da·vy Jones (dā′ vē jōnz′) the spirit of the sea; the sailor's devil.

Davy Jones's locker the grave of those who die at sea; the bottom of the ocean.

daw (do or dô) *n.* jackdaw. [ME *dawe*]

daw·dle (do′dəl or dô′dəl) *v.* **-dled, -dling,** *n.* —*v.* waste time; idle; loiter: *Don't dawdle over your work.* —*n.* **1** a person who dawdles. **2** the act of dawdling. [origin uncertain] —**daw′dler,** *n.*

dawn (don or dôn) *n.* **1** the break of day; the first light in the east. **2** the beginning: *before the dawn of history.* —*v.* **1** grow bright or clear: *Day dawns in the east.* **2** grow clear to the eye or mind: *It dawned on me that she was expecting a gift.* **3** begin; appear: *A new era is dawning.* [ME *dawnen* < *dawning* daybreak, probably < ON; replacing ME *dawen* < OE *dagian* become day]

day (dā) *n.* **1** the time between sunrise and sunset. **2** the light of day; daylight. **3** the 24 hours of day and night. **4** a certain day on which something happened, set aside for a particular purpose or for celebration: *Christmas Day.* **5** the hours for work: *an eight-hour day.* **6** a certain period of time: *the present day, in days of old.* **7** a period of life, activity, power, or influence: *He has had his day.* **8** a conflict; contest: *The day went well for our team. The day is ours.* **9 call it a day,** *Informal.* stop work. **10 day by day,** each day. **11 day in, day out,** every day. **12 from day to day,** each day. **13 pass the time of day,** take part in small talk. **14 the time of day, a** the time. **b** a greeting; salutation. **15 win the day,** be victorious. [OE *dæg*]

day bed or **day·bed** (dā′bed′) *n.* a bed, usually narrow, having a low headboard and a footboard of equal height. A day bed can be used as a couch by day.

day book 1 in bookkeeping, a book in which a record is kept of each day's business. **2** a diary.

day·break (dā′brāk′) *n.* dawn; the time when it first begins to get light in the morning.

day camp a summer camp for children, held during the daytime only.

hat, āge, cãre, fär; let, ēqual, tėrm; it, īce
hot, ōpen, ôrder; oil, out; cup, pu̇t, rüle, ūse
əbove, takən, pencəl, lemən, circəs
ch, child; ng, long; sh, ship
th, thin; ᴛʜ, then; zh, measure

day·dream (dā′drēm′) *n. v.* **-dreamed** or **-dreamt, -dream·ing.** —*n.* **1** a dreamy thought about pleasant things. **2** a pleasant plan or fancy, unlikely to come true. —*v.* think dreamily about pleasant things. —**day′dream′er,** *n.*

day laborer or **labourer** an unskilled or manual worker who is paid by the day.

day letter a telegram sent during the day for delivery later the same day. Service is slower for a day letter than for a regular telegram but cheaper.

day·light (dā′līt′) *n.* **1** the light of day. **2** the daytime. **3** dawn; daybreak. **4** publicity; openness. **5** open space; a gap. **6 see daylight,** *Informal.* **a** understand. **b** approach the end of a hard or tiresome job.

daylight-saving time time that is one hour in advance of standard time and gives more daylight after working hours. Clocks are set ahead one hour in the spring and back one hour in the fall.

day lily 1 any of a group of plants of the lily family having large yellow, orange, or red flowers that last about a day. **2** the plantain lily.

day·lin·er (dā′lī′nər) *n.* a railway train which runs express between two cities, or between suburbs and a city during the day.

day·long (dā′long′) *adj. adv.* through the whole day.

day nursery a nursery for the care of small children during the day.

Day of Atonement Yom Kippur.

Day of Judgment the day of God's final judgment of mankind at the end of the world.

day school 1 a school held in the daytime. **2** a private school for students who live at home.

days of grace the extra days (usually three) allowed for payment after a bill or note falls due.

day·spring (dā′spring′) *n. Poetic.* the dawn; daybreak.

day·star (dā′stär′) *n.* **1** the morning star. **2** *Poetic.* the sun.

day·time (dā′tīm′) *n.* the time when it is day.

daze (dāz) *v.* **dazed, daz·ing,** *n.* —*v.* **1** confuse; bewilder; cause to feel stupid; stun: *He was so dazed by the blow on his head that he could not find his way home.* **2** dazzle. —*n.* a dazed condition; a state of bewilderment. [ME *dase(n)* < ON; cf. Icelandic *dasask* become weary]

daz·ed·ly (dā′zid lē) *adv.* in a dazed, confused, or stupid manner.

daz·zle (daz′əl) *v.* **-zled, -zling,** *n.* —*v.* **1** confuse, dim, or overpower (the eyes) with too bright light or with quick-moving lights. **2** overcome (the sight or the mind) by brightness, display, etc.: *The girl was dazzled by the rich décor of her new home.* —*n.* the act or fact of dazzling; a bewildering brightness. [< *daze*] —**daz′zler,** *n.* —**daz′zling·ly,** *adv.*

D.B.E. Dame (Commander of the Order) of the British Empire.

dbl. double.

DBS Dominion Bureau of Statistics, the former name of Statistics Canada.

DC, D.C., or **d.c.** direct current.

D.C. 1 District of Columbia. **2** Doctor of Chiropractic. **3** in music, return to beginning. (for Ital. *da capo*)

D.C.L. 1 Doctor of Canon Law. **2** Doctor of Civil Law.

D.C.M. Distinguished Conduct Medal.

D.C.V.O. Distinguished Commander of the Victorian Order.

D.D. Doctor of Divinity.

D-day (dē′dā′) *n.* **1** the day when the Allies landed in France in World War II; June 6, 1944. **2** the day on which a previously planned military attack is to be made, or on which an operation is to be started.

D.D.S. Doctor of Dental Surgery.

DDT *dichloro-diphenyl-trichloroethane*, an odorless, powerful insecticide.

DE Destroyer Escort.

de- *prefix.* **1** do the opposite of, as in *decamp, deforest, decentralize, demobilize.* **2** down, as in *depress, descend.* **3** away; off, as in *deport, detract.* **4** cause to leave something, as in *derail.* **5** entirely; completely (intensive), as in *despoil.* **6** remove, as in *defrost.* [< L *de-* < *de* from, away]

dea·con (dē′kən) *n.* **1** an officer of a church who helps the minister in church duties other than preaching. **2** a member of the clergy immediately below a priest in rank. [OE *diacon* < L *diaconus* < Gk. *diakonos* servant]

dea·con·ess (dē′kən is) *n.* a woman who is an official assistant in church work, especially in caring for the sick and the poor.

dea·con·ry (dē′kən rē) *n.* **-ries. 1** the position of deacon. **2** deacons.

dead (ded) *adj.* **1** no longer living; that has died. **2** without life; inanimate. **3** like death. **4** not active or productive; dull; quiet. **5** without force, power, spirit, or feeling. **6** of wire, telephone lines, etc., not alive; shut off. **7** no longer in use: *dead languages.* **8** out of play; not in the game: *a dead ball.* **9** *Informal.* very tired; worn-out. **10** sure; certain: *a dead shot.* **11** complete; absolute: *a dead loss.* **12** carrying no electric current; not connected to a source of power: *a dead circuit. The telephone line is dead.* **13** not radio-active: *dead rocks.* **14** in law, deprived of civil rights. **15** in printing, that has been used or is no longer needed: *dead type.*
—*adv.* **1** completely; absolutely. **2** directly, straight.
—*n.* **1** a dead person or persons. **2** the time of greatest darkness, quiet, cold, etc.: *the dead of night.* [OE *dēad*]
—**dead′ness,** *n.*
Syn. *adj.* **1, 2 Dead, deceased, lifeless** = without life. **Dead** emphasizes the idea of dying, and applies particularly to someone or something that was living or alive, but no longer is: *The flowers in my garden are dead.* **Deceased,** a technical word, applies only to a dead person: *The deceased man left no will.* **Lifeless** emphasizes the idea of being without life, and is used both of what now is or seems to be without life of any kind and of things that never had life: *He lifted the lifeless body.*

dead air 1 air that is trapped between two walls for insulation. **2** in radio and television, a period of no broadcasting.

dead beat *Slang.* **1** a person who avoids paying for what he gets. **2** a lazy person; loafer.

dead-beat (ded′bēt′) *adj. Informal.* worn out; exhausted.

dead centre or **center** in an engine, the position of the crank and connecting rod at which the connecting rod has no power to turn the crank. Dead centre occurs at each end of a stroke, when the crank and the connecting rod are in the same straight line.

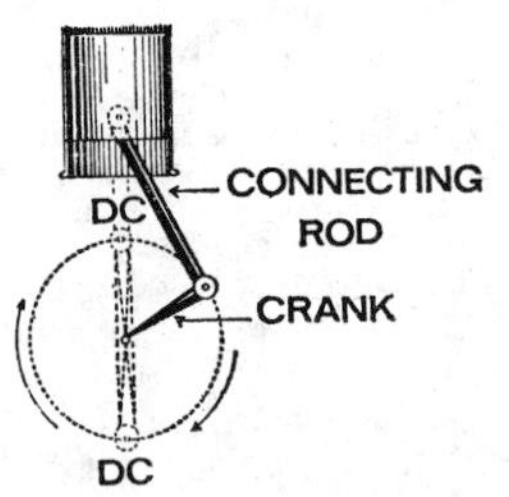

DC, dead centre

dead duck *Informal.* **1** a person or thing that is completely exhausted and without further strength or usefulness. **2** one whose fate is sealed: *The boss said, "Make another mistake like that, and you're a dead duck."*

dead·en (ded′ən) *v.* **1** make dull or weak; lessen the intenseness or force of. **2** reduce the sound of.
—**dead′en·er,** *n.*

dead end 1 a street, passage, etc. closed at one end. **2** a point beyond which progress, advancement, etc. is impossible: *The discussion reached a dead end.*

dead-end (ded′end′) *adj.* **1** closed at one end. **2** having no opportunity for progress, advancement, etc.; fruitless: *a dead-end job.*

dead·eye (ded′ī′) *n.* a round, flat, wooden block used to fasten the shrouds of a ship. See the picture below.

dead·fall (ded′fol′ or -fôl′) *n.* **1** a trap for animals made so that a heavy weight falls upon and holds or kills the animal. **2** a mass of fallen trees and underbrush. **3** a dead tree that has been blown to the ground.

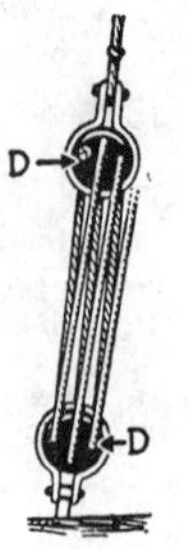

D, a deadeye

dead·head (ded′hed′) *n.* **1** *Informal.* **a** a person who rides on a bus, sees a game, etc. without paying. **b** a train, railway car, bus, etc. travelling without passengers or freight. **2** a water-soaked log, partly or entirely submerged in a river, lake, etc.

dead heat a race that ends in a tie.

dead letter 1 an unclaimed letter; a letter that cannot be delivered because of a wrong address, etc. **2** a law, rule, etc. that is not enforced.

dead·line (ded′līn′) *n.* **1** a time limit; the latest possible time to do something. **2** a line or boundary that must not be crossed.

dead·lock (ded′lok′) *n.* a complete standstill: *Employers and strikers have reached a deadlock.*
—*v.* bring or come to a complete standstill.

dead·ly (ded′lē) *adj.* **-li·er, -li·est,** *adv.* —*adj.* **1** causing death; liable to cause death; fatal: *a deadly wound.* **2** like death: *deadly paleness.* **3** filled with hatred that lasts till death: *The two chiefs were deadly enemies.* **4** causing death of the spirit: *deadly sin.* **5** *Informal.* extreme; intense. **6** dull: *The party was a deadly affair.*
—*adv.* **1** *Informal.* extremely. **2** like death. **3** as if dead.
—**dead′li·ness,** *n.* —**Syn.** *adj.* **1** mortal, lethal. See **fatal.**

deadly sins pride, covetousness, lust, anger, gluttony, envy, and sloth.

dead march funeral march.

dead·pan (ded′pan′) *n. adj. adv. v.* **-panned, -pan·ning.** *Slang.* —*n.* an expressionless face, person, or manner.
—*adj.* without expression or feeling: *a deadpan face, deadpan clowns.* —*adv*. in a deadpan manner. —*v.* act, tell, or behave in a deadpan manner: *deadpan a joke. The clown deadpanned all through the scene.*

dead point dead centre.

dead reckoning the calculation of the location of a ship or aircraft without observations of the sun, stars, etc. by using a compass and studying the record of the voyage.

Dead Sea Scrolls the name given to a number of parchment, leather, and copper scrolls found in 1947 and later in caves near the Dead Sea. They date approximately from between 100 B.C. and A.D. 100, and contain Hebrew and Aramaic texts of Biblical writings, explanation, etc.

dead weight 1 the heavy weight of anything inert. **2** a very great or oppressive burden.

dead·wood (ded′wu̇d′) *n.* **1** dead branches or trees. **2** useless people or things. **3** wording that adds nothing to the meaning of a sentence.

deaf (def) *adj.* **1** not able to hear. **2** not able to hear well. **3** not willing to hear; heedless: *A miser is deaf to all requests for money.* **4 deaf and dumb,** unable to hear and speak. [OE *dēaf*] —**deaf′ly,** *adv.* —**deaf′ness,** *n.*

deaf·en (def′ən) *v.* **1** make deaf. **2** stun with noise. **3** drown out by a louder sound. **4** make soundproof.
—**deaf′en·ing·ly,** *adv.*

deaf-mute (def′mūt′) *n.* a person who is deaf and dumb.

deal[1] (dēl) *v.* **dealt, deal·ing,** *n.* —*v.* **1** have to do (*with*): *Arithmetic deals with numbers.* **2** occupy oneself; take action: *The courts deal with those who break the laws.* **3** act; behave: *Deal fairly with everyone.* **4** do business; buy and sell: *A butcher deals in meat.* **5** give: *One fighter dealt the other a blow.* **6** give a share of to each; distribute. **7** distribute (playing cards). **8 deal out,** to give out or distribute.
—*n.* **1** *Informal.* a business arrangement; bargain. **2** *Informal.* a distribution; arrangement; plan: *a new deal.* **3** in cardplaying: **a** the distribution of cards. **b** a player's turn to deal. **c** the time during which one deal of cards is being played. **d** the cards held by a player; hand. **4** a quantity; amount: *I took a deal of trouble.* **5** a dealing; distributing. **6 a good deal** or **a great deal, a** a large amount: *He spends a great deal of money.* **b** to a great extent or degree; much: *He smokes a good deal.* **7 a square deal,** an honest business transaction; a fair arrangement. [OE *dælan*]

deal[2] (dēl) *n.* **1** a board of pine or fir wood, usually more than 7 inches wide and 6 feet long. **2** pine or fir wood. *—adj.* made of deal. [< MLG or MDu. *dele* plank]

deal·er (dēl′ər) *n.* **1** a man who trades; any person engaged in buying and selling. **2** a person who distributes the cards to the players.

deal·er·ship (dē′lər ship′) *n.* the business, franchise, or territory of a dealer.

deal·ing (dēl′ing) *n.* **1** a way of doing business: *The storekeeper is respected for his honest dealing.* **2** a way of acting; behavior toward others. **3** the distribution of playing cards, etc. **4 dealings,** *pl.* **a** business relations. **b** friendly relations.

dealt (delt) *v.* pt. and pp. of **deal**[1].

dean (dēn) *n.* **1** the head of a school or faculty in a college or university. **2** a member of the faculty of a college or university who has charge of the behavior or studies of the students. **3** a high official of a church, often in charge of a cathedral. **4** the member who has belonged to a group longest. [ME < OF *deien* < LL *decanus* master of ten < *decem* ten]

dean·er·y (dēn′ər ē) *n.* **-er·ies. 1** the position or authority of a dean. **2** the residence of a dean.

dean·ship (dēn′ship) *n.* the position, office, or rank of a dean.

dear (dēr) *adj.* **1** much loved; precious. **2** much valued; highly-esteemed. *Dear* is used as a form of polite address at the beginning of letters: *Dear Sir, Dear Isabel.* **3** high-priced; costly.
—n. a dear one.
—adv. **1** with affection; fondly: *He held his wife dear.* **2** at a high price; at a great cost.
—interj. an exclamation of surprise, trouble, etc. [OE *dēore*] **—dear′ly,** *adv.* **—dear′ness,** *n.* **—Syn.** *adj.* **1** beloved. **3** See **expensive.**

dear·ie or **dear·y** (dēr′ē) *n.* **dear·ies.** *Informal.* a dear one; darling.

dearth (dėrth) *n.* **1** a scarcity; lack; too small a supply. **2** a scarcity of food; famine. [ME *derthe* < *dere* hard, grievous < OE *dēor*]

death (deth) *n.* **1** the act or fact of dying; the end of life in human beings, animals, or plants. **2** Often, **Death.** the power that destroys life, often represented as a skeleton dressed in black and carrying a scythe. **3** any ending that is like dying: *the death of an empire.* **4** the state or condition of being dead. **5** any condition like being dead. **6** a cause of death. bloodshed; murder. **8 at death's door,** dying; about to die; almost dead. **9 do to death, a** kill; murder. **b** do, act, or say the same thing so often that it becomes boring. **10 put to death, a** kill. **b** killed. **11 to the death,** to the last resource or extremity: *to fight tyranny to the death.* [OE *dēath*] **—death′like′,** *adj.*

death·bed (deth′bed′) *n.* **1** a bed on which a person dies. **2** the last hours of life. *—adj.* during the last hours of life: *The murderer made a deathbed confession.*

death·blow (deth′blō′) *n.* **1** a blow that kills. **2** anything that puts an end (to something else).

death cup a poisonous mushroom that has a cuplike enlargement at the base of the stem.

death duty succession duty.

death·ful (deth′fəl) *adj.* **1** deadly. **2** like death. **3** like that of death. **4** mortal.

death·less (deth′lis) *adj.* never dying; living forever; immortal; eternal. **—death′less·ness,** *n.*

death·ly (deth′lē) *adj.* **1** like that of death: *Her face was a deathly white.* **2** causing death; deadly. **3** *Poetic.* of death. *—adv.* **1** as if dead. **2** extremely: *deathly ill.*

death mask a clay, wax, or plaster likeness of a person's face made from a cast taken after his death.

death penalty punishment by death.

death rate the proportion of the number of deaths per year to the total population or to some other stated number.

death sand in military use, radio-active dust that may be scattered over vast areas. It would kill all, or most, of the life it touched.

death's-head (deths′hed′) *n.* a human skull, used as a symbol of death.

death·trap (deth′trap′) *n.* **1** an unsafe building or structure where the risk of fire or other hazard is great. **2** a very dangerous situation.

hat, āge, cãre, fär; let, ēqual, tėrm; it, īce
hot, ōpen, ôrder; oil, out; cup, pu̇t, rüle, ūse
əbove, takən, pencəl, lemən, circəs
ch, child; ng, long; sh, ship
th, thin; ᴛʜ, then; zh, measure

death warrant an official order for a person's death.

death·watch (deth′woch′) *n.* **1** a watch kept beside a dying or dead person. **2** a guard for a person about to be put to death. **3** a small destructive beetle that lives in wood and makes a ticking sound that is supposed to be an omen of death.

de·ba·cle (dā bä′kəl or di bak′əl) *n.* **1** a disaster; overthrow; downfall. **2** the breaking up of ice in a river. **3** a violent rush of waters carrying debris. [< F *débâcle* < *débâcler* free < *dé-* un- + *bâcler* to bar]

de·bar (di bär′) *v.* **-barred, -bar·ring.** bar out; shut out; prevent; prohibit. [< F *débarrer* < LL *debarrare* < L *de-* from + *barrare* bar] **—de·bar′ment,** *n.*

de·bark[1] (di bärk′) *v.* go or put ashore from a ship or aircraft; disembark. [< *débarquer* < *dé-* from + *barque* bark[3] < LL *barca*]

de·bark[2] (dē bärk′) *v.* remove bark from (a tree). [< *de-* + *bark*[1]] **—de·bark′er,** *n.*

de·bar·ka·tion (dē′bär kā′shən) *n.* a debarking or being debarked; a landing from a ship or aircraft.

de·base (di bās′) *v.* **-based, -bas·ing.** make low or lower; lessen the value of: *He debased his character by evil actions. The country's paper money was debased when the government no longer had sufficient gold or silver to back it.* [< *de-* down + (*a*)*base*] **—de·base′ment,** *n.* **—de·bas′er,** *n.*

de·bat·a·ble (di bāt′ə bəl) *adj.* **1** capable of being debated; open to debate. To be debatable, a topic must have at least two sides. **2** not decided; in dispute.

de·bate (di bāt′) *v.* **-bat·ed, -bat·ing,** *n.* *—v.* **1** discuss reasons for and against (something). **2** argue about (a question, topic, etc.) in a public meeting. **3** think over in one's mind; consider. *—n.* **1** a discussion of reasons for and against. **2** a public argument for and against a question in a meeting. A formal debate is a contest between two sides to see which one has more skill in speaking and reasoning. **3** in Parliament, the discussion of a motion that is to be voted on. [ME < OF *debatre* < VL *debattere* < L *de-* (intensive) + *battuere* beat] **—de·bat′er,** *n.* **—Syn.** *v.* **1** deliberate. See **discuss.** *-n.* **1** argument.

de·bauch (di boch′ or di bôch′) *v.* **1** lead away from duty, virtue, or morality; corrupt morally; seduce: *Bad companions had debauched the boy.* **2** corrupt; pervert; deprave: *Cheap novels had debauched his taste.* **3** indulge excessively in sensual pleasures, eating, drinking, etc.
—n. **1** excessive indulgence in sensual pleasures; excess in eating or drinking. **2** a bout or period of debauchery. [< F *débaucher* entice from duty] **—de·bauch′er,** *n.* **—de·bauch′ment,** *n.*

deb·au·chee (deb′o chē′ or deb′ô chē′, deb′o shē′ or deb′ô shē′) *n.* an intemperate, dissipated, or depraved person.

de·bauch·er·y (di boch′ər ē or di bôch′ər ē) *n.* **-er·ies. 1** excessive indulgence in sensual pleasures. **2** a seduction from duty, virtue, or morality.

de·ben·ture (di ben′chər) *n.* a written acknowledgment of a debt. A common kind of debenture is a bond issued by a company acknowledging indebtedness for a sum on which interest is due until the principal is paid. [ME < L *debentur* there are owing, 3rd person pl. present passive of *debere*]

de·bil·i·tate (di bil′ə tāt′) *v.* **-tat·ed, -tat·ing.** weaken: *A hot, wet climate is often debilitating to people not accustomed to it.* [< *debilitare* < *debilis* weak] **—de·bil′i·ta′tion,** *n.* **—Syn.** See **weaken.**

de·bil·i·ty (di bil′ə tē) *n.* **-ties.** a weakness. [ME < OF *debilite* < L *debilitas* < *debilis* weak]

deb·it (deb′it) *n.* **1** in accounting: **a** the entry of something owed in an account. **b** the left-hand side of an account where such entries are made. **c** the amount entered or shown on this side. **2** the money owed by a person on an account. —*v.* **1** enter on the debit side of an account. **2** charge with or as a debt: *Debit his account $500.* **3** enter as a debit in a bank account, etc. [< L *debitum* (thing) owed, pp. neut. of *debere.* Doublet of DEBT.]

deb·o·nair or **deb·o·naire** (deb′ə nãr′) *adj.* **1** gay; cheerful. **2** pleasant; courteous. [ME < OF *debonaire* < *de bon aire* of good disposition] —**deb′o·nair′ly,** *adv.*

de·bouch (di büsh′) *v.* **1** come out from a narrow or confined place into open country: *The soldiers debouched from the gorges into the plain.* **2** come out; emerge; issue: *A horde of children debouched from the bus.* [< F *déboucher* < *dé-* from + *bouche* mouth < L *bucca*]

de·bouch·ment (di büsh′mənt) *n.* **1** an act of debouching. **2** a mouth; outlet: *the debouchment of a river.*

de·bris or **dé·bris** (də brē′, dā′brē, or deb′rē; *French,* dā brē′) *n.* **1** scattered fragments; ruins; rubbish: *The street was covered with debris from the explosion.* **2** in geology, a mass of fragments of rock, etc.: *the debris left by a glacier.* [< F *débris* < OF *debrisier* < *de-* away + *brisier* break]

debt (det) *n.* **1** something owed to another. **2** a liability or obligation to pay or render something: *be in debt to the grocer, get out of debt.* **3** the state or condition of being under such an obligation. **4** a sin. **5** *Cdn.* **a** credit given at a trading post to hunters and trappers in the form of supplies to be paid for out of the next season's catch. **b** the amount of credit given. **c** in the North, credit taken at any store, especially by Indians. [ME < OF *dette* < L *debitum* (thing) owed, pp. neut. of *debere.* Doublet of DEBIT.] —**Syn. 2** indebtedness.

debt of honor or **honour** a betting or gambling debt.

debt·or (det′ər) *n.* **1** a person who owes something to someone else. **2** *Cdn.* a person owing or taking debt at a trading post, etc.

de·bunk (di bungk′) *v. Informal.* **1** expose the bogus or sentimental claims of (a person, cult, institution, etc.). **2** prove false or incorrect. —**de·bunk′er,** *n.*

de·but or **dé·but** (dā′bū or dā bū′) *n.* **1** a first public appearance: *an actor's debut on the stage; the debut of a new magazine.* **2** a first formal appearance in society. [< F *début* < *débuter* make the first stroke < *de-* from + *but* mark (in game or sport)]

deb·u·tante or **dé·bu·tante** (deb′yů tänt′, deb′yů tant′, or deb′yů tänt′) *n.* **1** a girl during her first season in society. **2** a woman making a debut. [< F *débutante,* ppr. fem. of *débuter.* See DEBUT.]

Dec. December.

dec. 1 deceased. **2** decimetre. **3** declension. **4** decrease.

deca- ten: *decagram = ten grams.* [< Gk. combining form *deka-* < *deka* ten]

dec·ade (dek′ād) *n.* **1** a period of ten years. **2** a group of ten. [< F < LL *decas, decadis* < Gk. *dekas* group of ten < *deka* ten]

de·ca·dence (dek′ə dəns) *n.* a falling off; decline; decay: *the decadence of manners.* [< F < Med.L *decadentia* < L *de-* down + *cadere* fall]

de·ca·dent (dek′ə dənt) *adj.* falling off; declining; growing worse. —*n.* a decadent person. —**de′ca·dent·ly,** *adv.*

dec·a·gon (dek′ə gon′) *n.* a plane figure having 10 angles and 10 sides. [< Med.L *decagonum* < Gk. *dekagonon* < *deka* ten + *gōnia* corner, angle]

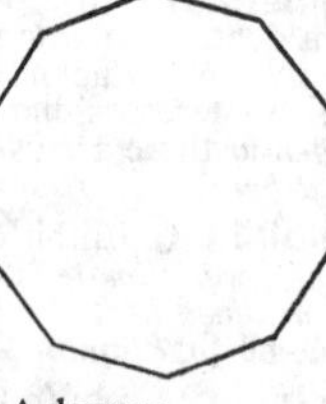
A decagon

dec·a·gram or **dec·a·gramme** (dek′ə gram′) *n.* 10 grams equal to 0.3527 ounce. [< F *décagramme*]

dec·a·he·dron (dek′ə hē′drən) *n.* **-drons, -dra** (-drə). a solid figure having ten flat, sharp-angled surfaces. [< NL < Gk. *deka* ten + Gk. *hedra* base]

de·cal (dē′kal, dek′əl or di kal′) *n.* decalcomania.

de·cal·co·ma·ni·a (di kal′kə mā′nē ə) *n.* **1** a design or picture treated so that it will stick to glass, wood, etc. **2** a process of decorating glass, wood, etc. by applying these designs or pictures. [< F *décalcomanie* < *décalquer* transfer a tracing + *manie* mania]

dec·a·li·tre or **dec·a·li·ter** (dek′ə lē′tər) *n.* 10 litres equal to approximately 2.2 imperial gallons. Also, **dekalitre** or **dekaliter.** [< F *décalitre*]

Dec·a·logue (dek′ə log′) *n.* **1** in the Bible, the Ten Commandments. Exod. 20:2-17. Also, **Decalog. 2 decalogue,** any set of ten commandments. Also, **decalog.** [< F *décalogue* < LL < Gk. *dekalogos* < *deka* ten + *logos* word]

dec·a·me·tre or **dec·a·me·ter** (dek′ə mē′tər) *n.* 10 metres, equal to 32.8 feet. Also, **dekametre** or **dekameter.** [< F *décamètre*]

de·camp (di kamp′) *v.* **1.** depart quickly, secretly, or without ceremony. **2** leave a camp. [< F *décamper* < *dé-* departing from + *camp* camp] —**de·camp′ment** *n.*

dec·a·nal (dek′ə nəl or di kā′nəl) *adj.* of a dean or deanery. [< LL *decanus* dean]

de·cant (di kant′) *v.* **1** pour off (liquor or a solution) gently without disturbing the sediment. **2** pour from one container to another. [< Med.L *decanthare* < *de-* from + *canthus* lip (of container) < Gk. *kanthos* corner of the eye] —**de′can·ta′tion,** *n.*

de·cant·er (di kan′tər) *n.* a glass bottle with a stopper, used for serving wine or liquor.

A decanter

de·cap·i·tate (di kap′ə tāt′) *v.* **-tat·ed, -tat·ing.** cut off the head of; behead. [< LL *decapitare* < L *de-* away + *caput, capitis* head] —**de·cap′i·ta′tor,** *n.* —**de·cap′i·ta′tion,** *n.*

dec·a·pod (dek′ə pod′) *n.* **1** a crustacean having ten legs or arms, such as lobsters and crabs. **2** a mollusc having ten arms or tentacles, such as a squid or cuttlefish. —*adj.* having ten legs or arms. [< *deca-* ten + Gk. *pous, podos* foot]

de·car·bon·ate (dē kär′bə nāt′) *v.* **-at·ed, -at·ing.** remove carbon dioxide or carbonic acid from. —**de·car′bon·a′tor,** *n.*

de·car·bon·ize (dē kär′bə nīz′) *v.* **-ized, -iz·ing.** remove carbon from: *Iron is decarbonized in making steel.* —**de·car′bon·iz′er,** *n.*

dec·are (dek′ãr or de kãr′) *n.* a metric unit of square measure equal to 10 ares, 1,000 square metres, or about 1,196 square yards. [< F *décare* < Gk. *deka* ten + F *are* are[2]]

dec·a·syl·lab·ic (dek′ə sə lab′ik) *adj.* having ten syllables. —*n.* a decasyllable.

dec·a·syl·la·ble (dek′ə sil′ə bəl) *n.* a line of verse having ten syllables.

de·cath·lon (di kath′lon) *n.* an athletic contest having ten parts, such as racing, jumping, throwing the javelin, etc. [< *deca-* + Gk. *athlon* contest]

de·cay (di kā′) *v.* **1** become rotten: *The fruit and vegetables began to decay.* **2** cause to rot. **3** grow less in power, strength, wealth, beauty, etc.
—*n.* **1** a rotting condition. **2** a loss of power, strength, wealth, beauty, etc. **3** in physics, a loss in quantity of a radio-active substance through disintegration of its component nuclei. [ME < OF *decair* < *de-* down + *cair* < L *cadere* fall]

Syn. *v.* **1 Decay, rot, decompose** = change from a good or healthy condition to a bad. **Decay** emphasizes the idea of changing little by little through natural processes: *Some diseases cause the bones to decay.* **Rot,** more emphatic, emphasizes the idea of spoiling, and applies especially to plant and animal matter: *The fruit rotted on the vines.* **Decompose** emphasizes the idea of breaking down into original parts, by natural or chemical processes: *Bodies decompose after death.* **2** deteriorate, decline.

de·cease (di sēs′) *n. v.* **-ceased, -ceas·ing.** —*n.* death: *His decease was unexpected.* —*v.* die. [ME < OF *deces* < L *decessus* < *decedere* < *de-* away + *cedere* go]

de·ceased (di sēst′) *adj.* dead. —*n.* **the deceased, 1** a (particular) dead person. **2** dead people. —**Syn.** *adj.* **See dead.**

de·ce·dent (di sē′dənt) *n.* in law, a dead person. [< L *decedens, -entis,* ppr. of *decedere.* See DECEASE.]

de·ceit (di sēt′) *n.* **1** the act of making a person believe as true something that is false; a deceiving, lying, or cheating. **2** a dishonest trick; a lie spoken or acted. **3** a deceitful quality; deceitfulness. [ME < OF *deceite* < *deceveir.* See DECEIVE.]
Syn. 1 Deceit, deception, guile = false or misleading representation. **Deceit** suggests a habit of trying to mislead others by covering up or twisting the truth and giving wrong ideas of things: *The trader was truthful and without deceit.* **Deception** applies to the act that gives a false or wrong idea, but does not always suggest a dishonest purpose: *A magician uses deception.* **Guile** suggests craftiness and slyness and deception by means of tricks: *He got what he wanted by guile, not work.*

de·ceit·ful (di sēt′fəl) *adj.* **1** ready or willing to deceive or lie. **2** deceiving; fraudulent. **3** meant to deceive. **—de·ceit′ful·ly,** *adv.* **—de·ceit′ful·ness,** *n.*

de·ceive (di sēv′) *v.* **-ceived, -ceiv·ing. 1** make (a person) believe as true something that is false; mislead. **2** lie; use deceit. [ME < OF *deceveir* < L *decipere* < *de-* away + *capere* take] **—de·ceiv′a·ble,** *adj.* **—de·ceiv′er,** *n.* **—de·ceiv′ing·ly,** *adv.* **—Syn. 1** delude, beguile. See **cheat.**

de·cel·er·ate (dē sel′ər āt′) *v.* **-at·ed, -at·ing.** decrease the velocity of; slow down. [< *de-* + *(ac)celerate*] **—de·cel′er·a′tion,** *n.* **—de·cel′er·a′tor,** *n.*

De·cem·ber (di sem′bər) *n.* the twelfth and last month of the year. It has 31 days. [ME < OF *decembre* < L *December* < *decem* ten; because it was the tenth month in the early Roman calendar]

de·cem·vir (di sem′vər) *n.* **-virs, -vi·ri** (-və rī′ or -və rē′). **1** in ancient Rome, a member of a council of ten men. The decemvirs in 451 and 450 B.C. prepared the earliest Roman law code. **2** a member of a council of ten. [< L *decemvir,* sing. of *decemviri* < *decem* ten + *viri* men]

de·cem·vi·rate (di sem′vər it or di sem′və rāt′) *n.* **1** the office or government of decemvirs. **2** a group or council of ten men or decemvirs.

de·cen·cy (dē′sən sē) *n.* **-cies. 1** the state or quality of being decent. **2** propriety of behavior; a conforming to the standards of good taste. **3** a proper regard for modesty or delicacy. **4 decencies,** *pl.* **a** the proper and admirable qualities of civilized life. **b** suitable acts; proper observances. **c** the things required for a proper standard of living.

de·cen·ni·al (di sen′ē əl) *adj.* **1** of or for ten years. **2** happening every ten years. *—n.* a tenth anniversary. [< L *decennium* decade < *decem* ten + *annus* year]

de·cent (dē′sənt) *adj.* **1** proper and right: *It is not decent to laugh during a funeral.* **2** modest; free from vulgarity; not obscene: *Uncle never told stories that were not decent.* **3** respectable: *decent people.* **4** good enough; fairly good: *He gets decent marks at school.* **5** suitable to one's position; adequate: *He earns a decent living.* **6** not severe; rather kind: *My boss was very decent about my being away from work when my mother was ill.* [< L *decens, -entis* becoming, fitting, ppr. of *decere*] **—de′cent·ly,** *adv.* **—de′cent·ness,** *n.* **—Syn. 1** suitable, appropriate. **4** tolerable.

de·cen·tral·i·za·tion (dē sen′trəl ə zā′shən or dē sen′trəl ī zā′shən) *n.* the act of decentralizing or the state of being decentralized.

de·cen·tral·ize (dē sen′trəl īz′) *v.* **-ized, -iz·ing. 1** spread or distribute (authority, power, etc.) among several groups or local governments. **2** reorganize (a large industry, business, etc.) into smaller units of management and operation: *decentralize a department store.*

de·cep·tion (di sep′shən) *n.* **1** the act of deceiving. **2** the state of being deceived. **3** something that deceives; an illusion. **4** a trick meant to deceive; fraud; sham. [< LL *deceptio, -onis* < *decipere.* See DECEIVE.] **—Syn. 1** imposture, subterfuge, trickery. See **deceit. 4** hoax, ruse.

de·cep·tive (di sep′tiv) *adj.* **1** deceiving. **2** meant to deceive: *The player scored on a deceptive shot.* **—de·cep′tive·ly,** *adv.* **—de·cep′tive·ness,** *n.*

décharge (dā shärzh′) *n. Cdn.* **1** a shallow stretch in a water course, where it is necessary to unload a canoe, etc. in order to make way by tracking or paddling. **2 make a décharge,** unload in order to pass through a shallow stretch of water. [< Cdn.F < *décharger* unload]

deci- *combining form.* one tenth of: *decigram = one tenth of a gram.* [< L *decem* ten, *decimus* tenth]

hat, āge, cãre, fär; let, ēqual, tėrm; it, īce
hot, ōpen, ôrder; oil, out; cup, pu̇t, rüle, ūse
əbove, takən, pencəl, lemən, circəs
ch, child; ng, long; sh, ship
th, thin; ᴛʜ, then; zh, measure

dec·i·are (des′ē ãr′) *n.* a metric unit of area equal to 1/10 of an are, 10 square metres, or 11.96 square yards. [< F *déciare* < *déci-* deci + *are* are[2]]

dec·i·bel (des′ə bel′) *n.* a unit for measuring the loudness of sounds. [< *deci-* + *bel,* a unit of measure in physics, after A. G. *Bell,* 1847-1922, the inventor of the telephone]

de·cide (di sīd′) *v.* **-cid·ed, -cid·ing. 1** settle (a question, dispute, etc.) by giving victory to one side; give a judgment or the decision. **2** make up one's mind; resolve. **3** cause (a person) to reach a decision. [< L *decidere* cut off < *de-* away + *caedere* cut]
Syn. 2 Decide, determine, resolve = make up one's mind. **Decide** emphasizes the idea of coming to a conclusion after some talk or thinking over: *I decided to take the position at the bank.* **Determine** suggests fixing one's mind so firmly on doing something that nothing could shake one loose from his decision or purpose: *I am determined to make a success of it.* **Resolve** = make up one's mind positively to do or not to do something: *He resolved to do good work.*

de·cid·ed (di sīd′id) *adj.* **1** clear; definite; unquestionable. **2** firm; determined. **—de·cid′ed·ness,** *n.*
☛ **decided, decisive.** There is a distinction between *decided,* meaning definite or unquestionable, and *decisive,* meaning having or giving a clear result: *His height gave him a decided advantage. In World War II the Battle of El Alamein was a decisive victory.*

de·cid·ed·ly (di sīd′id lē) *adv.* **1** clearly; definitely; unquestionably. **2** firmly; in a determined manner.

de·cid·u·ous (di sij′ü əs) *adj.* **1** falling off at a particular season or stage of growth: *deciduous leaves, deciduous horns.* **2** of trees, shrubs, etc., shedding leaves annually. Maples, elms, and most oaks are deciduous trees. [< L *deciduus* < *decidere* < *de-* + *cadere* fall] **—de·cid′u·ous·ly,** *adv.* **—de·cid′u·ous·ness,** *n.*

dec·i·gram or **dec·i·gramme** (des′ə gram′) *n.* 1/10 of a gram, equal to 1.5432 grains, or .003527 ounce. [< F *décigramme*]

dec·i·li·tre or **dec·i·li·ter** (des′ə lē′tər) *n.* 1/10 of a litre, equal to 6.102 cubic inches, or about 3.38 fluid ounces. [< F *décilitre*]

de·cil·lion (di sil′yən) *n.* **1** in Canada, the United States, and France, a numeral consisting of 1 with 33 zeros following it. **2** in the English and German numerical systems, a numeral consisting of 1 with 60 zeros following it. [< *deci-* < *(mi)llion*]

dec·i·mal (des′ə məl) *adj.* based upon ten or tenths; increasing by tens: *The metric system is a decimal system of measurement.* *—n.* **1** a decimal fraction; a fraction like .04 or 4/100, .2 or 2/10. **2** a number like 75.24, 3.062, .7, or .091. [< L *decimus* tenth]

decimal fraction a fraction whose denominator is ten or some power of ten, like .2, .02, etc.

dec·i·mal·ly (des′ə məl ē) *adv.* **1** by means of decimals. **2** by tens.

decimal point a period placed before a fraction expressed in decimal figures, as in 2.03, .623.

dec·i·mate (des′ə māt′) *v.* **-mat·ed, -mat·ing. 1** destroy much of; kill a large part of: *War had decimated the tribe.* **2** select by lot and execute every tenth man of. **3** take or destroy one tenth of. [< L *decimare* take a tenth, ult. < *decem* ten] **—dec′i·ma′tion,** *n.* **—dec′i·ma′tor,** *n.*

dec·i·me·tre or **dec·i·me·ter** (des′ə mē′tər) *n.* 1/10 of a metre, equal to 3.937 inches. [< F *décimètre*]

de·ci·pher (di sī′fər) *v.* **1** make out the meaning of (bad writing, an unknown language, or anything puzzling). **2** interpret (secret writing) by using a key; change (a message) from code to ordinary language. **—de·ci′pher·a·ble,** *adj.* **—de·ci′pher·er,** *n.*

de·ci·sion (di sizh′ən) *n.* **1** the deciding or settling of a question, dispute, etc. by giving judgment to one side. **2** a judgment reached or given. **3** the act of making up one's mind; resolution. **4** firmness; determination: *A man of decision makes up his mind what to do and then* *does it.* **5** in boxing, the winning of a match on points or by the verdict of the referee and judges, rather than by a knockout. [< L *decisio, -onis* < *decidere.* See DECIDE.] —**Syn. 2** verdict, decree.

de·ci·sive (di sī′siv) *adj.* **1** having or giving a clear result; settling something beyond question. **2** having or showing decision: *a decisive answer.* —**de·ci′sive·ly,** *adv.* —**de·ci′sive·ness,** *n.* —**Syn. 1** conclusive. ☛ See **decided** for usage note.

deck (dek) *n.* **1** a floor or platform extending from side to side of a ship. Often the upper deck has no roof over it. **2** a part or floor resembling the deck of a ship: *a sun deck, the deck of an airplane.* **3** a pack of playing cards. **4 clear the deck** or **decks, a** remove unnecessary objects from the decks of a warship to prepare for action. **b** make ready for any action. **5 on deck,** *Informal.* **a** present; on hand. **b** in baseball, next in the batting order. A player on deck usually waits at an assigned spot away from the batter's box. **6 stack the deck,** *Informal.* **a** arrange a pack of cards dishonestly. **b** prepare circumstances in advance.
—*v.* **1** provide with a deck. **2** adorn; cover. **3 deck out,** dress; adorn: *Grace was decked out in white linen.* [< MDu. *dek* roof]

deck chair a light folding chair, usually having a canvas cover, for use in the open air.

deck hand a sailor who works on deck; an ordinary sailor.

deck·house (dek′hous′) *n.* a cabin or compartment built on the deck of a ship.

deck·le (dek′əl) *n.* **1** in papermaking, a frame that regulates the size of a sheet. **2** deckle edge. [< G *Deckel,* dim. of *Decke* cover]

deckle edge 1 the rough edge of untrimmed paper. **2** an imitation of it. —**deck′le-edged′,** *adj.*

deck tennis a game similar to tennis, usually played on board a passenger ship, in which a ring of rope, rubber, etc. is tossed back and forth over a net.

de·claim (di klām′) *v.* **1** recite in public; make a formal speech. **2** speak in a loud and emotional manner; speak or write for effect. [< L *declamare* < *de-* (intensive) + *clamare* cry] —**de·claim′er,** *n.*

dec·la·ma·tion (dek′lə mā′shən) *n.* **1** the act or art of reciting in public; making a formal speech or speeches. **2** a selection of poetry, prose, etc. for reciting; formal speech. **3** the act of talking loudly and emotionally. **4** loud and emotional talk.

de·clam·a·to·ry (di klam′ə tô′rē) *adj.* **1** having to do with declamation. **2** loud and emotional.

dec·la·ra·tion (dek′lə rā′shən) *n.* **1** the act of declaring. **2** the thing declared. **3** a document containing a declaration. **4** a statement of goods, etc. for taxation. **5** a formal announcement. **6** a strong statement. **7** in bridge, a bid, especially the winning bid. **8** in cricket, a tactical decision by one side to close its innings.

Declaration of Independence in the United States, the public statement adopted by the Continental Congress on July 4, 1776, in which the American colonies were declared free and independent of Great Britain.

de·clar·a·tive (di klar′ə tiv or di kler′ə tiv) *adj.* making a statement. —**de·clar′a·tive·ly,** *adv.*
☛ Declarative sentences, as opposed to imperative, interrogative, and exclamatory sentences, make plain statements: *That was the most delicious breakfast we had ever tasted.*

de·clar·a·to·ry (di klar′ə tô′rē) *adj.* declarative.

de·clare (di klãr′) *v.* **-clared, -clar·ing. 1** announce publicly or formally; make known; proclaim: *That company has just declared a dividend on its stock. Peace was declared at last.* **2** say openly or strongly: *The boy declared that he would never go back to school again.* **3** make a declaration; proclaim oneself: *Both teams declared themselves against cheating.* **4** acknowledge being in possession of (income, assets, goods, etc.) for income tax, customs charges, etc. **5** in bridge, announce what suit will be played as trumps. [ME < L *declarare* < *de-* (intensive) + *clarare* make clear < *clarus* clear] —**de·clar′er,** *n.*
Syn. 1 See **announce. 2 Declare, assert** = say something positively. **Declare** = state something openly, strongly, and confidently, sometimes in spite of possible contradiction: *The weather bureau declares that the rain will stop.* **Assert** = state something positively, usually without proof and sometimes in spite of proof that one is wrong, but often because one believes he is right: *He asserts that he was not there, but ten people saw him.*

de·clas·si·fy (dē klas′ə fī′) *v.* **-fied, -fy·ing.** remove (documents, codes, etc.) from the list of restricted, confidential, or secret information.

de·clen·sion (di klen′shən) *n.* **1** in the grammar of certain languages: **a** a systematic arrangement of the forms of nouns, pronouns, and adjectives according to their case, number, and gender. The declension of *who* is: nominative case, *who*; possessive case, *whose*; objective case, *whom.* **b** a group of words whose endings for the different cases, etc. are alike. Latin nouns are usually grouped in five declensions. **c** the act of giving the variant forms of a word. **2** a downward movement, bend, or slope. **3** a sinking into a lower or inferior condition; decline. **4** a turning away (from one's religion, faith, etc.); deviation from a standard. [irregularly < OF < L *declinatio, -onis* < *declinare.* See DECLINE.]

de·clin·a·ble (di klīn′ə bəl) *adj.* **1** in the grammar of certain languages, of nouns, pronouns, and adjectives, capable of being given in different cases; that has different forms for its different cases. **2** that can be declined or refused.

dec·li·na·tion (dek′lə nā′shən) *n.* **1** a downward bend or slope. **2** a polite refusal. **3** the deviation of the needle of a compass from true north or south. **4** in astronomy, the angular distance of a star, planet, etc. from the celestial equator. The declination of a star is used to locate its north or south position in the heavens. **5** a turning aside; deviation from a standard.

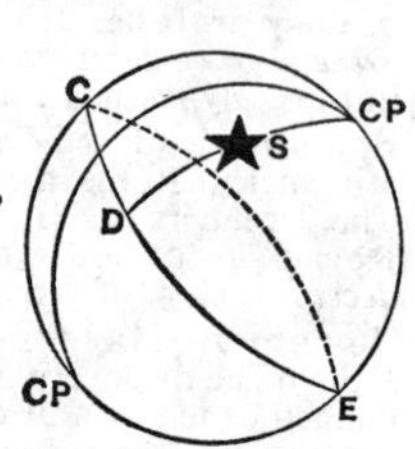

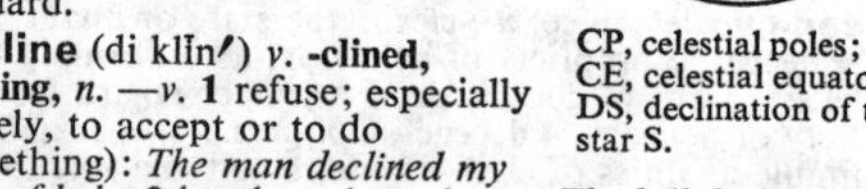
CP, celestial poles; CE, celestial equator; DS, declination of the star S.

de·cline (di klīn′) *v.* **-clined, -clin·ing,** *n.* —*v.* **1** refuse; especially politely, to accept or to do (something): *The man declined my offer of help.* **2** bend or slope down: *The hill declines to a fertile valley.* **3** grow less in strength, power, value, etc.; grow worse; decay: *Great nations have risen and declined.* **4** in the grammar of certain languages, give the different cases, etc. of (a noun, pronoun, or adjective). See **declension** (def. 1a).
—*n.* **1** a falling; a sinking: *a decline in prices.* **2** a losing of strength, power, value, etc.; a growing worse: *the decline of the Roman Empire.* **3** the last part of anything: *in the decline of a person's life.* **4** a wasting disease; consumption; tuberculosis of the lungs. **5** a downward slope. [< L *declinare* < *de-* from + *clinare* bend] —**de·clin′er,** *n.* —**Syn.** *v.* **1** reject. See **refuse. 4** deteriorate, degenerate. –*n.* **2** decay, deterioration. **5** declivity.

de·cliv·i·tous (di kliv′ə təs) *adj.* rather steep.

de·cliv·i·ty (di kliv′ə tē) *n.* **-ties.** a downward slope. [< L *declivitas* < *declivus* sloping downward < *de-* down + *clivus* slope]

de·clutch (dē kluch′) *v.* disengage the clutch of a car, truck, etc.

de·coct (di kokt′) *v.* extract desired substances from (herbs, etc.) by boiling. [< L *decoctus,* pp. of *decoquere* < *de-* away + *coquere* cook]

de·coc·tion (di kok′shən) *n.* **1** the act of boiling to extract some desired substance. **2** a preparation made by boiling a substance in water or other liquid; an extract obtained by boiling.

de·code (dē kōd′) *v.* **-cod·ed, -cod·ing.** translate (coded messages) into ordinary language. —**de·cod′er,** *n.*

dé·colle·tage (dā′kol ə täzh′; *French,* dā kôl täzh′) *n.* **1** the neck of a dress, blouse, etc. cut low so as to leave the neck and shoulders exposed. **2** a dress, blouse, etc. cut in this way. [< F]

dé·colle·té (dā′kol ə tā′; *French,* dā kôl tā′) *adj.* **1** low-necked. **2** wearing a low-necked dress, blouse, etc. [< F *décolleté,* pp. of *décolleter* bare the neck of]

de·com·pose (dē′kəm pōz′) *v.* **-posed, -pos·ing. 1** decay; rot. **2** separate (a substance) into what it is made of: *A prism decomposes sunlight into its various colors.* **3** of a substance, become separated into its parts.

—de′com·pos′er, *n.* —Syn. 1 See **decay.**

de·com·po·si·tion (dē′kom pə zish′ən) *n.* 1 the act or process of decomposing. 2 decay; rot.

de·com·press (dē′kəm pres′) *v.* 1 release from pressure. 2 remove pressure from (a diver, etc.) gradually by means of an air lock or decompression chamber.

de·com·pres·sion (dē kəm presh′ən) *n.* the removal or lessening of pressure, especially of air pressure.

decompression chamber an airtight compartment used for the gradual readjustment of persons from abnormal to normal air pressure or for the simulation of low air pressure in training flyers for high-altitude flight.

decompression sickness aeroembolism; the bends.

de·con·ges·tant (dē′kən jest′ənt) *n.* a drug to relieve congestion.

de·con·tam·i·nate (dē′kən tam′ə nāt′) *v.* **-nat·ed, -nat·ing.** 1 make free from poison gas or harmful radioactive agents. 2 free from any sort of contamination. **—de′con·tam′i·na′tion,** *n.*

de·con·trol (dē′kən trōl′) *v.* **-trolled, -trol·ling,** *n.* —*v.* remove controls from: *decontrol the price of meat.* —*n.* a removing of controls.

dé·cor (dā kôr′) *n.* 1 decoration. 2 the scenery and furnishings on a stage setting. 3 the overall arrangement of the decoration and furnishings of a room, etc. [< F *décor* < *décorer* decorate]

dec·o·rate (dek′ə rāt′) *v.* **-rat·ed, -rat·ing.** 1 make beautiful; adorn. 2 paint or paper (a room, etc.). 3 give a medal, ribbon, etc. to (a person) as an honor: *The Queen decorated the explorer for bravery.* [< L *decorare* < *decus, decoris* adornment]

Syn. 1 Decorate, ornament, adorn = add something to give or increase beauty. **Decorate** = put on ornaments or other trimming to add finish, color, or a festive appearance to something: *We decorated the Christmas tree.* **Ornament** suggests adding, often permanently, something that especially suits a thing and adds to its general effect and beauty: *Stained glass windows ornament the church.* **Adorn** suggests adding something that is beautiful itself and therefore increases the beauty of a thing or person: *She adorned her hair with flowers.*

dec·o·ra·tion (dek′ə rā′shən) *n.* 1 the act of decorating. 2 anything used to decorate; an ornament. 3 the arrangement of ornaments, furnishings, etc. 4 a medal, ribbon, etc. given as an honor.

dec·o·ra·tive (dek′ə rə tiv, dek′rə tiv, or dek′ə rā′tiv) *adj.* decorating; helping to adorn; ornamental: *The flowered curtains were highly decorative.* **—dec′o·ra′tive·ly,** *adv.* **—dec′o·ra′tive·ness,** *n.*

dec·o·ra·tor (dek′ə rā′tər) *n.* 1 a person who decorates. 2 a person who plans and arranges the furnishings of homes, clubs, offices, etc.; interior decorator. 3 a person whose work is painting or papering rooms, etc.

dec·o·rous (dek′ə rəs or di kô′rəs) *adj.* well-behaved; acting properly; in good taste; dignified. [< L *decorus* < *decor* seemliness, comeliness] **—dec′o·rous·ly,** *adv.* **—dec′o·rous·ness,** *n.*

de·co·rum (di kô′rəm) *n.* 1 propriety of action, speech, dress, etc.: *You behave with decorum when you do what is proper.* 2 an observance or requirement of polite society. [< L *decorum,* neut. of *decorus* seemly]

de·coy (*v.* di koi′; *n.* dē′koi or di koi′) *v.* 1 lure (wild birds, animals, etc.) into a trap or within gunshot. 2 lead or tempt into danger. 3 *Cdn.* draw a player out of position by faking a play in one direction or way and then making it in another. [< n.]
—*n.* 1 an artificial bird used to lure real birds into a trap or within gunshot. 2 a bird or other animal trained to lure others of its kind into a trap. 3 any place into which wild birds or animals are lured. 4 any person or thing used to lead or tempt into danger. [< MDu. *de kooi* the cage < L *cavea* cave] **—de·coy′er,** *n.*

de·crease (*v.* di krēs′; *n.* dē′krēs or di krēs′) *v.* **-creased, -creas·ing,** *n.* —*v.* 1 become less: *Hunger decreases as one eats.* 2 make less: *decrease prices.*
—*n.* 1 a becoming less: *Toward night there was a decrease of heat.* 2 the amount by which a thing becomes or is made less. 3 **on the decrease,** decreasing. [ME < OF *de(s)creiss-,* a stem of *descreistre* < L *decrescere* < *de-* down + *crescere* grow] **—de·creas′ing·ly,** *adv.*

Syn. *v.* **1, 2 Decrease, diminish, dwindle** = become or make less. **Decrease** suggests steadily going down little by little: *The outputo the factory is decreasing.* **Diminish** suggests becoming smaller in size, amount, or importance because someone or something keeps taking away a part: *The medical bills during his long sickness have diminished his savings.* **Dwindle** emphasizes the idea of wasting away, or becoming smaller and smaller until almost nothing is left: *Our savings have dwindled.*

hat, āge, cãre, fär; let, ēqual, tėrm; it, īce
hot, ōpen, ôrder; oil, out; cup, pu̇t, rüle, ūse
əbove, takən, pencəl, lemən, circəs
ch, child; ng, long; sh, ship
th, thin; ᴛʜ, then; zh, measure

de·cree (di krē′) *n. v.* **-creed, -cree·ing.** —*n.* 1 something ordered or settled by authority; an official decision. 2 in ecclesiastical use, a law of a church council, especially one settling a disputed point of doctrine or discipline. 3 in law, a decision or order of a court or judge.
—*v.* 1 order or settle by authority: *Fate decreed that Ulysses should travel long and far.* 2 decide; determine. [ME < OF *decre,* var. of *decret* < L *decretum,* pp. neut. of *decernere* < *de-* from + *cernere* sift, decide] **—de·cree′er,** *n.*

decree ni·si (nī′sī or nē′sē) in law, a conditional granting of a divorce. The decree becomes final, or absolute, after a given period unless cause to the contrary is shown in the interim. [< L *nisi* unless]

dec·re·ment (dek′rə mənt) *n.* 1 a gradual decrease; slow loss. 2 the amount lost by gradual decrease. 3 in mathematics, the amount by which a variable decreases. [< L *decrementum* < *decrescere.* See DECREASE; compare INCREMENT.]

de·crep·it (di krep′it) *adj.* broken down or weakened by old age; old and feeble. [< L *decrepitus* broken down < *de-* + *crepare* creak] **—de·crep′it·ly,** *adv.* **—Syn.** See **weak.**

de·crep·i·tude (di krep′ə tūd′ or di krep′ə tüd′) *n.* feebleness, usually from old age, a decrepit condition; weakness.

decresc. decrescendo.

de·cre·scen·do (dē′krə shen′dō or dā′krə shen′dō) *n.* **-dos,** *adj. adv.* in music: —*n.* 1 a gradual decrease in force or loudness; diminuendo. The sign for a decrescendo is >. 2 a passage to be played or sung with a decrescendo. —*adj. adv.* with a gradual decrease in force or loudness. *Abbrev.*: decresc. [< Ital.]

de·cre·tal (di krē′təl) *n.* in the Roman Catholic Church, a papal decree or reply settling some question of doctrine or ecclesiastical law. [ME < OF < Med.L *decretale,* ult. < L *decretum.* See DECREE.]

de·cri·al (di krī′əl) *n.* the act of decrying.

de·cry (di krī′) *v.* **-cried, -cry·ing.** 1 condemn: *The minister decried gambling in all its forms.* 2 make little of; try to lower the value of: *The lumber dealer decried the use of concrete for houses.* [< F *decrier* < *de-* away, apart + *crier* cry < L *quiritare*] **—de·cri′er,** *n.*

de·cum·bent (di kum′bənt) *adj.* 1 of stems, branches, etc., lying or trailing on the ground with the end tending to climb. 2 lying down; reclining. [< L *decumbens, -entis,* ppr. of *decumbere* lie down]

de·cur·rent (di kėr′ənt) *adj.* of leaves, extending down the stem. [< L *decurrens, -entis,* ppr. of *decurrere* < *de-* down + *currere* run]

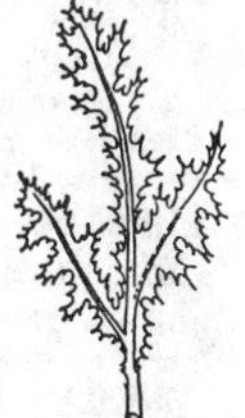
A decurrent leaf

ded·i·cate (ded′ə kāt′) *v.* **-cat·ed, -cat·ing.** 1 set apart for a sacred or solemn purpose; consecrate: *The new altar was dedicated at a special service.* 2 give up wholly or earnestly to some person or purpose: *The scientist is dedicated to the search for truth.* 3 address (a book, poem, etc.) to a friend or patron as a mark of affection, respect, gratitude, etc. 4 celebrate the opening of (a bridge, institution, meeting, etc.) with an official ceremony. [< L *dedicare* proclaim, affirm < *de-* (intensive) + *dicare* proclaim] **—ded′i·ca′tor,** *n.* **—Syn. 2** See **devote.**

ded·i·ca·tion (ded′ə kā′shən) *n.* 1 a setting apart or being set apart for a sacred or solemn purpose: *the dedication of a church.* 2 a giving up wholly or earnestly to some person or purpose. **3** the words dedicating a book, poem, etc. to a friend or patron. **4** a ceremony attending the official opening of something, as a building, institution, or convention: *the dedication of a new library wing.*

ded·i·ca·tive (ded′ə kə tiv or ded′ə kā′tiv) *adj.* dedicatory.

ded·i·ca·to·ry (ded′ə kə tô′rē) *adj.* of dedication; as a dedication.

de·duce (di dūs′ or di düs′) *v.* **-duced, -duc·ing. 1** infer from a general rule or principle; reach (a conclusion) by reasoning: *After looking at the evidence, the firemen deduced the cause of the fire.* **2** trace the course, descent, or origin of. [< L *deducere* < *de-* down + *ducere* lead]

de·duc·i·ble (di dūs′ə bəl or di düs′ə bəl) *adj.* capable of being deduced or inferred.

de·duct (di dukt′) *v.* take away; subtract. [< L *deductus*, pp. of *deducere.* See DEDUCE.] **—Syn.** See **subtract.**

de·duct·i·ble (di duk′tə bəl) *adj.* that can be deducted.

de·duc·tion (di duk′shən) *n.* **1** the act of taking away; subtraction: *No deduction in pay is made for absence due to illness.* **2** the amount deducted. **3** in logic, inference from a general rule or principle. A person using deduction reasons from general laws to particular cases. **4** a conclusion reached by this method of reasoning.

☛ **Deduction** and **induction** are the names of two opposite processes of logical reasoning. **Deduction** is the process by which one starts with a general principle, or premise, applies it to a particular case, and arrives at a conclusion that is true provided the premise is true: *All animals die; this is an animal; therefore, this will die.* **Induction** applies to the process by which one collects many particular cases, finds out by experiment what is common to all of them, and forms a general rule or principle that is probably true of the whole class: *Every animal I have tested died; therefore, all animals die.*

de·duc·tive (di duk′tiv) *adj.* of or using deduction; reasoning by deduction. **—de·duc′tive·ly,** *adv.*

deed (dēd) *n.* **1** something done; act. **2** a brave, skilful, or unusual act. **3** an action; doing; performance. **4** a written or printed document, sealed and signed, containing some contract. A buyer of real estate receives a deed legally transferring the ownership. **5 in deed,** in fact; actually.
—*v.* transfer by deed. [OE *dǣd*] **—Syn.** *n.* **2** feat, exploit.

deem (dēm) *v.* think; believe; consider: *The lawyer deemed it unwise to take the case to court.* [OE *dēman* < *dōm* judgment]

deep (dēp) *adj.* **1** going far down or back: *a deep well, a deep recess.* **2** from far down or back: *Take a deep breath.* **3** far down or back: *a deep cut.* **4** far on. **5** in depth: *a tank 8 feet deep.* **6** low in pitch: *a deep voice.* **7** strong and dark in color: *a deep red.* **8** strong; great; intense; extreme: *deep sorrow, a deep sleep.* **9** requiring much thought and study; hard to understand: *a deep book.* **10** with the mind fully taken up: *deep in thought.* **11** wise; shrewd. **12** sly; crafty. **13** grave; serious: *be in deep trouble.* **14** involved: *Because he was already deep in debt, he couldn't buy a new car.*
—*adv.* **1** far down or back: *The men dug deep before they found water.* **2** of time, far on: *He studied deep into the night.*
—*n.* **1** a deep place. **2** the most intense part: *the deep of winter.* **3 the deep,** the sea. [OE *dēop*] **—deep′ly,** *adv.* **—deep′ness,** *n.* **—Syn.** *adj.* **8** heartfelt, profound. **9** abstruse. **10** absorbed. **11** astute.

deep-chest·ed (dēp′ches′tid) *adj.* having a thick chest.

deep·en (dēp′ən) *v.* make or become deeper.

deep-freeze (*n.* dēp′frēz′; *v.* dēp′frēz′) *n. v.* **-froze** or **-freezed, -fro·zen** or **-freezed, -freez·ing.** —*n.* **1** a box or container for freezing and storing food. **2** the state of being deep-frozen: *The government kept the controversial report in deep-freeze.* —*v.* **1** freeze (food) and store it for later use. **2** keep as if frozen: *deep-freeze a plan.* **—deep′-freez′er,** *n.*

deep-fry (dēp′frī′) *v.* **-fried, -fry·ing.** fry in deep fat or oil. **—deep′-fry′er,** *n.*

deep-laid (dēp′lād′) *adj.* planned secretly and carefully: *deep-laid schemes.*

deep-root·ed (dēp′rüt′id) *adj.* **1** deeply rooted. **2** firmly fixed: *deep-rooted traditions, a deep-rooted dislike.*

deep-sea (dēp′sē′) *adj.* of or in the deeper parts of the sea: *a deep-sea diver.*

deep-seat·ed (dēp′sēt′id) *adj.* **1** far below the surface. **2** firmly fixed: *The disease was so deep-seated that it could not be cured.*

deep-set (dēp′set′) *adj.* **1** set deeply. **2** firmly fixed.

deep South or **Deep South** in the United States, generally, Georgia, Alabama, Mississippi, Louisiana, and part of South Carolina.

deep·wat·er (dēp′wo′tər or -wô′tər) *adj.* of or having to do with deep water; deep-sea.

deer (dēr) *n.* **deer. 1** a swift, graceful mammal of a group that have hoofs and chew the cud. A male deer has horns, or antlers, which are shed and grow again every year. **2** any of a group of mammals including deer, elk, moose. **3** *Cdn. North.* the caribou. **4** *Obsolete.* any beast, especially a wild beast. [OE *dēor* animal]

deer fly any of a group of bloodsucking flies similar to the horsefly but smaller.

deer·hound (dēr′hound′) *n.* **1** a Scottish breed of dog, resembling a greyhound but larger and having a shaggy coat. **2** a dog of this breed.

deer lodge a lodge or camp to accommodate deer hunters, especially one that may be rented by hunters visiting the area during the open season.

deer mouse a small North American mouse having white feet and large ears.

deer·skin (dēr′skin′) *n.* **1** the skin of a deer. **2** the leather made from this skin.

deer·stalk·er (dēr′stok′ər or -stôk′ər) *n.* **1** a person who hunts deer by stalking. **2** a close-fitting cap with earflaps, originally worn by hunters.

def. 1 definition. **2** defined. **3** defendant. **4** deferred. **5** defective.

de·face (di fās′) *v.* **-faced, -fac·ing.** spoil the appearance of; mar. [< obs. F *defacer* < *de-* away, apart + *face* face < L *facies* form] **—de·fac′er,** *n.*

Syn. Deface, disfigure = spoil the appearance of someone or something. **Deface** = spoil the surface of something by blotting out an important detail, by scratching something in, etc.: *Scribbled pictures and remarks defaced the pages of the library book.* **Disfigure** suggests spoiling the beauty of a person or thing by permanent injury too deep or serious to remove: *The accident left her face disfigured.*

de·face·ment (di fās′mənt) *n.* **1** the act of defacing. **2** the state of being defaced. **3** anything that defaces.

de fac·to (dē′fak′tō or dā′fak′tō) **1** in fact; in reality. **2** actually existing, whether legal or not: *a de facto government.* [< L *de facto* from the fact]

de·fal·cate (di fal′kāt, di fol′kāt, or di fôl′kāt) *v.* **-cat·ed, -cat·ing.** steal or misuse money trusted to one's care. [< Med.L *defalcare*, literally, to cut off with a sickle < *de-* away + *falx, -cis* sickle] **—de·fal′ca·tor,** *n.*

de·fal·ca·tion (dē′fal kā′shən, dē′fol kā′shən, or dē′fôl kā′shən) *n.* **1** the theft or misuse of money entrusted to one's care. **2** the amount stolen or misused.

def·a·ma·tion (def′ə mā′shən or dē′fə mā′shən) *n.* a defaming or being defamed; slander; libel.

de·fam·a·to·ry (di fam′ə tô′rē) *adj.* defaming; slanderous.

de·fame (di fām′) *v.* **-famed, -fam·ing.** attack the good name of; harm the reputation of; speak evil of; slander; libel: *Men in public life are sometimes defamed by opponents.* [ME < OF *diffamer* < L *diffamare* damage by rumor < *de-* down, from (confused with *dis-*) + *fama* rumor] **—de·fam′er,** *n.*

de·fault (di folt′ or -fôlt′) *n.* **1** a failure to do something or to appear somewhere when due; neglect. If, in any contest, one side does not appear, it loses by default. **2** a failure to pay when due. **3** in law, a failure to appear in court at the time specified for a legal proceeding. **4 in default of,** in the absence of; lacking: *In default of tools, she used a hairpin and a needle.*
—*v.* **1** fail to do something or appear somewhere when due. **2** fail to pay when due. **3** in law: **a** fail to appear in court at a specified time. **b** declare (a person) in default. **c** lose a case by default. [ME < OF *defaute* < *defaillir* < *de-* de- + *faillir*, ult. < L *fallere* deceive]

de·fault·er (di fol′tər or -fôl′tər) *n.* **1** a person who defaults. **2** a person who steals or misuses money trusted to his care.

de·feat (di fēt′) *v.* **1** win a victory over; overcome. **2** make useless: *defeat someone's plans.* **3** do out of; deprive: *His bad temper defeated him of ultimate success.* **4** in law, make null and void; annul.
—*n.* **1** a defeating. **2** a being defeated. **3** a making useless. [ME < OF *de(s)fait,* pp. of *desfaire* < LL *diffacere* < L *dis-* un- + *facere* do] **—de·feat′er,** *n.*
Syn. *v.* **1 Defeat, conquer, overcome** = win a victory over someone or something. **Defeat** = win a victory, at least for the moment: *We defeated Laurier Collegiate in basketball yesterday.* **Conquer,** more formal, emphasizes the idea of winning control over people, things, or feelings: *Some countries may be defeated, but never conquered.* **Overcome** emphasizes the idea of getting the better of things or, especially, feelings: *He could not overcome his dislike for that man.*

de·feat·ism (di fēt′iz əm) *n.* the attitude or behavior of a defeatist.

de·feat·ist (di fēt′ist) *n.* a person who expects, wishes for, or admits the defeat of his country, cause, party, etc.

def·e·cate (def′ə kāt′) *v.* **-cat·ed, -cat·ing.** have a movement of the bowels. [< L *defaecare* < *de-* from + *faeces,* pl. dregs, solid excrement] **—def′e·ca′tion,** *n.*

de·fect (*n.* dē′fekt or di fekt′; *v.* di fekt′) *n.* **1** a fault; blemish; imperfection. **2** the lack of something essential to completeness; a falling short. —*v.* forsake one's own country, group, etc. for another, especially another that is opposed to it in political or social doctrine. [< L *defectus* want < *deficere* fail. See DEFICIENT.]
—de·fec′tor, *n.*
Syn. 1 Defect, flaw = an imperfection or fault. **Defect** is the general word, applying to any imperfection on the surface or in the make-up of a person or thing: *A hearing aid helps to overcome defects in hearing. No person is without defects.* **Flaw** applies to a defect in structure, suggesting a crack or break when used literally, a fault in character when used figuratively: *That bubble is a flaw in the glass. Jealousy is the great flaw in his character.* **2** want, deficiency.

de·fec·tion (di fek′shən) *n.* **1** a falling away from loyalty, duty, religion, etc.; desertion. **2** a failure.

de·fec·tive (di fek′tiv) *adj.* **1** having a flaw or blemish; not perfect; not complete. **2** in grammar, lacking one or more of the usual forms of inflection. *Ought* is a defective verb. **3** in psychology, below normal in behavior or intelligence.
—*n.* **1** a defective person or thing. **2** in grammar, a defective word. **3** in psychology, a person who has some defect of body or mind. **—de·fec′tive·ly,** *adv.*
—de·fec′tive·ness, *n.* **—Syn.** *adj.* **1** faulty, imperfect.

de·fence or **de·fense** (di fens′) *n.* **1** the act of defending or protecting; a guarding against attack or harm: *The armed forces are responsible for the defence of the country.* **2** anything that defends or protects; something used to guard against attack or harm: *A wall around a city used to be a defence against enemies. A well-built house or a warm coat is a defence against cold weather.* **3** in boxing or fencing, the act of defending oneself. **4** the team or players defending a goal in a game. **5** an action, speech, or writing in favor of something. **6** in law: **a** the answer of a defendant to an accusation or lawsuit against him. **b** the arguments, etc. presented by a defendant or his lawyer in contesting a case. **c** a defendant and his lawyers. [ME < OF < L *defensa* < *defendere* ward off]

de·fence·less or **de·fense·less** (di fens′lis) *adj.* having no defence; unprotected; helpless against attack or harm: *A baby is defenceless.* **—de·fence′less·ly** or **de·fense′less·ly,** *adv.* **—de·fence′less·ness** or **de·fense′less·ness,** *n.*

de·fence·man or **de·fense·man** (di fens′mən) *n.* **-men** (-mən). in hockey, football, etc., a player whose job is to prevent the opposing players from approaching the goal.

defence mechanism **1** any self-protective reaction by an organism. **2** in psychology, an unconscious adjustment of behavior or mental attitude designed to shut out unpleasant emotions.

de·fend (di fend′) *v.* **1** guard from attack or harm; protect. **2** act, speak, or write in favor of: *The lawyer defended his client so ably that the case was dismissed.* **3** in law, resist (a claim); contest (a lawsuit). **4** make or enter a defence. [ME < OF < L *defendere* ward off]
—de·fend′a·ble, *adj.* **—Syn. 1** See **guard. 2** uphold.

hat, āge, cãre, fär; let, ēqual, tėrm; it, īce
hot, ōpen, ôrder; oil, out; cup, pu̇t, rüle, ūse
əbove, takən, pencəl, lemən, circəs
ch, child; ng, long; sh, ship
th, thin; ᴛʜ, then; zh, measure

de·fend·ant (di fen′dənt) *n.* a person accused or sued in a law court.

de·fend·er (di fen′dər) *n.* **1** a protector; guardian. **2** in sports, a person or team that stands ready to defend its championship.

de·fense (di fens′) *n.* defence.

de·fense·less (di fens′lis) *adj.* defenceless.

de·fense·man (di fens′mən) *n.* **-men** (-mən). defenceman.

de·fen·si·ble (di fen′si bəl) *adj.* **1** capable of being defended. **2** justifiable; proper. **—de·fen′si·bly,** *adv.*

de·fen·sive (di fen′siv) *adj.* **1** ready to defend; defending. **2** for defence. **3** of defence. —*n.* **1** a position or attitude of defence. **2** anything that defends. **—de·fen′sive·ly,** *adv.* **—de·fen′sive·ness,** *n.*

de·fer[1] (di fėr′) *v.* **-ferred, -fer·ring.** put off; delay. [< L *differe.* Doublet of DIFFER.] **—Syn.** postpone. See **delay.**

de·fer[2] (di fėr′) *v.* **-ferred, -fer·ring.** yield in judgment or opinion; submit courteously: *I will defer to your wishes.* [< F *déférer* < L *deferre* < *de-* down + *ferre* carry]

def·er·ence (def′ər əns) *n.* **1** a yielding to the judgment or opinion of another; courteous submission. **2** great respect. **3 in deference to,** out of respect for the wishes or authority of. **—Syn. 2** See **honor.**

def·er·ent (def′ər ənt) *adj.* deferential.

def·er·en·tial (def′ər en′shəl) *adj.* showing defence; respectful. **—def′er·en′tial·ly,** *adv.*

de·fer·ment (di fėr′mənt) *n.* a putting off; delay.

de·ferred (di·fėrd′) *adj.* **1** postponed. **2** with benefits withheld for a certain time. **3** *Esp.U.S.* exempted for a time from induction into the armed services.

de·fi·ance (di fī′əns) *n.* **1** a defying; a standing up against authority and refusing to recognize or obey it; open resistance. **2** a challenge to meet in a contest, to do something, or to prove something. **3 bid defiance to,** defy. **4 in defiance of,** without regard for; in spite of.

de·fi·ant (di fī′ənt) *adj.* showing defiance; challenging; openly resisting. [< F *défiant,* ppr. of *défier* defy]
—de·fi′ant·ly, *adv.* **—de·fi′ant·ness,** *n.*

de·fi·cien·cy (di fish′ən sē) *n.* **-cies. 1** a lack or absence of something needed or required; incompleteness. **2** the amount by which something falls short or is too small.

de·fi·cient (di fish′ənt) *adj.* **1** incomplete; defective. **2** not sufficient in quantity, force, etc. —*n.* a person or thing that is deficient: *a mental deficient.* [< L *deficiens, -entis* failing, ppr. of *deficere* < *de-* from + *facere* make, do] **—de·fi′cient·ly,** *adv.*

def·i·cit (def′ə sit) *n.* the amount by which a sum of money falls short; shortage: *Since the club owed $15 and had only $10 in the treasury, there was a deficit of $5.* [< L *deficit* it is wanting. See DEFICIENT.]

de·fi·er (di fī′ər) *n.* a person who defies.

de·file[1] (di fīl′) *v.* **-filed, -fil·ing. 1** make filthy or dirty; make disgusting in any way. **2** destroy the purity or cleanness of; corrupt. **3** violate the sanctity of: *During the war many shrines and churches were defiled by marauding raiders.* **4** stain; dishonour: *Charges of corruption defiled the reputation of the government.* [alteration of ME *defoul* (< OF *defouler* trample down, violate) after obs. *file* befoul < OE *fȳlan* < *ful* foul]
—de·fil′er, *n.*

de·file[2] (di fīl′ or dē′fīl) *v.* **-filed, -fil·ing,** *n.* —*v.* march in a line. —*n.* **1** a narrow way or passage through which troops can march only in narrow columns. **2** a steep and narrow valley. [< F *défilé,* special use of pp. of *défiler* march by files < *dé-* off + *file* file[1]]

de·file·ment (di fīl′mənt) *n.* **1** the act of defiling. **2** the state of being defiled. **3** something tha t defiles. [< *defile*[1]]

de·fine (di fīn′) *v.* **-fined, -fin·ing. 1** make clear the meaning of; explain: *A dictionary defines words.* **2** make clear; make distinct. **3** fix; settle. **4** settle the limits of. **5** be a distinguishing feature of; characterize: *Perseverance usually defines success.* [ME < OF < L *definire* to limit < *de-* from + *finis* boundary] **—de·fin′a·ble,** *adj.* **—de·fin′er,** *n.*

def·i·nite (def′ə nit) *adj.* **1** clear; exact; not vague. **2** limited; restricted. **3** limiting; restricting. The English **definite article** is *the.* [< L *definitus,* pp. of *definire.* See DEFINE.] **—def′i·nite·ness,** *n.*

☛ **Definite, definitive** are not synonyms, although both suggest "leaving no doubt." **Definite** is a synonym of *distinct* and means "perfectly clear and exact," leaving no doubt about either what is meant or what is not meant: *I expect a definite answer, either yes or no.* **Definitive** is a synonym of *decisive,* and means "final and complete," putting an end to doubt or uncertainty: *We have appealed to the Supreme Court for a definitive answer.*

def·i·nite·ly (def′ə nit lē or def′nət lē) *adv.* **1** in a definite manner. **2** certainly: *Will you go? Definitely.*

def·i·ni·tion (def′ə nish′ən) *n.* **1** the act of explaining; the act of making clear the meaning of a word; explanation. **2** a statement or explanation of the precise nature of anything. **3** the power of making clear and distinct. The capacity of a lens to give a clear, distinct image of an object is called its definition. **4** clearness; distinctness. **5** in radio and television, the accuracy with which sound is reproduced by a receiver.

de·fin·i·tive (di fin′ə tiv) *adj.* **1** conclusive; final. **2** authoritative; completely reliable: *That book is the definitive work on marine biology.* **3** limiting; defining. *—n.* in grammar, a word that limits or defines a noun. *The, this, all, none,* etc. are definitives. **—de·fin′i·tive·ly,** *adv.* **—de·fin′i·tive·ness,** *n.* ☛ See **definite** for usage note.

de·flate (di flāt′) *v.* **-flat·ed, -flat·ing. 1** let air or gas out of (a balloon, tire, football, etc.). **2** reduce the amount of; reduce: *deflate prices, deflate currency.* **3** become reduced. **4** injure or destroy the conceit or confidence of: *Our laughter soon deflated him.* [< L *deflare* < *de-* off + *flare* blow] **—de·fla′tor,** *n.*

de·fla·tion (di flā′shən) *n.* **1** the act of deflating: *the deflation of a tire, the deflation of a prig.* **2** a reduction. **3** the reduction of the amount of available money in circulation so that prices go down. **4** in geology, the removal of solid particles by the wind, leaving the rocks exposed to the weather.

de·fla·tion·ar·y (di flā′shən er′ē) *adj.* of or having to do with deflation.

de·flect (di flekt′) *v.* bend or turn aside; change the direction of. [< L *deflectere* < *de-* away + *flectere* bend] **—de·flec′tor,** *n.*

de·flec·tion (di flek′shən) *n.* **1** a bending or turning aside. **2** the amount of bending or turning. **3** a bending downward. **4** in physics, the movement of the needle or indicator of a scientific instrument from its zero or normal position.

de·flec·tive (di flek′tiv) *adj.* **1** causing deflection. **2** tending to deflect.

de·flex·ion (di flek′shən) *n. Esp.Brit.* deflection.

de·flow·er (dē flou′ər) *v.* **1** strip flowers from. **2** spoil; ruin; ravish. **—de·flow′er·er,** *n.*

de·fo·li·ant (di fō′lē ənt) *n.* a chemical agent that defoliates.

de·fo·li·ate (di fō′lē āt′) *v.* **-at·ed, -at·ing.** of a tree or plant, strip or be stripped of leaves. **—de·fo′li·a′tor,** *n.*

de·for·est (dē fôr′ist) *v.* clear of trees: *The land had to be deforested before the settlers could farm it.* **—de·for′est·a′tion,** *n.* **—de·for′est·er,** *n.*

de·form (di fôrm′) *v.* **1** spoil the form or shape of: *Shoes that are too tight deform the feet.* **2** mar the beauty of: *The ravages of hunger had deformed her appearance.* **3** become altered in shape or form. **4** in physics, change the shape of by stress. **—de·form′er,** *n.*

de·for·ma·tion (dē′fôr mā′shən or def′ər mā′shən) *n.* **1** the act of deforming. **2** a deformed condition. **3** a change of form. **4** a changed form. **5** in physics, a change in the shape or dimensions of a body, resulting from stress; strain. **6** in geology: **a** any change in the original state or size of rock masses, especially as produced by faulting. **b** an instance of this.

de·formed (di fôrmd′) *adj.* **1** not properly formed. **2** ugly.

de·form·i·ty (di fôr′mə tē) *n.* **-ties. 1** a part that is not properly formed. **2** the condition of being improperly formed. **3** an improperly formed person or thing. **4** ugliness.

de·fraud (di frod′ or -frôd′) *v.* take money, rights, etc. away from by fraud; cheat: *The dishonest lawyer defrauded the widow of her savings.* [ME < MF < L *defraudare* < *de-* completely + *fraus, fraudis* fraud] **—de·fraud′er,** *n.*

de·fray (di frā′) *v.* pay (costs or expenses): *The expenses of national parks are defrayed by the taxpayers.* [< F *défrayer* < *de-* (intensive) + *frai* cost] **—de·fray′er,** *n.*

de·fray·al (di frā′əl) *n.* a payment (of expenses, etc.).

de·fray·ment (di frā′mənt) *n.* defrayal.

de·frost (dē frost′) *v.* **1** remove frost or ice from. **2** thaw out (frozen foods).

de·frost·er (dē fros′tər) *n.* a device that removes ice, either through heat or mechanically. Defrosters are used on automobile windshields and in refrigerators.

deft (deft) *adj.* skilful; nimble: *The fingers of a violinist or surgeon are deft.* [var. of *daft*] **—deft′ly,** *adv.* **—deft′ness,** *n.* **—Syn.** See **dexterous.**

de·funct (di fungkt′) *adj.* dead; extinct. *—n.* **the defunct,** the dead person. [< L *defunctus,* pp. of *defungi* finish < *de-* (intensive) + *fungi* perform]

de·fy (di fī′) *v.* **-fied, -fy·ing. 1** resist boldly or openly. **2** withstand; resist: *This strong fort defies capture.* **3** challenge (a person) to do or prove something. [ME < OF *de(s)fier* < VL < L *dis-* away, apart + *fidus* faithful] **—Syn. 1** brave. **3** dare.

deg. degree; degrees.

de·gauss (di gous′, di gos′, or di gôs′) *v.* equip (a steel ship) with a device preventing the explosion of magnetic mines. [< Karl Friedrich *Gauss* (1777-1855), a German mathematician]

de·gen·er·a·cy (di jen′ər ə sē) *n.* a degenerate condition.

de·gen·er·ate (*v.* di jen′ər āt′; *adj. n.* di jen′ər it) *v.* **-at·ed, -at·ing,** *adj. n. —v.* **1** decline in physical, mental, or moral qualities; grow worse. **2** in biology, sink to a lower type; lose the normal or more highly developed characteristics of its race or kind.
—adj. **1** that has degenerated; showing a decline in physical, mental, or moral qualities: *The thief was a degenerate member of a fine family.* **2** in biology, that has lost the normal or more highly developed characteristics of its kind.
—n. **1** a person who shows degraded or debased physical, mental, or moral qualities. **2** a sexual pervert: *Only a degenerate could have committed such a horrible crime.* [< L *degenerare,* ult. < *de-* down + *genus* race, kind] **—de·gen′er·ate·ly,** *adv.*

de·gen·er·a·tion (di jen′ər ā′shən) *n.* **1** the process of degenerating. **2** a degenerate condition. **3** in medicine, a deterioration in tissues or organs caused by disease, injury, etc. **4** in biology, a gradual change to a less highly developed or lower type.

de·gen·er·a·tive (di jen′ər ə tiv or di jen′ər ā′tiv) *adj.* **1** tending to degenerate. **2** characterized by degeneration; showing degeneration.

de·glu·ti·tion (dē′glü tish′ən or deg′lü tish′ən) *n.* the act or power of swallowing. [< F *déglutition* < L *deglutire* swallow down]

deg·ra·da·tion (deg′rə dā′shən) *n.* **1** a degrading. **2** a being degraded: *Failure to obey orders caused the captain's degradation to the rank of a private.* **3** a degraded condition: *The drunkard, filthy and half-starved, lived in degradation.* **4** in geology, the wearing down of land, rocks, etc. by erosion.

de·grade (di grād′) *v.* **-grad·ed, -grad·ing. 1** reduce to a lower rank; take away a position, an honor, etc. from. **2** make worse; lower; debase: *You degrade yourself when you tell a lie.* **3** lower in price, quality, value, etc. **4** in geology, wear down by erosion. **5** in biology, reduce to a lower classification. **6** in chemistry, reduce systematically the molecule of (a compound) into others of less complex structure. [ME < OF *degrader* < LL *degradare* < L

hat, āge, cãre, fär; let, ēqual, tėrm; it, īce
hot, ōpen, ôrder; oil, out; cup, pu̇t, rüle, ūse
əbove, takən, pencəl, lemən, circəs
ch, child; ng, long; sh, ship
th, thin; ᴛʜ, then; zh, measure

de- down + *gradus* step, grade] **—de·grad′er,** *n.*

de·gree (di grē′) *n.* **1** a stage or step in a scale or process. **2** a step in direct line of descent: *a cousin two degrees removed.* **3** the amount; extent: *To what degree are you interested in reading?* **4** a unit for measuring temperature. The freezing point of water is 32 degrees (32°) Fahrenheit. A degree on the centigrade scale is 1.8 times a degree on the Fahrenheit scale. **5** a unit for measuring angles or arcs. A degree is 1/90 of a right angle or 1/360 of the circumference of a circle. Forty-five degrees (45°) is half a right angle or one eighth of the line bounding a circle. **6** rank: *A princess is a lady of high degree.* **7** a rank or title given by a college or university to a student whose work fulfils certain requirements, or to a person as an honor: *an M.A. degree, a D.D. degree.* **8** in grammar, one of the three stages in the comparison of adjectives or adverbs. *Fast* is the positive degree; *faster,* the comparative degree; *fastest,* the superlative degree. **9** in algebra, the rank as determined by an exponent or sum of exponents. a^3 and a^2b are terms of the third degree. $x^2y^2z^3$ is a term of the seventh degree. **10** a relative condition, manner, way, or respect: *A bond and a stock may both be wise investments, each in its degree.* **11** *U.S.* in law, the relative measure of guilt: *murder in the first degree.* **12** in music: **a** an interval between any note of the scale and the next note. **b** a line or space on the staff showing the position of the notes. **c** the interval between two of these. **13 by degrees,** gradually. **14 to a degree, a** to a large amount; to a great extent. **b** somewhat; rather. [ME < OF *degre* < VL *degradus* < *degradare* divide into steps < L *de-* down + *gradus* step, grade]

Degrees (def. 5)

☛ **degrees.** Academic degrees, when given with a person's name, are separated from the name by a comma: *Harry James, M.A.; Harry Paynter, D.Sc.* When the institution granting the degree is named or when the year of granting is given, the following forms are used: *George Smith, B.A. (Alberta), M.A. (McGill), Ph.D. (Toronto); Helen Lawrence, B.A. '35, M.A. '38.*

de·hisce (dē his′) *v.* **-hisced, -hisc·ing.** in biology, (of an organ, seed pod, etc.) burst open along a definite line, to provide for the discharge of the contents. [< L *dehiscere,* ult. < *de-* down + *hiare* gape]

de·his·cence (dē his′əns) *n.* in biology, the bursting open of pods, anthers, etc. to discharge seeds, pollen, etc.

de·his·cent (dē his′ənt) *adj.* of seed pods, capsules, etc., bursting open to scatter seeds.

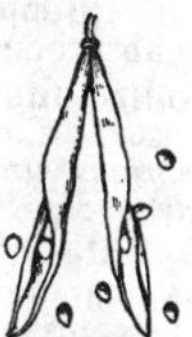

Dehiscent pods

de·horn (dē hôrn′) *v.* remove the horns from.

de·hu·man·ize (dē hū′mən īz′) *v.* **-ized, -iz·ing.** deprive of human qualities, interest, sympathy, etc. **—de·hu′man·i·za′tion,** *n.*

de·hy·drate (dē hī′drāt) *v.* **-drat·ed, -drat·ing. 1** deprive (a chemical compound) of water or the elements of water. **2** take moisture from; dry. **3** lose water or moisture.

de·hy·dra·tion (dē′hī drā′shən) *n.* the removal of water from a chemical compound or from vegetables, fruits, etc.

de-ice (dē īs′) *v.* **-iced, -ic·ing.** prevent formation of ice on; remove ice from (an aircraft, etc.). **—de-ic′er,** *n.*

de·i·fi·ca·tion (dē′ə fə kā′shən) *n.* **1** a deifying. **2** a being deified.

de·i·fy (dē′ə fī′) *v.* **-fied, -fy·ing. 1** make a god of. **2** worship or regard as a god. [ME < OF *deifier* < LL *deificare* < *deus* god + *facere* make] **—de′i·fi′er,** *n.*

deign (dān) *v.* **1** condescend; think fit: *So great a man would never deign to notice us.* **2** condescend to give (an answer, a reply, etc.). [ME < OF *deignier* < L *dignari* < *dignus* worthy]

De·i gra·ti·a (dē′ī grā′shē ē or dā′ē grä′tē ə) *Latin.* by the grace of God.

de·ism (dē′iz əm) *n.* **1** a belief that God exists entirely apart from our world and does not influence the lives of human beings. **2** a belief in God without accepting any particular religion. [< L *deus* god]

de·ist (dē′ist) *n.* a person who believes in deism.

de·i·ty (dē′ə tē) *n.* **-ties. 1** a god or goddess. **2** a divine nature; the state of being a god. **3 the Deity,** God. [ME < OF *deite* < L *deitas* < *deus* god]

de·ject·ed (di jek′tid) *adj.* in low spirits; sad; discouraged. **—de·ject′ed·ly,** *adv.* **—de·ject′ed·ness,** *n.* **—Syn. See sad.**

de·jec·tion (di jek′shən) *n.* lowness of spirits; sadness; discouragement: *Her face showed her dejection at missing the party.* [< L *dejectio, -onis* < *dejicere* < *de-* down + *jacere* throw]

dé·jeu·ner (dā zhœ nā′) *n. French.* **1** a breakfast. **2** a luncheon.

de ju·re (dē jür′ē or dā jür′ā) *Latin.* by right; according to law.

dek·a·li·tre or **dek·a·li·ter** (dek′ə lē′tər) *n.* decalitre.

dek·a·me·tre or **dek·a·me·ter** (dek′ə mē′tər) *n.* decametre.

deke (dēk) *v.* **deked, dek·ing,** *n. Cdn. Slang.* in hockey: *—n.* a kind of fake shot or movement intended to draw a defending player out of position. *—v.* **1** draw (a defending player) out of position by feinting. **2** manoeuvre (oneself or the puck) by feinting so as to outsmart a defending player. [< *decoy*]

Del. Delaware.

del. 1 delete. **2** delegate. **3** delivery.

de·lay (di lā′) *v.* **1** put off till a later time: *We will delay the party for a week.* **2** make late; keep waiting; hinder the progress of: *The accident delayed the train for two hours. Ignorance delays progress.* **3** be late; wait; go slowly; stop along the way: *Do not delay in coming.* *—n.* **1** the act of delaying. **2** the fact of being delayed. [ME < OF *delaier* postpone < *de-* away + *laier* leave, let, probably < Celtic] **—de·lay′er,** *n.* **—de·lay′ing·ly,** *adv.*

Syn. *v.* **1 Delay, defer, postpone** = put off doing something. **Delay** emphasizes the idea of putting off, and suggests either holding off for some reason but planning to act at some later time or, often, putting off indefinitely: *I delayed seeing the dentist.* **Defer** usually suggests deciding to put off until a better time, with the intention of acting then: *I deferred going until I had more time.* **Postpone** suggests deferring until a definite time, after something has been done, learned, etc.: *I postponed going until next week.* **2** retard.

de·le (dē′lē) *v.* **-led, -le·ing.** in printing, cross out; delete. [< L *dele,* imperative of *delere* delete]

de·lec·ta·ble (di lek′tə bəl) *adj.* very pleasing; delightful. [ME < OF < L *delectabilis* < *delectare.* See DELIGHT.] **—de·lec′ta·ble·ness,** *n.* **—de·lec′ta·bly,** *adv.*

de·lec·ta·tion (dē′lek tā′shən) *n.* delight; pleasure; entertainment: *The magician did many tricks for our delectation.*

del·e·ga·cy (del′ə gə sē) *n.* **-cies.** delegation.

del·e·gate (*n.* del′ə git or del′ə gāt′; *v.* del′ə gāt′) *n.* *v.* **-gat·ed, -gat·ing.** *—n.* a person given power or authority to act for others; representative. *—v.* **1** appoint or send (a person) as a delegate: *Each club delegated one member to attend the provincial meeting.* **2** give over (one's power or authority) to another as agent or deputy: *The provinces have delegated some of their rights to the Federal Government.* [< L *delegatus,* pp. of *delegare* < *de-* (intensive) + *legare* send with a commission]

del·e·ga·tion (del′ə gā′shən) *n.* **1** a delegating. **2** the fact of being delegated. **3** a group of delegates: *Each province sent a delegation to the national convention.*

de·lete (di lēt′) *v.* **-let·ed, -let·ing. 1** strike out or take out (anything written or printed); remove; cross out. **2** erase; wipe out: *Shock deleted all recollection of the accident from her mind.* [< L *deletus,* pp. of *delere* destroy]

del·e·te·ri·ous (del′ə tēr′ē əs) *adj.* harmful; injurious. [< NL *deleterius* < Gk. *dēlētērios,* ult. < *dēleesthai* hurt] **—del′e·te′ri·ous·ly,** *adv.*

de·le·tion (di lē′shən) *n.* **1** the act of deleting. **2** the fact of being deleted. **3** a deleted part.

delft (delft) *n.* **1** a kind of earthenware made in the Netherlands, having an opaque white glaze and decorated, usually, in blue. **2** any pottery having a similar glaze and color. [< *Delft*, a city in the S.W. Netherlands]

delft·ware (delft′wãr′) *n.* delft.

de·lib·er·ate (*adj.* di lib′ər it or di lib′rit; *v.* di lib′ər āt′) *adj. v.* **-at·ed, -at·ing.** —*adj.* **1** carefully thought out; made or done on purpose: *His excuse was a deliberate lie.* **2** slow and careful in deciding what to do: *A deliberate person takes a long time to make up his mind.* **3** not hurried; slow: *The old man walked with deliberate steps.* —*v.* **1** think over carefully; consider. **2** discuss reasons for and against something; debate. [< L *deliberatus*, pp. of *deliberare* < *de-* (intensive) + *librare* weigh] **—de·lib′er·ate·ly,** *adv.* **—de·lib′er·ate·ness,** *n.* **—de·lib′er·a′tor,** *n.*

Syn. *adj.* **1 Deliberate, intentional** = done on purpose. **Deliberate** suggests that what it describes was thought over in advance and done with a clear idea of what one is doing: *His attempt to deceive the customs authorities was deliberate.* **Intentional** emphasizes the idea of a purpose, and means "done with a definite end in mind": *His mean remark was intentional; he wanted to make you angry.* **2** thoughtful, cautious. **3** See **slow.**

de·lib·er·a·tion (di lib′ər ā′shən) *n.* **1** careful thought. **2** a discussion of reasons for and against something; debate: *the deliberations of the Legislative Assembly.* **3** slowness and care: *The hunter aimed his gun with great deliberation.*

de·lib·er·a·tive (di lib′ər ə tiv or di lib′ər ā′tiv) *adj.* **1** for deliberation; having to do with deliberation; discussing reasons for and against something: *Parliament is a deliberative body.* **2** characterized by deliberation; coming as a result of deliberation. **—de·lib′er·a′tive·ly,** *adv.*

del·i·ca·cy (del′ə kə sē) *n.* **-cies. 1** a delicate quality or nature; slightness and grace: *the delicacy of lace, the delicacy of a flower, the delicacy of a baby's skin.* **2** fineness of feeling for small differences; sensitiveness: *delicacy of hearing or touch.* **3** need of care, skill, or tact: *a matter of great delicacy.* **4** thought or regard for the feelings of others. **5** a shrinking from what is offensive or not modest. **6** weakness; the condition of being easily hurt or made ill: *The child's delicacy was the result of a long illness.* **7** a choice kind of food; a dainty.

del·i·cate (del′ə kit) *adj.* **1** pleasing to the taste; lightly flavored; mild; soft: *delicate foods, delicate colors, delicate fragrance.* **2** of fine weave, quality, or make; easily torn; thin: *A spider's web is very delicate.* **3** requiring careful handling: *delicate flowers, a delicate situation, a delicate question.* **4** very rapidly responding to slight changes of condition; finely sensitive: *delicate instruments, a delicate sense of touch.* **5** easily hurt or made ill: *a delicate child.* **6** hard to appreciate: *a delicate point in reasoning.* **7** careful of the feelings of others; considerate. **8** avoiding anything that is offensive or immodest. [ME < L *delicatus* pampered] **—del′i·cate·ly,** *adv.* **—del′i·cate·ness,** *n.*

Syn. 1, 2 Delicate, dainty = fine in quality and pleasing to the senses and taste. **Delicate** suggests fineness or softness of texture, lightness in quality, or exactness and fineness in the making that especially pleases any of the five senses or the mind: *Roses have a delicate fragrance. He does delicate work with water colors.* **Dainty** suggests smallness, perfection in the making, and a delicate beauty that especially pleases the sense of sight or taste: *The baby wore a dainty dress.* **5** frail, fragile. **7** tactful.

del·i·ca·tes·sen (del′ə kə tes′ən) *n.* **1** a store that sells prepared foods, such as cooked meats, smoked fish, cheese, salads, pickles, etc. **2** the foods sold at such a store. [< G *Delikatessen*, pl. of *Delikatesse* delicacy < F]

☛ **Delicatessen** = a store that sells prepared foods, is singular in use: *The delicatessen closes at nine o'clock.* When *delicatessen* means the foods sold at such a store, it is usually plural in use: *Delicatessen usually require little preparation for serving.*

de·li·cious (di lish′əs) *adj.* **1** very pleasing to taste or smell. **2** very pleasing; delightful: *a delicious color combination.* **3 Delicious,** a kind of red or yellow apple having a fine flavor. [ME < OF *delicieus* < LL *deliciosus* < *deliciae* delight < *delicere* entice. See DELIGHT.] **—de·li′cious·ly,** *adv.* **—de·li′cious·ness,** *n.*

Syn. 1 Delicious, luscious = delighting the senses. **Delicious** is used chiefly to mean pleasing in flavor, less often in fragrance or aroma: *This dessert is delicious. The coffee smells delicious.* **Luscious** adds to *delicious* the suggestion of richness or sweetness, and when applied to fruit, ripeness or juiciness: *She makes luscious apple pie.*

de·light (di līt′) *n.* **1** great pleasure; joy. **2** something that gives great pleasure. —*v.* **1** please greatly. **2** have great pleasure: *Children delight in surprises.* [ME < OF *delit* < *delitier* < L *delectare* to charm < *delicere* entice < *de-* (intensive) + *lacere* entice; spelling influenced by *light*] **—de·light′er,** *n.* **—Syn.** *n.* **1** ecstasy, rapture. See **pleasure.** –*v.* **1** gladden.

de·light·ed (di līt′id) *adj.* greatly pleased; joyful; glad. **—de·light′ed·ly,** *adv.*

de·light·ful (di līt′fəl) *adj.* very pleasing; giving joy. **—de·light′ful·ly,** *adv.* **—de·light′ful·ness,** *n.* **—Syn.** enjoyable, pleasurable.

de·light·some (di līt′səm) *adj.* delightful. **—de·light′some·ly,** *adv.* **—de·light′some·ness,** *n.*

De·lil·ah (di lī′lə) *n.* **1** in the Bible, the Philistine woman who was loved by Samson and who betrayed him. See **Samson. 2** any false, treacherous woman.

de·lim·it (di lim′it) *v.* fix the limits of; mark the boundaries of. **—de·lim′i·ta′tion,** *n.*

de·lin·e·ate (di lin′ē āt′) *v.* **-at·ed, -at·ing. 1** trace the outline of. **2** draw; sketch. **3** describe in words. [< L *delineare* < *de-* (intensive) + *linea* line] **—de·lin′e·a′tor,** *n.*

de·lin·e·a·tion (di lin′ē ā′shən) *n.* **1** a drawing; sketch. **2** a description.

de·lin·quen·cy (di ling′kwən sē) *n.* **-cies. 1** the failure to do what is required by law or duty; guilt. **2** a fault; offence. **3** the condition or habit of behaving unlawfully: *Juvenile delinquency is greatly increased by wartime conditions.*

de·lin·quent (di ling′kwənt) *adj.* **1** failing to do what is required by law or duty; guilty of a fault or an offence. **2** due and unpaid; overdue: *The owner lost his house when it was sold for delinquent taxes.* **3** having to do with delinquents. —*n.* a delinquent person; offender; criminal. [< L *delinquens, -entis*, ppr. of *delinquere* fail < *de-* down + *linquere* leave] **—de·lin′quent·ly,** *adv.*

del·i·quesce (del′ə kwes′) *v.* **-quesced, -quesc·ing.** become liquid by absorbing moisture from the air. [< L *deliquescere* < *de-* + *liquescere* become fluid < *liquere* be liquid]

del·i·ques·cence (del′ə kwes′əns) *n.* the act or process of deliquescing.

del·i·ques·cent (del′ə kwes′ənt) *adj.* becoming liquid by absorbing moisture from the air.

de·lir·i·ous (di lir′ē əs) *adj.* **1** temporarily out of one's senses; wandering in mind; raving. **2** wildly excited: *delirious with joy.* **3** caused by delirium. **—de·lir′i·ous·ly,** *adv.* **—de·lir′i·ous·ness,** *n.*

de·lir·i·um (di lir′ē əm) *n.* **-lir·i·ums, -lir·i·a** (-lir′ē ə). **1** a temporary disorder of the mind that occurs during fevers, insanity, drunkenness, etc. Delirium is characterized by excitement, irrational talk, and hallucinations. **2** any wild excitement that cannot be controlled. [< L *delirium* < *delirare* rave, be crazy < *de lira* (*ire*) (go) out of the furrow (in ploughing)]

delirium tre·mens (trē′mənz) delirium characterized by violent tremblings and terrifying hallucinations, usually caused by prolonged excessive drinking of alcoholic liquor. *Abbrev.*: d.t.'s [< NL *delirium tremens* trembling delirium]

de·liv·er (di liv′ər) *v.* **1** carry and give out; distribute: *The postman delivers letters.* **2** hand over; give up: *deliver a fort to the enemy.* **3** give forth in words: *The traveller delivered an interesting talk about his journey. The jury delivered its verdict.* **4** strike; throw: *deliver a blow.* **5** set free; rescue; save from evil or trouble: "*Deliver us from evil.*" **6** help give birth: *The farmer delivered his prize cow of a calf.* **7** help in the birth of: *The doctor delivered the baby at noon.* **8 deliver oneself of, a** speak; give out: *He delivered himself of a carefully prepared statement to the press.* **b** unburden oneself of (ideas, feelings, etc.) [ME < OF *delivrer* < L *deliberare* set free < *de-* (intensive) + *liber* free] **—de·liv′er·a·ble,** *adj.* **—de·liv′er·er,** *n.* **—Syn. 2** surrender. **5** liberate. See **rescue.**

de·liv·er·ance (di liv′ər əns or di liv′rəns) *n.* **1** the act of setting free or the state of being set free; a rescue; release. **2** a formal opinion or judgment.

de·liv·er·y (di liv′ər ē or di liv′rē) *n.* **-er·ies. 1** the act of carrying and giving out letters, goods, etc.; act of distributing: *There are two deliveries of mail a day in our city.* **2** a giving up; handing over: *The captive was released upon the delivery of his ransom.* **3** a manner of speaking; way of giving a speech, lecture, etc.: *Our minister has an excellent delivery.* **4** an act or way of striking, throwing, etc. **5** a rescue; release. **6** the act of giving birth; childbirth. **7** the act of assisting at a birth. **8** anything that is delivered; goods to be delivered.
—**Syn. 2** surrender.

dell (del) *n.* a small, sheltered glen or valley, usually with trees in it. [OE]

de·louse (dē lous′ or -louz′) *v.* **-loused, -lous·ing.** remove lice from.

Del·phi (del′fī) *n.* a town in ancient Greece where a famous oracle of Apollo was located.

Del·phi·an (del′fē ən) *adj.* Delphic.

Del·phic (del′fik) *adj.* **1** having to do with the oracle of Apollo at Delphi. **2** obscure; having a double meaning.

Delphic oracle the oracle of Apollo at Delphi. The oracle often gave ambiguous answers to questions.

del·phin·i·um (del fin′ē əm) *n.* the larkspur. [< NL < Gk. *delphinion* < *delphin* dolphin; from the shape of the nectar gland of the flower]

del·ta (del′tə) *n.* **1** a deposit of earth and sand, usually three-sided, that collects at the mouths of some rivers. **2** the fourth letter of the Greek alphabet (*Δ*, *δ*). **3** any triangular space or figure. [< Gk.]

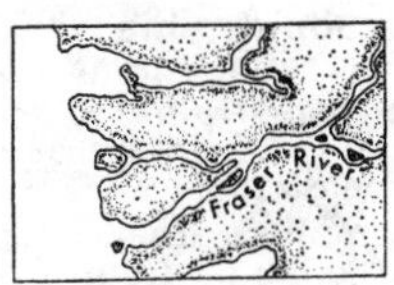

The delta of the Fraser River

Del·ta-wing or **del·ta-wing** (del′tə wing′) *adj.* of an aircraft, having wings in the shape of a Greek delta or triangle.

del·toid (del′toid) *adj.* **1** shaped like the Greek delta (Δ); triangular. **2** of or having to do with the deltoid muscle. —*n.* the deltoid muscle. [< NL *deltoides* < Gk. *deltoeidēs* < *delta* delta + *eidos* form]

deltoid muscle in physiology, a large, triangular muscle of the shoulder. It lifts the arm away from the side of the body.

de·lude (di lüd′) *v.* **-lud·ed, -lud·ing.** mislead; deceive: *He deluded himself into believing he would pass his examinations.* [< L *deludere* < *de-* (to the detriment of) + *ludere* play] —**de·lud′er,** *n.* —**de·lud′ing·ly,** *adv.*

del·uge (del′ūj) *n. v.* **-uged, -ug·ing.** —*n.* **1** a great flood. **2** a heavy fall of rain. **3** any overwhelming rush: *Most stores have a deluge of orders just before Christmas.* **4 the Deluge,** in the Bible, the great flood in the days of Noah. Gen. 7. —*v.* **1** flood. **2** overwhelm: *The movie star was deluged with requests for his autograph.* [ME < OF < L *diluvium* < *diluere* < *dis-* away + *luere* wash] —**Syn.** *n.* **1** See **flood.**

de·lu·sion (di lü′zhən) *n.* **1** the act of deluding. **2** the state of being deluded. **3** a false notion or belief: *The voyages of Columbus disproved the common delusion of his time that the earth was flat.* **4** a fixed belief maintained in spite of unquestionable evidence to the contrary: *The mental patient had the delusion that he was king.* [ME < LL *delusio, -onis* < *deludere.* See DELUDE.] —**Syn. 1** deception. **3** See **illusion.**

de·lu·sive (di lü′siv) *adj.* misleading; deceptive; false. —**de·lu′sive·ly,** *adv.* —**de·lu′sive·ness,** *n.*

de·lu·so·ry (di lü′sə rē) *adj.* delusive; deceptive.

de luxe or **de·luxe** (də lůks′ or də luks′) *adj.* of exceptionally good quality; elegant. [< F]

delve (delv) *v.* **delved, delv·ing. 1** search carefully for information: *The scholar delved in many libraries for facts.* **2** *Archaic or dialect.* dig. [OE *delfan*] —**delv′er,** *n.*

de·mag·net·ize (dē mag′nə tīz′) *v.* **-ized, -iz·ing.** deprive of magnetism. —**de·mag′net·i·za′tion,** *n.*

dem·a·gog (dem′ə gog′) *n.* demagogue.

dem·a·gog·ic (dem′ə goj′ik or dem′ə gog′ik) *adj.* **1** of or having to do with a demagogue. **2** like a demagogue or demagogues.

dem·a·gogue (dem′ə gog′) *n.* a popular leader who stirs up the people by appealing to their emotions and prejudices. The chief aim of most demagogues is to get money, power, etc. for themselves alone. [< Gk. *dēmagōgos* < *dēmos* people + *agōgos* leader < *agein* lead]

hat, āge, cãre, fär; let, ēqual, tėrm; it, īce
hot, ōpen, ôrder; oil, out; cup, pu̇t, rüle, ūse
əbove, takən, pencəl, lemən, circəs
ch, child; ng, long; sh, ship
th, thin; ᴛʜ, then; zh, measure

dem·a·gogu·er·y (dem′ə gog′ər ē) *n.* **1** the principles and practices of a demagogue. **2** government by a demagogue. **3** demagogues as a group.

dem·a·go·gy (dem′ə gō′jē, dem′ə goj′ē, or dem′ə gog′ē) *n.* demagoguery.

de·mand (di mand′) *v.* **1** ask for as a right: *The prisoner demanded a trial.* **2** ask for with authority: *The policeman demanded the boys' names.* **3** ask to know or to be told: *demand an answer.* **4** call for; require; need: *Training a puppy demands patience.*
—*n.* **1** the act of demanding. **2** the thing demanded. **3** a claim; requirement: *A busy person has many demands on his time.* **4** the desire and ability to buy: *Because of the large crop, the supply of apples was greater than the demand.* **5 in demand,** wanted. **6 on demand,** upon request; on being claimed: *a note payable on demand.* [ME < OF < L *demandare* < *de-* from + *mandare* to order] —**de·mand′er,** *n.*
Syn. *v.* **1, 4 Demand, claim, require** = ask or call for something as a right or need. **Demand** emphasizes insisting, sometimes in a domineering way, on getting something a person or thing has the authority, right, or need to call for: *I demand an answer immediately.* **Claim** emphasizes having, or stating one has, the right to get what is demanded: *He claimed the inheritance.* **Require** emphasizes the need for what is demanded: *This letter requires an answer.*

de·mar·cate (dē′mär kāt′ or di mär′kāt) *v.* **-cat·ed, -cat·ing. 1** set and mark the limits of. **2** separate; distinguish. [< *demarcation*] —**de′mar·ca′tor,** *n.*

de·mar·ca·tion (dē′mär kā′shən) *n.* **1** the act of setting and marking the limits. **2** a separation; distinction. [< Sp. *demarcación* < *de-* off + *marcar* mark]

de·mean[1] (di mēn′) *v.* lower in dignity or standing; humble: *The prince demeaned himself by mixing with thieves and robbers.* [< *de-* down + *mean*[2]; formed after *debase*]

de·mean[2] (di mēn′) *v.* behave or conduct oneself (in a certain manner): *He demeaned himself well.* [ME < OF *demener* < *de-* (intensive) + *mener* lead < L *minare* drive]

de·mean·or or **de·mean·our** (di mēn′ər) *n.* the way a person looks and acts; behavior; conduct; manner. [ME *demenure* < *demenen* behave < OF *demener.* See DEMEAN[2].]

de·ment·ed (di men′tid) *adj.* insane; crazy. [< L *dementare* < *demens* mad < *de-* out of + *mens, mentis* mind] —**de·ment′ed·ly,** *adv.* —**de·ment′ed·ness,** *n.*

de·men·tia (di men′shə) *n.* a condition characterized by a partial or complete deterioration of mental powers, the ability to reason, etc.

dementia prae·cox (prē′koks or prī′koks) a mental illness that usually occurs or begins in late adolescence. It is now more properly called schizophrenia. [< L *dementia praecox* precocious insanity]

de·mer·it (dē mer′it) *n.* **1** a fault; defect. **2** a mark against a person's record for poor work or unsatisfactory behavior.

de·mesne (di mān′ or di mēn′) *n.* **1** in law, the possession of land as one's own. **2** the land or land and buildings possessed as one's own; real estate. **3** the house and land belonging to a lord and used by him. **4** a domain; realm. **5** a region. [ME < AF *demesne,* a respelling of OF *demeine* domain. Doublet of DOMAIN.]

De Meurons (də mü′rənz) a group of disbanded mercenaries belonging to a Swiss-German regiment, many of whom settled in Lord Selkirk's Red River Colony in 1820. [< Col. de *Meuron,* commander of the regiment]

demi- *prefix.* **1** half: *demigod* = *half god.* **2** smaller than usual in size, power, etc.: *demitasse* = *a small cup.* [< F *demi* half < VL < L *dimidius* < *dis-* apart + *medius* middle]

dem·i·god (dem′ē god′) *n.* **1** a god that is partly human. Hercules was a demigod. **2** a minor or lesser god. **3** a person so outstanding as to seem like a god.

dem·i·john (dem′ē jon′) *n.* a large bottle of glass or earthenware enclosed in wicker. [< F *dame-jeanne* Lady Jane, playful personification]

A demijohn

de·mil·i·tar·ize (dē mil′ə tə rīz′) *v.* **-ized, -iz·ing.** free from military control. —**de·mil′i·ta·ri·za′tion,** *n.*

dem·i·monde (dem′ē mond′ or dem′ē mond′) *n.* a class of women whose reputation and morals are doubtful. [< F *demi-monde* half-world]

de·mise (di mīz′) *n. v.* **-mised, -mis·ing.** —*n.* **1** death. **2** in law, the transfer of an estate by a will or lease. **3** the transfer of royal power by death or abdication. —*v.* **1** in law, transfer (an estate) by a will or lease. **2** transfer (royal power) by death or abdication. [apparently < AF *demise,* pp. of *desmettre* put away < *des-* away + *mettre* put < L *mittere* let go, send]

dem·i·sem·i·qua·ver (dem′ē sem′ē kwā′vər) *n.* in music, a thirty-second note.

dem·i·tasse (dem′ē tas′) *n.* **1** a small cup for serving black coffee. **2** a small cup of black coffee. [< F *demi-tasse* half-cup]

de·mo·bi·lize (dē mō′bə līz′) *v.* **-lized, -liz·ing.** **1** disband: *After the war, it took several months to demobilize the armed services.* **2** discharge from one of the armed services. —**de·mo′bi·li·za′tion,** *n.*

de·moc·ra·cy (di mok′rə sē) *n.* **-cies.** **1** a government that is run by the people who live under it. Under a democracy the people rule either by direct vote or indirectly through the election of certain representatives to govern them. **2** the ideals and principles of such a government. **3** a country, state, or community having such a government. **4** the treatment of others as one's equals. [< F *démocratie* < Gk *dēmokratia* < *dēmos* people + *kratos* rule]

dem·o·crat (dem′ə krat′) *n.* **1** a person who believes that a government should be run by the people who live under it. **2** a person who holds, or acts on, the belief that all people are his equals. **3** a light, four-wheeled, horse-drawn vehicle having two double seats, one behind the other. **4 Democrat,** *U.S.* a member of the Democratic Party.

dem·o·crat·ic (dem′ə krat′ik) *adj.* **1** of a democracy; like a democracy. **2** treating all classes of people as one's equals: *The queen's democratic ways made her dear to her people.* **3 Democratic,** *U.S.* of or having to do with the Democratic Party. —**dem′o·crat′i·cal·ly,** *adv.*

Democratic Party in the United States, one of the two main political parties.

de·moc·ra·tize (di mok′rə tīz′) *v.* **-tized, -tiz·ing.** make or become democratic. —**de·moc′ra·ti·za′tion,** *n.*

de·mo·graph·ic (dē′mə graf′ik or dem′ə graf′ik) *adj.* of or having to do with demography. —**de′mo·graph′i·cal·ly,** *adv.*

de·mog·ra·phy (di mog′rə fē) *n.* the science dealing with the statistics of births, deaths, diseases, etc. of a community. —**de·mog′ra·pher,** *n.*

dem·oi·selle (dem′wä zel′) *n.* **1** a damsel. **2** a crane of Asia, Europe, and northern Africa, having long white plumes behind the eyes. **3** a type of dragonfly. **4** hoodoo (def. 3). [< F < OF *dameisele.* Doublet of DAMSEL.]

de·mol·ish (di mol′ish) *v.* pull or tear down; destroy: *demolish a building. His reputation was demolished by slander.* [< F *démoliss-,* a stem of *démolir* < L *demoliri* tear down < *de-* down + *moles* mass] —**de·mol′ish·er,** *n.* —**de·mol′ish·ment,** *n.* **Syn.** See **destroy.**

dem·o·li·tion (dem′ə lish′ən or dē′mə lish′ən) *n.* destruction; ruin.

demolition bomb a bomb with a relatively large explosive charge, used especially for destroying buildings and other important objects.

de·mon (dē′mən) *n.* **1** an evil spirit; devil; fiend. **2** a very wicked or cruel person. **3** an evil influence: *The demon of greed ruined the miser's happiness.* **4** an attendant or guiding spirit. **5** a person who has great energy or vigor. **6** in Greek mythology, an inferior or minor god. [< L < Gk. *daimonion* divine (thing); in Christian writings, evil spirit < *daimōn* divinity, spirit]

de·mon·e·tize (dē mon′ə tīz′ or -mun′ə tīz′) *v.* **-tized, -tiz·ing.** **1** deprive of its standard value as money. **2** withdraw from use as money. —**de·mon′e·ti·za′tion,** *n.*

de·mo·ni·ac (di mō′nē ak′) *adj.* **1** of demons. **2** devilish; fiendish. **3** raging; frantic. **4** possessed by an evil spirit. —*n.* a person supposed to be possessed by an evil spirit.

de·mo·ni·a·cal (dē′mə nī′ə kəl) *adj.* demoniac. —**de′mo·ni′a·cal·ly,** *adv.*

de·mon·ic (di mon′ik) *adj.* **1** of evil spirits; caused by evil spirits. **2** influenced by a guiding spirit; inspired.

de·mon·ism (dē′mən iz′əm) *n.* **1** belief in demons. **2** the worship of demons.

de·mon·ol·a·try (dē′mən ol′ə trē) *n.* the worship of demons.

de·mon·ol·o·gy (dē′mən ol′ə jē) *n.* the study of demons or of beliefs about demons.

de·mon·stra·bil·i·ty (di mon′strə bil′ə tē or dem′ən strə bil′ə tē) *n.* a demonstrable quality or condition.

de·mon·stra·ble (di mon′strə bəl or dem′ən strə bəl) *adj.* capable of being proved.

de·mon·stra·bly (di mon′strə blē or dem′ən strə blē) *adj.* **1** in a manner that can be proved; clearly. **2** by demonstration.

dem·on·strate (dem′ən strāt′) *v.* **-strat·ed, -strat·ing.** **1** establish the truth of; prove. **2** explain by using examples, experiments, etc.; show how (something) is done. **3** show the merits of (a thing for sale); advertise or make known by exhibiting a process in public: *The salesman came to the house and demonstrated a new type of electric floor polisher.* **4** show openly: *He demonstrated his love for his niece by giving her a big hug.* **5** exhibit feelings or attitudes by conducting a parade, holding a public meeting, etc.: *An angry mob demonstrated in front of the city hall.* **6** display military strength to frighten or deceive an enemy. [< L *demonstrare* < *de-* (intensive) + *monstrare* show] —**Syn. 1** attest.

dem·on·stra·tion (dem′ən strā′shen) *n.* **1** a clear proof: *a demonstration that the earth is round.* **2** an explanation with the use of examples, experiments, etc. **3** a showing of the merits of a thing for sale; advertising or making known some new product or process in a public place: *the demonstration of a washing machine.* **4** an open show or expression: *The mother greeted her long lost son with every demonstration of joy.* **5** an exhibition of feelings or attitudes by means of a parade, meeting, etc. **6** a display of military strength to frighten or deceive an enemy. **7** in logic, an argument or series of propositions that leads to a conclusion. **8** in mathematics, the process of proving that certain assumptions necessarily produce a certain result.

de·mon·stra·tive (di mon′strə tiv) *adj.* **1** expressing one's affections freely and openly: *The girl's demonstrative greetings embarrassed her shy brother.* **2** showing clearly; explanatory. **3** giving proof; conclusive. **4** in grammar, pointing out. *This* and *that* are demonstrative pronouns and also demonstrative adjectives. —*n.* in grammar, a pronoun or adjective that points out. —**de·mon′stra·tive·ly,** *adv.* —**de·mon′stra·tive·ness,** *n.*

☛ *This, that, these, those* are called **demonstrative adjectives** or **pronouns** according to their use in a sentence. Adjective: *This car we bought in May.* Pronoun: *This costs a good bit more than those.*

dem·on·stra·tor (dem′ən strā′tər) *n.* **1** a person who demonstrates. **2** a person who takes part in a demonstration. **3** a vehicle, machine, etc. used by a seller to demonstrate the qualities of his product: *He bought the demonstrator at a reduced price.* **4** an instructor who teaches by practical demonstration, as in a medical or dental school.

de·mor·al·i·za·tion (di môr′əl ə zā′shən or di môr′əl ī zā′shən) *n.* **1** a demoralizing. **2** a being demoralized.

de·mor·al·ize (di môr′əl īz′) *v.* **-ized, -iz·ing.** **1** corrupt the morals of: *The drug habit demoralizes people.* **2** weaken the spirit, courage, or discipline of; dishearten: *Lack of food and ammunition demoralized the besieged soldiers.*

3 throw into confusion or disorder: *Threats of war demoralized the stock market.* —**de·mor′a·liz′er,** *n.*

de·mote (di mōt′) *v.* **-mot·ed, -mot·ing.** put back to a lower grade; reduce in rank. [< *de-* + *(pro)mote*]

de·mot·ic (di mot′ik) *adj.* of the common people; popular. —*n.* a simplified form of ancient Egyptian writing. [< Gk. *demotikos* < *dēmos* the people]

de·mo·tion (di mō′shən) *n.* **1** the act of demoting. **2** the fact of being demoted.

de·mount (dē mount′) *v.* remove from a mounting.

de·mount·a·ble (dē moun′tə bəl) *adj.* that can be removed: *a demountable wheel rim.*

de·mul·cent (di mul′sənt) *adj.* soothing. —*n.* a soothing ointment or medicine. [< L *demulcens, -entis,* ppr. of *demulcere* < *de-* + *mulcere* soothe]

de·mur (di mėr′) *v.* **-murred, -mur·ring,** *n.* —*v.* **1** object: *The clerk demurred at working overtime.* **2** in law, enter a demurrer. —*n.* an objection. [< OF *demurer* < L *demorari* < *de-* (intensive) + *morari* delay]

de·mure (di mūr′) *adj.* **-mur·er, -mur·est.** **1** quiet and modest in behavior: *a demure young lady.* **2** artificially proper; assuming an air of modesty; coy: *the demure smile of a flirt.* [< obs. *mure,* adj., demure < OF *meür* < L *maturus* mature] —**de·mure′ly,** *adv.* —**de·mure′ness,** *n.* —**Syn. 1** See **modest.**

de·mur·rage (di mėr′ij) *n.* **1** the failure to load or unload a ship, railway car, etc. within the time specified. **2** the payment made for this failure. [< *demur*]

de·mur·rer (di mėr′ər) *n.* **1** a person who objects. **2** an objection. **3** in law, a plea that a lawsuit be dismissed (even if the facts are as alleged by the opposite party) because the facts do not sustain his claim.

den (den) *n.* *v.* **denned, den·ning.** —*n.* **1** the place where a wild animal lives: *The bear's den was a cave.* **2** a place where thieves, etc. have their headquarters. **3** a small dirty room. **4** a private room for reading, writing, or relaxation, usually small and cosy. **5** a group of eight to ten Cub Scouts.
—*v.* **1** live in or as if in a den. **2** escape into or hide in a den. [OE *denn*] —**den′like′,** *adj.*

Den. Denmark.

de·nar·i·us (di nãr′ē əs) *n.* **-nar·i·i** (-nãr′ē ī′ or -nãr′ē ē′). in ancient Rome: **1** a silver coin. **2** a gold coin. [< L *denarius* containing ten (here, ten times the value of an *as*[2]) < *deni* ten at a time. Doublet of DINAR, DENIER[2].]

de·na·tion·al·ize (dē nash′ən əl īz′ or -nash′nəl īz′) *v.* **-ized, -iz·ing. 1** deprive of national rights, scope, or character. **2** of industries, return from national to private control or ownership. —**de·na′tion·al·i·za′tion,** *n.*

de·nat·u·ral·ize (dē nach′ə rəl īz′ or -nach′rəl īz′) *v.* **-ized, -iz·ing. 1** make unnatural. **2** withdraw citizenship from (a naturalized citizen).
—**de·nat′u·ral·i·za′tion,** *n.*

de·na·ture (dē nā′chər) *v.* **-tured, -tur·ing. 1** change the nature of. **2** make (alcohol, food, etc.) unfit for drinking or eating without destroying its usefulness for other purposes. —**de·na′tur·a′tion,** *n.*

de·na·zi·fy (dē nät′sə fī′ or -nat′sə fī′) *v.* **-fied, -fy·ing.** rid of Nazi doctrines or Nazi influences.
—**de·na′zi·fi·ca′tion,** *n.*

den·drite (den′drīt) *n.* **1** in geology: **a** a stone or mineral with branching, tree-like markings. **b** a tree-like marking. **2** in anatomy, the branching part at the receiving end of a nerve cell. [< Gk. *dendritēs* of a tree < *dendron* tree]

A dendrite (def. 1)

Den·eb (den′eb) *n.* a first magnitude star in the constellation Cygnus. [< Arabic *dhanab* tail]

de·neu·tral·ize (dē nū′trəl īz′ or -nü′trəl īz′) *v.* **-ized, -iz·ing.** abolish the neutral status of (a country, territory, etc.). —**de·neu′tral·i·za′tion,** *n.*

den·gue (deng′gā or deng′gē) *n.* an infectious fever with skin rash and severe pain in the joints and muscles. [< Sp. < Swahili *kidinga popo*]

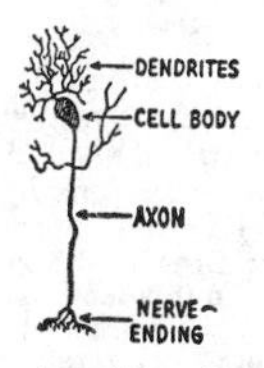

Dendrites (def. 2)

hat, āge, cãre, fär; let, ēqual, tėrm; it, īce
hot, ōpen, ôrder; oil, out; cup, pu̇t, rüle, ūse
əbove, takən, pencəl, lemən, circəs
ch, child; ng, long; sh, ship
th, thin; ᴛʜ, then; zh, measure

de·ni·al (di nī′əl) *n.* **1** the act of saying that something is not true. **2** the act of saying that one does not hold to or accept something: *a public denial of communism.* **3** a refusing. **4** a disowning; a refusing to acknowledge. **5** a doing without things that one wants; self-denial.

de·ni·er[1] (di nī′ər) *n.* a person who denies. [< *deny*]

den·ier[2] (den′yər or də nēr′ *for 1;* də nēr′ *for 2 and 3*) *n.* **1** a unit of weight used to express the fineness of silk, rayon, or nylon yarn. **2** formerly, in France, a coin having little value. **3** a very small sum. [< OF < L *denarius.* Doublet of DINAR, DENARIUS.]

den·i·grate (den′ə grāt′) *v.* **-grat·ed, -grat·ing. 1** defame; blacken the reputation of (someone). **2** make black; blacken. [< L *denigrare* blacken thoroughly < *de-* (intensive) + *nigrare* blacken < *niger* black]
—**Syn. 1** sully, stain.

den·i·gra·tion (den′ə grā′shən) *n.* the act of blackening a reputation; defamation.

den·im (den′əm) *n.* **1** a heavy, coarse cotton cloth with a diagonal weave, used for work pants, upholstery, sports clothes, etc. **2 denims,** *pl.* overalls or pants made of denim. [short for F *serge de Nîmes* serge of Nîmes]

de·ni·tri·fy (dē nī′trə fī′) *v.* **-fied, -fy·ing.** in chemistry: **1** remove nitrogen or its compounds from. **2** change (nitrates) by reduction into nitrites, nitrogen, or ammonia.

den·i·zen (den′ə zən) *n.* **1** an inhabitant; occupant: *Fish are denizens of the sea.* **2** a foreigner who is given certain rights of citizenship. **3** a foreign word, plant, animal, etc. that has been naturalized: *The common English sparrow is a denizen of North America; it was first brought from Europe about 1850.* [ME < AF *denzein* < *denz* within < LL < L *de* from + *intus* within]

de·nom·i·nate (*v.* di nom′ə nāt′; *adj.* di nom′ə nit′ or -nom′ə nāt′) *v.* **-na·ted, -nat·ing,** *adj.* —*v.* give a name to; name. —*adj.* called by a specific name. 6 ft., 4 oz., 10 in., and 9 lb. are **denominate numbers.** [< L *denominare* < *de-* (intensive) + *nomen* name]

de·nom·i·na·tion (di nom′ə nā′shən) *n.* **1** a name for a group or class of things; name. **2** a religious group or sect: *Presbyterians and Baptists are two large Protestant denominations.* **3** a class or kind of units: *Reducing 5 ft. and 10 in. to the same denomination gives 70 in. Reducing 5/12, 1/3, and 1/6 to the same denomination gives 5/12, 4/12, and 2/12. The Canadian coin of the lowest denomination is the cent.* **4** the act of naming.

de·nom·i·na·tion·al (di nom′ə nā′shən əl or di nom′ə nāsh′nəl) *adj.* having to do with some religious denomination or denominations; controlled by a religious denomination; sectarian. —**de·nom′i·na′tion·al·ly,** *adv.*

de·nom·i·na·tion·al·ism (di nom′ə nā′shən əl iz′əm or di nom′ə nāsh′nəl iz′əm) *n.* **1** denominational principles. **2** a division into denominations.

de·nom·i·na·tive (di nom′ə nə tiv or -nom′ə nā′tiv) *adj.* **1** giving a distinctive name; naming. **2** in grammar, formed from a noun or an adjective. *Centre* and *whiten* are denominative verbs. —*n.* in grammar, a word formed from a noun or an adjective. —**de·nom′i·na′tive·ly,** *adv.*

de·nom·i·na·tor (di nom′ə nā′tər) *n.* **1** in mathematics, the number below the line in a fraction, stating the size of the parts in their relation to the whole. In 3/4, 4 is the denominator, and 3 is the numerator. **2** a person or thing that names.

de·no·ta·tion (dē′nō tā′shən) *n.* **1** a meaning, especially the exact, literal meaning. **2** an indication; a denoting or marking out. **3** a mark or sign; symbol. **4** in logic: **a** the class, type, or number of things included in a given term; extension. **b** a value, quantity, etc. represented by a symbol.

☛ The **denotation** of a word is the exact, literal meaning of that word as contrasted with its **connotation,** the additional meaning suggested or implied by the word. The choice of words having certain connotations often indicates the intention of the speaker or writer to influence his hearers, either favorably or otherwise towards what he is describing. The denotation of *slender* and *skinny* is "thin," but *slender* connotes approval and *skinny* disapproval.

de·note (di nōt′) *v.* **-not·ed, -not·ing. 1** be the sign of; indicate: *A fever usually denotes sickness.* **2** be a name for; mean. **3** stand for as a symbol: *The sign '×' denotes multiplication.* [< F *dénoter* < L *denotare* < *de-* down + *nota* mark] ☛ See **denotation** for usage note.

de·noue·ment or **dé·noue·ment** (dā nü′mon; *French,* dā nü mäN′) *n.* the solution or unravelling of a plot in a play, a story, etc.; outcome; end. [< F *dénouement* < *dénouer* untie < L *de* down from + *nodare* tie]

de·nounce (di nouns′) *v.* **-nounced, -nounc·ing. 1** condemn publicly; express strong disapproval of. **2** inform against; accuse: *He denounced his own brother to the military police as a spy.* **3** give formal notice of the termination of (a treaty, etc.). [ME < OF *denoncier* < L *denuntiare* < *de-* (intensive) + *nuntius* messenger] **—de·nounc′er,** *n.*

de·nounce·ment (di nouns′mənt) *n.* the act of denouncing; denunciation.

de nou·veau (də nü vō′) *French.* again; afresh; anew.

de no·vo (dē nō′vō) *Latin.* anew; starting again.

D. en Ph. Docteur en Philosophie; Doctor of Philosophy.

dense (dens) *adj.* **den·ser, dens·est. 1** closely packed together; thick: *a dense fog.* **2** profound; intense; impenetrable: *dense ignorance.* **3** stupid. **4** in photography, (of a developed negative) relatively opaque, with strong contrasts of light and shade. [< L *densus*] **—dense′ly,** *adv.* **—dense′ness,** *n.* **—Syn. 1** compact.

den·si·ty (den′sə tē) *n.* **-ties. 1** a dense condition or quality; having parts very close together; compactness; thickness: *The density of the forest prevented us from seeing more than a little way ahead.* **2** the quantity of anything per unit area: *population density.* **3** in physics, the quantity of matter in a unit of volume; the ratio of the mass of a given volume of a substance to that of an equal volume of a standard substance. Water is the standard for solids and liquids, and hydrogen or air for gases. **4** in electricity: **a** the quantity of electricity per unit of area on a charged surface. **b** current density. **5** in photography, the relative opaqueness of a developed negative. **6** stupidity.

dent[1] (dent) *n.* **1** a hollow made by a blow or pressure: *Bullets had made dents in the steel helmet.* **2** an impression, especially one that weakens or damages: *The purchase of a new television set made a bad dent in our bank account.* —*v.* **1** make a dent in. **2** become dented. [ME *dente,* var. of *dint*]

dent[2] (dent) *n.* **1** a toothlike part, as in a gearwheel, comb, etc. **2** a notch; indentation. [< OF *dent* tooth < L *dens, dentis*]

den·tal (den′təl) *adj.* **1** of or for the teeth. **2** of or for a dentist's work. **3** in phonetics, of speech sounds, produced by placing the tip of the tongue against or near the back of the upper front teeth: *French speakers pronounce the consonants* (t) *and* (d) *as dental sounds, whereas in English* (t) *and* (d) *are alveolar.*
—*n.* in phonetics, a consonantal sound produced by placing the tip of the tongue against or near the back of the upper front teeth. [< L *dens, dentis* tooth]

den·tate (den′tāt) *adj.* having toothlike projections; toothed; notched. [< L *dentatus* < *dens, dentis* tooth]

A dentate leaf

den·ti·frice (den′tə fris) *n.* a paste, powder, or liquid for cleaning the teeth. [< F < L *dentifricium* < *dens, dentis* tooth + *fricare* rub]

den·tin (den′tin) *n.* dentine.

den·tine (den′tēn or den′tin) *n.* the hard, bony material beneath the enamel of a tooth, forming the main part of a tooth. [< L *dens, dentis* tooth]

den·tist (den′tist) *n.* a doctor whose work is the care of teeth. A dentist fills cavities in teeth, cleans, straightens, and extracts them, and supplies artificial teeth. [< F *dentiste* < *dent* tooth < L *dens, dentis*]

den·tist·ry (den′tis trē) *n.* the work, art, or profession of a dentist.

den·ti·tion (den tish′ən) *n.* **1** the growth of teeth; teething. **2** the kind, number, and arrangement of the teeth: *Dogs and wolves have the same dentition.* [< L *dentitio, -onis* < *dens, dentis* tooth]

den·toid (den′toid) *adj.* like a tooth.

den·ture (den′chər) *n.* **1** a set of artificial teeth. **2** an artificial tooth or group of teeth. [< F *denture* < *dent* tooth < L *dens, dentis*]

den·tur·ist (den′chər ist) *n.* a person trained to make and fit dentures.

de·nu·da·tion (dē′nyü dā′shən or den′yü dā′shən) *n.* **1** a denuding. **2** a denuded condition. **3** in geology, the laying bare of rock, especially by erosion.

de·nude (di nüd′ or -nüd′) *v.* **-nud·ed, -nud·ing. 1** make bare; strip of clothing, covering, etc. **2** in geology, lay (a rock, etc.) bare by removing what lies above, especially by erosion. [< L *denudare* < *de-* (intensive) + *nudus* bare]

de·nun·ci·a·tion (di nun′sē ā′shən) *n.* **1** public condemnation; expression of strong disapproval. **2** the act of informing against; accusation. **3** a formal notice of the intention to end a treaty, etc. **4** a declaration of a curse, revenge, etc.; warning; threat. [< L *denuntiatio, -onis* < *denuntiare.* See DENOUNCE.] **—de·nun′ci·a′tor,** *n.*

de·nun·ci·a·to·ry (di nun′sē ə tô′rē or di nun′shē ə tô′rē) *adj.* condemning; accusing; threatening.

Den·ver sandwich (den′vər) western sandwich. [< *Denver,* the capital of Colorado]

de·ny (di nī′) *v.* **-nied, -ny·ing. 1** declare (something) is not true: *The prisoner denied the charges against him. They denied the existence of disease in the town.* **2** say that one does not hold to or accept: *deny a political party.* **3** refuse: *I could not deny her so small a favor.* **4** refuse to acknowledge; disown: *He denied his signature.* **5 deny oneself,** do without the things one wants. **6 deny oneself to,** refuse to see: *Illness forced Mrs. Smith to deny herself to all callers.* [< F *dénier* < L *denegare* < *de-* completely + *negare* say no]
Syn. 1 Deny, contradict = declare something not true. **Deny** = state definitely or emphatically that something is untrue or cannot be true: *He denied that he planned to leave town.* **Contradict** suggests a more positive speaking against what has been said and stating emphatically that the opposite is true: *He contradicts everything I say, even if he has to insist that black is white.* **4** repudiate, disclaim.

de·o·dar (dē′ə där′) *n.* a cedar tree of the Himalayas, cultivated for shade. [< Hind. < Skt. *devadaru* wood of the gods]

de·o·dor·ant (dē ō′dər ənt) *n.* a preparation that destroys or prevents odors. —*adj.* that destroys or prevents odors.

de·o·dor·ize (dē ō′dər īz′) *v.* **-ized, -iz·ing. 1** destroy or prevent the odor of. **2** free from odor. **—de·o′dor·i·za′tion,** *n.* **—de·o′dor·iz′er,** *n.*

De·o gra·ti·as (dē′ō grā′shē as or grä′tē əs) *Latin.* thanks to God.

De·o vo·len·te (dē′ō vō len′tē or vō len′tā) *Latin.* if God is willing.

de·ox·i·dize (dē ok′sə dīz′) *v.* **-dized, -diz·ing.** remove oxygen from. **—de ox′i·di·za′tion,** *n.* **—de·ox′i·diz′er,** *n.*

de·ox·y·gen·ate (dē ok′sə jə nāt′) *v.* **-at·ed, -at·ing.** remove oxygen from; deoxygenize. **—de·ox′y·gen·a′tion,** *n.*

de·ox·y·ri·bo·nu·cle·ic acid (dē ok′sə rī′bō nū klē′ik or -nü klē′ik) in biochemistry, a complex nucleic acid contained in genes and known to have an important effect on the genetic activity of the chromosomes. *Abbrev.:* DNA [< *de-* from, away + *oxy*(*gen*) + *ribonucleic acid*]

dep. *pl.* **deps. 1** deputy. **2** department. **3** deponent. **4** deposit. **5** depot.

de·part (di pärt′) *v.* **1** go away; leave: *The train departs at 6:15.* **2** turn away; change (*from*): *He departed from his usual manner.* **3** go away from (chiefly used of *life*): *He departed this life at the age of seventy.* **4** die. [ME < OF < LL *departire* divide < L *de-* away + *pars* part]
Syn. 1 Depart, withdraw, retire = go away or leave; all are formal words in this sense. **Depart** suggests parting or separating oneself from a person, place, or thing: *He departed from his home.* **Withdraw** and **retire** = go apart or remove oneself from a place or someone's presence, usually for a good reason: *I withdrew* (*retired*) *while they discussed my qualifications.* **2** diverge, deviate.

hat, āge, cãre, fär; let, ēqual, tėrm; it, īce
hot, ōpen, ôrder; oil, out; cup, pu̇t, rüle, ūse
əbove, takən, pencəl, lemən, circəs
ch, child; ng, long; sh, ship
th, thin; ᴛʜ, then; zh, measure

de·part·ed (di pär′tid) *n.sing.* or *pl.* a dead person or persons. —*adj.* **1** dead. **2** gone; past.

de·part·ment (di pärt′mənt) *n.* **1** a separate part; a special branch; division: *the fire department of a municipal government.* **2** a main division of governmental administration. **3** a special division within a company, store, etc.: *the legal department, the furniture department.* **4** a section within a university, college, or school, giving instruction in a certain field: *the history department.* **5** one of the administrative districts into which France is divided.

de·part·men·tal (dē′pärt men′təl) *adj.* **1** having to do with a department. **2** divided into departments.

de·part·men·tal·ize (dē′ pärt men′tə līz′) *v.* **-ized, -iz·ing. 1** divide into departments. **2** arrange, classify, or restrict as if in departments. **—de′part·men′ta·li·za′tion,** *n.*

department store a store that is organized into departments where many different kinds of merchandise and services are sold.

de·par·ture (di pär′chər) *n.* **1** the act of going away; the act of leaving. **2** a turning away; change: *a departure from our old custom.* **3** a starting on a new course of action or thought. **4** death.

de·pend (di pend′) *v.* **1** rely; trust: *You can depend on the word of your friends.* **2** rely for support or help: *Children depend on their parents.* **3** result from another thing; be controlled or influenced by something else: *The success of our picnic will depend partly upon the weather.* **4** hang down. **5 depend on,** be a result of. **6 that depends,** the answer will be determined by certain conditions or actions that are not yet definitely known or understood: "*That depends,*" *answered the cook.* [ME < OF *dependre* < L *dependere* < *de-* from + *pendere* hand] **—de·pend′er,** *n.* **—Syn. 1, 2** See **rely.**

de·pend·a·bil·i·ty (di pen′də bil′ə tē) *n.* reliability; trustworthiness.

de·pend·a·ble (di pen′də bəl) *adj.* reliable; trustworthy. **—de·pend′a·ble·ness,** *n.* **—de·pend′a·bly,** *adv.*

de·pend·ant (di pen′dənt) *n.* a person who depends on someone else for support: *A man's wife and children are usually his dependants.* —*adj.* dependent.

de·pend·ence (di pen′dəns) *n.* **1** reliance on another for support or help. **2** reliance; trust. **3** the condition of being a result of another thing; the fact of being controlled or influenced by something else: *the dependence of crops on the weather.* **4** a person or thing relied on.

de·pend·en·cy (di pen′dən sē) *n.* **-cies. 1** a country or territory controlled by another country: *Gibraltar is a dependency of the United Kingdom.* **2** dependence. **3** a thing that depends on another for existence or help.

de·pend·ent (di pen′dənt) *adj.* **1** relying on another for support or help: *A child is dependent on its parents.* **2** resulting from another thing; controlled or influenced by something else: *Good crops are dependent on the right kind of weather.* **3** hanging down. **4** in grammar, subordinate: *a dependent clause.* —*n.* a dependant. **—de·pend′ent·ly,** *adv.* **—Syn.** *adj.* **2** contingent, conditional.

de·pict (di pikt′) *v.* **1** represent by drawing, painting, or carving; picture. **2** describe in words, music, etc.; portray. [< L *depictus,* pp. of *depingere* < *de-* + *pingere* paint] **—de·pict′er,** *n.*

de·pic·tion (di pik′shən) *n.* **1** the act of depicting; description. **2** a picture, carving, etc. **3** a description in words, music, etc.

dep·i·late (dep′ə lāt′) *v.* **-lat·ed, -lat·ing.** remove hair from. [< L *depilare* < *de-* from + *pilus* hair] **—dep′i·la′tion,** *n.*

de·pil·a·to·ry (di pil′ə tô′rē) *adj. n.* **-ries.** —*adj.* capable of removing hair. —*n.* a paste, liquid, or other preparation for removing hair.

de·plete (di plēt′) *v.* **-plet·ed, -plet·ing.** empty; exhaust: *The traveller went home because his funds were depleted.* [< L *depletus,* pp. of *deplere* empty < *de-* + *-plere* fill]

de·ple·tion (di plē′shən) *n.* **1** a depleting. **2** the state of being depleted.

de·plor·a·ble (di plôr′ə bəl) *adj.* **1** to be deplored; regrettable; lamentable: *a deplorable accident.* **2** wretched; miserable. **—de·plor′a·ble·ness,** *n.* **—de·plor′a·bly,** *adv.*

de·plore (di plôr′) *v.* **-plored, -plor·ing.** be very sorry about; regret deeply; lament. [< L *deplorare* < *de-* + *plorare* weep] **—Syn.** bewail, bemoan.

de·ploy (di ploi′) *v.* **1** spread out (troops, military units, etc.) from a column into a long battle line. **2** distribute (personnel, resources, etc.) in convenient positions for future use. [< F *déployer* < *dé-* + *ployer* < L *plicare* fold] **—de·ploy′ment,** *n.*

de·po·lar·ize (dē pō′lər īz′) *v.* **-ized, -iz·ing.** destroy or neutralize the polarity or polarization of. **—de·po′lar·i·za′tion.** *n.*

de·pone (di pōn′) *v.* **-poned, -pon·ing.** testify in writing under oath. [< L *deponere* put down (in Med.L, testify) < *de-* down + *ponere* put]

de·po·nent (di pō′nənt) *n.* **1** a person who testifies, especially in writing, under oath. **2** in Greek and Latin grammar, a verb passive in form but active in meaning. —*adj.* having passive form but active meaning. [< L *deponens, -entis,* ppr. of *deponere* < *de-* away, down + *ponere* put]

de·pop·u·late (dē pop′yu̇ lāt′) *v.* **-lat·ed, -lat·ing.** deprive of inhabitants: *The conquerors depopulated the enemy's country, driving the inhabitants away or killing them.* **—de·pop′u·la′tor,** *n.*

de·pop·u·la·tion (dē pop′yu̇ lā′shən) *n.* **1** a depopulating. **2** a being depopulated.

de·port (di pôrt′) *v.* **1** banish; expel; remove. When an alien is deported, he is sent out of the country, usually back to his native land. **2** behave or conduct (oneself) in a particular manner: *The boys were trained to deport themselves like gentlemen.* [< F *déporter* < L *deportare* < *de-* away + *portare* carry] **—de·port′er,** *n.* **—Syn. 1** See **banish.**

de·por·ta·tion (dē′pôr tā′shən) *n.* banishment; expulsion; removal: *Deportation of criminals from England to Australia was once common.*

de·port·ment (di pôrt′mənt) *n.* **1** the way a person acts; behavior; conduct: *A gentleman is known by his deportment.* **2** good bearing; graceful movement: *Young ladies once took lessons in deportment as a part of their regular studies.*

de·pos·al (di pōz′əl) *n.* deposing; deposition.

de·pose (di pōz′) *v.* **-posed, -pos·ing. 1** put out of office or a position of authority: *The king was deposed by the revolution.* **2** declare under oath; testify: *He deposed that he had seen the prisoner on the day of the murder.* [ME < OF *deposer* < *de-* down (< L) + *poser* put. See POSE[1].] **—de·pos′able,** *adj.* **—de·pos′er,** *n.*

de·pos·it (di poz′it) *v.* **1** put down; lay down; leave lying: *The flood deposited a layer of mud in the streets.* **2** put in a place for safe-keeping: *People deposit money in banks.* **3** pay as a pledge to do something or to pay more later. If you deposit part of the price, most stores will keep an article for you until you can pay the rest. —*n.* **1** something laid down or left lying: *There is often a deposit of mud and sand at the mouth of a river.* **2** something put in a place for safe-keeping: *Money put in a bank is a deposit.* **3** a sum of money paid as a pledge or security: *In the election, one of the candidates lost his deposit.* **4** the act of depositing. **5** a mass of some mineral in rock or in the ground. **6 on deposit, a** in a place for safe-keeping. **b** in a bank. [< L *depositus,* pp. of *deponere* < *de-* away + *ponere* put]

de·pos·i·tar·y (di poz′ə ter′ē) *n.* **-tar·ies. 1** a person or company that receives something for safe-keeping; trustee. **2** a depository; storehouse.

dep·o·si·tion (dē′pə zish′ən or dep′ə zish′ən) *n.* **1** the act of putting out of office or a position of authority. **2** in law: **a** the act of testifying under oath. **b** the testimony so given. **c** a sworn statement in writing: *A deposition made before the witness left town was used as evidence in the trial.* **3** an act of depositing. **4** something deposited; deposit.

de·pos·i·tor (di poz′ə tər) *n.* **1** a person who deposits. **2** a person who deposits money in a bank.

de·pos·i·to·ry (di poz′ə tô′rē) *n.* **-ries. 1** a place where a thing is put for safe-keeping; storehouse. **2** depositary; trustee.

dep·ot (dep′ō or dē′pō) *n.* **1** a bus or railway station. **2** a storehouse, especially for military supplies. **3** a military recruiting and distribution centre. [< F *dépôt* < L *depositum* < *deponere.* See DEPOSIT.]

de·prave (di prāv′) *v.* **-praved, -prav·ing.** make bad; corrupt: *Too much liquor often depraves a person's character.* [ME < L *depravare* < *de-* + *pravus* crooked, wrong] **—de·pra·va′tion,** *n.* **—de·prav′er,** *n.*

de·praved (di prāvd′) *adj.* corrupt; perverted. **—Syn.** See **corrupt.**

de·prav·i·ty (di prav′ə tē) *n.* **-ties. 1** wickedness; corruption. **2** a corrupt act; bad practice.

dep·re·cate (dep′rə kāt′) *v.* **-cat·ed, -cat·ing.** express strong disapproval of; plead against; protest against: *Lovers of peace deprecate war.* [< LL *deprecari* plead in excuse, avert by prayer < *de-* + *precari* pray] **—dep′re·cat′ing·ly,** *adv.* **—dep′re·ca′tor,** *n.*

☛ **deprecate, depreciate.** Do not confuse *deprecate* = express strong disapproval of, with *depreciate* = lessen in value or price. Contrast these sentences: *I feel I must deprecate the course the club is following. Naturally a car depreciates after a number of years of service.*

dep·re·ca·tion (dep′rə kā′shən) *n.* a strong expression of disapproval; a pleading or protesting against something.

dep·re·ca·to·ry (dep′rə kə tô′rē) *adj.* **1** deprecating. **2** *Informal.* apologetic.

de·pre·ci·ate (di prē′shē āt′) *v.* **-at·ed, -at·ing. 1** lessen the value or price of. **2** lessen in value: *Certain goods depreciate if they are kept very long.* **3** speak slightingly of; belittle: *He depreciates the value of exercise.* [< L *depretiare* < *de-* + *pretium* price] **—de·pre′ci·at′ing·ly,** *adv.* **—de·pre′ci·a′tor,** *n.* ☛ See **deprecate** for usage note.

de·pre·ci·a·tion (di prē′shē ā′shən) *n.* **1** a lessening or lowering in value: *Machinery undergoes depreciation as it is used or becomes obsolete.* **2** the amount of such loss of value, or the allowance made for it in accounting. **3** a speaking slightingly of; a belittling.

de·pre·ci·a·to·ry (di prē′shē ə tô′rē) *adj.* tending to depreciate, disparage, or undervalue.

dep·re·da·tion (dep′rə dā′shən) *n.* the act of plundering; robbery; a ravaging. [< L *depraedatio, -onis* < *depraedare* pillage < *de-* + *praeda* booty]

de·press (di pres′) *v.* **1** make sad or gloomy; cause to have low spirits: *She was depressed by the bad news from home.* **2** press down; push down; lower: *depress the keys of a piano.* **3** lower in amount or value. **4** reduce the activity of; weaken: *Some medicines depress the action of the heart.* [< OF *depresser* < L *depressus,* pp. of *deprimere* < *de-* + *premere* press] **—de·press′ing·ly,** *adv.* **—de·press′or,** *n.* **—Syn. 1** deject, sadden.

de·pres·sant (di pres′ənt) *adj.* decreasing the rate of vital activities; quieting. **—***n.* a medicine that lessens pain or excitement; sedative or tranquillizer.

de·pressed (di prest′) *adj.* **1** gloomy; low-spirited; sad. **2** pressed down; lowered. **3** in botany and zoology, flattened down; broader than high. **—Syn. 1** See **sad.**

depressed area a region characterized by unemployment, poverty, etc.

de·pres·sion (di presh′ən) *n.* **1** the act of pressing down; a sinking; a lowering: *A rapid depression of the mercury in a barometer usually indicates a storm.* **2** a depressed condition. **3** a low place; hollow: *The roads were dry, but water still filled depressions in the ground.* **4** sadness; gloominess; low spirits: *In a fit of depression the invalid killed himself.* **5** in medicine, a lowering of the vital functions or powers. **6** a reduction of activity; dullness of trade: *Many men lose their jobs during times of business depression.* **7 the Depression,** the economic depression that, in North America and W. Europe, followed the financial crisis of 1929 and lasted almost ten years. **8** in meteorology, an area of low barometric pressure; low. **—Syn. 4** dejection, melancholy.

dep·ri·va·tion (dep′rə vā′shən) *n.* **1** the act of depriving. **2** the state of being deprived; loss; privation.

de·prive (di prīv′) *v.* **-prived, -priv·ing. 1** take away from by force: *The people deprived the cruel tyrant of his power.* **2** keep from having or doing: *Worrying deprived him of sleep.* [ME < OF *depriver* < *de-* (intensive) + *priver* deprive < L *privare,* originally, exempt] **—de·priv′er,** *n.* **—Syn. 1** dispossess, divest.

de pro·fun·dis (dē′prō fun′dis or dā′ prō fůn′dis) *Latin.* from the depths (of sorrow, misery, despair, etc.). [initial words of Psalm cxxx]

dept. *pl.* **depts. 1** department. **2** deputy.

depth (depth) *n.* **1** the quality of being deep; deepness. **2** the distance from top to bottom: *the depth of a hole.* **3** the distance from front to back: *The depth of our house is 125 feet.* **4** a deep place. **5** the deepest part: *in the depths of the earth.* **6** the most central part; middle: *in the depth of the forest.* **7** intensity (of feelings, etc.). **8** profoundness: *A philosopher should have depth of mind.* **9** lowness of pitch. **10** intensity of color, etc. **11 be out of one's depth, a** be in water so deep that one cannot touch bottom. **b** try to study or talk about something that one cannot understand. [ME *depth(e)* < OE *dēop* deep]

depth bomb depth charge.

depth charge an explosive charge dropped from a ship or airplane and set to explode at a certain depth under water.

depts. 1 departments. **2** deputies.

dep·u·ta·tion (dep′yů tā′shən) *n.* **1** the act of deputing. **2** a group of persons appointed to act for others.

de·pute (di pūt′) *v.* **-put·ed, -put·ing. 1** appoint (someone) to do one's work or to act in one's place: *The teacher deputed a pupil to take charge of the room while she was gone.* **2** give (work, authority, etc.) to another. [ME < OF < LL *deputare* assign < L *deputare* consider as < *de-* + *putare* think, count]

dep·u·tize (dep′yů tīz′) *v.* **-tized, -tiz·ing. 1** appoint as deputy. **2** act as deputy.

dep·u·ty (dep′yů tē) *n.* **-ties,** *adj.* **—***n.* **1** a person appointed to do the work of or to act in the place of another: *A deputy minister is an assistant to a minister in the cabinet.* **2** a representative to or in certain assemblies. In Quebec, the members of the Legislative Assembly are often called **deputies.** In France, the citizens elect deputies to the lower house of the national legislative body, formerly called the **Chamber of Deputies.**
—*adj.* acting as a deputy. [< F *député,* originally pp. of *députer* < LL *deputare.* See DEPUTE.] **—Syn.** *n.* **1** proxy, delegate.

der. 1 derivation. **2** derivative. **3** derived.

de·rail (dē rāl′) *v.* **1** cause (a train, etc.) to run off the rails. **2** run off the rails. **—de·rail′ment,** *n.*

de·range (di rānj′) *v.* **-ranged, -rang·ing. 1** disturb the order or arrangement of; throw into confusion. **2** make insane. [< F *déranger* < *dé-* away + *ranger* range]

de·range·ment (di rānj′mənt) *n.* **1** a disturbance of order or arrangement. **2** a mental disorder; insanity.

der·by (dėr′bē) *n.* **-bies. 1** a stiff hat that has a rounded crown and narrow brim; a bowler hat. **2** a contest or race: *a fishing derby, a dog derby.* [< *Derby*]

Der·by (dėr′bē; *Brit.,* där′bē *for 1*) *n.* **-bies. 1** a famous horse race in England, founded by the Earl of Derby in 1780 and run every year at Epsom Downs, near London. **2** any horse race of similar importance: *the Kentucky Derby.*

der·e·lict (der′ə likt′) *adj.* **1** abandoned; deserted; forsaken: *a derelict ship.* **2** failing in one's duty; negligent. **—***n.* **1** a ship abandoned at sea. **2** any worthless, deserted person or thing: *The ragged old derelict was begging for money to buy a meal.* [< L *derelictus,* pp. of *derelinquere* abandon < *de-* (intensive) + *re-* behind + *linquere* leave]

der·e·lic·tion (der′ə lik′shən) *n.* **1** a failure in one's duty; negligence. **2** an abandonment; desertion; forsaking.

de·ride (di rīd′) *v.* **-rid·ed, -rid·ing.** make fun of; laugh at in scorn; ridicule with contempt. [< L *deridere* < *de-* down + *ridere* laugh] **—de·rid′er,** *n.* **—de·rid′ing·ly,** *adv.* **—Syn.** jeer, scoff, mock. See **ridicule.**

de ri·gueur (də rē gœr′) *French.* required by etiquette; according to custom; proper.

hat, āge, cãre, fär; let, ēqual, tėrm; it, īce
hot, ōpen, ôrder; oil, out; cup, pu̇t, rüle, ūse
əbove, takən, pencəl, lemən, circəs
ch, child; ng, long; sh, ship
th, thin; ᴛʜ, then; zh, measure

de·ri·sion (di rizh′ən) *n.* 1 scornful laughter; ridicule; contempt. 2 an object of ridicule. [< L *derisio, -onis* < *deridere*. See DERIDE.]

de·ri·sive (di rī′siv) *adj.* mocking; ridiculing. **—de·ri′sive·ly,** *adv.* **—de·ri′sive·ness,** *n.*

de·ri·so·ry (di rī′sə rē) *adj.* 1 derisive. 2 laughable; deserving contempt.

deriv. 1 derivation. 2 derivative.

der·i·va·tion (der′ə vā′shən) *n.* 1 the act or fact of deriving. 2 the state of being derived. 3 the source; origin. 4 the system used by some languages for making new words from old, through use of prefixes and suffixes and other methods. *Example*: *quickness* = *quick* + suffix *-ness*. 5 a statement of how a word was formed.

de·riv·a·tive (di riv′ə tiv) *adj.* derived; not original. *—n.* 1 something derived. Words formed by adding prefixes and suffixes, etc. to other words are called derivatives. 2 in chemistry, a substance obtained from another by modification or by partial substitution of components. **—de·riv′a·tive·ly,** *adv.*

de·rive (di rīv′) *v.* **-rived, -riv·ing.** 1 get; receive; obtain: *A scholar derives knowledge from reading books.* 2 trace back to: *We derive the word "table" ultimately from the Latin word "tabula."* 3 come from a source or origin; originate. 4 trace (a word, custom, etc.) from or to a source of origin. 5 obtain by reasoning. 6 obtain (a chemical compound) from another by substituting a different element. [< MF < LL *derivare* lead off, draw off < L *de-* from + *rivus* stream] **—de·riv′a·ble,** *adj.* **—de·riv′er,** *n.*

der·ma (dėr′mə) *n.* 1 the sensitive layer of skin beneath the epidermis. See **epidermis** for diagram. 2 the skin. [< Gk. *derma* skin]

der·mal (dėr′məl) *adj.* of the skin.

der·ma·to·log·i·cal (dėr′mə tə loj′ə kəl) *adj.* of or having to do with dermatology.

der·ma·tol·o·gist (dėr′mə tol′ə jist) *n.* an expert in dermatology.

der·ma·tol·o·gy (dėr′mə tol′ə jē) *n.* the science that deals with the skin and its diseases.

der·ma·to·sis (dėr′mə tō′sis) *n.* any skin disease. [< Gk. *derma, -atos* skin + E *-osis*]

der·mis (dėr′mis) *n.* derma.

der·o·gate (der′ə gāt′) *v.* **-gat·ed, -gat·ing.** 1 take away; detract: *The king felt that summoning a parliament would derogate from his authority.* 2 become worse; degenerate. [< L *derogare* < *de-* down from + *rogare* ask]

der·o·ga·tion (der′ə gā′shən) *n.* 1 a lessening or impairment (of power, law, position, etc.); detraction. 2 the state of becoming worse; deterioration; debasement.

de·rog·a·tive (di rog′ə tiv) *adj.* derogatory. **—de·rog′a·tive·ly,** *adv.*

de·rog·a·to·ry (di rog′ə tô′rē) *adj.* 1 disparaging; belittling; showing an unfavorable opinion of some person or thing: *The word "skinny" has a derogatory connotation, but "slender" has not.* 2 lessening the value; detracting. **—de·rog′a·to′ri·ly,** *adv.*

der·rick (der′ik) *n.* 1 a machine for lifting and moving heavy objects. A derrick has a long arm that swings at an angle from the base of an upright post or frame. 2 a towerlike framework over an oil well, gas well, etc. which holds the drilling and hoisting machinery. [after *Derrick*, a 17th-century hangman at Tyburn, London]

A derrick (def. 1)

der·ring-do (der′ing dü′) *n.* *Archaic.* heroic daring; daring deeds. [alteration of ME *dorryng don* daring to do]

der·rin·ger (der′ən jər) *n.* a short pistol of relatively large calibre. [after H. *Derringer*, an American inventor]

der·ris (der′is) *n.* any of a group of climbing tropical plants of the pea family. The roots of some E. Indian species produce rotenone, a fish poison and insecticide. [< NL *Derris* < Gk. *derris* leather cover]

der·vish (dėr′vish) *n.* 1 a Moslem monk or friar. **Dancing dervishes** have a religious ceremony in which they dance and spin about violently. **Howling dervishes** chant and shout loudly. 2 a member of any of the tribes of upper Egypt and the Sudan who revolted against the British and Egyptians between 1880 and 1885. [< Turkish *dervīsh* < Persian *darvīsh*]

de·sal·i·nate (dē sal′ə nāt′) *v.* **-nat·ed, -nat·ing.** remove salt from, especially from sea water. **—de·sal′i·na′tion,** *n.*

des·cant (*v.* des kant′; *n.* des′kant) *v.* 1 talk at great length; discourse: *She descanted upon the wonders of her trip to Europe.* 2 in music, sing or play a melody with one or more additional melodies.
—n. 1 in music: **a** a composition having various parts. **b** the art of composing or performing descants. **c** a melody to be played or sung with one or more additional melodies. **d** the highest part or melody. 2 any song or melody. 3 an extended comment; discourse. [ME < OF *deschanter* < Med.L *discantare* < L *dis-* away + *cantus* song < *canere* sing]

de·scend (di send′) *v.* 1 go or come down from a higher place to a lower place: *The river descends to the sea.* 2 go from earlier to later time. 3 go from greater to smaller: *75-50-25 forms a series that descends.* 4 slope downward. 5 make a sudden attack (*on*): *The bandits descended on the people and took their money.* 6 be handed down from parent to child; pass by inheritance: *This land has belonged to our family for 150 years, descending from father to son.* 7 have as ancestors: *John is descended from a pioneer family.* 8 lower oneself; stoop: *Dishonest persons descend to cheating, lying, and stealing.* [ME < OF < L *descendere* < *de-* down + *scandere* climb]

de·scend·ant (di sen′dənt) *n.* 1 a person born of a certain family or group: *a descendant of the United Empire Loyalists.* 2 an offspring; child; great-grandchild, etc. You are a direct descendant of your parents, grandparents, great-grandparents, etc. *—adj.* descending; going or coming down.

de·scend·ent (di sen′dənt) *adj.* descending.

de·scent (di sent′) *n.* 1 a coming down or going down from a higher to a lower place: *the descent of a balloon.* 2 a downward slope. 3 a way or passage down; means of descending. 4 a handing down from parent to child; descending or coming down in a family line. 5 a family line; ancestry: *We can trace our descent to before 1750.* 6 a decline; sinking to a lower condition; fall. 7 a lowering of oneself. 8 a sudden attack. [ME < OF *descente* < *descendre* < L *descendere*. See DESCEND.]

de·scribe (di skrīb′) *v.* **-scribed, -scrib·ing.** 1 tell or write about: *The reporter described the accident in detail.* 2 give a picture of in words, music, etc. 3 draw the outline of; trace: *The skater described a figure 8.* [< L *describere* < *de-* from + *scribere* write] **—de·scrib′a·ble,** *adj.* **—de·scrib′er,** *n.*

Syn. 1 Describe, narrate = tell or write about something. **Describe** = tell what a person, place, or thing looks like or is like, by giving details of appearance, character, etc. and arranging them so that the hearer or reader will get a clear picture: *He described the people he saw from the window.* **Narrate** = tell a story, by arranging details of events so the hearer or reader will understand what happened: *He narrated the history of the Yukon gold rush.* 2 depict.

de·scrip·tion (di skrip′shən) *n.* 1 the act of describing; the act of giving a picture or account in words. 2 a composition or account that describes. 3 a picture in words, music, etc. 4 a kind or sort: *In the crowd there were people of every description.* 5 the act of tracing; the act of drawing in outline.

de·scrip·tive (di skrip′tiv) *adj.* 1 describing; that tells about by using description. 2 in grammar: **a** describing In the phrase *cold water*, *cold* is a descriptive adjective. **b** adding descriptive detail; non-restrictive. 3 of or having to do with an objective, factual description: *descriptive biology, descriptive linguistics.* **—de·scrip′tive·ly,** *adv.* **—de·scrip′tive·ness,** *n.*

de·scry (di skrī′) *v.* **-scried, -scry·ing.** catch sight of;

be able to see; make out: *The shipwrecked sailor at last descried an island far away on the horizon.* [ME < MF *descrier* proclaim < *des-* away + *crier* cry < L *quiritare*]

des·e·crate (des′ə krāt′) *v.* **-crat·ed, -crat·ing.** treat or use without respect; disregard the sacredness of: *The enemy desecrated the church by using it as a stable.* [< *de-* (do the opposite of) + (*con*)*secrate*] —**des′e·crat′er, des′e·cra′tor,** *n.*

des·e·cra·tion (des′ə krā′shən) *n.* **1** the act of desecrating: *The Puritans thought that work or amusement was a desecration of the Sabbath.* **2** the fact or state of being desecrated.

de·seg·re·gate (dē seg′rə gāt′) *v.* **-gat·ed, -gat·ing.** abolish segregation in.

de·seg·re·ga·tion (dē seg′rə gā′shən) *n.* the abolishment of the practice of segregating one race from another, especially Negroes from whites.

de·sen·si·tize (dē sen′sə tīz′) *v.* **-tized, -tiz·ing. 1** make less sensitive. **2** in photography, make less sensitive to light. —**de·sen′si·ti·za′tion,** *n.* —**de·sen′si·tiz′er,** *n.*

des·ert[1] (dez′ərt) *n.* **1** a dry, barren region, usually sandy and without trees. **2** a region that is not inhabited or cultivated; wilderness. **3** a place or environment that provides no stimulus to the intellect or imagination.
—*adj.* **1** dry; barren. **2** not inhabited or cultivated; wild: *Robinson Crusoe was shipwrecked on a desert island.* [ME < OF < LL *desertum* (thing) abandoned, pp. neut. of *deserere.* See DESERT[2].]

Syn. *n.* **1, 2 Desert, wilderness** = an uninhabited or uncultivated region. **Desert** emphasizes dryness and barrenness and applies to a region that is usually sandy and without water, trees, or inhabitants: *Great sections of desert in Arizona and California have been turned into rich agricultural areas by irrigation.* **Wilderness** emphasizes lack of trails and roads and applies particularly to a region where few men have ever been and that is covered with dense vegetation: *Large areas in northern Ontario are wilderness.*

de·sert[2] (di zėrt′) *v.* **1** go away and leave; abandon; forsake: *The man was guilty of deserting his family.* **2** run away from duty. **3** leave military service without permission. **4** fail; leave: *The boy's courage deserted him when he met the angry dog.* [< F < LL *desertare* < L *deserere* abandon < *de-* dis- + *serere* join]

Syn. 1 Desert, forsake, abandon = leave someone or something completely. **Desert** emphasizes breaking a promise, oath, etc. or running away from a duty, and therefore implies blame: *He deserted his country and helped the enemy.* **Forsake** emphasizes breaking off sentimental attachments and thus has emotional connotations, but does not necessarily suggest blame: *He forsook sports to study medicine.* **Abandon** emphasizes that the action is final and complete, though it may be voluntary or involuntary, necessary or resulting from a desire to avoid duty: *They abandoned the wrecked plane.*

de·sert[3] (di zėrt′) *n.* Usually, **deserts,** *pl.* what is deserved; a suitable reward or punishment: *The robber got his just deserts when he was sentenced to five years in prison.* [ME < OF *deserte,* pp. of *deservir* < L *deservire.* See DESERVE.]

de·sert·er (di zėr′tər) *n.* **1** a person who deserts. **2** a member of the armed services who runs away from duty or leaves military service without permission.

de·ser·tion (di zėr′shən) *n.* **1** a deserting. **2** a being deserted. **3** in law, a deliberate abandoning of one's husband or wife and of the related moral and legal obligations. **4** a running away from duty. **5** the leaving of military service without permission.

de·serve (di zėrv′) *v.* **-served, -serv·ing. 1** have a claim or right to; be worthy of: *Good work deserves good pay.* **2** be worthy: *He deserves well.* [ME < OF < L *deservire* serve well < *de-* (intensive) + *servire* serve] —**de·serv′er,** *n.* —**Syn. 1** merit.

de·serv·ed·ly (di zėr′vid lē) *adv.* according to what is deserved; justly; rightly: *deservedly punished.*

de·serv·ing (di zėr′ving) *adj.* **1** that deserves; worthy (of something). **2** worth helping. —**de·serv′ing·ly,** *adv.*

des·ha·bille (dez′ə bēl′; *French,* dā zä bē′) *n.* dishabille.

des·ic·cate (des′ə kāt′) *v.* **-cat·ed, -cat·ing. 1** dry thoroughly. **2** make dry. **3** preserve by drying thoroughly. **4** make or become intellectually or emotionally dry. [< L *desiccare* < *de-* out + *siccus* dry] —**des′ic·ca′tion,** *n.* —**des′ic·ca′tor,** *n.*

☛ **desiccate.** Observe the proper meaning of this word. Because desiccated foods have often been cut into small pieces, people sometimes suppose that *desiccate* means "cut up or shred."

de·sid·er·a·ta (di sid′ər ā′tə or di sid′ər at′ə) *n.* pl. of **desideratum.**

de·sid·er·a·tive (di sid′ər ə tiv or di sid′ə rā′tiv) *adj.* expressing, implying, or having desire. —*n.* in grammar, expressing the desire to perform the action signified by another verb from which it is derived.

de·sid·er·a·tum (di sid′ər ā′təm or di sid′ər at′əm) *n.* **-ta.** something desired or needed: *His consent is a desideratum.* [< L *desideratum,* pp. neut. of *desiderare* long for]

de·sign (di zīn′) *n.* **1** a drawing, plan, or sketch made to serve as a pattern from which to work: *a design for a machine.* **2** in painting, weaving, building, etc., an arrangement of detail, form, and color: *a wallpaper design in tan and brown.* **3** the art of making designs: *a school of design.* **4** a piece of artistic work. **5** a plan in mind to be carried out. **6** a scheme of attack; evil plan: *The thief had designs upon the safe.* **7** a purpose; aim; intention: *Whether by accident or design, he overturned the lamp.* **8** the underlying plan or conception; organization of parts in relation to the whole and to its purpose: *the evidence of design in a communication satellite, unity of design in a novel.* **9 by design,** on purpose; by intention. [< MF *desseign* < Ital. *disegno* < *disegnare* < L *designare.* See verb.]
—*v.* **1** make a first sketch of; plan out; arrange the form and color of; draw in outline: *design a dress.* **2** make drawings, sketches, plans, etc.: *He designs for a firm of dressmakers.* **3** plan out; form in the mind; contrive: *The author of this detective story has designed a good plot.* **4** have in mind to do; purpose: *Did you design this, or did it just happen?* **5** set apart; intend: *His parents designed him for the ministry.* [< F *désigner* < L *designare* < *de-* (intensive) + *signum* mark] —**Syn.** *n.* **5** See **plan. 7** See **intention.**

des·ig·nate (*v.* dez′ig nāt′; *adj.* dez′ig nit or dez′ig nāt′) *v.* **-nat·ed, -nat·ing,** *adj.* —*v.* **1** mark out; point out; indicate definitely: *Red lines designate main roads on this map. His uniform designates his rank.* **2** name; entitle: *The ruler of the country was designated king.* **3** select for duty, office, etc.; appoint: *That is the man designated to succeed the present Governor General.*
—*adj.* appointed; selected. [< L *designare.* See DESIGN.] —**des′ig·na′tor,** *n.*

des·ig·na·tion (dez′ig nā′shən) *n.* **1** the act of marking out; the act of pointing out; a definite indication: *The designation of places on a map should be clear.* **2** a descriptive title; name: *"Your Majesty" is a designation given to the Queen.* **3** the appointment or selection for a duty, office, position, etc.: *The designation of Cabinet officers is one of the powers of the Prime Minister.*

de·sign·ed·ly (di zīn′id lē) *adv.* purposely; intentionally.

de·sign·er (di zīn′ər) *n.* **1** a person who designs: *The dress designer completed his patterns and sketches for his spring showing of women's clothes.* **2** a plotter; schemer.

de·sign·ing (di zīn′ing) *adj.* scheming; plotting; cunning: *a designing woman.* —*n.* the art of making designs, patterns, sketches, etc.: *She studies dress designing at school.* —**de·sign′ing·ly,** *adv.*

de·sir·a·bil·i·ty (di zīr′ə bil′ə tē) *n.* the state or quality of being desirable.

de·sir·a·ble (di zīr′ə bəl) *adj.* worth wishing for; worth having; pleasing; good; excellent. —**de·sir′a·ble·ness,** *n.* —**de·sir′a·bly,** *adv.*

de·sire (di zīr′) *v.* **-sired, -sir·ing,** *n.* —*v.* **1** wish for; wish strongly for. **2** express a wish for; ask for or request, especially in a formal manner: *The Governor General desires your presence.*
—*n.* **1** a wish; strong wish. **2** an expressed wish; request. **3** something desired. **4** sensual appetite; lust. [ME < OF *desirer* < L *desiderare* long for] —**de·sir′er,** *n.*

Syn. *v.* **1** long (*for*), yearn (*for*), crave. See **wish.** –*n.* **1 Desire, longing, craving** = a strong wish. **Desire** applies to any strong wish, good or bad, for something a person thinks or hopes he can get: *His desire is to travel.* **Longing** applies to an earnest desire, sometimes for something a person thinks he can get if he tries or wishes hard enough, but often for something that seems beyond reach: *His longing for a bicycle is pathetic.* **Craving** applies to a desire so strong that it amounts to a need or hunger: *She has a craving for candy.*

de·sir·ous (di zīr′əs) *adj.* having or showing desire; full of desire; desiring; eager: *desirous of going to France.*

de·sist (di sist′ or di zist′) *v.* stop; cease: *The judge ordered him to desist from fighting.* [< MF *desister* < L *desistere* < *de-* from + *sistere* stop]

desk (desk) *n.* **1** a piece of furniture with a flat or sloping top on which to write or to rest books for reading. **2** a department of work at a certain location or at a desk: *the information desk of a library, the copy desk of a newspaper office.* [< Med.L *desca* < Ital. *desco* < L *discus* quoit, dish < Gk. *diskos.* Doublet of DAIS, DISCUS, DISH, and DISK.]

D. ès L. Docteur ès Lettres; Doctor of Letters.

des·o·late (*adj.* des′ə lit; *v.* des′ə lāt′) *adj. v.* **-lat·ed, -lat·ing.** —*adj.* **1** laid waste; devastated; barren: *desolate land.* **2** not lived in; deserted: *a desolate house.* **3** left alone; solitary; lonely. **4** unhappy; wretched; forlorn: *The ragged, hungry child looked desolate.* **5** dreary; dismal: *a desolate life.*
—*v.* **1** make unfit to live in; lay waste: *The Vikings desolated the land they attacked.* **2** deprive of inhabitants. **3** make lonely, unhappy, or forlorn: *He was desolated to hear that his old friend was going away.* [ME < L *desolatus,* pp. of *desolare* < *de-* completely + *solus* alone] —**des′o·late·ly,** *adv.* —**des′o·late·ness,** *n.* —**des′o·lat′er, des′o·la′tor,** *n.*

Syn. *adj.* **1** ravaged. **3** forsaken. **4 Desolate, disconsolate** = unhappy and forlorn. **Desolate** = unhappy because feeling left alone, deserted by everyone or, especially, separated from someone: *She was desolate when he went away.* **Disconsolate** = wretched because broken-hearted, without hope, and unable to be consoled or comforted: *She was disconsolate when her former boy friend married another girl.*

des·o·la·tion (des′ə lā′shən) *n.* **1** the act of making desolate. **2** a ruined, lonely, or deserted condition. **3** a desolate place. **4** sadness; lonely sorrow: *There was desolation in the eyes of the condemned man.*

de·spair (di spãr′) *n.* **1** a loss of hope; the state of being without hope; hopelessness; feeling that nothing good can happen. **2** a person or thing that causes despair. [ME < OF *despeir* (later *despoir*) < *desperer.* See verb.]
—*v.* lose hope; be without hope: *The doctors despaired of saving the sick man's life.* [ME < OF *desperer* < L *desperare* < *de-* out of, without + *sperare* to hope]

Syn. *n.* **1 Despair, desperation** = hopelessness. **Despair** emphasizes loss of hope and usually suggests sinking into a state of discouragement: *In his despair over losing his job he sold all his precious possessions and left town.* **Desperation** suggests a recklessness that is caused by despair and is expressed in rash or frantic action as a last resort: *He had no job and no money, and in desperation he robbed a bank.*

de·spair·ing (di spãr′ing) *adj.* feeling, showing, or expressing despair; hopeless. —**de·spair′ing·ly,** *adv.* —**de·spair′ing·ness,** *n.* —**Syn.** See **hopeless.**

des·patch (dis pach′) *v. n.* dispatch.

des·patch·er (dis pach′ər) *n.* dispatcher.

des·per·a·do (des′pər ā′dō or des′pər ä′dō) *n.* **-does** or **-dos.** a bold or reckless criminal; a dangerous outlaw. [< OSp. *desperado* < L *desperatus.* Doublet of DESPERATE.]

des·per·ate (des′pər it or des′prit) *adj.* **1** reckless because of despair; willing to run any risk. **2** showing recklessness caused by despair; violent: *Suicide is a desperate act.* **3** with little or no hope of improvement; very dangerous or serious. **4** hopeless. **5** causing despair: *desperate circumstances.* **6** extreme; intense: *a desperate craving for water.* [ME < L *desperatus,* pp. of *desperare.* See DESPAIR. Doublet of DESPERADO.] —**des′per·ate·ly,** *adv.* —**des′per·ate·ness,** *n.* —**Syn. 4** See **hopeless.**

des·per·a·tion (des′pər ā′shən) *n.* recklessness caused by despair; willingness to run any risk: *When he saw that the stairs were on fire, he jumped out of the window in desperation.* —**Syn.** See **despair.**

des·pic·a·ble (des pik′ə bəl or des′pi kə bəl) *adj.* fit to be despised; contemptible: *Cowards and liars are despicable.* [< LL *despicabilis* < L *despicari* despise] —**des·pic′a·ble·ness,** *n.* —**des·pic′a·bly,** *adv.*

de·spise (di spīz′) *v.* **-spised, -spis·ing.** look down on; feel contempt for; scorn: *Honest people despise those who lie.* [ME < OF *despis-,* a stem of *despire* < L *despicere* < *de-* down + *specere* look at] —**de·spis′er,** *n.*

de·spite (di spīt′) *prep.* in spite of: *The boys went for a walk despite the rain.*
—*n.* **1** insult; injury. **2** *Archaic.* malice; spite. **3** *Archaic.* contempt; scorn. **4 in despite of,** in spite of. [ME < OF *despit* < L *despectus* a looking down upon < *despicere* < *de-* down + *specere* look at]

hat, āge, cãre, fär; let, ēqual, tėrm; it, īce
hot, ōpen, ôrder; oil, out; cup, pu̇t, rüle, ūse
əbove, takən, pencəl, lemən, circəs
ch, child; ng, long; sh, ship
th, thin; ᴛʜ, then; zh, measure

de·spite·ful (di spīt′fəl) *adj. Archaic.* spiteful; malicious. —**de·spite′ful·ly,** *adv.* —**de·spite′ful·ness,** *n.*

de·spoil (di spoil′) *v.* rob; plunder. [ME < OF *despoillier* < L *despoliare* < *de-* completely + *spolium* armor, booty]

de·spoil·ment (di spoil′mənt) *n.* despoliation.

de·spo·li·a·tion (di spō′lē ā′shən) *n.* robbery; pillage.

de·spond (di spond′) *v.* lose heart, courage, or hope. —*n. Archaic.* despondency. [ME < L *despondere* < *de-* away + *spondere* lose heart] —**de·spond′ing·ly,** *adv.*

de·spond·ence (di spon′dəns) *n.* despondency.

de·spond·en·cy (di spon′dən sē) *n.* **-cies.** loss of courage or hope; discouragement; dejection.

de·spond·ent (di spon′dənt) *adj.* without courage or hope; discouraged; dejected. —**de·spond′ent·ly,** *adv.*

des·pot (des′pot or des′pət) *n.* **1** a tyrant; oppressor. **2** a monarch having unlimited power; an absolute ruler. **3** any person who uses his power to get his own way: *Some fathers are despots in the eyes of their children.* **4** in medieval Italy, a noble, prince, or military leader in Italian cities. [< MF < Gk. *despotēs* master]

des·pot·ic (des pot′ik) *adj.* of a despot; tyrannical; having unlimited power.

des·pot·i·cal·ly (des pot′ik lē) *adv.* in a despotic manner; with absolute power.

des·pot·ism (des′pət iz′əm) *n.* **1** tyranny; oppression. **2** government by a monarch having unlimited power. **3** despotic rule or control.

des·sert (di zėrt′) *n.* **1** a course served at the end of a meal. **2** a food, such as fruit, cake, or ice cream, served at this course. [< F *dessert* < *desservir* clear the table < *des-* from + *servir* serve < L *servire*]

des·sert·spoon (di zėrt′spün′) *n.* a spoon larger than a teaspoon and smaller than a tablespoon.

des·sert·spoon·ful (di zėrt′spün′fu̇l) *n.* **-fuls.** the amount that a dessertspoon can hold.

des·ti·na·tion (des′tə nā′shən) *n.* **1** a place to which a person or thing is going or is being sent. **2** a setting apart for a particular purpose or use; intention.

des·tine (des′tən) *v.* **-tined, -tin·ing.** **1** set apart for a particular purpose or use; intend: *The prince was destined from birth to be a king.* **2** cause by fate: *My letter was destined never to reach him.* **3 destined for,** **a** intended to go to; bound for: *ships destined for England.* **b** intended for: *My brother is destined for the ministry.* [ME < OF < L *destinare* make fast < *de-* (intensive) + *stare* stand]

des·ti·ny (des′tə nē) *n.* **-nies.** **1** one's lot or fortune; what becomes of a person or thing in the end. **2** what will happen in spite of all efforts to change or prevent it. **3** the power that foreordains; overruling necessity; fate. —**Syn. 1** See **fate.**

des·ti·tute (des′tə tūt′ or des′tə tüt′) *adj.* **1** lacking such necessities as food, clothing, and shelter. **2 destitute of,** having no trace of; without: *The tyrant was destitute of pity.* [< L *destitutus,* pp. of *destituere* forsake < *de-* away + *statuere* put, place] —**Syn. 1** needy.

des·ti·tu·tion (des′tə tū′shən or des′tə tü′shən) *n.* **1** a destitute condition; extreme poverty. **2** the state of being without; lack. —**Syn. 1** See **poverty.**

de·stroy (di stroi′) *v.* **1** break to pieces; make useless; ruin; spoil. **2** put an end to; do away with. **3** deprive of life; kill. **4** counteract the effect of; make void. [ME < OF *destruire* < VL < L *destruere* < *de-* un- + *struere* pile, build]

Syn. 1 Destroy, demolish = pull down. **Destroy** suggests bringing to nothing or making useless by breaking to pieces, taking apart, killing, or in any other of many ways: *Some children destroy all* *their toys.* **Demolish** = tear down, and applies only to things thought of as having been built up, such as buildings or, figuratively, arguments and theories: *The city demolished many buildings to make room for the speedway.* **2** abolish, extinguish.

de·stroy·er (di stroi′ər) *n.* **1** a person or thing that destroys. **2** a small, fast warship equipped with guns, torpedoes, and other weapons: *In wartime, the Royal Canadian Navy used destroyers for hunting submarines.*

de·struct·i·bil·i·ty (di struk′tə bil′ə tē) *n.* the quality of being destructible.

de·struct·i·ble (di struk′tə bəl) *adj.* capable of being destroyed. **—de·struct′i·ble·ness,** *n.*

de·struc·tion (di struk′shən) *n.* **1** the act of destroying. **2** the state of being destroyed. **3** anything that destroys; a cause or means of destroying. **4** ruin. [ME < OF < L *destructio, -onis* < *destruere* destroy. See DESTROY.] **—Syn. 4** See **ruin.**

de·struc·tive (di struk′tiv) *adj.* **1** tending to destroy; liable to cause destruction: *Termites are destructive insects.* **2** destroying; causing destruction. **3** guilty of destroying; in the habit of causing destruction: *Destructive children should be corrected.* **4** not helpful: *His destructive criticism showed things to be wrong, but did not show how to correct them.* **—de·struc′tive·ly,** *adv.* **—de·struc′tive·ness,** *n.*

des·ue·tude (des′wə tūd′ or des′wə tüd′) *n.* disuse: *Many words once commonly used have fallen into desuetude.* [< F < L *desuetudo* < *de-* dis- + *suescere* accustom]

des·ul·to·ry (des′əl tô′rē) *adj.* jumping from one thing to another; unconnected; without aim or method: *The careful and systematic study of a few books is better than the desultory reading of many.* [< L *desultorius* of a leaper, ult. < *de-* down + *salire* leap] **—des′ul·to′ri·ly,** *adv.* **—des′ul·to′ri·ness,** *n.*

de·tach (di tach′) *v.* **1** loosen and remove; unfasten; separate: *He detached his watch from the chain.* **2** separate a number of men, ships, tanks, etc. from the main body for some special duty: *One squad of soldiers was detached to guard the camp.* [< F *détacher*, formed with *dé-* away + OF *tache* nail] **—de·tach′a·ble,** *adj.* **—de·tach′er,** *n.*

de·tached (di tacht′) *adj.* **1** separate from others; isolated: *A detached house is not in a solid row with others.* **2** not influenced by others or by one's own interests and prejudices; impartial; aloof. **—de·tach′ed·ly** (di tach′id lē), *adv.* **—de·tach′ed·ness** (di tach′id nis), *n.*

de·tach·ment (di tach′mənt) *n.* **1** a separation. **2** a group of men, ships, tanks, etc. sent on or assigned to some special duty: *He belonged to the machine-gun detachment.* **3** the state of being on special duty: *a platoon of soldiers on detachment.* **4** a standing apart; aloofness. **5** a freedom from prejudice or bias; impartial attitude: *Students were surprised at the professor's air of detachment in talking about his own books.*

de·tail (dē′tāl or di tāl′) *n.* **1** a small or particular part; item: *The details of your report must be accurate.* **2** a dealing with small things one by one: *An engineer must have a grasp of detail. I will give you the broad outlines of the situation in Australia; there is not space to go into detail.* **3** a minute account; report of particulars. **4** a minor decoration or subordinate part. **5** the parts of a design taken together: *The detail of the heavily carved ceiling was more ornate than the walls.* **6** a picture, or a part (often enlarged) of a larger picture, showing a detail: *The photograph showed a detail from Michelangelo's painting "The Last Judgment."* **7** a small group selected for or sent on some special duty: *The captain sent a detail of six soldiers to guard the road.* **8 in detail,** part by part. —*v.* **1** tell fully; give the particulars of. **2** select for or send on special duty: *Policemen were detailed to hold back the crowd watching the parade.* [< F *détail* < *détaillir* cut in pieces < *de-* completely + *tailler* cut] **—de·tail′er,** *n.* **—Syn.** *n.* **1** See **item. 7** squad, detachment, party.

☛ **detail.** The noun may be pronounced in two ways: (dē′tāl or di tāl′). The second is older; the first especially common in situations where the word is used a great deal (army life, architecture, etc.). The pronunciation (dē′tāl) is also frequently used for def. 2 of the verb.

de·tain (di tān′) *v.* **1** hold back; keep from going; delay. **2** keep in custody; confine: *The police detained the suspected thief for further questioning.* **3** *Archaic.* withhold. [ME < OF *detenir* < L *detinere* < *de-* away + *tenere* hold] **—Syn. 1** retard.

de·tain·ee (dē tā′nē′) *n.* a person held in custody; prisoner.

de·tain·ment (di tān′mənt) *n.* detention.

de·tect (di tekt′) *v.* **1** find out; discover. **2** discover the existence of: *Could you detect any odor in the room?* **3** in radio, change (alternating currents) by a detector; rectify. [< L *detectus*, pp. of *detegere* < *de-* un- + *tegere* cover]

de·tect·a·ble (di tek′tə bəl) *adj.* capable of being detected.

de·tect·i·ble (di tek′tə bəl) *adj.* detectable.

de·tec·tion (di tek′shən) *n.* **1** a finding out; discovery. **2** a being found out or discovered. **3** in radio, the change of alternating currents; rectification.

de·tec·tive (di tek′tiv) *n.* a policeman or other person whose work is finding information, discovering who committed a crime, etc. —*adj.* **1** having to do with detectives and their work: *detective stories.* **2** used in discovering or finding out: *Scientific detective methods are more accurate than guessing.*

de·tec·tor (di tek′tər) *n.* **1** a person or thing that detects. **2** a device for detecting the presence of electricity or radio-activity. **3** in radio, a vacuum tube or crystal that helps in the change of radio waves into sound waves; rectifier. **4** a device for causing the diaphragm in a telephone, etc. to vibrate when a high-frequency current passes through. **5** a device for indicating the depth of water in a boiler.

dé·tente (dā täNt′) *n. French.* the easing of tensions, especially between nations or political groups: *a détente in the cold war.*

de·ten·tion (di ten′shən) *n.* **1** the act of detaining; the act of holding back. **2** the state of being detained; delay. **3** the act of keeping in custody; confinement: *A jail is used for the detention of persons who have been arrested.* [< LL *detentio, -onis* < L *detinere.* See DETAIN.]

de·ter (di tėr′) *v.* **-terred, -ter·ring.** discourage; keep back; hinder: *The extreme heat deterred us from going downtown.* [< L *deterrere* < *de-* from + *terrere* frighten]

de·ter·gent (di tėr′jənt) *adj.* cleansing. —*n.* a synthetic substance used for cleansing. [< L *detergens, -entis*, ppr. of *detergere* < *de-* off + *tergere* wipe]

de·te·ri·o·rate (di tēr′ē ə rāt′) *v.* **-rat·ed, -rat·ing. 1** become worse; lessen in value; depreciate: *Machinery deteriorates if it is not given good care.* **2** make worse. [< L *deteriorare* < *deterior* worse]

de·te·ri·o·ra·tion (di tēr′ē ə rā′shən) *n.* **1** a deteriorating. **2** the condition of having deteriorated.

de·ter·ment (di tėr′mənt) *n.* **1** a deterring. **2** something that deters.

de·ter·mi·na·ble (di tėr′mə nə bəl) *adj.* **1** capable of being settled or decided. **2** capable of being found out exactly.

de·ter·mi·nant (di tėr′mə nənt) *n.* **1** something that determines. **2** in mathematics, the sum of all the products that can be formed according to special laws from a certain number of quantities arranged in a square block. —*adj.* determining.

de·ter·mi·nate (di tėr′mə nit) *adj.* **1** with exact limits; fixed; definite. **2** settled; positive. **3** determined; resolute. **4** in botany, having the primary and each secondary axis of a plant ending in a flower or bud. A forget-me-not has determinate inflorescence. **—de·ter′mi·nate·ly,** *adv.* **—de·ter′mi·nate·ness,** *n.*

de·ter·mi·na·tion (di tėr′mə nā′shən) *n.* **1** the act of deciding; the act of settling beforehand. **2** a finding out of the exact amount or kind, by weighing, measuring, or calculating: *the determination of the amount of gold in a sample of ore.* **3** the result of finding out exactly; a conclusion. **4** the state of being determined; a settlement; decision. **5** fixed purpose; great firmness in carrying out a purpose: *The boy's determination was not weakened by the difficulties he met.* **6** in logic: **a** the making of an idea, concept, etc. more concise in its outline by the addition of restrictive attributes or other qualifying features. **b** the defining of a concept by specifying its parts.

de·ter·mi·na·tive (di tėr′mə nə tiv or di tėr′mə nā′tiv) *adj.* determining. —*n.* something that determines. **—de·ter′mi·na·tive·ly,** *adv.* **—de·ter′mi·na·tive·ness,** *n.*

hat, āge, cãre, fär; let, ēqual, tėrm; it, īce
hot, ōpen, ôrder; oil, out; cup, pu̇t, rüle, ūse
əbove, takən, pencəl, lemən, circəs
ch, child; ng, long; sh, ship
th, thin; ᴛʜ, then; zh, measure

de·ter·mine (di tėr′mən) *v.* **-mined, -min·ing. 1** make up one's mind firmly; resolve: *He determined to become the best Scout in his troop.* **2** settle; decide. **3** find out exactly; fix: *The captain determined the latitude and longitude of his ship's position.* **4** in geometry, fix the position of. **5** be the deciding factor in reaching a certain result: *Tomorrow's events will determine whether we are to go or stay.* **6** fix or settle beforehand. **7** give an aim to; direct; impel: *Let hope determine your thinking.* **8** limit; define: *The meaning of a word is partly determined by its use in a particular sentence.* **9** put an end to; conclude. **10** come to an end. **11** *Archaic.* take a course to a definite point or end. [ME < OF < L *determinare* set limits to < *de-* completely + *terminus* end] **—Syn. 1** See **decide. 3** ascertain, establish.

de·ter·mined (di tėr′mənd) *adj.* **1** with one's mind firmly made up; resolved: *The determined explorer kept on his way in spite of the storm.* **2** firm; resolute: *His determined look showed that he had made up his mind.*

de·ter·mined·ly (di tėr′mənd lē or di tėr′mən id lē) *adv.* in a determined manner.

de·ter·min·er (di tėr′mə nər) *n.* **1** a person or thing that determines; determinant. **2** in grammar, a limiting adjective or other modifier that precedes a noun or noun phrase. *Examples: the* boy, *that* big house, *some* people. **3** in biology, a gene.

de·ter·min·ism (di tėr′mən iz′əm) *n.* **1** the doctrine that human actions are the necessary results of antecedent causes. **2** the doctrine that all events are determined by antecedent causes.

de·ter·min·ist (di tėr′mən ist) *n.* a person who believes in determinism.

de·ter·rence (di ter′əns) *n.* **1** the act or process of deterring. **2** something that deters; a restraint.

de·ter·rent (di tėr′ənt or di ter′ənt) *adj.* deterring; restraining. *—n.* something that deters: *Fear of consequences is a common deterrent from wrongdoing.*

de·test (di test′) *v.* dislike very much; hate. [< F *détester* < L *detestari* curse while calling the gods to witness < *de-* (intensive) + *testari* to witness] **—de·test′er,** *n.* **—Syn.** abhor, loathe. See **hate.**

de·test·a·ble (di tes′tə bəl) *adj.* deserving to be detested; hateful. **—de·test′a·ble·ness,** *n.* **—de·test′a·bly,** *adv.*

de·tes·ta·tion (dē′tes tā′shən) *n.* **1** a very strong dislike; hatred. **2** a detested person or thing.

de·throne (di thrōn′) *v.* **-throned, -thron·ing.** deprive of the power to rule; remove from a throne; depose.

de·throne·ment (di thrōn′mənt) *n.* **1** a dethroning. **2** a being dethroned.

det·o·nate (det′ə nāt′) *v.* **-nat·ed, -nat·ing. 1** cause to explode with a loud noise: *The workmen detonated the dynamite.* **2** explode with a loud noise: *The bomb detonated.* [< L *detonare* < *de-* (intensive) + *tonare* thunder]

det·o·na·tion (det′ə nā′shən) *n.* **1** an explosion with a loud noise. **2** a loud noise.

det·o·na·tor (det′ə nā′tər) *n.* **1** a fuse, percussion cap, etc. used to set off an explosive. **2** any explosive.

de·tour (dē′tür or di tür′) *n.* **1** a road that is used when the main or direct road cannot be travelled. **2** a roundabout way. *—v.* **1** use a roundabout way; make a detour: *We detoured around the flooded part of the highway.* **2** cause to use a detour. [< F *détour* < *détourner* turn aside < *dé-* away from + *tourner* turn]

de·tract (di trakt′) *v.* take away (*from*) the quality, value, etc. of something: *The ugly frame detracts from the beauty of the picture.* [< L *detractus,* pp. of *detrahere* < *de-* away + *trahere* draw]

de·trac·tion (di trak′shən) *n.* **1** the act of speaking evil; belittling. **2** a taking away; detracting.

de·trac·tive (di trak′tiv) *adj.* **1** tending to detract. **2** speaking evil; belittling. **—de·trac′tive·ly,** *adv.*

de·trac·tor (di trak′tər) *n.* a person who speaks evil of or belittles another.

de·train (dē trān′) *v.* **1** get off a railway train. **2** put off from a railway train.

det·ri·ment (det′rə mənt) *n.* **1** damage; injury; harm: *No one can tell lies without detriment to his character.* **2** something that causes damage or harm. [ME < L *detrimentum* < *deterere* < *de-* away + *terere* wear]

det·ri·men·tal (det′rə men′təl) *adj.* damaging; injurious; harmful: *Lack of sleep is detrimental to one's health.* **—det′ri·men′tal·ly,** *adv.*

de·tri·tus (di trī′təs) *n.* **1** particles of rock or other material worn away from a mass. **2** any disintegrated material; debris: *The detritus left by the flood covered the highway.* [< L *detritus* a rubbing away]

de trop (də trō′) *French.* **1** too much; too many. **2** unwelcome; in the way.

deuce[1] (dūs or düs) *n.* **1** in a game of cards or dice, the number two. **2** a playing card marked with a *2.* **3** the side of a die having two spots. **4** a dice throw of two aces. **5** in tennis, a tie score at 40 each in a game, or five games each in a set. [< OF *deus* two < L *duos,* accus. of *duo* two]

deuce[2] (dūs or düs) *interj. Informal.* an exclamation of annoyance meaning "bad luck," "the mischief," "the devil." [probably < LG *duus* deuce[1], an unlucky throw at dice]

deu·ced (dūst or düst, dū′sid or dü′sid) *Informal. —adj.* devilish; excessive. *—adv.* devilishly; excessively.

deu·ced·ly (dū′sid lē or dü′sid lē) *adv. Informal.* devilishly; excessively.

de·us ex ma·chi·na (dē′əs eks mak′ə nə) *Latin.* **1** a person, god, or event that comes just in time to solve a difficulty in a story, play, etc. **2** a person or event that solves any difficulty in a dramatic manner. [literally, god from the machinery (with reference to a stage device in the ancient theatre)]

Deut. Deuteronomy.

deu·te·ri·um (dū tēr′ē əm or dü tēr′ē əm) *n.* an isotope of hydrogen; heavy hydrogen. Its molecules weigh about twice as much as those of ordinary hydrogen. *Symbol:* D [< NL < Gk. *deutereion,* neut., having second place < *deuteros* second]

deuterium oxide in chemistry, heavy water. *Formula:* D_2O

deu·ter·on (dū′tə ron′ or dü′tə ron′) *n.* in chemistry, the nucleus of a deuterium atom, consisting of one proton and one electron. [< *deuter*ium + *-on,* as in *proton*]

Deu·ter·on·o·my (dū′tər on′ə mē or dü′tər on′ə mē) *n.* the fifth book of the Old Testament. [< L < Gk. *Deuteronomion* < *deuteros* second + *nomos* law]

deu·to·plasm (dū′tə plaz′əm or dü′tə plaz′əm) *n.* in biology, the yolk or other material that provides nourishment for the embryo in an egg or cell. [< Gk. *deuteros* second + *plasma.* See PLASMA.]

Deutsche mark (doi′chə) **1** a unit of money in West Germany (Federal Republic). See table at **money. 2** a coin worth one Deutsche mark.

Deut·sches Reich (doi′chəs rīн′) *German.* the former official name of Germany.

Deutsch·land (doich′länt′) *n. German.* Germany.

de·val·u·ate (dē val′ū āt′) *v.* **-at·ed, -at·ing. 1** lessen the value of. **2** fix a lower legal value on (a currency that has depreciated): *devaluate the pound.*

de·val·u·a·tion (dē val′ū ā′shən) *n.* **1** a devaluating. **2** a being devaluated.

de·val·ue (dē val′ū) *v.* **-val·ued, -val·uing.** devaluate.

dev·as·tate (dev′əs tāt′) *v.* **-tat·ed, -tat·ing.** make desolate; destroy; ravage: *A long war devastated the border towns.* [< L *devastare* < *de-* (intensive) + *vastus* waste] **—dev′as·tat′or,** *n.*

dev·as·ta·tion (dev′əs tā′shən) *n.* destruction; the act of laying waste or destroying; a being laid waste.

de·vel·op (di vel′əp) *v.* **1** bring or come into being or activity; grow: *Swimming will develop many different muscles. Plants develop from seeds.* **2** change or cause to change in character through successive periods; evolve: *Land animals are believed to have developed from sea animals. The modern power loom has been developed from an ancient and simpler machine.* **3** work out in detail: *Gradually we developed our plans for the boys' club.* **4** in music, painting, etc., elaborate a theme or motive by artistic devices. **5 a** bring forth; make available: *We must develop the country's copper.* **b** build on: *develop land.* **6** make or become known; reveal: *The detective's inquiry did not develop any new facts.* **7** in photography, treat or be treated with chemicals to bring out a visible image: *We shall print all the films we developed. This type of film develops in twenty minutes.* [< F *développer* unwrap] —**Syn. 1** generate, unfold.

de·vel·op·er (di vel′əp ər) *n.* **1** a person or thing that develops. **2** a chemical used to bring out the picture on an exposed photographic film, plate, print, etc.

de·vel·op·ment (di vel′əp mənt) *n.* **1** a developing; a gradual unfolding; a working out in detail: *The development of an airplane that would fly took many years of experimenting.* **2** growth; evolution: *The doctor followed the child's development closely.* **3 a** a group of houses, apartment blocks, etc. built either on previously open land or to replace old buildings. **b** a piece of land developed for any purpose. **4** a stage of advancement. **5** a happening; outcome; result: *This newspaper gives news about the latest developments in world affairs.* **6** a more elaborate form. **7** a developing of a photograph.

de·vel·op·men·tal (di vel′əp men′təl) *adj.* having to do with development.

development road *Cdn.* in the North, a road or one of a system of access roads intended to help the exploitation of natural resources.

de·vi·ate (*v.* dē′vē āt′; *n.* dē′vē ət or dē′vē āt′) *v.* **-at·ed, -at·ing,** *n.* —*v.* **1** turn aside (from a way, course, rule, truth, etc.); diverge: *His statements sometimes deviated slightly from the truth.* **2** cause to turn aside. —*n.* an individual who shows a marked deviation from the norm. [< LL *deviare* < *de-* aside + *via* way] —**de′vi·a′tor,** *n.* —**Syn.** See **diverge.**

de·vi·a·tion (dē′vē ā′shən) *n.* a turning aside from a way, course, rule, truth, etc.; divergence: *The iron in the ship caused a deviation of the magnetic needle of the compass.* See **angle of deviation** for diagram.

de·vi·a·tion·ism (dē′vē ā′shə niz′əm) *n.* a turning aside from strict principles, especially from official Communist policy.

de·vi·a·tion·ist (dē′vē ā′shən ist) *n.* a person who turns aside from strict principles, especially from official Communist policy.

de·vice (di vīs′) *n.* **1** a mechanical invention used for a special purpose; machine; apparatus: *a device for lighting a gas stove.* **2** a plan; scheme; trick: *By some device or other he got the boy to let him into the house.* **3** a drawing or figure used in a pattern or as an ornament. **4** in literature or music, a stylistic or technical feature introduced to achieve a particular effect. **5** a picture or design on a coat of arms, often accompanied by a motto. **6** a motto. **7 leave someone to his own devices,** leave him to do as he thinks best. [fusion of ME *devis* separation, talk + *devise* design, emblem, plan; both < OF < L *divisus*, pp. of *dividere* divide] —**Syn. 1** contrivance. **2** ruse, wile.

☛ **device, devise.** Do not confuse *device*, meaning a mechanical invention used for a specific purpose or a scheme or trick, with *devise*, meaning "think out": *He tried to perfect a device for removing clinkers. By one unfair device after another, he amassed a huge fortune. Ann devised a new plan for the organization.*

dev·il (dev′əl) *n. v.* **-illed** or **-iled, -il·ling** or **-il·ing,** *interj.* —*n.* **1 the Devil,** the supreme spirit of evil; the enemy of goodness; Satan. **2** an evil spirit; fiend; demon. **3** a wicked or cruel person. **4** a very clever, energetic, or reckless person. **5** an unfortunate or wretched person. **6** something very bad; an evil influence or power. **7** a person who does literary work for another, for which the latter gets the credit or pay. **8** the errand boy in a printing office. **9** a machine that has sharp teeth or spikes for tearing, cleaning, etc. **10 between the devil and the deep (blue) sea,** between two equally dangerous and unpleasant alternatives; in a dilemma. **11 give the devil his due,** be fair even to a bad or disliked person. **12 go to the devil,** go to ruin, degenerate morally. **13 raise the devil,** *Slang.* make a great disturbance. **14 The devil take the hindmost.** Do not worry about what happens to the slowest or last one. **15 the devil to pay,** much trouble ahead.
—*v.* **1** *Informal.* bother; tease; torment. **2** prepare (food) with hot seasoning: *devil ham.* **3** treat harshly. **4** tear (rags, etc.) to pieces with a devil; subject to the cleaning action of a devil. **5** act or serve as a literary devil. **6** produce (a literary work) for another who gets the credit or pay for it.
—*interj.* **the devil!** exclamation used to express disgust, anger, surprise, etc. [OE *deofol* < L < Gk. *diabolos* slanderer < *diaballein* slander < *dia-* across, against + *ballein* throw]

dev·iled (dev′əld) *adj.* devilled.

dev·il·fish (dev′əl fish′) *n.* **-fish** or **-fish·es. 1** a large, odd-shaped fish related to the shark; a giant ray. **2** octopus.

de·vil·ish (dev′əl ish or dev′lish) *adj.* **1** like a devil; like a devil's; very cruel or wicked. **2** mischievous; daring. **3** *Informal.* very great; extreme. —*adv. Informal.* very; extremely. —**dev′il·ish·ly,** *adv.* —**dev′il·ish·ness,** *n.*

dev·illed or **dev·iled** (dev′əld) *adj.* highly seasoned: *devilled eggs.*

dev·il·ment (dev′əl mənt) *n.* **1** an evil action; wicked behavior. **2** daring behavior. **3** mischief.

dev·il·ry (dev′əl rē) *n.* **-ries.** deviltry.

devil's advocate 1 in the Roman Catholic Church, an official appointed to argue against a proposed beatification or canonization. **2** a critic who argues either against a popular cause or for an unpopular cause.

devil's club a shrub of the Rocky Mountain region, having large maple-like leaves, a thick, prickly stem, and red berries. Also, **Devil's Club.**

devil's darning needle dragonfly.

devil's food cake a rich, dark, chocolate cake.

dev·il·try (dev′əl trē) *n.* **-tries. 1** an evil action; wicked behavior. **2** daring behavior. **3** mischief. **4** great cruelty or wickedness.

de·vi·ous (dē′vē əs) *adj.* **1** winding; twisting; roundabout: *We took a devious route through side streets and alleys to avoid the crowded main streets.* **2** straying from the right course; not straightforward; going astray: *His devious nature was shown in half lies and acts of petty dishonesty.* [< L *devius* < *de-* out of + *via* the way] —**de′vi·ous·ness,** *n.* —**de′vi·ous·ly,** *adv.*

de·vise (di vīz′) *v.* **-vised, -vis·ing.** *n.* —*v.* **1** think out; plan; contrive; invent: *The boys devised a scheme for earning money during the summer vacation.* **2** in law, give or leave (land, buildings, etc.) by a will.
—*n.* in law: **1** a giving or leaving of land, buildings, etc. by a will. **2** a will or part of a will doing this. **3** land, buildings, etc. given or left in this way. [ME < OF *deviser* dispose in portions, arrange, ult. < L *dividere* divide] —**de·vis′a·ble,** *adj.* ☛ See **device** for usage note.

de·vis·ee (di vīz′ē′ or dev′ə zē′) *n.* in law, a person to whom land, buildings, etc. are given or left by a will.

de·vis·er (di vīz′ər) *n.* one who devises; an inventor.

de·vi·sor (di vī′zər or di vī′zôr) *n.* in law, a person who gives or leaves land, buildings, etc. by a will.

de·vi·tal·i·za·tion (dē vī′təl ə zā′shən or dē vī′təl ī zā′shən) *n.* **1** a devitalizing. **2** a being devitalized.

de·vi·tal·ize (dē vī′təl īz′) *v.* **-ized, -iz·ing. 1** kill; take the life of. **2** weaken; exhaust; make less vital.

de·void (di void′) *adj.* lacking; without: *devoid of sense.* [ME; originally *devoided*, pp. of *devoid* cast out < OF *desvoidier* < *des-* away + *voidier* to empty < *voide* empty, ult. < var. of L *vacuus*]

dev·o·lu·tion (dev′ə lü′shən or dē′və lü′shən) *n.* **1** a progression from stage to stage. **2** the transmitting or passing of property from person to person; the passing on to a successor of an unexercised right. **3** the delegating (of duty, responsibility, etc.) to another. **4** in biology, reversed evolution; degeneration. [< Med.L *devolutio, -onis* < *devolvere.* See DEVOLVE.]

de·volve (di volv′) *v.* **-volved, -volv·ing. 1** transfer (duty, work, etc.) to someone else. **2** be handed down to someone else; be transferred: *If the president is unable to handle his duties, they devolve upon the vice-president.* [< L *devolvere* < *de-* down + *volvere* roll]

De·vo·ni·an (də vō′nē ən) *adj.* **1** of or having to do with Devonshire, a county in S.W. England. **2** in geology, of or having to do with a period of the Paleozoic era. —*n.* **1** a native of Devonshire, England. **2** in geology: **a** the period of the Paleozoic era coming between the Carboniferous and the Silurian. See **geology** for chart. **b** the rocks formed during this period.

Devonshire cream (dev′ən shər) a rich, thickened cream; clotted cream.

de·vote (di vōt′) *v.* **-vot·ed, -vot·ing. 1** give up (oneself, one's money, time, or efforts) to some person, purpose, or service: *The mother devoted herself to her children.* **2** set apart and consecrate to God or to a sacred purpose. **3** set apart for any particular purpose: *That museum devotes one wing to modern art.* [< L *devotus*, pp. of *devovere* < *de-* entirely + *vovere* vow. Doublet of DEVOUT.]
Syn. 1 Devote, dedicate, consecrate = give something or someone up to a purpose. **Devote** emphasizes giving up seriously to a single purpose, shutting out everything else: *He devoted his time to study.* **Dedicate** emphasizes giving up or setting apart earnestly or solemnly for a serious or sacred use: *He dedicated his life to science. They dedicated the hospital.* **Consecrate** = set a person or thing apart as sacred or glorified, by a solemn vow or ceremony: *A bishop consecrated the burial ground.*

de·vot·ed (di vōt′id) *adj.* **1** loyal; faithful: *a devoted friend.* **2** set apart for some purpose; dedicated; consecrated. **—de·vot′ed·ly,** *adv.* **—de·vot′ed·ness,** *n.*

dev·o·tee (dev′ə tē′) *n.* **1** a person deeply devoted to something. **2** a person earnestly devoted to religion.

de·vo·tion (di vō′shən) *n.* **1** a deep, steady affection; a feeling of loyalty; faithfulness: *the devotion of a mother to her child.* **2** the act of devoting or the state of being devoted: *the devotion of much time to study.* **3** the act of devoting or setting apart to a sacred use or purpose. **4** earnestness in religion; devoutness. **5** religious worship or observance; divine worship. **6 devotions,** *pl.* religious worship; prayers.

de·vo·tion·al (di vō′shən əl) *adj.* having to do with devotion; used in worship. **—de·vo′tion·al·ly,** *adv.*

de·vour (di vour′) *v.* **1** of animals, eat. **2** eat like an animal; eat hungrily: *The hungry boy was devouring his dinner.* **3** consume; waste; destroy: *devoured by disease.* **4** swallow up; engulf. **5** take in with eyes or ears in a hungry, greedy way: *devour a new book.* **6** absorb wholly: *She was devoured by anxiety.* [ME < OF *devorer* < L *devorare* < *de-* down + *vorare* gulp] **—de·vour′er,** *n.* **—de·vour′ing·ly,** *adv.*

de·vout (di vout′) *adj.* **1** active in worship and prayer; religious. **2** showing devotion: *a devout prayer.* **3** earnest; sincere; hearty: *devout thanks, a devout follower.* [ME < OF *devot* < L *devotus*, pp. of *devovere.* Doublet of DEVOTE.] **—de·vout′ly,** *adv.* **—de·vout′ness,** *n.* **—Syn. 1** See **pious.**

dew (dū or dü) *n.* **1** the moisture from the air that condenses and collects in small drops on cool surfaces during the night. **2** moisture in small drops. **3** anything fresh or refreshing like dew. —*v.* make wet with dew; moisten. [OE *dēaw*] **—dew′less,** *adj.*

dew·ber·ry (dū′ber′ē or dü′-) *n.* **-ries. 1** any of several blackberry-like vines that grow along the ground. **2** the fruit of one of these vines.

dew·claw (dū′klo′ or -klô′, dü′klo′ or -klô′) *n.* a small, useless hoof or toe on the feet of deer, pigs, dogs, etc.

dew·drop (dū′drop′ or dü′-) *n.* a drop of dew.

Dew·ey decimal system (dū′ē or dü′ē) a system for classifying books, pamphlets, etc. in libraries. Each subject and its subdivisions are assigned specific numbers and decimals. *Examples*: Literature 800, History 900, Canadian History 971, Canadian Northwest History 971.2. [< Melvil *Dewey*, 1851-1931, an American librarian, who devised the system]

dew·lap (dū′lap′ or dü′-) *n.* **1** a loose fold of skin under the throat of cattle and some other animals. **2** a similar fold of skin under the throat of certain birds. [< *dew* (origin and meaning uncertain) + *lap* < OE *læppa* pendulous piece]

hat, āge, cãre, fär; let, ēqual, tėrm; it, īce
hot, ōpen, ôrder; oil, out; cup, pu̇t, rüle, ūse
əbove, takən, pencəl, lemən, circəs
ch, child; ng, long; sh, ship
th, thin; ᴛʜ, then; zh, measure

dew point the temperature of the air at which dew begins to form.

dew-worm (dū′wėrm′ or dü′-) *n. Cdn.* a large earthworm that comes to the surface at night when there is dew on the grass: *Dew-worms make excellent fish bait.*

dew·y (dū′ē or dü′ē) *adj.* **dew·i·er, dew·i·est. 1** wet with dew. **2** of dew. **3** like dew; refreshing; sparkling; coming gently; vanishing quickly. **—dew′i·ly,** *adv.* **—dew′i·ness,** *n.*

dex·ter (deks′tər) *adj.* **1** of or on the right-hand side. **2** in heraldry, situated on that part of an escutcheon to the right of the bearer, and hence to the left of the observer. [< L *dexter* right]

dex·ter·i·ty (deks ter′ə tē) *n.* **1** skill in using the body, especially the hands. **2** skill in using the mind; cleverness.

dex·ter·ous (deks′tər əs or deks′trəs) *adj.* **1** having or showing skill in using the body, especially the hands. **2** having or showing skill in using the mind; clever. Also, **dextrous. —dex′trous·ly,** *adv.* **—dex′ter·ous·ness,** *n.*
Syn. 1 Dexterous, deft, adroit = skilful in using the hands and body. **Dexterous** suggests easy, quick, smooth movements and lightness and sureness of touch coming from practice: *Mary is a dexterous pianist.* **Deft** adds to *dexterous* the idea of neatness and exceptional lightness and swiftness: *A surgeon has to be deft.* **Adroit** adds to *dexterous* the idea of being quick-witted, and is used less often of physical skill than of mental quickness, resourcefulness, and cleverness in handling situations: *The adroit lawyer got the truth out of the witness.*

dex·tral (deks′trəl) *adj.* **1** of the right hand; right-hand. **2** right-handed. **3** having the spire or whorl rising from left to right when viewed from above, as with most snail shells.

dex·tran (deks′tran) *n.* in chemistry, a white, slimy carbohydrate, produced in sugar solutions by bacterial action. It is administered instead of blood plasma to persons in a state of shock. [< L *dexter* right hand, from its plane of polarization]

dex·trin (deks′trin) *n.* dextrine.

dex·trine (deks′trin or deks′trēn) *n.* a gummy substance obtained from starch, used as an adhesive, for sizing paper, etc. [< F]

dex·trose (deks′trōs) *n.* a sugar that is less sweet than cane sugar; a form of glucose. *Formula*: $C_6H_{12}O$ [< *dexter* + (*gluc*)*ose*]

dex·trous (deks′trəs) *adj.* dexterous.

dey (dā) *n.* **deys.** formerly, a title for rulers of Algiers, Tunis, and Tripoli. [< F < Turkish *dāī*, originally, maternal uncle]

D.F. Defender of the Faith.

D.F.C. Distinguished Flying Cross.

D.F.M. Distinguished Flying Medal.

dg. decigram; decigrams.

D.G. Deo gratias.

dhar·ma (där′mə) *n.* **1** in Buddhism, the law. **2** in Hinduism, virtue; righteousness; correct behavior. [< Skt. *dharma* decree, custom, right course of conduct]

dhole (dōl) *n.* **dholes** or **dhole.** a fierce, wild dog of India that usually hunts in packs. [native name]

dho·ti (dō′tē) *n.* **1** a large unstitched piece of white cloth, tied round the waist and loosely wrapping the legs down to the ankles, worn by male Indians, especially Hindus. **2** a fabric used for dhotis. [< Hind.]

dhow (dou) *n.* a lateen-rigged sailing ship that is used along the coasts of the Arabian peninsula and E. Africa. [cf. Arabic *dāw*]

A dhow

di (dē) *n.* in music, a note intermediate between do and re.

di-[1] *prefix.* twice; double; twofold, as in *dioxide, dicotyledon.* Also, **dis-**, before *s.* [< Gk. *di-* < *dis*]

di-[2] the form of **dis-**[1] before *b, d, l, m, n, r, s, v,* and sometimes before *g* and *j,* as in *direct, divert.*

di-[3] the form of **dia-** before vowels, as in *diorama.*

dia- *prefix.* through; across; thoroughly, as in *diaphragm.* Also, **di-** before vowels. [< Gk. *dia-* < *dia,* prep.]

di·a·be·tes (dī′ə bē′tis or dī′ə bē′tēz) *n.* any of several diseases characterized by an excessive quantity of urine and abnormal thirst, especially diabetes mellitus. [NL < Gk. *diabētēs* a passer-through < *dia-* through + *bainein* go]

diabetes mel·li·tus (mel ē′təs or mel ī′təs) a form of diabetes characterized by excessive sugar in the urine and by the inability of the body to absorb normal amounts of sugar and starch. [NL *diabetes mellitus* honey diabetes]

di·a·bet·ic (dī′ə bet′ik or dī′ə bē′tik) *adj.* **1** of or having to do with diabetes. **2** having diabetes.
—*n.* a person having diabetes.

di·a·ble·rie (dē ä′blə rē) *n.* **1** diabolic magic or art; sorcery; witchcraft. **2** deviltry; reckless mischief. **3** a domain or realm of devils. [< F]

di·a·bol·ic (dī′ə bol′ik) *adj.* **1** devilish; like the Devil; very cruel or wicked; fiendish. **2** having to do with the Devil or devils. [< LL *diabolicus* < Gk. *diabolikos* < *diabolos.* See DEVIL.] —**di′a·bol′i·cal·ly,** *adv.*

di·a·bol·i·cal (dī′ə bol′ə kəl) *adj.* diabolic.

di·ab·o·lism (dī ab′ə liz′əm) *n.* **1** sorcery; witchcraft. **2** a diabolical action; deviltry. **3** belief in or worship of a devil or devils. **4** the character or condition of a devil.

di·a·chron·ic (dī′ə kron′ik) *adj.* **1** extending through the course of time or history; chronological. **2** treating a subject from a historical rather than a descriptive viewpoint; opposed to *synchronic.*

di·a·chron·i·cal·ly (dī′ə kron′ə klē) *adv.* in a diachronic manner; chronologically.

di·ac·o·nal (dī ak′ə nəl) *adj.* of or having to do with a deacon. [< Med.L *diaconalis* < L *diaconus.* See DEACON.]

di·ac·o·nate (dī ak′ə nit or dī ak′ə nāt′) *n.* **1** the rank or position of a deacon. **2** a group of deacons.

di·a·crit·ic (dī′ə krit′ik) *adj.* diacritical. —*n.* a diacritical mark. [< Gk. *diakritikos* < *diakrinein* < *dia-* apart + *krinein* separate]

di·a·crit·i·cal (dī′ə krit′ə kəl) *adj.* **1** distinguishing: *diacritical marks.* **2** capable of seeing distinctions: *a man of superior diacritical powers.* —**di′a·crit′i·cal·ly,** *adv.*

diacritical mark a mark like ¨ ^ ¯ ′ or ` placed over or under a letter to indicate pronunciation, etc.

di·a·dem (dī′ə dem′) *n.* **1** a crown. **2** an ornamental band of cloth formerly worn as a crown. **3** royal power, authority, or dignity. [< L < Gk. *diadēma* < *diadeein* < *dia-* across + *deein* bind]

A diadem

di·aer·e·sis (dī er′ə sis) *n.* **-ses** (-sēz′). a dieresis.

di·ag·nose (dī′əg nōs′ or dī′əg nōz′) *v.* **-nosed, -nos·ing.** make a diagnosis of; find out the nature of by an examination: *The doctor diagnosed the child's disease as measles.*

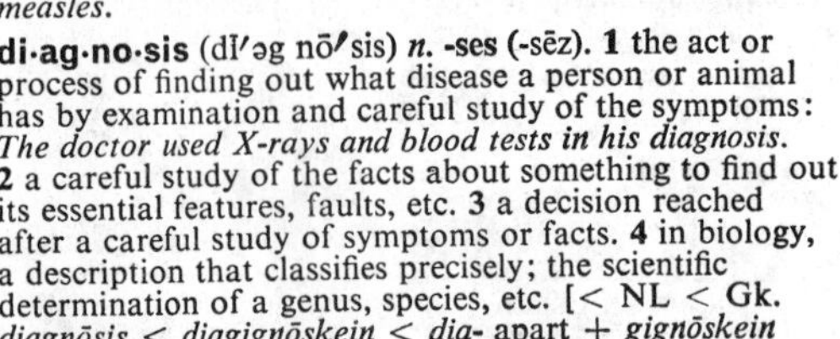

di·ag·no·sis (dī′əg nō′sis) *n.* **-ses** (-sēz). **1** the act or process of finding out what disease a person or animal has by examination and careful study of the symptoms: *The doctor used X-rays and blood tests in his diagnosis.* **2** a careful study of the facts about something to find out its essential features, faults, etc. **3** a decision reached after a careful study of symptoms or facts. **4** in biology, a description that classifies precisely; the scientific determination of a genus, species, etc. [< NL < Gk. *diagnōsis* < *diagignōskein* < *dia-* apart + *gignōskein* learn to know]

di·ag·nos·tic (dī′əg nos′tik) *adj.* **1** of or having to do with diagnosis: *a diagnostic survey of the problem.* **2** helping in diagnosis: *diagnostic tests.* —**di·ag·nos′ti·cal·ly,** *adv.*

di·ag·nos·ti·cian (dī′əg nos tish′ən) *n.* a person who is expert in making diagnoses.

di·ag·o·nal (dī ag′ə nəl) *n.* **1** a straight line that cuts across in a slanting direction, often from corner to corner. **2** any slanting line, row, course, etc. —*adj.* **1** taking the direction of a diagonal; slanting; oblique. **2** having slanting lines, ridges, etc. **3** in geometry, connecting two corners that are not next to each other. [< L *diagonalis* < Gk. *diagōnios* from angle to angle < *dia-* across + *gōnia* angle]

A B
The line AB is a diagonal

di·ag·o·nal·ly (dī ag′ə nəl ē) *adv.* in a diagonal direction.

di·a·gram (dī′ə gram′) *n. v.* **-grammed** or **-gramed, gram·ming** or **gram·ing.** —*n.* a drawing or sketch showing important parts of a thing. A diagram may be an outline, a plan, a drawing, a figure, a chart, or a combination of any of these, made to show clearly what a thing is or how it works: *He drew a diagram to show us how to get to his house. The engineer drew a diagram of the bridge.* —*v.* put on paper, a blackboard, etc. in the form of a drawing or sketch; make a diagram of. [< L < Gk. *diagramma* < *dia-* apart, out + *graphein* mark]

di·a·gram·mat·ic (dī′ə grə mat′ik) *adj.* **1** in the form of a diagram. **2** in outline only; sketchy.

di·a·gram·mat·i·cal (dī′ə grə mat′ə kəl) *adj.* diagrammatic.

di·a·gram·mat·i·cal·ly (dī′ə grə mat′ik lē) *adv.* in the form of a diagram.

di·al (dī′əl or dīl) *n. v.* **-alled** or **-aled, -al·ling** or **-al·ing.** —*n.* **1** a marked surface on which a moving pointer shows how much there is of something. The face of a clock or of a compass is a dial. A dial may show the amount of water in a tank or the amount of steam pressure in a boiler. **2** the plate, disk, etc. of a radio or television set with numbers, letters, etc. on it for tuning in to a radio or television station. **3** the part of an automatic telephone used in making telephone calls. **4** a sundial. **5** *Slang.* the face.
—*v.* **1** tune in by using a radio or television dial. **2** call by means of a telephone dial. **3** measure or record with or as if with a dial. [apparently < Med.L (*rota*) *dialis* daily (wheel) < L *dies* day]

dial. **1** dialect. **2** dialectal.

di·a·lect (dī′ə lekt′) *n.* **1** a form of speech characteristic of a fairly definite region or class: *The Scottish dialect, the dialect spoken in Lunenberg, Nova Scotia.* **2** one of a group of closely related languages: *Some of the dialects descended from the Latin language are French, Italian, Spanish, and Portuguese.* **3** the words and pronunciations used by certain professions, classes of people, etc.: *thieves' dialect.* **4** a distinct form or variety of a language: *the Sicilian dialect of Italian.* —*adj.* having to do with a dialect: *a dialect dictionary.* [< L *dialectus* < Gk. *dialektos,* ult. < *dia-* between + *legein* speak] —**Syn. 1** See **language.**

☛ **Dialects** exist because of the separation of groups of speakers either regionally or socially. Where several regional dialects exist, one may attain the highest status because it may be spoken in the area which contains the centre of government, education, or trade. A dialect is not to be confused with a form of a language that contains errors in grammar or pronunciation or vocabulary.

di·a·lec·tal (dī′ə lek′təl) *adj.* of or having to do with a dialect; like that of a dialect. —**di′a·lec′tal·ly,** *adv.*

di·a·lec·tic (dī′ə lek′tik) *n.* **1** the art or practice of logical discussion employed in finding out the truth of a theory or opinion. **2** logical argumentation; a discussion of the logical truth of an opinion or theory. **3** in logic, a branch that consists of formal rhetorical reasoning. **4** in logic, a method based on the resolution of contradictory opposites, thesis and antithesis, leading to synthesis. —*adj.* **1** having to do with logical discussion: *dialectic criticism.* **2** dialectal.

di·a·lec·ti·cal (dī′ə lek′tə kəl) *adj.* dialectic.

dialectical materialism a socialist doctrine formulated by Karl Marx and Friedrich Engels, using the philosopher Hegel's dialectic method, that advocates a classless society emerging as the result of a long struggle between economic classes. It is the official communist philosophy.

di·a·lec·ti·cian (dī′ə lek tish′ən) *n.* **1** a person skilled in dialectic; logician. **2** a dialectologist.

di·a·lec·tics (dī′ə lek′tiks) *n.* dialectic.

di·a·lec·tol·o·gist (dī′ə lek tol′ə jist) *n.* an expert in the study of dialects.

di·a·lec·tol·o·gy (dī′ə lek tol′ə jē) *n.* the study of dialects.

di·a·logue (dī′ə log′) *n.* **1** a conversation. **2** a literary work in the form of a conversation. **3** a conversation in a play, story, etc. **4** in music, a composition for two voices or instruments or two groups of voices or instruments, thought of as resembling a conversation. Also, **dialog.** [ME < OF *dialoge* < L < Gk. *dialogos* < *dia-* between + *logos* speech]

dial tone the humming sound that is heard on a dial telephone when the receiver is lifted. It indicates that a number may be dialled.

di·a·lyse or **di·a·lyze** (dī′ə līz′) *v.* **-lysed** or **-lyzed, -lys·ing** or **-lyz·ing.** in chemistry: **1** apply dialysis to. **2** separate or procure by dialysis. **—di′a·lys′er** or **di′a·lyz′er,** *n.*

di·al·y·sis (dī al′ə sis) *n.* **-ses** (-sēz′). in chemistry, the separation of crystalloids from colloids in solution by the application of the principle that crystalloids diffuse readily through a membrane, and colloids not at all or very slightly. [< Gk. *dialysis* < *dia-* apart + *lyein* loose]

di·a·lyt·ic (dī′ə lit′ik) *adj.* having to do with or like dialysis.

diam. diameter.

di·a·mag·net·ic (dī′ə mag net′ik) *adj.* repelled by a magnet; taking a position at right angles to the lines of force of a magnet. —*n.* a diamagnetic body or substance. **—di′a·mag·net′i·cal·ly,** *adv.*

di·a·mag·net·ism (dī′ə mag′nə tiz′əm) *n.* **1** a diamagnetic quality. **2** diamagnetic phenomena. **3** the science dealing with diamagnetic phenomena.

dia·man·té (dyä mäɴ tā′) *n. French.* a fabric set with rhinestones, paste, etc. so that it sparkles. —*adj.* set with diamonds or diamond chips: *diamanté buttons.*

di·am·e·ter (dī am′ə tər) *n.* **1** a straight line passing from one side to the other through the centre of a circle, sphere, etc. **2** the length of such a line; measurement from one side to the other through the centre; width; thickness: *The tree trunk was almost 2 feet in diameter.* [< OF *diametre* < L < Gk. *diametros* < *dia-* across + *metron* measure]

A B

The line AB is a diameter

di·a·met·ric (dī′ə met′rik) *adj.* **1** of or along a diameter. **2** direct; absolute; exactly opposite.

di·a·met·ri·cal (dī′ə met′rə kəl) *adj.* diametric.

di·a·met·ri·cal·ly (dī′ə met′rik lē) *adv.* **1** as a diameter. **2** directly; exactly; entirely. **3 diametrically opposed,** directly opposite; exactly contrary.

dia·mond (dī′mənd or dī′ə mənd) *n.* **1** a colorless or tinted precious stone, formed of pure carbon in crystals. Diamond is the hardest substance known. **2** a piece of this stone, or a gem made from it. Inferior diamonds are used to cut glass. **3** a tool with a diamond tip for cutting. **4** a plane figure shaped like this ◇. **5 a** a playing card with one or more red diamond-shaped designs on it. **b diamonds,** *pl.* the suit of cards marked with this design. **6** in baseball, the space inside the lines that connect the bases. **7** in printing, a very small size of type; 4½ point. This sentence is in diamond. **8 diamond cut diamond,** a dispute or struggle between two well-matched opponents. **9 diamond in the rough, a rough diamond,** a person who has good qualities but poor manners. [ME < OF *diamant* < Med.L *diamas, -antis,* alteration of L *adamas, -antis* adamant]

dia·mond·back terrapin (dī′mənd bak′ or dī′ə mənd-) a turtle that has diamond-shaped markings on its shell. It lives in salt marshes along the southeastern coast of North America.

diamond hitch a hitch used in fastening a load to a pack-animal, in which the rope is thrown back and forth across the animal in such a way that it forms a diamond pattern on top of the pack.

diamond wedding the 60th or 75th anniversary of a wedding.

Di·an·a (dī an′ə) *n.* **1** in Roman mythology, the goddess who was worshipped primarily as the protectress and helper of women. She also was the goddess of the

hat, āge, cãre, fär; let, ēqual, tėrm; it, īce
hot, ōpen, ôrder; oil, out; cup, pu̇t, rüle, ūse
əbove, takən, pencəl, lemən, circəs
ch, child; ng, long; sh, ship
th, thin; ᴛʜ, then; zh, measure

hunt and of the moon, and was identified with the Greek goddess Artemis. **2** *Poetic.* the moon. **3** any young woman of fine physique and easy, graceful carriage.

di·a·net·ic (dī′ə net′ik) *adj.* of or having to do with dianetics.

di·a·net·ics (dī′ə net′iks) *n.* a system of mental treatment that seeks to alleviate certain apparently physical ailments that are supposedly caused primarily by a mental attitude, etc. The theory of dianetics is based on the idea that a person can be taken back, in memory, to his prenatal life, and thus cured of his physical ailments. [apparently < *dianoetic* pertaining to reasoning < Gk. *dianoētikos,* ult. < *dia-* through + *noos* mind]

di·an·thus (dī an′thəs) *n.* any of various plants of the pink family, as the carnation and sweet william; pink. [< NL *Dianthus* < Gk. *Dios,* genitive of *Zeus* Zeus + *anthos* flower]

di·a·pa·son (dī′ə pā′zən or dī′ə pā′sən) *n.* **1** *Poetic.* harmony. **2** a melody; strain. **3** a swelling musical sound. **4** the whole range of a voice or instrument. **5** range; gamut; entire scope: *the diapason of emotional experience.* **6** a fixed standard of pitch. **7** a tuning fork. **8** in an organ, either of two principal stops: **a open diapason,** a stop giving full, majestic tones. **b stopped diapason,** a stop giving powerful flutelike tones. **9** in Greek music, an octave. [< L < Gk. *diapasōn* octave < *dia pasōn* (*chordōn*) across all (the notes of the scale)]

di·a·per (dī′ə pər or dī′pər) *n.* **1** a piece of cloth or other soft material folded and used as underpants for a baby; napkin. **2** a pattern of small, constantly repeated geometric figures. **3** a white cotton or linen cloth woven with such a pattern. —*v.* **1** put a diaper on a baby. **2** ornament with a diaper pattern. [ME < OF *diapre,* var. of *diaspre* < Med.Gk. *diaspros* < *dia-* (intensive) + *aspros* white]

A diaper design (def. 2)

di·aph·a·nous (dī af′ə nəs) *adj.* transparent: *Gauze is a diaphanous fabric.* [< Med.L *diaphanus* < Gk. *diaphanēs* < *dia-* through + *phainein* show] **—di·aph′a·nous·ly,** *adv.* **—di·aph′a·nous·ness,** *n.*

di·a·pho·re·sis (dī′ə fə rē′sis) *n.* in medicine, perspiration, especially when artificially induced. [< LL < Gk. *diaphorēsis* < *dia-* through + *phorein* carry]

di·a·phragm (dī′ə fram′) *n.* **1** in anatomy, a partition of muscles and tendons separating the cavity of the chest from the cavity of the abdomen. **2** a thin partition, as in a galvanic cell, in some shellfish, etc. **3** a thin disk or cone that moves rapidly to and fro when sounds are directed at it, used in telephone receivers, loudspeakers, earphones, and in similar instruments. **4** a device for controlling the amount of light entering a camera, microscope, etc. **5** a type of contraceptive. —*v.* **1** furnish with a diaphragm. **2** act upon by a diaphragm. [< LL < Gk. *diaphragma* < *dia-* across + *phragma* fence < *phrassein* to fence]

di·a·phrag·mat·ic (dī′ə frag mat′ik) *adj.* having to do with a diaphragm; like a diaphragm.

di·ar·chy (dī′är kē) *n.* **-chies.** government by two people or two ruling authorities. Also, **dyarchy.** [< Gk. *di-* twice + *archos* ruler (< *archein* to rule) + E *-y*[3]]

di·a·rist (dī′ə rist) *n.* a person who keeps a diary.

di·ar·rhe·a or **di·ar·rhoe·a** (dī′ə rē′ə) *n.* the condition of having too many and too loose movements of the bowels. [< LL *diarrhoea* < Gk. *diarrhọia* < *dia-* through + *rheein* flow]

di·a·ry (dī′ə rē) *n.* **-ries. 1** an account written down each day, of what one has done, thought, etc. during the day. **2** a book for keeping such an account. [< L *diarium* < *dies* day]

Di·as·po·ra (dī as′pə rə) *n.* **1** the scattering of the Jews after their captivity in Babylon. **2** the Jews thus scattered. **3** the early Jewish Christians living outside Palestine. **4** Jews living outside modern Israel. [< Gk. *diaspora* a scattering < *dia-* through + *speirein* sow]

di·a·stase (dī′ə stās′) *n.* an enzyme that changes starch into dextrine and maltose during digestion, germination of seeds, etc. [< F < Gk. *diastasis* separation < *dia-* apart + *sta-* stand]

di·as·to·le (dī as′tə lē′) *n.* the normal, rhythmical dilation of the heart, especially that of the ventricles. [< LL < Gk. *diastolē* expansion < *dia-* apart + *stellein* send]

di·as·tol·ic (dī′əs tol′ik) *adj.* having to do with diastole.

di·a·ther·mic (dī′ə thėr′mik) *adj.* having to do with diathermy. [< F *diathermique* < Gk. *dia-* through + *thermē* heat]

di·a·ther·my (dī′ə thėr′mē) *n.* a method of treating disease by heating the tissues beneath the skin with an electric current.

di·a·tom (dī′ə tom′) *n.* any of numerous microscopic, unicellular, aquatic algae that have hard shells composed mostly of silica. [< NL *Diatoma*, genus name < Gk. *diatomos* cut in half < *diatemnein* cut through]

di·a·to·ma·ceous (dī′ə tə mā′shəs) *adj.* of or having to do with diatoms; consisting of or containing diatoms or their fossil remains: *diatomaceous earth.*

di·a·tom·ic (dī′ə tom′ik) *adj.* in chemistry: **1** containing only two atoms. **2** containing two replaceable atoms. **3** bivalent.

di·a·ton·ic (dī′ə ton′ik) *adj.* in music, of or using only the eight tones of a standard major or minor scale. [< L *diatonicus* < Gk. *diatonikos* < *dia-* through + *tonos* tone]

diatonic scale in music, a standard major or minor scale of eight tones in the octave.

di·a·tribe (dī′ə trīb′) *n.* a bitter and violent denunciation of some person or thing. [< L *diatriba* < Gk. *diatribē* pastime, study, discourse < *dia-* away + *tribein* wear]

dib (dib) *n.* **1** a small marble, usually made of clay: *He bought some dibs at the store.* **2 dibs, a** the game played with these marbles. **b** *Slang.* money made, especially in small amounts. **c** *Slang.* one's share or shares in any profitable venture. [origin uncertain]

di·ba·sic (dī bā′sik) *adj.* in chemistry, having two hydrogen atoms that can be replaced by two atoms or radicals of a base in forming salts.

dib·ble (dib′əl) *n. v.* **-bled, -bling.** —*n.* a pointed tool that makes holes in the ground for seeds, young plants, etc. —*v.* **1** make a hole in (the soil) with or as if with a dibble. **2** sow or plant (seeds, etc.) in this way. [origin uncertain]

dice (dīs) *n.* pl. of **die**², *v.* **diced, dic·ing.** —*n.* **1** small cubes with a different number of spots (one to six) on each side, used in playing games and gambling. **2** a game played with dice. **3** small cubes. —*v.* **1** play dice, tossing them to see how many spots there will be on the sides turned up. **2** lose or throw away by gambling with dice. **3** cut into small cubes: *dice carrots.* —**dic′er,** *n.*

dic·ey (dī′sē) *adj. Slang.* **1** chancy; risky; uncertain. **2** dangerous; on the point of erupting into a dangerous situation.

di·chlo·ride (dī klô′rīd or -klô′rid) *n.* a chloride whose molecules contain two atoms of chlorine; bichloride.

di·chot·o·mous (dī kot′ə məs) *adj.* **1** divided or dividing into two parts. **2** in botany, branching by repeated divisions into two.

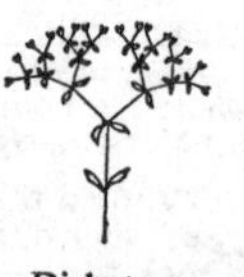
Dichotomy (def. 2)

di·chot·o·my (dī kot′ə mē) *n.* **-mies. 1** a division into two parts. **2** in botany, branching by repeated divisions into two parts. **3** in zoology, a form of branching in which each successive axis divides into two. **4** in logic, classification by division, or by successive subdivision, into two groups or sections: *the dichotomy in the universe of the living and the nonliving.* [< Gk. *dichotomia* a cutting in half < *dicha* in two + *temnein* cut]

di·chro·mate (dī krō′māt) *n.* a chromate whose molecules have two atoms of chromium; bichromate.

di·chro·mat·ic (dī′krō mat′ik) *adj.* **1** having two colors. **2** in zoology, showing two color phases independent of phases correlated with age, sex, or season. **3** of, having to do with, or affected with dichromatism (def. 2).

di·chro·ma·tism (dī krō′mə tiz′əm) *n.* **1** a dichromatic quality or condition. **2** color blindness in which a person can distinguish only two of the primary colors. [see DI-¹, CHROMATIC]

dick·ens (dik′ənz) *n. interj.* **1** the devil; deuce. **2 the dickens!** an exclamation expressing surprise or annoyance.

Dick·en·si·an (di ken′zē ən or di ken′sē ən) *adj.* **1** of or having to do with Charles Dickens (1812-1870), an English novelist. **2** of or suggestive of his style, writings, characters, etc. —*n.* a person who studies or admires Charles Dickens or his works.

dick·er (dik′ər) *v.* trade by barter or by petty bargaining. —*n.* **1** a petty bargain. **2** the act of bargaining. [< *dicker*, n., a lot of ten hides]

dick·ey¹ (dik′ē) *n.* **-eys. 1** a shirt front that can be detached. **2** a high collar on a shirt. **3** a child's bib or pinafore. **4** a vestee. **5** the driver's seat on the outside of a carriage. **6** a seat at the back of a carriage for servants. **7** a small bird. **8** a donkey. [< *Dick*, proper name]

dick·ey² (dik′ē) *n. Cdn.* a pull-over garment for the upper body, having a hood and made of duffle or skins; parka; atigi (def. 2). Also, **dickie, dicky.** [< Eskimo *atigi*]

dick·ie (dik′ē) *n.* **-ies.** dickey².

dick·y (dik′ē) *n.* **dick·ies.** dickey².

di·cot·y·le·don (dī kot′ə lē′dən) *n.* in botany, a flowering plant that has two cotyledons or seed leaves; any of a group of plants having two seed leaves. Many trees and most of the cultivated plants are dicotyledons. See **cotyledon** for picture.

di·cot·y·le·don·ous (dī kot′ə lē′dən əs) *adj.* having two seed leaves; belonging to the dicotyledons.

dict. 1 dictionary. **2** dictator.

dic·ta (dik′tə) *n.* a pl. of **dictum.**

Dic·ta·phone (dik′tə fōn′) *n. Trademark.* an instrument that records and reproduces sounds, used for dictating and transcribing. [< *dicta(te)* + *-phone*]

dic·tate (*v.* dik′tāt or dik tāt′; *n.* dik′tāt) *v.* **-tat·ed, -tat·ing,** *n.* —*v.* **1** say or read (something) aloud for another person or other persons to write down: *The teacher dictated a spelling list.* **2** command with authority; give orders that must be obeyed: *No one shall dictate to me.* —*n.* a direction or order that is to be carried out or obeyed: *An honest man follows the dictates of his conscience.* [< L *dictare* say often < *dicere* tell, say] —**Syn.** *v.* **2** order, decree. -*n.* command.

dic·ta·tion (dik tā′shən) *n.* **1** the act of saying or reading (something) aloud for another person or other persons to write down: *The pupils wrote at the teacher's dictation.* **2** the words said or read aloud to be written down: *We have dictation during the first five minutes of our French class.* **3** the act of commanding with authority; act of giving orders that must be obeyed: *The slave acted at the dictation of his master.*

dic·ta·tor (dik′tā tər or dik tā′tər) *n.* **1** a person exercising absolute authority; especially, a person who, without having any claim through inheritance or free popular election, seizes control of a government: *The dictator of the country had complete power over its people.* **2** a person who says or reads words aloud to another who writes them down.

dic·ta·to·ri·al (dik′tə tô′rē əl) *adj.* **1** of or like that of a dictator: *dictatorial government.* **2** imperious; domineering; overbearing: *The soldiers disliked the dictatorial manner of the new officer.* —**dic′ta·to′ri·al·ly,** *adv.*

dic·ta·tor·ship (dik′tā tər ship′ or dik tā′tər ship′) *n.* **1** the position or rank of a dictator. **2** the period during which a dictator rules. **3** absolute authority; the power to give orders that must be obeyed. **4** a country under the rule of a dictator.

dic·tion (dik′shən) *n.* **1** the manner of expressing ideas in words; style of speaking or writing. Good diction

implies grammatical correctness, a wide vocabulary, and skill in the choice and arrangement of words. **2** the manner of speaking or singing; articulation or enunciation. [< L *dictio, -onis* saying < *dicere* say]
Syn. Diction, phraseology, wording = words and the way of using them. **Diction** applies to words and emphasizes the choice of words used to express ideas and feelings and the way in which they convey meaning: *John's diction is poor; he uses too much slang and too many colorless words.* **Phraseology** applies to the grouping of words, particularly in the way peculiar to a person, group, profession, etc.: *I don't understand legal phraseology.* **Wording** applies to words and grouping but emphasizes their special suitability for a purpose: *I like the wording of that greeting.*

dic·tion·ar·y (dik′shən er′ē) *n.* **-ar·ies.** a book containing the words, or a selection of the words of a language or of some special subject, arranged alphabetically, with explanations of their meanings and with other information about them. [< Med.L *dictionarium* < L *dictio.* See DICTION.]

Dic·to·graph (dik′tə graf′) *n. Trademark.* a telephone with a very sensitive transmitter, used for secretly listening to or obtaining a record of conversation. [< L *dictum* (thing) said + E *-graph*]

dic·tum (dik′təm) *n.* **-tums** or **-ta. 1** a formal comment; an authoritative opinion: *The dictum of the critics was that the play was excellent.* **2** a maxim; saying. [< L *dictum* (thing) said, pp. neut. of *dicere* say]

did (did) *v.* pt. of **do**¹.

di·dac·tic (dī dak′tik or di dak′tik) *adj.* **1** intended to instruct: *Aesop's "Fables" are didactic stories; each one has an instructive moral.* **2** inclined to instruct others; teacherlike: *The older brother was called "Professor" because of his didactic manner.* [< Gk. *didaktikos* < *didaskein* teach] **—di·dac′ti·cal·ly,** *adv.*

di·dac·ti·cal (dī dak′tə kəl or di dak′tə kəl) *adj.* didactic.

di·dac·ti·cism (dī dak′tə siz′əm or di dak′tə siz′əm) *n.* a didactic quality, character, or manner.

di·dac·tics (dī dak′tiks or di dak′tiks) *n.* the science or art of giving instruction.

did·dle (did′el) *v.* **-dled, -dling.** *Informal.* **1** cheat; swindle. **2** waste (time). **3** ruin. [origin uncertain]

did·n't (did′ənt) did not.

di·do (dī′dō) *n.* **-dos** or **-does.** *Informal.* a prank; trick; a mischievous or disorderly action. [origin uncertain]

didst (didst) *v. Archaic or poetic.* 2nd pers. sing. past tense of **do**¹. "Thou didst" means "You did" (sing.).

die¹ (dī) *v.* **died, dy·ing. 1** cease to live; stop living; become dead. **2** come to an end; lose force or strength; stop. **3** *Informal.* want very much; be very desirous (usually a present participle with a form of *to be,* followed by an infinitive or by *for*): *I'm dying to go to the Rockies. We are dying for a home in the country.* **4 die away** or **down,** stop or end little by little; lose force or strength gradually: *The music died away.* **5 die hard,** struggle until death; resist to the very end; refuse to give in. **6 die off,** die one after another until all are dead. **7 die out, a** stop or end little by little. **b** cease or end completely. [OE *diegan*]
Syn. 1, 2 Die, perish = stop living or existing. **Die,** the general word meaning "to stop living," is also used figuratively of things that have been active in any way: (fig.) *The noisy conversation of the class died down suddenly when the teacher came into the room.* **Perish,** more formal or literary than *die,* emphasizes losing life through violence or hardship, and used figuratively means "to go out of existence permanently": *Many perished in the great fire.* (fig.) *The forces of evil may cause civilization to perish.*
☛ **Die** is generally used with *of* before an illness: *He died of* (not *from* or *with*) *cancer.* However, *from* is sometimes used: *He died from a wound.*

die² (dī) *n.* **dies.** any tool or apparatus for shaping, cutting, or stamping things. It is usually a metal block or plate cut in a certain way. [< *die*³]

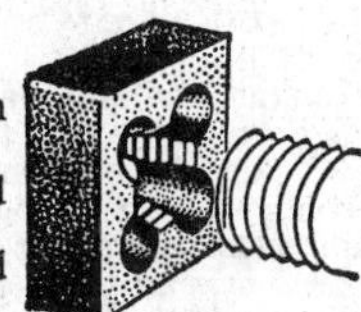
A die for cutting the threads of bolts

die³ (dī) *n.* **dice. 1** a small cube used in games of chance. See **dice. 2 The die is cast.** The decision is made and cannot be changed. [ME < OF *de* < L *datum* (thing) given (i.e., by fortune), pp. neut. of *dare* give. Doublet of DATUM.]

die·back (dī′bak′) *n.* a disease that kills trees, the outer or topmost parts dying first.

hat, āge, cãre, fär; let, ēqual, tėrm; it, īce
hot, ōpen, ôrder; oil, out; cup, pu̇t, rüle, ūse
əbove, takən, pencəl, lemən, circəs
ch, child; ng, long; sh, ship
th, thin; ᴛʜ, then; zh, measure

die-cast (dī′kast′) *adj.* made by the process of die-casting: *a die-cast engine block.*

die caster a person who makes die castings.

die casting 1 a process by which metal is cast to a desired shape by being forced into a mould, or **die,** when molten. **2** a metal object made in this way.

di·e·cious (dī ē′shəs) *adj.* dioecious.

die-hard (dī′härd′) *adj.* resisting to the very end; refusing to give in. *—n.* a person who refuses to give in.

di·e·lec·tric (dī′i lek′trik) *adj.* non-conducting. *—n.* a dielectric substance, such as glass, rubber, or wood.

di·er·e·sis or **di·aer·e·sis** (dī er′ə sis) *n.* **-ses** (-sēz′). two dots (¨) placed over the second of two consecutive vowels to indicate that the second vowel is to be pronounced in a separate syllable. *Example:* naïve. [< L *diaeresis* < Gk. *diairesis* separation, division < *diaireein* divide < *dia-* apart + *haireein* take]

die·sel (dē′zəl or dē′səl) *n.* a Diesel engine or motor. *—adj.* **1** powered by a Diesel engine or motor: *a diesel train.* **2** of or having to do with Diesel engines: *diesel fuel, a diesel mechanic.*

Diesel engine an internal-combustion engine that burns oil with heat caused by the compression of air. [after R. *Diesel,* 1858-1913, its inventor]

Diesel motor Diesel engine.

diesel oil a light fuel oil burned by Diesel engines and obtained from crude oil after the distillation of gasoline and kerosene.

die·sink·er (dī′singk′ər) *n.* a person who makes dies for shaping or stamping.

Di·es I·rae (dī′ēz ī′rē or dē′ās ē′rī) **1** a medieval Latin hymn describing the Day of Judgment and usually sung at masses for the dead. **2** a musical setting for such a hymn. [< L *dies irae* day of wrath]

di·et¹ (dī′ət) *n. v.* **-et·ed, -et·ing.** *—n.* **1** the usual food and drink for a person or animal. **2** a special selection of food and drink eaten during illness or in an attempt to lose or gain weight. **3** something provided habitually or repeatedly: *Anyone gets tired of a steady diet of good advice.*
—v. eat or cause to eat special food and drink. [ME < OF *diete(r)* < L < Gk. *diaita* way of life]
—di′et·er, *n.*

di·et² (dī′ət) *n.* **1** a formal assembly. **2** the national lawmaking body in certain countries. [< Med.L *dieta* day's work, session of councillors, ult. identical with *diet*¹ but influenced by L *dies* day]

di·e·tar·y (dī′ə ter′ē) *adj. n.* **-tar·ies.** *—adj.* having to do with diet: *Dietary rules tell us what food to eat for healthy living and how to prepare it.* *—n.* **1** an allowance of food in a prison, hospital, etc. **2** a system of diet.

di·e·tet·ic (dī′ə tet′ik) *adj.* of or having to do with diet. **—di·e·tet′i·cal·ly,** *adv.*

di·e·tet·ics (dī′ə tet′iks) *n.* the science that deals with the amount and kinds of food needed by the body.

di·e·ti·tian or **di·e·ti·cian** (dī′ə tish′ən) *n.* a person trained to plan meals that have the proper proportion of various kinds of food.

dif- the form of **dis-**¹ before *f,* as in *diffuse.*

diff. 1 difference. **2** different.

dif·fer (dif′ər) *v.* **1** be unlike; be different. **2** have or express a different opinion; disagree. [ME < OF < L *differre* set apart, differ < *dis-* apart + *ferre* carry. Doublet of DEFER¹.] **—Syn. 2** dissent.
☛ **Differ** is followed by *from* when it means "be unlike or different": *My answers to the algebra problems differed from Mary's.* When the meaning is "disagree," *differ* is followed **by with** or *from*: *I differed from him in the solution he offered. She never differs with my plans.*

dif·fer·ence (dif′rəns or dif′ər əns) *n.* **1** the condition of being different. **2** the way of being different; point in which people or things are different. **3** the amount by which one quantity is different from another; what is left after subtracting one number from another. **4** the condition of having a different opinion; disagreement. **5** a dispute. **6 make a difference, a** give or show different treatment. **b** matter; be important; have an effect or influence. **7 split the difference, a** divide what is left in half. **b** meet halfway; compromise.

Syn. *n.* **1 Difference, discrepancy, disparity** = unlikeness between two things. **Difference** applies to lack of sameness or any unlikeness, large or small, in a detail, quality, etc.: *There is a difference in John's and Mary's heights.* **Discrepancy** applies to a lack of agreement between things that should be alike or balance: *There was a discrepancy between the two reports of the accident.* **Disparity** applies to a lack of equality: *There is a disparity between my expenses and my income.*

dif·fer·ent (dif′rənt or dif′ər ənt) *adj.* **1** not alike; not like. **2** not the same; separate; distinct: *I saw her three different times today.* **3** not like others or most others; unusual. **—dif′fer·ent·ly,** *adv.* **—Syn. 1** dissimilar, unlike.

☛ **different.** In formal English, the standard idiom is *different from*: *His second book was entirely different from his first.* Informal usage is divided, using *from* occasionally, sometimes *to* (which is a common British idiom), and more often *than*: *She was different than any other girl he had ever known. Different than* is becoming more common when the object is a clause: *The house was a good deal different than he remembered it.*

dif·fer·en·ti·a (dif′ər en′shē ə) *n.* **-ti·ae** (-shē ē′ or -shē ī′). in logic, the quality or condition that distinguishes one species from all the others of the same genus or class. [< L *differentia* difference]

dif·fer·en·tial (dif′ər en′shəl) *adj.* **1** of a difference; showing a difference; depending on a difference: *Differential duties, rates, charges, etc. are those that differ according to circumstances.* **2** distinguishing; distinctive. **3** having to do with distinguishing characteristics or specific differences: *A differential diagnosis attempts to distinguish between two similar diseases or objects of natural history.* **4** in mathematics, having to do with or involving differentials. **5** in physics and mechanics, concerning the difference of two or more motions, pressures, etc. **6** in geology, producing different or selective effects on formations or constituents of rocks, soils, etc.: *differential erosion, differential weathering.*

A differential (def. 5); A, ring gear; B, axle; C, pinion gear; D, drive shaft; E, drive shaft gear. The shape of the gears changes the direction of motion between the drive shaft and the axle. When the car turns, power is transmitted only to the outside rear wheel.

—*n.* **1** a differential duty or rate; the difference involved. **2** in mathematics, an infinitesimal difference between consecutive values of a variable quantity. **3** in an automobile, an arrangement of gears that allows one of the rear wheels to turn faster than the other in going round a corner or curve.
—dif′fer·en′tial·ly, *adv.*

differential calculus the branch of higher mathematics that investigates differentials and their relations.

dif·fer·en·ti·ate (dif′ər en′shē āt′) *v.* **-at·ed, -at·ing. 1** make different: *Consideration for others differentiates good manners from mere politeness.* **2** become different: *This genus of plants differentiates into many species.* **3** perceive the difference in; make a distinction between: *The trained botanist can differentiate many varieties of plants.* **4** note differences. **—dif′fer·en′ti·a′tor,** *n.* **—Syn. 3, 4** See **distinguish.**

dif·fer·en·ti·a·tion (dif′ər en′shē ā′shən) *n.* the act or process of differentiating; alteration; modification; distinction.

dif·fi·cult (dif′ə kult′ or dif′ə kəlt) *adj.* **1** hard to do or understand: *Higher mathematics is difficult.* **2** hard to deal with, get along with, or please: *The secretary found her new employer difficult.* **—Syn. 1** arduous. **2** trying.

dif·fi·cul·ty (dif′ə kul′tē or dif′ə kəl tē) *n.* **-ties. 1** the fact or condition of being difficult: *the difficulty of a job.* **2** hard work; much effort. **3** trouble. **4** financial trouble. **5** something that is difficult; something in the way; an obstacle. **6** a disagreement; quarrel. **7 make a difficulty,** be unwilling; object. [ME< L *difficultas* < *difficilis* hard < *dis-* not + *facilis* easy] **—Syn. 3** hardship, dilemma, predicament. **5** hindrance.

dif·fi·dence (dif′ə dəns) *n.* lack of self-confidence; shyness.

dif·fi·dent (dif′ə dənt) *adj.* lacking in self-confidence; shy. [< L *diffidens, -entis,* ppr. of *diffidere* < *dis-* away + *fidere* trust] **—dif′fi·dent·ly,** *adv.*

dif·fract (di frakt′) *v.* break up by diffraction. [< L *diffractus,* pp. of *diffringere* < *dis-* up + *frangere* break]

dif·frac·tion (di frak′shən) *n.* in physics: **1** a breaking up of a ray of light into a series of light and dark bands or into the colored bands of the spectrum. **2** a similar breaking up of sound waves, electricity, etc.

dif·frac·tive (di frak′tiv) *adj.* having to do with diffraction; tending to diffract. **—dif·frac′tive·ly,** *adv.* **—dif·frac′tive·ness,** *n.*

dif·fuse (*v.* di fūz′; *adj.* -fūs′) *v.* **-fused, -fus·ing,** *adj.* —*v.* **1** spread out so as to cover a larger space or surface; scatter widely. **2** in physics, mix together by spreading into one another, as one gas with another or one liquid with another; spread by diffusion. [< L *diffusus.* See adj.]
—*adj.* **1** not concentrated at a single point; spread out: *diffuse light.* **2** using many words where a few would do: *a diffuse writer.* [ME < L *diffusus,* pp. of *diffundere* < *dis-* in every direction + *fundere* pour]
—dif·fuse′ly, *adv.* **—dif·fuse′ness,** *n.* **—dif·fus′er,** *n.*
—Syn. *v.* **1** disseminate, disperse. —*adj.* **1** widespread, scattered, dispersed. **2** wordy.

dif·fus·i·ble (di fūz′ə bəl) *adj.* capable of being diffused.

dif·fu·sion (di fū′zhən) *n.* **1** the act or fact of diffusing; a spreading widely; a scattering: *The invention of printing greatly increased the diffusion of knowledge.* **2** a being widely spread or scattered; a diffused condition. **3** in physics, a mixing together of the molecules or atoms of gases or of liquids by spreading into one another. **4** the use of too many words; wordiness.

dif·fu·sive (di fū′siv) *adj.* **1** tending to diffuse. **2** showing diffusion. **3** using too many words; wordy. **—dif·fu′sive·ly,** *adv.* **—dif·fu′sive·ness,** *n.*

dig (dig) *v.* **dug** or (*Archaic*) **digged, dig·ging,** *n.* —*v.* **1** use a shovel, a spade, the hands, the claws, or the snout in making a hole or in turning over the ground. **2** break up and turn over (ground) with a spade, etc. **3** make (a hole, cellar, etc.) by removing material. **4** make a way by digging: *dig under the mountain; dig through the hill.* **5** get by digging: *dig potatoes, dig clams.* **6** make a thrust or stab into; prod: *The rider dug his spurs into the horse.* **7** make a careful search or inquiry (for information or into the works of some author). **8** *Slang.* **a** understand; appreciate. **b** notice; observe. **c** like; admire. **9 dig in, a** work hard. **b** make a protective trench. **c** secure one's position: *He has really dug in at the factory.* **d** *Informal.* eat heartily. **10 dig into,** *Informal.* work hard at. **11 dig up, a** unearth. **b** excavate. **c** find out.
—*n.* **1** the act of digging. **2** *Informal.* a thrust or poke: *a dig in the ribs.* **3** *Informal.* a sarcastic remark: *The speaker made a dig at sports.* **4** *Informal.* an archaeological excavation. **5 digs,** *Esp. Brit. Informal.* diggings (def. 3). [ME *dygge(n),* probably < MF *diguer* < Gmc.] **—Syn.** *v.* **1** delve, spade, grub.

di·gam·ma (dī gam′ə) *n.* a letter in the early Greek alphabet (Ϝ), with the phonetic value of English (w).

Dig·by chicken (dig′bē) *Cdn.* a small smoke-cured herring. [< *Digby,* N.S.]

di·gest (*v.* dī jest′ or di jest′; *n.* dī′jest) *v.* **1** change (food) in the stomach and intestines so that it can be taken into the blood and used as nourishment. **2** undergo this process. **3** promote the digestion of (food). **4** understand and absorb mentally; make part of one's thoughts. **5** condense and arrange according to some system; summarize. **6** endure; tolerate: *I find it difficult to digest his bad manners.* **7** in chemistry, soften by heat or moisture; dissolve.
—*n.* **1** information condensed according to some system; a summary: *a digest of law.* **2** a collection of summaries or condensations: *a book-review digest, a digest of great novels.* [ME < L *digestus,* pp. of *digerere* separate,

dissolve < *dis-* apart + *gerere* carry] —**Syn.** *v.* **4** assimilate. *-n.* See **summary.**

di·gest·er (dī jes′tər or di jes′tər) *n.* **1** a person who makes a digest. **2** a heavy, covered kettle, etc. for softening or dissolving a substance by heat and moisture.

di·gest·i·bil·i·ty (dī jes′tə bil′ə tē or di jes′tə bil′ə tē) *n.* a digestible quality.

di·gest·i·ble (dī jes′tə bəl or di jes′tə bəl) *adj.* capable of being digested; easily digested. **—di·gest′i·ble·ness,** *n.* **—di·gest′i·bly,** *adv.*

di·ges·tion (dī jes′chən or di jes′chən) *n.* **1** the digesting of food. **2** the ability to digest. **3** the act of digesting.

di·ges·tive (dī jes′tiv or di jes′tiv) *adj.* **1** of or for digestion. **2** helping digestion. *—n.* something that aids digestion. **—di·gest′ive·ly,** *adv.*

dig·ger (dig′ər) *n.* **1** a person that digs. **2** the part of a machine that turns up the ground. **3** any tool for digging. **4 Digger,** a nickname for an Australian.

digger wasp a wasp that digs its nest in the ground.

dig·gings (dig′ingz) *n.pl.* **1** a mine or place where digging is being done: *The archaeologists examined the new diggings.* **2** the material that is dug out. **3** *Informal.* a place to live.

dight (dīt) *v.* **dight** or **dight·ed, dight·ing.** *Archaic.* **1** dress; adorn. **2** equip. [OE *dihtan* compose, arrange < L *dictare* dictate]

dig·it (dij′it) *n.* **1** a finger or toe. **2** any of the figures 0, 1, 2, 3, 4, 5, 6, 7, 8, 9. Sometimes 0 is not called a digit but is known as a cipher. [ME < L *digitus* finger]

dig·it·al (dij′ə təl) *adj.* **1** of a digit or digits, especially a finger. **2** having digits. **3** like a digit or digits. *—n.* **1** a finger. **2** a key of an organ, piano, etc. played with the finger.

digital computer a type of electronic calculating machine using numbers expressed as digits of some numerical system to solve problems that can be expressed mathematically.

dig·i·tal·is (dij′ə tal′is or dij′ə tā′lis) *n.* **1** a medicine used for stimulating the heart, obtained from the leaves and seeds of the purple foxglove. **2** a foxglove. [< L *digitalis* pertaining to the finger < *digitus* finger; from the shape of the corolla]

dig·i·tate (dij′ə tāt′) *adj.* **1** having fingers or toes. **2** in botany, having radiating divisions like fingers. **3** in zoology, having digits or digitlike parts. **—dig′i·tate′ly,** *adv.*

A digitate leaf

dig·i·ti·grade (dij′ə tə grād′) *n.* an animal having feet shaped so that the toes are on the ground, but not the heels. Dogs, cats, and horses are digitigrades. *—adj.* having feet like this. [F < L *digitus* finger, toe + *gradi* walk]

dig·ni·fied (dig′nə fīd′) *adj.* having dignity; noble; stately. **—dig′ni·fied′ly,** *adv.*

dig·ni·fy (dig′nə fī′) *v.* **-fied, -fy·ing. 1** give dignity to; make noble, worth-while, or worthy: *The little farmhouse was dignified by the great elms around it.* **2** give a high-sounding name to. [< OF *dignifier* < LL *dignificare* < L *dignus* worthy + *facere* make]

dig·ni·tar·y (dig′nə ter′ē) *n.* **-tar·ies.** a person who has a position of honor: *A bishop is a dignitary of the church.*

dig·ni·ty (dig′nə tē) *n.* **-ties. 1** a proud and self-respecting character or manner; stateliness. **2** a quality of character or ability that wins the respect and high opinion of others; worth; a being noble, worthy, or stately: *A judge should maintain the dignity of his position.* **3** a high office, rank, or title: *Mr. Vincent Massey attained the dignity of Governor General.* **4** a person of high office, rank, or title. **5** worth; nobleness: *Honest work has dignity.* [ME < OF *dignete* < L *dignitas* < *dignus* worthy. Doublet of DAINTY.]

di·graph (dī′graf) *n.* two letters used together to spell a single sound. *Examples: ea* in *each, th* in *with, sh* in *shop.* [< *di-*[1] double, twice + Gk. *graphē* a writing]

di·gress (dī gres′ or di gres′) *v.* turn aside; get off the main subject in talking or writing. [< L *digressus,* pp. of *digredi* deviate < *dis-* aside < *gradi* to step] **—di·gress′er,** *n.* **—Syn.** See **diverge.**

hat, āge, cãre, fär; let, ēqual, tėrm; it, īce
hot, ōpen, ôrder; oil, out; cup, pu̇t, rüle, ūse
əbove, takən, pencəl, lemən, circəs
ch, child; ng, long; sh, ship
th, thin; ᴛʜ, then; zh, measure

di·gres·sion (dī gresh′ən or di gresh′ən) *n.* a turning aside; a getting off the main subject in talking or writing.

di·gres·sive (dī gres′iv or di gres′iv) *adj.* tending to digress; digressing. **—di·gres′sive·ly,** *adv.* **—di·gres′sive·ness,** *n.*

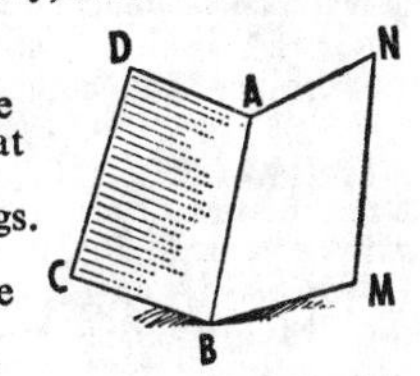

The angle between the planes ABCD and ABMN is a dihedral angle.

di·he·dral (dī hē′drəl) *adj.* **1** having or formed by two plane surfaces: *a dihedral angle.* **2** set at a dihedral angle to each other. Some aircraft have dihedral wings. *—n.* **1** the angle formed by two plane surfaces meeting along one edge. **2** the angle at which the wings of some aircraft incline to each other. [< *di-*[1] two + Gk. *hedra* seat; base + E *-al*[1]]

dike (dīk) *n. v.* **diked, dik·ing.** *—n.* **1** a bank of earth or a dam built as a defence against flooding by a river or the sea. **2** a ditch or channel for water. **3** a bank of earth thrown up in digging. **4** a low wall of earth or stone; causeway. **5** a barrier; obstacle. **6** in geology, a long, usually narrow mass of igneous rock that was thrust, while molten, into a fissure in older rock. *—v.* **1** provide with dikes. **2** drain with a ditch or channel for water. Also, **dyke.** [ME < ON *dík.* Akin to DITCH.]

dike·land (dīk′lənd) *n.* land, usually below sea level, that is protected from flooding by a system of embankments.

di·lan·tin (dī lan′tin) *n.* a white, powdery drug used in treating epilepsy. [*di*pheny*l*hyd*antoin* sodium]

dilantin sodium dilantin.

di·lap·i·dat·ed (di lap′ə dāt′id) *adj.* falling to pieces; partly ruined or decayed through neglect: *a dilapidated house.* [< L *dilapidatus,* pp. of *dilapidare* demolish, destroy (with stones) < *dis-* (intensive) + *lapis, lapidis* stone]

di·lap·i·da·tion (di lap′ə dā′shən) *n.* a falling to pieces; decay; ruin; tumble-down condition: *The house was in the last stage of dilapidation.*

dil·a·ta·tion (dī′lə tā′shən or dil′ə tā′shən) *n.* dilation.

di·late (dī lāt′ or di lāt′) *v.* **-lat·ed, -lat·ing. 1** make or become larger or wider: *The pupils of John's eyes dilated when the light dimmed.* **2** speak or write in a very complete or detailed manner. [< L *dilatare* < *dis-* apart + *latus* wide] **—Syn. 1** See **expand.**

di·lat·ed (dī lāt′id or di lāt′id) *adj.* widened; expanded.

di·la·tion (dī lā′shən or di lā′shən) *n.* **1** the act of dilating; enlargement; widening. **2** a dilated condition. **3** a dilated part.

di·la·tor (dī lā′tər or di lā′tər) *n.* **1** a person or thing that dilates. **2** in physiology, a muscle that dilates some part of the body. **3** a surgical instrument for dilating wounds, canals of the body, etc.

dil·a·to·ry (dil′ə tô′rē) *adj.* **1** tending to delay; not prompt. **2** causing delay. [< L *dilatorius* < *dilator* delayer < *dilatus,* pp. to *differre* defer, delay. See DIFFER.] **—dil′a·to′ri·ly,** *adv.* **—dil′a to′ri·ness,** *n.*

di·lem·ma (di lem′ə) *n.* **1** a situation requiring a choice between two evils; any embarrassing or perplexing situation; a difficult choice: *Her dilemma was whether to go to the party in her old dress or to stay at home.* **2** an argument forcing an opponent to choose one of two alternatives equally unfavorable to him. [< LL < Gk. *dilemma* < *di-* two + *lemma* premise] **—Syn. 1** See **predicament.**

dil·et·tan·te (dil′ə tan′tē or dil′ə tänt′) *n.* **-tes** (-tēz), **-ti** (-tē). **1** a lover of the fine arts. **2** a person who follows some art or science as an amusement or in a trifling way. **3** a trifler. [< Ital. *dilettante* < *dilettare* < L *delectare.* See DELIGHT.]

dil·et·tan·te·ism (dil′ə tan′tē iz′əm or dil′ə tän′tē iz′əm) *n.* dilettantism.

dil·et·tan·ti (dil′ə tan′tē or dil′ə tän′tē) *n.* a pl. of **dilettante.**

dil·et·tant·ism (dil′ə tan′tiz əm or dil′ə tän′tiz əm) *n.* the quality or practice of a dilettante.

dil·i·gence[1] (dil′ə jəns) *n.* the quality of being diligent; careful effort; the ability to work hard and steadily; industry: *The student's diligence was rewarded with high marks.* [< F < L *diligentia* < *diligere.* See DILIGENT.]

dil·i·gence[2] (dil′ə jəns) *n.* a public stagecoach formerly used in some parts of Europe. [special use of *diligence*[1]]

dil·i·gent (dil′ə jənt) *adj.* **1** hard-working; industrious. **2** careful and steady. [< L *diligens, -entis,* ppr. of *diligere* value highly, love < *dis-* apart + *legere* choose] **—dil′i·gent·ly,** *adv.* **—Syn. 1** See **busy.**

dill (dil) *n.* **1** the spicy seeds or leaves of a plant of the parsley family used to flavor pickles. **2** the plant that they grow on. [OE *dile*]

dill pickle a cucumber pickle flavored with dill.

dil·ly (dil′ē) *n.* **-lies.** *Slang.* a person or thing thought of as extraordinary, unique, odd, outstanding, etc.: *a dilly of a game.* [apparently < *del*ightful + *-y*[2]]

dil·ly-dal·ly (dil′ē dal′ē) *v.* **-lied, -ly·ing.** waste time; loiter; trifle.

di·lute (di lüt′ or dī lüt′) *v.* **-lut·ed, -lut·ing.** *adj.* —*v.* **1** make weaker or thinner by adding water or some other liquid. **2** weaken; lessen. **3** become diluted. —*adj.* weakened or thinned by the addition of water or other liquid. [< L *dilutus,* pp. of *diluere* < *dis-* apart + *luere* wash]

di·lut·ed (di lüt′id or dī lüt′id) *adj.* weakened; thinned.

di·lu·tion (di lü′shən or dī lü′shən) *n.* **1** the act of diluting. **2** the fact or state of being diluted. **3** something diluted.

di·lu·vi·al (di lü′vē əl or dī lü′vē əl) *adj.* **1** of or having to do with a flood. **2** made up of debris left by a flood or glacier. [< L *diluvialis* < *diluvium.* See DELUGE.]

di·lu·vi·an (di lü′vē ən or dī lü′vē ən) *adj.* diluvial.

dim (dim) *adj.* **dim·mer, dim·mest,** *v.* **dimmed, dim·ming.** —*adj.* **1** not bright; not clear; not distinct: *dim light.* **2** not clearly seen, heard, or understood: *a dim outline, a dim voice.* **3** not clear to the mind; vague: *a dim recollection.* **4** without lustre; dull. **5** not seeing, hearing, or understanding clearly: *My eyesight is getting dim.* **6** *Informal.* unfavorable: *He takes a dim view of his chances of winning the race.*
—*v.* **1** make or become dim. **2 dim out,** make nearly but not absolutely dark, by allowing light to appear only through slits, by use of blue lights, etc. [OE *dimm*] **—dim′ly,** *adv.* **—dim′ness,** *n.* **—Syn.** *adj.* **1** See **dark.**

dim. 1 diminuendo. **2** diminutive.

dime (dīm) *n.* a silver coin of Canada and the United States, worth 10 cents. [< OF *disme* < L *decima* (*pars*) tenth (part) < *decem* ten]

dime novel a sensational story that has no literary merit, of a type originally sold for a dime.

di·men·sion (di men′shən or dī men′shən) *n.* **1** the measurement of length, breadth, or thickness: *He ordered wallpaper for a room of the following dimensions: 16 ft. long, 12 ft. wide, 9 ft. high.* **2** the size; extent. **3** a characteristic; quality; part. [ME < MF < L *dimensio, -onis* < *dis-* out + *metiri* measure]

di·men·sion·al (di men′shən əl or dī men′shən əl) *adj.* having to do with dimension or dimensions. **—di·men′sion·al·ly,** *adv.*

di·mer (dī′mər) *n.* in chemistry, a compound in which two molecules of the same substance are present, especially as produced by polymerization. [< *di-*[1] two + Gk. *meros* part]

dim·er·ous (dim′ə rəs) *adj.* consisting of two parts, divisions, or members.

dime store a store selling a large variety of articles in a low price-range.

dim·e·ter (dim′ə tər) *n.* a line of verse having two metrical feet. *Examples*: The hóoded bát/Twirls sóftly bý (Walter de la Mare). [< L *dimetrus* < Gk. *dimetros* < *di-* two + *metron* meter]

dimin. 1 diminuendo. **2** diminutive.

di·min·ish (di min′ish) *v.* **1** make or become smaller in size, amount, or importance; lessen; reduce: *The heat diminished as the sun went down.* **2** in music, reduce a minor interval by a half-tone. [blend of *diminue* (< L *diminuere* < *dis-* (intensive) + *minuere* lessen) and *minish* (< OF *menuisier* make small < VL *minutiare,* ult. < L *minutus* small)] **—di·min′ish·ing·ly,** *adv.* **—Syn.** See **decrease.**

di·min·u·en·do (di min′ū en′dō) *n.* **-dos,** *adj. adv. v.* in music: —*n.* **1** a gradual decrease of loudness. The sign in music for a diminuendo is >. **2** a passage to be played or sung with a diminuendo. —*adj., adv.* with a diminuendo. —*v.* decrease gradually in force or loudness. *Abbrev.*: dim. or dimin. [< Ital. *diminuendo,* ppr. of *diminuire* diminish]

dim·i·nu·tion (dim′ə nū′shən or dim′ə nü′shən) *n.* a diminishing; a lessening; reduction; decrease. [ME < OF < L *diminutio, -onis*]

di·min·u·tive (di min′yů tiv) *adj.* **1** small; little; tiny. **2** expressing smallness. —*n.* **1** a small person or thing. **2** in grammar, a word or part of a word expressing smallness, as the suffixes *-let* and *-kin.* [< Med.L *diminutivus* < L *diminutus,* pp. of *diminuere* lessen] **—di·min′u·tive·ly,** *adv.* **—di·min′u·tive·ness,** *n.* **—Syn.** *adj.* **1** See **little.**

dim·i·ty (dim′ə tē) *n.* **-ties. 1** a thin cotton cloth woven with heavy threads at intervals in striped or cross-barred arrangement, used for dresses, curtains, etc. **2** a strong cotton cloth with raised patterns used for draperies, coverings for furniture, etc. [ME < Ital. *dimito* < Gk. *dimitos* of double thread < *di-* double + *mitos* warp thread]

dim·mer (dim′ər) *n.* **1** a person or thing that dims. **2** a device that dims an electric light or automobile headlight.

dim·out (dim′out′) *n.* a lessening or concealing of light at night.

dim·ple (dim′pəl) *n. v.* **-pled, -pling.** —*n.* **1** a small hollow, usually in the cheek or chin. **2** any small, hollow place. —*v.* **1** make or show dimples in. **2** form dimples. [ME *dympull,* cognate with MHG *tümpfil* pool]

din (din) *n. v.* **dinned, din·ning.** —*n.* a loud, confused noise. —*v.* **1** make a din. **2** strike with a din. **3** say over and over: *He was always dinning into our ears the importance of hard work.* [OE *dynn*; cf. ON *dynr*] **—Syn.** *n.* See **noise.**

di·nar (dē när′) *n.* **1** a unit of money in Algeria, Bahrain, Iraq, Kuwait, Jordan, Tunisia, and Yugoslavia. See table at **money. 2** a unit of money in Iran, worth 1/100 of a rial. **3** a coin worth one dinar. **4** any of various gold coins used in ancient Arab countries. [< Arabic or Persian < LGk. *denarion* < L *denarius*]

dine (dīn) *v.* **dined, din·ing. 1** eat dinner. **2** give a dinner to or for. **3 dine out,** eat dinner away from home. [ME < OF *disner* < VL *disjejunare* to breakfast < *dis* apart (cessation) + *jejunium* fast[2]]

din·er (dīn′ər) *n.* **1** a person who is eating dinner. **2** dining car. **3** a restaurant shaped like such a car. **4** a small eating place, usually near a main highway.

di·nette (dī net′) *n.* a small dining room.

ding (ding) *v.* **1** make a sound like a bell; ring continuously. **2** *Informal.* say over and over. —*n.* the sound made by a bell. [imitative]

ding-dong (ding′dong′) *n.* **1** the sound made by a bell or anything like a bell with alternating strokes; any persistent or monotonous ringing. **2** a jingle; rhyme in verse or song. —*adj.* **1** ringing with alternating strokes. **2** *Informal.* in which each side has the advantage in turns; closely contested: *a ding-dong contest, a ding-dong race.* [imitative]

din·gey (ding′gē or ding′ē) *n.* **-geys.** dinghy.

din·ghy (ding′gē or ding′ē) *n.* **-ghies. 1** a small rowboat. **2** a small boat used as a tender by a large boat. **3** a small sailboat. [< Hind. *dingi*]

din·gle (ding′gəl) *n.* a small, deep, shady valley. [origin uncertain]

din·go (ding′gō) *n.* **-goes.** **1** a species of wolf-like wild dogs of Australia. **2** a dog of this species. [< native Australian name]

ding·us (ding′əs) *n. Slang.* a thing, gadget, or device of which the name is unknown, unfamiliar, or forgotten. [< Du. *dinges* < *ding* thing, object]

din·gy[1] (din′jē) *adj.* **-gi·er, -gi·est.** dirty-looking; not bright and fresh; dull. [origin uncertain] **—din′gi·ly,** *adv.* **—din′gi·ness,** *n.*

din·gy[2] (ding′gē) *n.* **-gies.** dinghy.

dining car a railway car in which meals are served.

dining room a room in which dinner and other meals are served.

dink·ey (dingk′ē) *n.* **-eys.** *Informal.* a small locomotive, used for pulling freight cars around in a railway yard, for hauling logs, etc. [< *dinky*]

dink·y (dingk′ē) *adj.* **dink·i·er, dink·i·est.** *Slang.* small; insignificant; cute. [< Scottish or N. English dial. *dink* trim + *-y*]

din·ner (din′ər) *n.* **1** the main meal of the day. **2** a formal meal in honor of some person or occasion. [ME < OF *disner* dine; infinitive used as noun] **—din′ner·less,** *adj.*

dinner jacket a tuxedo.

din·ner·time (din′ər tīm′) *n.* the time at which dinner is eaten.

din·ner·ware (din′ər wãr′) *n.* plates, serving dishes, etc. for serving dinner.

di·no·saur (dī′nə sôr′ or din′ə sôr′) *n.* any of a group of extinct reptiles, often of huge size. [< NL *dinosaurus* < Gk. *deinos* terrible + *sauros* lizard]

di·no·sau·ri·an (dī′nə sô′rē ən or din′ə sô′rē ən) *adj.* of or like a dinosaur. *—n.* a dinosaur.

dint (dint) *n. v.* **1** a hollow made by the force of a blow or by pressure; dent. **2 by dint of,** by the force of; by means of: *By dint of hard work the job was completed on schedule.* *—v.* make a dent in. [OE *dynt*; cf. ON *dyntr*]

di·oc·e·san (dī os′ə sən or dī′ə sē′sən) *adj.* of or having to do with a diocese. *—n.* a bishop of a diocese.

di·o·cese (dī′ə sis or dī′ə sēs′) *n.* the district over which a bishop has authority. [ME < OF *diocise* < L < Gk. *dioikēsis* province, diocese < *oikeein* inhabit]

di·ode (dī′ōd) *n.* in electronics, a vacuum tube having two electrodes, especially a rectifier that allows electrons to pass in one direction only.

di·oe·cious (dī ē′shəs) *adj.* in botany, having male and female flowers in separate plants. Also, *diecious.* [< NL *dioecia,* genus name < Gk. *di-* double + *oikos* house]

Di·o·ny·si·a (dī′ə nish′ē ə or dī′ə nis′ē ə) *n.pl.* a set of festivals in honor of the Greek god Dionysus.

Di·o·nys·i·ac (dī′ə nis′ē ak′) *adj.* Dionysian.

Di·o·ny·sian (dī′ə nish′ən or dī′ə nis′ē ən) *adj.* **1** of or having to do with Dionysus. **2** highly exuberant; frenzied.

Di·o·ny·sus or **Di·o·ny·sos** (dī′ ə nī′ səs) *n.* in Greek mythology, the god of wine and fertility, identified by the Romans with Bacchus.

di·o·ram·a (dī′ə ram′ə) *n.* **1** a picture that is usually looked at through a small opening. It is lighted in such a way as to be very realistic. **2** a scene to be viewed through a window-like opening, showing a painted background and a foreground occupied by sculptured figures (life-size or smaller) of animals, men, etc. and appropriate accessory objects. [< F < Gk. *dia-* through + *horama* sight]

di·o·rite (dī′ə rīt′) *n.* a coarse-grained igneous rock consisting essentially of hornblende and feldspar. [< F *diorite* < Gk. *diorizein* distinguish (< *dia-* through + *orizein* mark a boundary) + F *-ite* ite[1]]

Di·os·cu·ri (dī′əs kūr′ī or dī′əs kū′rē) *n.pl.* the twins Castor and Pollux. [< Gk. *Dioskouroi* < *Dios,* gen. of *Zeus* Zeus + *kouros* boy, son]

di·ox·ide (dī ok′sīd or -ok′sid) *n.* in chemistry, an oxide having two atoms of oxygen per molecule.

dip (dip) *v.* **dipped** or **dipt, dip·ping,** *n.* *—v.* **1** put under water or any liquid and lift quickly out again: *Mary dipped her feet into the clear pool.* **2** go under water and come quickly out again. **3** dye by dipping in a liquid. **4** wash or clean by dipping in a liquid. **5** immerse in a solution for plating or galvanizing. **6** make (a candle) by putting a wick into hot tallow or wax. **7** take up in the hollow of the hand or with a pail, pan, or other container: *dip up water from a well, dip up a sample of wheat.* **8** put (one's hand, a spoon, etc.) into to take out something. **9** lower and raise again quickly: *The ship's flag was dipped as a salute.* **10** make a curtsy. **11** sink or drop down: *The bird dipped in its flight.* **12** slope downward: *The road dips.* **13** in aeronautics, make a short, sudden dive to gain momentum for a climb. **14 dip into, a** read or look at for a short time; glance at. **b** engage in superficially: *dip into astronomy.*
—n. **1** a dipping of any kind, especially a plunge into and out of a tub of water, the ocean, etc. **2** a liquid in which to dip something: *sheep dip.* **3** a candle made by dipping. **4** that which is taken out or up by dipping. **5** a sudden drop. **6** the degree of slope down. **7** a sinking down and out of sight; setting: *the dip of the sun.* **8** a creamy mixture of cheese and other foods served as an hors d'oeuvre and eaten by dipping a cracker, a piece of bread, etc. in it: *a cheese dip, a lobster dip.* **9** in surveying and astronomy, the angular distance of the visible horizon below the horizontal plane through the observer's eye. **10** the downward inclination of the magnetic needle at any particular place; the angle which the direction of the needle makes with the horizontal. [OE *dyppan.* Cognate with DEEP.]
Syn. *v.* **1 Dip, plunge, immerse** = put into a liquid. **Dip** emphasizes taking right out again after putting or lowering partly in or wholly under: *I dipped my handkerchief in the cool water.* **Plunge** emphasizes throwing or putting completely under, suddenly or with force: *I plunged the vegetables into boiling water.* **Immerse** emphasizes keeping completely under long enough to get thoroughly soaked: *I immersed my clothes in the soapy water.*

hat, āge, cãre, fär; let, ēqual, tėrm; it, īce
hot, ōpen, ôrder; oil, out; cup, pu̇t, rüle, ūse
əbove, takən, pencəl, lemən, circəs
ch, child; ng, long; sh, ship
th, thin; TH, then; zh, measure

diph·the·ri·a (dif thēr′ē ə or dip thēr′ē ə) *n.* an acute, infectious disease of the throat, usually accompanied by a high fever and by the formation of membranes that hinder breathing. [< F *diphthérie* < Gk. *diphthera* hide, leather; with reference to the tough membrane developed on the affected parts]

diph·the·ri·al (dif thēr′ē əl or dip thēr′ē əl) *adj.* having to do with diphtheria; diphtheritic.

diph·the·rit·ic (dif′thə rit′ik or dip′thə rit′ik) *adj.* **1** of diphtheria; like diphtheria. **2** suffering from diphtheria.

diph·thong (dif′thong or dip′thong) *n.* **1** in phonetics, a vowel sound made up of two identifiable vowel sounds in immediate sequence and pronounced in one syllable, as *ou* in *house, oi* in *noise.* **2** several letters joined together in printing, such as *ffi, æ,* and *œ,* properly called **a** ligature. **3** two vowel letters representing a single vowel sound, properly called a digraph, as *ea* in *eat.* [< F *diphthongue* < LL < Gk. *diphthongos* < *di-* double + *phthongos* sound]
☛ Sometimes a **diphthong** is represented by only one letter, as *i* in *ice* or *u* in *abuse.* The commonest English diphthongs are: ī (ä + i), oi (ô + i), ou (ä + u̇), and ū (i + ü) or (y + ü).

diph·thon·gal (dif thong′gəl or dip thong′gəl) *adj.* of or like a diphthong.

diph·thong·ise (dif′thong īz′ or dip′thong īz′) *v.* **-ised, -is·ing.** diphthongize.

diph·thong·ize (dif′thong īz′ or dip′thong īz′) *v.* **-ized, -iz·ing.** **1** change (a vowel or vowels) into a diphthong. **2** become a diphthong.

di·plo·ma (də plō′mə) *n.* **-mas** or **-ma·ta** (-mə tə). **1** a certificate given by a school, college, or university to its graduating students. **2** any certificate that bestows certain rights, privileges, honors, etc. [< L < Gk. *diplōma* paper folded double, ult. < *diploos* double]

di·plo·ma·cy (də plō′mə sē) *n.* **-cies.** **1** the management of relations between nations. The making of treaties, international agreements, etc. is an important part of diplomacy. **2** skill in managing such relations. **3** skill in dealing with others; tact: *Our son showed diplomacy in being very helpful at home the day he wanted to use the car.* [< F *diplomatie* < *diplomate* diplomat]

dip·lo·mat (dip′lə mat′) *n.* 1 a person employed in diplomacy, especially a representative of a nation who is located in a foreign country with the duty of looking after the interests of his own nation in the foreign country. 2 a person who is skilful in dealing with others; a tactful person. [back-formation < F *diplomatique.* See DIPLOMATIC.]

dip·lo·mat·ic (dip′lə mat′ik) *adj.* 1 of or having to do with diplomacy: *Ambassadors are the highest-ranking members of the diplomatic service.* 2 skilful in dealing with others; tactful: *a diplomatic policeman, a diplomatic answer.* [<NL *diplomaticus,* F *diplomatique* < Gk. *diplōma, -atos.* See DIPLOMA.]

dip·lo·mat·i·cal·ly (dip′lə mat′ik lē) *adv.* in a diplomatic manner; with diplomacy.

diplomatic corps all of the ambassadors, ministers, etc. of foreign nations at the capital of a country.

di·plo·ma·tist (de plō′mə tist) *n.* diplomat.

dip·per (dip′ər) *n.* 1 a person or thing that dips. 2 a long-handled cup or larger vessel for dipping water or other liquids. 3 any of various diving birds, such as the kingfisher. 4 **Dipper,** in astronomy, either of two groups of stars in the northern sky resembling dippers in shape; the Big Dipper or the Little Dipper.

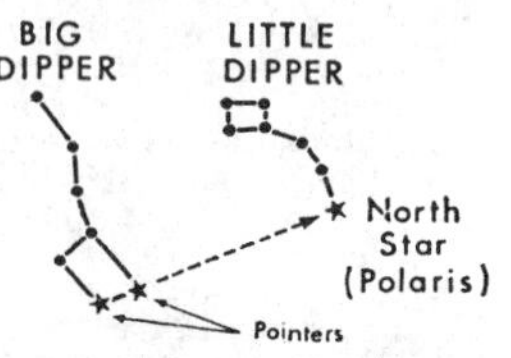

The Big Dipper and the Little Dipper

dipping needle a magnetic needle balanced to swing vertically and indicate by its dip the direction of the earth's magnetic field.

dip·py (dip′ē) *adj.* **-pi·er, -pi·est.** *Slang.* 1 foolish; half-witted. 2 light-headed; giddy; intoxicated.

dip·so·ma·ni·a (dip′sə mā′nē ə) *n.* an abnormal, uncontrollable craving for alcoholic liquor. [< NL < Gk. *dipsa* thirst + *mania* mania]

dip·so·ma·ni·ac (dip′sə mā′nē ak′) *n.* a person who has dipsomania.

dip·stick (dip′stik′) *n.* a rod for measuring the level of liquid in a container, such as the oil in the crankcase of a car.

dip·sy-do or **dip·sy-doo** (dip′sē dü′) *n. Slang.* 1 in baseball, a curved ball that is hard to hit. 2 tricky or complicated manoeuvring: *the dipsy-do of a magician.*

dip·sy-doo·dle (dip′sē dü′dəl) *n. v.* **-dled, -dling.** *Slang.* —*n.* 1 in baseball: **a** a dipsy-do. **b** a pitcher who is expert at throwing a dipsy-do. 2 a deceptive person; tricky thing. —*v.* deceive; trick.

dipt (dipt) *v.* a pt. and a pp. of **dip.**

Dip·ter·a (dip′tər ə) *n.pl.* a large group of insects that, except for some wingless parasitic forms, have one pair of membranous wings, the usual second pair of wings being replaced by small club-shaped organs. Mosquitoes, gnats, and houseflies belong to the Diptera.

dip·ter·ous (dip′tər əs) *adj.* 1 of insects, having one pair of wings. 2 belonging to the Diptera. [< NL *dipterus* two-winged < Gk. *dipteros* < *di-* two + *pteron* wing]

dip·tych (dip′tik) *n.* 1 in ancient times, a writing tablet consisting of two pieces of wood or ivory hinged together with the inner sides waxed for writing on with a stylus. 2 a pair of paintings or carvings on two panels hinged together. 3 anything folded so as to have two matching parts. [< LL *diptycha,* neut. pl. < Gk. *diptychos* folded double < *di-* twice + *ptychē* fold]

A diptych

dire (dīr) *adj.* **dir·er, dir·est.** causing great fear or suffering; dreadful: *His disobedience was followed by dire consequences.* [< L *dirus*] —**dire′ly,** *adv.* —**dire′ness,** *n.*

di·rect (di rekt′ or dī rekt′) *v.* 1 manage; control; guide: *The teacher directs the work of the pupils.* 2 plan, guide, and rehearse the staging of a play, opera, motion picture, television or radio program, etc. See **director** (def. 3). 3 order; command: *The captain directed his men to advance.* 4 tell or show the way; give information about where to go, what to do, etc.: *Can you direct me to the railway station?* 5 point (*to*); aim (*at*): *We should direct our efforts to a useful end.* 6 put the address on (a letter, package, etc.). 7 address (words, etc.) to a person: *direct a request to the king.* 8 turn (something) straight to or at; point (*to*); aim (*at*).
—*adj.* 1 proceeding in a straight line; straight: *a direct route.* 2 in an unbroken line of descent: *a direct descendant of Queen Victoria.* 3 immediate: *He took direct charge of the library.* 4 without anyone or anything in between; by oneself or itself; not through others: *a direct tax.* 5 straightforward; frank; plain; truthful: *a direct answer. He made a direct denial of the charge of cheating.* 6 exact; absolute: *the direct opposite.* —*adv.* directly. [< L *directus,* pp. of *dirigere* set straight < *dis-* apart + *regere* guide] —**di·rect′ing·ly,** *adv.* —**di·rect′ness,** *n.*
Syn. *v.* 1 See **manage.** 2 See **command.** *-adj.* 1 **Direct, immediate** = proceeding from one to another without a break. **Direct** = going straight from one to another in an unbroken line, though there may be many steps between: *Overwork and too much strain were the direct cause of his death.* **Immediate** = going from one thing to the next, without anything between: *A heart attack was the immediate cause of his death.*
☛ **direct address.** The name or descriptive term by which one addresses a person or persons in speaking, reading, or writing: *My friends, I wish you would forget this night. It's all right, Mrs. Williams, for you to come in now.* As these examples show, the term denoting the person or persons addressed is set off from the rest of the sentence by a comma, or, if it is in the middle of the sentence, by two commas.

direct current a steady electric current that flows in one direction. *Abbrev.:* DC., D.C., or d.c.

direct discourse a quoting of what a person says in his exact words. *Example:* He said, "Let's go now."

di·rec·tion (di rek′shən or dī rek′shən) *n.* 1 guidance; management; control: *the direction of a play or movie.* 2 an order; command. 3 a knowing or telling what to do, how to do, where to go, etc.; instruction: *Can you give me directions how to reach Montreal?* 4 the address on a letter or package. 5 the course taken by a moving body, such as a ball or a bullet. 6 any way in which one may face or point. North, south, east, and west are directions. 7 a line of action, tendency, etc.: *The town shows improvement in many directions.* 8 in music, a word, phrase, or sign indicating the tempo or style in which a score or part of a score should be played.
Syn. 7 **Direction, trend, tendency** = line or course of action. **Direction** applies to the line followed in the course of progress or an aim guiding the course of action: *The crime investigation has taken a new direction.* **Trend,** used figuratively, applies particularly to a general direction followed by, but in spite of, twistings and turnings: *The trend is toward fewer required subjects in school.* **Tendency** applies to movement in a certain direction or an inclination to act in a definite direction: *The tendency is toward higher taxes.*

di·rec·tion·al (di rek′shən əl or dī rek′shən əl) *adj.* 1 of or having to do with direction in space. 2 in radio, fitted for determining the direction from which signals come, or for sending signals in one direction only. 3 having to do with direction: *a directional tendency, directional signals.*

direction finder a receiving device, usually having a loop aerial, by which the direction of incoming radio signals may be determined.

di·rec·tive (di rek′tiv or dī rek′tiv) *n.* an order or instruction as to procedure. —*adj.* directing. —**di·rec′tive·ly,** *adv.* —**di·rec′tive·ness,** *n.*

di·rect·ly (di rekt′lē or dī rekt′lē) *adj.* 1 in a direct line or manner; straight. 2 exactly; absolutely: *directly opposite.* 3 immediately; at once.

direct object in grammar, a term for a word showing the person or thing undergoing the action expressed by the verb. In "The car struck me," *me* is the direct object.

Di·rec·toire (dē rek twär′) *n.* the Directory. —*adj.* 1 of the time of the Directory. 2 of or resembling the ornate styles of the Directory period: *a Directoire table, Directoire dresses.*

di·rec·tor (di rek′tər or dī rek′tər) *n.* 1 a manager;

person in control; leader. 2 one of the persons chosen to direct the affairs of a company or institution. 3 the person who plans, guides, and rehearses the staging of a play, opera, motion picture, television or radio program, etc. 4 a gun sight that co-ordinates the fire of a number of guns.

☛ **director** (def. 3), **producer.** Usually, the producer initiates a show and controls the business side of the production, while the director has overall responsibility for the artistic side. In the British theatre the director used to be, and sometimes still is, called *producer*, while the producer is known as *manager*.

di·rec·tor·ate (di rek′tər it or dī rek′tər it) *n.* 1 the position of a director. 2 a group of directors.

di·rec·to·ri·al (di rek′tô′rē əl or dī′rek tô′rē əl) *adj.* having to do with a director or directorate.

di·rec·tor·ship (di rek′tər ship′ or dī rek′tər ship′) *n.* the position or term of office of a director.

di·rec·to·ry (di rek′tə rē or dī rek′tə rē) *n.* **-ries,** *adj.* —*n.* 1 a list of names and addresses: *A telephone book is one kind of directory.* 2 a book of rules or instructions. 3 a group of directors; directorate. 4 **Directory,** a group of five men that governed France 1795-1799.
—*adj.* directing; advisory: *legislation of a directory character.*

direct question a question quoted in the enquirer's exact words. *Example*: He asked, "Shall we go now?"

di·rec·tress (di rek′tris or dī rek′tris) *n.* a woman director.

direct tax a tax demanded of the persons who must pay it. Income taxes, property taxes, and succession duties are direct taxes. The federal sales tax is an indirect tax.

dire·ful (dīr′fəl) *adj.* dire; dreadful; terrible. —**dire′ful·ly,** *adv.* —**dire′ful·ness,** *n.*

dirge (dėrj) *n.* 1 a funeral song or tune. 2 in the Roman Catholic Church: **a** the Office of the Dead; the choral funeral service. **b** a funeral hymn or requiem mass. [contraction of L *dirige* direct (imperative of *dirigere*), first word in office for the dead]

dir·ham (də ram′) *n.* 1 a unit of money in Morocco. See table at **money.** 2 a coin worth one dirham. [< Arabic *dirham* < L < Gk. *drachmē*]

dir·i·gi·bil·i·ty (dir′ə jə bil′ə tē) *n.* the fact or quality of being dirigible.

dir·i·gi·ble (dir′ə jə bəl or di rij′ə bəl) *n.* a kind of balloon that can be steered; an airship. —*adj.* capable of being directed. [< L *dirigere* direct]

dirk (dėrk) *n.* a dagger. —*v.* stab with a dirk. [origin unknown]

dirn·dl (dėrn′dəl) *n.* 1 an Alpine peasant girl's costume consisting of a blouse, a tight bodice, and a full, bright-colored skirt, gathered at the waist. 2 a dress imitating such a costume. 3 a skirt of this type. [< South G dial. *dirndl* girl, dim. of *dirne* maid]

dirt (dėrt) *n.* 1 mud, dust, earth, or anything of this nature. Dirt soils whatever it gets on. 2 loose earth; soil. 3 uncleanness in action, thought, or speech. 4 meanness. 5 *Informal.* anything worthless. 6 *Slang.* gossip; scandal: *Do you know the latest dirt?* 7 in mining, the earth, gravel, or other material from which gold is separated by washing. 8 **eat dirt,** *Informal.* submit to degrading treatment; make a humiliating apology or retraction. [ME *drit* < ON *drit* excrement] —**dirt′less,** *adj.*

dirt-cheap (dėrt′chēp′) *adj.* very cheap.

dirt farmer *Informal.* a person who has practical experience in doing his own farming.

dirt·y (dėr′tē) *adj.* **dirt·i·er, dirt·i·est,** *v.* **dirt·ied, dirt·y·ing.** —*adj.* 1 soiled by dirt; unclean. 2 that makes dirty; soiling: *a dirty job.* 3 unpleasant; disagreeable: *hire someone to do the dirty work.* 4 not clear or pure in color; clouded: *a dirty red.* 5 low; mean; vile. 6 unclean in action, thought, or speech: *a dirty joke.* 7 stormy; windy: *dirty weather.* 8 causing a great amount of radio-active fallout: *a dirty bomb.*
—*v.* 1 make dirty; soil. 2 become dirty. —**dirt′i·ness,** *n.*

Syn. *adj.* **1 Dirty, filthy, foul** = unclean. **Dirty** = soiled in any way: *Children playing in mud get dirty.* **Filthy,** often expressing a disgusted attitude toward a person or thing, emphasizes the idea of being entirely too dirty, covered or stained with greasy or sticky dirt or littered with trash: *In some cities and towns the streets are filthy.* **Foul,** expressing a strong reaction of disgust, suggests being filled or covered with filth or something unhealthy, impure, or rotten: *The water in the swamp is foul.*

hat, āge, cãre, fär; let, ēqual, tėrm; it, īce
hot, ōpen, ôrder; oil, out; cup, put, rüle, ūse
əbove, takən, pencəl, lemən, circəs
ch, child; ng, long; sh, ship
th, thin; ꟻH, then; zh, measure

Dis (dis) *n.* 1 in Roman mythology, the god of the lower world, identified with the Greek god Pluto. 2 the lower world; Hades.

dis-[1] *prefix.* 1 opposite of, as in *discontent.* 2 reverse of, as in *disentangle.* 3 apart; away, as in *dispel.* 4 not, as in *dishonest.* 5 completely (intensive), as in *disembowel.* Also, **di-,** before *b, d, l, m, n, r, s, v,* and sometimes before *g* and *j*; **dif-** before *f.* [< L]

dis-[2] a form of **di-**[1] before *s,* as in *dissyllable.*

dis·a·bil·i·ty (dis′ə bil′ə tē) *n.* **-ties.** 1 a disabled condition: *The player's disability was caused by illness.* 2 something that disables. 3 something that disqualifies.

dis·a·ble (dis ā′bəl) *v.* **-bled, -bling.** 1 deprive of ability or power; make useless; cripple. 2 disqualify legally. —**dis·a′ble·ment,** *n.* —**Syn. 1** See **cripple.**

dis·a·bled (dis ā′bəld) *adj.* deprived of ability or power; crippled.

dis·a·buse (dis′ə būz′) *v.* **bused, bus·ing.** free from deception or error: *Education should disabuse people of prejudice.*

dis·ac·cord (dis′ə kôrd′) *v.* disagree; be out of harmony. —*n.* disagreement; lack of harmony.

dis·ad·van·tage (dis′əd van′tij) *n.* 1 a lack of advantage; unfavorable condition: *The deaf child was at a disadvantage in school.* 2 harm; loss: *The candidate's enemies spread rumors to his disadvantage.*

dis·ad·van·ta·geous (dis ad′vən tā′jəs) *adj.* causing disadvantage; unfavorable. —**dis·ad′van·ta′geous·ly,** *adv.* —**dis·ad′van·ta′geous·ness,** *n.*

dis·af·fect·ed (dis′ə fek′tid) *adj.* 1 unfriendly; discontented. 2 no longer loyal; disloyal: *a disaffected Communist.*

dis·af·fec·tion (dis′ə fek′shən) *n.* 1 unfriendliness; discontent: *Lack of food and supplies caused disaffection among the soldiers.* 2 disloyalty; desertion: *The government party was seriously weakened by the disaffection of many of its members.*

dis·a·gree (dis′ə grē′) *v.* **-greed, -gree·ing.** 1 fail to agree; differ: *The witness disagreed with the lawyer about the time of the accident.* 2 quarrel; dispute. 3 have a bad effect; be harmful: *Strawberries disagree with him.*

dis·a·gree·a·ble (dis′ə grē′ə bəl) *adj.* 1 not to one's liking; unpleasant. 2 bad-tempered; cross. —**dis′a·gree′a·ble·ness,** *n.* —**dis′a·gree′a·bly,** *adv.*

dis·a·gree·ment (dis′ə grē′mənt) *n.* 1 a failure to agree; difference of opinion. 2 a quarrel or dispute. 3 a difference; unlikeness: *There is a striking disagreement between the two species.*

dis·al·low (dis′ə lou′) *v.* 1 refuse to allow; deny the truth or value of. 2 in law, reject: *The request for a new trial was disallowed.* 3 *Cdn.* of the Federal Government, nullify an act of a provincial legislature.

dis·al·low·ance (dis′ə lou′əns) *n.* 1 a disallowing: *The trial proceeded after the disallowance of the Crown Attorney's request.* 2 *Cdn.* the power of the Federal Government to annul provincial legislation. 3 *Cdn.* an act of the Federal Government exercising this power.

dis·ap·pear (dis′ə pēr′) *v.* 1 pass from sight. 2 pass from existence; be lost. —**dis′ap·pear′er,** *n.*

Syn. 1 Disappear, vanish, fade = pass from sight. **Disappear** is the general word, meaning pass out of sight slowly or quickly, gradually or suddenly: *He disappeared into the night.* **Vanish** = disappear without a trace, usually suddenly, often in some strange or mysterious way: *The stranger vanished from town.* **Fade** = die away, disappear slowly: *The ship faded into the fog.*

dis·ap·pear·ance (dis′ə pēr′əns) *n.* the act of disappearing.

dis·ap·point (dis′ə point′) *v.* 1 fail to satisfy or please; leave (one) wanting or expecting something. 2 fail to keep a promise to (someone). 3 keep from happening; oppose and defeat. —**dis′ap·point′er,** *n.*

dis·ap·point·ment (dis′ə point′mənt) *n.* **1** the state of being or feeling disappointed. **2** a person or thing that causes disappointment. **3** the act or fact of disappointing.

dis·ap·pro·ba·tion (dis′ap rə bā′shən) *n.* disapproval.

dis·ap·prov·al (dis′ə prüv′əl) *n.* **1** an opinion or feeling against; an expression of an opinion against; dislike. **2** a refusal to consent; rejection.

dis·ap·prove (dis′ə prüv′) *v.* **-proved, -prov·ing. 1** have or express an opinion against. **2** show dislike (*of*): *The boy disapproved of going to school in the summer.* **3** refuse consent to; reject: *The judge disapproved the verdict.* **—dis′ap·prov′ing·ly,** *adv.*

dis·arm (dis ärm′) *v.* **1** take weapons away from: *The police captured the bandits and disarmed them.* **2** stop having armed services; reduce or limit the size of the armed services. **3** remove suspicion from; make friendly; calm the anger of: *The speaker's frankness disarmed the angry mob, and they soon began to cheer him.* **4** make harmless: *The soldiers disarmed the big bomb.* **—dis·arm′er,** *n.* **—dis·arm′ing·ly,** *adv.*

dis·ar·ma·ment (dis är′mə mənt) *n.* **1** the act of disarming. **2** the reduction or limitation of armed services and their equipment.

dis·ar·range (dis′ə rānj′) *v.* **-ranged, -rang·ing.** disturb the arrangement of; put out of order: *The wind disarranged her hair.* **—dis′ar·range′ment,** *n.* **—dis′ar·rang′er,** *n.*

dis·ar·ray (dis′ə rā′) *n.* **1** a disorder; confusion. **2** a disorder of clothing. —*v.* **1** put into disorder or confusion. **2** *Archaic.* undress; strip.

dis·as·sem·ble (dis′ə sem′bəl) *v.* **-bled, -bling.** take apart.

dis·as·so·ci·ate (dis′ə sō′shē āt′) *v.* **-at·ed, -at·ing.** dissociate.

dis·as·ter (də zas′tər) *n.* an event that causes much suffering or loss; great misfortune: *A destructive fire, flood, earthquake, or shipwreck is a disaster.* [< F *désastre* < Ital. *disastro* (lack of a lucky star) < L *dis-* without + *astrum* star < Gk. *astron*]

Syn. Disaster, calamity, catastrophe = a great misfortune. **Disaster** applies to an event that happens suddenly or unexpectedly, through human fault, mechanical or structural failure, or the forces of nature, and causes much loss and suffering: *The lack of rain for so many weeks was a disaster for the farmers.* **Calamity** applies to a disaster that causes intense suffering and grief, often to a great number: *The flooding of the river last year was a calamity.* **Catastrophe** suggests a disaster that is final and complete, causing loss that can never be made up: *A nuclear war would be a catastrophe.*

disaster area 1 an area that has suffered a disaster. **2** an area that, having suffered some severe disaster, becomes entitled to special government assistance: *The flooded section of the province was designated a disaster area.*

dis·as·trous (di zas′trəs) *adj.* bringing disaster; causing great danger, suffering, loss, pain, or sorrow. **—dis·as′trous·ly,** *adv.*

dis·a·vow (dis′ə vou′) *v.* deny that one knows about, approves of, or is responsible for; disclaim: *The prisoner disavowed the confession bearing his signature.*

dis·a·vow·al (dis′ə vou′əl) *n.* a disavowing; denial of knowledge, approval, or responsibility.

dis·band (dis band′) *v.* **1** dismiss from service: *Most of the army was disbanded after the war.* **2** break ranks; become scattered. **—dis·band′ment,** *n.*

dis·bar (dis bär′) *v.* **-barred, -bar·ring.** deprive (a lawyer) of the right to practise his profession. **—dis·bar′ment,** *n.*

dis·be·lief (dis′bi lēf′) *n.* a lack of belief; refusal to believe. **—Syn.** See **unbelief.**

dis·be·lieve (dis′bi lēv′) *v.* **-lieved, -liev·ing.** have no belief in. **—dis′be·liev′er,** *n.*

dis·bur·den (dis bėr′dən) *v.* relieve of a burden: *The boy disburdened his mind to his brother by confessing what he had done.*

dis·burse (dis bėrs′) *v.* **-bursed, -burs·ing.** pay out; expend. [MF < OF *desbourser* < *des-* away from + *bourse* purse < LL *bursa* < Gk. *byrsa* leather, wineskin] **—dis·burs′er,** *n.* **—Syn.** See **spend.**

dis·burse·ment (dis bėrs′mənt) *n.* **1** the act of paying out: *Our treasurer attends to the disbursement of funds.* **2** the money paid out; expenditure.

disc (disk) *n. v.* disk.

disc. 1 discount. **2** discovered.

dis·card (*v.* dis kärd′; *n.* dis′kärd) *v.* **1** give up as useless or worn out; throw aside. **2** in card games: **a** get rid of (useless or unwanted playing cards) by throwing them aside or playing them. **b** play (a card) that is neither a trump nor of the suit led. **3** throw out an unwanted card.
—*n.* **1** the act of throwing aside as useless. **2** something thrown aside as useless or not wanted: *That old book is a discard from the library.* **3** the unwanted cards thrown aside; a card played as useless. **4 into the discard,** among things thrown aside or not wanted: *The scientist's discovery threw old theories into the discard.* [< *dis-*[1] + *card*[1]] **—dis·card′er,** *n.*

dis·cern (di sėrn′ or di zėrn′) *v.* perceive; see clearly; distinguish; recognize. [ME < OF *discerner* < L *discernere* < *dis-* off + *cernere* separate] **—dis·cern′er,** *n.*

dis·cern·i·ble (di sėr′nə bəl or di zėr′nə bəl) *adj.* capable of being discerned. **—dis·cern′i·bly,** *adv.*

dis·cern·ing (di sėr′ning or di zėr′ning) *adj.* shrewd; acute; discriminating. **—dis·cern′ing·ly,** *adv.*

dis·cern·ment (di sėrn′mənt or di zėrn′mənt) *n.* **1** keenness in perceiving and understanding; good judgment; shrewdness. **2** the act of discerning. **—Syn. 1** See **insight.**

dis·charge (*v.* dis chärj′; *n.* dis chärj′ or dis′chärj) *v.* **-charged, -charg·ing,** *n.* —*v.* **1** unload (a ship); unload (cargo) from a ship; unload. **2** fire; shoot: *discharge a gun.* **3** release; let go; dismiss: *discharge a patient from a hospital, discharge a committee, discharge a servant.* **4** give off; let out: *The wound discharges pus.* **5** come or pour forth: *The river discharged into a bay.* **6** rid of an electric charge; withdraw electricity from. **7** pay (a debt, etc.). **8** release from an obligation; exempt: *discharge a debtor from his debts.* **9** perform (a duty). **10** in law, cancel or set aside (a court order or an obligation). **11** remove or bleach (a dye or color) from a textile, cloth, etc.
—*n.* **1** an unloading. **2** a firing off of a gun, a blast, etc.: *The dynamite discharge could be heard for a mile.* **3** a release; the act of letting go; a dismissing: *the discharge of a convict from prison.* **4** a piece of writing that shows a person's release or dismissal; certificate of release: *Members of the armed services got discharges when the war ended.* **5** a giving off; a letting out: *His father explained that lightning is a discharge of electricity from the clouds.* **6** something given off or let out: *the watery discharge from a sore.* **7** the rate of flow: *The discharge from the pipe is ten gallons a second.* **8** the transference of electricity between two charged bodies when placed in contact or near each other. **9** a payment. **10** a performance: *A public official should be honest in the discharge of his duties.* [< *dis-*[1] + *charge*] **—dis·charg′er,** *n.* **—Syn.** *v.* **3** See **dismiss. 8** See **perform.**

dis·ci·ple (də sī′pəl) *n.* **1** a believer in the thought and teaching of a leader; follower. **2** one of the followers of Jesus, especially one of the twelve Apostles. **3 Disciple,** a member of the Disciples of Christ. [ME < OF < L *discipulus* pupil (*discere* learn)] **—Syn. 1** See **follower.**

dis·ci·ple·ship (di sī′pəl ship′) *n.* **1** the state of being a disciple. **2** the time during which one is a disciple.

Disciples of Christ a religious sect founded in U.S. in 1809, that rejects all creeds and seeks to unite Christians on the basis of the New Testament alone.

dis·ci·plin·a·ble (dis′ə plin ə bəl) *adj.* **1** that can be disciplined. **2** deserving discipline.

dis·ci·pli·nar·i·an (dis′ə plə nãr′ē ən) *n.* a person who enforces discipline or who believes in strict discipline. —*adj.* disciplinary.

dis·ci·pli·nar·y (dis′ə plə ner′ē) *adj.* **1** having to do with discipline. **2** for discipline; intended to improve discipline: *After the attempted jailbreak the prison governor took disciplinary measures.* **3** of or having to do with a particular field of study.

dis·ci·pline (dis′ə plin) *n. v.* **-plined, -plin·ing.** —*n.* **1** training, especially of the mind or character. **2** the training effect of experience, misfortune, etc. **3** a trained

condition of order and obedience. **4** order among school pupils, members of the armed services, or members of any group. **5** a particular system of rules for conduct. **6** the methods or rules for regulating the conduct of members of a church. **7** the control exercised over members of a church. **8** punishment; chastisement. **9** a branch of instruction or education; a field of study: *the discipline of science.* [ME < OF < L *disciplina.* See v.]
—*v.* **1** train; bring to a condition of order and obedience; bring under control: *A good officer must know how to discipline men.* **2** punish: *discipline a child for bad behavior.* [ME < LL *disciplinare* < L *disciplina* < *discipulus.* See DISCIPLE.] **—dis′ci·plin·er,** *n.*

dis·claim (dis klām′) *v.* **1** refuse to recognize as one's own; deny connection with: *The motorist disclaimed responsibility for the accident.* **2** give up all claim to: *She disclaimed any share in the invention.*

dis·claim·er (dis klām′ər) *n.* **1** a disclaiming; denial; rejection. **2** a person who disclaims.

dis·close (dis klōz′) *v.* **-closed, -clos·ing. 1** open to view; uncover. **2** make known; reveal. **—dis·clos′er,** *n.* **—Syn. 2** See **reveal.**

dis·clo·sure (dis klō′zhər) *n.* **1** the act of disclosing. **2** the thing disclosed.

dis·col·or or **dis·col·our** (dis kul′ər) *v.* **1** change or spoil the color of; stain: *Smoke had discolored the new paint work.* **2** become changed in color.

dis·col·or·a·tion or **dis·col·our·a·tion** (dis kul′ər ā′shən) *n.* **1** the act of discoloring. **2** the state of being discolored. **3** a stain.

dis·com·fit (dis kum′fit) *v.* **1** overthrow completely; defeat; rout. **2** defeat the plans or hopes of; frustrate. **3** embarrass greatly; confuse; disconcert. [ME < OF *desconfit,* pp. of *desconfire* < *des-* away + *confire* make, accomplish < L *conficere*] **—dis·com′fit·er,** *n.* **—Syn. 1** vanquish. **3** baffle, abash.

dis·com·fi·ture (dis kum′fi chər) *n.* **1** a complete overthrow; defeat; rout. **2** the defeat of plans or hopes; frustration. **3** confusion.

dis·com·fort (dis kum′fərt) *n.* **1** lack of comfort; a feeling of uneasiness. **2** something that causes discomfort. —*v.* make uncomfortable or uneasy.

dis·com·mode (dis′kə mōd′) *v.* **-mod·ed, -mod·ing.** disturb; trouble; inconvenience.

dis·com·pose (dis′kəm pōz′) *v.* **-posed, -pos·ing.** disturb the self-possession of; make uneasy; bring into disorder.

dis·com·po·sure (dis′kəm pō′zhər) *n.* the state of being disturbed; uneasiness; embarrassment.

dis·con·cert (dis′kən sėrt′) *v.* **1** disturb the self-possession of; embarrass greatly; confuse: *The policeman was disconcerted at finding that he had arrested the wrong man.* **2** upset; disorder: *The chairman's plans were disconcerted by the late arrival of the speaker.* **—dis′con·cert′ing·ly,** *adv.* **—Syn. 1** See **confuse.**

dis·con·cert·ed (dis′kən sėr′tid) *adj.* disturbed; confused. **—dis′con·cert′ed·ly,** *adv.* **—dis′con·cert′ed·ness,** *n.*

dis·con·nect (dis′kə nekt′) *v.* undo or break the connection of; unfasten; separate: *He disconnected the electric fan by pulling out the plug.* **—Syn.** detach.

dis·con·nect·ed (dis′kə nek′tid) *adj.* **1** not connected; separate. **2** without order or connection; incoherent; broken: *The injured man could give only a disconnected account of the accident.* **—dis′con·nect′ed·ly,** *adv.* **—dis′con·nect′ed·ness,** *n.*

dis·con·nec·tion (dis′kə nek′shən) *n.* **1** the act of disconnecting. **2** the state of being disconnected; separation.

dis·con·nex·ion (dis′kə nek′shən) *n. Esp.Brit.* disconnection.

dis·con·so·late (dis kon′sə lit) *adj.* without hope; forlorn; unhappy; cheerless. [ME < Med.L *disconsolatus* < L *dis-* not + *consolatus,* pp. of *consolari* < *com-* together + *solari* soothe] **—dis′con′so·late·ly,** *adv.* **—dis·con′so·late·ness,** *n.* **—Syn.** dejected, sad. See **desolate.**

dis·con·tent (dis′kən tent′) *n.* **1** dislike of what one has and a desire for something different; restlessness. **2** an uneasy feeling of dissatisfaction. —*v.* dissatisfy; displease.

hat, āge, cãre, fär; let, ēqual, tėrm; it, īce
hot, ōpen, ôrder; oil, out; cup, pu̇t, rüle, ūse
əbove, takən, pencəl, lemən, circəs
ch, child; ng, long; sh, ship
th, thin; ᴛʜ, then; zh, measure

dis·con·tent·ed (dis′kən ten′tid) *adj.* not contented; not satisfied; displeased and restless; disliking what one has and wanting something different: *She was discontented with life in the country.* **—dis′con·tent′ed·ly,** *adv.* **—dis′con·tent′ed·ness,** *n.* **—Syn.** dissatisfied.

dis·con·tent·ment (dis′kən tent′mənt) *n.* discontent.

dis·con·tin·u·ance (dis′kən tin′ū əns) *n.* **1** a stopping. **2** a being stopped.

dis·con·tin·u·a·tion (dis′kən tin′ū ā′shən) *n.* **1** a breaking off; a stopping; a ceasing. **2** a break; interruption.

dis·con·tin·ue (dis′kən tin′ū) *v.* **-tin·ued, -tin·u·ing. 1** cause to cease; put an end or stop to: *The morning train has been discontinued. After the patient got well, the doctor discontinued his visits.* **2** cease from; cease to take, use, etc. **3** in law, terminate (a lawsuit) at the request of the plaintiff or by his failure to continue it. **—dis′con·tin′u·er,** *n.* **—Syn. 2** stop, quit.

dis·con·ti·nu·i·ty (dis′kon tə nū′ə tē or -kon tə nü′ə tē) *n.* lack of connection or cohesion: *The discontinuity of the plot made the novel seem clumsy and difficult to understand.*

dis·con·tin·u·ous (dis′kən tin′ū əs) *adj.* not continuous; broken; interrupted. **—dis′con·tin′u·ous·ly,** *adv.*

dis·co·phile (dis′kə fīl′) *n.* a lover of phonograph records.

dis·cord (dis′kôrd) *n.* **1** a difference of opinion; unfriendly relations; a disagreement. **2** in music: **a** a lack of harmony in tones sounded at the same time. **b** an inharmonious combination of tones. **3** harsh, clashing sounds. [ME < OF *discord* < *discorder* < L *discordare* < *discors, -cordis* discordant < *dis-* apart + *cor, cordis* heart] **—Syn. 1** dissension.

dis·cord·ance (dis kôr′dəns) *n.* **1** a discord of sounds. **2** a disagreement.

dis·cord·an·cy (dis kôr′dən sē) *n.* discordance.

dis·cord·ant (dis kôr′dənt) *adj.* **1** not in harmony: *a discordant note in music.* **2** not in agreement; not fitting together: *Many discordant views were expressed.* **3** harsh; clashing: *The sound of some automobile horns is discordant.* **—dis·cord′ant·ly,** *adv.*

disc·o·thèque (dis′kə tek′) *n.* a type of night club where one may listen and dance to music on records. [< F; originally, record library]

dis·count (*v.* dis′kount or dis kount′; *n.* dis′kount) *v.* **1** deduct (a certain percentage) of the amount or cost: *The store discounts 3 per cent on all bills paid when due.* **2** allow for exaggeration, prejudice, or inaccuracy in; believe only part of. **3** make less effective by anticipation: *The price of the stock fell before its dividend was reduced, for the reduction had already been discounted.* **4** buy, sell, or lend money on (a note, bill of exchange, etc.), deducting a certain percentage to allow for unpaid interest. **5** lend money, deducting the interest in advance. **6** sell goods at a discount.
—*n.* **1** a deduction from the amount or cost: *During the sale the dealer allowed a 10 per cent discount on all cash purchases.* **2** a percentage charged for buying, selling, or lending money on (a note, bill of exchange, etc.). **3** the interest deducted in advance. **4** the act of discounting. **5 at a discount, a** at less than the regular price; below par. **b** easy to get because not in demand. [< MF *desconter* < *des-* away + *conter* count < L *computare*] **—dis′count·a·ble,** *adj.*

dis·coun·te·nance (dis koun′tə nəns) *v.* **-nanced, -nanc·ing. 1** refuse to approve; discourage: *This school discountenances secret societies.* **2** abash; disconcert.

discount house 1 discount store. **2** *Esp.Brit.* a financial firm which trades in discounted rates, loans, etc.

discount rate the percentage charged for discounting notes.

discount store a retail store that sells merchandise for less than the current average retail price, making its profit from a big sales volume with low overhead.

dis·cour·age (dis kėr′ij) *v.* **-aged, -ag·ing. 1** take away the courage of; lessen the hope or confidence of: *Repeated failures discouraged him.* **2** try to prevent by disapproving; frown upon. **3** prevent or hinder through fear, loss of incentive, etc.: *Lack of recognition discouraged him from publishing more novels.* **4** make unattractive; make to seem not worthwhile: *The chill of winter soon discouraged our picnics.* [ME < OF *descoragier* < *des-* away + *corage.* See COURAGE.] **—dis·cour′ag·er,** *n.* **—dis·cour′ag·ing·ly,** *adv.* **—Syn. 1** dishearten, depress, daunt.

dis·cour·age·ment (dis kėr′ij mənt) *n.* **1** the state of being or feeling discouraged. **2** the thing that discourages. **3** the act of discouraging.

dis·course (*n.* dis′kôrs; *v.* dis kôrs′) *n. v.* **-coursed, -cours·ing.** *—n.* **1** a formal speech or writing: *Lectures and sermons are discourses.* **2** a conversation; talk. *—v.* **1** speak or write formally. **2** converse; talk. [< F *discours* < Med.L < L *discursus* < *dis-* in different directions + *currere* run] **—dis·cours′er,** *n.*

dis·cour·te·ous (dis kėr′tē əs) *adj.* not courteous; rude; impolite. **—dis·cour′te·ous·ly,** *adv.* **—dis·cour′te·ous·ness,** *n.* **—Syn.** uncivil, disrespectful.

dis·cour·te·sy (dis kėr′tə sē) *n.* **-sies. 1** lack of courtesy; rudeness; impoliteness. **2** a rude or impolite act.

dis·cov·er (dis kuv′ər) *v.* **1** see or learn of for the first time; find out. **2** *Archaic.* make known; reveal. [ME < OF *descovrir* < *des-* away + *covrir* cover < L *cooperire*] **—dis·cov′er·a·ble,** *adj.* **—dis·cov′er·er,** *n.*

Syn. 1 Discover, invent = find something not known before. **Discover** = find or find out something that already existed, but was not known about or had not been seen: *Pierre and Marie Curie discovered radium.* **Invent** = make or work out something that did not exist before: *Alexander Graham Bell invented the telephone.*

dis·cov·er·y (dis kuv′ər ē or dis kuv′rē) *n.* **-er·ies. 1** the act of discovering. **2** the thing discovered. **3** a person whose special talent has just been discovered, especially an actor, writer, athlete, etc.

dis·cred·it (dis kred′it) *v.* **1** cast doubt on; destroy belief, faith, or trust in: *The lawyer discredited the witness by proving that he had been bribed.* **2** refuse to believe; decline to trust or have faith in. **3** damage the reputation of; disgrace.
—n. **1** a loss of belief, faith, or trust; doubt. **2** the loss of good name or standing: *The young thief brought discredit to his family.* **3** something that causes loss of good name or standing; disgrace: *Jim's behavior was a discredit to the school.* **—Syn.** *v.* **1** dishonor.

dis·cred·it·a·ble (dis kred′ə tə bəl) *adj.* bringing discredit. **—dis·cred′it·a·bly,** *adv.* **—Syn.** disgraceful, dishonorable.

dis·creet (dis krēt′) *adj.* careful and sensible in speech and action; wisely cautious; showing good sense. [ME < OF *discret* < Med.L < L *discretus* separated, pp. of *discernere.* Doublet of DISCRETE. See DISCERN.] **—dis·creet′ly,** *adv.* **—dis·creet′ness,** *n.* **—Syn.** prudent, wary.

dis·crep·an·cy (dis krep′ən sē) *n.* **-cies. 1** lack of consistency; difference; disagreement. **2** an example of inconsistency: *The lawsuit was lost because of discrepancies in the statements of the witnesses.* **—Syn. 1** See **difference.**

dis·crep·ant (dis krep′ənt) *adj.* differing; disagreeing; different; inconsistent. [< L *discrepans, -antis,* ppr. of *discrepare* < *dis-* differently + *crepare* sound] **—dis·crep′ant·ly,** *adv.*

dis·crete (dis krēt′) *adj.* **1** separate; distinct. **2** consisting of distinct parts. [ME < L *discretus,* separated, pp. of *discernere.* Doublet of DISCREET. See DISCERN.] **—dis·crete′ly,** *adv.* **—dis·crete′ness,** *n.*

dis·cre·tion (dis kresh′ən) *n.* **1** the freedom to judge or choose: *Making final plans was left to the president's discretion.* **2** the quality of being discreet; good judgment; carefulness in speech or action; wise caution. **—Syn. 1** choice.

dis·cre·tion·ar·y (dis kresh′ən er′ē) *adj.* with freedom to decide or choose; left to one's own judgment.

dis·crim·i·nate (*v.* dis krim′ə nāt′; *adj.* dis krim′ə nit) *v.* **-nat·ed, -nat·ing,** *adj.* *—v.* **1** make or see a difference: *It is often difficult to discriminate between mere exaggeration and a deliberate falsehood.* **2** make a distinction: *The law ought not to discriminate against any race, creed, or color.* **3** make or see a difference between; distinguish: *The study of literature helps a person to discriminate good books from poor ones.* *—adj.* having discrimination; making fine distinctions. [< L *discriminare* < *discrimen* separation < *discernere.* See DISCERN.] **—dis·crim′i·nate·ly,** *adv.* **—dis·crim′i·na′tor,** *n.* **—Syn.** *v.* **1, 3.** See **distinguish.**

dis·crim·i·nat·ing (dis krim′ə nāt′ing) *adj.* **1** that discriminates. **2** able to discriminate well. **3** in business, differential: *Manufacturers wanted a discriminating duty on imports.* **—dis·crim′i·nat′ing·ly,** *adv.*

dis·crim·i·na·tion (dis krim′ə nā′shən) *n.* **1** the act of making or recognizing differences and distinctions. **2** the ability to make fine distinctions. **3** the act of making a difference in favor of or against. **—Syn. 2** discernment, insight, acumen.

dis·crim·i·na·tive (dis krim′ə nə tiv or dis krim′ə nā′tiv) *adj.* **1** discriminating. **2** showing discrimination.

dis·crim·i·na·to·ry (dis krim′ə nə tô′ rē) *adj.* discriminative; showing partiality.

dis·crown (dis kroun′) *v.* deprive of royal power; depose.

dis·cur·sive (dis kėr′siv) *adj.* wandering or shifting from one subject to another; rambling: *His carefully planned speech was not discursive, but developed one topic.* **—dis·cur′sive·ly,** *adv.* **—dis·cur′sive·ness,** *n.*

dis·cus (dis′kəs) *n.* **-cus·es** or **-ci** (-kī or -kē). **1** a heavy, circular plate of stone or metal, used in athletic games as a test of skill and strength in throwing. **2** the act of throwing the discus. [< L < Gk. *diskos* quoit. Doublet of DAIS, DESK, DISH, and DISK.]

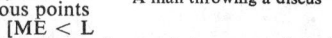

A man throwing a discus

dis·cuss (dis kus′) *v.* consider from various points of view; talk over. [ME < L *discussus,* pp. of *discutere* < *dis-* apart + *quatere* shake] **—dis·cuss′er,** *n.*

Syn. Discuss, argue, debate = talk something over with others. **Discuss** emphasizes considering all sides of a question: *We discussed the best road to take.* **Argue** suggests taking one side and bringing forward facts and reasons for it and against the others: *I argued for taking the new highway.* **Debate** suggests more formal arguing, often publicly, between clearly drawn up sides: *The Oxford students debated against two Canadian students in Toronto last week.*

dis·cus·sion (dis kush′ən) *n.* a going over reasons for and against; discussing things; talk.

dis·dain (dis dān′) *v.* look down on; consider beneath oneself; scorn: *He took a taxi, disdaining to go by bus.* *—n.* the act of disdaining; scorn. [ME < OF *desdeignier* < *des-* away + *deignier* deign < L *dignari*] **—Syn.** *v.* despise, spurn. *—n.* See **scorn.**

dis·dain·ful (dis dān′fəl) *adj.* feeling or showing disdain. **—dis·dain′ful·ly,** *adv.* **—dis·dain′ful·ness,** *n.* **—Syn.** contemptuous, scornful.

dis·ease (də zēz′) *n.* **1** sickness; illness; *Disease must be controlled.* **2** any particular illness: *Measles and chicken pox are two diseases of children.* **3** an unhealthy condition of a plant or a product: *the diseases of grain.* **4** a disordered or bad condition of mind, morals, public affairs, etc. [ME < OF *desaise* < *des-* away + *aise* ease, opportunity < VL *adjacens* neighbourhood < L *adjacens* adjacent] **—dis·ease′less,** *adj.*

dis·eased (də zēzd′) *adj.* **1** having a disease; showing signs of sickness or illness; being diseased: *a diseased hand.* **2** disordered: *a diseased mind.*

dis·em·bark (dis′em bärk′) *v.* go or put ashore from a ship or airplane; land from a ship or airplane.

dis·em·bar·ka·tion (dis′em bär kā′shən) *n.* **1** the act of disembarking. **2** the state of being disembarked.

dis·em·bar·rass (dis′em bar′əs) *v.* **1** free from something that holds back or entangles; disengage. **2** relieve; rid. **3** free from embarrassment or uneasiness.

dis·em·bod·y (dis′em bod′ē) *v.* **-bod·ied, -bod·y·ing.** separate (a soul, spirit, etc.) from the body: *Ghosts are usually thought of as disembodied spirits.* —**dis′em·bod′i·ment,** *n.*

dis·em·bow·el (dis′em bou′əl) *v.* **-elled** or **-eled, -el·ling** or **-el·ing.** take or rip out the bowels of. —**dis′em·bow′el·ment,** *n.*

dis·en·chant (dis′en chant′) *v.* free from a magic spell or illusion. —**dis′en·chant′er,** *n.* —**dis′en·chant′ing·ly,** *adv.* —**dis′en·chant′ment,** *n.*

dis·en·cum·ber (dis′en kum′bər) *v.* free from a burden, annoyance, or trouble.

dis·en·fran·chise (dis′en fran′chīz) *v.* **-chised, -chis·ing.** disfranchise.

dis·en·fran·chise·ment (dis′en fran′chiz mənt) *n.* disfranchisement.

dis·en·gage (dis′en gāj′) *v.* **-gaged, -gag·ing.** **1** free from an engagement, pledge, obligation, etc. **2** detach; loosen: *The mother disengaged her hand from that of the sleeping child.* **3** in military use, go away from combat or contact with (an enemy). —**dis′en·gage′ment,** *n.* —**Syn. 1** release.

dis·en·gaged (dis′en gājd′) *adj.* **1** not busy; free from appointments. **2** released; detached.

dis·en·tan·gle (dis′en tang′gəl) *v.* **-tan·gled, -tan·gling.** free from tangles or complications; untangle. —**dis′en·tan′gle·ment,** *n.*

dis·en·throne (dis′en thrōn′) *v.* **-throned, -thron·ing.** dethrone.

dis·en·twine (dis′en twīn′) *v.* **-twined, -twin·ing.** disentangle.

dis·es·tab·lish (dis′es tab′lish) *v.* deprive of the character of being established; especially, withdraw state recognition or support from (a church). —**dis′es·tab′lish·ment,** *n.*

dis·es·teem (dis′es tēm′) *v. n.* scorn; dislike.

dis·fa·vor or **dis·fa·vour** (dis fā′vər) *n.* **1** dislike; disapproval: *The workers looked with disfavor on any attempt to lower their wages.* **2** the state of being regarded with dislike or disapproval. —*v.* regard with dislike; disapprove.

dis·fig·ure (dis fig′ər or -fig′yər) *v.* **-ured, -ur·ing.** spoil the appearance of; mar the beauty of: *Large billboards disfigured the countryside.* —**dis·fig′ur·er,** *n.* —**Syn.** See **deface.**

dis·fig·ure·ment (dis fig′ər mənt or -fig′yər mənt) *n.* **1** the act of disfiguring. **2** a disfigured condition. **3** something that disfigures; a defect.

dis·fran·chise (dis fran′chīz) *v.* **-chised, -chis·ing.** **1** take the rights of citizenship away from. A disfranchised person cannot vote or hold office. **2** take a right or privilege from. Also, **disenfranchise.**

dis·fran·chise·ment (dis fran′chiz mənt) *n.* **1** a disfranchising. **2** a being disfranchised. Also, **disenfranchisement.**

dis·gorge (dis gôrj′) *v.* **-gorged, -gorg·ing.** **1** throw up (what has been swallowed); vomit forth. **2** pour forth; discharge: *Swollen streams disgorged their waters into the river.* **3** give up unwillingly: *The robbers were forced to disgorge their plunder.* [ME < OF *desgorger* < *des-* reverse of + *gorge* gorge < LL *gurges* throat, jaws < L *gurges* abyss, whirlpool] —**dis·gorg′er,** *n.*

dis·grace (dis grās′) *n. v.* **-graced, -grac·ing.** —*n.* **1** a loss of honor or respect; shame. **2** a cause of disgrace. **3** a loss of favor or trust: *The king's former adviser is now in disgrace.* —*v.* **1** cause disgrace to. **2** dismiss in disgrace: *The cowardly officer was disgraced for failing to do his duty.* [< F *disgrâce* < Ital. *disgrazia* < *dis-* opposite of + *grazia* grace < L *gratia*] —**dis·grac′er,** *n.*

Syn. *n.* **1 Disgrace, dishonor, ignominy** = loss of good name or respect. **Disgrace** suggests losing the respect and approval of others: *He was in disgrace after his ungentlemanly behavior.* **Dishonor** suggests losing one's honor and self-respect or reputation, or having them taken from one: *For neglect of duty he was stripped of his rank with dishonor.* **Ignominy** means public disgrace or dishonor and suggests being put to shame and held in contempt: *He brought on himself the ignominy of being caught cheating in the game.*

hat, āge, cãre, fär; let, ēqual, tėrm; it, īce
hot, ōpen, ôrder; oil, out; cup, pu̇t, rüle, ūse
əbove, takən, pencəl, lemən, circəs
ch, child; ng, long; sh, ship
th, thin; ᴛʜ, then; zh, measure

dis·grace·ful (dis grās′fəl) *adj.* causing loss of honor or respect; shameful. —**dis·grace′ful·ly,** *adv.* —**dis·grace′ful·ness,** *n.*

dis·grun·tle (dis grun′təl) *v.* **-tled, -tling.** put in bad humor; dissatisfy: *a disgruntled customer.* [< *dis-*[1] apart + obs. *gruntle*, frequentative of *grunt*]

dis·grun·tled (dis grun′təld) *adj.* in bad humor; discontented; disgusted; displeased. [< *dis-* + obs. *gruntle* grunt, grumble]

dis·guise (dis gīz′) *v.* **-guised, -guis·ing,** *n.* —*v.* **1** make a change in the clothes and appearance of (someone) for concealment or for looking like someone else: *The spy disguised himself as an old man.* **2** hide what (something) really is; make (something) seem like something else: *The pirates had disguised their ship. He disguised his handwriting. He disguised his hate by a false show of friendliness.*
—*n.* **1** the use of a changed or unusual dress and appearance in order not to be recognized: *The criminal resorted to disguise to escape from jail.* **2** clothes, actions, etc. used to hide who one really is or to make a person look like someone else: *Woman's clothes and a wig formed his disguise.* **3** a false or misleading appearance; deception; concealment. **4** the state or condition of being disguised. [ME < OF *desguisier* < *des-* down + *guise* guise < Gmc.] —**dis·guis′ed·ly,** *adv.* —**dis·guise′ment,** *n.* —**dis·guis′er,** *n.*

dis·gust (dis gust′) *n.* a strong dislike; sickening dislike. [< MF *desgoust* < *desgouster.* See DISGUST, v.] —*v.* **1** arouse disgust in. **2** cause distaste by offensive conduct: *The practice of cursing disgusts most women.* [< MF *desgouster* < *des-* apart + *goust* taste < L *gustus*] —**dis·gust′ing·ly,** *adv.* —**Syn.** *n.* distaste, loathing, repugnance. See **dislike.**

dis·gust·ed (dis gus′tid) *adj.* filled with disgust. —**dis·gust′ed·ly,** *adv.* —**dis·gust′ed·ness,** *n.*

dis·gust·ing (dis gus′ting) *adj.* that disgusts; unpleasant; distasteful. —**dis·gust·ing·ly,** *adv.*

dish (dish) *n.* **1** anything to serve food in, such as a plate, platter, bowl, cup, or saucer. **2** the amount of food served in a dish. **3** the food served: *Sliced peaches and cream is the dish I like best.* **4** something shaped like a dish. **5** *Slang.* anything that is in accord with one's tastes or desires; preference. **6** *Slang.* a pretty girl.
—*v.* **1** serve (food) by putting it in a dish. **2** shape like a dish. **3** *Slang.* defeat; ruin. **4 dish it out,** *Slang.* abuse or punish someone physically or verbally: *If you dish it out, you must learn to take it as well.* **5 dish out, a** serve (food): *The chef dished out the salad.* **b** *Informal.* give out; dispense: *Some firms dish out thousands of dollars in Christmas bonuses.* **c** *Informal.* inflict; administer; give: *dish out a series of knockout blows.* **6 dish up, a** serve (food). **b** present (facts, etc.) neatly. [OE *disc* < L *discus* dish, discus < Gk. *diskos.* Doublet of DAIS, DESK, DISCUS, and DISK.]

dis·ha·bille (dis′ə bēl′) *n.* **1** informal, careless dress. **2** a garment or costume worn carelessly. **3** the condition of being only partly dressed. Also, **deshabille.** [< F *déshabillé*, pp. of *déshabiller* < *dés-* away + *habiller* dress]

dis·har·mo·ny (dis här′mə nē) *n.* **-nies.** lack of harmony; discord.

dish·cloth (dish′kloth′) *n.* a cloth to wash dishes with.

dis·heart·en (dis här′tən) *v.* discourage; depress: *A long drought disheartens a farmer.* —**dis·heart′en·ing·ly,** *adv.* —**dis·heart′en·ment,** *n.*

di·shev·el (də shev′əl) *v.* **-elled** or **-eled, -el·ling** or **-el·ing.** disarrange or rumple (hair, clothing, etc.).

di·shev·elled or **di·shev·eled** (də shev′əld) *adj.* **1** rumpled; mussed; disordered; untidy: *a dishevelled appearance.* **2** hanging loosely or in disorder: *dishevelled hair.* [ME < OF *descheveler* < *des-* away + *chevel* hair < L *capillus*]

dish·ful (dish′ful) *n.* **-fuls.** as much as a dish can hold.

dis·hon·est (dis on′ist) *adj.* **1** not honest: *Lying, stealing, and cheating are the dishonest acts of dishonest people.* **2** arranged to work or function in an unfair way: *a dishonest card game, dishonest scales.* —**dis·hon′est·ly,** *adv.* —**Syn.** corrupt, fraudulent.

dis·hon·es·ty (dis on′is tē) *n.* **-ties. 1** lying, cheating, or stealing; lack of honesty. **2** a dishonest act.

dis·hon·or or **dis·hon·our** (dis on′ər) *n.* **1** a loss of honor or reputation; shame; disgrace. **2** the cause of dishonor. **3** a refusal or failure to pay a cheque, bill, etc. —*v.* **1** cause or bring dishonor to. **2** refuse or fail to pay (a cheque, bill, etc.). —**dis·hon′or·er** or **dis·hon′our·er,** *n.* —**Syn.** *n.* **1** See **disgrace.**

dis·hon·or·a·ble or **dis·hon·our·a·ble** (dis on′ər ə bəl) *adj.* **1** causing loss of honor; shameful; disgraceful **2** without honor. —**dis·hon′or·a·ble·ness** or **dis·hon′our·a·ble·ness,** *n.* —**dis·hon′or·a·bly** or **dis·hon′our·a·bly,** *adv.*

dis·hon·our (dis on′ər) *n. v.* dishonor.

dish·pan (dish′pan′) *n.* a pan in which to wash dishes.

dish·rag (dish′rag′) *n.* **1** a cloth to wash dishes with. **2** anything wet and limp.

dish·tow·el (dish′tou′əl) *n.* a towel to dry dishes with.

dish·wash·er (dish′wosh′ər) *n.* **1** a machine for washing dishes, glasses, pots, pans, etc. **2** a person who washes dishes, especially in a restaurant, canteen, etc.

dish·wa·ter (dish′wot′ər or -wô′tər) *n.* water for washing dishes; water in which dishes have been washed.

dis·il·lu·sion (dis′i lü′zhən) *v.* free from illusion: *He thought he could trust everyone; but soon he was disillusioned.* —*n.* a freeing or being freed from illusion.

dis·il·lu·sion·ment (dis′i lü′zhən mənt) *n.* a disillusioning or being disillusioned.

dis·in·cli·na·tion (dis in′klə nā′shən) *n.* unwillingness.

dis·in·cline (dis′in klīn′) *v.* **-clined, -clin·ing.** make or be unwilling.

dis·in·clined (dis′in klīnd′) *adj.* unwilling.

dis·in·fect (dis′in fekt′) *v.* destroy the disease germs in. —**dis′in·fec′tor,** *n.*

dis·in·fect·ant (dis′in fek′tənt) *n.* a means for destroying disease germs. Alcohol, iodine, and carbolic acid are disinfectants. —*adj.* destroying disease germs.

dis·in·fec·tion (dis′in fek′shən) *n.* the destruction of disease germs.

dis·in·gen·u·ous (dis′in jen′ū əs) *adj.* insincere, not frank. —**dis′in·gen′u·ous·ly,** *adv.* —**dis′in·gen′u·ous·ness,** *n.*

dis·in·her·it (dis′in her′it) *v.* prevent from inheriting; deprive of an inheritance: *A father who leaves none of his property to his son is said to have disinherited him.*

dis·in·her·it·ance (dis′in her′ə təns) *n.* **1** the act of disinheriting. **2** the state of being disinherited.

dis·in·te·grate (dis in′tə grāt′) *v.* **-grat·ed, -grat·ing. 1** break up; separate into small parts or bits: *Time had caused the old books to disintegrate into a pile of fragments and dust.* **2** in physics, change in nuclear structure through bombardment by charged particles.

dis·in·te·gra·tion (dis in′tə grā′shən) *n.* **1** a breaking up; separation into small parts or bits: *Rain and frost had caused the gradual disintegration of the rock.* **2** in physics, the emission of an alpha or beta particle by the nucleus of a radio-active element.

dis·in·te·gra·tor (dis in′tə grā′tər) *n.* **1** a person or thing that causes disintegration. **2** a machine for disintegrating a substance.

dis·in·ter (dis′in tėr′) *v.* **-terred, -ter·ring. 1** take out of a grave or tomb; dig up. **2** bring to light; discover and reveal.

dis·in·ter·est (dis in′trist or -in′tər ist) *n.* lack of interest; indifference.

dis·in·ter·est·ed (dis in′tris tid, -in′tər is tid, or -in′tər es′tid) *adj.* **1** not affected by selfish motives; not concerned with one's own interests. **2** impersonal. —**dis·in′ter·est·ed·ly,** *adv.* —**dis·in′ter·est·edness,** *n.*

☛ **Disinterested** and **uninterested** should not be confused. *Disinterested* = having no selfish interest or personal feelings in a matter and therefore having no reason or desire to be anything but strictly impartial and fair: *A judge should be disinterested. Uninterested* = not interested in any way, having no concern or feelings about the matter and paying no attention: *An uninterested boy can spoil a class.*

dis·in·ter·ment (dis′in tėr′mənt) *n.* **1** the act of disinterring. **2** the state of being disinterred. **3** something disinterred.

dis·join (dis join′) *v.* separate; keep from joining; prevent from being joined.

dis·joint (dis joint′) *v.* **1** take apart at the joints: *disjoint a chicken.* **2** break up; disconnect; put out of order: *The boy's speech was stumbling and disjointed.* **3** put out of joint; dislocate. **4** come apart; be put out of joint.

dis·joint·ed (dis join′tid) *adj.* **1** taken apart at the joints. **2** broken up; disconnected; incoherent. **3** out of joint. —**dis·joint′ed·ly,** *adv.* —**dis·joint′ed·ness,** *n.*

disjoint set in mathematics, one of two or more sets having no numbers in common.

dis·junc·tion (dis jungk′shən) *n.* **1** the act of disjoining or state of being disjoined; a separation. **2** in logic, the relation between the terms of a disjunctive proposition.

dis·junc·tive (dis jungk′tiv) *adj.* **1** causing separation; separating. **2** in grammar, showing a choice or contrast between two ideas, words, etc. *But, yet, either . . .or,* etc. are disjunctive conjunctions. *Otherwise, else,* etc. are disjunctive adverbs. **3** in logic, involving alternatives. A disjunctive proposition asserts that one or the other of two things is true but both cannot be true. —*n.* **1** in logic, a statement involving alternatives. **2** in grammar, a disjunctive conjunction. —**dis·junc′tive·ly,** *adv.*

disk or **disc** (disk) *n.* **1** a round, flat, thin object. **2** a round, flat surface, or one that is apparently so: *the sun's disk.* **3** a roundish, flat part in certain plants. The yellow centre of a daisy is a disk. **4** in anatomy and zoology, any round, flat part or structure, especially the masses of fibrous cartilage between the bodies of the vertebrae. **5** anything resembling a disk. **6** a phonograph record. **7** discus. —*v.* cultivate ground with disks. [< L *discus* discus < Gk. *diskos.* Doublet of DAIS, DESK, DISCUS, and DISH.] —**disk′like′** or **disc′like′**, *adj.* —**disk′er** or **disc′er,** *n.*

A disk (def. 1)

disk harrow or **disc harrow** a harrow with a row of sharp, revolving disks used in preparing ground for planting or sowing.

disk jockey or **disc jockey** *Informal.* an announcer for a radio or television program that consists chiefly of recorded music.

dis·like (dis līk′) *n. v.* **-liked, -lik·ing.** —*n.* a feeling of not liking; a feeling against. —*v.* not like; object to; having a feeling against.

Syn. *n.* **Dislike, distaste, disgust** = a feeling of not liking someone or something. **Dislike** is the general word, applying to any degree of this feeling, but always suggesting a turning away or being against a person or thing: *Bob has a dislike for study and would rather play baseball.* **Distaste** applies to a fixed dislike for something one finds unpleasant or disagreeable: *He has a distaste for chocolate.* **Disgust** applies to a strong dislike for something that is disagreeable, sickening, or bad: *We feel disgust for bad odors and tastes.*

dis·lo·cate (dis′lō kāt′) *v.* **-cat·ed, -cat·ing. 1** put out of joint: *The football player dislocated his shoulder when he fell.* **2** put out of order; disturb; upset: *Our plans for the picnic were dislocated by the bad weather.* —**dis′lo·ca′tor,** *n.*

dis·lo·ca·tion (dis′lō kā′shən) *n.* **1** the act of dislocating. **2** the state of being dislocated.

dis·lodge (dis loj′) *v.* **-lodged, -lodg·ing. 1** drive or force out of a place, position, etc.: *The workman used a crowbar to dislodge a heavy stone from the wall. Heavy gunfire dislodged the enemy from the fort.* **2** leave a lodging place.

dis·lodg·ment (dis loj′mənt) *n.* **1** the act of dislodging. **2** the state of being dislodged.

dis·loy·al (dis loi′əl) *adj.* not loyal; unfaithful: *A disloyal servant let robbers into the house.* —**dis·loy′al·ly,** *adv.* —**Syn.** false, traitorous.

dis·loy·al·ty (dis loiʹəl tē) *n.* **-ties. 1** lack of loyalty; unfaithfulness: *The traitor was shot for disloyalty to his country.* **2** a disloyal act.
Syn. 1 Disloyalty, treachery, treason = faithlessness. **Disloyalty** = unfaithfulness, felt or shown, to anyone or anything to whom one owes allegiance or is bound by promises, love, or friendship: *Refusing to defend parents, school, or country is disloyalty.* **Treachery** = dishonest faithlessness, and suggests some definite act of betraying trust while pretending to be loyal: *Secretly working to the detriment of a friend is treachery.* **Treason** applies to treachery to one's country, shown by doing something specifically to help the enemy: *Deliberately broadcasting enemy propaganda to our troops is treason.*

dis·mal (dizʹməl) *adj.* **1** dark; gloomy: *Damp caves or rainy days are dismal.* **2** dreary; miserable: *Sickness often makes a person feel dismal.* [ME *dismall* < AF *dis mal* evil days < L *dies mali*] **—disʹmal·ly,** *adv.* **—Syn. 1** sombre. **2** cheerless, sad.

dis·man·tle (dis manʹtəl) *v.* **-tled, -tling. 1** strip of covering, equipment, furniture, guns, rigging, etc.: *The warship was dismantled before the hull was sold for scrap metal.* **2** pull down; take apart: *We had to dismantle the bookcases to move them.* [< MF *desmanteler* < *des-* away + *mantel* mantle < L *mantellum*]

dis·mast (dis mastʹ) *v.* take the mast or masts from; break down the mast or masts of: *The storm dismasted the ship.*

dis·may (dis māʹ) *n.* a loss of courage because of fear of what is about to happen. [< v.] *—v.* trouble greatly; make afraid: *The thought that she might fail the history test dismayed her.* [ME < OF **desmaier* < VL *dismagare* deprive of strength < L *dis-* (reverse) + Frankish **magan* have strength] **—dis·mayʹing·ly,** *adv.*
Syn. *n.* **Dismay, consternation** = a feeling of being unnerved or overwhelmed by the thought of what is going to happen next. **Dismay** suggests loss of ability to face or handle something frightening, baffling, or upsetting that comes as a surprise or shock: *The mother was filled with dismay when her son confessed he had robbed a store.* **Dismay** is often used in a weakened sense: *To my dismay, my son gave up literature for mathematics.* **Consternation** = dismay and dread so great that a person cannot think clearly or, sometimes, move: *To our consternation the child darted out in front of the speeding car.*

dis·mem·ber (dis memʹbər) *v.* **1** pull apart; cut to pieces; separate or divide into parts: *The Austro-Hungarian Empire was dismembered after the First World War.* **2** cut or tear the limbs from. **—dis·memʹber·ment,** *n.*

dis·miss (dis misʹ) *v.* **1** send away; allow to go: *At noon the teacher dismissed the class.* **2** remove from office or service: *We dismissed the cook because her cooking was poor.* **3** put out of mind; stop thinking about: *Dismiss your troubles and be happy.* **4** in law, refuse to consider (a complaint, plea, etc.) in a court, refuse to grant the relief sought. **5** give brief or scant attention to: *She dismissed the article with a laugh, saying that it was worthless.* [< L *dismissus,* var. of *dimissus* < *dis-* away + *missus,* pp. of *mittere* send]
Syn. 1, 2 Dismiss, discharge, release = let go from responsibility, employment, etc. **Dismiss** emphasizes the idea of not keeping, both when it means to set free from the duty of staying and when, as usually, it means to force to leave: *After five days in the hospital, the patient was dismissed. The firm dismissed the man who struck his foreman.* **Discharge** emphasizes getting rid of a person, only in military and legal use suggesting giving formal permission to leave: *We discharged the maid.* **Release** emphasizes setting a person free from something that holds him: *The soldier was released from duty for two days.*

dis·miss·al (dis misʹəl) *n.* **1** the act of dismissing. **2** the state or fact of being dismissed. **3** a written or spoken order dismissing someone.

dis·mis·sion (dis mishʹən) *n.* dismissal.

dis·mount (dis mountʹ) *v.* **1** get off a horse, bicycle, etc. **2** knock, throw, or otherwise remove from a horse; unhorse. **3** take (a thing) from its setting or support: *The cannon were dismounted for shipping to another fort.* **4** take apart; take to pieces. **5** deprive (troops) of horses or mounts: *The Indians dismounted the troops by stealing their horses.*

dis·o·be·di·ence (disʹə bēʹdē əns or disʹə bēʹdyəns) *n.* a refusal to obey; failure to obey.

dis·o·be·di·ent (disʹə bēʹdē ənt or disʹə bēʹdyənt) *adj.* refusing to obey; failing to obey. **—disʹo·beʹdi·ent·ly,** *adv.*

dis·o·bey (disʹə bāʹ) *v.* refuse to obey; fail to obey. **—disʹo·beyʹer,** *n.* **—Syn.** defy.

dis·o·blige (disʹə blījʹ) *v.* **-bliged, -blig·ing. 1** neglect to oblige; refuse to oblige; refuse to do a favor for. **2** give offence to.

hat, āge, cãre, fär; let, ēqual, tėrm; it, īce
hot, ōpen, ôrder; oil, out; cup, pu̇t, rüle, ūse
əbove, takən, pencəl, lemən, circəs
ch, child; ng, long; sh, ship
th, thin; ᴛʜ, then; zh, measure

dis·or·der (dis ôrʹdər) *n.* **1** lack of order; confusion: *The records were in such a state of disorder that it will take hours to reorganize them.* **2** a public disturbance; riot. **3** a sickness; disease: *a disorder of the stomach.* *—v.* **1** destroy the order of; throw into confusion. **2** cause sickness in: *The bad food disordered my stomach.* **—Syn.** *n.* **1** jumble. **2** commotion, tumult.

dis·or·dered (dis ôrʹdərd) *adj.* **1** not in order; disturbed. **2** sick.

dis·or·der·ly (dis ôrʹdər lē) *adj.* **1** not orderly; in confusion: *An untidy, messy room is disorderly.* **2** causing disorder; making a disturbance; breaking rules; unruly: *a disorderly mob.* **3** against the law; contrary to good morals or decency. *—adv.* in a disorderly manner. **—dis·orʹder·li·ness,** *n.*

dis·or·gan·ize (dis ôrʹgən īzʹ) *v.* **-ized, -iz·ing.** throw into confusion and disorder; upset the order and arrangement of: *Heavy snowstorms disorganized the train schedule.* **—dis·orʹgan·i·zaʹtion,** *n.*

dis·o·ri·ent (dis ôrʹē entʹ) *v.* disorientate.

dis·o·ri·en·tate (dis ôrʹē en tātʹ) *v.* cause to lose sense of direction or time; mix up; disconcert: *His sudden rise to fame and fortune disorientated him at first.* **—dis·o·ri·en·taʹtion,** *n.*

dis·own (dis ōnʹ) *v.* refuse to recognize as one's own; cast off: *He disowned his disobedient son. The politician disowned his former views on the subject.*

dis·par·age (dis parʹij) *v.* **-aged, -ag·ing. 1** speak slightingly of; try to lessen the importance or value of; belittle: *The coward disparaged the hero's brave attempt to rescue the drowning child.* **2** lower the reputation of; discredit. [ME < OF *desparagier* match unequally < *des-* apart + *parage* rank, lineage < L *par* equal] **—dis·parʹag·er,** *n.* **—dis·parʹag·ing·ly,** *adv.* **—Syn. 1** depreciate.

dis·par·age·ment (dis parʹij mənt) *n.* **1** the act of disparaging. **2** something that lowers a thing or person in worth or importance. **3** a lessening in esteem or standing: *Say nothing that will be to Joe's disparagement.*

dis·pa·rate (disʹpə rit) *adj.* distinct in kind; essentially different; unlike. [< L *disparatus,* pp. of *disparare* < *dis-* apart + *parare* get] **—disʹpa·rate·ly,** *adv.* **—disʹpa·rate·ness,** *n.*

dis·par·i·ty (dis parʹə tē) *n.* **-ties.** inequality; difference: *There will be disparities in the accounts of the same event given by several people.* **—Syn.** See **difference.**

dis·part (dis pärtʹ) *v.* separate; divide into parts.

dis·pas·sion (dis pashʹən) *n.* freedom from emotion or prejudice; calmness; impartiality.

dis·pas·sion·ate (dis pashʹən it) *adj.* free from emotion or prejudice; calm; impartial: *To a dispassionate observer, the drivers of both cars seemed equally at fault.* **—dis·pasʹsion·ate·ly,** *adv.* **—dis·pasʹsion·ate·ness,** *n.*

dis·patch or **des·patch** (dis pachʹ) *v.* **1** send off to some place or for some purpose: *He dispatched a messenger to tell the general what had happened.* **2** get (something) done promptly or speedily. **3** give the death blow to; kill. **4** *Informal.* eat up. **5** dismiss; send away; get rid of: *The housewife dispatched the salesman.* *—n.* **1** a sending off (of a letter, a messenger, etc.): *Please hurry up the dispatch of this telegram.* **2** a written message, such as special news or government business. **3** promptness; speed. **4** a putting to death; a killing. **5** an agency for conveying goods, etc. **6 mention in dispatches,** in the armed services: **a** commend (someone) for bravery, distinguished service, etc. in the official report of an action. **b** the fact of being commended in this way: *He was promoted twice and received three mentions in dispatches.* [< Ital. *dispacciare* hasten or Sp. *despachar*]

dispatch box 1 a dispatch case. **2** in the British House of

Commons, either of two boxes, one of which rests on each side of a central table, from behind which a member of the Government or of the Opposition may speak.

dis·patch·er or **des·patch·er** (dis pach′ər) *n.* a person who dispatches: *An alert dispatcher is essential to the smooth working of a taxi company.*

dis·pel (dis pel′) *v.* **-pelled, -pel·ling.** drive away and scatter; disperse: *The captain's cheerful laugh dispelled our fears.* [< L *dispellere* < *dis-* away + *pellere* drive] **—dis·pel′ler,** *n.* **—Syn.** See **scatter.**

dis·pen·sa·ble (dis pen′sə bəl) *adj.* **1** that may be done without; unimportant. **2** capable of being dispensed or administered. **—dis·pen′sa·ble·ness,** *n.*

dis·pen·sa·ry (dis pen′sə rē) *n.* **-ries. 1** a place where medicines and medical advice are given free or for a small charge. **2** that part of a hospital where medicines are prepared and stored.

dis·pen·sa·tion (dis′pən sā′shən) *n.* **1** the act of giving out; act of distributing: *the dispensation of charity to the poor.* **2** the thing given out or distributed: *They gave thanks for the dispensations of Providence.* **3** rule; management: *England under the dispensation of Elizabeth I.* **4** the management or ordering of the affairs of the world by Providence or Nature. **5** a religious system: *the Christian dispensation.* **6** in the Roman Catholic Church: **a** official permission to disregard a law, obligation, etc. without penalty. **b** the writing giving such permission.

dis·pen·sa·to·ry (dis pen′sə tô′rē) *n.* **-ries. 1** a book that tells how to prepare and use medicines. **2** *Archaic.* a dispensary.

dis·pense (dis pens′) *v.* **-pensed, -pens·ing. 1** give out; distribute: *The Red Cross dispensed food and clothing to the sufferers.* **2** carry out; put in force; apply: *In our country judges and law courts dispense justice.* **3** prepare and give out: *Druggists must dispense medicine with the greatest care.* **4** release; excuse. **5 dispense with, a** do away with; make unnecessary. **b** do without; get along without. [ME < OF *despenser* < L *dispensare* weigh out < *dis-* out < *pendere* weigh] **—dis·pens′er,** *n.* **—Syn. 1** allot, apportion. See **distribute.**

☛ Dispense is followed by *with* when it means "do without, get along without," and by *from* when it means "release, excuse": *Let's dispense with this constant complaining. He was dispensed from payment of the heavy fine.*

dis·peo·ple (dis pē′pəl) *v.* **-pled, -pling.** deprive of all or many people or inhabitants.

dis·per·sal (dis pėr′səl) *n.* a dispersion; the act of scattering or state of being scattered: *the dispersal of a crowd.*

dis·perse (dis pėrs′) *v.* **-persed, -pers·ing. 1** spread in different directions; scatter: *The crowd dispersed when the Mounties arrived.* **2** distribute; circulate: *Children went through the crowd dispersing handbills.* **3** disappear or cause to disappear; dispel; dissipate: *The swelling on his arm was dispersed by cold compresses.* **4** in physics, divide (white light) into its colored rays. **5** in chemistry, scatter (the particles of a colloid) throughout another substance or a mixture. [ME < MF *disperser* < L *dispersus,* pp. of *dispergere* < *dis-* in every direction + *spargere* scatter] **—Syn. 1** See **scatter.**

dis·per·sion (dis pėr′zhən or dis pėr′shən) *n.* **1** a dispersing. **2** a being dispersed. **3** in physics: **a** the separation of light into its different colors. **b** a similar separation of electromagnetic waves, etc. **4** in chemistry: **a** a substance that has been dispersed. **b** the system consisting of the dispersed colloidal particles and the medium in which they are dispersed.

dis·per·sive (dis pėr′siv) *adj.* dispersing; tending to disperse.

dis·pir·it (dis pir′it) *v.* depress; discourage; dishearten. **—dis·pir′it·ed·ly,** *adv.* **—dis·pir′it·ed·ness,** *n.*

dis·place (dis plās′) *v.* **-placed, -plac·ing. 1** put something else in the place of; take the place of: *The automobile has almost displaced the horse and buggy.* **2** remove from a position of authority. **3** put out of place; move from its usual place or position: *A floating body displaces its own weight of liquid.*

displaced person a person forced out of his own country by war, famine, political disturbance, etc. *Abbrev.*: DP or D.P.

dis·place·ment (dis plās′mənt) *n.* **1** the act of displacing **2** a being displaced. **3** the weight of the volume of water displaced by a ship or other floating object. This weight is equal to that of the floating object. **4** the volume in a pump or engine cylinder displaced by a stroke of the piston. **5** the distance of movement of rocks or strata in a geological fault.

dis·play (dis plā′) *v.* **1** expose to view; show: *Many old Indian weapons are displayed in the museum.* **2** show in a special way, so as to attract attention: *The boys' suits were displayed in the big window of the store.* **3** let appear; reveal: *He displayed his good nature by answering all our questions.* **4** spread out; unfold: *display a newspaper.* —*n.* **1** a displaying; exhibition: *He did not like the boy's display of bad temper.* **2** a showing off; ostentation: *Her fondness for display led her to buy showy clothes.* **3** in printing, the choice and arrangement of type so as to make certain words, etc. prominent. **4** a planned showing of a thing for some special purpose; an exhibition: *There will be a display of the art students' drawings next week.* [ME < OF *despleier* < L *displicare* scatter < *dis-* apart + *plicare* fold]

Syn. *v.* **1 Display, exhibit, evince** = show. **Display** = put out in view for others, especially the public, to look at: *The stores are displaying new spring clothes.* **Exhibit** = show as something especially worth looking at in a way that draws attention: *She exhibited her wedding presents on the table.* **Evince** = show in some way something that cannot be seen with the eyes, such as a feeling or quality: *He evinced obvious displeasure when he learned he would have to stay after school.* *-n.* **1** See **show.**

dis·please (dis plēz′) *v.* **-pleased, -pleas·ing.** not please; offend; annoy. **—dis·pleas′ing·ly,** *adv.* **—Syn.** anger.

dis·pleas·ure (dis plezh′ər) *n.* **1** the feeling of being displeased; slight anger; annoyance; dislike. **2** *Archaic.* discomfort; uneasiness. **3** *Archaic.* offence; injury.

dis·port (dis pôrt′) *v.* amuse (oneself); sport, play: *People laughed at the clumsy bears disporting themselves in the water.* —*n. Archaic.* a pastime; amusement. [ME < OF *desporter* < *des-* away from + *porter* carry < L *portare*]

dis·pos·a·ble (dis pōz′ə bəl) *adj.* **1** capable of being disposed of. **2** at one's disposal; available.

dis·pos·al (dis pōz′əl) *n.* **1** the act of getting rid (of something): *the disposal of garbage.* **2** the act of giving away: *His will provided for the disposal of his property after his death.* **3** a sale. **4** the power or authority to dispose of or use something. **5** an arranging of matters; a settling of affairs. **6** an act of putting in a certain order or position; arrangement: *The disposal of the chairs around the sides of the room left plenty of space in the middle.* **7 at** or **in one's disposal,** ready for one's use or service at any time; under one's control or management.

dis·pose (dis pōz′) *v.* **-posed, -pos·ing. 1** put in a certain order or position; arrange: *The battleships were disposed in a straight line.* **2** arrange (matters); settle (affairs); determine. **3** make ready or willing; incline: *More pay and shorter hours of work disposed him to take the new job.* **4** make liable or subject: *Getting your feet wet disposes you to catching cold.* **5 dispose of, a** get rid of. **b** give away. **c** sell. **d** eat or drink. **e** arrange; settle. [ME < OF *disposer* < *dis-* variously + *poser* place. See POSE[1].] **—dis·pos′er,** *n.*

dis·posed (dis pōzd′) *adj.* **1** willing; inclined. **2 well-disposed toward,** favorable toward; friendly toward.

dis·po·si·tion (dis′pə zish′ən) *n.* **1** one's habitual ways of acting toward others or of thinking about things; nature: *a cheerful disposition, a selfish disposition.* **2** a tendency; inclination: *a disposition to argue.* **3** the act of putting in order or position; an arrangement: *the disposition of troops in battle.* **4** management; settlement: *the satisfactory disposition of a difficult problem.* **5** a disposal.

Syn. 1 Disposition, temperament, temper = the qualities that characterize a person as an individual. **Disposition** applies to the controlling mental or emotional quality that determines a person's natural or usual way of thinking and acting: *He has a quarrelsome disposition.* **Temperament** applies to the combined physical, emotional, and mental qualities that determine a person's whole nature: *He has an artistic temperament.* **Temper** applies to the combined natural and acquired qualities that determine the state of mind in which a person meets problems and troubles: *He is calm in temper.* **Temper** may also be applied to a more temporary state: *I found him in a good temper.*

dis·pos·sess (dis′pə zes′) *v.* **1** force to give up the possession of a house, land, etc.; oust: *The farmer was dispossessed for not paying his rent.* **2** deprive: *Fear dispossessed him of his senses.* **—dis′pos·ses′sion,** *n.* **—dis′pos·ses′sor,** *n.* **—Syn. 1** evict, remove.

dis·praise (dis prāz′) *v.* **-praised, -prais·ing,** *n.* **—***v.* express disapproval of; speak against; blame. **—***n.* an expression of disapproval; blame. **—dis·prais′er,** *n.*

dis·prize (dis prīz′) *v.* **-prized, -priz·ing.** *Archaic.* disdain.

dis·proof (dis prüf′) *n.* **1** a disproving; refutation. **2** a fact, reason, etc. that disproves something.

dis·pro·por·tion (dis′prə pôr′shən) *n.* a lack of proportion; lack of proper proportion; lack of symmetry. **—***v.* make disproportionate.

dis·pro·por·tion·al (dis′prə pôr′shən əl) *adj.* not in proportion; disproportionate.

dis·pro·por·tion·al·ly (dis′prə pôr′shən ə lē) *adv.* without proportion; unequally.

dis·pro·por·tion·ate (dis′prə pôr′shən it) *adj.* out of proportion; lacking in proper proportion.

dis·pro·por·tion·ate·ly (dis′prə pôr′shən it lē) *adv.* in a disproportionate degree; inadequately or excessively.

dis·prove (dis prüv′) *v.* **-proved, -prov·ing.** prove false or incorrect; refute. **—dis·prov′a·ble,** *adj.*

dis·put·a·ble (dis pūt′ə bəl or dis′pyů tə bəl) *adj.* liable to be disputed; uncertain; questionable.

dis·pu·tant (dis′pyů tənt or dis pūt′ənt) *n.* a person who takes part in a dispute or debate.

dis·pu·ta·tion (dis′pyů tā′shən) *n.* **1** a debate; controversy. **2** a dispute.

dis·pu·ta·tious (dis′pyů tā′shəs) *adj.* fond of disputing; inclined to argue. **—dis′pu·ta′tious·ly,** *adv.* **—dis′pu·ta′tious·ness,** *n.* **—Syn.** quarrelsome.

dis·put·a·tive (dis pūt′ə tiv) *adj.* disputatious.

dis·pute (dis pūt′) *v.* **-put·ed, -put·ing,** *n.* **—***v.* **1** discuss; argue; debate. **2** quarrel. **3** disagree with (a statement); declare not true; call in question: *The insurance company disputed his claim for damages done to his car.* **4** fight against; oppose; resist. **5** fight for; fight over: *The soldiers disputed every inch of ground when the enemy attacked.* **6** contend for; try to win: *The losing team disputed the victory until the very end of the game.* **—***n.* **1** an argument; debate. **2** a quarrel. **3 beyond dispute, a** not to be disputed. **b** final; settled. **4 in dispute,** being disputed. [< L *disputare* examine, discuss, argue < *dis-* item by item + *putare* calculate] **—dis·put′er,** *n.* **—Syn.** *n.* **1** See **argument.**

dis·qual·i·fi·ca·tion (dis kwol′ə fə kā′shən) *n.* **1** a disqualifying. **2** a being disqualified. **3** something that disqualifies.

dis·qual·i·fy (dis kwol′ə fī′) *v.* **-fied, -fy·ing. 1** make unfit; make unable to do something: *His lameness disqualified him from playing football.* **2** declare unfit or unable to do something; deprive of a right or privilege: *The school coach disqualified two football players because they had low marks.*

dis·qui·et (dis kwī′ət) *v.* make uneasy or anxious; disturb: *Rumors of a revolution disquieted the dictator.* **—***n.* uneasiness; anxiety.

dis·qui·et·ing (dis kwī′ə ting) *adj.* disturbing.

dis·qui·e·tude (dis kwī′ə tūd′ or -kwī′ə tüd′) *n.* uneasiness; anxiety.

dis·qui·si·tion (dis′kwə zish′ən) *n.* a long or formal speech or writing about a subject. [< L *disquisitio, -onis,* ult. < *dis-* (intensive) + *quaerere* seek]

dis·re·gard (dis′ri gärd′) *v.* **1** pay no attention to; take no notice of: *Disregarding the child's screams, the doctor cleaned and bandaged the cut.* **2** treat without proper regard or respect; slight. **—***n.* **1** a lack of attention; neglect: *The reckless driver was arrested for his complete disregard of the traffic laws.* **2** a lack of proper regard or respect. **—dis·re·gard′er,** *n.*

dis·re·gard·ful (dis′ri gärd′fəl) *adj.* lacking in regard; neglectful; careless.

dis·rel·ish (dis rel′ish) *v. n.* dislike.

dis·re·mem·ber (dis′ri mem′bər) *v. Informal.* fail to remember; forget.

hat, āge, cãre, fär; let, ēqual, tėrm; it, īce
hot, ōpen, ôrder; oil, out; cup, pu̇t, rüle, ūse
əbove, takən, pencəl, lemən, circəs
ch, child; ng, long; sh, ship
th, thin; ᴛʜ, then; zh, measure

dis·re·pair (dis′ri păr′) *n.* a bad condition; need of repairs: *The house was in disrepair.*

dis·rep·u·ta·ble (dis rep′yů tə bəl) *adj.* **1** having a bad reputation. **2** not respectable. **—dis·rep′u·ta·bly,** *adv.*

dis·re·pute (dis′ri pūt′) *n.* disgrace; discredit; disfavor: *Many remedies formerly used are now in disrepute.*

dis·re·spect (dis′ri spekt′) *n.* a lack of respect; rudeness; impoliteness: *Older people disliked the boy because of his disrespect toward his parents.* **—Syn.** discourtesy.

dis·re·spect·ful (dis′ri spekt′fəl) *adj.* rude; showing no respect; lacking in courtesy to elders or superiors. **—dis′re·spect′ful·ly,** *adv.* **—dis′re·spect′ful·ness,** *n.*

dis·robe (dis rōb′) *v.* **-robed, -rob·ing.** undress. **—dis·rob′er,** *n.*

dis·rupt (dis rupt′) *v.* break up; split: *A violent quarrel disrupted the meeting.* [< L *disruptus,* pp. of *disrumpere* < *dis-* apart + *rumpere* break]

dis·rup·tion (dis rup′shən) *n.* **1** a breaking up; a splitting. **2** a being broken up; a being split.

dis·rup·tive (dis rup′tiv) *adj.* tending to break up; causing disruption: *a disruptive influence.*

dis·sat·is·fac·tion (dis′sat is fak′shən) *n.* discontent; displeasure.

dis·sat·is·fac·to·ry (dis′sat is fak′tə rē or -sat is fak′trē) *adj.* causing discontent; unsatisfactory.

dis·sat·is·fied (dis sat′is fīd′) *adj.* **1** discontented; displeased. **2** showing discontent or displeasure.

dis·sat·is·fy (dis sat′is fī′) *v.* **-fied, -fy·ing.** fail to satisfy; make discontented; displease.

dis·sect (di sekt′ or dī sekt′) *v.* **1** cut in pieces; divide into parts. **2** separate or divide the parts of (an animal, plant, etc.) in order to examine or study the structure. **3** examine carefully part by part; analyse: *The lawyer dissected the testimony to show where the witnesses had contradicted themselves.* [< L *dissectus,* pp. of *dissecare* < *dis-* apart + *secare* cut]

dis·sect·ed (di sek′tid or dī sek′tid) *adj.* cut or divided into many parts: *These plants have dissected leaves.*

dis·sec·tion (di sek′shən or dī sek′shən) *n.* **1** the act of separating or dividing an animal or plant into parts in order to examine or study its structure. **2** an animal, plant, etc. that has been dissected. **3** an analysis; consideration of something in detail or point by point.

dis·sec·tor (di sek′tər or dī sek′tər) *n.* **1** a person who dissects. **2** an instrument used in dissecting.

dis·sem·ble (di sem′bəl) *v.* **-bled, -bling. 1** disguise or hide (one's real feelings, thoughts, plans, etc.): *She dissembled her anger with a smile.* **2** conceal one's motives, etc.; be a hypocrite. **3** pretend; feign: *The bored listener dissembled an interest he didn't feel.* **4** pretend not to see or notice; disregard; ignore. [alteration, after *resemble,* of obs. *dissimule* dissimulate < OF *dissimuler* < L *dissimulare*] **—dis·sem′bler,** *n.* **—dis·semb′ling·ly,** *adv.*

dis·sem·i·nate (di sem′ə nāt′) *v.* **-nat·ed, -nat·ing.** scatter widely; spread abroad: *Missionaries disseminate Christian beliefs all over the world.* [< L *disseminare* < *dis-* in every direction + *semen* seed] **—dis·sem′i·na′tion,** *n.* **—dis·sem′i·na′tor,** *n.*

dis·sen·sion (di sen′shən) *n.* a disputing; a quarrelling; hard feelings caused by a difference in opinion: *Their political disagreement caused dissension.* **—Syn.** disagreement, contention.

dis·sent (di sent′) *v.* **1** differ in opinion; disagree: *Two of the judges dissented from the decision of the other three.* **2** refuse to conform to the rules and beliefs of an established church.
—*n.* **1** a difference of opinion; disagreement: *Dissent among the members broke up the club meeting.* **2** a refusal to conform to the rules and beliefs of an established

church: *The Puritans' dissent caused their separation from the Church of England.* [ME < L *dissentire* < *dis-* differently + *sentire* think, feel] **—dis·sent′ing·ly,** *adv.*

dis·sent·er (di sen′tər) *n.* **1** a person who dissents. **2 Dissenter,** in England and Scotland, a Protestant who belongs to some church other than the state church.

dis·sen·tient (di sen′shənt) *adj.* dissenting, especially from the opinion of the majority. *—n.* a person who dissents.

dis·ser·ta·tion (dis′ər tā′shən) *n.* a formal discussion of a subject, especially a thesis submitted by a candidate for a doctoral or other higher degree; treatise. [< L *dissertatio, -onis* < *dissertare,* frequentative of *disserere* < *dis-* apart (distribution) + *serere* join words]

dis·serv·ice (dis sėr′vis or di sėr′vis) *n.* bad treatment; harm; injury.

dis·sev·er (di sev′ər) *v.* sever; separate.

dis·si·dence (dis′ə dəns) *n.* disagreement; dissent.

dis·si·dent (dis′ə dənt) *adj.* disagreeing; dissenting. *—n.* a person who disagrees or dissents. [< L *dissidens, -entis,* ppr. of *dissidere* < *dis-* apart + *sedere* sit]

dis·sim·i·lar (di sim′ə lər) *adj.* not similar; unlike; different. **—dis·sim′i·lar·ly,** *adv.*

dis·sim·i·lar·i·ty (di sim′ə lar′ə tē) *n.* **-ties.** lack of similarity; unlikeness; difference.

dis·sim·i·late (di sim′ə lāt′) *v.* **-lated, -lat·ing.** make or become unlike.

dis·sim·i·la·tion (di sim′ə lā′shən) *n.* **1** the act or process of making or becoming unlike. **2** in biology, the breaking down of organic substances into simpler ones; catabolism. **3** in phonetics, the changing of one of two similar, neighboring speech sounds so that one becomes unlike the other. *Example:* The Latin word *peregrinus* became Italian *pellegrino,* changing the first (r) to (l). See the etymologies for *peregrine* and *pilgrim.*

dis·si·mil·i·tude (dis′sə mil′ə tüd ′or -sə mil′ə tüd′) *n.* unlikeness; difference.

dis·sim·u·late (di sim′yů lāt′) *v.* **-lat·ed, -lat·ing.** disguise or hide under a pretence; dissemble. [< L *dissimulare*] **—dis·sim′u·la′tor,** *n.*

dis·sim·u·la·tion (di sim′yů lā′shən) *n.* the act of dissembling; hypocrisy; pretence; deceit.

dis·si·pate (dis′ə pāt′) *v.* **-pat·ed, -pat·ing. 1** spread in different directions; scatter. **2** disappear or cause to disappear; dispel: *The sun dissipated the mists.* **3** spend foolishly; waste on things of little value: *The extravagant son soon dissipated his father's fortune.* **4** indulge too much in foolish pleasures. [< L *dissipare* < *dis-* in different directions + *sipare* throw] —**Syn. 3** squander.

dis·si·pat·ed (dis′ə pāt′id) *adj.* **1** indulging too much in foolish pleasures; dissolute. **2** scattered. **3** wasted.

dis·si·pa·tion (dis′ə pā′shən) *n.* **1** a dissipating or being dissipated. **2** an amusement; diversion, especially harmful amusements. **3** too much indulgence in foolish pleasures; intemperance.

dis·so·ci·ate (di sō′shē āt′) *v.* **-at·ed, -at·ing. 1** break the connection or association with; separate: *When the man discovered that his companions were dishonest, he soon dissociated himself from them.* **2** in chemistry, separate or decompose by dissociation. [< L *dissociare* < *dis-* apart + *socius* ally]

dis·so·ci·a·tion (di sō′sē ā′shən or di sō′shē ā′shən) *n.* **1** the act of dissociating or state of being dissociated. **2** in chemistry: **a** the separation of molecules of an electrolyte into constituent ions; ionization. Sodium and chlorine ions are formed by the dissociation of sodium chloride molecules in water. **b** reversible decomposition. If water is heated to a very high temperature and gradually decomposes into hydrogen and oxygen in such a way that upon subsequent lowering of the temperature the liberated elements recombine into water, dissociation has occurred. **3** in psychology, the separation of an idea or feeling from the main stream of consciousness.

dis·so·ci·a·tive (di sō′shē ə tiv or di sō′shē ā′tiv) *adj.* having to do with or causing dissociation.

dis·sol·u·bil·i·ty (di sol′yů bil′ə tē) *n.* the fact or quality of being dissoluble.

dis·sol·u·ble (di sol′yů bəl) *adj.* capable of being dissolved. **—dis·sol′u·ble·ness,** *n.*

dis·so·lute (dis′ə lüt′) *adj.* living a wicked life; lewd; immoral. [< L *dissolutus,* pp. of *dissolvere.* See DISSOLVE.] **—dis′so·lute·ly,** *adv.* —**Syn.** dissipated.

dis·so·lu·tion (dis′ə lü′shən) *n.* **1** a breaking up; termination: *The partners arranged for the dissolution of their partnership.* **2** the ending of an assembly, especially of a parliament prior to an election. **3** ruin; destruction. **4** death. **5** a breaking down; decomposition: *the dissolution of water by electrolysis.* **6** the act or process of changing into a liquid state. **7** the state of being liquid.

dis·solve (di zolv′) *v.* **-solved, -solv·ing,** *n.* *—v.* **1** make or become liquid, especially by putting or being put into a liquid; form into a solution in a liquid: *Salt or sugar will dissolve in water.* **2** break up legally; terminate: *dissolve a partnership, dissolve Parliament.* **3** fade away: *The dream dissolved when she woke up.* **4** solve; explain; clear up. **5** separate into parts; decompose. **6** in motion pictures and television, fade or cause to fade gradually from the screen while the succeeding scene slowly appears. **7 dissolved in tears,** shedding many tears.
—n. **1** a breaking up; termination. **2** in motion pictures and television, the gradual disappearing of the figures of a scene while those of a succeeding scene slowly take their place. [ME < L *dissolvere* < *dis-* (intensive) + *solvere* loose] **—dis·solv′a·ble,** *adj.* **—dis·solv′er,** *n.* —**Syn.** *v.* **1** thaw. See **melt.**

dis·so·nance (dis′ə nəns) *n.* **1** a combination of sounds that is not harmonious; harshness and unpleasantness of sound; discord. **2** disagreement; lack of harmony. **3** in music, the relationship or sound of two or more tones in a combination which is conventionally considered to be in a condition of unrest needing resolution or completion; discord.

dis·so·nant (dis′ə nənt) *adj.* **1** harsh in sound; clashing; not harmonious. **2** out of harmony with other views or persons; disagreeing. [ME < L *dissonans, -antis,* ppr. of *dissonare* < *dis-* differently + *sonare* sound] **—dis′so·nant·ly,** *adv.*

dis·suade (di swād′) *v.* **-suad·ed, -suad·ing.** persuade not to do something: *The father dissuaded his son from leaving school.* [ME < L *dissuadere* < *dis-* against + *suadere* to urge]

dis·sua·sion (di swā′zhən) *n.* the act of dissuading.

dis·sua·sive (di swā′siv) *adj.* attempting to dissuade; tending to dissuade. **—dis·sua′sive·ly,** *adv.* **—dis·sua′sive·ness,** *n.*

dis·syl·lab·ic (dis′sə lab′ik) *adj.* having two syllables.

dis·syl·la·ble (dis′sil′ə bəl or di sil′ə bəl) *n.* a word having two syllables, such as *about, bandage, candy.* [< F *dissylabe* < L < Gk. *disyllabos* < *di-* two + *syllabē* syllable]

dist. 1 district. **2** distance. **3** distinguish. **4** distinguished.

dis·taff (dis′taf) *n.* **1** a stick, split at the tip, to hold wool, flax, etc. so that it may be spun into thread. **2** the staff on a spinning wheel for holding flax. **3** woman's work or affairs. **4** the female sex; woman or women. **5** the female branch of a family. [OE *distæf* < *dis-* (akin to MLG *dise* bunch of flax on a distaff) + *stæf* staff]

distaff side 1 the mother's side of a family. **2** the female sex; opposed to *spear side.*

dis·tain (dis tān′) *v. Archaic.* **1** discolor; stain. **2** dishonor; disgrace. [ME < OF *desteindre* < *des-* apart + *teindre* dye, color < L *tingere*]

dis·tal (dis′təl) *adj.* in anatomy, away from the place of attachment or origin; terminal: *Fingernails are at the distal ends of fingers.* [< *distant*]

dis·tance (dis′təns) *n. v.* **-tanced, -tanc·ing.** *—n.* **1** the space in between: *The distance from the farm to town is five miles.* **2** a long way; far away: *The farm is situated quite a distance from the road.* **3** a place far away: *a light in the distance.* **4** the time in between; interval. **5** in music, the interval or difference between two tones. **6** a lack of friendliness or familiarity; coldness of manner; reserve. **7** in painting: **a** the distant part of a landscape: *One sees cattle grazing in the distance.* **b** the part of a picture that represents this: *There is no distance in his*

paintings, which are all flat and two-dimensional. **8** in horse racing, a space measured back from the winning post. In order to qualify for further heats, a horse must be within this space when the winner finishes. **9 go the distance,** in sports: **a** play an entire game without substitution. **b** of a boxer, fight or last an entire match without being knocked out. **10 keep at a distance,** refuse to be friendly or familiar with; treat coldly. **11 keep one's distance,** be not too friendly or familiar.
—*v.* **1** leave far behind; do much better than. **2** in horse racing, beat by a distance. [ME < MF *destance* < L *distantia* < *distare.* See DISTANT.]

dis·tant (dis′ tənt) *adj.* **1** far away in space: *Vancouver is distant from Quebec City. The moon is distant from the earth.* **2** away: *The town is three miles distant.* **3** far apart in time, relationship, likeness, etc.; not close: *A third cousin is a distant relative.* **4** not friendly: *She gave him only a distant nod.* [ME < MF < L *distans, -antis,* ppr. of *distare* < *dis-* off + *stare* stand] —**dis′tant·ly,** *adv.*
Syn. 1, 2 Distant, far, remote = not near. **Distant** = standing away in space, and suggests a considerable space unless the exact measure is stated: *He lives in a distant city. Kingston is 158 miles distant from Toronto.* **Far** = a long way off; **remote** = far removed, especially from the centre of things: *The Canadian North is not so remote as it used to be.* **4** aloof, reserved.

dis·taste (dis tāst′) *n.* dislike; aversion: *His distaste for her behavior showed plainly on his face.* —**Syn.** See **dislike.**

dis·taste·ful (dis tāst′fəl) *adj.* unpleasant; disagreeable; offensive. —**dis·taste′ful·ly,** *adv.* —**dis·taste′ful·ness,** *n.*

dis·tem·per[1] (dis tem′pər) *n.* **1** an infectious disease of dogs and other animals, accompanied by a short, dry cough and a loss of strength. **2** any sickness of the mind or body; disorder; disease. **3** a disturbance. [< v.]
—*v.* make unbalanced; disturb; disorder. [ME < LL *distemperare* mix improperly < L *dis-* not + *temperare* mix in proper proportion]

dis·tem·per[2] (dis tem′pər) *n.* **1** paint made by mixing the colors with eggs or glue instead of oil. Distemper is often used for painting on plaster walls. **2** a method of painting with such a mixture. **3** a painting done in distemper. [< v.] —*v.* **1** mix (ingredients) to produce distemper. **2** paint with such a mixture. [< OF *destemprer* soak < LL *distemperare* mix thoroughly < L *dis-* completely + *temperare* mix]

dis·tend (dis tend′) *v.* **1** stretch out; swell out; expand: *The balloon was distended to the bursting point.* **2** become distended. [< L *distendere* < *dis-* apart + *tendere* stretch]

dis·ten·si·ble (dis ten′sə bəl) *adj.* capable of being distended.

dis·ten·sion or **dis·ten·tion** (dis ten′shən) *n.* **1** the act of distending. **2** the state of being distended.

dis·tich (dis′tik) *n.* **-tichs.** two lines of verse forming a stanza, and usually making complete sense; couplet. *Example:*

Those who in quarrels interpose
Must often wipe a bloody nose.

[< L < Gk. *distichon* < *di-* two + *stichos* line]

dis·til or **dis·till** (dis til′) *v.* **-tilled, -til·ling. 1** heat (a liquid or other substance) and condense the vapor given off. Water obtained by distilling dirty water is clean and pure because the steam given off contains no impurities. **2** obtain by distilling: *Gasoline is distilled from crude oil.* **3** extract; refine: *A jury must distil the truth from the testimony of witnesses.* **4** give off in drops: *Flowers distil nectar.* **5** fall or let fall in drops; drip. **6** undergo distillation. [< L *distillare* < *de-* down + *stilla* drop]

dis·til·late (dis′tə lit or dis′tə lāt′) *n.* a distilled liquid; something obtained by distilling.

dis·til·la·tion (dis′tə lā′shən) *n.* **1** a distilling. **2** the process of distilling. **3** something distilled; extract; essence.

dis·tilled (dis tild′) *adj.* obtained by distilling.

dis·till·er (dis til′ər) *n.* **1** a person or thing that distils. **2** a person or corporation that makes whisky, rum, brandy, etc.

dis·till·er·y (dis til′ər ē or dis til′rē) *n.* **-er·ies. 1** a place where distilling is done. **2** a place where whisky, rum, brandy, etc. are made.

dis·tinct (dis tingkt′) *adj.* **1** not the same; separate. **2** different in quality or kind: *Mice are distinct from rats.*

hat, āge, cãre, fär; let, ēqual, tėrm; it, īce
hot, ōpen, ôrder; oil, out; cup, pu̇t, rüle, ūse
əbove, takən, pencəl, lemən, circəs
ch, child; ng, long; sh, ship
th, thin; ᴛʜ, then; zh, measure

3 clear; plain: *distinct writing.* **4** unmistakable; definite; decided: *a distinct advantage.* [< L *distinctus,* pp. of *distinguere.* See DISTINGUISH.] —**dis·tinct′ness,** *n.*
—**Syn. 2** dissimilar. **3** obvious.

dis·tinc·tion (dis tingk′shən) *n.* **1** the act of distinguishing; the making of a difference: *He gave every servant ten dollars without distinction.* **2** a difference. **3** a point of difference; special quality or feature. **4** honor: *The soldier served with distinction.* **5** a mark or sign of honor. **6** excellence; superiority. **7 distinction without a difference,** a false distinction; artificial difference.

dis·tinc·tive (dis tingk′tiv) *adj.* **1** distinguishing from others; special; characteristic: *Policemen wear a distinctive uniform.* **2** of speech sounds, serving to distinguish significantly: *The difference between "p" and "b" is distinctive in English because it alone distinguishes words such as "pat" from "bat."* —**dis·tinc′tive·ly,** *adv.* —**dis·tinc′tive·ness,** *n.*

dis·tinct·ly (dis tingkt′lē) *adv.* **1** clearly; plainly: *Speak distinctly.* **2** unmistakably; decidedly: *The prisoner was distinctly unhappy.*

dis·tin·gué (dis′tang gā′ or dis tang′gā) *adj.* looking important or superior; distinguished. [< F]

dis·tin·guish (dis ting′gwish) *v.* **1** tell apart; see or show the difference between. **2** see or show the difference. **3** see or hear clearly; make out plainly: *It is much too dark for me to distinguish the outline of the house.* **4** make different; be a special quality or feature of: *The ability to talk distinguishes human beings from animals.* **5** make famous or well known: *He distinguished himself by winning three prizes.* **6** separate into different groups. [< L *distinguere* mark with a prick < *dis-* between + *stinguere* to prick]
Syn. 1 Distinguish, differentiate, discriminate = see or show the differences in or between things. **Distinguish** = see and know the qualities and features of a thing that give it its special character and set it off from others: *He distinguished the violins in the orchestra.* **Differentiate** = show the exact differences between one thing and others of the same class: *The teacher differentiated between Shakespeare's sonnets and Milton's.* **Discriminate** = see the fine shades of difference between things: *Sometimes only experts can discriminate between counterfeit bills and genuine money.*

dis·tin·guish·a·ble (dis ting′gwish ə bəl) *adj.* capable of being distinguished. —**dis·tin′guish·a·bly,** *adv.*

dis·tin·guished (dis ting′gwisht) *adj.* **1** famous; well-known. **2** having the appearance of an important person. —**Syn. 1.** See **eminent.**

dis·tort (dis tôrt′) *v.* **1** pull or twist out of shape; change the normal appearance of: *Rage distorted his face.* **2** change from the truth: *The man distorted the facts of the accident to escape blame.* [< L *distortus,* pp. of *distorquere* < *dis-* (intensive) + *torquere* twist] —**Syn. 1** contort. **2** misrepresent, falsify.

dis·tor·tion (dis tôr′shən) *n.* **1** a distorting: *A lie is a distortion of the truth.* **2** the fact or state of being distorted **3** anything distorted.

dis·tract (dis trakt′) *v.* **1** draw away (the mind, attention etc.): *Noise distracts my attention from study.* **2** confuse; disturb; bewilder. **3** put out of one's mind; make insane. [< L *distractus,* pp. of *distrahere* < *dis-* away + *trahere* draw] —**dis·tract′ed·ly,** *adv.* —**dis·tract′ing·ly,** *adv.*

dis·trac·tion (dis trak′shən) *n.* **1** the act of drawing away the attention, mind, etc. **2** anything that draws away the attention, mind, etc. **3** confusion of mind; disturbance of thought: *The mother of the lost children scarcely knew what she was doing in her distraction.* **4** insanity; madness. **5** confusion; perplexity; dissension. **6** a relief from continued thought, grief, or effort; amusement: *Movies and TV are popular distractions.*

dis·train (dis trān′) *v.* in law, seize (goods) for unpaid rent or other debts. [ME < OF *destreindre* < L *distringere* < *dis-* apart + *stringere* draw] —**dis·train′er** or **dis·train′or,** *n.*

dis·traint (dis trānt′) *n.* in law, an act of distraining.

dis·trait (dis trā′) *adj.* not paying attention; absentminded. [< F *distrait,* pp. of *distraire* distract]

dis·traught (dis trot′ or dis trôt′) *adj.* **1** in a state of mental conflict and confusion. **2** crazed. [var. of obs. *distract,* adj. See DISTRACT.]

dis·tress (dis tres′) *n.* **1** great pain or sorrow; anxiety; trouble. **2** something that causes distress; misfortune. **3** a dangerous condition; difficult situation: *A ship sinking or burning at sea is in distress.*
—*v.* **1** cause pain, grief, or suffering to; make miserable or troubled. **2** subject to pressure, stress, or strain. [ME < OF *distrece,* ult. < L *districtus,* pp. of *distringere* < *dis-* apart + *stringere* draw] **—dis·tress′ing·ly,** *adv.*
—Syn. *n.* **1** grief, agony, anguish. See **sorrow.**

distressed area a region characterized by an abnormally low standard of living because of unemployment, poverty, etc.

dis·tress·ful (dis tres′ fəl) *adj.* **1** causing distress; painful. **2** feeling or showing distress; suffering. **—dis·tress′ful·ly,** *adv.* **—dis·tress′ful·ness,** *n.*

dis·trib·ute (dis trib′yůt) *v.* **-ut·ed, -ut·ing. 1** give (some of) to each; divide and give out in shares: *distribute candy.* **2** spread; scatter: *Distribute the paint evenly over the wall.* **3** divide into parts. **4** arrange; classify: *A post-office clerk distributes mail when he puts each letter into the proper bag.* **5** in logic, use (a term) so that it includes every member of a class. *Example*: *dogs* in the sentence "All dogs are animals." **6** in printing, take apart and return (composed type) to the proper compartments in the case. [< L *distributus,* pp. of *distribuere* < *dis-* individually + *tribuere* assign]
Syn. 1 Distribute, dispense = give out shares. **Distribute** = divide the amount one has into shares, usually definite but not necessarily equal, and give them out according to some plan: *The teacher distributed paper to the class.* **Dispense** = give to each of a group the amount that has been measured out as his right or proper share: *The club dispensed new clothing to the children in the orphanage.* **4** sort.

dis·tri·bu·tion (dis′trə bū′shən) *n.* **1** the act or process of distributing: *After the contest the distribution of prizes to the winners took place.* **2** a way of being distributed: *If some get more than others, there is an uneven distribution.* **3** anything distributed. **4** in economics, the distributing to consumers of goods grown or made by producers. **5** division and arrangement; classification. **6** in statistics, a systematic arrangement of numerical data.

dis·tri·bu·tion·al (dis′trə bū′shə nəl) *adj.* of or having to do with distribution.

dis·trib·u·tive (dis trib′yů tiv) *adj.* **1** of or having to do with distribution; distributing. **2** in grammar, referring to each individual of a group considered separately. *Each, every, either,* and *neither* are distributive words.
—*n.* a distributive word.

distributive curve in statistics, a graph showing how the frequencies expressed are distributed.

dis·trib·u·tive·ly (dis trib′yů tiv lē) *adv.* **1** by distribution; not collectively. **2** in a distributive sense.

dis·trib·u·tor (dis trib′yů tər) *n.* **1** a person or thing that distributes. **2** a person or company that distributes to consumers the goods grown or made by producers. **3** a part of a gasoline engine that distributes electric current to the spark plugs.

dis·trict (dis′trikt) *n.* **1** a portion of a larger area; region: *Northern Ontario is the leading gold-mining district in Canada. They lived in a fashionable district of the city.* **2** a portion of a country, a province, or a city marked off for a special purpose, such as providing schools, electing officials, etc.: *a school district, a local improvement district. The Northwest Territories are divided into three districts*: *Mackenzie, Keewatin, and Franklin.* —*v.* divide into districts. [< LL *districtus* district < L *distringere.* See DISTRESS.]

district attorney a lawyer who is the prosecuting officer for a federal or state judicial district.

dis·trust (dis trust′) *v.* not trust; have no confidence in; be suspicious of. —*n.* a lack of trust or confidence; suspicion: *She could not overcome her distrust of the stranger.* **—Syn.** *n.* doubt, mistrust. See **suspicion.**

dis·trust·ful (dis trust′fəl) *adj.* **1** not trusting; suspicious. **2 distrustful of,** lacking confidence in. **—dis·trust′ful·ly,** *adv.* **—dis·trust′ful·ness,** *n.*

dis·turb (dis tėrb′) *v.* **1** destroy the peace, quiet, or rest of. **2** break in upon with noise or other distraction: *Do not disturb the baby; he is asleep.* **3** put out of order: *Someone has disturbed all my papers.* **4** make uneasy; trouble: *He was disturbed to hear of her illness.* **5** inconvenience: *Don't disturb yourself; I can do it.* [< L *disturbare* < *dis-* (intensive) + *turba* commotion] **—dis·turb′er,** *n.* **—dis·turb′ing·ly,** *adv.* **—Syn. 1** agitate, perturb.

dis·turb·ance (dis tėr′bəns) *n.* **1** a disturbing or being disturbed. **2** anything that disturbs. **3** confusion; disorder: *The police were called to quell the disturbance.* **4** uneasiness; trouble; worry.

di·sul·phide or **di·sul·fide** (dī sul′fīd or -sul′fid) *n.* in chemistry, a compound consisting of two atoms of sulphur combined with another element or radical. Also, **bisulphide.**

dis·un·ion (dis ūn′yən) *n.* **1** a separation; division. **2** a lack of unity; disagreement; unfriendliness.

dis·u·nite (dis′yů nīt′) *v.* **-nit·ed, -nit·ing. 1** separate; divide. **2** destroy the unity of; cause to disagree or to become unfriendly.

dis·u·ni·ty (dis ū′nə tē) *n.* lack of unity; disunion.

dis·use (*n.* dis ūs′; *v.* dis ūz′) *n. v.* **-used, -us·ing.**
—*n.* lack of use; not being used: *The old tools were rusted from disuse. Many words common in Shakespeare's time have fallen into disuse.* —*v.* stop using.

ditch (dich) *n.* a long, narrow trench dug in the earth, usually used to carry off water.
—*v.* **1** dig a ditch in. **2** run or throw into a ditch: *The careless driver ditched his car.* **3** land (an airplane not equipped for the purpose) on water. **4** abandon, especially an airplane in flight: *The pilot had to ditch the airplane because one of the engines was on fire.* **5** *Slang.* **a** get rid of. **b** leave in the lurch. [OE *dīc*] **—ditch′er,** *n.*

ditch·dig·ger (dich′dig′ər) *n.* a person or machine that digs ditches.

ditch·dig·ging (dich′dig′ing) *n.* the job of digging ditches. —*adj.* of or for the digging of ditches.

dith·er (diᴛʜ′ər) *n.* **1** a tremble; shiver; quiver. **2** *Informal.* a confused, excited condition. —*v.* **1** be in such a condition. **2** hesitate. [origin uncertain]

dith·y·ramb (dith′ə ram′ or dith′ə ramb′) *n.* **1** a Greek choral song in honor of Dionysus. **2** a poem that is full of wild emotion, enthusiasm, etc. **3** any speech or writing like this. [< L < Gk. *dithyrambos*]

dith·y·ram·bic (dith′ə ram′bik) *adj.* **1** of or like a dithyramb. **2** wildly enthusiastic.

dit·to (dit′ō) *n.* **-tos,** *v.* **-toed, -to·ing,** *adv. interj.* —*n.* **1** the same; exactly the same as appeared before. **2** a ditto mark or abbreviation (do.) that stands for ditto. **3** a copy; duplicate. —*v.* copy; duplicate. —*adv. Informal.* as said before; likewise. —*interj. Informal.* the same; "I agree!" [< Ital. *ditto* said < L *dictus,* pp. of *dicere* say]

ditto mark in itemized lists, etc., a mark (usually double quotes) placed under something written to show that it is to be repeated. *Example*:

6 lb. butter at 75c. = $4.50
4 ,, ,, ,, ,, = $3.00

dit·ty (dit′ē) *n.* **-ties.** a short, simple song or poem. [ME < OF *dite* < L *dictatum* (thing) dictated, pp. neut. of *dictare* dictate]

ditty bag a small bag, used especially by sailors, to hold sewing things and other odds and ends. [origin uncertain]

ditty box a small box used as a ditty bag.

di·u·ret·ic (dī′yů ret′ik) *adj.* causing an increase in the flow of urine. —*n.* any drug that causes an increase in the flow of urine. [ME < LL *diureticus* < Gk. *diourētikos* < *dia-* through + *oureein* urinate]

di·ur·nal (dī ėr′nəl) *adj.* **1** occurring every day; daily. **2** of or belonging to the daytime. **3** lasting a day. [ME < LL *diurnalis* < L *dies* day. Doublet of JOURNAL.]

di·ur·nal·ly (dī ėr′nəl ē) *adv.* **1** daily; every day. **2** by day; during the daytime.

div. 1 dividend. 2 division. 3 divided.

di·va (dē′və) *n.* **-vas.** a prima donna; famous woman opera singer. [< Ital. < L *diva* goddess]

di·va·gate (dī′və gāt′) *v.* **-gat·ed, -gat·ing.** wander; stray. [< L *divagari* < *dis-* about + *vagari* wander]

di·va·ga·tion (dī′və gā′shən) *n.* a wandering.

di·va·lent (dī vā′lənt) *adj.* in chemistry, having a valence of two.

di·van (dī′van or də van′) *n.* 1 a long, low, soft couch or sofa. 2 in Turkey and other oriental countries, court or council. 3 a room where a court or council meets; council chamber. 4 a smoking room. [< Turkish *divan* < Persian *devan*]

dive (dīv) *v.* **dived** or **dove, dived, div·ing,** *n.* —*v.* 1 plunge headfirst into the water. 2 go down or out of sight suddenly: *He dived into an alley.* 3 plunge the hand suddenly into anything: *He dived into his pocket and fished out a dollar.* 4 of an aircraft, missile, etc., plunge downward at a steep angle. 5 of a submarine, plunge downward into the water; submerge. 6 penetrate with the mind: *John has been diving into the history of the Incas.* —*n.* 1 the act of diving. 2 the downward plunge of an aircraft, submarine, etc. 3 *Informal.* a cheap, disreputable place for drinking and gambling. [OE *dȳfan*] ☛ See **dove**[2] for usage note.

dive-bomb (dīv′bom′) *v.* bomb at close range using a dive bomber.

dive bomber a bomber that releases its bomb load just before it pulls out of a dive toward the target.

div·er (dīv′ər) *n.* 1 a person or thing that dives. 2 a person whose occupation is to work under water. 3 a diving bird: *The loon is a well-known Canadian diver.*

di·verge (di vėrj′ or dī vėrj′) *v.* **-verged, -verg·ing.** 1 move or lie in different directions from the same point; branch off; *Their paths diverged at the fork in the road.* 2 differ; vary; deviate. 3 cause to diverge. 4 in mathematics, (of a series) increase indefinitely as more terms are added. [< LL *divergere* < *dis-* in different directions + *vergere* slope]

Syn. 1 Diverge, deviate, digress = turn or move in a different direction. **Diverge** = branch out in different directions like a Y from a main or old path or way: *Our paths diverged when we left school.* **Deviate** = turn aside in one direction from a normal or regular path, way of thinking or acting, rule, etc.: *The teacher deviated from her custom and gave us no homework.* **Digress** applies chiefly to turning aside from the main subject while speaking or writing: *I lose interest if an author digresses too much.*

di·ver·gence (di vėr′jəns or dī vėr′jəns) *n.* 1 the act or state of diverging; difference: *The committee couldn't come to an agreement because of the wide divergence of opinion among its members.* 2 in mathematics, the fact of diverging.

di·ver·gen·cy (di vėr′jən sē or dī vėr′jən sē) *n.* **-cies.** divergence.

di·ver·gent (di vėr′jənt or dī vėr′jənt) *adj.* 1 diverging; different. 2 causing divergence. **—di·ver′gent·ly,** *adv.*

di·vers (dī′vərz) *adj.* several different; various. [ME < OF < L *diversus*, pp. of *divertere*. See DIVERT.]

di·verse (di vėrs′, dī vėrs′, or dī′vėrs) *adj.* 1 different; completely unlike. 2 varied: *A person of diverse interests can talk on many subjects.* [var. of *divers*; now regarded as immediately from L *diversus*] **—di·verse′ness,** *n.*

di·verse·ly (di vėrs′lē or dī vėrs′lē) *adv.* in different ways or directions; differently; variously.

di·ver·si·fi·ca·tion (di vėr′sə fə kā′shən or dī vėr′sə fə kā′shən) *n.* 1 the act or process of diversifying. 2 the state of being diversified.

di·ver·si·fy (di vėr′sə fī′ or dī vėr′sə fī′) *v.* **-fied, -fy·ing.** give variety to; vary: *Investors should diversify their investments.* [< Med.L *diversificare* < L *diversus* diverse + *facere* make] **—di·ver′si·fi′er,** *n.*

di·ver·sion (di vėr′zhən or dī vėr′zhən) *n.* 1 a turning aside: *High tariffs often cause a diversion of trade from one country to another.* 2 an amusement; entertainment; pastime: *Golf is my father's favorite diversion.* 3 an attack or feint intended to distract an opponent's attention from a main operation. **—Syn. 1** deviation. **2** sport, recreation.

di·ver·sion·ar·y (di vėr′zhən er′ē or dī vėr′zhən er′ē) *adj.* of or like a diversion or feint, especially in military tactics.

di·ver·si·ty (di vėr′sə tē or dī vėr′sə tē) *n.* **-ties.**

hat, āge, cãre, fär; let, ēqual, tėrm; it, īce
hot, ōpen, ôrder; oil, out; cup, pu̇t, rüle, ūse
əbove, takən, pencəl, lemən, circəs
ch, child; ng, long; sh, ship
th, thin; ᴛʜ, then; zh, measure

1 complete difference; unlikeness. 2 variety: *Diversity of opinion is encouraged in a democracy.* **—Syn. 2** See **variety.**

di·vert (di vėrt′ or dī vėrt′) *v.* 1 turn aside: *A ditch diverted water from the stream into the fields.* 2 amuse; entertain: *Music diverted him after work.* [< MF *divertir* < L *divertere* < *dis-* aside + *vertere* turn]

di·ver·ti·men·to (di ver′tē men′tō) *n.* **-ti** (-tē). in music: 1 an instrumental composition, usually in several movements, intended to amuse and entertain. 2 an instrumental composition, usually light and entertaining, consisting of variations on a previously existing theme. [< Ital.]

di·ver·tisse·ment (dē ver tēs mäɴ′) *n.* 1 an amusement; entertainment. 2 a short ballet. 3 in music: **a** a collection of songs and dances inserted into an opera, ballet, etc. **b** a divertimento. **c** a light, entertaining composition for use between the acts of an opera, ballet, etc. [< F]

Dives (dī′vēz) *n.* 1 in the Bible, the rich man in the parable of the rich man and the beggar. Luke 16:19-31. 2 any rich man.

di·vest (di vest′ or dī vest′) *v.* 1 strip; rid; free: *The police divested the impostor of his stolen uniform and fake decorations.* 2 force to give up; deprive: *Citizens were divested of their right to vote.* 3 in law, take away (property). [< Med.L *divestire* < OF *desvestir* < *des-* away + *vestir* < L *vestire* clothe]

di·vide (di vīd′) *v.* **-vid·ed, -vid·ing,** *n.* —*v.* 1 separate into parts: *A brook divides the field. The river divides and forms two streams.* 2 in mathematics, separate into equal parts: *Divide 8 by 2, and you get 4.* 3 give some of to each; share: *The children divided the candy among them.* 4 disagree or cause to disagree; differ or cause to differ in feeling, opinion, etc.: *The school divided on the choice of a motto. Jealousy divided us.* 5 separate or cause to separate into two groups in voting. 6 mark off in parts; graduate (a scale, instrument, etc.).
—*n.* a ridge of land between two regions drained by different river systems: *The Continental Divide.* [ME < L *dividere*] **—Syn.** *v.* **1** sever, split. See **separate.**

di·vid·ed (di vīd′id) *adj.* 1 separated. 2 of a leaf, cut to the base so as to form distinct portions.

☛ **divided usage.** Usage is said to be *divided* when two or more forms are used by the members of a speech community, both of reputable standing in the same dialect or at the same social level. *Divided usage* is not applied, for example, to localisms, like *sack, bag, poke* (when referring to the same object), or to differences, like *ain't* and *isn't*, which belong to separate levels of the language. It applies to spellings, pronunciations, or constructions on which speakers and writers of similar education might differ. The two pronunciations of *either* (ē′ ᴛʜər and ī′ ᴛʜər), the two spellings of *honor* (*honor* and *honour*), and the two past tenses of *dive* (*dived* and *dove*) are examples of divided usage.

divided highway a road, such as an expressway, having a median strip or boulevard between lanes of traffic going in opposite directions.

divided skirt a woman's garment that looks like a flared skirt but actually has trouserlike legs.

div·i·dend (div′ə dend′) *n.* 1 in mathematics, a number or quantity to be divided by another: *In 8 ÷ 2, 8 is the dividend.* 2 money to be shared by those to whom it belongs. If a company makes a profit, it declares a dividend to the owners of the company. 3 a share of such money. 4 a part of the profits of an insurance company given to a person holding an insurance policy. [< L *dividendum* (thing) to be divided]

Dividers

di·vid·er (di vīd′er) *n.* 1 a person or thing that divides. 2 a device for partitioning an area into several sections. 3 a piece of cardboard for separating sections of a notebook. 4 **dividers,** *pl.* an instrument for measuring distances, dividing lines, etc.; compasses.

di·vi·na·tion (div′ə nā′shən) *n.* **1** the act of foreseeing the future or foretelling the unknown. **2** a skilful guess or prediction.

di·vine (di vīn′) *adj. n. v.* **-vined, -vin·ing.**—*adj.* **1** of God or a god. **2** by or from God. **3** to or from God; sacred; holy. **4** like God or a god; heavenly. **5** *Informal.* excellent; unusually good or great.
—*n.* a clergyman skilled in theology. [ME < OF < L *divinus* of a deity < *divus* deity]
—*v.* **1** find out or foretell by inspiration, by magic, or by guessing; predict. **2** interpret; explain. [ME < MF < L *divinare* < *divinus.* See n.] **—di·vine′ness,** *n.*

di·vine·ly (di vīn′lē) *adv.* **1** in a divine or godlike manner. **2** by the agency or influence of God. **3** supremely: *The orchestra played divinely at its first concert.*

di·vin·er (di vīn′ər) *n.* **1** a person who foresees the future or perceives the unknown, or professes to do these things. **2** a person who makes a skilful guess or prediction: *The water diviner told us where to sink the well.*

divine right of kings the right to rule, thought to have been given to kings by God.

diving bell a large, hollow, air-filled container in which people can work under water.

diving suit a waterproof suit with a helmet into which air can be pumped through a tube. Diving suits are worn by persons working under water.

divining rod a forked stick supposed to be useful in locating water, oil, metal, and other things underground. The forks are held in two hands, and the rod is supposed to dip downward when held over a deposit of the substance sought.

di·vin·i·ty (di vin′ə tē) *n.* **-ties. 1** a divine being; a god. **2 the Divinity,** God. **3** divine nature or quality. **4** the study of God, religion, and divine things; theology. **5** a creamy fudge.

di·vis·i·bil·i·ty (di viz′ə bil′ə tē) *n.* the quality of being divisible.

di·vis·i·ble (di viz′ə bəl) *adj.* **1** capable of being divided **2** capable of being divided without leaving a remainder: *Any even number is divisible by 2.*

di·vi·sion (di vizh′ən) *n.* **1** a dividing or being divided. **2** the act of giving some to each; a sharing: *a minute division of labor.* **3** in mathematics, the process of dividing one number by another. **4** something that divides. A boundary or a partition is a division. **5** a part; group; section: *a division of the animal kingdom.* **6** in the army, a formation usually consisting of three infantry brigades supported by artillery, armored, and other supporting units. A division is usually commanded by a major-general. **7** in the navy: **a** a company stationed on shore. **b divisions,** *pl.* a shore station. **8** a difference of opinion, thought, or feeling; disagreement. **9** in a legislative body, the process of separating into two groups for voting. [< L *divisio, -onis* < *dividere* divide] **—Syn. 2** allotment, distribution, apportionment.

di·vi·sion·al (di vizh′ən əl) *adj.* of a division; having to do with a division; belonging to a division.

division of labor or **labour 1** a condition under which the work of a society is divided among various trades and professions, as those of priest, soldier, shoemaker, etc. **2** a distribution of separate small parts of a process among many workers, as in a modern shoe factory.

di·vi·sive (di vī′siv) *adj.* **1** tending or serving to divide, disunite, etc. **2** causing or tending to cause strife, disunity, etc.

di·vi·sor (di vī′zər) *n.* **1** a number or quantity by which another is divided: *In 8 ÷ 2, 2 is the divisor.* **2** a number or quantity that divides another without a remainder.

di·vorce (di vôrs′) *n. v.* **-vorced, -vorc·ing.** —*n.* **1** the legal ending of a marriage. **2** a complete separation: *In this country there is a complete divorce of government and church.* —*v.* **1** end a marriage legally. **2** release from marriage by getting a divorce. *Mrs. Smith divorced her husband.* **3** separate: *In sports, exercise and play are not divorced.* [ME < OF < L *divortium* separation < *divertere.* See DIVERT.] **—di·vorc′er,** *n.*

di·vor·cé (di vôr′sā′) *n.* a divorced man.

di·vor·cee (di vôr′sē′) *n.* a divorced person.

di·vor·cée (di vôr′sā′) *n.* a divorced woman.

di·vorce·ment (di vôrs′mənt) *n.* divorce.

div·ot (div′ət) *n.* a small piece of turf or earth dug up by a golf club in making a stroke. [origin uncertain]

di·vulge (di vulj′ or dī vulj′) *v.* **-vulged, -vulg·ing.** make known; make public; tell; reveal: *The traitor divulged secret plans to the enemy.* [< L *divulgare* publish < *dis-* away + *vulgus* common people] **—di·vulg′er,** *n.* —**Syn.** disclose.

div·vy (div′ē) *v.* **div·vied, div·vy·ing,** *n. Slang.* —*v.* **1** divide or share. **2 divvy up,** make a division into shares. —*n.* a share or portion. [var. of *divide*]

dix (dēs) *n.* **1** in bezique and some other card games, the lowest trump. **2** in pinochle, a score of ten points. [< F *dix* ten]

Dix·ie (dik′sē) *n.* the southern states of the United States, especially those that united to form the Confederacy in 1860-61.

Dix·ie·land (dik′sē land′) *n.* **1** a style of jazz played originally in New Orleans, marked by fast tempo and improvization. **2** a piece of music played in this style.

diz·en (diz′ən or dī′zən) *v.* dress with gaudy clothes, ornaments, etc.; bedizen. [cf. MDu. *disen* wind up flax, MLG *dise* bunch of flax on distaff]

diz·zy (diz′ē) *adj.* **-zi·er, -zi·est,** *v.* **-zied, -zy·ing.** —*adj.* **1** disposed to fall, stagger, or spin around; not steady. **2** having the sensation that things about one are whirling: *Riding on a merry-go-round makes some people feel dizzy.* **3** confused; bewildered. **4** likely to make dizzy; causing dizziness: *The airplane climbed to a dizzy height.* **5** *Informal.* foolish; silly.
—*v.* make dizzy. [OE *dysig* foolish] **—diz′zi·ly,** *adv.* **—diz′zi·ness,** *n.*

djinn (jin) *n.* jinn.

dl. decilitre; decilitres.

D.Litt. or **D.Lit.** Doctor of Letters or of Literature. (for L *Doctor Lit(t)erarum*)

D.L.S. Doctor of Library Science.

DM or **Dm.** Deutsche mark.

dm. decimetre; decimetres.

DNA deoxyribonucleic acid.

DNB Dictionary of National Biography.

DND or **D.N.D.** Department of National Defence.

do[1] (dü) *v. pres. sing. 1* **do,** *2* **do** or (*Archaic*) **do·est** or **dost,** *3* **does** or (*Archaic*) **do·eth** or **doth;** *pl.* **do;** *pt.* **did;** *pp.* **done;** *ppr.* **do·ing,** *n.* —*v.* **1** carry out; perform: *She did her work.* **2** act; work: *Do or die.* **3** complete; finish; end: *My assignment is done.* **4** make; produce: *Walt Disney did a movie about wild life in the Arctic.* **5** be the cause of; bring about: *Do good. Your work does you credit.* **6** act; behave: *Do wisely.* **7** render: *do homage, do justice.* **8** deal with as the case may require; put in order: *do the dishes, do one's hair; have one's hair done.* **9** get along; manage; fare: *How do you do?* **10** be satisfactory; be enough; serve: *That hat will do.* **11** work out; solve: *do a puzzle, do a sum.* **12** cook: *The roast will be done in an hour.* **13** cover; traverse: *We did 80 miles in an hour.* **14** *Informal.* cheat; trick. **15** *Do* has special uses where it has no definite meaning: **a** in asking questions: *Do you like milk?* **b** in emphasizing a verb: *I do want to go.* **c** in standing for a verb already used: *My dog goes where I do.* **d** in negative expressions: *People talk; animals do not.* **e** in inverted constructions after the adverbs *rarely, hardly, little,* etc.: *Rarely did she laugh.*
do away with, a abolish: *do away with a rule.* **b** kill.
do by, act or behave toward; treat.
do for, a ruin; damage. **b** *Informal.* act as housekeeper for. **c** provide for; manage.
do in, a cheat. **b** ruin. **c** *Informal.* kill.
do over, a do once again. **b** redecorate.
do up, a wrap or tie up. **b** clean and get ready for use. **c** *Informal.* wear out; exhaust.
do without, get along without the thing mentioned or implied: *We can do without luxuries if we have to.*
have to do with, relate to; deal with: *Abstract art has little to do with everyday experience.*

it isn't done, custom, good manners, or good taste forbids it.
—*n. Informal.* a celebration. [OE *dōn*]
Syn. 1 Do, perform, accomplish = carry out work, etc. **Do** is the general word and may be used, at least informally, of every kind of act: *He did nothing today.* **Perform,** the formal word, often interchangeable with *do,* particularly means carry an action through to the end, and often suggests regular activities: *He performed none of his duties today.* **Accomplish** = carry out successfully to the desired end: *He worked, but accomplished very little today.* **9** prosper. **10** suffice, answer.

do[2] (dō) *n.* in music, a syllable used for the first and last tones of an eight-tone scale. The eight syllables are do, re, mi, fa, sol, la, ti, do. [substituted for *ut.* See GAMUT.]

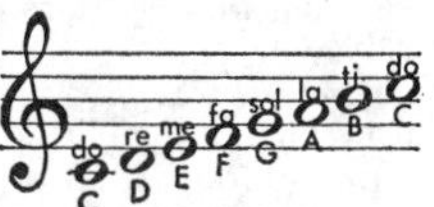

do. ditto.

DOA dead on arrival.

do·a·ble (dü′ə bəl) *adj.* that can be done.

dob·bin (dob′ən) *n.* a farm horse, especially a quiet plodding one. [var. of *Robin,* traditional name for a farm horse]

Do·ber·man pin·scher (dō′bər mən pin′shər) **1** a breed of medium-sized, slender, alert dog having short, dark hair. **2** a dog of this breed. [< Ludwig *Doberman,* a German dog breeder + G *Pinscher* terrier]

dob·son fly (dob′sən) a large winged insect whose larva is often used as bait by anglers. [origin uncertain]

do·cent (dō′sənt) *n.* **1** a lecturer, especially at a college or university. **2** a person trained as a guide and lecturer to conduct groups through a picture gallery, museum, etc. [< G < L *docens, -entis,* ppr. of *docere* teach]

do·cile (dō′sīl, dos′īl, or dos′əl) *adj.* **1** easily managed; obedient. **2** easily taught; willing to learn. [ME < L *docilis* < *docere* teach] —**do′cile·ly,** *adv.* —**Syn. 1** See **obedient.**

do·cil·i·ty (dō sil′ə tē) *n.* a docile quality.

dock[1] (dok) *n.* **1** a large basin equipped with floodgates to receive ships for loading, unloading, and repairs. **2** a platform built on the shore or out from the shore; a wharf or pier. **3** the water between two piers, permitting the entrance of ships. **4** a drydock.
—*v.* **1** bring (a ship) to a dock: *The sailors docked the ship and began to unload it.* **2** come into a dock. [< MDu. or MLG *docke*]

dock[2] (dok) *n.* **1** the solid, fleshy part of an animal's tail. **2** the part of a tail left after cutting or clipping.
—*v.* **1** cut short; cut the end off: *Horses' and dogs' tails are sometimes docked.* **2** cut down; take away part of: *The company docked the men's wages when they came late to work.* [OE *-docca,* as in *finger-docca* finger muscle]

dock[3] (dok) *n.* the place where an accused person stands in a law court. [cf. Flemish *dok* pen]

dock[4] (dok) *n.* a large, coarse weed of the buckwheat family, having sour or bitter leaves. [OE *docce*]

dock·age[1] (dok′ij) *n.* **1** a place to dock ship. **2** a charge for using a dock. **3** the docking of ships. [< *dock*[1]]

dock·age[2] (dok′ij) *n.* **1** an act of cutting down or cutting off. **2** a cut or deduction made, as from wages. **2** easily removable foreign material that is added to grain in processing. [< *dock*[2]]

dock·er[1] (dok′ər) *n. Esp.Brit.* a laborer who works on a dock; longshoreman.

dock·er[2] (dok′ər) *n.* a person or thing that docks, cuts off, or cuts short.

dock·et (dok′it) *n. v.* **-et·ed, -et·ing.** —*n.* **1** a list of lawsuits to be tried by a court. **2** a summary or list of law-court decisions. **3** any list of matters to be considered by some group of people. **4** a label or ticket giving the contents of a package, document, etc.
—*v.* **1** enter on a docket. **2** make a summary or list of (law-court decisions). **3** mark with a docket. [origin uncertain]

dock·yard (dok′yärd′) *n.* a place where ships are built, equipped, and repaired. A dockyard contains docks, workshops, and warehouses for supplies.

doc·tor (dok′tər) *n.* **1** a person licensed to treat diseases and physical or mental disorders; physician. **2** a dentist. **3** a veterinary surgeon. **4** any person who treats diseases: *a witch doctor.* **5** a person who has received one of the highest degrees given by a university: *a Doctor of Laws, a Doctor of Philosophy.* **6** the academic degree held by such a person. **7** *Archaic.* a learned man; teacher. **8** any of various mechanical devices, especially one designed to remedy something. **9** in fishing, a brightly-colored artificial fly. *Abbrev.:* Dr.
—*v. Informal.* **1** treat diseases in (a person, animal, etc.). **2** be a doctor; practise medicine. **3** take medicine. **4** tamper with: *The whisky had been doctored with water. The dishonest cashier doctored the accounts.* **5** repair; mend. [ME < OF *doctour* < L *doctor* teacher < *docere* teach]

doc·tor·al (dok′tər əl) *adj.* **1** having to do with a doctor or doctorate. **2** having a doctorate.

doc·tor·ate (dok′tər it) *n.* the degree of Doctor given by a university.

doc·tri·naire (dok′trə nãr′) *n.* an impractical theorist; a person who tries to apply a theory rigidly, without considering the actual circumstances or consequences. —*adj.* impractical; stubbornly theoretical.

doc·tri·nal (dok′trī′nəl or dok′trə nəl) *adj.* of or having to do with doctrine. —**doc·tri′nal·ly,** *adv.*

doc·trine (dok′trən) *n.* **1** what is taught as the belief of a church, nation, or group of persons. **2** what is taught; teachings. **3** a belief, especially a religious one. [ME < OF < L *doctrina* < *doctor.* See DOCTOR.]

doc·u·ment (*n.* dok′yu̇ mənt; *v.* dok′yu̇ ment′) *n.* something written, printed, etc. that gives information or proof of some fact; any object used as evidence. Letters, maps, and pictures are documents. —*v.* **1** provide with documents. **2** prove or support by means of documents. **3** provide (a book, etc.) with references as proof of the facts stated in it. [< L *documentum* example, proof < *docere* show] —**doc′u·men·ta′tion,** *n.*

doc·u·men·ta·ry (dok′yu̇ men′tə rē or dok′yu̇ men′trē) *adj. n.* **-ries.** —*adj.* **1** consisting of documents; in writing, print, etc.: *The man's own letters were documentary evidence of his guilt.* **2** presenting or recording factual information in an artistic fashion: *a documentary film.*
—*n.* a documentary book, motion picture, radio or television program.

dod·der[1] (dod′ər) *v.* shake; tremble; totter: *The man dodders about as if he were ninety years old.* [origin uncertain] —**dod′der·er,** *n.*

dod·der[2] (dod′ər) *n.* a plant without leaves, roots, or chlorophyl, that lives as a parasite by twining its thread-like stems around other plants and absorbing food from them. [ME *doder*]

do·dec·a·gon (dō dek′ə gon′) *n.* a geometrical figure having 12 angles and 12 sides. [< Gk. *dōdekagonon* < *dōdeka* twelve + *gōnia* angle]

do·dec·a·he·dron (dō′dek ə hē′drən) *n.* **-drons, -dra** (-drə). a solid object having 12 faces. [< Gk. *dōdekaedron* < *dōdeka* twelve + *hedra* seat, base]

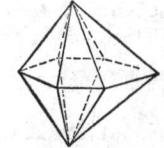

A dodecahedron

dodge (doj) *v.* **dodged, dodg·ing,** *n.*
—*v.* **1** move quickly to one side: *He dodged into the shadow of the house.* **2** move quickly in order to get away from (a person, a blow, or something thrown): *He dodged the ball as it came flying toward his head.* **3** get away by some trick; use trickery.
—*n.* **1** a sudden movement to one side. **2** *Informal.* a trick to cheat. [origin uncertain]

dodge·ball (doj′bol′ or -bôl′) *n.* a game in which players forming a circle or two opposite lines try to hit opponents in the centre with a large ball.

dodg·er (doj′ər) *n.* **1** a person who dodges. **2** a shifty or dishonest person. **3** a small handbill.

do·do (dō′dō) *n.* **-dos** or **-does.** a large, clumsy bird unable to fly. Dodos are now extinct. [< Pg. *doudo* fool]

doe (dō) *n.* a female deer, antelope, rabbit, hare, or other animal of which the male is called a buck. [OE *dā*]

Doe (dō) *n.* John. See **John Doe.**

doe-eyed (dō′īd′) *adj.* having eyes as naïve, shy, and soft as those of a doe.

do·er (dü′ər) *n.* a person who does something, especially with energy and enthusiasm.

does (duz) *v.* 3rd pers. sing. present tense of **do.**

doe·skin (dō′skin′) *n.* **1** the skin of a female deer. **2** the leather made from it. **3** a smooth, soft woollen cloth, sometimes used for gloves, men's suits, etc.

does·n't (duz′ənt) *v.* does not.

do·est (dü′ist) *v. Archaic.* 2nd pers. sing. present tense of **do**[1]. "Thou doest" means "You do" (sing.).

do·eth (dü′ith) *v. Archaic.* does.

doff (dof) *v.* **1** take off; remove: *He doffed his hat as the women passed by.* **2** get rid of; throw aside. [contraction of *do off*]

dog (dog) *n. v.* **dogged, dog·ging.** —*n.* **1** a domesticated mammal, related to wolves, foxes, and jackals, that is kept as a pet, for hunting, or for guarding property. Two well-known breeds are the cocker spaniel and the greyhound. **2** any animal of the same family as the dog, which includes wolves, foxes, and jackals. **3** a male dog, fox, wolf, etc. **4** any of various animals resembling a dog, such as the prairie dog. **5** a low, worthless man. **6** *Informal.* a man; fellow: *He is a gay dog.* **7** *Informal.* outward show; assumed airs. **8** a device to hold or grip something. See also **canthook** for picture. **9** a firedog; andiron. **10 Dog,** in astronomy, either of two constellations, Canis Major **(Great Dog)** or Canis Minor **(Little Dog). 11** *Slang.* a person or thing that is inferior or unattractive.

A dog for gripping

dog eat dog, a killing or injuring one another. **b** cut-throat competition.
dog in the manger, one who prevents others from using or enjoying something of no value to himself.
Every dog has his day. Everyone gets some attention or luck sometime in his life.
go to the dogs, be ruined; deteriorate rapidly.
put on the dog, *Informal.* behave or dress in a showy, affected manner.
teach an old dog new tricks, get an older person to accept new ideas or ways of doing things.
throw to the dogs, throw away as worthless; abandon.
—*v.* **1** hunt or follow like a dog: *The police dogged the thief's footsteps until they caught him.* **2** worry as if by a dog; beset: *The company was dogged by financial crises for several years.* **3** fasten or secure (a log, etc.) by means of a dog (def. 8). [OE *docga*] —**dog′like′,** *adj.*

do·gan (dō′gən) *n. Cdn. Slang.* a Roman Catholic, especially one of Irish background. [origin uncertain]

dog·bane (dog′bān′) *n.* any of various poisonous plants having clusters of small, white or pink, bell-shaped flowers.

dog·ber·ry (dog′ber′ē) *n.* **-ries. 1** the berry or fruit of such plants as the European dogwood or mountain ash. **2** the plant.

dog·cart (dog′kärt′) *n.* **1** a small cart pulled by dogs. **2** a small, open, horse-drawn carriage with two seats that are placed back to back.

dog days in the northern hemisphere, a period of very hot, humid, and uncomfortable weather during July and August. [with reference to the rising of Sirius, the Dog Star]

doge (dōj; *Italian,* dō′jā) *n.* the chief magistrate of Venice or Genoa when they were republics. [< Venetian Ital. < L *dux* leader. Doublet of DUCE, DUKE.]

dog-ear (dog′ēr′) *n.* a folded-down corner of a page in a book: *I made a dog-ear to mark the page where I stopped reading.* —*v.* fold down the corner of. Also, **dog's-ear.** —**dog′-eared′,** *adj.*

dog·fight (dog′fīt′) *n. v.* **-fought, -fight·ing.** *Informal.* —*n.* **1** a combat between individual fighter planes. **2** a fierce fight; brawl. —*v.* engage in a dogfight.

dog·fish (dog′fish′) *n.* **-fish** or **-fishes. 1** any of several kinds of small shark. **2** any of certain other fishes, such as the mudfish, the black fish, and the wrasse.

dog·ged (dog′id) *adj.* stubborn; persistent; not giving up: *In spite of failures, he kept on with dogged determination to succeed.* [< *dog*] —**dog′ged·ly,** *adv.* —**dog′ged·ness,** *n.* —**Syn.** obstinate, headstrong.

dog·ger[1] (dog′ər) *n.* **1** a person who dogs. **2** in lumbering, a workman who ties dogs or hooks to a log for hauling by cable.

dog·ger[2] (dog′ər) *n.* a broad boat with two masts, used by fishermen in the North Sea. [ME; origin uncertain]

dog·ger·el (dog′ər əl) *n.* poor poetry; verse that is not artistic in form or meaning. —*adj.* **1** of or like doggerel; not artistic; poor. **2** of verse, comic in style and irregular in form. [ME; origin uncertain]

dog·gie (dog′ē) *n.* **1** a little dog. **2** a pet name for a dog.

dog·gone (dog′gon) *adj. adv. v.* **-goned, -gon·ing.** *Slang.* —*adj.* darned; damned. —*adv.* very; much. —*v.* darn; damn.

dog·gy (dog′ē) *adj.* **-gi·er, -gi·est,** *n.* **-gies.** —*adj.* **1** like a dog. **2** *Informal.* outwardly showy. —*n.* doggie.

dog·house (dog′hous′) *n.* **1** a small house or shelter for a dog. **2 be in the doghouse,** *Slang.* be in disfavor with somebody.

do·gie (dō′gē) *n.* in the western parts of Canada and the United States, a motherless calf on the range or in a range herd. Also, **dogy.** [origin uncertain]

dog·ma (dog′mə) *n.* **-mas, -ma·ta** (-mə tə). **1** a belief taught or held as true, especially by the authority of a church. **2** a doctrine. **3** an opinion asserted in a positive manner as if it were authoritative. [< L < Gk. *dogma* opinion < *dokeein* think]

dog·mat·ic (dog mat′ik) *adj.* **1** having to do with dogma; doctrinal. **2** asserting opinions as if one were the highest authority; positive; overbearing. **3** asserted without proof. —**dog·mat′i·cal·ly,** *adv.*

dog·mat·i·cal (dog mat′ə kəl) *adj.* dogmatic.

dog·ma·tism (dog′mə tiz′əm) *n.* a positive or authoritative assertion of opinion.

dog·ma·tist (dog′mə tist) *n.* **1** a person who asserts opinions as if they were authoritative. **2** a person who states dogmas.

dog·ma·tize (dog′mə tīz′) *v.* **-tized, -tiz·ing.** assert opinions in a positive or authoritative manner; speak or write in a dogmatic way.

do-good·er (dü′gu̇d′ər) *n. Informal.* a person who is too eager to correct or set things right.

Dog-Rib (dog′rib) *n.* **-Rib** or **-Ribs. 1** a tribe of Indians living in the Northwest Territories. **2** a member of this tribe. **3** the Athapascan language of this tribe.

dog rose a wild rose of Europe having pink flowers and hooked spines.

dog salmon chum salmon.

dog's-ear (dogz′ēr′) *n. v.* dog-ear.

dog-sled (dog′sled′) *n. Cdn.* a sled that is pulled by dogs. See **sled** for picture.

dog-sledge (dog′slej′) *n. Cdn.* a dog-sled.

dog's life a miserable life.

Dog Star 1 Sirius. **2** Procyon.

dog's-tooth violet (dogz′tüth′) *n.* dogtooth violet.

dog tag *Informal.* **1** an identification disk worn on a neck chain by a member of the armed services. **2** a metal disk attached to a dog's collar.

dog-tired (dog′tīrd′) *adj.* very tired.

dog·tooth violet (dog′tüth′) a small plant of the lily family that has a single flower, and, in some varieties, mottled leaves. Also, **dog's-tooth violet.**

dog-train (dog′trān′) *n. Cdn.* a sled pulled by a team of dogs.

dog·trot (dog′trot′) *n.* a gentle, easy trot.

dog·watch (dog′woch′) *n.* a two-hour period of work on a ship. There are two dogwatches a day, one from 4 to 6 p.m. and the other from 6 to 8 p.m.

dog·wood (dog′wu̇d′) *n.* 1 a tree having large white or pinkish flowers in the spring, which develop into red berries, called **dogwood berries,** in the fall. The dogwood flower is the floral emblem of British Columbia. 2 its hard wood. 3 any tree of the same family as the dogwood.

do·gy (dō′gē) *n.* **-gies.** dogie.

doi·ly (doi′lē) *n.* **-lies.** 1 a small piece of linen, lace, paper, etc. used to cover plates, dishes, etc. or placed underneath them as a mat. 2 a small dessert napkin. Also, **doyley, doyly.** [after a 17th-century London dry-goods dealer]

do·ings (dü′ingz) *n.pl.* 1 things done; actions. 2 behavior; conduct.

doit (doit) *n.* 1 a former Dutch copper coin worth about 1/4 cent. 2 a small sum; trifle; bit: *No one cares a doit what he thinks.* [< Du. *duit*]

do-it-your·self (dü′it yər self′) *adj.* designed for use, construction, or assembly by amateurs: *a do-it-yourself construction kit.*

dol·ce (dōl′chā) *adj. Italian.* sweet; soft.

dol·ce far nien·te (dōl′chā fär nyen′tā) *Italian.* pleasant idleness (literally, sweet to do nothing).

dol·drums (dol′drəmz or dōl′-) *n.pl.* 1 certain regions of the ocean near the equator where the wind is very light or constantly shifting; regions of calms: *When a sailing ship gets in the doldrums, it makes hardly any headway.* 2 the calm or windless weather characteristic of these regions. 3 dullness; a gloomy feeling; low spirits: *She seems to be always in the doldrums.* [probably related to *dull*]

dole[1] (dōl) *n. v.* **doled, dol·ing.** —*n.* 1 a portion of money, food, etc. given in charity. 2 a small portion. 3 relief money given by a government to unemployed workers. 4 **go** or **be on the dole,** receive relief money from the government. 5 *Archaic.* lot; fate.
—*v.* 1 deal out in portions to the poor. 2 give in small portions. [OE *dāl* part. Related to DEAL[1].]

dole[2] (dōl) *n. Archaic.* sorrow; grief. [ME < OF *doel* < VL *dolus* grief < L *dolere* grieve]

dole·ful (dōl′fəl) *adj.* sad; mournful; dreary; dismal. —**dole′ful·ly,** *adv.* —**dole′ful·ness,** *n.* —**Syn.** sorrowful, woeful, plaintive.

dole·some (dōl′səm) *adj. Archaic.* doleful.

dol·i·co·ce·phal·ic (dol′ə kō sə fal′ik) *adj.* long-headed; having a long, narrow skull; having a skull whose breadth is less than eighty per cent of its length; opposed to *brachycephalic.*

doll (dol) *n.* 1 a child's plaything made to look like a baby, child, or grown person. 2 a pretty girl or woman, especially one without much intelligence. 3 a pretty child. —*v. Slang.* dress (*up* or *out*) in a stylish or showy way. [pet name for *Dorothy*] —**doll′-like′,** *adj.*

dol·lar (dol′ər) *n.* 1 a unit of money in Canada and the United States. See table at **money.** 2 a unit of money in Australia, Ethiopia, Hong Kong, Guyana, and some other countries. 3 West Indian dollar. 4 a note or coin worth one dollar. [earlier *daler* < LG < G (*Joachims*)*thaler* coin of St. Joachim's valley (in Bohemia)]

dollar crisis the situation arising when a country's reserve of dollars becomes dangerously low through failure to balance its imports from the United States by its exports.

dollar diplomacy *Informal.* a rich country's use of economic aid to needy nations in order to advance its own financial interests or to gain allies for its foreign policy.

dollar gap the shortage of dollars (for exchange) in a country suffering from a dollar crisis.

dollar imperialism the extending of control and authority into foreign countries through the buying power of the dollar.

dollar sign or **mark** the symbol $, meaning dollar or dollars: *Five dollars can be written $5.*

dol·lop (dol′əp) *n. Informal.* a portion or serving, large or small: *a dollop of ice cream.* —*v.* apply or spread on heavily. [? < Scand.; cf. Norwegian *dolp* lump]

doll·y (dol′ē) *n.* **doll·ies.** 1 a child's name for a doll. 2 a small, low frame on wheels, used to move heavy objects: *The fridge was moved on a dolly.* 3 a small truck on which a motion-picture or television camera can be moved about. 4 a small locomotive run on narrow-gauge tracks, used in switching, construction jobs, etc. 5 in mining, a device for shaking and washing ore in a vessel. 6 a bar with a flat or cup-shaped piece set at an angle on one end, used to form or hold the head of a rivet. 7 a block placed on the top of a pile while it is being driven. [< *doll*]

hat, āge, cãre, fär; let, ēqual, tėrm; it, īce
hot, ōpen, ôrder; oil, out; cup, pu̇t, rüle, ūse
əbove, takən, pencəl, lemən, circəs
ch, child; ng, long; sh, ship
th, thin; ᴛʜ, then; zh, measure

Dolly Var·den (vär′dən) 1 a speckled trout, or char, of western N. America. 2 a long flower-printed dress having the skirt tied in loops to show the petticoat. 3 a woman's wide-brimmed hat trimmed with flowers and turned down at one side. [< *Dolly Varden,* a character in Dickens' *Barnaby Rudge*]

dol·man (dol′mən or dōl′mən) *n.* **-mans.** 1 a woman's coat with capelike flaps instead of sleeves. 2 a long Turkish robe, open at the front. 3 a hussar's gold-braided uniform jacket worn like a cape with the sleeves hanging free. [ult. < Turkish *dōlāmān*]

dolman sleeve a sleeve that tapers from narrow at the wrist to wide at the shoulder.

dol·men (dol′mən) *n.* a prehistoric monument, generally regarded as a tomb, consisting of a large, flat stone laid across upright stones. [< F < Breton *tol* table + *men* stone]

A dolmen

dol·o·mite (dol′ə mīt′) *n.* 1 a rock consisting mainly of calcium and magnesium carbonate. Much so-called white marble is really dolomite. 2 calcium and magnesium carbonate. *Formula:* $CaCO_3 \cdot MgCO_3$ [after D. G. de *Dolomieu* (1750-1801), a French geologist]

dol·o·mit·ic (dol′ə mit′ik) *adj.* containing or consisting of dolomite.

do·lor or **do·lour** (dō′lər) *n. Poetic.* sorrow; grief. [ME < OF < L *dolor*]

do·lo·ro·so (dō′lō rō′sō) *adj.* in music, plaintive, soft, sorrowful. [< Ital.]

dol·or·ous (dol′ər əs or dō′lər əs) *adj.* 1 mournful; sorrowful. 2 grievous; painful. —**dol′or·ous·ly,** *adv.* —**dol′or·ous·ness,** *n.*

do·lour (dō′lər) *n.* dolor.

dol·phin (dol′fən) *n.* 1 a sea mammal related to the whale, but smaller and having a beaklike snout. 2 a large edible, salt-water fish remarkable for its changes of color when taken from the water. 3 the porpoise. 4 a buoy or piling used to mark a channel for ships. [ME < OF *daulphin* < L < Gk. *delphis*]

dolphin striker on a ship, a small spar under the bowsprit that helps support the jib boom.

dolt (dōlt) *n.* a dull, stupid person. [apparently a var. of obs. *dold,* pp. of ME **dole*(*n*) to dull, OE *dol* dull]

dolt·ish (dōl′tish) *adj.* dull and stupid.

-dom *suffix.* 1 the position, rank, or realm of a ——: *kingdom = realm of a king.* 2 the condition of being ——: *martyrdom = condition of being a martyr.* 3 all those who are ——: *heathendom = all those who are heathen.* [OE *-dōm* state, condition < *dōm.* See DOOM.]

dom. 1 domestic. 2 dominion.

Dom. 1 Dominion. 2 Dominican.

do·main (dō mān′) *n.* 1 the territory under the control of one ruler or government. 2 the land owned by one person; an estate. 3 a field of thought, action, etc.: *Sir John A. Macdonald was a leader in the domain of politics.* [< F *domaine* < OF < L *dominium* < *dominus,* lord, master < *domus* house. Doublet of DEMESNE.]

dome (dōm) *n. v.* **domed, dom·ing.** —*n.* 1 in architecture, a large, rounded roof or ceiling on a circular or many-sided base. 2 something high and rounded: *the dome of the sky, the dome of a hill.* 3 in crystallography, a prism whose faces meet in a horizontal edge, like the roof of a house. 4 a dome car. 5 in geology, an anticlinal formation, circular or elliptical in structure, characteristic of oil and salt deposits, extrusions of volcanic lava, etc.
—*v.* 1 cover with a dome. 2 shape like a dome. 3 rise or swell like a dome. [< F *dôme* < Provençal *doma* < LL *doma* roof, house < Gk.] —**dome′like′,** *adj.*

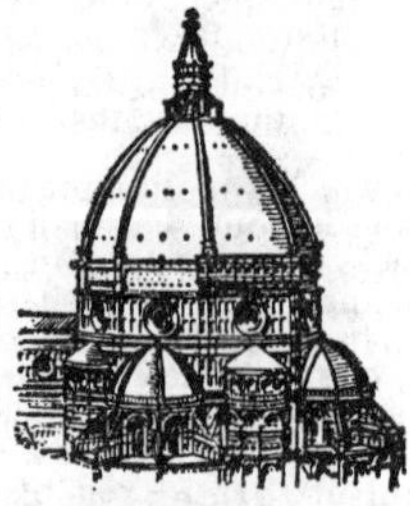
The dome of a church

dome car a railway car having a glass-enclosed upper level that resembles a dome and affords a wide view.

Domesday Book (dümz′dā′) a record of the value and ownership of the lands in England, made in 1086 at the order of William the Conqueror.

do·mes·tic (də mes′tik) *adj.* 1 of the home, household, or family affairs: *domestic cares, a domestic scene.* 2 fond of home and family life. 3 not wild; tame: *Cats, dogs, cows, horses, sheep, and pigs are domestic animals.* 4 of one's own country; not foreign: *This newspaper publishes both domestic and foreign news.* 5 made in one's own country; native: *domestic cheese.*
—*n.* a servant in a household: *Cooks and maids are domestics.* [< L *domesticus* < *domus* house]

do·mes·ti·cal·ly (də mes′tik lē) *adv.* in a domestic manner; so far as concerns domestic affairs.

do·mes·ti·cate (də mes′tə kāt′) *v.* **-cat·ed, -cat·ing.** 1 change (animals, savages, or plants) from a wild to a tame or cultivated state; tame. 2 make fond of home and family life. 3 cause to be or feel at home.

do·mes·ti·ca·tion (də mes′tə kā′shən) *n.* 1 a domesticating. 2 a being domesticated.

do·mes·tic·i·ty (dō′mes tis′ə tē) *n.* **-ties.** 1 home and family life. 2 fondness for home and family life. 3 **domesticities,** *pl.* domestic affairs.

domestic science home economics.

dom·i·cile (dom′ə sīl′ or dom′ə səl) *n. v.* **-ciled, -cil·ing.** —*n.* 1 a house; home; residence. 2 in law, one's place of permanent residence. One may have several residences, but only one legal domicile at a time.
—*v.* 1 settle in a domicile. 2 dwell; reside. [ME < MF < L *domicilium* < *domus* house]

dom·i·cil·i·ar·y (dom′ə sil′ē er′ē) *adj.* having to do with a domicile.

dom·i·cil·i·ate (dom′ə sil′ē āt′) *v.* **-at·ed, -at·ing.** 1 settle in a domicile. 2 dwell; reside.

dom·i·nance (dom′ə nəns) *n.* a being dominant; rule; control.

dom·i·nan·cy (dom′ə nən sē) *n.* **-cies.** dominance.

dom·i·nant (dom′ə nənt) *adj.* 1 most influential; controlling; ruling; governing. 2 rising high above its surroundings; occupying a commanding position: *A dominant cliff rose at the bend of the river.* 3 in music, based on or having to do with the fifth note in a standard major or minor scale. 4 in biology, of or having to do with a dominant member of a pair or series of genetic factors present in a germ plasm; opposed to *recessive.*
—*n.* in music, the fifth note in a standard major or minor scale. G is the dominant in the key of C. [< F < L *dominans, -antis,* ppr. of *dominari.* See DOMINATE.] —**dom′i·nant·ly,** *adv.*

Syn. *adj.* 1 **Dominant, predominant, paramount** = uppermost. **Dominant** = ruling, and therefore having the most influence, power, or authority: *Efficiency is the dominant idea in many businesses.* **Predominant** = before others in influence, power, authority, and therefore principal or superior: *Love of liberty is predominant in struggles for independence.* **Paramount** = first in importance, authority, or rank, and therefore supreme: *It is of paramount importance that we finish the work on time.*

dominant character a hereditary trait resulting from a dominant factor. *Example:* If a child inherits a gene for brown eyes from one parent and a gene for blue eyes from the other, it will have brown eyes, as brown eyes are dominant and blue eyes are recessive.

dom·i·nate (dom′ə nāt′) *v.* **-nat·ed, -nat·ing.** 1 control or rule by strength or power; prevail: *A man of strong will often dominates others.* 2 rise high above; hold a commanding position over: *The mountain dominates the harbor.* [< L *dominari* < *dominus* lord, master] —**dom′i·na′tor,** *n.*

dom·i·na·tion (dom′ə nā′shən) *n.* control; rule: *The tyrant's domination was challenged by the rebels.*

dom·i·neer (dom′ə nēr′) *v.* rule (over) at one's own will; tyrannize; be overbearing in asserting one's authority. [< Du. *domineren* < F < L *dominari.* See DOMINATE.]

dom·i·neer·ing (dom′ə nēr′ing) *adj.* inclined to domineer; arrogant. —**dom′i·neer′ing·ly,** *adv.*

Do·min·i·can (də min′ə kən) *adj.* 1 of Saint Dominic or the religious orders founded by him. 2 of or having to do with the Dominican Republic. —*n.* 1 a friar or nun belonging to the Dominican order. 2 a native or inhabitant of the Dominican Republic.

dom·i·nie (dom′ə nē *for 1;* dom′ə nē or dō′mə nē *for 2*) *n.* 1 *Esp.Scottish.* schoolmaster. 2 *Informal.* clergyman. [< L *domine* (vocative) lord, master]

do·min·ion (də min′yən) *n.* 1 supreme authority; rule; control. 2 a territory under the control of one ruler or government: *British dominions.* 3 a self-governing territory. 4 **Dominion,** a name given to certain self-governing countries in the British Commonwealth of Nations. Canada, Australia, and New Zealand are Dominions. —*adj.* Often, **Dominion.** 1 of or having to do with a dominion: *to achieve dominion status.* 2 in Canada: **a** relating to the country as a whole; national in scope: *the Dominion Drama Festival.* **b** under the control or authority of the federal government: *The company has a dominion permit to drill for oil; the Dominion Weather Bureau.* [< obs. F < Med.L *dominio, -onis,* alteration of L *dominium* ownership]

Dominion Day a national holiday commemorating the establishment of the Dominion of Canada on July 1, 1867.

dom·i·no[1] (dom′ə nō′) *n.* **-noes** or **-nos.** 1 a loose cloak, hood, and a small mask that covers the upper part of the face, worn as a disguise, especially at masquerades. 2 the small mask. 3 a person wearing a domino. [< F < L *domino* (dative of *dominus* master), short for some such phrase, jestingly used, as *benedicamus Domino* let us praise the Lord]

dom·i·no[2] (dom′ə nō′) *n.* **-noes.** 1 **dominoes,** *pl.* a game played with flat, oblong pieces having a varying number of dots marked on one side. Players try to match pieces having the same number of dots. 2 any of the pieces of bone or wood marked with spots and used in playing dominoes. [special use of *domino*[1]; so called from the solid black of the backs of the pieces]

☛ **Dominoes** meaning the game, is plural in form and singular in use: *Dominoes is played with 28 flat, oblong pieces of bone or wood.*

don[1] (don or dōn) *n.* 1 Mr.; Sir (a Spanish title). 2 a Spanish gentleman; Spaniard. 3 a distinguished person. 4 *Informal.* a head, fellow, or tutor of a college at Oxford or Cambridge University. 5 in some Canadian universities, an official in charge of a residence or dormitory. [< Sp. < L *dominus* lord, master]

don[2] (don) *v.* **donned, don·ning.** put on. [contraction of *do on*]

do·ña (don′yä or dō′nyä) *n.* 1 Lady; Madam (a Spanish title). 2 a Spanish lady. [< Sp. < L *domina* mistress. Doublet of DONNA.]

do·nate (dō′nāt or dō nāt′) *v.* **-nat·ed, -nat·ing.** give; contribute, especially to a fund or institution: *He donated ten dollars to the church.* [< L *donare* < *donum* gift] —**do·nat′or,** *n.*

☛ **donate.** As a rule, this word is a rather pretentious substitute for *give.*

do·na·tion (dō nā′shən) *n.* 1 the act of giving or contributing. 2 a gift; contribution.

done (dun) *adj.* 1 completed; finished; ended; through. 2 *Informal.* worn out; exhausted. 3 cooked enough. 4 proper; fitting; conforming to custom or convention:

This is the done thing. Eating peas with a knife is not done. —*v.* pp. of **do**[1].

☛ **Done with** is used in informal speech to mean finished, completed: *I'd like to get done with this.*

don·jon (dun′jən or don′jən) *n.* a large, strongly fortified tower of a castle. [var. of *dungeon*]

Don Juan (don wän′, don hwän′, or don jü′ən) **1** a legendary Spanish nobleman who led a dissolute and immoral life. **2** any person leading an immoral life; libertine.

☛ **Don Juan.** This name is usually pronounced (don wän′) or (don hwän′) in imitation of the Spanish pronunciation (dōng ʜwän′), but Byron's poem *Don Juan* and its hero are always pronounced (don jü′ən).

don·key (dong′kē or dung′kē) *n.* **-keys. 1** a small animal resembling a horse but having longer ears, a shorter mane, and a tuft of hair on the end of its tail; ass. **2** a stubborn person. **3** a silly or stupid person. **4** a donkey engine. [? a nickname form of *Duncan*]

donkey engine a small steam engine. Donkey engines are used on ships for hoisting anchor, etc.

don·na (don′ə; *Italian,* dôn′nä) *n.* **1** a lady. **2 Donna,** lady; madam (an Italian title). [< Ital. < L *domina* mistress. Doublet of DOÑA.]

don·nish (don′ish) *adj.* of or like a type of university don; pedantic; formal. —**don′nish·ly,** *adv.* —**don′nish·ness,** *n.*

Don·ny·brook (don′ə brůk′) *n. Informal.* a riot; a brawl: *The players engaged in a terrific Donnybrook after the hockey game.* Also, **donnybrook.** [< *Donnybrook,* a town in the Irish Republic, site of an annual fair. The 1855 fair was suppressed because of wild brawls.]

do·nor (dō′nər) *n.* a person who contributes; giver: *The Canadian Red Cross Society welcomes blood donors.* [ME < AF *donour* < L *donator* < *donare.* See DONATE.]

do-nothing (dü′nuth′ing) *n.* **1** one who does nothing; idler. **2** a person unwilling to take action because it may upset the existing order.

Don Qui·xo·te (don kē hō′ tē or don kwik′sət; *Spanish,* dōng kē ʜō′te) **1** the hero of a story by Cervantes that satirizes chivalric romances, published in two parts in 1605 and 1615. Don Quixote is chivalrous and idealistic but ridiculously impractical. **2** any person of high but impractical ideals.

don't (dōnt) do not.

☛ **Don't** is universally used in conversation and often in informal writing when *do not* would seem too emphatic or when rhythm seems more comfortable with the shorter form. In substandard usage *don't* = *doesn't: He don't look as well as he used to.*

doo·dad (dü′dad) *n. Informal.* a fancy, trifling ornament.

doo·dle (dü′dəl) *v.* **-dled, -dling,** *n.* —*v.* make drawings, etc. absent-mindedly while talking or thinking. —*n.* a drawing or mark made absent-mindedly.

doo·dle·bug[1] (dü′dəl bug′) *n. U.S.* larva of the ant lion. The doodlebug digs a pit to catch other insects. [< *doodle* simpleton (cf. LG *dudeltopf*) + *bug*]

doo·dle·bug[2] (dü′dəl bug′) *n. Informal.* **1** any of various devices with which it is claimed mineral and oil deposits can be located. **2** a buzz bomb. [apparently special use of *doodlebug*[1]]

doo·hick·ey (dü′hik ē) *n. Informal.* **1** any small mechanical device; a gadget. **2** any small device, the name of which escapes one: *Pass that doohickey for opening windows.* [a humorous coinage based on *do*]

doom (düm) *n.* **1** fate. **2** an unhappy or terrible fate; ruin; death: *The soldiers marched to their doom in battle.* **3** judgment; sentence: *The judge pronounced the guilty man's doom.* **4** the end of the world; God's final judgment of mankind.
—*v.* **1** condemn to some fate: *Her hopes were doomed to disappointment.* **2** destine to an unhappy or terrible fate: *the doomed men.* **3** condemn (to punishment): *The prisoner was doomed to death.* [OE *dōm* law, judgment]
—**Syn.** *n.* **1** destiny, lot, portion. See **fate.**

dooms·day (dümz′dā′) *n.* the end of the world; day of God's final judgment of mankind.

Doomsday Book Domesday Book.

door (dôr) *n.* **1** a movable slab of wood, stone, or metal, intended for closing an opening in a wall of a building. A door may turn on hinges or slide open and shut. Most rooms have doors. **2** any movable part that

hat, āge, cãre, fär; let, ēqual, tėrm; it, īce
hot, ōpen, ôrder; oil, out; cup, půt, rüle, ūse
əbove, takən, pencəl, lemən, circəs
ch, child; ng, long; sh, ship
th, thin; ᴛʜ, then; zh, measure

suggests a door. **3** an opening where a door is; doorway: *He walked into the room through the door.* **4** a room, house, or building to which a door belongs: *His house is three doors down the street.* **5** any means by which to go in or out; a way to get something; access: *an open door to the Yukon.* **6 in doors,** in a house or building, inside. **7 lay at the door of,** blame for. **8 out of doors,** not in a house or building; outside. **9 show a person the door,** ask a person to leave. [OE *duru*] —**door′like′,** *adj.*

door·bell (dôr′bel′) *n.* a bell inside the house to be rung by pressing a button or pulling a handle on the outside of a door as a signal that someone has arrived.

door·jamb (dôr′jam′) *n.* the upright piece forming the side of a doorway.

door·keeper (dôr′kēp′ər) *n.* **1** a person who guards a door or entrance. **2** a doorman.

door·knob (dôr′nob′) *n.* a handle on a door.

door·man (dôr′mən or -man′) *n.* **-men** (-mən or -men′). **1** a man whose work is opening the door of a hotel, store, apartment house, etc. for people going in or out. **2** a man who guards a door.

door·mat (dôr′mat′) *n.* **1** a mat for wiping dirt off shoes, usually placed by an outside door of a house. **2** *Informal.* a person who is easily imposed upon. **3** knotgrass.

door·nail (dôr′nāl′) *n.* **1** a nail with a large head. **2 dead as a doornail,** entirely dead.

door·plate (dôr′plāt′) *n.* a metal plate on a door with a name, number, etc. on it.

door·post (dôr′pōst′) *n.* doorjamb.

door·sill (dôr′sil′) *n.* a threshold.

door·step (dôr′step′) *n.* a step leading from an outside door to the ground.

door·stop (dôr′stop′) *n.* a device to hold a door open or to prevent it from opening too far.

door-to-door (dôr′tə dôr′) *adj.* **1** going from one apartment, house, office, etc. to another: *a door-to-door salesman.* **2** proceeding from starting point to destination: *door-to-door haulage.* —*adv.* **1** from one apartment, house, office, etc. to the next. **2** from starting point to destination.

door·way (dôr′wā′) *n.* an opening to be closed by a door.

door·yard (dôr′yärd′) *n.* a yard near the door of a house; yard around a house.

dope (dōp) *n. v.* **doped, dop·ing.** —*n.* **1** *Slang.* **a** a harmful, narcotic drug, such as opium, morphine, etc. **b** a drug addict. **2** oil, grease, etc., used to make machinery run smoothly. **3** a varnish formerly put on the cloth parts of an airplane to make them stronger, waterproof, and airtight. **4** *Slang.* information; forecast; prediction. **5** *Slang.* a very stupid person. **6** *Slang.* a stimulating drug illegally given to a horse before a race.
—*v.* **1** *Slang.* apply or give dope to. **2** use dope. **3** *Slang.* work out; forecast; predict. [< Du. *doop* dipping sauce < *doopen* dip] —**dop′er,** *n.*

dope·y or **dop·y** (dōp′ē) *adj. Slang.* **1** drugged; drowsy; as if affected by drugs. **2** very stupid.

dop·pler or **Dop·pler** (dop′lər) *adj.* of or having to do with the Doppler effect.

Doppler effect in physics, the apparent shift in the frequency of sound, light, and other waves caused by relative movement between the source and the observer. [< Christian *Doppler,* 1803-1853, an Austrian physicist]

Doppler shift Doppler effect.

dor (dôr) *n.* a kind of large beetle. [OE *dora*]

do·ré (dô′rā or dô′rē) *n. Cdn.* yellow pickerel; pike-perch; wall-eyed pike. [< F. See DORY[2].]

Do·ri·an (dô′rē ən) *adj.* of or having to do with Doris or its inhabitants; Doric. —*n.* a native or inhabitant of Doris.

Dor·ic (dôr′ik) *adj.* 1 in architecture: **a** of or having to do with the earliest of the three orders of ancient Greek architecture, characterized by simplicity, strength, and solidity. The Parthenon in Athens, dedicated to the goddess Athena, is a Doric temple. **b** of or having to do with the type of column characteristic of Doric architecture. The Doric column consists of a tapering circular shaft, slightly fluted, and a severely plain capital. 2 Dorian. —*n.* the Greek dialect spoken in Doris.

Dor·king (dôr′king) *n.* 1 a breed of domestic chickens that have long, heavy bodies and five toes on each foot. 2 a chicken of this breed. [after *Dorking*, a town in Surrey, England]

dorm (dôrm) *n. Informal.* dormitory.

dor·man·cy (dôr′mən sē) *n.* a dormant condition.

dor·mant (dôr′mənt) *adj.* 1 sleeping. 2 quiet as if asleep. 3 inactive: *The plant bulbs were dormant during the cold winter.* 4 in heraldry, (of an animal) lying down with its head on its forepaws. [ME < OF *dormant*, ppr. of *dormir* sleep < L *dormire*] —**Syn. 3** See **inactive.**

dor·mer (dôr′mər) *n.* 1 an upright window that projects from a sloping roof. 2 the projecting part of a roof that contains such a window. [originally, a sleeping room; < OF *dormeor* < L *dormitorium.* Doublet of DORMITORY.]

A dormer (def. 2) and window

dormer window dormer (def. 1).

dor·mi·to·ry (dôr′mə tô′rē) *n.* **-ries.** 1 a building with many sleeping rooms: *Many colleges have dormitories for students.* 2 a sleeping room containing several beds. [< L *dormitorium* < *dormire* sleep. Doublet of DORMER.]

dor·mouse (dôr′mous′) *n.* **-mice.** a small, hibernating rodent that resembles a squirrel. [apparently < E dial. *dorm* sleep, doze (< F *dormir* < L *dormire*) + mouse]

dor·sal (dôr′səl) *adj.* of, on, or near the back: *a dorsal fin, a dorsal nerve.* [< LL *dorsalis* < L *dorsum* back]

dor·sal·ly (dôr′səl ē) *adv.* 1 on the back; by the back. 2 toward the back.

Dor·set (dôr′sit) *n.* an Eskimo culture of N.E. Canada and N. Greenland, lasting approximately from A.D. 100 to 1000, characterized by skill in carving and by the hunting of seal and caribou. [< Cape *Dorset*, Baffin Island]

do·ry[1] (dô′rē) *n.* **-ries.** a rowboat with a flat bottom and high sides, often used by ocean fishermen. [< Central Am.Ind. *dóri* dugout]

do·ry[2] (dô′rē) *n.* **-ries.** 1 John Dory, an edible sea fish. 2 walleyed pike; yellow pickerel; doré. [< F *dorée*, literally, gilded; with reference to its color]

dos·age (dōs′ij) *n.* 1 the size and frequency of a dose. 2 the giving of medicine in doses. 3 the intensity or length of application of X-rays in certain methods of therapy.

dose (dōs) *n. v.* **dosed, dos·ing.** —*n.* 1 the amount of a medicine to be taken at one time. 2 a portion; the amount of anything given at one time as a remedy, treatment, etc.: *a dose of flattery.* 3 a certain amount of brandy, sugar, etc. added to wine to give it strength or flavor. 4 anything unpleasant or disagreeable to take or endure.
—*v.* 1 give medicine to in doses; treat with medicine: *The doctor dosed the boy with quinine.* 2 blend; adulterate: *dose wine with sugar.* [< F < LL < Gk. *dosis* a giving < *didonai* give] —**dos′er,** *n.*

do·sim·e·ter (dō sim′ə tər) *n.* a device for measuring the dosage or amount of radiation received over a given period of time. [< Gk. *dosis* dose + E *-meter*]

doss (dos) *n. Slang.* 1 a bed in a cheap lodging house. 2 a doss house. 3 sleep. —*v.* bed down in any convenient spot; sleep. [probably < F *dos* the back < VL *dossum* < L *dorsum*]

doss house *Slang.* a cheap lodging house.

dos·si·er (dos′ē ā or dos′ē ər) *n.* a collection of papers or documents about some subject or person. [< F]

dost (dust) *v. Archaic.* doest.

dot[1] (dot) *n. v.* **dot·ted, dot·ting.** —*n.* 1 a tiny, round mark; a very small spot; point. 2 a small spot: *a blue necktie with white dots.* 3 in music: **a** a tiny, round mark after a note or rest that makes it half again as long. **b** a similar mark placed over or under a note to indicate that it is to be played or sung staccato. 4 a short sound used in sending messages by telegraph or radio. 5 **on the dot,** *Informal.* at exactly the right time; at the specified time.
—*v.* mark with a dot or dots.

dot[2] (dot) *n.* dowry. [< F < L *dos, dotis*]

DOT or **D.O.T.** Department of Transport.

dot·age (dōt′ij) *n.* an enfeebled and childish mental condition that sometimes accompanies old age. [< *dote*]

do·tard (dō′tərd) *n.* a person who is mentally enfeebled and childish because of old age; one in his dotage. [< *dote*]

dote (dōt) *v.* **dot·ed, dot·ing.** 1 be feeble-minded and childish because of old age. 2 **dote on** or **upon,** be foolishly fond of; be too fond of: *The old lady dotes on her grandson.* [ME *doten*] —**dot′er,** *n.*

doth (duth) *v. Archaic.* does. "He doth" means "he does." Also, **doeth.**

dot·ing (dōt′ing) *adj.* 1 foolishly fond; too fond. 2 in botany, (of trees) decaying from age. —**dot′ing·ly,** *adv.*

dot·ted (dot′id) *adj.* 1 marked with or as with a dot or dots. 2 formed of dots: *Sign on the dotted line.* 3 in music, (of a note or rest) followed by a dot, thus making it half again as long: *a dotted eighth.*

dotted swiss a sheer, crisp cotton fabric having an overall design of raised dots. [< *Swiss* (muslin)]

dot·ter·el (dot′ər əl) *n.* 1 a short-billed shore bird that is easily caught; European plover. 2 *Dialect.* a stupid person who is easily fooled or cheated. [< *dote*]

dot·tle (dot′əl) *n.* the plug of tobacco left in a pipe after smoking. [ME *dottel* a plug, ? dim. of *dot* small piece]

dot·ty (dot′ē) *adj.* **-ti·er, -ti·est.** 1 *Informal.* feebleminded; half-witted; partly insane. 2 *Informal.* unsteady; shaky; feeble. 3 *Informal.* very enthusiastic. 4 full of dots. —**dot′ti·ness,** *n.*

Dou·ay Bible (dü′ā) an English translation of the Latin Vulgate Bible, made by a group of Roman Catholic scholars. The New Testament was published at Reims in 1582, the Old Testament at Douai in 1609–1610. The Douay Bible is the version traditionally used by English-speaking Roman Catholics. [< *Douai*, a town in N. France]

Douay Version Douay Bible.

dou·ble (dub′əl) *adj. adv. n. v.* **-bled, -bling.** —*adj.* 1 twice as much, as many, as large, as strong, etc.: *double pay, a double letter.* 2 for two: *a double bed.* 3 made of two similar parts; in a pair: *double doors.* 4 made of two unlike parts; combining two in one. *Bear* has a double meaning: *carry* and a certain animal. 5 insincere; deceitful; false: *a double tongue.* 6 in botany, having more than one set of petals: *Some roses are double, others are single.* 7 in music: **a** having two beats or a multiple of two beats to the measure. **b** (of an instrument) producing a tone an octave lower than the ordinary instrument: *a double trumpet.*
—*adv.* 1 twice. 2 two (of everything) instead of one: *The blow made him see double.*
—*n.* 1 a number or amount that is twice as much. 2 a person or thing just like another: *I saw your double in the streetcar yesterday.* In a motion picture an actor often has a double to do the dangerous parts. 3 a fold; bend. 4 a sharp backward bend or turn; shift. 5 in baseball, the hit by which a batter gets to second base. 6 in bridge, the act of doubling a bid. 7 **doubles,** *pl.* game with two players on each side. 8 **on the double, a** quickly; at the run. **b** in double time.
—*v.* 1 make twice as much or twice as many. 2 become twice as much or as many. 3 be used for another; be the double of. 4 take another's place: *Tom doubled for me when I couldn't get to the meeting.* 5 serve two purposes; play two parts: *The maid doubled as cook.* 6 fold; bend: *He doubled his fists in anger.* 7 bend or turn sharply backward: *The fox doubled on his track to get away from the dogs.* 8 go around: *The ship doubled the Cape.* 9 in

bridge, increase the points or penalties of (an opponent's bid). **10** move at the run: *We doubled over to the barracks.* **11** make move at the run: *The corporal doubled his men around the building.* **12** in baseball, make a two-base hit. **13 double back, a** fold over. **b** go back the same way that one came. **14 double up, a** fold up; curl up. **b** draw the knees up to the chest. **c** share room, bed, or quarters with another. **d** move at the double; run. [ME < OF < L *duplus.* Doublet of DUPLE.] —**dou′bler,** *n.*

☛ **double letter.** In abbreviations, a double letter often indicates plurality: *pp.* = *pages;* LL.B. = *Bachelor of Laws.*

☛ **double negative.** The use of two negatives for one is no longer acceptable in formal or informal educated usage, though it is often found in substandard speech and writing. Substandard: *There wasn't no answer to my call.* Formal and Informal: *There was no answer to my call. There wasn't any answer to my call.* But two negatives cancelling each other out may be used for special effects: *He isn't unaware of it.*

double bar in music, a double line on a staff that marks the end of a movement or of an entire piece of music.

dou·ble-bar·relled or **dou·ble-bar·reled** (dub′əl bar′əld) *adj.* **1** having two barrels: *a double-barrelled shotgun.* **2** having a two-fold purpose. **3** having a double meaning: *a double-barrelled question.*

double bass a stringed musical instrument shaped like a cello but much larger, and having a very low bass tone; bass viol. One plays it standing up.

double bassoon a large bassoon, an octave lower in pitch than the ordinary bassoon.

double bill two plays, movies, etc. presented on one program.

double boiler a pair of pans, one of which fits down into the other. The food in the upper pan is cooked gently by the heat from the boiling water in the lower pan.

dou·ble-breast·ed (dub′əl bres′tid) *adj.* of clothing, overlapping enough to make two thicknesses cross the breast and having two rows of buttons.

dou·ble-check (dub′əl chek′) *v.* check twice: *The police double-checked the vagrant's story before releasing him.* —*n.* a checking of something twice.

double chin a soft fold of flesh under the chin.

double cross *Informal.* an act of treachery.

dou·ble-cross (dub′əl kros′) *v. Informal.* promise to do one thing and then do another; be treacherous to. —**dou′ble-cross′er,** *n.*

double dagger a mark (‡) used for reference from one place in a book to another.

dou·ble-deal·er (dub′əl dēl′ər) *n.* a person guilty of double-dealing.

dou·ble-deal·ing (dub′əl dēl′ing) *n. adj.* pretending to do one thing and then doing another; deceiving.

double-deck (dub′əl dek′) *adj.* having or consisting of two decks, floors, levels, sections, etc.: *double-deck beds.* —*v.* arrange or construct in two decks, floors, etc.

dou·ble-deck·er (dub′əl dek′ər) *n.* **1** a structure having two decks, floors, levels, sections, etc.: *Some railway cars are double-deckers.* **2** a sandwich having two layers of filling between three slices of bread.

dou·ble-edged (dub′əl ejd′) *adj.* **1** two-edged. **2** as much against as for: *a double-edged compliment.*

dou·ble-en·ten·dre (du′bəl on ton′drə; *French,* dü blän tän′drə) *n.* a word or expression with two meanings. One is often indelicate or improper. [< obs. F *double entendre,* literally, to be taken two ways]

double entry a system of bookkeeping in which each transaction is written down twice, once on the credit side of the account and once on the debit side.

dou·ble-faced (dub′əl fāst′) *adj.* **1** pretending to be what one is not; hypocritical; deceitful. **2** having two faces or aspects.

double feature a motion-picture program with two full-length films.

dou·ble-head·ed (dub′əl hed′id) *adj.* **1** two-fold; double. **2** having two heads: *a double-headed tool.* **3** having both good and bad qualities.

dou·ble-head·er (dub′əl hed′ər) *n.* **1** two baseball games on the same day, one right after the other. **2** a railway train pulled by two engines.

double indemnity in life insurance, a clause binding the insurance company to pay twice the face value of the policy in case of the accidental death of the insured.

hat, āge, cãre, fär; let, ēqual, tėrm; it, īce
hot, ōpen, ôrder; oil, out; cup, pu̇t, rüle, ūse
əbove, takən, pencəl, lemən, circəs
ch, child; ng, long; sh, ship
th, thin; ᴛʜ, then; zh, measure

dou·ble-joint·ed (dub′əl join′tid) *adj.* having joints that let fingers, arms, legs, etc. bend in unusual ways.

dou·ble-park (dub′əl pärk′) *v.* park (a car, etc.) beside another car that is occupying the area where parking is allowed: *It is usually illegal to double-park.*

double play in baseball, a play in which two base runners are put out. —**double′-play′,** *adj.*

dou·ble-quick (dub′əl kwik′) *n.* in marching, the next quickest step to a run. —*adj.* very quick. —*adv.* in double-quick time. —*v.* march in double-quick step.

dou·ble-reed (dub′əl rēd′) *adj.* in music, having two reeds bound together and made to vibrate against each other. The oboe and the bassoon are double-reed instruments.

double sharp in music, a sign (× or ✻) to indicate that a note must be raised two half tones above the natural pitch.

double star two stars so close together that they look like one to the naked eye.

dou·blet (dub′lit) *n.* **1** a man's close-fitting jacket. Men in Europe wore doublets in the 15th, 16th, and 17th centuries. **2** a pair of two similar or equal things. **3** one of a pair. **4** one of two or more words in a language, derived from the same original source but coming by different routes. *Example: fragile* and *frail.*

double tackle a pulley with two grooved wheels.

dou·ble-take (dub′əl tāk′) *n.* a delayed reaction to a situation, joke, etc., often used for comic effect by actors.

double talk talk that is purposely made confusing so as to cloak ignorance or deceit.

double time **1** payment at twice the normal rate: *The workers in the factory demanded double time for Sunday work.* **2** a rate of marching in which 180 paces, each of 36 inches, are taken in a minute. **3** double-quick.

dou·ble·tree (dub′əl trē′) *n.* a crossbar on a carriage, wagon, plough, etc. When two horses are used, the singletrees of their harness are attached to this crossbar.

double window storm window.

dou·bloon (dub lün′) *n.* an old Spanish gold coin. Its value varied from about $5 to about $16. [< F *doublon* or < Sp. *doblón* < *doble* double]

dou·bly (dub′lē) *adv.* **1** twice; twice as. **2** two at a time. **3** *Archaic.* deceitfully.

doubt (dout) *v.* **1** not believe; not to be sure of; feel uncertain about. **2** be uncertain. **3** *Archaic.* be afraid; fear; suspect.
—*n.* **1** a lack of belief or sureness; uncertainty. **2** a feeling of uncertainty. **3** an uncertain condition or situation: *In such a case, the defendant is entitled to the benefit of the doubt.* **4** *Obsolete.* fear; apprehension. **5 beyond doubt,** surely; certainly. **6 in doubt,** not sure; uncertain. **7 no doubt, a** surely; certainly. **b** probably. **8 without doubt,** surely; certainly. [ME < OF *douter* < L *dubitare*] —**doubt′er,** *n.* —**doubt′ing·ly,** *adv.* —**Syn.** *n.* **1** See **suspicion.**

☛ **doubt.** The idioms with *doubt* are: a negative (where there is no real doubt), *doubt that: I do not doubt that he means well.* **b** positive (where doubt exists), *doubt that, whether* (in formal use): *I doubt whether he meant it that way. I doubt that he meant it that way* (indicating unbelief really more than doubt), *if* (in general use): *I doubt if he meant it that way.*

doubt·ful (dout′fəl) *adj.* **1** in doubt; not sure; uncertain. **2** causing doubt; open to question or suspicion. —**doubt′ful·ly,** *adv.* —**doubt′ful·ness,** *n.*

doubting Thomas a person who doubts everything. [< St. *Thomas,* the disciple who doubted Christ's resurrection. John 20: 24-29.]

doubt·less (dout′lis) *adv.* **1** surely; certainly. **2** probably. —*adj.* having no doubts; sure; certain. —**doubt′less·ly,** *adv.* —**doubt′less·ness,** *n.*

douche (düsh) *n.* *v.* **douched, douch·ing.** —*n.* **1** a jet of water applied on or into any part of the body: *A douche of salt water up my nose helped relieve my cold in the head.* **2** an application of a douche. **3** a spray, syringe, or other device for applying a douche.
—*v.* **1** apply a douche to. **2** take a douche. [< F < Ital. *doccia,* ult. < L *ducere* lead]

dough (dō) *n.* **1** a soft, thick mixture of flour, liquid, and other materials for baking. Bread, biscuits, cake, pie crust, etc. are made from dough. **2** any soft, thick mass like this. **3** *Informal.* money. [OE *dāg*] **—dough′like′,** *adj.*

dough·boy (dō′boi′) *n.* *U.S. Informal.* an infantryman in the United States army.

dough·nut (dō′nut′) *n.* a small cake, often ring-shaped, fried in deep fat.

dough·ty (dou′tē) *adj.* **-ti·er, -ti·est.** *Archaic.* brave; valiant; strong: *doughty knights.* [OE *dohtig* < *dugan* be good] **—dought′i·ly,** *adv.* **—dough′ti·ness,** *n.*

dough·y (dō′ē) *adj.* **dough·i·er, dough·i·est.** of dough; like dough; soft and thick; pale and flabby.

Douglas fir an evergreen tree, often over 200 feet high, common in British Columbia and the western United States. [after David *Douglas,* 1798–1834, a Scottish botanist and explorer]

Douk (dük) *n.* *Slang.* a Doukhobor.

Douk·ho·bor or **Douk·ho·bour** (dük′ə bôr′) *n.* a member of a Christian sect that had its origin in Russia about 200 years ago. Several thousand Doukhobors left Russia in 1898 and settled in Western Canada. Also, **Dukhobor.** [< Russian *dukhoborcy* < *dukh* spirit + *borcy* wrestlers]

Dou·ma (dü′mä) *n.* Duma.

dour (dür or dour) *adj.* **1** gloomy; sullen. **2** stern; severe. **3** stubborn. [< L *durus* hard, stern] **—dour′ly,** *adv.* **—dour′ness,** *n.*

douse (dous) *v.* **doused, dous·ing.** **1** plunge or be plunged into water or any other liquid. **2** throw water over; drench. **3** *Informal.* put out (a light); extinguish. **4** *Informal.* take off; doff. **5** lower or slacken (a sail) in haste. **6** close (a porthole). [origin uncertain] **—dous′er,** *n.*

dove[1] (duv) *n.* **1** a bird having a thick body, short legs, and a beak enlarged at the tip; pigeon. The dove is often a symbol of peace. **2 Dove,** the Holy Ghost. **3** a gentle, innocent, or loving person. **4** a person who advocates peace (opposed to *hawk*). [OE *dūfe.* Related to DIVE.]

dove[2] (dōv) *v.* a pt. of **dive.**

☛ **dove, dived.** In formal usage many educated speakers prefer *dived* for the past tense of *dive*; informal English commonly uses *dove.* Formal: *He dived into the lake when he heard her screams.* Informal: *He dove from the platform.*

dove·cot (duv′kot′) *n.* dovecote.

dove·cote (duv′kōt′) *n.* a small house or shelter for doves or pigeons.

dove·kie or **dove·key** (duv′kē) *n.* **1** a small black and white auk having a short, stout bill, common in the north Atlantic and Arctic regions. **2** the black guillemot. [Scottish dim. of *dove*[1]]

dove·tail (duv′tāl′) *n.* **1** a projection at the end of a piece of wood, metal, etc. that can be fitted into a corresponding opening at the end of another piece to form a joint. **2** the joint formed in this way. —*v.* **1** fasten, join, or fit together with projections that fit into openings. **2** fit together exactly: *The various bits of evidence dovetailed so completely that the mystery was solved at once.*

Dovetails (def. 1)

dow·a·ger (dou′ə jər) *n.* **1** a woman who holds some title or property from her dead husband: *The queen and her mother-in-law, the queen dowager, were both present.* **2** *Informal.* a dignified, elderly lady. [< OF *douagere* (def. 1) < *douage* dower < *douer* endow < L *dotare*]

dow·dy (dou′dē) *adj.* **-di·er, -di·est,** *n.* **-dies.** —*adj.* poorly dressed; not neat; not stylish; shabby: *The old lady wore a dowdy coat and a shapeless hat.* —*n.* a woman whose clothes are dowdy. [origin uncertain] **—dow′di·ly,** *adv.* **—dow′di·ness,** *n.*

dow·el (dou′əl) *n.* *v.* **-elled** or **-eled, -el·ling** or **-el·ing.** —*n.* a peg on a piece of wood, metal, etc. to fit into a corresponding hole on another piece, and so form a joint fastening the two pieces together. —*v.* fasten with dowels. [probably akin to MLG *dovel,* G *Döbel* plug, tap (of a cask)]

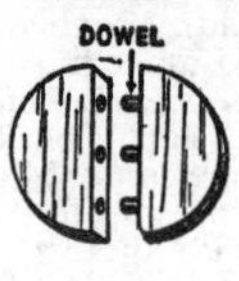

dow·er (dou′ər) *n.* **1** in law, a widow's share of her dead husband's property. **2** a dowry. **3** a natural gift, talent, or quality; endowment. —*v.* provide with a dower; endow. [ME < OF *douaire* < Med.L *dotarium* < L *dotare* endow < *dos, dotis* dowry] **—dow′er·less,** *adj.*

down[1] (doun) *adv.* **1** from a higher to a lower place or condition: *The soldiers laid down their arms. They ran down from the top of the hill.* **2** in a lower place or condition: *Down in the valley the fog still lingers.* **3** to or in a place or condition thought of as lower: *down river; down East. He lives in the Yukon, but goes down to Vancouver every winter.* **4** to a position or condition that is difficult, dangerous, etc.: *The dogs ran the fox down.* **5** from an earlier to a later time or person: *The house was handed down from father to son.* **6** from a larger to a smaller amount, degree, station, etc.: *everyone from the hotel manager down to the shoeshine boy. The temperature has gone down.* **7** actually; really: *Stop talking, and get down to work.* **8** on paper; in writing: *Take down what I say.* **9** when bought: *You can pay part of the price down and the rest later.* **10** into a heavier or more concentrated form: *boil down to a thick syrup.* **11 down with, a** put down. **b** get rid of.
—*prep.* down along, through, or into: *ride down a hill, walk down a street, sail down a river.*
—*adj.* **1** in a lower place or condition. **2** going or pointed down: *the down train.* **3** sick; ill: *She is down with a cold.* **4** sad; discouraged: *He felt down about his failure.* **5** of a football, no longer in play. **6** behind an opponent by a certain number. **7** in baseball, out. **8 down and out, a** completely without health, money, friends, etc. **b** in boxing, knocked out. **9 down on,** *Informal.* **a** angry at; having a grudge against. **b** attacking; criticizing.
—*v.* **1** put down; get down: *He downed the medicine at one swallow.* **2** defeat: *down the favorite team.* **3** lie down: *Down, Fido!*
—*n.* **1** a downward movement. **2** a piece of bad luck: *the ups and downs of life.* **3** in football, a chance to move a ball forward. In Canadian football, a team is allowed three downs in which to move the ball forward ten yards. **4** *Informal.* a grudge: *have a down on someone.* [var. of *adown,* OE *adūne,* earlier *of dūne* from (the) hill. Cf. *down*[3].]

down[2] (doun) *n.* **1** soft feathers. **2** soft hair or fluff: *The down on a boy's chin develops into a beard.* [ME < ON *dúnn*]

down[3] (doun) *n.* **1** Usually **downs,** *pl.* a stretch of rolling, grassy land. **2** a mound or ridge of sand heaped up by the wind; dune. [OE *dūn* hill]

down-beat (doun′bēt′) *n.* in music: **1** the first beat in a measure. **2** the downward gesture of the conductor's hand to indicate this beat.

down·cast (doun′kast′) *adj.* **1** directed downward: *Ashamed of his mistake, he stood with downcast eyes.* **2** dejected; sad; discouraged: *A life of failure had made her downcast.* —*n.* **1** a downcast look. **2** a casting down; overthrow.

down·fall (doun′fol′ or -fôl′) *n.* **1** a bringing to ruin; a sudden overthrow of a great person through a change in fortune: *the downfall of a hero, the downfall of an empire.* **2** a heavy fall of rain or snow; a downpour.

down·fall·en (doun′fol′ən or -fôl′ən) *adj.* fallen; overthrown; ruined.

down·fold (doun′fōld′) *n.* in geology, a downward fold or depression; syncline.

down·grade (doun′grād′) *n.* *v.* **-grad·ed, -grad·ing.** —*n.* a downward slope. —*v.* **1** move to a lower position with a smaller salary. **2** move to a lower status, level of importance, etc.: *The poor quality of his latest book downgraded his reputation as a writer.*

down·heart·ed (doun′här′tid) *adj.* discouraged; dejected; depressed. **—down′heart′ed·ly,** *adv.* **—down′heart′ed·ness,** *n.*

down·hill (doun′hil′) *adv.* down the slope of a hill; downward. —*adj.* 1 sloping downward. 2 worse.

Down·ing Street (doun′ing) 1 in London, a street where several important offices of the British government are located, including the official residence (at No. 10) of the Prime Minister. 2 the British government.

down payment in instalment buying, a deposit or initial payment made at the time of a purchase.

down·pour (doun′pôr′) *n.* a heavy rainfall.

down·right (doun′rīt′) *adj.* 1 thorough; complete: *a downright thief, a downright lie.* 2 plain; positive: *His downright answer left no doubt as to what he thought.* 3 plain and direct in speech or behavior: *a downright person.*
—*adv.* 1 thoroughly; completely: *He was downright rude to me.* 2 plainly; definitely. **—down′right′ly,** *adv.* **—down′right′ness,** *n.*

down·stage (doun′stāj′) *adj. adv.* in a theatre, toward or at the front of the stage.

down·stairs (doun′stãrz′) *adv.* 1 down the stairs. 2 on a lower floor. 3 to a lower floor: *I went downstairs for breakfast.*
—*adj.* on a lower floor.
—*n.* the lower floor or floors.

down·stream (doun′strēm′) *adv. adj.* with the current of a stream; down a stream.

down-to-earth (doun′tə ėrth′) *adj.* practical; realistic: *He would rather have down-to-earth planning than visionary theories.*

down·town (doun′toun′) *adv. adj.* 1 to, toward, or in the lower part of a town. 2 to or in the main part or business section of a town: *His office is in downtown Toronto. The traffic downtown gets heavier every day.*
—*n.* the business section or main part of a town.

down·trod (doun′trod′) *adj.* downtrodden.

down·trod·den (doun′trod′ən) *adj.* 1 tyrannized over; oppressed. 2 trodden down.

down under the region of Australia, New Zealand, etc. [with reference to the antipodes, in relation to the British Isles]

down·ward (doun′wərd) *adv. adj.* 1 toward a lower place or condition. 2 toward a later time.
—down′ward·ly, *adv.* **—down′ward·ness,** *n.*

down·wards (doun′wərdz) *adv* . downward.

down·y (doun′ē) *adj.* **down·i·er, down·i·est.** 1 of soft feathers or hair. 2 covered with soft feathers or hair. 3 like down; soft; fluffy. **—down′i·ly,** *adv.* **—down′i·ness,** *n.*

dow·ry (dou′rē) *n.* **-ries.** 1 the money, property, etc. that a bride brings to her husband. 2 a natural gift, talent, or quality; endowment from nature: *Good health and intelligence make a useful dowry.* Also, **dower.** [ME < AF *dowarie* < OF *douaire.* See DOWER.]

dowse (douz) *v.* **dowsed, dows·ing.** use a divining rod to locate water, minerals, etc. **—dows′er,** *n.*

dox·ol·o·gy (doks ol′ə jē) *n.* **-gies.** a hymn or statement praising God. One of the best-known doxologies begins: "Glory to God in the highest." [< Med.L < Gk. *doxologia* < *doxologos* < *doxa* glory, praise + *logos* speaking]

dox·y[1] (dok′sē) *n. Informal.* a doctrine or belief. [abstracted from *orthodoxy, heterodoxy,* etc.]

dox·y[2] (dok′sē) *n. Slang.* a prostitute or mistress. [origin uncertain]

doy·en (doi′ən or dwä′yən; *French,* dwä yaɴ′) *n.* the senior member of a group. [< F *doyen* dean < OF *deien.* See DEAN.]

doy·ley (doi′lē) *n.* **-lies.** doily.

doy·ly (doi′lē) *n.* **-lies.** doily.

doz. dozen; dozens.

doze (dōz) *v.* **dozed, doz·ing,** *n.* —*v.* 1 sleep lightly; be half asleep: *After supper, my father dozes in his chair.* 2 **doze off,** fall into a doze. —*n.* a light sleep; a nap. [< Scand.; cf. Danish *döse* make dull] **—doz′er,** *n.*

doz·en (duz′ən) *n.* **-ens** or (*after a number*) **-en.** a group of 12. [ME < OF *dozeine* < *douse* twelve < L *duodecim*]

doz·enth (duz′ənth) *adj.* the twelfth.

hat, āge, cãre, fär; let, ēqual, tėrm; it, īce
hot, ōpen, ôrder; oil, out; cup, pu̇t, rüle, ūse
əbove, takən, pencəl, lemən, circəs
ch, child; ng, long; sh, ship
th, thin; ᴛʜ, then; zh, measure

doz·er (dō′zər) *n. Informal.* bulldozer.

doz·y (dō′zē) *adj.* **doz·i·er, doz·i·est.** drowsy; sleepy. **—doz′i·ly,** *adv.* **—doz′i·ness,** *n.*

DP or **D.P.** displaced person.

D. Paed. Doctor of Paedagogy. (for L *Doctor Paedagogiae*)

D. Péd. Docteur de Pédagogie.

DPH Department of Public Health.

D.P.H. Diploma of Public Health.

D.Phil. Doctor of Philosophy.

dpt. 1 department. 2 deponent.

dr. 1 dram; drams. 2 debtor. 3 drawer. 4 debit.

Dr. or **Dr** 1 Doctor. 2 Drive.

drab[1] (drab) *adj.* **drab·ber, drab·best,** *n.* —*adj.* 1 dull; monotonous; unattractive: *the drab houses of the mining town.* 2 dull brownish-gray. —*n.* 1 a dull, brownish gray. 2 a khaki drill uniform: *the soldiers wore drab on manoeuvres.* [apparently var. of *drap* cloth < F. See DRAPE.] **—drab′ly,** *adv.* **—drab′ness,** *n.*

drab[2] (drab) *n.* 1 a dirty, untidy woman. 2 a prostitute. [cf. Irish *drabóg* slattern]

drachm (dram) *n.* dram.

drach·ma (drak′mə) *n.* 1 a unit of money in Greece. See table at **money.** 2 a coin worth one drachma. 3 in ancient times: **a** a Greek silver coin varying in value. **b** a small Greek weight. [< L *drachma* < Gk. *drachmē* handful]

Dra·co (drā′kō) *n.* a northern constellation, a part of which forms a semicircle around the Little Dipper. [< L *Draco* dragon]

drae·ger·man (drag′ər mən or drā′gər-) *n.* **-men** (-mən). a mine-rescue worker who wears special oxygen equipment developed in Germany. [< Alexander B. *Dräger,* 1870-1928, a German scientist who devised the special equipment used by these men + *man*]

draft (draft) *n.* 1 a current of air. 2 a device for regulating a current of air: *When I opened the draft of the furnace the fire burned faster.* 3 a plan; a sketch. 4 a rough copy: *He made three different drafts of his speech before he had it in final form.* 5 a selection of persons for some special purpose: *The United States government supplied men to the army and navy by draft.* 6 the persons selected for some special purpose. 7 the act of pulling loads. 8 the quantity pulled. 9 Usually, **draught. a** the pulling in of a net to catch fish. **b** the quantity of fish caught in a net at one time. 10 a written order from one person or bank to another, requiring the payment of a stated amount of money. 11 a heavy demand or drain on anything: *Her long illness was a draft on her resources.* 12 Usually, **draught.** the depth of water that a ship needs for floating; depth to which a ship sinks in water. 13 Usually, **draught. a** the act of drinking: *He emptied the glass at one draught.* **b** the amount taken in one drink. **c** the breathing in of air, smoke, etc. **d** the air, smoke, etc. breathed in. **e** the drawing of beer, ale, etc. from a barrel when ordered. Beer is sold on draught and in bottles. 14 the area of an opening for a flow of water, as in a sluice gate.
—*v.* 1 make a plan or sketch of. 2 write out a rough copy of. 3 select for some special purpose; especially, conscript persons for military service. 4 draw off or away.
—*adj.* 1 for pulling loads: *A big, strong horse or ox is a draft animal.* 2 drawn from a barrel when ordered: *draught beer.* [var. of *draught*] **—draft′er,** *n.* ☛ See **draught** for usage note.

draft·ee (draf tē′) *n. U.S.* a person who is drafted for military service.

drafts·man (drafts′mən) *n.* **-men** (-mən). 1 a person who makes plans or sketches. A draftsman draws designs or diagrams from which buildings and machines are made. 2 a person who writes out rough copies of documents, speeches, etc. **3** a person who draws up legal or official documents. Also, **draughtsman.** See **draught** for usage note.

drafts·man·ship (drafts′mən ship′) *n.* the work of a draftsman. Also, **draughtsmanship.**

draft·y (draf′tē) *adj.* **draft·i·er, draft·i·est. 1** in a current of air. **2** having many currents of air. **3** causing a current of air. Also, **draughty. —draft′i·ly,** *adv.* **—draft′i·ness,** *n.*

drag (drag) *v.* **dragged, drag·ging,** *n.* —*v.* **1** pull or move along heavily or slowly; pull or draw along the ground: *A team of horses dragged the big log out of the forest.* **2** go too slowly: *Time drags when you have nothing to do.* **3** pull a net, hook, harrow, etc. over or along for some purpose: *drag a lake for fish or for a drowned person's body.* **4** use a drag. **5** *Slang.* take part in a drag race. **6 drag in,** bring (something irrelevant) into a discussion: *Whatever we talk about, you drag in stamp-collecting.* **7 drag on** or **out, a** make or be too slow. **b** make or last too long. **8 drag one's feet,** *U.S. Informal.* work slowly on purpose.
—*n.* **1** a net, hook, etc. used in dragging. **2** the act of dragging. **3** anything dragged. **4** anything that holds back; obstruction; hindrance: *Some old ideas and ways are a drag on progress.* **5** a low, strong sled for carrying heavy loads. **6** a big coach with seats inside and on top. **7** a heavy harrow or other implement drawn over land to level it and break up clods. **8** a device for slowing down the rotation of the wheels of a vehicle. **9** the force acting on a body in motion through a fluid in a direction opposite to the body's motion and produced by friction. **10** in hunting: **a** an animal's trail or scent. **b** an artificial scent dragged on the ground to leave a trail for hounds. **c** a drag hunt. **11** in fishing: **a** a brake to prevent excessive spin in a reel. **b** a pull on a line caused by a water current. **12** a drift anchor. **13** *Slang.* influence. **14** *Slang.* a pull or suck; a smoke: *a drag on a cigarette.* **15** *Slang.* a street: *the main drag.* [ME < ON *draga,* if not a dial. var. of *draw,* OE *dragan*] **—Syn.** *v.* **1** haul, tug, trail. See **draw.** *–n.* **4** impediment.

drag·ger (drag′ər) *n.* **1** a person or thing that drags. **2** a boat used in fishing; trawler.

drag·gle (drag′əl) *v.* **-gled, -gling. 1** make or become wet or dirty by dragging through mud, water, dust, etc. **2** follow slowly; lag behind; straggle.

drag·hound (drag′hound′) *n.* a hound trained to follow an artificial scent or drag.

drag hunt a hunt using an artificial scent or drag.

drag·line (drag′līn′) *n.* **1** a rope dragging from something, such as the guide line on a dirigible. **2** an excavating or dredging machine having an endless belt of scoops or buckets that are drawn towards the machine in the digging operation. **3** a rope for pulling anything.

drag·net (drag′net′) *n.* **1** a net pulled over the bottom of a river, pond, etc. or along the ground: *Fish and small birds can be caught in a dragnet.* **2** a means of catching or gathering in: *Twenty of the criminals were caught in the police dragnet.*

drag·o·man (drag′ə mən) *n.* **-mans** or **-men** (-mən). in the Near East, an interpreter. [< F < Med.Gk. *dragomanos* < Arabic *targumān*]

drag·on (drag′ən) *n.* **1** in legend, a huge, fierce animal supposed to look like a snake but equipped with wings and claws. Dragons breathe out fire and smoke. **2** a fierce, violent person. **3** a very strict and watchful woman; a stern chaperon. **4** a lizard with winglike membranes. [ME < OF < L *draco* < Gk. *drakōn*] **—drag′on-like′,** *adj.*

drag·on·fly (drag′ən flī′) *n.* **-flies.** a large, harmless insect, having a long, slender body and two pairs of gauzy wings. It darts about, catching flies and other insects.

drag·on·nade (drag′ə nād′) *n.* **1** the persecution of the French Protestants by the troops of Louis XIV. **2** any persecution by soldiers. [< F *dragonnade* < *dragon.* See DRAGOON.]

dra·goon (drə gün′) *n.* a heavily armed cavalry soldier. Dragoons formerly rode horses to the battlefield, but sometimes fought on foot. Most dragoon regiments are now equipped with tanks or other armored vehicles. —*v.* **1** oppress or persecute by dragoons. **2** compel by oppression or persecution: *He was dragooned into signing a false statement.* [< F *dragon* dragon, pistol, (later) soldier]

drag race a race between cars, usually hot rods, to see which has the fastest acceleration.

drag·ster (drag′stər) *n. Slang.* a car used in a drag race.

drag strip a straight stretch of asphalt or concrete road set aside or built for drag races.

drain (drān) *v.* **1** draw off or flow off slowly: *That ditch drains water from the swamp. The water drains into a river.* **2** draw water or other liquid from; empty or dry by draining: *The farmers drained the swamps to get more land for crops.* **3** dry; lose moisture by dripping or flowing: *I left the umbrella outside to drain.* **4** take away from slowly; use up little by little; deprive: *The war drained the country of its manpower and money.* **5** empty by drinking; drink dry: *He drained his glass.*
—*n.* **1** a channel or pipe for carrying off water or other liquid. **2** anything that drains: *The student nurse learned to use strips of gauze as drains to take the pus from wounds.* **3** a slow taking away; a using up little by little: *Working or playing too hard is a drain on a person's strength.* **4 down the drain,** to nothing: *His savings went down the drain on a bad investment.* [OE *drēahnian.* Related to DRY.] **—Syn.** *v.* **4** exhaust.

drain·age (drān′ij) *n.* **1** the act or process of draining; a gradual flowing off. **2** a system of channels or pipes for carrying off water or waste of any kind. **3** what is drained off. **4** the area that is drained.

drainage basin the area that is drained by a river and its tributaries.

drain·board (drān′bôrd′) *n.* **1** a board set at a downward angle into one side of a sink for draining off the water from washed dishes. **2** a rubber mat or tray used for the same purpose.

drain·er (drān′ər) *n.* **1** a person who makes channels or lays pipes for draining land. **2** a pan, vat, etc. for draining off liquid.

drain·pipe (drān′pīp′) *n.* a pipe for carrying off water or other liquid.

drake (drāk) *n.* a male duck. [OE *draca* < L *draco.* Doublet of DRAGON.]

dram[1] (dram) *n.* **1** a small weight. In apothecaries' weight, 8 drams make one ounce; in avoirdupois weight, 16 drams make one ounce. **2** a fluid dram. **3** a small drink of intoxicating liquor. **4** a small amount of anything. Also, *Brit.* **drachm.** [ME < OF *drame* < L *drachma.* Doublet of DRACHMA.]

dram[2] (dram) *n. Cdn.* formerly, in lumbering, a section of a timber raft, made up of several cribs lashed together. [origin uncertain]

dra·ma (dram′ə or drä′mə) *n.* **1** a story written to be acted out by actors on a stage; a play such as one sees in a theatre. **2** a series of happenings that seem like those of a play: *The history of the world is a great and thrilling drama.* **3** the art of writing, acting, or producing plays; the branch of literature having to do with plays: *He is studying drama.* [< LL < Gk. *drama* play, deed < *draein* do]

Dram·a·mine (dram′ə mēn′) *n. Trademark.* a drug used against seasickness, airsickness, etc. It is also useful against hives.

dra·ma·tic (drə mat′ik) *adj.* **1** of drama; having to do with plays. **2** seeming like a drama or play; full of action or feeling; exciting: *The hostess made a dramatic entrance into the room.* **—dra·mat′i·cal·ly,** *adv.*
Syn. 2 Dramatic, theatrical, melodramatic, as applied to situations in real life, mean "having qualities suitable to plays or the stage." **Dramatic** emphasizes genuineness, and suggests exciting the imagination as well as deeply moving the feelings: *The reunion of the veterans with their wives was dramatic.* **Theatrical** emphasizes show and unreality, and suggests artificial or cheap effects and calling directly on the feelings: *Her show of gratitude was theatrical.* **Melodramatic** emphasizes falseness and exaggeration, especially in trying to stir up the feelings: *The paper gave a melodramatic account of the child's murder.*

dra·mat·ics (drə mat′iks) *n.* **1** the art of acting or producing plays. **2** plays given by amateurs. **3** *Informal.* dramatic behavior; tendency to show off.

☞ **Dramatics,** meaning "the art of acting or producing plays," is singular in use: *Dramatics is taught in some colleges.* When *dramatics* means "plays given by amateurs," it is plural in use: *Dramatics are presented in many theatres in the summer.*

dram·a·tis per·so·nae (dram′ə tis pər sō′ nē or pər sō′ nī) the characters or actors in a play. [< L]

dram·a·tist (dram′ə tist) *n.* a writer of plays; playwright.

dram·a·ti·za·tion (dram′ə tə zā′ shən or dram′ə tī zā′ shən) *n.* **1** the act of dramatizing. **2** what is dramatized.

dram·a·tize (dram′ə tīz′) *v.* **-tized, -tiz·ing. 1** make a drama of; arrange in the form of a play: *dramatize a novel.* **2** show or express in a dramatic way; make exciting and thrilling. —**dram′a·tiz′er,** *n.*

dram·a·tur·gic (dram′ə tėr′jik) *adj.* having to do with dramaturgy. —**dram′a·tur′gi·cal·ly,** *adv.*

dram·a·tur·gy (dram′ə tėr′jē) *n.* the art of writing or producing dramas. [< Gk. *dramatourgia* < *drama* drama + *-ourgos* making < *ergon* work]

drank (drangk) *v.* pt. and a pp. of **drink.**

drape (drāp) *v.* **draped, drap·ing,** *n.* —*v.* **1** cover or hang with cloth falling loosely in graceful folds: *The buildings were draped with red, white, and blue bunting.* **2** arrange (clothes, hangings, etc.) in graceful folds: *The designer draped the robe around the model's shoulders.* —*n.* **drapes,** large curtains that are made to hang in folds; draperies: *There are drapes on the large windows in the living room.* [ME < OF *draper* < *drap* cloth < LL *drappus*]

drap·er (drāp′ər) *n.* **1** a person that drapes. **2** *Esp.Brit.* a dealer in cloth or dry goods.

drap·er·y (drā′ pər ē or drāp′ rē) *n.* **-per·ies. 1** clothing or hangings arranged in graceful folds. **2** the graceful arrangement of hangings or clothing. **3** cloth or fabric. **4** the business of a draper.

dras·tic (dras′tik) *adj.* acting with force or violence; extreme: *The police took drastic measures to put a stop to the crime wave.* [< Gk. *drastikos* effective < *draein* do] —**dras′ti·cal·ly,** *adv.*

draught (draft) *n. v. adj.* draft. [ME *draht* < OE *dragan* draw] —**draught′er,** *n.*

☞ **draft, draught.** The spelling of *draught* has gradually come to represent its pronunciation (draft). In Canadian usage, *draft* is usually the spelling for a *bank draft,* a *draft of a composition,* a *draft of air. Draught* is more common for a *ship's draught,* a *draught of fish,* and for a *draught of ale* or *beer on draught* —though *draft* is rapidly gaining in all these senses. Usage is divided on the word in the sense of a maker of drawings —*draftsman* or *draughtsman.*

draughts (drafts) *n.pl. Brit.* the game of checkers.

draughts·man (drafts′mən) *n.* **-men** (-mən). draftsman.

draughts·man·ship (drafts′mən ship′) *n.* draftsmanship.

draughty (draf′tē) *adj.* **draught·i·er, draught·i·est.** drafty.

drave (drāv) *v. Archaic.* a pt. of **drive.**

Dra·vid·i·an (drə vid′ē ən) *adj.* of or having to do with the non-Aryan peoples in S. India and in Ceylon. —*n.* **1** a member of any of these peoples. **2** their languages.

draw (dro or drô) *v.* **drew, drawn, draw·ing,** *n.* —*v.* **1** pull; drag: *The horse drew the wagon.* **2** pull out; pull up; pull back: *He drew the cork from the bottle.* **3** bring out; take out; get out: *Draw a pail of water from the well.* **4** take out a pistol, sword, etc. for action. **5** take; get; receive: *I drew another idea from the story.* **6** make; cause; bring: *Your actions draw praise or blame on yourself.* **7** move; come; go: *We drew near the fire to get warm.* **8** attract: *The Canadian National Exhibition draws huge crowds.* **9** make a picture or likeness of with pencil, pen, chalk, crayon, etc.; represent by lines. **10** make pictures or likenesses with pen, pencil, chalk, crayon, etc.; make drawings: *He draws very well for a six-year-old.* **11** mark out; distinguish: *He cannot draw the line between a loan and a gift.* **12** describe; depict: *The characters in this novel are not fully drawn; they seem unreal.* **13** write out in proper form; frame; draft: *draw up a deed.* **14** write (an order to pay money). **15** make a demand; be a drain: *Poor health may draw on one's income.* **16** make a current of air to carry off smoke: *A chimney draws.* **17** breathe in; inhale; take in. **18** utter: *draw a sigh.* **19** make the same score in (a game); finish with neither side winning. **20** make or become longer; stretch: *The men drew the rope taut.* **21** make or become smaller; shrink. **22** (of a ship) sink to a specified depth in floating: *A ship draws more water when it is loaded than when it is empty.* **23** take out the insides of; eviscerate: *The cook drew the chicken before cooking it.* **24** make (tea) by extracting the essence. **25** draw lots. **26** draw by lot; get by chance. **27** empty; drain: *draw a lake.* **28** in curling, slide a stone so that it comes to rest within the target area without hitting another stone. **29 draw on,** come near; approach. **30 draw oneself up,** stand up straight. **31 draw out, a** make or become longer; stretch. **b** persuade to talk. **32 draw up, a** arrange in order. **b** write out. **c** stop.
—*n.* **1** the act of drawing. **2** anything that attracts. **3** a tie in a game: *If neither side wins, it is a draw.* **4** a lottery; a drawing of lots. **5** the lot drawn. **6** a part of a drawbridge that can be moved. **7** a small land basin into or through which water drains; valley: *The rancher found his strayed cattle grazing in a draw.* **8** in curling, a shot in which the stone comes to rest within the target area without hitting another stone. [OE *dragan*]

Syn. *v.* **1 Draw, drag, haul** = pull. **Draw** suggests smoothness or ease of movement: *He drew a chair to the table.* **Drag** suggests resistance and means to pull with force, sometimes slowly: *He dragged the piano across the room.* **Haul** suggests pulling or dragging something very heavy, slowly and with great effort, now often in a heavy vehicle: *Two engines are needed to haul trains over the mountains.* **3** extract. **5** obtain, derive, infer. **8** entice, allure. **9** trace, sketch, depict. **13** formulate. **20** lengthen, prolong.

draw·back (dro′bak′ or drô′-) *n.* **1** something unfavorable or unpleasant; something that lessens satisfaction or success; a disadvantage; hindrance: *Our trip was interesting, but the rainy weather was a drawback.* **2** the money paid back from a charge made: *A drawback is made on customs duties on imported goods when they are later exported.*

draw·bridge (dro′brij′ or drô′-) *n.* a bridge that can be wholly or partly lifted, lowered, or moved to one side. In old castles drawbridges were lifted to keep out enemies. A drawbridge over a river is lifted to let boats pass.

draw·ee (dro ē′ or drô ē′) *n.* a person for whom an order to pay money is written.

draw·er[1] (dro′ər or drô′ər) *n.* **1** a person or thing that draws. **2** a person who writes an order to pay money.

draw·er[2] (drôr) *n.* a box built to slide in and out of a table, dresser, desk, etc.: *He kept his shirts in the dresser drawer.*

drawers (drôrz) *n.pl.* long undergarments fitting over the legs and around the waist.

draw·ing (dro′ing or drô′-) *n.* **1** a picture or likeness made with pencil, pen, chalk, crayon, etc.; lines representing a person or thing. **2** the making of such pictures or likenesses; the act of representing objects by lines.

drawing knife drawknife.

drawing room 1 a room for receiving or entertaining guests; parlor. **2** the guests assembled in a drawing room. **3** a private compartment in a Pullman car. **4** a formal reception. [for *withdrawing room*]

draw·knife (dro′nīf′or drô′-) *n.* **-knives.** a blade with a handle at each end, used to shave off surfaces. The workman pulls a drawknife toward him. Also, **drawshave.**

A man using a drawknife

drawl (drol or drôl) *v.* talk in a slow, lazy way. —*n.* a slow, lazy way of talking. [apparently related to *draw*] —**drawl′er,** *n.* —**drawl′ing·ly,** *adv.*

draw·mas·ter (dro′mas′tər or drô′-) *n.* in curling, the official in charge of organizing

hat, āge, cãre, fär; let, ēqual, tėrm; it, īce
hot, ōpen, ôrder; oil, out; cup, pu̇t, rüle, ūse
əbove, takən, pencəl, lemən, circəs
ch, child; ng, long; sh, ship
th, thin; ᴛʜ, then; zh, measure

a bonspiel, drawing teams, arranging schedules of play, etc.

drawn (dron or drôn) *v.* pp. of **draw.**

drawn work ornamental work done by drawing threads from a fabric, the remaining portions usually being formed into patterns by needlework.

draw·shave (dro′shāv′ or drô′-) *n.* drawknife.

draw·string (dro′string′ or drô′-) *n.* a cord, ribbon, or string running through a hem, eyeholes, etc. so that it can be drawn tight: *a hood with a drawstring, a drawstring at the top of a duffel bag.*

dray (drā) *n.* a low, strong cart for hauling heavy loads. —*v.* transport or carry on a cart. [OE *dræge* dragnet < *dragan* draw]

dray·age (drā′ij) *n.* **1** the act of hauling a load on a dray. **2** a charge for hauling a load on a dray.

dray·man (drā′mən) *n.* **-men** (-mən). a man who drives a dray.

DRB or **D.R.B.** Defence Research Board.

dread (dred) *v.* **1** look forward to with fear; fear greatly: *We dread visits to the dentist. My cat dreads water.* **2** regard with awe. **3** feel great fear.
—*n.* **1** fear; especially, fear of something that will or may happen. **2** a person or thing inspiring fear.
—*adj.* **1** dreaded; dreadful. **2** held in awe; awe-inspiring. [OE *drædan*] —**Syn.** *v.* apprehend. -*n.* **1** See **fear.**

dread·ful (dred′fəl) *adj.* **1** causing dread; fearful; terrible; awe-inspiring. **2** *Informal.* very bad; very unpleasant: *I have a dreadful cold.* —**dread′ful·ness**, *n.* —**Syn. 1** dire.

dread·ful·ly (dred′fəl ē) *adv.* **1** in a dreadful manner. **2** very; exceedingly.

dread·nought or **dread·naught** (dred′not′ or -nôt′) *n.* a big, powerful battleship with heavy armor and large guns. [< *Dreadnought*, the first such ship, built in 1906]

dream (drēm) *n. v.* **dreamed** or **dreamt, dream·ing.** —*n.* **1** something thought, felt, seen, or heard during sleep. **2** something as unreal as a dream. **3** the state in which a person has dreams. **4** something having great beauty or charm. **5** a daydream; reverie.
—*v.* **1** have dreams. **2** see in a dream. **3** think of (something) as possible; suppose in a vague way; imagine. **4** have daydreams. **5** spend in dreaming. **6 dream up,** *Informal.* create (an invention, etc.) mentally. [OE *drēam* joy, music; meaning influenced by ON *draumr* dream] —**dream′less**, *adj.* —**dream′like′**, *adj.* —**Syn.** *n.* **2** vision, fantasy.

dream·boat (drēm′bōt′) *n. Slang.* **1** a very imaginative invention, idea, etc.: *Today's commonplaces are often yesterday's dreamboats.* **2** a very attractive person.

dream·er (drēm′ər) *n.* **1** a person who has dreams. **2** a person whose ideas do not fit real conditions; impractical person.

dream·land (drēm′land′) *n.* **1** a place where a person seems to be when he is dreaming. **2** a beautiful and desirable place. **3** an ideal place existing only in the imagination. **4** sleep.

dreamt (dremt) *v.* a pt. and a pp. of **dream.**

dream·y (drēm′ē) *adj.* **dream·i·er, dream·i·est. 1** full of dreams: *a dreamy sleep.* **2** like a dream; vague; dim: *a dreamy recollection.* **3** fond of thinking about pleasant things that are unreal; impractical: *a dreamy person.* **4** causing dreams; soothing: *dreamy songs.* **5** *Slang.* wonderful; exciting; attractive. —**dream′i·ly**, *adv.* —**dream′i·ness**, *n.*

drear (drēr) *adj. Poetic.* dreary.

drear·y (drēr′ē) *adj.* **drear·i·er, drear·i·est. 1** dull; gloomy; cheerless; depressing. **2** *Archaic.* sad; sorrowful. **3** uninteresting; boring: *We heard a dreary sermon last Sunday.* [OE *drēorig*] —**drear′i·ly**, *adv.* —**drear′i·ness**, *n.* —**Syn. 1** dismal. **3** tedious, tiresome.

dredge[1] (drej) *n. v.* **dredged, dredg·ing.** —*n.* **1** a machine with a scoop, series of buckets, etc. for removing mud, sand, or other materials from the bottom of a river, harbor, etc. **2** an apparatus with a net, used for gathering oysters, etc. It is dragged along the bottom of the sea.
—*v.* **1** clean out or deepen (a channel, harbor, etc.) with a dredge; use a dredge. **2** bring up or gather with a dredge. **3** dig up; gather: *The lawyer dredged up all the facts he could find to support his case.* [ME *dreg.* Related to DRAG.] —**dredg′er**, *n.*

dredge[2] (drej) *v.* **dredged, dredg·ing.** sprinkle: *dredge meat with flour.* [apparently < *dredge*, n., grain mixture < OF *dragie* < L < Gk. *tragēmata* spices] —**dredg′er**, *n.*

dregs (dregz) *n.pl.* **1** the solid bits of matter that settle to the bottom of a liquid: *After pouring the tea, she rinsed the dregs out of the teapot.* **2** the most worthless part: *Thieves and murderers are the dregs of humanity.* [ME < Scand.; cf. Icel. *dreggjar*]

drench (drench) *v.* **1** wet thoroughly; soak: *A heavy rain drenched the campers, and they had to dry out their clothing.* **2** cause to drink; compel (an animal) to swallow a medicine: *drench a cow.*
—*n.* **1** a thorough wetting; a soaking. **2** something that drenches; a solution for soaking. **3** a draft of medicine given to an animal. [OE *drencan* < *drincan* drink] —**drench′er**, *n.* —**drench′ing·ly**, *adv.* —**Syn.** *v.* See **wet.**

Dresden (drez′dən) *n.* **1** a kind of fine porcelain, noted for its delicacy of design. **2** something made of this porcelain. [< *Dresden*, a city in East Germany, near which this ware was originally made]

dress (dres) *n. adj. v.* **dressed** or **drest, dress·ing.**
—*n.* **1** an outer garment worn by women, girls, and babies. **2** an outer covering. **3** clothes. **4** formal clothes. [< *v.*]
—*adj.* **1** of or for a dress. **2** of formal dress; characterized by formal dress. [< v.]
—*v.* **1** put clothes on. **2** wear clothes properly and attractively: *Some girls don't know how to dress.* **3** put formal clothes on. **4** decorate; trim; adorn: *The store windows were dressed for Christmas.* **5** make ready for use; prepare: *The butcher dressed the chickens by pulling out the feathers, cutting off the head and feet, and taking out the insides.* **6** care for and arrange (hair): *Mother has her hair dressed each week.* **7** put a medicine, bandage, etc. on (a wound or sore): *The nurse dressed the wound every day.* **8** form in a straight line: *The captain ordered the soldiers to dress their ranks.* **9** smooth; finish: *dress leather.* **10 dress down,** *Informal.* **a** scold; rebuke. **b** beat; thrash. **11 dress up, a** put on one's best clothes. **b** put on formal clothes. [ME < OF *dresser* arrange, ult. < L *directus* straight. See DIRECT.]
Syn. *n.* **1** frock, gown. **3 Dress, apparel, attire** = clothing. **Dress** is the general word for outer clothing, dresses and suits, etc.: *I can't go camping without the proper dress.* **Apparel,** more formal and impersonal, applies to outer clothing for men, women, or children: *You can't buy underwear in that store; it carries only apparel.* **Attire,** rather formal, emphasizes the general impression made by clothes: *We need neat, not fine, attire.* -*v.* **1** attire, garb. See **clothe.**

dres·sage (dres′ij; *French*, dre säzh′) *n.* the process of guiding a horse without reins through various manoeuvres, the riding using barely perceptible signals of leg pressure, body weight, etc. [< F]

dress coat a man's coat with an open front and two long tails, worn on formal occasions, especially in the evening.

dress·er[1] (dres′ər) *n.* **1** a person who dresses (himself, another person, a shop window, or a wound). **2** a person who dresses properly and attractively. **3** an implement or machine to prepare things for use. [< *dress*]

dress·er[2] (dres′ər) *n.* **1** a piece of furniture with drawers for clothes and a mirror; bureau. **2** a piece of furniture with shelves for dishes. **3** a table on which to get food ready for serving. [ME < OF. See DRESS.]

dress·ing (dres′ing) *n.* **1** what is put on or in something to prepare it for use. **2** a sauce for salads, fish, meat, etc. **3** a stuffing of bread crumbs, seasoning, etc. for roast chicken, turkey, etc. **4** the medicine, bandage, etc. put on a wound or sore. **5** a fertilizer. **6** formation: *The soldiers are noted for their dressing on parade.* **7** preparations before and during getting dressed: *She took care with her dressing before the dance.* **8** preparation for display: *the dressing of a store window.*

dress·ing-down (dres′ing doun′) *n. Informal.* **1** a scolding; rebuke. **2** a beating; a thrashing.

dressing gown a loose robe worn while dressing or resting.

hat, āge, cãre, fär; let, ēqual, tėrm; it, īce
hot, ōpen, ôrder; oil, out; cup, pu̇t, rüle, ūse
əbove, takən, pencəl, lemən, circəs
ch, child; ng, long; sh, ship
th, thin; ᴛʜ, then; zh, measure

dressing table a table with a mirror.

dress·mak·er (dres′māk′ər) *n.* a person whose work is making dresses, etc. *—adj.* of women's clothing, having delicate or flowing lines and decoration: *a dressmaker suit.*

dress·mak·ing (dres′māk′ing) *n.* the act or occupation of making dresses, etc.

dress parade a formal parade of servicemen in dress uniform.

dress rehearsal a rehearsal of a play with costumes and scenery just as for a regular performance.

dress suit a suit worn by men on formal occasions, especially in the evening.

dress·y (dres′ē) *adj.* **dress·i·er, dress·i·est.** *Informal.* **1** fond of wearing showy clothes. **2** stylish; fashionable. **—dress′i·ness,** *n.*

drest (drest) *v.* a pt. and a pp. of **dress.**

drew (drü) *v.* pt. of **draw.**

drib·ble (drib′əl) *v.* **-bled, -bling,** *n.* *—v.* **1** flow or let flow in drops, small amounts, etc.; trickle: *Gasoline dribbled from the leak in the tank.* **2** let saliva run from the mouth. **3** move (a ball) along by bouncing it or giving it short kicks.
—n. **1** a dropping; dripping; trickle. **2** a very light rain. **3** the act of dribbling a ball. [< *drib,* var. of *drip*] **—drib′bler,** *n.*

drib·let (drib′lit) *n.* a small amount: *He paid off the debt in driblets, a dollar or two a week.*

dried (drīd) *v.* pt. and pp. of **dry.**

dri·er (drī′ər) *adj. comparative of* **dry.** *—n.* **1** a person or thing that dries. **2** a device or machine that removes water by heat, air, etc.; dryer. **3** the substance put in paint, varnish, etc. to make it dry more quickly; dryer.

drift (drift) *v.* **1** carry or be carried along by currents of water or air: *The wind drifted the boat onto rocks. A raft drifts if it is not steered.* **2** move or appear to move aimlessly: *People drifted in and out of the meeting.* **3** go along without knowing or caring where one is going: *Some people have a purpose in life; others just drift.* **4** pass without special intention. **5** move or appear one at a time or in small groups as drift does on a beach: *The students drifted into class.* **6** heap or be heaped up by the wind: *The wind is so strong it's drifting the snow. The snow is drifting badly.* [< n.]
—n. **1** a drifting. **2** the direction of drifting. **3** a tendency; trend. *The drift of opinion was against war.* **4** the direction of thought; meaning: *Explain that again; I did not get the drift of your words.* **5** snow, sand, etc. heaped up by the wind. **6** floating matter driven by currents of water, as a log or a mass of wood. **7** a current of water or air caused by the wind. **8** the sideways movement of an aircraft or ship off its projected course due to cross-currents of air or water. **9** the distance that a ship or aircraft is off its course because of currents. **10** in geology, sand, gravel, rocks, etc. moved from one place and left in another by a river, glacier, etc. **11** an almost horizontal passageway in a mine along a vein of ore, coal, etc. [ME *drift* a driving < OE *drīfan* drive. Related to DRIVE.] **—drift′ing·ly,** *adv.* **—Syn.** *v.* **1** float. *–n.* **4** intent.

drift·age (drif′tij) *n.* **1** a drifting. **2** the distance drifted. **3** what has drifted; material that drifts around in water or is washed up on the shore.

drift·wood (drift′wu̇d′) *n.* wood drifting in the water or washed ashore by water.

drill[1] (dril) *n.* **1** an implement or machine for boring holes. **2** group instruction and training in physical exercises or in marching, handling a rifle, etc. **3** the process of teaching or training by having the learners do a thing over and over again: *The teacher gave the class plenty of drill in arithmetic.* **4** *Informal.* a correct or approved procedure for doing something: *This leaflet gives the drill for putting the machine together.* **5** a snail that bores into and destroys oysters.
—v. **1** bore a hole in; pierce with a drill. **2** teach by having learners do a thing over and over again. **3** be taught or trained in this way. **4** do or cause to do military or physical exercises. [< MDu. *dril* (n.) < *drillen* (v.) bore] **—drill′er,** *n.* **—Syn.** *n.* **3** practice. See **exercise.**

A drill (def. 1). The cutting part, or bit, works like an auger.

drill[2] (dril) *n.* **1** a machine for planting seeds in rows. It makes a small furrow, drops the seed, and then covers the furrow. **2** a small furrow to plant seeds in. **3** a row of planted seeds. *—v.* plant in small furrows. [origin uncertain]

drill[3] (dril) *n.* a strong, twilled cotton or linen cloth, used for overalls, linings, etc. [short for *drilling* < G *Drillich* < L *trilix* of three threads < *tri-* three + *licium* thread]

drill[4] (dril) *n.* a black-faced baboon of W. Africa, smaller than the mandrill. [probably < African name]

drill·ing (dril′ing) *n.* drill[3].

drill·mas·ter (dril′mas′tər) *n.* **1** an instructor who drills soldiers in marching, handling rifles, etc. **2** a person who drills others in anything.

dri·ly (drī′lē) *adv.* dryly.

drink (dringk) *v.* **drank** or (*formerly*) **drunk, drunk.** (*formerly or as pred. adj.*) **drunk·en** or (*sometimes*) **drank, drink·ing,** *n.* *—v.* **1** swallow (liquid). **2** take and hold; absorb: *The dry ground drank up the rain.* **3** drink liquor. **4** drink in honor of. **5** drink liquor to excess. **6 drink in,** take in eagerly with the senses. **7 drink to,** drink in honor of; drink with good wishes for.
—n. **1** any liquid swallowed or to be swallowed. **2** liquor. **3** excessive drinking of liquor. **4** *Slang.* a body of water; ocean, lake, pool, etc. [OE *drincan*] **—drink′less,** *adj.*
Syn. *v.* **1 Drink, sip, imbibe** = swallow a liquid. **Drink** is the general word: *A person or animal must drink water in order to stay alive.* **Sip** = drink little by little in very small quantities: *One should sip, not gulp, very cold or hot liquids.* **Imbibe,** formal, is now for the most part used humorously in the literal sense of drinking; used figuratively, it means "absorb": *His one desire is to imbibe more knowledge.*
☛ **drunk, drank.** Although **drunk** is the usual past participle, many educated North Americans use **drank** in speech: *He's drank several glasses of milk already.* In writing, **drunk** should be used, except perhaps when writing dialogue. **Drank** is now the proper form for the past tense.
☛ See **drunk** for another usage note.

drink·a·ble (drink′ə bəl) *adj.* fit to drink. *—n.* something to drink.

drink·er (dringk′ər) *n.* **1** a person who drinks. **2** a person who drinks liquor often or too much.

drip (drip) *v.* **dripped** or **dript, drip·ping,** *n.* *—v.* **1** fall or let fall in drops. **2** be so wet that drops fall.
—n. **1** a falling in drops. **2** the liquid that falls in drops. **3** a part that projects to keep water off the parts below. **4** *Slang.* a person considered to be objectionable. [OE *dryppan* < *dropa* a drop]

drip-dry (drip′drī′) *adj. v.* **-dried, -dry·ing.** *—adj.* made to be dried by being let drip after washing, then needing little or no ironing: *drip-dry curtains.* *—v.* let drip until dry.

drip·ping (drip′ing) *n.* **1** liquid that has dripped down. **2** the melted fat and juice that drip down from meat while roasting: *Some people like beef dripping spread on bread.*

dripping pan a pan put under roasting meat to catch the dripping.

dript (dript) *v.* a pt. and a pp. of **drip.**

drive (drīv) *v.* **drove** or (*Archaic*) **drave, driv·en, driv·ing,** *n.* *—v.* **1** make go: *Drive the dog away. Drive the nails into the board. Grief drove her insane.* **2** force (into or out of some place, condition, act, etc.): *Hunger drove him to steal.* **3** direct the movement of (an automobile, a horse-drawn vehicle, etc.). **4** go or carry in an automobile, carriage, etc. **5** carry out with vigor; bring about: *drive a bargain.* **6** work hard or compel to work hard. **7** dash or rush with force: *The ship drove on the rocks.* **8** set in motion; supply power for: *The wind drives the windmill.* **9** in mining, excavate horizontally; make a drift. **10** go through an area and herd or direct (game) toward waiting hunters with guns. **11** in sports, hit very hard and fast: *drive a golf ball.* **12** aim; strike. **13** get or

make by drilling, boring, etc.: *drive a well.* **14** move logs in large numbers by a water route such as a river. **15 drive at,** mean; intend. **16 let drive,** aim; strike.
—*n.* **1** a trip in an automobile, carriage, etc. **2** a road to drive on, often a private road from the street to a house. **3** vigor; energy. **4** an impelling force; pressure: *The craving for approval is a strong drive in mankind.* **5** a special effort of a group for some purpose: *The town had a drive to get money for charity.* **6** a very hard, fast hit. **7** a military attack, often a large-scale, forceful attack. **8** a driving. **9** a thing or things driven: *a drive of logs.* **10** a part that drives machinery: *a chain drive.* **11** the special way in which a motor, transmission, etc. generates or controls a vehicle's power or motion: *fluid drive, four-wheel drive.* **12** in mining, a drift; a horizontal or inclined tunnel or passage. **13** the act of floating a great many logs down a river: *Many lumberjacks took part in the spring drive.* **14** a great many logs floating down a river. [OE *drīfan*] —**Syn.** *v.* **2** impel, push.
–*n.* **1** See **ride.**

drive-in (drīv′in′) *n.* a place where customers may make purchases, eat, or attend movies, etc. while seated in their cars.

driv·el (driv′əl) *v.* **-elled** or **-eled, -el·ling** or **-el·ing,** *n.* —*v.* **1** let saliva run from the mouth. **2** flow like saliva running from the mouth. **3** talk or say in a stupid, foolish manner; talk silly nonsense. **4** waste (time, energy, etc.) in a stupid, foolish way.
—*n.* **1** saliva running from the mouth. **2** stupid, foolish talk. [OE *dreflian*]

driv·el·ler or **driv·el·er** (driv′əl ər) *n.* a person who drivels.

driv·en (driv′ən) *v.* pp. of **drive.** —*adj.* carried along and gathered into heaps by the wind; drifted.

driv·er (drīv′ər) *n.* **1** a person or thing that drives. **2** a person who directs the movement of an engine, automobile, horses, etc. **3** a person who makes the people under him work very hard. **4** a golf club with a large wooden head, used in hitting the ball from the tee. **5** a part of a machine, such as a gear or wheel, that transmits motion to another part or parts. —**driv′er·less,** *adj.*

drive·way (drīv′wā′) *n.* **1** a private road. A driveway usually leads from a house to the public street or road. **2** a road, usually one that is lined with trees and lawns.

driz·zle (driz′əl) *v.* **-zled, -zling,** *n.* —*v.* **1** rain in very small drops resembling mist. **2** fall in very small drops; sprinkle with very small drops. **3** shed or let fall in very small drops. —*n.* rain that falls in very small drops. [? < ME *drese* to fall < OE *drēosan*]

driz·zly (driz′lē) *adj.* drizzling.

DRO in elections, deputy returning officer.

dro·gher (drō′gər) *n.* a slow, clumsy sailing boat used in the West Indies. [< F *drogeur* < Du. *drogher* drier, from the drying of fish in these boats]

drogue (drōg) *n.* **1** a device shaped like a large funnel at the end of the hose used to refuel airplanes in flight. The pilot of the plane being refuelled guides the nose of his plane into the drogue. **2** a parachute for decelerating or stabilizing an aircraft while in flight. **3** a type of small sea anchor. [? var. of *drag,* n.]

droit (droit; *French,* drwä) *n.* **1** in law, a right or claim. **2** something to which a person has a right or claim; a due.

droll (drōl) *adj.* amusingly odd; humorously quaint; laughable: *We smiled at the monkey's droll tricks.*
—*n.* a funny person; jester; buffoon. —*v.* joke; jest. [< F *drôle* (originally n.) good fellow < Du. *drol* little fat fellow]

droll·er·y (drōl′ər ē or drōl′rē) *n.* **-er·ies. 1** something odd and amusing; a laughable trick. **2** quaint humor. **3** jesting.

drom·e·dar·y (drom′ə der′ē or drum′ə der′ē) *n.* **-dar·ies.** a swift camel for riding, especially the one-humped Arabian camel. [ME < OF *dromedaire* < LL *dromedarius* < Gk. *dromas, -ados* runner]

drone[1] (drōn) *n. v.* **droned, dron·ing.** —*n.* **1** a male bee, especially a male honeybee. Drones do not sting, gather honey, or help in the upkeep of a hive. **2** a person not willing to work; idler; loafer. **3** a target towed by an airplane. **4** a pilotless aircraft or vessel directed by remote control. —*v.* spend time idly; loaf. [OE *drān*]

drone[2] (drōn) *v.* **droned, dron·ing,** *n.* —*v.* **1** make a deep, continuous, humming sound: *Bees droned among the flowers.* **2** talk or say in a monotonous voice: *drone a prayer.* —*n.* **1** a deep, continuous, humming sound: *the drone of airplane motors.* **2** the bass pipe of a bagpipe. [related to DRONE[1]]

drool (drül) *v.* **1** let saliva run from the mouth as a baby does. **2** *Slang.* talk or say foolishly. —*n.* **1** saliva running from the mouth. **2** *Slang.* foolish talk. [contraction of *drivel*]

droop (drüp) *v.* **1** hang down; bend down. **2** become weak; lose strength and energy. **3** become discouraged or depressed; be sad and gloomy. —*n.* **1** a bending position; the act or condition of hanging down. **2** *Slang.* an anti-social person; a drip. [ME < ON *drúpa*] —**droop′ing·ly,** *adv.* —**droop′y,** *adj.* —**Syn.** *v.* **2** fade, wilt, flag, fail.

drop (drop) *n. v.* **dropped** or **dropt, drop·ping.** —*n.* **1** a small amount of liquid in a roundish shape: *a drop of rain.* **2** a very small amount of liquid: *Drink a drop of this.* **3** a very small amount of anything: *a drop of kindness.* **4** anything roundish like a drop: *Some earrings or pieces of candy are called drops.* **5** a sudden fall. **6** the distance down; length of a fall: *From the top of the cliff to the water is a drop of 200 feet.* **7** something arranged to fall or let fall: *A letter drop is a slot, usually with a hinged cover.* **8** in baseball, a pitch that suddenly dips downward as it reaches the plate. **9** the act of letting bombs, supplies, etc. fall from an airplane. **10 drops,** *pl.* liquid medicine given in drops. **11 at the drop of a hat, a** when a signal is given. **b** at once; willingly. **12 drop in the bucket,** a very small amount compared to the rest. **13 get** or **have the drop on,** *Slang.* **a** point a gun at (a person) before he can point one at you. **b** get or have an advantage over.
—*v.* **1** fall or let fall in drops. **2** fall suddenly; let fall suddenly. **3** fall or cause to fall. **4** fall dead, wounded, or tired out. **5** cause to fall dead; kill. **6** go or make lower; sink. **7** pass into a less active or a worse condition: *She finally dropped off to sleep.* **8** let go; dismiss: *Members who do not pay will be dropped from the club.* **9** leave out; omit: *Drop the "e" in "drive" before adding "ing."* **10** stop; end: *The matter is not important; let it drop.* **11** send (a letter, etc.). **12** come casually or unexpectedly: *Drop over to our house for a visit sometime.* **13** give or express casually: *drop a hint.* **14** go along gently with the current or tide: *The raft dropped down the river.* **15** in cooking, poach (an egg). **16** set down from a ship, automobile, carriage, etc.: *He dropped his passengers at Broadway and Main.* **17 a** in rugger, make (a goal) by a drop kick. **b** in football, drop-kick (a ball). **18** *Slang.* lose: *The team dropped four straight games.* **19 drop in,** come casually or unexpectedly. **20 drop off, a** go away; disappear. **b** go to sleep. **c** become less; fall; sink. **21 drop out,** leave school, a training program, etc. without completing the course. —**drop′like′,** *adj.* [OE *dropa*]

drop cake 1 a small, sweet cake for which the batter is dropped onto a greased pan or into boiling oil. **2** a small, sweet cake baked in a muffin tin as an individual serving.

drop cookie or **cooky** a cookie for which the dough is dropped onto a flat sheet for baking.

drop-forge (drop′fôrj′) *v.* **-forged, -forg·ing.** beat (hot metal) into shape with a very heavy hammer or weight. —**drop′-forg′er,** *n.*

drop-front (drop′frunt′) *adj.* of furniture, having a front that opens out on hinges and lies flat to form a shelf or writing surface: *a drop-front desk.*

drop hammer a very heavy weight lifted by machinery and then dropped on the metal that is to be beaten into shape.

drop kick a kick given to a football just as it touches the ground after being dropped from the hands.

drop-kick (drop′kik′) *v.* give (a football) a drop kick. —**drop′-kick′er,** *n.*

drop leaf a hinged section of the surface of a table. Such a leaf can be folded down when not in use.

drop-leaf (drop′lēf′) *adj.* having a drop leaf: *a drop-leaf dining table.*

hat, āge, cãre, fär; let, ēqual, tėrm; it, īce
hot, ōpen, ôrder; oil, out; cup, pu̇t, rüle, ūse
əbove, takən, pencəl, lemən, circəs
ch, child; ng, long; sh, ship
th, thin; ᴛʜ, then; zh, measure

drop·let (drop′lit) *n.* a tiny drop.

drop light an electric or gas lamp connected with a fixture above by a tube or wire.

drop-off (drop′of′) *n.* **1** a lessening or decline: *a drop-off in sales.* **2** a sudden, sharp slope.

drop-out (drop′out′) *n.* **1** a person who leaves school, a training program, etc. without completing the course. **2** the act or fact of dropping out.

dropped goal in rugger, a goal made by a drop kick.

drop·per (drop′ər) *n.* **1** a person or thing that drops. **2** a small glass tube with a hollow rubber cap at one end and a small opening at the other end from which a liquid can be made to fall in drops.

drop·pings (drop′ingz) *n.pl.* **1** what is dropped. **2** the dung of animals and birds.

drop·si·cal (drop′sə kəl) *adj.* **1** of or like dropsy. **2** having dropsy.

drop·sy (drop′sē) *n.* an abnormal accumulation of watery fluid in certain tissues or cavities of the body. [ME, var. of *hydropsy* < OF *idropisie* < L *hydropisis* < Gk. *hydrōps* < *hydōr* water]

dropt (dropt) *v.* a pt. and a pp. of **drop.**

drosh·ky or **dros·ky** (drosh′kē) *n.* **-kies.** a low, open, four-wheeled Russian carriage. [< Russian *drozhki*, dim. of *drogi* wagon]

dro·soph·i·la (drō sof′ə lə) *n.* **-lae** (-lē′ or -lī′). a small fly whose larvae feed on fruit and decaying plants; fruit fly. [< NL < Gk. *drosos* dew + *philos* loving]

dross (dros) *n.* **1** the waste or scum that comes to the surface of molten metals. **2** waste material; rubbish. [OE *drōs*]

drought (drout) *n.* **1** a long period of dry weather; continued lack of rain. **2** lack of moisture; dryness. **3** *Archaic or dialect.* thirst. [OE *drūgath.* Related to DRY.]

☛ **drought, drouth.** Both forms are in good use, though *drought* is more usual in formal English.

drought·y (drout′ē) *adj.* **1** showing or suffering from drought. **2** dry; lacking moisture. **3** *Archaic or dialect.* thirsty.

drouth (drouth) *n.* drought.

drouth·y (drouth′ē) *adj.* droughty.

drove[1] (drōv) *v.* pt. of **drive.**

drove[2] (drōv) *n.* **1** a group of cattle, sheep, pigs, etc. moving or driven along together; a herd or flock. **2** many people moving along together; a crowd. [OE *drāf*]

dro·ver (drō′vər) *n.* **1** a man who drives cattle, sheep, pigs, etc. to market. **2** a dealer in cattle.

drown (droun) *n.* **1** suffocate under water or other liquid. **2** kill by keeping under water or some other liquid. **3** cover with water; flood. **4** be stronger or louder than; keep from being heard: *The boat's whistle drowned what she was trying to tell us.* **5** get rid of: *He tried to drown his sorrow in drink.* [OE *druncnian.* Related to DRINK.] **—drown′er,** *n.* **—drown′ing·ly,** *adv.*

drowse (drouz) *v.* **drowsed, drows·ing,** *n.* **—***v.* **1** be sleepy; be half asleep: *She drowsed, but she did not quite fall asleep.* **2** make or be inactive or dull, as if asleep. **3** pass (time) in drowsing: *She drowsed the day away.* **—***n.* the state of being half asleep; sleepiness. [OE *drūs(i)an* sink, become slow]

drow·sy (drou′zē) *adj.* **-si·er, -si·est. 1** half asleep; sleepy. **2** causing sleepiness or half sleep; lulling. **3** inactive; lethargic. **—drow′si·ly,** *adv.* **—drow′si·ness,** *n.* **—Syn. 1** See **sleepy.**

drub (drub) *v.* **drubbed, drub·bing. 1** beat with a stick; thrash; whip soundly. **2** in a fight, game, contest, etc. defeat by a large margin. [? < Arabic *daraba* beat] **—drub′ber,** *n.* **—Syn.** *v.* **1** thrash; cudgel.

drudge (druj) *n. v.* **drudged, drudg·ing. —***n.* a person who does hard, tiresome, or disagreeable work. [apparently < v.] **—***v.* do hard, tiresome, or disagreeable work. [ME *drugge(n)*; probably related to OE *drēogan* work, suffer]

drudg·er·y (druj′ər ē or druj′rē) *n.* **-er·ies.** hard, uninteresting, or disagreeable work.

drug (drug) *n. v.* **drugged, drug·ging. —***n.* **1** a substance (other than food) used as a medicine or as a component of a medicine, especially one listed in an official pharmacopoeia. Such a substance increases or retards the activity of the cells, organs, etc. that it affects. **2** a narcotic. **3** something resembling a narcotic in its effect. **4 drug on the market,** an article that is too abundant, is no longer in demand, or has too slow a sale.
—*v.* **1** give drugs to, particularly drugs that cause sleep. **2** put a harmful or poisonous drug in (food or drink). **3** affect or overcome (the body or senses) as if by a drug: *The wine had drugged him. She was drugged by the soothing music.* [ME < MF *drogue* < MLG *droge-fate* dry barrels, with *droge-* wrongly taken as the name of the contents] **—drug′less,** *adj.*

drug·get (drug′it) *n.* **1** a coarse, thick woollen fabric used for rugs. **2** a rug or carpet made of this fabric. **3** a woollen or mixed fabric used for clothing. [< F *droguet*]

drug·gist (drug′ist) *n.* **1** a person who sells drugs, medicines, etc. **2** a person licensed to fill prescriptions; pharmacist.

drug·store (drug′stôr′) *n.* a store where drugs and other medicines are sold. A drugstore often sells soft drinks, cosmetics, magazines, etc. as well as drugs.

Dru·id or **dru·id** (drü′id) *n.* a member of a religious order of priests, prophets, poets, etc. among the ancient Celts of Britain, Ireland, and Gaul where they were powerful as leaders and judges until the advent of the Christian religion. [< F *druide* < L *druidae*, pl. < Gaulish; cf. Old Irish *drui* sorcerer]

Dru·id·ess or **dru·id·ess** (drü′ə dis) *n.* a female Druid; a Druidic prophetess.

Dru·id·ic or **dru·id·ic** (drü id′ik) *adj.* of or having to do with the Druids.

dru·id·i·cal (drü id′ə kəl) *adj.* druidic.

Dru·id·ism (drü′ə diz′əm) *n.* the religion of the Druids, or their beliefs and practices.

drum (drum) *n. v.* **drummed, drum·ming. —***n.* **1** a musical percussion instrument that makes a sound when it is beaten. A drum is hollow with a covering, usually of parchment or leather, stretched tightly over the ends and is played with sticks, brushes, or the hands. **2** the sound made when a drum is beaten; any sound like this. **3** anything shaped like a drum. **4** the part around which something is wound in a machine. **5** a drum-shaped container to hold oil, food, etc. **6** in anatomy and zoology: **a** the membrane covering the hollow part of the ear. **b** the hollow part of the middle ear. **7** in architecture: **a** a circular or polygonal structure upon which a dome is erected. **b** the block of stone making up one section of the shaft of a column. **8** a natural organ by which an animal produces a loud or bass sound. **9 beat the drums for,** *Informal.* support vigorously; promote; advocate.

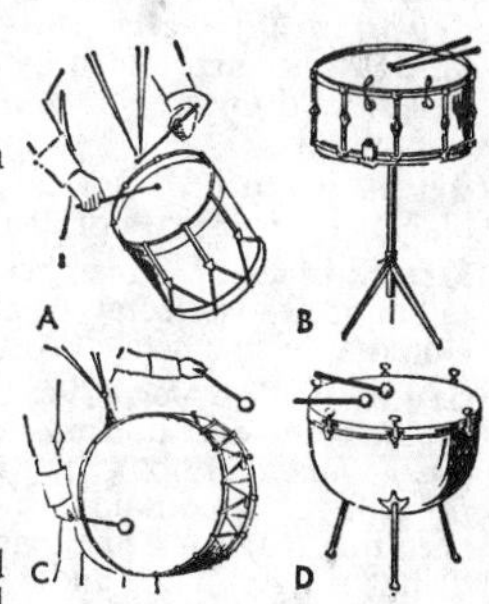

Drums: A, B, side drums; C, bass drum; D, kettledrum or timpano.

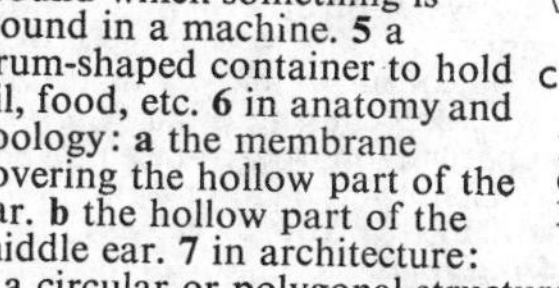

—*v.* **1** beat or play a drum; make a sound like this. **2** beat, tap, or strike again and again: *Stop drumming on the table with your fingers.* **3** force into one's mind by repeating over and over: *His lessons had to be drummed into him because he did not like school.* **4** sound like a drum; resound: *The noise drummed in his ears.* **5** (of birds and insects) make a hollow, reverberating sound, as by quivering the wings: *The gnats drummed around him.* **6** call or summon by or as if by beating a drum. **7 drum out of,** send away from in disgrace. **8 drum up, a** call together. **b** get by asking again and again. [< *drumslade* drummer < Du. or LG *trommelslag* drumbeat] **—drum′like′,** *adj.*

drum·beat (drum′bēt′) *n.* the sound made when a drum is beaten.

drum·fish (drum′fish′) *n.* any of several kinds of large, carnivorous fishes of the Atlantic coast that make a drumming sound.

drum·head (drum′hed′) *n.* the parchment or membrane stretched tightly over the end of a drum.

drumhead court-martial a court-martial on the battlefield or while troops are moving, held in order to try offenders without delay.

drum·lin (drum′lən) *n.* a ridge or oval hill formed by deposit from a glacier. [for *drumling*, dim. of *drum* ridge < Scottish Gaelic and Irish *druim* ridge]

drum major the leader or director of a marching band.

drum ma·jo·rette (mā′jə ret′) a girl who leads parades, twirling a baton.

drum·mer (drum′ər) *n.* **1** a person who plays a drum. **2** *Informal.* a travelling salesman.

drum·stick (drum′stik′) *n.* **1** a stick for beating a drum. **2** the lower half of the leg of a cooked chicken, turkey, or other edible bird.

drunk (drungk) *adj.* **1** overcome by liquor; intoxicated. **2** very much excited or affected: *drunk with power.*
—*n. Slang.* **1** a person who is often drunk; a drunkard. **2** a drinking bout.
—*v.* **1** pp. of **drink. 2** *Archaic.* a pt. of **drink.**
☛ **drunk, drunken.** As an adjective standing before the noun, the form *drunken* is preferred.

drunk·ard (drungk′ərd) *n.* a person who is often drunk; person who drinks too much liquor.

drunk·en (drungk′ən) *adj.* **1** drunk. **2** caused by or resulting from being drunk. **3** often drinking too much liquor. —*v. Archaic.* a pp. of **drink.** —**drunk′en·ly,** *adv.* —**drunk′en·ness,** *n.* —**Syn.** *adj.* **1** intoxicated. ☛ See **drunk** for usage note.

drunk·om·e·ter (drungk om′ ə tər) *n.* an instrument for measuring the alcohol in the blood by analysis of the breath. The person to be tested breathes into the machine.

dru·pa·ceous (drü pā′shəs) *adj.* in botany: **1** like a drupe. **2** producing drupes.

drupe (drüp) *n.* a fruit whose seed is contained in a hard pit or stone surrounded by soft, pulpy flesh. Cherries and olives are drupes. [< NL *drupa* < L < Gk. *dryppa* very ripe olive]

drupe·let (drüp′lit) *n.* a small drupe. A raspberry or blackberry is a mass of drupelets.

Druse (drüz) *n.* a member of a sect in Syria and Lebanon whose secret, basically Moslem religion contains Christian elements. [< Arabic *Durūz*, pl.]

dry (drī) *adj.* **dri·er, dri·est,** *v.* **dried, dry·ing,** *n.* **drys.**
—*adj.* **1** not wet; not moist. **2** having little or no rain: *a dry climate.* **3** not giving milk: *That cow has been dry for a month.* **4** containing no water or other liquid. **5** not shedding tears or accompanied by tears. **6** wanting a drink; thirsty. **7** not under, in, or on water: *dry land.* **8** not liquid; solid: *dry measure.* **9** causing thirst: *Cutting the lawn is dry work.* **10** apparently matter-of-fact but actually ironic: *dry humor.* **11** not interesting; dull. **12** without butter: *dry toast.* **13** free from sweetness or fruity flavor: *dry wine.* **14** *Informal.* having or favoring laws against making and selling alcoholic drinks. **15** abstaining from drinking alcoholic beverages. **16** bald; plain; unadorned: *a list of dry facts.*
—*v.* **1** make or become dry. **2 dry up, a** make or become completely dry. **b** *Slang.* stop talking. **c** of a writer, artist, etc., lose one's creative ability.
—*n. Informal.* a person who favors laws against making and selling alcoholic drinks. [OE *drӯge*] —**dry′ness,** *n.*
Syn. *adj.* **1 Dry, arid** = without moisture. **Dry** is the general word, meaning "not wet or moist," and may or may not mean "completely without moisture": *This bread is dry.* **Arid** = completely dry or dried out, and adds the idea of barrenness, particularly when applied to land: *No crops will grow in this arid soil.* **2** droughty. -*v.* **1** evaporate.

dry·ad or **Dry·ad** (drī′əd or drī′ad) *n.* **-ads, -a·des** (-ə dēz′). in Greek mythology, a nymph that lives in a tree; wood nymph. [< L < Gk. *Dryades*, pl. < *drys* tree]

dry battery 1 a set of dry cells connected to produce electric current. **2** a dry cell.

dry cell an electric cell in which the chemical agent is made into a paste with gelatin, sawdust, etc. so that its contents cannot spill.

dry cereal any breakfast cereal that does not require cooking but is sold ready for eating.

dry-clean (drī′klēn′) *v.* clean (clothes, etc.) with naphtha, benzine, etc. instead of water.

dry cleaner 1 naphtha, benzine, etc. used in dry cleaning. **2** a person or establishment that does dry cleaning.

dry cleaning the cleaning of fabrics without water, using liquids like naphtha, benzine, and carbon tetrachloride.

dry dock a dock built watertight so that the water may be kept high or pumped out. Dry docks are used for building or repairing ships.

dry-dock (drī′dok′) *v.* **1** place in a dry dock. **2** go into dry dock.

dry·er or **dri·er** (drī′ər) *n.* **1** a device or machine that removes water by heat, air, etc. **2** a substance put in paint, varnish, etc. to make it dry more quickly.

dry-farm (drī′färm′) *v.* farm (land) where there is no irrigation and little rain.

dry farmer a person who engages in dry farming.

dry farming in areas that lack irrigation, farming by use of methods that save soil moisture and by raising crops that survive drought.

dry fly an artificial fishing lure made to resemble a fly or other insect floating on the water.

dry goods cloth, ribbon, lace, etc.

Dry Ice *Trademark.* a very cold, white solid formed when carbon dioxide is compressed and then cooled. It is used for cooling because it changes from solid back to gas without becoming liquid.

dry law a law prohibiting the making and selling of alcoholic liquor.

dry·ly or **dri·ly** (drī′lē) *adv.* in a dry manner: *He spoke dryly of his experiences at election time.*

dry measure a system for measuring such things as grain, vegetables, or fruit:

2 pints = 1 quart
8 quarts = 1 peck
4 pecks = 1 bushel

dry nurse a nurse who takes care of a baby, but does not suckle it.

dry-nurse (drī′nėrs′) *v.* **-nursed, -nurs·ing.** act as dry nurse to.

dry point 1 a picture made from a copper plate into which lines have been engraved with a hard needle without using acid. **2** the needle used. **3** this method of engraving.

dry rot 1 the decay of seasoned wood, causing it to crumble to a dry powder by the action of various fungi. **2** a disease of plants caused by the fungi that produce dry decay. **3** any of these fungi. **4** inner decay: *Lack of new people and new ideas often causes dry rot in an organization.*

dry run 1 a practice test or session. **2** in military use, any simulated firing practice, bombing approach, etc. without use of live ammunition.

dry-shod (drī′shod′) *adj., adv.* having dry shoes; without getting the feet wet.

dry-stone (drī′stōn′) *adj.* built of stone without the use of mortar.

dry wash clothes, linens, etc. that have been washed and dried, but not ironed.

Ds dysprosium.

d.s. 1 daylight saving. **2** in business, days after sight. **3** in music, from the (repeat) sign.

D.S. 1 Doctor of Science. **2** Dental Surgeon. **3** in music, from the (repeat) sign. (for Ital. *dal segno*)

D.Sc. Doctor of Science. (for L *Doctor Scientiae*)

D.S.C. Distinguished Service Cross.

D.S.M. Distinguished Service Medal.

D.S.O. Distinguished Service Order.

D.S.T., DST, or **d.s.t.** Daylight Saving Time.

D.Th. or **D.Theol.** Doctor of Theology. (for L *Doctor Theologiae*)

d.t.'s delirium tremens.

Du. Dutch.

du·al (dū′əl or dü′əl) *adj.* 1 of two; showing two. 2 consisting of two parts; double; twofold: *The airplane had dual controls, one set for each pilot.* 3 in grammar, signifying or implying two persons or things. —*n.* 1 the dual number. 2 a word in the dual number. [< L *dualis* < *duo* two]

du·al·ism (dū′əl iz′əm or dü′əl iz′əm) *n.* 1 a dual condition; duality. 2 in philosophy, the doctrine that all the phenomena of the universe can be explained by two separate and distinct substances or principles, such as mind and matter. 3 in theology: **a** the doctrine that Christ consisted of two personalities. **b** the doctrine that two distinct elements are constituted in man, as body and spirit.

du·al·ist (dū′əl ist or dü′əl ist) *n.* a believer in dualism.

du·al·is·tic (dū′əl is′tik or dü′əl is′tik) *adj.* 1 having to do with dualism; based on dualism. 2 dual. —**du′al·is′ti·cal·ly,** *adv.*

du·al·i·ty (dū al′ə tē or dü al′ə tē) *n.* **-ties.** a dual condition or quality.

dub[1] (dub) *v.* **dubbed, dub·bing.** 1 make (a man) a knight by striking his shoulder lightly with a sword. 2 give a title to; call; name. 3 smooth by cutting, rubbing, scraping, etc. 4 dress, trim or crop. [OE *dubbian*]

dub[2] (dub) *n. v.* **dubbed, dub·bing.** *Slang.* —*n.* 1 a clumsy, unskilful person. 2 in sports, an awkward, clumsy player. —*v.* do or play awkwardly; bungle. [? related to *dub*[1]]

dub[3] (dub) *v.* **dubbed, dub·bing,** *n.* —*v.* 1 push; thrust. 2 beat a drum. —*n.* 1 a thrust or push. 2 the beat of a drum. [origin uncertain]

dub[4] (dub) *v.* **dubbed, dub·bing,** *n.* —*v.* 1 add music, voices, or sound effects to (a motion-picture film, a radio or television broadcast, a recording, etc.) by making a new sound track: *The Italian film was dubbed with English dialogue.* 2 add (sounds) to. 3 make a record of (a previously made recording).
—*n.* the sounds added. [short for *double*]

du·bi·e·ty (dū bī′ə tē or dü bī′ə tē) *n.* **-ties.** 1 doubtfulness; uncertainty. 2 something that is doubtful.

du·bi·ous (dū′bē əs or dü′bē əs) *adj.* 1 doubtful; uncertain: *a dubious compliment, dubious authorship, a dubious friend.* 2 of questionable character; probably bad: *a dubious scheme for making money.* [< L *dubiosus* < *dubius* doubtful < *du-* two] —**du′bi·ous·ly,** *adv.* —**du′bi·ous·ness,** *n.*

du·cal (dū′kəl or dü′kəl) *adj.* of or having to do with a duke or dukedom. [< LL *ducalis* < L *dux, ducis* leader]

duc·at (duk′ət) *n.* 1 a gold or silver coin formerly used in some European countries. 2 *Slang.* a ticket. [ME < Ital. *ducato* < Med.L < L *dux, ducis* leader]

du·ce (dü′chā) *n. Italian.* 1 a leader. 2 **Duce,** the title given to Benito Mussolini (1883-1945), dictator of Italy from 1922 to 1943. [< Ital. < L *dux, ducis* leader. Doublet of DOGE, DUKE.]

duch·ess (duch′is) *n.* 1 the wife or widow of a duke. 2 a woman with a rank equal to that of a duke. [ME < OF *duchesse* < *duc* duke. See DUKE.]

duch·y (duch′ē) *n.* **duch·ies.** the territory under the rule of a duke or duchess; a dukedom.

duck[1] (duk) *n.* 1 a wild or tame swimming bird having a short neck, short legs, and webbed feet. Most ducks have broad, flat bills. 2 the female of this bird. A male duck is called a drake. 3 the flesh of a duck used for food. 4 *Informal.* a darling; pet. 5 *Slang.* a fellow; chap. 6 **like water off a duck's back,** without having any effect. 7 **make ducks and drakes of** or **play ducks and drakes with,** handle recklessly; squander foolishly. [OE *dūce.* Related to DUCK[2].] —**duck′like′,** *adj.*

duck[2] (duk) *v.* 1 dip or plunge suddenly under water and out again. 2 lower the head or bend the body suddenly to keep from being hit, seen, etc. 3 lower (the head) or bend (the body) suddenly. 4 *Informal.* get or keep away from by ducking; avoid. 5 *Slang.* get away; withdraw; make off: *He ducked out of town to avoid paying his bills.*

hat, āge, cãre, fär; let, ēqual, tėrm; it, īce
hot, ōpen, ôrder; oil, out; cup, pu̇t, rüle, ūse
əbove, takən, pencəl, lemən, circəs
ch, child; ng, long; sh, ship
th, thin; ᴛʜ, then; zh, measure

—*n.* 1 a sudden dip or plunge under water and out again. 2 a sudden lowering of the head or bending of the body to keep from being hit, seen, etc. [ME *duke(n)*] —**duck′er,** *n.*

duck[3] (duk) *n.* 1 a strong cotton or linen cloth with a lighter and finer weave than canvas. Duck is used to make small sails and clothes for sailors or people living in hot climates. 2 **ducks,** *pl. Informal.* trousers made of duck. [< Du. *doek* cloth]

duck[4] (duk) *n.* a military vehicle that resembles a truck, but has a watertight body so that it may move through the water like a boat. [for DUKW, its code name]

duck·bill (duk′bil′) *n.* a small water mammal of Australia and Tasmania that lays eggs and has webbed feet and a beak somewhat like a duck's; platypus.

duckbilled platypus duckbill.

ducking stool in former times, a stool on which a person was tied and ducked into water as a punishment.

duck·ling (duk′ling) *n.* a young duck.

duck·pins (duk′pinz′) *n.* a game that resembles bowling but is played with smaller balls and pins.

duck soup *Slang.* something that is easily done; a cinch: *This job will be duck soup to us.*

duck·weed (duk′wēd′) *n.* a very small plant that grows in water, often forming a dense green scum on the surface.

duct (dukt) *n.* 1 a tube, pipe, or channel for carrying liquid, air, wires, etc. 2 a tube in the body for carrying a bodily fluid: *tear ducts.* [< L *ductus* < *ducere* lead] —**duct′less,** *adj.*

duc·tile (duk′tīl or duk′təl) *adj.* 1 capable of being hammered out thin or drawn out into a wire: *Gold and copper are ductile metals.* 2 easily moulded or shaped: *Wax is ductile.* 3 easily managed or influenced; docile. [< F < L *ductilis* < *ducere* lead]

duc·til·i·ty (duk til′ə tē) *n.* **-ties.** a ductile quality.

ductless gland a gland without a duct whose secretion passes directly into the blood or lymph circulating through it. The thyroid, the spleen, and the thymus are ductless glands.

dud[1] (dud) *n.* 1 *Obsolete.* an article of clothing. 2 **duds,** *pl. Informal.* **a** clothes. **b** old ragged clothes. **c** possessions; belongings. [ME *dudde* cloak; origin uncertain]

dud[2] (dud) *n.* 1 a person or thing that is useless or inefficient. 2 *Slang.* a shell or bomb that fails to explode. 3 *Slang.* a failure. —*adj.* 1 useless; inefficient; valueless: *a dud cheque.* 2 out of order. [probably related to DUB[2]]

dude (dūd or düd) *n.* 1 in the western parts of Canada and the United States, a city-bred person, especially one who spends a holiday on a ranch. 2 a man who pays too much attention to his clothes; dandy. [origin unknown]

dude ranch a ranch that is run as a tourist resort.

dudg·eon (duj′ən) *n. Archaic.* 1 anger; resentment. 2 **in high dudgeon,** very angry; resentful. [origin unknown]

dud·ish (dūd′ish or düd′ish) *adj.* like that of a dude.

due (dū or dü) *adj.* 1 owed as a debt; to be paid or given to as a right: *Money is due to him for his work. Respect is due to older people.* 2 proper; suitable; rightful: *Good deeds deserve due reward; bad deeds deserve due punishment.* 3 as much as needed; enough: *Use due care when crossing streets.* 4 promised to come or be ready; looked for; expected: *The train is due at noon. Your report is due tomorrow.* 5 of notes, bills, etc., becoming payable; having reached maturity; mature. 6 of dates, on which notes, bills, etc. become mature. 7 **become due,** be required to be paid. 8 **due to,** caused by: *The accident was due to his careless use of the gun.* 9 **fall due,** be required to be paid.
—*n.* 1 something owed as a debt or to be paid or given as a right: *Courtesy is a person's due as long as he is your guest.* 2 **dues,** *pl.* **a** the amount of money owed or to be

paid; a fee; tax. **b** the amount of money owed or to be paid to a club, etc. by a member. **3 give a person his due,** be fair to a person.
—*adv.* straight; directly; exactly: *The wind is due east.* [ME < OF *deü*, pp. of *devoir* owe < L *debere*] —**Syn.** *adj.* **1** payable. **2** appropriate, fitting. **3** adequate, sufficient.
☛ Due was originally used only as an adjective, and in formal English it is still restricted by many writers to this use: *Economic depressions are due to uncontrolled inflation* (modifies *depressions*). *Due to* as a preposition (*Due to his bad temper most people avoid him*) is in general use and appears in the writing of many North American and British authors, although some users of formal English do not approve of the construction. If you wish, you can easily avoid using *due to* as a preposition by substituting *because of* or *on account of* or by recasting the sentence. General: *Due to the storm he postponed his canoe trip.* Formal: *Because of the storm he postponed his canoe trip. The postponement of his canoe trip was due to the storm.*

du·el (dū′əl or dü′əl) *n. v.* **-elled** or **-eled, -el·ling** or **-el·ing.** —*n.* **1** a formal fight between two men armed with swords or firearms. Duels are arranged to settle quarrels, avenge insults, etc., and are fought in the presence of witnesses, called seconds. **2** any fight or contest between two opponents: *The two opposing lawyers fought a duel of wits in the law court.*
—*v.* fight in a duel or duels. [< Med.L *duellum* a combat between two < L *duellum* (early form of *bellum*) war]

du·el·list or **du·el·ist** (dū′əl ist or dü′əl ist) *n.* a person who fights a duel or duels.

du·en·na (dū en′ə or dü en′ə) *n.* **1** an elderly woman who is the governess and chaperone of young girls in a Spanish or Portuguese family. **2** a governess; chaperone. [< Sp. *dueña* < L *domina* mistress]

du·et (dū et′ or dü et′) *n.* **1** a piece of music to be sung or played by two people. **2** two singers or players performing together. [< Ital. *duetto*, dim. of *duo*. See DUO.]

duff[1] (duf) *n.* a flour pudding boiled in a cloth bag: *plum duff.* [var. of *dough*]

duff[2] (duf) *n.* the decaying vegetable matter that covers the ground in a forest. [origin uncertain]

duffel or **duffle** (duf′əl) *n.* **1** a coarse woollen cloth having a thick nap. **2** the personal belongings of a hunter, camper, soldier, etc. **3** a duffel sock. **4** a duffel bag. [< Du. < *Duffel*, a town near Antwerp]

duffel bag or **duffle bag 1** a large bag of heavy cloth or canvas, used by campers, hunters, soldiers, etc. for carrying personal belongings. **2** any bag of stout material.

duffel coat or **duffle coat** a knee-length, usually hooded coat made of duffel.

duffel sock or **duffle sock** in the North: **1** one of a pair of wrap-around leggings made of long strips of duffel or blanketing, worn as a protection against intense cold. **2** an outer sock or liner made of duffel, worn between a sock and a boot or mukluk, etc.

duff·er (duf′ər) *n. Informal.* a useless, clumsy, or stupid person. [origin uncertain]

duf·fle (duf′əl) *n.* duffel.

dug[1] (dug) *v.* pt. and pp. of **dig.**

dug[2] (dug) *n.* a teat or nipple of a female animal. [< Scand.; cf. Danish *dægge*, Swedish *dägga* suckle]

du·gong (dü′gong) *n.* a large, fish-shaped mammal of the coastal waters of S. Asia and Australia, having flipperlike forelimbs and a paddle-like tail. [< Malay *dūyong*]

dug·out (dug′out′) *n.* **1** a rough shelter made by digging into the side of a hill, trench, etc. During war, soldiers use dugouts for protection against bullets and bombs. **2** a small shelter at the side of a baseball field, used by players who are not at bat or not in the game. **3** a boat made by hollowing out a large log. **4** *Cdn.* especially on the Prairies, a large excavation used to hold water collected there from the spring thaw and from rainfall: *Some dugouts are used for watering livestock; others are used for watering land.*

du·i (dū′ē or dü′ē) *n.* a pl. of **duo.**

duke (dūk or dük) *n.* **1** a nobleman ranking next below a prince and above a marquis. **2** a prince who rules a small state or country called a duchy. **3 dukes,** *pl. Slang.* hands; fists. [ME < OF *duc* < L *dux, ducis* leader. Doublet of DOGE, DUCE.]

duke·dom (dūk′dəm or dük′-) *n.* **1** the territory under the rule of a duke; duchy. **2** the title or rank of a duke.

Duk·ho·bor (dü′kə bôr′) *n.* Doukhobor.

dul·cet (dul′sit) *adj.* soothing, especially to the ear; sweet; pleasing. [< F *doucet*, dim. of *doux*, earlier *dulz* sweet < L *dulcis*]

dul·ci·mer (dul′sə mər) *n.* a musical instrument with metal strings, played by striking the strings with two hammers. [< MF *doulcemer*, var. of *doulcemele* < L *dulcis* sweet + *melos* song (< Gk.)]

Dul·cin·e·a (dul sin′ ē ə or dul′sə nē′ ə) *n.* **1** the name given by Don Quixote to the coarse peasant girl whom he supposed to be a beautiful lady and whom he chose for his sweetheart. **2** any idolized sweetheart.

dull (dul) *adj.* **1** not sharp or pointed: *a dull knife.* **2** not bright or clear: *dull eyes, a dull day.* **3** slow in understanding; stupid: *a dull mind.* **4** lacking keenness of perception in the senses or feelings; insensitive. **5** not interesting; tiresome; boring: *a dull book.* **6** having little life, energy, or spirit; not active: *The coal business is dull this summer.* **7** not felt sharply: *a dull pain.*
—*v.* **1** make dull. **2** become dull. [ME *dul*] —**dull′ness** or **dul′ness,** *n.*
Syn. *adj.* **1 Dull, blunt** = with the edge or point not sharp. **Dull** suggests that the object described has lost the sharpness it had or is not as sharp as it should be: *This knife is dull.* **Blunt** suggests that the edge or point is not intended to be sharp or keen: *The blunt side of a knife will not cut meat. The weapon used by the murderer was a blunt instrument, possibly a poker.* **2** dim, clouded, dingy. **3** dense, slow. See **stupid. 5** uninteresting, colorless. **6** lifeless, sluggish.

dull·ard (dul′ərd) *n.* a person who is stupid and who learns very slowly.

dull·ish (dul′ish) *adj.* rather dull.

dul·ly (dul′ē) *adv.* in a dull manner.

dulse (duls) *n.* any of several coarse, edible seaweeds that have reddish-brown fronds. [< Irish and Scots Gaelic *duileasg*]

du·ly (dū′lē or dü′lē) *adv.* **1** according to what is due; as due; properly; suitably; rightfully: *The documents were duly signed before a lawyer.* **2** as much as is needed; enough. **3** when due; at the proper time: *The debt was duly paid.*

Du·ma (dü′mä) *n.* in Imperial Russia, the national lawmaking body, established in 1905 and discontinued in 1917. Also, **Douma.** [< Russian *duma* thought, counsel, ult. < Gmc. Related to DEEM, DOOM.]

dumb (dum) *adj.* **1** not able to speak: *dumb animals.* **2** silenced for the moment by fear, surprise, shyness, etc. **3** that does not speak; silent. **4** *Informal.* stupid; dull: *a dumb blonde.* [< (defs. 1-3) OE *dumb*; (def. 4) influenced by G *dumm* stupid] —**dumb′ly,** *adv.* —**dumb′ness,** *n.*
Syn. 1 Dumb, mute, speechless = without speech. **Dumb** = without the power of speech, and although often used interchangeably with *mute* and *speechless*, it is the term applied particularly to animals: *Even intelligent animals are dumb.* **Mute** emphasizes being silent for some strong reason, and applies particularly to people who have never been able to speak because they were born deaf or became deaf in very early life and have never or almost never heard sounds: *Many mute children are now taught to speak.* **Speechless** = without speech, usually temporarily and as the result of emotion, surprise, etc.: *I was speechless with rage.*

dumb-bell (dum′bel′) *n.* **1** a short bar of wood or iron with large, heavy, round ends. Dumb-bells are generally used in pairs and are lifted or swung around to exercise the muscles of the arms, back, etc. **2** *Slang.* a stupid person.

A dumb-bell

dumb·found (dum′found′) *v.* dumfound.

dumb show gestures without words; pantomime: *He indicated by dumb show that he wanted to speak to me privately.*

dumb·wait·er (dum′wāt′ər) *n.* **1** a small box with shelves, pulled up and down in a shaft to send dishes, food, rubbish, etc. from one floor of a building to another. **2** a small stand placed near a dining table, for holding dishes, etc.

dum·dum (dum′dum) *n.* a bullet that spreads out when

it strikes, causing a serious wound. [< *Dum Dum*, a town near Calcutta, India, where it was first made]

dumdum bullet dumdum.

dum·found (dum′found′) *v.* amaze and make unable to speak; bewilder; confuse. [< *dumb* + con*found*]

dum·my (dum′ē) *n.* **-mies,** *adj.* —*n.* **1** a figure of a person, used to display clothing in store windows, to shoot at in rifle practice, to tackle in football, etc. **2** an empty or imitation package or article used for display or advertisement: *All the articles in this window are dummies.* **3** *Informal.* a stupid person; blockhead. **4** an imitation; counterfeit. **5** a person supposedly acting for himself, but really acting for another. **6** a person who has nothing to say or who takes no active part in affairs. **7** in card games: **a** a player whose cards are laid face up on the table and played by his partner. **b** a hand of cards played in this way. **8** in printing: **a** a sample volume bound or unbound, and usually either blank or only partly printed, to show the size and general appearance of a book, etc. in preparation (in Great Britain called a *size copy*). **b** a format for parts or the whole of a magazine, book, etc. made up of printer's proofs pasted down upon empty pages to show the general arrangement of the material; layout.
—*adj.* **1** imitation; counterfeit; sham: *The boys played soldier with dummy swords made of wood.* **2** acting for another while supposedly acting for oneself. **3** in card games, played with a hand of cards exposed. [< *dumb* + *-y*[1]]

dump (dump) *v.* **1** empty out; throw down; unload in a mass: *The truck backed up to the curb and dumped the coal on the sidewalk.* **2** unload rubbish. **3** put (goods) on the market in large quantities and at a low price, especially, in a foreign country at a price below that in the home country. **4** *Slang.* get rid of; abandon; reject: *dump an unpopular candidate.*
—*n.* **1** a place for unloading rubbish. **2** a heap of rubbish. **3** a place for storing military supplies: *an ammunition dump.* **4** *Slang.* a shabby, ill-kept, untidy or otherwise depressing house, town, or locality: *Life in this dump is unbearable.* **5** in lumbering, a place at water's edge where cut logs are piled before being rolled into the water and driven downstream. **6** in placer mining, a pile of dirt waiting to be put through the sluice box to separate any gold that may be there. [ME ? < Scand; cf. Danish *dumpe* fall with a thud]

dump cart a cart that opens at the bottom or tips to dump its contents.

dump·ling (dump′ling) *n.* **1** a rounded piece of dough, boiled or steamed and served with meat. **2** a small pudding made by enclosing fruit in a piece of dough and baking or steaming it. **3** a dumpy animal or person, short and of rounded outlines. [< *dump* a badly shaped piece + *-ling*]

dumps (dumps) *n.pl. Informal.* **1** low spirits; gloomy feelings. **2** **(down) in the dumps,** feeling gloomy or sad.

dump·y (dump′ē) *adj.* **dump·i·er, dump·i·est.** short and fat. —**dump′i·ly,** *adv.* —**dump′i·ness,** *n.*

dun[1] (dun) *v.* **dunned, dun·ning,** *n.* —*v.* demand payment of a debt from (someone) again and again. —*n.* **1** a demand for payment of a debt. **2** a person constantly demanding payment of a debt. [var. of *din,* with reference to making a din for money due]

dun[2] (dun) *n. adj.* dull grayish-brown. [OE *dunn*]

Duncan Phyfe (dung′kən fīf′) **1** of, like, or having to do with a style of gracefully proportioned and soundly constructed furniture. **2** this style of furniture. **3** a piece of furniture of this style. [after *Duncan Phyfe* (1768-1854), an American furniture designer]

dunce (duns) *n.* **1** a child slow at learning his lessons in school. **2** a stupid person. [< *Duns(man),* name applied by his attackers to any follower of *Duns Scotus,* a medieval theologian]

dunce cap or **dunce's cap** a tall, cone-shaped cap formerly worn as a punishment by a child who was slow in learning his lessons in school.

dun·der·head (dun′dər hed′) *n.* a stupid, foolish person; dunce; blockhead. [*dunder* of uncertain origin]
—**dun′der·head′ed·ness,** *n.*

dune (dūn or dün) *n.* a mound or ridge of loose sand heaped up by the wind. [< F < MDu. *dune.* Akin to DOWN[3].]

hat, āge, cãre, fär; let, ēqual, tėrm; it, īce
hot, ōpen, ôrder; oil, out; cup, pu̇t, rüle, ūse
əbove, takən, pencəl, lemən, circəs
ch, child; ng, long; sh, ship
th, thin; ᴛʜ, then; zh, measure

dune buggy a small, usually roofless vehicle, often a converted car, for use on sand dunes or rough terrain.

dung (dung) *n.* waste matter from the bowels of animals; manure: *Dung is much used as a fertilizer.* —*v.* put dung on as a fertilizer. [OE]

dun·ga·ree (dung′gə rē′ or dung′gə rē′) *n.* **1** a coarse cotton cloth, used for work clothes, sails, etc. **2** **dungarees,** *pl.* trousers or clothing made of this cloth. [< Hind. *dungrī*]

dun·geon (dun′jən) *n.* **1** a dark underground room to keep prisoners in. **2** a donjon. —*v.* confine in a dungeon; imprison. [ME < OF *donjon* < Gmc.]

dung·hill (dung′hil′) *n.* **1** a heap of dung. **2** a vile place or person.

dunk (dungk) *v.* **1** dip (something to eat) into a liquid: *dunk doughnuts in coffee.* **2** *Informal.* push somebody into water. [< LG *dunken* dip] —**dunk′er,** *n.*

Dunk·ard (dungk′ərd) *n.* a member of the Church of the Brethren. [variant of *Dunker* < Pennsylvania Du. *Dunker* < LG *dunken* dip, baptize]

Dunk·er (dungk′ər) *n.* Dunkard.

dun·lin (dun′lən) *n.* **-lin** or **-lins.** a small wading bird that has a broad black stripe across the abdomen during the breeding season. [dim. of *dun*[2]]

dun·nage (dun′ij) *n.* **1** personal belongings; kit; baggage. **2** branches, mats, etc. placed around a cargo to protect it from damage by water or chafing. [origin uncertain]

du·o (dū′ō or dü′ō) *n.* **duos, dui. 1** in music, a duet. **2** *Informal.* a pair. [< Ital. < L *duo* two]

du·o·dec·i·mal (dū′ō des′ə məl or dü′ō-) *adj.* having to do with twelfths or twelve; proceeding by twelves. —*n.* **1** a twelfth part. **2** one of a system of numerals, the base of which is twelve instead of ten. **3** **duodecimals,** *pl.* a system of counting by twelves.

du·o·dec·i·mo (dū′ō des′ə mō′ or dü′ō-) *n.* **-mos,** *adj.* —*n.* **1** the page size of a book in which each leaf is one twelfth of a whole sheet of paper, or about 5 by 7½ inches. **2** a book having pages of this size. —*adj.* having pages of this size. [< L *in duodecimo* in a twelfth]

du·o·de·nal (dū′ō dē′nəl or dü′ō-) *adj.* having to do with the duodenum: *a duodenal ulcer.*

du·o·de·num (dū′ō dē′nəm or dü′ō-) *n.* **-na** (-nə). in anatomy and zoology, the first part of the small intestine, just below the stomach. See **intestine** for diagram. [ME < Med.L < L *duodeni* twelve each; with reference to its length, about twelve finger breadths]

du·o·tone (dū′ə tōn′ or dü′ə tōn′) *adj.* in printing, printed in two tones of the same color. —*n.* a method by which illustrations are reproduced in two tones of the same color. [< L *duo* two + E *tone*]

dup. duplicate.

dupe (dūp or düp) *n. v.* **duped, dup·ing.** —*n.* **1** a person easily deceived or tricked. **2** one who is being deluded or tricked: *The young politician's inexperience is making him the dupe of some unscrupulous schemers.*
—*v.* deceive; trick. [< F < OF *duppe,* earlier *d'uppe* < L *upupa* hoopee (a bird thought to be stupid)]
—**dup′er,** *n.*

du·ple (dū′pəl or dü′pəl) *adj.* **1** double. **2** in music, having two or a multiple of two beats to the measure. [< L *duplus* double. Doublet of DOUBLE.]

du·plet (dū′plit or dü′plit) *n.* in chemistry, a pair of electrons that is shared by two atoms.

duple time two-part time.

du·plex (dū′pleks or dü′pleks) *adj.* double; twofold. —*n.* **1** a duplex house or duplex apartment. **2** one half of a duplex house. [< L *duplex* < *du-* two + *plicare* fold]

duplex house a single house built to accommodate two families.

du·pli·cate (*adj., n.* dū′plə kit or dü′plə kit; *v.*

dū′plə kāt′ or dü′plə kāt′) *adj. n. v.* **-cat·ed, -cat·ing.** —*adj.* **1** exactly like something else; corresponding to something else: *We have duplicate keys for the front door.* **2** double. **3** having two corresponding parts; twofold: *A person's lungs are duplicate, but he has only one heart.* **4** in card games, having the same hands played by different players: *duplicate bridge.*
—*n.* **1** one of two things exactly alike; an exact copy. **2 in duplicate,** in two forms exactly alike.
—*v.* **1** make an exact copy of; repeat exactly. **2** make double or twofold; double. [< L *duplicatus,* pp. of *duplicare* to double < *du-* two + *plicare* fold]

du·pli·ca·tion (dū′plə kā′shən or dü′plə kā′shən) *n.* **1** a duplicating. **2** a being duplicated. **3** a duplicate copy.

du·pli·ca·tor (dū′plə kā′tər or dü′plə kā′tər) *n.* a machine for making many exact copies of anything written or typed; a duplicating machine.

du·plic·i·ty (dū plis′ə tē or dü plis′ə tē) *n.* **-ties.** deceitfulness; treachery; secretly acting one way and openly acting another in order to deceive. [< LL *duplicitas* doubleness < L *duplex.* See DUPLEX.]

du·ra·bil·i·ty (dūr′ə bil′ə tē or dür′ə bil′ə tē) *n.* **-ties.** lasting quality; ability to stand wear.

du·ra·ble (dūr′ə bəl or dür′ə bəl) *adj.* lasting a long time; not soon injured or worn out. [ME < OF < L *durabilis* < *durare* to last, harden < *durus* hard] **—du′ra·ble·ness,** *n.* **—du′ra·bly,** *adv.* **—Syn.** permanent, stable, enduring, strong.

Du·ral·u·min (dū ral′yů min′ or dü ral′yů min′) *n. Trademark.* a light, strong, hard metal that is an alloy of aluminum containing copper, manganese, and sometimes magnesium. [< *dur*able + *alumin*um]

du·rance (dūr′əns or dür′əns) *n.* imprisonment. [< MF *durance* duration]

du·ra·tion (dū rā′shən or dü rā′shən) *n.* **1** length of time; the time during which anything continues. **2 for the duration,** until the end, especially of a war. [ME < LL *duratio, -onis* < L *durare* to last]

dur·bar (dėr′bär) *n.* in India: **1** an official court or reception held by an Indian prince or, formerly, by a British monarch, viceroy, governor, etc. **2** a hall where such a reception is held. [< Hind., Persian *darbār* court]

du·ress (dū res′ or dü res′, dūr′es or dür′es) *n.* **1** compulsion. A person cannot be legally forced to fulfil a contract signed under duress. **2** imprisonment. [ME < OF *duresse* < L *duritia* hardness < *durus* hard]

Dur·ham (dėr′əm) *n.* **1** a breed of short-horned cattle. **2** a cow of this breed. [< *Durham,* a county in England, where this breed originated]

Durham boat a boat used for river transport by early settlers in the east of Canada and the United States. It could be propelled by pole or sail. [after Robert *Durham,* an 18th-century American boat builder]

Durham report, the *Report on the Affairs of British North America,* issued in 1839 by Lord Durham (1792-1840), Governor-in-Chief of British North America from May to December, 1838. The report led to the union of Upper and Lower Canada in 1841 and to the introduction of responsible government and municipal government in Canada.

dur·ing (dūr′ing or dür′ing) *prep.* **1** throughout: *The boys played during the afternoon.* **2** at some time in; in the course of: *Come to see me during the afternoon.* **3** while something lasts: *The girls play tag during recess.* [ppr. of obs. *dure* endure < OF < L *durare*]

Du·roc (dūr′ok or dür′ok) *n.* **1** a large, red breed of pigs having drooping ears. **2** a pig of this breed.

Du·roc-Jer·sey (dūr′ok jėr′zē or dür′ok-) *n.* Duroc.

dur·ra (dür′ə) *n.* a kind of sorghum with slender stalks that produces grain. [< Arabic *dhura*]

durst (dėrst) *v.* a pt. of **dare.**

du·rum (dūr′əm or dür′əm) *n.* a hard wheat from which the flour used in macaroni, spaghetti, etc. is made. [< L *durum,* neut. of *durus* hard]

durum wheat durum.

dusk (dusk) *n.* **1** the time just before dark. **2** shade; gloom. —*adj.* dark-colored; dusky. —*v.* make or become dusky. [var. of OE *dux, dox* dark] **—Syn.** *n.* **1** twilight.

dusk·y (dus′kē) *adj.* **dusk·i·er, dusk·i·est. 1** somewhat dark; dark-coloured. **2** dim; obscure. **3** sad; gloomy. **—dusk′i·ly,** *adv.* **—dusk′i·ness,** *n.*
Syn. 1 Dusky, swarthy = rather dark. **Dusky,** the general word, means rather dark and dim, but not completely without light or color: *It was dusky in the old warehouse.* **Swarthy** = very dark-colored, and applies only to complexion: *He has a swarthy skin.*

dust (dust) *n.* **1** fine, dry earth. **2** any fine powder. **3** the earth; ground. **4** what is left of a dead body after decay. **5** a low or humble condition. **6** a worthless thing or person. **7** a cloud of dust floating in the air: *The car raised a great dust.* **8** confusion; disturbance; turmoil: *raise a dust about nothing.* **9** *Brit.* ashes or refuse. **10** *Slang.* money. **11 bite the dust,** *Slang.* **a** fall dead or wounded. **b** be defeated or dismissed; be vanquished. **c** be thoroughly humiliated. **12 lick the dust, a** fall dead or wounded. **b** humble oneself slavishly. **13 shake the dust off one's feet,** go away feeling angry or scornful. **14 throw dust in someone's eyes,** deceive or mislead a person.
—*v.* **1** brush or wipe the dust from; get dust off. **2** get dust on; soil with dust. **3** sprinkle (with dust, powder, etc.). **4 dust off, dust.** *Informal.* get rid of; eliminate. [OE *dūst*] **—dust′like′,** *adj.*

dust·bin (dust′bin′) *n. Brit.* a receptacle for refuse or trash; garbage can.

dust bowl an area, especially in the western parts of Canada and the United States, where dust storms are frequent and violent: *Because of improved farming, dust bowls are quite rare.*

dust devil a small whirlwind that stirs up a column of dust, leaves, etc. as it moves along.

dust·er (dus′tər) *n.* **1** a person or thing that dusts. **2** a cloth, brush, etc. used to get dust off things. **3** a contrivance for removing dust by sifting; sieve. **4** an apparatus for sifting or blowing dry poisons on plants to kill insects. **5** a long, lightweight coat worn over the clothes to keep dust off them. **6** a similar garment worn without a belt, as a woman's coat or bathrobe. **7** *Informal.* a dust storm.

dusting powder 1 an antiseptic powder for dusting over wounds, etc. **2** a fine, usually perfumed, powder for dusting on the body after a bath, etc.

dust jacket a loose outer covering for a book, made of paper and folded over the hard cover.

dust·less (dust′lis) *adj.* **1** without dust. **2** not causing dust.

dust·pan (dust′pan′) *n.* a flat, broad pan into which dust can be swept from the floor.

dust·proof (dust′prüf′) *adj.* impervious to dust.

dust sheet a large sheet to protect articles of furniture from dust.

dust storm a strong wind carrying clouds of dust across or from a dry region.

dust·up (dust′up′) *n. Slang.* a violent quarrel; commotion; disturbance.

dust·y (dus′tē) *adj.* **dust·i·er, dust·i·est. 1** covered with dust; filled with dust. **2** like dust; dry and powdery. **3** having the color of dust; grayish. **—dust′i·ly,** *adv.* **—dust′i·ness,** *n.*

Dutch (duch) *adj.* **1** of or having to do with the Netherlands, its people, or their language. **2** *Informal.* German. **3 go Dutch,** *Informal.* have each person pay for himself.
—*n.* **1 the Dutch, a** the people of the Netherlands. **b** *Informal.* the people of Germany. The ancestors of the Pennsylvania Dutch came from Germany, not from the Netherlands. **2** the language of the Netherlands. **3** *Informal* the German language. **4 beat the Dutch,** *Informal.* be very strange or surprising; outdo anything considered remarkable. **5 in Dutch,** *Slang.* **a** in disgrace. **b** in trouble. [< MDu. *dutsch* Dutch, German]
☛ The numerous derogatory expressions compounded of *Dutch,* such as **Dutch courage** and **Dutch uncle,** are a legacy from the Dutch-English commercial rivalry of the 17th and 18th centuries.

Dutch courage *Informal.* courage brought on by alcohol.

Dutch elm disease a killing disease of elm trees,

caused by a fungus and carried by insects.

Dutch·man (duch′mən) *n.* **-men** (-mən). **1** a native or inhabitant of the Netherlands. **2** a Dutch ship. **3** *Informal.* a German.

Dutch·man's-breech·es (duch′mənz brich′iz) *n.sing. or pl.* **1** a spring wild flower shaped rather like breeches. **2** the plant that bears it.

Dutch oven 1 a metal box that opens in front, used for roasting meat, etc. before an open fire or on top of a stove. **2** a heavy kettle with a close-fitting cover. Some Dutch ovens are covered with hot coals and used for baking. **3** a brick oven in which the walls are first heated, and food is put in to cook after the fire goes out or is removed.

Dutch treat *Informal.* a meal or entertainment in which each person pays for himself.

Dutch uncle *Informal.* a person who sternly or severely criticizes or scolds another.

du·te·ous (dū′tē əs or dü′tē əs) *adj.* dutiful; obedient. **—du′te·ous·ly,** *adv.* **—du′te·ous·ness,** *n.*

du·ti·a·ble (dū′tē ə bəl or dü′tē ə bəl) *adj.* on which a duty or tax must be paid: *Perfumes imported into Canada are dutiable goods.*

du·ti·ful (dū′tə fəl or dü′tə fəl) *adj.* **1** performing the duties one owes; obedient: *a dutiful daughter.* **2** required by duty; proceeding from or expressing a sense of duty: *dutiful words.* **—du′ti·ful·ly,** *adv.* **—du′ti·ful·ness,** *n.*

du·ty (dū′tē or dü′tē) *n.* **-ties. 1** the thing that a person ought to do; something that is right to do: *It is your duty to obey the laws.* **2** the binding force of what is right: *A sense of duty makes a person do what he thinks is right.* **3** the thing that a person has to do in his work; action required by one's occupation or position: *A policeman's duties include enforcing the laws and arresting people who break them.* **4** the proper behavior owed to an older or superior person; obedience; respect. **5** a tax on articles brought into or taken out of a country, made, sold, etc. **6** a tax on the performance of certain transactions, the execution of various deeds and documents, etc. **7 do duty for,** serve in place of. **8 in duty bound,** compelled to do something as a duty. **9 off duty,** not at one's work or occupation. **10 on duty,** at one's work or occupation. [ME < AF *duete* < *du,* var. of OF *deü.* See DUE.]

Syn. 1 Duty, obligation = what a person ought to do. **Duty** applies to what a person ought to do because conscience, piety, or law demands it: *I have a duty to help my parents.* **Obligation** applies to something incidental to social living, to specific actions demanded by usage, customs, etc.: *I have obligations to my neighbors.*

duty-bound (dū′tē bound′ or dü′tē-) *adj.* bound by duty; obligated: *He was duty-bound to pay his share of the cost.*

duty-free (dū′tē frē or dü′tē-) *adj.* exempt from custom duty.

du·um·vir (dū um′vər or dü um′vər) *n.* **-virs, -vi·ri** (-və rī or -və rē). in ancient Rome, either of two men who shared the same governmental position. [< L *duumvir* man of two]

du·um·vir·ate (dū um′vər it or dü um′vər it) *n.* **1** a governmental position shared by two men simultaneously: *The consulship in ancient Rome was a duumvirate.* **2** a union or partnership of two men.

du·ve·tyn (dü′və tēn′) *n.* a soft, closely woven woollen cloth having a velvety finish. [< *duvet* down quilt < F]

D.V. 1 Deo volente. **2** Douai Version.

DVA Department of Veterans Affairs.

dwarf (dwôrf) *n.* **dwarfs** or **dwarves** (dwôrvz). **1** a person, animal, or plant much smaller than the usual size for its kind. **2** in fairy tales, an ugly little man with magic power.
—adj. much smaller than the usual size of its kind; checked in growth.
—v. **1** keep from growing large; check in growth. **2** cause to seem small by contrast or by distance: *That tall building dwarfs the other.* [OE *dweorg*]

Syn. *n.* **1 Dwarf, midget** = a person very much smaller than normal. **Dwarf** applies particularly to a very small person whose growth has been stunted, usually by glandular deficiency, and who often has a head large enough for a normal person of his age, or larger, or a body deformed in some way. **Dwarf** may be applied to a stunted animal or plant. With plants, however, *dwarf* usually refers not to the individual but to a *kind* or *variety* smaller than related varieties, either because of natural differentiation or because of breeding: *dwarf marigolds, the dwarf birch.* **Midget** applies to a tiny person who is perfectly shaped and normal in every way except size. A pygmy is one of a diminutive race found in Africa; but the word may be used as a synonym for both **dwarf** and **midget.** *–v.* **1** stunt.

dwarf·ish (dwôr′fish) *adj.* like a dwarf; smaller than usual. **—dwarf′ish·ly,** *adv.* **—dwarf′ish·ness,** *n.*

dwell (dwel) *v.* **dwelt** or **dwelled, dwell·ing. 1** make one's home; live. **2 dwell on, a** think, write, or speak about for a long time. **b** put stress on. [OE *dwellan* delay] **—Syn. 1** reside, abide.

dwell·er (dwel′ər) *n.* a person who lives in a place: *a city dweller.*

dwell·ing (dwel′ing) *n.* a house to live in; the place in which one lives. **—Syn.** residence, abode, habitation.

dwelling house a house in which people live.

dwelling place dwelling.

dwelt (dwelt) *v.* a pt. and a pp. of **dwell.**

dwin·dle (dwin′dəl) *v.* **-dled, -dling.** make or become smaller and smaller; shrink; diminish. [dim. of obs. *dwine* < OE *dwīnan* waste away] **—Syn.** lessen, decline, wane. See **decrease.**

dwt. pennyweight; pennyweights.

DX or **D.X.** in radio, distance; distant.

Dy dysprosium.

Dy·ak (dī′ak) *n.* **1** a primitive people living in central Borneo. **2** a member of this people.

dyb·buk (dib′uk) *n.* in Jewish folklore, a spirit, either a demon or the soul of a dead person, that takes possession of a living human being. Also, **dibbuk.** [< Hebrew *dibbuq,* originally, cement, glue]

dye (dī) *n. v.* **dyed, dye·ing.** *—n.* **1** a coloring matter used to color cloth, hair, etc. Some dyes are vegetable, others chemical. **2** a liquid containing such coloring matter: *We bought some blue dye.* **3** a color produced by such coloring matter; tint; hue. **4 of deepest** or **blackest dye,** of the lowest or vilest kind.
—v. **1** color (cloth, hair, etc.) by putting it in a liquid containing coloring matter. **2** become colored when treated with a dye: *This material dyes evenly.* **3** color; stain: *The wounded soldier's blood dyed the ground red.* [OE *dēag*]

dyed-in-the-wool (dīd′in ᴛʜə wůl′) *adj.* **1** of people, thorough-going, especially in a political sense; complete. **2** of materials, dyed before being woven into cloth.

dye·ing (dī′ing) *n.* the coloring of fabrics with dye.

dy·er (dī′ər) *n.* a person whose business is dyeing fabrics.

dye·stuff (dī′stuf′) *n.* any substance, such as indigo or cochineal, yielding a dye or used as a dye.

dy·ing (dī′ing) *adj.* **1** about to die. **2** coming to an end. **3** of death; at death. *—n.* death. *—v.* ppr. of **die**[1].

dyke (dīk) *n. v.* **dyked, dyk·ing.** dike.

dy·nam·ic (dī nam′ik) *adj.* **1** of or having to do with energy or force in motion. **2** of or having to do with dynamics. **3** active; energetic; forceful: *Many successful salesmen have dynamic personalities.* [< Gk. *dynamikos* < *dynamis* power]

dy·nam·i·cal (dī nam′ə kəl) *adj.* dynamic.

dy·nam·i·cal·ly (dī nam′ik lē) *adv.* in a dynamic manner.

dy·nam·ics (dī nam′iks) *n.* **1** the branch of physics dealing with the action of force on bodies either in motion or at rest. Dynamics includes kinematics, kinetics, and, sometimes, statics. **2** the science of force acting in any field. **3** forces, physical or moral, at work in any field. **4** the variation and contrast of force or loudness in the production of musical sounds.

dy·na·mism (dī′nə miz′əm) *n.* **1** any of various doctrines or philosophical systems which seek to explain the

hat, āge, cãre, fär; let, ēqual, tėrm; it, īce
hot, ōpen, ôrder; oil, out; cup, pu̇t, rüle, ūse
əbove, takən, pencəl, lemən, circəs
ch, child; ng, long; sh, ship
th, thin; ᴛʜ, then; zh, measure

phenomena of nature by the action of some force. 2 dynamic quality; energetic quality.

dy·na·mist (dī′nə mist) *n.* a person who believes in dynamism.

dy·na·mite (dī′nə mīt′) *n. v.* **-mit·ed, -mit·ing.** —*n.* a powerful explosive used in blasting rock, tree stumps, etc., made of nitroglycerine mixed with an absorbent material and pressed into round sticks.
—*v.* **1** blow up or destroy with dynamite. **2** mine or charge with dynamite. [< Gk. *dynamis* power; named by Alfred Nobel (1833-1896), the inventor] —**dy′na·mit′er,** *n.*

dy·na·mo (dī′nə mō′) *n.* **-mos. 1** a machine that changes mechanical energy into electric energy and produces electric current; generator. **2** *Informal.* a very active or energetic person. [short for *dynamo-electric machine*]

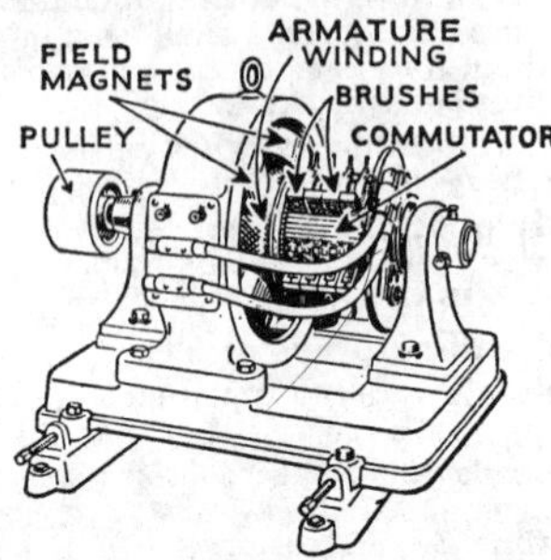

A dynamo or generator. When a conductor (such as copper wire) is moved through lines of magnetic force, electrons flow along the conductor. This flow is electric current. The armature, rotated by the pulley, turns through the lines of force of the magnets; electric current is generated in the wires wound on the armature; and the current is transferred to an outside circuit by means of the brushes and commutator.

dy·na·mo-e·lec·tric (dī′nə mō i lek′trik) *adj.* having to do with the transformation of mechanical energy into electric energy, or electric energy into mechanical energy. [< *dynamo-* (< Gk. *dynamis* power) + *electric*]

dy·na·mom·e·ter (dī′nə mom′ə tər) *n.* an apparatus to measure force. [< F *dynamomètre*]

dy·na·mom·e·try (dī′nə mom′ə trē) *n.* the act or art of using a dynamometer.

dy·na·mo·tor (dī′nə mō′tər) *n.* a combined electric motor and dynamo for changing the voltage of an electric current.

dy·nast (dī′nast or din′ast) *n.* **1** a member of a dynasty; hereditary ruler. **2** any ruler. [< L < Gk. *dynastēs* < *dynasthai* be powerful]

dy·nas·tic (dī nas′tik or di nas′tik) *adj.* having to do with a dynasty.

dy·nas·ty (dī′nəs tē or din′əs tē) *n.* **-ties. 1** a succession of rulers who belong to the same family: *The Bourbon dynasty ruled France for more than 200 years.* **2** the period of time during which a dynasty rules.

dy·na·tron (dī′nə tron′) *n.* **1** a vacuum tube that uses the secondary emission of electrons caused by an increase in the plate voltage to decrease the plate current. Dynatrons are often used in radio as oscillators. **2** in physics, a meson. [< Gk. *dyna*mis + elec*tron.* See DYNAMIC, ELECTRIC.]

dyne (dīn) *n.* in physics, the amount of force that, acting on a mass of one gram for one second, gives it a velocity of one centimetre per second. [< F < Gk. *dynamis* power < *dynasthai* be powerful]

dys·en·ter·y (dis′ən ter′ē or dis′ən trē) *n.* a painful disease of the intestines, producing diarrhea with blood and mucus. [ME < OF *dissenterie* < L < Gk. *dysenteria* < *dys-* bad + *entera* intestines]

dys·func·tion (dis fungk′shən) *n.* a functional abnormality or impairment, as of a body organ.

dys·func·tion·al (dis fungk′shə nəl) *adj.* **1** having to do with dysfunction. **2** performing badly or improperly; malfunctioning.

dys·gen·ic (dis jen′ik) *adj.* having to do with or causing degeneration in the type of offspring produced; opposed to *eugenic.* [< Gk. *dys-* bad + *gen-* produce]

dys·pep·si·a (dis pep′sē ə or dis pep′shə) *n.* poor digestion; indigestion. [< L < Gk. *dyspepsia* < *dys-* bad + *pep-* cook, digest]

dys·pep·tic (dis pep′tik) *adj.* **1** having to do with dyspepsia. **2** suffering from dyspepsia. **3** gloomy; pessimistic. —*n.* a person who has dyspepsia.

dys·pep·ti·cal·ly (dis pep′tik lē) *adv.* **1** with dyspepsia. **2** as a dyspeptic.

dys·pha·si·a (dis fā′zē ə or dis fā′zhə) *n.* difficulty in speaking or in understanding speech, as a result of brain damage. [< NL < Gk. *dys-* bad + *-phasis.* See APHASIA.]

dys·pho·ri·a (dis fôr′ē ə) *n.* in medicine, a chronic feeling of general discontent and illness. [< Gk. *dysphoria* discomfort, ult. < *dys-* ill, bad + *phorein* to bear, suffer]

dys·pro·si·um (dis prō′sē əm or dis prō′shē əm) *n.* a rare chemical element, the most magnetic substance known. *Symbol:* Dy; *at.no.* 66; *at.wt.* 162.50. [< NL < Gk. *dysprositos* hard to get at]

dys·tro·phy (dis′trə fē) *n.* in medicine: **1** defective nutrition. **2** defective development or degeneration: *muscular dystrophy.* [< Gk. *dys-* bad + *trophē* nourishment]

dz. dozen; dozens.

hat, āge, cãre, fär; let, ēqual, tėrm; it, īce
hot, ōpen, ôrder; oil, out; cup, pu̇t, rüle, ūse
əbove, takən, pencəl, lemən, circəs
ch, child; ng, long; sh, ship
th, thin; ᴛʜ, then; zh, measure

E or **e** (ē) *n.* **E's** or **e's. 1** the fifth letter of the English alphabet. **2** any speech sound represented by this letter. **3** the fifth in a series or group designated alphabetically. **4** in music: **a** the third tone of the scale of C major. **b** a symbol representing this tone. **c** a key or string that produces this tone. **d** the scale or key that has E as its keynote. See **do**[2] for diagram.

e 1 in physics, erg. **2** in baseball, an error.

e. 1 east. **2** eastern. **3** entrance.

e- *prefix.* out of; from, as in *educe, emerge, erase, evoke.* It is the form of **ex-**[1] used before consonants except *c, f, p, q, s, t.*

E 1 East. **2** Eastern. **3** English. **4** excellent.
E. 1 East. **2** Eastern. **3** Earl. **4** Engineering. **5** English. **6** Earth.

EA educational age.

ea. each.
each (ēch) *adj.* every single one: *Each dog has a name.* —*pron.* every one: *Each went his way.*
—*adv.* for each; to each; apiece: *These pencils are a penny each.* [OE ǣlc < ā ever + gelīc alike]
Syn. *adj.* **Each, every** = one and all (of a number or group). **Each** emphasizes that one and all of a number, or one and the other of two are thought of singly, as individuals: *Each dog has a name* means that, as individuals, all the dogs in the group have names of their own. **Every,** relating to a group, means that one and all are included, with no exceptions: *Every dog has a name* = none of the dogs was left without a name. In a more inclusive sense, **every** refers to one and all everywhere: *Every dog has his day.*
☛ **each. a** As a pronoun, *each* is singular: *Each of the three students has a different instructor.* **b** As an adjective, *each* does not affect the number of a verb; when the subject modified by *each* is plural, the verb is plural: *Each applicant has to fill out the blanks* (sing.). *The three top students each receive a scholarship* (pl.).

each other 1 each the other: *They struck each other,* that is, they struck, *each* striking *the other.* **2** one another: *The three boys struck at each other.*
☛ **Each other** is in good use for more than two, although formal usage frequently has *one another.* General: *The boys in the class were shouting to each other.* Formal: *The boys in the class were shouting to one another.*

ea·ger (ē′gər) *adj.* **1** wanting very much; desiring strongly; anxious to do or get something: *The child is eager to have the candy.* **2** characterized by or showing keenness of desire or feeling: *eager looks.* [ME < OF *aigre* keen < L *acer, acris*] —**ea′ger·ly,** *adv.* —**ea′ger·ness,** *n.*
Syn. 1 Eager, keen, anxious = desirous, or wanting very much. **Eager** suggests enthusiasm with a touch of impatience: *The boys were eager to start building the clubhouse.* **Keen** suggests intensity of desire and quickness in action: *keen on learning golf.* **Anxious** implies desire overhung with fear about what may happen: *They were anxious to do their best.*

eager beaver *Informal.* an especially hard-working person.

ea·gle (ē′gəl) *n.* **1** a large, strong bird of prey that has keen eyes and powerful wings. Eagles live on flesh. **2** a picture of an eagle, or an object shaped like an eagle, used as an emblem on a flag, coat of arms, coin, stamp, etc.: *The eagle is the symbol of the United States.* **3** a standard bearing the figure of an eagle as an emblem. **4** in golf, two strokes less than par for any hole on a course. **5 Eagle,** the constellation Aquila. [ME < OF *aigle* < L *aquila*]

ea·gle-eyed (ē′gəl īd′) *adj.* able to see far and clearly.

ea·glet (ē′glit) *n.* a young eagle. [< F *aiglette,* dim. of *aigle* eagle]

ear[1] (ēr) *n.* **1** the part of the body by which human beings and animals hear, usually consisting of three parts **(external ear, middle ear,** and **inner ear)**; organ of hearing. **2** the external ear; visible part of the ear. **3** the sense of hearing. **4** the ability to distinguish small differences in sounds: *That musician has a very good ear for pitch and tone.* **5** favorable attention; listening; attention. **6** anything shaped like the external part of an ear.

MALLEUS
INCUS
STAPES
SEMICIRCULAR CANALS
AUDITORY NERVE
COCHLEA
VESTIBULE
EARDRUM
EUSTACHIAN TUBE

The ear of a man

be all ears, *Informal.* listen eagerly; pay careful attention.
believe one's ears, credit what one hears.
be wet behind the ears, *Informal.* be quite immature.
by the ears, in a state of discord or contention.
fall on deaf ears, not be listened to; receive no attention.
gain the ear of, induce someone to listen favorably.
go in one ear and out the other, make no impression.
have or **keep an ear to the ground,** *Informal.* pay attention to what people are thinking and saying so that one can act accordingly.
lend an ear, listen; pay attention.
play by ear, a play (an instrument or a composition) without using written music. **b** deal with difficulties or problems as they arise.
set by the ears, cause to disagree or quarrel; stir up trouble between.
turn a deaf ear, refuse to listen; pay no attention.
up to the ears, *Informal.* deeply taken up; thoroughly involved; almost overcome.
[OE *ēare*] —**ear′less,** *adj.* —**ear′like′,** *adj.*

ear[2] (ēr) *n.* the part of cereal plants that contains the grains. The grains of corn, wheat, oats, barley, and rye are formed on ears. —*v.* develop into ears; form ears. [OE *ēar*]

An ear of corn

ear·ache (ēr′āk′) *n.* pain in the ear.

ear·drop (ēr′drop′) *n.* an earring, especially one with an ornament hanging from the ear.

ear·drum (ēr′drum′) *n.* **1** the thin membrane across the middle ear that vibrates when sound waves strike it; tympanic membrane. See **ear**[1] for diagram. **2** the middle ear.

eared (ērd) *adj.* having ears or earlike parts.

-eared *combining form.* having a specific number or kind of ears: *long-eared, one-eared.*

eared seal any of a family of seals having small external ears, including the sea lions and fur seals.

ear·flap (ēr′flap′) *n.* a part of a cap that can be turned down over the ear to keep it warm.

earl (ėrl) *n.* **1** in the United Kingdom, a nobleman ranking below a marquis and above a viscount. The wife or widow of an earl is called a countess. **2** in England, formerly, a noble who was the governor of a county or shire. **3** the title of an earl. [OE *eorl*]

ear·lap (ēr′lap′) *n.* **1** an earflap. **2** the lobe of the ear. **3** the external ear; visible part of the ear.

earl·dom (ėrl′dəm) *n.* **1** the territory under the rule of an earl. **2** the rank or dignity of an earl.

ear·ly (ėr′lē) *adv. adj.* **-li·er, -li·est.** —*adv.* **1** near the beginning; in the first part: *The sun is not hot early in the day.* **2** before the usual or expected time: *Call me early.* **3** long ago; far back in time; in ancient times: *The plough was invented early in the history of man.* **4** before very long; in the near future; soon.
—*adj.* **1** of or occurring in the first part: *In his early years he liked ships.* **2** occurring before the usual or expected time: *We had an early dinner.* **3** happening far back in time. **4** occurring in the near future: *Let us have an early reply.* [OE *ǣrlīce* < *ǣr* ere + *-līce* -ly[1]]
—**ear′li·ness,** *n.*

early bird a person who gets up or arrives early.

ear·mark (ēr′märk′) *n.* **1** *Informal.* a mark made on the ear of an animal to show who owns it. **2** a special mark, quality, or feature that gives information about a person or thing; sign.
—*v.* **1** make an earmark on. **2** identify or give information about: *Careful work earmarks a good student.* **3** set aside for some special purpose: *Five hundred dollars is earmarked to buy books for the library.*

ear·muffs (ēr′mufs′) *n.pl.* a pair of coverings to put over the ears to keep them warm.

earn (ėrn) *v.* **1** receive for work or service; be paid: *She earns ten dollars a day.* **2** do enough work for; deserve; be worth: *He is paid more than he really earns.*

3 bring or get as deserved: *Her unselfish acts earned her the respect of all who knew her.* 4 gain as a profit or return: *Money well invested earns good interest.* [OE *earnian*] —**earn′er,** *n.*

ear·nest[1] (ėr′nist) *adj.* 1 sincerely zealous; strong and firm in purpose; serious. 2 important: "*Life is real, life is earnest.*" —*n.* **in earnest, 1** seriously: *I speak in earnest.* 2 sincerely zealous; serious. [OE *eornost*] —**ear′nest·ly,** *adv.* —**ear′nest·ness,** *n.* —**Syn.** *adj.* 1 sincere, diligent.

ear·nest[2] (ėr′nist) *n.* 1 the part given or done in advance as a pledge for the rest: *Take this as an earnest of what is to come.* 2 anything that shows what is to come; pledge; token. [ME *ernes,* apparently alteration (by association with *-ness*) of *erres* < OF *erres,* pl. < L *arra* < Gk. *arrhabōn* < Hebrew *'ērābōn*]

earnest money money paid as a pledge.

earn·ings (ėr′ningz) *n.pl.* money earned; wages; profits.

ear·phone (ēr′fōn′) *n.* a receiver for a telephone, telegraph, radio, hearing aid, etc. that is fastened over one or both ears; headphone.

ear·piece (ēr′pēs′) *n.* 1 a part of something that is connected to, held to, or supported by the ear; *the earpiece of a telephone.* 2 an earflap.

ear·plug (ēr′plug′) *n.* 1 a round piece of rubber, plastic, etc. inserted into the ear to keep out noise or water. 2 an earphone connected to a radio, television set, etc. for private listening.

ear·ring (ēr′ring′) *n.* an ornament for the lobe of the ear, held in place either by a screw or clip or by a metal ring passed through a hole in the lobe of the ear.

ear·shot (ēr′shot′) *n.* the distance at which a sound can be heard; range of hearing: *He was out of earshot and could not hear our shouts.*

earth (ėrth) *n.* 1 the planet on which we live; the third planet from the sun, and the fifth in size. 2 all the people who live on this planet. 3 this world (often in contrast to heaven and hell). 4 dry land. 5 ground; soil; dirt. 6 the ground: *The arrow fell to the earth 100 yards away.* 7 the hole of a fox or other burrowing animal. 8 worldly matters. 9 in chemistry, a metallic oxide from which it is difficult to remove the oxygen, such as alumina. 10 in electricity, the connection of a conductor with the earth. **11 come back to earth,** stop dreaming and get back to practical matters. **12 down to earth,** seeing things as they really are; practical. **13 how, why,** etc. **on earth,** how, why, etc. ever: *How on earth can one accomplish such a feat?* **14 run to earth, a** hunt or chase until caught. **b** look for until found.
—*v.* 1 connect (an electrical wire or other conductor) with the earth; ground. 2 cover with soil: *earth up a plant or its roots.* 3 drive (a fox, etc.) to its burrow. 4 hide in the earth: *The fox earthed.* [OE *eorthe*]
Syn. *n.* 1, 3 **Earth, world, globe** = the planet on which we live. **Earth** applies to this planet covered by land and water, in contrast to the other planets and sun, stars, etc. or, sometimes, to heaven and hell. **World** applies to the earth as the home of man, usually suggesting all mankind and human affairs. In the works of older writers, **world** sometimes means the visible universe, including sun, stars, etc. **Globe** applies to the earth as our world, and emphasizes its roundness: *Nowadays everyone on earth should try to understand the people of the world all over the globe.*

earth·born (ėrth′bôrn′) *adj.* 1 sprung from the earth. 2 human; mortal.

earth·bound (ėrth′bound′) *adj.* bound or limited to this earth.

earth·en (ėr′thən) *adj.* 1 made of earth. 2 made of baked clay.

earth·en·ware (ėr′thən wãr′) *n.* 1 dishes, containers, etc. made of baked clay, fired to a lower temperature than stoneware or porcelain; pottery or crockery. 2 baked clay —*adj.* made of earthenware.

earth·ling (ėrth′ling) *n.* 1 an inhabitant of the earth; human being. 2 a worldly person.

earth·ly (ėrth′lē) *adj.* **-li·er, -li·est.** 1 having to do with the earth, not with heaven. 2 possible; conceivable: *That rubbish is of no earthly use.* —**earth′li·ness,** *n.*
Syn. 1 **Earthly, terrestrial, worldly** = having to do with the earth. **Earthly** describes things connected with life in this world, in contrast to heavenly things: *He thinks only of earthly affairs.* **Terrestrial** is the formal word, meaning "earthly," contrasted with *celestial* and is used particularly to describe things on the earth regarded as a planet: *Of all terrestrial beings man is the most adaptable.* **Worldly,** in contrast to *spiritual,* emphasizes thinking only of human affairs, especially pleasures, success, vanity, etc.: *She enjoys parties, dances, and other worldly pleasures.*

earth·man (ėrth′man′ or ėrth′mən) *n.* **-men** (-men′ or -mən). a man considered as an inhabitant of the planet earth; human being.

earth·nut (ėrth′nut′) *n.* 1 the underground part of certain plants, such as root, tuber, or underground pod: *Peanuts are earthnuts.* 2 a plant producing such a root, tuber, etc.

earth·quake (ėrth′kwāk′) *n.* a shaking of the earth's surface, caused by the sudden movement of masses of rock or by changes beneath the earth's surface.

earth satellite a satellite of the earth, especially a metal sphere or other structure launched by rockets into an orbit outside the earth's atmosphere.

earth science any of a group of sciences concerned with the origin and physical features of the earth. *Examples*: geology, geography, seismology.

earth-shak·ing (ėrth′shāk′ing) *adj.* of extreme importance or significance.

earth tide a modification of the earth's crust, similar to the ocean tide, due to gravitation. The rigidity of the earth can be calculated from the distortions thus caused in solid rock.

earth·ward (ėrth′wərd) *adv. adj.* toward the earth.

earth·wards (ėrth′wərdz) *adv.* earthward.

earth·work (ėrth′wėrk′) *n.* 1 a bank of earth piled up for a fortification. 2 the moving of earth in engineering operations.

earth·worm (ėrth′wėrm′) *n.* a reddish-brown or grayish worm that lives in the soil; angleworm.

earth·y (ėr′thē) *adj.* **earth·i·er, earth·i·est.** 1 of earth or soil. 2 like earth or soil. 3 not spiritual; worldly. 4 not refined; coarse. 5 natural; simple and frank; unsophisticated. —**earth′i·ly,** *adv.* —**earth′i·ness,** *n.*

ear trumpet a trumpet-shaped instrument held to the ear as an aid in hearing.

ear·wax (ēr′waks′) *n.* the sticky, yellowish substance that collects in the canal of the outer ear.

ear·wig (ēr′wig′) *n.* 1 a beetle-like insect once supposed to creep into people's ears. 2 a kind of long, narrow-bodied centipede. [OE *ēarwicga* < *ēare* ear + *wicga* beetle, worm]

ease (ēz) *n. v.* **eased, eas·ing.** —*n.* 1 freedom from pain or trouble; comfort. 2 freedom from trying hard; lack of effort; readiness. 3 freedom from constraint; natural or easy manner. **4 at ease, a** free from pain or trouble; comfortable. **b** with the body relaxed and the feet apart: *The soldiers were ordered to stand at ease.* **5 take one's ease,** make oneself comfortable; rest. **6 with ease,** without having to try hard; with little effort.
—*v.* 1 make free from pain or trouble; give relief or comfort to. 2 lessen; lighten: *This medicine eased my pain.* 3 make easy; loosen: *The belt is too tight; ease it a little.* 4 move slowly and carefully: *He eased the big box through the narrow door.* 5 become less rapid, less tense, etc. 6 make (money, credit, etc.) available at low rates of interest. 7 of securities, goods, etc., tend to decline in prices. **8 ease in,** break in with light work. **9 ease off** or **up, a** lessen; lighten. **b** loosen. **10 ease out,** dismiss from or leave quietly (a job, an office, etc.). [ME < OF *aisier* < *aise* comfort, elbow-room < VL *adjacens* neighborhood < L *adjacens* adjacent. Doublet of ADJACENT.]
Syn. *n.* 1 **Ease, comfort** = freedom from strain. **Ease** = freedom from hard work, trouble, pain, or any pressure, and suggests being relaxed or at rest: *When the holidays come, I am going to live a life of ease.* **Comfort** = freedom from all strain, pain, hardship, and unhappiness, and emphasizes feeling well and perfectly content: *Let others have money and fame; I want only comfort.* –*v.* 1 relieve, soothe.

ea·sel (ē′zəl) *n.* a support or upright frame for holding a picture, blackboard, etc. [< Du. *ezel* easel, literally, ass < L *asinus*]

ease·ment (ēz′mənt) *n.* 1 in law, a right held by one person in land owned by another. 2 an easing; relief: *an easement of political tension.* 3 a convenience.

eas·i·ly (ēz′ə lē) *adv.* 1 in an easy manner. 2 without trying hard; with little effort. 3 without pain or trouble; comfortably. 4 smoothly; freely. 5 by far; beyond question: *She is easily the best singer in the choir.* 6 very likely: *A war may easily begin.*

eas·i·ness (ēz′ē nis) *n.* 1 the quality, condition, or state of being easy. 2 carelessness; indifference.

east (ēst) *n.* 1 the direction of the sunrise: point of the compass to the right as one faces north. 2 Also, **East.** the part of any country toward the east. 3 **the East,** a the eastern part of Canada and the United States. b the countries in Asia; the Orient. c the Soviet Union and the countries allied with it; the communist world. d the Eastern Roman Empire. 4 **down East,** in Canada: a any point to the east of Winnipeg, especially that part east of Quebec. b in or towards any place east of Winnipeg, especially that part east of Quebec.
—*adj.* 1 toward the east. 2 from the east. 3 in the east. 4 **east of,** farther east than.
—*adv.* toward the east: *They travelled east.* [OE *ēast*]

East African shilling 1 a unit of money in Kenya, Tanzania, and Uganda. See table at **money.** 2 a coin or note worth one East African shilling.

east·bound (ēst′bound′) *adj.* going toward the east.

East·er (ēs′tər) *n.* 1 the yearly Christian celebration commemorating Christ's rising from the dead. In most Christian churches, Easter comes between March 21 and April 26 on the first Sunday after the first full moon after March 21. 2 the season of Easter. —*adj.* of or having to do with Easter: *Easter music.* [OE *ēastre,* originally, the name of a dawn goddess < *ēast* east]

Easter egg a colored egg, either real or artificial, used as a gift or for decoration at Easter.

east·er·ly (ēs′tər lē) *adj. adv.* 1 toward the east. 2 from the east: *an easterly wind.*

east·ern (ēs′tərn) *adj.* 1 toward the east. 2 from the east. 3 of or in the east; of or in the eastern part of the country. 4 of or in the Orient, or Asia; Oriental. 5 of or having to do with the Soviet Union and its East European satellites.

Eastern Church 1 a group of Christian churches in E. Europe, W. Asia, and Egypt that do not recognize the Pope as head of the church, but follow the ceremonies used by the patriarch of Constantinople; Orthodox Church. 2 Uniat Church.

East·ern·er (ēs′tər nər) *n.* a native or inhabitant of the eastern part of the country: *In the West, Ontario people are referred to as Easterners. In Ontario, Maritimers are referred to as Easterners.*

east·ern·most (ēs′tərn mōst′) *adj.* farthest east.

Eastern Townships most of that part of Quebec lying south of the St. Lawrence River Valley and west of a line drawn southeast from Quebec City to the United States border: *The Eastern Townships were first settled by United Empire Loyalists.*

East·er·tide (ēs′tər tīd′) *n.* Easter time.

East·main (ēst′mān′) *n. Cdn.* the eastern shore of Hudson Bay.

east·ward (ēst′wərd) *adv. adj.* toward the east.

east·ward·ly (ēst′wərd lē) *adj. adv.* 1 toward the east. 2 of winds, from the east.

east·wards (ēst′wərdz) *adv.* eastward.

eas·y (ēz′ē) *adj.* eas·i·er, eas·i·est, *adv.* —*adj.* 1 requiring little effort; not hard: *easy work.* 2 free from pain, discomfort, trouble, or worry: *an easy life.* 3 giving comfort or rest: *an easy chair.* 4 fond of comfort or rest; lazy. 5 not harsh; not severe; not strict: *easy terms.* 6 not hard to influence; ready to agree with, believe in, or help anyone: *Choose whichever one you wish: I'm easy.* 7 smooth and pleasant; not awkward: *easy manners.* 8 not tight; loose: *an easy fit.* 9 not fast; slow: *an easy pace.* 10 not much in demand; not hard to get. 11 of a money market, favorable to borrowers. 12 of aces or honors in card games, divided evenly between the competing sides. 13 **on easy street,** in comfortable circumstances.
—*adv. Informal.* in an easy manner; with ease. [ME < OF *aisie,* pp. of *aisier* set at ease. See EASE.]

hat, āge, cãre, fär; let, ēqual, tėrm; it, īce
hot, ōpen, ôrder; oil, out; cup, pu̇t, rüle, ūse
əbove, takən, pencəl, lemən, circəs
ch, child; ng, long; sh, ship
th, thin; ᴛʜ, then; zh, measure

Syn. *adj.* 1 Easy, simple, effortless = requiring little effort. Easy = not hard because not too much work is needed: *Dinner was easy to prepare.* Simple = not complicated: *I can work out simple crossword puzzles.* Effortless = without effort, but suggests seeming to be easy or simple either by nature or by training: *Watch the effortless movements of a cat.* 2 tranquil, comfortable.

easy chair a comfortable chair, usually having arms and cushions.

eas·y·go·ing (ēz′ē gō′ing) *adj.* taking matters easily; not worrying.

easy mark *Informal.* a person who is easily imposed on.

eat (ēt) *v.* **ate, eat·en, eat·ing** (see note below). 1 chew and swallow. 2 have a meal: *Where shall we eat?* 3 gnaw; devour: *Termites have eaten the posts and ruined them.* 4 destroy as if by eating; corrode; wear away: *The sea has eaten into the north shore. The acid has eaten through the metal.* 5 make by eating: *Moths ate holes in my wool coat.* 6 *Informal.* bother; annoy. 7 **eat one's words,** *Informal.* take back what one has said; retract. 8 **eat out of another's hand,** be completely submissive to him or her. 9 **eat up,** a eat all of. b use up; waste away: *Extravagance ate up his inheritance.* c. *Slang.* receive eagerly or greedily: *Mary is eating up the course in algebra. They lavished the most absurd flattery on him, and he ate it up.* [OE *etan*] —**eat′er,** *n.* —**Syn. 4** consume, waste.

☛ eat. The principal parts of *eat* are: *eat* (ēt), *ate* (āt), *eaten* (ēt′ən). The British pronunciation of ate (et) is not uncommon in the Maritimes, although it is rarely heard elsewhere in Canada.

eat·a·ble (ēt′ə bəl) *adj.* fit to eat. —*n.* Usually, **eatables,** *pl.* food.

ea·ten (ēt′ən) *v.* pp. of **eat.**

eat·er·y (ē′tər ē) *n.* **-er·ies.** *Informal.* a restaurant.

Eau de Co·logne (ō′ də kə lōn′) *Trademark.* cologne. [< F *eau de Cologne* water of Cologne, Germany, where it was first made]

eau de vie (ō′ də vē′) *French.* brandy; literally, water of life.

eaves (ēvz) *n.pl.* the lower edges of a roof projecting beyond the wall of a building. [OE *efes*]

☛ Eaves, originally singular, is now understood as plural, and a new singular, *eave,* is sometimes found.

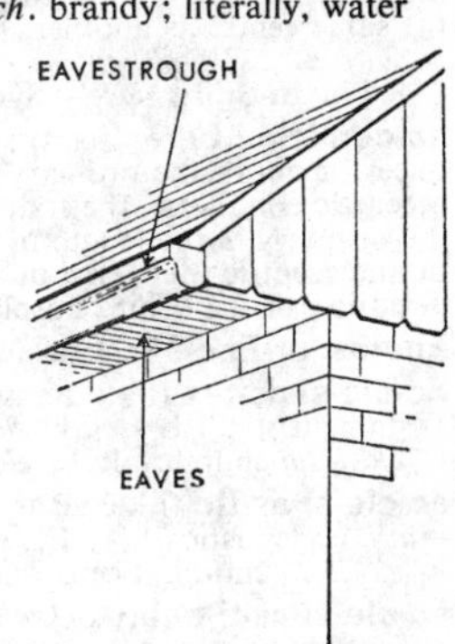

eaves·drop (ēvz′drop′) *v.* **-dropped, -drop·ping.** listen to what one is not supposed to hear; listen secretly to private conversation. [OE *efesdrype* the dripping of water from the eaves, the ground on which the water drips; hence to stand there, especially to listen to private conversation] —**eaves′drop′per,** *n.*

eaves·trough (ēvz′trof′) *n.* a gutter placed under the eaves of a roof to catch rain water and carry it away.

ebb (eb) *n.* 1 a flowing of the tide away from the shore; fall of the tide. 2 a growing less or weaker; decline. 3 a point of decline: *His fortunes were at their lowest ebb.*
—*v.* 1 flow out; fall: *We waded farther out as the tide ebbed.* 2 grow less or weaker; decline: *His courage began to ebb as he neared the haunted house.* [OE *ebba*] —**Syn.** *v.* 2 wane, decrease.

ebb and flow 1 the falling and rising of the tide. 2 constantly changing circumstances; a period of growth followed by a period of decline: *The ebb and flow of business.*

ebb tide the flowing of the tide away from the shore.

eb·on (eb′ən) *Poetic.* —*n.* ebony. —*adj.* 1 made of ebony. 2 dark; black.

eb·on·ite (eb′ən īt′) *n.* a hard, black substance made by heating rubber together with a large quantity of sulphur; vulcanite. Ebonite is used in making combs and buttons and for electric insulation. [< *ebony* + *-ite*[1]]

eb·on·y (eb′ən ē) *n.* **-on·ies,** *adj.* —*n.* **1** a hard, heavy, durable wood, used for the black keys of a piano, the backs and handles of brushes, ornamental woodwork, etc. **2** a tropical tree that yields this wood.
—*adj.* **1** made of ebony. **2** like ebony; black; dark. [ME *hebeny* < L *ebeninus* of ebony < Gk. < Egyptian]

e·bul·lience (i bul′yəns or i bul′ē əns) *n.* **1** an overflow of excitement, liveliness, etc.; great enthusiasm. **2** a bubbling up like a boiling liquid: *the ebullience of the river below the falls.*

e·bul·lient (i bul′yənt or i bul′ē ənt) *adj.* **1** overflowing with excitement, liveliness, etc.; very enthusiastic. **2** boiling; bubbling. [< L *ebulliens, -entis,* ppr. of *ebullire* < *ex-* out + *bullire* boil] —**e·bul′lient·ly,** *adv.*

eb·ul·li·tion (eb′ə lish′ən) *n.* **1** a boiling; a bubbling up. **2** an outburst (of feeling, etc.).

ec- the form of **ex-**[2] before consonants, as in *eccentric, eclectic, ecstasy.*

é·car·té (ā′kär tā′) *n.* a card game for two people, played with 32 cards. [< F *écarté,* pp. of *écarter* discard < *é-* out + *carte* card[1]]

ec·ce ho·mo (ek′sē hō′mō or ek′e) **1** Latin for "Behold the man!" John 19 : 5. **2** a picture, statue, etc. of Christ crowned with thorns.

ec·cen·tric (ek sen′trik) *adj.* **1** out of the ordinary; odd, peculiar. **2** in mathematics, not having the same centre: *These circles* ◎ *are eccentric.* **3** in astronomy, not moving in a circle but in a related line. The orbit of an eccentric planet is not circular. **4** off centre; having its axis set off centre: *an eccentric wheel.*

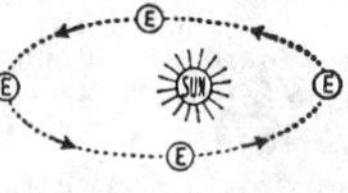

An eccentric

—*n.* **1** a person who behaves in an unusual manner. **2** a disk or wheel set off centre so that it can change circular motion into back-and-forth motion. **3** a circle not having the same centre as another. [< Med.L *eccentricus* < L *eccentrus* < Gk. *ekkentros* < *ek-* out + *kentron* centre] —**ec·cen′tri·cal·ly,** *adv.* —**Syn.** *adj.* **1** irregular, queer.

ec·cen·tric·i·ty (ek′sen tris′ə tē) *n.* **-ties. 1** something queer or out of the ordinary; oddity; peculiarity. **2** an eccentric condition; the state of being unusual or out of the ordinary. **3** the length of the back-and-forth stroke of an eccentric (def. 2). **4** in astronomy, the amount of deviation of the orbit of a planet from a perfect circle.

Eccles. or **Eccl.** Ecclesiastes.

Ec·cle·si·as·tes (i klē′zē as′tēz) *n.* a book of the Old Testament. [< LL < Gk. *ekklēsiastēs* preacher < *ekklēsia* church, ult. < *ek-* out + *kaleein* call]

ec·cle·si·as·tic (i klē′zē as′tik) *n.* a clergyman.
—*adj.* ecclesiastical. [< LL *ecclesiasticus* < Gk., ult. < *ekklēsia* church. See ECCLESIASTES.]

ec·cle·si·as·ti·cal (i klē′zē as′tə kəl) *adj.* of or having to do with the church or the clergy. —**ec·cle′si·as′ti·cal·ly,** *adv.*

Ec·cle·si·as·ti·cus (i klē′zē as′tə kəs) *n.* a book of proverbs included in the Douay Version of the Bible and in the Apocrypha.

Ecclus. Ecclesiasticus.

ec·dys·i·ast (ek diz′ē ast′) *n.* a strip-teaser. [< Gk. *ekdysis* stripping]

ECG in medicine, electrocardiogram.

ech·e·lon (esh′ə lon′) *n.* **1** an arrangement of troops, ships, etc. in a steplike formation. **2** the level of command. **3** a unit performing a special task or stationed in a certain position: *a maintenance echelon, a support echelon.*
—*adj.* **1** of or having to do with an echelon. **2** in the form of an echelon.

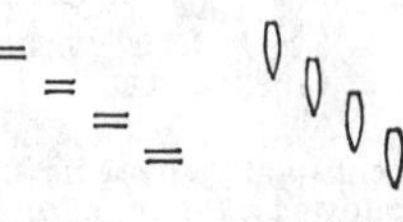

Echelons

—*v.* form into a steplike arrangement. [< F *échelon* rung of a ladder < *échelle* ladder < L *scala*]

e·chid·na (i kid′nə) *n.* **-nas, -nae** (-nē or -nī). a small, egg-laying, ant-eating mammal of Australia having a covering of spines and a long, slender snout. [< L < Gk. *echidna* viper]

e·chi·no·derm (i kī′nə dėrm′ or ek′ə nə dėrm′) *n.* a starfish, sea urchin, or other similar small sea animal having a spiny, stony shell and a body whose parts are arranged radially. [< NL *Echinodermata* < Gk. *echinos* sea urchin, originally, hedgehog + *derma* skin]

e·chi·nus (i kī′nəs) *n.* **-ni** (-nī or -nē). **1** a sea urchin. **2** in architecture, a rounded moulding at the top of a Doric column. [< L < Gk. *echinos* sea urchin, originally hedgehog]

ech·o (ek′ō) *n.* **ech·oes,** *v.* **ech·oed, ech·o·ing.** —*n.* **1** a sounding again; repeating of a sound. An echo is heard when a sound is sent back by a cliff or hill. **2** a person who repeats the words or imitates the feelings, acts, etc. of another. **3** the act of repeating the words or imitating the feelings, acts, etc. of another. **4** a sympathetic response: *Patriotic sentiments evoke an echo in every breast.* **5** in music: **a** a very soft repetition of a phrase. **b** a stop of an organ for producing soft or echolike tones. **6** a cardplayer's response to a signal from his partner or by a signal to his partner's lead. **7** a radio wave which has been reflected. Such echoes are the basis of radar, sonar, etc.
—*v.* **1** sound again; repeat or be repeated in sound; reflect sounds. **2** repeat (the words) or imitate (the feelings, acts, etc.) of another: *That girl is always echoing her mother.* [ME < L < Gk.; cf. *ēchē* sound] —**ech′o·er,** *n.*

Ech·o (ek′ō) *n.* in Greek legend, a nymph who pined away with love for Narcissus until only her voice was left.

e·cho·ic (e kō′ik) *adj.* **1** like an echo. **2** in imitation of natural sounds; onomatopoeic: *"Buzz," "caw," and "moo" are echoic words.*

ech·o·ism (ek′ō iz′əm) *n.* onomatopoeia.

é·clair (ē klãr′ or ā klãr′) *n.* an oblong piece of puff pastry filled with whipped cream or custard and covered with icing. [< F *éclair,* literally, lightning < *éclairer* lighten < L *exclarare* < *ex-* out + *clarus* clear]

é·clat (ā klä′) *n.* **1** a brilliant success. **2** fame; glory. **3** a burst of applause or approval. [< F *éclat* < *éclater* burst out]

ec·lec·tic (ek lek′tik) *adj.* **1** selecting and using what seems best from various sources. **2** made up of selections from various sources.
—*n.* a follower of an eclectic method. [< Gk. *eklektikos* < *eklegein* < *ek-* out of + *legein* pick] —**ec·lec′ti·cal·ly,** *adv.*

ec·lec·ti·cism (ek lek′tə siz′əm) *n.* **1** the use or advocacy of an eclectic method. **2** an eclectic system of philosophy, medicine, etc.

e·clipse (i klips′) *n.* *v.* **e·clipsed, e·clips·ing.** —*n.* **1** a darkening of the sun, moon, etc. when some other heavenly body is in a position that partly or completely cuts off its light as seen from some part of the earth's surface. A **solar eclipse** occurs when the moon passes between the sun and the earth. A **lunar eclipse** occurs when the moon enters the earth's shadow. **2** a loss of importance or reputation; failure for a time: *The former champion has suffered an eclipse.*
—*v.* **1** cut off or obscure the light from; darken. **2** obscure the importance or reputation of; make less outstanding by comparison; surpass: *Napoleon eclipsed all the other generals of his time.* [ME < OF < L < Gk. *ekleipsis* < *ek-* out + *leipein* leave] —**e·clips′er,** *n.*
—**Syn.** *v.* **2** outshine, excel.

e·clip·tic (i klip′tik) *n.* **1** the path that the sun appears to travel in one year. It is that great circle of the celestial sphere which is cut by the plane containing the orbit of the earth. **2** the great circle on the terrestrial sphere which at any given moment lies in the plane of the celestial ecliptic.
—*adj.* **1** of this circle. **2** having to do with the eclipses.

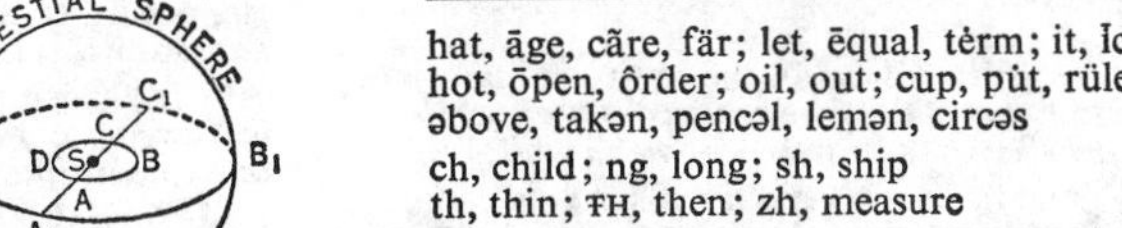

ABCD, the orbit of the earth: $A_1B_1C_1D_1$, an ecliptic; S, the sun.

e·clip·ti·cal (i klip′tə kəl) *adj.* ecliptic.

ec·logue (ek′log) *n.* a short poem about country life, often written as a dialogue between shepherds. [< L *ecloga* < Gk. *eklogē* a selection < *eklegein.* See ECLECTIC.]

ECM European Common Market.

é·cole (ā kol′) *n. French.* a school.

ec·o·log·i·cal (ek′ə loj′ə kəl or ē′kə loj′ə kəl) *adj.* of or having to do with ecology. —**ec′o·log′i·cal·ly,** *adv.*

e·col·o·gist (ē kol′ə jist) *n.* a person skilled in ecology.

e·col·o·gy (ē kol′ə jē) *n.* **1** the branch of biology that deals with the relation of living organisms to their environment and to each other. **2** the branch of sociology that deals with the relations between human beings and their environment. [< Gk. *oikos* house + E *-logy*]

econ. 1 economic. **2** economics. **3** economy.

e·co·nom·ic (ē′kə nom′ik or ek′ə nom′ik) *adj.* **1** having to do with economics. Economic problems have to do with the production, distribution, and consumption of wealth. **2** having to do with the management of the income, supplies, and expenses of a household, community, government, etc. **3** having to do with the material welfare of a community or nation; practical; utilitarian: *economic geography.* **4** economical; saving; thrifty.

e·co·nom·i·cal (ē′kə nom′ə kəl or ek′ə nom′ə kəl) *adj.* **1** avoiding waste; saving; thrifty: *An efficient engine is economical of fuel.* **2** having to do with economics.
Syn. 1 Economical, frugal, thrifty = saving. **Economical** = avoiding waste of money, time, work, or any other resources by careful planning and making the best and fullest possible use of what is spent: *He does more than others because he is economical of time and energy.* **Frugal** emphasizes saving by living simply and needing or using little: *The frugal widow bought and used food carefully.* **Thrifty** = avoiding waste by planning well, spending carefully, and working hard: *Successful farmers are thrifty.*

e·co·nom·i·cal·ly (ē′kə nom′ik lē or ek′ə nom′ik lē) *adv.* **1** in an economical manner. **2** from the point of view of economics.

e·co·nom·ics (ē′kə nom′iks or ek′ə nom′iks) *n.* the science of the production, distribution, and consumption of wealth. Economics deals with the material welfare of mankind and the problems of capital, labor, wages, prices, tariffs, taxes, etc.

e·con·o·mist (i kon′ə mist) *n.* **1** an expert in economics. **2** a person who is economical.

e·con·o·mize (i kon′ə mīz′) *v.* **-mized, -miz·ing. 1** manage so as to avoid waste; use to the best advantage. **2** cut down expenses. —**e·con′o·miz′er,** *n.*

e·con·o·my (i kon′ə mē) *n.* **-mies. 1** making the most of what one has; freedom from waste in the use of anything; thrift. **2** an instance of this. **3** the managing of affairs and resources to the best advantage; management. **4** an efficient arrangement of parts; organization; system. **5** a system of managing the production, distribution, and consumption of goods: *feudal economy.* [< L < Gk. *oikonomia* < *oikos* house + *nemein* manage]

ec·ru or **é·cru** (ek′rü or ā′krü) *n. adj.* pale brown; light tan. [< F *écru* raw, unbleached, var. of *cru* raw < L *crudus*]

ec·sta·sy (ek′stə sē) *n.* **-sies. 1** state of great joy; thrilling or overwhelming delight; rapture: *Speechless with ecstasy, the little boy gazed at the toys.* **2** any strong feeling that completely absorbs the mind; uncontrollable emotion. **3** a trance. [< L *extasis* < Gk. *ekstasis* trance, distraction < *existanai* < *ek-* out + *histanai* to place]

ec·stat·ic (ek stat′ik) *adj.* **1** full of ecstasy; showing ecstasy. **2** caused by ecstasy. **3** likely to show ecstasy.
—*n.* **1** a person subject to fits of ecstasy. **2 ecstatics,** *pl.* fits of ecstasy; raptures. —**ec·stat′i·cal·ly,** *adv.*

hat, āge, cãre, fär; let, ēqual, tėrm; it, īce
hot, ōpen, ôrder; oil, out; cup, pu̇t, rüle, ūse
əbove, takən, pencəl, lemən, circəs
ch, child; ng, long; sh, ship
th, thin; ᴛʜ, then; zh, measure

ecto- *combining form.* to or on the outside: *Ectoderm = the outer cellular layer of an embryo.* [< Gk. *ekto-* < *ektos* outside]

ec·to·derm (ek′tə dėrm′) *n.* in biology, the outer layer of cells formed during the development of the embryos of animals. Skin, hair, nails, the enamel of teeth, and essential parts of the nervous system, grow from the ectoderm. [< *ecto-* + *-derm* skin (< Gk. *derma*)]

ec·to·plasm (ek′tə plaz′əm) *n.* **1** in biology, the outer portion of the cytoplasm of a cell. **2** a supposed emanation from the body of a medium in a trance. [< *ecto-* + *-plasm* something moulded (< Gk. *plasma*)]

é·cu (ā kʏ′) *n.* **é·cus** (ā kʏ′). *French.* **1** in the Middle Ages, a short triangular shield carried by a mounted soldier. **2** any of several French gold or silver coins of varying value, in use from the 13th century on, especially a silver coin of the 17th and 18th centuries.

Ec·ua·do·re·an or **Ec·ua·do·ri·an** (ek′wə dôr′ē ən) *adj.* of Ecuador or its people. —*n.* a native or inhabitant of Ecuador.

ec·u·men·ic (ek′yu̇ men′ik) *adj.* ecumenical.

ec·u·men·i·cal (ek′yu̇ men′ə kəl) *adj.* **1** general; universal. **2** of or representing the whole Christian Church. **3** promoting unity among all Christians or Christian denominations. Also, **oecumenical.** [< L < Gk. *oikoumenikos* < *oikoumenē* (*gē*) inhabited (world), ult. < *oikos* dwelling] —**ec′u·men′i·cal·ly,** *adv.*

ec·u·me·nism (ek′yu̇ mə niz′əm) *n.* ecumenical principles or a church movement in support of them.

ec·ze·ma (ek′sə mə or eg zē′mə) *n.* an inflammation of the skin with redness, itching, and the formation of patches of scales. [< NL < Gk. *ekzema* < *ek-* out + *zeein* to boil]

-ed¹ *suffix.* forming the past tense of most English verbs. [OE *-de, -ede, -ode, -ade*]
☛ **-ed.** Pronounced as a separate syllable (id) after (t) or (d): *wanted, loaded:* otherwise, as (d) after a vowel or voiced consonant: *vowed, lagged*; and as (t) after a voiceless consonant: *dressed, washed.*

-ed² *suffix.* **1** forming the past participle. **2** with various meanings: **a** having; supplied with, as in *bearded, long-legged, pale-faced, tender-hearted.* **b** having the characteristics of, as in *honeyed.* [OE *-ed, -od, -ad*]
☛ **-ed.** Pronunciation as for *-ed¹* except that, in certain participles used adjectivally, *-ed²* may be pronounced (id) instead of (d) or (t): *aged* (ā′jid), *learned* (lėrn′id), *crooked* (kru̇k′id).

ed. 1 editor. **2** edition. **3** edited. **4** educated at.

E.D. (Canadian) Efficiency Decoration (for officers of Military Auxiliary Forces).

E·dam (ē′dam or ē′dəm) *n.* Edam cheese.

Edam cheese 1 a round, yellow cheese made in the Netherlands, and usually having red wax on the outside. **2** any cheese resembling this. [< a village in the Netherlands]

E.D.C. or **EDC** European Defence Community (France, Italy, West Germany, and Benelux united for mutual defence).

Ed·da (ed′ə) *n.* **Ed·das.** either of two books written in Icelandic about 1200 to 1230, one in prose, the other in verse. They relate some of the old Norse myths and legends and give rules for the writing of poetry. [< ON < Gmc. *wōth- exaltation of spirits, poetry, song]

ed·dy (ed′ē) *n.* **-dies,** *v.* **-died, -dy·ing.** —*n.* **1** water, air, etc. moving against the main current, especially when having a whirling motion; small whirlpool or whirlwind. **2** any similar current, as of fog or dust, or of thought or opinion: *Eddies of controversy grew around the new theory.*
—*v.* **1** move against the main current in a whirling motion; whirl: *The water eddied out of the sink.* **2** move in circles. [? < OE *ed-* turning + *ēa* stream]

e·del·weiss (ā′dəl vīs′) *n.* a small Alpine plant that

has heads of tiny white flowers in the centre of star-shaped clusters of leaves that are covered with a white fuzz. [< G *Edelweiss* < *edel* noble + *weiss* white]

e·de·ma (i dē′mə) *n.* **-ma·ta** (-mə tə). a swelling caused by an abnormal accumulation of watery fluid in the tissues of the body. [< NL < Gk. *oidēma* < *oidos* tumor]

E·den (ē′dən) *n.* **1** in the Bible, the garden where Adam and Eve lived at first. **2** a delightful spot; paradise. [< Hebrew *'edēn*, literally, pleasure, delight]

e·den·tate (ē den′tāt) *adj.* **1** toothless. **2** of or having to do with the edentates. —*n.* one of a group of mammals that are toothless or that lack incisors. Armadillos, sloths, and some anteaters are edentates. [< L *edentatus* < *ex-* without + *dens, dentis* tooth]

edge (ej) *n. v.* **edged, edg·ing.** —*n.* **1** a line or place where something ends; part farthest from the middle; side. **2** a brink; verge. **3** a thin, sharp side that cuts. The blade of a knife, axe, or razor has an edge. **4** sharpness; keenness. **5** *Informal.* an advantage: *We have a slight edge on the second team in the league.* **6 on edge, a** disturbed; excited; irritable. **b** tense with eagerness; anxious; impatient. **7 set on edge, a** disturb; cause to feel excited or irritable. **b** make eager, anxious, or impatient. **8 take the edge off,** deprive of force, strength, or enjoyment.

—*v.* **1** put an edge on; form an edge on. **2** move in a sideways manner: *She edged through the crowd.* **3** move little by little: *He edged his chair nearer to the fire.* **4** *Informal.* win a narrow victory over: *Our team edged the visitors 3-2.* **5** tilt a ski so that the edge cuts the snow. **6 edge in,** manage to get in. **7 edge out,** *Informal.* win by a narrow margin: *Montreal edged out Toronto in the playoffs.* [OE *ecg*] —**edg′er,** *n.*

edge·ways (ej′wāz′) *adv.* **1** with the edge forward; in the direction of the edge. **2 get a word in edgeways,** manage to say something to a talkative person or in a talkative group.

edge·wise (ej′wīz′) *adv.* edgeways.

edg·ing (ej′ing) *n.* **1** anything forming an edge or put on along an edge. **2** a border or trimming for an edge.

edg·y (ej′ē) *adj.* **edg·i·er, edg·i·est. 1** having an edge; sharp; sharply defined: *edgy outlines.* **2** impatient; irritable. —**edg′i·ly,** *adv.* —**edg′i·ness,** *n.*

ed·i·bil·i·ty (ed′ə bil′ə tē) *n.* fitness for eating.

ed·i·ble (ed′ə bəl) *adj.* fit to eat. —*n.* Usually, **edibles,** *pl.* things to eat. [< LL *edibilis* < L *edere* eat]

e·dict (ē′dikt) *n.* a public order or command by some authority; decree. [< L *edictum* < *edicere* < *ex-* out + *dicere* say] —**Syn.** See **proclamation.**

Edict of Nantes the decree signed at Nantes in 1598 by Henry IV of France, giving religious freedom to the French Protestants. It was repealed in 1685 by Louis XIV.

ed·i·fi·ca·tion (ed′ə fə kā′shən) *n.* moral improvement; spiritual benefit; instruction.

ed·i·fice (ed′ə fis) *n.* a building, especially a large or imposing building. [ME < OF *edifice* < L *aedificium* < *aedificare* build < *aedis* temple (pl., house) + *facere* make] —**Syn.** See **building.**

ed·i·fy (ed′ə fī′) *v.* **-fied, -fy·ing.** improve morally; benefit spiritually; instruct. [ME < OF *edifier* < L *aedificare* build (up). See EDIFICE.]

e·dile (ē′dīl) *n.* aedile.

ed·it (ed′it) *v.* **1** prepare for publication, correcting errors, checking facts, etc. **2** have charge of (a newspaper, magazine dictionary, etc.) and decide what shall be printed in it. **3** revise or give final form to (motion-picture film, tape recordings, etc.) by such means as cutting and splicing. [< L *editus*, pp. of *edere* < *ex-* out + *dare* give; partly < *editor*]

edit. 1 edition. **2** edited. **3** editor.

e·di·tion (i dish′ən) *n.* **1** all the copies of a book, newspaper, etc. printed alike and issued at or near the same time: *In the second edition of the book many of the errors in the first edition had been corrected.* **2** the form in which a book is printed or published: *The reading matter in the cheap one-volume edition was exactly the same as in the three-volume edition. Some books appear in pocket editions.* **3** an issue of the same newspaper, book, etc. published at different times with additions, changes, alterations, etc.: *the afternoon edition, a foreign edition.*

ed·i·tor (ed′ə tər) *n.* **1** a person who edits. **2** a person who writes editorials. **3** a device or instrument that helps one to edit films, tape recordings, etc. [< L]

ed·i·to·ri·al (ed′ə tô′rē əl) *n.* an article in a newspaper or magazine written by the editor or under his direction, giving the opinion or attitude of the paper regarding some subject. —*adj.* of or having to do with an editor; by an editor.

ed·i·to·ri·al·ist (ed′ə tôr′ē ə list) *n.* a person who writes editorials.

ed·i·to·ri·al·ize (ed′ə tô′rē əl īz′) *v.* **-ized, -iz·ing. 1** write news articles as if they were editorials, including comment and criticisms in the articles. **2** write an editorial.

ed·i·to·ri·al·ly (ed′ə tô′rē əl ē) *adv.* **1** in an editorial manner. **2** in an editorial.

ed·i·tor·ship (ed′ə tər ship′) *n.* the position, duties, or authority of an editor.

E·dom (ē′dəm) *n.* in the Bible, a region in Palestine south of the Dead Sea. Num. 20:14-21.

E·dom·ite (ē′dəm īt′) *n.* a native or inhabitant of Edom.

E.D.P. or **EDP** electronic data processing.

EDT, E.D.T., or **e.d.t.** Eastern Daylight Time.

ed·u·ca·ble (ej′ů kə bəl) *adj.* capable of being educated, taught, or trained.

ed·u·cate (ej′ů kāt′) *v.* **-cat·ed, -cat·ing. 1** develop in knowledge, skill, ability, or character by training, study, or experience; teach; train. **2** send to school. [< L *educare* bring up, raise; related to *educere.* See EDUCE.] —**Syn. 1** instruct.

ed·u·ca·tion (ej′ů kā′shən) *n.* **1** a development in knowledge, skill, ability, or character by teaching, training, study, or experience; teaching; training. **2** the knowledge, skill, ability, or character developed by teaching, training, study, or experience. **3** the science and art that deals with the principles, problems, etc. of teaching and learning.

Syn. 2 Education, enlightenment, culture = the qualities and knowledge a person gets from study, teaching, and experience. **Education** emphasizes the training, knowledge, and abilities a person gets through teaching and study: *A person with education knows how to speak, write, and read well.* **Enlightenment** emphasizes the insight and understanding that make a person free from prejudice and ignorance: *A person with enlightenment knows the value of education.* **Culture** applies to the combination of enlightenment and fineness of feeling and taste that results from complete education: *A person of culture appreciates music and art.*

ed·u·ca·tion·al (ej′ů kā′shən əl or ej′ů kāsh′nəl) *adj.* **1** of or having to do with education: *an educational association.* **2** giving education; tending to educate: *an educational motion picture.* —**ed′u·ca′tion·al·ly,** *adv.*

ed·u·ca·tion·al·ist (ej′ů kā′shə nə list) *n.* an expert on the methods and principles of education; educator.

ed·u·ca·tion·ist (ej′ů kā′shə nist) *n.* an educationalist.

ed·u·ca·tive (ej′ů kā′tiv) *adj.* **1** that educates; instructive. **2** of or having to do with education.

ed·u·ca·tor (ej′ů kā′tər) *n.* **1** a person whose profession is education; teacher. **2** a leader in education; authority on methods and principles of education.

e·duce (i dūs′ or i düs′) *v.* **e·duced, e·duc·ing.** bring out; draw forth; elicit; develop. [< L *educere* < *ex-* out + *ducere* lead]

-ee *suffix.* **1** a person who is ——: *absentee = person who is absent.* **2** a person who is ——ed: *appointee = person who is appointed.* **3** a person to whom something is ——ed: *mortgagee = person to whom something is mortgaged.* **4** a person who ——s: *standee = a person who stands.* [< F *-é*, masc. pp. ending]

E.E. Electrical Engineer.

EEC European Economic Community.

EEG in medicine, electroencephalogram.

eel (ēl) *n.* **1** a long, slippery fish, shaped like a snake and lacking ventral fins. **2** any of various similar fishes, such as the electric eel and lamprey. [OE *ǣl*] —**eel′-like′,** *adj.*

hat, āge, cãre, fär; let, ēqual, tėrm; it, īce
hot, ōpen, ôrder; oil, out; cup, pu̇t, rüle, ūse
əbove, takən, pencəl, lemən, circəs
ch, child; ng, long; sh, ship
th, thin; ᴛʜ, then; zh, measure

eel·grass (ēl′gras′) *n.* **1** a sea plant having long, narrow leaves, growing under water along the North Atlantic and North Pacific coasts of North America. **2** a fresh-water plant with ribbonlike leaves springing directly from the root, growing in shallow ponds; wild celery.

eel·pout (ēl′pout′) *n.* **1** a small, eel-like salt-water fish. **2** a burbot. [OE *ǣlepūte*]

e'en (ēn) *adv. Poetic.* even.

e'er (ãr) *adv. Poetic.* ever.

-eer *suffix.* **1** a person who is concerned with, works with, or deals with, as in *auctioneer, charioteer.* **2** a person who produces, as in *pamphleteer, sonneteer.* **3** be concerned or deal with, as in *electioneer.* [< F *-ier*]

ee·rie (ēr′ē) *adj.* **-ri·er, -ri·est. 1** causing fear; strange; weird: *an eerie scream.* **2** timid because of superstition. [ME *eri,* var. of *erg,* OE *earg* cowardly] **—ee′ri·ly,** *adv.* **—ee′ri·ness,** *n.* **—Syn. 1** See **weird.**

ee·ry (ēr′ē) *adj.* **-ri·er, -ri·est.** eerie.

ef- the form of **ex-**[1] before *f,* as in *effect.*

EFC Eastern Football Conference.

ef·face (ə fās′) *v.* **-faced, -fac·ing. 1** rub out; blot out; do away with; destroy; wipe out: *The inscriptions on many ancient monuments have been effaced by time. It takes many years to efface the unpleasant memories of a war.* **2** keep (oneself) from being noticed; make inconspicuous: *The shy boy effaced himself by staying in the background.* [< F *effacer* < *es-* away + *face* face < L *facies* form] **—ef·face′a·ble,** *adj.* **—ef·fac′er,** *n.* **—Syn. 1** See **erase.**

ef·face·ment (ə fās′mənt) *n.* **1** an effacing. **2** a being effaced.

ef·fect (i fekt′) *n.* **1** whatever is produced by a cause; something made to happen by a person or thing; result. **2** the power to produce results; force; validity. **3** influence: *The medicine had an immediate effect.* **4** the impression produced. **5** the combination of color or form in a picture, etc.: *Sunshine coming through leaves creates a lovely effect.* **6** purport; intent; meaning. **7 effects,** *pl.* personal property; belongings; goods.
for effect, for show; to impress or influence others.
give effect to, put in operation, make active.
in effect, a in result; in fact; really. **b** in operation; active.
into effect, in operation, in action; in force.
of no effect, with no results; useless.
take effect, begin to operate; become active.
to the effect, with the meaning or purpose.
—*v.* **1** produce as an effect; make happen; get done; bring about. **2** *Rare.* make; construct. [ME < L *effectus* < *efficere* < *ex-* out + *facere* make]
Syn. *n.* **1 Effect, consequence, result** = something produced by a cause. **Effect** applies to whatever is produced by a cause, particularly what happens or occurs directly and immediately: *The effect of raising the speed limit was a number of bad accidents.* **Consequence** applies to something that follows, but is not always closely or directly connected with the cause: *As a consequence, there was a provincial investigation of highway conditions.* **Result** applies to what happens as a final effect or consequence: *The result was a new set of traffic regulations.* **7** See **property.** *-v.* **1** accomplish, achieve, realize.
☛ See **affect** for usage note.

ef·fec·tive (i fek′tiv) *adj.* **1** producing an effect. **2** producing the desired effect. **3** in operation; active: *These laws will become effective on New Year's Day.* **4** striking; impressive. **5** in the armed services, equipped and ready for fighting.
—*n.* **1** a member of the armed services equipped and ready for fighting. **2** a military force equipped and ready for fighting. **—ef·fec′tive·ly,** *adv.* **—ef·fec′tive·ness,** *n.* **—ef·fect′less,** *adj.*
Syn. *adj.* **1 Effective, effectual, efficient** = producing an effect. **Effective,** usually describing things, emphasizes producing a wanted or expected effect: *Several new drugs are effective in treating serious diseases.* **Effectual,** describing things, emphasizes having produced or having the power to produce the exact effect or result intended: *The Christmas Seal campaign is an effectual means of teaching the public about tuberculosis.* **Efficient,** often describing people, emphasizes being able to produce the effect wanted or intended without wasting energy, time, etc.: *A skilled surgeon is highly efficient.*

ef·fec·tor (ə fek′tər) *n.* in physiology: **1** a muscle or gland capable of responding to a nerve impulse. **2** the part of a nerve that transmits an impulse.

ef·fec·tu·al (i fek′chü əl) *adj.* **1** producing the effect desired; capable of producing the effect desired: *Quinine is an effectual preventive of malaria.* **2** valid. **—ef·fec′tu·al·ness,** *n.* **—Syn. 1** See **effective.**

ef·fec·tu·al·ly (i fek′chü əl ē) *adv.* with a desired effect; thoroughly.

ef·fec·tu·ate (i fek′chü āt′) *v.* **-at·ed, -at·ing.** cause; make happen; bring about; accomplish. [< F *effectuer* < L *effectus.* See EFFECT.]

ef·fem·i·na·cy (ə fem′ə nə sē) *n.* lack of manly qualities; unmanly weakness or delicacy.

ef·fem·i·nate (ə fem′ə nit) *adj.* lacking in manly qualities; showing unmanly weakness or delicacy. [< L *effeminatus,* pp. of *effeminare* make a woman out of < *ex-* out + *femina* woman] **—ef·fem′i·nate·ly,** *adv.* **—ef·fem′i·nate·ness,** *n.* **—Syn.** womanish.

ef·fen·di (ə fen′dē) *n.* **-dis.** in Turkey: **1** a title of respect similar to "Sir" or "Master." **2** a person having this title; doctor, official, scholar, etc. [< Turkish *efendi* < Gk. *authentēs* master, doer < *auto-* by oneself + *hentēs* one who acts]

ef·fer·ent (ef′ər ənt) *adj.* in anatomy and physiology, conveying outward from a central organ or point. Efferent nerves carry impulses from the brain to the muscles.
—*n.* an efferent nerve. [< L *efferens, -entis,* ppr. of *efferre* < *ex-* out + *ferre* carry]

ef·fer·vesce (ef′ər ves′) *v.* **-vesced, -vesc·ing. 1** give off bubbles of gas; bubble: *Ginger ale effervesces.* **2** be lively and gay; be excited. [< L *effervescere* boil up < *ex-* out + *fervescere* begin to boil < *fervere* be hot]

ef·fer·ves·cence (ef′ər ves′əns) *n.* **1** the act or process of bubbling. **2** liveliness; gaiety.

ef·fer·ves·cent (ef′ər ves′ənt) *adj.* **1** giving off bubbles of gas; bubbling. **2** lively; gay. **—ef′fer·ves′cent·ly,** *adv.*

ef·fete (i fēt′) *adj.* no longer able to produce; worn out; exhausted. [< L *effetus* worn out by bearing < *ex-* out + *fe-* breed, bear] **—ef·fete′ly,** *adv.* **—ef·fete′ness,** *n.*

ef·fi·ca·cious (ef′ə kā′shəs) *adj.* producing the desired results; effective: *Vaccination for smallpox is efficacious.* **—ef′fi·ca′cious·ly,** *adv.* **—ef′fi·ca′cious·ness,** *n.*

ef·fi·ca·cy (ef′ə kə sē) *n.* **-cies.** the power to produce a desired effect or result; effectiveness. [< L *efficacia* < *efficere* accomplish. See EFFICIENT.]

ef·fi·cien·cy (ə fish′ən sē) *n.* **-cies. 1** the ability to produce the effect wanted without waste of time, energy, etc. **2** efficient operation: *Friction lowers the efficiency of a machine.*

efficiency expert a person whose profession is to devise more effective, economical methods of doing things in factories, offices, etc.

ef·fi·cient (ə fish′ənt) *adj.* **1** able to produce the effect wanted without waste of time, energy, etc. **2** actually producing an effect: *Heat is the efficient cause in changing water to steam.* [< L *efficiens, -entis,* ppr. of *efficere* < *ex-* out of + *facere* do, make] **—ef·fi′cient·ly,** *adv.* **—Syn. 1** competent, capable. See **effective.**

ef·fi·gy (ef′ə jē) *n.* **-gies. 1** a statue, etc. of a person; image: *The dead man's monument bore his effigy.* **2 burn** or **hang in effigy,** burn or hang an image of a person to show hatred or contempt. [< F *effigie* < L *effigies* < *effingere* < *ex-* out + *fingere* form]

ef·flo·resce (ef′lə res′) *v.* **-resced, -resc·ing. 1** burst into bloom; blossom out. **2** in chemistry: **a** change either throughout or on the surface to a powder by loss of water of crystallization when exposed to air. **b** become covered with a crusty deposit when water evaporates. [< L *efflorescere* < *ex-* out + *flos, floris* flower]

ef·flo·res·cence (ef′lə res′əns) *n.* **1** the act or process of blooming; a flowering. **2** the period or state of flowering: *The efflorescence of Romantic music occurred during the nineteenth century.* **3** a mass of flowers.

4 anything resembling a mass of flowers. **5** in chemistry: **a** a change that occurs when crystals lose their water of crystallization and become powder. **b** a powder formed in this way. **c** a deposit formed in this way. **d** the formation of a crusty deposit when water evaporates from a solution. **6** an eruption on the skin; rash.

ef·flo·res·cent (ef′lə res′ənt) *adj.* **1** blooming; flowering. **2** in chemistry: **a** that changes from crystals into powder by losing water of crystallization when exposed to air. **b** covered with a deposit formed by efflorescence.

ef·flu·ence (ef′lü əns) *n.* **1** an outward flow. **2** the thing that flows out; emanation.

ef·flu·ent (ef′lü ənt) *adj.* flowing out or forth. —*n.* **1** that which flows out or forth; outflow. **2** a stream flowing out of another stream, lake, etc. [< L *effluens, -entis,* ppr. of *effluere* < *ex-* out + *fluere* flow]

ef·flu·vi·a (i flü′vē ə) *n.* a pl. of **effluvium.**

ef·flu·vi·al (i flü′vē əl) *adj.* of or having to do with effluvia.

ef·flu·vi·um (i flü′vē əm] *n.* **-vi·a** or **-vi·ums. 1** an unpleasant vapor or odor. **2** a vapor; odor. [< L *effluvium* a flowing out < *effluere.* See EFFLUENT.]

ef·fort (ef′ərt) *n.* **1** the use of energy and strength to do something; a trying hard: *Climbing a steep hill takes effort.* **2** a hard try; strong attempt. **3** the result of effort; anything done with effort; achievement. Works of literature or art are often called literary or artistic efforts. [< F < OF *esfort* < *esforcier* force, exert < L *ex-* out + *fortis* strong]
Syn. 1 Effort, endeavor, application = active use of physical or mental power to do something. **Effort** emphasizes using energy and strength and trying hard, but usually suggests a single act or action: *John made an effort to finish his work today.* **Endeavor,** more formal, applies to sincere and serious effort continued over some time: *By constant endeavor, he realized his ambition.* **Application** emphasizes continued effort and close attention to what one is doing: *By application to his work he makes good grades.*

ef·fort·less (ef′ərt lis) *adj.* requiring or involving no effort; easy. —**ef′fort·less·ly,** *adv.* —**ef′fort·less·ness,** *n.* —**Syn.** See **easy.**

ef·fron·ter·y (ə frun′tər ē or ə frun′trē) *n.* **-ter·ies.** shameless boldness; impudence: *The politician had the effrontery to ask the people he had insulted to vote for him.* [< F *effronterie* < OF < LL *effrons* barefaced, shameless < *ex-* without + *frons, frontis* forehead, ability to blush, hence, without blushing] —**Syn.** presumption, insolence.

ef·ful·gence (i ful′jəns) *n.* brightness; radiance.

ef·ful·gent (i ful′jənt) *adj.* shining brightly; radiant. [< L *effulgens, -entis,* ppr. of *effulgere* < *ex-* forth + *fulgere* shine] —**ef·ful′gent·ly,** *adv.*

ef·fuse (i fūz′) *v.* **-fused, -fus·ing.** pour out; spill; shed. [< L *effusus,* pp. of *effundere* < *ex-* out + *fundere* pour]

ef·fu·sion (i fū′zhən) *n.* **1** a pouring out: *the effusion of blood.* **2** an unrestrained expression of feeling, etc. in talking or writing.

ef·fu·sive (i fū′siv) *adj.* showing too much feeling; too emotional in expression. —**ef·fu′sive·ly,** *adv.* —**ef·fu′sive·ness,** *n.*

eft[1] (eft) *n.* **1** a newt in the land stage. **2** formerly, a small newt or lizard. [OE *efete.* Cf. NEWT.]

eft[2] (eft) *adv. Obsolete.* again. [OE]

eft·soon (eft sün′) *adv. Archaic.* **1** soon afterward. **2** again. [OE *eftsōna* < *eft* again + *sōna* at once]

eft·soons (eft sünz′) *adv. Archaic.* eftsoon.

e.g. exempli gratia.
☛ E.g. is not usually italicized, that is, not underlined in writing, but should always have abbreviation periods. In all but expository prose or technical writing, the English phrase "for example" is stylistically preferable. In formal writing *e.g.* is preceded by some punctuation mark.

e·gad (ē gad′) *interj.* a mild oath, like "by Jove." [alteration of *a God!* Oh God!]

e·gal·i·tar·i·an (ē gal′ə tãr′ē ən) *n.* a person who believes in equality, especially in social equality. —*adj.* of or relating to equality, especially social equality.

e·gal·i·tar·i·an·ism (ē gal′ə tãr′ē ə niz′əm) *n.* belief in equality, especially in social equality.

egg[1] (eg) *n.* **1** a roundish body, covered with a shell or membrane, that is laid by the female of birds, fishes, and other animals that do not bring forth their young. **2** in biology, a female reproductive cell. **3** anything shaped like a hen's egg. **4** *Slang.* an aerial bomb. **5 have** or **put all one's eggs in one basket,** risk everything that one has on one chance. **6 bad egg,** a person or plan that comes to no good. **7 good egg,** a promising person or thing. [ME < ON] —**egg′less,** *adj.* —**egg′like′,** *adj.*

egg[2] (eg) *v.* urge; encourage (*on*): *The other boys egged him on to fight.* [ME < ON *eggja* < *egg* edge, point]

egg cell in biology, the reproductive cell produced by a female plant or animal. A new animal or plant develops from a fertilized egg cell.

egg·head (eg′hed′) *n. Informal. Often derogatory.* an intellectual, especially one who is committed to cultural and intellectual interests and who pays no attention to popular fads; highbrow.

egg·nog (eg′nog′) *n.* a drink made of eggs beaten up with milk and sugar, often containing whisky, brandy, or wine. [< *egg*[1] + *nog* strong ale]

egg·plant (eg′plant′) *n.* **1** a plant having a large, oval, purple-skinned fruit. **2** the fruit, used as a vegetable.

egg·shell (eg′shel′) *n.* the shell covering an egg. —*adj.* like an eggshell; very thin and delicate.

e·gis (ē′jis) *n.* aegis.

eg·lan·tine (eg′lən tīn′ or eg′lən tēn′) *n.* a wild rose having a tall, prickly stem and single pink flowers; sweetbrier. [< F *eglantine,* dim. of OF *aiglent* < VL *aculentus* < L *acus* needle]

e·go (ē′gō or eg′ō) *n.* **e·gos. 1** the individual as a whole in his capacity to think, feel, and act; self. **2** *Informal.* conceit. **3** in philosophy, the element of being that consciously and continuously enables an individual to think, feel, and act. **4** in psychoanalysis, the part of the personality that is conscious of the environment and adapts itself to it. [< L *ego* I]

e·go·cen·tric (ē′gō sen′trik or eg′ō-) *adj.* looking upon oneself as the focus and object of all experience and events; seeing everything in relation to oneself; self-centred; egoistic; —*n.* an egocentric person.

e·go·ism (ē′gō iz′əm or eg′ō iz′əm) *n.* **1** the state of seeking the welfare of oneself only; selfishness. **2** talking too much about oneself; conceit. **3** the ethical doctrine that morality lies in the pursuit of individual self-interest, and that self-interest motivates all conduct.
☛See **egotism** for usage note.

e·go·ist (ē′gō ist or eg′ō ist) *n.* **1** a person who seeks the welfare of himself only; selfish person. **2** a person who talks too much about himself; conceited person. **3** a believer in egoism as a principle of human conduct.

e·go·is·tic (ē′gō is′tik or eg′ō is′tik) *adj.* **1** seeking the welfare of oneself only; selfish. **2** talking too much about oneself; conceited. —**e′go·is′ti·cal·ly,** *adv.*

e·go·tism (ē′gə tiz′əm or eg′ə tiz′əm) *n.* **1** the excessive use of *I, my,* and *me*; habit of thinking, talking, or writing too much of oneself. **2** self-conceit. **3** selfishness. [< *ego* + *-t* + *-ism*]
☛ **Egotism, egoism** = a habit of thinking too much about self. **Egotism** emphasizes conceit, boasting, and selfishness, and means always talking about oneself and one's own affairs and trying to get attention: *Henry's egotism drives away friends.* **Egoism** emphasizes being self-centred and looking at everyone and everything only as it affects oneself and one's own welfare, but does not suggest boasting or annoying conceit, nor always selfishness: *We forget the natural egoism of a genius if he is charming.*

e·go·tist (ē′gə tist or eg′ə tist) *n.* **1** a person who thinks and talks about himself a great deal; conceited, boastful person. **2** a selfish person.

e·go·tis·tic (ē′gə tis′tik or eg′ə tis′tik) *adj.* **1** characterized by egotism; conceited. **2** selfish.

e·go·tis·ti·cal (ē′gə tis′tə kəl or eg′ə tis′tə kəl) *adj.* egotistic.

e·go·tis·ti·cal·ly (ē′gə tis′tik lē or eg′ə tis′tik lē) *adv.* in an egotistic manner.

e·gre·gious (i grē′jəs) *adj.* **1** remarkably or extraordinarily bad; outrageous; flagrant: *an egregious* *lie.* **2** remarkable; extraordinary. [< L *egregius* < *ex-* out + *grex, gregis* herd, flock] —**e·gre′gious·ly,** *adv.*

e·gress (ē′gres) *n.* **1** a going out: *The enemy blocked the narrow pass so that no egress was possible for our soldiers.* **2** a way out; exit. **3** the right to go out. [< L *egressus* < *egredi* < *ex-* out + *gradi* step, go]

e·gret (ē′gret or eg′ret) *n.* **1** any of various herons having tufts of beautiful, long plumes. **2** the plume of an egret; aigrette. [< F *aigrette*]

E·gyp·tian (i jip′shən) *adj.* **1** of or having to do with Egypt or its people. **2** Gypsy. —*n.* **1** a native or inhabitant of Egypt. **2** the language of the ancient Egyptians. **3** a Gypsy.

Egyptian cotton a type of cotton having long fibres, much grown in Egypt.

E·gyp·tol·o·gist (ē′jip tol′ə jist) *n.* an expert in Egyptology.

E·gyp·tol·o·gy (ē′jip tol′ə jē) *n.* the science or study of the monuments, history, language, etc. of ancient Egypt.

eh (ā) *interj.* **1** an exclamation expressing doubt, surprise, or failure to hear exactly. **2** an exclamation suggesting "Yes" for an answer or assuming that the answer will be affirmative: *You're going home now, eh?*

EIB Export-Import Bank.

ei·der (ī′dər) *n.* **1** a large duck, usually black and white, having very soft feathers on its breast. **2** its down. [< Icel. *æthr*]

ei·der-down (ī′dər doun′) *n.* **1** the soft feathers from the breasts of eiders, used to stuff pillows, bed quilts, as trimming, etc. **2** a quilt stuffed with these feathers.

eider duck eider (def. 1).

eight (āt) *n.* **1** one more than seven; 8. **2** a playing card having eight spots. **3** a crew of eight rowers. —*adj.* being one more than seven. [OE *eahta*]

eight ball **1** in pool, a black ball bearing a figure 8, which in certain varieties of the game carries a penalty if hit or pocketed. **2 behind the eight ball,** *Slang.* in an unfavorable position; an awkward or threatening situation.

eight·een (ā′tēn′) *n. adj.* eight more than ten; 18. [OE *eahtatēne*]

eight·eenth (ā′tēnth′) *adj. n.* **1** next after the 17th; last in a series of 18. **2** one, or being one, of 18 equal parts.

eighth (ātth) *adj.* **1** next after the seventh; last in a series of 8. **2** being one of 8 equal parts. —*n.* **1** the next after the seventh; last in a series of 8. **2** one of 8 equal parts. **3** in music, one octave.

eighth note in music, a short note; one eighth of a whole note; quaver.

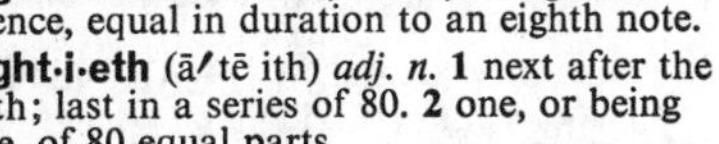
An eighth note

eighth rest in music, a rest, or sign for silence, equal in duration to an eighth note.

eight·i·eth (ā′tē ith) *adj. n.* **1** next after the 79th; last in a series of 80. **2** one, or being one, of 80 equal parts.

eight·y (ā′tē) *n.* **eight·ies,** *adj.* eight times ten; 80. [OE *eahtatig*]

ei·kon (ī′kon) *n.* icon.

Einstein equation (īn′stīn) an equation expressing the relation of mass and energy: $E = MC^2$. E = the energy in ergs; M = the mass in grams; C = the velocity of light in centimetres per second.

ein·stein·i·um (īn stīn′ē əm) *n.* a rare, artificial chemical element that is radio-active and is produced as a by-product of nuclear fission. *Symbol*: Es; *at.no.* 99; *at.wt.* 254 (most stable isotope) [after Albert *Einstein*]

eis·tedd·fod (ā steᴛʜ′vod) *n.* **eis·tedd·fod·au** (ā′steᴛʜ vod′ī). an annual assembly of Welsh poets and musicians. [< Welsh *eisteddfod* session < *eistedd* sit, akin to E *sit*]

ei·ther (ē′ᴛʜər or ī′ᴛʜər) *adj.* **1** one or the other of two: *Either hat is becoming.* **2** each of two: *On either side of the river lie cornfields.*
—*pron.* one or the other of two: *Either of the hats is becoming.*
—*adv.* **1** any more than another; also: *If you do not go, I shall not go either.* **2** *Informal.* a word used to strengthen a negative in contradiction or retraction: *I've not finished all my homework; no, I haven't either.*
—*conj.* one or the other of two: *Either come in or go out.* [OE *ǣgther* < *ǣghwæther* each of two < *ā* always + *gehwæther* each of two]
☛ In formal writing, **either** is always construed as singular (though its informal use as a plural is increasing): *Either is good enough for me. Either Grace or Phyllis is expected.*

e·jac·u·late (i jak′yu̇ lāt′) *v.* **-lat·ed, -lat·ing.** **1** say suddenly and briefly; exclaim. **2** eject; discharge. [< L *ejaculari* < *ex-* out + *jaculum* javelin < *jacere* throw]

e·jac·u·la·tion (i jak′yu̇ lā′shən) *n.* **1** something said suddenly and briefly; exclamation. **2** an ejection; discharge.

e·jac·u·la·to·ry (i jak′yu̇ lə tô′rē) *adj.* **1** said suddenly and briefly; containing exclamations. **2** ejecting; discharging.

e·ject (i jekt′) *v.* **1** throw out: *The volcano ejected lava and ashes.* **2** force out; expel: *The landlord ejected the tenant who did not pay his rent.* [< L *ejectus,* pp. of *ejicere* throw out < *ex-* out + *jacere* throw]

e·jec·tion (i jek′shən) *n.* **1** an ejecting. **2** a being ejected. **3** something ejected: *Lava is a volcanic ejection.*

ejection capsule a cockpit or cabin that can be ejected from an airplane and parachuted to earth.

ejection seat in an airplane, a seat that, with its occupant, can be instantly ejected and parachuted to earth.

e·ject·ment (i jekt′mənt) *n.* an ejecting; a dispossessing; an ousting.

e·jec·tor (i jek′tər) *n.* a person or thing that ejects.

eke[1] (ēk) *v.* **eked, ek·ing.** **1** *Archaic* and *Dialect.* increase; enlarge; lengthen. **2 eke out, a** supply what is lacking to; supplement: *The clerk eked out his regular wages by working evenings and Sundays.* **b** barely make (a living) by various schemes or makeshifts. [dial. var. of obs. *eche* augment, OE *ēcan* < OE *ēaca* addition]

eke[2] (ēk) *adv. conj. Archaic.* also; moreover. [OE *ēac*]

EKG in medicine, electrocardiogram.

el (el) *n.* **1** ell[1]. **2** ell[2]. **3** *Informal.* an elevated railway.

e·lab·o·rate (*adj.* i lab′ə rit or i lab′rit; *v.* i lab′ə rāt′) *adj. v.* **-rat·ed, -rat·ing.** —*adj.* worked out with great care; having many details; complicated.
—*v.* **1** work out with great care; add details to: *The inventor spent months in elaborating his plans for a new engine.* **2** talk, write, etc. in great detail; give added details: *The witness was asked to elaborate upon one of his statements.* **3** make with labor; produce. [< L *elaboratus,* pp. of *elaborare* < *ex-* out + *labor* work]
—**e·lab′o·rate·ly,** *adv.* —**e·lab′o·rate·ness,** *n.*
—**e·lab′o·rat·or,** *n.*
Syn. *adj.* **Elaborate, studied, labored** = worked out in detail. **Elaborate** emphasizes the idea of details, and means having many details all worked out with great care and exactness: *The scientists made elaborate preparations for studying the eclipse.* **Studied** emphasizes care in working out details, and means being thought out beforehand and done on purpose: *His studied politeness was insulting.* **Labored** emphasizes great effort to work out details, and means showing effort by being strained and unnatural: *The boy gave a labored excuse for arriving late at school.*

e·lab·o·ra·tion (i lab′ə rā′shən) *n.* **1** an elaborating. **2** a being elaborated. **3** something elaborated.

E·lam·ite (ē′ləm īt′) *n.* a native or inhabitant of Elam, an ancient country in what is now W. Iran, just east of ancient Babylonia.

é·lan (ā lon′; *French,* ā läɴ′) *n.* enthusiasm; liveliness. [< F *élan* < *élancer* dart]

e·land (ē′lənd) *n.* a large, heavily built African antelope having twisted horns. [< Du. *eland* elk]

e·lapse (i laps′) *v.* **e·lapsed, e·laps·ing.** slip away; glide by; pass: *Hours elapsed while he slept like a log.* [< L *elapsus,* pp. of *elabi* < *ex-* away + *labi* glide]

e·las·mo·branch (i las′mə brangk′ or i laz′mə brangk′) *n.* any of a group of fishes whose skeletons are formed of cartilage and whose gills are thin and platelike.

Sharks and rays are elasmobranchs. [< NL *Elasmobranchii*, pl. < Gk. *elasmos* metal plate + *branchia* gills]

e·las·tic (i las′tik) *adj.* **1** having the quality of springing back to its original size, shape, or position after being stretched, squeezed, bent, etc.: *Toy balloons, sponges, and steel springs are elastic.* **2** springing back; springy: *an elastic step.* **3** recovering quickly from weariness, low spirits, or misfortune; buoyant: *His elastic spirits never let him be discouraged for long.* **4** easily altered to suit changed conditions; flexible; adaptable.
—*n.* **1** elastic tape, cloth, etc., especially when woven partly of rubber. **2** a rubber band. [< NL *elasticus* < Gk. *elastikos* driving, propulsive < *elaunein* drive]
—**e·las′ti·cal·ly,** *adv.*

e·las·tic·i·ty (i las′tis′ə tē or ē′las tis′ə tē) *n.* **1** an elastic quality: *Rubber has great elasticity.* **2** flexibility: *"Good" and "evil" are words having great elasticity of meaning.*

e·las·ti·cized (i las′ti sīzd′) *adj.* woven or made with elastic: *The dress has an elasticized belt.*

e·las·to·mer (i las′tə mər) *n.* in chemistry, any elastic, rubberlike substance. [< *elastic* + Gk. *meros* part]

e·late (i lāt′) *v.* **e·lat·ed, e·lat·ing.** put in high spirits; make joyful or proud. [< L *elatus* < *ex-* out, away + *latus,* pp. to *ferre* carry]

e·lat·ed (i lāt′id) *adj.* in high spirits; joyful; proud.
—**e·lat′ed·ly,** *adv.* —**e·lat′ed·ness,** *n.*

e·la·tion (i lā′shən) *n.* high spirits; joyous pride; exultant gladness.

E layer the Heaviside layer.

El·ber·ta (el bėr′tə) *n.* a variety of freestone peach grown in eastern North America. [< *Elberta,* the name of the wife of the originator of this variety]

el·bow (el′bō) *n.* **1** the joint between the upper and lower arm. **2** anything resembling a bent elbow in shape or position. A sharp turn in a road or river may be called an elbow. **3** a bent joint for connecting pipes. **4** the raised arm of a chair or the end of a sofa, for supporting the elbow. **5 at one's elbow,** close to one. **6 out at the elbow,** worn out; ragged; shabby; poor. **7 rub elbows with,** mingle with (people, especially of a different social level). **8 up to the elbows, a** very busy. **b** deeply involved.
—*v.* **1** push with the elbow, jostle. **2** make one's way by pushing: *He elbowed his way through the crowd.* [OE *elnboga* < *eln* length of lower arm + *boga* bow[2]]

elbow grease *Informal.* hard work; energy.

elbow room or **el·bow·room** (el′bō rüm′ or -rům′) *n.* plenty of room; enough space to move or work in.

eld (eld) *n. Archaic.* **1** old age. **2** old times; former times. [OE *eldo* < *eald* old]

eld·er[1] (el′dər) *adj.* **1** born, produced, or formed before something else; older; senior: *my elder brother, an elder statesman.* **2** prior in rank, validity, etc.: *an elder title to an estate.* **3** earlier; former: *in elder times.*
—*n.* **1** an older person: *Children should respect their elders.* **2** an aged person. **3** an ancestor. **4** one of the older and more influential men of a tribe or community; a chief, ruler, member of council, etc. **5** any of various important officers of certain churches. [OE *eldra,* comparative of *eald* old]

☛ **elder, eldest.** These archaic forms of *old* survive in formal English and are used, when speaking of persons, chiefly for members of the same family: *the elder brother, our eldest daughter;* and in some phrases: *the elder statesman.*

el·der[2] (el′dər) *n.* elderberry. [OE *ellærn*]

el·der·ber·ry (el′dər ber′ē) *n.* **-ries. 1** a shrub or tree having flat clusters of white flowers and black or red berries, used in making wine, pies, etc. **2** the berry of such a plant.

eld·er·ly (el′dər lē) *adj.* somewhat old; beyond middle age; near old age. —*n.* **the elderly,** people who are old.
—Syn. See **old.**

eld·er·ship (el′dər ship′) *n.* **1** the office or position of an elder in a church. **2** a group or court of elders; presbytery.

eld·est (el′dist) *adj.* oldest. [OE *eldest(a),* superlative of *eald* old] ☛ See **elder** for usage note.

El·do·ra·do (el′də rä′dō) *n.* **-dos. 1** a legendary city of great wealth sought by early explorers in South America. **2** any fabulously wealthy place. Also, **El Dorado.** [< Sp. *El Dorado* the gilded]

elec. or **electr. 1** electricity. **2** electrical. **3** electrician.

e·lect (i lekt′) *v.* **1** choose or select for an office by voting: *The club members elect a new president each year.* **2** choose. **3** in theology, select for salvation and eternal life.
—*adj.* **1** elected but not yet in office. **2** specially chosen; selected. **3** chosen by God for salvation and eternal life.
—*n.* **the elect, a** the people supposedly selected or chosen by God for salvation and eternal life because He foresees their merit. **b** people who belong to a group with special rights and privileges. [< L *electus,* pp. of *eligere* < *ex-* out + *legere* choose] —**Syn.** *v.* **2** select, pick.

e·lec·tion (i lek′shən) *n.* **1** a choice. **2** a choosing by vote. **3** a selection by God for salvation. **4** a general election. —**Syn. 1** selection, preference.

e·lec·tion·eer (i lek′shən ēr′) *v.* work for the success of a candidate or party in an election. —**e·lec′tion·eer′er,** *n.*

e·lec·tive (i lek′tiv) *adj.* **1** chosen by an election: *Aldermen are elective officials.* **2** filled by an election: *an elective office.* **3** having the right to vote in an election. **4** having to do with the principle of electing to office. **5** in chemistry, tending to combine with certain substances in preference to others. **6** open to choice; not required: *German is an elective subject in many high schools.*
—*n.* a subject or course of study that may be taken, but is not required. —**e·lec′tive·ly,** *adv.* —**e·lec′tive·ness,** *n.*

e·lec·tor (i lek′tər) *n.* **1** a person who has the right to vote in an election. **2** *U.S.* a member of the electoral college. **3** one of the princes who had the right to elect the emperor of the Holy Roman Empire.

e·lec·tor·al (i lek′tər əl) *adj.* **1** of electors. **2** of or having to do with an election.

electoral college *U.S.* a group of people chosen by the voters to elect the President and Vice-President of the United States.

e·lec·tor·ate (i lek′tər it) *n.* **1** the persons having the right to vote in an election. **2** a territory under the rule of an elector of the Holy Roman Empire. **3** the rank of an elector of the Holy Roman Empire.

E·lec·tra (i lek′trə) *n.* in Greek legend, the daughter of Agamemnon and Clytemnestra. Electra urged her brother, Orestes, to kill their mother and her lover in order to avenge the murder of their father.

Electra complex in psychiatry, the repressed desire of a daughter for her father, parallel to the Oedipus complex in males.

e·lec·tric (i lek′trik) *adj.* **1** of electricity; having to do with electricity. **2** charged with electricity: *an electric battery.* **3** capable of giving an electric shock: *an electric eel.* **4** run by electricity. **5** exciting; thrilling.
—*n. Informal.* **1** a car or railway run by electricity. **2** a substance, such as amber or glass, that can exhibit electricity when rubbed. [< NL *electricus* < LGk. *ēlektron* amber (which, under friction, has the property of attracting)] —**Syn.** *adj.* **5** stimulating, stirring.

e·lec·tri·cal (i lek′trə kəl) *adj.* electric.

e·lec·tri·cal·ly (i lek′trik lē) *adv.* by electricity.

electrical storm electric storm.

electrical transcription 1 the system of radio broadcasting from a special phonograph record. **2** a special phonograph record used for such broadcasting.

electric brain electronic brain.

electric chair a chair used in electrocuting criminals.

electric eel a large eel-like fish of South America that can give strong electric shocks.

electric eye a photo-electric cell. An electric eye can operate a mechanism so as to open a door when its invisible beam is interrupted by the approach of a person, car, etc. Electric eyes are much used in industry, scientific research, etc.

electric fish any fish that can give an electric shock, such as the electric eel.

electric heater a portable device that furnishes heat by means of small electric coils.

e·lec·tri·cian (i lek′trish′ən or ē′lek trish′ən) *n.* a person whose work is installing or repairing electric wires, lights, motors, etc.

e·lec·tric·i·ty (i lek′tris′ə tē or ē′lek tris′ə tē) *n.* **1** a form of energy that can produce light, heat, magnetism, and chemical changes, and that can be generated by friction, induction, or chemical changes. **2** an electric current; flow of electrons. **3** the branch of physics that deals with electricity.

electric ray one of various flat-bodied fish that stun or kill their prey by means of an electric shock; torpedo.

electric storm or **electrical storm** a storm accompanied by thunder and lightning.

e·lec·tri·fi·ca·tion (i lek′trə fə kā′shən) *n.* **1** an electrifying. **2** a being electrified.

e·lec·tri·fy (i lek′trə fī′) *v.* **-fied, -fy·ing. 1** charge with electricity. **2** equip to use electricity: *Some railways once operated by steam are now electrified.* **3** give an electric shock to. **4** excite; thrill. **5** provide with electric power service: *Many rural areas will soon be electrified.*

electro- *combining form.* **1** electric, as in *electromagnet.* **2** electrically, as in *electropositive.* **3** electricity. [< Gk. *ēlektron* amber]

e·lec·tro·bi·ol·o·gy (i lek′trō bī ol′ə jē) *n.* the branch of biology that deals with electrical phenomena in living organisms.

e·lec·tro·car·di·o·gram (i lek′trō kär′dē ə gram′) *n.* a tracing made by an electrocardiograph. *Abbrev.*: ECG, EKG

e·lec·tro·car·di·o·graph (i lek′trō kär′dē ə graf′) *n.* in medicine, an instrument that records the electric current produced by the action of the heart muscle, used in the diagnosis and treatment of heart disease.

e·lec·tro·chem·i·cal (i lek′trō kem′ə kəl) *adj.* of or having to do with electrochemistry.

e·lec·tro·chem·is·try (i lek′trō kem′is trē) *n.* the branch of chemistry that deals with chemical changes produced by electricity and the production of electricity by chemical changes.

e·lec·tro·cute (i lek′trə kūt′) *v.* **-cut·ed, -cut·ing.** kill by an electric current. [< *electro-* + exe*cute*]

e·lec·tro·cu·tion (i lek′trə kū′shən) *n.* a killing by electricity.

e·lec·trode (i lek′trōd) *n.* either of the two terminals of a battery or any other source of electricity; anode or cathode. [< *electro-* + Gk. *hodos* way]

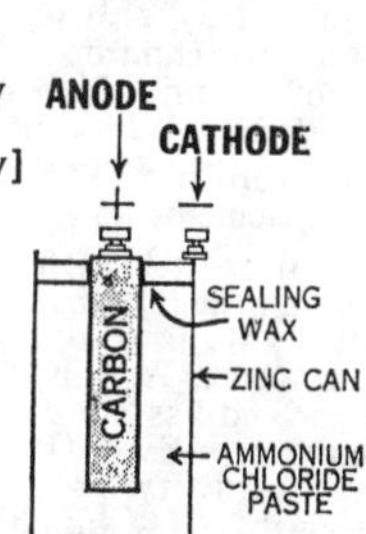

The electrodes of a dry cell: +, positive; −, negative. Chemical reaction between the paste and the zinc causes a flow of electrons toward the zinc, and of positive ions toward the carbon. When the electrodes are connected, the flow of electrons (electric current) leaves the cell at − and returns to it at +

e·lec·tro·dy·nam·ic (i lek′trō dī nam′ik) *adj.* **1** of or having to do with the force of electricity in motion. **2** of or having to do with electrodynamics. —**e·lec′tro·dy·nam′i·cal·ly,** *adv.*

e·lec·tro·dy·nam·ics (i lek′trō dī nam′iks) *n.* the branch of physics that deals with the action of electricity or with electric currents.

e·lec·tro·en·ceph·a·lo·gram (i lek′trō en sef′ə lə gram′) *n.* a tracing made by an electroencephalograph. *Abbrev.*: EEG

e·lec·tro·en·ceph·a·lo·graph (i lek′trō en sef′ə lə graf′) *n.* in medicine, an instrument for measuring the electrical activity of the brain, used in the diagnosis and treatment of brain disorders.

e·lec·tro·lier (i lek′trə lēr′) *n.* a chandelier or other support for electric lights. [< *electro-* + chande*lier*]

e·lec·trol·y·sis (i lek′trol′ə sis or ē′lek trol′ə sis) *n.* **1** the decomposition of a chemical compound into ions by the passage of an electric current through a solution of it. **2** the removal of excess hair, moles, etc. by destruction with an electrified needle. [< *electro-* + *-lysis* a loosing (< Gk. *lysis* < *lyein* loose)]

hat, āge, cãre, fär; let, ēqual, tėrm; it, īce
hot, ōpen, ôrder; oil, out; cup, pu̇t, rüle, ūse
əbove, takən, pencəl, lemən, circəs
ch, child; ng, long; sh, ship
th, thin; ᴛʜ, then; zh, measure

e·lec·tro·lyte (i lek′ trə līt′) *n.* **1** a solution that will conduct an electric current. **2** in chemistry, a compound whose water solution will conduct an electric current. Acids, bases, and salts are electrolytes. [< *electro-* + Gk. *lytos* loosed < *lyein* loose]

e·lec·tro·lyt·ic (i lek′trə lit′ik) *adj.* having to do with electrolysis or with an electrolyte.

e·lec·tro·lyt·i·cal·ly (i lek′trə lit′ik lē) *adv.* by means of electrolysis.

e·lec·tro·lyze (i lek′trə līz′) *v.* **-lyzed, -lyz·ing.** decompose by electrolysis. —**e·lec′tro·ly·za′tion,** *n.* —**e·lec′tro·lyz′er,** *n.*

e·lec·tro·mag·net (i lek′trō mag′nit) *n.* a piece of iron that becomes a strong magnet when an electric current is passed through wire coiled around it.

An electromagnet

e·lec·tro·mag·net·ic (i lek′trō mag net′ik) *adj.* **1** of or caused by an electromagnet. **2** of electromagnetism.—**e·lec′tro·mag·net′i·cal·ly,** *adv.*

e·lec·tro·mag·net·ism (i lek′trō mag′nə tiz′əm) *n.* **1** the magnetism produced by a current of electricity. **2** the branch of physics that deals with this.

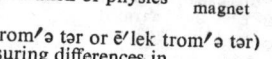

e·lec·trom·e·ter (i lek′trom′ə tər or ē′lek trom′ə tər) *n.* an instrument for measuring differences in electrical charge or potential.

e·lec·tro·met·ric (i lek′trə met′rik) *adj.* of or having to do with electrometry.

e·lec·tro·mo·tive (i lek′trə mō′tiv) *adj.* **1** producing a flow of electricity. **2** of or having to do with electromotive force.

electromotive force the amount of energy derived from an electric source in one second when one unit of current is passing through the source, commonly measured in volts. Electromotive force is produced by differences in electrical charge or potential. *Abbrev.*: EMF, e.m.f., or emf

electromotive series in chemistry, an arrangement of the metallic elements so that each is positive with reference to those that follow it and negative with reference to those that precede it.

e·lec·tro·mo·tor (i lek′trə mō′tər) *n.* **1** a machine producing electric current. **2** a motor run by electricity.

e·lec·tron (i lek′tron) *n.* the unit charge of an elementary particle, the electricity found outside the nucleus of all atoms, especially when a negative particle. All atoms are composed of electrons, protons, and neutrons. [< Gk. *ēlektron.* See ELECTRIC.]

electron beam a stream of electrons moving in the same direction at the same speed. The electron beam inside the picture tube of a television set inscribes the picture on the screen.

e·lec·tro·neg·a·tive (i lek′trō neg′ə tiv) *adj.* **1** charged with negative electricity. **2** tending to pass to the positive pole in electrolysis. **3** non-metallic; acid.

electron gun a device that guides the flow and greatly increases the speed of atomic particles. Electron guns are used in oil refining and in various other industries.

e·lec·tron·ic (i lek′tron′ik or ē′lek tron′ik) *adj.* of or having to do with an electron or electrons. —**e·lec′tron′i·cal·ly,** *adv.*

electronic brain a complex electric calculating machine. Also, **electric brain.**

electronic music music created, usually on magnetic tape, from sound made by electronic generators and filters.

e·lec·tron·ics (i lek′tron′iks or ē′lek tron′iks) *n.* the branch of physics that deals with the study of electrons in motion. Radio, radar, television, etc. are based on the principles of electronics.

electron microscope a microscope that uses beams of electrons instead of beams of light, and has much higher power than any ordinary microscope. Its enlarged images are not observable directly by the eye, but are projected upon a fluorescent surface or photographic plate.

electron tube vacuum tube.

e·lec·troph·o·rus (i lek′trof′ə rəs or ē′lek trof′ə rəs) *n.* **-ri** (-rī′ or -rē′). a simple device for producing charges of electricity by means of induction. [< NL *electrophorus* < *electro-* + Gk. *-phoros* bearing]

e·lec·tro·plate (i lek′trə plāt′) *v.* **-plat·ed, -plat·ing,** *n.* —*v.* cover with a coating of metal by means of electrolysis. —*n.* **1** silverware, etc. covered in this way. **2** in printing, a plate made by this process. —**e·lec′tro·plat′er,** *n.*

e·lec·tro·pos·i·tive (i lek′trō poz′ə tiv) *adj.* **1** charged with positive electricity. **2** tending to pass to the negative pole (cathode) in electrolysis. **3** metallic; basic. —*n.* an electropositive substance.

e·lec·tro·scope (i lek′trə skōp′) *n.* a device that indicates the presence of minute charges of electricity and shows whether they are positive or negative.

e·lec·tro·stat·ic (i lek′trə stat′ik) *adj.* having to do with electricity at rest or with stationary electric charges. —**e·lec′tro·stat′i·cal·ly,** *adv.*

e·lec·tro·stat·ics (i lek′trə stat′iks) *n.* the branch of physics that deals with objects charged with electricity.

e·lec·tro·ther·a·py (i lek′trō ther′ə pē) *n.* the treatment of disease by electricity.

e·lec·tro·type (i lek′trə tīp′) *n. v.* **-typed, -typ·ing.** —*n.* **1** in printing, a metal or composition plate. **2** a print made from such a plate. —*v.* make such a plate or plates of. —**e·lec′tro·typ′er,** *n.*

e·lec·tro·va·lence (i lek′trō vā′ləns) *n.* the number of electrons gained or lost by an atom when it becomes an ion in a compound. —**e·lec′tro·va′lent,** *adj.*

e·lec·trum (i lek′trəm) *n.* a pale-yellow alloy of gold and silver, used by the ancients. [< L < Gk. *ēlektron*]

e·lec·tu·ar·y (i lek′chü er′ē) *n.* **-ar·ies.** a medicinal paste of powdered drugs and syrup or honey. [ME < LL *electuarium* < Gk. *ekleikton* < *ekleichein* lick out < *ex-* out + *leichein* lick]

el·ee·mos·y·nar·y (el′ə mos′ə ner′ē or el′ē mos′ə ner′ē) *adj.* **1** of or for charity; charitable. **2** provided by charity; free. **3** dependent on charity; supported by charity. [< LL *eleemosynarius* < L *eleemosyna* < Gk. *eleēmosynē* compassion < *eleos* mercy]

el·e·gance (el′ə gəns) *n.* **1** refined grace and richness; luxury free from coarseness. **2** something elegant. —**Syn. 1** fineness, choiceness.

el·e·gan·cy (el′ə gən sē) *n.* **-cies.** elegance.

el·e·gant (el′ə gənt) *adj.* **1** having or showing good taste; gracefully and richly refined: *The palace had elegant furnishings.* **2** expressed with taste; correct and polished in expression or arrangement: *an elegant speech.* **3** *Informal.* fine; excellent; superior. [< F < L *elegans, -antis*] —**el′e·gant·ly,** *adv.* —**Syn. 1** See **fine.**

el·e·gi·ac (el′ə jī′ək) *adj.* **1** of or suitable for an elegy. **2** sad; mournful; melancholy. **3** written in elegiacs. —*n.* in Greek and Latin verse, a dactylic hexameter couplet, the second line having only a long or accented syllable in the third and sixth feet like this:

— ∪ ∪ ∣ — ∪ ∪ ∣ — ∪ ∪ ∣ — ∪ ∪ ∣ — ∪ ∪ ∣ — ∪
— ∪ ∪ ∣ — ∪ ∪ ∣ — ∣ — ∪ ∪ ∣ — ∪ ∪ ∣ —

el·e·gize (el′ə jīz′) *v.* **-gized, -giz·ing. 1** write an elegy about. **2** write an elegy; lament.

el·e·gy (el′ə jē) *n.* **-gies. 1** a mournful or melancholy poem; poem that is a lament for the dead. Milton's *Lycidas* and Shelley's *Adonais* are elegies. **2** a poem written in elegiac verses. [< F *élégie* < L < Gk. *elegeia,* ult. < *elegos* mournful poem]

elem. 1 element; elements. **2** elementary.

el·e·ment (el′ə mənt) *n.* **1** one of the simple substances, such as gold, iron, carbon, sulphur, oxygen, and hydrogen, that have not yet been separated into simpler parts; a substance composed of atoms that are chemically alike. **2** one of the parts of which anything is made up: *Honesty, industry, and kindness are elements of good living.* **3** one of the four substances—earth, water, air, and fire—that were once thought to make up all other things. **4** the environment, activities, etc. to which a person or thing is best suited; natural or suitable surroundings: *The boy was in his element when taking apart an old car.* **5** in military use, any unit or part of a larger group, formation, or manoeuvre. **6** in Canada, one of the three basic branches of the armed forces: Sea (S), Land (L), and Air (A). **7 be in one's element,** be where one can live and thrive. **8 the elements, a** the simple, necessary parts to be learned first; first principles. **b** the atmospheric forces: *The storm seemed a war of the elements.* **c** bread and wine used in the Eucharist. [< L *elementum* rudiment, first principle]

Syn. 2 Element, component, constituent = one of the parts of which something is made up. **Element** is the general word, applying to a part of any thing, but sometimes suggests an essential or basic part: *Kindness is an element of courtesy.* **Component** = a part of something that is put together as a compound or mixture: *Ice cream and syrup are components of a sundae.* **Constituent,** often used interchangeably with *component*, differs in suggesting active helping to form the whole instead of just being a part: *Syrup is a necessary constituent of a sundae.*

el·e·men·tal (el′ə men′təl) *adj.* **1** of the four elements —earth, water, air, and fire. **2** of the forces of nature: *Primitive peoples usually worship elemental gods, such as the sun, earth, thunder, etc.* **3** as found in nature; simple but powerful: *Survival is an elemental instinct.* **4** being a necessary or essential part. **5** elementary. —**el′e·men′tal·ly,** *adv.*

el·e·men·ta·ry (el′ə men′tə rē or el′ə men′trē) *adj.* **1** of or dealing with the simple, necessary parts to be learned first; having to do with first principles; introductory. **2** in chemistry: **a** made up of only one chemical element; not a compound: *Silver is an elementary substance.* **b** having to do with a chemical element or elements. **3** elemental. **4** of or having to do with elementary schools. —**el′e·men′tar·i·ly,** *adv.*

Syn. 1 Elementary, rudimentary, primary = having to do with the beginnings of something. **Elementary** emphasizes the idea of basic things and means having to do with the first steps or beginning facts and principles of anything: *John learned simple addition and subtraction when he began elementary arithmetic.* **Rudimentary** is a formal word emphasizing the idea of an undeveloped beginning and used particularly to mean "consisting of the first parts and principles of knowledge or a subject studied": *She has only a rudimentary knowledge of mathematics.* **Primary** emphasizes coming first in order or time: *Children attend primary school before high school.*

elementary school a school of six, seven, or eight grades, for children aged six and over, followed by high school or junior high school: *Some elementary schools include kindergartens.*

el·e·men·toid (el′ə men′toid) *adj.* having the appearance of an element: *an elementoid compound.*

el·e·phant (el′ə fənt) *n.* **-phants** or (*esp. collectively*) **-phant.** a huge, heavy mammal, having a long snout called a trunk; the largest four-footed animal now living. Ivory comes from its tusks. The African elephant is larger and has more prominent ears than the Indian elephant. [ME < OF *olifant* < L < Gk. *elephas, -antis* elephant, ivory, probably < Egyptian]

el·e·phan·ti·a·sis (el′ə fan tī′ə sis) *n.* a disease in which parts of the body, usually the legs, become greatly enlarged and the skin thickened and broken. It is caused by parasitic worms that block the flow of lymph. [< L < Gk. *elephantiasis* < *elephas, -antis* elephant]

el·e·phan·tine (el′ə fan′tīn or el′ə fan′tēn) *adj.* **1** like an elephant; huge; heavy; clumsy; slow. **2** of elephants.

el·e·phant's-ear (el′ə fənts ēr′) *n.* a plant having large leaves shaped like elephant's ears; caladium.

El·eu·sin·i·an mysteries (el′yù sin′ē ən) in ancient Greece, the secret, religious ceremonies held yearly at Eleusis in honor of the goddesses Demeter and Persephone.

E·leu·sis (i lü′sis) *n.* a city in ancient Greece, near Athens.

el·e·vate (el′ə vāt′) *v.* **-vat·ed, -vat·ing. 1** lift up; raise. **2** raise in rank or station: *The soldier was elevated to knighthood for bravery.* **3** raise in quality: *Good books elevate the mind.* **4** put in high spirits; make joyful or proud; elate. [< L *elevare* < *ex-* out + *levare* lighten, raise] —**Syn. 1** hoist. **2, 3** promote, advance, exalt. See **raise.**

el·e·vat·ed (el′ə vāt′id) *adj.* **1** lifted up; raised; high.

2 dignified; lofty; noble. 3 in high spirits; joyful; proud. —*n. Informal.* an elevated railway.

elevated railway a railway raised above the ground on a supporting frame high enough for streetcars, automobiles, etc. to pass underneath.

el·e·va·tion (el′ə vā′shən) *n.* **1** a raised place; high place: *A hill is an elevation.* **2** the height above the earth's surface: *The airplane cruised at an elevation of 35,000 feet.* **3** the height above sea level: *The elevation of Calgary is 3,450 feet.* **4** dignity; loftiness; nobility. **5** a raising; a lifting up: *the elevation of Caesar to be the ruler of Rome.* **6** a being raised or lifted up. **7** a flat drawing of the front, rear, or side of a building. **8** in astronomy, the altitude of the pole or of any heavenly body above the horizon. **9** in surveying, the angular distance of an object above the horizontal plane through the point of observation.

el·e·va·tor (el′ə vā′tər) *n.* **1** anything that raises or lifts. **2** a moving platform or cage to carry people and freight up and down in a building, mine, etc. **3** a building for storing grain. **4** an adjustable flat piece that causes an aircraft to go up or down. See **airplane** for picture. [< LL]

Elevators (def. 3)

elevator shaft a vertical passageway for an elevator.

e·lev·en (i lev′ən) *n.* **1** one more than ten; 11. **2** in soccer, cricket, and certain other sports, a team of eleven players. —*adj.* being one more than ten. [OE *endleofan* one left (over ten)]

e·lev·enth (i lev′ənth) *adj. n.* **1** next after the 10th; last in a series of 11. **2** one, or being one, of 11 equal parts.

eleventh hour the latest possible moment; time just before it is too late.

elf (elf) *n.* **elves. 1** a tiny, mischievous fairy. **2** a small, mischievous person. [OE *ælf*] —**elf′like′**, *adj.*

elf·in (el′fən) *adj.* of or suitable for elves; like an elf's: *The child's elfin smile was very charming.* —*n.* an elf.

elf·ish (el′fish) *adj.* elflike; elfin; mischievous. —**elf′ish·ly**, *adv.* —**elf′ish·ness**, *n.*

elf·lock (elf′lok′) *n.* a tangled lock of hair, supposedly caused by elves.

e·lic·it (i lis′it) *v.* draw forth: *elicit a reply, elicit applause, elicit the truth.* [< L *elicitus*, pp. of *elicere* < *ex-* out + *lacere* entice] —**e·lic′it·or**, *n.*

☛ **Elicit, illicit** are not synonymous, but are sometimes confused because they sound alike. **Illicit** is a formal adjective meaning unlawful or improper: *The police are trying to stop the illicit sale of drugs.*

e·lic·i·ta·tion (i lis′ə tā′shən) *n.* a drawing forth or being drawn forth.

e·lide (i līd′) *v.* **e·lid·ed, e·lid·ing.** omit or slur over in pronunciation. The *e* in *the* is elided in "th' inevitable hour." [< L *elidere* < *ex-* out + *laedere* dash]

el·i·gi·bil·i·ty (el′ə jə bil′ə tē) *n.* **-ties.** fitness; qualification; desirability.

el·i·gi·ble (el′ə jə bəl) *adj.* fit to be chosen; properly qualified; desirable: *Players had to pass in all subjects to be eligible for the school team.* —*n.* an eligible person. [< F < LL < L *eligere* pick out, choose. See ELECT.] —**el′i·gi·ble·ness**, *n.* —**el′i·gi·bly**, *adv.*

e·lim·i·nate (i lim′ə nāt′) *v.* **-nat·ed, -nat·ing. 1** get rid of; remove: *The new bridge over the railway tracks eliminated the danger in crossing.* **2** pay no attention to; leave out of consideration; omit: *The architect eliminated furniture, rugs, etc. in figuring the cost of the house.* **3** in mathematics, get rid of (an unknown quantity) by combining algebraic equations. **4** put out of a championship competition by reason of defeat: *The Toronto team was eliminated in the first round of the hockey playoffs.* **5** in physiology, expel (waste) from the body; excrete. [< L *eliminare* < *ex-* out + *limen* threshold] —**e·lim′i·na′tor**, *n.* —**Syn. 1** See **exclude. 2** dismiss, rule out.

e·lim·i·na·tion (i lim′ə nā′shən) *n.* **1** an eliminating. **2** a being eliminated.

E·lis (ē′lis) *n.* an ancient division of W. Greece. Olympic games were held on the plains of Olympia in Elis.

hat, āge, cãre, fär; let, ēqual, tėrm; it, īce
hot, ōpen, ôrder; oil, out; cup, pu̇t, rüle, ūse
əbove, takən, pencəl, lemən, circəs
ch, child; ng, long; sh, ship
th, thin; ᴛʜ, then; zh, measure

e·li·sion (i lizh′ən) *n.* the suppression of a vowel or a syllable in pronouncing. Elision is often used in poetry, and generally consists in cutting off a vowel at the end of one word when the next begins with a vowel. [< L *elisio, -onis* < *elidere.* See ELIDE.]

e·lite or **é·lite** (i lēt′ or ā lēt′) *n.* **1** the choice or distinguished part; the best people: *The elite of society attended the reception for the visiting queen.* **2** a size of typewriter type corresponding to 10-point printing type. There are 12 elite characters to the inch. —*adj.* **1** of or having to do with an elite. **2** choice; superior; distinguished. **3** of or having to do with elite type. [< F *élite*, fem. pp. of *élire* pick out < L *eligere.* See ELECT.]

e·lix·ir (i lik′sər) *n.* **1** a substance supposed to have the power of changing lead, iron, etc. into gold or of lengthening life indefinitely, sought by the alchemists of the Middle Ages. **2** a universal remedy; cure-all. **3** a medicine made of drugs or herbs mixed with alcohol and syrup. **4** the quintessence of a thing; chief principle. [ME < Med.L < Arabic *al-iksīr* (def. 1), probably < Gk. *xērion* drying powder used on wounds < *xēros* dry]

E·liz·a·be·than (i liz′ə bē′thən) *adj.* of the time of Queen Elizabeth I (1533-1603). —*n.* a person, especially a writer, of the time of Queen Elizabeth I.

Elizabethan sonnet a type of sonnet used by Shakespeare and many other Elizabethans. It has a rhyme scheme *abab cdcd efef gg.*

elk (elk) *n.* **elks** or (*esp. collectively*) **elk. 1** a large deer of N. Europe and Asia, having antlers resembling those of a moose. **2** a large, reddish deer of North America; wapiti. **3** a soft leather made from elk hide, or from calfskin or cowhide in imitation of this. [apparently < AF form of OE *eolh*]

elk·hound (elk′hound′) *n.* **1** a breed of Norwegian hunting dog having a short body, pointed ears, curly tail, and gray coat. It is used for tracking elk, etc. **2** a dog of this breed.

ell[1] (el) *n.* an old measure of length, chiefly used in measuring cloth. In England it was equal to 45 inches. Also, **el.** [OE *eln* length of lower arm]

ell[2] (el) *n.* **1** the letter L, l. **2** something shaped like a capital L. **3** an extension of a building at right angles to it.

el·lipse (i lips′) *n.* in geometry, an oval having both ends alike. It is the path of a point that moves so that the sum of its distances from two fixed points remains the same. Any conic section formed by a cutting plane inclined to the base but not passing through the base is an ellipse. See also **conic section** for diagram. [< L *ellipsis.* See ELLIPSIS.]

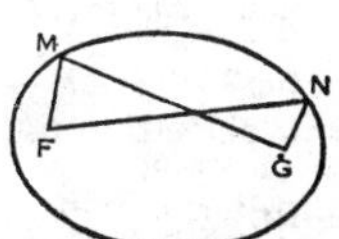

Showing the rule for making an ellipse. F and G are the two foci. The sum of the distances of any point of the ellipse from F and G is always the same. FM + GM equals FN + GN.

el·lip·ses (i lip′siz *for 1*; i lip′sēz *for 2*) *n.* **1** pl. of **ellipse. 2** pl. of **ellipsis.**

el·lip·sis (i lip′sis) *n.* **-ses** (-sēz). **1** in grammar, the omission of a word or words that could complete the construction of a sentence. *Example*: In "She is as tall as her brother," there is a permissible ellipsis of *is tall* after *brother.* **2** in writing or printing, marks (. . . or * * *) used to show an omission. [< L < Gk. *elleipsis* < *elleipein* come short, leave out]

el·lip·soid (i lip′soid) *n.* in mathematics: **1** a solid of which all plane surfaces are ellipses or circles. **2** any such surface. —*adj.* of or in the form of an ellipsoid.

el·lip·tic (i lip′tik) *adj.* elliptical.

el·lip·ti·cal (i lip′tə kəl) *adj.* **1** shaped like an ellipse; of an ellipse. **2** showing ellipsis; having a word or words omitted. —**el·lip′ti·cal·ly**, *adv.*

elm (elm) *n.* 1 a tall, graceful shade tree. 2 its hard, heavy wood. [OE]

el·o·cu·tion (el′ə kū′shən) *n.* 1 the art of speaking or reading clearly and effectively in public; art of public speaking, including the correct use of the voice, gestures, etc. 2 a manner of speaking or reading in public. [< L *elocutio, -onis* < *eloqui* < *ex-* out + *loqui* speak]

el·o·cu·tion·ar·y (el′ə kū′shən er′ē) *adj.* of or having to do with elocution.

el·o·cu·tion·ist (el′ə kū′shən ist) *n.* 1 a person skilled in elocution. 2 a teacher of elocution.

E·lo·him (e lō′him) *n.* a Hebrew name for God. [< Hebrew *elohim,* pl.]

e·lon·gate (i long′gāt) *v.* **-gat·ed, -gat·ing,** *adj.* —*v.* lengthen; extend; stretch: *A rubber band can be elongated to several times its normal length.* —*adj.* 1 lengthened. 2 long and thin: *the elongate leaf of a willow.* [< L *elongare* < *ex-* out + *longus* long]

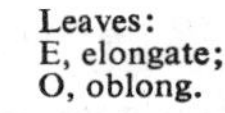

Leaves: E, elongate; O, oblong.

e·lon·ga·tion (ē′long gā′shən) *n.* 1 a lengthening; extension. 2 a lengthened part; continuation.

e·lope (i lōp′) *v.* **e·loped, e·lop·ing.** 1 run away with a lover. 2 run away; escape. [< AF *aloper,*? < ME *lope(n)* run, probably < ON *hlaupa* leap] —**e·lope′ment,** *n.* —**e·lop′er,** *n.*

el·o·quence (el′ə kwəns) *n.* 1 a flow of speech that has grace and force: *The eloquence of the speaker moved all hearts.* 2 the power to win by speaking; the art of speaking so as to stir the feelings. —**Syn. 2** elocution, oratory.

el·o·quent (el′ə kwənt) *adj.* 1 having eloquence. 2 highly expressive. [ME < OF < L *eloquens, -entis,* ppr. of *eloqui* < *ex-* out + *loqui* speak] —**el′o·quent·ly,** *adv.* —**Syn. 1** voluble, fluent, glib.

else (els) *adj.* 1 other; different; instead: *What else could I say?* 2 in addition: *The Browns are here; do you expect anyone else?* —*adv.* 1 differently: *How else can it be done?* 2 otherwise; if not: *Hurry, else you will be late.* 3 **or else,** otherwise; if not. [OE *elles*]

☛ The possessive ending is now usually transferred to **else** in phrases compounded with pronouns: *someone else's, who else's* (not *whose else*).

else·where (els′hwãr′ or -wãr′) *adv.* somewhere else; in or to some other place.

else·whith·er (els′hwiᴛʜ′ər or -wiᴛʜ′ər) *adv. Archaic.* elsewhere.

e·lu·ci·date (i lü′sə dāt′) *v.* **-dat·ed, -dat·ing.** make clear; explain: *The scientist elucidated his theory by a few simple experiments.* [< LL *elucidare* < L *ex-* out + *lucidus* bright] —**e·lu′ci·da′tor,** *n.*

e·lu·ci·da·tion (i lü′sə dā′shən) *n.* a making clear; explanation.

e·lude (i lüd′) *v.* **e·lud·ed, e·lud·ing.** 1 slip away from; avoid or escape by cleverness, quickness, etc.: *The sly fox eluded the dogs.* 2 escape discovery by; baffle: *The cause of cancer will not long elude research.* [< L *eludere* < *ex-* out + *ludere* play] —**e·lud′er,** *n.* —**Syn. 1** avoid, evade, shun. See **escape. 2** foil.

E·lul (e lül′) *n.* in the Hebrew calendar, the sixth month of the ecclesiastical year and the twelfth month of the civil year.

e·lu·sion (i lü′zhən) *n.* an eluding; clever avoidance. [< Med.L *elusio, -onis* < *eludere.* See ELUDE.]

e·lu·sive (i lü′siv) *adj.* 1 hard to describe or understand; baffling. 2 tending to elude: *an elusive enemy.* —**e·lu′sive·ly,** *adv.* —**e·lu′sive·ness,** *n.*

e·lu·so·ry (i lü′sə rē) *adj.* elusive.

e·lu·vi·um (i lü′vē əm) *n.* **-vi·a** (-vē ə). in geology, the deposit of soil and dust that remains after the decomposition of rock; opposed to *alluvium.* [< NL < L *ex* out + *luere* wash]

el·ver (el′vər) *n.* a young eel. [var. of *eelfare,* the passing of young eels up a stream < *eel* + *fare* journey (blend of OE *fær* and *faru*)]

elves (elvz) *n.* pl. of elf.

elv·ish (el′vish) *adj.* elfish; elflike.

E·lys·i·an (i liz′ē ən or i lizh′ən) *adj.* 1 of or having to do with Elysium. 2 happy; delightful.

Elysian Fields in Greek mythology, Elysium.

E·lys·i·um (i liz′ē əm or i lizh′əm) *n.* 1 in Greek mythology, a place where heroes and virtuous people lived after death. 2 any place or condition of perfect happiness; paradise. [< L < Gk. *Elysion (pedion)* Elysian (field)]

el·y·tra (el′ə trə) *n.* pl. of **elytron.**

el·y·tron (el′ə tron′) *n.* **-tra.** either of a pair of hardened front wings that form a protective covering for the hind pair. Beetles and certain other insects have elytra. [< NL < Gk. *elytron* sheath < *elyein* roll around]

em[1] (em) *n.* **ems.** 1 the letter M, m. 2 in printing, the square of any size of type; unit for measuring the amount of print in a line, page, etc. It was originally the portion of a line occupied by the letter *m.*

'em or **em**[2] (əm) *pron.pl. Informal.* them. [probably < OE *hem* them]

em-[1] the form of **en-**[1] before *b, p,* and sometimes *m,* as in *embark, employ.*

em-[2] the form of **en-**[2] before *b, m, p, ph,* as in *emblem, emphasis.*

E.M. 1 Efficiency Medal. 2 Edward Medal.

e·ma·ci·ate (i mā′shē āt′ or i mā′sē āt′) *v.* **-at·ed, -at·ing.** make unnaturally thin; cause to lose flesh or waste away: *A long illness had emaciated the invalid.* [< L *emaciare* < *ex-* (intensive) + *macies* leanness]

e·ma·ci·a·tion (i mā′shē ā′shən or i mā′sē ā′shən) *n.* an unnatural thinness from loss of flesh; wasting away.

em·a·nate (em′ə nāt′) *v.* **-nat·ed, -nat·ing.** come forth: *Fragrance emanated from the flowers. The rumor emanated from Ottawa.* [< L *emanare* < *ex-* out + *manare* flow] —**Syn.** See **issue.**

em·a·na·tion (em′ə nā′shən) *n.* 1 a coming forth. 2 anything that comes forth from a source: *Light and heat are emanations from the sun.* 3 in chemistry, a gas given off by a disintegrating radio-active substance.

e·man·ci·pate (i man′sə pāt′) *v.* **-pat·ed, -pat·ing.** release from slavery or restraint; set free. [< L *emancipare* < *ex-* away + *manceps* purchaser < *manus* hand + *capere* take]

e·man·ci·pa·tion (i man′sə pā′shən) *n.* a release from slavery or restraint; a setting free.

e·man·ci·pa·tor (i man′sə pā′tər) *n.* 1 a person who emancipates. 2 **the Great Emancipator,** Abraham Lincoln.

e·mas·cu·late (*v.* i mas′kyu̇ lāt′; *adj.* i mas′kyu̇ lit or i mas′kyu̇ lāt′) *v.* **-lat·ed, -lat·ing,** *adj.* —*v.* 1 remove the male glands of; castrate. 2 destroy the force of; weaken: *The editor emasculated the speech by cutting out its strongest passages.* —*adj.* deprived of vigor; weakened; effeminate. [< L *emasculare* < *ex-* away + *masculus* male] —**e·mas′cu·la′tion,** *n.* —**e·mas′cu·la′tor,** *n.*

em·balm (em bom′ or em bäm′) *v.* 1 treat (a dead body) with drugs, chemicals, etc. to keep it from decaying. 2 keep in memory; preserve: *Many fine sentiments are embalmed in poetry.* 3 fill with sweet scent; perfume: *Roses embalmed the June air.* Also, **imbalm.** [ME < OF *embaumer* < *en-* in + *baume* balm < L *balsamum*] —**em·balm′er,** *n.* —**em·balm′ment,** *n.*

em·bank (em bangk′) *v.* protect, enclose, or confine with a raised bank of earth, stones, etc.

em·bank·ment (em bangk′mənt) *n.* 1 a raised bank of earth, stones, etc., used to hold back water, support a roadway, etc. 2 a protecting, enclosing, or confining with a bank of this kind.

em·bar·go (em bär′gō) *n.* **-goes,** *v.* **-goed, -go·ing.** —*n.* 1 an order of a government forbidding ships to enter or leave its ports: *During the war, an embargo was placed on certain vessels.* 2 any restriction put on commerce by law. 3 a restriction; restraint; hindrance.
—*v.* lay an embargo on; forbid to enter or leave port. [< Sp. *embargo* < *embargar* restrain < VL *in-* in + *barra* bar]

em·bark (em bärk′) *v.* 1 go on board ship: *Many people embark for Europe in Montreal.* 2 enter a plane, bus,

hat, āge, cãre, fär; let, ēqual, tėrm; it, īce
hot, ōpen, ôrder; oil, out; cup, pu̇t, rüle, ūse
əbove, takən, pencəl, lemən, circəs
ch, child; ng, long; sh, ship
th, thin; ꟻH, then; zh, measure

train, etc. as a passenger. **3** put on board ship: *The general embarked his troops.* **4** set out; start: *After leaving college, the young man embarked on a business career.* **5** involve (a person) in an enterprise; invest (money) in an enterprise: *He foolishly embarked much money in the swindler's scheme and so lost it all.* [< F *embarquer* < *en-* in + *barque* bark³]

em·bar·ka·tion (em′bär kā′shən) *n.* an embarking.

em·bar·rass (em bar′əs) *v.* **1** disturb (a person); make self-conscious: *Meeting strangers embarrassed the shy boy so that he blushed and stammered.* **2** complicate; mix up; make difficult: *He embarrasses discussion of the simplest subject by use of technical terms.* **3** involve in difficulties; hinder: *Heavy equipment embarrassed the army's movements.* **4** burden with debt; involve in financial difficulties. [< F *embarrasser*, literally, to block < Ital. *imbarazzare* (< VL *barra* bar), literally, put a block into] —**Syn. 1** discomfit, disconcert, abash. See **confuse. 3** hamper, impede.

em·bar·rass·ing (em bar′əs ing) *adj.* that embarrasses. —**em·bar′rass·ing·ly,** *adv.*

em·bar·rass·ment (em bar′əs mənt) *n.* **1** an embarrassing. **2** a being embarrassed. **3** something that embarrasses.

em·bas·sa·dor (em bas′ə dər or em bas′ə dôr′) *n.* ambassador.

em·bas·sy (em′bə sē) *n.* **-sies. 1** an ambassador and his staff of assistants. An embassy ranks next above a legation. **2** the official residence, office, etc. of an ambassador in a foreign country. **3** the position or duties of an ambassador. **4** a person or group officially sent to a foreign government with a special errand. **5** a special errand; important mission; official message. [< OF *ambassee* < Ital. < Provençal < Gmc; cf. Gothic *andbahti* service]

em·bat·tle¹ (em bat′əl) *v.* **-tled, -tling. 1** prepare for battle; form into battle order. **2** fortify (a town, etc.). [ME < OF *embatailler* < *en-* into + *bataille* battle < L *battuere* beat]

em·bat·tle² (em bat′əl) *v.* **-tled, -tling.** provide with battlements; fortify. [< *em-*¹ + obs. *battle*, v., furnish with battlements]

em·bay (em bā′) *v.* **1** put or bring into a bay for shelter; force into a bay. **2** shut in; surround.

em·bed (em bed′) *v.* **-bed·ded, -bed·ding. 1** plant in a bed: *He embedded the bulbs in a box of sand.* **2** fix or enclose in a surrounding mass: *Precious stones are found embedded in rock.* **3** fix firmly (in the mind): *Every detail of the accident is embedded in my memory.* Also, **imbed.**

em·bel·lish (em bel′ish) *v.* **1** decorate; adorn; ornament. **2** make more interesting by adding real or imaginary details; elaborate: *He embellished the old stories so that they sounded new.* [ME < OF *embelliss-*, a stem of *embellir* < *en-* in (intensive) + *bel* handsome < L *bellus*]

em·bel·lish·ment (em bel′ish mənt) *n.* **1** a decoration; adornment; ornament. **2** a detail, often imaginary, added to make a story, account, etc. more interesting.

em·ber¹ (em′bər) *n.* **1** a piece of wood or coal still glowing in the ashes of a fire. **2 embers,** *pl.* ashes in which there is still some fire. [OE *æmerge*]

em·ber² (em′bər) *adj.* having to do with the Ember days. [OE *ymbren, ymbryne* course, literally, running around < *ymb* around + *ryne* a running]

Ember day in the Roman Catholic, Anglican, and some other churches, one of four series of three days each set apart for fasting and prayer. The Ember days are the Wednesday, Friday, and Saturday following the first Sunday in Lent, Whitsunday, and including or following September 14 and December 13.

em·bez·zle (em bez′əl) *v.* **-zled, -zling.** steal by putting to one's own use money held in trust for some other person or group of persons: *The treasurer embezzled $2,000 from the club's funds.* [< AF *enbesiler* < OF *besillier* maltreat, of uncertain origin] —**em·bez′zle·ment,** *n.* —**em·bez′zler,** *n.*

em·bit·ter (em bit′ər) *v.* make bitter; make more bitter: *The old man was embittered by the loss of his money.* —**em·bit′ter·ment,** *n.*

em·bla·zon (em blā′zən) *v.* **1** display conspicuously; picture in bright colors. **2** decorate; adorn: *The knight's shield was emblazoned with his coat of arms.* **3** praise highly; honor publicly; make known the fame of: *King Arthur's exploits were emblazoned in song and story.* —**em·bla′zon·er,** *n.* —**em·bla′zon·ment,** *n.*

em·bla·zon·ry (em blā′zən rē) *n.* **-ries. 1** a brilliant decoration; adornment; conspicuous display. **2** a display of coats of arms, etc.; heraldic decoration.

em·blem (em′bləm) *n.* **1** an object or representation that stands for an invisible quality, idea, etc. by some connection of thought; sign of an idea; symbol: *The dove is an emblem of peace.* **2** a heraldic device. **3** a picture suggesting a moral, often with an accompanying explanation, proverb, etc. [< L *emblema* inlaid work < Gk. *emblēma* insertion < *en-* in + *ballein* throw]
Syn. 1 Emblem, symbol = an object or sign that represents something else. The two words are interchangeable in current usage; but **symbol** strictly means something naturally associated in the mind with the thing symbolized: *The crown is the symbol of kingship.* **Emblem** is usually something that is chosen arbitrarily to represent the nature of the object in mind: *The beaver and the maple leaf are both emblems of Canada.*

em·blem·at·ic (em′blə mat′ik) *adj.* used as an emblem; symbolical: *The Cross is emblematic of Christianity.*

em·blem·at·i·cal (em′blə mat′ə kəl) *adj.* emblematic. —**em′blem·at′i·cal·ly,** *adv.*

em·bod·i·ment (em bod′ē mənt) *n.* **1** an embodying. **2** a being embodied. **3** that in which something is embodied; person or thing symbolizing some idea, quality, etc. **4** something embodied.

em·bod·y (em bod′ē) *v.* **-bod·ied, -bod·y·ing. 1** put into visible form; express in definite form: *The building embodied the idea of the architect.* **2** bring together and include in a single book, law, system, etc.; organize: *The British North America Act embodies the conditions of Confederation.* **3** make part of an organized book, law, system, etc.; incorporate: *The new engineer's suggestions were embodied in the revised plan of the bridge.* —**Syn. 1** incarnate, materialize, externalize. **3** include, embrace, assimilate.

em·bold·en (em bōl′dən) *v.* make bold; encourage. —**em·bold′en·er,** *n.*

em·bol·ic (em bol′ik) *adj.* **1** in medicine, of or caused by an embolus or embolism. **2** in biology, pushing or growing inwards.

em·bo·lism (em′bə liz′əm) *n.* in medicine, the obstruction of a blood vessel by a clot, a bit of fat, or other obstacle carried there by the blood. [< L < Gk. *embolismos* < *emballein* < *en-* in + *ballein* throw]

em·bo·lus (em′bə ləs) *n.* **-li** (-lī′ or -lē′). in medicine, an air bubble, clot, etc. that is carried in the blood stream and sometimes obstructs a blood vessel. [< L < Gk. *embolos* peg; < *emballein* put in. See EMBOLISM.]

em·bon·point (äɴ bôɴ pwaɴ′) *n. French.* fatness; plumpness.

em·bos·om (em bu̇z′əm or em bü′zəm) *v.* **1** surround; enclose; envelop. **2** embrace; cherish.

em·boss (em bos′) *v.* **1** decorate with a design, pattern, etc. that stands out from the surface: *Our coins are embossed with letters and figures.* **2** cause to stand out from the surface: *He ran his finger over the letters to see if they had been embossed.* [ME < OF *embocer* < *en-* in + *boce* swelling, boss²]

em·boss·ment (em bos′mənt) *n.* **1** an embossing. **2** a figure carved or moulded in relief. **3** a part that sticks out; bulge.

em·bou·chure (äm′bü shür′) *n.* **1** the mouth of a river. **2** the widening of a river valley into a plain. **3** in music: **a** the mouthpiece of a wind instrument. **b** the shaping and use of the lips, tongue, etc. in playing such an instrument; lip. [< F *embouchure* < *emboucher* put into or discharge from a mouth < *en-* in + *bouche* mouth < L *bucca*]

em·bow·er (em bou′ər) *v.* enclose in a shelter of leafy branches.

em·brace (em brās′) *v.* **-braced, -brac·ing,** *n.* —*v.* **1** clasp or hold in the arms to show love or friendship; hug. **2** hug one another: *The two lovers embraced.* **3** take up; take for oneself; accept: *She eagerly embraced the chance to make a trip to Europe. Many Indians have embraced the Christian religion.* **4** include; contain: *The cat family embraces lions, tigers, leopards, and many other animals.* **5** surround; enclose.
—*n.* an embracing; a hug. [ME < OF *embracer* take into one's arms < VL < L *in-* in + *brachium* arm < Gk. *brachion*] **—em·brace′a·ble,** *adj.* **—Syn.** *v.* **3** adopt, espouse. **4** comprise.

em·bra·sure (em brā′zhər) *n.* **1** an opening in a wall for a gun, with sides that spread outward to permit the gun to swing through a greater arc. **2** in architecture, a slanting of the wall at an oblique angle on the inner sides of a window or door. [< F *embrasure* < *embraser* widen an opening]

An embrasure for a gun

em·bro·cate (em′brō kāt′) *v.* **-cat·ed, -cat·ing.** bathe and rub with liniment or lotion. [< LL *embrocare* < *embroc(h)a* < Gk. *embrochē* lotion < *en-* in + *brechein* wet]

em·bro·ca·tion (em′brō kā′shən) *n.* **1** a bathing and rubbing with liniment or lotion. **2** the liniment or lotion used.

em·broi·der (em broi′dər) *v.* **1** ornament (cloth, leather, etc.) with a raised design, pattern, etc. of stitches. **2** make (a design, pattern, etc.) on cloth, leather, etc. with stitches: *She embroidered dainty flowers on her blue dress.* **3** do embroidery. **4** add imaginary details to; exaggerate: *He didn't exactly tell lies, but he did embroider his stories.* [< *em-*[1] + *broider* embroider < OF *broder*] **—em·broi′der·er,** *n.* **—Syn. 1** embellish, beautify, decorate.

em·broi·der·y (em broi′dər ē or em broi′drē) *n.* **-der·ies. 1** the art of working raised and ornamental designs in cloth, leather, etc. with a needle; embroidering. **2** embroidered work or material. **3** imaginary details; exaggeration.

em·broil (em broil′) *v.* **1** involve (a person, country, etc.) in a quarrel: *He did not wish to become embroiled in the dispute.* **2** throw (affairs, etc.) into a state of confusion. [< F *embrouiller* < *en-* in + *brouiller* to disorder] **—em·broil′er,** *n.* **—em·broil′ment,** *n.*

em·brown (em broun′) *v.* tan; darken.

em·bry·o (em′brē ō) *n.* **-bry·os,** *adj.* —*n.* **1** an animal during the period of its growth from the fertilized egg until its organs have developed so that it can live independently. A chicken within an egg is an embryo. A human embryo more than three months old is usually called a fetus. **2** in botany, an undeveloped plant within a seed. **3** a beginning or undeveloped state of something. **4 in embryo,** in an undeveloped state.
—*adj.* embryonic; undeveloped; not mature. [< Med.L < Gk. *embryon* < *en-* in + *bryein* swell]

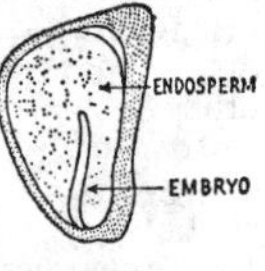

An embryo (def. 2)

em·bry·o·log·ic (em′brē ə loj′ik) *adj.* embryological.

em·bry·o·log·i·cal (em′brē ə loj′ə kəl) *adj.* of or having to do with embryology.

em·bry·ol·o·gist (em′brē ol′ə jist) *n.* a person trained in embryology.

em·bry·ol·o·gy (em′brē ol′ə jē) *n.* the branch of biology that deals with the formation and development of embryos.

em·bry·on·ic (em′brē on′ik) *adj.* **1** of the embryo. **2** undeveloped; not mature. **—em·bry·on′i·cal·ly,** *adv.*

em·cee (*n.* em′sē′; *v.* em′sē′) *n. v.* **-ceed, -cee·ing.** *Informal.* —*n.* master of ceremonies. —*v.* act as master of ceremonies of; be master of ceremonies. Also, **M.C.**

e·meer (ə mēr′) *n.* emir.

e·mend (i mend′) *v.* suggest changes to free (a faulty text, document, etc.) from errors; correct. [< L *emendare* < *ex-* out of + *mendum, menda* fault. Doublet of AMEND.] **—e·mend′a·ble,** *adj.* **—e·mend′er,** *n.*

e·men·date (ē′men dāt′) *v.* **-dat·ed, -dat·ing.** emend.

e·men·da·tion (ē′men dā′shən or em′en dā′shən) *n.* **1** a correction; improvement. **2** a suggested change to free a faulty text, document, etc. from errors.

em·er·ald (em′ər əld or em′rəld) *n.* **1** a bright-green precious stone; transparent green beryl. **2** a piece of this stone or a gem made from it. **3** a bright green. **4** in printing, a size of type; 6½ point.
—*adj.* bright-green. [ME < OF *esmeralde* < L < Gk. *smaragdos*]

Emerald Isle *Poetic.* Ireland.

e·merge (i mėrj′) *v.* **e·merged, e·merg·ing.** come out; come up; come into view: *The sun emerged from behind a cloud. Many facts emerged as a result of the investigation.* [< L *emergere* < *ex-* out + *mergere* dip] **—Syn.** See **issue.**

e·mer·gence (i mėr′jəns) *n.* the act or fact of emerging; a coming into view.

e·mer·gen·cy (i mėr′jən sē) *n.* **-cies,** *adj.* —*n.* a sudden need for immediate action: *I keep a fire extinguisher in my car for use in an emergency.* —*adj.* for a time of sudden need: *an emergency brake, an emergency operation.*
Syn. *n.* **Emergency, crisis** = a trying or dangerous time or state of affairs. **Emergency** suggests a sudden or unexpected happening or situation that calls for action without delay: *The failure of the city's electric power caused an emergency.* **Crisis** emphasizes the life-or-death nature of a happening or situation that marks a turning point in the life of a person, country, etc.: *The floods brought a crisis into the lives of the valley's inhabitants.*

emergency brake an auxiliary brake, usually hand-operated, to hold a vehicle in place when parked, stopped on a hill, etc.

e·mer·gent (i mėr′jənt) *adj.* emerging.

e·mer·i·tus (i mer′ə təs) *adj.* honorably discharged; retired from active service, but still holding one's rank and title: *At the age of seventy, Professor Arnold became professor emeritus.* —*n.* a person honorably discharged or retired from service. [< L *emeritus*, pp. of *emerere* + *ex-* to the end + *merere* serve]

e·mer·sion (i mėr′zhən or i mėr′shən) *n.* an emerging. [< L *emersio, -onis* < *emergere.* See EMERGE.]

em·er·y (em′ər ē or em′rē) *n.* a hard, dark mineral, an impure corundum, used for grinding, smoothing, and polishing. [< F *émeri* < Ital. < VL *smericulum* < Med.Gk. *smēris* < Gk. *smyris* abrasive powder]

e·met·ic (i met′ik) *adj.* causing vomiting. —*n.* something that causes vomiting. [< L *emeticus* < Gk. *emetikos* < *emeein* vomit]

E.M.F., e.m.f., or **emf** electromotive force.

em·i·grant (em′ə grənt) *n.* a person who leaves his own country or region to settle in another. —*adj.* leaving one's own country or region to settle in another. See **emigrate** for usage note.

em·i·grate (em′ə grāt′) *v.* **-grat·ed, -grat·ing.** leave one's own country or region to settle in another. [< L *emigrare* < *ex-* out + *migrare* move]
☛ **emigrate, immigrate.** *Emigrate* = move out of a country or region; *immigrate* = move into a country. An *emigrant* from Norway might be an *immigrant* to Canada.

em·i·gra·tion (em′ə grā′shən) *n.* **1** the act of leaving one's own country or region to settle in another: *In recent years there has been much emigration from Italy to Canada.* **2** a movement of emigrants.

é·mi·gré (em′ə grā′; *French,* ā mē grā′) *n.* **-grés** (-grāz′; *French,* -grā′). *French.* **1** an emigrant. **2** a royalist refugee from France during the French Revolution. **3** a refugee from Russia during and after the Russian Revolution.

em·i·nence (em′ə nəns) *n.* **1** a rank or position above all or most others; high standing; greatness; fame. **2** a high place; lofty hill. **3 Eminence,** in the Roman Catholic Church, the title of honor given to a cardinal. **—Syn. 1** distinction, prominence, renown.

em·i·nent (em′ə nənt) *adj.* **1** distinguished; exalted: *The Governor General is an eminent man.* **2** conspicuous; noteworthy: *The judge was a man of eminent fairness.* **3** high; lofty. **4** prominent; projecting. [< L *eminens, -entis,* ppr. of *eminere* be prominent < *ex-* out + *minere* jut] **—em′i·nent·ly,** *adv.*
Syn. 1 Eminent, prominent, distinguished = well-known. **Eminent** = standing high among or above all others of the same kind because of excellence in something: *Wolfe and Montcalm*

were eminent generals. **Prominent** = standing out from the crowd, and suggests being well-known at least locally: *The president of that bank is a prominent man in his home town.* **Distinguished** = set off from others of the same kind because of outstanding qualities, and suggests being well-known to the public: *Lieutenant-generals are distinguished officers.*

☛ **eminent, imminent.** *Eminent* = distinguished, exalted: *Parkinson proved himself valuable in the diplomatic service, but he was not the eminent statesman his predecessor had been. Imminent* = likely to happen soon: *Convinced that bankruptcy was imminent, the chairman called a meeting of the directors.*

eminent domain in law, the right of the government to take private property for public use. The owner must be paid for the property taken.

e·mir (ə mēr′) *n.* **1** in the Arabian peninsula, parts of Africa, etc., a chief, prince, or military leader. **2** the title of the descendants of Mohammed. **3** in Turkey, the title of certain officials. Also, **emeer.** [< Arabic *amir* commander]

e·mir·ate (ə mēr′it) *n.* **1** the rank or authority of an emir. **2** the territory governed by an emir.

em·is·sar·y (em′ə ser′ē) *n.* **-sar·ies.** a person sent on a mission or errand, especially one sent secretly. [< L *emissarius* < *emittere.* See EMIT.]

e·mis·sion (i mish′ən) *n.* **1** the act or fact of emitting. **2** the thing emitted. **3** in electronics: **a** the streaming out of electrons from the heated cathode of a vacuum tube. **b** the streaming out of electrons from an electrode subjected to irradiation or to the impact of electrons or ions. [< L *emissio, -onis* < *emittere.* See EMIT.]

e·mis·sive (i mis′iv) *adj.* emitting.

e·mit (i mit′) *v.* **e·mit·ted, e·mit·ting. 1** give off; send out; discharge: *The sun emits light and heat. Volcanoes emit lava.* **2** put into circulation; issue. **3** utter; express: *The trapped lion emitted roars of rage.* [< L *emittere* < *ex-* out + *mittere* send] **—Syn. 1** exude, expel, eject.

Em·man·u·el (i man′ū əl) *n.* Christ. Also, **Immanuel.**

Em·men·ta·ler (em′ən tä′lər) *n.* a pale-yellow Swiss cheese made from whole milk. [< G *Emmentaler* < *Emmenthal,* a town in Switzerland]

Em·men·thal (em′ən täl′) *n.* Emmentaler.

em·met (em′it) *n. Archaic.* ant. [OE *æmete*]

Em·my (em′ē) *n.* **-mies.** an annual award presented in the United States by the Academy of Television Arts and Sciences for outstanding achievement in the field of television. The Emmy is a gold-plated statuette. [origin uncertain]

EMO Emergency Measures Organization.

e·mol·lient (i mol′yənt or i mol′ē ənt) *adj.* softening; soothing. *—n.* something that softens and soothes: *Cold cream is an emollient for the skin. His encouragement was an emollient to her troubled mind.* [< L *emolliens, -entis,* ppr. of *emollire* soften < *ex-* (intensive) + *mollis* soft]

e·mol·u·ment (i mol′yu̇ mənt) *n.* the profit from a job, office, or position; salary; fee. [< L *emolumentum* profit, ult. < *ex-* out + *molere* grind]

e·mote (i mōt′) *v.* **e·mot·ed, e·mot·ing.** *Informal.* **1** act, especially in an exaggerated manner. **2** show emotion. **—e·mot′er,** *n.*

e·mo·tion (i mō′shən) *n.* a strong feeling. Fear, anger, love, joy, and grief are emotions. [< F *émotion* (after *motion*) < *émouvoir* stir up < L *emovere* < *ex-* out + *movere* move] **—Syn.** sentiment, passion. See **feeling.**

e·mo·tion·al (i mō′shən əl or i mōsh′nəl) *adj.* **1** of or having to do with the emotions. **2** showing emotion. **3** appealing to the emotions: *The guest speaker made an emotional plea for money to help crippled children.* **4** easily affected by emotion: *Emotional people are likely to cry if they hear sad music or read sad stories.* **—e·mo′tion·al·ly,** *adv.*

e·mo·tion·al·ism (i mō′shən əl iz′əm or i mōsh′nəl iz′əm) *n.* **1** an emotional quality or character. **2** an appeal to the emotions. **3** a tendency to display emotion too easily.

e·mo·tion·al·ist (i mō′shə nə list or i mōsh′nə list) *n.* **1** a person whose emotions are easily aroused. **2** a person who uses the emotions to try to influence others. **3** a person who bases theories of conduct on the emotions.

e·mo·tive (i mō′tiv) *adj.* **1** showing or causing emotion. **2** having to do with the emotions. **—e·mo′tive·ly,** *adv.* **—e·mo′tive·ness,** *n.*

em·pan·el (em pan′əl) *v.* **-elled** or **-eled, -el·ling** or **-el·ing.** impanel.

hat, āge, cãre, fär; let, ēqual, tėrm; it, īce
hot, ōpen, ôrder; oil, out; cup, pu̇t, rüle, ūse
əbove, takən, pencəl, lemən, circəs
ch, child; ng, long; sh, ship
th, thin; ᴛʜ, then; zh, measure

em·pa·thy (em′pə thē) *n.* in psychology, the quality or process of entering fully, through imagination, into another's feelings or motives, into the meaning of a work of art, etc. [< Gk. *empatheia* < *en-* in + *pathos* feeling]

em·pen·nage (em pen′ij) *n.* in aeronautics, the tail assembly of an aircraft. [< F *empennage* feathering of an arrow < OF *empenner* to feather (an arrow)]

em·per·or (em′pər ər) *n.* a man who is the sovereign ruler of an empire. [ME < OF *empereor* < L *imperator* commander < *imperare* command < *in-* in + *parare* order] **—Syn.** kaiser, czar.

em·pha·sis (em′fə sis) *n.* **-ses** (-sēz′). **1** special force; stress; importance: *emphasis on scientific studies.* **2** special force or loudness given to particular syllables, words, or phrases; stress. [< L < Gk. < *emphainein* indicate < *en-* in + *phainein* show] **—Syn. 2** accent, accentuation.

em·pha·size (em′fə sīz′) *v.* **-sized, -siz·ing. 1** give special force to; stress; make important: *He emphasized that word by saying it very loudly.* **2** call attention to: *Accidents emphasize the need for careful driving.*

em·phat·ic (em fat′ik) *adj.* **1** spoken or done with force or stress; strongly expressed: *Her answer was an emphatic "No!"* **2** speaking with force or stress; expressing oneself strongly: *The emphatic speaker kept pounding the table and shouting.* **3** attracting attention; very noticeable; striking: *The club made an emphatic success of their party.* [< Gk. *emphatikos* < *emphainein.* See EMPHASIS.] **—em·phat′i·cal·ly,** *adv.* **—Syn. 1** expressive, positive, energetic, forcible.

em·phy·se·ma (em′fə sē′mə) *n.* in medicine, a condition, especially of the lung, in which body tissue becomes bloated by air. [< NL < Gk. *emphysēma* bodily inflation] **—em′phy·se·mat′ic,** *adj.*

em·pire (em′pīr) *n.* **1** a group of countries or states under the same ruler or government, one country having some measure of control over the rest: *the British Empire.* **2** a country ruled by an emperor or empress: *the Japanese Empire.* **3** absolute power; supreme authority. [ME < OF < L *imperium*] **—Syn. 1** realm, domain. **3** sovereignty, dominion, rule, sway.

Em·pire (em′pīr) *adj.* **1** of or having to do with the first French Empire (1804-1815). **2 a** of, like, or having to do with a style of massive, ornate furniture in fashion during the Empire period. **b** of, like, or having to do with a style of high-waisted, short-sleeved woman's dress in fashion during this period.

Empire Day Victoria Day.

em·pir·ic (em pir′ik) *n.* **1** a person who lacks theoretical or scientific knowledge and relies entirely on practical experience. **2** a person without regular or proper training; quack. *—adj.* empirical. [< L *empiricus* < Gk. *empeirikos* < *en-* in + *peira* experience, experiment]

em·pir·i·cal (em pir′ə kəl) *adj.* **1** based on experiment and observation: *Chemistry is largely an empirical science.* **2** based entirely on practical experience, without regard to science or theory: *The quack doctor had only an empirical knowledge of medicine.* **—em·pir′i·cal·ly,** *adv.*

em·pir·i·cism (em pir′ə siz′əm) *n.* **1** the use of methods based on experiment and observation. **2** undue reliance upon experience; quackery. **3** in philosophy, the theory that all knowledge is based on experience.

em·pir·i·cist (em pir′ə sist) *n.* **1** a person who uses methods based on experiment and observation; experimenter. **2** a person who relies too much upon mere experience; quack. **3** a person who believes the philosophical doctrine of empiricism.

em·place·ment (em plās′mənt) *n.* **1** a space or platform for a heavy gun or guns. **2** a placing in position: *the emplacement of windows into a wall.*

em·plane (em plān′) *v.* **-planed, -plan·ing. 1** get on an airplane. **2** put (someone or something) on an airplane.

em·ploy (em ploi′) *v.* **1** use the services of; give work

and pay to: *That big factory employs many workers.* 2 use: *You employ a knife, fork, and spoon in eating.* 3 engage the attention of; keep busy; occupy: *Instead of wasting time, she employed herself in reading.*
—*n.* a being employed; service for pay; employment: *There are many workers in the employ of the government.* [< F *employer* < L *implicare* < *in-* in + *plicare* fold. Doublet of IMPLICATE, IMPLY.] —**em·ploy′a·ble,** *adj.*
Syn. *v.* **1 Employ, hire** = give work and pay to someone. **Employ** emphasizes a certain regularity and dignity in the work even though it is done for pay: *The steel mill employs most of the men in the town.* **Hire,** the more everyday word, emphasizes the fact of the work being paid: *She hired a man to mow the lawn.* **2** See **use.**

em·ploy·e or **em·ploy·é** (em ploi′ē or em′ploi ē′) *n.* employee.

em·ploy·ee (em ploi′ē or em′ploi ē′) *n.* a person who works for some person or firm for pay. [< F *employé,* pp. of *employer* employ]

em·ploy·er (em ploi′ər) *n.* **1** a person or firm that employs one or more persons. **2** a user.

em·ploy·ment (em ploi′mənt) *n.* **1** an employing or being employed. **2** what a person is doing; work. **3** a use. —**Syn. 2** business, trade, profession, See **occupation.**

em·po·ri·um (em pô′rē əm) *n.* **-ri·ums, -ri·a** (-rē ə). **1** a centre of trade; market place. **2** a large store selling many different things. [< L < Gk. *emporion* < *emporos* merchant, traveller < *en-* on + *poros* voyage]

em·pow·er (em pou′ər) *v.* **1** give power or authority to: *The secretary was empowered to sign certain contracts.* **2** enable; permit: *Man's erect position empowers him to use his hands freely.* Also, **impower.** —**Syn. 1** authorize, commission, license.

em·press (em′pris) *n.* **1** the wife of an emperor. **2** a woman who is the sovereign ruler of an empire.

em·prise or **em·prize** (em prīz′) *n. Archaic.* **1** an adventure; daring undertaking. **2** knightly daring. [ME < OF *emprise,* originally fem. pp. of *emprendre* undertake < *en-* in + *prendre* take < L *prehendere*]

emp·ty (emp′tē) *adj.* **-ti·er, -ti·est,** *v.* **-tied, -ty·ing,** *n.* **-ties.** —*adj.* **1** with nothing or no one in it: *The birds had gone and their nest was empty.* **2** vacant; unoccupied: *an empty room or house.* **3** having no cargo; unloaded: *an empty ship.* **4** not real; meaningless: *An empty promise is insincere. An empty threat has no force behind it.* **5** lacking knowledge or sense; foolish; frivolous. **6** *Informal.* hungry. **7 empty of,** without; lacking.
—*v.* **1** pour out or take out the contents of; make empty: *Empty the box of rubbish into the fire.* **2** become empty: *The hall emptied as soon as the concert was over.* **3** flow out; discharge: *The St. Lawrence River empties into the Gulf of St. Lawrence.*
—*n. Informal.* something that is empty; an empty bottle, container, freight car, etc. [OE *ǣmtig* < *ǣmetta* leisure] —**emp′ti·ly,** *adv.* —**emp′ti·ness,** *n.* —**Syn.** *adj.* **2** hollow, unsubstantial. *-v.* **1** unload, unburden, evacuate.

emp·ty-hand·ed (emp′tē han′did) *adj.* having nothing in the hands; bringing or taking nothing: *We expected our uncle to bring a present for each of us, but he arrived empty-handed.*

emp·ty-head·ed (emp′tē hed′id) *adj.* silly; stupid.

empty set in mathematics, a set that has no members.

em·pur·pled (em pėr′pəld) *adj.* made purple; colored with purple.

em·pyr·e·al (em pir′ē əl, em pī′ē əl, or em′pə rē′əl) *adj.* of the empyrean; celestial; heavenly.

em·py·re·an (em′pī rē′ən or em′pə rē′ən) *n.* **1** the highest heaven; region of pure light. **2** the sky; firmament; the vault of the heavens. —*adj.* empyreal. [< LL *empyreus* < Gk. *empyrios, empyros* < *en-* in + *pyr* fire]

e·mu (ē′mū) *n.* a large Australian bird resembling an ostrich but smaller. Emus cannot fly, but they can run very fast. [< Pg. *ema* ostrich, crane]

e.m.u., emu, or **E.M.U.** electromagnetic unit.

em·u·late (em′yů lāt′) *v.* **-lat·ed, -lat·ing.** try to equal or excel: *The proverb tells us to emulate the industry of the ant.* [< L *aemulari* < *aemulus* striving to equal] —**em′u·la′tor,** *n.*

em·u·la·tion (em′yů lā′shən) *n.* imitation in order to equal or excel; ambition or desire to equal or excel.

em·u·la·tive (em′yů lə tiv or em′yů lā′tiv) *adj.* **1** tending to emulate. **2** of or caused by emulation. —**em′u·la′tive·ly,** *adv.*

em·u·lous (em′yů ləs) *adj.* wishing to equal or excel. [< L *aemulus*] —**em′u·lous·ly,** *adv.* —**em′u·lous·ness,** *n.*

e·mul·si·fi·ca·tion (i mul′sə fə kā′shən) *n.* **1** an emulsifying. **2** a being emulsified.

e·mul·si·fy (i mul′sə fī′) *v.* **-fied, -fy·ing.** make into an emulsion. —**e·mul′si·fi′er,** *n.*

e·mul·sion (i mul′shən) *n.* **1** a liquid that is a mixture of liquids that do not dissolve in each other. In an emulsion, one of the liquids contains minute droplets of the other, which are evenly distributed throughout. **2** in pharmacy, a milky liquid containing very tiny drops of fat, oil, etc. Cod-liver oil is made into an emulsion to improve its taste. **3** in photography, a coating on a camera film, plate, etc. that is sensitive to light. [< NL *emulsio, -onis* < L *emulgere* < *ex-* out + *mulgere* milk]

en (en) *n.* **1** the letter N, n. **2** in printing, half the width of an em.

en-[1] *prefix.* **1** cause to be; make, as in *enable, enfeeble.* **2** put in; put on, as in *encircle, enthrone.* **3** other meanings, as in *enact, encourage, entwine.* The addition of *en-* rarely changes the meaning of a verb except to make it more emphatic. Also, **em-,** before *b, p,* and sometimes *m.* [< OF < L *in-* < *in* in, into]

en-[2] *prefix.* in; on, as in *energy.* Also, **em-,** before *b, m, p, ph.* [< Gk.]

-en[1] *suffix.* **1** cause to be; make, as in *blacken, sharpen.* **2** cause to have, as in *heighten, strengthen.* **3** become, as in *sicken, soften.* **4** come to have; gain, as in *lengthen.* [OE *-nian*]

-en[2] *suffix.* made of, as in *silken, wooden, woollen.* [OE]

-en[3] *suffix.* *-en* (or *-n*) ends the past participles of many strong verbs, as in *fallen, shaken, written, sworn.* [OE]

-en[4] *suffix.* *-en* is used to form the plural of a few nouns, as in *children, oxen.* [OE *-an*]

en·a·ble (en ā′bəl) *v.* **-bled, -bling.** give ability, power, or means to; make able: *Airplanes enable people to travel through the air.* —**Syn.** empower, permit, authorize.

en·act (en akt′) *v.* **1** pass (a bill) giving it validity as law; make into a law. **2** decree; order. **3** play the part of; act out; play: *In his time, the famous actor had enacted many characters from Shakespeare.*

en·act·ment (en akt′mənt) *n.* **1** an enacting. **2** a being enacted. **3** a law.

e·nam·el (i nam′əl) *n. v.* **-elled** or **-eled, -el·ling** or **-el·ing.** —*n.* **1** a glasslike substance melted and then cooled to make a smooth, hard surface. Different colors of enamel are used to cover or decorate metal, pottery, etc. **2** a paint or varnish used to make a smooth, hard, glossy surface. **3** the smooth, hard, glossy outer layer of the teeth. **4** anything covered or decorated with enamel. **5** any smooth, hard, shiny coating or surface. [< v.]
—*v.* **1** cover or decorate with enamel. **2** form an enamel-like surface upon. **3** adorn with various colors; decorate as if with enamel. [ME < AF *enamayller* < *en-* on + *amayl* enamel < Gmc.] —**e·nam′el·ler** or **e·nam′el·er,** *n.*

e·nam·el·ware (i nam′əl wãr′) *n.* pots, pans, etc. that are made of metal coated with enamel.

en·am·or or **en·am·our** (en am′ər) *v.* arouse to love; cause to fall in love; charm: *Her beauty enamored the prince.* [< OF *enamourer* < *en-* in + *amour* love < L *amor*]

en·am·ored or **en·am·oured** (en am′ərd) *adj.* **1** very much in love; very fond; charmed: *The enamored prince gave up his throne to marry the beautiful peasant girl.* **2 enamored of** or **enamoured of,** in love with; very fond of; charmed by.

en a·vant (äN nä väN′) *French.* forward.

en bloc (en′blok′ or än′blok′; *French,* äN blôk′) all together; in one lump. [< F]

en·camp (en kamp′) *v.* **1** make a camp: *It took the soldiers only an hour to encamp.* **2** stay in a camp: *They encamped all night.* **3** put in a camp: *They were encamped in tents.* —**en·camp′ment,** *n.*

en·case (en kās′) *v.* **-cased, -cas·ing.** incase.

en·caus·tic (en kos′tik or en kôs′tik) *n.* **1** in painting, decorating, etc., a method or art of burning in the colors. **2** a painting, etc. produced by this method. —*adj.* prepared by heat; burnt in. Encaustic tile is decorated by burning in colored clays.

-ence *suffix.* **1** the act, fact, quality, or state of ——ing, as in *abhorrence, dependence, indulgence.* **2** the quality or state of being ——ent, as in *absence, confidence, competence, independence, prudence.* See also **-ency.** [< L *-entia*]

en·ceinte (en sent′; *French,* äN saNt′) *adj.* pregnant. [< F]

en·ce·phal·ic (en′sə fal′ik) *adj.* of or having to do with the brain. [< Gk. *enkephalos* brain]

en·ceph·a·lit·ic (en sef′ə lit′ik) *adj.* having to do with or suffering from encephalitis.

en·ceph·a·li·tis (en sef′ə lī′tis) *n.* an inflammation of the brain caused by injury, infection, poison, etc. Sleeping sickness is one kind of encephalitis. [< NL < Gk. *enkephalos* brain + Gk. *-itis*]

en·ceph·a·lo·gram (en sef′ə lə gram′) *n.* an X-ray photograph of the brain.

en·ceph·a·lo·my·e·li·tis (en sef′ə lō mī′ə lī′təs) *n.* an inflammation of the brain and spine, found in humans and certain animals, especially horses.

en·ceph·a·lon (en sef′ə lon′) *n.* the brain. [< NL < Gk. *enkephalos* < *en-* in + *kephalē* head]

en·chain (en chān′) *v.* **1** put in chains; fetter. **2** attract and fix firmly; hold fast: *The speaker's earnestness enchained the attention of his audience.*

en·chant (en chant′) *v.* **1** use magic on; put under a spell: *The witch enchanted the princess.* **2** delight greatly; charm. [< F *enchanter* < L *incantare* < *in-* against + *cantare* chant] **—en·chant′er,** *n.* **—Syn. 2** fascinate, captivate, enrapture.

en·chant·ing (en chan′ting) *adj.* **1** very delightful; charming. **2** bewitching.

en·chant·ment (en chant′mənt) *n.* **1** the use of magic; the act of putting under a spell. **2** the condition of being put under a magic spell. **3** a magic spell. **4** delight; rapture. **5** something that delights or charms; great delight; charm.

en·chan·tress (en chan′tris) *n.* **1** a woman who enchants; witch. **2** a very delightful, charming woman.

en·chase (en chās′) *v.* **-chased, -chas·ing. 1** engrave: *His initials were enchased on the back of the watch.* **2** ornament with engraved designs; decorate with gems, inlay, etc.: *The shield was enchased with gold and silver.* **3** place in a setting; mount; frame. [< F *enchâsser* < *en-* in + *châsse* frame, case < L *capsa* box]

en·chi·la·da (en′chi lä′də) *n.* a tortilla rolled around a filling of meat, cheese, etc., served with a peppery sauce. [< Mexican Sp., ult. < Sp. *en-* in + Nahuatl *chili* chili]

en·cir·cle (en sėr′kəl) *v.* **-cled, -cling. 1** form a circle around; surround: *Trees encircled the pond.* **2** go in a circle around: *The moon encircles the earth.* **—Syn. 1** encompass, gird.

en·cir·cle·ment (en sėr′kəl mənt) *n.* **1** an encircling. **2** a being encircled.

en·clave (en′klāv) *n.* **1** a country or district surrounded by the territory of another country. **2** a separate unit enclosed within a larger one. [< F *enclave* < *enclaver* enclose]

en·clit·ic (en klit′ik) *n.* a word or contraction that, having no stress, is pronounced as part of the preceding word. *Examples: s* in *Bert's here* (= *Bert is here*), *not* in *I cannot tell.* [< LL *encliticus* < Gk. *enklitikos* < *enklinein* lean on < *en-* in, on + *klinein* lean, incline]

en·close (en klōz′) *v.* **-closed, -clos·ing. 1** shut in on all sides; surround. **2** put a wall or fence around. **3** put in an envelope along with something else: *A cheque was enclosed with the letter.* **4** contain. Also, **inclose.** [< *en-*[1] in + *close,* v., ME, after OF *enclos,* pp. of *enclore*]

en·clo·sure (en klō′zhər) *n.* **1** an enclosing or being enclosed. **2** an enclosed place: *Those cages are enclosures for the monkeys.* **3** something that encloses. A wall or fence is an enclosure. **4** anything enclosed with something else, especially in an envelope: *There was a ten-dollar enclosure with the letter.* Also, **inclosure.**

hat, āge, cãre, fär; let, ēqual, tėrm; it, īce
hot, ōpen, ôrder; oil, out; cup, pu̇t, rüle, ūse
əbove, takən, pencəl, lemən, circəs
ch, child; ng, long; sh, ship
th, thin; ᴛʜ, then; zh, measure

en·code (en kōd′) *v.* **-cod·ed, -cod·ing.** put into code; *The spy encoded his message before mailing it.* **—en·cod′er,** *n.*

en·co·mi·ast (en kō′mi ast′) *n.* a writer or speaker of encomiums; eulogist. [< Gk. *enkōmiastēs* < *enkōmion.* See ENCOMIUM.]

en·co·mi·um (en kō′mē əm) *n.* **-mi·ums, -mi·a** (-mē ə). an elaborate expression of praise; high praise; eulogy. [< LL < Gk. *enkōmion,* neut., laudatory < *en-* in + *kōmos* revelry]

en·com·pass (en kum′pəs) *v.* **1** surround completely; shut in on all sides; encircle: *The atmosphere encompasses the earth.* **2** enclose; contain. **—en·com′pass·ment,** *n.*

en·core (ong′kôr or on′kôr) *interj. n. v.* **-cored, -cor·ing.** —*interj.* once more; again.
—*n.* **1** a demand by the audience for the repetition of a song, a piece of music, etc., or for another appearance of the performer or performers. **2** the repetition of a song, etc. in response to such a demand. **3** an additional song, etc. given in response to such a demand. **4** in sports, the arts, etc., another appearance, match, bout, etc. involving the same people.
—*v.* call for a repetition of (a song, etc.); call for an encore from (a performer, etc.) by applauding: *The audience encored the singer.* [< F]

en·coun·ter (en koun′tər) *v.* **1** meet unexpectedly: *I encountered an old friend on the train.* **2** meet with (difficulties, opposition, etc.); be faced with. **3** meet as an enemy; meet in a fight or battle.
—*n.* **1** a meeting; unexpected meeting. **2** a meeting of two opposed forces, teams, etc.; a fight; battle. [ME < OF *encontrer* < VL < L *in-* in + *contra* against]
—Syn. *n.* **2** conflict, combat, skirmish.

en·cour·age (en kėr′ij) *v.* **-aged, -ag·ing. 1** give courage to; increase the hope or confidence of; urge on: *Success encourages you to go ahead and do better.* **2** be favorable to; help; support: *High prices for farm products encourage farming.* [ME < OF *encoragier* < *en-* in + *corage* courage, ult. < L *cor* heart] **—en·cour′ag·er,** *n.* **—en·cour′ag·ing·ly,** *adv.* **—Syn. 1** hearten, inspirit. **2** promote, advance.

en·cour·age·ment (en kėr′ij mənt) *n.* **1** an encouraging. **2** the state of being or feeling encouraged. **3** something that encourages.

en·croach (en krōch′) *v.* **1** go beyond proper or usual limits: *The sea encroached upon the shore and submerged the beach.* **2** trespass upon the property or rights of another; intrude: *He is a good salesman and will not encroach upon his customer's time.* [< OF *encrochier* < *en-* in + *croc* hook < Gmc.] **—en·croach′er,** *n.* **—Syn. 2** See **intrude.**

en·croach·ment (en krōch′mənt) *n.* **1** an encroaching. **2** something taken by encroaching.

en·crust (en krust′) *v.* incrust.

en·cum·ber (en kum′bər) *v.* **1** hold back (from running, doing, etc.); hinder; hamper: *Heavy shoes encumber the wearer in the water.* **2** make difficult to use; fill; obstruct: *Rubbish and old boxes encumbered the fire escape.* **3** weigh down; burden: *The farm was encumbered with a heavy mortgage.* Also, **incumber.** [ME < OF *encombrer* < *en-* in + *combre* barrier, probably < Celtic]

en·cum·brance (en kum′brəns) *n.* **1** anything that encumbers; a hindrance; obstruction. **2** an annoyance; trouble; burden. **3** a dependent person; child. **4** in law, a claim, mortgage, etc. on property. Also, **incumbrance.**

-ency *suffix.* **1** the act, fact, quality, or state of ——ing, as in *dependency.* **2** the quality or state of being ——ent, as in *clemency, frequency.* **3** other meanings, as in *agency, currency.* See also **-ence.** [< L *-entia*]
☛ See **-ance** for usage note.

encyc. or **ency.** encyclopedia.

en·cyc·li·cal (en sik′lə kəl or en sī′klə kəl) *n.* in the

Roman Catholic Church, a letter from the Pope to his clergy. *—adj.* intended for wide circulation. [< LL *encyclicus* < Gk. *enkyklios* < *en-* in + *kyklos* circle]

en·cy·clo·pe·di·a or **en·cy·clo·pae·di·a** (en sī′klə pē′dē ə) *n.* **1** a book or series of books giving information, usually arranged alphabetically, on all branches of knowledge. **2** a book treating one subject very thoroughly, with its articles arranged alphabetically. [< LL *encyclopaedia* < Gk. *enkyklopaideia*, for *enkyklios paideia* well-rounded education]

en·cy·clo·pe·dic or **en·cy·clo·pae·dic** (en sī′klə pē′dik) *adj.* **1** covering a wide range of subjects; possessing wide and varied information. **2** of or having to do with an encyclopedia.

en·cy·clo·pe·dist or **en·cy·clo·pae·dist** (en sī′klə pē′dist) *n.* a person who makes or compiles an encyclopedia.

en·cyst (en sist′) *v.* enclose or become enclosed in a cyst or sac. **—en·cyst′ment,** *n.*

end (end) *n.* **1** the last part; conclusion: *He read through to the end of the book.* **2** the point where something stops or ceases to be: *Drive to the end of this road.* **3** a purpose; object: *The end of work is to get something done.* **4** a result; outcome: *It is hard to tell what the end will be.* **5** death; destruction. **6** a cause of death or destruction. **7** a part left over; remnant; fragment. **8** in football, the player at either end of the line. **9** the furthest or most distant part; extreme point: *The police will hunt the murderer to the ends of the earth.* **10** limit; boundary: *There was no end to her patience.* **11** in curling, one of the divisions of a game: *Our team was beaten in the last end.*
at loose ends, a not settled or established. **b** in confusion or disorder.
jump or **go off the deep end,** *Slang.* act suddenly and rashly without deliberation.
keep or **hold up one's end,** sustain one's part or bear one's share fully in an undertaking or performance.
make an end of, stop; do no more.
make both ends meet, a spend no more than one has. **b** just manage to live on what one has.
no end, *Informal.* very much; very many.
on end, a upright. **b** one after another: *It snowed for days on end.*
put an end to, stop; do away with; destroy; kill.
—v. **1** bring or come to an end; stop; finish: *Let us end this fight.* **2** destroy; kill. **3** form the end of; be the end of. [OE *ende*] **—end′er,** *n.*
Syn. *n.* **1** termination, close, finish, expiration. **3** intention, design, goal, aim. **4** issue, consequence. **5** extermination, annihilation. **7** remainder. *–v.* **1 End, conclude, finish** = bring or come to a close. **End** suggests a sudden stop or natural close: *My holidays ended when school started.* **Conclude** is a formal word and suggests a formal ending of a speech, essay, action, piece of business, etc.: *Singing the national anthem will conclude the meeting.* **Finish** suggests ending only after getting everything done that should be done: *I never finish my homework on time.*

end-all (end′ol′ or -ôl′) *n.* the ultimate; the end of everything.

en·dan·ger (en dān′jər) *v.* cause danger to; expose to loss or injury: *Fire endangered the hotel's guests, but no lives were lost.*

en·dear (en dēr′) *v.* make dear: *Her kindness endeared her to all of us.* **—en·dear′ing·ly,** *adv.*

en·dear·ment (en dēr′mənt) *n.* **1** an endearing. **2** the thing that endears. **3** an act or word showing love or affection; caress.

en·deav·or or **en·deav·our** (en dev′ər) *v.* try hard; attempt earnestly; make an effort; strive. *—n.* an earnest attempt; effort. [ME < *-en-*[1] + *devoir* < *dever* duty < OF *deveir* < L *debere* owe]
—en·deav′or·er or **en·deav·our·er,** *n.* **—Syn.** *v.* struggle, labor, essay. See **try.** *–n.* exertion, struggle. See **effort.**

en·dem·ic (en dem′ik) *adj.* regularly found in a particular people or locality: *Cholera is endemic in India.* *—n.* an endemic disease. [< Gk. *endēmos* native < *en-* in + *dēmos* people] **—en·dem′i·cal·ly,** *adv.*

en dés·ha·bil·lé (äɴ dā zä bē yā′) *French.* partly or carelessly dressed.

end·ing (en′ding) *n.* **1** the last part; end. **2** death. **3** in grammar, a letter or syllable added to a word or stem to change its meaning or to show how it is used in relation to other words. The common plural ending in English is *-s* or *-es*, as in *kings, dresses.*

en·dive (en′dīv or on′dīv; *French,* äɴ dēv′) *n.* **1** a kind of chicory having finely divided, curly leaves, used for salads. **2** a kind of chicory that has broad leaves and looks like smooth white celery, also used for salads; escarole. [ME < OF < Med.L *endivia* < L *intibus* < Gk. *entybon*]

end·less (end′lis) *adj.* **1** having no end; never stopping; lasting or going on forever: *Doing housework is an endless task.* **2** with the ends joined for continuous action: *The chain that turns the rear wheel of a bicycle is an endless chain.* **—end′less·ly,** *adv.* **—end′less·ness,** *n.* **—Syn.** **1** boundless, limitless, immeasurable, interminable, incessant, unceasing, continual, perpetual, everlasting.

end man 1 the man at the end of a row or line. **2** in a minstrel show, a man at either end of a line of performers.

end·most (end′mōst) *adj.* nearest to the end; last; farthest.

endo- *word element.* within; inside; inner, as in *endocarp, endoderm, endogamy.* [< Gk. *endo-* < *endon*]

en·do·car·di·al (en′dō kär′dē əl) *adj.* **1** in the heart. **2** of or having to do with the endocardium.

en·do·car·di·um (en′dō kär′dē əm) *n.* the delicate, smooth membrane that lines the chambers of the heart. [< NL *endocardium* + Gk. *endon* within + *kardia* heart]

en·do·carp (en′dō kärp′) *n.* in botany, the inner layer of a fruit or ripened ovary of a plant. A peach stone is an endocarp. [< *endo-* + Gk. *karpos* fruit]

en·do·crin (en′dō krin) *adj. n.* endocrine.

en·do·crine (en′dō krīn′, en′dō krin, or en′dō krēn′) *adj.* **1** producing secretions that pass directly into the blood or lymph instead of into a duct. The thyroid is an endocrine gland. **2** of or having to do with the endocrine glands or the hormones they secrete. *—n.* **1** an endocrine gland. **2** its secretion. [< *endo-* + Gk. *krinein* separate]

endocrine gland any of various ductless glands that secrete hormones that influence other organs in the body.

en·do·derm (en′dō dėrm′) *n.* in biology, the inner layer of cells formed during development of animal embryos. The lining of the organs of the digestive system develops from the endoderm. [< *endo-* + Gk. *derma* skin]

end of steel *Cdn.* **1** the limit to which tracks have been laid for a railway. **2** a town at the end of a railway line; the terminus of a northern railway: *A road will soon connect us with the end of steel.*

en·dog·a·my (en dog′ə mē) *n.* the custom of marrying only within one's own tribe. [< *endo-* + *-gamy*]

en·dog·e·nous (en doj′ə nəs) *adj.* in biology, growing from the inside, originating within. [< *endo-* + *-genous* born, produced (< Gk. *-genēs*)]

en·dog·e·ny (en doj′ə nē) *n.* in biology, a growing from within, as in cell formation.

en·do·lymph (en′dō limf′) *n.* the fluid of the inner ear.

end-on (end′on′) *adj.* of or on the end: *an end-on collision.*

en·do·plasm (en′dō plaz′əm) *n.* in biology, the inner portion of the cytoplasm of a cell. [< *endo-* + Gk. *plasma* something formed or moulded]

en·dor·sa·tion (en′dôr sā′shən) *n. Cdn.* approval; support: *The mayor's proposals received wide endorsation.*

en·dorse (en dôrs′) *v.* **-dorsed, -dors·ing. 1** write one's name, instructions, etc. on the back of (a cheque, money order, or other document): *He had to endorse the cheque before the bank would cash it.* **2** approve; support: *Parents heartily endorsed the plan for a school playground.* Also, **indorse.** [alteration of ME *endosse(n)* < OF *endosser* < *en-* on + *dos* back < L *dorsum*]
—en·dors′able, *adj.* **—en·dors′er,** *n.*

en·dor·see (en dôr′sē′ or en′dôr sē′) *n.* a person to whom a cheque, note, or other document is assigned by endorsement. Also, **indorsee.**

en·dorse·ment (en dôrs′mənt) *n.* **1** the act of writing on the back of a cheque or other document. **2** a name, comment, or instructions, etc. written on the back of a cheque or other document. **3** approval; support: *The* proposal for a new stadium has our endorsement. 4 an additional provision or clause in an insurance contract by which the coverage described in the contract may be increased or diminished. Also, **indorsement.**

en·do·skel·e·ton (en′dō skel′ə tən) *n.* in zoology, the internal skeleton characteristic of vertebrates and allied forms.

en·do·sperm (en′dō spėrm′) *n.* in botany, nourishment for the embryo enclosed with it in the seed of a plant. See **embryo** for picture.

en·dow (en dou′) *v.* **1** give money or property to provide an income for: *The rich man endowed the college he had attended.* **2** furnish at birth; provide with some ability, quality, or talent; favor: *Nature endowed her with both beauty and brains.* [ME < OF *endouer* < *en-* in + *douer* endow < L *dotare*] —**en·dow′er,** *n.* —**Syn. 2** furnish, equip, invest.

en·dow·ment (en dou′mənt) *n.* **1** an endowing. **2** the money or property given to provide an income: *This college has a large endowment.* **3** a gift from birth; ability; talent: *A good sense of rhythm is a natural endowment.*

end·pa·per (end′pā′pər) *n.* a folded sheet of paper half of which is pasted to the inside of either cover of a book, the other half acting as a flyleaf.

end product 1 the part remaining after something is processed. **2** in nuclear physics, the last stable member of a series of isotopes, each produced by the radio-active decay of the preceding isotope.

en·due (en dū′ or en dü′) *v.* **-dued, -du·ing. 1** provide with a quality or power; furnish; supply: *The wisest man is not endued with perfect wisdom.* **2** put on. **3** clothe. Also, **indue.** [ME < OF *enduire* < L *inducere* lead into; confused with L *induere* put on]

en·dur·ance (en dūr′əns or en dür′əns) *n.* **1** the power to last or keep on: *A man must have great endurance to run 30 miles in a day. Cheap, shoddy cloth lacks endurance.* **2** the power to put up with, bear, or stand: *His endurance of the pain was remarkable.* **3** an act or instance of enduring pain, hardship, etc. **4** duration. —**Syn. 2** fortitude, patience, forbearance, tolerance.

en·dure (en dūr′ or en dür′) *v.* **-dured, -dur·ing. 1** keep on; last: *A gold ring will endure for a thousand years.* **2** undergo; bear; tolerate: *Those Indians endured much pain.* [ME < OF *endurer* < L *indurare* make hard < *in-* in (causative) + *durus* hard] —**en·dur′a·ble,** *adj.* —**en·dur′a·bly,** *adv.* —**en·dur′er,** *n.* —**Syn. 1** remain. **2** suffer, stand, experience. See **bear.**

en·dur·ing (en dūr′ing or en dür′ing) *adj.* lasting; permanent. —**en·dur′ing·ly,** *adv.* —**Syn.** abiding, unchangeable. See **lasting.**

end use the particular function that a manufactured product serves or to which it is limited.

end·ways (end′wāz′) *adv.* **1** on end; upright. **2** with the end forward; in the direction of the end. **3** lengthwise. **4** end to end.

end·wise (end′wīz′) *adv.* endways.

En·dym·i·on (en dim′ē ən) *n.* in Greek legend, a beautiful youth loved by Selene, the goddess of the moon.

end zone 1 in football, the part of the field between each goal line and the corresponding end of the field. **2** in hockey, the ice between each blue line and the corresponding end of the rink.

E.N.E., ENE or **e.n.e.** east-northeast, a direction halfway between east and northeast.

en·e·ma (en′ə mə) *n.* **en·e·mas, e·nem·a·ta** (i nem′ə tə). **1** an injection of liquid into the rectum to flush the bowels. **2** the apparatus used. [< Gk. *enema* < *en-* in + *hienai* send]

en·e·my (en′ə mē) *n.* **-mies,** *adj.* —*n.* **1** a person or group that hates and tries to harm another. **2** a hostile force, nation, fleet, army, or air force; person, ship, etc. of a hostile nation. **3** anything harmful: *Frost is an enemy of plants.* —*adj.* of an enemy. [ME < OF *enemi* < L *inimicus* < *in-* not + *amicus* friendly]

Syn. *n.* **1, 2 Enemy, foe** = a hostile person, group, country, army, etc. **Enemy** is the common and general word, applying to any person or group who wants or tries to harm another person or group in any way: *Because of his unfair methods that businessman has many enemies.* **Foe,** now chiefly poetic or literary, means a very dangerous and actively opposed enemy.

en·er·get·ic (en′ər jet′ik) *adj.* **1** full of energy; eager to work. **2** full of force; active. —**en′er·get′i·cal·ly,** *adv.* —**Syn.** vigorous, strenuous.

hat, āge, cãre, fär; let, ēqual, tėrm; it, īce
hot, ōpen, ôrder; oil, out; cup, pu̇t, rüle, ūse
əbove, takən, pencəl, lemən, circəs
ch, child; ng, long; sh, ship
th, thin; ŧh, then; zh, measure

en·er·gize (en′ər jīz′) *v.* **-gized, -giz·ing.** give energy to; make active.

en·er·giz·er (en′ər jī′zər) *n.* **1** any one of several drugs used to give energy or to relieve severe mental depression. **2** a device that stores chemical energy and can operate small mechanisms.

en·er·gy (en′ər jē) *n.* **-gies. 1** active strength or force; healthy power; vigor: *Young men have more energy than old people.* **2** strength; force; power. **3** in physics, the capacity for doing work, such as lifting or moving an object. Energy is measured in ergs. [< LL < Gk. *energeia* < *energos* active < *en-* in + *ergon* work]

en·er·vate (en′ər vāt′) *v.* **-vat·ed, -vat·ing.** lessen the vigor or strength of; weaken: *A hot, damp climate enervates people who are not used to it.* [< L *enervare* < *ex-* away + *nervus* sinew, nerve] —**en′er·va′tion,** *n.* —**en′er·va′tor,** *n.*

en fa·mille (äɴ fä mē′) *French.* with one's family; at home; informally.

en·fant (äɴ fäɴ′) *n. French.* a child.

en·fant ter·ri·ble (äɴ fäɴ te rē′blə) *French.* **1** a child whose behavior, questions, remarks, etc. embarrass older people. **2** a person who is indiscreet or lacks a sense of responsibility.

en·fee·ble (en fē′bəl) *v.* **-bled, -bling.** make feeble; weaken. —**en·fee′ble·ment,** *n.* —**en·fee′bler,** *n.*

en·fi·lade (en′fə lād′) *n. v.* **-lad·ed, -lad·ing.** —*n.* gunfire directed from the side at a line of troops or a position held by them. —*v.* fire guns at (a line of troops or the position held by them) from the side. [< F *enfilade* < *enfiler* thread, pierce < *en-* on + *fil* thread < L *filum*]

en·fold (en fōld′) *v.* **1** fold in; wrap up: *The old lady was enfolded in a shawl.* **2** embrace; clasp: *The mother enfolded her baby in her arms.* Also, **infold.**

en·force (en fôrs′) *v.* **-forced, -forc·ing. 1** force obedience to; put into force: *Policemen and judges enforce the laws.* **2** force; compel: *The robbers enforced obedience to their demand by threats of violence.* **3** urge with force; emphasize: *The teacher enforced the principle by examples.* [ME < OF *enforcier,* ult. < L *in-* + *fortis* strong] —**en·force′a·ble,** *adj.* —**en·forc′er,** *n.* —**Syn. 1** execute, administer.

en·force·ment (en fôrs′mənt) *n.* an enforcing; putting into force: *Strict enforcement of the laws against speeding will reduce automobile accidents.*

en·fran·chise (en fran′chīz) *v.* **-chised, -chis·ing. 1** give the right to vote: *Canadian citizens are enfranchised at the age of 21 years. When a Canadian Indian is enfranchised, he loses his treaty rights.* **2** set free; release from slavery or restraint. —**en·fran′chis·er,** *n.*

en·fran·chise·ment (en fran′chiz mənt) *n.* **1** an enfranchising. **2** a being enfranchised.

eng. 1 engineer. **2** engineering. **3** engraving. **4** engraved. **5** engraver.

Eng. 1 England. **2** English. **3** Engineer.

en·gage (en gāj′) *v.* **-gaged, -gag·ing. 1** bind oneself; promise; pledge: *I will engage to be there on time.* **2** promise or pledge to marry: *John is engaged to Mary.* **3** keep busy; occupy: *Work engages much of his time.* **4** keep oneself busy; be occupied; be active; take part: *He engages in politics. His wife engages in social work.* **5** hire; employ; take for use or work; reserve (seats, rooms, a taxi, etc.): *She engaged a cook for the summer.* **6** catch and hold; attract: *Bright colors engaged the baby's attention.* **7** fit into; lock together: *The teeth of one gear engage with the teeth of another. The teeth engage*

Cogwheels engaged

each other. **8** start a battle with; attack: *Our soldiers engaged the enemy.* [< F *engager* < *en gage* under pledge] —**en·gag′er,** *n.*

en·ga·gé (äɴ gä zhā′) *n. Cdn.* formerly, one hired by a fur company for inland service in the trade. [< Cdn.F < F *engagé* enlisted]

en·gaged (en gājd′) *adj.* **1** promised or pledged to marry. **2** busy; occupied: *Engaged in conversation, they did not see us.* **3** taken for use or work; hired. **4** fitted together. **5** involved in a fight or battle. —**Syn. 1** betrothed, affianced.

en·gage·ment (en gāj′mənt) *n.* **1** the act of engaging. **2** the fact or condition of being engaged. **3** a promise; pledge: *An honest person fulfils all his engagements.* **4** a promise to marry. **5** a meeting with someone at a certain time; appointment. **6** the period of being hired; time of use or work. **7** a fight; battle. —**Syn. 3** agreement. **4** betrothal. **7** encounter, combat, conflict. See **battle.**

en·gag·ing (en gāj′ing) *adj.* very attractive; pleasing; charming. —**en·gag′ing·ly,** *adv.* —**en·gag′ing·ness,** *n.*

En·gel·mann spruce (eng′gəl mən) **1** a large mountain spruce tree of western North America. **2** the light, soft wood of this tree, much used for lumber, pulpwood, etc. [< George *Engelmann* (1809-1884), a German-born physicist and botanist]

en·gen·der (en jen′dər) *v.* bring into existence; produce; cause: *Filth engenders disease.* [ME < OF *engendrer* < L *ingenerare* < *in-* in + *generare* create]

en·gine (en′jən) *n.* **1** a machine that applies power to some work, especially a machine that can start others moving. **2** a machine that pulls a railway train. **3** a machine; device; instrument: *Those big guns are engines of war.* [ME < OF *engin* < L *ingenium* inborn qualities, talent < *in-* in + *gen-*, root of *gignere* create, produce, beget. Related to GENIUS.]

en·gi·neer (en′jə nēr′) *n.* **1** a man who runs an engine. **2** a person who plans, builds, or manages engines, machines, roads, bridges, canals, railways, forts, etc.; an expert in engineering. **3** in the armed services, a member of a group of men who do engineering work.
—*v.* **1** plan, build, direct, or work as an engineer. **2** manage cleverly; guide skilfully: *Although many opposed his insurance plan, he engineered it through to final approval.*

en·gi·neer·ing (en′jə nēr′ing) *n.* **1** the science, work, or profession of an engineer. **2** the planning, building, or managing of engines, machines, roads, bridges, canals, railways, forts, etc. **3** manoeuvring; skilful contrivance.

engine house a station for a fire engine.

en·gine·ry (en′jən rē) *n.* engines; machines.

Eng·land·er (ing′glən dər) *n.* an English person.

Eng·lish (ing′glish) *adj.* of or having to do with England, its people, or their language.
—*n.* **1** the people of England collectively. **2** the English language, including Old English or Anglo-Saxon (before 1100), Middle English (about 1100-1500), and Modern English (from about 1500). As well as in the British Isles, English is also spoken in Canada, the United States, the Republic of South Africa, Australia, New Zealand, and many other places. **3** in printing, a large size of type; 14 point. **4** Sometimes, **english.** a spinning motion imparted to a ball by hitting on one side of its centre.
—*v.* **1** translate into English; express in plain English. **2** Sometimes, **english.** *U.S.* give a spinning motion to (a billiard ball). [OE *Englisc* < *Engle* the English people] —**Eng′lish·ness,** *n.*

English cocker spaniel 1 a breed of hunting dog, resembling the cocker spaniel but larger. A dog weighs from 26 to 34 pounds. **2** a dog of this breed.

English horn a wooden musical instrument resembling an oboe, but larger and having a lower tone. [a mistranslation of F *cor anglé* angled, cornered horn, *anglé* being confused with *anglais* English]

Eng·lish·man (ing′glish mən) *n.* **-men** (-mən). **1** a man who is a native or inhabitant of England. **2** one whose ancestry is English.

English setter 1 a breed of setter, having black and white markings, and sometimes tan spots. **2** a dog of this breed.

English sonnet Elizabethan sonnet.

English sparrow a small, brownish-gray bird, a European finch now very common in North America. See **sparrow** for picture.

English walnut 1 a walnut tree from Asia, cultivated in Europe and North America. **2** its edible nut, used in candy, cakes, etc.

Eng·lish·wom·an (ing′glish wům′ən) *n.* **-wom·en. 1** a woman who is a native or inhabitant of England. **2** a woman whose ancestry is English.

en·gorge (en gôrj′) *v.* **-gorged, -gorg·ing. 1** swallow greedily. **2** glut; gorge. **3** feed greedily. **4** in medicine, congest with blood.

engr. 1 engineer. **2** engraved. **3** engraver.

en·graft (en graft′) *v.* **1** insert or graft a shoot from one tree or plant into or on another: *Peach trees can be engrafted on plum trees.* See **graft** for picture. **2** add permanently; implant: *Honesty and thrift are engrafted in his character.* Also, **ingraft.**

en·grave (en grāv′) *v.* **-graved, -grav·ing. 1** cut in; carve artistically; decorate by engraving: *The jeweller engraved the boy's initials on the back of the watch.* **2** in printing: **a** cut in lines on a metal plate, block of wood, etc., for printing. **b** print from such a plate, block, etc. **3** impress deeply; fix firmly: *His mother's face was engraved on his memory.* [< *en-*[1] + *grave*[3]] —**Syn. 1** chisel.

en·grav·er (en grāv′ər) *n.* a person who engraves metal plates, blocks of wood, etc. for printing.

en·grav·ing (en grāv′ing) *n.* **1** the art of an engraver; cutting lines in metal plates, blocks of wood, etc. for printing. **2** a picture printed from an engraved plate, block, etc. **3** an engraved plate, block, etc.; engraved design or pattern.

en·gross (en grōs′) *v.* **1** occupy wholly; take up all the attention of: *She was engrossed in a story.* **2** copy or write in large letters; write a beautiful copy of. **3** write out in formal style; express in legal form. **4** in business, buy all or much of (the supply of some commodity) so as to control prices. [(defs. 1, 4) < *in gross* < F *en gros* in a lump, in large amounts; (defs. 2, 3) < AF *engrosser* < *en-* in + *grosse* large writing, document] —**en·gross′er,** *n.* —**en·gross′ment,** *n.*

en·gulf (en gulf′) *v.* swallow up; overwhelm; submerge: *A wave engulfed the small boat.* Also, **ingulf.**

en·hance (en hans′) *v.* **-hanced, -hanc·ing.** make greater; add to; heighten: *The gardens enhanced the beauty of the house.* [ME < AF *enhauncer* raise, ult. < L *altus* high. Related to HAWSER.] —**en·hance′ment,** *n.* —**en·hancer,** *n.* —**Syn.** increase, augment.

en·har·mon·ic (en′här mon′ik) *adj.* in music: **1** having to do with or designating a scale, a style of music, or an instrument employing intervals smaller than a semitone, especially quarter tones. **2** of different notes on the scale that have the same tone or key on an instrument. *Example*: C sharp and D flat.

en haut (äɴ ō′) *French.* above; on high.

e·nig·ma (i nig′mə) *n.* **1** a puzzling statement; riddle: *To most of the audience the philosopher seemed to speak in enigmas.* **2** a baffling or puzzling problem, situation, person, etc.: *The queer behavior of the child was an enigma even to its parents.* [< L < Gk. *ainigma* < *ainissesthai* speak darkly < *ainos* fable]

en·ig·mat·ic (en′ig mat′ik or ē′nig mat′ik) *adj.* enigmatical.

en·ig·mat·i·cal (en′ig mat′ə kəl or ē′nig mat′ə kəl) *adj.* like a riddle; baffling; puzzling; mysterious. —**en′ig·mat′i·cal·ly,** *adv.*

en·jamb·ment or **en·jambe·ment** (en jam′mənt or en jamb′mənt; *French,* äɴ zhäɴb mäɴ′) *n.* in prosody, the continuation of a sentence without pause from one line or couplet to the next. [< F *enjambement* < MF *enjamber* encroach, stride < *en-* on + OF *jambe* leg < L *gamba*]

en·join (en join′) *v.* **1** order; direct; urge: *Parents enjoin good behavior on their children.* **2** in law, issue an authoritative command. Through an injunction a judge may enjoin a person not to do some act. [ME < OF *enjoindre* < L *injungere* attack, charge < *in-* on

+ *jungere* join] **—en·join′er,** *n.* **—en·join′ment,** *n.* **—Syn. 1** prescribe, command, charge, bid.

en·joy (en joi′) *v.* **1** have or use with joy; be happy with; take pleasure in. **2** have as an advantage or benefit: *He enjoyed good health.* **3 enjoy oneself,** be happy; have pleasure; have a good time. [ME < OF *enjoir* < *en-* in (intensive) + *joir* rejoice < L *gaudere*] **—en·joy′er,** *n.*

en·joy·a·ble (en joi′ə bəl) *adj.* capable of being enjoyed; giving enjoyment; pleasant. **—en·joy′a·bly,** *adv.*

en·joy·ment (en joi′mənt) *n.* **1** an enjoying. **2** something enjoyed. **3** joy; happiness; pleasure. **4** the condition of having as an advantage or benefit; possession; use: *Laws protect the enjoyment of our rights.* **—Syn. 3** delight, felicity.

en·kin·dle (en kin′dəl) *v.* **-dled, -dling. 1** arouse; excite; stir up. **2** light up; brighten.

en·lace (en lās′) *v.* **-laced, -lac·ing. 1** wind about; encircle; enfold. **2** twine together; interlace. [< F *enlacer*]

en·large (en lärj′) *v.* **-larged, -larg·ing. 1** make or become larger; increase in size. **2 enlarge on,** talk or write more about. [ME < OF *enlarger* < *en-* in (causative) + *large* large < L *largus* copious] **—en·larg′er,** *n.* **—Syn. 1** augment, broaden, extend, expand. See **increase.**

en·large·ment (en lärj′mənt) *n.* **1** an enlarging or being enlarged. **2** anything that is an enlarged form of something else. **3** in photography, a print that is made larger than the negative. **4** anything that enlarges something else; an addition.

en·light·en (en līt′ən) *v.* give the light of truth and knowledge to; free from prejudice, ignorance, etc. **—en·light′en·er,** *n.* **—Syn.** instruct, teach, inform.

en·light·en·ment (en līt′ən mənt) *n.* **1** an enlightening of the mind. **2** the fact or state of being enlightened. **—Syn.** See **education.**

En·light·en·ment (en līt′ən mənt) *n.* a philosophical movement in Europe in the 18th century, characterized by rationalism, by scepticism about existing political and social beliefs, and by emphasis on intellectual freedom.

en·list (en list′) *v.* **1** join the navy, army, or air force. **2** enrol in some branch of the armed services. **3** induce to join in some cause or undertaking; secure the help or support of: *The mayor enlisted the churches and schools of the city to work for more parks.* **4** join in some cause or undertaking; give help or support. **—en·list′er,** *n.*

enlisted man *Esp.U.S.* a member of the armed services who is not a commissioned officer or cadet.

en·list·ment (en list′mənt) *n.* **1** an enlisting. **2** a being enlisted. **3** the time for which a person enlists.

en·liv·en (en līv′ən) *v.* make lively, active, gay, or cheerful: *The speaker enlivened his talk with humor. Bright curtains enliven a room.* **—en·liv′en·er,** *n.* **—en·liv′en·ing·ly,** *adv.*

en masse (on′ mas′ or en′ mas′; *French,* äN mäs′) in a group; all together. [< F]

en·mesh (en mesh′) *v.* catch in a net; enclose in meshes; entangle. **—en·mesh′ment,** *n.*

en·mi·ty (en′mə tē) *n.* **-ties.** the feeling that enemies have for each other; hatred. [ME < OF *ennemistie* < VL < L *inimicus.* See ENEMY.] **—Syn.** hostility, hatred, animosity, ill will, antipathy.

en·no·ble (en nō′bəl) *v.* **-bled, -bling. 1** give a title or rank of nobility to; raise to the rank of nobleman. **2** raise in the respect of others; dignify; exalt: *A good deed ennobles the person who does it.* **3** make finer or more noble in nature: *His character had been ennobled through suffering.* **—en·no′ble·ment,** *n.* **—en·no′bler,** *n.*

en·nui (on′wē; *French,* äN nwē′) *n.* a feeling of weariness and discontent from lack of occupation or interest; boredom. [< F. Related to ANNOY.]

e·nor·mi·ty (i nôr′mə tē) *n.* **-ties. 1** extreme wickedness; outrageousness: *The murderer finally realized the enormity of his crime.* **2** an extremely wicked crime; outrageous offence.

e·nor·mous (i nôr′məs) *adj.* **1** extremely large; huge: *Long ago enormous animals lived on the earth.* **2** extremely wicked; outrageous. [< L *enormis* < *ex-* out of + *norma* pattern] **—e·nor′mous·ness,** *n.* **—Syn. 1** immense, colossal, gigantic, vast, mammoth, prodigious, stupendous. See **huge. 2** abominable, atrocious.

hat, āge, cãre, fär; let, ēqual, tėrm; it, īce
hot, ōpen, ôrder; oil, out; cup, pu̇t, rüle, ūse
əbove, takən, pencəl, lemən, circəs
ch, child; ng, long; sh, ship
th, thin; ᴛʜ, then; zh, measure

e·nor·mous·ly (i nôr′məs lē) *adv.* in or to an enormous degree; extremely; vastly; beyond measure.

e·nough (i nuf′) *adj.* as much or as many as needed or wanted: *Buy enough food for the picnic.*
—n. an adequate quantity or number: *I have had enough to eat.*
—adv. **1** sufficiently; adequately: *Have you played enough?* **2** quite; fully: *He is willing enough to take a tip.* **3** rather; fairly: *She talks well enough for a baby.*
—interj. stop! no more! [OE *genōg*]
Syn. *adj.* **Enough, sufficient, adequate** = as much as is needed. **Enough** is the general word, and is often used interchangeably with *sufficient,* but it means "as much as is needed to satisfy a desire": *A growing boy never has enough time to play.* **Sufficient** = as much as is required to satisfy a need: *She is not getting sufficient food.* **Adequate** = as much as is needed to meet special, sometimes minimum, requirements: *To be healthy one must have an adequate diet.* -*n.* sufficiency, plenty.
☛ **enough.** In sentences having a plural subject, the predicate adjective *enough* may be preceded by a plural or singular verb: *Five boxes of apples are enough for the camp.* There is a strong tendency to place the adjective *enough* after a noun it modifies, and the adverb *enough* must be placed after an adjective or adverb it modifies: *We have room enough. Martha's sewing is good enough for me. You don't get up early enough.*

e·nounce (i nouns′) *v.* **e·nounced, e·nounc·ing. 1** proclaim; make a public or formal statement. **2** speak; pronounce; enunciate.

e·now (i nou′) *adj. n. adv. Archaic.* enough.

en pas·sant (äN pä säN′) *French.* in passing; by the way; incidentally.

en·quire (en kwīr′) *v.* **-quired, -quir·ing.** inquire.

en·quir·y (en kwīr′ē or en′kwə rē) *n.* **-quir·ies.** inquiry.

en·rage (en rāj′) *v.* **-raged, -rag·ing.** put into a rage; make very angry; make furious. [< OF *enrager* < *en-* in (causative) + *rage* rage < VL *rabia* < L *rabies*] **—Syn.** infuriate, exasperate, incense, anger.

en rap·port (äN rä pôr′) *French.* in sympathy; in agreement.

en·rapt (en rapt′) *adj.* rapt; filled with great delight.

en·rap·ture (en rap′chər) *v.* **-tured, -tur·ing.** fill with great delight; entrance: *The audience was enraptured by the singer's beautiful voice.*

en·rich (en rich′) *v.* **1** make rich or richer: *An education enriches your mind. Decorations enrich a room. Fertilizers enrich the soil.* **2** raise the nutritive value of (a food) by adding vitamins and minerals in processing. **3** make (a radio-active element) more fissionable by increasing the content of fissionable material: *Uranium that has its content of the isotope U235 increased is called enriched uranium.* **4** in schools, expand the range or content of a course of study: *an enriched program.* [ME < OF *enrichir* < *en-* in (causative) + *riche* rich] **—en·rich′er,** *n.*

en·rich·ment (en rich′mənt) *n.* **1** an enriching. **2** a being enriched. **3** anything that enriches.

en·rol or **en·roll** (en rōl′) *v.* **-rolled, -rol·ling. 1** write in a list. **2** have one's name written in a list. **3** make a member. **4** become a member. **5** enlist. [ME < OF *enroller* < *en-* in + *rolle* roll, n., ult. < L *rota* wheel]

en·rol·ment or **en·roll·ment** (en rōl′mənt) *n.* **1** an enrolling. **2** the number enrolled: *The school has an enrolment of 200 students.*

en route (on rüt′; *French,* äN rüt′) on the way: *We shall stop at Toronto en route from Montreal to Winnipeg.* [< F]

en·sam·ple (en sam′pəl) *n. Archaic.* example.

en·san·guine (en sang′gwin) *v.* **-guined, -guin·ing.** stain with blood.

en·sconce (en skons′) *v.* **-sconced, -sconc·ing. 1** shelter safely; hide: *The soldiers were ensconced in strongly fortified trenches.* **2** settle comfortably and firmly: *The cat ensconced itself in the armchair.* [< *en-*[1] + *sconce* fortification, probably < Du. *schans*]

en·sem·ble (on som′bəl) *n.* **1** all the parts of a thing considered together; general effect. **2** in music: **a** a united performance of the full number of singers, instrumentalists, etc.: *After the solo all the singers joined in the ensemble.* **b** a group of musicians or the musical instruments used in taking part in such a performance: *Two violins, a cello, and a harp made up the string ensemble.* **3** a set of clothes of which each item is chosen to match or complement the others; a complete, harmonious costume. [< F < VL < L *in-* + *simul* at the same time]

en·shrine (en shrīn′) *v.* **-shrined, -shrin·ing. 1** enclose in a shrine: *A fragment of the Cross is enshrined in the cathedral.* **2** keep sacred; cherish: *Memories of happier days were enshrined in the old beggar's heart.*

en·shrine·ment (en shrīn′mənt) *n.* **1** an enshrining. **2** anything that enshrines or surrounds.

en·shroud (en shroud′) *v.* cover; hide; veil: *Fog enshrouded the ship, but we could hear its siren.*

en·sign (en′sīn or en′sən *for 1, 3, and 4*; en′sən *for 2*) *n.* **1** a flag; banner: *the Red Ensign.* **2** *U.S.* in the navy, a commissioned officer junior to a lieutenant, junior grade. An ensign is the lowest commissioned officer in the United States navy. **3** formerly, a British army officer whose duty was carrying the flag. **4** the sign of one's rank, position, or power; symbol of authority. [ME < OF *enseigne* < L *insignia* insignia. Doublet of INSIGNIA.]

en·sign·ship (en′sən ship′) *n.* the rank or position of an ensign.

en·si·lage (en′sə lij) *n.* **1** the preservation of green fodder by packing it in a silo or pit. **2** green fodder preserved in this way. Ensilage is used to feed cattle in winter. [< F]

en·slave (en slāv′) *v.* **-slaved, -slav·ing.** make a slave or slaves of; take away freedom from.

en·slave·ment (en slāv′mənt) *n.* **1** an enslaving. **2** a being enslaved.

en·snare (en snãr′) *v.* **-snared, -snar·ing.** catch in a snare; trap. **—en·snare′ment,** *n.* **—en·snar′er,** *n.* Also, **insnare.**

en·sue (en sü′ or en sū′) *v.* **-sued, -su·ing. 1** come after; follow: *The ensuing year means the next year.* **2** happen as a result: *In his anger he hit the man, and a fight ensued.* [ME < OF *ensuivre* < L *insequi* < *in-* upon + *sequi* follow] **—Syn.** succeed, result. See **follow.**

en·sure (en shür′) *v.* **-sured, -sur·ing. 1** make sure or certain: *Careful planning and hard work ensured the success of the party.* **2** make sure of getting; secure: *A letter of introduction will ensure you an interview.* **3** make safe; protect: *Proper clothing ensured us against suffering from the cold.* [< AF *enseurer* < *en-* in (causative) + *seür* sure < L *securus*]

☛ **ensure, insure.** *Ensure* is the usual spelling for "make sure or certain"; *insure,* for "arrange for money payment in case of loss, accident, or death": *These letters ensure your claims. He should insure his car before he has an accident.*

-ent *suffix.* **1** ——ing, as in *absorbent, indulgent, coincident.* **2** one that ——s, as in *correspondent, president, superintendent.* **3** other meanings, as in *competent, confident.* [< L *-ens, -entis*]

en·tab·la·ture (en tab′lə chür′ or en tab′lə chər) *n.* in architecture, a part of a building resting on the top of columns. [< Ital. *intavolatura* < *in-* on + *tavola* board, tablet < L *tabula*]

CORNICE
FRIEZE
ARCHITRAVE
ENTABLATURE

en·tail (en tāl′) *v.* **1** impose; require: *Owning an automobile entailed greater expense than he had expected.* **2** limit the inheritance of (property, etc.) to a specified line of heirs so that it cannot be left to anyone else. An entailed estate usually passes to the eldest son.
—n. **1** an entailing. **2** an entailed inheritance. **3** the order of descent specified for an entailed estate. [ME < *en-*[1] + OF *taille* cutting, tax < *taillier* cut] **—en·tail′er,** *n.*

en·tail·ment (en tāl′mənt) *n.* **1** an entailing. **2** a being entailed.

en·tan·gle (en tang′gəl) *v.* **-gled, -gling. 1** get twisted up and caught; tangle: *Loose string is easily entangled.* **2** get into difficulty; involve: *The villain tried to entangle the hero in an evil scheme.* **3** perplex; confuse. **—en·tan′gler,** *n.* **—en·tan′gling·ly,** *adv.* **—Syn. 1** snarl, knot, mat. **2** implicate, ensnare. **3** bewilder, embarrass.

en·tan·gle·ment (en tang′gəl mənt) *n.* **1** an entangling. **2** a being entangled. **3** anything that entangles: *The trench was protected by a barbed-wire entanglement.*

en·tente (on tont′; *French,* äN täNt′) *n.* **1** an understanding; agreement between two or more governments. **2** the parties to an understanding; governments that have made an agreement.

en·tente cor·diale (äN täNt′ kôr dyäl′) *French.* a friendly understanding or agreement.

en·ter (en′tər) *v.* **1** go into; come into: *He entered the house.* **2** go in; come in: *Let them enter.* **3** become a part or member of; join: *The men entered the army.* **4** cause to join; enrol; obtain admission for: *Parents enter their children in school.* **5** begin upon; start on: *After years of training, the doctor entered the practice of medicine.* **6** write or print in a book, list, etc.: *A dictionary enters words in alphabetical order.* **7** put in regular form; record: *The injured man entered a complaint in court.* **8** report (a ship or its cargoes) at the custom house. **9** in the theatre, come on stage. **10 enter into, a** take part in; form a part of. **b** consider; discuss. **11 enter on** or **upon, a** begin; start. **b** take possession of. [ME < OF *entrer,* ult. < L *intra* within] **—en′ter·er,** *n.*

en·ter·ic (en ter′ik) *adj.* intestinal. [< Gk. *enterikos* < *entera* intestines]

enteric fever typhoid fever.

en·ter·i·tis (en′tər ī′tis) *n.* an inflammation of the intestines, usually accompanied by diarrhea, fever, etc. [< Gk. *entera* intestines + E *-itis*]

en·ter·prise (en′tər prīz′) *n.* **1** an important, difficult, or dangerous undertaking. **2** an undertaking; project: *a business enterprise.* **3** readiness to start projects; courage and energy in starting projects. **4** the carrying on of enterprises; a taking part in enterprises. See **private enterprise.** [ME < OF *entreprise* < *entre-* between + *prendre* take < L *prehendere*] **—Syn. 2** plan, venture.

en·ter·pris·ing (en′tər prīz′ing) *adj.* ready to try new, important, difficult, or dangerous plans; courageous and energetic in starting projects. **—Syn.** bold, venturesome.

en·ter·tain (en′tər tān′) *v.* **1** interest; please; amuse: *The circus entertained the children.* **2** have as a guest: *She entertained ten people at dinner.* **3** have guests; invite people to one's home: *She entertains a great deal.* **4** take into the mind; consider: *entertain an idea.* **5** hold in the mind; maintain: *Even after failing twice, we still entertained a hope of success.* [< F *entretenir* < *entre-* among + *tenir* hold < L *tenere*] **—en·ter·tain·a·ble,** *adj.* **—Syn. 1** divert, beguile, delight. See **amuse.**

en·ter·tain·er (en′tər tān′ər) *n.* **1** a person who entertains. **2** a singer, musician, reciter, etc. who takes part in public entertainments.

en·ter·tain·ing (en′tər tān′ing) *adj.* very interesting; pleasing; amusing. **—en′ter·tain′ing·ly,** *adv.*

en·ter·tain·ment (en′tər tān′mənt) *n.* **1** an entertaining. **2** a being entertained. **3** something that interests, pleases, or amuses. A show or play is an entertainment. **4** hospitality; the act or practice of paying attention to the comfort and desires of guests: *The hostess devoted herself to the entertainment of her guests.* **—Syn. 3** amusement, diversion, recreation, pastime.

en·thal·py (en thal′pē or en′thəl pē) *n.* in physics, the heat content per unit mass of substance. [< Gk. *enthalpein* to warm in]

en·thral or **en·thrall** (en throl′ or -thrôl′) *v.* **-thralled, -thrall·ing. 1** captivate; fascinate; charm: *The explorer enthralled the audience with the story of his exciting adventures.* **2** make a slave of; enslave. Also, **inthral** or **inthrall. —en·thral′ment** or **en·thrall′ment,** *n.*

en·throne (en thrōn′) *v.* **-throned, -thron·ing. 1** set on a throne. **2** place highest of all; exalt: *"Mercy is enthroned in the hearts of men."* **3** invest with authority, especially as a sovereign or as a bishop. Also, **inthrone. —en·throne′ment,** *n.*

en·thuse (en thüz′ or en thūz′) *v.* **-thused, -thus·ing.** *Esp.U.S. Informal.* **1** show enthusiasm. **2** fill with enthusiasm. [< *enthusiasm*]

☞ Although many people object to **enthuse**, it is now often heard in the U.S. and, less often, in Canada. It is wise to avoid the word in formal writing.

en·thu·si·asm (en thü′zē az′əm or en thūz′ē az′əm) *n.* eager interest; zeal: *The great leader filled his followers with enthusiasm.* [< LL *enthusiasmus* < Gk. *enthousiasmos* < *entheos* god-possessed < *en-* in + *theos* god] —**Syn.** eagerness, ardor, fervor.

en·thu·si·ast (en thü′zē ast′ or en thūz′ē ast′) *n.* **1** a person who is filled with eager interest or zeal: *a baseball enthusiast.* **2** a person who is carried away by his feelings for a cause. —**Syn. 2** zealot, fanatic, devotee.

en·thu·si·as·tic (en thü′zē as′tik or en thūz′ē as′tik) *adj.* full of enthusiasm; eagerly interested. —**Syn.** zealous, eager.

en·thu·si·as·ti·cal·ly (en thü′zē as′tik lē or en thūz′ē as′tik lē) *adv.* with enthusiasm; in an enthusiastic way.

en·tice (en tīs′) *v.* **-ticed, -tic·ing.** tempt by arousing hopes or desires; attract by offering some pleasure or reward: *The robber enticed his victims into a cave by promising to show them a gold mine.* [ME < OF *enticier* stir up, incite ? < *en-* in + L *titio* firebrand] —**en·tic′er,** *n.* —**en·tic′ing·ly,** *adv.* —**Syn.** inveigle, decoy. See **lure.**

en·tice·ment (en tīs′mənt) *n.* **1** an enticing. **2** a being enticed. **3** anything that entices.

en·tire (en tīr′) *adj.* **1** having all the parts or elements; whole; complete: *The entire platoon was wiped out.* **2** not broken; in one piece. **3** of leaves, not indented. **4** not castrated or gelded: *an entire horse.* [ME < OF *entier* < L *integer* < *in-* not + *tag-* a base of *tangere* touch. Doublet of INTEGER.] —**Syn. 1** total, full. See **complete. 2** intact, unimpaired.

en·tire·ly (en tīr′lē) *adv.* **1** wholly; completely; fully. **2** solely.

en·tire·ty (en tīr′tē or en tīr′ə tē) *n.* **-ties. 1** wholeness; completeness. **2** a complete thing; the whole. **3 in its entirety,** wholly; completely.

en·ti·tle (en tī′təl) *v.* **-tled, -tling. 1** give the title of; call by the name of: *She read a poem entitled "Trees."* **2** give a claim or right to; provide with a reason to ask or get something: *Their age and experience entitle old people to the respect of young people.* Also, **intitle.** [ME < OF *entituler* < LL *intitulare* < L *in-* in + *titulus* title] —**Syn. 1** name, denominate, designate. **2** empower, qualify, enable.

en·ti·tle·ment (en tī′təl mənt) *n.* something to which one is entitled.

en·ti·ty (en′ti tē) *n.* **-ties. 1** something that has a real and separate existence either actually or in the mind; anything real in itself: *Persons, mountains, languages, and beliefs are entities.* **2** a state of being; existence. [< LL *entitas* < L *ens, entis,* ppr. of *esse* be]

en·tomb (en tüm′) *v.* **1** place in a tomb; bury. **2** shut up as if in a tomb. Also, **intomb.** [ME < OF *entomber* < *en-* in + *tombe* tomb < LL *tumba* < Gk. *tymbos*] —**en·tomb′ment,** *n.*

en·to·mo·log·ic (en′tə mə loj′ik) *adj.* entomological.

en·to·mo·log·i·cal (en′tə mə loj′ə kəl) *adj.* of or having to do with entomology.

en·to·mol·o·gist (en′tə mol′ə jist) *n.* a person skilled in entomology.

en·to·mol·o·gy (en′tə mol′ə jē) *n.* the branch of zoology that deals with insects. [< Gk. *entomon* insect + E *-logy*]

en·tou·rage (on′tü räzh′) *n.* a group of attendants or people usually accompanying a person. [< F *entourage* < *entourer* surround]

en·tr'acte (än trakt′) *n.* **1** an interval between two acts of a play, ballet, opera, etc. **2** the music, dancing, or any entertainment performed during this interval. [< F *entr'acte* between-act]

en·trails (en′trālz or en′trəlz) *n.pl.* **1** the inner parts of a man or animal. **2** the intestines; bowels. **3** any inner parts. [ME < OF *entrailles* < LL *intralia* < L *interanea* < *inter* within]

en·train (en trān′) *v.* **1** get on a train. **2** put on a train: *The soldiers were entrained at night.*

en·trance[1] (en′trəns) *n.* **1** the act of entering: *The actor's entrance was greeted with applause.* **2** a place by which to enter; door, passageway, etc. **3** the freedom or right to enter; permission to enter. [< MF *entrance* < *entrer* enter < L *intrare.* See ENTER.] —**Syn. 1** entry, ingress. **2** opening, inlet, gate, portal.

hat, āge, cãre, fär; let, ēqual, tėrm; it, īce
hot, ōpen, ôrder; oil, out; cup, pu̇t, rüle, ūse
əbove, takən, pencəl, lemən, circəs
ch, child; ng, long; sh, ship
th, thin; ᴛʜ, then; zh, measure

en·trance[2] (en trans′) *v.* **-tranced, -tranc·ing. 1** put into a trance. **2** fill with joy; delight; charm. [< *en-*[1] + *trance*] —**en·tranc′ing·ly,** *adv.*

en·trance·ment (en trans′mənt) *n.* **1** an entrancing. **2** a being entranced. **3** something that entrances.

en·trance·way (en′trəns wā′) *n.* a place by which to enter.

en·trant (en′trənt) *n.* **1** a person who enters. **2** a new member in a profession, club, association, etc. **3** a person who takes part in a contest. [< F *entrant,* ppr. of *entrer* enter]

en·trap (en trap′) *v.* **-trapped, -trap·ping. 1** catch in a trap. **2** bring into difficulty or danger; deceive; trick: *By clever questioning, the lawyer entrapped the witness into contradicting himself.* [< MF *entraper* < *en-* in (intensive) + *trape* trap]

en·treat (en trēt′) *v.* ask earnestly; beg and pray; implore: *The captives entreated the savages not to kill them.* Also, **intreat.** [ME < OF *entraitier* < *en-* in (intensive) + *traitier* treat < L *tractare*] —**en·treat′er,** *n.* —**en·treat′ing·ly,** *adv.* —**Syn.** beseech, supplicate.

en·treat·y (en trēt′ē) *n.* **-treat·ies.** an earnest request; prayer: *The savages paid no attention to their captives' entreaties for mercy.* —**Syn.** supplication, appeal, solicitation, suit, petition.

en·tre·chat (äɴ trə shä′) *n.* in ballet, a leap in which the dancer repeatedly crosses his pointed feet. [< F *entrechat,* a respelling of Ital. (*capriola*) *intrecciata* complicated (leap) < *intrecciare* intertwine < *in-* in + *treccia* tress, plait]

en·tree or **en·trée** (on′trā; *French,* äɴ trā′) *n.* **1** the freedom or right to enter; access. **2** the main dish of food at dinner or lunch. **3** a dish of food served before the roast or between the main courses at dinner. [< F *eutrée,* fem. pp. of *entrer* enter]

en·trench (en trench′) *v.* **1** surround with a trench; fortify with trenches. **2** establish firmly: *Exchanging gifts at Christmas is a custom entrenched in people's minds.* **3** trespass; encroach; infringe: *Do not entrench upon the rights of others.* Also, **intrench.**

en·trench·ment (en trench′mənt) *n.* **1** an entrenching. **2** an entrenched position. **3** a defence consisting of a trench and a rampart of earth or stone. Also, **intrenchment.**

en·tre nous (äɴ′trə nü′) *French.* between ourselves; confidentially.

en·tre·pôt (on′trə pō′) *n.* **1** a place where goods are stored; warehouse. **2** a place where goods are sent for distribution; commercial centre. [< F]

en·tre·pre·neur (on′trə prə nėr′) *n.* a person who organizes and manages a business or industrial enterprise, attempting to make a profit but taking the risk of a loss. [< F *entrepreneur* < *entreprendre* undertake]

en·tre·sol (en′tər sol′ or on′trə sol′) *n.* a low storey between the first two floors of a building; mezzanine. [< F]

en·tro·py (en′trə pē) *n.* **1** in physics: **a** in a thermodynamic system, a measure of the energy that is not available for conversion into mechanical work. **b** a measure of the degree of molecular disorder in a system. **2 a** the tendency of the universe toward increasing disorder. **b** the probable outcome of this tendency. **3** in communications, a statistical measure of the predictable accuracy of a system in transmitting information. [< G *Entropie,* probably influenced by Gk. *entropia* a turning in < *en-* + *tropē* a turning < *trepein* to turn]

en·trust (en trust′) *v.* **1** charge with a trust; trust: *The club entrusted the newly elected treasurer with all its* *money.* **2** give the care of; hand over for safekeeping: *While travelling, they entrusted their children to a nurse.* Also, **intrust.** —**Syn. 2** See **commit.**

en·try (en′trē) *n.* **-tries. 1** the act of entering. **2** a place by which to enter; a way to enter. A vestibule is an entry. **3** something written or printed in a book, list, etc. Each word explained in a dictionary is an entry. A bookkeeper makes entries in a ledger. **4** a person or thing that takes part in a contest. **5** in law, the act of taking possession of lands or buildings by entering or setting foot on them. **6** a giving of an account of a ship's cargo at a custom house to obtain permission to land the goods. [ME < OF *entree* < *entrer.* See ENTER.]

entry word 1 in a dictionary, a word listed in alphabetical order and followed by information concerning its pronunciation, meanings, etc. Entry words are printed in heavy black type. **2** in other reference books, a word giving the subject of the following article. **3** the word under which a book, pamphlet, etc. is entered in a list or catalogue.

en·twine (en twīn′) *v.* **-twined, -twin·ing. 1** twine together. **2** twine around: *Roses entwined the little cottage.* —**en·twine′ment,** *n.*

en·twist (en twist′) *v.* twist together.

e·nu·mer·ate (i nū′mər āt′ or i nü′mər āt′) *v.* **-at·ed, -at·ing. 1** name one by one; give a list of: *He enumerated the provinces of Canada.* **2** count. [< L *enumerare* < *ex-* out + *numerus* number] —**Syn. 1** recount, rehearse, detail.

e·nu·mer·a·tion (i nū′mər ā′shən or i nü′mər ā′shən) *n.* **1** an enumerating; a listing; a counting. **2** a list.

e·nu·mer·a·tive (i nū′mər ə tiv or i nü′mər ə tiv, i nū′mər ā′tiv or i nü′ mər ā′tiv) *adj.* that enumerates; having to do with enumeration.

e·nu·mer·a·tor (i nū′mər ā′tər or i nü′mər ā′tər) *n.* **1** *Cdn.* a person appointed to list, prior to an election, the eligible voters in a polling area. **2** one who enumerates.

e·nun·ci·ate (i nun′sē āt′ or i nun′shē āt′) *v.* **-at·ed, -at·ing. 1** pronounce (words): *He is a well-trained actor and enunciates very distinctly.* **2** state definitely; announce: *After performing many experiments, the scientist enunciated a new theory.* [< L *enuntiare* < *ex-* out + *nuntius* messenger] —**e·nun′ci·a′tor,** *n.*

e·nun·ci·a·tion (i nun′sē ā′shən) *n.* **1** one's manner of pronouncing words. **2** a definite statement; announcement.

en·vel·op (en vel′əp; *n. also,* en′və lōp′ or on′və lōp′) *v.* **-oped, -op·ing,** *n.* —*v.* **1** wrap; cover. **2** surround: *Our soldiers enveloped the enemy and captured them.* **3** hide; conceal: *Fog enveloped the village.*
—*n.* envelope. [ME < OF *enveloper* < *en-* in (intensive) + *voloper* wrap] —**Syn.** *v.* **1** enfold. **2** encompass, encircle.

en·ve·lope (en′və lōp′ or on′və lōp′) *n.* **1** a paper cover in which a letter or anything flat and fairly thin can be mailed, filed, etc. It can usually be folded over and sealed by wetting a gummed edge. **2** a covering; wrapper. **3** in botany, a surrounding or enclosing part, as of leaves. **4** in biology, any enclosing covering, such as membrane or shell; integument. **5** in geometry, a curve or surface touching a continuous series of curves or surfaces. **6** in astronomy, a nebulous mass surrounding the nucleus of a comet on the side nearest the sun. **7** a bag that holds the gas in a balloon or airship. **8** the outer covering of a rigid airship. [< F *enveloppe* < *envelopper* envelop]

en·vel·op·ment (en vel′əp mənt) *n.* **1** an enveloping. **2** a being enveloped. **3** something that envelops; wrapping; covering.

en·ven·om (en ven′əm) *v.* **1** make poisonous. **2** fill with bitterness, hate, etc.: *The wicked boy envenomed his father's mind against his half brother.* [ME < OF *envenimer* < *en-* in + *venim* venom < L *venenum*]

en·vi·a·ble (en′vē ə bəl) *adj.* to be envied; desirable; worth having: *She has an enviable school record.* —**en′vi·a·ble·ness,** *n.* —**en′vi·a·bly,** *adv.*

en·vi·ous (en′vē əs) *adj.* full of envy; feeling or showing envy. [ME < AF *envious,* var. of OF *envieus* < *envie.* See ENVY.] —**en′vi·ous·ly,** *adv.* —**en′vi·ous·ness,** *n.*

en·vi·ron (en vī′rən) *v.* surround; enclose. [ME < OF *environner* < *environ* around < *en-* in + *viron* circle]

en·vi·ron·ment (en vī′rən mənt) *n.* **1** all of the surrounding conditions and influences that affect the development of a living thing. A person's character is influenced by his environment. Differences in environment often account for differences in plants of the same kind. **2** surroundings: *Banff has a beautiful environment.* **3** the act or fact of surrounding.

en·vi·ron·men·tal (en vī′rən men′təl) *adj.* having to do with environment.

en·vi·rons (en vī′rənz) *n.pl.* surrounding districts; suburbs.

envisage (en viz′ij) *v.* **-aged, -ag·ing. 1** foresee; visualize: *I envisage no difficulty with our plans.* **2** *Archaic.* look in the face of; confront: *He finally envisaged the realities of the situation.* [< F *envisager* < *en-* in + *visage* face]

en·vi·sion (en vizh′ən) *v.* have a mental picture of; imagine, especially something that does not yet exist; picture to oneself; look forward to: *It is difficult to envision a state of permanent peace.*

en·voy[1] (en′voi) *n.* **1** a messenger. **2** a diplomat ranking next below an ambassador and next above a minister. [< F *envoyé,* pp. of *envoyer* send < OF *envoier.* See ENVOY[2].]

en·voy[2] (en′voi) *n.* **1** a short stanza ending a poem. **2** a postscript to a literary work, often addressed to a friend or patron of the author. [ME < OF *envoy* < *envoier* send < VL < L *in via* on the way]

en·vy (en′vē) *n.* **-vies,** *v.* **-vied, -vy·ing.** —*n.* **1** discontent or ill will at another's good fortune because one wishes it were one's own; dislike for a person who has what one wants. **2** the object of such feeling: *She was the envy of the younger girls in the school.* —*v.* **1** feel envy toward: *Some people envy the rich.* **2** feel envy because of: *James envied his friend's success.* [ME < OF *envie* < L *invidia,* ult. < *invidere* look with enmity at < *in-* against + *videre* see]

☞ **Envy, covet** may each suggest the meaning of the other as part of its own. **Envy** = feel discontent, jealousy, or, sometimes, hatred or resentment because another has something one wishes one had oneself. *John envies famous people.* **Covet** = feel a great desire for something, especially something belonging to someone else, and may suggest feeling envy as well as desire: *He covets his neighbor's new car.*

en·womb (en wüm′) *v.* enclose in, or as if in, a womb.

en·wrap (en rap′) *v.* **-wrapped, -wrap·ping.** wrap. Also, **inwrap.**

en·wreathe (en rēᴛʜ′) *v.* **-wreathed, -wreath·ing.** wreathe around; encircle; surround. Also, **inwreathe.**

en·zy·mat·ic (en′zī mat′ik or en′zi mat′ik) *adj.* of or having to do with an enzyme or enzymes.

en·zyme (en′zīm or en′zim) *n.* a chemical substance, produced in living cells, that can cause changes in other substances within the body without being changed itself. Pepsin is an enzyme. [< Med.Gk. *enzymos* leavened < *en-* in + *zymē* leaven]

en·zy·mol·o·gist (en′zī mol′ə jist or en′zi mol′ə jist) *n.* an expert in enzymology.

en·zy·mol·o·gy (en′zī mol′ə jē or en′zi mol′ə jē) *n.* the study of enzymes.

E·o·cene (ē′ə sēn′) *n.* in geology: **1** the earliest division of the Tertiary period, beginning approximately 60 million years ago, when the lowest rocks were formed. **2** the rocks formed during this period. See **geology** for chart. —*adj.* having to do with this period or group of rocks. [< Gk. *ēōs* dawn + *kainos* recent]

e·o·hip·pus (ē′ō hip′əs) *n.* the prehistoric ancestor of the horse. It was about 15 inches high and 3½ feet long, and it had toes instead of hoofs. [< NL *Eohippus* < Gk. *ēōs* dawn + *hippos* horse]

E·o·li·an (ē ō′lē ən) *adj.* Aeolian.

e·o·lith (ē′ə lith′) *n.* a roughly-shaped stone tool belonging to a very early stage of human culture. [< Gk. *ēōs* dawn + *lithos* stone]

e·o·lith·ic or **E·o·lith·ic** (ē′ə lith′ik) *adj.* having to do with a very early stage of human culture, characterized by the use of the most primitive stone instruments. —*n.* this stage, the earliest part of the Stone Age.

e·on (ē′ən or ē′on) *n.* a very long period of time; many thousands of years: *Eons passed before life existed on the earth.* Also, **aeon.** [< L *aeon* < Gk. *aiōn* lifetime, age]

E·os (ē′os) *n.* in Greek mythology, the goddess of the dawn, identified with the Roman goddess Aurora. [< L < Gk.]

e·o·sin (ē′ə sin) *n.* **1** a rose-red dye or stain made from coal tar. *Formula*: $C_{20}H_8Br_4O_5$ **2** its reddish-brown potassium or sodium salt. [< Gk. *ēōs* dawn]

E·o·zo·ic (ē′ə zō′ik) *n.* in geology: **1** the era in which living things first appeared. See the chart under **geology.** **2** the rocks formed during this era. *—adj.* of or having to do with this era or the rocks formed during it. [< Gk. *ēōs* dawn + *zōē* life + E *-ic*]

EP of records, Extended Play.

Ep. Epistle; Epistles.

ep- form of **epi-** before vowels and *h*, as in *epode, ephemeral.*

An epaulette

ep·au·lette or **ep·au·let** (ep′ə let′) *n.* an ornament on the shoulder of a uniform. Epaulettes are usually worn only by officers in the armed services. [< F *épaulette*, dim. of *épaule* shoulder]

é·pée (ā pā′) *n.* a sword used in fencing, especially one with a sharp point and no cutting edge. [< F *épée* < OF *espee* < L *spatha* < Gk. *spathē* blade, sword]

e·phah (ē′fə) *n.* a Hebrew dry measure equal to a little more than a bushel. [< Hebrew]

e·phed·rin (i fed′rin; *in chemistry*, ef′ə drin) *n.* ephedrine.

e·phed·rine (i fed′rin; *in chemistry also*, ef′ə drēn′ or ef′ə drin) *n.* a drug used to relieve hay fever, asthma, head colds, etc. It is a plant alkaloid. *Formula*: $C_{10}H_{15}ON$ [< NL *ephedra* < L *ephedra* horsetail (a plant) < Gk.]

e·phem·er·a (i fem′ər ə) *n.* **-er·ae** (-ə rē′ or -ə rī′) or **-er·as. 1** any short-lived or transitory person or thing: *Of the many books published in a year, the majority are ephemerae.* **2** an ephemerid; May fly. **3** a brief fever. [< Gk. *ephēmeros* living only a day < *epi-* upon + *hēmera* day]

e·phem·er·al (i fem′ər əl) *adj.* lasting for only a day; lasting for only a very short time; very short-lived. [< Gk. *ephēmeros* lasting only a day < *epi-* upon, over + *hēmera* day] —**Syn.** transient; fleeting.

e·phem·er·id (i fem′ər id) *n.* the May fly, a type of insect having a delicate body and two pairs of gauzy wings, the fore pair being much larger than the rear pair. Ephemerids live a day or two in the adult form but from one to three years in the immature stages.

E·phe·sian (i fē′zhən) *adj.* of Ephesus, an ancient Greek city in Asia Minor, or its people. *—n.* **1** a native or inhabitant of Ephesus. **2 Ephesians,** *pl.* a book of the New Testament written in the name of the Apostle Paul to the Christians at Ephesus.

eph·od (ef′od or ē′fod) *n.* a vestment worn by Hebrew priests when performing sacred duties. [< Hebrew]

eph·or (ef′ôr or ef′ər) *n.* **-ors, -o·ri** (-ə rī′ or -ə rē′). in ancient Sparta, one of the five leading magistrates, elected yearly by the people to advise the king. [< L < Gk. *ephoros* <*epi-* over + *horaein* see]

epi- *prefix.* on; over; upon; in addition; to; among, as in *epidemic.* Also, **ep-,** before vowels and *h.* [< Gk. *epi-* < *epi*, prep., adv.]

ep·ic (ep′ik) *n.* **1** a long poem that tells of the adventures of one or more great heroes. An epic is written in a dignified, majestic style, and often gives expression to the ideals of a nation or race. The *Iliad*, the *Aeneid*, and *Paradise Lost* are epics. **2** any writing having the qualities of an epic. **3** any story or series of events worthy of being the subject of an epic. **4** *Informal.* a spectacular motion picture or other entertainment. *—adj.* **1** of or having to do with an epic. **2** like an epic; grand in style; heroic. [< L *epicus* < Gk. *epikos* < *epos* word, story] —**ep′i·cal·ly,** *adv.*

ep·i·cal (ep′ə kəl) *adj.* epic.

ep·i·ca·lyx (ep′ə kā′liks or -kal′iks) *n.* in botany, a ring of bracts at the base of a flower that looks like an outer calyx.

ep·i·carp (ep′ə kärp′) *n.* in botany, the outer layer of a fruit or ripened ovary of a plant. The skin of a pear is its epicarp. [< *epi-* on + Gk. *karpos* fruit]

hat, āge, cãre, fär; let, ēqual, tėrm; it, īce
hot, ōpen, ôrder; oil, out; cup, pu̇t, rüle, ūse
əbove, takən, pencəl, lemən, circəs
ch, child; ng, long; sh, ship
th, thin; ᴛʜ, then; zh, measure

ep·i·cene (ep′ə sēn′) *adj.* **1** in grammar: **a** having only one gender for both sexes. The Latin noun *leo* is epicene, for it is masculine in gender but stands for both *lion* and *lioness.* **b** of common gender. English nouns such as *fish, human,* etc. are epicene. **2** belonging to or having the characteristics of both sexes. **3** not clearly of either sex; sexless. **4** effeminate.
—n. **1** an epicene person. **2** an epicene noun. [< L <Gk. *epikoinos* common gender < *epi-* upon + *koinos* common]

ep·i·cen·tre or **ep·i·cen·ter** (ep′ə sen′tər) *n.* **1** the point from which earthquake waves seem to go out. It is situated directly above the true centre of the earthquake. **2** any point of great tension, disturbance, etc.: *the epicentre of a revolt.*

ep·i·cure (ep′ə kūr′) *n.* a person who has a refined taste in eating and drinking and cares much about foods and drinks. [Anglicized var. of *Epicurus*] —**Syn.** gourmet.

ep·i·cu·re·an (ep′ə kyu̇ rē′ən) *adj.* **1** like an epicure; fond of pleasure and luxury. **2** fit for an epicure. **3 Epicurean,** of Epicurus or his philosophy.
—n. **1** a person fond of pleasure and luxury; epicure. **2 Epicurean,** a believer in the philosophy of Epicurus.

Ep·i·cu·re·an·ism (ep′ə kyu̇ rē′ən iz′əm) *n.* **1** the philosophy or principles of Epicurus (342?-270 B.C.), a Greek philosopher who taught that pleasure is the highest good and that virtue alone produces pleasure. **2** Also, **epicureanism.** the belief in or practice of this philosophy.

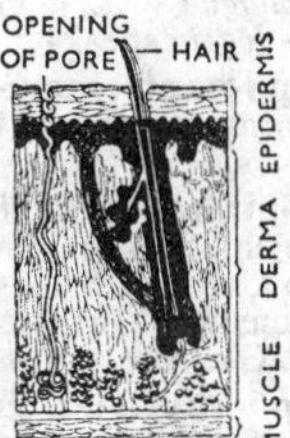

A section showing layers of the skin

ep·i·dem·ic (ep′ə dem′ik) *n.* **1** a rapid spreading of a disease so that many people have it at the same time: *All the schools in the city were closed because of an epidemic of scarlet fever.* **2** the rapid spread of an idea, fashion, etc. *—adj.* affecting many people at the same time; widespread. [< F *épidémique* < *épidémie* < Med.L < Gk. *epidēmia* stay, visit, prevalence (of a disease) < *epi-* among + *dēmos* people]

ep·i·dem·i·cal (ep′ə dem′ə kəl) *adj.* epidemic. —**ep·i·dem′i·cal·ly,** *adv.*

ep·i·der·mal (ep′ə dėr′məl) *adj.* of or having to do with the epidermis.

ep·i·der·mis (ep′ə dėr′mis) *n.* **1** the outer layer of the skin of vertebrates. **2** the outer covering on the shells of many molluscs. **3** any of various other outer layers of invertebrates. **4** a skinlike layer of cells in seed plants and ferns. [< LL < Gk. *epidermis* < *epi-* on + *derma* skin]

ep·i·dote (ep′ə dōt′) *n.* a mineral consisting chiefly of aluminium, iron, and lime silicate. [< F *épidote* < Gk. *epididonai* to increase < *epi-* over + *didonai* give (because it is longer in the base of the crystal than allied minerals)]

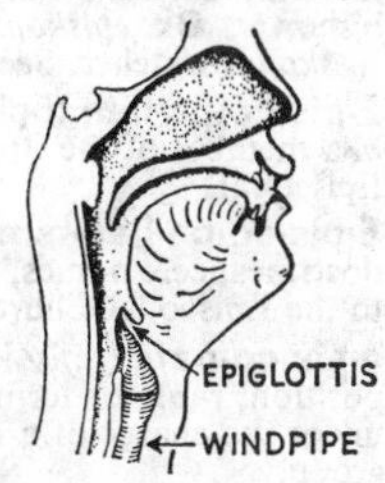

ep·i·glot·tis (ep′ə glot′is) *n.* a thin, triangular plate of cartilage that covers the entrance to the windpipe during swallowing, so that food, etc. does not get into the lungs. [< LL < Gk. *epiglottis* < *epi-* on + *glotta* tongue]

ep·i·gram (ep′ə gram′) *n.* **1** a short, pointed, witty saying. *Example*: "The only way to get rid of temptation is to yield to it." **2** a short poem ending in a witty or clever turn of thought. *Example*:

"Here lies our Sovereign Lord the King
Whose word no man relied on,
Who never said a foolish thing,
Nor ever did a wise one."

[< L < Gk. *epigramma* < *epigraphein* < *epi-* on + *graphein* write]

☛ **epigrams.** An *epigram* is a short, pointed, witty saying. A special type of epigram is the *paradox*, which makes a statement that, as it stands, contradicts fact or common sense or itself, and yet suggests a truth or at least a half truth: *All generalizations are false, including this one.* Closely related to epigrams are *aphorisms*—pithy statements but more likely to be abstract and not necessarily witty: *A living dog is better than a dead lion.* Proverbs are the often quoted, concrete expressions of popular wisdom. They are likely to make observations on character or conduct: *Still waters run deep.*

ep·i·gram·mat·ic (ep′ə grə mat′ik) *adj.* **1** of epigrams; full of epigrams. **2** like an epigram; terse and witty. **—ep′i·gram·mat′i·cal·ly,** *adv.*

ep·i·graph (ep′ə graf′) *n.* **1** an inscription on a building, monument, tomb, etc. **2** a quotation or motto at the beginning of a book or chapter. [< Gk. *epigraphē* inscription < *epigraphein* < *epi-* on + *graphein* write]

e·pig·ra·phy (i pig′rə fē) *n.* **1** inscriptions. **2** the branch of knowledge that deals with the deciphering and interpretation of inscriptions. [< *epigraph* inscription < Gk. *epigraphē* < *epigraphein.* See EPIGRAM.]

ep·i·lep·sy (ep′ə lep′sē) *n.* a chronic disorder of the nervous system whose attacks cause convulsions and unconsciousness. [< LL < Gk. *epilepsia* seizure, ult. < *epi-* on + *lambanein* take]

ep·i·lep·tic (ep′ə lep′tik) *adj.* **1** of or having to do with epilepsy. **2** having epilepsy. *—n.* a person who has epilepsy.

ep·i·log (ep′ə log′) *n.* epilogue.

ep·i·logue (ep′ə log′) *n.* **1** a concluding section added to a novel, poem, etc. and serving to round out or interpret the work. **2** a speech or poem after the end of a play, addressed to the audience and spoken by one of the actors. **3** the actor who speaks an epilogue. [< F *épilogue* < L < Gk. *epilogos,* ult. < *epi-* in addition + *legein* speak]

ep·i·neph·rine (ep′ə nef′rin or ep′ə nef′rēn) *n.* a hormone secreted by the adrenal gland; adrenalin. [< *epi-* + Gk. *nephros* kidney + E *-ine*[2]]

E·piph·a·ny (i pif′ə nē) *n.* the yearly Christian celebration commemorating the coming of the Wise Men to Christ at Bethlehem; in most Christian churches, January 6. [ME < OF < LL < LGk. *epiphania,* ult. < Gk. *epi-* to + *phainein* show]

ep·i·phyte (ep′ə fīt′) *n.* in botany, any of various plants that grow on other plants for support, but do not derive nourishment from their host. Many mosses, lichens, and orchids are epiphytes. [< *epi-* on + Gk. *phyton* plant]

ep·i·phyt·ic (ep′ə fit′ik) *adj.* being an epiphyte; having the characteristics of an epiphyte. **—ep′i·phyt′i·cal·ly,** *adv.*

Epis. 1 Episcopal. 2 Episcopalians. 3 Epistle.

Episc. Episcopal.

e·pis·co·pa·cy (i pis′kə pə sē) *n.* **-cies. 1** the government of a church by bishops. **2** bishops as a group. **3** the position, rank, or term of office of a bishop; episcopate.

e·pis·co·pal (i pis′kə pəl) *adj.* **1** of or having to do with bishops. **2** governed by bishops. **3 Episcopal,** of or having to do with the Church of England, the Anglican Church of Canada, the Protestant Episcopal Church in the United States, etc. [< LL *episcopalis* < L *episcopus* bishop < Gk. *episkopos* overseer < *epi-* on, over + *skopos* watcher. See BISHOP.]

E·pis·co·pa·lian (i pis′kə pāl′yən or i pis′kə pā′lē ən) *n.* a member of the Protestant Episcopal Church. *—adj.* Episcopal.

E·pis·co·pa·lian·ism (i pis′kə pāl′yə niz′əm) *n.* **1** the doctrines, ceremonies, etc. of Episcopalians. **2** adherence to the Episcopal Church or Episcopal principles.

e·pis·co·pate (i pis′kə pit or i pis′kə pāt′) *n.* **1** the position, rank, or term of office of a bishop. **2** a district under the charge of a bishop; bishopric. **3** bishops as a group.

ep·i·sode (ep′ə sōd′) *n.* **1** an incident or experience that stands out from others: *The year he spent in France was an important episode in the artist's life.* **2 a** a set of events or actions separate from the main plot of a novel, story, etc. **b** in music, a similar digression in a composition. **3** in classical Greek tragedy, the part between two choric songs. [< Gk. *episodion,* neut., coming in besides, ult. < *epi-* on + *eis* into + *hodos* way]

ep·i·sod·ic (ep′ə sod′ik) *adj.* **1** like an episode; incidental; occasional. **2** consisting of a series of episodes: *This novel is loosely episodic.* **—ep′i·sod′i·cal·ly,** *adv.*

ep·i·sod·i·cal (ep′ə sod′ə kəl) *adj.* episodic.

e·pis·te·mo·log·i·cal (i pis′tə mə loj′ə kəl) *adj.* of or having to do with epistemology. **—e·pis′te·mo·log′i·cal·ly,** *adv.*

e·pis·te·mol·o·gist (i pis′tə mol′ə jist) *n.* an expert in epistemology.

e·pis·te·mol·o·gy (i pis′tə mol′ə jē) *n.* the part of philosophy that deals with the origin, nature, and limits of knowledge. [< Gk. *epistēmē* knowledge + E *-logy*]

e·pis·tle (i pis′əl) *n.* **1** a letter. Epistles are usually long, instructive letters written in formal or elegant language. **2** a literary work, usually in verse, written in the form of a letter. **3 Epistle, a** a letter written by one of Christ's Apostles. The Epistles make up 21 books of the New Testament. **b** a selection from one of these, read as part of certain Christian church services. [OE *epistole* < L < Gk. *epistolē,* ult. < *epi-* to + *stellein* send] **—Syn. 1** See **letter.**

e·pis·to·lar·y (i pis′tə ler′ē) *adj.* **1** carried on by letters; contained in letters. **2** of letters; suitable for writing letters.

ep·i·style (ep′i stīl′) *n.* in architecture, the part of a building resting directly on top of columns; architrave. See **entablature** for picture. [< L < Gk. *epistylion* < *epi-* on + *stylos* pillar]

ep·i·taph (ep′ə taf′) *n.* **1** a short statement in memory of a dead person, usually put on his tombstone. **2** any brief writing resembling such an inscription. [< L < Gk. *epitaphion* funeral oration < *epi-* at + *taphos* tomb]

ep·i·tha·la·mi·um (ep′ə thə lā′mē əm) *n.* **-mi·ums, -mi·a** (-mē ə). a poem or song in honor of a bride, bridegroom, or newly married couple. [< L < Gk. *epithalamion* < *epi-* at + *thalamos* bridal chamber]

ep·i·the·li·al (ep′ə thē′lē əl) *adj.* of the epithelium.

ep·i·the·li·um (ep′ə thē′lē əm) *n.* **-li·ums, -li·a** (-lē ə). in biology, a thin layer of cells forming a tissue that covers surfaces and lines hollow organs. [< NL < Gk. *epi-* on + *thēlē* nipple]

ep·i·thet (ep′ə thet′) *n.* **1** a descriptive expression; an adjective or noun, or sometimes a clause, expressing some quality or attribute. In *crafty Ulysses* and *Richard the Lion-Hearted* the epithets are *crafty* and *the Lion-Hearted.* **2** a word or phrase (sometimes highly insulting) used in place of a person's name. **3** that part of the scientific name of an animal or plant which denotes a species, variety, or other division of a genus. [< L < Gk. *epitheton* added < *epi-* on + *tithenai* place]

e·pit·o·me (i pit′ə mē′) *n.* **1** a condensed account; summary. An epitome contains only the most important points of a literary work, subject, etc. **2** a person or thing that is typical or representative of a quality: *Solomon is often spoken of as the epitome of wisdom.* [< L < Gk. *epitomē* < *epitemnein* cut short < *epi-* into + *temnein* cut]

e·pit·o·mize (i pit′ə mīz′) *v.* **-mized, -miz·ing.** make an epitome of; summarize. **—Syn.** abridge, condense.

ep·i·zo·ot·ic (ep′ə zō ot′ik) *adj.* temporarily prevalent among animals. *—n.* an epizootic disease. [< *epi-* among + Gk. *zōion* animal]

ep·och (ē′pok or ep′ək) *n.* **1** a period of time; era. **2** a period of time in which striking things happened. **3** the starting point of such a period: *The invention of the steam engine marked an epoch in the evolution of industry.* **4** one of the divisions of time into which a geological period is divided: *the Recent epoch of the Quaternary period.* [< Med.L < Gk. *epochē* a stopping, fixed point in time < *epechein* < *epi-* up + *echein* hold] **—Syn. 1** age.

ep·och·al (ep′ək əl or ē′pok əl) *adj.* **1** having to do with an epoch. **2** epoch-making.

ep·och-mak·ing (ē′pok māk′ing or ep′ək-) *adj.* beginning an epoch; causing important changes.

ep·ode (ep′ōd) *n.* in classical verse: **1** a lyric poem in which a long line is followed by a shorter one. **2** a part of a lyric ode following the strophe and antistrophe. [< F < L *epodos* < Gk. *epoidos* < *epi-* after + *aidein* sing]

ep·o·nym (ep′ō nim′) *n.* **1** a person from whom a nation, tribe, place, etc. gets or is reputed to get its name: *Romulus is the eponym of Rome.* **2** a person whose name is a synonym for something: *Ananias is the eponym of liar.* [< Gk. *epōnymos* < *epi-* to + *onyma* (dial.) name]

ep·on·y·mous (ep on′ə məs) *adj.* giving one's name to a nation, tribe, place, etc.

ep·ox·y (ep ok′sē) *adj. n.* **-ox·ies.** —*adj.* containing oxygen as a bond between two different atoms already united in another way. Epoxy resins are extremely durable plastics used for adhesives, varnishes, etc. —*n.* an epoxy resin. [< *ep-* + *oxygen*]

ep·si·lon (ep′sə lon′ or ep sī′lən) *n.* the fifth letter of the Greek alphabet (Ε, ε), corresponding to *e* (as in *get*) in English. [< Med.Gk. *epsilon* < Gk. *e psilon* simple *e*]

Epsom Downs (ep′səm) the track near the town of Epsom where England's famous horse race, the Derby, is run.

Epsom salt or **salts** hydrated magnesium sulphate, a bitter, white, crystalline powder used in medicine, especially as a laxative. *Formula*: $MgSO_4 \cdot 7H_2O$ [< *Epsom,* a town in S.E. England]

eq. 1 equal. **2** equivalent. **3** equator. **4** equation.

eq·ua·bil·i·ty (ek′wə bil′ə tē or ē′kwə bil′ə tē) *n.* an equable condition or quality.

eq·ua·ble (ek′wə bəl or ē′kwə bəl) *adj.* changing little; uniform; even; tranquil. [< L *aequabilis* < *aequare* make uniform < *aequus* even, just] —**eq′ua·bly,** *adv.* —**eq′ua·ble·ness,** *n.* —**Syn.** unvarying, steady, smooth. See **even.**

e·qual (ē′kwəl) *adj. n. v.* **e·qualled** or **e·qualed, e·qual·ling** or **e·qual·ing.** —*adj.* **1** the same in amount, size, number, value, degree, rank, etc.; (*to*) as much (as); neither more nor less than: *Ten dimes are equal to one dollar.* **2** the same throughout; even; uniform. **3** evenly matched; with no advantage on either side: *an equal contest.* **4 equal to,** able to; strong enough for; brave enough for; etc.: *He was equal to the task.* **5** *Archaic.* just; fair.
—*n.* **1** a person or thing that is similar in rank or excellence: *In spelling she had no equal.* **2** something that is equal: *7 + 3 is the equal of 5 × 2. Add equals to equals.*
—*v.* **1** be equal to. *Four times five equals twenty.* **2** make or do something equivalent to; match: *He tried hard to equal the scoring record.* [< L *aequalis* < *aequus* even, just]
Syn. *adj.* **1 Equal, equivalent, tantamount** = as much as another or each other. **Equal** = exactly the same in size, amount, value, or any quality that can be measured or weighed: *The pieces of pie are equal.* **Equivalent,** applying to things otherwise different, means equal in value or in a quality that cannot be physically measured, such as meaning, importance, effect, etc.: *A Grade XIII course in high school may be regarded as equivalent to a first year course in university.* **Tantamount,** formal, applying only to immaterial things, means equivalent to another in effect: *His answer was tantamount to an insult.* –*n.* peer, match.

e·qual·i·ty (i kwol′ə tē) *n.* **-ties.** a being equal; sameness in amount, size, number, value, degree, rank, etc.

e·qual·i·za·tion (ē′kwəl ə zā′shən or ē′kwəl ī zā′shən) *n.* **1** an equalizing. **2** a being equalized.

equalization grant or **payment** in Canada, one of a series of grants paid by the Federal Government to the poorer provinces in order to bring their standard of living nearer to that of the wealthier provinces.

e·qual·ize (ē′kwəl īz′) *v.* **-ized, -iz·ing. 1** make equal. **2** make even or uniform.

e·qual·iz·er (ē′kwə lī′zər) *n.* **1** a person or thing that equalizes. **2** a device for equalizing strain, pressure, etc. **3** in electricity: **a** any network of coils, resistors, or capacitors introduced into a circuit to change its response, especially its frequency response. **b** a conductor of low resistance used to equalize voltages.

e·qual·ly (ē′kwəl ē) *adv.* in an equal manner; in or to an equal degree; so as to be equal.

e·qua·nim·i·ty (ē′kwə nim′ə tē or ek′wə nim′ə tē) *n.* evenness of mind or temper; calmness: *A wise man bears misfortune with equanimity.* [< L *aequanimitas* < *aequus* even + *animus,* mind, temper] —**Syn.** composure.

hat, āge, cãre, fär; let, ēqual, tėrm; it, īce
hot, ōpen, ôrder; oil, out; cup, pu̇t, rüle, ūse
əbove, takən, pencəl, lemən, circəs
ch, child; ng, long; sh, ship
th, thin; ᴛʜ, then; zh, measure

e·quate (i kwāt′) *v.* **e·quat·ed, e·quat·ing. 1** state to be equal; put in the form of an equation. **2** consider, treat, or represent as equal. **3** make equal. **4** reduce to an average. [< L *aequare* make equal < *aequus* equal]

e·qua·tion (i kwā′zhən or i kwā′shən) *n.* **1** a statement of equality between two quantities. *Examples*: $(4 \times 8) + 12 = 44$. $C = 2\pi r$. **2** an expression using chemical formulas and symbols showing the substances used and produced in a chemical reaction. *Example*: $HCl + NaOH = NaCl + H_2O$. **3** an equating or being equated.

e·qua·tor (i kwā′tər) *n.* **1** an imaginary circle around the middle of the earth, halfway between the North Pole and the South Pole. **2** a similarly situated circle on any heavenly body. **3** a great circle (**celestial equator**) of the celestial sphere, the plane of which is perpendicular to the axis of the earth. [< Med.L *aequator* (*diei et noctis*) equalizer (of day and night) < L *aequare* make equal. See EQUATE.]

e·qua·to·ri·al (ē′kwə tô′rē əl or ek′wə tô′rē əl) *adj.* **1** of, at, or near the equator. **2** similar to conditions at or near the equator.

eq·uer·ry (ek′wər ē) *n.* **-ries. 1** an officer of a royal or noble household who has charge of the horses or who accompanies his master's carriage. **2** an attendant on a royal or noble person. [short for *groom of the equerry*; < F *écurie* stable < Gmc.; influenced by L *equus* horse]

e·ques·tri·an (i kwes′trē ən) *adj.* **1** of horsemen or horsemanship; having to do with horseback riding: *Jockeys need to have equestrian skill.* **2** on horseback; mounted on horseback. An equestrian statue shows a person riding a horse. —*n.* a rider or performer on horseback. [< L *equestris* of a horseman < *equus* horse]

e·ques·tri·enne (i kwes′trē en′) *n.* a woman rider or performer on horseback. [< F]

equi- *combining form.* **1** equal, as in *equivalence.* **2** equally, as in *equiangular, equidistant.* [< L *aequus* equal]

e·qui·an·gu·lar (ē′kwē ang′gyu̇ lər) *adj.* having all angles equal: *A square is equiangular.*

e·qui·dis·tant (ē′kwə dis′tənt) *adj.* equally distant: *All points of the circumference of a circle are equidistant from the centre.* —**e′qui·dis′tant·ly,** *adv.*

e·qui·lat·er·al (ē′kwə lat′er əl) *adj.* having all sides equal. —*n.* **1** a figure having all sides equal. **2** a side equal to others. [< LL *aequilateralis* < L *aequus* equal + *latus, lateris* side] —**e′qui·lat′er·al·ly,** *adv.*

An equilateral triangle

e·quil·i·brant (i kwil′ə brənt) *n.* in physics, a force able to balance a specified force or set of forces.

e·qui·li·brate (ē′kwə lī′brāt or i kwil′ə brāt′) *v.* **-brat·ed, -brat·ing.** balance. [< LL *aequilibratus* in equilibrium < L *aequus* equal + *libra* balance] —**e′qui·li′bra·tor,** *n.*

e·qui·li·bra·tion (ē′kwə lī brā′shən or i kwil′ə brā′shən) *n.* **1** a balancing evenly. **2** a being balanced evenly.

e·qui·lib·ri·um (ē′kwə lib′rē əm) *n.* **1** a state of balance; condition in which opposing forces exactly balance or equal each other: *Scales are in equilibrium when the weights on each side are equal.* **2** the state of a chemical system when no further change occurs in it. **3** a condition of balance between powers of any kind. **4** mental poise: *She is a sensible person and will not let petty annoyances upset her equilibrium.* [< L *aequilibrium,* ult. < *aequus* equal + *libra* balance]

e·qui·mo·lec·u·lar (ē′kwə mə lek′yə lər) *adj.* having an equal number of molecules.

e·quine (ē′kwīn or ek′wīn) *adj.* of horses; like a horse; like that of a horse. —*n.* a horse. [< L *equinus* < *equus* horse]

e·qui·noc·tial (ē′kwə nok′shəl) *adj.* **1** having to do with either equinox. Equinoctial points are the two imaginary

points in the sky where the sun crosses the celestial equator. 2 occurring at or near the equinox: *equinoctial gales.* 3 at or near the earth's equator: *Borneo is an equinoctial island.*
—*n.* 1 the celestial equator. 2 a storm occurring at or near the equinox.

equinoctial line the celestial equator. See **equator** (def. 3).

e·qui·nox (ē′kwə noks′) *n.* either of the two times in the year when the centre of the sun crosses the celestial equator, and day and night are of equal length all over the earth. The **vernal** (spring) **equinox** occurs about March 21, the **autumnal equinox** about September 22. [< Med.L *equinoxium* < L *aequinoctium* < *aequus* equal + *nox* night]

e·quip (i kwip′) *v.* **e·quipped, e·quip·ping.** furnish with all that is needed; fit out; provide: *The fort was equipped with guns, ammunition, and food. He was equipped with a good mind and a keen sense of humor.* [< F *équipper* < OF *esquiper* < ON *skipa* man (a ship) < *skip* ship. Akin to SHIP.] —**Syn.** See **furnish.**

eq·ui·page (ek′wə pij) *n.* 1 a carriage. 2 a carriage with its horses, driver, and servants. 3 equipment; outfit.

e·quip·ment (i kwip′mənt) *n.* 1 the act of equipping. 2 the state of being equipped. 3 what a person or thing is equipped with; an outfit. 4 knowledge or skill; ability.

e·qui·poise (ē′kwə poiz′ or ek′wə-) *n.* 1 a state of balance. 2 a balancing force; counterbalance.

eq·ui·se·tum (ek′wə sē′təm) *n.* **-tums, -ta** (-tə). 1 a genus of plants with jointed, green, cylindrical stems, either simple or branched, rough to the touch, and having leaves reduced to scales. 2 the horsetail. [< NL < L *equisaetum* < *equus* horse + *saeta* (coarse) hair]

eq·ui·ta·ble (ek′wə tə bəl) *adj.* 1 fair; just: *Paying a person what he has earned is equitable.* 2 in law, having to do with or dependent upon equity; valid in equity, as distinguished from common law and statute law.
—**eq′ui·ta·ble·ness,** *n.* —**eq′ui·ta·bly,** *adv.*

eq·ui·ta·tion (ek′wə tā′shən) *n.* horseback riding; horsemanship. [< L *equitatio, -onis,* ult. < *equus* horse]

eq·ui·tes (ek′wə tēz′) *n.pl.* in ancient Rome: 1 originally, the class of citizens serving in the cavalry. 2 later, a privileged class of citizens. [< L *equites,* pl. of *eques* horseman, knight < *equus* horse]

eq·ui·ty (ek′wə tē) *n.* **-ties.** 1 fairness; justice. 2 what is fair and just. 3 in law: **a** a system of rules and principles based on fairness and justice. Equity covers cases in which fairness and justice require a settlement not covered by common law. **b** a claim or right according to equity. 4 the amount that a property, business, etc. is worth beyond what is owed on it. [< L *aequitas* < *aequus* even, just]

e·quiv·a·lence (i kwiv′ə ləns or i kwiv′ləns) *n.* 1 a being equivalent; equality in value, force, significance, etc. 2 in chemistry: **a** the quality of having equal valence. **b** valence. 3 in geometry, the fact of being equal in extent, but not in form.

e·quiv·a·lent (i kwiv′ə lənt or i kwiv′lənt) *adj.* 1 equal in value, measure, force, effect, meaning, etc.: *Nodding your head is equivalent to saying yes.* 2 in chemistry, equal in combining or reacting value to a (stated) quantity of another substance. 3 having the same extent: *A triangle and a square may be equivalent in area.*
—*n.* 1 something equivalent. 2 a word, expression, sign, etc. of equal meaning or import. [< LL *aequivalens, -entis,* ppr. of *aequivalere* < L *aequus* equal + *valere* be worth] —**e·quiv′a·lent·ly,** *adv.* —**Syn.** *adj.* 1 See **equal.**

e·quiv·o·cal (i kwiv′ə kəl) *adj.* 1 having two or more meanings; intentionally vague or ambiguous: *His equivocal answer left us uncertain as to his real opinion.* 2 undecided; uncertain: *The result of the experiment was equivocal.* 3 questionable; rousing suspicion: *The stranger's equivocal behavior made everyone distrust him.* [< LL *aequivocus* ambiguous < L *aequus* equal + *vocare* call] —**e·quiv′o·cal·ly,** *adv.* —**e·quiv′o·cal·ness,** *n.* —**Syn.** 1 doubtful.

e·quiv·o·cate (i kwiv′ə kāt′) *v.* **-cat·ed, -cat·ing.** use expressions of double meaning in order to mislead. [< LL *aequivocare* call by the same name < *aequivocus* ambiguous. See EQUIVOCAL.] —**e·quiv′o·cat′ing·ly,** *adv.* —**e·quiv′o·ca′tor,** *n.*

e·quiv·o·ca·tion (i kwiv′ə kā′shən) *n.* 1 the use of equivocal expressions in order to mislead. 2 an equivocal expression.

-er[1] *suffix.* 1 a person or thing that ——s: *admirer = a person who admires; burner = a thing that burns.* 2 a person living in ——: *Newfoundlander = a person living in Newfoundland; villager = a person living in a village.* 3 a person that makes or works with ——: *hatter = a person who makes hats.* 4 a person or thing that is or has ——: *six-footer = a person who is six feet tall.* [OE *-ere,* ult. < L *-arius*]

☞ **-er, -or.** Names of persons or things performing an act (nouns of agent) and some other nouns are generally formed in English by adding *-er* to a verb (*doer, killer, painter, heater, thinker*), but many, chiefly nouns taken from Latin or French (*assessor, prevaricator*), end in *-or*. With a few words (*exhibitor or exhibiter, adviser or advisor*) either ending may be used.

-er[2] *suffix.* a person or thing connected with ——, as in *officer.* [< AF, OF < L *-arius, -arium*]

-er[3] *suffix forming the comparative degree.* 1 of certain adjectives, as in *softer, smoother.* [OE *-ra* (masc.), *-re* (fem., neut.)] 2 of certain adverbs, as in *slower.* [OE *-or*]

-er[4] *suffix.* frequently; again and again, as in *flicker, patter.* [OE *-rian*]

Er erbium.

E.R. Queen Elizabeth. (for L *Elizabeth Regina*)

e·ra (ēr′ə) *n.* 1 a historical period distinguished by certain important or significant happenings; an age in history. The decade from 1929 to 1939 is often called the Depression Era. 2 a period of time starting from some important or significant happening, date, etc.: *the A-bomb era.* 3 a system of reckoning time from some important or significant happening, given date, etc. The Christian era is the period of time reckoned from about four years after the Birth of Christ. 4 one of five very extensive periods of time in geological history. See table at **geology.** [< LL *era,* var. of *aera* number, epoch; probably same word as L *aera* counters (for reckoning), pl. of *aes* brass]

e·rad·i·ca·ble (i rad′ə kə bəl) *adj.* that can be eradicated.

e·rad·i·cate (i rad′ə kāt′) *v.* **-cat·ed, -cat·ing.** 1 get rid of entirely; destroy completely: *Yellow fever has been eradicated in many countries.* 2 pull out by the roots: *eradicate weeds from a garden.* [< L *eradicare* < *ex-* out + *radix, radicis* root] —**e·rad′i·ca′tor,** *n.*

e·rad·i·ca·tion (i rad′ə kā′shən) *n.* an eradicating; complete destruction.

e·rase (i rās′) *v.* **e·rased, e·ras·ing.** 1 rub out; scrape out: *He erased the wrong answer and wrote in the right one.* 2 remove all trace of; blot out: *The blow on his head erased from his memory the details of the accident.* [< L *erasus,* pp. of *eradere* < *ex-* out + *radere* scrape] —**e·ras′a·ble,** *adj.*

Syn. 1, 2 Erase, expunge, efface = remove everything from a record of some kind. **Erase** = remove all trace of something by scraping or rubbing, literally as from paper or figuratively as from memory: *I erased him from my mind.* **Expunge** = blot out so that the thing seems never to have existed: *The judge ordered certain charges expunged from the record.* **Efface** = wipe out identity or existence by or as if by rubbing away the face: *Rain and wind effaced the inscription on the monument.*

e·ras·er (i rās′ər) *n.* a piece of rubber or any other substance for erasing marks made with pencil, ink, chalk. etc.

e·ra·sure (i rā′shər or i rā′zhər) *n.* 1 an erasing. 2 an erased word, letter, etc. 3 a place where a word, letter, etc. has been erased.

Er·a·to (er′ə tō′) *n.* in Greek mythology, the Muse of lyric poetry.

er·bi·um (ėr′bē əm) *n.* a rare metallic chemical element of the yttrium group. *Symbol:* Er; *at.no.* 68; *at.wt.* 167.26. [< NL *erbium* < *Ytterby,* a town in Sweden]

ere (ãr) *Archaic.* —*prep.* before. —*conj.* 1 before. 2 sooner than; rather than. [OE *ǣr*]

Er·e·bus (er′ə bəs) *n.* in Greek mythology, a dark, gloomy place through which the dead passed on their way to Hades.

e·rect (i rekt′) *adj.* 1 straight up; upright: *That flagpole stands erect.* 2 raised; bristling: *The cat faced the dog with fur erect.*

hat, āge, cãre, fär; let, ēqual, tėrm; it, īce
hot, ōpen, ôrder; oil, out; cup, pu̇t, rüle, ūse
əbove, takən, pencəl, lemən, circəs
ch, child; ng, long; sh, ship
th, thin; ᴛʜ, then; zh, measure

—*v.* **1** put straight up; set upright: *They erected a television antenna on the roof. The mast was erected on a firm base.* **2** build; put up: *That house was erected forty years ago.* **3** put together; set up: *When the missing parts arrived, we erected the machine.* [ME < L *erectus*, pp. of *erigere* < *ex-* up + *regere* direct] —**e·rect′ly,** *adv.* —**e·rect′ness,** *n.* —**e·rect′or,** *n.* —**Syn.** *adj.* **1** See **upright.**

e·rec·tion (i rek′shən) *n.* **1** an erecting. **2** a being erected. **3** something erected; a building or other structure.

ere·long (ãr′long′) *adv. Archaic.* before long; soon.

er·e·mite (er′ə mīt′) *n. Archaic.* hermit. [ME < L *eremita* < Gk. *erēmitēs* dweller in a desert < *erēmos* uninhabited. Doublet of HERMIT.]

ere·while (ãr′hwīl′ or -wīl′) *adv. Archaic.* a while before; a short time ago.

erg (ėrg) *n.* a unit for measuring work or energy. It is the amount of work done by one dyne acting through a distance of one centimetre. *Abbrev.*: e [< Gk. *ergon* work]

er·go (ėr′gō) *adv. conj. Latin.* therefore.

er·got (ėr′gət or ėr′got) *n.* **1** a disease of rye and other cereals in which the grains are replaced by blackish fungus growths. **2** any fungus producing this disease. **3** the growth produced by this disease. **4** a medicine made from these growths, used to stop bleeding and to contract muscles. [< F < OF *argot* cock's spur]

E·rie (ēr′ē) *n.* **E·rie** or **E·ries. 1** a tribe of Indians formerly living along the southern and eastern shores of Lake Erie. **2** a member of this tribe.

Er·in (er′ən) *n. Poetic.* Ireland.

E·rin·y·es (i rin′ē ēz′) *n.* pl. of **Erinys.** in Greek mythology, the Furies, three female spirits with snakelike hair who avenged unpunished crimes.

E·rin·ys (i rin′is or i rī′nis) *n.* **E·rin·y·es.** one of the Erinyes.

erl·king (ėrl′king′) *n.* in German and Scandinavian legend, a spirit or personification of natural forces, such as cold, storm, etc. that does harm, especially to children. [< G *Erlkönig* alder-king, a mistranslation of Danish *ellerkonge* king of the elves]

er·mine (ėr′mən) *n.* **-mines** or (*esp. collectively*) **-mine. 1** any of several kinds of weasel of northern climates that are brown in summer but white with a black-tipped tail in winter. **2** the soft, white fur of the winter phase, used for women's coats, trimming, etc. The official robes of English judges are trimmed with ermine as a symbol of purity and fairness. **3** a coat or other garment made of this fur. **4** the position, rank, or duties of a judge. [ME < OF < Gmc. or < L *Armenius* (*mus*) Armenian (rat)]

erne (ėrn) *n.* a kind of eagle that lives near the sea. [OE *earn*]

e·rode (i rōd′) *v.* **e·rod·ed, e·rod·ing. 1** eat into; eat or wear away gradually: *Running water erodes soil and rocks. The channel had probably eroded for a million years.* **2** form by a gradual eating or wearing away: *The stream eroded a channel in the solid rock.* [< L *erodere* < *ex-* away + *rodere* gnaw]

E·ros (ēr′os or er′os) *n.* in Greek mythology, the god of love, son of Aphrodite, identified by the Romans with Cupid.

e·ro·sion (i rō′zhən) *n.* **1** a gradual eating or wearing away by glaciers, running water, waves, or wind: *By absorbing water, trees help prevent the erosion of soil.* **2** the condition of being eaten or worn away. [< L *erosio, -onis* < *erodere.* See ERODE.]

e·ro·sive (i rō′siv) *adj.* eroding; causing erosion.

e·rot·ic (i rot′ik) *adj.* of or having to do with sexual love. [< Gk. *erōtikos* of Eros] —**e·rot′i·cal·ly,** *adv.*

ERP European Recovery Plan; also called the *Marshall Plan.*

err (ėr or er) *v.* **1** go wrong; make mistakes: *Everyone errs at some time or other.* **2** be wrong; be mistaken or incorrect. **3** do wrong; sin: *To err is human; to forgive, divine.* [ME < OF < L *errare* wander] —**Syn. 1** stray, deviate, blunder.

☛ **err.** In the past regularly pronounced (ėr); but there is a growing tendency to pronounce it (er), probably by analogy with *error* (er′ər).

er·rand (er′ənd) *n.* **1** a trip to do something for someone else: *The little boy goes to the stores and runs other errands for his parents.* **2** what one is sent to do. **3** the purpose or object of a trip. [OE *ǣrende*]

errand boy **1** a boy who does errands. **2** *Informal.* a person who acts entirely under others, without using his own initiative or intelligence.

er·rant (er′ənt) *adj.* **1** travelling in search of adventure; wandering; roving. **2** of thoughts, conduct, etc., straying from the regular path. [< F *errant*, ppr. of OF *errer* travel, blended with F *errant*, ppr. of *errer* err]

er·rant·ry (er′ənt rē) *n.* **-ries.** the conduct or action of a knight-errant.

er·ra·ta (ə rā′tə or ə rä′tə) *n.* pl. of **erratum.**

er·rat·ic (ə rat′ik) *adj.* **1** not steady; uncertain; irregular: *An erratic mind jumps from one idea to another.* **2** queer; odd: *erratic behavior.* [< L *erraticus* < *errare* err] —**Syn. 2** eccentric.

er·rat·i·cal·ly (ə rat′ik lē) *adv.* in an erratic manner.

er·ra·tum (ə rā′təm or ə rä′təm) *n.* **-ta.** in writing or printing, an error or mistake. [< L *erratum*, neut. pp. of *errare* err]

er·ro·ne·ous (ə rō′nē əs) *adj.* wrong; mistaken; incorrect: *Years ago many people held the erroneous belief that the earth was flat.* [< L *erroneus* < *errare* err] —**er·ro′ne·ous·ly,** *adv.* —**er·ro′ne·ous·ness,** *n.*

er·ror (er′ər) *n.* **1** something wrong; what is incorrect; a mistake: *A false belief is an error.* **2** the condition of being wrong, mistaken, or incorrect: *You are in error.* **3** wrongdoing; sin. **4** in baseball, a faulty play that permits the batter to remain at bat or allows a runner who should have been put out to advance. **5** in mathematics, the difference between the observed or approximate amount and the correct amount. [ME < OF < L *error* < *errare* err]

Syn. 1 Error, mistake = something incorrect or wrong. **Error** implies a straying or deviation, usually blameworthy: *I failed my test because of errors in spelling.* **Mistake** applies to an error in judging or understanding, usually due to taking one thing for another: *I used your towel by mistake.*

er·satz (er′zäts or er′zats) *adj. n.* substitute. [< G]

Erse (ėrs) *n.* **1** the Celtic language of the Scottish Highlanders; Scots Gaelic. **2** less accurately, the Celtic language of Ireland; Irish Gaelic. —*adj.* of either of these languages. [Scottish var. of *Irish*]

erst (ėrst) *adv. Archaic.* formerly; long ago. [OE *ǣrst*, superlative of *ǣr* ere]

erst·while (ėrst′hwīl′ or -wīl′) *adv. Archaic.* some time ago; in time past; formerly. —*adj.* former; past.

e·ruct (i rukt′) *v.* belch. [< L *eructare* < *ex-* out + *ructare* belch]

e·ruc·tate (i ruk′tāt) *v.* **-tat·ed, -tat·ing.** belch.

e·ruc·ta·tion (i ruk′tā′shən or ē′ruk tā′shən) *n.* **1** a belching. **2** that which is belched up.

er·u·dite (er′yu̇ dīt′ or er′u̇ dīt′) *adj.* scholarly; learned. [< L *eruditus*, pp. of *erudire* instruct < *ex-* away + *rudis* rude] —**er′u·dite′ly,** *adv.* —**er′u·dite′ness,** *n.*

er·u·di·tion (er′yu̇ dish′ən or er′u̇ dish′ən) *n.* acquired knowledge; scholarship; learning.

e·rupt (i rupt′) *v.* **1** burst forth: *Hot water erupted from the geyser.* **2** throw forth: *The volcano erupted lava and ashes.* **3** break out in a rash: *Her skin erupted when she had measles.* **4** break through the gums: *When the baby was seven months old, its teeth started to erupt.* [< L *eruptus*, pp. of *erumpere* < *ex-* out + *rumpere* burst]

e·rup·tion (i rup′shən) *n.* **1** a bursting forth. **2** a throwing forth of lava, etc. from a volcano or of hot water from a geyser. **3** in medicine: **a** a breaking out in a rash: *When a person has measles, his skin is in a state of eruption.* **b** red spots on the skin; rash: *Scarlet fever causes an eruption on the body.* **4** a breaking through the gums: *The eruption of teeth made the baby fretful.* **5** an outbreak; outburst: *eruptions of racial or national hatred.*

e·rup·tive (i rup′tiv) *adj.* 1 bursting forth; tending to burst forth. 2 causing the skin to break out: *Measles is an eruptive disease.* 3 in geology, of or formed by volcanic eruptions. —*n.* in geology, a rock formed or forced up by eruption.

-ery *suffix.* 1 a place for ——ing, as in *cannery, hatchery.* 2 a place for ——s, as in *nunnery.* 3 the occupation or business of a ——, as in *cookery.* 4 the state or condition of a ——, as in *slavery.* 5 the qualities, actions, etc. of a ——, as in *knavery.* 6 ——s as a group, as in *machinery.* [< OF *-erie* < *-ier* (< L *-arius*) + *-ie* (< LL *-ia* < Gk. *-ia*)]

er·y·sip·e·las (er′ə sip′ə ləs or ēr′ə sip′ə ləs) *n.* 1 an acute infectious disease characterized by fever and a deep-red inflammation of the skin. 2 an acute or chronic bacterial disease of swine, and less commonly of turkeys and sheep, characterized by enteritis, red patches on the skin, and arthritis. [< Gk.]

e·ryth·ro·my·cin (i rith′rō mī′sin) *n.* a drug related to streptomycin, used against certain bacteria. *Formula:* $C_{37}H_{67}NO_{13}$ [< Gk. *erythros* red + *mykēs* fungus]

Es einsteinium.

-es *suffix.* a form of -s used after such letters as *s, z, sh,* and *ch,* as in *masses, buzzes, rushes, lunches.*

E·sau (ē′so or ē′sô) *n.* in the Bible, the older son of Isaac and Rebecca, who sold his birthright to his brother Jacob. Gen. 25:21-34.

es·ca·drille (es′kə dril′) *n.* formerly, a small fleet of airplanes or warships, together with their equipment and men. [< F *escadrille,* dim. of *escadre* squadron; form influenced by Sp. *escuadrilla,* dim. of *escuadra*]

es·ca·lade (es′kə lād′) *n.* the climbing of the walls of a fortified place with the help of ladders. —*v.* scale or attack over (a wall, rampart, etc.) by means of ladders. [< F < Ital. *scalata,* ult. < L *scala* ladder]

es·ca·late (es′kə lāt′) *v.* **-lat·ed, -lat·ing. 1 a** cause prices, wages, etc. to increase or decrease in accordance with some standard, such as the cost of living index. **b** increase or decrease in accordance with some standard: *As prices go up, costs escalate.* 2 increase or expand by stages: *small battles can easily escalate into major wars.* [back formation < *escalator*] **—es′ca·la′tion,** *n.*

es·ca·la·tor (es′kə lā′tər) *n.* a continuous moving stairway. Many department stores have escalators to carry the customers from one floor to another. [< *Escalator,* a blend of *escalade* and *elevator,* a trademark]

escalator clause a provision in a contract allowing an increase or decrease in wages, royalties, etc. under specified conditions.

es·cal·lop (es kol′əp or es kal′əp) *v.* bake in a cream sauce or with bread crumbs. —*n.* 1 food cooked in this way: *escallop of veal.* 2 a scallop (def. 1). [(originally n.) < OF *escalope* shell < Gmc.]

es·ca·pade (es′kə pād′ or es′kə pād′) *n.* 1 a breaking loose from rules or restraint. 2 a wild adventure or prank. [< F < Ital. *scappata* < *scappare* escape]

es·cape (es kāp′) *v.* **-caped, -cap·ing,** *n. adj.* —*v.* 1 get free; get out and away: *escape from prison.* 2 get free from: *He thinks he will never escape hard work.* 3 keep free or safe from; avoid: *We all escaped the measles.* 4 avoid capture, trouble, etc.: *The thief has escaped.* 5 come out of without being intended: *A cry escaped her lips.* 6 fail to be noticed or remembered by: *I knew his face, but his name escaped me.*
—*n.* 1 an escaping. 2 a way of escaping: *There was no escape from the trap.* 3 relief from boredom, trouble, etc.: *find escape in mystery stories.* 4 an outflow or leakage of gas, water, etc.
—*adj.* providing a way of escape or avoidance. [ME < AF *escaper,* ult. < L *ex-* out of + *cappa* cloak]
Syn. *v.* 1 flee, abscond. 3 **Escape, evade, elude** = keep free from someone or something. **Escape** = miss possible or threatened unpleasantness or danger by being out of its way or by managing to keep free: *He escaped being killed in the blast because he had not gone to work.* **Evade** emphasizes cleverness or trickery in managing to stay free: *Some boys try to evade doing chores around the home.* **Elude** suggests slipperiness and quickness in getting away from trouble that is close or in keeping free: *The bandit eluded the posse that was following him.*

escape clause a clause that frees a signer of a contract from certain responsibilities under specified circumstances.

escape mechanism 1 in psychiatry, a thought or action, usually unconscious, that permits avoidance of an unpleasant reality. 2 any device or apparatus, such as an ejection seat in an aircraft, designed to permit escape or release in an emergency.

es·cape·ment (es kāp′mənt) *n.* 1 a device in a timepiece by which the motion of the wheels and of the pendulum or balance wheel are accommodated to each other so that one tooth of the wheel escapes at each swing of the pendulum. 2 the mechanism that controls the movement of a typewriter carriage.

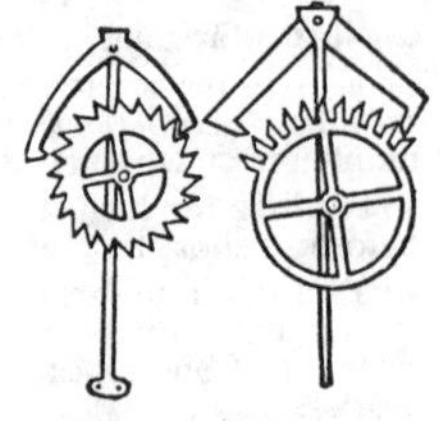
Two forms of escapement

escape velocity in physics, the minimum speed an object must attain to get free of a gravitational field. An escape velocity of approximately 25,000 miles per hour is needed to overcome the gravitational pull of the earth.

es·cap·ism (es kāp′iz əm) *n.* a habitual avoidance of unpleasant realities by recourse to imagination or to entertainment.

es·cap·ist (es kāp′ist) *n.* a person who seeks escape from reality in daydreams, amusements, etc. —*adj.* providing a way of escaping from reality: *escapist literature.*

es·ca·role (es′kə rōl′) *n.* a kind of endive that has broad leaves, used for salads. [< F]

es·carp (es kärp′) *n.* an escarpment.

es·carp·ment (es kärp′mənt) *n.* 1 a steep slope; cliff. 2 the ground made into a steep slope as part of a fortification. [< F *escarpement* < *escarper* form into a steep slope < *escarpe* a steep slope < Ital. *scarpa* < Gmc.]

es·cha·to·log·i·cal (es′kə tə loj′ə kəl) *adj.* of or having to do with eschatology.

es·cha·tol·o·gy (es′kə tol′ə jē) *n.* 1 the body of doctrines concerning the four last things, death, judgment, heaven, and hell. 2 the branch of theology that deals with these things. [< Gk. *eschatos* last, final + E *-logy*]

es·cheat (es chēt′) *n.* in law: 1 a reverting of the ownership of property to the state or to the lord of a manor when there are no legal heirs. 2 the property whose ownership has so reverted. —*v.* in law: 1 revert to the state or the lord of the manor. 2 confiscate; transfer (the ownership of property) to the state. [ME < OF *eschete,* ult. < L *ex-* out + *cadere* fall]

es·chew (es chü′) *v.* avoid; shun; keep away from: *A wise person eschews bad company.* [ME < OF *eschiver* < Gmc.] **—es·chew′er,** *n.*

Es·co·ri·al (es kô′rē əl) *n.* a huge structure near Madrid, containing a palace and tomb for the kings of Spain, a church, a college, and a monastery.

es·cort (*n.* es′kôrt; *v.* es kôrt′) *n.* 1 one or a group going with another to give protection, show honor, etc.: *an escort of ten airplanes.* 2 one or more ships, airplanes, etc. serving as a guard: *During World War II Canada's destroyers served as escorts to many convoys.* 3 the act of going with another as an escort.
—*v.* go with as an escort: *Warships escorted the royal yacht. He enjoyed escorting his pretty cousin to the movies.* [< F *escorte* < Ital. *scorta* < *scorgere* guide < L *ex-* out + *corrigere* set right] **—Syn.** *v.* See **accompany.**

es·cri·toire (es′krə twär′ or es′krə twär′) *n.* a writing desk. [< F < LL *scriptorium* < L *scribere* write]

es·crow (es′krō or es krō′) *n.* in law: 1 a deed, bond, or other written agreement put in charge of a third person until certain conditions are fulfilled by two other parties. 2 **in escrow,** held by a third party in accordance with an agreement. [< AF var. of OF *escroue* scrap, scroll < Gmc.]

es·cu·do (es kü′dō) *n.* **-dos.** 1 a unit of money in Chile and Portugal. See table at **money.** 2 a coin worth one escudo. [< Pg. < L *scutum* shield]

es·cu·lent (es′kyů lənt) *adj.* suitable for food; edible. [< L *esculentus* < *esca* food]

Es·cu·ri·al (es kūr′ē əl) *n.* Escorial.

hat, āge, cãre, fär; let, ēqual, tėrm; it, īce
hot, ōpen, ôrder; oil, out; cup, pu̇t, rüle, ūse
əbove, takən, pencəl, lemən, circəs
ch, child; ng, long; sh, ship
th, thin; ᴛʜ, then; zh, measure

es·cutch·eon (es kuch′ən) *n.* **1** a shield or shield-shaped surface on which a coat of arms is put. **2** a protective metal plate around a keyhole. **3** the panel on a ship's stern bearing her name. **4 blot on the escutcheon,** a disgrace to honor or reputation. [< ONF *escuchon* < L *scutum* shield]

-ese *suffix.* **1** of, belonging to, or having to do with: *Japanese = of, belonging to, or having to do with Japan.* **2** a native or inhabitant of: *Portuguese = a native or inhabitant of Portugal.* **3** the language of: *Chinese = the language of China.* **4** the typical style or vocabulary of: *journalese = newspaper style.* [< OF *-eis* < L *-ensis*]

E.S.E., ESE, or **e.s.e.** east-southeast, a direction halfway between east and southeast.

es·ker (es′kər) *n.* a winding ridge of sand, gravel, etc. believed to have been deposited by meltwater streams flowing inside the retreating glaciers of the Ice Age. Also, **eskar.** [< Irish *eiscir*]

Es·ki·mo (es′kə mō′) *n.* **-mos** or **-mo. 1** a people living on the Arctic shores of North America and N.E. Asia. Eskimos are short and stocky, and have broad, flat faces, yellowish skin, and black hair. **2** a member of this people. **3** their language. [< Danish < F < Algonquian *eskimantsis* eaters of raw flesh]

Eskimo dog 1 a breed of strong, broad-chested, northern work dog, much used by the Eskimos for pulling sleds. **2** a dog of this breed.

Eskimo pie a chocolate-coated ice-cream bar.

e·so·phag·e·al (ē′sə faj′ē əl) *adj.* of, having to do with, or connected with the esophagus.

e·soph·a·gus (ē sof′ə gəs or i sof′ə gəs) *n.* **-gi** (-jī or -gē′). in anatomy and zoology, the passage for food from the mouth to the stomach; gullet. Also **oesophagus.** [< NL < Gk. *oisophagos* < *oiso-* carry + *phagein* eat]

es·o·ter·ic (es′ə ter′ik) *adj.* **1** understood only by the select few; intended for an inner circle of disciples, scholars, etc. **2** private; secret; confidential; opposed to *exoteric.* [< Gk. *esōterikos,* ult. < *esō* within] **—es′o·ter′i·cal·ly,** *adv.*

E.S.P. or **ESP** extrasensory perception.

esp. or **espec.** especially.

es·pal·ier (es pal′yər) *n.* **1** a framework of stakes upon which fruit trees and shrubs are trained. **2** a plant or row of plants trained to grow this way. —*v.* trail or furnish with an espalier. [< F < Ital. *spalliera* support < *spalla* shoulder]

Es·pa·ña (es pä′nyä) *n. Spanish.* Spain.

es·par·to (es pär′tō) *n.* a tough grass of S. Spain and N. Africa, used to make paper, cord, baskets, etc. [< Sp. < L < Gk. *spartos*]

espec. especially.

es·pe·cial (es pesh′əl) *adj.* special; particular; exceptional: *my especial friend; of no especial value.* [ME < OF < L *specialis* belonging to a particular species. Doublet of SPECIAL.]

es·pe·cial·ly (es pesh′əl ē or es pesh′lē) *adv.* particularly; chiefly; unusually.

Syn. Especially, particularly, principally = in a special manner or degree, first or most of all. **Especially** emphasizes the idea of over and above all others: *This book is designed especially for young students.* **Particularly** singles out the foremost case or example from others of the same class or kind: *All my arithmetic problems are hard, but particularly this one.* **Principally** emphasizes the idea of before all others or for the most part: *Robberies occur principally at night.*

☛ **especially, specially. Especially** = pre-eminently or exceptionally. **Specially** = for that purpose and no other. You should say, *I came specially to see John*; but, *I came especially to see John* if you would see others after seeing John, or if you have other business in mind besides visiting. A parallel distinction exists between **especial** and **special,** although the latter word now replaces **especial** for most purposes.

Es·pe·ran·to (es′pə rän′tō or es′pə ran′tō) *n.* an artificial language for international use, whose vocabulary and grammar are based on forms common to the principal European languages. [< the pseudonym "Dr. *Esperanto*" used by its inventor, Dr. Zamenhof]

es·pi·al (es pī′əl) *n.* **1** the act of spying. **2** the act of watching. **3** a discovery.

es·pi·o·nage (es′pē ə nij or es′pē ə näzh′) *n.* the use of spies, especially the use of spies by one country to find out the military, political, etc. secrets of another; spying. [< F *espionnage* < *espionner* to spy < *espion* spy < Ital. *spione* < *spia* spy < Gmc.]

es·pla·nade (es′plə nād′ or es′plə näd′) *n.* **1** any open, level space used for public walks or drives. **2** an open space separating a fortress from the houses of a town. [< F < Sp. *esplanada* < *esplanar* < L *explanare* < *ex-* out + *planus* level]

es·pous·al (es pouz′əl) *n.* **1** an espousing; adoption (of a cause, etc.). **2** the ceremony of becoming engaged or married. **3 espousals,** *pl.* **a** a betrothal; betrothal ceremony. **b** a marriage; wedding. [ME < OF *espousailles,* pl. < L *sponsalia,* neut. pl. of *sponsalis* having to do with betrothal < *sponsus* betrothed. See ESPOUSE.]

es·pouse (es pouz′) *v.* **-poused, -pous·ing. 1** marry. **2** take up or make one's own: *Late in life he espoused a new religion.* [ME < OF *espouser* < L *sponsare* < *sponsus* betrothed, pp. of *spondere* betroth] **—es·pous′er,** *n.*

es·pres·so (es pres′ō) *n.* **-sos.** a very strong coffee made from dark-roasted, finely powdered beans and brewed under steam pressure. [< Ital. *espresso,* pp. of *esprimere* < L *exprimere.* See EXPRESS.]

espresso bar a coffee shop that specializes in espresso.

es·prit (es prē′) *n.* lively wit; spirit. [< F *esprit* < L *spiritus* spirit, originally, breath < *spirare* breathe. Doublet of SPIRIT, SPRITE.]

esprit de corps (es prē′ də kôr′) *French.* a sense of union and of common interests and responsibilities in some group: *The regiment has a strong esprit de corps.*

es·py (es pī′) *v.* **-pied, -py·ing. 1** see; catch sight of. **2** *Archaic.* spy on. [ME < OF *espier* < Gmc.]

☛ Usually espy suggests that a thing is hard to see because it is far away, small, or hidden.

Esq. Esquire.

☛ **Esq., Esquire.** Written after a man's name in the inside and outside address of a letter, *Esq.* or *Esquire* is formal and is no longer widely used in Canada except in official and professional circles. Many people consider the usage British, or archaic, or both. No other title (such as *Mr., Dr., Hon.*) should be used with the word: *Harry A. Kinne, Esq.*

-esque *suffix.* **1** in the —— style; resembling the —— style, as in *Romanesque.* **2** like a ——; like that of a ——, as in *statuesque.* [< F < Ital. *-esco* < Gmc. Akin to -ISH.]

Es·qui·mau (es′kə mō′) *n.* **-maux** (-mō′ or -mōz′). *Esp.Brit.* Eskimo.

es·quire (es kwīr′ or es′kwīr) *n.* **1** in the Middle Ages, a young man of noble family who attended a knight until he himself was made a knight. **2** an Englishman ranking next below a knight. **3** *Archaic.* an English country gentleman; squire. **4 Esquire,** a title of respect (for birth, position or education) placed after a man's last name instead of placing *Mr.* before the name: *John Jones, Esquire = Mr. John Jones.* [ME < OF *esquier* < L *scutarius* shieldbearer < *scutum* shield] ☛ See **Esq.** for usage note.

ess (es) *n.* **1** the 19th letter of the alphabet (S, s). **2** anything shaped like an S.

-ess *suffix.* female, as in *heiress, hostess, lioness.* [< F *-esse* < L < Gk. *-issa*]

es·say (*n.* es′ā *for 1,* es′ā or e sā′ *for 3*; *v.* e sā′) *n.* **1** a literary composition on a certain subject. An essay is usually shorter and more personal, but less methodical than a treatise. **2** a written composition, theme, term paper, etc. assigned as an exercise in a high school, college, etc. **3** a try; attempt.
—*v.* try; attempt. [< OF *essai* < L *exagium* a weighing] **—es·say′er,** *n.* **—Syn.** *n.* **2** effort, endeavor.

es·say·ist (es′ā ist) *n.* a writer of essays.

es·sence (es′əns) *n.* **1** that which makes a thing what it is; the necessary part or parts; important feature or features: *Kindness is the essence of politeness.* **2** any concentrated substance that has the characteristic flavor, fragrance, or effect of the plant, fruit, etc. from which it is obtained. Atropine is the essence of the belladonna plant. 3 a solution of such a substance in alcohol. Essence of peppermint is oil of peppermint dissolved in alcohol. 4 a perfume. 5 something that is, especially a spiritual or immaterial entity. [ME < OF < L *essentia* < *esse* be]

es·sen·tial (ə sen′shəl) *adj.* 1 needed to make a thing what it is; necessary; very important: *Good food and enough rest are essential to good health.* 2 of, like, or constituting the essence of a substance. 3 being or containing the essence, or fragrance, flavor, and medicinal qualities, of a plant or other material: *essential odors.* 4 being such by its essence or very nature, or in the highest sense: *essential happiness, essential poetry.* —*n.* an absolutely necessary element or quality; fundamental feature: *Learn the essentials first; then learn the details.* [ME < Med.L *essentialis* < L *essentia.* See ESSENCE.] —**Syn.** *adj.* 1 indispensable, requisite, vital. See **necessary.**

es·sen·tial·ly (ə sen′shəl ē) *adv.* in essence; in essentials; in an essential manner.

essential oil a volatile oil having the characteristic fragrance or flavor of the plant or fruit from which it is extracted. It is used in making perfumes and in flavoring.

-est *suffix forming the superlative degree.* 1 of adjectives, as in *warmest.* 2 of adverbs, as in *slowest.* [OE *-est, -ost*]

est. 1 established. 2 estate. 3 estuary.

EST, E.S.T., or **e.s.t.** Eastern Standard Time.

es·tab·lish (es tab′lish) *v.* 1 set up permanently: *establish a government or a business.* 2 settle in a position; set up in a business: *He established himself in the most comfortable chair. A new doctor has established himself on this street.* 3 bring about permanently; cause to be accepted: *establish a custom.* 4 show beyond dispute; prove: *establish a fact.* 5 make (a church) a national institution recognized and supported by the government. [ME < OF *establiss-,* a stem of *establir* < L *stabilire* make stable < *stabilis* stable] —**es·tab′lish·er,** *n.* —**Syn.** 1 See fix. 4 verify, substantiate.

established church a church that is a national institution, recognized and supported by the government.

es·tab·lish·ment (es tab′lish mənt) *n.* 1 an establishing. 2 a being established. 3 something established. A household, business, church, or army is an establishment. 4 the recognition of a church by the state as the official church. 5 **the Establishment, a** the Church of England or the Presbyterian Church of Scotland. **b** the prevailing order in a country; the people with controlling influence. 6 the number of men in a regiment, a ship's company, etc., as set by regulations: *The regiment needed three officers to complete its establishment.* 7 a steady income; secure livelihood. 8 a secure, settled position in life.

es·tate (es tāt′) *n.* 1 a large piece of land belonging to a person; landed property: *He has a beautiful estate with a country house and a swimming pool on it.* 2 what a person owns; property; possessions. Land and buildings are real estate. When a person dies, his estate is divided up among those to whom he has left it. 3 a condition or stage in life: *A boy attains man's estate at 21.* 4 a class or group of people in a nation: *The press is often called the fourth estate.* 5 **the three estates,** the noblemen, clergymen, and common people. [ME < OF *estat* < L *status* state. Doublet of STATE.]

Es·tates-Gen·er·al (es tāts′jen′ər əl or -jen′rəl) *n.* States-General (def. 1).

es·teem (es tēm′) *v.* 1 have a very favorable opinion of; regard highly: *We esteem men of good character.* 3 think; consider: *Men have often esteemed happiness the greatest good.* —*n.* a very favorable opinion; high regard: *Courage is held in esteem.* [ME < OF *estimer* < L *aestimare* value] —**Syn.** *v.* 1 See **value.** *-n.* estimation, respect.

es·ter (es′tər) *n.* a compound resulting from the reaction of an acid with an alcohol, so that the acid hydrogen of the acid is replaced by the hydrocarbon radical of the alcohol. Animal and vegetable fats and oils are esters. [coined by L. Gmelin (1788-1853), a German chemist]

Es·ther (es′tər) *n.* 1 the Jewish wife of a Persian king, who saved her people from massacre. 2 the book of the Old Testament that tells her story.

es·thete (es′thēt or ēs′thēt) *n.* aesthete.

es·thet·ic (es thet′ik or ēs thet′ik) *adj.* aesthetic. —**es·thet′i·cal·ly,** *adv.*

es·thet·i·cism (es thet′ə siz′əm or ēs thet′ə siz′əm) *n.* aestheticism.

es·thet·ics (es thet′iks or ēs thet′iks) *n.* aesthetics.

Es·tho·ni·an (es thō′nē ən) *adj. n.* Estonian.

es·ti·ma·ble (es′tə mə bəl) *adj.* 1 worthy of esteem; deserving high regard. 2 capable of being estimated or calculated. —**es′ti·ma·bly,** *adv.*

es·ti·mate (*n.* es′tə mit or es′tə māt′; *v.* es′tə māt′) *n. v.* **-mat·ed, -mat·ing.** —*n.* 1 a judgment or opinion about (how much, how many, how good, etc.): *My estimate of the length of the room was 15 feet; it actually measured 14 feet, 9 inches.* 2 a statement of what a certain job will cost, made by one willing to do the work: *The painter's estimate for painting the house was $850.* —*v.* 1 form a judgment or opinion about (how much, how many, how good, etc.). 2 fix the worth, size, amount, etc., especially in a rough way; calculate approximately. 3 draw up or submit a statement of the cost of doing a specified piece of work or the price at which a contractor is prepared to undertake it. [< L *aestimatus,* pp. of *aestimare* value] —**es′ti·ma′tor,** *n.*

Syn. *v.* 1 **Estimate, appraise, evaluate** = judge the measure, weight, or value of someone or something. **Estimate** suggests a personal opinion based on personal knowledge, experience, or taste, and emphasizes that the result given may not be correct: *I estimated the room to be 15 feet long without measuring it.* **Appraise** emphasizes expert opinion, and suggests that the result given is correct or cannot be questioned: *appraise property for taxation.* **Evaluate** especially suggests trying to find the value or amount of a thing or person in terms of something besides money: *She evaluates people by their clothes.* 2 reckon, gauge.

es·ti·ma·tion (es′tə mā′shən) *n.* 1 judgment; opinion: *In my estimation, your plan will not work.* 2 esteem; respect. 3 the act or process of estimating.

es·ti·val (es′tə vəl or es tī′vəl) *adj.* of or having to do with summer. Also, **aestival.** [< L *aestivalis* < *aestivus,* adj. of *aestas* summer]

es·ti·vate (es′tə vāt′) *v.* **-vat·ed, -vat·ing.** 1 spend the summer. 2 in zoology, spend the summer in a dormant or torpid condition. Some snakes estivate. Also, **aestivate.**

es·ti·va·tion (es′tə vā′shən) *n.* 1 in zoology, the state of being in a dormant or torpid condition during the summer. 2 in biology, the arrangement of the parts of a flower in the bud.

Es·to·ni·an (es tō′nē ən) *adj.* of or having to do with Estonia or its people. —*n.* 1 a native or inhabitant of Estonia. 2 the language of Estonia. Also, **Esthonian.**

es·top (es top′) *v.* **-topped, -top·ping.** 1 in law, prevent from asserting or doing something contrary to a previous assertion or act. 2 *Archaic.* stop; bar; obstruct. [< OF *estoper* < *estoupe* tow < L *stuppa*]

es·top·pel (es top′əl) *n.* an estopping.

es·trange (es trānj′) *v.* **-tranged, -trang·ing.** 1 turn (a person) from affection to indifference, dislike, or hatred; make unfriendly; separate: *A quarrel had estranged him from his family.* 2 keep apart; keep away. [ME < OF *estranger* < L *extraneare* < *extraneus* strange, foreign. Related to STRANGE.] —**es·trang′er,** *n.*

es·trange·ment (es trānj′mənt) *n.* 1 an estranging. 2 a being estranged: *A misunderstanding between the two friends had caused their estrangement.*

es·tray (es trā′) *n.* a stray person, animal, or thing.

es·tro·gen (es′trə jən) *n.* any of three hormones that induce a series of physiological changes in females, especially in the reproductive or sexual organs. [< L *oestrus* frenzy + E *-gen* producing]

es·tu·ar·y (es′chü er′ē) *n.* **-ar·ies.** 1 the broad mouth of a river into which the tide flows. 2 an inlet of the sea. [< L *aestuarium* < *aestus* tide]

-et *suffix.* —— little: *owlet* = *little owl; islet* = *little isle.* [< OF]

e·ta (ā′tə or ē′tə) *n.* the seventh letter of the Greek alphabet (H, η).

ETA estimated time of arrival.

et al. *Latin.* 1 and others. 2 and elsewhere. [(def. 1) < L *et alii;* (def. 2) < L *et alibi*]

☛ Et alii in Latin means "and other (people)." Do not use *et al.* in the sense "and other things," which may be suitably expressed by *etc.*

etc. et cetera.

☛ **etc., et cetera.** *Etc.*, usually read *and so forth*, is sometimes a convenient way to end a series that samples rather than completes an enumeration, but it belongs primarily to reference and business usage: *The case is suitable for prints, maps, blueprints, etc.* It is inappropriate in a sentence like this: *A student's professors can be of immense aid to him because of their knowledge of boys and their habits, customs, needs, ideals, etc.* Writing out *et cetera* now seems an affectation. In consecutive writing most people prefer the English "and so forth." It is better to avoid these end tags by rephrasing the list, preceding it by *such as* or some other warning that the list you are giving is not complete. *And etc.* shows the writer doesn't realize that the *et* of *etc.* means *and*, so that he is really writing *and and so forth.*

et cet·er·a (et set′ər ə or set′rə) *Latin.* **1** and other things; and the rest; and so forth; and so on. **2** and the like. [< L] ☛ See **etc.** for usage note.

et·cet·er·as (et set′ər əz or -set′rəz) *n.pl.* extra things; usual additions.

etch (ech) *v.* **1** engrave (a drawing, etc.) by using acid to eat a design into a printing plate of metal, glass, etc. **2** engrave a drawing or sign on by means of acid: *The artist etched only a few copper plates.* **3** make drawings or designs by this method. [< Du. *etsen* < G *ätzen.* Akin to EAT.] **—etch′er,** *n.*

etch·ing (ech′ing) *n.* **1** a picture or design printed from an etched plate. **2** an etched plate; an etched drawing or design. **3** the art of an etcher; the process of engraving a drawing or design on metal, glass, etc. by means of acid.

e·ter·nal (i tėr′nəl) *adj.* **1** without beginning or ending; lasting throughout all time. **2** always and forever the same. **3** seeming to go on forever; occurring very frequently. *—n.* **the Eternal,** God. [ME < OF < L *aeternalis*, ult. < *aevum* age]

Syn. *adj.* **1** Eternal, everlasting = lasting forever. **Eternal** emphasizes having neither a beginning nor an end: *God is eternal.* **Everlasting** emphasizes having no end, but going on and on forever: *We wish for everlasting peace.*

Eternal City Rome.

e·ter·nal·ly (i tėr′nəl ē) *adv.* **1** without beginning or ending; throughout all time. **2** always and forever. **3** constantly; incessantly.

e·ter·ni·ty (i tėr′nə tē) *n.* **-ties. 1** time without beginning or ending; all time. **2** an eternal quality; endlessness. **3** the endless period after death; future life. **4** a seemingly endless period of time. [ME < OF *eternite* < L *aeternitas* < *aeternus* eternal, ult. < *aevum* age]

e·ter·nize (i tėr′nīz) *v.* **-nized, -niz·ing.** make eternal; perpetuate; immortalize. **—e·ter′ni·za′tion,** *n.*

eth·ane (eth′ān) *n.* colorless, odorless, inflammable hydrocarbon of the methane series, present in natural gas and coal gas. *Formula*: C_2H_6 [< *ether*]

eth·a·nol (eth′ə nōl′ or eth′ə nol′) *n.* ethyl alcohol. [< *ethan*e + alcoh*ol*]

e·ther (ē′thər) *n.* **1** a colorless, strong-smelling liquid that burns and evaporates readily. Its fumes cause unconsciousness when deeply inhaled. Ether is used as an anesthetic, a solvent for fats and resins, etc. *Formula*: $(C_2H_5)_2O$ **2** the upper regions of space beyond the earth's atmosphere; clear sky; aether. **3** the invisible, elastic substance formerly supposed to be distributed evenly through all space and to conduct light waves, electric waves, etc.; aether. [< L *aether* < Gk. *aithēr* upper air]

e·the·re·al (i thēr′ē əl) *adj.* **1** light; airy; delicate: *Her ethereal beauty made her seem more like a spirit than a human being.* **2** not of the earth; heavenly. **3** of or having to do with the upper regions of space. **4** of or having to do with the ether diffused through space. Also, **aethereal. —e·the′re·al·ly,** *adv.* **—Syn. 1** intangible.

e·the·re·al·ize (i thēr′ē əl īz′) *v.* **-ized, -iz·ing.** make ethereal.

e·ther·i·za·tion (ē′thər ə zā′shən or ē′thər ī zā′shən) *n.* **1** a being or becoming etherized. **2** a giving of ether as an anesthetic.

e·ther·ize (ē′thər īz′) *v.* **-ized, -iz·ing. 1** make unconscious with ether fumes. **2** change into ether.

eth·ic (eth′ik) *adj.* ethical. *—n.* ethics; a system of ethics. [< L *ethicus* < Gk. *ēthikos* < *ēthos* moral character]

eth·i·cal (eth′ə kəl) *adj.* **1** having to do with standards of right and wrong; of ethics or morality. **2** in accordance

hat, āge, cãre, fär; let, ēqual, tėrm; it, īce
hot, ōpen, ôrder; oil, out; cup, pu̇t, rüle, ūse
əbove, takən, pencəl, lemən, circəs
ch, child; ng, long; sh, ship
th, thin; ᴛʜ, then; zh, measure

with formal or professional rules of right and wrong: *It is not considered ethical for a doctor to disclose a patient's confidences.* **—eth′i·cal·ly,** *adv.* **—Syn. 1** See **moral.**

eth·ics (eth′iks) *n.* **1** (*sing. in use*) the study of standards of right and wrong; that part of science and philosophy dealing with moral conduct, duty, and judgment. **2** (*sing. in use*) a book about ethics. **3** (*pl. in use*) formal or professional rules of right and wrong; system of conduct or behavior: *Medical ethics do not permit doctors and surgeons to advertise.*

☛ **Ethics** is singular in use when the meaning is the study of standards of right and wrong or a book about this study: *Ethics deals with moral conduct. Ethics* is plural in use when it means professional rules of right and wrong: *The ethics of his profession do not permit him to do that.*

E·thi·op (ē′thē op′) *adj. n.* Ethiopian.

E·thi·o·pi·an (ē′thē ō′pē ən) *adj.* **1** of or having to do with Ethiopia or its people. **2** Negro. *—n.* **1** a native or inhabitant of Ethiopia. **2** a Negro.

E·thi·o·p·ic (ē′thē op′ik or ē′thē ō′pik) *adj.* of or having to do with the ancient Semitic language of Ethiopia or the church using this language. *—n.* the ancient Semitic language of Ethiopia.

eth·moid (eth′moid) *adj.* in anatomy, having to do with certain bones situated in the walls and septum of the nose and containing numerous perforations for the filaments of the olfactory nerve. *—n.* in anatomy, an ethmoid bone. [< Gk. *ēthmoeidēs* < *ēthmos* sieve + *eidos* form]

eth·nic (eth′nik) *adj.* **1** of or having to do with various cultural groups of people and the characteristics, language, and customs of each; of, having to do with, or peculiar to a people. **2** of or having to do with people of foreign birth or descent: *the ethnic groups of Toronto, ethnic newspapers.* **3** heathen; pagan; not Christian; not Jewish. [< L *ethnicus* < Gk. *ethnikos* < *ethnos* nation]

☛ **ethnic** (def. 2). The use of *ethnic* to mean *foreign* has become widespread in Canada though it is considered unacceptable usage by many and is resented as being condescending and inaccurate by others.

eth·ni·cal (eth′nə kəl) *adj.* ethnic.

ethno- *combining form.* race; nation, as in *ethnology.* [< Gk. *ethno-* < *ethnos*]

eth·nog·ra·pher (eth nog′rə fər) *n.* an expert in ethnography.

eth·no·graph·ic (eth′nə graf′ik) *adj.* having to do with ethnography. **—eth′no·graph′i·cal·ly,** *adv.*

eth·nog·ra·phy (eth nog′rə fē) *n.* the scientific description and classification of the various cultural groups of people.

eth·no·log·ic (eth′nə loj′ik) *adj.* ethnological.

eth·no·log·i·cal (eth′nə loj′ə kəl) *adj.* having to do with ethnology.

eth·no·log·i·cal·ly (eth′nə loj′ik lē) *adv.* from the point of view of ethnology.

eth·nol·o·gist (eth nol′ə jist) *n.* a person trained in ethnology.

eth·nol·o·gy (eth nol′ə jē) *n.* the branch of anthropology that deals with the various cultural groups of people, their origin, distribution, and characteristics.

e·thos (ē′thos) *n.* **1** the essential and distinctive character or spirit of a race, or people, or of a system, culture, institution, etc. **2** in aesthetics, the objective or universal qualities in a work of art as distinguished from the subjective or emotional. [< NL < Gk. *ēthos* character, nature]

eth·yl (eth′əl) *n.* **1** a univalent radical present in many organic compounds. Ordinary alcohol contains ethyl. *Formula*: C_2H_5 **2 Ethyl,** *Trademark.* **a** a poisonous, colorless lead compound used in gasoline to reduce knocking; tetraethyl lead. *Formula*: $Pb(C_2H_5)_4$ **b** a gasoline containing this compound. [< *ether*]

ethyl alcohol ordinary alcohol, made by the fermentation of grain, sugar, etc. *Formula*: C_2H_5OH

eth·yl·ene (eth′ə lēn′) *n.* a colorless, inflammable gas with an unpleasant odor, used as an anesthetic, in making organic compounds, and for coloring and ripening citrus fruits. *Formula:* C_2H_4

e·ti·o·late (ē′tē ə lāt′) *v.* **-lat·ed, -lat·ing. 1** in botany, make (a plant) pale or colorless by depriving it of light; blanch. **2** of a plant, become pale or colorless through lack of sunlight. **3** make weak, dull, colorless: *His literary style was bland and etiolated.* [< F *étioler* blanch + E *-ate*] **—e′ti·o·la′tion,** *n.*

e·ti·ol·o·gy (ē′tē ol′ə jē) *n.* **1** the assigning of a cause. **2** the science that deals with origins or causes. **3** the theory of the causes of disease. Also, **aetiology.** [< L *aetiologia* < Gk. *aitiologia* < *aitia* cause + *-logos* treating of]

et·i·quette (et′ə ket′ or et′ə kət) *n.* **1** the conventional rules for conduct or behavior in polite society. **2** the formal rules or conventions governing conduct in a profession, official ceremony, etc.: *medical etiquette.* [< F < Gmc.]

Eton collar a broad, stiff collar worn outside the coat collar.

Eton jacket a short, black coat with broad lapels. The jacket comes to the waist and is not made to button.

E·tru·ri·an (i trür′ē ən) *adj. n.* Etruscan.

E·trus·can (i trus′kən) *adj.* of or having to do with Etruria, an ancient country in W. Italy, its people, their language, art, or customs. *—n.* **1** a native or inhabitant of Etruria. **2** the language of Etruria. [< L *Etruscus*]

et seq. and the following; and that which follows. [for L *et sequens*]

-ette *suffix.* **1** small, as in *kitchenette, statuette.* **2** female, as in *farmerette, suffragette.* **3** substitute for, as in *leatherette.* [< F *-ette,* fem. of *-et* -et]

é·tude (ā tūd′ or ā tüd′) *n.* **1** a study. **2 a** a piece of music intended to develop skill in technique. **b** a composition of a similar type, having artistic quality, and intended for public performance: *Chopin's "Harp" Etude.* [< F *étude* study < L *studium.* Doublet of STUDIO, STUDY.]

et·y·mo·log·i·cal (et′ə mə loj′ə kəl) *adj.* having to do with the origin and history of words.

et·y·mo·log·i·cal·ly (et′ə mə loj′ik lē) *adv.* according to etymology; by etymology; with respect to the origin and history of words.

et·y·mol·o·gist (et′ə mol′ə jist) *n.* a person skilled in etymology.

et·y·mol·o·gy (et′ə mol′ə jē) *n.* **-gies. 1** the derivation of a word. **2** an account or explanation of the origin and history of a word. **3** the branch of linguistics dealing with word origins. [< L < Gk. *etymologia* < *etymon* the original sense or form of a word (neut. of *etymos* true, real) + *-logos* treating of]

et·y·mon (et′ə mon′) *n.* the original form of a word that is the basis of later derivatives. [< Gk. *etymon* (neut. adj.) what is true]

eu- *prefix.* good; well, as in *eulogy, euphony.* [< Gk.]

Eu europium.

eu·ca·lypt (ū′kə lipt′) *n.* eucalyptus.

eu·ca·lyp·tus (ū′kə lip′təs) *n.* **-tus·es, -ti** (-tī or -tē). a tall evergreen tree that is native to Australia and other subtropical countries. It is valued for its timber and for an oil made from its leaves. Also, **eucalypt.** [< NL < Gk. *eu-* well + *kalyptos* covered; with reference to bud covering]

Eu·cha·rist (ū′kə rist) *n.* in the Christian church: **1** the sacrament of the Lord's Supper; Holy Communion. **2** the consecrated bread and wine used in this sacrament. [< LL < Gk. *eucharistia* thankfulness, the Eucharist]

Eu·cha·ris·tic (ū′kə ris′tik) *adj.* having to do with the Eucharist.

eu·chre (ū′kər) *n. v.* **-chred, -chring.** *—n.* **1** a simple card game for two, three, or four players, using the 32 (or 28, or 24) highest cards in the pack. **2** a social gathering during which people play euchre. **3** the failure of the side that declared the trump to win three tricks. *—v.* **1** defeat (the side that declared the trump) at euchre. **2** *Informal.* outwit; defeat. [origin uncertain]

Eu·clid·e·an or **Eu·clid·i·an** (ū klid′ē ən) *adj.* **1** of or having to do with Euclid, a Greek mathematician who wrote a book on geometry about 300 B.C. **2** of or about his principles of geometry.

eu·gen·ic (ū jen′ik) *adj.* **1** having to do with improvement of the race; improving the race; improving the offspring produced: *eugenic breeding.* **2** coming of good stock. [< Gk. *eugenēs* well-born < *eu-* well + *genos* birth]

eu·gen·i·cal·ly (ū jen′ik lē) *adv.* in a eugenic manner; with respect to racial improvement.

eu·gen·ics (ū jen′iks) *n.sing. or pl.* **1** the science of improving the human race by a careful selection of parents in order to develop healthier and more intelligent children. **2** the science of improving offspring.

eu·la·chon (ū′lə kən) *n.* oolichan.

eu·lo·gist (ū′lə jist) *n.* a person who eulogizes.

eu·lo·gis·tic (ū′lə jis′tik) *adj.* praising highly.

eu·lo·gis·ti·cal (ū′lə jis′tə kəl) *adj.* eulogistic. **—eu′lo·gis′ti·cal·ly,** *adv.*

eu·lo·gi·um (ū lō′jē əm) *n.* **-gi·ums, -gi·a** (-jē ə). eulogy; praise. [< Med.L *eulogium,* var. of L *eulogia* < Gk. *eulogia.* See EULOGY.]

eu·lo·gize (ū′lə jīz′) *v.* **-gized, -giz·ing.** praise very highly. **—eu′lo·giz′er,** *n.*

eu·lo·gy (ū′lə jē) *n.* **-gies. 1** a speech or writing in praise of a person, action, etc.: *He pronounced a eulogy upon the hero.* **2** high praise. [< Gk. *eulogia* < *eu-* well + *legein* speak]

Eu·men·i·des (ū men′ə dēz′) *n.pl.* in Greek mythology, the Furies; Erinyes. Literally, the kindly (goddesses), a name used for the Furies to avoid offending them.

eu·nuch (ū′nək) *n.* **1** a castrated man. **2** a castrated man in charge of a harem or the household of an Oriental ruler. [< L *eunuchus* < Gk. *eunouchos* < *eunē* bed + *echein* keep]

eu·pep·si·a (ū pep′sē ə or ū pep′shə) *n.* good digestion; opposed to *dyspepsia.* [< NL < Gk. *eupepsia* < *eupeptos* having a good digestion < *eu-* well + *peptein* digest]

eu·pep·tic (ū pep′tik) *adj.* **1** having good digestion. **2** aiding digestion.

eu·phe·mism (ū′fə miz′əm) *n.* **1** the use of a mild or indirect expression instead of one that is harsh or unpleasantly direct. **2** a mild or indirect expression used in this way. "Pass away" is a common euphemism for "die." The name *Eumenides,* meaning *kindly goddesses,* for the Furies was a euphemism. [< Gk. *euphēmismos* < *euphemizein* speak with fair words < *eu-* good + *phēmē* speaking]

eu·phe·mist (ū′fə mist) *n.* a person who uses euphemisms.

eu·phe·mis·tic (ū′fə mis′tik) *adj.* of or showing euphemism; containing a euphemism.

eu·phe·mis·ti·cal·ly (ū′fə mis′tik lē) *adv.* by way of euphemism; using euphemism.

eu·phon·ic (ū fon′ik) *adj.* **1** having to do with euphony. **2** euphonious.

eu·pho·ni·ous (ū fō′nē əs) *adj.* sounding well; pleasing to the ear; harmonious. **—eu·pho′ni·ous·ly,** *adv.* **—eu·pho′ni·ous·ness,** *n.*

eu·pho·ni·um (ū fō′nē əm) *n.* a brass musical instrument resembling a tuba and having a loud, deep tone. [< NL < Gk. *euphōnos* well-sounding < *eu-* good + *phōnē* sound]

eu·pho·ny (ū′fə nē) *n.* **-nies. 1** agreeableness of sound; pleasing effect to the ear; harmony of speech sounds as uttered or combined in utterance. **2** a tendency to change sounds so as to favor ease of utterance. [< LL < Gk. *euphōnia* < *eu-* good + *phōnē* sound]

eu·phor·bi·a (ū fôr′bē ə) *n.* any of a variety of plants having acrid, milky juice and small, inconspicuous flowers; spurge. Some euphorbia resemble cactuses. [< L *euphorbea* < *Euphorbus,* a Greek physician]

eu·pho·ri·a (ū fô′rē ə) *n.* in psychology, a feeling of well-being. [< NL < Gk. *euphoria* < *eu-* good + *pherein* bear]

eu·phor·ic (ū fôr′ik) *adj.* having to do with or characterized by euphoria.

hat, āge, cãre, fär; let, ēqual, tėrm; it, īce
hot, ōpen, ôrder; oil, out; cup, pu̇t, rüle, ūse
əbove, takən, pencəl, lemən, circəs
ch, child; ng, long; sh, ship
th, thin; ᴛʜ, then; zh, measure

eu·phu·ism (ū′fū iz′əm) *n.* 1 an affected style of speaking and writing English that was fashionable around 1600, characterized by long series of antitheses, frequent similes, and alliteration. *Example*: ". . . the milk of the Tygresse, that the more salt there is thrown into it the fresher it is." 2 any affected, elegant style of writing; flowery, artificial language. [< *Euphues*, the main character in two works of John Lyly, a 16th-century English dramatist and romance writer]

eu·phu·ist (ū′fū ist) *n.* a person who uses euphuism.

eu·phu·is·tic (ū′fū is′tik) *adj.* using or containing euphuism; like euphuism. —**eu′phu·is′ti·cal·ly,** *adv.*

Eur. 1 Europe. 2 European.

Eur·a·sian (ūr ā′zhən or ūr ā′shən) *adj.* 1 of or having to do with Europe and Asia or its people. 2 of mixed European and Asian parentage. —*n.* a person of mixed European and Asian parentage.

Eur·at·om (ūr at′əm) *n.* an organization to pool the nuclear-power research and developments of six European countries (France, West Germany, Italy, Belgium, the Netherlands, and Luxemburg); European Atomic Energy Community.

eu·re·ka (ū rē′kə) *interj.* I have found it! An exclamation of triumph about some discovery. [< Gk.]

eu·rhyth·mic (ū riᴛʜ′mik or ū rith′mik) *adj.* 1 of or having to do with eurhythmics. 2 pleasingly proportioned, especially in architecture. Also, **eurythmic.** —**eu·rhyth′mi·cal·ly,** *adv.*

eu·rhyth·mics (ū riᴛʜ′miks or ū rith′miks) *n.* a system for the development of rhythm and grace by the performing of bodily movements in response to music.

Eu·ro·pe·an (ūr′ə pē′ən) *adj.* of or having to do with Europe or its people. —*n.* a native or inhabitant of Europe.

European Common Market European Economic Community.

European Economic Community a trading and political association of W. European countries for eliminating tariffs between each other and working toward a complete customs union. The original member countries are Belgium, France, Italy, Luxembourg, the Netherlands, and W. Germany.

Eu·ro·pe·an·ize (ūr′ə pē′ən īz′) *v.* **-ized, -z·ing.** make European in appearance, habit, way of life, etc.

European plan a hotel system by which guests pay for only room and service, meals being extra; opposed to *American plan.*

eu·ro·pi·um (ū rō′pē əm) *n.* a rare, metallic chemical element of the same group as cerium. *Symbol*: Eu; *at.no.* 63; *at.wt.* 151.96. [< NL < L *Europa* Europe < Gk.]

eu·ryth·mic (ū riᴛʜ′mik or ū rith′mik) *adj.* eurhythmic.

eu·ryth·mics (ū riᴛʜ′miks or ū rith′miks) *n.* eurhythmics.

Eu·sta·chi·an tube (ū stā′kē ən or ū stā′shən) in anatomy, a slender canal between the pharynx and the middle ear, which equalizes the air pressure on the two sides of the eardrum. See **ear** for diagram. [< Bartolommeo *Eustachio*, a 16th-century Italian anatomist]

eu·tha·na·sia (ū thə nā′zē ə or ū′thə nā′zhə) *n.* 1 an easy, painless death. 2 a painless killing, especially to end a painful and incurable disease; mercy killing. [< Gk. *euthanasia* < *eu-* easy + *thanatos* death]

eu·then·ics (ū then′iks) *n.* the science of improving biologically the human race by controlling the environment or living conditions. [< Gk. *euthēnia* well-being]

ev or **e.v.** electron volts.

e·vac·u·ant (i vak′ū ənt) *adj.* in medicine, producing evacuation; cathartic; purgative. —*n.* an evacuant medicine, drug, etc., especially a purgative.

e·vac·u·ate (i vak′u āt′) *v.* **-at·ed, -at·ing.** 1 leave empty; withdraw from: *The soldiers evacuated the fort.* 2 withdraw; remove: *evacuate all foreign residents from the war zone.* 3 make empty: *evacuate the bowels.* [< L *evacuare* < *ex-* out + *vacuus* empty] —**e·vac′u·a′tor,** *n.*

e·vac·u·a·tion (i vak′ū ā′shən) *n.* 1 a leaving empty; a withdrawal from occupation or possession; the act or process of evacuating. 2 a removal. 3 a making empty. 4 a discharge.

e·vac·u·ee (i vak′ū ē′ or i vak′ū ē′) *n.* one who is removed to a place of greater safety.

e·vade (i vād′) *v.* **e·vad·ed, e·vad·ing.** 1 get away from by trickery; avoid by cleverness. 2 avoid the truth by indefinite or misleading statements. [< L *evadere* < *ex-* away + *vadere* go] —**Syn. 1** elude, dodge. See **escape.**

e·vad·er (i vād′ər) *n.* one who evades.

e·val·u·ate (i val′ū āt′) *v.* **-at·ed, -at·ing.** find the value or the amount of; fix the value of: *An expert will evaluate the old furniture in this house.* [< F *évaluer*] —**e·val′u·a′tor,** *n.* —**Syn.** See **estimate.**

e·val·u·a·tion (i val′ū ā′shən) *n.* 1 an evaluating. 2 an estimated value; valuation.

ev·a·nesce (ev′ə nes′) *v.* **-nesced, -nes·cing.** disappear gradually; fade away; vanish. [< L *evanescere* < *ex-* out + *vanescere* vanish < *vanus* insubstantial]

ev·a·nes·cence (ev′ə nes′əns) *n.* 1 a gradual disappearance; a fading away; vanishing. 2 a tendency to disappear or fade away; inability to last long.

ev·a·nes·cent (ev′ə nes′ənt) *adj.* tending to disappear or fade away; able to last only a short time.

e·van·gel (i van′jəl) *n.* 1 the Gospel; good news of the saving of mankind through Christ. 2 good news. 3 an evangelist. 4 **Evangel,** in the Bible, one of the four gospels; Matthew, Mark, Luke, or John. [< L *evangelium* < Gk. *euangelion* good tidings, ult. < *eu-* good + *angellein* announce]

e·van·gel·ic (ē′van jel′ik or ev′ən jel′ik) *adj.* evangelical.

e·van·gel·i·cal (ē′van jel′ə kəl or ev′ən jel′ə kəl) *adj.* 1 of, concerning, or according to the four Gospels of the New Testament. 2 of or having to do with the Protestant churches that emphasize Christ's atonement and salvation by faith as the most important parts of Christianity. Methodists and Baptists are evangelical; Unitarians and Universalists are not. 3 evangelistic. 4 **Evangelical, a** designating those Protestant churches deriving from Lutheranism, rather than Calvinism (contrasted with *Reformed*). **b** (in some parts of Europe) Protestant. —**e′van·gel′i·cal·ly,** *adv.*

e·van·gel·i·cal·ism (ē′van jel′ə kəl iz′əm or ev′ən jel′ə kəl iz′əm) *n.* 1 the doctrines of an evangelical church. 2 the adherence to such doctrines.

e·van·gel·ism (i van′jə liz′əm) *n.* 1 a preaching of the Gospel; earnest effort for the spread of the Gospel. 2 the work of an evangelist. 3 the belief in the doctrines of an evangelical church or party.

e·van·gel·ist (i van′jə list) *n.* 1 a preacher of the Gospel. 2 a travelling preacher who stirs up religious feeling in revival services or camp meetings. 3 **Evangelist,** any one of the four apostles, Matthew, Mark, Luke, or John, who wrote the Gospels bearing their names.

e·van·gel·is·tic (i van′jə lis′tik) *adj.* 1 of the Evangelists. 2 of or by evangelists. —**e·van′gel·is′ti·cal·ly,** *adv.*

e·van·gel·ize (i van′jə līz′) *v.* **-ized, -iz·ing.** 1 preach the Gospel to. 2 convert to Christianity by preaching. —**e·van′gel·i·za′tion,** *n.*

e·vap·o·rate (i vap′ə rāt′) *v.* **-rat·ed, -rat·ing.** 1 change from a liquid or solid into a vapor: *Boiling water evaporates rapidly. Some solids, such as moth balls and Dry Ice, evaporate without melting.* 2 remove water or other liquid from: *Heat is used to evaporate milk.* 3 give off moisture. 4 vanish; disappear: *His good resolutions evaporated soon after New Year's Day.* [< L *evaporare* < *ex-* out + *vapor* vapor]

evaporated milk a thick, unsweetened, canned milk, prepared by evaporating some of the water from ordinary milk.

e·vap·o·ra·tion (i vap′ə rā′shən) *n.* 1 a changing of a liquid or solid into vapour. 2 a being changed into vapor.

3 the removal of water or other liquid. 4 disappearance.

e·vap·o·ra·tor (i vap′ə rā′tər) *n.* an apparatus for evaporating water or other liquid.

e·va·sion (i vā′zhən) *n.* 1 a getting away from something by trickery; an avoiding by cleverness: *Evasion of one's duty is contemptible.* 2 an attempt to escape an argument, a charge, a question, etc.: *The prisoner's evasions of the lawyer's questions convinced the jury of his guilt.* 3 a means of evading; trick or excuse used to avoid something. [ME < OF < LL *evasio, -onis* < L *evadere.* See EVADE.]

e·va·sive (i vā′siv or i vā′ziv) *adj.* tending or trying to evade: *"Perhaps" is an evasive answer.* —**e·va′sive·ly,** *adv.* —**e·va′sive·ness,** *n.* —**Syn.** shifty, misleading.

eve (ēv) *n.* 1 the evening or day before a holiday or some other special day: *Christmas Eve.* 2 the time just before. *Everything was quiet on the eve of the battle.* 3 *Poetic.* evening. [var. of *even*[2]]

Eve (ēv) *n.* 1 in the Bible, the first woman. Tempted by Satan, she ate the forbidden fruit and afterwards induced her husband Adam to do the same. Genesis 2 : 21-25; 3-20. 2 **daughter of Eve,** any woman.

e·ven[1] (ē′vən) *adj.* 1 level; flat; smooth: *Even country has no hills.* 2 at the same level; in the same plane or line: *The snow was even with the window.* 3 always the same; regular; uniform: *An even motion does not change.* 4 equal: *They divided the money into even shares.* 5 leaving no remainder when divided by 2: *2, 4, 6, 8, and 10 are even numbers.* 6 neither more nor less; exact: *Twelve apples make an even dozen.* 7 owing nothing: *When he had paid all of his debts, he was even.* 8 not easily disturbed or angered; calm: *A person with an even temper is seldom excited.* 9 not favoring one more than another; fair: *Justice is even treatment.* 10 **be even, a** owe nothing. **b** have revenge.
—*v.* make even; make level or equal: *She evened the edges by trimming them.*
—*adv.* 1 in an even manner. 2 just; exactly: *She left even as you came.* 3 indeed: *He is ready, even eager, to go.* 4 fully; quite: *He was faithful even unto death.* 5 though one would not expect it; as one would not expect: *Even the least noise disturbs her.* 6 still; yet: *You can do even better if you try.* 7 **break even,** *Informal.* have equal gains and losses. 8 **even if,** *Informal.* in spite of the fact that; although. 9 **even though,** *Informal.* although. 10 **get even, a** owe nothing. **b** have revenge. [OE *efen*] —**e′ven·er,** *n.* —**e′ven·ly,** *adv.* —**e′ven·ness,** *n.*
Syn. *adj.* 1 plane. See **level.** 3 **Even, uniform, equable** = always the same. **Even** emphasizes being regular and steady, never changing in motion, action, quality, etc.: *The even hum of the motor stopped.* **Uniform** emphasizes being always the same in form or character, never changing from the normal or regular: *We should have uniform traffic laws.* **Equable** is a formal word used interchangeably with *even,* but suggesting a quality in the thing or person that makes it likely to be even or uniform: *A watch has equable movement.* 8 unruffled.

e·ven[2] (ē′vən) *n. Poetic.* evening. [OE *ǣfen*]

e·ven-hand·ed (ē′vən han′did) *adj.* impartial; fair; just: *The judge meted out even-handed justice to all.* —**e′ven-hand′ed·ly,** *adv.* —**e′ven-hand′ed·ness,** *n.*

eve·ning (ēv′ning) *n.* 1 the last part of day and early part of night; the time between day and night. 2 the time between sunset and bedtime. 3 the last part: *Old age is the evening of life.* —*adj.* in the evening; of the evening; for the evening. [OE *ǣfnung* < *ǣfnian* become evening < *ǣfen* evening]

evening dress formal clothes worn in the evening.

evening gown a woman's evening dress.

evening primrose a tall plant having spikes of fragrant yellow flowers that open in the evening.

evening star a bright planet seen in the western sky after sunset. Venus is often the evening star.

e·ven·song (ē′vən song′) *n.* 1 in certain Christian churches, service said or sung in the late afternoon or early evening; vespers. 2 *Archaic.* evening. [OE *ǣfensang*]

e·vent (i vent′) *n.* 1 a happening. 2 an important happening: *The discovery of oil in Alberta was a great event.* 3 the result; outcome: *We made careful plans and awaited the event.* 4 an item or contest in a program of sports: *The broad jump was the last event.* 5 **at all events** or **in any event,** in any case; whatever happens. 6 **in the event of,** in case of; if there is; if there should be. 7 **in the event that,** if it should happen that; supposing: *In the event that the roads are icy, we shall not come.* [< L *eventus* < *evenire* < *ex-* out + *venire* come]
Syn. 1 **Event, incident, occurrence** = happening. **Event** applies particularly to a happening of some importance, usually resulting from what has gone before: *Graduation from high school is an event that most students eagerly look forward to.* **Incident** applies to a happening of less or little importance taking place between events, but not always in connection with them: *The unexpected meeting with a boy I used to know was an amusing incident.* **Occurrence** is the general word for any happening, event, or incident: *Going to school is an everyday occurrence.* 2 consequence.

e·ven-tempered (ē′vən tem′pərd) *adj.* not easily disturbed or angered; calm.

e·vent·ful (i vent′fəl) *adj.* 1 full of events; having many unusual events: *World War II was an eventful period in history.* 2 having important results; important. —**e·vent′ful·ly,** *adv.* —**e·vent′ful·ness,** *n.*

e·ven·tide (ē′vən tīd′) *n. Poetic.* evening.

e·ven·tu·al (i ven′chü əl) *adj.* 1 coming in the end; final: *After his many failures, his eventual success surprised us.* 2 depending on uncertain events; possible.

e·ven·tu·al·i·ty (i ven′chü al′ə tē) *n.* **-ties.** a possible occurrence or condition; possibility: *We hope for peace, but are ready for all the eventualities of war.*

e·ven·tu·al·ly (i ven′chü əl ē) *adv.* in the end; finally.

e·ven·tu·ate (i ven′chü āt′) *v.* **-at·ed, -at·ing.** come out in the end; happen finally; result. —**e·ven′tu·a′tion,** *n.*

ev·er (ev′ər) *adv.* 1 at any time: *Is she ever at home?* 2 at all times; always: *ever at your service.* 3 at all; by any chance; in any case: *What did you ever do to make him so angry?* 4 **ever so,** *Informal.* very. 5 **for ever and a day,** always. [OE *ǣfre*] —**Syn.** 2 forever.

ev·er·glade (ev′ər glād′) *n. U.S.* a large tract of low, wet ground partly covered with tall grass; a large swamp or marsh.

ev·er·green (ev′ər grēn′) *adj.* 1 of trees, shrubs, etc., having green leaves all the year. 2 of leaves, lasting until the next season.
—*n.* 1 an evergreen plant or tree. Pine, spruce, cedar, ivy, box, rhododendrons, etc. are evergreens. 2 **evergreens,** *pl.* evergreen twigs or branches used for decoration, especially at Christmas.

ev·er·last·ing (ev′ər las′ting) *adj.* 1 lasting forever; never ending or stopping. 2 lasting a long time. 3 lasting too long; repeated too often; tiresome: *his everlasting complaints.*
—*n.* 1 an eternity. 2 any of various plants whose flowers keep their shape and color when dried. 3 **the Everlasting,** God. —**ev′er·last′ing·ly,** *adv.* —**ev′er·last′ing·ness,** *n.* —**Syn.** *adj.* 1 See **eternal.**

ev·er·more (ev′ər môr′) *adv. n.* always; forever.

e·ver·sion (i vėr′zhən or i vėr′shən) *n.* 1 a turning of an organ, structure, etc. inside out. 2 a being turned inside out. [< L *eversio, -onis* < *evertere.* See EVERT.]

e·vert (i vėrt′) *v.* turn inside out. [< L *evertere* < *ex-* out + *vertere* turn]

eve·ry (ev′rē) *adj.* 1 all, regarded singly or separately; each and all: *Every written word is made of letters.* 2 all possible: *We showed him every consideration.* 3 **every now and then,** from time to time; again and again. 4 **every other,** each first, third, fifth, etc. or second, fourth, sixth, etc.: *Every other prisoner was shot.* 5 **every which way,** *Informal.* in all directions; in disorder. [OE *ǣfre* ever + *ǣlc* each] —**Syn.** 1 See **each.**

eve·ry·bod·y (ev′rē bud′ē or -bod′ē) *pron.* every person; everyone: *Everybody likes the new minister.*
☞ **everybody, everyone. a** Both these pronouns are grammatically singular: *Everybody was thrilled when our troops marched past. Everyone who wishes to attend is invited.* In informal speech, the pronouns are sometimes used as collectives. A verb immediately following either of them is usually singular, but another pronoun referring back from a little distance is likely to be plural: *Everybody dresses in their best clothes.* To make such expressions accord with formal written usage, it is often better to change the *everybody* or *everyone* to a more specific plural or collective than to change the later pronoun. **b** The pronoun *everybody* is always written as one word.

eve·ry·day (ev′rē dā′) *adj.* 1 of every day; daily: *Accidents are everyday occurrences.* 2 for every ordinary day; not for Sundays or holidays: *She wears everyday clothes to work.* 3 not exciting; usual.

☛ Everyday is one word when it is an adjective, two words when *day* is a noun modified by *every*: *This was an everyday occurrence. Every day seemed a year.*

Every·man (ev′rē man′) *n.* **1** an early sixteenth-century morality play symbolizing man's journey through life. **2** the chief character in this play, personifying humanity. **3** the average man; a typical human being.

eve·ry·one (ev′rē wun′ or ev′rē wən) *pron.* every person; everybody: *Everyone took his purchases home.* Also, **every one.**

☛ **everyone. a** See usage note under **everybody. b** *Everyone* is usually one word, but when *one* is stressed or emphasized, it is written as two words: *Everyone wants to attend the concert. Winning this game depends upon every one of you.*

eve·ry·thing (ev′rē thing′) *pron.* every thing; all things. —*n.* something extremely important; a very important thing: *This news means everything to us.*

☛ **Everything** is one word when it is a noun or pronoun, two words when *thing* is stressed or emphasized: *Everything was in its place. She meant everything to him. Food, water, clothes—every thing that Midas touched turned to gold.*

eve·ry·where (ev′rē hwãr′ or -wãr′) *adv.* in every place; in all places: *We looked everywhere for our lost dog.*

e·vict (i vikt′) *v.* **1** expel by a legal process from land, a building, etc.; eject (a tenant): *Because he had not paid his rent, the tenant was evicted by the sheriff.* **2** expel or put out by force: *The soldiers evicted the enemy from the occupied building.* [< L *evictus*, pp. of *evincere*. See EVINCE.] —**e·vic′tor,** *n.*

e·vic·tion (i vik′shən) *n.* an evicting or being evicted; expulsion.

ev·i·dence (ev′ə dəns) *n. v.* **-denced, -denc·ing.** —*n.* **1** whatever makes clear the truth or falsehood of something: *The evidence showed that he had not been near the place of the crime.* **2** in law: **a** facts established and accepted in a court of law. Before deciding a case, the judge or jury hears all the evidence given by both sides. **b** a person who gives testimony in a court of law: *queen's evidence.* **3** an indication; sign: *A smile gives evidence of pleasure.* **4 in evidence,** easily seen or noticed: *A crying baby is much in evidence.* **5 turn king's** (or **queen's**) **evidence** (in the United States, **turn state's evidence**), of an accomplice in a crime, offer oneself as a witness against the others implicated. —*v.* make easy to see or understand; show clearly; prove: *His smiles evidenced his pleasure.*

Syn. *n.* **1 Evidence, testimony, proof** = something that makes clear that a thing is true or false. **Evidence** applies to any facts that point toward, but do not fully prove, the truth or falsehood of something: *Running away was evidence of his guilt.* **Testimony** = something said or done to show or prove something true or false: *His speech was clear testimony of his good intentions.* **Proof** = complete evidence that leaves no doubt: *His actions were proof that he was telling the truth.*

ev·i·dent (ev′ə dənt) *adj.* easy to see or understand; clear; plain: *He has brought Betty a kitten, to her evident joy.* [< L *evidens, -entis* < *ex-* out + *videns*, ppr. of *videre* see] —**Syn.** apparent. See **obvious.**

ev·i·den·tial (ev′ə den′shəl) *adj.* **1** serving as evidence; of evidence; based on evidence. **2** like evidence; giving evidence.

ev·i·dent·ly (ev′ə dənt lē) *adv.* plainly; clearly; apparently.

e·vil (ē′vəl) *adj.* **1** morally bad; wrong; sinful; wicked: *an evil life, an evil character.* **2** causing harm or injury: *an evil plan.* **3** unfortunate. **4** due to bad character or conduct: *an evil reputation.*
—*n.* **1** something bad; sin; wickedness. **2** something that causes harm or injury. [OE *yfel*] —**e′vil·ly,** *adv.* —**e′vil·ness,** *n.* —**Syn.** *adj.* **1** depraved, vicious, corrupt. See **bad. 2** harmful, pernicious.

e·vil·do·er (ē′vəl dü′ər) *n.* a person who does evil.

e·vil·do·ing (ē′vəl dü′ing) *n.* the doing of evil.

evil eye the power that some people are supposed to have of causing harm or bringing bad luck to others by looking at them. —**e′vil-eyed′,** *adj.*

e·vil-mind·ed (ē′vəl mīn′did) *adj.* having an evil mind; wicked; malicious.

Evil One the Devil; Satan.

e·vince (i vins′) *v.* **e·vinced, e·vinc·ing. 1** show clearly: *The dog evinced its dislike of strangers by growling.* **2** show that one has (a certain quality, trait, etc.). [< LL *evincere* claim for oneself < *ex-* out + *vincere* conquer] —**e·vince′ment,** *n.* —**Syn. 1** See **display.**

hat, āge, cãre, fär; let, ēqual, tėrm; it, īce
hot, ōpen, ôrder; oil, out; cup, pu̇t, rüle, ūse
əbove, takən, pencəl, lemən, circəs
ch, child; ng, long; sh, ship
th, thin; ᴛʜ, then; zh, measure

e·vin·ci·ble (i vin′sə bəl) *adj.* able to be proved; demonstrable.

e·vis·cer·ate (i vis′ər āt′) *v.* **-at·ed, -at·ing. 1** remove the bowels from; disembowel. **2** deprive of something essential: *The abridgement leaves the book somewhat eviscerated.* [< L *eviscerare* < *ex-* out + *viscera* viscera] —**e·vis′cer·a′tion,** *n.*

ev·o·ca·tion (ev′ō kā′shən) *n.* an evoking.

e·voc·a·tive (i vok′ə tiv) *adj.* tending to produce or arouse an emotional response. —**e·voc′a·tive·ly,** *adv.* —**e·voc′a·tive·ness,** *n.*

e·voke (i vōk′) *v.* **e·voked, e·vok·ing.** call forth; bring out: *A good joke evokes a laugh.* [< L *evocare* < *ex-* out + *vocare* call] —**e·vok′er,** *n.*

ev·o·lu·tion (ev′ə lü′shən or ē′və lü′shən) *n.* **1** any process of formation or growth; gradual development: *the evolution of the modern steamship from the first crude boat.* **2** something evolved; a product of development; not a sudden discovery or creation. **3** the theory that all living things developed from a few simple forms of life or from a single form. **4** a movement of ships or soldiers, planned beforehand. **5** a movement that is a part of a definite plan, design, or series: *A clumsy person could never achieve the graceful evolutions of that ballet dancer.* **6** a releasing; giving off; setting free: *the evolution of heat from burning coal.* **7** in mathematics, the extraction of roots from powers. [< L *evolutio, -onis* < *evolvere.* See EVOLVE.]

ev·o·lu·tion·al (ev′ə lü′shən əl or ē′və lü′shən əl) *adj.* evolutionary.

ev·o·lu·tion·ar·y (ev′ə lü′shən er′ē or ē′və lü′shən er′ē) *adj.* **1** having to do with evolution or development. **2** in accordance with the theory of evolution. **3** performing evolutions; having to do with evolutions.

ev·o·lu·tion·ist (ev′ə lü′shən ist or ē′və lü′shən ist) *n.* a student of, or believer in, the theory of evolution.

e·volve (i volv′) *v.* **e·volved, e·volv·ing. 1** develop gradually; work out: *The boys evolved a plan for earning money during their summer vacation.* **2** in biology, develop by a process of growth and change to a more highly organized condition. **3** release; give off; set free. **4** be developed by evolution. [< L *evolvere* < *ex-* out + *volvere* roll] —**e·volv′er,** *n.*

e·volve·ment (i volv′mənt) *n.* **1** an evolving. **2** a being evolved.

ev·zone (ev′zōn) *n.* in the Greek army, a member of a corps of infantrymen famous for its valor. Evzones wear a picturesque uniform that includes a short kilt. [< Gk. *euzōnos* dressed for exercise < *eu-* well + *zōnē* girdle]

ewe (ū) *n.* a female sheep. [OE *ēowu*]

ew·er (ū′ər) *n.* a wide-mouthed water pitcher: *The ewer and basin are on the washstand.* [ME < AF var. of OF *eviere, aiguiere* < VL *aquaria* < L *aquarius* of or for water < *aqua* water]

A ewer and a basin

ex[1] (eks) *prep.* **1** out of. "Ex elevator" means free of charges until the time of removal from the grain elevator. **2** without; not including. "Ex-dividend stocks" are stocks on which the purchaser will not receive the next dividend to be paid. [< L]

ex[2] (eks) *n.* **1** the 24th letter of the alphabet (X, x). **2** anything shaped like an X.

Ex (eks) *n. Informal.* an exhibition, especially the Canadian National Exhibition held annually in Toronto.

ex-[1] *prefix.* **1** out of; from; out, as in *exclude, exit, export.* **2** utterly; thoroughly, as in *excruciating, exasperate.* **3** former; formerly, as in *ex-member,* *ex-president, ex-soldier.* Also: **e-**, before consonants except *c, f, p, q, s, t;* **ef-**, before *f.* [< L *ex-* < *ex* out of]

ex-[2] *prefix.* from, out of, as in *exodus.* Also, **ec-**, before consonants. [< Gk.]

ex. **1** example. **2** examined. **3** exchange. **4** exercise.

Ex. Exodus.

ex·ac·er·bate (eg zas′ər bāt′ or eks as′ər bāt′) *v.* **-bat·ed, -bat·ing. 1** make worse; aggravate (pain, disease, anger). **2** irritate (a person's feelings). [< L *exacerbare* < *ex-* completely + *acerbus* harsh, bitter]

ex·ac·er·ba·tion (eg zas′ər bā′shən or eks as′ər bā′shən) *n.* **1** aggravation. **2** irritation.

ex·act (eg zakt′) *adj.* **1** without any error or mistake; strictly correct; accurate; precise: *an exact measurement, the exact amount.* **2** strict; severe; rigorous. **3** characterized by or using strict accuracy: *A scientist should be an exact thinker.* —*v.* **1** demand and get; force to be paid: *If he does the work, he can exact payment for it.* **2** call for; need; require: *A hard piece of work exacts effort and patience.* [< L *exactus,* pp. of *exigere* weigh accurately < *ex-* out + *agere* weigh] —**ex·act′a·ble,** *adj.* —**ex·act′ness,** *n.* —**ex·act′or,** *n.* —**Syn.** *adj.* **1** See **correct.**

ex·act·ing (eg zak′ting) *adj.* **1** requiring much; making severe demands; hard to please: *an exacting employer.* **2** requiring effort, care, or attention: *Flying an airplane is exacting work.* —**ex·act′ing·ly,** *adv.* —**ex·act′ing·ness,** *n.*

ex·ac·tion (eg zak′shən) *n.* **1** an exacting: a demanding and getting; an enforcing of a payment considered arbitrary: *The ruler's exactions of money left the people very poor.* **2** a being exacted; extortion. **3** thing exacted. Taxes, fees, etc., forced to be paid, are exactions.

ex·act·i·tude (eg zak′tə tüd′ or eg zak′tə tūd′) *n.* exactness.

ex·act·ly (eg zakt′lē) *adv.* **1** in an exact manner; accurately; precisely. **2** just so; quite right.

exact science a science in which facts can be accurately observed and results can be accurately predicted. Mathematics and physics are exact sciences.

ex·ag·ger·ate (eg zaj′ər āt′) *v.* **-at·ed, -at·ing. 1** make (something) greater than it is; overstate: *He exaggerated the dangers of the trip in order to frighten them into not going.* **2** increase or enlarge abnormally. **3** say or think something is greater than it is; go beyond the truth: *He always exaggerates when he tells about things he has done.* [< L *exaggerare* < *ex-* out, up + *agger* heap] —**ex·ag′ger·a′tor,** *n.* —**Syn. 1** stretch, magnify.

ex·ag·ger·a·tion (eg zaj′ər ā′shən) *n.* **1** a statement that goes beyond the truth: *It is an exaggeration to say that you would rather die than touch a snake.* **2** the act of going beyond the truth: *His constant exaggeration made people distrust him.* **3** a being exaggerated.

ex·alt (eg zolt′ or eg zôlt′) *v.* **1** raise in rank, honor, power, character, quality, etc.: *We exalt a man when we elect him to high office.* **2** fill with pride, joy, or noble feeling. **3** praise, honor; glorify. [< L *exaltare* < *ex-* out, up + *altus* high] —**Syn. 1** elevate, promote, ennoble.

ex·al·ta·tion (eg′zol tā′shən or eg′zôl tā′shən) *n.* **1** an exalting. **2** a being exalted. **3** an elation of mind or feeling; rapture.

ex·am (eg zam′) *n. Informal.* an examination.

ex·am·i·na·tion (eg zam′ə nā′shən) *n.* **1** an examining or being examined. **2** a test of knowledge or qualifications; a list of questions; test. **3** the answers given in such a test. **4** in law, an interrogation, especially of a witness. —**Syn. 1** See **investigation.**

ex·am·ine (eg zam′ən) *v.* **-ined, -in·ing. 1** look at closely and carefully. **2** test the knowledge or qualifications of; ask questions of; test. **3** question (a witness) formally. [< F *examiner* < L *examinare* < *examen* a weighing < *exigere.* See EXACT.] —**ex·am′in·a·ble,** *adj.* —**ex·am′in·er,** *n.* —**Syn. 1** scrutinize, investigate. **3** interrogate.

ex·am·i·nee (eg zam′ə nē′) *n.* a person who is being examined.

ex·am·ple (eg zam′pəl) *n.* **1** one thing taken to show what others are like; a case that shows something; sample: *Vancouver is an example of a busy city.* **2** a person or thing to be imitated; model; pattern: *A father should try to be a good example to his sons.* **3** a problem in arithmetic, etc. **4** a warning to others: *The captain made an example of the shirkers by making them clean up the camp.* **5 set an example,** behave so that others may profitably imitate; be a model or pattern of conduct. **6 without example,** with nothing like it before. [ME < OF *essample* < L *exemplum,* originally, that which is taken out (i.e., a sample) < *eximere.* See EXEMPT.]

Syn. 1 Example, sample = a part or thing taken to show the nature of something. **Example** applies to an individual thing, fact, happening, situation, etc. that shows what the type or kind is like or how a general rule works: *This chair is an example of period furniture.* **Sample** applies to a part taken out of a thing or class to show the quality of the whole, which is considered to be exactly like it: *She looked carefully at all the samples of material before buying any.* **2** paragon, ideal. See **model.**

ex·as·per·ate (eg zas′pər āt′) *v.* **-at·ed, -at·ing.** irritate very much; annoy extremely; make angry: *The child's endless questions exasperated her father.* [< L *exasperare* < *ex-* thoroughly + *asper* rough] —**ex·as′per·at′ed·ly,** *adv.* —**ex·as′per·at′er,** *n.* —**Syn.** incense, anger, nettle, vex, provoke. See **irritate.**

ex·as·per·a·tion (eg zas′pər ā′shən) *n.* **1** the act of exasperating. **2** extreme annoyance, irritation, or anger.

exc. except.

Exc. Excellency.

Ex·cal·i·bur (eks kal′ə bər) *n.* the magic sword of King Arthur. [ME < OF *Escalibor* < Med.L *Caliburnus,* probably < Celtic]

ex ca·the·dra (eks′kə thē′drə or kath′ə drə) **1** with authority; from the seat of authority. **2** spoken with authority; authoritative. [< L *ex cathedra* from the chair]

ex·ca·vate (eks′kə vāt′) *v.* **-vat·ed, -vat·ing. 1** make hollow; hollow out. **2** make by digging; dig: *The tunnel was excavated through solid rock.* **3** dig out; scoop out: *Steam shovels excavated the dirt.* **4** get or uncover by digging: *They excavated an ancient buried city.* [< L *excavare* < *ex-* out + *cavus* hollow]

ex·ca·va·tion (eks′kə vā′shən) *n.* **1** a digging; a digging out or up. **2** a hole or hollow made by digging.

ex·ca·va·tor (eks′kə vā′tər) *n.* a person or thing that excavates. A steam shovel is an excavator.

ex·ceed (ek sēd′) *v.* **1** go beyond; be more or greater than; do more than; surpass: *The sum of 5 and 7 exceeds 10.* **2** be more or greater than others. [< F < L *excedere* < *ex-* out + *cedere* go] —**Syn. 2** excel.

ex·ceed·ing (ek sēd′ing) *adj.* surpassing; very great; unusual; extreme. —*adv. Archaic.* exceedingly.

ex·ceed·ing·ly (ek sēd′ing lē) *adv.* extremely; unusually, very: *Yesterday was an exceedingly hot day.*

ex·cel (ek sel′) *v.* **-celled, -cel·ling. 1** be better than; do better than: *He excelled his classmates in history.* **2** be better than others; do better than others; *excel in wisdom.* [< F < L *excellere*]

Syn. 1, 2 Excel, surpass, outdo = be better in quality or action. **Excel** emphasizes standing out above others in fineness, merit, or doing things: *He excels in mathematics.* **Surpass** = be better in comparison with others or a definite standard: *Mary surpasses her sister in history.* **Outdo** emphasizes doing more or better than others, especially more or better than has been done before: *The runner outdid his previous record for the race.*

ex·cel·lence (ek′sə ləns) *n.* **1** a being better than others; superiority: *the pursuit of excellence.* **2** an unusually good quality: *The inn was famous for the excellence of its food.* **3 Excellence,** Excellency; Your Excellency.

ex·cel·len·cy (ek′sə lən sē) *n.* **-cies. 1** excellence. **2 Excellency,** a title of honor used in speaking to or of the Governor General, an ambassador, a bishop, etc. *Abbrev.*: Exc.

ex·cel·lent (ek′sə lənt) *adj.* unusually good; better than others. [< L *excellens, -entis,* ppr. of *excellere* excel] —**ex′cel·lent·ly,** *adv.* —**Syn.** superior, meritorious, worthy, estimable, choice.

ex·cel·si·or (*adj.* ek sel′sē ôr; *n.* ek sel′sē ər) *adj. Latin.* ever upward; higher. —*n.* **1** short, fine, curled shavings of soft wood used as a stuffing for cushions and mattresses, and as a packing material. **2** a size of printing type (3 point). This sentence is set in excelsior. [< L *excelsior,* comparative of *excelsus* high, pp. of *excellere* excel]

ex·cept (ek sept′) *prep.* leaving out; but; other than: *every day except Sunday.*
—*v.* **1** take out; leave out; exclude: *Those who passed the first test were excepted from the second.* **2** make an objection; object.
—*conj. Archaic.* unless. [< L *exceptus*, pp. of *excipere* < *ex-* out + *capere* take]
Syn. *prep.* **Except, but** = leaving out. **Except** emphasizes the idea of leaving out, keeping out, or even shutting out: *Everyone was invited to the party except me.* **But** is unemphatic, and suggests more the idea of not taking in than of keeping out: *Everyone was invited but me.* ☞ See **accept** for usage note.

ex·cept·ing (ek sep′ting) *prep.* except; leaving out; other than. —*conj. Archaic.* unless.

ex·cep·tion (ek sep′shən) *n.* **1** a leaving out: *I like my studies, with the exception of German.* **2** a person or thing left out: *She praised them all, with two exceptions.* **3** an unusual instance; a case that does not follow the rule. **4** an objection. **5 take exception, a** object. **b** be offended: *The woman took exception to his remark.*

ex·cep·tion·a·ble (ek sep′shən ə bəl) *adj.* liable to exception; objectionable.

ex·cep·tion·al (ek sep′shən əl) *adj.* out of the ordinary; unusual: *This warm weather is exceptional for January.* —**ex·cep′tion·al·ly,** *adv.* —**Syn.** uncommon, singular, extraordinary.

ex·cerpt (*n.* ek′sėrpt; *v.* ek sėrpt′) *n.* a selected passage; quotation; extract: *The doctor read excerpts from several medical books.* —*v.* take out; select (passages) from; quote; make extracts from. [< L *excerptum*, pp. of *excerpere* < *ex-* out + *carpere* pluck]

ex·cess (*n.* ek ses′; *adj.* ek′ses or ek ses′) *n.* **1** more than enough; the part that is too much: *Pour off the excess.* **2** the amount or degree by which one thing is more than another: *The excess of 7 over 5 is 2.* **3** an action that goes beyond what is necessary or just: *The invaders burned and robbed houses and committed other excesses.* **4** the act or practice of eating or drinking too much; overindulgence; intemperance: *His excesses shortened his life.* **5** an extra charge. **6 in excess of,** more than. **7 to excess,** too much.
—*adj.* extra; more than the desirable amount: *excess baggage on a train.* [ME < OF < L *excessus* < *excedere.* See EXCEED.] —**Syn.** *n.* **1** surplus, superfluity. **4** dissipation, immoderation.

ex·ces·sive (ek ses′iv) *adj.* too much; too great; going beyond what is necessary or right: *Wise people will not buy when prices are excessive.* —**ex·cess′ive·ness,** *n.*
Syn. Excessive, exorbitant, inordinate = too much or too great. **Excessive** = going beyond what is right or normal in amount or extent: *Mary spends an excessive amount of time telephoning.* **Exorbitant** also = excessive, beyond what is proper or reasonable, and particularly describes demands: *He asked an exorbitant rent for the house.* **Inordinate** = going beyond what is in order, and suggests lack of restraint: *He has an inordinate appetite.*

ex·ces·sive·ly (ek ses′iv lē) *adv.* too much; too greatly.

excess profits tax a government tax on all business profits above a certain average for a specified term of years, or above a certain percentage of capital.

ex·change (eks chānj′) *v.* **-changed, -chang·ing,** *n.* —*v.* **1** give (for something else): *She would not exchange her house for a palace.* **2** give in trade for something regarded as equivalent: *I will exchange ten dimes for a dollar.* **3** give and receive (things of the same kind): *exchange letters.* **4** replace or have replaced (a purchase): *We can exchange no yard goods.* **5** make an exchange. **6** pass or be taken in exchange or as an equivalent.
—*n.* **1** an exchanging. **2** what is exchanged. **3** a place where things are exchanged. Stocks are bought, sold, and traded in a stock exchange. **4** a central office. A telephone exchange handles telephone calls. **5** a system of settling accounts in different places by exchanging bills of exchange that represent money instead of exchanging money itself. **6** the changing of the money of one country into the money of another. **7** a fee charged for settling accounts or changing money. **8** the rate of exchange; varying rate or sum in one currency given for a fixed sum in another currency. [ME < OF *eschangier* < VL *excambiare* < *ex-* out + *cambiare* change (< Celtic)] —**ex·chang′er,** *n.*
Syn. *v.* **2 Exchange, interchange** = give and take. **Exchange** emphasizes the idea of trading, or giving one thing and getting back another: *We exchanged blows.* **Interchange** emphasizes the idea of an even exchange, of taking turns giving and receiving or of giving back something equal in value or amount: *Delegates from different countries interchanged ideas.*

hat, āge, cãre, fär; let, ēqual, tėrm; it, īce
hot, ōpen, ôrder; oil, out; cup, pu̇t, rüle, ūse
əbove, takən, pencəl, lemən, circəs
ch, child; ng, long; sh, ship
th, thin; ᴛʜ, then; zh, measure

ex·change·a·bil·i·ty (eks chān′jə bil′ə tē) *n.* the state of being exchangeable.

ex·change·a·ble (eks chān′jə bəl) *adj.* capable of being exchanged.

exchange reaction in chemistry, a process in which atoms of the same element exchange positions within a molecule or between molecules.

ex·cheq·uer (eks chek′ər or eks′chek ər) *n.* **1** the treasury of a state or nation. **2** a treasury. **3** *Informal.* finances; funds. **4 Exchequer, a** the department of the British government in charge of its finances and the public revenues. **b** the offices of this department of the British government. **c** the funds of the British government. [ME < OF *eschequier* chessboard; because accounts were kept on a table marked in squares]

Exchequer Court a court having jurisdiction to hear legal actions brought by or against the Federal Government, absorbed in 1971 by the Federal Court of Canada.

ex·cise[1] (ek′sīz or ek sīz′) *n.* a tax on the manufacture, sale, or use of certain articles made, sold, or used within a country. There is an excise on tobacco. [apparently < MDu. *excijs* < OF *acceis* tax, ult. < L *ad-* to + *census* tax]

ex·cise[2] (ek sīz′) *v.* **-cised, -cis·ing.** cut out; remove: *The editor excised the objectionable passages from the book.* [< L *excisus*, pp. of *excidere* < *ex-* out + *caedere* cut]

ex·ci·sion (ek sizh′ən) *n.* **1** a cutting out; removal. **2** the state of being excised.

ex·cit·a·bil·i·ty (ek sīt′ə bil′ə tē) *n.* **1** the quality of being easily excited. **2** in physiology, the capacity to respond to a stimulus; irritability.

ex·cit·a·ble (ek sīt′ə bəl) *adj.* **1** capable of being excited; easily excited. **2** in physiology, sensitive to or capable of excitement. —**ex·cit′a·ble·ness,** *n.* —**ex·cit′a·bly,** *adv.*

ex·cit·ant (ek sī′tənt) *n.* **1** something that arouses or excites; stimulant. **2** the liquid that produces a magnetic field in an electric cell. —*adj.* stimulating; tending to arouse or excite.

ex·ci·ta·tion (ek′sī tā′shən) *n.* **1** an exciting. **2** a being excited. **3** the production of a magnetic field by means of electricity.

ex·cite (ek sīt′) *v.* **-cit·ed, -cit·ing. 1** stir up the feelings of: *The news of war excited everybody.* **2** arouse: *Her new dress excited envy.* **3** stir to action; stimulate: *If you do not excite the dog, he will keep still.* **4** in physiology, affect (an organ, tissue, etc.) so that its usual activity is aroused or intensified; stimulate. **5** produce an electric or magnetic field in (a dynamo, cyclotron, etc.). **6** displace an electron of (an atom) to a more distant orbit. [ME < L *excitare*, ult. < *ex-* out + *ciere* set in motion] —**ex·cit′ed·ly,** *adv.* —**Syn. 1** rouse, animate, kindle.

excited atom in nuclear physics, an atom having a higher energy level than is normal.

ex·cite·ment (ek sīt′mənt) *n.* **1** an exciting; arousing. **2** the state of being excited. **3** something that excites. —**Syn. 2** agitation, perturbation, commotion, ado.

ex·cit·er (ek sī′tər) *n.* **1** a person or thing that excites. **2** a dynamo, battery, etc. used to produce a magnetic field in another dynamo or motor. **3** a device for producing Hertzian waves.

ex·cit·ing (ek sīt′ing) *adj.* arousing; stirring.

ex·claim (eks klām′) *v.* say or speak suddenly in surprise or strong feeling; cry out. [< F < L *exclamare* < *ex-* + *clamare* cry out] —**Syn.** shout, ejaculate.

ex·cla·ma·tion (eks′klə mā′shən) *n.* **1** an exlaiming. **2** something exclaimed. *Ah!* and *oh!* are exclamations.

exclamation mark or **exclamation point** a mark of punctuation (!) used after exclamations. The exclamation mark is also used, within square brackets or, informally, parentheses, to suggest that some statement or situation is remarkable, absurd, or the like: "*William the Conqueror was born in Moose Jaw.*" (!)

ex·clam·a·to·ry (eks klam′ə tô′rē) *adj.* using, containing, or expressing exclamation.

ex·clude (eks klüd′) *v.* **-clud·ed, -clud·ing. 1** shut out; keep out. **2** drive out and keep out; expel: *Perfect faith excludes doubt.* **3** give no place to; prevent the existence, occurrence, or use of. **4** reject from consideration, notice, or use: *exclude a bid.* [ME < L *excludere* < *ex-* out + *claudere* shut] —**ex·clud′er,** *n.*

Syn. 1 Exclude, eliminate = keep out. **Exclude** emphasizes keeping someone or something from coming in to a place, thought, rights, etc.: *Closing the windows excludes street noises.* **Eliminate** emphasizes putting out something already in, by getting rid of it or shutting it off from attention: *He eliminated fear from his thinking.* **2** eject, exile.

ex·clu·sion (eks klü′zhən) *n.* **1** an excluding. **2** a being excluded. **3 to the exclusion of,** so as to shut out or keep out. [< L *exclusio, -onis* < *excludere.* See EXCLUDE.]

ex·clu·sive (eks klü′siv or eks klü′ziv) *adj.* **1** each shutting out the other. "Baby" and "adult" are exclusive terms since a person cannot be both. **2** shutting out all or most: *This school is exclusive; only very bright children can go to it.* **3** not divided or shared with others; single; sole: *An inventor has an exclusive right for a certain number of years to make what he has invented and patented.* **4** very selective in choosing friends, members, patrons, etc.: *It is hard to get admitted to an exclusive club.* **5 exclusive of,** excluding; leaving out; not counting or considering: *There are 26 days in that month, exclusive of Sundays.* —**ex·clu′sive·ly,** *adv.* —**ex·clu′sive·ness,** *n.* —**Syn. 4** select, clannish, snobbish.

ex·com·mu·ni·cate (eks′kə mū′nə kāt′) *v.* **-cat·ed, -cat·ing.** cut off from membership in a church; expel formally from the fellowship of a church; prohibit from participating in any of the rites of a church. [< LL *excommunicare,* literally, put out of the fellowship (of the Church) < L *ex-* out of + *communis* common]

ex·com·mu·ni·ca·tion (eks′kə mū′nə kā′shən) *n.* **1** a formal expulsion from the fellowship of a church; prohibition from participating in any of the rites of a church. **2** the formal, official statement announcing excommunication. **3** the condition or state of a person who has been excommunicated.

ex·co·ri·ate (eks kô′rē āt′) *v.* **-at·ed, -at·ing. 1** strip or rub off the skin of; make raw and sore. **2** denounce violently. [< LL *excoriare* < *ex-* off + *corium* hide, skin] —**ex·co′ri·a′tion,** *n.*

ex·cre·ment (eks′krə mənt) *n.* waste matter that is discharged from the body, especially from the bowels. [< L *excrementum,* ult. < *excernere* < *ex-* out + *cernere* sift]

ex·cre·men·tal (eks′krə men′təl) *adj.* of or like excrement.

ex·cres·cence (eks kres′əns) *n.* **1** an unnatural growth; a disfiguring addition. Warts are excrescences on the skin. **2** a natural outgrowth. Fingernails are excrescences. **3** an abnormal increase; outflow (of anything).

ex·cres·cent (eks kres′ənt) *adj.* **1** forming an unnatural growth or a disfiguring addition. **2** in phonetics, (of a sound) present for no historical or grammatical reason, as *b* in *thimble,* derived from Old English *thymle.* [< L *excrescens, -entis,* ppr. of *excrescere* < *ex-* out + *crescere* grow]

ex·cre·ta (eks krē′tə) *n.pl.* waste matter discharged from the body, such as sweat or urine. [< L *excreta,* neut. pl. of *excretus,* pp. of *excernere.* See EXCREMENT.]

ex·crete (eks krēt′) *v.* **-cret·ed, -cret·ing.** discharge (waste matter) from the body; separate (waste matter) from the blood or tissues. The skin excretes sweat. [< L *excretus,* pp. of *excernere.* See EXCREMENT.]

ex·cre·tion (eks krē′shən) *n.* **1** the discharge of waste matter from the body; the separation of waste matter from the blood or tissues. **2** the waste matter discharged from the body: waste matter separated from the blood or tissues. Sweat is an excretion.

ex·cre·tive (eks krē′tiv) *adj.* excreting; serving to excrete.

ex·cre·to·ry (eks′krə tô′rē) *adj.* of or having to do with excretion; that excrete: *The kidneys are excretory organs.*

ex·cru·ci·at·ing (eks krü′shē āt′ing) *adj.* very painful; torturing; causing great suffering. [< *excruciate* crucify, torture < L *excruciare* < *ex-* utterly + *cruciare* torture, crucify < *crux, crucis* cross] —**ex·cru′ci·at′ing·ly,** *adv.*

ex·cul·pate (eks′kəl pāt′ or eks kul′pāt) *v.* **-pat·ed, -pat·ing.** free from blame; prove innocent. [< Med.L **exculpare* < L *ex-* out + *culpa* guilt]

ex·cul·pa·tion (eks′kəl pā′shən) *n.* **1** a freeing from blame; a proving innocent. **2** a vindication; proof of innocence; excuse.

ex·cur·sion (eks kėr′zhən or eks kėr′shən) *n.* **1** a short journey made with the intention of returning; a pleasure trip: *Our club went on an excursion to the mountains.* **2** a trip on an aircraft, a train, ship, etc. at lower fares than are usually charged. **3** a group of people who go on an excursion. **4** a sally; raid. **5** a wandering from the subject; deviation; digression. [< L *excursio, -onis* < *excurrere* < *ex-* out + *currere* run] —**Syn. 1** expedition, tour, jaunt.

ex·cur·sion·ist (eks kėr′zhən ist or eks kėr′shən ist) *n.* a person who goes on an excursion.

ex·cur·sive (eks kėr′siv) *adj.* off the subject; wandering; rambling. —**ex·cur′sive·ly,** *adv.*

ex·cuse (*v.* eks kūz′; *n.* eks kūs′) *v.* **-cused, -cus·ing,** *n.* —*v.* **1** overlook (a fault, etc.); pardon; forgive. **2** give a reason or apology for; try to clear of blame: *She excused her own faults by blaming others.* **3** be a reason or explanation for; clear of blame: *Sickness excused his absence from school.* **4** free from duty or obligation; let off: *Those who passed the first test are excused from the second one.* **5** not demand or require; dispense with: *We will excuse your presence.* **6** seek or obtain exemption or release for. **7 excuse oneself, a** ask to be pardoned. **b** ask permission to leave.

—*n.* **1** a real or pretended reason or explanation. **2** an apology given. **3** the act of excusing. [ME < OF < L *excusare* < *ex-* away + *causa* cause] —**ex·cus′a·ble,** *adj.* —**ex·cus′a·bly,** *adv.* —**ex·cus′er,** *n.*

Syn. *v.* **1 Excuse, pardon, forgive** = free from blame or punishment. **Excuse** = overlook, or let off with only disapproval, less important errors and faults: *This time he excused my carelessness.* **Pardon,** more formal in tone, means free from punishment due for serious faults, wrongdoing, or crimes: *The governor pardoned the thief.* **Forgive** suggests more personal feeling, and emphasizes giving up all wish to punish for a wrong done: *He forgave his brother for leaving home.* **3** justify, extenuate. –*n.* **1** justification. **2 Excuse, apology** = something said to explain an offence or failure. **Excuse** suggests trying to justify a mistake or failure or to make it seem less serious, in order to escape being blamed or punished: *He is always late, and always has an excuse.* **Apology** suggests admitting that one has, or seems to have, done or been wrong and expressing regret: *He offered his apology for damaging my car.*

☛ **excuse, pardon.** "Pardon me" is sometimes considered more elegant than "Excuse me" in upper-class social situations. "I beg (your) pardon" or "Pardon me" is a standard formula meaning "I didn't hear what you said." *Excuse* has also the special meaning of "give permission to leave."

exec. 1 executive. **2** executor.

ex·e·cra·ble (ek′sə krə bəl) *adj.* abominable; detestable. —**ex′e·cra·ble·ness,** *n.* —**ex′e·cra·bly,** *adv.*

ex·e·crate (ek′sə krāt′) *v.* **-crat·ed, -crat·ing. 1** abhor; loathe; detest. **2** curse. [< L *ex(s)ecrare* < *ex-* completely + *sacer* accursed] —**ex′e·crat′or,** *n.*

ex·e·cra·tion (ek′sə krā′shən) *n.* **1** abhorrence; loathing; detestation. **2** a cursing. **3** a curse: *The mob shouted angry execrations.* **4** a person or thing execrated.

ex·e·cute (ek′sə kūt′) *v.* **-cut·ed, -cut·ing. 1** carry out; do: *The nurse executed the doctor's orders.* **2** put into effect; enforce: *The will was executed by the lawyer.* **3** put to death according to law: *The murderer was executed.* **4** make according to a plan or design: *An artist executes a painting or statue.* **5** perform or play (a piece of music). **6** make (a deed, lease, contract, will, etc.) legal by signing, sealing, or doing whatever else is necessary. [ME < OF < Med.L *ex(s)ecutare* < *ex(s)ecutus,* pp. of *exsequi* < *ex* out + *sequi* follow] —**Syn. 1** accomplish, fulfil, complete. See **perform. 3** kill, hang, electrocute, behead.

ex·e·cu·tion (ek′sə kū′shən) *n.* **1** a carrying out; a doing; a performing. **2** a putting into effect; an enforcing. **3** a way of carrying out or doing; skill. **4** a manner of performing or playing a piece of music. **5** a putting to death according to law. **6** a making according to a plan or design. **7** a making legal by signing, sealing, or doing what is necessary. **8** a written order from a court directing a judgment to be carried out. **9 do execution,** have a destructive effect; have an effective action.

ex·e·cu·tion·er (ek′sə kū′shən ər or ek′sə kūsh′nər) *n.* a person who puts criminals to death according to law.

ex·ec·u·tive (eg zek′yů tiv) *adj.* **1** having to do with carrying out or managing affairs: *an executive committee. The head of a school has an executive position.* **2** having the duty and power of putting the laws into effect: *The Cabinet is the executive branch of our government.*
—*n.* **1** a person who carries out or manages affairs: *The president of a company is an executive.* **2** a person, group, or branch of government that has the duty and power of putting the laws into effect. **3** a group of people responsible for running the affairs of a society, association, etc. —**ex·ec′u·tive·ly,** *adv.*

Executive Council in Canada, the cabinet of a provincial government, consisting of the Premier and his ministers.

ex·ec·u·tor (eg zek′yů tər *for 1*; ek′sə kū′tər *for 2*) *n.* **1** a person named in a will to carry out the provisions of the will. **2** a person who performs or carries out things. [ME < AF *executour* < L *ex(s)ecutor* < *exsequi.* See EXECUTE.]

ex·ec·u·trix (eg zek′yů triks′) *n.* a female executor.

ex·e·ge·sis (ek′sə jē′sis) *n.* **-ses** (-sēz). **1** a scholarly explanation or interpretation of the Bible or of a passage in the Bible: *The minister gave an exegesis of the parable of the Good Samaritan.* **2** an explanation or interpretation of a word, sentence, etc.; explanatory note. [< Gk. *exēgēsis* < *ex-* out + *hēgeesthai* lead, guide]

ex·e·get·ic (ek′sə jet′ik) *adj.* having to do with exegesis; expository.

ex·e·get·i·cal (ek′sə jet′ə kəl) *adj.* exegetic.

ex·em·plar (eg zem′plər or eg zem′plär) *n.* **1** a person or thing worth imitating; model; pattern: *He is the exemplar of all parents.* **2** a typical case; example. [ME < L *exemplar* < *exemplum.* See EXAMPLE.]

ex·em·pla·ry (eg zem′plə rē or eg′zəm pler′ē) *adj.* **1** worth imitating; being a good model or pattern: *exemplary conduct.* **2** serving as a warning to others: *exemplary punishment of the ringleaders.* **3** serving as an example; typical. [< L *exemplaris* < *exemplum.* See EXAMPLE.]

ex·em·pli·fi·ca·tion (eg zem′plə fə kā′shən) *n.* **1** a showing by example; a being an example. **2** an example.

ex·em·pli·fy (eg zem′plə fī′) *v.* **-fied, -fy·ing.** show by example; be an example of: *The knights exemplified courage and courtesy.* [< Med.L *exemplificare* < L *exemplum* example + *facere* make]

ex·em·pli gra·ti·a (eg zem′plī grā′shē ə or eg zem′plē gra′tē ə) *Latin.* for example; for instance. *Abbrev.*: e.g.

ex·empt (eg zempt′) *v.* make free (from a duty, obligation, rule, etc.); release: *Students who get very high marks will be exempted from the final examination.*
—*adj.* freed from a duty, obligation, rule, etc.; released: *The school property is exempt from taxes.*
—*n.* an exempt person. [ME < OF < L *exemptus,* pp. of *eximere* < *ex-* out + *emere* take]

ex·emp·tion (eg zemp′shən) *n.* **1** the act of exempting. **2** freedom from a duty, obligation, rule, etc.; release. **3** such a release or a cause permitting one: *income-tax exemptions.*
Syn. 2 Exemption, immunity = freedom from obligation or duty. **Exemption** emphasizes freeing a person or thing from some obligation, rule, etc. required of or applied to others: *Churches have exemption from taxes.* **Immunity** emphasizes being protected from obligations, restrictions, and penalties to which other people are liable: *Members of Parliament have immunity from jury duty.*

ex·er·cise (ek′sər sīz′) *n. v.* **-cised, -cis·ing.** —*n.* **1** active use to give practice and training or to cause improvement: *Exercise of the body is needed for health.* **2** something that gives practice and training or causes improvement: *Study the lesson, and then do the exercises at the end.* **3** an active use: *Road safety requires the exercise of care in driving.* **4** Often, **exercises,** *pl.* a ceremony.
—*v.* **1** give exercise to; train. **2** take exercise. **3** use actively: *Exercise care in crossing streets.* **4** carry out in action; perform: *The mayor exercises the duties and powers of his office.* **5** have as an effect: *What others think exercises a great influence on most of us.* **6** occupy the attention of. **7** make uneasy; worry; trouble; annoy: *When her plan failed, she was greatly exercised.* [ME < OF *exercice* < L *exercitium* < *exercere* not allow to rest < *ex-* + *arcere* keep away] —**ex′er·cis′er,** *n.*
Syn. *n* **1 Exercise, practice, drill** = active use of physical or mental power for training or improvement. **Exercise** emphasizes repeated use of mental or physical powers to develop strength, health, and energy: *Exercise of the mind increases its power.* **Practice** applies to action repeated often and regularly to develop skill or gain perfection, especially in the use of a particular power: *Learning to play the piano well takes much practice.* **Drill** = constant repetition of a particular kind of exercise to discipline the body or mind and develop correct habits: *Children need drill in spelling.*
3 employment, application. –*v.* **1** discipline, drill. **3** employ, apply.

hat, āge, cãre, fär; let, ēqual, tėrm; it, īce
hot, ōpen, ôrder; oil, out; cup, pův, rüle, ūse
əbove, takən, pencəl, lemən, circəs
ch, child; ng, long; sh, ship
th, thin; ᴛʜ, then; zh, measure

ex·ert (eg zėrt′) *v.* **1** use; use actively; put into action: *A clever fighter exerts both strength and skill. A ruler exerts authority.* **2 exert oneself,** make an effort; try hard; strive. [< L *ex(s)ertus,* pp. of *ex(s)erere* thrust out < *ex-* out + *serere* attach]

ex·er·tion (eg zėr′shən) *n.* **1** effort: *The exertions of the firemen kept the fire from spreading.* **2** a putting into action; active use; use: *Unwise exertion of authority may cause rebellion.* —**Syn. 1** endeavor, struggle, attempt.

ex·e·unt (ek′sē ənt or ek′sē ůnt) *v. Latin.* in stage directions, the signal for actors to leave the stage. It is the plural of **exit** and means "They go out."

ex·ha·la·tion (eks′hə lā′shən) *n.* **1** an exhaling. Breathing out is an exhalation of air. **2** something exhaled; air, vapor, smoke, odor, etc.

ex·hale (eks hāl′) *v.* **-haled, -hal·ing. 1** breathe out: *Exhale air from the lungs.* **2** give off (air, vapor, smoke, odor, etc.). **3** pass off as vapor; rise like vapor: *Sweet odors exhale from the flowers.* **4** change into vapor; evaporate. [< F < L *exhalare* < *ex-* out + *halare* breathe]

ex·haust (eg zost′ or eg zôst′) *v.* **1** empty completely: *exhaust a well.* **2** use up: *exhaust one's money.* **3** tire very much: *The climb up the hill exhausted us.* **4** drain of strength, resources, etc.: *The long war exhausted the country.* **5** draw off: *exhaust the air in a jar.* **6** leave nothing important to be found out or said about; study or treat thoroughly: *Her book about tulips exhausted the subject.* **7** be discharged; go forth: *Gases from an automobile exhaust through a pipe.* **8** deprive wholly of useful or essential properties: *exhaust the soil.* **9** deprive of ingredients by the use of solvents.
—*n.* **1** the escape of used steam, gasoline, etc. from a machine. **2** a means or way for used steam, gasoline, etc. to escape from an engine. **3** the used steam, gasoline, etc. that escapes. [< L *exhaustus,* pp. of *exhaurire* < *ex-* out, off + *haurire* draw] —**ex·haust′er,** *n.* —**Syn.** *v.* **1** drain, deplete. **2** consume. **3** fatigue.

ex·haust·ed (eg zos′tid or eg zôs′tid) *adj.* **1** used up. **2** worn out; very tired. —**ex·haust′ed·ly,** *adv.* —**Syn. 2** See **tired.**

ex·haust·i·bil·i·ty (eg zos′tə bil′ə tē or eg zôs′tə bil′ə tē) *n.* the quality of being exhaustible; capability of being exhausted.

ex·haust·i·ble (eg zos′tə bəl or eg zôs′tə bəl) *adj.* capable of being exhausted.

ex·haus·tion (eg zos′chən or eg zôs′chən) *n.* **1** an exhausting. **2** a being exhausted. **3** extreme fatigue. —**Syn. 3** weariness, lassitude, languor.

ex·haus·tive (eg zos′tiv or eg zôs′tiv) *adj.* leaving out nothing important; thorough; comprehensive: *The students were given an exhaustive examination.*
—**ex·haust′ive·ly,** *adv.* —**ex·haust′ive·ness,** *n.*
☛ Do not confuse **exhaustive** with **exhausting.** An *exhaustive* lecture on Vitamin A would be *exhausting* to an eighth-grade class, but appropriate in a medical school.

ex·haust·less (eg zost′lis or eg zôst′lis) *adj.* that cannot be exhausted.

ex·hib·it (eg zib′it) *v.* **1** show; display. **2** show publicly. **3** show in court as evidence; submit for consideration or inspection.
—*n.* **1** a show; display. **2** the thing or things shown publicly. **3** a public show; small exhibition; part of an exhibition. **4** a document or other thing shown in court and referred to in written evidence. [< L *exhibitus,* pp. of *exhibere* < *ex-* out + *habere* hold]
Syn. *v.* **1** manifest, evince, reveal, disclose. See **display.**
-n. **2, 3 Exhibit, exhibition** = a public show. **Exhibit** applies particularly to an object or collection of things put on view at a fair, exhibition, or other public show: *His lambs were part of the school's exhibit at the county fair.* **Exhibition** applies to a public show of works of art, rare objects of any kind, commercial objects, etc.: *The city holds an exhibition of all its different products every year.*

ex·hi·bi·tion (ek′sə bish′ən) *n.* **1** a showing; display: *Such an exhibition of bad manners I never saw.* **2** a public show: *The art school holds an exhibition every year.* **3** a thing or things shown publicly; exhibit. **4** a public showing of livestock, produce, manufactured goods, etc., accompanied by amusements such as sideshows, rides, games, and other forms of entertainment; a big fair: *the Canadian National Exhibition.* —**Syn. 2** exposition. See **exhibit.**

ex·hi·bi·tion·ism (ek′sə bish′ən iz′əm) *n.* **1** an excessive tendency to seek attention or to show off one's abilities. **2** a morbid tendency toward the indecent exposure of the body.

ex·hi·bi·tion·ist (ek′sə bish′ən ist) *n.* **1** a person who tends to seek attention or show off his abilities excessively. **2** one given to the indecent exposure of the body.

ex·hib·i·tor or **ex·hib·it·er** (eg zib′ə tər) *n.* a person, company, or group that exhibits.

ex·hil·a·rate (eg zil′ə rāt′) *v.* **-rat·ed, -rat·ing.** make merry or lively; put into high spirits; stimulate. [< L *exhilarare* < *ex-* thoroughly + *hilaris* merry]
—**ex·hil′a·rat·or,** *n.*

ex·hil·a·ra·tion (eg zil′ə rā′shən) *n.* **1** an exhilarating. **2** a being or feeling exhilarated; high spirits; stimulation.

ex·hort (eg zôrt′) *v.* urge strongly; advise or warn earnestly: *The preacher exhorted his congregation to live better lives.* [< L *exhortari* < *ex-* + *hortari* urge strongly] —**ex·hort′er,** *n.*

ex·hor·ta·tion (eg′zôr tā′shən or ek′sôr tā′shən) *n.* **1** a strong urging; earnest advice or warning. **2** a speech, sermon, etc. that exhorts.

ex·hor·ta·tive (eg zôr′tə tiv) *adj.* exhortatory.

ex·hor·ta·to·ry (eg zôr′tə tô′rē) *adj.* urging; intended to exhort; admonitory.

ex·hu·ma·tion (eks′hū mā′shən) *n.* an exhuming.

ex·hume (eks hūm′ or eg zūm′) *v.* **-humed, -hum·ing.** **1** take out of a grave or out of the ground; dig up. **2** reveal. [< Med.L *exhumare* < L *ex-* out of + *humus* ground]

ex·i·gence (ek′sə jəns) *n.* exigency.

ex·i·gen·cy (ek′sə jən sē) *n.* **-cies. 1** Usually, **exigencies,** *pl.* an urgent need; demand for immediate action or attention: *The exigencies of business kept him from leaving town.* **2** a situation demanding immediate action or attention; urgent case.

ex·i·gent (ek′sə jənt) *adj.* **1** demanding immediate action or attention; urgent: *The exigent pangs of hunger sent him on a search for food.* **2** demanding a great deal; exacting. [< L *exigens, -entis,* ppr. of *exigere.* See EXACT.]

ex·i·gu·i·ty (ek′sə gū′ə tē) *n.* scantiness; smallness.

ex·ig·u·ous (eg zig′ū əs or ek sig′ū əs) *adj.* scanty; small. [< L *exiguus* scanty, originally, weighed out (sparingly) < *exigere.* See EXACT.] —**ex·ig′u·ous·ly,** *adv.* —**ex·ig′u·ous·ness,** *n.*

ex·ile (eg′zīl or ek′sīl) *v.* **-iled, -il·ing,** *n.* —*v.* force (a person) to leave his country or home; banish: *After the revolution many people were exiled from the country.*
—*n.* **1** a being exiled; banishment: *Napoleon's exile to Elba was brief.* **2** an exiled person. **3** any prolonged absence from one's own country. [ME < OF *exilier* < LL *exiliare* < L *ex(s)ilium*] —**Syn.** *v.* expel, expatriate. See **banish.** *-n.* **1** expulsion.

ex·im·port (eks′im pôrt) *n. Cdn. Slang.* in football, a non-Canadian, who, after playing in the country for a certain number of years, qualifies as a Canadian player.

ex·ist (eg zist′) *v.* **1** have actual existence; be; be real. **2** continue to be; live; have life. **3** be present; occur. **4** be recorded; be known as a matter of record. [< F *exister* < L *ex(s)istere* < *ex-* forth + *sistere* stand]

ex·ist·ence (eg zis′təns) *n.* **1** real or actual being; being. **2** continued being; living; life. **3** an occurrence; presence. **4** all that exists. **5** something that exists.

ex·ist·ent (eg zis′tənt) *adj.* **1** existing. **2** existing now; of the present time.

ex·is·ten·tial (eg′zis ten′shəl or ek′sis ten′shəl) *adj.* **1** of or having to do with existence. **2** of or having to do with existentialism: *an existential play.* —**ex′is·ten′tial·ly,** *adv.*

ex·is·ten·tial·ism (eg′zis ten′shəl iz′əm or ek′sis ten′shəl iz′əm) *n.* a system of philosophy that avoids thought-out theories on life and holds that man is free, and responsible to himself alone, and that reality consists in living.

ex·is·ten·tial·ist (eg′zis ten′shə list or ek′sis ten′shə list) *adj.* having to do with or resembling existentialism. —*n.* a person who supports or follows the philosophy of existentialism.

ex·it (eg′zit or ek′sit) *n.* **1** a way out: *The theatre had six exits.* **2** a going out; departure. **3** the act of leaving the stage: *The actor made a graceful exit.* **4** opportunity to go out. **5** death.
—*v.* **1** go out; depart. **2** in stage directions, the signal for an actor to leave the stage. [< L *exit* goes out; also < L *exitus* a going out; both < *ex-* out + *ire* go]

ex li·bris (eks′ lī′bris or lē′bris) *Latin.* **1** from among the books (of). **2** an inscription or device in or on a book to indicate the owner; bookplate.

ex·o·bi·ol·o·gy (ek′sō bī ol′ə jē) *n.* the study of life on other planets or celestial bodies.

Exod. Exodus.

ex·o·dus (ek′sə dəs) *n.* **1** a going out; departure: *Every summer there is an exodus from the city.* **2** Often, **Exodus.** the departure of the Israelites from Egypt under Moses. **3 Exodus,** the second book of the Old Testament, containing an account of this departure. [< L < Gk. *exodos* < *ex-* out + *hodos* way]

ex of·fi·ci·o (eks′ ə fish′ē ō) because of one's office: *The secretary is, ex officio, a member of all committees.* [< L]

ex·og·e·nous (eks oj′ə nəs) *adj.* **1** in botany, having stems that grow by the addition of layers of wood on the outside under the bark. **2** originating from the outside; caused by external conditions. [< NL *exogenus* growing on the outside < Gk. *exō-* outside + *-genēs* born, produced]

ex·on·er·ate (eg zon′ər āt′) *v.* **-at·ed, -at·ing. 1** free from blame; prove or declare innocent: *Witnesses of the accident completely exonerated the driver of the truck.* **2** relieve from a duty, task, obligation, etc. [< L *exonerare* < *ex-* off + *onus, oneris* burden]
—**ex·on′er·a′tion,** *n.* —**ex·on′er·a′tor,** *n.*

ex·or·bi·tance (eg zôr′bə təns) *n.* a being exorbitant.

ex·or·bi·tant (eg zôr′bə tənt) *adj.* exceeding what is customary, proper, or reasonable; excessive: *Two dollars is an exorbitant price for a dozen eggs.* [< L *exorbitans, -antis,* ppr. of *exorbitare* go out of the track < *ex-* out of + *orbita* track] —**Syn.** See **excessive.**

ex·or·bi·tant·ly (eg zôr′bə tənt lē) *adv.* **1** extravagantly. **2** in an excessive degree or amount; beyond reasonable limits.

ex·or·cise (ek′sôr sīz′) *v.* **-cised, -cis·ing. 1** drive out (an evil spirit) by prayers, ceremonies, etc. **2** free (a person or place) from an evil spirit. [< LL *exorcizare* < Gk. *exorkizein* bind by oath, conjure, exorcise < *ex-* + *horkos* oath] —**ex′or·cis′er,** *n.*

ex·or·cism (ek′sôr siz′əm) *n.* **1** an exorcising. **2** the prayers, ceremonies, etc. used in exorcising.

ex·or·cist (ek′sôr sist) *n.* a person who exorcises.

ex·or·cize (ek′sôr sīz′) *v.* **-cized, -ciz·ing.** exorcise.

ex·or·di·um (eg zôr′dē əm or ek sôr′dē əm) *n.* **-di·ums, -di·a** (-dē ə). **1** the beginning. **2** the introductory part of a speech, treatise, etc. [< L *exordium* < *ex-* + *ordiri* begin, originally, begin a web]

ex·o·skel·e·tal (ek′sō skel′ə təl) *adj.* of or having to do with the exoskeleton.

ex·o·skel·e·ton (ek′sō skel′ə tən) *n.* in zoology, any hard, external, protective covering or structure, such as the shells of turtles and lobsters. [< Gk. *exo-* outside + E *skeleton*]

ex·o·sphere (eks′ō sfēr′) *n.* the outermost rim of the earth's atmosphere; the layer of the atmosphere in which the ionosphere begins to merge with interplanetary space.

ex·o·ter·ic (ek′sə ter′ik) *adj.* **1** capable of being understood by the general public. **2** not belonging to an inner circle of disciples, scholars, etc. **3** popular; well-known; commonplace; opposed to *esoteric.* [< LL *exotericus* < Gk. *exōterikos* < *exō-* outside < *ek* out of]

ex·ot·ic (eg zot′ik) *adj.* **1** foreign; strange; not native: *We saw many exotic plants at the Flower Show.* **2** *Informal.* beautiful or fascinating because of strangeness. *—n.* anything exotic. [< L *exoticus* < Gk. *exōtikos* < *exō-* outside < *ek* out of] **—ex·ot′i·cal·ly,** *adv.*

ex·ot·i·cism (eg zot′ə siz′əm) *n.* **1** the state or quality of being exotic. **2** something such as a foreign word or phrase.

exp. 1 export. **2** exportation. **3** express. **4** expenses. **5** expired.

ex·pand (eks pand′) *v.* **1** increase in size; enlarge; swell: *The balloon expanded as it filled with air.* **2** spread out; open out; unfold; extend: *A bird expands its wings before flying.* **3** express in fuller form or greater detail: *The writer expanded one sentence into a paragraph.* [< L *expandere* < *ex-* out + *pandere* spread. Doublet of SPAWN.] **—ex·pand′er,** *n.* **—ex·pand′ing·ly,** *adv.*

Syn. 1 Expand, swell, dilate = make or become larger. **Expand** emphasizes spreading out or opening out in any or all directions: *Our interests expand as we grow.* **Swell** emphasizes growing bigger, getting higher or bigger around than normal, usually from pressure inside or from having something added: *His abscessed tooth made his face swell.* **Dilate** = widen, and applies particularly to circular or hollow things: *The pupils of her eyes dilated in the darkness.* **2** unfurl.

ex·panse (eks pans′) *n.* **1** a large, unbroken space or stretch; wide, spreading surface: *The Pacific Ocean is a vast expanse of water.* **2** the amount or distance of expansion. [< L *expansum,* pp. neut. of *expandere.* See EXPAND.]

ex·pan·si·bil·i·ty (eks pan′sə bil′ə tē) *n.* a capacity for expanding.

ex·pan·si·ble (eks pan′sə bəl) *adj.* capable of being expanded.

ex·pan·sile (eks pan′sīl or eks pan′səl) *adj.* **1** capable of expanding; of such a nature as to expand. **2** of or having to do with expansion.

ex·pan·sion (eks pan′shən) *n.* **1** an expanding: *Heat caused the expansion of the gas.* **2** a being expanded; increase in size, volume, etc.: *The expansion of the factory made room for more machines.* **3** the amount or degree of expansion. **4** an expanded part or form. **5** in an engine, the increase in bulk of the power medium which takes place in a cylinder. **6** in mathematics, the fuller development of an indicated operation: *The expansion of* $(a + b)^3$ *is* $a^3 + 3a^2b + 3ab^2 + b^3$. [< LL *expansio, -onis* < *expandere.* See EXPAND.]

ex·pan·sion·ar·y (ek span′shə ner′ē) *adj.* **1** having to do with or tending to expansion or expansionism. **2** inflationary.

ex·pan·sion·ism (ek span′shə niz′əm) *n.* a policy of territorial or commercial expansion, usually at the expense of weaker rivals.

ex·pan·sion·ist (ek span′shən ist) *n.* a supporter or advocate of expansionism. *—adj.* of, having to do with, or favoring expansionism.

ex·pan·sive (eks pan′siv) *adj.* **1** capable of expanding; tending to expand. **2** wide; spreading. **3** taking in much or many things; broad; extensive. **4** showing one's feelings freely and openly; unrestrained; effusive. **—ex·pan′sive·ly,** *adv.* **—ex·pan′sive·ness,** *n.*

ex par·te (eks′ pär′tē) *Latin.* **1** from one side only. **2** in the interest of only one side.

hat, āge, cãre, fär; let, ēqual, tėrm; it, īce
hot, ōpen, ôrder; oil, out; cup, pu̇t, rüle, ūse
əbove, takən, pencəl, lemən, circəs
ch, child; ng, long; sh, ship
th, thin; ᴛʜ, then; zh, measure

ex·pa·ti·ate (eks pā′shē āt′) *v.* **-at·ed, -at·ing. 1** write or talk much (*on*): *She expatiated on the thrills of her trip.* **2** roam or wander freely. [< L *ex(s)patiari* walk about < *ex-* out + *spatium* space] **—ex·pa′ti·a′tor,** *n.*

ex·pa·ti·a·tion (eks pā′shē ā′shən) *n.* **1** the act of writing or talking much. **2** an extended talk, description, etc.

ex·pa·tri·ate (*v.* eks pā′trē āt′; *adj. n.* eks pā′trē it or eks pā′trē āt′) *v.* **-at·ed, -at·ing,** *adj. n.* *—v.* **1** banish; exile. **2** withdraw (oneself) from one's country; renounce one's citizenship. *—adj.* expatriated. *—n.* an expatriated person; exile or emigrant. [< LL *expatriare* < L *ex-* out of + *patria* fatherland]

ex·pa·tri·a·tion (eks pā′trē ā′shən) *n.* **1** a banishment; exile. **2** a withdrawal from one's country; renunciation of one's citizenship.

ex·pect (eks pekt′) *v.* **1** look forward to; think likely to come or happen. **2** look forward to with reason or confidence; desire and feel sure of getting. **3** count on as necessary or right. **4** *Informal.* think; suppose; guess. [< L *ex(s)pectare* < *ek-* out + *specere* look]

ex·pect·ance (eks pek′təns) *n.* expectation.

ex·pect·an·cy (eks pek′tən sē) *n.* **-cies. 1** expectation; anticipation. **2** something expected or that can be expected: *Medical science is constantly raising our life expectancy.*

ex·pect·ant (eks pek′tənt) *adj.* **1** having expectations; anticipating pleasure; expecting. **2** showing expectation: *She opened her Christmas present with an expectant smile.* **3 expectant mother,** one who is expecting a baby. **—*n.*** a person who expects something. **—ex·pect′ant·ly,** *adv.*

ex·pec·ta·tion (eks′pek tā′shən) *n.* **1** an expecting or being expected; anticipation of pleasure. **2** something expected. **3** a ground for expecting something; prospect: *He has expectations of inheriting money from a rich uncle.* **—Syn. 1** hope.

expectation of life the average number of years that a person of a certain age can expect to live.

ex·pec·to·rant (eks pek′tə rənt) *adj.* causing or helping the discharge of phlegm, etc. *—n.* a medicine that promotes expectoration.

ex·pec·to·rate (eks pek′tə rāt′) *v.* **-rat·ed, -rat·ing.** cough up and spit out (phlegm, etc.); spit. [< L *expectorare* < *ex-* out of + *pectus, pectoris* breast] **—ex·pec′to·ra′tor,** *n.*

ex·pec·to·ra·tion (eks pek′tə rā′shən) *n.* **1** the act of expectorating. **2** the expectorated matter.

ex·pe·di·ence (eks pē′dē əns) *n.* expediency.

ex·pe·di·en·cy (eks pē′dē ən sē) *n.* **-cies. 1** usefulness; suitability for bringing about a desired result; desirability or fitness under the circumstances. **2** personal advantage; self-interest: *The dishonest lawyer was influenced more by expediency than by love of justice.*

ex·pe·di·ent (eks pē′dē ənt) *adj.* **1** fit for bringing about a desired result; desirable or suitable under the circumstances. **2** giving or seeking personal advantage; based on self-interest.
—n. **1** a means of bringing about a desired result: *Having no ladder or rope, the prisoner tied sheets together and escaped by this expedient.* **2** a cunning way of doing something. [< L *expediens, -entis,* ppr. of *expedire* free from a net, set right < *ex-* out + *pes, pedis* foot] **—ex·pe′di·ent·ly,** *adv.* **—Syn.** *adj.* **1** advantageous, profitable, advisable. *-n.* **1** shift device.

ex·pe·dite (eks′pə dīt′) *v.* **-dit·ed, -dit·ing. 1** make easy and quick; speed up: *If everyone will help, it will expedite matters.* **2** do quickly. **3** issue officially. [< L *expeditus,* pp. of *expedire.* See EXPEDIENT.]

ex·pe·dit·er (eks′pə dīt′ər) *n.* **1** a person who is responsible for supplying raw materials or delivering finished products on schedule. **2** a person who issues official statements and decisions.

ex·pe·di·tion (eks′pə dish′ən) *n.* **1** a journey for some special purpose. A voyage of discovery or a military march against the enemy is an expedition. **2** the group of people, ships, etc. that make such a journey. **3** efficient and prompt action; speed: *He completed his work with expedition.* —**Syn. 1** voyage, trip, excursion. **3** promptness, haste, quickness.

ex·pe·di·tion·ar·y (eks′pə dish′ən er′ē) *adj.* of, concerning, or making up an expedition.

ex·pe·di·tious (eks′pə dish′əs) *adj.* quick; speedy; efficient and prompt. —**ex′pe·di′tious·ly,** *adv.* —**ex′pe·di′tious·ness,** *n.*

ex·pel (eks pel′) *v.* **-pelled, -pel·ling. 1** force out; force to leave: *When the gunpowder exploded, the bullet was expelled from the gun.* **2** put out; dismiss permanently: *A lazy pupil may be expelled from school.* [< L *expellere* < *ex-* out + *pellere* drive] —**ex·pel′ler,** *n.*

ex·pel·lant or **ex·pel·lent** (eks pel′ənt) *adj.* tending to force out or expel. —*n.* an expellant medicine.

ex·pend (eks pend′) *v.* spend; use up. [< L *expendere* < *ex-* out + *pendere* weigh, pay. Doublet of SPEND.] —**ex·pend′er,** *n.* —**Syn.** disburse, consume. See **spend.**

ex·pend·a·ble (eks pen′də bəl) *adj.* **1** that may be expended or used up. **2** in military use: **a** normally used up in service. **b** worth giving up or sacrificing to the enemy or to destruction for strategic reasons. —*n.* Usually, **expendables,** *pl.* expendable persons or things.

ex·pend·i·ture (eks pen′də chür′ or eks pen′də chər) *n.* **1** a spending; a using up: *Such a complicated enterprise requires the expenditure of much money, time, and effort.* **2** the amount of money, time, energy, etc. spent or used up: *Limit your expenditures to what is necessary.*

ex·pense (eks pens′) *n.* **1** the cost; charge: *The expense of the trip was slight. He travelled at his uncle's expense. We had many a laugh at his expense.* **2** a cause of spending: *Running an automobile is an expense.* **3** an expending; the paying out of money; outlay: *A boy at college puts his father to considerable expense.* **4** loss; sacrifice. **5 at the expense of, a** so as to be paid for by. **b** with the loss or sacrifice of. **6 expenses,** *pl.* **a** the charges incurred in doing something. **b** the money to repay such charges: *The salesman gets expenses besides his salary.* [ME < AF < LL *expensa* < L *expensus,* pp. of *expendere.* See EXPEND.] —**Syn. 1** price.

ex·pen·sive (eks pen′siv) *adj.* costly; high-priced. —**ex·pen′sive·ly,** *adv.* —**ex·pen′sive·ness,** *n.*
Syn. Expensive, costly, dear = costing much. **Expensive,** the general word, means "high-priced," sometimes suggesting more than a person can afford, sometimes more than a thing is worth, and applies to cost in money or in time, effort, etc.: *He had a very expensive pocketknife that cost $10.* **Costly** = of very high price, but usually because rare, precious, luxurious, etc., and is often used of cost in effort, etc.: *An emerald or a victory may be costly.* **Dear** = too expensive: *Meat is dear this week.*

ex·pe·ri·ence (eks pēr′ē əns) *n. v.* **-enced, -enc·ing.** —*n.* **1** what has happened to one; what is or has been met with or felt; anything or everything observed, done, or lived through: *We had several pleasant experiences on our trip.* **2** all of the actions, events, states, feelings, etc., which make up the life of a person, a community, a a race, etc.: *No parallel for such wickedness can be found in human experience.* **3** an observing, doing, or living through things: *People learn by experience.* **4** skill, practical knowledge, or wisdom gained by observing, doing, or living through things.
—*v.* have happen to one; meet with; feel; live through: *In life you experience both joy and sorrow.* [ME < OF < L *experientia* < *experiri* test, try out] —**ex·pe′ri·enc·er,** *n.*
Syn. *v.* **Experience, undergo** = go through something in life. **Experience** emphasizes having something happen to one, but does not suggest whether it is pleasant or unpleasant, brief or long-lasting, important or unimportant: *Visiting the Calgary Stampede was the greatest thrill I ever experienced.* **Undergo** suggests having to suffer or live through something unpleasant, painful, or dangerous: *I had to undergo many disappointments and failures before experiencing success.*

ex·pe·ri·enced (eks pēr′ē ənst) *adj.* **1** having had experience. **2** taught by experience. **3** skilful or wise because of experience. —**Syn. 3** expert, practised.

ex·pe·ri·en·tial (eks pēr′ē en′shəl) *adj.* having to do with experience; based on or coming from experience.

ex·per·i·ment (*v.* eks per′ə ment′; *n.* eks per′ə mənt) *v.* try in order to find out; make trials or tests: *That man is experimenting with dyes to get the color he wants.* [< n.]
—*n.* **1** a test or trial to find out something: *a cooking experiment.* **2** a conducting of such tests or trials: *Scientists test out their theories by a series of experiments.* [< L *experimentum* < *experiri.* See EXPERIENCE.] —**ex·per′i·ment′er,** *n.* —**Syn.** *n.* **1** examination. See **trial.**

ex·per·i·men·tal (eks per′ə men′təl) *adj.* **1** based on experiments: *Chemistry is an experimental science.* **2** used for experiments: *an experimental room.* **3** based on experience, not on theory or authority. **4** for testing or trying out: *A new variety of wheat was developed at the experimental farm.*

ex·per·i·men·tal·ly (eks per′ə men′təl ē) *adv.* **1** by making experiments. **2** as an experiment.

ex·per·i·men·ta·tion (eks per′ə men tā′shən) *n.* an experimenting: *A cure for the disease was found by experimentation.*

ex·pert (*n.* eks′pėrt; *adj.* eks′pėrt or eks pėrt′) *n.* a very skilful person; person who knows a great deal about some special thing or topic.
—*adj.* **1** very skilful; knowing a great deal about some special field of knowledge. **2** from an expert; requiring or showing knowledge about some special field of knowledge. [< L *expertus,* pp. of *experiri* test. See EXPERIENCE.] —**ex′pert·ly** or **ex·pert′ly,** *adv.* —**ex·pert′ness,** *n.*
Syn. *n.* authority, specialist. -*adj.* **1 Expert, proficient, skilled** = having the training and knowledge to do a special thing well. **Expert** = having mastery or unusual ability as the result of experience in addition to training and practice: *He is an expert chemist.* **Proficient** = very good at doing something, especially as the result of training and practice: *She is proficient at sewing.* **Skilled** = knowing thoroughly how to do something and being unusually proficient at doing it: *He is a skilled mechanic.*

ex·per·tise (eks′pər tēz′) *n.* **1** an overall grasp of a subject, process, etc., produced by ability, experience, and skill. **2** the state or quality of being an expert; skill. [< F]

ex·pi·a·ble (eks′pē ə bəl) *adj.* that can be expiated.

ex·pi·ate (eks′pē āt′) *v.* **-at·ed, -at·ing.** make amends for (a wrong, sin, etc.); atone for: *The thief expiated his theft by giving back the amount stolen and by reforming.* [< L *expiare* < *ex-* completely + *piare* appease < *pius* devout] —**ex′pi·a′tor,** *n.*

ex·pi·a·tion (eks′pē ā′shən) *n.* **1** a making amends for a wrong, sin, etc.; atonement: *He made a public apology in expiation of his error.* **2** amends; a means of atonement.

ex·pi·a·to·ry (eks′pē ə tô′rē) *adj.* intended to expiate; expiating; atoning.

ex·pi·ra·tion (ek′spə rā′shən) *n.* **1** a coming to an end: *the expiration of a lease.* **2** a breathing out: *the expiration of used air from the lungs.* **3** the sound made in breathing out.

ex·pir·a·to·ry (ek spīr′ə tô′rē) *adj.* having to do with breathing out air from the lungs.

ex·pire (ek spīr′) *v.* **-pired, -pir·ing. 1** come to an end: *You must obtain a new automobile licence before your old one expires.* **2** die. **3** breathe out: *expire used air from the lungs.* [< L *ex(s)pirare* < *ex-* out + *spirare* breathe] —**ex·pir′er,** *n.* —**Syn. 2** perish.

ex·pi·ry (ek spī′rē or ek′spə rē) *n.* **-ries.** expiration.

ex·plain (eks plān′) *v.* **1** make plain or clear; tell how to do. **2** tell the meaning of; interpret. **3** give reasons for; account for. **4** give an explanation. **5 explain away,** get rid of by giving reasons. **6 explain oneself, a** make one's meaning plain or clear. **b** give reasons for one's behavior. [< L *explanare* < *ex-* out + *planus* flat] —**ex·plain′a·ble,** *adj.* —**ex·plain′er,** *n.*
Syn. 1 Explain, interpret = make plain or understandable. **Explain** = make clear and plain something that is not understood: *He explained all the difficult mathematical problems to me.* **Interpret** = explain or bring out the meaning of something especially difficult, by using special knowledge or, sometimes, unusual understanding or imagination: *She interpreted the symbolism of the poem for us.*

ex·pla·na·tion (eks′plə nā′shən) *n.* **1** the act of explaining or clearing up a difficulty or mistake: *The teacher's explanation of electricity was not hard to follow.*

2 something that explains: *The book contains a good explanation of the principles of atomic fission.* —**Syn.** 1 elucidation, exposition, definition.

ex·plan·a·to·ry (eks plan′ə tô′rē) *adj.* explaining; serving or helping to explain: *Read the explanatory part of the lesson before you try to do the problems.*

ex·ple·tive (eks′plə tiv or eks plē′tiv) *adj.* filling out a sentence or line of verse; completing.
—*n.* 1 something that fills out a sentence or line. In "There is a book on the table," *there* is an expletive. 2 an oath or meaningless exclamation. "Damn" and "My goodness" are expletives. [< LL *expletivus* < *expletus,* pp. of *explere* < *ex-* out + *plere* fill]

ex·pli·ca·ble (eks plik′ə bəl or eks′plə kə bəl) *adj.* capable of being explained. [< L *explicabilis* < *explicare.* See EXPLICIT.]

ex·pli·cate (eks′plə kāt′) *v.* **-cat·ed, -cat·ing.** 1 develop (a principle, doctrine, etc.). 2 explain. [< L *explicare.* See EXPLICIT.] —**ex′pli·ca′tor,** *n.*

ex·pli·ca·tion (eks′plə kā′shən) *n.* 1 an explanation. 2 a detailed statement or description.

ex·pli·ca·to·ry (eks′plə kə tô′rē) *adj.* that explains.

ex·plic·it (eks plis′it) *adj.* 1 clearly expressed; distinctly stated; definite: *He gave such explicit directions that everyone understood them.* 2 not reserved; frank; outspoken. [< L *explicitus,* pp. of *explicare* unfold, explain < *ex-* un- + *plicare* fold] —**ex·plic′it·ly,** *adv.* —**ex·plic′it·ness,** *n.* —**Syn.** 1 precise, exact, unequivocal.

ex·plode (eks plōd′) *v.* **-plod·ed, -plod·ing.** 1 blow up; burst with a loud noise: *The building was destroyed when the defective boiler exploded.* 2 cause to explode: *Many boys explode firecrackers on the 24th of May.* 3 burst forth noisily: *The speaker's mistake was so funny the audience exploded with laughter.* 4 cause to be rejected; destroy belief in: *Columbus helped to explode the theory that the earth was flat.* 5 in phonetics, end the articulation of (a stop) by audibly releasing the breath. The first *p* in *pop* is always exploded, the final *p* is often not. 6 of a stop, be articulated with such a release of breath. 7 of states, situations, etc., suddenly get out of control or burst out: *Racial tensions explode into riots.* [< L *explodere* drive out by clapping < *ex-* out + *plaudere* clap] —**ex·plod′er,** *n.* —**Syn.** 4 discredit, disprove.

ex·ploit (*n.* eks′ploit or eks ploit′; *v.* eks ploit′) *n.* a bold, unusual act; daring deed: *Old stories tell about the exploits of famous heroes.*
—*v.* 1 make use of; turn to practical account: *A mine is exploited for its minerals.* 2 make unfair use of; use selfishly for one's own advantage: *Some nations exploit their colonies, taking as much wealth out of them as they can.* [ME < OF *esploit* < VL *explicitum* achievement < L *explicitum,* pp. neut. of *explicare* unfold, settle. See EXPLICIT.] —**ex·ploit′a·ble,** *adj.* —**ex·ploit′er,** *n.*
Syn. *n.* **Exploit, feat, achievement** = a great or unusual deed. **Exploit** emphasizes daring or great courage or bravery in accomplishing something in the face of danger or against odds: *The pilot won the Victoria Cross for his exploits in the Battle of Britain.* **Feat** emphasizes use of great skill or strength in accomplishing something unusual: *Climbing Mount Everest is a tremendous feat.* **Achievement** emphasizes continued hard work in spite of difficulties and obstacles in accomplishing something outstanding: *Two Canadians, F. G. Banting and J. J. R. Macleod, won the Nobel Prize in 1923 for their achievements in medicine.*

ex·ploi·ta·tion (eks′ploi tā′shən) *n.* 1 use. 2 selfish or unfair use.

ex·plo·ra·tion (eks′plə rā′shən) *n.* 1 a travelling in little-known lands or seas for the purpose of discovery. 2 a going over carefully; a looking into closely; examining. 3 in medicine, the examination of parts or organs concealed within the body.

ex·plor·a·tive (eks plôr′ə tiv) *adj.* 1 exploratory. 2 inclined to make explorations.

ex·plor·a·to·ry (eks plôr′ə tô′rē) *adj.* having to do with exploration; for discovery.

ex·plore (eks plôr′) *v.* **-plored, -plor·ing.** 1 travel in (little-known lands or seas) for the purpose of discovery. 2 go over carefully; look into closely; examine. 3 in medicine, examine with the fingers, a probe, etc.: *The surgeon explored the wound.* [< L *explorare* investigate, spy out, originally, cry out (at sight of game or enemy) < *ex-* out + *plorare* weep] —**ex·plor′ing·ly,** *adv.* —**Syn.** 2 investigate, scrutinize. See **search.**

ex·plor·er (eks plôr′ər) *n.* 1 a person who explores. 2 any instrument for exploring a wound, a dental cavity, etc.

hat, āge, cãre, fär; let, ēqual, tėrm; it, īce
hot, ōpen, ôrder; oil, out; cup, pu̇t, rüle, ūse
əbove, takən, pencəl, lemən, circəs
ch, child; ng, long; sh, ship
th, thin; ᴛʜ, then; zh, measure

ex·plo·sion (eks plō′zhən) *n.* 1 a blowing up; a bursting with a loud noise: *the explosion of a bomb.* 2 a loud noise caused by something blowing up: *People five miles away heard the explosion.* 3 a noisy bursting forth: *an explosion of laughter.* 4 in phonetics, the sudden audible release of the breath at the end of the articulation of a stop. 5 an outbreak or bursting forth of anything capable of development: *an explosion of anger, the population explosion.* [< L *explosio, -onis* < *explodere.* See EXPLODE.]

ex·plo·sive (eks plō′siv or eks plō′ziv) *adj.* 1 of or for explosion; tending to explode: *Gunpowder is explosive.* 2 tending to burst forth noisily: *The irritable old man had an explosive temper.* 3 in phonetics, pronounced with a slight pop or sudden release of breath. The consonants *p, b, t, d, k,* and *g* (as in *go*) are explosive. 4 of or having to do with sudden outbursts: *explosive evolution, an explosive situation.*
—*n.* 1 an explosive substance. Explosives are used in making fireworks. 2 in phonetics, an explosive consonant. —**ex·plo′sive·ly,** *adv.* —**ex·plo′sive·ness,** *n.*

ex·po·nent (eks pō′nənt) *n.* 1 a person or thing that explains, interprets, etc. 2 a person or thing that stands as an example, type, or symbol of something: *This man is a famous exponent of self-education.* 3 in algebra, an index or small number written above and to the right of a symbol or quantity to show how many times the symbol or quantity is to be used as a factor. *Examples:* $2^2 = 2 \times 2$; $a^3 = a \times a \times a$. [< L *exponens, -entis,* ppr. of *exponere.* See EXPOUND.]

ex·po·nen·tial (eks′pō nen′shəl) *adj.* having to do with algebraic exponents; involving unknown or variable quantities as exponents.

ex·port (*v.* eks pôrt′ or eks′pôrt; *n.* eks′pôrt) *v.* send (goods) out of one country for sale and use in another: *Canada exports millions of bushels of wheat each year.*
—*n.* 1 the article exported: *Asbestos is an important export of Quebec.* 2 an exporting; exportation. [< L *exportare* < *ex-* away + *portare* carry]

ex·por·ta·tion (eks′pôr tā′shən) *n.* 1 an exporting. 2 an article exported; export.

ex·port·er (eks pôr′tər or eks′pôr tər) *n.* a person or company whose business is exporting goods.

ex·pose (eks pōz′) *v.* **-posed, -pos·ing.** 1 lay open; leave unprotected; uncover: *The soldiers in the open field were exposed to the enemy's gunfire. His foolish actions exposed him to ridicule.* 2 show openly; display: *expose goods for sale in a store.* 3 make known; show up; reveal: *He exposed the plot to the police.* 4 abandon; put out without shelter: *The ancient Spartans used to expose the babies they did not want.* 5 in photography, allow light to reach and act on (a film or plate). [< OF *exposer* < *ex-* forth (< L *ex-*) + *poser* put. See POSE[1].] —**ex·pos′er,** *n.* —**Syn.** 2 exhibit. 3 disclose.

ex·po·sé (eks′pō zā′) *n.* the showing up of a crime, of dishonesty, fraud, etc. [< F *exposé,* originally pp. of *exposer* expose]

ex·posed (eks pōzd′) *adj.* 1 left unprotected; uncovered. 2 open to view; not concealed. 3 of a photographic film or plate, acted on by light; used and ready to develop.

ex·po·si·tion (eks′pə zish′ən) *n.* 1 a public show or exhibition. The Canadian National Exhibition is a well-known annual exposition. 2 a detailed explanation. 3 a speech or a piece of writing explaining a process or idea. 4 in music: **a** the first section of a movement, as of a sonata, in which the principal and secondary subjects are presented. **b** the first entry, in a fugue, of the theme or themes in each part or voice. —**Syn.** 1 display, fair.

ex·pos·i·tor (eks poz′ə tər) *n.* a person or thing that explains; expounder; interpreter. [< LL < L *exponere.* See EXPOUND.]

ex·pos·i·to·ry (eks poz′ə tô′rē) *adj.* explaining; serving or helping to explain.

ex post fac·to (eks′ pōst′ fak′tō) made or done after something, but applying to it. An **ex post facto law** applies to actions done before the law was passed. [< Med.L *ex post facto* from what is done afterwards]

ex·pos·tu·late (eks pos′chù lāt′) *v.* **-lat·ed, -lat·ing.** reason earnestly with a person, protesting against something he means to do or has done; remonstrate: *The father expostulated with his son about the foolishness of leaving school before graduating.* [< L *expostulare* < *ex-* (intensive) + *postulare* demand] —**ex·pos′tu·la′tor,** *n.*

ex·pos·tu·la·tion (eks pos′chù lā′shən) *n.* an earnest protest; remonstrance: *Expostulations having failed, the teacher resorted to threats.*

ex·pos·tu·la·to·ry (eks pos′chù lə tô′rē) *adj.* of or containing expostulation.

ex·po·sure (eks pō′zhər) *n.* **1** an exposing: *The exposure of the real criminal cleared the innocent man.* **2** a being exposed: *Exposure to the rain has spoiled this machinery.* **3** a position in relation to the sun and wind. A house with a southern exposure is open to sun and wind from the south. **4** in photography, **a** the time during which light reaches and acts on a film or plate. **b** the part of a film used for one picture. **c** the total amount of light on a film in making a picture. **5** a putting out without shelter; abandoning.

exposure meter in photography, an instrument for measuring the amount of light falling on a subject, thus indicating the proper exposure.

ex·pound (eks pound′) *v.* **1** make clear; explain; interpret. **2** set forth or state in detail. [ME < OF *espondre* < L *exponere* < *ex-* forth + *ponere* put]

ex·press (eks pres′) *v.* **1** put into words: *Express your ideas clearly.* **2** show by look, voice, or action; reveal: *Your smile expresses joy.* **3** show by a sign, figure, etc.; indicate: *The sign × expresses multiplication.* **4** send by express. **5** press out; squeeze out: *The juice is expressed from grapes to make wine.* **6 express oneself,** say what one thinks.
—*adj.* **1** clear; plain; definite: *It was his express wish that we should go without him.* **2** for a particular purpose; special: *She came for the express purpose of seeing you.* **3** exact: *He is the express image of his father.* **4** having to do with express: *an express agency or company.* **5** travelling fast and making few stops: *an express train.* **6** for fast travelling: *an express highway.*
—*n.* **1** a special messenger or message sent for a particular purpose. **2** a quick or direct means of sending things. Packages and money can be sent by express in trains or airplanes. **3** a system or company for sending parcels, money, etc.: *Canadian National Express.* **4** things sent by express. **5** a train, bus, elevator, etc. travelling fast and making few stops.
—*adv.* by express; directly. [< L *expressus,* pp. of *exprimere* < *ex-* out + *premere* press] —**ex·press′er,** *n.* —**Syn.** *v.* **1** utter, declare, state, say. **3** signify.

ex·press·age (eks pres′ij) *n.* **1** the business of carrying parcels, money, etc. by express. **2** a charge for carrying parcels, etc. by express.

ex·press·i·ble (eks pres′ə bəl) *adj.* capable of being expressed.

ex·pres·sion (eks presh′ən) *n.* **1** a putting into words: *Clarity of expression is important in style.* **2** a word or group of words used as a unit: "*Swell guy*" *is a slang expression.* **3** a showing by look, voice, or action: *His sigh was an expression of anxiety.* **4** an indication of feeling, spirit, character, etc.; look that shows feeling: *He had a silly expression on his face.* **5** a bringing out the meaning or beauty of something read, spoken, played, sung, etc.: *Try to read with more expression.* **6** a showing by a sign, figure, etc. **7** a symbol or group of symbols expressing some mathematical process or quantity. **8** a pressing out: *the expression of oil from plants.* —**Syn. 1** utterance.

ex·pres·sion·ism (eks presh′ən iz′əm) *n.* **1** in art and literature, a movement of the late 19th and 20th centuries, marked by the attempt to express the artist's subjective feelings without regard to accepted forms or tradition. It began as a revolt against naturalism and impressionism. **2** a similar movement in music.

ex·pres·sion·ist (eks presh′ə nist) *n.* a writer, artist, etc. who follows the principles of expressionism. —*adj.* of, like, or having to do with expressionism.

ex·pres·sion·is·tic (eks presh′ə nis′tik) *adj.* of or having to do with expressionism or expressionists.

ex·pres·sion·less (eks presh′ən lis) *adj.* without expression: *an expressionless face, an expressionless voice.*

ex·pres·sive (eks pres′iv) *adj.* **1** serving as a sign or indication; expressing: "*Alas*" *is a word expressive of sadness.* **2** full of expression; having much feeling, meaning, etc. —**ex·pres′sive·ly,** *adv.* —**ex·pres′sive·ness,** *n.*
Syn. 1 indicative. **2 Expressive, significant, suggestive** = full of meaning. **Expressive** emphasizes showing in a strikingly clear or lively way the meaning or feeling in what is described: *She gave an expressive shrug.* **Significant** emphasizes being full of meaning, which may be expressed, but often is only pointed to: *Graduation Day is a significant event in every student's life.* **Suggestive** emphasizes conveying meaning in an indirect way, as by expressing part of the meaning or by hinting: *The teacher gave an interesting and suggestive list of composition topics.*

ex·press·ly (eks pres′lē) *adv.* **1** clearly; plainly; definitely: *You are expressly forbidden to touch it.* **2** specially; on purpose: *She came expressly to see you.*

ex·press·man (eks pres′mən) *n.* **-men** (-mən). a person who works in the express business, especially one who collects or delivers articles.

ex·press·way (eks pres′wā′) *n.* an express highway; a highway that stretches for long distances with few intersections: *A modern expressway runs between Toronto and Fort Erie.*

ex·pro·pri·ate (eks prō′prē āt′) *v.* **-at·ed, -at·ing. 1** take (land, etc.) out of the owner's possession, especially for public use: *Often a city must expropriate land for a public park.* **2** put (a person) out of possession; dispossess. [< Med.L *expropriare* < *ex-* away from + *proprius* one's own] —**ex·pro′pri·a′tion,** *n.* —**ex·pro′pri·a′tor,** *n.*

ex·pul·sion (eks pul′shən) *n.* **1** an expelling; forcing out: *the expulsion of air from the lungs.* **2** a being expelled or forced out: *Expulsion from school was his punishment for bad behavior.* [< L *expulsio, -onis* < *expellere.* See EXPEL.]

ex·pul·sive (eks pul′siv) *adj.* expelling; forcing out.

ex·punge (eks punj′) *v.* **-punged, -pung·ing.** remove completely; blot out; erase: *The secretary was directed to expunge certain accusations from the record.* [< L *expungere* < *ex-* out + *pungere* prick] —**ex·pung′er,** *n.* —**Syn.** See **erase.**

ex·pur·gate (eks′pər gāt′) *v.* **-gat·ed, -gat·ing.** remove objectionable passages or words from (a book, letter, etc.); purify. [< L *expurgare* < *ex-* out + *purgare* purge] —**ex′pur·ga′tor,** *n.*

ex·pur·ga·tion (eks′pər gā′shən) *n.* the removing or removal from a book, etc. of something that seems objectionable.

ex·qui·site (eks′kwi zit or eks kwiz′it) *adj.* **1** very lovely; delicate: *Those violets are exquisite.* **2** sharp; intense: *exquisite pain, exquisite joy.* **3** of the highest excellence; the most admirable: *She has exquisite taste and manners.* **4** keenly sensitive: *an exquisite ear for music.* [< L *exquisitus,* pp. of *exquirere* < *ex-* out + *quaerere* seek] —**ex′qui·site·ly,** *adv.* —**ex′qui·site·ness,** *n.* —**Syn. 1** dainty, fine, beautiful. **2** acute, keen.

ex-serv·ice (eks′sėr′vis) *adj.* having formerly served in the navy, army, or air force.

ex-serv·ice·man (eks′sėr′vis mən) *n.* **-men** (-mən). a man who formerly served in the navy, army, or air force.

ex·tant (eks′tənt or eks tant′) *adj.* still in existence: *Some of Captain Vancouver's charts are extant.* [< L *ex(s)tans, -antis,* ppr. of *ex(s)tare* < *ex-* out, forth + *stare* stand]

ex·tem·po·ral (eks tem′pə rəl) *adj. Archaic.* extemporaneous.

ex·tem·po·ra·ne·ous (eks tem′pə rā′nē əs) *adj.* **1** spoken or done without preparation; offhand: *an extemporaneous speech.* **2** made for the occasion: *an extemporaneous shelter against a storm.* **3** inclined and able to make speeches without preparation: *an extemporaneous speaker.* [< LL *extemporaneus* < L *ex tempore* according to the moment] —**ex·tem′po·ra′ne·ous·ly,** *adv.* —**ex·tem′po·ra′ne·ous·ness,** *n.*

☛ **extemporaneous.** In general usage, as defined above, an "extemporaneous speech" is one made without any preparation, usually on the spur of the moment. In the terminology of speech teachers, however, such a speech as this is called an "impromptu speech," and an extemporaneous speech is one that is carefully prepared, but which is usually not written out and is never committed to memory. It may be given with or without notes.

ex·tem·po·rar·y (eks tem′pə rer′ē) *adj.* extemporaneous. **—ex·tem′po·rar′i·ly,** *adv.*

ex·tem·po·re (eks tem′pə rē or eks tem′pə rā) *adv.* on the spur of the moment; without preparation; offhand: *Each pupil will be called on to speak extempore.* —*adj.* made, done, or said on the spur of the moment; impromptu. Also, **ex tempore.** [< L *ex tempore* according to the moment]

ex·tem·po·rize (eks tem′pə rīz′) *v.* **-rized, -riz·ing.** **1** speak, play, sing, or dance, composing as one proceeds: *The pianist was extemporizing.* **2** compose offhand; make for the occasion: *The campers extemporized a shelter for the night.* **—ex·tem′po·ri·za′tion,** *n.* **—ex·tem′po·riz′er,** *n.*

ex·tend (eks tend′) *v.* **1** stretch out: *extend your hand.* **2** continue or be continued in time, space, or direction: *The beach extends for miles in both directions. The conference extends from Wednesday to Saturday.* **3** straighten out: *Extend your arms in front of you.* **4** widen; enlarge: *The farmer is planning to extend his barn.* **5** become longer or larger. **6** give; grant: *extend help to poor people.* **7** exert (oneself); strain. **8** cause to put out greater or maximum effort: *The competition was not strong enough to extend him.* [< L *extendere* < *ex-* out + *tendere* stretch] **—ex·tend′er,** *n.* **—Syn. 4** prolong, protract. See **lengthen.**

ex·tend·ed (eks ten′did) *adj.* **1** extensive; widespread. **2** stretched out; prolonged. **3** widened. **4** spread out; outstretched.

ex·ten·si·ble (eks ten′sə bəl) *adj.* capable of being extended.

ex·ten·sile (eks ten′sīl or eks ten′səl) *adj.* **1** capable of being stretched out: *extensile claws.* **2** extensible.

ex·ten·sion (eks ten′shən) *n.* **1** an extending: *the extension of one's arm.* **2** a being extended: *The building will undergo an extension.* **3** an extended part; addition: *The new extension to the old school will make room for more students.* **4** a telephone connected with a main telephone or switchboard but in a different location: *Our telephone is in the living room, but we have an extension in the kitchen.* **5** the provision of courses of study by a university or college to people unable to take courses in the regular session: *Evening classes and correspondence courses may be provided by a department of extension.* **6** range; extent. **7** in physics, that property of a body by which it occupies a portion of space. **8** the straightening of a part by the action of an extensor muscle. **9** the condition of being straightened in this way. **10** the pulling or stretching of a fractured or dislocated part to enable the bones to be restored to their natural relative positions. [< LL *extensio, -onis* < L *extendere.* See EXTEND.] **—ex·ten′sion·less,** *adj.* **—Syn. 1** stretching, expansion, enlargement. **3** projection.

extension ladder a ladder having a movable part or parts enabling it to be extended to varying heights as needed.

ex·ten·si·ty (eks ten′sə tē) *n.* spatial quality.

ex·ten·sive (eks ten′siv) *adj.* **1** of great extent; wide; broad; large: *an extensive park.* **2** far-reaching; affecting many things; comprehensive: *extensive changes.* **3** depending on the use of large areas: *extensive agriculture.* **—ex·ten′sive·ly,** *adv.* **—ex·ten′sive·ness,** *n.* **—Syn. 1** extended, ample.

ex·ten·sor (eks ten′sər or eks ten′sôr) *n.* in physiology, a muscle that extends or straightens out a limb or other part of the body. [< LL *extensor* one who stretches]

ex·tent (eks tent′) *n.* **1** the size, space, length, amount, or degree to which a thing extends: *Railways carry people and goods through the whole extent of the country. The extent of a judge's power is limited by law.* **2** something extended; an extended space: *a vast extent of prairie.* **3** in physics, anything that has extension; an object or body having length, area, or volume. **4** in mathematics, a continuous magnitude of dimensions: *A plane figure is 2-extent.* **5** in logic, extension. [< AF *extente, estente,* fem. pp., used as a noun, of *estendre* extend < L *extendere.* See EXTEND.] **—Syn. 1** magnitude, area, scope, compass, range.

hat, āge, cãre, fär; let, ēqual, tėrm; it, īce
hot, ōpen, ôrder; oil, out; cup, pu̇t, rüle, ūse
əbove, takən, pencəl, lemən, circəs
ch, child; ng, long; sh, ship
th, thin; ᴛʜ, then; zh, measure

ex·ten·u·ate (eks ten′yü āt′) *v.* **-at·ed, -at·ing.** **1** make (guilt, a fault, offence, etc.) seem less; excuse in part: *His foreign origin extenuates his faulty pronunciation of English.* **2** make thin or weak; diminish. [< L *extenuare* < *ex-* out + *tenuis* thin] **—ex·ten′u·at′ing·ly,** *adv.* **—ex·ten′u·a′tor,** *n.*

ex·ten·u·a·tion (eks ten′yü ā′shən) *n.* **1** an extenuating: *The lawyer pleaded his client's youth in extenuation of the crime.* **2** extenuated condition. **3** something that lessens the seriousness of guilt, a fault, an offence, etc.; a partial excuse.

ex·te·ri·or (eks tēr′ē ər) *n.* **1** an outer surface or part; outward appearance; outside: *The exterior of the house was of brick. The gruff old man has a harsh exterior but a kind heart.* **2** an outdoor scene on the stage. **3** a motion picture made outdoors.
—*adj.* **1** on the outside; outer: *The skin of an apple is its exterior covering.* **2** coming from without; happening outside: *exterior influences.* [< L *exterior,* comparative of *exterus* outside < *ex-* out of] **—Syn.** *adj.* **1** outward, external.

exterior angle in geometry: **1** any of the four angles formed outside the intersections of a straight line with two parallel lines. **2** an angle formed by a side of a polygon and the extension of an adjacent side.

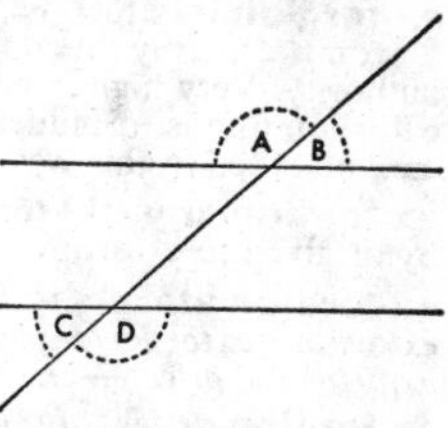

Angles A, B, C, and D are exterior angles.

ex·ter·mi·nate (eks tėr′mə nāt′) *v.* **-nat·ed, -nat·ing.** destroy completely: *This poison will exterminate rats.* [< LL *exterminare* destroy < L *exterminare* drive out < *ex-* out of + *terminus* boundary]

ex·ter·mi·na·tion (eks tėr′mə nā′shən) *n.* complete destruction: *This poison is useful for the extermination of rats.*

ex·ter·mi·na·tor (eks tėr′mə nā′tər) *n.* **1** a person or thing that exterminates. **2** a person whose business is exterminating fleas, lice, bedbugs, rats, etc.

ex·ter·nal (eks tėr′nəl) *adj.* **1** on the outside; outer. **2** to be used on the outside of the body: *Liniment and rubbing alcohol are external remedies.* **3** entirely outside; coming from without. **4** having existence outside one's mind. **5** having to do with outward appearance or show; superficial: *Going to church is an external act of worship.* **6** having to do with international affairs; foreign: *external affairs. War affects a nation's external trade.*
—*n.* **1** an outer surface or part; outside. **2 externals,** *pl.* clothing, manners, outward acts, or appearances: *He judges people by mere externals.* [< L *externus* outside < *exterus* outside < *ex-* out of] **—Syn.** *adj.* **1** outward, exterior.

external ear the fleshy part of the ear next to the head, including the opening to the vestibule.

ex·ter·nal·ise (eks tėr′nə līz′) *v.* externalize.

ex·ter·nal·i·ty (eks′tər nal′ə tē) *n.* **-ties.** **1** the quality of being external. **2** an external thing.

ex·ter·nal·ize (eks tėr′nə līz′) *v.* **-ized, -iz·ing.** give shape or form to; make external. Also, **externalise.**

ex·ter·nal·ly (eks tėr′nəl ē) *adv.* in an external manner; on the outside.

ex·tinct (eks tingkt′) *adj.* **1** no longer in existence: *The dinosaur is an extinct animal.* **2** no longer active; extinguished: *an extinct volcano.* [< L *ex(s)tinctus,* pp. of *ex(s)tinguere.* See EXTINGUISH.] **—Syn. 1** dead.

ex·tinc·tion (eks tingk′shən) *n.* **1** an extinguishing: *The sudden extinction of the lights left the room in darkness.* **2** a being extinguished; extinct condition. **3** a suppression; a doing away with completely; wiping out; destruction: *The war caused the extinction of many pacifist organizations.*

ex·tin·guish (eks ting′gwish) *v.* **1** put out; quench: *Water extinguished the fire.* **2** put an end to; do away with; wipe out; destroy: *One failure after another extinguished her hope.* **3** eclipse or obscure by superior brilliancy. [< L *ex(s)tinguere* < *ex-* out + *stinguere* quench] —**ex·tin′guish·able,** *adj.* —**Syn. 2** See **abolish.**

ex·tin·guish·er (eks ting′gwi shər) *n.* **1** a person or thing that extinguishes. **2** a device for quenching fires.

ex·tir·pate (eks′tər pāt′ or eks tėr′pāt) *v.* **-pat·ed, -pat·ing. 1** remove completely; destroy totally: *Kidnapping must be extirpated.* **2** tear up the roots. [< L *ex(s)tirpare* < *ex-* out + *stirps* root) —**ex′tir·pa′tor,** *n.*

ex·tir·pa·tion (eks′tər pā′shən) *n.* **1** a complete removal; total destruction. **2** a tearing up by the roots.

ex·tir·pa·to·ry (ek stėr′pə tôr′ē) *adj.* extirpating; serving to root out or destroy.

ex·tol or **ex·toll** (eks tōl′) *v.* **-tolled, -tol·ling.** praise highly. [< L *extollere* < *ex-* up + *tollere* raise] —**Syn.** commend, laud, eulogize.

ex·tort (eks tôrt′) *v.* obtain (money, a promise, etc.) by threats, force, fraud, or illegal use of authority. Blackmailers try to extort money from their victims. [< L *extortus,* pp. of *extorquere* < *ex-* out + *torquere* twist] —**ex·tort′er,** *n.* —**Syn.** See **extract.**

ex·tor·tion (eks tôr′shən) *n.* **1** an obtaining of money, a promise, etc. by threats, force, fraud, or illegal use of authority. Very high interest on loans is considered extortion and is forbidden by law. **2** the money, promise, etc., obtained in this way.

ex·tor·tion·ar·y (eks tôr′shən er′ē) *adj.* characterized by or given to extortion.

ex·tor·tion·ate (eks tôr′shən it) *adj.* **1** characterized by extortion: *extortionate demands.* **2** much too great: *an extortionate price.* —**ex·tor′tion·ate·ly,** *adv.*

ex·tor·tion·er (eks tôr′shən ər) *n.* a person who is guilty of extortion.

ex·tor·tion·ist (eks tôr′shən ist) *n.* extortioner.

ex·tra (eks′trə) *adj.* more, greater, or better than what is usual, expected, or needed: *extra pay, extra favors.* —*n.* **1** something in addition to what is usual, expected, or needed. **2** an additional charge. **3** a special edition of a newspaper. **4** a person who is employed by the day to play minor parts in motion pictures. **5** an additional worker.
—*adv.* **1** more than usually: *extra-fine quality.* **2** in addition to the usual amount: *The larger edition contains three maps extra.* [probably short for *extraordinary*] —**Syn.** *adj.* additional, supplemental, supplementary.

extra- *prefix.* outside; beyond; besides, as in *extraordinary.* [< L]

ex·tract (*v.* eks trakt′; *n.* eks′trakt) *v.* **1** pull out or draw out, usually with some effort: *extract a tooth, extract a confession.* **2** obtain by pressure, suction, etc.: *extract oil from olives.* **3** deduce: *extract a principle from a collection of facts.* **4** derive: *extract pleasure from a situation.* **5** take out; select (a passage) from a book, speech, etc. **6** calculate or find (the root of a number). —*n.* **1** something drawn out or taken out; a passage taken from a book, speech, etc. **2** a concentrated preparation of a substance. Vanilla extract, made from vanilla beans, is often used as a flavoring in ice cream. [< L *extractus,* pp. of *extrahere* < *ex-* **out** + *trahere* draw] —**ex·trac′tor,** *n.*
Syn. *v.* **1 Extract, extort** = draw out with force. **Extract** emphasizes pulling out something hard to get loose: *The dentist extracted her wisdom tooth.* **Extort** suggests wringing something from a person who does not want to give it up: *Not even torture could extort from him the names of his companions.* -*n.* **1** excerpt, citation, quotation, selection.

ex·tract·a·ble (eks trak′tə bəl) *adj.* capable of being extracted.

ex·tract·i·ble (eks trak′tə bəl) *adj.* extractable.

ex·trac·tion (eks trak′shən) *n.* **1** an extracting. **2** a being extracted. **3** descent; origin: *Miss del Rio is of Spanish extraction.* **4** something that has been extracted; extract.

ex·trac·tive (eks trak′tiv) *adj.* **1** extracting; tending to extract. **2** capable of being extracted.

ex·tra·cur·ric·u·lar (eks′trə kə rik′yù lər) *adj.* outside the regular course of study: *Football and debating are extra-curricular activities in high school.*

ex·tra·dit·a·ble (eks′trə dīt′ə bəl) *adj.* **1** that can be extradited. A person accused of murder in the United States is extraditable if he is caught in Canada. **2** for which a person can be extradited: *Murder is extraditable.*

ex·tra·dite (eks′trə dīt′) *v.* **-dit·ed, -dit·ing. 1** give up or deliver (a fugitive or prisoner) to another nation or legal authority for trial or punishment: *If an escaped prisoner from Canada is caught in the United States, he can be extradited to Canada.* **2** obtain the extradition of (such a person). [< *extradition*]

ex·tra·di·tion (eks′trə dish′ən) *n.* the surrender of a fugitive or prisoner by one state, nation, or legal authority to another for trial or punishment. [< F < L *ex-* out + *traditio* a delivering up < *tradere* hand over]

ex·tra·le·gal (eks′trə lē′gəl) *adj.* beyond the control or influence of law.

ex·tra·mar·i·tal (eks′trə mar′ə təl) *adj.* outside the limits or bonds of marriage.

ex·tra·mu·ral (eks′trə mūr′əl) *adj.* **1** occurring outside the boundaries of a school, college, etc.: *extramural hockey.* **2** of or having to do with a university course of study available to persons not attending the university. **3** beyond the boundaries or walls of a city. [< L *extra muros* outside the walls + E *-al*]

ex·tra·ne·ous (eks trā′nē əs) *adj.* **1** from outside; not belonging; foreign: *Sand or some other extraneous matter had got into the butter.* **2** not part of what is under consideration; external: *The speaker made many extraneous remarks.* [< L *extraneus* < *extra* outside < *ex* out of. Doublet of STRANGE.]

ex·traor·di·nar·i·ly (eks trôr′də ner′ə lē or eks′trə ôr′də ner′ə lē) *adv.* in an extraordinary manner; to an extraordinary degree; most unusually.

ex·traor·di·nar·y (eks trôr′də ner′ē or eks′trə ôr′də ner′ē) *adj.* **1** beyond what is ordinary; most unusual; very remarkable: *Seven feet is an extraordinary height for a person.* **2** outside of, additional to, or ranking below the regular class of officials; special. An **envoy extraordinary** is one sent on a special mission; he ranks below an ambassador. [< L *extraordinarius* < *extra ordinem* out of the (usual) order] —**Syn. 1** uncommon, exceptional, singular.

ex·tra·po·late (ek strap′ə lāt′ or eks′trə pə lāt′) *v.* **-lat·ed, -lat·ing. 1** in mathematics, project new values or terms of a series from those already known. **2** infer something by projecting from known facts on the assumption that they form part of a series. [< *extra* + inter*polate*] —**ex′tra·po·la′tion,** *n.* —**ex·trap′o·la′tor,** *n.*

ex·tra·sen·so·ry (eks′trə sen′sər ē) *adj.* beyond the normal scope or range of the senses: *Mental telepathy is one kind of extrasensory perception.*

extrasensory perception the perceiving of thoughts, actions, etc. in other than a normal fashion; mental telepathy.

ex·tra·ter·ri·to·ri·al (eks′trə ter′ə tô′rē əl) *adj.* **1** outside the laws of the country that a person is living in. Any ambassador to a foreign country has certain extra-territorial privileges. **2** beyond territorial limits or jurisdiction.

ex·trav·a·gance (eks trav′ə gəns) *n.* **1** careless and lavish spending; wastefulness: *His extravagance kept him always in debt.* **2** a going beyond the bounds of reason; excess: *The extravagance of the salesman's claims caused us to doubt the worth of his product.* **3** an extravagant action, idea, purchase, etc. —**Syn. 1** dissipation.

ex·trav·a·gant (eks trav′ə gənt) *adj.* **1** spending carelessly and lavishly; wasteful: *An extravagant person usually has extravagant tastes and habits.* **2** beyond the bounds of reason; excessive: *People laughed at the inventor's extravagant praise of his invention. He refused to buy the ring because of its extravagant price.* [< Med.L *extravagans, -antis,* ppr. of *extravagari* < L *extra-* outside + *vagari* wander] —**ex·trav′a·gant·ly,** *adv.* —**Syn. 1** prodigal, lavish. **2** immoderate, inordinate, exorbitant.

ex·trav·a·gan·za (eks trav′ə gan′zə) *n.* a fantastic play, piece of music, literary composition, etc. Musical comedies having elaborate scenery, gorgeous costumes, etc. are extravaganzas. [< Ital. *stravaganza* peculiar behavior, influenced by E *extra*]

hat, āge, cãre, fär; let, ēqual, tėrm; it, īce
hot, ōpen, ôrder; oil, out; cup, pu̇t, rüle, ūse
ən above, takən, pencəl, lemən, circəs
ch, child; ng, long; sh, ship
th, thin; ᴛʜ, then; zh, measure

ex·treme (eks trēm′) *adj.* **-trem·er, -trem·est,** *n.* —*adj.* **1** much more than usual; very great; very strong. **2** very severe; very violent. **3** farthest from the centre; outermost: *the extreme outlying districts of the city.* **4** of persons, opinions, etc., going beyond usual limits; opposed to *moderate.*
—*n.* **1** something extreme; one of two things as far or as different as possible from each other: *Love and hate are two extremes of feeling.* **2** an extreme degree or condition: *Joy is happiness in the extreme.* **3** in mathematics, the first or last term in a proportion or series: *In the proportion, 2 is to 4 as 8 is to 16, 2 and 16 are the extremes; 4 and 8 are the means.* **4 go to extremes,** do or say too much; resort to extreme measures. [< L *extremus,* superlative of *exterus* outside < *ex-* out of] —**ex·treme′ness,** *n.* —**Syn.** *adj.* **1** immoderate, excessive, radical, fanatical. **3** outermost, utmost, final, ultimate.
☞ **extreme.** While *extremer* and *extremest* are used as the comparative and superlative of *extreme, more extreme* and *most extreme* are found more frequently in general usage.

ex·treme·ly (eks trēm′ lē) *adv.* much more than usual; very.

extreme unction in the Roman Catholic Church, the sacrament given by a priest to a dying person or one in danger of death.

ex·trem·ist (eks trēm′ ist) *n.* **1** a person who goes to extremes. **2** a person who has extreme ideas or favors extreme measures.

ex·trem·i·ty (eks trem′ ə tē) *n.* **-ties. 1** the very end; the farthest possible place; the last part or point. **2** an extreme need, danger, suffering, etc.: *In their extremity the people on the sinking ship bore themselves bravely.* **3** an extreme degree. **4** an extreme action: *The soldiers were forced to the extremity of firing their rifles to scatter the angry mob.* **5 the extremities,** *pl.* the hands and feet. —**Syn. 1** termination.

ex·tri·ca·ble (eks′ trə kə bəl) *adj.* capable of being extricated.

ex·tri·cate (eks′ trə kāt′) *v.* **-cat·ed, -cat·ing.** set free (from entanglements, difficulties, embarrassing situations, etc.); release: *Tom extricated his younger brother from the barbed-wire fence.* [< L *extricare* < *ex-* out of + *tricae* perplexities] —**ex′tri·ca′tion,** *n.*

ex·trin·sic (eks trin′ sik) *adj.* **1** not essential or inherent; caused by external circumstances. **2** being outside of a thing; coming from without; external. [< later L *extrinsecus* outer < earlier L *extrinsecus* from outside < OL **extrim* from outside + *secus* following]

ex·trin·si·cal·ly (eks trin′ sik lē) *adv.* in an extrinsic manner; from without; externally.

ex·trorse (eks trôrs′) *adj.* in botany, turned or facing outward. [< LL *extrorsus* in an outward direction < *extra-* outside + *versus* towards]

ex·tro·ver·sion (eks′ trə vėr′ zhən or -vėr′ shən) *n.* the tendency to be more interested in what is going on around one than in one's own thoughts and feelings; tendency to show off.

ex·tro·vert (eks′ trə vėrt′) *n.* a person more interested in what is going on around him than in his own thoughts and feelings; person tending to act rather than think; person who shows off. [< *extro-* outside (var. of *extra-*) + L *vertere* turn]

ex·trude (eks trüd′) *v.* **-trud·ed, -trud·ing. 1** thrust out; push out. **2** stick out; protrude. [< L *extrudere* < *ex-* out + *trudere* thrust]

ex·tru·sion (eks trü′ zhən) *n.* an extruding. **2** a being extruded. [< L *extrudere.* See EXTRUDE.]

ex·tru·sive (eks trü′ siv) *adj.* tending to extrude.

ex·u·ber·ance (eg zü′ bər əns) *n.* **1** the fact, quality, state, or condition of being exuberant. **2** great abundance. **3** luxurious growth.

ex·u·ber·an·cy (eg zü′ bər ən sē) *n.* **-cies.** exuberance.

ex·u·ber·ant (eg zü′ bər ənt) *adj.* **1** very abundant; overflowing; lavish: *exuberant health, good nature, or joy; an exuberant welcome.* **2** profuse in growth; luxuriant: *the exuberant vegetation of the jungle.* [< L *exuberans, -antis,* ppr. of *exuberare* grow luxuriantly < *ex-* thoroughly + *uber* fertile] —**ex·u′ber·ant·ly,** *adv.*

ex·u·da·tion (eks′ yu̇ dā′ shən) *n.* **1** an exuding. **2** something exuded, such as sweat.

ex·ude (eks ūd′ or eg züd′) *v.* **-ud·ed, -ud·ing. 1** come or send out in drops; ooze: *Sweat exudes from the skin.* **2** give forth: *Some successful men exude self-confidence.* [< L *ex(s)udare* < *ex-* out + *sudare* sweat]

ex·ult (eg zult′) *v.* be very glad; rejoice greatly: *The winners exulted in their victory.* [< L *ex(s)ultare,* frequentative of *exsilire* leap out or up < *ex-* forth + *salire* leap]

ex·ult·ant (eg zul′ tənt) *adj.* rejoicing greatly; exulting; triumphant: *He gave an exultant shout.*

ex·ul·ta·tion (eg′zul tā′ shən or ek′sul tā′ shən) *n.* the act of exulting; great rejoicing; triumph: *There was exultation over the army's victory.*

ex·ur·ban (eks′ ėr′ bən) *adj.* of, about, or in a region between the suburbs and the country.

ex·ur·ban·ite (eks′ ėr′ bən īt′) *n.* a person who has moved out of a large city to the region between the suburbs and the country, and whose way of living is a mixture of urban and rural elements. [< *ex-* + sub*urbanite*]

-ey *suffix.* full of; containing; like, as in *clayey, skyey,* etc. [var. of *-y*[1]]

ey·as (ī′ əs) *n.* **1** a young hawk taken from the nest for training as a falcon. **2** a nestling. [ME *a nyas* (mistaken as *an eyas*) < OF *niais,* literally, fresh from the nest; ult. < L *nidus* nest]

eye (ī) *n. v.* **eyed, ey·ing** or **eye·ing.** —*n.* **1** the organ of the body by which people and animals see; the organ of sight. **2** the colored part of the eye; iris. **3** the region surrounding the eye: *The blow he got gave him a black eye.* **4** any organ that is sensitive to light. **5** the sense of seeing; vision; sight. **6** the ability to see small differences in things: *A good artist must have an eye for color.* **7** a look; glance: *He cast an eye in her direction.* **8** a watchful look. **9** a way of thinking or considering; view; opinion; judgment: *Stealing is a crime in the eye of the law.* **10** something shaped like, resembling, or suggesting an eye. The little spots on potatoes, the hole for thread in a needle, and the loop to fasten a hook are all called eyes. **11** the calm, clear area at the centre of a hurricane, cyclone, etc.

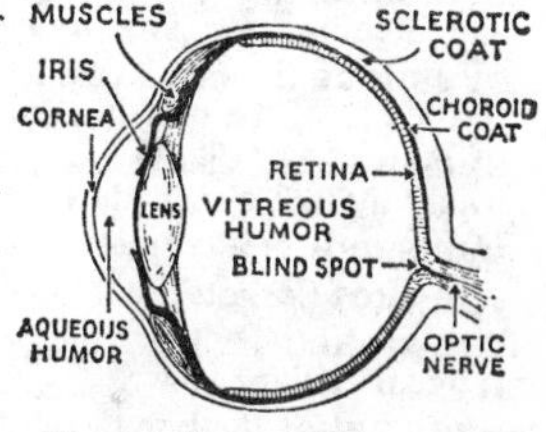

The eye of a man

an eye for an eye, a punishment or retaliation as severe as the offence.
catch one's eye, attract one's attention.
eyes right or **eyes left,** a military order to turn the head to the right or to the left as a salute while marching.
have an eye to, look out for; pay attention to.
in the public eye, a often seen in public. **b** widely known.
keep an eye on, look after; watch carefully.
make eyes at, look at in an inviting or loving way.
open a person's eyes, make him see what is really happening.
see eye to eye, agree entirely; have exactly the same opinion.
set eyes on, see; look at.
shut one's eyes to, refuse to see or consider.
with an eye to, for; considering.
—*v.* look at; watch: *The dog eyed the stranger.* [OE *ēage*]

eye·ball (ī′bol′ or -bôl′) *n.* the ball-shaped part of the eye without the lids and bony socket.

eye·brow (ī′brou′) *n.* **1** the arch of hair above the eye. **2** the bony ridge that it grows on.

eye-catch·er (ī′kach′ər) *n. Informal.* anything striking; an attraction.

eye-catch·ing (ī′kach′ing) *adj. Informal.* **1** striking; appealing. **2** conspicuous; clearly visible.

eye·cup (ī′kup′) *n.* a small cup with a rim shaped to fit over the eye, used in washing the eyes or putting medicine in them.

-eyed *combining form.* having a —— eye or eyes: *brown-eyed = having brown eyes.*

eye·ful (ī′fu̇l) *n.* **1** as much as the eye can see at one time. **2** *Informal.* a good look. **3** *Slang.* a good-looking girl or woman.

eye·glass (ī′glas′) *n.* **1** a glass lens to aid poor vision. **2** an eyecup. **3** an eyepiece. **4 eyeglasses,** *pl.* a pair of glass lenses to help vision: *Eyeglasses are often called spectacles.*

eye·hole (ī′hōl′) *n.* **1** the bony socket for the eyeball. **2** a hole to look through. **3** a round opening for a pin, hook, rope, etc. to go through.

eye·lash (ī′lash′) *n.* **1** one of the hairs on the edge of the eyelid. **2** the fringe of such hairs. **3 by an eyelash,** by a narrow margin; by very little.

eye·less (ī′lis) *adj.* without eyes; blind.

eye·let (ī′lit) *n.* **1** a small, round hole for a lace or cord to go through. **2** a metal ring that is set around such a hole to strengthen it. **3** a hole to look through. **4** a small, round hole with stitches around it, used to make a pattern in embroidery. [< OF *œillet*, dim. of *œil* eye < L *oculus*; influenced by E *eye* and *-let*]

eye·lid (ī′lid′) *n.* the movable fold of skin over the eye.

eye opener **1** a surprising happening or discovery; a startling piece of information. **2** a drink of liquor taken early in the day.

eye-o·pen·ing (ī′ō′pə ning or -ōp′ning) *adj.* enlightening; revealing: *an eye-opening report.*

eye·piece (ī′pēs′) *n.* the lens or set of lenses nearest to the eye of the user in a telescope, microscope, etc.

eye·shade (ī′shād′) *n.* **1** a visor to shield the eyes in bright light. **2** eye shadow.

eye shadow a cosmetic for coloring the eyelids.

eye·shot (ī′shot′) *n.* the range of vision.

eye·sight (ī′sīt′) *n.* **1** the power of seeing; sight. **2** the range of vision; view.

eye socket the bony cavity in which the eyeball is set.

eye·sore (ī′sôr′) *n.* something unpleasant to look at: *An untidy garbage heap is an eyesore.*

eye·spot (ī′spot′) *n.* the simplest kind of organ for seeing in many lower animals.

eye·stalk (ī′stok′ or -stôk′) *n.* in zoology, the stalk or peduncle upon which the eye is borne in lobsters, shrimp, etc.

eye·strain (ī′strān′) *n.* a tired or weak condition of the eyes caused by using them too much, reading in a dim light, etc.

eye·tooth (ī′tüth′) *n.* **-teeth.** either of the two pointed, upper teeth between the incisors and the bicuspids; upper canine tooth.

eye·wash (ī′wosh′) *n.* **1** a liquid preparation to clean or heal the eyes. **2** *Slang.* deceiving flattery; insincere excuse. **3** *Slang.* nonsense.

eye·wit·ness (ī′wit′nis) *n.* a person who actually sees or has seen some act or happening, and thus can give testimony concerning it.

ey·rie or **ey·ry** (ãr′ē or ėr′ē) *n.* **-ries.** **1** the lofty nest of an eagle or other bird of prey. **2** young eagles or the young of other birds of prey. **3** a house, castle, etc. built in a high place. Also, **aerie, aery.** [< Med.L *aeria* < OF ? < L *area* or *atrium* atrium]

ey·rir (ā′rir) *n.* **au·rar** (ou′rär). **1** a unit of money in Iceland, worth 1/100 of a krona. **2** a coin worth one eyrir. [< Icelandic]

Ez. or **Ezr.** Ezra.

Ezek. Ezekiel.

F or **f** (ef) *n.* **F's** or **f's.** **1** the sixth letter of the English alphabet. **2** any speech sound represented by this letter. **3** the sixth in a series designated alphabetically: *F is the lowest or failing grade in certain schools.* **4** in music: **a** the fourth tone in the scale of C major. **b** a symbol representing this tone. **c** a key, string, etc. that produces this tone. **d** the scale or key that has F as its keynote.

f. **1** female. **2** feminine. **3** forte. **4** franc. **5** farthing. **6** in mathematics, function. **7** in photography, f number. **8** folio. **9** frequency. **10** frame.

F fluorine.

F. or **F** **1** Fahrenheit. **2** French. **3** Friday. **4** February.

fa (fä) *n.* in music, a syllable used for the fourth tone of an eight-tone scale. See **do**[2] for diagram. [See GAMUT.]

Fa·bi·an (fā′bē ən) *adj.* **1** using stratagem and delay to wear out an opponent; cautious; slow. **2** of or having to do with the Fabian Society. —*n.* a member or supporter of the Fabian Society. [< *Fabius Maximus*, a Roman general who successfully harassed Hannibal's army without risking a battle]

Fa·bi·an·ism (fā′bē ən iz′əm) *n.* **1** especially in politics, the practice of using stratagem and delay to wear out an opponent. **2** a moderate form of socialism; the principles and methods of the Fabian Society.

Fabian Society an English socialist society, founded in 1884, that favors the adoption of socialism by gradual reform rather than by revolution.

fa·ble (fā′bəl) *n. v.* **-bled, -bling.** —*n.* **1** a story made up to teach a lesson. **2** an untrue story; falsehood. **3** a legend; myth. —*v.* tell or write fables. [ME < OF < L *fabula* < *fari* speak] ☛ See **allegory** for usage note.

fa·bled (fā′bəld) *adj.* **1** told about in fables, legends, or myths. **2** having no real existence; made up; fictitious.

fab·li·au (fab′lē ō′) *n.* **-aux (-ōz′).** a medieval poem, usually French or English, relating a short tale that deals with real or possible (often comic) incidents of ordinary human life. [< F *fabliau*, dim. of *fable* fable]

fab·ric (fab′rik) *n.* **1** any woven or knitted material; cloth. Velvet, canvas, linen, and flannel are fabrics. **2** texture, whether smooth or rough, loose or close, etc.: *suits and dresses made of cloths of different fabric.* **3** a structure; something constructed of combined parts; framework: *Unwise loans weakened the financial fabric of the bank.* [< F *fabrique* < L *fabrica* workshop. Doublet of FORGE[1].]

fab·ri·cate (fab′rə kāt′) *v.* **-cat·ed, -cat·ing.** **1** build; construct; manufacture. **2** make by fitting together standardized parts: *Automobiles are fabricated from parts made in different factories.* **3** make up; invent (stories, lies, excuses, etc.). **4** forge (a document). [< L *fabricare* build < *fabrica* workshop] —**fab′ri·ca′tor,** *n.*

fab·ri·ca·tion (fab′rə kā′shən) *n.* **1** manufacture; fabricating. **2** something fabricated, such as a story, lie, excuse, etc.

fab·u·list (fab′yu̇ list) *n.* **1** a person who tells, writes, or makes up fables. **2** a liar.

fab·u·lous (fab′yu̇ ləs) *adj.* **1** not believable; amazing: *That antique shop asks fabulous prices.* **2** of or belonging to a fable; imaginary: *The phoenix is a fabulous bird.* **3** like a fable. **4** *Slang.* wonderful; exciting: *We had a fabulous time at the party.* [< L *fabulosus* < *fabula.* See FABLE.] —**fab′u·lous·ly,** *adv.* —**fab′u·lous·ness,** *n.* —**Syn.** **1** incredible, astonishing. **2** legendary, mythical.

fa·çade (fə säd′) *n.* **1** the front part of a building. **2** any side of a building that faces a street or other open space. **3** a front or outward part of anything, especially when thought of as concealing something, as an error, weakness, or scheme: *a façade of honesty.* [< F *façade* < *face.* See FACE.]

face (fās) *n. v.* **faced, fac·ing.** —*n.* **1** the front part of the head. **2** a look; expression: *His face was sad.* **3** an ugly or peculiar look made by distorting the face. **4** outward appearance. **5** the front part; surface: *the face of a wall.* **6** the side of a watch, playing card, printing plate, etc. that bears the symbols or other markings: *He turned one of the cards face upwards.* **7** in mining, the surface at the end of a tunnel, drift, or excavation where work is in progress. **8** in printing, a particular style or size of type. **9** *Informal.* boldness; impudence. **10** personal importance; dignity; self-respect: *To most people, loss of face is humiliating.* **11** the stated value: *The face value of*

the note was $100, but $73 was all that anybody would pay for it.
face to face, a with faces toward each other. **b** in the actual presence.
in the face of, a in the presence of. **b** in spite of.
lose face, lose dignity or self-respect; be humiliated.
on the face of it, by its own evidence; obviously.
pull a long face, look sad, unhappy, or disapproving.
put a good, brave, etc. **face on,** make the best of; face cheerfully, bravely, etc.
set one's face against, oppose and resist.
show one's face, appear; be seen.
to one's face, a in one's presence. **b** openly; boldly.
—*v.* **1** have the face (toward); be opposite (to). **2** turn the face (toward). **3** cause to face. **4** meet face to face; stand before. **5** meet bravely or boldly; oppose and resist: *The soldiers faced the enemy.* **6** present itself to: *A crisis faced us.* **7** cover or line with a different material: *a wooden house faced with brick.* **8** apply a piece of material along an edge of a garment for protection or trimming: *She faced the sleeves with silk.* **9** smooth the surface of (stone, etc.). **10 face off,** in hockey, lacrosse, etc., put a puck, ball, etc. into play by dropping or placing it between the sticks of two players facing each other: *The referee starts a hockey game by facing off the puck at centre ice.* [< F *face* < VL *facia* < L *facies* form]
Syn. *n.* **1 Face, countenance, visage** = the front part of the head. **Face** is the common word, but especially emphasizes the physical nature or the features: *That girl has a pretty face.* **Countenance** is formal and emphasizes the looks, especially as they show a person's thoughts, feelings, or character: *He has a cheerful countenance.* **Visage** is a literary word meaning either face or countenance, but emphasizing the general look of the face: *The courtiers were awed by the emperor's sombre visage.* **3** grimace. **7** assurance, effrontery, audacity. –*v.* **4** front, confront. **5** brave, defy, oppose.

face card of playing cards, the king, queen, or jack.

face-cloth (fās′kloth′) *n.* a small cloth, usually made of towelling, for washing the face.

-faced *combining form.* having a —— face or look: *round-faced = having a round face; satin-faced garments = garments having a satin face; gloomy-faced = having a gloomy face.*

face·less (fās′lis) *adj.* **1** without a face: *a faceless clock.* **2** anonymous; without individual character.

face·lift (fās′lift′) *n.* **1** an operation designed to improve the appearance of a face by tightening the skin, removing wrinkles, etc. **2** *Informal.* a change in appearance or manner of operation, designed to improve or bring up-to-date: *The whole company needs a facelift.* —*v.* give a facelift to. —**face′lift′er,** *n.*

face-off (fās′of′) *n.* in hockey, lacrosse, etc., the act of putting the puck, ball, etc. into play; a facing off: *The last goal was scored from the face-off.*

fac·er (fās′ər) *n.* **1** one that faces. **2** a blow in the face. **3** a violent check; a sudden serious difficulty.

fac·et (fas′it) *n. v.* **-et·ted** or **-et ed, -et·ting** or **-et·ing.** —*n.* **1** any one of the small, polished surfaces of a cut gem. **2** anything like the facet of a gem. **3** any one of several sides or views, as of a character or personality: *Selfishness was a facet of his character that we seldom saw.* —*v.* cut facets on. [< F *facette,* dim. of *face.* See FACE.]

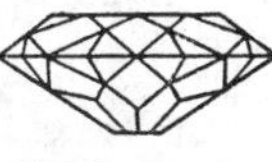
The facets of a diamond

fa·ce·tious (fə sē′shəs) *adj.* **1** having the habit of joking. **2** said in fun; not to be taken seriously. [< L *facetia* jest < *facetus* witty] —**fa·ce′tious·ly,** *adv.* —**fa·ce′tious·ness,** *n.*

face value 1 the value stated on a bond, cheque, note, bill, etc. **2** the apparent worth, meaning, etc.

fa·cial (fā′shəl) *adj.* **1** of the face. **2** for the face. —*n. Informal.* a massage or treatment of the face.

fac·ile (fas′il, fas′ēl, or fas′əl) *adj.* **1** easily done, used, etc.: *a facile task, facile methods.* **2** moving, acting, working, etc. with ease: *a facile hand, a facile tongue, a facile pen.* **3** having easy manners or temper; agreeable; yielding: *Her facile nature adapted itself to any company.* [< L *facilis* easy < *facere* do] —**fac′ile·ly,** *adv.* —**fac·ile′ness,** *n.*
☞ **Facile** often has a pejorative connotation so that it means "too easy" or "working too easily": *facile methods* could be naïve and superficial; *a facile tongue* could refer to a way of speaking that seemed too smooth and charming to be convincing or sincere.

hat, āge, cãre, fär; let, ēqual, tėrm; it, īce
hot, ōpen, ôrder; oil, out; cup, pu̇t, rüle, ūse
əbove, takən, pencəl, lemən, circəs
ch, child; ng, long; sh, ship
th, thin; ᴛʜ, then; zh, measure

fa·cil·i·tate (fə sil′ə tāt′) *v.* **-tat·ed, -tat·ing.** make easy; lessen the labor of; help forward; assist: *A vacuum cleaner facilitates housework.* —**Syn.** expedite.

fa·cil·i·ty (fə sil′ə tē) *n.* **-ties. 1** the absence of difficulty, ease: *The facility of communication is far greater now than it was a hundred years ago.* **2** the power to do anything easily, quickly, and smoothly. **3** something that makes an action easy; an aid; convenience: *Ropes, swings, and sand piles are facilities for play.* **4** Often, **facilities,** *pl.* anything built or installed for a special purpose or to facilitate something: *washroom facilities. At the opening of the cafeteria, the workers thanked the management for the new facility provided.* **5** an easy-going quality; a tendency to yield to others. —**Syn. 1** easiness. **2** knack, readiness.

fac·ing (fās′ing) *n.* **1** a covering of different material for ornament, protection, etc.: *A wooden house sometimes has a brick facing.* **2** any material applied inside or outside, along an edge of a garment to protect or trim it.
3 facings, *pl.* the cuffs, collar, and trimmings of a coat or jacket.

facsim. facsimile.

fac·sim·i·le (fak sim′ə lē) *n. v.* **-led** (-lid), **-le·ing.** —*n.* **1** an exact copy or likeness; a perfect reproduction. **2** a process for transmitting printed matter and photographs by radio and reproducing them on paper at the receiving set. **3 in facsimile,** exactly. —*v.* make a facsimile of. [< L *fac* (imperative) make + *simile* (neut.) like]

fact (fakt) *n.* **1** anything known to be true or to have really happened: *scientific facts.* **2** what is true or has really happened; truth; reality: *The fact of the matter is, I did not go.* **3** something said or supposed to be true or to have really happened: *We doubted his facts.* **4** in law, anything that is known or alleged to have occurred in connection with a case (as distinguished from a principle or rule): *A question of fact is decided by the jury, a question of law by the court.* **5** *Obsolete.* a deed; act. **6 in fact,** truly; really. **7 in point of fact,** truly; really. [< L *factum* (thing) done, pp. neut. of *facere* do. Doublet of FEAT.] —**Syn. 2** actuality.
☞ **fact.** *The fact that* is very often a circumlocution for which *that* alone would be more direct and more acceptable stylistically: *He was quite conscious (of the fact) that his visitor had some special reason for coming.*

fac·tion (fak′shən) *n.* **1** a group of people in a political party, church, club, etc. acting together, usually against the interests of the group as a whole. **2** a selfish or unscrupulous group: *A faction in our club tried to use its prestige for their own purposes.* **3** strife or quarrelling among the members of a political party, church, club, etc. [< L *factio, -onis* party, originally, a doing < *facere* do. Doublet of FASHION.] —**Syn. 1** party, group, clique, cabal.

fac·tion·al (fak′shən əl) *adj.* **1** of or having to do with factions; partisan. **2** causing faction.

fac·tious (fak′shəs) *adj.* **1** fond of causing strife or faction. **2** of or caused by strife or faction. [< L *factiosus* < *factio.* See FACTION.] —**fac′tious·ly,** *adv.* —**fac′tious·ness,** *n.*

fac·ti·tious (fak tish′əs) *adj.* developed by effort; not natural; forced; artificial: *Extensive advertising can cause a factitious demand for an article.* [< L *facticius* artificial < *facere* do, make. Doublet of FETISH.] —**fac·ti′tious·ly,** *adv.* —**fac·ti′tious·ness,** *n.*

fac·ti·tive (fak′tə tiv) *adj.* in grammar: **1** denoting a verb that takes a direct object and an objective complement. *Examples:* They *made* him captain. They *called* him a fool. **2** of or having to do with such a verb. [< NL *factitivus* < L *factitare* make or declare to be < *factare* make (frequentative) < *facere* make, do] —**fac′ti·tive·ly,** *adv.*

fac·tor (fak′tər) *n.* **1** any element, condition, quality, etc. that helps to bring about a result: *Endurance is an important factor of success in sports.* **2** in mathematics, any of the numbers, algebraic expressions, etc. that produce a given number or quantity when multiplied together: *5, 3, and 4 are factors of 60.* **3** a person who acts as a representative of a company; agent: *The Hudson's Bay Company formerly employed many factors, now usually called managers, in its fur-trading posts throughout the Northland.* **4** in biology, a gene. [< L *factor* doer < *facere* do]

fac·tor·age (fak′tər ij) *n.* **1** the business of a factor or agent; buying and selling on commission. **2** a commission paid to a factor or agent.

fac·tor·ize (fak′tə rīz′) *v.* **-rized, -riz·ing.** in mathematics, separate into factors.

fac·to·ry (fak′tə rē or fak′trē) *n.* **-ries. 1** a building or group of buildings where things are manufactured. **2** a trading post. [< Med.L *factoria* < L *factor.* See FACTOR.] —**Syn. 1** mill.

fac·to·tum (fak tō′təm) *n.* a person employed to do all kinds of work. [< Med.L < L *fac* (imperative) do + *totum* the whole]

fac·tu·al (fak′chü əl) *adj.* concerned with fact; consisting of facts. —**fac′tu·al·ly,** *adv.* —**fac′tu·al·ness,** *n.*

fac·ul·ty (fak′əl tē) *n.* **-ties. 1** a power of the mind or body: *the faculty of hearing, the faculty of memory. Old people sometimes lose their faculties.* **2** the power to do some special thing, especially a power of the mind: *Nell has a remarkable faculty for arithmetic.* **3** the teachers of a college, or university, and less often of a school. **4** a department of learning in a university: *the faculty of arts and science, of law, of medicine.* **5** the members of a profession: *The medical faculty is made up of doctors, surgeons, etc.* [< L *facultas* < *facilis.* See FACILE.] —**Syn. 1** capacity, capability.

fad (fad) *n.* **1** something everybody is very much interested in for a short time; a craze; rage: *Crossword puzzles became a fad several years ago.* **2** a hobby: *Collecting stamps is an interesting fad.* [origin uncertain]

fad·dish (fad′ish) *adj.* **1** inclined to follow fads. **2** like a fad. —**fad′dish·ness,** *n.*

fad·dist (fad′ist) *n.* a person devoted to a fad; person who takes up fads.

fade (fād) *v.* **fad·ed, fad·ing. 1** lose color or brightness: *My colored dress faded when it was washed.* **2** lose freshness or strength; wither: *The flowers in her garden faded at the end of the summer.* **3** die away; disappear: *The sound of the train faded away.* **4** cause to fade: *Sunlight faded my new dress.* **5** in motion pictures, radio, and television: **a fade in,** slowly become more distinct or louder. **b fade out,** slowly become less perceptible. [ME < OF *fader* < *fade* pale, weak < VL *fatidus* < L *fatuus* silly, tasteless; influenced by L *sapidus* (cf. OF *sade*) tasty] —**Syn. 1** blanch, bleach, pale. **2** droop. **3** See **disappear.**

fade-in (fād′in′) *n.* in movies, radio, television, a gradual increase in brightness or sound.

fade·less (fād′lis) *adj.* not fading; permanent.

fade-out (fād′out′) *n.* **1** in a motion picture, or on television, a scene that slowly disappears. **2** a gradual disappearance.

fae·cal (fē′kəl) *adj.* fecal.

fae·ces (fē′sēz) *n.pl.* feces.

fa·er·ie (fā′ər ē or fãr′ē) *n.* **-ies,** *adj. Archaic.* —*n.* **1** fairyland. **2** fairy. —*adj.* fairy. [var. of *fairy*]

fa·er·y (fā′ər ē or fãr′ē) *n.* **fa·er·ies,** *adj.* faerie.

fag[1] (fag) *v.* **fagged, fag·ging,** *n.* —*v.* **1** work hard or until wearied: *Tom fagged away at his arithmetic.* **2** tire by work: *The horse was fagged.* **3** act as a fag. —*n.* **1** a hard, uninteresting job; drudgery. **2** a person who does hard work; drudge. **3** *Brit.* a boy who waits on an older boy in certain schools. [origin uncertain]

fag[2] (fag) *n. Esp.Brit. Slang.* a cigarette. [origin uncertain]

fag end 1 the last and poorest part of anything; remnant. **2** the coarse, unfinished end of a piece of cloth. **3** an untwisted end of rope.

fag·got or **fag·ot** (fag′ət) *n. v.* —*n.* **1** a bundle of sticks or twigs tied together: *He built the fire with faggots.* **2** a bundle of iron rods or pieces of iron or steel to be welded. —*v.* **1** tie or fasten together into bundles; make into a faggot. **2** ornament with faggoting. [< OF]

fag·got·ing or **fag·ot·ing** (fag′ət ing) *n.* **1** an ornamental stitch made by drawing horizontal threads out of the cloth and tying groups of the cross threads together in the middle. **2** an open, zigzag stitch used for loosely joining two finished edges.

fag·ot (fag′ət) *n. v.* faggot.

fag·ot·ing (fag′ət ing) *n.* **faggoting.**

Fahr. Fahrenheit.

Fahr·en·heit (far′ən hīt′) *adj.* of, based on, or according to the Fahrenheit scale for measuring temperature, on which 32 degrees marks the freezing point of water and 212 degrees the boiling point. *Abbrev.*: F., F, or Fahr. —*n.* a Fahrenheit thermometer or its scale. [< Gabriel Daniel *Fahrenheit,* 1686-1736, the German physicist who introduced this scale]

Fahrenheit thermometer a thermometer marked according to the Fahrenheit scale. See **thermometer** for diagram.

fai·ence (fī ons′ or fā äns′; *French,* fä yäns′) *n.* a glazed earthenware or porcelain, usually of fine quality. [< F; said to be named after and to have been invented in *Faenza,* Italy, in 1299]

fail (fāl) *v.* **1** not succeed; be unable to do or become what is wanted, expected, or attempted; come out badly: *After a long drought, the crops failed.* **2** not do; neglect: *He failed to follow our advice.* **3** be of no use or help to: *When we needed him, he failed us.* **4** be lacking or absent; be not enough; fall short: *When our supplies failed, we starved.* **5** lose strength; become weak; die away: *The sick man's heart was failing.* **6** be unable to pay what one owes: *That company will fail.* **7** be unsuccessful in an examination, etc.; receive a mark of failure. **8** give the mark of failure to (a student). **9 fail of,** be unable to have or get; lack. —*n.* **without fail,** without failing to do, happen, etc.; surely; certainly. [ME < OF *faillir,* ult. < L *fallere* deceive] —**fail′er,** *n.* —**Syn.** *v.* **5** decline, sink, wane, deteriorate.

fail·ing (fāl′ing) *n.* **1** a failure. **2** a fault; weakness; defect. —*prep.* in the absence of; lacking; without: *Failing good weather, the party will be held indoors.* —**Syn.** *n.* **2** See **fault.**

faille (fīl or fāl) *n.* a soft, ribbed cloth of silk, rayon, acetate, etc. [< F < MDu. *falie* scarf]

fail·ure (fāl′yər) *n.* **1** a being unable to do or become; failing. **2** a not doing; neglecting. **3** a lack or absence; falling short. **4** a loss of strength; becoming weak; dying away. **5** the state of being unable to pay what one owes. **6** a person or thing that has failed: *The picnic was a failure because it rained.* —**Syn. 4** decline, decay, deterioration. **5** bankruptcy.

fain (fān) *Archaic and poetic.* —*adv.* by choice; gladly; willingly. —*adj.* **1** willing, but not eager; forced by circumstances. **2** glad; willing. **3** eager; desirous. [OE *fægen*]

faint (fānt) *adj.* **1** not clear or plain; dim: *faint colors.* **2** weak; feeble: *a faint voice.* **3** done feebly or without zest: *a faint attempt.* **4** ready to faint; about to faint. **5** lacking courage; cowardly. **6** oppressive. —*v.* **1** lose consciousness temporarily. **2** *Archaic.* grow weak; lose courage: "*Ye shall reap, if ye faint not.*" —*n.* a temporary lack of consciousness caused by an insufficient flow of blood to the brain. In this condition, a person lies for a time as if asleep and does not know what is going on around him. [ME < OF *faint, feint,* pp. of *faindre, feindre.* See FEIGN.] —**faint′ly,** *adv.* —**faint′ness,** *n.* —**Syn.** *adj.* **1** indistinct, faded. **2** faltering, languid.

faint·heart (fānt′härt′) *n.* a faint-hearted person.

faint-heart·ed (fānt′här′tid) *adj.* lacking courage; cowardly; timid. —**faint′-heart′ed·ly,** *adv.* —**faint′-heart′ed·ness,** *n.*

fair[1] (fãr) *adj.* **1** not favoring one more than the other or others; just; honest: *a fair judge.* **2** according to the rules: *fair play.* **3** pretty good; not bad; average: *There is a fair crop of wheat this year.* **4** favorable; likely; promising: *He is in a fair way to succeed.* **5** not dark; light: *A blond person has fair hair and skin.* **6** not cloudy

hat, āge, cãre, fär; let, ēqual, tėrm; it, īce
hot, ōpen, ôrder; oil, out; cup, pút, rüle, ūse
əbove, takən, pencəl, lemən, circəs
ch, child; ng, long; sh, ship
th, thin; ᴛʜ, then; zh, measure

or stormy; clear; sunny: *The weather will be fair today.* **7** pleasing to look at; beautiful: *a fair lady.* **8** civil; courteous: *fair words.* **9** without spots or stains; clean: *She made a fair copy of her essay.* **10** easily read; plain: *fair handwriting.* **11** unobstructed; open: *a fair view of the ocean.* **12** seeming good at first, but not really so: *His fair promises proved false.* **13 fair and square,** *Informal.* just; honest. **14 fair to middling,** moderately good; average. **15 the fair sex,** women.
—*adv.* **1** in a fair manner. **2** directly; straight: *The stone hit him fair on the head.* **3 bid fair,** seem likely; have a good chance.
—*n. Archaic.* a woman; sweetheart. [OE *fæger*]
—**fair′ness,** *n.*
Syn. *adj.* **1 Fair, just, impartial** = not showing favor in making judgments. **Fair** emphasizes putting all on an equal footing: *He is fair event o people he dislikes.* **Just** emphasizes paying attention only to what is right or lawful: *Our teacher is always just in her grading.* **Impartial** emphasizes complete absence of favor or feeling for or against either side: *We need someone impartial to settle this quarrel.* **3** middling, passable, tolerable. **4** propitious. **7** pretty, comely, attractive. **9** spotless, untarnished, pure.

fair² (fãr) *n.* **1** a display of goods, products, etc.; an exhibition: *The Royal Winter Fair. At the county fair last year, prizes were given for the best farm products and livestock.* **2** a gathering of people to buy and sell, often held in a certain place at regular times during the year. **3** an entertainment and sale of articles: *Our church held a fair to raise money.* [ME < OF *feire* < LL *feria* holiday]

fair ball **1** in baseball, a batted ball that is not a foul. **2** *Slang.* a fair deal; an acceptable arrangement.

fair game **1** animals or birds that it is lawful to hunt. **2** a suitable object of attack.

fair·ground (fãr′ground′) *n.* a place out of doors, usually with equipment for exhibitions and entertainment, where fairs are held.

fair-haired (fãr′härd′) *adj.* having light-colored hair.

fair-haired boy *Informal.* a favorite.

fair·ish (fãr′ish) *adj.* fairly good, well, or large.

fair·ly (fãr′lē) *adv.* **1** in a fair manner. **2** to a fair degree. **3** justly; honestly. **4** rather; somewhat: *A fairly good pupil is neither very bad nor very good.* **5** actually. **6** clearly. —**Syn. 2** tolerably. **3** impartially. **5** positively. **6** legibly, distinctly, plainly.

fair-mind·ed (fãr′mīn′did) *adj.* not prejudiced; just; impartial. —**fair′-mind′ed·ly,** *adv.* —**fair′-mind′ed·ness,** *n.*

fair play **1** an abiding by the rules of a game; fair dealings in any contest. **2** just and equal treatment of all.

fair shake *Esp.U.S. Informal.* an honest arrangement; fair treatment.

fair-spo·ken (fãr′spō′kən) *adj.* speaking smoothly and pleasantly; civil; courteous.

fair·way (fãr′wā′) *n.* **1** an unobstructed passage or way. The fairway in a harbor is the channel for ships. **2** the part in a golf course where the grass is kept short, between the tee and the putting green.

fair-weath·er (fãr′weᴛʜ′ər) *adj.* **1** of or fitted for fair weather. **2** weakening or failing in time of need: *He is only a fair-weather friend.*

fair·y (fãr′ē) *n.* **fair·ies,** *adj.* —*n.* an imaginary supernatural being with magic powers, able to help or harm human beings. In recent legend, fairies have been pictured as very small, and sometimes very lovely and delicate. In medieval story, however, fairies were often of full human size. —*adj.* **1** of fairies. **2** like a fairy; lovely; delicate. [ME < OF *faerie* < *fae.* See FAY¹.]
—**fair′y-like′,** *adj.* —**Syn.** *n.* elf, fay, sprite, brownie.

fair·y·land (fãr′ē land′) *n.* **1** the imaginary place where the fairies live. **2** an enchanting and pleasant place.

fairy ring a circle formed on the grass by certain fungi. It used to be thought that it was made by fairies when dancing.

fairy tale **1** a story about fairies or other beings with magic powers. **2** *Informal.* an untrue story; falsehood; lie. —**fair′y-tale′,** *adj.*

fait ac·com·pli (fet′ə kom′plē; *French,* fe tä kôɴ plē′) something done and so no longer worth opposing. [< F]

faith (fāth) *n.* **1** a believing without proof; trust. **2** belief in God, religion, or spiritual things. **3** what is believed. **4** a religion. **5** a being faithful; loyalty: *Good faith is honesty of intention; bad faith is intent to deceive.* **6 in faith,** truly; indeed. **7 in bad faith,** dishonestly. **8 in good faith,** honestly; sincerely. **9 keep faith,** keep one's promise. —*interj. Archaic.* truly; indeed. [ME < OF *feid* < L *fides.* Doublet of FAY².] —**Syn.** *n.* **1** confidence, reliance. **3** doctrine, tenet, creed. See **belief.** **5** fidelity, constancy, faithfulness.

faith·ful (fāth′fəl) *adj.* **1** worthy of trust; doing one's duty; keeping one's promise; loyal: *a faithful friend, a faithful servant.* **2** true; accurate: *The witness gave a faithful account of what happened.* **3** *Archaic.* full of faith. —*n.* **the faithful,** a true believers. b loyal followers or supporters. —**faith′ful·ly,** *adv.* —**faith′ful·ness,** *n.*
Syn. *adj.* **1 Faithful, loyal, constant** = true to a person or thing. **Faithful** emphasizes being true to a person, group, belief, duty, or trust to which one is bound by a promise, pledge, honor, or love: *He is a faithful friend.* **Loyal** adds to *faithful* the idea of wanting to stand by and fight for the person or thing, even against heavy odds: *She was loyal during his trial.* **Constant** emphasizes steadfast devotion to friends or loved ones: *One could not find a more constant friend.* **2** precise, exact.

faith·less (fāth′lis) *adj.* **1** unworthy of trust; failing in one's duty; breaking one's promise; not loyal: *A traitor is faithless.* **2** not reliable. **3** without faith; unbelieving. —**faith′less·ly,** *adv.* —**faith′less·ness,** *n.* —**Syn. 1** disloyal, false, inconstant, fickle. **3** doubting, sceptical.

fake (fāk) *v.* **faked, fak·ing,** *n. adj.* —*v.* **1** make to seem satisfactory; falsify; counterfeit: *The picture was faked by pasting together two photographs.* **2** intentionally give a false appearance of; simulate: *to fake an illness.*
—*n.* a fraud; deception: *The beggar's limp was a fake.*
—*adj.* intended to deceive; false: *The firm forbids its salesman to use fake testimonials.* [origin uncertain]
—**fak′er,** *n.*

fa·kir (fä′kər or fə kēr′) *n.* **1** a Moslem holy man who lives by begging. **2** a dervish. **3** a Hindu ascetic. Some fakirs lie on beds of nails. [< Arabic *faqir* poor]

Fa·lange (fā′lanj or fə lanj′; *Spanish,* fä läng′hä) *n.* the political party holding power in Spain since the Civil War (1936-1939). [< Sp. < L *phalanx* phalanx < Gk.]

Fa·lan·gist (fə lan′jist) *n.* a member of the Falange.

fal·cate (fal′kāt) *adj.* curved like a sickle; hooked. [< L *falcatus* < *falx, falcis* sickle]

fal·chion (fol′chən or fôl′chən) *n.* **1** a broad, short sword with an edge that curves to a point. **2** *Poetic.* any sword. [ME < OF Ital. *falcione,* ult. < L *falx, falcis* sickle]

A falchion (def. 1)

fal·con (fol′kən or fôl′kən) *n.* **1** a hawk or hawk-like bird trained to hunt and kill birds and small game. In the Middle Ages, hunting with falcons was a popular sport. **2** a swift-flying hawk having a short, curved, notched bill, and long claws and wings. [ME < OF < LL *falco, -onis* for L *falx, falcis* sickle; from the hooked talons]

fal·con·er (fol′kən ər or fôl′kən ər) *n.* **1** a man who hunts with falcons. **2** a breeder and trainer of falcons.

fal·con·ry (fol′kən rē or fôl′kən rē) *n.* **1** the sport of hunting with falcons. **2** the training of falcons to hunt.

fal·de·ral (fol′də rol′) *n.* **1** a flimsy thing; a trifle. **2** nonsense; rubbish. **3** a meaningless refrain in songs. Also, **falderol, folderol.**

fal·de·rol (fol′də rol′) *n.* falderal.

fall (fol or fôl) *v.* **fell, fall·en, fall·ing,** *n.* —*v.* **1** drop or come down from a higher place: *The snow is falling fast. The leaves are falling from the trees.* **2** come down suddenly from an erect position: *He fell on his knees.* **3** hang down: *Her curls fell upon her shoulders.* **4** droop: *His spirits fell at the bad news.* **5** yield to temptation: *He was tempted and fell.* **6** lose position, power, dignity, etc.: *The dictator fell from the people's favor.* **7** be captured, overthrown, or destroyed: *The fort fell to the enemy.* **8** drop wounded or dead; be killed: *Many men fell in battle.* **9** pass into a certain condition; become: *He fell asleep. The rent falls due on Monday.* **10** come; arrive: *When night falls, the stars appear.* **11** come by chance or lot: *Our choice fell on him.* **12** come to pass; happen; occur: *Christmas falls on Sunday this year.* **13** pass by inheritance: *The money fell to the only son.* **14** be placed: *The principal stress of "farmer" falls on the first syllable.* **15** become lower or less: *Prices fell sharply. The water in the river has fallen two feet. The pitch of the voice often falls at the end of a statement.* **16** be divided: *The story falls into five parts.* **17** look sad or disappointed: *His face fell at the bad news.* **18** slope downward: *The land falls gradually to the beach.* **19** be directed: *The light falls on my book.*

fall across, or **among,** come upon or among by chance; meet with.

fall apart, crumble; break down; disintegrate.

fall away, a withdraw support or allegiance. **b** become bad or worse. **c** be overthrown or destroyed. **d** become thin.

fall back, go toward the rear, retreat.

fall back on, a go back to for safety. **b** turn to for help or support.

fall behind, fail to keep up.

fall down on, *Informal.* prove a failure at.

fall flat, fail completely; have no effect or interest: *The poor performance fell flat.*

fall for, *Slang.* **a** be deceived by. **b** fall in love with.

fall foul (of or **upon), a** become entangled. **b** come into conflict; quarrel with. **c** come into collision, as ships.

fall from, *Obsolete.* **a** disagree with. **b** forsake allegiance to. **c** give up.

fall from grace, a *Informal.* lose favor. **b** revert to sin or evildoing; backslide.

fall heir to, inherit.

fall in, a take a place in a military formation and come to a position of attention. **b** meet. **c** agree. **d** collapse toward the inside: *The building fell in.*

fall off, a drop; become less. **b** (of health) deteriorate.

fall on, a attack: *The Indians fell on the sleeping settlement.* **b** come across; light on.

fall out, a leave a place in a military formation. **b** stop being friends; quarrel. **c** turn out; happen.

fall short (of), a fail. **b** fail to equal: *Income fell short of expenditures.*

fall through, fail.

fall to, a begin. **b** begin to attack, eat, etc. **c** go into place; close by itself: *The lid of the chest fell to.*

fall under, belong under; be classified as.

fall upon, attack.

—*n.* **1** a falling; dropping from a higher place. **2** the amount that falls: *We had a heavy fall of snow last winter.* **3** the distance that anything falls. **4** a waterfall. **5** a coming down suddenly from an erect position: *The child had a bad fall.* **6** a hanging down; dropping. **7** a giving in to temptation. **8** a loss of position, power, dignity, etc. **9** a capture; overthrow; destruction. **10** the proper place: *the fall of a stress.* **11** a lowering; becoming less. **12** a downward slope. **13** the season of the year between summer and winter; autumn. **14** in wrestling: **a** a being thrown on one's back. **b** a contest. **15 falls,** *pl.* **a** a waterfall; cataract; cascade. **b** an apparatus used in lowering and raising a ship's boat. **16 ride for a fall,** act so as to be in danger or get into trouble. **17 the Fall,** the sin of Adam and Eve in yielding to temptation and eating the forbidden fruit. [OE *feallan*] **—Syn.** *v.* **1** descend.

☛ **Falls,** though plural in form, is really singular (or collective) in meaning. We speak of *a falls* but ordinarily use it with a plural verb: *The falls are almost dry in August.* In proper names *falls* is frequently used with a singular verb: *Niagara Falls is receding.*

fal·la·cious (fə lā′shəs) *adj.* **1** deceptive; misleading. **2** logically unsound; erroneous: *It is fallacious reasoning to base a general rule on just two or three examples.* **—fal·la′cious·ly,** *adv.* **—fal·la′cious·ness,** *n.*

fal·la·cy (fal′ə sē) *n.* **-cies. 1** a false idea; mistaken belief; error: *It is a fallacy to suppose that riches always bring happiness.* **2** a mistake in reasoning; misleading or unsound argument. **3** unsoundness; falsity; delusive character. [< L *fallacia* < *fallax* deceptive < *fallere* deceive]

fal·lal (fal′lal′) *n.* a useless bit of finery. [coined word]

fall·en (fol′ən or fôl′ən) *v.* pp. of **fall.** —*adj.* **1** dropped. **2** on the ground; down flat. **3** degraded. **4** overthrown; destroyed. **5** dead. **6** shrunken; decreased: *fallen cheeks.* —*n.* dead: *The battlefield was covered with the fallen.* **—Syn.** *adj.* **1** decreased, depreciated. **3** debased. **4** ruined.

fallen angel any one of the angels who were cast out of heaven when Satan rebelled against God.

fall guy *Slang.* **1** the member of a comic act who takes all the knocks. **2** any person left in a difficult situation, especially a scapegoat.

fal·li·bil·i·ty (fal′ə bil′ə tē) *n.* a fallible quality or nature.

fal·li·ble (fal′ə bəl) *adj.* **1** liable to be deceived or mistaken; liable to err. **2** liable to be erroneous, inaccurate, or false. [< Med.L *fallibilis* < *fallere* deceive]

falling sickness epilepsy.

falling star meteor.

fall line a line that marks the end of layers of hard rock of a plateau and the beginning of a softer rock layer of a coastal plain. Many falls and rapids mark this line.

Fal·lo·pi·an tubes (fə lō′pē ən) a pair of slender tubes through which ova from the ovaries pass to the uterus. [after *Fallopius,* a 16th-century Italian anatomist]

fall-out (fol′out′ or fôl′-) *n.* the radio-active particles or dust that fall to the earth after an atomic explosion.

fal·low[1] (fal′ō) *adj.* ploughed and left unseeded for a season or more; uncultivated; inactive. —*n.* **1** land ploughed and left unseeded for a season or more: *Half the farm lay fallow in summer.* **2** the ploughing of land without seeding it for a season in order to destroy weeds, improve the soil, etc. [OE *fealg*]

fal·low[2] (fal′ō) *n. adj.* pale yellowish-brown. [OE *fealu*]

fallow deer a small European deer having a yellowish coat that is spotted with white in the summer.

false (fols or fôls) *adj.* **fals·er, fals·est,** *adv.* —*adj.* **1** not true; not correct; wrong: *false statements, false testimony.* **2** not truthful; lying. **3** not loyal; not faithful: *a false friend.* **4** used to deceive; deceiving: *false weights.* **5** in music, not true in pitch: *a false note.* **6** not real; artificial: *false diamonds.* **7** based on wrong notions; ill-founded: *False pride kept the poor man from accepting money from his rich brothers.* **8** in biology, improperly called or named. The false acacia is really a locust tree.

—*adv.* **1** in a false manner. **2 play false,** deceive; cheat; trick; betray. [< L *falsus* < *fallere* deceive] **—false′ly,** *adv.* **—false′ness,** *n.*

Syn. *adj.* **1** erroneous, mistaken, incorrect. **2** untruthful, mendacious. **3** disloyal, unfaithful, inconstant, treacherous, traitorous. **4** misleading, deceptive, fallacious. **6 False, counterfeit** = not real or genuine. **False,** describing something made to look like the real thing, emphasizes pretending to be what it really is not, and sometimes suggests being intended to deceive others: *Most false teeth really look natural.* **Counterfeit** emphasizes passing as the real thing, and always suggests being meant to deceive or cheat: *Counterfeit money occasionally gets into circulation.*

false alarm 1 a warning signal, such as a fire alarm, air raid siren, etc., given when no danger exists. **2** a situation that arouses some strong reaction, as of hope, fear, etc., which proves to be unjustified.

false bottom the bottom of a trunk, suitcase, drawer etc. that forms a secret or a supplementary compartment.

false colors or **colours 1** a flag of another country, used for deception: *The raiding ship was flying false colors.* **2** false pretences.

false face 1 a funny or ugly mask; mask. **2 put on a false face,** assume a certain appearance or behavior in order to deceive.

false·hood (fols′hůd or fôls′-) *n.* **1** the quality of being false; falsity. **2** something false. **3** a making of false statements: lying. **4** a false statement; lie. **5** an attempt to deceive; pretence. **—Syn. 1** falseness, untruthfulness, mendacity. **4** untruth, fib. See **lie.**

false pride a pride based on mistaken ideas.

false ribs the ribs not attached to the breastbone. Human beings have five pairs of false ribs.

false step 1 a wrong step; stumble. **2** a blunder; mistake.

false teeth artificial teeth used after the real teeth have been removed.

fal·set·to (fol set′o or fôl set′ō) *n.* **-tos,** *adj. adv.*

—*n.* 1 an unnaturally high-pitched voice, especially in a man. 2 a person who sings with a falsetto.
—*adj.* of or for a falsetto; that sings in a falsetto.
—*adv.* in a falsetto. [< Ital. *falsetto*, dim. of *falso* false < L *falsus*. See FALSE.]

false·work (fols′wėrk′ or fôls′-) *n.* a temporary structure that supports a bridge, etc. until the main structure is completed.

fal·sies (fol′sēz or fôl′sēz) *n.pl. Informal.* a type of padded brassiere, worn to give a full-bosomed appearance.

fal·si·fi·ca·tion (fol′sə fə kā′shən or fôl′sə fə kā′shən) *n.* a falsifying or being falsified.

fal·si·fy (fol′sə fī′ or fôl′sə fī′) *v.* **-fied, -fy·ing. 1** make false; change in order to deceive; misrepresent. **2** make false statements; lie. **3** prove to be false; disprove. [< LL *falsificare* < L *falsificus* acting falsely < *falsus* (see FALSE) + *facere* make] —**fal′si·fi′er,** *n.*

fal·si·ty (fol′sə tē or fôl′sə tē) *n.* **-ties. 1** a being false; incorrectness: *Education showed him the falsity of his superstitions.* **2** untruthfulness; deceitfulness; treachery. **3** that which is false.

Fal·staff·i·an (fol staf′ē ən or fôl staf′ē ən) *adj.* **1** of or having to do with Falstaff, a soldier in Shakespeare's *Henry IV* and *Merry Wives of Windsor*, or his group of ragged soldiers. **2** fat, jolly, and brazen, as Falstaff was.

fal·ter (fol′tər or fôl′tər) *v.* **1** lose courage; draw back; hesitate; waver: *The soldiers faltered for a moment as their captain fell.* **2** move unsteadily; stumble; totter. **3** speak in hesitating, broken words; stammer: *Greatly embarrassed, he faltered out his thanks.* **4** come forth in hesitating, broken sounds: *His voice faltered.*
—*n.* **1** the act of faltering. **2** a faltering sound. [ME *falteren*; cf. ON *faltrask* be burdened] —**fal′ter·er,** *n.*
—**Syn.** *v.* **1** vacillate. See **hesitate. 2** stagger, tremble.

fame (fām) *n.* **1** a being very well known; having much said or written about one. **2** what is said about one; reputation. [< obs. F < L *fama* < *fari* speak]
—**Syn. 1** notoriety, celebrity, renown, eminence.

famed (fāmd) *adj.* famous; celebrated; well-known.

Fa·meuse (fə mūz′; *French,* fä mœz′) *n.* a late autumn apple having red stripes; snow apple. [< F *fameuse*]

fa·mil·ial (fə mil′yəl or fə mil′ē əl) *adj.* **1** of, having to do with, or characteristic of a family. **2** in genetics, transmitted within the family: *a familial snub nose.*

fa·mil·iar (fə mil′yər) *adj.* **1** well-known; common: *a familiar tune, a familiar face. A knife is a familiar tool.* **2** well acquainted: *He is familiar with French.* **3** close; personal; intimate: *Familiar friends know each other very well.* **4** not formal; friendly. **5** too friendly; presuming; forward.
—*n.* **1** a familiar friend or acquaintance. **2** a spirit or demon supposed to serve a particular person. A witch was formerly supposed to have a familiar in the shape of a black cat. **3** in the Roman Catholic Church, a person who belongs to the household of a bishop, and renders domestic, though not menial, service. **4** an officer of the Inquisition whose chief duty was to arrest the accused or suspected. [ME < OF < L *familiaris* < *familia.* See FAMILY.] —**fa·mil′iar·ly,** *adv.*
Syn. *adj.* **2** conversant, versed. **3 Familiar, intimate, confidential** = personally near or close. **Familiar** suggests the free and easy relationship that comes when people are closely acquainted or have known each other a long time: *I am not familiar with my cousin.* **Intimate** suggests a close relationship that develops when people know each other and each other's thoughts and feelings very well: *They are intimate friends.* **Confidential** emphasizes the trust people place in each other, and suggests that neither will divulge the other's secrets and private affairs: *She is the manager's confidential secretary.* **4** unceremonious, informal.

fa·mil·iar·i·ty (fə mil′yar′ə tē) *n.* **-ties. 1** close acquaintance. **2** a freedom of behavior suitable only to friends; lack of formality or ceremony. **3** an instance of such behavior: *She dislikes such familiarities as the use of her first name by people she has just met.* —**Syn. 1** intimacy, friendship, fellowship. **2** informality, lack of constraint.

fa·mil·iar·ize (fə mil′yər īz′) *v.* **-ized, -iz·ing. 1** make well acquainted: *Before playing the new game, familiarize yourself with the rules.* **2** make well-known: *The publicity given to nuclear research has familiarized a whole new vocabulary.* —**fa·mil′iar·i·za′tion,** *n.*

fam·i·ly (fam′ə lē or fam′lē) *n.* **-lies. 1** a father, mother, and their children. **2** the children of a father and mother. **3** a group of related people living in the same house. **4** all of a person's relatives. **5** a group of related people; tribe. **6** good or noble descent; descent. **7** a group of related or similar things. **8** in biology, a group of related animals or plants ranking below an order and above a genus. Lions, tigers, and leopards belong to the cat family. [< L *familia* household < *famulus* servant]
—**Syn. 5** clan, race. **6** ancestry, stock, lineage.
☛ **Family,** though singular, may take a plural verb when the emphasis is on the individual members: *Her family is opposed to the marriage. The family were gathered in the living room.*

hat, āge, cãre, fär; let, ēqual, tėrm; it, īce
hot, ōpen, ôrder; oil, out; cup, pu̇t, rüle, ūse
əbove, takən, pencəl, lemən, circəs
ch, child; ng, long; sh, ship
th, thin; ᴛʜ, then; zh, measure

family allowance 1 an allowance paid to members of the armed services, often to cover living expenses overseas. **2** an allowance paid by a government to parents for each of their children under a stipulated age. **3 Family Allowance,** in Canada, an allowance paid to mothers by the Federal Government for each child under 16 years of age.

family circle the immediate members of a family; adults and children of a particular household.

Family Compact in Canada, the name applied to the governing class of Upper Canada before 1837, and, in particular, to the executive and legislative councils of Upper Canada.

family man 1 a man who has a family. **2** a man who takes pleasure in his family and enjoys domestic life.

family name the last name of all the members of a certain family; surname.

family skeleton a cause of shame that a family tries to keep secret: *They tried to ignore their family skeleton, the desertion of their grandfather to the enemy.*

family tree 1 a diagram showing the relationships and descent of all the members and ancestors of a family; genealogical chart. **2** all the members of a family line.

fam·ine (fam′ən) *n.* **1** starvation. **2** a lack of food in a place; time of starving: *Many people have died during famines in India.* **3** a very great shortage of anything: *a coal famine.* [< F *famine* < *faim* hunger < L *fames*]
—**Syn. 3** scarcity, insufficiency, deficiency.

fam·ish (fam′ish) *v.* be or make extremely hungry; starve. [ME *famen* famish < OF *afamer* < L *ad* (intensive) + *fames* hunger; modelled after verbs in *-ish*]
—**Syn.** See **hungry.**

fa·mous (fā′məs) *adj.* **1** very well known; noted: *a famous general.* **2** *Informal.* first-rate; excellent. [< AF < L *famosus* < *fama.* See FAME.] —**fa′mous·ly,** *adv.*
Syn. 1 Famous, renowned, noted = very well known. **Famous** applies to a person, place, thing, or happening widely known to the public either during or after its lifetime or existence, always in a good way if still living: *A great crowd of people greeted the famous cosmonaut.* **Renowned** suggests great or long-lasting fame, often great praise and honor: *Shakespeare is renowned.* **Noted** = well known for a particular thing, but not always for something good or for a long time: *The noted gangster was deported.* ☛ See **notorious** for usage note.

fam·u·lus (fam′yu̇ ləs) *n.* **-li** (-lī′ or -lē′). a servant; attendant. [< L]

fan[1] (fan) *n. v.* **fanned, fan·ning.** —*n.* **1** an instrument or device with which to stir the air in order to cool or ventilate a room, to cool one's face, or to blow dust away. **2** anything spread out like an open fan. **3** of machinery: **a** any of various devices consisting essentially of a series of radiating flat or curved blades attached to and revolving with a central hublike part. **b** such a device turned by a belt from the driveshaft for cooling the radiator of an automobile. **c** such a device turned by an electric motor for cooling a room. **4** a winnowing machine.
—*v.* **1** make a current of (air) with a fan, etc. **2** direct a current of air toward with a fan, etc.: *Fan the fire to make it burn faster.* **3** drive away with a fan, etc.: *She fanned the flies from the sleeping child.* **4** stir up; arouse: *Cruel treatment fanned their dislike into hate.* **5** spread out like an open fan. **6** blow gently and refreshingly upon; cool: *The breeze fanned their hot faces.* **7** winnow.

8 *Slang.* in baseball, strike out. [OE *fann* < L *vannus* fan for winnowing grain] **—fan′like′,** *adj.* **—fan′ner,** *n.*

fan² (fan) *n. Informal.* **1** a person extremely interested (in baseball, motion pictures, radio, etc.). **2** an admirer of an actor, writer, etc. [short for *fanatic*]

fa·nat·ic (fə nat′ik) *n.* a person who is carried away beyond reason by his feelings or beliefs. *—adj.* enthusiastic or zealous beyond reason. [< L *fanaticus* inspired by divinity < *fanum* temple]

fa·nat·i·cal (fə nat′ə kəl) *adj.* unreasonably enthusiastic; extremely zealous. **—fa·nat′i·cal·ly,** *adv.*

fa·nat·i·cism (fə nat′ə siz′əm) *n.* an unreasonable enthusiasm; extreme zeal.

fan·cied (fan′sēd) *adj.* imagined; imaginary.

fan·ci·er (fan′sē ər) *n.* a person who is especially interested in something: *A dog fancier is interested in breeding and raising dogs.*

fan·ci·ful (fan′sē fəl) *adj.* **1** showing fancy; quaint; odd: *a fanciful decoration.* **2** influenced by fancy; imaginative. **3** suggested by fancy; imaginary; unreal: *He gave a fanciful account of the events.* **—fan′ci·ful·ly,** *adv.* **—fan′ci·ful·ness,** *n.*

fan·cy (fan′sē) *n.* **-cies,** *v.* **-cied, -cy·ing,** *adj.* **-ci·er, -ci·est.** *—n.* **1** one's power to imagine; imagination: *Dragons, fairies, and giants are creatures of fancy.* **2** something imagined. **3** something supposed; an idea; notion. **4** a liking; fondness: *They took a great fancy to each other.* **5** a liking that lasts only a short time.
—v. **1** imagine. **2** have an idea or belief; suppose: *I fancy she is about forty.* **3** be fond of; like. **4 fancy oneself,** think highly of oneself: *That girl really fancies herself.*
—adj. **1** showy: *a fancy dancer.* **2** decorated; ornamental. **3** of high quality: *fancy pears.* **4** excessively high: *fancy prices.* **5** bred for special excellence. [contraction of *fantasy*] **—Syn.** *n.* **1** fantasy. See **imagination. 3** conception, whim, caprice. *-v.* **1** conceive, picture. **2** presume, conjecture.

fancy dress 1 costumes such as those worn at a masquerade: *People who go to parties dressed as clowns, historical personages, etc. are wearing fancy dress.* **2** a particular costume of this nature.

fan·cy-free (fan′sē frē′) *adj.* **1** not in love. **2** carefree; not restrained.

fancy man *Slang.* a man who is supported by a woman, especially by a prostitute.

fancy woman *Slang.* a mistress or prostitute.

fan·cy·work (fan′sē wėrk′) *n.* ornamental needlework; embroidery, crocheting, etc.

F. and A. M. Free and Accepted Masons.

fan·dan·go (fan dang′gō) *n.* **-gos. 1** a lively Spanish dance in three-quarter time. **2** the music for such a dance. [< Sp.]

fane (fān) *n. Archaic and poetic.* temple; church. [< L *fanum* temple]

fan·fare (fan′fãr) *n.* **1** a short tune or call sounded by trumpets, bugles, hunting horns, etc. **2** a loud show of activity, talk, etc.; showy flourish. [< F *fanfare* < *fanfarer* blow a fanfare < Sp. < Arabic *farfâr* talkative]

fang (fang) *n.* **1** a long, pointed tooth of a dog, wolf, snake, etc. Poisonous snakes have hollow or grooved fangs through which they inject venom into their victims. **2** a long, slender, tapering part of anything, such as the root of a tooth or the prong of a fork. [OE]

fan hitch *Cdn.* a method of harnessing sled dogs first used by Eskimos, with a lead dog up in front and others on shorter traces fanning out behind him.

fan·light (fan′līt′) *n.* **1** a semicircular window with bars spread out like an open fan. **2** any semicircular or other window over a door.

fan mail the mail received by a celebrity from fans.

fan·tail (fan′tāl′) *n.* **1** a tail, end, or part spread out like an open fan. **2** a pigeon whose tail spreads out like an open fan. **3** any of various animals whose tail spreads out like an open fan. **4** in architecture, a fan-shaped structure or part.

fan-tan (fan′tan′) *n.* **1** a Chinese gambling game played by betting on the number of coins under a bowl. **2** a card game in which the player who gets rid of his cards first wins the game. [< Chinese *fan t'an* repeated divisions]

fan·ta·si·a (fan tā′zhē ə, fan tā′zhə, or fan tā′zē ə) *n.* in music: **1** a composition in which form depends on the composer's fancy. **2** a medley of popular tunes with interludes. [< Ital. *fantasia* < L < Gk. *phantasia.* Doublet of FANTASY.]

fan·tas·tic (fan tas′tik) *adj.* **1** very odd or queer; wild and strange in shape; showing unrestrained fancy: *The firelight cast weird, fantastic shadows on the walls.* **2** very fanciful; capricious; eccentric; irrational: *A hundred years ago, the idea that machines could be made to fly seemed fantastic.* **3** existing only in the imagination; unreal: *Superstition causes fantastic fears.* **4** *Informal.* unbelievably good, quick, high, etc.: *That store charges fantastic prices.* [ME < OF < LL < Gk. *phantastikos* < *phantazesthai* appear] **—fan·tas′ti·cal·ly,** *adv.* **—Syn. 1** freakish, bizarre, grotesque.

fan·tas·ti·cal (fan tas′tə kəl) *adj.* fantastic.

fan·ta·sy (fan′tə sē or fan′tə zē) *n.* **-sies. 1** the play of the mind; imagination; fancy. **2** a wild, strange fancy. **3** a picture existing only in the mind; queer illusion. Fantasies seem real to a delirious person. **4** a caprice; whim. **5** in music, a fantasia. Also, **phantasy.** [ME < OF *fantasie* < L < Gk. *phantasia* appearance, image, ult. < *phainein* show. Doublet of FANTASIA.]

fan tracery in architecture, tracery used in fan vaulting.

fan vaulting in architecture, a style of vaulting in which the ribs flare out like those of a fan.

fan·wise (fan′wīz′) *adv.* as a fan; spread out like an open fan.

FAO in the United Nations, Food and Agricultural Organization.

far (fär) *adj.* **far·ther, far·thest,** *adv. —adj.* **1** distant; not near: *a far country.* **2** more distant: *the far side of the hill.* **3** extending to a great distance; long: *a far look ahead, a far journey.*
—adv. **1** a long way off in time or space: *far distant.* **2** very much: *It is far better to be overcautious than to be careless in driving.* **3** to an advanced point, distance, or degree: *He studied far into the night. The explorers penetrated far into the jungle.*
as far as, to the distance, point, or degree that.
by far, very much.
far and away, very much.
far and near, everywhere.
far and wide, everywhere; even in distant parts.
far be it from me, I do not dare or want.
far from it, by no means; not at all: *Agree with you? Far from it!*
far out, *Slang.* **a** fine; excellent. **b** experimental.
go far, a last long. **b** tend very much. **c** get ahead.
how far, to what distance, point, or degree.
in so far as, to the extent that.
so far, a to this or that point. **b** until now or then: *Our team has won every game so far this season.*
so far as, to the extent that.
so far so good, until now everything has been safe or satisfactory. [OE *feorr*] **—Syn.** *adj.* **1** remote. See **distant.**

far·ad (far′əd) *n.* a unit of electrical capacity. It is the capacity of a condenser that, when charged with one coulomb, gives a pressure of one volt. [after Michael *Faraday.* See FARADAY.]

far·a·day (far′ə dā′ or far′ə dē) *n.* a unit of electricity equal to about 96,500 coulombs. In electrolysis, it is the amount needed to deposit one gram-atom of a univalent element. [< Michael *Faraday,* 1791-1867, an English physicist and chemist]

fa·rad·ic (fə rad′ik) *adj.* of or having to do with induced currents of electricity.

far·an·dole (far′ən dōl′) *n.* **1** a fast Provençal dance in six-eight time, in which the dancers whirl in a circle. **2** the music for this dance. [< F < Provençal *farandoulo*]

far·a·way (fär′ə wā′) *adj.* **1** distant. **2** dreamy: *A faraway look in her eyes showed that she was thinking of something else.*

farce (färs) *n.* **1** a play intended merely to make people laugh, full of ridiculous happenings, absurd actions, and improbable situations. **2** such plays as a class; branch of drama concerned with such plays. **3** the kind of humor

found in such plays; broad humor. **4** ridiculous mockery; absurd pretence: *The trial was a mere farce.*
—*v.* spice (a composition or speech); season: *He farced his essay with anecdotes.* [< F *farce*, literally, stuffing < *farcir* < L *farcire* stuff; originally applied to comic interludes]

far·ci·cal (fär′sə kəl) *adj.* of or like a farce; ridiculous; absurd; improbable. —**far′ci·cal·ly,** *adv.* —**far′ci·cal·ness,** *n.*

far cry a long way.

far·del (fär′dəl) *n. Archaic.* bundle; burden. [ME < OF *fardel*, dim. of *farde* bundle < Arabic *farda*]

fare (fãr) *n. v.* **fared, far·ing.** —*n.* **1** the sum of money paid to ride in an aircraft, a train, car, bus, etc. **2** the passenger on an aircraft, a train, car, bus, etc. **3** food provided or eaten: *dainty fare.* [blend of OE *fær* and *faru*]
—*v.* **1** eat food; be fed. **2** get along; do: *If you fare well, you have good luck or success.* **3** turn out; happen: *It will fare hard with the thief if he is caught.* **4** *Archaic.* go; travel. [OE *faran*] —**far′er,** *n.*

Far East China, Japan, and other parts of E. Asia.

fare·well (fãr′wel′) *interj.* **1** an expression of good wishes at parting. **2** good-bye; good luck.
—*n.* **1** an expression of good wishes at parting. **2** good-bye; good luck. **3** a departure; leave-taking.
—*adj.* of farewell; parting; last: *The singer gave a farewell performance.*

far-fetched (fär′fecht′) *adj.* not coming naturally; forced; strained.

far-flung (fär′flung′) *adj.* widely spread; covering a large area.

fa·ri·na (fə rē′nə) *n.* **1** flour or meal made from grain, potatoes, beans, nuts, etc. **2** starch. **3** a coarse, white corn meal. [< L *farina* < *far* grits]

far·i·na·ceous (far′ə nā′shəs) *adj.* consisting of flour or meal; starchy; mealy. Cereals, bread, and potatoes are farinaceous foods.

farm (färm) *n.* **1** the buildings and land used in raising crops or animals. **2** anything like a farm. A sheet of water for cultivating oysters is an oyster farm. **3** in sports, a farm club. **4** *Archaic.* **a** a fixed yearly amount payable in the form of rent, taxes, etc. **b** a fixed yearly amount accepted from a person instead of taxes, or the like, that he is authorized to collect. **5 a** the letting out of the collection of public taxes. **b** the condition of being let out at a fixed amount: *a district in farm.* **c** a district let out for the collection of taxes.
—*v.* **1** raise crops or animals on a farm. **2** cultivate (land). **3** take proceeds or profits of (a tax, undertaking, etc.) on paying a fixed sum. **4** let out (taxes, revenues, an enterprise, etc.) to another for a fixed sum or percentage. **5** let the labor or services of (a person) for hire. **6** contract for the maintenance of (paupers, children, etc.). **7 farm out, a** in sports, send a professional athlete to a less advanced league so that he can gain experience. **b** turn over to a person, company, etc. for a special purpose: *The children were farmed out with neighbors during the summer.* **c** to exhaust land by farming. [ME < OF *ferme* lease, leased farm < *fermer* make a contract < L *firmare* < *firmus* firm]

farm club or **team** in sports, a minor-league team that trains players for the major leagues.

farm·er (fär′mər) *n.* **1** a person who raises crops or animals on a farm. **2** a person who takes a contract for the collection of taxes by agreeing to pay a certain sum to the government. —**Syn. 1** agriculturist.

farm·er·ette (fär′mər et′) *n. Informal.* a woman or girl who works on a farm.

farm hand a person employed to work on a farm.

farm·house (färm′hous′) *n.* the house on a farm.

farm·ing (fär′ming) *n.* **1** the business of raising crops or animals on a farm; agriculture. **2** the practice of letting out the collection of a public revenue. **3** the condition of being let out at a fixed sum. —**Syn. 1** husbandry, tillage.

farm·land (färm′land′ or färm′lənd) *n.* land suitable for or used for raising crops or grazing.

farm·out (färm′out′) *n.* a sublease for drilling oil, granted by one company to another.

farm·stead (färm′stəd) *n.* a farm with its buildings.

hat, āge, cãre, fär; let, ēqual, tėrm; it, īce
hot, ōpen, ôrder; oil, out; cup, pu̇t, rüle, ūse
əbove, takən, pencəl, lemən, circəs
ch, child; ng, long; sh, ship
th, thin; ᴛʜ, then; zh, measure

farm system in sports, an organization of clubs or teams that train players for a major-league club.

farm·yard (färm′yärd′) *n.* the yard connected with farm buildings or enclosed by them.

far North in Canada, the Arctic and sub-Arctic regions; the territories lying north of the provinces.

far·o (fãr′ō) *n.* a gambling game played by betting on the order in which certain cards will appear. [apparently alteration of *Pharaoh*]

far-off (fär′of′) *adj.* distant.

far·ra·go (fə rā′gō or fə rä′gō) *n.* **-goes.** a confused mixture; hodgepodge; jumble. [< L *farrago* mixed fodder, ult. < *far* grits]

far-rang·ing (fär′rān′jing) *adj.* **1** able to travel over a great length or distance: *far-ranging missiles.* **2** covering a wide area (of thought, influence, subject matter, etc.): *a far-ranging debate, a far-ranging inspection.*

far-reaching (fär′rēch′ing) *adj.* having a wide influence or effect; extending far.

far·ri·er (far′ē ər) *n.* **1** a blacksmith who shoes horses. **2** *Archaic.* a horse doctor; veterinarian. [< MF *ferrier* < L *ferrarius* < *ferrum* iron]

far·ri·er·y (far′ē ər ē) *n.* **-er·ies. 1** the work of a farrier. **2** the place where a farrier works. **3** *Archaic.* the care and treatment of horses.

far·row (far′ō) *n.* a litter of pigs. —*v.* **1** give birth to a litter of pigs. **2** give birth to (pigs). [OE *fearh*]

far·ru·ca (fär rü′kä) *n.* an Andalusian gypsy dance. [< Sp., ultimately < a dim. of *Francisco* Francis]

far-see·ing (fär′sē′ing) *adj.* **1** able to see far. **2** looking ahead; planning wisely for the future.

far-sight·ed (fär′sīt′id) *adj.* **1** able to see far. **2** seeing distant things more clearly than near ones. **3** looking ahead; planning wisely for the future. —**far′-sight′ed·ly,** *adv.* —**far′-sight′ed·ness,** *n.*

far·ther (fär′ᴛʜər) *the comparative of* **far.** —*adj.* more distant: *Three miles is farther than two.*
—*adv.* **1** at or to a greater distance: *Go no farther.* **2** at or to a more advanced point: *He has investigated the subject farther than any other man.* **3** in addition; also. [ME *ferther*]

☛ **farther, further.** In formal English some people make a distinction between *farther* and *further*, confining the first to expressions of physical distance and the second to abstract relationships of degree or quantity: *We went on twenty miles farther. He went farther than I, but neither of us reached the town. He carries that sort of thing further than I would. He went further into his family history.* In informal English the distinction is not kept and there seems to be a definite tendency for *further* to be used in all senses.

far·ther·most (fär′ᴛʜər mōst′) *adj.* most distant; farthest.

far·thest (fär′ᴛʜist) *the superlative of* **far.** —*adj.* **1** most distant. **2** longest: *His last trip was the farthest he had ever undertaken.*
—*adv.* **1** to or at the greatest distance. **2** most. [ME *ferthest*]

far·thing (fär′ᴛʜing) *n.* **1** formerly, a British coin, worth a fourth of a British penny or about half a cent in Canadian money. **2** something having a very low value; a small amount. [OE *fēorthung* < *fēortha* fourth]

A farthingale

far·thin·gale (fär′ᴛʜing gāl′) *n.* a hoop skirt or framework for extending a woman's skirt at the hip line, worn in England from about 1550 to about 1650. [< MF *verdugale* < Sp. *verdugado* < *verdugo* rod, ult. < L *viridis* green]

fas·ces (fas′ēz) *n.* pl. of **fas·cis** (fas′is). in ancient Rome, a bundle of rods or sticks containing an axe with the blade projecting, carried before a magistrate as a symbol of authority. [< L *fasces,* pl. of *fascis* bundle]

fas·ci·a (fash′ē ə) *n.* **-ci·ae** (-ē ē′ or -ē ī′). band; fillet; a long flat strip. [< L]

fas·ci·cle (fas′ə kəl) *n.* **1** a small bundle. **2** part of a volume published in instalments. **3** in botany, a close cluster of flowers, leaves, etc. [< L *fasciculus,* dim. of *fascis* bundle]

fas·ci·cule (fas′ə kūl) *n.* fascicle.

fas·ci·nate (fas′ə nāt′) *v.* **-nat·ed, -nat·ing.** **1** attract very strongly; enchant by charming qualities: *The actress's charm and beauty fascinated everyone.* **2** hold motionless by strange power, terror, etc.: *Snakes are said to fascinate small birds.* [< L *fascinare* < *fascinum* spell] —**Syn. 1** entrance, enrapture, captivate.

An ancient Roman holding fasces

fas·ci·nat·ing (fas′ə nāt′ing) *adj.* captivating; enchanting; charming. —**fas′ci·nat′ing·ly,** *adv.*

fas·ci·na·tion (fas′ə nā′shən) *n.* **1** a fascinating or being fascinated. **2** a very strong attraction; charm; enchantment.

fas·ci·na·tor (fas′ə nā′tər) *n.* **1** a person or thing that fascinates. **2** a crocheted scarf worn by women as a head covering.

fas·cine (fa sēn′) *n.* **1** a bundle of sticks tied together, used to line trenches, strengthen earthworks, etc. **2** a large, circular trap, resembling a palisade enclosure, for catching fish. [< F < L *fascina* bundle of sticks < *fascis* bundle]

fas·cism (fash′iz əm) *n.* **1** Also, **Fascism.** the doctrines, principles, or methods of the Fascists. **2** any system of government in which property is privately owned, but in which all industry and labor are regulated by a strong national government, while all opposition is rigorously suppressed. [< Ital. *fascismo* < *fascio* bundle (as political emblem) < L *fascis*]

☛ **Fascism, Fascist** are capitalized when they refer to the Italian movement or party, as we capitalize *Liberal* and *Conservative* in this country. When the word refers to a movement in another country in which the party has a different name, it need not be capitalized but often is. When it refers to the general idea of fascist politics, or an unorganized tendency, it is not capitalized. Compare **Nazi.**

fas·cist (fash′ist) *n.* **1 Fascist,** a member of a strongly nationalistic political party that seized control of the Italian government in 1922 under the leadership of Mussolini. **2** Also, **Fascist.** a member of any similar political party in other countries. **3** a person who favors and supports fascism. —*adj.* Also, **Fascist.** of or having to do with fascism or fascists. ☛ See **fascism** for usage note.

fash·ion (fash′ən) *n.* **1** a manner; way: *Crabs walk in a peculiar fashion.* **2** the prevailing style; current custom in dress, manners, speech, etc. **3** polite society; fashionable people. **4 after** or **in a fashion,** in some way or other; not very well. **5 set the fashion,** fix the fashion, method, etc. for others to follow.
—*v.* make; shape; form: *He fashioned a whistle out of a piece of wood.* [ME < AF *fachon* < L *factio* a doing or making. Doublet of FACTION.]

Syn. *n.* **2 Fashion, style** = custom in dress, manners, living, speech, etc. **Fashion** applies to the custom prevailing at a particular time or among a particular group: *She likes to read about the latest fashions.* **Style** is often used in place of *fashion,* but now particularly emphasizes good taste, regardless of the fashion: *That dress is in such good style that it will last for years.* -*v.* frame, construct. See **make.**

fash·ion·a·ble (fash′ən ə bəl or fash′nə bəl) *adj.* **1** following the fashion; in fashion; stylish. **2** of, like, or used by people of fashion. —**fash′ion·a·ble·ness,** *n.*

fash·ion·a·bly (fash′ən ə blē or fash′nə blē) *adv.* in a fashionable manner.

-fashioned *combining form.* in fashion or style: *old-fashioned* = *old in fashion or style.*

fast[1] (fast) *adj.* **1** quick; rapid; swift: *a fast runner.* **2** indicating a time ahead of the correct time: *My watch is fast.* **3** not restrained in pleasures; too gay; wild. **4** firm; secure; tight: *a fast hold on a rope.* **5** loyal; steadfast: *They have been fast friends for years.* **6** not fading easily: *This cloth is dyed with fast color.* **7** adapted for speed; helping to produce or increase speed: *a fast track.* **8** with greater than average speed, force, etc.: *a fast pitcher.* **9** firmly fixed or attached; tightly shut or locked: *a fast window or door.* **10** in photography, (of a film, lens, etc.) making a short exposure possible.
—*adv.* **1** quickly; rapidly; swiftly. **2** firmly; securely; tightly. **3** thoroughly; completely; soundly: *He was fast asleep.* **4** *Archaic.* close; near. **5 play fast and loose,** say one thing and do another; be tricky, insincere, or unreliable. [OE *fæst*] —**Syn.** *adj.* **1** fleet, speedy, hasty. See **quick. 3** dissipated, dissolute, profligate, immoral. **4** fixed, immovable, tenacious.

fast[2] (fast) *v.* go without food; eat little or nothing; go without certain kinds of food. Members of some religious faiths fast on certain days. —*n.* **1** a fasting. **2** a day or time of fasting. **3 break one's fast,** eat the first meal of the day. [OE *fæstan*]

fast·ball (fast′bol′ or -bôl′) *n.* a variety of softball having a number of features to add speed and action, making the game more like baseball.

fast day a day observed by fasting, especially a day regularly set apart by a religious organization.

fas·ten (fas′ən) *v.* **1** fix firmly in place; tie; lock; shut: *fasten a dress, fasten a door.* **2** attach; connect: *He tried to fasten the blame upon his companions.* **3** direct; fix: *The dog fastened his eyes on the stranger.* **4 fasten on** or **upon,** take hold of; seize. [OE *fæstnian* < *fæst* fast[1]] —**Syn. 1** link, hook, clasp, clamp, secure, bind.

fas·ten·er (fas′ən ər) *n.* **1** a person who fastens. **2** an attachment, device, etc. used to fasten a door, garment, etc.

fas·ten·ing (fas′ən ing) *n.* a device used to fasten things together: *Locks, bolts, clasps, hooks, buttons, etc. are all fastenings.*

fas·tid·i·ous (fas tid′ē əs) *adj.* **1** hard to please. **2** extremely refined or critical: *a fastidious dresser.* **3** easily disgusted: *a fastidious eater.* [< L *fastidiosus* < *fastidium* loathing] —**fas·tid′i·ous·ly,** *adv.* —**fas·tid′i·ous·ness,** *n.*

fast·ness (fast′nis) *n.* **1** a strong, safe place; stronghold: *The bandits hid in their mountain fastness.* **2** a being fast.

fast time daylight-saving time.

fat (fat) *n. adj.* **fat·ter, fat·test,** *v.* **fat·ted, fat·ting.** —*n.* **1** a type of white or yellow oily substance formed in the bodies of animals and also in some seeds. **2** any animal tissue mainly composed of such a substance. **3** in chemistry, any of a class of organic compounds of which the natural fats are mixtures. **4** the richest, best, or most nourishing part of anything. **5 The fat is in the fire.** It is too late to prevent unpleasant results; matters have been made worse. **6 the fat of the land,** the best of everything. [< adj.]
—*adj.* **1** consisting of or containing fat; oily: *fat meat.* **2** abounding in some element; fertile: *fat land.* **3** yielding much money; profitable: *a fat job.* **4** affording good opportunities. **5** plentifully supplied; large. **6** fleshy; plump; round and well-fed. **7** thick; broad. **8** dull; stupid. **9** too fat; corpulent; obese. **10** *Slang.* not much; little; small: *A fat chance you have of catching him now. A fat lot of help you are to me.*
—*v.* make fat; become fat. [OE *fætt,* originally pp., fatted] —**fat′like′,** *adj.* —**fat′ly,** *adv.* —**fat′ness,** *n.*

Syn. *adj.* **1** greasy, unctuous. **3** lucrative, remunerative. **6, 9 Fat, stout, portly** = having too much flesh. **Fat** is the general word, in common use applying to any degree from healthy, well-fed plumpness to ugly, unhealthy obesity, but when describing people usually suggests flabbiness, oiliness, etc.: *That boy is too fat.* **Stout** emphasizes thickness and bulkiness, but sometimes suggests firm rather than flabby flesh and is often used as a euphemism for too fat: *She calls herself stylishly stout.* **Portly** = stout and stately: *The retired admiral is a portly old gentleman.*

fa·tal (fā′təl) *adj.* **1** causing death: *fatal accidents.* **2** causing destruction or ruin: *The loss of all our money was fatal to our plans.* **3** decisive; fateful: *At last the fatal day for the contest arrived.* **4** influencing fate: *Fates, the three goddesses who controlled the fate of mankind, were sometimes called the fatal sisters.* [ME < L *fatalis* < *fatum.* See FATE.]

Syn. 1 Fatal, deadly, mortal = causing death. **Fatal** emphasizes the idea of certain death and applies to anything that is sure to cause death or that has caused it: *Many diseases are no longer fatal.* **Deadly** applies to something that is likely to cause death and usually does: *Cyanide is a deadly poison.* **Mortal** applies to something that is the direct cause of death, but cannot apply to a weapon used to cause the injury that actually killed the person: *His wound was mortal.* **2** destructive, disastrous.

fa·tal·ism (fā′təl iz′əm) *n.* **1** the belief that fate controls everything that happens. 2 submission to everything that happens as inevitable.

fa·tal·ist (fā′təl ist) *n.* a believer in fatalism.

fa·tal·is·tic (fā′təl is′tik) *adj.* 1 of or having to do with fatalism. 2 believing that fate controls everything; accepting things and events as inevitable. —**fa′tal·is′ti·cal·ly,** *adv.*

fa·tal·i·ty (fə tal′ə tē or fā tal′ə tē) *n.* **-ties.** 1 a fatal accident or happening; death: *Automobiles cause thousands of fatalities every year.* 2 a fatal influence or effect; deadliness: *Doctors are trying to reduce the fatality of diseases.* 3 liability to disaster. 4 the condition of being controlled by fate; inevitable necessity: *We struggle against fatality in vain.* 5 the belief that everything is predestined: *Abandon the pessimistic doctrine of fatality.*

fa·tal·ly (fā′təl ē) *adv.* 1 in a manner leading to death or disaster: *He was fatally wounded.* 2 according to fate.

Fatal Sisters the Fates.

Fa·ta Mor·ga·na (fä′tə môr gä′nə) Morgan le Fay, the fairy half-sister of King Arthur.

fate (fāt) *n.* 1 a power supposed to fix beforehand and control everything that happens. Fate is beyond any person's control. 2 what is caused by fate. 3 one's lot or fortune. 4 what becomes of a person or thing: *The jury settled the fate of the accused.* 5 death; ruin. [ME < L *fatum* (thing) spoken (i.e., by the gods), pp. neut. of *fari* speak]

Syn. 1, 3 Fate, destiny, doom = a person's fortune or lot in life. **Fate** suggests some power or force that determines what becomes of a person or thing, and emphasizes an outcome that cannot be avoided, escaped, or changed: *World history describes the fate of many nations.* **Destiny,** often used interchangeably with *fate,* emphasizes a fate all prearranged and not to be altered: *Death is every man's destiny.* **Doom** applies to an unhappy or awful end: *The condemned man went to his doom.*

fat·ed (fāt′id) *adj.* 1 controlled by fate. 2 destined; predestined.

fate·ful (fāt′fəl) *adj.* 1 controlled by fate. 2 determining what is to happen; decisive. 3 showing what fate decrees; prophetic. 4 causing death, destruction, or ruin; disastrous. —**fate′ful·ly,** *adv.* —**fate′ful·ness,** *n.*

Fates (fāts) *n.pl.* in Greek and Roman mythology, the three goddesses supposed to control human life. They were Clotho, who spins the thread of life; Lachesis, who decides how long it shall be; and Atropos, who cuts it off.

fat·head (fat′hed′) *n. Slang.* a dolt; a stupid or slow person.

fa·ther (fo′ᴛʜər) *n.* 1 a male parent. 2 a person who is like a father. 3 a male ancestor; forefather. 4 a person who helped to make something, such as a founder, inventor, author, oldest member, etc.: *Fathers of Confederation.* 5 a title of respect used in addressing priests or other clergymen. 6 a clergyman having this title. 7 a title of respect to an old man. 8 in ancient Rome, a senator. 9 **the Father,** God. 10 **the fathers,** *pl.* the chief writers and teachers of the Christian Church during the first six centuries A.D.
—*v.* 1 be the father of. 2 take care of as a father does; act as a father to. 3 make; originate. 4 acknowledge oneself as the father of. [OE *fæder*]

father confessor 1 a priest to whom one confesses. 2 a person to whom one confides everything.

fa·ther·hood (fo′ᴛʜər hůd′) *n.* the condition of being a father.

fa·ther-in-law (fo′ᴛʜər in lo′ or -lô′) *n.* **fa·thers-in-law.** the father of one's husband or wife.

fa·ther·land (fo′ᴛʜər land′) *n.* one's native country; the land of one's ancestors.

fa·ther·less (fo′ᴛʜər lis) *adj.* 1 without a father living. 2 without a known father.

fa·ther·ly (fo′ᴛʜər lē) *adj.* 1 of a father. 2 like a father; kindly. —**fa′ther·li·ness,** *n.*

Fathers of Confederation the men, led by Sir John A. Macdonald, who brought about the confederation of the original provinces of Canada in 1867.

fath·om (faᴛʜ′əm) *n.* **fath·oms** or (*esp. collectively*) **fath·om,** *v.* —*n.* a unit of measure equal to six feet, used mostly in measuring the depth of water and the length of ships' ropes, cables, etc. *Abbrev.:* fm., fth., or fthm.
—*v.* 1 measure the depth of. 2 get to the bottom of; understand fully. [OE *fæthm* width of the outstretched arms]

hat, āge, cãre, fär; let, ēqual, tėrm; it, īce
hot, ōpen, ôrder; oil, out; cup, pů t, rüle, ūse
əbove, takən, pencəl, lemən, circəs
ch, child; ng, long; sh, ship
th, thin; ᴛʜ, then; zh, measure

fath·om·a·ble (faᴛʜ′əm ə bəl) *adj.* 1 that can be measured. 2 understandable.

fath·om·less (faᴛʜ′əm lis) *adj.* 1 too deep to be measured. 2 impossible to be fully understood.

fa·tigue (fə tēg′) *n. v.* **-tigued, -ti·guing,** *adj.* —*n.* 1 weariness. 2 any task or exertion producing weariness: *The doctor has not yet recovered from the fatigues of the epidemic.* 3 a weakening (of metal) caused by long-continued use or strain. 4 in physiology, a temporary decrease in the capacity of an organ or cell to function after excessive activity. 5 fatigue duty. 6 **fatigues,** *pl.* clothes worn during fatigue duty.
—*v.* 1 cause fatigue in; weary. 2 weaken (metal) by much use or strain.
—*adj.* having to do with fatigue. [< F *fatigue* < *fatiguer* < L *fatigare* tire] —**Syn.** *n.* 1 lassitude, languor, exhaustion. -*v.* 1 tire, exhaust.

fatigue duty non-military work done by members of the armed services. Cleaning up the camp or repairing roads is fatigue duty.

Fa·ti·ma (fə tē′mə or fat′ə mə) *n.* A.D. 606?-632, the favorite daughter of Mohammed.

fat·ling (fat′ling) *n.* a calf, lamb, kid, or pig fattened to be killed for food.

fat·ten (fat′ən) *v.* 1 make fat; become fat. 2 enrich soil. 3 in poker, add more chips to (a pot). 4 **fatten up,** feed animals for market. —**fat′ten·er,** *n.*

fat·ty (fat′ē) *adj.* **-ti·er, -ti·est.** 1 of fat; containing fat: *fatty tissues.* 2 like fat; oily; greasy. —**fat′ti·ly,** *adv.* —**fat′ti·ness,** *n.*

fatty acid in chemistry, any of a group of organic acids, some of which, such as stearic acid, are found in animal and vegetable fats and oils. *Formula:* $C_nH_{2n}O_2$

fa·tu·i·ty (fə tū′ə tē or fə tü′ə tē) *n.* **-ties.** self-satisfied stupidity; folly; silliness. [< L *fatuitas* < *fatuus* foolish]

fat·u·ous (fach′ü əs) *adj.* stupid but self-satisfied; foolish; silly. [< L *fatuus* foolish] —**fat′u·ous·ly,** *adv.* —**fat′u·ous·ness,** *n.* —**Syn.** See **foolish.**

fau·bourg (fō′bür or fō′bürg; *French,* fō bür′) *n.* 1 a suburb. 2 a district in a city.

fau·cal (fo′kəl or fô′kəl) *adj.* of, having to do with, or produced in the fauces. —*n.* in phonetics, a sound produced in the fauces. [< L *fauces* throat + E *-al*[1]]

fau·ces (fo′sēz or fô′sēz) *n.pl.* in anatomy, the cavity at the back of the mouth, leading into the pharynx. [< L]

fau·cet (fo′sit or fô′sit) *n.* 1 a device for controlling the flow of water or other liquid in a pipe, tank, barrel, etc.; tap. 2 the enlarged end of a pipe into which the end of another pipe fits. [< F *fausset* < *fausser* bore through, originally, break < L *falsare* corrupt]

faugh (fo or fô) *interj.* an exclamation of disgust.

fault (folt or fôlt) *n.* 1 something that is not as it should be; a flaw; defect. 2 a mistake. 3 a cause for blame; responsibility: *Whose fault was it?* 4 in geology, a break in a mass of rock with the segment on one side of the break pushed up or down. See **stratum** for picture. 5 in tennis and similar games, a failure to serve the ball into the right place. 6 an accidental defect in an electric circuit. 7 **at fault, a** deserving blame; wrong. **b** puzzled; perplexed. 8 **find fault,** pick out faults; complain. 9 **find fault with,** object to; criticize. 10 **in fault,** deserving blame; wrong. 11 **to a fault,** too much; very. [ME < OF *faute,* ult. < L *fallere* deceive]
—*v.* 1 in tennis and similar games, fail to serve the ball into the right place. 2 find fault with: *They could not fault him on his knowledge of algebra.* 3 in geology, (of rock strata) cause or undergo a fault or faults.

Syn. 1 Fault, failing = a defect in character, mental attitude, emotional make-up, conduct, or habits. **Fault** particularly suggests a lack of something essential to perfection, but not necessarily a cause for blame: *Sloppiness is his greatest fault.* **Failing** suggests a falling short of perfection, and applies particularly to a weakness in character, often excusable: *Extravagance is her failing.* **2** error, slip, lapse.

fault·find·er (folt′fīn′dər or fôlt′-) *n.* **1** a person who finds fault; complainer. **2** a device for locating defects, as in an electric circuit.

fault·find·ing (folt′fīn′ding or fôlt′-) *n. adj.* finding fault; complaining; pointing out faults.

fault·less (folt′lis or fôlt′-) *adj.* without a single fault; free from blemish or error; perfect. **—fault′less·ly,** *adv.* **—fault′less·ness,** *n.*

fault·y (fol′tē or fôl′tē) *adj.* **fault·i·er, fault·i·est.** having faults; containing blemishes or errors; wrong; imperfect. **—fault′i·ly,** *adv.* **—fault′i·ness,** *n.* **—Syn.** defective, incomplete.

faun (fon or fôn) *n.* a minor Roman deity that helped farmers and shepherds. A faun is represented as a man, but with the ears, horns, tail, and sometimes the legs, of a goat. [ME < L *Faunus* a rural deity]

fau·na (fo′nə or fô′nə) *n.* all the animals of a given region or time: *the fauna of Australia, the fauna of the carboniferous age.* [< NL *Fauna* a rural goddess, wife of Faunus]

Faust (foust) *n.* a German astrologer and magician, 1488?-1541?, who was reputed to have sold his soul to the Devil in exchange for all he wanted on earth. He is the hero of dramas by Marlowe and Goethe. Also, **Faustus. —Faust′i·an,** *adj.*

Faust·us (fous′təs) *n.* Faust. Marlowe's play on Faust is called *The Tragedy of Dr. Faustus.*

Fauves (fōvz) *n.pl.* a group of French painters, including Henri Matisse, whose work in the period from 1905 to 1920 is characteristic of Fauvism. [< F *fauves* wild beasts]

Fau·vism (fō′viz əm) *n.* in painting, a style that was an extreme form of expressionism, developed in France in the early 20th century and characterized by simplicity and boldness of design, vivid clashing colors, and individuality of approach.

faux pas (fō′ pä′ or fō′pä′) *pl.* **faux pas** (fō′ päz′ or fō′ päz′). a slip in speech, conduct, manners, etc.; breach of etiquette; blunder. [< F]

fa·vor or **fa·vour** (fā′vər) *n.* **1** an act of kindness: *Will you do me a favor?* **2** liking; approval: *They are sure to look with favor on your plan.* **3** the condition of being liked or approved: *A fashion in favor this year may be out of favor next year.* **4** more than fair treatment; too great kindness. **5 a** a gift; token: *The knight wore his lady's favor on his arm.* **b** a small token given to every guest at a party, dinner, etc. **6** *Now rare.* a letter; note: *We acknowledge your favor of the 15th.* **7 in favor of, a** on the side of; supporting. **b** to the advantage of; helping. **c** to be paid to: *write a cheque in favor of the bank.* **8 in his favor,** for him; to his benefit.
—*v.* **1** show kindness to. **2** like; approve. **3** give more than fair treatment to. **4** be on the side of; support. **5** be to the advantage of; help. **6** treat gently: *The dog favors his sore foot when he walks.* **7** look like: *The girl favors her mother.* [ME < OF < L *favor* < *favere* show kindness to] **—fa′vor·er** or **fa′vour·er,** *n.*
Syn. *n.* **2 Favor, good will** = kindly or friendly feeling. **Favor** emphasizes having kindly or friendly thoughts or giving approval: *The manager looked on the new clerk with favor.* **Good will** emphasizes greater friendliness and desire or effort to be helpful: *The audience showed its good will toward the singer by its applause.*

fa·vor·a·ble or **fa·vour·a·ble** (fā′vər ə bəl or fāv′rə bəl) *adj.* **1** favoring; approving. **2** being to one's advantage; helping: *a favorable wind.* **3** boding well; promising. **—fa′vor·a·ble·ness** or **fa′vour·a·ble·ness,** *n.*
Syn. 1 kindly. **2** advantageous, helpful. **3 Favorable, auspicious** = promising or giving signs of turning out well. **Favorable** = promising because conditions or people having to do with an event or situation show they will be helpful: *It was a favorable time for our trip, since business was light.* **Auspicious** = promising because all the signs point to a lucky or successful outcome: *The popularity of his first book was an auspicious beginning of his career.*

fa·vor·a·bly or **fa·vour·a·bly** (fā′vər ə blē or fāv′rə blē) *adv.* with consent or approval; kindly.

fa·vored or **fa·voured** (fā′vərd) *adj.* **1** treated with favor. **2** having special advantages; talented.

fa·vor·ite or **fa·vour·ite** (fā′vər it or fāv′rit) *adj.* liked better than others; liked very much.
—*n.* **1** one liked better than others; person or thing liked very much. **2** a person treated with special favor. **3** in sports, a person, horse, etc. expected to win a contest. [ME < MF *favorit* (fem. *favorite*) < Ital. *favorito,* ult. < *favore* favor < L *favor*]

fa·vor·it·ism or **fa·vour·it·ism** (fā′vər ə tiz′əm or fāv′rə tiz′əm) *n.* **1** a favoring of one or some more than others; having favorites. **2** the state of being a favorite.

fa·vour (fā′vər) *n. v.* favor.

fawn[1] (fon or fôn) *n.* **1** a deer less than a year old. **2** a light yellowish brown.
—*adj.* light yellowish-brown.
—*v.* of deer, give birth to young. [ME < OF *faon,* ult. < L *fetus* fetus] **—fawn′like′,** *adj.*

fawn[2] (fon or fôn) *v.* **1** cringe and bow; act slavishly: *Many flattering relatives fawned on the rich old man.* **2** of dogs, etc., show fondness by crouching, wagging the tail, licking the hand, etc. [OE *fagnian* < *fægen* fain] **—fawn′er,** *n.* **—fawn′ing·ly,** *adv.* **—Syn. 1** shrink, cower, truckle.

fay[1] (fā) *n.* fairy. [ME < OF *fae, fee,* ult. < L *fatum.* See FATE.]

fay[2] (fā) *n. Archaic.* faith: *By my fay!* [ME < OF *fei* < L *fides.* Doubled of FAITH.]

faze (fāz) *v.* **fazed, faz·ing.** *Informal.* disturb; worry; bother; put out. [var. of *feeze,* OE *fēsian* drive]
☛ **Faze,** an informal term meaning "worry, bother, or disturb," is almost always used negatively: *His original failure did not faze him. Nothing we said fazed her—she did just as she pleased.*

FBI *U.S.* Federal Bureau of Investigation.

F clef in music, the bass clef. See **clef** for diagram.

F.D. Fire Department.

Fe iron. [< L *ferrum*]

F.E. Forest Engineer.

fe·al·ty (fē′əl tē) *n.* **-ties. 1** in the Middle Ages, the loyalty and duty owed by a vassal to his feudal lord: *The nobles swore fealty to the king.* **2** loyalty; faithfulness; allegiance. [ME < OF *feaulte* < L *fidelitas.* Doublet of FIDELITY.]

fear (fēr) *n.* **1** a being afraid; feeling that danger or evil is near; dread. **2** a cause for fear; danger: *There is no fear of our losing.* **3** an uneasy feeling; anxious thought; concern: *fear for one's life.* **4** awe; reverence. **5 for fear of** (a thing), in order to prevent (that thing) from occurring. **6 without fear or favor,** impartially; justly.
—*v.* **1** feel fear. **2** feel fear of. **3** have an uneasy feeling or anxious thought; feel concern. **4** have awe or reverence for. [OE *fǣr* peril]
Syn. *n.* **1 Fear, dread, alarm** = the disagreeable feeling that comes over a person when danger or harm threatens. **Fear** is the general word, meaning "being afraid": *The knight felt no fear in the midst of battle.* **Dread** applies to the fear that comes from knowing something unpleasant or frightening will happen or from expecting danger, often unknown or uncertain: *He has a constant dread of losing his job.* **Alarm** applies to startled or excited fear, coming from the sudden appearance of danger: *The explosion caused widespread alarm.*

fear·ful (fēr′fəl) *adj.* **1** causing fear; terrible; dreadful: *The conflagration was a fearful sight.* **2** full of fear; afraid. **3** showing fear; caused by fear. **4** *Informal.* very bad, unpleasant, ugly, etc.: *a fearful cold.* **—fear′ful·ly,** *adv.* **—fear′ful·ness,** *n.* **—Syn. 1** awful, frightful, horrible. **2** frightened, alarmed.

fear·less (fēr′lis) *adj.* without fear; afraid of nothing; brave; daring. **—fear′less·ly,** *adv.* **—fear′less·ness,** *n.*

fear·some (fēr′səm) *adj.* **1** causing fear; frightful: *a fearsome sight.* **2** timid; afraid: *She was fearsome of danger.* **—fear′some·ly,** *adv.* **—fear′some·ness,** *n.*

fea·sance (fē′zəns) *n.* in law, the doing or performance of a condition, obligation, duty, etc.

fea·si·bil·i·ty (fē′zə bil′ə tē) *n.* the quality of being easily done or carried out.

fea·si·ble (fē′zə bəl) *adj.* **1** capable of being done or carried out easily; practicable: *The committee selected the plan that seemed most feasible.* **2** likely; probable: *The witness's explanation of the accident sounded feasible.* **3** suitable; convenient: *The road was too rough to be feasible for travel by automobile.* [ME < OF *faisable,* ult. < L *facere* do] **—fea′si·ble·ness,** *n.* **—fea′si·bly,** *adv.* **—Syn. 1** See **possible.**

hat, āge, cãre, fär; let, ēqual, tėrm; it, īce
hot, ōpen, ôrder; oil, out; cup, pu̇t, rüle, ūse
əbove, takən, pencəl, lemən, circəs
ch, child; ng, long; sh, ship
th, thin; ᴛʜ, then; zh, measure

feast (fēst) *n.* **1** an elaborate meal prepared for a number of guests on some special occasion. **2** an unusually delicious or abundant meal. **3** something that gives pleasure or joy: *a feast for the eyes.* **4** a religious festival or celebration: *Christmas and Easter are the most important Christian feasts.*
—*v.* **1** have a feast. **2** provide with a feast. **3** give pleasure or joy to: *We feasted our eyes on the beautiful picture.* [ME < OF < L *festa* festal ceremonies] —**feast′er,** *n.*
Syn. *n.* **1 Feast, banquet** = an elaborate meal with many guests. Feast emphasizes the abundance, fineness, and richness of the food and drink, served to a large number in celebration of a special occasion: *We went to the wedding feast.* **Banquet** emphasizes the formality of the celebration and applies particularly to a formal dinner given in rich surroundings: *A banquet was given by the town to honor the returning hero.*

feast day a day set aside as a celebration of some religious festival, or in honor of some person, event, or thing.

feat (fēt) *n.* a great or unusual deed; an act showing great skill, strength, etc. [ME < OF *fait* < L *factum* (thing) done. Doublet of FACT.] —**Syn.** achievement. See **exploit.**

feath·er (feᴛʜ′ər) *n.* **1** one of the light, thin growths that cover a bird's skin. Because feathers are soft and light, they are used to fill pillows. **2** something like a feather in shape or lightness. **3** the act of feathering an oar. **4 feather in one's cap,** something to be proud of. **5 in feather,** covered with feathers. **6 in fine, good,** or **high feather,** in good health, high spirits, etc. **7** in archery: **a** a feather or feathers attached to the end of an arrow to direct its flight. **b** the end of an arrow to which the feathers are attached.
—*v.* **1** supply or cover with feathers. **2** grow like feathers. **3** move like feathers. **4 a** turn (an oar) after a stroke so that the blade is flat and keep it that way until the next stroke begins. **b** turn (the blade of an airplane propeller) to decrease wind resistance. **5** touch or apply pressure lightly: *The driver feathered his brakes to slow down on the slippery road.* **6** touch (the strings of a violin, etc.) very lightly with a bow. **7 feather one's nest,** take advantage of chances to get rich. [OE *fether*]
—**feath′er·less,** *adj.* —**feath′er·like′,** *adj.*

feather bed a soft, warm mattress filled with feathers.

feath·er·bed·ding (feᴛʜ′ər bed′ing) *n.* the requiring of an employer to pay more employees than he considers are needed, or to pay full wages for unnecessary work or for restricted output.

feath·er·brain (feᴛʜ′ər brān′) *n.* a silly, foolish, weak-minded person.

feath·er·brained (feᴛʜ′ər brānd′) *adj.* silly; foolish; weak-minded.

feath·ered (feᴛʜ′ərd) *adj.* **1** having feathers; covered with feathers. **2** swift; rapid.

feath·er·edge (feᴛʜ′ər ej′) *n.* a very thin edge.

feath·er·edged (feᴛʜ′ər ejd′) *adj.* having a very thin edge.

feath·er·stitch (feᴛʜ′ər stich′) *n.* a zigzag embroidery stitch. —*v.* **1** make zigzag embroidery stitches. **2** decorate with such stitches.

feath·er·weight (feᴛʜ′ər wāt′) *n.* **1** a very light thing or person. **2** a boxer who weighs less than 126 pounds and more than 118 pounds. **3** an unimportant person or thing. —*adj.* **1** very light. **2** of or having to do with featherweights. **3** unimportant.

feath·er·y (feᴛʜ′ər ē) *adj.* **1** having feathers; covered with feathers. **2** like feathers; soft. **3** light; flimsy. —**feath′er·i·ness,** *n.*

feat·ly (fēt′lē) *adv. Archaic.* **1** nimbly; skilfully. **2** suitably; properly. **3** neatly; elegantly.

fea·ture (fē′chər) *n. v.* **-tured, -tur·ing.** —*n.* **1** a part of the face. The eyes, nose, mouth, chin, and forehead are features. **2 features,** *pl.* the face. **3** a distinct part or quality; something that stands out and attracts attention. **4** a main attraction, especially a full-length motion picture. **5** a special article, comic strip, etc. in a newspaper or magazine.
—*v.* **1** be a feature of. **2** make a feature of; give special prominence to: *The movie featured an outstanding actor. The store was featuring radios in its sale.* **3** be like in features. [ME < OF *feture* < L *factura* < *facere* do]
Syn. *n.* **3 Feature, characteristic, trait** = a quality of a person or thing. **Feature** applies to a quality or detail that stands out and attracts attention: *The main features of the resort are its climate and scenery.* **Characteristic** applies to a quality or feature that expresses or shows the character or nature of a person, thing, or class or distinguishes it from others: *Ruggedness was a characteristic of the early pioneers in Canada.* **Trait** applies particularly to a distinguishing feature of the character or mind of a person: *Cheerfulness is his outstanding trait.*

-featured *combining form.* having —— features: *cruel-featured = having cruel features.*

fea·ture·less (fē′chər lis) *adj.* without features; not interesting or impressive.

Feb. February.

feb·ri·fuge (feb′rə fūj′) *n.* **1** a medicine to reduce fever. **2** a cooling drink. —*adj.* curing or lessening fever. [< F. Cf. FEVERFEW.]

fe·brile (fē′brīl or fē′brəl, feb′rīl or feb′rəl) *adj.* **1** of fever; feverish. **2** caused by fever. [< Med.L *febrilis* < *febris* fever]

Feb·ru·ar·y (feb′rü er′ē or feb′ū er′ē) *n.* **-ar·ies.** the second month of the year. It has 28 days except in leap years, when it has 29. [< L *Februarius* < *februa,* pl., the feast of purification celebrated on Feb. 15]

fe·cal (fē′kəl) *adj.* having to do with feces. Also, **faecal.**

fe·ces (fē′sēz) *n.pl.* **1** the waste matter discharged from the intestines. **2** dregs; sediment. Also, **faeces.** [< L *faeces,* pl., dregs]

feck·less (fek′lis) *adj.* futile; ineffective. [< *feck* vigor, var. of *fect* < *effect*]

fe·cund (fē′kənd or fek′ənd) *adj.* fruitful; productive; fertile: *Edison had a fecund mind.* [< F < L *fecundus*]

fe·cun·di·ty (fi kun′də tē) *n.* fruitfulness; fertility.

fed (fed) *v.* pt. and pp. of **feed.**

Fed·a·yeen (fed′ä yēn′) *n.* **-yeen.** in Egypt, a commando or guerrilla fighter. [< Arabic *fidā'īn,* pl. of *fidā'ī* (literally) one who sacrifices himself < *fidā'* redemption; sacrifice]

fed·er·al (fed′ər əl or fed′rəl) *adj.* **1** formed by an agreement between groups establishing a central organization to handle their common affairs while the parties to the agreement keep control of local affairs: *The Canadian Federation of Agriculture is a federal organization of farm representatives.* **2** of or having to do with the central government formed in this way: *Parliament is the federal lawmaking body of Canada.* **3** Also, **Federal.** of or having to do with the central government. **4 Federal,** in the United States: **a** of or having to do with the Federal Party. **b** supporting the central government during the Civil War.
—*n.* **Federal,** in the United States, a supporter or soldier of the central government during the Civil War. [< L *foedus, foederis* compact] —**fed′er·al·ly,** *adv.*

Federal Bureau of Investigation a United States government bureau that investigates crimes.

Federal Court of Canada a court, having trial and appeal divisions, established in 1971 to hear legal actions brought by or against the Federal Government.

Federal Government 1 the government of Canada, located in Ottawa. Its responsibilities are specified by the British North America Act. **2** the Prime Minister and his Cabinet. **3** the government of a federation.

fed·er·al·ism (fed′ər əl iz′əm or fed′rəl iz′əm) *n.* the federal principle of government.

fed·er·al·ist (fed′ər əl ist or fed′rəl ist) *n.* a person who favors the federal principle of government.

fed·er·al·ize (fed′ər əl īz′ or fed′rəl īz′) *v.* **-ized, -iz·ing. 1** put under the control of the federal government. **2** unite into a federal union. —**fed′er·al·i·za′tion,** *n.*

fed·er·ate (*v.* fed′ər āt′; *adj.* fed′ər it or fed′rit) *v.* **-at·ed, -at·ing,** *adj.* —*v.* **1** form into a federation. **2** organize on a federal basis. —*adj.* formed into a federation. [< L *foederare* league together < *foedus, -deris* compact]

fed·er·a·tion (fed′ər ā′shən) *n.* **1** the act or process of federating. **2** a union in a league; the formation of a political unity out of a number of separate provinces, states, etc. **3** a league; union by agreement, often a union of states or nations: *a federation of students.*

fed·er·a·tive (fed′ər ə tiv or fed′ər ā′tiv) *adj.* of or having to do with a federation; like a federation; forming a federation.

fe·do·ra (fi dô′rə) *n.* a man's soft felt hat with a curved brim and a crown creased lengthwise. [apparently from the play *Fédora* by the French playwright Sardou]

fee (fē) *n. v.* **feed, fee·ing.** —*n.* **1** a sum of money asked or paid for a service or privilege; charge: *Doctors and lawyers get fees for their services.* **2** a small present of money; tip. **3** in the Middle Ages: **a** the right to keep and use land. **b** a fief. **4** an inherited estate in land. **5** ownership. **6 hold in fee,** own. **7** in law: **a** an estate of land that may be passed on to the owner's heirs. **Fee simple** is an estate that may be inherited by any heirs; when there is a restriction on those who may inherit, the estate is a **fee tail. b** any such estate; possession. —*v.* give a fee to. [ME < AF var. of OF *fieu* < Med.L *feudum* fief ? < Gmc.; cf. OE *feoh* money, cattle] —**Syn.** *n.* **1** pay, compensation, payment, recompense.

fee·ble (fē′bəl) *adj.* **-bler, -blest. 1** lacking strength; weak: *a feeble old man.* **2** weak intellectually or morally: *a feeble mind.* **3** lacking in force; ineffective: *a feeble attempt.* **4** lacking in volume, brightness, etc.: *a feeble cry.* [ME < OF *feble* < L *flebilis* lamentable < *flere* weep] —**fee′ble·ness,** *n.* —**fee′bly,** *adv.* —**Syn. 1** infirm, frail, doddering. See **weak. 4** slight, faint.

fee·ble-mind·ed (fē′bəl mīn′did) *adj.* weak in mind; lacking normal intelligence. —**fee′ble-mind′ed·ly,** *adv.* —**fee′ble-mind′ed·ness,** *n.*

feed (fēd) *v.* **fed, feed·ing,** *n.* —*v.* **1** give food to. **2** give as food to: *Feed this grain to the chickens.* **3** eat. **4** supply with material: *feed a machine.* **5** satisfy; gratify: *Praise fed his vanity.* **6** nourish: *He fed his anger with thoughts of revenge.* **7** in the theatre, supply (another actor) with cues. **8** in sports, pass or give (the puck, ball, etc.) to a teammate. **9 fed up,** *Slang.* **a** fed too much. **b** bored; tired. **10 feed on** or **upon, a** live at the expense of; prey on. **b** derive satisfaction, support, etc. from. —*n.* **1** food for animals; an allowance of food for an animal. **2** *Informal.* a meal for a person. **3** a supplying with material. **4** the material supplied. **5** the part of a machine that supplies material. **6** in the theatre: **a** a line or cue to which a comedian replies with a line that gets a laugh. **b** a person who gives such cues. **7** in sports, a pass of the puck, ball, etc. [OE *fēdan* < *fōda* food]
Syn. *v.* **6** sustain. —*n.* **1 Feed, fodder** = food for animals. **Feed** is the general word applying to food for animals and fowls: *Give the chicken their feed.* **Fodder** applies to coarse or dried feed, like alfalfa, hay, corn, or other plants fed to horses, cattle, pigs, or sheep: *Put some fodder in the bins.*

feed·back (fēd′bak′) *n.* **1** in electronics, the return of part of the output of a system to its input so as to modify or control the input. **2** in biology, psychology, etc., the modification of a reaction or process by the activity of some of its products. **3** *Informal.* news; information: *There was no feedback from the usual sources.*

feed·bag (fēd′bag′) *n.* **1** a bag that can be hung over a horse's head for holding oats, etc.; nose bag. **2 put on the feedbag,** *Slang.* eat.

feed·box (fēd′boks′) *n.* **1** a box used to hold food for livestock. **2** a box containing the mechanism for feeding a machine.

feed·er (fēd′ər) *n.* **1** a person or thing that feeds. **2** a person or device that supplies food to a person or animal. **3** anything that supplies something else with material. A brook is a feeder for a river. A branch that brings traffic to the main line is a feeder. **4** a wire or cable used to conduct electricity from a source to a distribution point.

feeder line a branch airline, railway, pipeline, etc.

feed·lot (fēd′lot) *n.* a plot of land for feeding and fattening livestock for the market.

feel (fēl) *v.* **felt, feel·ing,** *n.* —*v.* **1** touch: *Feel this cloth.* **2** try to find or make (one's way) by touch: *He felt his way across the room when the lights went out.* **3** test or examine by touching: *feel a person's pulse, feel a child's forehead to see if he has a fever.* **4** search by touch; grope: *He felt in his pockets for a dime.* **5** find out by touching: *Feel how cold my hands are.* **6** be aware of: *feel the cool breeze.* **7** have the feeling of being; be: *She feels well.* **8** give the feeling of being; seem: *The air feels cold.* **9** have in one's mind; experience: *He feels joy.* **10** have pity or sympathy: *She feels for all who suffer.* **11** be influenced or affected by: *The ship feels her helm.* **12** think; believe; consider: *I feel that we shall win.* **13 feel out,** find out about in a cautious way. —*n.* **1** the touch: *I like the feel of silk.* **2** the way in which something feels to the touch: *Wet soap has a greasy feel.* **3** the sense of touch. **4** the act of feeling. [OE *fēlan*] —**Syn.** *v.* **1** handle. **2** grope. **8** appear.

feel·er (fēl′ər) *n.* **1** a special part of an animal's body for touching with. An insect's antennae are its feelers. **2** a suggestion, remark, hint, question, etc. made to find out what others are thinking or planning. **3** a person or thing that feels.

feel·ing (fēl′ing) *n.* **1** the act or condition of one that feels. **2** the sense of touch. **3** a being conscious; awareness. **4** emotion: *Joy, sorrow, fear, and anger are feelings.* **5** the capacity for emotion; sensibility: *She was guided by feeling rather than thought.* **6** sensitivity to the higher or more refined emotions: *His work shows both feeling and taste.* **7** pity; sympathy. **8** an opinion; sentiment: *Her feeling was that right would win.* **9** the quality felt to belong to anything: *There is a weird feeling about the place.* **10 feelings,** *pl.* sympathies, susceptibilities: *hurt one's feelings.* —*adj.* full of feeling; sensitive, emotional. —**feel′ing·ly,** *adv.*
Syn. *n.* **3** sensation, impression. **4 Feeling, emotion, passion** = a pleasant or painful mental state produced in a person in reaction to a stimulus of some kind. **Feeling** is the general word: *He had a vague feeling of hope.* **Emotion** = a strong and moving feeling, such as love, fear, sorrow, joy, etc.: *She was so overwhelmed with emotion that she couldn't speak for a moment.* **Passion** = violent emotion, usually overcoming the power to think clearly and taking complete possession of a person: *In a passion of rage he smashed the watch.*

fee simple See fee, def. 7.

feet (fēt) *n.* pl. of **foot. 1 carry off one's feet, a** make very enthusiastic. **b** impress. **2 sit at one's feet,** be a pupil or admirer of. **3 stand on one's own feet,** be independent.

fee tail See fee, def. 7.

feign (fān) *v.* **1** put on a false appearance of; make believe; pretend: *Some animals feign death when in danger.* **2** make up to deceive; invent falsely: *feign an excuse.* **3** represent fictitiously. **4** imagine: *The phoenix is a feigned bird.* [ME < OF *feign-*, a stem of *feindre* < L *fingere* form] —**feign′er,** *n.* —**Syn. 1** assume, affect, simulate.

feigned (fānd) *adj.* **1** imagined; not real. **2** pretended: *a feigned attack.* **3** invented to deceive: *a feigned headache.* —**feign′ed·ly,** *adv.*

feint (fānt) *n.* **1** a movement intended to deceive; pretended blow; sham attack. **2** a false appearance; pretence. —*v.* make a pretended blow or sham attack. *The fighter feinted with his right hand and struck with his left.* [< F *feinte* < *feindre* feign]

feld·spar (feld′spär′) *n.* any of several crystalline minerals composed mostly of aluminum silicates. Also **felspar.** [< *feld-* (< G *Feldspat*, literally, field spar) + *spar*[3]]

fe·lic·i·tate (fə lis′ə tāt′) *v.* **-tat·ed, -tat·ing.** formally express good wishes to; congratulate: *John's friends felicitated him on his engagement to marry.* [< LL *felicitare* < *felix* happy]

fe·lic·i·ta·tion (fə lis′ə tā′shən) *n.* a formal expression of good wishes; congratulation.

fe·lic·i·tous (fə lis′ə təs) *adj.* **1** well chosen for the occasion; unusually appropriate: *The poem was full of striking and felicitous similes.* **2** having a gift for apt speech. —**fe·lic′i·tous·ly,** *adv.* —**fe·lic′i·tous·ness,** *n.*

fe·lic·i·ty (fə lis′ə tē) *n.* **-ties. 1** happiness; bliss. **2** good fortune; blessing. **3** a pleasing aptness in expression; appropriateness; grace: *The famous writer phrased his ideas with felicity.* **4** a happy turn of thought; well-chosen phrase. [ME < OF < L *felicitas* < *felix* happy] —**Syn. 1** See **happiness.**

fe·line (fē′līn) *adj.* **1** of or belonging to the cat family. **2** catlike; stealthy; sly: *With noiseless, feline movements the Indian stalked the deer.* —*n.* any animal belonging to the cat family. Lions, tigers, leopards, and panthers are felines. [< L *felis* cat]

fell[1] (fel) *v.* pt. of **fall.**

fell[2] (fel) *v.* **1** cause to fall; knock down: *One blow felled him to the ground.* **2** cut down (a tree). **3** turn down and stitch one edge of (a seam) over the other. —*n.* **1** all the trees cut down in one season. **2** a seam made by felling. [OE *fellan* < *feallan* fall]

fell[3] (fel) *adj.* **1** cruel; fierce; terrible: *a fell blow.* **2** deadly; destructive: *a fell disease.* [ME < OF *fel* < VL *fello.* See FELON[1].]

fell[4] (fel) *n.* the skin or hide of an animal. [OE. Related to FILM.]

fell[5] (fel) *n.* **1** a stretch of high moorland. **2** a hill; mountain. [< ON *fiall*]

fel·la (fel′ə) *n. Slang.* fellow.

fel·la·gha (fə lä′ gə) *n.* **-has** or **-ha.** an Arab guerrilla fighting in Algeria or Tunisia. [< Arabic *fallaq* (literally) outlaw]

fel·lah[1] (fel′ə) *n.* **fel·la·hin** (fel′ə hēn′). a peasant or laborer in Egypt and other Arabic-speaking countries. [< Arabic *fallāh* husbandman]

fel·lah[2] (fel′ə) *n. Slang.* fellow.

fell·er[1] (fel′ər) *n.* **1** a person or thing that fells. **2** a part attached to a sewing machine to fell seams.

fell·er[2] (fel′ər) *n. Slang.* fellow.

fel·loe (fel′ō) *n.* the circular rim of a wheel into which the outer ends of the spokes are inserted. Also, **felly.** [var. of FELLY]

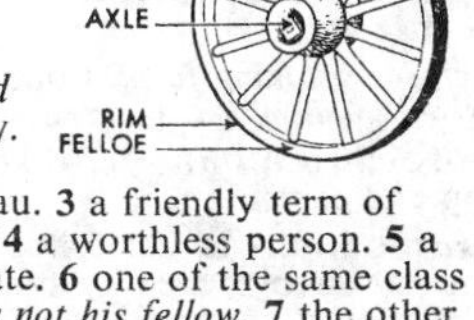

fel·low (fel′ō; *for defs. 2 and 4, often* fel′ə) *n.* **1** a man; boy. **2** *Informal.* a young man courting a young woman; beau. **3** a friendly term of address for a dog, horse, etc. **4** a worthless person. **5** a companion; comrade; associate. **6** one of the same class or rank; equal: *The world has not his fellow.* **7** the other one of a pair; mate. **8** a graduate student who has a fellowship in a university or college. **9** an honored member of a learned society. **10 hail fellow well met,** very friendly.
—*adj.* belonging to the same class; united by the same work, interests, aims, etc.; being in the same or a like condition: *fellow citizens, fellow sufferers.* [OE *fēolaga* < ON *felagi* partner (literally, fee-layer)]

fellow feeling sympathy.

fel·low·ship (fel′ō ship′) *n.* **1** companionship; friendliness. **2** a taking part with others; sharing. **3** a group of people having similar tastes, interests, etc.; brotherhood; corporation. **4** a position or sum of money given to a graduate student in a university or college to enable him to go on with his studies. **5** the relationship existing among those holding the same religious beliefs; communion. —**Syn. 1** comradeship, friendship.

fellow traveller or **traveler** a person sympathizing with, though not a member of, a political movement or party, especially the Communist Party.

fel·ly (fel′ē) *n.* **-lies.** felloe. [OE *felg*]

fel·on[1] (fel′ən) *n.* a person who has committed a serious crime; criminal: *Murderers and thieves are felons.*
—*adj.* wicked; cruel. [ME < OF *felon* < L; ultimate origin uncertain]

fel·on[2] (fel′ən) *n.* a painful infection on a finger or toe, usually near the nail; whitlow. [origin uncertain]

fe·lo·ni·ous (fə lō′ nē əs) *adj.* **1** that is a felony; criminal. **2** wicked; villainous. —**fe·lo′ni·ous·ly,** *adv.* —**fe·lo′ ni·ous·ness,** *n.*

fel·o·ny (fel′ə nē) *n.* **-nies.** in law, a crime of a more serious nature than a misdemeanor. Murder and burglary are felonies.

fel·spar (fel′spär′) *n.* feldspar.

felt[1] (felt) *v.* pt. and pp. of **feel.**

felt[2] (felt) *n.* **1** a kind of cloth that is not woven but made by rolling and pressing together wool, hair, or fur, used to make hats, slippers, and pads. **2** something made of felt. **3** in papermaking, a belt, usually of textile material, that carries the freshly formed paper through the machine.
—*adj.* made of felt.

hat, āge, cãre, fär; let, ēqual, tėrm; it, īce
hot, ōpen, ôrder; oil, out; cup, pu̇t, rüle, ūse
əbove, takən, pencəl, lemən, circəs
ch, child; ng, long; sh, ship
th, thin; ꟸH, then; zh, measure

—*v.* **1** make into felt. **2** cover with felt. [OE]

fe·luc·ca (fə luk′ə) *n.* a long, narrow ship with oars, or lateen sails, or both, used in the coastal waters of the Mediterranean Sea and the Red Sea. [< Ital. < Arabic *fulk* ship]

A felucca

fem. **1** female. **2** feminine.

fe·male (fē′māl) *n.* **1** a woman or girl. **2** an animal belonging to the sex that brings forth young or produces eggs. **3** in botany: **a** a flower having a pistil or pistils and no stamens. **b** a plant bearing only flowers with pistils.
—*adj.* **1** of or having to do with women or girls. **2** belonging to the sex that brings forth young. **3** in botany: **a** indicating or having to do with any reproductive structure that produces or contains elements that need fertilization from the male element; having pistils. **b** having flowers that contain a pistil or pistils but no stamens. **4** designating some part of a machine, connection, etc. into which a corresponding part fits. [ME < OF < *femelle* < L *femella,* dim. of *femina* woman; form influenced by *male*]
Syn. *n.* **1 Female, woman, lady** = member of the feminine sex. **Female,** applicable to baby, child, adolescent, or adult, emphasizes sex, and except when used in science or statistics, expresses an attitude of contempt: *Girls' schools once were called academies for females.* **Woman** is the general word for the feminine adult: *men, women, and children.* **Lady** applies particularly to a woman who stands above others in nobility of character, gentleness, dignity, fineness of feeling and habits: *She is always a lady.*

fem·i·nine (fem′ə nin) *adj.* **1** of women or girls. **2** like a woman; womanly; gentle. **3** like that of a woman; not suited to a man. **4** of or belonging to the female sex. **5** in grammar, of the gender to which names of females belong. *Actress, queen,* and *cow* are feminine nouns.
—*n.* **1** the feminine gender. **2** a word or form in the feminine gender. [ME < OF < L *femininus* < *femina* woman] —**fem′i·nine·ly,** *adv.* —**fem′i·nine·ness,** *n.*

feminine rhyme a rhyme of two syllables of which the second is unstressed (as, *motion, notion*), or of three syllables of which the second and third are unstressed (as, *happily, snappily*).

fem·i·nin·ity (fem′ə nin′ə tē) *n.* **1** a feminine quality or condition. **2** women.

fem·i·nism (fem′ə niz′əm) *n.* a doctrine that favors increased rights and activities for women.

fem·i·nist (fem′ə nist) *n.* a person who believes in or favors feminism.

femme fa·tale (fäm′ fä täl′) *pl.* **femmes fa·tales** (fäm′ fä täl′). *French.* a disastrously seductive woman; siren.

fem·o·ral (fem′ə rəl) *adj.* of the femur. [< L *femur, femoris* thigh]

fe·mur (fē′mər) *n.* **fe·murs, fem·o·ra** (fem′ə rə). **1** in anatomy, the thighbone. **2** a corresponding bone in the leg or hind limb of other animals. See **skeleton** for picture. [< L *femur* thigh]

fen[1] (fen) *n. Brit.* a marsh; swamp; bog. [OE *fenn*]

fen[2] (fen) *n.* **1** a unit of money in China, worth 1/100 of a yuan. **2** a coin worth one fen. [< Chinese]

fence (fens) *n. v.* **fenced, fenc·ing.** —*n.* **1** a railing, wall, or other means of enclosing a yard, garden, field, farm, etc. to show where the property ends or to keep people or animals out or in. **2** fencing. **3** skill or adroitness in argument or repartee. **4** a person who buys and sells stolen goods. **5** a place where stolen goods are bought and sold. **6** a guard, guide, or gauge designed to regulate the movements of a tool or machine. **7 mend one's fences,** *Informal.* **a** look after one's political interests at home, as in preparation for renomination. **b** improve one's relations and popularity in any area. **8 on the fence,** *Informal.* not having made up one's mind which side to take; doubtful. —*v.* **1** put a fence around; enclose with a fence; keep out or in with a fence. **2** separate as by a fence; keep apart or at a distance: *The patents were used to fence in and block off other manufacturers.* **3** fight with swords or foils. **4** parry; evade. **5** defend; protect. **6 fence with,** avoid giving a direct answer to. [var. of *defence*]

fenc·er (fen′sər) *n.* **1** a person who knows how to fight with a sword or foil. **2** a person who makes or mends fences. **3** a horse that jumps fences; steeplechaser.

fenc·ing (fen′sing) *n.* **1** the art of fighting with swords or foils. **2** the act or practice of parrying the points of one's opponent in a debate, discussion, or argument. **3** the material for making fences. **4** fences.

fend (fend) *v.* **1** defend; resist. **2 fend for oneself,** *Informal.* provide for oneself; get along by one's own efforts. **3 fend off,** ward off; keep off. [var. of *defend*]

fend·er (fen′dər) *n.* **1** anything that keeps or wards something off. **2** a guard or protection over the wheel of an automobile, motorcycle, etc.; mudguard: *The fenders prevent mud from splashing when the vehicle is moving over a wet, dirty road.* **3** a metal bar or frame placed on the front or rear of a locomotive, streetcar, etc. to lessen damage in case of collision. **4** a cowcatcher or other device at the front of a locomotive, etc. to reduce injury to an animal or person in case of collision. **5** a metal guard, frame, or screen in front of a fireplace to keep hot coals and sparks from the room. **6** a rope pad or cushion, log, etc. to prevent damage to the side of a ship when docking: *Fenders may be attached to the side of the boat or to the dock.* [var. of DEFENDER]

fen·es·tra·tion (fen′is trā′shən) *n.* **1** the arrangement of windows in a building. **2** in medicine, the operation of making an opening into the labyrinth or semicircular canal of the ear to eliminate deafness caused by obstruction of sound waves. [< L *fenestrare* provide with windows < *fenestra* window]

Fe·ni·an (fē′nē ən or fēn′yən) *n.* **1** a member of an Irish secret organization founded in the United States about 1858 for the purpose of overthrowing English rule in Ireland. **2** a member of a group of warriors in Irish legend. —*adj.* of or having to do with the Fenians. [< OIrish *fēne*, a name of the ancient inhabitants of Ireland, confused with Irish *fianna*, a legendary body of warriors]

fen·nel (fen′əl) *n.* a tall perennial plant with yellow flowers. Its aromatic seeds are used in medicine and cooking. [OE *fenol* < VL **fenuclum*, ult. < L *fenum* hay]

fen·ny (fen′ē) *adj.* **1** marshy; swampy; boggy. **2** growing or living in fens. [OE *fennig* < *fenn* fen]

feoff (fēf) *n.* fief.

fe·ral[1] (fēr′əl) *adj.* **1** wild; untamed. **2** brutal; savage. [< L *fera* beast]

fe·ral[2] (fē′rəl) *adj.* **1** deadly or fatal: *a feral disease.* **2** gloomy; funereal. [< L *feralis* of the dead, of funeral rites]

fer·ment (*v.* fər ment′; *n.* fėr′ment) *v.* **1** undergo a gradual chemical change, giving off bubbles of gas, and changing in character. Vinegar is formed when cider ferments. **2** cause this chemical change in (something). **3** cause unrest in; excite; agitate. **4** be excited; seethe with agitation or unrest.
—*n.* **1** a substance causing fermentation: *Yeast is used as a ferment in brewing beer.* **2** excitement; agitation; unrest. [< L *fermentare* < *fermentum* leaven < *fervere* boil] —**fer·ment′a·ble,** *adj.* —**fer·ment′er,** *n.*

fer·men·ta·tion (fėr′men tā′shən) *n.* **1** the act or process of fermenting. **2** excitement; agitation; unrest. **3** a chemical change caused by a ferment.

fer·mi·um (fėr′mē əm) *n.* a rare, radio-active, artificial chemical element, produced as a by-product of nuclear fission. *Symbol*: Fm; *at.no.* 100; *at.wt.* 253 (most stable isotope). [< Enrico *Fermi*, an Italian-born American physicist]

fern (fėrn) *n.* any of a group of plants that have roots, stems, and leaves, but no flowers, and reproduced by spores instead of seeds. Maidenhair, adder's-tongue, bracken, club mosses, etc. are ferns. [OE *fearn*] —**fern′like′,** *adj.*

fern·er·y (fėr′nər ē or fėrn′rē) *n.* **-er·ies. 1** a place where ferns are grown for ornament. **2** a container in which ferns are grown for ornament.

fern·y (fėr′nē) *adj.* **1** of ferns. **2** like ferns. **3** overgrown with ferns.

fe·ro·cious (fə rō′shəs) *adj.* savagely cruel; fierce. [< L *ferox, -ocis* fierce] —**fe·ro′cious·ly,** *adv.* —**Syn.** ruthless, brutal, murderous. See **fierce.**

fe·roc·i·ty (fə ros′ə tē) *n.* **-ties. 1** savage cruelty; fierceness. **2** a savage or cruel act. [< L *ferocitas* < *ferox* fierce]

-ferous *suffix.* producing; containing; conveying, as in *metalliferous.* [< *-fer* (< *ferre* bear) + E *-ous*]

fer·rate (fer′āt) *n.* a salt of ferric acid.

fer·ret (fer′it) *n.* a European white or yellowish-white weasel used for killing rats, hunting rabbits, etc.
—*v.* **1** hunt with ferrets. **2** hunt; search: *The detectives ferreted out the criminal.* [ME < OF *fuiret*, ult. < L *fur* thief]

fer·ric (fer′ik) *adj.* of or containing iron, especially trivalent iron. [< L *ferrum* iron]

ferric oxide a reddish-brown compound of iron and oxygen found naturally as hematite and produced chemically as a powder for use as a pigment, abrasive, etc. *Formula*: Fe_2O_3

Fer·ris wheel (fer′is) a large, revolving, wheel-like framework of steel equipped with swinging seats that hang from its rim: *Ferris wheels are found in the amusement areas of fairs, exhibitions, and carnivals.* [< G. W. G. *Ferris* (1859-1896), an American engineer, the inventor]

ferro- *combining form.* iron; derivation from iron, as in *ferrochromium.* [< L *ferrum* iron]

fer·ro·chro·mi·um (fer′ō krō′mē əm) *n.* an alloy of iron and chromium.

fer·ro·con·crete (fer′ō kon′krēt or -kon krēt′) *n.* concrete strengthened by a metal framework embedded in it; reinforced concrete.

fer·ro·man·ga·nese (fer′ō mang′gə nēz′ or -mang′gə nēs′) *n.* an alloy of iron, manganese, and sometimes carbon, used for making tough steel.

fer·rous (fer′əs) *adj.* of or containing divalent iron. [< L *ferrum* iron]

fer·ru·gi·nous (fə rü′jə nəs) *adj.* **1** of or containing iron; like that of iron. **2** reddish-brown like rust. [< L *ferruginus* < *ferrugo* iron rust < *ferrum* iron]

fer·rule (fer′ül or fer′əl) *n.* a metal ring or cap put around the end of a cane, wooden handle, umbrella, etc. to strengthen and protect it. Also, **ferule.** [earlier *verrel*, < OF *virelle* < L *viriola*, dim. of *viriae* bracelets; form influenced by L *ferrum* iron]

fer·ry (fer′ē) *n.* **-ries,** *v.* **-ried, -ry·ing.** —*n.* **1** a place where boats carry people and goods across a river or narrow stretch of water. **2** the boat used; ferryboat. **3** a system for flying airplanes to a destination for delivery. [< v.]
—*v.* **1** carry (people and goods) in a boat back and forth across a river or narrow stretch of water. **2** go across in a ferryboat. **3** carry back and forth across a wide stretch of water in an airplane. **4** fly an airplane to a destination for delivery. [OE *ferian* < *fær* fare]

fer·ry·boat (fer′ē bōt′) *n.* a boat used for ferrying.

fer·ry·man (fer′ē mən) *n.* **-men** (-mən). **1** a man who owns or has charge of a ferry. **2** a man who works on a ferry.

fer·tile (fėr′tīl or fėr′təl) *adj.* **1** able to produce much; rich in things that aid growth, development, etc.: *Fertile soil produces good crops.* **2** producing many offspring. **3** capable of reproduction; able to produce seeds, fruit, young, etc. **4** in biology, capable of developing into a new individual; fertilized: *Chicks hatch from fertile eggs.* **5** productive of ideas; artistically creative: *Keats had a fertile imagination. Einstein had a fertile mind.* [< L *fertilis* < *ferre* bear] —**fer′tile·ness,** *n.*

Syn. **1 Fertile, productive** = able to produce much. **Fertile** emphasizes containing within itself the things needed to nourish what is brought forth and maintain its life and development, and describes things in which seeds or ideas can take root and grow: *The seed fell on fertile ground. He has a fertile imagination.* **Productive** emphasizes bringing forth, especially in abundance: *Those fruit trees are very productive. He is a productive writer.*

hat, āge, cãre, fär; let, ēqual, tėrm; it, īce
hot, ōpen, ôrder; oil, out; cup, pu̇t, rüle, ūse
əbove, takən, pencəl, lemən, circəs
ch, child; ng, long; sh, ship
th, thin; TH, then; zh, measure

Fertile Crescent a fertile, crescent-shaped strip of land on the eastern shore of the Mediterranean. See **Babylonia** for map.

fer·til·i·ty (fėr til′ə tē) *n.* the condition of being fertile.

fer·ti·li·za·tion (fėr′tə lə zā′shən or fėr′tə lī zā′shən) *n.* **1** a fertilizing or being fertilized. **2** in biology, the union of male and female reproductive cells to form a cell that will develop into a new individual.

fer·ti·lize (fėr′tə līz′) *v.* **-lized, -liz·ing. 1** make fertile; make able to produce much: *A crop of alfalfa fertilized the soil by adding nitrates to it.* **2** put fertilizer on. **3** in biology, unite with (an egg cell) in fertilization; impregnate.

fer·ti·liz·er (fėr′tə līz′ər) *n.* **1** a substance put on land to make it able to produce more. Manure is a common fertilizer. **2** a person or thing that fertilizes.

fer·ule[1] (fer′ül or fer′əl) *n. v.* **-uled, -ul·ing.** —*n.* a stick or ruler used for punishing children by striking them, especially on the hand. —*v.* punish with a stick or ruler. [< L *ferula* rod]

fer·ule[2] (fer′ül or fer′əl) *n.* ferrule.

fer·ven·cy (fėr′vən sē) *n.* warmth of feeling; great earnestness.

fer·vent (fėr′vənt) *adj.* **1** showing warmth of feeling; very earnest: *a fervent plea.* **2** hot; glowing. [< F < L *fervens, -entis,* ppr. of *fervere* boil] —**fer′vent·ly,** *adv.* —**fer′vent·ness,** *n.* —**Syn. 1** ardent, zealous, passionate.

fervid (fėr′vid) *adj.* **1** showing great warmth of feeling; intensely emotional. **2** intensely hot. [< L *fervidus* < *fervere* boil] —**fer′vid·ly,** *adv.* —**fer′vid·ness,** *n.*

fer·vor or **fer·vour** (fėr′vər) *n.* **1** great warmth of feeling; intense emotion: *The patriot's voice trembled from the fervor of his emotion.* **2** intense heat. [ME < OF < L *fervor* < *fervere* boil] —**Syn. 1** zeal, ardor.

fes·cue (fes′kū) *n.* **1** a tough grass used for pasture. **2** a small stick, straw, etc. for pointing out the letters in teaching a child to read. [ME < OF *festu* < L *festuca*]

fess or **fesse** (fes) *n.* in heraldry, a wide, horizontal band across the middle of a shield. [ME < OF *fesse, faisse* < L *fascia* band]

A fess

fes·ta (fes′tə) *n. Italian.* a holiday; feast; festival; party.

fes·tal (fes′təl) *adj.* of a feast, festival, or holiday; gay; joyous; festive: *A wedding or a birthday is a festal occasion.* [< MF < LL < L *festum* feast]

fes·ter (fes′tər) *v.* **1** form pus: *The neglected wound festered and became very painful.* **2** cause pus to form. **3** cause soreness or pain; rankle: *Resentment festered in his mind.* **4** decay; rot. [< n.] —*n.* a sore that forms pus; small ulcer. [ME < OF *festre* < L *fistula* pipe, ulcer. Doublet of FISTULA.]

fes·ti·val (fes′tə vəl) *n.* **1** a day or special time of rejoicing or feasting, often in memory of some great happening: *Christmas and Easter are two festivals of the Christian Church.* **2** a celebration; entertainment: *Every year the city has a music festival during the first week in May.* **3** a competition among drama groups, orchestras, etc. for recognition as the best in the region: *the Dominion Drama Festival.* **4** merry-making; revelry. —*adj.* having to do with a festival. [< Med.L *festivalis,* ult. < L *festum* feast]

fes·tive (fes′tiv) *adj.* of or for a feast, festival, or holiday; gay; joyous; merry: *A birthday or wedding is a festive occasion.* —**fes′tive·ly,** *adv.* —**fes′tive·ness,** *n.*

fes·tiv·i·ty (fes tiv′ə tē) *n.* **-ties. 1** a festive activity; something done to celebrate: *The festivities on Dominion Day included a parade and fireworks.* **2** gaiety; merriment. **3** a festival.

fes·toon (fes tün′) *n.* **1** a hanging curve of flowers, leaves, ribbons, etc.: *The flags were hung on the wall in colorful festoons.* **2** a carved or moulded ornament like this on furniture, pottery, etc. —*v.* **1** decorate with festoons: *The Christmas tree was festooned with tinsel.* **2** form into festoons; hang in curves: *Draperies were festooned over the window.* [< F *feston* < Ital. *festone* < *festa* festival, feast]

fe·tal or **foe·tal** (fē′təl) *adj.* **1** of a fetus. **2** like that of a fetus.

fetch (fech) *v.* **1** go and get; bring. **2** cause to come; succeed in bringing. **3** be sold for: *These eggs will fetch a good price.* **4** *Informal.* attract; charm: *Flattery will fetch her.* **5** *Informal.* hit; strike: *He fetched him one on the nose.* **6** give (a groan, sigh, etc.). **7** reach; arrive at: *They tried to fetch the harbor but the storm broke too soon.* **8** of ships, take a course; move; go: *The boat was fetching to windward.* **9 fetch and carry,** do small jobs. **10 fetch up,** arrive; stop.
—*n.* **1** the act of fetching. **2** a trick. [OE *feccan*] —**fetch′er,** *n.* —**Syn.** *v.* **1** See **bring.**

fetch·ing (fech′ing) *adj. Informal.* attractive; charming. —**fetch′ing·ly,** *adv.*

fete or **fête** (fāt; *French,* fet) *n. v.* **fet·ed** or **fêt·ed, fet·ing** or **fêt·ing.** —*n.* a festival; a gala entertainment or celebration, usually held outdoors: *A large fete was given for the benefit of the town hospital.* —*v.* honor with a fete; entertain: *The engaged couple were feted by their friends.* [< F *fête* feast]

fet·ich (fet′ish or fē′tish) *n.* fetish.

fet·id (fet′id or fē′tid) *adj.* smelling very bad; stinking. [< L *foetidus* < *foetere* to smell. —**fet′id·ly,** *adv.* —**fet′id·ness,** *n.*

fet·ish (fet′ish or fē′tish) *n.* **1** any material object supposed to have magic power. **2** anything regarded with unreasoning reverence or devotion: *Some people make a fetish of style.* [< F *fétiche* < Pg. *feitiço* charm, originally adj., artificial < L *facticius.* Doublet of FACTITIOUS.]

fet·ish·ism (fet′ish iz′əm or fē′tish iz′əm) *n.* a belief in fetishes; worship of fetishes.

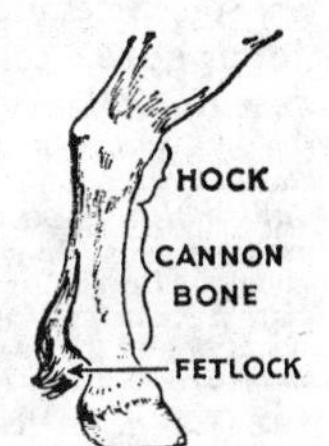

fet·lock (fet′lok) *n.* **1** the tuft of hair above a horse's hoof on the back part of the leg. **2** the part of a horse's leg where this tuft grows. **3** the joint at this spot. [ME *fetlok*]

fe·tor (fē′tər) *n.* a strong, offensive smell. [< L *foetor* < *foetere* to smell]

fet·ter (fet′ər) *n.* **1** a chain or shackle for the feet to prevent escape. **2** Usually, **fetters,** *pl.* anything that shackles or binds; restraint. —*v.* **1** bind with fetters; chain the feet of. **2** bind; restrain: *The boy had to learn to fetter his temper.* [OE *feter.* Related to FOOT.] —**Syn.** *v.* **2** confine, hamper, impede.

fet·tle (fet′əl) *n.* condition; trim: *The horse is in fine fettle and should win the race.* [? < ME *fettel(en)* gird up < OE *fetel* belt]

fe·tus or **foe·tus** (fē′təs) *n.* an animal embryo during the later stages of its development. [< L]

feud[1] (fūd) *n.* **1** a long and deadly quarrel between families, tribes, etc., often passed down from generation to generation. **2** continued strife between two persons, groups, etc. **3** a quarrel.
—*v.* engage in a deadly quarrel, especially one involving families: *They have been feuding with their neighbors for years.* [var. of ME *fede* < OF *fe(i)de* < OHG *fehida* enmity] —**Syn. 3** See **quarrel.**

feud[2] (fūd) *n.* a feudal estate; fief. [< Med.L *feudum* < Gmc.]

feu·dal (fū′dəl) *adj.* **1** of or having to do with feudalism. **2** of or having to do with feuds or fiefs. [< Med.L *feudalis* < *feudum.* See FEUD[2].]

feu·dal·ism (fū′dəl iz′əm) *n.* **1** the social, economic, and political system of Western Europe in the Middle Ages. Under this system vassals held land on condition of giving military and other services to the lord owning it in return for his protection and the use of the land. **2** any social, economic, or political system that suggests or resembles this.

feu·dal·is·tic (fū′dəl is′tik) *adj.* **1** of or having to do with feudalism. **2** tending toward feudalism: favoring feudalism.

feu·dal·i·ty (fū dal′ə tē) *n.* **-ties. 1** feudalism. **2** a feudal estate; fief.

feudal system feudalism.

feu·da·to·ry (fū′də tô′rē) *adj. n.* **-ries.** *—adj.* **1** owing feudal services to a lord. **2** holding or held as a feudal estate or fief. *—n.* **1** a feudal vassal: *The duke summoned his feudatories to aid him in war.* **2** a feudal estate; fief.

feu de joie (fœ də zhwä′) *pl.* **feux de joie. 1** a salute made by a line of troops firing their rifles in rapid succession. **2** *French.* a bonfire. [< F, literally, fire of joy]

feud·ist (fūd′ist) *n.* a person engaging in a feud.

fe·ver (fē′vər) *n.* **1** an unhealthy condition of the body in which the temperature is higher than normal. **2** any of various diseases that cause fever, such as scarlet fever and typhoid fever. **3** an excited, restless condition. **4** a current fad or enthusiasm for something or for some person.
—v. **1** affect with fever; heat; excite as if with fever. **2** become feverish. [OE *fefer* < L *febris*] **—fe′ver·less,** *adj.*

fe·vered (fē′vərd) *adj.* **1** having fever. **2** excited; restless.

fe·ver·few (fē′vər fū′) *n.* a perennial plant of the aster family having small, white, daisy-like flowers, formerly used in medicine. [OE *fēferfūg(i)e* < LL *febrifug(i)a* < L *febris* fever + *fugare* drive away]

fe·ver·ish (fē′vər ish or fēv′rish) *adj.* **1** having fever. **2** having a slight degree of fever. **3** causing fever. **4** infested with fever: *a feverish swamp.* **5** excited; restless. **—fe′ver·ish·ly,** *adv.* **—fe′ver·ish·ness,** *n.*

fe·ver·ous (fē′vər əs or fēv′rəs) *adj.* feverish.

fever pitch a state of intense excitement or frenzied activity.

fe·ver·root (fē′vər rüt′) *n.* a coarse plant whose roots are sometimes used for medicine.

fever sore a cold sore.

few (fū) *adj.* not many: *There are few women more than six feet tall.* *—n.* **1** a small number: *Only a few of the boys had bicycles.* **2 the few,** the minority. **3 quite a few,** *Informal.* a good many. [OE *fēawe*] **—few′ness,** *n.*

☛ **fewer, less.** *Fewer* refers only to number and things that are counted: *Fewer cars were on the road. There were fewer than sixty present.* In formal usage *less* refers only to amount or quantity and things measured: *There was a good deal less tardiness in the second term. There was even less hay than the summer before.*

fez (fez) *n.* **fez·zes.** a felt cap, usually red, ornamented with a long, black tassel. It was formerly the national head-dress of the Turks. [< Turkish; after *Fez,* Morocco]

A man wearing a fez

ff fortissimo.

ff. **1** folios following; and the following pages, sections, etc. **2** folios.

F.I. Falkland Islands.

fi·a·cre (fi ä′kər; *French,* fyä′ krə) *n.* a small four-wheeled horse-drawn hackney coach. [< St. *Fiacre,* the name of the hotel in Paris where they were first hired]

fi·an·cé (fē′än sā′ or fē′än sā′) *n.* a man to whom a woman is engaged to be married. [< F *fiancé,* pp. of *fiancer* betroth]

fi·an·cée (fē′än sā′ or fē′än sā′) *n.* a woman to whom a man is engaged to be married. [< F]

fi·as·co (fē as′kō) *n.* **-cos** or **-coes.** a failure; breakdown. [< F < Ital. *fiasco,* literally, flask; development of meaning uncertain]

fi·at (fī′ət or fī′at, fē′ət or fē′at) *n.* **1** an authoritative order or command; decree. **2** sanction. [< L *fiat* let it be done]

fib (fib) *n. v.* **fibbed, fib·bing.** lie about some small matter. [? < *fibble-fable* < *fable*] **—fib′ber,** *n.* **—Syn. See lie.**

fi·ber (fī′bər) *n.* fibre.

Fi·ber·glas (fī′bər glas′) *n. Trademark.* fibreglass.

fi·bre or **fi·ber** (fī′bər) *n.* **1** a threadlike part; thread: *A muscle is made up of many fibres.* **2** a substance made up of threads or threadlike parts: *Hemp fibre can be spun into rope or woven into a coarse cloth.* **3** texture: *cloth of coarse fibre.* **4** character; nature: *A person of strong moral fibre can resist temptation.* **5** a slender, threadlike root of a plant. [< F *fibre* < L *fibra*]

fi·bre·board or **fi·ber·board** (fī′bər bôrd′) *n.* a building material made by compressing fibres, especially wood fibres, into flat sheets.

fi·bre·glass or **fi·ber·glass** (fī′bər glas′) *n.* very fine, flexible threads of glass that can be made into insulating materials, fabrics, boats, etc.

fi·bril (fī′brəl) *n.* **1** a small or very slender fibre. **2** one of the hairs on the roots of some plants. [< NL *fibrilla* < L *fibra* fibre]

fi·brin (fī′brən) *n.* **1** a tough, elastic, yellowish protein formed when blood clots. **2** the gluten in plants. [< L *fibra* fibre]

fi·brin·o·gen (fī brin′ə jen′) *n.* a protein found in the blood, lymph, etc. and yielding fibrin in the coagulation of blood. [< *fibrin* + *-gen*]

fi·bri·no·sis (fī′brə nō′sis) *n.* a condition marked by too much fibrin in the blood.

fi·brin·ous (fī′brə nəs) *adj.* of or like fibrin.

fi·broid (fī′broid) *adj.* made up of fibres; of fibrelike structure. *—n.* a tumor made up of fibres or fibrous tissue.

fi·bro·sis (fī brō′sis) *n.* an excessive growth of fibrous connective tissue in the body. [< NL *fibrosis* < L *fibra* fibre + *-osis* -osis]

fi·bro·si·tis (fī′brə sī′tis) *n.* inflammation of fibrous tissue in the muscle sheaths.

fi·brous (fī′brəs) *adj.* made up of fibres; having fibres; like fibre. **—fi′brous·ly,** *adv.*

fib·u·la (fib′yů lə) *n.* **-lae** (-lē′) or **-las. 1** in anatomy, the outer and thinner of the two bones in the lower leg. It extends from knee to ankle. See **skeleton** for picture. **2** in zoology, a similar bone in the hind leg of animals. **3** in archaeology, a clasp or brooch, often highly ornamented. [< L *fibula* clasp, brooch]

fib·u·lar (fib′yů lər) *adj.* of or having to do with the fibula.

-fic *adjective suffix.* making; causing, as in *scientific, terrific.* [< L *-ficus* < *facere* do, make]

-fication *noun suffix.* a making or doing; corresponding to verbs ending in *-fy,* as in *falsification, purification.* [< L *-ficatio, -onis* < *-ficare* < *facere* do, make]

fich·u (fish′ü) *n.* a three-cornered piece of muslin, lace, or other soft material worn by women about the neck, with the ends drawn together or crossed on the breast. [< F]

fick·le (fik′əl) *adj.* likely to change without reason; changing; not constant: *fickle fortune, a fickle friend.* [OE *ficol* deceitful] **—fick′le·ness,** *n.* **—Syn.** unstable, unsteady.

fic·tion (fik′shən) *n.* **1** novels, short stories, and other prose writings that tell about imaginary, and sometimes real, people and happenings. Both characters and events in fiction may sometimes be partly real. **2** what is imagined or made up; imaginary happenings; make-believe: *The explorer exaggerated so much in telling about his adventures that it was impossible to separate fact from fiction.* **3** an imaginary account or statement; made-up story. **4** an inventing of imaginary accounts, stories, etc.; a feigning. **5** in law, something acted upon as a fact, in spite of its possible falsity. It is a legal fiction that a corporation is a person. [< L *fictio, -onis* < *fingere* to form, fashion]

fic·tion·al (fik′shən əl) *adj.* of or having to do with fiction. **—fic′tion·al·ly,** *adv.*

fic·ti·tious (fik tish′əs) *adj.* **1** not real; imaginary; made-up: *Characters in novels are usually fictitious.* **2** assumed in order to deceive; false: *The criminal used a fictitious name.* [< L *ficticius* artificial < *fingere* form, fashion] **—fic·ti′tious·ly,** *adv.* **—fic·ti′tious·ness,** *n.* **—Syn. 2** counterfeit, sham, feigned.

fid (fid) *n.* **1** on a ship, a square bar used to support a topmast. **2** a bar or pin used to support or steady anything. **3** a hard pin like a spike for separating strands of rope in splicing. [origin uncertain]

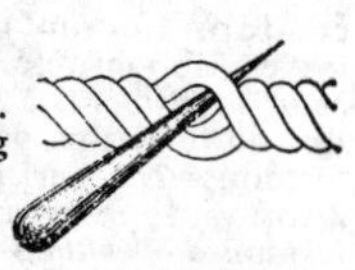

A fid (def. 3)

-fid *adjective suffix.* split; cleft; lobed, as in *bifid.* [< L *-fidus* < *findere* cleave, split]

fid·dle (fid′əl) *n. v.* **-dled, -dling.** *—n.* **1** *Informal.* a violin. **2** something resembling a violin. **3** on a ship, a

low railing on the edge of a table to prevent dishes, etc. from sliding off when the ship rolls or pitches. **4** *Slang.* deception; fraud; artifice. **5 fit as a fiddle,** in excellent physical condition. **6 play second fiddle,** take a secondary part.
—*v.* **1** *Informal.* play on a violin. **2** make aimless movements; play nervously; toy: *The embarrassed boy fiddled with his hat.* **3** trifle: *He fiddled away the whole day doing absolutely nothing.* **4** *Slang.* cheat; swindle; falsify. [OE *fithele* (recorded in *fithelere* fiddler); probably akin to Med.L *vitula.* See VIOL.] —**fid′dler,** *n.*

fid·dle-de-dee (fid′əl dē dē′) *n. interj.* nonsense.

fid·dle-fad·dle (fid′əl fad′əl) *n. interj. v.* **-dled, -dling.** *Informal.* —*n.* trifling speech or action. —*interj.* nonsense. —*v.* busy oneself about trivial things. [? reduplication of *fiddle*]

fid·dle·head (fid′əl hed′) *n.* **1** the young leaves, or fronds, of certain ferns, eaten as a delicacy. Fiddleheads are found especially in Nova Scotia and New Brunswick. **2** a scroll-shaped ornament on a ship's bow, resembling the head of a violin.

Fiddleheads on a fern

fid·dle·neck (fid′əl nek′) *n.* fiddlehead.

fiddler crab a small burrowing crab common along the Atlantic coast of the United States.

fid·dle·stick (fid′əl stik′) *n.* **1** a violin bow. **2** a mere nothing; trifle.

fid·dle·sticks (fid′əl stiks′) *interj.* nonsense! rubbish!

Fi·de·i De·fen·sor (fī dē ī or fē′dā ē di fen′sôr) *Latin.* Defender of the Faith, one of the titles of the British Sovereign.

fi·del·i·ty (fə del′ə tē or fī del′ə tē) *n.* **-ties.** **1** faithfulness to a trust or vow; steadfast faithfulness; loyalty. **2** strictness or thoroughness in the performance of duty: *His fidelity and industry brought him speedy promotion.* **3** exactness, as in a copy; accuracy: *The reporter wrote his story with absolute fidelity.* **4** the ability of a device, as a radio transmitter or receiver, to transmit or reproduce an electric signal or sound accurately. [< L *fidelitas,* ult. < *fides* faith. Doublet of FEALTY.]

fidg·et (fij′it) *v.* **1** move about restlessly; be uneasy: *A child fidgets if he has to sit still for a long time.* **2** make uneasy. —*n.* **1** the condition of being restless or uneasy. **2** a person who moves about restlessly. **3 the fidgets,** a fit of restlessness or uneasiness. [< obs. *fidge* move restlessly]

fidg·et·y (fij′ə tē) *adj.* restless; uneasy.

fi·du·ci·ar·y (fə dū′shē er′ē or fə dü′shē er′ē) *adj. n.* **-ar·ies.** —*adj.* **1** held in trust: *fiduciary estates.* **2** holding in trust. A fiduciary possessor is legally responsible for what belongs to another. **3** of a trustee; of trust and confidence: *A guardian acts in a fiduciary capacity.* **4** depending upon public trust and confidence for its value. Paper money that cannot be redeemed in gold or silver is fiduciary currency. —*n.* a trustee. [< L *fiduciarius* < *fiducia* trust]

fie (fī) *interj.* for shame! shame! [< OF]
☛ The disgust, disapproval, or impatience conveyed by this word is now often ironical.

fief (fēf) *n.* in feudal times, a piece of land held from a lord in return for military and other services as required; feudal estate. Also, **feoff.** [< F < Gmc.]

field (fēld) *n.* **1** land with few or no trees. **2** a piece of land used for crops or pasture. **3** a piece of land used for some special purpose: *a flying field.* **4** land yielding some product: *a coal field.* **5** in military use: **a** the place where a battle is or has been fought. **b** a battle: *The English won the field at Poitiers.* **c** a region where certain military operations are carried on. **6** in sports: **a** an area for athletics, games, etc. **b** the part of this area used for contests in jumping, etc. **c** the sports contested in this area. **d** all those participating in a game, contest, or outdoor sport. **e** all those participating in a game or contest except one or more specified: *bet on one horse against the field.* **f** a defensive football, baseball, etc. team. **7** in baseball: **a** the playing field, including both infield and outfield. **b** the outfield. **8** a range of opportunity or interest; sphere of activity or operation: *Many great discoveries have been made in the field of science.* **9** a flat space; broad surface: *A field of ice surrounds the North Pole.* **10** the surface on which some emblem is pictured or painted: *the field of a coat of arms.* **11** the ground of each division of a flag. **12** in physics, the space throughout which a force operates. A magnet has a magnetic field about it. **13** the space or area in which things can be seen through a telescope, microscope, etc. without moving it: *the field of vision.* **14** in television, the entire screen area occupied by an image. **15 play the field, a** *Informal.* take a broad sphere of action or operation. **b** *Slang.* go with many different persons of the opposite sex. **16 take the field,** begin a battle, campaign, game, etc.
—*v.* **1** in baseball, cricket, etc: **a** stop or catch and return (a ball). **b** act as a fielder. **2** put into the field; have as players: *We field a strong team.* **3** *Informal.* answer skilfully (difficult or controversial questions). **4** protect; defend: *He fielded his political position gracefully.* [OE *feld*]

hat, āge, cãre, fär; let, ēqual, tėrm; it, īce
hot, ōpen, ôrder; oil, out; cup, pu̇t, rüle, ūse
əbove, takən, pencəl, lemən, circəs
ch, child; ng, long; sh, ship
th, thin; ᴛʜ, then; zh, measure

field artillery **1** artillery mounted on carriages for easy movement by armies in the field. **2** that branch of the artillery equipped with light mobile guns.

field day **1** a day for athletic contests and outdoor sports. **2** a day when soldiers perform drills, mock fights, etc. **3** a day of unusual activity or display.

field·er (fēl′dər) *n.* **1** in baseball, a player who is stationed around or outside the diamond to stop the ball and throw it in. **2** in cricket, a person playing a similar position.

field event any one of the events at an athletic meet that are held on the field as opposed to on the track. Jumping, pole-vaulting, shot-putting, and discus-throwing are field events.

field·fare (fēld′fãr′) *n.* a European thrush having a gray head, black tail, and brown-and-white body. [OE *feldefare*]

field glasses or **field glass** a small binocular telescope.

Field glasses

field goal in rugby football, a goal counting three points scored by kicking the ball between the uprights and above the bar of the goal post.

field gun an artillery gun.

field hockey a game played on a grass field by two teams whose players use curved sticks and try to drive a ball into the opposing team's goal.

field hospital a temporary hospital near a battlefield.

field house a building near an athletic field, used for storing equipment, for dressing rooms, etc.

field jacket a light, waterproof cotton jacket designed to be worn by soldiers in combat.

field kitchen a portable kitchen that can be set up in the open to cook food for a large number of people, such as an army unit.

field magnet an electromagnet used in a generator or motor to make a strong electric field.

field·man (fēld′man′ or fēld′mən) *n.* **-men** (-men′ or -mən). a salesman, researcher, or government agent who has direct contact with customers, research subjects, etc. and usually works at a distance from his head office.

field marshal in the army, a commissioned officer of the highest rank. *Abbrev.*: F.M.

field mouse any variety of mouse living in fields and meadows.

field officer in the army, a commissioned officer senior to a captain and junior to a brigadier: *Colonels, lieutenant-colonels, and majors are field officers.*

field of fire the area that a gun or battery covers effectively.

field·piece (fēld′pēs′) *n.* field gun.

field·stone (fēld′stōn′) *n.* rough stones used for houses, walls, etc. especially when found in the area near the construction site. *—adj.* of or resembling fieldstone.

field trial 1 a test of the performance of hunting dogs in the field. 2 a test of a new product under actual conditions of use.

field trip a trip to give students special opportunities for observing facts relating to a particular field of study.

field work the scientific or technical work done in the field by surveyors, geologists, linguists, sociologists, etc.

field·work (fēld′wėrk′) *n.* a temporary fortification for defence made by soldiers in the field.

field·work·er (fēld′wėrk′ər) *n.* one engaged in field work. Also, **field worker.**

fiend (fēnd) *n.* 1 an evil spirit; devil. 2 an extremely wicked or cruel person. 3 *Informal.* a person who indulges excessively in some habit, practice, game, etc.: *An opium fiend cannot get along without opium.* 4 **the Fiend,** the Devil. [OE *fēond,* originally ppr. of *fēogan* hate]
—**fiend′like′,** *adj.*

fiend·ish (fēn′dish) *adj.* extremely cruel or wicked; devilish: *fiendish tortures, a fiendish yell.* —**fiend′ish·ly,** *adv.* —**fiend′ish·ness,** *n.*

fierce (fērs) *adj.* **fierc·er, fierc·est.** 1 savage; wild: *a fierce lion.* 2 raging; violent: *a fierce wind.* 3 very eager or active; ardent: *fierce efforts to get ahead.* 4 *Slang.* very bad, unpleasant, etc. [ME < OF *fers, fiers* < L *ferus* wild] —**fierce′ly,** *adv.* —**fierce′ness,** *n.*
Syn. 1 **Fierce, ferocious, savage** = wild and harsh. **Fierce** emphasizes having a pitiless or unfeeling nature, showing a readiness to harm or kill, or being given to wild rage, especially in manner or actions: *He was a fierce fighter.* **Ferocious** suggests being wildly fierce or cruel, or showing wild force, especially in looks, disposition, or actions: *That man looks ferocious.* **Savage** adds the idea of showing an uncivilized lack of restraint on the emotions or passions and an inhuman lack of feeling for pain caused to others: *He has a savage temper.*

fier·y (fīr′ē or fī′ər ē) *adj.* **fier·i·er, fier·i·est.** 1 consisting of fire; containing fire; burning; flaming. 2 like fire; very hot; flashing; glowing. 3 full of feeling or spirit; ardent: *a fiery speech.* 4 easily aroused or excited: *a fiery temper.* 5 inflamed: *a fiery sore.* —**fier′i·ly,** *adv.* —**fier′i·ness,** *n.*
—**Syn.** 3 fervent, fervid, spirited.

fi·es·ta (fē es′tə) *n.* 1 a religious festival; saint's day. 2 a holiday; festivity. [< Sp. *fiesta* feast]

fife (fīf) *n. v.* **fifed, fif·ing.** —*n.* a small, shrill musical instrument like a flute: *Fifes and drums are used in playing marches.* —*v.* play on a fife. [< G *Pfeife* pipe]
—**fif′er,** *n.*

fif·teen (fif′tēn) *n. adj.* five more than ten; 15. [OE *fīftēne*]

fif·teenth (fif′tēnth′) *adj. n.* 1 next after the 14th; last in a series of 15. 2 one, or being one, of 15 equal parts.

fifth (fifth) *adj.* 1 next after the fourth; last in a series of 5. 2 being one of 5 equal parts.
—*n.* 1 the next after the fourth; last in a series of 5. 2 one of 5 equal parts. 3 in music: **a** the fifth tone from the keynote of a scale; the dominant. **b** the interval between such tones. **c** a combination of such tones. [alteration of OE *fīfta*]

fifth column any persons within a country who secretly aid its enemies. Originally, the term was applied to the Franco supporters in Madrid during the Spanish Civil War, who constituted an additional, or fifth, column to the four military columns that attacked the city from outside.

fifth columnist a member of the fifth column.

fifth·ly (fifth′lē) *adv.* in the fifth place.

fifth wheel *Informal.* a person or thing that is not needed.

fif·ti·eth (fif′tē ith) *adj. n.* 1 next after the 49th; last in a series of 50. 2 one, or being one, of 50 equal parts.

fif·ty (fif′tē) *n.* **-ties.** *adj.* five times ten; 50. [OE *fīftig*]

fif·ty-fif·ty (fif′tē fif′tē) *adv. adj. Informal.* half-and-half; in or with equal shares.

fig[1] (fig) *n.* 1 a small, soft, sweet fruit that grows in warm regions: *Figs are usually dried like dates and raisins.* 2 the tree that figs grow on. 3 a very small amount: *I don't care a fig for your opinion.* [ME < OF *figue* < Provençal *figa,* ult. < L *ficus* fig]

fig[2] (fig) *n. Informal.* 1 dress; equipment. 2 **in full fig,** fully dressed or equipped. [origin uncertain]

fig. 1 figure. 2 figurative. 3 figuratively.

fight (fīt) *n. v.* **fought, fight·ing.** —*n.* 1 a struggle; battle; conflict; combat; contest. 2 an angry dispute. 3 the power or will to fight. 4 **show fight,** resist; be ready to fight. [OE *feoht*]
—*v.* 1 take part in a fight. 2 take part in a fight against; war against. 3 carry on (a fight, conflict, etc.). 4 get or make by fighting. 5 cause to fight. 6 disagree angrily; quarrel: *The brothers were always fighting about one thing or another.* 7 **fight back,** offer resistance; show fight: *They had no heart to fight back.* 8 **fight it out,** fight until one side wins. 9 **fight shy of,** keep away from; avoid. [OE *feohtan*]
Syn. *n.* 1 **Fight, combat, conflict** = battle or struggle. **Fight** = a struggle for victory or mastery between two or more people, animals, or forces, and particularly suggests hand to hand fighting: *When boys fight, they often hurt one another.* **Combat** applies particularly to a battle between two armed men or forces: *The gladiators were ordered into combat in the arena.* **Conflict** emphasizes clashing, and applies to a battle or fight or to a mental or moral struggle between two beliefs, duties, etc.: *We all undergo mental conflicts.*

fight·er (fīt′ər) *n.* 1 one that fights. 2 a professional boxer. 3 a fighter plane.

fight·er-bomb·er (fī′tər bom′ər) *n.* an aircraft used both as a fighter and as a bomber.

fighter plane a highly manoeuvrable and heavily armed airplane used mainly for attacking enemy aircraft or strafing ground forces.

fighting chance *Informal.* the possibility of success after a long, hard struggle.

fighting cock 1 a gamecock. 2 *Informal.* a pugnacious person.

fig·ment (fig′mənt) *n.* something imagined; a made-up story. [< L *figmentum* < *fingere* form, fashion]

fig·ur·ate (fig′ər it or fig′yər it) *adj.* 1 having a characteristic or well-defined form, shape, or pattern. 2 in music, full of embellishments; ornate.

fig·ur·a·tion (fig′ər ā′shən or fig′yər ā′shən) *n.* 1 a form; shape. 2 a forming; shaping. 3 a representation by a likeness or symbol. 4 the act of marking or adorning with figures or designs. 5 in music: **a** the use of transitional tones, ornaments, etc. that are essential to the harmony. **b** the indicating of harmonics with figures above the bass part.

fig·ur·a·tive (fig′ər ə tiv or fig′yər ə tiv) *adj.* 1 in writing or speech, using words out of their literal meaning to add beauty or force. 2 having many figures of speech. Much poetry is figurative. 3 representing by a likeness or symbol: *A globe is a figurative model of the world.*
—**fig′ur·a·tive·ly,** *adv.* —**fig′ur·a·tive·ness,** *n.*

fig·ure (fig′ər or fig′yər) *n. v.* **-ured, -ur·ing.** —*n.* 1 a symbol for a number. The symbols 1, 2, 3, etc. are called figures. 2 an amount or value given in figures: *The price is too high; ask a lower figure.* 3 a form or shape: *In the darkness she saw dim figures moving.* 4 a form enclosing a surface or space: *Circles, triangles, squares, cubes, and spheres are geometrical figures.* 5 a person; character: *Samuel de Champlain is a great figure in Canadian history.* 6 a human form; a person considered from the point of view of appearance, manner, etc.: *The poor old woman was a figure of distress.* 7 an artificial representation of the human form in sculpture, painting, drawing, etc., usually of the whole or greater part of the body. 8 an image; likeness. 9 a picture; drawing; diagram; illustration: *This dictionary makes use of many figures to help explain the meaning of words.* 10 a design; pattern: *Cloth or wallpaper often has figures on it.* 11 in music, a motif (def. 3). 12 an outline traced by movements: *figures made by an airplane.* 13 in dancing or skating, a set of movements. 14 a figure of speech. 15 in logic, any of the forms of a syllogism that differ only in the position of the middle term. 16 **figures,** calculations using figures, arithmetic: *She was never very good at figures.*
—*v.* 1 use figures to find the answer to a problem; reckon; compute; show by figures. 2 be conspicuous; appear: *The names of great leaders figure in the story of human progress.* 3 show by a figure; represent in a

diagram. **4** decorate with a figure or pattern. **5** think; consider. **6** *Informal.* make sense: *That figures.* **7** in music: **a** write figures over and under (the bass) to indicate the intended harmony. **b** use transitional tones, ornaments, etc. in; embellish. **8** picture mentally; imagine: *Figure to yourself a happy family, secure in their own home.* **9 figure on,** *Informal.* **a** depend on; rely on. **b** consider as part of a plan or undertaking. **10 figure out,** *Informal.* **a** find out by using figures: *She soon figured out how much it would cost.* **b** think out; understand: *She couldn't figure out what was meant.* [< F < L *figura* < *fingere* form] **—fig′ur·er,** *n.* **—Syn.** *n.* **3** conformation, outline. See **form. 7** effigy, statue. *–v.* **1** calculate, cipher.

fig·ured (fig′ərd or fig′yərd) *adj.* **1** decorated with a design or pattern; not plain. **2** shown by a figure, diagram, or picture. **3** formed; shaped: *figured in bronze.* **4** in music: **a** ornamented; florid. **b** having accompanying chords of the bass part indicated by figures.

fig·ure·head (fig′ər hed′ or fig′yər-) *n.* **1** a person who is the head in name only, and has no real authority or responsibility. **2** on a ship, a statue or carving decorating the bow.

figure of speech an expression in which words are used out of their literal meaning or in exceptional combinations to add beauty or force. Similes and metaphors are figures of speech.

fig·ure-skate (fig′ər skāt′ or fig′yər-) *v.* **-skat·ed, -skat·ing.** engage in figure skating.

fig·ure-skat·er (fig′ər skā′tər or fig′yər-) *n.* a person who figure-skates.

figure skating the art or practice of performing figures and balletic programs on ice skates, often to music.

fig·ur·ine (fig′ər ēn′ or fig′yər ēn′) *n.* a small ornamental figure made of stone, pottery, metal, etc.; statuette. [< F < Ital. *figurina,* dim. of *figura* figure]

fig·wort (fig′wėrt′) *n.* **1** a tall, coarse plant having small, greenish-purple or yellow flowers that have a disagreeable odor. **2** any similar plant.

Fi·ji (fē′jē) *n.* a native of the Fiji Islands, a group of islands in the S. Pacific.

Fi·ji·an (fē′jē ən or fi jē′ən) *adj.* of or having to do with the Fiji Islands, their people, or their language. *—n.* **1** a Fiji. **2** the language of the Fijis.

fil (fil) *n.* **1** a unit of money in Iraq, Kuwait, and Jordan, worth 1/1000 of a dinar. **2** a coin worth one fil. [< Arabic *fils*]

fil·a·ment (fil′ə mənt) *n.* **1** a very fine thread. **2** a very slender, threadlike part. The wire that gives off light in an electric light bulb is a filament. **3** in botany, the stalklike part of a stamen that supports the anther. **4** the wire in a vacuum tube through which current passes to generate the heat necessary for electrons to be emitted. In some vacuum tubes, the filament also acts as the cathode. **5** a continuous strand of yarn of a synthetic, as acetate, which may be used in weaving without spinning. [< LL *filamentum* < L *filum* thread]

fil·a·men·tous (fil′ə men′təs) *adj.* **1** threadlike. **2** having filaments.

fil·bert (fil′bərt) *n.* **1** a hazelnut, the thick-shelled, sweet, edible nut of any of the varieties of hazel. **2** a tree or shrub that bears such nuts. [after St. *Philibert,* because the nuts ripen about the time of his day, August 22]

filch (filch) *v.* steal in small quantities; pilfer: *He filched pencils from the teacher's desk.* [origin uncertain] **—filch′er,** *n.* **—Syn.** See **steal.**

file[1] (fīl) *n. v.* **filed, fil·ing.** *—n.* **1** a place for keeping papers in order. **2** a set of papers kept in order. **3** a line of persons, animals, or things one behind another. **4** a small detachment of soldiers. **5** one of the lines of squares extending across a chessboard, checkerboard, etc. from player to player. **6** a collection of news stories sent by wire. **7 in file,** one after another; in succession. **8 on file,** in a file; put away and kept in order.
—v. **1** put away (papers, etc.) in order. **2** march or move in a file. **3** make application. **4** send (a news story) by wire: *The reporter immediately filed his story of the explosion.* [< F *fil* thread (< L *filum*) and F *file* row (ult. < LL *filare* spin a thread)] **—fil′er,** *n.*

hat, āge, cãre, fär; let, ēqual, tėrm; it, īce
hot, ōpen, ôrder; oil, out; cup, pu̇t, rüle, ūse
əbove, takən, pencəl, lemən, circəs
ch, child; ng, long; sh, ship
th, thin; ᴛʜ, then; zh, measure

file[2] (fīl) *n. v.* **filed, fil·ing.** *—n.* a steel tool with many small ridges or teeth on it: *The rough surface of a file is used to cut through or wear away hard materials or to make rough materials smooth.*
—v. smooth or wear away with a file. [OE *fīl*] **—fil′er,** *n.*

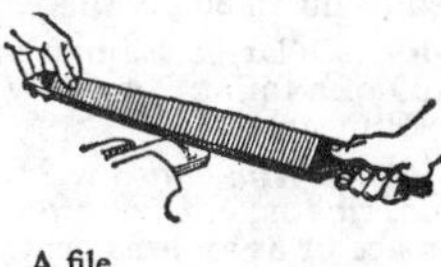

A file

file clerk a person whose work is taking care of the files in an office.

file·fish (fīl′fish′) *n.* **-fish** or **-fish·es.** fish whose skin is covered with many very small spines instead of scales, and whose front dorsal fin is a long spine.

fi·let (fi lā′, fil′ā or fē′lā) *n.* **1** a net or lace having a square mesh. **2** a fillet (def. 3). [< F. See FILLET.]

filet mignon a small, round, thick piece of choice beef, cut from the tenderloin.

fil·i·al (fil′ē əl) *adj.* of a son or daughter; due from a son or daughter: *The children treated their parents with filial respect.* [< LL *filialis* < L *filius* son, *filia* daughter] **—fil′i·al·ly,** *adv.*

fil·i·bus·ter (fil′ə bus′tər) *n.* **1 a** in a legislature, the deliberate hindering of the passage of a bill by long speeches or other means of delay. **b** a member of a legislature who hinders the passage of a bill by such means. **2** a person who fights against another country without the authorization of his government; freebooter.
—v. **1** deliberately hinder the passage of a bill by long speeches or other means of delay. **2** fight against another country without the authorization of one's government; act as a freebooter. [< Sp. *filibustero* < Du. *vrijbuiter.* See FREEBOOTER.] **—fil′i·bus′ter·er,** *n.*

fil·i·gree (fil′ə grē′) *n. v.* **-greed, -gree·ing,** *adj. —n.* **1** very delicate, lacelike ornamental work of gold or silver wire. **2** a lacy, delicate, or fanciful pattern in any material: *The frost made a beautiful filigree on the window pane. —v.* decorate with or form into filigree. *—adj.* ornamented with filigree; made into filigree. [for *filigrane* < F < Ital. *filigrana* < L *filum* thread + *granum* grain]

Filigree around a gem

filing cabinet a set of steel or wooden drawers for storing files of letters or other papers, records, etc.

fil·ings (fīl′ingz) *n.pl.* the small pieces of iron, wood, etc. that have been removed by a file.

Fil·i·pine (fil′ə pēn′) *adj.* Philippine.

Fil·i·pi·no (fil′ə pē′nō) *n.* **-nos,** *adj. —n.* a native of the Philippines, a group of islands in the W. Pacific. *—adj.* Philippines.

fill (fil) *v.* **1** put into until there is room for no more; make full: *fill a cup.* **2** become full: *The hall filled rapidly.* **3** take up all the space in: *The crowd filled the hall.* **4** satisfy the hunger or appetite of. **5** supply what is needed for: *A store fills orders, prescriptions, etc.* **6** stop up or close by putting something in: *A dentist fills decayed teeth.* **7** hold and do the duties of (a position, office, etc.). **8** supply a person for or appoint a person to (a position, office, etc.). **9 fill in, a** fill with something put in. **b** complete by filling. **c** put in to complete something. **d** acquaint with; bring up to date: *Would you be good enough to fill me in as to what happened during my absence?* **10 fill out, a** make larger; grow larger; swell. **b** make rounder, grow rounder. **c** complete by filling. **d** complete (a questionnaire, etc.), enter requested information on a form. **11 fill the bill,** come up to requirements. **12 fill up,** fill; fill completely.
—n. **1** enough to fill something. **2** all that is needed or wanted: *Eat and drink your fill; there is plenty for all of us.* **3** something that fills: *Earth or rock used to make uneven land level is called fill.* [OE *fyllan* < *full* full] **—Syn.** *v.* **7** occupy. **10 a** inflate, expand, distend.

fill·er (fil′ər) *n.* **1** a person or thing that fills. **2** an implement used to fill something, such as a funnel. **3** anything put in to fill something. A pad of paper for a notebook, a preparation put on wood before painting it, and the tobacco inside cigars are all fillers. **4** something used to fill an empty space.

fil·lér (fēl′lăr) *n.* **1** a unit of money in Hungary, worth 1/100 of a forint. **2** a coin worth one fillér. [< Hungarian]

fil·let (fil′it; *n. 3 and v. 2, usually* fi lā′) *n.* **1** a narrow band, ribbon, etc. put around the head to keep the hair in place or as an ornament. **2** a narrow band or strip of any material. Fillets are often used between mouldings, the flutes of a column, etc. **3** a slice of fish, meat, etc. without bones or fat; filet.
—*v.* **1** bind or decorate with a narrow band, ribbon, strip, etc. **2** cut (fish, meat, etc.) into fillets. [< F *filet, dim.* of *fil* < L *filum* thread]

fill-in (fil′in′) *n.* **1** a person or thing used to fill a vacancy or omission. **2** an activity that occupies spare time between more important events. **3** information that brings (someone) up to date on a situation; a briefing.

fill·ing (fil′ing) *n.* **1** anything put in to fill something. A dentist puts a filling in a decayed tooth. **2** the threads running from side to side across a woven fabric. **3** a making full; a becoming full.

filling station a place where gasoline and oil for motor vehicles are sold.

fil·lip (fil′əp) *v.* **1** strike with the fingernail as it is snapped quickly outwards after being bent and held back against the thumb. **2** toss or cause to move by striking in this way: *He filliped a coin into the beggar's cup.* **3** rouse; revive; stimulate.
—*n.* **1** a quick, light blow given by striking with the fingernail as it is snapped quickly outwards after being bent and held back against the thumb. **2** anything that rouses, revives, or stimulates: *Relishes serve as fillips to the appetite.* [probably imitative]

fil·ly (fil′ē) *n.* **-lies. 1** a young female horse; a mare that is less than four or five years old. **2** *Informal.* a lively girl. [< ON *fylja.* Akin to FOAL.]

film (film) *n.* **1** a very thin layer, sheet, surface, or coating: *Oil poured on water will spread and make a film.* **2** a roll or sheet of thin, flexible material, such as cellulose nitrate or cellulose acetate, used in making photographs. This roll or sheet is coated with an emulsion that is sensitive to light. **3 a** a motion-picture film. **b** a motion picture. **4** a very thin sheet or leaf of metal or other material. **5** a thin skin or membranous layer.
—*v.* **1** cover or become covered with a film: *Her eyes filmed with tears.* **2** make a motion picture of: *They filmed the scene three times.* **3** photograph or be photographed for motion pictures. [OE *filmen.* Related to FELL[4].]
—**film′like′,** *adj.*

film·strip (film′strip′) *n.* a series of still pictures on one theme or subject, put on film to be projected in sequence.

film·y (fil′mē) *adj.* **film·i·er, film·i·est. 1** of or like a film, very thin. **2** covered with or as if with a film. —**film′i·ly,** *adv.* —**film′i·ness,** *n.*

fil·ter (fil′tər) *n.* **1** a device for straining out substances from a liquid or gas by passing it slowly through felt, paper, sand, charcoal, etc. A filter is used to remove impurities from drinking water. **2** the felt, paper, sand, charcoal, or other porous material used in such a device. **3** any of various devices for removing dust, smoke, germs, etc. from the air. **4** a device for controlling certain light rays, electric currents, etc. Putting a yellow filter in front of a camera lens causes less blue light to reach the film.
—*v.* **1** pass through a filter; strain. **2** act as a filter for. **3** pass or flow very slowly: *Water filters through the sandy soil and into the well.* **4** remove or control by a filter: *Filter out all the dirt before using this water.* [< Med.L *filtrum* felt < Gmc.] —**fil′ter·er,** *n.*

fil·ter·a·ble (fil′tər ə bəl) *adj.* **1** that can be filtered. **2** capable of passing through a filter that arrests bacteria: *a filterable virus.*

filter tip 1 a cigarette with an attached filter, for removing impurities from the smoke before it is inhaled. **2** the filter itself.

filth (filth) *n.* **1** foul, disgusting dirt: *The alley was littered with garbage and other filth.* **2** obscene words or thoughts; vileness; moral corruption. [OE *fȳlth* < *fūl* foul]

filth·y (fil′thē) *adj.* **filth·i·er, filth·i·est. 1** disgustingly dirty; foul. **2** vile. —**filth′i·ly,** *adv.* —**filth′i·ness,** *n.*
—**Syn. 1** squalid, nasty. See **dirty. 2** obscene, indecent.

fil·tra·ble (fil′trə bəl) *adj.* filterable.

fil·trate (fil′trāt) *n. v.* **-trat·ed, -trat·ing.** —*n.* liquid that has been passed through a filter. —*v.* pass through a filter.

fil·tra·tion (fil trā′shən) *n.* **1** a filtering. **2** a being filtered.

fin (fin) *n.* **1** a movable winglike part of a fish's body. Moving the fins enables the fish to swim, guide, and balance itself in the water. **2** anything shaped or used like a fin. Some aircraft have fins to help balance them in flight. See **airplane** for diagram. **3** any of certain thin, flat, lateral projections in various mechanisms, as the cooling fins of a radiator. [OE *finn*] —**fin′less,** *adj.* —**fin′like′,** *adj.*

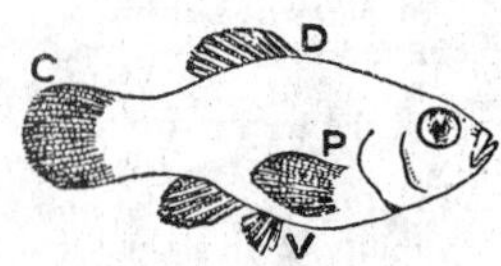

Fins: C, caudal; D, dorsal; P, pectoral; V, ventral.

fi·na·gle (fə nā′gəl) *v.* **-gled, -gling.** *Informal.* **1** manage craftily or cleverly: *He finagled his way into the job.* **2** cheat; swindle. [var. of *Brit. dial. fainaigue* renege at cards; origin uncertain] —**fi·na′gler,** *n.*

fi·nal (fī′nəl) *adj.* **1** at the end; last; with no more after it. **2** deciding; settling the question; not to be changed: *The decisions of the judge will be final.* **3** having to do with purpose: *a final clause.*
—*n.* **1** something final: *The last examination of a school term is a final.* **2 finals,** *pl.* the last or deciding set in a series of contests, examinations, etc. [ME < L *finalis* < *finis* end] —**Syn.** *adj.* **1** ultimate, eventual, terminal. See **last[1]. 2** definitive.

fi·na·le (fə nal′ē or fə nä′lē) *n.* **1** the last part of a piece of music or a play. **2** the last part; end. [< Ital. *finale* final]

fi·nal·ist (fī′nəl ist) *n.* a person who takes part in the last or deciding set in a series of contests, etc.

fi·nal·i·ty (fī nal′ə tē or fə nal′ə tē) *n.* **-ties. 1** a being final, finished, or settled: *He spoke with an air of finality.* **2** something final; a final act, speech, etc.

fi·nal·ize (fī′nəl īz′) *v.* bring to a conclusion; complete or finish in such a manner as to be final: *The committee hopes to finalize its report next week.*
☛ This word, though well established, is considered jargon by many people.

fi·nal·ly (fī′nəl ē) *adv.* **1** at the end; at last. **2** so as to decide or settle the question.

fi·nance (fī′nans, fə nans′, or fī nans′) *n. v.* **-nanced, -nanc·ing.** —*n.* **1** money matters. **2** the management of large sums of public or private money. **Public finance** is the management of government revenue and expenditure. **3 finances,** *pl.* money matters; money; funds; revenues.
—*v.* **1** provide money for: *His friends helped him finance a new business.* **2** manage the finances of. [ME < OF *finance* ending, settlement of a debt, ult. < *fin* end < L *finis.* Related to FINE[2].]

finance company a firm whose business is lending money for repayment by instalments with interest.

fi·nan·cial (fī nan′shəl or fə nan′shəl) *adj.* **1** having to do with money matters. **2** having to do with the management of large sums of public or private money.
Syn. 1 Financial, monetary, fiscal = having to do with money. **Financial** = having to do with money matters in general: *His financial affairs are in bad condition.* **Monetary** = of or directly connected with money itself: *His work brought him fame, but little monetary reward.* **Fiscal** = having to do with the funds and financial affairs of a government, institution, or corporation: *The fiscal year of the Canadian government begins on April 1.*

fi·nan·cial·ly (fī nan′shəl ē or fə nan′shəl ē) *adv.* in relation to finances or money matters.

fin·an·cier (fī′nən sēr′, fin′ən sēr′, or fə nan′sēr) *n.* **1** a person skilled in finance. **2** a person who is active in matters involving large sums of money. [< F]

fin·back (fin′bak′) *n.* a kind of whale having a fin on its back; rorqual.

finch (finch) *n.* any of a group of small songbirds that have cone-shaped bills. Sparrows, buntings, grosbeaks, canaries, and cardinals are finches. [OE *finc*]

find (fīnd) *v.* **found, find·ing,** *n.* —*v.* **1** come upon; happen on; meet with: *He found a silver dollar in the road.* **2** look for and get: *Please find my hat for me.* **3** discover; learn: *We found that he could not swim.* **4** see; know; feel; perceive: *He found that he was growing sleepy.* **5** get; get the use of: *Can you find time to do this?* **6** arrive at; reach: *Water finds its level.* **7** in law, decide and declare: *The jury found the accused man guilty.* **8** provide; supply: *find food and lodging for a friend.* **9** come to have; receive: *The book found many readers.* **10 find oneself,** learn one's abilities and make good use of them. **11 find out,** learn about; come to know; discover.
—*n.* **1** a finding. **2** something found, especially something exciting or valuable. [OE *findan*]

find·er (fīn′dər) *n.* **1** a person or thing that finds. **2** a small extra lens on the outside of a camera that shows what is being photographed. **3** a small telescope attached to a larger one to help find objects more easily.

fin de siè·cle (faɴ də sye′klə) *French.* the end of the century. From about 1880 to 1910, *fin de siècle* was used to mean "up-to-date," connoting also "over-elegant" or "decadent."

find·ing (fīn′ding) *n.* **1** a discovering. **2** the thing found. **3** the decision reached after an examination or inquiry: *After a short absence the jury returned and announced its finding.* **4 findings,** *pl.* **a** the tools, materials, supplies, etc. provided by a worker. **b** small tools and materials other than leather used in making shoes. **c** results of any research or inquiry: *the census takers' findings.*

fine[1] (fīn) *adj.* **fin·er, fin·est,** *adv. v.* **fined, fin·ing.** —*adj.* **1** of very high quality; very good; excellent: *a fine sermon, a fine view, a fine young man.* **2** very small or thin: *fine wire.* **3** in very small particles: *fine sand.* **4** sharp: *a tool with a fine edge.* **5** not coarse or heavy; delicate: *fine linen.* **6** refined; elegant: *fine manners.* **7** subtle: *The law makes fine distinctions.* **8** too highly decorated; showy: *fine language or writing.* **9** handsome; good-looking: *a fine horse.* **10** clear; bright: *fine weather.* **11** without impurities. Fine gold is gold not mixed with any other metal. **12** having a stated proportion of gold or silver in it. A gold alloy that is 925/1000 fine is 92.5 gold. **13** well; in good health: *I feel fine.*
—*adv. Informal.* very well; excellently.
—*v.* make fine or finer; become fine or finer. [ME < OF *fin,* ult. < L *finire* finish] —**fine′ly,** *adv.*
Syn. *adj.* **1 Fine, choice, elegant** = very high quality. **Fine** is the general word: *He does fine work.* **Choice** = of fine or the best quality, usually carefully picked by or for a taste that can tell and appreciate differences in quality or value: *He selected a choice piece of jade.* **Elegant** = showing fine taste, rich or luxurious but graceful and refined: *She selected elegant drapes.* **2** slender, minute. **4** dainty. **8** handsome.

fine[2] (fīn) *n. v.* **fined, fin·ing.** —*n.* **1** a sum of money paid as a punishment. **2 in fine, a** finally. **b** in a few words; briefly. —*v.* cause to pay a fine. [ME < OF *fin* < L *finis* end; in Med.L, settlement, payment]

fi·ne[3] (fē′nā) *n.* the end; in music, a direction marking the end of a passage that has to be repeated. [< Ital.]

fine arts the arts depending upon taste and appealing to the sense of beauty; painting, drawing, sculpture, and architecture. Literature, music, dancing, and acting are also usually included in the fine arts.

fine-drawn (fīn′dron′ or -drôn′) *adj.* **1** drawn out until very small or thin. **2** very subtle: *Fine-drawn distinctions are difficult to understand.*

fine-grained (fīn′grānd′) *adj.* having a fine, close grain: *Mahogany is a fine-grained wood.*

fine·ness (fīn′nis) *n.* **1** a being fine. **2** the proportion of gold or silver in an alloy.

fin·er·y (fīn′ər ē) *n.* **-er·ies.** showy clothes, ornaments, etc. [< FINE[1]]

fine-spun (fīn′spun′) *adj.* **1** spun or drawn out until very small or thin. **2** very subtle.

fi·nesse (fə nes′) *n. v.* **-nessed, -ness·ing.** —*n.* **1** delicacy of execution; skill: *That artist shows wonderful finesse.* **2** the skilful handling of a delicate situation to one's advantage; craft; stratagem: *a master of finesse.* **3** in bridge, whist, etc., an attempt to take a trick with a lower card while holding a higher card, in the hope that the card or cards between may not be played.

hat, āge, cãre, fär; let, ēqual, tėrm; it, īce
hot, ōpen, ôrder; oil, out; cup, pu̇t, rüle, ūse
əbove, takən, pencəl, lemən, circəs
ch, child; ng, long; sh, ship
th, thin; ᴛʜ, then; zh, measure

—*v.* **1** use finesse. **2** bring or change by finesse. **3** make a finesse with (a card). [< F *finesse* < *fin* fine[1]] —**Syn.** *n.* **2** artifice, strategy.

fine-toothed (fīn′ tütht′) *adj.* **1** having fine, very closely set teeth: *a fine-toothed saw.* **2 go over with a fine-toothed comb,** examine carefully.

fin·ger (fing′gər) *n.* **1** one of the five end parts of the hand, especially the four besides the thumb. **2** the part of a glove that covers a finger. **3** anything shaped or used like a finger. **4** the breadth of a finger; ¾ inch. **5** the length of a finger; 4½ inches. **6 burn one's fingers,** get into trouble by meddling. **7 have a finger in the pie, a** take part or have a share in doing something. **b** meddle; interfere. **8 put one's finger on,** point out exactly. **9 put the finger on,** *Slang.* single out for slaying (by a gang). **10 twist around one's little finger,** manage easily; control completely.
—*v.* **1** touch or handle with the fingers; use the fingers on. **2** perform or mark (a passage of music) with a certain fingering. **3** pilfer; filch; steal. **4** *Slang.* point out; betray; inform upon. **5** make vague grasping movements with the fingers. [OE] —**fin′ger·er,** *n.*

finger board 1 on a violin, guitar, etc., a strip of wood on the neck against which the strings are pressed by the fingers of the player. **2** on a piano or organ, the keyboard.

finger bowl a small bowl to hold water for rinsing the fingers during or after a meal.

fin·ger·hold (fing′gər hōld′) *n.* **1** anything that offers a grip for the fingers. **2** a grip using the fingers only. **3** a weak support or grip.

fin·ger·ing (fing′gər ing or fing′gring) *n.* **1** a touching or handling with the fingers; way of using the fingers. In playing certain musical instruments the fingering is important. **2** the signs marked on a piece of music to show which fingers are to be used in playing particular notes.

fin·ger·ling (fing′gər ling) *n.* **1** a small fish no longer than a finger. **2** something very small.

fin·ger·mark (fing′gər märk′) *n.* a smudge or stain left by a finger.

fin·ger·nail (fing′gər nāl′) *n.* the hard layer of hornlike substance at the end of a finger.

finger paint any of various thickened water colors used in finger painting.

fin·ger·paint (fing′gər pānt′) *v.* paint with the fingers, palms, etc. instead of with brushes.

finger painting 1 a technique of applying paint using fingers, palms, etc. instead of brushes. **2** a design or picture so painted.

finger post a guidepost having a sign shaped like a finger or hand to show the direction.

fin·ger·print (fing′gər print′) *n.* an impression of the markings on the inner surface of the last joint of a finger or thumb: *The murderer was identified by the fingerprints he left on the gun.* —*v.* take the fingerprints of.

fin·ger·tip (fing′gər tip′) *n.* the very end or tip of the finger.

fin·i·al (fin′ē əl or fī′nē əl) *n.* **1** in architecture, an ornament on the top of a roof, the corner of a tower, the end of a pew in church, etc. **2** the highest point. [< Med.L *finium* final settlement (probably originally, end) < L *finis*]

fin·i·cal (fin′ə kəl) *adj.* too dainty or particular; too precise; fussy. [apparently < *fine*[1]] —**fin′i·cal·ly,** *adv.* —**Syn.** overnice, fastidious, squeamish.

fin·ick·ing (fin′ə king) *adj.* finical.

fin·ick·y (fin′ə kē) *adj.* finical.

fin·is (fin′is) *n.* end. [< L]

fin·ish (fin′ish) *v.* **1** bring (action, speech, etc.) to an end; end. **2** bring (work, affairs, etc.) to completion; complete: *He started the race but did not finish it.* **3** come to an end: *There was so little wind that the sailing race didn't finish until after dark.* **4** use up completely: *finish a*

spool of thread. **5** *Informal.* overcome completely: *My answer finished him.* **6** *Informal.* destroy; kill: *finish a wounded animal.* **7** perfect; polish. **8** prepare the surface in some way: *finish cloth with nap.* **9 finish off, a** complete. **b** overcome completely; destroy; kill. **10 finish up, a** complete. **b** use up completely. **11 finish with, a** complete. **b** stop being friends with; have nothing to do with. **c** finish using; come to the end of one's need of: *Have you finished with my book yet?*
—*n.* **1** the end. **2** a polished condition or quality; perfection. **3** the way in which a surface is prepared. **4** something used to finish something else. **5** cultivated manners or speech; social polish. **6** the work done on a building after the main structure is finished, such as the window and door trim, etc. **7** the material used for such work. **8 in at the finish,** present at the end. [ME < OF *feniss-*, a stem of *fenir* < L *finire*] **—fin′ish·er,** *n.* **—Syn.** *v.* **1** See **end.**

fin·ished (fin′isht) *adj.* **1** ended. **2** completed. **3** *Informal.* exhausted; defeated; completely overcome: *By the third round the boxer was finished.* **4** perfected; polished.

finishing school a private school that prepares young women for social life rather than for business or a profession.

fi·nite (fī′nīt) *adj.* **1** having limits or bounds; not infinite: *Death ends man's finite existence.* **2** in grammar, having a definite person, number, and tense; not an infinitive or participle. In "To write the letter seemed a tiresome task," the finite verb is "seemed." **3** in mathematics: **a** of a number, capable of being reached or passed in counting. **b** of a magnitude, less than infinite and greater than infinitesimal. —*n.* what is finite; something finite. [< L *finitus*, pp. of *finire* finish]

☛ A finite verb is a verb that has definite grammatical tense, person, and number. In the following example *stopped* is a finite verb; *going* and *to mail* are not: *Before going to the game, he stopped to mail the letter.*

fink (fingk) *n. Slang.* **1** an informer. **2** a strikebreaker. **3** any unpleasant person.

Finn (fin) *n.* **1** a native or inhabitant of Finland, a country in northern Europe. **2** a member of those peoples that speak a language similar to Finnish.

fin·nan had·die (fin′ən had′ē) smoked haddock. [for *Findhorn haddock*; from the name of a town in Scotland]

Finn·ish (fin′ish) *adj.* of or having to do with Finland, its people, or their language. —*n.* the language of Finland.

Finn·mark (fin′märk′) *n.* markka.

Fin·no-U·gric (fin′ō ū′grik or -ü′grik) *adj.* **1** of or having to do with the Finns and the Ugrians. **2** of or having to do with a family of languages of Eastern Europe and Western Asia, including Finnish, Estonian, and Hungarian. —*n.* this language family.

fin·ny (fin′ē) *adj.* **1** abounding with fish: *The sea is sometimes called the finny deep.* **2** having fins. **3** like a fin.

fiord (fyôrd) *n.* a long narrow bay of the sea between high banks or cliffs. Norway has many fiords. Also **fjord.** [< Norwegian *fiord*, earlier *fjorthr.* Akin to FIRTH.]

fir (fėr) *n.* **1** an evergreen tree that belongs to the same family as the pine. **2** the wood of this tree. [OE **fyrh* (cf. *furhwudu* fir-wood) or < ON *fyri-*]

fire (fīr) *n. v.* **fired, fir·ing.** —*n.* **1** the flame, heat, and light caused by burning. **2** something burning. **3** destruction by burning. **4** a preparation that will burn: *Red fire is used in signalling.* **5** fuel burning or arranged so that it will burn quickly: *A fire was laid in the fireplace.* **6** something that suggests a fire because it is hot, glowing, brilliant, or light: *the fire of lightning, an insane fire in his eye, the fire in a diamond.* **7** any feeling that suggests fire; passion, fervor, enthusiasm, excitement, etc. **8** a burning pain; fever; inflammation: *the fire of a wound.* **9** a severe trial or trouble. **10** the shooting or discharge of guns, etc.: *enemy fire.*
between two fires, attacked from both sides.
catch fire, begin to burn.
go through fire and water, endure many troubles or dangers.
hang fire, a be slow in going off. **b** be slow in acting. **c** be delayed.
lay a fire, build a fire so that it is ready to be lit.
on fire, a burning. **b** full of a feeling or spirit like fire.
play with fire, meddle with something dangerous.
set fire to, cause to burn.
set on fire, a cause to burn. **b** fill with a feeling or spirit like fire.
take fire, begin to burn.
under fire, a exposed to shooting from enemy guns. **b** attacked; blamed.
—*v.* **1** cause to burn. **2** begin to burn; burst into flame. **3** supply with fuel; tend the fire of: *fire a furnace.* **4** dry with heat; bake: *Bricks are fired to make them hard.* **5** grow or make hot, red, glowing, etc. **6** arouse; excite; inflame: *Stories of adventure fire the imagination.* **7** discharge (a gun, bomb, gas mine, etc.). **8** shoot: *The soldiers fired from the fort. The hunter fired small shot at the birds.* **9** *Informal.* dismiss from a job, etc. **10** of grain, turn yellow before ripening as a result of drought or disease. **11** of pottery, etc., respond in a specified manner to baking in a kiln: *This clay fires a deep red.* **12 fire away,** *Informal.* begin; start; go ahead. **13 fire up, a** start a fire in a furnace, boiler, etc. **b** become angry, lose one's temper. **c** set a machine or other device in operation. [OE *fȳr*] **—fir′er,** *n.* **—Syn.** *n.* **1** blaze, combustion, conflagration. **7** ardor, enthusiasm.

fire alarm 1 the signal that a fire has broken out. **2** a device that gives such a signal.

fire·arms (fīr′ärmz′) *n.pl.* rifles, pistols, and other weapons to shoot with, usually such as a man can carry.

fire·ball (fīr′bol′ or -bôl′) *n.* **1** anything that looks like a ball of fire, such as a ball of lightning. **2** a large, brilliant meteor. **3** the great billowing mass of fire produced by an atomic explosion. **4** in baseball, a very fast pitch to the batter. **5** *Informal.* a person who possesses great energy and enthusiasm.

fire·boat (fīr′bōt′) *n.* a boat equipped with apparatus for putting out fires on a dock, ship, etc.

fire-bomb·er (fīr′bom′ər) *n.* an airplane used in fire-fighting, designed to carry water and discharge it over a burning area.

fire·box (fīr′boks′) *n.* **1** the place for the fire in a furnace, boiler, etc. **2** the furnace of a steam boiler, especially that of a steam locomotive.

fire·brand (fīr′brand′) *n.* **1** a piece of burning wood. **2** a person who stirs up unrest, strife, rebellion, etc.; hothead.

fire·break (fīr′brāk′) *n.* a strip of land that has been cleared of trees or on which the sod has been turned over so as to prevent the spreading of a forest fire or a prairie fire.

fire·brick (fīr′brik′) *n.* a brick capable of standing great heat, and used to line furnaces and fireplaces.

fire brigade 1 a body of men organized, often privately or temporarily, to fight fires. **2** *Esp.Brit.* a fire department.

fire·bug (fīr′bug′) *n. Informal.* a person who has a mania for setting houses or property on fire; pyromaniac.

fire clay clay capable of resisting high temperatures, used for making crucibles, firebricks, etc.

fire company a group of men organized to put out fires.

fire·crack·er (fīr′krak′ər) *n.* a paper roll containing gunpowder and a fuse: *A firecracker explodes with a loud noise.*

fire·damp (fīr′damp′) *n.* methane, a gas formed in coal mines, dangerously explosive when mixed with certain proportions of air.

fire department a municipal department in charge of the fighting and prevention of fires.

fire·dog (fīr′dog′) *n.* andiron.

fire drill drill for firemen, a ship's crew, pupils in a school, etc. to train them for duties or for orderly exit in case of fire.

fire-eat·er (fīr′ēt′ər) *n.* **1** an entertainer who pretends to eat fire. **2** a person who is too ready to fight or quarrel.

fire engine a machine for throwing water, chemicals, etc. to put out fires.

fire escape a stairway, ladder, etc. in or on a building, to use in case of fire.

fire extinguisher a container filled with chemicals that can be sprayed upon fire to extinguish it.

fire·fight·er (fīr′fīt′ər) *n.* **1** a member of a fire department; a fireman. **2** a person who fights forest fires.

fire·fight·ing (fīr′fīt′ing) *n.* the act or process of fighting fires.

fire·find·er (fīr′fīn′dər) *n.* an instrument consisting of a sighting device and a map, for finding the position of a forest fire.

fire·fly (fīr′flī′) *n.* **-flies.** a small beetle that gives off flashes of light that can be seen in the dark.

fire·guard (fīr′gärd′) *n.* **1** fire screen. **2** fire break.

fire hall **1** a building in which fire-fighting equipment is kept. **2** the headquarters of a fire department: *Permits for burning rubbish may be obtained at the fire hall.*

fire insurance insurance against damage or loss caused by fire.

fire irons tools, such as a poker, tongs, and shovel, needed for tending a fire.

fire·less (fīr′lis) *adj.* **1** without a fire. **2** without enthusiasm or animation.

fireless cooker a container that stays hot a long time without heat from outside, used to cook food or keep it hot.

fire·light (fīr′līt′) *n.* the light from a fire.

fire line **1** a firebreak. **2** the front edge of a forest fire or a prairie fire.

fire·lock (fīr′lok′) *n.* an old type of gun, fired by a spark falling on the gunpowder; flintlock.

fire·man (fīr′mən) *n.* **-men** (-mən). **1** a man whose work is putting out fires. **2** a man whose work is taking care of the fire in a furnace, boiler, locomotive, etc.

fire·place (fīr′plās′) *n.* a place built in the wall of a room or out of doors to hold a fire.

fire plug hydrant.

fire pot the part of a stove, furnace, etc. that holds the fire.

fire·pow·er (fīr′pou′ər) *n.* **1** the amount of fire delivered by a military unit, by a particular weapon, etc. **2** the ability to deliver fire.

fire·proof (fīr′prüf′) *adj.* that will not burn; almost impossible to burn: *A building made entirely of steel and concrete is fireproof.* —*v.* make fireproof.

fire·rang·er (fīr′rān′jər) *n.* a government employee engaged in preventing and putting out forest fires on Crown lands.

fire-reels (fīr′ rēlz′) *n.* fire engine.

fire screen a screen to be placed in front of a fire as protection against heat or flying sparks.

fire ship a ship loaded with explosives and inflammable materials, set adrift among enemy ships.

fire·side (fīr′sīd′) *n.* **1** the space around a fireplace or hearth. **2** the home. **3** home life. —*adj.* beside the fire.

fire-spot·ter (fīr′spot′ər) *n.* a person who works as an agent of the firefighting authorities by watching for and locating forest fires.

fire tower a tower from which to keep watch for forest fires.

fire·trap (fīr′trap′) *n.* **1** a building hard to get out of in case of fire. **2** a building that will burn very easily.

fire wall **1** a fireproof wall for confining a possible fire. **2** a fireproof plate or shield behind the engine of an automobile or airplane.

fire·ward·en (fīr′wôr′dən) *n.* an official whose duty is preventing and putting out fires in forests, camps, etc.

fire·wa·ter (fīr′wot′ər or -wô′tər) *n. Humorous.* any strong alcoholic drink: *The North American Indians called whisky, gin, rum, etc. firewater.*

fire·weed (fīr′wēd′) *n.* any of various weeds that often appear on land recently burned.

fire·wood (fīr′wu̇d′) *n.* the wood to make a fire.

fire·work (fīr′wėrk′) *n.* **1** a firecracker, bomb, rocket, etc. that makes a loud noise or a beautiful, fiery display, especially at night. **2 fireworks,** a firework display.

firing line **1** any line where soldiers are stationed to shoot at the enemy, a target, etc. **2** the soldiers on such a line. **3** the foremost position in a controversy, campaign for a cause, etc.

hat, āge, cãre, fär; let, ēqual, tėrm; it, īce
hot, ōpen, ôrder; oil, out; cup, pu̇t, rüle, ūse
əbove, takən, pencəl, lemən, circəs
ch, child; ng, long; sh, ship
th, thin; ᴛʜ, then; zh, measure

firing range **1** an area used for shooting practice. **2** the distance within which specific weapons are effective: *The robber was within firing range.*

firing squad **1** a small detachment of troops assigned to shoot to death a condemned person. **2** a detachment assigned to fire a salute.

fir·kin (fėr′kən) *n.* **1** a quarter of a barrel, used as a measure of capacity. **2** a small wooden cask for butter, etc. [ME *ferdekyn* < MDu. *verdelkijn,* dim. of *verdel,* literally, fourth part]

firm[1] (fėrm) *adj.* **1** not yielding easily to pressure or force; solid; hard: *firm flesh.* **2** not easily moved or shaken; tightly fastened or fixed: *a tree firm in the earth.* **3** steady in motion or action: *a firm step, a firm grasp.* **4** not easily changed; determined; resolute; positive: *a firm purpose.* **5** not changing; staying the same; steady: *a firm price.*
—*v.* make or become firm. [< L *firmus*] **—firm′ly,** *adv.* **—firm′ness,** *n.*

Syn. *adj.* **1 Firm, hard, solid** = not yielding easily to pressure or force. **Firm** = so strong, tough, or compact in composition or structure that it is not easy to squeeze or pull out of shape, bend, or dig or cut into: *His muscles are firm.* **Hard** = so strong, stiff, or thick as to be almost impossible to squeeze, pull, etc.: *The ground is too hard to dig.* **Solid** = so strongly built, uniformly dense, firm, or hard as to withstand all pressure or force: *We build houses on solid ground.* **2** fast, secure, immovable. **4** enduring, constant.

firm[2] (fėrm) *n.* a business company or partnership. [< Ital. < Sp., Pg. *firma* signature, ult. < L *firmus* firm[1]]

fir·ma·ment (fėr′mə mənt) *n.* the arch of the heavens; sky. [< L *firmamentum,* ult. < *firmus* firm[1]]

firn (fėrn) *n.* névé. [< G *firn* of last year]

first (fėrst) *adj.* **1** before all others; before anything else: *John is first in his class.* **2** in music: **a** highest in pitch. **b** playing or singing the part highest in pitch. **3 in the first place,** first; firstly; before anything else. **4 (the) first thing,** at the earliest possible moment: *He is going first thing in the morning.*
—*adv.* **1** before all others; before anything else: *The good die first.* **2** before some other thing or event: *First bring me the chalk.* **3** for the first time: *when I first visited Italy.* **4** rather; sooner: *I'll go to jail first.*
—*n.* **1** a person, thing, place, etc. that is first. **2** the winning position in a race, etc. **3** the beginning. **4** in an automobile or similar machine, the first, or lowest, gear; low. **5 firsts,** *pl.* articles of the best quality. **6 at first,** in the beginning. **7 first and last,** taking all together. **8 from the first,** since the beginning. [OE *fyrst*] **—Syn.** *adj.* earliest, original, initial, chief, foremost, principal, leading.

☛ **first. a** When used with a numeral, *first* precedes the numeral: *For tomorrow I want you to do the first six problems.* **b first, last, latest.** *First* and *last* refer to items in a series, usually of more than two: *His first act in office was to appoint a new secretary. We felt let down at the end of the last act. Latest* refers to a series that is still continuing: *Have you read the latest instalment of the new serial story? Last* refers either to the final item of a completed series or to the most recent item of a continuing series: *His last jump proved fatal. I was pleased with the last election.*

first aid the emergency treatment given to an injured person before a doctor comes. **—first′-aid′,** *adj.*

first base **1** in baseball, the base that must be touched first by a runner. **2** a first baseman. **3 get to first base,** *Informal.* make the first step toward success: *The new secretary will never get to first base if she is not punctual.*

first-born (fėrst′bôrn′) *adj.* born first; oldest. —*n.* the first-born child.

first-class (fėrst′klas′) *adj.* **1** of the highest class or best quality; excellent. **2** of or having to do with the class of mail that includes letters, post cards, etc.: *It would be expensive to send a heavy parcel by first-class mail.*
—*adv.* **1** on a first-class ship, train, airplane, etc.; in or on the first-class section. **2** by first-class mail.

first day Sunday.

first-day cover (fėrst′dā′) in stamp collecting, an envelope bearing a commemorative stamp, cancelled on its first day of issue by the post office that issued it.

first finger the finger next to the thumb.

first fruits **1** the earliest fruits of the season. **2** the first products or results.

first-hand (fėrst′hand′) *adj. adv.* from the original source; direct: *first-hand information. He got the information first-hand.*

first lieutenant in the army, a commissioned officer junior to a captain and senior to a second lieutenant.

first·ling (fėrst′ling) *n.* **1** the first of its kind. **2** the first product or result. **3** the first offspring of an animal.

first·ly (fėrst′lē) *adv.* in the first place; first.

first person in grammar, the form of a pronoun or verb used to refer to the speaker and those he includes with himself. *I, me, mine* and *we, us, ours* are pronouns of the first person.

first quarter **1** the period between the new moon and the first half moon. **2** the phase of moon represented by the first half moon after the new moon.

first-rate (fėrst′rāt′) *adj.* **1** of the highest class. **2** *Informal.* excellent; very good. —*adv. Informal.* excellently; very well.

firth (fėrth) *n.* a narrow arm of the sea; estuary of a river. [< ON *fjörthr.* Akin to FIORD.]

fisc (fisk) *n.* a royal or state treasury; exchequer. [< L *fiscus* purse]

fis·cal (fis′kəl) *adj.* **1** financial. **2** having to do with a treasury or exchequer: *Important changes were made in the government's fiscal policy.* —*n.* in some countries, a public prosecutor. [< L *fiscalis* < *fiscus* purse]
—**fis′cal·ly,** *adv.* —**Syn.** *adj.* **1** See **financial.**

fiscal year the time between one yearly settlement of financial accounts and another. The fiscal year of the Canadian government ends March 31.

fish (fish) *n.* **fish** or **fish·es** (see usage note), *v.* —*n.* **1** a vertebrate that lives in water and has gills instead of lungs for breathing. Fish are usually covered with scales and have fins for swimming. Some fish lay eggs in the water; others produce living young. **2** the flesh of fish used for food. **3** *Informal.* a person; fellow. **4** a long strip of iron, wood, etc. used to strengthen a joint, etc. **5 fish out of water,** a person who is uncomfortable or ill at ease as a result of being out of his usual environment. **6 other fish to fry,** *Informal.* other things to do. **7 the Fishes,** in astrology, the twelfth sign of the zodiac; Pisces.
—*v.* **1** catch fish; try to catch fish. **2** try to catch fish in: *to fish a pool.* **3** search: *She fished in her purse for a coin.* **4** find and take out: *He fished the map from the back of the drawer.* **5 fish for, a** look for; try to find: *He was fishing for some papers in the file.* **b** try to get, often by indirect or underhand means: *He is always fishing for information.* **6 fish in troubled waters,** take advantage of confusion or trouble to get what one wants. **7 fish out,** use up the supply of fish in. [OE *fisc*] —**fish′less,** *adj.* —**fish′like′,** *adj.*

☛ **fish.** The plural is usually *fish* except in speaking definitely of different kinds or species of fish: *He had a string of eight fish. Most of the income of the island is from these fishes: cod, halibut, and salmon.*

fish eagle osprey.

fish·er (fish′ər) *n.* **1** *Archaic.* a fisherman. **2** an animal or bird that catches fish for food. **3** a slender mammal like a weasel or marten but larger. **4** its dark-brown fur.

fish·er·man (fish′ər mən) *n.* **-men** (-mən). **1** a man who fishes for a living or for pleasure. **2** a ship used in fishing.

fish·er·y (fish′ər ē) *n.* **-er·ies.** **1** the business or industry of catching fish. **2** a place for catching fish: *Salmon is the main catch in the Pacific fisheries.*

Fish·es (fish′iz) *n.* a constellation and the twelfth sign of the zodiac; Pisces.

fish flake a slatted platform used for drying fish: *Fish flakes are a familiar sight in Newfoundland fishing villages.*

fish flour a tasteless, odorless, high-protein flour produced by pulverizing dried fish.

fish glue a strong glue made from waste parts of fish.

fish-hawk (fish′hok′ or -hôk′) *n.* a large bird that feeds on fish; osprey.

fish-hook (fish′hůk′) *n.* a hook used for catching fish.

fish house a hut or small building on the shore, where fishermen store their gear, catch, etc. Fish houses are sometimes used also for smoking and curing fish.

fish·ing (fish′ing) *n.* the catching of fish for a living or for pleasure.

fishing ground a place where fish are plentiful.

fishing hole a hole cut through the ice of a lake, river, etc. to catch fish in winter.

fishing line a line used in fishing.

fishing pole fishing rod.

fishing rod a slender rod, made of bamboo, plastics, etc. for fishing.

fishing smack a small ship used in fishing at sea.

fishing tackle rods, lines, hooks, etc. used in catching fish.

fish ladder fishway.

fish line fishing line.

fish·mon·ger (fish′mung′gər or -mong′gər) *n. Esp.Brit.* a dealer in fish.

fish oil oil obtained from fish.

fish pass fishway.

fish·plate (fish′plāt′) *n.* a plate used to fasten two rails or beams together end to end. The rails of a railway track are usually joined by fishplates.

fish pole fishing rod.

fish stick **1** frozen fish fillets packaged in the form of a short, oblong stick for ease in shipping and handling: *Each year, thousands of fish sticks are shipped from the Maritimes to markets in Central Canada.* **2** a portion of fish, often breaded and pre-cooked, frozen and packaged for retail sale.

fish story *Informal.* an exaggerated, unbelievable story.

fish·tail (fish′tāl′) *adj.* like a fish's tail in shape or action. —*v.* **1** swing the tail of an airplane from side to side to reduce its speed. **2** swing or sway in this way.

fish·way (fish′wā′) *n.* a waterway built as an ascending series of little pools to enable fish to pass over a dam or falls on their way to spawning grounds upstream.

fish·wife (fish′wīf′) *n.* **-wives.** **1** a woman who sells fish. **2** a woman who uses coarse and abusive language.

fish·y (fish′ē) *adj.* **fish·i·er, fish·i·est.** **1** like a fish in smell, taste, or shape. **2** of fish. **3** full of fish. **4** *Informal.* doubtful; unlikely; suspicious. **5** without expression or lustre; dull. —**fish′i·ly,** *adv.* —**fish′i·ness,** *n.*

fis·sile (fis′īl or fis′əl) *adj.* **1** easily split. **2** capable of nuclear fission. [< L *fissilis* < *findere* cleave]

fis·sion (fish′ən) *n.* **1** a splitting apart; division into parts. **2** in biology, a method of reproduction in which the body of the parent divides to form two or more independent individuals. Many simple plants and animals reproduce by fission. **3** the splitting that occurs when the nucleus of an atom under bombardment absorbs a neutron. Nuclear fission releases tremendous amounts of energy when heavy elements, especially plutonium and uranium, are involved. [< L *fissio, -onis* < *findere* cleave]

fis·sion·a·ble (fish′ən ə bəl) *adj.* capable of nuclear fission.

fission bomb an atomic bomb that derives its force solely from the splitting of atoms. The original atomic bombs were fission bombs; hydrogen bombs are fusion bombs.

fis·sure (fish′ər) *n. v.* **-sured, -sur·ing.** —*n.* **1** a split or crack; a long, narrow opening: *a fissure in a rock.* **2** a splitting apart; a division into parts. **3** a natural cleft or opening in an organ or part of the body.
—*v.* split apart; divide into parts; become split. [< F < L *fissura* < *findere* cleave]

fist (fist) *n.* **1** the hand closed tightly. **2** *Informal.* the hand. **3** *Informal.* handwriting. **4** in printing, a symbol (☛). [OE *fȳst*] —**fist′like′,** *adj.*

-fisted *combining form.* having —— fists: *quick-fisted* = *having quick fists.*

fist·ic (fis′tik) *adj. Informal.* having to do with fighting with the fists; done with the fists.

fist·i·cuffs (fis′ti kufs′) *n.pl.* **1** a fight with the fists. **2** blows with the fists: *It soon came to fisticuffs between them.*

fist·note (fist′nōt′) *n.* in printed texts, a special note preceded by a fist (def. 4).

fis·tu·la (fis′chů lə) *n.* **-las, -lae** (-lē′ or -lī′). **1** a tube or pipe. **2** a tubelike sore connecting the surface of the body with an internal organ or cavity. [< L *fistula* pipe, ulcer. Doublet of FESTER, n.]

fis·tu·lar (fis′chů lər) *adj.* **1** tubelike; tubular. **2** made up of tubelike parts. **3** having to do with a fistula.

fit[1] (fit) *adj.* **fit·ter, fit·test,** *v.* **fit·ted, fit·ting,** *n. adv.*
—*adj.* **1** having the necessary qualities; suitable: *Grass is fit food for cows; it is not fit for men.* **2** right; proper. **3** ready; prepared: *fit for active service.* **4** in good health; in good physical condition: *He is now well and fit for work.*
—*v.* **1** be fit; be fit for. **2** have the right size or shape; have the right size or shape for. **3** cause to fit; make fit: *Mother was trying to fit too small a cover on our chesterfield.* **4** install; attach: *It took two hours to fit the new radio in the car.* **5** make ready; prepare. **6** supply with what is needed; equip. **7** suit; make suitable: *to fit the action to the word.* **8 fit out** or **up,** provide with what is needed.
—*n.* **1** the manner in which one thing fits another: *the fit of a coat, a tight fit.* **2** something that fits: *This coat is a good fit.*
—*adv.* **see** or **think fit,** decide. [ME *fyt;* origin uncertain]
—**fit′ness,** *n.*
Syn. *adj.* **1 Fit, suitable, appropriate** = having the right qualities for something. **Fit** = having the qualities needed for the purpose, work, or use of the person or thing: *That shack is not fit to live in.* **Suitable** = having the qualities right or proper for a definite occasion, purpose, position, condition, or situation: *The lawyer found a suitable office.* **Appropriate** = unusually fit or suitable for the particular person, purpose, position, occasion, etc.: *A tailored suit is appropriate for a secretary.* **2** seemly, meet, becoming. -*v.* **6** furnish, provide.

fit[2] (fit) *n.* **1** a sudden, sharp attack of illness: *a fit of colic.* **2** a sudden attack of illness characterized by loss of consciousness or by convulsions: *a fainting fit, a fit of epilepsy.* **3** any sudden, sharp attack: *In a fit of anger he hit his friend.* **4** a short period of doing one thing. **5 by fits and starts,** irregularly; starting, stopping, beginning again, and so on. [OE *fitt* conflict]

fitch (fich) *n.* **1** the polecat of Europe. **2** its fur, yellowish with dark markings. [? < MDu. *fisse*]

fitch·et (fich′it) *n.* fitch.

fitch·ew (fich′ü) *n.* fitch.

fit·ful (fit′fəl) *adj.* going on and then stopping awhile; irregular: *a fitful sleep, a fitful conversation.* [< *fit*[2]] —**fit′ful·ly,** *adv.* —**fit′ful·ness,** *n.* —**Syn.** spasmodic.

fit·ly (fit′lē) *adv.* **1** in a suitable manner. **2** at a proper time.

fit·ter (fit′ər) *n.* **1** a person who fits. **2** a person who fits dresses, suits, etc. on people. **3** a man who adjusts parts of machinery. **4** a man who supplies and fixes anything necessary for some purpose: *a pipe fitter.*

fit·ting (fit′ing) *adj.* right; proper; suitable. —*n.* **1** a trying on of unfinished clothes to see if they will fit. **2 fittings,** *pl.* furnishings; fixtures. —**fit′ting·ly,** *adv.*
Syn. *adj.* **Fitting, becoming, seemly** = suitable. **Fitting** = suiting the purpose or nature of a thing, character or mood of a person, atmosphere or spirit of a time, place, or occasion, etc.: *It is a fitting evening for a dance.* **Becoming** = fitting or suitable in conduct or speech, suiting a person's character, position, or personal standards: *Gentleness is becoming in a nurse.* **Seemly** = pleasing and fitting or becoming, as judged by rigid rules for conduct or behavior as well as by good taste: *Swearing is not seemly in a girl.*

five (fīv) *n.* **1** one more than four; 5. **2** in basketball, a team of five players. **3** a playing card, die, etc. having five spots. —*adj.* being one more than four. [OE *fīf*]

five·fold (fīv′fōld′) *adj.* **1** five times as much or as many. **2** having five parts. —*adv.* five times as much or as many.

Five Nations a former confederacy of Iroquois Indian tribes, consisting of the Mohawks, Oneidas, Onondagas, Cayugas, and Senecas. Members of the Five Nations (now the Six Nations) lived in Ontario and Quebec.

five·pin (fīv′pin′) *n.* **1 fivepins,** a bowling game in which a large ball is rolled down a long indoor alley with the aim of knocking down all of the five pins arranged upright at the other end: *Fivepins is a popular Canadian game.* **2** one of the pins used in this game.

hat, āge, cãre, fär; let, ēqual, tėrm; it, īce
hot, ōpen, ôrder; oil, out; cup, pût, rüle, ūse
əbove, takən, pencəl, lemən, circəs
ch, child; ng, long; sh, ship
th, thin; ᴛʜ, then; zh, measure

fives (fīvz) *n.* an English game like handball.

Five-Year Plan 1 in the Soviet Union, any of the six government plans for the economic development of the country, the first of which was adopted in 1928. **2** any similar plan in various other countries.

fix (fiks) *v.* **fixed, fix·ing,** *n.* —*v.* **1** make firm; become firm; fasten tightly; be fastened tightly: *We fixed the post in the ground.* **2** settle; set: *He fixed the price at one dollar.* **3** direct or hold steady (eyes, attention, etc.); be directed or held steadily. **4** attract and hold (the eye, attention, etc.). **5** make or become rigid. **6** put definitely: *She fixed the blame on the leader.* **7** treat to keep from changing or fading: *A dye or photograph is fixed with chemicals.* **8** mend; repair. **9** *Informal.* put in order; arrange. **10** *Informal.* put in a condition or position favorable to oneself or unfavorable to one's opponents; bribe. **11** *Informal.* get revenge upon; get even with; punish. **12** in chemistry, make stable; change into a more permanent form or state. **13** prearrange or influence the outcome of a game, race, trial, etc. by payment or other inducement: *The jury had been fixed.* **14 fix on** or **upon,** decide on; choose; select. **15 fix up,** *Informal.* **a** mend; repair. **b** put in order; arrange. **c** provide with something needed: *I will fix you up in that house.*
—*n. Informal.* **1** a position hard to get out of; awkward state of affairs. **2** the position of a ship, aircraft, radio transmitter, etc. as determined by obtaining radio signals or other signals from two or more given points. **3** an arrangement for dodging the law, especially one made by bribery. **4** money thus paid. **5** a sports contest whose outcome is prearranged. **6** a dose of a narcotic. [< F *fixer,* ult. < L *fixus,* pp. of *figere* fix] —**fix′a·ble,** *adj.*
Syn. *v.* **1, 2 Fix, establish, settle** = set something or someone firmly in position. **Fix** emphasizes setting so firmly, solidly, or definitely in a position, place, or condition that it is hard to change or move: *We fixed the stove in place.* **Establish** emphasizes making firm, steady, and lasting, and means "set up or fix firmly or permanently": *They established a partnership.* **Settle** = put in a steady, ordered, or permanent position, place, or condition: *He settled his daughter in a business of her own.*

fix·a·tion (fiks ā′shən) *n.* **1** the act of fixing or condition of being fixed. **2** a treatment to keep something from changing or fading: *the fixation of a photographic film.* **3** in chemistry, the process of changing into a more stable form. **4** a morbid attachment or prejudice.

fix·a·tive (fik′sə tiv) *n.* a substance used to keep something from fading or changing. —*adj.* that prevents fading or change.

fixed (fikst) *adj.* **1** not movable; firm. **2** settled; set; definite: *fixed charges for taxicabs.* **3** steady; not moving. **4** made stiff or rigid. **5** *Informal.* prearranged privately or dishonestly: *a fixed horse race.* **6** in chemistry: **a** entering into a stable compound. **b** not volatile: *a fixed acid.*
—**Syn. 1** stationary. **2** established.

fix·ed·ly (fik′sid lē) *adv.* in a fixed manner; without change; intently: *stare fixedly.*

fix·ed·ness (fik′sid nis) *n.* a being fixed; intentness.

fixed star a star whose position in relation to other stars appears not to change.

fix·er (fik′sər) *n.* **1** one who fixes something. **2** a thing that makes permanent; fixative. **3** *Informal.* a person who dishonestly arranges the outcome of a game, contest, etc.

fix·ings (fik′singz) *n.pl. Informal.* **1** furnishings; trimmings. **2** ingredients.

fix·i·ty (fik′sə tē) *n.* **-ties. 1** a fixed condition or quality; permanence; steadiness; firmness. **2** something fixed.

fix·ture (fiks′chər) *n.* **1** something put in place to stay: *bathroom fixtures, electric-light fixtures.* **2** a person or thing that stays in one place, job, etc.: *After twenty-five years of service, he is considered a fixture in the factory.*

3 a game or some other sports event for which a date has been fixed. [var. of obs. *fixure* (< L *fixura* a fastening < *figere* fasten); influenced by *mixture*]

fiz (fiz) *v.* **fizzed, fiz·zing,** *n.* fizz.

fizz (fiz) *v.* make a hissing sound. —*n.* **1** a hissing sound. **2** a bubbling drink, such as champagne, soda water, etc. [imitative]

fiz·zle (fiz′əl) *v.* **-zled, -zling,** *n.* —*v.* **1** hiss or sputter weakly: *The firecracker fizzled instead of exploding with a bang.* **2** *Informal.* fail. **3 fizzle out,** end in failure. —*n.* **1** a hissing; sputtering. **2** *Informal.* a failure. [< obs. *fise* the breaking of wind; cf. OE *fīsting*]

fizz·y (fiz′ē) *adj.* **fizz·i·er, fizz·i·est.** that fizzes.

fjord (fyôrd) *n.* fiord.

fl. **1** fluid. **2** flourished. **3** florin. **4** floor. **5** in music, the flute.

Fl fluorine.

F.L. or **F/L** Flight Lieutenant.

Fla. Florida.

flab·ber·gast (flab′ər gast′) *v. Informal.* make speechless with surprise; astonish greatly; amaze. [? blend of *flap* or *flabby* + *aghast*]

flab·by (flab′ē) *adj.* **-bi·er, -bi·est.** lacking firmness or force; soft; weak: *flabby cheeks.* [var. of earlier *flappy* < *flap*] —**flab′bi·ly,** *adv.* —**flab′bi·ness,** *n.* —**Syn.** See **limp**[2].

flac·cid (flak′sid) *adj.* limp; weak: *flaccid muscles, a flaccid will.* [< L *flaccidus* < *flaccus* flabby] —**flac′cid·ly,** *adv.*

flac·cid·i·ty (flak sid′ə tē) *n.* a flaccid quality or condition.

flack (flak) *n. Slang.* a publicity or press agent. [origin uncertain]

fla·con (flä kon′; *French,* flä kôN′) *n.* a small bottle with a stopper, used for perfume, smelling salts, etc. [< F < OF *flascon.* See FLAGON.]

flag[1] (flag) *n. v.* **flagged, flag·ging.** —*n.* **1** a piece of cloth, often rectangular, that shows the emblem of a country, of a unit of the armed forces, or of some other organization: *the Canadian flag, the regimental flag.* **2** a piece of cloth, often rectangular and of gay color, used as a decoration: *The hall was decorated with many flags.* **3** a piece of cloth of a certain shape, color, or design that has a special meaning: *A red flag is often a sign of danger, a white flag of surrender, a black flag of disaster.* **4** something that suggests a flag. The tail of a deer or of a setter dog is a flag. **5** something like a flag. **6** a large cloth used to keep lights from interfering with a television camera. **7 flags,** *pl.* **a** the feathers on the second joint of a bird's wing. **b** the long feathers on the lower parts of certain birds' legs.
—*v.* **1** put a flag or flags over or on; decorate with flags. **2** stop or signal by a flag: *flag a train.* **3** communicate by a flag: *flag a message.* **4** decoy (game) by waving a flag or something like it to excite attention or curiosity. [? < *flag*[3]] —**Syn.** *n.* **1** ensign, standard, banner.

flag[2] (flag) *n.* **1** an iris having blue, purple, yellow, or white flowers and sword-shaped leaves. **2** the sweet flag, a plant having a sweet-smelling rootstalk. **3** the flower of either of these plants. **4** the leaf of either of these plants. [cf. Danish *flæg*]

flag[3] (flag) *v.* **flagged, flag·ging.** get tired; grow weak; droop: *After doing the same thing for a long time, one's interest flags.* [cf. earlier Du. *vlaggheren* flutter] —**Syn.** decline, languish, fail.

flag[4] (flag) *n. v.* **flagged, flag·ging.** —*n.* flagstone. —*v.* pave with flagstones. [? var. of *flake*]

flag·el·lant (flaj′ə lənt or flə jel′ənt) *n.* **1** a person who whips or is whipped. **2** a religious fanatic who whips himself for religious discipline or for penance. —*adj.* having the habit of whipping.

flag·el·late (flaj′ə lāt′) *v.* **-lat·ed, -lat·ing,** *adj.* —*v.* whip; flog. —*adj.* **1** long, slender, and flexible, as a flagellum or whiplash. **2** having flagella. **3** in botany, having runners or runnerlike branches. [< L *flagellare* < *flagellum,* dim. of *flagrum* whip] —**flag′el·la′tor,** *n.*

flag·el·la·tion (flaj′ə lā′shən) *n.* a whipping; flogging.

fla·gel·lum (flə jel′əm) *n.* **-la** (-lə) or **-lums.** **1** in biology, a long, whiplike tail or part, which is an organ of locomotion in certain cells, bacteria, protozoa, etc. **2** a whip. **3** in botany, a runner of a plant. [< L *flagellum,* dim. of *flagrum* whip]

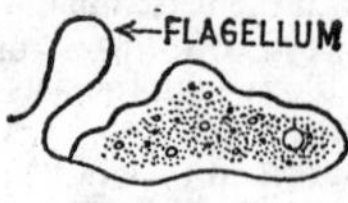

A flagellum (def. 1)

flag·eo·let (flaj′ə let′) *n.* a small wind musical instrument resembling a flute, with a mouthpiece at one end, six main finger holes, and sometimes keys. [< F *flageolet,* dim. of OF *flajol* flute, ult. < L *flare* blow]

flag·ging[1] (flag′ing) *adj.* drooping; tired; weak. [< *flag*[3]]

flag·ging[2] (flag′ing) *n.* **1** flagstones. **2** a pavement made of flagstones. [< *flag*[4]]

fla·gi·tious (flə jish′əs) *adj.* scandalously wicked; shamefully vile. [< L *flagitiosus* < *flagitium* shame] —**fla·gi′tious·ly,** *adv.* —**fla·gi′tious·ness,** *n.*

flag·man (flag′mən) *n.* **-men** (-mən). **1** a person who has charge of or carries a flag. **2** a person who signals with a flag or lantern at a railway crossing, etc.

flag officer in the navy, an officer entitled to display a flag on his ship indicating his rank or command. An admiral, vice-admiral, rear admiral, or officer in command of a fleet or squadron is a flag officer.

flag of truce a white flag used as a sign of surrender or of a desire to confer with the enemy.

flag·on (flag′ən) *n.* **1** a container for liquids, usually having a handle and a spout, and often a cover. **2** a large bottle, holding about two quarts. **3** the contents of a flagon. [ME < OF *flascon.* Akin to FLASK.]

flag·pole (flag′pōl′) *n.* a pole from which a flag is flown.

fla·gran·cy (flā′grən sē) *n.* a flagrant nature or quality.

fla·grant (flā′grənt) *adj.* notorious; outrageous; scandalous. [< L *flagrans, -antis,* ppr. of *flagrare* burn] —**fla′grant·ly,** *adv.* —**Syn.** glaring.

fla·gran·te de·lic·to (flə gran′tā di lik′tō) in law, in the very act of committing the crime; in the performance of the deed. [< L *in flagrante delicto,* literally, while the crime is blazing]

flag·ship (flag′ship′) *n.* the ship that carries the officer in command of a fleet or squadron and displays his flag.

flag·staff (flag′staf′) *n.* a pole from which a flag is flown.

flag station or **stop** a railway station where trains stop only when a signal is given.

flag·stone (flag′stōn′) *n.* a large, flat stone, used for paving walks, etc.

flail (flāl) *n.* an instrument for threshing grain by hand. A flail consists of a wooden handle with a short, heavy stick fastened at one end by a thong. —*v.* **1** strike with a flail. **2** beat; thrash. [OE *flīgel.* Related to FLY[2], v.]

flair (flãr) *n.* **1** a keen perception: *That trader had a flair for bargains.* **2** a natural talent: *The poet had a flair for making clever rhymes.* [< F *flair* scent < *flairer* smell < L *fragrare*]

flak (flak) *n.* **1** gunfire from the ground, directed against airplanes. **2** anti-aircraft guns. [for *Fl.A.K.,* an abbreviation of G *Fliegerabwehrkanone* anti-aircraft gun]

flake[1] (flāk) *n. v.* **flaked, flak·ing.** —*n.* **1** a small, light mass; a soft, loose bit: *a flake of snow.* **2** a thin, flat piece or layer: *flakes of rust, flakes of ice floating on the pond, corn flakes.*
—*v.* **1** come off in flakes; take off, chip, or peel in flakes: *Dirty spots showed where the paint had flaked off.* **2** break or separate into flakes. **3** cover or mark with flakes; make spotted. **4** form into flakes. **5 flake out,** *Slang.* drop with exhaustion; lose consciousness. [ME ? < Scand.; cf. ON *flaki*] —**flake′like′,** *adj.* —**flak′er,** *n.*

flake[2] (flāk) *n.* a slatted platform used for drying fish; fish flake. [ME < ON *flake, fleke* a hurdle, wicker shield]

flak·y (flāk′ē) *adj.* **flak·i·er, flak·i·est.** **1** consisting of flakes: *Mica is a flaky substance.* **2** easily broken or separated into flakes. —**flak′i·ly,** *adv.* —**flak′i·ness,** *n.*

hat, āge, cãre, fär; let, ēqual, tėrm; it, īce
hot, ōpen, ôrder; oil, out; cup, pu̇t, rüle, ūse
əbove, takən, pencəl, lemən, circəs
ch, child; ng, long; sh, ship
th, thin; ᴛʜ, then; zh, measure

flambé (fläɴ bā′) *adj.* **-bés** or **-bées,** *v.* **-béd** or **-béed, -bé·ing.** —*adj.* **1** flaming, especially of food served by pouring alcoholic liquor over it and setting it aflame. **2** iridescent china or porcelain ware: *a flambé vase.* —*v.* pour liquor over and set aflame. [< F]

flam·beau (flam′bō) *n.* **-beaux** (-bōz) or **-beaus. 1** a flaming torch. **2** a large, decorated candlestick. [< F < OF *flambe* flame, ult. < L *flamma*]

flam·boy·ance (flam boi′əns) *n.* a flamboyant nature or quality.

flam·boy·ant (flam boi′ənt) *adj.* **1** gorgeously brilliant; flaming: *flamboyant colors.* **2** very ornate; excessively decorated: *flamboyant architecture.* **3** given to display; ostentatious; showy: *a flamboyant person.* **4** having wavy lines or flamelike curves: *flamboyant designs.* [< F *flamboyant*, ppr. of *flamboyer* flame] **—flam·boy′ant·ly,** *adv.*

flame (flām) *n. v.* **flamed, flam·ing,** *adj.* —*n.* **1** one of the glowing red or yellow tongues of light that shoot out from a blazing fire. **2** a burning gas or vapor. **3** a burning with flames; blaze. **4** a thing or condition, such as love or anger, that suggests flame. **5** a bright light. **6** a patch or streak of color. **7** a burning feeling; ardor; zeal. **8** *Informal.* a sweetheart. **9** a bright reddish yellow or reddish orange.
—*v.* **1** burn with flames; blaze. **2** grow hot, red, etc.: *Her cheeks flamed.* **3** shine brightly; give out a bright light. **4** have or show a burning feeling. **5** burst out quickly and hotly; be or act like a flame. **6 flame out, up,** or **forth, a** burst out quickly and hotly. **b** of jet engines, fail to function.
—*adj.* bright reddish-yellow or reddish-orange. [ME < OF < L *flamma*] **—flame′less,** *adj.* **—flame′like′,** *adj.*
Syn. *n.* **1, 3 Flame, blaze** = a bright burning or fire. **Flame** applies to either a single glowing tongue of fire, such as from a candle, or to a fire burning brightly and quickly, and is often used in the plural to suggest a fire with many bright tongues darting or shooting up: *The dying fire suddenly burst into flame. The house burst into flames.* **Blaze** applies to a hotter, brighter, and steadier fire: *The whole room was lighted by the blaze in the fireplace.* -*v.* **1** flare, glow, flash.

fla·men (flā′men) *n.* a priest devoted to one particular Roman god: *a flamen of Jupiter.* [< L]

fla·men·co (flə meng′kō) *n.* **1** a style of Spanish Gypsy dance performed with castanets to fast, fiery, vigorous rhythms. **2** a song or piece of music in this style, or for such a dance. [< Sp. *flamenco* Flemish (applied to the Gypsies' dance celebrating their departure from Germany, later confused with Flanders)]

flame·out (flām′out′) *n.* the sudden failure of a jet engine to function, especially while the aircraft containing it is in flight.

flame·proof (flām′prüf′) *adj.* **1** not liable to combustion. **2** not liable to burn when in contact with flames: *flameproof curtains.*

flame-re·sist·ant (flām′ri zis′tənt) *adj.* resistant to flame; not easily burned.

flame thrower 1 a weapon or device that directs a jet of burning gasoline mixture, napalm, etc. through the air. **2** a person who operates such a weapon or device. [translation of G *Flammenwerfer*]

flam·ing (flām′ing) *adj.* **1** burning with flames. **2** like a flame; very bright; brilliant. **3** showing or arousing strong feeling; violent; vehement.

fla·min·go (flə ming′gō) *n.* **-gos** or **-goes.** a tropical wading bird having very long legs and neck, and feathers that vary from pink to scarlet. [< Pg. < Sp. *flamenco* < Provençal *flamenc* < *flama* < L *flamma* flame]

Fla·min·i·an Way (flə min′ē ən) an old Roman road leading north from Rome, built in 220 B.C.

flam·ma·ble (flam′ə bəl) *adj.* easily set on fire; inflammable.
☛ **Flammable and inflammable mean the same though inflammable is more usual in Canada. Note that the opposite is non-flammable, not non-inflammable.**

flan (flan) *n.* **1** *Brit.* a tart or open pastry filled with fruit, custard, etc. **2** a blank piece of metal, ready to be stamped and made into a coin. [< MF *flaon* tart < Gmc.]

flange (flanj) *n. v.* **flanged, flang·ing.** —*n.* a projecting edge, rim, collar, etc. on an object for keeping it in place, attaching it to another object, strengthening it, etc. Railway cars and locomotives have wheels with flanges to keep them on the track. —*v.* provide with a flange. [var. of *flanch*, n., < *flanch*, v., < OF *flanchir* bend]

Flanges

flank (flangk) *n.* **1** of animals or people, the part of the body between the hip and the ribs. See **beef** for diagram. **2** a piece of beef cut from this part of a steer. **3** the side of a mountain, building, etc. **4** the far right or left side of an army, fleet, etc.
—*v.* **1** be at the side of: *High buildings flanked the dark, narrow alley.* **2** get around the far right or left side of. **3** attack from or on the side. **4** occupy a position on the flank or side. **5** present the flank or side. [ME < OF *flanc* < Gmc.] **—flank′er,** *n.*

flan·nel (flan′əl) *n.* **1** a soft, warm woollen cloth. **2** flannelette. **3** a face-cloth. **4 flannels,** *pl.* **a** clothes, especially trousers, made of flannel. **b** woollen underwear. —*adj.* made of flannel.

flan·nel·ette or **flan·nel·et** (flan′əl et′) *n.* a soft, warm, cotton cloth with a fuzzy nap, that looks like flannel.

flap (flap) *v.* **flapped, flap·ping,** *n.* —*v.* **1** swing or sway about loosely: *The curtains flapped in the open windows.* **2** cause to swing or sway loosely: *The breeze noisily flapped the sheets on the clothes line.* **3** move (wings, arms, etc.) up and down. **4** fly by moving wings up and down: *The large bird flapped away.* **5** strike noisily with something broad and flat. **6** *Slang.* become excited, confused, or alarmed.
—*n.* **1** a flapping motion. **2** a noise caused by flapping. **3** a blow from something broad and flat. **4** a broad, flat piece, usually hanging or fastened at one edge only: *His coat had flaps on the pockets.* **5** a hinged section on an airfoil of an airplane, especially a wing, which can be moved to assist a take-off or a landing. **6** *Slang.* excitement or anger; commotion. **7** in surgery, a piece of flesh partially detached from adjacent tissue, as for later use in grafting. **8** in phonetics, a type of trill in which the vibrating organ gives only a single tap, as in some British pronunciations of *merry, very,* etc. [ME; probably imitative]

flap·doo·dle (flap′dü′dəl) *n. Slang.* nonsense; rubbish; humbug. [a coined word]

flap·jack (flap′jak′) *n.* a pancake; griddlecake.

flap·per (flap′ər) *n.* **1** something broad and flat to strike with. **2** a broad, flat, hanging piece; flap. **3** a young bird just able to fly. **4** *Informal.* especially, in the 1920's, a young girl; girl who is rather forward and unconventional.

flare (flãr) *v.* **flared, flar·ing,** *n.* —*v.* **1** flame up briefly or unsteadily, sometimes with smoke: *A gust of wind made the torches flare.* **2** signal by lights: *The rockets flared a warning.* **3** spread out in the shape of a bell: *The sides of a ship flare from the keel to the deck. The skirt should be flared at the bottom.* **4** burst out: *Suddenly, his temper flared.* **5 flare up** or **out,** flame up; burst out into anger, violence, etc.
—*n.* **1** a bright, unsteady light or blaze that lasts only a short time: *The flare of a match showed us his face.* **2** a dazzling light that burns for a short time, used for signalling, lighting up a battlefield, etc. **3** a sudden outburst. **4** a spreading out into a bell shape. **5** a part that spreads out: *the flare of a skirt.* [cf. Norwegian *flara* blaze]

flare·pot (flãr′pot′) *n.* a metal sphere, usually containing kerosene, that may be lit as a warning signal.

flare-up (flãr′up′) *n.* **1** an outburst of flame. **2** *Informal.* a sudden outburst of anger, violence, etc.

flar·ing (flãr′ing) *adj.* **1** flaming. **2** gaudy. **3** spreading gradually outward in form or shape.

flash (flash) *n.* **1** a sudden, brief light or flame: *a flash of lightning.* **2** a sudden, brief feeling or display: *a flash of*

hope, a flash of wit. **3** a very brief time; instant. **4** a brief news report, usually received by teletype, or given over the radio or television. **5** a showy display. **6** **flash in the pan,** a sudden, showy attempt or effort that often fails or is not followed by further efforts.
—*v.* **1** give out a sudden, brief light or flame. **2** come suddenly; pass quickly. **3** cause to flash. **4** give out or send out like a flash. **5** communicate by flashes; send by telegraph, radio, etc. **6** **a** a rush of water, as produced by a dam or sluiceway, used to float a boat over shoals or for other purposes. **b** the device, as a lock or sluice, used for this purpose. **7** *Informal.* show off.
—*adj.* flashy. [apparently imitative] —**flash′er,** *n.*
Syn. *n.* **1** **Flash, glitter, sparkle** = a sudden or unsteady light. **Flash** = a sudden, bright light that disappears immediately: *We saw a single flash of light from the signal tower.* **Glitter** = a bright and wavering light that off and on sends out brilliant flashes as light is reflected from a shining, hard surface: *We saw the glitter of swords in the moonlight.* **Sparkle** = light shooting out in many tiny, brief, brilliant flashes like sparks: *We looked at the sparkle of the little dancing waves in the sunlight.*

flash-back (flash′bak′) *n.* **1** in a novel, play, movie, etc., the introduction of some event or scene that took place or is supposed to have taken place at an earlier time. **2** the scene thus introduced.

flash bulb **1** a bulb, often containing magnesium, used to give a bright light for taking photographs indoors, in shadow, or at night. **2** a portable electric device used to make bright flashes for taking photographs.

flash burn a severe burn caused by instantaneous thermal radiation, such as that from an atomic bomb.

flash card one of a set of cards displaying letters, words, figures, pictures, etc., intended to be shown briefly for drills in reading, arithmetic, and other school subjects, or to be used for various other purposes.

flash flood a very sudden, violent flooding of a river, stream, etc.

flash gun in photography, an apparatus for holding and setting off a flash bulb.

flash·i·ness (flash′ē nis) *n.* a flashy quality.

flash·ing (flash′ing) *n.* **1** the pieces of sheet metal used to cover and protect the joints and angles of a building to make them watertight. **2** the process of suddenly letting in a rush of water so as to produce an artificial flood, as for cleaning a sewer.

flash·light (flash′līt′) *n.* **1** a light that flashes, used in a lighthouse or for signalling. **2** a portable electric light, usually operated by batteries. **3** a flash bulb.

flash·y (flash′ē) *adj.* **flash·i·er, flash·i·est.** **1** very bright for a short time; flashing. **2** showy; gaudy. —**flash′i·ly,** *adv.* —**Syn.** **1** glittering, dazzling. **2** tawdry.

flask (flask) *n.* **1** any bottle-shaped container, especially one having a narrow neck: *Flasks of thin glass are used in chemical laboratories for heating liquids.* **2** a small glass, plastic or metal bottle with flat sides, made to be carried in the pocket. **3** a box or frame for holding the sand, etc. used as a mould in a foundry. [OE *flasce*; cf. LL *flasca* < Gmc.]

flat[1] (flat) *adj.* **flat·ter, flat·test,** *n. adv. v.* **flat·ted, flat·ting.** —*adj.* **1** smooth and level; even: *flat land.* **2** spread out; at full length: *The storm left the trees flat.* **3** not very deep or thick: *A plate is flat.* **4** with little air in it: *a flat tire.* **5** not to be changed; positive: *A flat refusal is complete. A flat rate involves no extra charges.* **6** without much life, interest, flavor, etc.; dull: *flat food, a flat voice, flat beer.* **7** not shiny or glossy: *a flat yellow.* **8** not clear or sharp in sound. **9** in music: **a** below the true pitch. **b** one half step or half note below natural pitch. **c** marked with or having flats. **10** of feet, having the arches fallen. **11** **That's flat,** I mean it.
—*n.* **1** something flat. **2** a flatboat. **3** a shallow box or basket. **4** a flatcar. **5** a piece of theatrical scenery. **6** *Informal.* a tire with little air in it. **7** a flat part: *The front of an open hand is the flat.* **8** flat land. **9** land covered with shallow water; marsh; swamp. **10** in music: **a** a tone or note that is one half step or half note below natural pitch. **b** the sign (♭) that shows such a tone or note. **11** in horse racing: **a** a race on a flat course in contrast to a steeplechase or other jumping race. **b** **flat racing,** on a track without jumps or obstacles.
—*adv.* **1** in music, below the true pitch. **2** in a flat manner. **3** in or into a flat position; horizontally. **4** directly; exactly. **5** **fall flat,** fail completely; have no effect or interest. **6** **flat out,** at maximum speed or effort.
—*v.* **1** make or become flat. **2** in music, make or sound flat. [ME < ON *flatr*] —**flat′ly,** *adv.* —**flat′ness,** *n.*
—**Syn.** *adj.* **1** plane. **2** prostrate, prone, supine. **5** downright, absolute. **6** monotonous.

flat[2] (flat) *n.* an apartment or set of rooms on the same floor and not generally self-contained. [alteration of *flet,* OE *flett*]

flat·boat (flat′bōt′) *n.* a large boat with a flat bottom, often used for carrying goods on a river or canal.
—*v.* transport in a flatboat.

flat-bot·tomed (flat′bot′əmd) *adj.* having a flat bottom.

flat·car (flat′kär′) *n.* a railway freight car without a roof or sides.

flat·fish (flat′fish′) *n.* **-fish** or **-fish·es.** any of a group of fishes having flat bodies, and with both eyes on the side kept uppermost when lying flat: *Halibut, flounder, and sole are flatfish.*

flat·foot (flat′fu̇t′) *n.* **-feet.** **1** a foot with a flattened arch. **2** a condition in which the feet have flattened arches. **3** *Slang.* a policeman.

flat-foot·ed (flat′fu̇t′id) *adj.* **1** having feet with flattened arches. **2** *Informal.* not to be changed or influenced; firm; uncompromising. —**flat′foot′ed·ly,** *adv.* —**flat′foot′ed·ness,** *n.*

Flat·head (flat′hed′) *n.* **1** a Chinook Indian. **2** a tribe of North American Indians living in W. Montana. **3** a member of this tribe. [from their supposed practice of flattening the heads of their children]

flat·i·ron (flat′ī′ərn) *n.* an iron with a flat surface, which, when heated, is used for smoothing wrinkles out of cloth.

flat·ten (flat′ən) *v.* **1** make or become flat. **2** **flatten out,** **a** spread out flat. **b** in aeronautics, return to a level position from a dive or climb; level off. —**flat′ten·er,** *n.*

flat·ter (flat′ər) *v.* **1** praise too much or beyond what is true; praise insincerely. **2** show to be better looking than is actually the case: *This picture flatters her.* **3** try to please or win over by flattering. **4** cause to be pleased or feel honored. **5** **flatter oneself,** **a** be pleased to know or think. **b** overestimate oneself. [? extended use of ME *flateren* float. Related to FLUTTER.] —**flat′ter·er,** *n.* —**flat′ter·ing·ly,** *adv.* —**Syn.** **1** compliment. **3** cajole, blandish.

flat·ter·y (flat′ər ē) *n.* **-ter·ies.** **1** the act of flattering. **2** words of praise, usually untrue or overstated.

flat·tish (flat′ish) *adj.* somewhat flat.

flat·top (flat′top′) *n.* **1** *Esp.U.S. Informal.* an aircraft carrier. **2** a haircut similar to a crew cut but completely flat across the top.

flat·u·lence (flach′u̇ ləns) *n.* **1** gas in the stomach or intestines. **2** pompous speech or behavior; vanity; emptiness.

flat·u·lent (flach′u̇ lənt) *adj.* **1** having gas in the stomach or intestines. **2** causing gas in the stomach or intestines. **3** pompous in speech or behavior; vain; empty. [< F < L *flatus* a blowing < *flare* blow]

fla·tus (flā′təs) *n.* **-tus·es.** gas in the stomach, intestines, etc. [< L]

flat·ware (flat′wãr′) *n.* **1** knives, forks, and spoons. **2** plates, platters, saucers, etc.

flat·ways (flat′wāz′) *adv.* with the flat side forward, upward, or touching.

flat·worm (flat′wėrm′) *n.* a flat-bodied worm that lives in water or as a parasite on some animals: *Tapeworms and planarians are flatworms.*

flaunt (flont or flônt) *v.* **1** show off. **2** wave proudly: *banners flaunting in the breeze.* —*n.* a flaunting. [? < Scand.; cf. Norwegian *flanta* gad about] —**flaunt′er,** *n.* —**flaunt′ing·ly,** *adv.*

flau·tist (flo′tist or flô′tist) *n.* flutist.

fla·vor or **fla·vour** (flā′vər) *n.* **1** a taste, especially a characteristic taste: *Chocolate and vanilla have different flavors.* **2** anything used to give a certain taste to food or drink; flavoring. **3** a characteristic quality: *Many stories by Joseph Conrad have a flavor of the sea.* **4** an aroma; odor.
—*v.* **1** give an added taste to; season: *We use salt,*

pepper, and spices to flavor food. **2** give a characteristic quality to: *Many exciting adventures flavor an explorer's life.* [ME < OF *flaur*, ult. < L *fragrare* emit odor] **—fla′vor·er** or **fla′vour·er,** *n.* **—fla′vor·less** or **fla′vour·less,** *adj.* **—Syn.** *n.* **1** savor, smack, tang, relish. See **taste.**

fla·vor·ing or **fla·vour·ing** (flā′vər ing or flāv′ring) *n.* something used to give a certain taste to food or drink: *vanilla flavoring, chocolate flavoring.*

fla·vour (flā′vər) *n. v.* flavor.

flaw[1] (flo or flô) *n.* **1** a defective place; crack: *A flaw in the dish caused it to break.* **2** a fault; defect. —*v.* make or become defective; crack. [ME < Scand.; cf. Swedish *flaga*] **—Syn.** *n.* **1** chink, rent, breach. **2** imperfection, blemish. See **defect.**

flaw[2] (flo or flô) *n.* a gust of wind; sudden squall. [< Scand.; cf. Norwegian *flaga* gust]

flaw·less (flo′lis or flô′lis) *adj.* perfect; without a flaw. **—flaw′less·ly,** *adv.* **—flaw′less·ness,** *n.*

flax (flaks) *n.* **1** a plant with small, narrow leaves, blue flowers, and slender stems about two feet tall. Linseed oil is made from its seeds. **2** the fibres from the stems of this plant prepared for spinning. Flax is spun into linen thread for making linen cloth. [OE *fleax*]

flax·en (flak′sən) *adj.* **1** made of flax. **2** like the color of flax; pale yellow: *flaxen hair.*

flax·seed (flaks′sēd′) *n.* the seed of flax; linseed: *Flaxseed is used to make linseed oil and some medicines.*

flay (flā) *v.* **1** strip the skin or outer covering from by whipping or lashing: *The tyrant had his enemies flayed alive.* **2** scold severely; criticize without pity or mercy: *The angry man flayed his servant with his tongue.* **3** rob; cheat. [OE *flēan*] **—flay′er,** *n.*

fld. field.

flea (flē) *n.* **1** a small, wingless, jumping insect that lives as a parasite on animals, sucking their blood. **2 flea in one's ear, a** a severe scolding; rebuff. **b** a sharp hint. [OE *flēah*]

flea·bane (flē′bān′) *n.* any of various plants supposed to drive away fleas.

flea-bit·ten (flē′bit′ən) *adj.* **1** bitten by fleas. **2** having reddish-brown spots on a light-colored hide: *a flea-bitten horse.*

flea market a market selling a mixture of cheap or odd items, junk, antiques, etc.

fleck (flek) *n.* **1** a spot or patch of color, light, etc.: *Freckles are brown flecks on the skin.* **2** a small particle; flake. —*v.* sprinkle with spots or patches of color, light, etc.; speckle: *Sunlight coming through the branches flecked the shadow cast by the tree.* [ME < ON *flekkr*]

flecked (flekt) *adj.* sprinkled with spots or patches of color, light, etc.; speckled: *The bird's breast is flecked with brown.*

flec·tion (flek′shən) *n.* **1** a bending: *Every flection of his arm caused the muscles to bulge.* **2** a bent part; bend. **3** in grammar, inflection. **4** in physiology, flexion. Also, *Esp.Brit.* **flexion.** [< L *flexio, -onis* < *flectere* bend]

fled (fled) *v.* pt. and pp. of **flee.**

fledge (flej) *v.* **fledged, fledg·ing. 1** grow the feathers needed for flying. **2** bring up (a young bird) until it is able to fly. **3** provide or cover with feathers. [cf. OE *unfligge* unfledged, unfit to fly]

fledg·ling or **fledge·ling** (flej′ling) *n.* **1** a young bird just able to fly. **2** a young, inexperienced person.

flee (flē) *v.* **fled, flee·ing. 1** run away; try to get away by running. **2** run away from; try to get away from by running. **3** go quickly; move swiftly: *The clouds are fleeing before the wind.* **4** pass away; cease; vanish: *The shadows flee as day breaks.* [OE *flēon*] **—fle′er,** *n.*

fleece (flēs) *n. v.* **fleeced, fleec·ing.** —*n.* **1** the wool that covers a sheep or similar animal. **2** the quantity of wool cut from a sheep at one time. **3** something like a fleece: *a fleece of hair, the fleece of new-fallen snow.* **4** a fabric with a soft, silky pile, used for lining outer garments. **5** the pile of such a fabric. —*v.* **1** cut the fleece from. **2** strip of money or belongings; rob; cheat: *The gamblers fleeced him of a large sum.* [OE *flēos*] **—fleec′er,** *n.* **—fleece′like,** *adj.*

fleec·y (flēs′ē) *adj.* **fleec·i·er, fleec·i·est. 1** like a fleece; soft and white: *Fleecy clouds floated in the blue sky.* **2** covered with fleece. **3** made of fleece. **—fleec′i·ly,** *adv.* **—fleec′i·ness,** *n.*

hat, āge, cãre, fär; let, ēqual, tėrm; it, īce
hot, ōpen, ôrder; oil, out; cup, pu̇t, rüle, ūse
əbove, takən, pencəl, lemən, circəs
ch, child; ng, long; sh, ship
th, thin; ᴛʜ, then; zh, measure

fleer (flēr) *v. n.* jeer; sneer; jibe. [ME *flery(e)*, *flire*; cf. Norwegian *flira* grin]

fleet[1] (flēt) *n.* **1** a group of warships under one command; navy. **2** any group of ships or boats sailing together: *a fleet of fishing boats.* **3** a group of airplanes, automobiles, etc. moving or working together. [OE *flēot* ship, vessel < *flēotan* float]

fleet[2] (flēt) *adj.* swift; rapid. [< ON *fljótr*. Akin to verb.] —*v.* pass swiftly; move rapidly. [OE *flēotan*. Akin to FLOAT.] **—fleet′ly,** *adv.* **—fleet′ness,** *n.*

fleet·ing (flēt′ing) *adj.* passing swiftly; moving rapidly; soon gone. **—fleet′ing·ly,** *adv.* **—Syn.** transitory, momentary, temporary.

Fleet Street in London, England: **1** a very old street, now the location of many newspaper offices. **2** the newspaper industry.

Flem·ing (flem′ing) *n.* **1** a native of Flanders, a district in W. Belgium, N. France, and S.W. Netherlands. **2** a Belgian whose native language is Flemish.

Flem·ish (flem′ish) *adj.* of or having to do with Flanders, a district in W. Belgium, N. France, and S.W. Netherlands, its people, or their language. —*n.* **1** the people of Flanders. **2** their language.

flense (flens) *v.* **flensed, flens·ing.** strip skin or blubber from a seal or whale. [< Du. *flensen* or Danish and Norwegian *flense*] **—flens′er,** *n.*

flesh (flesh) *n.* **1** the soft substance of a human or animal body that covers the bones and is covered by skin. Flesh consists mostly of muscles and fat. **2** the tissue or muscles of animals. **3** fatness. **4** meat, especially of a sort not usually eaten by human beings. **5** the body, not the soul or spirit. **6** the physical side of human nature, as distinguished from the spiritual or moral side. **7** the human race; people as a group. **8** all living creatures. **9** one's family or relatives by birth. **10** the soft or edible part of fruits or vegetables: *The McIntosh apple has crisp, juicy, white flesh.* **11** the color of a white person's skin; pinkish white with a little yellow. **12 in the flesh, a** alive. **b** in person. —*v.* **1** plunge (a weapon) into the flesh. **2** feed (a hound or hawk) with flesh. **3** excite (to passion, bloodshed, etc.) by a foretaste. **4** make or become fleshy; fatten. **5** remove flesh, tissue, etc. from (hides). **6 flesh out, a** put on flesh in the process of growth: *Sam has fleshed out a lot lately.* **b** fill up or fill out: *The show time outside of the feature film was fleshed out with cartoons.* [OE *flǣsc*] **—flesh′less,** *adj.*

flesh and blood 1 the body; the material composing man's physical frame. **2** an individual person or persons. **3** human nature: *The temptation was more than flesh and blood could resist.* **4** one's family or relatives by birth; a child or relative by birth.

flesh-and-blood (flesh′ən blud′) *adj.* having human existence; real: *a flesh-and-blood heroine.*

flesh-col·ored or **-col·oured** (flesh′kul′ərd) *adj.* pinkish-white with a tinge of yellow.

-fleshed *combining form.* having —— flesh: *solid-fleshed = having solid flesh.*

flesh fly a fly whose larvae feed on decaying flesh.

flesh·ly (flesh′lē) *adj.* **-li·er, -li·est. 1** of the flesh; bodily. **2** sensual. **3** of or having to do with the material body; mortal; human. **4** worldly. **—flesh′li·ness,** *n.*

flesh·pot (flesh′pot′) *n.* **1** a pot for cooking meat. **2 fleshpots,** *pl.* good food and living; luxuries.

flesh wound a wound that merely injures the flesh; slight wound.

flesh·y (flesh′ē) *adj.* **flesh·i·er, flesh·i·est. 1** having much flesh: *The calf is the fleshy part of the lower leg.* **2** plump; fat. **3** of flesh; like flesh. **4** pulpy. **—flesh′i·ly,** *adv.* **—flesh′i·ness,** *n.*

fleur-de-lis (flėr′də lē′ or flėr′də lēs′) *n.* **fleurs-de-lis** (flėr′də lēz′ or flėr′də lē′). **1** a design or device used in heraldry representing a lily. **2** the former royal coat of arms of France. **3** the unofficial floral emblem of the province of Quebec. **4** the iris flower or plant; blue flag. [< F *fleur-de-lis* lily flower]

A fleur-de-lis design

flew (flü) *v.* pt. of **fly**[2].

flews (flüz) *n.pl.* the overhanging part of the lip of certain dogs, especially hounds. [origin uncertain]

flex (fleks) *v.* **1** bend: *He slowly flexed his stiff arm.* **2** of muscles, tighten and relax alternately. —*n.* **1** flexibility. **2** a bend or contraction of a muscle. **3** *Esp.Brit.* flexible insulated wire used to connect electric appliances or lamps; cord. [< L *flexus*, pp. of *flectere* bend]

flex·i·bil·i·ty (flek′sə bil′ə tē) *n.* a flexible quality.

flex·i·ble (flek′sə bəl) *adj.* **1** easily bent; not stiff; bending without breaking: *Leather, rubber, and wire are flexible materials.* **2** easily adapted to fit various uses, purposes, etc.: *The actor's flexible voice accommodated itself to every emotion.* **3** easily managed; willing to yield to influence or persuasion. [< F < L < *flexibilis* < *flexus.* See FLEX.] —**flex′i·bly,** *adv.*

Syn. 1, 3 Flexible, pliant, limber = easily bent. **Flexible** = capable of being bent or twisted easily and without breaking, or, used figuratively of people and their minds, etc., capable of being turned or managed with little trouble if handled skilfully: *Great thinkers have flexible minds.* **Pliant,** literally and figuratively, emphasizes having the quality of bending or adapting itself easily rather than of being easily affected by outside force: *English is a pliant language.* **Limber,** used chiefly of the body, means "having flexible muscles and joints": *A jumper has limber legs.*

flex·ile (flek′səl) *adj.* flexible.

flex·ion (flek′shən) *n.* **1** in physiology: **a** a bending of some part of the body by the action of flexors. **b** a being bent in this way. **2** *Esp.Brit.* flection (def. 3). [var. of *flection*]

flex·or (flek′sər) *n.* in physiology, any muscle that bends some part of the body. [< NL]

flex·ure (flek′shər) *n.* **1** a bending; curving. **2** a bend; curve. [< L *flexura* < *flexus.* See FLEX.]

flib·ber·ti·gib·bet (flib′ər tē jib′it) *n.* **1** a frivolous, flighty person. **2** a chatterbox. —**flib′ber·ti·gib′bet·y,** *adj.*

flick (flik) *n.* **1** a quick, light blow; sudden, snapping stroke: *By a flick of his whip, he drove the fly from the horse's head.* **2** the light, snapping sound of such a blow or stroke. **3** a streak; splash; fleck. **4** *Slang.* a movie. —*v.* **1** strike lightly with a quick, snapping blow: *He flicked the dust from his shoes with a handkerchief.* **2** make a sudden, snapping stroke with: *The boys flicked wet towels at each other.* **3** flutter; move quickly and lightly. [probably imitative]

flick·er[1] (flik′ər) *v.* **1** shine with a wavering light; burn with an unsteady flame: *A dying fire flickered on the hearth.* **2** move quickly and lightly in and out or back and forth: *The tongue of a snake flickers.* **3** cause to flicker: *There was just enough breeze to flicker the candle.* —*n.* **1** a wavering, unsteady light or flame. **2** a brief flame; spark. **3** a quick, light movement. [OE *flicorian*]

flick·er[2] (flik′ər) *n.* any of various types of North American woodpecker: *The yellowhammer is one kind of flicker.* [? imitative of its note]

fli·er (flī′ər) *n.* flyer.

flight[1] (flīt) *n.* **1** the act or manner of flying. **2** the distance a bird, bullet, aircraft, etc. can fly. **3** a group of things flying through the air together: *a flight of six birds.* **4** an air-force unit of either planes or personnel. **5** a trip in an aircraft. **6** a swift movement. **7** a soaring above or beyond what is ordinary. **8** a set of stairs or steps between landings or storeys of a building. [OE *flyht.* Related to FLY[2].]

flight[2] (flīt) *n.* **1** the act of fleeing or running away: *The defeated army was in flight.* **2** escape: *The flight of the prisoners was soon discovered.* **3 put to flight,** force to flee. **4 take to flight,** flee. [ME *fliht* < OE *flēon* flee]

flight·less (flīt′lis) *adj.* unable to fly.

flight lieutenant in the air force, a commissioned officer senior to a flying officer and junior to a squadron leader. *Abbrev.*: F/L., F.L., or Flt.Lt.

flight·path (flīt′path′) *n.* in aeronautics: **1** the course taken by an aircraft, missile, etc. **2** a course indicated by an electronic beam as a navigation aid.

flight sergeant in the air force, a non-commissioned officer senior to a sergeant and junior to a warrant officer. *Abbrev.*: Flt. Sgt.

flight·y (flīt′ē) *adj.* **flight·i·er, flight·i·est. 1** likely to have sudden fancies; full of whims; frivolous. **2** slightly crazy; light-headed. —**flight′i·ly,** *adv.* —**flight′i·ness,** *n.*

flim·flam (flim′flam′) *n. v.* **-flammed, -flam·ming.** *Informal.* —*n.* **1** nonsense; rubbish. **2** deception; a low trick. —*v.* cheat (a person) out of money; trick. —**flim′ flam′ mer,** *n.*

flim·sy (flim′zē) *adj.* **-si·er, -si·est,** *n.* **-sies.** —*adj.* **1** light and thin; frail: *Muslin is too flimsy to be used for sails.* **2** not serious or convincing: *a flimsy excuse.*
—*n.* **1** a thin paper used by reporters. **2** a newspaper report on this paper. **3** a sheet of very thin paper for typing or writing. [? < alteration of *film* + *-sy*, adj. suffix] —**flim′si·ly,** *adv.* —**flim′si·ness,** *n.* —**Syn.** *adj.* **2** shallow, feeble, weak.

flinch (flinch) *v.* draw back from difficulty, danger, or pain; shrink. —*n.* **1** a drawing back: *He took his punishment without a flinch.* **2** a game played with cards bearing numbers from 1 to 14. [probably < OF *flenchir* < Frankish **hlankjan* bend; cf. G *lenken*]
—**flinch′ing·ly,** *adv.* —**Syn.** *v.* wince, quail. See **shrink.**

flin·ders (flin′dərz) *n.pl.* small pieces; fragments; splinters: *The box was smashed into flinders.* [cf. Norwegian *flindra*]

fling (fling) *v.* **flung, fling·ing,** *n.* —*v.* **1** throw with force; throw: *fling a stone.* **2** rush; dash: *She flung out of the room.* **3** plunge; kick. **4** put suddenly or violently: *Fling him into jail.* —*n.* **1** a sudden throw. **2** a plunge; kick. **3** a time of doing as one pleases: *He had his fling when he was young; now he must work.* **4** a lively Scottish dance: *the Highland fling.* **5 have** or **take a fling at, a** try; attempt. **b** make scornful remarks about. [? akin to ON *flengja* flog]

flint (flint) *n.* **1** a very hard gray or brown stone, a kind of quartz, that makes a spark when struck against steel. **2** a piece of this stone used with steel to light fires, explode gunpowder, etc. **3** anything very hard or unyielding: *He had a heart of flint.* [OE]

flint glass a brilliant glass containing lead, potassium or sodium, and silicon. It is used for lenses, dishes, etc.

flint·lock (flint′lok′) *n.* **1** a gunlock in which a flint striking against steel makes sparks that explode the gunpowder. **2** an old-fashioned gun with such a lock.

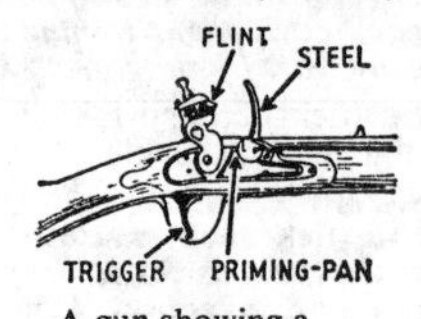

A gun showing a flintlock

flint·y (flin′tē) *adj.* **flint·i·er, flint·i·est. 1** consisting of flint; containing flint. **2** like flint; very hard; unyielding. —**flint′i·ly,** *adv.* —**flint′i·ness,** *n.*

flip[1] (flip) *v.* **flipped, flip·ping,** *n. adj.* **flip·per, flip·pest.** —*v.* **1** toss or move with a snap of a finger and thumb: *He flipped a coin on the counter.* **2** jerk; turn or move with a jerk: *She flipped her fan shut. The branch flipped back.* **3** flick: *The driver flipped his whip at a fly.* **4 flip up,** flip a coin in the air to decide a chance.
—*n.* **1** a smart tap; snap: *The cat gave the kitten a flip on the ear.* **2** a sudden jerk. [probably imitative]

flip[2] (flip) *n.* a hot drink containing beer, ale, cider, or the like, with sugar and spice. [nominal use of *flip*[1], v.]

flip[3] (flip) *adj. Informal.* flippant.

flip·pan·cy (flip′ən sē) *n.* **-cies. 1** a being flippant. **2** flippant speech or conduct.

flip·pant (flip′ənt) *adj.* smart or pert in speech; not respectful: *a flippant answer.* [? < *flip*[1] + *-ant*] —**flip′pant·ly,** *adv.* —**Syn.** impertinent, saucy.

flip·per (flip′ər) *n.* **1** a broad, flat fin especially adapted for swimming: *Seal flippers are a popular food in Newfoundland.* See picture on the opposite page. **2** a piece of rubber or plastic that fits onto the foot and has a broad, flat blade extending from the toe, used by swimmers to give extra power, especially when swimming underwater: *A pair of flippers is part of every skindiver's equipment.* **3** a person or thing that flips: *a pancake flipper.* **4** a stabilizing fin on an ocean liner. **5** *Slang.* the hand.

flirt (flėrt) *v.* **1** pretend to be in love with someone; try to win a person's attention and affection by pretending to be attracted to the person: *The girl's father advised her not to flirt with boys.* **2** trifle; toy: *He flirted with the idea of going to Europe, though he couldn't afford it.* **3** move quickly to and fro; flutter: *She flirted her fan impatiently.* **4** toss; jerk.
—*n.* **1** a person who flirts. **2** a quick movement or flutter: *With a flirt of its tail, the bird flew away.* **3** a toss; jerk. [ult. imitative (see v. def. 4)] —**flirt′er,** *n.*

flir·ta·tion (flėr tā′shən) *n.* **1** a pretending to be in love with someone. **2** a love affair that is not serious. **3** a flirting or toying.

flir·ta·tious (flėr tā′shəs) *adj.* **1** inclined to flirt. **2** having to do with flirtation. —**flir·ta′tious·ly,** *adv.* —**flir·ta′tious·ness,** *n.*

flit (flit) *v.* **flit·ted, flit·ting,** *n.* —*v.* **1** fly lightly and quickly; flutter: *Birds flitted from tree to tree.* **2** pass lightly and quickly: *Many idle thoughts flitted through his mind as he lay in the sun.* —*n.* a light, quick movement. [ME < ON *flytja.* Akin to FLEET[2].] —**flit·ter,** *n.*

flitch (flich) *n.* a side of a pig salted and cured; side of bacon. [OE *flicce*]

flit·ter (flit′ər) *v. n.* flutter. [< *flit*]

fliv·ver (fliv′ər) *n. Slang.* a small, cheap automobile. [origin unknown]

float (flōt) *v.* **1** stay on top of or be held up by air, water, or other liquid. **2** move with a moving liquid; drift: *The boat floated out to sea.* **3** rest or move in a liquid, the air, etc. **4** cause to float. **5** cover with liquid; flood. **6** set going as a company. **7** sell (securities): *float an issue of stock.* **8** move effortlessly or drift: *A vision floated before her eyes. He floats from job to job.*
—*n.* **1** anything that stays up or holds up something else in water, such as a raft. **2** a cork on a fish line. **3** an air-filled organ that supports a fish. **4** an air-filled, water-tight part on an aircraft for landing or floating on water; pontoon. **5** a hollow, metal ball that regulates the level, supply, or outlet of a liquid. **6** a flat board of a water wheel or paddle wheel. **7** a low, flat car that carries something to be shown in a parade. **8** a drink consisting of ginger ale or a similar beverage with ice cream in it. **9** in geology: **a** fragments of rock, mineral, or ore loosened from their source and deposited elsewhere: *iron ore float.* **b** fine mineral particles floating in water: *They have located the source of the float coal.* **10 floats,** in the theatre, footlights. [OE *flotian* < *flēotan.* Related to FLEET[2].] —**float′a·ble,** *adj.*

float·er (flōt′ər) *n.* **1** a person or thing that floats. **2** *Informal.* a person who often changes his place of living, working, etc. **3** in sports, a ball thrown or hit so as to travel slowly and appear to hang in the air, usually on a slightly arched course. **4** an insurance policy covering a category of goods, as household furnishings, rather than specific items, as a particular gem.

float·ing (flōt′ing) *adj.* **1** that floats. **2** not fixed; not staying in one place; moving around. **3** in use or circulation; not permanently invested. **4** not funded; changing: *The floating debt of a business consists of notes, drafts, etc. payable within a short time.* **5** in medicine, not in the normal position; displaced: *a floating kidney.* **6** of or having to do with a machine part, such as a connecting rod or coupler, that is connected or hung in such a way that it functions without causing vibration. —**float′ing·ly,** *adv.*

floating ribs the ribs not attached to the breastbone; last two pairs of ribs.

float·stone (flōt′stōn′) *n.* **1** a stone used to smooth the surface of bricks used in curved work. **2** a whitish-gray spongy variety of opal, light enough to float.

FLIPPER

Flipper (def. 1)

floc·cu·lent (flok′yů lənt) *adj.* **1** like bits of wool. **2** made up of soft, woolly masses. **3** covered with a soft, woolly substance. [< L *floccus* tuft of wool]

hat, āge, cãre, fär; let, ēqual, tėrm; it, īce
hot, ōpen, ôrder; oil, out; cup, pu̇t, rüle, ūse
əbove, takən, pencəl, lemən, circəs
ch, child; ng, long; sh, ship
th, thin; ᴛʜ, then; zh, measure

flock[1] (flok) *n.* **1** animals of one kind that feed and move about in a group, especially sheep, goats, or birds. **2** a large group; crowd. **3** people of the same church group; band; company. —*v.* go or gather in a flock; come crowding: *The children flocked around the Christmas tree.* [OE *flocc*] —**Syn.** *n.* **1** herd, drove.

flock[2] (flok) *n.* **1** a tuft of wool. **2** waste wool or cotton used to stuff mattresses and cushions. **3** finely powdered wool or cloth used in making wallpaper. —*v.* **1** stuff with flock. **2** cover or coat with flock. [ME < OF *floc* < L *floccus*]

floe (flō) *n.* **1** a field or sheet of floating ice. **2** a floating piece broken off from such a field or sheet. [? < Norwegian *flo*]

flog (flog) *v.* **flogged, flog·ging.** whip very hard; beat with a whip, stick, etc. [? English school slang for L *flagellare* whip] —**flog′ger,** *n.*

flood (flud) *n.* **1** a flow of water over what is usually dry land. **2** *Poetic.* a large amount of water; ocean; sea; lake; river. **3** a great outpouring of anything: *a flood of light, a flood of words.* **4** a flowing of the tide toward the shore; rise of the tide. **5 in flood,** filled to overflowing with an unusual amount of water: *The river was in flood.* **6 the Flood,** in the Bible, the water that deluged the earth in the time of Noah. Gen. 7.
—*v.* **1** flow over or into: *When the snows melted last spring, the river rose and flooded our fields.* **2** fill much fuller than usual. **3** become covered or filled with water: *During the thunderstorm, our cellar flooded.* **4** cover the surface of something with water: *The attendants flooded the ice before every hockey game.* **5** pour out or stream like a flood: *Sunlight flooded into the room.* **6** fill, cover, or overcome like a flood: *The rich man was flooded with requests for money.* **7** flow like a flood. **8** cause or allow too much fuel into (a carburetor) so that it fails to start; receive too much fuel into the carburetor. [OE *flōd*] —**flood′er,** *n.*

Syn. *n.* **1 Flood, deluge, inundation** = a great flow of water. **Flood** applies particularly to a great flow of water over land usually dry, caused by the rising and overflowing of a river or other body of water: *Floods followed the melting of mountain snow.* **Deluge** applies to a great flood that washes away everything in its path, or, sometimes, to a heavy, continuous rain that causes a flood: *Livestock drowned in the deluge.* **Inundation,** formal, means an overflow covering everything around: *Crops were destroyed by the inundation of the fields.*

flood control the control of floods and the prevention of damage caused by them, by means of dams, levees, dikes, extra outlets, reforestation, etc.

flood·gate (flud′gāt′) *n.* **1** a gate in a canal, river, stream, etc. to control the flow of water. **2** something that controls any flow or passage.

flood·light (flud′līt′) *n. v.* **-light·ed** or **-lit, -light·ing.** —*n.* **1** a lamp that gives a broad beam of light: *Several floodlights were used to illuminate the stage.* **2** the broad beam of light from such a lamp. —*v.* illuminate with floodlights.

flood plain a plain bordering a river and made of soil deposited by floods.

flood tide the flowing of the tide toward the shore; the rise of the tide.

floor (flôr) *n.* **1** the inside bottom covering of a room. **2** a storey of a building. **3** a flat surface at the bottom of anything. **4** the part of a room or hall where members of a lawmaking body, etc. sit and from which they speak: *the floor of the House of Commons.* **5** the right or privilege to speak in a lawmaking body, etc.: *The chairman decides who has the floor.* **6** the main part of an exchange, where buying and selling of stocks, bonds, etc. is done. **7** *Informal.* of prices, amounts, etc., the lowest level. **8** in mining, an underlying stratum on which a seam of coal, etc. lies.
—*v.* **1** put a floor in or over. **2** knock down. **3** *Informal.*

defeat. **4** *Informal.* confuse or puzzle completely: *The last question on the exam floored us all.* **5** place upon a floor; base. [OE *flōr*] —**floor′er,** *n.*

floor·board (flôr′bôrd′) *n.* **1** one of the strips of wood used in a wooden floor. **2** Usually, **floorboards,** *pl.* the floor of an automobile.

floor hockey an indoor hockey game, using hooked sticks and a ball.

floor·ing (flôr′ing) *n.* **1** a floor. **2** floors collectively. **3** material for making floors.

floor price a minimum price set by the government on a commodity to protect the producer against sudden declines in price.

floor show an entertainment consisting of music, singing, dancing, etc. presented at a night club, hotel, etc.

floor·walk·er (flôr′wok′ər or -wôk′ər) *n.* a person employed in a large store to oversee sales, direct customers, etc.

flooz·ie or **flooz·y** (flü′zē) *n.* **flooz·ies.** *Slang.* a woman or girl, especially one of loose morals, such as a prostitute. [? variant of *Flossie,* a nickname for *Florence,* a woman's name]

flop (flop) *v.* **flopped, flop·ping,** *n.* —*v.* **1** move loosely or heavily; flap around clumsily: *The fish flopped helplessly on the deck.* **2** fall, drop, throw, or move heavily or clumsily: *He flopped down into a chair.* **3** change or turn suddenly. **4** *Informal.* fail.
—*n.* **1** a flopping. **2** the sound made by flopping. **3** *Informal.* a failure: *The new play was a flop.* [imitative var. of *flap*] —**flop′per,** *n.*

flop·house (flop′hous′) *n.* a cheap, run-down hotel or rooming house, especially one used by down-and-outs, etc.

flop·py (flop′ē) *adj.* **-pi·er, -pi·est.** *Informal.* flopping; tending to flop. —**flop′pi·ly,** *adv.* —**flop′pi·ness,** *n.*

flo·ra (flô′rə) *n.* **1** the plants of a particular region or time: *the flora of the West Indies.* **2** a work that systematically describes such plants. [< L]

Flo·ra (flô′rə) *n.* in Roman mythology, the goddess of flowers and spring.

flo·ral (flô′rəl) *adj.* **1** of flowers; having to do with flowers. **2** resembling flowers.

floral envelope in botany, the floral leaves (petals or sepals, or both) of a flower, collectively.

Flor·ence flask (flôr′əns) **1** a thin glass bottle with a long neck, usually covered with straw or something similar, for holding olive oil or wine. **2** a bottle of this shape used in a laboratory for heating chemicals.

Flor·en·tine (flôr′ən tēn′) *adj.* of or having to do with Florence, a city in Italy. —*n.* **1** a native or inhabitant of Florence. **2 florentine,** a twilled silk cloth, used for wearing apparel.

flo·res·cence (flô res′əns) *n.* **1** the act of blossoming. **2** the condition of blossoming. **3** the period of blossoming. [< NL *florescentia,* ult. < L *florere* flourish]

flo·res·cent (flô res′ənt) *adj.* blossoming.

flo·ret (flô′rit) *n.* **1** a small flower. **2** in botany, one of the small flowers in a flower head of a composite plant, such as an aster. [< OF *florete,* dim. of *flor* flower < L *flos, floris*]

flor·i·bun·da (flôr′ə bun′də) *n.* a low-growing hybrid rose having abundant blossoms. [< NL *floribunda* < L *flos, floris* flower]

flor·id (flôr′id) *adj.* **1** highly colored; ruddy: *a florid complexion.* **2** elaborately ornamented; flowery; showy; ornate. [< L *floridus* < *flos, floris* flower] —**flor′id·ly,** *adv.* —**flor′id·ness,** *n.*

flor·in (flôr′ən) *n.* **1** a former British coin worth two shillings. **2** a gold coin issued at Florence in 1252. **3** any of various gold or silver coins used in different countries of Europe since then. [< F < Ital. *fiorino* a Florentine coin marked with a lily < *fiore* flower < L *flos, floris*]

flo·rist (flô′rist) *n.* a person who raises or sells flowers.

floss (flos) *n.* **1** short, loose silk fibres. **2** a shiny, untwisted silk thread made from such fibres. Floss is used for embroidery. Waxed floss is used for cleaning between the teeth. **3** soft, silky fluff or fibres. Milkweed pods contain white floss. [apparently related to FLEECE]

floss·y (flos′ē) *adj.* **floss·i·er, floss·i·est.** **1** of floss. **2** like floss. **3** *Informal.* fancy; glamorous; highly decorated.

flo·ta·tion (flō tā′shən) *n.* **1** a floating or launching. **2** a getting started or established. **3** a selling or putting on sale. [var. of *floatation* < *float,* v.]

flo·til·la (flō til′ə) *n.* **1** a small fleet. **2** a fleet of small ships. [< Sp., dim. of *flota* fleet < F < ON *floti* fleet]

flot·sam (flot′səm) *n.* **1** the wreckage of a ship or its cargo found floating on the sea. **2 flotsam and jetsam, a** wreckage or cargo found floating on the sea or washed ashore. **b** odds and ends; useless things. **c** people without steady work or permanent homes. [< AF *floteson* < *floter* float. Akin to FLOAT.]

flounce[1] (flouns) *v.* **flounced, flounc·ing,** *n.* —*v.* **1** go with an angry or impatient fling of the body: *She flounced out of the room in a rage.* **2** twist; turn; jerk.
—*n.* **1** an angry or impatient fling of the body. **2** a twist; turn; jerk. [? < Scand.; cf. Swedish *flunsa* plunge]

flounce[2] (flouns) *n. v.* **flounced, flounc·ing.** —*n.* a wide strip of cloth, gathered along the top edge and sewed to a dress, skirt, etc. as trimming; a wide ruffle. —*v.* trim with a flounce or flounces. [var. of *frounce* < OF *fronce* wrinkle < Gmc.]

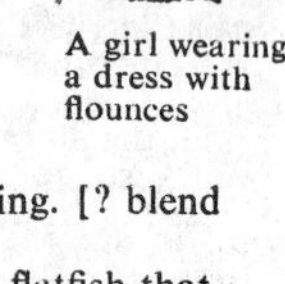
A girl wearing a dress with flounces

flounc·ing (floun′sing) *n.* **1** fabric for flounces. **2** a flounce or flounces.

floun·der[1] (floun′dər) *v.* **1** struggle awkwardly without making much progress; plunge about: *Men and horses were floundering in the deep snowdrifts.* **2** be clumsy or confused and make mistakes: *The frightened girl could only flounder through her song.* —*n.* a floundering. [? blend of *founder*[1] and *blunder*]

floun·der[2] (floun′dər) *n.* **-der** or **-ders.** a flatfish that has a large mouth. [< AF *floundre* < Scand.; cf. Swedish *flundra*]

flour (flour) *n.* **1** a fine, powdery substance made by grinding and sifting wheat or other grain. **2** any fine soft powder. —*v.* **1** cover with flour. **2** grind and sift (grain) into flour. [special use of *flower;* i.e., the flower (best) of the meal]

flour·ish (flėr′ish) *v.* **1** grow or develop with vigor; thrive; do well. **2** be in the best time of life or activity. **3** wave (a sword, stick, arm, etc.) in the air. **4** make a showy display.
—*n.* **1** a waving in the air. **2** a showy decoration in handwriting. **3** in music, a showy trill or passage: *a flourish of trumpets.* **4** a showy display of enthusiasm, heartiness, etc. **5** an expression used for effect in speech or writing. **6** the state of being in the best time of life: *in full flourish.* [ME < OF *floriss-,* a stem of *florir* < L *florere* bloom < *flos, floris* flower] —**flour′ish·ing·ly,** *adv.* —**Syn.** *v.* **1** succeed, prosper. **3** brandish.

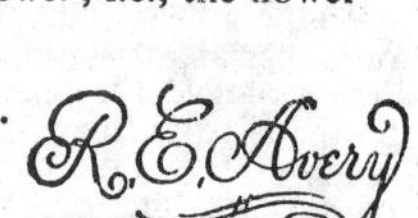

Flourishes in handwriting

flour mill **1** a machine for grinding wheat or other grain into flour. **2** a place or establishment where there is such a machine or machines.

flour·y (flour′ē) *adj.* **1** of or like flour. **2** covered or white with flour.

flout (flout) *v.* **1** treat with contempt or scorn; mock; scoff at: *The disobedient boy flouted his mother's advice.* **2** show contempt or scorn; scoff. —*n.* a contemptuous speech or act; insult; mockery; scoffing. [var. of *flute,* v.] —**flout′er,** *n.* —**flout′ing·ly,** *adv.* —**Syn.** *v.* **1** taunt. **2** jeer.

flow (flō) *v.* **1** run like water; move in a current or stream. **2** pour out; pour along. **3** move easily or smoothly; glide. **4** hang loosely and waving. **5** be plentiful; be full and overflowing. **6** flow in; rise.
—*n.* **1** the act or way of flowing. **2** any continuous movement like that of water in a river: *a rapid flow of speech.* **3** the rate of flowing. **4** something that flows; current; stream. **5** the flowing of the tide toward the shore; rise of the tide. **6** in physics, the directional

movement in a current or stream that is a characteristic of all fluids as air or electricity. [OE *flōwan*]
Syn. *v.* **1, 2 Flow, gush, stream** = run or pour out or along. **Flow** emphasizes the continuous forward movement of running or pouring water, whether fast or slow, in great or small quantity: *Water flowed in the streets.* **Gush** = rush out or flow forth suddenly in considerable quantity from an opening: *Oil gushed from the new well.* **Stream** = pour forth steadily from a source or flow steadily, always in the same direction: *Tears streamed from her eyes.*

flow·age (flō′ij) *n.* **1** a flowing or flooding. **2** the state of being flooded. **3** the liquid that flows or floods. **4** the rate at which a liquid flows or floods. **5** in physics, the gradual structural alteration of a solid, such as asphalt, by intermolecular movement.

flow·er (flou′ər) *n.* **1** the part of a plant that produces the seed; blossom. A flower is a shortened branch with modified leaves called petals. **2** a plant grown for its blossoms. **3** any of several kinds of reproductive structures in lower plants, such as the mosses. **4** the finest part: *The flower of England's manhood was killed in the war.* **5** the time of being at one's best. **6** an ornament representing a flower; ornament; adornment: *A diamond flower glittered in her hair.* **7 flowers,** *pl.* a chemical substance in the form of a fine powder. **8 in flower,** flowering. **9 in full flower,** at the peak of attainment.
—*v.* **1** have flowers; produce flowers. **2** cover or decorate with flowers. **3** cause to blossom or bloom. **4** be at one's best. [ME < OF *flour* < L *flos, floris*] —**flow′er·er** *n.* —**flow′er·less,** *adj.* —**flow′er·like′,** *adj.*

flow·ered (flou′ərd) *adj.* **1** having flowers. **2** covered or decorated with flowers.

flow·er·et (flou′ər it) *n.* **1** a small flower. **2** a floret.

flow·er·ing (flou′ər ing) *adj.* having flowers.

flow·er·pot (flou′ər pot′) *n.* a pot to hold earth for a plant to grow in.

flow·er·y (flou′ər ē) *adj.* **-er·i·er, -er·i·est. 1** having many flowers. **2** containing many fine words and fanciful expressions. —**flow′er·i·ly,** *adv.* —**flow′er·i·ness,** *n.*

flow·ing (flō′ing) *adj.* **1** moving in a current or stream: *flowing water.* **2** moving easily or smoothly: *flowing words.* **3** hanging loosely: *flowing robes.* —**flow′ing·ly,** *adv.* —**flow′ing·ness,** *n.*

flow·me·ter (flō′mē′tər) *n.* any apparatus designed to measure and record the rate of flow of a liquid or gas.

flown (flōn) *v.* pp. of **fly**[2].

FLQ or **F.L.Q.** Front de Libération du Québec.

Flt.Lt. Flight Lieutenant.

Flt.Sgt. Flight Sergeant.

flu (flü) *n. Informal.* influenza.

flub (flub) *v.* **flubbed, flub·bing,** *n.* —*v.* do (something) very clumsily; make a mess of. —*n.* a failure in performance; botch; mistake; error.

fluc·tu·ate (fluk′chü āt′) *v.* **-at·ed, -at·ing. 1** rise and fall: change continually; vary irregularly: *The temperature fluctuates from day to day.* **2** move in waves. [< L *fluctuare* < *fluctus* wave] —**Syn. 1** oscillate, vacillate.

fluc·tu·a·tion (fluk′chü ā′shən) *n.* **1** a rising and falling; continual change; irregular variation. **2** a wavelike motion.

flue (flü) *n.* **1** a tube, pipe, or other enclosed passage for conveying smoke, hot air, etc.: *Our chimney has several flues.* **2** in an organ, a flue pipe. **3** the air passage in such a pipe. [origin uncertain]

flue·cured (flü′kūrd′) *adj.* of tobacco, cured by being hung for several days in a place heated through flues, without smoke.

flu·en·cy (flü′ən sē) *n.* **1** a smooth, easy flow: *The orator had great fluency of speech.* **2** easy, rapid speaking or writing.

flu·ent (flü′ənt) *adj.* **1** flowing smoothly or easily: *Long practice had enabled the traveller to speak fluent French.* **2** speaking or writing easily and rapidly. **3** not fixed or stable; fluid. [< L *fluens, -entis,* ppr. of *fluere* flow] —**flu′ent·ly,** *adv.*
Syn. 2 Fluent, glib, voluble = speaking easily. **Fluent** suggests being ready, either because properly prepared or because willing or eager, and therefore speaking or writing easily and rapidly: *He is a fluent lecturer.* **Glib** = speaking too easily and smoothly, suggests lack of sincerity behind the words or superficial talk: *He is a glib liar.* **Voluble** = speaking fluently and continuously, often suggesting an uncheckable flood of words: *Detained by my voluble friend, I was late.*

hat, āge, cãre, fär; let, ēqual, tėrm; it, īce
hot, ōpen, ôrder; oil, out; cup, pu̇t, rüle, ūse
əbove, takən, pencəl, lemən, circəs
ch, child; ng, long; sh, ship
th, thin; ᴛʜ, then; zh, measure

flue pipe in an organ, a pipe in which the sound is made by a current of air striking its mouth or opening.

fluff (fluf) *n.* **1** soft, light, downy particles: *Woollen blankets often have fluff on them.* **2** a soft, light, downy mass: *The little kitten looked like a ball of fluff.* **3** *Slang.* a mistake in reading, speaking, etc. on the stage or on radio or television.
—*v.* **1** shake or puff out (hair, feathers, etc.) into a soft, light, downy mass. **2** become fluffy. **3** move or float softly like fluff. **4** *Slang.* make a mistake in reading one's lines, etc. [apparently var. of *flue* downy matter (? OE *flug-* in *flugol* fleeting, related to *flēogan* to fly); influenced by *puff*]

fluff·y (fluf′ē) *adj.* **fluff·i·er, fluff·i·est. 1** soft and light like fluff: *Whipped cream is fluffy.* **2** covered with fluff; downy: *fluffy baby chicks.* —**fluff′i·ly,** *adv.* —**fluff′i·ness,** *n.*

flü·gel·horn or **flu·gel·horn** (flü′gəl hôrn′) *n.* one of several brass wind instruments similar in design to a cornet but having a more mellow tone. [< G *Flügelhorn* < *Flügel* wing + *Horn* horn]

flu·id (flü′id) *n.* any liquid or gas; any substance that flows: *Water, mercury, air, and oxygen are fluids.*
—*adj.* **1** in the state of a fluid; like a fluid; flowing. **2** of or having to do with fluids. **3** changing easily; not fixed. [< L *fluidus* < *fluere* flow] —**flu′id·ly,** *adv.* —**flu′id·ness,** *n.* —**Syn.** *n.* See **liquid.**

fluid dram one-eighth of a fluid ounce.

flu·id·i·ty (flü id′ə tē) *n.* a fluid condition or quality.

fluid ounce a measure for liquids. In Canada, 20 fluid ounces = 1 pint.

fluke[1] (flük) *n.* **1** either of the two triangular points of an anchor that catch in the ground. **2** the barbed head or barb of an arrow, harpoon, etc. **3** either half of a whale's tail. [? special use of *fluke*[3]]

An anchor showing flukes (def. 1)

fluke[2] (flük) *n. v.* **fluked, fluk·ing.** *Informal.* —*n.* **1** in billiards or pool, a lucky shot. **2** a lucky chance; fortunate accident. —*v.* **1** in billiards or pool, make or hit by a lucky shot. **2** get by chance or accident. [origin uncertain]

fluke[3] (flük) *n.* **1** a flatfish. **2** a parasitic flatworm shaped like a flatfish; trematode. [OE *flōc*]

fluk·ey or **fluk·y** (flük′ē) *adj.* **fluk·i·er, fluk·i·est.** *Informal.* **1** obtained by chance rather than by skill. **2** uncertain: *flukey weather.*

flume (flüm) *n.* **1** a deep, narrow valley with a stream running through it. **2** a large, inclined trough or chute for carrying water. Flumes are used to transport logs and to furnish water for power or irrigation. [ME < OF *flum* < L *flumen* river < *fluere* flow]

flum·mer·y (flum′ər ē) *n.* **-mer·ies. 1** pudding made of milk, eggs, flour, sugar, etc. **2** an empty compliment; empty trifling; nonsense. [< Welsh *llymru*]

flum·mox (flum′əks) *v. Informal.* confuse; bewilder; confound. [? < dial. *flummocks* to maul, mangle] —**flum′mox·er,** *n.*

flung (flung) *v.* pt. and pp. of **fling.**

flunk (flungk) *Informal. v.* **1** fail in school work: *He flunked his chemistry examination but passed all the others.* **2** cause to fail. **3** mark or grade as having failed. **4** give up; back out. **5 flunk out,** dismiss or be dismissed from school, college, etc. because of inferior work. —*n.* a failure. [origin uncertain]

flunk·ey (flungk′ē) *n.* **-eys. 1** a man servant who wears livery; footman. **2** a flattering, fawning person. **3** *Dialect.* a farm hand; cook's assistant. Also, **flunky.** [? alteration of *flanker* one posted on the flank of a person or group < *flank*, v. < *flank*, n. < OF *flanc* < Gmc.]

flunk·y (flungk′ē) *n.* **flunk·ies.** flunkey.

flu·or (flü′ôr) *n.* fluorite. [< L *fluor* a flowing < *fluere* flow]

flu·o·resce (flü′ə res′) *v.* **-resced, -resc·ing.** give off light by fluorescence. [< *fluorescence*]

flu·o·res·cence (flü′ə res′əns) *n.* **1** a giving off of light from a substance while exposed to certain rays (X rays and ultraviolet rays). **2** the property of a substance that causes this. Fluorescence is an ability to transform light so as to emit rays of a different wave length or color. **3** the light given off in this way. [< *fluor* (*spar*) + *-escence*, as in *phosphorescence*]

flu·o·res·cent (flü′ə res′ənt) *adj.* that gives off light by fluorescence. Fluorescent substances glow in the dark when exposed to X rays.

fluorescent lamp a type of electric lamp, usually a cathode-ray tube containing a gas or vapor that produces light **(fluorescent light)** when acted on by an electric current.

flu·or·ic (flü ôr′ik) *adj.* of, having to do with, or obtained from fluorite or fluorine.

flu·o·rid (flü′ə rid) *n.* fluoride.

fluor·i·date (flůr′ə dāt′ or flü′ə rə dāt′) *v.* **-dat·ed, -dat·ing.** add small amounts of a fluoride to drinking water, especially to prevent tooth decay in children. [back formation < *fluoridation*]

fluor·i·da·tion (flůr′ə dā′shən or flü′ə rə dā′shən) *n.* the act or process of fluoridating. [< *fluoride*]

flu·o·ride (flü′ə rīd′ or flü′ə rid′) *n.* a compound of fluorine and another element or radical.

flu·o·rin (flü′ə rin) *n.* fluorine.

flu·o·rine (flü′ə rēn′ or flü′ə rin) *n.* a poisonous, greenish-yellow gaseous chemical element similar to chlorine. *Symbol*: F or Fl; *at.no.* 9; *at.wt.* 18.9984. [< *fluor*(*ite*); because found in *fluorite*]

flu·o·rite (flü′ə rīt′) *n.* a transparent, crystalline mineral that occurs in many colors; calcium fluoride. It is used for fusing metals, making glass, etc. *Formula*: CaF_2 [< *fluor*]

fluor·o·scope (flůr′ə skōp′ or flü′ə rə skōp′) *n.* a device containing a fluorescent screen for examining objects exposed to X rays or other radiations. The parts of the object not penetrated by the rays cast shadows on the screen. [< *fluor*(*escence*) + *-scope*]

fluor·o·scop·ic (flůr′ə skop′ik or flü′ə rə skop′ik) *adj.* of or having to do with the fluoroscope or with fluoroscopy. **—fluor′o·scop′i·cal·ly,** *adv.*

fluor·spar (flü′ər spär′) *n.* fluorite.

flur·ry (flėr′ē) *n.* **-ries,** *v.* **-ried, -ry·ing.** *—n.* **1** a sudden gust of wind: *A flurry upset the small sailboat.* **2** a light fall of snow or, less usually, rain: *snow flurries.* **3** a sudden excitement, confusion, or disturbance.
—v. excite; confuse; disturb: *Noise in the audience flurried the actor so that he forgot his lines.* [? blend of *flutter* and *hurry*]

flush[1] (flush) *v.* **1** blush; glow. **2** cause to blush or glow: *Exercise flushed his face.* **3** rush suddenly; flow rapidly: *Embarrassment caused the blood to flush to her cheeks.* **4** wash or cleanse with a rapid flow of water: *The city streets were flushed every night.* **5** empty out; drain: *flush water from flooded land.* **6** make joyful and proud; excite: *The team was flushed with its first victory.* **7** of a plant, send out shoots.
—n. **1** a blush; glow. **2** a sudden rush; rapid flow. **3** an excited condition or feeling; sudden rush of joyous pride, etc. **4** a sudden, fresh growth: *April brought the first flush of grass.* **5** glowing vigor; freshness: *the first flush of youth.* **6** a fit of feeling very hot. [? blend of *flash* and *blush*]

flush[2] (flush) *adj.* **1** even; level: *The edge of the new shelf must be flush with the old one.* **2** well supplied; having plenty: *The rich man was always flush with money.* **3** abundant; plentiful: *Money is flush when times are good.* **4** liberal; lavish. **5** prosperous. **6** glowing; ruddy. **7** direct; square.
—adv. **1** so as to be level; evenly. **2** directly; squarely: *The fighter hit him flush on the nose.*
—v. make even; level. [? extended use of *flush*[1]]

flush[3] (flush) *v.* **1** fly or start up suddenly. **2** cause to fly or start up suddenly: *The hunter's dog flushed a partridge in the woods.* [origin uncertain] **—flush′er,** *n.*

flush[4] (flush) *n.* in cards, a hand all of one suit. [< OF *flus, flux* < L *fluxus* flow]

flus·ter (flus′tər) *v.* make nervous and excited; confuse.
—n. nervous excitement; confusion. [< Scand.; cf. Icelandic *flaustr* bustle and *flaustra* be flustered]

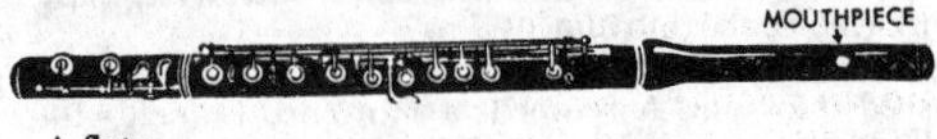

A flute

flute (flüt) *n. v.* **flut·ed, flut·ing.** *—n.* **1** a long, slender musical instrument, played by blowing across a hole near one end. Different notes are made on a flute by opening and closing holes along the tube with the fingers or with keys. **2** a long, rounded groove. Some pillars have flutes.
—v. **1** play on a flute. **2** sing or whistle so as to sound like a flute. **3** make long, rounded grooves in. [ME < OF *fleüte, flaüte* < Provençal *flauta*, ult. < L *flatus* pp. of *flare* blow] **—flute′like′,** *adj.*

flut·ing (flüt′ing) *n.* a type of decoration consisting of long, round grooves.

Fluting

flut·ist (flüt′ist) *n.* a person who plays a flute. Also, **flautist.**

flut·ter (flut′ər) *v.* **1** wave back and forth quickly and lightly. **2** flap the wings; flap. **3** come or go with a fluttering motion. **4** move about restlessly; flit. **5** be in a state of excitement: *The crowd fluttered with expectation.* **6** beat feebly and irregularly: *Her pulse fluttered.* **7** confuse, excite.
—n. **1** a fluttering. **2** a confused or excited condition: *The appearance of the Queen caused a great flutter in the crowd.* **3** unstable vibration of some part of an aircraft: *wing flutter.* **4** in high-fidelity sound reproduction, a change in pitch caused by variations in the speed of a record turntable or reel of tape. Also, **flitter.** [ME *floteren* < OE *flotorian* < *flēotan* float. Related to FLEET[1].] **—flut′ter·er,** *n.* **—flut′ter·ing·ly,** *adv.*
—Syn. *v.* **3** hover, flicker, flit.

flu·vi·al (flü′vē əl) *adj.* of, found in, or produced by a river: *A delta is a fluvial deposit.* [< L *fluvialis* < *fluvius* river]

flux (fluks) *n.* **1** a flow; flowing. **2** a flowing in of the tide. **3** continuous change: *New words and meanings keep the English language in a state of flux.* **4** an unnatural discharge of blood or liquid matter from the body. **5** a substance used to help metals or minerals fuse together: *Rosin is used as a flux in soldering.* **6** the rate of flow of a fluid, heat, etc. across a certain surface or area.
—v. **1** cause an unnatural discharge of blood or liquid matter in; purge. **2** fuse together. **3** heat with a substance that helps metals or minerals fuse together. [< L *fluxus* < *fluere* flow]

flux·ion (fluk′shən) *n.* **1** a flowing; flow. **2** a discharge. **3** in mathematics, the rate of change of a continuously varying quantity; differential.

fly[1] (flī) *n.* **flies. 1** a housefly. **2** any of a large group of insects that have two wings, including houseflies, mosquitoes, gnats, etc. **3** any insect having transparent wings, such as a May fly. **4** a fish-hook with feathers, silk, tinsel, etc. on it to make it look like an insect: *Some fishermen make their own flies.* **5 fly in the ointment,** a small thing that spoils something else or lessens its value. [OE *flēoge* < *flēogan* fly[2]]

fly[2] (flī) *v.* **flew, flown, fly·ing** *for 1-12, 14-18*; **flied, fly·ing** *for 13*; *n.* **flies.** *—v.* **1** move through the air with wings. **2** float or wave in the air. **3** cause to float or wave in the air: *fly a kite.* **4** travel through the air in an aircraft. **5** manage an aircraft: *The pilot has to fly long hours.* **6** move through the air in bits or shreds: *The bottle flew into a thousand pieces.* **7 a** hunt with a falcon. **b** attack by flying, as a hawk does. **8** travel over in an aircraft. **9** manage (an aircraft). **10** carry in an aircraft. **11** move swiftly; go rapidly. **12** run away; flee; flee from; shun. **13** in baseball, hit a ball high into the air with a bat.

14 fly at, attack violently. **15 fly in the face of,** disobey openly; defy. **16 fly off,** leave suddenly; break away. **17 fly off the handle,** get very excited. **18 fly up,** be promoted from Brownie to Girl Guide. **19 let fly, a** aim; shoot; throw: *The hunter let fly an arrow.* **b** say violently. —*n.* **1** a flap or opening in a garment, especially in the front of trousers. **2** a piece of canvas that serves as an extra, outer flap or roof for a tent. **3** in baseball, a ball hit high into the air with a bat. **4 flies,** *pl.* in a theatre, the space above a stage. **5 on the fly,** while still in the air: before touching the ground. [OE *flēogan*] —**Syn.** *v.* **12** abscond.

fly·a·way (flī′ə wā′) *adj.* **1** fluttering; streaming. **2** frivolous; flighty. **3** produced and packaged for shipment by air: *flyaway supplies.*

fly·blown (flī′blōn′) *adj.* **1** tainted by the eggs or larvae of flies. **2** spoiled. **3** covered with fly specks.

fly-by-night (flī′bī nīt′) *adj.* not reliable; not to be trusted. —*n. Informal.* **1** a person who avoids paying his debts by leaving secretly at night. **2** an unreliable or irresponsible person.

fly·catch·er (flī′kach′ər) *n.* any of a family of songless perching birds having small, weak feet, short necks, and large heads with broad, flattened bills hooked at the tip. The kingbird, phoebe, and crested flycatcher are common types of flycatcher.

fly·er or **fli·er** (flī′ər) *n.* **1** a person or thing that flies. **2** an aviator. **3** a very fast train, ship, bus, etc. **4** *Slang.* a reckless financial venture. **5** *Informal.* a try; an experimental venture into something. **6** a small handbill, used for advertising. **7** one step of a straight flight of stairs.

fly-fish (flī′fish′) *v.* fish with flies, natural or artificial, as bait.

fly-fish·ing (flī′fish′ing) *n.* fishing with natural or artificial flies as bait.

fly-in (flī′in′) *adj.* designed for flying into; having landing facilities: *a fly-in fishing camp.*

fly-in camp *Cdn.* a fishing or hunting camp that is accessible only by airplane.

fly·ing (flī′ing) *adj.* **1** that flies; moving through the air. **2** floating or waving in the air. **3** swift. **4** short and quick; hasty: *Aunt Mary paid us a flying visit last week.* **5** of cattle brands, wavy.

flying boat a type of seaplane having a boatlike hull.

flying buttress an arched support or brace built against the wall of a building to resist outward pressure. See **buttress** for picture.

flying colors or **colours** success; victory: *He passed all the tests with flying colors.*

Flying Dutchman **1** a legendary Dutch sea captain condemned to sail the seas until the day of judgment. **2** his ghostlike ship, supposed to appear at sea and to be a bad omen.

flying fish a tropical sea fish that has winglike pectoral fins which help it to glide for some distance through the air after leaping from the water.

flying jib a small, triangular sail set in front of the regular jib.

flying machine aircraft.

flying officer **1** in the air force, a commissioned officer senior to a pilot officer and junior to a flight lieutenant. **2** an officer of similar rank. *Abbrev.*: F.O. or F/O

flying saucer or **disk** a disklike object that some people claim to have seen flying in the sky at great speed over various parts of the world.

flying spot in television, a moving beam of light that produces a succession of thin lines against a surface containing an image. The areas of lightness and darkness are electronically picked up and transmitted to receiving sets where the image is reproduced.

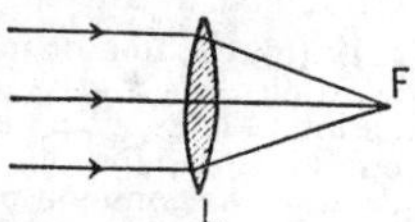

Rays of light brought to a focus at F by the lens, L

flying squirrel a squirrel that can make long, gliding leaps through the air. Its front and hind legs are connected by winglike folds of skin.

flying wing **1** in rugby football, a player whose position is variable behind the line of scrimmage: *There is no flying wing on American football teams.* **2** a type of airplane in which the motors, fuselage, etc. are inside the wing structure.

hat, āge, cãre, fär; let, ēqual, tėrm; it, īce
hot, ōpen, ôrder; oil, out; cup, pu̇t, rüle, ūse
əbove, takən, pencəl, lemən, circəs
ch, child; ng, long; sh, ship
th, thin; ᴛʜ, then; zh, measure

fly·leaf (flī′lēf′) *n.* **-leaves.** a blank sheet of paper at the beginning or end of a book, pamphlet, etc.

fly·man (flī′mən) *n.* **-men** (-mən). in the theatre, a stagehand who works in the flies above the stage.

fly·o·ver (flī′ō′vər) *n.* **1** flypast. **2** *Esp.Brit.* a highway overpass.

fly·pa·per (flī′pā′pər) *n.* a paper coated with a sticky substance to catch flies.

fly·past (flī′past′) *n.* an air-force display in which aircraft in formation fly over a reviewing stand located on the ground: *We enjoyed the flypast at the air show.*

fly specks the tiny, dark spots left by flies on windows, light bulbs, etc.; fly dung.

fly swatter a device for killing flies, usually consisting of a long wooden or wire handle to which is attached a broad, flat piece of perforated rubber, plastic, etc.

fly·trap (flī′trap′) *n.* **1** a plant that traps insects. **2** a trap to catch flies.

fly-up (flī′up′) *n.* a ceremony at which Brownies are promoted to Girl Guides.

fly·way (flī′wā′) *n.* a route usually followed by migrating birds.

fly·weight (flī′wāt′) *n.* a boxer who weighs not more than 112 pounds.

fly·wheel (flī′hwēl′ or -wēl′) *n.* a heavy wheel attached to machinery to keep the speed even.

fm. fathom.

Fm fermium.

FM, F.M., or **f.m.** frequency modulation.

F.M. Field-Marshal.

f number in photography, the number obtained by dividing the focal length of a lens by its effective diameter.

foal (fōl) *n.* **1** a young horse, donkey, etc.; colt or filly. **2 in** or **with foal,** of a mare, pregnant. —*v.* give birth to (a foal). [OE *fola*]

foam (fōm) *n.* **1** a mass of very small bubbles. **2** a frothy mass formed in the mouth as saliva or on the skin of animals as sweat: *The dog with foam around its mouth is suffering from rabies.* **3** a spongy, flexible material made from plastics, rubber, etc.
—*v.* **1** form or gather foam. **2** cause to foam. **3** break into foam: *The stream foams over the rocks.* **4** cover with foam. **5 foam at the mouth,** be greatly enraged. [OE *fām*] —**foam′less,** *adj.* —**foam′like′,** *adj.*

foam rubber a firm, spongy foam of natural or synthetic rubber, used especially for mattresses and upholstery.

foam·y (fōm′ē) *adj.* **foam·i·er, foam·i·est. 1** covered with foam; foaming. **2** made of foam. **3** like foam. —**foam′i·ly,** *adv.* —**foam′i·ness,** *n.*

fob[1] (fob) *n.* **1** a small pocket in trousers to hold a watch, etc. **2** a short watch chain, ribbon, etc. that hangs out of a watch pocket. **3** an ornament worn at the end of such a chain, ribbon, etc. [cf. dial. HG *fuppe* pocket]

fob[2] (fob) *v.* **fobbed, fob·bing,** *n.* —*v.* **1** trick; deceive; cheat. **2 fob off, a** put off or deceive by a trick. **b** palm off or get rid of by a trick. —*n.* a trick. [? extended use of *fob*[1]]

f.o.b. or **F.O.B.** free on board.

fo·cal (fō′kəl) *adj.* of a focus; having to do with a focus. The **focal length** of a lens is the distance of its focus from the optical centre of the lens.

fo·cal·ize (fō′kəl īz′) *v.* **-ized, -iz·ing. 1** focus. **2** bring or come into focus. —**fo′cal·i·za′tion,** *n.*

fo·ci (fō′sī or fō′sē) *n.* a pl. of **focus.** focuses.

fo·cus (fō′ kəs) *n.* **-cus·es** or **-ci,** *v.* **-cus·ses** or **-cus·es, -cussed** or **-cused, -cus·sing** or **-cus·ing.** —*n.* **1** a point where rays of light, heat, etc. meet, appear to meet, or should meet after being bent by a lens, curved mirror, etc. See picture on the previous page. **2** the distance of this point from the lens, curved mirror, etc.; focal distance: *A near-sighted eye has a shorter focus than a normal eye.* **3** the correct adjustment of a lens, the eye, etc. to make a clear image: *If my camera is not brought into focus, the photograph will be blurred.* **4** the central point of attention, activity, disturbance, etc.: *The focus of a disease is the part of the body where it is most active.* **5** in geometry: **a** either of two fixed points used in determining an ellipse. **b** a point used in determining some other curve. **6 in focus,** clear; distinct. **7 out of focus,** blurred; indistinct.
—*v.* **1** bring (rays of light, heat, etc.) to a point. **2** adjust (a lens, the eye, etc.) to make a clear image: *A near-sighted person cannot focus accurately on distant objects.* **3** make (an image, etc.) clear by adjusting a lens, the eye, etc. **4** concentrate: *When studying, he focussed his mind on his lessons.* [< L *focus* hearth] —**fo′cus·ser** or **fo′cus·er,** *n.*

fod·der (fod′ər) *n.* coarse food for horses, cattle, etc.: *Hay and cornstalks are fodder.* —*v.* give fodder to (horses, cattle, etc.). [OE *fōdor* < *fōda* food] —**Syn.** See **feed.**

foe (fō) *n.* an enemy. [OE *fāh* hostile] —**Syn.** See **enemy.**

foehn (fān; *German,* fœn) *n.* in meteorology, a warm, dry wind that blows down the slopes of a mountain and across a valley, especially in the Alps. Also, **föhn.** [< dial. G *föhn,* ult. < L *Favonius* the west wind]

foe·man (fō′ mən) *n.* **-men** (-mən). *Archaic.* an enemy.

foe·tal (fē′ təl) *adj.* fetal.

foe·tus (fē′ təs) *n.* fetus.

fog (fog) *n. v.* **fogged, fog·ging.** —*n.* **1** a cloud of fine drops of water that forms just above the earth's surface; thick mist. **2** a darkened condition; dim, blurred state. **3** a confused or puzzled condition.
—*v.* **1** cover with fog. **2** darken; dim; blur. **3** become covered or filled with fog. **4** confuse; puzzle. [< *foggy*]

fog bank a dense mass of fog.

fog·bound (fog′bound′) *adj.* kept from travelling, especially from sailing, by fog.

fo·gey (fō′ gē) *n.* **-geys.** one who is behind the times or lacks enterprise. Also, **fogy.** [origin uncertain]

fog·gy (fog′ē) *adj.* **-gi·er, -gi·est. 1** having much fog; misty. **2** not clear; dim; blurred: *His understanding of geography was rather foggy.* **3** confused; puzzled. [< *fog* long grass; originally, marshy] —**fog′gi·ly,** *adv.* —**fog′gi·ness,** *n.*

fog·horn (fog′hôrn′) *n.* **1** a horn that warns ships in foggy weather. **2** a loud, harsh voice.

fo·gy (fō′ gē) *n.* **-gies.** fogey.

foi·ble (foi′bəl) *n.* a weak point; a weakness in character: *Talking too much is one of her foibles.* [< F *foible,* older form of modern *faible* feeble] —**Syn.** failing, frailty.

foil[1] (foil) *v.* **1** prevent (someone) from carrying out (plans, attempts, etc.); get the better of; turn aside or hinder: *The hero foiled the villain.* **2** prevent (a scheme, plan, etc.) from being carried out or from succeeding. **3** spoil (a trace or scent) by crossing it. [< OF *fouler* trample, full (cloth) < VL *fullare* < L *fullo* a fuller; with reference to spoiling a trace or scent by crossing it] —**Syn.** frustrate.

foil[2] (foil) *n.* **1** metal beaten, hammered, or rolled into a very thin sheet: *tin foil, aluminum foil.* **2** anything that makes something else look or seem better by contrast. **3** a very thin layer of polished metal, placed under a gem to give it more color or sparkle. **4** in architecture, a leaflike ornament; arc or rounded space between cusps.
—*v.* **1** coat or back with foil. **2** set off by contrast. [ME < OF < L *folia* leaves]

foil[3] (foil) *n.* **1** a long, narrow sword with a knob or button on the point to prevent injury, used in fencing. **2 foils,** *pl.* fencing. [origin uncertain]

foist (foist) *v.* **1** palm off as genuine; impose slyly: *The dishonest shopkeeper foisted inferior goods on his customers.* **2** put in secretly or slyly: *The author discovered that the translator had foisted several passages into his book.* [probably < dial. Du. *vuisten* take in hand < *vuist* fist]

fol. 1 folio. **2** following.

fold[1] (fōld) *v.* **1** bend or double over on itself. **2** bring together with the parts in or around one another. **3** bring close to the body. **4** put the arms around and hold tenderly. **5** wrap; enclose. **6** *Informal.* bring or come to a halt; close up; terminate: *They folded the business after only two months and with great loss.* **7 fold in,** add to a mixture in cooking by gently turning one part over another with strokes of a spoon: *Fold in beaten egg whites.* **8 fold up, a** make or become smaller by folding. **b** break down; collapse. **c** *Informal.* fail.
—*n.* **1** a layer of something folded. **2** a hollow place made by folding. **3** something that is or can be folded. **4** the act or process of folding. **5** in geology, a bend in a layer of rock. [OE *fealdan*]

fold[2] (fōld) *n.* **1** a pen to keep sheep in. **2** sheep kept in a pen. **3** a church group; congregation; church. **4 return to the fold, a** return to active membership of one's church. **b** return to the place or group of people to which one naturally belongs.
—*v.* put or keep (sheep) in a pen. [OE *falod*]

-fold *suffix.* **1** times as many; times as great, as in *tenfold.* **2** formed or divided into —— parts, as in *manifold.* [OE *-feald.* Related to FOLD[1].]

fold·er (fōl′dər) *n.* **1** a person or thing that folds. **2** a holder for papers, made by folding a piece of cardboard. **3** a pamphlet made of one or more folded sheets.

fol·de·rol (fol′ də rol′) *n.* falderal.

folding doors doors having one part hinged to another so that they open and close by folding and unfolding.

folding money *Informal.* paper money, as opposed to coins.

fo·li·a·ceous (fō′lē ā′shəs) *adj.* **1** leaflike; leafy. **2** made of leaflike plates or thin layers. [< L *foliaceus* < *folia* leaves]

fol·i·age (fō′ lē ij) *n.* **1** leaves. **2** a decoration made of carved or painted leaves, flowers, etc. [alteration of F *feuillage* < *feuille* leaf < L *folia* leaves]

fo·li·ate (*adj.* fō′lē it or fō′lē āt′; *v.* fō′lē āt′) *adj. v.* **-at·ed, -at·ing.** —*adj.* **1** having leaves; covered with leaves. **2** resembling a leaf; leaflike.
—*v.* **1** put forth leaves. **2** split into leaflike plates or thin layers. **3** shape like a leaf. **4** decorate with leaflike ornaments. [< L *foliatus* < *folia* leaves]

fo·li·a·tion (fō′lē ā′shən) *n.* **1** a growing of leaves; putting forth of leaves: *foliation of trees in the spring.* **2** a being in leaf. **3** a decoration with leaflike ornaments or foils. **4** in geology: **a** the property of splitting up into leaflike layers. **b** the leaflike plates or layers into which crystalline rocks are divided.

folic acid (fō′ lik) in biochemistry, a crystalline compound of the vitamin complex, found in green leaves, mushrooms, and some animal tissue and used in the treatment of anemia. *Formula:* $C_{19}H_{19}N_7O_6$ [< L *folium* leaf + E *-ic*]

fo·li·o (fō′lē ō′) *n.* **-li·os,** *adj.* —*n.* **1** a large sheet of paper folded once to make two leaves, or four pages, of a book, etc. **2 a** a book of the largest size, having pages made by folding large sheets of paper once; large volume. A folio is usually any book more than 11 inches in height. **b** the size of a folio book. **3** in printing, a page number of a book, etc. **4** a leaf of a book, manuscript, etc. numbered on the front side only. **5** a case for loose papers, etc. **6 in folio,** of folio size or form.
—*adj.* of the largest size; made of large sheets of paper folded once: *The encyclopedia was in twenty volumes folio.*
—*v.* number the pages or folios of (a book, etc.); page. [< L *folio,* ablative of *folium* leaf]

folk (fōk) *n.* **folk** or **folks,** *adj.* —*n.* **1** people as a group: *Most city folk know very little about farming.* **2** a tribe; nation. **3 folks,** *pl.* **a** people. **b** *Informal.* the members of one's own family; one's relatives. —*adj.* of or having to do with the common people, their beliefs, legends, customs, etc. [OE *folc*]

folk·a·thon (fōk′ə thon′) *n. Slang.* a gathering for the singing of folk songs for a long period of time. [< *folk songs* + *marathon*]

folk dance 1 a dance originating and handed down among the common people. 2 the music for such a dance.

folk etymology popular misconception of the origin of a word that often results in a modification of its sound or spelling. Thus, ME *crevice* became E *crayfish*, influenced by *fish*.

folk·lore (fōk′lôr′) *n.* the beliefs, legends, customs, etc. of a people, tribe, etc. —**folk′lor′ist,** *n.*

folk music music originating and handed down among the common people.

folk·nik (fōk′nik) *n. Slang.* a person keen on singing or listening to folk songs. [< *folk* songs + beat*nik*]

folk-rock (fōk′rok′) *n.* rock-and-roll music with folk-song themes or lyrics.

folk song 1 a song originating among the common people and handed down from generation to generation. 2 a song imitating a genuine folk song.

folk speech the dialect spoken by the common people of a particular area.

folk·sy (fōk′sē) *adj.* **-si·er, -si·est.** *Informal.* 1 friendly; sociable. 2 plain and unpretentious. 3 artificially or affectedly simple or familiar: *The movie was full of folksy stupidity.* —**folk′si·ness,** *n.*

folk tale a story or legend originating among the common people and handed down from generation to generation.

folk·way (fōk′wā′) *n.* a custom or habit that has grown up within a social group and is very common among the members of this group.

fol·li·cle (fol′ə kəl) *n.* 1 a small cavity, sac, or gland. Hair grows from follicles. 2 a one-celled seed vessel. It is a dry fruit that splits open along one seam only. Milkweed pods are follicles. [< L *folliculus*, dim. of *follis* bellows]

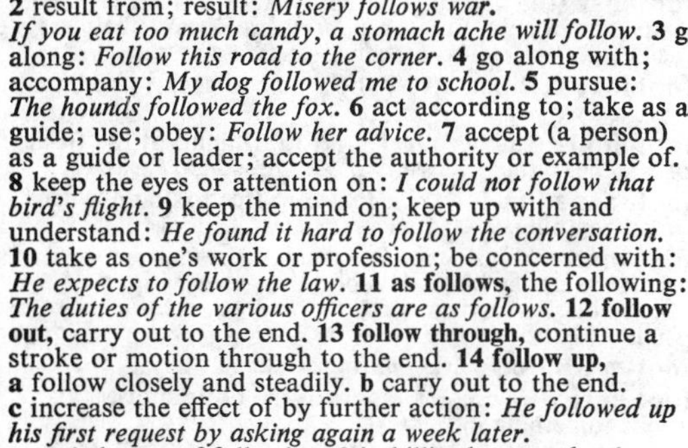
Follicles (def. 2)

fol·lic·u·lar (fə lik′yu̇ lər) *adj.* 1 of or resembling a follicle or follicles. 2 in medicine, affecting the follicles: *follicular tonsillitis.*

fol·low (fol′ō) *v.* 1 go or come after: *Night follows day. He leads; we follow.* 2 result from; result: *Misery follows war. If you eat too much candy, a stomach ache will follow.* 3 go along: *Follow this road to the corner.* 4 go along with; accompany: *My dog followed me to school.* 5 pursue: *The hounds followed the fox.* 6 act according to; take as a guide; use; obey: *Follow her advice.* 7 accept (a person) as a guide or leader; accept the authority or example of. 8 keep the eyes or attention on: *I could not follow that bird's flight.* 9 keep the mind on; keep up with and understand: *He found it hard to follow the conversation.* 10 take as one's work or profession; be concerned with: *He expects to follow the law.* 11 **as follows,** the following: *The duties of the various officers are as follows.* 12 **follow out,** carry out to the end. 13 **follow through,** continue a stroke or motion through to the end. 14 **follow up,** a follow closely and steadily. b carry out to the end. c increase the effect of by further action: *He followed up his first request by asking again a week later.*
—*n.* 1 the act of following. 2 in billiards, a stroke that causes the player's ball to roll on after the ball struck by it. [OE *folgian*]

Syn. *v.* 1, 2 **Follow, succeed, ensue** = come after. **Follow** is the general word meaning "come or go after": *He has come to take his new position, but his wife will follow later.* **Succeed** = come next in order of time, and usually suggests taking the place of someone or something: *He succeeded his father as president of the company.* **Ensue**, formal, means "follow as a result or conclusion": *A lasting friendship ensued from our working together during the war.* 4 attend.

☛ **follow.** The idiom is *followed by*, not *followed with: Supper was followed by games and dancing.*

fol·low·er (fol′ō ər) *n.* 1 a person or thing that follows. 2 a person who follows the ideas or beliefs of another. 3 an attendant; servant.

Syn. 2 **Follower, adherent, disciple** = someone who follows another, his beliefs, a cause, etc. **Follower** is the general word: *Men who promise security always find followers among unthinking people.* **Adherent**, more formal, means a faithful follower who gives active and loyal support to a belief, cause, party, sometimes personal devotion to the leader: *Socialized medicine has many adherents.* **Disciple** emphasizes both devotion to the person as leader and teacher and firm belief in his teachings: *He is a disciple of Einstein.*

fol·low·ing (fol′ō ing) *n.* 1 followers; attendants. 2 **the following,** the persons, things, items, etc. now to be named, related, described, etc. —*adj.* that follows; next after.

hat, āge, cãre, fär; let, ēqual, tėrm; it, īce
hot, ōpen, ôrder; oil, out; cup, pu̇t, rüle, ūse
əbove, takən, pencəl, lemən, circəs
ch, child; ng, long; sh, ship
th, thin; ᴛʜ, then; zh, measure

follow-through (fol′ō thrü′) *n.* 1 in sports, the smooth completion of a movement, especially of a stroke in golf or tennis after the ball has been hit. 2 any logical continuation and completion.

fol·low-up (fol′ō up′) *n.* 1 the act of following up. 2 any action or thing, such as a second or third visit, appeal, letter, etc., designed to be a further effort in achieving some goal. —*adj.* sent or used as a follow-up: *a follow-up circular.*

fol·ly (fol′ē) *n.* **-lies.** 1 a being foolish; lack of sense; unwise conduct. 2 a foolish act, practice, or idea; something silly. 3 a costly but foolish undertaking. [ME < OF *folie* < *fol* foolish. See FOOL.]

fo·ment (fō ment′) *v.* 1 promote; foster (trouble, rebellion, etc.). 2 apply warm water, hot cloths, etc. to (a hurt or pain). [< LL *fomentare* < *fomentum* a warm application < L *fovere* warm] —**fo·ment′er,** *n.*

fo·men·ta·tion (fō′men tā′shən) *n.* 1 a stirring up; instigation; encouragement. 2 the application of moist heat. 3 a hot, moist application.

fond (fond) *adj.* 1 **fond of,** having a liking for: *fond of children.* 2 loving: *a fond look.* 3 loving foolishly or too much. 4 cherished: *fond hopes.* 5 *Archaic.* foolish; foolishly ready to believe or hope. [ME *fonned*, pp. of *fonne(n)* be foolish; origin uncertain] —**fond′ly,** *adv.* —**fond′ness,** *n.* —**Syn.** 2 affectionate, amorous.

fon·dant (fon′dənt) *n.* 1 a creamy sugar candy used as a filling or coating for other candies. 2 a candy consisting mainly of fondant. [< F *fondant*, literally, melting, ppr. of *fondre* melt. See FOUND[3].]

fon·dle (fon′dəl) *v.* **-dled, -dling.** pet; caress lovingly: *Mothers like to fondle their babies.* [< *fond*, v., special use of *fond*, adj.] —**fon′dler,** *n.*

fon·due (fon′dü or fon dü′) *n.* a dish made of melted cheese, eggs, butter, etc. [< F *fondue*, fem. pp. of *fondre* melt. See FOUND[3].]

font[1] (font) *n.* 1 a basin holding water for baptism. 2 a basin for holy water. 3 *Archaic.* a fountain. 4 a source; origin: *the font of truth.* [< L *fons, fontis* spring]

font[2] (font) *n.* in printing, a complete set of type of one size and style. [< F *fonte* < *fondre* melt. See FOUND[3].]

fon·ta·nel (fon′tə nel′) *n.* a membrane-covered spot on the growing skull of an infant or fetus. [< F *fontanelle*, dim. of *fontaine.* See FOUNTAIN.]

food (füd) *n.* 1 what an animal or plant takes in to enable it to live and grow. 2 what is eaten: *Give him food and drink.* 3 a particular kind or article of food. 4 what helps anything to live and grow. 5 what sustains or serves for consumption in any way: *food for thought.* [OE *fōda*]

Syn. 1 **Food, provisions, rations** = what human beings and animals eat. **Food** is the general word for what is taken in by people, animals, or plants to keep them alive and help them grow: *Milk is a valuable food.* **Provisions** = a supply of food, either for immediate use or stored away: *I must buy provisions for the holidays.* **Rations** = fixed allowances of food set for one day's use or allowed under some system of rationing: *The survivors lived for three days on small rations of water and chocolate.*

food·stuff (füd′stuf′) *n.* 1 any material for food: *Grain and meat are foodstuffs.* 2 any nutritionally valuable element in food, as protein or carbohydrate.

foo·fa·raw or **foo·fe·raw** (fü′fə ro′ or -rô′) *n.* 1 unnecessary ornamentation, as frills, fringes, bows, etc. 2 *Slang.* a loud disturbance caused by something of no importance. [origin uncertain]

fool (fül) *n.* 1 a person without sense; unwise or silly person. 2 formerly, a clown kept by a king or lord to amuse people; jester. 3 a person who has been deceived or tricked; dupe.
—*v.* 1 act like a fool for fun; play; joke: *The teacher told*

him not to fool during class. **2** make a fool of; deceive; trick. **3 fool around,** *Informal.* waste time foolishly. **4 fool away,** *Informal.* waste foolishly. **5 fool with,** *Informal.* meddle foolishly with. [ME < OF *fol* madman, probably < LL *follis* empty-headed < L *follis* bag, bellows]

Syn. *n.* **1 Fool, idiot, imbecile,** in non-technical use, mean "a foolish person." **Fool** suggests absence of any sign of intelligence, and expresses contempt for someone who acts without good sense or judgment: *She is a fool to leave school when her grades are so high.* **Idiot** is used of someone acting as if he were totally feeble-minded: *She was such an idiot that she walked in the deep snow without her boots.* **Imbecile** is used of someone the speaker considers half-witted: *Look at that imbecile grinning at nothing.*

fool·er·y (fül′ər ē) *n.* **-er·ies.** a foolish action.

fool·har·dy (fül′här′dē) *adj.* **-di·er, -di·est.** foolishly bold; rash. **—fool′har′di·ness,** *n.*

fool hen any of various grouse or quail, especially the bush partridge, or spruce grouse. The fool hen is so called because of its foolish indifference to danger: *The hunter walked up to the sitting fool hen and dropped a noose over its neck.*

fool·ish (fül′ish) *adj.* **1** like a fool; without sense; unwise; silly. **2** ridiculous. **—fool′ish·ly,** *adv.* **—fool′ish·ness,** *n.*

Syn. 1 Foolish, silly, fatuous = without sense. **Foolish** = like a fool, showing lack of common sense and judgment: *The foolish girl insists on having her own way.* **Silly** = seeming weakminded, doing and saying things without sense or point, often making oneself ridiculous: *It is silly to giggle at everything.* More contemptuous, **fatuous** = silly, empty-headed, and stupid, but completely self-satisfied: *After his boring speech, the fatuous speaker waited for applause.*

fool·proof (fül′prüf′) *adj. Informal.* so safe or simple that even a fool can use or do it: *The car had a foolproof safety catch on the door.*

fool's cap 1 formerly, a cap or hood worn by the fool or jester of a king or lord. **2** a dunce cap.

fools·cap (fülz′kap′ or fülz′-) *n.* writing paper in sheets from 12 to 13½ inches wide and 15 to 17 inches long. [from the watermark]

fool's errand a foolish or useless undertaking.

fool's gold a mineral that looks like gold; iron pyrites or copper pyrites.

fool's paradise a condition of happiness based on false beliefs or hopes.

foot (fůt) *n.* feet, *v.* —*n.* **1** the end part of a leg; the part that a person, animal, or thing stands on. **2** the part near the feet; the end toward which the feet are put. **3** the lowest part; bottom; base. **4** the part of a stocking, etc. that covers the foot. **5** soldiers that go on foot; infantry. **6** a measure of length, height, or depth equalling 12 inches: *Three feet equal one yard.* **7** one of the parts into which a line of verse is divided. This line has four feet: The boy | stood on | the burn | ing deck. **8** the last of a list or series.
on foot, a standing or walking. **b** going on; in progress.
put one's best foot forward, *Informal.* **a** do one's best. **b** try to make a good impression.
put one's foot down, *Informal.* make up one's mind and act firmly.
put one's foot in it, *Informal.* get into trouble by meddling; blunder.
under foot, a in the way. **b** in one's power; in subjection.
with one foot in the grave, almost dead; dying.
—*v.* **1** make or renew the foot of (a stocking, etc.). **2** walk. **3** dance. **4** add. **5** *Informal.* pay (a bill, etc.). [OE *fōt*]

foot·age (fůt′ij) *n.* **1** the length in feet. **2** quantity of lumber expressed in board feet: *The footage of the lumber used in this house amounts to 200,000 board feet.*

foot-and-mouth disease a dangerous, contagious virus disease of cattle and some other animals, causing blisters in the mouth and around the hoofs.

foot·ball (fůt′bol′ or -bôl′) *n.* **1** an air-filled, leather-covered ball used in games that involve kicking: *Footballs of different shapes are used in soccer and rugby football.* **2** a game in which a football is kicked, passed, or carried toward the opponents' goal; rugby football. The rules of Canadian football are somewhat different from those of the American game. See **rugby** for usage note. **3** a game in which the ball must be played toward the opponents' goal without the use of the hands; soccer.

foot·board (fůt′bôrd′) *n.* **1** a board or small platform to be used as a support for the feet. **2** an upright piece across the foot of a bed.

foot·bridge (fůt′brij′) *n.* a bridge for pedestrians only.

foot-can·dle (fůt′kan′dəl) *n.* a unit for measuring illumination. It is the amount of light produced by a standard candle at a distance of one foot.

-footed *combining form.* having a certain kind or number of feet: *a four-footed animal.*

-footer *combining form.* a person or thing —— feet in height or length: *six-footer = a person or thing six feet in height or length.*

foot·fall (fůt′fol′ or -fôl′) *n.* **1** the sound of steps coming or going. **2** a footstep.

foot fault in tennis, a failure to keep both feet behind the base line when serving, or to keep one foot on the ground.

foot·gear (fůt′gēr′) *n.* shoes, boots, etc.

foot·hill (fůt′hil′) *n.* a low hill at the base of a mountain or mountain range: *Calgary lies in the foothills of the Rockies.*

foot·hold (fůt′hōld′) *n.* **1** a place to put a foot; support for the feet; surface to stand on: *He climbed the steep cliff by finding footholds in cracks in the rock.* **2** a firm footing or position: *It is hard to break a habit that has gained a foothold.*

foot·ing (fůt′ing) *n.* **1** a firm and secure placing of the feet: *He lost his footing and fell down on the ice.* **2** the position of the feet: *When he changed his footing, he lost his balance.* **3** a place to put the feet; support for the feet; a surface to stand on. **4** a firm place or position: *The newly rich family struggled for a footing in society.* **5** a basis of understanding; relationship: *Canada and the United States are on a friendly footing.* **6** an adding. **7** the amount found by adding; sum; total. **8** the act of moving on the feet; walking, dancing, etc. **9** the manner of placing or using the feet; footwork. **10 footings,** *pl.* the concrete foundations of a building, wall, etc.

foot·less (fůt′lis) *adj.* **1** without a foot or feet. **2** without support; not substantial. **3** *Informal.* awkward; helpless; inefficient. **—foot′less·ly,** *adv.* **—foot′less·ness,** *n.*

foot·let (fůt′lit) *n.* a very short type of sock sometimes worn by women.

foot·lights (fůt′līts′) *n.pl.* **1** a row of lights at the front of a stage. **2** the profession of acting; stage; theatre.

foot·loose (fůt′lüs′) *adj. Informal.* free to go anywhere or do anything.

foot·man (fůt′mən) *n.* **-men** (-mən). **1** a male servant who answers the bell, waits on table, goes with an automobile or carriage to open the door, etc. Footmen usually wear a kind of uniform. **2** *Archaic.* a foot soldier.

foot·mark (fůt′märk′) *n.* footprint.

foot·note (fůt′nōt′) *n.* a note at the bottom of a page about something in the text.

foot·pace (fůt′pās′) *n.* walking pace; speed of ordinary walking.

foot·pad (fůt′pad′) *n. Archaic.* a highway robber who goes on foot only.

foot·path (fůt′path′) *n.* a path for pedestrians only.

foot·pound (fůt′pound′) *n.* the amount of energy needed to raise a weight of one pound to a height of one foot. *Abbrev.:* F.P., f.p., or fp

foot·print (fůt′print′) *n.* the mark made by a foot.

foot·rest (fůt′rest′) *n.* a support on which to rest the feet.

foot rule a wooden or metal ruler one foot long.

foot soldier a soldier who fights on foot; infantryman.

foot·sore (fůt′sôr′) *adj.* having sore feet, especially from much walking.

foot·stalk (fůt′stok′ or -stôk′) *n.* **1** the stem of a leaf, flower, or flower cluster. **2** a stemlike part of an animal, by which it is supported or attached to something.

foot·step (fůt′step′) *n.* **1** a person's step. **2** the distance covered in one step. **3** the sound of steps coming or going. **4** the mark made by a foot; footprint. **5** a step on which to go up or down. **6 follow in someone's footsteps,** do as another has done.

foot·stool (fu̇t′stül′) *n.* a low stool on which to rest the feet when one is sitting in a chair, etc.

foot·way (fu̇t′wā′) *n.* a path for pedestrians only; sidewalk.

foot·wear (fu̇t′wãr′) *n.* shoes, slippers, stockings, gaiters, etc.

foot·work (fu̇t′ wėrk′) *n.* the way of using the feet: *Footwork is important in boxing and dancing.*

foot·worn (fu̇t′wôrn′) *adj.* **1** worn by feet: *a footworn path.* **2** having tired feet.

foo·zle (fü′zəl) *v.* **-zled, -zling,** *n.* —*v.* do clumsily; bungle (a stroke in golf, etc.). —*n.* **1** a clumsy failure; in golf, a badly played stroke. **2** *Informal.* a dull, old-fashioned person. **3** *Informal.* a man who is easily fooled. [cf. dial. G *fuseln* work badly or slowly]

fop (fop) *n.* a vain man who is very fond of fine clothes and has affected manners; empty-headed dandy. [origin uncertain]

fop·per·y (fop′ər ē) *n.* **-per·ies.** foppish behavior; fine clothes, affected manners, etc. suitable for a fop.

fop·pish (fop′ish) *adj.* **1** of a fop; suitable for a fop. **2** vain; empty-headed; affected. —**fop′pish·ly,** *adv.* —**fop′pish·ness,** *n.*

for (fôr; *unstressed,* fər) *prep.* **1** in place of: *We used boxes for chairs.* **2** in support of; in favor of: *He voted for Laurier.* **3** representing; in the interest of: *A lawyer acts for his client.* **4** in return for: *These twelve apples were sold to me for a dollar.* **5** with the object or purpose of taking, achieving, or obtaining: *He went for a walk. He is looking for a job.* **6** in order to become, have, keep, etc.: *The navy trains men for sailors. She seeks for happiness. He ran for his life.* **7** in search of: *She is hunting for her cat.* **8** in order to get to: *He has just left for Toronto.* **9** meant to belong to or with, or to be used by or with; suited to: *a box for gloves, books for children.* **10** because of; by reason of: *He was punished for stealing.* **11** in honor of: *A party was given for her.* **12** with a feeling toward: *She has an eye for beauty. We longed for home.* **13** with respect or regard to: *It is warm for April. Eating too much is bad for one's health.* **14** as far or as long as; throughout; during: *We walked for a mile. He worked for an hour.* **15** as being: *They know it for a fact.* **16** in spite of: *For all his faults, we like him still.* **17** in proportion to: *For every poisonous snake there are many harmless ones.* **18** to the amount of: *His father gave him a cheque for $20.* **19 Oh! for,** I wish that I might have: *Oh! for the wings of a bird!*
—*conj.* because: *We can't go, for it is raining.* [OE]
☛ **for.** A comma is usually needed between two co-ordinate clauses joined by *for*; without it the *for* might be read as a preposition: *He was glad to go, for Mrs. Crane had been especially good to him.* (Not: *He was glad to go for Mrs. Crane ....*) ☛ See because for another usage note.

for- *prefix.* away; opposite; completely, as in *forbid, forswear.* [OE]

for. **1** foreign. **2** forestry.

for·age (fôr′ij) *n. v.* **-aged, -ag·ing.** —*n.* **1** food for horses, cattle, etc. **2** a hunting or searching for food: *We went on a forage for supplies.* —*v.* **1** supply with food; feed. **2** hunt or search for food: *The boys foraged in the kitchen till they found some cookies.* **3** get by hunting or searching about. **4** hunt; search about: *The man made a living by foraging for old metal.* **5** get or take food from. **6** plunder: *The soldiers foraged the villages near their camp.* [ME < OF *fourrager* < *fuerre* fodder < Gmc.] —**for′ag·er,** *n.*

fo·ra·men (fô rā′mən or fô ra′mən) *n.* **-ra·mens** (-rā′mənz) or **-ra·mi·na** (-ra′mə nə). in biology, a small hole or hollow, especially a natural cavity in a bone. [< L]

fo·ram·i·nif·er·a (fô ram′ə nif′ər ə) *n.pl.* a group of tiny, one-celled sea animals, most of which have shells with tiny holes in them. [< NL < L *foramen* a small opening + *ferre* bear]

for·as·much as (fôr′əz much′) in view of the fact that; because; since.

for·ay (fôr′ā) *n.* a raid for plunder. —*v.* plunder; lay waste; pillage. [ME < OF *fourrier* < *fuerre* fodder. See FORAGE.]

for·bade (fər bad′ or fər bād′) *v.* pt. of **forbid.**

hat, āge, cãre, fär; let, ēqual, tėrm; it, īce
hot, ōpen, ôrder; oil, out; cup, pu̇t, rüle, ūse
əbove, takən, pencəl, lemən, circəs
ch, child; ng, long; sh, ship
th, thin; ᴛʜ, then; zh, measure

for·bear[1] (fôr bãr′) *v.* **-bore, -borne, -bear·ing. 1** hold back; keep from doing, saying, using, etc.: *The boy forbore to hit back because the other boy was smaller.* **2** be patient; control oneself. [OE *forberan*] —**for·bear′er,** *n.* —**for·bear′ing·ly,** *adv.* —**Syn. 1** refrain, abstain.

for·bear[2] (fôr′bãr) *n.* forebear.

for·bear·ance (fôr bãr′əns) *n.* **1** the act of forbearing. **2** patience; self-control. —**Syn. 2** See **patience.**

for·bid (fər bid′) *v.* **-bade** or **-bad, -bid·den** or **-bid, -bid·ding. 1** order (someone) not to do something; make a rule against; prohibit. **2** keep from happening; prevent: *God forbid!* **3** command to keep away from; exclude from: *I forbid you the house.* [OE *forbēodan*]
Syn. 1 Forbid, prohibit = order not to do something. **Forbid** = give an order, often directly or personally, or make a rule that something must not be done, and suggests that obedience is expected: *His father forbade him to smoke.* **Prohibit** is formal, and means "to make a formal regulation against something" usually by law or official action, and suggests power to enforce it: *Smoking is often prohibited in theatres.*

for·bid·den (fər bid′ən) *adj.* not allowed; against the law or rules. —*v.* pp. of **forbid.**

for·bid·ding (fər bid′ing) *adj.* causing fear or dislike; looking dangerous or unpleasant: *The coast was rocky and forbidding.* —**for·bid′ding·ly,** *adv.* —**for·bid′ding·ness,** *n.* —**Syn.** disagreeable, displeasing, grim.

for·bore (fôr bôr′) *v.* pt. of **forbear**[1].

for·borne (fôr bôrn′) *v.* pp. of **forbear**[1].

for·by (fôr bī′) *Scottish and archaic.* —*prep.* **1** besides. **2** close by; near. —*adv.* besides.

force (fôrs) *n. v.* **forced, forc·ing.** —*n.* **1** strength; power. **2** strength used against a person or thing; violence. **3** the power to control, influence, persuade, convince, etc.; effectiveness; vividness: *He writes with force.* **4** a group of people working or acting together: *our office force.* **5** a group of sailors, soldiers, policemen, etc. **6** in physics, any cause that produces, changes, or stops the motion of a body. **7** an agency, influence or source of power likened to a physical force: *social forces.* **8** the meaning or significance (of a word, sentence, etc.). **9** binding power; validity, as of a law or contract: *The force of some laws has to be tested in court.* **10 by force of,** by dint of; by virtue of; by means of. **11 forces,** *pl.* the navy, army, and air force; the armed services. **12 in force, a** in effect or operation; binding; valid. **b** with full strength.
—*v.* **1** use force on. **2** make or drive by force. **3** get or take by force. **4** put by force. **5** impose or impress by force: *to force one's views on another.* **6** break open or through by force. **7** overpower by force. **8** urge to violent effort. **9** make by an unusual or unnatural effort; strain. **10** hurry the growth or development of: *He forced his rhubarb by growing it in a dark, warm place.* **11** in baseball, compel (a player) to leave one base and try in vain to reach the next. [< F, ult. < L *fortis* strong] —**force′less,** *adj.* —**forc′er,** *n.* —**Syn.** *n.* **1** might, vigor, energy. See **power. 2** coercion, compulsion, constraint. **7** significance, import.

forced (fôrst) *adj.* **1** made, compelled, or driven by force: *The work of slaves is forced labor.* **2** made by an unusual or unnatural effort: *She hid her dislike for him with a forced smile.* —**Syn. 1** compulsory, enforced. **2** strained.

forced march an unusually long, fast march.

force·ful (fôrs′fəl) *adj.* full of force; strong; powerful; vigorous; effective: *a forceful manner.* —**force′ful·ly,** *adv.* —**force′ful·ness,** *n.*
Syn. Forceful, forcible. Forcible suggests more force than **forceful,** which only indicates possession or use of vigor; **forcible** may also imply violence: *a forceful style* but *a forcible entry.*

force·meat (fôrs′mēt′) *n.* chopped and seasoned meat, used for stuffing, etc. [< *force,* var. of obs. *farce* stuffing + *meat*]

for·ceps (fôr′seps or fôr′səps) *n.* **-ceps.** a pair of small pincers or tongs used by surgeons, dentists, etc. for seizing, holding, and pulling. [< L *forceps* < *formus* hot + *capere* take]

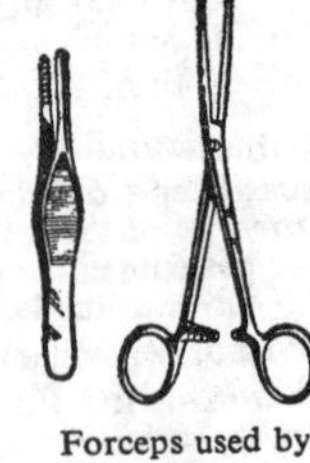
Forceps used by surgeons

force pump a pump with a valveless piston whose action forces liquid through a pipe; any pump which delivers liquid under pressure.

for·ci·ble (fôr′sə bəl) *adj.* **1** made or done by force; using force: *a forcible entrance into a house.* **2** having or showing force; strong; powerful; effective; convincing: *a forcible speaker.* —**for′ci·ble·ness,** *n.* —**for′ci·bly,** *adv.* —**Syn.** See **forceful.**

ford (fôrd) *n.* a place where a river or stream is shallow enough to be crossed by walking or driving through the water. —*v.* cross (a river, etc.) by walking or driving through the water: *They spent an hour looking for a place to ford the river.* [OE] —**ford′a·ble,** *adj.*

for·done (fôr dun′) *adj. Archaic.* worn out; exhausted.

fore[1] (fôr) *adj. adv.* at the front; toward the beginning or front; forward. [adj. < *fore-*; adv. < OE] —*n.* **1** the forward part; front. See **aft** for picture. **2 to the fore, a** in or into full view; in or into a conspicuous place or position. **b** at hand; ready. **c** alive. [< adj.]

fore[2] (fôr) *interj.* in golf, a shout of warning to persons ahead on the fairway who are liable to be struck by the ball. [? for *before*]

fore- *prefix.* **1** front; in front; at or near the front, as in *forecastle, foremast.* **2** before; beforehand, as in *foreknow, foresee.* [OE *fore* before]

fore and aft 1 at or toward both bow and stern of a ship. **2** on a ship, lengthwise; from bow to stern; placed lengthwise.

fore-and-aft (fôr′ənd aft′ or fôr ən aft′) *adj.* lengthwise on a ship; from bow to stern; placed lengthwise. A fore-and-aft-rigged ship has the sails set lengthwise.

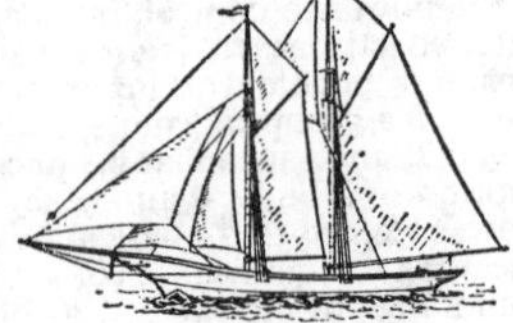
A fore-and-aft-rigged ship

fore·arm[1] (fôr′ärm′) *n.* the part of the arm between the elbow and wrist.

fore·arm[2] (fôr ärm′) *v.* prepare for trouble ahead of time; arm beforehand.

fore·bear (fôr′bãr) *n.* an ancestor; forefather. Also, **forbear.** [< *fore-* + *be* + *-er*[1]]

fore·bode (fôr bōd′) *v.* **-bod·ed, -bod·ing. 1** give warning of; predict: *Black clouds forebode a storm.* **2** have a feeling that something bad is going to happen. —**fore·bod′er,** *n.* —**Syn. 1** foretell.

fore·bod·ing (fôr bōd′ing) *n.* **1** a prediction; warning. **2** a feeling that something bad is going to happen: *As the lights went out, we were filled with foreboding.*

fore·brain (fôr′brān′) *n.* the front section of the brain, consisting of the cerebrum, the pituitary gland, and the pineal body.

fore·cast (fôr′kast′) *v.* **-cast** or **-cast·ed, -cast·ing,** *n.* —*v.* **1** prophesy; predict: *Cooler weather is forecast for tomorrow.* **2** be a prophecy or prediction of. **3** foresee; plan ahead. —*n.* **1** a prophecy; prediction. **2** a planning ahead; foresight. —**fore′cast′er,** *n.*

fore·cas·tle (fōk′səl or fôr′kas′əl) *n.* **1** the upper deck in front of the foremast. **2** the sailors' quarters in a merchant ship, formerly in the forward part of the ship.

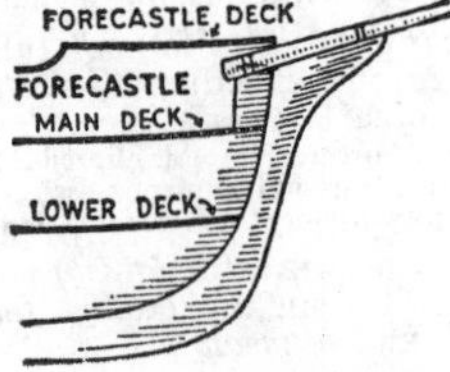

fore·check (fôr′chek′) *v.* in ice hockey, check an opposing player in his own defensive zone. —**fore′check′er,** *n.*

fore·close (fôr klōz′) *v.* **-closed, -clos·ing. 1** shut out; prevent; exclude. **2** in law: **a** take away the right to redeem (a mortgage): *When the conditions of a mortgage are not met, the holder can foreclose and have the property sold to satisfy his claim.* **b** take away the right of (a mortgager) to redeem his property. [ME < OF *forclos,* pp. of *forclore* exclude < *for-* out (< L *foris*) + *clore* shut < L *claudere*]

fore·clo·sure (fôr klō′zhər) *n.* the foreclosing of a mortgage.

fore·court (fôr′kôrt′) *n.* **1** an enclosed space in front of a building. **2** in tennis, basketball, hardball, etc., the area nearest the net, offensive basket, front wall, etc.

fore·done (fôr dun′) *adj. v. Archaic.* exhausted.

fore·doom (fôr düm′) *v.* doom beforehand.

fore·fa·ther (fôr′fo′ᴛʜər) *n.* an ancestor.

fore·fend (fôr fend′) *v.* forfend.

fore·fin·ger (fôr′fing′gər) *n.* the finger next to the thumb; first finger; index finger.

fore·foot (fôr′fu̇t′) *n.* **-feet. 1** one of the front feet of an animal. **2** the forward end of a ship's keel.

fore·front (fôr′frunt′) *n.* the place of greatest importance, activity, etc.; foremost part.

fore·gath·er (fôr gaᴛʜ′ər) *v.* forgather.

fore·go[1] (fôr gō′) *v.* **-went, -gone, -go·ing.** do without; give up: *She decided to forego the movies and do her essay.* Also, **forgo.** [OE *foregān*] —**fore·go′er,** *n.* —**Syn.** surrender, relinquish, sacrifice.

fore·go[2] (fôr gō′) *v.* **-went, -gone, -go·ing.** precede; go before. [OE *foregān*] —**fore·go′er,** *n.*

fore·go·ing (fôr′gō′ing) *adj.* preceding; previous.

fore·gone (*adj.* fôr′gon or fôr gon′; *v.* fôr gon′) *adj.* that has gone before; previous. —*v.* pp. of **forego.**

foregone conclusion a result that was expected with certainty; inevitable result.

fore·ground (fôr′ground′) *n.* **1** the part of a picture or scene nearest the observer; part toward the front. **2 in the foreground,** conspicuous.

fore·hand (fôr′hand′) *adj.* made with the palm of the hand turned forward. —*n.* **1** in tennis, etc., a stroke made with the palm of the hand turned forward. **2** a position in front or above; advantage.

fore·hand·ed (fôr′han′did) *adj.* **1** providing for the future; prudent; thrifty. **2** done beforehand; early; timely. —**fore′hand′ed·ness,** *n.*

fore·head (fôr′hed′ or fôr′id) *n.* **1** the part of the face above the eyes. **2** a front part. [OE *forhēafod*]

for·eign (fôr′ən) *adj.* **1** outside one's own country: *She has travelled much in foreign countries.* **2** of, characteristic of, or coming from outside one's own country: *a foreign ship, a foreign language, foreign money.* **3** having to do with other countries; carried on or dealing with other countries: *foreign trade.* **4** not belonging; not related: *Sitting still all day is foreign to a healthy boy's nature.* **5** not related to the matter that is being discussed or considered. **6** in law, falling outside the jurisdiction of a particular country. **7** not belonging naturally to the place where found: *a foreign object in the eye, a foreign substance in the blood.* [ME < OF *forain,* ult. < L *foras* outside]—**for′eign·ness,** *n.* —**Syn. 4** unfamiliar, strange.

foreign affairs a country's relations with other countries.

for·eign-born (fôr′ən bôrn′) *adj.* born in another country.

for·eign·er (fôr′ən ər) *n.* **1** a person from another country; alien. **2** *Informal.* a person strange to one's own customs, ideas, etc. **3** a foreign ship.

foreign legion part of an army made up largely of soldiers who are volunteers from other countries: *the French Foreign Legion.*

Foreign Office *Brit.* the government department in charge of foreign affairs.

fore·judge (fôr juj′) *v.* **-judged, -judg·ing.** judge beforehand.

fore·knew (fôr nü′ or -nū′) *v.* pt. of **foreknow.**

fore·know (fôr nō′) *v.* **-knew, -known, -know·ing.** know beforehand.

fore·knowl·edge (fôr′nol′ij) *n.* knowledge of a thing before it happens.

fore·known (fôr nōn′) *v.* pp. of **foreknow.**

fore·la·dy (fôr′lā′dē) *n.* **-dies.** a forewoman (def. 1).

fore·land (fôr′land′) *n.* a cape; headland; promontory.

fore·leg (fôr′leg′) *n.* one of the front legs of an animal.

fore·lock (fôr′lok′) *n.* **1** a lock of hair that grows just above the forehead. **2 take time by the forelock,** act promptly.

fore·man (fôr′mən) *n.* **-men** (-mən). **1** the man in charge of a group of workers or of some part of a factory. **2** the chairman of a jury.

fore·mast (fôr′mast or fôr′məst) *n.* on a ship, the mast nearest the bow.

fore·men·tioned (fôr men′shənd or fôr′men′shənd) *adj.* mentioned previously; aforementioned.

fore·most (fôr′mōst′) *adj.* **1** first. **2** chief; leading; most notable. —*adv.* first: *He stumbled and fell head foremost.* [OE *formest*; double superlative of *forma* first, superlative of *fore* before]

fore·name (fôr′nām′) *n.* the first name.

fore·noon (fôr′nün′) *n.* the time between early morning and noon. —*adj.* between early morning and noon.

fo·ren·sic (fə ren′sik) *adj.* of or suitable for a law court or public debate. —*n.* a spoken or written exercise in argumentation, as in a college or high-school class in speech or rhetoric. [< L *forensis* < *forum* forum]

forensic medicine the application of medical science to problems of law; medical jurisprudence.

fore·or·dain (fôr′ôr dān′) *v.* ordain beforehand; predestine. —**Syn.** predetermine.

fore·or·di·na·tion (fôr′ôr də nā′shən) *n.* an ordaining beforehand; predestination.

fore·part (fôr′pärt′) *n.* the front part.

fore·paw (fôr′po′ or -pô′) *n.* front paw.

fore·piece (fôr′pēs′) *n.* the front or first piece of something.

fore·quar·ter (fôr′kwôr′tər) *n.* a front leg, shoulder, and nearby ribs of beef, lamb, pork, etc.; front quarter.

fore·ran (fôr ran′) *v.* pt. of **forerun.**

fore·reach (fôr rēch′) *v.* **1** move ahead quickly, as a ship does after coming into the wind. **2** move ahead of; pass. **3** get the better of.

fore·run (fôr run′) *v.* **-ran, -run, -run·ning. 1** precede. **2** be a sign or warning of (something to come). **3** forestall.

fore·run·ner (fôr′run′ər) *n.* **1** a person going before or sent before to show that someone or something else is coming; herald. **2** a sign or warning of something to come: *Black clouds are often the forerunners of a storm.* **3** a predecessor; ancestor.

fore·sail (fôr′sāl′ or fôr′səl) *n.* **1** the principal sail on the foremast of a schooner. **2** the lowest sail on the foremast of a square-rigged ship.

fore·saw (fôr so′ or -sô′) *v.* pt. of **foresee.**

fore·see (fôr sē′) *v.* **-saw, -seen, -see·ing.** see or know beforehand: *Mother put up a big picnic lunch, because she foresaw how hungry we would be.* [OE *foresēon*] —**fore·see′a·ble,** *adj.* —**fore·see′a·bly,** *adv.* —**Syn.** anticipate, divine.

fore·seen (fôr sēn′) *v.* pp. of **foresee.**

fore·shad·ow (fôr shad′ō) *v.* indicate beforehand; be a warning of: *Black clouds foreshadow a storm.*

fore·shank (fôr′shangk′) *n.* the meat on the upper part of the forelegs of cattle. See **beef** for diagram.

fore·sheet (fôr′shēt′) *n.* **1** one of the ropes used to hold a foresail in place. **2 foresheets,** *pl.* the space in the forward part of an open boat.

fore·shore (fôr′shôr′) *n.* the part of the shore between the high-water mark and low-water mark.

fore·short·en (fôr shôr′tən) *v.* in a drawing or painting, represent (lines, etc.) as of less than true length in order to give the proper impression to the eye.

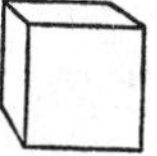

Foreshortening of lines in a cube

fore·show (fôr shō′) *v.* **-showed, -shown, -show·ing.** show beforehand; foretell; foreshadow. [OE *forescēawian*]

hat, āge, cãre, fär; let, ēqual, tėrm; it, īce
hot, ōpen, ôrder; oil, out; cup, pu̇t, rüle, ūse
əbove, takən, pencəl, lemən, circəs
ch, child; ng, long; sh, ship
th, thin; ᴛʜ, then; zh, measure

fore·shown (fôr shōn′) *v.* pp. of **foreshow.**

fore·sight (fôr′sīt′) *n.* **1** the power to see or realize beforehand what is likely to happen. **2** careful thought for the future; prudence. **3** a looking ahead; a view into the future. —**Syn. 2** See **prudence.**

fore·sight·ed (fôr′sīt′id or fôr′sīt′id) *adj.* having or showing foresight. —**fore′sight′ed·ness,** *n.*

fore·skin (fôr′skin′) *n.* the fold of skin that covers the end of the penis.

for·est (fôr′ist) *n.* **1** a large area of land covered with trees; thick woods, woodland. **2** the trees themselves. —*adj.* of a forest; in a forest. —*v.* plant with trees; change into a forest. [ME < OF *forest*, ult. < L *foris* out of doors] —**for′est·less,** *adj.*

fore·stall (fôr stol′ or -stôl′) *v.* **1** prevent by acting first: *The mayor forestalled a riot by having the police ready.* **2** deal with (a thing) in advance; anticipate; be ahead of. **3** buy up (goods, etc.) in advance in order to increase the price. [ME *forstalle(n)* < OE *foresteall* prevention] —**fore·stall′er,** *n.*

for·est·a·tion (fôr′is tā′shən) *n.* the planting or taking care of forests.

fore·stay (fôr′stā′) *n.* the rope or cable reaching from the top of a ship's foremast to the bowsprit. The forestay helps to support the foremast.

for·est·er (fôr′is tər) *n.* **1** a government official whose job it is to guard against fires and to protect timber in a forest. **2** a person, bird, animal, etc. that lives in a forest.

forest preserve a forest protected by the government from wasteful cutting, fires, etc.

for·est·ry (fôr′is trē) *n.* **1** the science of planting and taking care of forests. **2** the art of making and managing forests.

fore·taste (*n.* fôr′tāst′; *v.* fôr tāst′) *n. v.* **-tast·ed, -tast·ing.** —*n.* a preliminary taste; anticipation: *The boy got a foretaste of business life by working during his vacation.* —*v.* taste beforehand; anticipate.

fore·tell (fôr tel′) *v.* **-told, -tell·ing.** tell or show beforehand; predict; prophesy: *Who can foretell what a baby will do next?* —**fore·tell′er,** *n.*

fore·thought (fôr′thot′ or -thôt′) *n.* **1** previous thought or consideration; planning. **2** careful thought for the future; prudence; foresight: *A little forethought will often prevent mistakes.*

fore·to·ken (*v.* fôr tō′kən; *n.* fôr′tō′kən) *v.* indicate beforehand; be an omen of. [< n.] —*n.* an indication of something to come; omen. [OE *foretācn*]

fore·told (fôr tōld′) *v.* pt. and pp. of **foretell.**

fore·top (fôr′top′ or fôr′təp) *n.* a platform at the top of the foremast.

fore-top·gal·lant (fôr′top gal′ənt or -tə gal′ənt) *adj.* next above the fore-topmast; of or belonging to the mast, sails, yards, etc. next above the fore-topmast. The fore-topgallant mast is the third mast from the deck of the ship.

fore-top·mast (fôr′top′mast′ or -top′məst) *n.* the mast next above the foremast.

fore-top·sail (fôr′top′sāl′ or -top′səl) *n.* the sail set on the fore-topmast and next above the foresail.

for·ev·er (fər ev′ər) *adv.* **1** for always; without ever coming to an end. **2** all the time; always: *That woman is forever talking.* —*n. Informal.* an excessively long time; an eternity: *He is taking forever to write that book.* —**Syn. 1** ever, evermore, eternally, everlastingly. **2** continually.

for·ev·er·more (fər ev′ər môr′) *adv.* forever.

fore·warn (fôr wôrn′) *v.* warn beforehand.

fore·went (fôr went′) *v.* pt. of **forego.**

fore·wing (fôr′wing′) *n.* the front wing of an insect.

fore·wom·an (fôr′wům′ən) *n.* **-wom·en. 1** a woman who supervises a group of workers, as in a factory, etc. **2** a chairwoman of a jury.

fore·word (fôr′wėrd′) *n.* an introduction; preface. —**Syn.** See **introduction.**

for·feit (fôr′fit) *v.* lose or have to give up as a penalty for some act, neglect, fault, etc.: *He forfeited his deposit when he lost the library book* [< n.]
—*n.* **1** something lost or given up because of some act, neglect, or fault; penalty; fine: *A headache was the forfeit he paid for staying up late.* **2** the loss or giving up of something as a penalty.
—*adj.* lost or given up as a penalty. [ME < OF *forfait* < *forfaire* transgress < *for-* wrongly (< L *foris* outside) + *faire* do < L *facere*] —**for′feit·a·ble,** *adj.* —**for′feit·er,** *n.*

for·fei·ture (fôr′fi chər) *n.* **1** the loss or giving up of something as a penalty; a forfeiting. **2** the thing forfeited; penalty; fine.

for·fend (fôr fend′) *v. Archaic.* ward off; avert; prevent. Also, **forefend.**

for·gat (fər gat′) *v. Archaic.* a pt. of **forget.**

for·gath·er (fôr gaᴛʜ′ər) *v.* **1** gather together; assemble; meet. **2** meet by accident. **3** be friendly; associate. Also, **foregather.**

for·gave (fər gāv′) *v.* pt. of **forgive.**

forge[1] (fôrj) *n. v.* **forged, forg·ing.** —*n.* **1** a fireplace where metal is heated to a high temperature before being hammered into shape: *The blacksmith took the white-hot horseshoe out of the forge.* **2** a blacksmith's shop; smithy. **3** a place where iron or other metal is melted and refined.
—*v.* **1** heat (metal) to a high temperature and then hammer it into shape. **2** make; shape; form. **3** make or write (something false). **4** sign (another's name) falsely in order to deceive: *He was sent to jail for forging cheques.* [ME < OF *forge,* ult. < L *fabrica* workshop. Doublet of FABRIC.] —**forg′er,** *n.* —**Syn.** *v.* **3** counterfeit, falsify.

forge[2] (fôrj) *v.* **forged, forg·ing.** move forward slowly but steadily: *forge ahead.* [origin uncertain]

for·ger·y (fôr′jər ē) *n.* **-ger·ies. 1** the act of forging a signature, etc. **2** something made or written falsely to deceive: *The painting was a forgery. The signature on the cheque was not mine but a forgery.*

for·get (fər get′) *v.* **-got** or (*Archaic*) **-gat, -got·ten** or **-got, -get·ting. 1** let go out of the mind; fail to remember; be unable to remember. **2** omit or neglect without meaning to. **3** leave behind unintentionally: *She had to return home because she had forgotten her purse.* **4 forget oneself, a** not think of oneself and one's interests; be unselfish. **b** fail to consider what one should do or be; say or do something improper. [OE *forgietan* < *for-* (opposite) + ON *geta* get] —**for·get′ter,** *n.*

for·get·ful (fər get′fəl) *adj.* **1** apt to forget; having a poor memory. **2** heedless. **3** *Poetic.* causing to forget. —**for·get′ful·ly,** *adv.*

for·get·ful·ness (fər get′fəl nis) *n.* **1** the quality of being forgetful; the state of having a poor memory. **2** a neglect; lack of attention.

for·get-me-not (fər get′mē not′) *n.* any of several small plants of the same family as the borage, having hairy leaves and clusters of small blue, pink, or white flowers.

forg·ing (fôr′jing) *n.* something forged; a piece of metal that has been forged.

for·give (fər giv′) *v.* **-gave, -giv·en, -giv·ing. 1** give up the wish to punish or get even with; pardon; excuse; not have hard feelings about or toward. **2** give up all claim to; not demand payment for: *forgive a debt.* [OE *forgiefan* < *for-* away + *giefan* give] —**for·giv′a·ble,** *adj.* —**for·giv′a·bly,** *adv.* —**Syn. 1** absolve. See **excuse.**

for·giv·en (fər giv′ən) *v.* pp. of **forgive.**

for·give·ness (fər giv′nis) *n.* **1** the act of forgiving; pardon. **2** willingness to forgive.

for·giv·ing (fər giv′ing) *adj.* that forgives; willing to forgive. —**for·giv′ing·ly,** *adv.* —**for·giv′ing·ness,** *n.*

for·go (fôr gō′) *v.* **-went, -gone, -go·ing.** forego.

for·gone (fôr gon′) *v.* pp. of **forgo.**

for·got (fər got′) *v.* a pt. and a pp. of **forget.**

for·got·ten (fər got′ən) *v.* a pp. of **forget.**

for·int (fôr′int) *n.* **1** a unit of money in Hungary. See table at **money. 2** a coin worth one forint. [< Hungarian *forint,* prob. < Ital. *fiorino* florin]

fork (fôrk) *n.* **1** an instrument having a handle and two or more long, pointed prongs, or tines, at one end: *a table fork, a garden fork.* **2** anything shaped like a fork, such as a tuning fork or a divining rod. **3** the place where a tree, road, or stream divides into two branches: *They parted at the fork of the road.* **4** one of the branches into which anything is divided.
—*v.* **1** lift, throw, or dig with a fork. **2** make in the shape or form of a fork. **3** have a fork or forks; divide into branches. **4 fork up, out,** or **over,** *Slang.* hand over; pay out. [OE *forca* < L *furca*] —**fork′less,** *adj.* —**fork′like′,** *adj.*

forked (fôrkt; *Archaic and poetic,* fôr′kid) *adj.* **1** having a fork or forks; divided into branches. **2** zigzag: *forked lightning.* **3 speak with a forked tongue,** speak untruths; tell lies.

fork lift a loading, unloading, and stacking device, consisting of a movable machine having two prongs for raising and lowering a skid loaded with goods.

for·lorn (fôr lôrn′) *adj.* **1** left alone; neglected; deserted: *The lost kitten, a forlorn little animal, was wet and dirty.* **2** wretched in feeling or looks; unhappy. **3** hopeless; desperate. **4** bereft (*of*): *forlorn of hope.* [OE *forloren* lost, pp. of *forlēosan*] —**for·lorn′ly,** *adv.* —**for·lorn′ness,** *n.* —**Syn. 1** abandoned, forsaken.

forlorn hope 1 a desperate enterprise. **2** an undertaking almost sure to fail. **3** a party of soldiers engaged in a very dangerous job. [alteration of Du. *verloren hoop* lost troop]

form (fôrm) *n.* **1** appearance apart from color or materials; shape. **2** a shape of body; body of a person or animal. **3** something that gives shape to something else: *A mould is a form.* **4** an orderly arrangement of parts: *The effect of a work of literature, art, or music comes from its form as well as its content.* **5** a way of doing something; manner; method: *He is a fast runner, but his form in running is bad.* **6** a set way of doing something; set way of behaving according to custom or rule; formality; ceremony: *Shaking hands is a form. Many forms have little or no real meaning.* **7** a set order of words; formula: *A written agreement to buy, sell, or do something follows a certain form.* **8** a document with printing or writing on it and blank spaces to be filled in: *To get a licence, you must fill out a form.* **9** the way in which a thing exists, takes shape, or shows itself; condition; character; manifestation: *Water appears also in the forms of ice, snow, and steam.* **10** kind; sort; variety: *Heat, light, and electricity are forms of energy.* **11** a good condition of body or mind: *Athletes exercise to keep in form.* **12** in grammar, any of the ways in which a word is spelled or pronounced to express different ideas and relationships. *Boys* is the plural form of *boy. Saw* is the past form of *see. My* and *mine* are the possessive forms of *I.* **13** a grade in school, especially in high school. **14** a long seat; bench. **15** in printing, type fastened in a frame ready for printing or making plates. **16** in philosophy, the element or quality in a thing that makes it what it is. **17 bad form,** behavior contrary to accepted customs. **18 good form,** behavior in accord with accepted customs.
—*v.* **1** give shape to; make: *The cook formed the dough into loaves.* **2** be formed; take shape: *Clouds form in the sky.* **3** become: *Water forms ice when it freezes.* **4** make up; compose: *Parents and children form a family.* **5** organize; establish: *We formed a club.* **6** develop: *Form good habits while you are young.* **7** arrange in some order: *The soldiers formed themselves into lines.* [ME < OF < L *forma* form, mould] —**form′a·ble,** *adj.*

Syn. *n.* **1 Form, shape, figure** = the appearance of something apart from the color or the material of which it is made. **Form** particularly suggests that there is substance or structure under the surface, which gives rise to the special appearance seen: *There have been many improvements in the form of airplanes.* **Shape,** more informal, emphasizes definiteness of form and solidness of body or substance, and means the whole outline or mould of the person or thing: *His head has a strange shape.* **Figure** applies only to the outline of a form: *He drew figures of animals.* **6** convention. —*v.* **1** fashion, shape, mould.

-form *suffix.* **1** having the form of ——, as in *cruciform.* **2** having —— form or forms, as in *multiform.* [< L *-formis* < *forma* form]

for·mal (fôr′məl) *adj.* **1** with strict attention to outwar forms and ceremonies; not familiar and homelike; stiff: *The judge always had a formal manner in court.* **2** according to set customs or rules. **3** done with the proper forms; clear and definite: *A written contract is a formal agreement to do something.* **4** very regular; symmetrical; orderly. **5** having to do with the form, not the content. **6** of language, conforming to a studied style in vocabulary, syntax, and pronunciation, as accepted for dignified use. ☛ See **informal** for usage note. —*n.* **1** a social gathering at which formal dress is worn. **2** a gown worn to formal social gatherings: *She was dressed in her first formal.* [< L *formalis* < *forma* form] —**for′mal·ly,** *adv.*

Syn. 1, 2 Formal, conventional = according to outward forms and rules. **Formal** = showing strict attention to rules and set ways of doing things, and implies correctness, stiffness, and lack of warmth and naturalness: *The judge always had a formal manner in court.* **Conventional** = showing attention to generally accepted forms and customs, especially in social behavior, and emphasizes lack of originality: *She wrote a conventional note of sympathy.*

form·al·de·hyde (fôr mal′də hīd′) *n.* a colorless gas with a sharp, irritating odor, used in solution as a disinfectant and preservative. *Formula*: CH_2O [< *form(ic acid)* + *aldehyde*]

for·ma·lin (fôr′mə lin) *n.* a solution for formaldehyde in water.

for·mal·ism (fôr′məl iz′əm) *n.* strict attention to outward forms and ceremonies.

for·mal·ist (fôr′məl ist) *n.* a person inclined to formalism.

for·mal·is·tic (fôr′məl is′tik) *adj.* of formalism or formalists.

for·mal·i·ty (fôr mal′ə tē) *n.* **-ties. 1** a procedure required by custom or rule; outward form; ceremony. **2** attention to forms and customs: *Visitors at the court of a king are received with formality.* **3** stiffness of manner, behavior, or arrangement.

for·mal·ize (fôr′məl īz′) *v.* **-ized, -iz·ing. 1** make formal. **2** give a definite form to. —**for′mal·i·za′tion,** *n.* —**for′mal·iz·er,** *n.*

for·mat (fôr′mat) *n.* **1** the shape, size, and general arrangement of a book, magazine, etc. **2** the design, plan, or arrangement of anything: *the format of a legislative program, television show, etc.* [< F < L *(liber) formatus* (book) formed (in a special way)]

for·ma·tion (fôr mā′shən) *n.* **1** a forming or being formed: *Heat causes the formation of steam from water. The formation of words is a fascinating study.* **2** the way in which a thing is arranged; arrangement; order: *troops in battle formation.* **3** the thing formed: *Clouds are formations of tiny drops of water in the sky.* **4** in geology, a series of layers or deposits of the same kind of rock or mineral.

form·a·tive (fôr′mə tiv) *adj.* **1** having to do with formation or development; forming; moulding: *Home and school are the chief formative influences in a child's life.* **2** in grammar, used to form words. Words may be made from other words by adding formative endings, such as *-ly* and *-ness.* **3** in biology, that can produce new cells or tissues: *formative tissue, formative yolk.* —**for′ma·tive·ly,** *adv.* —**for′ma·tive·ness,** *n.*

for·mer[1] (fôr′mər) *adj.* **1** first of two. In "Jack and Jim" Jack is the former. **2** earlier; past; long past: *In former times people lived in caves.* [ME *formere,* comparative back-formation from *formest.* See FOREMOST.] —**Syn. 2** bygone.

for·mer[2] (fôr′mər) *n.* a person or thing that forms. [< *form*]

for·mer·ly (fôr′mər lē) *adv.* in the past; some time ago: *Mrs. Smith was formerly known as Miss Snell.* —**Syn.** previously, once.

for·mic acid (fôr′mik) a colorless liquid that is irritating to the skin. It occurs in ants, spiders, nettles, etc. and is used in dyeing, finishing textiles, etc. *Formula*: CH_2O_2 [< L *formica* ant]

for·mi·da·ble (fôr′mə də bəl) *adj.* hard to overcome; hard to deal with; to be dreaded. [< L *formidabilis* < *formidare* dread] —**for′mi·da·ble·ness,** *n.* —**for′mi·da·bly,** *adv.* —**Syn.** appalling, fearful.

hat, āge, cãre, fär; let, ēqual, tėrm; it, īce
hot, ōpen, ôrder; oil, out; cup, pu̇t, rüle, ūse
əbove, takən, pencəl, lemən, circəs
ch, child; ng, long; sh, ship
th, thin; ᴛʜ, then; zh, measure

form·less (fôrm′lis) *adj.* without definite or regular form; shapeless. —**form′less·ly,** *adv.* —**form′less·ness,** *n.*

form letter a letter so phrased that it may be sent to many different people; a letter copied from a pattern.

form sheet 1 a detailed information sheet having the names of the horses and jockeys in the day's races, records of past performances, weights carried, etc. **2** a list giving the records of participants in any match, contest, etc.

for·mu·la (fôr′myu̇ lə) *n.* **-las** or **-lae** (-lē′ or -lī′). **1** a set form of words, especially one that by much use has partly lost its meaning: *"How do you do?" is a formula of greeting.* **2** a statement of religious belief or doctrine: *The Apostles' Creed is a formula of the Christian faith.* **3** a rule for doing something, especially as used by those who do not know the reason on which it is based. **4** a recipe; prescription: *a formula for making soup.* **5** a mixture, especially one for feeding a baby, made according to a recipe or prescription. **6** in chemistry, an expression showing by symbols and figures the composition of a compound: *The formula for water is* H_2O. **7** an expression showing by algebraic symbols a rule, principle, etc. $(a + b)^2 = a^2 + 2ab + b^2$ is an algebraic formula. [< L *formula,* dim. of *forma* form]

for·mu·lae (fôr′myu̇ lē or fôr′myu̇ lī′) *n.* a pl. of **formula.**

for·mu·lar·y (fôr′myu̇ ler′ē) *n.* **-lar·ies,** *adj.* —*n.* **1** a collection of formulas. **2** a set form of words; formula. **3** in pharmacy, a book of formulas for standard preparations used in medicines. —*adj.* having to do with formulas.

for·mu·late (fôr′myu̇ lāt′) *v.* **-lat·ed, -lat·ing. 1** state definitely; express in systematic form. **2** express in a formula; reduce to a formula. —**for′mu·la′tor,** *n.*

for·mu·la·tion (fôr′myu̇ lā′shən) *n.* **1** a definite statement; an expression in systematic form. **2** expression in a formula.

for·mu·lism (for′myu̇ liz′əm) *n.* **1** reliance on, or adherence to, formulas. **2** a group or set of formulas.

for·ni·cate (fôr′nə kāt′) *v.* **-cat·ed, -cat·ing.** commit fornication. [< Ecclesiastical L *fornicari* < *fornix* brothel] —**for′ni·ca·tor,** *n.*

for·ni·ca·tion (fôr′nə kā′shən) *n.* **1** a sexual act between unmarried persons. **2** in the Bible: **a** adultery. **b** idolatry.

for·sake (fôr sāk′) *v.* **-sook, -sak·en, -sak·ing.** give up; leave alone; leave; abandon. [OE *forsacan* < *for-* away + *sacan* dispute, deny] —**Syn.** See **desert**[2].

for·sak·en (fôr sāk′ən) *v.* pp. of **forsake.** —*adj.* deserted; abandoned; *a forsaken house.* —**for·sak′en·ly,** *adv.*

for·sook (fôr su̇k′) *v.* pt. of **forsake.**

for·sooth (fôr süth′) *adv. Archaic.* in truth; indeed. [OE *forsōth* < *for* for + *sōth* sooth, truth]

for·swear (fôr swãr′) *v.* **-swore, -sworn, -swear·ing. 1** renounce on oath; swear or promise solemnly to give up. **2** deny solemnly or on oath. **3** be untrue to one's sworn word or promise; perjure (oneself). [OE *forswerian*]

for·swore (fôr swôr′) *v.* pt. of **forswear.**

for·sworn (fôr swôrn′) *adj.* untrue to one's sworn word or promise; perjured. —*v.* pp. of **forswear.**

for·syth·i·a (fôr sith′ē ə or fôr sī′thē ə) *n.* a shrub having many bell-shaped, yellow flowers in early spring before its leaves come out. [< NL; after William *Forsyth* (1737-1804), a British horticulturist]

fort (fôrt) *n.* **1** a strong building or place that can be defended against an enemy. **2** formerly, a trading post. In the early days of the fur trade, these posts were usually fortified: *Winnipeg is built on the site of Fort Garry, an old Hudson's Bay Company post.* **3 hold the fort,** make a defence. [< F < L *fortis* strong]

forte[1] (fôrt) *n.* something a person does very well; strong point: *Cooking is her forte.* [< F *forte,* fem. of *fort* strong < L *fortis*]

for·te[2] (fôr′tā) in music: —*adj. adv.* loud. —*n.* a loud passage or tone. [< Ital. *forte* strong < L *fortis*]

forth (fôrth) *adv.* **1** forward; onward. **2** into view or consideration; out. **3** away. **4 and so forth,** and so on; and the like. [OE]

forth·com·ing (fôrth′kum′ing or fôrth kum′ing) *adj.* **1** about to appear; approaching: *The forthcoming week will be busy.* **2** ready when wanted: *She needed help, but none was forthcoming.* **3** ready to meet or make advances; accommodating. —*n.* an appearance, approach.

forth·right (*adj.* fôrth′rīt′; *adv. also* fôrth′rīt′) *adj.* frank and outspoken; straightforward; direct.
—*adv.* **1** straight ahead; directly forward. **2** at once; immediately. —**forth′right′ly,** *adv.* —**forth′right′ness,** *n.*

fort hunter formerly, a hunter, usually an Indian, employed by a fur company to provide meat for a trading post, or fort.

forth·with (fôrth′with′ or -wiTH′) *adv.* at once; immediately.

for·ti·eth (fôr′tē ith) *adj. n.* **1** next after the 39th; last in a series of 40. **2** one, or being one, of 40 equal parts.

for·ti·fi·ca·tion (fôr′tə fə kā′shən) *n.* **1** a fortifying: *Soldiers were busy with the fortification of the village.* **2** anything used in fortifying; a fort, wall, ditch, etc. **3** a fortified place. **4** the enriching of foods with vitamins and minerals.

for·ti·fy (fôr′tə fī′) *v.* **-fied, -fy·ing. 1** build forts, walls, etc.; strengthen against attack; provide with forts, walls, etc. **2** give support to; strengthen. **3** enrich with vitamins and minerals: *fortify bread.* **4** strengthen with alcohol: *Port and sherry are fortified wines.* [ME < OF *fortifier* < LL *fortificare,* ult. < L *fortis* strong + *facere* make] —**for′ti·fi·er,** *n.*

for·tis·si·mo (fôr tis′ə mō′) in music: —*adj. adv.* very loud. —*n.* a very loud passage or tone. *Abbrev.*: ff [< Ital. *fortissimo,* superlative of *forte* strong]

for·ti·tude (fôr′tə tūd′ or fôr′tə tüd′) *n.* courage in facing pain, danger, or trouble; firmness of spirit. [< L *fortitudo* < *fortis* strong] —**Syn.** endurance, bravery, resolution. See **patience.**

for·ti·tu·di·nous (fôr′tə tū′də nəs or fôr′tə tü′də nəs) *adj.* having or characterized by fortitude: *a fortitudinous display of character.*

fort·night (fôrt′nīt) *n.* two weeks. [ME *fourtenight,* contraction of OE *fēowertīene niht* fourteen nights]

fort·night·ly (fôrt′nīt lē) *adv.* once every two weeks. —*adj.* appearing or happening once in every two weeks. —*n.* a periodical published every two weeks.

for·tress (fôr′tris) *n.* a fortified place; large and well-protected fort. [ME < OF *forteresse* < *fort* strong < L *fortis*] —**Syn.** citadel.

for·tu·i·tous (fôr tū′ə təs or fôr tü′ə təs) *adj.* happening by chance; accidental: *a fortuitous meeting, a fortuitous acquaintance.* [< L *fortuitus,* ult. < *fors, fortis* chance] —**for·tu′i·tous·ly,** *adv.* —**for·tu′i·tous·ness,** *n.*

☞ **Fortuitous** is sometimes used to refer to events that, besides being accidental and unintentioned, happen to be providential or fortunate. **Fortuitous** and **fortunate** have a common origin: L *fors, fortis* luck. However, not every **fortunate** happening may be correctly referred to as **fortuitous,** but only those that are accidentally so.

for·tu·i·ty (fôr tū′ə tē or fôr tü′ə tē) *n.* **-ties.** chance; accident.

for·tu·nate (fôr′chə nit) *adj.* **1** having good luck; lucky. **2** bringing good luck; having favorable results. [< L *fortunatus,* pp. of *fortunare* assign fortune to < *fortuna* fortune] —**for′tu·nate·ly,** *adv.*

Syn. 1, 2 Fortunate, lucky = having or bringing good luck. **Fortunate** suggests being favored by circumstances strongly to one's advantage or helpful in bringing about success that could not have been counted on or in bringing something wholly unexpected: *He made a fortunate decision when he went into advertising.* **Lucky** is less formal and emphasizes the idea of accident or pure chance: *It was lucky that he missed his train the day it was wrecked.*

for·tune (fôr′chən) *n.* **1** a great deal of money or property; riches; wealth. **2** what is going to happen to a person; fate: *Gypsies often claim that they can tell people's fortunes.* **3** good luck; prosperity; success. **4** what happens; luck; chance: *Fortune was against us; we lost.* [ME < OF < L *fortuna*] —**Syn. 2** destiny, lot.

fortune hunter 1 a person who tries to get a fortune by marrying someone rich. **2** anybody who seeks wealth.

for·tune·tell·er (fôr′chən tel′ər) *n.* a person who claims to be able to tell what is going to happen to other people.

for·ty (fôr′tē) *n.* **-ties,** *adj.* four times ten; 40. [OE *fēowertig*]

For·ty-Nin·er (fôr′tē nīn′ər) *n.* a person who went to California to seek gold in 1849. It had been discovered there in 1848.

forty winks *Informal.* a short nap.

fo·rum (fô′rəm) *n.* **1** in ancient Rome, the public square or market place. The forum in Rome was used for public assemblies and business. **2** an assembly for discussing questions of public interest. **3** a law court; tribunal. [< L]

for·ward (fôr′wərd) *adv.* **1** ahead; onward: *The men marched forward.* **2** toward the front. **3** out; into view or consideration: *In his talk he brought forward several new ideas.*
—*adj.* **1** toward the front: *the forward part of a ship.* **2** far ahead; advanced: *A child of four years that can read is forward for his age.* **3** ready; eager: *He knew his lesson and was forward with his answers.* **4** pert; bold.
—*v.* **1** send on further: *Please forward my mail to my new address.* **2** help along: *He forwarded his friend's plan.*
—*n.* in certain games, a player whose position is in the front line. [OE *forweard*] —**for′ward·er,** *n.* —**for′ward·ly,** *adv.*

Syn. *adv.* **1 Forward, onward** = toward the front or a position or point ahead. **Forward** especially suggests looking or moving toward what lies ahead, in front or in the future or at the end: *We must look forward, not backward.* **Onward,** often interchangeable with *forward,* emphasizes moving or progressing toward a definite point, place, or goal: *The boat sailed onward toward the shore.* —*adj.* **2** precocious. **4** impertinent, presumptuous. See **bold.**

for·ward·ness (fôr′wərd nis) *n.* **1** readiness; eagerness. **2** pertness; boldness.

forward pass the throwing of a football to a player on the same team in the direction of the opponents' goal.

for·wards (fôr′wərdz) *adv.* forward.

for·went (fôr went′) *v.* pt. of **forgo.**

fos·sa (fos′ə) *n.* **fos·sae** (fos′ē or fos′ī). in anatomy, a shallow depression or cavity in a bone, etc. [< L *fossa* ditch]

fosse (fos) *n.* a ditch; trench; canal; moat. [ME < OF < L *fossa* ditch]

fos·sil (fos′əl) *n.* **1** the hardened remains or traces of animals or plants of a former age: *Fossils of ferns are often found in coal.* **2** a very old-fashioned person, set in his ways.
—*adj.* **1** forming a fossil; of the nature of a fossil. **2** dug out of the earth: *fossil salt.* **3** belonging to the outworn past: *fossil ideas.* [< F < L *fossilis* dug up < *fodere* dig] —**fos′sil-like′,** *adj.*

fos·sil·if·er·ous (fos′ə lif′ər əs) *adj.* containing fossils.

fos·sil·ize (fos′ə līz′) *v.* **-ized, -iz·ing. 1** make into a fossil; change into a fossil; turn into stone. **2** make or become antiquated, set, stiff, or rigid. —**fos′sil·i·za′tion,** *n.*

fos·ter (fos′tər) *v.* **1** help the growth or development of; encourage: *Ignorance fosters superstition.* **2** care for fondly; cherish. **3** bring up; rear. —*adj.* in the same family but not related by birth: *a foster brother.* [OE *fōstrian* nourish, *fōster* nourishment. Related to FOOD.]
—**Syn.** *v.* **1** promote, further. **2** See **cherish.**

foster brother a boy brought up with another child or children of different parents.

foster child a child brought up by a person who is not his parent.

foster father a man who brings up a child or children of other parents.

foster mother a woman who brings up a child or children of other parents.

foster parent a person who brings up a child or children of other parents; a foster father or foster mother.

foster sister a girl brought up with another child or children of different parents.

fou·droy·ant (fü droi′ənt) *adj.* **1** striking like lightning; suddenly overwhelming. **2** in medicine, starting suddenly and severely: *a foudroyant TB case.* [< F *foudroyant* < *foudroyer* strike like lightning < OF *fouldre* lightning < LL *fulgere* < L *fulgur* lightning]

fouet·té (fwe tā′) *n. v.* **-téd, -té·ing.** in ballet: —*n.* a quick turn in which one leg acts as a pivot as the other leg is thrown sideways and then bent in with the toes pointing toward the other knee. —*v.* perform a fouetté. [< F *fouetté*, literally, a whipped step, pp. of *fouetter* whip, beat]

fought (fot or fôt) *v.* pt. and pp. of **fight.**

foul (foul) *adj.* **1** containing filth; covered with filth; very dirty; nasty; smelly: *Open the windows and let out the foul air.* **2** very wicked; vile: *Murder is a foul crime.* **3** obscene; indecent: *foul language.* **4** against the rules; unfair. **5** hitting against: *One boat was foul of the other.* **6** tangled up; caught: *The sailor cut the foul rope.* **7** clogged up: *The fire will not burn because the chimney is foul.* **8** of a ship, having the bottom covered with seaweed, barnacles, etc. **9** unfavorable; stormy: *Foul weather delayed the ship.* **10** contrary: *a foul wind.* **11** *Informal.* very unpleasant or objectionable. **12** in baseball, of or having to do with foul balls or foul lines.
—*v.* **1** make or become dirty; soil; defile: *Mud fouls things.* **2** dishonor; disgrace: *a name fouled by misdeeds.* **3** make a foul, make a foul against. **4** in baseball, hit a ball so that it falls outside the foul lines. **5** hit against: *One boat fouled the other.* **6** get tangled up with; catch: *The rope fouled the anchor chain.* **7** clog up: *Grease fouled the drain.* **8** cover (a ship's bottom) with seaweed, barnacles, etc. **9 foul out, a** in baseball, be put out by hitting a ball that is caught outside the foul lines. **b** in basketball, be put out of a game for having committed too many fouls. **10 foul up,** *Informal.* make a mess of; bungle.
—*n.* **1** something done contrary to the rules; unfair play. **2** in baseball, a foul ball.
—*adv.* **go, fall,** or **run foul of, a** hit against and get tangled up with. **b** get into trouble or difficulties with. [OE *fūl*] —**foul′ly,** *adv.* —**foul′ness,** *n.* —**Syn.** *adj.* **1** soiled, polluted, unclean. See **dirty.**

fou·lard (fü lärd′) *n.* **1** a soft, thin fabric made of silk, rayon, or cotton, usually with a printed pattern. It is used for neckties, dresses, etc. **2** a necktie or handkerchief made from this material. [< F < Swiss F *foulat* cloth that has been cleansed and thickened]

foul ball in baseball, a ball hit so that it falls outside the foul lines.

foul line 1 in baseball, either the line from home to first base, or from home to third base, with their marked or unmarked continuations. **2** in basketball, a line within the circle in front of each basket from which foul shots are made. **3** a line or mark which may not be stepped on or over in making a broad jump, throwing the javelin, etc.

foul-mouthed (foul′mouᴛʜd′ or -moutht′) *adj.* using vile language.

foul play 1 unfair play; a thing or things done against the rules. **2** treachery; violence.

foul shot in basketball: **1** a free shot awarded to one team for a foul by the opponent's team. **2** a score of one point for putting such a shot into the basket.

foul tip in baseball, a ball deflected by the bat back to the catcher.

foul-up (foul′up′) *n. Slang.* a disorder or muddle that interferes with a project or operation: *There was a last-minute foul-up in the sports program.*

found[1] (found) *v.* pt. and pp. of **find.**

found[2] (found) *v.* **1** establish; set up: *Champlain founded Quebec in 1608.* **2** rest for support; base: *He founded his claim on facts.* [ME < OF *fonder* < L *fundare* < *fundus* bottom] —**Syn. 1** settle.

found[3] (found) *v.* melt and mould (metal); make of molten metal; cast. [< F *fondre* < L *fundere* pour]

foun·da·tion (foun dā′shən) *n.* **1** the part on which the other parts rest for support; base: *the foundation of a house.* **2** a basis: *Anglo-Saxon common law is the foundation of our legal system.* **3** a founding or establishing. **4** a being founded or established. **5** an institution founded and endowed: *a charitable foundation.* **6** a fund given to support an institution. **7** a part over which something is laid: *Her full skirt swirled over a foundation of starched cotton petticoats.* **8** a foundation garment. **9** a cream or liquid cosmetic applied on the face as a base for rouge, powder, etc. —**Syn. 1** See **base**[1].

hat, āge, cãre, fär; let, ēqual, tėrm; it, īce
hot, ōpen, ôrder; oil, out; cup, pu̇t, rüle, ūse
əbove, takən, pencəl, lemən, circəs
ch, child; ng, long; sh, ship
th, thin; ᴛʜ, then; zh, measure

foundation garment a woman's corset, girdle, etc., usually having a brassiere attached.

foun·der[1] (foun′dər) *v.* **1** fill with water and sink: *The ship foundered in the storm.* **2** break down; go lame; stumble: *His horse foundered.* **3** become worn out; fail. **4** cause to fill with water and sink. **5** cause (a horse) to break down, fall lame, etc. **6** in golf, hit (the ball) into the ground. [ME < OF *fondrer*, ult. < L *fundus* bottom]

found·er[2] (foun′dər) *n.* a person who founds or establishes something. [< *found*[2]]

found·er[3] (foun′dər) *n.* a person who casts metals. [< *found*[3]]

found-in (found′in′) *n.* a person arrested for being present in a brothel, an illegal drinking or gambling establishment, etc.

found·ling (found′ling) *n.* a baby or child found abandoned. [ME *fundeling.* Related to FIND.]

found·ry (foun′drē) *n.* **-ries. 1** a place where metal is melted and moulded; place where things are made of molten metal. **2** the melting and moulding of metal; process of making things of molten metal. **3** things made of molten metal; castings. [< F *fonderie* < *fondre* found[3]]

fount (fount) *n.* **1** a fountain. **2** a source. [< L *fons, fontis* spring]

foun·tain (foun′tən) *n.* **1** a stream of water rising into the air. **2** the pipes through which water is forced and the basin that receives it. **3** a spring of water. **4** a place to get a drink: *a soda fountain.* **5** a source; origin: *Solomon was a fountain of wisdom.* **6** a container to hold a steady supply of ink, oil, etc. [ME < OF *fontaine* < LL *fontana*, originally fem. of *fontanus* of a spring < L *fons, fontis* spring]

foun·tain·head (foun′tən hed′) *n.* **1** the source of a stream. **2** an original source.

Fountain of Youth a legendary spring whose waters were supposed to cure any sickness and restore youth.

fountain pen a pen having a reservoir that gives a steady supply of ink while writing.

four (fôr) *n.* **1** one more than three; 4. **2** a set of four things or persons, such as a team of four horses, or the crew of a four-oared boat. **3** a boat with four oars. **4** a playing card, die, domino, etc. having four spots. **5** in cricket, a hit for which four runs are scored. **6 on all fours, a** on all four feet. **b** on hands and knees.
—*adj.* being one more than three. [OE *fēower*]

four flush 1 in poker, a four-card suit (instead of the five needed for a flush). **2** *Slang.* false pretence; bluff.

four-flush·er (fôr′flush′ər) *n. Slang.* a person who pretends to be more or other than he really is; bluffer.

four·fold (fôr′fōld′) *adj.* **1** four times as much or as many. **2** having four parts. —*adv.* four times as much or as many.

four-foot·ed (fôr′fu̇t′id) *adj.* having four feet.

four-four (fôr′fôr′) *adj.* in music, indicating or having four quarter notes in a bar or measure, the first and third of which are accented.

four freedoms freedom of speech, freedom of worship, freedom from want, and freedom from fear, set forth in 1941 by President Franklin D. Roosevelt of the United States.

four-hand·ed (fôr′han′did) *adj.* **1** having four hands. **2** for four players.

Four-H clubs or **4-H clubs** a national system of clubs to teach rural children agriculture and home economics. Their purpose is the improvement of head, heart, hands, and health.

Four Horsemen of the Apocalypse in the Bible, the riders of four different colored horses, seen in a prophetic vision, the red horse representing War, the black horse,

Famine, the pale horse, Death and Pestilence, the white horse, Christ or Victory. Rev. 6:1-8.

four-in-hand (fôr′in hand′) *n.* **1** a necktie tied in a slip knot with the ends left hanging. **2** a carriage pulled by four horses driven by one person. **3** a team of four horses.

four-letter word (fôr′let′ər) any of various short English words judged to be obscene and unfit to print.

four-o'clock (fôr′ə klok′) *n.* a small plant having red, white, or yellow trumpet-shaped flowers that open late in the afternoon and close in the morning.

four of a kind in poker, a hand having four cards of the same value.

four·score (fôr′skôr′) *adj. n.* four times twenty; 80.

four·some (fôr′səm) *n.* **1** a group of four people. **2** a game played by four people, two on each side. **3** the players.

four·square (*adj.* fôr′skwãr′; *n.* fôr′skwãr′) *adj.* **1** square. **2** frank; outspoken. **3** not yielding; firm. —*n.* a square.

four·teen (fôr′tēn′) *n. adj.* four more than ten; 14. [OE *fēowertēne*]

four·teenth (fôr′tēnth′) *adj. n.* **1** next after the 13th; last in a series of 14. **2** one, or being one, of 14 equal parts.

fourth (fôrth) *adj.* **1** next after the third; last in a series of 4. **2** being one of 4 equal parts.
—*n.* **1** the next after the third; last in a series of 4. **2** one of 4 equal parts. **3** in music: **a** the fourth tone from the keynote of a scale. **b** the interval between such tones. **c** a combination of such tones.

fourth dimension a dimension in addition to length, breadth, and depth: *Time has been thought of as a fourth dimension.*

fourth estate the press; newspapers and those who work for them.

fourth·ly (fôrth′lē) *adv.* in the fourth place.

Fourth of July in the United States, a holiday in memory of the adoption of the Declaration of Independence on July 4, 1776.

four-wheeled (fôr′hwēld′ or -wēld′) *adj.* having four wheels; running on four wheels.

fowl (foul) *n.* **fowls** or (*esp. collectively*) **fowl. 1** any bird. **2** any of several kinds of large birds used for food, such as chickens, geese, and turkeys. **3** the flesh of a fowl used for food. —*v.* hunt, shoot, catch, or trap wild birds. [OE *fugol*]

fowl·er (foul′ər) *n.* a person who hunts, shoots, catches, or traps wild birds.

fowling piece a light gun for shooting wild birds.

fox (foks) *n.* **1** a wild animal related to the dog, having a pointed muzzle and a bushy tail. Foxes are sly and crafty. **2** the fur of this animal. **3** a coat or other garment made of this fur. **4** a sly, crafty person; a person noted for his ability to get the better of other people.
—*v.* **1** *Informal.* trick in a sly and crafty way. **2** of beer, turn sour. **3** make (beer) sour. **4** discolor; stain (the pages of a book). **5** become discolored or stained. **6** make or repair (a boot, shoe, etc.) by covering with or adding upper leather. **7** hunt the fox. [OE] —**fox′like′**, *adj.*

Fox (foks) *n.* **Fox·es** or **Fox. 1** a tribe of Algonquian Indians, closely related to the Sauks, inhabiting the Fox River valley in Wisconsin. **2** a member of this tribe. **3** the language of this tribe.

fox·ber·ry (foks′ber′ē) *n.* a trailing evergreen of the heath family, having red berries and thick leaves.

fox·glove (foks′gluv′) *n.* a plant having tall stalks and many bell-shaped flowers. Digitalis is obtained from its leaves and seeds. [OE *foxes glōfa*]

fox·hole (foks′hōl′) *n.* a hole in the ground for protection against enemy fire.

fox·hound (foks′hound′) *n.* **1** either of two breeds of hound, English or American, having a keen sense of smell. **2** a dog of either of these breeds. Foxhounds are bred and trained to hunt foxes.

fox hunt a sport in which hunters on horseback follow dogs that chase the fox.

fox-hunt (foks′hunt′) *v.* pursue or hunt foxes with hounds. —**fox′-hunt′er**, *n.*

fox-hunt·ing (foks′hun′ting) *n.* the sport of hunting foxes with hounds. —*adj.* **1** having to do with the hunting of foxes. **2** having the habits and preferences of a fox hunter.

fox·tail (foks′tāl′) *n.* **1** the tail of a fox. **2** a kind of grass having soft, brushlike spikes of flowers.

fox terrier 1 a breed of small, active dog originally used to drive foxes from their holes. They are white with brown or black spots and may have smooth or rough coats. **2** a dog of this breed.

fox trot 1 a dance in two-four or four-four time with short, quick steps. **2** the music for this dance.

fox-trot (foks′trot′) *v.* **-trot·ted, -trot·ting.** dance the fox trot.

fox·y (fok′sē) *adj.* **fox·i·er, fox·i·est. 1** like a fox; sly; crafty. **2** discolored; stained. —**fox′i·ly,** *adv.* —**fox′i·ness,** *n.*

foy·er (foi′ər or foi′ā) *n.* **1** an entrance hall used as a lounging room in a theatre or hotel; lobby. **2** an entrance hall. [< F, ult. < L *focus* hearth]

F.P., f.p., or **fp 1** foot-pound. **2** freezing point.

fpm or **f.p.m.** feet per minute.

fps or **f.p.s.** feet per second.

fr. 1 franc. **2** from. **3** fragment.

Fr francium.

Fr. 1 France. **2** French. **3** Father. **4** Friday. **5** Friar.

Fra (frä) *n.* Brother. It is used as the title of a monk or friar. [< Ital. *fra,* abbreviation of *frate* brother < L *frater*]

fra·cas (frā′kəs) *n.* a noisy quarrel or fight; disturbance; uproar; brawl. [< F < Ital. *fracasso* < *fracassare* smash]

frac·tion (frak′shən) *n.* **1** in mathematics: **a** one or more of the equal parts of a whole. $\frac{1}{2}$, $\frac{2}{3}$, $\frac{3}{4}$, $\frac{5}{8}$, and $\frac{7}{8}$ are fractions. **b** a division of one mathematical expression by another, indicated by a line with one quantity above it and another below it. **2** a very small part, amount, etc.; fragment. **3** a breaking. **4** in chemistry, any of the components of a substance separated by distillation, crystallization, etc. [< LL *fractio, -onis* < L *frangere* break]

frac·tion·al (frak′shən əl) *adj.* **1** having to do with fractions. **2** forming a fraction: *440 yards is a fractional part of a mile.* **3** very small; insignificant. **4** in chemistry, of or designating a method for separating a mixture into its component parts based on certain differences in boiling points, solubility, etc. of these parts: *fractional crystallization, fractional oxidation.* **5** in stock exchanges, being less than the amount used as a standard unit of measurement, as less than 100 shares of stock, or $10,000 of bonds. —**frac′tion·al·ly,** *adv.*

frac·tion·ate (frak′shə nāt′) *v.* **-at·ed, -at·ing. 1** in chemistry, separate a mixture into components or properties by distillation, crystallization, etc. **2** acquire or obtain by this process. —**frac′tion·a′tion,** *n.*

frac·tious (frak′shəs) *adj.* **1** cross; fretful; peevish. **2** hard to manage; unruly. [< *fraction* (in obs. sense of discord, brawling), on the model of *captious,* etc.] —**frac′tious·ly,** *adv.* —**frac′tious·ness,** *n.* —**Syn. 1** irritable, snappish. **2** refractory, intractable.

frac·ture (frak′chər) *v.* **-tured, -tur·ing,** *n.* —*v.* break; crack: *The boy fell from a tree and fractured his arm.* —*n.* **1** a break; crack. **2** a breaking or being broken. **3** a breaking of a bone or cartilage. **4** the surface of a freshly broken mineral. [< F < L *fractura* < *frangere* break]

frae (frā) *Scottish.* —*prep.* from. —*adv.* fro.

frag·ile (fraj′īl or fraj′əl) *adj.* easily broken, damaged, or destroyed; delicate; frail. [< L *fragilis* (related to *frangere* break). Doublet of FRAIL.] —**frag′ile·ly,** *adv.* —**frag′ile·ness,** *n.* —**Syn.** breakable, weak.

fra·gil·i·ty (frə jil′ə tē) *n.* a fragile quality.

frag·ment (*n.* frag′mənt; *v.* frag ment′) *n.* **1** a broken piece; part broken off. **2** an incomplete or disconnected part: *He could hear only fragments of the conversation.* **3** a part of an incomplete or unfinished work. —*v.* **break**

or divide into fragments. [< L *fragmentum* < *frangere* break] —**Syn. 1** chip, scrap, bit.

frag·men·tal (frag men′ təl) *adj.* **1** fragmentary. **2** in geology, formed from older rocks.

frag·men·tar·y (frag′ mən ter′ ē) *adj.* **1** made up of fragments; incomplete; disconnected: *fragmentary remains of a temple, fragmentary evidence, a fragmentary account.* **2** in geology, fragmental.

frag·men·ta·tion (frag′ mən tā′ shən) *n.* the actual process of breaking into many pieces.

fragmentation bomb a bomb, grenade, etc. that throws bits of metal in all directions as it bursts.

fra·grance (frā′ grəns) *n.* a sweet smell; pleasing odor.

fra·grant (frā′ grənt) *adj.* having or giving off a pleasing odor; sweet-smelling. [< L *fragrans, -antis,* ppr. of *fragrare* emit odor] —**fra′ grant·ly,** *adv.*

frail (frāl) *adj.* **1** slender and not very strong; weak. **2** easily broken, damaged, or destroyed. **3** morally weak; liable to yield to temptation. [ME < OF *fraile* < L *fragilis* fragile. Doublet of FRAGILE.] —**frail′ly,** *adv.* —**frail′ness,** *n.* —**Syn. 1** delicate. **2** brittle.

frail·ty (frāl′ tē) *n.* **-ties. 1** a being frail. **2** moral weakness; liability to yield to temptation. **3** a fault or sin caused by moral weakness.

frame (frām) *n. v.* **framed, fram·ing.** —*n.* **1** a supporting structure over which something is stretched or built: *the frame of a house.* **2** anything made of parts fitted and joined together; structure. **3** the body; the build of the body: *a man of heavy frame.* **4** a skeleton. **5** the way in which a thing is put together. **6** an established order; plan; system. **7** a shape; form. **8** the border in which a thing is set: *a window frame, a picture frame.* **9** one of a series of pictures on a strip of film. **10** one image transmitted by television. **11** one turn at bowling. **12** in programmed learning, a single item or statement presented at one time. **13** in pool: **a** the triangular form used to arrange the balls at the start of a game. **b** the triangle of balls thus placed. **c** the period of play between the placing of the balls. [< v.]
—*v.* **1** shape; form: *frame one's life according to a noble pattern.* **2** put together; plan; make: *Laws are framed in Parliament.* **3** put a border around; enclose with a frame. **4** *Slang.* prearrange falsely; make seem guilty. [OE *framian* to profit < *fram* forth] —**fram′er,** *n.* —**Syn.** *v.* **1** fashion. **2** devise, fabricate, concoct.

frame house a house made of a wooden framework covered with boards.

frame of mind a way of thinking or feeling; disposition; mood.

frame-up (frām′ up′) *n. Slang.* **1** a secret and dishonest arrangement made beforehand. **2** a prearranged scheme made to have a person falsely accused.

frame·work (frām′ wėrk′) *n.* **1** a support over which a thing is stretched or built; stiff part that gives shape to a thing. **2** the way in which a thing is put together; structure; system. **3** the branches of a fruit tree.

franc (frangk) *n.* **1** the unit of money in Burundi, France, Belgium, Luxembourg, Rwanda, Switzerland, and countries of the French Community. See table at **money**. **2** a note or coin worth one franc. [ME < OF *franc* < *Francorum Rex* king of the Franks, on an early gold coin first struck in 1360]

fran·chise (fran′ chīz) *n.* **1** a privilege or right granted by a government: *The city granted the company a franchise to operate buses on the city streets.* **2** the right to vote: *In 1920 Canada established a universal franchise for persons of 21 years and over.* **3** the privilege, often exclusive, of selling the products of a manufacturer or providing a company's service in a given area. [ME < OF *franchise* a freeing < *franc* free. See FRANK.]

Fran·cis·can (fran sis′ kən) *n.* a member of a religious order founded by Saint Francis of Assisi (1182-1226) in 1209. —*adj.* of or having to do with this religious order.

fran·ci·um (fran′ sē əm) *n.* a rare radio-active chemical element. *Symbol*: Fr; *at.no.* 87; *at.wt.* 223. [< NL; after *France*]

Fran·co- *combining form.* French: *Francophile.*

Fran·co·phone (frangk′ ə fōn′) *n. Cdn.* a French-speaking inhabitant of a bilingual or multilingual country.

franc-ti·reur (fräN tē rœr′) *n.* **francs-ti·reurs** (fräN tē rœr′) *French.* a sharpshooter in the French army.

hat, āge, cãre, fär; let, ēqual, tėrm; it, īce
hot, ōpen, ôrder; oil, out; cup, pu̇t, rüle, ūse
əbove, takən, pencəl, lemən, circəs
ch, child; ng, long; sh, ship
th, thin; ᴛʜ, then; zh, measure

fran·gi·ble (fran′ jə bəl) *adj.* breakable. [< F < L *frangere* break]

fran·gi·pan·i (fran′ jə pan′ ē) *n.* **1** a perfume derived from, or resembling the odor of, the red jasmine flower. **2** the West Indian red jasmine. [< Muzio *Frangipani,* a 16th-century Italian marquis, supposed inventor of the perfume]

Fran·glais (fräng glā′) *n.* French spoken with many English words and expressions. [< F *français* French + *anglais* English]

frank[1] (frangk) *adj.* **1** free in expressing one's real thoughts, opinions, and feelings; not hiding what is in one's mind; not afraid to say what one thinks. **2** clearly manifest; undisguised; plain; downright: *frank mutiny.*
—*v.* **1** send (a letter, package, etc.) without charge. **2** mark (a letter, package, etc.) for free mailing.
—*n.* **1** a mark to show that a letter, package, etc. is to be sent without charge. **2** the right to send letters, packages, etc. without charge. **3** a letter, package, etc. sent without charge. [< OF *franc* free, sincere (originally, a Frank, freedom in early France being confined to the Franks, the dominant tribe) < Gmc.] —**frank′ly,** *adv.* —**frank′ness,** *n.*
Syn. *adj.* **1 Frank, outspoken, candid** = not afraid to say what one thinks or feels. **Frank** = free in expressing or showing, by manner or looks or actions, one's real thoughts and feelings: *His eyes are frank and honest.* **Outspoken** = speaking out frankly and openly, hiding or keeping back nothing even when it involves giving offence: *He was outspoken in his criticism.* **Candid** = frank and sincere and, above all, completely truthful and impartial: *His candid account of his best friend's dishonesty surprised some people.*

frank[2] (frangk) *n. Informal.* frankfurter.

Frank (frangk) *n.* **1** a member of a group of W. Germanic tribes that crossed the Rhine from the north and settled along the river in the third century A.D. **2** in the Near East, a name for any European. [? named for their national weapon; cf. OE *franca* spear]

Frank·en·stein (frangk′ ən stīn′) *n.* **1** in a novel by Mary Shelley (1797-1851), a man who creates a monster that he cannot control. **2** a thing that causes the ruin of its creator. **3** erroneously, a monster.

frank·furt (frangk′ fərt) *n.* frankfurter.

frank·furt·er (frangk′ fėr tər) *n.* a wiener. [< G *Frankfurter* of Frankfort]

frank·in·cense (frangk′ in sens′) *n.* a fragrant resin from certain Asiatic or African trees that gives off a sweet, spicy odor when burned. [ME < OF *franc encens* pure incense]

Frank·ish (frangk′ ish) *adj.* of or having to do with the Franks. —*n.* the language of the Franks (def. 1).

frank·lin (frangk′ lən) *n.* in England: **1** a freeholder. **2** in the 14th and 15th centuries, a landowner of free birth who ranked next below the gentry. [ME *francoleyn,* ult. < Med.L *francus* free < Gmc.]

fran·tic (fran′ tik) *adj.* very much excited; wild with rage, fear, pain, grief, etc. [ME < OF *frenetique* < L < Gk. Doublet of PHRENETIC.] —**fran′ ti·cal·ly,** *adv.* —**Syn.** mad, distracted.

frap·pé (fra pā′) *adj.* iced; cooled. —*n.* **1** fruit juice sweetened and frozen. **2** any frozen or iced food or drink. [< F *frappé,* pp. of *frapper* chill, beat]

fra·ter·nal (frə tėr′ nəl) *adj.* **1** brotherly. **2** having to do with a fraternal order. **3** of twins, coming from two separately fertilized egg cells, as distinguished from identical twins. [< L *fraternus* brotherly < *frater* brother] —**fra·ter′ nal·ly,** *adv.*

fraternal order a group organized for mutual aid and fellowship; secret society; fraternity.

fra·ter·ni·ty (frə tėr′ nə tē) *n.* **-ties. 1** a group of men or women joined together for fellowship or for some specific purpose; society: *There are student fraternities in many Canadian colleges.* **2** a group having the same interests, kind of work, etc. **3** fraternal feeling; brotherhood. **4 a** an ecclesiastical order. **b** in the Roman Catholic

Church, an organization of laymen for pious or charitable purposes. [< L *fraternitas* brotherhood]

frat·er·nize (frat′ər nīz′) *v.* **-nized, -niz·ing. 1** associate in a brotherly way; be friendly. **2** associate in a friendly way with citizens of a hostile nation during occupation of their territory. —**frat′er·ni·za′tion,** *n.* —**frat′er·niz′er,** *n.*

frat·ri·cid·al (frat′rə sīd′əl) *adj.* **1** having to do with fratricide. **2** having to do with the killing of relatives or fellow citizens: *A civil war is a fratricidal struggle.*

frat·ri·cide[1] (frat′rə sīd′) *n.* the act of killing one's brother or sister. [< L *fratricidium* < *frater* brother + *-cidium* act of killing]

frat·ri·cide[2] (frat′rə sīd′) *n.* a person who kills his brother or sister. [< L *fratricida* < *frater* brother + *-cida* killer]

frau (frou) *n.* **fraus;** *Slang.* wife.

Frau (frou) *n.* **Fraus** or (*German*) **Frau·en** (frou′ən). *German.* **1** Mrs. **2** a wife.

fraud (frod or frôd) *n.* **1** deceit; cheating; dishonesty: *Any intent to deceive is considered as fraud.* **2** a dishonest act, statement, etc.; something done to deceive or cheat; trick. **3** *Informal.* a person who is not what he pretends to be. [ME < OF *fraude* < L *fraus, fraudis* cheating] —**Syn. 2** dodge, sham, fake. **3** cheat, impostor.

fraud·u·lence (froj′ů ləns or frôj′ů ləns) *n.* a being fraudulent.

fraud·u·len·cy (froj′ů lən sē or frôj′ů lən sē) *n.* **-cies.** fraudulence.

fraud·u·lent (froj′ů lənt or frôj′ů lənt) *adj.* **1** deceitful; cheating; dishonest. **2** intended to deceive. **3** done by fraud; obtained by trickery. [ME < OF < L *fraudulentus*] —**fraud′u·lent·ly,** *adv.*

fraught (frot or frôt) *adj.* loaded; filled: *A battlefield is fraught with horror.* [pp. of obs. *fraught* load, verbal use of noun, < MDu. or MLG *vracht* freight]

fräu·lein (froi′līn) *n. Slang.* a young unmarried German woman.

Fräu·lein (froi′līn) *n.* **Fräu·leins;** *German,* **Fräu·lein.** *German.* **1** Miss. **2** an unmarried woman; young lady.

fray[1] (frā) *n.* a noisy quarrel; fight. [var. of *affray*]

fray[2] (frā) *v.* **1** separate into threads; make or become ragged or worn along the edge. **2** wear away; rub. [< F *frayer* < L *fricare* rub]

frazil (fraz′əl or frə zil′) *n. Cdn.* ice crystals or flakes formed in the turbulent waters of rivers, rapids, etc. and often accumulating as icebanks along the shore. Also, **frazil ice.** [< Cdn.F < F *fraisil* coal cinders, ult. < L *fax, facis,* torch]

fraz·zle (fraz′əl) *v.* **-zled, -zling,** *n. Informal.* —*v.* **1** tear to shreds; fray; wear out. **2** tire out; weary.
—*n.* a frazzled condition. [blend of *fray*[2] and obs. *fazle,* ME *faselyn* unravel < OE *fæs* a fringe]

freak (frēk) *n.* **1** something very queer or unusual: *A green leaf growing in the middle of a rose would be called a freak of nature.* **2** an abnormally developed animal, plant, or person; monstrosity: *A circus often has a sideshow of freaks.* **3** a sudden change of mind without reason; odd notion or fancy. —*adj.* very queer or unusual. —*v.* **freak out,** *Slang.* escape, especially by abandoning reality with the use of drugs. [cf. OE *frīcian* dance] —**Syn.** *n.* **2** whim, vagary, caprice.

freak·ish (frēk′ish) *adj.* full of freaks; very queer or unusual. —**freak′ish·ly,** *adv.* —**freak′ish·ness,** *n.*

freck·le (frek′əl) *n. v.* **-led, -ling.** —*n.* a small, light-brown spot on the skin. —*v.* **1** cover with freckles. **2** become marked or spotted with freckles. [probably alteration of *frecken* < ON *freknur,* pl.]

freck·ly (frek′lē) *adj.* covered with freckles.

free (frē) *adj.* **fre·er, fre·est,** *adv. v.* **freed, free·ing.**
—*adj.* **1** not under another's control; having liberty; able to do, act, or think as one pleases. **2** showing liberty; caused by liberty. **3** not held back, fastened, or shut up; released; loose. **4** not hindered. **5** clear (*of* or *from*); exempt from; not marred or bothered by: *free of error, free from taxes. The whole community was free of disease.* **6** allowed; permitted (*to*); *You are free to speak.* **7** clear; open. **8** open to all: *a free port.* **9** without cost or payment. **10** without paying a tax or duty. **11** done, given, or made willingly or spontaneously: *a free offer.* **12** giving or using much. **13** abundant. **14** not following rules, forms, or words exactly; not strict. **15** saying what one thinks; frank. **16** not restrained enough by manners or morals. **17** in chemistry, not combined with something else: *Oxygen exists free in the atmosphere.* **18 free and easy,** paying little attention to rules or customs; unrestrained. **19 free from** or **of,** without; lacking. **20 free with,** giving or using freely. **21 make free with,** use as if one owned or had complete rights; act uninhibitedly. **22 set free,** make free; let loose; release.
—*adv.* **1** without cost or payment. **2** in a free manner.
—*v.* **1** relieve from any kind of burden, bondage, or slavery; make free. **2** let loose; release: *free a boat from weeds.* **3** clear: *He will have to free himself of this charge of stealing.* [OE *frēo, frīo*] —**free′ly,** *adv.* —**free′ness,** *n.*
—**Syn.** *adj.* **1** independent. **3** movable, unfastened. **9** generous, liberal, lavish. –*v.* **1** liberate, emancipate. **2** See **release.**

free·board (frē′bôrd′) *n.* **1** that part of a ship's side between the water line and the deck or gunwale. **2** the distance between the ground and the under part of the frame of an automobile.

free·boot (frē′büt′) *v.* act as a freebooter; plunder.

free·boot·er (frē′büt′ər) *n.* a pirate; buccaneer. [< Du. *vrijbuiter* < *vrij* free + *buit* booty]

free·boot·ing (frē′büt′ing) *n.* piracy; buccaneering.

free·born (frē′bôrn′) *adj.* **1** born free, not in slavery. **2** of or suitable for people born free.

Free Church a Presbyterian church, known as the "Free Church of Scotland" that seceded from the established Presbyterian Church in 1843.

free city a city forming an independent state.

freed·man (frēd′mən) *n.* **-men** (-mən). a man freed from slavery.

free·dom (frē′dəm) *n.* **1** the state or condition of being free. **2** the condition of not being under another's control; power to do, say, or think as one pleases; liberty. **3** free use: *We give all guests the freedom of our home.* **4** lack of restraint; frankness. **5** ease of movement or action. **6 freedom of the seas,** the right of ships to come and go on the high seas, no state having any jurisdiction over foreign vessels except within its own territorial waters. [OE *frēodōm*]
Syn. 2 Freedom, liberty, independence = not being under the rule or control of another. **Freedom** emphasizes the power to make one's own laws, impose one's own restraints, control one's own life. **Liberty** emphasizes the right or power to do as one pleases, without restraint: *Freedom of speech does not mean liberty to gossip or tell lies.* **Independence** emphasizes the power to stand alone, sometimes supported by, but never subject to or dependent on, someone or something else: *Parents generally try to teach their children independence.*

Free·dom·ite (frē′dəm īt′) *n.* a member of the Sons of Freedom, a Doukhobor sect.

freed·wom·an (frēd′wům′ən) *n.* **-wom·en.** a woman freed from slavery.

free enterprise an economic system based on the right of a private individual to run a business for profit, with a minimum of government control.

free fall 1 the floating motion of a body when in space and not acted upon by gravity: *A body is weightless during free fall.* **2** in parachute jumping, the period between jumping off and the opening of a parachute.

free-for-all (frē′fər ol′ or -ôl′) *adj.* open to all.
—*n.* a fight, race, etc. open to all or in which everybody participates.

Free French the French people who continued resistance to the Nazis during World War II after the Franco-German armistice of 1940.

free·hand (frē′hand′) *adj.* done by hand without using instruments, measurements, etc.: *freehand drawing.*

free·hand·ed (frē′han′did) *adj.* generous; liberal.

free·hold (frē′hōld′) *n.* in law: **1** a piece of land held for life or with the right to transfer it to one's heirs. **2** the holding of land in this way.

free·hold·er (frē′hōl′dər) *n.* a person who has a freehold.

free lance 1 a writer, artist, etc. who works independently and sells his work to anyone who will buy it. **2** in the Middle Ages, a soldier who fought for any

hat, āge, cãre, fär; let, ēqual, tėrm; it, īce
hot, ōpen, ôrder; oil, out; cup, pu̇t, rüle, ūse
əbove, takən, pencəl, lemən, circəs
ch, child; ng, long; sh, ship
th, thin; ᴛʜ, then; zh, measure

person, group, or state that would pay him. **3** a person who fights or works for any cause that he chooses.

free-lance (frē′lans′) *adj.* *v.* **-lanced, -lanc·ing.** —*adj.* working as a free lance. —*v.* work as a free lance.

free·load or **free-load** (frē′lōd′) *v. Slang.* **1** attend a party, convention, etc. chiefly for the free food and drink. **2** take liberally, without contributing anything of one's own. —**free′load′er,** *n.*

free·man (frē′mən) *n.* **-men** (-mən). **1** a person who is not a slave or a serf. **2** a person who has civil or political freedom; citizen.

free·ma·son (frē′mā′sən) *n.* **1** formerly, a member of a skilled stoneworkers' guild, having its own passwords and secret signs. **2 Freemason,** a member of a world-wide society called Free and Accepted Masons; Mason. The purpose of the society of Freemasons is mutual aid and fellowship.

Free·ma·son·ry (frē′mā′sən rē) *n.* **1** the principles, doctrines, etc. of the society of Freemasons; Masonry. **2** the members of this society. **3 freemasonry,** common understanding and sympathy based on similar experiences.

free on board delivered free of charge on a train, ship, etc. *Abbrev.*: f.o.b. or F.O.B.

free port 1 a port open to traders of all countries on the same conditions. **2** a port where no taxes or duties have to be paid.

free press a press not censored or controlled by the government of the country where it operates.

free·sia (frē′zhə) *n.* a plant of the same family as the iris having clusters of fragrant white or yellow flowers. Freesias are grown from bulbs. [< NL; after F. H. T. *Freese* (1795?-1876), a German botanist]

free-spo·ken (frē′spō′kən) *adj.* speaking freely; saying what one thinks; frank.

free·stone (frē′stōn′) *n.* **1** any stone, such as limestone or sandstone, that can easily be cut without splitting. **2** any fruit having a stone that is easily separated from the pulp; opposed to *clingstone.* Certain kinds of peaches and plums are freestones. —*adj.* of fruit, having a stone that is easily separated from the pulp.

free·think·er (frē′thingk′ər) *n.* a person who forms his religious opinions independently of authority or tradition.

free thought religious opinions formed independently of authority or tradition.

free trade 1 international trade free from protective duties and subject only to tariffs for revenue. **2** the system, principles, or practice of maintaining such trade. **3** trade unrestricted by taxes, customs, duties, or differences of treatment.

free·trad·er (frē′trād′ər) *n.* **1** a person who favors the system of free trade. **2** *Cdn.* formerly, a man who traded in furs independently of such companies as the Hudson's Bay Company.

free verse poetry not restricted by the usual conventions of metre, rhyme, etc.

free·way (frē′wā′) *n.* a high-speed highway on which no tolls are charged.

free·wheel (frē′ hwēl′ or -wēl′) *n.* **1** in the transmission of an automobile, etc., a device that permits the drive shaft to run freely when it is turning faster than the engine shaft. **2** on a bicycle, a device that enables the wheels to continue turning while the pedals are held still. —*v.* coast.

free·wheel·ing (frē′hwēl′ing or -wēl′ing) *adj.* **1** using or having a freewheel. **2** independent or unhampered: *a freewheeling operator.*

free will a voluntary choice; freedom of decision.

free·will (frē′wil′) *adj.* voluntary: *a freewill offering.*

free world in the mid-20th century, the non-communist nations. —**free′world′,** *adj.*

freeze (frēz) *v.* **froze, fro·zen, freez·ing,** *n.* —*v.* **1** turn into ice; harden by cold. **2** make very cold. **3** become very cold. **4** be of the degree of cold at which water becomes ice: *It is freezing tonight.* **5** kill or injure by frost. **6** be killed or injured by frost. **7** cover or become covered with ice; clog with ice. **8** fix or become fixed to something by freezing. **9** make or become stiff and unfriendly. **10** chill or be chilled with fear, etc. **11** become motionless. **12** fix (prices, wages, etc.) at a definite amount, usually by governmental decree. **13** make (funds, bank balances, etc.) unusable and inaccessible by governmental decree. **14** prohibit the further use of (a raw material) in any way: *Cobalt was frozen during the war.* **15** make numb by injecting or applying an anesthetic: *The dentist froze my gum before extracting the decayed tooth.* **16 freeze on to,** *Informal.* hold on tightly to. **17 freeze out,** *Informal.* force out; exclude: *The clique's unfriendliness froze out all newcomers.*
—*n.* **1** a freezing or being frozen. **2** a period during which there is freezing weather. [OE *frēosan*]

freez·er (frēz′ər) *n.* **1** a machine to freeze ice cream. **2** a refrigerator cabinet or compartment within which a temperature below the freezing point is maintained.

freeze-up (frēz′up′) *n.* the time of year when rivers and lakes freeze over; onset of winter: *Freeze-up came late last year.*

freezing point the temperature at which a liquid freezes. The freezing point of water at sea level is 32 degrees Fahrenheit or 0 degrees centigrade. *Abbrev.*: F.P., f.p., or fp

F region the part of the ionosphere comprising the two layers above the E layer. The two sections, both of which reflect radio waves, are known as the *F 1 layer* and *F 2 layer.*

freight (frāt) *n.* **1** the load of goods carried on a train, ship, etc.: *It took a whole day to unload the freight.* **2** the carrying of goods on a train, ship, etc. **3** the charge for this. **4** anything carried for pay by land, water, or air; goods in transit. **5** a train for carrying goods. **6** a load; burden.
—*v.* **1** load with freight. **2** carry as freight. **3** send as freight. **4** load; burden. [ME < MDu. or MLG *vrecht*]

freight·age (frāt′ij) *n.* **1** the carrying of goods on a train, ship, etc. **2** charge for this. **3** freight; cargo.

freight car a railway car for carrying freight.

freight·er (frāt′ər) *n.* a ship or aircraft for carrying freight.

French (french) *adj.* **1** of or having to do with France, its people, or their language. **2** French Canadian; of or having to do with French Canada, French Canadians, or their language.
—*n.* **1** the people of France. **2** the people of French Canada. **3** the French language: *The kind of French spoken in Canada is called Canadian French.* [OE *Frencisc* < *Franca* Frank]

French and Indian War the part of the Seven Years' War fought in North America between Great Britain and France, with Indian allies (1754-1763).

French Canada 1 French Canadians as a group; all French Canadians. **2** that part of Canada inhabited mainly or entirely by French Canadians, especially the province of Quebec.

French Canadian 1 a Canadian whose ancestors came from France. **2** of or having to do with French Canada or French Canadians. **3** the language of the French Canadians; Canadian French.

French chalk talc used for marking lines on cloth or removing grease.

French Community an association formed in 1958 of France and her dependent territories, and many of her former colonies.

French cuff a sleeve cuff that is folded back at the wrist and fastened with a cuff link instead of a button.

French doors a pair of doors hinged at the sides and opening in the middle. They have panes of glass like a window.

French dressing a salad dressing made of olive oil, vinegar, salt, spices, etc.

French fries potatoes that have been **French fried,** that is, cut into long square-sided strips and cooked in boiling fat until crisp on the outside.

French horn a brass wind instrument that has a mellow tone.

A French horn

French·i·fy (fren′chə fī′) *v.* **-fied, -fy·ing.** make French or like the French.

French leave 1 the act of leaving without ceremony, permission, or notice; secret or hurried departure. **2** originally, the custom of going away from a reception, etc., without taking leave of the host or hostess.

French·man (french′mən) *n.* **-men** (-mən). **1** a native or inhabitant of France. **2** a citizen of France. **3** a French Canadian.

French pastry 1 small, individual, rich cakes, tarts, eclairs, etc. **2** one of these cakes.

French Provincial 1 of, like, or having to do with a style of furniture, architecture, or fabric design that originated in the 17th and 18th century French provinces. **2** this style of furniture.

French Revolution the revolution in France from 1789 to 1799, which ousted the monarchy and set up a republic.

French seam a seam stitched first on the right side of the material, then on the wrong side, to cover the raw edges.

French Shore 1 the west coast of Newfoundland, where the French held fishing and other rights from 1713 till 1904. **2** an area originally settled by the Acadian French, located on the southwest coast of Nova Scotia.

French toast slices of bread dipped in a mixture of egg and milk and then fried in a small quantity of fat.

French windows a pair of long windows like doors, hinged at the sides and opening in the middle.

French·wom·an (french′wům′ən) *n.* **-wom·en. 1** a woman who is a native or inhabitant of France. **2** a French-Canadian woman.

fre·net·ic (frə net′ik) *adj.* **1** frenzied. **2** insane. Also, **phrenetic.** [var. of *phrenetic*] **—fre·net′i·cal·ly,** *adv.*

fren·zied (fren′zēd) *adj.* greatly excited; frantic. **—fren′zied·ly,** *adv.*

fren·zy (fren′zē) *n.* **-zies. 1** a brief fury. **2** a state of near madness: *She was in a frenzy of grief when she heard of her son's death.* **3** a state of very great excitement: *The spectators were in a frenzy after the home team scored the winning goal.* [ME < OF *frenesie* < L *phrenesis*, ult. < Gk. *phrēn* mind] **—Syn.** rage, furor, delirium.

fre·quen·cy (frē′kwən sē) *n.* **-cies. 1** in physics: **a** the number of times that any regularly repeated event, as a vibration, occurs in a given unit of time. **b** the rate of occurrence. **2** a frequent occurrence. **3** the number of complete cycles per second of an alternating current or any type of wave motion: *Different radio stations broadcast at different frequencies so that their signals can be heard distinctly.* **4** in mathematics, the ratio of the number of times an event actually occurs to the number of times it might occur in a given period. **5** in statistics, the number of cases of the data under consideration falling within a particular class interval.

frequency band in television, radio, etc., a certain range of wave lengths; channel.

frequency modulation 1 in broadcasting, a deliberate modulation of the frequency of the transmitting wave. **2** a broadcasting system, relatively free of static, using this method of modulation. Compare **amplitude modulation.** *Abbrev.*: FM, F.M., or f.m.

fre·quent (*adj.* frē′kwənt; *v.* fri kwent′) *adj.* **1** occurring often, near together, or every little while. **2** regular; habitual: *He is a frequent caller at our house.* —*v.* go often to; be often in: *Frogs frequent ponds, streams, and marshes.* [< L *frequens, -entis* crowded] **—Syn.** *v.* haunt.

fre·quen·ta·tive (fri kwen′tə tiv) *adj.* in grammar, expressing frequent repetition of an action. *Waggle* is a frequentative verb from *wag.* —*n.* a frequentative verb.

fre·quent·er (fri kwen′tər) *n.* a habitual visitor.

fre·quent·ly (frē′kwənt lē) *adv.* often; repeatedly; every little while. **—Syn.** See **often.**

fres·co (fres′kō) *n.* **-coes** or **-cos,** *v.* **-coed, -co·ing.** —*n.* **1** the act or art of painting with water colors on damp, fresh plaster. **2** a picture or design so painted. —*v.* paint in fresco. [< Ital. *fresco* cool, fresh]

fresh (fresh) *adj.* **1** newly made, arrived, or obtained: *fresh footprints.* **2** not known, seen, or used before; new; recent. **3** additional; further; another: *After her failure she made a fresh start.* **4** not salty: *There is fresh water in the Great Lakes.* **5** not spoiled; newly grown, produced, or gathered; not stale. **6** not artificially preserved. **7** not wearied; vigorous; lively. **8** not faded or worn; bright. **9** looking healthy or young. **10** clean; newly washed: *a fresh shirt.* **11** pure; cool; refreshing: *a fresh breeze.* **12** fairly strong; brisk: *a fresh wind.* **13** not experienced. **14** *Slang.* too bold; impudent. [OE *fersc*; but influenced in form by OF *fresche*, fem. of *freis* < Gmc.] **—fresh′ly,** *adv.* **—fresh′ness,** *n.* **—Syn. 2** novel. **13** untrained.

fresh·en (fresh′ən) *v.* make fresh; become fresh.

fresh·et (fresh′it) *n.* **1** a flood caused by heavy rains or melted snow. **2** a rush of fresh water flowing into the sea. [< *fresh* flood, stream, or pool of fresh water + *-et*]

fresh·ette (fresh et′) *n.* a girl student in the first year of a university course.

fresh·man (fresh′mən) *n.* **-men** (-mən), *adj.* —*n.* **1** a student in the first year of a university course. **2** a beginner. —*adj.* of or concerning students in the first year of a university course.

fresh-wa·ter (fresh′wo′tər or -wô′tər) *adj.* **1** of or living in water that is not salty: *The catfish is a fresh-water fish.* **2** not used to sailing on the sea. **3** having little experience; unskilled.

fres·no (frez′nō) *n.* **fres·noes.** buck scraper. [< *Fresno* Agricultural Works, California]

fret[1] (fret) *v.* **fret·ted, fret·ting,** *n.* —*v.* **1** be peevish, unhappy, discontented, or worried: *A baby frets in hot weather. Don't fret about your mistake.* **2** make peevish, unhappy, discontented, or worried. **3** eat away; wear; rub. **4** roughen; disturb.
—*n.* a peevish complaining; worry; a discontented condition. [OE *fretan* eat] **—fret′ter,** *n.* **—Syn.** *v.* **2** harass, vex, provoke.

fret[2] (fret) *n. v.* **fret·ted, fret·ting.** —*n.* an ornamental pattern made of straight lines bent or combined at angles. —*v.* decorate with fretwork. [ME < OF *frete* trellis work]

fret[3] (fret) *n.* on a guitar, banjo, etc., any of a series of ridges of wood, ivory, or metal, showing where to put the fingers in order to produce certain tones. [origin uncertain]

fret·ful (fret′fəl) *adj.* **1** inclined to fret; peevish; unhappy; discontented. **2** agitated; seething: *the fretful sea.* **3** gusty: *the fretful wind.* **—fret′ful·ly,** *adv.* **—fret′ful·ness,** *n.*

fret saw a saw with a long, slender blade and fine teeth, used to cut thin wood into patterns.

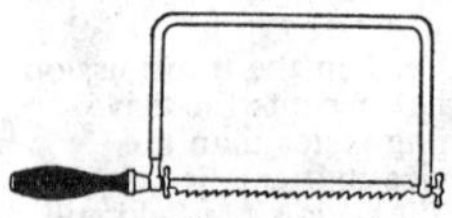
A fret saw

Two examples of fretwork

fret·ted (fret′id) *adj.* having frets. —*v.* pt. and pp. of **fret**[1] and **fret**[2].

fret·work (fret′wėrk′) *n.* ornamental openwork or carving.

Freud·i·an (froid′ē ən) *adj.* of or having to do with Sigmund Freud (1856-1939), an Austrian physician, who developed a theory and technique of psychoanalysis, or his teachings. —*n.* a person who believes in Freud's teachings or follows his technique of psychoanalysis.

F.R.G.S. Fellow of the Royal Geographical Society.

Fri. Friday.

fri·a·bil·i·ty (frī′ə bil′ə tē) *n.* the state of being friable.

fri·a·ble (frī′ə bəl) *adj.* easily crumbled: *Dry soil is friable.* [< L *friabilis* < *friare* crumble]

fri·ar (frī′ər) *n.* a member of certain religious orders, especially the Roman Catholic mendicant orders, the Franciscans, Dominicans, Carmelites, and Augustinians.

hat, āge, cãre, fär; let, ēqual, tėrm; it, īce
hot, ōpen, ôrder; oil, out; cup, pu̇t, rüle, ūse
əbove, takən, pencəl, lemən, circəs
ch, child; ng, long; sh, ship
th, thin; ᴛʜ, then; zh, measure

[ME < OF *frere* < L *frater* brother] ☛ See **monk** for usage note.

fri·ar·y (frī′ər ē) *n.* **-ar·ies. 1** a building or buildings where friars live; monastery. **2** a brotherhood of friars.

fric·an·deau (frik′ən dō′) *n.* veal or other meat larded, braised, or fried, and served with a sauce. [< F *fricandeau*, related to *fricassée*. See FRICASSEE.]

fric·as·see (frik′ə sē′) *n. v.* **-seed, -see·ing.** —*n.* meat cut up, stewed, and served in a sauce made with its own gravy. —*v.* prepare (meat) in this way. [< F *fricassée* < *fricasser* mince and cook in sauce]

fric·a·tive (frik′ə tiv) *adj.* in phonetics, of consonants, pronounced by forcing the breath through a narrow opening. The English fricative consonants are (f), (v), (th), (ᴛʜ), (s), (z), (sh), (zh), and (h). —*n.* a fricative consonant. [< NL < L *fricare* to rub]

fric·tion (frik′shən) *n.* **1** a rubbing of one object against another; rubbing: *Matches are lighted by friction.* **2** in physics, the resistance to motion of surfaces that touch; resistance of a moving body to water, air, etc. through which it travels or to the surface on which it moves: *A sled moves more easily on smooth ice than on rough ground because there is less friction.* **3** conflict of differing ideas, opinions, etc.; disagreement: *Political differences caused friction between the two countries.* [< L *frictio, -onis* < *fricare* rub]

fric·tion·al (frik′shən əl) *adj.* having to do with friction; caused by friction. —**fric′tion·al·ly,** *adv.*

Fri·day (frī′dē or frī′dā) *n.* **1** the sixth day of the week, following Thursday. **2** the servant of Robinson Crusoe. **3** any faithful servant or devoted follower. [OE *Frīgedæg* Frigg's day < gen. of *Frīg* + *dæg* day; based on L *dies Veneris* Venus' day]

fridge (frij) *n. Informal.* refrigerator. Also, **frig.** [shortening of *refrigerator* or *Frigidaire* (a trade mark)]

fried (frīd) *adj.* cooked in fat. —*v.* pt. and pp. of **fry**[1].

fried cake a small cake fried in deep fat.

friend (frend) *n.* **1** a person who knows and likes another. **2** a person who favors and supports. **3** a person who belongs to the same side or group: *Are you friend or foe?* **4 Friend,** a member of the Society of Friends, a religious group opposed to war and to taking oaths; Quaker: *The Friends favor simplicity in clothes and manners.* **5 be friends with,** be a friend of. **6 make friends with,** become a friend of. [OE *frēond,* originally ppr. of *frēogan* love] —**Syn. 1** comrade, chum, crony, companion, pal. **2** supporter, patron, advocate.

friend at court a person who can help one to influence others; influential friend.

friend·less (frend′lis) *adj.* without friends. —**friend′less·ness,** *n.*

friend·ly (frend′lē) *adj.* **-li·er, -li·est,** *adv.* —*adj.* **1** of a friend; having the attitude of a friend; kind: *a friendly greeting.* **2** like a friend; like a friend's. **3** on good terms; not hostile: *friendly relations between countries.* **4** wanting to be a friend: *a friendly dog.* **5** favoring and supporting; favorable.
—*adv.* in a friendly manner; as a friend. [OE *frēondlīc*] —**friend′li·ness,** *n.*

friend·ship (frend′ship) *n.* **1** the state of being friends. **2** a liking between friends. **3** a friendly feeling; friendly behavior: *His smile radiated friendship.*

frieze[1] (frēz) *n.* **1** a horizontal band of decoration around a room, building, mantel, etc. **2** in architecture, a horizontal band, often ornamented with sculpture, between the cornice and architrave of a building. See **entablature** for diagram. [< F *frise* < Med.L *frisium* < L *Phrygium* of Phrygia]

frieze[2] (frēz) *n.* a thick woollen cloth with a shaggy nap on one side. —*v.* raise a nap on (cloth). [ME < OF (*drap de*) *frise* Frisian (cloth)]

frig (frij) *n. Informal.* refrigerator.

frig·ate (frig′it) *n.* **1** a modern warship smaller than a destroyer. The Royal Canadian Navy has frigates as escort vessels. **2** formerly, a three-masted sailing warship of medium size. [< F *frégate* < Ital. *fregata*]

frigate bird a tropical sea bird that has powerful wings. It steals other birds' food.

Frigg (frig) *n.* in Norse mythology, the wife of Odin and goddess of the sky.

fright (frīt) *n.* **1** sudden fear; sudden terror. **2** *Informal.* a person or thing that is ugly, shocking, or ridiculous: *She looked a fright in that hat.* —*v. Poetic.* frighten. [OE *fryhto*] —**Syn.** *n.* **1** dismay, consternation, alarm.

fright·ed (frīt′id) *adj.* frightened; terrified.

fright·en (frīt′ən) *v.* **1** fill with fright; make afraid; scare. **2** become afraid. —**fright′en·er,** *n.*
Syn. 1 Frighten, scare, alarm = fill with fear. **Frighten** = fill with a sudden, startling, often very great fear: *The rattlesnake frightened me.* **Scare,** often used as an informal substitute for *frighten,* particularly suggests suddenly giving sharp fear or terror to a timid person or animal, making him shrink and tremble or turn and run: *The firecrackers scared the puppy.* **Alarm** = fill suddenly with intense fear and anxiety: *Her failure to come home at midnight alarmed us.*

fright·ened (frīt′ənd) *adj.* filled with fright; afraid. —**Syn.** See **afraid.**

fright·en·ing (frīt′ning or frīt′ən ing) *adj.* capable of causing fright or fear: *a frightening experience.* —**fright′en·ing·ly,** *adv.*

fright·ful (frīt′fəl) *adj.* **1** causing fright or horror; dreadful; terrible: *a frightful thunderstorm.* **2** ugly; shocking. **3** *Informal.* disagreeable; unpleasant: *a frightful person, a frightful trip.* **4** *Informal.* very great. —**fright′ful·ly,** *adv.* —**fright′ful·ness,** *n.*

frig·id (frij′id) *adj.* **1** very cold: *a frigid climate.* **2** cold in feeling or manner; stiff; chilling: *a frigid reception.* [< L *frigidus* < *frigere* be cold < *frigus* cold] —**frig′id·ly,** *adv.* —**frig′id·ness,** *n.*

fri·gid·i·ty (fri jid′ə tē) *n.* a being frigid.

Frigid Zone a region within the Arctic or the Antarctic Circle. See **zone** for diagram.

frill (fril) *n.* **1** a ruffle. **2** *Informal.* anything added merely for show; useless ornament; affectation of dress, manner, speech, etc. **3** a fringe of feathers, hair, etc. around the neck of a bird or animal. —*v.* **1** decorate with a ruffle; adorn with ruffles. **2** form into a ruffle. [origin uncertain]

fril·ly (fril′ē) *adj.* **1** having ruffles or frills. **2** like frills.

fringe (frinj) *n. v.* **fringed, fring·ing,** *adj.* —*n.* **1** a border or trimming made of threads, cords, etc., either loose or tied together in small bunches: *The chesterfield had a fringe along the bottom edge.* **2** anything like this; border: *A fringe of hair over her forehead.* **3** anything thought of as marginal rather than central: *He belongs to the radical fringe of the labor movement.*
—*v.* **1** make a border for. **2** be a border for; border: *Bushes fringed the road.*
—*adj.* **1** of the border or outside: *Even the fringe areas of the city are becoming residential.* **2** apart from the main purpose; secondary: *fringe benefit.* [ME < OF *frenge* < L *fimbria*]

Fringes

fringe benefit any employment benefit given to an employee over and above his regular wages: *Pensions and medical insurance are fringe benefits.*

fringe land *Cdn.* in the North, land that is relatively far from a railway.

frip·per·y (frip′ər ē) *n.* **-per·ies. 1** cheap, showy clothes; gaudy ornaments. **2** a cheap, showy article of clothing; gaudy ornament. **3** a showing off; foolish display; pretended refinement: *Affectations of manner and speech are mere frippery.* [< F *friperie,* ult. < *frepe* rag]

Fri·sian (frizh′ən) *adj.* of or having to do with Friesland (a district in N. Netherlands), its people, or their language. —*n.* **1** a native or inhabitant of Friesland or certain nearby islands. **2** the language spoken in Friesland and certain nearby islands: *Frisian is a West Germanic dialect, closely akin to English.*

frisk (frisk) *v.* **1** run and jump about playfully; skip and dance joyously; frolic. **2** *Slang.* search (a person) for concealed weapons, stolen goods, etc. by running a hand quickly over his clothes. 3 *Slang.* steal from (a person) in this way. [originally adj., < OF *frisque* < Gmc.; cf. G *frisch*]

frisk·y (fris′kē) *adj.* **frisk·i·er, frisk·i·est.** playful; lively. —**frisk′i·ly,** *adv.* —**frisk′i·ness,** *n.*

frith (frith) *n.* firth. [var. of *firth*]

frit·il·lar·y (frit′ə ler′ē) *n.* **-lar·ies. 1** a small plant having drooping, bell-shaped flowers usually spotted with dark green or purple. **2** a butterfly having many-colored spots. [< NL *fritillaria* < L *fritillus* dice box; with reference to the checkered markings on the petals]

frit·ter[1] (frit′ər) *v.* **1** waste little by little. **2** cut or tear into small pieces; break into fragments. —*n.* a small piece; fragment. [< OF *freture, fraiture* < L *fractura.* See FRACTURE.] —**frit′ter·er,** *n.*

frit·ter[2] (frit′ər) *n.* a small cake of batter, sometimes containing fruit or other food, fried in fat: *corn fritters.* [ME < OF *friture,* ult. < L *frigere* fry]

fri·vol·i·ty (fri vol′ə tē) *n.* **-ties. 1** a being frivolous. **2** a frivolous act or thing.

friv·o·lous (friv′ə ləs) *adj.* **1** lacking in seriousness or sense; silly: *Frivolous behavior is out of place in church.* **2** of little worth or importance; trivial: *He wasted his time on frivolous matters.* [< L *frivolus*] —**friv′o·lous·ly,** *adv.* —**friv′o·lous·ness,** *n.* —**Syn. 1** foolish. **2** trifling, unimportant, petty.

frizz or **friz** (friz) *v.* **frizzed, friz·zing,** *n.* **friz·zes.** —*v.* form into small, crisp curls; curl. —*n.* hair curled in small, crisp curls or a very close crimp. [apparently < F *friser*]

friz·zle[1] (friz′əl) *v.* **-zled, -zling,** *n.* —*v.* form into small, crisp curls; curl. —*n.* **1** a being frizzled. **2** a small, crisp curl. [? related to OE *frīs* curly] —**friz′zler,** *n.*

friz·zle[2] (friz′əl) *v.* **-zled, -zling,** *n.* —*v.* **1** make a hissing, sputtering noise when cooking; sizzle. **2** fry or broil until crisp. —*n.* a sizzle. [? < *fry* and *sizzle*]

friz·zly (friz′lē) *adj.* **-zli·er, -zli·est.** full of small, crisp curls; curly.

friz·zy (friz′ē) *adj.* **-zi·er, -zi·est.** frizzly.

fro (frō) *adv.* **1** from; back. **2 to and fro,** first one way and then back again; back and forth. [< ON *frá.* Akin to FROM.]

frock (frok) *n.* **1** a gown; dress. **2** a loose outer garment. **3** a robe worn by a clergyman. —*v.* **1** clothe in a frock. **2** invest with clerical authority. [ME < OF *froc*]

frock coat a man's coat reaching approximately to the knees, and equally long in front and at the back.

frog[1] (frog) *n.* **1** a small, leaping amphibian having webbed feet. **2** an animal like this: *A tree frog lives in trees.* **3** the arrangement of a rail where a railway track crosses or branches from another. **4** a pad of horny substance in the middle of the bottom of a foot of a horse, donkey, etc. **5** a small perforated or spiked device for holding flowers upright in a vase, bowl, etc. **6 frog in the throat,** *Informal.* a slight hoarseness caused by soreness or swelling in the throat. [OE *frogga*]

frog[2] (frog) *n.* **1** an ornamental fastening for a coat or dress. **2** an attachment or loop on a belt, for carrying a sword, bayonet, etc. [? < Pg. *froco* < L *floccus* flock[2]]

F, Frogs on a cloak

frog·man (frog′man′ or frog′mən) *n.* **-men** (-men′ or -mən). a skindiver, especially one employed in military or naval operations.

frol·ic (frol′ik) *n. v.* **-icked, -ick·ing,** *adj.* —*n.* **1** a gay prank; fun. **2** a merry game or party. **3** formerly, a gathering for work, such as a husking bee or a barn raising. [< v. or adj.]
—*v.* play; have fun; make merry. [< adj.]
—*adj.* full of fun; gay; merry. [< Du. *vrolijk* < MDu. *vrō* glad + *-lijk* -ly] —**frol′ick·er,** *n.*

frol·ic·some (frol′ik səm) *adj.* full of fun; gay; merry.

from (frum or from; *unstressed,* frəm) *prep.* **1** out of: *He arrived on the train from Montreal.* **2** out of the control or possession of: *Take the book from her.* **3** starting at; beginning with: *from that time forward.* **4** caused by; because of; by reason of: *act from a sense of duty.* **5** as being unlike: *Anyone can tell apples from oranges.* **6** off: *He took a book from the table.* [OE *fram, from*]

frond (frond) *n.* **1** a divided leaf of a fern, palm, etc. **2** a leaflike part of a seaweed, lichen, etc. [< L *frons, frondis* leaf]

front (frunt) *n.* **1** the first part; foremost part: *the front of a car.* **2** the part that faces forward: *the front of a dress.* **3** something fastened or worn on the front. **4** in war, the place where fighting is going on; line of battle: *He spent many weeks at the front.* **5** a sphere of activity combining different groups in a political or economic battle: *the labor front.* **6** the forces fighting for some political or social aim. **7** the land facing a street, river, lake, etc. **8** a manner of looking or behaving. **9** *Informal.* an outward appearance of wealth, importance, etc. **10** *Informal.* a person appointed to add respectability or prestige to an enterprise. **11** *Informal.* a person or thing that serves as a cover for illegal activities. **12** the forehead. **13** the face. **14** *Cdn.* **a** the settled, civilized part of the country at the edge of the frontier. **b** in Newfoundland and Nova Scotia, the area where the spring seal hunt takes place, at the edge of the Arctic ice-fields. **15 in front of,** in a place or position before (a person or thing): *He stood in front of me.* **16** the dividing surface between two dissimilar air masses: *The weather report says there is a cold front approaching from the northwest.*
—*adj.* **1** of, on, in, or at the front. **2** in phonetics, pronounced by raising the tongue against or near the forward part of the hard palate. The *e* (*ē*) in *she* is a front vowel.
—*v.* **1** have the front toward; face. **2** be in front of. **3** furnish with a front. **4** meet face to face; defy; oppose. **5** *Informal.* serve as a cover for a pressure group, an illegal activity, or the like: *Some claimed that the dockers' union fronted for the smuggling ring.*
—*adv.* **eyes front!** look forward! direct the eyes ahead! [< L *frons, frontis,* literally, forehead]

front·age (frun′tij) *n.* **1** the front of a building or of a lot. **2** the length of this front. **3** the direction that the front of a building or lot faces. **4** the land facing a street, river, etc. **5** the land between a building and a street, river, etc.

frontage road a road paralleling an expressway or freeway to provide access for local traffic.

fron·tal (frun′təl *adj.* **1** of, on, in, or at the front. **2** of the forehead. —*n.* a bone of the forehead. [< NL *frontalis* < L *frons, frontis,* literally, forehead]

front bench 1 in a legislative chamber, the front seats on either side, reserved for the party leaders. **2** the party leaders.

front bencher in a legislative body, one of the leading members of a political party: *Cabinet ministers are the government front benchers.*

fron·tier (fron tēr′, frun tēr′, or fron′tēr) *n.* **1** the farthest part of a settled country, where the wilds begin: *The Yukon is part of Canada's present-day frontier.* **2** a part of one country that touches on the border of another; boundary line or border between two countries. **3** an uncertain or undeveloped region: *the frontiers of science.* —*adj.* of or on the frontier: *Frontier life is often harsh.* [ME < OF *frontiere* < *front* front < L *frons, frontis,* literally, forehead]

Frontier College a famous Canadian educational body serving isolated mining and lumber camps.

fron·tiers·man (fron tērz′mən or frun tērz′-) *n.* **-men** (-mən). a man who lives on the frontier.

fron·tis·piece (frun′tis pēs′ or fron′tis pēs′) *n.* **1** a picture facing the title page of a book or of a division of a book. **2** in architecture: **a** the main part or the decorated entrance of a building. **b** a pediment over a door, gate, etc. [< F *frontispice* < LL *frontispicium,* literally, looking at the forehead < L *frons, frontis* forehead + *specere* look]

front·let (frunt′lit) *n.* **1** a band or ornament worn on the forehead. **2** the forehead of an animal.

front line in warfare, the operational area nearest to enemy positions.

front man 1 one who officially represents a group or organization. **2** one who fronts for another: *The pleasant storekeeper was front man for a gang of jewel smugglers.*

front matter in printing, the pages of a book that precede the actual text. The preface and table of contents belong to the front matter.

front-page (frunt′pāj′) *adj. v.* **-paged, -pag·ing.** *—adj.* suitable for the front page of a newspaper; important: *front-page news.* *—v.* put on the front page; play up; emphasize.

frost (frost) *n.* **1** a freezing condition; very cold weather; temperature below the point at which water freezes: *There was frost in the air last night.* **2** the moisture frozen on or in a surface; feathery crystals of ice that are formed when water vapor in the air condenses at a temperature below freezing: *frost on windows, frost on the grass.* **3** a coldness of manner or feeling. **4** *Informal.* a falling off of, or coolness in, friendship; estrangement. **5** *Slang.* a failure.
—v. **1** cover or become covered with frost. **2** cover with anything that suggests frost; cover with frosting: *The cook frosted the cake with a mixture of sugar and white of eggs.* **3** kill or injure by frost. [OE] **—frost′less,** *adj.* **—frost′like′,** *adj.*

frost·bite (frost′bīt′) *n. v.* **-bit, -bit·ten, -bit·ing.** *—n.* an injury to a part of the body caused by severe cold.
—v. injure (a part of the body) by severe cold.

frost·bit·ten (frost′bit′ən) *adj.* injured by severe cold. *—v.* pp. of **frostbite.**

frost boil in a paved road, a defective place where the pavement has heaved as a result of the expansion of trapped moisture frozen during the cold weather; a frost heave.

frost·ed (fros′tid) *adj.* **1** covered with frost: *a frosted window.* **2** having a surface like frost: *frosted glass.* **3** iced: *a frosted cake.* **4** frozen.

frost heave frost boil.

frost·ing (fros′ting) *n.* **1** a mixture of sugar and some liquid, with or without the whites of eggs, flavoring, etc. used to cover and decorate a cake. **2** a dull finish on glass, metal, etc.

frost·line (frost′līn′) *n.* in geology, the depth to which frost penetrates into the ground.

frost·y (fros′tē) *adj.* **frost·i·er, frost·i·est.** **1** cold enough for frost; freezing: *a frosty morning.* **2** covered with frost: *The glass is frosty.* **3** covered with anything like frost. **4** cold in manner or feeling; unfriendly: *a frosty greeting.* **5** hoary; gray. **6** of or like old age. **—frost′i·ly,** *adv.* **—frost′i·ness,** *n.*

froth (froth) *n.* **1** foam. **2** foaming saliva coming from the mouth, caused by disease, exertion, etc.: *There was froth on the mad dog's lips.* **3** something light and trifling; trivial notions, talk, etc. *—v.* **1** give out froth; foam. **2** cover with foam. **3** cause to foam by beating, pouring, etc. [ME < ON *frotha*] **—Syn.** *n.* **1** spume, lather, scum, suds.

froth·y (froth′ē) *adj.* **froth·i·er, froth·i·est.** **1** of or like froth; foamy. **2** light; trifling, shallow, unimportant. **—froth′i·ly,** *adv.* **—froth′i·ness,** *n.*

frou-frou (frü′frü′) *n.* **1** a swishing sound; rustling, especially of clothes. **2** *Informal.* fancy or fussy trimmings or the like; frills. [< F]

fro·ward (frō′wərd or frō′ərd) *adj.* not easily managed; willful; contrary. [< *fro* + *-ward*] **—fro′ward·ly,** *adv.* **—fro′ward·ness,** *n.* **—Syn.** perverse, obstinate, refractory.

frown (froun) *n.* **1** a drawing together of the brows, in concentrating or to express displeasure. **2** any expression or show of disapproval. [< v.]
—v. **1** draw the brows together, as in concentrating or in displeasure. **2** look displeased or irritated. **3** express by frowning. **4 frown on,** disapprove of: *Many people frown on gambling.* [ME < OF *froignier* < Celtic] **—frown′ing·ly,** *adv.*
Syn. *v.* **1, 2 Frown, scowl** = draw the eyebrows together, usually to express feeling or attitude. **Frown** = draw the eyebrows tightly together, sometimes in looking closely at something or concentrating, but usually to express irritation or displeasure: *The teacher frowned when the boy came in late.* **Scowl** = look sullen or sour out of discontent or ill-temper: *He is a disagreeable person, always scowling.*

frows·y (frouz′ē) *adj.* **frows·i·er, frows·i·est.** frowzy.

frowz·y (frouz′ē) *adj.* **frowz·i·er, frowz·i·est.** **1** slovenly; dirty; untidy. **2** smelling bad. [cf. obs. *frowze* frizz, ruffle, rumple, and dial. Brit. *frowsty* musty] **—frowz′i·ly,** *adv.* **—frowz′i·ness,** *n.*

froze (frōz) *v.* pt. of **freeze.**

hat, āge, cãre, fär; let, ēqual, tėrm; it, īce
hot, ōpen, ôrder; oil, out; cup, pu̇t, rüle, ūse
əbove, takən, pencəl, lemən, circəs
ch, child; ng, long; sh, ship
th, thin; ᴛʜ, then; zh, measure

fro·zen (frō′zən) *adj.* **1** turned into ice; hardened by cold. **2** very cold. **3** killed or injured by frost. **4** covered or clogged with ice. **5** cold and unfeeling: *a frozen heart.* **6** too frightened or stiff to move: *frozen to the spot in horror.* **7** temporarily forbidden to be sold or exchanged: *frozen assets.* **8** of prices, wages, etc., fixed at a particular amount or level; unchanged. *—v.* pp. of **freeze.**

F.R.S. Fellow of the Royal Society.

F.R.S.C. Fellow of the Royal Society of Canada.

frt. freight.

fruc·ti·fi·ca·tion (fruk′tə fə kā′shən) *n.* **1** a forming or bearing of fruit. **2** the fruit.

fruc·ti·fy (fruk′tə fī′) *v.* **-fied, -fy·ing.** **1** bear fruit. **2** make fruitful; fertilize. [< F < L *fructificare* < *fructus* fruit + *facere* make]

fruc·tose (fruk′tōs) *n.* a sugar occurring in three different forms, especially the sweet form found in fruit juices, honey, etc.; levulose. *Formula:* $C_6H_{12}O_6$ [< L *fructus* fruit]

fru·gal (frü′gəl) *adj.* **1** avoiding waste; saving; tending to avoid unnecessary spending: *A frugal housekeeper buys and uses food carefully.* **2** costing little; barely sufficient: *He ate a frugal supper of bread and milk.* [< L *frugalis,* ult. < *frux, frugis* fruit] **—fru′gal·ly,** *adv.* **—Syn.** **1** sparing, thrifty. See **economical.**

fru·gal·i·ty (frü gal′ə tē) *n.* **-ties.** thrift; avoidance of waste; a tendency to avoid unnecessary spending.

fruit (früt) *n.* **1** the product of a tree, bush, shrub, or vine that is good to eat: *Apples and oranges are fruits.* **2** in botany, the part of a plant that contains the seeds. A fruit is the ripened ovary of a flower and the tissues connected with it. Pea pods, acorns, grains of wheat, etc. are fruits. **3** the useful product of plants: *the fruits of the earth.* **4** a product; result: *His invention was the fruit of much effort.*
—v. have or produce fruit. [ME < OF < L *fructus* < *frui* enjoy] **—fruit′er,** *n.* **—fruit′like′,** *adj.*

fruit·age (früt′ij) *n.* **1** the having or producing of fruit. **2** fruit; crop of fruit. **3** a product; result.

fruit cake a rich cake containing raisins, currants, spices, etc.

fruit cup mixed fruits served in a cup or glass as an appetizer or a dessert.

fruit·er·er (früt′ər ər) *n.* a dealer in fruit.

fruit fly a small fly whose larvae feed on decaying fruits and vegetables.

fruit·ful (früt′fəl) *adj.* **1** producing much fruit. **2** producing much of anything. **3** favorable to the growth of fruit or useful vegetation in general: *fruitful showers.* **4** having good results; bringing benefit or profit: *The new plan promises to be fruitful.* **—fruit′ful·ly,** *adv.* **—fruit′ful·ness,** *n.* **—Syn.** **2** productive, prolific, fertile.

fru·i·tion (frü ish′ən) *n.* **1** the condition of having results; fulfilment; attainment: *After years of hard work his plans came to fruition.* **2** the pleasure that comes from possession or use. **3** the condition of producing fruit. [< LL *fruitio, -onis* < *frui* enjoy]

fruit·less (früt′lis) *adj.* **1** having no results; useless; unsuccessful. **2** producing no fruit; barren. **—fruit′less·ly,** *adv.* **—Syn.** **1** abortive, futile, vain.

fruit nappie or **fruit nappy** a small bowl or dish in which dessert such as fruit may be served.

fruit ranch a ranch or farm where fruit is raised.

fruit stand a small store or stand where fruit is sold.

fruit sugar **1** levulose. **2** a finely powdered form of cane sugar.

fruit tree a tree whose fruit is good to eat.

fruit·wood (früt′wu̇d′) *n.* the wood of fruit trees used in carvings, furniture, etc. *—adj.* **1** of fruitwood. **2** related to the patterns or color of fruitwood.

fruit·y (früt′ē) *adj.* **fruit·i·er, fruit·i·est. 1** tasting or smelling like fruit. **2** *Informal.* full of rich or strong quality; highly interesting, attractive, or suggestive: *His description was fruity but embarrassing.* **—fruit′i·ness,** *n.*

fru·men·ty (frü′mən tē) *n.* hulled wheat boiled in milk and flavored with sugar, cinnamon, etc. [ME < OF *frumentee* < *frument* < L *frumentum* grain]

frump (frump) *n.* a woman who is shabby and out of style in dress. [origin uncertain]

frump·ish (frump′ish) *adj.* shabby and out of style in dress. **—frump′ish·ly,** *adv.*

frump·y (frump′ē) *adj.* **frump·i·er, frump·i·est.** frumpish. **—frump′i·ly,** *adv.* **—frump′i·ness,** *n.*

frus·trate (frus′trāt) *v.* **-trat·ed, -trat·ing. 1** bring to nothing; make useless or worthless; foil; defeat. **2** thwart; oppose: *The great artist had never been frustrated in his ambition to paint.* [< L *frustrari* < *frustra* in vain] **—frus′trat·er,** *n.*

Syn. 1, 2 Frustrate, thwart, baffle = keep from doing something. **Frustrate** emphasizes making all efforts and plans useless and vain, and thus keeping a person from achieving his aim: *The boy's waywardness frustrated his father's plans for his future.* **Thwart** = block someone's effort by some contrary action: *The sudden storm thwarted the men who were trying to reach the wrecked plane.* **Baffle** suggests causing confusion or bewilderment: *The absence of clues baffled the police.*

frus·tra·tion (frus trā′shən) *n.* a frustrating or being frustrated.

frus·tum (frus′təm) *n.* **-tums, -ta** (-tə). **1** in geometry, the part of a cone-shaped solid left after the top has been cut off by a plane parallel to the base. **2** the part of a solid between two cutting planes. [< L *frustum* piece]

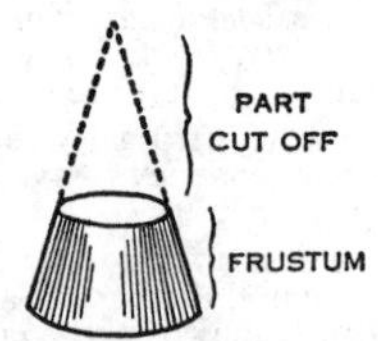

fry[1] (frī) *v.* **fried, fry·ing,** *n.* **fries.** *—v.* cook or be cooked over direct heat, with or without using fat or oil. *—n.* **1** fried food; a dish of fried meat, fish, etc. **2** an outdoor social gathering at which food, usually fish, is fried and eaten. [ME < OF *frire* < L *frigere*]

fry[2] (frī) *n.* **1** the young of fish. **2** small adult fish that live together in large groups or schools: *Sardines are classed as fry.* **3** young creatures; offspring; children. **4 small fry, a** children: *This movie is not for small fry.* **b** people or things having little importance. [ME < ON *frjó* seed]

fry·er (frī′ər) *n.* **1** a chicken, usually not over three lbs. in weight, intended for frying. **2** a person or thing that fries. **3** a pan used for frying.

frying pan 1 a shallow pan with a long handle, used for frying food. **2 out of the frying pan into the fire,** straight from one danger or difficulty into a worse one.

ft. 1 foot. **2** feet. **3** fort.

fth. or **fthm.** fathom.

fuch·sia (fū′shə) *n.* a shrub having handsome pink, red, or purple flowers that droop from the stems. [< NL; after Leonhard *Fuchs* (1501-1566), a German botanist]

fud·dle (fud′əl) *v.* **-dled, -dling. 1** make stupid with alcohol; intoxicate. **2** confuse; muddle. [origin uncertain]

fud·dy-dud·dy (fud′ē dud′ē) *n.* **-dies,** *adj. Informal.* *—n.* a fussy or stuffy old-fashioned person. *—adj.* obsolete; old-fashioned. [origin uncertain]

fudge[1] (fuj) *n. interj. v.* **fudged, fudg·ing.** *—n.* **1** a soft candy made of sugar, milk, butter, etc. **2** *Informal.* nonsense.
—interj. Informal. nonsense! bosh!
—v. Informal. put together in a clumsy or dishonest way; fake. [origin uncertain]

fudge[2] (fuj) *n.* **1** in printing, a small insert that can be patched on to a type page or printing plate without resetting the whole. **2** an item of news or other material added to the type page already set. **3** a machine for printing this kind of insert. [? < obs. *fadge* make fit]

Fueh·rer (fū′rər; *German,* fʏ′rər) *n. German.* Führer.

fu·el (fū′əl) *n. v.* **-elled** or **-eled, -el·ling** or **-el·ing.** *—n.* **1** something that can be burned to make a fire. **2** any substance used to produce heat energy. **3** atomic matter producing heat by fission or fusion, as in a nuclear reactor. **4** anything that keeps up or increases a feeling: *His insults were fuel to her hatred.*
—v. **1** supply with fuel. **2** get fuel. [ME < OF *fouaille,* ult. < L *focus* hearth]

fu·gal (fū′gəl) *adj.* of, having to do with, or in the style of a fugue.

fu·gi·tive (fū′jə tiv) *n.* a person who is fleeing or who has fled: *The murderer became a fugitive from justice.*
—adj. **1** fleeing; having fled; runaway. **2** lasting only a very short time; passing swiftly: *the fugitive hours.* **3** dealing with subjects of temporary interest. **4** roving; shifting. [ME < OF < L *fugitivus* < *fugere* flee] **—fu′gi·tive·ly,** *adv.* **—fu′gi·tive·ness,** *n.*

fugue (fūg) *n.* in music, a contrapuntal composition based on one or more short themes in which different voices or instruments repeat the same melody with slight variations. [< F < Ital. < L *fuga* flight]

Füh·rer (fū′rər; *German,* fʏ′rər) *n. German.* the title given to Adolf Hitler (1889-1945), the German dictator. Führer means leader.

-ful *suffix.* **1** full of, as in *cheerful.* **2** having; characterized by, as in *careful, thoughtful.* **3** having a tendency to, as in *harmful, mournful.* **4** enough to fill, as in *cupful, handful.* **5** other meanings, as in *manful, useful.* [OE; representing *full,* adj.]

ful·crum (fůl′krəm or ful′krəm) *n.* **-crums, -cra** (-krə). a support on which a lever turns or rests in moving or lifting something. [< L *fulcrum* bedpost < *fulcire* support]

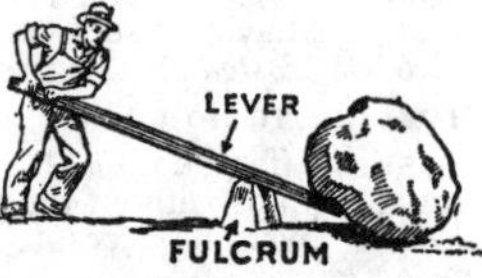

A man lifting a stone with a lever resting on a fulcrum. The closer the fulcrum is to the stone, the more lift he gets by pushing down on the lever at the other end.

ful·fil or **ful·fill** (fůl fil′) *v.* **-filled, -fill·ing. 1** carry out (a promise, prophecy, etc.); cause to happen or take place. **2** do or perform (a duty); obey (a command, law, etc.). **3** satisfy (a requirement, condition, etc.); serve (a purpose). **4** finish; complete. [OE *fullfyllan*] **—ful·fill′er,** *n.* **—Syn. 1** accomplish, realize. **2** execute, discharge.

ful·fil·ment or **ful·fill·ment** (fůl fil′mənt) *n.* a fulfilling; completion; performance; accomplishment: *Winning the race brought him a feeling of fulfilment.*

full[1] (fůl) *adj.* **1** able to hold no more; filled; with no empty space: *a full cup.* **2** complete; entire: *a full supply.* **3** of the greatest size, amount, extent, volume, etc.: *He ran a full mile.* **4** more than enough to satisfy; well supplied; abundant: *He ate three full meals a day.* **5** well filled out; plump; round: *a full face.* **6** made with wide folds or much cloth: *a full skirt.* **7** strong, sonorous, and distinct: *An orator should have a full voice.* **8 full of, a** filled with. **b** absorbed by; completely taken up with.
—adv. **1** completely; entirely. **2** straight; squarely; directly: *The blow hit him full in the face.* **3 full well,** *Archaic.* very well. **4 full many,** *Archaic.* very many.
—n. **1** the greatest size, amount, extent, volume, etc. **2 at the full,** at the time or point of fullness. **3 in full, a** to or for the complete amount. **b** written or said with all the words; not abbreviated or shortened. **4 to the full,** completely; entirely.
—v. make with wide folds or much cloth. [OE] **—Syn.** *adj.* **1** replete, sated. **2** whole. **4** ample, plentiful, copious.

full[2] (fůl) *v.* clean and thicken (cloth). [< *fuller*]

full·back (fůl′bak′) *n.* in football and other games, a player whose position is farthest behind the front line.

full blast *Informal.* in full operation; at highest speed or largest capacity.

full-blood·ed (fůl′blud′id) *adj.* **1** of pure race, breed, or strain; thoroughbred. **2** vigorous; hearty.

full-blown (fůl′blōn′) *adj.* **1** in full bloom. **2** completely developed or matured.

full-bod·ied (fůl′bod′ēd) *adj.* having considerable strength, flavor, etc.

full dress 1 the formal clothes worn in the evening or on important occasions. **2** in the armed services, full ceremonial dress.

full-dress (fu̇l′dres′) *adj.* **1** having to do with or requiring full dress; formal: *a full-dress reception.* **2** utilizing all resources; all-out; exhaustive: *a full-dress report, a full-dress debate.*

full·er (fu̇l′ər) *n.* a person whose work is cleaning and thickening cloth. [OE *fullere* < L *fullo* fuller]

fuller's earth a soft, clay-like mixture used for removing grease from cloth and for purifying oil.

full-fash·ioned (fu̇l′fash′ənd) *adj.* knitted to fit the shape of the foot, leg, or body.

full-fledged (fu̇l′flejd′) *adj.* **1** fully developed. **2** of full rank or standing.

full-grown (fu̇l′grōn′) *adj.* fully grown; mature.

full house 1 in a theatre, etc., the fact or state of every seat being occupied. **2** in poker, a hand made up of three cards of one kind and two of another, such as three sixes and two kings.

full-length (fu̇l′length′ or -lengkth′) *adj.* **1** showing the whole figure: *a full-length portrait.* **2** of traditional size, recognized length, or duration, etc.: *a full-length novel.* **3** reaching almost to the floor: *full-length windows, a full-length dress.* **4** of a woman's coat, reaching to the hem of a dress. —*adv.* lengthwise.

full moon 1 the moon seen with the whole disk illuminated. **2** the period when this occurs. See **moon** for picture.

full nelson in wrestling, a hold applied by hooking both arms under the opponent's with the hands gripped behind his neck.

full·ness (fu̇l′nis) *n.* **1** the state or condition of being full. **2 in the fullness of time,** in due course. Also, **fulness.**

full-rigged (fu̇l′rigd′) *adj.* **1** of a sailing ship, completely equipped with masts and sails. **2** completely equipped.

full sail 1 with all sails set. **2** with all possible power and energy.

full-scale (fu̇l′skāl′) *adj.* **1** drawn to actual size. **2** in a blue-print, scaled to correspond exactly. **3** thorough; all-out: *a full-scale investigation; a full-scale offensive.*

full swing 1 full operation; vigorous activity or movement: *The party was in full swing.* **2** with vigor: *He ran full swing.*

full-throat·ed (fu̇l′thrōt′id) *adj.* **1** clamorous and loud; vociferous. **2** rich and full in sound; sonorous.

full-time (fu̇l′tīm′) *adj. adv.* for the usual or normal length of time: *Full-time clerk wanted* (adj.). *The plant employs men full-time only* (adv.).

ful·ly (fu̇l′ē) *adv.* **1** completely; entirely. **2** abundantly; plentifully. **3** quite; exactly.

ful·mar (fu̇l′mər) *n.* a sea bird related to the petrel. [< ON *full* foul + *már* gull; from the foul-smelling liquid it ejects in self-defence]

ful·mi·nate (ful′mə nāt′) *v.* **-nat·ed, -nat·ing,** *n.* —*v.* **1** thunder forth (censure, threats, decrees, etc.): *The churches and the newspapers fulminated against the crime wave.* **2** denounce violently; censure strongly. **3** explode violently. **4** of a disease, develop suddenly and severely. **5** thunder and lighten.
—*n.* **1** a violent explosive. **2** a salt of fulminic acid. The fulminates, chiefly mercury and silver, are very unstable compounds, exploding with great violence by percussion or heating. [< L *fulminare* < *fulmen* lightning]
—**ful′mi·na′tor,** *n.*

ful·mi·na·tion (ful′mə nā′shən) *n.* **1** a violent denunciation; strong censure. **2** a violent explosion.

fulminic acid in chemistry, an acid encountered only in its salts, the fulminates, which are highly explosive. *Formula*: CNOH

ful·ness (fu̇l′nis) *n.* fullness.

ful·some (fu̇l′səm or ful′səm) *adj.* so much as to be disgusting; offensive. [< *full* + *-some*[1]; influenced in meaning by *foul*] —**ful′some·ly,** *adv.* —**ful′some·ness,** *n.*

fu·ma·gil·lin (fū′mə gil′in) *n.* an antibiotic derived from a fungus, used especially against amoebic infections. *Formula*: $C_{26}H_{31}O_7$

fu·ma·role (fū′mə rōl′) *n.* in volcanic areas, an opening in the earth's crust from which steam and gases issue: *There are many fumaroles near Katmai volcano in Alaska.* [< F *fumarolle* < Ital. *fumaruolo* < LL *fumariolum* smoke hole, ult. < L *fumus* smoke]

hat, āge, cãre, fär; let, ēqual, tėrm; it, īce
hot, ōpen, ôrder; oil, out; cup, pu̇t, rüle, ūse
əbove, takən, pencəl, lemən, circəs
ch, child; ng, long; sh, ship
th, thin; ᴛʜ, then; zh, measure

fum·ble (fum′bəl) *v.* **-bled, -bling,** *n.* —*v.* **1** grope awkwardly: *He fumbled about in his pockets for the ticket. Jane fumbled for words to express her thanks.* **2** handle awkwardly. **3** in sports, fail to catch and hold (a ball).
—*n.* **1** an awkward groping or handling. **2** in sports, a failure to catch and hold a ball. [cf. LG *fummeln*]
—**fum′bler,** *n.* —**fum′bling·ly,** *adv.*

fume (fūm) *n. v.* **fumed, fum·ing.** —*n.* **1** Usually, **fumes,** *pl.* a vapor, gas, or smoke, especially if harmful, strong, or odorous: *The strong fumes of the acid nearly choked him.* **2** a fit of anger; angry or irritable mood.
—*v.* **1** give off fumes. **2** pass off in fumes. **3** make angry complaints, show anger or irritation: *Mr. Smith always fumed about the slowness of the trains.* **4** treat with fumes. [ME < OF *fum* < L *fumus* smoke] —**fum′er,** *n.* —**Syn.** *v.* **1** smoke. **3** chafe, fret.

fumed oak oak darkened and colored by exposure to ammonia fumes.

fu·mi·gate (fū′mə gāt′) *v.* **-gat·ed, -gat·ing.** disinfect with fumes; expose to fumes: *They fumigated the building to kill the vermin.* [< L *fumigare* to smoke < *fumus* smoke, fume] —**fu′mi·ga′tion,** *n.*

fu·mi·ga·tor (fū′mə gā′tər) *n.* **1** a person who fumigates. **2** an apparatus for fumigating.

fun (fun) *n. adj. v.* **funned, fun·ning.** —*n.* **1** playfulness; merry play; amusement; joking. **2 for** or **in fun,** playfully; as a joke. **3 make fun of** or **poke fun at,** laugh at; ridicule.
—*adj. Informal.* providing amusement; for fun; full of fun: *a fun show.*
—*v. Informal.* act or speak in fun. [? originally v., var. of obs. *fon* befool] —**Syn. 1** sport; diversion.

func·tion (fungk′shən) *n.* **1** proper work; normal action or use; purpose: *The function of the stomach is to digest food.* **2** a formal public or social gathering for some purpose: *All the local dignitaries attended the great function to welcome the Queen.* **3** a mathematical quantity whose value depends on, or varies with, the value given to one or more related quantities: *The volume of a sphere is a function of the radius.* **4** anything likened to a mathematical function. **5** in grammar, the position or positions in which a linguistic form occurs in an utterance.
—*v.* work; be used; act. [< L *functio, -onis* < *fungi* perform] —**Syn.** *n.* **1** office, capacity, duty.

func·tion·al (fungk′shən əl) *adj.* **1** having to do with a function or functions. **2** having a function; working; acting. **3** useful in many ways. **4** of buildings, furniture, etc., having the intended use as the main basis of design. **5** in medicine, of or having to do with the function of an organ rather than its structure. —**func′tion·al·ly,** *adv.*

functional illiterate a person whose ability to read is too poor for practical purposes.

func·tion·al·ism (fungk′shə nə liz′əm) *n.* in architecture and design, the principle that the design of a structure should be determined primarily by its purpose or function.

func·tion·ar·y (fungk′shən er′ē) *n.* **-ar·ies,** *adj.* official.

fund (fund) *n.* **1** a sum of money set aside for a special purpose: *The school has a fund of $1,000 to buy books with.* **2** a stock or store ready for use; supply: *There is a fund of information in a dictionary.* **3 funds,** *pl.* **a** money ready to use. **b** money.
—*v.* **1** set aside a sum of money to pay the interest on (a debt). **2** change (a debt) from a short term to a long term. **3** put into a fund or store; collect; store up. [< L *fundus* bottom, a piece of land]

fun·da·ment (fun′də mənt) *n.* the part of the body used in sitting; buttocks. [< L *fundamentum,* ult. < L *fundus* bottom]

fun·da·men·tal (fun′də men′təl) *adj.* **1** of the foundation or basis; forming a foundation or basis; essential. **2** in music, having to do with the lowest note of a chord.
—*n.* **1** a principle, rule, law, etc. that forms a foundation or basis; essential part: *the fundamentals of grammar.* **2** in music, the lowest note of a chord. **3** in physics, the component of a wave that has the greatest wave length.

[< NL *fundamentalis* < L *fundamentum* foundation, ult. < *fundus* bottom] —**fun′da·men′tal·ly,** *adv.* —**Syn.** *adj.* 1 basic, indispensable.

fun·da·men·tal·ism (fun′də men′təl iz′əm) *n.* **1** the belief that the words of the Bible were inspired by God and should be believed and followed literally. **2** Often, **Fundamentalism.** a movement in certain churches upholding this belief.

fun·da·men·tal·ist (fun′də men′təl ist) *n.* a person who believes in fundamentalism. Fundamentalists refuse to accept any teaching that conflicts with the Bible.

fu·ner·al (fū′nər əl or fūn′rəl) *n.* **1** the ceremonies that accompany the burial or burning of the dead, usually including a religious service and a procession to the place of burial. **2** the procession taking a dead person's body to the place where it is to be buried or burned.
—*adj.* of a funeral; suitable for a funeral: *A funeral march is very slow.* [< LL *funeralis* of a funeral < L *funus, funeris* funeral, death]

fu·ner·ar·y (fū′nər er′ē) *adj.* of a funeral or burial: *A funerary urn holds the ashes of a dead person's body.*

fu·ne·re·al (fū nēr′ē əl) *adj.* **1** of or suitable for a funeral. **2** sad; gloomy; dismal. [< L *funereus* < *funus, -neris* funeral] —**fu·ne′re·al·ly,** *adv.* —**Syn. 2** solemn, mournful.

fun fair 1 a local fund-raising bazaar offering many attractions for children. **2** *Brit.* an amusement park.

fun·gal (fung′gəl) *adj.* fungous. —*n.* a fungus.

fun·gi (fung′gī; fung′gē, fun′jī or fun′jē) *n.* pl. of **fungus.**

fun·gi·cid·al (fung′gə sīd′əl or fun′jə sīd′əl) *adj.* that destroys fungi.

fun·gi·cide (fung′gə sīd′ or fun′jə sīd′) *n.* any substance that destroys fungi. [< L *fungus* + E *-cide*²]

fun·goid (fung′goid) *adj.* resembling a fungus; having spongy, unhealthful growths.

fun·gous (fung′gəs) *adj.* **1** of a fungus or of fungi; like a fungus; spongy. **2** growing or springing up suddenly, but not lasting. **3** caused by a fungus. [< L *fungosus* < *fungus* fungus]

fun·gus (fung′gəs) *n.* **fun·gi** or **fun·gus·es,** *adj.* —*n.* **1** any of a group of plants without flowers, leaves, or green coloring matter: *Mushrooms, toadstools, moulds, smuts, and mildews are fungi.* **2** something that grows or springs up rapidly like a mushroom. **3** a diseased, spongy growth on the skin. —*adj.* fungous. [< L; probably akin to Gk. *sphongos* sponge]

Fungi growing on a tree

fu·nic·u·lar (fū nik′yù lər) *adj.* of a rope; hanging from or operated by a rope. A **funicular railway** is a railway system in which the cars are moved by cables. [< L *funiculus,* dim. of *funis* rope]

funk (fungk) *Informal.* —*n.* fear; panic. —*v.* **1** be afraid of. **2** frighten. **3** shrink from; shirk. [origin uncertain]

fun·nel (fun′əl) *n. v.* **-nelled** or **-neled, -nel·ling** or **-nel·ing.** —*n.* **1** a small, tapering tube with a wide, cone-shaped mouth: *He used a funnel to pour the gas into the tank.* **2** anything shaped like a funnel. **3** a cylindrical metal chimney; smokestack: *The steamship had two funnels.* **4** a flue.
—*v.* pass or feed through or as if through a funnel. [ME < OF *fonel* < LL *fundibulum* < L *infundibulum* < *in-* in + *fundere* pour]

A funnel (def. 1) for pouring

fun·ny (fun′ē) *adj.* **-ni·er, -ni·est,** *n.* **-nies.** —*adj.* **1** causing laughter; amusing. **2** *Informal.* strange; peculiar; odd. **3** having to do with the part of a newspaper containing comic strips.
—*n.* **funnies,** *pl. Informal.* **a** a comic strips. **b** a section of a newspaper devoted to comic strips. [< *fun*] —**fun′ni·ly,** *adv.* —**fun′ni·ness,** *n.*

Syn. *adj.* **1 Funny, laughable** = such as to cause laughter or amusement. **Funny** in common informal use is interchanged with any word meaning "causing or fit to cause amusement, smiles, or laughter," but particularly suggests being queer or extraordinary in a way that causes amusement or laughter: *The funny little man and his funny little children keep our neighborhood smiling.* **Laughable** is the general word meaning "ridiculous, fit to cause or causing laughter": *His fine airs are laughable.*

funny bone the part of the elbow over which a nerve passes. When the funny bone is struck, a sharp, tingling sensation is felt in the arm and hand.

fur (fėr) *n. v.* **furred, fur·ring.** —*n.* **1** the soft hair covering the skin of certain animals. **2** skin with such hair on it: *Fur is used to make, cover, trim, or line clothing.* **3** Usually, **furs,** *pl.* a garment made of fur. **4** a coating of foul or waste matter like fur: *A sick person often has fur on his tongue.* **5 make the fur fly,** *Informal.* cause trouble; quarrel; fight. **6 stroke a person's fur the wrong way,** irritate him. [< v.]
—*v.* **1** make, cover, trim, or line with fur. **2** coat with foul or waste matter like fur. **3** put furring on. [ME < OF *forrer* line, encase < *forre* sheath < Gmc.] —**fur′less,** *adj.*

fur. 1 furlong. **2** furnished.

fur·be·low (fėr′bə lō′) *n.* a bit of elaborate trimming: *There were many frills and furbelows on her dress.*
—*v.* trim in an elaborate way. [var., by folk etymology, of F dial. *ferbalaw, farbala,* var. of F *falbala*]

fur·bish (fėr′bish) *v.* **1** brighten by rubbing or scouring; polish: *He furbished up the rusty sword.* **2** restore to good condition; make usable again: *Before going to France, he furbished up his half-forgotten French.* [ME < OF *forbiss-,* a stem of *forbir* polish < Gmc.] —**fur′bish·er,** *n.*

fur brigade *Cdn.* formerly, a convoy of freight canoes, dog sleds, etc. that carried furs and other goods to and from remote trading posts.

fur·cate (fėr′kāt or fėr′kit) *adj.* forked. [< Med.L *furcatus* cloven < L *furca* fork]

fur·fur·al (fėr′fə ral′ or fėr′fə ral′) *n.* a liquid aldehyde made by distilling corn cobs, oat hulls, etc. It is used in manufacturing dyes and plastics, in refining oil, etc. *Formula*: $C_5H_4O_2$ [< *furfur*ane + *al*dehyde]

Fu·ries (fūr′ēz) *n.pl.* in Greek and Roman mythology, the three spirits of revenge; Erinyes.

fu·ri·ous (fūr′ē əs) *adj.* **1** intensely violent; raging: *a furious storm.* **2** full of wild, fierce anger. **3** of unrestrained energy, speed, etc.: *furious activity.* [< L *furiosus* < *furia* fury] —**fu′ri·ous·ly,** *adv.* —**fu′ri·ous·ness,** *n.*

furl (fėrl) *v.* roll up; fold up; curl: *furl a sail, furl a flag.*
—*n.* **1** the act of furling. **2** the manner in which a sail, flag, etc. is furled. **3** a roll, coil, or curl of anything furled. [< F *ferler* < OF *ferlier* < *fer* firm (< L *firmus*) + *lier* bind < L *ligare*] —**furl′er,** *n.*

fur·long (fėr′long) *n.* a measure of distance equal to one-eighth of a mile. *Abbrev.*: fur. [OE *furlang* < *furh* furrow + *lang* long]

fur·lough (fėr′lō) *n.* a leave of absence, especially for a soldier. —*v.* give leave of absence to. [< Du. *verlof*]

fur·nace (fėr′nis) *n.* **1** an enclosed structure to make a very hot fire in: *Furnaces are used to heat buildings, melt metals, make glass, etc.* **2** a very hot place. **3** a severe test. [ME < OF *fornais, fornaise* < L *fornax, -acis* < *fornus* oven]

fur·nish (fėr′nish) *v.* **1** supply; provide: *The sun furnishes heat.* **2** supply (a room, house, etc.) with furniture, equipment, etc. [< OF *furniss-,* a stem of *furnir* accomplish < Gmc.] —**fur′nish·er,** *n.*

Syn. 1, 2 Furnish, equip = provide or supply. **Furnish** = provide things or services necessary for existence or wanted for use or comfort: *We furnished the living room. The caterer furnished both food and waiters. Furnish one good reason.* **Equip** = fit out with what is needed to do work or to work with: *We equipped the kitchen. He is not equipped to translate Latin.*

fur·nish·ings (fėr′nish ingz) *n.pl.* **1** the furniture or equipment for a room, house, etc. **2** accessories of dress; articles of clothing: *That store sells men's furnishings.*

fur·ni·ture (fėr′nə chər) *n.* **1** the movable articles needed in a room, house, etc.: *Beds, chairs, tables, and desks are furniture.* **2** *Archaic.* articles needed; equipment: *The harness and ornamental coverings for a horse were called furniture in the Middle Ages.* **3** apparatus, appliances, or instruments for work, now especially the tools, **utensils,** rigging, stores, and tackle of a ship. **4** in printing, strips or blocks of wood or metal, lower than type-high, set in and about pages of type to fill out large white areas such as margins. [< F *fourniture*]

fu·ror (fūr′ôr) *n.* **1** an outburst of wild enthusiasm or excitement: *His speech roused the crowd to a furor.* **2** a craze; mania. **3** fury; madness; frenzy. [< F *fureur* < L *furor* < *furere* rage]

fu·rore (fū′rôr or fyu̇ rôr′ē) *n.* furor. [< Ital. *furore* < L *furor*]

furred (fėrd) *adj.* **1** having fur. **2** made, covered, trimmed, or lined with fur. **3** wearing fur. **4** coated with foul or waste matter: *The sick man's tongue was furred.* **5** with furring on it.

fur·ri·er (fėr′ē ər) *n.* **1** a dealer in furs. **2** a person whose work is preparing furs or making and repairing fur coats, etc. **3** a store that sells or repairs fur coats, etc.

fur·ri·er·y (fėr′ē ər ē) *n.* **-er·ies.** **1** furs. **2** the business or work of a furrier.

fur·ring (fėr′ing) *n.* **1** fur used to make, cover, trim, or line clothing. **2** a coating of foul or waste matter like fur. **3** thin strips of wood fastened to beams, walls, etc. to make a level support for laths, etc. or to provide air spaces.

fur·row (fėr′ō) *n.* **1** a long, narrow groove or track cut in the ground by a plough. **2** any long, narrow groove or track: *Heavy trucks made deep furrows in the muddy road.* **3** a wrinkle. —*v.* **1** plough. **2** make furrows in. **3** wrinkle: *The old man's face was furrowed with age.* [OE *furh*]

fur·ry (fėr′ē) *adj.* **-ri·er, -ri·est.** **1** of fur; consisting of fur. **2** covered with fur; wearing fur. **3** looking or feeling like fur. **4** coated or covered as if with fur: *a furry tongue.* —**fur′ri·ness,** *n.*

fur·ther (fėr′ᴛʜər) *adj.* **1** farther; more distant: *on the further side.* **2** more: *Have you any further need of me?* —*adv.* **1** at or to a greater distance. **2** to a greater extent. **3** moreover; also; besides: *say further.* —*v.* help forward; promote. [OE *furthra,* adj., *furthor,* adv. < *forth* forth] —**Syn.** *v.* See **promote.** ☛ See **farther** for usage note.

fur·ther·ance (fėr′ᴛʜər əns) *n.* an act of furthering; helping forward; advancement; promotion.

fur·ther·more (fėr′ᴛʜər môr′) *adv.* moreover; also; besides.

fur·ther·most (fėr′ᴛʜər mōst′) *adj.* furthest.

fur·thest (fėr′ᴛʜist) *adv.* farthest; most distant. —*adj.* **1** farthest; most distant. **2** to the greatest degree or extent. [ME]

fur·tive (fėr′tiv) *adj.* **1** done stealthily; secret: *a furtive glance into the forbidden room.* **2** sly; stealthy; shifty: *The thief had a furtive manner.* [< L *furtivus* < *fur* thief] —**fur′tive·ly,** *adv.* —**fur′tive·ness,** *n.*

fu·run·cle (fūr′ung kəl) *n.* in medicine, a boil; inflammatory sore. [< L *furunculus,* dim. of *fur* thief]

fu·ry (fūr′ē) *n.* **-ries.** **1** wild, fierce anger; a rage. **2** violence; fierceness. **3** a raging or violent person. **4 like fury,** *Informal.* violently; very rapidly. **5** unrestrained energy, speed, etc.: *work with fury.* **6 Fury,** in Greek and Roman mythology, any one of the three spirits of revenge. [< L *furia*] —**Syn. 1** ire, wrath. See **rage.** **2** vehemence.

furze (fėrz) *n.* a low, prickly, evergreen shrub having yellow flowers, common on waste lands; gorse. [OE *fyrs*]

fuse[1] (fūz) *n. v.* **fused, fus·ing.** —*n.* **1** the part of an electric circuit that melts, thus breaking the connection when the current becomes dangerously strong. **2** a slow-burning wick or other device to detonate dynamite, a shell, a bomb, etc. Also, **fuze.** —*v. Informal.* of an electric light, be extinguished because of the melting of a fuse. [< Ital. *fuso* < L *fusus* spindle]

fuse[2] (fūz) *v.* **fused, fus·ing.** **1** melt; melt together: *The wax from the two candles fused as they burned.* **2** blend; unite. [< L *fusus,* pp. of *fundere* pour, melt]

fu·see (fū zē′) *n.* **1** a large-headed match that will burn in a wind. **2** a flare used by railways as a signal: *A fusee burns with a red or green light.* Also, **fuzee.** [< F *fusée* spindleful < OF **fus* spindle < L *fusus*]

fu·se·lage (fū′zə läzh′ or fū′zə lij) *n.* the framework of the body of an aircraft that holds passengers, cargo, etc. See **airplane** for picture. [< F *fuselage* < *fuselé* spindle-shaped]

fu·sel oil (fū′zəl) an acrid, oily liquid that occurs in alcoholic liquors when they are not distilled enough. [*fusel* < G *Fusel* bad liquor]

hat, āge, cãre, fär; let, ēqual, tėrm; it, īce
hot, ōpen, ôrder; oil, out; cup, pu̇t, rüle, ūse
əbove, takən, pencəl, lemən, circəs
ch, child; ng, long; sh, ship
th, thin; ᴛʜ, then; zh, measure

fu·si·bil·i·ty (fū′ze bil′ə tē) *n.* the quality of being fusible.

fu·si·ble (fū′zə bəl) *adj.* that can be fused or melted. —**fu′si·ble·ness,** *n.*

fu·si·form (fū′zə fôrm′) *adj.* rounded and tapering from the middle toward each end: *A milkweed pod is fusiform.* [< L *fusus* spindle + E *-form*]

fu·sil (fū′zəl) *n.* a light flintlock musket. [< F *fusil* steel for tinder box, ult. < L *focus* hearth]

fu·sil·eer (fū′zə lēr′) *n.* fusilier.

fu·sil·ier (fū′zə lēr′) *n.* **1** formerly, a soldier armed with a light flintlock musket called a fusil. **2** a private soldier in a regiment that used to be armed with fusils. [< F *fusilier* < *fusil* musket]

fu·sil·lade (fū′zə lād′) *n. v.* **-lad·ed, -lad·ing.** —*n.* **1** the simultaneous or continuous discharge of many firearms. **2** something that resembles a fusillade: *The reporters greeted the mayor with a fusillade of questions.* —*v.* attack or shoot down by a fusillade. [< F *fusillade* < *fusiller* shoot < *fusil* musket]

fu·sion (fū′zhən) *n.* **1** a melting; melting together; fusing: *Bronze is made by the fusion of copper and tin.* **2** a blending; union: *A new party was formed by the fusion of two political groups.* **3** a fused mass. **4** in nuclear physics, the combining of two nuclei to create a nucleus of greater mass: *The fusion of atomic nuclei releases tremendous amounts of energy, which can be used in such things as the hydrogen or fusion bomb.* [< L *fusio, -onis* < *fundere* pour, melt]

fusion bomb hydrogen bomb.

fu·sion·ist (fū′zhən ist) *n.* a person taking part in a union of political parties or factions.

fuss (fus) *n.* **1** too much bother about small matters; useless talk and worry; attention given to something not worth it. **2** a person who fusses too much. —*v.* **1** make a fuss: *Nervously she fussed about her work.* **2** make nervous or worried; bother. [origin uncertain] —**fuss′er,** *n.* —**Syn.** *n.* **1** bustle, ado, commotion.

fuss·y (fus′ē) *adj.* **fuss·i·er, fuss·i·est.** **1** inclined to fuss; hard to please; very particular: *A sick person is likely to be fussy about his food.* **2** much trimmed; elaborately made: *Some girls like fussy dresses.* **3** full of details; requiring much care: *a fussy job.* —**fuss′i·ly,** *adv.* —**fuss′i·ness,** *n.*

fus·tian (fus′chən) *n.* **1** a coarse, heavy cloth made of cotton and flax: *Fustian was used for clothing in Europe throughout the Middle Ages.* **2** a thick cotton cloth like corduroy. **3** pompous, high-sounding language; would-be eloquence. —*adj.* **1** made of fustian. **2** pompous and high-sounding, but cheap. [ME < OF *fustaigne* < LL *fustaneum* < L *fustis* stick of wood]

fus·tic (fus′tik) *n.* **1** a tropical American tree of the mulberry family. **2** the wood of this tree. **3** the dye. [< F *fustoc* < Sp. < Arabic *fustuq.* Akin to PISTACHIO.]

fust·y (fus′tē) *adj.* **fust·i·er, fust·i·est.** **1** having a stale smell; musty; mouldy; stuffy. **2** old-fashioned; out-of-date. [< *fust,* n., < OF *fust* wine cask < L *fustis* staff] —**fust′i·ly,** *adv.* —**fust′i·ness,** *n.*

fut. future.

fu·tile (fū′tīl or fū′təl) *adj.* **1** not successful; useless. **2** not important; trifling. **3** occupied with things of no value or importance; lacking in purpose: *a futile life.* [< L *futilis* pouring easily, worthless < *fundere* pour] —**fu′tile·ly,** *adv.* —**fu′tile·ness,** *n.* —**Syn. 1** ineffectual, profitless. See **vain. 2** frivolous, idle, trivial.

fu·til·i·ty (fū til′ə tē) *n.* **-ties.** **1** uselessness. **2** unimportance. **3** a futile action, event, etc.

fut·tock (fut′ək) *n.* one of the curved timbers that form the middle of a rib in a ship. [? for *foot hook*]

fu·ture (fū′chər) *n.* **1** the time to come; what is to come; what will be. **2** a chance of success or prosperity: *a young*

man with a future. **3** in grammar, a future tense or verb form. **4 futures,** *pl.* **a** things bought or sold to be received or delivered at a future date. **b** a buying or selling of such things for future delivery.
—adj. **1** that is to come; that will be; coming. **2** in grammar, expressing or indicating time to come. [< L *futurus,* future participle of *esse* be] **—fu′ture·less,** *adj.*

future perfect **1** in grammar, a verb tense formed by adding "will have" or "shall have" to the past participle, to express action to be completed in the future: *By next week, he will have gone.* **2** designating this tense. **3** a verb form or verb phrase in this tense.

future tense a verb tense that expresses occurrence in time to come.

fu·tur·ism (fū′chər iz′əm) *n.* in art, literature, music, etc., a movement that originated in Italy early in the 20th century, rejecting traditional forms and methods in an attempt to express the violence, speed, and noise of contemporary civilization.

fu·tur·ist (fū′chər ist) *n.* a person who favors futurism.

fu·tur·is·tic (fū′chə ris′tik) *adj.* **1** of or like futurism. **2** of or relating to the future; untraditional; advanced. **—fu′tur·is′ti·cal·ly,** *adv.*

fu·tu·ri·ty (fū tūr′ə tē or fū tür′ə tē) *n.* **-ties. 1** future. **2** a future state or event. **3** the quality of being future.

fuze (fūz) *n.* fuse[1].

fu·zee (fū zē′) *n.* fusee.

fuzz (fuz) *n.* **1** loose, light fibres or hairs; down: *Caterpillars and peaches are covered with fuzz.* **2** *Slang.* **a the fuzz,** the police. **b** a policeman. *—v.* **1** make fuzzy. **2** become fuzzy. **3** fly out in fuzz.

fuzz·y (fuz′ē) *adj.* **fuzz·i·er, fuzz·i·est. 1** of fuzz. **2** like fuzz. **3** covered with fuzz: *The kitten was a fuzzy little creature.* **4** blurred; indistinct: *His eyes were so weak that everything looked fuzzy.* **—fuzz′i·ly,** *adv.* **—fuzz′i·ness,** *n.*

fwd. forward.

-fy *suffix.* **1** make; cause to be; change into, as in *simplify, intensify.* **2** become, as in *solidify.* [< F *-fier* < L *-ficare* < *facere* do, make]

FY fiscal year.

fyl·fot (fil′fot) *n.* swastika. [? < *fill foot,* a design for filling the foot of a painted window]

G or **g** (jē) *n.* **G's** or **g's. 1** the seventh letter of the English alphabet. **2** any speech sound represented by this letter. **3** the seventh of a series designated alphabetically. **4** in music: **a** the fifth tone of the scale of C major. **b** a symbol representing this tone. **c** a key string, etc. that produces this tone. **d** the scale or key that has G for its keynote.

g. or **g** **1** gram. **2** guinea. **3** gauge. **4** genitive. **5** gender. **6** goalkeeper.

G[1] **1** German. **2** gravitational force expressed in G's.

G[2] (jē) *n.* **G's** or **Gs.** *U.S. Slang.* a thousand dollars. [< *grand* a thousand dollars]

G. **1** gravity. **2** German. **3** gulf.

Ga gallium.

Ga. Georgia.

G.A. **1** in the United Nations, General Assembly. **2** General Agent.

gab (gab) *n. v.* **gabbed, gab·bing.** *Informal. —n.* **1** chatter; gabble; idle talk. **2 gift of gab** or **gift of the gab,** fluency of speech; glibness.
—v. talk too much; chatter; gabble. [probably imitative]

gab·ar·dine (gab′ər dēn′ or gab′ər dēn′) *n.* **1** a closely woven, woollen, cotton, or rayon cloth having small, diagonal ribs on its surface, used for raincoats, suits, etc. **2** gaberdine (def. 1). [var. of *gaberdine*]

gab·ble (gab′əl) *v.* **-bled, -bling,** *n. —v.* **1** talk rapidly with little or no meaning; jabber. **2** make rapid, meaningless sounds: *The geese gabbled. —n.* rapid talk or sounds with little or no meaning. [< *gab,* var. of *gob* < Gaelic *gob* mouth] **—gab′bler,** *n.*

gab·by (gab′ē) *adj.* **-bi·er, -bi·est.** *Informal.* very talkative.

gab·er·dine (gab′ər dēn′ or gab′ər·dēn′) *n.* **1** a man's long, loose, outer garment or cloak. Gaberdines were worn by the Jews in the Middle Ages. **2** gabardine (def. 1). [< Sp. *gabardina*]

ga·bi·on (gā′bē ən) *n.* **1** in military use, a cylinder of wicker filled with earth, formerly used as a defence. In modern warfare sandbags are used in place of gabions. **2** a similar cylinder made of metal, etc. and filled with stones, used in building dams, supporting bridge foundations, etc. [< F < Ital. *gabbione,* ult. < L *cavea* cage]

ga·ble (gā′bəl) *n.* **1** the end of a ridged roof, with the three-cornered piece of wall that it covers. **2** an end wall with a gable. **3** a triangular ornament or canopy over a door, window, etc. *—v.* **1** make (a roof) end with a gable or gables. **2** form gables. [ME < OF *gable* < ON *gafl*]

Gables of a house

ga·bled (gā′bəld) *adj.* built with a gable or gables; having or forming gables.

gable roof a roof that forms a gable at one or both ends.

ga·by (gā′bē) *n.* **-bies.** *Informal.* a fool; simpleton. [origin uncertain]

gad[1] (gad) *v.* **gad·ded, gad·ding. 1** go about looking for pleasure or excitement: *She was always gadding about town.* **2** move about restlessly. *—n.* **1** the act of gadding. **2** a gadabout: *He is a born gad.* [? back formation < obs. *gadling* companion < OE *gædeling* < *gæd* fellowship + *-ling*] **—gad′der,** *n.*

gad[2] (gad) *n. v.* **gad·ded, gad·ding.** *—n.* **1** a goad. **2** a pointed mining tool for breaking up rock, coal, ore, etc. *—v.* **1** goad. **2** break up (rock or ore) with a gad. [< Scand.; cf. Icelandic *gaddr*]

Gad or **gad**[3] (gad) *n. interj. Archaic.* a word used as a mild oath, exclamation of surprise, etc. [euphemistic var. of *God*]

gad·a·bout (gad′ə bout′) *n. Informal.* a person who wanders about looking for pleasure or excitement; person fond of going from place to place. [< *gad*[1]]

gad·fly (gad′flī′) *n.* **-flies. 1** a fly that stings cattle, horses, etc. The horsefly and botfly are two kinds of gadfly. **2** a person who irritates others by calling attention to their faults. [< *gad*[2] + *fly*]

gadg·et (gaj′it) *n. Informal.* a small mechanical or electrical device or contrivance; any ingenious device:

My brother is always buying new gadgets for his car. [origin uncertain]

gadg·et·ry (gaj′ə trē) *n.* **1** gadgets: *electronic gadgetry.* **2** the inventing, making, and using of gadgets.

gad·o·lin·i·um (gad′ə lin′ē əm) *n.* a rare metallic chemical element. *Symbol*: Gd; *at.no.* 64; *at.wt.* 157.25. [after Johann *Gadolin* (1760-1852), a Finnish chemist]

Gae·a (jē′ə) *n.* in Greek mythology, the earth goddess and mother of the Titans.

Gael (gāl) *n.* **1** a Scottish Highlander. **2** a Celt born or living in Scotland or the Isle of Man, or, in some cases, in Ireland. [< Scots Gaelic *Gaidheal* < OIrish *Goidhel*]

Gael·ic (gā′lik or gal′ik) *adj.* of or having to do with the Gaels or their language, in Scotland or Ireland. —*n.* the language of the Gaels.

gaff (gaf) *n.* **1** a strong hook or barbed spear for pulling large fish out of the water. **2** a sharp metal spur fastened to the leg of a gamecock. **3** a spar or pole extending along the upper edge of a fore-and-aft sail. **4** something uncomfortable or hard to take. **5 bring to gaff,** draw (a hooked fish) with the line within reach of the gaff. **6 stand the gaff,** *Slang.* hold up well under strain or punishment of any kind. **7 throw a gaff into,** *Slang.* break up; disrupt. —*v.* hook or pull (a fish) out of the water with a gaff. [< F *gaffe* < Celtic.; cf. Irish Gaelic *gaf, gafa*]

A gaff (def. 3)

gaf·fer (gaf′ər) *n. Informal.* an old man. [alteration of *godfather*]

☛ **Gaffer is now normally used in a humorous or unfavorable sense; it is the masculine counterpart of gammer, an old gossip.**

gaff·top·sail (gaf′top′sāl′ or -top′səl) *n.* a topsail set above a gaff.

gag (gag) *n. v.* **gagged, gag·ging.** —*n.* **1** something thrust into a person's mouth to keep him from talking, crying out, etc. **2** anything used to silence a person; a restraint or hindrance to free speech. **3** *Slang.* an amusing remark or trick; something said or done to cause a laugh; a joke: *The comedian's gags made the audience laugh.* **4** in a legislative body, a law or ruling designed to restrict or prevent discussion on a particular subject. —*v.* **1** put a gag into; keep from talking, crying out, etc. by means of a gag: *The bandits tied the watchman's arms and gagged his mouth.* **2** force to keep silent; restrain or hinder from free speech. **3** say something to cause a laugh. **4** choke or strain in an effort to vomit. **5** cause to choke or strain in an effort to vomit. [probably imitative] —**gag′ger,** *n.* —**Syn.** *v.* **2** silence, suppress.

ga·ga (gä′gä′) *adj. Slang.* **1** foolish; crazy; silly. **2** wildly or foolishly enthusiastic: *They went quite gaga over the show.* [< F *gaga* old fool]

gage[1] (gāj) *n. v.* **gaged, gag·ing.** —*n.* **1** a pledge to fight; challenge: *The knight threw down his gauntlet as a gage of battle.* **2** a pledge; security. —*v. Archaic.* offer as a pledge or security; wager. [ME < OF *gage* < Frankish **wadja-*. Doublet of WAGE.]

gage[2] (gāj) *n. v.* **gaged, gag·ing.** gauge. —**gag′er,** *n.*

gage·a·ble (gāj′ə bəl) *adj.* gaugeable.

gag·gle (gag′əl) *v.* **-gled, -gling,** *n.* —*v.* make a sound like the cackle of a goose; cackle. —*n.* **1** the sound that a goose makes; cackle. **2** a flock of geese. **3** *Informal.* a group of people, especially women.

gag·man (gag′man′) *n.* **-men** (-men′). a man who invents comic lines and situations for comedians.

gai·e·ty (gā′ə tē) *n.* **-ties. 1** a being gay; cheerful liveliness; merriment. **2** gay entertainment. **3** bright appearance; showiness; finery: *gaiety of dress.* Also, **gayety.** [< F *gaieté*]

gai·ly (gā′lē) *adv.* **1** as if gay; happily; merrily. **2** brightly; showily. Also, **gayly.**

gain (gān) *v.* **1** get; obtain; secure: *The king gained possession of more lands.* **2** get as an increase, addition, advantage, or profit. **3** make progress; advance; improve: *The sick child is gaining and will soon be well.* **4** be the victor in; win: *The stronger army gained the battle.* **5** get to; arrive at; reach: *The swimmer gained the shore.* **6 gain on,** come closer to; get nearer to: *One boat is gaining on the other.* **7 gain over,** persuade to join one's side. —*n.* **1** the act of gaining or getting anything. **2** what is gained; increase; addition; advantage; profit. **3** getting wealth: *Greed is love of gain.* **4** in a radio, phonograph, etc., amplification of a signal, or of the volume of sound. **5 gains,** *pl.* profits; earnings; winnings. [< F *gagner* < Gmc.] —**Syn.** *v.* **1** acquire, earn. **5** attain. –*n.* **2** benefit, acquisition.

hat, āge, cãre, fär; let, ēqual, tėrm; it, īce
hot, ōpen, ôrder; oil, out; cup, pu̇t, rüle, ūse
əbove, takən, pencəl, lemən, circəs
ch, child; ng, long; sh, ship
th, thin; ᴛʜ, then; zh, measure

gain·er (gān′ər) *n.* **1** one that gains. **2** in swimming, a fancy dive in which the diver turns a back somersault in the air.

gain·ful (gān′fəl) *adj.* bringing in money or advantage; profitable. —**gain′ful·ly,** *adv.*

gain·said (gān′sed′) *v.* a pt. and a pp. of **gainsay.**

gain·say (gān′sā′) *v.* **-said** or **-sayed, -saying.** deny; contradict; dispute: *We could not gainsay his opinion.* [< obs. *gain-* against + *say*] —**gain′say′er,** *n.*

gainst or **'gainst** (genst or gānst) *prep. conj. Poetic.* against.

gait (gāt) *n.* **1** the kind of step used in walking or running. A gallop is one of the gaits of a horse. **2** a way of walking or running; carriage or bearing of the body in moving: *He has a lame gait because of an injured foot.* [ME < ON *gata* way]

gait·ed (gāt′id) *adj.* having a certain gait: *heavy-gaited oxen.*

gai·ter (gā′tər) *n.* **1** a covering for the lower leg, made of cloth, leather, etc. **2** a shoe with an elastic strip in each side. [< F *guêtre*]

gal. gallon; gallons.

Gal. 1 Galatians. **2** Galway.

ga·la (gā′lə or gal′ə) *n.* a festive occasion; festival. —*adj.* of festivity; for a festive occasion; with festivities. [< F < Ital.; cf. OF *gale* merriment]

ga·lac·tic (gə lak′tik) *adj.* **1** in astronomy, of or having to do with a number of stars forming one system, especially the Milky Way. **2** of milk; obtained from milk. [< Gk. *galaktikos* < *gala, -aktos* milk]

galactic circle in astronomy, the great circle whose plane passes almost centrally along the Milky Way.

galactic cluster any diffuse group of stars, usually numbering over a hundred, such as the Pleiades.

Gal·a·had (gal′ə had′) *n.* **1 Sir,** in Arthurian legend, the son of Lancelot and Elaine. He was the noblest and purest knight of the Round Table and the only one to see the Holy Grail. **2** any man as noble and pure as Sir Galahad.

gal·an·tine (gal′ən tēn′) *n.* veal, chicken, or other white meat boned, tied up, boiled, and then served cold with its own jelly. [< F]

Gal·a·te·a (gal′ə tē′ə) *n.* in Greek legend, an ivory statue of a maiden, carved by Pygmalion. When he fell in love with the statue, Aphrodite gave it life.

Ga·la·tian (gə lā′shən) *adj.* of or having to do with Galatia, an ancient country in central Asia Minor that later became a Roman province. —*n.* **1** an inhabitant of Galatia. **2 Galatians,** a book of the New Testament, consisting of an epistle of St. Paul to the Christians of Galatia.

gal·ax·y (gal′ək sē) *n.* **-ax·ies. 1** in astronomy, a great number of stars forming one system. **2** a brilliant or splendid group: *The queen was followed by a galaxy of brave knights and fair ladies.* **3 Galaxy,** the Milky Way. [< OF < LL < Gk. *galaxias* < *gala, -aktos* milk]

gale[1] (gāl) *n.* **1** a very strong wind. **2** in meteorology, a wind with a velocity of 32 to 63 miles per hour. **3** *Poetic.* a breeze. **4** a noisy outburst: *gales of laughter.* [origin uncertain]

gale[2] (gāl) *n.* a shrub of the same family as the wax myrtle, having fragrant leaves, and growing in marshy places. [OE *gagel*]

ga·le·na (gə lē′nə) *n.* a gray metallic ore containing much lead sulphide; lead sulphide. It is the most important source of lead. *Formula*: PbS [< L]

ga·le·nite (gə lē′nīt) *n.* galena.

Ga·li·cian (gə lish′ən) *adj.* of or having to do with Galicia, a region in central Europe. —*n.* an inhabitant of Galicia.

Gal·i·le·an (gal′ə lē′ən) *adj.* of or having to do with Galilee, a region in N. Palestine that was a Roman province in the time of Christ, or its people. —*n.* **1** a native or inhabitant of Galilee. **2** a Christian. **3 the Galilean,** Jesus.

gal·i·ot or **gal·li·ot** (gal′ē ət) *n.* **1** a small, fast galley equipped both with oars and sails that was used until the end of the 18th century. **2** a heavy, single-masted, Dutch cargo vessel or fishing boat. [ME < OF *galiote*, dim. of *galie*, ult. < Med.Gk. *galea*]

gall[1] (gol or gôl) *n.* **1** a bitter, yellow, brown, or greenish liquid secreted by the liver and stored in the gall bladder; bile of animals. **2** the gall bladder. **3** anything very bitter or harsh. **4** bitterness; hate: *His heart was filled with gall.* **5** *Informal.* excessive boldness; impudence: *He had a lot of gall to talk to his employer in such a nasty way.* [OE *gealla*]

gall[2] (gol or gôl) *v.* **1** make or become sore by rubbing: *The rough strap galled the horse's skin.* **2** annoy; irritate. —*n.* **1** a sore spot on the skin caused by rubbing. **2** a cause of annoyance or irritation. [extended use of *gall*[1]]

gall[3] (gol or gôl) *n.* a lump or ball that forms on the leaves, stems, or roots of plants where they have been injured by insects or fungi. The galls of oak trees contain tannin, used in making ink, in medicine, etc. [< F *galle* < L *galla*]

Gal·la (gal′ə) *n.* **1** a member of one of the Hamitic tribes of Ethiopia and other countries of northeast Africa. **2** the language of the Gallas.

gal·lant (*adj. 1-3* gal′ənt; *adj. 4, 5* gə lant′ or gal′ənt; *n.* gal′ənt or gə lant′) *adj.* **1** noble; brave; daring: *King Arthur was a gallant knight.* **2** grand; fine; stately: *A ship with all of its sails spread is a gallant sight.* **3** gay; showy: *Our garden was a gallant sight.* **4** very polite and attentive to women. **5** amorous.
—*n.* **1** a spirited or courageous man. **2** a man who is gay or wears showy clothes; man of fashion. **3** a man who is very polite and attentive to women. **4** a lover. [ME < OF *galant*, ppr. of *galer* make merry < *gale*. See GALA.] —**gal′lant·ly,** *adv.* —**gal′lant·ness,** *n.* —**Syn.** *adj.* **1** valiant, heroic. **4** chivalrous, courtly.

gal·lant·ry (gal′ən trē) *n.* **-ries. 1** noble spirit or conduct; bravery; dashing courage. **2** great politeness and chivalrous attention to women. **3** a gallant act or speech. **4** *Archaic.* a gay appearance; showy display.

gall bladder a sac attached to the liver, in which excess gall or bile is stored until needed.

A galleon

gal·le·ass (gal′ē as′) *n.* formerly, a heavy, low-built warship larger than a galley and equipped with both oars and sails. It was used in the 16th and 17th centuries. [< MF *galeasse* < Ital. *galeazza* < *galea* < Med.Gk.]

gal·le·on (gal′yən or gal′ē ən) *n.* a large, tall sailing ship, usually with three or four decks, formerly used by the Spaniards and others. [< Sp. *galeón* < *galea* < Med.Gk.]

gal·ler·y (gal′ər ē or gal′rē) *n.* **-ler·ies. 1** a long, narrow platform or passage projecting from the wall of a building. **2** in a church, theatre, or hall, a projecting upper floor with seats or room for part of the audience; balcony. **3** the highest floor of this kind in a theatre. **4** the people who sit in the highest balcony of a theatre. **5** a group of people watching or listening; audience. **6** a long, narrow room or passage; hall. **7** a covered walk or porch. **8** an underground passage. **9** a room or building where works of art are shown. **10** a collection of works of art. **11** a room or building for use as a shooting range, etc. **12 play to the gallery,** *Informal.* try to get the praise or favor of the common people by doing or saying what will please them, in the manner of actors who used to style their performance to suit the tastes of the people watching from the gallery. [< Ital. *galleria*]

gal·ley (gal′ē) *n.* **-leys. 1** a long, narrow ship of former times, having oars and sails. Galleys were often rowed by slaves or convicts. **2** the kitchen of a ship. **3** in printing: **a** a long, narrow tray for holding type that has been set. **b** galley proof. [ME < OF *galee*, ult. < Med.Gk. *galea*]

A galley (def. 1)

galley proof in printing, a proof printed from type in a galley.

galley slave 1 a person compelled or condemned to row a galley. **2** a drudge.

gall·fly (gol′flī′ or gôl′-) *n.* **-flies.** an insect that causes galls on plants.

gal·liard (gal′yərd) *n.* **1** a lively dance in triple time, popular in the 16th and 17th centuries. **2** the music for this dance. **3** *Archaic.* a strong, valiant, or gallant man.

gal·lic (gal′ik) *adj.* in chemistry: **1** of gallium. **2** containing gallium, especially with a valence of three.

Gal·lic (gal′ik) *adj.* **1** of or having to do with Gaul or its people. **2** French. [< L *Gallicus* < *Gallus* a Gaul]

gal·lic acid an acid obtained especially from galls on plants, used in making ink, dyes, etc. *Formula*: $C_7H_6O_5 \cdot H_2O$

Gal·li·cism or **gal·li·cism** (gal′ə siz′əm) *n.* **1** a French idiom or expression. **2** such an idiom or expression literally translated into another language. *Example*: "that leaps to the eyes," from French *ça saute aux yeux*, meaning "that is obvious." **3** a French trait or characteristic.

Gal·li·cize or **gal·li·cize** (gal′ə sīz′) *v.* **-cized, -ciz·ing.** make or become French in character, habits, language, etc. —**Gal′li·ci·za′tion** or **gal′li·ci·za′tion,** *n.*

gal·li·gas·kins (gal′ə gas′kinz) *n.pl.* **1** loose breeches. **2** leggings. [formerly *garragascoynes* < MF *garguesque*, var. of (*à la*) *greguesque* < Ital. *alla grechesca* in the Greek fashion < *greco* Greek < L *Graecus*; influenced by earlier *Gascoyne* Gascon]

gal·li·na·ceous (gal′ə nā′shəs) *adj.* **1** belonging to a large group of birds that nest on the ground and fly only short distances. Chickens, turkeys, pheasants, grouse, partridges, etc. are gallinaceous birds. **2** of, having to do with, or like domestic fowl. [< L *gallinaceus* < *gallina* hen]

gall·ing (gol′ing or gôl′-) *adj.* bitterly disappointing; annoying; chafing; irritating.

gal·li·nule (gal′ə nūl′ or gal′ə nül′) *n.* any of certain long-toed wading birds of the same family as the rail. [< NL *gallinula* < L *gallina* hen, ult. < *gallus* cock]

Gal·li·o (gal′ē ō′) *n.* **1** in the Bible, a Roman proconsul who, when the Jews accused St. Paul, refused to take action against him. **2** any person, especially an official, who avoids becoming involved in matters which are not his immediate concern; an easygoing, indifferent person.

gal·li·pot (gal′ə pot′) *n.* a small pot or jar of glazed earthenware used especially by druggists to hold medicine, salve, etc. [< *galley* + *pot*]

gal·li·um (gal′ē əm) *n.* a shining, white, metallic chemical element, similar to mercury, with a low melting point. *Symbol*: Ga; *at.no.* 31; *at.wt.* 69.72. [< NL, ? < L *gallus* cock, translation of *Lecoq* (de Boisbaudran), the discoverer]

gal·li·vant (gal′ə vant′) *v.* **1** go about seeking pleasure; gad about. **2** flirt. [? < *gallànt*]

gall·nut (gol′nut′ or gôl′-) *n.* a nutlike gall on plants.

gal·lon (gal′ən) *n.* a measure for liquids, equal to 4 quarts. The imperial gallon used in Canada equals 277.274 cubic inches. The United States gallon equals 231 cubic inches. *Abbrev.*: gal. [ME < ONF *galon*]

hat, āge, cãre, fär; let, ēqual, tėrm; it, īce
hot, ōpen, ôrder; oil, out; cup, pu̇t, rüle, ūse
əbove, takən, pencəl, lemən, circəs
ch, child; ng, long; sh, ship
th, thin; ᴛʜ, then; zh, measure

gal·loon (gə lün′) *n.* a narrow braid of gold, silver, or silk thread used in trimming uniforms, furniture, etc. [< F *galon* < *galonner* dress the hair with ribbons < OF *gale* merriment. See GALA.]

gal·lop (gal′əp) *n.* **1** the fastest gait of horses and other four-footed animals. In a gallop, all four feet are off the ground together once in each stride. **2** a ride at a gallop. **3** *Informal.* any rapid rate: *Mother always does her housework at a gallop.* [< F *galop*]
—*v.* **1** ride at a gallop. **2** go at a gallop. **3** cause to gallop. **4** go very fast; hurry. [< F *galoper* < Gmc.] —**gal′lop·er,** *n.*

gal·lous (gal′əs) *adj.* in chemistry, containing gallium, especially with a valence of two.

gal·lows (gal′ōz) *n.* **-lows** or **-lows·es. 1** a wooden structure usually consisting of a crossbar on two upright posts, used for hanging criminals. **2** a similar structure used in gymnastics. **3** hanging or being hanged as a punishment. **4 cheat the gallows,** escape the death penalty for a crime. [OE *galga*]

gallows bird *Informal.* a person who deserves to be hanged.

gall·stone (gol′stōn′ or gôl′-) *n.* a pebble-like mass that sometimes forms in the gall bladder or its duct. When one or more gallstones stop the flow of bile, a painful illness results.

Gal·lup poll (gal′əp) a poll or opinion on social and political issues, etc., taken from a selected group of people and intended to reflect the opinion of the general public. [< George *Gallup*, an American statistician, born 1901]

gal·op (gal′əp; *French,* gä lō′) *n.* **1** a lively dance in two-four time. **2** the music for this dance. —*v.* dance a galop. [< F]

ga·lore (gə lôr′) *adv.* in abundance: *Over Christmas we had parties galore.* [< Irish *go leōr* to sufficiency]

ga·losh (gə losh′) *n.* Usually, **galoshes,** *pl.* a rubber-soled overshoe often having a rubber top as well, worn in wet or snowy weather. Also, **golosh.** [< F *galoche*]

gals. gallons.

gal·van·ic (gal van′ik) *adj.* **1** producing an electric current by chemical action. **2** of or caused by an electric current. **3** affecting or affected as if by galvanism; startling.

gal·va·nism (gal′və niz′əm) *n.* **1** electricity produced by chemical action. **2** the branch of physics dealing with this. **3** the use of such electricity for medical purposes. **4** any power or quality that arouses a sudden or forceful reaction: *We were overwhelmed by the galvanism of the actor's performance.* [after Luigi *Galvani*]

gal·va·nize (gal′və nīz′) *v.* **-nized, -niz·ing. 1** apply an electric current to. **2** arouse suddenly; startle. **3** cover (iron or steel) with a thin coating of zinc to prevent rust. —**gal′va·ni·za′tion,** *n.* —**gal′va·niz′er,** *n.*

galvanized iron iron covered with a thin coating of zinc, to resist rust.

gal·va·nom·e·ter (gal′və nom′ə tər) *n.* an instrument for detecting, measuring, and determining the direction of an electric current. [< *galvano-*, combining form of *galvanic* + *-meter*]

gal·va·no·met·ric (gal′və nə met′rik or gal van′ə met′rik) *adj.* **1** having to do with a galvanometer. **2** measured by a galvanometer.

gal·va·nom·e·try (gal′və nom′ə trē) *n.* the detection, measurement, and determination of the direction of electric currents by a galvanometer.

gal·va·no·scope (gal′və nə skōp′ or gal van′ə skōp′) *n.* an instrument for detecting very small electric currents and showing their direction. [< *galvano-*, combining form of *galvanic* + *-scope*]

gam (gam) *n. Slang.* a leg, especially a woman's leg. [prob. < F dial. *gambe* < ONF; ult. < LL *gamba* leg]

gam·bit (gam′bit) *n.* **1** in chess, a way of opening a game by purposely risking a pawn or a piece to gain some advantage. **2** any calculated opening move or preliminary manoeuvre, especially a risky one: *His opening gambit was to call for an investigation.* [< F < Provençal *cambi* an exchange < Ital. cambio < LL *cambiare* to change ?< Celtic]

gam·ble (gam′bəl) *v.* **-bled, -bling,** *n.* —*v.* **1** play games of chance for money. **2** take a risk; take great risks in business, speculation, etc. **3** bet; wager. **4** lose or squander by gambling.
—*n. Informal.* **1** a risky venture or undertaking. **2** an act of gambling. [probably related to GAME, *v.*]

gam·bler (gam′blər) *n.* **1** a person who gambles. **2** a person who gambles a great deal, especially one whose occupation is gambling.

gam·bling (gam′bling) *n.* **1** the playing of games of chance for money. **2** betting; wagering; taking great risks in business, speculation, etc.

gam·boge (gam bōj′ or gam büzh′) *n.* a gum resin from certain tropical trees, used as a yellow pigment and as a cathartic. [< NL *gambogium* < *Cambodia*]

gam·bol (gam′bəl) *n. v.* **-bolled** or **-boled, -bol·ling** or **-bol·ing.** —*n.* a playful running and jumping about; caper; frolic. —*v.* frisk about; run and jump about in play: *Lambs gambolled in the meadow.* [< F *gambade* < Ital. *gambata* < *gamba* leg]

gam·brel (gam′brəl) *n.* **1** the hock of a horse or other animal. **2** a gambrel roof. [< ONF *gamberel* < *gambe* leg < LL *gamba, camba* < Gk. *kampē* bend]

A gambrel roof

gambrel roof a roof having two slopes on each side, the lower slope usually being steeper than the upper one.

game[1] (gām) *n. adj.* **gam·er, gam·est,** *v.* **gamed, gam·ing.** —*n.* **1** a way of playing; pastime; amusement. **2** the things needed to play a game: *This store sells games.* **3** a contest with certain rules: *Our team did their best to win the game.* **4** a single round in a game: *The winner won three games out of five.* **5** the condition of the score in a game: *At the end of the first period the game was 6 to 3 in our favor.* **6** the number of points required to win. **7** a particular manner of playing: *He plays a good game.* **8** any activity or undertaking that is carried on under set rules like a game: *the game of diplomacy.* **9** *Informal.* any business venture, profession, etc.: *the acting game.* **10** a plan; scheme: *He tried to trick us, but we saw through his game.* **11** what is hunted or pursued. **12** wild animals, birds, or fish hunted or caught for sport or for food. **13** flesh of wild animals or birds used for food. **14** courage; endurance. **15 ahead of the game,** winning rather than losing. **16 be off one's game,** play badly. **17 be on one's game,** play well. **18 make game of,** make fun of; laugh at; ridicule. **19 play the game,** *Informal.* follow the rules; be a good sport. **20 The game is up.** *Informal.* The plan or scheme has failed.
—*adj.* **1** having to do with game, hunting, or fishing: *Game laws protect wild life.* **2** brave; plucky: *The losing team put up a game fight.* **3** having spirit or will enough: *The explorer was game for any adventure.* **4 die game,** die fighting; die bravely.
—*v.* gamble. [OE *gamen* joy] —**game′ly,** *adv.* —**game′ness,** *n.* —**Syn.** *n.* **1** See **play.**

game[2] (gām) *adj. Informal.* lame; crippled; injured: *a game leg.* [origin uncertain]

game bag 1 a bag for carrying game that has been killed. **2** the amount of game killed.

game bird a bird hunted for sport or food.

game·cock (gām′kok′) *n.* **1** a rooster bred and trained for fighting: *Fighting with gamecocks is illegal in Canada.* **2** a courageous, spirited person.

game fish a fish that fights to get away when hooked.

game fowl a fowl of a breed trained for fighting.

game·keep·er (gām′kēp′ər) *n.* a person whose work is taking care of the wild animals and birds on an estate and preventing anyone from stealing them or from killing them without permission.

game law a law intended to protect wild animals, birds, and fish by restricting hunting and fishing to certain seasons and by limiting the size, sex, and number of animals, birds, and fish that can be killed or caught.

game misconduct in hockey, a penalty banishing a player from the ice for the remainder of a game, awarded for gross misconduct or after the player has received three major penalties in the same game.

game of chance any game depending on luck, not skill.

game reserve or **preserve** a large tract of land set aside by the government for the protection of wild life.

game·some (gām′səm) *adj.* full of play; sportive; ready to play. —**game′some·ly,** *adv.*

game·ster (gām′stər) *n.* a gambler.

gam·ete (gam′ēt or gə mēt′) *n.* in biology, a reproductive cell capable of uniting with another to form a fertilized cell that can develop into a new plant or animal. [< NL *gameta* < Gk. *gametē* wife, *gametēs* husband, ult. < *gamos* marriage]

ga·me·to·phyte (gə mē′ tə fīt′) *n.* in botany, the part or structure of a plant that produces gametes. [< *gameto-*, combining form of *gamete* + *-phyte*]

game warden an official whose duty it is to enforce the game laws in a certain district.

gam·ey or **gam·y** (gām′ē) *adj.* **gam·i·er, gam·i·est.** 1 having a strong taste or smell like the flesh of wild animals or birds. 2 abounding in game. 3 brave; plucky. 4 indecent; improper: *a gamey joke.* —**gam′i·ly,** *adv.* —**gam′i·ness,** *n.*

gam·in (gam′ən) *n.* 1 a neglected boy left to roam about the streets; urchin. 2 a small lively person of either sex. —*adj.* like an urchin; impudent. [< F]

gam·ing (gām′ing) *n.* the playing of games of chance for money; gambling.

gam·ma (gam′ə) *n.* 1 the third letter of the Greek alphabet (Γ, γ = English G, g). 2 the third in any series or group.

gamma globulin a constituent of the human blood. Gamma globulin contains antibodies that are used against infantile paralysis and other diseases.

gamma rays penetrating electromagnetic radiations of very high frequency given off by radium and other radio-active substances, that are similar to X rays but have a shorter wave length. Deadly gamma rays are emitted by the nuclei of excited atoms in atomic explosions. Gamma rays are used in the treatment of certain diseases.

gam·mer (gam′ər) *n. Archaic.* an old woman. [alteration of *godmother*] ☛ See **gaffer** for usage note.

gam·mon[1] (gam′ən) *n. Brit. Informal.* nonsense; humbug. —*v.* 1 talk nonsense, especially with intent to deceive. 2 deceive; hoax: *We were gammoned into sounding the fire alarm.* [cf. ME *gamen* game[1]] —**gam′mon·er,** *n.*

gam·mon[2] (gam′ən) *n.* 1 the lower end of a side of bacon. 2 a smoked or cured ham. [< ONF *gambon* < *gambe* leg < LL *gamba.* See GAMBREL.]

gam·o·pet·al·ous (gam′ə pet′əl əs) *adj.* in botany, having the petals joined to form a tube-shaped corolla. [< Gk. *gamos* marriage + E *petal* + *-ous*]

gam·o·sep·al·ous (gam′ə sep′əl əs) *adj.* in botany, having the sepals joined together. [< Gk. *gamos* marriage + E *sepal* + *-ous*]

-gamous *word element.* marrying; uniting, as in *bigamous.* [< Gk. *-gamos* < *gamos* marriage + *-ous*]

gam·ut (gam′ət) *n.* 1 in music: **a** the whole series of recognized notes. **b** the major scale. 2 the entire range of anything: *In one minute I ran the gamut of feeling from hope to despair.* [contraction of Med.L *gamma ut* < *gamma G*, the lowest tone, + *ut*, later *do*; notes of the scale were named from syllables in a Latin hymn: *Ut* queant laxis *re*sonare fibris, *Mi*ra gestorum *fa*muli tuorum, *Sol*ve polluti *la*bii reatum, *S*ancte *I*ohannes]

-gamy *word element.* union; marriage, as in *bigamy.* [< Gk. *-gamia* < *gamos* marriage]

gan or **'gan** (gan) *v. Archaic and poetic.* began, pt. of **gin**[4].

gan·der (gan′dər) *n.* 1 the male of the goose family. 2 a fool; simpleton. 3 *Slang.* a long look, like that of a gander. 4 **take a gander,** *Slang.* take a look. [OE *gandra*]

gan·dy dancer (gan′dē) a member of a railway section gang, especially a seasonal or itinerant laborer. [? < former *Gandy* Manufacturing Company of Chicago, Ill. that made tools used by railway laborers]

gang[1] (gang) *n.* 1 a group of people acting or going around together: *Criminals often form gangs.* 2 a group of people working together under one foreman: *Two gangs of workmen were mending the road.* 3 a set of similar tools or machines arranged to work together. —*v.* 1 *Informal.* **a** form a gang. **b** attack in a gang. 2 **gang up on,** oppose as a group. [OE *gang* a going]

gang[2] (gang) *v. Scottish.* go; walk.

gan·gli·a (gang′glē ə) *n.* pl. of **ganglion.**

gan·gling (gang′gling) *adj.* awkwardly tall and slender; lank and loosely built. [apparently ult. < *gang*, v.]

gan·gli·on (gang′glē ən) *n.* **-gli·a** or **-gli·ons.** 1 in anatomy, a mass or group of nerve cells forming a nerve centre, especially outside the brain or spinal cord. 2 a centre of force, activity, etc. 3 in medicine, a cyst or swelling in the sheath of a tendon. [< LL *ganglion* a type of swelling < Gk.]

gan·gly (gang′glē) *adj.* gangling.

gang·plank (gang′plangk′) *n.* a movable bridge used by persons or animals in getting on and off a ship, etc.

A gangplank

gang plough or **gang plow** a set of ploughs arranged to work together.

gan·grene (gang′grēn or gang grēn′) *n. v.* **-grened, -gren·ing.** —*n.* the decay of a part of a living person or animal when the blood supply is interfered with by injury, infection, freezing, etc. —*v.* cause gangrene in; be or become affected with gangrene; decay: *The wounded leg gangrened and had to be amputated.* [< L *gangraena* < Gk. *gangraina*]

gan·gre·nous (gang′grə nəs) *adj.* of or having gangrene; decaying.

gang·ster (gang′stər) *n.* a member of a gang of criminals, roughs, etc.

gang·ster·ism (gang′stə riz′əm) *n.* 1 the committing of crimes by members of an organized gang. 2 gangsters or their crimes: *The fight against gangsterism never stops.* 3 crime of the type committed by gangs or gangsters.

gang·way (gang′wā′) *n.* 1 a passageway. 2 a passageway on a ship. 3 a gangplank. —*interj.* get out of the way, please! stand aside and make room!

gan·net (gan′it) *n.* a large, fish-eating sea bird resembling a pelican, but having long, pointed wings and a shorter tail. [OE *ganot*]

gan·oid (gan′oid) *adj.* of fishes, having hard scales of bone overlaid with enamel. —*n.* a ganoid fish: *Sturgeons and gar pikes are ganoids.* [< Gk. *ganos* brightness]

gant·let (gont′lit or gônt′lit) *n.* gauntlet[2].

gan·try (gan′trē) *n.* **-tries.** a bridgelike framework, often mobile, for supporting a travelling crane, block signals over railway tracks, etc. [< ONF *gantier* < L *canterius* beast of burden, rafter, framework < Gk. *kanthēlios* pack ass]

A gantry

Gan·y·mede (gan′ə mēd′) *n.* in Greek and Roman mythology, a handsome youth, cupbearer to the gods of Olympus.

gaol (jāl) *n. Brit.* jail.

gaol·er (jāl′ər) *n. Brit.* jailer.

gap (gap) *n.* 1 a broken place; opening. 2 an empty part; unfilled space; blank: *My diary is not complete; there are several gaps in it.* 3 a wide difference of opinion, character, etc. 4 a pass through mountains. 5 **stop, fill,** or **supply a gap,** make up a deficiency; supply a want; fill a vacant space: *stop a gap in our balance of payments.* [ME < ON. Related to GAPE.]

gape (gāp) *v.* **gaped, gap·ing,** *n.* —*v.* 1 open wide: *A deep hole in the earth gaped before us* 2 open the mouth

wide; yawn. **3** stare with the mouth open: *The savages gaped when they saw an airplane for the first time.*
—*n.* **1** a wide opening. **2** the act of opening the mouth wide; yawning. **3** an open-mouthed stare. **4 the gapes, a** a fit of yawning. **b** a disease of birds and poultry. [ME < ON *gapa*] —**gap′er,** *n.*

gar (gär) *n.* **gar** or **gars.** garfish.

ga·rage (gə rozh′, gə razh′, or gə raj′) *n. v.* **-raged, -rag·ing.** —*n.* **1** a place where automobiles, trucks, etc. are kept. **2** a shop for repairing automobiles, trucks, etc. —*v.* put or keep in a garage. [< F *garage* < *garer* put in shelter]

garb (gärb) *n.* **1** the way one is dressed. **2** clothing. **3** the outward covering, form, or appearance. —*v.* clothe: *The doctor was garbed in white from head to toe.* [< F *garbe* < Ital. *garbo* grace]

gar·bage (gär′bij) *n.* **1** waste animal or vegetable matter from a kitchen, store, etc. **2** scraps of food to be thrown away. **3** trash; rubbish. **4** *Informal.* anything of no value. [ME, animal entrails; origin uncertain]

gar·ble (gär′bəl) *v.* **-bled, -bling. 1** make unfair or misleading selections from (facts, statements, writings, etc.); omit parts of, often in order to misrepresent: *Foreign newspapers gave a garbled account of the ambassador's speech.* **2** confuse or mix up (statements, words, etc.) unintentionally. [< Ital. *garbellare* < Arabic *gharbala* sift, probably < LL *cribellare,* ult. < *cribrum* sieve] —**gar′bler,** *n.* —**Syn. 1** distort, misquote.

gar·çon (gär sôN′) *n.* **-çons** (-sôN′). *French.* **1** a young man; boy. **2** a servant. **3** a waiter.

gar·den (gär′dən) *n.* **1** a piece of ground used for growing vegetables, herbs, flowers, or fruits. **2** a park or place where people go for amusement or to see things on display. **3** a fertile and delightful spot; well-cultivated region.
—*v.* **1** take care of a garden; make a garden; work in a garden. **2 lead up the garden path,** *Slang.* lead on; lure.
—*adj.* **1** growing or grown in a garden; for a garden. **2** common; ordinary. [ME < ONF *gardin* < Gmc.] —**gar′den·like′,** *adj.*

gar·den·er (gärd′nər or gär′də nər) *n.* **1** a person whose occupation is taking care of a garden, lawn, etc. **2** a person who makes a garden or works in a garden.

gar·de·nia (gär dēn′yə or gär dē′nē ə) *n.* **1** a fragrant, roselike, white or yellow flower having waxy petals. **2** the shrub on which these flowers grow. [< NL; after Alexander *Garden* (1730-1791), an American botanist]

gar·fish (gär′fish′) *n.* **-fish** or **-fish·es.** an edible fish having a long slender body covered with thin scales, and long narrow jaws. [< *gar* (OE *gār* spear) + *fish*]

Gar·gan·tu·an (gär gan′chü ən) *adj.* enormous; gigantic: *a Gargantuan meal, appetite.* [< *Gargantua,* a good-natured giant of enormous appetite in a satire by Rabelais]

gar·get (gär′git) *n.* **1** in cattle and pigs, an inflamed condition of the head or throat. **2** in cows, ewes, etc., an inflammation of the udder. [< OF *gargate*]

gar·gle (gär′gəl) *v.* **-gled, -gling,** *n.* —*v.* **1** wash or rinse (the inside of the throat) with a liquid kept in motion by the outgoing breath: *He treated his sore throat by gargling with salt water.* **2** make a gargling sound. —*n.* a liquid used for gargling. [probably imitative and influenced by OF *gargouiller* < *gargoule* throat < L *gurgulio* windpipe]

gar·goyle (gär′goil) *n.* **1** a spout for carrying off rain water, ending in a grotesque head that projects from the gutter of a building. **2** a projection or ornament on a building resembling a gargoyle. [ME < MF *gargouille* (imitative); cf. L *gurgulio* gullet]

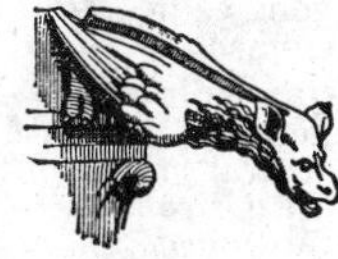
A gargoyle

gar·ish (gãr′ish) *adj.* **1** unpleasantly bright; glaring. **2** showy; gaudy. [ult. < obs. *gaure* stare] —**gar′ish·ly,** *adv.* —**gar′ish·ness,** *n.*

gar·land (gär′lənd) *n.* **1** a wreath of flowers, leaves, etc. **2** a collection of short poems, ballads, etc.; anthology. **3** on ships: **a** a band, loop, or collar, as of rope, used on a mast for various purposes, such as to prevent chafing. **b** a net for holding provisions high up, away from rats, etc.

hat, āge, cãre, fär; let, ēqual, tėrm; it, īce
hot, ōpen, ôrder; oil, out; cup, pu̇t, rüle, ūse
əbove, takən, pencəl, lemən, circəs
ch, child; ng, long; sh, ship
th, thin; ᴛʜ, then; zh, measure

—*v.* **1** decorate with garlands. **2** form into garlands. [ME < OF *garlande*]

gar·lic (gär′lik) *n.* **1** a plant resembling an onion whose strong-smelling bulb is composed of small sections called cloves. **2** a bulb or clove of this plant, used to season meats, salads, etc. [OE *gārlēac* < *gār* spear + *lēac* leek]

gar·lick·y (gär′lik ē) *adj.* smelling or tasting of garlic.

gar·ment (gär′mənt) *n.* **1** any article of clothing. **2** an outer covering. —*v.* clothe. [ME < OF *garnement* < *garnir* fit out. See GARNISH.] —**gar′ment·less,** *adj.*

gar·ner (gär′nər) *v.* gather and store away: *Wheat is cut and garnered at harvest time. Squirrels garner nuts in the fall.* [< n.] —*n.* **1** a storehouse for grain. **2** a store of anything. [ME < OF *gernier, grenier* < L *granarium* < *granum* grain]

gar·net (gär′nit) *n.* **1** a hard, vitreous silicate mineral occurring in a number of varieties. A common, deep-red, transparent variety is used for gems. **2** a piece of this stone, or a gem made from it. **3** a deep red.—*adj.* deep-red. [ME *gernet* < OF *grenat* grained (stone) < LL *granatum* < L *granum* grain, seed. See GRENADE.] —**gar′net·like′,** *adj.*

gar·nish (gär′nish) *n.* **1** something laid on or around food as a decoration: *The turkey was served with a garnish of cranberries and parsley.* **2** a decoration; trimming. [< v.] —*v.* **1** decorate (food). **2** decorate; trim. **3** in law, warn or notify by a garnishment. [ME < OF *garniss-,* a stem of *garnir* provide, defend < Gmc.] —**gar′nish·er,** *n.* —**Syn.** *v.* **2** adorn.

gar·nish·ee (gär′nish ē′) *v.* **-nish·eed, -nish·ee·ing,** *n.* —*v.* in law: **1** attach (money or property) by legal authority in payment of a debt. If a creditor garnishees a debtor's salary, a certain portion of the salary is withheld and paid to the creditor. **2** notify (a person) not to hand over money or property belonging to the defendant in a lawsuit until the plaintiff's claims have been settled: *The debtor's employer was garnisheed.* —*n.* in law, a person notified to hold the defendant's money or property as a trustee until the lawsuit is settled.

gar·nish·ment (gär′nish mənt) *n.* **1** decoration; trimming. **2** in law: **a** a legal notice warning a person to hold in his possession property that belongs to the defendant in a lawsuit until the plaintiff's claims have been settled. **b** a summons to a third person to appear in court while a lawsuit between others is being heard.

gar·ni·ture (gär′nə chər) *n.* decoration; trimming; garnish. [< F]

ga·rotte (gə rot′ or gə rōt′) *n. v.* **-rot·ted, -rot·ting.** garrote. —**ga·rot′ter,** *n.*

gar pike garfish.

gar·ret (gar′it) *n.* **1** a space in a house just below a sloping roof; attic. **2** a room or apartment in such a place. [ME < OF *garite* watchtower < *garir* defend < Gmc.]

gar·ri·son (gar′ə sən) *n.* **1** the soldiers stationed in a fort, town, etc., usually for the purpose of defending it. **2** a place that has a garrison.
—*v.* **1** station soldiers in (a fort, town, etc.) to defend it. **2** take over or occupy (a fort, town, etc.) as a garrison.
—*adj.* of or associated with a garrison: *Kingston is a well-known garrison town.* [ME < OF *garison* < *garir.* See GARRET.]

gar·rote (gə rot′ or gə rōt′) *n. v.* **-rot·ed, -rot·ing.** —*n.* **1** a Spanish method of executing a person by strangling him with an iron collar. The collar is fastened to a post and tightened by a screw. **2** the iron collar used for this type of execution. **3** strangulation, especially in order to rob. **4** any device used to strangle. —*v.* **1** execute by garroting. **2** strangle and rob; strangle. [< Sp. *garrote* stick for twisting cord] —**gar·rot′er,** *n.*

gar·rotte (gə rot′ or gə rōt′) *n. v.* **-rot·ted, -rot·ting.** garrote. —**gar·rot′ter,** *n.*

gar·ru·li·ty (gə rü′lə tē) *n.* the quality or state of being garrulous.

gar·ru·lous (gar′yů ləs or gar′ə ləs) *adj.* **1** talking too much about trifles. **2** using too many words. [< L *garrulus* < *garrire* chatter] —**gar′ru·lous·ly,** *adv.* —**gar·ru′lous·ness,** *n.* —**Syn. 1** talkative, loquacious.

gar·ter (gär′tər) *n.* **1** a band or strap, usually of elastic, intended to hold up a stocking or sock. **2 Garter, a Order of the Garter,** the oldest and most important order of knighthood in Great Britain, established about 1344. **b** the badge of this order. **c** membership in it.
—*v.* fasten with a garter. [ME < OF *gartier* < *garet* bend of the knee < Celtic]

garter snake a small, harmless, brownish or greenish snake having yellow stripes along its back.

gas[1] (gas) *n.* **gas·es,** *v.* **gassed, gas·sing.** —*n.* **1** any fluid substance that can expand without limit; not a solid or liquid. Oxygen and nitrogen are gases. **2** any gas or mixture of gases except air. **3** any mixture of gases that can be burned, usually obtained from coal but occasionally from other substances. Gas was once much used for lighting, but is now used chiefly for cooking and heating. **4** any gas used as an anesthetic, such as nitrous oxide (laughing gas). **5** in mining, an explosive mixture of methane with air. **6** a substance that vaporizes and then poisons, suffocates, or stupefies: *The police used tear gas to dispel the mob.* **7** *Informal.* flatulence; wind: *gas on the stomach.* **8** *Slang.* empty or boasting talk.
—*v.* **1** supply with gas. **2** treat with gas; use gas on. Some kinds of seeds are gassed to hasten sprouting. **3** give off gas. **4** attack with gas in warfare; injure or kill by poisonous gas. **5** *Slang.* talk idly, emptily, or boastfully. [alteration of Gk. *chaos* chaos; coined by Jean B. van Helmont (1577-1644), a Flemish physicist] —**gas′less,** *adj.*

gas[2] (gas) *n. v.* **gassed, gas·sing.** *Informal.* —*n.* **1** gasoline. **2 step on the gas, a** push down the gas pedal. **b** go faster.
—*v.* **1** supply with gasoline. **2 gas up,** fill the tank of a motor vehicle with gasoline: *You'd better gas up before you leave on your trip.*

gas bag 1 a container to hold gas. **2** an inflatable bag used to plug a gas pipe during repairs. **3** *Slang.* a person who talks too much; windbag.

gas burner the small nozzle of a gas fixture from which gas comes out and is burned.

Gas·con (gas′kən) *n.* **1** a native of Gascony, a region in S.W. France. Gascons were formerly noted for their boastfulness. **2 gascon,** a boaster. —*adj.* **1** of Gascony or its people. **2 gascon,** boastful. [< F]

gas·con·ade (gas′kən ād′) *n. v.* **-ad·ed, -ad·ing.** —*n.* extravagant boasting. —*v.* boast extravagantly. [< F *gasconnade* < *gascon* Gascon]

gas engine 1 an internal-combustion engine run by illuminating gas, natural gas, or some other gas supplied from without. **2** any internal-combustion engine.

gas·e·ous (gas′ē əs or gās′ē əs) *adj.* in the form of gas; of or like a gas: *Steam is water in a gaseous condition.*

gas fitter a person whose work is putting in and repairing pipes and fixtures for the use of gas in buildings.

gash (gash) *n.* a long, deep cut or wound. [< v.]
—*v.* make a long, deep cut or wound in. [earlier *garsh* < ONF *garser* scarify]

gas·i·fy (gas′ə fī′) *v.* **-fied, -fy·ing.** change into a gas. —**gas′i·fi·ca′tion,** *n.* —**gas′i·fi′er,** *n.*

gas jet 1 a small nozzle of a gas fixture where gas comes out. **2** a flame of gas.

gas·ket (gas′kit) *n.* **1** a ring or strip of rubber, metal, plaited hemp, etc. packed around a piston, pipe, joint, etc. to keep steam, gas, etc. from escaping. **2** a cord or small rope used to secure a furled sail on a yard. [origin uncertain]

A gasket (def. 2)

gas·light (gas′līt′) *n.* **1** light made by burning gas. **2** a gas burner or gas jet.

gas main a large underground pipe to carry gas.

gas·man (gas′man′) *n.* **-men** (men′). **1** a man whose work is to read consumers' gas meters and report the amount of gas used. **2** a man who manufactures or supplies gas. **3** a gas fitter. **4** in coal mining, a man who inspects mines for firedamp.

gas mantle a lacelike tube around a gas flame that glows and gives off light when heated.

gas mask a helmet or mask that covers the mouth and nose and is supplied with a filter containing chemicals to neutralize poisons. The wearer breathes only filtered air.

gas·o·line or **gas·o·lene** (gas′ə lēn′ or gas′ə lēn′) *n.* a colorless liquid consisting of a mixture of hydrocarbons. Gasoline, which evaporates and burns very easily, is made by distilling petroleum. It is used as a fuel, solvent, cleansing agent, etc. [< *gas* + *-ol,* suffix meaning "oil" (< L *oleum*) + *-ine*[2]]

gas·om·e·ter (gas om′ə tər) *n.* **1** a container for holding and measuring gas. **2** a gas tank. [< F *gazomètre* < *gaz* gas + *mètre* measure < Gk. *metron*; influenced by *gas*]

gasp (gasp) *n.* **1** a catching of the breath with open mouth, as if out of breath or surprised. **2 at the last gasp, a** about to die. **b** about to come to an end: *The election campaign was almost at its last gasp.* [< v.]
—*v.* **1** catch the breath with difficulty. **2** breathe with gasps. **3** utter with gasps. **4** wish (for); long (for). [ME < ON *geispa* yawn] —**Syn.** *v.* **2** pant.

gasp·er (gas′pər) *n. Slang.* a cigarette.

gas·pe·reau (gas′pə rō′) *n.* **gas·pe·reaux.** *Cdn.* a species of herring commonly found along the N. Atlantic coast; alewife. [< Cdn.F]

Gas·pe·sian (gas pā′zhən or gas pē′zhən) *Cdn. n.* a native or inhabitant of the Gaspé Peninsula in E. Quebec. [< Cdn.F *Gaspésien*] —*adj.* of or having to do with the Gaspé or its inhabitants.

gas·ser (gas′ər) *n.* **1** a person or thing that gasses. **2** a natural gas-well. **3** *Slang.* something of more than usual merit; a huge success.

gas station a place that sells gasoline, oil, etc., provides service, and sometimes makes minor repairs, etc. to motor vehicles.

gas·sy (gas′ē) *adj.* **-si·er, -si·est. 1** full of gas; containing gas. **2** like gas.

gas·tric (gas′trik) *adj.* of or near the stomach. [< Gk. *gastēr, gastros* stomach]

gastric juice the thin, nearly clear digestive fluid secreted by glands in the lining of the stomach. It contains pepsin and other enzymes and hydrochloric acid.

gas·tri·tis (gas trī′tis) *n.* in medicine, an inflammation of the stomach, especially of its mucous membrane. [< Gk. *gastēr, gastros* stomach + E *-itis*]

gastro- *combining form.* **1** the stomach: *gastrotomy = surgical incision into the stomach.* **2** the stomach and ——: *gastrohepatic = of or having to do with the stomach and liver.* Also, **gastr-** before vowels. [< Gk. *gastēr, gastros*]

gas·tro·en·ter·i·tis (gas′trō en′tə rī′tis) *n.* in medicine, inflammation of the membranes of the stomach and intestines.

gas·tro·nome (gas′trə nōm′) *n.* a person who is expert in gastronomy; epicure. [< F *gastronome,* back formation < *gastronomie.* See GASTRONOMY.]

gas·tro·nom·ic (gas′trə nom′ik) *adj.* of or having to do with gastronomy.

gas·tro·nom·i·cal (gas′trə nom′ə kəl) *adj.* gastronomic.

gas·tron·o·my (gas tron′ə mē) *n.* the art or science of good eating. [< F < Gk. *gastronomia* < *gastēr, gastros* stomach + *nomos* law]

gas·tro·pod (gas′trə pod′) *n.* any of a group of molluscs that have a disklike organ of locomotion on the ventral surface of their bodies. Snails, slugs, and whelks are gastropods. —*adj.* of such molluscs. [< NL *Gastropoda,* pl. < Gk. *gastēr, gastros* stomach + *-podos* footed < *pous, podos* foot]

gas·tru·la (gas′trů lə) *n.* **-lae** (-lē′ or -lī′). in biology, the stage in the development of all many-celled animals when the embryo is usually saclike and composed of two layers of cells. [< NL *gastrula,* dim. of Gk. *gastēr, gastros* stomach]

gat[1] (gat) *v. Archaic.* a pt. of get.

gat[2] (gat) *n. Slang.* a gun; revolver; pistol. [shortened form of *Gatling gun*]

gate (gāt) *n.* **1** a movable part or frame for closing an opening in a wall or fence. It turns on hinges or slides open and shut. **2** an opening in a wall, usually fitted with a door, turnstile, or some other barrier; gateway. **3** the part of a building containing the gate or gates, with the adjoining towers, walls, etc. **4** a way to go in or out; a way to get to something. **5** a barrier intended to prevent entrance, stop traffic, etc.: *Level crossings are often equipped with gates to keep cars off the track when a train is passing.* **6** a door, valve, etc. to stop or control the flow of water in a pipe, dam, lock, etc. **7** the number of people who pay to see a contest, exhibition, performance, etc. **8** the total amount of money received from these people: *The two teams divided a gate of $3,250.* **9 get the gate,** *Slang.* be dismissed. **10 give the gate to,** *Informal.* **a** dismiss or turn away. **b** in hockey, award a player a penalty, thus putting him off the ice. [OE *gatu,* pl. of *geat*] —**gate′less,** *adj.* —**gate′like′,** *adj.*

gate·crash (gāt′krash′) *v. Slang.* attend a party, social function, or entertainment without being invited or without a ticket.

gate crasher *Informal.* a person who attends parties, gatherings, etc. without an invitation; an uninvited guest.

gate·house (gāt′hous′) *n.* **1** a house at or over a gate, used as the keeper's quarters. **2** a structure at the gate of a reservoir, dam, etc., with machinery for regulating the flow of water.

gate·post (gāt′pōst′) *n.* one of the posts on either side of a gate. A swinging gate is fastened to one gatepost and closes against the other.

gate·way (gāt′wā′) *n.* **1** an opening in a wall, fence, etc., intended for a gate or some other barrier. **2** a way to go in or out; way to get to or attain something. **3** a frame or arch in which a gate is hung. **4** a structure built at or over a gate.

gath·er (gaᴛʜ′ər) *v.* **1** bring into one place or group: *He gathered his books and papers and started off to school.* **2** come together; assemble: *A crowd gathered at the scene of the accident.* **3** get together from various places or sources, or gradually: *gather sticks for a fire.* **4** form a mass; collect: *Tears gathered in her eyes.* **5** pick and collect; take: *Farmers gather their crops.* **6** get or gain little by little: *The train gathered speed as it left the station.* **7** collect (oneself, one's strength, energies, thoughts, etc.) for an effort. **8** put together in the mind; conclude; infer: *I gathered from his words that he was really much upset.* **9** pull together in folds; wrinkle: *She gathered her brow in a frown.* **10** pull together in little folds and stitch: *The skirt is gathered at the waist.* **11** draw together or closer: *Gather your robe around you.* **12** come to a head and form pus: *A boil is a painful swelling that gathers under the skin.* **13** in bookbinding, collect and place in order (the printed, folded sheets of a book). **14 be gathered to one's fathers,** die and be buried. **15 gather up, a** pick up and put together. **b** pull together; bring into a smaller space.
—*n.* **1** one of the little folds between the stitches when cloth is pulled together in folds. **2** a contraction; drawing together. **3** in glassmaking, a blob of glass collected on the end of a blowpipe. [OE *gaderian* < *geador* (to)gether]

Syn. *v.* **Gather, collect, assemble** = bring or come together. **Gather,** the general word, is interchangeable with **collect,** though the former is the more colloquial and idiomatic. **Collect** is of Latin origin and has a formal and professional air: *collect stamps, collect taxes;* but *gather wealth, gather honey.* **Assemble,** also formal, has the special sense of "bringing or coming together according to a definite plan or purpose": *assemble a watch. Parliament assembles.*

gath·er·ing (gaᴛʜ′ər ing or gaᴛʜ′ring) *n.* **1** the act of one that gathers. **2** that which is gathered. **3** a meeting; assembly; party; crowd. **4** a swelling that comes to a head and forms pus. —**Syn. 3** See **meeting.**

Gat·ling gun (gat′ling) an early type of machine gun consisting of a revolving cluster of barrels around a central axis. [after Richard J. *Gatling* (1818-1903), an American inventor]

GATT General Agreement on Tariff and Trade.

gauche (gōsh) *adj.* awkward; clumsy; tactless. [< F *gauche* left-handed] —**gauche′ly,** *adv.* —**gauche′ness,** *n.*

gau·che·rie (gō′shə rē′ or gō′shə rē′) *n.* **1** awkwardness; tactlessness. **2** an awkward or tactless movement, act, etc. [< F]

hat, āge, cãre, fär; let, ēqual, tėrm; it, īce
hot, ōpen, ôrder; oil, out; cup, pu̇t, rüle, ūse
əbove, takən, pencəl, lemən, circəs
ch, child; ng, long; sh, ship
th, thin; ᴛʜ, then; zh, measure

gau·cho (gou′chō) *n.* **-chos.** a cowboy of mixed Spanish and Indian descent in the southern plains of South America. [< Sp.]

gaud (god or gôd) *n.* a cheap, showy ornament; trinket: *beads, mirrors, and such gauds.* [apparently < AF *gaude* < *gaudir* rejoice < L *gaudere*]

gaud·y (god′ē or gôd′ē) *adj.* **gaud·i·er, gaud·i·est.** too bright and gay to be in good taste; cheap and showy. —**gaud′i·ly,** *adv.* —**gaud′i·ness,** *n.*

gauge (gāj) *n. v.* **gauged, gaug·ing.** —*n.* **1** a standard measure; scale of standard measurements; measure. There are gauges of the capacity of a barrel, the thickness of sheet iron, the diameter of wire, etc. **2** an instrument for measuring. A **steam gauge** measures the pressure of steam. **3** a means of estimating or judging. **4** size; capacity; extent. **5** the diameter of the bore of a firearm, especially a shotgun. **6** the distance between rails of a railway track or between the right and left wheels of a wagon, automobile, etc. In North America, the standard gauge is 56½ inches. **7** the position of one sailing ship with reference to another and to the wind. A ship having the weather gauge of another is to the windward of it. **8** the length of the exposed part of shingles, tiles, etc. when laid in rows. **9** in knitting, the number of needles per 1½ inches of the needlebar of a knitting machine, used as a standard of the fineness of a fabric: *51-gauge stockings.*
—*v.* **1** measure accurately; find out the exact measurement of (something) with a gauge. **2** estimate; judge: *It is difficult to gauge the character of a stranger.* Also, **gage.** [ME < ONF]

A gauge for measuring wire. Size nine wire fits the hole marked 9.

gauge·a·ble (gāj′ə bəl) *adj.* that may be gauged. Also, **gage·a·ble.**

gaug·er (gāj′ər) *n.* **1** a person or thing that gauges. **2** an official who measures the contents of barrels of taxable liquor. **3** a collector of excise taxes. Also, **gager.**

Gaul (gol or gôl) *n.* **1** one of the Celtic inhabitants of Gaul, an ancient country in W. Europe. **2** a Frenchman. [(def. 1) < F *Gaule* < L *Gallia* < *Gallus* a Gaul; (def. 2) < L *Gallus*]

Gau·lei·ter (gou′lī tər) *n.* **1** in the Nazi party, a high official who acted as governor of a district in Germany or German-occupied territory. **2 gauleiter,** any subordinate who carries out harsh or criminal orders.

gaunt (gont or gônt) *adj.* **1** very thin and bony; with hollow eyes and a starved look: *Hunger and suffering make people gaunt.* **2** looking bare and gloomy; desolate; forbidding; grim. [origin uncertain] —**gaunt′ly,** *adv.* —**gaunt′ness,** *n.* —**Syn. 1** lean, spare, lank. See **thin.**

gaunt·let[1] (gont′lit or gônt′lit) *n.* **1** a stout, heavy glove, usually of leather covered with plates of iron or steel, that was part of a knight's armor. See **armor** for picture. **2** a stout, heavy glove with a wide, flaring cuff. **3** the wide, flaring cuff. **4 take up the gauntlet, a** accept a challenge. **b** take up the defence of a person, opinion, etc. **5 throw down the gauntlet,** challenge. [ME < OF *gantelet,* dim. of *gant* glove < Gmc.]

gaunt·let[2] (gont′lit or gônt′lit) *n.* **1** formerly, a military punishment in which the offender had to run between two rows of men who struck him with clubs or other weapons as he passed. **2 run the gauntlet, a** pass between two rows of men each of whom strikes the runner as he passes. **b** carry out an action in spite of danger threatening on all sides: *During the war, convoys ran the gauntlet of enemy submarines.* **c** be exposed to unfriendly attacks, criticism, etc. Also, **gantlet.** [< Swedish *gatlopp* < *gata* lane + *lopp* course]

Gau·ta·ma (got′ə mə, gô′tə mə or gou′tə mə) *n.* Buddha. Also, **Gotama.**

gauze (goz or gôz) *n.* **1** a very thin, light cloth, easily seen through: *Gauze is often used for bandages.* **2** a thin haze. [< F *gaze*; after *Gaza*, the capital of the Gaza Strip, S.W. of Israel] **—gauze′like′,** *adj.*

gauz·y (goz′ē or gôz′ē) *adj.* **gauz·i·er, gauz·iest.** like gauze; thin and light as gauze. **—gauz′i·ly,** *adv.* **—gauz′i·ness,** *n.*

gave (gāv) *v.* pt. of **give.**

gav·el (gav′əl) *n.* a small mallet used by a presiding officer to signal for attention and order or by an auctioneer to announce that the bidding is over. [origin uncertain]

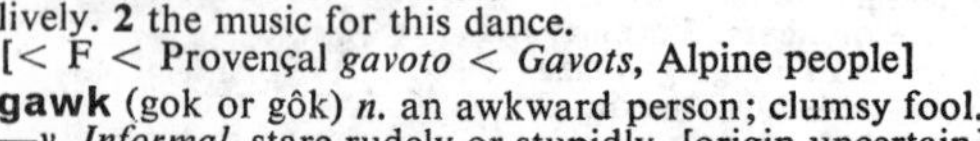

A judge holding a gavel

ga·vi·al (gā′vē əl) *n.* a large crocodile of India that has a long, slender snout. [< F < Hind. *ghariyāl*]

ga·votte (gə vot′) *n.* **1** a dance like a minuet but much more lively. **2** the music for this dance. [< F < Provençal *gavoto* < *Gavots*, Alpine people]

gawk (gok or gôk) *n.* an awkward person; clumsy fool. —*v. Informal.* stare rudely or stupidly. [origin uncertain] **—gawk′er,** *n.*

gawk·y (gok′ē or gôk′ē) *adj.* **gawk·i·er, gawk·i·est.** awkward; clumsy. **—gawk′i·ly,** *adv.* **—gawk′i·ness,** *n.*

gay (gā) *adj.* **gay·er, gay·est. 1** happy and full of fun; merry. **2** bright-colored; showy. **3** fond of pleasures. **4** dissipated; immoral. **5** *Slang.* homosexual. [< F *gai*] **—gay′ness,** *n.*

Syn. 1 Gay, merry = lively and light-hearted. **Gay** emphasizes being free from care and full of life, joy, and high spirits; **merry** emphasizes being full of laughter and lively pleasure and fun: *The gay young people were merry as they danced.*

gay·e·ty (gā′ə tē) *n.* **-ties.** gaiety.

gay·ly (gā′lē) *adv.* gaily.

gaz. 1 gazette. **2** gazetteer.

gaze (gāz) *v.* **gazed, gaz·ing,** *n.* —*v.* look long and steadily. —*n.* a long, steady look. [cf. Norwegian and Swedish dial. *gasa*] **—gaz′er,** *n.* **—gaz′ing·ly,** *adv.*

Syn. *v.* **Gaze, stare** = look long and steadily at someone or something. **Gaze** emphasizes looking steadily and intently, chiefly in wonder, delight, or interest: *For hours he sat gazing at the stars.* **Stare** emphasizes looking with wide-open eyes steadily and directly at someone or something or off into space, chiefly in curiosity, rudeness, surprise, or stupidity: *The little girl stared at the stranger briefly before answering his question.*

ga·ze·bo (gə zē′bō) *n.* **-bos** or **-boes.** a summer-house, balcony, etc. that commands a wide view. [supposedly < *gaze*, on the pattern of Latin future tenses in *-bo*]

ga·zelle (gə zel′) *n.* a small, graceful antelope of Africa and Asia that has soft, lustrous eyes. [< F < Arabic *ghazāl*] **—ga·zelle′-like′,** *adj.*

ga·zette (gə zet′) *n. v.* **-zet·ted, -zet·ting.** —*n.* **1** a newspaper. **2** an official government journal containing lists of appointments, promotions, etc. —*v.* publish, list, or announce in a gazette. [< F < Ital. *gazzetta*, originally, coin; from the price of a paper]

gaz·et·teer (gaz′ə tēr′) *n.* **1** a dictionary of geographical names. **2** a writer for a gazette. **3** an official appointed to publish a gazette. [< F *gazettier*]

G.B. Great Britain.

G.B.E. (Knight or Dame) Grand (Cross or Order) of the British Empire.

G.C. George Cross.

G.C.B. (Knight) Grand Cross of the (Order of the) Bath.

G.C.D., g.c.d., or **gcd 1** greatest common denominator. **2** greatest common divisor.

G.C.F., g.c.f., or **gcf** greatest common factor.

G clef in music, the treble clef. See **clef** for diagram.

G.C.M., g.c.m., or **gcm** greatest common measure.

G.C.V.O. (Knight) Grand Cross of the (Royal) Victorian Order.

Gd gadolinium.

Ge germanium.

gear (gēr) *n.* **1** a wheel having teeth that fit into the teeth of another wheel of the same kind. If the wheels are of different sizes, they will turn at different speeds. See **cogwheel** for picture. **2** an arrangement of fixed and moving parts for transmitting or changing motion; mechanism; machinery: *The car ran off the road when the steering gear broke.* **3** working order; adjustment: *His watch got out of gear and would not run.* **4** the equipment needed for some purpose. Harness, clothes, household goods, tools, tackle, and rigging are various kinds of gear. **5 in gear, a** connected to the motor, etc. **b** in working order. **6 out of gear,** disconnected from the motor, etc. **7 shift gears,** change from one gear to another; connect a motor, etc. to a different set of gears.
—*v.* **1** connect by gears. An automobile moves when the motor is geared to the driving wheels. **2** fit or work together; mesh: *The cogs gear smoothly.* **3** provide with gear; equip; harness. **4** put into gear. **5** make subordinate to in order to serve: *The steel industry was geared to the needs of war.* [ME < ON *gervi*] **—gear′less,** *adj.*

gear·ing (gēr′ing) *n.* **1** a set of gears, chains, etc. for transmitting motion or power; gears. **2** the act of fitting a machine with gears. **3** the way in which a machine is fitted with gears.

gear·shift (gēr′shift′) *n.* a device for connecting a motor, etc. to any of several sets of gears.

gear·wheel (gēr′hwēl′ or -wēl′) *n.* a wheel having teeth that fit into the teeth of another wheel of the same kind.

geck·o (gek′ō) *n.* **geck·os** or **geck·oes.** a small, nocturnal insect-eating lizard found in the tropics, having suction pads on its toes for climbing. [< Malay *gekok*; imitative of its cry]

gee[1] (jē) *interj. v.* **geed, gee·ing.** —*interj.* a command to horses, oxen, etc. directing them to turn to the right. "Haw" is used for "left." —*v.* turn to the right.

gee[2] (jē) *interj.* an exclamation or mild oath. [a shortened form of *Jesus*]

geese (gēs) *n.* pl. of **goose.**

gee·zer (gē′zər) *n. Slang.* a fellow, usually an odd person and especially an elderly one. [dial. pronunciation of *guiser* someone in disguise, mummer]

Ge·hen·na (gə hen′ə) *n.* **1** hell. **2** a place of torment or misery. [< L < Gk. *geenna* < Hebrew *gehinnom*, originally, valley of Hinnom where children used to be sacrificed. See Jer. 19:5.]

Gei·ger counter (gī′gər) a device that detects and counts ionizing particles. It is used to measure radio-activity, test cosmic-ray particles, etc. [after Hans *Geiger*, a German physicist]

Geiger-Mül·ler counter (mul′ər; *German*, mʏl′ər) an improved, more sensitive form of the Geiger counter.

Gei·gers (gī′gərz) *n.pl. Informal.* radio-active particles and radiation collectively.

gei·sha (gā′shə or gē′shə) *n.* **-sha** or **-shas.** a specially trained Japanese singing and dancing girl. [< Japanese]

gel (jel) *n. v.* **gelled, gel·ling.** —*n.* a jelly-like or solid material formed from a colloidal solution. When glue sets, it forms a gel. —*v.* form a gel. Egg white gels when it is cooked. [shortened form of *gelatin*]

gel·a·tin (jel′ə tən) *n.* **1** an odorless, tasteless substance obtained by boiling animal tissues, bones, hoofs, etc. It dissolves easily in hot water and is used in making jellied desserts, camera film, glue, etc. **2** any of various vegetable substances having similar properties. **3** a preparation or product in which gelatin is the essential constituent. [< F < Ital. *gelatina* < *gelata* jelly < L *gelare* freeze]

gel·a·tine (jel′ə tən or jel′ə tēn′) *n.* gelatin.

ge·lat·i·nous (jə lat′ə nəs) *adj.* **1** jelly-like; of the consistency of jelly. **2** of gelatin; containing gelatin.

geld (geld) *v.* **geld·ed** or **gelt, geld·ing.** remove the male glands of (a horse or other animal); castrate. [ME < ON *gelda* castrate < *geldr* barren]

geld·ing (gel′ding) *n.* a gelded horse or other animal.

gel·id (jel′id) *adj.* cold as ice; frosty. [< L *gelidus* < *gelum* cold]

gelt (gelt) *v.* a pt. and a pp. of **geld.**

gem (jem) *n. v.* **gemmed, gem·ming.** —*n.* **1** a precious stone; jewel. Diamonds and rubies are gems. **2** a person or thing that is very precious, beautiful, etc.: *The gem of his collection was a rare Persian stamp.* **3** a kind of muffin made of coarse flour. —*v.* set or adorn with gems, or set as if with gems: *Stars gem the sky.* [< F < L *gemma* gem, bud] —**gem′like′**, *adj.*

Ge·ma·ra (gə mä′rə or gə mô′rə) *n.* a rabbinical commentary on the Mishnah. The Mishnah and Gemara together make up the Talmud. [< Aramaic *gemara* completion]

gem·i·nate (*v.* jem′ə nāt′; *adj.* jem′ə nit or jem′ə nāt′) *v.* **-nat·ed, -nat·ing,** *adj.* —*v.* make or become double; combine in pairs. —*adj.* combined in a pair or pairs; coupled. [< L *geminare* < *geminus* twin] —**gem′i·na′tion,** *n.*

Gem·i·ni (jem′ə nī′ or jem′ə nē′) *n.pl.* **1** in astronomy, a northern constellation containing the two bright stars, Castor and Pollux. **2** in astrology, the third sign of the zodiac; Twins. The sun enters Gemini about May 21. See **zodiac** for diagram. **3** Castor and Pollux, the twin sons of Zeus. [< L *gemini* twins]

gem·ma (jem′ə) *n.* **gem·mae** (jem′ē). **1** in botany, a bud. **2** in biology, a budlike growth that can develop into a new plant or animal. [< L *gemma* bud]

gem·mate (jem′āt) *v.* **-mat·ed, -mat·ing.** put forth buds; reproduce by budding. [< L *gemmare* < *gemma* bud] —**gem·ma′tion,** *n.*

gem·mol·o·gist or **gem·ol·o·gist** (jem ol′ə jist) *n.* an expert in gemmology.

gem·mol·o·gy or **gem·ol·o·gy** (jem ol′ə jē) *n.* the study of gems, their origins, uses, etc.

gem·mule (jem′ūl) *n.* a small gemma. [< L *gemmula*, dim. of *gemma* bud]

gems·bok (gemz′bok′) *n.* a large antelope of South Africa, having long, straight horns and a long, tufted tail. [< Afrikaans < G *Gemsbock* < *gemse* chamois + *bock* buck]

gem·stone (jem′stōn′) *n.* a precious or semiprecious stone, capable of being cut and polished to make a gem.

gen (jen) *n. v.* **genned, gen·ning.** *Slang.* —*n.* authentic, detailed information. —*v.* give authentic, detailed information to. [originally Royal Air Force slang, perhaps < *gen*uine information]

-gen *suffix.* producing; born; produced, as in *acrogen, nitrogen.* [< F < Gk. *-genēs*, ult. < *gignesthai* be born]

gen. 1 gender. **2** general. **3** genitive. **4** genus. **5** generator.

Gen. 1 General. **2** Genesis.

gen·darme (zhon′därm; *French,* zhäN därm′) *n.* **-darmes** (-därmz). in France and several other European countries, a policeman who has had military training. [< F *gendarme* < *gens d'armes* men of arms]

gen·der (jen′dər) *n.* **1** in grammar: **a** a system of grouping words (such as nouns, pronouns, and adjectives) into two or more categories classified variously in different languages according to criteria that are either arbitrary or based on such distinctions as sex, social rank, shape, size, or kind of existence (living things as opposed to non-living). **b** any such category. **c** a form or inflection used to indicate such a category. **2** *Informal.* sex. [ME < OF *gendre* < L *genus, -neris* kind, sort]

☛ **gender.** Many languages have special endings for masculine, feminine, and neuter nouns and for adjectives modifying them, but English lost such formal distinctions several hundred years ago. Now, except in pronouns and a few nouns with endings such as *-ess, -us, -a, -or, -trix, -e, -eur, -euse* (*actress, mistress, alumnus, alumna, actor, aviatrix, blonde, masseur, masseuse*), gender is indicated only by the meaning of the word: *man—woman, nephew—niece, rooster—hen.*

gene (jēn) *n.* in biology, a minute part of a chromosome that determines the nature and development of an inherited characteristic. The genes inherited from its parents determine what kind of plant or animal will develop from a fertilized egg cell. [< Gk. *genea* breed, kind]

ge·ne·a·log·i·cal (jē′nē ə loj′ə kəl or jen′ē ə loj′ə kəl) *adj.* having to do with genealogy. A genealogical table or chart shows the descent of a person or family from an ancestor. —**ge′ne·a·log′i·cal·ly,** *adv.*

ge·ne·al·o·gist (jē′nē al′ə jist or jē′nē ol′ə jist, jen′ē al′ə jist or jen′ē ol′ə jist) *n.* a person who traces genealogies; person who makes a study of genealogies.

hat, āge, cãre, fär; let, ēqual, tėrm; it, īce
hot, ōpen, ôrder; oil, out; cup, pu̇t, rüle, ūse
əbove, takən, pencəl, lemən, circəs
ch, child; ng, long; sh, ship
th, thin; ᴛʜ, then; zh, measure

ge·ne·al·o·gy (jē′nē al′ə jē or jē′nē ol′ə jē, jen′ē al′ə jē or jen′ē ol′ə jē) *n.* **-gies. 1** an account of the descent of a person or family from an ancestor or ancestors. **2** the descent of a person or family from an ancestor; pedigree; lineage. **3** the making or investigation of accounts of descent; study of pedigrees. [< L < Gk. *genealogia*, ult. < *genea* generation + *-logos* treating of]

gen·er·a (jen′ər ə) *n.* pl. of **genus.**

gen·er·al (jen′ər əl or jen′rəl) *adj.* **1** of all; for all; from all: *A government takes care of the general welfare.* **2** common to many or most; not limited to a few; widespread: *There is a general interest in sports.* **3** not special; not limited to one kind, class, department, or use: *A general reader reads different kinds of books.* **4** not detailed; sufficient for practical purposes: *general instructions.* **5** indefinite; vague: *She referred to her trip in a general way.* **6** of or for all those forming a group: "*Cat*" *is a general term for cats, lions, and tigers.* **7** in chief; of highest rank: *The Postmaster General is the head of the Post Office Department.*
—*n.* **1** in the army: **a** a commissioned officer senior to a lieutenant-general and junior to a field marshal. **b** any commissioned officer ranking above a colonel and entitled to command a force larger than a regiment, such as a lieutenant-general, a major-general, etc. **2** any officer in command of many soldiers: *Sir Arthur Currie was a famous Canadian general.* **3 in general, a** referring to all those mentioned. **b** usually; for the most part. **4** a general fact, idea, principle, or statement. **5** the head of a religious order. **6** *Archaic.* people as a group; the public. *Abbrev.*: gen. [< L *generalis* of a whole class < *genus, -neris* class, race]

Syn. *adj.* **1, 2 General, common, popular** = belonging or relating to all. **General** = belonging to or existing among all, or almost all, of a group or class of people or things thought of as a whole: *Laws are made for the general good.* **Common** = shared by all the members of a group or class: *English is the common language in the United States.* **Popular** = belonging to, existing among, or representing the general public: *Various polls are devised to find out popular opinions.*

General Assembly the legislative body of the United Nations.

general election 1 an election involving all the voters of a country. **2** in Canada, an election in which either a new federal Parliament or a new provincial legislative assembly is elected.

gen·er·al·is·si·mo (jen′ər əl is′ə mō or jen′rəl is′ə mō) *n.* **-mos. 1** the commander-in-chief of all the military forces of a country. **2** the commander-in-chief of several armies in the field. [< Ital. *generalissimo*, superlative of *generale* general]

gen·er·al·i·ty (jen′ər al′ə tē) *n.* **-ties. 1** a general statement; a word or phrase not definite enough to have much meaning or value: *The candidate spoke only in generalities; not once did he mention definite laws that he and his party would try to pass.* **2** a general principle or rule: "*Nothing happens without a cause*" *is a generality.* **3** the greater part; main body; mass: *The generality of people must work for a living.* **4** general quality or condition: *A rule of great generality has very few exceptions.*

gen·er·al·i·za·tion (jen′ər əl ə zā′shən or jen′ər əl ī zā′shən; jen′rəl ə zā′shən or jen′rəl ī zā′shən) *n.* **1** the act or process of generalizing: *Don't be hasty in generalization; be sure you have the necessary facts first.* **2** a general idea, statement, principle, or rule.

gen·er·al·ize (jen′ər əl īz′ or jen′rəl īz′) *v.* **-ized, -iz·ing. 1** make into one general statement; bring under a common heading, class, or law. **2** infer (a general rule) from particular facts: *If you have seen cats, lions, leopards, and tigers eat meat, you can generalize and say, "Animals of the cat family eat meat."* **3** state in a more general form; extend in application. The statement that $5 + 3 = 8$ and $50 + 30 = 80$ can be generalized to the form $5a + 3a = 8a$. **4** talk indefinitely or vaguely; use generalities. **5** make general; bring into general use or knowledge. **6** make general inferences.

gen·er·al·ly (jen′ər əl ē or jen′rəl ē) *adv.* **1** in most cases; usually: *He is generally on time.* **2** for the most part; widely: *It was once generally believed that the earth was flat.* **3** in a general way; without giving details; not specially: *Generally speaking, our coldest weather comes in January.*

General of the Army in the United States, a general of the highest rank.

gen·er·al·ship (jen′ər əl ship′ or jen′rəl-) *n.* **1** ability as a general; skill in commanding an army. **2** skilful management; leadership. **3** the rank, commission, authority, or term of office of a general.

general staff a group of high army officers who make plans for war or national defence.

general store a store that carries a wide variety of goods for sale: *Most villages and small towns have one or more general stores.*

gen·er·ate (jen′ər āt′) *v.* **-at·ed, -at·ing. 1** produce; cause to be: *Rubbing generates heat. Steam can be used to generate power or electricity.* **2** produce (offspring). **3** in mathematics, form (a line, surface, figure, or solid) by moving a point, line, etc. [< L *generare* < *genus, -neris* race]

gen·er·a·tion (jen′ər ā′shən) *n.* **1** all the people born about the same time. Your parents and their friends belong to one generation; you and your friends belong to the following generation. **2** the time from the birth of one generation to the birth of the next generation; about 30 years. **3** one step or degree in the descent of a family: *The picture showed four generations: great-grandmother, grandmother, mother, and baby.* **4** the production of offspring. **5** production; a causing to be; generating: *Steam and water power are used for the generation of electricity.* **6** in biology, a form or stage of a plant or animal, with reference to its method of reproduction: *the asexual generation of a fern.* **7** in mathematics, the formation of a line, surface, figure, or solid by moving a point, line, etc.

gen·er·a·tive (jen′ər ə tiv or jen′ər ā′tiv) *adj.* **1** having to do with the production of offspring. **2** having the power of producing. **—gen′er·a·tive·ly,** *adv.* **—gen′er·a·tive·ness,** *n.*

gen·er·a·tor (jen′ər ā′tər) *n.* **1** a machine that changes mechanical energy into electrical energy; dynamo. **2** a piece of apparatus for generating or producing gas or steam. **3** a person or thing that generates. [< L]

gen·er·a·trix (jen′ər ā′triks) *n.* **gen·er·a·tri·ces** (jen′ər ə trī′sēz). in mathematics, a point, line, etc. whose motion produces a line, surface, figure, or solid. [< L]

ge·ner·ic (jə ner′ik) *adj.* **1** having to do with or characteristic of a genus of plants or animals: *Cats and lions show generic differences.* **2** having to do with a class or group of similar things; inclusive; not specific: *Liquid is a generic term.* **3** applied to, or referring to, a group or class; general; not special. [< L *genus, generis* kind] **—ge·ner′i·cal·ly,** *adv.*

gen·er·os·i·ty (jen′ər os′ə tē) *n.* **-ties. 1** a being generous; willingness to share with others; unselfishness. **2** nobleness of mind; absence of meanness. **3** a generous act.

gen·er·ous (jen′ər əs or jen′rəs) *adj.* **1** willing to share with others; unselfish. **2** having or showing a noble mind; willing to forgive; not mean. **3** large; plentiful: *A quarter of a pie is a generous serving.* **4** fertile: *generous fields.* **5** rich and strong: *a generous wine.* [< L *generosus* of noble birth < *genus, -neris* race, stock] **—gen′er·ous·ly,** *adv.* **—gen′er·ous·ness,** *n.* **—Syn. 1** liberal, bountiful, lavish. **2** high-minded, magnanimous. **3** ample, abundant.

gen·e·sis (jen′ə sis) *n.* **-ses** (-sēz′). **1** origin; creation; coming into being. **2 Genesis,** the first book of the Old Testament. Genesis gives an account of the creation of the world. [< L < Gk.]

gen·et (jen′it) *n.* jennet.

ge·net·ic (jə net′ik) *adj.* **1** having to do with origin and natural growth. **2** of or having to do with genetics. [< Gk. *genētikos* < *genesis* origin, creation]

ge·net·i·cal·ly (jə net′ik lē) *adv.* **1** with respect to genesis or origin. **2** according to the laws of genetics.

ge·net·i·cist (jə net′ə sist) *n.* a person trained in genetics.

ge·net·ics (jə net′iks) *n.* the branch of biology dealing with the principles of heredity and variation in animals and plants of the same or related kinds.

Ge·ne·va Convention (jə nē′və) an agreement between nations providing for the neutrality of the members and buildings of the medical departments on battlefields. It was first formulated at Geneva, Switzerland, in 1864.

Ge·ne·van (jə nē′vən) *adj.* of Geneva, a city in S.W. Switzerland, or its people. *—n.* a native or inhabitant of Geneva.

gen·ial (jē′nē əl or jēn′yəl) *adj.* **1** smiling and pleasant; cheerful and friendly; kindly: *a genial welcome.* **2** helping growth; pleasantly warming; comforting: *genial sunshine.* [< L *genialis,* literally, belonging to the genius < *genius.* See GENIUS.] **—gen′ial·ly,** *adv.* **—gen′ial·ness,** *n.*

ge·ni·al·i·ty (jē′nē al′ə tē) *n.* a genial quality.

gen·ic (jen′ik) *adj.* in biology, of, relating to, or like a gene; genetic.

-genic *combining form.* **1** producing; having to do with production: *carcinogenic = producing cancer.* **2** of or having to do with a gene or genes. **3** suitable for; suitable for production or reproduction by: *photogenic = suitable for photography.*

ge·nie (jē′nē) *n.* a spirit; jinni: *When Aladdin rubbed his lamp, the genie came and did whatever Aladdin asked.* [< F *génie*]

ge·ni·i (jē′nē ī′) *n.* a pl. of **genius.**

gen·i·tal (jen′ə təl) *adj.* having to do with reproduction or the sex organs. [< L *genitalis,* ult. < *gignere* beget]

gen·i·tals (jen′ə təlz) *n.pl.* the external sex organs.

gen·i·ti·val (jen′ə tī′vəl) *adj.* of or in the genitive case.

gen·i·tive (jen′ə tiv) *n.* in certain languages: **1** a case that indicates possession, source, origin, etc. The genitive corresponds in part to the possessive case in English. **2** a word or construction in this case. *—adj.* of this case; in this case; having to do with its forms or constructions. [< L *genitivus* of origin]

gen·ius (jē′nē əs or jēn′yəs) *n.* **gen·ius·es** *for 1-4, 7,* **ge·ni·i** *for 5, 6, 8.* **1** very great natural power of mind. **2** a person having such power: *Shakespeare was a genius.* **3** a great natural ability of some special kind: *Mozart played the piano well, but he had a genius for composing.* **4** the special character or spirit of a person, nation, age, language, etc.: *Shakespeare gave expression to the genius of Elizabethan England.* **5** a guardian spirit of a person, place, institution, etc.: *the genius of the hill.* **6** either of two spirits, one good and one evil, supposed to influence a person's fate. **7** a person who powerfully influences another. **8** a spirit; genie; jinni. [< L *genius* god presiding over birth, ult. < *genere* beget]

gen·o·cid·al (jen′ə sīd′əl) *adj.* having to do with genocide.

gen·o·cide (jen′ə sīd′) *n.* systematic measures for the extermination of a national, cultural, religious, or racial group. [< Gk. *genos* race + *-cide*[1]; coined by R. Lemkin in 1944]

Gen·o·ese (jen′ō ēz′) *adj. n.* **-ese.** *—adj.* of Genoa, a seaport in N.W. Italy, or its people. *—n.* a native or inhabitant of Genoa.

gen·o·type (jen′ə tīp′) *n.* in biology: **1** the arrangement or combination of genes in an organism. **2** a group of organisms each having the same combinations of hereditary characteristics. [< Gk. *genos* race + E *type*]

gen·re (zhon′rə; *French,* zhäN′rə) *n.* kind; sort; style: *Poe was the originator of a genre of detective story.* [< F < L *genus* kind]

genre painting a style of painting that shows scenes from ordinary life.

gens[1] (jenz) *n.* **gen·tes** (jen′tēz). **1** in ancient Rome, a group of families that claimed the same ancestor and were united by a common name and common religious ceremonies: *Julius Caesar was a member of the Julian gens.*

2 a tribe; clan. 3 in ethnology, a group or tribe of people descended through their fathers from a common ancestor. [< L]

gens² (zhäN) *n.pl. French.* any group of people following the same occupation, engaged in the same business, or inhabiting the same region. **Gens de chantier** are lumberjacks.

Gent. or **gent.** gentleman; gentlemen.

gen·teel (jen tēl′) *adj.* 1 belonging or suited to polite society. 2 polite; well-bred; fashionable; elegant. 3 trying to be aristocratic, but not really being so. [< F *gentil* < L *gentilis.* Doublet of GENTILE, GENTLE, JAUNTY.] **—gen·teel′ly,** *adv.* **—gen·teel′ness,** *n.* **—Syn. 2** refined.

gen·tian (jen′shən) *n.* any of a large family of plants having funnel-shaped flowers, stemless leaves, and bitter juice. Gentians have blue, white, red, or yellow flowers. [< L *gentiana;* said to be named for *Gentius,* king of Illyria (ancient country on the Adriatic)]

gen·tile or **Gen·tile** (jen′tīl) *n.* 1 a person who is not a Jew. 2 a heathen; pagan. 3 among Mormons or Moslems, a person who is not a Mormon or Moslem. *—adj.* 1 not Jewish. 2 heathen; pagan. 3 among Mormons or Moslems, of or having to do with those outside of the Mormon or Moslem community. [ME < LL *gentilis* foreign < L *gentilis* of a people, national. Doublet of GENTEEL, GENTLE, JAUNTY.]

gen·til·i·ty (jen til′ə tē) *n.* **-ties.** 1 membership in the aristocracy or upper class. 2 good manners. 3 refinement: *The lady had an air of gentility.* 4 Usually, **gentilities,** *pl.* pretended refinements.

gen·tle (jen′təl) *adj.* **-tler, -tlest.** 1 not severe, rough, or violent; mild: *a gentle tap.* 2 soft; low: *a gentle sound.* 3 moderate: *gentle heat, a gentle slope.* 4 kindly; friendly: *a gentle disposition.* 5 easily handled or managed: *a gentle dog.* 6 of good family and social position; well-born. 7 honorable; good; superior. 8 *Archaic.* noble; gallant: *a gentle knight.* 9 refined; polite.
—v. treat in a soothing way; make quiet or gentle: *The rider gentled his excited horse.* [ME < OF *gentil* < L *gentilis* of the (same) family, national < *gens, gentis* family, nation. Doublet of GENTEEL, GENTILE, JAUNTY.]
Syn. *adj.* **1 Gentle, mild, meek** = agreeable, not harsh, rough, or violent. **Gentle** emphasizes control of strength or force, and suggests being pleasant or pleasing or being soft, tender, calm, or kindly: *My nurse is gentle in touch, manner, and voice.* **Mild** emphasizes being by nature not disagreeable, lacking in harshness, severity, etc.: *He is a mild man and seldom gets angry.* **Meek,** applying only to people, and meaning mild or gentle in disposition, emphasizes being patient and humble: *This meek little clerk tries to please everyone.* 5 docile, tame.

gen·tle·folk (jen′təl fōk′) *n.pl.* people of good family and social position.

gen·tle·man (jen′təl mən) *n.* **-men** (-mən). 1 a man of good family and social position. 2 a man who is honorable and well-bred. 3 a man of fine feelings or instincts, shown by behavior and consideration for others. 4 a polite term for any man. **—gen′tle·man·like′,** *adj.* ☛ See **man** for usage note.

gen·tle·man-in-wait·ing (jen′təl mən in wāt′ing) *n.* a man of good family who attends a king or prince.

gen·tle·man·ly (jen′təl mən lē) *adj.* like a gentleman; suitable for a gentleman; polite; well-bred. **—gen′tle·man·li·ness,** *n.*

gentleman's agreement or **gentlemen's agreement** an informal agreement. Because it is not written, the people or countries that make it are bound only by their promise to keep it.

gen·tle·ness (jen′təl nis) *n.* a being gentle.

gen·tle·wom·an (jen′təl wu̇m′ən) *n.* **-wom·en.** 1 a woman of good family and social position. 2 a well-bred woman; lady. 3 formerly, a woman attendant of a lady of rank. **—gen′tle·wom′an·ly,** *adv.*

gen·tly (jen′tlē) *adv.* 1 in a gentle way; tenderly; softly. 2 gradually: *a gently sloping hillside.*

gen·try (jen′trē) *n.* 1 people of good family and social position. 2 people of any particular class. [alteration of *gentrice* < OF *genterise,* ult. < *gentil.* See GENTLE.]

gen·u·flect (jen′yu̇ flekt′) *v.* bend the knee as an act of reverence or worship. [< Med.L *genuflectere* < L *genu* knee + *flectere* bend]

gen·u·flec·tion (jen′yu̇ flek′shən) *n.* a bending of the knee as an act of reverence or worship.

hat, āge, cãre, fär; let, ēqual, tėrm; it, īce
hot, ōpen, ôrder; oil, out; cup, pu̇t, rüle, ūse
əbove, takən, pencəl, lemən, circəs
ch, child; ng, long; sh, ship
th, thin; ᴛʜ, then; zh, measure

gen·u·flex·ion (jen′yu̇ flek′shən) *n. Esp.Brit.* genuflection.

gen·u·ine (jen′ū ən) *adj.* 1 actually being what it seems or is claimed to be; real; true: *genuine leather, a genuine diamond.* 2 without pretence; sincere; frank: *genuine sorrow.* [< L *genuinus* native, natural, ult. < *gignere* beget] **—gen′u·ine·ly,** *adv.* **—gen′u·ine·ness,** *n.*
Syn. 1 Genuine, authentic = what it is claimed to be. **Genuine** refers to something that is real, pure, actually having the nature or quality it is supposed to have: *The table is genuine mahogany, not wood stained to look like mahogany.* **Authentic** = of genuine origin or authorship: *That is his authentic signature, not a forgery.* 2 unaffected.
☛ The pronunciation (jen′ū īn′) is frequently heard even among educated Canadians. However, many consider it a vulgarism.

ge·nus (jē′nəs or jen′əs) *n.* **gen·er·a** or **ge·nus·es.** 1 kind; sort; class. 2 in biology, a group of related animals or plants ranking below a family and above a species. The scientific name of an animal or plant consists of the genus written with a capital letter and the species written with a small letter. *Example:* Homo sapiens. 3 in logic, a class or group of individuals divided into subordinate groups called species. [< L]

geo- *combining form.* earth; land, as in *geocentric.* [< Gk. *geō* < *gē* earth]

Geo. George.

ge·o·cen·tric (jē′ō sen′trik) *adj.* 1 as viewed or measured from the earth's centre. 2 having or representing the earth as a centre. [< *geo-* + Gk. *kentron* centre] **—ge′o·cen′tri·cal·ly,** *adv.*

ge·o·cen·tri·cal (jē′ō sen′trə kəl) *adj.* geocentric.

ge·ode (jē′ōd) *n.* 1 a rock having a cavity lined with crystals. 2 the cavity itself. [< F *géode* < L < Gk. *geōdēs* earthy < *gē* earth + *eidos* form]

ge·o·des·ic (jē′ə des′ik or jē′ə dē′sik) *adj.* 1 of or having to do with geodesy; geodetic. 2 having a curve like the curvature of the earth: *geodesic dome.* **—***n.* a geodesic line.

geodesic line the shortest possible line connecting two points on a surface, which it follows.

ge·od·e·sy (jē od′ə sē) *n.* the branch of applied mathematics dealing with the shape and dimensions of the earth, the determination of the shape and area of large tracts on its surface, variations in terrestrial gravity, and the exact position of geographical points. [< NL < Gk. *geodaisia* < *gē* earth + *daiein* divide]

ge·o·det·ic (jē′ə det′ik) *adj.* having to do with geodesy. **—ge′o·det′i·cal·ly,** *adv.*

ge·og·no·sy (jē og′nə sē) *n.* the branch of geology that deals with the structure of the earth, its rocks and minerals, and the water and air surrounding it. [< F < Gk. *gē* earth + *gnōsis* knowledge]

ge·og·ra·pher (jē og′rə fər) *n.* a person trained in geography.

ge·o·graph·ic (jē′ə graf′ik) *adj.* geographical.

ge·o·graph·i·cal (jē′ə graf′ə kəl) *adj.* 1 of or having to do with geography. 2 of, having to do with, or characteristic of a particular region.

ge·o·graph·i·cal·ly (jē′ə graf′ik lē) *adv.* 1 in geographical respects. 2 according to geography.

geographical mile about 6,080 feet.

ge·og·ra·phy (jē og′rə fē) *n.* **-phies.** 1 the study of the earth's surface, climate, continents, countries, peoples, industries, and products. 2 the surface features of a place or region. 3 a book about geography. [< L < Gk. *geōgraphia* < *gē* earth + *graphein* describe]

geol. 1 geology. 2 geologic.

ge·o·log·ic (jē′ə loj′ik) *adj.* geological.

ge·o·log·i·cal (jē′ə loj′ə kəl) *adj.* of or having to do with geology. **—ge′o·log′i·cal·ly,** *adv.*

ge·ol·o·gist (jē ol′ə jist) *n.* a person trained in geology.

TIME IN GEOLOGY

Eras and their durations	Periods and their beginnings	Changes and characteristics
Cenozoic (age of mammals) Has lasted 50 million years.	**Quaternary**	
	Recent (began 10,000-25,000 years ago)	Glaciers are melted and Great Lakes are formed. Climate is warm. Man found in most parts of the earth. He domesticates animals and develops agriculture.
	Pleistocene 1 million)	Great ice sheets cover the northern hemisphere. Extensive deposits of gravel. Mammals are widespread. Early man reaches Europe and North America.
	Tertiary	
	Pliocene (12 million)	Mountains continue to rise in western America. Mammals migrate between continents.
	Miocene (28 million)	Rocky Mountains and Sierra Nevada are forming.
	Oligocene (35 million)	Land becomes lower. Alps and Himalayas begin to rise.
	Eocene (50 million)	Climates are mild. Seas cover only a little of the land. Early horses and elephants appear.
	Paleocene (60 million)	Mountains become higher. Climates are less uniform. Mammals become common.
Mesozoic (age of reptiles) Lasted 150 million years.	Cretaceous (130 million)	Seas spread over the land. Flowering plants appear. Dinosaurs die out. Most chalk deposits made.
	Jurassic (170 million)	Dinosaurs dominate the earth. Flying reptiles and birds appear.
	Triassic (200 million)	Continents are high and have many deserts. Reptiles dominate the earth.
Paleozoic (age of fishes) Lasted 300 million years.	Permian (230 million)	Appalachian mountains and other ranges in Europe and Asia have been formed. Reptiles are developing.
	Carboniferous Pennsylvanian (270 million) Mississippian (290 million)	Warm, moist climate produces great forests that later become coal beds. First reptiles and insects appear.
	Devonian (330 million)	First amphibians and forests of fernlike trees appear.
	Silurian (360 million)	First air-breathing animals and land plants appear.
	Ordovician (420 million)	Much land is covered by water. First fishes appear.
	Cambrian (500 million)	Seas spread over the land. Greatest development of invertebrates occurs.
Proterozoic Lasted 500 million years.	**Pre-Cambrian** Keweenawan (750 million) Huronian (1,000 million)	Laurentian mountains are formed, but great eruptions of lava occur; there is much erosion. Sponges appear.
Archeozoic (first living things) Lasted 1,300 million years.	**Pre-Cambrian** Timiskaming (1,420 million) Keewatin (2,300 million)	Laurentian mountains are forming in area of modern Canadian Shield. There is much volcanic activity. Simple one-celled plants and animals exist.
Azoic (no life)	Lasted over 2,000 million years.	The earth's crust is cooling and rock is being formed.

ge·ol·o·gy (jē ol′ə jē) *n.* **-gies. 1** the science that deals with the earth's crust, the layers of which it is composed, and their history. See the chart opposite. **2** the features of the earth's crust in a place or region; rocks, rock formation, etc. of a particular area. **3** a book about geology. [< NL *geologia* < Gk. *gē* earth + *-logos* treating of]

geom. 1 geometry. **2** geometric.

ge·o·mag·net·ic (jē′ō mag net′ik) *adj.* of or having to do with the magnetism of the earth.

geo·mag·net·ism (jē′ō mag′nə tiz′əm) *n.* **1** the magnetism of the earth. **2** the science concerned with the magnetism of the earth.

ge·om·e·ter (jē om′ə tər) *n.* geometrician. [< L < Gk. *geōmetrēs* < *gē* earth + *metrēs* measurer]

ge·o·met·ric (jē′ə met′rik) *adj.* **1** of geometry; according to the principles of geometry: *geometric proof.* **2** consisting of straight lines, circles, triangles, etc.; regular and symmetrical: *a geometric design.*

ge·o·met·ri·cal (jē′ə met′rə kəl) *adj.* geometric.

ge·om·e·tri·cian (jē om′ə trish′ən or jē′ə mə trish′ən) *n.* a person trained in geometry.

geometric progression a series, such as 2, 4, 8, 16, or 5, 1/5, 1/25, in which the ratio of each term to its predecessor is always constant.

ge·om·e·trid (jē om′ə trid) *n.* any of a group of gray or greenish moths having slender bodies whose larvae are called measuring worms or inchworms. Geometrids move by bringing the rear end of the body forward, thus forming a loop, and then advancing the front end. [< NL *Geometridae*, pl. < L < Gk. *geōmetrēs*. See GEOMETER.]

ge·om·e·try (jē om′ə trē) *n.* **-tries. 1** the branch of mathematics that deals with lines, angles, surfaces, and solids. Geometry includes the definition, comparison, and measurement of squares, triangles, circles, cubes, cones, spheres, etc. **2** a book about geometry. [< L < Gk. *geōmetria* < *gē* earth + *-metria* measuring]

ge·o·mor·phic (jē′ə môr′fik) *adj.* **1** of or having to do with the form of the earth or the configuration of its surface. **2** resembling the earth.

ge·o·mor·pho·log·i·cal (jē′ō môr′fə loj′ə kəl) *adj.* of or having to do with geomorphology.

ge·o·mor·phol·o·gist (jē′ō môr fol′ə jist) *n.* an expert in geomorphology.

ge·o·mor·phol·o·gy (jē′ō môr fol′ə jē) *n.* the study of the surface features of the earth, their origins, development, etc.

ge·o·phys·i·cal (jē′ō fiz′ə kəl) *adj.* of or having to do with geophysics.

ge·o·phys·ics (jē′ō fiz′iks) *n.* the science dealing with the relations between the features of the earth and the forces that produce them; physics of the earth.

ge·o·po·lit·i·cal (jē′ō pə lit′ə kəl) *adj.* having to do with or involved in geopolitics.

ge·o·pol·i·ti·cian (jē′ō pol′ə tish′ən) *n.* a person who has special skill in, or knowledge of, geopolitics.

ge·o·pol·i·tics (jē′ō pol′ə tiks) *n.* the study of government and its policies as affected by physical geography.

George (jôrj) *n.* **1** a part of the insignia of the Order of the Garter, representing Saint George slaying the dragon. It may be a piece set with jewels or a single carved gem. **2** *Brit. Slang.* the automatic pilot of an airplane.

George Cross in the British Commonwealth, the highest award for courage that can be awarded to a civilian, established by King George VI, King of England from 1936 to 1952. *Abbrev.*: G.C.

The George Cross

geor·gette (jôr jet′) *n.* a thin, fine, transparent, silk cloth with a slightly wavy surface, used for dresses, etc. [from the name of a French modiste]

Geor·gian (jôr′jən) *adj.* **1** of or having to do with the four Georges, kings of England from 1714 to 1830. **2** having to do with the style of architecture, art, or decoration during this period. **3** of or having to do with, especially, George V, King of England from 1910 to 1936, or with George VI, King from 1936 to 1952. **4** of or having to do with the state of Georgia in the United

hat, āge, cãre, fär; let, ēqual, tėrm; it, īce
hot, ōpen, ôrder; oil, out; cup, pu̇t, rüle, ūse
əbove, takən, pencəl, lemən, circəs
ch, child; ng, long; sh, ship
th, thin; ᴛʜ, then; zh, measure

States. **5** of or having to do with the Soviet Republic of Georgia, its people, or their language.
—*n.* **1** a native or inhabitant of the state of Georgia in the United States. **2** a native or inhabitant of the Soviet Republic of Georgia. **3** the South Caucasian language of the Republic of Georgia. **4** a person, such as a writer, of either of the Georgian periods in England.

ge·o·sphere (jē′ə sfēr′) *n.* the solid matter that comprises the earth.

ge·o·trop·ic (jē′ə trop′ik) *adj.* in biology, affected by geotropism; responding to gravity. [< *geo-* + Gk. *tropikos* < *tropē* turning]

ge·ot·ro·pism (jē ot′rə piz′əm) *n.* in biology, a response to gravity. **Positive geotropism** is a tendency to move down into the earth, as roots do. **Negative geotropism** is a tendency to move upward.

ger. gerund.

Ger. 1 German. **2** Germany. **3** Germanic.

ge·ra·ni·um (jə rā′nē əm) *n.* **1** a cultivated plant having large clusters of showy flowers and fragrant leaves. It is often grown in pots and in window boxes. **2** a wild plant having pink or purple flowers, deeply notched leaves, and long, pointed pods. [< L < Gk. *geranion* < *geranos* crane; from the resemblance of the pod to a crane's bill]

ger·bil (jėr′bəl) *n.* any of a group of rodents having long hind legs, native to Asia and Africa. Gerbils are used in scientific research and are kept as pets. [< F *gerbille* < NL *gerbillus*, dim. of *gerbo* jerboa]

ger·fal·con (jėr′fol′kən or -fôl′kən) *n.* any of various large falcons of the Arctic. Also, **gyrfalcon.** [ME < OF *gerfaucon* < Gmc.]

ger·i·at·rics (jer′ē at′riks) *n.* the science that deals with the study of old age and its diseases. [< Gk. *gēras* old age + *iatreia* healing]

germ (jėrm) *n.* **1** a microscopic animal or plant that causes disease. **2** the earliest form of a living thing; seed; bud. **3** the beginning of anything; origin. [< F < L *germen* sprout] —**germ′less,** *adj.* —**germ′like′,** *adj.*

ger·man[1] (jėr′mən) *adj.* **1** having the same parents. Children of the same father and mother are **brothers-german** or **sisters-german. 2** being a child of one's uncle or aunt. A **cousin-german** is a first cousin. [ME < OF *germain* < L *germanus*]

ger·man[2] (jėr′mən) *n.* **1** a dance with complicated steps and frequent changing of partners; cotillion. **2** a party at which it is danced. [short for *German cotillion*]

Ger·man (jėr′mən) *adj.* of Germany, its people, or their language. —*n.* **1** a native or inhabitant of Germany. **2** a citizen of Germany. **3** the language of Germany. See also **High German** and **Low German.** [< L *Germanus*]

ger·man·der (jėr man′dər) *n.* **1** a plant like mint. It usually has dense spikes of small flowers. **2** speedwell, a plant with bright blue flowers. [< LL *germandra* < Gk. *chamaidryas*, alteration of *chamaidrys* ground oak]

ger·mane (jėr mān′) *adj.* closely connected; to the point; pertinent: *Your statement is not germane to the discussion.* [var. of *german*[1]]

Ger·man·ic (jėr man′ik) *adj.* **1** German. **2** Teutonic. —*n.* a branch of the Indo-European language family, customarily divided into **East Germanic** (Gothic), **North Germanic** (the Scandinavian languages), and **West Germanic** (English, Frisian, Dutch, German).

ger·ma·ni·um (jėr mā′nē əm) *n.* a rare, grayish white metallic chemical element whose compounds resemble those of tin. *Symbol*: Ge; *at.no.* 32; *at.wt.* 72.59. [< NL < L *Germania* Germany]

German measles a contagious disease resembling measles, but much less serious.

German shepherd dog 1 a breed of large, intelligent dog developed in Germany, often trained to work with soldiers or police, to guide the blind, etc.; police dog; Alsatian. **2** a dog of this breed.

German silver a white alloy of copper, zinc, and nickel, used for ornaments, utensils, wire, etc.

germ cell in biology, a cell that can produce a new individual, usually after union with another cell of the opposite sex; egg or sperm cell.

ger·mi·cid·al (jėr′mə sīd′əl) *adj.* capable of killing germs.

ger·mi·cide (jėr′mə sīd′) *n.* any substance that kills germs, especially disease germs. [< *germ* + *-cide*[2]]

ger·mi·nal (jėr′mə nəl) *adj.* **1** of germs or germ cells. **2** like germs; like that of germs or germ cells. **3** in the earliest stage of development.

ger·mi·nate (jėr′mə nāt′) *v.* **-nat·ed, -nat·ing. 1** start growing or developing; sprout: *Seeds germinate in the spring.* **2** cause to develop: *Warmth and moisture germinate seeds.* [< L *germinare* < *germen* sprout] **—ger′mi·na′tion,** *n.* **—ger′mi·na′tor,** *n.*

germ plasm a substance in germ cells that transmits hereditary characteristics to the offspring.

germ warfare the spreading of germs to produce disease among the enemy in time of war.

ger·on·tol·o·gy (jer′ən tol′ə jē) *n.* the branch of science dealing with the phenomena and problems of old age.

ger·ry·man·der (ger′ē man′dər or jer′ē-) *n.* an arrangement of the political boundaries of a riding, constituency, etc. that gives the party in power an undue advantage in an election. —*v.* **1** arrange the political boundaries of a riding, constituency, etc. so as to give the party in power an undue advantage in an election. **2** manipulate unfairly. [< *Gerry* + sala*mander*; Governor Gerry's party rearranged the districts of Massachusetts in 1812, and Essex County was divided so that one district became roughly salamander-shaped]

ger·und (jer′ənd) *n.* in grammar, a verb form used as a noun. *Abbrev.*: ger. [< LL *gerundium*, ult. < L *gerere* bear]

☛ The English **gerund** ends in *-ing*. It has the same form as the present participle but differs in use. Gerund: *Running a hotel appealed to him.* Participle: *Running around the corner, he bumped into a cop.* A gerund may take an object (*running a hotel*) or a complement (*being a hero*), and it may serve in any of the functions of a noun: Subject: *Looking for an apartment always fascinated her.* Object: *He taught dancing.* Predicate noun: *Seeing is believing.* Adjective use: *a fishing boat* (a boat for fishing, not a boat that fishes). When not in one of these constructions a gerund is related to the rest of the sentence by a preposition.

ge·run·di·al (jə run′dē əl) *adj.* **1** of a gerund. **2** used as a gerund.

ge·run·dive (jə run′div) *n.* a Latin verb form used as an adjective, frequently expressing the idea of necessity.

gest or **geste** (jest) *n. Archaic.* **1** a story or romance in verse. **2** a story; tale. **3** a deed; exploit. [ME < OF < L *gesta* deeds < *gerere* carry on, accomplish]

Ges·talt (gə shtält′) *n.* in psychology, the total structure or pattern of various acts, experiences, and elements, so integrated as to constitute a whole that is greater than the sum of its parts. [< G *Gestalt* form, configuration]

Ge·sta·po (gə stap′ō or gə stä′pō) *n.* in Nazi Germany, an official organization of secret police and detectives. [< G *Ge*heime *Sta*ats *Po*lizei secret state police]

ges·ta·tion (jes tā′shən) *n.* **1** the act or period of carrying young in the uterus from conception to birth; pregnancy. **2** the formation and development of a project, etc. in the mind. [< L *gestatio, -onis* < *gestare* carry]

ges·tic·u·late (jes tik′yů lāt′) *v.* **-lat·ed, -lat·ing.** make or use gestures, especially vehement gestures. [< L *gesticulari*, ult. < *gestus* gesture] **—ges·tic′u·la′tor,** *n.*

ges·tic·u·la·tion (jes tik′yů lā′shən) *n.* **1** the act of gesticulating. **2** a gesture. **—Syn. 2** See **gesture.**

ges·tic·u·la·tive (jes tik′yů lə tiv or jes tik′yů lā′tiv) *adj.* making or using gestures.

ges·ture (jes′ chər) *n. v.* **-tured, -turing.** —*n.* **1** a movement of the hands, arms, or any part of the body, used instead of words or with words to help express an idea or feeling: *A speaker often gestures with his hands or arms to stress something that he is saying.* **2** any action made for effect or to impress others: *Her refusal was merely a gesture; she really wanted to go.* —*v.* make or use gestures. [< Med.L *gestura* < L *gerere* to bear, conduct]

Syn. *n.* **1 Gesture, gesticulation** = movement of the head, shoulders, hands, or arms to express thought or feeling. **Gesture** applies to any such movement or motion used to take the place of words or add to the meaning expressed by the words: *He did not speak, but with a gesture indicated that I should follow him.* **Gesticulation** applies only to wild, excited, or clumsy gestures: *His gesticulations suggested he was losing his temper rapidly.*

get (get) *v.* **got** or (*Archaic*) **gat, got** or **got·ten, get·ting. 1** come to have; obtain; receive; gain: *I got a new coat yesterday. He got first prize in the spelling contest.* **2** reach: *I got home early last night. Your letter got here yesterday.* **3** catch; get hold of: *I have got a bad cold.* **4** cause to be or do: *He got his hair cut yesterday. They got the fire under control.* **5** *Informal.* be obliged (used with some form of **have**): *We have got to win.* **6** become: *get sick, get old.* **7** be: *Don't get nervous when you have to take the test.* **8** go; come: *His boat got in yesterday.* **9** persuade; influence: *We got him to speak.* **10** prepare: *Jane helped her mother get dinner.* **11** begin; start: *We soon got talking about our days at camp.* **12** possess; have (used with some form of **have**): *She has got black hair.* **13** usually of animals, beget. **14** *Informal.* hit; strike: *The bullet got the soldier in the arm.* **15** *Informal.* kill. **16** *Informal.* puzzle; annoy. **17** *Informal.* understand: *I don't get what you mean.*

get about, a go from place to place. **b** spread, become widely known.

get across, *Informal.* **a** make clear or convincing. **b** succeed.

get after, a scold. **b** urge.

get ahead, advance one's position, career, etc.; be successful.

get along, a go away. **b** advance. **c** manage. **d** succeed; prosper. **e** agree.

get around, a go from place to place. **b** become widely known; spread. **c** overcome. **d** deceive; trick.

get at, a reach. **b** find out. **c** *Informal.* tamper with; influence with money or threats.

get away, a go away. **b** escape. **c** start.

get away with, *Informal.* succeed in taking or doing something and escaping safely.

get back, a return. **b** recover. **c** *Slang.* get revenge.

get back at, *Slang.* get revenge on.

get behind, a support; endorse. **b** fail to keep up to schedule.

get by, *Informal.* **a** pass. **b** not be noticed or caught. **c** make a living: *just get by in hard times.*

get in, a go in. **b** put in. **c** arrive. **d** become friendly or familiar (with).

get into, a find out about. **b** get control of. **c** come to be in; result in being in: *get into trouble.*

get off, a come down from or out of. **b** take off. **c** escape. **d** help to escape. **e** start. **f** put out; issue. **g** say or express (a joke or funny remark). **h** deliver (a speech).

get on, a go up on or into. **b** put on. **c** advance. **d** manage. **e** succeed. **f** agree.

get on to, a learn; grasp. **b** communicate with.

get out, a go out. **b** take out. **c** go away. **d** escape. **e** help to escape. **f** become known. **g** publish. **h** find out.

get over, a recover from. **b** overcome. **c** *Slang.* make clear or convincing. **d** *Slang.* succeed.

get over with, come to grips with and dispose of (something unpleasant).

get set, get ready; prepare.

get there, succeed.

get through, a reach the end of: *I got through some correspondence today.* **b** reach a destination or desired end successfully: *I tried to phone you, but could not get through. I got through in the examination. The bill got through.* **c** cause to reach an end successfully: *I got him through the examination. Finally, they got the bill through parliament.* **d** become or make oneself understood: *Am I getting through (to you)?*

get together, *Informal.* **a** bring or come together; meet; assemble. **b** come to an agreement.

get up, a get out of bed, etc. **b** stand up. **c** prepare; arrange. **d** dress up. **e** go ahead.

[ME *gete(n)* < ON *geta*]

Syn. 1 Get, obtain, acquire = come to have something. **Get** = come to have something in some way or by some means, whether or not one wants or tries to gain it: *I got a new car. He got a bad reputation.* **Obtain** usually suggests working hard or trying to get something one wants: *I obtained permission to go.* **Acquire** emphasizes getting possession of something, usually by one's own efforts or actions: *I acquired a reading knowledge of German.*

☛ Get is increasingly used as an informal emphatic passive auxiliary: *We all got punished.* ☛ **get up.** See **rise** for usage note.

get·a·way (get′ə wā′) *n. Informal.* **1** the act of getting away; escape. **2** the start of a race.

Geth·sem·a·ne (geth sem′ə nē) *n.* in the Bible, a garden near Jerusalem, the scene of Jesus' agony, betrayal, and arrest. Matt. 26:36. [< Gk. *Gethsēmanē* < Aramaic]

getter (get′ər) *n.* **1** one that gets. **2** a chemically active substance such as magnesium, used in vacuum tubes to clear gases. **3** a sire, especially a begetter of superior offspring. **4** *Cdn.* poisoned bait used in exterminating wolves, gophers, etc.

get-to·geth·er (get′tů geтн′ər) *n. Informal.* an informal social gathering or party.

get-up (get′up′) *n. Informal.* **1** the way a thing is put together; arrangement; style. **2** dress; costume.

get-up-and-go (get′up′ən gō′) *Informal. n.* energy; initiative. *—adj.* full of energy and initiative; enterprising.

gew·gaw (gū′go or gū′gô) *n.* a showy trifle; gaudy, useless ornament or toy; bauble. *—adj.* showy but trifling.

gey·ser (gī′zər, gī′sər, or gā′zər) *n.* **1** a spring that sends a column of hot water and steam into the air at intervals. **2** anything that spurts or gushes like a geyser. *—v.* spurt or cause to spurt like a geyser. [< Icel. *Geysir*, the name of a spring in Iceland < *geysa* gush]

A geyser

G force (jē′ fôrs′) the force exerted on a body by gravity or by reaction to changes of speed.

Gha·nai·an or **Gha·ni·an** (gä′nē ən) *adj.* of or having to do with Ghana or its people. *—n.* a native or inhabitant of Ghana.

ghast·ly (gast′lē) *adj.* **-li·er, -li·est,** *adv.* *—adj.* **1** horrible: *Murder is a ghastly crime.* **2** like a dead person or ghost; deathly pale: *The sick man's face was ghastly.* **3** *Informal.* shocking: *a ghastly failure.* *—adv.* in a ghastly manner. [OE *gāstlic* < *gāst* ghost + *-lic* -ly] **—ghast′li·ness,** *n.*

Syn. *adj.* **1 Ghastly, grisly, horrible** refer to something that causes terror or horror. **Ghastly** suggests a connection or association with death, and emphasizes the frightening or horrifying appearance or nature of what is described: *We saw a ghastly accident.* **Grisly** emphasizes being so ghastly or horrible, and sometimes unearthly or weird, as to cause a person to shudder with horror or dread: *Robbing graves is a grisly occupation.* **Horrible** emphasizes the feeling of horror or abhorrence caused by what is decribed: *It was a horrible murder.* **2** deathlike, pallid, lurid.

ghat or **ghaut** (got or gôt) *n.* in India: **1** steps or a stairway leading down to a river; landing place. **2** a mountain pass. [< Hind.]

ghee (gē) *n.* in India, a liquid butter clarified by boiling, made from the milk of buffaloes and cows. [< Hind.]

gher·kin (gėr′kən) *n.* **1** a small, prickly cucumber often used for pickles. **2** a young, green cucumber used for pickles. [< earlier Du. *agurkje*, dim. of *agurk* < G < Slavic < Med.Gk., ult. < Persian *angorah* watermelon]

ghet·to (get′ō) *n.* **-tos. 1** formerly, a part of some cities where Jews were required to live. **2** a part of a city where many Jews live. **3** a part of a city inhabited by a racial, national, or religious minority. [< Ital.]

ghost (gōst) *n.* **1** the spirit of a dead person. It is supposed to live in another world and appear to living people as a pale, dim, shadowy form. **2** anything pale, dim, or shadowy like a ghost; a faint image; the slightest suggestion: *the ghost of a smile, not a ghost of a chance.* **3 give up the ghost,** die. **4** *Informal.* a ghost writer. **5** in television, a secondary or multiple image resulting from the reflection of a transmitted signal.
—v. **1** *Informal.* be a ghost writer (for). **2** of a television set, show a secondary or multiple image resulting from wave reflection.
—adj. designating a habitation, town, etc. that is deserted: *a ghost town.* [OE *gāst*] **—ghost′like′,** *adj.*

Syn. *n.* **1 Ghost, spectre, apparition** = an appearance or visible form of someone or something not really present. **Ghost** applies chiefly to the spirit of a dead person: *He saw his father's ghost.* **Spectre** applies to a ghostly, mysterious, usually frightening shape, something appearing as if by magic: *A spectre flitted through the graveyard.* **Apparition** applies especially to an appearance, often of someone dead or about to die, seeming very real to the person seeing it and impossible to explain or understand: *The apparition of his mother startled him.*

hat, āge, cãre, fär; let, ēqual, tėrm; it, īce
hot, ōpen, ôrder; oil, out; cup, pu̇t, rüle, ūse
əbove, takən, pencəl, lemən, circəs
ch, child; ng, long; sh, ship
th, thin; тн, then; zh, measure

ghost·ly (gōst′lē) *adj.* **-li·er, -li·est. 1** like a ghost; pale, dim, and shadowy: *In the darkness he seemed to see ghostly forms.* **2** of or having to do with a ghost. **3** *Archaic.* spiritual; religious. **—ghost′li·ness,** *n.*

ghost-write (gōst′rīt′) *v.* **-wrote, -writ·ten, -writ·ing.** write (something) for another who is nominally the author.

ghost writer a person who writes something for another who is nominally the author.

ghoul (gül) *n.* **1** in Oriental stories, a horrible demon, believed to feed on corpses. **2** a person who robs graves or corpses. **3** a person who enjoys what is revolting, brutal, and horrible. [< Arabic < *ghūl* ogre, monster]

ghoul·ish (gül′ish) *adj.* like a ghoul; revolting, brutal, and horrible. **—ghoul′ish·ly,** *adv.* **—ghoul′ish·ness,** *n.*

GHQ General Headquarters.

G.I. or **GI** (jē′ī′) *adj. n.* **G.I.'s, GI's,** or **GIs** (jē′īz′). *U.S.* *—adj.* **1** government issue: *G.I. shoes, G.I. socks.* **2** *Informal.* conforming to regulations; standard: *G.I. uniform.* *—n. Informal.* a soldier. [< the initial letters of the phrase "Government Issue"]

gi·ant (jī′ənt) *n.* **1** an imaginary being having human form, but larger and more powerful than a man. **2** a person or thing of unusual size, strength, importance, etc. *—adj.* like a giant; unusually big and strong; huge. [ME < OF *geant* < L *gigas, gigantis* < Gk.]

gi·ant·ess (jī′ən tis) *n.* a woman giant.

giant panda panda (def. 1).

giant powder an explosive resembling dynamite, used in blasting.

giaour (jour) *n.* a Moslem term for a person who does not believe in the Moslem religion. [< Turkish *giaur* < Persian *gaur*]

gib·ber (jib′ər or gib′ər) *v.* chatter senselessly; talk rapidly and indistinctly: *The monkeys gibbered angrily at each other.* *—n.* senseless chattering; rapid indistinct talking. [imitative] **—Syn.** *v.* babble, prattle.

gib·ber·ish (jib′ər ish or gib′ər ish) *n.* senseless chatter; rapid, indistinct talk; jargon.

gib·bet (jib′it) *n. v.* **-bet·ed, -bet·ing.** *—n.* **1** an upright post with a projecting arm at the top, from which the bodies of criminals were hung after execution. **2** a gallows. *—v.* **1** hang on a gibbet. **2** hold up to public scorn or ridicule. **3** put to death by hanging. [ME < OF *gibet*, dim. of *gibe* club]

gib·bon (gib′ən) *n.* a small, long-armed ape of S.E. Asia and the East Indies. Gibbons live in trees. [< F]

gib·bous (gib′əs) *adj.* **1** curved out; humped. A gibbous moon is more than half full but less than full. See **moon** for picture. **2** humpbacked. [< L *gibbosus* < *gibbus* hump] **—gib′bous·ly,** *adv.* **—gib′bous·ness,** *n.*

gibe or **jibe** (jīb) *v.* **gibed, gib·ing,** *n.* jeer; scoff; sneer. [? < OF *giber* handle roughly < *gibe* staff] **—gib′er,** *n.* **—gib′ing·ly,** *adv.* **—Syn.** *v.* mock, taunt.

gib·let (jib′lit) *n.* Usually, **giblets,** *pl.* the heart, liver, or gizzard of a fowl. [< OF *gibelet* stew of game]

gid·dy (gid′ē) *adj.* **-di·er, -di·est. 1** having a confused, whirling feeling in one's head; dizzy. **2** likely to make dizzy; causing dizziness: *The couples whirled around in their giddy dance.* **3** rarely or never serious; flighty; heedless: *Nobody can tell what that giddy girl will do next.* [OE *gydig* mad, possessed (by an evil spirit) < *god* a god] **—gid′di·ly,** *adv.* **—gid′di·ness,** *n.* **—Syn.** *adj.* **1** light-headed. **3** frivolous, fickle.

gift (gift) *n.* **1** something given; a present: *a Christmas gift.* **2** the act of giving: *The house came to him by gift from an uncle.* **3** the power or right of giving: *The job is within his gift.* **4** a natural ability; special talent: *a gift for painting.* [ME < ON *gipt*. Akin to GIVE.]

Syn. 1 Gift, present = something given. **Gift** is the general word, applying to an object, sum of money, or something like friendship, given or presented to a person, organization, or institution: *The university received a gift of a million dollars.* **Present** always suggests a personal connection between giver and receiver, and applies to something material, often of little monetary value, given a friend, relative, or other person: *We bought a wedding present for Betty.* **4** aptitude.

gift·ed (gif′tid) *adj.* having natural ability or special talent: *a gifted musician.*

gift horse **look a gift horse in the mouth,** question the value of a gift.

gift-wrap (gift′rap′) *v.* **-wrapped, -wrap·ping,** *n.* —*v.* wrap (a parcel, gift, etc.) in fancy paper and with decorative trimmings. —*n.* fancy wrappings suitable for gifts.

gig[1] (gig) *n. v.* **gigged, gig·ging.** —*n.* **1** a light, two-wheeled carriage drawn by one horse. **2** a long, light ship's boat moved by oars or sails. **3** a machine for raising nap on cloth.
—*v.* **1** travel in a gig. **2** raise the nap of (cloth) with a gig. [origin uncertain]

gig[2] (gig) *n. v.* **gigged, gig·ging.** —*n.* a fish spear; harpoon. —*v.* spear (fish) with a gig. [short for *fishgig,* ult. < Sp. *fisga* harpoon]

gi·gan·tic (jī gan′tik) *adj.* **1** like a giant: *Paul Bunyan was a gigantic lumberjack.* **2** huge; enormous: *a gigantic building project.* [< L *gigas, gigantis* giant. See GIANT.] **—gi·gan′ti·cal·ly,** *adv.* —**Syn.** immense, colossal.

gi·gan·tism (jī gan′tiz əm) *n.* **1** abnormal growth or size. **2** in medicine, pathological overdevelopment caused by malfunction of the pituitary gland; acromegaly.

gig·gle (gig′əl) *v.* **-gled, -gling,** *n.* —*v.* laugh in a silly or undignified way. —*n.* a silly or undignified laugh. [imitative] **—gig′gler,** *n.* **—gig′gling·ly,** *adv.*

gig·gly (gig′lē) *adj.* having the habit of giggling.

gig·let (gig′lit) *n.* a flighty, giggly girl.

gig·o·lo (jig′ə lō′) *n.* **-los.** a man who is paid for being a dancing partner or escort for a woman. [< F]

gig·ot (jig′ət) *n.* **1** a leg-of-mutton sleeve. **2** a leg of mutton, veal, etc. [< F]

Gi·la monster (hē′lə) a large, poisonous lizard of Arizona and New Mexico having a short, stumpy tail and a heavy, clumsy body covered with beadlike orange-and-black scales. [after *Gila* River, Arizona]

gild[1] (gild) *v.* **gild·ed** or **gilt, gild·ing. 1** cover with a thin layer of gold or similar material; make golden. **2** make (a thing) look bright and pleasing. **3** make (a thing) seem better than it is. **4 gild the lily, a** adorn something that is beautiful enough not to need adornment; adorn unnecessarily. **b** praise something fine or beautiful excessively or unnecessarily. [OE *gyldan* < *gold* gold]

gild[2] (gild) *n.* guild.

gild·ing (gil′ding) *n.* **1** a thin layer of gold or similar material with which a thing is gilded. **2** the thing gilded.

gil·guy (gil′gī) *n.* **1** in ships, a temporary rope or rigging. **2** a gaudy, useless trinket; gimcrack. [? < *guy*[1]]

gill[1] (gil) *n.* **1** one of the breathing organs of certain animals that live under water: *Fish, tadpoles, and crabs have gills.* **2 gills,** *pl.* **a** the fine, thin leaflike structures on the under side of a mushroom. **b** the flesh under a person's jaws. **c** the red, hanging flesh under the throat of a fowl.
—*v.* **1** catch (fish) by the gills in a gill net. **2** clean (fish). **3** cut away the gills of (a mushroom). [ME < ON; cf. Swedish *gäl*]

gill[2] (jil) *n.* a measure for liquids, equal to one fourth of a pint. [ME < OF *gille* wine measure]

gil·lie (gil′ē) *n.* **1** a man who goes with and helps a hunter or fisherman in the Scottish Highlands. **2** a follower; servant. [< Scots Gaelic *gille* lad]

gill net a net in which fish trying to pass through are caught by their gills.

gill-net (gil′net′) *v.* **-nett·ed, -net·ting.** catch fish by using a gill net.

gill-net·ter (gil′net′ər) *n.* **1** one who uses a gill net. **2** a boat used for gillnetting.

gil·ly (gil′ē) *n.* **-lies.** gillie.

gil·ly·flow·er (jil′ē flou′ər) *n.* any of various flowers that have a spicy fragrance, such as the wallflower, stock, and clove pink. [ME < OF *gilofre* < L < Gk. *karyophyllon* clove tree < *karyon* clove + *phyllon* leaf]

gilt (gilt) *v.* a pt. and a pp. of **gild**[1]. —*adj.* gilded.
—*n.* **1** a thin layer of gold or similar material with which a thing is gilded. **2 gilt on the gingerbread,** an additional adornment to something that is already sufficiently attractive.

gilt-edged (gilt′ejd′) *adj.* **1** having gilded edges. **2** of the very best quality.

gim·bals (jim′bəlz or gim′bəlz) *n.pl.* an arrangement for keeping an object horizontal. A ship's compass is supported on gimbals made of a pair of rings pivoted to swing, one within the other, on axes at right angles to each other. [ult. < OF *gemel* twin < L *gemellus*]

gim·crack (jim′krak′) *n.* a showy, useless trifle. —*adj.* showy but useless. [origin uncertain]

gim·let[1] (gim′lit) *n.* a small tool with a screw point, for boring holes. [ME < OF *guimbelet*]

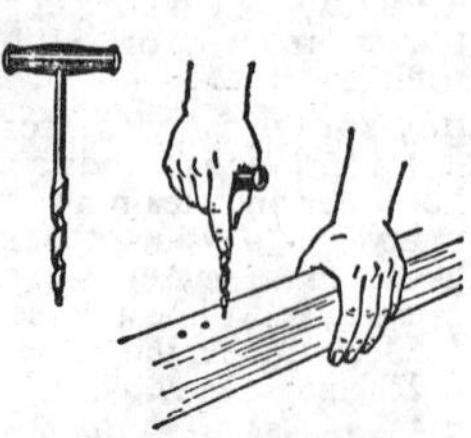
A gimlet[1]. It works like an auger but is used with one hand instead of two.

gim·let[2] (gim′lit) *n.* a cocktail made with vodka or gin, lime-juice, and sugar. [< *gimlet*[1], coined on model of *screwdriver,* another cocktail]

gim·let-eyed (gim′lit īd′) *adj.* having sharp and piercing eyes.

gim·mick (gim′ik) *n.* **1** *Slang.* any small device, especially one used secretly or in a tricky manner. **2** a deceptive thing or quality; trick. **3** something to attract attention; stunt. —*v.* fit with gimmicks or gadgets. [origin uncertain] **—gim′mick·y,** *adj.*

gimp (gimp) *n.* a braidlike trimming made of silk, worsted, or cotton, sometimes stiffened with wire, used on garments, curtains, furniture, etc. [< F *guimpe* < OF < Gmc. Doublet of GUIMPE.]

gin[1] (jin) *n.* a strong, colorless alcoholic drink, made from grain and usually flavored with juniper berries. [shortened form of *geneva* liquor]

gin[2] (jin) *n. v.* **ginned, gin·ning.** —*n.* **1** a machine for separating cotton from its seeds. **2** a trap; snare.
—*v.* **1** separate (cotton) from its seeds. **2** trap; snare. [ME < OF (*en*)*gin* engine] **—gin′ner,** *n.*

gin[3] (jin) *n.* gin rummy.

gin[4] (gin) *v.* **gan, gun, gin·ning.** *Archaic and poetic.* begin. [OE *ginnan,* short for *aginnan,* var. of *onginnan*]

gin·ger (jin′jər) *n.* **1** a spice made from the root of a tropical plant, used for flavoring and in medicine. **2** the root. Ginger is sometimes preserved in syrup and sometimes candied. **3** the plant. **4** *Informal.* liveliness; energy: *That horse has plenty of ginger.* **5** a light, reddish or brownish yellow.
—*adj.* light reddish- or brownish-yellow.
—*v.* **1** treat or flavor with ginger. **2** *Informal.* make spirited or enliven: *The new manager soon gingered up the company.* [OE *gingiber* < LL < L *zingiber* < Gk. *zingiberis* < Prakrit *singabēra* ?< Malayalam *inchi-ver*]

ginger ale a non-alcoholic, bubbling drink flavored with ginger.

ginger beer a drink similar to ginger ale, but made with fermenting ginger.

gin·ger·bread (jin′jər bred′) *n.* **1** a cake flavored with ginger and sweetened with molasses. **2** something showy and elaborate, but not in good taste, such as cheap carvings glued on furniture; tasteless and useless ornamentation of a building. —*adj.* showy; gaudy.

gin·ger·ly (jin′jər lē) *adv. adj.* with extreme care or caution. **—gin′ger·li·ness,** *n.*

gin·ger·snap (jin′jər snap′) *n.* a thin, crisp, cookie flavored with ginger.

gin·ger·y (jin′jər ē) *adj.* **1** like ginger; hot and sharp; spicy. **2** light reddish- or brownish-yellow. **3** alert; full of vigor.

ging·ham (ging′əm) *n.* a cotton cloth made from colored threads. Its patterns are usually in stripes, plaids, or checks. —*adj.* made of gingham. [< F *guingan* < Malay *ginggang*, originally, striped]

gin·gi·val (jin′jə vəl or jin jī′vəl) *adj.* **1** of or having to do with the gums. **2** in phonetics, referring to the ridge behind and above the upper front teeth; alveolar. [< NL *gingivalis* < L *gingiva* gum]

gin·giv·i·tis (jin′jə vī′tis) *n.* inflammation of the gums.

gink·go (ging′kō or jing′kō) *n.* **-goes.** a large, ornamental tree of China and Japan having fan-shaped leaves and edible nuts. [< Japanese]

gin rummy (jin) a kind of rummy in which players form sequences and matching combinations and lay down their hands when having ten or fewer points. [origin uncertain]

gin·seng (jin′seng) *n.* **1** a low plant having a thick, branched root. **2** this root, much used in medicine by the Chinese. [< Chinese *jên shên* (*jên* man, from a frequent shape of the root)]

Gi·o·con·da (jē′ə kon′də; *Italian*, jō kōn′dä) *n.* **La,** a famous portrait usually called the Mona Lisa, painted by Leonardo da Vinci (1452-1519), Italian painter and scientist.

Gip·sy or **gip·sy** (jip′sē) *n.* **-sies,** *adj.* Gypsy.

gipsy moth gypsy moth.

gi·raffe (jə raf′) *n.* a large African mammal having a very long neck and legs and a spotted skin. Giraffes are the tallest of living animals. [< F < Arabic *zarāfah*]

gir·an·dole (jir′ən dōl′) *n.* **1** a decorative branched candlestick. **2** a rotating jet of water. **3** a rotating firework. [< F *girandole* < Ital. *girandola* fireworks circle, dim. of *giranda* fire circle < *girare* turn in a circle < LL *gyrare* turn < Gk. *gyros* ring]

gird[1] (gėrd) *v.* **girt** or **gird·ed, gird·ing. 1** put a belt or girdle around. **2** fasten with a belt or girdle. **3** surround; enclose. **4** get ready for action: *Soldiers gird themselves for battle.* **5** clothe; furnish; endue. [OE *gyrdan*]

gird[2] (gėrd) *v. n.* jeer; sneer; scoff. [origin uncertain]

gird·er (gėr′dər) *n.* a main supporting beam. Steel girders are often used for the framework of bridges and tall buildings. [< *gird*[1]]

gir·dle (gėr′dəl) *n. v.* **-dled, -dling.** —*n.* **1** a belt, sash, cord, etc. worn around the waist. **2** anything that surrounds or encloses: *a girdle of trees around the pond.* **3** a support like a corset worn about the hips or waist. **4** a ring made around a tree trunk, etc. by cutting the bark.
—*v.* **1** form a girdle around; encircle: *Wide roads girdle the city.* **2** cut away the bark so as to make a ring around (a tree, branch, etc.). **3** put a girdle on or around. [OE *gyrdel* < *gyrdan* gird[1]] —**gir′dler,** *n.*

girl (gėrl) *n.* **1** a female child. **2** a young, unmarried woman. **3** a female servant. **4** *Informal.* a sweetheart. **5** *Informal.* a woman of any age. [ME *gurle, girle* child, young person; origin uncertain]

girl Friday a female assistant or aid.

Girl Guide a member of the Girl Guides.

Girl Guides an organization for girls that seeks to develop health and character as well as a knowledge of homemaking.

girl·hood (gėrl′hůd) *n.* the time or condition of being a girl: *The old woman recalled her girlhood with pleasure.*

girl·ie (gėr′lē) *n. Informal.* a little girl.

girl·ish (gėr′lish) *adj.* **1** of a girl. **2** like that of a girl. **3** proper or suitable for girls: *Her mother made her wear girlish clothes.* —**girl′ish·ly,** *adv.* —**girl′ish·ness,** *n.*

Gi·ron·dist (jə ron′dist) *n.* a member of a French political party of moderate republicans from 1791 to 1793.

girt[1] (gėrt) *v.* a pt. and a pp. of **gird**[1].

girt[2] (gėrt) *v.* **1** put a belt, girdle, or girth around; gird. **2** fasten with a belt, girdle, or girth.

girth (gėrth) *n.* **1** the measure around anything: *a man of large girth, the girth of a tree.* **2** a strap or band that keeps a saddle, pack, etc. in place on a horse's back. See **harness** for picture. **3** a girdle.
—*v.* **1** measure in girth. **2** fasten with a strap or band. **3** girdle. [ME < ON *gjörth* girdle. Akin to GIRD[1].]

gist (jist) *n.* the essential part; real point; main idea; substance of a longer statement. [< OF *gist* (it) consists (in), depends (on) < L *jacet* it lies] —**Syn.** essence, pith.

hat, āge, cãre, fär; let, ēqual, tėrm; it, īce
hot, ōpen, ôrder; oil, out; cup, pu̇t, rüle, ūse
əbove, takən, pencəl, lemən, circəs
ch, child; ng, long; sh, ship
th, thin; ᴛʜ, then; zh, measure

git·tern (git′ərn) *n.* an old musical instrument with wire strings, resembling a guitar. [ME < OF *guiterne*]

give (giv) *v.* **gave, giv·en, giv·ing,** *n.* —*v.* **1** hand over as a present: *My brother gave me his watch.* **2** hand over; deliver: *give a person into custody, give one's word. Please give me a drink.* **3** hand over in return for something: *I gave it to him for $5.* **4** let have; cause to have: *Give me permission to leave.* **5** deal; administer: *Some boys give hard blows even in play. He gave the ball a kick.* **6** offer; present: *This newspaper gives a full story of the game.* **7** put forth; make; do; utter: *He gave a cry of pain.* **8** furnish; supply: *give aid to the enemy.* **9** produce; deliver: *give a lecture.* **10** cause; create: *Don't give the teacher any trouble.* **11** relinquish; surrender: *give ground.* **12** yield to pressure or force: *The lock gave when he battered the door.* **13** provide a view or passage; open; lead: *This window gives upon the courtyard.*
give and take, exchange evenly or fairly.
give away, *Informal.* **a** give as a present. **b** give as a bride: *The bride's father gave her away at a wedding ceremony.* **c** cause to become known; reveal; betray: *The spy gave away secrets to the enemy.*
give back, return.
give in, a stop fighting and admit defeat; yield. **b** hand in.
give it to, *Informal.* **a** beat; punish. **b** scold.
give off, send out; put forth.
give or take, add or subtract (a few): *The distance is two miles, give or take a few yards.*
give out, a send out; put forth. **b** distribute. **c** make known. **d** become used up or worn out.
give over, a hand over; deliver. **b** stop.
give up, a hand over; deliver; surrender. **b** stop having or doing. **c** stop trying. **d** have no more hope for. **e** devote entirely: *He gave himself up to his studies.*
—*n.* a yielding to force or pressure; elasticity. [ME *give*(*n*) < *yive*(*n*); initial *g* in ME form influenced by ON *gefa* give] —**giv′er,** *n.*
Syn. *v.* **1 Give, present, confer** = hand over or bestow something as a gift. **Give** is the general word: *He gave me these books.* **Present** = give in a formal way, often with ceremony: *The Board of Trade presented a trophy to the football team.* **Confer** = give in a kindly or courteous way, as to an inferior, or to present as an honor or favor: *She conferred her smiles on the admiring crowd.*

give-and-take (giv′ən tāk′) *n.* **1** an even or fair exchange; mutual concession. **2** good-natured banter; exchange of talk.

give·a·way (giv′ə wā′) *n. Informal.* **1** an unintentional revelation; exposure; betrayal. **2** a radio or television show in which contestants participate and receive prizes. **3** anything given away or sold at a cheap price to promote business, good relations, etc.

giveaway show or **program** giveaway (def. 2).

giv·en (giv′ən) *adj.* **1** stated; fixed; specified: *You must finish the test in a given time.* **2** inclined; disposed; having a fondness or habit: *A conceited person is often given to boasting.* **3** assigned as a basis of calculating, reasoning, etc.: *Given that the radius is 4 ft., find the circumference.* —*v.* pp. of **give.**

given name a name given to a person in addition to his family name. *John* is the given name of *John Smith.*

giz·zard (giz′ərd) *n.* **1** a bird's second stomach, where the food from the first stomach is ground up fine. **2** in insects and earthworms, a muscular organ that is posterior to the crop and serves to grind the food. [ME < OF *giser*, ult. < L *gigeria* cooked entrails of a fowl]

Gk. Greek.

Gl glucinum.

gla·brous (glā′brəs) *adj.* without hair or down; smooth: *Nasturtiums have glabrous stems.* [< L *glaber* smooth]

gla·cé (gla sā′) *adj.* **1** covered with sugar, frosting, or icing. **2** frozen. **3** finished with a glossy surface. [< F *glacé*, pp. of *glacer* impart a gloss to]

gla·cial (glā′shəl) *adj.* 1 of ice or glaciers; having much ice or many glaciers. 2 relating to a glacial epoch or period. 3 made by the pressure and movement of ice or glaciers. 4 like ice; very cold; icy. 5 in chemistry, having an icelike form: *glacial acetic acid.* [< L *glacialis* < *glacies* ice] **—gla′cial·ly,** *adv.*

glacial epoch in geology: 1 any of the times when much of the earth was covered with glaciers. 2 the most recent time when much of the northern hemisphere was covered with glaciers.

glacial period a period that includes the glacial epochs; ice age.

gla·ci·ate (glā′shē āt′) *v.* **-at·ed, -at·ing.** 1 cover with ice or glaciers. 2 act on by ice or glaciers. 3 freeze. **—gla′ci·a′tion,** *n.*

gla·cier (glā′shər or glās′yər) *n.* a large mass of ice formed from snow on high ground wherever winter snowfall exceeds summer melting. It moves very slowly down a mountain or along a valley. [< F *glacier* < *glace* ice < L *glacies*]

gla·ci·o·log·i·cal (glā′shē ə loj′ə kəl or glā′sē ə loj′ə kəl) *adj.* of or having to do with glaciers or glaciology.

gla·ci·ol·o·gist (glā′shē ol′ə jist or glā′sē ol′ə jist) *n.* a specialist in the science of glaciology.

gla·ci·ol·o·gy (glā′shē ol′ə jē or glā′sē ol′ə jē) *n.* the science that deals with glaciers and glaciation. [< F < L *glacies* + E *-logy*]

gla·cis (glā′sis or glas′is) *n.* 1 a gentle slope. 2 in fortification, a bank of earth in front of a counterscarp, having a gradual slope toward the field or open country. [< F *glacis,* originally, slippery place < *glacer* freeze, make icy < *glace* ice]

glad[1] (glad) *adj.* **glad·der, glad·dest.** 1 happy; pleased: *She is glad to be well again.* 2 bringing joy; pleasant: *The glad news made her happy.* 3 bright; gay. [OE *glæd* bright, shining] **—glad′ness,** *n.*

Syn. 1 **Glad, happy** = feeling pleasure or joy. **Glad,** which is not used before the noun when describing people (as distinct from their looks, etc.), particularly suggests feeling contented and filled with pleasure or delight: *She was glad to see him.* **Happy** particularly suggests feeling deeply and fully contented or satisfied and at peace, or filled with joy: *He will never be happy until he has paid all his debts.* 3 joyful, joyous, cheerful, merry.

glad[2] (glad) *n. Informal.* a gladiolus.

glad·den (glad′ən) *v.* make or become glad: *His heart was gladdened by the good news.* **—glad′den·er,** *n.* **—Syn.** enliven, delight. See **cheer.**

glade (glād) *n.* 1 an open space in a wood or forest. 2 a marshy tract of low ground covered with grass. [probably related to GLAD[1]]

glad·i·a·tor (glad′ē ā′tər) *n.* 1 in ancient Rome, a slave, captive, or paid fighter who fought at the public shows. 2 a person who argues, fights, wrestles, etc. with great skill. [< L *gladiator* < *gladius* sword]

glad·i·a·to·ri·al (glad′ē ə tô′rē əl) *adj.* of or having to do with gladiators.

glad·i·o·la (glad′ē ō′lə) *n.* gladiolus.

glad·i·o·lus (glad′ē ō′ləs) *n.* **-li** (-lī or -lē) or **-lus·es.** a kind of iris that grows from bulblike underground stems and has spikes of large, handsome flowers in various colors. [< L *gladiolus,* dim. of *gladius* sword]

glad·ly (glad′lē) *adv.* in a glad manner; cheerfully; with gladness; willingly.

glad rags *Slang.* one's best clothes.

glad·some (glad′səm) *adj.* 1 glad; joyful; cheerful. 2 causing gladness; pleasant; delightful. **—glad′some·ly,** *adv.* **—glad′some·ness,** *n.*

Glad·stone bag (glad′stōn or glad′stən) a travelling bag that opens flat into two equal compartments. [after William Ewart *Gladstone* (1809-1898), a British statesman]

glair (glãr) *n.* 1 the raw white of an egg or any similar viscous substance. 2 a glaze or size made from it. [ME < OF *glaire,* ult. < L *clarus* clear]

glaive (glāv) *n. Archaic.* a sword; broadsword. [ME < OF < L *gladius* sword]

glam·or or **glam·our** (glam′ər) *n.* 1 a mysterious fascination; alluring charm: *The glamor of Hollywood draws many young people there every year. She uses perfume to enhance her glamor.* 2 a magic spell or influence; enchantment. [alteration of *grammar* or its var. *gramarye* occult learning; originally, a spell]

☛ **glamor, glamour.** See -or for usage note.

glam·or·ize (glam′ər īz′) *v.* **-ized, -iz·ing.** make someone or something glamorous. **—glam′or·i·za′tion,** *n.*

glam·or·ous (glam′ər əs or glam′rəs) *adj.* full of glamor; fascinating; charming. **—glam′or·ous·ly,** *adv.*

glam·our (glam′ər) *n.* glamor.

glam·our·ize (glam′ər īz′) *v.* glamorize.

glam·our·ous (glam′ər əs or glam′rəs) *adj.* glamorous.

glance (glans) *n. v.* **glanced, glanc·ing.** *—n.* 1 a quick look. 2 a flash of light; gleam. 3 a glancing off; deflected motion; swift, oblique movement. 4 a passing reference; brief allusion. [< v.]
—v. 1 look quickly; cause to look quickly. 2 flash with light; gleam. 3 hit and go off at a slant: *The spear glanced off his armor and hit the wall.* 4 make a short reference and go on to something else. [var. of ME *glace(n)* strike a glancing blow < OF *glacier* to slip, ult. < L *glacies* ice] **—glanc′ing·ly,** *adv.*

Syn. *n.* 1 **Glance, glimpse** = a quick look. **Glance** applies to a look directed at someone or something: *I gave him only a glance.* **Glimpse** applies to what is seen, a short, quick, imperfect view such as can be seen in a glance: *I caught a glimpse of him as he turned the corner.*

gland (gland) *n.* 1 an organ in the body by which certain substances are separated from the blood and changed into some secretion for use in the body, such as bile, or into a product to be discharged from the body, such as sweat. The liver, the kidneys, the pancreas, and the thyroid are glands. 2 any of various structures similar to glands, such as the lymph nodes. 3 in botany, a secreting organ or structure, generally on or near a surface. [< F *glande* < OF *glandre* < L *glandula,* dim. of *glans, glandis* acorn]

glan·ders (glan′dərz) *n.* a serious contagious disease of horses, mules, etc., accompanied by swellings beneath the lower jaw and a profuse discharge from the nostrils. [< OF *glandre* gland < L *glandula.* See GLAND.]

glan·du·lar (glan′jů lər or glan′dyů lər) *adj.* of or like a gland; having glands; made up of glands. **—glan′du·lar·ly,** *adv.*

glan·du·lous (glan′jů ləs or glan′dyů ləs) *adj.* glandular.

glare[1] (glãr) *n. v.* **glared, glar·ing.** *—n.* 1 a strong, bright light; light that shines so brightly that it hurts the eyes: *The glare from the ice made his eyes sore.* 2 a fierce, angry stare. 3 too great brightness and showiness. [< v.]
—v. 1 give off a strong, bright light; shine so brightly as to hurt the eyes. 2 stare fiercely and angrily: *The angry man glared at his defiant son.* 3 express by a fierce, angry stare. 4 be too bright and showy. [ME *glaren;* cf. OE *glæren* glassy]

glare[2] (glãr) *n.* 1 a bright, smooth surface. 2 **glare ice,** *Cdn.* ice that has a smooth, glassy surface. *—adj.* bright and smooth. [extended use of *glare*[1]]

glar·ing (glãr′ing) *adj.* 1 very bright; shining so brightly that it hurts the eyes; dazzling. 2 staring fiercely and angrily. 3 too bright and showy. 4 very easily seen; conspicuous: *The student made a glaring error in spelling.* **—glar′ing·ly,** *adv.* **—glar′ing·ness,** *n.* **—Syn.** 1 brilliant.

glar·y (glãr′ē) *adj.* glaring.

glass (glas) *n.* 1 a hard, brittle substance that is usually transparent, made by melting sand with soda, potash, lime, or other substances. 2 a drinking vessel made of glass: *He knocked a glass off the table.* 3 *Informal.* a similar container made of plastic, aluminum, etc. 4 the amount that a glass can hold. 5 a glass and its contents. 6 something made of glass. A piece of glass for a picture frame, a windowpane, a mirror, a watch crystal, a lens to correct defective eyesight, a telescope, a thermometer, a barometer, or an hourglass is called a glass. 7 things made of glass. 8 **glasses,** *pl.* **a** a pair of lenses to correct defective eyesight; eyeglasses; spectacles. **b** field glasses; binoculars. 9 **see through rose-colored glasses,** be very, often unduly, optimistic about something.
—v. 1 put glass in; cover or protect with glass. 2 reflect. 3 make or become glassy.
—adj. 1 made of glass. 2 with glass put in it; covered with glass. 3 having to do with glass: *the glass industry.* [OE *glæs*]

glass blower a person who shapes glass by blowing it while it is still hot and soft.

glass blowing the art or process of shaping glass by blowing it while it is still hot and soft.

glass·ful (glas′fu̇l) *n.* **-fuls.** as much as a glass holds.

glass·house (glas′hous′) *n.* a greenhouse; hothouse.

glass·ine (gla sēn′) *n.* a thin, tough, glazed, almost transparent paper, used in packaging.

glass·ware (glas′wãr′) *n.* articles made of glass.

glass wool glass spun in very fine threads, with a texture resembling loose fibres of wool, used for insulation, etc.

glass·work (glas′wėrk′) *n.* **1** the manufacture of glass or glassware. **2** objects or articles made of glass; glassware. **3** the fitting of window glass; glazing.

glass·wort (glas′wėrt′) *n.* a plant having juicy, leafless stems, and growing in salt-water marshes. Its ashes were formerly used as a source of soda in making glass.

glass·y (glas′ē) *adj.* **glass·i·er, glass·i·est. 1** like glass; smooth; easily seen through. **2** having a fixed, stupid stare: *The dazed man's eyes were glassy.* **—glass′i·ly,** *adv.* **—glass′i·ness,** *n.*

Glau·ber's salt (glou′bərz, glo′bərz, or glô′bərz) sodium sulphate, used as a cathartic, etc. [after Johann R. *Glauber* (1604-1668), a German chemist]

glau·co·ma (glo kō′mə, glô kō′mə, or glou kō′mə) *n.* a disease of the eye, characterized by hardening of the eyeball and gradual loss of sight. [< Gk. *glaukoma* < *glaukos* gray]

glau·cous (glo′kəs or glô′kəs) *adj.* **1** light bluish-green. **2** covered with whitish powder as plums and grapes are. [< L *glaucus* < Gk. *glaukos* gray]

glaze (glāz) *v.* **glazed, glaz·ing,** *n.* **—*v.* 1** put glass in; cover with glass. Pieces of glass cut to the right size are used to glaze windows and picture frames. **2** make a smooth, glassy surface or glossy coating on (china, food, etc.). **3** become smooth, glassy, or glossy.
—*n.* 1 a smooth, glassy surface or glossy coating: *the glaze on a china cup, a glaze of ice.* **2** a substance used to make such a surface or coating on things. [ME *glase(n)* < *glas* glass, OE *glæs*] **—glaz′er,** *n.*

gla·zier (glā′zhər or glā′zhē ər) *n.* a person whose work is putting glass in windows, picture frames, etc. [ME *glasier* < *glas* glass, OE *glæs*]

glaz·ing (glāz′ing) *n.* **1** the work of a glazier. **2** glass set or to be set in frames. **3** a substance used to make a smooth, glassy surface or glossy coating on things. **4** such a surface or coating.

gleam (glēm) *n.* **1** a flash or beam of light. **2** a short or faint light. **3** a short appearance; faint show: *After one gleam of hope, they all became discouraged.* **—*v.* 1** flash or beam with light: *A cat's eyes gleam in the dark.* **2** shine with a short or faint light. **3** appear suddenly; be shown briefly. [OE *glǣm*]
Syn. *n.* **1, 2 Gleam, glimmer** = an unsteady or not bright light. **Gleam** applies to a light that comes out of the darkness and disappears soon, or is softened or toned down: *We saw the gleam of headlights through the rain.* **Glimmer** applies to a faint gleam, a light shining feebly or with varying intensity: *We saw the glimmer of a distant light through the trees.*

glean (glēn) *v.* **1** gather (grain) left on a field by reapers. **2** gather little by little or slowly: *glean information.* [ME < OF *glener* < LL *glennare* < Celtic] **—glean′er,** *n.*

glebe (glēb) *n.* **1** *Poetic.* soil; earth; field. **2** a portion of land assigned to a clergyman as part of his living. [< L *gleba*]

glee (glē) *n.* **1** joy; delight; mirth. **2** a song for three or more voices singing different parts, usually without instrumental accompaniment. [OE *glēo*] **—Syn. 1** gaiety, jollity.

glee club a group organized for singing songs.

glee·ful (glē′fəl) *adj.* filled with glee; merry; joyous. **—glee′ful·ly,** *adv.* **—glee′ful·ness,** *n.* **—Syn.** gay.

glee·man (glē′mən) *n.* **-men** (-mən). *Archaic.* a singer; minstrel.

glee·some (glē′səm) *adj.* gleeful.

glen (glen) *n.* a small, narrow valley. [< Scots Gaelic *gle(a)nn*]

hat, āge, cãre, fär; let, ēqual, tėrm; it, īce
hot, ōpen, ôrder; oil, out; cup, pu̇t, rüle, ūse
əbove, takən, pencəl, lemən, circəs
ch, child; ng, long; sh, ship
th, thin; ᴛʜ, then; zh, measure

glen·gar·ry (glen gar′ē) *n.* **-ries.** a Scottish cap with straight sides and a creased top, often having short ribbons at the back. [after *Glengarry*, a valley in Scotland]

A glengarry

glib (glib) *adj.* **glib·ber, glib·best. 1** speaking or spoken smoothly and easily: *The glib salesman sold the woman some dishes she did not really need.* **2** speaking or spoken too smoothly and easily to be sincere: *No one believed his glib excuses.* [short for *glibbery* slippery; cf. Du. *glibberig*] **—glib′ly,** *adv.* **—glib′ness,** *n.* **—Syn. 1** smooth-tongued. See **fluent.**

glide (glīd) *v.* **glid·ed, glid·ing,** *n.* **—*v.* 1** move along smoothly, evenly, and easily. Birds, ships, dancers, and skaters glide. **2** pass gradually, quietly, or imperceptibly: *The years glided past.* **3** of aircraft, come down slowly at a slant without using a motor. Under favorable circumstances, an airplane can glide about a mile for every thousand feet that it is above the ground. **4** in music, pass from one tone to another without a break; slur. **5** in phonetics, produce a glide.
—*n.* 1 a smooth, even, easy movement. **2** of an airplane, a coming down slowly at a slant without using a motor. **3** in music, a slur. **4** in phonetics: **a** a sound made in passing from one speech sound to another, such as the *y* often heard between the *i* and *r* in *hire.* **b** a semivowel. **5** in dancing: **a** a step made by sliding rather than raising the foot. **b** a waltz or other dance using such steps. **6** a metal or plastic attachment under a piece of furniture to make it easy to move. [OE *glīdan*] **—Syn.** *v.* **1** See **slide.**

glid·er (glīd′ər) *n.* **1** a motorless aircraft that is kept in the air by rising air currents. **2** a person or thing that glides.

glim (glim) *n. Slang.* **1** a light; lamp; candle. **2** an eye. [related to GLEAM, GLIMMER]

glim·mer (glim′ər) *n.* **1** a faint, unsteady light. **2** a vague idea; dim notion; faint glimpse. **—*v.* 1** shine with a faint, unsteady light: *The candle glimmered and went out.* **2** appear faintly or dimly. [ME. Related to GLEAM.] **—Syn.** *n.* **1** See **gleam.**

glim·mer·ing (glim′ər ing or glim′ring) *n.* **1** a faint, unsteady light; glimmer. **2** a vague idea; dim notion; faint glimpse.

glimpse (glimps) *n. v.* **glimpsed, glimps·ing. —*n.* 1** a short, quick view: *I caught a glimpse of the falls as our train went by.* **2** a short, faint appearance. **—*v.* 1** catch a short quick view of. **2** look quickly; glance. [ME. Related to GLIM, GLIMMER.] **—Syn.** *n.* **1** See **glance.**

glint (glint) *v. n.* gleam; flash: *His eyes glinted fiercely in the light.* (*v.*) *There was a glint of steel as the man swung his axe.* (*n.*) [cf. dial. Swedish *glinta*]

glis·sade (gli sad′ or gli säd′) *n. v.* **-sad·ed, -sad·ing. —*n.* 1** in ballet, a gliding step, often ending in a leap. **2** a sliding down any smooth, sloping surface. **—*v.*** perform a glissade; slide. [< F *glissade* < *glisser* slide]

glis·san·do (gli sän′dō) *adj. n.* **-di** (dē). in music: **—*adj.*** performed with a gliding effect. A pianist plays a glissando passage by running the fingers rapidly over the keys. **—*n.* 1** a gliding effect. **2** a glissando passage. [in imitation of Italian, < F *glissant*, ppr. of *glisser* slide]

glis·ten (glis′ən) *v. n.* sparkle; shine. [OE *glisnian*]

glis·ter (glis′tər) *v. n. Archaic.* glisten; glitter; sparkle. [? < *glisten*; cf. MDu. *glisteren*]

glit·ter (glit′ər) *v.* **1** glisten, sparkle; shine with a bright, sparkling light: *Jewels and new coins glitter.* **2** be bright and showy. **3** become covered with ice after a freezing rain. **—*n.* 1** a bright, sparkling light. **2** brightness; showiness; a bright display. **3** the bright, sparkling ice that forms on everything outdoors after a rain that freezes. [ME < ON *glitra*] **—glit′ter·er,** *n.* **—Syn.** *n.* **1** See **flash.**

glit·ter·y (glit′ər ē) *adj.* glittering.

gloam·ing (glōm′ing) *n.* evening twilight; dusk. [OE *glōmung* < *glōm* twilight; influenced by *glow*]

gloat (glōt) *v.* gaze intently; ponder with pleasure; stare: *The miser gloated over his gold.* [cf. ON *glotta* smile scornfully] **—gloat′er,** *n.* **—gloat′ing·ly,** *adv.*

glob·al (glōb′əl) *adj.* **1** of the earth as a whole; world-wide: *the threat of global war.* **2** shaped like a globe. **—glob′al·ly,** *adv.*

glo·bate (glō′bāt) *adj.* shaped like a globe.

globe (glōb) *n. v.* **globed, glob·ing.** *—n.* **1** anything round like a ball; sphere. **2** the earth; world. **3** a sphere with a map of the earth or sky on it. **4** anything rounded like a globe. An electric light bulb is a globe. *—v.* gather or form into a globe. [< F < L *globus*] **—Syn.** *n.* **1** See **ball. 2** See **earth.**

globe·fish (glōb′fish′) *n.* **-fish** or **-fish·es.** a tropical fish that when disturbed can inflate itself into a ball-shaped form.

globe·flow·er (glōb′flou′ər) *n.* a plant of the same family as the buttercup, having globe-shaped, yellow flowers.

globe·trot·ter (glōb′trot′ər) *n.* a person who travels widely over the world for the purpose of sightseeing.

globe·trot·ting (glōb′trot′ing) *n.* travelling widely throughout the world, especially as a tourist.

glo·bose (glō′bōs or glō bōs′) *adj.* globular. [< L *globosus* < *globus* globe]

glob·u·lar (glob′yù lər) *adj.* **1** shaped like a globe or globule; round; spherical. **2** consisting of globules. **—glob′u·lar·ly,** *adv.*

glob·ule (glob′yùl) *n.* a very small ball; tiny drop: *globules of sweat.* [< F < L *globulus,* dim. of *globus* globe]

glob·u·lin (glob′yù lin) *n.* in biochemistry, any of a group of proteins, found in plant and animal tissues, that are soluble in weak salt solutions but insoluble in water.

glock·en·spiel (glok′ən spēl′) *n.* a musical instrument consisting of a series of small, tuned bells, metal bars, or tubes mounted in a frame and struck by two little hammers. [< G *Glockenspiel* < *Glocke* bell + *Spiel* play]

glom·er·ate (glom′ər it) *adj.* clustered together; collected into a rounded mass. [< L *glomeratus,* pp. of *glomerare* < *glomus, -meris* ball]

glom·er·ule (glom′ər ül′) *n.* any compact cluster. [< NL *glomerulus,* dim. of L *glomus* ball]

gloom (glüm) *n.* **1** deep shadow; darkness; dimness. **2** low spirits; sadness. **3** a dejected or sad look. [< *gloomy*] *—v.* **1** be or become dark, dim, or dismal. **2** be in low spirits; feel miserable. **3** look sad or dismal. [ME *gloume(n)* look sullen, lower[2]] —**Syn.** *n.* **1** obscurity, shade. **2** despondency, dejection, depression, melancholy.

gloom·y (glüm′ē) *adj.* **gloom·i·er, gloom·i·est. 1** dark; dim. **2** in low spirits; sad; melancholy. **3** causing low spirits; discouraging; dismal. [< *gloom,* v.] **—gloom′i·ly,** *adv.* **—gloom′i·ness,** *n.* **—Syn. 1** shadowy, sombre. **2** dejected, downhearted.

glo·ri·a (glô′rē ə) *n.* **1** a Christian song of praise to God, or its musical setting. **2 Gloria,** one of three Christian songs of praise to God, beginning "Glory be to God on high," "Glory be to the Father," and "Glory be to Thee, O Lord." **3** a halo. **4** a fabric made of silk and some other material, used for umbrellas. [< L]

glo·ri·fi·ca·tion (glô′rə fə kā′shən) *n.* **1** a glorifying. **2** a being glorified. **3** *Informal.* a celebration; festivity.

glo·ri·fy (glô′rə fī′) *v.* **-fied, -fy·ing. 1** give glory to; make glorious. **2** praise; honor; worship. **3** make more beautiful or splendid. **4** exalt to the glory of heaven. [ME < OF *glorifier* < L *glorifieare* < *gloria* glory + *facere* make] **—glo′ri·fi′er,** *n.*

glo·ri·ous (glô′rē əs) *adj.* **1** having or deserving glory; illustrious. **2** giving glory: *Our army won a glorious victory.* **3** magnificent; splendid. **4** admirable; delightful; fine: *have a glorious time. Isn't it a glorious day?* [ME < AF < L *gloriosus* < *gloria* glory] **—glo′ri·ous·ly,** *adv.* **—Syn. 1** famous, renowned. **3** brilliant.

glo·ry (glô′rē) *n.* **-ries,** *v.* **-ried, -ry·ing.** *—n.* **1** great praise and honor; fame; renown. **2** that which brings praise and honor; a source of pride and joy. **3** adoring praise and thanksgiving. **4** radiant beauty; brightness; magnificence; splendor. **5** a condition of magnificence, splendor, or greatest prosperity. **6** the splendor and bliss of heaven; heaven. **7** a halo. **8 go to glory,** die. **9 in one's glory,** *Informal.* in a state of greatest satisfaction or enjoyment: *He's in his glory with a dish of ice cream.* *—v.* be proud; rejoice: *The mother gloried in the success of her son.* [ME < OF *glorie* < L *gloria*] **—Syn.** *n.* **1** distinction.

gloss[1] (glos) *n.* **1** a smooth, shiny surface; lustre: *Varnished furniture has a gloss.* **2** an outward appearance or surface that covers faults underneath. *—v.* **1** put a smooth, shiny surface on. **2 gloss over,** explain away (faults, errors, etc.): *He wished to gloss over the errors in his essay.* [cf. ON *glossi* flame] **—Syn.** *n.* **1** sheen, polish.

gloss[2] (glos) *n.* **1** an explanation; comment. **2** a glossary. **3** a translation inserted between the lines of a text printed in a foreign language. *—v.* comment on; explain. [< L < Gk. *glōssa,* literally, tongue] **—gloss′er,** *n.*

glos·sar·i·al (glo sãr′ē əl) *adj.* having to do with a glossary; like a glossary.

glos·sa·ry (glos′ə rē) *n.* **-ries.** a list of special, technical, or difficult words with explanations or comments: *a glossary to Shakespeare's plays, a glossary of terms used in chemistry. Textbooks sometimes have glossaries at the end.* [< L *glossarium* < *glossa.* See GLOSS[2].]

gloss·y (glos′ē) *adj.* **gloss·i·er, gloss·i·est,** *n.* *—adj.* smooth and shiny. *—n. Informal.* a photograph printed on glossy paper. **—gloss′i·ly,** *adv.* **—gloss′i·ness,** *n.* **—Syn.** lustrous, polished, sleek.

glot·tal (glot′əl) *adj.* **1** of the glottis. **2** in phonetics, produced in the glottis. *H* in *hope* is often a glottal sound.

glot·tis (glot′is) *n.* the opening in the upper part of the windpipe, between the vocal cords. [< NL < Gk. *glōttis,* ult. < *glōtta* tongue]

glove (gluv) *n. v.* **gloved, glov·ing.** *—n.* **1** a covering for the hand, usually having separate places for each of the four fingers and the thumb. **2** a boxing glove. **3 fit like a glove,** fit perfectly or tightly. **4 handle with kid gloves,** treat gently. **5 handle without gloves,** treat roughly. *—v.* **1** cover with a glove; provide with gloves. **2** serve as a glove for. [OE *glōf*] **—glove′less,** *adj.*

glov·er (gluv′ər) *n.* a person who makes or sells gloves.

glow (glō) *n.* **1** the shine from something that is red-hot or white-hot. **2** any similar shine. **3** brightness: *the glow of sunset.* **4** a warm feeling or color of the body: *the glow of health on his cheeks.* **5** an eager look on the face: *a glow of interest or excitement.* [< v.] *—v.* **1** shine as if red-hot or white-hot. **2** show a warm color; be red or bright. **3** be hot; burn. **4** be eager or animated. [OE *glōwan*]

glow·er (glou′ər) *v.* stare angrily; scowl: *The fighters glowered at each other.* *—n.* an angry or sullen look. [? < obs. *glow,* v., stare] **—glow′er·ing·ly,** *adv.*

glow·ing (glō′ing) *adj.* **1** shining from something that is red-hot or white-hot. **2** bright: *glowing colors.* **3** showing a warm color: *glowing cheeks.* **4** eager; animated: *a glowing description.* **—glow′ing·ly,** *adv.*

glow-worm (glō′wėrm′) *n.* any insect larva or worm-like insect that glows in the dark. Fireflies develop from glow-worms.

glox·in·i·a (glok sin′ē ə) *n.* a tropical American plant having large, white, red, or purple, bell-shaped flowers, frequently cultivated as a house plant. [< NL; after Benjamin P. *Gloxin,* a German botanist]

gloze (glōz) *v.* **glozed, gloz·ing. 1** smooth over; explain away: *His friends glozed over his faults.* **2** talk speciously or flatteringly. **3** *Obsolete.* make glosses upon. [ME < OF *gloser* < *glose* < L *glossa.* See GLOSS.[2]]

glu·cin·i·um (glü sin′ē əm) *n.* glucinum.

glu·ci·num (glü sī′nəm) *n.* beryllium. *Symbol:* Gl [< NL < Gk. *glykys* sweet]

glu·cose (glü′kōs) *n.* **1** a kind of sugar occurring in fruits. It is about half as sweet as cane sugar. *Formula:* $C_6H_{12}O_6$ **2** a syrup made from starch. [< F < Gk. *glykys* sweet]

glue (glü) *n. v.* **glued, glu·ing.** —*n.* **1** a substance used to stick things together, often made by boiling the hoofs, skins, and bones of animals in water. **2** any similar sticky substance. —*v.* **1** stick together with glue. **2** fasten tightly; attach firmly: *During the ride down the mountain his hands were glued to the steering wheel.* **3** regard or look at fixedly: *He walked on, his eyes glued to the road.* [ME < OF *glu* < LL *glus, glutis*] —**glu′er,** *n.*

glue·y (glü′ē) *adj.* **glu·i·er, glu·i·est. 1** like glue; sticky. **2** full of glue; smeared with glue.

glum (glum) *adj.* **glum·mer, glum·mest.** gloomy; dismal; sullen: *a glum look.* [cf. LG *glum* turbid, muddy. Akin to GLOOM.] —**glum′ly,** *adv.* —**Syn.** See **sullen.**

glut (glut) *v.* **glut·ted, glut·ting,** *n.* —*v.* **1** fill full; feed or satisfy fully: *Years of war had glutted his appetite for adventure.* **2** fill too full; supply too much for: *The prices for wheat dropped when the market was glutted with it.* —*n.* **1** a full supply; great quantity. **2** too great a supply. [< obs. *glut,* n., glutton < OF]

glu·tam·ic acid (glü tam′ik) a white crystalline amino acid obtained from proteins. *Formula:* $C_5H_9NO_4$ [*gluten* + *amide* + *-ic*]

glu·ta·mine (glü′tə mēn′ or glü′tə min) *n.* a crystalline amine derived from glutamic acid. *Formula:* $C_5H_{10}N_2O_3$ [< *glutam*ic acid + *-ine*[2]]

glu·ten (glü′tən) *n.* a tough, sticky substance that remains in flour when the starch is taken out. [< L *gluten* glue]

glu·te·nous (glü′tə nəs) *adj.* **1** like gluten. **2** containing much gluten.

glu·ti·nous (glü′tə nəs) *adj.* sticky. —**glu′ti·nous·ly,** *adv.* —**glu′ti·nous·ness,** *n.*

glut·ton[1] (glut′ən) *n.* **1** a greedy eater; a person who eats too much. **2** a person who never seems to have enough of something: *That boxer is a glutton for punishment.* [ME < OF *glouton* < L *glutto*]

glut·ton[2] (glut′ən) *n.* a clumsy, heavily built mammal of northern regions; wolverine. [translation of G *Vielfrass,* literally, great eater, by popular etymology from Swedish *fjällfräs* mountain cat]

glut·ton·ous (glut′ən əs) *adj.* **1** greedy about food; having the habit of eating too much. **2** greedy. —**glut′ton·ous·ly,** *adv.* —**glut′ton·ous·ness,** *n.*

glut·ton·y (glut′ən ē) *n.* **-ton·ies.** greediness about food; the habit of eating too much.

glyc·er·in (glis′ər in) *n.* a colorless, syrupy, sweet liquid obtained from fats and oils, used in ointments, lotions, antifreeze solutions, explosives, etc. *Formula:* $C_3H_8O_3$ [< F *glycérine* < Gk. *glykeros* sweet]

glyc·er·ine (glis′ər in or glis′ər ēn′) *n.* glycerin.

glyc·er·ol (glis′ər ōl′ or glis′ər ol′) *n.* glycerin.

gly·co·gen (glī′kə jən) *n.* a starchlike substance in the liver and other animal tissues that is changed into glucose when needed. [< Gk. *glykys* sweet + E *-gen*]

gly·col (glī′kol or glī′kōl) *n.* in chemistry: **1** a colorless liquid obtained from certain ethylene compounds and used as an antifreeze, solvent, etc. *Formula:* $C_2H_6O_2$ **2** any of a similar group of alcohols. [< *glyc*erin + *-ol*]

gm. gram; grams.

G.M. George Medal.

G-man (jē′man′) *n.* **-men** (-men′). *U.S. Informal.* a special agent of the United States Department of Justice; an agent of the FBI. [for *Government man*]

Gmc. Germanic.

G.M.T. or **GMT** Greenwich mean time.

gnarl (närl) *n.* a knot in wood; hard, rough lump. Wood with gnarls is hard to cut. —*v.* make knotted and rugged like an old tree; contort; twist. [< *gnarled*]

gnarled (närld) *adj.* covered with knots or hard, rough lumps; knotted; twisted; rugged: *The farmer's gnarled hands grasped the plough firmly.* [var. of *knurled*]

gnash (nash) *v.* **1** strike or grind (the teeth) together; grind together. **2** bite by gnashing the teeth. [var. of ME *gnast,* apparently < ON *gnastan* a gnashing]

gnat (nat) *n.* **1** any of various small, two-winged insects or flies. Most gnats are bloodsucking and make bites that itch. **2 strain at a gnat,** object to some small or very trifling thing. [OE *gnætt*] —**gnat′like′,** *adj.*

gnaw (no or nô) *v.* **gnawed, gnawed** or **gnawn, gnaw·ing. 1** bite at and wear away. **2** make by biting: *A rat gnaws a hole.* **3** wear away; consume; corrode. **4** torment. [OE *gnagan*] —**gnaw′er,** *n.* —**gnaw′ing·ly,** *adv.*

gnawn (non or nôn) *v.* a pp. of **gnaw.**

gneiss (nīs) *n.* a metamorphic rock composed of quartz, feldspar, and mica or hornblende. It is distinguished from granite by its layered structure. [< G]

gnome (nōm) *n.* **1** in folklore, a dwarf supposed to live underground and guard treasures of precious metals and stones. **2** an odd-looking, dwarfish person: *a little gnome of a man.* [< F < NL *gnomus;* invented by Paracelsus (16th c.)]

gno·mic (nō′mik or nom′ik) *adj.* full of maxims or instructive sayings; aphoristic; sententious. [< Gk. *gnōmikos* < *gnōmē* judgment, opinion]

gno·mon (nō′mon) *n.* **1** a rod, pointer, or triangular piece on a sundial, etc. that shows the time of day by casting its shadow on a marked surface. **2** in geometry, what is left of a parallelogram after a similar parallelogram has been taken away at one corner. [< Gk. *gnōmōn* indicator < *gignōskein* know]

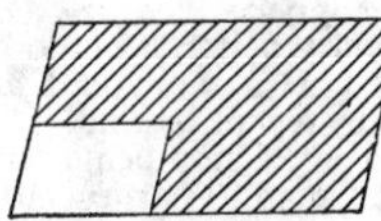
The shaded area is a gnomon (def. 2).

gno·mon·ic (nō mon′ik) *adj.* **1** of or having to do with a gnomon or sundial. **2** having to do with the measuring of time, etc. by a sundial.

gnos·tic (nos′tik) *adj.* of, having to do with, or possessing knowledge, especially of spiritual things. [< *Gnostic*]

Gnos·tic (nos′tik) *n.* a believer in Gnosticism. —*adj.* of Gnosticism or Gnostics. [< Gk. *gnōstikos* of knowledge < *gignōskein* know]

Gnos·ti·cism (nos′tə siz′əm) *n.* a mystical religious and philosophical doctrine of pre-Christian and early Christian times.

GNP gross national product.

gnu (nū or nü) *n.* **gnu** or **gnus.** a large, African antelope having an oxlike head, curved horns, and a long tail; wildebeest. [< Hottentot]

go (gō) *v.* **went, gone, go·ing,** *n.* **goes.** —*v.* **1** move along: *Go straight home.* **2** move away; leave: *It is time for us to go.* **3** be in motion; act; work; run: *Does your watch go well?* **4** get to be; become: *go mad.* **5** be habitually; be: *go hungry.* **6** proceed; advance: *go to Edmonton.* **7** attend on a regular basis: *He goes to the vocational school.* **8** be current: *A rumor went through the town.* **9** be known: *She went under a false name.* **10** put oneself: *Don't go to any trouble for me.* **11** extend; reach: *His memory does not go back that far.* **12** pass: *The summer holidays go quickly.* **13** be given: *First prize goes to the winner.* **14** be sold: *The painting goes to the highest bidder.* **15** tend; lead: *This goes to show that you must work harder.* **16** turn out; have a certain result: *How did the game go?* **17** have its place; belong: *This book goes on the top shelf.* **18** make a certain sound: *The cork went "Pop!"* **19** have certain words; be said: *How does that poem go?* **20** refer; appeal: *go to court.* **21** stop being; be given up, used up, or lost: *His eyesight is going.* **22** die: *His wife went first.* **23** break down; give way: *The engine in the old car finally went.* **24** *Informal.* put up with; stand: *I can't go tea.*

as people or **things go,** considering how others are.

go about, a be busy at; work on. **b** move from place to place. **c** turn around; change direction.

go ahead, a continue; proceed: *He went ahead with his plan.* **b** advance or improve one's position.

go all out, strive to the utmost extent.

go along, agree; co-operate.

go around, a move from place to place. **b be enough to** give some to all.

go at, attack.
go back on, *Informal.* not be faithful or loyal to.
go behind, investigate the real or hidden reasons for.
go by, a pass. **b** be guided by; follow. **c** be controlled by. **d** be known by.
go down, a descend; decline; sink. **b** be defeated; lose. **c** lose violence; subside: *The wind went down in the evening.* **d** be accepted by: *His motion did not go down with the assembly.* **e** in contract bridge, fail to fulfill one's contract.
go for, *Informal.* **a** try to get. **b** favor; support. **c** be attracted to. **d** attack.
go in for, *Informal.* try to do; take part in; spend time and energy at.
go into, a be contained in. **b** investigate.
go in with, join; share with.
go it, *Informal.* go fast.
go it alone, act without assistance; act independently or solely.
go off, a leave; depart. **b** be fired; explode. **c** lose quality; deteriorate. **d** take place; happen.
go on, a go ahead; go forward. **b** manage. **c** behave. **d** happen: *What goes on here?*
go one better, a outdo or excel to some extent in quality or fitness of action. **b** accept a bet and offer to increase it by a unit in kind.
go out, a stop being; end. **b** stop burning: *Let the fire go out.* **c** go to parties, etc. **d** give sympathy. **e** go on strike. **f** cease to be fashionable. **g** in golf, play the first nine holes of a course.
go over, *Informal.* **a** look at carefully. **b** do again. **c** read again. **d** succeed. **e** change sides, political party, etc. **f** *Slang.* beat up.
go through, a go to the end of; do all. **b** undergo; experience. **c** search. **d** be accepted or approved. **e** exhaust as a fortune: *He soon went through his inheritance.*
go through with, complete; carry out to the end.
go together, keep steady company: *John and Mary have been going together all this year; in fact, they consider themselves engaged.*
go under, a be overwhelmed or sunk. **b** be ruined; fail.
go up, a ascend; rise. **b** increase. **c** be built; be raised: *New houses are going up quickly. The curtain goes up at 7 p.m.*
go with, a accompany. **b** keep company with. **c** be in harmony with: *That tie doesn't go with your suit.*
go without, do without the thing stated or implied.
let go, a allow to escape. **b** give up one's hold. **c** give up. **d** fail to keep in good condition.
let oneself go, a give way to one's feelings or desires. **b** fail to keep oneself in good condition.
—*n.* **1** the act of going. **2** *Informal.* spirit; energy. **3** *Informal.* the state of affairs; way things are. **4** *Informal.* a fashion; style; rage. **5** *Informal.* a try; attempt; chance. **6** something successful. **7** *Informal.* a bargain; anything agreed on: *It's a go.* **8 no go,** *Informal.* not to be done or had; impossible; useless; worthless. **9 on the go,** *Informal.* always moving or acting.
—*adj. Slang.* in the launching of space capsules, missiles, etc., in perfect order and ready to proceed; A-one: *All systems are go.* [OE *gān*] —**go′er,** *n.*
Syn. *v.* **2 Go, leave** = move away from a point or place. **Go,** the opposite of *come,* emphasizes the movement involved: *He comes and goes as he pleases.* **Leave** emphasizes the departure from the place where one is (or has been): *He has left home. The boat left yesterday.*
☛ **Go and** is an informal way of emphasizing a verb: *Go and try it yourself* (no actual movement meant). *She went and shot the bear herself.* Sometimes the speaker implies that the action was ill-advised: *He went and bought a cheap used car.* These are primarily colloquial expressions, but they would be appropriate in some informal writing.

go·a (gō′ə) *n.* an antelope of the Tibetan plateau. [< Tibetan *dgoba*]

goad (gōd) *n.* **1** a sharp-pointed stick for driving cattle, etc.; gad. **2** anything that drives or urges one on.
—*v.* drive or urge on; act as a goad to: *Hunger goaded him to steal a loaf of bread.* [OE *gād*] —**Syn.** *v.* stimulate, spur, impel.

go-a·head (gō′ə hed′) *Informal. n.* **1** the action of going forward; ambition; spirit. **2** authority to proceed.
—*adj.* **1** disposed to push ahead; ambitious. **2** giving authority to proceed: *a go-ahead signal.*

goal (gōl) *n.* **1** in certain games: **a** the space between two posts into which a player tries to shoot a puck, kick a ball, etc. in order to score. **b** the act of scoring in such a manner. **c** the point or points counted for scoring a goal. **2** the finish line of a race. **3** a goalkeeper. **4** something for which an effort is made; something wanted; one's aim or object in doing something: *His goal was to be a great doctor.* **5 play goals,** *Informal.* be the goalkeeper. [ME *gol*; origin uncertain] —**goal′-less,** *adj.*

goal·er (gōl′ər) *n.* goalie.

goal·ie (gōl′ē) *n.* in hockey, lacrosse, etc., the player who guards the goal to prevent scoring; goalkeeper.

goal·keep·er (gōl′kēp′ər) *n.* goalie.

goal line the line marking the goal in a game.

goal-mouth (gōl′mouth′) *n.* in soccer, hockey, etc., the area just in front of the goal.

goal post in football, lacrosse, hockey, etc., one of a pair of posts with a bar across them, forming a goal.

goal tender goalie.

goat (gōt) *n.* **goat** or **goats. 1** a cud-chewing mammal having hollow horns and long, usually straight, hair, closely related to the sheep. Goats are stronger, less timid, and more active than sheep. **2** *Slang.* a person made to take the blame or suffer for the mistakes of others; scapegoat. **3 Goat,** in astrology, the tenth sign of the zodiac; Capricorn. **4 get one's goat,** *Slang.* make a person angry or annoyed; tease him. [OE *gāt*] —**goat′like′,** *adj.*

goat·ee (gō tē′) *n.* a pointed beard on a man's chin.

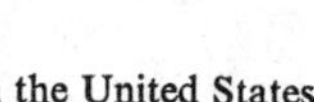
A goatee

goat·herd (gōt′hėrd′) *n.* a person who tends goats.

goat·skin (gōt′skin′) *n.* **1** the skin of a goat. **2** the leather made from the skin of goats: *a goatskin bag.*

goat·suck·er (gōt′suk′ər) *n.* a bird having a flat head, wide mouth, and long wings, that flies at night and feeds on flying insects. A whip-poor-will is a goatsucker.

gob[1] (gob) *n. U.S. Slang.* a sailor in the United States navy. [origin uncertain]

gob[2] (gob) *n. Informal.* a lump; mass. [apparently < OF *gobe*]

gob·bet (gob′it) *n.* a lump; mass. [ME < OF *gobet,* dim. of *gobe* gob[2]]

gob·ble[1] (gob′əl) *v.* **-bled, -bling. 1** eat fast and greedily; swallow quickly in big pieces. **2 gobble up,** *Informal.* **a** seize upon eagerly. **b** devour; eat away; eat up. [< *gob*[2]] —**Syn. 1** gulp, bolt, devour.

gob·ble[2] (gob′əl) *v.* **-bled, -bling,** *n.* —*v.* make the throaty sound that a male turkey does. —*n.* the throaty sound that a turkey makes. [imitative]

gob·ble·dy·gook or **gob·ble·de·gook** (gob′əl dē gůk′) *n. Informal.* speech or writing that is unnecessarily complicated or involved: *Official documents are often full of gobbledygook.* [coined by Maury Maverick, U.S. Congressman, in 1944]

gob·bler (gob′lər) *n.* a male turkey.

Gob·e·lin (gob′ə lin) *adj.* **1** made at the factory of the Gobelins in Paris: *Gobelin tapestry or upholstery.* **2** of or having to do with such tapestry or upholstery.

go-be·tween (gō′bi twēn′) *n.* a person who goes back and forth between people with messages, proposals, suggestions, etc.; intermediary.

gob·let (gob′lit) *n.* **1** a drinking glass with a base and stem. **2** *Archaic.* a hollow dish to drink from, usually without a handle. [ME < OF *gobelet,* dim. of *gobel* cup]

A goblet

gob·lin (gob′lən) *n.* a mischievous elf in the form of an ugly dwarf. [ME < MF *gobelin* ? < MHG *kobold* sprite]

go·by (gō′bē) *n.* **-by** or **-bies.** a bony fish living near seacoasts. The ventral fins of gobies are united to form a cup-shaped suction pad with which they cling to rocks. [< L *gobius, cobius,* a kind of fish < Gk. *kōbios*]

go-by (gō′ bī′) *n. Informal.* a going by or casting off; a slight; intentional neglect: *He gave her the go-by.*

hat, āge, cãre, fär; let, ēqual, tėrm; it, īce
hot, ōpen, ôrder; oil, out; cup, pu̇t, rüle, ūse
əbove, takən, pencəl, lemən, circəs
ch, child; ng, long; sh, ship
th, thin; ᴛʜ, then; zh, measure

go·cart or **go-cart** (gō′kärt′) *n.* **1** a low seat on wheels to take a small child around on. **2** a small framework with casters in which children sometimes learn to walk. **3** a light carriage. **4** go-kart.

god (god) *n.* **1** a being thought of as superior to nature and to human beings and considered worthy of worship. **2** a male god. **3** an image of a god; idol. **4** any person or thing worshipped like a god. [OE]

God (god) *n.* in the Christian, Jewish, Moslem, and certain other religions, the creator and ruler of the world; Supreme Being.

god·child (god′chīld′) *n.* **-chil·dren.** a child for whom an adult takes vows at its baptism.

god·daugh·ter (god′do′tər or -dô′tər) *n.* a female godchild.

god·dess (god′is) *n.* **1** a female god. **2** a very beautiful or charming woman.

go-devil (gō′dev′əl) *n.* **1** in mining and lumbering, a type of sleigh used to move ore, logs, etc. **2** a stoneboat or drag. **3** a device flushed through a pipeline to clean the inside of the pipe.

god·fa·ther (god′fo′ᴛʜər) *n.* a man who takes vows for a child when it is baptized.

god·for·sak·en (god′fər sāk′ən) *adj.* **1** Often, **Godforsaken.** apparently forsaken by God. **2** completely given over to evil; totally depraved. **3** desolate; wretched.

God-giv·en (god′giv′ən) *adj.* **1** given by God. **2** very welcome and suitable.

God·head (god′hed′) *n.* **1** God. **2 godhead,** divine nature; divinity.

god·hood (god′hu̇d) *n.* divine character; divinity.

god·less (god′lis) *adj.* **1** not believing in God; not religious. **2** wicked; evil. **—god′less·ly,** *adv.* **—god′less·ness,** *n.* **—Syn. 1** ungodly, impious.

god·like (god′līk′) *adj.* **1** like God or a god; divine. **2** suitable for God or a god.

god·ly (god′lē) *adj.* **-li·er, -li·est. 1** obeying God's laws; religious; pious; devout. **2** *Archaic.* of or from God; divine. **—god′li·ness,** *n.*

god·moth·er (god′muᴛʜ′ər) *n.* a woman who takes vows for a child when it is baptized.

god·par·ent (god′pãr′ənt) *n.* a godfather or godmother.

God's acre a churchyard with graves in it; a burial ground; cemetery.

god·send (god′send′) *n.* something unexpected and very welcome, as if sent from God.

god·ship (god′ship) *n.* the character of a god; divinity.

god·son (god′sun′) *n.* a male godchild.

God·speed (god′spēd′) *n.* a wish of success to a person starting on a journey or undertaking.

god·wit (god′wit) *n.* a wading bird resembling a snipe, having a long bill and slender legs. [origin uncertain]

goe·thite or **go·thite** (gō′tīt or gœ′tīt) *n.* a mineral consisting of a hydrous oxide of iron. [< Johann W. von *Goethe,* 1749-1832, German writer, noted also for studies in mineralogy]

go-get·ter (gō′get′ər) *n. Slang.* an aggressive person who tries hard for, and usually gets, what he wants.

gog·gle (gog′əl) *n. v.* **-gled, -gling,** *adj.* **—***n.* Usually, **goggles,** *pl.* a pair of large, close-fitting spectacles to protect the eyes from light, dust, etc.: *He wore goggles while welding the broken steel rod.* [< v.]
—*v.* **1** roll one's eyes; stare with bulging eyes. **2** roll; bulge: *The children's eyes goggled as the magician pulled a rabbit out of the empty hat.* **3** be goggle-eyed with surprise, wonder, or disbelief.
—*adj.* rolling; bulging: *A frog has goggle eyes.* [ME *gogel(en)*; origin uncertain]

gog·gle-eyed (gog′əl īd′) *adj.* having rolling, bulging, or staring eyes.

Goid·el (goi′dəl) *n.* **1** any member of the Gaelic branch of the Celts. **2** a speaker of a Goidelic language.

Goid·el·ic (goi del′ik) *adj.* **1** of or having to do with the Goidels. **2** of, having to do with, or denoting the Celtic language group to which Scots Gaelic, Irish, and Manx belong. **—***n.* one of the two main divisions of the Celtic language (the other being *Brythonic*), including Scots Gaelic, Irish, and Manx.

go·ing (gō′ing) *n.* **1** a going away; leaving: *His going was sudden.* **2** the condition of the ground or road for walking, riding, etc.: *The going is bad on a muddy road.*
—*adj.* **1** moving; acting; working; running: *The clock is going.* **2** that goes; that can or will go. **3** in existence; existing; to be had; current or prevalent: *the going price for gold.* **4 be going to,** will; be about to. **5 going on,** almost; nearly: *It is going on four o'clock.*

going concern a company, store, etc. that is doing good business.

go·ings on (gō′ingz) actions; behavior; conduct: *There were some strange goings on at the party.*

go·ing-o·ver (gō′ing ō′vər) *n.* **1** *Informal.* a thorough study; intense and critical examination. **2** *Slang.* **a** a scolding. **b** a beating.

goi·tre or **goi·ter** (goi′tər) *n.* **1** a disease of the thyroid gland, which often produces a large swelling in the neck, usually caused by iodine deficiency. **2** the swelling itself. [< F *goitre,* ult. < L *guttur* throat]

go-kart (gō′kärt′) *n.* a small four-wheeled racing vehicle that consists of a bare chassis and a low-powered engine.

Gol·con·da (gol kon′də) *n.* a mine or source of wealth. [after an ancient city in S. India, famed for its wealth and for its diamond cutting]

gold (gōld) *n.* **1** a shiny, bright-yellow, precious metallic chemical element, used for making coins and jewellery. *Symbol*: Au (for L *aurum*); *at.no.* 79; *at.wt.* 196.967. **2** coins made of gold. **3** money in large sums; wealth; riches. **4** a bright, beautiful, or precious thing or material: *Wheat is prairie gold.* **5** a bright yellow.
—*adj.* **1** made of gold. **2** of or like gold. **3** bright-yellow. [OE]

gold·beat·er (gōld′bēt′ər) *n.* a person whose work is beating gold into very thin sheets.

gold brick *Informal.* anything that looks good at first, but turns out to be worthless.

gold-brick (gōld′brik′) *Slang.* **—***v.* **1** swindle, as by means of a gold brick. **2** pretend illness to avoid duties.
—*n.* a person, especially in the armed forces, who avoids duty or shirks work. **—gold′-brick′er,** *n.*

gold digger 1 a person who digs for or mines gold. **2** *Slang.* a woman who is interested in men for what she can get out of them.

gold dust very tiny bits of gold; gold in a fine powder.

gold·en (gōl′dən) *adj.* **1** made or consisting of gold. **2** containing or yielding gold. **3** shining like gold; bright-yellow. **4** very good; most excellent; extremely favorable, valuable, or important: *a golden opportunity.* **5** resembling gold in value; most excellent, important, or precious: *golden deeds.* **6** very happy and prosperous; flourishing. **7** having to do with the fiftieth year or event in a series: *a golden wedding anniversary.*

Golden Age 1 in classical mythology, the first age of mankind, an era of idyllic peace, prosperity, and happiness. **2** a legendary and imaginary age, long past, of perfect human happiness and innocence. **3 golden age,** the finest or most flourishing period.

golden calf 1 in the Bible, an idol made of gold, set up by the Israelites in the wilderness. **2** wealth too highly esteemed.

golden eagle a large eagle having dark-brown feathers on the back of its neck.

gold·en·eye (gōl′dən ī′) *n.* **-eye** or **-eyes.** a diving duck with black and white feathers, found in northern regions.

Golden Fleece 1 in Greek legend, a fleece of gold taken from a ram, and guarded by a dragon until Jason and the Argonauts carried it away with the help of Medea. **2** an order of knighthood that existed in Spain and Austria, founded in 1430 by Philip, Duke of Burgundy.

golden glow a tall plant having globe-shaped yellow flowers.

golden mean the avoidance of extremes; a safe, sensible way of doing things; moderation.

golden retriever 1 a breed of dog of medium size, having a golden, water-resistant coat and used in hunting to retrieve game, especially waterfowl. 2 a dog of this breed.

gold·en·rod (gōl′dən rod′) *n.* a plant of the aster family that blooms in the autumn and has many small, yellow flowers on tall, branching stalks.

golden rule a rule of conduct common to most great religions, set forth by Jesus as: "As ye would that men should do to you, do ye also to them likewise." Luke 6:31.

golden wedding the 50th anniversary of a wedding.

gold·eye (gōld′ī′) *n.* **-eye** or **-eyes.** *Cdn.* an edible freshwater fish that is native to rivers and lakes from Ontario to the Northwest Territories. Goldeye is smoked and dyed for marketing as a table delicacy.

gold-filled (gōld′fild′) *adj.* made of cheap metal covered with a layer of gold.

gold·finch (gōld′finch′) *n.* 1 a small American songbird. The male is yellow marked with black. 2 a European songbird having yellow on its wings. [OE *goldfinc*]

gold·fish (gōld′fish′) *n.* **-fish** or **-fish·es.** a small, reddish-golden fish. Goldfish are often kept in garden pools or glass bowls.

gold·i·locks (gōl′dē loks′) *n.* 1 a person with yellow hair. 2 a plant having many small, yellow flowers.

gold leaf gold beaten into very thin sheets.

gold mine 1 a mine where ore yielding gold is obtained. 2 the source of something of great value: *His special knowledge made him a gold mine of information. His real-estate business is a gold mine.*

gold rush a sudden rush of people to a place where gold has just been found.

gold·smith (gōld′smith′) *n.* a man whose work is making articles of gold. [OE]

gold standard the use of gold as the standard of value for the money of a country. The nation's unit of money value is declared by the government to be equal to and exchangeable for a certain amount of gold.

golf (golf) *n.* an outdoor game played with a small, hard ball and a set of long-handled clubs having wooden or iron heads. The player tries to drive his ball into each of a number of holes with as few strokes as possible. —*v.* play the game of golf: *He golfs every Saturday.* [origin uncertain] —**golf′er,** *n.*

golf club 1 a long-handled club having a wooden or iron head, used in playing golf. 2 a group of people joined together for the purpose of playing golf. 3 the buildings, land, etc. used by such a group.

golf course a place where golf is played, having tees, greens, and fairway.

golf links golf course.

Gol·go·tha (gol′gə thə or gol goth′ə) *n.* 1 the place of Christ's crucifixion; Calvary. 2 a place of burial. [< Gk. < Aramaic *gūlgūlthā* place of skulls < Hebrew]

Go·li·ath (gə lī′əth) *n.* 1 in the Bible, a giant whom David killed with a stone from a sling. I Sam. 17:4-51. 2 any huge, extremely strong man.

go·losh (gə losh′) *n.* galosh.

Go·mor·rah or **Go·mor·rha** (gə môr′ə) *n.* 1 in the Bible, a wicked city destroyed, together with Sodom, by fire from heaven. Gen. 18 and 19. 2 any extremely wicked place.

gon·ad (gō′nad or gon′ad) *n.* an organ in which reproductive cells develop. Ovaries and testes are gonads. [< NL < Gk. *gonē* seed < *gignesthai* be produced]

gon·do·la (gon′də lə) *n.* 1 a long, narrow boat with a high peak at each end, used on the canals of Venice. 2 a large flat-bottomed river boat with pointed ends. 3 a freight car that has low sides and no top. 4 a car that hangs under a dirigible and holds the motors, passengers, etc. 5 a broadcasting booth built up near the roof of a hockey arena. 6 a car that hangs from and moves along a cable: *We went up the mountain in the gondola.* [< dial. Ital. *gondola* < *gondolar* to rock]

A gondola (def. 1)

gon·do·lier (gon′də lēr′) *n.* a man who rows or poles a gondola. [< F < Ital. *gondoliere* < *gondola* gondola]

gone (gon) *adj.* 1 moved away; left. 2 lost: *a gone case.* 3 dead. 4 used up. 5 failed; ruined. 6 weak; faint: *a gone feeling.* 7 *Slang.* a very good; great: *the gone blues sung by Bessie Smith.* b that carries strong feeling; transported; inspired: *a gone look on his face, gone music.* 8 **far gone,** much advanced; deeply involved. 9 **gone on,** *Informal.* in love with. —*v.* pp. of **go.**

gon·er (gon′ər) *n. Informal.* a person or thing that is dead, ruined, past help, etc.

gon·fa·lon (gon′fə lən) *n.* a flag or banner hung from a crossbar instead of a pole, often having several streamers. Gonfalons were used by medieval Italian republics. [< Ital. *gonfalone,* ult. < OHG *gundfano,* literally, war banner]

gong (gong) *n.* 1 in music, a metal disk with a turned-up rim, which makes a loud noise when struck. 2 a bell shaped like a shallow bowl or saucer. [< Malay]

gon·or·rhe·a or **gon·or·rhoe·a** (gon′ə rē′ə) *n.* a contagious venereal disease that causes inflammation of the genital, urinary, and certain other organs. [< LL < Gk. *gonorrhoia* < *gonos* seed + *rhoia* flow]

goo (gü) *n. Slang.* any thick, sticky substance. [origin uncertain] —**goo′ey,** *adj.*

good (gůd) *adj.* **bet·ter, best,** *n. interj.* —*adj.* 1 having the right qualities; admirable; desirable: *a good book, a good game.* 2 as it ought to be; right; proper: *Do what seems good to you.* 3 well-behaved: *a good boy.* 4 kind; friendly: *Say a good word for me.* 5 benevolent; gracious: *a good king.* 6 honorable; worthy: *my good friend.* 7 reliable; dependable: *good judgment.* 8 real; genuine: *It is hard to tell counterfeit money from good money.* 9 agreeable; pleasant: *Have a good time.* 10 beneficial; advantageous; useful: *drugs good for a fever.* 11 well-suited to its purpose: *A craftsman insists on good tools.* 12 satisfying; enough; full: *a good meal.* 13 skilful; clever: *a good manager, be good at arithmetic.* 14 fairly great; more than a little: *a good while.* **15 as good as,** almost the same as; almost; practically. **16 feel good,** *Informal.* feel well or elated. **17 good for,** a able to do, live, or last. b able to pay. c worth: *a coupon good for a free ride.* **18 make good,** a make up for; give or do in place of; pay for. b carry out; fulfil. c succeed in doing. d succeed. e prove. —*n.* 1 benefit; advantage; use: *work for the common good.* 2 that which is good: *He always looked for the good in people.* 3 a good thing. 4 good people. **5 for good** or **for good and all,** forever; finally; permanently. **6 to the good,** on the side of profit or advantage; in one's favor. —*interj.* that is good! [OE *gōd*]

☛ **good, well.** Careful speakers maintain the distinction between *good* and *well,* using the former as adjective only.

Good Book the Bible.

good-by (gůd′bī′) *interj. n.* **-bys.** good-bye.

good-bye (gůd′bī′) *interj. n.* **-byes.** farewell. [contraction of *God be with ye*]

good cheer 1 feasting and merrymaking. 2 good food. 3 courage.

good day a form of greeting or farewell said in the daytime.

good deal 1 much; many. 2 a favorable business transaction. 3 *Slang.* very good.

good evening a form of greeting or farewell said in the evening.

good-for-noth·ing (gůd′fər nuth′ing) *adj.* worthless; useless. —*n.* a person who is worthless or useless.

Good Friday the Friday before Easter, observed by Christians in commemoration of Christ's crucifixion.

good-heart·ed (gůd′här′tid) *adj.* kind and generous. —**good′-heart′ed·ly,** *adv.* —**good′heart′ed·ness,** *n.*

good humor or **good humour** a cheerful, pleasant disposition or mood.

good-hu·mored or **good-hu·moured** (gůd′hū′mərd or gůd′ū′mərd) *adj.* cheerful; pleasant. —**good′-**

hu′mored·ly or **good′-hu′moured·ly,** *adv.* **—good′-hu′mored·ness** or **good′-hu′moured·ness,** *n.*

good·ish (gůd′ish) *adj.* **1** pretty good. **2** fairly great; considerable.

good-look·er (gůd′lůk′ər) *adj. Informal.* a person or animal of attractive or handsome appearance.

good-look·ing (gůd′lůk′ing) *adj.* having a pleasing appearance; handsome.

good looks a handsome or pleasing personal appearance.

good·ly (gůd′lē) *adj.* **-li·er, -li·est. 1** considerable: *a goodly quantity.* **2** *Archaic.* **a** excellent; fine: *a goodly land.* **b** good-looking: *a goodly youth.* **—good′li·ness,** *n.*

good·man (gůd′mən) *n.* **-men** (-mən). *Archaic.* **1** the master of a household; husband. **2** a title for a man ranking below a gentleman: *Goodman Brown.*

good morning a form of greeting or farewell said in the morning.

good nature pleasant or kindly disposition; amiability.

good-na·tured (gůd′nā′chərd) *adj.* pleasant; kindly; cheerful; agreeable. **—good′-na′tured·ly,** *adv.* **—good′-na′tured·ness,** *n.*

good·ness (gůd′nis) *n.* **1** the quality or state of being good. **2** excellence; virtue. **3** kindness; friendliness. **4** the valuable quality; best part.
—interj. an exclamation of surprise.
Syn. *n.* **2 Goodness, virtue** = excellence in character. **Goodness** applies to the inner quality in a person that makes him kind, generous, fair, sympathetic, and otherwise acceptable in character and conduct: *His goodness is shown by the many kind deeds he does.* **Virtue** applies to moral excellence that is acquired by consciously developing particular qualities of character, such as moral courage, justice, wise judgment, etc., or by consciously following the principles of right and wrong: *He is a man of the highest virtue.*

good night a form of farewell said at night.

goods (gůdz) *n.pl.* **1** personal property; belongings. **2** things for sale; wares. **3** material for clothing; cloth. **4** *Slang.* what is needed to do something. **5** *Brit.* freight. **6 catch with the goods, a** catch with stolen goods. **b** catch in the act of committing a crime. **7 deliver the goods,** *Slang.* do what is expected or wanted. **8 get** or **have the goods on,** *Slang.* find out or know something bad about. **—Syn. 1** See **property.**

Good Samaritan 1 in the Bible, a traveller who rescued and cared for another traveller who had been beaten and robbed by thieves. Luke 10:30-37. **2** any person who is unselfish in helping others.

good-sized (gůd′sīzd′) *adj.* large; fairly large.

good speed a farewell expressing a wish for success or good luck.

goods train *Brit.* freight train.

good-tem·pered (gůd′tem′pərd) *adj.* easy to get along with; cheerful; agreeable. **—good′-tem′pered·ly,** *adv.*

good turn a kind or friendly act; favor.

good·wife (gůd′wīf′) *n.* **-wives.** *Archaic.* **1** the mistress of a household. **2** a title for a woman ranking below a lady: *Goodwife Brown.*

good will 1 a kindly or friendly feeling. **2** cheerful consent; willingness. **3** the reputation and steady trade that a business has with its customers. **—Syn. 1** See **favor.**

good·y[1] (gůd′ē) *n.* **good·ies,** *interj. adj. Informal.* *—n.* something very good to eat; a piece of candy or cake. *—interj.* an exclamation of pleasure. *—adj.* making too much of being good; good in a weak way. [< *good*]

good·y[2] (gůd′ē) *n.* **good·ies.** an old woman of humble station. [var. of *goodwife*]

good·y-good·y (gůd′ē gůd′ē) *adj. n.* **-good·ies.** *—adj.* making too much of being good; good in a weak way. *—n.* a person who makes too much of being good.

goof (güf) *Slang. n.* **1** a stupid or foolish person. **2** a blunder; an obvious or careless error. *—v.* **1** make a mistake; blunder. **2** fumble; make a complete hash of (an undertaking, deal, etc.). **3 goof off,** *Slang.* waste time; loaf; shirk work or duty. [apparently < dial. var. of earlier *goff* dunce]

goof·ball (güf′bol′ or -bôl′) *n. Slang.* **1** a barbiturate pill, especially one taken with alcohol. **2** an odd, peculiar, or crazy person.

goo·gol (gü′gəl) *n.* one followed by a hundred zeros; 10^{100}. [coined by Dr. Edward Kasner (1878-1955), an American mathematician, on the basis of a child's word for a very large number]

hat, āge, cãre, fär; let, ēqual, tėrm; it, īce
hot, ōpen, ôrder; oil, out; cup, půt, rüle, ūse
əbove, takən, pencəl, lemən, circəs
ch, child; ng, long; sh, ship
th, thin; ᴛʜ, then; zh, measure

goo·gol·plex (gü′gəl pleks′) *n.* one followed by googol zeros; $10^{10^{100}}$.

goon (gün) *n. Slang.* **1** a ruffian hired to disrupt labor disputes. **2** a stupid person. [from semihuman characters in a comic strip of the 1930's]

goose (güs) *n.* **geese** *for 1-4,* **goos·es** *for 5.* **1** a wild or tame web-footed swimming bird resembling a duck, but larger and having a longer neck. **2** the female of this bird. A male goose is called a gander. **3** the flesh of this bird used as food. **4** a silly person: *What a goose you are!* **5** a tailor's smoothing iron that has a long, curved handle like a goose's neck. **6 cook someone's goose,** ruin someone's reputation, plan, chances, etc. **7 The goose hangs high.** All is well. Prospects are good. [OE *gōs*] **—goose′like′,** *adj.*

goose·ber·ry (güs′ber′ē or güz′-) *n.* **-ries. 1** a small, sour berry some varieties of which are bristly or spiny, used to make pies, tarts, jam, etc. **2** the thorny bush that this berry grows on. [? alteration of F *groseille* + E *berry*]

goose flesh skin that has become rough like that of a plucked goose, from cold or fright.

goose·foot (güs′fůt′) *n.* **-foots.** a plant having coarse leaves, clusters of very small flowers, and dry, seedlike fruits. Beets and spinach are goosefoots.

goose·herd (güs′hėrd′) *n.* a person who tends geese.

goose·neck (güs′nek′) *n.* anything long and curved like a goose's neck, such as an iron hook, a movable support for a lamp, or a curved, connecting pipe.

goose pimples goose flesh.

goose step a marching step in which the leg is swung high with straight, stiff knee.

goose-step (güs′step′) *v.* **-stepped, -step·ping.** march with a goose step.

go·pher (gō′fər) *n.* **1** a burrowing rodent having large cheek pouches. **2** a ground squirrel. [< N.Am.F *gaufre,* literally, honeycomb; with reference to burrowing]

Gor·di·an knot (gôr′dē ən) **1** a knot tied by Gordius, King of Phrygia, to be undone only by the person who should rule Asia. Alexander the Great cut the knot after failing to untie it. **2** an intricate or baffling problem. **3 cut the Gordian knot,** solve a perplexity or vexing problem by some quick and drastic means.

Gor·don setter (gôr′dən) **1** a breed of setter having a black coat with tan or red markings. **2** a dog of this breed. [< 4th Duke of *Gordon,* who maintained hunting kennels]

gore[1] (gôr) *n.* blood that is shed; thick blood; clotted blood: *The battlefield was covered with gore.* [OE *gor* dirt, dung]

gore[2] (gôr) *v.* **gored, gor·ing.** wound with a horn or tusk: *The savage bull gored the farmer to death.* [ME *gorre(n)*; origin uncertain]

gore[3] (gôr) *n. v.* **gored, gor·ing.** *—n.* **1** a tapering or triangular piece of cloth put or made in a skirt, sail, etc. to give greater width or change the shape. **2** *Cdn.* an unassigned tract of land remaining after the surveying and marking out of a township into lots.
—v. put or make a gore in. [OE *gāra* point < *gār* spear]

gorge (gôrj) *n. v.* **gorged, gorg·ing.** *—n.* **1** a deep, narrow valley, usually steep and rocky. **2** a gorging; gluttonous meal. **3** the contents of a stomach. **4** a feeling of disgust, indignation, resentment, etc. **5** a narrow rear entrance from a fort into an outwork or outer part. **6** a mass stopping up a narrow passage: *An ice gorge blocked the river.* **7** *Archaic.* the throat; gullet.
—v. **1** eat greedily until full; stuff with food. **2** fill full; stuff. [ME < OF *gorge* throat, ult. < LL *gurges* throat, jaws < L *gurges* abyss, whirlpool] **—gorg′er,** *n.*

gor·geous (gôr′jəs) *adj.* richly colored; splendid: *a gorgeous sunset.* [< OF *gorgias* fashionable, with reference to the ruff for the throat < *gorge* throat. See GORGE.] —**gor′geous·ly,** *adv.* —**gor′geous·ness,** *n.* —**Syn.** magnificent.

gor·get (gôr′jit) *n.* **1** a piece of armor for the throat. See **armor** for picture. **2** a covering for the neck and breast, formerly worn by women. [< OF *gorgete,* dim. of *gorge.* See GORGE.]

Gor·gon (gôr′gən) *n.* **1** in Greek legend, any of three horrible sisters who had snakes for hair and whose look turned the beholder to stone. Medusa is the best-known of the three Gorgons. **2 gorgon,** any very ugly or terrible woman. [< L *Gorgo, -onis* < Gk. *Gorgō* < *gorgos* terrible]

Gor·gon·zo·la (gôr′gən zō′lə) *n.* a strong, white Italian cheese that looks and tastes much like Roquefort cheese. [< *Gorgonzola,* a town in Italy]

go·ril·la (gə ril′ə) *n.* **1** a very large, fierce, powerful manlike ape of Africa. **2** *Slang.* a strong and brutal man. [< NL < Gk. < W. African word, according to a traveller in the 5th century B.C.]

gor·mand (gôr′mənd) *n.* gourmand.

gor·mand·ize (gôr′mən dīz′) *v.* **-ized, -iz·ing.** stuff oneself with food; eat very greedily; gorge. [originally n., < F *gourmandise* gluttony] —**gor′mand·iz′er,** *n.*

gorse (gôrs) *n.* furze. [OE *gorst*]

gor·y (gôr′ē) *adj.* **gor·i·er, gor·i·est. 1** bloody. **2** characterized by violence, bloodshed, etc. —**gor′i·ly,** *adv.* —**gor′i·ness,** *n.*

gosh (gosh) *interj.* **1** an exclamation or mild oath. **2 by gosh,** by God. [euphemism for *God*]

gos·hawk (gos′hok′ or -hôk′) *n.* a powerful short-winged hawk, formerly much used in falconry. [OE *gōshafoc* < *gōs* goose + *hafoc* hawk]

Go·shen (gō′shən) *n.* **1** in the Bible, a fertile part of Egypt where the Israelites were permitted to live. Exod. 8:20-22. **2** a land of plenty and comfort.

gos·ling (goz′ling) *n.* a young goose.

go-slow (gō′slō′) *n. Informal.* **1** a change, development, etc. that progresses at a slow pace. **2** a deliberate slowing down of the rate of work, production, etc.; slowdown.

gos·pel (gos′pəl) *n.* **1** the teachings of Jesus and the Apostles. **2** Usually, **Gospel. a** any one of the first four books of the New Testament, by Matthew, Mark, Luke, and John. **b** a part of one of these books read during a religious service. **3** *Informal.* anything earnestly believed or taken as a guide for action. **4** the absolute truth. [OE *gōdspel* good tidings (i.e., of the Nativity) < *gōd* good + *spel* spell[2]]

gos·sa·mer (gos′ə mər or goz′ə mər) *n.* **1** a film or thread of cobweb. **2** a very thin, light cloth. **3** a thin, light, waterproof cloth or coat. **4** anything very light and thin.
—*adj.* like gossamer; very light and thin; filmy. [ME *gossomer* goose summer, name for Indian summer, the season for goose and cobwebs]

gos·san (gos′ən or goz′ən) *n.* in mining, decomposed rock that often indicates an ore-bearing vein, because of its rusty-red color resulting from oxidized iron pyrites. [< Cornish *gossen* < *gōs* blood]

gos·sip (gos′ip) *n. v.* **-siped, -sip·ing.** —*n.* **1** idle talk, not always truthful, about people and their affairs. **2** a person who gossips a good deal. **3** *Archaic.* a friend. **4** *Archaic.* a godparent.
—*v.* repeat what one knows, or the idle talk that one hears, about people and their affairs. [OE *godsibb,* originally, godparent < *god* God + *sibb* relative] —**gos′sip·er,** *n.* —**Syn.** *n.* **1** tattle.

gos·sip·mon·ger (gos′ip mung′gər or -mong′gər) *n.* a person who spreads gossip.

gos·sip·y (gos′ip ē) *adj.* **1** fond of gossip. **2** full of gossip.

gos·soon (go sün′) *n. Archaic.* **1** a boy. **2** a male servant. [an Irish alteration of F *garçon*

got (got) *v.* a pt. and a pp. of **get.**

☛ **Got** is frequently used as a way of intensifying *have* in the sense of "possess" or "be obligated": *Have you got a pencil? I've got to study now.* However, this usage is inappropriate in formal English. See also gotten.

Go·ta·ma (go′tə mə or gô′tə mə) *n.* Gautama or Buddha.

Goth (goth) *n.* **1** a member of a Teutonic tribe that overran the Roman Empire in the third, fourth, and fifth centuries A.D. The Goths settled in S. and E. Europe. **2** an uncivilized person; barbarian. [ME < LL *Gothi,* pl.]

Goth·ic (goth′ik) *n.* **1** in architecture, a style characterized by pointed arches and high, steep roofs, developed in W. Europe during the Middle Ages. **2** the language of the Goths. **3** in printing, a kind of type. **This sentence is in Gothic.**
—*adj.* **1** of Gothic architecture. **2** of the Goths or their language. **3** uncivilized; crude; barbarous. **4** medieval. **5** of or having to do with a type of literature that emphasizes the supernatural and the grotesque, usually having a medieval setting. [< LL *Gothicus*]

got·ten (got′ən) *v.* a pp. of **get.**

☛ **Gotten** is frequent in North America for *got* (pp.), the British form. Usage varies, however, according to sentence rhythm and individual habit: *He could have gotten* (or *got*) *here by now. In the past I have gotten* (or *got*) *a good meal here.*

gouache (gwäsh) *n.* **1** a method of painting with opaque water colors obtained by mixing pigments with water and gum. **2** a color made in this way. **3** a painting using this medium. [< F *gouache* < Ital. *guazzo* water colors, mire; earlier, watering place < L *aquatio* watering place]

Gou·da (gou′də or gü′də) *n.* a mild, yellow cheese made in Holland. [< *Gouda,* a city in the Netherlands]

gouge (gouj) *n. v.* **gouged, goug·ing.** —*n.* **1** a chisel with a curved blade used for cutting round grooves or holes in wood. **2** a groove or hole made by gouging. **3** *Informal.* a cutting with or as if with a gouge. **4** *Informal.* a trick; cheat; swindle.
—*v.* **1** cut with a gouge. **2** dig out; tear out; force out. **3** *Informal.* trick; cheat; swindle. [< F < LL *gulbia*] —**goug′er,** *n.*

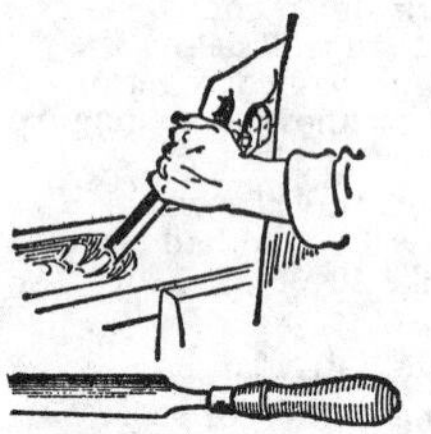

A gouge

Gourds

gou·lash (gü′lash) *n.* a stew made of beef or veal and vegetables, usually highly seasoned. [< Hungarian *gulyás* (*hús*) herdsman's (meat)]

gou·ra·mi (gůr′ə mē or gů rä′mē) *n.* **-mis. 1** a large edible fresh-water fish of S. E. Asia. **2** any of various much smaller but related fish, bred for home aquariums. [< Malay *gurami*]

gourd (gôrd or gůrd) *n.* **1** the hard-shelled fruit of certain vines. Gourds are dried and hollowed out to be used as cups, bowls, etc. **2** the vine that gourds grow on. **3** a bowl, bottle, etc. made from the dried shell of a gourd. **4** any plant of the family to which cucumbers, pumpkins, and muskmelons belong. [ME < F *gourde* < OF *cohorde* < L *cucurbita*]

gourde (gürd) *n.* **1** a unit of money in Haiti. See table at **money. 2** a coin worth one gourde. [< F]

gour·mand (gür′mənd) *n.* **1** a person who is fond of good eating. **2** a person who is greedy; glutton. Also, **gormand.** [< F *gourmand* gluttonous < *gourmet* gourmet]

gour·met (gür′mā) *n.* a person who is expert in judging and choosing fine foods, wines, etc.; epicure. [< F < OF *gourmet, groumet* wine taster < *gromet* servant]

gout (gout) *n.* **1** a painful disease of the joints, often characterized by a painful swelling of the big toe. **2** a drop; splash; clot: *gouts of blood.* [ME < OF *goute* < L *gutta* a drop, with reference to the medieval theory of the flow of body humors]

goût (gü) *n. French.* taste.

gout·y (gout′ē) *adj.* **gout·i·er, gout·i·est. 1** diseased or swollen with gout. **2** of gout; caused by gout. **3** causing gout. —**gout′i·ly,** *adv.* —**gout′i·ness,** *n.*

Gov. or **gov. 1** governor. **2** government.

gov·ern (guv′ərn) *n.* **1** rule; control; manage. **2** exercise a directing or restraining influence over; determine: *the motives governing a person's decision.* **3** hold back; restrain; check. **4** be a rule or law for: *the principles governing a case.* **5** in grammar, require (a word) to be in a certain case, number, or mood; require (a certain case, number, or mood). [ME < OF *governer* < L *gubernare* < Gk. *kybernaein* steer] —**gov′ern·a·ble,** *adj.* —**Syn. 1** direct, conduct. See **rule. 3** curb, bridle.

gov·ern·ance (guv′ər nəns) *n.* government; rule; control.

gov·ern·ess (guv′ər nis) *n.* a woman who teaches children in a private house.

gov·ern·ment (guv′ərn mənt or guv′ər mənt) *n.* **1** the rule or authority over a country, province, district, etc.; direction of the affairs of state. **2** the person or persons ruling a country, state, district, etc.; administration. **3** a system of ruling: *Canada has a democratic government.* **4** the country, province, district, etc. ruled. **5** rule; control. **6** in grammar, the relationship by which one word determines the case, number, or mood of another depending on it.

gov·ern·men·tal (guv′ərn men′təl or guv′ər men′təl) *adj.* of or having to do with government. —**gov′ern·men′tal·ly,** *adv.*

Government House 1 the official residence of the Governor General in Ottawa, also known as Rideau Hall. **2** in some provinces, the official residence of the Lieutenant-Governor.

gov·er·nor (guv′ər nər) *n.* **1** the appointed ruler of a colony; the representative of a monarch in a colony. **2** an official appointed to govern a province, city, fort, etc. **3** in the United States, an official elected as the executive head of a state. **4** a person who manages or directs a club, society, institution, etc. A club often has a board of governors. **5** an automatic device that controls the supply of steam, gas, etc. and keeps a machine going at a certain speed. [ME < OF *governeor* < L *gubernator* steersman]

governor general *pl.* **governors general. 1** a governor who has subordinate or deputy governors under him. **2 Governor General, a** in Canada, the representative of the Crown, appointed on the advice of the Prime Minister for a term of five years. **b** the representative of the Crown in certain other independent countries of the British Commonwealth.

gov·er·nor·ship (guv′ər nər ship′ or guv′nər ship′) *n.* the position or term of office of governor.

Govt. or **govt.** government.

gow·an (gou′ən) *n. Scottish.* the wild daisy. [< dial. *gowlan,* var. of *golding* gold-colored]

gown (goun) *n.* **1** a woman's dress, especially a formal or evening dress. **2** a loose outer garment. Judges, clergymen, members of a university, and students graduating from college wear gowns to show their position, profession, etc. **3** a nightgown or dressing gown. **4** the members of a university: *arguments between town and gown.* —*v.* put a gown on; dress in a gown. [ME < OF *goune* < LL *gunna*] —**gown′less,** *adj.*

The gown of a college graduate

gowns·man (gounz′mən) *n.* **-men** (-mən). **1** a person such as a lawyer or clergyman who wears a gown as a mark of his profession. **2** a member of a university; wearer of an academic gown.

goy (goi) *n.* **goy·im.** *Yiddish. Derogatory.* **1** a non-Jew; gentile. **2** a Jew who does not observe the law. [originally < Hebrew]

gp. *pl.* **gps.** group.

G.P. in medicine, General Practitioner.

GPM, gpm, or **g.p.m.** gallons per minute.

G.P.O. General Post Office.

gr. 1 gram; grams. **2** grain; grains. **3** gross. **4** grade. **5** grammar. **6** group. **7** great.

Gr. 1 Greek. **2** Grecian. **3** Greece.

G.R. King George. (for L *Georgius Rex*)

grab (grab) *v.* **grabbed, grab·bing,** *n.* —*v.* **1** seize suddenly; snatch: *The dog grabbed the meat and ran.* **2** take possession of in an unscrupulous manner: *grab land.* **3** *Informal.* capture; arrest: *The police grabbed the robbers after a long chase.* **4** get or take in a hurry: *grab a sandwich.*
—*n.* **1** a snatching; a sudden seizing. **2** that which is grabbed. **3** a mechanical device for firmly holding something that is to be lifted or raised. [cf. MDu. *grabben*] —**grab′ber,** *n.*

hat, āge, cãre, fär; let, ēqual, tėrm; it, īce
hot, ōpen, ôrder; oil, out; cup, pu̇t, rüle, ūse
əbove, takən, pencəl, lemən, circəs
ch, child; ng, long; sh, ship
th, thin; ᴛʜ, then; zh, measure

grab bag 1 a bag or other receptacle filled with an assortment of articles, one of which may be selected, sight unseen, by a person paying a certain price. **2** *Informal.* any varied assortment.

grace (grās) *n. v.* **graced, grac·ing.** —*n.* **1** beauty of form, movement, or manner; a pleasing or agreeable quality. **2** good will; favor. **3** mercy; pardon. **4** in theology: **a** God's free and undeserved favor to and love for mankind; the influence of God operating in man to improve or strengthen him. **b** the condition of being influenced and favored by God. **5** a short prayer of thanks said before or after a meal. **6** the favor shown by granting a postponement. **7** an allowance of time: *The bank gave him three days' grace.* **8** virtue; merit; excellence. **9** Usually, **Grace.** a title used in speaking to or of a duke, duchess, or archbishop: *He spoke a few words to his Grace the Duke of Bedford.* **10** a grace note. **11 Graces,** *pl.* three Greek sister goddesses controlling beauty and charm in people and in nature.
have the grace, show a sense of what is right or proper.
in the bad graces of, disfavored or disliked by.
in the good graces of, favored or liked by.
with bad grace, unpleasantly; unwillingly.
with good grace, pleasantly; willingly.
—*v.* **1** give or add grace to; set off with grace. **2** do a favor or honor to: *The Queen graced the ball with her presence.* **3** in music, add grace notes to. [< F < L *gratia* < *gratus* pleasing] —**Syn.** *n.* **1** charm, ease, elegance. **2** kindness. *–v.* **1** adorn, decorate. **2** honor.

grace·ful (grās′fəl) *adj.* having or showing grace; beautiful in form, movement, or manner; pleasing; agreeable: *A good dancer must be graceful. She thanked him with a graceful speech.* —**grace′ful·ly,** *adv.* —**grace′ful·ness,** *n.*

grace·less (grās′lis) *adj.* **1** without grace. **2** not caring for what is right or proper: *That boy is a graceless rascal.* —**grace′less·ly,** *adv.* —**grace′less·ness,** *n.*

grace note in music, a note or group of notes added for ornament and not essential to the harmony or melody.

gra·cious (grā′shəs) *adj.* **1** pleasant; kindly; courteous: *The bride's gracious manner pleased everyone.* **2** pleasant, kindly, and courteous to people of lower social position: *The Queen greeted the crowd with a gracious smile.* **3** merciful; kindly. —*interj.* an exclamation of surprise. [ME < OF < L *gratiosus*] —**gra′cious·ly,** *adv.* —**gra′cious·ness,** *n.* —**Syn. 1, 2** See **kind**[1].

grack·le (grak′əl) *n.* a kind of blackbird that has black feathers with a metallic lustre. [< L *graculus* jackdaw]

grad. 1 graduate. **2** graduated.

gra·da·tion (grā dā′shən or grə dā′shən) *n.* **1** a change by steps or stages; gradual change: *Our acts show gradation between right and wrong.* **2** Usually, **gradations,** *pl.* a step, stage, or degree in a series: *There are many gradations between poverty and wealth. The rainbow shows gradations of color.* **3** the act or process of grading. [< L *gradatio, -onis* < *gradus* step, degree]

grade (grād) *n. v.* **grad·ed, grad·ing.** —*n.* **1** in schools: **a** any one division, or class, arranged according to the pupil's progress. **b** the pupils in any such division. **2** a step or stage in a course or process. **3** a degree in a scale of rank, quality, value, etc.: *grade A milk.* **4** a group of people or things having the same rank, quality, value, etc. **5 the grades,** *U.S.* elementary school. **6** a number or letter that shows how well one has done: *Her grade in English is B.* **7** the slope of a road, railway track, etc.

8 the amount of slope. 9 in farming, an animal having one purebred parent. **10 at grade,** on the same level. **11 down grade, a** going down. **b** getting worse. **12 make the grade, a** ascend a steep slope. **b** overcome difficulties. **13 up grade, a** going up. **b** getting better.
—*v.* **1** arrange in classes; arrange according to size, value, etc.; sort: *These apples are graded by size.* **2** be of a particular grade or quality. **3** give a grade to: *The teacher graded the papers.* **4** often **grade up,** in farming, improve a breed by crossing with a superior one. **5** make more nearly level: *The workmen graded the land around the new house.* **6** change gradually; go through a series of steps, stages, or degrees: *Red and yellow grade into orange.* [< F < L *gradus* step, degree]

grade crossing level crossing.

grad·er (grād′ər) *n.* **1** a person or thing that grades. **2** a machine that levels uneven or bumpy ground. **3** a person who is in a certain grade at school: *a sixth-grader.*

grade school *U.S.* elementary school.

gra·di·ent (grā′dē ənt) *n.* **1** the rate at which a road, railway track, etc. rises. **2** the sloping part of a road, etc. **3** in physics, the rate at which temperature or pressure changes. **4** a curve or graph representing such a rate.
—*adj.* **1** going up or down gradually. **2** moving by taking steps; walking. [< L *gradiens, -entis,* ppr. of *gradi* walk, go < *gradus* step, degree]

grad·u·al (graj′ü əl) *adj.* changing by degrees too small to be separately noticed; little by little: *The hill had a gradual slope.* [< Med.L *gradualis* < L *gradus* step, degree] **—grad′u·al·ly,** *adv.*

grad·u·and (graj′ü and′) *n.* a student who is about to graduate. [< Med.L *graduandus* < *graduare.* See GRADUATE.]

grad·u·ate (*v.* graj′ü āt′; *n.* graj′ü it′ or graj′ü āt; *adj.* graj′ü it) *v.* **-at·ed, -at·ing,** *n. adj.* —*v.* **1** finish a course of study at a school, college, or university and be awarded a diploma. **2** give a diploma to for finishing a course of study. **3** mark with degrees for measuring: *A thermometer is graduated.* **4** arrange in regular steps, stages, or degrees: *An income tax is graduated so that the people who make the most money pay the highest rate of taxes.* **5** change gradually.
—*n.* **1** a person who has graduated. **2** a container marked with degrees for measuring.
—*adj.* **1** that is a graduate: *a graduate student.* **2** of or for graduates: *a graduate school.* [< Med.L *graduare* < L *gradus* step, degree] **—grad′u·a′tor,** *n.*

grad·u·a·tion (graj′ü ā′shən) *n.* **1** a graduating or being graduated from a school, college, or university. **2** the ceremony of graduating; graduating exercises. **3** a marking with degrees for measuring. **4** a mark or set of marks to show degrees for measuring. **5** an arrangement in regular steps, stages, or degrees.

graf·fi·to (grə fē′tō) *n.* **-ti** (-tē). a drawing or inscription on a wall, fence, etc. [< Ital. *graffito* scribbling < *graffio* a scratch, scribble < Gk. *gráphein* draw, write]

graft[1] (graft) *v.* **1** insert (a shoot, bud, etc.) from one tree or plant into a slit in another so that it will grow there permanently. **2** produce or improve (a fruit, flower, etc.) by grafting. **3** do grafting on. **4** transfer (a piece of skin, bone, etc.) from one part of the body to another so that it will grow there permanently. **5** insert or fix as if by grafting. **6** become grafted. [< n.]
—*n.* **1** the shoot, bud, etc. used in grafting. **2** the place on a tree or plant where the shoot, bud, etc. is inserted. **3** the tree or plant that has had a shoot bud, etc. grafted on it. **4** the act of grafting. **5** a piece of skin, bone, etc. transferred in grafting. [earlier *graff* < OF *grafe* < L *graphium* < Gk. *grapheion* stylus (< *graphein* write); from similarity of shape] **—graft′er,** *n.*

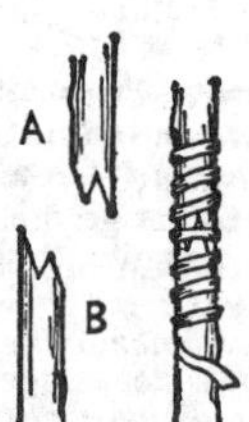

The process of grafting. The branch (A) is grafted on the main stem (B) by making a jagged split in both pieces and fitting them together.

graft[2] (graft) *n.* **1** the taking of money dishonestly, especially in connection with city or government business; political dishonesty, corruption, etc. **2** a method of getting money dishonestly. **3** money dishonestly taken or obtained. —*v. Informal.* make money dishonestly through one's job, especially in political positions. [origin uncertain] **—graft′er,** *n.*

gra·ham (grā′əm) *adj.* made from whole-wheat flour. Graham flour is wheat flour that has not been sifted. [after Sylvester *Graham* (1794-1851), an American reformer of dietetics]

Grail (grāl) *n.* the cup or dish supposed to have been used by Christ at the Last Supper, in which one of His followers received the last drops of blood from Christ's body on the cross; Holy Grail. [ME < OF *graal* < Med.L *gradale* plate, or < VL *cratale* < *crater* bowl < Gk. *kratēr*]

grain (grān) *n.* **1** a single seed or seedlike fruit of wheat, corn, oats, and similar cereal grasses. **2** the seeds or seedlike fruits of such plants in the mass. **3** the plants that these seeds or seedlike fruits grow on. **4** a tiny, hard particle of sand, salt, sugar, etc. **5** the smallest unit of weight in North American and British systems of weighing. One pound avoirdupois equals 7,000 grains; one pound troy equals 5,760 grains. **6** the smallest possible amount; tiniest bit: *a grain of truth.* **7** the arrangement or direction of fibres in wood, layers in stone, etc. Wood and stone split along the grain. **8** the little lines and other markings in wood, marble, etc. **9** the rough surface of leather, originally, the hairy side of the skin. **10 a** the plane of cleavage in coal, stone, etc.; lamination. **b** the directions in which cleavage occurs in diamond polishing. **11** the quality of a substance due to the size, character, or arrangement of its constituent particles; texture: *a stone or salt of coarse grain.* **12** natural character; disposition: *For him, to apologize goes against the grain.* **13** in photography, any of the small, separate particles of light-sensitive material emulsified and deposited on photographic film. The size of the particle limits the possible enlargement of the image and affects the speed of exposure.
—*v.* **1** form into grains. **2** paint in imitation of the grain in wood, marble, etc. **3** remove the hair from (a skin or skins). **4** soften and raise the grain of (leather). [ME < OF < L *granum* grain, seed] **—grain′less,** *adj.*

grain alcohol ethyl alcohol, often made from grain.

grained (grānd) *adj.* **1** having little lines and markings. **2** painted in imitation of the grain in wood, marble, etc. **3** with the hair removed; roughened on the surface.

grain elevator a building for storing grain.

grain·field (grān′fēld′) *n.* a field in which grain grows.

grain·ing (grān′ing) *n.* painting in imitation of the grain in wood, marble, etc.

gram or **gramme** (gram) *n.* in the metric system, unit of weight. Twenty-eight grams weigh about one ounce avoirdupois. *Abbrev.:* g, gr., or gm. [< F *gramme* < LL < Gk. *gramma* small marked weight < *graphein* mark, write]

-gram[1] *combining form.* something written; message, as in *cablegram, telegram, monogram.* [< Gk. *-gramma* something written, ult. < *graphein* write]

-gram[2] or **-gramme** *combining form.* grams; of a gram, as in *kilogram, milligram.* [see GRAM]

gra·mer·cy (grə mėr′sē or gram′ər sē) *interj. Archaic.* **1** many thanks; thank you. **2** an exclamation of surprise. [ME < OF *grant merci* (God give you) great reward]

gram·mar (gram′ər) *n.* **1** the scientific study and classification of a language with reference to the sounds and forms of words and the structure of sentences. **2** a systematic study comparing the forms and constructions of two or more languages. **3** a systematic study comparing present with past forms and usage of a language. **4** a treatise or book on one of these subjects. **5** a manner of speech or writing with reference to conformity to established usage. **6** statements about the use of words. **7** the elements of any subject: *the grammar of painting.* [ME < OF *grammaire* < L *grammatica* < Gk. *grammatikē* (*technē*) (art) of letters, ult. < *graphein* write]

gram·mar·i·an (grə mãr′ē ən) *n.* an expert in grammar.

grammar school 1 a public school having the grades between primary school and high school. **2** in the United Kingdom, a secondary school that prepares students for university.

hat, āge, cãre, fär; let, ēqual, tėrm; it, īce
hot, ōpen, ôrder; oil, out; cup, pu̇t, rüle, ūse
əbove, takən, pencəl, lemən, circəs
ch, child; ng, long; sh, ship
th, thin; ᴛʜ, then; zh, measure

gram·mat·i·cal (grə mat′ə kəl) *adj.* **1** having the correct use of words. **2** of or having to do with grammar.

gram·mat·i·cal·ly (grə mat′ik lē) *adv.* according to the principles and rules of grammar; as regards grammar.

gramme (gram) *n.* gram.

gram-mo·lec·u·lar (gram′mə lek′yu̇ lər) *adj.* of or having to do with a gram molecule.

gram-molecular weight gram molecule.

gram molecule the amount of a chemical element or compound that equals its molecular weight expressed in grams.

gram·o·phone (gram′ə fōn′) *n.* a record player; phonograph. [inversion of *phonogram* < Gk. *phōnē* sound + *-gram*[1]]

gram·pus (gram′pəs) *n.* **1** a large dolphin of the northern Atlantic and Pacific Oceans. **2** a killer whale. **3** *Informal.* a person who breathes loudly. [*graundepose* < earlier *grapeys* < OF *graspeis* < L *crassus piscis* fat fish]

gran·a·ry (gran′ə rē or grān′ə rē) *n.* **-ries. 1** a place or building where grain is stored. **2** a region in which much grain is grown. [< L *granarium* < *granum* grain]

grand (grand) *adj.* **1** large and of fine appearance: *grand mountains.* **2** fine; noble; dignified; stately; splendid: *a very grand palace, grand music, a grand old man.* **3** highest or very high in rank; chief: *grand jury, grand duke.* **4** great; important; main: *the grand staircase.* **5** complete; comprehensive: *grand total.* **6** *Informal.* very pleasing: *a grand time.* **7** in names of relationship, in the second degree of ascent or descent: *grandmother, grandson.* —*n.* **1** *Slang.* a thousand dollars. **2** a grand piano. [< MF *grant, grand* < L *grandis* big] —**grand′ness,** *n.*
Syn. *adj.* **1** great, lofty. **2 Grand, stately, noble** = great, dignified, fine, and impressive. **Grand** emphasizes greatness that makes the person or thing described stand out, and suggests impressive dignity or splendor: *Under the leadership of that grand old man, the nation withstood its peril.* **Stately** emphasizes impressive dignity, sometimes also appearance: *He was moved by the stately rhythm of processional music.* **Noble** emphasizes an imposing greatness, splendor, or stateliness in appearance: *The Rocky Mountains are a noble sight.*

gran·dam (gran′dam) *n.* **1** a grandmother. **2** an old woman. [ME < AF *graund dame*]

gran·dame (gran′dām) *n.* grandam.

grand·aunt (grand′ant′) *n.* an aunt of one's father or mother; great-aunt.

grand·child (gran′chīld′ or grand′-) *n.* **-chil·dren.** a child of one's son or daughter.

grand·chil·dren (gran′chil′drən or grand′-) *n.* pl. of **grandchild.**

grand·daugh·ter (gran′do′tər or grand′-, gran′dô′tər or grand′-) *n.* a daughter of one's son or daughter.

grand duchess 1 the wife or widow of a grand duke. **2** a lady equal in rank to a grand duke. **3** in Russia before 1917, a princess of the ruling house.

grand duchy the territory under the rule of a grand duke or grand duchess.

grand duke 1 a prince who rules a small state or country called a grand duchy. A grand duke ranks just below a king. **2** in Russia before 1917, a prince of the ruling house.

gran·dee (gran dē′) *n.* **1** in Spain or Portugal, a nobleman of the highest rank. **2** a person of high rank or great importance. [< Sp., Pg. *grande*]

gran·deur (gran′jər or gran′ju̇r) *n.* greatness; majesty; nobility; dignity; splendor. [< F *grandeur* < *grand* grand]

grand·fa·ther (gran′fo′ᴛʜər or grand′-) *n.* **1** the father of one's father or mother. **2** a forefather.

grand·fa·ther·ly (gran′fo′ᴛʜər lē or grand′-) *adj.* **1** of a grandfather. **2** like or characteristic of a grandfather.

grandfather's clock or **grandfather clock** a clock in a tall, wooden case that stands on the floor.

gran·di·flo·ra (gran′də flôr′ə) *n.* **1** any of a group of tall rosebushes bearing clusters of large flowers. **2** any plant developed to bear large, showy blooms. **3** a flower from such a rosebush or other plant. —*adj.* large-flowered. [< NL *Grandiflora* < L *grandis* grand + *flos, floris* flower]

gran·dil·o·quence (gran dil′ə kwəns) *n.* the use of lofty or pompous words.

gran·dil·o·quent (gran dil′ə kwənt) *adj.* using lofty or pompous words. [< L *grandiloquus* < *grandis* grand + *loqui* speak; influenced by the form of E *eloquent*] —**gran·dil′o·quent·ly,** *adv.*

gran·di·ose (gran′dē ōs′) *adj.* **1** grand in an imposing or impressive way; magnificent. **2** grand in an affected or pompous way; trying to seem magnificent. [< F < Ital. *grandioso*] —**gran′di·ose·ly,** *adv.*

grand jury a jury of from 12 to 23 persons chosen to investigate accusations of crime. A hearing before a grand jury may be followed by an indictment before an ordinary jury.

Grand Lama Dalai Lama.

grand larceny *U.S.* a theft in which the value of the property taken equals or is more than a certain amount, in most states, between $25 and $50.

grand·ly (grand′lē) *adv.* in a grand manner.

grand·ma (gran′mä′, gram′mä′, or grand′mä′) *n.* *Informal.* grandmother.

grand march a ceremony at a ball in which the guests march around the ballroom in couples.

Grand Master the head of an order of knighthood, a lodge, etc.

grand·moth·er (gran′muᴛʜ′ər or grand′-) *n.* **1** the mother of one's father or mother. **2** an ancestress.

grand·moth·er·ly (gran′muᴛʜ′ər lē or grand′-) *adj.* **1** of a grandmother. **2** like or characteristic of a grandmother.

grand·neph·ew (gran′nef′ū or grand′-) *n.* the son of one's nephew or niece.

grand·niece (gran′nēs′ or grand′-) *n.* the daughter of one's nephew or niece.

grand opera a musical drama, having a serious and often tragic theme, in which all the speeches are sung or recited to the accompaniment of an orchestra.

grand·pa (gran′pä′, gram′pä′, or grand′pä′) *n. Informal.* a grandfather.

grand·par·ent (gran′pãr′ənt or grand′-) *n.* a grandfather or grandmother.

grand piano a large piano mounted on legs and having horizontal strings in a flat, harp-shaped wooden case.

grand·sire (gran′sīr′ or grand′-) *n. Archaic.* **1** a grandfather. **2** a forefather. **3** an old man.

grand slam in bridge, the winning of all the tricks in a hand.

grand·son (gran′sun′ or grand′-) *n.* a son of one's son or daughter.

grand·stand (gran′stand′ or grand′-) *n.* the principal seating place for spectators at an athletic field, race track, etc.: *Grandstands are usually covered.*

grand·un·cle (grand′ung′kəl) *n.* the uncle of one's father or mother; great-uncle.

grange (grānj) *n.* **1** a farm with its buildings; farmstead. **2 Grange, a** an organization of farmers to promote agricultural interests, founded in U.S. in 1867. **b** a local branch of this organization. [ME < OF < VL *granica* < L *granum* grain]

grang·er (grān′jər) *n.* **1** a farmer. **2 Granger,** a member of the Grange.

gran·ite (gran′it) *n.* a hard igneous rock made of grains of other rocks, chiefly quartz, feldspar, and mica. Granite is much used for buildings and monuments. [< Ital. *granito* grained, pp. of *granire* < *grano* grain < L *granum*]

gran·ite·ware (gran′it wãr′) *n.* ironware covered with gray enamel.

gra·nit·ic (grə nit′ik) *adj.* of or like granite.

gran·nie or **gran·ny** (gran′ē) *n.* **-nies.** *Informal.* **1** a grandmother. **2** an old woman. **3** a fussy person.

grannie knot or **granny knot** a knot differing from a square knot in having the ends crossed in the opposite way. See **knot** for picture.

grant (grant) *v.* **1** give what is asked; allow: *grant a request, grant permission.* **2** admit to be true; accept without proof; concede: *I grant that you are right.* **3** bestow or confer (a right, etc.) by formal act; transfer or convey (the ownership of property), especially by deed or writing. **4 take for granted,** assume to be true; accept as proved or as agreed to.
—*n.* **1** something granted, such as a privilege, right, sum of money, or tract of land: *The companies that built the railways received large grants of land from the government.* **2** the act of granting. [ME < OF *graanter,* var. of *creanter,* promise, authorize, ult. < L *credens,* ppr. of *credere* trust] —**grant′a·ble,** *adj.* —**grant′er,** *n.*
—**Syn.** *n.* **1** gift, appropriation.

grant·ee (gran′tē′) *n.* a person to whom a grant is made.

grant·or (gran′tər or gran′tôr′) *n.* a person who makes a grant.

gran·u·lar (gran′yù lər) *adj.* **1** consisting of or containing grains or granules. **2** resembling grains or granules. —**gran′u·lar·ly,** *adv.*

gran·u·late (gran′yù lāt′) *v.* **-lat·ed, -lat·ing. 1** form into grains or granules. **2** roughen on the surface. **3** become granular; develop granulations. Wounds granulate in healing. —**gran′u·la′tor,** *n.*

gran·u·lat·ed (gran′yù lāt′id) *adj.* **1** formed into grains or granules: *granulated sugar.* **2** roughened on the surface. **3** having granulations.

gran·u·la·tion (gran′yù lā′shən) *n.* **1** a formation into grains or granules. **2** a roughening on the surface. **3** a granule on a roughened surface. **4** the formation of small, grainlike bodies, especially in the process of healing. **5** a small, grainlike body or elevation, especially one of those that form on the surface of wounds during healing.

gran·ule (gran′ūl) *n.* **1** a small grain. **2** a small bit or spot like a grain. [< LL *granulum,* dim. of *granum* grain]

gran·u·lose (gran′yù lōs′) *n.* that part of a starch granule on which diastase and saliva act.

grape (grāp) *n.* **1** a small, round, red, purple, or pale-green fruit that grows in bunches on a vine. Grapes may be eaten raw, dried so that they become raisins, or crushed and their juice made into wine. **2** a grapevine. **3** a dark purplish red. **4** the juice of the grape; wine. **5** *Obsolete.* grapeshot. [ME < OF *grape* bunch of grapes < *graper* pick grapes < *grape* hook < Gmc.] —**grape′like′,** *adj.*

grape·fruit (grāp′früt′) *n.* **-fruit** or **-fruits.** a pale-yellow, roundish, citrus fruit like an orange, but larger and not as sweet.

grape·shot (grāp′shot′) *n.* a cluster of small iron balls formerly used as a charge for cannon.

grape sugar a sugar formed in all green plants, but especially in grapes; dextrose.

grape·vine (grāp′vīn′) *n.* **1** a vine that bears grapes. **2** *Informal.* a way by which reports are mysteriously spread.

graph (graf) *n.* **1** a line or diagram showing how one quantity depends on or changes with another. **2** in mathematics, any line or lines representing the relations of equations or functions.—*v.* draw such a line or diagram; draw a line representing some change, equation, or function. [for *graphic formula.* See GRAPHIC.]

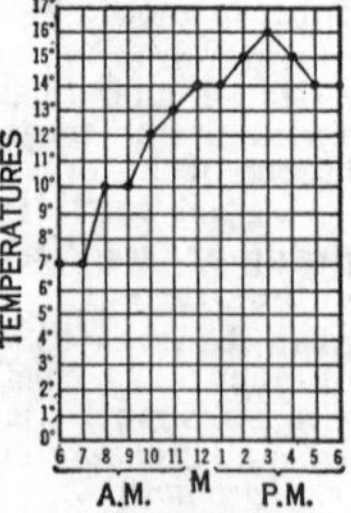

A graph of the temperature of a winter day for 12 hours

-graph *combining form.* **1** make a picture, draw, or write, as in *photograph.* **2** a machine that makes a picture, draws, or writes, as in *seismograph.* **3** drawn or written, as in *autograph.* **4** something drawn or written, as in *lithograph.* [< Gk. *-graphos.* < *graphein* write]

graph·ic (graf′ik) *adj.* **1** lifelike; vivid: *a graphic account of the battle.* **2** of or about diagrams and their use. **3** shown by a graph: *a graphic record of school attendance for a month.* **4** of or about drawing, painting, engraving, or etching: *the graphic arts.* **5** of or used in handwriting: *graphic symbols.* **6** written; inscribed. [< L *graphicus* < Gk. *graphikos* < *graphein* write]

graph·i·cal (graf′ə kəl) *adj.* graphic.

graph·i·cal·ly (graf′ik lē) *adv.* by a diagram or pictures; vividly.

graphic arts drawing, painting, engraving, etching, etc.

graph·ite (graf′īt) *n.* a soft, black form of carbon with a metallic lustre, used for lead in pencils, for lubricating machinery, etc. [< G *Graphit* < Gk. *graphein* write]

graph·o·log·i·cal (graf′ə loj′ə kəl) *adj.* of or having to do with graphology: *graphological analysis.*

graph·ol·o·gist (gra fol′ə jist) *n.* an expert in graphology.

graph·ol·o·gy (gra fol′ə jē) *n.* the study of handwriting, especially as a means of analysing a person's character. [< Gk. *graphē* writing + E *-logy*]

-graphy *combining form.* **1** a writing, describing, or recording, as in *telegraphy.* **2** a descriptive science, as in *geography.* [< Gk. *-graphia* < *graphein* write]

grap·nel (grap′nəl) *n.* **1** an instrument with one or more hooks for seizing and holding something. **2** a small anchor with three or more hooks. [ME *grapenel,* dim. of OF *grapin* hook, dim. of *grape* hook < Gmc. Related to GRAPE.]

A grapnel (def. 2)

grap·ple (grap′əl) *v.* **-pled, -pling,** *n.*
—*v.* **1** seize and hold fast; grip or hold firmly. **2** struggle; fight: *The wrestlers grappled in the centre of the ring.* **3** use a grappling iron; search with a grappling iron. [< n.]
—*n.* **1** a seizing and holding fast; a firm grip or hold. **2** an iron bar with hooks at one end for seizing and holding fast an object; grappling iron; grapnel. [< OF *grapil* hook < Gmc. Related to GRAPE.] —**grap′pler,** *n.*
—**Syn.** *v.* **1** grasp, clinch. **2** wrestle.

grappling iron grapnel.

grasp (grasp) *v.* **1** seize and hold fast by closing the fingers around. **2** seize greedily: *grasp an opportunity.* **3** understand. **4 grasp at, a** try to grasp; try to take hold of. **b** accept eagerly: *Joan grasped at the opportunity.*
—*n.* **1** a seizing and holding tightly; clasp of the hand. **2** the power of seizing and holding; reach. **3** control; possession. **4** understanding: *He has a good grasp of mathematics.* [ME *graspe(n).* Related to GROPE.]
—**grasp′a·ble,** *adj.* —**grasp′er,** *n.* —**Syn.** *v.* **1** grip, clutch, grab, snatch. See **seize. 2** comprehend.

grasp·ing (gras′ping) *adj.* eager to get all that one can; greedy. —**grasp′ing·ly,** *adv.* —**grasp′ing·ness,** *n.*

grass (gras) *n.* **1** any of various plants that cover fields, lawns, pastures, etc. Horses, cows, and sheep eat grass. **2** land covered with grass; pasture. **3** in botany, any of a group of plants that have jointed stems and long, narrow leaves. Wheat, corn, sugar cane, and bamboo are grasses. **4 at grass, a** out to pasture. **b** out of work; at leisure. **5 go to grass, a** graze; go to pasture. **b** take a rest. **6 let the grass grow under one's feet,** waste time; lose chances. **7 put, send,** or **turn out to grass, a** turn (an animal) out to pasture. **b** *Informal.* dismiss (a person) from a position; force into retirement.
—*v.* **1** cover with grass. **2** feed on growing grass; graze. [OE *gærs, græs.* Related to GREEN, GROW.] —**grass′less,** *adj.* —**grass′like′,** *adj.*

grass hockey *Informal.* field hockey.

grass·hop·per (gras′hop′ər) *n.* **1** a winged insect having strong hind legs for jumping. Locusts and katydids are grasshoppers. **2** a small airplane, designed for flying at low altitudes, especially one used for scouting and for directing fire from artillery units.

grass·land (gras′land′) *n.* land with grass on it, used for pasture.

grass roots 1 in politics, people and party organizations at the local level, especially in rural communities. **2** soil near or at the surface. **3** the beginning or source. —**grass-roots,** *adj.*

grass snake a kind of harmless, grayish-green snake.

grass widow *Informal.* a woman divorced or separated from her husband.

grass·y (gras′ē) *adj.* **grass·i·er, grass·i·est. 1** covered with grass. **2** of grass. **3** like grass. **—grass′i·ness,** *n.*

grate[1] (grāt) *n. v.* **grat·ed, grat·ing.** *—n.* **1** a framework of iron bars to hold a fire. A coal furnace has a grate. **2** a fireplace. **3** a framework of bars over a window or opening; grating. **4** in mining, a screen used for separating or grading ore. *—v.* furnish with a grate or grating. [< Med.L *grata* < L *cratis* hurdle] **—grate′like′,** *adj.*

A grate for an open fire

grate[2] (grāt) *v.* **grat·ed, grat·ing. 1** have an annoying or unpleasant effect; annoy: *His rude manners grate on other people.* **2** rub harshly together: *grate the teeth.* **3** make a grinding sound; sound harshly. **4** rub with a harsh sound: *The door grated on its old, rusty hinges.* **5** wear down or grind off in small pieces: *grate cheese.* **6** *Archaic.* wear away by rubbing. [< OF *grater* < Gmc.]

grate·ful (grāt′fəl) *adj.* **1** feeling gratitude; thankful. **2** pleasing; welcome: *A breeze is grateful on a hot day.* [< obs. *grate* agreeable (< L *gratus*) + *-ful*] **—grate′ful·ly,** *adv.* **—grate′ful·ness,** *n.*

Syn. 1 Grateful, thankful = feeling or expressing gratitude. **Grateful** emphasizes recognizing and gladly acknowledging favors or kindness shown to one by others: *I am grateful to the friends who have helped me.* **Thankful,** often used as if it were a less formal substitute for *grateful*, emphasizes giving thanks to some higher being or power, fate, or some force of nature, for one's good fortune: *I am thankful that I have good friends.*

grat·er (grā′tər) *n.* **1** one that grates. **2** an instrument with a rough surface for rubbing off small particles.

grat·i·fi·ca·tion (grat′ə fə kā′shən) *n.* **1** a gratifying. **2** a being gratified. **3** something that satisfies or pleases. **4** a reward; fee.

grat·i·fy (grat′ə fī′) *v.* **-fied, -fy·ing. 1** give pleasure or satisfaction to; please: *Flattery gratifies a vain person.* **2** satisfy; indulge: *A drunkard gratifies his craving for liquor.* **3** give a fee to. [< F < L *gratificari* < *gratus* pleasing + *facere* make, do] **—grat′i·fi′er,** *n.* **—grat′i·fy′ing·ly,** *adv.* **—Syn. 1** delight. **2** See **humor.**

grat·ing[1] (grāt′ing) *n.* a framework of bars over a window or opening. Windows in a prison, bank, or ticket office usually have gratings over them. [< *grate*[1]]

grat·ing[2] (grāt′ing) *adj.* **1** unpleasant; annoying; irritating. **2** harsh or jarring in sound. [< *grate*[2]]

grat·is (grat′is or grā′tis) *adv. adj.* for nothing; free of charge. [< L *gratis*, ult. < *gratia* favor]

grat·i·tude (grat′ə tūd′ or grat′ə tüd′) *n.* a kindly feeling because of a favor received; desire to do a favor in return; thankfulness. [< LL *gratitudo* < *gratus* thankful]

gra·tu·i·tous (grə tū′ə təs or grə tü′ə təs) *adj.* **1** freely given or obtained; free. **2** without reason or cause; unnecessary; uncalled for. **—gra·tu′i·tous·ly,** *adv.* **—gra·tu′i·tous·ness,** *n.* **—Syn. 2** unwarranted.

gra·tu·i·ty (grə tū′ə tē or grə tü′ə tē) *n.* **-ties. 1** a present of money in return for service; tip. Gratuities are given to waiters, porters, servants, etc. **2** a present; gift. **3** a payment given to members of the armed services on being discharged or at retirement. [< Med.L *gratuitas* gift, apparently < L *gratuitus* free]

grat·u·la·tion (grach′ů lā′shən) *n.* **1** congratulation. **2** rejoicing; joy. [< L **gratulatio, -onis,** ult. < *gratus* pleasing, thankful]

gra·va·men (grə vā′mən) *n.* **-vam·i·na** (-vam′ə nə). **1** a grievance. **2** in law, the part of an accusation that weighs most heavily against the accused. [< L *gravamen* < *gravare* load < *gravis* heavy]

grave[1] (grāv) *n.* **1** a hole dug in the ground in which a dead body is to be buried. **2** a mound or monument over it. **3** any place that becomes the receptacle of what is dead: *a watery grave.* **4** death. **5 make** (a person) **turn in his grave,** say or do something that a dead person would have found offensive. **6 one foot in the grave,** near death. **7 secret as the grave,** kept as a close secret. [OE *græf.* Related to GRAVE[3].]

grave[2] (grāv *for adj. 1-4*; gräv or grāv *for adj. 5, n.*) *adj.* **grav·er, grav·est,** *n. —adj.* **1** important; weighty; momentous: *grave cares.* **2** serious; threatening: *grave questions, doubts, symptoms, news.* **3** dignified; sober; solemn: *a grave face, a grave ceremony.* **4** sombre: *grave colors.* **5** in phonetics: **a** low in pitch; not acute. **b** having a grave accent. *—n.* a grave accent. [< F < L *gravis* serious] **—grave′ly,** *adv.* **—grave′ness,** *n.*

Syn. *adj.* **3 Grave, serious, sober** = thoughtful and free from frivolity or gaiety in mood, looks, behavior, etc. **Grave** emphasizes dignity and lack of gaiety, especially in looks, behavior, and attitude, and suggests having a great problem on one's mind: *His expression was grave.* **Serious** emphasizes being thoughtful, concerned with important things, and free from frivolity or giddiness, especially in disposition and manner: *He became serious when he spoke of finding a job.* **Sober** suggests a settled or self-restrained seriousness or gravity, especially in looks, behavior, and speech: *His words were sober and wise.*

hat, āge, cãre, fär; let, ēqual, tėrm; it, īce
hot, ōpen, ôrder; oil, out; cup, pů̇t, rüle, ūse
əbove, takən, pencəl, lemən, circəs
ch, child; ng, long; sh, ship
th, thin; ᴛʜ, then; zh, measure

grave[3] (grāv) *v.* **graved, graved** or **grav·en, grav·ing. 1** *Archaic.* engrave; carve; sculpture. **2** impress deeply; fix firmly. [OE *grafan*] **—grav′er,** *n.*

grave[4] (grāv) *v.* **graved, grav·ing.** clean (a ship's bottom) and cover with tar. [origin uncertain]

gra·ve[5] (grä′vā) in music: *—adj.* slow and solemn in tempo. *—adv.* slowly and solemnly. [< Ital. *grave*, learned borrowing from L *gravis* serious, heavy]

grave accent a mark (`) placed over a vowel to indicate stress, pitch, quality of sound (as in French *père*), or syllabic value (as in *belovèd*).

grave·dig·ger (grāv′dig′ər) *n.* a person whose work is digging graves.

grav·el (grav′əl) *n. v.* **-elled** or **-eled, -el·ling** or **-el·ing.** *—n.* **1** pebbles and rock fragments coarser than sand. Gravel is much used for roads and walks. **2** a road surfaced with gravel. **3** in medicine: **a** small, hard substances formed in the bladder and kidneys. **b** the disease causing them. *—v.* **1** lay or cover with gravel. **2** puzzle; perplex. [ME < OF *gravele*, dim. of *grave* sand, seashore < Celtic]

grav·el·ly (grav′əl ē) *adj.* **1** having much gravel. **2** consisting of or like gravel. **3** rough; rasping; grating: *a gravelly voice.*

grav·en (grāv′ən) *adj.* **1** engraved; carved; sculptured. **2** deeply impressed; firmly fixed. *—v.* a pp. of **grave**[3].

graven image 1 a statue. **2** an idol.

grav·er (grāv′ər) *n.* **1** a tool for cutting, engraving, etc. **2** an engraver.

grave·stone (grāv′stōn′) *n.* a stone that marks a grave.

grave·yard (grāv′yärd′) *n.* **1** a place for burying the dead; cemetery; burial ground. **2** a lot, yard, etc. in which old or useless objects are discarded. **3** *Slang.* the graveyard shift: *He has been working on graveyard for a month now.*

graveyard shift *Slang.* the working hours between midnight and the morning shift.

gra·vim·e·ter (grə vim′ə tər) *n.* a device used to measure gravity at the earth's surface; a gravity meter. [< F *gravimètre* < L *gravis* heavy + F *mètre* measure]

grav·i·met·ric (grav′ə met′rik) *adj.* **1** of or having to do with gravimetry. **2** in chemistry, of or having to do with measurement by weight. **3** of or having to do with the use of gravity measurements to calculate distances and draw maps.

gra·vim·e·try (grə vim′ə trē) *n.* the measurement of weight, specific gravity, or density.

grav·i·tate (grav′ə tāt′) *v.* **-tat·ed, -tat·ing. 1** move or tend to move by gravitation. **2** settle down; sink; fall: *The sand and dirt in the water gravitated to the bottom of the bottle.* **3** tend to go; be strongly attracted. [< NL *gravitare*, ult. < L *gravis* heavy]

grav·i·ta·tion (grav′ə tā′shən) *n.* **1** in physics, the fact that the earth pulls any object toward it and that the sun, moon, stars, and other such bodies in the universe do the same; the force or pull that makes bodies in the universe tend to move toward one another. **2** a moving or tendency to move caused by this force. **3** a settling down;

sinking; falling. **4** a natural tendency toward some point or object of influence: *the gravitation of population to the cities.*

grav·i·ta·tion·al (grav′ə tā′shən əl or grav′ə tāsh′nəl) *adj.* of gravitation; having to do with gravitation.
—**gra′vi·ta′tion·al·ly,** *adv.*

grav·i·ty (grav′ə tē) *n.* **-ties. 1** in physics: **a** the natural force that causes objects to move or tend to move toward the centre of the earth. Gravity causes objects to have weight. **b** the natural force that makes objects move or tend to move toward each other; gravitation. **2** heaviness; weight: *He balanced the long pole at its centre of gravity.* **3** a serious manner; serious behavior: *The look of gravity on the child's face was rather amusing.* **4** a serious or critical character; importance: *The gravity of the situation was greatly increased by threats of war.* **5** lowness of pitch. [< L *gravitas* < *gravis* heavy]

gra·vure (grə vūr′ or grā′vūr) *n.* **1** a photogravure. **2** a plate or print produced by photogravure. [< F *gravure* < *graver* engrave < Gmc.]

gra·vy (grā′vē) *n.* **-vies. 1** the juice that comes out of meat in cooking. **2** a sauce for meat, potatoes, etc. made from this juice. **3** *Slang.* easy gain or profit. [ME *grave,* a misreading of OF *grané* sauce, originally, properly grained, seasoned, ult. < L *granum* grain]

gravy train *Slang.* **1** a situation in which good profits can be realized with little effort. **2 ride a gravy train, a** realize easy profits. **b** enjoy an easy life.

gray or **grey** (grā) *n.* **1** the color made by mixing black and white. **2** gray cloth or clothing. **3** a gray horse. **4** something gray.
—*adj.* **1** having a color between black and white: *Ashes and lead are gray.* **2** having gray hair. **3** old; ancient. **4** dark; gloomy; dismal.
—*v.* make or become gray. [OE *grǣg*] —**gray′ly** or **grey′ly,** *adv.* —**gray′ness** or **grey′ness,** *n.*

gray·beard or **grey·beard** (grā′bērd′) *n.* an old man.

Gray Friar or **Grey Friar** a Franciscan friar.

gray-head·ed or **grey-head·ed** (grā′hed′id) *adj.* having gray hair.

gray·hound (grā′hound′) *n.* greyhound.

gray·ish or **grey·ish** (grā′ish) *adj.* somewhat gray.

gray jay or **grey jay** Canada jay.

gray·lag or **grey·lag** (grā′lag′) *n.* a wild, gray goose that is common in Europe. [< *gray* + *lag;* because these birds migrate south at a very late date]

gray·ling (grā′ling) *n.* **1** a fresh-water fish resembling a trout, but having a longer and higher dorsal fin. **2** a gray-and-brown butterfly.

gray market or **grey market** the buying and selling of products at prices considered exorbitant.

gray matter or **grey matter 1** the grayish tissue in the brain and spinal cord that contains nerve cells and some nerve fibres. **2** *Informal.* intelligence; brains.

gray mullet or **grey mullet** any of a group of bluish-silver food fishes of salt and fresh water.

gray squirrel or **grey squirrel** a large, gray squirrel of North America.

gray wolf or **grey wolf** a large, gray wolf that lives in the western parts of North America; timber wolf.

graze[1] (grāz) *v.* **grazed, graz·ing. 1** feed on growing grass. Cattle and sheep graze. **2** put (cattle, sheep, etc.) to feed on growing grass or a pasture. **3** tend or look after (cattle, sheep, etc.) while they are grazing.
—*n.* a grazing or feeding on grass. [OE *grasian* < *græs* grass] —**graz′er,** *n.*

graze[2] (grāz) *v.* **grazed, graz·ing,** *n.* —*v.* **1** touch lightly in passing; rub lightly (against). **2** scrape the skin from: *The bullet grazed his shoulder.* —*n.* **1** a grazing. **2** a slight wound made by grazing. [origin uncertain]

gra·zier (grā′zhər) *n.* a person who grazes cattle for market.

graz·ing (grāz′ing) *n.* the growing grass that cattle, sheep, etc. feed on; pasture.

Gr.Br. or **Gr.Brit.** Great Britain.

grease (grēs) *n. v.* **greased, greas·ing.** —*n.* **1** soft animal fat. **2** any thick, oily substance. **3** in hunting, the fat or fatness of game, with reference to the season for killing. **4** shorn, uncleaned wool.
—*v.* **1** smear with grease; put grease on. **2** cause to run smoothly by greasing. **3** *Slang.* give money to as a bribe or tip. [ME < OF *graisse* < L *crassus* fat]

grease cup a small cup to hold oil or grease, fastened on machinery to supply grease to parts that need it.

greas·er (grēs′ər) *n.* **1** one that greases. **2** *U.S. Derogatory slang.* a Mexican or Spanish American.

grease·wood (grēs′wůd′) *n.* a stiff, prickly shrub having narrow leaves, growing in alkaline regions in the western parts of Canada and the United States.

greas·y (grēs′ē) *adj.* **greas·i·er, greas·i·est. 1** smeared with grease; having grease on it. **2** containing much grease. **3** like grease; smooth; slippery. **4** disagreeably unctuous; oily. —**greas′i·ly,** *adv.* —**greas′i·ness,** *n.*

great (grāt) *adj.* **1** big; large: *a great house, a great crowd.* **2** more than usual; much: *great ignorance.* **3** important; remarkable; famous: *a great composer.* **4** most important; main; chief: *the great seal.* **5** noble; generous. **6** much in use; favorite: *That is a great habit of his.* **7** very much of a: *a great talker.* **8** *Informal.* very good; fine: *We had a great time at the party.* **9** *Informal.* skilful; expert: *He's great at skiing.* **10** in names of relationship, of the next generation before or after: *great-grandmother, great-grandson.* **11 go great guns,** *Slang.* move vigorously ahead; advance at full speed.
—*n.* Usually, **greats,** *pl. Informal.* a great or outstanding person; celebrity: *All the greats of show business have appeared at the Palace.* [OE *grēat*] —**great′ly,** *adv.* —**great′ness,** *n.*

Syn. 1, 2 Great, large, big = above average in size or measure. **Great** chiefly means "more than usual" (in degree), but sometimes is used to describe physical size that is impressive in some way: *We saw the great redwoods* (size). *They are trees of great age* (degree). **Large** = of great size, amount, etc. but never degree: *We saw many large trees.* **Big** particularly emphasizes weight and bulk: *A redwood is a big tree, very heavy and thick.* **3** renowned, eminent, distinguished. **5** magnanimous. **8** first-rate, excellent.

great-aunt (grāt′ant′) *n.* an aunt of one's father or mother; grandaunt.

Great Bear in astronomy, the constellation Ursa Major, containing the seven bright stars forming the Big Dipper.

great circle 1 any circle on the surface of a sphere having its plane passing through the centre of the sphere. The equator is one of the great circles of the earth. **2** an arc of such a circle; the line of shortest distance between two points on the earth's surface.

great·coat (grāt′kōt′) *n.* a heavy overcoat, especially one worn by members of the armed services.

Great Dane 1 a breed of large, powerful, short-haired dog. **2** a dog of this breed.

great-grand·child (grāt′gran′chīld′ or -grand′-) *n.* **-children.** a grandchild of one's son or daughter.

great-grand·daugh·ter (grāt′gran′do′tər or -grand′do′tər, -gran′dô′tər or -grand′dô′tər) *n.* a granddaughter of one's son or daughter.

great-grand·fa·ther (grāt′gran′fo′ᴛʜər or -grand′-) *n.* a grandfather of one's father or mother.

great-grand·moth·er (grāt′gran′muᴛʜ′ər or -grand′-) *n.* a grandmother of one's father or mother.

great-grand·par·ent (grāt′gran′pãr′ənt or -grand′-) *n.* a grandfather or grandmother of one's mother or father.

great-grand·son (grāt′gran′sun′ or -grand′-) *n.* a grandson of one's son or daughter.

great-heart·ed (grāt′här′tid) *adj.* **1** noble; generous. **2** brave; fearless. —**great′-heart′ed·ness,** *n.*

great horned owl a North American owl that has two hornlike tufts of feathers on its head.

great·ly (grāt′lē) *adv.* **1** in a great manner. **2** much.

Great Mogul 1 the emperor of Delhi, of the Mogul dynasty that ruled over a large part of India from 1526 to 1857. **2 great mogul,** a great or important person, especially a tycoon.

great-neph·ew (grāt′nef′ū) *n.* a son of one's nephew or niece; grandnephew.

great-niece (grāt′nēs′) *n.* a daughter of one's nephew or niece; grandniece.

Great Russians a Slavic people living in central northern and N.E. Russia.

great seal the most important seal of a country, province, etc. stamped on official documents as proof of their approval by the government.

Great Spirit a deity worshipped by certain tribes or groups of North American Indians.

great-un·cle (grāt′ung′kəl) *n.* an uncle of one's father or mother; granduncle.

Great Wall of China a stone wall between China and Mongolia, about 1,500 miles long. It was begun in the third century B.C. for the defence of China against attack by nomads from the north.

Great War the First World War, from 1914 to 1918.

Great White Way the brightly lighted theatre district along Broadway, a street in New York City.

greave (grēv) *n.* armor for the leg below the knee. [ME < OF *greves,* pl.; origin uncertain]

grebe (grēb) *n.* **1** a diving bird resembling a loon, having feet not completely webbed and a pointed bill. **2** its breast feathers, used to trim hats, etc. [< F *grèbe*]

Gre·cian (grē′shən) *adj.* Greek. —*n.* **1** a Greek. **2** a person who is thoroughly familiar with the Greek language or literature.

Grecian nose a straight nose; a nose that does not dip at the forehead.

Greco- *combining form.* **1** Greece; Greek things: *Grecophile = a lover of Greece or Greek things.* **2** Greek and ——: *Greco-Roman = Greek and Roman.* [< L *Graeco-* < Gk. *Graikos* a Greek]

Gre·co·phile (grē′kō fīl′ or grē′kō fil) *n.* a person who loves Greece and Greek things.

Gre·co-Ro·man (grē′kō rō′mən) *adj.* Greek and Roman.

greed (grēd) *n.* the wanting of more than one's share; extreme or excessive desire: *a miser's greed for money.* [< *greedy*] —**Syn.** avidity, avarice, cupidity.

greed·y (grēd′ē) *adj.* **greed·i·er, greed·i·est. 1** wanting to get more than one's share; having a very great desire to possess something. **2** wanting to eat or drink a great deal in a hurry; piggish. [OE *grǣdig*] —**greed′i·ly,** *adv.* —**greed′i·ness,** *n.*

Greek (grēk) *adj.* **1** of Greece, its people, or their language. **2** in architecture, of or having to do with a style developed by the ancient Greeks, characterized by symmetry and graceful proportion, plain or fluted pillars, and pediments. [< n.]
—*n.* **1** a native or inhabitant of Greece. **2** a citizen of Greece. **3** the language of Greece. **Ancient** or **classical Greek,** the language until about A.D. 200; **late Greek,** the language until about A.D. 700; **medieval Greek,** the language during the Middle Ages until about A.D. 1500; **modern Greek,** the language from about 1500 on. **4** a member of the Greek Orthodox Church. **5 It's Greek to me.** I can't understand it. [OE *grēcas* (earlier *Crēcas*), pl. < L *Graeci,* pl. of *Graecus* a Greek < Gk. *Graikos*]

Greek Catholic 1 a member of the Greek Orthodox Church. **2** a Greek or Byzantine who adheres to the Roman Catholic faith, including the doctrine of papal supremacy, but observes the Greek Orthodox rites, liturgy, etc.; Uniat.

Greek cross a cross whose four arms are of the same length and form right angles.

Greek fire a substance easily set on fire whose flames could not be put out by water, used in warfare in ancient and medieval times.

Greek gift a gift offered to conceal treachery or as part of a treacherous plan. [< the story of the Trojan horse]

Greek Orthodox Church 1 a group of Christian churches that are in communion or doctrinal agreement with the patriarchs of Constantinople, Alexandria, Antioch, and Jerusalem; Eastern Church. **2** the part of this church that constitutes the established church in Greece.

Greek rite the ceremony of the Eucharist, Mass, etc. as used in the Greek Orthodox Church.

green (grēn) *n.* **1** the color of most growing plants, grass, and leaves; the color in the spectrum between yellow and blue. **2** green coloring matter, dye, paint, etc. **3** green cloth or clothing. **4** grassy land or a plot of grassy

hat, āge, cãre, fär; let, ēqual, tėrm; it, īce
hot, ōpen, ôrder; oil, out; cup, pu̇t, rüle, ūse
əbove, takən, pencəl, lemən, circəs
ch, child; ng, long; sh, ship
th, thin; ᴛʜ, then; zh, measure

ground. **5** a putting green on a golf course. **6 greens,** *pl.* **a** green leaves and branches used for decoration. **b** leaves and stems of plants used as food: *salad greens.* **7 the Green,** the national color of the Irish Republic.
—*adj.* **1** having the color green. **2** covered with growing plants, grass, leaves, etc.: *green fields.* **3** characterized by growing grass, etc.: *a green Christmas.* **4** undecayed: *green old age.* **5** not dried, cured, seasoned, or otherwise prepared for use: *green tobacco.* **6** not ripe; not fully grown: *green apples.* **7** not trained or experienced; not mature in age, judgment, etc.: *a green girl.* **8** easily fooled; easy to trick or cheat. **9** recent; fresh; new: *a green wound.* **10** having a pale, sickly color because of fear, jealousy, or sickness.
—*v.* make or become green. [OE *grēne* Related to GRASS, GROW.] —**green′ness,** *n.* —**Syn.** *adj.* **6** immature, unripe. **7** inexperienced, untrained, unsophisticated, callow. **8** gullible.

green·back (grēn′bak′) *n.* **1** *U.S.* a piece of United States paper money having the back printed in green. **2** *Slang.* paper money.

green·bri·er (grēn′brī′ər) *n.* a climbing smilax having prickly stems and green leaves.

Green Chamber a name given to the Canadian House of Commons because of the color of the rugs, draperies, etc. in the room in which the House meets.

green corn Indian corn, especially the ears in the milky stage; roasting ears.

green·er·y (grēn′ər ē or grēn′rē) *n.* **-er·ies. 1** green plants, grass, or leaves; verdure. **2** a place where green plants are grown or kept.

green-eyed (grēn′īd′) *adj.* **1** having green eyes. **2** jealous.

green·gage (grēn′gāj′) *n.* a large plum having a light-green skin and pulp. [after Sir William *Gage,* who introduced it into England c. 1725]

green·gro·cer (grēn′grō′sər) *n. Brit.* a person who sells fresh vegetables and fruit.

green·gro·cer·y (grēn′grō′sər ē or -grōs′rē) *n.* **-cer·ies.** *Brit.* a store that sells fresh vegetables and fruit.

green·heart (grēn′härt′) *n.* **1** a large laurel tree of tropical America, whose tough wood is used in ship-building, and whose bark yields a substance resembling quinine. **2** any of various other tropical American trees used for timber. **3** the durable, greenish wood of any of these trees.

green·horn (grēn′hôrn′) *n. Informal.* **1** a person without experience. **2** a person easy to trick or cheat. [with reference to the green horns of young oxen]

green·house (grēn′hous′) *n.* a building with a glass roof and glass sides, kept warm for the growing of plants; hothouse.

green·ing (grēn′ing) *n.* an apple having a yellowish-green skin when ripe.

green·ish (grēn′ish) *adj.* somewhat green.

green light *Informal.* permission to proceed on a particular task or undertaking.

green manure 1 green, leafy plants ploughed under to enrich the soil. **2** manure that has not decayed.

green·room (grēn′rüm′ or -ru̇m′) *n.* in a theatre, a room for the use of actors and actresses when not on the stage.

green·stone (grēn′stōn′) *n.* **1** in geology, any of various igneous rocks having a greenish color. **2** a variety of jade. **3** a piece of this stone.

green·sward (grēn′swôrd′) *n.* green grass; turf.

green tea tea made from leaves dried by machine without fermentation, thus retaining some of the green color.

green thumb a remarkable ability to grow flowers, vegetables, etc., especially as a hobby: *When Aunt Mary* *saw our garden, she said Mother must certainly have a green thumb.*

green turtle a large sea turtle with a green shell.

Green·wich mean time (grin′ij, grin′ich, or gren′ich) the basis for setting standard time in England and elsewhere, reckoned from the meridian passing through Greenwich. Also, **Greenwich Time.** *Abbrev.*: G.M.T.

Green·wich Village (gren′ich) a section of New York City, famous as a district where artists, writers, etc. live.

green·wood (grēn′wu̇d′) *n.* the forest in spring and summer when the trees are green with leaves.

greet (grēt) *v.* **1** speak or write to in a friendly, polite way; address in welcome. **2** address; salute: *She greeted him sternly.* **3** receive: *His speech was greeted with cheers.* **4** present itself to; meet: *A strange sight greeted her eyes.* [OE *grētan*] **—greet′er,** *n.* **—Syn. 1** welcome. **2** hail, accost.

greet·ing (grēt′ing) *n.* **1** the act or words of a person who greets another; welcome. **2 greetings,** *pl.* friendly wishes on a special occasion: *Christmas greetings.*

gre·gar·i·ous (grə gãr′ē əs) *adj.* **1** living in flocks, herds, or other groups: *Sheep and cattle are gregarious.* **2** fond of being with others. **3** of or having to do with a flock or crowd. [< L *gregarius* < *grex, gregis* flock] **—gre·gar′i·ous·ly,** *adv.* **—gre·gar′i·ous·ness,** *n.*

Gre·go·ri·an (grə gô′rē ən) *adj.* **1** of or having to do with Pope Gregory I, pope from A.D. 590 to 604: *Gregorian music.* **2** of or introduced by Pope Gregory XIII, pope from 1572 to 1585.

Gregorian calendar the calendar now in use in most countries, introduced by Pope Gregory XIII in 1582 as an improvement on the Julian calendar.

Gregorian chant vocal music having free rhythm and a limited scale, introduced by Pope Gregory I, 540?-604, and still used in the Roman Catholic Church. It is usually sung without an accompaniment.

grem·lin (grem′lən) *n.* an imaginary mischievous spirit or goblin, especially one supposed to trouble airplane pilots. [origin uncertain]

gre·nade (grə nād′) *n.* **1** a small bomb, usually thrown by hand: *The soldiers threw grenades into the enemy's trenches.* **2** a round, glass bottle filled with chemicals that scatter as the glass breaks. Fire grenades are thrown on fires to extinguish them. [< F < OF (*pume*) *grenate* pomegranate, fruit full of seeds; ult. < L *granum* seed, grain]

gren·a·dier (gren′ə dēr′) *n.* **1** originally, a soldier who threw grenades. **2** today, a soldier in any one of several infantry regiments. [< F *grenadier* < *grenade.* See GRENADE.]

gren·a·dine[1] (gren′ə dēn′ or gren′ə dēn′) *n.* a thin, openwork fabric used for women's dresses. [< F, ? named for *Granada,* Spain]

gren·a·dine[2] (gren′ə dēn′ or gren′ə dēn′) *n.* a syrup made from pomegranate or currant juice. [< F *grenadin* < *grenade.* See GRENADE.]

Gret·na Green (gret′nə) a village in S. Scotland in which many runaway couples from England used to be married.

grew (grü) *v.* pt. of **grow.**

grew·some (grü′səm) *adj.* gruesome. **—grew′some·ness,** *n.*

grey (grā) *n. adj. v.* gray. **—grey′ly,** *adv.* **—grey′ness,** *n.*

grey·beard (grā′bērd′) *n.* graybeard.

Grey Cup *Cdn.* **1** a trophy awarded to the champion professional rugby-football team each year in Canada. It is competed for annually in a single game by the winning teams of the Eastern Football Conference and the Western Football Conference. **2** the game played to decide the winner of this trophy. [< Earl *Grey,* Governor General of Canada 1904-1911, who first presented the cup in 1909]

grey-head·ed (grā′hed′id) *adj.* gray-headed.

grey·hound (grā′hound′) *n.* **1** a breed of tall, slender, swift dog having a smooth coat and sharp sight. **2** a dog of this breed. **3** a swift ship. Also, **grayhound.** [OE *grīghund*; not connected with *gray*; cf. ON *greyhunda* < *grey* bitch]

grey·ish (grā′ish) *adj.* grayish.

grid (grid) *n.* **1** a framework of parallel iron bars; grating; gridiron. **2** in military use, the numbered squares drawn on maps and used for map references. **3** in surveying: **a** the system of survey lines running parallel to lines of latitude and longitude, used in the division of an area into counties, sections, lots, etc. **b** one of these lines. **4** the lead plate in a storage battery. **5** an electrode in a vacuum tube that controls the flow of current between the filament and the plate. **6** a network of electric lines and connections. **7** a gridiron in a theatre. [shortened form of *gridiron*]

grid·dle (grid′əl) *n. v.* **-dled, -dling.** **—***n.* a heavy flat plate of metal or soapstone, used for cooking bacon, pancakes, etc. **—***v.* cook on a griddle. [ME < OF **gredil* (cf. OF *grediller* singe) < L *craticulum.* See GRILL.]

grid·dle·cake (grid′əl kāk′) *n.* a thin, flat cake of batter cooked on a griddle; pancake; flapjack.

grid·i·ron (grid′ ī′ərn) *n.* **1** a metal framework, often with a handle, used for broiling meat, fish, etc. **2** any framework or network that looks like a gridiron. **3** a football field. **4** in a theatre, a structure above the stage, from which scenery is hung and manipulated. [ME *gredire* griddle, var. of *gredile* < OF **gredil* (see GRIDDLE); final element assimilated to *iron*]

A gridiron (def. 1) for broiling

grid leak a very high resistance placed in a vacuum tube to permit the escape of excess electrons.

grid road *Cdn.* a municipal road that follows a grid line established by survey. In Saskatchewan, these roads are built two miles apart from north to south and one mile from east to west.

grief (grēf) *n.* **1** deep sadness caused by trouble or loss; heavy sorrow. **2 come to grief,** have trouble; fail. **3** a cause of sadness or sorrow. [ME < OF *grief* < *grever.* See GRIEVE.] **—Syn. 1** anguish, heartache. See **sorrow.**

griev·ance (grēv′əns) *n.* a real or imagined wrong; reason for being angry or annoyed; cause for complaint. **—Syn.** injustice, injury.

grieve (grēv) *v.* **grieved, griev·ing.** **1** feel grief; be very sad: *She grieved over her kitten's death.* **2** cause to feel grief; make very sad; afflict. [ME < OF *grever,* ult. < L *gravis* heavy] **—griev′er,** *n.* **—griev′ing·ly,** *adv.*

griev·ous (grēv′əs) *adj.* **1** hard to bear; causing great pain or suffering: *grievous cruelty.* **2** flagrant; atrocious: *Wasting food when people are starving is a grievous wrong.* **3** causing grief. **4** full of grief; showing grief: *a grievous cry.* **—griev′ous·ly,** *adv.* **—griev′ous·ness,** *n.* **—Syn. 1** distressing, severe.

grif·fin (grif′ən) *n.* a mythical creature with the head, wings, and forelegs of an eagle, and the body, hind legs, and tail of a lion. Also, **griffon, gryphon.** [ME < OF *grifon* < L *gryphus,* var. of *gryps* < Gk.]

grif·fon[1] (grif′ən) *n.* **1** a breed of small, sturdy, rough or smooth-coated dog developed in Belgium. **2** a dog of this breed. [< F *griffon,* an English breed of dog < OF *grifon.* See GRIFFIN.]

grif·fon[2] (grif′ən) *n.* griffin.

grift·er (grif′tər) *n. Slang.* a swindler, especially one who operates a dishonest game of chance at a fair, circus, etc. [perhaps var. of *grafter*]

grig (grig) *n. Dialect.* **1** a small or young eel. **2** a cricket. **3** a grasshopper. **4** a cheerful, lively person. [origin uncertain]

grill (gril) *n.* **1** a cooking utensil consisting of a metal framework for broiling meat, fish, etc.; gridiron. **2** a dish of broiled meat, fish, etc. **3** a grillroom. **—***v.* **1** broil. **2** torture with heat. **3** question severely and persistently: *The detectives grilled the prisoner until he confessed.* [< F *gril* < OF *greil,* earlier *grail* < L *craticulum,* var. of *craticula* gridiron, dim. of *cratis* latticework. Doublet of GRIDDLE.] **—grill′er,** *n.*

hat, āge, cãre, fär; let, ēqual, tėrm; it, īce
hot, ōpen, ôrder; oil, out; cup, pu̇t, rüle, ūse
əbove, takən, pencəl, lemən, circəs
ch, child; ng, long; sh, ship
th, thin; ᴛʜ, then; zh, measure

grille (gril) *n.* an openwork, metal structure, or screen, used as a gate, door, or window; grating. [< F < L *craticula* < *cratis* hurdle]

Grilles

grill·room (gril′rüm′ or -ru̇m′) *n.* a restaurant or dining room that specializes in serving broiled meat, fish, etc.

grilse (grils) *n.* **grilse** or **gril·ses.** a salmon that is returning from the sea to fresh water for the first time. [ME; ? var. of *grisle* grayish]

grim (grim) *adj.* **grim·mer, grim·mest.** **1** without mercy; stern; harsh; fierce. **2** not yielding; not relenting. **3** looking stern, fierce, or harsh. **4** horrible; ghastly: *He made grim jokes about death and ghosts.* [OE *grimm* fierce] —**grim′ly,** *adv.* —**grim·ness,** *n.* —**Syn. 1** cruel, merciless. **2** relentless, unyielding. **3** hard, forbidding, severe.

gri·mace (grə mās′ or grim′is) *n. v.* **-maced, -mac·ing.** —*n.* a twisting of the face; an ugly or funny smile. —*v.* make grimaces. [< F < Sp. *grimazo* panic] —**gri·mac′er,** *n.*

gri·mal·kin (grə mal′kən) *n.* **1** a cat. **2** an old female cat. **3** a spiteful old woman. [probably < gray + *Malkin,* dim. of *Maud,* proper name]

grime (grīm) *n. v.* **grimed, grim·ing.** —*n.* dirt rubbed deeply and firmly into a surface: *the grime on a coal miner's hands.* —*v.* cover with grime; make very dirty. [? OE *grīma* mask]

grim·y (grīm′ē) *adj.* **grim·i·er, grim·i·est.** covered with grime; very dirty. —**grim′i·ly,** *adv.* —**grim′i·ness,** *n.*

grin (grin) *v.* **grinned, grin·ning,** *n.* —*v.* **1** smile broadly. **2** show, make or express by smiling broadly: *He grinned approval.* **3** draw back the lips and show the teeth in anger, pain, scorn, etc.: *A snarling dog grins.*
—*n.* **1** a broad smile. **2** the act of showing the teeth in anger, pain, scorn, etc. [OE *grennian*] —**grin′ner,** *n.*

grind (grīnd) *v.* **ground** or (*Rare*) **grind·ed, grind·ing,** *n.* —*v.* **1** crush into bits or into powder: *Our back teeth grind food.* **2** crush by harshness or cruelty: *The slaves were ground down by their masters.* **3** sharpen, smooth, or wear by rubbing on something rough: *An axe is ground on a grindstone.* **4** rub harshly (on, into, against, or together): *grind one's heel into the earth, grind one's teeth in anger.* **5** work by turning a crank: *grind a coffee mill.* **6** produce by turning a crank: *grind out music on a hand organ.* **7** *Informal.* work or study long and hard.
—*n.* **1** the act of grinding. **2** a grinding sound. **3** *Informal.* long, hard work or study. **4** a dull and laborious task. **5** *Informal.* a person who works long and hard at his studies. [OE *grindan*] —**Syn.** *v.* **1** pulverize. **2** oppress. **4** grit, grate.

grind·er (grīn′dər) *n.* **1** a person or thing that grinds: *a coffee grinder.* **2** a man or machine that sharpens tools. **3** a back tooth for grinding food; molar.

grind·stone (grīn′stōn′ or grīnd′-) *n.* **1** a flat, round stone set in a frame and turned by a crank, treadle, etc. It is used to sharpen tools, such as axes and knives, or to smooth and polish things. **2 have, keep, or put one's nose to the grindstone,** work long and hard.

grin·go (gring′gō) *n.* **-gos.** *Derogatory.* an American, Englishman, or North European (a term used by Spanish Americans). [< Mexican Sp. < Sp. *gringo* gibberish, alteration of *griego* Greek, stranger]

grip (grip) *n. v.* **gripped, grip·ping.** —*n.* **1** a firm hold; seizing and holding tight; tight grasp. **2** the power of gripping. **3** something for gripping something else. **4** a part to take hold of; handle. **5** a special way of shaking hands. **6** a small suitcase; handbag. **7** firm control. **8** mental grasp. **9** a sudden, sharp pain. **10** grippe; influenza. **11 come to grips,** fight hand to hand; struggle close together. **12 lose one's grip,** lose control.
—*v.* **1** take a firm hold on; seize and hold tight. **2** get and keep the interest and attention of: *An exciting story grips you.* [OE *gripe* < *grīpan* grasp] —**grip′less,** *adj.* —**grip′per,** *n.*

gripe (grīp) *v.* **griped, grip·ing,** *n.* —*v.* **1** clutch; pinch. **2** oppress; distress. **3** cause or have pain in the bowels. **4** *Informal.* complain: *He was always griping about something.*
—*n.* **1** a fast hold; gripping; clutch. **2** grasp; control: *The empire held many small nations in its gripe.* **3** *Informal.* a complaint. **4 gripes,** *pl.* a clutching pain in the bowels; colic. [OE *grīpan*] —**grip′er,** *n.*

grippe (grip) *n.* a contagious disease like a very severe cold with fever; influenza. [< F < Russian *khrip* hoarseness]

grip·ping (grip′ing) *adj.* that grips; especially, that holds the attention or interest. —**grip′ping·ly,** *adv.*

Gri·sel·da (grə zel′də) *n.* a very meek, patient woman. [< *Griselda,* the heroine of several medieval romances, including Chaucer's *Clerk's Tale,* famed for her meekness and patience when cruelly treated by her husband]

gri·sette (gri zet′) *n.* a French working girl, especially a flirtatious seamstress or shop assistant. [< F *grisette* < *gris* gray; from usual color of their dresses]

gris·ly (griz′lē) *adj.* **-li·er, -li·est.** frightful; horrible; ghastly. [OE *grislic*] —**gris′li·ness,** *n.* —**Syn.** See **ghastly.**

grist (grist) *n.* **1** grain to be ground. **2** grain that has been ground; meal or flour. **3 grist to someone's mill,** source of profit to someone. [OE *grīst* < *grindan* grind]

gris·tle (gris′əl) *n.* cartilage; firm, tough, elastic tissue. Babies have gristle instead of bone in some parts of the skull. [OE]

gris·tly (gris′lē) *adj.* **-tli·er, -tli·est.** of, containing, or like gristle.

grist mill a mill for grinding grain.

grit (grit) *n. adj. v.* **grit·ted, grit·ting.** —*n.* **1** very fine gravel or sand. **2** a coarse sandstone. **3** the grain or texture of a stone with respect to fineness, coarseness, etc. **4** the abrasive quality of a sanding disk, cloth, paper, etc. **5** *Informal.* courage; pluck: *The fighter showed plenty of grit.* **6 Grit,** *Informal.* a member of the Liberal party in Canada. —*adj.* **Grit,** *Informal.* of or associated with the Liberals.
—*v.* **1** grate; grind: *He gritted his teeth and plunged into the cold water.* **2** put grit into or over. **3** make or cause to make a grating or gritty sound. [OE *grēot*]

grits (grits) *n.pl.* **1** coarsely ground corn, oats, etc., with the husks removed. **2** *U.S.* coarse hominy. [OE *grytte*]

grit·ty (grit′ē) *adj.* **-ti·er, -ti·est. 1** of or containing grit; like grit; sandy. **2** *Informal.* courageous; plucky. —**grit′ti·ly,** *adv.* —**grit′ti·ness,** *n.*

griz·zle[1] (griz′əl) *n. adj. v.* **-zled, -zling.** —*n.* **1** graying hair. **2** a wig. **3** the color gray. **4** a gray animal, especially a horse. —*adj.* gray; grizzled. —*v.* make or become gray. [ME < MF *grisel,* dim. of *gris* gray < Gmc.]

griz·zled (griz′əld) *adj.* **1** gray; grayish. **2** gray-haired.

griz·zly (griz′lē) *adj.* **-zli·er, -zli·est,** *n.* **-zlies.** —*adj.* **1** grayish; gray. **2** gray-haired.
—*n.* **1** a grizzly bear. **2** in mining, a screening device made of iron bars or rails and used to separate ore from gravel.

grizzly bear a large, fierce, gray, or brownish-gray bear of western North America.

groan (grōn) *n.* a deep-throated sound expressing grief, pain, or disapproval; deep, short moan. [< v.]
—*v.* **1** give a groan or groans. **2** be loaded or overburdened: *The table groaned with food.* **3** express by groaning. **4** suffer greatly. [OE *grānian*] —**groan′er,** *n.*
Syn. *n.* **Groan, moan** = a low sound expressing painful feelings. **Groan** suggests a heavier sound than **moan** and implies suffering too hard to bear and, often, rebelliousness: *the groans of people caught in the wreckage; the groans of slaves under a yoke.* **Moan** implies a more continuous and involuntary cry of pain or some similar sound: *the moan of the wind.*

groat (grōt) *n.* **1** an old English silver coin worth about six cents. **2** a very small sum. [< MDu. *groot,* literally, thick (coin)]

groats (grōts) *n.pl.* hulled grain; hulled and crushed grain. [OE *grotan,* pl.]

gro·cer (grō′sər) *n.* a merchant who sells food and household supplies. [ME < OF *grossier*, originally, one who sells in bulk; ult. < L *grossus* thick]

gro·cer·y (grō′sər ē or grōs′rē) *n.* **-cer·ies. 1** a store that sells food and household supplies. **2** the business or trade of a grocer. **3 groceries,** *pl.* **a** food and household supplies sold by a grocer. **b** the business of a grocer.

gro·ce·te·ri·a (grō′sə tēr′ē ə) *n.* a self-service grocery store. [*grocery* + *cafeteria*]

grog (grog) *n.* **1** a drink made of rum or any other strong alcoholic liquor diluted with water. **2** any strong alcoholic liquor. [short for *grogram*, nickname of British Admiral Vernon, from his *grogram* cloak]

grog·gy (grog′ē) *adj.* **-gi·er, -gi·est.** *Informal.* **1** shaky; unsteady. **2** drunk; intoxicated. **—grog′gi·ly,** *adv.* **—grog′gi·ness,** *n.*

grog·ram (grog′rəm) *n.* a coarse cloth made of silk, wool, or combinations of these with mohair. [< F *gros grain* coarse grain]

grog·shop (grog′shop′) *n.* *Esp.Brit.* a saloon.

groin (groin) *n.* **1** the hollow on either side of the body where the thigh joins the abdomen. **2** in architecture, a curved line where two vaults of a roof cross. —*v.* form or build with groins. [ME *grynde*, influenced by *loin*]

A, groins (def. 2)

grom·met (grom′it) *n.* **1** a metal eyelet. **2** a ring of rope, used as an oarlock, to hold a sail on its stays, etc. [< obs. F *gromette* curb of bridle < *gourmer* curb]

groom (grüm) *n.* **1** a man or boy who has charge of horses. **2** a man just married or about to be married; bridegroom. **3** in England, any of several officers of the royal household. **4** *Archaic.* a manservant.
—*v.* **1** feed and take care of (horses); rub down and brush. **2** take care of the appearance of; make neat and tidy. **3** prepare (a person) to run for a political office. [ME *grom(e)* boy; origin uncertain; cf. OF *gromet* servant] **—groom′er,** *n.*

grooms·man (grümz′mən) *n.* **-men** (-mən). the man who attends the bridegroom at a wedding.

groove (grüv) *n. v.* **grooved, groov·ing.** —*n.* **1** a long, narrow channel or furrow, especially one cut by a tool: *The plate rests in a groove on the rack.* **2** any similar channel; rut: *Wheels leave grooves in a dirt road.* **3** a fixed way of doing things: *It is hard to get out of a groove.* **4 in the groove,** *Slang.* **a** in music, playing or played smoothly and with great skill. **b** perfect; perfectly.
—*v.* make a groove in: *The sink shelf is grooved so that the water will run off.* [< MDu. *groeve* furrow, ditch] **—groov′er,** *n.*

grope (grōp) *v.* **groped, grop·ing. 1** feel about with the hands: *He groped for a flashlight when the lights went out.* **2** search blindly and uncertainly: *The detectives groped for some clue to the murder.* **3** find by feeling about with the hands; feel (one's way) slowly: *The blind man groped his way to the door.* —*n.* the act of groping. [OE *grāpian.* Related to GRASP, GRIP, GRIPE.] **—grop′er,** *n.* **—grop′ing·ly,** *adv.*

gros·beak (grōs′bēk′) *n.* a finch having a large, stout, cone-shaped bill. [< F *grosbec* < *gros* large + *bec* beak]

gro·schen (grō′shən) *n.* **1** a unit of money in Austria, worth 1/100 of a schilling. **2** a coin worth one groschen. [< G < ML (*denarius*) *grossus* thick denarius]

gros·grain (grō′grān′) *n.* a closely woven silk or rayon cloth with heavy cross threads and a dull finish. —*adj.* having heavy cross threads and a dull finish. [var. of *grogram*]

gros point (grōs′point′; *French,* grō pwäN′) *n.* in embroidery, a raised tapestry stitch; a coarse cross stitch. [< F *gros* large + *point* stitch]

gross (grōs) *adj. n.* **gross·es** *for 1,* **gross** *for 2.* —*adj.* **1** with nothing taken out; whole; entire. The gross receipts are all the money taken in before costs are deducted. **2** very bad; conspicuously bad: *She makes gross errors in pronunciation.* **3** coarse; vulgar: *Her manners are too gross for a lady.* **4** too big and fat; overfed. **5** thick; heavy; dense: *the gross growth of a jungle.* **6** concerned with large masses or outlines; general. —*n.* **1** the whole sum; total amount. **2** a unit consisting of twelve dozen; 144. **3 in the gross, a** as a whole; in bulk. **b** wholesale.
—*v.* make a gross profit of; earn a total of: *He grosses $20,000 per year.* [ME < OF *gros* < L *grossus* thick] **—gross′er,** *n.* **—gross′ly,** *adv.* **—Syn.** *adj.* **1** aggregate, total. **2** flagrant, outrageous, glaring. **3** broad, indecent, low. **5** rank.

gross national product the total market value of a nation's goods and services, before allowances or deductions. *Abbrev.*: GNP or G.N.P.

gross·ness (grōs′nis) *n.* a being gross.

gross profit the difference between the cost and the selling price of goods, before deductions.

gross ton 2,240 pounds.

gross weight the total weight, including wastage, packaging, etc.

grosz (grōsh) *n.* **gro·sze** (grō′shə), **gro·szy** (grō′shē). **1** a unit of money in Poland, worth 1/100 of a zloty. **2** a coin worth one grosz. [< Polish]

grot (grot) *n.* *Poetic.* grotto.

gro·tesque (grō tesk′) *adj.* **1** odd or unnatural in shape, appearance, manner, etc.; fantastic; queer: *The book had pictures of hideous dragons and other grotesque monsters.* **2** ridiculous; absurd: *The monkey's grotesque antics made the children laugh.* **3** of painting or sculpture, in or resembling the grotesque. —*n.* a painting, sculpture, etc. combining designs, ornaments, figures of persons or animals, etc. in a fantastic or unnatural way. [< F < Ital. *grottesco* < *grotta.* See GROTTO.] **—gro·tesque′ly,** *adv.* **—gro·tesque′ness,** *n.* **—Syn.** *adj.* **1** bizarre, strange.

grot·to (grot′ō) *n.* **-toes** or **-tos. 1** a cave. **2** an artificial cave made for coolness or pleasure. **3** a shrine in or like a cave. [< Ital. *grotta* < L *crypta* < Gk. *kryptē* vault. Doublet of CRYPT.]

grouch (grouch) *Informal.* —*v.* be sulky or ill-tempered; complain. —*n.* **1** a sulky person. **2** a sulky, discontented feeling. [var. of obs. *grutch* < OF *groucher* murmur, grumble. Doublet of GROUSE², GRUDGE.]

grouch·y (grouch′ē) *adj.* **grouch·i·er, grouch·i·est.** *Informal.* sulky; sullen; discontented. **—grouch′i·ly** *adv.* **—grouch′i·ness,** *n.*

ground¹ (ground) *n.* **1** the solid part of the earth's surface: *Snow covered the ground.* **2** earth; soil; dirt: *The ground was hard.* **3** a particular piece of land; land for some special purpose: *The Cariboo was his favorite hunting ground.* **4** the foundation for what is said, thought, claimed, or done; basis; reason. **5** underlying surface; background: *The cloth has a blue pattern on a white ground.* **6** Often, **grounds,** *pl.* land or area for some purpose or special use. **7 grounds,** *pl.* the land, lawns, and gardens around a house, college, etc. **8 grounds,** *pl.* the small bits that sink to the bottom of a drink such as coffee or tea; dregs; sediment. **9 grounds,** *pl.* foundation; basis. **10** the connection of an electrical conductor with the earth. **11** in a radio, television set, etc., the connection for the conductor that leads to the ground.
above ground, alive.
break ground, a dig; plough. **b** begin building.
break new ground, a do something for the first time. **b** do something in a new and original manner.
cover ground, a go over a certain distance or area. **b** travel. **c** do a certain amount of work, etc.
cut the ground from under one's feet, spoil a person's defence or argument by disposing of it in advance.
fall to the ground, fail; be given up.
from the ground up, completely; entirely; thoroughly.
gain ground, a go forward; advance; progress. **b** become more common or widespread.
give ground, retreat; yield.
hold one's ground, keep one's position; not retreat or yield.
lose ground, a go backward; retreat; yield. **b** become less common or widespread.

on the grounds of, because of; by reason of.
run into the ground, *Informal.* overdo; overwork.
shift one's ground, change one's position; use a different defence or argument.
stand one's ground, keep one's position; refuse to retreat or yield.
—*adj.* of, on, at, or near the ground; living or growing in, on, or close to the ground.
—*v.* **1** put on the ground; cause to touch the ground. **2** run aground; hit the bottom or shore: *The boat grounded in shallow water.* **3** put on a firm foundation or basis; establish firmly. **4** instruct in the first principles or elements: *The class is well grounded in grammar.* **5** furnish with a background. **6** connect (an electric wire or other conductor) with the earth. **7** prohibit (an aviator or an aircraft) from flying. **8** in baseball, hit a grounder. [OE *grund* bottom] —**Syn.** *n.* **2** loam, mould. **4** premise, motive.

ground[2] (ground) *v.* pt. and pp. of **grind.**

ground crew 1 the non-flying personnel responsible for the conditioning and maintenance of airplanes. **2** any group of men responsible for maintaining a baseball field or other playing field.

ground·er (groun′dər) *n.* in baseball, a ball hit or thrown so as to bound or roll along the ground.

ground·fish (ground′fish′) *n.* any of the various fish that swim at or near the bottom of the sea. Cod and haddock are groundfish.

ground floor 1 the first floor of a building. **2** the beginning of a venture: *get in on the ground floor.* **3** *Informal.* the best position in relation to a business deal, etc.

ground glass 1 glass with the surface roughened so that it is not transparent. **2** glass that has been ground to powder.

ground·hog (ground′hog′) *n.* a North American burrowing animal of the marmot family; woodchuck. Groundhogs hibernate in their burrows all winter, nourished by fat accumulated in summer.

Groundhog Day February 2, when the groundhog is supposed to come out of his burrow to see whether the sun is shining; if the sun is shining and he sees his shadow, he returns to his burrow for six more weeks of winter. Clouds would mean an early spring.

ground ice ice formed below the surface of a stream, lake, etc., either at the bed or attached to submerged objects. Also, **anchor ice.**

ground·less (ground′lis) *adj.* without foundation, basis, or reason. —**ground′less·ly,** *adv.* —**ground′less·ness,** *n.* —**Syn.** baseless.

ground·ling (ground′ling) *n.* **1** a plant or animal that lives close to the ground. **2** a fish that lives at the bottom of the water. **3** a spectator or reader who has poor taste. **4** formerly, a spectator of a play who sat or stood in the pit.

ground·nut (ground′nut′) *n.* **1** any of various plants having edible tubers or nutlike underground seeds, such as the peanut. **2** the edible tuber, pod, etc. of such a plant.

ground pine 1 a low, creeping evergreen, a kind of club moss, used for Christmas decorations, etc. **2** a European herb with resinous smell.

ground plan 1 the plan of a floor of a building. **2** the first or fundamental plan.

ground·sel (groun′səl or ground′-) *n.* a plant having small heads of yellow flowers. The seeds of some kinds are used for bird food. [OE *g(r)undeswelge* < *grund* ground or *gund* pus + *swelgan* swallow[1]; variously explained as meaning "ground-swallower" because it spreads rapidly, or "pus absorber" because it was used to reduce abscesses]

ground·sill (ground′sil′) *n.* a horizontal timber used as a foundation; lowest part of a wooden framework; sill. [ME *gronsel* < OE *grund* ground + *syll(e)* sill; the modern form has been influenced by its components *ground* and *sill*]

ground squirrel any one of various burrowing rodents belonging to the same family as the squirrel, especially the chipmunk.

ground swell 1 the broad, deep waves caused by a distant storm, earthquake, etc. **2** a great rise or increase in the amount, degree, or force of anything.

ground water water that flows or seeps through the ground into springs and wells.

ground wire a wire connecting electric wiring, a radio, etc. with the ground.

ground·work (ground′wėrk′) *n.* a foundation; basis.

ground zero the exact point where a bomb strikes the ground or, in an atomic explosion, the area directly beneath the core of radiation.

group (grüp) *n.* **1** a number of persons or things together: *A group of children were playing tag.* **2** a number of persons or things belonging or classed together: *Wheat, rye, and oats belong to the grain group.* **3** in the air force, a unit corresponding to a regiment in the army.
—*v.* **1** form into a group. **2** put in a group. **3** arrange in groups. [< F < Ital. *gruppo* < Gmc.] —**Syn.** *n.* **1** cluster, aggregation, assemblage.

group captain in the air force, a commissioned officer senior to a wing commander and junior to an air commodore. *Abbrev.*: G.C. or G/C

group·er (grüp′ər) *n.* **-er** or **-ers.** a large food fish of warm seas. [< Pg. *garupa*]

group·ing (grüp′ing) *n.* a placing or manner of being placed in a group or groups.

grouse[1] (grous) *n.* **grouse.** a game bird having feathered legs. The prairie chicken and sage hen are different kinds of grouse. [origin uncertain]

grouse[2] (grous) *v.* **groused, grous·ing,** *n. Informal.* —*v.* grumble; complain. —*n.* **1** a complaint. **2** a person who complains; grumbler. [apparently < OF *groucer,* var. of *groucher* murmur, grumble. Doublet of GROUCH, GRUDGE.]

grous·er[1] (grou′sər) *n. Informal.* a grouch or complainer.

grous·er[2] (grou′sər) *n.* **1** a pole driven into a river bottom, etc. to keep a boat or other floating object in place. **2** on a tractor, one of a set of cleats attached to a wheel or track to prevent slipping. [origin unknown]

grout (grout) *n.* thin mortar used to fill cracks, etc. —*v.* fill up or finish with this mortar. [OE *grūt*]

grove (grōv) *n.* a group of trees standing together. An orange grove is an orchard of orange trees. [OE *grāf*]

grov·el (grov′əl or gruv′əl) *v.* **-elled** or **-eled, -el·ling** or **-el·ing. 1** lie or crawl face downward at someone's feet; humble oneself: *The frightened slaves grovelled before their cruel master.* **2** enjoy low, mean, or contemptible things. [back formation from ME *grovelinge* (adv.) on the face < *on grufe* prone < ON *á grúfu*] —**grov′el·ler** or **grov′el·er,** *n.* —**Syn. 1** cringe, fawn.

grow (grō) *v.* **grew, grown, grow·ing. 1** become bigger by taking in food, as plants and animals do. **2** exist; sprout; spring; arise: *a tree growing only in the tropics.* **3** become greater; increase: *His fame grew.* **4** become gradually attached or united by growth: *The vine has grown fast to the wall.* **5** become: *grow cold, grow rich.* **6 grow on** or **upon,** have an increasing effect or influence on: *The habit grew on me.* **7 grow up, a** advance to or arrive at full growth and maturity. **b** come into being; be produced; develop. **8** cause to grow; produce; raise: *grow corn.* **9** allow to grow: *grow a beard.* **10** develop. [OE *grōwan.* Related to GRASS, GREEN.] —**Syn. 3** expand, develop, flourish. **8** cultivate.

grow·er (grō′ər) *n.* **1** a person who grows something: *a fruit grower.* **2** a plant that grows in a certain way: *a quick grower.*

growing pains 1 pains during childhood and youth, supposed to be caused by growing. **2** troubles that arise when something new is just developing.

growl (groul) *v.* **1** make a deep, low, angry sound: *The dog growled at the tramp.* **2** express by growling: *He growled his thanks.* **3** complain angrily: *The soldiers growled about the poor food.* **4** rumble.
—*n.* **1** a deep, low, angry sound; deep, warning snarl.

2 an angry complaint. 3 a rumble. [probably imitative] —**Syn.** *v.* 3 grumble.

growl·er (groul′ər) *n.* 1 a person or animal that growls. 2 a floating piece of ice resembling a small iceberg, broken off from a glacier or larger iceberg.

grown (grōn) *adj.* 1 arrived at full growth. 2 covered with a growth. —*v.* pp. of **grow.**

grown-up (grōn′up′) *adj.* 1 adult. 2 characteristic of or suitable for adults. —*n.* an adult: *The boy went to church with the grown-ups.*

growth (grōth) *n.* 1 the process of growing; development. 2 the amount of growing or developing; increase: *one year's growth.* 3 what has grown or is growing: *A thick growth of bushes covered the ground.* 4 an unhealthy mass of tissue formed in or on the body. Cancer causes a growth. —**Syn.** 2 expansion, enlargement.

grub (grub) *n. v.* **grubbed, grub·bing.** —*n.* 1 a wormlike form or larva of an insect. A grub is usually the smooth, thick larva of a beetle. 2 a drudge. 3 *Slang.* food. [probably < v.]
—*v.* 1 dig: *Pigs grub for roots.* 2 root out of the ground; dig up: *It took the farmer weeks to grub the stumps on his land.* 3 rid (ground) of roots, etc. 4 drudge; toil. 5 search (for); rummage. 6 *Slang.* eat. [ME *grubbe(n)*] —**grub′ber,** *n.*

grub·by (grub′ē) *adj.* **-bi·er, -bi·est.** 1 dirty; grimy. 2 like a grub. 3 infested with grubs. —**grub′bi·ness,** *n.*

grub·stake (grub′stāk′) *n. v.* **-staked, -stak·ing.** —*n.* 1 the food, outfit, money, etc. supplied to a prospector on the condition of sharing in whatever he finds. 2 the arrangement by which this is done. 3 *Cdn.* the money or the means to buy food and other provisions for a certain period. 4 *Cdn.* a store of food or provisions. —*v.* provide with a grubstake. —**grub′stak′er,** *n.*

Grub Street 1 a former street in London where poor, struggling writers lived. 2 writers of little ability who write merely to earn money; hack writers.

grudge (gruj) *n. v.* **grudged, grudg·ing.** —*n.* 1 ill will; a sullen feeling against; dislike of long standing. 2 **bear a grudge,** have and keep a grudge. [< v.]
—*v.* 1 feel anger or dislike toward (a person) because of (something); envy the possession of: *He grudged me my little prize even though he had won a bigger one.* 2 give or let have unwillingly: *The mean man grudged his horse the food that it ate.* [earlier meaning, grumble, complain; var. of obs. *grutch* < OF *groucher* murmur, grumble. Doublet of GROUCH, GROUSE².] —**Syn.** *n.* 1 resentment. See **spite.** -*v.* 1 envy, begrudge.

grudg·ing·ly (gruj′ing lē) *adv.* unwillingly.

gru·el (grü′əl) *n. v.* **-elled** or **-eled, -el·ling** or **-el·ing.** —*n.* a thin, almost liquid food made by boiling oatmeal, etc. in water or milk. Gruel is often given to those who are sick or old. —*v. Informal.* tire out completely; exhaust. [ME < OF *gruel,* ult. < Gmc.]

gru·el·ing (grü′əl ing) *adj. n.* gruelling.

gru·el·ling (grü′əl ing) *Informal.* —*adj.* exhausting; very tiring: *a gruelling contest.* —*n.* an exhausting or very tiring experience.

grue·some (grü′səm) *adj.* horrible; frightful; revolting. Also, **grewsome.** [< *grue* shudder; cf. MDu., MLG *gruwen*] —**grue′some·ly,** *adv.* —**grue′some·ness,** *n.*

gruff (gruf) *adj.* 1 deep and harsh; hoarse. 2 rough; rude; unfriendly; bad-tempered: *a gruff manner.* [< MDu. *grof*] —**gruff′ly,** *adv.* —**gruff′ness,** *n.* —**Syn.** 2 grumpy, brusque, impolite.

grum·ble (grum′bəl) *v.* **-bled, -bling,** *n.* —*v.* 1 mutter in discontent; complain in a bad-tempered way. 2 express by grumbling. 3 rumble. —*n.* 1 a mutter of discontent; bad-tempered complaint. 2 a rumble. [related to OE *grymettan* roar, and *grim*] —**grum′bler,** *n.* —**Syn.** *v.* 1, 2 growl, murmur. See **complain.**

grump·y (grump′ē) *adj.* **grump·i·er, grump·i·est.** surly; ill-humored; gruff: *The grumpy old man found fault with everything.* [origin uncertain] —**grump′i·ly,** *adv.* —**grump′i·ness,** *n.*

Grun·dy (grun′dē) *n.* **Mrs.** the social censorship of manners and morals: *Mrs. Grundy would not approve of these scanty swim suits.* [from a character in Thomas Morton's play *Speed the Plough* (1798). She was referred to in the question, "What will Mrs. Grundy say?"]

grunt (grunt) *n.* 1 the deep, hoarse sound that a pig makes. 2 a sound like this: *The old man got out of his chair with a grunt.* 3 an edible sea fish that grunts when taken out of the water. [< v.] —*v.* 1 make the deep, hoarse sound of a pig. 2 say with a sound like this: *The sullen boy grunted his apology.* [OE *grunnettan* < *grunian* grunt] —**grunt′er,** *n.*

Gru·yère (gri yăr′ or grü yăr′) *n.* a variety of firm, light-yellow cheese made from whole milk. [< *Gruyère,* a district in Switzerland]

gryph·on (grif′ən) *n.* griffin.

G.S. General Staff.

G string 1 on a musical instrument, a string tuned to G. 2 a narrow loincloth held up by a cord around the waist. 3 a similar covering worn by striptease artists. 4 a single-wire method of television transmission.

gt. 1 drop. (for L *gutta*) 2 great.

Gt.Br. or **Gt.Brit.** Great Britain.

gtd. guaranteed.

guai·a·cum (gwī′ə kəm) *n.* 1 any of various tropical shrubs or trees having bluish flowers, capsular fruit, and tough wood. 2 the hard, greenish-brown wood of such a tree. 3 a resin obtained from this wood, formerly used medicinally. [< NL *Guaiacum* the genus name < Sp. *guayacán* < Arawak (West Indies) *guayacan*]

gua·na·co (gwä nä′kō) *n.* **-cos.** a wild South American mammal like a small camel without a hump. Llamas and alpacas are thought to have been domesticated from guanacos. [< Sp. < Quechua (Indian lang. of Peru) *huancau*]

gua·no (gwä′nō) *n.* **-nos.** 1 the manure of sea birds, found especially on islands near Peru. Guano is an excellent fertilizer. 2 an artificial fertilizer made from fish. [< Sp. < Quechua (Indian lang. of Peru) *huanu*]

gua·ra·ni (gwär′ə nē) *n.* 1 a unit of money in Paraguay. See table at **money.** 2 a coin worth one guarani. [< *Guarani,* a group of Indians from Central South America]

guar·an·tee (gar′ən tē′) *n. v.* **-teed, -tee·ing.** —*n.* 1 a promise to pay or do something if another fails; a pledge to replace goods if they are not as represented; backing. 2 a person who so promises. 3 one to whom such a pledge is made. 4 something given or taken as security; guaranty. 5 something having the force or effect of a guaranty: *Wealth is no guarantee of happiness.*
—*v.* 1 stand behind; give a guarantee for; assure genuineness or permanence of; answer for fulfilment of (a contract, etc.): *This company guarantees its clocks for a year. The father guaranteed his son's future behavior.* 2 undertake to secure for another: *He will guarantee us possession of the house by May.* 3 secure (against or from): *His insurance guaranteed him against money loss in case of fire.* 4 engage (to do something): *I will guarantee to prove every statement I made.* 5 ensure that (something) has been or will be: *The advance payment of money guarantees the good faith of the purchaser.* [probably var. of *guaranty*] —**Syn.** *n.* 1 warrant, security, surety.

guar·an·tor (gar′ən tôr′) *n.* a person who makes or gives a guarantee.

guar·an·ty (gar′ən tē) *n.* **-ties,** *v.* **-tied, -ty·ing.** —*n.* 1 the act or fact of giving security. 2 a pledge or promise given as security; security. —*v.* guarantee. [< OF *guarantie* < *guarantir* to warrant < *guarant* a warrant < Gmc. Doublet of WARRANTY.]

guard (gärd) *v.* 1 keep safe; watch over carefully; take care of: *The dog guards the house.* 2 defend; protect: *The goalie guards the goal.* 3 keep from escaping: *The soldiers guarded the prisoners day and night.* 4 keep in check; hold back; keep under control: *Guard your tongue.* 5 take precautions (against).
—*n.* 1 a person or group that guards. A soldier or group of soldiers guarding a person or place is a guard. 2 anything that gives protection; contrivance or appliance to protect against injury, loss, etc.: *A guard was placed in front of the fire.* 3 a careful watch: *A soldier kept guard over the prisoners.* 4 a picked body of soldiers: *a guard of honor.* 5 defence; protection. 6 in boxing, fencing, or cricket, a position of defence. 7 arms or weapons held in a position of defence. 8 in football, a player on either side of the

centre. **9** in basketball, either of the two players serving as defencemen. **10** *Brit.* a person in charge of a railway train; brakeman. **11** in former times, the man in charge of a stagecoach. **12 the Guards, a** certain British regiments whose duties include guarding the sovereign. **b** certain Canadian regiments: *the Governor General's Horse Guards.* **13 off one's guard,** unprepared to meet a sudden attack; unwary. **14 on guard,** ready to defend or protect; watchful. [< F *garder* (earlier *guarder*), v., *garde* (earlier *guarde*), n. < Gmc. Doublet of WARD.] **—guard′er,** *n.*
Syn. *v.* **1 Guard, defend, protect** = keep safe. **Guard** = keep safe by watching over carefully: *The dog guarded the child night and day.* **Defend** = guard from harm by keeping away, turning aside, or resisting danger or attack: *He defended the child against the big boys.* **Protect** = keep safe by means of something that serves as a shield and keeps away danger or harm: *Proper food protects a person's health.* **5** safeguard, preserve. *-n.* **1** defender, protector, sentry, sentinel. **5** bulwark, shield.

guard·ed (gär′did) *adj.* **1** kept safe; carefully watched over; protected. **2** careful; cautious: "*Maybe*" *is a guarded answer to a question.* **—guard′ed·ness,** *n.* **—Syn. 1** defended. **2** circumspect.

guard·ed·ly (gär′did lē) *adv.* in a guarded manner.

guard·house (gärd′hous′) *n.* **1** a building used as a jail for soldiers. **2** a building used by soldiers on guard.

guard·i·an (gär′dē ən) *n.* **1** a person who takes care of another or of some special thing. **2** a person appointed by law to take care of the affairs of someone who is young or cannot take care of them himself. *—adj.* protecting: *a guardian angel.* [ME < AF *gardein,* var. of OF *g(u)arden* < *guarde* < Gmc. Doublet of WARDEN.] **—Syn.** *n.* **1** protector, defender. **2** trustee, warden, keeper, guard.

guard·i·an·ship (gär′dē ən ship′) *n.* the position or care of a guardian.

guard·rail (gärd′rāl′) *n.* a rail or railing for protection.

guard·room (gärd′rüm′ or -rům′) *n.* **1** a room used by soldiers on guard. **2** a room used as a jail for soldiers.

guards·man (gärdz′mən) *n.* **-men** (-mən). **1** a guard. **2** a private in any one of the Guards regiments. **3** any man serving in such a regiment.

gua·va (gwä′və) *n.* **1** a tropical American tree or shrub having a yellowish, pear-shaped fruit. **2** the fruit, used for jelly, jam, etc. [< Sp. *guayaba* < native name]

gu·ber·na·to·ri·al (gū′bər nə tô′rē əl or gü′bər nə tô′rē əl) *adj. Esp.U.S.* of a governor; having to do with a governor. [< L *gubernator,* originally, pilot < *gubernare.* See GOVERN.]

guck (guk) *n. Slang.* anything oozy, slimy, or similarly distasteful. [? < goo + m*uck*]

gudg·eon (guj′ən) *n.* **1** a small European fresh-water fish that is easy to catch and is often used for bait. **2** a minnow. **3** a person easily fooled or cheated. [ME < OF *goujon,* ult. < L *gobius* a kind of fish < Gk.]

guer·don (gėr′dən) *n. v. Poetic.* a reward. [ME < OF *guerdon,* var. of *werdon* < Med.L *widerdonum* < OHG *widarlōn* repayment, influenced by L *donum* gift]

gue·ril·la (gə ril′ə) *n.* guerrilla.

Guern·sey (gėrn′zē) *n.* **-seys. 1** a breed of dairy cattle resembling the Jersey, but somewhat larger. **2** an animal of this breed. **3 guernsey,** a close-fitting knitted woollen shirt or sweater worn by sailors. [< *Guernsey,* one of the Channel Islands, where this breed of cattle originated]

guer·ril·la (gə ril′ə) *n.* **1** a member of a small independent band of fighters who harass the enemy by sudden raids, ambushes, etc. **2** warfare carried on by such fighters. *—adj.* of or by guerrillas: *a guerrilla attack.* [< Sp. *guerrilla,* dim. of *guerra* war]

guess (ges) *v.* **1** form an opinion (of) without really knowing: *guess the height of a tree.* **2** get the right answer to by guessing: *guess a riddle.* **3** think; believe; suppose. *—n.* **1** an opinion formed without really knowing. **2** a guessing. [n. < v., ME; cf. Swedish *gissa*] **—guess′er,** *n.*
Syn. *v.* **1 Guess, conjecture, surmise** = form an opinion without knowing enough. **Guess,** the least formal word, suggests forming an opinion on the basis of what one thinks likely, without really knowing for certain: *He guessed the distance to the nearest town.* **Conjecture** suggests having some evidence, but not enough for proof: *Scientists conjecture the value of a new drug.* **Surmise** = form a conjecture more on what one suspects might be true than on facts one knows: *He surmised her thoughts.* *-n.* **1** estimate, supposition, surmise, conjecture.

guess·work (ges′wėrk′) *n.* work, action, or result based on guessing; guessing.

hat, āge, cãre, fär; let, ēqual, tėrm; it, īce
hot, ōpen, ôrder; oil, out; cup, půt, rüle, ūse
əbove, takən, pencəl, lemən, circəs
ch, child; ng, long; sh, ship
th, thin; ᴛʜ, then; zh, measure

guest (gest) *n.* **1** a person who is received and entertained at one's home, club, etc. **2** a person who is not a regular member; visitor. **3** a person staying at a hotel, motel, boarding house, etc. *—adj.* **1** of or for guests: *a guest room, guest towels.* **2** being a guest: *a guest conductor, a guest lecturer.* [OE *giest* stranger (friend or foe)? < ON *gestr.* Akin to HOST[2].] **—Syn.** *n.* **1** See **visitor.**

guff (guf) *n. Informal.* foolish talk, especially when used in an attempt to hide the real facts. [probably imitative]

guf·faw (gu fo′ or gu fô′) *n.* a loud, coarse burst of laughter. *—v.* laugh loudly and coarsely. [imitative]

guid·ance (gīd′əns) *n.* **1** a guiding; leadership; direction: *Under her mother's guidance Nan learned to cook.* **2** something that guides. **3** in education, studies and counselling to help students understand their school environment, make the most of their opportunities, and plan for the future. **4** in aeronautics, the regulation of the path of rockets, missiles, etc. in flight.

guide (gīd) *v.* **guid·ed, guid·ing,** *n. —v.* **1** show the way; lead; conduct; direct. **2** manage; control; regulate. *—n.* **1** a person or thing that shows the way, leads, conducts, or directs: *Tourists and hunters sometimes hire guides.* **2** a part of a machine for directing or regulating motion or action. **3** a guidebook. **4** a Girl Guide. [ME < OF *guider* < Gmc.] **—guid′er,** *n.* **—guide′less,** *adj.*
Syn. *v.* **1 Guide, lead, conduct** = show the way. **Guide** emphasizes knowing the way and all the points of interest or danger along it, and means to go along to point these out: *The Indian guided the hunters.* **Lead** emphasizes going ahead to show the way, expecting the person or thing to follow: *The dog led his master to the injured man.* **Conduct** emphasizes going with the person or thing to guide or assist him: *He conducted a party of tourists to Europe.* **2** govern. *-n.* **1** leader, conductor, director, pilot.

guide·board (gīd′bôrd′) *n.* a board or sign with directions for travellers, often attached to a guidepost.

guide·book (gīd′bůk′) *n.* a book of directions and information, especially one for travellers, tourists, etc.

guided missile a projectile that can be guided accurately, usually by means of transmitted electronic impulses.

guide·line (gīd′līn′) *n.* a principle or instruction set forth as a guide.

guide·post (gīd′pōst′) *n.* a post with signs and directions on it for travellers. A guidepost where roads meet tells travellers what places each road goes to and how far it is to each place.

Guid·er (gīd′ər) *n.* an adult who is associated in some way with the Girl Guides or Brownies.

guide rope 1 a rope that is used to steady and guide something. **2** a long rope hanging from a dirigible or balloon for regulating its speed and altitude.

guide word in dictionaries and similar reference works, either of two words appearing at the top of a page, one indicating the first entry word on the page and the other showing the last entry word on the page.

gui·don (gī′dən or gī′don) *n.* **1** a small flag or streamer carried as a guide by soldiers, or used for signalling. **2** a soldier who carries the guidon. [< F < Ital. *guidone*]

guild (gild) *n.* **1** a society for mutual aid or for some common purpose: *the Ladies' Auxiliary Guild.* **2** in the Middle Ages, a union of the men in a particular trade to keep standards high and to safeguard the interests of their trade. Also, **gild.** [ME < ON *gildi*]

guil·der (gil′dər) *n.* **1** a unit of money in the Netherlands and Surinam. See table at **money. 2** a coin worth one guilder. Also, **gulden.** [alteration of *gulden*]

guild·hall (gild′hol′ or -hôl′) *n.* **1** the hall in which a guild meets. **2** a town hall; city hall.

guilds·man (gildz′mən) *n.* **-men** (-mən). a member of a guild.

guile (gīl) *n.* crafty deceit; craftiness; sly tricks: *A* *swindler uses guile; a robber uses force.* [ME < OF < Gmc. Akin to WILE.] —**Syn.** cunning, wiliness, trickery. See **deceit.**

guile·ful (gīl′fəl) *adj.* crafty and deceitful; sly and tricky. —**guile′ful·ly,** *adv.* —**guile′ful·ness,** *n.* —**Syn.** cunning, wily, artful.

guile·less (gīl′lis) *adj.* without guile; honest; frank; sincere. —**guile′less·ly,** *adv.* —**guile′less·ness,** *n.*

guil·le·mot (gil′ə mot′) *n.* any of several narrow-billed arctic diving birds of the auk family. [< F *guillemot,* probably < *Guillaume* William]

guil·lo·tine (*n.* gil′ə tēn′; *v.* gil′ə tēn′) *n. v.* **-tined, -tin·ing.** —*n.* **1** a machine for beheading persons by means of a heavy blade that slides down between two grooved posts. The guillotine was much used during the French Revolution. **2** a machine for cutting paper.
—*v.* **1** behead with a guillotine. **2** cut with a guillotine. [< F, after Joseph I. *Guillotin* (1738-1814), a French physician and advocate of its use] —**guil′lo·tin′er,** *n.*

guilt (gilt) *n.* **1** the fact or state of having done wrong; a being guilty; a being blameworthy. **2** guilty action or conduct; a crime; offence. [OE *gylt* offence] —**Syn. 1** guiltiness, culpability. **2** wrongdoing.

guilt·less (gilt′lis) *adj.* not guilty; free from guilt; innocent. —**Syn.** See **innocent.**

guilt·y (gil′tē) *adj.* **guilt·i·er, guilt·i·est. 1** having done wrong; deserving to be blamed and punished: *The jury pronounced the prisoner guilty of murder.* **2** knowing or showing that one has done wrong: *The one who did the crime had a guilty conscience and a guilty look.* [OE *gyltig*] —**guilt′i·ly,** *adv.* —**guilt′i·ness,** *n.* —**Syn. 1** culpable, sinful, criminal.

guimpe (gimp or gamp) *n.* a blouse worn under a dress and showing at the neck or at the neck and arms. [< F < Gmc. Doublet of GIMP.]

guin·ea (gin′ē) *n.* **1** an amount equal to 21 shillings, used in the British Isles in stating prices, fees, etc. **2** a former British gold coin worth 21 shillings, so-called because originally made of gold from Guinea. **3** a guinea fowl.

guinea fowl a domestic fowl resembling a pheasant, having dark-gray feathers with small white spots.

guinea hen 1 a guinea fowl. **2** a female guinea fowl.

guinea pig 1 a short-eared animal resembling a big, fat, harmless rat. Guinea pigs make good pets. **2** any person or thing serving as a subject for experiment or observation.

Guin·e·ver (gwin′ə vər) *n.* Guinevere.

Guin·e·vere (gwin′ə vēr′) *n.* in Arthurian legend, King Arthur's wife.

guise (gīz) *n.* **1** a style of dress; garb: *The soldier went into the village in the guise of a monk so that he would not be recognized.* **2** external appearance; aspect; semblance: *His theory is nothing but an old idea in a new guise.* **3** an assumed appearance; pretence: *Under the guise of friendship he plotted treachery.* [ME < OF < Gmc. Akin to WISE².]

gui·tar (gə tär′) *n.* a musical instrument having six strings, played with the fingers. [< Sp. *guitarra* < Gk. *kithara* cithara. Doublet of CITHARA and ZITHER.]

A guitar

gulch (gulch) *n.* a deep, narrow ravine with steep sides, especially one marking the course of a stream or torrent. [origin unknown]

gul·den (gůl′dən) *n.* **-dens** or **-den.** guilder. [< Du. and G *Gulden,* literally, golden]

gules (gūlz) *n. adj.* in heraldry, red. [ME < OF *goules* red fur neck-piece (originally, pieces of neck fur) < *goule* throat < L *gula*]

gulf (gulf) *n.* **1** a large bay; an arm of an ocean or sea extending into the land. **2** a very deep break or cut in the earth. **3** any wide separation: *The quarrel left a gulf between the two friends.* **4** something that swallows up; whirlpool. [ME < OF *golfe* < Ital. *golfo,* ult. < Gk. *kolpos,* originally, bosom] —**gulf′like′,** *adj.*

gulf·weed (gulf′wēd′) *n.* an olive-brown seaweed having many berry-like sacs that keep it afloat.

gull¹ (gul) *n.* a graceful, gray-and-white bird having long wings, webbed feet, and a thick, strong beak, living on or near large bodies of water. [ME ? < Welsh *gŵylan*]

gull² (gul) *v.* deceive; cheat. —*n.* a person who is easily deceived or cheated. [origin uncertain]

Gul·lah (gul′ə) *n.* **1** a group of Negroes living along the coast of South Carolina and Georgia and on the islands off the coast. **2** a member of this group. **3** a dialect of English spoken by the Gullahs.

gull·er·y (gul′ər ē) *n.* a breeding place of gulls.

gul·let (gul′it) *n.* **1** a passage for food from the mouth to the stomach; esophagus. **2** the throat. [ME < OF *goulet,* ult. < L *gula* throat]

gul·li·bil·i·ty (gul′ə bil′ə tē) *n.* a being gullible; tendency to be easily deceived or cheated.

gul·li·ble (gul′ə bəl) *adj.* easily deceived or cheated. [< *gull²*] —**gul′li·bly,** *adv.*

gul·ly (gul′ē) *n.* **-lies,** *v.* **-lied, -ly·ing.** —*n.* **1** a narrow gorge; a small ravine. **2** a channel or ditch made by heavy rains or running water: *After the storm, the newly-seeded lawn was covered with gullies.* **3** in cricket: **a** the part of the playing field behind the slips. **b** a fielder stationed in the gully.
—*v.* make gullies in. [? var. of *gullet*]

gulp (gulp) *v.* **1** swallow eagerly or greedily. **2** keep in; choke back; repress: *The disappointed boy gulped down a sob.* **3** gasp; choke. —*n.* **1** the act of swallowing. **2** the amount swallowed at one time; mouthful. [imitative] —**gulp′er,** *n.*

gum¹ (gum) *n. v.* **gummed, gum·ming.** —*n.* **1** a sticky juice, obtained from or given off by certain trees and plants, that hardens in the air and dissolves in water. Gum is used to make candy, medicine, and mucilage. **2** any similar secretion, such as resin, gum resin, etc. **3** a preparation of such a substance for use in industry or the arts. **4** chewing gum. **5** the substance on the back of a stamp, the flap of an envelope, etc.; mucilage; glue. **6** rubber. **7** a gum tree; eucalyptus.
—*v.* **1** smear, stick together, or stiffen with gum. **2** give off gum; form gum. **3** make or become sticky; clog with something sticky. **4 gum up,** *Slang.* mess up; put out of order. [ME < OF *gomme* < L *gummi* < Gk. *kommi*]

gum² (gum) *n.* Often, **gums,** *pl.* the flesh around the teeth. [OE *gōma* palate]

gum ammoniac a natural mixture of gum and resin, used in medicine; ammoniac.

gum arabic the gum obtained from acacia trees, used in making candy, medicine, mucilage, etc.

gum·bo (gum′bō) *n.* **-bos. 1** the okra plant. **2** its sticky pods. **3** soup thickened with okra pods: *chicken-gumbo soup.* **4** soil that contains much silt and becomes very sticky when wet, especially that found on the western prairies: *It took him an hour to clean the gumbo off his boots.* [of African origin]

gum·boil (gum′boil′) *n.* a small abscess on the gums.

gum·drop (gum′ drop′) *n.* a stiff, jelly-like piece of candy made of gum arabic, gelatin, etc. sweetened and flavored.

gum·my (gum′ē) *adj.* **-mi·er, -mi·est. 1** sticky; like gum. **2** covered with gum. **3** giving off gum. —**gum′mi·ness,** *n.*

gump·tion (gump′shən) *n. Informal.* **1** initiative; energy; resourcefulness. **2** common sense; good judgment. [< Scots dial.; origin uncertain]

gum resin a natural mixture of gum and resin, obtained from certain plants.

gum·shoe (gum′shü′) *n. v.* **-shoed, -shoe·ing.** —*n.* **1** a rubber overshoe. **2 gumshoes,** *pl.* sneakers. **3** *Slang.* a detective. —*v. Slang.* go around quietly and secretly.

gum tree a tree that yields gum. The sweet gum, sour gum, and eucalyptus are gum trees.

gum·wood (gum′wůd′) *n.* the wood of a gum tree.

gun¹ (gun) *n. v.* **gunned, gun·ning.** —*n.* **1** a weapon with a long metal tube for shooting shells, bullets, shot, etc. An artillery piece or a cannon is properly a gun; rifles, pistols, and revolvers are commonly called guns.

hat, āge, cãre, fär; let, ēqual, tėrm; it, īce
hot, ōpen, ôrder; oil, out; cup, pu̇t, rüle, ūse
əbove, takən, pencəl, lemən, circəs
ch, child; ng, long; sh, ship
th, thin; ᴛʜ, then; zh, measure

2 anything resembling a gun in use or shape. 3 the firing of a gun as a signal or salute. 4 **beat the gun,** begin before the signal to start. 5 **give it the gun,** *Informal.* speed up; go faster. 6 **jump the gun,** start too soon; start before the signal to do so; get a head start on one's opposition. 7 **spike someone's guns,** make a person powerless; defeat him. 8 **stick to one's guns,** keep one's position; refuse to retreat or yield.
—*v.* 1 shoot with a gun; hunt with a gun. 2 *Slang.* put at high speed; accelerate: *The pilot of the airplane gunned his engine for a sharp climb.* [ME ? < ON *Gunna,* shortened form of *Gunnhildr,* a woman's name applied to engines of war]

gun[2] (gun) *v. Archaic and poetic.* pp. of **gin[4].**

gun barrel the metal tube of a gun.

gun·boat (gun′bōt′) *n.* a small warship, often one that can be used in shallow water.

gun carriage a structure on which a gun is mounted or moved and on which it is fired.

gun·cot·ton (gun′kot′ən) *n.* an explosive made by treating cotton with nitric and sulphuric acids.

gun·dog (gun′dog′) *n.* a dog trained to locate, flush, or retrieve game for hunters who use guns. Pointers and setters are gundogs.

gun·fight (gun′fīt′) *n.* a fight in which guns are used.

gun·fire (gun′fīr′) *n.* the shooting of a gun or guns.

gunk hole (gungk) *Cdn.* a tiny, rocky-sided cove with deep water, making an excellent fishing spot.

gun·lock (gun′lok′) *n.* the part of a gun by which the charge is fired.

gun·man (gun′mən) *n.* **-men** (-mən). a man who uses a gun to rob, kill, etc.

gun metal 1 a dark-gray alloy used for chains, buckles, handles, etc. 2 a dark gray. 3 a kind of bronze formerly used for making guns. **—gun′-met′al,** *adj.*

gun·nel[1] (gun′əl) *n.* gunwale.

gun·nel[2] (gun′əl) *n.* a small fish resembling a perch, found in the N. Atlantic Ocean. [origin uncertain]

gun·ner (gun′ər) *n.* 1 a man trained to fire artillery pieces; a soldier who handles and fires big guns. 2 a naval officer in charge of a ship's guns. 3 a private soldier in the artillery. 4 any man serving in the artillery. 5 a person who hunts with a shotgun, rifle, etc.

gun·ner·y (gun′ər ē) *n.* 1 the art and science of constructing and managing big guns. 2 the use of guns; the shooting of guns. 3 guns collectively.

gun·ning (gun′ing) *n.* the act of shooting with a gun; hunting with a gun.

gun·ny (gun′ē) *n.* **-nies.** 1 a strong, coarse fabric used for sacks, bags, etc. 2 a sack, bag, etc. made of this fabric. [< Hind. *goni*]

gunny sack a sack or bag made of gunny.

gun pit an excavation where artillery is placed.

gun·point (gun′point′) *n.* 1 the tip or point of a gun barrel. 2 **at gunpoint,** being threatened by a gun; having a gun pointed at one.

gun·pow·der (gun′pou′dər) *n.* a powder that explodes with force when brought into contact with fire. Gunpowder is used in guns, fireworks, and blasting. One kind of gunpowder is made of saltpetre, sulphur, and charcoal.

gun room 1 a room where guns are kept. 2 a room for junior officers on a warship.

gun·run·ning (gun′run′ing) *n.* the bringing of guns and ammunition into a country illegally.

gun·shot (gun′shot′) *n.* 1 a shot fired from a gun. 2 the shooting of a gun. 3 the distance that a gun will shoot.

gun·sight (gun′sīt′) *n.* a device on a gun to help in taking aim.

gun·smith (gun′smith′) *n.* a person whose work is making or repairing small guns.

gun·stock (gun′stok′) *n.* the wooden support or handle to which the barrel of a gun is fastened.

Gun·ter's chain (gun′tərz) a surveyor's chain consisting of 100 links, each 7.92 inches or 12 inches long. [named after Edmund *Gunter* (1581-1626), an English mathematician]

gun·wale (gun′əl) *n.* the upper edge of a ship's or boat's side. Also, **gunnel.** [< *gun[1]* + *wale* a plank; because formerly used to support guns]

GUNWALE

gup·py (gup′ē) *n.* **-pies.** a very small, brightly colored fish of tropical fresh water. The female bears young instead of producing eggs. [after Robert J. L. *Guppy* of Trinidad, who supplied the first specimens]

gur·gle (gėr′gəl) *v.* **-gled, -gling,** *n.* —*v.* 1 flow or run with a bubbling sound: *Water gurgles when it is poured out of a bottle or when it flows over stones.* 2 make a bubbling sound: *The baby gurgled happily.* 3 express with a gurgle. —*n.* a bubbling sound. [? imitative]

Gurk·ha (gu̇r′kə) *n.* a member of a Nepalese Hindu people famous for its soldiers.

gu·ru (gü′rü or gu̇ ru̇′) *n.* 1 in Hinduism, a personal religious adviser or teacher. 2 a person who guides others, especially in a spiritual way. [< Hind. *gurū*]

gush (gush) *v.* 1 rush out suddenly; pour out. 2 *Informal.* talk in a silly way about one's affections or enthusiasms. 3 give forth suddenly or very freely. 4 have an abundant flow of blood, tears, etc.
—*n.* 1 a rush of water or other liquid from an enclosed place: *If you get a deep cut, there is usually a gush of blood.* 2 *Informal.* silly, emotional talk. 3 a sudden and violent outbreak; burst: *a gush of anger.* [probably imitative] —**Syn.** *v.* 1 spurt, spout. See **flow.**

gush·er (gush′ər) *n.* 1 an oil well that flows copiously without being pumped. 2 *Informal.* a gushy person.

gush·ing (gush′ing) *adj.* 1 that gushes. 2 effusive.

gush·y (gush′ē) *adj.* **gush·i·er, gush·i·est.** showing one's feelings in a silly way; effusive; sentimental. **—gush′i·ly,** *adv.* **—gush′i·ness,** *n.*

gus·set (gus′it) *n.* 1 a triangular piece of material inserted in a dress, etc. to give greater strength or more room. 2 a bracket or plate used to reinforce the joints of a structure. [ME < OF *gousset* < *gousse* husk]

gus·sy (gu′sē) *v. Slang.* make seemly or attractive; spruce (*up*): *The girls gussied themselves up for the party.* [origin uncertain]

gust (gust) *n.* 1 a sudden, violent rush of wind: *A gust upset the small sailboat.* 2 a sudden burst of rain, smoke, sound, etc. 3 an outburst of anger, enthusiasm, etc. [< ON *gustr*]

gus·ta·to·ry (gus′tə tô′rē) *adj.* of the sense of taste; having to do with tasting: *Eating fine foods gives gustatory pleasure.* [< L *gustatus,* pp. of *gustare* taste]

gus·to (gus′tō) *n.* **-tos.** 1 keen relish; hearty enjoyment: *The hungry boy ate his dinner with gusto.* 2 a liking or taste. [< Ital. *gusto,* originally, taste < L *gustus*]

gust·y (gus′tē) *adj.* **gust·i·er, gust·i·est.** 1 coming in gusts; windy; stormy. 2 marked by outbursts: *gusty laughter.* **—gust′i·ly,** *adv.* **—gust′i·ness,** *n.*

gut (gut) *n. v.* **gut·ted, gut·ting.** —*n.* 1 the intestine. 2 **guts,** *pl.* **a** entrails; bowels. **b** *Slang.* pluck; courage; endurance. 3 a tough string made from the dried and twisted intestines of sheep or other animals; catgut. Gut is used for the strings in certain musical instruments and tennis rackets. 4 a narrow channel or gully.
—*v.* 1 remove the entrails of; disembowel. 2 plunder or destroy the inside of: *Fire gutted the building and left only the brick walls standing.*
—*adj. Slang.* vital; basic: *The gut issue is the demand for higher wages.* [OE *guttas,* pl.]

gut·ta-per·cha (gut′ə pėr′chə) *n.* a substance resembling rubber, obtained from the thick milky juice of certain tropical trees and used in dentistry, etc. [< Malay]

gut·ter (gut′ər) *n.* 1 a channel or ditch along the side of a street or road to carry off water; the low part of a

street beside the sidewalk. **2** a channel or trough along the lower edge of a roof to carry off rain water. See **eaves** for picture. **3** any channel; groove. **4** a low, poor, or wretched place: *a child of the gutter.* **5** in printing, the white space formed by the inner margins of two facing pages of a book.
—*v.* **1** form gutters in. **2** flow or melt in streams: *A candle gutters when the melted wax runs down its sides.* **3** become channelled. [ME < AF *gotere*, ult. < L *gutta* drop]

gut·ter·snipe (gut′ər snīp′) *n. Informal.* **1** an urchin who lives in the streets. **2** any ill-bred person.

gut·tur·al (gut′ər əl or gut′rəl) *adj.* **1** of the throat. **2** formed in the throat; harsh: *The man spoke in a guttural voice.* **3** in phonetics, formed between the back of the tongue and the soft palate, or velum; velar. The *g* in *go* is sometimes called a guttural sound. —*n.* in phonetics, a sound formed between the back of the tongue and the soft palate. [< NL *gutturalis* < L *guttur* throat] —**gut′tur·al·ly,** *adv.* —**gut′tur·al·ness,** *n.*

guy[1] (gī) *n. v.* **guyed, guy·ing.** —*n.* a rope, chain, wire, etc. attached to something to steady or secure it. —*v.* steady or secure with a guy or guys. [< OF *guie* < *guier* to guide, ult. < Gmc.]

guy[2] (gī) *n. v.* **guyed, guy·ing.** —*n.* **1** a fellow; chap. **2** a queer-looking person. —*v. Informal.* make fun of; tease. [< *Guy* Fawkes, a leader of the Gunpowder Plot (1605) to blow up the British king and parliament]

Guy·a·nese (gī′ə nēz′) *adj. n.* **-ese.** —*adj.* of or having to do with Guyana, a country in South America, formerly British Guiana. —*n.* a native or inhabitant of Guyana.

guy rope one of several ropes attached to a tent, marquee, etc. for pegging it to the ground as a means of support.

guz·zle (guz′əl) *v.* **-zled, -zling.** drink greedily; drink too much. [probably < OF *gosiller* vomit (? originally, pass through the throat); cf. F *gosier* throat] —**guz′zler,** *n.*

gym (jim) *n.* gymnasium.

gym·na·si·a (jim nā′zē ə) *n.* a pl. of **gymnasium.**

gym·na·si·um (jim nā′zē əm) *n.* **-si·ums** or **-si·a.** a room, building, etc. fitted up for physical exercise or training and for indoor athletic sports. [< L < Gk. *gymnasion* < *gymnazein* exercise (naked) < *gymnos* naked]

Gym·na·si·um (jim nā′zē əm; *German*, gim nä′zē ům) *n.* in Germany, etc., a secondary school that prepares students for the universities.

gym·nast (jim′nast) *n.* an expert in gymnastics. [< Gk. *gymnastēs* < *gymnazein* exercise. See GYMNASIUM.]

gym·nas·tic (jim nas′tik) *adj.* having to do with bodily exercise or activities. —**gym·nas′ti·cal·ly,** *adv.*

gym·nas·tics (jim nas′tiks) *n.pl.* physical exercises for developing the muscles, such as are performed in a gymnasium.

gym·no·sperm (jim′nə spėrm′) *n.* in botany, any of a large group of plants having the seeds exposed, not enclosed in ovaries. The pine, fir, and spruce, which bear seeds on the surface of cone scales instead of in pods, are gymnosperms. [< NL < Gk. *gymnospermos* < *gymnos* naked + *sperma* seed]

gym·no·sper·mous (jim′nə spėr′məs) *adj.* belonging to the gymnosperms; having the seeds exposed.

gy·nae·col·o·gist (gī′nə kol′ə jist, jī′nə kol′ə jist, or jin′ə kol′ə jist) *n.* gynecologist.

gy·nae·col·o·gy (gī′nə kol′ə jē, jī′nə kol′ə jē, or jin′ə kol′ə jē) *n.* gynecology.

gy·nan·drous (ji nan′drəs or jī nan′drəs) *adj.* in botany, having stamens and pistil joined as one, as in an orchid. [< Gk. *gynandros* of doubtful sex < *gynē* woman + *anēr, andros* man]

gy·ne·co·log·ic (gī′nə kə loj′ik, jī′nə kə loj′ik or jin′ə kə loj′ik) *adj.* of or having to do with gynecology. —**gy′ne·co·log′i·cal·ly,** *adv.*

gy·ne·col·o·gist (gī′nə kol′ə jist, jī′nə kol′ə jist, or jin′ə kol′ə jist) *n.* a doctor who specializes in gynecology. Also, **gynaecologist.**

gy·ne·col·o·gy (gī′nə kol′ə jē, jī′nə kol′ə jē, or jin′ə kol′ə jē) *n.* the branch of medical science that deals with the functions and diseases of women. Also, **gynaecology.** [< Gk. *gynē, gynaikos* woman + E *-logy*]

gy·noe·ci·um (jī nē′sē əm or jə nē′sē əm) *n.* **-ci·a** (-sē ə). in botany, the pistil or pistils of a flower. [< NL < Gk. *gynē* woman + *oikion* house]

-gynous *combining form.* female; woman; female organs: *misogynous = hating women.* [< Gk. *-gynos* < *gynē* woman]

gyp (jip) *v.* **gypped, gyp·ping,** *n. Slang.* —*v.* cheat; swindle. —*n.* **1** a cheat; swindle. **2** a cheat; swindler. [shortened form of *gypsy*] —**gyp′per,** *n.*

gyp·sif·er·ous (jip sif′ər əs) *adj.* having or yielding gypsum.

gyp·soph·i·la (jip sof′ə lə) *n.* a plant having many small, fragrant, white or pink flowers on delicate branching stalks with few leaves. [< NL < Gk. *gypsos* gypsum + *philos* fond of]

gyp·sum (jip′səm) *n.* a mineral used for making plaster of Paris, fertilizer, etc.; hydrated calcium sulphate. Alabaster is one form of gypsum. *Formula*: $CaSO_4 \cdot 2H_2O$ [< L < Gk. *gypsos* chalk, plaster]

Gyp·sy (jip′sē) *n.* **-sies,** *adj.* —*n.* **1** Also, **gypsy. a** a wandering group of people having dark skin and black hair, who probably came from N. India originally. **b** a member of this group. **2** the language of the Gypsies. **3 gypsy,** a person who looks or lives like a Gypsy. —*adj.* **gypsy, 1** of or having to do with the Gypsies: *a gypsy girl, gypsy music.* **2** resembling a Gypsy or gypsy. —*v.* **gypsy, 1** live or act like Gypsies. **2** picnic. Also, **Gipsy, gipsy.** [ult. < *Egyptian*]

gypsy moth a brownish or white moth whose larvae eat the leaves of trees. Also, **gipsy moth.**

gy·rate (jī′rāt or jī rāt′) *v.* **-rat·ed, -rat·ing.** move in a circle or spiral; whirl; rotate: *A top gyrates.* [< L *gyrare* < *gyrus* circle < Gk. *gyros*] —**gy·ra′tor,** *n.*

gy·ra·tion (jī rā′shən) *n.* a circular or spiral motion; whirling; rotation.

gy·ra·to·ry (jī′rə tô′rē) *adj.* gyrating.

gyr·fal·con (jėr′fol′kən or -fôl′kən) *n.* gerfalcon.

gyro- *combining form.* circle; spiral, as in *gyroscope.* [< Gk. *gyro-* < *gyros*]

gy·ro·com·pass (jī′rō kum′pəs) *n.* a compass using a motor-driven gyroscope instead of a magnetic needle to point to the north. It points to the geographic North Pole instead of to the magnetic pole.

gy·ro·pi·lot (jī′rō pī′lət) *n.* in aeronautics, a device that automatically keeps an aircraft on course; automatic pilot.

gy·ro·plane (jī′rō plān′) *n.* an aircraft that is kept in the air by means of horizontal blades rapidly rotating around a vertical axis.

A gyroscope. Once spinning, the wheel will continue to rotate in the same plane and in the same direction, regardless of magnetic force.

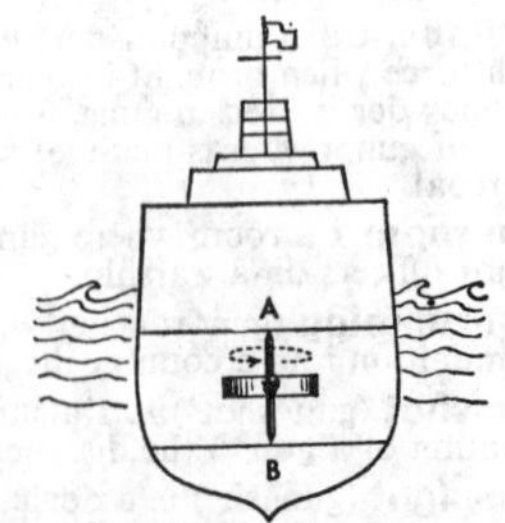

A gyrostabilizer. The spinning of the wheel, W, creates gyroscopic inertia along the axis AB, thus preventing the ship from rolling.

gy·ro·scope (jī′rə skōp′) *n.* a heavy wheel or disk mounted so that its axis can turn freely in one or more directions. A spinning gyroscope tends to resist change in the direction of its axis, and is used to keep ships and airplanes balanced.

gy·ro·scop·ic (jī′rə skop′ik) *adj.* having to do with a gyroscope.

gy·ro·sta·bi·liz·er (jī′rō stā′bə līz′ər) *n.* a device for stabilizing a seagoing vessel by counteracting its rolling motion. See picture on the opposite page.

gy·ro·stat·ics (jī′rə stat′iks) *n.* the branch of physics that deals with the laws governing the rotation of solid bodies.

gyve (jīv) *n. v.* **gyved, gyv·ing.** —*n.* fetter; shackle, especially for the leg. —*v.* put fetters or shackles on. [ME; origin uncertain]

hat, āge, cãre, fär; let, ēqual, tėrm; it, īce
hot, ōpen, ôrder; oil, out; cup, pu̇t, rüle, ūse
əbove, takən, pencəl, lemən, circəs
ch, child; ng, long; sh, ship
th, thin; ᴛʜ, then; zh, measure

H or **h** (āch) *n.* **H's** or **h's. 1** the eighth letter of the English alphabet. **2** any speech sound represented by this letter. **3** the eighth of a series designated alphabetically. **4** anything shaped like **H.**

h. 1 hour. **2** harbor. **3** hard. **4** high. **5** height. **6** hundred. **7** husband. **8** in baseball, hit or hits.

H 1 hydrogen. **2** in physics: **a** intensity of magnetic field. **b** the earth's horizontal component of magnetic field. **3** in electricity, henry.

H. 1 harbor. **2** high.

ha (ho, hä, or ha) *interj.* **1** an exclamation of surprise, joy, triumph, etc.: *"Ha! I've caught you!" cried the giant to Jack.* **2** in writing, a way of indicating laughter: *"Ha! ha! ha!" laughed the boys.*

Hab. Habakkuk.

ha·be·as cor·pus (hā′bē əs kôr′pəs) in law, a writ or order requiring that a prisoner be brought before a judge or into court to decide whether he is being held lawfully. The right of habeas corpus is a protection against unjust imprisonment. [< L *habeas corpus* you may have the person]

hab·er·dash·er (hab′ər dash′ər) *n.* **1** a dealer in men's furnishings, such as hats, ties, shirts, socks, etc. **2** a dealer in small articles, such as buttons, needles, and trimmings. [? < AF *hapertas*, a kind of cloth]

hab·er·dash·er·y (hab′ər dash′ər ē or hab′ər dash′rē) *n.* **-er·ies. 1** the articles sold by a haberdasher. **2** the shop of a haberdasher.

hab·er·geon (hab′ər jən) *n.* **1** a short coat of mail without sleeves; haubergeon. **2** a hauberk. [ME < OF *haubergeon*, dim. of *hauberc.* See HAUBERK.]

ha·bil·i·ment (hə bil′ə mənt) *n.* **1 habiliments,** *pl.* articles of clothing. **2** dress; attire. [ME < OF (*h*)*abillement* < *abiller* prepare, fit out; originally, reduce (a tree) to a trunk by stripping off branches < *bille* long stock, log < Celtic]

hab·it (hab′it) *n.* **1** a tendency to act in a certain way or to do a certain thing; usual way of acting; custom; practice. **2** the distinctive dress or costume worn by members of a religious order. Monks and nuns wear habits. **3 take the habit,** become a nun. **4** a woman's riding dress. **5** the characteristic form, mode of growth, etc., of an animal or plant: *The honeysuckle is of a twining habit.*
—*v.* put a habit on; dress. [ME < OF < L *habitus* < *habere* hold, live in, stay] —**Syn.** *n.* **1** usage, use, wont. See **custom.**

hab·it·a·ble (hab′ə tə bəl) *adj.* fit to live in. —**hab′it·a·ble·ness,** *n.* —**hab′it·a·bly,** *adv.*

hab·it·ant (*n. 1* hab′ə tənt; *n. 2, adj.* hab′ə tont′; *French,* ä bē täɴ′) *n.* **1** an inhabitant. **2** *Cdn.* a French-Canadian farmer. —*adj. Cdn.* of or having to do with French Canadians or French Canada, especially with regard to country life. [< Cdn.F < F < L *habitans, -antis,* ppr. of *habitare* live in < *habere*]

hab·i·tat (hab′ə tat′) *n.* **1** the place where an animal or plant naturally lives or grows: *The jungle is the habitat of tigers.* **2** a place of living; dwelling place. [< L *habitat* it inhabits]

hab·i·ta·tion (hab′ə tā′shən) *n.* **1** a place to live in. **2** an inhabiting. —**Syn. 1** home, dwelling, residence.

ha·bit·u·al (hə bich′ü əl) *adj.* **1** done by habit; caused by habit: *a habitual smile, habitual courtesy.* **2** being or doing something by habit: *A habitual reader reads a great deal.* **3** often done, seen, or used; usual; customary: *Ice and snow are a habitual sight in arctic regions.* —**ha·bit′u·al·ly,** *adv.* —**ha·bit′u·al·ness,** *n.* —**Syn. 2** chronic, inveterate. **3** accustomed.

ha·bit·u·ate (hə bich′ü āt′) *v.* **-at·ed, -at·ing. 1** make used (*to*); accustom: *Lumbermen are habituated to hard work.* **2** go to (a place) frequently. [< LL *habituari* be in a state of, be characterized by (? passive of

habituare bring into a state) < L *habitus* condition (*see* HABIT); influenced in meaning by E *habit*]
—**ha·bit′u·a′tion,** *n.* —**Syn.** familiarize, acclimatize.

hab·i·tude (hab′ə tūd′ or hab′ə tüd′) *n.* **1** a characteristic condition of body or mind. **2** a habit; custom; practice. [< F < L *habitudo* condition]

ha·bit·u·é (hə bich′ü ā′) *n.* a person who has the habit of going to a place frequently: *a habitué of the theatre.* [< F *habitué*, pp. of *habituer* accustom]

Habs·burg (haps′bėrg; *German*, häps′bůrk) *n.* Hapsburg.

ha·ci·en·da (hä′sē en′də) *n. Spanish American.* a large ranch; landed estate; country house. [< Sp. < L *facienda* (things) to be done < *facere* do]

hack[1] (hak) *v.* **1** cut roughly or unevenly; deal cutting blows: *He hacked the box apart with a dull axe.* **2** give short dry coughs. **3** in basketball, hit the arm of (an opponent who has the ball).
—*n.* **1** a rough cut. **2** a tool or instrument for hacking or cutting, such as an axe, pick, hoe, etc. **3** in curling, a notch cut in the ice at one end of a rink, used as a foothold when a player throws his rock. **4** a short dry cough. **5** in basketball, a personal foul committed by striking the arm of a player who has the ball. [OE *haccian*] —**hack′er,** *n.* —**Syn.** *v.* **1** See **cut.**

hack[2] (hak) *n.* **1** a carriage for hire. **2** *Informal.* a taxi. **3** an old or worn-out horse. **4** a horse for ordinary riding. **5** a person hired to do routine literary work; drudge. **6** a plodding, faithful, but undistinguished worker in an organization, as a political party: *an old party hack.*
—*v.* **1** ride on horseback over roads. **2** *Informal.* drive a taxi. **3** write or act as a hack.
—*adj.* working or done merely for money; hired; drudging. [short for *hackney*]

hack·a·more (hak′ə môr′) *n.* a halter (def. 1). [< Sp. *jáquima*]

hack·ber·ry (hak′ber′ē) *n.* **-ries. 1** a tree related to the elm that has small, cherry-like fruit. **2** the fruit. [var. of *hagberry* < Scand.; cf. Danish *hæggebær*]

hack·le[1] (hak′əl) *n. v.* **-led, -ling.** —*n.* **1** a comb used in dressing flax, hemp, etc. **2** one of the long, slender feathers on the neck of certain male birds. **3** the neck plumage of certain birds. **4** in fishing: **a** the part of an artificial fly corresponding to the legs of an insect, made from feathers from the neck of a rooster. **b** a hackle fly. **5 hackles,** the erectile hairs on the back of a dog's neck. **6 raise the hackles,** *Informal.* arouse suspicion or anger.
—*v.* comb (flax, hemp, etc.) with a hackle. [ME *hakell.* Related to HECKLE.]

hack·le[2] (hak′əl) *v.* **-led, -ling.** cut roughly; hack; mangle. [< *hack*[1]]

hackle fly a wingless artificial fly used in fishing.

hack·man (hak′mən) *n.* **-men** (-mən). the driver of a hack or carriage for hire.

hack·ma·tack (hak′mə tak′) *n.* any of several evergreen trees, including the larch and the juniper. [< Algonquian]

hack·ney (hak′nē) *n.* **-neys,** *adj. v.* **-neyed, -ney·ing.**
—*n.* **1** a horse for ordinary riding. **2** a carriage for hire.
—*adj.* hired; let out, employed, or done for hire.
—*v.* use too often; make commonplace. [ME *hakeney* < *Hackney*, a town in England]

hack·neyed (hak′nēd) *adj.* used too often; commonplace: "*White as snow*" *is a hackneyed comparison.* —**Syn.** trite, stale, banal.

hack·saw (hak′so′ or -sô′) *n.* a saw for cutting metal, consisting of a narrow, fine-toothed blade fixed in a frame.

HACKSAW

hack·work (hak′wėrk′) *n.* **1** routine literary work done by a hack. **2** any similar work of a routine or unstimulating nature.

had (had; *unstressed*, həd or əd) *v.* pt. and pp. of **have.**
☛ **had better, had rather.** *Had better* is the usual idiom for giving advice or making an indirect command: *You had better take cover before she sees you.* Informally, a shorter form without *had* is common: *If he asks you to do it, you better do it.*

had·dock (had′ək) *n.* **-dock** or **-docks.** a food fish of the N. Atlantic Ocean, resembling a cod, but smaller. [ME *haddok*; origin uncertain]

Ha·des (hā′dēz) *n.* **1** in Greek mythology: **a** the god of the lower world, identified by the Romans with Pluto. **b** home of the dead, below the earth. **2 hades,** *Informal.* hell. [< Gk. *Haidēs*]

had·n't (had′ənt) had not.

hadst (hadst) *v. Archaic.* 2nd pers. sing. pt. of **have.** "Thou hadst" means "you had" (sing.).

haema- *combining form.* hema-.

haem·a·tite (hem′ə tīt′ or hē′mə tīt′) *n.* hematite.

haemato- *combining form.* hemato-.

haem·a·tol·o·gist (hem′ə tol′ə jist or hē′mə-) *n.* hematologist.

haem·a·tol·o·gy (hem′ə tol′ə jē or hē′mə-) *n.* hematology.

haemo- *combining form.* hemo-.

hae·mo·glo·bin (hē′mə glō′bən or hem′ə-) *n.* hemoglobin.

hae·mo·phil·i·a (hē′mə fil′ē ə or hem′ə-) *n.* hemophilia.

hae·mo·phil·i·ac (hē′ mə fil′ē ak′ or hem′ə-) *n.* hemophiliac.

haem·or·rhage (hem′ə rij or hem′rij) *n. v.* **-rhaged, -rhaging.** hemorrhage.

haem·or·rhoid (hem′ ə roid′) *n.* hemorrhoid.

haem·or·rhoi·dal (hem′ə roi′dəl) *adj.* hemorrhoidal.

haf·ni·um (haf′nē əm) *n.* a rare metallic chemical element somewhat like zirconium. *Symbol*: Hf; *at.no.* 72; *at.wt.* 178.49. [< *Hafnia*, L name for Copenhagen]

haft (haft) *n.* the handle (of a knife, sword, dagger, etc.). —*v.* furnish with a handle or hilt; set in a haft. [OE *hæft*]

hag (hag) *n.* **1** a very ugly old woman, especially one who is vicious or malicious. **2** a witch. [ME *hagge*, related to OE *hægtesse* witch, fury]

Hag. Haggai.

Ha·gen (hä′gən) *n.* in the *Nibelungenlied*, the murderer of Siegfried. [< G]

hag·fish (hag′fish′) *n.* **-fish** or **-fish·es.** a small, parasitic, eel-shaped sea animal, related to the lamprey. It attaches itself to fish by its round mouth and bores into them with its horny teeth.

Hag·ga·dah or **Hag·ga·da** (hə gä′də) *n.* **-doth** (-dōth′). **1** in the Talmud: **a** a story or legend that explains or illustrates the Jewish law. **b** the section containing such stories and legends. **2 a** the text of the Seder service on the first, or the first two, evenings of Passover. **b** a book containing this text. [< Hebrew *haggadah* story < *higgid* relate]

hag·gard (hag′ərd) *adj.* wild-looking from pain, fatigue, worry, hunger, etc.; gaunt; careworn. [< MF *hagard* of the hedges, untamed (hawk) ? < MHG *hag* hedge]
—**hag′gard·ly,** *adv.* —**hag′gard·ness,** *n.* —**Syn.** emaciated.

hag·gis (hag′is) *n. Scottish.* the heart, lungs, and liver of a sheep mixed with suet and oatmeal and boiled in the stomach of the animal. [ME ? < Scottish *hag* chop; cf. ON *höggva.* Akin to HEW.]

hag·gle (hag′əl) *v.* **-gled, -gling. 1** dispute about a price or the terms of a bargain; wrangle. **2** mangle in cutting; hack. —*n.* the act of haggling; a wrangle or dispute about terms. [< Scottish *hag* chop, hack < ON *höggva*]
—**hag′gler,** *n.*

hag·i·og·ra·pher (hag′ē og′rə fər or hā′jē og′rə fər) *n.* **1** a writer of lives of the saints. **2** any writer on sacred subjects.

hag·i·o·graph·ic (hag′ē ə graf′ik or hā′jē ə graf′ik) *adj.* of or having to do with hagiography.

hag·i·og·ra·phy (hag′ē og′rə fē or hā′jē og′rə fē) *n.* the writing of lives of the saints; hagiology. [< LL < Gk. *hagios* holy + *graphos* thing written]

hag·i·o·log·ic (hag′ē ə loj′ik or hā′jē ə loj′ik) *adj.* of or having to do with hagiology.

hag·i·ol·o·gy (hag′ē ol′ə jē or hā′jē ol′ə jē) *n.* **-gies.** 1 literature that deals with the lives and legends of saints. 2 a book on this subject. 3 a list of saints. [< Gk. *hagios* holy + E *-logy*]

hag·rid·den (hag′rid′ən) *adj.* worried or tormented, as if by witches; harassed.

hah (hä) *interj.* ha.

Hai·da (hī′də) *n.* **Hai·da.** 1 a tribe of Indians living in northern British Columbia. 2 a member of this tribe. 3 the language of this tribe.

hai·ku (hī′kü) *n.* a Japanese verse form consisting of three lines of five, seven, and five syllables respectively. [< Japanese]

hail[1] (hāl) *v.* 1 shout in welcome to; greet; cheer: *The crowd hailed the winner.* 2 greet as; call: *They hailed him leader.* 3 call loudly to; shout to: *The captain hailed the passing ship.* 4 **hail from,** come from. [< interj.]
—*n.* 1 a greeting; cheer; shout of welcome. 2 a loud call; shout. 3 **within hail,** near enough to hear a call or shout. [< v. and interj.]
—*interj.* 1 *Poetic.* greetings! welcome!: *Hail to the winner!* 2 **hail fellow well met,** very friendly. [earlier *be hail!* < ON *heill* healthy] **—hail′er,** *n.* **—Syn.** *v.* 1 address, salute.

hail[2] (hāl) *n.* 1 small, roundish piece of ice coming down from the clouds in a shower; frozen rain. 2 a shower resembling hail: *A hail of bullets met the soldiers.*
—*v.* 1 come down in hail: *Sometimes it hails during a summer thunderstorm.* 2 pour down in a shower like hail: *The angry mob hailed blows on the thief.* [OE *hægel*]

hail·stone (hāl′stōn′) *n.* a small, roundish piece of ice coming down from the clouds.

hail·storm (hāl′stôrm′) *n.* a storm with hail.

hair (hãr) *n.* 1 a fine, threadlike outgrowth from the skin of human beings and animals. 2 a mass of such growths. 3 the hair of the human head: *I must get my hair cut.* 4 a fine, threadlike growth from the outer layer of plants. 5 a very narrow space; something very small; least degree: *He won the race by a hair.* 6 **get in one's hair,** annoy; be a nuisance to. 7 **let one's hair down,** be informal or unconventional in behavior. 8 **not turn a hair,** not show any sign of being disturbed or embarrassed. 9 **split hairs,** make excessively fine distinctions. 10 **to a hair,** exactly; just right.
—*adj.* made of or with hair. [OE *hǣr*]

hair·breadth (hãr′bredth′ or -bretth′) *adj.* very narrow; extremely close: *a hairbreadth escape.*
—*n.* a very narrow space; a very small distance.

hair·brush (hãr′brush′) *n.* a brush for the hair.

hair·cloth (hãr′kloth′) *n.* a cloth made of horsehair or camel's hair, used to cover furniture, stiffen garments, etc.

hair·cut (hãr′kut′) *n.* 1 the act or manner of cutting the hair of the head. 2 a trimming of head hair: *He needs a haircut.*

hair·do (hãr′dü′) *n.* **-dos.** 1 a way of arranging women's hair: *a smart hairdo.* 2 an arranging of hair: *She needs a hairdo.*

hair·dress·er (hãr′dres′ər) *n.* a person whose work is cutting and taking care of people's, especially women's, hair.

hair·dress·ing (hãr′dres′ing) *n.* 1 the act or process of cutting and arranging someone's hair. 2 the business or occupation of a hairdresser.

hair·less (hãr′lis) *adj.* without hair.

hair·line (hãr′līn′) *n.* 1 a very thin line. 2 in printing, a very fine line, especially a stroke or part of a letter thinner than other parts. 3 the irregular outline where hair growth ends on the head or forehead.

hair net a net worn to keep one's hair in place.

hair·pin (hãr′pin′) *n.* 1 a pin, usually a U-shaped piece of wire, shell, or plastic, used by women to keep the hair in place. 2 a sharp bend in a road, river, etc., likened to a hairpin in shape. —*adj.* shaped like a hairpin: U-shaped: *a hairpin bend.*

hair-rais·ing (hãr′rāz′ing) *adj. Informal.* making the hair seem to stand on end; terrifying.

hair's-breadth or **hairs·breadth** (hãrz′bredth′ or -bretth′) *n. adj.* hairbreadth.

hat, āge, cãre, fär; let, ēqual, tėrm; it, īce
hot, ōpen, ôrder; oil, out; cup, pu̇t, rüle, ūse
əbove, takən, pencəl, lemən, circəs
ch, child; ng, long; sh, ship
th, thin; ᴛʜ, then; zh, measure

hair seal any of various rough-coated seals, whose fur has little or no commercial value.

hair shirt a rough shirt or girdle made of horsehair, worn as a penance.

hair·split·ting (hãr′split′ing) *n.* the making of excessively fine distinctions. —*adj.* being excessively subtle.

hair·spring (hãr′spring′) *n.* a fine, hairlike spring that regulates the balance wheel in a watch or clock.

hair trigger a trigger that operates by very slight pressure.

hair-trigger (hãr′trig′ər) *adj.* 1 having a hair trigger. 2 set off by the slightest pressure: *a hair-trigger temper.*

hair·y (hãr′ē) *adj.* **hair·i·er, hair·i·est.** 1 covered with hair; having much hair. 2 of or like hair. 3 *Slang.* difficult; disturbing; dismaying: *a hairy situation.*
—hair′i·ly, *adv.* **—hair′i·ness,** *n.* **—Syn.** 1 shaggy, hirsute.

Hai·sla (hī′slə) *n.* **Hai·sla** or **Hai·slas.** 1 a group of Kwakiutl Indians of the northern branch, living in British Columbia. 2 a member of this group.

Hai·ti·an (hā′tē ən or hā′shən) *adj.* of or having to do with Haiti or its people. —*n.* 1 a native or inhabitant of Haiti. 2 the language spoken in Haiti, a creolized dialect of French.

hake (hāk) *n.* **hake** or **hakes.** a sea fish related to the cod but slenderer and inferior as food. [dial. var. of *hook*; from the hooklike growth under the lower jaw; cf. Norwegian *hakefisk*]

ha·kim[1] (hə kēm′) *n.* among Moslems: 1 a wise or learned man. 2 a doctor. [< Arabic *ḥakīm* wise man]

ha·kim[2] (hä′kim) *n.* among Moslems, a ruler; judge; governor. [< Arabic *hākim* ruler]

hal·berd (hal′bərd) *n.* a weapon that was both a spear and a battle-axe, used in warfare in the 15th and 16th centuries. [< F *hallebarde* < Ital. *alabarda* < Gmc.]

hal·berd·ier (hal′bər dēr′) *n.* formerly, a soldier armed with a halberd.

hal·bert (hal′bərt) *n.* halberd.

hal·cy·on (hal′sē ən) *adj.* 1 calm; peaceful; happy. 2 of or having to do with the halcyon. [< n.]
—*n. Archaic or poetic.* a bird that was supposed to calm the waves; kingfisher. [< L < Gk. *halkyon*, var. of *alkyon* kingfisher]

hale[1] (hāl) *adj.* **hal·er, hal·est.** strong and well; healthy. [OE *hāl*] **—hale·ness,** *n.* **—Syn.** sound, robust.

hale[2] (hāl) *v.* **haled, hal·ing.** 1 drag by force. 2 compel to go: *The man was haled into court.* [ME < OF *haler* < Gmc. Doublet of HAUL.]

half (haf) *n.* **halves,** *adj. adv.* —*n.* 1 one of two equal parts. 2 in certain games, one of two equal periods. 3 in golf, a score equal to that of one's opponent, on any hole or on a round. 4 one of two nearly equal parts: *Which is the bigger half?* 5 in football, a halfback. 6 **by half,** by far.
—*adj.* 1 forming a half; being or making half of. 2 not complete; being only part of: *A half-truth is often no better than a lie.*
—*adv.* 1 to half of the full amount or degree: *a glass half full of milk.* 2 partly: *speak half aloud.* 3 almost: *The beggar was half dead from hunger.* 4 **not half, a** to a very slight extent. **b** *Informal.* not at all; the reverse of: *not half bad.* [OE *healf*]

☛ **half.** The more formal idiom is *a half*, the general *half a*: Formal: *He walked a half mile in a half hour.* General: *He walked half a mile in half an hour. A half a* (as in *a half a mile*) is a redundancy, characteristic of careless informal or substandard usage.

half-and-half (haf′ənd haf′) *adj.* 1 half one thing and half another. 2 not clearly one thing or the other.
—*adv.* in two equal parts.
—*n.* 1 a mixture of milk and cream. 2 *Brit.* a beverage consisting of two drinks, especially ale and porter, mixed together.

half·back (haf′bak′) *n.* in football, soccer, etc., a player whose position is behind the forward line.

half-baked (haf′bākt′) *adj.* **1** not cooked enough. **2** *Informal.* not fully worked out; incomplete. **3** *Informal.* not experienced; showing poor judgment.

half blood the relationship between persons who are related through one parent only.

half-blood (haf′blud′) *n.* **1** a half-breed. **2** a person related to another through one parent only.

half-blood·ed (haf′blud′id) *adj.* **1** having parents of different races. **2** related through only one parent.

half boot a boot reaching about halfway to the knee.

half-breed (haf′brēd′) *n.* **1** a person whose parents are of different races, especially a person of mixed white and American-Indian blood. **2** a person whose parents are half-breeds: *There are many half-breeds in the Canadian North.* —*adj.* of or having to do with half-breeds.

half brother a brother related through one parent only.

half-caste (haf′kast′) *n.* **1** a child of one European parent and one Asian parent. **2** a half-breed.

half cock **1** the position of the hammer of a gun when it is pulled back halfway. At half cock the trigger is locked and the gun cannot be fired. **2 go off at half cock,** a fire too soon. b act or speak without sufficient thought or preparation.

half crown a former British silver coin worth two shillings and sixpence.

half dollar a silver coin of Canada and the United States, worth 50 cents.

half eagle a former gold coin of the United States, worth $5.

half-heart·ed (haf′här′tid) *adj.* lacking courage, interest, or enthusiasm. —**half′-heart′ed·ly,** *adv.* —**half′-heart′ed·ness,** *n.* —**Syn.** indifferent, perfunctory, lukewarm.

half hitch a knot formed by passing the end of a rope under and over its standing part and then inside the loop.

A half hitch

half-hour (haf′our′) *n.* **1** thirty minutes. **2** the halfway point in an hour. —*adj.* of a half-hour; lasting a half-hour. —**half′-hour′ly,** *adv.*

half-life (haf′līf′) *n.* in nuclear physics, the time in which half of the original radiant energy of a radio-active substance is given off, used to distinguish one such substance from another and as a measurement of radio-activity.

half-mast (haf′mast′) *n.* a position halfway or part way down from the top of a mast, staff, etc.: *When the Governor General died, flags were lowered to half-mast as a mark of respect.* —*v.* put (a flag) at half-mast: *They have half-masted the flag.*

half moon **1** the moon when only half of its surface appears bright. **2** something shaped like a half moon or crescent.

half nelson in wrestling, a hold, applied by hooking one arm under an opponent's armpit and putting a hand on the back of his neck.

half note in music, a note held half as long as a whole note; minim.

A half note

half·pence (hā′pəns) *n.* a pl. of **halfpenny.**

half·pen·ny (hā′pə nē or hāp′nē) *n.* **half·pen·nies** (hā′pə nēz or hāp′nēz) or **half·pence,** *adj.* —*n.* **1** a former British bronze coin worth half a penny. **2** a new halfpenny. —*adj.* **1** worth only a halfpenny. **2** having little value; trifling.

half rest in music, a rest lasting as long as a half note.

half sister a sister related through one parent only.

half sole the sole of a shoe or boot from the toe to the instep.

half-sole (haf′sōl′) *v.* **-soled, -sol·ing.** put a new half sole or half soles on (shoes, etc.).

half sovereign a British gold coin worth ten shillings.

half-staff (haf′staf′) *n. v. Esp.U.S.* half-mast.

half step in music, the difference in pitch between two adjacent keys on a piano; a semitone.

half-tim·bered (haf′tim′bərd) *adj.* having walls of wooden framework with the spaces filled by plaster, stone, or brick.

A half-timbered house

half-time (haf′tīm′) *n.* the time between two halves of a game. —*adj.* having to do with this period.

half tone in music, an interval equal to half a tone on the scale; half step.

half-tone (haf′tōn′) *n.* **1** in photo-engraving: **a** a process used in making pictures for books and magazines. **b** a picture made by this process. **2** in paintings, a tone between the high light and deep shades.

half-track or **half·track** (haf′trak′) *n.* an army motor vehicle that has wheels in front and short tracks in the rear for driving, used to carry personnel and weapons.

half-truth (haf′trüth′) *n.* an assertion or statement that is only partly true.

half·way (haf′wā′) *adv.* **1** half the way; half the required distance: *The rope reached only halfway to the boat.* **2 go** or **meet halfway,** do one's share toward reaching an agreement or toward patching up a quarrel. —*adj.* **1** midway: *The inn served as a halfway house between the two towns.* **2** not going far enough; incomplete; inadequate: *Halfway measures are never satisfactory.*

half-wit (haf′wit′) *n.* **1** a feeble-minded person. **2** a stupid, foolish person.

half-wit·ted (haf′wit′id) *adj.* **1** feeble-minded. **2** very stupid; foolish. —**half′-wit′ted·ly,** *adv.* **-half′-wit′ted·ness,** *n.*

hal·i·but (hal′ə bət) *n.* **-but** or **-buts.** a large flatfish much used for food, often weighing several hundred pounds. [ME *halybutte* < *haly* holy + *butte* flatfish; eaten on holy days]

hal·ide (hal′īd, hal′id, hā′līd, or hā′lid) *n.* any compound of a halogen with another element or radical. Sodium chloride is a halide. —*adj.* haloid. [< *hal(ogen)* + *ide*]

hal·i·dom (hal′ə dəm) *n. Archaic.* **1** a holy place; sanctuary. **2** something regarded as holy; a holy relic. [OE *hāligdōm* < *hālig* holy + *-dōm* position, condition]

hal·i·dome (hal′ə dōm′) *n. Archaic.* halidom.

Hal·i·go·ni·an (hal′i gō′nē ən) *n.* **1** a native or inhabitant of Halifax, Nova Scotia. **2** a native or inhabitant of Halifax, a city in Yorkshire, England. —*adj.* of or having to do with Halifax.

hal·ite (hal′īt or hā′līt) *n.* native rock salt. [< NL *halites* < Gk. *hals* salt]

hal·i·to·sis (hal′ə tō′sis) *n.* bad or offensive breath. [< NL < L *halitus* breath]

hall (hol or hôl) *n.* **1** a way to go through a building; passageway; corridor. **2** a passageway or room at the entrance of a building. **3** a large room for holding meetings, parties, banquets, etc. **4** a building for public business: *The mayor's office is in the town hall.* **5** a building of a school, college, or university. **6** in England, the residence of a landowner. [OE *heall*]

hal·le·lu·jah or **hal·le·lu·iah** (hal′ə lü′yə) *interj.* praise ye the Lord! —*n.* a song of praise to God. Also, **alleluia.** [< Hebrew *halleluyah* praise ye Yah (Jehovah)]

Halley's comet (ha′lēz) the comet that Halley predicted could be seen about every 75 years, last seen in 1910. [after Edmund *Halley* (1656-1742), an English astronomer]

hal·liard (hal′yərd) *n.* halyard.

hall·mark (hol′märk′ or hôl′-) *n.* **1** an official mark indicating standard of purity, put on gold and silver articles. **2** a mark or sign of genuineness or good quality: *Courtesy and self-control are the hallmarks of a gentleman.* —*v.* put a hallmark on. [from Goldsmiths' *Hall* in London, the seat of the Goldsmiths' Company, by whom the stamping was legally regulated in Britain]

hal·lo (hə lō′) *interj. n.* **-los,** *v.* **-loed, -lo·ing.** —*interj.* hello.

hal·loa (hə lō′) *interj. n. v.* hello.

hal·loo (hə lü′) *interj. n.* **-loos,** *v.* **-looed, -loo·ing.** —*interj.* **1** in hunting, a shout to make hounds run faster. **2** a call or shout to attract attention.
—*n.* **1** in hunting, a shout to make hounds run faster. **2** a call or shout to attract attention. **3** a shout; call.
—*v.* shout; call. [ME < OF *halloer* chase with shouts, var. of *haler* < *hale, hare* (the shout). Cf. HARASS.]

hal·low[1] (hal′ō) *v.* **1** make holy; make sacred. **2** honor as holy or sacred. [OE *hālgian* < *hālig* holy]

hal·low[2] (hə lō′) *interj. n. v.* halloo.

hal·lowed (hal′ōd; *in church use, often* hal′ō id) *adj.* **1** made holy; sacred; consecrated: *A churchyard is hallowed ground.* **2** honored or observed as holy.

Hal·low·een or **Hal·low·e'en** (hal′ō ēn′, hal′ə wēn′, hol′ə wēn′, or hol′ō ēn′) *n.* the evening of October 31. The next day is Allhallows or All Saints' Day. [for *Allhallow-even* < *all* + obs. *hallow* (ME *halwe* < OE *hālga* saint) + *even*[2]. See HALLOW[1].]

Hal·low·mas (hal′ō məs or hol′ō məs, hal′ō mas or hol′ō mas) *n.* a former name of the Christian church feast of Allhallows or All Saints' Day, observed on November 1.

hal·lu·ci·na·tion (hə lü′sə nā′shən) *n.* **1** a seeing or hearing things that have no basis outside a person's brain. A person alone in a perfectly quiet room suffers from hallucinations if he sees people around him or hears voices. **2** a thing seen or heard when there is no external cause for it. [< L *hallucinatio, -onis* < *hallucinari* wander (of the mind), ult. < Gk. *haluein* be beside oneself; form influenced by L *vaticinari* rave]

hal·lu·cin·o·gen (hə lü′sə nə jən) *n.* a drug or substance that produces hallucinations.

hal·lu·cin·o·gen·ic (hə lü′sə nə jen′ik) *adj.* of, producing, or tending to produce, hallucinations.

hall·way (hol′wā′ or hôl′-) *n.* **1** a way to go through a building; passageway; corridor. **2** a passageway or room at the entrance of a building. —**Syn. 1** passage.

ha·lo (hā′lō) *n.* **-los** or **-loes,** *v.* **-loed, -lo·ing.** —*n.* **1** a ring of light around a luminous body such as the sun, the moon, or a star. **2** a golden circle or disk of light represented about the head of a holy person, as in pictures of saints and angels. **3** the glory or glamor that surrounds an idealized person or thing: *A halo of glory surrounds King Arthur and his knights.* —*v.* surround with a halo. [< L *halo* < Gk. *halōs* disk, threshing floor (with reference to circular path of the oxen)]

hal·o·gen (hal′ə jən or hāl′ə jən) *n.* any one of the chemical elements, iodine, bromine, chlorine, fluorine, and astatine, that combine directly with metals to form salts. The halogens are the most active elements. [< Gk. *hals, halos* salt + E *-gen*]

hal·oid (hal′oid or hā′loid) *adj.* **1** of or like a salt. **2** formed from a halogen. —*n.* halide. [< Gk. *hals, halos* salt + E *-oid*]

halt[1] (holt or hôlt) *v.* **1** stop for a time. **2** cause to stop for a time. [< n.]
—*n.* **1** a stop for a time; a stopping. **2 call a halt,** order a stop.
—*interj.* a command to stop or come to a halt. [< F *halte* < G *halt* < *halten* stop, hold]

halt[2] (holt or hôlt) *v.* **1** be in doubt; hesitate; waver: *Shyness made her halt as she talked.* **2** be faulty or imperfect: *A poor argument halts.* **3** *Archaic.* be lame or crippled; limp. —*adj. Archaic.* lame; crippled; limping. —*n.* **1** *Archaic.* lameness; crippled condition; limping walk. **2 the halt,** persons who halt, limp, or hesitate. [OE *healt*, adj., *haltian*, v.] —**halt′ing·ly,** *adv.*

A halter

hal·ter (hol′tər or hôl′tər) *n.* **1** a rope, strap, etc. for leading or tying an animal. **2** a rope for hanging a person; noose. **3** death by hanging. **4** an abbreviated blouse for women that fastens behind the neck and across the back. —*v.* put a halter on; tie with a halter. [OE *hælftre*]

hat, āge, cãre, fär; let, ēqual, tėrm; it, īce
hot, ōpen, ôrder; oil, out; cup, pu̇t, rüle, ūse
əbove, takən, pencəl, lemən, circəs
ch, child; ng, long; sh, ship
th, thin; ᴛʜ, then; zh, measure

halve (hav) *v.* **halved, halv·ing. 1** divide into two equal parts; share equally. **2** reduce to half: *The new machine halves the time of doing the work.* [< *half*]

halves (havz) *n.* pl. of **half. 1 by halves, a** not completely; partly. **b** in a half-hearted way. **2 go halves,** share equally.

hal·yard (hal′yərd) *n.* on a ship, a rope or tackle used to raise or lower a sail, yard, flag, etc. Also, **halliard.** [ME *hallyer* < *hale*[2]; form influenced by *yard*[2]]

ham (ham) *n.* **1** salted and smoked meat from the upper part of a pig's hind leg. **2** the upper part of an animal's hind leg, used for food. See **pork** for picture. **3** Often, **hams,** *pl.* the back of the thigh; thigh and buttock. **4** the part of the leg back of the knee. **5** *Slang.* in the theatre, **a** a person who overacts or exaggerates his part in a play or show: *That actor is a ham.* **b** insincere, exaggerated acting. **6** *Slang.* an amateur radio operator. —*v. Slang.* in the theatre, act in an insincere exaggerated manner; overact. [OE *hamm*]

Ham (ham) *n.* in the Bible, the second son of Noah, supposed by legend to be the ancestor of the African races. Gen. 10:6-20.

ham·a·dry·ad (ham′ə drī′əd or ham′ə drī′ad) *n.* **1** in Greek mythology, a wood nymph supposed to live and die with the tree she dwelt in; dryad. **2** a large baboon of Ethiopia. [< L < Gk. *Hamadryas, -adis* < *hama* together (with) + *drys* tree]

ham·burg (ham′bėrg) *n.* hamburger.

ham·burg·er (ham′bėr gər) *n.* **1** ground beef, usually shaped into round, flat cakes and fried or broiled. **2** a split roll containing this meat. [< G *Hamburger* pertaining to Hamburg]

Hamburg steak or **hamburg steak** hamburger (def. 1).

hame (hām) *n.* either of two curved pieces on either side of the collar in a horse's harness. The traces are fastened to the hames. [OE *hama* covering]

Ham·ite (ham′īt) *n.* **1** a descendant of Ham. **2** a member of various peoples in N. and E. Africa.

Ham·it·ic (ham it′ik or hə mit′ik) *adj.* **1** of or having to do with the Hamites. **2** of or having to do with a group of languages in N. and E. Africa, including ancient Egyptian, Berber, Ethiopian, etc.

ham·let (ham′lit) *n.* a small village; a little group of houses in the country. [< OF *hamelet*, dim. of *hamel* village < Gmc. Akin to HOME.]

ham·mer (ham′ər) *n.* **1** a tool with a metal head and a handle, used to drive nails and beat metal into shape. **2** a machine in which a heavy block of metal is used for beating, striking, etc.: *a steam hammer, trip hammer.* **3** a small mallet used by auctioneers to indicate by a rap the sale of an article. **4** one of the padded mallets for striking the string of a piano. **5** a lever with a hard head for striking a bell, as in a clock. **6** the part of the firing mechanism of a gun that is released by the tripper so that it strikes the percussion cap of a cartridge or pushes the firing pin and explodes the charge. **7** the malleus of the ear. **8** in track and field, a metal ball attached to a length of steel wire with a handle on the other end by which it is twirled around in a circle and thrown for distance. **9** anything shaped or used like a hammer. **10 come** or **go under the hammer,** be sold at auction. **11 hammer and tongs,** with all one's force and strength.
—*v.* **1** drive, hit, or work with a hammer. **2** beat into shape with a hammer. **3** fasten by using a hammer. **4** hit again and again. **5** force by many efforts. **6** work out with much effort. **7 hammer at,** work hard at; keep working at.

8 hammer away, keep working hard. **9 hammer out, a** beat into shape with a hammer. **b** flatten or spread with a hammer. **c** remove with a hammer. **d** work out with much effort. **e** make clear by much thinking or talking. [OE *hamor*] —**ham′mer·er,** *n.* —**ham′mer·like′,** *adj.*

hammer and sickle the Soviet emblem of a crossed hammer and sickle, standing for the laborer and the farmer, that symbolizes Russian communism.

ham·mer·head (ham′ər hed′) *n.* a fierce shark whose wide head resembles a double-headed hammer.

ham·mer·less (ham′ər lis) *adj.* **1** having no hammer. **2** of firearms, having no visible hammer. A hammerless pistol has its hammer covered.

hammer lock in wrestling, a hold in which an opponent's arm is twisted and held behind his back.

ham·mock (ham′ək) *n.* a hanging bed or couch made of canvas, netted cord, etc. [< Sp. *hamaca* < Carib]

ham·per[1] (ham′pər) *v.* hold back; hinder. [ME *hampre(n)*; origin uncertain] —**Syn.** restrain, restrict.

ham·per[2] (ham′pər) *n.* a large basket, usually with a cover: *a picnic hamper.* [var. of *hanaper* < OF *hanapier* < *hanap* cup < Gmc.]

ham·ster (ham′stər) *n.* **1** a small, short-tailed rodent with large cheek pouches, often kept as a pet. **2** its fur. [< G]

ham·string (ham′string′) *n. v.* **-strung** or (*rare*) **-stringed, -string·ing.** —*n.* **1** in a human being, one of the tendons at the back of the knee. **2** in a four-footed animal, the great tendon at the back of the hock.
—*v.* **1** cripple by cutting the hamstring. **2** cripple; disable; destroy the activity, efficiency, etc. of.

ham·strung (ham′strung′) *v.* pt. and pp. of **hamstring.**

hand (hand) *n.* **1** the end part of the arm; part that a person grasps and holds things with. **2** the end of any limb that grasps, holds, or clings. We call a monkey's feet hands. **3** something resembling a hand in shape, appearance, or use: *The hands of a clock or watch show the time.* **4** a hired worker who uses his hands: *a factory hand, a farm hand.* **5** a member of a ship's crew; sailor. **6** Often, **hands,** *pl.* possession; control: *The property is no longer in my hands.* **7** a part or share in doing something: *He had no hand in the matter.* **8** side: *At her left hand stood two men.* **9** source: *She heard his story at first hand.* **10** one's style of handwriting: *He writes in a clear hand.* **11** a person's signature. **12** skill; ability: *The artist's work showed a master's hand.* **13** a person, with reference to action, skill, or ability: *She is a great hand at thinking up new games.* **14** a round of applause or clapping: *The crowd gave the winner a big hand.* **15** a promise of marriage. **16** a measure used in giving the height of horses, etc.; a breadth of a hand; 4 inches. **17** in cardplaying: **a** the cards held by a player in one round of a card game. **b** one round of a card game. **c** a player in a card game.
all hands, a all sailors of a ship's crew. **b** *Informal.* all members of a group.
at first hand, from direct knowledge or experience.
at hand, a within reach; near; close. **b** ready.
at second hand, from a source other than the original source: *The story he heard at second hand proved to be an exaggeration.*
at the hand (or hands) of, from (a person, as giver, doer, etc.): *We have received many favors at his hands.*
bear a hand, help.
by hand, by using the hands, not machinery.
change hands, pass from one person to another.
clean hands, freedom from crime or dishonesty.
eat out of one's hand, follow one's ideas, leadership, etc.; submit to one's authority.
force one's hand, a make a person do something. **b** make a person show what he is going to do.
from hand to mouth, spending all one receives: *He was living from hand to mouth, having used his savings to pay his bills.*
give a hand, assist; help: *Please give me a hand with this trunk.*
hand and glove (with), intimate; in close relations.
hand in glove (with), intimate; in close relations.
hand in hand, a holding hands. **b** together.
hands down, easily: *He won the contest hands down.*
hand to hand, close together; at close quarters: *to fight hand to hand.*
have one's hands full, be very busy; be able to do no more; have all one can do.
in hand, a under control. **b** in possession. **c** going along; being done.
in one's hands, in one's care or charge.
join hands, a become partners. **b** marry.
keep one's hand in, keep up one's skill; keep in practice.
lay hands on, a seize; take; get. **b** arrest. **c** attack; harm. **d** bless by touching with the hands.
lend a hand, help; assist.
off one's hands, out of one's care or charge.
on hand, a within reach; near; close. **b** ready. **c** present.
on one's hands, in one's care or charge.
on the one hand, considering this side; from this point of view: *On the one hand I feel that to buy this house would be a good investment in the long run.*
on the other hand, considering the other side of the question or argument; from the opposite point of view: *I want the bicycle very much; on the other hand, I can't afford to buy it.*
out of hand, a out of control. **b** at once. **c** finished; done with.
show one's hand, reveal one's real intentions.
sit on one's hands, *Informal.* **a** applaud feebly; show little enthusiasm for a play, performance, etc. **b** do nothing.
take a hand, a bring under control. **b** consider; deal with. **c** attempt.
tie one's hands, make one unable to do something.
to hand, a within reach; near; close. **b** in one's possession.
try one's hand, try to do; test one's ability: *After trying his hand at politics, he soon went back into business.*
turn one's hand to, work at.
wait on hand and foot, serve diligently.
wash one's hands of, have no more to do with; refuse to be responsible for.
—*v.* **1** give with the hand; pass; pass along: *Please hand me the butter.* **2** help with the hand: *The young man handed the lady into her car.* **3 hand down, a** pass along. **b** in law, announce (a decision, opinion, etc.). **4 hand in,** give; deliver. **5 hand it to,** *Informal.* acknowledge as superior: *You've got to hand it to him; he's quite a salesman.* **6 hand on,** pass along. **7 hand out,** give out; distribute. **8 hand over,** give to another; deliver.
—*adj.* of, for, by, or in the hand. [OE] —**hand′like′,** *adj.*

hand·bag (han′bag′ or hand′-) *n.* **1** a woman's small bag for money, keys, cosmetics, etc.; purse. **2** a small travelling bag to hold clothes, etc.

hand·ball (han′bol′ or hand′-, han′bôl′ or hand′-) *n.* **1** a game played by hitting a small ball against a wall with the hand. **2** the ball used in this game.

hand·bar·row (han′bar′ō or hand′-) *n.* **1** a frame with two handles at each end by which it is carried. **2** a handcart.

hand·bill (han′bil′ or hand′-) *n.* a printed notice, announcement, advertisement, etc. to be handed out to people.

hand·book (han′bu̇k′ or hand′-) *n.* **1** a small book of reference on some field of study; manual: *a handbook of engineering.* **2** a guidebook for tourists. **3** a book for recording bets.

hand brake a brake operated by a manual lever. The emergency brake on some automobiles is a hand brake.

hand·breadth (han′bredth′ or hand′-, han′bretth′ or hand′-) *n.* the breadth of a hand, used as a measure. It varies from $2\frac{1}{2}$ to 4 inches.

hand·car (hand′kär′) *n.* a small car used on railway tracks by maintenance men and driven by a hand lever that is pumped up and down.

hand·cart (han′kärt′ or hand′-) *n.* a small cart pulled or pushed by hand.

hand·clap (hand′klap′) *n.* a striking together of the hands to signal, mark rhythm, applaud, etc.

hand·cuff (han′kuf′ or hand′-) *n.* Usually, **handcuffs,** *pl.* a device to keep a person from using his hands, usually a pair of metal clasps joined by a short chain and fastened around the wrists. —*v.* put handcuffs on.

Handcuffs and key

-handed *combining form.* **1** having a hand or hands. **2** having a certain kind or number of hands, as in *left-handed*. **3** using a certain number of hands: *a two-handed stroke.*

hand·ful (han′fu̇l or hand′-) *n.* **-fuls. 1** as much or as many as the hand can hold. **2** a small number or quantity. **3** *Informal.* a person or thing that is hard to handle or control: *That boy is quite a handful.*

hand grenade a small bomb designed to be thrown by hand.

hand·grip (hand′grip′) *n.* **1** a grip or grasping of the hand, used in greeting. **2** a handle. **3 come to handgrips,** get into a hand-to-hand fight.

hand·hold (hand′hōld′) *n.* a place to put the hands.

hand·i·cap (han′di kap′ or han′dē-) *n. v.* **-capped, -cap·ping.** —*n.* **1** a race, contest, game, etc. in which the better contestants are given certain disadvantages, or the poorer ones certain advantages, so that all have an equal chance to win. **2** the disadvantage or advantage given: *A runner with a 5-yard handicap in a 100-yard race has to run either 105 yards or 95 yards.* **3** something that puts a person at a disadvantage; hindrance: *A sore throat is a handicap to a singer.*
—*v.* **1** give a handicap to. **2** put at a disadvantage; hinder: *The pitcher was handicapped by a lame arm.* [for *hand in cap*; apparently with reference to an old game] **—hand′i·cap′per,** *n.*

hand·i·craft (han′di kraft′ or han′dē-) *n.* **1** skill with the hands. **2** a trade or art requiring skill with the hands: *Basket weaving is a handicraft.* [alteration of *handcraft*, patterned after *handiwork*]

hand·i·crafts·man (han′di krafts′mən or han′dē-) *n.* **-men** (mən). a person skilled with his hands in a trade or art; craftsman.

hand·i·work (han′di wėrk′ or han′dē-) *n.* **1** work done with the hands. **2** work that a person has done himself. **3** the result of a person's action. [OE *handgeweorc* handwork]

hand·ker·chief (hang′kər chif) *n.* **1** a piece of fine cotton, linen, silk, etc., generally square, used especially for wiping the nose. **2** a piece of cloth worn over the head or around the neck; kerchief.

han·dle (han′dəl) *n. v.* **-dled, -dling.** —*n.* **1** the part of a thing made to be held or grasped by the hand. **2** a chance; opportunity; occasion: *Don't let your conduct give any handle for gossip.* **3 fly off the handle,** *Slang.* get angry or excited; lose one's temper or self-control. **4** *Slang.* a name or title.
—*v.* **1** touch, feel, hold, or move with the hand; use the hands on. **2** manage; direct; control: *The captain handles his soldiers well.* **3** behave or act when handled: *This car handles easily.* **4** deal with; treat: *The cruel boy handled his kitten roughly.* **5** deal in; trade in: *The store handles meat and groceries.* [OE *handle* < *hand* hand]

han·dle·bars (han′dəl bärz′) *n. pl.* the bars, usually curved, in front of the rider, by which a bicycle, etc. is guided.

-handled *combining form.* having a —— handle: *a black-handled pot* = *a pot having a black handle.*

han·dler (han′dlər) *n.* **1** a person or thing that handles. **2** a person who helps to train a boxer, or who acts as his second during a boxing match. **3** a person who shows dogs or cats in a contest.

hand·made (han′mād′ or hand′-) *adj.* made by hand, not by machinery; not machine-made.

hand·maid (han′mād′ or hand′-) *n.* **1** a female servant. **2** a female attendant.

hand·maid·en (han′mād′ən or hand′-) *n.* handmaid.

hand-me-down (hand′mē doun′) *Informal.* —*n.* **1** a second-hand article, especially a garment, passed from one person to another. **2** any cheap, badly tailored coat, suit, etc. —*adj.* having been passed on or handed down.

hand organ a large music box that is made to play tunes by turning a crank.

hand·out (hand′out′) *n. Slang.* **1** a portion of food handed out: *The tramp was given a handout.* **2** a news story or piece of publicity issued to the press by a business organization, government agency, etc. **3** a set of mimeographed notes issued to students in connection with their courses, to people attending a public lecture, etc.

hand-picked (han′pikt′ or hand′-) *adj.* **1** picked by hand. **2** carefully selected. **3** unfairly selected.

hat, āge, cãre, fär; let, ēqual, tėrm; it, īce
hot, ōpen, ôrder; oil, out; cup, pu̇t, rüle, ūse
əbove, takən, pencəl, lemən, circəs
ch, child; ng, long; sh, ship
th, thin; ᴛʜ, then; zh, measure

hand·rail (hand′rāl′) *n.* a railing used as a guard or support on a stairway, platform, etc.

hand·saw (han′so′ or hand′-, han′sô′ or hand′-) *n.* a saw used with one hand.

hand·sel (han′səl) *n. v.* **-selled** or **-seled, -sel·ling** or **-sel·ing.** —*n.* **1** a gift given in token of good wishes, as at New Year's, to one entering a new job or house, etc. **2** a first payment; the first money taken in by a dealer in the morning, or on opening a new store. **3** a first experience of anything; foretaste.
—*v.* **1** give a handsel to. **2** inaugurate. **3** be the first to use, try, taste, etc. Also, **hansel.** [OE *handselen* giving of the hand (i.e., to confirm a bargain)]

hand·set (hand′set′) *n.* a telephone that has the receiver and mouthpiece on the same handle.

hand·shake (han′shāk′ or hand′-) *n.* a clasping and shaking of hands by two people as a sign of friendship when meeting, parting, or sealing a bargain.

hand·some (han′səm) *adj.* **-som·er, -som·est. 1** good-looking; pleasing in appearance. We usually say that a man is handsome, but that a woman is pretty or beautiful. **2** fairly large; considerable: *Ten thousand dollars is a handsome amount of money.* **3** generous: *a handsome gift.* **4** gracious; proper. [ME *handsom* easy to handle, ready at hand < *hand* + *-some*[1]] **—hand′some·ly,** *adv.* **—hand′some·ness,** *n.* **—Syn. 1** See **beautiful.**

hand·spike (han′spīk′ or hand′-) *n.* a bar used as a lever, especially on a ship.

hand·spring (han′spring′ or hand′-) *n.* a spring or leap in which a person turns his heels over his head while balancing on one or both hands.

hand-to-hand (han′tə hand′ or hand′-) *adj. adv.* close together; at close quarters: *a hand-to-hand fight.*

hand-to-mouth (han′tə mouth′ or hand′-) *adj.* having nothing to spare; being unable to save or provide for the future; not thrifty.

hand·work (hand′wėrk′) *n.* work done by hand, not by machinery.

hand·writ·ing (hand′rīt′ing) *n.* **1** writing done by hand; writing done with pen, pencil, etc. **2** a manner or style of writing: *He recognized his mother's handwriting on the envelope.* **3 handwriting on the wall, a** in the Bible, a cryptic handwriting seen by Belshazzar, King of Babylon, on the wall of his palace, which Daniel interpreted as a prophecy of the fall of Babylon. Daniel 5:26-28. **b** a portent of doom. **4 see** or **read the handwriting on the wall, a** perceive that an institution, order, way of life, etc. is coming to an end. **b** see things as they really are.

hand·y (han′dē) *adj.* **hand·i·er, hand·i·est. 1** easy to reach or use; saving work; useful; convenient. **2** skilful with the hands. **3** easy to handle or manage. **—hand′i·ly,** *adv.* **—hand′i·ness,** *n.*

hand·y·man (han′dē man′) *n.* **-men** (-men′). a man who does odd jobs.

hang (hang) *v.* **hung** or (*for defs. 3, 4, see usage note*) **hanged, hang·ing,** *n.* —*v.* **1** fasten or be fastened to something above. **2** fasten or be fastened so as to swing or turn freely: *hang a door on its hinges.* **3** put or be put to death by hanging with a rope around the neck: *He was hanged several weeks after being sentenced.* **4** die by hanging. **5** cover or decorate with things that hang: *hang a window with curtains. The walls were hung with pictures.* **6** bend down; droop: *He hung his head in shame.* **7** fasten in position. **8** attach (paper, etc.) to walls. **9** depend. **10** be wearisome or tedious: *Time hangs on his hands.* **11** hold fast; cling. **12** be doubtful or undecided; hesitate; waver. **13** keep (a jury) from making a decision or reaching a verdict. One member can hang a jury by refusing to agree with the others. **14** loiter; linger: *Don't hang about!* **15** hover.
hang back, be unwilling to go forward; be backward.
hang it! an expression of annoyance.
hang on, a hold tight: *The dying man hung on to life for*

several days. **b** be unwilling to let go, stop, or leave. **c** depend on. **d** consider or listen to very carefully: *She hung on the teacher's every word.*
hang out, a show by hanging outside. **b** lean out. **c** *Slang.* live; stay.
hang over, a be about to happen to; threaten. **b** *Informal.* remain from an earlier time or condition.
hang together, a stick together. **b** be coherent or consistent: *The story does not hang together.*
hang up, a put on a hook, peg, etc. **b** put a telephone receiver back in place. **c** hold back; delay; detain.
—*n.* **1** the way a thing hangs: *She changed the hang of her skirt.* **2** *Informal.* the way of using or doing (something): *Riding a bicycle is easy after you get the hang of it.* **3** *Informal.* the idea; meaning: *After studying an hour he finally got the hang of the lesson.* **4** a trifle: *not care a hang.* [OE *hōn* (with past *hēng*) suspend, and OE *hangian* be suspended, blended with ON *hengja* suspend]

☛ **hanged, hung.** In formal English the principal parts of *hang* when referring to the death penalty are *hang, hanged, hanged*; in other senses they are *hang, hung, hung*: *They hanged the renegade from the ship's yardarm. They hung the rifle over the fireplace mantel.* Informal usage does not keep this distinction, using *hang, hung, hung* in all senses.

hang·ar (hang′ər) *n.* **1** a shed for aircraft. **2** a shed. [< F < Med. L *angarium* shed for shoeing horses, ? < Gmc.]

hang·bird (hang′bėrd′) *n.* any bird that builds a hanging nest, especially the Baltimore oriole.

hang·dog (hang′dog′) *adj.* ashamed; sneaking; degraded.

hang·er (hang′ər) *n.* **1** a person who hangs things. A paper hanger puts on wallpaper. **2** a tool or machine that hangs things. **3** anything on which something else is hung: *a coat hanger.* **4** a loop, ring, etc. attached to something to hang it up by. **5** a kind of short, light sword formerly worn by sailors on their belts.

hang·er-on (hang′ər on′) *n.* **hang·ers-on. 1** a follower; dependent. **2** an undesirable follower. **3** a person who often goes to a place.

hang·ing (hang′ing) *n.* **1** death by hanging with a rope around the neck. **2** Often, **hangings,** *pl.* something that hangs from a wall, bed, etc.: *Curtains are hangings.*
—*adj.* **1** deserving to be punished by hanging: *a hanging crime.* **2** fastened to something above. **3** leaning over or down. **4** located on a height or steep slope.

hang·man (hang′mən) *n.* **-men** (-mən). a man who puts condemned persons to death by hanging them.

hang·nail (hang′nāl′) *n.* a bit of skin that hangs partly loose near the edge of a fingernail. [alteration of *agnail,* OE *angnægl* (< *ang-* compressed, painful + *nægl* nail, corn), under the influence of *hang*]

hang·out (hang′out′) *n. Slang.* **1** a place one lives in or goes to often. **2** a rendezvous, especially for criminals.

hang·o·ver (hang′ō′vər) *n.* **1** *Informal.* something that remains from an earlier time or condition. **2** *Slang.* a condition resulting from the consumption of too much alcohol the previous night.

hang-up (hang′up′) *n. Slang.* a personal or emotional difficulty; a fixation.

hank (hangk) *n.* **1** a coil; loop. **2** a skein. **3** a skein of yarn containing a definite number of yards. There are 840 yards in a hank of cotton yarn, and 560 yards in a hank of worsted yarn. [< ON *hönk*]

han·ker (hang′kər) *v.* wish; crave. [origin uncertain]

han·ker·ing (hang′kər ing or hang′kring) *n.* a longing; craving: *I have a hankering for a large, juicy steak.*

Han·o·ve·ri·an (han′ō vēr′ē ən) *adj.* **1** of or having to do with Hanover, Germany. **2** of or having to do with Hanover, the English royal house from 1714 to 1901.
—*n.* **1** a native or inhabitant of Hanover. **2** a supporter of the House of Hanover.

Han·sard (han′sərd) *n.* the printed record of the proceedings of the Canadian or British House of Commons. [after Luke *Hansard* (1752-1828), first compiler]

hanse (hans) *n.* in the Middle Ages, a merchant guild of a town. [ME < OF < MHG *hanse* merchants' guild < OHG *hansa* band]

Han·se·at·ic (han′sē at′ik) *adj.* of or having to do with the Hanseatic League.

Hanseatic League in the Middle Ages, a league of towns in Germany and nearby countries for the promotion and protection of commerce.

han·sel (han′səl) *n. v.* **-selled** or **-seled, -sel·ling** or **-sel·ing.** handsel.

han·som (han′səm) *n.* a two-wheeled cab for two passengers drawn by one horse. [after Joseph *Hansom,* an early designer of such cabs]

Ha·nuk·kah or **Ha·nuk·ka** (hä′nů kä′; *Hebrew,* HÄ′nů kä′) *n.* the Feast of Dedication or the Feast of Lights, an eight-day Jewish festival, falling in December. Also, **Chanukah.** [< Hebrew *hannukah* dedication]

hap (hap) *n. v.* **happed, hap·ping.** *Archaic.* —*n.* chance; luck. —*v.* happen. [ME < ON *happ*]

hap·haz·ard (*n.* hap′haz′ərd; *adj. adv.* hap′haz′ərd) *n.* chance: *Events seemed to happen at haphazard.*
—*adj.* random; casual; not planned: *Haphazard answers are usually wrong.*
—*adv.* by chance; at random; casually: *He took a card haphazard from the deck.* —**hap′haz′ard·ly,** *adv.* —**hap′haz′ard·ness,** *n.* —**Syn.** *adj.* See **random.**

hap·less (hap′lis) *adj.* unlucky; unfortunate. —**hap′less·ly,** *adv.* —**hap′less·ness,** *n.*

hap·ly (hap′lē) *adv. Archaic.* perhaps; by chance.

hap·pen (hap′ən) *v.* **1** take place; occur: *Nothing interesting happens here.* **2** be or take place by chance: *Accidents will happen.* **3** have the fortune (*to*); chance: *I happened to sit next to a famous hockey player.* **4** be done (*to*); go wrong with: *Something has happened to this lock; the key won't turn.* **5 as it happens,** by chance; as it turns out: *As it happens, I have no money with me.* **6 happen on, a** meet by chance. **b** find by chance: *She happened on a dime while looking for her ball.* [ME *happene(n)* < *hap*]

hap·pen·ing (hap′ən ing or hap′ning) *n.* anything that happens; event; occurrence.

hap·pi·ly (hap′ə lē) *adv.* **1** in a happy manner; with pleasure, joy, and gladness: *She lives happily.* **2** luckily; fortunately: *Happily I saved her from falling.* **3** aptly; appropriately.

hap·pi·ness (hap′ē nis) *n.* **1** a being happy; gladness. **2** good luck; good fortune. **3** aptness.
Syn. 1 Happiness, felicity, bliss = a feeling of satisfaction and pleasure. **Happiness** is the general word, applying to a feeling of contentment coming from being and doing well or of satisfaction at having got what one wanted: *His promotion brought him happiness.* **Felicity,** formal, means great or joyous happiness: *I wish you every felicity in your marriage.* **Bliss** suggests feeling lifted to the heights of happiness or joy: *They are in a state of bliss now that they are engaged.*

hap·py (hap′ē) *adj.* **-pi·er, -pi·est. 1** feeling or showing pleasure and joy; glad; pleased; contented. **2** lucky, fortunate: *By a happy chance, I found the lost money.* **3** clever and fitting; apt; successful and suitable: *a happy way of expressing an idea.* [ME *happy* < *hap*] —**Syn. 1** joyful; delighted. See **glad. 2** favorable. **3** appropriate, felicitous.

hap·py-go-luck·y (hap′ē gō luk′ē) *adj.* taking things easily; trusting to luck.

happy hunting ground 1 the North American Indian paradise. **2** any paradise. **3** any pleasant place with which one is particularly associated: *He returns every summer to his happy hunting ground in California.*

Haps·burg (haps′bėrg; *German,* häps′bůrk) *n.* a German princely family, prominent since about 1100. The Hapsburgs were rulers of the Holy Roman Empire from 1438 to 1806, of Austria from 1804 to 1918, of Hungary from 1526 to 1918, and of Spain from 1516 to 1700. Also, **Habsburg.** [< *Habsburg,* shortening of *Habichtsburg* (meaning hawk's castle), name of a castle in Aargau, Switzerland]

har·a·ki·ri (har′ə kēr′ē or hä′rə kēr′ē) *n.* suicide committed by ripping open the abdomen with a knife, the national form of honorable suicide in Japan. Also, **hara-kari** or **hari-kari.** [< Japanese < *hara* belly + *kiri* cutting]

ha·rangue (hə rang′) *n. v.* **-rangued, -rangu·ing.** —*n.* **1** a noisy speech. **2** a long, pompous speech. —*v.* **1** address in a harangue. **2** deliver a harangue. [ME < OF *arenge* < Gmc.] —**ha·rangu′er,** *n.*

har·ass (har′əs or hə ras′) *v.* **1** troubled by repeated attacks; harry: *Pirates harassed the villages along the coast.* **2** disturb; worry; torment. [< F *harasser* < OF *harer* set a dog on] —**Syn. 2** plague, bother. See **worry.**

har·ass·ment (har′əs mənt or hə ras′mənt) *n.* **1** a harassing. **2** a being harassed; worry. **3** something that harasses.

har·bin·ger (här′bin jər) *n.* one that goes ahead to announce another's coming; forerunner: *The robin is a harbinger of spring.* —*v.* announce beforehand; announce. [ME < OF *herbergere* provider of shelter (hence, one who goes ahead), ult. < *herberge* lodging < Gmc. Akin to HARBOR.]

har·bor or **har·bour** (här′bər) *n.* **1** a naturally or artificially sheltered area of deep water where ships may dock or anchor. A harbor may have loading and unloading facilities for passengers and cargo. **2** any place of shelter. —*v.* **1** give shelter to; give a place to hide: *The dog's shaggy hair harbors fleas.* **2** take shelter or refuge. **3** keep or nourish in the mind: *Don't harbor unkind thoughts.* [OE *herebeorg* lodgings < *here* army + *beorg* shelter] —**har′bor·er** or **har′bour·er,** *n.* —**har′bor·less** or **har′bour·less,** *adj.*

Syn. *n.* **1 Harbor, port** = place of shelter for ships. **Harbor** emphasizes shelter, and applies to a protected part of the sea, or other large body of water, where land or breakwaters shield against wind and heavy waves: *Many yachts are lying at anchor in the harbor.* **Port** emphasizes the idea of a place to put in to land or unload at the end of a voyage, and applies particularly to a harbor where commercial ships dock for loading and unloading: *The ship arrived in port.* **2** refuge. -*v.* **3** See **cherish.**

har·bor·age or **har·bour·age** (här′bər ij or här′brij) *n.* **1** a shelter for ships and boats. **2** any shelter.

harbor master or **harbour master** an officer who has charge of a harbor or port and enforces its regulations.

har·bour (här′bər) *n. v.* harbor.

hard (härd) *adj.* **1** solid and firm to the touch; not soft: *Rocks are hard.* **2** firmly formed; tight: *His muscles were hard.* **3** needing much ability, effort, or time; difficult: *a hard problem.* **4** causing much pain, trouble, care, etc.; severe: *a hard illness.* **5** stern; unfeeling: *a hard master.* **6** not pleasant; harsh: *a hard face, a hard laugh.* **7** acting or done with energy, persistence, etc.: *a hard worker.* **8** vigorous; violent: *a hard storm, a hard run.* **9** containing mineral salts that interfere with the action of soap: *hard water.* **10** containing much alcohol: *hard liquor.* **11** *Informal.* real and significant: *hard facts, hard news.* **12** in phonetics, pronounced by stopping and then releasing the breath. The *c* and *g* in *corn* and *get* are "hard"; in *city* and *gem* they are "soft." **13 hard and fast,** that cannot be changed or broken; strict. **14 hard of hearing,** rather deaf. **15 hard put to it,** in much difficulty or trouble. **16 hard up,** *Informal.* needing money or anything very badly.
—*adv.* **1** so as to be hard, solid, or firm: *frozen hard.* **2** firmly; tightly: *Don't hold hard.* **3** with difficulty: *breathe hard.* **4** so as to cause trouble, pain, care, etc.: harshly; severely: *taxes that bear hard upon us.* **5** with effort or energy: *They try hard.* **6** with vigor or violence: *He hit hard.* **7** earnestly; intently: *look hard at a person.* **8** close; near: *The house stands hard by the bridge.* **9** to the extreme limit; fully. [OE *heard*] —**hard′ness,** *n.*

hard-bit·ten (härd′bit′ən) *adj.* stubborn; unyielding.

hard·board (härd′bôrd′) *n.* a strong kind of wallboard made by compressing ground wood fibres under heat.

hard-boiled (härd′boild′) *adj.* **1** boiled until hard: *hard-boiled eggs.* **2** *Slang.* not easily influenced by the feelings; tough; rough.

hard·bound (härd′bound′) *adj.* of books, bound in leather, boards, or cloth, rather than in flexible paper.

hard cash **1** metal coins. **2** cash.

hard cider fermented cider, containing alcohol.

hard coal anthracite.

hard core the permanent or most lasting part of any thing or any group; the central or vital part.

hard currency currency that has full backing in gold or silver and is unlikely to fluctuate in value.

hard·en (här′dən) *v.* **1** make or become hard. **2** make or become capable of endurance. **3** make or become unfeeling or pitiless. **4** temper or make (metals and alloys, especially steel) hard by raising to a high temperature and then cooling in oil, water, or air. **5** of prices of stocks, commodities, etc., become higher; rise. —**hard′en·er,** *n.* —**Syn. 1** solidify. **2** accustom.

hat, āge, cãre, fär; let, ēqual, tėrm; it, īce
hot, ōpen, ôrder; oil, out; cup, pu̇t, rüle, ūse
əbove, takən, pencəl, lemən, circəs
ch, child; ng, long; sh, ship
th, thin; ᴛʜ, then; zh, measure

hard·hack (härd′hak′) *n.* a shrub of the rose family, a kind of spirea, having clusters of small pink, purple, or white flowers and woolly leaves and branches.

hard hat a type of helmet worn by construction workers as protection against falling objects.

hard·head (härd′hed′) *n.* **1** a person not easily moved; a shrewd, unemotional person. **2** any of various fishes, including the salmon trout and the alewife. **3** any of various durable sponges.

hard-head·ed (härd′hed′id) *adj.* **1** not easily excited or deceived; practical; shrewd. **2** stubborn; obstinate. —**hard′-head′ed·ly,** *adv.* —**hard′-head′ed·ness,** *n.*

hard-heart·ed (härd′här′tid) *adj.* without pity; cruel; unfeeling. —**hard′-heart′ed·ly,** *adv.* —**hard′-heart′ed·ness,** *n.*

har·di·hood (här′dē hu̇d′) *n.* boldness; daring.

har·di·ness (här′dē nis) *n.* **1** endurance; strength. **2** hardihood.

hard labor or **labour** hard work in addition to imprisonment.

hard·ly (härd′lē) *adv.* **1** only just; barely: *We hardly had time for breakfast.* **2** not quite: *hardly strong enough.* **3** probably not: *He will hardly come now.* **4** with trouble or effort: *money hardly earned.* **5** in a hard manner; harshly; severely: *deal hardly with a person.*

Syn. 1 Hardly, barely, scarcely = only just or almost not what is named or stated, and are often used interchangeably. But **hardly** = near or close to the minimum limit, with little to spare: *I had hardly reached there when it began to rain.* **Barely** = just enough, with nothing to spare: *He eats barely enough.* **Scarcely** = almost not at all: *He has scarcely anything to eat.*

☛ **hardly.** Formal and informal English avoid a concealed double negative when using *hardly* with the meaning "not quite." Formal and informal: *The biology films showed hardly anything that was new to us.* Substandard: *The biology films showed hardly nothing that was new to us.*

hard palate the front, bony part of the roof of the mouth.

hard·pan (härd′pan′) *n.* hard, firm, underlying earth.

hard·rock (härd′rok′) *n.* **1** in mining, rock, such as quartz, that can be removed only by drilling or blasting. **2** *Slang.* a strong, rough person. —*adj.* Often, **hard-rock. 1** of or having to do with hardrock: *hardrock miners.* **2** *Slang.* characterized by hardness and strength: *That hockey player was feared for his hardrock checking.*

hard sauce a sauce made by creaming sugar, butter, and flavoring together, used on cakes, puddings, etc.

hard sell *Informal.* a forceful and direct method of advertising a product; high-pressure salesmanship: *More and more companies are using the hard sell.*

hard-shell (härd′shel′) *adj.* **1** having a hard shell. **2** *Informal.* strict; uncompromising.

hard·ship (härd′ship) *n.* something hard to bear; hard condition of living: *Hunger, cold, and sickness are hardships.* —**Syn.** trial, affliction.

hard sledding difficult going; unfavorable conditions.

hard·tack (härd′tak′) *n.* a very hard, dry biscuit.

hard·top (härd′top′) *n. Informal.* an automobile, having a body design similar to that of a convertible except that the top is rigid.

hard·ware (härd′wãr′) *n.* **1** articles made from metal: *Locks, hinges, nails, and tools are hardware.* **2** in military use, manufactured equipment such as guns, tanks, aircraft, or missiles. **3** the mechanical, electronic, or structural parts of computers or of a computer, teaching machine, etc. (opposed to *software*).

hard wheat wheat having a hard kernel and high gluten content, used in making bread, macaroni, etc.

hard·wood (härd′wu̇d′) *n.* **1** any hard, compact wood. **2** in forestry, any tree that has broad leaves or does not have needles. 3 the wood of such a tree. Oak, cherry, maple, etc. are hardwoods; pine and fir are softwoods.

har·dy (här′dē) *adj.* **-di·er, -di·est. 1** able to bear hard treatment, fatigue, etc.; strong; robust. **2** able to withstand the cold of winter in the open air: *hardy plants.* **3** bold; daring. **4** too bold; rash. [ME < OF *hardi*, pp. of *hardir* harden < Gmc.] **—har′di·ly,** *adv.* **—Syn. 1** hale, hearty. **3** courageous, intrepid.

hare (hãr) *n.* **hare** or **hares,** *v.* **hared, har·ing.** *—n.* a gnawing animal resembling a rabbit but larger. It has long ears, long hind legs, a short tail, and a divided upper lip. *—v.* hurry; run: *They hared off after the thief.* [OE *hara*] **—hare′like′,** *adj.*

hare·bell (hãr′bel′) *n.* a slender plant having blue, bell-shaped flowers; bluebell.

hare·brained (hãr′brānd′) *adj.* giddy; heedless; reckless.

hare·lip (hãr′lip′) *n.* **1** a deformity caused when parts of the lip fail to grow together before birth. **2** a lip that is deformed in this way. **—hare′lipped′,** *adj.*

har·em (hãr′əm) *n.* **1** the part of a Moslem house where the women live. **2** its occupants; the wives, female relatives, female servants, etc. of a Moslem household. **3** of fur seals, wild horses, and certain other animals, a number of females controlled by one male. [< Arabic *haram, harim* forbidden]

har·i·cot (har′ə kō′) *n.* a string bean. [< F]

har·i-kar·i (har′ē kar′ē or hä′rē kä′rē) *n.* hara-kiri.

hark (härk) *v.* **1** listen. **2 hark back, a** go back; turn back: *His ideas hark back twenty years.* **b** return to a previous point or subject; revert: *Whenever we chat together, he is always harking back to his time in the army.* [ME *herkien*]

hark·en (här′kən) *v.* hearken. [OE *heorcnian*]

Har·le·quin (här′lə kwin′ or här′lə kin′) *n.* **1** in traditional Italian comedy and in pantomime, the lover of Columbine. He is usually masked, wears a costume of varied colors, and carries a wooden sword. **2 harlequin,** a mischievous person; buffoon. *—adj.* varied in color; many-colored. [< F < OF var. of *Herlequin* < ME *Herle King* King Herla (mythical figure); modern meaning in French is from Ital. *arlecchino* < OF *Harlequin*]

Harlequin

har·le·quin·ade (här′lə kwi nād′ or här′lə ki nād′) *n.* **1** a pantomime or play in which the harlequin and the clown are the leading players. **2** buffoonery; clownish antics.

har·lot (här′lət) *n.* a prostitute. [ME < OF *harlot* vagabond]

har·lot·ry (här′lət rē) *n.* prostitution.

harm (härm) *n.* **1** hurt; damage: *The accident did a lot of harm to the car.* **2** evil; wrong. *—v.* damage; injure; hurt. [OE *hearm*] **—harm′er,** *n.*

Syn. *v.* **Harm, damage** = hurt or injure a person or thing. **Harm** = injure, but is a more informal word, and especially suggests injuring a person or his mind, health, rights, business, etc. so as to cause pain, loss, or suffering of some kind: *Unfounded and malicious rumors harmed his reputation.* **Damage** = hurt or harm so as to lessen the value, usefulness, or appearance of a person or thing: *The furniture was damaged in the fire.*

harm·ful (härm′fəl) *adj.* causing harm; injurious; hurtful. **—harm′ful·ly,** *adv.* **—harm′ful·ness,** *n.* **—Syn.** detrimental, deleterious, pernicious.

harm·less (härm′lis) *adj.* causing no harm; that would not harm anyone or anything. **—harm′less·ly,** *adv.* **—harm′less·ness,** *n.* **—Syn.** innocuous, inoffensive.

har·mon·ic (här mon′ik) *adj.* **1** in music: **a** of or having to do with harmony as distinguished from melody and rhythm. **b** of or having to do with overtones that are heard along with the main tone. **c** musical. **2** having to do with or marked by harmony, agreement, or concord; concordant; consonant. **3** in physics, of or having to do with any of the frequencies making up a wave or alternating current, that are integral multiples of the fundamental frequency. **4** in mathematics, having relations similar in some way to those of musical concords. 1, $\frac{1}{2}$, $\frac{1}{3}$, $\frac{1}{4}$, etc. are in harmonic progression. *—n.* **1** in music: **a** a tone produced on a stringed instrument by a light pressure at a point on a string. **b** an overtone whose rate of vibration is an integral multiple of the main tone. Harmonics have a higher pitch and lower volume than main tones. **2** a fainter and higher tone heard along with the main tone; overtone. [< L *harmonicus* < Gk. *harmonikos* harmonic, musical < *harmonia.* See HARMONY.]

har·mon·i·ca (här mon′ə kə) *n.* a small, oblong musical instrument having several metal reeds which are caused to vibrate by air from the player's mouth controlled by the tongue and lips; mouth organ. [< L *harmonica* fem. of *harmonicus.* See HARMONIC.]

har·mon·ics (här mon′iks) *n.* the science of musical sounds.

har·mo·ni·ous (här mō′nē əs) *adj.* **1** agreeing in feelings, ideas, or actions; getting along well together: *The children played together in a harmonious group.* **2** arranged so that the parts are orderly or pleasing; going well together: *This picture is remarkable for its harmonious colors.* **3** sweet-sounding; musical. **—har·mo′ni·ous·ly,** *adv.* **—har·mo′ni·ous·ness,** *n.* **—Syn. 1** peaceable, amicable. **2** congruous, consonant, consistent. **3** melodious.

har·mo·ni·um (här mō′nē əm) *n.* a small musical organ with metal reeds. [< F *harmonium* < *harmonie.* See HARMONY.]

har·mo·nize (här′mə nīz′) *v.* **-nized, -niz·ing. 1** bring into harmony or agreement. **2** be in harmony or agreement: *The colors in the room harmonize.* **3** in music, add tones to (a melody) to make successive chords. **—har′mo·ni·za′tion,** *n.* **—har′mo·niz′er,** *n.*

har·mo·ny (här′mə nē) *n.* **-nies. 1** an agreement of feeling, ideas, or actions; getting along well together: *The two brothers lived and worked in perfect harmony.* **2** an orderly or pleasing arrangement of parts; going well together: *In this picture there is harmony between the different colors.* **3** in music: **a** a sounding together of tones in a chord. **b** the study of chords and of relating them to successive chords. **4** a sweet or musical sound; music. **5** the act of harmonizing, especially of singing voices: *The quartet achieved excellent harmony.* **6** a grouping of passages on the same subject from different stories or accounts, showing their points of agreement: *a harmony of the Gospels.* [< F *harmonie* < L < Gk. *harmonia* concord, a joining < *harmos* joint] **—Syn. 1** unity, friendship. **2** congruity.

har·ness (här′nis) *n.* **1** the leather straps, bands, and pieces of various other shapes used to hitch a horse or other animal to a carriage, wagon, plough, etc. See picture on the opposite page. **2** the straps by which a parachute is attached to a person. **3** the straps attached to an infant or young child to prevent his falling out of a crib or carriage or to control him in walking. **4** any similar arrangement of straps. **5** *Archaic.* the armor for a knight, soldier, or horse. **6 in harness,** in or at one's regular work: *The old man died in harness.* *—v.* **1** put harness on. **2** cause to produce power. Water in a stream is harnessed by allowing it to accumulate behind a dam and installing turbines that it can drive. **3** *Archaic.* put armor on. [ME < OF *harneis,* ? < Scand.]

harp (härp) *n.* **1** a musical instrument with strings set in a triangular frame, played by plucking the strings with the fingers. **2** harp seal. *—v.* **1** play on a harp. **2 harp on,** keep on tiresomely talking or writing about; refer continually to. [OE *hearpe*] **—harp′er,** *n.*

A harp

harp·ist (här′pist) *n.* a person who plays the harp.

har·poon (här pün′) *n.* a barbed spear with a rope tied to it, used for catching whales and other sea animals. It is either hurled by the hand or fired from a gun. *—v.* strike, catch, or kill with a harpoon. [< F *harpon* < MF *harper* grip < Gmc.] **—har·poon′er,** *n.*

harp seal a type of large gray seal found off northeastern Canada. The harp seal has a dark, harp-shaped marking on its back.

harp·si·chord (härp′sə kôrd′) *n.* a stringed musical instrument resembling a piano, used especially from about 1550 to 1750. It produces a tinkling sound because the strings are plucked by leather or quill points instead of being struck by hammers. [< obs. F *harpechorde* < *harpe* harp (< Gmc.) + *chorde* string of a musical instrument < L < Gk.]

Har·py (här′pē) *n.* **-pies. 1** in Greek legend, any of several filthy, greedy monsters having women's heads and birds' bodies, wings, and claws. **2 harpy,** a very greedy person; a person who preys upon others. [< L *Harpyia* < Gk., probably related to *harpazein* snatch]

har·que·bus (här′kwə bəs) *n.* a form of portable firearm used before muskets were invented. Also, **arquebus.** [< F *(h)arquebuse* < Ital. *archibuso* < Du. *haakbus,* literally, hook gun]

har·ri·dan (har′ə dən) *n.* a bad-tempered, disreputable old woman. [probably < F *haridelle* a worn-out horse]

har·ri·er[1] (har′ē ər) *n.* **1** a breed of small hound resembling the English foxhound, used to hunt hares. **2** a dog of this breed. **3** a cross-country runner. [apparently < *hare*]

har·ri·er[2] (har′ē ər) *n.* **1** a person who harries. **2** a hawk that preys on small animals. [< *harry*]

Harris tweed hand-woven tweed of very high quality, originally made on the Island of Harris in the Hebrides.

har·row (har′ō) *n.* a heavy frame with iron teeth or upright disks. Harrows are drawn over ploughed land to break up clods, cover seeds, etc. —*v.* **1** draw a harrow over (land, etc.). **2** hurt; wound. **3** arouse uncomfortable feelings in; distress; torment. [ME *harwe*] —**har′row·er,** *n.*

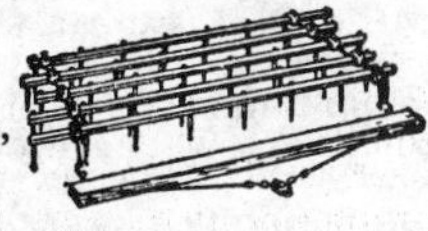

A harrow

har·ry (har′ē) *v.* **-ried, -ry·ing. 1** raid and rob with violence: *The pirates harried the towns along the coast.* **2** keep troubling; worry; torment: *Fear of losing his job harried the clerk.* [OE *hergian* < *here* army]

harsh (härsh) *adj.* **1** rough to the touch, taste, eye, or ear; sharp and unpleasant: *a harsh voice, a harsh climate.* **2** without pity; cruel; severe: *a harsh man.* **3** stern; grim; forbidding: *a harsh expression.* [var. of ME *harsk*; cf. Danish *harsk* rancid] —**harsh′ly,** *adv.* —**harsh′ness,** *n.* —**Syn. 1** grating, rasping, acrid, sour, inharmonious, discordant, strident, raucous. **2** unfeeling, unkind, rigorous, strict.

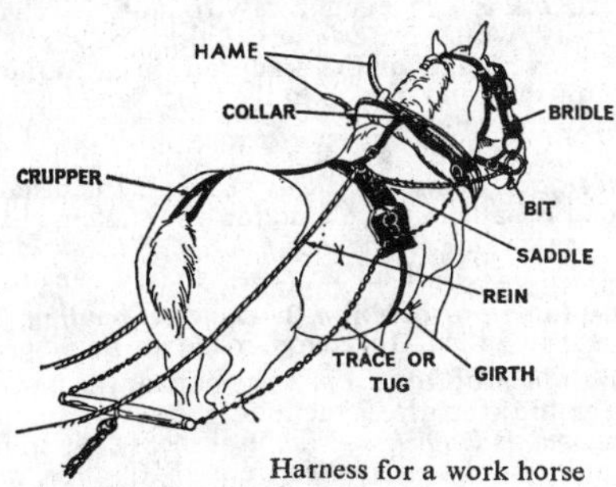

Harness for a work horse

hart (härt) *n.* **hart** or **harts.** a male deer; stag. A hart is usually a male red deer after its fifth year. [OE *heorot*]

har·te·beest (här′tə bēst′ or härt′bēst′) *n.* **-beest** or **-beests.** a large, swift African antelope having ringed, curved horns bent backward at the tips. [< Afrikaans *hartebeest* hart beast]

harts·horn (härts′hôrn′) *n.* **1** ammonia dissolved in water. **2** smelling salts; sal volatile.

har·um-scar·um (hãr′əm skãr′əm) *adj.* reckless; rash; thoughtless: *What a harum-scarum child you are!* —*adv.* recklessly; wildly: *The car rushed harum-scarum down the main street.* —*n.* a reckless person. [apparently < *hare* frighten + *scare*]

ha·rus·pex (hə rus′peks or har′əs peks′) *n.* **ha·rus·pi·ces** (hə rus′pə sēz′). in ancient Rome, a member of a class of minor priests or soothsayers who made predictions by examining the entrails of animals killed in sacrifice, by observing lightning, etc. [< L *haruspex* < **haru-* entrails + *specere* inspect]

hat, āge, cãre, fär; let, ēqual, tėrm; it, īce
hot, ōpen, ôrder; oil, out; cup, pu̇t, rüle, ūse
əbove, takən, pencəl, lemən, circəs
ch, child; ng, long; sh, ship
th, thin; ᴛʜ, then; zh, measure

har·vest (här′vist) *n.* **1** a reaping and gathering in of grain and other food crops, usually in the late summer or early autumn. **2** the time or season when grain, fruit, etc. are gathered in. **3** one season's yield of any natural product; a crop: *The oyster harvest was small this year.* **4** the result; consequences: *He is reaping the harvest of his mistakes.*
—*v.* **1** gather in and bring home for use: *to harvest wheat.* **2** gather a crop. **3** win or undergo as a result or consequence. [OE *hærfest*] —**Syn.** *n.* **3** See **crop.**

har·vest·er (här′vis tər) *n.* **1** a person who works in a harvest field; reaper. **2** a machine for harvesting crops, especially grain.

harvest home 1 the end of harvesting. **2** a festival to celebrate the end of harvesting. **3** a harvest song.

harvest moon the full moon at harvest time, or about September 23.

harvest mouse a tiny European mouse that nests on the stalks of growing grain.

has (haz; *unstressed,* hez or əz) *v.* 3rd pers. sing. present tense of **have.**

has-been (haz′bin′ or -bēn′) *n. Informal.* a person or thing whose best days are past.

hash (hash) *n.* **1** a mixture of cooked meat, potatoes, etc. chopped into small pieces and fried or baked. **2** a mixture; jumble. **3** a mess; muddle. **4 settle one's hash,** *Informal.* subdue or silence someone completely; put an end to someone. [< v.]
—*v.* **1** chop into small pieces. **2** make a mess or muddle of. **3** *Informal.* talk about in detail; discuss or review thoroughly: *The two leaders hashed over their dispute for hours.* [< F *hacher* < *hache* hatchet]

hash·eesh (hash′ēsh) *n.* hashish.

hash·ish (hash′ēsh or hash′ish) *n.* the dried flowers, top leaves, and tender parts of Indian hemp prepared for use as a narcotic. In the Orient, hashish is smoked or chewed for its intoxicating effect. [< Arabic *hashish* dried hemp leaves]

has·n't (haz′ənt) *v.* has not.

hasp (hasp) *n.* a clasp or fastening for a door, window, trunk, box, etc., especially a hinged metal clasp that fits over a staple or into a hole and is fastened by a peg, padlock, etc. [var. of OE *hæpse*]

has·sle (has′əl) *n.* a struggle; contest.

has·sock (has′ək) *n.* **1** a padded footstool or thick cushion to rest the feet on, sit on, or kneel on. **2** a tuft or bunch of coarse grass. [OE *hassuc* coarse grass]

hast (hast) *v. Archaic.* 2nd pers. sing. present tense of **have.** "Thou hast" means "you have" (sing.).

has·tate (has′tāt) *adj.* shaped like the head of a spear. [< L *hastatus* < *hasta* spear]

haste (hāst) *n. v.* **hast·ed, hast·ing.** —*n.* **1** a trying to be quick; hurrying: *The king's business required haste.* **2** quickness without thought or care: *Haste makes waste.* **3 in haste, a** in a hurry; quickly. **b** without careful thought; rashly. **4 make haste,** hurry; be quick.
—*v. Poetic.* hasten. [ME < OF < Gmc.; cf. OE *hǣst* violence] —**Syn.** *n.* **1** celerity, swiftness, speed. See **hurry.**

has·ten (hās′ən) *v.* **1** cause to be quick; speed; hurry: *She hastened the children off to bed.* **2** be quick; go fast: *Let me hasten to explain.* —**Syn. 1** quicken, accelerate.

has·ten·er (hās′ən ər) *n.* a follow-up note or letter to hurry delivery of an order, payment of a bill, etc.

hast·y (hās′tē) *adj.* **hast·i·er, hast·i·est. 1** hurried; quick: *a hasty visit.* **2** not well thought out; rash: *His hasty decisions caused many mistakes.* **3** easily angered; quick-tempered: *He should not be so hasty.* —**hast′i·ly,** *adv.* —**hast′i·ness,** *n.*

hasty pudding 1 a mush of meal or flour made with boiling water (or milk) and seasoning. **2** *U.S.* a mush made with corn meal.

hat (hat) *n. v.* **hat·ted, hat·ting.** —*n.* **1** a covering for the head, usually with a brim. **2** in the Roman Catholic Church: **a** a red head covering worn by a cardinal. **b** the dignity or office of a cardinal.
hat in hand, with the head uncovered in respect; obsequiously; servilely.
pass the hat, take up a collection.
take off one's hat to, doff or remove the hat, as a salute or sign of respect; honor; hail.
talk through one's hat, talk without knowing what one is talking about; talk foolishly.
throw one's hat into the ring, *Informal.* enter a contest, especially for election to a public office.
under one's hat, *Informal.* as a secret; to oneself.
—*v.* cover or furnish with a hat. [OE *hætt*] —**hat′less,** *adj.* —**hat′like′**, *adj.*

hat·band (hat′band′) *n.* a band around the crown of a hat, just above the brim.

hatch[1] (hach) *v.* **1** bring forth (young) from an egg or eggs: *A hen hatches chickens.* **2** keep (an egg or eggs) warm until the young come out: *The heat of the sun hatches turtles' eggs.* **3** come out from the egg: *Three chickens hatched today.* **4** develop to be young animals: *Not all eggs hatch properly.* **5** arrange; plan. **6** plan secretly; plot.
—*n.* **1** the act of hatching. **2** the brood hatched. **3** something that is hatched. [ME *hæche(n)*] —**hatch′er,** *n.* —**Syn.** *v.* **6** scheme, contrive.

hatch[2] (hach) *n.* **1** an opening in a ship's deck through which the cargo is loaded. **2** the trap door covering such an opening: *The hatches were closed tightly during the storm.* **3** an opening in the floor or roof of a building, etc. **4** the lower half of a divided door. [OE *hæcc*]

hatch[3] (hach) *v.* draw, cut, or engrave fine parallel lines on: *With a sharp pencil the artist hatched certain parts of the picture to darken and shade them.* —*n.* one of such a set of lines. [< F *hacher* chop, hatch. See HASH.]

hatch·el (hach′əl) *n. v.* **-elled** or **-eled, -el·ling** or **-el·ing.** —*n.* a comb used in cleaning flax, hemp, etc.
—*v.* **1** comb (flax, hemp, etc.) with a hatchel. **2** annoy; torment; heckle. [var. of *hackle*[1]] —**hatch′el·ler** or **hatch′el·er,** *n.*

hatch·er·y (hach′ər ē or hach′rē) *n.* **-er·ies.** a place for hatching eggs of fish, hens, etc.

hatch·et (hach′it) *n.* **1** a small axe with a handle about a foot long, for use with one hand. **2** a tomahawk. **3 bury the hatchet,** make peace. **4 dig up the hatchet,** make war. [ME < OF *hachette*, dim. of *hache* axe]

hatch·ing (hach′ing) *n.* fine, parallel lines drawn, cut, or engraved close together. See **crosshatch** for picture. [< *hatch*[3]]

hatch·ment (hach′mənt) *n.* a square tablet set diagonally, bearing the coat of arms of a dead person. [earlier *atcheament, achement,* contraction of *achievement*]

A hatchment

hatch·way (hach′wā′) *n.* **1** an opening in the deck of a ship to the lower part. **2** a similar opening in a floor, roof, etc.

hate (hāt) *v.* **hat·ed, hat·ing,** *n.* —*v.* **1** dislike very strongly. **2** dislike: *I hate study.* —*n.* **1** a strong dislike. **2** an object of hatred. [OE *hatian*] —**hat′er,** *n.*
Syn. *v.* **1 Hate, detest, abhor** = dislike someone or something very much. **Hate,** the general word, suggests very strong dislike and a feeling of hostility, often a desire to hurt or harm: *The prisoners hated the wicked guards.* **Detest** suggests strong or deep fixed dislike mixed with scorn for something or someone disagreeable or disgusting: *I detest a coward.* **Abhor** suggests a dislike that makes one shudder or shrink away from someone or something extremely disagreeable, disgusting, or shocking: *I abhor filth of any kind.*

hate·ful (hāt′fəl) *adj.* **1** causing hate; to be hated. **2** feeling hate; showing hate. —**hate′ful·ly,** *adv.* —**hate′ful·ness,** *n.*
Syn. 1 Hateful, odious, obnoxious = causing strong dislike or hate. **Hateful** emphasizes the hatred caused, a feeling of strong dislike and hostility combined with anger, fear, spite, a feeling of injury, etc.: *A bully does hateful things.* **Odious,** formal, emphasizes having qualities that cause hatred or strong dislike, and suggests being disagreeable, irritating, or disgusting: *Conditions in the slums are odious.* **Obnoxious** = being so disagreeable or annoying to a person that he cannot stand the sight or thought of what is described: *His disgusting table manners made him obnoxious to us.*

hat·ful (hat′fůl) *n.* **1** the amount a hat can hold. **2** a great deal; considerable amount.

hath (hath) *v. Archaic.* 3rd pers. sing. present tense of **have.** "He hath" means "he has."

hat·pin (hat′pin′) *n.* a long pin used by women to fasten a hat to the hair.

hat·rack (hat′rak′) *n.* a rack, shelf, or arrangement of hooks or pegs to put hats on.

ha·tred (hā′trid) *n.* very strong dislike; hate. [ME *hatred, hatereden* < *hate* hate + *-reden,* OE *ræden* condition, state] —**Syn.** loathing, aversion, animosity, ill will.

hat·ter (hat′ər) *n.* a person who makes or sells hats.

hat trick 1 in hockey and soccer, three goals scored in a single game by the same player. **2** in cricket, the taking of three wickets with three successive balls. **3** *Informal.* any feat consisting of three or more victories in a row. [< the fact of a *hat* formerly being the prize for this feat in cricket]

hau·ber·geon (ho′bər jən or hô′bər jən) *n.* habergeon (def. 1).

hau·berk (ho′bėrk or hô′bėrk) *n.* a long coat of mail. [ME < OF *hauberc* < Gmc.; cf. OE *healsbeorg*, literally, neck cover]

haugh·ti·ness (ho′tē nis or hô′tē nis) *n.* a haughty manner or spirit; an arrogant looking down on other people.

haugh·ty (ho′tē or hô′tē) *adj.* **-ti·er, -ti·est. 1** too proud of oneself and too scornful of others. **2** showing too great pride of oneself and scorn for others: *a haughty smile.* [< *haut* or *haught* < OF *haut* < L *altus* high; French form influenced by OHG *hoh* high]
—**haugh′ti·ly,** *adv.* —**haugh′ti·ness,** *n.*
Syn. 1 Haughty, arrogant = too proud. **Haughty** = feeling oneself superior to others and showing it by treating them with cold indifference and scorn: *A haughty girl is always unpopular at school.* **Arrogant** = thinking oneself more important than one is and showing it by treating others in a domineering and slighting manner: *He was so arrogant that he lost his job.*

haul (hol or hôl) *v.* **1** pull or drag with force: *The logs were hauled to the mill by horses.* **2 haul up, a** turn a ship nearer to the direction of the wind. **b** change the course of (a ship). **3** change; shift: *The wind hauled around to the east.* **4 haul off, a** turn a ship away from an object. **b** draw away; withdraw. **c** *Informal.* draw back one's arm to give a blow. **5 haul on the wind,** sail closer to the direction of the wind. **6 haul to the wind,** sail closer to the direction of the wind.
—*n.* **1** the act of hauling; hard pull. **2** the load hauled: *Powerful trucks are used for heavy hauls.* **3** the distance that a load is hauled. **4** the amount won, taken, etc. at one time; catch: *a good haul of fish.* [< F *haler* < Gmc. Doublet of HALE[2].] —**haul′er,** *n.* —**Syn.** *v.* **1** See **draw.**

haul·age (hol′ij or hôl′ij) *n.* **1** the act of hauling. **2** the force used in hauling. **3** a charge made for hauling.

haunch (honch or hônch) *n.* **1** the part of the body around the hip; the hip. **2** the hind quarter of an animal: *A dog sits on his haunches.* **3** a cut of meat consisting of the leg and loin of a deer, sheep, etc. [ME < OF *hanche* < Gmc.]

haunt (hont or hônt) *v.* **1** go often to; visit frequently. **2** be often with; come often to: *Memories of his youth haunted the old man.*
—*n.* **1** Often, **haunts,** *pl.* a place frequently gone to or often visited: *The swimming pool was the favorite haunt of the boys in the summer.* **2** the usual feeding place of deer, game, wild fowl, etc. **3** a place frequented by criminals. **4** *Dialect.* a ghost. [ME < OF *hanter* < OE *hāmettan* shelter (cf. *home*)] —**haunt′er,** *n.* —**haunt′ing·ly,** *adv.*

haunt·ed (hon′tid or hôn′tid) *adj.* **1** visited by ghosts. **2** harried or harassed, as if by ghosts; troubled; worried.

Hau·sa (hou′sä) *n.* **1** a negroid people of the Sudan and northern Nigeria. **2** a member of this people. **3** the Chad language of this people.

haut·boy (hō′boi or ō′boi) *n.* oboe. [< F *hautbois* < *haut* high + *bois* wood; with reference to its high notes]

haute cou·ture (ōt kü TYR′) *French.* **1** the best-known fashion houses and designers. **2** the clothes made by leading designers and dressmakers.

haute cui·sine (ōt kwē zēn′) *French.* **1** cooking as a fine art, especially as practised by acknowledged master chefs. **2** food that is prepared in this way.

hau·teur (hō tėr′ or ō tėr′) *n.* haughtiness; a haughty manner or spirit. [< F *hauteur* < *haut* high]

Ha·van·a (hə van′ə) *n.* a cigar made from Cuban tobacco. [< *Havana,* the capital of Cuba]

have (hav; *unstressed,* həv or əv) *v. pres. 1* **have,** *2* **have** or (*Archaic*) **hast,** *3* **has** or (*Archaic*) **hath,** *pl.* **have;** *pt. and pp.* **had;** *ppr.* **hav·ing. 1** hold: *I have a book in my hand.* **2** possess; own: *He has a big house and farm.* **3** have as a part, quality, etc.: *The house has many windows. He has a pleasant face.* **4** cause to: *Have him shut the door.* **5** be obliged: *Men have to eat.* **6** obtain; receive; take; get: *Have a seat.* **7** show by action: *have the courage to.* **8** experience: *have a pain, have fear.* **9** engage in; carry on; perform: *Have a talk with him.* **10** allow; permit: *Ann won't have any noise while she is reading.* **11** maintain; assert: *They will have it so.* **12** keep; retain: *He has the directions in mind.* **13** know; understand: *He has no Latin.* **14** hold in the mind: *have an idea.* **15** be in a certain relation to: *She has three brothers.* **16** *Informal.* hold an advantage over: *You have him there.* **17** *Slang.* outwit or cheat. **18** become the father or mother of. **19** *Have* is used with past participles to express completed action: *They have come.*
have at, attack; hit.
have done, stop; be through.
have had it, *Slang.* **a** become disgusted; become fed up. **b** reach an end; lose something that one has had.
have it, a will; make happen: *As luck would have it, we missed the train.* **b** gain a victory or advantage. **c** receive a thrashing or punishment: *If he catches you, he'll let you have it.* **d** discover or hit upon an answer, solution, etc.: *Eureka! I have it!* **e** *Informal.* find oneself in certain (good or bad) circumstances: *You never had it so good.*
have it in for, *Informal.* have a grudge against; try to get revenge on.
have it out, fight or argue until a question is settled.
have nothing on, have no advantage of or superiority over.
have to do with, a be connected with; be related to. **b** be a companion, partner, or friend of; associate with.
to have and to hold, to keep and possess. [OE *habban*]
Syn. 1 Have, hold, own = possess or be in possession of something. **Have** is the general word: *He has many friends.* **Hold** emphasizes having control over or keeping: *He holds the office of treasurer. He cannot hold a friend long.* **Own** suggests having a right, especially a legal right, to hold a thing as property: *He owns a farm.*

have·lock (hav′lok) *n.* a white cloth covering for a cap. It falls over the back of the neck and gives protection against the sun. [after Henry *Havelock,* a British general]

ha·ven (hā′vən) *n.* **1** a harbor, especially one providing shelter from a storm. **2** a place of shelter and safety. —*v.* shelter in a haven. [OE *hæfen*]

have-not (hav′not′) *n. Informal.* a person or country that has little or no property or wealth.

have·n't (hav′ənt) *v.* have not.

hav·er·sack (hav′ər sak′) *n.* a bag used by soldiers and hikers to carry food, utensils, etc. [< F *havresac* < LG *Habersack* oat sack]

A haversack

hav·oc (hav′ək) *n.* **1** very great destruction or injury: *Tornadoes, severe earthquakes, and plagues create widespread havoc.* **2 play havoc with,** injure severely; ruin; destroy. [< AF var. of OF *havot* plundering, devastation (especially in phrase *crier havot* cry havoc) < Gmc.] —**Syn. 1** devastation, ruin.

haw[1] (ho or hô) *n.* **1** the red berry of the hawthorn. **2** the hawthorn. [OE *haga*]

haw[2] (ho or hô) *interj. n.* a stammering sound between words. —*v.* make this sound; stammer. [imitative]

haw[3] (ho or hô) *interj. n.* a word of command to horses, oxen, etc. directing them to turn to the left. "Gee" is used for "right." —*v.* turn to the left. [origin uncertain]

Ha·wai·ian (hə wī′yən) *adj.* of or having to do with Hawaii, its people, or their language. —*n.* **1** a native or

hat, āge, cãre, fär; let, ēqual, tėrm; it, īce
hot, ōpen, ôrder; oil, out; cup, pu̇t, rüle, ūse
əbove, takən, pencəl, lemən, circəs
ch, child; ng, long; sh, ship
th, thin; ᴛʜ, then; zh, measure

inhabitant of Hawaii. **2** the Polynesian language of Hawaii.

hawk[1] (hok or hôk) *n.* **1** a bird of prey having a strong hooked beak, large curved claws, short rounded wings, and a long tail. Falcons, ospreys, etc. are called hawks, distinguishing them from larger birds of prey, such as eagles. **2** a bird of prey like a hawk, such as buzzards, kites, etc. **3** a person who preys on others. **4** a person who is eager for war or advocates war as a policy. —*v.* **1** hunt with trained hawks. **2** hunt or pursue like a hawk. [OE *hafoc*] —**hawk′like′,** *adj.*

hawk[2] (hok or hôk) *v.* **1** carry (goods) about for sale as a street peddler does. **2** advertise by shouting that goods are for sale. **3** spread (a report) around. [< *hawker*[1]]

hawk[3] (hok or hôk) *v.* clear the throat noisily. —*n.* **1** a noisy effort to clear the throat. **2** the noise made in such an effort. [probably imitative]

hawk·er[1] (hok′ər or hôk′ər) *n.* a person who carries his wares around and offers them for sale by shouting; peddler. [probably < MLG *hoker.* Akin to HUCKSTER.]

hawk·er[2] (hok′ər or hôk′ər) *n.* a person who hunts with a hawk. [< *hawk*[1]]

hawk-eyed (hok′īd′ or hôk′-) *adj.* having sharp eyes like a hawk.

hawk·ing (hok′ing or hôk′ing) *n.* the act of hunting with hawks; falconry.

hawk moth a large moth having a long, stout body and narrow wings.

hawk's-bill or **hawks·bill** (hoks′bil′ or hôks′-) *n.* hawksbill turtle.

hawksbill turtle a sea turtle whose mouth is shaped like a hawk's beak. Tortoise shell is made from the overlapping, horny plates of its shell.

hawk·weed (hok′wēd′ or hôk′-) *n.* a weed that has small, yellow or orange flowers in summer and autumn.

hawse (hoz or hôz, hos or hôs) *n.* **1** the part of a ship's bow having holes for hawsers or cables to pass through. **2** one of these holes. **3** the space between the bow of a ship at anchor and her anchors. [< ON *hals*]

A hawse (def. 1)

hawse·hole (hoz′hōl′ or hôz′-, hos′hōl′ or hôs′-) *n.* a hole in a ship's bow for a hawser or cable to pass through.

haw·ser (ho′zər or hô′zər, ho′sər or hô′sər) *n.* a stout rope or a thin steel cable, used for mooring or towing ships. [ME < OF *haucier* hoist, ult. < L *altus* high]

haw·thorn (ho′thôrn or hô′-) *n.* a thorny shrub or tree having clusters of white, red, or pink blossoms and small red berries called haws. [OE *hagathorn* < *haga* hedge + *thorn* thorn]

hay (hā) *n.* **1** grass, alfalfa, clover, etc. that has been cut and dried for use as food for cattle, horses, etc. **2** grass ready for mowing. **3 hit the hay,** *Slang.* go to bed. **4 make hay, a** cut and dry grass, alfalfa, clover, etc. for hay. **b** *Informal.* take advantage of some opportunity. **5 make hay while the sun shines,** make hay (def. b). —*v.* **1** cut and dry grass, alfalfa, clover, etc. for hay: *The men are haying in the east field.* **2** supply with hay. [OE *hēg.* Related to HEW.]

hay·cock (hā′kok′) *n.* a small, cone-shaped pile of hay in a field.

hay·coil (hā′koil′) *n.* haycock.

hay fever an allergy affecting the respiratory tract and the eyes as a severe cold does, caused by the pollen of ragweed and other plants.

hay·field (hā′fēld′) *n.* a field where crops such as grass, alfalfa, or clover are grown or cut for hay.

hay·fork (hā′fôrk′) *n.* **1** a pitchfork. **2** a mechanically operated device for loading hay into or out of a hayloft.

hay·loft (hā′loft′) *n.* a place in a stable or barn where hay is stored.

hay·mak·er (hā′māk′ər) *n.* **1** a person who tosses and spreads hay to dry after it is cut. **2** an apparatus for shaking up and drying hay. **3** *Slang.* in boxing, a hard, swinging, upward blow with the fist.

hay·mow (hā′mou′ or -mō′) *n.* **1** a place in a barn where hay is stored; hayloft. **2** a heap of hay stored in a barn.

hay·rack (hā′rak′) *n.* **1** a rack or frame used for holding hay to be eaten by cattle, horses, etc. **2** a framework on a wagon used in hauling hay, straw, etc. **3** the wagon and framework together.

hay·rick (hā′rik′) *n.* haystack.

hay·seed (hā′sēd′) *n.* **1** grass seed, especially that shaken out of hay. **2** the chaff that falls from hay. **3** *Slang.* a person from the country; farmer.

hay·stack (hā′stak′) *n.* a large pile of hay outdoors.

hay·wire (hā′wīr′) *n.* wire used to tie up bales of hay. *—adj.* **1** out of order; tangled up. **2** emotionally disturbed or upset. **3** *Slang.* shoddy; stop-gap; flimsy: *a haywire repair job.* **4 go haywire,** get out of order; act in an excited or confused manner.

haz·ard (haz′ərd) *n.* **1** a risk; danger; peril: *The life of an aviator is full of hazards.* **2** a chance. **3** in golf, any obstruction on a course that can trap a ball. **4** in billiards and pool, a stroke by which the player sends the object ball or his own ball (after it hits another) into a pocket. **5** an old and complicated dice game from which craps developed. **6 at all hazards,** whatever the risk; in spite of great danger or peril.
—*v.* **1** take a chance with; risk; venture: *I would hazard my life on his honesty.* **2** expose to risk. [ME < OF *hasard* < Arabic *al-zahr* the die²] **—Syn.** *n.* **1** jeopardy.

haz·ard·ous (haz′ər dəs) *adj.* dangerous; risky; perilous. **—haz′ard·ous·ly,** *adv.* **—haz′ard·ous·ness,** *n.*

haze¹ (hāz) *n.* **1** a small amount of mist, smoke, dust, etc. in the air: *A thin haze veiled the hills.* **2** a vague condition of the mind during which one sees things indistinctly: *After he was hit on the head, everything was a haze.* **3** general vagueness; a slight confusion of the mind. [origin uncertain; cf. E dial. *haze* drizzle, be foggy]

haze² (hāz) *v.* **hazed, haz·ing. 1** in schools, colleges, etc., force newcomers to do unpleasant tasks; bully. **2** harass cattle, horses, etc. to drive them. [? < OF *haser* irritate, harass] **—haz′er,** *n.*

ha·zel (hā′zəl) *n.* **1** a shrub or small tree of the same family as the birch, whose light-brown nuts are edible. **2** the wood of this shrub or tree. **3** a hazelnut. **4** a light brown. *—adj.* light-brown. [OE *hæsel*]

ha·zel·nut (hā′zəl nut′) *n.* the nut of a hazel.

ha·zy (hā′zē) *adj.* **-zi·er, -zi·est. 1** full of haze; misty; smoky: *hazy air.* **2** rather confused; vague; obscure: *hazy ideas.* **—ha′zi·ly,** *adv.* **—ha′zi·ness,** *n.*

H.B.C. Hudson's Bay Company.

H-bomb (āch′bom′) *n.* the hydrogen bomb.

H.C. House of Commons.

H.C.F., h.c.f., or **hcf** highest common factor.

h.c.l. *Informal.* high cost of living.

hd. *pl.* **hds.** head.

hdbk. *pl.* **hdbks.** handbook.

hdkf. *pl.* **hdkfs.** handkerchief.

hdqrs. headquarters.

hds. heads.

he (hē; *unstressed,* ē or i) *pron. nom.* **he**; *poss.* **his**; *obj.* **him**; *pl. nom.* **they**; *poss.* **theirs**; *obj.* **them**; *n.* **he's.**
—pron. **1** a boy, man, or male animal: *John has to work hard, but he likes his job and it pays him well.* **2** anyone: *He who hesitates is lost.*
—n. a boy; man; male animal: *Is it a he or a she?* [OE *hē*]

He helium.

HE or **H.E.** high explosive.

H.E. 1 His Eminence. **2** His Excellency.

head (hed) *n.* **heads** (*for 1-7, 9-23*) or **head** (*for 8*), *adj. v.*
—n. **1** the top part of the human body where the eyes, ears, and mouth are. **2** the corresponding part of an animal's body. **3** the top part of anything: *the head of a pin, the head of a page.* **4** the foremost part or end of anything; the front: *the head of a procession.* **5** the chief person; leader; commander; director. **6** the position of head; chief authority; leadership; command; direction. **7** a person; an individual: *Kings and queens are crowned heads.* **8** a unit, used in counting animals: *He sold fifty head of cattle and ten head of horses.* **9** anything rounded like a head: *a head of cabbage or lettuce.* **10** in botany, a cluster of flowers in which the flowers or florets do not have individual stems, but grow close together from the main stem; flower head. **11** the part of a boil or pimple where pus is about to break through the skin. **12** the striking part of a tool or implement: *the head of a hammer.* **13** a piece of skin stretched tightly over the end of a drum, tambourine, etc. **14** either end of a barrel or cask. **15** the end of a bed, couch, etc. at which a person's head is placed. **16** mind; understanding; intelligence; intellect: *The old man has a wise head.* **17** a topic; point: *He arranged his speech under four main heads.* **18** a decisive point; crisis; conclusion: *His sudden refusal brought matters to a head.* **19** strength or force gained little by little: *As more people joined, the movement gathered head.* **20** pressure of water, steam, etc. **21** the source of a river or stream. **22** foam; froth. **23** in nautical use: **a** the forward part of a ship. **b** a toilet. **24 heads,** *pl.* the top side of a coin.
come to a head, a of boils, pimples, etc., reach the stage where they are about to break through the skin. **b** reach a decisive stage: *The international crisis came to a head and war was declared.*
eat one's head off, a eat very much. **b** cost more to feed than one is worth.
give someone his head, let him go as he pleases.
go to one's head, a affect one's mind. **b** make one dizzy or intoxicated. **c** make one conceited.
hang one's head, be ashamed and show that one is so.
head over heels, a in a somersault. **b** hastily; rashly. **c** completely; thoroughly.
heads up!, watch out! take care!
hide one's head, be ashamed and show that one is so.
keep one's head, not get excited; stay calm.
keep one's head above water, a stay afloat. **b** avoid failure, loss, defeat, death, etc.
lay heads together, a confer; consult. **b** plot; conspire.
lose one's head, get excited; lose one's self-control.
make head, move forward; make progress; advance.
make head or tail of, understand.
off or **out of one's head,** *Informal.* crazy, insane.
on or **upon one's head,** on one's responsibility.
over one's head, a beyond one's power to understand or manage. **b** to a person higher in authority: *He threatened to go to the manager over the foreman's head.* **c** so as to pass over or ignore a person who has a senior status, a prior claim, or a better right: *An outsider has now been promoted over their heads.*
put heads together, a confer; consult. **b** plot; conspire.
take it into one's head, a get the idea. **b** plan; intend.
talk one's head off, talk endlessly.
turn one's head, a affect the mind. **b** make one dizzy. **c** make one conceited.
—adj. **1** at the head, top, or front: *the head division of a parade.* **2** coming from in front: *a head wind.* **3** chief; leading; commanding, directing. **4** of, having to do with, or for the head.
—v. **1** be or go at the head, top, or front of: *head a parade.* **2** cause to move or face in a certain direction: *head a boat toward shore.* **3** move or go in a certain direction: *It's getting late; we'd better head for home.* **4** be the head or chief of; lead; command; direct: *head a business.* **5** put a head on; furnish with a head. **6** form a head; come to a head. **7** cut off the head of. **8 head off, a** get in front of and turn back or aside: *The cowboys tried to head off the stampeding herd.* **b** prevent; forestall: *He tried to head off possible trouble for himself by extreme care in what he did.* [OE *hēafod*] **—head′like′,** *adj.*

head·ache (hed′āk′) *n.* **1** pain in the head. **2** *Informal.* any thing, situation, etc. that is the cause of great bother, annoyance, etc.

head·band (hed′band′) *n.* **1** a band of cloth, ribbon, etc worn around the head; fillet. **2** a decorative strip of material at the top and sometimes at the bottom of the spine of a book. **3** a decorative printed strip at the head of a page or chapter in a book. **4** the band that connects a pair of earphones.

head·board (hed′bôrd′) *n.* a board or frame that forms the head of a bed.

head·cheese (hed′chēz′) *n.* a jellied loaf formed of parts of the head and feet of pigs cut up, cooked, and seasoned.

head·dress (hed′dres′) *n.* **1** a covering or decoration for the head. **2** a way of wearing or arranging the hair.

head·ed (hed′id) *adj.* **1** having a head. **2** having a heading. **3** grown or shaped into a head.

-headed *combining form.* **1** having a certain kind of head, as in *long-headed, bareheaded.* **2** having a specified number of heads, as in *two-headed.*

head·er (hed′ər) *n.* **1** a person, tool, or machine that puts on or takes off heads of grain, barrels, pins, nails, etc. **2** *Informal.* a plunge or dive headfirst: *He took a header into the water.* **3** a brick or stone laid with its length across the thickness of a wall. **4** a beam forming part of the framework around an opening in a floor or roof, placed so as to fit between two long beams and support the ends of short ones. **5** in soccer, the act of hitting the ball with the head.

HEADER

A header (def. 4)

head·first (hed′fėrst′) *adv.* **1** with the head first. **2** hastily; rashly.

head·fore·most (hed′fôr′mōst) *adv.* headfirst.

head·frame (hed′frām′) *n.* in mining, the structure over a shaft to support the hoisting equipment.

head gate 1 an upstream gate of a lock in a canal or river. **2** the floodgate of a race, sluice, etc.

head·gear (hed′gēr′) *n.* **1** a covering for the head; hat, cap, etc. **2** the harness for an animal's head.

head-hunt·er (hed′hun′tər) *n.* a person who practises head-hunting.

head-hunt·ing (hed′hunt′ing) *n.* the practice, among certain primitive tribes, of trying to get the heads of enemies as a sign of victory, manhood, etc. *—adj.* of or having to do with head-hunters.

head·ing (hed′ing) *n.* **1** the part forming the head, top, or front. **2** something written or printed at the top of a page. **3** the title of a page, chapter, etc.; topic.

head·lamp (hed′lamp′) *n.* **1** a small lamp worn on the cap or the forehead. **2** a headlight on a train, automobile, etc.

head·land (hed′lənd or -land′) *n.* a point of land jutting out into water; cape.

head·less (hed′lis) *adj.* **1** having no head. **2** without a leader. **3** without brains; stupid.

head·light (hed′līt′) *n.* **1** of vehicles such as automobiles, one of two large lights at the front. **2** a large single light at the front of a locomotive, streetcar, etc. **3** on a ship, a light at a masthead.

head·line (hed′līn′) *n. v.* **-lined, -lin·ing.** *—n.* **1** the words printed at the top of an article in a newspaper or magazine to indicate the topic dealt with. **2** a line printed at the top of a page giving the running title, page number, etc. **3 headlines,** publicity: *He's the kind of man who gets plenty of headlines.* **4 make headlines,** receive publicity: *The new discovery made headlines everywhere.*
—v. furnish with a headline.

head·lock (hed′lok′) *n.* in wrestling, a hold in which a person's head is held between the body and arm of his opponent.

head·long (hed′long) *adv. adj.* **1** headfirst. **2** with great speed and force. **3** in too great a rush; without stopping to think: *The boy was always rushing headlong into trouble.* **4** rash; rashly. [ME *hedlong,* alteration of earlier *hedlyng* < *hed* head + *-ling,* adv. suffix expressing direction, OE *-ling*]

head·man (hed′man′ or hed′mən) *n.* **-men** (-men′ or -mən). a chief; leader.

head·mas·ter (hed′mas′tər) *n.* a person in charge of a school, especially of a private school; principal.

head·mas·ter·ship (hed′mas′tər ship′) *n.* the position or authority of a headmaster.

hat, āge, cãre, fär; let, ēqual, tėrm; it, īce
hot, ōpen, ôrder; oil, out; cup, pu̇t, rüle, ūse
əbove, takən, pencəl, lemən, circəs
ch, child; ng, long; sh, ship
th, thin; ᴛʜ, then; zh, measure

head·most (hed′mōst′) *adj.* first; most advanced.

head of steel *Cdn.* end of steel.

head-on (hed′on′) *adj.* with the head or front first: *a head-on collision.*

head·phone (hed′fōn′) *n.* a telephone or radio receiver held on the head, against the ears.

head·piece (hed′pēs′) *n.* **1** a piece of armor for the head; helmet. **2** a hat, cap, or other covering for the head. **3** a headphone. **4** *Informal.* the head; mind; intellect. **5** in printing, a decoration at the head of a page, chapter, etc.

head pin in bowling and tenpins, the front pin of the triangle of pins.

head·quar·ters (hed′kwôr′tərz) *n.pl. or sing.* **1** the place from which the chief or commanding officer of an army, police force, etc. sends out orders. **2** the centre from which any organization is controlled and directed; main office: *The headquarters of the Canadian Red Cross Society is in Toronto.*

head·rest (hed′rest′) *n.* a support for the head: *The dentist's chair has a headrest.*

head·room (hed′rüm′ or -ru̇m′) *n.* a clear space above; clearance; headway: *Some bridges do not have enough headroom to allow high trucks to pass underneath.*

head·set (hed′set′) *n.* a pair of earphones.

head·ship (hed′ship) *n.* the position of head; chief authority. —**Syn.** leadership.

head·shrink·er (hed′shring′kər) *n.* **1** *Slang.* a psychiatrist. **2** a head-hunter who cuts off and shrinks the heads of his enemies.

heads·man (hedz′mən) *n.* **-men** (-mən). a man who puts condemned persons to death by cutting off their heads.

head·stall (hed′stol′ or -stôl′) *n.* **1** the part of a bridle or halter that fits over a horse's head. **2** a halter.

head start 1 an advantage or lead allowed someone at the beginning of a race: *The smaller boy was given a head start.* **2** an advantage gained by beginning something before somebody else: *That team is playing better hockey than we are because they had a head start in practising.*

head·stock (hed′stok′) *n.* **1** the part of a machine that contains the revolving or working parts. **2** the part of a lathe that holds the spindle.

head·stone (hed′stōn′) *n.* **1** a stone set at the head of a grave; tombstone. **2** the principal stone in a foundation; cornerstone.

head·stream (hed′strēm′) *n.* a stream that is the source of a larger stream.

head·strong (hed′strong′) *adj.* **1** rashly or foolishly determined to have one's own way; hard to control or manage; obstinate. **2** showing rash or foolish determination to have one's own way: *a headstrong action.* —**Syn. 1** willful.

head tone 1 a note produced in the second or third register of the voice. **2** in singing, a tone that causes vibration in the cavities of the head.

head·wait·er (hed′wāt′ər) *n.* a man in charge of the waiters in a restaurant, hotel, etc.

head·wa·ters (hed′wot′ərz or -wô′tərz) *n.pl.* the sources or upper parts of a river.

head·way (hed′wā′) *n.* **1** forward motion: *The ship could make no headway against the strong wind and tide.* **2** progress with work, etc. **3** a clear space overhead in a doorway or under an arch, bridge, etc; clearance. **4** the interval of time between two trains, streetcars, ships, etc. going in the same direction over the same route.

head wind a wind blowing straight against the front of a ship, etc.

head·work (hed′wėrk′) *n.* mental work; effort with the mind; thought.

head·y (hed′ē) *adj.* **head·i·er, head·i·est. 1** hasty; rash. **2** apt to affect the head and make one dizzy; intoxicating. [ME *hevedi* headlong] —**head′i·ly,** *adv.* —**head′i·ness,** *n.*

heal (hēl) *v.* **1** make whole, sound, or well; bring back to health; cure (a disease or wound). **2** become whole or sound; get well; return to health; be cured: *His cut finger healed in a few days.* **3** free from anything bad. **4** get rid of (anything bad). [OE *hǣlan* < *hāl* well, whole] —**heal′er,** *n.* —**Syn. 1** See **cure.**

health (helth) *n.* **1** a being well; freedom from sickness. **2** a condition of body or mind: *She is in poor health.* **3** a toast drunk in honor of a person with a wish that he may be healthy and happy: *We all drank a health to the bride.*
—*interj.* **your health,** a phrase used in drinking a person's health. [OE *hǣlth* < *hāl* well, whole]

health·ful (helth′fəl) *adj.* giving health; good for the health: *healthful exercise, a healthful diet.* —**health′ful·ly,** *adv.* —**health′ful·ness,** *n.*
☛ **healthful, healthy.** Formal usage tends to distinguish between these words, using *healthful* to mean "giving health," and *healthy* to mean "having good health." Places and food are *healthful*; persons and animals are *healthy.*

healthy (hel′thē) *adj.* **health·i·er, health·i·est. 1** having good health: *a healthy baby.* **2** showing good health: *a healthy appearance.* **3** healthful. —**health′i·ly,** *adv.* —**health′i·ness,** *n.*
Syn. 1, 2 Healthy, wholesome = having or showing health. **Healthy** emphasizes energy, strength, and freedom from sickness, both when used literally to describe the physical condition of people or things or the mental or emotional condition of people when used figuratively of ideas, society, etc.: *He has a healthy appearance.* **Wholesome** emphasizes soundness and freedom from weakness, decay, or harmfulness physically or, particularly, emotionally or morally, and usually suggests having a good effect: *Our uncle gave us some wholesome advice.* **3** nourishing, salutary.
☛ See **healthful** for usage note.

heap (hēp) *n.* **1** a pile of many things thrown or lying together: *a heap of stones, a sand heap.* **2** *Informal.* a large amount.
—*v.* **1** form into a heap; gather in heaps: *She heaped the dirty clothes besides the washing machine.* **2** give generously or in large amounts. **3** fill to the point of overflowing; load: *His mother heaped potatoes on his plate. His friends heaped praise on him after he won his victory.* [OE *hēap*] —**Syn.** *n.* **1** mass, stack, accumulation.

hear (hēr) *v.* **heard, hear·ing,** *interj.* —*v.* **1** perceive by the ear: *hear sounds, hear voices.* **2** be able to perceive by the ear: *He cannot hear well.* **3** listen to: *hear a person's explanation.* **4** listen. **5** give a chance to be heard; give a formal hearing to, as a king, a judge, a teacher, or an assembly does. **6** find out by hearing: *hear news.* **7** be told; receive news or information: *I don't know the plans for the meeting; I haven't heard yet.* **8** listen to with favor: *Lord, hear my prayer.* **9 hear from, a** receive news or information from: *Have you heard from your friend?* **b** receive a reprimand from. **10 hear out,** listen to till the end. **11 will not hear of it,** will not listen to, think of, agree to, or allow it.
—*interj.* **hear! hear!** shouts of approval; cheering. [OE *hēran*] —**hear′er,** *n.*
Syn. *v.* **1 Hear, listen** = perceive by the ear. **Hear** applies to the physical act of receiving sound through the ear: *Do you hear a noise?* **Listen** = pay attention to a sound and try to hear or understand it: *I heard him talking, but did not listen to what he said.*

heard (hėrd) *v.* pt. and pp. of **hear.**

hear·ing (hēr′ing) *n.* **1** the sense by which sound is perceived: *The old man's hearing is poor.* **2** the act or process of perceiving sound: *Hearing the good news made him happy.* **3** a formal or official listening: *The Royal Commission has set a date for its next hearing.* **4** the trial of an action: *The judge gave both sides a hearing in court.* **5** a chance to be heard: *Give us a hearing.* **6** the distance that a sound can be heard: *be within hearing of the baby, talk freely in the hearing of others.*

hearing aid an electrical device to amplify sound, consisting usually of an earphone connected to a microphone and amplifier inside a small case.

heark·en (här′kən) *v. Archaic.* listen; listen attentively. Also, **harken.** [OE *hercnian, heorcnian*]

hear·say (hēr′sā′) *n.* common talk; gossip.

hearsay evidence in law, evidence based on the testimony of another person, rather than on the first-hand knowledge of the witness. Such evidence is usually not admissible.

hearse (hėrs) *n.* an automobile, carriage, etc. used in funerals to carry a dead person to his grave. [ME < OF *herce* < L *hirpex, -picis,* harrow; originally, a frame like a harrow]

heart (härt) *n.* **1** a hollow, muscular organ that pumps the blood throughout the body by contracting and dilating. **2** the region of the heart; breast; bosom: *She clasped her hands to her heart.* **3** the feelings; mind; soul: *She has a kind heart.* **4** the source of the emotions, especially of love: *give one's heart.* **5** a person, especially one who is loved or praised: *a group of stout hearts.* **6** kindness, sympathy: *have no heart.* **7** spirit; courage; enthusiasm: *The losing team showed plenty of heart.* **8** the innermost part; middle; centre: *in the heart of the forest.* **9** the main part; vital or most important part: *the very heart of the matter.* **10** a figure shaped like a heart: *There was a big red heart on the front of the valentine.* **11 a** a playing card with one or more red heart-shaped figures. **b hearts,** *pl.* a suit of playing cards with red heart-shaped designs on them. **c hearts,** *pl.* a game in which the players try to get rid of cards of this suit.

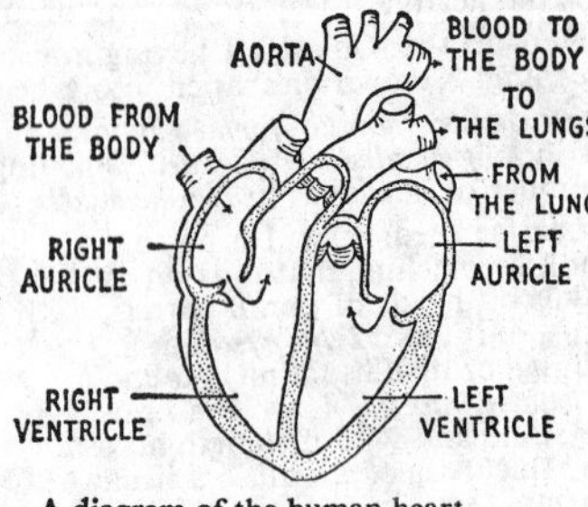

A diagram of the human heart

A heart (def. 10)

after one's own heart, just as one likes it; pleasing one perfectly.
at heart, in one's deepest thoughts or feelings; really.
break the heart of, crush with sorrow or grief.
by heart, a by memory. **b** from memory.
eat one's heart out, feel great sorrow, grief, or worry.
from one's heart, with deepest feeling; sincerely.
get to the heart of, find out the secret or hidden meaning of.
have one's heart in one's boots or mouth, be very frightened.
have one's heart in the right place, mean well; have good intentions.
have the heart, a be courageous or spirited enough (to do something). **b** be hard-hearted enough: *He hadn't the heart to refuse his son's request.*
heart and soul, with all one's affections and energies.
heart of gold, an extremely kind, generous and sympathetic nature.
in one's heart of hearts, in one's deepest thoughts or feelings.
lay to heart, a keep in mind; remember. **b** think seriously about.
near one's heart, of great value or interest to one.
take heart, be encouraged.
take to heart, think seriously about; be deeply affected by; grieve over.
to one's heart's content, as much as one wants.
wear one's heart on one's sleeve, show one's feelings too plainly.
with all one's heart, a sincerely. **b** gladly. [OE *heorte*]
☛ **Hearts,** meaning the card game (def. 11c), is plural in form and singular in use: *Hearts is an interesting game.*

heart·ache (härt′āk′) *n.* sorrow; grief.

heart attack a sudden, sometimes fatal, failure of the heart to beat, caused by arteriosclerosis, high blood pressure, etc.

heart·beat (härt′bēt′) *n.* a pulsation of the heart, including one complete contraction and dilation.

heart·break (härt′brāk′) *n.* a crushing sorrow or grief.

heart·break·ing (härt′brāk′ing) *adj.* crushing with sorrow or grief. —**heart′break′ing·ly,** *adv.*

heart·brok·en (härt′brō′kən) *adj.* crushed with sorrow or grief. —**heart′bro′ken·ly,** *adv.* —**heart′brok′en·ness,** *n.*

heart·burn (härt′bėrn′) *n.* **1** a burning feeling in the esophagus, often accompanying indigestion. **2** envy; jealousy.

heart·burn·ing (härt′bėr′ning) *n.* a feeling of envy or jealousy.

-hearted *combining form.* having a —— heart: *good-hearted = having a good heart.*

heart·en (här′tən) *v.* encourage; cheer up: *Good news heartens you.* —**heart·en·er,** *n.*

heart·felt (härt′felt′) *adj.* sincere; genuine.

hearth (härth) *n.* **1** the floor of a fireplace. **2** the home; fireside: *The soldier longed for his own hearth.* **3** the lowest part of a blast furnace. [OE *heorth*]

hearth·side (härth′sīd′) *n.* **1** the side of a hearth. **2** the home.

hearth·stone (härth′stōn′) *n.* **1** a stone forming a hearth. **2** the home; fireside.

heart·i·ly (här′tə lē) *adv.* **1** sincerely; genuinely; in a warm, friendly way: *express good wishes very heartily.* **2** with enthusiasm; with a good will; vigorously: *set to work heartily.* **3** with a good appetite. **4** very; completely; thoroughly.

heart·i·ness (här′tē nis) *n.* a being hearty.

heart·land (härt′land′) *n.* **1** any area or region that is the centre of, or vital to, an institution, industry, country, etc. **2** in geopolitics, an economically and militarily self-sufficient land mass, located centrally in and controlling the world island (Eurasia and Africa), and relatively invulnerable to attack.

heart·less (härt′lis) *adj.* **1** without kindness or sympathy; unfeeling; cruel. **2** without courage, spirit, or enthusiasm. —**heart′less·ly,** *adv.* —**heart′less·ness,** *n.*

heart-lung machine or **pump** (härt′lung′) in medicine, a device used during heart surgery to pump blood through the body, thus temporarily taking the place of the heart.

heart-rend·ing (härt′ren′ding) *adj.* causing mental anguish; very distressing. —**heart′-rend′ing·ly,** *adv.*

hearts·ease or **heart's-ease** (härts′ēz′) *n.* **1** peace of mind. **2** a pansy.

heart·sick (härt′sik′) *adj.* sick at heart; very much depressed; very unhappy.

heart·sore (härt′sôr′) *adj.* feeling or showing grief; grieved.

heart-strick·en (härt′strik′ən) *adj.* struck to the heart with grief; shocked with fear; dismayed.

heart·strings (härt′stringz′) *n.pl.* deepest feelings; strongest affections.

heart-to-heart (härt′tə härt′) *adj.* without reserve; frank; sincere.

heart-whole (härt′hōl′) *adj.* **1** not in love. **2** hearty; sincere.

heart·wood (härt′wu̇d′) *n.* the hard, central wood of a tree.

heart·y (här′tē) *adj.* **heart·i·er, heart·i·est,** *n.* **heart·ies.** —*adj.* **1** warm and friendly; genuine; sincere: *a hearty welcome.* **2** strong and well; vigorous: *The old man was still hale and hearty.* **3** full of energy and enthusiasm; not restrained: *He burst out in a loud, hearty laugh.* **4** with plenty to eat; nourishing: *A hearty meal satisfied his hunger.* **5** requiring or using much food: *a hearty eater.*
—*n.* **1** a fellow sailor; a brave and good comrade. **2** an excessively hearty and effusive person; backslapper. [< *heart*] —**Syn.** *adj.* **1** cordial, genial. **2** hale, healthy, robust.

heat (hēt) *n.* **1** the quality or state of being hot; hotness; high temperature. **2** the degree of hotness; temperature. **3** the sensation or perception of hotness or warmth. **4** in physics, a form of energy that consists of the motion of the molecules of a substance. The rate at which the molecules move determines the temperature. **5** the hot weather. **6** warmth or intensity of feeling; anger; violence; excitement; eagerness; ardor. **7** the hottest point; most violent or active state: *In the heat of the fight he lost his temper.* **8** *Slang.* pressure; coercion; torture. **9** one trial in a race: *He won the first heat, but lost the final race.* **10** one operation of heating in a furnace or a forge.

hat, āge, cãre, fär; let, ēqual, tėrm; it, īce
hot, ōpen, ôrder; oil, out; cup, pu̇t, rüle, ūse
əbove, takən, pencəl, lemən, circəs
ch, child; ng, long; sh, ship
th, thin; ᴛʜ, then; zh, measure

11 a periodically recurring condition of sexual excitement in female mammals. **12** the time during which this excitement lasts. **13 in heat,** in such a condition of excitement, and so able to be mated.
—*v.* **1** make hot or warm; become hot or warm. **2** fill with strong feeling; inflame; excite; become excited. [OE *hǣtu.* Related to HOT.] —**heat′er,** *n.*

heat barrier the point of speed beyond which the wings and fuselage of an airplane are made dangerously hot by friction with the atmosphere.

heat·ed·ly (hēt′id lē) *adv.* in a vigorous, angry, or excited manner.

heat exchanger a device by means of which heat is transferred from one medium to another in order that it may be utilized as a source of power, as in an atomic power plant, certain gas turbine engines, etc.

heath (hēth) *n. Brit.* **1** open waste land with heather or low bushes growing on it; moor. It has few or no trees. **2** a low bush growing on such land. **3** any of a group of low, evergreen shrubs with needlelike leaves. **4 one's native heath,** the place where one was born or brought up. [OE *hǣth*]

hea·then (hē′ᴛʜən) *n.* **-thens** or **-then,** *adj.* —*n.* **1** a person who does not believe in the God of the Bible; a person who is not a Christian, Jew, or Moslem. **2** people who are heathen. **3** in the Old Testament, the Gentiles, or people who did not worship Jehovah, the God of the Jews. **4** an irreligious or unenlightened person.
—*adj.* **1** of or having to do with the heathen. **2** irreligious; unenlightened. [OE *hǣthen,* probably originally, heath dweller < *hǣth* heath]
Syn. *n.* **Heathen, pagan** were formerly applied to people outside the Christian, Jewish, and Moslem faiths, with the connotation of "rude" and "unenlightened." But, with the development of international relations, these terms are going out of general use as being too exclusive and derogatory. (Followers of ancient faiths such as the Hindus and the Chinese resent being referred to as "heathen" and "pagan"). However, it is proper to use these terms in appropriate historical settings: *Julius Caesar was a pagan. The Goths were heathens.*

hea·then·dom (hē′ᴛʜən dəm) *n.* **1** heathen worship or ways. **2** heathen lands or people.

hea·then·ish (hē′ᴛʜən ish) *adj.* **1** having to do with the heathen. **2** like the heathen. —**hea′then·ish·ly,** *adv.* —**hea′then·ish·ness,** *n.*

hea·then·ism (hē′ᴛʜən iz′əm) *n.* **1** heathen worship or ways. **2** the lack of religion or culture; barbarism.

heath·er (heᴛʜ′ər) *n.* a low, evergreen shrub having stalks of small, rosy-pink flowers, covering many heaths, especially in the northern parts of the British Isles. [? < *heath*]

heath·er·y (heᴛʜ′ər ē) *adj.* **1** of or like heather. **2** covered with heather.

heating element the part of an electrical heating device that gets hot.

heat lightning flashes of light without any thunder, seen near the horizon, especially on hot summer evenings.

heat·stroke (hēt′strōk′) *n.* a collapse or sudden illness caused by too much heat.

heat wave a long period of very hot weather.

heave (hēv) *v.* **heaved** or (*esp. nautical*) **hove, heav·ing,** *n. interj.* —*v.* **1** lift with force or effort: *He heaved the heavy box into the wagon.* **2** lift and throw: *The sailors heaved the anchor overboard.* **3** pull with force or effort; haul: *They heaved on the rope.* **4** give (a sigh, groan, etc.) with a deep, heavy breath. **5** rise and fall alternately: *Waves heave in a storm.* **6** breathe hard; pant. **7** try to vomit; vomit. **8** move in some direction; move. **9** rise; swell; bulge: *The ground heaved during the earthquake.* **10** in geology, thrust (a vein, etc.) out of place horizontally. **11 heave in sight,** come into view. **12 heave to,** of ships, come to a stop.
—*n.* **1** the act or fact of heaving. **2** in geology, a

horizontal displacement or dislocation of a vein or stratum at a fault. **3 heaves,** *pl.* a disease of horses characterized by difficult breathing, coughing, and heaving of the flanks.
—*interj.* **heave ho!** a sailor's cry when pulling up the anchor, or pulling on any rope or cable. [OE *hebban*] —**heav′er,** *n.*

☛ Heaves, the disease of horses (def. 3), is plural in form and singular in use: *Heaves is difficult to cure.*

heav·en (hev′ən) *n.* **1** in religious use, the place where God and His angels live and where the blessed go after death. **2 Heaven,** God; Providence. **3** the place or condition of greatest happiness. **4** Usually, **heavens,** *pl.* the upper air; sky: *Millions of stars were shining in the heavens.* **5 for heaven's sake** or **good heavens!** an exclamation of surprise or protest. **6 move heaven and earth,** do everything possible. [OE *heofon*]

heav·en·ly (hev′ən lē) *adj.* **1** of or in heaven; divine; holy: *God is our heavenly Father.* **2** like heaven; suitable for heaven; very happy, beautiful, or excellent: *a heavenly spot, heavenly peace.* **3** of or in the heavens; in the sky or upper air. —**heav′en·li·ness,** *n.* —**Syn. 2** blissful.

heav·en·ward (hev′ən wərd) *adv. adj.* toward heaven.

heav·en·wards (hev′ən wərdz) *adv.* heavenward.

Heav·i·side layer (hev′ē sīd′) the ionosphere's second layer, which reflects radio waves of frequencies produced in short-wave broadcasting. [after Oliver *Heaviside* (1850-1925), a British physicist]

heav·y (hev′ē) *adj.* **heav·i·er, heav·i·est,** *n.* **heav·ies,** *adv.* —*adj.* **1** hard to lift or carry; of great weight: *a heavy load.* **2** having much weight for its size: *heavy metal.* **3** of more than usual weight for its kind: *heavy silk.* **4** of great amount, force, or intensity; greater than usual; large: *a heavy vote, heavy strain, heavy sea, heavy sleep, heavy rain, heavy meal, heavy crop.* **5** being such to an unusual degree or extent: *a heavy buyer, a heavy smoker.* **6** hard to bear or endure: *heavy taxes.* **7** hard to deal with; trying or difficult in any way: *A heavy road is muddy, sandy, etc. and is thus hard to travel over. A heavy slope is a steep one. Heavy food is hard to digest. Heavy soil is hard to work.* **8** weighted down; laden: *air heavy with moisture, eyes heavy with sleep.* **9** causing sorrow; sorrowful; gloomy: *heavy news.* **10** grave; serious; sober; sombre: *a heavy part in a play.* **11** cloudy: *a heavy sky.* **12** broad; thick; coarse: *a heavy line, heavy features.* **13** clumsy; sluggish; slow: *a heavy walk.* **14** ponderous; dull: *heavy reading.* **15** loud and deep: *the heavy roar of cannon.* **16** in military use: **a** heavily armed or equipped: *heavy tanks.* **b** of large size: *heavy artillery.* **17** not risen enough: *heavy bread.* **18** in physics, indicating an isotope possessing a greater atomic weight than another of the same element: *heavy water.* **19** pregnant.
—*n.* **1** a heavy person or thing. **2** *Informal.* in the theatre: **a** the villain in a play. **b** an actor who plays villains or takes similar parts.
—*adv.* **1** in a heavy manner; heavily. **2 hang heavy,** pass slowly and tediously. [OE *hefig* < *hebban* heave] —**heav′i·ly,** *adv.* —**heav′i·ness,** *n.*

Syn. *adj.* **1 Heavy, weighty, burdensome** = of great weight. **Heavy** emphasizes being hard to lift or carry, and used figuratively suggests something pressing down on or weighing down the mind or feelings: *He has heavy responsibilities.* **Weighty** = having great weight, but is used chiefly figuratively, applying to something of great importance: *He made a weighty announcement.* **Burdensome** suggests something very heavy that interferes with freedom of movement and puts a strain on the person or thing carrying it: *The extra work was burdensome.* **9** sad. **13** lumbering.

heav·y-armed (hev′ē ärmd′) *adj.* equipped with heavy weapons or armor.

heavy-duty (hev′ē dū′tē or -dü′tē) *adj.* **1** durably built to stand hard use, strain, etc. **2** taxed by a high tariff.

heav·y-hand·ed (hev′ē han′did) *adj.* **1** clumsy; awkward: *heavy-handed humor.* **2** harsh; cruel. —**heav′y-hand′ed·ly,** *adv.* —**heav′y-hand′ed·ness,** *n.*

heav·y-heart·ed (hev′ē här′tid) *adj.* sad; gloomy; in low spirits.

heavy hydrogen deuterium. *Symbol:* H^2 or D

heavy water water formed of oxygen and heavy hydrogen; deuterium oxide. Heavy water is about 1.1 times as heavy as ordinary water and has a higher freezing point. It occurs in very small amounts in ordinary water. *Formula:* D_2O

heav·y·weight (hev′ē wāt′) *n.* **1** a person or thing of much more than average weight. **2** a boxer or wrestler who weighs 175 pounds or more. **3** *Informal.* a person who has much intelligence or importance.

Heb. or **Hebr.** Hebrew; Hebrews.

heb·dom·a·dal (heb dom′ə dəl) *adj.* weekly. [< LL *hebdomadalis* < *hebdomas, -adis* seven, seven days < Gk.]

He·bra·ic (hi brā′ik or hē′brā′ik) *adj.* of or having to do with the Hebrews or their language or culture; Hebrew. [< LL *Hebraicus* < Gk. *Hebraikos*]

He·bra·ism (hē′brā iz′əm) *n.* **1** a linguistic structure or idiom peculiar to Hebrew. **2** such a structure or idiom translated literally into another language. **3** Hebrew character, spirit, thought, or practice.

He·bra·ist (hē′brā ist) *n.* **1** a scholar skilled in the Hebrew language and literature. **2** a person imbued with the Hebraic spirit.

He·bra·is·tic (hē′brā is′tik) *adj.* of or having to do with Hebraism or Hebraists; Hebraic.

He·brew (hē′brü) *n.* **1** a Jew; Israelite. **2** the ancient language of the Jews, in which the Old Testament was recorded. **3** one of the present-day official languages of Israel. The other is Arabic.
—*adj.* Jewish. [ME < OF *Ebreu* < L *Hebraeus* < Gk. *Hebraios* < Aramaic *'ebrai* < Hebrew *'ibri,* literally, one from beyond (the river)]

Hec·a·te (hek′ə tē) *n.* in Greek mythology, the goddess of the moon, earth, and infernal regions. She was later associated with magic and witchcraft.

hec·a·tomb (hek′ə tōm′, -tüm′, or -tom′) *n.* **1** in ancient Greece and Rome, the sacrifice of 100 oxen at one time. **2** any great slaughter. [< L < Gk. *hekatombē* sacrifice of 100 oxen < *hekaton* hundred + *bous* ox]

heck·le (hek′əl) *v.* **-led, -ling.** harass and annoy (a speaker, etc.) by asking bothersome questions, etc. Also, **hatchel.** [< *heckle* comb for flax or hemp, ME *hekele.* Related to HACKLE[1].] —**heck′ler,** *n.*

hec·tare (hek′tãr or hek′tär) *n.* in the metric system, a measure of area equal to 100 ares, 10,000 square metres, or 2.471 acres. Also, **hektare.** [< F *hectare* < Gk. *hekaton* hundred + F *are* are[2]]

hec·tic (hek′tik) *adj.* **1** flushed. **2** feverish. **3** *Informal.* much excited. **4** *Informal.* very exciting: *He leads a hectic life.* **5** showing the signs of tuberculosis; consumptive.
—*n.* **1** a flush. **2** a fever. [ME < OF *etique* < LL < Gk. *hektikos* habitual, consumptive < *hexis* habit]

hecto- *combining form.* hundred, as in *hectogram.* [< F < Gk. *hekaton*]

hec·to·gram or **hec·to·gramme** (hek′tə gram′) *n.* 100 grams, equal to 3.527 ounces. Also, **hektogram.**

hec·to·graph (hek′tə graf′) *n.* a machine for making many copies of a page of writing, a drawing, etc. The original writing is transferred to a surface coated with gelatin, and the copies are made from this. —*v.* make copies of with a hectograph.

hec·to·li·tre or **hec·to·li·ter** (hek′tə lē′tər) *n.* a measure of capacity in the metric system, equal to 100 litres, 2.750 bushels or 22 imperial gallons.

hec·to·me·tre or **hec·to·me·ter** (hek′tə mē′tər) *n.* 100 metres, equal to 0.1 kilometre or 328.08 feet.

hec·tor (hek′tər) *n.* a bragging, bullying fellow.
—*v.* **1** bluster; bully. **2** tease. [< *Hector,* a Trojan hero]

he'd (hēd; *unstressed,* ēd, id, or hid) **1** he had. **2** he would.

hedge (hej) *n. v.* **hedged, hedg·ing.** —*n.* **1** a thick row of bushes or small trees, planted as a fence or boundary. **2** any barrier or boundary. **3** a means of protection or defence. **4** the act of hedging.
—*v.* **1** put a hedge around. **2** enclose or separate with a hedge. **3** avoid giving a direct answer; evade questions; avoid taking a definite stand. **4** protect oneself from losing money on (a bet, risk, etc.) by an opposite bet, risk, etc. **5 hedge in, a** hem in; surround on all sides. **b** keep from getting away or moving freely. [OE *hecg*]

hedge·hog (hej′hog′) *n.* **1** the porcupine of North America. **2** any of a group of small European mammals that have spines on the back. When attacked, hedgehogs roll up into a bristling ball. 3 in military use: a an X-shaped portable obstacle, usually laced with barbed wire. b an area defended by pillboxes, mines, and lanes for machine-gun fire.

hedge-hop (hej′hop′) *v.* **-hopped, -hop·ping.** fly an airplane very low. —**hedge′-hop′per,** *n.*

hedge-hop·ping (hej′hop′ing) *n.* the act of flying an airplane very low.

hedge·row (hej′rō′) *n.* a thick row of bushes or small trees forming a hedge.

hedge sparrow a small European warbler that frequents hedges.

he·don·ism (hē′dən iz′əm) *n.* the doctrine that pleasure or happiness is the highest good. [< Gk. *hēdonē* pleasure]

he·don·ist (hē′dən ist) *n.* a person who believes in or practises hedonism.

heed (hēd) *v.* give careful attention to; take notice of: *Now heed what I say.* —*n.* careful attention; notice: *She pays heed to her clothes.* [OE *hēdan*] —**heed′er,** *n.* —**Syn.** *v.* regard, note, consider, mind. —*n.* regard.

heed·ful (hēd′fəl) *adj.* careful; attentive. —**heed′ful·ly,** *adv.* —**heed′ful·ness,** *n.* —**Syn.** mindful, watchful.

heed·less (hēd′lis) *adj.* careless; thoughtless. —**heed′less·ly,** *adv.* —**heed′less·ness,** *n.*

hee·haw (hē′ho′ or -hô′) *n.* 1 the braying sound made by a donkey. 2 a loud, coarse laugh. —*v.* 1 make the braying sound of a donkey. 2 laugh loudly and coarsely.

heel[1] (hēl) *n.* 1 the back part of a person's foot, below the ankle. 2 the part of a stocking or shoe that covers the heel. 3 the part of a shoe or boot that is under the heel or raises the heel. 4 the part of an animal's hind leg that corresponds to a person's heel. 5 anything shaped, used, or placed at an end like a heel, such as an end crust of bread, the rind of cheese, the rear end of a ship's keel, or the lower end of a mast. 6 *Informal.* a despicable person.
at heel, near the heels; close behind.
cool one's heels, *Informal.* be kept waiting a long time.
down at the heel or **heels, a** with the heel of the shoe worn down. **b** shabby. **c** slovenly.
drag one's heels, a hold back or slow up on purpose. **b** agree reluctantly; work (at) without interest or enthusiasm.
kick one's heels, a be kept waiting for a very long time. **b** wait impatiently.
lay by the heels, put in prison or in stocks.
out at the heels, a with the heel of the stocking or shoe worn through. **b** shabby. **c** slovenly.
show a clean pair of heels, run away.
take to one's heels, run away.
to heel, a near a person's heels; close behind: *The dog walked to heel.* **b** under control: *He soon brought the mutineers to heel.*
—*v.* 1 follow closely. 2 put a heel or heels on. 3 touch the ground or floor with the heel. 4 of dogs, follow one's master closely. 5 perform (a dance) with the heels. 6 in golf, strike (the ball) with the heel of the club. [OE *hēla*] —**heel′less,** *adj.*

heel[2] (hēl) *v.* lean over to one side; tilt; tip: *The ship heeled as it turned.* —*n.* the act of heeling. [alteration of earlier *heeld* < OE *h(i)eldan* < *heald* inclined]

heeled (hēld) *adj.* 1 having a heel or heel-like projection. 2 *Slang.* a provided with money. b armed with a revolver or other weapon.

heel·er (hēl′ər) *n.* 1 a person who puts heels on shoes. 2 *Esp.U.S. Slang.* a follower or hanger-on of a political boss.

heel·tap (hēl′tap′) *n.* 1 a layer of leather, etc. in the heel of a shoe. 2 a small amount of liquor left in a glass after drinking.

heft (heft) *Informal.* —*n.* 1 weight; heaviness. 2 the greater part; bulk. —*v.* 1 judge the weight or heaviness of by lifting. 2 lift; heave. [< *heave*]

heft·y (hef′tē) *adj.* **heft·i·er, heft·i·est.** *Informal.* 1 weighty; heavy: *a hefty load.* 2 substantial; considerable: *a hefty bill for repairs. Investors made a hefty profit.* 3 big and strong. [< *heft*]

hat, āge, cãre, fär; let, ēqual, tėrm; it, īce
hot, ōpen, ôrder; oil, out; cup, pu̇t, rüle, ūse
əbove, takən, pencəl, lemən, circəs
ch, child; ng, long; sh, ship
th, thin; ᴛʜ, then; zh, measure

he·gem·o·ny (hi jem′ə nē or hej′ə mō′nē) *n.* **-nies.** political domination, especially the leadership or domination of one state in a group; leadership. [< Gk. *hēgemonia* < *hēgemōn* leader < *hēgeesthai* lead]

He·gi·ra (hi jī′rə or hej′ə rə) *n.* 1 the flight of Mohammed from Mecca to Medina in A.D. 622. The Moslems use a calendar reckoned from this date. 2 the Moslem era. 3 **hegira,** a departure; flight. Also, **Hejira.** [< Med.L < Arabic *hijrah* flight, departure]

heif·er (hef′ər) *n.* a young cow that has not yet had a calf. [OE *hēahfore*]

heigh (hī or hā) *interj.* a sound used to attract attention, give encouragement, express surprise, etc.

heigh-ho (hī′hō′ or hā′-) *interj.* a sound made to express surprise, joy, sadness, or weariness.

height (hīt) *n.* 1 the measurement from top to bottom; the tallness of anyone or anything; the point to which anything rises above ground: *Seven feet is an unusual height for a man.* 2 the distance above sea level. 3 a fairly great distance up: *rising at a height above the valley.* 4 a high point or place; hill: *on the mountain heights.* 5 the highest part; top. 6 the highest point; greatest degree: *Being reckless in an automobile is the height of folly.* 7 high rank; high degree. [OE *hīehthu* < *hēah* high]

height·en (hīt′ən) *v.* 1 make or become higher. 2 make or become stronger or greater; increase: *She put rouge on her cheeks to heighten their color.* —**height′en·er,** *n.*

height of land 1 a region higher than its surroundings. 2 a watershed: *A height of land marks the boundary between Labrador and Quebec.*

hei·nous (hā′nəs) *adj.* very wicked; extremely offensive; hateful. [ME < OF *haïnos,* ult. < *hair* to hate < Gmc.] —**hei′nous·ly,** *adv.* —**hei′nous·ness,** *n.* —**Syn.** odious, infamous, atrocious.

heir (ãr) *n.* 1 a person who receives, or has the right to receive, someone's property or title after the death of its owner; a person who inherits property. 2 a person who inherits anything; a person who receives or has something from someone who lived before him. [ME < OF < L *heres* heir]

heir apparent *pl.* **heirs apparent.** a person who is first in the line of succession: *The monarch's oldest son is heir apparent to the throne.*

heir·ess (ãr′is) *n.* 1 a female heir. 2 a female heir to great wealth.

heir·loom (ãr′lüm′) *n.* a possession handed down from generation to generation. [< *heir* + *loom,* originally, implement]

heir presumptive *pl.* **heirs presumptive.** a person who will be heir unless someone with a stronger claim is born.

heir·ship (ãr′ship) *n.* the position or rights of an heir; right of inheritance; inheritance.

heist (hīst) *Slang.* —*v.* rob or steal. —*n.* a theft or robbery. [alteration of *hoist*]

He·ji·ra (hi jī′rə or hej′ə rə) *n.* Hegira.

hek·tare (hek′tãr or hek′tär) *n.* hectare.

hek·to·gram or **hek·to·gramme** (hek′tə gram′) *n.* hectogram.

Hel (hel) *n.* in Norse mythology: 1 the goddess of death and of the lower world. 2 the lower world, inhabited by those who did not die in battle.

held (held) *v.* pt. and pp. of **hold**[1].

heli- *combining form.* the form of *helio-* used before vowels, as in *heliac.*

he·li·an·thus (hē′lē an′thəs) *n.* a sunflower. [< NL < Gk. *hēlios* sun + *anthos* flower]

hel·i·cal (hel′ə kəl) *adj.* having to do with, or having the form of, a helix; spiral. —**hel′i·cal·ly,** *adv.*

hel·i·ces (hel′ə sēz′) *n.* a pl. of **helix.**

hel·i·coid (hel′ə koid′) *n.* in geometry, a surface generated by a straight line moving along a fixed helix and maintaining a constant angle with its axis. —*adj.* like a helix; spiral, as in certain univalve shells.

hel·i·con (hel′ə kon′ or hel′ə kən) *n.* a large bass tuba.

hel·i·cop·ter (hel′ə kop′tər or hē′lə kop′tər) *n.* an aircraft lifted from the ground and kept in the air by horizontal propellers. [< F *hélicoptère* < Gk. *helix, -ikos,* spiral + *pteron* wing]

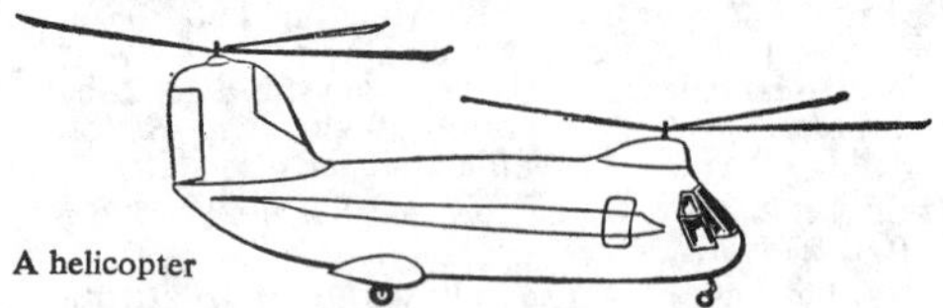
A helicopter

helio- *combining form.* the sun, as in *heliograph.* [< Gk. *hēlios* sun]

he·li·o·cen·tric (hē′lē ō sen′trik) *adj.* **1** viewed or measured from the centre of the sun. **2** having or representing the sun as a centre. [< *helio-* + Gk. *kentron* centre]

he·li·o·gram (hē′lē ə gram′) *n.* a message transmitted by heliograph.

he·li·o·graph (hē′lē ə graf′) *n.* **1** a device for signalling by means of a movable mirror that flashes beams of light to a distance. The flashes of the mirror represent the dots and dashes of the Morse code. **2** an apparatus for taking photographs of the sun. —*v.* communicate or signal by heliograph.

He·li·os (hē′lē os′) *n.* in Greek mythology, the sun god, son of Hyperion, represented as driving a chariot across the heavens. He was afterwards identified with Apollo and with the Roman god Sol.

he·li·o·scope (hē′lē ə skōp′) *n.* **1** a device for looking at the sun without injury to the eye. **2** a telescope having such a device.

he·li·o·ther·a·py (hē′lē ō ther′ə pē) *n.* the treatment of disease by means of sunlight.

he·li·o·trope (hē′lē ə trōp′ or hēl′yə-) —*n.* **1** a plant having clusters of small, fragrant purple or white flowers. **2** a pinkish purple. **3** a bloodstone. —*adj.* pinkish-purple. [< L < Gk. *hēliotropion* < *hēlios* sun + *-tropos* turning]

he·li·ot·ro·pism (hē′lē ot′rə piz′əm) *n.* an involuntary response to the sun's rays; a tendency that makes a plant turn toward the light. **Negative heliotropism** makes an organism turn or move away from the light. [< *heliotrope* any plant that turns toward the sun]

he·li·o·type (hē′lē ə tīp′) *n.* **1** a picture or print produced by a photomechanical process in which the impression in ink is taken directly from a prepared gelatin film that has been exposed under a negative. **2** such a process.

hel·i·port (hel′ə pôrt′) *n.* an airport for use by helicopters. Heliports may be built on the tops of buildings or in other small areas in cities.

he·li·um (hē′lē əm) *n.* a rare, gaseous chemical element, first discovered in the sun's atmosphere. It is a very light, inert gas that will not burn, much used in balloons and dirigibles. *Symbol*: He; *at.no.* 2; *at.wt.* 4.0026. [< NL < Gk. *hēlios* sun]

he·lix (hē′liks) *n.* **hel·i·ces** or **he·lix·es. 1** a spiral. A screw thread or a watch spring is a helix. **2** in architecture, a spiral ornament. **3** in anatomy, the rim of the outer ear. **4** in geometry, the curve traced by a straight line, on a plane that is wrapped around a cylinder, as the thread of a screw. [< L < Gk. *helix* a spiral]

Helixes in a Corinthian capital

hell (hel) *n.* **1** in religious use, a place where wicked persons are punished after death. **2** the powers of evil. **3** the persons in hell. **4** the abode of the dead; Hades. **5** any place or state of wickedness, torment, or misery. [OE]

he'll (hēl; *unstressed,* hil) **1** he will. **2** he shall.

hell·bent (hel′bent′) *Slang.* —*adj.* strongly determined; reckless. —*adv.* recklessly, wildly.

hell·cat (hel′kat′) *n.* **1** a mean, spiteful woman. **2** a witch.

hel·le·bore (hel′ə bôr′) *n.* **1** a European plant of the same family as the buttercup, having showy flowers that bloom before spring. One kind is called **black hellebore. 2** a cathartic made from the roots of black hellebore. **3** a tall plant having clusters of purple, green, or white flowers. One kind is called **white hellebore. 4** an insecticide made from the roots of white hellebore. **5** a cardiac medicine made from the roots of white hellebore. [< L < Gk. *helleboros*]

Hel·lene (hel′ēn) *n.* Greek. [back-formation singular of Gk. *Hellēnes,* literally, descendants of Hellen, mythical father of the Greeks]

Hel·len·ic (he len′ik or he lē′nik) *adj.* **1** Greek. **2** of Greek history, language, or culture from about 776 B.C. to the death of Alexander the Great in 323 B.C. —*n.* **1** the Greek language. **2** the branch of the Indo-European languages that includes the various dialects of Greek.

Hel·len·ism (hel′ən iz′əm) *n.* **1** the ancient Greek culture or ideals. **2** the adoption or imitation of Greek speech, ideals, etc. **3** an idiom or expression peculiar to the Greek language. **4** such an idiom or expression translated literally into another language.

Hel·len·ist (hel′ən ist) *n.* **1** a scholar skilled in the ancient Greek language, literature, and culture. **2** a person who uses or imitates Greek language, ideals, or customs.

Hel·len·is·tic (hel′ə nis′tik) *adj.* **1** of or having to do with Hellenists. **2** of or having to do with Greek history, language, and culture after the death of Alexander the Great in 323 B.C.

Hel·len·ize (hel′ən īz′) *v.* **-ized, -iz·ing. 1** make Greek in character. **2** use or imitate the Greek language, ideals, or customs. —**Hel′len·i·za′tion,** *n.* —**Hel′len·iz′er,** *n.*

hel·ler[1] (hel′ər) *n.* **1** a unit of money in Czechoslovakia, worth 1/100 of a koruna. **2** a coin worth one heller. [< earlier *haller* < MHG *haller* or *häller,* supposedly from Schwäbisch*hall,* where hellers were first coined]

hel·ler[2] (hel′ər) *n. Slang.* a mischievous, trouble-making person; hellion.

hel·ler·y (hel′ə rē) *n. Slang.* mischief; wild behavior.

hell·fire (hel′fīr′) *n.* the fire of hell; punishment in hell.

hell·gram·mite (hel′grə mīt′) *n.* the larva of a dobson fly, often used for fish bait. [origin uncertain]

hell·hound (hel′hound′) *n.* **1** in mythology, Cerberus, the watch-dog of Hades. **2** a dog or hound of hell. **3** a cruel, fiendish person.

hel·lion (hel′yən) *n. Informal.* a mischievous, troublesome person. [origin uncertain]

hell·ish (hel′ish) *adj.* **1** fit to have come from hell; devilish; fiendish. **2** of hell. —**hell′ish·ly,** *adv.* —**hell′ish·ness,** *n.* —**Syn. 1** diabolical, wicked.

hel·lo (he lō′ or hə lō′) *interj. n.* **-los,** *v.* **-loed, -lo·ing.** —*interj.* **1** an exclamation to express a greeting or attract attention. **2** an exclamation of surprise. —*n.* **1** a call of greeting or surprise. **2** a call to attract attention. —*v.* shout; call. Also, **hallo, hollo, hullo.**

helm[1] (helm) *n.* **1** the handle or wheel by which a ship is steered. **2** a position of control or guidance: *The Prime Minister is at the country's helm.* [OE *helma*] —**helm′less,** *adj.*

helm[2] (helm) *Archaic.* —*n.* helmet. —*v.* put a helmet on. [OE. Akin to HELMET.]

A football helmet

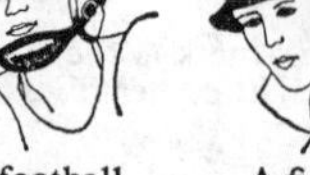
A fireman's helmet

Soldiers' helmets

hel·met (hel′mit) *n.* **1** a covering to protect the head. Soldiers wear steel helmets; firemen wear leather helmets.

2 a piece of armor for the head: *Knights wore helmets as part of their armor.* See **armor** for picture. 3 anything that resembles a helmet in shape, appearance, or position. [ME < OF *helmet*, dim. of *helme* helm[2] < Gmc.]

hel·minth (hel′minth) *n.* an intestinal worm, such as the tapeworm, roundworm, etc. [< Gk. *helmins, -inthos*]

helms·man (helmz′mən) *n.* **-men** (-mən). the man who steers a ship.

Hel·ot (hel′ət or hē′lət) *n.* **1** in ancient Sparta, a slave or serf. **2 helot,** a slave; serf. [< L *Helotes*, pl. < Gk. *Heilōs*, probably related to Gk. *haliskesthai* be captured]

hel·ot·ism (hel′ət iz′əm or hē′lət iz′əm) *n.* serfdom like that of ancient Sparta.

hel·ot·ry (hel′ət rē or hē′lət rē) *n.* **1** helots; slaves. **2** serfdom; slavery.

help (help) *v.* **helped** or (*Archaic*) **holp, helped** or (*Archaic*) **holp·en, help·ing,** *n.* —*v.* **1** provide with what is needed or useful: *help a person with one's money.* **2** aid; assist: *help someone with his work.* **3** give aid or assistance: *We could finish the job faster if he would help.* **4** make better; relieve: *This medicine will help your cough.* **5** prevent; stop: *It can't be helped.* **6** avoid; keep from: *He can't help yawning.* (See usage note.) **7** give food to; serve with food: *Help her to some cake.* **8 help oneself to** take when one wants. **9 help out,** help; help in doing or getting. **10 so help me God!** a formula concluding a solemn oath.
—*n.* **1** anything done or given in helping. **2** aid; assistance. **3** a person or thing that helps; helper. **4** a hired helper or group of hired helpers: *The storekeeper treats his help well.* **5** a means of making better; remedy: *The medicine was a help.* **6** a means of preventing or stopping. [OE *helpan*]

☛ **can't help (but).** There are three possible idioms. General: *I can't help feeling sorry for him.* Formal: *I cannot but feel sorry for him.* Informal: *I can't help but feel sorry for him.* The last is an established idiom, though avoided by many writers.

Syn. *v.* **1, 2 Help, aid, assist** = give support to someone or something by providing something needed or useful. **Help** emphasizes actively providing whatever physical, moral, or material support another needs for any purpose: *She helps her mother at home.* **Aid** particularly suggests helping in a less personal way or working together with another to do or get something: *She aids the children's hospital.* **Assist** suggests standing by to help or serve in any way needed or useful, especially in doing something: *A nurse assists a doctor.* **4** remedy, heal.

help·er (hel′pər) *n.* **1** a person who helps; assistant; supporter. **2** something that helps.

help·ful (help′fəl) *adj.* giving help; useful. —**help′ful·ly,** *adv.* —**help′ful·ness,** *n.* —**Syn.** serviceable, beneficial.

help·ing (hel′ping) *n.* **1** the portion of food served to a person at one time. **2** a portion: *The program included a generous helping of contemporary music.*

help·less (help′lis) *adj.* **1** not able to help oneself; weak. **2** without help, protection, etc. —**help′less·ly,** *adv.*

help·less·ness (help′lis nis) *n.* a being helpless: *the helplessness of a little baby.*

help·mate (help′māt′) *n.* a companion and helper; wife or husband.

help·meet (help′mēt′) *n.* helpmate. [from a misinterpretation of "an *help meet* for him," Gen. 2:18, 20; *meet* = suitable]

hel·ter-skel·ter (hel′tər skel′tər) *adv.* with headlong, disorderly haste: *The children ran helter-skelter when the dog rushed at them.* —*n.* noisy and disorderly haste, confusion, etc. —*adj.* carelessly hurried; disorderly; confused.

helve (helv) *n.* the handle of an axe, hammer, etc. [OE *hielfe*]

hem[1] (hem) *n. v.* **hemmed, hem·ming.** —*n.* **1** a border or edge on a garment; an edge made by folding over the cloth and sewing it down. **2** a border; edge.
—*v.* **1** fold over and sew down the edge of (cloth). **2** border; edge. **3 hem in, around,** or **about, a** surround on all sides. **b** keep from getting away or moving freely. [OE *hemm*]

hem[2] (hem) *interj. n. v.* **hemmed, hem·ming.** —*interj. n.* an exclamation imitating a clearing of the throat, used to attract attention or show doubt or hesitation. —*v.* **1** make a sound like that of clearing the throat. **2** hesitate in speaking. [imitative]

hema- *combining form.* blood: *hematite = bloodstone.*

hat, āge, cãre, fär; let, ēqual, tėrm; it, īce
hot, ōpen, ôrder; oil, out; cup, pu̇t, rüle, ūse
əbove, takən, pencəl, lemən, circəs
ch, child; ng, long; sh, ship
th, thin; ᴛʜ, then; zh, measure

[< Gk. *haima, -atos* blood]

he-man (hē′man′) *Informal.* —*n.* a virile, rugged man. —*adj.* tough; masculine; rugged.

hem·a·tite (hem′ə tīt′ or hē′mə tīt′) *n.* an important iron ore that is reddish-brown when powdered. *Formula:* Fe_2O_3 Also, **haematite.** [< L *haematites* < Gk. *haimatitēs* bloodlike < *haima, -matos* blood]

hemato- *combining form.* blood: *hematogenesis = the formation of blood.* [< Gk. *haima, -atos* blood]

hem·a·tol·o·gist (hem′ə tol′ə jist or hē′mə-) *n.* a person who studies blood, or an expert in the diseases of the blood. Also, **haematologist.**

hem·a·tol·o·gy (hem′ə tol′ə jē or hē′mə-) *n.* the branch of physiology that deals with the structure, function, and diseases of the blood. Also, **haematology.**

hemi- *prefix.* half, as in hemisphere. [< Gk.]

hem·i·ple·gi·a (hem′ə plē′jē ə) *n.* paralysis of one side of the body. [< Gk. *hēmi-* half + *plēgē* stroke]

hem·i·ple·gic (hem′ə plē′jik or -plej′ik) *adj.* **1** suffering from hemiplegia. **2** having to do with hemiplegia. —*n.* a person suffering from hemiplegia.

he·mip·ter·ous (hi mip′tər əs) *adj.* belonging to a large group of insects that have pointed beaks for piercing and sucking and usually two pairs of wings. Bedbugs, lice, and aphids belong to this group. [< *hemi-* + Gk. *pteron* wing]

hem·i·sphere (hem′ə sfēr′) *n.* **1** a half of a sphere or globe. **2** a half of the earth's surface. North America and South America are in the Western Hemisphere. Europe, Asia, Africa, and Australia are in the Eastern Hemisphere. All countries north of the equator are in the Northern Hemisphere. **3** a half of the celestial sphere, as divided by the celestial equator, the ecliptic, or the horizon. [< F < L < Gk. *hēmisphairion* < *hēmi-* half + *sphaira* sphere]

hem·i·spher·i·cal (hem′ə sfer′ə kəl) *adj.* **1** shaped like a hemisphere. **2** of a hemisphere.

hem·i·stich (hem′ə stik′) *n.* **1** a half line of verse, especially the part of a verse preceding or following the main caesura. **2** an incomplete line or line of verse having less than the usual length. [< L < Gk. *hēmistichion* < *hēmi-* half + *stichos* row]

hem·lock (hem′lok) *n.* **1** an evergreen tree of the pine family having small cones and drooping branches. Bark from hemlock is used in tanning. **2** the wood of this tree. **3** a poisonous plant having spotted stems, finely divided leaves, and small white flowers. It belongs to the same family as the carrot. **4** a poison made from it. [OE *hymlice*]

hem·mer (hem′ər) *n.* **1** a person or thing that hems. **2** an attachment to a sewing machine for hemming.

hemo- *combining form.* blood. [< Gk. *haima* blood]

he·mo·glo·bin (hē′mə glō′bən or hem′ə-) *n.* the protein matter in the red corpuscles of the blood, which carries oxygen from the lungs to the tissues and carbon dioxide from the tissues to the lungs. Also, **haemoglobin.** [for *hematoglobulin*, ult. < Gk. *haima* blood + L *globulus*, dim. of *globus* globe]

he·mo·phil·i·a (hē′mə fil′ē ə or hem′ə-) *n.* an inherited condition in which the blood does not clot normally. Excessive bleeding results from the slightest cut. Also, **haemophilia.** [< NL *haemophilia* < Gk. *haima* blood + *philia* affection, tendency]

he·mo·phil·i·ac (hē′mə fil′ē ak′ or hem′ə-) *n.* a person who has hemophilia; bleeder. Also, **haemophiliac.**

hem·or·rhage (hem′ə rij or hem′rij) *n. v.* **-rhaged, -rhag·ing.** —*n.* discharge of blood. A nosebleed is a mild hemorrhage. —*v.* bleed. Also, **haemorrhage.** [< L *haemorrhagia* < Gk. *haimorrhagia*, ult. < *haima* blood + *rhēgnynai* break, burst]

hem·or·rhoid (hem′ə roid′) *n.* a painful swelling formed by the dilation of blood vessels near the anus; in the plural, piles. Also, **haemorrhoid.** [< L *haemorrhoida* < Gk. *haimorrhois,* ult. < *haima* blood + *-rhoos* flowing]

hem·or·rhoi·dal (hem′ə roi′dəl) *adj.* **1** of or having to do with hemorrhoids. **2** suffering from hemorrhoids. Also, **haemorrhoidal.**

hemp (hemp) *n.* **1** a tall Asiatic plant whose tough fibres are made into heavy string, rope, coarse cloth, etc. **2** the tough fibres of this plant. **3** hashish or some other drug obtained from some kinds of hemp. [OE *henep*]

hemp·en (hem′pən) *adj.* **1** made of hemp. **2** like hemp.

hemp nettle a coarse, prickly weed of the mint family.

hem·stitch (hem′stich′) *v.* make a hem along a line from which threads have been drawn out, gathering the cross threads into a series of little groups. —*n.* **1** the stitch used. **2** ornamental needlework made by hemstitching.

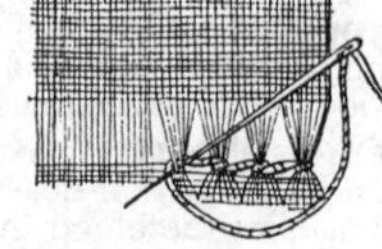

Hemstitching

hen (hen) *n.* **1** a female chicken. **2** the female of certain other birds and a few animals: *a hen sparrow, a hen lobster.* [OE *henn*] —**hen′like′,** *adj.*

hen·bane (hen′bān′) *n.* a coarse, bad-smelling plant having sticky, hairy leaves and clusters of yellowish-brown flowers. It is poisonous to fowls.

hence (hens) *adv.* **1** as a result of this; therefore: *It is very late, hence you must go to bed.* **2** from now; from this time onward: *years hence.* **3** from this source or origin. **4** from here. **5** from this world.
—*interj. Archaic.* **1 hence!** go away! **2 hence with!** take away! [ME *hennes* < OE *heonan* + *-s,* adv. ending]
☛ Hence is a formal word for the less formal *consequently, therefore,* and the general *so that*: *He has not answered our last letter; hence it would seem he is not interested. Hence* is rare in current informal writing.

hence·forth (hens′fôrth′) *adv.* from this time on; from now on.

hence·for·ward (hens′fôr′wərd) *adv.* henceforth.

hench·man (hench′mən) *n.* **-men** (-mən). **1** a trusted attendant or follower. **2** an obedient, unscrupulous follower. [ME *henxtman* < OE *hengest* horse + *man* man; originally, a groom]

hen·coop (hen′küp′) *n.* a coop for hens.

hen·dec·a·gon (hen dek′ə gon′) *n.* a plane figure having 11 sides and 11 angles. [< Gk. *hendeka* eleven + *gōnia* angle]

hen·e·quen or **hen·e·quin** (hen′ə kin) *n.* **1** a yellow fibre from the leaves of an agave of Yucatán, used for making binder twine, ropes, coarse fabrics, etc. **2** the plant that yields this fibre. [< Sp. < native Yucatán word]

hen·house (hen′hous′) *n.* a house for poultry.

hen·na (hen′ə) *n. adj. v.* **-naed, -na·ing.** —*n.* **1** a dark, reddish-orange dye used on the hair. **2** a small thorny tree of Asia and Africa from whose leaves this dye is made. **3** a reddish brown. —*adj.* reddish-brown.
—*v.* dye or color with henna. [< Arabic *henna*ʻ]

hen·ner·y (hen′ər ē) *n.* **-ner·ies.** a place where poultry is kept.

hen·pecked (hen′pekt′) *adj. Informal.* ruled by one's wife: *a henpecked husband.*

hen·ry (hen′rē) *n.* **-ries** or **-rys.** in electricity, a unit inductance. When a current varying at the rate of one ampere per second induces an electromotive force of one volt, the circuit has an inductance of one henry. *Abbrev.*: H [after Joseph *Henry* (1797-1878), an American physicist]

hep (hep) *adj. Slang.* informed; having intimate and up-to-date knowledge. [origin uncertain]

he·pat·ic (hi pat′ik) *adj.* **1** of or having to do with the liver. **2** acting on the liver as a medicine. **3** liver-colored. **4** in botany, of or belonging to the liverworts.
—*n.* **1** a medicine that acts on the liver. **2** in botany, a liverwort. [< L < Gk. *hēpatikos* < *hēpar* liver]

he·pat·i·ca (hi pat′ə kə) *n.* a low plant having delicate purple, pink, or white flowers that bloom early in the spring. [< NL, ult. < Gk. *hēpar* liver; the leaf is thought to resemble the liver in shape]

hep·a·ti·tis (hep′ə tī′tis) *n.* inflammation of the liver. [< Gk. *hēpar, hēpatos* liver + E *-itis*]

hep·cat (hep′kat′) *n. Slang.* **1** an informed admirer of swing music. **2** a performer in a swing band.

Hep·ple·white (hep′əl hwīt′ or -wīt′) *adj.* of, like, or having to do with a style of furniture having graceful curves and slender lines. —*n.* **1** this style of furniture. **2** a piece of furniture in this style. [after George *Hepplewhite* (?-1786), an English furniture designer]

hept- the form of **hepta-** before vowels, as in *heptarchy.*

hepta- *combining form.* seven, as in *heptagon.* [< Gk. *hepta*]

hep·ta·gon (hep′tə gon′) *n.* a plane figure having seven angles and seven sides. [< LL < Gk. *heptagonon* < *hepta* seven + *gōnia* angle]

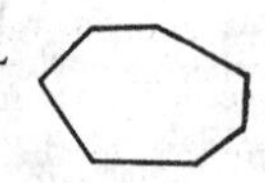

A heptagon

hep·tag·o·nal (hep tag′ə nəl) *adj.* having the form of a heptagon.

hep·tam·e·ter (hep tam′ə tər) *n.* a line of verse having seven feet. *Example*:

> And thríce | he róut|ed áll | his fóes,
> and thríce | he sléw | the sláin.

[< LL < Gk. *heptametron* < *hepta* seven + *metron* measure]

hep·tar·chy (hep′tär kē) *n.* **-chies. 1** a government by seven persons. **2** a group of seven states, each under its own ruler. **3 the Heptarchy,** the seven principal Anglo-Saxon kingdoms between A.D. 449 and A.D. 838. [< *hept-* + Gk. *-archia* rule < *archos* ruler]

hep·ta·stich (hep′tə stik′) *n.* a group of seven lines forming a strophe, stanza, or poem. [< *hepta-* + Gk. *stichos* line of verse]

her (hėr; *unstressed,* hər or ər) *pron.* the objective case of **she**: *I like her.* —*adj.* the possessive form of **she**: of her; belonging to her; done by her: *her look, her book, her work.* [OE *hire*]

her. 1 heraldry. **2** heraldic.

He·ra (hēr′ə) *n.* in Greek mythology, the wife of Zeus and queen of gods and men, identified by the Romans with Juno. She was the special goddess of women and marriage. Also, **Here.**

Her·a·cles (her′ə klēz′) *n.* Hercules.

her·ald (her′əld) *n.* **1** formerly, an officer who carried messages, made announcements, arranged and supervised tournaments and other public ceremonies, and regulated the use of armorial bearings. **2** a person who carries messages and makes announcements; messenger. **3** a forerunner; harbinger: *Dawn is the herald of day.* **4** in Great Britain, etc., an official who has authority over coats of arms and keeps a record of families that have them.
—*v.* **1** bring news of; announce: *The robins heralded the arrival of spring.* **2** go before and announce the coming of. [ME < OF < W.Gmc. **heriwald* army chief] —**Syn.** *n.* **3** precursor.

he·ral·dic (he ral′dik) *adj.* of or having to do with heraldry or heralds.

her·ald·ry (her′əld rē) *n.* **-ries. 1** the science or art dealing with coats of arms. Heraldry deals with a person's right to use a coat of arms, the tracing of family descent, the creating of a coat of arms for a new country, etc. **2** a heraldic device; collection of such devices. **3** a coat of arms. **4** the ceremony or pomp connected with the life of noble families.

herb (ėrb or hėrb) *n.* **1** a plant whose leaves or stems are used for medicine, seasoning, food, or perfume. Sage, mint, and lavender are herbs. **2** a flowering plant whose stems live only one season. Herbs do not form woody tissue as shrubs and trees do, though their roots may live many years. Peonies, buttercups, corn, wheat, cabbage, lettuce, etc. are herbs. [ME < OF < L *herba*]

her·ba·ceous (hėr bā′shəs) *adj.* **1** of an herb; like an herb; having stems that are soft and not woody. **2** like a leaf; green. [< L *herbaceus*]

herb·age (ėr′bij or hėr′bij) *n.* **1** herbs collectively. **2** grass. **3** the green leaves and soft stems of plants.

herb·al (hėr′bəl or ėr′bəl) *adj.* of herbs. *—n.* a book about herbs.

herb·al·ist (hėr′bəl ist or ėr′bəl ist) *n.* a person who gathers herbs or deals in them.

her·bar·i·um (hėr bãr′ē əm) *n.* **-bar·i·ums, -bar·i·a** (-bãr′ē ə). **1** a collection of dried plants systematically arranged. **2** a room or building where such a collection is kept. [< LL *herbarium* < L *herba* herb. Doublet of ARBOR[1].]

her·bi·cide (hėr′bə sīd′) *n.* a poisonous chemical weed killer, such as 2,4-D. [< L *herba* herb + *-cidium* act of killing]

her·bi·vore (hėr′bə vôr′) *n.* any animal, such as a cow or horse, that feeds mainly on grass or other vegetation.

her·biv·o·rous (hėr biv′ə rəs) *adj.* feeding on grass or other plants. Cattle are herbivorous animals. [< NL *herbivorus* < L *herba* herb + *vorare* devour]

herb·y (ėr′bē or hėr′bē) *adj.* **1** having many herbs; grassy. **2** of or like herbs.

her·cu·le·an or **Her·cu·le·an** (hėr′kyů lē′ən or hėr kū′lē ən) *adj.* **1** of great strength, courage, or size; very powerful. **2** requiring great strength, courage, or size; very hard to do.

Her·cu·les (hėr′kyů lēz′) *n.* **1** in Greek and Roman mythology, a hero of immense strength who performed twelve extraordinary tasks or labors imposed on him by the goddess Hera. **2** in astronomy, a northern constellation. **3** any man of great strength. Also, **Heracles.** [< L < Gk. *Hēraklēs*, literally, the glory of Hera < *Hēra* + *kleos* glory]

herd[1] (hėrd) *n.* **1** a number of animals together, especially large animals: *a herd of cows, a herd of horses, a herd of elephants.* **2** a large number of people. **3** the common people; rabble. *—v.* **1** join together; flock together. **2** form into a flock, herd, or group. [OE *heord*]

herd[2] (hėrd) *n.* the keeper of a herd, as in *cowherd, goatherd.* *—v.* drive, tend, or take care of (cattle, sheep, etc.). [OE *hierde* < *heord* herd[1]]

herd·er (hėr′dər) *n.* herdsman.

herds·man (hėrdz′mən) *n.* **-men** (-mən). a man who takes care of a herd.

here (hēr) *adv.* **1** in this place; at this place: *Place it here. Here the speaker paused.* **2** to this place: *Come here.* **3** at this time; now. **4** in this life.
here and there, in this place and that; at intervals.
here below, on earth; in this life.
here goes! *Informal.* announcement of something bold about to be done.
here's to, a wish for health, happiness, or success to.
here you are, *Informal.* here is what you want.
neither here nor there, not to the point; off the subject; unimportant.
—n. **1** this place. **2** this life.
—interj. here! **1** an answer showing that one is present when roll is called. **2** a call to attention or to introduce a command: *Here, take away the dishes.* [OE *hēr*]

He·re (hēr′ē) *n.* Hera.

here·a·bout (hēr′ə bout′) *adv.* around here; about this place; near here.

here·a·bouts (hēr′ə bouts′) *adv.* hereabout.

here·af·ter (hēr af′tər) *adv.* **1** after this; in the future. **2** in life after death. *—n.* **1** the future. **2** the life after death.

here·at (hēr at′) *adv.* **1** when this happened; at this time. **2** because of this.

here·by (hēr bī′) *adv.* by this means; in this way: *I hereby certify that I am over 21 years of age.*

he·red·i·ta·ble (hə red′ə tə bəl) *adj.* that can be inherited.

he·red·i·tar·y (hə red′ə ter′ē) *adj.* **1** coming by inheritance: *"Prince" is a hereditary title.* **2** holding a position by inheritance: *The Queen of England is a hereditary ruler.* **3** transmitted or caused by heredity: *Color blindness is hereditary.* **4** having to do with inheritance or heredity. [< L *hereditarius* < *hereditas.* See HEREDITY.] **—Syn. 3** inherited.

he·red·i·ty (hə red′ə tē) *n.* **-ties. 1** in biology, the genetic transmission of physical or mental characteristics from parent to offspring. **2** the qualities that have come to offspring from parents. **3** the tendency of offspring to be like the parents. **4** the transmission from one generation to another of property, titles, customs, etc. by inheritance or tradition.

hat, āge, cãre, fär; let, ēqual, tėrm; it, īce
hot, ōpen, ôrder; oil, out; cup, půt, rüle, ūse
əbove, takən, pencəl, lemən, circəs
ch, child; ng, long; sh, ship
th, thin; ᴛʜ, then; zh, measure

Here·ford (her′ə fərd or hėr′fərd) *n.* **1** a breed of beef cattle having a red body, white face, and white markings under the body. **2** an animal of this breed. [< *Herefordshire,* England]

here·in (hēr in′) *adv.* **1** in this place, book, document, etc. **2** in this matter; in this way.

here·in·af·ter (hēr′in af′tər) *adv.* afterward in this document, statement, etc.

here·in·be·fore (hēr in′bi fôr′) *adv.* before in this document, statement, etc.

here·in·to (hēr in′tü) *adv.* **1** into this place. **2** into this matter.

here·of (hēr ov′ or hēr uv′) *adv.* of this; about this.

here·on (hēr on′) *adv.* **1** on this. **2** immediately after this.

her·e·sy (her′ə sē) *n.* **-sies. 1** a belief different from the accepted belief of a church, school, profession, etc. **2** the holding of such a belief. [ME < OF < LGk. *hairesis* a taking, choosing < *haireein* take]

her·e·tic (her′ə tik) *n.* a person who holds a belief that is different from the accepted belief of his church, school, profession, etc. *—adj.* holding such a belief. [< F *hérétique* < LL *haereticus* < Gk. *hairetikos* able to choose] **—Syn.** *n.* dissenter.

he·ret·i·cal (hə ret′ə kəl) *adj.* **1** of or having to do with heresy or heretics. **2** containing heresy; characterized by heresy. **—he·ret′i·cal·ly,** *adv.*

here·to (hēr tü′) *adv.* to this place, thing, etc.

here·to·fore (hēr′tə fôr′) *adv.* before this time; until now.

here·un·to (hēr′un tü′) *adv.* to this.

here·up·on (hēr′ə pon′) *adv.* **1** upon this. **2** immediately after this.

here·with (hēr wiᴛʜ′ or -with′) *adv.* **1** with this. **2** by this means; in this way.

her·it·a·bil·i·ty (her′ə tə bil′ə tē) *n.* a heritable quality or condition.

her·it·a·ble (her′ə tə bəl) *adj.* **1** capable of being inherited. **2** capable of inheriting.

her·it·age (her′ə tij) *n.* what is or may be handed on to a person from his ancestors; inheritance. [ME < OF *heritage* < *heriter* inherit < LL *hereditare,* ult. < L *heres, -redis* heir]

her·maph·ro·dite (hėr maf′rə dīt′) *n.* **1** an animal or plant having the reproductive organs of both sexes. **2** a hermaphrodite brig. *—adj.* of or like a hermaphrodite. [< L < Gk. *Hermaphroditos* Hermaphroditus, a son of Hermes and Aphrodite, who became united in body with a nymph]

hermaphrodite brig a sailing ship with two masts, square-rigged forward and schooner-rigged aft.

her·maph·ro·dit·ic (hėr maf′rə dit′ik) *adj.* of or like a hermaphrodite.

Her·mes (hėr′mēz) *n.* in Greek mythology, the messenger of Zeus and the other gods, represented as wearing a winged cap and shoes

A hermaphrodite brig

and carrying a caduceus. He was the god of boundaries and roads, science and invention, eloquence, luck, and cunning; and he was the patron of thieves. The Romans identified him with Mercury.

her·met·ic (hėr met′ik) *adj.* **1** closed tightly so that air cannot get in; airtight. **2** of a poem, having a meaning that is difficult to decipher; obscure. **3** magical; alchemical. [< Med.L *hermeticus* < *Hermes* Trismegistus, supposed author of a work on magic and alchemy]

her·met·i·cal (hėr met′ə kəl) *adj.* hermetic. **—her·met′i·cal·ly,** *adv.*

her·mit (hėr′mit) *n.* **1** a person who goes away from other people and lives by himself. He often lives a religious life. **2** any of various animals of solitary habits, such as the hermit crab. **3** a spiced, brown sugar, drop cooky, usually containing raisins and nuts. [ME < OF < LL < Gk. *erēmitēs* < *erēmia* desert < *erēmos* uninhabited. Doublet of EREMITE.] **—her′mit·like′,** *adj.*

her·mit·age (hėr′mə tij) *n.* **1** the home of a hermit. **2** any place in which to live away from other people.

hermit crab a soft-bodied crab of solitary habits. It uses the empty shells of snails, whelks, etc. as portable shelters.

hermit thrush a brown thrush of N. America, having a spotted breast and reddish tail, noted for its song.

her·ni·a (hėr′nē ə) *n.* **-ni·as, -ni·ae** (-nē ē′ or -nē ī′). the protrusion of a part of the intestine or some other organ through a break in its surrounding walls; a rupture. [< L]

her·ni·al (hėr′nē əl) *adj.* of or having to do with hernia.

he·ro (hēr′ō) *n.* **-roes. 1** a man or boy admired for his bravery, great deeds, or noble qualities. **2** the most important male person in a story, play, poem, etc. **3** in Greek legend, a man of more than human qualities, favored by the gods. Hercules and Achilles were heroes. [ult. < L *heros* < Gk.]

He·ro (hēr′ō) *n.* in Greek legend, a priestess of Aphrodite, whose lover Leander swam the Hellespont every night to visit her. One night he drowned, and, on learning of his death, Hero killed herself.

he·ro·ic (hi rō′ik) *adj.* **1** like a hero, his deeds, or his qualities; brave; great; noble. **2** of or about heroes and their deeds: *The "Iliad" and the "Odyssey" are heroic poems.* **3** resembling the language or style of heroic poetry: *heroic prose.* **4** unusually daring or bold: *Only heroic measures could save the town from the flood.* **5** unusually large; larger than life size.
—*n.* 1 a heroic poem. **2 heroics,** *pl.* **a** high-sounding language. **b** words, feelings, or actions that seem grand or noble but are only for effect. **c** heroic verse. **—he·ro′i·cal·ly,** *adv.*

heroic age the period of the legendary heroes of a nation or folk: *the heroic age of Greece.*

he·ro·i·cal (hi rō′ə kəl) *adj.* heroic.

heroic couplet two successive and rhyming lines of verse in iambic pentameter.

heroic verse a poetic form used in heroic and other long poems. In English, German, and Italian, it is iambic pentameter. In French it is the Alexandrine. In Greek and Latin, it is dactylic hexameter.

her·o·in (her′ō in) *n.* a poisonous habit-forming drug made from morphine. *Formula*: $C_{21}H_{23}NO_5$

her·o·ine (her′ō in) *n.* **1** a woman admired for her bravery, great deeds, or noble qualities. **2** the most important female character in a story, play, poem, etc. **3** in Greek legend, a woman of more than human qualities, favored by the gods. [< L < Gk. *hērōinē*, fem. of *hērōs* hero]

her·o·ism (her′ō iz′əm) *n.* **1** the actions and qualities of a hero or heroine; great bravery; daring courage. **2** a very brave act or quality. **—Syn. 1** valor, gallantry, intrepidity.

her·on (her′ən) *n.* a wading bird having a long neck, long bill, and long legs. [ME < OF *hairon* < Gmc.]

her·on·ry (her′ən rē) *n.* **-ries.** a place where many herons come in the breeding season.

he·ro-wor·ship (hēr′ō wėr′ship) *v.* **-shipped** or **-shiped, -ship·ping** or **-ship·ing,** *n.* **—*v.*** idolize; worship as a hero. **—*n.*** Also, **hero worship. 1** in ancient Greece and Rome, the worship of ancient heroes as gods. **2** the idolizing of great men, or of persons thought of as heroes. **—he′ro-wor′ship·per** or **-wor′ship·er,** *n.*

her·pes (hėr′pēz) *n.* a disease of the skin or mucous membrane characterized by clusters of blisters. [< L < Gk. *herpēs* shingles < *herpein* creep]

her·pe·tol·o·gy (hėr′pə tol′ə jē) *n.* the branch of zoology dealing with reptiles. [< Gk. *herpeton* reptile (< *herpein* creep) + E *-logy*]

Herr (her) *n.* **Her·ren** (her′ən). *German.* **1** Mr.; Sir. **2** a gentleman.

her·ring (her′ing) *n.* **-ring** or **-rings.** a small food fish of the northern hemisphere. Herring are bony fish that have spineless fins, the ventral fins back of the pectorals, no scales on the head, and no fleshy fin back of the dorsal fin. [OE *hǣring*]

her·ring·bone (her′ing bōn′) *adj.* having a zigzag pattern or arrangement.
—*n.* 1 a zigzag pattern, stitch, or arrangement. **2** the spine of a herring. **3** in skiing, a type of ascent made by walking with the skis at an angle to each other and the outer edge turned up. The tracks form a herringbone pattern.
—*v.* embroider or sew with a herringbone stitch; make a herringbone pattern.

H

H, herringbone masonry

herringbone stitch in embroidery, a stitch consisting of crosses in a herringbone design.

herring choker *Slang.* a person from the Maritime Provinces, especially one from New Brunswick.

herring gull a large gray and white gull, commonly found in northern regions around sea and ocean ports, and sometimes inland.

hers (hėrz) *pron.* **1** of her; belonging to her: *This money is hers.* **2** the one or ones belonging to her: *Your answers are wrong; hers are right.*

her·self (hėr self′; *unstressed,* ər self′) *pron.* **1** the emphatic form of **she** or **her**: *Mary bought the book herself. She herself did it.* **2** the reflexive form of **her**: *She hurt herself.* **3** her real self: *In those fits she is not herself.*

hertz (hėrtz) *n.* in physics, a unit of frequency, equivalent to one cycle per second. *Symbol*: Hz [See HERTZIAN WAVES.]

Hertz·i·an waves (hėrt′sē ən) electromagnetic radiation, such as the waves used in communicating by radio. Hertzian waves are produced by irregular fluctuations of electricity in a conductor. [first investigated by Heinrich Rudolph *Hertz* (1857-1894), a German physicist]

he's (hēz; *unstressed,* ēz, iz, or hiz) he is.

Hesh·van (hesh′van) *n.* in the Hebrew calendar, the eighth month of the ecclesiastical year, and the second month of the civil year. Also **Heshwan, Hesvan.**

hes·i·tance (hez′ə təns) *n.* hesitancy.

hes·i·tan·cy (hez′ə tən sē) *n.* **-cies.** hesitation; doubt; indecision.

hes·i·tant (hez′ə tənt) *adj.* hesitating; doubtful; undecided. **—hes′i·tant·ly,** *adv.*

hes·i·tate (hez′ə tāt′) *v.* **-tat·ed, -tat·ing. 1** fail to act promptly; hold back because one feels doubtful; be undecided; show that one has not yet made up one's mind. **2** feel that perhaps one should not; be unwilling; not want: *I hesitated to ask you because you were so busy.* **3** stop for an instant; pause. **4** speak with stops or pauses. [< L *haesitare* < *haerere* stick fast]
Syn. 1 Hesitate, falter, waver = show doubt or lack of firmness in deciding or acting. **Hesitate** emphasizes holding back, unable to make up one's mind firmly or to act promptly: *I hesitated about taking the position.* **Falter** suggests losing courage and hesitating or giving way after starting to act: *I went to apologize, but faltered at the door.* **Waver** suggests being unable to stick firmly to a decision and giving way or drawing back: *My confidence in him wavers.* **4** stammer, stutter.

hes·i·tat·ing·ly (hez′ə tāt′ing lē) *adv.* with hesitation.

hes·i·ta·tion (hez′ə tā′shən) *n.* **1** a hesitating; doubt; indecision. **2** a speaking with short stops or pauses.

Hes·per·i·an (hes pēr′ē ən) *adj.* **1** western. **2** of or having to do with the Hesperides.

hat, āge, cãre, fär; let, ēqual, tėrm; it, īce
hot, ōpen, ôrder; oil, out; cup, pu̇t, rüle, ūse
əbove, takən, pencəl, lemən, circəs
ch, child; ng, long; sh, ship
th, thin; ᴛʜ, then; zh, measure

Hes·per·i·des (hes per′ ə dēz′) *n.pl.* in Greek mythology: **a** the four nymphs who guarded the golden apples of Hera. **b** the garden where these apples were kept.

Hes·per·us (hes′ pər əs) *n.* the evening star; Venus. [< L < Gk. *Hesperos*, originally adj., pertaining to the evening, western]

hes·sian (hesh′ ən) *n.* a coarse fabric of jute and hemp, used in making bags, etc. [< *Hessian*]

Hes·sian (hesh′ ən) *adj.* of Hesse, a district in West Germany, or its people. *—n.* **1** a native or inhabitant of Hesse. **2** a German mercenary soldier in the British army that fought against the Americans during the American Revolution. **3** a mercenary. [< *Hesse*, a state in West Germany]

Hessian boots high boots with tassels, popular in England during the 19th century.

Hessian fly a small two-winged insect whose larvae are destructive to wheat.

hest (hest) *n. Archaic.* behest; command. [alteration of OE *hǣs*]

Hes·van (hes′ van) *n.* Heshvan.

he·tae·ra (hi tēr′ ə) *n.* **-tae·rae** (-tēr′ ē or -tēr′ ī). in ancient Greece, a courtesan. [< Gk. *hetaira*, fem., companion]

he·tai·ra (hi tī′ rə) *n.* **-rai** (-rī). hetaera.

hetero- *combining form.* other; different, as in *heterogenous.* [< Gk. *hetero-* < *heteros*]

het·er·o·dox (het′ ər ə doks′ or het′ rə doks′) *adj.* rejecting the regularly accepted beliefs or doctrines; differing from an acknowledged standard; not orthodox. [< LL < Gk. *heterodoxos* < *heteros* other + *doxa* opinion]

het·er·o·dox·y (het′ ər ə dok′ sē or het′ rə dok′ sē) *n.* **-dox·ies. 1** the rejection of regularly accepted beliefs or doctrines; departure from an acknowledged standard; the opposite of orthodoxy. **2** a belief, doctrine, or opinion not in agreement with what is regularly accepted.

het·er·o·dyne (het′ ər ə dīn′ or het′ rə dīn′) *adj.* having to do with the production of sounds by combining radio oscillations of slightly different frequencies. [< *hetero-* + *-dyne* force (< F < Gk. *dynamos* power)]

het·er·o·ge·ne·i·ty (het′ ər ə jə nē′ ə tē or het′ rə jə nē′ ə tē) *n.* **-ties. 1** a being heterogeneous; wide dissimilarity. **2** a heterogeneous element or part.

het·er·o·ge·ne·ous (het′ ər ə jē′ nē əs or het′ ər ə jēn′ yəs, het′ rə jē′ nē əs or het′ rə jēn′ yəs) *adj.* **1** different in kind; unlike; not at all similar; varied. **2** made up of unlike elements or parts; miscellaneous. **3** in mathematics, of different kinds and having no common integral divisor except 1. **4** of different degrees or dimensions. [< Med.L *heterogeneus*, ult. < Gk. *heteros* other + *genos* kind] **—het′ er·o·ge′ ne·ous·ly,** *adv.* **—het′ er·o·ge′ ne·ous·ness,** *n.*

het·er·o·nym (het′ ər ə nim′) *n.* a word spelled the same as another but having a different sound and meaning. *Example*: *lead*, to conduct, and *lead*, a metal. [< *hetero-* + Gk. dial. *onyma* name; formed on the pattern of *homonym*]

het·er·o·sex·u·al (het′ ər ə sek′ shü əl or het′ rə-) *adj.* **1** in biology, of or having to do with the different sexes. **2** of, having to do with, or characterized by sexual feeling for a person of the opposite sex. *—n.* a heterosexual person.

het·man (het′ mən) *n.* **-mans** (-mənz). a Cossack leader or chief. [< Polish < G *Hauptmann* chief < *Haupt* head + *Mann* man]

heu·ris·tic (hū ris′ tik) *adj.* **1** guiding or helping one to discover: *heuristic reasoning.* **2** in education, having to do with a method that encourages a student to use personal investigation, observation, etc. so that he may find things out for himself. [< Gk. *heuristein* to find + E *-ist* + *-ic*]

hew (hū) *v.* **hewed, hewed** or **hewn, hew·ing. 1** cut with an axe, sword, etc.: *He hewed down the tree.* **2** cut into shape; form by cutting with an axe, etc.: *hew stone for building, hew logs into beams.* **3** make or produce with cutting blows: *The knight hewed his way through the enemy.* [OE *hēawan*]

hew·er (hū′ ər) *n.* a person or thing that hews.

hewn (hūn) *v.* a pp. of **hew.**

hex (heks) *Informal.* *—v.* practise witchcraft on; bewitch. [< n.] *—n.* **1** a witch. **2** a magic spell. [< Pennsylvania G < G *Hexe* witch]

hex- the form of **hexa-** before vowels.

hexa- *combining form.* six, as in *hexagon.* [< Gk. *hex* six]

hex·a·gon (hek′ sə gon′) *n.* a plane figure having six angles and six sides. [< L < Gk. *hexagōnon*, neut. of *hexagōnos* hexagonal, ult. < *hex* six + *gōnia* angle]

Hexagons

hex·ag·o·nal (heks ag′ ə nəl) *adj.* **1** of a hexagon. **2** having the form of a hexagon. **3** having a hexagon as base or cross section. **—hex·ag′ o·nal·ly,** *adv.*

hex·a·gram (hek′ sə gram′) *n.* a six-pointed star formed of two equilateral triangles: ✡

hex·a·he·dral (hek′ sə hē′ drəl) *adj.* having six faces.

hex·a·he·dron (hek′ sə hē′ drən) *n.* **-drons, -dra** (-drə). a solid figure having six faces. [< Gk. *hexaedron*, neut. of *hexaedros* < *hex* six + *hedra* base, surface]

hex·am·e·ter (heks am′ ə tər) *adj.* of verse, consisting of six feet or measures. *—n.* a line of verse consisting of six feet or measures. *Example*: "This′ is the|for′ est pri|me′ val. The|mur′ muring pines′ and the|hem′ locks." [< L < Gk. *hexametros* < *hex* six + *metron* measure]

hex·an·gu·lar (heks ang′ gyü lər) *adj.* having six angles.

hex·a·pod (hek′ sə pod′) *n.* a true insect; an arthropod having six feet. *—adj.* having six feet. [< Gk. *hexapous, -podos* < *hex* six + *pous, podos* foot]

hex·a·stich (hek′ sə stik′) *n.* a group of six lines forming a strophe, stanza, or a poem. [< *hexa-* + Gk. *stichos* line of verse]

hey (hā) *interj.* a sound made to attract attention, to express surprise or other feeling, or to ask a question.

hey·day (hā′ dā′) *n.* the period of greatest strength, vigor, spirits, prosperity, etc. [origin uncertain]

hf. half.

Hf hafnium.

HF, H.F., or **h.f.** high frequency.

hg. hectogram.

Hg mercury. (for L *hydrargyrum*)

HG High German.

H.G. 1 His (or Her) Grace. **2** Holy Ghost.

H.H. 1 His Highness. **2** Her Highness. **3** His Holiness.

hhd. *pl.* **hhds.** hogshead.

H.I. Hawaiian Islands.

hi·a·tus (hī ā′ təs) *n.* **-tus·es** or **-tus. 1** an empty space; gap; a space that needs to be filled. **2** a slight pause between two vowels that come together in successive syllables or words. There is a hiatus between the *e*'s in *pre-eminent.* [< L *hiatus* gap < *hiare* gape]

hi·ba·chi (hē bä′ chē) *n.* a cast-iron or similar container in which charcoal is burnt for cooking, heating, etc. [< Japanese *hibachi* < *hi* fire + *bachi* bowl]

hi·ber·nal (hī bėr′ nəl) *adj.* of or having to do with winter; wintry. [< L *hibernus* wintry]

hi·ber·nate (hī′ bər nāt′) *v.* **-nat·ed, -nat·ing. 1** spend the winter in sleep or in an inactive condition, as bears, groundhogs, and some other wild animals do. **2** spend the winter. [< L *hibernare* < *hibernus* wintry]

hi·ber·na·tion (hī′ bər nā′ shən) *n.* the condition of hibernating.

Hi·ber·ni·a (hī bėr′ nē ə) *n. Poetic.* Ireland. [< L] **—Hi·ber′ ni·an,** *n. adj.*

Hi·ber·ni·an (hī bėr′ nē ən) *adj.* Irish. *—n.* a native of Ireland; Irishman.

hi·bis·cus (hə bis′kəs or hī bis′kəs) *n.* a plant, shrub, or tree of the mallow family having large, red, pink, or white, bell-shaped flowers. [< L]

hic·cough (hik′up) *n. v.* hiccup.

hic·cup (hik′up or hik′əp) *n. v.* **hic·cupped, hic·cup·ping.** —*n.* **1** an involuntary catching of the breath. **2 hiccups,** a seizure of one hiccup after another. —*v.* **1** catch the breath in this way. **2** make the sound of a hiccup. [probably imitative]

hic ja·cet (hik jā′sit) **1** *Latin.* here lies. **2** an epitaph.

hick (hik) *Slang.* —*n.* **1** a farmer or farm worker. **2** an unsophisticated person. —*adj.* of or like hicks. [< *Hick,* a form of *Richard,* a man's name]

hick·ey (hik′ē) *n. Informal.* **1** a pimple or other blemish. **2** a gadget; dingus.

hick·o·ry (hik′ə rē or hik′rē) *n.* **-ries,** *adj.* —*n.* **1** a North American tree having hard, edible nuts, of the same family as the walnut. **2** the tough, hard wood of this tree. **3** a rod, stick, etc. made of this wood. —*adj.* made of hickory. [< Algonquian]

hid (hid) *v.* pt. and a pp. of **hide**[1].

hi·dal·go (hi dal′gō) *n.* **-gos.** a Spanish nobleman of the second class, not as high in rank as a grandee. [< Sp. < OSp. *hijo de algo* son of someone (important)]

hid·den (hid′ən) *adj.* concealed; secret; mysterious; obscure. —*v.* a pp. of **hide**[1]. —**Syn.** *adj.* covert, clandestine, occult, esoteric, latent.

hide[1] (hīd) *v.* **hid, hid·den** or **hid, hid·ing. 1** put or keep out of sight; conceal: *Hide it where no one else will know how to find it.* **2** cover up; shut off from sight: *Clouds hide the sun.* **3** keep secret: *She hid her anxiety.* **4** conceal oneself. [OE *hȳdan*] —**hid′er,** *n.*

Syn. 1 Hide, conceal = put or keep out of sight. **Hide** is the general word: *I hid the present in my closet.* **Conceal** is more formal and usually suggests hiding with a purpose or keeping under cover: *She concealed the note in her dress.*

hide[2] (hīd) *n. v.* **hid·ed, hid·ing.** —*n.* **1** the skin of an animal, either raw or tanned. **2** a person's skin. **3 neither hide nor hair,** nothing at all. —*v. Informal.* beat; thrash. [OE *hȳd*] —**Syn.** *n.* **1** See **skin.**

hide[3] (hīd) *n.* an old English measure of land, probably about 120 acres. [OE *hīgid*]

hide-and-seek (hīd′ən sēk′) *n.* a children's game in which some of the players hide and others try to find them.

hide·a·way (hīd′ə wā′) *n.* **1** a place of concealment or hiding. **2** a retreat; an isolated spot.

hide·bound (hīd′bound′) *adj.* **1** with the skin sticking close to the bones. **2** narrow-minded and stubborn.

hid·e·ous (hid′ē əs) *adj.* **1** very ugly; frightful; horrible: *a hideous monster.* **2** terrible; revolting; abominable: *a hideous crime.* [ME < OF *hide* fear, horror] —**hid′e·ous·ly,** *adv.* —**hid′e·ous·ness,** *n.*

hide-out or **hide·out** (hīd′out′) *n.* a place for hiding or being alone.

hid·ing[1] (hīd′ing) *n.* **1** a being hidden; concealment. **2** a place to hide. [< *hide*[1]]

hid·ing[2] (hīd′ing) *n. Informal.* a beating. [< *hide*[2]]

hie (hī) *v.* **hied, hie·ing** or **hy·ing.** hasten; cause to hasten; go quickly. [OE *hīgian*]

hi·er·arch (hī′ər ärk′) *n.* a chief priest.

hi·er·ar·chic (hī′ər är′kik) *adj.* hierarchical.

hi·er·ar·chi·cal (hī′ər är′kə kəl) *adj.* of a hierarchy; having to do with or belonging to a hierarchy. —**hi′er·ar′chi·cal·ly,** *adv.*

hi·er·ar·chy (hī′ər är′kē) *n.* **-chies. 1** the order of higher and lower ranks in an organization or system. **2** government by priests, church officials, etc. **3** a group of church officials of different ranks. The church hierarchy is composed of archbishops, bishops, priests, etc. **4** one of the three divisions of angels, each made up of three orders. [< Med.L < Gk. *hierarchia* < *hieros* sacred + *archos* ruler]

hi·er·at·ic (hī′ər at′ik) *adj.* **1** having to do with the priestly caste; used by the priestly class; priestly. **2** designating or having to do with a form of Egyptian writing used by the early priests in their records. Hieratic writing is a simplified form of hieroglyphics. **3** of or having to do with certain styles in art, such as the Egyptian or Greek, in which earlier types or methods, fixed by religious tradition, are conventionally followed. [< *hieraticus* < Gk. *hieratikos,* ult. < *hieros* sacred]

hi·er·at·i·cal (hī′ər at′ə kəl) *adj.* hieratic. —**hi′er·at′i·cal·ly,** *adv.*

hi·er·o·glyph (hī′ər ə glif′) *n.* hieroglyphic.

hi·er·o·glyph·ic (hī′ər ə glif′ik) *n.* **1** a picture of an object standing for a word, idea, or sound; a character or symbol standing for a word, idea, or sound. The ancient Egyptians used hieroglyphics instead of an alphabet like ours. **2** a secret symbol. **3** a letter or word that is hard to read. **4 hieroglyphics,** *pl.* **a** any system of writing that uses hieroglyphics. **b** *Informal.* writing that is hard to read. —*adj.* **1** of or written in hieroglyphics. **2** symbolical. **3** hard to read. [< LL < Gk. *hieroglyphikos* < *hieros* sacred + *glyphē* carving]

1. A kingly 2. gift of an 3. offering table 4. to 5. Ra= 6. Horus 7. the great 8. God 9. Lord of 10. Heaven

Egyptian hieroglyphics (def. 1)

hi·er·o·glyph·i·cal (hī′ər ə glif′ə kəl) *adj.* hieroglyphic. —**hi′er·o·glyph′i·cal·ly,** *adv.*

hi·er·o·phant (hī′ər ə fant′ or hī er′ə fant′) *n.* a demonstrator of sacred mysteries or religious knowledge. [< L < Gk. *hierophantes* < *hieros* sacred + *phainein* show]

hi-fi (*adj.* hī′fī′; *n.* hī′fī′) *Informal.* —*adj.* high-fidelity. —*n.* high-fidelity reproduction of music, etc. or the equipment for such reproduction.

hig·gle (hig′əl) *v.* **-gled, -gling.** dispute about terms in a petty way; haggle. [? akin to HAGGLE]

hig·gle·dy-pig·gle·dy (hig′əl dē pig′əl dē) *adv.* in jumbled confusion. —*adj.* jumbled; confused. —*n.* a jumble; confusion.

high (hī) *adj.* **1** of more than usual height; tall: *a high building.* **2** rising to a specified extent: *The mountain is 20,000 feet high.* **3** far above the ground or some base: *an airplane high in the air.* **4** extending to or done from a height: *a high leap, a high dive.* **5** above others in rank, quality, character, etc.: *a high official.* **6** greater, stronger, or better than average; great: *high temperature.* **7** most important; chief; main: *the high altar.* **8** extreme of its kind: *high crimes.* **9** costly: *Strawberries are high in winter.* **10** not low in pitch; shrill; sharp: *a high voice.* **11** advanced to its peak: *high summer.* **12** stinking as a result of decay; tainted: *Some people prefer to eat game after it has become high.* **13** haughty: *a high manner.* **14** *Informal.* excited by alcohol or drugs. **15** of a system of gears, having a driving gear larger than the driven gear, so as to cause the driven gear to revolve more rapidly than the other: *the high gear of an automobile.* **16** having extreme or rigid political or religious opinions, usually ultraconservative: *a high ritualist, a high Tory.* **17** of or belonging to high or inland regions: *High German, high Asia.* **18** in biology, highly developed; more advanced in structure, intelligence, etc.: *the higher algae, the higher apes.*

—*adv.* **1** at or to a high point, place, rank, amount, degree, price, pitch, etc.: *The eagle flies high.* **2 fly high,** have big ideas, plans, hopes, ambitions, etc. **3 high and dry, a** up and out of the water. **b** all alone; without help. **4 high and low,** everywhere. **5 run high, a** be strong or rough: *The tide runs high.* **b** become heated; reach a high pitch: *Tempers ran high at election time.*

—*n.* **1** something that is high. **2** in automobiles and similar machines, an arrangement of gears to give the greatest speed. **3** a high point, level, position, etc.: *Food prices reached a new high last month.* **4** in meteorology, an area of relatively high barometric pressure; anticyclone: *The weatherman reports that a high is approaching.* **5 from high, a** from a high place or position. **b** from **heaven. 6 on high, a** high above; up in the air. **b** in heaven. [OE *hēah*]

Syn. *adj.* **1 High, tall, lofty** = of more than usual height. **High,** the general word, describes things, not people, that rise to more than usual height: *High hills surround the valley.* **Tall** = higher than the average of its kind, and is used to describe people or something that is or grows both high and narrow or slender: *He is a tall*

hat, āge, cãre, fär; let, ēqual, tėrm; it, īce
hot, ōpen, ôrder; oil, out; cup, pủt, rüle, ūse
əbove, takən, pencəl, lemən, circəs
ch, child; ng, long; sh, ship
th, thin; ᴛʜ, then; zh, measure

man. The corn grows tall here. **Lofty,** more literary, means "very high, rising to an impressive height": *We saw the lofty Mount Robson, snow-capped and rising over 12,972 feet.* **5** eminent, elevated, exalted, noble.

high·ball (hī′bol′ or -bôl′) *n.* **1** a railway signal to proceed. **2** whisky, brandy, etc. mixed with soda water or ginger ale and served with ice in a tall glass. —*v. Slang.* **1** move or drive at high speed. **2** run on a speeded-up schedule.

high·born (hī′bôrn′) *adj.* of noble birth.

high·boy (hī′boi′) *n.* a tall chest of drawers on legs.

high·bred (hī′bred′) *adj.* **1** of superior breeding or stock. **2** well-mannered; very refined.

high·brow (hī′brou′) *Informal.* —*n.* a person who cares or claims to care a great deal about knowledge and culture. —*adj.* of or suitable for a highbrow.

High Church a party in the Anglican Communion, laying great stress on church authority, ceremonial observances, etc.

A highboy

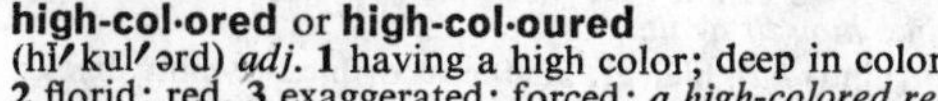

high-col·ored or **high-col·oured** (hī′kul′ərd) *adj.* **1** having a high color; deep in color. **2** florid; red. **3** exaggerated; forced: *a high-colored report of the event.*

high comedy comedy dealing with polite society and depending more on witty dialogue and well-drawn characters than on comic situations.

High Commissioner the chief representative of one Commonwealth country in another.

high-energy physics (hī′en′ər jē) the branch of physics that studies matter and energy in their most elementary forms, especially the study of particles that appear only at high speeds.

high·er-up (hī′ər up′) *n. Informal.* a person occupying a superior position.

high·fa·lu·tin or **high·fa·lu·ting** (hī′fə lü′tən) *adj. Informal.* pompous; bombastic.

high-fi·del·i·ty (hī′fī del′ə tē or hī′fə del′ə tē) *adj.* **1** in electronics, indicating reproduction of the full audio range of a transmitted signal with a minimum of distortion. **2** of or having to do with high-fidelity reproduction, equipment, recordings, etc.

high·fli·er (hī′flī′ər) *n.* **1** a person or thing that flies high. **2** a person who is extravagant or has pretentious ideas, ambitions, etc.

high-flown (hī′flōn′) *adj.* **1** aspiring; extravagant. **2** attempting to be elegant or eloquent: *high-flown compliments.*

high·fly·er (hī′flī′ər) *n.* highflier.

high-fre·quen·cy (hī′frē′kwən sē) *adj.* in electronics, having or concerning a frequency of from 3 to 30 megacycles per second. *Abbrev.:* HF, H.F., or h.f.

High German the literary and official language of Germany and Austria and one of the official languages of Switzerland. It developed from the dialects of the highlands in central and southern Germany.

high-grade (hī′grād′) *n. v.* **-grad·ed, -grad·ing.** *adj.* —*n.* **1** gold nuggets or rich ore. **2** gold nuggets or rich ore stolen in small quantities from a mine. —*v.* **1** steal small quantities of gold or ore from a mine. **2** in lumbering, take only the best timber from a stand. —*adj.* **1** of fine quality; superior. **2** of or having to do with high-grading.

high hand the use of bold, arbitrary, domineering, or over-bearing ways.

high-hand·ed (hī′han′did) *adj.* arbitrary; domineering; overbearing. —**high′-hand′ed·ly,** *adv.* —**high′-hand′ed·ness,** *n.* —**Syn.** tyrannical, autocratic.

high hat a tall black silk hat; top hat.

high-hat (hī′hat′) *v.* **-hat·ted, -hat·ting,** *adj. Slang.* —*v.* treat as inferior; snub. —*adj.* **1** stylish; grand. **2** snobbish.

high·jack (hī′jak′) *v. Informal.* hijack.

high·jack·er (hī′jak′ər) *n. Informal.* hijacker.

high jinks (jingks) boisterous merrymaking; lively fun and sport.

high jump 1 an athletic contest or event in which the contestants try to jump as high as possible. **2** the jump itself.

high·land (hī′lənd) *n.* a country or region that is higher and hillier than the neighboring country. —*adj.* of or in such country.

High·land (hī′lənd) *adj.* of or having to do with the Scottish Highlands.

Highland cattle 1 a breed of small cattle from the Scottish Highlands, having shaggy fur and long, curved, widely set horns. **2** an animal of this breed.

High·land·er (hī′lən dər) *n.* **1** a native or inhabitant of the Highlands of Scotland. **2** a soldier of a regiment from the Highlands of Scotland. **3** a soldier in an allied British or Canadian regiment.

Highland fling a lively dance originating in the Highlands of Scotland.

high·light (hī′līt′) *n. v.* **-light·ed, -light·ing.** —*n.* Also, **high light. 1** the effect or representation of bright light. **2** the part of a painting, photograph, etc. in which light is represented as falling with full force. **3** the most conspicuous or interesting part, event, scene, etc. —*v.* **1** cast a bright light on. **2** emphasize (parts of a painting, photograph, etc.) with lighting, certain colors, etc. **3** make prominent.

high·line (hī′līn′) *n.* highliner.

high·lin·er (hī′līn′ər) *n.* in a Maritime fishing fleet: **1** the boat making the largest catch within a specified time. **2** the captain of such a boat.

high·ly (hī′lē) *adv.* **1** in a high degree; very; very much. **2** favorably; with much approval; with great praise or honor. **3** at a high price.

High Mass a complete ritual of the Mass sung by the priest, with musical and choral accompaniment.

high-mind·ed (hī′mīn′did) *adj.* **1** having or showing high principles and feelings. **2** *Archaic.* proud. —**high′mind′ed·ly,** *adv.* —**high′mind′ed·ness,** *n.* —**Syn. 1** noble.

high·ness (hī′nis) *n.* **1** a being high; height. **2 Highness,** a title of honor given to members of royal families. The Prince of Wales is addressed as "Your Highness" and spoken of as "His Royal Highness."

high noon fully noon; exactly midday.

high-oc·tane (hī′ok′tān) *adj.* of gasoline, having a high percentage of octane or a high octane number.

high-pitched (hī′picht′) *adj.* **1** of high tone or sound; shrill. **2** having a steep slope.

high-pow·ered (hī′pou′ərd) *adj.* having much power: *a high-powered car, rifle, etc.*

high-pres·sure (hī′presh′ər) *adj. v.* **-sured, -sur·ing.** —*adj.* **1** having or using more than the usual pressure. **2** *Informal.* using strong, vigorous methods: *a high-pressure salesman.* —*v. Informal.* use strong, vigorous methods in selling, etc.

high-priced (hī′prīst′) *adj.* expensive.

high priest 1 a chief priest. **2** in ancient times, the head of the Jewish priesthood.

high relief carving or sculpture in which the figures project well out from the background.

high-rise (hī′rīz′) *adj.* having many storeys: *high-rise apartments.*

high·road (hī′rōd′) *n.* **1** a main road; highway. **2** a direct and easy way: *There is no highroad to success.*

high school a school attended after the elementary or public school. Some provinces have junior high schools intermediate between elementary and high school. —**high′-school′,** *adj.*

☛ **high school.** Capitalize only when referring to a particular school: *He graduated from high school at seventeen. I graduated from Collins Bay High School in 1951.*

high seas the open ocean. The high seas are outside the jurisdiction of any country.

high-sound·ing (hī′soun′ding) *adj.* having an imposing or pretentious sound.

high-spir·it·ed (hī′spir′ə tid) *adj.* 1 proud. 2 courageous. 3 spirited; fiery. —**high′-spir′it·ed·ly,** *adv.* —**high′-spir′it·ed·ness,** *n.*

high spirits happiness; cheerfulness; gaiety.

high spot 1 the main part; the climax. 2 an attraction or place of interest for sightseers.

high·stick (hī′stik′) *v.* in hockey, check (an opposing player) illegally by striking or hindering him with the stick carried above shoulder level.

high·stick·ing (hī′stik′ing) *n.* in hockey: 1 the act of carrying one's stick above shoulder level. 2 an illegal check made by striking or hindering an opponent with the stick so carried.

high-strung (hī′strung′) *adj.* very sensitive; easily excited; nervous.

hight (hīt) *v. pt. and pp. Archaic.* named; called: *The knight was hight Gawain.* [OE *heht,* pt. of *hātan* be called]

high-tail (hī′tāl′) *v. Slang.* 1 run away at full speed; hurry. 2 **high-tail it,** hurry or run fast.

high-ten·sion (hī′ten′shən) *adj.* having or accommodating a high voltage: *high-tension wiring.*

high-test (hī′test′) *adj.* 1 passing very difficult requirements and tests. 2 having a very low boiling point.

high tide 1 the highest level of the tide. 2 the time when the tide is highest. 3 the highest point.

high time 1 the time just before it is too late: *It is high time he began to study.* 2 *Informal.* a gay, jolly time at a party, etc.

high-toned (hī′tōnd′) *adj.* 1 high in tone or pitch. 2 having a high character or high principles; dignified. 3 *Informal.* fashionable; stylish.

high treason treason against one's ruler, state, or government.

high water 1 the highest level of water. 2 high tide.

high-water mark 1 the highest level reached by a body of water. 2 any highest point.

high·way (hī′wā′) *n.* 1 a public road. 2 a main road or route. 3 a direct line or way to some end.

high·way·man (hī′wā′mən) *n.* **-men** (-mən). a man who robs travellers on a public road.

H.I.H. 1 His Imperial Highness. 2 Her Imperial Highness.

hi·jack (hī′jak′) *v. Informal.* 1 rob or take by force, especially goods, liquor, etc. being transported illegally. 2 force the pilot of an aircraft to make an unscheduled flight. Also, **highjack.** [origin uncertain]

hi·jack·er (hī′jak′ər) *n. Informal.* 1 a robber, especially one who robs bootleggers of liquor in transit. 2 a person who forces a pilot to make an unscheduled flight. Also, **highjacker.**

hike (hīk) *v.* **hiked, hik·ing,** *n. Informal.* —*v.* 1 take a long walk; tramp; march. 2 move, draw, or raise with a jerk. 3 raise; increase: *The company is going to hike wages.* —*n.* 1 a long walk; a march or tramp. 2 an increase: *a hike in prices.* [? related to HITCH] —**hik′er,** *n.*

hi·lar·i·ous (hə lãr′ē əs) *adj.* 1 very merry; noisily gay: *It was a hilarious party.* 2 very funny: *The joke was hilarious.* [< L *hilaris.* See HILARITY.] —**hi·lar′i·ous·ly,** *adv.* —**hi·lar′i·ous·ness,** *n.* —**Syn.** 1 rollicking.

hi·lar·i·ty (hə lar′ə tē) *n.* great mirth; noisy gaiety. [< L *hilaritas* < *hilaris, hilarus* gay < Gk. *hilaros*]

hill (hil) *n.* 1 a raised part on the earth's surface, not so big or so high as a mountain. 2 a little heap or pile. Ants and moles make hills. The soil put over and around the roots of a plant is a hill. 3 a plant with a little heap of soil over and around its roots. —*v.* 1 put a little heap of soil over and around. 2 form into a little heap. [OE *hyll*] —**hill′er,** *n.*

hill·bil·ly (hil′bil′ē) *n.* **-lies,** *adj. Informal.* —*n.* a person who lives in the backwoods or a mountain region, especially in the southern United States. —*adj.* of, having to do with, or characteristic of a hillbilly: *hillbilly music.*

hill·ock (hil′ək) *n.* a little hill.

hill·side (hil′sīd′) *n.* the side of a hill.

hill·top (hil′top′) *n.* the top of a hill.

hill·y (hil′ē) *adj.* **hill·i·er, hill·i·est.** 1 having many hills. 2 like a hill; steep. —**hill′i·ness,** *n.*

hilt (hilt) *n.* 1 the handle of a sword, dagger, etc. See **sword** for picture. 2 **up to the hilt,** thoroughly; completely. [OE]

hi·lum (hī′ləm) *n.* **-la** (-lə). in botany, the mark or scar on a seed at the point of attachment to the seed vessel. The eye of a bean is a hilum. [< L *hilum* trifle]

him (him; *unstressed,* im) *pron.* the objective case of **he**: *Take him home.* [OE *him,* dative of *hē* he]

H.I.M. His (or Her) Imperial Majesty.

Him·a·la·yan (him′ə lā′ən or hə mäl′yən) *adj.* of or having to do with the Himalayas, a mountain range in India. —*n.* 1 a breed of cat having a thick, fluffy, long-haired body and massive head. It is a cross between a Persian cat and a Siamese. 2 a cat of this breed.

him·self (him self′; *unstressed,* im self′) *pron.* 1 the emphatic form of **he** or **him**: *He himself did it.* 2 the reflexive form of **him**: *He hurt himself.* 3 his real self: *He feels like himself again.*

hind[1] (hīnd) *adj.* **hind·er, hind·most** or **hind·er·most.** back; rear: *The mule kicked up his hind legs.* [see HINDER[2]]

hind[2] (hīnd) *n.* **hind** or **hinds.** a female deer, usually a female red deer after its third year. [OE]

Hind. 1 Hindustan. 2 Hindustani. 3 Hindu. 4 Hindi.

hind·brain (hīnd′brān′) *n.* the back part of the brain, including the cerebellum and medulla oblongata.

hin·der[1] (hin′dər) *v.* keep back; hold back; get in the way of; make difficult; stop; prevent. [OE *hindrian*] —**hin′der·er,** *n.* —**Syn.** impede, encumber, retard, hamper. See **prevent.**

hind·er[2] (hīn′dər) *adj.* hind; back; rear. [cf. OE *hinder* and *hindan* in back, behind]

hind·er·most (hīn′dər mōst′) *adj.* hindmost.

Hin·di (hin′dē) *n.* an Indo-European language, the most widely spoken in India. Hindi has been given official status in the country's constitution. [< Hind. *Hindi* < *Hind* India < Persian *Hind.* See HINDU.]

hind·most (hīnd′mōst′) *adj.* farthest back; nearest the rear; last.

Hin·doo (hin′dü) *n.* **-doos,** *adj.* Hindu.

hind·quar·ter (hīnd′kwôr′tər) *n.* the hind leg and loin of a carcass of beef, lamb, etc.

hin·drance (hin′drəns) *n.* 1 a person or thing that hinders; obstacle. 2 the act of hindering. —**Syn.** 1 See **obstacle.**

hind·sight (hīnd′sīt′) *n. Informal.* the ability to see, after the event is over, what should have been done.

Hin·du (hin′dü) *n.* **-dus,** *adj.* —*n.* 1 a person who believes in Hinduism. 2 loosely, a person from India. —*adj.* 1 of, or having to do with Hinduism. 2 loosely, of or having to do with India. [< Persian *Hindū* < *Hind* India < OPersian *Hindu*]

Hindu. Hindustani.

Hindu-Arabic numerals (hin′dü ar′ə bik) the figures 1, 2, 3, 4, 5, 6, 7, 8, 9, 0. Also, **Arabic numerals.**

Hin·du·ism (hin′dü iz′əm) *n.* one of the great religions of the world, the chief religion and social system of the Hindus.

Hin·du·sta·ni (hin′dů stä′nē or hin′dů stan′ē) *adj.* having to do with India, its people, or their languages. —*n.* a dialect of Hindi having an admixture of Persian and Arabic. [< Hind., Persian *Hindūstānī* Indian < *Hindūstān* India < *Hindū* Hindu + *stan* place, country]

hinge (hinj) *n. v.* **hinged, hing·ing.** —*n.* 1 a joint on which a door, gate, cover, lid, etc. moves back and forth. 2 a natural joint doing similar work: *the hinge of the knee, the hinge of a clam.* 3 that on which something turns or depends; central principle; critical point. 4 a small piece of gummed paper with a fold, by which stamps can be mounted in an album without gluing them to the pages. —*v.* 1 furnish with hinges; attach by hinges. 2 hang or turn on a hinge. 3 depend: *The success of the picnic hinges on the kind of weather we get.* [ME *heng.* Related to HANG.]

hat, āge, cãre, fär; let, ēqual, tėrm; it, īce
hot, ōpen, ôrder; oil, out; cup, pu̇t, rüle, ūse
əbove, takən, pencəl, lemən, circəs
ch, child; ng, long; sh, ship
th, thin; ᴛʜ, then; zh, measure

hinged (hinjd) *adj.* having a hinge or hinges.

hin·ny (hin′ē) *n.* **-nies.** an animal resembling a mule, the offspring of a male horse and a female donkey. [apparently dim. of *hin < L *hinnus* (influenced by *hinnire* neigh) < Gk. *innos*]

hint (hint) *n.* a slight sign; indirect suggestion: *A black cloud gave a hint of the coming storm.*
—*v.* **1** give a slight sign of; suggest indirectly. **2 hint at,** give a hint of; suggest. [apparently < *hent,* v., seize, OE *hentan*] **—hint′er,** *n.* **—hint′ing·ly,** *adv.*
Syn. *n.* allusion, inkling, innuendo, insinuation.
-v. **1 Hint, insinuate** = suggest indirectly. **Hint** = say something in a roundabout way, not openly, directly, or frankly: *She hinted that it was time to go to bed by saying, "Do you often stay up this late?"* **Insinuate** = suggest or hint something unkind or nasty in a sly or underhand way: *Are you insinuating that I am a liar?*

hin·ter·land (hin′tər land′) *n.* **1** the land or district behind a coast; back country. **2** remote parts; background. [< G]

hip[1] (hip) *n. v.* **hipped, hip·ping.** —*n.* **1** in human beings: **a** the joint formed by the upper thighbone and pelvis. **b** the part of the body surrounding this joint. **2** in animals, a similar part of the body, where the hind leg joins the body. **3** in architecture, the ridge formed by two sloping sides of a roof. **4 on the hip,** at a disadvantage. —*v.* in architecture, form with a hip or hips. [OE *hype*] **—hip′less,** *adj.* **—hip′like′,** *adj.*

hip[2] (hip) *n.* a pod containing the ripe seed of a rose bush. [OE *hēope*]

hip[3] (hip) *adj. Slang.* **1** aware; up-to-date; hep. **2** of or having to do with hipsters, their language, style, etc. [var. of *hep*]

hip·bone (hip′bōn′) *n.* **1** either the left or the right lower part of the pelvis. **2** the ilium. **3** the ischium.

hipped[1] (hipt) *adj.* in architecture, formed with hips. [< *hip*[1]]

hipped[2] (hipt) *adj. Slang.* obsessed. [var. of *hypt* < *hyp,* n., for *hypochondria*]

-hipped *combining form.* having —— hips: *wide-hipped = having wide hips.*

hip·pie (hip′ē) *n. Slang.* **1** a person who believes in freedom of expression and a philosophy of love and fellowship. **2** any beatnik. [< *hip*[3] + *-ie*]

hip·po (hip′ō) *n. Informal.* a hippopotamus.

Hip·po·crat·ic (hip′ə krat′ik) *adj.* of or having to do with Hippocrates. [< *Hippocrates* (460?-377? B.C.), a Greek physician]

Hippocratic oath an oath describing the duties and obligations of a physician, usually taken by those about to become physicians.

Hip·po·crene (hip′ə krēn′ or hip′ə krē′nē) *n.* a fountain on Mt. Helicon, sacred to the Muses and regarded as a source of poetic inspiration. [< L < Gk. *Hippokrēnē* < *hippos* horse + *krēnē* fountain]

hip·po·drome (hip′ə drōm′) *n.* **1** in ancient Greece and Rome, an oval track for horse races and chariot races, surrounded by tiers of seats for spectators. **2** an arena or building for a circus, rodeo, etc. [< L < Gk. *hippodromos* < *hippos* horse + *dromos* course]

Hip·pol·y·tus (hi pol′ə təs) *n.* in Greek legend, the son of Theseus. Falsely accused by his stepmother Phaedra, he was cursed by his father, and killed when his chariot overturned.

hip·po·pot·a·mus (hip′ə pot′ə məs) *n.* **-mus·es, -mi** (-mī′ or -mē′). a huge, thick-skinned, hairless mammal often weighing as much as four tons, found in and near the rivers of tropical Africa. Hippopotamuses feed on plants and can stay under water for a long time. [< L < Gk. *hippopotamos* < *hippos* horse + *potamos* river]

hip roof a roof with sloping ends and sides.

A hip roof

hip·ster (hip′stər) *n. Slang.* **1** one who is unconventional in regard to music, sex, religion, the use of drugs, etc.; a person who is hep. **2** a beatnik. **3** a jazz fan. [< *hip*[3] + *-ster*]

hir·cine (hėr′sīn or hėr′sən) *adj.* **1** of or having to do with goats; resembling a goat, especially in having a strong, unpleasant odor. **2** lustful. [< L *hircinus* < *hircus* he-goat]

hire (hīr) *v.* **hired, hir·ing,** *n.* —*v.* **1** pay for the use of (a thing) or the work or services of (a person). **2** take on as an employee; engage: *He has hired a new secretary.* **3** give the use of (a thing) or the work or services of (a person) in return for payment. **4 hire out,** give one's work in return for payment. [OE *hȳrian,* < n.]
—*n.* **1** payment for the use of a thing or the work or services of a person. **2** a hiring. **3 for hire,** for use or work in return for payment. **4 on hire,** for use or work in return for payment. [OE *hȳr*] **—Syn.** *v.* **1** lease, rent. See **employ.**

hire·ling (hīr′ling) *n.* **1** a person who works only for money, without interest or pride in the task. **2** a person hired to do whatever another orders him to do. —*adj.* to be had for hire; mercenary.

hir·sute (hėr′süt) *adj.* hairy. [< L *hirsutus*]

his (hiz; *unstressed,* iz) *pron.* **1** of him; belonging to him: *This is his.* **2** the one or ones belonging to him: *The others are not his.* —*adj.* of him; belonging to him: *This is his book.* [OE *his,* genitive of *hē* he]

His·pa·ni·a (his pā′nē ə or his pān′yə) *n. Poetic.* Spain.

hiss (his) *v.* **1** make a sound like that of the *s* in *see*: *The snake hissed as we approached.* **2** make this sound as a sign of disapproval. **3** force or drive by hissing: *They hissed him off the stage.* **4** say or show by hissing.
—*n.* **1** the sound of hissing: *There was a loud hiss as the water boiled over onto the hot stove.* **2** the sound of hissing to express disapproval: *The actor was upset by the hisses of the crowd.* [imitative] **—hiss′er,** *n.*

hist (hist) *interj.* be still! listen!

hist. 1 history. **2** historian. **3** histology.

his·ta·mine (his′tə mēn′ or his′tə min) *n.* an amine released by the body in allergic reactions. It lowers the blood pressure and is used in the diagnosis and treatment of various allergies. *Formula:* $C_5H_9N_3$ [< *hist(idine),* an amino acid (< Gk. *histion* tissue) + *amine*]

his·ti·dine (his′tə dēn′ or his′tə din) *n.* a basic amino acid found in many proteins. It is important in diet control. *Formula:* $C_6H_9N_3O_2$ [< *Histidin* < Gk. *histion* tissue, web + *-ide* + *-ine*[2]]

his·to·log·i·cal (his′tə loj′ə kəl) *adj.* of or having to do with histology. **—his′to·log′i·cal·ly,** *adv.*

his·tol·o·gist (his tol′ə jist) *n.* a person skilled in histology.

his·tol·o·gy (his tol′ə jē) *n.* **1** the branch of biology that deals with the tissues of animals and plants; study of organic tissues with a microscope. **2** the tissue structure of an animal or plant. [< Gk. *histos* web + E *-logy*]

his·to·ri·an (his tô′rē ən) *n.* **1** a person who writes about history. **2** a scholar who is an authority on history.

his·tor·ic (his tôr′ik) *adj.* **1** famous or important in history: *Halifax and Kingston are historic cities.* **2** historical.

his·tor·i·cal (his tôr′ə kəl) *adj.* **1** of history; having to do with history. **2** according to history; based on history. **3** known to be real or true; in history, not in legend. **4** historic. [< L < Gk. *historikos* < *historia.* See HISTORY.] **—his·tor′i·cal·ly** (-ik lē), *adv.*

historical present the present tense used in describing past events to make them seem more vivid.

his·to·ri·og·ra·pher (his tô′rē og′rə fər) *n.* **1** a historian. **2** the official historian of a court, public institution, etc. [< LL < Gk. *historiographos* < *historia* history + *graphein* write]

his·to·ry (his′tə rē or his′trē) *n.* **-ries. 1** a statement of what has happened. **2** the story of a man, a nation, movement, etc.; a systematic written account. **3** a known past: *This ship has an interesting history.* **4** all past events considered together; the course of human affairs. **5** the branch of knowledge or study that deals with the record and interpretation of past events: *a course in history.* **6** a statement or record of all the facts or events having to do with a person being treated by a doctor, social worker, etc.; a case history. **7** a textbook on history. **8** a historical play. **9 make history, a** influence or guide the course of history. **b** do something spectacular or worthy of remembrance. [< L *historia* < Gk. *historia* inquiry, record, history. Doublet of STORY¹.]

his·tri·on·ic (his′trē on′ik) *adj.* **1** having to do with actors or acting. **2** theatrical; insincere. [< L *histrionicus* < *histrio, -onis* actor] **—his′tri·on′i·cal·ly,** *adv.*

his·tri·on·ics (his′trē on′iks) *n.sing. or pl.* **1** dramatic representation; theatricals; dramatics. **2** a theatrical or insincere manner, expression, etc.

hit (hit) *v.* **hit, hit·ting,** *n.* —*v.* **1** give a blow to; strike; knock: *He hit the ball with the bat. He hit out against his opponents.* **2** get to (what is aimed at): *His second arrow hit the bull's-eye.* **3** come on; meet with; get to; reach; find: *We hit the right road in the dark.* **4** have a painful effect on; affect severely: *The stockbroker was hard hit by the fall in stocks.* **5** attack or criticize sharply: *The reviews hit the new play.* **6** please; appeal to: *This hits my fancy.* **7** in baseball, make a base hit. **8 hit at,** criticize; make fun of; ridicule. **9 hit below the belt,** be unfair to an opponent. **10 hit it off,** *Informal.* agree or get along well with someone: *Tom hit it off well with his new friend.* **11 hit off, a** imitate. **b** represent or describe cleverly. **12 hit on** or **upon, a** come on; meet with; get to. **b** find, especially by accident; guess correctly. **13 hit or miss,** whether one succeeds or fails; regardless of results; by chance; at random. **14 hit the nail on the head,** be apt or to the point: *The solution he proposed hit the nail on the head.*
—*n.* **1** a blow; stroke. **2** a successful attempt, performance, or production. A play, book, or song that becomes popular is a hit. **3** a getting to what is aimed at. **4** a sharp attack or criticism. **5** in baseball, a ball so struck that the batter can get at least to first base safely; base hit. [OE *hittan* < ON *hitta* meet with] **—hit′ter,** *n.* **—Syn.** *v.* **1** See **beat.**

hit-and-run (hit′ ən run′) *adj.* **1** of or caused by a driver who runs into another person or vehicle and drives away without stopping. **2** of or suggesting any similar act: *a hit-and-run attack.* —*n.* in baseball, a play in which the batter tries to hit the ball to protect a runner who has already left base.

hitch (hich) *v.* **1** fasten with a hook, ring, rope, strap, etc.: *He hitched his horse to a post.* **2** harness to a wagon, carriage, etc.: *The farmer hitched up his team and drove to town.* **3** become fastened or caught; fasten; catch. **4** move or pull with a jerk; move jerkily: *He hitched his chair nearer the fire.* **5** limp; hobble. **6** tie a hitch (def. 5): *He hitched a rope around the spar.* **7** *Informal.* hitchhike. **8 be** or **get hitched,** *Slang.* be or get married.
—*n.* **1** a fastening; catch: *The hitch joining the plough to the tractor is broken.* **2** a short, sudden pull or jerk; jerky movement: *The sailor gave his pants a hitch.* **3** a limp; hobble. **4** an obstacle; hindrance; a going wrong: *A hitch in their plans made them miss the train.* **5** a kind of knot used for temporary fastening: *He put a hitch in the rope.* **6** *Informal.* a free ride from a passing automobile. **7** *Slang.* a period of time, especially a period of service in the armed forces. **8 without a hitch,** smoothly; successfully. [ME *hyche(n)*; origin uncertain] **—hitch′er,** *n.* **—Syn.** *v.* **1** attach, tie, hook, tether, harness.

hitch-hike (hich′hīk′) *v.* **-hiked, -hik·ing,** *n. Informal.* —*v.* travel by walking and getting free rides in cars or trucks. —*n.* a journey made in this way. **—hitch′-hik′er,** *n.*

hitching post (hich′ing) a stand or post for hitching horses, etc.

hith·er (hiᴛʜ′ər) *adv.* **1** to this place; toward this place; here. **2 hither and thither,** here and there. —*adj.* on this side; nearer. [OE *hider.* Related to HERE.]

hith·er·most (hiᴛʜ′ər mōst′) *adj.* nearest.

hith·er·to (hiᴛʜ′ər tü′) *adv.* up to this time; until now.

hith·er·ward (hiᴛʜ′ər wərd) *adv.* toward this place; hither.

hith·er·wards (hiᴛʜ′ər wərdz) *adv.* hitherward.

Hit·ler·ism (hit′lər iz′əm) *n.* the program and teachings of the political regime in Germany under Adolf Hitler (1889-1945), Chancellor of Germany from 1933 to 1945.

Hit·tite (hit′īt) *n.* **1** a member of an ancient people of Asia Minor and Syria. Their civilization existed from about 2000 B.C. until about 1200 B.C. **2** the language of the Hittites.
—*adj.* of or having to do with the Hittites or their language. [< Hebrew *Hittīm*]

hive (hīv) *n. v.* **hived, hiv·ing.**
—*n.* **1** a house or box for bees to live in. **2** a large number of bees living together. **3** a busy, swarming place full of people or animals. **4** a swarming crowd.
—*v.* **1** put (bees) in a hive. **2** enter a hive. **3** store up (honey) in a hive. **4** lay up for future use. **5** live close together like bees. [OE *hȳf*]

Hives (def. 1)

hives (hīvz) *n.* a disease in which the skin itches and shows slightly swollen patches, properly called urticaria. [Scottish; origin unknown]

H.J. hic jacet.

hkf. *pl.* **hkfs.** handkerchief.

hl. hectolitre; hectolitres.

h'm (həm) hem; hum.

hm. hectometre; hectometres.

H.M. His (or Her) Majesty.

H.M.C.S. 1 His (or Her) Majesty's Canadian Ship. **2** His (or Her) Majesty's Canadian Service.

H.M.S. 1 His (or Her) Majesty's Ship. **2** His (or Her) Majesty's Service.

ho (hō) *interj.* **1** an exclamation of scornful laughter, joy, or surprise. **2** an exclamation to attract attention.

ho. house.

Ho holmium.

hoar (hôr) *adj.* hoary. [OE *hār*]

hoard (hôrd) *n.* what is saved and stored away; things stored. —*v.* save and store away: *A squirrel hoards nuts for the winter.* [OE *hord*] **—hoard′er,** *n.* **—Syn.** *v.* treasure, amass, accumulate.

hoard·ing¹ (hôr′ding) *n.* **1** the act of one who hoards. **2** something hoarded.

hoard·ing² (hôr′ding) *n. Brit.* **1** a temporary board fence around a building that is being put up or repaired. **2** a billboard. [< *hoard* fence, apparently < AF *hurdis,* ult. < Gmc.]

hoar·frost (hôr′frost′) *n.* white frost.

hoar·hound (hôr′hound′) *n.* horehound.

hoarse (hôrs) *adj.* **hoars·er, hoars·est. 1** sounding rough and deep: *the hoarse sound of the bullfrog.* **2** having a rough voice. [OE *hās*; influenced by ON **hārs*] **—hoarse′ly,** *adv.* **—hoarse′ness,** *n.*

hoar·y (hôr′ē) *adj.* **hoar·i·er, hoar·i·est. 1** white or gray. **2** white or gray with age. **3** old; ancient. **—hoar′i·ness,** *n.*

hoar·y-head·ed (hôr′ē hed′id) *adj.* having white or gray hair.

hoary marmot a large gray marmot of W. Canada and N.W. United States.

hoax (hōks) *n.* a mischievous trick, especially one based on a made-up story: *The report of an attack from Mars was a hoax.* —*v.* play a mischievous trick on; deceive. [probably an alteration of *hocus*] **—hoax′er,** *n.*

hob¹ (hob) *n.* **1** a shelf at the back or side of a fireplace. **2** a peg at which quoits, etc. are thrown. **3** a hobnail. [var. of *hub*; origin uncertain]

hob² (hob) *n.* **1** a hobgoblin; elf. **2** *Informal.* **play hob** or **raise hob,** cause trouble. [ME, for *Rob* (*Robert* or *Robin*)]

hob·ble (hob′əl) *v.* **-bled, -bling,** *n.* —*v.* **1** walk awkwardly; limp. **2** cause to walk awkwardly or limp. **3** move unsteadily. **4** tie the legs of (a horse, etc.) together. **5** hinder.
—*n.* **1** an awkward walk; limp. **2** a rope or strap used to hobble a horse, etc. **3** an awkward or difficult situation. [ME *hobelen*; cf. Du. *hobbelen* rock] **—hob′bler,** *n.*

hob·ble·de·hoy (hob′əl dē hoi′) *n.* **1** a youth between boyhood and manhood. **2** an awkward, clumsy boy. [origin uncertain]

hobble skirt a woman's skirt that is very narrow below the knees.

hob·by (hob′ē) *n.* **-bies. 1** something a person especially likes to work at or study apart from his main business; any favorite pastime, topic of conversation, etc. **2 ride a hobby,** give too much time or attention to one's hobby. [short for *hobbyhorse*] **—hob′ by·ist,** *n.*

hob·by·horse (hob′ē hôrs′) *n.* **1** a stick with a horse's head, used as a toy by children. **2** a rocking horse. **3** a favorite idea or topic: *Father is again on his hobbyhorse of cutting costs.* [*hobby*, ME *hobyn* small horse]

hob·gob·lin (hob′gob′lən) *n.* **1** a goblin; elf. **2** a bogey; ghost. [< *hob*[2] + *goblin*]

hob·nail (hob′nāl′) *n.* a short nail with a large head. Hobnails are used to protect the soles of heavy shoes. [< *hob* peg + *nail*]

Hobnails

hob·nob (hob′nob′) *v.* **-nobbed, -nob·bing.** *Informal.* **1** associate intimately; talk together on familiar terms. **2** drink together. [from drinking phrase *hob or nob* give or take, ult. < OE *hæbbe* have + *næbbe* not have]

ho·bo (hō′bō) *n.* **-bos** or **-boes.** a tramp. [origin uncertain]

Hob·son's choice (hob′sənz) the choice of taking the thing offered or nothing. [< Thomas *Hobson* (?-1631), an English stablekeeper, who would rent only the horse nearest his stable door or none]

hock[1] (hok) *n.* **1** the joint in the hind leg of a horse, cow, etc. above the fetlock joint. See **fetlock** for picture. **2** the corresponding joint in the leg of a fowl. *—v.* cripple by cutting the tendons of the hock; hamstring. Also, **hough.** [OE *hōh*]

hock[2] (hok) *n. Esp.Brit.* a kind of white Rhine wine. [for *Hockamore*, alteration of *Hochheimer* (from *Hochheim*, Germany)]

hock[3] (hok) *Slang. —v.* pawn: *He hocked his watch to buy a ticket. —n.* **1** pawn. **2 in hock, a** in another's possession as security; in pawn. **b** in debt. **3 out of hock, a** no longer in another's possession as security. **b** no longer in debt. [originally, n.; cf. Du. *hok* pen, jail]

A hockey game in progress

hock·ey (hok′ē) *n.* **1** a winter game played on ice by two teams of six players wearing skates and carrying hooked sticks with which they try to shoot a black rubber disk, the puck, into the opposing team's goal. **2** a field game played with curved sticks and a small ball. Field hockey is not as well known to Canadians as ice hockey. [< *hock* hooked stick, var. of *hook*]

hockey stick a hooked or curved stick used in playing hockey.

hock·shop (hok′shop′) *n. Informal.* a store where goods may be pawned.

ho·cus (hō′kəs) *v.* **-cussed** or **-cused, -cus·sing** or **-cus·ing. 1** play a trick on; hoax; cheat. **2** stupefy with drugs. **3** put drugs in (alcoholic drink). [short for *hocus-pocus*]

ho·cus-po·cus (hō′kəs pō′kəs) *n.* **1** a form of words used in conjuring. **2** sleight of hand; magic. **3** trickery; deception. [sham Latin used by jugglers, etc.; probably alteration of *hoc est corpus* (this is the Body) from the Eucharist]

hod (hod) *n.* **1** a trough or tray with a long handle, used for carrying bricks, mortar, etc. on the shoulder. **2** a coal scuttle. [< MDu. *hodde*]

A hod for mortar

hat, āge, cãre, fär; let, ēqual, tėrm; it, īce
hot, ōpen, ôrder; oil, out; cup, pu̇t, rüle, ūse
əbove, takən, pencəl, lemən, circəs
ch, child; ng, long; sh, ship
th, thin; ᴛʜ, then; zh, measure

hod carrier a laborer who carries bricks, mortar, etc. in a hod.

hod·den (hod′ən) *n. Scottish.* a coarse cloth of undyed wool. [probably Northern dial. *hodden*, var. of *holden* (old pp. of *hold*) held, kept (at home, handed down)]

hodge·podge (hoj′poj′) *n.* a disorderly mixture; a mess or jumble. [var. of *hotchpotch*, var. of *hotchpot* < OF *hochepot* ragout < *hocher* shake (< Gmc.) + *pot* pot]

hoe (hō) *n. v.* **hoed, hoe·ing.** *—n.* an implement with a small blade set across the end of a long handle, used to loosen soil and cut weeds. *—v.* **1** loosen, dig, or cut with a hoe. **2** use a hoe. [ME < OF *houe* < Gmc.] **—ho′er,** *n.*

hoe·down (hō′doun′) *n.* **1** a lively, noisy square dance. **2** the music for such a dance.

hog (hog) *n. v.* **hogged, hog·ging.** *—n.* **1** a pig. **2** a full-grown pig, raised for food. **3** *Informal.* a selfish, greedy, or dirty person. **4 go the whole hog,** go to the limit; do something thoroughly. *—v. Slang.* take more than one's share of. [OE *hogg*]

hog·back (hog′bak′) *n.* **1** in geology, a low, sharp ridge with steep sides. **2** an arching back like that of a hog.

hog·gish (hog′ish) *adj.* **1** like a hog; very selfish; greedy. **2** dirty; filthy. **—hog′gish·ly,** *adv.* **—hog′gish·ness,** *n.*

hog·ma·nay (hog′mə nā′) *n.* in Scotland and northern England, New Year's eve, when children knock on doors for presents, cakes, etc. [origin uncertain]

hogs·head (hogz′hed′) *n.* **1** a large barrel or cask that contains from 50 to 120 gallons. **2** a liquid measure equal to 52½ imperial gallons. [? from shape of cask]

hog·wash (hog′wosh′) *n.* **1** refuse given to hogs; swill. **2** *Slang.* worthless stuff; nonsense.

hog-wild (hog′wīld′) *adj. Slang.* frenzied; wildly aroused; berserk.

Hoh·en·stau·fen (hō′ən stou′fən; *German,* hō′ən shtou′fən) *n.* a German princely family to which some of the German kings and Holy Roman emperors between 1138 and 1254 belonged.

Hoh·en·zol·lern (hō′ən zol′ərn; *German,* hō′ən tsôl′ərn) *n.* the German princely family that included the kings of Prussia from 1701 to 1918, and the emperors of Germany from 1871 to 1918.

hoi·den (hoi′dən) *n.* hoyden.

hoi·den·ish (hoi′dən ish) *adj.* hoydenish.

hoi pol·loi (hoi′ pə loi′ or pol′oi) ordinary people. [< Gk. *hoi polloi* the many]

hoist (hoist) *v.* raise on high; lift up, often with ropes and pulleys: *hoist sails, hoist blocks of stone. —n.* **1** a hoisting; lift. **2** an elevator or other apparatus for hoisting heavy loads. **3** on a ship: **a** the perpendicular height of a sail or flag. **b** a signal or message sent by means of flags hoisted. [earlier *hoise* < Du. *hijschen*] **—hoist′er,** *n.*

hoi·ty-toi·ty (hoi′tē toi′tē) *interj.* an exclamation of surprise mixed with contempt or annoyance. *—adj.* **1** giddy; flighty. **2** inclined to put on airs; haughty. *—n.* **1** giddy behavior; flightiness. **2** haughtiness.

ho·key-po·key (hō′kē pō′kē) *n.* **1** trickery; hocus-pocus. **2** a cheap kind of ice cream sold by street vendors.

ho·kum (hō′kəm) *n. Slang.* **1** elements of low comedy or crude humor introduced into a play, etc. for the sake of the laughs they may bring. **2** sentimental matter similarly introduced merely for effect. **3** humbug; nonsense; bunk. [? < *hocus*]

hold[1] (hōld) *v.* **held, held** or (*Archaic*) **hold·en, hold·ing,** *n. —v.* **1** take in the hands or arms and keep; not let go; keep from getting away: *Please hold my hat. Hold my watch while I play this game.* **2** keep in some position or condition; force to keep: *He will hold the paper steady while you draw.* **3** keep from falling; support: *He held his head in his hands.* **4** not break, loosen, or give way: *The*

dike held during the flood. **5** keep from acting; keep back: *Hold your breath.* **6** keep; retain: *This package will be held until called for.* **7** oblige (a person) to adhere to a promise, etc.: *They held him to his promise.* **8** keep by force against an enemy; defend: *Hold the fort.* **9** keep or have within itself; contain: *This theatre holds 500 people.* **10** have and keep as one's own; possess; occupy: *hold an office.* **11** have and take part in; carry on together: *Shall we hold a meeting of the club?* **12** keep or have in mind: *hold a belief.* **13** think; consider: *People once held that the earth was flat.* **14** remain faithful or firm: *He held to his promise.* **15** be true; be in force or effect: *The rule holds in all cases.* **16** keep on; continue: *The weather held warm.* **17** decide legally: *The court holds him guilty.* **18** in music, keep on singing or playing (a note).
hold back, a keep back; keep from acting. **b** avoid disclosing: *hold back the truth.* **c** withhold money, wages, etc.
hold down, a keep down; keep under control. **b** *Slang.* have and keep: *hold down a job.*
hold forth, a talk; preach (often used disparagingly). **b** offer.
hold in, a keep in; keep back. **b** restrain oneself.
hold off, a keep at a distance. **b** keep from acting or attacking.
hold on, *Informal.* **a** keep one's hold. **b** keep on; continue. **c** stop! wait a minute!
hold one's own, a maintain one's position against opposition; stand one's ground; make no concessions. **b** of an invalid, maintain one's strength or state of health; lose no ground.
hold out, a continue; last. **b** stretch forth; extend: *Hold out your hand.* **c** keep resisting; not give in. **d** offer. **e** *Slang.* keep back (something expected or due).
hold over, a keep for future action or consideration. **b** retain or remain beyond the expected time. **c** in music, hold (a tone) from one bar to the next.
hold up, a keep from falling; support. **b** show; display. **c** continue; last; endure. **d** stop. **e** *Informal.* stop by force and rob.
hold with, a side with. **b** agree with. **c** approve of.
—*n.* **1** the act of holding: *release one's hold.* **2** the manner of grasping or holding: *You must take a better hold if you are to pull your weight.* **3** something to hold by. **4** something to hold something else with. **5** a holding back; delay: *a hold in the launching of a missile.* **6** an order to delay or temporarily halt something. **7** a controlling force or influence: *A habit has a hold on you.* **8** in wrestling, a way of holding one's opponent. **9** in music, a sign for a pause. **10** a prison cell. **11** *Archaic.* a fort; stronghold. **12 lay** or **take hold of, a** seize; grasp. **b** get control or possession. [OE *healdan*] —**Syn.** *v.* **3** sustain, bear. **9** See **contain. 10** See **have. 13** regard, deem.

hold² (hōld) *n.* the interior of a ship below the deck. A ship's cargo is carried in its hold. [var. of *hole*]

hold·back (hōld′bak′) *n.* **1** a restraining or preventing of action. **2** something that holds back; restraint; hindrance. **3** an iron or strap on the shaft of a wagon, carriage, etc. to which the harness is attached, enabling a horse to hold back or to back the wagon, carriage, etc. **4** money, wages, etc withheld.

hold·en (hōl′dən) *v. Archaic.* a pp. of **hold¹**.

hold·er (hōl′dər) *n.* **1** a person or thing that holds. **2** a person who owns, possesses, or occupies property, such as an owner, possessor, or tenant. **3** anything to hold something else with. Pads of cloth are used as holders for lifting hot dishes. **4** a person legally entitled to receive payment on, or negotiate, a note, bill, etc.

hold·fast (hōld′fast′) *n.* anything used to hold something else in place. A catch, hook, or clamp is a holdfast.

hold·ing (hōl′ding) *n.* **1** land; a piece of land. **2** Often, **holdings,** *pl.* property in stocks or bonds.

holding company a company that owns stocks or bonds of other companies and thus often controls them.

hold·out (hold′out′) *n. Informal.* **1** a person or group that resists or refuses a settlement. **2** refusal to settle or comply; continued resistance. **3** a hiding place or stronghold.

hold·o·ver (hōld′ō′vər) *n.* **1** a person or thing that is held over from another time or place: *He was a holdover from last year's team.* **2** a person who remains in office beyond the regular time.

hold·up (hōld′up′) *n.* **1** *Informal.* the act of stopping by force and robbing. **2** a stopping.

hole (hōl) *n. v.* **holed, hol·ing.** —*n.* **1** an open place: *a hole in a stocking.* **2** a hollow place: *Rabbits dig holes in the ground to live in.* **3** a small, dark, dirty place. **4** *Informal.* a flaw; defect. **5** *Informal.* a position hard to get out of; embarrassing position. **6** in golf: **a** a small, round hollow to hit a ball into. **b** the part of a golf course leading from a tee to such a place. A regular golf course has 18 holes. **7** a cove; small harbor. **8 burn a hole in one's pocket,** of money, make one want badly to spend: *His Christmas gift is burning a hole in his pocket.* **9 in the hole,** in debt or financial difficulties. **10 make a hole in,** use up a large amount of. **11 pick holes in,** find fault with; criticize.
—*v.* **1** make holes in. **2** in golf, hit or drive (a ball) into a hole. **3 hole out,** hit a golf ball into a hole. **4 hole up, a** of animals, hibernate. **b** *Slang.* go into hiding or seclusion. [OE *hol*]
Syn. *n.* **1, 2 Hole, cavity** = an open or hollow place in something. **Hole** is the common word applying to an opening in or through anything, or to a hollow space in something solid: *Fire burned a hole in the roof. He bored a hole in the tree.* **Cavity** is chiefly scientific or technical, and applies only to a hollow space inside a solid mass or body, often with an opening at the surface: *The dentist filled several cavities in my teeth.*

hole-and-corner (hōl′ ən kôr′ nər) *adj. Informal.* furtive; underhand.

hole-in-the-wall (hōl′ in ᴛʜə wol′ or -wôl′) *adj. Informal.* insignificant; shabby; grubby.

hol·i·day (hol′ə dā′) *n.* **1** a day free of work; day for pleasure and enjoyment. **2** a day on which, either by law or custom, general business is suspended: *Labor Day and Christmas Day are holidays.* **3** Often, **holidays,** *pl.* a vacation; a period of rest or recreation. **4** a holy day; religious festival.
—*adj.* suited to a holiday; gay. [OE *hāligdæg* holy day]

ho·li·er-than-thou (hō′lē ər ᴛʜən ᴛʜou′) *Informal.* —*adj.* hypocritical; self-righteous. —*n.* a self-righteous person.

ho·li·ness (hō′lē nis) *n.* **1** a being holy. **2 Holiness,** a title used in speaking to or of the Pope. [OE *hālignes*]

hol·la (hə lä′ or hol′ə) *interj. n. v.* hollo.

hol·land (hol′ənd) *n.* a linen, or linen and cotton cloth used for window shades, upholstery, etc. It is usually light-brown and sometimes glazed. [first made in *Holland*]

hol·lan·daise sauce (hol′ən dāz′) a creamy sauce made from egg yolks, butter, lemon juice, and seasoning. [< F *hollandaise,* fem. of *hollandais* Dutch]

Hol·land·er (hol′ən dər) *n.* a native or inhabitant of Holland; Dutchman.

Holland gin (hol′ənd) Hollands.

Hol·lands (hol′əndz) *n.* a strong gin made in Holland.

hol·ler (hol′ər) *Informal.* —*v.* shout. —*n.* a loud cry or shout.

hol·lo (hə lō′ or hol′ō) *interj. n.* **-los,** *v.* **-loed, -lo·ing.** —*interj. n.* **1** hello. **2** a shout of exultation or triumph. —*v.* hello. [var. of *halloo*]

hol·loa (hə lō′ or hol′ō) *interj. n. v.* hollo.

hol·low (hol′ō) *adj.* **1** having nothing, or only air, inside; empty; with a hole inside; not solid: *A tube or pipe is hollow.* **2** bowl-shaped; cup-shaped: *a hollow dish for vegetables.* **3** as if coming from something hollow; dull: *a hollow voice, a hollow groan.* **4** not real or sincere; false; worthless: *hollow promises, hollow joys.* **5** deep and sunken: *A starving person has hollow eyes and cheeks.* **6** hungry.
—*n.* **1** a hollow place; hole: *a hollow in the road.* **2** a valley: *Sleepy Hollow.*
—*v.* **1** make hollow; bend or dig out to a hollow shape. **2** become hollow. **3 hollow out,** form by hollowing.
—*adv. Informal.* **1** thoroughly. **2 beat (all) hollow,** beat completely. [OE *holh,* n.; influenced in use by *hol,* adj.] —**hol′low·ly,** *adv.* —**hol′low·ness,** *n.* —**Syn.** *adj.* **1** void, unfilled. **4** idle, vain, insincere.

hol·low-eyed (hol′ō īd′) *adj.* **1** having eyes set deep in the head. **2** *Informal.* appearing very weary.

hol·ly (hol′ē) *n.* **-lies. 1** a tree or shrub having shiny, sharp-pointed, green leaves and bright-red berries. **2** the

hat, āge, cãre, fär; let, ēqual, tėrm; it, īce
hot, ōpen, ôrder; oil, out; cup, pu̇t, rüle, ūse
əbove, takən, pencəl, lemən, circəs
ch, child; ng, long; sh, ship
th, thin; ᴛʜ, then; zh, measure

leaves and berries, used as Christmas decorations. [OE *holegn*]

hol·ly·hock (hol′ē hok′) *n.* a tall plant of the mallow family, having clusters of large, showy flowers of various colors. [ME *holihoc* < *holi* holy (OE *hālig*) + *hoc* mallow (OE *hocc*)]

Hol·ly·wood (hol′ē wu̇d′) *n.* the American motion-picture industry. [< *Hollywood*, a section of Los Angeles, California, centre of the United States motion-picture industry]

holm[1] (hōm) *n.* **1** low, flat land by a stream. **2** a small island in a river or lake near a large island or the mainland. [OE]

holm[2] (hōm) *n.* holm oak.

hol·mi·um (hōl′mē əm) *n.* a rare metallic chemical element belonging to the yttrium group. *Symbol*: Ho; *at.no.* 67; *at.wt.* 164.930. [< NL; < Stock*holm*]

holm oak (hōm) an evergreen oak of S. Europe having leaves that look like holly. [OE *holegn* holly + *āc* oak]

hol·o·caust (hol′ə kost′ or hol′ə kôst′) *n.* **1** a sacrificial offering, all of which is burned. **2** complete destruction by fire, especially of animals or human beings. **3** great or wholesale destruction. [< L < Gk. *holokauston*, neut. of *holokaustos* < *holos* whole + *kaustos* burned]

hol·o·gram (hol′ə gram′) *n.* a photograph obtained by exposing a photographic plate near an object illuminated by a laser beam.

hol·o·graph (hol′ə graf′) *adj.* wholly written in the handwriting of the person in whose name it appears: *a holograph will.* —*n.* a holograph manuscript, letter, document, etc. [< LL < Gk. *holographos* < *holos* whole + *graphē* writing] —**hol·o·graph·ic,** *adj.*

ho·log·ra·phy (hə log′rə fē) *n.* a photographic process for making three-dimensional pictures without the use of lenses, in which a split beam of laser light waves causes a diffraction pattern that is reconstructed in visible light.

holp (hōlp) *v. Archaic.* a pt. of **help.**

hol·pen (hōl′pən) *v. Archaic.* a pp. of **help.**

Hol·stein (hōl′stīn or hōl′stēn) *n.* **1** a breed of large black-and-white dairy cattle, originating in Schleswig-Holstein, a state in Germany. **2** an animal of this breed.

Hol·stein-Frie·sian (hōl′stīn frē′zhən or hōl′stēn-) *n.* Holstein.

hol·ster (hōl′stər) *n.* a leather case for a pistol, usually attached to a belt. [< Du. *holster*]

ho·lus-bo·lus (hō′ləs bō′ləs) *adv. Informal.* all at once; altogether. [humorous Latinization of E *whole bolus*]

ho·ly (hō′lē) *adj.* **-li·er, -li·est,** *n.* **-lies.** —*adj.* **1** belonging to God; set apart for God's service; coming from God; sacred. **2** declared sacred by religious use and authority: *a holy day.* **3** like a saint; spiritually perfect; very good; pure in heart. **4** worthy of reverence. —*n.* a holy place. [OE *hālig*] —**Syn.** *adj.* **3** pious, saintly.

Holy Alliance a league formed by the rulers of Russia, Austria, and Prussia in 1815, supposedly uniting their governments in a Christian brotherhood.

Holy City **1** a city considered sacred by the adherents of a religion. Jerusalem, Rome, and Mecca are Holy Cities. **2** heaven.

Holy Communion in the Christian church: **1** a sharing in the Lord's Supper as a part of church worship; a receiving of the Holy Eucharist. **2** the celebration of the Lord's Supper.

holy day a religious festival, especially one not occurring on a Sunday. Ash Wednesday and Good Friday are holy days.

Holy Father a title of the Pope.

Holy Ghost **1** the spirit of God. **2** the third person of the Trinity.

Holy Grail Grail.

Holy Land Palestine.

Holy Office **1** in the Roman Catholic church, the papal Congregation of the Holy Office, charged with the supervision and protection of Catholic faith and morals. **2** formerly, the Inquisition.

holy of holies **1** the holiest place. **2** the inner shrine of the Jewish tabernacle and temple.

holy orders **1** the rite or sacrament of ordination. **2** the rank or position of an ordained Christian minister or priest. **3** in the Roman Catholic and Anglican churches, the three higher ranks or positions of the clergy. Bishops, priests, and deacons are members of holy orders. **4 take holy orders,** become ordained as a Christian minister or priest.

Holy Roman Empire an empire in western and central Europe regarded both as the continuation of the Roman Empire and as the temporal form of a universal dominion whose spiritual head was the Pope. It began in A.D. 962, or, according to some, in A.D. 800, and ended in 1806.

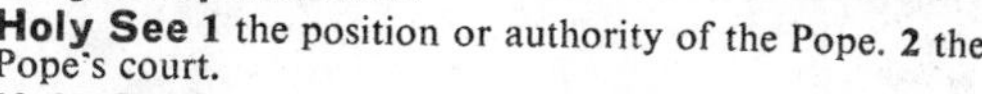

Holy Rood **1** the cross on which Jesus died. **2** a representation of it.

Holy Saturday the Saturday before Easter.

Holy Scripture Bible.

Holy See **1** the position or authority of the Pope. **2** the Pope's court.

Holy Spirit Holy Ghost.

ho·ly·stone (hō′lē stōn′) *n. v.* **-stoned, -ston·ing.** —*n.* a piece of soft sandstone used for scrubbing the wooden decks of ships. —*v.* scrub with a holystone.

Holy Synod the church council that governs an Orthodox church.

Holy Thursday **1** in the Roman Catholic Church, the Thursday before Easter. **2** in Anglican churches, the 40th day after Easter; Ascension Day.

holy water water blessed by a priest.

Holy Week the week before Easter.

Holy Writ the Bible; the Scriptures.

hom·age (hom′ij) *n.* **1** respect; reverence; honor: *Everyone paid homage to the great leader.* **2** in feudal times: **a** a formal acknowledgment by a vassal that he owed loyalty and service to his lord. **b** anything done or given to show such acknowledgment. **3** a formal statement, or oath, of loyalty and service owed to one's sovereign. [ME < OF *homage* < *hom* man, vassal < L *homo*] —**Syn. 1** deference. See **honor.**

hom·bre (om′brā or om′brē; *Spanish,* ōm′brā) *n.* man. [< Sp.]

Hom·burg (hom′bėrg) *n.* a man's felt hat having a slightly rolled brim and a crown creased lengthwise. [< *Homburg*, a German resort where it was first worn]

home (hōm) *n. adj. adv. v.* **homed, hom·ing.** —*n.* **1** the place where a person or family lives; one's own house. **2** the place where a person was born or brought up; one's own town or country. **3** a private house; a house, especially a new house built for occupation by one family: *There are some lovely homes for sale in the new subdivision.* **4** the place where an animal or plant lives: *A beaver makes his home at the water's edge.* **5** a place where a thing is very common: *The Canadian tundra is the home of the musk-ox.* **6** any place where a person can rest and be safe. **7** a place where people who are homeless, poor, old, sick, blind, etc. may live. **8** in many games, the goal. **9** in baseball, the home plate. **10 at home, a** in one's own home or country. **b** in a friendly place or familiar condition; at ease; comfortable. **c** ready to receive visitors. **d** a reception.

—*adj.* **1** having to do with one's own home or country. **2** reaching its goal; effective. **3** of or belonging to headquarters; principal: *the home office of a company.* **4** in various games: **a** having to do with, or situated at or near, home. **b** reaching, or enabling a player to reach, home.

—*adv.* 1 at, to, or toward one's own home or country: *Go home.* 2 to the place where it belongs; to the thing aimed at: *strike home.* 3 to the heart or centre; deep in: *drive a nail home.* 4 directly and effectively: *speak home.* 5 **bring home,** make clear, emphatic, or realistic. 6 **come home to,** be understood or realized by. 7 **see one home,** escort to one's home.
—*v.* 1 go home. 2 bring, carry, or send home. 3 have a home. 4 furnish with a home. 5 **home (in) on,** of a guided missile, locate and move in a straight line toward (the target). [OE *hām*] —**Syn.** *n.* 1 residence, dwelling, abode.
☛ **home, house.** In general usage *home* refers to any place that is the centre of one's family life; *house* refers only to a building. In real-estate advertising, etc. *home* is frequently used in place of *house* because of its favorable connotations.

home·bred (hōm′bred′) *adj.* 1 bred or reared at home; native; domestic. 2 not polished or refined; crude; unsophisticated. —*n. Slang.* in sports, a homebrew.

home·brew (hōm′brü′) *n.* 1 beer brewed at home. 2 *Slang.* in sports: **a** a professional athlete who is a native of the country he is playing in. **b** an athlete, usually a professional, who is a native of the region, city, etc. that his team represents.

home economics the science and art that deals with the management of a household.

home-guard Indian *Cdn.* formerly, an Indian who was employed at a fur-trading post.

home Indian a home-guard Indian.

home·land (hōm′land′) *n.* one's own or native land.

home·less (hōm′lis) *adj.* having no home. —**home′less·ness,** *n.*

home·like (hōm′līk′) *adj.* like home; friendly; familiar; comfortable. —**home′like′ness,** *n.*

home·ly (hōm′lē) *adj.* **-li·er, -li·est.** 1 not good-looking; plain: *She was rather a homely girl.* 2 suited to home life; simple; everyday: *homely pleasures, homely food.* 3 of plain manners; unpretending: *a simple, homely man.* —**home′li·ness,** *n.* —**Syn. 3** See **ugly.**

home·made (hōm′mād′) *adj.* made at home.

home·mak·er (hōm′māk′ər) *n.* a woman who manages a home and its affairs; housewife.

home·mak·ing (hōm′māk′ing) *n.* the art or practice of managing a home and looking after a family.

ho·me·o·path (hō′mē ə path′ or hom′ē ə path′) *n.* a person who practises or advocates homeopathic treatment.

ho·me·o·path·ic (hō′mē ə path′ik or hom′ē ə path′ik) *adj.* of or like homeopathy; practising or believing in homeopathy. —**ho′me·o·path′i·cal·ly,** *adv.*

ho·me·op·a·thist (hō′mē op′ə thist or hom′ē op′ə thist) *n.* homeopath.

ho·me·op·a·thy (hō′mē op′ə thē or hom′ē op′ə thē) *n.* a method of treating disease by drugs, given in very small doses, which in large doses would produce in a healthy person symptoms similar to those of the disease. [< Gk. *homoios* similar + E *-pathy*]

home-own·er (hōm′ōn′ər) *n.* a person who owns his own home.

home plate in baseball, the block or slab beside which a player stands to hit the ball, and to which he must return, after hitting the ball and rounding the bases, in order to score.

hom·er (hōm′ər) *Informal.* —*n.* 1 in baseball, a home run. 2 a homing pigeon. —*v.* hit a home run.

Ho·mer·ic (hō mer′ik) *adj.* 1 by Homer, the epic poet of Ancient Greece. 2 of or having to do with Homer or his poems. 3 in the style of Homer; having some characteristics of Homer's poems. 4 of or having to do with the age in Greek life from about 1200 to about 800 B.C.

Homeric laughter loud, hearty laughter.

home rule the management of the affairs of a country, district, or city by its own people; local self-government.

home run in baseball, a run made by a player on a hit that enables him, without aid from fielding errors of the opponents, to make the entire circuit of the bases without a stop.

home·sick (hōm′sik′) *adj.* ill or depressed because one is away from home; longing for home. —**home′sick′ness,** *n.*

home·spun (hōm′spun′) *adj.* 1 spun or made at home. 2 made of homespun cloth. 3 not polished; plain; simple: *homespun manners.* —*n.* 1 cloth made of yarn spun at home. 2 a strong, loosely woven cloth similar to homespun.

home·stead (hōm′sted′) *n.* 1 a house with its land and other buildings; a farm with its buildings. 2 in the west, a parcel of public land, usually consisting of 160 acres (a quarter section), granted to a settler under certain conditions by the federal government. —*v.* 1 settle on such land: *His father homesteaded in Saskatchewan.* 2 settle and work a farm, land, etc.: *They homesteaded a quarter section west of the river.*

Homestead Act the Act of 1872 under which settlers became homesteaders in the Canadian West.

home·stead·er (hōm′sted′ər) *n.* 1 a person who has a homestead. 2 a settler granted a homestead by the federal government.

home stretch 1 the part of a track over which the last part of a race is run. 2 the last part.

home·ward (hōm′wərd) *adv. adj.* toward home.

home·wards (hōm′wərdz) *adv.* homeward.

home·work (hōm′wėrk′) *n.* 1 work done at home. 2 a lesson or lessons to be studied or prepared outside the classroom.

home·y (hōm′ē) *adj.* **hom·i·er, hom·i·est.** *Informal.* 1 like home; cosy and comfortable. 2 homely (def. 1): *She was a homey person.*

hom·i·cid·al (hom′ə sīd′əl or hō′mə sīd′əl) *adj.* 1 having to do with homicide. 2 murderous. —**hom′i·cid′al·ly,** *adv.*

hom·i·cide[1] (hom′ə sīd′ or hō′mə sīd′) *n.* the killing of one human being by another. Intentional homicide is murder. [ME < OF < L *homicidium* < *homo* man + *-cidium* act of killing]

hom·i·cide[2] (hom′ə sīd′ or hō′mə sīd′) *n.* a person who kills a human being. [ME < OF < L *homicida* < *homo* man + *-cida* killer]

hom·i·let·ic (hom′ə let′ik) *adj.* having to do with sermons or the art of preaching. [< LL < Gk. *homilētikos* affable, ult. < *homileein* associate with < *homilos*. See HOMILY.]

hom·i·let·ics (hom′ə let′iks) *n.* the art of composing and preaching sermons.

hom·i·ly (hom′ə lē) *n.* **-lies.** 1 a sermon, usually based on some part of the Bible. 2 a serious moral talk or writing. [ME < OF *omelie* < LL < Gk. *homilia* < *homilos* throng < *homou* together + *ilē* crowd]

hom·i·nes (hom′ə nēz′) *n.* pl. of **homo.**

homing pigeon a pigeon trained to fly home from great distances. Homing pigeons are often used in racing or for carrying written messages.

hom·i·nid (hom′ə nid) *adj.* resembling or having to do with any of the group of primates that includes man. Man is the only hominid still extant. —*n.* a hominid animal. [< NL *Hominidae*, the family name]

hom·i·noid (hom′ə noid′) *adj.* like a man; of the form of a man. —*n.* a hominoid animal. [< L *homo, -inis* man + E *-oid*]

hom·i·ny (hom′ə nē) *n.* corn hulled and coarsely ground or crushed, usually eaten boiled. [< short for *rockahominy* < Algonquian]

ho·mo (hō′mō) *n.* **hom·i·nes** (hom′ə nēz′). man. [< L]

homo- *combining form.* the same, as in *homopterous.* [< Gk. *homo-* < *homos* same]

ho·mo·ge·ne·i·ty (hō′mə jə nē′ə tē or hom′ə-) *n.* the state of being homogeneous.

ho·mo·ge·ne·ous (hō′mə jē′nē əs or hō′mə jēn′yəs hom′ə jē′nē əs or hom′ə jēn′yəs) *adj.* 1 of the same kind; similar. 2 composed of similar elements or parts. 3 in mathematics: **a** of the same kind and commensurable. **b** of the same degree or dimensions. [< Med.L < Gk. *homogenēs* < *homos* same + *genos* kind] —**ho′mo·ge′ne·ous·ly,** *adv.*

ho·mog·e·nize (hə moj′ə nīz′) *v.* **-nized, -niz·ing.** make homogeneous. In **homogenized milk** the fat is distributed evenly throughout the milk and does not rise to the top in the form of cream.

hat, āge, cãre, fär; let, ēqual, tėrm; it, īce
hot, ōpen, ôrder; oil, out; cup, pu̇t, rüle, ūse
əbove, takən, pencəl, lemən, circəs
ch, child; ng, long; sh, ship
th, thin; ᴛʜ, then; zh, measure

hom·o·graph (hom′ə graf′ or hō′mə-) *n.* a word having the same spelling as another, but a different origin and meaning. *Mail,* meaning "letters," and *mail,* meaning "armor," are homographs. [< Gk. *homographos* < *homos* same + *graphē* writing]

ho·mol·o·gous (hō mol′ə gəs) *adj.* **1** corresponding in position, proportion, value, structure, etc. **2** in biology, corresponding in type of structure and in origin. The wing of a bird and the foreleg of a horse are homologous. **3** in chemistry, differing in composition successively by a constant amount of certain constituents, and showing a gradation of chemical and physical properties. [< Gk. *homologos* agreeing < *homos* same + *logos* reasoning, relation]

hom·o·logue (hom′ə log′) *n.* a homologous thing, organ, or part.

ho·mol·o·gy (hō mol′ə jē) *n.* **-gies. 1** correspondence in position, proportion, value, structure, etc. **2** in biology, correspondence in type of structure and in origin. **3** in chemistry, the relation of the compounds forming a homologous series. [< Gk. *homologia* agreement < *homologos.* See HOMOLOGOUS.]

hom·o·nym (hom′ə nim′ or hō′mə nim′) *n.* a word having the same pronunciation as another, but a different meaning. *Meat* and *meet* are homonyms. [< L < Gk. *homonymos* < *homos* same + dial. *onyma* name]

ho·mon·y·mous (hō mon′ə məs) *adj.* **1** of the nature of homonyms; alike in spelling and sound but not in meaning. **2** having, or being called by, the same name.

hom·o·phone (hom′ə fōn′ or hō′mə-) *n.* **1** a letter or symbol having the same sound as another. The letters *c* and *k* are homophones in the word *cork.* **2** a homonym. [< Gk. *homophonos* < *homos* same < *phōnē* sound]

hom·o·phon·ic (hom′ə fon′ik or hō′mə-) *adj.* **1** having the same sound. **2** in music: **a** in unison. **b** having one part or melody predominating.

ho·moph·o·nous (hō mof′ə nəs) *adj.* homophonic.

ho·moph·o·ny (hō mof′ə nē or hom′ə fō′nē) *n.* **1** sameness of sound. **2** homophonic music.

ho·mop·ter·ous (hō mop′tər əs) *adj.* belonging to a group of insects that have mouth parts adapted to sucking and wings of the same texture throughout. Aphids and cicadas are homopterous insects. [< *homo-* + Gk. *pteron* wing]

Ho·mo sa·pi·ens (hō′mō sā′pē enz or sa′pē enz) man; a human being; the species including all existing races of mankind. [< L *homo sapiens,* literally, man having wisdom]

ho·mo·sex·u·al (hō′mə sek′shü əl) *adj.* having to do with or manifesting sexual feelings for one of the same sex. *—n.* a homosexual person.

ho·mo·sex·u·al·i·ty (hō′mə sek′shü al′ə tē) *n.* the fact or quality of being homosexual.

ho·mun·cu·lus (hō mung′kyu̇ ləs) *n.* **-li** (-lī′ or -lē′). **1** a little man; dwarf. **2** a model of a little man used for demonstrating anatomy, etc. [< L *homunculus,* dim. of *homo* man]

hon. 1 honorary. **2** honorable or honourable.

Hon. 1 Honorable or Honourable. **2** Honorary. **3** Honors or Honours.

hone (hōn) *n. v.* **honed, hon·ing.** *—n.* a fine-grained whetstone on which to sharpen cutting tools, especially razors. *—v.* sharpen on a hone. [OE *hān* a stone]

hon·est (on′ist) *adj.* **1** not lying, cheating, or stealing; fair and upright; truthful: *an honest man.* **2** obtained by fair and upright means; without lying, cheating, or stealing: *honest profits.* **3** not hiding one's real nature; frank; open: *honest opposition.* **4** not mixed with something of less value; genuine; pure: *honest goods.* **5** *Archaic.* chaste; virtuous. [ME < OF < L *honestus* < *honos* honor] **—hon′est·ly,** *adv.* **—Syn. 1** just, incorruptible. **3** sincere, candid.

hon·est-to-good·ness (on′is tə gu̇d′nis) *adj. Informal.* sincere; genuine.

hon·es·ty (on′is tē) *n.* **1** fairness and uprightness. **2** truthfulness. **3** freedom from deceit or fraud. **4** a garden herb of the mustard family, with large, purple flowers and flat, round, semitransparent, satiny pods. **5** *Archaic.* chastity.

Syn. 1 Honesty, integrity = the quality of being honorable and upright in character and actions. **Honesty** emphasizes fairness and uprightness in relations with others, and refusal to steal, lie, cheat, or misrepresent: *He shows honesty in all his business affairs.* **Integrity** applies more directly to character than to actions, and means soundness of character, having very high standards of right and wrong, and refusing to do anything that does not measure up to them: *A man of integrity can be trusted.*

hon·ey (hun′ē) *n.* **hon·eys,** *adj. v.* **hon·eyed** or **hon·ied, hon·ey·ing.** *—n.* **1** a thick, sweet, yellow liquid, good to eat, that bees make out of the nectar they collect from flowers. **2** any of various similar substances produced by insects or in other ways. **3** the nectar of flowers: *Honey attracts bees to flowers.* **4** sweetness. **5** a darling; dear: *I won't be long, honey.* **6** a person or thing that is attractive: *She's a honey. His new car is a honey.* *—adj.* **1** of or like honey; sweet. **2** lovable; dear. *—v.* **1** sweeten with or as with honey. **2** talk sweetly; flatter. [OE *hunig*] **—hon′ey-like′,** *adj.*

hon·ey·bee (hun′ē bē′) *n.* a bee that makes honey.

hon·ey·comb (hun′ē kōm′) *n.* **1** a structure of wax containing rows of six-sided cells formed by bees, in which they store honey, pollen, and their eggs. **2** anything like this. *—adj.* like a honeycomb: *a honeycomb weave of cloth, a honeycomb pattern in knitting.* *—v.* **1** make or decorate like a honeycomb. **2** pierce with many holes: *The rock was honeycombed with passages.* **3** weaken or harm by spreading through: *That city is honeycombed with crime.* [OE *hunigcamb*]

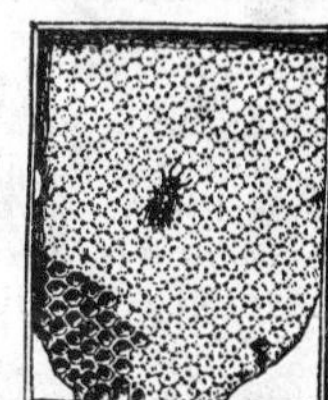

A honeycomb

hon·ey·dew (hun′ē dū′ or -dü′) *n.* **1** a sweet substance on the leaves of certain plants in hot weather. **2** a sweet substance on leaves and stems, secreted by tiny insects called aphids. **3** a honeydew melon.

honeydew melon a variety of melon having sweet, green flesh and a smooth, whitish skin.

hon·eyed or **hon·ied** (hun′ēd) *adj.* **1** sweetened with honey. **2** laden with honey. **3** sweet as honey.

honey locust a thorny North American tree having long, divided leaves and large, flat pods containing sweet pulp.

hon·ey·moon (hun′ē mün′) *n.* **1** the holiday spent together by a newly married couple. **2** the first month of marriage. **3** a period of good feeling or good relations. *—v.* spend or have a honeymoon. **—hon′ey·moon′er,** *n.*

hon·ey·suck·le (hun′ē suk′əl) *n.* **1** any of various upright or climbing shrubs or vines. Some kinds have fragrant white, yellow, or red tubular flowers. **2** any of various similar plants. [ME *hunisuccle,* dim. of OE *hunisūce* privet, literally, honey-suck < *hunig* honey + *sūcan* suck]

hon·ied (hun′ēd) *v.* a pt. and a pp. of **honey.** *—adj.* honeyed.

honk (hongk) *n.* **1** the cry of the wild goose. **2** any similar sound: *the honk of an automobile.* *—v.* make the cry of the wild goose or a similar sound. [imitative] **—honk′er,** *n.*

hon·ky-tonk (hong′kē tongk′) *Slang.* *—n.* **1** a cheap bar or drinking place. **2** a low-class dance hall, night club, etc. *—adj.* of or having to do with the entertainment or music in a low-class dance hall, etc. [? imitative of the music typically found there]

hon·or or **hon·our** (on′ər) *n.* **1** glory; fame; renown. **2** credit for acting well; good name: *It was greatly to his honor that he refused the reward.* **3** a source of credit; cause of honor. **4** a nice sense of what is right or proper; sticking to action that is right or that is usual and expected. **5** great respect; high regard: *held in honor.* **6** an act of respect: *funeral honors.* **7** rank; dignity; distinction: *Knighthood is an honor.* **8** chastity; virtue. **9** in golf, the privilege of teeing off first, awarded to the player or side winning the previous hole. **10 Honor** or **Honour,** a title used in speaking to or of a judge, mayor, etc. **11 honors**

or **honours,** *pl.* **a** special favors or courtesies. **b** a special mention, grade, or credit given to a student for unusually excellent work. **c** an honors course. **d** in the game of bridge, the ace, king, queen, jack, and ten of trumps, or the four aces in no-trump. **12 do honor** or **honour to, a** show honor to; treat with great respect. **b** cause honor to; bring honor to. **13 do the honors** or **honours,** act as host or hostess. **14 upon** (or **on**) **one's honor,** pledged to speak the truth and to do what is right: *put students on their honor not to cheat in examinations.*
—*v.* **1** respect greatly, regard highly. **2** show respect to. **3** confer dignity upon; be an honor to; favor: *be honored by a royal visit.* **4** adore or worship. **5** accept and pay (a bill, draft, note, etc.) when due. [ME < OF < L *honos, honor*] —**hon′or·er** or **hon′our·er,** *n.*
Syn. *n.* **4** integrity, uprightness. **5 Honor, deference, homage** = respect shown to someone. **Honor** = respect felt or shown in acknowledgment or appreciation of a person's high character or position or something he has done with high courage or ability: *We pay honor to heroes.* **Deference** = respect shown a person, or his age, position, or accomplishments, by putting his wishes or opinions before one's own: *In deference to his mother's wishes, he stopped smoking at the table.* **Homage** applies to honor paid with reverence or an attitude of deference: *He bowed in homage to the Unknown Soldier.* **7** eminence.

hon·or·a·ble or **hon·our·a·ble** (on′ər ə bəl) *adj.* **1** having or showing a sense of what is right and proper; honest; upright. **2** causing honor; bringing honor to the one that has it; suffered under creditable circumstances. **3** accompanied by honor or honors: *an honorable discharge.* **4** worthy of honor; to be respected; noble. **5** showing honor or respect. **6** having a title, rank, or position of honor. **7 Honorable,** Honourable.
—**hon′or·a·ble·ness** or **hon′our·a·ble·ness,** *n.*
—**hon′or·a·bly** or **hon′our·a·bly,** *adv.*

hon·o·rar·i·um (on′ə rãr′ē əm) *n.* **-rar·i·ums, -rar·i·a** (-rãr′ē ə). an honorary fee for professional services on which no fixed price is set. [< L *honorarium,* originally neut. of *honorarius* honorary]

hon·or·ar·y (on′ər er′ē) *adj.* **1** given or done as an honor. **2** as an honor only; without pay or regular duties. Some associations have honorary secretaries, etc. as well as those who are regularly employed. **3** of an obligation, depending on one's honor for fulfillment, but not enforceable otherwise. [< L *honorarius* < *honos, honor* honor]

honor course or **honour course** honors course.

honor degree or **honour degree** honors degree.

hon·or·if·ic (on′ər if′ik) *adj.* **1** doing or giving honor. **2** showing respect or deference. —*n.* a title of respect. "Sir" is an honorific.

honors course or **honours course** a university program of study, usually taking a year more than a pass course, offered to superior scholars for specialization in certain major subjects. Also, **honor course** or **honour course.**

honors degree or **honours degree** the university degree awarded to candidates successful in an honors course. Also, **honor degree** or **honour degree.**

honors list or **honours list 1** a list of persons receiving special honors or recognition. **2** *Esp.Brit.* a list of persons honored by the sovereign with titles or other distinctions.

honors of war or **honours of war** special favors or courtesies shown to a brave but defeated enemy.

honor system or **honour system** in schools and other institutions, a system of trusting people to obey the rules and do their work without being watched or forced.

hon·our (on′ər) *n. v.* honor.

Hon·our·a·ble or **Hon·or·a·ble** (on′ər ə bəl) *adj.* **1** in Canada, a title given to members of the Privy Council (which includes the Federal Cabinet), to the Speakers of both the House of Commons and the provincial legislative assemblies, and to certain senior judges. **2** in Great Britain and elsewhere, a title of respect used under various conditions.
☛ **Honourable, Honorable.** The spelling *Honourable* is usually retained in Canada as an official title for Cabinet ministers, etc. *Abbrev.*: Hon.

hooch (hüch) *n.* hootch.

hood[1] (hůd) *n.* **1** a soft covering for the head and neck, either separate or as part of a cloak. **2** anything like a hood in shape or use. **3** a metal covering over the engine of an automobile. **4** in falconry, a cover for the head of a hawk, used to blind the hawk when not pursuing game. **5** a fold of cloth, banded with distinguishing colors to show what degrees are held, that hangs down over the gown worn by graduates of universities and colleges. **6** a crest or other part on a bird's or animal's head that suggests a hood in shape, color, etc. **7** hood seal.
—*v.* cover or furnish with a hood. [OE *hōd*] —**hood′less,** *adj.* —**hood′like′,** *adj.*

hood[2] (hůd or hüd) *n. Slang.* **1** hoodlum (def. 1). **2** a criminal, especially one who uses force; thug; gunman; gangster.

-hood *suffix.* **1** the state or condition of being ——, as in *boyhood, likelihood.* **2** the character or nature of ——, as in *manhood, sainthood.* **3** a group, body of ——, as in *priesthood, a sisterhood of noble women.* [OE *-hād* < *hād* state]

hood·ed (hůd′id) *adj.* **1** having a hood. **2** shaped like a hood.

hooded seal hood seal.

hood·lum (hüd′ləm) *n. Informal.* **1** a young rowdy; street ruffian. **2** a criminal or gangster. [probably < G (Bavarian dial.) *Hodalum, Huddellump*]

hoo·doo (hü′dü) *n.* **-doos,** *v.* **-dooed, -doo·ing.** —*n.* **1** Negro magic; voodoo. **2** *Informal.* a person or thing that brings bad luck. **3** a strangely shaped formation of earth resulting from erosion. **4** *Informal.* bad luck.
—*v. Informal.* bring or cause bad luck to. [? < var. of *voodoo*]

hood seal a type of large seal found off eastern Greenland. The male has an inflatable sac on its head. Also, **hooded seal.**

hood·wink (hůd′wingk′) *v.* **1** mislead by a trick; deceive. **2** blindfold. [< *hood* + *wink,* make one wink (close the eyes) by covering with a hood] —**hood′wink·er,** *n.*

hoof (hüf or hůf) *n.* **hoofs** or (*rare*) **hooves,** *v.* —*n.* **1** a hard, horny covering on the feet of horses, cattle, sheep, pigs, and some other animals. **2** the whole foot of such animals. **3** *Humorous.* the human foot. **4 on the hoof,** alive; not killed and butchered.
—*v.* Also, **hoof it. 1** *Informal.* walk. **2** *Slang.* dance. **3** strike with the hoof. [OE *hōf*] —**hoof′less,** *adj.* —**hoof′like′,** *adj.*

hoof·beat (hüf′bēt′ or hůf′-) *n.* the sound made by an animal's hoofs.

hoofed (hüft or hůft) *adj.* having hoofs.

hoof·er (hüf′ər or hůf′ər) *n. Slang.* a professional dancer.

hook (hůk) *n.* **1** a piece of metal, wood, or other stiff material, curved or having a sharp angle for catching hold of something or for hanging things on. **2** a curved piece of wire, usually with a barb at the end, for catching fish. **3** a snare; trap. **4** anything curved or bent like a hook. **5** a large, curved knife for cutting down grass or grain. **6** a sharp bend. **7** a point of land. **8** the act of hooking. **9** in baseball, the curve made by a thrown ball. **10** in golf, a ball's path of flight curving to the left away from a right-handed player. **11** in boxing, a short, swinging blow. **12** in music, a line on the stem of certain notes. **13** in hockey, an instance of hooking. **14 by hook or by crook,** in any way at all; by fair means or foul. **15 get the hook,** *Slang.* be dismissed; lose one's job. **16 off the hook,** *Informal.* free of responsibility; out of a predicament. **17 on one's own hook,** *Informal.* independently.
—*v.* **1** attach or fasten with a hook or hooks. **2** join; fit; be fastened. **3** catch or take hold of with a hook. **4** catch (fish) with a hook. **5** give the form of a hook to. **6** be curved or bent like a hook. **7** catch by a trick. **8** *Informal.* steal. **9** make (rugs, etc.) by pulling loops of yarn or strips of cloth through canvas, burlap, etc. with a hook. **10** in baseball, throw (a ball) so that it curves. **11** in golf, hit (a ball) widely to the left. **12** in boxing, hit with a short, swinging blow. **13** in hockey, impede the progress of a puck-carrier illegally by catching at his body from the side or rear with one's hockey stick. **14 hook it,** *Slang.* run away. **15 hook up, a** attach or fasten with a hook or hooks. **b** arrange and connect the parts of (a radio set, telephone, etc.). [OE *hōc*] —**hook′like′,** *adj.*

hook·a (hůk′ə) *n.* hookah.

hook·ah (hůk′ə) *n.* a tobacco pipe with a long tube by which the smoke is drawn through water for cooling. Hookahs are used in the Orient. [< Arabic *ḥuqqah* vase, pipe]

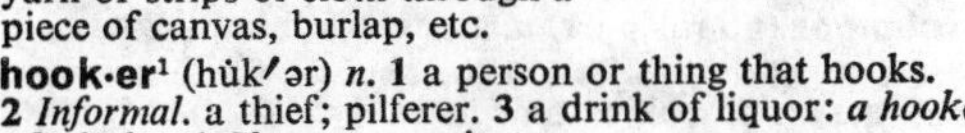

A man smoking a hookah

hook and eye a small hook and loop used as a fastener on clothing.

hooked (hůkt) *adj.* **1** curved or bent like a hook. **2** having hooks. **3** made with a hook. **4** *Slang.* addicted, especially to narcotics.

hooked rug a rug made by pulling yarn or strips of cloth through a piece of canvas, burlap, etc.

hook·er[1] (hůk′ər) *n.* **1** a person or thing that hooks. **2** *Informal.* a thief; pilferer. **3** a drink of liquor: *a hooker of whisky.* **4** *Slang.* a prostitute.

hook·er[2] (hůk′ər) *n.* **1** a small fishing boat. **2** an old-fashioned or clumsy ship. [apparently < Du. *hoeker, hoeckerschip* < *hoeck* hook; allusion uncertain]

hook·up (hůk′up′) *n.* the arrangement and connection of the parts of a radio or television set, telephone, broadcasting facilities, etc.

hook·worm (hůk′wėrm′) *n.* **1** a worm that gets into the intestines and causes a disease characterized by weakness and drowsiness. **2** the disease.

hook·y (hůk′ē) *n.* **play hooky,** *Informal.* stay away from school without permission; play truant.

hoo·li·gan (hü′lə gən) *n. Informal.* one of a gang of street ruffians; hoodlum. [? < an Irish surname]

hoo·li·gan·ism (hü′lə gən iz′əm) *n. Informal.* rough, noisy behavior; lawless fun.

hoop (hüp) *n.* **1** a ring or flat band in the form of a circle: *A hoop holds together the staves of a barrel.* **2** a large wooden, metal or plastic ring used as a toy: *The boy rolled his hoop along the sidewalk.* **3** a circular frame formerly used to hold out a woman's skirt. **4** in croquet, an iron arch or piece of wire shaped like an arch. **5** anything shaped like a hoop. —*v.* fasten together with hoops. [OE *hōp*] —**hoop′like′,** *adj.*

hoop·er (hůp′ər) *n.* a man who makes or repairs hoops on casks, barrels, etc.; cooper.

hoop·la (hůp′lä) *n. Slang.* **1** uproar; hullabaloo. **2** sensational advertising; ballyhoo. [originally, a coach driver's exclamation]

hoo·poe (hü′pü) *n.* a bright-colored bird of Europe having a long, sharp bill and a fanlike crest on its head. [earlier *hoop* < F *huppe* < L *upupa* (imitative of its cry)]

hoop skirt 1 an arrangement of flexible hoops connected by tapes, worn to expand a woman's skirt. **2** a skirt worn over such a frame.

A hoop skirt

hoo·ray (hů rā′) *interj. n. v.* hurrah.

hoot (hüt) *n.* **1** the sound that an owl makes. **2** a sound like that made by an owl: *the hoot of an automobile horn.* **3** a sound to show disapproval or scorn. **4** a damn: *I don't give a hoot.* [< v.]
—*v.* **1** make the sound that an owl makes or one like it. **2** make a sound to show disapproval or scorn. **3** show disapproval of, or scorn for, by hooting: *The audience hooted the speaker's plan.* **4** force or drive by hooting: *They hooted him off the platform.* **5** say or show by hooting. [ME *hute(n)*; ? imitative] —**hoot′er,** *n.*

hootch (hüch) *n.* **1** hootchinoo. **2** *Slang.* any alcoholic liquor, especially cheap whisky. [shortening of *hootchinoo*]

hoo·tchi·noo (hü′chi nü′) *n.* in the Yukon and Alaska, a potent alcoholic liquor distilled illegally. [< *Hootchinoo,* an Indian people of S. Alaska < Tlingit *khutsnuwu* (literally, grizzly bear fort)]

hoo·te·nan·ny (hüt′nan′ē) *n.* **-nies.** an informal party or jamboree featuring folk-singing. [developed from *hoot*]

hooves (hüvz or hůvz) *n.* a pl. of **hoof.**

hop[1] (hop) *v.* **hopped, hop·ping,** *n.* —*v.* **1** spring, or move by springing, on one foot. **2** spring, or move by springing, with all feet at once: *Many birds hop.* **3** jump over: *hop a ditch.* **4** *Informal.* jump on (a train, car, etc.). **5** *Informal.* fly across in an airplane. **6** dance. **7 hop it,** *Slang.* depart; go away. **8 hop off,** *Informal.* **a** get off or out of quickly or with a jump: *He hopped off the ladder.* **b** rise from the ground in an airplane. **9 hop on,** *Informal.* get on or into quickly or with a jump: *He hopped on the bus.*
—*n.* **1** a hopping; spring. **2** *Informal.* a flight in an airplane. **3** *Informal.* a dancing party; a dance. **4** *Informal.* a dance. [OE *hoppian*]

hat, āge, cãre, fär; let, ēqual, tėrm; it, īce
hot, ōpen, ôrder; oil, out; cup, půt, rüle, ūse
əbove, takən, pencəl, lemən, circəs
ch, child; ng, long; sh, ship
th, thin; ᴛʜ, then; zh, measure

hop[2] (hop) *n. v.* **hopped, hop·ping.** —*n.* **1** a vine having flower clusters that look like small, yellow pine cones. **2 hops,** *pl.* the dried, ripe, flower clusters of the hop vine, used to flavor beer and other malt drinks.
—*v.* **1** pick hops. **2** flavor with hops. [< MDu. *hoppe*]

hope (hōp) *n. v.* **hoped, hop·ing.** —*n.* **1** an expectation that what one desires will happen. **2** a person or thing in which one places hope: *He is the hope of the family.* **3** something hoped for. **4** *Archaic.* trust; reliance.
—*v.* **1** wish and expect. **2** *Archaic.* trust; rely. **3 hope against hope,** keep on hoping even though there is no good reason to have hope. [OE *hopa*] —**Syn.** *n.* **1** expectation, anticipation, optimism.

hope chest a chest in which a young woman collects articles that will be useful after she marries.

hope·ful (hōp′fəl) *adj.* **1** feeling or showing hope; expecting to receive what one wants. **2** causing hope; giving hope; likely to succeed. —*n.* **1 young hopeful,** a boy or girl thought likely to succeed. **2** a person who hopes to obtain or achieve something. —**hope′ful·ly,** *adv.* —**hope′ful·ness,** *n.*

hope·less (hōp′lis) *adj.* **1** feeling no hope. **2** giving no hope: *a hopeless illness.* —**hope′less·ly,** *adv.* —**hope′less·ness,** *n.*

Syn. 1 Hopeless, desperate, despairing = without hope. **Hopeless** suggests giving up completely and being willing to take patiently whatever comes: *He was disappointed so often that he became hopeless.* **Desperate** suggests a rash hopelessness, being without real hope but willing to run any risk to improve the situation: *The desperate gunman tried to shoot his way out of the trap.* **Despairing** = completely hopeless because unable to think of anything else to do or anywhere else to look for help: *Despairing of saving his business, he shot himself.*

Ho·pi (hō′pē) *n.* **-pis. 1** a tribe of Pueblo Indians living mainly in stone-built towns in N. Arizona. **2** a member of this tribe. **3** the language of this tribe.

hop·lite (hop′līt) *n.* in ancient Greece, a heavily armed foot soldier. [< Gk. *hoplītēs* < *hopla* arms]

hopped-up (hopt′up′) *adj. Slang.* **1** exhilarated; excited. **2** stimulated by drugs; high. **3** of engines, supercharged.

hop·per (hop′ər) *n.* **1** a person or thing that hops. **2** a grasshopper or other hopping insect. **3** a container into which substances are put before being fed or emptied into something else; the part of a machine into which substances are put so that they may be fed into another part of the machine: *Some cement mixers are equipped with hoppers. There is a hopper at the top of a coffee grinder.*

hop·scotch (hop′skoch′) *n.* a children's game in which the players hop over the lines of a figure drawn on the ground. [< *hop*[1] + *scotch* a scratch, line]

Ho·ra·tian (hə rā′shən) *adj.* of, like, or having to do with the Roman poet and satirist Horace (65-8 B.C.) or his poetry.

Ho·ra·tius (hə rā′shəs) *n.* in Roman legend, a Roman hero who held back an invading Etruscan army until a bridge behind him was destroyed.

horde (hôrd) *n.* **1** a crowd; swarm. **2** a wandering tribe or troop: *Hordes of Mongols and Turks invaded Europe during the Middle Ages.* —*v.* gather in a horde; live in a horde. [< F < G < Polish < Turkish *ordu* camp]

hore·hound (hôr′hound′) *n.* **1** a plant of the same family as the mint, having woolly, whitish leaves and clusters of small, whitish flowers. **2** a bitter extract made from the leaves of this plant. **3** candy or cough medicine flavored with this extract. Also, **hoarhound.** [OE *hārhūne* < *hār* hoar + *hūne*, the name of a plant]

ho·ri·zon (hə rī′zən) *n.* **1** the line where the earth and sky seem to meet. You cannot see beyond the horizon. **2** the limit of one's thinking, experience, interest, or outlook. **3** the actual or imaginary horizontal line in perspective drawing, etc., toward which receding parallel lines converge. It represents the eye level of the observer. **4** in geology, a distinct layer or group of layers of rock or soil. [ME < OF *orizonte* < L < Gk. *horizōn* (*kyklos*) bounding (circle), ult. < *horos* limit] **—ho·ri·zon·less,** *adj.*

hor·i·zon·tal (hôr′ə zon′təl) *adj.* **1** parallel to the horizon; at right angles to a vertical line. **2** flat; level. **3** placed, acting, or working wholly or mainly in a horizontal direction. **4** of or having to do with the horizon; on, at, or near the horizon. **5** so organized as to include only one stage in production or one group of people or crafts: *a horizontal union, horizontal trusts.*

VERTICAL

HORIZONTAL

—*n.* a horizontal line, plane, direction, position, etc. **—hor′i·zon′tal·ly,** *adv.*

horizontal bar in gymnastics, a bar hung horizontally a few feet from the floor for chinning and other exercises.

hor·mone (hôr′mōn) *n.* **1** in physiology, a substance formed in certain parts of the body, which enters the blood stream and influences the activity of some organ. Adrenalin and insulin are hormones. **2** in botany, a substance carried in the sap of plants that acts similarly. [< Gk. *hormōn* setting in motion, ult. < *hormē* impulse] **—hor·mo′nal,** *adj.*

horn (hôrn) *n.* **1** a hard growth, usually curved and pointed, on the heads of cattle, sheep, goats, and certain other animals. **2** one of a pair of branching growths on the head of a deer, which fall off and grow afresh each year. **3** anything that sticks up on the head of an animal: *a snail's horns, an insect's horns.* **4** the substance or material of horns. **5** any similar material, as that of hoofs, nails, etc. **6** something made, or formerly made, of horn. **7** a container made by hollowing out a horn: *a drinking horn, a powder horn.* **8** any one of several musical instruments resembling a horn in shape and sounded by blowing into the smaller end: *a hunting horn, a French horn, an English horn.* **9** a device sounded as a warning signal: *a foghorn, an automobile horn.* **10** anything that projects like a horn or is shaped like a horn: *a saddle horn, the horn of a bay.* **11** either pointed tip of a new or old moon, or of some other crescent. **12 draw** or **pull in one's horns, a** restrain oneself. **b** back down; withdraw. **13 horns of a dilemma,** two unpleasant choices, one of which must be taken.
—*adj.* made of horn.
—*v.* **1** hit or wound with horns; gore. **2** furnish with horns. **3** make horn-shaped. **4 horn in,** *Slang.* meddle; intrude. [OE] **—horn′less,** *adj.* **—horn′like′,** *adj.*

horn·beam (hôrn′bēm′) *n.* a tree or shrub of the same family as the birch, having very hard wood.

horn·bill (hôrn′bil′) *n.* a large bird having a very large bill with a horn or horny lump on it.

horn·blende (hôrn′blend′) *n.* a common black, dark-green, or brown mineral found in granite and other rocks. [< F]

horn·book (hôrn′bu̇k′) *n.* **1** a page with the alphabet, etc. on it, covered with a sheet of transparent horn and fastened in a frame with a handle, formerly used in teaching children to read. **2** a primer.

horned (hôrnd) *adj.* having a horn or horns.

horned toad a small lizard having a broad, flat body, short tail, and many spines on its head and back.

hor·net (hôr′nit) *n.* a large wasp that can give a painful sting. [OE *hyrnet*(*u*); form influenced by E *horn*]

hornet's nest 1 trouble in store; a situation likely to be troublesome. **2 stir up a hornet's nest,** cause an outburst or angry reaction.

horn of plenty 1 a horn-shaped container overflowing with fruits, vegetables, and flowers. **2** a horn-shaped container or ornament; cornucopia. See **cornucopia** for picture.

horn·pipe (hôrn′pīp′) *n.* **1** a lively dance done by one person, formerly popular among sailors. **2** the music for it. **3** in former times, a musical wind instrument consisting of a wooden pipe with a bell-shaped end.

horn·worm (hôrn′wėrm′) *n.* a caterpillar, the larva of a hawk moth, having a hornlike tailpiece.

horn·y (hôr′nē) *adj.* **horn·i·er, horn·i·est. 1** made of horn or a substance like it. **2** hard like horn: *A farmer's hands are horny from work.* **3** having a horn or horns.

hor·o·loge (hôr′ə lōj′ or hôr′ə loj′) *n.* a timepiece; clock, sundial, hourglass, etc. [ME < OF *orloge* < L < Gk. *hōrologion* < *hōra* hour + *-logos* -telling]

ho·rol·o·ger (hô rol′ə jər) *n.* an expert in horology.

ho·rol·o·gy (hô rol′ə jē) *n.* **1** the science of measuring time. **2** the art of making timepieces. [< Gk. *hōra* time + E *-logy*]

hor·o·scope (hôr′ə skōp′) *n.* in astrology: **1** the position of the planets and stars relative to each other at the hour of a person's birth, regarded as influencing his life. **2** a diagram of the heavens at given times, used in telling fortunes by the planets and the stars. **3** a fortune told by this means. **4 cast a horoscope,** discover the influence that the stars and planets are supposed to have upon a person's life. [< L < Gk. *hōroskopos* < *hōra* time + *skopos* watcher]

ho·ros·co·py (hô ros′kə pē) *n.* **1** the practice of casting horoscopes. **2** the position of the planets, especially at a person's birth.

hor·ren·dous (hô ren′dəs) *adj.* horrible; terrible; frightful. [< L *horrendus*] **—hor·ren′dous·ly,** *adv.*

hor·ri·ble (hôr′ə bəl) *adj.* **1** causing horror; terrible; dreadful; frightful; shocking: *a horrible crime, a horrible disease.* **2** *Informal.* extremely unpleasant or amazing: *a horrible noise.* [ME < OF < L *horribilis* < *horrere* bristle] **—hor′ri·ble·ness,** *n.* **—hor′ri·bly,** *adv.* **—Syn. 1** hideous, grim, horrid. See **ghastly.**

hor·rid (hôr′id) *adj.* **1** terrible; frightful. **2** *Informal.* very unpleasant: *a horrid little boy, a horrid day.* [< L *horridus*] **—hor′rid·ly,** *adv.* **—hor′rid·ness,** *n.*

hor·rif·ic (hô rif′ik) *adj.* producing horror; horrifying.

hor·ri·fy (hôr′ə fī′) *v.* **-fied, -fy·ing. 1** cause to feel horror. **2** *Informal.* shock very much. [< L *horrificare*]

hor·ror (hôr′ər) *n.* **1** a shivering, shaking fear and dislike; terror and disgust caused by something frightful or shocking. **2** a very strong dislike; very great disgust. **3** the quality of causing horror. **4** a cause of horror. **5** *Informal.* something very bad or unpleasant. **6 the horrors,** *Informal.* **a** a fit of horror, as in delirium tremens. **b** extreme depressions; the blues. [ME < OF < L *horror* < *horrere* bristle] **—Syn. 1** dread. **2** loathing, abhorrence, aversion.

hors de com·bat (ôr də kôɴ bä′) *French.* out of the fight; disabled.

hors d'oeu·vre (ôr′ dėrv′; *French,* ôr dœ′vr) *pl.* **hors d'oeu·vres** (dėrvz′; *French,* dœ′vr). a relish or light dish served before the regular courses of a meal: *Olives, celery, anchovies, etc. are hors d'oeuvres.* [< F *hors d'œuvre,* literally, apart from (the main) work]

horse (hôrs) *n.* **hors·es** or (*esp. collectively*) **horse,** *v.* **horsed, hors·ing,** *adj.* —*n.* **1** a four-legged mammal with solid hoofs and flowing mane and tail, used from very early times to draw loads, carry riders, etc. **2** a full-grown male horse. **3** any animal of the same family as the horse, including asses and zebras. **4** any of various extinct animal species thought to be ancestors of the present horse, such as the eohippus. **5** soldiers on horses; cavalry: *six thousand horse.* **6** a piece of gymnasium apparatus to jump or vault over. **7** a frame with legs to support something; trestle. **8 a horse of a different color,** something different. **9 to horse!** mount horses! get on horseback!
—*v.* **1** provide with a horse or horses. **2** put or go on horseback. **3** set or carry on a person's back; carry on one's own back. **4** *Informal.* make fun of; play jokes on. **5** *Slang.* perform boisterously, as a part or a scene in a play. **6 horse around,** *Slang.* fool around; get into mischief.
—*adj.* **1** having to do with horses. **2** on horses. [OE *hors*]

horse-and-bug·gy (hôrs′ ən bug′ē) *adj.* out-dated; old-fashioned: *horse-and-buggy ideas.*

hat, āge, cãre, fär; let, ēqual, tėrm; it, īce
hot, ōpen, ôrder; oil, out; cup, pu̇t, rüle, ūse
əbove, takən, pencəl, lemən, circəs
ch, child; ng, long; sh, ship
th, thin; ᴛʜ, then; zh, measure

horse·back (hôrs′bak′) *n.* the back of a horse. —*adv.* on the back of a horse.

horse-boat (hôrs′bōt′) *n.* a kind of ferry boat in use before the steamboat. Horses, carried in the horse-boat, turned the paddle wheel.

horse·car (hōrs′kär′) *n.* **1** a streetcar pulled by a horse or horses. **2** a car used for transporting horses.

horse chestnut **1** a shade tree having spreading branches, large leaves, clusters of showy, white flowers, and glossy, brown nuts. **2** the nut. **3** any tree or shrub of the same family as the horse chestnut.

horse·draw·ing (hôrs′dro′ing or -drô′ing) *n.* a contest in which horses or teams of horses draw increasingly heavier loads on a stoneboat until all but the strongest are eliminated. Also, **horse-hauling.**

horse·flesh (hôrs′flesh′) *n.* **1** horses for riding, driving, and racing. **2** meat from horses.

horse·fly (hôrs′flī′) *n.* **-flies.** a large fly that bites mammals, especially horses.

horse·hair (hôrs′hãr′) *n.* **1** the hair from the mane or tail of a horse. **2** a stiff fabric made of this hair. **3** a similar fabric made of a synthetic material. —*adj.* made of horsehair; covered with material made of horsehair; stuffed with horsehair.

horse-haul·ing (hôrs′hol′ing or -hôl′ing) *n.* horsedrawing.

horse·hide (hôrs′hīd′) *n.* **1** the hide of a horse. **2** leather made from this hide.

horse latitudes two regions where there is often very calm weather and that extend around the world at about 30° north and 30° south of the equator.

horse laugh *Informal.* a loud, boisterous laugh.

horse·leech (hôrs′lēch′) *n.* a large leech, supposed to attack the mouths of horses while they are drinking.

horse·less (hôrs′lis) *adj.* **1** without a horse. **2** not requiring a horse; self-propelled: *Automobiles used to be called horseless carriages.*

horse·man (hôrs′mən) *n.* **-men** (-mən). **1** a man who rides on horseback. **2** a man skilled in riding or managing horses.

horse·man·ship (hôrs′mən ship′) *n.* the art of riding on horseback; skill in riding or managing horses.

horse marine *Humorous.* **1** a member of an imaginary corps of marines mounted on horseback, or cavalrymen doing duty on shipboard. **2** a person out of his natural surroundings.

horse·meat (hôrs′mēt′) *n.* the meat or flesh of a horse, especially when used for food.

horse opera *Slang.* a motion picture, radio or television drama, etc. about cowboys, horses, etc.; western.

horse pistol a large pistol formerly carried by horsemen.

horse·play (hôrs′plā′) *n.* rough, boisterous fun.

horse·pow·er (hôrs′pou′ər) *n.* a unit for measuring the power of engines, motors, etc.; 1 horsepower = 550 foot-pounds per second. *Abbrev.*: HP, H.P., or h.p.

horse·rad·ish (hôrs′rad′ish) *n.* **1** a tall plant having a white, hot-tasting root that is ground up and used as a relish with meat, oysters, etc. **2** the root of this plant. **3** a relish made of this root.

horse sense *Informal.* common sense; plain, practical good sense.

horse·shoe (hôrs′shü′ or hôrsh′-) *n. v.* **-shoed, -shoe·ing.** —*n.* **1** a U-shaped metal plate nailed to a horse's hoof to protect it. **2** anything shaped like a horseshoe: *a horseshoe of flowers.* **3** **horseshoes,** *pl.* a game in which the players try to throw horseshoes over or near a stake 40 feet away. —*v.* put a horseshoe or horseshoes on.

☛ Horseshoes (def. 3), is plural in form and singular in use: *Horseshoes is often played by men.*

A horseshoe

horseshoe crab a crablike sea animal having a body shaped like a horseshoe and a long, spiny tail; king crab.

horse·sho·er (hôrs′shü′ər or hôrsh′-) *n.* a man who puts horseshoes on horses.

horse·tail (hôrs′tāl′) *n.* **1** a horse's tail. **2** in Turkey, a horse's tail formerly used as a military standard or to show the rank of a pasha. **3** a flowerless plant having hollow, jointed stems and scale-like leaves at each joint.

horse trader **1** a buyer or seller of horses. **2** a shrewd negotiator.

horse·whip (hôrs′hwip′ or -wip′) *n. v.* **-whipped, -whip·ping.** —*n.* a whip for driving or controlling horses. —*v.* beat with a horsewhip.

horse·wom·an (hôrs′wu̇m′ən) *n.* **-wom·en. 1** a woman who rides on horseback. **2** a woman skilled in riding or managing horses.

hors·y (hôr′sē) *adj.* **hors·i·er, hors·i·est. 1** of, like, or having to do with horses. **2** fond of horses or horse racing. **3** dressing or talking like people who spend much time with horses. **4** *Slang.* large and awkward in appearance. **—hors′i·ly,** *adv.* **—hors′i·ness,** *n.*

hor·ta·tive (hôr′tə tiv) *adj.* tending to exhort or encourage; hortatory. —*n.* an exhortation. **—hor′ta·tive·ly,** *adv.*

hor·ta·to·ry (hôr′tə tô′rē) *adj.* serving to urge or encourage; giving advice; exhorting. [< LL *hortatorius* < L *hortari* exhort]

hor·ti·cul·tur·al (hôr′tə kul′chər əl) *adj.* having to do with the growing of flowers, fruits, vegetables, plants, etc. **—hor′ti·cul′tur·al·ly,** *adv.*

hor·ti·cul·ture (hôr′tə kul′chər) *n.* **1** the science of growing flowers, fruits, vegetables, etc. **2** the cultivation of a garden. [< L *hortus* garden + E *culture*]

hor·ti·cul·tur·ist (hôr′tə kul′chər ist) *n.* a person skilled in horticulture.

Ho·rus (hô′rəs) *n.* a sun god of ancient Egypt, son of Osiris and Isis. Horus was represented as having the head of a hawk.

Hos. Hosea.

ho·san·na (hō zan′ə) *interj. n.* **1** a shout of praise to the Lord. **2** a shout of praise, adoration, etc. [< LL < Gk. < Hebrew *hoshi'ahnna* save now, we pray]

hose (hōz) *n.* **hose,** (*Archaic*) **ho·sen** (hō′zən) *for 1 and 2,* **hos·es** *for 3, v.* **hosed, hos·ing.** —*n.* **1** socks or, especially stockings. **2** a close-fitting outer garment extending from the waist to the toes, formerly worn by men. **3** a tube made of rubber, plastic, canvas, or other material that will bend, used to carry water or other liquids for short distances. —*v.* **1** put water on with a hose. **2** *Slang.* **a** get the better of. **b** cheat; trick. [OE *hosa*]

ho·sier (hō′zhər) *n.* a person who makes or sells hosiery.

ho·sier·y (hō′zhər ē or hōzh′rē) *n.* **1** hose; stockings. **2** the business of a hosier.

hos·pice (hos′pis) *n.* a house where travellers can lodge, often kept by monks. [< F < L *hospitium* < *hospes, -pitis* guest, host[1]]

hos·pi·ta·ble (hos′pi tə bəl or hos pit′ə bəl) *adj.* **1** giving or liking to give a welcome, food and shelter, and friendly treatment to guests or strangers: *a hospitable family, reception, etc.* **2** willing and ready to entertain; favorably receptive or open: *a person hospitable to new ideas.* [ME < L *hospitari* stay as a guest < *hospes, -pitis* guest, host[1]] **—hos′pi·ta·bly,** *adv.* **—hos′pi·ta·ble·ness,** *n.*

hos·pi·tal (hos′pi təl) *n.* **1** a place where sick or injured people are cared for. **2** a similar place for sick or injured animals. [ME < OF < Med.L *hospitale* inn, sing. of L *hospitalia* guest rooms, ult. < *hospes, -pitis* guest, host[1]. Doublet of HOSTEL, HOTEL.]

Hos·pi·tal·er or **Hos·pi·tal·ler** (hos′pi tə lər) *n.* **1** a member of a military religious order, the Knights of the Hospital of St. John of Jerusalem (or the Knights Hospitalers), founded by Crusaders in the 11th century. **2** a member of any religious order founded to take care of the sick, or for other charitable purposes.

hos·pi·tal·i·ty (hos′pə tal′ə tē) *n.* **-ties.** friendly, generous reception and treatment of guests or strangers. [< L *hospitalitas* < *hospes* guest, host[1]]

hos·pi·tal·ize (hos′ pi tәl īz′) *v.* **-ized, -iz·ing. 1** put in a hospital. **2** accustom to hospital treatment.
—hos′ pi·tal·i·za′ tion, *n.*

host[1] (hōst) *n.* **1** a person who receives another at his house as his guest. **2** the keeper of an inn or hotel. **3** in biology, a plant or animal in or on which a parasite lives: *The oak tree is the host of the mistletoe that grows on it.* **4 reckon without one's host, a** overlook the chances of one's plans going wrong. **b** calculate one's bill or score without consulting the host or landlord.
—*v.* act as host. [ME < OF < L *hospes, -pitis* guest, host]

host[2] (hōst) *n.* **1** a large number; multitude: *A host of stars glittered in the sky.* **2** an army. [ME < OF < LL *hostis* army < L *hostis* enemy (originally, stranger)]

Host (hōst) *n.* in the Roman Catholic Church, the bread or wafer used in the Mass. [ME < OF *oiste* < L *hostia* animal sacrificed; form influenced by *host*[1]]

hos·tage (hos′ tij) *n.* **1** a person given up to another or held by an enemy as a pledge that certain promises, agreements, etc. will be carried out. **2** the state or condition of such a person. **3** a pledge; security. **4 give hostages to fortune,** have persons or things that one may lose. [ME < OF *hostage, ostage* status of guest, status of hostage, hostage < *oste* guest < L *hospes, -pitis*]

hos·tel (hos′ tәl) *n.* **1** a lodging place, especially a supervised lodging place for travellers. **2** an inn; hotel. [ME < OF *hostel, ostel* < Med.L *hospitale* inn. Doublet of HOSPITAL, HOTEL.]

hos·tel·ry (hos′ tәl rē) *n.* **-ries.** an inn; hotel.

hostel school *Cdn.* in the North, a boarding school run by the federal government for Indian and Eskimo children.

host·ess (hōs′ tis) *n.* **1** a woman who receives another person as her guest. **2** a woman who keeps an inn or hotel, or helps her husband to do so. **3** a woman paid to greet, entertain, or dance with guests, travellers, etc.

hos·tile (hos′ tīl or hos′ tәl) *adj.* **1** of or having to do with an enemy or enemies. **2** opposed; unfriendly; unfavorable. [< L *hostilis* < *hostis* enemy]
—hos′ tile·ly, *adv.*

Syn. 2 Hostile, unfriendly, inimical = not friendly or favorable. **Hostile,** describing people or things, emphasizes being opposed, either actively unfriendly in purpose or spirit or openly acting against a person or thing: *Their hostile looks showed that he was unwelcome.* **Unfriendly** places less emphasis on active ill will, and suggests being unwilling to be agreeable, kindly, helpful, or encouraging in any way: *A cold, damp climate is unfriendly to tuberculosis.* **Inimical,** a formal word meaning "hostile," particularly suggests having harmful effects: *Jealousy is inimical to friendship.*

hos·til·i·ty (hos til′ ә tē) *n.* **-ties. 1** the feeling that an enemy has; the state of being an enemy; unfriendliness. **2** the state of being at war. **3** opposition; resistance. **4** a hostile act. **5 hostilities,** *pl.* acts of war; warfare; fighting.

hos·tler (os′ lәr or hos′ lәr) *n.* a person who takes care of horses at an inn or stable. Also, **ostler.** [var. of *ostler* < OF *hostelier* < *hostel.* See HOSTEL.]

hot (hot) *adj.* **hot·ter, hot·test,** *adv.* —*adj.* **1** much warmer than the body; having much heat: *That fire is hot.* **2** having a relatively high temperature: *This food is too hot to eat.* **3** having a sharp, burning taste: *Pepper and mustard are hot.* **4** full of any strong feeling; passionate, violent, angry, etc.: *hot with rage.* **5** full of great interest or enthusiasm; very eager. **6** intense; violent: *a hot fight.* **7** new; fresh: *a hot scent or trail.* **8** near or approaching an object or answer sought. **9** following closely: *in hot pursuit.* **10** charged with radio-activity; radio-active: *the hot debris left by an atomic explosion.* **11** electrically charged. **12** of jazz, played or playing with exciting variations from the score. **13** open and ready for instantaneous use: *the hot line between the White House and the Kremlin.* **14** *Slang.* obtained illegally; stolen: *hot diamonds.* **15** *Slang.* wanted by the police. **16** *Slang.* likely to win or succeed; difficult to beat, stop, or hinder: *a hot favorite, a hot team.* **17 make it hot for,** *Informal.* make trouble for; make things unpleasant or uncomfortable for.
—*adv.* **1** in a hot manner. **2 blow hot and cold,** waver in mind or opinion: vacillate. [OE *hāt*] **—hot′ ly,** *adv.* **—hot′ ness,** *n.* **—Syn.** *adj.* **1** scorching, scalding. **3** pungent, peppery. **5** ardent, fervent, fervid.

hot air *Slang.* empty, showy talk or writing.

hot atom an atom whose nucleus is radio-active.

hot·bed (hot′ bed′) *n.* **1** a bed of earth covered with glass and kept warm for the growing of plants. **2** any place favorable to rapid growth: *These slums are a hotbed of crime.*

hot-blood·ed (hot′ blud′ id) *adj.* **1** easily excited or angered. **2** rash; reckless. **3** passionate.

hot·box (hot′ boks′) *n.* an overheated bearing on a shaft or axle.

hot cake 1 a flapjack or pancake. **2 go** or **sell like hot cakes, a** be sold quickly. **b** be in great demand.

hotch·potch (hoch′ poch′) *n.* hodgepodge.

hot cross bun a bun marked with a cross, eaten during Lent, especially on Good Friday.

hot dog 1 a wiener. **2** a sandwich made of a hot wiener enclosed in a long roll and usually served with mustard, relish, etc.

ho·tel (hō tel′) *n.* **1** a building where rooms may be rented and meals bought on a day-to-day basis. **2** a place where beer and wine are sold for drinking on the premises; beer parlor. [< F *hôtel* < OF *hostel* < Med.L *hospitale* inn. Doublet of HOSPITAL, HOSTEL.]

hô·tel de ville (ō tel dә vēl′) *French.* city hall; town hall.

hot·foot (hot′ fu̇t′) *Informal.* —*adv.* in great haste.
—*v.* go in great haste; hurry.

hot·head (hot′ hed′) *n.* a hot-headed person.

hot-head·ed (hot′ hed′ id) *adj.* **1** having a fiery temper; easily angered. **2** impetuous; rash. **—hot′ -head′ ed·ly,** *adv.* **—hot′ -head′ ed·ness,** *n.*

hot·house (hot′ hous′) *n.* a building with a glass roof and sides, kept warm for the growing of plants; greenhouse.

hot laboratory or **lab** a laboratory exposed to radiations of more than one curie.

hot plate 1 a small, portable, gas or electric stove for cooking. **2** a plate of hot food. **3** a covered plate to keep food hot. **4** a heating unit on the top of a stove.

hot potato *Slang.* something too controversial or too complex to handle.

hot·press (hot′ pres′) *n.* a machine in which heat and pressure are applied together.

hot rod *Slang.* a rebuilt or modified automobile with a supercharged engine.

hot rodder (rod′ әr) *Slang.* a person who drives a hot rod.

hot·spur (hot′ spėr′) *n.* an impetuous or reckless person. [< *Hotspur*, the nickname of Sir Henry Percy (1364-1403), portrayed as an impetuous character in Shakespeare's *Henry IV, Part I*]

hot-tem·pered (hot′ tem′ pәrd) *adj.* having a quick temper; easily angered.

Hot·ten·tot (hot′ әn tot′) *n.* **1** a South African race having a dark, yellowish-brown complexion. **2** a member of this people. **3** their language. —*adj.* of the Hottentots or their language. [native word]

hot war a war involving actual fighting; opposed to *cold war.*

hot water *Informal.* trouble.

hou·dah (hou′ dә) *n.* howdah.

hough (hok) *n.* hock[1].

hound (hound) *n.* **1** any of various breeds of hunting dog that chase their quarry. Some hounds, such as bloodhounds and foxhounds, follow a foot scent; others, such as greyhounds and Afghans, hunt by sight. **2** a dog of any of these breeds. **3** any dog. **4** a contemptible person. **5** *Slang.* a person who is very fond of something. **6 follow the hounds** or **ride to hounds,** go hunting on horseback with hounds.
—*v.* **1** hunt; chase: *The police hounded the thief until they caught him.* **2** urge (on): *His parents hounded him to do his homework.* [OE *hund*]

hound's tooth or **hounds-tooth** (houndz′ tüth′) *adj.* in textiles, having a pattern of broken checks.

hat, āge, cãre, fär; let, ēqual, tėrm; it, īce
hot, ōpen, ôrder; oil, out; cup, pût, rüle, ūse
əbove, takən, pencəl, lemən, circəs
ch, child; ng, long; sh, ship
th, thin; ᴛʜ, then; zh, measure

hour (our) *n.* **1** 60 minutes; 1/24 of a day. **2** one of the 12 points that measure time from noon to midnight and from midnight to noon: *Some clocks strike the hours and the half-hours.* **3** the time of day: *The hour is 7.30.* **4** a particular or fixed time: *Our breakfast hour is at seven o'clock.* **5** a short or limited space of time: *After his hour of glory, he was soon forgotten.* **6** a period in a classroom, often less than a full hour. **7** the present time: *questions of the hour, the man of the hour.* **8** 15 degrees of longitude. **9 hours,** *pl.* **a** the time for work, study, etc.: *Our school hours are 9 to 12 and 1 to 4.* **b** the usual times for going to bed and getting up. **c** seven special times of the day set aside for prayer and worship. **d** the prayers or services for these times. **e Hours,** the Greek goddesses of the seasons, orderliness, justice, and peace. **10 in an evil hour,** at a bad or unlucky time. [ME < OF *hure* < L < Gk. *hōra* season, time, hour]

☛ **hours.** In very formal writing, hours are written in words: *four o'clock.* In most informal writing, figures are used with the abbreviations "a.m." and "p.m.," especially if several times are mentioned.

hour·glass (our′glas′) *n.* a device for measuring time, requiring just an hour for its contents, sand or mercury, to go from a glass bulb or container on top to one on the bottom. —*adj.* shaped like an hourglass, with a very narrow central section swelling outward at each end.

An hourglass

hour hand the short hand on a clock or watch, which moves around the whole dial once in twelve hours.

hou·ri (hür′ē or hou′rē) *n.* **-ris.** one of the young, eternally beautiful maidens promised in the Koran to the faithful in the Moslem paradise. [< F < Persian *huri* < Arabic *ḥaura* (*ḥawira* with eyes like gazelle's)]

hour·ly (our′lē) *adj.* **1** done, happening, or counted every hour. **2** coming very often; frequent. —*adv.* **1** every hour; hour by hour. **2** very often; frequently.

house (*n.* hous; *v.* houz) *n.* **hous·es** (houz′iz), *v.* **housed, hous·ing.** —*n.* **1** a building in which people live. **2** the people living in a house; household. **3** an abode; habitation. **4** a building to hold anything: *an engine house.* **5** an assembly for making laws and considering questions of government; lawmaking body: *the House of Commons.* **6** the building in which such an assembly meets. **7** a place of business. **8** a business firm. **9** a place of entertainment; theatre. **10** an audience; attendance: *A large house heard the singer.* **11** a family regarded as consisting of ancestors, descendants, and kindred, especially a noble or royal family: *He was a prince of the house of Hanover.* **12** a religious order. **13** in curling, the goal or target. **14 bring down the house,** *Informal.* be loudly applauded. **15 clean house, a** set a house in order. **b** get rid of bad conditions; set a business, institution, etc. in order. **16 keep house,** manage a home and its affairs; do housework. **17 on the house,** paid for by the owner of the business; free. **18 put** or **set one's house in order,** arrange one's affairs in good order.
—*v.* **1** put or receive into a house; provide with a house; put under cover. **2** give shelter to; lodge. **3** place in a secure or protected position. **4** take shelter. [OE *hūs*]
☛ See **home** for usage note.

house·boat (hous′bōt′) *n.* a boat that can be used as a place to live in.

house·break·er (hous′brāk′ər) *n.* a person who breaks into a house to steal or commit some other crime.

house·break·ing (hous′brāk′ing) *n.* the act of breaking into a house to steal or commit some other crime.

house·bro·ken (hous′brō′kən) *adj.* of a dog, cat, etc., trained to live indoors.

house·coat (hous′kōt′) *n.* a woman's loose garment worn indoors instead of a robe or dress.

house·fly (hous′flī′) *n.* **-flies.** a two-winged fly that lives around and in houses, feeding on food and garbage. Its larvae or maggots develop in decaying organic matter.

house·hold (hous′hōld′) *n.* **1** all the people living in a house; family; family and servants. **2** a home and its affairs. **3** a royal household. —*adj.* of a household; having to do with a household; domestic: *household expenses, household cares.*

house·hold·er (hous′hōl′dər) *n.* **1** a person who owns or lives in a house. **2** the head of a family.

household word any very familiar word or phrase.

house·keep·er (hous′kēp′ər) *n.* **1** a woman who manages a home and its affairs and does the housework. **2** a woman who directs the servants that do housework.

house·keep·ing (hous′kēp′ing) *n.* **1** the managing of a home and its affairs; doing the housework. **2** the act of directing the servants that do housework.

house·leek (hous′lēk′) *n.* a plant having thick, juicy leaves and pink flowers, that grows on roofs and walls.

house·maid (hous′mād′) *n.* a woman servant who does housework.

housemaid's knee *Informal.* an inflammation near the knee, usually caused by kneeling.

house·mas·ter (hous′mas′tər) *n.* a teacher in charge of a residence hall in a boarding school.

house·moth·er (hous′muᴛʜ′ər) *n.* a woman who supervises and takes care of a group of people living together as a family.

House of Assembly in Newfoundland, the provincial legislature consisting of 36 elected members.

house of cards anything that can be easily knocked down; flimsy structure.

House of Commons 1 in Canada, the body of elected representatives who meet in Ottawa to make laws and debate questions of government: *In 1965 there were 265 members of the House of Commons.* **2** the chamber in which the representatives, or members, meet. **3** in the United Kingdom, the elected members of Parliament. **4** the buildings in which these members meet.

house of correction a place of confinement and reform for persons convicted of minor offences and not regarded as confirmed criminals.

house of God a place of worship; church; temple.

House of Lords in the United Kingdom, the upper, non-elective branch of the lawmaking body, composed of nobles and clergymen of high rank.

House of Representatives 1 in the United States: **a** the lower branch of the federal lawmaking body. **b** the chamber in which the representatives meet. **c** the lower branch of the lawmaking body of certain states. **2** the lower branch of the Parliament of Australia, or of the General Assembly of New Zealand.

house·par·ent (house′pãr′ənt) *n.* one of a married couple in charge of a residence at a school, college, or other institution.

house party 1 the entertainment of guests in a home, especially for a few days. **2** a group of guests thus entertained.

house physician a resident physician of a hotel, hospital, etc.

house plant a small plant in a pot or box, kept inside the house. Ferns are often used as house plants.

house·room (hous′rüm′ or -rům′) *n.* room or space in a house.

house·top (hous′top′) *n.* the top of a house; roof.

house·warm·ing (hous′wôr′ming) *n.* a party given when a person or family moves into a new residence.

house·wife (hous′wīf′ *for 1 and 2*; huz′if, *also* hous′wīf′, *for 3*) *n.* **-wives** (huz′ifs *for 3*). **1** a woman who manages a home and its affairs. **2** a woman who is the head of a household. **3** a small case for needles, thread, etc.

house·wife·ly (hous′wīf′lē) *adj.* of or like a housewife; thrifty or skilled in household affairs.

house·wif·er·y (hous′wīf′ər ē or -wīf′rē) *n.* the work of a housewife; housekeeping.

house·work (hous′wėrk′) *n.* the work to be done in housekeeping, such as washing, ironing, cleaning, sweeping, and cooking.

hous·ing[1] (houz′ing) *n.* **1** the act of sheltering;

providing houses as homes. **2** houses. **3** a shelter; covering. **4** a frame or plate for holding together and protecting the parts of a machine.

hous·ing[2] (houz′ing) *n.* an ornamental covering for a horse: *Under the saddle was a housing of red velvet.* [< *house* covering < OF *houce* < Gmc.]

hove (hōv) *v.* a pt. and a pp. of **heave.**

hov·el (hov′əl or huv′əl) *n.* **1** a house that is small, miserable, and unpleasant to live in. **2** an open shed for sheltering cattle, tools, etc. [ME; origin uncertain]

hov·er (hov′ər or huv′ər) *v.* **1** stay in or near one place in the air: *The two birds hovered over their nest.* **2** stay in or near one place; wait nearby. **3** be in an uncertain condition; waver: *The sick man hovered between life and death.* [ME *hover(en)* < *hoven* hover; origin uncertain]

hov·er·craft (hov′ər kraft′ or huv′ər-) *n.* a vehicle that can travel on a cushion of jet-propelled air a short distance above any surface. [< a trade name]

how (hou) *adv.* **1** in what way; by what means: *Tell her how to do it.* **2** to what degree, extent, etc.: *How long will it take you to do this?* **3** at what price: *How do you sell these apples?* **4** in what state or condition: *Tell me how Mrs. Jones is.* **5** for what reason; why: *How is it you are late?* **6** to what effect; with what meaning; by what name: *How do you mean?* **7 how now?** what does this mean? **8 how so?** why is it so? **9 how then?** what does this mean?
—*n.* a way or manner of doing: *She considered all the hows and wherefores.* [OE *hū*]
☛ **How come** is an informal shortening of "How does (did) it come that . . . ": *How come you didn't call me last night?*

how·be·it (hou bē′it) *adv. Archaic.* however it may be; nevertheless; however.

how·dah (hou′də) *n.* a seat for persons riding on the back of an elephant. Also, **houdah.** [< Hind. *haudah* < Arabic *haudaj*]

A howdah

how·e'er (hou ãr′) *conj. adv.* however.

how·ev·er (hou ev′ər) *conj.* nevertheless; yet; in spite of all that: *It is his; however, you may borrow it.* —*adv.* **1** to whatever degree or amount; no matter how: *However you do it, the effect will be the same.* **2** in whatever way; by whatever means: *However did you manage to get here?* —**Syn.** *conj.* See **but.**

how·itz·er (hou′it sər) *n.* a short artillery piece for firing shells in a high curve. [earlier *howitz* < Du. < G *Haubitze* < Czech *houfnice* catapult]

howl (houl) *v.* **1** give a long, loud, mournful cry: *Dogs and wolves howl.* **2** give a long, loud cry of pain, rage, scorn, etc. **3** yell; shout: *It was so funny that we howled with laughter.* **4** force or drive by howling: *The angry mob howled the speaker off the platform.* **5 howl down,** drown out the words of by howling.
—*n.* **1** a long, loud, mournful cry. **2** a loud cry of pain, rage, etc. **3** a yell of scorn, amusement, etc. **4** a yell; shout. [ME *houle(n)*]

howl·er (houl′ər) *n.* **1** a person or thing that howls. **2** *Informal.* a ridiculous mistake; stupid blunder.

how·so·ev·er (hou′sō ev′ər) *adv.* **1** to whatever extent, degree, or amount; however. **2** in whatever way; by whatever means; however.

hoy·den (hoi′dən) *n.* a boisterous, romping girl; tomboy. Also, **hoiden.** [origin uncertain]

hoy·den·ish (hoi′dən ish) *adj.* of or like a hoyden; boisterous; romping. Also, **hoidenish.**

Hoyle (hoil) *n.* **1** a book of rules and instructions for playing card games. **2 according to Hoyle,** according to the rules or customs; fair; correct. [< Edmond *Hoyle,* 1672-1769, an English writer on card games]

HP, H.P., hp., or **h.p. 1** horsepower. **2** high pressure.

HQ headquarters.

hr. *pl.* **hrs.** hour; hours.

h.r. in baseball, home run.

HRC or **H.R.C.** Humanities Research Council.

H.R.H. His (or Her) Royal Highness.

H.S. or **HS** High School.

ht. 1 height. **2** heat.

H.T. Hawaiian Territory, now the U.S. state of Hawaii.

Hts. Heights.

hub (hub) *n.* **1** the central part of a wheel. See **felloe** for picture. **2** any centre of interest, importance, activity, etc.: *London is the hub of the Commonwealth.* [var. of *hob*[1]; origin uncertain]

hub·ble (hub′əl) *n.* a small hump. [< *hubbly* rough, uneven, var. of E dial. *hobbly* < *hobble,* in the meaning "move unsteadily up and down"]

hub·bub (hub′ub) *n.* a noisy tumult; uproar. [imitative]

hu·bris (hū′bris) *n.* insolence; arrogance; wanton or contemptuous pride. [< Gk. *hybris*]

huck·a·back (huk′ə bak′) *n.* a heavy, coarse, linen or cotton cloth with a rough surface, used for towels. [origin uncertain]

huck·le·ber·ry (huk′əl ber′ē) *n.* **-ries. 1** a small berry like a blueberry, but darker. **2** the shrub that it grows on. [apparently alteration of *hurtleberry* < **hurtle* (dim. of E dial. *hurt,* OE *horte* whortleberry) + *berry*]

huck·ster (huk′stər) *n.* **1** a peddler. **2** a person who sells small articles. **3** *Esp.U.S. Informal.* a person who is in the advertising business. **4** a mean and unfair trader.
—*v.* sell; peddle; haggle. [cf. MDu. *hokester,* originally fem. Akin to HAWKER[1].]

hud·dle (hud′əl) *v.* **-dled, -dling,** *n.* —*v.* **1** crowd close: *The sheep huddled in a corner of the pen.* **2** crowd or put close together: *She huddled all four boys into one bed.* **3** curl oneself up: *The rescued swimmer sat huddled in a blanket by the fire.* **4** put on (clothes) with careless haste. **5** of football players, group together behind the line of scrimmage to receive signals.
—*n.* **1** a confused heap mass, or crowd. **2** slovenly hurry; confusion. **3** in football, a grouping of players behind the line of scrimmage to receive signals. **4** *Informal.* a secret conference. **5 go into a huddle,** *Informal.* confer secretly. [cf. ME *hodre(n),* of the same meaning]

Hudson's Bay Company a British trading company chartered in 1670 to carry on the fur trade with the Indians of N. America. The Hudson's Bay Company played a great part in the exploration and development of Canada's Northwest. [< Henry *Hudson,* died 1611, an English navigator and explorer]

Hudson seal a muskrat fur that is dyed and plucked to look like seal.

hue[1] (hū) *n.* **1** that property of color by which it can be distinguished from gray of equal brightness; color; shade: tint: *all the hues of the rainbow.* **2** a variety of a color; a particular color. [OE *hīw*] —**Syn.** See **color.**

hue[2] (hū) *n.* **1** a shouting. **2 hue and cry, a** shouts of alarm or protest. **b** an outcry or alarm formerly raised to call people to pursue a criminal, in which they were obliged by law to join. **c** the pursuit of a criminal in this way: *The hue and cry ended in the capture of the thief.* [< F *hu* < *huer* shout]

huff (huf) *n.* a fit of anger or peevishness.
—*v.* **1** make angry; offend. **2** *Dialect.* puff; blow. [imitative]

huff·y (huf′ē) *adj.* **huff·i·er, huff·i·est. 1** offended. **2** easily offended; touchy. **—huff′i·ly,** *adv.* **—huff′i·ness,** *n.*

hug (hug) *v.* **hugged, hug·ging,** *n.* —*v.* **1** put the arms around and hold close, especially in affection. **2** squeeze tightly with the arms, as a bear does. **3** cling firmly or fondly to: *hug an opinion.* **4** keep close to: *The boat hugged the shore.*
—*n.* **1** a tight clasp with the arms. **2** a tight squeeze with the arms especially as a grip in wrestling. [apparently < ON *hugga* to comfort]

huge (hūj) *adj.* **hug·er, hug·est. 1** extremely large in size, quantity, etc.: *A whale or an elephant is a huge animal.* **2** unusually great in extent, scope, degree, or capacity: *a huge undertaking.* [ME < OF *ahuge*] **—huge′ly,** *adv.* **—huge′ness,** *n.*

Syn. huge, enormous, immense. Huge is the most general word:

A St. Bernard is a huge dog. **Enormous** implies "abnormally or excessively large or great": *enormous dimensions.* **Immense** often carries the original sense of being so large or great as to be impossible to measure by ordinary standards: *an immense body of water.*

hug·ger-mug·ger (hug′ər mug′ər) *Informal. n.* confusion; disorder. —*adj.* confused, disorderly. —*adv.* in a confused, disorderly manner. [origin uncertain]

Hu·gue·not (hū′gə not′ or hū′gə nō′) *n.* **1** a Calvinistic French Protestant of the 16th and 17th centuries. **2** any member of a church founded by John Calvin. [< F *huguenot*, earlier *eigenot* (< Swiss G *Eidgenoss* confederate < *Eid* oath + *Genoss* comrade), influenced by the name of *Hugues* Besançon, a party leader; originally applied to Genevans who were partisans against the Duke of Savoy]

huh (hu) *interj.* a sound made to express surprise, contempt, etc. or to ask a question.

hu·la (hü′lə) *n.* **1** a native Hawaiian dance that tells a story in mime. **2** the music for such a dance. [< Hawaiian]

hula hoop a plastic hoop designed to be rotated around the body by swinging the hips.

hu·la-hu·la (hü′lə hü′lə) *n.* hula.

hulk (hulk) *n.* **1** the body of an old or worn-out ship. **2** a ship used as a prison. **3** a big, clumsy ship. **4** a big, clumsy person or thing. —*v.* **1** be bulky or unwieldy; loom bulkily. **2** lounge or slouch clumsily or boorishly. [OE *hulc*, ? < Med.L < Gk. *holkas* merchant ship]

hulk·ing (hul′king) *adj.* big and clumsy.

hull[1] (hul) *n.* **1** the outer covering of a seed. **2** the calyx of some fruits. We call the green frill of a strawberry its hull. **3** any outer covering.
—*v.* remove the hull or hulls from. [OE *hulu*] —**hull′er,** *n.*

hull[2] (hul) *n.* **1** the body or frame of a ship. Masts, sails, and rigging are not part of the hull. **2** the main body or frame of a seaplane, airship, etc. **3 hull down,** of ships, so far away that the hull is below the horizon.
—*v.* strike or pierce the hull of (a ship) with a shell, torpedo, etc. [? extended use of *hull*[1]]

hul·la·ba·loo (hul′ə bə lü′) *n.* a loud noise or disturbance; uproar. [imitative, probably < reduplication of *hullo*]

hul·lo (hə lō′) *interj. n.* **-los,** *v.* **-loed, -lo·ing.** hello.

hum (hum) *v.* **hummed, hum·ming,** *n. interj.* —*v.* **1** make a continuous murmuring sound like that of a bee or of a spinning top: *The sewing machine hums busily.* **2** make a low sound like that symbolized by the letter *m,* in hesitation, embarrassment, dissatisfaction, etc. **3** sing with closed lips, not sounding words. **4** put or bring by humming: *The mother hummed her baby to sleep.* **5** *Informal.* be busy and active: *The new president made things hum.*
—*n.* **1** a continuous murmuring sound: *the hum of the bees, the hum of the city street.* **2** a low sound like that symbolized by the letter *m,* used to express hesitation, disagreement, etc. **3** a singing with closed lips, not sounding words.
—*interj.* a low sound like that symbolized by the letter *m,* used to express hesitation, disagreement, etc. [imitative] —**hum′mer,** *n.* —**Syn.** *v.* **1** drone, buzz, murmur.

hu·man (hū′mən) *adj.* **1** of or proper to man: *Selfishness is a human weakness.* **2** being a person or persons; having the form or qualities of people: *Men, women, and children are human beings.* **3** having or showing qualities (good or bad) natural to people: *He is more human than his brother.* **4** having to do with people: *human affairs.* **5** having to do with people and what they can or cannot do: *To know what will happen in the future is beyond human power.*
—*n.* a human being; person. [ME < OF *humain* < L *humanus*] —**hu′man·ly,** *adv.*

Syn. *adj.* **3 Human, humane** = having or showing qualities belonging to man. **Human** describes or suggests any quality, good or bad, belonging specially to man as distinct from animals or God, but particularly suggests his feelings or faults: *He is a very human person, warm and understanding and not too perfect.* **Humane** chiefly suggests man's tender and compassionate feelings and actions toward animals or people who are helpless, troubled, or suffering: *We believe in the humane treatment of prisoners.*

human being a man, woman, or child; person: *Human beings are the only animals able to reason.*

hu·mane (hū mān′) *adj.* **1** kind; merciful; not cruel or brutal. **2** tending to humanize and refine: *humane studies.* [var. of *human*] —**hu·mane′ly,** *adv.* —**hu·mane′ness,** *n.* —**Syn. 1** tender, compassionate. See **human.**

hat, āge, cãre, fär; let, ēqual, tėrm; it, īce
hot, ōpen, ôrder; oil, out; cup, pu̇t, rüle, ūse
əbove, takən, pencəl, lemən, circəs
ch, child; ng, long; sh, ship
th, thin; ᴛʜ, then; zh, measure

hu·man·ism (hū′mən iz′əm) *n.* **1** any system of thought or action mainly concerned with human interests. **2** the study of the humanities; literary culture. Humanism spread throughout Europe in the Middle Ages when scholars began to study Latin and Greek culture. As a result there was the great revival of art and learning that is called the Renaissance.

hu·man·ist (hū′mən ist) *n.* **1** a follower of any philosophy or field of study mainly concerned with human interests and values. **2** a student of the humanities or of Latin and Greek culture.

hu·man·is·tic (hū′mən is′tik) *adj.* of humanism or humanists.

hu·man·i·tar·i·an (hū man′ə tãr′ē ən) *adj.* **1** helpful to humanity; philanthropic. **2** of or having to do with humanitarianism, especially in theology. —*n.* **1** a person who is devoted to the welfare of all human beings. **2** a believer in theological or ethical humanitarianism. [< *humanity*; patterned after *unitarian,* etc.]

hu·man·i·tar·i·an·ism (hū man′ə tãr′ē ən iz′əm) *n.* **1** humanitarian principles or practices. **2** in theology, the doctrine that Jesus Christ was human, not divine. **3** the ethical doctrine that man's obligations are concerned wholly with human relations and the welfare of the human race.

hu·man·i·ty (hū man′ə tē) *n.* **-ties. 1** human beings taken as a group; people: *Advances in medical science help all humanity.* **2** the fact of being human; human character or quality. **3** the fact of being humane; humane treatment; kindness; mercy: *Treat animals with humanity.* **4 the humanities, a** the Latin and Greek languages and literatures. **b** languages, literatures, philosophies, art, etc. **c** the branches of learning concerned with human ideas and their values. [< F *humanité* < L *humanitas*]

hu·man·ize (hū′mən īz′) *v.* **-ized, -iz·ing. 1** make human; give a human character or quality to. **2** make humane; cause to be kind or merciful. —**hu′man·i·za′tion,** *n.* —**hu′man·iz′er,** *n.*

hu·man·kind (hū′mən kīnd′) *n.* human beings; people; the human race; mankind.

hu·man·oid (hū′mə noid′) *adj.* having human characteristics; manlike. —*n.* a manlike or almost human creature: *A Neanderthal man was a humanoid.*

hum·ble (hum′bəl) *adj.* **-bler, -blest,** *v.* **-bled, -bling.** —*adj.* **1** low in position or condition; not important or grand: *A one-room log cabin is a humble place to live in.* **2** having or showing a feeling that one is unimportant, weak, poor, etc.; modest in spirit; not proud. **3** deeply or courteously respectful: *in my humble opinion.*
—*v.* **1** make humble; bring down. **2** make lower in position, condition, or pride. [ME < OF < L *humilis* low < *humus* ground] —**hum′ble·ness,** *n.* —**hum′bler,** *n.* —**hum′bly,** *adv.*

Syn. *adj.* **1** unpretentious, common, poor. **2 Humble, lowly, meek** = not proud in spirit or behavior. **Humble** in a good sense means modest, "without wrongful pride in oneself or one's accomplishments," but now chiefly suggests "feeling inferior and belittling oneself": *Defeat and failure make people humble.* **Lowly,** more literary, means "humble" in the good sense, but is now seldom used to describe people: *The saint had a lowly heart.* **Meek** = patient and mild in disposition, but now often suggests "being without proper pride or spirit, submitting tamely to abuse" *The little fellow was meek when the other boys made fun of him.*

hum·ble·bee (hum′bəl bē′) *n.* bumblebee. [ME *humbylbee,* ult. < *hum*]

humble pie 1 an inferior pie made of the inward parts of an animal, formerly served to the huntsmen and servants after a hunt. **2 eat humble pie, a** be forced to do something very disagreeable and humiliating. **b** admit one's mistake and apologize. [var. of *umble pie* < *umbles,* var. of *numbles* entrails < OF, pl. < L *lumbulus,* dim. of *lumbus* loin]

hum·bug (hum′bug′) *n. v.* **-bugged, -bug·ging.** —*n.* **1** a person who pretends to be what he is not; fraud. **2** a cheat. **3** pretence; sham. **4** a hard candy, usually brown with light stripes. —*v.* deceive with a sham; cheat. [origin unknown] —**hum′ bug′ ger,** *n.*

hum·drum (hum′drum′) *adj.* without variety; commonplace; dull. —*n.* **1** a humdrum routine. **2** anything that is dull or tiresome. **3** a dull person. [varied reduplication of *hum,* v.]

hu·mer·al (hū′mər əl) *adj.* **1** of or near the humerus. **2** of or near the shoulder.

hu·mer·us (hū′mər əs) *n.* **-mer·i** (-mər ī′ or -mər ē′). **1** the long bone in the upper part of the forelimb or arm, reaching from the shoulder to the elbow. **2** the upper part of the forelimb or arm. See **skeleton** for diagram. [< L *umerus*]

hu·mid (hū′mid) *adj.* moist; damp: *The air is very humid here.* [< L *umidus* < *umere* be moist] —**hu′mid·ly,** *adv.* —**hu′ mid·ness,** *n.* —**Syn.** See **damp.**

hu·mi·dex (hū′mi deks′) *n. Cdn.* a combined measurement of temperature and humidity got by adding the Fahrenheit figure to vapor pressure in millibars minus 10. It indicates the dry-air temperature that would cause the same level of discomfort. Humidex values above 85 stand for increasingly uncomfortable combinations of heat and humidity. [< *humid*ity + ind*ex*; first used by the Toronto Weather Office in 1965]

hu·mid·i·fi·ca·tion (hū mid′ə fə kā′shən) *n.* a humidifying.

hu·mid·i·fi·er (hū mid′ə fī′ər) *n.* a device for keeping air moist.

hu·mid·i·ty (hū mid′ə tē) *n.* **1** moistness; dampness. **2** the amount of moisture in the air. The **relative humidity** is the ratio between the amount of water vapor present in the air and the greatest amount the air could contain at the same temperature.

hu·mi·dor (hū′mə dôr′) *n.* **1** a box, jar, etc. for keeping tobacco moist. **2** any similar device.

hu·mil·i·ate (hū mil′ē āt′) *v.* **-at·ed, -at·ing.** lower the pride, dignity, or self-respect of. [< L *humiliare* < *humilis.* See HUMBLE.] —**hu·mil′ i·at′ ing·ly,** *adv.* —**hu·mil′ i·a·tor,** *n.* —**Syn.** humble, mortify, chagrin, disgrace, shame. See **ashamed.**

hu·mil·i·a·tion (hū mil′ē ā′shən) *n.* **1** a lowering of pride, dignity, or self-respect. **2** the state or feeling of being humiliated.

hu·mil·i·ty (hū mil′ə tē) *n.* **-ties.** humbleness of mind; lack of pride; meekness. [< F *humilité* < *humilitas*] —**Syn.** lowliness, modesty.

hu·mit (hū′mit) *n.* a unit of measurement used in expressing humiture. If the temperature is 80° and relative humidity is 60%, the humiture is 70 humits. [< *humiture*]

hu·mi·ture (hū′mə chər) *n.* a combined measurement of temperature and humidity arrived at by adding degrees of temperature to percentage of relative humidity and dividing by two. [< *humid*ity + tempera*ture*; coined by O.F. Hevener of New York in 1937]

hum·ming·bird (hum′ing bėrd′) *n.* a very small, brightly colored bird of N. and S. America having a long, narrow bill and narrow wings that move so rapidly they make a humming sound.

hum·mock (hum′ək) *n.* **1** a very small, rounded hill; knoll; hillock. **2** a bump or ridge in a field of ice. [origin unknown]

hum·mock·y (hum′ək ē) *adj.* **1** full of hummocks. **2** like a hummock.

hu·mor or **hu·mour** (hū′mər or ū′mər) *n.* **1** a funny or amusing quality: *I see no humor in your tricks.* **2** the ability to see or show the funny or amusing side of things. **3** speech, writing, etc. showing this ability. **4** a state of mind; mood; disposition: *Success puts you in good humor.* **5** a fancy; whim. **6** any of various body fluids formerly supposed to determine a person's health and disposition. They were blood, phlegm, choler (yellow bile), and melancholy (black bile). **7 out of humor** or **humour,** angry; displeased; in a bad mood. **8 sense of humor** or **humour,** the ability to see the amusing side of things.
—*v.* **1** give in to the fancies or whims of (a person); indulge. **2** adapt oneself to; act so as to agree with. [ME < AF < L *umor* fluid] —**hu′mor·less** or **hu′ mour·less,** *adj.*

Syn. *n.* **2** See wit. **4** See **mood.** —*v.* **1 Humor, indulge, gratify** = give someone what he wants. **Humor** = give in to someone's whims, changing moods, unreasonable demands, or purely imaginary desires, in order to quiet or comfort him: *Unless the little boy is humored, he has tantrums.* **Indulge** = give way, often too easily, to someone's wishes, especially ones that should not be granted, in order to please: *Many parents indulge their children by giving them too much candy and ice cream.* **Gratify** = make someone happy by providing what he likes or longs for: *Praise gratifies most people.*

hu·mor·esque (hū′mər esk′) *n.* a light, playful, or humorous piece of music. [< G *Humoreske*]

hu·mor·ist (hū′mər ist or ū′mər ist) *n.* **1** a person with a strong sense of humor. **2** a humorous talker; a writer of jokes and funny stories.

hu·mor·ous (hū′mər əs or ū′mər əs) *adj.* full of humor; funny; amusing. —**hu′ mor·ous·ly,** *adv.* —**hu′ mor·ous·ness,** *n.*

hu·mour (hū′mər or ū′mər) *n. v.* humor.

hump (hump) *n.* **1** a rounded lump that sticks out: *Some camels have two humps on their backs.* **2** a mound; a hill. **3** a long, gradual hill in a railway yard where cars are uncoupled and allowed to roll down into the classification yard, where switches sort them onto different tracks. **4 over the hump,** past a difficult period or crucial test.
—*v.* **1** raise or bend up into a hump: *The cat humped her back when she saw the dog.* **2** move (a railway car) over the hump for sorting in the classification yard. **3** *Slang.* exert oneself; make an effort. [cf. Du. *homp* lump]

hump·back (hump′bak′) *n.* **1** a hunchback. **2** a back having a hump on it. **3** a large whale that has a humplike dorsal fin. **4** a species of Pacific salmon; pink salmon.

hump·backed (hump′bakt′) *adj.* hunchbacked.

humph (humpf) *interj. n.* an exclamation expressing doubt, disgust, contempt, etc.

hump·y (hump′ē) *adj.* **hump·i·er, hump·i·est. 1** full of humps. **2** humplike.

hu·mus (hū′məs) *n.* soil made from decayed leaves and other vegetable matter, containing valuable plant foods. [< L *humus* earth]

Hun (hun) *n.* **1** a member of a warlike Asiatic people who overran eastern and central Europe between about A.D. 375 and 453. Attila was a famous king and leader of the Huns. **2** a barbarous, destructive person. **3** *Informal.* a Hungarian partridge. **4** *Derogatory.* **a** a German. **b** the German forces, used especially during World War I. [OE (pl.) *Hūne, Hūnas*; probably < the native name of the people]

hunch (hunch) *v.* **1** hump. **2** draw, bend, or form into a hump: *He sat hunched up with his chin on his knees.* **3** move, push, or shove by jerks. —*n.* **1** a hump. **2** *Informal.* a vague feeling or suspicion: *I had a hunch we would win the game.* **3** a thick slice or piece; chunk. [origin unknown]

hunch·back (hunch′bak′) *n.* **1** a person with a hump on his back; humpback. **2** a back having a hump on it.

hunch·backed (hunch′bakt′) *adj.* having a hump on the back; humpbacked.

hun·dred (hun′drəd) *n.* **-dreds** or (*as after a numeral*) **-dred,** *adj.* —*n.* **1** ten times ten; 100: *five hundred.* **2** formerly, a division of an English county. —*adj.* being ten times ten: *a hundred men.* [OE *hund* 100 + *red* reckoning]

Hundred Days the period of Napoleon's return to power in France in 1815, between his escape from Elba and his defeat, abdication, and final exile.

hun·dred·fold (hun′drəd fōld′) *adj. adv. n.* a hundred times as much or as many.

hun·dredth (hun′drədth) *adj. n.* **1** next after the 99th; last in a series of 100. **2** one, or being one, of 100 equal parts.

hun·dred·weight (hun′drəd wāt′) *n.* **-weights** or (as after a numeral) **-weight.** a measure of weight, equal to 100 pounds in Canada and the United States or 112 pounds in Great Britain.

Hundred Years' War a series of wars between England and France from 1337 to 1453.

hung (hung) *v.* a pt. and a pp. of **hang.** ☞ See **hang** for usage note.

Hun·gar·i·an (hung gãr′ ē ən) *adj.* of Hungary, a country in central Europe, its people, or their language. —*n.* **1** a native or inhabitant of Hungary. **2** the language of Hungary.

Hungarian partridge a game bird introduced into the prairies from Europe.

hun·ger (hung′ gər) *n.* **1** an uncomfortable or painful feeling or weak condition caused by lack of food. **2** a desire or need for food. **3** a strong desire: *a hunger for kindness.* —*v.* **1** feel hunger; be hungry. **2** *Archaic.* starve. **3** have a strong desire. [OE *hungor*] —**hun′ger·er,** *n.*

hunger strike a refusal to eat until certain demands are granted.

hun·gry (hung′ grē) *adj.* **-gri·er, -gri·est. 1** feeling a desire or need for food. **2** showing hunger: *a hungry look.* **3** causing hunger. **4** having a strong desire or craving; eager: *hungry for knowledge.* **5** not rich or fertile: *hungry soil.* [OE *hungrig*] —**hun′ gri·ly,** *adv.* —**hun′ gri·ness,** *n.*
Syn. 1 Hungry, famished = needing food. **Hungry** is the general word: *Boys are always hungry.* **Famished** = brought to a serious state of physical exhaustion, sometimes even to the point of dying, by lack of food: *We try to feed and save famished war orphans.* But in informal use, it often means no more than "very hungry."

hunk (hungk) *n. Informal.* a big lump, piece, or roughly-cut slice. [cf. Flemish *hunke* hunk]

hun·ker (hung′ kər) *v. Dialect.* squat on one's haunches. [origin uncertain]

hun·kers (hung′ kərs) *n.pl. Dialect.* haunches.

hunk·y[1] (hung′ kē) *adj. Slang.* all right; safe and sound.

hunk·y[2] (hung′ kē) *n. Slang. Usually derogatory.* a central European immigrant, especially a Hungarian. [prob. < earlier *hunk* foreigner < *Bohunk*]

hunk·y-do·ry (hung′ kē dôr′ ē) *adj. Slang.* fine; just right; satisfactory.

hunt (hunt) *v.* **1** chase (wild animals, game birds, etc.) for food or sport. **2** chase or go out after wild animals or game. **3** search through (a region) in pursuit of game. **4** use (horses or dogs) in the chase. **5** drive (out, away); pursue; harry; persecute. **6** try to find: *hunt a clue.* **7** look thoroughly; search carefully: *hunt through drawers.* **8 hunt down, a** hunt for until caught or killed. **b** look for until found. **9 hunt out,** seek and find. **10 hunt up, a** look carefully for. **b** find by search.
—*n.* **1** the act of hunting. **2** a group of persons hunting together. **3** an attempt to find something; thorough look; careful search. [OE *huntian*] —**Syn.** *v.* **7** ransack, rummage.

hunt·er (hun′ tər) *n.* **1** a person who hunts. **2** a horse or dog trained and used for hunting.

hunt·ing (hun′ ting) *n.* the act of a person or animal that hunts.

hunting case a watchcase with a hinged cover to protect the crystal.

hunting ground 1 a place or region for hunting. **2** See **happy hunting ground.**

hunting horn a horn used in a hunt.

hunt·ress (hun′ tris) *n.* a woman who hunts.

hunts·man (hunts′ mən) *n.* **-men** (-mən). **1** a hunter. **2** the manager of a hunt.

hur·dle (hėr′ dəl) *n. v.* **-dled, -dling.** —*n.* **1** in a race, a barrier for people or horses to jump over. **2 hurdles,** *pl.* a race in which the runners jump over hurdles. **3** an obstacle, difficulty, etc. **4** a frame made of sticks used as a temporary fence. **5** *Brit.* formerly, a portable frame resembling a stoneboat or sled, used for dragging traitors to a place of execution.
—*v.* **1** jump over: *The horse hurdled both the fence and the ditch.* **2** overcome (an obstacle, difficulty, etc.). **3** enclose with a frame of sticks. [OE *hyrdel*]

hur·dler (hėr′ dlər) *n.* a person who jumps over hurdles in a race.

hur·dy (hėr′ dē) *n. Slang.* hurdy-gurdy girl.

hur·dy-gur·dy (hėr′ dē gėr′ dē) *n.* **-dies. 1** a barrel organ or street piano played by turning a handle. **2** formerly, an instrument shaped like a guitar, played by turning a wheel. [probably imitative]

hurdy-gurdy girl *Cdn.* formerly, a dancing girl,

hat, āge, cãre, fär; let, ēqual, tėrm; it, īce
hot, ōpen, ôrder; oil, out; cup, pu̇t, rüle, ūse
əbove, takən, pencəl, lemən, circəs
ch, child; ng, long; sh, ship
th, thin; ᴛʜ, then; zh, measure

especially one of a number imported into British Columbia mining communities as dancing partners.

hurl (hėrl) *v.* **1** throw with much force: *The man hurled his spear at one bear; the dogs hurled themselves at the other.* **2** throw forth (words, cries, etc.) violently; utter with vehemence. —*n.* a forcible or violent throw. [cf. LG *hurreln*] —**hurl′ er,** *n.*

hurl·y-burl·y (hėr′ lē bėr′ lē) *n.* **-burl·ies.** disorder and noise; tumult. [< earlier *hurling and burling,* varied reduplication of *hurling* in obs. sense of "commotion" < *hurl*]

Hu·ron (hūr′ ən) *n.* **1** a tribe of Iroquois Indians formerly living in Huronia, an area in Ontario S.E. of Georgian Bay. **2** a member of this tribe. **3** the language of this tribe. [< F *huron* unkempt person, ruffian < *hure* dishevelled head of hair; a name applied to these Indians from about 1600]

Hu·ro·ni·an (hū rō′ nē ən) in geology: —*adj.* **1** of or having to do with a rock system north of Lake Huron. **2** of or having to do with the period of the Proterozoic era in which these rocks originated. See **geology** for chart. —*n.* **1** a geological period of the Proterozoic era. **2** the rocks formed during this period.

hur·rah (hə rä′ or hə ro′) *interj. n.* a shout of joy, approval, etc. —*v.* shout hurrahs; cheer. Also, **hooray.**

hur·ray (hə rā′) *interj. n. v.* hurrah.

hur·ri·cane (hėr′ ə kān′) *n.* **1** a tropical cyclone. **2** in meteorology, a storm with winds having a velocity of over 75 miles per hour and, usually, very heavy rain. **3** a sudden, violent outburst. [< Sp. *huracán* < Carib] —**Syn.** See **cyclone.**

hurricane deck the upper deck on a river boat, etc.

hur·ried (hėr′ ēd) *adj.* **1** forced to hurry: *The burglar made a hurried departure before the police arrived.* **2** done or made in a hurry; hasty: *a hurried reply.* —**hur′ ried·ly,** *adv.*

hur·ry (hėr′ ē) *v.* **-ried, -ry·ing,** *n.* **-ries.** —*v.* **1** drive, carry, send, or move quickly. **2** move or act with more than an easy or natural speed. **3** urge to act soon or too soon. **4** urge to great speed or to too great speed. **5** cause to go on or occur more quickly; hasten.
—*n.* **1** a hurried movement or action. **2** an eagerness to have quickly or do quickly. **3** need of haste: *There is no hurry for this.* [origin uncertain]
Syn. *v.* **3** quicken, accelerate, expedite. —*n.* **1 Hurry, haste, speed** = quickness or swiftness in action or movement. **Hurry** = action that is quicker than is easy or natural, sometimes quicker than necessary, and often suggests bustling or rushing: *In her hurry she dropped the eggs.* **Haste** emphasizes trying to be quick, and often suggests hurried or rushed action, sometimes too rushed to get the desired results: *All this haste was of no use.* **Speed** = swift or rapid movement of people or things: *They did the work with speed.*

hur·ry-scur·ry or **hur·ry-skur·ry** (hėr′ ē skėr′ ē) *n.* **-ries,** *adj. adv. Informal.* —*n.* a hurrying and confusion. —*adj.* hurried and confused. —*adv.* with hurrying and confusion.

hurt (hėrt) *v.* **hurt, hurt·ing,** *n.* —*v.* **1** cause pain, harm, or damage. **2** cause pain to; give a wound to; injure. **3** suffer pain; be the source of pain: *My sprained ankle hurts terribly.* **4** have a bad effect on; do damage or harm to. **5** give mental pain to; grieve; distress: *He hurt his mother's feelings.*
—*n.* **1** a pain; injury; wound. **2** a bad effect; damage, harm, or injury: *His failing was a great hurt to his pride.* [apparently < OF *hurter* strike < Gmc.] —**hurt′ er,** *n.* —**Syn.** *v.* **2, 4** See **injure.**

hurt·ful (hėrt′ fəl) *adj.* causing hurt, harm, or damage; injurious. —**hurt′ ful·ly,** *adv.* —**Syn.** harmful, pernicious.

hur·tle (hėr′ təl) *n.* **-tled, -tling,** *n.* —*v.* **1** dash or drive violently; rush suddenly; come with a crash: *Spears hurtled against shields.* **2** move with a clatter; rush noisily or violently: *The express train hurtled past.*

3 dash or drive violently; fling: *The impact of the crash hurtled the driver against the windshield of the car.* 4 dash against; collide with.
—*n.* the act or fact of hurtling; clash; clatter. [ME, frequentative of *hurten* strike < OF < Gmc.; cf. ON *hrutr* a ram]

hus·band (huz′bənd) *n.* **1** the man married to a particular woman; married man. **2** *Archaic.* a manager.
—*v.* **1** manage carefully; be saving of: *husband one's strength or resources.* **2** marry. **3** *Archaic.* till (soil); cultivate (plants). [OE *hūsbonda* < *hūs* house + *bonda* head of family (< ON *bóndi*)]

hus·band·ly (huz′bənd lē) *adj.* of, like, or befitting a husband.

hus·band·man (huz′bənd mən) *n.* **-men** (-mən). a farmer.

hus·band·ry (huz′bənd rē) *n.* **1** farming. **2** the management of one's affairs or resources. **3** careful management; thrift.

hush (hush) *v.* **1** stop making a noise; make or become silent or quiet. **2** soothe; calm. **3 hush up, a** keep from being told; stop discussion of. **b** *Informal.* be silent!
—*n.* a stopping of noise; silence; quiet.
—*interj.* stop the noise! be silent! keep quiet! [ME *hussht* silent, originally interj., silence!]

hush-hush (hush′hush′) *adj. Informal.* secret; confidential: *hush-hush plans.*

hush money *Informal.* money paid to keep a person from telling something.

husk[1] (husk) *n.* **1** the dry outer covering of certain seeds or fruits. An ear of corn has a husk. **2** the dry or worthless outer covering of anything. —*v.* remove the husk from. [ME *huske*; origin uncertain; cf. MDu. *huyskijn*, dim. of *huus* house] —**husk′er,** *n.*

husk[2] (husk) *n.* a husky condition or quality of the voice. [back formation from *husky*]

husk·y (hus′kē) *adj.* **husk·i·er, husk·i·est. 1** dry in the throat; hoarse; rough of voice: *a husky tone.* **2** of, like, or having husks. **3** big and strong. [< *husk*[1], n.] —**husk′i·ly,** *adv.* —**husk′i·ness,** *n.*

Husk·y (hus′kē) *n.* **-ies. 1** *Informal.* **a** an Eskimo. **b** the Eskimo language. **2** Usually, **husky. a** Siberian husky. **b** *Informal.* any northern work dog. [ult. from a variant of *Eskimo*]

hus·sar (hù zär′) *n.* **1** a light-armed cavalry soldier. **2** a member of certain armored regiments. [< Hungarian *huszár*, originally, freebooter < Old Serbian *husar*, var. of *kursar* < Ital. *corsaro* runner < VL *cursarius* < L *cursus* a run. Doublet of CORSAIR.]

Huss·ite (hus′īt) *n.* a follower of John Huss (1369?-1415), a Bohemian religious reformer and martyr.
—*adj.* of or having to do with John Huss or his teachings.

hus·sy (huz′ē or hus′ē) *n.* **-sies. 1** a bad-mannered or pert girl. **2** a worthless woman. [ME *huswif* housewife]

hus·tings (hus′tingz) *n.pl. or sing.* **1** in Great Britain, a platform from which candidates for Parliament were formerly nominated and from which they addressed the voters. **2** a platform from which speeches are made in a political campaign. **3** the proceedings at an election. [OE < ON *hústhing* council < *hús* house + *thing* assembly]

hus·tle (hus′əl) *v.* **-tled, -tling,** *n.* —*v.* **1** hurry. **2** force hurriedly or roughly: *The police hustled the tramps out of town.* **3** push or shove roughly; jostle rudely: *The other boys hustled him along the street.* **4** *Informal.* work with tireless energy. **5** *Slang.* sell or solicit, especially in an aggressive or deceitful way.
—*n.* **1** a hurry. **2** a rough pushing or shoving; rude jostling. **3** *Informal.* tireless energy. [< MDu. *hutselen* shake] —**hus′tler,** *n.*

hut (hut) *n.* **1** a small, roughly built house; a small cabin. **2** a temporary wooden or metal structure for quartering troops. [< F *hutte* < MHG *hütte*] —**hut′like′,** *adj.*

hutch (huch) *n.* **1** a pen for rabbits, etc. **2** a hut. **3** a box; chest; bin. **4** a cupboard with open shelves on the upper part for holding dishes, etc. —*v.* put in a hutch; lay up, as in a chest. [ME < OF *huche* < Med.L *hutica* chest]

Hut·ter·ite (hut′ər īt′) *n.* a member of an originally Austrian religious and ethnic group living mainly in Alberta and Manitoba. —*adj.* of or having to do with these people: *Hutterite communities.* [< Jacob *Hutter* (? -1536), who founded the group in 1528 + *-ite*[1]]

huz·za (hə zä′) *interj. n.* **-zas,** *v.* **-zaed, -za·ing.** —*interj. n.* a loud shout of joy, encouragement, or applause; hurrah. —*v.* shout huzzas; cheer.

H.V., h.v., or **hv** high voltage.

h.w. high water.

hwan (hwän or wän) *n.* **1** a unit of money in Korea, revalued in 1962. **2** a coin worth one hwan. [< Korean]

hy·a·cinth (hī′ə sinth′) *n.* **1** a plant of the lily family that grows from a bulb and has a spike of small, fragrant, bell-shaped flowers. **2** its flower. **3** a reddish-orange gem; jacinth. **4** a purplish blue. [< L *hyacinthus* < Gk. *hyakinthos*, a kind of flower. Doublet of JACINTH.]

hy·a·cin·thine (hī′ə sin′thən or hī′ə sin′thīn) *adj.* **1** of or like the hyacinth. **2** adorned with hyacinths.

Hy·a·des (hī′ə dēz′) *n.pl.* **1** in astronomy, a group of stars in the constellation Taurus. In ancient times, they were supposed to be a sign of rain when they rose with the sun. **2** in Greek mythology, the daughters of Atlas, nymphs who supplied the earth with moisture and who were placed in the sky by Zeus.

hy·ae·na (hī ē′nə) *n.* hyena.

hy·a·line (hī′ə lin or hī′ə līn′) *adj.* glassy; transparent. A hyaline cartilage contains little fibre. —*n.* something glassy or transparent. [< LL *hyalinus* < Gk. *hyalinos* < *hyalos* glass]

hy·a·lite (hī′ə līt′) *n.* a colorless variety of opal, sometimes transparent like glass and sometimes whitish and translucent. [< Gk. *hyalos* glass]

hy·a·loid (hī′ə loid′) *adj.* glassy; transparent; crystalline.

hy·brid (hī′brid) *n.* **1** the offspring of two animals or plants of different species, varieties, etc. **2** anything of mixed origin. **3** a word formed of parts from different languages. *Example*: starvation (E *starve* + L *-ation*).
—*adj.* **1** bred from two different species, varieties, etc.: *A mule is a hybrid animal.* **2** of mixed origin. [< L *hybrida*, var. of *ibrida* mongrel, *hybrid*]

hy·brid·ism (hī′brid iz′əm) *n.* **1** the production of hybrids; crossbreeding. **2** a hybrid character, nature, or condition.

hy·brid·i·za·tion (hī′brid ə zā′shən or hī′brid ī zā′shən) *n.* the production of hybrids; crossing of different species.

hy·brid·ize (hī′brid īz′) *v.* **-ized, -iz·ing. 1** cause to produce hybrids. Botanists hybridize different kinds of plants to get new varieties. **2** produce hybrids. —**hy′brid·iz′er,** *n.*

Hyde (hīd) *n.* **Mr.** See **Jekyll.**

hydr- *combining form.* the form of **hydro-** before vowels, as in *hydraulic.*

hy·dra (hī′drə) *n.* **-dras, -drae** (-drē or -drī). **1 Hydra, a** in Greek mythology, a monstrous serpent having nine heads, each of which, after being cut off, was replaced by two heads unless the wound was cauterized. The Hydra was slain by Hercules. **b** in astronomy, a southern constellation represented as a serpent. **2** any persistent evil. **3** a kind of freshwater polyp, so called because when the tubelike body is cut into pieces, each piece forms a new individual. [< L < Gk. *hydra* water serpent < *hydōr* water]

hy·dran·gea (hī drān′jə) *n.* a shrub having opposite leaves and large, showy clusters of small white, pink, or blue flowers. [< NL < Gk. *hydōr* water + *angeion* vessel, capsule; with reference to its cup-shaped seed capsule]

hy·drant (hī′drənt) *n.* an upright cylinder or street fixture with a valve for drawing water directly from a main. Hydrants are used to get water to put out fires, wash the streets, etc. [< Gk. *hydōr* water]

hy·drate (hī′drāt) *n. v.* **-drat·ed, -drat·ing.** in chemistry: —*n.* a compound produced when certain substances unite with water, represented in formulas as containing molecules of water. Washing soda ($Na_2CO_3 \cdot 10H_2O$) is a hydrate. —*v.* become or cause to become a hydrate; combine with water to form a hydrate. Blue vitriol is hydrated copper sulphate. [< Gk. *hydōr* water]

hy·dra·tion (hī drā′shən) *n.* the act or process of combining with water, usually to form a hydrate.

hy·drau·lic (hī dro′lik or hī drô′lik) *adj.* **1** having to do with water or other liquids in motion. **2** operated by water or other liquid: *a hydraulic press, hydraulic brakes.* **3** hardening under water: *hydraulic cement.* [< L *hydraulicus* < Gk. *hydraulikos*, ult. < *hydōr* water + *aulos* pipe]

hy·drau·li·cal·ly (hī dro′lik lē or hī drô′lik lē) *adv.* by hydraulic power.

hy·drau·lics (hī dro′liks or hī drô′liks) *n.* the science dealing with water or other liquids in motion, their uses in engineering, the laws of their actions, etc.

hy·dra·zine (hī′drə zēn′ or hī′drə zin) *n.* **1** in chemistry, a colorless, fuming, toxic liquid used in organic synthesis, and as rocket fuel. *Formula*: N_2H_4 **2** any of various compounds obtained from this liquid by replacing one or more hydrogen atoms with an organic radical.

hy·dric (hī′drik) *adj.* of or containing hydrogen.

hy·drid (hī′drid) *n.* hydride.

hy·dride (hī′drīd or hī′drid) *n.* in chemistry, a compound of hydrogen with another element or radical.

hy·dri·od·ic (hī′dri od′ik) *adj.* containing hydrogen and iodine. Hydriodic acid (HI) is a colorless gas with a suffocating odor.

hy·dro (hī′drō) *n. Cdn.* **1** hydro-electric power: *Niagara Falls provides hydro for many factories.* **2** electricity as a utility distributed by a power company or commission: *The hydro was off for two hours during the storm.* **3 Hydro,** a company or commission producing and distributing electricity as a utility.

hydro- *combining form.* **1** of or having to do with water, as in *hydrometer, hydrostatics.* **2** combined with hydrogen, as in *hydrochloric, hydrosulphuric.* Also, **hydr-**, before vowels. [< Gk. *hydro-* < *hydōr* water]

hy·dro·car·bon (hī′drō kär′bən) *n.* any of a class of compounds containing only hydrogen and carbon. Methane benzene, and acetylene are hydrocarbons. Gasoline is a mixture of hydrocarbons.

hy·dro·ce·phal·ic (hī′drə sə fal′ik) *adj.* affected with or having to do with hydrocephalus.

hy·dro·ceph·a·lous (hī′drə sef′ə ləs) *adj.* hydrocephalic.

hy·dro·ceph·a·lus (hī′drō sef′ə ləs) *n.* an accumulation of fluid within the cranium, especially in infancy, often causing great enlargement of the head. [< *hydro-* + Gk. *kephalē* head]

hy·dro·chlo·ric (hī′drə klô′rik) *adj.* containing hydrogen and chlorine.

hydrochloric acid a clear, colorless solution of hydrogen chloride, that has a strong, sharp odor and is highly corrosive. It is used in various industrial processes, in dyeing, and in medicine. *Formula*: HCl

hy·dro·cor·ti·sone (hī′drō kôr′tə zōn′) *n.* an adrenal hormone similar to cortisone, used in treating arthritis.

hy·dro·cy·an·ic (hī′drō sī an′ik) *adj.* containing hydrogen and cyanogen.

hydrocyanic acid a colorless, volatile solution of hydrogen cyanide, that has an odor like that of bitter almonds and is highly poisonous; prussic acid. It is used as a fumigant and in the manufacture of dyes, plastics, etc. *Formula*: HCN

hy·dro·dy·nam·ic (hī′drō dī nam′ik) *adj.* having to do with the force or motion of fluids, or with hydrodynamics.

hy·dro·dy·nam·ics (hī′drō dī nam′iks) *n.* the branch of physics dealing with the forces that water and other liquids exert; hydraulics.

hy·dro-e·lec·tric (hī′drō′i lek′trik) *adj.* of or having to do with the generation of electricity by water power, or by the friction of water or steam: *There is a large hydro-electric power plant on the St. Lawrence Seaway.*

hy·dro-e·lec·tric·i·ty (hī′drō i lek′tris′ə tē) *n.* electricity produced from water power, etc.

hy·dro·flu·or·ic (hī′drō flü ôr′ik) *adj.* containing hydrogen and fluorine.

hydrofluoric acid a colorless, corrosive, volatile solution of hydrogen fluoride, used for etching glass. *Formula*: HF

hy·dro·foil (hī′drə foil′) *n.* **1** a flat or curved surface designed to lift a moving boat or seaplane just above the water. **2** a boat equipped with hydrofoils.

hat, āge, cãre, fär; let, ēqual, têrm; it, īce
hot, ōpen, ôrder; oil, out; cup, pu̇t, rüle, ūse
əbove, takən, pencəl, lemən, circəs
ch, child; ng, long; sh, ship
th, thin; ᴛʜ, then; zh, measure

hy·dro·gen (hī′drə jən) *n.* a colorless, odorless, gaseous chemical element, that burns easily and weighs less than any other known element. Hydrogen combines chemically with oxygen to form water. *Symbol*: H; *at.no.* 1; *at.wt.* 1.00797. [< F *hydrogène*, ult. < Gk. *hydōr* water + *-genēs* born]

hy·dro·gen·ate (hī′drə jən āt′ or hī droj′ən āt′) *v.* **-at·ed, -at·ing.** combine with hydrogen; treat with hydrogen.

hy·dro·gen·a·tion (hī′drə jə nā′shən) *n.* the process of combining with hydrogen. Hydrogenation changes vegetable oils into solid fats.

hydrogen bomb a bomb that uses the fusion of atoms to cause an explosion of tremendous force; fusion bomb. It is many times more powerful than the atomic bomb. Also, **H-bomb.**

hydrogen chloride a colorless, strong-smelling, poisonous gas, a compound of hydrogen and chlorine. It is soluble in water, forming hydrochloric acid. *Formula*: HCl

hydrogen cyanide a colorless, highly poisonous gas, a compound of hydrogen and cyanogen. It has an odor of bitter almonds and dissolves in water to form hydrocyanic acid. *Formula*: HCN

hydrogen fluoride a colorless, corrosive, poisonous liquid or gas, a compound of hydrogen and fluorine. It is soluble in water, forming hydrofluoric acid. *Formula*: HF

hy·dro·gen·ize (hī′drə jən īz′ or hī droj′ən īz′) *v.* **-ized, -iz·ing.** hydrogenate.

hy·drog·e·nous (hī droj′ə nəs) *adj.* of or containing hydrogen.

hydrogen peroxide a colorless, unstable liquid often used in dilute solution as an antiseptic, a bleaching agent, etc. *Formula*: H_2O_2

hydrogen sulphide or **sulfide** an inflammable, poisonous gas having an odor like that of rotten eggs. *Formula*: H_2S

hy·dro·graph (hī′drə graf′) *n.* a hydrographic diagram, chart, or record.

hy·drog·ra·pher (hī drog′rə fər) *n.* an expert in hydrography.

hy·dro·graph·ic (hī′drə graf′ik) *adj.* of or having to do with hydrography. **—hy′dro·graph′i·cal·ly,** *adv.*

hy·drog·ra·phy (hī drog′rə fē) *n.* the science of the measurement and description of seas, lakes, rivers, etc., with special reference to their use for navigation and commerce.

hy·droid (hī′droid) *n.* a very simple form of hydrozoan that grows into branching colonies by budding; polyp. [< *hydra*]

hy·dro·ki·net·ic (hī′drō ki net′ik) *adj.* of or having to do with hydrokinetics.

hy·dro·ki·net·ics (hī′drō ki net′iks) *n.* the branch of physics dealing with the motion, or kinetics, of fluids; hydraulics.

hy·dro·log·ic (hī′drə loj′ik) *adj.* of or having to do with hydrology.

hy·drol·o·gist (hī drol′ə jist) *n.* an expert in hydrology.

hy·drol·o·gy (hī drol′ə jē) *n.* the branch of physical geography that deals with the laws, properties, distribution, etc. of water.

hy·drol·y·sis (hī drol′ə sis) *n.* **-ses** (-sēz′). a chemical decomposition that changes a compound into other compounds by taking up the elements of water. [< *hydro-* + Gk. *lysis* a loosening]

hy·dro·lyze (hī′drə līz′) *v.* **-lyzed, -lyz·ing.** decompose by hydrolysis. **—hy′dro·ly·za′tion,** *n.*

hy·dro·me·chan·ics (hī′drō mə kan′iks) *n.* the branch

of physics dealing with the mechanics of fluids, or of their laws of equilibrium or motion.

hy·drom·e·ter (hī drom′ə tər) *n.* a graduated instrument for finding the specific gravities of liquids.

hy·dro·met·ric (hī′drə met′rik) *adj.* **1** of or having to do with hydrometry. **2** of or having to do with a hydrometer.

hy·dro·met·ri·cal (hī′drə met′rə kəl) *adj.* hydrometric.

hy·drom·e·try (hī drom′ə trē) *n.* the determination of specific gravity, purity, etc. by means of a hydrometer.

hy·dro·path·ic (hī drə path′ik) *adj.* of or using hydropathy. —*n.* a sanitarium that specializes in hydropathy.

hy·drop·a·thy (hī drop′ə thē) *n.* the treatment of disease by using quantities of water externally and internally.

hy·dro·pho·bi·a (hī′drə fō′bē ə) *n.* **1** an infectious disease of dogs and other flesh-eating mammals that causes convulsions, frothing at the mouth, madness, and, usually, death; rabies. The disease can be transmitted to man and other animals by the bite of an infected animal. **2** a morbid dread of water.

hy·dro·pho·bic (hī′drə fō′bik) *adj.* **1** of or having to do with hydrophobia. **2** suffering from hydrophobia.

hy·dro·phone (hī′drə fōn′) *n.* **1** an instrument for detecting the position and source of sounds under water. **2** an instrument detecting water flowing in a pipe, used in finding leaks. **3** in medicine, a listening instrument for detecting sounds through a column of water.

hy·dro·phyte (hī′drə fīt′) *n.* any plant that can grow only in water or very wet soil. Most algae are hydrophytes.

hy·dro·plane (hī′drə plān′) *n.* **1** a motorboat that glides on the surface of the water. **2** a finlike surface that lifts a motorboat or seaplane slightly above the level of the water; hydrofoil. **3** an aircraft that can take off from or come down on the water; seaplane.

hy·dro·pon·ic (hī′drə pon′ik) *adj.* of, produced, or grown by hydroponics.

hy·dro·pon·ics (hī′drə pon′iks) *n.* the growing of plants in water without soil. [< *hydro-* + L *ponere* to place]

hy·dro·qui·none (hī′drō kwi nōn′ or -kwin′ōn) *n.* a white, sweetish, crystalline compound, used in photographic developers and in medicine. *Formula*: $C_6H_4(OH)_2$

hy·dro·sol (hī′drə sol′ or -sōl′) *n.* in chemistry, a colloid in a water solution.

hy·dro·sphere (hī′drə sfēr′) *n.* **1** the water on the surface of the globe. **2** the water vapor in the atmosphere.

hy·dro·stat (hī′drə stat′) *n.* **1** any of various devices for preventing injury to a steam boiler as a result of lack of water. **2** an electrical device for detecting the presence of water from overflow, leakage, etc. [< *hydro-* + Gk. *-statos* that stands]

hy·dro·stat·ic (hī′drə stat′ik) *adj.* of or having to do with hydrostatics.

hy·dro·stat·ics (hī′drə stat′iks) *n.* the branch of physics that deals with the equilibrium and pressure of water and other liquids.

hy·dro·ther·a·peu·tics (hī′drō ther′ə pū′tiks) *n.* hydropathy.

hy·dro·ther·a·py (hī′drō ther′ə pē) *n.* the treatment of various diseases by means of water; hydropathy.

hy·dro·trop·ic (hī′drə trop′ik) *adj.* having the tendency to turn or move toward, or away from, water.

hy·drot·ro·pism (hī drot′rə piz′əm) *n.* a tendency to turn or move toward or away from water. Hydrotropism causes roots to grow toward water.

hy·drous (hī′drəs) *adj.* containing water, usually in combination. A hydrous salt is a crystalline compound. [< Gk. *hydōr* water]

hy·drox·id (hī drok′sid) *n.* hydroxide.

hy·drox·ide (hī drok′sīd or hī drok′sid) *n.* in chemistry, any compound consisting of an element or radical combined with one or more hydroxyl radicals. Hydroxides of metals are bases; those of non-metals are acids.

hy·drox·yl (hī drok′səl) *n.* in chemistry, a univalent radical, —OH. It is found in all hydroxides.

hy·dro·zo·an (hī′drə zō′ən) *n.* any of a group of invertebrate water animals including hydras, polyps, many jellyfishes, etc. [< NL *Hydrozoa*, the genus name < Gk. *hydōr* water + *zōon* animal]

hy·e·na (hī ē′nə) *n.* a wolflike flesh-eating mammal of Africa and Asia. Also, **hyaena.** [< L *hyaena* < Gk. *hyaina* < *hys* pig]

Hy·ge·ia (hī jē′ə) *n.* in Greek mythology, the goddess of health.

hy·giene (hī′jēn) *n.* the rules of health; science of keeping well. [< F < NL (*ars*) *hygieina* the healthful art < Gk. *hygieinē* < *hygiēs* healthy]

hy·gien·ic (hī jē′nik or hī jen′ik) *adj.* **1** healthful; sanitary. **2** having to do with health or hygiene. **—hy′gi·en′i·cal·ly,** *adv.*

hy·gien·ist (hī′jēn ist) *n.* a person who is trained in hygiene.

hygro- *combining form.* wet; moist; moisture, as in *hygrometer.* [< Gk. *hygro-* < *hygros* wet]

hy·grom·e·ter (hī grom′ə tər) *n.* an instrument for determining the amount of moisture in the air.

hy·gro·met·ric (hī′grə met′rik) *adj.* **1** of or having to do with hygrometry. **2** absorbing moisture readily; sensitive to moisture.

hy·grom·e·try (hī grom′ə trē) *n.* the science of determining the amount of moisture in the air.

hy·gro·scope (hī′grə skōp′) *n.* an instrument that shows the variations in the humidity of the air.

hy·gro·scop·ic (hī′grə skop′ik) *adj.* **1** having to do with or perceptible by the hygroscope. **2** absorbing or attracting moisture from the air.

hy·ing (hī′ing) *v.* ppr. of **hie.**

Hyk·sos (hik′sos or hik′sōs) *n.pl.* Shepherd Kings, the foreign rulers of Egypt from about 1750 B.C. to about 1600 B.C.

hy·la (hī′lə) *n.* a tree toad. [< NL < Gk. *hylē* wood]

Hy·men (hī′mən) *n.* in Greek mythology, the god of marriage.

hy·men (hī′mən) *n.* in anatomy, a fold of mucous membrane extending partly across the opening into the vagina. [< LL < Gk.]

hy·me·ne·al (hī′mə nē′əl) *adj.* having to do with marriage. —*n.* a wedding song.

hy·me·nop·ter·ous (hī′mə nop′tər əs) *adj.* belonging to a group of insects including ants, bees, and wasps. Winged hymenopterous insects have four membranous wings. [< Gk. *hymenopteros* < *hymēn* membrane + *pteron* wing]

hymn (him) *n.* **1** a song in praise or honor of God. **2** any song of praise. —*v.* praise or honor with a hymn. [< L < Gk. *hymnos*] **—hymn′like′,** *adj.*

hym·nal (him′nəl) *n.* a book of hymns.

hym·nar·y (him′ner′ē or him′nər ē) *n.* **-ies.** a book of hymns; hymnal.

hym·nol·o·gist (him nol′ə jist) *n.* **1** an expert in hymnology. **2** a composer of hymns.

hym·nol·o·gy (him nol′ə jē) *n.* **1** the study of hymns, their history, classification, etc. **2** hymns collectively. **3** the composing of hymns.

hy·oid (hī′oid) *n.* **1** in anatomy, the U-shaped bone at the root of the tongue. **2** in zoology, a corresponding bone or collection of bones. —*adj.* of or having to do with this bone. [< F < NL < Gk. *hyoeidēs* U-shaped < Υ (upsilon) + *eidos* form]

hyp. **1** hypothesis. **2** hypotenuse.

hyper- *prefix.* over; above; beyond; exceedingly; to excess, as in *hyperacidity, hypersensitive.* [< Gk. *hyper-* < *hyper*]

hy·per·a·cid·i·ty (hī′pər ə sid′ə tē) *n.* excessive acidity.

hy·per·bo·la (hī pėr′bə lə) *n.* **-las.** in geometry, a curve formed when a cone is cut by a plane making a larger angle with the base than the side of the cone makes. See **conic section** for diagram. [< NL < Gk. *hyperbolē*, ult. < *hyper-* beyond + *ballein* throw]

hat, āge, cãre, fär; let, ēqual, tėrm; it, īce
hot, ōpen, ôrder; oil, out; cup, pu̇t, rüle, ūse
əbove, takən, pencəl, lemən, circəs
ch, child; ng, long; sh, ship
th, thin; ᴛʜ, then; zh, measure

hy·per·bo·le (hī pėr′bə lē) *n.* exaggeration for effect. *Example*: Waves high as mountains broke over the reef. [< L < Gk. *hyperbolē*. See HYBERBOLA.]

hy·per·bol·ic (hī′pər bol′ik) *adj.* **1** of, like, or using hyperbole; exaggerated; exaggerating. **2** of or having to do with hyperbolas. —**hy′per·bol′i·cal·ly,** *adv.*

Hy·per·bo·re·an (hī′pər bô′rē ən) *n.* **1** in Greek legend, one of a group of people described as living in a land of perpetual sunshine and plenty beyond the north wind. **2 hyperborean,** an inhabitant of the far north. —*adj.* **hyperborean,** of the far north; arctic; frigid. [< LL *Hyperboreanus* < L *Hyperboreus* < Gk. *Hyperboreos* beyond the north < *hyper-* beyond + *boreios* northern < *boreas* the north wind]

hy·per·crit·i·cal (hī′pər krit′ə kəl) *adj.* excessively critical. —**hy′per·crit′i·cal·ly,** *adv.*

Hy·pe·ri·on (hī pēr′ē ən) *n.* in Greek mythology: **1** a Titan, father of the sun god Helios. **2** Helios. **3** Apollo.

hy·per·o·pi·a (hī′pər ō′pē ə) *n.* far-sightedness. [< NL < Gk. *hyper-* beyond + *ōps* eye]

hy·per·op·ic (hī′pər op′ik) *adj.* far-sighted.

hy·per·sen·si·tive (hī′pər sen′sə tiv) *adj.* excessively sensitive. —**hy′per·sen′si·tive·ness,** *n.*

hy·per·sen·si·tiv·i·ty (hī′pər sen′sə tiv′ə tē) *n.* excessive sensitiveness.

hy·per·son·ic (hī′pər son′ik) *adj.* **1** of or denoting speed five or more times faster than that of sound. **2** able to travel at this speed.

hy·per·ten·sion (hī′pər ten′shən) *n.* an abnormally high blood pressure.

hy·per·thy·roid (hī′pər thī′roid) *n.* **1** an overactive thyroid gland. **2** a person having such a gland. —*adj.* relating to an overactive thyroid gland.

hy·per·tro·phy (hī pėr′trə fē) *n.* **-phies,** *v.* **-phied, -phy·ing.** —*n.* the enlargement of a part or organ; a growing too big. —*v.* grow too big. [< NL *hypertrophia* < Gk. *hyper-* over + *trophē* nourishment]

hy·phen (hī′fən) *n.* a mark (-) used to connect the parts of certain words, such as *tail-less, radio-active, re-enter,* or the parts of a word divided at the end of a line, etc. —*v.* hyphenate. [< LL < Gk. *hyphen* in one, hyphen < *hypo-* under + *hen* one]

hy·phen·ate (hī′fən āt′) *v.* **-at·ed, -at·ing.** connect by a hyphen; write or print with a hyphen.

hy·phen·a·tion (hī′fən ā′shən) *n.* the act of connecting by or writing with a hyphen.

hyp·nol·o·gy (hip nol′ə jē) *n.* the branch of science dealing with the phenomena of sleep.

hyp·no·sis (hip nō′sis) *n.* **-ses** (-sēz). a state resembling deep sleep, but more active, in which a person has little will of his own and little feeling, and acts according to the suggestions of the person who induced the hypnosis. [< NL]

hyp·not·ic (hip not′ik) *adj.* **1** of hypnosis. **2** easily hypnotized. **3** in a hypnotized state. **4** causing or tending to cause sleep. —*n.* **1** a person who is hypnotized or easily hypnotized. **2** a drug or other means of causing sleep. [< LL *hypnoticus* < Gk. *hypnotikos* putting to sleep < *hypnoein* put to sleep < *hypnos* sleep]

hyp·not·i·cal·ly (hip not′ik lē) *adv.* in a hypnotic manner.

hyp·no·tism (hip′nə tiz′əm) *n.* **1** the inducing of hypnosis; hypnotizing. **2** the science dealing with hypnosis.

hyp·no·tist (hip′nə tist) *n.* a person who hypnotizes.

hyp·no·tize (hip′nə tīz′) *v.* **-tized, -tiz·ing. 1** put into a hypnotic state; cause hypnosis. **2** *Informal.* dominate or control the will of by suggestion. —**hyp′no·tiz′a·ble,** *adj.* —**hyp′no·ti·za′tion,** *n.* —**hyp′no·tiz′er,** *n.*

hy·po[1] (hī′pō) *n.* a colorless crystalline salt used as a fixing agent in photography; sodium thiosulphate or sodium hyposulphite. *Formula*: $Na_2S_2O_3{\cdot}5H_2O$ [short for *hyposulphite*]

hy·po[2] (hī′pō) *n.* **-pos.** *Informal.* hypodermic.

hypo- *prefix.* **1** under; beneath; below, as in *hypodermic.* **2** less than; less than normal, as in *hypothyroid.* [< Gk. *hypo-* < *hypo*]

hy·po·chlo·rite (hī′pə klô′rīt) *n.* a salt of hypochlorous acid.

hy·po·chlo·rous acid (hī′pə klô′rəs) a yellow solution with an irritating odor, used as a bleach, disinfectant, etc. *Formula*: HClO

hy·po·chon·dri·a (hī′pə kon′drē ə) *n.* **1** unnatural anxiety about one's health; imaginary illness. **2** low spirits without any real reason. [< LL *hypochondria* abdomen < Gk. *hypochondria,* neut. pl. < *hypo-* under + *chondros* cartilage (of the breastbone); from the supposed seat of melancholy]

hy·po·chon·dri·ac (hī′pə kon′drē ak′) *n.* a person suffering from hypochondria. —*adj.* suffering from hypochondria.

hy·po·cot·yl (hī′pə kot′əl) *n.* the part of the stem below the cotyledons in the embryo of a plant. [< *hypo-* + *cotyl(edon)*]

hy·poc·ri·sy (hi pok′rə sē) *n.* **-sies. 1** the act or fact of putting on a false appearance of goodness or religion. **2** a pretending to be what one is not; pretence. [ME < OF *ypocrisie* < LL < Gk. *hypokrisis* acting, dissimulation, ult. < *hypo-* under + *krinein* judge]

hyp·o·crite (hip′ə krit′) *n.* **1** a person who puts on a false appearance of goodness or religion. **2** a person who pretends to be what he is not; pretender. [ME < OF *ypocrite* < L < Gk. *hypokritēs* actor. Related to HYPOCRISY.]

hyp·o·crit·i·cal (hip′ə krit′ə kəl) *adj.* of or like a hypocrite; insincere. —**hyp′o·crit′i·cal·ly,** *adv.*

hy·po·der·mic (hī′pə dėr′mik) *adj.* **1** under the skin. **2** injected or for injecting under the skin: *The doctor used a hypodermic needle.* —*n.* **1** a dose of medicine injected under the skin: *The doctor gave her a hypodermic to make her sleep.* **2** a syringe used to inject medicine under the skin. [< NL *hypoderma* < Gk. *hypo-* under + *derma* skin]

A hypodermic needle being withdrawn after an injection. The "needle" actually consists of a hollow needle, which pierces the skin, a tube for the medicine, and a plunger that forces the medicine through the needle.

hy·po·der·mi·cal·ly (hī′pə dėr′mik lē) *adv.* by injection under the skin.

hypodermic injection an injection of medicine under the skin.

hy·po·gas·tric (hī′pə gas′trik) *adj.* of or having to do with the lower middle region of the abdomen.

hy·po·phos·phate (hī′pə fos′fāt) *n.* a salt of hypophosphoric acid.

hy·po·phos·phite (hī′pə fos′fīt) *n.* a salt of hypophosphorous acid, used in medicine as a tonic.

hy·po·phos·phor·ic (hī′ pō fos fôr′ik) *adj.* of or having to do with an acid, $H_4P_2O_6$, produced by the slow oxidation of phosphorus in moist air.

hy·po·phos·pho·rous (hī′pə fos′fə rəs) *adj.* of or having to do with an acid of phosphorus, H_3PO_2, having salts which are used in medicine.

hy·poph·y·sis (hī pof′ə sis) *n.* **-ses** (-sēz′). the pituitary gland. [< Gk. *hypophysis* attachment underneath < *hypo-* under + *physis* a growing < *phyein* cause to grow]

hy·po·sul·phite or **hy·po·sul·fite** (hī′pə sul′fīt) *n.* a salt of hyposulphurous acid.

hy·po·sul·phur·ous or **hy·po·sul·fur·ous** (hī′pō sul′fər əs, -sul′fū rəs, or -sul fūr′əs) *adj.* of or having to do with an acid, $H_2S_2O_4$, used as a reducing and bleaching agent.

hy·pot·e·nuse (hī pot′ə nūz′ or hī pot′ə nüz′, hī pot′ə-nūs′ or hī pot′ə nüs′) *n.* the side of a right-angled triangle opposite the right angle. See diagram on the next page.

[< LL *hypotenusa* < Gk. *hypoteinousa* subtending, ppr. of *hypoteinein* < *hypo-* under + *teinein* stretch]

HYPOTENUSE 90°

hy·po·thal·a·mic (hī′pə thə lam′ik or hip′ə-) *adj.* of or having to do with the hypothalamus.

hy·po·thal·a·mus (hī′pə thal′ə məs or hip′ə-) *n.* the part of the brain beneath the thalamus. It controls hunger, thirst, temperature, and growth.

hy·poth·e·cate (hī poth′ə kāt′) *v.* **-cat·ed, -cat·ing.** pledge (property, stock, etc.) to a creditor as security for a loan or debt; mortgage. [< Med.L *hypothecare* < L < Gk. *hypothēkē* pledge < *hypo-* under + *tithenai* place] —**hy·poth′e·ca′tor,** *n.*

hy·poth·e·ca·tion (hī poth′ə kā′shən) *n.* **1** the act or fact of depositing as security. **2** a claim against property deposited as security.

hy·poth·e·nuse (hī pot′ə nūz′ or hī pot′ə nüz′, hī poth′ə nūs′ or hī poth′ə nüs′) *n.* hypotenuse.

hy·poth·e·ses (hī poth′ə sēz′) *n.* pl. of **hypothesis.**

hy·poth·e·sis (hī poth′ə sis) *n.* **-ses. 1** something assumed because it seems likely to be a true explanation; theory. **2** a proposition assumed as a basis for reasoning. [< NL < Gk. *hypothesis* < *hypo-* under + *thesis* a placing] —Syn. **1** See **theory.**

hy·poth·e·size (hī poth′ə sīz′) *v.* **-sized, -siz·ing. 1** make a hypothesis. **2** assume; suppose.

hy·po·thet·ic (hī′pə thet′ik) *adj.* hypothetical.

hy·po·thet·i·cal (hī′pə thet′ə kəl) *adj.* **1** of or based on a hypothesis; assumed; supposed. **2** in logic: **a** of a proposition, involving a hypothesis or condition; conditional. **b** of a syllogism, having a hypothetical proposition for one of its premises. **3** fond of making hypotheses: *a hypothetical scientist.* [< L < Gk. *hypothetikos*] —**hy′po·thet′i·cal·ly,** *adv.*

hy·po·thy·roid (hī′pə thī′roid) *n.* **1** an underactive thyroid gland. **2** a person having such a gland. —*adj.* relating to an underactive thyroid gland.

hy·rax (hī′raks) *n.* any of various small, timid, rabbitlike mammals of Asia and Africa. [< NL *Hyrax* the generic name < Gk. *hyrax* shrew-mouse]

hy·son (hī′sən) *n.* a Chinese green tea. [< Chinese *hsi-ch'un* blooming spring]

hys·sop (his′əp) *n.* **1** a fragrant, bushy plant of the same family as mint, used for medicine, flavoring, etc. **2** in the Bible, a plant whose twigs were used in certain Jewish ceremonies. Psalms 51:7. [ME < OF < L < Gk. *hyssōpos* < Semitic]

hys·ter·ec·to·my (his′tə rek′tə mē) *n.* in surgery, removal of the uterus. [< Gk. *hystera* uterus + *ektomē* a cutting]

hys·te·ri·a (his tēr′ē ə or his ter′ē ə) *n.* **1** a nervous disorder that causes violent fits of laughing and crying, imaginary and, often, real illnesses, or general lack of self-control. **2** senseless excitement. [< NL < Gk. *hystera* uterus; because it was formerly thought that women are more often affected than men]

hys·ter·ic (his ter′ik) *adj.* hysterical.

hys·ter·i·cal (his ter′ə kəl) *adj.* **1** unnaturally excited. **2** showing an extreme lack of control; unable to stop laughing, crying, etc.; suffering from hysteria: *She was hysterical with grief.* [< L < Gk. *hysterikos* < *hystera* uterus] —**hys·ter′i·cal·ly,** *adv.*

hys·ter·ics (his ter′iks) *n.pl.* a fit of hysterical laughing and crying.

I[1] or **i** (ī) *n.* **I's** or **i's. 1** the ninth letter of the English alphabet. **2** any speech sound represented by this letter. **3** the ninth of a series designated alphabetically.

I[2] (ī) *pron. nom.* **I**; *poss.* **mine**; *obj.* **me**; *pl.nom.* **we**; *poss.* **ours**; *obj.* **us**; *n.* **I's.** the person who is speaking or writing. [OE *ic*]

☛ The pronoun *I* is written with a capital simply because in the old handwritten manuscripts a small *i* was likely to be lost or to get attached to a neighboring word, and a capital helped keep it a distinct word.

i- *prefix.* the form of **in-**[1] before *gn*, as in *ignore.*

i a Roman numeral for 1.

i. 1 intransitive. **2** island. **3** interest. **4** incisor.

I 1 a Roman numeral for 1. **2** iodine.

I. 1 Island; Islands. **2** Isle; Isles. **3** in politics, Independent.

Ia. Iowa.

IAEA International Atomic Energy Agency (of the United Nations).

-ial *suffix.* a form of **-al,** used in *adverbial, facial,* etc.

i·amb (ī′amb) *n.* an iambic foot or measure. [< F < L < Gk. *iambos*]

i·am·bic (ī am′bik) *n.* **1** in verse, a measure consisting of two syllables, a weakly stressed followed by a strongly stressed or a short syllable followed by a long one. **2** Usually, **iambics,** *pl.* a verse of iambics.
—*adj.* of or containing iambic measures. *Example*:

> "The sún | that bríef | Decém | ber dáy
> Rose chéer | less ó | ver hílls | of gráy."

i·am·bus (ī am′bəs) *n.* **-bi** (-bī or -bē) or **-bus·es.** iamb.

-ian *suffix.* a form of **-an,** used in *Canadian, Presbyterian,* etc.

-iana *suffix.* a form of *-ana,* as in *Canadiana.*

IATA International Air Transport Association.

ib. ibidem.

I·be·ri·an (ī bēr′ē ən) *adj.* **1** of or having to do with Iberia, a peninsula of S.W. Europe, or its people. **2** of or having to do with the Iberian people. **3** of or having to do with ancient Iberia (south of the Caucasus in Asia) or its people.
—*n.* **1** an inhabitant of ancient Iberia. The Basques are supposed to be descended from the Iberians. **2** the language of ancient Iberia. **3** a member of a dark, long-headed people inhabiting a great part of S. Europe and parts of N. Africa. **4** an inhabitant of ancient Iberia in Asia.

i·bex (ī′beks) *n.* **i·bex·es, ib·i·ces** (ib′ə sēz′ or ī′bə sēz′), or (*esp. collectively*) **i·bex.** a wild goat of Europe, Asia, or Africa. The male ibex has very large horns. [< L]

ibid. ibidem.

☛ **Ibid** is used in a footnote to refer to the book, article, etc. mentioned in the immediately preceding footnote.

i·bi·dem (i bī′dem) *adv. Latin.* in the same place; in the same book, chapter, page, passage, etc. *Abbrev.*: ibid. or ib.

i·bis (ī′bis) *n.* **i·bis·es** or (*esp. collectively*) **i·bis.** a long-legged wading bird resembling a heron. The ancient Egyptians regarded the ibis as sacred. [< L < Gk. < Egyptian]

-ible *suffix.* that can be ——ed, as in *impressible, perfectible, reducible.* [< OF < L *-ibilis*] ☛ See **-able** for usage note.

-ic *suffix.* **1** of or having to do with, as in *atmospheric, Icelandic.* **2** having the nature of, as in *artistic, heroic.* **3** constituting or being, as in *bombastic, monolithic.* **4** characterized by; containing; made up of, as in *alcoholic, iambic.* **5** made by; caused by, as in *phonographic.* **6** like; like that of; characteristic of, as in *meteoric, antagonistic, idyllic, sophomoric.* Many words ending in *-ic* have two or more of these meanings (1 to 6). **7** in chemical terms, *-ic* implies a smaller proportion of the element that *-ous* implies, as in *boric, chloric, ferric, sulphuric.* [< F *-ique* or L *-icus* or Gk. *-ikos*]

-ical *suffix.* **1** *-ic,* as in *geometrical, parasitical, hysterical.* **2** *-ic,* specialized or differentiated in meaning, as in *economical.* **3** *-ical* sometimes arises from *-al* added to nouns ending in *-ic,* as in *critical, musical.* [< L *-icalis*]

-ically *suffix.* *-ic* + *-ly.* Instead of *artistic-ly* we write *artistically*; instead of *alphabetic-ly* we write *alphabetically.* In speaking, the suffix is ordinarily pronounced in two syllables (-ik lē).

ICAO International Civil Aviation Organization (of the United Nations).

I·car·i·an (i kãr′ē ən or ī kãr′ē ən) *adj.* rash; carelessly bold. [< *Icarus*]

Ic·a·rus (ik′ə rəs or ī′kə rəs) *n.* in Greek legend, the son of Daedalus. When he and his father were escaping from Crete, using wings that Daedalus had made, Icarus flew so high that the sun melted the wax which held the wings on, and he fell to his death in the sea.

ICBM Intercontinental Ballistic Missile.

ice (īs) *n. adj. v.* **iced, ic·ing.** **—*n.*** **1** water made solid by freezing; frozen water. **2** a layer or surface of ice. **3** a frozen area of sea or land: *Icebreakers cut through ice. Baby seals are found on the ice.* **4** a natural or artificially frozen surface for skating, hockey, curling, etc. **5** especially in Newfoundland, the seal-hunting grounds on the edge of the Arctic icefields. **6** something that looks or feels like ice: *camphor ice.* **7** a frozen dessert, usually made of sweetened fruit juice. **8** icing. **9** *Slang.* diamonds. **10** coldness of manner. **11 break the ice,** *Informal.* **a** make a beginning; start something dangerous or difficult. **b** overcome first difficulties in taking or getting acquainted. **12 cut no ice,** *Informal.* have little or no effect. **13 on thin ice,** in a dangerous or difficult position.
—*adj.* **1** of ice; having to do with ice. **2** made or consisting of ice.
—*v.* **1** cool with ice; put ice in or around. **2** cover with ice. **3** turn to ice; freeze. **4** cover with icing. **5** in hockey: **a** shoot (a puck) from the defensive zone past the red line at the opposite end of the rink: *No player may ice the puck when his team is at full strength.* **b** put a team into play: *Our town iced a good hockey team.* [OE *īs*]
—ice′less, *adj.*

ice age a glacial epoch.

ice·berg (īs′bėrg′) *n.* a large mass of ice floating in the sea. [? < Du. *ijsberg,* literally, ice mountain]

ice·boat (īs′bōt′) *n.* **1** a triangular frame on runners, fitted with sails for sailing on ice. **2** an icebreaker.

ice·bound (īs′bound′) *adj.* **1** held fast by ice; frozen in. **2** shut in or obstructed by ice.

ice-box or **ice·box** (īs′boks′) *n.* **1** an insulated cabinet containing ice, used to keep food from spoiling. **2** a refrigerator.

ice·break·er (īs′brāk′ər) *n.* **1** a ship designed for breaking a passage through ice. **2** a structure for protection against moving ice.

ice bridge **1** a winter road over a frozen river, lake, etc. **2** a bridge of ice formed by the jamming of ice in a river or other channel.

ice·cap (īs′kap′) *n.* a permanent covering of ice over an area, sloping down on all sides from an elevated centre.

ice cream (īs′krēm′ or īs′krēm′) a frozen dessert made of cream or custard sweetened and flavored.

ice cube a small piece of ice, usually having six sides, used for chilling drinks or food.

iced (īst) *adj.* **1** cooled with ice. **2** covered with ice. **3** covered with icing.

ice field **1** a large sheet of ice floating in the sea, smaller than a floe. **2** a large sheet of ice on land.

ice-fish·er·man (īs′fish′ər mən) *n.* a person who goes ice fishing.

ice fishing the act or practice of fishing through a hole or holes cut through ice.

ice hockey the game of hockey played on ice. See **hockey.**

ice·house (īs′hous′) *n.* **1** a building where ice is stored and kept from melting. **2** a structure or pit having insulated walls and roof and used as a cold storage for meat and other perishables which are stored with blocks of ice or snow. **3** a snow house.

ice island an iceberg several miles wide and hundreds of feet thick that has its top flattish.

ice-jam (īs′jam′) *n.v.* **-jammed, -jam·ming.** **—*n.*** Also, **ice jam.** the damming up of a river or other watercourse with masses of ice that cannot float down owing to some obstruction. **—*v.*** block by an ice-jam.

Ice·land·er (īs′lan′dər or īs′lən dər) *n.* a native or

hat, āge, cãre, fär; let, ēqual, tėrm; it, īce
hot, ōpen, ôrder; oil, out; cup, pu̇t, rüle, ūse
əbove, takən, pencəl, lemən, circəs
ch, child; ng, long; sh, ship
th, thin; ᴛʜ, then; zh, measure

inhabitant of Iceland, a large island in the N. Atlantic.

Ice·lan·dic (īs lan′dik) *adj.* of or having to do with Iceland, its people, or their language. **—*n.*** the Scandinavian language of Iceland.

Iceland moss a lichen of the arctic regions, used as a food, in medicine, etc.

ice·man (īs′man′ or īs′mən) *n.* **-men** (-men′ or -mən). a man who sells, delivers, or handles ice.

ice pack **1** a large area of floating ice, consisting of separate masses more or less packed together. **2** a bag containing ice for application to the body.

ice pick a sharp-pointed tool for breaking up ice.

ice road ice bridge (def. 1).

ice sheet a broad, thick sheet of ice covering a very large area for a long time.

ice-skate (īs′skat′) *v.* **-skat·ed, -skat·ing.** skate on ice. **—ice′-skat′er,** *n.*

ice skates **1** a pair of metal runners to be attached to boots for skating on ice. **2** the runners and boots together.

ice water **1** water cooled with ice. **2** melted ice.

ice worm **1** *Cdn.* in the North: **a** a fictional creature, thought up as a joke. **b ice-worm cocktail,** a cocktail having bits of spaghetti in it. **2** a worm found on mountain snow and ice fields. [coined during the Klondike gold rush]

ich·neu·mon (ik nū′mən or ik nü′mən) *n.* **1** a small, brownish mammal of Egypt, resembling the weasel. **2** the ichneumon fly. [< L < Gk. *ichneumōn,* literally, searcher (supposedly of crocodile's eggs), ult. < *ichnos* track]

ichneumon fly an insect that looks like a wasp but does not sting. The larvae of this fly live as parasites in or on other insects, usually killing them.

i·chor[1] (ī′kôr or ī′kər) *n.* in Greek mythology, the fluid supposed to flow in the veins of the gods. [< Gk.]

i·chor[2] (ī′kôr or ī′kər) *n.* in medicine, an acrid, watery discharge from ulcers, wounds, etc. [< NL < Gk.]

ich·thy·ol·o·gist (ik′thē ol′ə jist) *n.* an expert in ichthyology.

ich·thy·ol·o·gy (ik′thē ol′ə jē) *n.* the branch of zoology dealing with fishes. [< Gk. *ichthys* fish + E *-logy*]

ich·thy·o·saur (ik′thē ə sôr′) *n.* an extinct fishlike marine reptile having four paddle-like flippers. [< NL *ichthyosaurus* < Gk. *ichthys* fish + *sauros* lizard]

ich·thy·o·sau·rus (ik′thē ə sô′rəs) *n.* **-sau·ri** (-sô′rī or -sô′rē). ichthyosaur.

i·ci·cle (ī′si kəl) *n.* **1** a pointed, hanging stick of ice formed by the freezing of dripping water. **2** anything resembling this, such as tinsel for trimming a Christmas tree. **3** *Informal.* a cold or unemotional person. [ME *isykle* < OE *īs* ice + *gicel* icicle]

ic·ing (īs′ing) *n.* a mixture of fine sugar, flavoring, a liquid, and, sometimes, the whites of eggs; frosting.

i·con or **i·kon** (ī′kon) *n.* **i·cons, i·co·nes** (ī′kə nēz′). **1** a sacred picture or image of Christ, an angel, a saint, etc. **2** a picture; image. Also, **eikon.** [< L < Gk. *eikōn*]

i·con·o·clasm (ī kon′ ə klaz′əm) *n.* the belief or practice of iconoclasts.

i·con·o·clast (ī kon′ə klast′) *n.* **1** a person opposed to worshipping images. **2** a person who attacks cherished beliefs or institutions. [< Med.L *ikonoklastes* < Med.Gk. *eikonoklastēs* < Gk. *eikōn* image + *klaein* break]

i·con·o·clas·tic (ī kon′ə klas′tik) *adj.* of or having to do with iconoclasts.

i·co·nog·ra·phy (ī′kə nog′rə fē) *n.* **-phies.** **1** the art or study of illustrating by means of icons, symbols, etc. **2** the representation of an individual in portraits, statues, etc. [< Med.L < Gk. *eikonographia.* See **icon, -graphy.**]

-ics *suffix.* **1** facts, principles, science, as in *physics.* **2** methods, system, activities, as in *tactics.* [originally pl. of *-ic* < L *-ica* < Gk. *-ika,* neut. pl.]

ic·tas (ik′təs) *n.pl.* iktas.

ic·ter·ic (ik ter′ik) *n.* **1** a remedy for jaundice. **2** one who is affected with jaundice. —*adj.* of or having to do with icterus.

ic·ter·us (ik′tər əs) *n.* **1** jaundice. **2** in botany, the yellowing of certain plants, caused by too much cold or moisture. [< L *icterus* jaundice < Gk. *ikteros* a yellow bird believed to cure jaundice]

ic·tus (ik′təs) *n.* **-tus·es** or **-tus.** rhythmical or metrical stress. [< L *ictus* a blow < *icere* to hit]

i·cy (ī′sē) *adj.* **i·ci·er, i·ci·est. 1** like ice; very cold; slippery. **2** having much ice; covered with ice. **3** of ice. **4** without warm feeling; cold and unfriendly. —**i′ci·ly,** *adv.* —**i′ci·ness,** *n.* —**Syn. 1** frosty, frigid.

I'd (īd) **1** I should. **2** I would. **3** I had.

id. idem.

Id. Idaho.

Ida. Idaho.

ID card identification card.

-ide or **-id** *suffix.* compound of ——, as in *chloride, sulphide.* [< *oxide*]

i·de·a (ī dē′ə) *n.* **1** a mental concept or abstraction: *the idea of immortality.* **2** an opinion: *to force one's ideas on others.* **3** resourcefulness; creative thinking: *a man of ideas.* **4** a plan, scheme: *a bright idea.* **5** the point or purpose: *The idea of a vacation is to relax.* **6** in exclamations, something outrageous: *The very idea!* **7** a premonition; fancy; notion: *I had an idea you would be here for dinner.* **8 get ideas into one's head,** expect too much. **9 the young idea,** the child's way of thinking. [< L < Gk. *idea* form, kind < base *id-* see]

Syn. Idea, notion, thought = something understood or formed in the mind. **Idea** is the general word applying to something existing in the mind as the result of understanding, thinking, reasoning, imagining, etc.: *Learn to express your ideas clearly.* Historically, **idea** has been the subject of many philosophical theories. **Notion** applies to an idea not fully, clearly, plainly, or completely formed or understood: *I have only a notion of what you mean.* **Thought** applies to an idea formed by reflection or reasoning, rather than by the imagination: *Tell me your thoughts on this proposal.*

☛ **idea.** With a dependent verb, the idiom is *idea of* plus a gerund: *They got the happy idea of climbing Sugarloaf Hill.* Not: *They got the happy idea to climb Sugarloaf Hill.*

i·de·al (ī dē′əl) *n.* a perfect type; model to be imitated; what one would wish to be: *Florence Nightingale is the nurse's ideal. Religions set high ideals for us to follow.* —*adj.* **1** just as one would wish; perfect: *A warm, sunny day is ideal for a picnic.* **2** existing only in thought: *A point without length, breadth, or thickness is an ideal object.* **3** not practical; visionary. **4** having to do with ideas; representing an idea. [< LL *idealis* < L *idea.* See IDEA.] —**i·de′al-less,** *adj.* —**Syn.** *adj.* **3** unreal, fanciful.

i·de·al·ism (ī dē′əl iz′əm) *n.* **1** an acting according to one's ideals of what ought to be, regardless of circumstances or of the approval or disapproval of others. **2** a cherishing of fine ideals. **3** in art or literature, the representing of imagined types rather than an exact copy of any one person, instance, or situation. Idealism is opposed to realism. **4** in philosophy, the belief that all our knowledge is a knowledge of ideas and that it is impossible to know whether there really is a world of objects on which our ideas are based. Idealism is opposed to materialism, which holds that objects really exist apart from our ideas about them.

i·de·al·ist (ī dē′əl ist) *n.* **1** a person who acts according to his ideals; a person who has fine ideals. **2** a person who neglects practical matters in following ideals. **3** in art, literature, or philosophy, an adherent of idealism.

i·de·al·is·tic (ī′dē əl is′tik or ī dē′əl is′tik) *adj.* **1** having high ideals and acting according to them. **2** forgetting or neglecting practical matters in trying to follow out one's ideals; not practical. **3** of idealism or idealists. —**i·de′al·is′ti·cal·ly,** *adv.*

i·de·al·i·ty (ī′dē al′ə tē) *n.* **-ties. 1** an ideal quality or character. **2** an ability to idealize. **3** something ideal or imaginary.

i·de·al·i·za·tion (ī dē′əl ə zā′shən or ī dē′əl ī zā′shən) *n.* **1** the process of idealizing. **2** the state of being idealized. **3** the result of idealizing.

i·de·al·ize (ī dē′əl īz′) *v.* **-ized, -iz·ing. 1** make ideal; think of or represent as perfect rather than as is actually the case: *Mary idealized her older sister and thought that everything she did was right.* **2** imagine or form an ideal or ideals. —**i·de′al·iz′er,** *n.*

i·de·al·ly (ī dē′əl ē) *adv.* **1** according to an ideal; perfectly. **2** in idea or theory.

i·de·a·tion (ī′dē ā′shən) *n.* the formation of ideas.

i·de·a·tion·al (ī′dē ā′shən əl) *adj.* having to do with the process of forming ideas.

i·dée fixe (ē dā fēks′) *French.* a fixed idea; obsession.

idem (ī′dem or id′em) *pron. adj. Latin.* the same as previously given or mentioned.

i·den·tic (ī den′tik) *adj.* identical.

i·den·ti·cal (ī den′tə kəl) *adj.* **1** the same: *Both events happened on the identical day.* **2** exactly alike: *6 feet 2 inches and 74 inches are identical amounts.* **3** of twins, coming from a single fertilized egg cell, as distinguished from fraternal twins. [< Med.L *identicus* < L *idem* same] —**i·den′ti·cal·ly,** *adv.* —**i·den′ti·cal·ness,** *n.* —**Syn. 1** See **same.**

i·den·ti·fi·ca·tion (ī den′tə fə kā′shən) *n.* **1** an identifying. **2** the state of being identified. **3** something used to identify a person or thing.

i·den·ti·fy (ī den′tə fī′) *v.* **-fied, -fy·ing. 1** recognize as being, or show to be, a certain person or thing; prove to be the same: *Fred identified the bag as his by what it contained.* **2** make the same; treat as the same: *He identified his own ambitions with those of his brother.* **3** connect closely; link; associate: *He identified himself with the revolutionary movement.* —**i·den′ti·fi′able,** *adj.* —**i·den′ti·fi′er,** *n.*

i·den·ti·ty (ī den′tə tē) *n.* **-ties. 1** individuality; who a person is; what a thing is: *The writer concealed his identity under an assumed name.* **2** exact likeness; sameness: *The identity of the two crimes led the police to think that the same person had committed them.* **3** the state or fact of being the same one: *You must establish the identity of the person you saw today with the one you saw yesterday.* [< LL *identitas,* ult. < L *idem* same]

ideo- *combining form.* idea: *ideogram = a written symbol that represents an idea.*

id·e·o·gram (id′ē ə gram′ or ī′dē ə gram′) *n.* ideograph.

id·e·o·graph (id′ē ə graf′ or ī′dē ə-) *n.* a graphic symbol that represents a thing or an idea directly, without representing the sounds of the word for the thing or idea. Most Egyptian hieroglyphics and some Chinese characters are ideographs.

i·de·ol·o·gy (ī′dē ol′ə jē or id′ē ol′ə jē) *n.* **-gies. 1** a set of doctrines; a body of opinions. **2** the combined doctrines, assertions, and intentions of a social or political movement. **3** abstract speculation, especially theorizing or speculation of a visionary or unpractical nature. **4** the science of ideas.

ides (īdz) *n.pl.* in the ancient Roman calendar, the 15th day of March, May, July, and October, and the 13th day of the other months. [< OF < L *idus*]

id·i·o·cy (id′ē ə sē) *n.* **-cies. 1** the state of being an idiot. **2** an acting like an idiot. **3** very great stupidity or folly.

id·i·om (id′ē əm) *n.* **1** a phrase or expression whose meaning cannot be understood from the ordinary meanings of the words in it: *"How do you do?" and "I have caught cold" are English idioms.* **2** dialect: *He spoke in the idiom of the Ottawa Valley.* **3** a people's way of expressing themselves: *In the French idiom, one can say "of a rapidity" for "rapid."* **4** in music, arts, etc., an individual manner of expression. [< LL < Gk. *idioma,* ult. < *idios* one's own] —**Syn. 2, 3** See **language.**

id·i·o·mat·ic (id′ē ə mat′ik) *adj.* **1** using an idiom or idioms. **2** of idioms; concerning idioms. **3** showing the individual character of a language; characteristic of a particular language. —**id′i·o·mat′i·cal·ly,** *adv.*

id·i·o·syn·cra·sy (id′ē ə sing′krə sē) *n.* **-sies.** a personal peculiarity of taste, behavior, opinion, etc.: *He was an eccentric person with many idiosyncrasies.* [< Gk. *idiosynkrasia* < *idios* one's own + *synkrasis* temperament < *syn* together + *kerannynai* mix]

id·i·o·syn·crat·ic (id′ē ə sin krat′ik) *adj.* having to do with or due to idiosyncrasy.

id·i·ot (id′ē ət) *n.* **1** a person born without the ability to learn. **2** a very stupid or foolish person: *He was an idiot to behave like that.* [< L < Gk. *idiōtēs*, originally, private person < *idios* one's own] —**Syn. 2** See **fool.**

id·i·ot·ic (id′ē ot′ik) *adj.* of or like an idiot; very stupid or foolish. —**id′i·ot′i·cal·ly,** *adv.*

i·dle (ī′dəl) *adj.* **i·dler, i·dlest,** *v.* **i·dled, i·dling.** —*adj.* **1** doing nothing; not busy; not working: *idle hands.* **2** not willing to do things; lazy. **3** useless; worthless: *He wasted his time in idle pleasures.* **4** without any good reason, cause, or foundation: *idle fears, idle rumors.* —*v.* **1** be idle; do nothing: *He spent his whole vacation idling.* **2** waste (time); spend wastefully: *She idled away the hours.* **3** move or saunter idly. **4** run slowly without transmitting power: *A motor idles when it is out of gear and running slowly.* **5** cause (a person or thing) to be idle; take out of work or use. [OE *īdel*] —**i′dle·ness,** *n.* —**i′dly,** *adv.*

Syn. *adj.* **1, 2 Idle, lazy, indolent** = not active or working. **Idle** = not busy or working at the moment, and does not always suggest cause for blame: *The long drought made many farm workers idle.* **Lazy,** usually suggesting cause for blame, means "not liking to work," and "not industrious when at work": *Lazy people are seldom successful.* **Indolent** = by nature or habit fond of ease and opposed to work or activity: *Too much idleness sometimes makes a man indolent.*

i·dler (ī′dlər) *n.* **1** a lazy person. **2** a device allowing a motor to idle. **3** an idle wheel.

idle wheel 1 a gear wheel placed between two others to transfer motion from one axis to another without change in direction or speed. **2** a pulley for taking up slack in a belt; idle pulley.

i·dol (ī′dəl) *n.* **1** an image or other object worshipped as a god. **2** in the Bible, a false god. **3** a person or thing worshipped or loved very much; object of extreme devotion. [ME < OF < L *idolum* < Gk. *eidōlon* image < *eidos* form]

i·dol·a·ter (ī dol′ə tər) *n.* **1** a person who worships idols. **2** an admirer; adorer; devotee.

i·dol·a·tress (ī dol′ə tris) *n.* **1** a woman who worships idols. **2** an adorer; devotee.

i·dol·a·trous (ī dol′ə trəs) *adj.* **1** worshipping idols. **2** having to do with idolatry. **3** blindly adoring. —**i·dol′a·trous·ly,** *adv.*

i·dol·a·try (ī dol′ə trē) *n.* **-tries. 1** the worship of idols. **2** worship of a person or thing; great love or admiration; extreme devotion. [< OF < L < Gk. *eidōlolatreia* < *eidōlon* image + *latreia* service]

i·dol·ize (ī′dəl īz′) *v.* **-ized, -iz·ing. 1** worship as an idol; make an idol of: *The ancient Hebrews idolized the golden calf.* **2** love or admire very much; be extremely devoted to: *The boy idolizes his mother.* —**i′dol·i·za′tion,** *n.*

i·dyll or **i·dyl** (ī′dəl or id′əl) *n.* **1** in poetry or prose, a short description of a simple and charming scene or event, especially one connected with country life. **2** a simple and charming scene, event, or experience suitable for such a description. **3** a short musical composition in a pastoral or sentimental mood. [< L *idyllium* < Gk. *eidyllion*, dim. of *eidos* form]

i·dyl·lic (ī dil′ik or i dil′ik) *adj.* suitable for an idyll; simple and charming. —**i·dyl′li·cal·ly,** *adv.*

i.e. that is. (for L *id est*)

-ie *suffix.* little; darling, as in *dearie, lassie.* [var. of *-y*[2]]

IE Indo-European.

-ier *suffix.* a person occupied or concerned with ——, as in *financier, clothier.* [< F < L *-arius*]

if (if) *conj.* **1** supposing that; in case that: *If you are going, leave now.* **2** on condition that: *I'll go if you will.* **3** whether: *I wonder if he will go.* **4** *Informal.* although; even though: *If he is little, he is strong.* **5 as if,** as it would be if. —*n.* a condition; supposition. [OE *gif*]

☛ **if, whether.** In formal usage *if* is used to express conditions: *If the gasoline holds out, he will reach Jasper before dawn. If* is not used with *or. Whether,* usually with *or,* is used, though not consistently, in: **a** conditions of two parts: *Whether it rains or not, they are det r nined to go.* **b** indirect questions: *He asked whether they should go or stay.* **c** expressions of doubt: *They wondered whether their decision had been wise.* In informal usage *if* would commonly take the place of *whether* in sentences **b** and **c** above.

IF, if, or **i-f** intermediate frequency.

I.F.S. or **IFS** Irish Free State.

ig·loo (ig′lü) *n.* **-loos. 1** an Eskimo dwelling, especially a domed structure built of blocks of snow. **2** any structure

hat, āge, cãre, fär; let, ēqual, tėrm; it, īce
hot, ōpen, ôrder; oil, out; cup, pu̇t, rüle, ūse
əbove, takən, pencəl, lemən, circəs
ch, child; ng, long; sh, ship
th, thin; ᴛʜ, then; zh, measure

resembling this in shape. [< Eskimo *iglu, igdlu* abode, dwelling (irrespective of material and style of structure)]

ig·ne·ous (ig′nē əs) *adj.* **1** of fire; having to do with fire. **2** in geology, produced by fire, intense heat, or volcanic action: *Granite is an igneous rock.* [< L *igneus* < *ignis* fire]

ig·nis fat·u·us (ig′nis fach′ü əs) *pl.* **ig·nes fat·u·i** (ig′nēz fach′ü ī′ or fach′ü ē′). **1** a flitting phosphorescent light seen at night chiefly over marshy ground; will-o'-the-wisp. **2** something deluding or misleading. [< NL *ignis fatuus*, literally, foolish fire]

ig·nite (ig nīt′) *v.* **-nit·ed, -nit·ing. 1** set on fire. **2** make intensely hot; cause to glow with heat. **3** take fire; begin to burn. **4** in chemistry, heat to the point of combustion or chemical change. [< L *ignire* < *ignis* fire] —**ig·nit′er,** *n.* —**Syn. 1** See **kindle.**

ig·ni·tion (ig nish′ən) *n.* **1** a setting on fire. **2** a catching fire. **3** a means of igniting or setting on fire. **4** the apparatus for igniting the explosive vapor in the cylinders of an internal-combustion engine. **5** any chemical or mechanical device used to ignite a rocket propellant or a fuel mixture in a jet engine.

ig·no·ble (ig nō′bəl) *adj.* **1** mean; base; without honor: *To betray a friend is ignoble.* **2** of low birth. [< L *ignobilis* < *in-* not + OL *gnobilis* noble] —**ig·no′ble·ness,** *n.* —**ig·no′bly,** *adv.* —**Syn. 1** degraded, dishonorable, contemptible.

ig·no·min·i·ous (ig′nə min′ē əs) *adj.* **1** shameful; disgraceful; dishonorable; humiliating. **2** contemptible. [< L *ignominiosus* < *ignominia.* See IGNOMINY.] —**ig′no·min′i·ous·ly,** *adv.* —**ig′no·min′i·ous·ness,** *n.*

ig·no·min·y (ig′nə min′ē) *n.* **-min·ies. 1** loss of one's good name; public shame and disgrace; dishonor. **2** shameful action or conduct. [< L *ignominia* < *in-* not + *nomen* name; form influenced by OL *gnoscere* come to know] —**Syn. 1** See **disgrace.**

ig·no·ra·mus (ig′nə rā′məs or ig′nə ram′əs) *n.* **-mus·es.** an ignorant person. [< L *ignoramus* we do not know]

ig·no·rance (ig′nə rəns) *n.* a lack of knowledge; the quality or condition of being ignorant.

ig·no·rant (ig′nə rənt) *adj.* **1** knowing little or nothing; without knowledge: *A person who has not had much opportunity to learn may be ignorant without being stupid.* **2** caused by lack of knowledge. **3** showing lack of knowledge: *an ignorant remark.* **4** uninformed; unaware: *He was ignorant of the fact that his house had been burned.* [< L *ignorans, -antis,* ppr. of *ignorare* not know. See IGNORE.] —**ig′no·rant·ly,** *adv.*

Syn. 1 Ignorant, illiterate, uneducated = without knowledge. **Ignorant** = without general knowledge, sometimes without knowledge of some particular subject: *People who live in the city are often ignorant of farm life.* **Illiterate** = unable to read or write: *There are many illiterate people in the underdeveloped countries.* **Uneducated** = without systematic training or learning, in schools or from books: *Because of the shortage of schools, many people in the world's backward countries are uneducated.* **2** unknowing.

ig·nore (ig nôr′) *v.* **-nored, -nor·ing.** pay no attention to; disregard. [< L *ignorare* not know < *ignarus* unaware < *in-* not + OL *gnarus* aware; form influenced by *ignotus* unknown] —**Syn.** overlook, neglect.

i·gua·na (i gwä′nə) *n.* a large climbing lizard that has small scales and a fringelike crest of skin along the back. It is found in tropical America. [< Sp. < Carib]

IGY International Geophysical Year.

IHS in Greek, the first three letters of "Jesus."

I.H.S. 1 Jesus the Saviour of men. [for L *Iesus Hominum Salvator*] **2** In this sign (thou shalt conquer). [for L *In Hoc Signo* (*Vinces*)] **3** In this (cross) is salvation. [for L *In Hac* (*Cruce*) *Salus*]

i·kon (ī′kon) *n.* icon.

il-[1] a form of **in-**[1] before *l,* as in *illegal.*

il-[2] a form of **in-**[2] before *l,* as in *illuminate.*

Il illinium.

il·e·ac (il′ē ak′) *adj.* iliac.

il·e·i·tis (il′ē ī′tis) *n.* an inflammation of the ileum, due to infection, a tumor, etc. and involving partial or complete blocking of the passage of food through the small intestine.

il·e·um (il′ē əm) *n.* in anatomy, the lowest part of the small intestine. [< LL *ileum,* var. of *ilium,* sing. of L *ilia* loins, entrails]

i·lex (ī′leks) *n.* **1** holm oak. **2** holly. [< L]

il·i·ac (il′ē ak′) *adj.* **1** of or having to do with the ilium; near the ilium. **2** of or having to do with the ileum.

Il·i·ad (il′ē əd) *n.* a Greek epic poem, by Homer, about the siege of Ilium (Troy). [< L < Gk. *Ilias, -iados* < *Ilion* Ilium]

Il·i·on (il′ē ən) *n. Poetic.* Ilium.

il·i·um (il′ē əm) *n.* **il·i·a** (il′ē ə). in anatomy, the broad upper portion of the hipbone. [< NL < LL *ilium,* sing. L *ilia* loins, entrails]

Il·i·um (il′ē əm) *n. Poetic.* ancient Troy.

ilk (ilk) *adj. Archaic.* same. —*n.* **1** *Informal.* family; kind; sort. **2 of that ilk,** *Informal.* **a** of the same place or name. **b** of that kind or sort. [OE *ilca* same]

ill (il) *adj.* **worse, worst,** *n. adv.* —*adj.* **1** having some disease; not well; sick. **2** bad; evil; harmful: *an ill deed.* **3** unfavorable; unfortunate: *an ill wind.* **4** unkind; harsh; cruel. **5 ill at ease,** uneasy; uncomfortable.
—*n.* **1** a sickness; disease. **2** an evil; a harm; a trouble: *Poverty is an ill.*
—*adv.* **1** badly; harmfully. **2** unfavorably; unfortunately. **3** in an unkind manner; harshly; cruelly. **4** with trouble or difficulty; scarcely: *You can ill afford to waste your money.* **5 take ill,** fall sick; become ill. **6 take** (something) **ill,** take offence at or be offended by (something). [ME < ON *illr*] ☛ See **sick** for usage note.

ill. **1** illustration. **2** illustrated.

I'll (īl) I will.

Ill. Illinois.

ill-ad·vised (il′əd vīzd′) *adj.* acting or done without enough consideration; unwise.

ill-bred (il′bred′) *adj.* badly brought up; impolite; rude.

ill breeding bad manners; lack of a good upbringing; impoliteness; rudeness.

ill-con·sid·ered (il′kən sid′ərd) *adj.* not well considered; unwise; unsuitable.

ill-de·fined (il′di fīnd′) *adj.* not clear; not clearly indicated or explained; hazy.

ill-dis·posed (il′dis pōzd′) *adj.* unfriendly; unfavorable.

il·le·gal (i lē′gəl) *adj.* not lawful; against the law; forbidden by law: *illegal parking.* —**il·le′gal·ly,** *adv.* —**Syn.** unlawful, illicit.

il·le·gal·i·ty (il′ē gal′ə tē) *n.* **-ties.** **1** unlawfulness. **2** an illegal act; act contrary to law.

il·leg·i·bil·i·ty (i lej′ə bil′ə tē) *n.* **-ties.** an illegible quality or condition.

il·leg·i·ble (i lej′ə bəl) *adj.* very hard or impossible to read. —**il·leg′i·ble·ness,** *n.* —**il·leg′i·bly,** *adv.*

il·le·git·i·ma·cy (il′ə jit′ə mə sē) *n.* **-cies.** the fact or condition of being illegitimate.

il·le·git·i·mate (il′ə jit′ə mit) *adj.* **1** born of parents who are not married to each other. **2** not according to the law or the rules. **3** not logical; not according to good usage; improper. —**il′le·git′i·mate·ly,** *adv.*

ill-fat·ed (il′fāt′id) *adj.* **1** sure to have a bad fate or end. **2** bringing bad luck; unlucky.

ill-fa·vored or **ill-fa·voured** (il′fā′vərd) *adj.* **1** not pleasant to look at; ugly. **2** unpleasant; offensive. —**ill′-fa′vored·ly** or **ill′-fa′voured·ly,** *adv.* —**ill′-fa′vored·ness** or **ill′-fa′voured·ness,** *n.*

ill-fit·ting (il′fit′ing) *adj.* fitting badly: *ill-fitting trousers.*

ill-found·ed (il′foun′did) *adj.* without a good reason or sound basis.

ill-got·ten (il′got′ən) *adj.* acquired by evil or unfair means; dishonestly obtained.

ill health poor health.

ill humor or **humour** a cross, unpleasant temper or mood.

ill-hu·mored or **ill-hu·moured** (il′hū′mərd or -ū′mərd) *adj.* cross; unpleasant. —**ill′-hu′mored·ly** or **ill′-hu′moured·ly,** *adv.* —**ill′-hu′mored·ness** or **ill′-hu′moured·ness,** *n.*

il·lib·er·al (i lib′ər əl or i lib′rəl) *adj.* **1** not liberal; narrow-minded; prejudiced. **2** stingy; miserly. **3** without liberal culture; unscholarly; ill-bred.

il·lib·er·al·i·ty (i lib′ər al′ə tē) *n.* **-ties.** a being illiberal.

il·lic·it (i lis′it) *adj.* not permitted by law; forbidden; improper. —**il·lic′it·ly,** *adv.* —**il·lic′it·ness,** *n.* ☛ See **elicit** for usage note.

il·lim·it·a·ble (i lim′ə tə bəl) *adj.* limitless; boundless; infinite. —**il·lim′it·a·ble·ness,** *n.* —**il·lim′it·a·bly,** *adv.*

il·lin·i·um (i lin′ē əm) *n.* a rare metallic chemical element of the cerium group, now known as promethium. *Symbol:* Il; *at.no.* 61. [< NL; after *Illinois*]

il·lit·er·a·cy (i lit′ər ə sē) *n.* **-cies.** **1** the inability to read or write. **2** lack of education; deficiency in cultural knowledge. **3** an error in speaking or writing, caused by a lack of education or knowledge.

il·lit·er·ate (i lit′ər it) *adj.* **1** unable to read or write. **2** not cultured: *He writes in a very illiterate way.* —*n.* **1** a person unable to read or write. **2** a person who lacks culture. —**il·lit′er·ate·ly,** *adv.* —**il·lit′er·ate·ness,** *n.* —**Syn** *adj.* **1** See **ignorant**

ill-judged (il′jujd′) *adj.* unwise; rash.

ill-man·nered (il′man′ərd) *adj.* having or showing bad manners; impolite; rude. —**ill′-man′nered·ly,** *adv.* —**ill′-man′nered·ness,** *n.*

ill nature crossness; disagreeableness; spite.

ill-na·tured (il′nā′chərd) *adj.* cross; disagreeable; spiteful. —**ill′-na′tured·ly,** *adv.*

ill·ness (il′nis) *n.* **1** a sickness; disease. **2** poor health; a sickly condition: *She suffered from long periods of illness.*

il·log·i·cal (i loj′ə kəl) *adj.* **1** not logical. **2** not reasonable. —**il·log′i·cal·ly,** *adv.* —**il·log′i·cal·ness,** *n.* —**Syn.** **1** unsound, fallacious.

ill-spent (il′spent′) *adj.* spent badly; wasted; misspent.

ill-starred (il′stärd′) *adj.* unlucky; unfortunate; disastrous.

ill-suit·ed (il′süt′id) *adj.* poorly suited; unsuitable.

ill temper bad temper or disposition; crossness.

ill-tem·pered (il′tem′pərd) *adj.* having or showing a bad temper; cross. —**ill′-tem′pered·ly,** *adv.* —**ill′-tem′pered·ness,** *n.*

ill-timed (il′tīmd′) *adj.* coming at a bad time; inappropriate.

ill-treat (il′trēt′) *v.* treat badly or cruelly; do harm to; abuse.

ill treatment bad or cruel treatment; harm; abuse.

ill turn **1** an action that is unkind, unfriendly, or spiteful. **2** a change for the worse.

il·lume (i lüm′) *v.* **-lumed, -lum·ing.** *Poetic.* illuminate.

il·lu·mi·nant (i lü′mə nənt) *n.* something that gives light. Electricity and oil are illuminants.

il·lu·mi·nate (i lü′mə nāt′) *v.* **-nat·ed, -nat·ing.** **1** light up; make bright: *The room was illuminated by four large lamps.* **2** make clear; explain: *Our teacher could illuminate almost any subject we studied.* **3** decorate with lights: *The streets were illuminated for the celebration.* **4** decorate with gold, colors, pictures, and designs. In former times books and manuscripts were often illuminated. **5** enlighten; inform; instruct. **6** make illustrious. [< L *illuminare* < *in-* in + *lumen* light]

il·lu·mi·na·tion (i lü′mə nā′shən) *n.* **1** an illuminating; a lighting up; a making bright. **2** the amount of light; light. **3** a making clear; explanation. **4** a decoration with lights. **5** the decoration of books and letters with gold, colors, pictures, and designs. **6** enlightenment.

il·lu·mi·na·tive (i lü′mə nə tiv or i lü′mə nā′tiv) *adj.* illuminating; tending to illuminate.

il·lu·mi·na·tor (i lü′mə nā′tər) *n.* **1** a person or thing that illuminates. **2** any instrument for illuminating, such as a lens for concentrating light or a mirror for reflecting light. **3** one who decorates manuscripts, books, etc. with color, gold, etc.

il·lu·mine (i lü′mən) *v.* **-mined, -min·ing.** make or become bright; illuminate; light up: *A smile can often illumine a homely face.* [< F *illuminer*]

illus. 1 illustration. **2** illustrated.

ill-us·age (il′ūs′ij or -ūz′ij) *n.* bad, cruel, or unfair treatment.

ill-use (*v.* il′ūz′; *n.* il′ūs′) *v.* **-used, -us·ing,** *n.* —*v.* treat badly, cruelly, or unfair. —*n.* bad, cruel, or unfair treatment.

il·lu·sion (i lü′zhən) *n.* **1** an appearance that is not in accordance with reality; misleading appearance. **2** a false impression or perception. **3** a false idea, notion, or belief: *Many people have the illusion that wealth is the chief cause of happiness.* **4** a delicate silk net or gauze, often used for veils and over dresses. [< L *illusio, -onis* < *illudere* mock < *in-* at + *ludere* play]

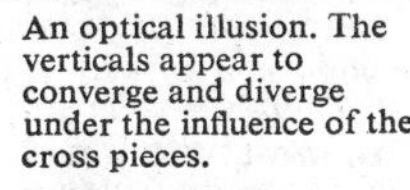

An optical illusion. The verticals appear to converge and diverge under the influence of the cross pieces.

Syn. 1 Illusion, delusion = something mistakenly or falsely believed to be true or real. **Illusion** applies to something appearing to be real or true, but actually not existing or being quite different from what it seems: *Good motion pictures create an illusion of reality.* **Delusion** applies to a false and often harmful belief about something that does exist: *The old woman had the delusion that the butcher was always trying to cheat her.*

☛ **Illusion, allusion** are sometimes confused. An *illusion* is a misleading appearance: *an illusion of wealth.* An *allusion* is an indirect reference or slight mention: *He made several allusions to recent novels.*

il·lu·sion·ist (i lü′zhən ist) *n.* **1** a person who produces illusions; conjurer. **2** a person who has illusions; dreamer.

il·lu·sive (i lü′siv) *adj.* due to an illusion; unreal; misleading; deceptive. —**il·lu′sive·ly,** *adv.* —**il·lu′sive·ness,** *n.*

il·lu·so·ry (i lü′sə rē) *adj.* illusive.

illust. 1 illustration. **2** illustrated.

il·lus·trate (il′əs trāt′ or i lus′trāt) *v.* **-trat·ed, -trat·ing. 1** make clear or explain by stories, examples, comparisons, etc.: *A model of a pump may be used to illustrate the action of the heart in sending blood around the body.* **2** provide with pictures, diagrams, maps, etc. that explain or decorate: *This book is well illustrated.* [< L *illustrare* light up, ult. < *in-* in + *lustrum,* originally, lighting] —**Syn. 1** demonstrate, elucidate, exemplify.

il·lus·tra·tion (il′əs trā′shən) *n.* **1** a picture, diagram, map, etc. used to explain or decorate something. **2** a story, example, comparison, etc. used to make clear or explain something: *The teacher cut an apple into four equal pieces as an illustration of what "quarter" means.* **3** the act or process of illustrating.

il·lus·tra·tive (i lus′trə tiv or il′əs trā′tiv) *adj.* illustrating; used to illustrate; helping to explain: *A good teacher uses illustrative examples to explain difficult ideas.* —**il·lus′tra·tive·ly,** *adv.*

il·lus·tra·tor (il′əs trā′tər) *n.* **1** an artist who makes pictures to be used as illustrations. **2** a person or thing that illustrates.

il·lus·tri·ous (i lus′trē əs) *adj.* **1** very famous; great; outstanding: *Canada's Governor General is an illustrious man.* **2** bringing or conferring glory; glorious. [< L *illustris* lighted up, bright] —**il·lus′tri·ous·ly,** *adv.* —**il·lus′tri·ous·ness,** *n.* —**Syn.** distinguished, renowned, eminent.

ill will unkind or unfriendly feeling; dislike; hate.

Il·lyr·i·a (i lir′ē ə) *n.* in ancient times, a country in the region east of the Adriatic. See **Roman Empire** for map. —**Il·lyr′i·an,** *adj. n.*

il·men·ite (il′mə nīt′) *n.* a luminous black mineral consisting of iron, titanium, and oxygen. *Formula*: $FeTiO_3$ [< *Ilmen* Mountains in the Urals, where it was first discovered + *-ite*[1]]

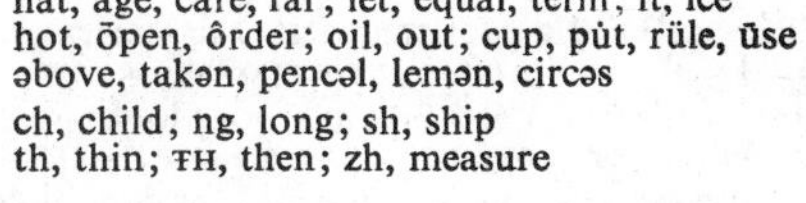

hat, āge, cãre, fär; let, ēqual, tėrm; it, īce
hot, ōpen, ôrder; oil, out; cup, pu̇t, rüle, ūse
əbove, takən, pencəl, lemən, circəs
ch, child; ng, long; sh, ship
th, thin; ᴛʜ, then; zh, measure

ILO in the United Nations, International Labor Organization.

ILS Instrument Landing System.

im-[1] a form of **in-**[1] before *b, m, p,* as in *imbalance, immoral, impatient.*

im-[2] a form of **in-**[2] before *b, m, p,* as in *imbibe, immure, impart.*

I'm (īm) I am.

im·age (im′ij) *n. v.* **-aged, -ag·ing.** —*n.* **1** an artificial likeness or representation of the form of an object, such as a painting or statue; idol: *The Greeks and Romans worshipped images of their gods.* **2** a person or thing resembling another; counterpart: *She is the very image of her mother.* **3** a mental picture: *Canada's image in the world's eye.* **4** a description or figure of speech that helps the mind to form forceful or beautiful pictures. Poetry often contains images. **5** in optics, the impression of an object produced by reflection, refraction, or by a small hole. A **real image** is projected by a lens (by refraction) and a **virtual image** is reflected in a mirror. **6** a television picture.
—*v.* **1** form an image of. **2** reflect as a mirror does. **3** picture in one's mind; imagine. **4** describe with images. [ME < OF < L *imago*]

im·age·ry (im′ij rē) *n.* **-ries. 1** pictures in the mind; things imagined. **2** descriptions and figures of speech that help the mind to form forceful or beautiful pictures. **3** images; statues.

i·mag·i·na·ble (i maj′ə nə bəl or i maj′nə bəl) *adj.* that can be imagined; possible. —**i·mag′i·na·bly,** *adv.*

i·mag·i·nar·y (i maj′ə ner′ē) *adj.* existing only in the imagination; not real: *Fairies are imaginary. The equator is an imaginary line circling the earth midway between the North and South Poles.*

i·mag·i·na·tion (i maj′ə nā′shən) *n.* **1** an imagining; the power of forming in the mind pictures of things not present to the senses. **2** the ability to create new things or ideas or to combine old ones in new forms. **3** a creation of the mind; fancy.

Syn. 1, 2 Imagination, fancy = the power of forming pictures in the mind. **Imagination** emphasizes power to create new pictures and ideas by putting together in new ways or giving new meaning to things seen or known before or by creating new pictures, complete and perfect, of things that never existed and making them seem real: *Poets, artists, and inventors make use of their imagination.* **Fancy** applies to ability to make unreal or unbelievable pictures, by inventing them or by putting things from reality together in unrealistic ways: *Many comic strips are products of fancy.*

i·mag·i·na·tive (i maj′ə nə tiv or i maj′ə nā′tiv) *adj.* **1** showing imagination: *Fairy tales are imaginative.* **2** able to imagine well; fond of imagining. **3** of imagination. —**i·mag′i·na·tive·ly,** *adv.* —**i·mag′i·na·tive·ness,** *n.* —**Syn. 1, 2** inventive, creative.

i·mag·ine (i maj′ən) *v.* **-ined, -in·ing. 1** picture in one's mind; have an idea: *We can hardly imagine life without electricity.* **2** suppose; guess: *I cannot imagine what you mean.* **3** think; believe: *She imagined someone was watching her.* [ME < OF < L *imaginari* < *imago, -ginis* image]

Syn. 1 Imagine, conceive = form in the mind. **Imagine** = form a clear and definite picture of something in the mind: *I like to imagine myself flying a plane.* **Conceive** = bring an idea into existence and give it an outline or pattern or shape in the mind: *The Wright brothers conceived the first successful motor-powered airplane.* **2** conjecture. **3** fancy.

im·ag·ism (im′ij iz′əm) *n.* an early 20th-century movement in poetry that advocates the use of clear and precise imagery and opposes symbolism and conventional metrical rhythm.

im·ag·ist (im′ij ist) *n.* a poet who practises imagism. Most imagists use free verse.

i·ma·go (i mā′gō) *n.* **i·ma·gos, i·mag·i·nes** (i maj′ə nēz′). **1** an insect in the final adult, especially winged, stage. **2** in psychoanalysis, an unconscious childhood concept of a parent or other person, carried over unchanged into adulthood. [< L *imago* image]

i·mam (i mäm′) *n.* 1 a Moslem priest. 2 a Moslem leader, chief, etc. [< Arabic *imam* < *amma* go before]

i·mam·ate (i mä′māt) *n.* 1 the rank or office of an imam. 2 the territory governed by an imam.

im·bal·ance (im bal′ əns) *n.* 1 the state or condition of lacking balance or of being out of balance. 2 in medicine, a lack or defect of co-ordination in glands, muscles, etc.

im·balm (im bom′ or -bäm′) *v.* embalm.

im·be·cile (im′bə səl) *n.* 1 a person of very weak mind. An imbecile is almost an idiot. 2 a very stupid or foolish person. —*adj.* 1 very weak in mind. 2 very stupid or foolish. [< F < L *imbecillus* weak, ult. < *in-* without + *baculum* staff] —**Syn.** *n.* 2 See **fool.**

im·be·cil·i·ty (im′bə sil′ə tē) *n.* **-ties.** 1 feebleness of mind; mental weakness. 2 great stupidity or dullness. 3 a very stupid or foolish action, remark, etc.

im·bed (im bed′) *v.* **-bed·ded, -bed·ding.** embed.

im·bibe (im bīb′) *v.* **-bibed, -bib·ing.** 1 drink; drink in. 2 absorb: *The roots of a plant imbibe moisture from the earth.* 3 take into one's mind: *Children often imbibe superstitions that last all their lives.* [< L *imbibere* < *in-* in + *bibere* drink] —**im·bib′er,** *n.* —**Syn.** 1 See **drink.**

im·bri·cate (*v.* im′brə kāt′; *adj.* im′brə kit′ or im′brə kāt′) *v.* **-cat·ed, -cat·ing,** *adj.* —*v.* overlap as tiles or shingles do. —*adj.* 1 like roof tiles in shape, composition, etc. 2 like the pattern of overlapping tiles. [< L *imbricare* cover with tiles < *imbrex, -ricis* hollow tile]

im·bri·cat·ed (im′brə kāt′id) *adj.* overlapping.

im·bri·ca·tion (im′brə kā′shən) *n.* 1 an overlapping like that of tiles, shingles, etc. 2 a decorative pattern in imitation of this.

An imbrication of tiles

im·bro·glio (im brōl′yō) *n.* **-glios.** 1 a complicated or difficult situation. 2 a complicated misunderstanding or disagreement. [< Ital.]

im·brue (im brü′) *v.* **-brued, -bru·ing.** wet; stain: *His sword was imbrued with blood.* [ME < OF *embreuver* give to drink, ult. < L *bibere* drink]

im·bue (im bū′) *v.* **-bued, -bu·ing.** 1 fill; inspire: *He imbued his son's mind with the ambition to succeed.* 2 fill with moisture or color. [< L *imbuere*]

im·i·ta·ble (im′ə tə bəl) *adj.* that can be imitated.

im·i·tate (im′ə tāt′) *v.* **-tat·ed, -tat·ing.** 1 try to be like; follow the example of: *The little boy imitated his father.* 2 make or do something like; copy: *A parrot imitates the sounds it hears.* 3 act like: *John amused us by imitating a bear.* 4 be like; look like; resemble: *wood painted to imitate stone.* [< L *imitari*] —**Syn.** 2 reproduce. See **copy.** 3 mimic, ape.

im·i·ta·tion (im′ə tā′shən) *n.* 1 an imitating: *We learn many things by imitation.* 2 a copy: *Give as good an imitation as you can of a rooster crowing.* 3 in music, the repetition of a melodic phrase or theme of a different pitch or key from the original, or in a different voice part, or with modifications of rhythm or intervals that do not destroy the resemblance. 4 **in imitation of,** imitating; in order to be like or look like. —*adj.* not real: *Imitation pearls are naturally cheaper than real ones.*

im·i·ta·tive (im′ə tā′tiv) *adj.* 1 fond of imitating; likely or inclined to imitate others: *Monkeys are imitative.* 2 imitating; showing imitation: "*Bang*" *and* "*whizz*" *are imitative words.* 3 not real. —**im′i·ta′tive·ly,** *adv.* —**im′i·ta′tive·ness,** *n.*

im·i·ta·tor (im′ə tā′tər) *n.* a person or animal that imitates.

im·mac·u·late (i mak′yů lit) *adj.* 1 without spot or stain; absolutely clean: *The newly laundered shirts were immaculate.* 2 without fault; in perfect order: *His appearance was immaculate.* 3 without sin; pure. 4 in biology, without colored marks or spots; unspotted. [< L *immaculatus* < *in-* not + *macula* spot] —**im·mac′u·late·ly,** *adv.* —**im·mac′u·late·ness,** *n.* —**Syn.** 1 spotless.

Immaculate Conception 1 in the Roman Catholic Church, the doctrine that the Virgin Mary was conceived free of original sin. 2 a feast observed on December 8 commemorating this.

im·ma·nence (im′ə nəns) *n.* the state of being immanent.

im·ma·nen·cy (im′ə nən sē) *n.* immanence.

im·ma·nent (im′ə nənt) *adj.* remaining within; inherent. [< L *immanens, -entis,* ppr. of *immanere* < *in-* in + *manere* stay]

Im·man·u·el (i man′ū əl) *n.* Christ. Also, **Emmanuel.** [< Hebrew '*Immānū'ēl,* literally, God with us]

im·ma·ter·i·al (im′ə tēr′ē əl) *adj.* 1 not important; insignificant. 2 not material; spiritual rather than physical. —**im′ma·te′ri·al·ly,** *adv.* —**im′ma·te′ri·al·ness,** *n.* —**Syn.** 1 unimportant, unessential.

im·ma·ture (im′ə chür′ or im′ə tūr′) *adj.* not mature; not ripe; not full-grown; not fully developed. —**im′ma·ture′ly,** *adv.*

im·ma·tu·ri·ty (im′ə chür′ə tē or im′ə tūr′ə tē) *n.* the state of being immature.

im·meas·ur·a·ble (i mezh′ər ə bəl) *adj.* too vast to be measured; boundless; without limits.

im·meas·ur·a·bly (i mezh′ər ə blē) *adv.* beyond measure; to an immeasurable extent or degree.

im·me·di·a·cy (i mē′dē ə sē) *n.* **-cies.** 1 the state or condition of being immediate. 2 topical significance; immediate importance.

im·me·di·ate (i mē′dē it) *adj.* 1 coming at once; without delay: *an immediate reply.* 2 with nothing between: *in immediate contact.* 3 direct: *the immediate result.* 4 closest; nearest: *my immediate neighbor.* 5 close; near: *the immediate neighborhood.* 6 having to do with the present: *our immediate plans.* 7 in philosophy, directly or intuitively perceived or known: *an immediate inference.* [< LL *immediatus,* ult. < L *in-* not + *medius* in the middle] —**im·me′di·ate·ness,** *n.* —**Syn.** 3 See **direct.**

im·me·di·ate·ly (i mē′dē it lē) *adv.* 1 at once; without delay. 2 with nothing between. 3 next. 4 directly. —*conj.* as soon as.

Syn. 1 **Immediately, instantly, presently** = with little or no delay. **Immediately** = without delay, with no noticeable time in between: *Please close your books immediately and answer these questions.* **Instantly** = right this instant, without a second's delay: *The driver was killed instantly.* **Presently,** less common, means "soon, before very long": *I will do the dishes presently, but I want to finish this story first.*

im·med·i·ca·ble (i med′ə kə bəl) *adj.* incapable of being healed; incurable: *immedicable wounds, immedicable wrongs.*

im·me·mo·ri·al (im′ə mô′rē əl) *adj.* extending back beyond the bounds of memory; extremely old: *time immemorial.* —**im′me·mo′ri·al·ly,** *adv.*

im·mense (i mens′) *adj.* 1 very big; huge; vast: *The Pacific Ocean is an immense body of water.* 2 *Slang.* very good; fine; excellent. [< L *immensus* < *in-* not + *mensus* pp. of *metiri* measure] —**im·mense′ness,** *n.* —**Syn.** 1 enormous. See **huge.**

im·mense·ly (i mens′lē) *adv.* very greatly.

im·men·si·ty (i men′sə tē) *n.* **-ties.** 1 a very great or boundless extent; vastness. 2 an infinite space or existence.

im·merge (i mėrj′) *v.* **-merged, -merg·ing.** immerse. [< L *immergere.* See IMMERSE.]

im·merse (i mėrs′) *v.* **-mersed, -mers·ing.** 1 plunge into a liquid. 2 baptize by dipping under water. 3 involve deeply; absorb: *immersed in business affairs, immersed in debts.* [< L *immersus,* pp. of *immergere* < *in-* in + *mergere* plunge] —**Syn.** 1 submerge, duck. See **dip.** 3 engross, occupy. —**im·mers′i·ble,** *adj.*

im·mer·sion (i mėr′zhən or i mėr′shən) *n.* 1 an immersing. 2 a being immersed. 3 a baptism by dipping a person under water.

im·mi·grant (im′ə grənt) *n.* a person who comes into a foreign country or region to live: *Canada has many immigrants from Europe.* —*adj.* immigrating.

im·mi·grate (im′ə grāt′) *v.* **-grat·ed, -grat·ing.** come into a foreign country or region to live. [< L *immigrare* < *in-* into + *migrare* move] —**im′mi·gra′tor,** *n.* ☞ See **emigrate** for usage note.

im·mi·gra·tion (im′ə grā′shən) *n.* 1 a coming into a foreign country or region to live: *There has been* *immigration to Canada from most of the countries of Europe.* **2** immigrants: *The immigration of 1956 included many people from Hungary.*

im·mi·nence (im′ə nəns) *n.* **1** the state or fact of being imminent. **2** something that is imminent; evil or danger about to occur.

im·mi·nen·cy (im′ə nən sē) *n.* imminence.

im·mi·nent (im′ə nənt) *adj.* likely to happen soon; about to occur: *The rapidly approaching black clouds show that a storm is imminent.* [< L *imminens, -entis,* ppr. of *imminere* overhang] —**im′mi·nent·ly,** *adv.*
Syn. Imminent, impending = likely to happen soon. **Imminent,** chiefly describing danger, death, etc., suggests "hanging threateningly over a person" and means "likely to happen any minute without further warning": *Swept along by the swift current, he was in imminent danger of going over the falls.* **Impending** suggests hanging over one, often indefinitely, and keeping him in suspense, and means "near and about to take place": *impending disaster.* ☛ See **eminent** for usage note.

im·mis·ci·ble (i mis′ə bəl) *adj.* incapable of being mixed: *Water and oil are immiscible.*

im·mo·bile (i mō′bīl or -mō′bəl) *adj.* **1** not movable; firmly fixed. **2** not moving; not changing; motionless.

im·mo·bil·i·ty (im′ō bil′ə tē) *n.* a being immobile.

im·mo·bi·lize (i mō′bə līz′) *v.* **-lized, -liz·ing.** make immobile. —**im·mo′bi·li·za′tion,** *n.*

im·mod·er·ate (i mod′ər it) *adj.* not moderate; too much; going too far; extreme; more than is right or proper. —**im·mod′er·ate·ly,** *adv.* —**im·mod′er·ate·ness,** *n.* —**im·mod′er·a′tion,** *n.* —**Syn.** excessive, intemperate, exorbitant, inordinate.

im·mod·est (i mod′ist) *adj.* **1** not modest; bold and rude. **2** indecent; improper. —**im·mod′est·ly,** *adv.* —**Syn. 1** forward, impudent. **2** lewd, obscene.

im·mod·es·ty (i mod′is tē) *n.* **1** a lack of modesty; boldness and rudeness. **2** a lack of decency; improper behavior.

im·mo·late (im′ə lāt′) *v.* **-lat·ed, -lat·ing. 1** kill as a sacrifice. **2** sacrifice. [< L *immolare* sacrifice; originally, sprinkle with sacrificial meal < *in-* on + *mola* sacrificial meal]

im·mo·la·tion (im′ə lā′shən) *n.* a sacrifice.

im·mo·la·tor (im′ə lā′tər) *n.* a person who offers sacrifice.

im·mor·al (i môr′əl) *adj.* **1** morally wrong; wicked: *Lying and stealing are immoral.* **2** lewd; unchaste. —**im·mor′al·ly,** *adv.*

im·mo·ral·i·ty (im′ə ral′ə tē) *n.* **-ties. 1** wickedness; wrongdoing; vice. **2** lewdness; unchastity. **3** an immoral act.

im·mor·tal (i môr′təl) *adj.* **1** living forever; never dying; everlasting. **2** of or having to do with immortal beings or immortality; divine. **3** likely to be remembered or famous forever.
—*n.* **1** an immortal being. **2** Usually **immortals,** *pl.* one of the gods of ancient Greek and Roman mythology. **3** a person likely to be remembered or famous forever: *Shakespeare is one of the immortals.* —**im·mor′tal·ly,** *adv.* —**Syn.** *adj.* **1** eternal, endless.

im·mor·tal·i·ty (im′ôr tal′ə tē) *n.* **-ties. 1** endless life; the fact or condition of living forever. **2** fame that is likely to last forever.

im·mor·tal·ize (i môr′təl īz′) *v.* **-ized, -iz·ing. 1** make immortal. **2** give everlasting fame to. —**im·mor′tal·i·za′tion,** *n.* —**im·mor′tal·iz′er,** *n.*

im·mor·telle (im′ôr tel′) *n.* a plant whose flowers keep their shape and color for a long time after they have entirely dried. [< F *immortelle* immortal]

im·mov·a·bil·i·ty (i müv′ə bil′ə tē) *n.* a being immovable.

im·mov·a·ble (i müv′ə bəl) *adj.* **1** that cannot be moved; firmly fixed. **2** not moving; not changing position; motionless. **3** firm; steadfast; unyielding. **4** unfeeling; impassive. —*n.* **immovables,** *pl.* land, buildings, and other property that cannot be carried from one place to another. —**im·mov′a·bly,** *adv.* —**Syn.** *adj.* **1** stationary. **3** resolute.

im·mune (i mūn′) *adj.* **1** protected from disease; not susceptible; inoculated. **2** exempt; being free from some duty or obligation, or from something unpleasant: *immune from taxes. Nobody is immune from criticism.* [< L *immunis,* originally, free from obligation]

hat, āge, cãre, fär; let, ēqual, tėrm; it, īce
hot, ōpen, ôrder; oil, out; cup, pu̇t, rüle, ūse
əbove, takən, pencəl, lemən, circəs
ch, child; ng, long; sh, ship
th, thin; ᴛʜ, then; zh, measure

im·mu·ni·ty (i mū′nə tē) *n.* **-ties. 1** resistance to disease, poison, etc.: *One attack of measles often gives a person immunity to that disease for a number of years.* **2** freedom; protection: *The law gives schools and churches immunity from taxation.* [< L *immunitas* < *immunis.* See IMMUNE.] —**Syn. 2** See **exemption.**

im·mu·nize (im′yu̇ nīz′) *v.* **-nized, -niz·ing.** give immunity to; make immune: *Vaccination immunizes people against smallpox.* —**im′mu·ni·za′tion,** *n.*

im·mu·nol·o·gist (im′yu̇ nol′ə jist) *n.* an expert in immunology.

im·mu·nol·o·gy (im′yu̇ nol′ə jē) *n.* the science of the nature and causation of immunity from diseases.

im·mure (i mūr′) *v.* **-mured, -mur·ing. 1** imprison. **2** confine closely. [< Med.L *immurare* < L *in-* in + *murus* wall] —**im·mure′ment,** *n.*

im·mu·ta·bil·i·ty (i mū′tə bil′ə tē) *n.* a being immutable.

im·mu·ta·ble (i mū′tə bəl) *adj.* never changing; unchangeable. —**im·mu′ta·ble·ness,** *n.* —**im·mu′ta·bly,** *adv.* —**Syn.** unalterable, permanent.

imp (imp) *n.* **1** a young or small devil or demon. **2** a mischievous child. [OE *impe* a shoot, graft, ult. < VL *imputus* < Gk. *emphytos* engrafted]

imp. **1** imperative. **2** import; imported. **3** imperfect. **4** imprimatur. **5** imperial. **6** imprimis.

im·pact (*n.* im′pakt; *v.* im pakt′) *n.* **1** a striking (of one thing against another); collision: *The impact of the two swords broke both of them.* **2** in physics, the single instantaneous blow of a moving body when it meets another body. **3** a forceful effect; dramatic effect: *the impact of automation on society.*
—*v.* drive or press closely or firmly into something; pack in. [< L *impactus* struck against, pp. of *impingere.* See IMPINGE.]

im·pact·ed (im pak′tid) *adj.* **1** firmly wedged in place. **2** of a tooth, pressed between the jawbone and another tooth. **3** closely packed; driven or pressed tightly together.

im·pair (im pãr′) *v.* make worse; damage; weaken: *Poor food impaired his health.* [ME < OF *empeirer,* ult. < L *in-* + *pejor* worse] —**Syn.** harm, hurt. See **injure.**

impaired driver one whose driving ability has been impaired by alcohol or narcotics.

im·pair·ment (im pãr′mənt) *n.* **1** an impairing. **2** a being impaired. **3** an injury; damage.

im·pale (im pāl′) *v.* **-paled, -pal·ing. 1** pierce through with something pointed; fasten upon something pointed: *The butterflies were impaled on small pins stuck in a sheet of cork.* **2** torture or punish by thrusting upon a pointed stake. **3** make helpless as if by piercing: *The judge impaled the flippant witness with a look of steel.* **4** in heraldry, combine (two coats of arms) side by side on one shield. [< F *empaler,* ult. < L *in-* on + *palus* stake] —**im·pale′ment,** *n.*

im·pal·pa·ble (im pal′pə bəl) *adj.* **1** that cannot be perceived by the sense of touch: *Sunbeams are impalpable. A thread of a spider's web is so thin as to be almost impalpable.* **2** very hard for the mind to grasp: *impalpable distinctions.* —**im·pal′pa·bly,** *adv.*

im·pan·el (im pan′əl) *v.* **-elled** or **-eled, -el·ling** or **-el·ing. 1** put on a list for duty on a jury. **2** select (a jury) from the list. Also, **empanel.**

im·par·a·dise (im par′ə dīs′) *v.* **-dised, -dis·ing. 1** put in paradise; make supremely happy. **2** make a paradise of.

im·part (im pärt′) *v.* **1** give a share in; give: *The furnishings imparted an air of elegance to the room.* **2** communicate; tell: *I will impart a secret to you.* [< L *impartire* < *in-* in + *pars, partis* part] —**Syn. 1** bestow, convey. 2 relate, reveal. See **communicate.**

im·par·tial (im pär′shəl) *adj.* showing no more favor to one side than to the other; fair; just. —**im·par′tial·ly,** *adv.* —**Syn.** unbiassed, unprejudiced. See **fair.**

im·par·ti·al·i·ty (im′pär shē al′ə tē) *n.* fairness; justice.

im·pass·a·bil·i·ty (im pas′e bil′ə tē) *n.* the state of being impassable.

im·pass·a·ble (im pas′ə bəl) *adj.* not passable; so that one cannot go through or across: *Deep mud made the road impassable.* —**im·pass′a·ble·ness,** *n.* —**im·pass′a·bly,** *adv.*

im·passe (im pas′ or im′pas) *n.* 1 a position from which there is no escape; deadlock. 2 a road or way closed at one end. [< F]

im·pas·si·bil·i·ty (im pas′ə bil′ə tē) *n.* the condition or quality of being impassible.

im·pas·si·ble (im pas′ə bəl) *adj.* 1 unable to suffer or feel pain. 2 that cannot be harmed. 3 without feeling; impassive. [< L *impassibilis,* ult. < *in-* not + *pati* suffer] —**im·pass′i·bly,** *adv.*

im·pas·sioned (im pash′ənd) *adj.* full of strong feeling; ardent; emotional: *The general made an impassioned speech to his soldiers.*

im·pas·sive (im pas′iv) *adj.* 1 without feeling or emotion; unmoved: *He listened with an impassive face.* 2 not feeling pain or injury; insensible: *The soldier lay as impassive as if he were dead.* 3 incapable of being injured. —**im·pas′sive·ly,** *adv.* —**im·pas′sive·ness,** *n.* —**Syn.** 1 indifferent, apathetic, passive.

im·pas·siv·i·ty (im′pa siv′ə tē) *n.* a being impassive.

im·pas·to (im päs′tō) *n.* in painting: 1 a technique in which the paint is thickly applied, often with a palette knife. 2 the paint thus applied. [< Ital. *impasto* < *impastare* beplaster]

im·pa·tience (im pā′shəns) *n.* 1 a lack of patience; being impatient. 2 uneasiness combined with eagerness.

im·pa·tient (im pā′shənt) *adj.* 1 not patient; not willing to bear delay, opposition, pain, bother, etc. 2 restless: *The horses were impatient to start.* 3 showing lack of patience: *an impatient answer.* 4 **impatient of,** unwilling to endure; not liking or wanting. —**im·pa′tient·ly,** *adv.*

im·peach (im pēch′) *v.* 1 call in question: *impeach a person's honor.* 2 charge with wrongdoing; accuse. 3 accuse before a competent tribunal (a public officer) of wrong conduct during office: *The judge was impeached for taking bribes.* [ME < OF *empeechier* hinder < LL *impedicare* < L *in-* on + *pedica* shackle]

im·peach·a·ble (im pēch′ə bəl) *adj.* 1 liable to be impeached. 2 likely to cause impeachment: *an impeachable offence.*

im·peach·ment (im pēch′mənt) *n.* 1 an impeaching. 2 a being impeached.

im·pearl (im pėrl′) *v.* 1 form into pearl-like drops. 2 adorn with pearls or pearl-like drops.

im·pec·ca·bil·i·ty (im pek′ə bil′ə tē) *n.* an impeccable quality; faultlessness.

im·pec·ca·ble (im pek′ə bəl) *adj.* 1 faultless. 2 sinless. [< LL *impeccabilis* < *in-* not + *peccare* sin] —**im·pec′ca·bly,** *adv.*

im·pe·cu·ni·ous (im′pi kū′nē əs) *adj.* having little or no money; penniless; poor. [< *in-* not + L *pecuniosus* rich < *pecunia* money < *pecu* head of cattle] —**im′pe·cu′ni·ous·ly,** *adv.*

im·ped·ance (im pēd′əns) *n.* 1 in electricity, the apparent resistance in an alternating-current circuit, made up of two components, reactance and true or ohmic resistance. 2 in physics, the ratio of pressure in a sound wave to the product of the particle velocity and the area of a cross section of the wave at a given point.

im·pede (im pēd′) *v.* **-ped·ed, -ped·ing.** hinder; obstruct. [< L *impedire* < *in-* on + *pes, pedis* foot] —**im·ped′er,** *n.* —**Syn.** hamper, retard. See **prevent.**

im·ped·i·ment (im ped′ə mənt) *n.* 1 a hindrance; obstruction. 2 a defect in speech: *Stuttering is an impediment.* 3 in law, a bar to the making of a valid marriage contract. [< L *impedimentum*]

im·ped·i·men·ta (im ped′ə men′tə) *n.pl.* 1 travelling equipment; baggage. 2 the military supplies carried along with an army. 3 any equipment that one carries and which obstructs one or hinders progress. 4 in law, obstacles; hindrances. [< L]

im·pel (im pel′) *v.* **-pelled, -pel·ling.** 1 drive; force; cause: *Hunger impelled the lazy man to work.* 2 cause to move; drive forward; push along: *The wind impelled the boat to shore.* [< L *impellere* < *in-* on + *pellere* push] —**Syn.** 1 See **compel.**

im·pel·ler (im pel′ər) *n.* 1 a person or thing that impels. 2 the rotating blades of a centrifugal pump or blower.

im·pel·lent (im pel′ənt) *adj.* tending to impel; impelling. —*n.* a person, force, or thing that impels.

im·pend (im pend′) *v.* 1 be likely to happen soon; be ready to occur; be near: *When war impends, wise men try to prevent it.* 2 hang; hang threateningly. [< L *impendere* < *in-* over + *pendere* hang]

im·pend·ent (im pen′dənt) *adj.* impending.

im·pend·ing (im pen′ding) *adj.* 1 likely to happen soon; threatening; about to occur. 2 overhanging: *Above him were impending cliffs.* —**Syn.** 1 See **imminent.**

im·pen·e·tra·bil·i·ty (im pen′ə trə bil′ə tē) *n.* a being impenetrable.

im·pen·e·tra·ble (im pen′ə trə bəl) *adj.* 1 that cannot be entered, pierced, or passed: *A thick sheet of steel is impenetrable by an ordinary bullet.* 2 not open to ideas, influences, etc. 3 impossible for the mind to understand; inscrutable. 4 in physics, of a body, excluding all other bodies from the space it occupies. —**im·pen′e·tra·bly,** *adv.*

im·pen·i·tence (im pen′ə təns) *n.* a lack of any sorrow or regret for doing wrong.

im·pen·i·tent (im pen′ə tənt) *adj.* not penitent; feeling no sorrow or regret for having done wrong. —**im·pen′i·tent·ly,** *adv.*

imper. imperative.

im·per·a·tive (im per′ə tiv) *adj.* 1 not to be avoided; urgent; necessary: *It is imperative that a very sick child stay in bed.* 2 expressing a command; commanding. 3 in grammar, denoting the mood of a verb that expresses a command, request, or advice. "Go!" and "Stop, look, listen!" are in the imperative mood.
—*n.* 1 a command: *The great imperative is "Love thy neighbor as thyself."* 2 in grammar: **a** the imperative mood. **b** a verb form in this mood. *Abbrev.:* imp. or imper. [< L *imperativus*< *imperare* command] —**im·per′a·tive·ly,** *adv.* —**im·per′a·tive·ness,** *n.*

im·pe·ra·tor (im′pə rā′tər) *n.* 1 an absolute or supreme ruler. 2 in ancient Rome: **a** a victorious military commander. **b** the emperor. [< L *imperator* < *imperare* command]

im·per·cep·ti·ble (im′pər sep′tə bəl) *adj.* 1 very slight; gradual. 2 that cannot be perceived or felt. —**im′per·cep′ti·ble·ness,** *n.* —**im′per·cep′ti·bly,** *adv.*

imperf. imperfect.

im·per·fect (im pėr′fikt) *adj.* 1 not perfect; having some defect or fault. 2 not complete; lacking some part. 3 in grammar, expressing continued or customary action in the past. 4 in music: **a** denoting a major or minor third or sixth. **b** of an interval, diminished.
—*n.* in grammar: 1 the imperfect tense. English has no imperfect, but such forms as *was studying* and *used to study* are similar to the imperfect in other languages. 2 a verb form in this tense. *Abbrev.:* imp. or imperf. —**im·per′fect·ly,** *adv.* —**im·per′fect·ness,** *n.*

im·per·fecti·on (im′pər fek′shən) *n.* 1 a lack of perfection; imperfect condition or character. 2 a fault; defect: *The costly vase proved to have several imperfections.*

im·per·fo·rate (im pėr′fə rit or im pėr′fə rāt′) *adj.* 1 not pierced through with holes. 2 of stamps, not separated from other stamps by perforations; having the margins whole. —**im·per′fo·ra′tion,** *n.*

im·pe·ri·al (im pēr′ē əl) *adj.* 1 of or having to do with an empire or its ruler. 2 of or having to do with the rule or authority of one country over other countries and colonies. 3 having the rank of an emperor. 4 supreme; majestic; magnificent. 5 of larger size or better quality. 6 according to the British standard of weights and measures.

hat, āge, cãre, fär; let, ēqual, tėrm; it, īce
hot, ōpen, ôrder; oil, out; cup, pu̇t, rüle, ūse
əbove, takən, pencəl, lemən, circəs
ch, child; ng, long; sh, ship
th, thin; ᴛʜ, then; zh, measure

—*n.* **1** a very small beard left growing beneath the lower lip. **2** a size of paper, 23 by 31 inches (in England, 22 by 30 inches). [< L *imperialis* < *imperium* empire] —**im·pe′ri·al·ly,** *adv.*

A man wearing an imperial (def. 1)

imperial gallon the British and Canadian gallon, equal to 160 fluid ounces or about 1⅕ United States gallons.

im·pe·ri·al·ism (im pēr′ē əl iz′əm) *n.* **1** the policy of extending the rule or authority of one country over other countries and colonies. **2** an imperial system of government. **3** the dominating of another nation's economic, political, and even military structure without actually taking governmental control.

im·pe·ri·al·ist (im pēr′ē əl ist) *n.* a person who favors imperialism. —*adj.* imperialistic.

im·pe·ri·al·is·tic (im pēr′ē əl is′tik) *adj.* **1** of imperialism or imperialists. **2** favoring imperialism. —**im·pe′ri·al·is′ti·cal·ly,** *adv.*

Imperial Order Daughters of the Empire an organization of women founded in 1900, whose purpose is to stimulate patriotism and promote good citizenship.

im·per·il (im per′əl) *v.* **-illed** or **-iled, -il·ling** or **-il·ing.** put in danger. —**Syn.** endanger, jeopardize.

im·pe·ri·ous (im pēr′ē əs) *adj.* **1** haughty; arrogant; domineering; overbearing. **2** imperative; necessary; urgent. [< L *imperiosus* commanding] —**im·pe′ri·ous·ly,** *adv.* —**im·pe′ri·ous·ness,** *n.* —**Syn. 1** dictatorial.

im·per·ish·a·bil·i·ty (im per′ish ə bil′ə tē) *n.* a being imperishable; enduring quality.

im·per·ish·a·ble (im per′ish ə bəl) *adj.* everlasting; not perishable; indestructible. —**im·per′ish·a·bly,** *adv.*

im·pe·ri·um (im pēr′ē əm) *n.* **-pe·ri·a** (-pēr′ē ə). **1** command; supreme power; empire. **2** in law, the right to use the force of the state in order to enforce the law. [< L]

im·per·ma·nence (im pėr′mə nəns) *n.* the state or condition of being impermanent.

im·per·ma·nent (im pėr′mə nənt) *adj.* not lasting; temporary. —**im·per′ma·nent·ly,** *adv.*

im·per·me·a·bil·i·ty (im pėr′mē ə bil′ə tē) *n.* an impermeable quality or condition.

im·per·me·a·ble (im pėr′mē ə bəl) *adj.* **1** that cannot be permeated; impassable. **2** in physics, not permitting the passage of fluid through the pores, interstices, etc.

impers. impersonal.

im·per·son·al (im pėr′sən əl or im pėrs′nəl) *adj.* **1** referring to all or any persons, not to any special one: "*First come, first served*" *is an impersonal remark. In the expression* "*One must do his best,*" *the word* "*one*" *is impersonal.* **2** having no existence as a person: *Electricity is an impersonal force.* **3** in grammar, of a verb, having nothing but an indefinite *it* for a subject. *Example*: *rained* in "It rained yesterday."

im·per·son·al·i·ty (im pėr′sən al′ə tē) *n.* **-ties. 1** an impersonal character; absence of personal quality. **2** an impersonal thing, force, etc.

im·per·son·al·ly (im pėr′sən əl ē or im pėrs′nəl ē) *adv.* in an impersonal manner; without personal reference or connection.

impersonal pronoun any of the words *it, one, they,* or *you* when used to refer to a person or thing not named or identified: *It is cold today. One must do his best. They say that life begins at forty. You should be careful when crossing the street.*

im·per·son·ate (im pėr′sən āt′) *v.* **-at·ed, -at·ing. 1** act the part of: *He impersonated Hamlet on the stage.* **2** pretend to be; mimic the voice, appearance, and manners of, especially with intent to deceive: *The thief impersonated a policeman.* **3** represent in personal form; personify; typify: *To many people Henry Hudson impersonates the spirit of adventure.*

im·per·son·a·tion (im pėr′sən ā′shən) *n.* **1** an impersonating. **2** a being impersonated. **3** a personification; type.

im·per·son·a·tor (im pėr′sən ā′tər) *n.* **1** one who impersonates. **2** an actor who impersonates particular persons or types; professional mimic.

im·per·ti·nence (im pėr′tə nəns) *n.* **1** an impertinent quality; impudence; insolence. **2** an impertinent act or speech. **3** a lack of pertinence; irrelevance. —**Syn. 1** impudence, insolence.

im·per·ti·nen·cy (im pėr′tə nən sē) *n.* **-cies.** impertinence.

im·per·ti·nent (im pėr′tə nənt) *adj.* **1** saucy; impudent; insolent; rude. **2** not pe tinent; not to the point; out of place. —**im·per′ti·nent·ly** *adv.*

Syn. 1 Impertinent, impudent, saucy = showing lack of proper respect. **Impertinent** = showing lack of respect for others' privacy or rights, by taking too much interest in what is not one's business or too many liberties with those deserving respect: *Talking back to older people is impertinent.* **Impudent** adds the idea of shamelessness and defiance: *The impudent boy made faces at the teacher.* **Saucy** suggests a disrespectful attitude shown by light and flippant manner or speech: *The saucy girl tossed her head when her father scolded her.* **2** inappropriate, incongruous, irrelevant.

im·per·turb·a·bil·i·ty (im′pər tėr′bə bil′ə tē) *n.* a being imperturbable; calmness.

im·per·turb·a·ble (im′pər tėr′bə bəl) *adj.* **1** not capable of being excited or disturbed. **2** not easily excited; calm. —**im′per·turb′a·bly,** *adv.*

im·per·vi·ous (im pėr′vē əs) *adj.* **1** not letting anything pass through; not allowing passage: *Rubber cloth is impervious to moisture.* **2** not open to or affected by argument, suggestions, etc.: *She is impervious to all the gossip about her.* —**im·per′vi·ous·ly,** *adv.* —**im·per′vi·ous·ness,** *n.*

im·pe·ti·go (im′pə tī′gō) *n.* an infectious skin disease causing pimples filled with pus. [< L *impetigo* < *impetere* attack < *in-* + *petere* aim for]

im·pet·u·os·i·ty (im pech′ü os′ə tē) *n.* **-ties. 1** sudden or rash energy; violence; ardor: *The impetuosity of the speaker stirred the audience.* **2** an impetuous action.

im·pet·u·ous (im pech′ü əs) *adj.* **1** moving with great force or speed: *the impetuous rush of water over Niagara Falls.* **2** acting hastily, rashly, or with sudden feeling: *Boys are more impetuous than old men.* [< LL *impetuosus* < L *impetus* attack] —**im·pet′u·ous·ly,** *adv.* —**im·pet′u·ous·ness,** *n.*

im·pe·tus (im′pə təs) *n.* **1** the force with which a moving body tends to maintain its velocity and overcome resistance: *the impetus of a cannon ball.* **2** a driving force; incentive: *Ambition is an impetus that impels some people toward success.* [< L *impetus* attack < *impetere* attack < *in-* + *petere* aim for] —**Syn. 1** momentum. **2** stimulus, impulse.

imp. gal. imperial gallon.

im·pi·e·ty (im pī′ə tē) *n.* **-ties. 1** lack of piety or reverence for God; wickedness. **2** lack of dutifulness or respect. **3** an impious act.

im·pinge (im pinj′) *v.* **-pinged, -ping·ing. 1** hit; strike: *Rays of light impinge on the eye.* **2** encroach; infringe. [< L *impingere* + *in-* on + *pangere* strike]

im·pinge·ment (im pinj′mənt) *n.* an impinging.

im·pi·ous (im′pē əs or im pī′əs) *adj.* not pious; not having or not showing reverence for God; wicked; profane. —**im′pi·ous·ly,** *adv.* —**im′pi·ous·ness,** *n.*

imp·ish (imp′ish) *adj.* **1** of an imp; like an imp. **2** mischievous. —**imp′ish·ly,** *adv.* —**imp′ish·ness,** *n.*

im·plac·a·bil·i·ty (im plak′ə bil′ə tē or im plā′kə bil′ə tē) *n.* the quality of being implacable.

im·plac·a·ble (im plak′ə bəl or im plā′kə bəl) *adj.* that cannot be placated, pacified, or appeased; relentless. —**im·pla′ca·bly,** *adv.* —**Syn.** unforgiving, inexorable.

im·plant (*v.* im plant′; *n.* im′plant) *v.* **1** instil; fix deeply: *A good teacher implants high ideals in children.* **2** insert: *A steel tube is then implanted in the socket.* **3** set in the ground; plant. **4** graft or set (a piece of skin, bone, etc.) into the body. —*n.* **1** tissue grafted into the body. **2** a small radio-active tube or needle inserted into the body, especially to treat cancer.

im·plan·ta·tion (im′plan tā′shən) *n.* **1** an implanting. **2** the state of being implanted.

im·plau·si·bil·i·ty (im plo′zə bil′ ə tē or im plô′ zə bil′ ə tē) *n.* the quality or condition of being implausible.

im·plau·si·ble (im plo′zə bəl or im plô′zə bəl) *adj.* not plausible; lacking the appearance of truth or trustworthiness. **—im·plau′si·bly,** *adv.*

im·ple·ment (*n.* im′plə mənt; *v.* im′plə ment′) *n.* a useful piece of equipment; tool; instrument; utensil: *Ploughs, axes, shovels, can openers, and brooms are all implements.* **—*v.* 1** provide with implements or other means to carry out a task. **2** provide the power and authority necessary to accomplish or put (something) into effect: *implement an order.* **3** carry out; get done: *Do not undertake a project unless you can implement it.* [< LL *implementum,* literally, that which fills a need < L *implere* < *in-* in + *-plere* fill] **—im′ple·men·ta′tion,** *n.* **—Syn.** *n.* See **tool.**

im·pli·cate (im′plə kāt′) *v.* **-cat·ed, -cat·ing. 1** show to have a part in or to be connected with (something); involve: *The thief's confession implicated two other men.* **2** imply. **3** entangle; fold or twist together. [< L *implicare* < *in-* in + *plicare* fold. Doublet of EMPLOY, IMPLY.] **—Syn. 1** See **involve.**

im·pli·ca·tion (im′plə kā′shən) *n.* **1** an implying or being implied. **2** something implied; an indirect suggestion; hint: *There was no implication of dishonesty in his failure in business.* **3** an implicating or being implicated.

im·plic·it (im plis′it) *adj.* **1** without doubting, hesitating, or asking questions; absolute: *A soldier must give implicit obedience to his officers.* **2** meant, but not clearly expressed or distinctly stated; implied: *Her silence gave implicit consent.* **3** involved as a necessary part or condition. [< L *implicitus,* pp. of *implicare.* See IMPLICATE.] **—Syn. 1** unquestioning, unreserved. **2** tacit.

im·plic·it·ly (im plis′it lē) *adv.* **1** unquestioningly. **2** by implication.

im·plied (im plīd′) *adj.* involved, indicated, suggested, or understood without express statement: *an implied contract, an implied rebuke.*

im·pli·ed·ly (im plī′id lē) *adv.* by implication.

im·plore (im plôr′) *v.* **-plored, -plor·ing. 1** beg earnestly for. **2** beg (a person to do something). [< L *implorare,* originally, invoke with weeping < *in-* toward + *plorare* cry] **—im·plor′er,** *n.* **—im·plor′ing·ly,** *adv.* **—Syn. 1** beseech, entreat. See **beg.**

im·ply (im plī′) *v.* **-plied, -ply·ing. 1** indicate without saying outright; express indirectly; suggest: *Silence often implies consent. Her smile implied that she had forgiven us.* **2** involve as a necessary part or condition: *Speech implies a speaker.* **3** signify; mean. [ME < OF *emplier* involve, put (in) < L *implicare.* Doublet of EMPLOY, IMPLICATE.] **—Syn. 1** insinuate.

☞ **Imply, infer** should not be treated as synonyms. A writer or speaker *implies* something in his words or manner; a reader or listener *infers* something from what he reads, sees, or hears: *She implied by the look in her eyes that she did not intend to keep the appointment. We inferred from the principal's announcement that he already knew who had broken the window.*

im·po·lite (im′pə līt′) *adj.* not polite; having or showing bad manners; rude. **—im′po·lite′ly,** *adv.* **—im′po·lite′ness,** *n.* **—Syn.** discourteous, disrespectful.

im·pol·i·tic (im pol′ə tik′) *adj.* not politic; not expedient; not judicious; unwise: *It is impolitic to offend people who could be of help to you.*

im·pon·der·a·ble (im pon′dər ə bəl) *adj.* without weight that can be felt or measured: *Faith and love are imponderable forces.* **—*n.*** something imponderable. **—im·pon′der·a·bly,** *adv.*

im·port (*v.* im pôrt′ or im′pôrt; *n.* im′pôrt) *v.* **1** bring in from a foreign country for sale or use: *Canada imports coffee from Brazil.* **2** mean; signify: *Tell me what your remark imports.* **3** be of importance or consequence. **—*n.* 1** anything imported: *Rubber is a useful import.* **2** an importing; importation: *The import of diseased animals is forbidden.* **3** meaning: *What is the import of your remark?* **4** importance: *It is a matter of great import.* **5** *Cdn. Slang.* **a** in professional football, a non-Canadian player who has not played five years in Canada. **b** in other sports, a player who is not a native of the country or area in which he is playing. [< L *importare* < *in-* in + *portare* carry]

im·por·tance (im pôr′təns) *n.* a being important; consequence; significance; value.

Syn. Importance, consequence = the quality of having much value, meaning, influence, etc. **Importance,** the general word, emphasizes being of great value, meaning, etc. in itself: *Anybody can see the importance of good health.* **Consequence** emphasizes having, or being likely to have, important or far-reaching results or effects: *The discovery of insulin was an event of great consequence for diabetics.*

im·por·tant (im pôr′ tənt) *adj.* **1** meaning much; worth noticing or considering; having value or significance. **2** having social position or influence. **3** acting as if important; seeming to be important; self-important: *An important little man rushed around giving orders.* [< F < Med.L *importans, -antis,* ppr. of *importare* be significant < L *importare* bring on or in. See IMPORT.] **—im·por′tant·ly,** *adv.* **—Syn. 1** significant, momentous, weighty.

im·por·ta·tion (im′pôr tā′shən) *n.* **1** the act of importing. **2** something imported.

im·port·er (im pôr′tər or im′pôr tər) *n.* a person or company whose business is importing goods.

im·por·tu·nate (im pôr′chə nit) *adj.* asking repeatedly; annoyingly persistent; urgent. **—im·por′tu·nate·ly,** *adv.* **—im·por′tu·nate·ness,** *n.*

im·por·tune (im′pôr tūn′ or im′pôr tün′) *v.* **-tuned, -tun·ing.** ask urgently or repeatedly; trouble with demands. [< MF < L *importunus* inconvenient] **—im′por·tune′ly,** *adv.* **—im′por·tun′er,** *n.*

im·por·tu·ni·ty (im′pôr tū′nə tē or im′pôr tü′nə tē) *n.* **-ties.** persistence in asking; the act of demanding again and again.

im·pose (im pōz′) *v.* **-posed, -pos·ing. 1** put (a burden, tax, punishment, etc.) on: *The judge imposed a fine of $500 on the guilty man.* **2** force or thrust one's authority or influence on another or others. **3** force or thrust (oneself or one's company) on another or others; obtrude; presume. **4** pass off (a thing upon a person) to deceive. **5** in ecclesiastical use, lay on (hands) in confirmation or ordination. **6** in printing, arrange (pages of type) in the correct order. **7 impose on** or **upon, a** take advantage of; use for selfish purposes: *to impose on the good nature of others.* **b** deceive; cheat; trick. [< F *imposer* < *in-* on + *poser* put, place] **—im·pos′er,** *n.*

im·pos·ing (im pōz′ing) *adj.* impressive because of size, appearance, or dignity: *The Peace Tower of the Parliament Buildings is an imposing landmark.* **—im·pos′ing·ly,** *adv.* **—Syn.** commanding, stately, majestic.

im·po·si·tion (im′pə zish′ən) *n.* **1** the act or fact of imposing. **2** a tax, duty, task, burden, etc. **3** an unfair tax, etc. **4** an imposing upon a person by taking advantage of his good nature: *Would it be an imposition to ask you to mail this parcel?* **5** a deception; fraud; trick. **6** in ecclesiastical use, a ceremonial laying on of hands, as in confirmation. **7** in printing, the act or process of arranging pages of type.

im·pos·si·bil·i·ty (im pos′ə bil′ə tē or im′pos ə bil′ə tē) *n.* **-ties. 1** the quality of being impossible. **2** something impossible.

im·pos·si·ble (im pos′ə bəl) *adj.* **1** that cannot be done or achieved: *an impossible task.* **2** that cannot exist or happen: *an impossible tale, an impossible character.* **3** that cannot be true: *an impossible rumor.* **4** not easy to endure; very objectionable: *an impossible person.* **—*n.* 1** something that is or seems impossible: *The sergeant always demanded the impossible of his men.* **2** an impossibility: *His statement is in the nature of an impossible.* **—Syn. 1** impracticable, unfeasible. **—im·pos′si·bly,** *adv.* **—im·pos′si·ble·ness,** *n.*

im·post¹ (im′pōst) *n.* **1** a tax on goods brought into a country; customs duty. **2** a tax; tribute. **3** in racing, the weight that a horse must carry in a handicap, assigned on the basis of age. [< OF, ult. < L *in-* on + *ponere* place, put]

im·post² (im′pōst) *n.* in architecture, the uppermost

part of a column, etc. on which the end of an arch rests. [< F < Ital. *imposta*, ult. < L *in-* on + *ponere* place, put]

im·pos·tor (im pos′tər) *n.* **1** a person who assumes a false name or character. **2** a deceiver; cheat. [< LL < L *imponere* impose < *in-* on + *ponere* place, put]

im·pos·ture (im pos′chər) *n.* deception; fraud. [< LL *impostura* < L *imponere* impose]

im·po·tence (im′pə təns) *n.* a lack of power; helplessness; the condition or quality of being impotent.

im·po·ten·cy (im′pə tən sē) *n.* impotence.

im·po·tent (im′pə tənt) *adj.* **1** not having power; helpless: *The cripple fell back in an impotent rage.* **2** incapable of having sexual intercourse. **—im′po·tent·ly,** *adv.* **—Syn. 1** weak, feeble, infirm.

im·pound (im pound′) *v.* **1** shut up in a pen or pound: *impound stray animals.* **2** shut up; enclose; confine: *A dam impounds water.* **3** seize and put in the custody of a law court: *The court impounded the documents to use as evidence.* **—im·pound′er,** *n.*

im·pov·er·ish (im pov′ər ish or im pov′rish) *v.* **1** make very poor. **2** exhaust the strength, richness, or resources of: *impoverish the soil.* [ME < OF *empoveriss-*, a stem of *empoverir*, ult. < L *in-* + *pauper* poor] **—im·pov′er·ish·er,** *n.*

im·pov·er·ished (im pov′ər isht or im pov′risht) *adj.* very poor. **—Syn.** See **poor.**

im·pov·er·ish·ment (im pov′ər ish mənt or im pov′rish mənt) *n.* **1** an impoverishing. **2** a being impoverished. **3** something that impoverishes.

im·pow·er (im pou′ər) *v.* empower.

im·prac·ti·ca·bil·i·ty (im prak′tə kə bil′ə tē) *n.* **-ties. 1** the quality of being impracticable. **2** something impracticable.

im·prac·ti·ca·ble (im prak′tə kə bəl) *adj.* **1** not working well in practice; difficult to put into practice: *His suggestions were impracticable.* **2** very hard to manage: *an impracticable horse.* **3** that cannot be used: *an impracticable road.* **—im·prac′ti·ca·bly,** *adv.* ☛ See **impractical** for usage note.

im·prac·ti·cal (im prak′tə kəl) *adj.* not practical; unrealistic: *To build a bridge across the Atlantic Ocean is an impractical scheme.* **—im·prac′ti·cal·ly,** *adv.*

☛ **Impractical, impracticable. Impractical** describes things that are useless or people who have a very unrealistic view of life or show little judgment or common sense in what they do: *Buying useless things because they are on sale is impractical.* **Impracticable** describes things that have been proved unusable in actual practice or that would be impossible to put into practice: *Most schemes to abolish poverty are impracticable.*

im·pre·cate (im′prə kāt′) *v.* **-cat·ed, -cat·ing.** call down (curses, evil, etc.): *The witch doctor imprecated ruin on his people's enemies.* [< L *imprecari* < *in-* on + *prex, precis* prayer] **—im′pre·ca′tor,** *n.*

im·pre·ca·tion (im′prə kā′shən) *n.* **1** the act of calling down curses, evil, etc. **2** a curse.

im·pre·cise (im′pri sīs′) *adj.* lacking precision; inexact. **—im′pre·ci′sion,** *n.*

im·preg·na·bil·i·ty (im preg′nə bil′ə tē) *n.* the quality of being impregnable.

im·preg·na·ble (im preg′nə bəl) *adj.* that cannot be overthrown by force; able to resist attack: *an impregnable fortress, an impregnable argument.* [ME < OF *imprenable* < *in-* not + *prenable* pregnable] **—im·preg′na·bly,** *adv.*

im·preg·nate (im preg′nāt) *v.* **-nat·ed, -nat·ing,** *adj.* **—***v.* **1** make pregnant; fertilize. **2** fill (*with*); saturate: *Sea water is impregnated with salt.* **3** instil into (the mind); inspire; imbue: *A great book impregnates the mind with new ideas.* **—***adj.* impregnated. [< LL *impraegnare* make pregnant < *in-* + *praegnans* pregnant] **—im·preg′na·tor,** *n.*

im·preg·na·tion (im′preg nā′shən) *n.* **1** an impregnating or being impregnated. **2** the thing, influence, etc. with which anything is impregnated.

im·pre·sa·ri·o (im′prə sä′rē ō′) *n.* **-sa·ri·os.** a person who presents or manages a concert tour, an opera or ballet company, or other, especially musical, entertainment. [< Ital. *impresario* < *impresa* undertaking, ult. < L *in-* on + *prehendere* take]

hat, āge, cãre, fär; let, ēqual, tėrm; it, īce
hot, ōpen, ôrder; oil, out; cup, pu̇t, rüle, ūse
əbove, takən, pencəl, lemən, circəs
ch, child; ng, long; sh, ship
th, thin; ᴛʜ, then; zh, measure

im·pre·scrip·ti·ble (im′prē skrip′tə bəl) *adj.* existing independently of law or custom; not justly to be taken away or violated: *imprescriptible rights.*

im·press[1] (*v.* im pres′; *n.* im′pres) *v.* **-pressed** or (*Archaic*) **-prest, -press·ing,** *n.* **—***v.* **1** have a strong effect on the mind or feelings of: *A hero impresses us with his courage.* **2** fix in the mind: *She repeated the words to impress them on her memory.* **3** make marks by pressing or stamping: *impress wax with a seal.* **4** imprint; stamp. **—***n.* an impression; mark; stamp: *An author leaves the impress of his personality on what he writes.* [ME < OF < L *impressus*, pp. of *imprimere* < *in-* in + *premere* press] **—im·press′er,** *n.*

im·press[2] (im pres′) *v.* **-pressed** or (*Archaic*) **-prest, -press·ing. 1** seize by force for public use: *The police impressed our car in order to pursue the escaping robbers.* **2** force (men) to serve in the navy or army. **3** bring in and use. [< *in-*[2] + *press*[2]]

im·press·i·ble (im pres′ə bəl) *adj.* impressionable.

im·pres·sion (im presh′ən) *n.* **1** an effect produced on a person: *Punishment seemed to make little impression on the child.* **2** an idea; notion: *I have a vague impression that I left the house unlocked.* **3** something produced by pressure as a mark, stamp, print, etc.: *The thief left an impression of his feet in the garden.* **4** the act of impressing. **5** the state of being impressed. **6** in dentistry, a mould of the teeth and the surrounding gums. **7** in printing: **a** the total number of copies of a book made at one time. **b** a printed copy.

im·pres·sion·a·bil·i·ty (im presh′ən ə bil′ə tē or im presh′nə bil′ə tē) *n.* an impressionable quality or condition.

im·pres·sion·a·ble (im presh′ən ə bəl or im presh′nə bəl) *adj.* sensitive to impressions; easily impressed or influenced.

im·pres·sion·ism (im presh′ən iz′əm) *n.* **1** in painting, a style developed by French painters of the late 19th century and characterized by the use of strong, bright colors applied in dabs to suggest the artist's general, rather than detailed, impressions of nature, etc. **2** in literature, a style of writing having a similar intention. **3** in music, a style characterized by the use of unusual and rich harmonies, tonal qualities, etc. to suggest the composer's impressions of nature, emotion, etc.

im·pres·sion·ist (im presh′ən ist) *n.* **1** an artist, writer, or composer who favors impressionism. **2** an entertainer who does impersonations or impressions, especially of famous persons.

im·pres·sion·is·tic (im presh′ən is′tik) *adj.* **1** of or characteristic of impressionism or impressionists. **2** giving only a general or hasty impression.

im·pres·sive (im pres′iv) *adj.* able to make an impression on the mind, feelings, conscience, etc.: *an impressive lecture, an impressive storm, an impressive ceremony.* **—im·pres′sive·ly,** *adv.* **—im·pres′sive·ness,** *n.* **—Syn.** imposing, commanding, striking.

im·press·ment (im pres′mənt) *n.* the act or practice of impressing men or property for public service or use.

im·pri·ma·tur (im′pri mā′tər) *n.* **1** an official licence to print or publish a book, etc., now generally used of works sanctioned by the Roman Catholic Church. **2** sanction; approval. [< NL *imprimatur* let it be printed]

im·pri·mis (im prī′mis) *adv. Latin.* in the first place; first.

im·print (*n.* im′print; *v.* im print′) *n.* **1** a mark made by pressure; print: *the imprint of a foot in the sand.* **2** an impression; mark: *Suffering left its imprint on her face.* **3** a publisher's name, with the place and date of publication, on the title page or at the end of a book; a printer's name and address as printed on his work. **—***v.* **1** mark by pressing or stamping; print: *imprint a postmark on an envelope, imprint a letter with a postmark.*

2 press or impress: *imprint a kiss on someone's cheek, a scene imprinted on the memory.* —**im·print′er,** *n.*

im·pris·on (im priz′ən) *v.* 1 put in prison; keep in prison. 2 confine closely; restrain.

im·pris·on·ment (im priz′ən mənt) *n.* 1 a putting or keeping in prison. 2 a being put or kept in prison. 3 close confinement; restraint.

im·prob·a·bil·i·ty (im prob′ə bil′ə tē) *n.* **-ties.** 1 a being improbable; unlikelihood. 2 something improbable.

im·prob·a·ble (im prob′ə bəl) *adj.* 1 not probable; not likely to happen. 2 not likely to be true: *an improbable story.*

im·prob·a·bly (im prob′ə blē) *adv.* with little or no probability.

im·promp·tu (im promp′tū or im promp′tü) *adv. adj.* without previous thought or preparation; offhand: *a speech made impromptu.* —*n.* something impromptu; improvisation. [< L *in promptu* in readiness] —**Syn.** *adj.* improvised.

im·prop·er (im prop′ər) *adj.* 1 not in accordance with accepted standards: *Among educated Canadians "ain't" is considered improper.* 2 not suitable. 3 not decent: *She was shocked by the boys' improper language.*
—**im·prop′er·ly,** *adv.*
Syn. 1, 3 Improper, indecent = not right or fitting according to accepted standards. **Improper** describes something that goes against or fails to observe standards of manners, morals, health, etc. set by those who know what is right or fitting: *Talking in church is improper.* **Indecent** = contrary to standards of good taste in behavior, modesty, and morals: *That fat girl looks indecent in those tight clothes.*

improper fraction a fraction equal to or greater than 1. *Examples*: 3/2, 4/3, 27/4, 8/5, 12/12.

im·pro·pri·e·ty (im′prə prī′ə tē) *n.* **-ties.** 1 a lack of propriety; the quality of being improper. 2 improper conduct. 3 an improper act, expression, etc. Using *learn* in speech or writing to mean *teach* is an impropriety.

im·prove (im prüv′) *v.* **-proved, -prov·ing.** 1 make better: *You could improve your handwriting if you tried.* 2 become better: *His health is improving.* 3 increase the value of (land or property). 4 formerly, in Upper Canada, clear virgin land of trees, underbrush, etc. in preparation for seeding. 5 use well; make good use of: *Improve your time by studying.* 6 **improve on,** make better; do better than. [< AF *emprouer* < OF *en-* in + *prou* profit]
—**im·prov′a·ble,** *adj.* —**im·prov′er,** *n.*

im·prove·ment (im prüv′mənt) *n.* 1 a making better or becoming better. 2 an increase in value. 3 a change or addition that increases value: *An old house can be made to look modern by judicious improvements.* 4 a better condition; anything that is better than another; advance. 5 formerly, in Upper Canada: **a** the condition of land cleared of trees and underbrush in preparation for seeding. **b** a piece of land in this condition: *an improvement of 50 acres.* 6 **improvements,** *pl.* buildings, fences, etc. added to land.

im·prov·i·dence (im prov′ə dəns) *n.* a lack of foresight; failure to look ahead; carelessness in providing for the future; lack of thrift.

im·prov·i·dent (im prov′ə dənt) *adj.* lacking foresight; not looking ahead; not careful in providing for the future; not thrifty. —**im·prov′i·dent·ly,** *adv.* —**Syn.** shiftless, imprudent, wasteful.

im·pro·vi·sa·tion (im′prə vī zā′shən or im′prov ə-zā′shən) *n.* 1 an improvising. 2 something improvised.

im·pro·vise (im′prə vīz′) *v.* **-vised, -vis·ing.** 1 compose or utter (verse, music, etc.) without preparation. 2 prepare or provide offhand; extemporize: *The boys improvised a tent out of two blankets and some long poles.* [< F Ital. *improvvisare,* ult. < L *in-* not + *pro-* beforehand + *videre* see] —**im′pro·vis′er,** *n.*

im·pru·dence (im prü′dəns) *n.* a lack of prudence; imprudent behavior.

im·pru·dent (im prü′dənt) *adj.* not prudent; rash; not discreet. —**im·pru′dent·ly,** *adv.* —**Syn.** indiscreet, ill-advised, heedless.

im·pu·dence (im′pyů dəns) *n.* 1 a lack of shame or modesty; rude boldness. 2 impudent conduct or language.

im·pu·dent (im′pyů dənt) *adj.* without shame or modesty; forward; rudely bold. [< L *impudens, -entis,* ult. < *in-* not + *pudere* be modest] —**im′pu·dent·ly,** *adv.* —**Syn.** presumptuous. See **impertinent.**

im·pugn (im pūn′) *v.* call in question; attack by words or arguments; challenge as false. [ME < OF < L *impugnare* assault < *in-* against + *pugnare* fight]
—**im·pugn′a·ble,** *adj.*

im·pulse (im′puls) *n.* 1 a sudden, driving force or influence; thrust; push: *the impulse of a wave, the impulse of hunger.* 2 the effect of a sudden, driving force or influence. 3 a sudden inclination or tendency to act. 4 the stimulating force of desire or emotion: *An angry mob is influenced more by impulse than by reason.* 5 in physiology, a stimulus that is transmitted, especially by nerve cells, and influences action in the muscle, gland, or other nerve cells that it reaches. 6 in mechanics, the product obtained by multiplying the value of a force by the time during which it acts. 7 the surge of electrical current in one direction. [< L *impulsus* < *impellere.* See IMPEL.] —**Syn. 1** impetus, drive.

im·pul·sion (im pul′shən) *n.* 1 an impelling; driving force. 2 an impulse. 3 an impetus.

im·pul·sive (im pul′siv) *adj.* 1 acting upon impulse; easily moved: *The impulsive child gave all his money to the beggar.* 2 driving onward; impelling; pushing.
—**im·pul′sive·ly,** *adv.* —**im·pul′sive·ness,** *n.* —**Syn. 1** rash, hasty, impetuous.

im·pu·ni·ty (im pū′nə tē) *n.* freedom from punishment, injury, or other unpleasant consequences: *If laws are not enforced, crimes are committed with impunity.* [< L *impunitas,* ult. < *in-* without + *poena* punishment]

im·pure (im pūr′) *adj.* 1 not pure; dirty; unclean. 2 mixed with something of lower value; adulterated. 3 not of one color, style, etc.; mixed. 4 forbidden by religion as unclean. —**im·pure′ly,** *adv.* —**im·pure′ness,** *n.*

im·pu·ri·ty (im pūr′ə tē) *n.* **-ties.** 1 a lack of purity; the state of being impure. 2 Often, **impurities,** *pl.* an impure thing or element; anything that makes something else impure: *Unfiltered water has impurities.*

im·pu·ta·tion (im′pyů tā′shən) *n.* 1 an imputing or being imputed. 2 a charge or hint of wrongdoing: *No imputation has ever been made against his good name.*

im·pute (im pūt′) *v.* **-put·ed, -put·ing.** consider as belonging; attribute; charge (a fault, etc.) to a person; blame: *I impute his failure to laziness.* [< L *imputare* < *in-* in + *putare* reckon] —**im·put′a·ble,** *adj.*

in (in) *prep. In* expresses inclusion, situation, presence, existence, position, and action within limits of space, time, state, circumstances, etc. 1 inside; within: *in an hour, in the box.* 2 into: *Put it in the fire.* 3 with; having; by: *wrap in paper, dressed in blue, be in trouble.* 4 of; made of; using: *a table in mahogany.* 5 surrounded by; in the midst of: *in the dust, in cold water.* 6 from among; out of: *one in a hundred.* 7 because of; for: *act in self-defence.* 8 about; concerning: *a book in Canadian history.* 9 at; during; after: *in the present time.* 10 while; when: *in crossing the street.* 11 **in that,** because.
—*adv.* 1 in or into some place, position, condition, etc.: *come in.* 2 present, especially in one's home or office: *The doctor is not in today.* 3 in fashion: *Short skirts are in again.* 4 **in for,** unable to avoid; sure to get or have. 5 **in with, a** friendly with. **b** partners with.
—*adj.* 1 that is in; being in. 2 coming or going in.
—*n.* 1 *Informal.* **a** a way of approach: *an in to a career in business.* **b** a position of familiarity or influence: *an in with the company president.* 2 **ins,** *pl.* people in office; the political party in power. 3 **ins and outs, a** the turns and twists; nooks and corners. **b** the different parts; details. [OE]
☛ **in, into.** *In* generally shows location (literal or figurative); *into* generally shows direction: *He was in the house. He came into the house. He was in a stupor. He fell into a deep sleep.* Informally, *in* is often used for *into*: *He fell in the creek.* ☛ See **at** for another usage note.

in-[1] *prefix.* not; the opposite of; the absence of, as in *inexpensive, inattention, inconvenient.* Also: **i-,** before *gn*; **il-,** before *l*; **im-,** before *b, m, p*; **ir-,** before *r.* [< L]
☛ **In-** or **un-** prefixed to many words gives them a negative meaning, as in *inconsiderate, incapable, uneven, unloved.* Some words take both prefixes and one of them may be the more current. Thus *indistinguishable* is preferred to *undistinguishable.*

in-[2] *prefix.* 1 in; into; on; upon, as in *inhale, inscribe.*

2 in- is also used to strengthen a meaning or change an intransitive verb to a transitive, usually with very little change in meaning. Also: **il-**, before *l*; **im-**, before *b, m, p*; **ir-**, before *r*. [< L *in-* < *in*, prep.]

in-[3] *prefix.* in; within; into; toward, as in *inborn, indoors, inland.* [OE]

-in *suffix.* a variant of *-ine*[2], sometimes used in chemical terms to denote neutral substances, as in *albumin, stearin.* [< NL < L *-ina*, fem. suffix to abstract nouns]

in. inch; inches.

In indium.

in·a·bil·i·ty (in′ə bil′ə tē) *n.* a lack of ability, power, or means; being unable.

in ab·sen·tia (in ab sen′shə) *Latin.* while absent.

in·ac·ces·si·bil·i·ty (in′ək ses′ə bil′ə tē) *n.* a lack of accessibility; being inaccessible.

in·ac·ces·si·ble (in′ək ses′ə bəl) *adj.* **1** not accessible; that cannot be reached or entered. **2** hard to get at; hard to reach or enter: *The fort on top of the steep hill is inaccessible.* **3** that cannot be obtained; hard to obtain. **—in′ac·ces′si·bly,** *adv.*

in·ac·cu·ra·cy (in ak′yů rə sē) *n.* **-cies. 1** a lack of accuracy; being inaccurate: *The inaccuracy of the report was not hard to prove.* **2** an error; mistake.

in·ac·cu·rate (in ak′yů rit) *adj.* not accurate; not exact; containing mistakes: *an inaccurate description.* **—in·ac′cu·rate·ly,** *adv.* **—Syn.** inexact, erroneous, faulty.

in·ac·tion (in ak′shən) *n.* an absence of action; idleness.

in·ac·tive (in ak′tiv) *adj.* not active; idle; sluggish. **—in·ac′tive·ly,** *adv.*

Syn. Inactive, inert, dormant = not in action or showing activity. **Inactive** = not acting or working, and suggests nothing more: *He is an inactive member of the club.* **Inert** = having by nature, condition, or habit no power or desire to move or act, and suggests being hard or impossible to set in motion or moving slowly: *He dragged the inert, unconscious body from the water.* **Dormant** suggests being asleep, and means "temporarily inactive": *Some animals and plants are dormant during the winter.*

in·ac·tiv·i·ty (in′ak tiv′ə tē) *n.* an absence of activity; idleness; sluggishness.

in·ad·e·qua·cy (in ad′ə kwə sē) *n.* a being inadequate.

in·ad·e·quate (in ad′ə kwit) *adj.* not adequate; not enough; not as much as is required: *inadequate preparation for an examination.* **—in·ad′e·quate·ly,** *adv.*

in·ad·mis·si·bil·i·ty (in′əd mis′ə bil′ə tē) *n.* the quality of being inadmissible.

in·ad·mis·si·ble (in′əd mis′ə bəl) *adj.* **1** not allowable. **2** not to be admitted. **—in′ad·mis′si·bly,** *adv.*

in·ad·vert·ence (in′əd vėr′təns) *n.* **1** a lack of attention; carelessness. **2** an oversight; mistake.

in·ad·vert·en·cy (in′əd vėr′tən sē) *n.* **-cies.** inadvertence.

in·ad·vert·ent (in′əd vėr′tənt) *adj.* **1** not attentive; heedless; negligent. **2** not done on purpose; caused by oversight. **—in′ad·vert′ent·ly,** *adv.* **—Syn. 1** thoughtless. **2** unintentional, accidental.

in·ad·vis·a·bil·i·ty (in′əd vī′zə bil′ə tē) *n.* the condition of being inadvisable.

in·ad·vis·a·ble (in′əd vīz′ə bəl) *adj.* not advisable; unwise; not prudent. **—in′ad·vis′a·bly,** *adv.*

in·al·ien·a·bil·i·ty (in ā′lē ən ə bil′ə tē or in āl′yən ə bil′ə tē) *n.* the quality of being inalienable.

in·al·ien·a·ble (in ā′lē ən ə bəl or in āl′yən ə bəl) *adj.* that cannot be given away or taken away: *Every person has the inalienable right of equality before the law.* **—in·al′ien·a·bly,** *adv.*

in·am·o·ra·ta (in am′ə rä′tə) *n.* **-tas.** the girl or woman with whom one is in love; sweetheart. [< Ital. *innamorata* ult. < L *in-* in + *amor* love]

in·ane (in ān′) *adj.* **1** silly; foolish: *an inane thing to do.* **2** empty of meaning; senseless: *We soon tired of his inane remarks.* **3** *Archaic.* empty; void. —*n.* something empty or without substance. [< L *inanis*] **—in·ane′ly,** *adv.*

in·an·i·mate (in an′ə mit) *adj.* **1** lifeless: *inanimate stones.* **2** seeming to be lifeless; unconscious: *The lifeguard pulled her inanimate body out of the pool.* **3** dull: *an inanimate face.* **—in·an′i·mate·ly,** *adv.* **—in·an′i·mate·ness,** *n.*

hat, āge, cãre, fär; let, ēqual, tėrm; it, īce
hot, ōpen, ôrder; oil, out; cup, půt, rüle, ūse
əbove, takən, pencəl, lemən, circəs
ch, child; ng, long; sh, ship
th, thin; ᴛʜ, then; zh, measure

in·a·ni·tion (in′ə nish′ən) *n.* **1** emptiness. **2** weakness from lack of food. [< LL *inanitio, -onis* < L *inanire* to empty < *inanis* empty]

in·an·i·ty (in an′ə tē) *n.* **-ties. 1** silliness; lack of sense. **2** a silly or senseless act, practice, remark, etc. **3** emptiness.

in·ap·pli·ca·bil·i·ty (in ap′lə kə bil′ə tē or in′ə plik′ə bil′ə tē) *n.* the quality of being inapplicable.

in·ap·pli·ca·ble (in ap′lə kə bəl or in′ə plik′ə bəl) *adj.* not applicable; not appropriate; not suitable. **—in·ap′pli·ca·bly,** *adv.* **—Syn.** unbecoming, unfitting.

in·ap·po·site (in ap′ə zit) *adj.* not pertinent; not suitable; inappropriate. **—in·ap′po·site·ly,** *adv.*

in·ap·pre·ci·a·ble (in′ə prē′shē ə bəl or in′ə prē′shə bəl) *adj.* too small to be noticed or felt; very slight. **—in′ap·pre′ci·a·bly,** *adv.*

in·ap·pro·pri·ate (in′ə prō′prē it) *adj.* not appropriate; not suitable; not fitting: *Jokes are inappropriate at a funeral.* **—in′ap·pro′pri·ate·ly,** *adv.***—in′ap·pro′pri·ate·ness,** *n.*

in·apt (in apt′) *adj.* **1** not apt; not suitable; unfit. **2** unskilful; awkward. **—in·apt′ly,** *adv.* **—in·apt′ness,** *n.* **—Syn. 1** inappropriate. **2** unhandy.

in·ap·ti·tude (in ap′tə tūd′ or in ap′tə tüd′) *n.* **1** unfitness. **2** lack of skill.

in·ar·tic·u·late (in′är tik′yů lit) *adj.* **1** not distinct; not like regular speech: *an inarticulate mutter or groan.* **2** unable to speak in words; unable to say what one thinks; dumb: *Cats and dogs are inarticulate.* **3** in zoology, not jointed: *A jellyfish's body is inarticulate.* [< LL *inarticulatus*] **—in′ar·tic′u·late·ly,** *adv.* **—in′ar·tic′u·late·ness,** *n.*

in·ar·tis·tic (in′är tis′tik) *adj.* **1** not artistic; lacking good taste. **2** having no appreciation for or love of art; unskilled in art. **—in′ar·tis′ti·cal·ly,** *adv.*

in·as·much as (in′əz much′) because; since; in view of the fact that: *Inasmuch as he was smaller than the other boys, he was given a head start in the race.*

in·at·ten·tion (in′ə ten′shən) *n.* a lack of attention; heedlessness; negligence. **—Syn.** disregard.

in·at·ten·tive (in′ə ten′tiv) *adj.* not attentive; careless; heedless; negligent. **—in′at·ten′tive·ly,** *adv.* **—in′at·ten′tive·ness,** *n.* **—Syn.** unmindful, preoccupied.

in·au·di·ble (in o′də bəl or in ô′də bəl) *adj.* that cannot be heard. **—in·au′di·bly,** *adv.*

in·au·gu·ral (in o′gyů rəl or in ô′gyů rəl) *adj.* of or for an inauguration: *The President of the United States gave an inaugural address when he took office.* —*n.* an inaugural address or speech. [< F *inaugural* < *inaugurer* inaugurate]

in·au·gu·rate (in o′gyů rāt′ or in ô′gyů rāt′) *v.* **-rat·ed, -rat·ing. 1** install in office with a ceremony: *The Vice-Chancellor of the University was inaugurated at the spring convocation.* **2** make a formal beginning of; begin: *The invention of the airplane inaugurated a new era in transportation.* **3** open or begin use of a public building, etc. with a ceremony. [< L *inaugurare* < *in-* for + *augur* taker of omens] **—in·au′gu·ra′tor,** *n.*

in·au·gu·ra·tion (in o′gyů rā′shən or in ô′gyů rā′shən) *n.* **1** the act or ceremony of installing a person in office. **2** a beginning, especially a formal one. **3** the opening or bringing into use of public buildings, etc. with a formal ceremony: *We were present at the inauguration of the new City Hall.*

in·aus·pi·cious (in′os pish′əs or in′ôs pish′əs) *adj.* showing signs of probable failure; unfavorable; unlucky. **—in′aus·pi′cious·ly,** *adv.* **—in′aus·pi′cious·ness,** *n.* **—Syn.** unpromising.

inbd. inboard.

in-be·tween (in′bi twēn′) *adj.* **1** coming or belonging in the middle; relating to the space or time separating two things: *He is at that in-between age, neither boy nor man.* **2** being neither one thing nor another; neutral;

indifferent. —*adv.* between. —*n.* a person or thing that is in-between.

in·board (in′bôrd′) *adv. adj.* inside the hull of a ship; in or toward the middle of a ship. —*n.* **1** a motorboat having its motor inside the hull. **2** the motor itself.

in·born (in′bôrn′) *adj.* born in a person; instinctive; natural: *an inborn love of rhythm.* —**Syn.** innate, inbred.

in·bound (in′bound′) *adj.* inward bound.

in·bred (in′bred′) *adj.* **1** inborn; natural: *an inbred courtesy.* **2** bred for generations from ancestors closely related.

in·breed (in′brēd′ or in brēd′) *v.* **-bred, -breed·ing.** **1** breed from closely related persons, animals, or plants. **2** produce or develop within.

in·breed·ing (in′brēd′ing) *n.* the practice of breeding from closely related persons, animals, or plants.

inc. 1 incorporated. **2** inclosure. **3** including. **4** included. **5** inclusive. **6** increase.

In·ca (ing′kə) *n.* **1** a member of certain tribes of South American Indians who held power in Peru before the Spanish conquest. **2** a member of any of these tribes. **3** a ruler of these tribes. [< Sp. < Quechua (S.Am.Ind.) *ynca* prince of the ruling family] —**In′can,** *n. adj.*

in·cal·cu·la·ble (in kal′kyů lə bəl) *adj.* **1** too great in number to be counted; numerous: *The sands of the beach are incalculable.* **2** not to be reckoned beforehand: *A flood in the valley would cause incalculable losses.* **3** not to be relied on; uncertain. —**in·cal′cu·la·bly,** *adv.*

in ca·me·ra (in kam′ər ə) **1** in law, in the privacy of a judge's chambers, rather than in open court. **2** behind closed doors; secret. [< L *in camera* in a room, chamber]

in·can·des·cence (in′kən des′əns) *n.* a red-hot or white-hot condition.

in·can·des·cent (in′kən des′ənt) *adj.* **1** glowing with heat; red-hot or white-hot. **2** intensely bright; brilliant. **3** having to do with or containing a material that gives light by incandescence. An **incandescent lamp** is an electric lamp with a filament of very fine wire that becomes white-hot when current flows through it. [< L *incandescens, -entis,* ppr. of *incandescere* begin to glow < *in-* in + *candere* be gleaming white]

in·can·ta·tion (in′kan tā′shən) *n.* **1** a set of words spoken as a magic charm or to cast a magic spell. "Double, double, toil and trouble, Fire burn and cauldron bubble," is an incantation. **2** the use of such words. **3** magical ceremonies; magic; sorcery. [< L *incantatio, -onis* < *incantare* chant a magic formula against < *in-* against + *cantare* chant]

in·ca·pa·bil·i·ty (in′kā pə bil′ə tē) *n.* an incapacity; unfitness.

in·ca·pa·ble (in kā′pə bəl) *adj.* **1** without ordinary ability; not efficient; not competent: *An employer cannot afford to hire incapable workers.* **2 incapable of, a** without the ability, power, or fitness for: *His honesty made him incapable of lying.* **b** not legally qualified for: *Certain beliefs make a man incapable of serving on a jury.* **c** not susceptible to; not capable of receiving or admitting: *incapable of exact measurement.* [< LL *incapabilis*] —**in·ca′pa·bly,** *adv.*

in·ca·pac·i·tate (in′kə pas′ə tāt′) *v.* **-tat·ed, -tat·ing.** **1** deprive of ability, power, or fitness; disable: *The man's injury incapacitated him for working.* **2** legally disqualify. —**in′ca·pac′i·ta′tion,** *n.*

in·ca·pac·i·ty (in′kə pas′ə tē) *n.* **-ties. 1** a lack of ability, power, or fitness; disability. **2** a legal disqualification. —**Syn. 1** unfitness, inability.

in·car·cer·ate (in kär′sər āt′) *v.* **-at·ed, -at·ing.** imprison. [< LL *incarcerare* < L *in-* in + *carcer* jail] —**in·car′cer·a·tor,** *n.*

in·car·cer·a·tion (in kär′sər ā′shən) *n.* imprisonment.

in·car·na·dine (in kär′nə dīn′, in kär′nə dēn′, or in kär′nə din) *adj. v.* **-dined, -din·ing.** —*adj.* **1** blood-red. **2** flesh-colored. —*v.* make blood-red or flesh-colored. [< F < Ital. *incarnadino,* ult. < L *in-* in + *caro, carnis* flesh]

in·car·nate (*adj.* in kär′nit or in kär′nāt; *v.* in kär′nāt) *adj. v.* **-nat·ed, -nat·ing.** —*adj.* **1** embodied in flesh, especially in human form: *The villain was an incarnate fiend.* **2** personified or typified: *evil incarnate.* **3** in botany, flesh-colored.
—*v.* **1** make incarnate; embody. **2** put into an actual form; realize: *The sculptor incarnated his vision in a beautiful statue.* **3** be the living embodiment of: *She incarnates all womanly virtues in her own person.* [< L *incarnatus,* pp. of *incarnare* < *in-* in + *caro, carnis* flesh]

in·car·na·tion (in′kär nā′shən) *n.* **1** the taking on of human form by a divine being. **2** an embodiment. **3** a person or thing that represents some quality or idea: *A miser is an incarnation of greed.* **4 the Incarnation,** the union of divine nature and human nature in the person of Jesus Christ; assumption of human form by the son of God.

in·case (in kās′) *v.* **-cased, -cas·ing. 1** put into a case. **2** cover completely; enclose: *Armor incased the knight's body.* Also, **encase.**

in·case·ment (in kās′mənt) *n.* **1** an incasing. **2** a being incased. **3** something that incases.

in·cau·tious (in ko′shəs or in kô′shəs) *adj.* not cautious; heedless; reckless; rash. —**in·cau′tious·ly,** *adv.* —**in·cau′tious·ness,** *n.* —**Syn.** imprudent, unwary.

in·cen·di·a·rism (in sen′dē ə riz′əm) *n.* **1** the crime of maliciously setting fire to property. **2** the deliberate stirring up of strife or rebellion.

in·cen·di·ar·y (in sen′dē er′ē) *adj. n.* **-ar·ies.** —*adj.* **1** having to do with the malicious setting on fire of property. **2** causing fires; used to start a fire: *The enemy town was set on fire with incendiary shells and bombs.* **3** deliberately stirring up strife or rebellion: *The agitator was arrested for making incendiary speeches.*
—*n.* **1** a person who maliciously sets fire to property. **2** a person who deliberately stirs up strife or rebellion. **3** a shell or bomb containing chemical agents that cause fire. [< L *incendiarius* < *incendium* fire]

in·cense[1] (in′sens) *n.* **1** a substance giving off a sweet smell when burned. **2** the perfume or smoke from it. **3** something sweet, such as the perfume of flowers, or the pleasure given by flattery or praise. [ME < OF < LL *incensus* < L *incendere* burn]

in·cense[2] (in sens′) *v.* **-censed, -cens·ing.** make very angry; fill with rage: *The lady was incensed by the boy's rudeness.* [< L *incensus,* pp. of *incendere* kindle] —**Syn.** enrage, madden, provoke.

in·cen·tive (in sen′tiv) *n.* something that urges a person on; the cause of action or effort; a motive; stimulus. [< L *incentivus* < *incinere* sound, cause to sound < *in-* in + *canere* sing] —**Syn.** spur, incitement.

in·cep·tion (in sep′shən) *n.* a beginning; commencement. [ME < L *inceptio, -onis* < *incipere* begin < *in-* on + *capere* take] —**Syn.** origin.

in·cep·tive (in sep′tiv) *adj.* **1** beginning; initial. **2** in grammar, expressing the beginning of an action or state. *Phosphoresce* is an inceptive verb. All verbs ending **-esce** and adjectives ending in **-escent** are inceptives.
—*n.* in grammar, an inceptive word or structure.

in·cer·ti·tude (in sėr′tə tūd′ or in sėr′tə tüd′) *n.* uncertainty; doubt. [< LL *incertitudo*]

in·ces·sant (in ses′ənt) *adj.* never stopping; continued or repeated without interruption: *The roar of Niagara Falls is incessant. The incessant noise of traffic kept me awake all night.* [< LL *incessans, -antis* < L *in-* not + *cessare* cease] —**in·ces′sant·ly,** *adv.* —**Syn.** ceaseless, continual, constant.

in·cest (in′sest) *n.* the crime of sexual intercourse between persons so closely related that their marriage is prohibited by law. [< L *incestum* < *incestus* unchaste < *in-* not + *castus* chaste]

in·ces·tu·ous (in ses′chü əs) *adj.* **1** involving incest. **2** guilty of incest. —**in·ces′tu·ous·ly,** *adv.* —**in·ces′tu·ous·ness,** *n.*

inch (inch) *n.* **1** a measure of length, 1/12 of a foot: *An inch of rainfall is the amount of water that would cover a surface to the depth of one inch.* **2** the smallest part, amount, or degree; very little bit: *He would not yield an inch.* **3 by inches,** slowly; little by little. **4 every inch,** in every way; completely. **5 inch by inch,** slowly; little by little. **6 within an inch of,** very near; very close to.
—*v.* move slowly or little by little: *The worm inched*

along. [OE *ynce* < L *uncia,* originally, a twelfth. Doublet of OUNCE[1].]

inch·meal (inch′mēl′) *adv.* little by little; slowly. —*adj.* very slow. —*n.* **by inchmeal,** little by little; slowly. [ME *inch* + *-mele* < OE *mælum* by measures < *mæl* measure]

in·cho·ate (in kō′it) *adj.* just begun; in an early stage; incomplete; undeveloped. [< L *inchoatus,* var. of *incohatus,* pp. of *incohare* begin, originally, harness < *in-* on + *cohum* yoke fastener] —**in·cho′ate·ly,** *adv.* —**in·cho′ate·ness,** *n.*

in·cho·a·tive (in kō′ə tiv) *adj.* **1** inchoate. **2** in grammar, inceptive. —*n.* in grammar, an inceptive word or structure.

inch·worm (inch′wėrm′) *n.* a measuring worm; the larva of a geometrid.

in·ci·dence (in′sə dəns) *n.* **1** the range of occurrence or influence; extent of effects; way of falling on or affecting: *In an epidemic the incidence of a disease is widespread. The incidence of a tax is limited if only a few people must pay the tax.* **2** a falling on; a striking. **3** the direction in which one thing falls on or strikes another. **4** angle of incidence. See **angle of incidence** for diagram.

in·ci·dent (in′sə dənt) *n.* **1** a happening; event. **2** an event that helps or adds to something else. **3** a distinct piece of action in a story, play, or poem.
—*adj.* **1** liable to happen; belonging: *Hardships are incident to the life of an explorer.* **2** falling or striking (*upon*): *rays of light incident upon a mirror.* [< L *incidens, -entis,* ppr. of *incidere* happen < *in-* on + *cadere* to fall] —**Syn.** *n.* **1** occurrence, episode. See **event.** —*adj.* **1** relating.

in·ci·den·tal (in′sə den′təl) *adj.* **1** happening or likely to happen along with something else more important: *Certain discomforts are incidental to camping out.* **2** occurring by chance. —*n.* **1** something of secondary importance: *On our trip we spent $52 for meals, room, and railway fare, and $1.50 for incidentals, such as candy, magazines, and stamps.* **2** in music, a tone not properly belonging to a chord, or a harmony foreign to a key. —**Syn.** *adj.* **1** See **accidental. 2** occasional, casual.

in·ci·den·tal·ly (in′sə dent′lē or in′sə den′təl ē) *adv.* **1** as an incident along with something else; by the way. **2** accidentally; by chance.

incidental music music played as accompaniment to a motion picture, play, etc. to help evoke an appropriate emotional climate or mood.

in·cin·er·ate (in sin′ər āt′) *v.* **-at·ed, -at·ing.** burn or be burned to ashes. [< Med.L *incinerare* < L *in-* into + *cinis, -neris* ashes] —**in·cin′er·a′tion,** *n.*

in·cin·er·a·tor (in sin′ər ā′tər) *n.* a furnace or other arrangement for burning things.

in·cip·i·ence (in sip′ē əns) *n.* the very beginning; the earliest stage.

in·cip·i·ent (in sip′ē ənt) *adj.* just beginning; in an early stage. [< L *incipiens, -entis,* ppr. of *incipere* begin < *in-* on + *capere* take] —**in·cip′i·ent·ly,** *adv.*

in·cise (in sīz′) *v.* **-cised, -cis·ing. 1** cut into. **2** carve; engrave. [< F *inciser* < L *incidere* < *in-* into + *caedere* cut]

in·cised (in sīzd′) *adj.* **1** cut into. **2** carved; engraved. **3** having notches around the edge: *an incised leaf.*

in·ci·sion (in sizh′ən) *n.* **1** a cut made in something; gash: *The doctor made an incision to take out the splinter in my hand.* **2** the act of incising. **3** an incisive quality.

in·ci·sive (in sī′siv) *adj.* sharp; penetrating; piercing; keen: *an incisive criticism.* [< Med.L *incisivus* < L *incidere.* See INCISE.] —**in·ci′sive·ly,** *adv.* —**in·ci′sive·ness,** *n.*

in·ci·sor (in sī′zər) *n.* a tooth having a sharp edge for cutting; one of the front teeth between the canine teeth in either jaw: *Man has eight incisors in all.* See **tooth** for diagram. [< NL]

in·ci·ta·tion (in′sī tā′shən or in′sə tā′shən) *n.* an inciting.

in·cite (in sīt′) *v.* **-cit·ed, -cit·ing.** urge on; stir up; rouse. [< L *incitare,* ult. < *in-* on + *ciere* cause to move] —**in·cit′er,** *n.* —**in·cit′ing·ly,** *adv.*

Syn. Incite, instigate = stir up or urge on to action. **Incite** = stir someone up or urge him on to do something good or bad: *Their captain's example incited the men to fight bravely.* **Instigate** = stir up to do something bad, or, more often, to bring about something bad, such as a plot or rebellion, by inciting others to act: *The police never discovered who instigated the looting.*

hat, āge, cãre, fär; let, ēqual, tėrm; it, īce
hot, ōpen, ôrder; oil, out; cup, pu̇t, rüle, ūse
əbove, takən, pencəl, lemən, circəs
ch, child; ng, long; sh, ship
th, thin; ᴛʜ, then; zh, measure

in·cite·ment (in sīt′mənt) *n.* **1** something that urges on, stirs up, or rouses: *Extreme poverty was their incitement to rebellion.* **2** the act of urging on, stirring up, or rousing.

in·ci·vil·i·ty (in′sə vil′ə tē) *n.* **-ties. 1** rudeness; lack of courtesy; impoliteness. **2** a rude or impolite act. —**Syn. 1** discourtesy, disrespect.

incl. 1 inclosure. **2** including. **3** inclusive.

in·clem·en·cy (in klem′ən sē) *n.* **-cies.** severity; harshness: *The inclemency of the weather kept us at home.*

in·clem·ent (in klem′ənt) *adj.* **1** rainy; rough and stormy. **2** severe; harsh: *an inclement ruler.* [< L *inclemens, -entis*] —**in·clem′ent·ly,** *adv.* —**Syn. 1** rigorous. **2** cruel.

in·cli·na·tion (in′klə nā′shən) *n.* **1** a preference; liking: *a strong inclination for sports.* **2** a tendency: *Many middle-aged men have an inclination to become fat.* **3** a leaning; bending; bowing: *A nod is an inclination of the head.* **4** a slope; slant: *the inclination of a roof.* **5** in geometry, the difference of direction of two lines, especially as measured by the angle between them. [< L *inclinatio, -onis* < *inclinare.* See INCLINE.] —**Syn. 1** bias; predilection. **2** proneness. **4** declivity.

in·cline (*v.* in klīn′; *n.* in′klīn or in klīn′) *v.* **-clined, -clin·ing,** *n.* —*v.* **1** be favorable or willing; tend: *Dogs incline to prefer meat as a food.* **2** make favorable or willing; influence: *Incline your hearts to obey God's laws.* **3** slope; slant. **4** lean; bend; bow. **5 incline one's ear,** listen favorably.
—*n.* **1** a slope; slant: *There is quite an incline to that roof.* **2** a sloping surface: *The side of a hill is an incline.* [ME < OF < L *inclinare* < *in-* in + *clinare* bend]

in·clined (in klīnd′) *adj.* **1** favorable; willing; tending. **2** sloping; slanting.

inclined plane a plane surface set at an oblique angle to a horizontal surface.

in·cli·nom·e·ter (in′klə nom′ə tər) *n.* **1** an instrument for measuring the slope of anything. **2** an instrument for measuring the angle that an aircraft makes with the horizontal. [< *incline* + *-meter*]

in·close (in klōz′) *v.* **-closed, -clos·ing.** enclose.

in·clo·sure (in klō′zhər) *n.* enclosure.

in·clude (in klüd′) *v.* **-clud·ed, -clud·ing. 1** put, hold, or enclose within limits: *The price includes both house and furniture.* **2** contain; comprise: *The farm includes 160 acres.* **3** put in a total, a class, or the like; reckon in a count: *All on board the ship were lost, including the captain.* [ME < L *includere* < *in-* in + *claudere* shut] —**in·clud′a·ble,** *adj.*

Syn. 2 Include, comprise, comprehend = contain or take in as a part or parts. **Include** emphasizes containing or taking in as an element or part of the whole: *The list includes my name.* **Comprise** emphasizes being made up of parts, or going together to make up the whole: *The list comprises the names of those who passed.* **Comprehend,** formal and applying to ideas, statements, outlines, etc., emphasizes holding or taking within the limits or scope of the whole: *The examination comprehended the whole course.*

in·clu·sion (in klü′zhən) *n.* **1** an including. **2** a being included. **3** the thing included. [< Med.L *inclusio, -onis* < *includere.* See INCLUDE.]

in·clu·sive (in klü′siv) *adj.* **1** including in consideration; including; comprising. *Read pages 10 to 20 inclusive* means *Read pages 10 and 20 and all those in between.* **2** including much; including everything concerned: *Make an inclusive list of your expenses.* **3 inclusive of,** including; taking in; counting on. —**in·clu′sive·ly,** *adv.* —**in·clu′sive·ness,** *n.*

in·cog (in kog′) *adj. adv. n. Informal.* incognito.

incog. incognito.

in·cog·ni·to (in kog′nə tō′ or in′kog nē′tō) *adj. adv. n.*

-tos. —*adj. adv.* with one's name, character, rank, etc. concealed: *The prince travelled incognito to avoid crowds and ceremonies.* —*n.* **1** a person who is incognito. **2** a disguised state or condition. [< Ital. < L *incognitus* unknown < *in-* not + *cognitus,* pp. of *cognoscere* come to know]

in·co·her·ence (in′kō hēr′əns) *n.* **1** a failure to stick together; looseness. **2** a lack of logical connection. **3** disconnected thought or speech: *the incoherence of a madman.*

in·co·her·en·cy (in′kō hēr′ən sē) *n.* **-cies.** incoherence.

in·co·her·ent (in′kō hēr′ənt) *adj.* **1** not sticking together. **2** disconnected; confused. —**in′co·her′ent·ly,** *adv.*

in·com·bus·ti·bil·i·ty (in′kəm bus′tə bil′ə tē) *n.* the quality of being incombustible.

in·com·bus·ti·ble (in′kəm bus′tə bəl) *adj.* that cannot be burned; fireproof. —*n.* an incombustible substance.

in·come (in′kum) *n.* what comes in from property, business, labor, etc.; receipts; returns. —**Syn.** revenue, proceeds, profit, salary.

income tax a government tax on a person's income.

in·com·ing (in′kum′ing) *adj.* coming in: *The incoming tenant will pay a higher rent.* —*n.* a coming in: *the incoming of the tide.*

in·com·men·su·ra·bil·i·ty (in′kə men′shə rə bil′ə tē or in′kə men′sə rə bil′ə tē) *n.* the quality of being incommensurable; absence of a common measure or standard of comparison.

in·com·men·su·ra·ble (in′kə men′shə rə bəl or in′kə men′sə rə bəl) *adj.* **1** that cannot be compared because not measurable in the same units or by the same scale: *Money and human life are incommensurable.* **2** in mathematics, having no common integral divisor except 1: *8, 17, and 11 are incommensurable numbers.* —**in′com·men′su·ra·bly,** *adv.*

in·com·men·su·rate (in′kə men′shə rit or in′kə men′sə rit) *adj.* **1** not in proportion; not adequate: *strength incommensurate to a task.* **2** having no common measure; incommensurable. —**in′com·men′su·rate·ly,** *adv.*

in·com·mode (in′kə mōd′) *v.* **-mod·ed, -mod·ing.** inconvenience; trouble. [< L *incommodare* < *incommodus* < *in-* not + *commodus* convenient] —**Syn.** disturb, annoy.

in·com·mo·di·ous (in′kə mō′dē əs) *adj.* **1** not roomy enough. **2** inconvenient; uncomfortable. —**in·com·mo′di·ous·ly,** *adv.*

in·com·mu·ni·ca·ble (in′kə mū′nə kə bəl) *adj.* not capable of being communicated or told. —**in·com·mu′ni·ca·bly,** *adv.*

in·com·mu·ni·ca·do (in′kə mū′nə kä′dō) *adj.* deprived of communication with others: *The prisoner was being held incommunicado.* [< Sp. *incomunicado*]

in·com·pa·ra·ble (in kom′pə rə bəl, in kom′prə bəl, or in kəm pär′ə bəl) *adj.* **1** without equal; matchless: *Helen of Troy had incomparable beauty.* **2** not to be compared; unsuitable for comparison. —**in·com′pa·ra·bly,** *adv.* —**Syn. 1** peerless, unequalled. ☛ See **comparable** for usage note on pronunciation.

in·com·pat·i·bil·i·ty (in′kəm pat′ə bil′ə tē) *n.* **-ties. 1** the quality of being incompatible; a lack of harmony. **2** an incompatible thing, quality, etc.

in·com·pat·i·ble (in′kəm pat′ə bəl) *adj.* **1** not able to live or act together peaceably; opposed in character: *My cat and dog are incompatible.* **2** inconsistent: *Late hours are incompatible with health.* **3** of or denoting drugs, blood types, etc. that cannot be combined or used together because of undesirable chemical or physiological reactions. —*n.* an incompatible person or thing. —**in′com·pat′i·bly,** *adv.*

in·com·pe·tence (in kom′pə təns) *n.* **1** a lack of ability, power, or fitness. **2** a lack of legal qualification.

in·com·pe·ten·cy (in kom′pə tən sē) *n.* incompetence.

in·com·pe·tent (in kom′pə tənt) *adj.* **1** not competent; lacking ability, power, or fitness. **2** not legally qualified. —*n.* an incompetent person. —**in·com′pe·tent·ly,** *adv.* —**Syn.** *adj.* **1** incapable, unfit.

in·com·plete (in′kəm plēt′) *adj.* not complete; lacking some part; unfinished. [< LL *incompletus*] —**in′com·plete′ness,** *n.* —**Syn.** imperfect, deficient.

in·com·plete·ly (in′kəm plēt′lē) *adv.* not fully; imperfectly.

in·com·pre·hen·si·bil·i·ty (in′kom pri hen′sə bil′ə tē) *n.* the fact or quality of being incomprehensible.

in·com·pre·hen·si·ble (in′kom pri hen′sə bəl) *adj.* impossible to understand. —**in′com·pre·hen′si·bly,** *adv.*

in·com·press·i·bil·i·ty (in′kəm pres′ə bil′ə tē) *n.* an incompressible condition or quality.

in·com·press·i·ble (in′kəm pres′ə bəl) *adj.* not capable of being squeezed into a smaller size.

in·con·ceiv·a·bil·i·ty (in′kən sēv′ə bil′ə tē) *n.* the quality of being inconceivable.

in·con·ceiv·a·ble (in′kən sēv′ə bəl) *adj.* impossible to imagine; unthinkable; incredible: *A circle without a centre is inconceivable.* —**in·con·ceiv′a·ble·ness,** *n.*

in·con·ceiv·a·bly (in′kən sēv′ə blē) *adv.* **1** in an inconceivable manner. **2** to an inconceivable degree.

in·con·clu·sive (in′kən klü′siv) *adj.* not convincing; not settling or deciding something doubtful: *The jury found the evidence against the prisoner inconclusive and acquitted him.* —**in′con·clu′sive·ly,** *adv.* —**in′con·clu′sive·ness,** *n.*

in·con·gru·i·ty (in′kən grü′ə tē) *n.* **-ties. 1** unfitness; inappropriateness; a being out of place. **2** a lack of agreement or harmony; inconsistency. **3** something that is incongruous.

in·con·gru·ous (in kong′grü əs) *adj.* **1** out of keeping; not appropriate; out of place: *Heavy walking shoes would be incongruous with evening dress.* **2** lacking in agreement or harmony; not consistent. [< L *incongruus*] —**in·con′gru·ous·ly,** *adv.* —**in·con′gru·ous·ness,** *n.* —**Syn. 1** inappropriate, unsuited. **2** inharmonious, inconsistent.

in·con·nu (in′kə nū′ or in′kə nü′) *n.* **-nu** or **-nus.** *Cdn.* a freshwater food fish, related to the whitefish, found in northern Canadian waters. [< F *inconnu* unknown, because little known to anglers]

in·con·se·quence (in kon′sə kwens′ or in kon′sə kwəns) *n.* a lack of logic or logical sequence; irrelevance; being inconsequent.

in·con·se·quent (in kon′sə kwent′ or in kon′sə kwənt) *adj.* **1** not logical; not logically connected: *an inconsequent argument.* **2** not to the point; off the subject: *an inconsequent remark.* **3** apt to think or talk without logical connection. —**in·con′se·quent·ly,** *adv.*

in·con·se·quen·tial (in′kon sə kwen′shəl or in kon′sə kwen′shəl) *adj.* **1** unimportant; trifling. **2** inconsequent.

in·con·sid·er·a·ble (in′kən sid′ər ə bəl) *adj.* not worthy of consideration; not important. —**in′con·sid′er·a·ble·ness,** *n.* —**in′con·sid′er·a·bly,** *adv.* —**Syn.** unimportant, insignificant, petty.

in·con·sid·er·ate (in′kən sid′ər it) *adj.* **1** not thoughtful of the rights and feelings of others. **2** thoughtless; heedless. —**in′con·sid′er·ate·ly,** *adv.* —**in′con·sid′er·ate·ness,** *n.* —**Syn. 2** rash.

in·con·sist·en·cy (in′kən sis′tən sē) *n.* **-cies. 1** a lack of agreement or harmony; variance. **2** a failure to keep to the same principles, course of action, etc.; changeableness. **3** the thing, act, etc. that is inconsistent.

in·con·sist·ent (in′kən sis′tənt) *adj.* **1** lacking in agreement or harmony; at variance: *The policeman's accepting the bribe was inconsistent with his reputation for honesty.* **2** lacking harmony between its different parts; not uniform. **3** failing to keep to the same principles, course of action, etc.; changeable: *An inconsistent person's opinions change frequently without reason.* —**in′con·sist′ent·ly,** *adv.* —**Syn. 1** discrepant, incongruous.

in·con·sol·a·ble (in′kən sōl′ə bəl) *adj.* not to be comforted; broken-hearted. —**in′con·sol′a·bly,** *adv.*

in·con·so·nant (in kon′sə nənt) *adj.* not harmonious; not in agreement or accord. —**in·con′so·nant·ly,** *adv.*

in·con·spic·u·ous (in′kən spik′ū əs) *adj.* not conspicuous; attracting little or no attention. —**in′con·spic′u·ous·ly,** *adv.* —**in′con·spic′u·ous·ness,** *n.*

hat, āge, cãre, fär; let, ēqual, tėrm; it, īce
hot, ōpen, ôrder; oil, out; cup, pu̇t, rüle, ūse
əbove, takən, pencəl, lemən, circəs
ch, child; ng, long; sh, ship
th, thin; ᴛʜ, then; zh, measure

in·con·stan·cy (in kon′stən sē) *n.* a lack of constancy; changeableness; fickleness.

in·con·stant (in kon′ stənt) *adj.* not constant; changeable; fickle. **—in·con′stant·ly,** *adv.* **—Syn.** variable.

in·con·test·a·ble (in′kən tes′tə bəl) *adj.* not to be disputed; unquestionable. **—in′con·test′a·bly,** *adv.* **—Syn.** indisputable, undeniable, certain.

in·con·ti·nence (in kon′tə nəns) *n.* **1** lack of self-restraint. **2** lack of chastity.

in·con·ti·nent (in kon′tə nənt) *adj.* **1** without self-restraint. **2** not chaste; licentious. **3** in medicine, unable to control natural evacuations. [< L *incontinens, -entis*] **—in·con′ti·nent·ly,** *adv.*

in·con·tro·vert·i·ble (in′kon trə vėr′tə bəl) *adj.* that cannot be disputed; too clear or certain to be argued about; unquestionable. **—in′con·tro·vert′i·bly,** *adv.*

in·con·ven·ience (in′kən vēn′yəns or in′kən vēn′ē əns) *n. v.* **-ienced, -ienc·ing.** **—***n.* **1** lack of convenience or ease; trouble; bother. **2** a cause of trouble, difficulty, or bother. **—***v.* cause trouble, difficulty, etc. to: *Would it inconvenience you to carry this package for me?*

in·con·ven·ient (in′kən vēn′yənt or in kən vēn′ ē ənt) *adj.* not convenient; troublesome; causing bother, difficulty, or discomfort. [< L *inconveniens, -entis*] **—in′con·ven′ient·ly,** *adv.* **—Syn.** embarrassing.

in·con·vert·i·bil·i·ty (in′kən vėr′tə bil′ə tē) *n.* the condition of being inconvertible.

in·con·vert·i·ble (in′kən vėr′tə bəl) *adj.* not convertible; incapable of being converted or exchanged: *Paper money is inconvertible when it cannot be exchanged for gold or silver.*

in·cor·po·rate (*v.* in kôr′pə rāt′; *adj.* in kôr′pə rit) *v.* **-rat·ed, -rat·ing,** *adj.* **—***v.* **1** make (something) a part of something else; join or combine (something) with something else: *We shall incorporate your suggestion in this new plan.* **2** form into a corporation: *When Mr. Smith's business expanded, he incorporated it.* **3** form a corporation. **4** unite or combine so as to form one body. **5** embody; give material form to: *incorporate one's thoughts in an article.*
—*adj.* united; combined; incorporated. [< L *incorporare* < *in-* into + *corpus, -poris* body] **—Syn.** *v.* **1** merge, unite.

in·cor·po·ra·tion (in kôr′pə rā′shən) *n.* **1** an incorporating: *The incorporation of air bubbles in the glass spoiled it.* **2** a being incorporated: *Incorporation gives a company the power to act as one person.*

in·cor·po·ra·tor (in kôr′pə rā′tər) *n.* **1** a person who incorporates. **2** one of the original members of a corporation.

in·cor·po·re·al (in′kôr pô′rē əl) *adj.* not made of any material substance; spiritual. **—in′cor·po′re·al·ly,** *adv.* **—Syn.** immaterial, disembodied.

in·cor·rect (in′kə rekt′) *adj.* **1** not correct; wrong; faulty. **2** not proper. **—in′cor·rect′ly,** *adv.* **—in′cor·rect′ness,** *n.* **—Syn. 1** erroneous, inaccurate.

in·cor·ri·gi·bil·i·ty (in kôr′ə jə bil′ə tē) *n.* the quality of being incorrigible.

in·cor·ri·gi·ble (in kôr′ə jə bəl) *adj.* **1** so firmly fixed (in bad ways, a bad habit, etc.) that nothing else can be expected: *an incorrigible liar.* **2** so fixed that it cannot be changed or cured: *an incorrigible habit of wrinkling one's nose.* **—***n.* an incorrigible person. **—in·cor′ri·gi·bly,** *adv.*

in·cor·rupt (in kə rupt′) *adj.* **1** not corruptible; honest. **2** free from decay; sound. **3** not marred by errors, alterations, etc.: *The manuscript appeared to be an incorrupt text of Chaucer's original poem.*

in·cor·rupt·i·ble (in′kə rup′tə bəl) *adj.* **1** not to be corrupted; honest: *The incorruptible judge could not be bribed.* **2** not capable of decay: *Diamonds are incorruptible.* **—in′cor·rupt′i·bly,** *adv.*

in·crease (*v.* in krēs′; *n.* in′krēs) *v.* **-creased, -creas·ing,** *n.* **—***v.* **1** make greater or more numerous; make richer, more prosperous, or more powerful: *The driver increased the speed of the car.* **2** become greater; grow in numbers, especially by propagation; advance in quality, success, power, etc.: *These flowers will increase every year.*
—*n.* **1** a gain in size, numbers, etc.; growth; multiplication by propagation. **2** an addition; result of increasing; increased product. **3 on the increase,** increasing. **4** the production of offspring. **5** offspring.
[ME < AF *encress-*, var. of OF *encreiss-*, a stem of *encreistre* < L *increscere* < *in-* in + *crescere* grow] **—in·creas′er,** *n.*

Syn. *v.* **1, 2 Increase, enlarge, augment** = make or become greater. **Increase** = make or grow greater in amount, number, wealth, power, etc.: *His weight has increased by ten pounds.* **Enlarge** = make or become larger, chiefly in size, extent, or capacity: *They enlarged the school auditorium.* **Augment,** more formal, means "increase by adding amounts or sums to what there is": *Many teachers do outside work to augment their salaries.* –*n.* **1, 2** enlargement, extension.

in·creas·ing·ly (in krēs′ing lē) *adv.* more and more.

in·cred·i·bil·i·ty (in kred′ə bil′ə tē) *n.* the quality of being incredible.

in·cred·i·ble (in kred′ə bəl) *adj.* seeming too extraordinary to be possible; unbelievable: *The hero fought with incredible bravery.* **—in·cred′i·ble·ness,** *n.* **—in·cred′i·bly,** *adv.*

☞ **incredible, incredulous.** *Incredible* = unbelievable; *incredulous* = not ready to believe or showing a lack of belief: *His story of having seen a ghost seemed incredible to his family. If they are incredulous, show them the evidence.*

in·cre·du·li·ty (in′krə dū′lə tē or in′krə dü′lə tē) *n.* lack of belief; doubt. **—Syn.** unbelief, distrust.

in·cred·u·lous (in krej′ u̇ ləs) *adj.* **1** not ready to believe; not credulous; doubting: *People nowadays are incredulous about ghosts and witches.* **2** showing a lack of belief. **—in·cred′u·lous·ly,** *adv.* **—in·cred′u·lous·ness,** *n.* ☞ See **incredible** for usage note.

in·cre·ment (in′krə mənt or ing′krə mənt) *n.* **1** an increase; growth. **2** the amount by which something increases. **3** in mathematics: **a** the amount, positive or negative, by which the value of an independent variable changes. **b** the amount by which the dependent function changes as a result. [< L *incrementum* < *increscere.* See INCREASE.]

in·crim·i·nate (in krim′ə nāt′) *v.* **-nat·ed, -nat·ing.** accuse of a crime, show to be guilty: *In his confession the thief incriminated two of his accomplices.* [< LL *incriminare* < L *in-* against + *crimen, -minis* charge] **—in·crim′i·na′tion,** *n.* **—in·crim′i·na′tor,** *n.*

in·crim·i·na·to·ry (in krim′ə nə tô′rē) *adj.* tending to incriminate.

in·crust (in krust′) *v.* **1** cover with a crust or hard coating: *The inside of a kettle is incrusted with lime.* **2** form a crust (*on*); form into a crust: *The extremely cold weather during the night had incrusted the snow so that it was able to bear our weight.* **3** decorate with a layer of costly material: *The gold crown was incrusted with precious gems.* Also, **encrust.** [< L *incrustare* < in- on + *crusta* crust]

in·crus·ta·tion (in′krus tā′shən) *n.* **1** an incrusting. **2** a being incrusted. **3** a crust or hard coating. **4** a decorative layer of costly material.

in·cu·bate (in′kyu̇ bāt′ or ing′kyu̇ bāt′) *v.* **-bat·ed, -bat·ing.** **1** sit on (eggs, etc.) in order to hatch them; brood. **2** keep (eggs, etc.) warm so that they will hatch or grow. **3** in medicine, of a disease, go through the process of incubation. [< L *incubare* < *in-* on + *cubare* lie]

in·cu·ba·tion (in′kyu̇ bā′shən or ing′kyu̇ bā′shən) *n.* **1** an incubating. **2** a being incubated. **3** in medicine, the stage of a disease from the time of infection until the appearance of the first symptoms.

in·cu·ba·tor (in′kyu̇ bā′tər or ing′kyu̇ bā′tər) *n.* **1** an apparatus for keeping eggs warm so that they will hatch. It has a box or chamber that can be kept at a certain temperature. **2** a similar apparatus for rearing children born prematurely. **3** an apparatus in which bacterial cultures are developed. [< L]

in·cu·bus (in′kyu̇ bəs or ing′kyu̇ bəs) *n.* **-bi** (-bī′ or -bē′) or **-bus·es.** **1** an evil spirit supposed to descend upon sleeping persons, especially women. **2** a nightmare. **3** an oppressive or burdensome thing: *This debt will be an incubus until I have paid it.* [< Med.L (def. 1), LL (def. 2) < L *incubare* < *in-* on + *cubare* lie]

in·cu·des (in kū′dēz) *n.* pl. of **incus.**

in·cul·cate (in kul′kāt or in′kul kāt′) *v.* **-cat·ed, -cat·ing.** impress by repetition; teach persistently. [< L *inculcare,* originally, trample in, ult. < *in-* in + *calx, calcis* heel] —**in·cul′ca·tor,** *n.*

in·cul·ca·tion (in′kul kā′shən) *n.* the act or process of impressing principles, etc. on the mind by persistent urging or teaching.

in·cul·pate (in kul′pāt or in′kul pāt′) *v.* **-pat·ed, -pat·ing. 1** blame; accuse. **2** involve in responsibility for wrongdoing; incriminate. [< LL *inculpare* < L *in-* in + *culpa* blame]

in·cum·ben·cy (in kum′bən sē) *n.* **-cies.** the holding of an office, position, etc. and performance of its duties; term of office: *During his incumbency as mayor, the city prospered.*

in·cum·bent (in kum′bənt) *adj.* **1** lying, leaning, or pressing (*on*). **2** resting (on a person) as a duty: *She felt it incumbent upon her to answer the letter at once.* **3** currently holding office: *the incumbent minister.* **4** *Poetic.* overhanging.
—*n.* a person holding an office, position, church living, etc. [< L *incumbens, -entis,* ppr. of *incumbere* lie down on]

in·cum·ber (in kum′bər) *v.* encumber.

in·cum·brance (in kum′brəns) *n.* encumbrance.

in·cu·nab·u·la (in′kyů nab′yů lə) *n.* pl. of **incunabulum** (in′kyů nab′yů ləm) **1** the earliest stages or first traces of anything; beginnings. **2** books printed before the year 1500. [< L *incunabula* swaddling clothes < *cunae* cradle]

in·cur (in kėr′) *v.* **-curred, -cur·ring. 1** acquire (something unpleasant): *He incurred a serious wound during the war.* **2** bring (blame, punishment, danger, etc.) on oneself: *The disobedient boy incurred his father's anger.* [< L *incurrere* < *in-* upon + *currere* run]

in·cur·a·bil·i·ty (in kūr′ə bil′ə tē) *n.* the quality of being incurable.

in·cur·a·ble (in kūr′ə bəl) *adj.* not capable of being cured or remedied: *an incurable invalid.* —*n.* a person having an incurable disease. —**in·cur′a·bly,** *adv.*

in·cu·ri·ous (in kūr′ē əs) *adj.* **1** not curious; inattentive; unobservant; indifferent. **2** deficient in interest or novelty. —**in·cu′ri·ous·ly,** *adv.*

in·cur·sion (in kėr′zhən or in kėr′shən) *n.* **1** an invasion; raid; sudden attack: *The pirates made incursions along the coast.* **2** a running or flowing in: *Dikes protected the lowland from incursions of the sea.* [ME < L *incursio, -onis* < *incurrere.* See INCUR.]

in·cur·sive (in kėr′siv) *adj.* making incursions.

in·curve (in′kėrv′) *n.* in baseball, a pitch that curves toward the batter.

in·cus (ing′kəs) *n.* **in·cu·des.** in anatomy, the middle one of a chain of three small bones in the middle ear of man and other animals: *The incus is shaped somewhat like an anvil.* See **ear** for picture. [< L *incus, -udis* anvil]

ind. 1 independent. **2** indicative. **3** industrial. **4** index. **5** indirect. **6** indigo.

Ind (ind) *n. Poetic.* **1** India. **2** Indies.

Ind. 1 Indiana. **2** India. **3** Indian. **4** in politics, Independent.

in·debt·ed (in det′id) *adj.* in debt; obliged; owing money or gratitude: *We are indebted to men of science for many of our comforts.*

in·debt·ed·ness (in det′id nis) *n.* **1** the condition of being in debt. **2** the amount owed; debts.

in·de·cen·cy (in dē′sən sē) *n.* **-cies. 1** lack of decency; the quality of being indecent. **2** an indecent act or word.

in·de·cent (in dē′sənt) *adj.* **1** not decent; in very bad taste; improper: *He showed an indecent lack of gratitude to the man who saved his life.* **2** not modest; morally bad; disgusting; obscene. —**in·de′cent·ly,** *adv.* —**Syn. 1** unbecoming, unseemly. See **improper. 2** coarse.

in·de·ci·pher·a·ble (in′di sī′fər ə bəl) *adj.* incapable of being deciphered; illegible.

in·de·ci·sion (in′di sizh′ən) *n.* lack of decision; a tendency to delay or to hesitate; tendency to put off deciding or to change one's mind. —**Syn.** hesitation, uncertainty.

in·de·ci·sive (in′di sī′siv) *adj.* **1** having the habit of hesitating and putting off decisions. **2** not deciding or settling the matter: *an indecisive battle, an indecisive answer.* —**in′de·ci′sive·ly,** *adv.* —**in′de·ci′sive·ness,** *n.*

in·de·clin·a·ble (in′di klīn′ə bəl) *adj.* of words, having the same form in all grammatical constructions. *None* is an indeclinable pronoun.

in·dec·o·rous (in dek′ə rəs or in′di kô′rəs) *adj.* not suitable; improper; unseemly. [< L *indecorus*] —**in·dec′o·rous·ly,** *adv.* —**in·dec′o·rous·ness,** *n.* —**Syn.** undignified.

in·de·co·rum (in′di kô′rəm) *n.* **1** lack of decorum. **2** improper behavior, speech, dress, etc. [< L *indecorum,* originally neut. of *indecorus* indecorous]

in·deed (in dēd′) *adv.* in fact; really; truly; surely: *War is indeed terrible.* —*interj.* an expression of surprise, incredulity, irony, or contempt.

indef. indefinite.

in·de·fat·i·ga·bil·i·ty (in′di fat′ə gə bil′ə tē) *n.* the quality of being indefatigable; tirelessness.

in·de·fat·i·ga·ble (in′di fat′ə gə bəl) *adj.* never getting tired or giving up; tireless. [< L *indefatigabilis* < *in-* not + *defatigare* tire out < *de-* completely + *fatigare* tire] —**in′de·fat′i·ga·bly,** *adv.* —**Syn.** untiring, persistent.

in·de·fea·si·ble (in′di fē′zə bəl) *adj.* not to be annulled or made void: *Kings were once believed to have an indefeasible right to rule.* [< *in-*[1] + *defeasible* that may be annulled < AF *defeasible* < OF *desfaire* undo < *des-* apart + *faire* < L *facere* do] —**in′de·fea′si·bly,** *adv.*

in·de·fen·si·ble (in′di fen′sə bəl) *adj.* **1** that cannot be defended: *an indefensible island.* **2** not justifiable: *an indefensible lie.* —**in′de·fen′si·ble·ness,** *n.* —**in′de·fen′si·bly,** *adv.*

in·de·fin·a·ble (in′di fīn′ə bəl) *adj.* that cannot be defined. —**in′de·fin′a·ble·ness,** *n.* —**in′de·fin′a·bly,** *adv.*

in·def·i·nite (in def′ə nit) *adj.* **1** not clearly defined; not precise; vague: *"Maybe" is a very indefinite answer.* **2** not limited: *We have an indefinite time to finish this work.* **3** not specifying precisely. An indefinite adjective, pronoun, etc. does not determine the person, thing, time, etc. to which it refers. *Some, many,* and *few,* are often indefinite pronouns. [< L *indefinitus*] —**in·def′i·nite·ly,** *adv.* —**in·def′i·nite·ness,** *n.* —**Syn. 1** obscure, ambiguous, equivocal, inexact.

in·de·his·cent (in′di his′ənt) *adj.* in botany, not opening at maturity: *Acorns are indehiscent fruits.*

in·del·i·bil·i·ty (in del′ə bil′ə tē) *n.* the quality of being indelible; permanence.

in·del·i·ble (in del′ə bəl) *adj.* **1** that cannot be erased or removed; permanent: *indelible ink, an indelible disgrace.* **2** capable of making an indelible mark: *an indelible pencil.* [< L *indelebilis* < *in-* not + *delebilis* able to be destroyed < *delere* destroy] —**in·del′i·bly,** *adv.* —**Syn. 1** fixed, fast, ineffaceable.

in·del·i·ca·cy (in del′ə kə sē) *n.* **-cies.** lack of delicacy; a being indelicate.

in·del·i·cate (in del′ə kit) *adj.* **1** not delicate; coarse; crude. **2** improper; immodest. —**in·del′i·cate·ly,** *adv.* —**Syn. 2** vulgar, indecent.

in·dem·ni·fi·ca·tion (in dem′nə fə kā′shən) *n.* **1** an indemnifying. **2** a being indemnified. **3** a compensation; recompense.

in·dem·ni·fy (in dem′nə fī′) *v.* **-fied, -fy·ing. 1** repay; make good; compensate for damage, loss, or expense incurred: *He promised to indemnify me for my losses.* **2** secure against damage or loss; insure. [< L *indemnis* unhurt (< *in-* not + *damnum* damage) + E *-fy*] —**in·dem′ni·fi·er,** *n.* —**Syn. 1** recompense, reimburse.

in·dem·ni·ty (in dem′nə tē) *n.* **-ties. 1** the payment for damage, loss, or expense incurred: *Money demanded by a victorious nation at the end of a war as a condition of peace is an indemnity.* **2** a security against damage or loss; insurance. **3** in Canada, the remuneration paid to an

M.P. or M.L.A. [< LL *indemnitas* < L *indemnis* unhurt < *in-* not + *damnum* damage]

in·dent[1] (*v.* in dent′; *n.* in′dent or in dent′) *v.* **1** cut (an edge) so that it looks like a row of teeth; notch. **2** form deep notches or bays in. **3** form a notch or recess. **4** begin (a line) farther from the edge of a page than the other lines: *We usually indent the first line of a paragraph.* **5** order (goods, etc.) by an indent. **6** draw an order upon (a source of supply).
—*n.* **1** a notch; indentation. **2** an official requisition for supplies. **3** an order for goods. [ME < OF *endenter,* ult. < L *in-* in + *dens, dentis* tooth]

Indented moulding

in·dent[2] (in dent′) *v.* **1** make a dent in; mark with a dent. **2** press in; stamp. [< *in-*[2] + *dent*]

in·den·ta·tion (in′dən tā′shən) *n.* **1** an indenting or being indented. **2** a dent; notch; cut. **3** an indention.

in·den·tion (in den′shən) *n.* **1** a beginning of a line farther from the edge of a page than the other lines. **2** the blank space left by doing this. **3** an indentation.

in·den·ture (in den′chər) *n. v.* **-tured, -tur·ing.** —*n.* **1** a written agreement. **2** a contract by which a person is bound to serve someone else. **3** an indentation. —*v.* bind by a contract to serve someone else. [ME < MF *endenteüre* indentation < OF *endenter.* See INDENT[1].]

in·de·pend·ence (in′di pen′dəns) *n.* **1** freedom from the control, influence, support, or help of another. **2** enough income to live on: *The young man received an independence from his rich uncle.* —**Syn. 1** See **freedom.**

Independence Day *U.S.* the Fourth of July.

in·de·pend·en·cy (in′di pen′dən sē) *n.* **-cies.** **1** independence. **2** an independent country, territory, etc.

in·de·pend·ent (in′di pen′dənt) *adj.* **1** needing, wishing, or getting no help from others: *independent work, independent thinking.* **2** acting, working, or especially, voting by one's own ideas, not as the crowd does. **3** guiding, ruling, or governing oneself; not under another's rule: *Canada is an independent country within the British Commonwealth of Nations.* **4** not depending on others: *Miss Jones has an independent fortune.* **5** not resulting from another thing; not controlled or influenced by something else; separate; distinct. **6** in mathematics, of a variable, that can be assigned any value. **7 independent of,** apart from; without regard to.
—*n.* **1** a person who is independent in thought or behavior. **2** a person who votes without regard to party. **3** a business that operates without any outside management or control by another company or companies.

In·de·pend·ent (in′di pen′dənt) *n.* a candidate for election or an elected representative not of any party.

in·de·pend·ent·ly (in′di pen′dənt lē) *adv.* **1** in an independent manner. **2 independently of,** apart from; without regard to.

in-depth (in′depth′) *adj.* going below the surface; deep; detailed: *an in-depth study.*

in·de·scrib·a·ble (in′di skrīb′ə bəl) *adj.* that cannot be described; beyond description. —**in′de·scrib′a·bly,** *adv.*

in·de·struct·i·bil·i·ty (in′di struk′tə bil′ə tē) *n.* the quality of being indestructible.

in·de·struct·i·ble (in′di struk′tə bəl) *adj.* that cannot be destroyed. —**in′de·struct′i·bly,** *adv.*

in·de·ter·mi·na·ble (in′di tėr′mə nə bəl) *adj.* **1** not capable of being settled or decided. **2** not capable of being found out exactly. —**in′de·ter′mi·na·bly,** *adv.*

in·de·ter·mi·nate (in′di tėr′mə nit) *adj.* not determined; not fixed; indefinite; vague. —**in′de·ter′mi·nate·ly,** *adv.*

in·de·ter·mi·na·tion (in′di tėr′mə nā′shən) *n.* **1** a lack of determination. **2** an unsettled state.

in·dex (in′deks) *n.* **-dex·es** or **-di·ces,** *v.* —*n.* **1** an alphabetical listing of the contents of a book, giving page, paragraph, or section references for each of the subjects discussed: *The index usually appears at the end of the book.* **2** something that points out or shows; sign: *A person's face is often an index of his mood.* **3** the index finger. **4** a pointer: *A dial or scale usually has an index.* **5** in printing, a sign (☛) used to point out a particular note, paragraph, etc. **6** in science, a number or formula expressing some property, ratio, etc. **7** in mathematics:

hat, āge, cãre, fär; let, ēqual, tėrm; it, īce
hot, ōpen, ôrder; oil, out; cup, pu̇t, rüle, ūse
əbove, takən, pencəl, lemən, circəs
ch, child; ng, long; sh, ship
th, thin; ᴛʜ, then; zh, measure

a an exponent. **b** the number indicating the root: *In* $\sqrt[3]{764}$ *the index is 3.* **8** a number that indicates the amount of business activity in relation to past levels of business activity: *the cost-of-living index.* **9 the Index, a** Index Expurgatorius. **b** Index Librorum Prohibitorum.
—*v.* **1** provide with an index; make an index of. **2** enter in an index. **3** work at an index; prepare an index. **4** serve to indicate. [< L *index,* originally, that which points out < *in-* toward + *dic-* point]

Index Ex·pur·ga·to·ri·us (eks pėr′gə tô′rē əs) a list of books that the Roman Catholic Church forbids its members to read until objectionable parts have been taken out or changed.

index finger the finger next to the thumb; forefinger.

Index Li·bro·rum Pro·hib·i·to·rum (lī brô′rəm prō hib′ə tô′rəm) a list of books that the Roman Catholic Church forbids its members to read.

India ink 1 a black pigment consisting of lampblack mixed with a binding material and moulded into sticks or cakes. India ink is made chiefly in China and Japan. **2** a liquid ink prepared from this pigment.

In·di·a·man (in′dē ə mən) *n.* **-men** (-mən). formerly, a ship in the trade with India, especially a large one belonging to the East India Company.

In·di·an (in′dē ən) *n.* **1** a member of the so-called red race living in N. and S. America long before the Europeans came; an American Indian. **2** any one of the languages of the American Indians. **3** a native of India or the East Indies.
—*adj.* **1** of or having to do with American Indians. **2** made of Indian corn or maize: *Indian pudding.* **3** of, living in, or belonging to India or the East Indies.

Indian agent in Canada, an official of the federal government who looks after Indian affairs on a reservation, etc.

Indian club a bottle-shaped wooden club that is swung for exercise.

Indian corn 1 a grain that grows on large ears; maize. **2** the plant that it grows on: *Indian corn is a cereal grass that Europeans found in use among the Indians.*

Indian devil 1 the carcajou or wolverine. **2** a malevolent spirit; werewolf.

Indian file single file.

Indian giver *Informal.* a person who, when offended, takes back a gift after having bestowed it.

Indian hall formerly, a building or room where Indians bringing fur and other goods for sale were received.

Indian hemp a plant having a tough bark, the fibre of which was used by the Indians for cordage and in medicine; a type of dogbane.

Indian horse or **pony** a smallish type of horse bred by the western Indians; a cayuse.

Indian ink India ink.

Indian list *Cdn.* **1** the official register of treaty Indians. **2** *Informal.* the list of persons barred by a legal interdict from buying liquor. **3 be on the Indian list,** *Informal.* **a** be barred by law from buying liquor. **b** be blacklisted.

Indian meal meal made from Indian corn; corn meal.

Indian paint fungus a tooth fungus of the Rocky Mountain region that attacks trees such as fir and spruce.

Indian pipe a leafless plant having a solitary flower that looks like a tobacco pipe.

Indian summer a time of mild, dry, hazy weather that sometimes occurs in October or early November, after the first frosts of autumn.

Indian tobacco a weed having small, blue flowers and swollen capsules, used in medicine.

Indian turnip jack-in-the-pulpit.

Indian wrestling any of several forms of wrestling formerly used as trials of strength by the Indians.

India paper 1 a thin, tough paper, used for Bibles, prayer books, etc. 2 a thin, soft paper, used for the first or finest impressions of engravings, etc.

India rubber or **india rubber** a substance of great elasticity obtained from the coagulated, milky juice of various tropical plants; rubber.

indic. indicative.

Indic (in′dik) *adj.* 1 of or having to do with India; Indian. 2 denoting or having to do with the Indian branch of the Indo-Iranian languages. [< L *Indicus* < Gk. *Indikos* < *India*]

in·di·cate (in′də kāt′) *v.* **-cat·ed, -cat·ing.** 1 point out; point to: *The arrow on the sign indicates the right way to go.* 2 show; make known: *A thermometer indicates temperature.* 3 be a sign or hint of: *The asterisk indicates a footnote.* 4 give a sign or hint of. 5 in medicine: **a** show to be needed as a remedy or treatment: *The examination indicated surgery.* **b** show the presence of (a disease). [< L *indicare* < *index, -dicis.* See INDEX.]
—**Syn.** 1 designate. 2 reveal, disclose. 3 signify, evidence.

in·di·ca·tion (in′də kā′shən) *n.* 1 an indicating. 2 something that indicates; a sign: *There was no indication that the house was occupied.* 3 the amount or degree indicated: *The speedometer indication was 45 miles.*

in·dic·a·tive (in dik′ə tiv) *adj.* 1 pointing out; showing; being a sign (*of*); suggestive: *A headache is sometimes indicative of eye strain.* 2 in grammar, expressing or denoting a state, act, or happening as actual; asking a question of simple fact. In "I go" and "Did I go?" the verbs are in the indicative mood.
—*n.* in grammar: **a** the indicative mood. **b** a verb form in this mood. —**in·dic′a·tive·ly,** *adv.*

in·di·ca·tor (in′də kā′tər) *n.* 1 a person or thing that indicates. 2 the pointer on the dial of an instrument that measures something. 3 a measuring or recording instrument. 4 a substance used to indicate chemical conditions or changes: *Litmus is an indicator.*

in·di·ces (in′də sēz′) *n.* a pl. of **index.**

in·dict (in dīt′) *v.* 1 charge with an offence or crime; accuse. 2 of a grand jury, find enough evidence against (an accused person) to justify a trial. [ME < AF *enditer* < OF. See INDITE.] —**in·dict′er** or **in·dict′or,** *n.*

in·dict·a·ble (in dīt′ə bəl) *adj.* 1 liable to be indicted. 2 rendering one liable to be indicted.

in·dict·ment (in dīt′mənt) *n.* 1 a formal accusation, especially the legal accusation presented by a grand jury. 2 an accusation.

in·dif·fer·ence (in dif′rəns or in dif′ər əns) *n.* 1 a lack of interest or attention. 2 little or no importance: *Where we ate was a matter of indifference to us.*
Syn. 1 **Indifference, unconcern, apathy** = lack of interest. **Indifference** emphasizes not caring one way or the other, showing no interest: *A lazy, careless person treats his work with indifference.* **Unconcern** emphasizes not caring enough to take a natural or proper interest, and suggests being unaware of any cause for anxiety or need for personal attention: *Nobody understands the unconcern of her parents.* **Apathy** suggests indifference to everything except one's own troubles, sorrow, or pain: *We have been worried about her apathy since her husband died.* 2 insignificance.

in·dif·fer·ent (in dif′rənt or in dif′ər ənt) *adj.* 1 having no feeling for or against: *indifferent to an admirer.* 2 impartial; neutral; without preference: *an indifferent decision.* 3 unimportant; not mattering much: *The time for starting is indifferent to me.* 4 neither good nor bad; just fair. 5 rather bad. 6 neutral in chemical, electrical, or magnetic quality. —**Syn.** 1 apathetic, unconcerned. 2 unbiassed, disinterested, fair.

in·dif·fer·ent·ly (in dif′rənt lē or in dif′ər ənt lē) *adv.* 1 with indifference. 2 without distinction; equally. 3 moderately; tolerably; passably. 4 poorly; badly; in an inferior manner: *He did his work indifferently.*

in·di·gence (in′də jəns) *n.* poverty.

in·dig·e·nous (in dij′ə nəs) *adj.* 1 originating in the region or country where found; native: *Musk-oxen are indigenous to Canada.* 2 innate; inherent. [< L *indigena* a native] —**in·dig′e·nous·ly,** *adv.*

in·di·gent (in′də jənt) *adj.* poor; needy. [< L *indigens, -entis,* ppr. of *indigere* need] —**in′di·gent·ly,** *adv.*

in·di·gest·i·bil·i·ty (in′də jes′tə bil′ə tē or in′dī jes′tə bil′ə tē) *n.* an indigestible nature or quality.

in·di·gest·i·ble (in′də jes′tə bəl or in′dī jes′tə bəl) *adj.* that cannot be digested; hard to digest. —**in′di·gest′i·bly,** *adv.*

in·di·ges·tion (in′də jes′chən or in′dī jes′chən) *n.* an inability to digest food; difficulty in digesting food.

in·dig·nant (in dig′nənt) *adj.* angry at something unworthy, unjust, or mean. [< L *indignans, -antis,* ppr. of *indignari* be indignant (at), regard as unworthy < *indignus* unworthy < *in-* not + *dignus* worthy] —**in·dig′nant·ly,** *adv.* —**Syn.** incensed, provoked, displeased.

in·dig·na·tion (in′dig nā′shən) *n.* anger at something unworthy, unjust, or mean; anger mixed with scorn; righteous anger: *Cruelty to animals arouses our indignation.* —**Syn.** See **anger.**

in·dig·ni·ty (in dig′nə tē) *n.* **-ties.** an injury to dignity; an insult; a slight. [< L *indignitas*] —**Syn.** See **insult.**

in·di·go (in′də gō′) *n.* **-gos** or **-goes,** *adj.* —*n.* 1 a blue dyestuff that can be obtained from certain plants, but is now usually made artificially. 2 the plant from which indigo is obtained. 3 a deep violet-blue. —*adj.* deep violet-blue. [< Sp. < L < Gk. *indikon,* originally *adj.,* Indian (dye)]

indigo bunting a small N. American finch. The male is a deep violet-blue; the female is brown.

in·di·rect (in′də rekt′ or in′dī rekt′) *adj.* 1 not direct; not straight: *an indirect route.* 2 not directly connected; secondary: *Happiness is an indirect consequence of doing one's work well.* 3 not straightforward and to the point: *The witness gave an indirect answer to the lawyer's question instead of a frank "Yes" or "No."* 4 dishonest; deceitful: *indirect methods.* —**in′di·rect′ly,** *adv.* —**in′di·rect′ness,** *n.* —**Syn.** 1 circuitous, roundabout. 2 incidental.

indirect discourse the repetition of the substance of a person's speech without directly quoting it. *Example:* "He said that he would come," instead of "He said, 'I will come.' "

in·di·rec·tion (in′də rek′shən or in′dī rek′shən) *n.* 1 a roundabout act, means, or method. 2 dishonesty; deceit.

indirect object the person or thing that is indirectly affected by the action of the verb. In English, the indirect object usually comes before the direct object and shows to whom or for whom something is done. *Example:* In "I gave John a book," *John* is the indirect object, and *book* is the direct object.

indirect tax a tax paid indirectly by the consumer and included in the price of an article.

in·dis·cern·i·ble (in′də sėr′nə bəl or in′də zėr′nə bəl) *adj.* not discernible; imperceptible. —**in·dis·cern′i·bly,** *adv.*

in·dis·creet (in′dis krēt′) *adj.* not discreet; not wise and judicious; imprudent: *The boy was indiscreet enough to irritate the stranger.* —**in′dis·creet′ly,** *adv.* —**in·dis·creet′ness,** *n.* —**Syn.** unwise, foolish, rash.

in·dis·cre·tion (in′dis kresh′ən) *n.* 1 lack of good judgment; imprudence. 2 an indiscreet act.

in·dis·crim·i·nate (in′dis krim′ə nit) *adj.* 1 confused: *He tipped everything out of his suitcase in an indiscriminate mass.* 2 not discriminating; with no feeling for differences: *He is an indiscriminate reader and likes both good books and bad ones.* —**in′dis·crim′i·nate·ly,** *adv.* —**in′dis·crim′i·na′tion,** *n.* —**Syn.** 2 See **miscellaneous.**

in·dis·pen·sa·bil·i·ty (in′dis pen′sə bil′ə tē) *n.* the state or quality of being indispensable; absolute necessity.

in·dis·pen·sa·ble (in′dis pen′sə bəl) *adj.* absolutely necessary: *Air is indispensable to life.* —**Syn.** See **necessary.**

in·dis·pen·sa·bly (in′dis pen′sə blē) *adv.* to an indispensable degree; necessarily.

in·dis·pose (in′dis pōz′) *v.* **-posed, -pos·ing.** 1 make unwilling; make averse: *Hot weather indisposes a person to work hard.* 2 make slightly ill. 3 make unfit or unable.

in·dis·posed (in′dis pōzd′) *adj.* 1 slightly ill. 2 unwilling; without inclination; averse: *The men were indisposed to work nights.* —**Syn.** 1 sick.

in·dis·po·si·tion (in′dis pə zish′ən) *n.* **1** a disturbance of health; slight illness. **2** an unwillingness; disinclination; aversion.

in·dis·put·a·bil·i·ty (in′dis pūt′ə bil′ə tē or in dis′pyů tə bil′ə tē) *n.* a being indisputable.

in·dis·put·a·ble (in′dis pūt′ə bəl or in dis′pyů tə bəl) *adj.* not to be disputed; undoubtedly true; unquestionable. **—in′dis·put′a·bly,** *adv.* **—Syn.** undeniable, certain.

in·dis·sol·u·bil·i·ty (in′di sol′yů bil′ə tē) *n.* a being indissoluble; stability.

in·dis·sol·u·ble (in′di sol′yů bəl) *adj.* not capable of being dissolved, undone, or destroyed; lasting; firm. **—in′dis·sol′u·bly,** *adv.*

in·dis·tinct (in′dis tingkt′) *adj.* not distinct; not clear to the eye, ear, or mind; confused. [< L *indistinctus*] **—in′dis·tinct′ly,** *adv.* **—in′dis·tinct′ness,** *n.* **—Syn.** undefined, vague.

in·dis·tin·guish·a·ble (in′dis ting′gwish ə bəl) *adj.* that cannot be distinguished. **—in′dis·tin′guish·a·bly,** *adv.*

in·dite (in dīt′) *v.* **-dit·ed, -dit·ing.** put in words or writing; compose: *indite a letter.* [ME < OF *enditer* make known < L *in-* in + *dictare* dictate, express in writing. Cf. INDICT.]

in·di·um (in′dē əm) *n.* a rare metallic chemical element that is soft, white, malleable, and easily fusible. *Symbol*: In; *at.no.* 49; *at.wt.* 114.82. [< NL < L *indicum.* See INDIGO.]

in·di·vid·u·al (in′də vij′ü əl) *n.* **1** a person. **2** one person, animal, or thing. *—adj.* **1** single; particular; separate: *an individual question.* **2** for one only: *We use individual salt-cellars.* **3** having to do with or peculiar to one person or thing: *individual tastes.* **4** marking off one person or thing specially: *Each girl has an individual style of arranging her hair.* [< Med.L *individualis* < L *individuus* < *in-* not + *dividuus* divisible] ☛ **See person** for usage note.

in·di·vid·u·al·ism (in′də vij′ü əl iz′əm) *n.* **1** a theory that individual freedom is as important as the welfare of the community or group as a whole. **2** any ethical, economic, or political theory that emphasizes the importance of individuals. **3** each for himself; the absence of co-operation; wanting a separate existence for oneself. **4** individuality.

in·di·vid·u·al·ist (in′də vij′ü əl ist) *n.* **1** one who goes his own way, independent of the views or interests of others. **2** a supporter of individualism.

in·di·vid·u·al·is·tic (in′də vij′ü əl is′tik) *adj.* of individualism or individualists. **—in′di·vid′u·al·is′ti·cal·ly,** *adv.*

in·di·vid·u·al·i·ty (in′də vij′ü al′ə tē) *n.* **-ties.** **1** individual character; the sum of the qualities that make a person himself, not someone else. **2** the state of being individual; existence as an individual. **3** an individual person or thing. **—Syn. 1** See **character.**

in·di·vid·u·al·ize (in′də vij′ü əl īz′) *v.* **-ized, -iz·ing.** **1** make individual; cause to be different from others; give a distinctive character to. **2** consider as individuals; list one by one; specify. **—in′di·vid′u·al·za′tion,** *n.*

in·di·vid·u·al·ly (in′də vij′ü əl ē) *adv.* **1** personally; one at a time; as individuals: *The teacher helps us individually.* **2** each from the others: *People differ individually.*

in·di·vis·i·bil·i·ty (in′də viz′ə bil′ə tē) *n.* the state o quality of being indivisible.

in·di·vis·i·ble (in′də viz′ə bəl) *adj.* **1** not capable of being divided. **2** not capable of being divided without a remainder. **—in′di·vis′i·bly,** *adv.*

Indo- *combining form.* **1** Indian; of Indian or the East Indies; *Indo-Aryan = of or having to do with the Aryans of India.* **2** Indian and: *Indo-European = of India and Europe.*

In·do-Ar·yan (in′dō ãr′ ē ən or -är′yən) *adj.* **1** of or having to do with the Aryans of India. **2** of or relating to the Indo-Iranian languages; Indic. *—n.* an Aryan native of India.

In·do-Chi·nese (in′dō chī nēz′) *adj.* **1** of or having to do with Indo-China, the southeastern peninsula of Asia, the Mongoloid peoples living there, or their languages. **2** of or having to do with the family of languages comprising these languages and the Tibetan and Chinese groups of languages.

hat, āge, cãre, fär; let, ēqual, tėrm; it, īce
hot, ōpen, ôrder; oil, out; cup, půt, rüle, ūse
əbove, takən, pencəl, lemən, circəs
ch, child; ng, long; sh, ship
th, thin; ᴛʜ, then; zh, measure

in·doc·tri·nate (in dok′trə nāt′) *v.* **-nat·ed, -nat·ing.** **1** teach a doctrine, belief, or principle to. **2** teach. [probably < Med.L *indoctrinare* < *in-* in + *doctrinare* teach < L *doctrina* doctrine] **—in·doc′tri·na′tion,** *n.* **—in·doc′tri·na′tor,** *n.*

In·do-Eu·ro·pe·an (in′dō ūr′ə pē′ən) *adj.* **1** of India and Europe. **2** of or having to do with a group of related languages spoken in India, western Asia, and Europe. English, German, Latin, Greek, Persian, and Sanskrit are Indo-European languages.
—n. **1** this group of languages. **2** the assumed prehistoric language from which they are derived; Aryan. **3** a member of an ethnological group that speaks an Indo-European language.

In·do-Ger·man·ic (in′dō jər man′ik) *adj.* Indo-European.

In·do-I·ra·ni·an (in′dō ī rā′nē ən) *adj.* of or having to do with a division of the Indo-European family of languages that comprises the Indic and Iranian branches.
—n. this division.

in·do·lence (in′də ləns) *n.* laziness; dislike of work; idleness.

in·do·lent (in′də lənt) *adj.* lazy; disliking work. [< LL *indolens, -entis* < L *in-* not + *dolens*, ppr. of *dolere* be in pain] **—in′do·lent·ly,** *adv.* **—Syn.** See **idle.**

in·dom·i·ta·bil·i·ty (in dom′ə tə bil′ə tē) *n.* the quality or state of being indomitable.

in·dom·i·ta·ble (in dom′ə tə bəl) *adj.* unconquerable; unyielding. [< LL *indomitabilis*, ult. < L *in-* not + *domare* tame] **—in·dom′i·ta·bly,** *adv.*

In·do·ne·sian (in′dō nē′zhən or in′dō nē′shən) *adj.* **1** of or having to do with Indonesia, a republic in the East Indies. **2** of or having to do with the Malay Archipelago, its people, or their language.
—n. **1** a native or inhabitant of Indonesia. **2** the official language of Indonesia, based on Malay. **3** an inhabitant of the Malay Archipelago. **4** a member of a race supposed to have been dominant on the Malay Archipelago before the Malays. [< Gk. *Indos* Indian + *nēsos* island]

in·door (in′dôr′) *adj.* **1** done, played, used, etc. in a house or building: *indoor tennis, indoor skating.* **2** that is indoors: *an indoor rink.*

in·doors (in′dôrz′) *adv.* in or into a house or building: *go indoors.*

in·dorse (in dôrs′) *v.* **-dorsed, -dors·ing.** endorse.

in·dor·see (in′dôr sē′) *n.* endorsee.

in·dorse·ment (in dôrs′mənt) *n.* endorsement.

In·dra (in′drə) *n.* in ancient times, the chief god of the Hindu religion.

in·draft (in′draft′) *n.* **1** a drawing in. **2** an inward flow or current of water, air, etc.

in·drawn (in′dron′ or -drôn′) *adj.* **1** drawn in. **2** preoccupied; introspective.

in·du·bi·ta·ble (in dū′bə tə bəl or in dü′bə tə bəl) *adj.* not to be doubted; certain. **—in·du′bi·ta·ble·ness,** *n.* **—in·du′bi·ta·bly,** *adv.*

in·duce (in dūs′ or in düs′) *v.* **-duced, -duc·ing.** **1** lead on; influence; persuade: *Advertising induces people to buy.* **2** cause; bring about: *Some drugs induce sleep.* **3** produce (an electric current, electric charge, or magnetic change) without direct contact. **4** infer by reasoning from particular facts to a general rule or principle. [< L *inducere* < *in-* in + *ducere* lead] **—in·duc′er,** *n.* **—Syn. 1** incite, impel.

in·duce·ment (in dūs′mənt or in düs′mənt) *n.* something that influences or persuades; incentive: *Prizes are inducements to work.*

in·duct (in dukt′) *v.* **1** bring in; introduce (into a place, seat, position, office, etc.). **2** put formally into a position, office, etc.: *They proposed to induct him as secretary.* 3 *U.S.* take into or enroll in military service. 4 initiate. [< L *inductus*, pp. of *inducere*. See INDUCE.]

in·duct·ance (in duk′təns) *n.* 1 the property of an electrical conductor or circuit that makes induction possible. 2 a circuit or a device having this property. 3 the lag in an electric circuit when the current goes on or off.

in·duc·tee (in duk′tē) *n.* a person who is soon to be inducted, especially, in the United States, into military service.

in·duc·tile (in duk′tīl or in duk′təl) *adj.* not ductile.

in·duc·tion (in duk′shən) *n.* 1 in electricity: **a** the process by which an object having electrical or magnetic properties produces similar properties in a nearby object, without direct contact. **b** a tendency exhibited by currents of electricity to resist change. 2 the act of reasoning from particular facts to a general rule or principle. 3 the conclusion reached in this way. 4 the act of inducting; act or ceremony of installing a person in office. 5 the act of bringing into existence or operation; producing; causing; inducing: *induction of a hypnotic state.* 6 in an internal-combustion engine, the taking of the explosive mixture or air into the cylinder. ☛ See **deduction** for usage note.

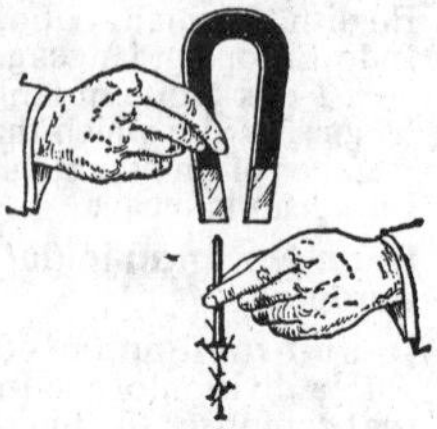

Magnetic induction. The tacks are sticking to the nail and to each other because of induced magnetism.

induction coil a device for producing a high, pulsating voltage from a current of low, steady voltage, such as that from a battery.

in·duc·tive (in duk′tiv) *adj.* 1 of or using induction; reasoning by induction. 2 having to do with electrical or magnetic induction. **—in·duc′tive·ly,** *adv.*

in·duc·tiv·i·ty (in′duk tiv′ə tē) *n.* **-ties.** an inductive property; capacity for induction.

in·duc·tor (in duk′tər) *n.* 1 a person who inducts another into office. 2 a part of an electrical apparatus that works or is worked by induction.

in·due (in dū′ or in dü′) *v.* **-dued, -du·ing. endue.** [< L *induere* put on]

in·dulge (in dulj′) *v.* **-dulged, -dulg·ing.** 1 yield to the wishes of; humor: *We often indulge a sick person.* 2 give way to: *We do not indulge all our desires.* 3 give way to one's pleasures; give oneself up to; allow oneself something desired: *He indulges in tobacco.* [< L *indulgere*] **—in·dulg′ing·ly,** *adv.* **—Syn. 1** gratify. See **humor.**

in·dul·gence (in dul′jəns) *n.* 1 an indulging. 2 something indulged in. 3 a favor; privilege. 4 in the Roman Catholic Church: **a** a remission of the punishment still due for a sin, after the guilt has been forgiven. **b** a dispensation.

in·dul·gent (in dul′jənt) *adj.* 1 indulging; kind; almost too kind. 2 lenient; making allowances; not critical. **—in·dul′gent·ly,** *adv.*

in·du·rate (*v.* in′dū rāt′ or in′dü rāt′; *adj.* in′dū rit or in′dü rit) *v.* **-rat·ed, -rat·ing,** *adj.* **—***v.* 1 harden. 2 make or become unfeeling. **—***adj.* 1 hardened. 2 unfeeling. [< L *indurare* < *in-* + *durus* hard] **—in′du·ra′tion,** *n.*

in·dus·tri·al (in dus′trē əl) *adj.* 1 of or resulting from industry or productive labor. 2 having to do with or connected with the industries, trades, or manufacturers: *industrial activity, an industrial exhibition, industrial workers.* 3 for use in industry. 4 of or having to do with the workers in industries: *industrial insurance.* **—***n.* a stock, bond, etc. of an industrial enterprise. [earlier < Med.L *industrialis* < L *industria* diligence; later < F *industriel* < L *industria*] **—in·dus′tri·al·ly,** *adv.*

in·dus·tri·al·ism (in dus′trē əl iz′əm) *n.* a system of social and economic organization in which large industries are very important and industrial activities or interests prevail.

in·dus·tri·al·ist (in dus′trē əl ist) *n.* 1 a person who conducts or owns an industrial enterprise. 2 an industrial worker.

in·dus·tri·al·i·za·tion (in dus′trē əl ə zā′shən or in dus′trē əl ī zā′shən) *n.* the development of large industries as an important feature in a country or a social or economic system.

in·dus·tri·al·ize (in dus′trē əl īz′) *v.* **-ized, -iz·ing.** 1 make industrial; develop industry in. 2 organize as an industry.

Industrial Revolution the change from an agricultural to an industrial civilization, especially that which took place in England from about the middle of the 18th century to the middle of the 19th century.

in·dus·tri·ous (in dus′trē əs) *adj.* hard-working. [< L *industriosus*] **—in·dus′tri·ous·ly,** *adv.* **—in·dus′tri·ous·ness,** *n.* **—Syn.** diligent. See **busy.**

in·dus·try (in′dəs trē) *n.* **-tries.** 1 any branch of business, trade, or manufacture: *the steel industry, the automobile industry.* 2 all such enterprises taken collectively: *Canadian industry is expanding.* 3 systematic work or labor. 4 steady effort; busy application: *Industry and thrift lead to success.* [< L *industria*] **—Syn. 4** diligence.

in·dwell·ing (in′dwel′ing) *adj.* dwelling within.

-ine[1] *suffix.* of; like; like that of; characteristic of; having the nature of; being, as in *crystalline, elephantine.* [< L *-inus*, sometimes < Gk. *-inos*]

-ine[2] *suffix.* used especially in the names of some chemicals, as in *chlorine, aniline.* [< F (< L *-ina*) or directly < L *-ina*]

in·e·bri·ate (*v.* in ē′brē āt′; *n. adj.* in ē′brē it) *v.* **-at·ed, -at·ing,** *n. adj.* **—***v.* make drunk; intoxicate. **—***n.* a habitual drunkard; intoxicated person. **—***adj.* intoxicated; drunk. [< L *inebriare* < *in-* + *ebrius* drunk]

in·e·bri·a·tion (in ē′brē ā′shən) *n.* drunkenness; intoxication.

in·e·bri·e·ty (in′i brī′ə tē) *n.* drunkenness.

in·ed·i·ble (in ed′ə bəl) *adj.* not fit to eat: *Some toadstools are inedible.*

in·ed·u·ca·ble (in ej′ů kə bəl) *adj.* incapable of being educated.

in·ef·fa·ble (in ef′ə bəl) *adj.* 1 not to be expressed in words; too great to be described in words. 2 that must not be spoken. [< L *ineffabilis*, ult. < *in-* not + *ex-* out + *fari* speak] **—in·ef′fa·ble·ness,** *n.* **—in·ef′fa·bly,** *adv.*

in·ef·face·a·ble (in′ə fās′ə bəl) *adj.* that cannot be rubbed out or wiped out. **—in′ef·face′a·bly,** *adv.*

in·ef·fec·tive (in′ə fek′tiv) *adj.* 1 not effective; of little use: *The medicine proved ineffective.* 2 unfit for work; incapable. **—in′ef·fec′tive·ly,** *adv.* **—in′ef·fec′tive·ness,** *n.*

in·ef·fec·tu·al (in′ə fek′chü əl) *adj.* 1 without effect; useless. 2 not able to produce the effect wanted. **—in′ef·fec′tu·al·ly,** *adv.* **—Syn. 1** ineffective, futile, vain.

in·ef·fi·ca·cious (in′ef ə kā′shəs) *adj.* not efficacious; not able to produce the effect wanted.

in·ef·fi·ca·cy (in ef′ə kə sē) *n.* a lack of efficacy; inability to produce the effect wanted.

in·ef·fi·cien·cy (in′ə fish′ən sē) *n.* a lack of efficiency; inability to get things done.

in·ef·fi·cient (in′ə fish′ənt) *adj.* 1 not efficient; not able to produce an effect without waste of time, energy, etc.: *A machine that uses too much power is inefficient.* 2 incapable; not able to get things done: *an inefficient housekeeper.* **—in′ef·fi′cient·ly,** *adv.* **—Syn. 1** incompetent, ineffective.

in·e·las·tic (in′i las′tik) *adj.* not elastic; stiff; inflexible; unyielding.

in·e·las·tic·i·ty (in′i las tis′ə tē) *n.* a lack of elasticity.

in·el·e·gance (in el′ə gəns) *n.* 1 a lack of elegance; lack of good taste. 2 something that is not elegant or graceful.

in·el·e·gan·cy (in el′ə gən sē) *n.* **-cies.** inelegance.

in·el·e·gant (in el′ə gənt) *adj.* not elegant; not in good taste; crude; vulgar. **—in·el′e·gant·ly,** *adv.* **—Syn.** rough, unrefined.

in·el·i·gi·bil·i·ty (in el′ə jə bil′ə tē) *n.* a lack of eligibility; being ineligible.

in·el·i·gi·ble (in el′ə jə bəl) *adj.* not suitable; not qualified: *His youth makes him ineligible for the post.* —*n.* a person who is not suitable or not qualified. —**in·el′i·gi·bly,** *adv.*

in·e·luc·ta·ble (in′i luk′tə bəl) *adj.* unable to be avoided; inevitable. [< L *ineluctabilis* < *eluctari* < *ex-* out + *luctari* struggle] —**in′e·luc′ta·bly,** *adv.*

in·ept (in ept′) *adj.* **1** not suitable; out of place: *He would be an inept choice as captain.* **2** absurd; foolish: *That was certainly an inept performance.* [< L *ineptus* < *in-* not + *aptus* apt] —**in·ept′ly,** *adv.* —**in·ept′ness,** *n.*

in·ept·i·tude (in ep′tə tūd′ or in ep′tə tüd′) *n.* **1** unfitness; foolishness. **2** a silly or inappropriate act or remark.

in·e·qual·i·ty (in′ē kwol′ə tē) *n.* **-ties. 1** lack of equality; the state or condition of being unequal in amount, size, value, rank, etc. **2** a lack of evenness, regularity, or uniformity. **3** in mathematics, an expression showing that two quantities are unequal, like $a > b$ or $c < d$. —**Syn. 1** disparity. **2** unevenness, variableness.

in·eq·ui·ta·ble (in ek′wə tə bəl) *adj.* unfair; unjust. —**in·eq′ui·ta·bly,** *adv.*

in·eq·ui·ty (in ek′wə tē) *n.* **-ties. 1** unfairness; injustice. **2** an unfair or unjust act.

in·e·rad·i·ca·ble (in′i rad′ə kə bəl) *adj.* that cannot be rooted out or got rid of. —**in′e·rad′i·ca·bly,** *adv.*

in·ert (in ėrt′) *adj.* **1** having no inherent power to move or act; lifeless: *A stone is an inert mass of matter.* **2** inactive; slow; sluggish. **3** in chemistry, with few or no active properties: *Helium and neon are inert gases.* [< L *iners, inertis* idle, unskilled < *in-* without + *ars, artis* art, skill] —**in·ert′ly,** *adv.* —**in·ert′ness,** *n.* —**Syn. 2** See **inactive.**

in·er·tia (in ėr′shə) *n.* **1** a tendency to remain in the state one is in and not start changes. **2** in physics, the tendency of all objects and matter in the universe to stay still if still, or if moving, to go on moving in the same direction unless acted on by some outside force. [< L *inertia* < *iners.* See INERT.]

in·er·tial (in ėr′shəl) *adj.* resembling inertia: *Inertial navigation is made possible by gyroscopic control.*

in·es·cap·a·ble (in′is kāp′ə bəl) *adj.* that cannot be escaped or avoided. —**in′es·cap′a·bly,** *adv.*

in·es·ti·ma·ble (in es′tə mə bəl) *adj.* too good, great, valuable, etc. to be measured or estimated: *Freedom is an inestimable privilege.* —**Syn.** invaluable, priceless.

in·es·ti·ma·bly (in es′tə mə blē) *adv.* so as to be inestimable.

in·ev·i·ta·bil·i·ty (in ev′ə tə bil′ə tē) *n.* the quality of being inevitable.

in·ev·i·ta·ble (in ev′ə tə bəl) *adj.* not avoidable; sure to happen; certain to come. [< L *inevitabilis* < *in-* not + *evitabilis* avoidable < *evitare* avoid < *ex-* + *vitare* avoid] —**in·ev′i·ta·bly,** *adv.*

in·ex·act (in′ig zakt′) *adj.* not exact; not accurate. —**in′ex·act′ly,** *adv.* —**in′ex·act′ness,** *n.*

in·ex·cus·a·ble (in′iks kūz′ə bəl) *adj.* that ought not to be excused; that cannot be justified. —**in′ex·cus′a·bly,** *adv.* —**Syn.** unpardonable, unjustifiable.

in·ex·haust·i·bil·i·ty (in′ig zos′tə bil′ə tē or in′ig zôs′tə bil′ə tē) *n.* an inexhaustible nature or quality.

in·ex·haust·i·ble (in′ig zos′tə bəl or in′ig zôs′tə bəl) *adj.* **1** that cannot be exhausted; very abundant. **2** tireless. —**in′ex·haust′i·bly,** *adv.*

in·ex·o·ra·bil·i·ty (in ek′sə rə bil′ə tē) *n.* an inexorable nature or quality.

in·ex·o·ra·ble (in ek′sə rə bəl) *adj.* relentless; unyielding; not influenced by prayers or entreaties: *The forces of nature are inexorable.* [< L *inexorabilis* < *in-* not + *ex-* (intensive) + *orare* entreat] —**in·ex′o·ra·bly,** *adv.* —**Syn.** unrelenting, implacable. See **inflexible.**

in·ex·pe·di·en·cy (in′iks pē′dē ən sē) *n.* lack of expediency; a being inexpedient.

in·ex·pe·di·ent (in′iks pē′dē ənt) *adj.* not expedient; not practicable, suitable, or wise. —**Syn.** inadvisable.

in·ex·pen·sive (in′iks pen′siv) *adj.* not expensive; cheap; low-priced. —**in′ex·pen′sive·ly,** *adv.* —**in′ex·pen′sive·ness,** *n.* —**Syn.** See **cheap.**

in·ex·pe·ri·ence (in′iks pēr′ē əns) *n.* lack of experience or practice; lack of skill or wisdom gained from experience.

hat, āge, cãre, fär; let, ēqual, tėrm; it, īce
hot, ōpen, ôrder; oil, out; cup, pu̇t, rüle, ūse
əbove, takən, pencəl, lemən, circəs
ch, child; ng, long; sh, ship
th, thin; ᴛʜ, then; zh, measure

in·ex·pe·ri·enced (in′iks pēr′ē ənst) *adj.* not experienced; without practice; lacking the skill and wisdom gained by experience. —**Syn.** unpractised, untrained.

in·ex·pert (in eks′pėrt or in′iks pėrt′) *adj.* not expert; unskilled. —**in·ex′pert·ly,** *adv.* —**in·ex′pert·ness,** *n.*

in·ex·pi·a·ble (in eks′pē ə bəl) *adj.* that cannot be atoned for: *Murder is an inexpiable crime.* [< L *inexpiabilis*]

in·ex·pli·ca·bil·i·ty (in′iks plik′ə bil′ə tē or in eks′plə kə bil′ə tē) *n.* an unexplainable nature or quality.

in·ex·pli·ca·ble (in′iks plik′ə bəl or in eks′plə kə bəl) *adj.* impossible to explain or understand; mysterious. [< L *inexplicabilis*] —**in·ex′pli·ca·bly,** *adv.*

in·ex·press·i·ble (in′iks pres′ə bəl) *adj.* that cannot be expressed; beyond expression. —**Syn.** unutterable.

in·ex·press·i·bly (in′iks pres′ə blē) *adv.* beyond expression; indescribably.

in·ex·pres·sive (in′iks pres′iv) *adj.* not expressive; lacking in expression. —**in′ex·pres′sive·ly,** *adv.* —**in′ex·pres′sive·ness,** *n.*

in ex·ten·so (in iks ten′sō) at full length; in full. [< L *in extenso,* literally, in an extended (state)]

in·ex·tin·guish·a·ble (in′iks ting′gwish ə bəl) *adj.* that cannot be put out or stopped: *An inextinguishable fire keeps on burning.* —**in′ex·tin′guish·a·bly,** *adv.*

in ex·tre·mis (in iks trē′mis) at the point of death. [< L *in extremis,* literally, amid the final things]

in·ex·tri·ca·ble (in eks′trə kə bəl) *adj.* **1** that one cannot get out of. **2** that cannot be disentangled or solved. —**in·ex′tri·ca·bly,** *adv.*

inf. 1 infantry. **2** infinitive. **3** inferior. **4** below. (for L *infra*) **5** information.

Inf. infantry.

in·fal·li·bil·i·ty (in fal′ə bil′ə tē) *n.* absolute freedom from error: *The infallibility of the Pope when speaking officially on matters of faith and morals was proclaimed by the Vatican Council in 1870.*

in·fal·li·ble (in fal′ə bəl) *adj.* **1** free from error; that cannot be mistaken: *an infallible rule.* **2** absolutely reliable; sure: *infallible obedience.* **3** in the Roman Catholic Church, incapable of error in the exposition of doctrine on faith and morals (said of the Pope as head of the Church). —**in·fal′li·bly,** *adv.*

in·fa·mous (in′fə məs) *adj.* **1** deserving or causing a very bad reputation; shamefully bad; extremely wicked. **2** having a very bad reputation; in public disgrace: *A traitor's name is infamous.* [< Med.L *infamosus,* in L *infamis*] —**in′fa·mous·ly,** *adv.* —**in·fa·mous·ness,** *n.* —**Syn. 1** odious. **2** notorious, disreputable.

in·fa·my (in′fə mē) *n.* **-mies. 1** an extremely bad reputation; public disgrace: *Traitors are held in infamy.* **2** shameful badness; extreme wickedness. **3** a shamefully bad or extremely wicked act. [< L *infamia* < *in-* without + *fama* (good) reputation]

in·fan·cy (in′fən sē) *n.* **-cies. 1** the condition or time of being an infant; babyhood; early childhood. **2** an early stage; beginning of development: *Space travel is in its infancy.* **3** the condition of being under the legal age of responsibility (in common law, under 21).

in·fant (in′fənt) *n.* **1** a baby; very young child. **2** a person under the legal age of responsibility; minor. —*adj.* **1** of or for an infant. **2** in an early stage; just beginning to develop. [< L *infans, infantis,* originally, not speaking < *in-* not + *fari* speak]

in·fan·ta (in fan′tə) *n.* **1** a daughter of a king of Spain or Portugal. **2** the wife of an infante. [< Sp., Pg. *infanta,* fem.]

in·fan·te (in fan′tā) *n.* a son of a king of Spain or Portugal, but not the heir to the throne. [< Sp., Pg.]

in·fan·ti·cide[1] (in fan′tə sīd′) *n.* the killing of a baby. [< L *infanticidium* < *infans, -antis* infant + *-cidium* act of killing < *caedere* kill]

in·fan·ti·cide[2] (in fan′tə sīd′) *n.* a person who kills a baby. [< L *infanticida* < *infans, -antis* < *-cida* killer < *caedere* kill]

in·fan·tile (in′fən tīl′ or in′fən təl) *adj.* 1 of an infant or infants; having to do with infants. 2 like an infant; babyish; childish: *Her father was annoyed at her infantile behavior.* 3 in an early stage; just beginning to develop.

infantile paralysis an acute infectious virus disease that destroys tissue in the brain and spinal cord, causing fever, paralysis of various muscles, and, sometimes, death; poliomyelitis. Infantile paralysis attacks children especially, often leaving them crippled.

in·fan·ti·lism (in fan′tə liz′əm) *n.* an abnormal persistence or appearance of childish traits in adults.

in·fan·tine (in′fən tīn′ or in′fən tin) *adj.* infantile; babyish; childish.

in·fan·try (in′fən trē) *n.* **-tries.** 1 soldiers trained, equipped, and organized to fight on foot. 2 the branch of an army made up of such soldiers. [< F *infanterie* < Ital. *infanteria* < *infante, fante* foot soldier; originally, a youth < L *infans, -fantis.* See INFANT.]

in·fan·try·man (in′fən trē mən) *n.* **-men** (-mən). a soldier who fights on foot.

in·fat·u·ate (*v.* in fach′ü āt′; *adj.* in fach′ü it or in fach′ü āt′) *v.* **-at·ed, -at·ing,** *adj.* —*v.* 1 make foolish. 2 inspire with a foolish or unreasoning passion. —*adj.* infatuated. [< L *infatuare* < *in-* in + *fatuus* foolish]

in·fat·u·at·ed (in fach′ü āt′id) *adj.* extremely adoring; foolishly in love: *He is infatuated with the girl.*

in·fat·u·a·tion (in fach′ü ā′shən) *n.* 1 an infatuating. 2 a being infatuated. 3 a foolish love; unreasoning fondness.

in·fect (in fekt′) *v.* 1 cause illness in (a person, animal, etc.) by the action of disease-producing organisms. 2 introduce such organisms into (a wound, part of the body, etc.): *Dirt may infect an open cut.* 3 influence in a bad way. 4 influence by spreading from one to another: *The captain's courage infected his soldiers.* 5 fill with something that affects quality, character, or condition, especially unfavorably. [< L *infectus,* pp. of *inficere* dye, originally, put in < *in-* in + *facere* make] **—in·fec′tor,** *n.* **—Syn.** 3 deprave, contaminate.

in·fec·tion (in fek′shən) *n.* 1 a causing of disease in people, animals, and plants by the action of disease-producing organisms: *Air, water, clothing, and insects are all means of infection.* 2 a disease caused in this way. 3 an influence, feeling, or idea spreading from one to another. 4 the fact or state of being infected.

in·fec·tious (in fek′shəs) *adj.* 1 spread by infection: *Measles is an infectious disease.* 2 causing infection; liable to cause infection: *That disease is infectious.* 3 apt to spread: *an infectious laugh.* **—in·fec′tious·ly,** *adv.* **—in·fec′tious·ness,** *n.* **—Syn.** 1 contagious, catching.

in·fec·tive (in fek′tiv) *adj.* infectious.

in·fe·lic·i·tous (in′fə lis′ə təs) *adj.* 1 unsuitable; not appropriate. 2 unfortunate; unhappy.

in·fe·lic·i·ty (in′fə lis′ə tē) *n.* **-ties.** 1 unsuitability; inappropriateness. 2 a misfortune; unhappiness. 3 something unsuitable; inappropriate word, remark, etc.

in·fer (in fėr′) *v.* **-ferred, -fer·ring.** 1 find out by reasoning; conclude: *Seeing the frown on my face, the boy inferred that I was displeased.* 2 indicate; imply: *Ragged clothing infers poverty.* 3 draw inferences. [< L *inferre* < *in-* in + *ferre* bring] ☛ See **imply** for usage note.

in·fer·ence (in′fər əns) *n.* 1 the process of inferring. 2 that which is inferred; conclusion: *What inference do you draw from smelling smoke?*

in·fer·en·tial (in′fər en′shəl) *adj.* having to do with inference; depending on inference.

in·fe·ri·or (in fēr′ē ər) *adj.* 1 lower in position or rank: *an inferior officer.* 2 not so good; lower in quality; worse. 3 below average: *an inferior mind, an inferior grade of coffee.* 4 in botany: a growing below some other organ. b belonging to the part of the flower that is farthest from the main stem. 5 of animal organs, below or posterior to others of the same kind, or to the usual or normal position: *the inferior vena cava.* 6 in printing, set below the main line of type, as letters or numerals in chemical formulas: In H_2O, the *2* is inferior. 7 **inferior to,** a below; lower than: *A lieutenant is inferior to a captain.* b not as good or as great as; worse than: *This cloth is inferior to silk.*
—*n.* 1 a person who is lower in rank or station. 2 an inferior thing. [< L *inferior,* comparative of *inferus,* adj., situated below]

in·fe·ri·or·i·ty (in fēr′ē ôr′ə tē) *n.* an inferior condition or quality.

inferiority complex an abnormal or morbid feeling of being inferior to other people resulting in timidity in certain cases and in aggressiveness in others.

in·fer·nal (in fėr′nəl) *adj.* 1 of hell; having to do with the lower world. 2 hellish; diabolical. 3 *Informal.* abominable; outrageous. [< LL *infernalis,* ult. < L *inferus* below] **—in·fer′nal·ly,** *adv.*

infernal machine a disguised bomb or other explosive apparatus intended for the malicious destruction of life and property.

in·fer·no (in fėr′nō) *n.* **-nos.** 1 hell. 2 a hell-like place or thing: *Firemen fought their way through a roaring inferno of flames.* [< Ital.]

in·fer·tile (in fėr′tīl or in fėr′təl) *adj.* not fertile; not fruitful; sterile.

in·fer·til·i·ty (in′fėr til′ə tē) *n.* a lack of fertility; being infertile.

in·fest (in fest′) *v.* trouble or disturb frequently or in large numbers: *Swamps are often infested by mosquitoes.* [< L *infestare* attack < *infestus* hostile] **—Syn.** overrun.

in·fes·ta·tion (in′fes tā′shən) *n.* 1 an infesting. 2 the condition of being infested.

in·fi·del (in′fə dəl) *n.* 1 a person who does not believe in religion. 2 a person who does not accept a particular faith: *Moslems call Christians infidels.* 3 a person who does not accept Christianity.
—*adj.* 1 not believing in religion. 2 not accepting a particular faith, especially Christianity or Mohammedanism. 3 rejecting the Christian religion. 4 of or like unbelievers or infidels. [< L *infidelis* < *in-* not + *fidelis* faithful < *fides* faith]

in·fi·del·i·ty (in′fə del′ə tē) *n.* **-ties.** 1 lack of religious faith. 2 lack of belief in Christianity. 3 unfaithfulness, especially of husband or wife; disloyalty. 4 an unfaithful or disloyal act.

in·field (in′fēld′) *n.* 1 in baseball: a the area of a field lying within the baseline. b the first, second, and third basemen and the shortstop of a team: *That team has a good infield.* 2 the part of farm lands nearest the buildings.

in·field·er (in′fēl′dər) *n.* in baseball, a player of the infield.

in·fight·ing (in′fīt′ing) *n.* 1 *Informal.* internal dissension or conflict: *Infighting among salesmen lost their company the contract.* 2 in boxing, fighting at close quarters.

in·fil·trate (in fil′trāt or in′fil trāt′) *v.* **-trat·ed, -trat·ing.** 1 pass into or through by, or as by, filtering: *Enemy troops infiltrated the front lines.* 2 filter into or through; permeate or cause to permeate.

in·fil·tra·tion (in′fil trā′shən) *n.* 1 an infiltrating or the condition of being infiltrated. 2 something that infiltrates. 3 a method of attack in which small groups of men penetrate the enemy's lines at various weak points.

infin. infinitive.

in·fi·nite (in′fə nit) *adj.* 1 without limits or bounds; endless. 2 extremely great: *Teaching little children takes infinite patience.* 3 in mathematics: a greater than any assignable quantity or magnitude of the sort in question b (of a magnitude) beyond any finite magnitude.
—*n.* 1 that which is infinite. 2 in mathematics, an infinite quantity or magnitude. 3 **the Infinite,** God. [< L *infinitus* < *in-* not + *finis* boundary] **—in′fi·nite·ness,** *n.* **—Syn.** *adj.* 1 boundless, unlimited. 2 immeasurable, immense.

in·fi·nite·ly (in′fə nit lē) *adv.* 1 to an infinite degree. 2 *Informal.* very or very much: *I'm infinitely obliged to you.*

in·fi·ni·tes·i·mal (in′fi nə tes′ə məl) *adj.* **1** so small as to be almost nothing: *A millionth of an inch is an infinitesimal length.* **2** in mathematics, less than any assignable quantity or magnitude of the sort in question. —*n.* **1** an infinitesimal amount. **2** in mathematics, a variable continually approaching zero as a limit. [< NL *infinitesimus* the "nth" < L *infinitus.* See INFINITE.]

in·fi·ni·tes·i·mal·ly (in′fi nə tes′ə mə lē) *adv.* to an infinitesimal degree.

in·fin·i·tive (in fin′ə tiv) *n.* a form of a verb, not limited by person and number. *Examples*: Let him *go.* We want *to go* now. *Abbrev.*: infin. [< LL *infinitivus* < L *infinitus* unrestricted. See INFINITE.]

☛ **infinitive.** The present infinitive is the simple form of the verb, often preceded by *to*: *I want* to buy *a hat. Let him* leave *if he wants* to leave. Infinitives are used as: **a** nouns: To swim *across the English Channel is his ambition.* **b** adjectives: *He had money* to burn. **c** adverbs: *He went home* to rest. **d** part of verb phrases: *Henry will* do *most of the work.* ☛ See also usage note under **split infinitive.**

in·fin·i·tude (in fin′ə tūd′ or in fin′ə tüd′) *n.* **1** the state of being infinite. **2** an infinite extent, amount, or number.

in·fin·i·ty (in fin′ə tē) *n.* **-ties. 1** the state of being infinite. **2** an infinite distance, space, time, or quantity. **3** an infinite extent, amount, or number: *the infinity of God's mercy.* **4** in mathematics, an infinite quantity or magnitude. **5 to infinity,** without limits or bounds; endlessly. [< L *infinitas*]

in·firm (in fėrm′) *adj.* **1** weak; feeble. **2** weak in will or character; not steadfast. **3** not firm; not stable. —**in·firm′ly,** *adv.* —**in·firm′ness,** *n.* —**Syn. 1** shaky, decrepit, debilitated.

in·fir·ma·ry (in fėr′mə rē) *n.* **-ries. 1** a place for the care of the infirm, sick, or injured; a hospital in a school or institution. **2** any small hospital.

in·fir·mi·ty (in fėr′mə tē) *n.* **-ties. 1** weakness; feebleness. **2** a sickness; illness. **3** a moral weakness or failing. —**Syn. 3** defect.

in·flame (in flām′) *v.* **-flamed, -flam·ing. 1** excite; make more violent: *His stirring speech inflamed the crowd.* **2** become excited with intense feeling. **3** make unnaturally hot, red, sore, or swollen: *The smoke had inflamed the fireman's eyes.* **4** become red or hot from disease, etc. [ME < OF *enflamer* < L *inflammare* < *in-* in + *flamma* flame] —**Syn. 1** arouse, fire.

in·flam·ma·bil·i·ty (in flam′ə bil′ə tē) *n.* an inflammable quality or condition.

in·flam·ma·ble (in flam′ə bəl) *adj.* **1** easily set on fire: *Paper and gasoline are inflammable.* **2** easily excited or aroused. —*n.* something inflammable. —**in·flam′ma·bly,** *adv.* ☛ See **flammable** for usage note.

in·flam·ma·tion (in′flə mā′shən) *n.* **1** a diseased condition of some part of the body, marked by heat, redness, swelling, and pain. **2** an inflaming. **3** the condition of being inflamed.

in·flam·ma·to·ry (in flam′ə tô′rē) *adj.* **1** tending to excite or arouse: *The leader of the opposition made an inflammatory speech attacking the government.* **2** of, causing, or accompanied by inflammation: *an inflammatory condition of the tonsils.*

in·flate (in flāt′) *v.* **-flat·ed, -flat·ing. 1** blow out or swell with air or gas: *inflate a balloon.* **2** swell or puff out: *inflate with pride.* **3** increase (prices or currency) beyond the normal amount. [< L *inflatus,* pp. of *inflare* < *in-* into + *flare* blow] —**in·flat′a·ble,** *adj.* —**in·flat′er, in·fla′tor,** *n.* —**Syn. 1** distend, expand.

in·fla·tion (in flā′shən) *n.* **1** a swelling (with air, gas, pride, etc.). **2** a swollen state; excessive expansion. **3** an increase of the currency of a country by issuing much paper money. **4** a sharp and sudden rise of prices resulting from an excessive expansion in paper money or bank credit.

in·fla·tion·ar·y (in flā′shən er′ē) *adj.* of or having to do with inflation; tending to inflate.

in·fla·tion·ist (in flā′shən ist) *n.* a person who favors inflation.

in·flect (in flekt′) *v.* **1** change the tone or pitch of (the voice). **2** in grammar, vary the form of (a word) to show case, number, gender, person, tense, mood, comparison, etc. By inflecting *who,* we have *whose* and *whom.* **3** undergo such variations: *Latin nouns inflect for case and number.* **4** bend; curve. [< L *inflectere* < *in-* in + *flectere* bend]

hat, āge, cãre, fär; let, ēqual, tėrm; it, īce
hot, ōpen, ôrder; oil, out; cup, pu̇t, rüle, ūse
əbove, takən, pencəl, lemən, circəs
ch, child; ng, long; sh, ship
th, thin; ᴛʜ, then; zh, measure

in·flec·tion (in flek′shən) *n.* **1** a change in the tone or pitch of the voice: *We end certain questions with a rising inflection.* **2** in grammar: **a** a variation in the form of a word to show case, number, gender, person, tense, mood, or comparison. **b** a suffix or other element used to indicate such a variation. **3** a bending; curving. **4** a bend; curve.

in·flec·tion·al (in flek′shən əl) *adj.* of, having to do with, or showing grammatical inflection.

in·flex·i·bil·i·ty (in flek′sə bil′ə tē) *n.* lack of flexibility; the state or quality of being inflexible.

in·flex·i·ble (in flek′sə bəl) *adj.* **1** firm; unyielding; steadfast: *Neither threats nor promises could change his inflexible determination.* **2** that cannot be changed; unalterable. **3** not easily bent; stiff; rigid. —**in·flex′i·bly,** *adv.*

Syn. 1 Inflexible, inexorable, unrelenting = unyielding in character or purpose. **Inflexible** = unbending, holding fast or doggedly to what one has made up one's mind to do, think, or believe: *It is a waste of time to argue with someone whose attitude is inflexible.* **Inexorable** = not to be influenced or affected by begging or pleading, but firm and pitiless: *The principal was inexorable in his decision.* **Unrelenting** = not softening in force, harshness, or cruelty: *He was unrelenting in his hatred.* **3** unbending, firm.

in·flex·ion (in flek′shən) *n. Esp.Brit.* inflection.

in·flict (in flikt′) *v.* **1** give or cause (a blow, wound, pain, etc.). **2** impose (a burden, suffering, anything unwelcome, etc.): *Their disagreeable aunt inflicted herself on them for a long visit.* [< L *inflictus,* pp. of *infligere* < *in-* on + *fligere* dash]

in·flic·tion (in flik′shən) *n.* **1** the act of inflicting. **2** something inflicted; pain; suffering; burden; punishment.

in·flo·res·cence (in′flô res′əns) *n.* **1** the flowering stage. **2** in botany: **a** the arrangement of flowers on the stem or axis. **b** a flower cluster. [< NL *inflorescentia* < L *in-* in + *flōs, floris* flower]

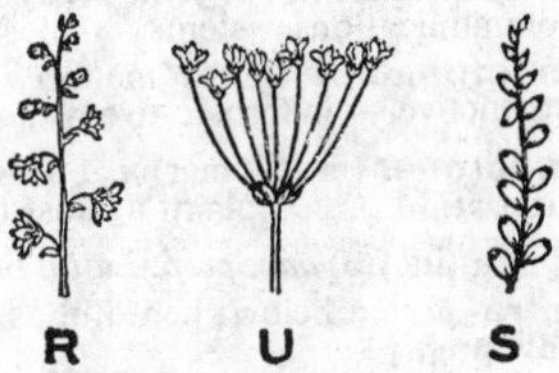

Common types of inflorescence: R, a raceme; U, an umbel; S, a spike.

in·flo·res·cent (in′flô res′ənt) *adj.* showing inflorescence; flowering.

in·flow (in′flō′) *n.* **1** a flowing in or into. **2** that which flows in.

in·flu·ence (in′flü əns) *n. v.* **-enced, -enc·ing.** —*n.* **1** the power of persons or things to act on others. **2** the power to produce an effect without using coercion: *A person may have influence by his ability, personality, position, or wealth.* **3** a person or thing that has such power. **4** in electricity, induction, especially electrostatic induction. **5** in astrology, the supposed power of the stars over the characters and destinies of men.
—*v.* have power over; change the nature or behavior of: *The moon influences the tides.* [ME < OF < Med.L *influentia,* originally, a flowing in < L *in-* in + *fluere* flow] —**Syn.** *n.* **1** See **authority.** –*v.* move, stir, sway, persuade.

in·flu·en·tial (in′flü en′shəl) *adj.* **1** having much influence; having influence: *Influential friends helped him to get a job.* **2** using influence; producing results.

in·flu·en·za (in′flü en′zə) *n.* an acute contagious virus disease, occasionally resembling a severe cold in some of its symptoms, but much more dangerous and exhausting; flu. [< Ital. *influenza* influence]

in·flux (in′fluks) *n.* **1** a flowing in; steady flow: *the influx of immigrants into a country.* **2** the point where a river or stream flows into another river, a lake, or the sea; mouth. [< LL *influxus,* ult. < L *in-* in + *fluere* flow]

in·fo (in′fō) *n. Slang.* information.

in·fold (in fōld′) *v.* enfold.

in·form (in fôrm′) *v.* **1** supply with knowledge, facts, or news; tell. **2** make an accusation or complaint: *One thief* *informed against the others.* 3 inspire; animate: *God informed their hearts with pity.* [< L *informare* < *in-* in + *forma* form]

Syn. 1 Inform, acquaint, notify = tell or let someone know something. **Inform** emphasizes telling or passing along directly to a person facts or knowledge of any kind: *Her letter informed us how and when she expected to arrive.* **Acquaint** emphasizes introducing someone to facts or knowledge that he has not known before: *He acquainted us with his plans.* **Notify** = inform someone, by an official announcement or formal notice, of something he ought to or needs to know: *The university notified him that he was awarded a scholarship.*

in·for·mal (in fôr′məl) *adj.* **1** not formal; not in the regular or prescribed manner. **2** done without ceremony. **3** used in everyday, common speech, but not used in formal speaking or writing. Such an expression as *kids* for *children* is informal. **—in·for′mal·ly,** *adv.* **—Syn. 2** unconventional, easy. **3** colloquial.

☛ **Informal English** is the kind of English used by educated people in informal speaking or writing, as distinguished from formal English, which is used in lectures, speeches, learned articles, legal documents, etc.

in·for·mal·i·ty (in′fôr mal′ə tē) *n.* **-ties. 1** the quality of being informal; lack of ceremony. **2** an informal act.

in·form·ant (in fôr′mənt) *n.* a person who gives information to another: *My informant saw the accident happen.*

in·for·ma·tion (in′fər mā′shən) *n.* **1** knowledge; facts; news: *A dictionary gives information about words. The general sent information of his victory to headquarters.* **2** an informing: *A guidebook is for the information of travellers.* **3** a person or office whose duty is to answer questions. **4** an accusation or complaint against a person. **5** any message or part of a message in coded form assembled by or fed to a computer. **—Syn. 1** See **knowledge.**

in·for·ma·tion·al (in′fər mā′shən əl or in′fər māsh′nəl) *adj.* giving information; instructive.

information theory the study of the efficiency of any communications system.

in·form·a·tive (in fôr′mə tiv) *adj.* giving information; instructive. **—in·form′a·tive·ly,** *adv.* **—in·form′a·tive·ness,** *n.*

in·form·er (in fôr′mər) *n.* **1** a person who makes an accusation or complaint against others. **2** an informant.

in·fra (in′frə) *adv. prep. Latin.* beneath; below.

infra- *prefix.* below; beneath, as in *infra-red.* [< L *infra,* adv. prep.]

in·frac·tion (in frak′shən) *n.* a breaking of a law or obligation; violation: *Reckless driving is an infraction of the law.* [< L *infractio, -onis* < *infringere.* See INFRINGE.]

in·fran·gi·ble (in fran′jə bəl) *adj.* **1** unable to be broken; unbreakable: *the infrangible laws of nature.* **2** inviolable: *an infrangible rule.* **—in·fran′gi·bly,** *adv.*

in·fra-red (in′frə red′) *adj.* of the invisible part of the spectrum whose rays have wave lengths longer than those of the red part of the visible spectrum. Most of the heat from sunlight, incandescent lamps, carbon arcs, resistance wires, etc. is from infra-red rays.

in·fra·struc·ture (in′frə struk′chər) *n.* the essential elements of a system or structure.

in·fre·quence (in frē′kwəns) *n.* infrequency.

in·fre·quen·cy (in frē′kwən sē) *n.* scarcity; rarity.

in·fre·quent (in frē′kwənt) *adj.* not frequent; occurring seldom or far apart; scarce; rare. [< L *infrequens, -entis*] **—in·fre′quent·ly,** *adv.*

in·fringe (in frinj′) *v.* **-fringed, -fring·ing. 1** violate: *A false label infringes the laws relating to food and drugs.* **2** trespass; encroach: *infringe upon the rights of another.* [< L *infringere* < *in-* in + *frangere* break] **—in·fring′er,** *n.* **—Syn. 1** break. **2** intrude.

in·fringe·ment (in frinj′mənt) *n.* **1** a violation. **2** a trespassing; encroachment.

in·fu·ri·ate (in fūr′ē āt′) *v.* **-at·ed, -at·ing.** put into a fury; make furious; enrage. [< Med.L *infuriare* < L *in-* into + *furia* fury] **—in·fu′ri·at′ing·ly,** *adv.* **—in·fu′ri·a′tion,** *n.*

in·fuse (in fūz′) *v.* **-fused, -fus·ing. 1** pour in; put in: *The captain infused his own courage into his soldiers.* **2** inspire: *The soldiers were infused with his courage.* **3** steep or soak in a liquid to get something out: *We infuse tea leaves in hot water to make tea.* [< L *infusus,* pp. of *infundere* < *in-* in + *fundere* pour] **—in·fus′er,** *n.*

in·fu·si·ble (in fū′zə bəl) *adj.* that cannot be fused or melted.

in·fu·sion (in fū′zhən) *n.* **1** the act or process of infusing. **2** something poured in or mingled; infused element. **3** a liquid extract obtained by steeping or soaking.

in·fu·so·ri·an (in′fyů sô′rē ən) *n.* one of a group of one-celled animals that move by vibrating filaments. *—adj.* of or belonging to this group. [< NL *Infusoria,* genus name < L *infusus,* pp. of *infundere* pour in. See INFUSE.]

-ing[1] *suffix.* **1** the action, result, product, material, etc. of some verb, as in *hard thinking, the art of painting, a beautiful drawing, fine sewing, a blue lining, rich trimming.* **2** an action, result, product, material, etc. of some other part of speech, as in *lobstering, smoking, shirting, over-coating.* **3** of one that ——s; of those that ——, as in *smoking habit, printing trade, drinking song.* [ME *-ing,* OE *-ing, -ung*]

-ing[2] *suffix.* **1** an element forming the present participle. **2** that ——s, as in *seeing eye, lasting happiness, growing child.* [ME *-ing(e),* var. of *-ind(e), -end(e),* OE *-ende*]

in·ge·ni·ous (in jē′nē əs or in jēn′yəs) *adj.* **1** clever; skilful in making; good at inventing: *The ingenious boy made a radio set for himself.* **2** cleverly planned and made: *This mousetrap is an ingenious device.* [< L *ingeniosus* < *ingenium* natural talent] **—in·gen′ious·ly,** *adv.* **—in·gen′ious·ness,** *n.* **—Syn. 1** inventive, resourceful. See **clever.**

☛ **ingenious, ingenuous. Ingenious** = clever; skilful; **ingenuous** = frank; sincere; simple: *Fay is so ingenious that she is sure to think of some way of doing this work more easily. The ingenuous child had never thought of being suspicious of what others told her.*

in·gé·nue (on′zhə nü′; *French,* aɴ zhā nʏ′) *n.* **-nues. 1** a simple, innocent girl or young woman, especially as represented on the stage, in films, etc. **2** an actress who plays such a part. [< F *ingénue,* originally fem. adj., ingenuous]

in·ge·nu·i·ty (in′jə nū′ə tē or in′jə nü′ə tē) *n.* **-ties. 1** skill in planning, inventing, etc.; cleverness. **2** a cleverly planned act, device, etc. [< L *ingenuitas* frankness < *ingenuus* ingenuous; influenced by association with *ingenious*]

in·gen·u·ous (in jen′ū əs) *adj.* **1** frank; open; sincere. **2** simple; natural; innocent. [< L *ingenuus,* originally, native, free born] **—in·gen′u·ous·ly,** *adv.* **—in·gen′u·ous·ness,** *n.* **—Syn. 1** candid. **2** naïve. ☛ See **ingenious** for usage note.

in·gest (in jest′) *v.* **1** take (food, etc.) into the body for digestion. **2** take in: *He ingested the new idea slowly.* [< L *ingestus,* pp. of *ingerere* < *in-* in + *gerere* carry] **—in·gest′ion,** *n.*

in·gle (ing′gəl) *n.* **1** a fireplace. **2** a fire burning on the hearth. [? < Scots Gaelic *aingeal* fire]

in·gle·nook (ing′gəl nůk′) *n.* a corner by the fire.

in·glo·ri·ous (in glô′rē əs) *adj.* **1** bringing no glory; shameful; disgraceful. **2** having no glory; not famous. **—in·glo′ri·ous·ness,** *n.* **—Syn. 1** ignoble. **2** humble, obscure.

in·got (ing′gət) *n.* a mass of metal, such as gold, silver or steel, cast into a convenient shape in a mould. [OE *in-* in + *goten,* pp. of *gēotan* pour]

in·graft (in graft′) *v.* engraft.

in·grain (*v.* in grān′; *adj. n.* in′grān′) *v.* **1** fix deeply and firmly; make an integral part of: *Certain habits are ingrained in one's nature.* **2** dye fibre before it is spun or woven.
—adj. **1** dyed before manufacture. **2** made of yarn dyed before weaving: *an ingrain rug.*
—n. yarn, wool, etc. dyed before manufacture.

in·grate (in′grāt) *n.* an ungrateful person. *—adj. Archaic.* ungrateful. [< L *ingratus* < *in-* not + *gratus* thankful]

in·gra·ti·ate (in grā′shē āt′) *v.* **-at·ed, -at·ing.** bring (oneself) into favor: *He tried to ingratiate himself with the teacher by giving her presents.* [apparently < Ital. *ingraziare,* ult. < L *in gratiam* into favor] **—in·gra′ti·at′ing·ly,** *adv.*

in·grat·i·tude (in grat′ə tūd′ or in grat′ə tüd′) *n.* lack of gratitude; being ungrateful.

in·gre·di·ent (in grē′dē ənt) *n.* one of the parts of a mixture: *the ingredients of a cake.* [< L *ingrediens, -entis,* ppr. of *ingredi* < *in-* in + *gradi* go] —**Syn.** constituent, component.

in·gress (in′gres) *n.* **1** a going in: *A high fence prevented ingress to the field.* **2** a way in; entrance. **3** a right to go in. [< L *ingressus* < *ingredi.* See INGREDIENT.]

in·grow·ing (in′grō′ing) *adj.* **1** growing within; growing inward. **2** growing into the flesh: *an ingrowing toenail.*

in·grown (in′grōn′) *adj.* **1** grown within; grown inward. **2** grown into the flesh.

in·gui·nal (ing′gwə nəl) *adj.* of the groin; in or near the groin. [< L *inguinalis* < *inguen* groin]

in·gulf (in gulf′) *v.* engulf.

in·hab·it (in hab′it) *v.* **1** live in (a place, region, house, cave, tree, etc.): *Fish inhabit the sea. Thoughts inhabit the mind.* **2** live; dwell. [< L *inhabitare* < *in-* in + *habitare* dwell < *habere* have, dwell]

in·hab·it·a·ble (in hab′ə tə bəl) *adj.* **1** capable of being inhabited. **2** fit to live in; habitable.

in·hab·it·ant (in hab′ə tənt) *n.* a person or animal that lives in a place. [< L *inhabitans, -antis,* ppr. of *inhabitare.* See INHABIT.] —**Syn.** dweller.

in·hal·ant (in hāl′ənt) *n.* **1** a medicine to be inhaled. **2** an apparatus for inhaling it. —*adj.* used for inhaling.

in·ha·la·tion (in′hə lā′shən) *n.* **1** the act of inhaling. **2** a medicine to be inhaled.

in·ha·la·tor (in′hə lā′tər) *n.* an apparatus for inhaling anaesthetics, medicine, etc.

in·hale (in hāl′) *v.* **-haled, -hal·ing.** draw into the lungs; breathe in (air, gas, fragrance, tobacco smoke, etc.). [< L *inhalare* < *in-* in + *halare* breathe]

in·hal·er (in hāl′ər) *n.* **1** an apparatus used in inhaling medicine, a gas, etc. **2** an apparatus for filtering dust, gases, etc. from air. **3** a person who inhales.

in·har·mon·ic (in′här mon′ik) *adj.* not harmonic; not musical.

in·har·mo·ni·ous (in′här mō′nē əs) *adj.* not harmonious; discordant; disagreeing. —**in′har·mo′ni·ous·ly,** *adv.*

in·here (in hēr′) *v.* **-hered, -her·ing.** exist; belong to as a quality or attribute: *Greed inheres in human nature. Power inheres in that ruler.* [< L *inhaerere* < *in-* in + *haerere* stick]

in·her·ence (in hēr′əns or in her′əns) *n.* the quality of being inherent.

in·her·ent (in hēr′ənt or in her′ənt) *adj.* existing; abiding; belonging to (a person or thing) as a quality or attribute: *In spite of flattery, she kept her inherent modesty.* [< L *inhaerens, -entis,* ppr. of *inhaerere.* See INHERE.]

in·her·ent·ly (in hēr′ənt lē or in her′ənt lē) *adv.* by its own nature; essentially.

in·her·it (in her′it) *v.* **1** receive as an heir: *Mr. Jones's widow inherited the farm.* **2** succeed as an heir to property, a right, title, privilege, etc.: *When the old bachelor dies, his nephew will inherit.* **3** get or possess from one's ancestors: *Mary inherits her father's blue eyes.* **4** receive (anything) as by succession from predecessors: *When we took the house, we inherited the previous owner's carpets. The new government inherited a financial crisis.* [ME < OF *enheriter* < LL *inhereditare* < L *in-* in, + *heres, -redis* heir]

in·her·it·a·ble (in her′ə tə bəl) *adj.* **1** capable of being inherited. **2** capable of inheriting; qualified to inherit.

in·her·it·ance (in her′ə təns) *n.* **1** the act of inheriting: *He obtained his house by inheritance from an aunt.* **2** the right of inheriting. **3** anything inherited: *Good health is a fine inheritance.* —**Syn. 3** heritage, legacy.

inheritance tax a tax on inherited property; succession duty.

in·her·i·tor (in her′ə tər) *n.* one who inherits; heir.

in·hib·it (in hib′it) *v.* **1** check; restrain; hinder by obstruction or restriction: *The soldier's sense of duty inhibited his impulse to run away.* **2** prohibit; forbid. [< L *inhibitus,* pp. of *inhibere* < *in-* in + *habere* hold] —**Syn. 1** repress, stop. **2** interdict.

in·hi·bi·tion (in′ə bish′ən or in′hi bish′ən) *n.* **1** the act of inhibiting. **2** the state of being inhibited. **3** an idea, emotion, attitude, habit, or other inner force that restrains natural impulses.

hat, āge, cãre, fär; let, ēqual, tėrm; it, īce
hot, ōpen, ôrder; oil, out; cup, pu̇t, rüle, ūse
əbove, takən, pencəl, lemən, circəs
ch, child; ng, long; sh, ship
th, thin; ᴛʜ, then; zh, measure

in·hib·i·tive (in hib′ə tiv) *adj.* inhibitory.

in·hib·i·tor (in hib′ə tər) *n.* **1** a person or thing that inhibits. **2** in chemistry, anything that checks or interferes with a chemical reaction: *Antifreeze is an inhibitor.*

in·hib·i·to·ry (in hib′ə tô′rē) *adj.* inhibiting; tending to inhibit.

in·hos·pi·ta·ble (in hos′pi tə bəl or in′hos pit′ə bəl) *adj.* **1** not hospitable. **2** providing no shelter; barren: *The colonists encountered a rocky, inhospitable shore.* —**in·hos′pi·ta·ble·ness,** *n.* —**in·hos′pi·ta·bly,** *adv.* —**Syn. 2** cheerless, uninviting.

in·hos·pi·tal·i·ty (in hos′pə tal′ə tē) *n.* a lack of hospitality; inhospitable behavior.

in·hu·man (in hū′mən) *adj.* **1** unfeeling; hard-hearted; brutal; cruel. **2** not human; not having the qualities natural to a human being. [ME < MF *inhumain* < L *inhumanus* < *in-* not + *humanus* human; later influenced in spelling by L *inhumanus*] —**in·hu′man·ly,** *adv.* —**Syn. 1** pitiless, merciless.

in·hu·mane (in′hū mān′) *adj.* not humane; lacking in compassion, humanity, or kindness. —**in′hu·mane′ly,** *adv.* —**Syn.** cruel, brutal.

in·hu·man·i·ty (in′hū man′ə tē) *n.* **-ties. 1** an inhuman quality; lack of feeling; cruelty; brutality. **2** an inhuman, cruel, or brutal act.

in·im·i·cal (in im′ə kəl) *adj.* **1** unfriendly; hostile. **2** adverse; unfavorable; harmful: *Lack of ambition is inimical to success.* [< LL *inimicalis* < L *inimicus* < *in-* not + *amicus* friendly] —**in·im′i·cal·ly,** *adv.* —**Syn. 1** antagonistic. See **hostile.**

in·im·i·ta·bil·i·ty (in im′ə tə bil′ə tē) *n.* the fact or quality of being inimitable.

in·im·i·ta·ble (in im′ə tə bəl) *adj.* that cannot be imitated or copied; matchless. —**in·im′i·ta·bly,** *adv.*

in·iq·ui·tous (in ik′wə təs) *adj.* very unjust; wicked. —**in·iq′ui·tous·ly,** *adv.* —**in·iq′ui·tous·ness,** *n.*

in·iq·ui·ty (in ik′wə tē) *n.* **-ties. 1** very great injustice; wickedness. **2** a wicked or unjust act. [< L *iniquitas* < *iniquus* < *in-* not + *aequus* just]

i·ni·tial (i nish′əl) *adj. n. v.* **-tialled** or **-tialed, -tial·ling** or **-tial·ing.** —*adj.* occurring at the beginning; first; earliest.
—*n.* **1** the first letter of a word or name. **2** an extra large letter, often decorated, at the beginning of a chapter or other division of a book or illuminated manuscript. **3 initials,** the first letters of one's surname and one or more given names used instead of one's signature.
—*v.* mark or sign with initials: *John Allen Smith initialled the note J.A.S.* [< L *initialis* < *initium* beginning < *inire* begin < *in* -in + *ire* go]

i·ni·tial·ly (i nish′əl ē) *adv.* at the beginning.

i·ni·ti·ate (*v.* i nish′ē āt′; *n. adj.* i nish′ē it or i nish′ē āt′) *v.* **-at·ed, -at·ing,** *n. adj.* —*v.* **1** be the first one to start; begin. **2** admit (a person) by special forms or ceremonies (into mysteries, secret knowledge, or a society). **3** introduce into the knowledge of some art or subject: *His uncle initiated him into modern business methods.*
—*n.* a person who is initiated.
—*adj.* initiated. [< L *initiare* < *initium* beginning < *inire* begin. See INITIAL.] —**i·ni′ti·a′tor,** *n.* —**Syn.** *v.* **1** commence, originate. **2** install, induct.

i·ni·ti·a·tion (i nish′ē ā′shən) *n.* **1** an initiating. **2** a being initiated. **3** a formal admission into a group or society. **4** the ceremonies by which one is admitted to a group or society.

i·ni·ti·a·tive (i nish′ē ə tiv, i nish′ə tiv or i nish′ē ā′tiv) *n.* **1** the active part in taking the first steps in any undertaking; the lead: *A shy person does not like to take the initiative in making acquaintances.* **2** the readiness and ability to be the one to start a course of action: *A leader must have initiative.* **3** the right to be the first to act, legislate, etc.

i·ni·ti·a·to·ry (i nish′ē ə tô′rē) *adj.* **1** first; beginning; introductory. **2** of initiation.

in·ject (in jekt′) *v.* **1** force (liquid) into a passage, cavity, or tissue: *inject a drug into the body.* **2** fill (a cavity, etc.) with fluid forced in. **3** throw in: *The stranger injected a remark into our conversation.* [< L *injectus,* pp. of *inicere* < *in-* in + *jacere* throw] **—in·jec′tor,** *n.*

in·jec·tion (in jek′shən) *n.* **1** the act or process of injecting: *Drugs are given by injection as well as through the mouth.* **2** the liquid injected.

in·ju·di·cious (in′jü dish′əs) *adj.* showing lack of judgment; unwise; not prudent. **—in′ju·di′cious·ly,** *adv.* **—in′ju·di′cious·ness,** *n.* **—Syn.** indiscreet.

in·junc·tion (in jungk′shən) *n.* **1** a command; order: *Injunctions of secrecy did not prevent the news from leaking out.* **2** in law, a formal order issued by a court or judge ordering a person or group to refrain from doing something; a prohibition. **3** the act of commanding or authoritatively directing. [< LL *injunctio, -onis* < L *injungere* enjoin < *in-* in + *jungere* join. Related to ENJOIN.]

in·jure (in′jər) *v.* **-jured, -jur·ing. 1** do damage to; harm; hurt: *Do not break or injure the bushes in the park.* **2** be unfair to; do wrong to. [< *injury*]

Syn. 1 Injure, hurt, impair = do harm or damage to someone or something. **Injure** is a general word meaning "to do something that harms, reduces, or takes away strength, health, perfection, rights, value, usefulness, etc.": *Dishonesty injures a business.* **Hurt,** a less formal substitute for *injure,* particularly means "to cause physical injury to a person or thing, or bodily or mental pain": *He hurt my hand by twisting it.* **Impair** = injure by weakening, diminishing, or decreasing strength or value: *Poor eating habits impair health.*

in·ju·ri·ous (in jür′ē əs) *adj.* **1** causing injury; harmful: *Hail is injurious to crops.* **2** unfair; unjust; wrongful. **—in·ju′ri·ous·ly,** *adv.* **—in·ju′ri·ous·ness,** *n.*

in·ju·ry (in′jər ē) *n.* **-ju·ries. 1** damage; harm; hurt: *She escaped from the train wreck without injury.* **2** a wound; hurt: *He received a serious injury in the accident.* **3** an act that harms or damages: *The accident will certainly be an injury to the reputation of the airline.* [< L *injuria* < *in-* not + *jus, juris* right]

in·jus·tice (in jus′tis) *n.* **1** a lack of justice; a being unjust. **2** an unjust act: *To send an innocent man to jail is an injustice.*

ink (ingk) *n.* **1** a colored substance, usually liquid, used for writing or printing. **2** a dark liquid thrown out for protection by cuttlefish, squids, etc. *—v.* put ink on; mark or stain with ink. [ME < OF *enque* < LL < Gk. *enkauston* < *en* in + *kaiein* burn] **—ink′er,** *n.* **—ink′like′,** *adj.*

ink·horn (ingk′hôrn′) *n. Archaic.* a small container formerly used to hold ink, often made of horn.

ink·ling (ingk′ling) *n.* a slight suggestion; vague notion; hint. [ME *inclen* whisper, hint < OE *inca* doubt]

ink·stand (ingk′stand′) *n.* **1** a stand to hold ink and pens. **2** a container used to hold ink.

ink·well (ingk′wel′) *n.* a container used to hold ink on a desk or table.

ink·y (ingk′ē) *adj.* **ink·i·er, ink·i·est. 1** like ink; dark; black. **2** covered with ink; marked or stained with ink. **3** of ink. **—ink′i·ly,** *adv.* **—ink′i·ness,** *n.*

in·laid (in′lād′) *adj.* **1** set in the surface as a decoration or design: *The desk had an inlaid design of light wood in dark.* **2** decorated with a design or material set in the surface: *The box had an inlaid cover.* *—v.* pt. and pp. of **inlay.**

in·land (*adj.* in′lənd; *n. adv.* in′land′ or in′lənd) *adj.* **1** away from the coast or the border; situated in the interior: *an inland sea.* **2** domestic; not foreign: *inland trade.* *—n.* the interior of a country; land away from the border or the coast. *—adv.* in or toward the interior.

inland boat *Cdn.* formerly, a York boat.

in-law (in′lo′ or -lô′) *n. Informal.* a relative by marriage.

in·lay (in′lā′) *v.* **-laid, -lay·ing,** *n.* *—v.* **1** set in the surface as a decoration or design: *inlay strips of gold.* **2** decorate with something set in the surface: *inlay a wooden box with silver.* **3** in horticulture, insert (a scion) into a slit in the bark of a stock.
—n. **1** an inlaid decoration, design, or material. **2** a shaped piece of gold, porcelain, etc. cemented in a tooth as a filling. **3** a graft made by inlaying. **—in′lay′er,** *n.*

in·let (in′let′ or in′lət) *n.* **1** a narrow strip of water extending from a larger body of water into the land or between islands. **2** an entrance.

in lo·co pa·ren·tis (in lō′kō pə ren′tis) *Latin.* in the place of a parent; as a parent.

in·ly (in′lē) *adv. Poetic.* **1** inwardly; within. **2** thoroughly; deeply. [OE *inlīce*]

in·mate (in′māt′) *n.* **1** a person confined in a prison, asylum, hospital, etc. **2** an occupant; inhabitant. [< *in-*[3] + *mate*[1]]

in me·di·as res (in me′dē as′rāz′) *Latin.* into the midst of things.

in me·mo·ri·am (in′mə mô′rē əm) *Latin.* in memory (of); to the memory (of).

in·most (in′mōst′) *adj.* **1** farthest in; deepest within: *We went to the inmost depths of the mine.* **2** most private; most secret: *Her inmost desire was to be an actress.* [OE *innemest,* double superlative of *inne* within; influenced by *most*]

inn (in) *n.* **1** a public house for lodging and caring for travellers: *Many old inns in England are still flourishing.* **2** a hotel. **3** a tavern. [OE *inn* lodging]

in·nards (in′ərdz) *n.pl. Informal.* **1** the internal organs of the body; insides; viscera. **2** the internal workings or parts of any complex mechanism, structure, etc. [var. of *inwards*]

in·nate (i nāt′ or in′āt) *adj.* natural; inborn: *an innate talent for drawing.* [< L *innatus* < *in-* in + *nasci* be born] **—in·nate′ly,** *adv.* **—in·nate′ness,** *n.*

in·ner (in′ər) *adj.* **1** farther in; inside: *an inner room.* **2** more private; more secret: *She kept her inner thoughts to herself.* **3** of the mind or soul: *a person's inner life.* [OE *innera,* comparative of *inne* within]

inner ear the cavity behind the three bones of the middle ear. In human beings it contains the semicircular canals, the cochlea, and part of the auditory nerve.

in·ner·most (in′ər mōst′) *adj.* farthest in; inmost: *the innermost parts.*

inner tube the circular rubber tube that holds the air inside a bicycle tire and inside some automobile tires.

in·ning (in′ing) *n.* **1** in baseball, the time when each team is at bat. **2** in certain other games, the turn of one side. **3** a chance to play. **4** the time a person or party is in power; chance for action: *After winning the election, the Conservatives had their inning.* [OE *innung* a taking in]

in·nings (in′ingz) *n.* **1** pl. of **inning. 2** in cricket, an inning.

inn·keep·er (in′kēp′ər) *n.* a person who owns, manages, or keeps an inn.

in·no·cence (in′ə səns) *n.* **1** freedom from sin, wrong, or guilt: *The accused man proved his innocence of the crime.* **2** simplicity: *the innocence of a little child.* **3** a tiny, blue flower; bluet.

in·no·cen·cy (in′ə sən sē) *n.* innocence.

in·no·cent (in′ə sənt) *adj.* **1** doing no wrong; free from sin or wrong; not guilty. **2** without knowledge of evil: *A baby is innocent.* **3** without evil effects; harmless: *innocent amusements.* **4** simple; artless. **5** lacking; devoid (*of*). **6** spotless, stainless.
—n. **1** an innocent person. **2** an idiot; fool. [< L *innocens, -entis* < *in-* not + *nocere* harm]
—in′no·cent·ly, *adv.*

Syn. *adj.* **1 Innocent, blameless, guiltless** = free from fault or wrong. **Innocent** emphasizes having intended or consciously done no wrong, having broken no moral, social, or statute law: *The truck driver was proved innocent of manslaughter.* **Blameless** = not to blame, not to be held responsible or punished, whether or not wrong has actually been done: *He was held blameless, although the child was killed.* **Guiltless** = without guilt in thought, intention, or act: *The other driver was not guiltless.* **4** naïve, guileless.

in·noc·u·ous (i nok′ū əs) *adj.* harmless; not injurious. [< L *innocuus* < *in-* not + *nocuus* hurtful < *nocere* to harm] **—in·noc′u·ous·ly,** *adv.*

in·no·vate (in′ə vāt′) *v.* **-vat·ed, -vat·ing.** make changes; bring in something new or new ways of doing things. [< L *innovare* < *in-* in + *novus* new]

in·no·va·tion (in′ə vā′shən) *n.* **1** a change made in the established way of doing things. **2** the making of changes; introduction of new things or of new ways of doing things.

in·no·va·tor (in′ə vā′tər) *n.* a person who makes changes or introduces new methods.

in·nu·en·do (in′ū en′dō) *n.* **-does. 1** an indirect hint or reference. **2** an indirect suggestion against somebody: *spread scandal by innuendo.* [< L *innuendo,* literally, by giving a nod to, ablative gerund of *innuere* < *in-* in + *-nuere* nod] **—Syn. 1** insinuation.

In·nu·it (in′ū it, in′ū it, or in′yə wit) *Cdn. n. pl.* Inuit.

in·nu·mer·a·ble (i nū′mər ə bəl or i nü′mər ə bəl) *adj.* too many to count; very many. **—in·nu′mer·a·ble·ness,** *n.* **—Syn.** countless, myriad. See **many.**

in·nu·mer·a·bly (i nū′mər ə blē or i nü′mər ə blē) *adv.* countlessly; in very great numbers.

in·oc·u·late (in ok′yů lāt′) *v.* **-lat·ed, -lat·ing. 1** infect (a person or animal) with organisms that will cause a very mild form of a disease, thus reducing the individual's chances of contracting the disease thereafter. **2** use disease-producing organisms to prevent or cure diseases. **3** put bacteria, serums, etc. into. Farmers inoculate the soil with bacteria that will take nitrogen from the air and change it so that it can be used by plants. **4** fill (a person's mind) with ideas, opinions, etc. [< L *inoculare* engraft < *in-* in + *oculus* bud, eye] **—in·oc′u·la′tor,** *n.*

in·oc·u·la·tion (in ok′yů lā′shən) *n.* an inoculating: *Inoculation has greatly reduced the number of deaths from diphtheria and typhoid fever.*

in·of·fen·sive (in′ə fen′siv) *adj.* not offensive; harmless; not arousing objections. **—in′of·fen′sive·ly,** *adv.* **—in′of·fen′sive·ness,** *n.*

in·op·er·a·ble (in op′ər ə bəl) *adj.* **1** unable to be cured by surgery: *an inoperable cancer.* **2** not operable; unworkable.

in·op·er·a·tive (in op′rə tiv or in op′ər ā′tiv) *adj.* not operative; not working; without effect.

in·op·por·tune (in op′ər tūn′ or in op′ər tün′) *adj.* not opportune; coming at a bad time; unsuitable: *An inopportune call delayed us.* **—in·op′por·tune′ly,** *adv.* **—in·op′por·tune′ness,** *n.* **—Syn.** untimely, unseasonable.

in·or·di·nate (in ôr′də nit) *adj.* much too great; excessive; unrestrained. [< L *inordinatus* < *in-* not + *ordo, -dinis* order] **—Syn.** See **excessive.**

in·or·di·nate·ly (in ôr′də nit lē) *adv.* excessively.

in·or·gan·ic (in′ôr gan′ik) *adj.* **1** not having the organized physical structure of animals and plants: *Minerals are inorganic.* **2** not produced by animal or plant activities. **3** not characterized by the processes peculiar to living animals and plants. **4** not belonging to the constitution or structure of a thing; not fundamental; extraneous. **—in′or·gan′i·cal·ly,** *adv.*

inorganic chemistry the branch of chemistry dealing with inorganic compounds and elements, primarily compounds not containing carbon.

in·put (in′půt′) *n.* **1** what is put in or taken in. **2** the power supplied to a machine. **3** information put into the storage unit of a computer.

in·quest (in′kwest) *n.* **1** a legal inquiry led by a coroner, usually with a jury, to determine the cause of a sudden death when there is a possibility that the death was the result of a crime or of a situation that could be dangerous to others. **2** a jury appointed to hold such an inquiry: *The inquest was told that one of the witnesses had been delayed.* **3** any investigation into the cause of an event, situation, etc. [ME < OF *enqueste,* ult. < L *inquirere.* See INQUIRE.]

in·qui·e·tude (in kwī′ə tūd′ or in kwī′ə tüd′) *n.* restlessness; uneasiness.

in·quire (in kwīr′) *v.* **-quired, -quir·ing. 1** try to find out by questions; ask. **2** make a search for information, knowledge, or truth; make an examination of facts or principles. Also, **enquire.** [< L *inquirere* < *in-* into + *quaerere* ask] **—in·quir′er,** *n.* **—in·quir′ing·ly,** *adv.* **—Syn. 1** See **ask.**

in·quir·y (in kwīr′ē or in′kwə rē) *n.* **-quir·ies. 1** an inquiring; an asking. **2** a question. **3** a search for information, knowledge, or truth; an examination of facts or principles. Also, **enquiry. —Syn. 3** See **investigation.**

hat, āge, cãre, fär; let, ēqual, tėrm; it, īce
hot, ōpen, ôrder; oil, out; cup, pů t, rüle, ūse
əbove, takən, pencəl, lemən, circəs
ch, child; ng, long; sh, ship
th, thin; ꟻH, then; zh, measure

in·qui·si·tion (in′kwə zish′ən) *n.* **1** a thorough investigation; searching inquiry. **2** an official investigation, a judicial inquiry. **3 the Inquisition, a** a court established by the Roman Catholic Church in 1229 to discover and suppress heresy and to punish heretics. During the 15th and 16th centuries, the powers of the Inquisition were tremendously enlarged, especially in Spain, Portugal, and parts of Italy. It was abolished in 1834. **b** the activities of this court. [< L *inquisitio, -onis* < *inquirere.* See INQUIRE.]

in·quis·i·tive (in kwiz′ə tiv) *adj.* **1** curious; asking many questions. **2** too curious; prying into other people's affairs. **—in·quis′i·tive·ly,** *adv.* **—in·quis′i·tive·ness,** *n.* **—Syn. 1** See **curious.**

in·quis·i·tor (in kwiz′ə tər) *n.* **1** a person who makes an inquisition; official investigator; judicial inquirer. **2 Inquisitor,** a member of the Inquisition.

in·quis·i·to·ri·al (in kwiz′ə tô′rē əl) *adj.* **1** of an inquisitor or inquisition. **2** making searching inquiry; thorough. **3** unduly curious.

in re (in rē′ or in rā′) *Latin.* concerning; in the matter of.

I.N.R.I. Jesus of Nazareth, King of the Jews. (for L *Iesus Nazarenus, Rex Iudaeorum*)

in·road (in′rōd′) *n.* **1** an attack; raid. **2** a forcible encroachment: *The expenses of her illness made inroads upon the money that she had saved.*

in·rush (in′rush′) *n.* a rushing in; inflow.

ins. 1 inches. **2** insurance. **3** insulated. **4** inspected.

in·sane (in sān′) *adj.* **1** not sane; mentally deranged; crazy. **2** in law, mentally unsound, temporarily or permanently, so as to be considered not competent or not responsible for one's actions. **3** for insane people: *an insane asylum.* **4** extremely foolish; completely lacking in common sense. **—in·sane′ly,** *adv.* **—Syn. 1** demented, lunatic, mad. See **crazy. 3** senseless, wild.

in·san·i·tar·y (in san′ə ter′ē) *adj.* unhealthful. **—in·san′i·tar′i·ness,** *n.*

in·san·i·ty (in san′ə tē) *n.* **-ties. 1** the state of being insane; madness; mental disease. **2** in law, any state of mental unsoundness, temporary or permanent, in which a person is not considered competent or held responsible for his actions. **3** extreme folly.

in·sa·tia·ble (in sā′shə bəl) *adj.* that cannot be satisfied; extremely greedy. **—in·sa′tia·bly,** *adv.* **—Syn** unquenchable.

in·sa·ti·ate (in sā′shē it) *adj.* never satisfied: *an insatiate desire for praise.* **—in·sa′ti·ate·ly,** *adv.* **—in·sa′ti·ate·ness,** *n.*

in·scribe (in skrīb′) *v.* **-scribed, -scrib·ing. 1** write, engrave, or mark (words, letters, etc.) on paper, metal, stone, etc. **2** mark or engrave (with words, letters, etc.): *His tombstone was inscribed with his name and the date of his death.* **3** address or dedicate (a book, etc.) informally to a person. **4** impress deeply: *My father's words are inscribed in my memory.* **5** put in a list; enrol. **6** in geometry, draw (one figure) within another figure so that the inner touches the outer at as many points as possible. [< L *inscribere* < *in-* on + *scribere* write] **—in·scrib′er,** *n.*

in·scrip·tion (in skrip′shən) *n.* **1** something inscribed; words, letters, etc. written or engraved on stone, metal, paper, etc. A monument or a coin has an inscription on it. **2** an informal dedication in a book, on a picture, etc. **3** the act of inscribing. [< L *inscriptio, -onis* < *inscribere.* See INSCRIBE.]

in·scru·ta·bil·i·ty (in skrü′tə bil′ə tē) *n.* **1** the quality of being inscrutable. **2** something inscrutable.

in·scru·ta·ble (in skrü′tə bəl) *adj.* that cannot be

understood; so mysterious or obscure that one cannot make out its meaning; incomprehensible. [< LL *inscrutabilis* < L *in-* not + *scrutari* examine, ransack < *scruta* trash] —**in·scru′ta·bly,** *adv.* —**Syn.** unfathomable, impenetrable. See **mysterious.**

in·sect (in′sekt) *n.* **1** any of a group of small invertebrate animals having the body divided into three parts (head, thorax, and abdomen), having three pairs of legs and, usually, two pairs of wings. Flies, mosquitoes, grasshoppers, and beetles are insects. See **abdomen** for picture. **2** any similar small animal with its body divided into several parts, having several pairs of legs. Spiders, centipedes, mites, and ticks are often called insects. **3** an insignificant or despicable person. [< L *insectum*, literally, divided, neut. pp. of *insecare* < *in-* into + *secare* cut]

insect bomb a bomb (def. 2) containing insecticide.

in·sec·ti·cide (in sek′tə sīd′) *n.* a substance for killing insects. [< L *insectum* + E *-cide*[2]]

in·sec·ti·vore (in sek′tə vôr′) *n.* **1** any animal or plant that feeds mainly on insects. **2** any of a group of small insect-eating mammals, including moles and hedgehogs. [< F < NL *insectivorus*. See INSECTIVOROUS.]

in·sec·tiv·o·rous (in′sek tiv′ə rəs) *adj.* **1** insect-eating; feeding mainly on insects. **2** of or belonging to the insectivores. [< NL *insectivorus* < L *insectum* insect + *vorare* devour; formed on the pattern of L *carnivorus* meat-eating]

in·se·cure (in′si kūr′) *adj.* **1** not secure; unsafe. **2** liable to give way; not firm: *an insecure lock.* **3** not well-adjusted; not sure of oneself: *an insecure person.* —**in′se·cure′ly,** *adv.* —**Syn. 1** See **uncertain.**

in·se·cu·ri·ty (in′si kūr′ə tē) *n.* **-ties. 1** lack of security; the state of being insecure; an unsafe condition. **2** something insecure.

in·sem·i·nate (in sem′ə nāt′) *v.* **-nat·ed, -nat·ing. 1** inject semen into; fertilize; impregnate. **2** sow; implant seeds into. **3** instil (ideas or opinions). [< L *inseminare* (with E *-ate*[1]) < *in-* not + *seminare* to sow < *semen, -inis* seed] —**in·sem′i·na′tion,** *n.* —**in·sem′i·na′tor,** *n.*

in·sen·sate (in sen′sāt or in sen′sit) *adj.* **1** without sensation. **2** unfeeling: *insensate cruelty.* **3** senseless; stupid: *insensate folly.* —**in·sen′sate·ly,** *adv.* —**in·sen′sate·ness,** *n.*

in·sen·si·bil·i·ty (in sen′sə bil′ə tē) *n.* **-ties. 1** lack of feeling. **2** lack of consciousness.

in·sen·si·ble (in sen′sə bəl) *adj.* **1** not sensitive; not able to feel or observe: *A blind man is insensible to colors.* **2** not aware: *The boys in the boat were insensible of their danger.* **3** not able to feel anything; unconscious: *The man hit by the truck was insensible for four hours.* **4** not easily felt or realized: *The room grew cold by insensible degrees.*

in·sen·si·bly (in sen′sə blē) *adv.* by imperceptible degrees; little by little.

in·sen·si·tive (in sen′sə tiv) *adj.* **1** not sensitive; having little or no power to feel or notice. **2** slow to feel or notice. —**in·sen′si·tive·ly,** *adv.* —**in·sen′si·tive·ness,** *n.*

in·sen·si·tiv·i·ty (in sen′sə tiv′ə tē) *n.* lack of sensitivity.

in·sen·ti·ent (in sen′shē ənt or in sen′shənt) *adj.* unable to feel; lifeless.

in·sep·a·ra·bil·i·ty (in sep′ə rə bil′ə tē or in sep′rə bil′ə tē) *n.* the state of being inseparable.

in·sep·a·ra·ble (in sep′ə rə bəl or in sep′rə bəl) *adj.* that cannot be separated. —*n.* **inseparables,** *pl.* inseparable persons or things. —**in·sep′a·ra·bly,** *adv.*

in·sert (*v.* in sėrt′; *n.* in′sėrt) *v.* put in; set in: *insert a key into a lock; insert a letter into a word.* —*n.* something set in or to be set in: *The newspaper had an insert of several pages of pictures.* [< L *insertus*, pp. of *inserere* < *in-* in + *serere* entwine]

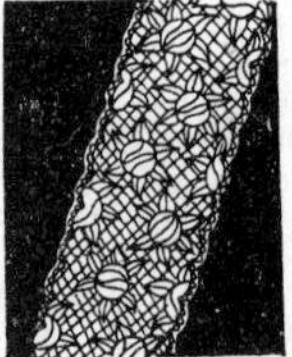
An insertion (def. 3) of lace

in·ser·tion (in sėr′shən) *n.* **1** an inserting. **2** the thing inserted. **3** a band of lace, embroidery, etc. to be sewed at each edge between parts of other material.

in·serv·ice (in′sėr′vis) *adj.* of or having to do with a program for the training of employees: *in-service courses for civil servants.*

in·set (*v.* in set′ or in′set′; *n.* in′set′) *v.* **-set, -set·ting,** *n.* —*v.* set in; insert. —*n.* **1** something inserted. **2** a small map, picture, etc. set within the border of a larger one. **3** an influx; inflow.

in·shore (in′shôr′) *adj.* **1** near the shore. **2** done or working near the shore: *the inshore fishermen of Newfoundland.* —*adv.* in toward the shore.

in·side (*n. adj.* in′sīd′; *adv. prep.* in′sīd′) *n.* **1** the side or surface that is within; inner part; contents: *the inside of a house.* **2** Often, **insides,** *pl. Informal.* the parts inside the body, especially the stomach and bowels. **3** *Informal.* those who are in a position to know about something or who are in a position of authority.
—*adj.* **1** being on the inside: *an inside seat.* **2** of or used for the inside: *an inside paint.* **3** *Slang.* **a** done or known by those inside; private; secret: *The police thought that the theft was an inside job and suspected the maid.* **b** working within a group or company as an emissary or spy: *an inside man.* **4** indoor. **5** that is nearer the centre of a curve: *the inside skate.* **6** in baseball: **a** of a pitch, close to the batter and missing the strike zone. **b** of a part of the home plate, on the same side as the batter.
—*adv.* **1** indoors: *go inside.* **2 inside out,** so that what should be inside is outside; with the inside showing.
—*prep.* in; within the limits of.
—**Syn.** *adj.* **1** internal, interior.
☛ **Inside of** is a doubling of prepositions common in informal expressions of time: *He'll be back inside of an hour.* The more formal idiom is *within: He will return within an hour.*

in·sid·er (in′sīd′ər) *n.* **1** a person who is inside some place, society, organization, etc. **2** *Informal.* a person who is so situated as to understand the actual conditions or facts of a case.

inside track 1 on a race track, the lane nearest the inside of the curve, and so the shortest way round. **2** *Informal.* an advantageous position or situation.

in·sid·i·ous (in sid′ē əs) *adj.* **1** wily; sly; crafty; tricky; treacherous. **2** working secretly or subtly: *an insidious disease.* [< L *insidiosus* < *insidiae* ambush < *insidere* < *in-* in + *sedere* sit] —**in·sid′i·ous·ly,** *adv.* —**in·sid′i·ous·ness,** *n.* —**Syn. 1** cunning.

in·sight (in′sīt′) *n.* **1** a viewing of the inside or inner parts (of something) with understanding. **2** wisdom and understanding in dealing with people or with facts. **3** in psychology: **a** the relatively sudden awareness of a solution to a problem. **b** understanding of oneself.
Syn. 2 Insight, discernment, penetration = ability to understand people or things. **Insight** suggests both the power to see deeply into the inner workings of things and of people's minds and feelings and the ability to understand them: *Good teachers have insight into the problems of their students.* **Discernment** = the ability to see below the surface clearly and sharply and to judge accurately: *In selecting employees he shows discernment.* **Penetration** emphasizes going deeply into things and seeing fine distinctions and relations: *Solving the mystery required penetration.*

in·sig·ni·a (in sig′nē ə) *n.pl.* **1** the emblems, badges, or other distinguishing marks of a high position, honor, etc.: *The crown, orb, and sceptre are the insignia of kings.* **2** the distinguishing badges, crests, etc. of a regiment, corps, or any other unit or branch of the armed services. [< L *insignia*, pl. of *insigne* badge < *in-* on + *signum* mark. Doublet of ENSIGN.]

in·sig·nif·i·cance (in′sig nif′ə kəns) *n.* **1** unimportance. **2** meaninglessness.

in·sig·nif·i·cant (in′sig nif′ə kənt) *adj.* **1** having little use or importance. **2** meaningless. —**in′sig·nif′i·cant·ly,** *adv.* —**Syn. 1** petty, trifling.

in·sin·cere (in′sin sēr′) *adj.* not sincere; not honest or candid; deceitful. —**in′sin·cere′ly,** *adv.* —**Syn.** hypocritical, dissembling, false.

in·sin·cer·i·ty (in′sin ser′ə tē) *n.* **-ties.** a lack of sincerity; hypocrisy.

in·sin·u·ate (in sin′ū āt′) *v.* **-at·ed, -at·ing. 1** suggest indirectly; hint: *To say "Fred can't do it; no coward can" is to insinuate that Fred is a coward.* **2** push in or get in by an indirect, twisting way: *The spy insinuated himself into the confidence of important army officers.* [< L *insinuare* < *in-* in + *sinus* a curve, winding] —**in·sin′u·a′tor,** *n.* —**Syn. 1** See **hint.**

in·sin·u·a·tion (in sin′ū ā′shən) *n.* **1** an insinuating. **2** an indirect suggestion against someone. **3** a hint;

suggestion. 4 an act or speech to gain favor.

in·sip·id (in sip′id) *adj.* 1 without much taste: *A mixture of milk and water is an insipid drink.* 2 dull; uninteresting; colorless; weak. [< LL *insipidus* < L *in-* not + *sapidus* tasty] **—in·sip′id·ly,** *adv.* **—in·sip′id·ness,** *n.* **—Syn.** 1 flat. 2 stupid, vapid.

in·si·pid·i·ty (in′sə pid′ə tē) *n.* **-ties.** 1 a lack of flavor; lack of interest. 2 something insipid.

in·sist (in sist′) *v.* keep firmly to some demand, some statement, or some position: *He insisted on following his own plan.* [< L *insistere* < *in-* on + *sistere* take a stand] **—Syn.** urge, persist, press.

in·sist·ence (in sis′təns) *n.* 1 the act of insisting. 2 the quality of being insistent.

in·sist·en·cy (in sis′tən sē) *n.* insistence.

in·sist·ent (in sis′tənt) *adj.* 1 insisting; continuing to make a strong, firm demand or statement: *In spite of the rain, he was insistent on going out.* 2 compelling attention or notice; pressing; urgent. **—in·sist′ent·ly,** *adv.*

in si·tu (in sī′tū or sē′tü) *Latin.* in its original place; in position.

in·snare (in snãr′) *v.* **-snared, -snar·ing.** ensnare.

in·so·bri·e·ty (in′sə brī′ə tē) *n.* intemperance; drunkenness.

in so far or **in·so·far** (in′sō fär′) *adv.* to such an extent, or degree (usually with *as*): *In so far as we can ascertain, the Prime Minister will not call an election.*

in·sole (in′sōl′) *n.* 1 the inner sole of a shoe or boot. 2 a shaped piece of warm or waterproof material laid on the sole inside a shoe or boot.

in·so·lence (in′sə ləns) *n.* bold rudeness; insulting behavior or speech.

in·so·lent (in′sə lənt) *adj.* boldly rude; insulting. [< L *insolens, -entis* originally, unusual < *in-* not + *solere* be wont] **—in′so·lent·ly,** *adv.* **—Syn.** arrogant, impudent.

in·sol·u·bil·i·ty (in sol′yu̇ bil′ə tē) *n.* a being insoluble.

in·sol·u·ble (in sol′yu̇ bəl) *adj.* 1 that cannot be dissolved: *Diamonds are insoluble.* 2 that cannot be solved: *an insoluble mystery.* **—in·sol′u·bly,** *adv.*

in·solv·a·ble (in sol′və bəl) *adj.* that cannot be solved.

in·sol·ven·cy (in sol′vən sē) *n.* **-cies.** the condition of not being able to pay one's debts; bankruptcy.

in·sol·vent (in sol′vənt) *adj.* 1 not able to pay one's debts; bankrupt. 2 of or having to do with bankrupt persons or bankruptcy. *—n.* an insolvent person.

in·som·ni·a (in som′nē ə) *n.* the inability to sleep; sleeplessness. [< L *insomnia* < *in-* not + *somnus* sleep]

in·so·much (in′sō much′) *adv.* to such an extent or degree; so.

in·sou·ci·ance (in sü′sē əns) *n.* freedom from care or anxiety; a carefree feeling.

in·sou·ci·ant (in sü′sē ənt) *adj.* free from care or anxiety. [< F *insouciant* < *in-* not (< L *in-*) + *souciant,* ppr. of *soucier* care, ult. < L *sollicitus* solicitous]

insp. 1 inspected. 2 inspector.

in·spect (in spekt′) *v.* 1 look over carefully; examine: *A dentist inspects the children's teeth twice a year.* 2 examine officially: *All factories and mines are inspected by government officials.* [< L *inspectus,* pp. of *inspicere* < *in-* upon + *specere* look]

in·spec·tion (in spek′shən) *n.* 1 an inspecting: *An inspection of the roof showed no leaks.* 2 a formal or official examination: *The soldiers lined up for their daily inspection by their officers.*

in·spec·tor (in spek′tər) *n.* 1 a person who inspects. 2 an officer appointed to inspect. 3 a police officer ranking next below a superintendent. [< L]

in·spi·ra·tion (in′spə rā′shən) *n.* 1 the influence of thought and strong feelings on actions, especially on good actions: *Many people get inspiration from nature.* 2 any influence that arouses effort to do well: *The captain was an inspiration to his men.* 3 an idea that is inspired. 4 a suggestion to another; the act of causing something to be told or written by another. 5 in theology, a divine influence directly and immediately exerted upon the mind or soul of man. 6 a breathing in; the drawing of air into the lungs.

in·spi·ra·tion·al (in′spə rā′shən əl or in′spə rāsh′nəl) *adj.* 1 inspiring. 2 inspired. 3 of or having to do with inspiration.

hat, āge, cãre, fär; let, ēqual, tėrm; it, īce
hot, ōpen, ôrder; oil, out; cup, pu̇t, rüle, ūse
əbove, takən, pencəl, lemən, circəs
ch, child; ng, long; sh, ship
th, thin; ᴛʜ, then; zh, measure

in·spire (in spīr′) *v.* **-spired, -spir·ing.** 1 put thought, feeling, life, force, etc. into: *The speaker inspired the crowd.* 2 cause (thought or feeling): *The leader's courage inspired confidence in others.* 3 affect; influence with a thought or feeling: *His sly ways inspire me with distrust.* 4 arouse or influence by a divine force. 5 suggest; cause to be told or written: *His enemies inspired false stories about him.* 6 breathe in; breathe in air. [< L *inspirare* < *in-* in + *spirare* breathe] **—in·spir′er,** *n.* **—in·spir′ing·ly,** *adv.*

in·spir·it (in spir′it) *v.* put spirit into; encourage; hearten. **—Syn.** animate, enliven, cheer.

in·spis·sate (in spis′āt) *v.* **-sat·ed, -sat·ing.** thicken, as by evaporation; condense. [< LL *inspissare* < L *in-* in + *spissus* thick] **—in·spis′sa·tion,** *n.*

inst. *Archaic.* instant. "The 10th inst." means "the tenth day of the present month."

☛ **inst.** Abbreviations such as *inst.* (of the current month) and *ult.* (of last month) are no longer considered good form in business correspondence.

Inst. 1 Institute. 2 Institution.

in·sta·bil·i·ty (in′stə bil′ə tē) *n.* lack of firmness; liability to fall, give way, or change.

in·stall (in stol′ or in stôl′) *v.* 1 place (a person) in office with ceremonies. 2 establish in a place: *The cat installed itself in an easy chair.* 3 put in position for use: *install a telephone.* [< Med.L *installare* < *in-* in (< L) + *stallum* stall[1] (< Gmc.)] **—in·stall′er,** *n.*

in·stal·la·tion (in′stə lā′shən) *n.* 1 an installing or being installed. 2 the thing installed; machinery placed in position for use. 3 a military organization including personnel, equipment, buildings, etc.

in·stal·ment[1] or **in·stall·ment**[1] (in stol′mənt or in stôl′-) *n.* 1 a part of a sum of money or of a debt to be paid at certain regular times: *The furniture cost $100; we paid for it in instalments of $10 a month for ten months.* 2 any of several parts furnished or issued at successive times: *This magazine has a serial story in six instalments.* [alteration of earlier *(e)stallment* < *stall* agree to the payment of (a debt) by instalments < OF *estaler* fix, place < *estal* position < Gmc.]

in·stal·ment[2] or **in·stall·ment**[2] (in stol′mənt or in stôl′-) *n.* an installing or being installed.

instalment plan or **installment plan** a system of paying for goods in instalments.

in·stance (in′stəns) *n. v.* **-stanced, -stanc·ing.** *—n.* 1 an example; case: *His rude question was an instance of bad manners.* 2 a stage or step in an action; occasion: *I went in the first instance because I was asked to go.* 3 a request; suggestion; urging: *He came at our instance.* 4 **for instance,** as an example. *—v.* 1 refer to as an example. 2 exemplify. [ME < OF < L *instantia* insistence < *instans* insistent. See INSTANT.] **—Syn.** *n.* 1 See **case**[1].

in·stant (in′stənt) *n.* 1 a particular moment: *Stop talking this instant!* 2 a moment of time: *He paused for an instant.* 3 **the instant,** just as soon as. *—adj.* 1 immediate; without delay: *The medicine gave instant relief from pain.* 2 pressing; urgent: *When there is a fire, there is an instant need for action.* 3 able to be prepared quickly: *instant coffee.* 4 of the present month; present: *"The 10th instant" means "the tenth day of the present month."* [< L *instans, -antis,* ppr. of *instare* insist, stand near < *in-* in + *stare* stand] **—Syn.** *n.* 2 See **minute.** ☛ See **inst.** for usage note.

in·stan·ta·ne·ous (in′stən tā′nē əs) *adj.* occurring, done, or made in an instant: *an instantaneous photograph.* **—in′stan·ta′ne·ous·ly,** *adv.* **—in′stan·ta′ne·ous·ness,** *n.*

in·stan·ter (in stan′tər) *adv.* at once; immediately. [< L *instanter* insistently < *instans.* See INSTANT.]

in·stant·ly (in′stənt lē) *adv.* in an instant; at once; immediately. —**Syn.** See **immediately.**

in·state (in stāt′) *v.* **-stat·ed, -stat·ing.** put into a certain state, position, or office; install.

in sta·tu quo (in stā′tū kwō′ or in stach′ü kwō′) *Latin.* in the same situation, condition, or state.

in·stead (in sted′) *adv.* **1** in place (*of*): *Instead of studying, she read a book.* **2** in one's or its place: *If you cannot go, let him go instead.* [earlier *in stead* in place]

in·step (in′step) *n.* **1** the upper surface of the human foot between the toes and the ankle. **2** the part of a shoe, stocking, etc. over the instep. **3** the front part of the hind leg of a horse between the hock and the pastern joint.

in·sti·gate (in′stə gāt′) *v.* **-gat·ed, -gat·ing.** urge on; stir up: *Foreign agents instigated a rebellion.* [< L *instigare*] —**Syn.** provoke, foment. See **incite.**

in·sti·ga·tion (in′stə gā′shən) *n.* **1** the act of instigating. **2 at the instigation of,** instigated by.

in·sti·ga·tor (in′stə gā′tər) *n.* a person who instigates; person who stirs up evil or trouble.

in·stil or **in·still** (in stil′) *v.* **-stilled, -still·ing. 1** put in little by little; impart gradually: *Reading good books instils a love for really fine literature.* **2** put in drop by drop. [< L *instillare* < *in-* in + *stilla* a drop] —**in·still′er,** *n.*

in·stil·la·tion (in′stə lā′shən) *n.* **1** an instilling. **2** something instilled.

in·stinct[1] (in′stingkt) *n.* **1** a natural feeling, knowledge, or power, such as guides animals; unlearned tendency: *An instinct leads birds to fly.* **2** a natural bent, tendency, or gift; talent. [< L *instinctus,* n. < *instinctus,* pp. of *instinguere* impel]

in·stinct[2] (in stingkt′) *adj.* charged or filled with something: *The picture is instinct with life and beauty.* [< L *instinctus,* pp. of *instinguere* impel]

in·stinc·tive (in stingk′tiv) *adj.* of or having to do with instinct; caused or done by instinct; born in an animal or person, not learned: *Climbing is instinctive in monkeys.* —**in·stinc′tive·ly,** *adv.* —**Syn.** intuitive, natural, innate.

in·sti·tute (in′stə tūt′ or in′stə tüt′) *v.* **-tut·ed, -tut·ing,** *n.* —*v.* set up; establish; begin: *The police instituted an inquiry into the causes of the accident.*
—*n.* **1** an established principle, law, custom, organization, or society. **2** an organization or society set up for some special purpose. An art institute teaches or displays art. A technical school is often called an institute. **3** a building used by such an organization or society. **4** a short program of instruction for a particular group. [< L *institutus,* pp. of *instituere* < *in-* in + *statuere* establish < *status* position] —**Syn.** *v.* found, organize.

in·sti·tu·tion (in′stə tū′shən or in′stə tü′shən) *n.* **1** an organization or society for some public or social purpose: *A church, school, college, hospital, asylum, or prison is an institution.* **2** a building used by such an organization or society. **3** an established law, custom, organization, or society: *Giving presents on Christmas is an institution.* **4** a setting up; establishing; beginning: *Many people favor the institution of more clubs for young people.* **5** *Informal.* a familiar person or thing.

in·sti·tu·tion·al (in′stə tū′shən əl or in′stə tü′shən əl) *adj.* **1** of or like an institution. **2** promoting reputation and establishing good will for a business rather than aiming at immediate sales: *institutional advertising.* —**in′sti·tu′tion·al·ly,** *adv.*

in·struct (in strukt′) *v.* **1** teach. **2** give directions or orders to; direct; order: *The owner instructed his agent to sell his property.* **3** inform; tell: *My lawyer instructs me that your last payment is due March first.* **4** of a judge, give (the jury) a final explanation of the points of law in a case. **5** of a solicitor, engage the services of (a barrister) on behalf of his client. [< L *instructus,* pp. of *instruere* arrange, furnish, instruct < *in-* on + *struere* to pile] —**Syn. 1** train, educate, tutor, coach. See **teach. 2** command.

in·struc·tion (in struk′shən) *n.* **1** a teaching; knowledge; education. **2** the knowledge or teaching given. **3 instructions,** *pl.* directions; orders.

in·struc·tion·al (in struk′shən əl) *adj.* of or for instruction; educational. —**in·struc′tion·al·ly,** *adv.*

in·struc·tive (in struk′tiv) *adj.* useful for instruction; instructing; giving knowledge or information: *A trip around the world is an instructive experience.* —**in·struc′tive·ly,** *adv.* —**in·struc′tive·ness,** *n.*

in·struc·tor (in struk′tər) *n.* **1** a teacher. **2** in some colleges and universities, a teacher ranking below an assistant professor. [< Med.L *instructor* teacher < L *instructor* preparer]

in·struc·tress (in struk′tris) *n.* a woman instructor or teacher.

in·stru·ment (in′strə mənt) *n.* **1** anything with or by which something is done; a person so made use of; means: *The master criminal used many men and women as instruments in his crimes.* **2** a tool or mechanical device: *a dentist's instruments.* **3** a device for producing musical sounds: *wind instruments, stringed instruments.* **4** a formal legal document, such as a contract, deed, or grant.
—*v.* equip with instruments, especially with scientific recording devices: *a fully instrumented missile.* [< L *instrumentum* < *instruere* arrange, furnish, instruct < *in-* on + *struere* pile]

in·stru·men·tal (in′strə men′təl) *adj.* **1** acting or serving as a means; useful; helpful: *My uncle was instrumental in getting me a job.* **2** played on or written for musical instruments: *An orchestra provided instrumental music to accompany the singing.* **3** of an instrument; made by a device or tool. —*n.* a piece of music composed for or played on a musical instrument. —**in′stru·men′tal·ly,** *adv.*

in·stru·men·tal·ist (in′strə men′təl ist) *n.* a person who plays on a musical instrument.

in·stru·men·tal·i·ty (in′strə mən tal′ə tē) *n.* **-ties.** the quality of being an instrument; agency; means.

in·stru·men·ta·tion (in′strə men tā′shən) *n.* **1** the arrangement or composition of music for instruments. **2** the use of instruments; work done with instruments. **3** the mechanized use of instruments, especially for scientific or technical purposes.

instrument board a board with instruments showing how the parts of a machine, etc. are working.

instrument flying the directing of an aircraft by instruments only.

in·sub·or·di·nate (in′sə bôr′də nit) *adj.* resisting authority; disobedient; unruly. —**in′sub·or′di·nate·ly,** *adv.* —**Syn.** mutinous.

in·sub·or·di·na·tion (in′sə bôr′də nā′shən) *n.* resistance to authority; disobedience; unruly behavior.

in·sub·stan·tial (in′səb stan′shəl) *adj.* **1** frail; flimsy; weak: *A cobweb is very insubstantial.* **2** unreal; not actual; imaginary: *Dreams and ghosts are insubstantial.* —**in′sub·stan′tial·ly,** *adv.*

in·suf·fer·a·ble (in suf′ər ə bəl or in suf′rə bəl) *adj.* intolerable; unbearable: *insufferable insolence.* —**in·suf′fer·a·ble·ness,** *n.* —**in·suf′fer·a·bly,** *adv.*

in·suf·fi·cien·cy (in′sə fish′ən sē) *n.* too small an amount; lack; deficiency.

in·suf·fi·cient (in′sə fish′ənt) *adj.* not enough. —**in′suf·fi′cient·ly,** *adv.* —**Syn.** inadequate.

in·su·lar (in′sə lər) *adj.* **1** of or having to do with islands or islanders. **2** living or situated on an island. **3** forming an island; standing alone like an island. **4** narrow-minded; prejudiced. [< LL *insularis* < L *insula* island]

in·su·lar·i·ty (in′sə lar′ə tē) *n.* **1** the fact or condition of being an island or of living on an island. **2** narrow-mindedness; prejudice.

in·su·late (in′sə lāt′) *v.* **-lat·ed, -lat·ing. 1** keep from losing or transferring electricity, heat, sound, etc., especially by covering or surrounding with a non-conducting material. Wires are often insulated by a covering of rubber. **2** pack with material that will not burn, so as to prevent the spread of fire. **3** set apart; separate from others; isolate. [< L *insula* island]

in·su·la·tion (in′sə lā′shən) *n.* **1** an insulating. **2** a being insulated. **3** the material used in insulating.

in·su·la·tor (in′sə lā′tər) *n.* that which insulates; something that prevents the passage of electricity or heat; a non-conductor.

hat, āge, cãre, fär; let, ēqual, tėrm; it, īce
hot, ōpen, ôrder; oil, out; cup, pu̇t, rüle, ūse
əbove, takən, pencəl, lemən, circəs
ch, child; ng, long; sh, ship
th, thin; ᴛʜ, then; zh, measure

in·su·lin (in′sə lin) *n.* **1** a hormone secreted by the pancreas that enables the body to use sugar and other carbohydrates. **2** a preparation containing this hormone, used especially in the treatment of diabetes. Insulin is obtained from the pancreas of slaughtered animals. [< L *insula* island (i.e., of the pancreas)]

in·sult (*v.* in sult′; *n.* in′sult) *v.* treat with scorn, abuse, or great rudeness: *The rebels insulted the flag by throwing mud on it.* —*n.* an insulting speech or action. [< L *insultare*, frequentative of *insilire* leap at or upon < *in-* on, at + *salire* leap] —**in·sult′ing·ly,** *adv.*
Syn. *n.* **Insult, affront, indignity** = something said or done to offend by showing disrespect or contempt. **Insult** emphasizes insolence and abuse, and intention to hurt or shame: *Stamping on the flag is an insult.* **Affront** applies to a deliberate and open show of disrespect: *Leaving during her song was an affront to my sister.* **Indignity** applies to an act that hurts a person's dignity, suggests lack of respect, but emphasizes the feelings of the victim: *Spanking is an indignity to a teen-ager.*

in·su·per·a·ble (in sü′pər ə bəl) *adj.* that cannot be passed over or overcome: *an insuperable barrier.* —**in·su′per·a·ble·ness,** *n.* —**in·su′per·a·bly,** *adv.* —**Syn.** insurmountable, impassable.

in·sup·port·a·ble (in′sə pôr′tə bəl) *adj.* unbearable; unendurable; intolerable. —**in′sup·port′a·ble·ness,** *n.* —**in′sup·port′a·bly,** *adv.*

in·sur·a·ble (in shür′ə bəl) *adj.* capable of being insured; fit to be insured.

in·sur·ance (in shür′əns) *n.* **1** an insuring of property, person, or life: *fire insurance, burglary insurance, accident insurance, life insurance, health insurance.* **2** the business of insuring property, life, etc. **3** the amount of money for which a person or thing is insured: *He has $10,000 insurance.* **4** the amount of money paid for insurance; premium: *His insurance is $300 a year.* **5** the contract made between insurer and insured; policy. **6** any means of insuring or protecting: *Good health habits are an insurance against illness.*

in·sure (in shür′) *v.* **-sured, -sur·ing. 1** make safe; protect; ensure: *More care will insure you against making so many mistakes.* **2** arrange for money payment in case of loss of (property, profit, etc.) or accident or death to (a person). An insurance company will insure your property, person, or life if you pay a certain amount of money. **3** make safe from financial loss by accident, death, etc. by paying money to an insurance company: *He insured his car against accident, theft, and fire.* **4** give or buy insurance. **5** make sure; ensure: *Check your work to insure its accuracy.* [ME; var. of *ensure* < AF *enseurer* < *en-* in + OF *seür* sure < L *securus.* Related to SURE.]
☛ See **ensure** for usage note.

in·sured (in shürd′) *n.* one who is insured.

in·sur·er (in shür′ər) *n.* **1** a person, company, etc. that insures. **2** something that insures or protects.

in·sur·gence (in sėr′jəns) *n.* a rising in revolt; rebellion.

in·sur·gen·cy (in sėr′jən sē) *n.* insurgence.

in·sur·gent (in sėr′jənt) *n.* a person who rises in revolt; rebel. —*adj.* rising in revolt; rebellious. [< L *insurgens, -entis*, ppr. of *insurgere* < *in-* against + *surgere* rise]

in·sur·mount·a·ble (in′sər moun′tə bəl) *adj.* that cannot be overcome. —**in′sur·mount′a·bly,** *adv.*

in·sur·rec·tion (in′sə rek′shən) *n.* a rising against established authority; revolt. [ME < OF< LL *insurrectio, -onis* < L *insurgere.* See INSURGENT.] —**Syn.** rebellion, revolution, riot. See **revolt.**

in·sur·rec·tion·ar·y (in′sə rek′shən er′ē) *adj.* **1** having a tendency to revolt. **2** having to do with revolt.

in·sur·rec·tion·ist (in′sə rek′shən ist) *n.* a person who takes part in or favors an insurrection; rebel.

in·sus·cep·ti·bil·i·ty (in′sə sep′tə bil′ə tē) *n.* the fact or quality of being insusceptible.

in·sus·cep·ti·ble (in′sə sep′tə bəl) *adj.* not susceptible; not easily influenced. —**in′sus·cep′ti·bly,** *adv.*

int. 1 interest. **2** international. **3** internal. **4** interior. **5** intransitive. **6** interval.

in·tact (in takt′) *adj.* with no part missing; untouched; uninjured; whole: *Strangely enough, the dishes were intact after the fall.* [< L *intactus* < *in-* not + *tactus*, pp. of *tangere* touch]

in·tagl·io (in tal′yō or in täl′yō) *n.* **in·tagl·ios. 1** the process of engraving by making cuts in the surface. **2** ornamentation by designs sunk below the surface. **3** a design engraved in this way. **4** a gem ornamented in this way. **5** a method of printing in which paper is pressed into inked lines below the surface of the plate or cylinder. The ink is wiped off the surface but remains in the recesses, as in etching, photogravure, etc. [< Ital. *intaglio* < *intagliare* engrave < *in-* into + *tagliare* cut]

in·take (in′tāk′) *n.* **1** a place where water, air, gas, etc. enters a channel, pipe, or other narrow opening. **2** a taking in. **3** the amount or thing taken in. **4** a narrowing or contraction in a tube, stocking, etc., or the point at which this begins.

in·tan·gi·bil·i·ty (in tan′jə bil′ə tē) *n.* the quality of being intangible.

in·tan·gi·ble (in tan′jə bəl) *adj.* **1** not capable of being touched: *Sound and light are intangible.* **2** not easily grasped by the mind; vague: *She had that intangible something called charm.* —*n.* something intangible. —**in·tan′gi·ble·ness,** *n.* —**in·tan′gi·bly,** *adv.* —**Syn.** *adj.* **1** insubstantial.

in·te·ger (in′tə jər) *n.* **1** a member of the set of positive and negative whole numbers and zero. **2** a thing complete in itself; something whole. [< L *integer* whole. Doublet of ENTIRE.]

in·te·gral (in′tə grəl or in teg′rəl) *adj.* **1** necessary to the completeness of the whole; essential: *Steel is an integral part of a modern skyscraper.* **2** entire; complete. **3** in mathematics, having to do with whole numbers; not fractional. —*n.* a whole; a whole number. [< LL *integralis* < L *integer* whole]

in·te·grate (in′tə grāt′) *v.* **-grat·ed, -grat·ing. 1** make into a whole; complete. **2** bring together (parts) into a whole. **3** make available an institution or facilities to people regardless of race, nationality, religion, etc. [< L *integrare* < *integer* whole] —**in′te·gra′tor,** *n.*

in·te·gra·tion (in′tə grā′shən) *n.* an integrating.

in·te·gra·tion·ist (in′tə grā′shə nist) *n.* a person who believes in, or practises, integration.

in·teg·ri·ty (in teg′rə tē) *n.* **1** honesty; sincerity; uprightness: *A man of integrity is respected.* **2** wholeness; completeness. **3** perfect condition; soundness. [< L *integritas* < *integer* whole] —**Syn. 1** See **honesty.**

in·teg·u·ment (in teg′yu̇ mənt) *n.* **1** a natural outer covering: *The skin or shell of an animal is its integument.* **2** any outer covering. [< L *integumentum* < *integere* cover < *in-* on + *tegere* cover]

in·tel·lect (in′tə lekt′) *n.* **1** the power of knowing; understanding. A man's actions are influenced by his intellect, will, and feelings. **2** great intelligence; high mental ability: *Isaac Newton was a man of intellect.* **3** a person having high mental ability: *Einstein was one of the greatest intellects of his time.* [< L *intellectus* < *intelligere.* See INTELLIGENT.] —**Syn. 1** See **mind.**

in·tel·lec·tu·al (in′tə lek′chü əl) *adj.* **1** of the intellect. **2** needing or using intelligence: *Reasoning is an intellectual process.* **3** possessing or showing intelligence. **4** directed or inclined toward things that involve the intellect. —*n.* a person who is well informed and intelligent.

in·tel·lec·tu·al·ism (in′tə lek′chü əl iz′əm) *n.* **1** the exercise of the intellect; a devotion to intellectual pursuits. **2** in philosophy, the doctrine that knowledge is wholly or chiefly derived from pure reason.

in·tel·lec·tu·al·i·ty (in′tə lek′chü al′ə tē) *n.* **-ties.** a being intellectual; intellectual nature or power.

in·tel·lec·tu·al·ly (in′tə lek′chü əl ē) *adv.* **1** in an intellectual way. **2** so far as intellect is concerned.

in·tel·li·gence (in tel′ə jəns) *n.* **1** the ability to learn and know; understanding; mind: *A dog has more intelligence than a worm.* **2** knowledge; news; information: *The general had secret intelligence of the plans of the enemy.* **3** the getting or distributing of information, especially secret information. **4** a group engaged in obtaining secret information. **5** Often, **Intelligence.** an intelligent being or spirit.

intelligence department a branch of the government that collects and studies information that will help its armed services or its foreign affairs department.

intelligence quotient the number used to measure a person's intelligence. It is 100 × the mental age shown in tests, divided by the actual age. *Abbrev.*: I.Q.

intelligence test a test used to measure mental development.

in·tel·li·gent (in tel′ə jənt) *adj.* having or showing intelligence; able to learn and know; quick at learning. [< L *intelligens, -entis,* ppr. of *intelligere* understand < *inter-* between + *legere* choose] **—in·tel′li·gent·ly,** *adv.* —**Syn.** bright, clever.

in·tel·li·gent·si·a (in tel′ə jent′sē ə or in tel′ə gent′sē ə) *n. sing.* or *pl.* the persons representing, or claiming to represent, the superior intelligence or enlightened opinion of a country; the intellectuals. [< Russian *intelligentsiya* < L *intelligentia* < *intelligens.* See INTELLIGENT.]

in·tel·li·gi·bil·i·ty (in tel′ə jə bil′ə tē) *n.* the fact or quality of being intelligible.

in·tel·li·gi·ble (in tel′ə jə bəl) *adj.* capable of being understood; comprehensible. [< L *intelligibilis* < *intelligere.* See INTELLIGENT.] **—in·tel′li·gi·bly,** *adv.* —**Syn.** understandable, plain, clear.

in·tem·per·ance (in tem′pər əns or in tem′prəns) *n.* **1** a lack of moderation or self-control; excess. **2** the excessive use of intoxicating liquor.

in·tem·per·ate (in tem′pər it or in tem′prit) *adj.* **1** not moderate; lacking in self-control; excessive. **2** drinking too much intoxicating liquor. **3** not temperate; severe: *an intemperate winter.* **—in·tem′per·ate·ly,** *adv.*

in·tend (in tend′) *v.* **1** have in mind as a purpose; plan: *We intend to go home soon.* **2** mean for a particular purpose or use: *That gift was intended for you.* **3** *Archaic.* direct: *intend one's course.* [ME < OF < L *intendere* < *in-* toward + *tendere* stretch] **—in·tend′er,** *n.*

Syn. 1 Intend, mean = have in mind as a purpose. **Intend** = have some definite purpose or plan and to be determined to carry it out: *I intend to finish this work before I go to bed.* **Mean** is sometimes used interchangeably with *intend,* but puts greater emphasis on having something in mind to do or get and less emphasis on the determination to carry it out or gain it: *I meant to get up early, but forgot to set the alarm.*

in·tend·an·cy (in ten′dən sē) *n.* **-cies. 1** the position or work of an intendant. **2** intendants. **3** a district under an intendant.

in·tend·ant (in ten′dənt) *n.* **1** a person in charge; superintendent; manager; director. **2** the most important administrative office in New France, eventually responsible for the administration of finance, justice, and police in the colony. **3** an official who held this office: *Jean Talon was the first and greatest intendant of New France.* [< F, ult. < L *intendere* attend to. See INTEND.]

in·tend·ed (in ten′did) *adj.* **1** meant; planned. **2** prospective: *a woman's intended husband.* —*n. Informal.* a prospective husband or wife.

in·tense (in tens′) *adj.* **1** very much; very great; very strong; *intense happiness, intense pain, intense light.* **2** full of vigorous activity, strong feelings, etc.: *An intense life is crowded with action, interests, etc.* **3** having or showing strong feeling: *an intense person, an intense face.* [< L *intensus,* pp. of *intendere* strain. See INTEND.] **—in·tense′ness,** *n.*

in·tense·ly (in tens′lē) *adv.* **1** in an intense manner. **2** exceedingly; extremely.

in·ten·si·fi·er (in ten′sə fī′ər) *n.* **1** in photography, a chemical used to increase contrast in a negative. **2** an intensive.

in·ten·si·fy (in ten′sə fī′) *v.* **-fied, -fy·ing. 1** make or become intense or more intense; strengthen; increase: *Blowing on a fire intensifies the heat.* **2** in photography, make (parts of a negative) more dense or opaque by treating with chemicals. **—in·ten′si·fi·ca′tion,** *n.* **—in·ten′si·fi′er,** *n.* —**Syn.** heighten.

in·ten·si·ty (in ten′sə tē) *n.* **-ties. 1** the quality of being intense; great strength; extreme degree. **2** a great strength or violence of feeling. **3** the strength of a color resulting from the degree to which it is lacking its complementary color. **4** in physics, the amount or degree of strength of heat, light, sound, etc. per unit of area, volume, etc. **5** in photography, of parts of a negative, density; opaqueness.

in·ten·sive (in ten′siv) *adj.* **1** deep and thorough: *An intensive study of a few books is more valuable than a superficial reading of many.* **2** having to do with a system of farming in which more money and work is spent on a small area to produce larger crops. **3** in grammar, giving force or emphasis; expressing intensity. In "He himself said it," *himself* is an intensive pronoun. —*n.* **1** something that makes intense. **2** an intensive word, prefix, etc. **—in·ten′sive·ly,** *adv.*

in·tent[1] (in tent′) *n.* **1** the purpose; intention: *The thief shot with intent to kill.* **2** meaning; significance: *What is the intent of that sentence?* **3 to all intents and purposes,** in almost every way; practically. [ME < OF *entent, entente* < L *intendere.* See INTEND.]

in·tent[2] (in tent′) *adj.* **1** very attentive; having the eyes or thoughts earnestly fixed on something; earnest: *an intent look.* **2** earnestly engaged; much interested: *He is intent on moneymaking.* [< L *intentus,* pp. of *intendere* strain. See INTEND.] **—in·tent′ly,** *adv.* **—in·tent′ness,** *n.*

in·ten·tion (in ten′shən) *n.* **1** a purpose; design; plan: *Good acts are better than good intentions.* **2** meaning. **3 intentions,** *pl. Informal.* purposes with respect to marrying.

Syn. 1 Intention, purpose, design = what a person intends or plans to get or do. **Intention** = what one has in mind to do, but does not always suggest determination or definite planning: *My intention was to arrive early.* **Purpose** = a definite thing a person intends to do or get and toward which he strives with determination: *My purpose was to avoid the crowd.* **Design** suggests deliberate intention, with definite planning or preparations, often underhand, for carrying out one's purpose: *I arrived early by design. He had designs on her fortune.*

in·ten·tion·al (in ten′shən əl) *adj.* done on purpose; meant; planned; intended: *His insult was intentional; he wanted to hurt your feelings.* —**Syn.** See **deliberate.**

in·ten·tion·al·ly (in ten′shən əl ē) *adv.* with intention; on purpose.

in·ter (in tėr′) *v.* **-terred, -ter·ring.** put (a dead body) into a grave or tomb; bury. [ME < OF *enterrer* + L *interrare* < *in-* in + *terra* earth]

inter- *prefix.* **1** together; one with the other: *intercommunicate* = *communicate with each other.* **2** between: *interpose* = *put between.* **3** among a group: *interscholastic* = *between or among schools.* [< L *inter-* < *inter,* prep. adv., among, between, during]

in·ter·act (in′tər akt′) *v.* act on each other.

in·ter·ac·tion (in′tər ak′shən) *n.* action on each other.

in·ter a·li·a (in′tər ā′lē ə) *Latin.* among other things.

in·ter-A·mer·i·can (in′tər ə mer′ə kən) *adj.* between or among countries of North, South, or Central America.

in·ter·bor·ough (in′tər bėr′ō) *adj.* between boroughs.

in·ter·breed (in′tər brēd′) *v.* **-bred, -breed·ing.** breed by the mating of different kinds; breed by using different varieties or species of animals or plants.

in·ter·ca·lar·y (in tėr′kə ler′ē) *adj.* **1** inserted in the calendar to make the calendar year agree with the solar year. February 29 is an intercalary day. **2** having an added day, month, etc. as a particular year. **3** put in between; interposed; intervening. [< L *intercalaris, intercalarius* < *intercalare.* See INTERCALATE.]

in·ter·ca·late (in tėr′kə lāt′) *v.* **-lat·ed, -lat·ing. 1** put into the calendar. **2** put between; interpolate. [< L *intercalare* < *inter-* between + *calare* proclaim]

in·ter·ca·la·tion (in tėr′kə lā′shən) *n.* **1** an intercalating. **2** something intercalated.

in·ter·cede (in′tər sēd′) *v.* **-ced·ed, -ced·ing. 1** plead or beg in another's behalf: *Friends of the condemned man interceded with the Governor General for a stay of execution.* **2** interfere in order to bring about an agreement. [< L *intercedere* < *inter-* between + *cedere* go]

in·ter·cel·lu·lar (in′tər sel′yu̇ lər) *adj.* situated between or among cells.

in·ter·cept (in′tər sept′) *v.* **1** take or seize on the way from one place to another: *intercept a letter or a messenger.* **2** check; stop: *intercept the flight of a criminal.* **3** especially in mathematics, mark off between two points or lines. [< L *interceptus*, pp. of *intercipere* < *inter-* between + *capere* catch] —**in′ter·cep′tion,** *n.*

The line intercepts the circle at A and B

in·ter·cep·tor (in′tər sep′tər) *n.* **1** one that intercepts. **2** an airplane designed to intercept enemy aircraft.

in·ter·ces·sion (in′tər sesh′ən) *n.* the act or fact of interceding. [< L *intercessio, -onis* < *intercedere.* See INTERCEDE.]

in·ter·ces·sor (in′tər ses′ər or in′tər ses′ər) *n.* a person who intercedes.

in·ter·ces·so·ry (in′tər ses′ə rē) *adj.* making or relating to intercession; interceding.

in·ter·change (*v.* in′tər chānj′; *n.* in′tər chānj′) *v.* **-changed, -chang·ing,** *n.* —*v.* **1** put each of (two or more persons or things) in the place of the other. **2** give and take; exchange: *interchange gifts.* **3** cause to happen by turns; alternate: *interchange severity with indulgence.*
—*n.* **1** the putting of each of two or more persons or things in the other's place: *The word "team" may be turned into "meat" by the interchange of the end letters.* **2** a road that permits traffic from one highway to change to another without crossing in front of other traffic; cloverleaf. **3** a giving and taking; exchanging. **4** an alternate succession; alternation: *an interchange of hard work with rest.* [ME *entrechange(n)* < OF *entrechangier* < *entre-* (< L *inter-*) + *changier* < L *cambiare* exchange; later influenced by *inter-*] —**Syn.** *v.* **2** See **exchange.**

in·ter·change·a·bil·i·ty (in′tər chān′jə bil′ə tē) *n.* the quality of being interchangeable.

in·ter·change·a·ble (in′tər chān′jə bəl) *adj.* capable of being used in place of each other. —**in′ter·change′a·bly,** *adv.*

in·ter·class (in′tər klas′) *adj.* between classes: *interclass swimming meets.*

in·ter·col·le·giate (in′tər kə lē′jit or -kə lē′jē it) *adj.* between colleges, universities, or high schools: *intercollegiate football games.*

in·ter·co·lo·ni·al (in′tər kə lō′nē əl) *adj.* between colonies; *intercolonial trade.*

in·ter·com (in′tər kom′) *n. Informal.* **1** a telephone apparatus with which members of the crew of an airplane, tank, ship, etc. can talk to each other. **2** a similar apparatus for use in offices, private homes, etc. [a shortened form of *intercommunication system*]

in·ter·com·mu·ni·cate (in′tər kə mū′nə kāt′) *v.* **-cat·ed, -cat·ing.** communicate with each other. —**in′ter·com·mu′ni·ca′tion,** *n.*

in·ter·con·nect (in′tər kə nekt′) *v.* connect with each other. —**in′ter·con·nec′tion,** *n.*

in·ter·con·ti·nen·tal (in′tər kon′tə nen′təl) *adj.* **1** for use between continents. **2** of more than one continent.

in·ter·cos·tal (in′tər kos′təl) *adj.* between the ribs. —*n.* in anatomy, a muscle or part situated between the ribs. [< NL *intercostalis* < L *inter-* between + *costa* rib]

in·ter·course (in′tər kôrs′) *n.* **1** communication; dealings between people; exchange of thoughts, services, feelings, etc. **2** sexual union. [ME *entercourse* < OF *entrecours* < L *intercursus* a running between, ult. < *inter-* between + *currere* run; later influenced by *inter-*]

in·ter·de·nom·i·na·tion·al (in′tər di nom′ə nā′shən əl or -di nom′ə nāsh′nəl) *adj.* between or involving different religious denominations.

in·ter·de·part·men·tal (in′tər dē′pärt men′təl) *adj.* between departments. —**in′ter·de′part·men′tal·ly,** *adv.*

in·ter·de·pend·ence (in′tər di pen′dəns) *n.* dependence on each other; mutual dependence.

in·ter·de·pend·ent (in′tər di pen′dənt) *adj.* dependent each upon the other. —**in′ter·de·pend′ent·ly,** *adv.*

in·ter·dict (*v.* in′tər dikt′; *n.* in′tər dikt′) *v.* **1** prohibit; forbid. **2** restrain. **3** in the Roman Catholic Church, cut off from certain church privileges.

hat, āge, cãre, fär; let, ēqual, tėrm; it, īce
hot, ōpen, ôrder; oil, out; cup, pu̇t, rüle, ūse
əbove, takən, pencəl, lemən, circəs
ch, child; ng, long; sh, ship
th, thin; ᴛʜ, then; zh, measure

—*n.* **1** a prohibition based on authority; a formal order forbidding something. **2** a cutting off from certain church privileges. **3** in law, a decree; order. **4** a person forbidden to purchase intoxicants. [ME < OF < L *interdictus*, pp. of *interdicere* prohibit < *inter-* between + *dicere* speak] —**in′ter·dic′tor,** *n.*

in·ter·dic·tion (in′tər dik′shən) *n.* **1** an interdicting. **2** the state of being interdicted.

in·ter·est (in′trist or in′tər ist) *n.* **1** a feeling of wanting to know, see, do, own, share in, or take part in: *Boys usually have an interest in sports.* **2** the power of arousing such a feeling: *A dull book lacks interest.* **3** something that stirs up such feelings. Any activity, pastime, or hobby can be an interest. **4** a share; part: *He bought a half interest in the farm.* **5** something in which a person has an interest, share, or part. Any business, activity, or pastime can be an interest. **6** a group of people having the same business, activity, etc. **7** advantage; benefit: *Each person should look after his own interest.* **8 in the interest of,** for; to help. **9** money paid for the use of money. Anyone who borrows money from a bank must pay interest on the loan. **10** something extra given in return: *She returned our favor with interest.*
—*v.* **1** arouse the attention, curiosity, etc. of: *An exciting story interests you.* **2** cause (a person) to take a share or interest in something: *The agent tried to interest us in buying a car.* [ME < AF < L *interest* it is of importance, it makes a difference, 3rd person sing. present of *interesse* < *inter-* between + *esse* be] —**Syn.** *v.* **1** engage, occupy, entertain.

in·ter·est·ed (in′tris təd, in′tər is təd, or in′tər es′təd) *adj.* **1** feeling or showing interest. **2** having an interest or share. **3** influenced by personal considerations; prejudiced: *interested motives.* —**in′ter·est·ed·ly,** *adv.* —**in′ter·est·ed·ness,** *n.*

☛ **interested.** The adjective *interested* has two opposites: *uninterested*, which is merely its negative, and *disinterested*, which means "free from selfish motives; impartial; fair": *He was uninterested in the outcome of the game. A disinterested spectator offered to referee.* See also **disinterested.**

in·ter·est·ing (in′tris ting, in′tər is ting, or in′tər es′ting) *adj.* arousing interest; holding one's attention. —**in′ter·est·ing·ly,** *adv.*

in·ter·face (in′tər fās′) *v.* provide with an interfacing.

in·ter·fa·cing (in′tər fā′sing) *n.* a piece of cloth sewn between the facing and outside of a garment for stiffening or retaining the shape, as in collars and cuffs.

in·ter·fere (in′tər fēr′) *v.* **-fered, -fer·ing.** **1** come into opposition; clash: *Because the two plans interfere with each other, one must be changed. I'll come on Saturday if nothing interferes.* **2** disturb the affairs of others; meddle: *That woman is always interfering in other people's business.* **3** intervene; take part for a purpose: *The police interfered to stop the riot.* **4 interfere with,** hinder. **5** in sports, obstruct the action of an opposing player in a way barred by the rules. **6** in physics, of waves, act one upon another. [< OF *entreferir* strike each other < *entre-* between (< L *inter-*) + *ferir* strike < L *ferire*] —**Syn.** **1** conflict. **2** See **meddle.** **3** intervene.

in·ter·fer·ence (in′tər fēr′əns) *n.* **1** an interfering. **2** in physics, the reciprocal action of waves by which they reinforce or neutralize one another. **3** in radio or television: **a** the interruption or scrambling of a desired signal by other signals. **b** the signals thus interfering. **4** in football: **a** the protecting of the player who has the ball by blocking opposing players. **b** the players protecting or blocking for the player with the ball. **5** in football, hockey, and other sports, the illegal obstruction of an opponent.

in·ter·fer·on (in′tər fēr′on) *n.* in biochemistry, a substance produced in virus-infected cells to counteract the infection.

in·ter·fold (in′tər fōld′) *v.* fold one with another; fold together.

in·ter·fuse (in′tər fūz′) *v.* **-fused, -fus·ing.** **1** be diffused through; permeate. **2** fuse together; blend. [< L *interfusus*, pp. of *interfundere* < *inter-* between + *fundere* pour] **—in′ter·fu′sion,** *n.*

in·ter·gla·cial (in′tər glā′shəl) *adj.* in geology, of or occurring in the period between two glacial epochs. —*n.* the period between two glacial epochs.

in·ter·im (in′tər im) *n.* meantime; time between. —*adj.* for the meantime; temporary. [< L *interim* in the meantime < *inter* between]

in·te·ri·or (in tēr′ē ər) *n.* **1** the inside; inner surface or part: *The interior of the house was beautifully decorated.* **2** the part of a region or country away from the coast or border. **3** a picture or stage setting of the inside of a room, house, etc. —*adj.* **1** on the inside; inner. **2** away from the coast or border. **3** having to do with affairs within a country; domestic. **4** private; secret. [< L *interior* inner]

interior angle in geometry: **1** any of the four angles formed inside the intersections of a straight line with two parallel lines. **2** an angle within a polygon, formed by any two adjacent sides.

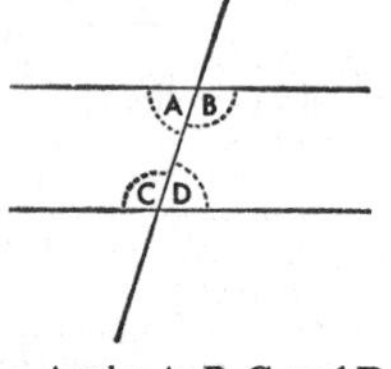

Angles A, B, C, and D are interior angles.

interior decoration **1** the art of planning furnishings, decorations, etc. for homes, offices, and other buildings. **2** the profession of an interior decorator. **3** the arrangement or the material used in interior decoration.

interj. interjection.

in·ter·ject (in′tər jekt′) *v.* throw in between other things; insert abruptly: *Every now and then the speaker interjected some witty remark.* [< L *interjectus*, pp. of *interjicere* < *inter-* between + *jacere* throw]

in·ter·jec·tion (in′tər jek′shən) *n.* **1** an exclamation of surprise, delight, or some other feeling. *Oh! ah! alas!* and *hurrah!* are interjections. **2** an interjecting. **3** something interjected; remark; exclamation.

in·ter·jec·tion·al (in′tər jek′shən əl) *adj.* **1** of an interjection; used as an interjection. **2** containing an interjection. **3** interjected. **—in′ter·jec′tion·al·ly,** *adv.*

in·ter·lace (in′tər lās′) *v.* **-laced, -lac·ing. 1** cross over and under each other; weave together; intertwine: *Baskets are made by interlacing reeds or fibres.* **2** cross in an intricate manner: *roads and streams that interlace.* **3** give variety to; intersperse: *meadows interlaced with streams.*

in·ter·lard (in′tər lärd′) *v.* give variety to; mix so as to give variety to; intersperse: *The speaker interlarded his long speech with amusing stories.* [< F *entrelarder* < *entre-* between (< L *inter-*) + *larder* lard < L *lardum* fat]

in·ter·leaf (in′tər lēf′) *n.* **-leaves.** a leaf of paper put between others.

in·ter·leave (in′tər lēv′) *v.* **-leaved, -leav·ing.** insert a leaf or leaves of paper between the pages of (a book, album, etc.).

in·ter·line[1] (in′tər līn′) *v.* **-lined, -lin·ing.** insert an interlining. [< *inter-* + *line*[2]]

in·ter·line[2] (in′tər līn′) *v.* **-lined, -lin·ing. 1** insert (words etc.) between the lines of. **2** write, print, or mark between the lines: *The teacher interlined corrections on the students' themes.* [< Med.L *interlineare*]

in·ter·lin·e·ar (in′tər lin′ē ər) *adj.* **1** inserted between the lines: *an interlinear translation.* **2** containing two different languages or versions in alternate lines. **—in′ter·lin′e·ar·ly,** *adv.*

in·ter·lin·e·a·tion (in′tər lin′ē ā′shən) *n.* **1** interlining; the insertion of matter between the lines of writing or print. **2** the matter thus inserted.

in·ter·lin·ing (in′tər līn′ing) *n.* **1** an extra lining of wool, chamois, etc. inserted between the outer cloth and the ordinary lining of a garment to add warmth. **2** a fabric used to interline.

in·ter·link (in′tər lingk′) *v.* link together.

in·ter·lock (in′tər lok′) *v.* lock or join with one another: *The antlers of the two stags were interlocked.*

in·ter·loc·u·tor (in′tər lok′yù tər) *n.* **1** a person who takes part in a conversation or dialogue. **2** in a minstrel show, the man who asks the end man questions. [< L *interlocutus*, pp. of *interloqui* converse < *inter-* between + *loqui* speak]

in·ter·loc·u·to·ry (in′tər lok′yù tô′rē) *adj.* **1** of or in conversation or dialogue. **2** in law: **a** made during a lawsuit or other action; not final: *The judge granted an interlocutory decree after the hearing.* **b** of or having to do with a decision made in this way. **3** inserted into a conversation, speech, etc: *interlocutory anecdotes.*

in·ter·lop·er (in′tər lōp′ər) *n.* an intruder. [probably < Du. *enterlooper* < *entre-* between (< L *inter-*) + *looper* runner < *loopen* run]

in·ter·lude (in′tər lüd′) *n.* **1** anything thought of as filling the time between two things; interval: *There were only a few interludes of fair weather during the rainy season.* **2** in music, a composition played between the parts of a song, church service, play, etc. **3** an entertainment between the acts of a play. **4** in early English drama: **a** a short, humorous play, commonly introduced between the parts of the long mystery plays or given as part of other entertainment. **b** a stage play of a popular nature; comedy; farce. [< Med.L *interludium* < L *inter-* between + *ludus* play]

in·ter·lu·nar (in′tər lü′nər) *adj.* between the old moon and the new moon.

in·ter·mar·riage (in′tər mar′ij) *n.* **1** marriage between members of different religious, social, or ethnic groups. **2** marriage between close blood relations.

in·ter·mar·ry (in′tər mar′ē) *v.* **-ried, -ry·ing. 1** of families, tribes, etc., become connected by marriage. **2** marry within the family or with close relations.

in·ter·med·dle (in′tər med′əl) *v.* **-dled, -dling.** interfere; meddle.

in·ter·me·di·ar·y (in′tər mē′dē er′ē) *n.* **-ar·ies,** *adj.* —*n.* **1** a person who acts for one person with another; go-between: *The teacher acted as intermediary for the students with the principal.* **2** a medium; means. **3** an intermediate form or stage. —*adj.* **1** acting between. **2** being between; intermediate: *A cocoon is an intermediary stage between caterpillar and butterfly.* [< L *intermedius* intermediate < *inter-* between + *medius* in the middle]

in·ter·me·di·ate (in′tər mē′dē it) *adj.* being or occurring between: *Gray is intermediate between black and white.* —*n.* **1** something in between. **2** a person who acts between others to bring about an agreement; mediator. **3** a compound formed between the initial and final stages in a chemical process. [< Med.L *intermediatus* < L *intermedius* < *inter-* between + *medius* in the middle] **—Syn.** *adj.* intervening.

in·ter·ment (in tėr′mənt) *n.* the act of putting a dead body into a grave or tomb; burial.

in·ter·mez·zo (in′tər met′sō or -med′zō) *n.* **-mez·zos, -mez·zi** (-met′sē or -med′zē). **1** a short dramatic, musical, or other entertainment of a light character between the acts of a drama or opera. **2** in music: **a** a short composition between the main divisions of an extended musical work. **b** an independent composition of similar character. [< Ital.]

in·ter·mi·na·ble (in tėr′mə nə bəl) *adj.* endless; so long as to seem endless. [ME < LL *interminabilis*, ult. < L *in-* not + *terminare* to end] **—in·ter′mi·na·ble·ness,** *n.* **—*Syn.*** unending, limitless.

in·ter·mi·na·bly (in tėr′mə nə blē) *adv.* without end.

in·ter·min·gle (in′tər ming′gəl) *v.* **-gled, -gling.** mix together; mingle.

in·ter·mis·sion (in′tər mish′ən) *n.* **1** a time between periods of activity; pause: *The band played from eight to twelve with a short intermission at ten.* **2** a stopping for a time; interruption: *The rain continued all day without intermission.* [< L *intermissio, -onis* < *intermittere.* See INTERMIT.] **—Syn. 1** interval.

in·ter·mit (in′tər mit′) *v.* **-mit·ted, -mit·ting.** stop for a time. [< L *intermittere* < *inter-* between + *mittere* leave]

in·ter·mit·tent (in′tər mit′ənt) *adj.* stopping and

beginning again; pausing at intervals. —**in′ter·mit′tent·ly,** *adv.*

in·ter·mix (in′tər miks′) *v.* mix or become mixed together; blend: *Oil and water do not intermix.*

in·ter·mix·ture (in′tər miks′chər) *n.* **1** a mixing together. **2** a mass of ingredients mixed together.

in·ter·mus·cu·lar (in′tər mus′kyu̇l ər) *adj.* found or set between muscles or muscle fibres.

in·tern[1] (in tėrn′) *v.* confine within a country; force to stay in a certain place: *Soldiers who enter a neutral country in wartime are interned there until the war is over.* —*n.* a person who is interned. [< F *interner* < *interne* inner, internal < L *internus* < *in* in]

in·tern[2] (in′tėrn) *n.* a medical doctor acting as a resident assistant in a hospital; interne. —*v.* act as an intern. [< F *interne* < *interne,* adj. See INTERN[1].]

in·ter·nal (in tėr′nəl) *adj.* **1** inner; on the inside: *internal injuries.* **2** to be taken inside the body: *internal remedies.* **3** entirely inside; coming from within: *Internal evidence of a book's date is evidence obtained from the book itself.* **4** having to do with affairs within a country; domestic: *internal disturbances.* **5** of the mind; subjective: *Thoughts are internal.* [< Med.L *internalis* < L *internus* within < *in* in]

internal-combustion engine 1 an engine in which the power comes from each piston being moved by explosions within its cylinder. **2** a gas-turbine engine that uses for its power the gas formed by burning or exploding fuel.

in·ter·nal·ly (in tėr′nəl ē) *adv.* **1** inside. **2** inside the body.

in·ter·na·tion·al (in′tər nash′ən əl or -nash′nəl) *adj.* **1** between or among nations: *A treaty is an international agreement.* **2** having to do with the relations between nations: *international law.* —*n.* **International,** one of several international socialist or communist organizations.

international candle a unit for measuring the intensity of light.

International Date Line date line (def. 1).

In·ter·na·tio·nale (in′tər nash′ə nəl or -nash′nəl; *French,* aN ter nä syô näl′) *n.* a workers' revolutionary song, the national anthem of the Soviet Union till 1944. [< F]

in·ter·na·tion·al·ism (in′tər nash′ən əl iz′əm or -nash′nə liz′əm) *n.* the principle of international co-operation for the good of all nations.

in·ter·na·tion·al·ist (in′tər nash′ən əl ist or -nash′nə list) *n.* a person who favors internationalism.

in·ter·na·tion·al·ize (in′tər nash′ən əl īz′ or -nash′nə līz′) *v.* **-ized, -iz·ing.** make international; bring (territory) under the control of several nations. —**in′ter·na′tion·al·i·za′tion,** *n.*

International Joint Commission a committee set up by Canada and the United States to settle possible disputes between the two countries concerning boundary waters.

in·ter·na·tion·al·ly (in′tər nash′ən əl ē or -nash′nə lē) *adv.* in an international manner; between or among nations.

in·terne (in′tėrn) *n.* intern[2].

in·ter·ne·cine (in′tər nē′sən or -nē′sīn) *adj.* **1** destructive to both sides. **2** deadly; destructive. [< L *internecinus* < *internecere* kill < *inter-* between + *nex, necis* slaughter]

in·tern·ee (in′tėr nē′) *n.* a person who is interned. In wartime, prisoners of war, enemy aliens, etc. may be internees.

in·tern·ment (in tėrn′mənt) *n.* **1** an interning. **2** a being interned.

in·tern·ship (in′tėrn ship′) *n.* a position or period of service as an intern.

in·ter·o·ce·an·ic (in′tər ō′shē an′ik) *adj.* between oceans.

in·ter·pel·late (in′tər pel′āt or in tėr′pə lāt′) *v.* **-lat·ed, -lat·ing.** make an interpellation. [< L *interpellare* interrupt]

in·ter·pel·la·tion (in′tər pə lā′shən or in tėr′-) *n.* in a legislature, a formal request for an explanation of official action or government policy.

in·ter·pen·e·trate (in′tər pen′ə trāt′) *v.* **-trat·ed, -trat·ing.** penetrate thoroughly; permeate. —**in′ter·pen′e·tra′tion,** *n.*

hat, āge, cãre, fär; let, ēqual, tėrm; it, īce
hot, ōpen, ôrder; oil, out; cup, pu̇t, rüle, ūse
əbove, takən, pencəl, lemən, circəs
ch, child; ng, long; sh, ship
th, thin; ᴛʜ, then; zh, measure

in·ter·phone (in′tər fōn′) *n.* intercom.

in·ter·plan·e·tar·y (in′tər plan′ə ter′ē) *adj.* **1** between planets; in the region of the planets: *interplanetary travel.* **2** within the solar system, but not within the atmosphere of the sun or any planet.

in·ter·play (in′tər plā′) *n.* the action or influence of things on each other: *the interplay of light and shadow.* —*v.* exert mutual influence; have reciprocal action.

In·ter·pol (in′tər pōl′ or in′tər pol′) *n.* the international police network that assists the police of its member nations in the investigation of crime. [*Inter*national *pol*ice]

in·ter·po·late (in tėr′pə lāt′) *v.* **-lat·ed, -lat·ing. 1** alter (a book, passage, etc.) by putting in new words or groups of words. **2** put in (new words, passages, etc.). **3** in mathematics, insert (intermediate terms) in a series. **4** insert or introduce (something additional or different) between other things, or in a series; interpose. [< L *interpolare* freshen up]

in·ter·po·la·tion (in tėr′pə lā′shən) *n.* **1** an interpolating. **2** something interpolated.

in·ter·pose (in′tər pōz′) *v.* **-posed, -pos·ing. 1** put between; insert. **2** come between other things; be between other things. **3** interrupt. **4** interfere in order to help; intervene. **5** put in as an interference or interruption. [< F *interposer* < *inter-* between (< L *inter-*) + *poser* place (see POSE[1])] —**in′ter·pos′er,** *n.* —**Syn. 4** intercede, mediate.

in·ter·po·si·tion (in′tər pə zish′ən) *n.* **1** an interposing. **2** the thing interposed.

in·ter·pret (in tėr′prit) *v.* **1** explain the meaning of: *interpret a difficult passage in a book, interpret a dream.* **2** bring out the meaning of: *interpret a part in a play.* **3** understand: *We interpret your silence as consent.* **4** serve as an interpreter; translate. [< L *interpretari* < *interpres, -pretis* negotiator] —**Syn. 1** expound, elucidate, unfold. See **explain.**

in·ter·pre·ta·tion (in tėr′prə tā′shən) *n.* **1** an interpreting; explanation: *different interpretations of the same facts.* **2** a bringing out of the meaning of a dramatic part, a piece of music, etc. **3** a translation.

in·ter·pre·ta·tive (in tėr′prə tā′tiv or in tėr′prə tə tiv) *adj.* used for interpreting; explanatory. —**in·ter′pre·ta·tive·ly,** *adv.*

in·ter·pret·er (in tėr′prə tər) *n.* **1** a person who interprets. **2** a person whose business is translating from a foreign language.

in·ter·pre·tive (in tėr′prə tiv) *adj.* interpretative. —**in·ter′pre·tive·ly,** *adv.*

in·ter·pro·vin·cial (in′tər prə vin′shəl) *adj.* between or among provinces.

in·ter·ra·cial (in′tər rā′shəl) *adj.* between or involving different races. —**in′ter·ra′cial·ly,** *adv.*

in·ter·reg·num (in′tər reg′nəm) *n.* **-nums, -na** (-nə). **1** the time between the end of one ruler's reign and the beginning of the next one. **2** any time during which a nation is without its usual ruler. **3** a period of inactivity; pause. [< L *interregnum* < *inter-* between + *regnum* reign]

in·ter·re·late (in′tər ri lāt′) *v.* **-lat·ed, -lat·ing.** relate to one another.

in·ter·ro·gate (in ter′ə gāt′) *v.* **-gat·ed, -gat·ing. 1** question thoroughly; examine by asking questions: *The lawyer took two hours to interrogate the witness.* **2** ask a series of questions. [< L *interrogare* < *inter-* between + *rogare* ask] —**Syn. 1, 2** See **question.**

in·ter·ro·ga·tion (in ter′ə gā′shən) *n.* **1** a questioning. The formal examination of a witness by asking questions is an interrogation. **2** a question.

interrogation mark or **point** a question mark (?).

in·ter·rog·a·tive (in′tə rog′ə tiv) *adj.* asking a question; having the form of a question: *an interrogative sentence, an interrogative look or tone of voice.* —*n.* in grammar, a word used in asking a question. *Who, why,* and *what* are interrogatives. —**in′ter·rog′a·tive·ly,** *adv.*

in·ter·ro·ga·tor (in ter′ə gā′tər) *n.* a questioner.

in·ter·rog·a·to·ry (in′tə rog′ə tô′rē) *adj. n.* **-to·ries.** —*adj.* questioning. —*n.* a formal question or set of questions.

in·ter·rupt (in′tə rupt′) *v.* **1** break in upon (talk, work, rest, a person speaking, etc.); hinder; stop. **2** make a break in: *A building interrupts the view from our window.* **3** cause a break; break in; cut in: *It is not polite to interrupt when someone is talking.* [ME< L *interruptus,* pp. of *interrumpere* < *inter-* between + *rumpere* break] —**in′ter·rupt′er,** *n.*

in·ter·rup·tion (in′tə rup′shən) *n.* **1** an interrupting. **2** a being interrupted. **3** something that interrupts. **4** an intermission.

in·ter·scho·las·tic (in′tər skə las′tik) *adj.* between schools: *interscholastic competition.* ☛ See **intramural** for usage note.

in·ter·sect (in′tər sekt′) *v.* **1** cut or divide by passing through or crossing: *A path intersects the field.* **2** cross each other: *Streets usually intersect at right angles.* [< L *intersectus,* pp. of *intersecare* < *inter-* between + *secare* cut]

A
B
The line AB intersects the parallel lines

in·ter·sec·tion (in′tər sek′shən or in′tər sek′shən) *n.* **1** an intersecting. **2** a point or line where one thing crosses another: *A stop sign means that vehicles must stop before entering the intersection.* In the diagram, there are two intersections where the line AB crosses the parallel lines.

in·ter·space (*n.* in′tər spās′; *v.* in′tər spās′) *n. v.* **-spaced, -spac·ing.** —*n.* a space between things; an interval. —*v.* **1** put a space between. **2** occupy or fill the space between.

in·ter·sperse (in′tər spėrs′) *v.* **-spersed, -spers·ing.** **1** vary with something put here and there: *The grass was interspersed with beds of flowers.* **2** scatter or place here and there among other things: *Bushes were interspersed among the trees.* [< L *interspersus* scattered < *inter-* between + *spargere* scatter]

in·ter·sper·sion (in′tər spėr′zhən or in′tər spėr′shən) *n.* an interspersing or being interspersed.

in·ter·state (in′tər stāt′) *adj.* between states: *an interstate highway.*

in·ter·stel·lar (in′tər stel′ər) *adj.* among or between the stars.

in·ter·stice (in tėr′stis) *n.* **-sti·ces** (-stə sēz′). a small or narrow space between things or parts; chink. [< LL *interstitium* < L *inter-* between < *stare* to stand]

in·ter·sti·tial (in′tər stish′əl) *adj.* of, in, or forming interstices. —**in′ter·sti′tial·ly,** *adv.*

in·ter·trib·al (in′tər trīb′əl) *adj.* between tribes. —**in′ter·trib′al·ly,** *adv.*

in·ter·twine (in′tər twīn′) *v.* **-twined, -twin·ing.** twine one with another.

in·ter·twist (in′tər twist′) *v.* twist one with another.

in·ter·ur·ban (in′tər ėr′bən) *adj.* between cities or towns.

in·ter·val (in′tər vəl) *n.* **1** the time or space between: *an interval of a week, intervals of freedom from pain.* **2 at intervals, a** now and then. **b** here and there. **3** in music, the difference in pitch between two tones. **4** intervale. [< L *intervallum,* originally, space between palisades < *inter-* between + *vallum* wall]

in·ter·vale (in′tər vāl′) *n.* a low-lying area of rich land between hills or by a river. [< *interval,* influenced by *vale*[1]]

in·ter·vene (in′tər vēn′) *v.* **-vened, -ven·ing.** **1** come between; be between: *A week intervenes between Christmas and New Year's.* **2** come in to help settle a dispute: *The Prime Minister was asked to intervene in the railway strike.* [< L *intervenire* < *inter-* between + *venire* come] —**in′ter·ven′er,** *n.* —**Syn. 2** mediate, intercede.

in·ter·ven·tion (in′tər ven′shən) *n.* **1** an intervening. **2** an interference by one nation in the affairs of another.

in·ter·ven·tion·ist (in′tər ven′ shə nist) *n.* **1** a person who supports interference in the affairs of another country. **2** in medicine, a person who prefers medical action rather than letting a disease take its course. —*adj.* **1** of or having to do with intervention or interventionists. **2** approving intervention.

in·ter·view (in′tər vū′) *n.* **1** a meeting, generally of persons face to face, to talk over something special: *John applied for the job and had an interview with the manager.* **2** a meeting between a reporter, writer, radio or television commentator, etc. and a person from whom information is sought. **3** a printed report or broadcast of such a meeting. —*v.* have an interview with; meet and talk with. [< F *entrevue* < *entrevoir* glimpse < L *inter-* between + *videre* see] —**in′ter·view′er,** *n.*

in·ter·weave (in′tər wēv′) *v.* **-wove** or **-weaved, -wo·ven** or **-wove** or **-weaved, -weav·ing.** **1** weave together. **2** intermingle; connect closely.

in·ter·wove (in′tər wōv′) *v.* a pt. and a pp. of **interweave.**

in·ter·wo·ven (in′tər wō′vən) *adj.* **1** woven together. **2** intermingled. —*v.* a pp. of **interweave.**

in·tes·ta·cy (in tes′tə sē) *n.* the condition of being intestate at death.

in·tes·tate (in tes′tāt or in tes′tit) *adj.* **1** having made no will. **2** not disposed of by a will. —*n.* a person who has died without making a will. [< L *intestatus* < *in-* not + *testari* make a will < *testis* witness]

in·tes·ti·nal (in tes′tə nəl) *adj.* of or in the intestines. —**in·tes′ti·nal·ly,** *adv.*

in·tes·tine (in tes′tən) *n.* **1** the part of the alimentary canal that extends from the stomach to the anus. Food from the stomach passes into the intestine for further digestion and for absorption. In grown people, the **small intestine** is about twenty-five feet long; the **large intestine** is about five feet long. **2 intestines,** *pl.* the intestine; the bowels. —*adj.* within a country; internal: *Intestine strife is civil war.* [< L *intestina,* neut. pl., internal < *intus* within < *in* in]

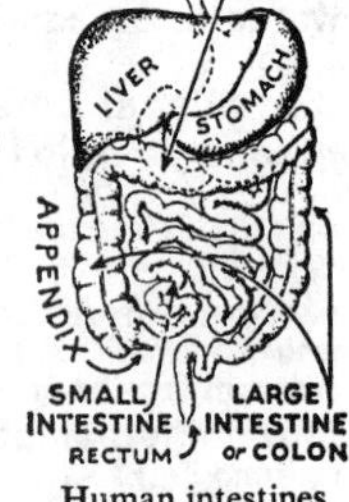

Human intestines

in·thral (in throl′ or in thrôl′) *v.* enthral.

in·throne (in thrōn′) *v.* **-throned, -thron·ing.** enthrone.

in·ti·ma·cy (in′tə mə sē) *n.* **-cies.** **1** the state of being intimate; close acquaintance. **2** a familiar or intimate act. —**Syn. 1** closeness. **2** familiarity.

in·ti·mate[1] (in′tə mit) *adj.* **1** very familiar; known very well; closely acquainted. **2** close. **3** very personal; most private. **4** far within; inmost. —*n.* a close friend. [earlier *intime* < L *intimus* inmost (and, as a noun, close friend), superlative, to *in* in; later altered under the influence of L *intimatus,* pp. of *intimare.* See INTIMATE[2].] —**in′ti·mate·ly,** *adv.* —**Syn.** *adj.* **1** See **familiar.**

in·ti·mate[2] (in′tə māt′) *v.* **-mat·ed, -mat·ing.** **1** suggest indirectly; hint. **2** announce; notify. [< L *intimare,* originally, press in < L *intimus* inmost. See INTIMATE[1].] —**in′ti·mat′er,** *n.* —**Syn. 1** See **hint.**

in·ti·ma·tion (in′tə mā′shən) *n.* **1** an indirect suggestion; hint: *A frown is often an intimation of disapproval.* **2** an announcement; notice.

in·tim·i·date (in tim′ə dāt′) *v.* **-dat·ed, -dat·ing.** **1** frighten; make afraid. **2** influence or force by fear. [< Med.L *intimidare* < L *in-* + *timidus* fearful] —**in·tim′i·da′tion,** *n.* —**in·tim′i·da′tor,** *n.*

in·ti·tle (in tī′təl) *v.* **-tled, -tling.** entitle.

in·to (in′tü; *before consonants, often* in′tə) *prep.* **1** to the inside of; toward the inside; within: *go into the house.* **2** to the condition of; to the form of: *a house divided into ten rooms.* **3** in mathematics, going into (implying or expressing division): *5 into 30 is 6.* ☛ See **in** for usage note.

in·tol·er·a·bil·i·ty (in tol′ər ə bil′ə tē) *n.* the quality of being intolerable.

in·tol·er·a·ble (in tol′ər ə bəl) *adj.* unbearable; too much, too painful, etc. to be endured. [< L *intolerabilis*] **—in·tol′er·a·ble·ness,** *n.* **—Syn.** unendurable, insufferable.

in·tol·er·a·bly (in tol′ər ə blē) *adv.* unbearably; beyond endurance.

in·tol·er·ance (in tol′ər əns) *n.* **1** lack of tolerance; unwillingness to let others do and think as they choose, especially in matters of religion. **2** inability to endure; unwillingness to endure.

in·tol·er·ant (in tol′ər ənt) *adj.* **1** not tolerant; unwilling to let others do and think as they choose, especially in matters of religion. **2 intolerant of,** not able to endure; unwilling to endure. **—in·tol′er·ant·ly,** *adv.* **—Syn. 1** bigoted, narrow, dogmatic.

in·tomb (in tüm′) *v.* entomb.

in·to·na·tion (in′tō nā′shən or in′tə nā′shən) *n.* **1** the act of intoning: *the intonation of a psalm.* **2** the production of musical notes. **3** the manner of speaking, singing, or playing in regard to tone variations: *a British intonation.* **4** in linguistics, the pattern of significant pitch differences and pauses in speech.

in·tone (in tōn′) *v.* **-toned, -ton·ing. 1** read or recite in a singing voice; chant. **2** utter with a particular tone. **3** make musical sounds, especially in a slow, drawn-out manner. [ME < Med.L *intonare,* ult. < L *in-* in + *tonus* tone]

in to·to (in′ tō′tō) *Latin.* as a whole; completely.

in·tox·i·cant (in tok′sə kənt) *n.* **1** alcoholic liquor. **2** any drug that intoxicates. *—adj.* intoxicating.

in·tox·i·cate (in tok′sə kāt′) *v.* **-cat·ed, -cat·ing. 1** make drunk: *Alcohol intoxicates people.* **2** excite beyond self-control. [< Med.L *intoxicare,* ult. < L *in-* in + *toxicum* poison < Gk. *toxicon* (*pharmakon*) (poison) for shooting arrows < *toxon* bow. Related to TOXIC.] **—in·tox′i·cat′ing·ly,** *adv.*

in·tox·i·cat·ed (in tok′sə kāt′id) *adj.* **1** drunk. **2** excited beyond self-control. **—in·tox′i·cat′ed·ly,** *adv.*

in·tox·i·ca·tion (in tok′sə kā′shən) *n.* **1** drunkenness. **2** great excitement. **3** in medicine, poisoning.

intr. intransitive.

intra- *prefix.* within; inside; on the inside, as in *intravenous.* [< L *intra-* < *intra,* prep. adv.]

in·trac·ta·bil·i·ty (in trak′tə bil′ə tē) *n.* the quality of being intractable; stubbornness.

in·trac·ta·ble (in trak′tə bəl) *adj.* hard to manage; stubborn. **—in·trac′ta·bly,** *adv.* **—Syn.** unruly, perverse.

in·tra·dos (in trā′dos) *n.* in architecture, the interior curve or surface of an arch or vault. [< F < L *intra-* within + F *dos* back]

in·tra·mu·ral (in′trə mūr′əl) *adj.* within the walls; inside. In intramural games, all the players belong to the same school.

☛ **Intramural is written without a hyphen. It is applied specifically to school activities carried on by groups belonging to the same school as contrasted with *intercollegiate,* applied to activities of groups belonging to different schools.**

intrans. intransitive.

in·tran·si·gence (in tran′sə jəns) *n.* the quality of being intransigent; uncompromising hostility.

in·tran·si·gen·cy (in tran′sə jən sē) *n.* intransigence.

in·tran·si·gent (in tran′sə jənt) *adj.* unwilling to agree or compromise. *—n.* a person who is unwilling to agree or compromise. [< F < Sp. *los intransigentes,* name for various extreme political parties, ult. < L *in-* not + *transigere* come to an agreement < *trans-* through + *agere* drive] **—in·tran′si·gent·ly,** *adv.*

in·tran·si·tive (in tran′sə tiv) *adj.* of verbs, not taking a direct object. The verbs *belong, go,* and *seem* are intransitive. *—n.* an intransitive verb. *Abbrev.:* intrans. **—in·tran′si·tive·ly,** *adv.* ☛ See **verb** for usage note.

in·tra·ve·nous (in′trə vē′nəs) *adj.* **1** within a vein or the veins. **2** into a vein: *an intravenous injection.* [< *intra-* + L *vena* vein] **—in′tra·ve′nous·ly,** *adv.*

in·treat (in trēt′) *v.* entreat.

in·trench (in trench′) *v.* entrench.

in·trench·ment (in trench′mənt) *n.* entrenchment.

hat, āge, cãre, fär; let, ēqual, tėrm; it, īce
hot, ōpen, ôrder; oil, out; cup, pu̇t, rüle, ūse
əbove, takən, pencəl, lemən, circəs
ch, child; ng, long; sh, ship
th, thin; ᴛʜ, then; zh, measure

in·trep·id (in trep′id) *adj.* fearless; dauntless; courageous; very brave. [< L *intrepidus* < *in-* not + *trepidus* alarmed] **—in·trep′id·ly,** *adv.* **—Syn.** bold, daring.

in·tre·pid·i·ty (in′trə pid′ə tē) *n.* fearlessness; dauntless courage; great bravery.

in·tri·ca·cy (in′trə kə sē) *n.* **-cies. 1** the quality or state of being intricate; complexity: *The intricacy of the plan made it hard to understand.* **2** a complication; something involved; intricate proceedings: *The plan was full of intricacies.*

in·tri·cate (in′trə kit) *adj.* **1** with many twists and turns; perplexing, entangled, or complicated: *an intricate knot, an intricate maze, an intricate plot.* **2** very hard to understand: *an intricate design, an intricate piece of machinery, intricate directions.* [< L *intricatus* < *intricare* entangle, ult. < *in-* in + *tricae* hindrances] **—in′tri·cate·ly,** *adv.* **—in′tri·cate·ness,** *n.* **—Syn. 1** involved, complex.

in·trigue (*n.* in trēg′ or in′trēg; *v.* in trēg′) *n. v.* **-trigued, -tri·guing.** *—n.* **1** underhand planning; secret scheming; plotting: *The royal palace was filled with intrigue.* **2** a crafty plot; a secret scheme. **3** a secret love affair. **4** the plot of a play, dramatic poem, etc., especially the development of a complex or involved situation. *—v.* **1** carry on an underhand plan; scheme secretly; plot. **2** excite the curiosity and interest of: *The book's unusual title intrigued me.* **3** have a secret love affair. **4** interest in a pleasing way: *That lady's hat intrigues me.* [< F < Ital. *intrigo* < *intrigare* < L *intricare* entangle. See INTRICATE.] **—in·tri′guing·ly,** *adv.* **—Syn.** *n.* **1** conspiracy.

in·trin·sic (in trin′sik) *adj.* **1** belonging to a thing by its very nature; essential; inherent: *The intrinsic value of a dollar bill is only that of the paper it is printed on.* **2** in anatomy, originating or being inside the part on which it acts: *the intrinsic muscles of the larynx.* [< F < Med.L *intrinsecus* internal < L *intrinsecus* inwardly]

in·trin·si·cal (in trin′sə kəl) *adj.* intrinsic.

in·trin·si·cal·ly (in trin′sik lē) *adv.* by its very nature; essentially; inherently.

intro- *prefix.* inwardly; within, as in *introvert.* [< L *intro-* < *intro,* adv.]

intro. or **introd. 1** introduction. **2** introductory.

in·tro·duce (in′trə dūs′ or in′trə düs′) *v.* **-duced, -duc·ing. 1** bring in: *introduce a new subject into the conversation.* **2** put in; insert: *The doctor introduced a long tube into the sick man's throat.* **3** bring into use, notice, knowledge, etc.: *introduce a new word.* **4** make known: *The chairman introduced the speaker to the audience.* **5** bring to acquaintance with something: *I introduced my country cousin to the city by showing him the sights.* **6** bring forward: *introduce a question for debate.* **7** begin: *He introduced his speech by telling a joke.* [< L *introducere* < *intro-* in + *ducere* lead] **—in′tro·duc′er,** *n.*

Syn. 4, 5 Introduce, present = make someone known to another or others. **Introduce** = make a person known, in a more or less formal way, to another or to a group, or to make two people acquainted with each other: *Mrs. Brown, may I introduce Mr. Smith?* **Present,** always suggesting formality, means "introduce, with more or less ceremony, a person or group to one regarded or treated as superior": *The new ambassador was presented to the Governor General.*

in·tro·duc·tion (in′trə duk′shən) *n.* **1** an introducing: *The introduction of steel made skyscrapers easy to build.* **2** a being introduced: *She was shy at her introduction to so many strangers.* **3** something that introduces; the first part of a book, speech, piece of music, etc. leading up to the main part. **4** a first book for beginners. **5** the thing introduced; thing brought into use: *Radios are a later introduction than telephones.* [ME < L *introductio, -onis* < *introducere.* See INTRODUCE.]

Syn. 3 Introduction, preface, foreword = a section at the beginning of a book, etc. **Introduction** applies to an actual part of the book, article, play, etc. that leads into or gives what is necessary for understanding the main part: *School editions of* *literary works usually have introductions.* **Preface** applies to a separate section coming before the actual book, explaining something, such as the purpose, method, importance, etc. **Foreword** may mean a short, simple preface but applies especially to an introductory note on the book or the author by a distinguished writer, scholar, or public figure: *A foreword by the President of the University came before the author's preface.*

in·tro·duc·to·ry (in′trə duk′tə rē or in′trə duk′trē) *adj.* used to introduce; serving as an introduction; preliminary.

in·tro·it (in trō′it) *n.* **1** in the Roman Catholic Church, a hymn or responsive anthem recited by the priest at the beginning of Mass or sung by the choir at High Mass. **2** in Anglican churches, a psalm, hymn, etc. at the beginning of the communion service. [ME < L *introitus* entrance < *introire* enter < *intro-* in + *ire* go]

in·trorse (in trôrs′) *adj.* in botany, turned or facing inward. A violet has introrse stamens. [< L *introrsus,* ult. < *intro-* inward + *versus* turned]

in·tro·spec·tion (in′trə spek′shən) *n.* an examination of one's own thoughts and feelings. [< L *introspectus,* pp. of *introspicere* < *intro-* into + *specere* look]

in·tro·spec·tive (in′trə spek′tiv) *adj.* inclined to examine one's own thoughts and feelings.
—**in′tro·spec′tive·ly,** *adv.*

in·tro·ver·sion (in′trə vėr′zhən or -vėr′shən) *n.* **1** a tendency to be more interested in one's own thoughts and feelings than in what is going on around one. **2** the act or fact of turning inward. [< *intro-* + *version,* as in *reversion,* etc.]

in·tro·vert (in′trə vėrt′) *n.* a person more interested in his own thoughts and feelings than in what is going on around him; a person tending to think rather than act. [< *intro-* within + L *vertere* turn]

in·trude (in trüd′) *v.* **-trud·ed, -trud·ing. 1** thrust oneself in; come unasked and unwanted. **2** thrust in; force in: *Do not intrude your opinions upon others.* [< L *intrudere* < *in-* in + *trudere* thrust] —**in·trud′er,** *n.*

Syn. 1 Intrude, trespass, encroach = thrust oneself into or upon the presence, possessions, territory, or rights of others. **Intrude** = thrust in, without permission, where uninvited, unwanted, or having no right to go: *He intrudes upon their hospitality.* **Trespass** = intrude unlawfully or by overstepping the limits of what is proper or right: *Joe trespassed on another boy's paper route.* **Encroach** adds the idea of gradually or secretly taking the property or rights of another: *Our neighbor's irrigation system is encroaching on our land.*

in·tru·sion (in trü′zhən) *n.* **1** the act of intruding; coming unasked and unwanted. **2** an unlawful entry or seizure of land or rights belonging to another. **3** in geology: **a** the forcing of molten rock into fissures or between strata. **b** the molten rock forced in and solidified in place. [ME < Med.L *intrusio, -onis* < L *intrusus,* pp. of *intrudere.* See INTRUDE.]

in·tru·sive (in trü′siv) *adj.* **1** intruding; coming unasked and unwanted. **2** in geology, forced into fissures or between strata while molten. **3** in phonetics, inserted without any etymological or historical basis. The (r) often heard in *khaki* (kär′kē) is intrusive. —**in·tru′sive·ly,** *adv.*

in·trust (in trust′) *v.* entrust.

in·tu·i·tion (in′tü ish′ən or in′tū ish′ən) *n.* **1** the perception of truths, facts, etc. without reasoning: *His intuition told him that the stranger was honest.* **2** something so perceived. [< LL *intuitio, -onis* a gazing at < L *intueri* < *in-* at + *tueri* look]

in·tu·i·tion·al (in′tü ish′ən əl or in′tü ish′ən əl) *adj.* of, having to do with, or characterized by, intuition; based on intuition. —**in′tu·i′tion·al·ly,** *adv.*

in·tu·i·tive (in tü′ə tiv or in tū′ə tiv) *adj.* **1** perceiving by intuition: *intuitive power.* **2** acquired by intuition: *intuitive knowledge.* **3** of the nature of an intuition: *an intuitive guess.*—**in·tu′i·tive·ly,** *adv.*

I·nu·it (in′ü it, in′yü it, or in′yə wit) *Cdn. n. pl.* a people living mainly in northern Canada, Greenland, Alaska, and eastern Siberia, who are the original inhabitants of the Arctic; the Eskimo people.
—*adj.* of or related to these people or their language: *Inuit customs.* [< Eskimo *inuit,* pl. of *inuk* man, person]

in·un·date (in′ən dāt′ or in un′dāt) *v.* **-dat·ed, -dat·ing.** overflow; flood. [< L *inundare* < *in-* onto + *undare* flow < *unda* wave]

in·un·da·tion (in′ən dā′shən) *n.* an overflowing; flood. —**Syn.** See **flood.**

in·ure (in ūr′) *v.* **-ured, -ur·ing. 1** toughen or harden; accustom; habituate: *Poverty has inured the beggar to hardships.* **2** have effect; be useful: *The agreement inures to the benefit of the employees.* [< *in* + obs. *ure* use, n. < AF *ure* < L *opera* work] —**in·ure′ment,** *n.*

inv. 1 invoice. **2** inventor. **3** invented. **4** inventory. **5** investment.

in va·cu·o (in′ vak′ū ō′) *Latin.* in a vacuum.

in·vade (in vād′) *v.* **-vad·ed, -vad·ing. 1** enter with force or as an enemy; attack: *Soldiers invaded the country. Diseases invade the body.* **2** enter as if to take possession: *Tourists invaded the city. Night invades the sky.* **3** interfere with; encroach upon; violate: *The law punishes people who invade the rights of others.* [< L *invadere* < *in-* in + *vadere* go, walk] —**in·vad′er,** *n.*

in·val·id[1] (in′və lid) *n.* a sick, weak person not able to get about and do things.
—*adj.* **1** not well; weak and sick. **2** of or for an invalid or invalids.
—*v.* **1** make weak or sick; disable. **2** release or retire from active service because of sickness or injury: *He was invalided out of the army.* [< L *invalidus* not strong; influenced by F *invalide* (< L *invalidus*). See INVALID[2].]

in·val·id[2] (in val′id) *adj.* not valid; without force or effect; worthless: *If a will is not signed, it is invalid.* < L *invalidus* < *in-* not + *validus* strong < *valere* be strong] —**in·val′id·ly,** *adv.* —**Syn.** worthless.

in·val·i·date (in val′ə dāt′) *v.* **-dat·ed, -dat·ing.** make valueless; deprive of force or effect: *A contract is invalidated if only one party signs it.* —**in·val′i·da′tion,** *n.* —**in′val·i·da′tor,** *n.*

in·va·lid·ism (in′və lid iz′əm) *n.* the condition of being an invalid; prolonged ill health.

in·va·lid·i·ty (in′və lid′ə tē) *n.* a lack of validity, force, or effect; worthlessness.

in·val·u·a·ble (in val′yů bəl or in val′ū ə bəl) *adj.* priceless; very precious; valuable beyond measure. —**in·val′u·a·bly,** *adv.* —**in·val′u·a·ble·ness,** *n.*

in·var·i·a·bil·i·ty (in vãr′ē ə bil′ə tē) *n.* unchangeableness; constancy; uniformity.

in·var·i·a·ble (in vãr′ē ə bəl) *adj.* always the same; unchangeable; unchanging. —**Syn.** uniform, constant. —**in·var′i·a·bly,** *adv.*

in·va·sion (in vā′zhən) *n.* **1** an invading; an attack. **2** an interference; encroachment, violation: *She objected to the invasion of her privacy.* [< LL *invasio, -onis* < *invadere.* See INVADE.]

in·vec·tive (in vek′tiv) *n.* a violent attack in words; abusive language. [ME < LL *invectivus* abusive < L *invehi.* See INVEIGH.]

in·veigh (in vā′) *v.* make a violent attack in words. [< L *invehi* launch an attack < *in-* against + *vehere* carry]

in·vei·gle (in vā′gəl or in vē′gəl) *v.* **-gled, -gling.** mislead by trickery; entice; allure: *The saleswoman inveigled the poor girl into buying four hats.* [apparently alteration of earlier **avegle* < F *aveugler* make blind < *aveugle* blind < VL *aboculus* < L *ab-* without + *oculus* eye] —**in·vei′gler** ,*n.* —**Syn.** ensnare, beguile, dupe.

in·vent (in vent′) *v.* **1** make, create, or think out (something new): *Bell invented the telephone.* **2** make up; think up: *invent an excuse.* [< L *inventus,* pp. of *invenire* < *in-* in + *venire* come] —**Syn. 1** See **discover.**

in·ven·tion (in ven′shən) *n.* **1** a making something new: *the invention of gunpowder.* **2** the thing invented: *Radio was a wonderful invention.* **3** the power of inventing: *To be a good novelist, a person needs invention.* **4** a made-up story; a false statement: *His testimony was pure invention.* **5** in music, a short instrumental composition consisting of one or two simple melodies developed in two- or three-part harmony.

in·ven·tive (in ven′tiv) *adj.* **1** good at inventing: *An inventive person thinks up ways to save time, money, and work.* **2** of invention. **3** showing power of inventing. —**in·ven′tive·ly,** *adv.* —**in·ven′tive·ness,** *n.*

in·ven·tor (in ven′tər) *n.* a person who invents: *Alexander Graham Bell was a great inventor.*

hat, āge, cãre, fär; let, ēqual, tėrm; it, īce
hot, ōpen, ôrder; oil, out; cup, pu̇t, rüle, ūse
əbove, takən, pencəl, lemən, circəs
ch, child; ng, long; sh, ship
th, thin; ᴛʜ, then; zh, measure

in·ven·tory (in′vən tô′rē) *n.* **-to·ries,** *v.* **-to·ried, -to·ry·ing.** —*n.* **1** a detailed list of articles with their estimated value. **2** a collection of articles that are or may be so listed; stock: *A storekeeper had a sale to reduce his inventory.* —*v.* make a detailed list of; enter in a list: *Some stores inventory their stock once a month.* [< Med.L *inventorium* < LL < *inventus,* pp. of *invenire.* See INVENT.]

in·ver·ness (in′vər nes′) *n.* an overcoat with a long removable cape. [< *Inverness,* Scotland]

An inverness cape

in·verse (in vėrs′ or in′vėrs) *adj.* reversed in position, direction, or tendency; inverted: *DCBA is the inverse order of ABCD.* —*n.* **1** something reversed: *The inverse of 3/4 is 4/3.* **2** direct opposite: *Evil is the inverse of good.* [< L *inversus,* pp. of *invertere.* See INVERT.] —**in·verse′ly,** *adv.*

in·ver·sion (in vėr′zhən or in vėr′shən) *n.* **1** an inverting. **2** the state of being inverted. **3** something inverted.

inversion layer in meteorology, a layer of air warmer than the air beneath it.

in·vert (in vėrt′) *v.* **1** turn upside down: *invert a glass.* **2** turn around or reverse in position, direction, order, etc.: *If you invert "I can," you have "Can I?"* **3** in music, change by making the lower or lowest note an octave higher or the higher or highest note an octave lower. [< L *invertere* < *in-* over, around + *vertere* turn] —**in·vert′er,** *n.* —**Syn. 1** See **reverse.**

in·ver·te·brate (in vėr′tə brit or in vėr′tə brāt′) *adj.* **1** without a backbone. **2** of or having to do with invertebrates. **3** lacking moral strength; without character, conviction, or purpose. —*n.* **1** an animal without a backbone. All animals except fish, amphibians, reptiles, birds, and mammals are invertebrates. **2** a person without moral strength or character.

in·vest (in vest′) *v.* **1** use (money) to buy something that is expected to produce a profit, or income, or both: *He invested his money in stocks, bonds, and land.* **2** invest money: *Learn to invest wisely.* **3** clothe; cover; surround: *Darkness invests the earth by night.* **4** give power, authority, or right to: *He invested his lawyer with complete power to act for him.* **5** install in office with a ceremony: *A king is invested by crowning him.* **6** surround with soldiers or ships; besiege: *The enemy invested the city and cut it off from our army.* [< L *investire* < *in-* in + *vestis* clothing]

in·ves·ti·gate (in ves′tə gāt′) *v.* **-gat·ed, -gat·ing.** search into; examine closely: *Detectives investigate crimes. Scientists investigate nature.* [< L *investigare* < *in-* in + *vestigare* track, trace] —**Syn.** explore, scrutinize.

in·ves·ti·ga·tion (in ves′tə gā′shən) *n.* a careful search; detailed or careful examination.

Syn. Investigation, examination, inquiry = a search for information or truth. **Investigation** emphasizes carefully tracking down everything that can be found out, in order to bring out hidden facts and learn the truth: *An investigation of the accident by the police put the blame on the drivers of both cars.* **Examination** emphasizes looking something or someone over closely or testing carefully in order to learn the facts about it, its condition, value, etc.: *The doctor gave him a physical examination.* **Inquiry** especially suggests a search made by asking questions: *Counsellors began an inquiry into the industrial needs of the region.*

in·ves·ti·ga·tor (in ves′tə gā′tər) *n.* a person who investigates.

in·ves·ti·ture (in ves′tə chür′ or in ves′tə chər) *n.* **1** a formal investing of a person with an office, dignity, power, right, etc. **2** clothing; apparel; covering.

in·vest·ment (in vest′mənt) *n.* **1** an investing; a laying out of money: *Getting an education is a wise investment of time and money.* **2** the amount of money invested: *His investments amount to thousands of dollars.* **3** something that is expected to yield money as income or profit or both: *Canada Savings Bonds are a safe investment.* **4** a surrounding with soldiers or ships; siege. **5** an investiture.

in·ves·tor (in ves′tər) *n.* a person who invests money.

in·vet·er·a·cy (in vet′ər ə sē) *n.* a settled, fixed condition; the nature of a fixed habit.

in·vet·er·ate (in vet′ər it) *adj.* **1** confirmed in a habit, practice, feeling, etc.; habitual: *an inveterate smoker.* **2** long and firmly established: *Cats have an inveterate dislike of dogs.* [< L *inveteratus,* pp. of *inveterascere* make old < *in-* in + *veterascere* grow old < *vetus, -teris* old] —**in·vet′er·ate·ly,** *adv.* —**Syn. 1** hardened, chronic.

in·vid·i·ous (in vid′ē əs) *adj.* likely to arouse ill will or resentment; giving offence because unfair or unjust: *Such comparisons are invidious.* [< L *invidiosus* < *invidia* envy. Related to ENVY.] —**in·vid′i·ous·ly,** *adv.* —**in·vid′i·ous·ness,** *n.* —**Syn.** hateful.

in·vig·or·ate (in vig′ər āt′) *v.* **-at·ed, -at·ing.** give vigor to; fill with life and energy. [< *in-* in + *vigor*] —**in·vig′or·at′ing·ly,** *adv.* —**Syn.** brace, refresh, stimulate, animate.

in·vig·or·a·tion (in vig′ər ā′shən) *n.* an invigorating or being invigorated.

in·vin·ci·bil·i·ty (in vin′sə bil′ə tē) *n.* the quality of being invincible.

in·vin·ci·ble (in vin′sə bəl) *adj.* not to be overcome; unconquerable. [ME < OF < L *invincibilis* < *in-* not + *vincere* conquer] —**in·vin′ci·bly,** *adv.* —**Syn.** indomitable.

in vi·no ve·ri·tas (in vē′nō ver′ə tas) *Latin.* intoxication makes men reveal their true thoughts; literally, in wine (there is) truth.

in·vi·o·la·bil·i·ty (in vī′ə lə bil′ə tē) *n.* the quality of being inviolable.

in·vi·o·la·ble (in vī′ə lə bəl) *adj.* **1** that must not be violated or injured; sacred: *an inviolable vow, an inviolable sanctuary.* **2** that cannot be violated or injured: *The gods are inviolable.* —**in·vi′o·la·bly,** *adv.*

in·vi·o·late (in vī′ə lit or in vī′ə lāt′) *adj.* not violated; uninjured; unbroken; not profaned. —**in·vi′o·late·ly,** *adv.*

in·vis·i·bil·i·ty (in viz′ə bil′ə tē) *n.* the state or quality of being invisible.

in·vis·i·ble (in viz′ə bəl) *adj.* **1** not visible; not capable of being seen: *Thought is invisible.* **2** not in sight; not to be seen: *The queen kept herself invisible in the palace.* **3** too small to be perceived: *Germs are invisible to the naked eye.* **4** so dark as to be hardly distinguishable from black: *invisible indigo.* **5** in commerce: **a** not listed in the regular financial statements: *an invisible asset.* **b** not appearing in returns of exports and imports, but from which payment is accepted or made to a foreign country. —*n.* **1** an invisible being or thing. **2 invisibles,** *pl.* invisible exports or imports: *Insurance, freight, royalties, investment earnings, etc. are invisibles.* **3 the invisible,** the unseen world. **4 the Invisible,** God.

in·vis·i·bly (in viz′ə blē) *adv.* without being seen; so as not to be seen.

in·vi·ta·tion (in′və tā′shən) *n.* **1** a request to come to some place or to do something. Formal invitations are written or printed. **2** the act of inviting. **3** attraction; enticement.

in·vite (*v.* in vīt′; *n.* in′vīt) *v.* **-vit·ed, -vit·ing,** *n.* —*v.* **1** ask (someone) politely to come to some place or to do something: *We invited her to join our club.* **2** make a polite request for: *The author invited our opinion of his story.* **3** give occasion for: *The letter invites some questions.* **4** attract; tempt: *The calm water invited us to swim.* —*n. Slang.* an invitation. [< L *invitare*] —**in·vit′er,** *n.* —**Syn.** *v.* **1** bid, request. See **call. 4** encourage, incite.

in·vit·ing (in vīt′ing) *adj.* attractive; tempting. —**in·vit′ing·ly,** *adv.*

in·vo·ca·tion (in′və kā′shən) *n.* **1** the act of calling upon in prayer; appeal for help or protection: *A church service often begins with an invocation to God.* **2** the form of words used in this. **3 a** a calling forth of spirits by magic. **b** a set of magic words used to call forth spirits; incantation. **4** a formal appeal at or near the beginning of a long poem, in which the poet asks a Muse to give him inspiration. **5** in law, a call for evidence, papers, etc. from another case.

in·voice (in′vois) *n. v.* **-voiced, -voic·ing.** —*n.* **1** a list of goods sent to a purchaser showing prices, amounts, shipping charges, etc. **2** a shipment of invoiced goods. **3** the form used for listing such goods. —*v.* make an invoice of; enter on an invoice. [earlier *invoyes,* pl. of *invoy,* var. of *envoy* < OF *envoy* < *envoier* send < VL < L *in via* on the way]

in·voke (in vōk′) *v.* **-voked, -vok·ing. 1** call on in prayer; appeal to for help or protection. **2** appeal to for confirmation or judgment: *invoke an authority.* **3** ask earnestly for; beg for: *The condemned criminal invoked the judge's mercy.* **4** call forth by magic. [< L *invocare* < *in-* on + *vocare* call] —**in·vok′er,** *n.*

in·vo·lu·cre (in′və lü′kər) *n.* in botany, a circle of small leaves or bracts around a flower or flower cluster. [< F < L *involucrum* a cover < *involvere.* See INVOLVE.]

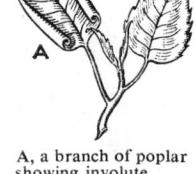

INVOLUCRE

in·vol·un·tar·y (in vol′ən ter′ē) *adj.* **1** not voluntary; not done of one's own free will; unwilling. **2** not done on purpose; not intended: *an involuntary injury.* **3** not controlled by the will: *Breathing is mainly involuntary.* —**in·vol′un·tar′i·ly,** *adv.* —**in·vol′un·tar′i·ness,** *n.* —**Syn. 1** compulsory, forced. **2** unintentional, inadvertent. **3** instinctive. See **automatic.**

in·vol·ute (in′və lüt′) *adj.* **1** involved; intricate. **2** rolled up on itself; curved spirally. **3** in botany, rolled inward from the edge: *an involute leaf.* **4** of shells, having the whorls closely wound. —*n.* something involved or intricate. [< L *involutus,* pp. of *involvere.* See INVOLVE.]

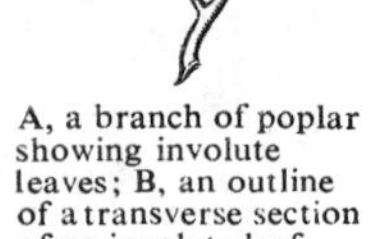

A, a branch of poplar showing involute leaves; B, an outline of a transverse section of an involute leaf.

in·vo·lu·tion (in′və lü′shən) *n.* **1** an involving. **2** a being involved; entanglement; complexity. **3** something involved; a complication. **4** in mathematics, the raising of a quantity to any power. **5** in biology, degeneration; retrograde change. **6** in botany: **a** a rolling inward from the edge. **b** a part thus formed.

in·volve (in volv′) *v.* **-volved, -volv·ing. 1** have as a necessary part, condition, or result; take in; include: *Housekeeping involves cooking, washing dishes, sweeping, and cleaning.* **2** have an effect on; affect: *These changes in the business involve the interests of all the owners.* **3** cause to be unpleasantly concerned; bring (into difficulty, danger, etc.): *One foolish mistake can involve you in a good deal of trouble.* **4** entangle; complicate: *A sentence that is involved is generally hard to understand.* **5** take up the attention of; occupy: *She was involved in working out a puzzle.* **6** wrap; enfold; envelop: *The outcome of the war is involved in doubt.* **7** wind spirally; coil: *The serpent involved his scaly folds.* **8** in mathematics, raise to a given power. [ME < L *involvere* < *in-* in + *volvere* roll] —**in·volv′er,** *n.*

Syn. 1 entail. **3 Involve, implicate** = draw someone or something into a situation hard to get out of. **Involve** = get someone or something caught in a situation that is unpleasantly embarrassing, mixed up, or complex and hard to solve or settle: *Buying an expensive car involved him in debt. Telling one lie usually involves you in many more.* **Implicate** = show that someone is involved in or closely connected with something, usually disgraceful or bad: *Having the stolen goods in his possession implicated him in the robbery.* **5** absorb. **6** surround.

in·volve·ment (in volv′mənt) *n.* **1** an involving. **2** the state of being involved.

in·vul·ner·a·bil·i·ty (in vul′nər ə bil′ə tē) *n.* the quality of being invulnerable.

in·vul·ner·a·ble (in vul′nər ə bəl) *adj.* **1** that cannot be wounded or injured: *Achilles was invulnerable except for his heel.* **2** proof against attack; not easily assailable: *an invulnerable argument.* —**in·vul′ner·a·bly,** *adv.*

in·ward (in′wərd) *adv.* **1** toward the inside: *a passage leading inward.* **2** into the mind or soul: *Turn your thoughts inward.* —*adj.* **1** placed within; internal: *the inward parts of the body.* **2** directed toward the inside: *an inward slant of the eyes.* **3** in mind or soul: *inward peace.* **4** intrinsic; inherent; essential: *the inward nature of a thing.* [OE *inweard*]

in·ward·ly (in′wərd lē) *adv.* **1** on the inside; within. **2** toward the inside. **3** in the mind or soul. **4** not aloud or openly.

in·ward·ness (in′wərd nis) *n.* **1** inner nature or meaning. **2** spirituality. **3** earnestness.

in·wards (*adv.* in′wərdz; *n.* in′ərdz) *adv.* inward. —*n.pl. Slang.* parts inside the body; stomach and intestines; innards.

in·weave (in wēv′) *v.* **-wove** or **-weaved, -wo·ven** or **-wove** or **-weaved, -weav·ing.** weave in; weave together; interweave.

in·wove (in wōv′) *v.* a pt. and a pp. of **inweave.**

in·wo·ven (in wō′vən) *v.* a pp. of **inweave.**

in·wrap (in rap′) *v.* **-wrapped, -wrap·ping.** enwrap.

in·wreathe (in rēᴛʜ′) *v.* **-wreathed, -wreath·ing.** enwreathe.

in·wrought (in rot′ or -rôt′) *adj.* **1** having a decoration worked in. **2** worked in. **3** mixed together; closely blended.

I·o (ī′ō) *n.* **1** in Greek mythology, a maiden loved by Zeus, who changed her into a white heifer to save her from the jealousy of Hera. Hera, however, sent a gadfly to torment Io and caused her to wander through many lands until she reached Egypt, where Zeus restored her to her natural form. **2** the Io moth.

Io ionium.

IODE or **I.O.D.E.** Imperial Order Daughters of the Empire.

i·o·did (ī′ə did) *n.* iodide.

i·o·dide (ī′ə dīd′ or ī′ə did) *n.* a compound of iodine with another element or radical.

i·o·din (ī′ə din) *n.* iodine.

i·o·dine (ī′ə dīn′ or ī′ə din; *in chemistry,* ī′ə dēn′) *n.* **1** a non-metallic chemical element consisting of blackish crystals that give off a dense, violet-colored vapor with an irritating odor. Iodine is used in medicine, in making dyes, in photography, etc. *Symbol:* I; *at.no.* 53; *at.wt.* 126.9044. **2** a brown liquid, **tincture of iodine,** used as an antiseptic. [< F *iode* iodine < Gk. *ioeidēs* violet-colored < *ion* violet]

i·o·dize (ī′ə dīz′) *v.* **-dized, -diz·ing.** combine or impregnate with iodine or an iodide: *iodized salt.* —**i′o·diz′er,** *n.*

i·o·do·form (ī ō′də fôrm′ or ī od′ə fôrm′) *n.* a crystalline compound of iodine, used as an antiseptic. *Formula:* CHI_3 [< *iodo-* iodine (< NL *iodum*) + *form(yl)* (< *formic acid*)]

IOF or **I.O.F.** Independent Order of Foresters.

Io moth (ī′ō) a yellow American moth having a bluish spot on each hind wing. [< *Io*]

i·on (ī′ən or ī′on) *n.* **1** either of the two substances into which a compound is broken up by the action of an electric current. **Positive ions** (cations) are formed in electrolysis by the loss of electrons. **Negative ions** (anions) are formed by the gain of electrons. **2** an electrically charged particle formed in a gas. [< Gk. *ion,* neut. ppr. of *ienai* go]

-ion *suffix.* **1** the act of ——ing, as in *attraction, calculation.* **2** the condition or state of being ——ed, as in *adoption, fascination.* **3** the result of ——ing, as in *abbreviation, collection, connection.* [< F < L *-io, -ionis,* or directly < L]

I·o·ni·an (ī ō′nē ən) *adj.* **1** of or having to do with Ionia, in ancient times a region of W. Asia Minor, or its people. **2** having to do with one of the main branches of the ancient Greek people or its language. The Athenians were of Ionian descent. —*n.* a Greek of this branch.

i·on·ic (ī on′ik) *adj.* having to do with ions.

I·on·ic (ī on′ik) *adj.* **1** in architecture: **a** of or having to do with the second of the three orders of ancient Greek architecture, characterized by height, lightness, and grace. **b** of or having to do with the type of column characteristic of Ionic architecture. The Ionic column consists of an ornate base, a tall, slender, deeply fluted shaft, with a capital featuring a projecting double scroll.

See **order** for picture. **2** of Ionia, in ancient times, a region of W. Asia Minor, or its people. —*n.* the dialect of ancient Greek spoken by the Ionians and including Homeric and Attic Greek. [< L *Ionicus* < Gk. *Iōnikos*]

i·o·ni·um (ī ō′nē əm) *n.* a radio-active isotope of thorium having a mass of 230. *Abbrev.*: Io; *half-life* 80,000 years. [< *ion* + uran*ium*; for its ionizing action]

i·on·i·za·tion (ī′ən ə zā′shən) *n.* a separation into ions; dissociation; formation of ions.

i·on·ize (ī′ən īz′) *v.* **-ized, -iz·ing.** separate into ions; produce ions in. Acids, bases, and salts ionize in solution. The gas in a neon light must be ionized before it can conduct an electric current. —**i′on·iz′er,** *n.*

i·on·o·sphere (ī on′ə sfēr′) *n.* a region of ionized layers of air above the stratosphere. Low pressure and solar radiation in the ionosphere help the transmission of radio waves over long distances by reflection.

IOOF or **I.O.O.F.** Independent Order of Odd Fellows.

i·o·ta (ī ō′tə) *n.* **1** the ninth letter of the Greek alphabet (Ι, ι). **2** a very small quantity: *There is not an iota of truth in the prisoner's story.* [< L < Gk. *iōta.* Doublet of JOT.] —**Syn. 2** bit, jot.

IOU or **I.O.U.** (ī′ō′ū′) an informal note acknowledging a debt: *Write me an IOU for ten dollars.* [for the phrase *I owe you*]

IPA or **I.P.A.** **1** International Phonetic Alphabet. **2** International Phonetic Association.

ip·e·cac (ip′ə kak′) *n.* **1** a medicine made from the dried roots of a S. American vine, used as an emetic or purgative. **2** the dried roots. **3** the vine. [< Pg. < Tupi-Guarani *ipe-kaa-guéne* creeping plant causing nausea]

ip·e·cac·u·an·ha (ip′ə kak′ū an′ə) *n.* ipecac.

Iph·i·ge·ni·a (if′ə jə nī′ə) *n.* in Greek mythology, the daughter of Agamemnon. He intended to sacrifice her to Artemis to obtain favorable winds for the Greek ships sailing to Troy, but Artemis put a hart in her place and carried Iphigenia off to Tauris to become her priestess.

ip·se dix·it (ip′sē dik′sit) a dogmatic assertion based merely on someone's authority. [< L *ipse dixit* he himself said (it)]

☛ **ipse dixit.** The Latin phrase, when used in English as a noun, takes the regular plural ending: *His argument was merely a succession of ipse dixits.*

ip·so fac·to (ip′sō fak′tō) *Latin.* by that very fact; by the fact itself.

IQ or **I.Q.** in psychology, intelligence quotient.

ir-[1] form of **in-**[1] before *r*, as in *irrational.*

ir-[2] form of **in-**[2] before *r*, as in *irrigate.*

Ir iridium.

Ir. **1** Ireland. **2** Irish.

I.R.A. or **IRA** Irish Republican Army.

I·ra·ni·an (i rā′nē ən or ī rā′nē ən) *adj.* of or having to do with Iran, a kingdom in S.W. Asia, its people, or their language. —*n.* **1** a native or inhabitant of Iran. **2** a citizen of Iran. **3** the language of Iran.

I·ra·qi (ē rä′kē) *n.* **1** a native of Iraq. **2** the Arabian dialect spoken in Iraq. —*adj.* of or having to do with Iraq, its people, or their dialect.

i·ras·ci·bil·i·ty (i ras′ə bil′ə tē) *n.* quickness of temper; irritability.

i·ras·ci·ble (i ras′ə bəl) *adj.* **1** easily made angry; irritable. **2** showing anger. [< LL *irascibilis* < L *irasci* grow angry < *ira* anger] —**i·ras′ci·bly,** *adv.* —**i·ras′ci·ble·ness,** *n.* —**Syn. 1** touchy, testy. See **irritable.**

i·rate (ī′rāt or ī rāt′) *adj.* angry. [< L *iratus* < *ira* anger] —**i′rate·ly,** *adv.*

IRBM Intermediate Range Ballistic Missile.

ire (īr) *n.* anger; wrath. [ME < OF < L *ira*]

Ire. Ireland.

ire·ful (īr′fəl) *adj.* angry; wrathful. —**ire′ful·ly,** *adv.*

ir·i·des·cence (ir′ə des′əns) *n.* a changing or play of colors, as in mother-of-pearl, opals, a peacock's feathers.

ir·i·des·cent (ir′ə des′ənt) *adj.* **1** displaying colors like those of the rainbow. **2** changing colors according to position. [< L *iris, iridis* rainbow < Gk.] —**ir′i·des′cent·ly,** *adv.*

i·rid·i·um (i rid′ē əm) *n.* a rare metallic chemical element that resembles platinum and is twice as heavy as lead, used for the points of pen nibs. *Symbol*: Ir; *at.no.* 77; *at.wt.* 192.2. [< NL < L *iris, -idis* rainbow; with reference to its iridescence in solution]

hat, āge, cãre, fär; let, ēqual, tėrm; it, īce
hot, ōpen, ôrder; oil, out; cup, pu̇t, rüle, ūse
əbove, takən, pencəl, lemən, circəs
ch, child; ng, long; sh, ship
th, thin; ᴛʜ, then; zh, measure

i·ris (ī′ris) *n.* **1** a plant having sword-shaped leaves and large flowers with three upright petals and three drooping petal-like sepals. **2** the flower of this plant. **3** the colored part around the pupil of the eye. See **eye** for diagram. **4 Iris,** in Greek mythology, the goddess of the rainbow and messenger of the gods. **5** the rainbow. [< L *iris* rainbow < Gk.]

I·rish (ī′rish) *adj.* of or having to do with Ireland, one of the British Isles, its people, or their language. —*n.* **1** the people of Ireland. **2** the Celtic language spoken in parts of Ireland; Gaelic. [ME *Irisc, Irish* < OE *Iras,* pl., the people of Ireland]

I·rish·man (ī′rish mən) *n.* **-men** (-mən). a man of Irish birth or descent.

Irish moss carrageen.

Irish potato the common white potato.

Irish setter **1** a breed of setter having silky, reddish-brown hair. **2** a dog of this breed.

Irish stew a stew made of meat, potatoes, and onions.

Irish terrier **1** a breed of small dog having wiry, brown hair, resembling a small Airedale. **2** a dog of this breed.

Irish wolfhound **1** a breed of very large, powerful dog, formerly used in hunting wolves. **2** a dog of this breed.

I·rish·wom·an (ī′rish wu̇m′ən) *n.* **-wom·en.** a woman of Irish birth or descent.

irk (ėrk) *v.* weary; disgust; annoy; trouble; bore: *It irks us to wait for people who are late.* [ME *irke(n)*]

irk·some (ėrk′səm) *adj.* tiresome; tedious. —**irk′some·ly,** *adv.* —**irk′some·ness.** *n.* —**Syn.** annoying.

IRO or **I.R.O.** International Refugee Organization.

i·ron (ī′ərn) *n.* **1** the commonest and most useful metal, from which tools, machinery, etc. are made. It is a very hard, strong, silver-white chemical element. *Symbol*: Fe; *at.no.* 26; *at.wt.* 55.847. **2** a tool, instrument, or weapon made from this metal. **3** great hardness and strength; firmness: *men of iron.* **4** a tool with a flat surface for smoothing cloth or pressing clothes. **5** a golf club with an iron or steel head. **6** *Slang.* a pistol; shooting iron. **7 a** a branding iron. **b** a harpoon. **8** in medicine, a preparation of or containing iron, used as a tonic. **9 irons,** *pl.* chains or bands of iron; handcuffs; shackles. **10 have too many irons in the fire,** try to do too many things at once. **11 strike while the iron is hot,** act while conditions are favorable.
—*adj.* **1** made of iron; having to do with iron. **2** like iron; hard or strong; unyielding: *an iron will.* **3** harsh or cruel.
—*v.* **1** smooth or press (cloth, etc.) with a heated iron. **2** furnish or cover with iron. **3** put in irons; fetter. **4 iron out,** straighten out; smooth away: *A tactful person can iron out many problems between people.* [OE *īren,* ? < Celtic] —**i′ron·er,** *n.*

Iron Age the period in man's history when iron began to be worked and used. It followed the Stone Age and the Bronze Age. In S.Europe, the Iron Age started around 1000 B.C.

i·ron·bark (ī′ərn bärk′) *n.* **1** any of the eucalyptus trees having hard, solid bark. **2** the wood of such a tree.

i·ron·bound (ī′ərn bound′) *adj.* **1** bound with iron. **2** hard; firm; rigid; unyielding. **3** rocky.

i·ron·clad (ī′ərn klad′) *adj.* **1** protected with iron plates. **2** very hard to change or get out of: *an ironclad agreement.* —*n.* a warship protected with iron plates.

Iron Cross a German medal given for services in war.

Iron Curtain or **iron curtain** an imaginary wall or dividing line separating the Soviet Union and the nations under her control or influence from the rest of the world. [coined by Sir Winston Churchill in a speech in 1946]

i·ron·fist·ed (ī′ərn fis′tid) *adj.* unyielding; cruel; despotic.

i·ron-gray or **i·ron-grey** (ī′ərn grā′) *adj.* having the color of freshly broken cast iron.

iron hand a firm, strict manner.

i·ron-hand·ed (ī′ərn han′did) *adj.* exercising stern discipline or tight control.

i·ron·ic (ī ron′ik) *adj.* ironical.

i·ron·i·cal (ī ron′ə kəl) *adj.* **1** expressing one thing and meaning the opposite: *"Speedy" would be an ironical name for a snail.* **2** contrary to what would naturally be expected: *It was ironical that the man was run over by his own automobile.* **3** using or given to using irony. [< LL *ironicus* < Gk. *eirōnikos* dissembling < *eirōneia.* See IRONY.] —**i·ron′i·cal·ly,** *adv.*

ironing board a board covered with a smooth cloth, used for ironing clothes on.

i·ro·nist (ī′rə nist) *n.* a person who takes an ironical view of life and things, especially as a writer.

iron lung a device that gives artificial respiration by rhythmically alternating the air pressure in a chamber enclosing the patient's chest.

i·ron·mon·ger (ī′ərn mung′gər or -mong′gər) *n. Brit.* a dealer in ironware or hardware.

iron pyrites pyrite.

i·ron·sides (ī′ərn sīdz′) *n.pl.* **1** a man of great strength or endurance. **2** an armor-plated warship. **3 Ironsides, a** the regiment led by Oliver Cromwell. **b** his army.

☛ **Ironsides,** meaning warship (def. 2), is plural in form and singular in use: *An ironsides is protected with iron plates.*

i·ron·stone (ī′ərn stōn′) *n.* any iron ore with clay or other impurities in it.

i·ron·ware (ī′ərn wãr′) *n.* articles made of iron, such as pots, kettles, tools, etc.; hardware.

i·ron·weed (ī′ərn wēd′) *n.* a plant of the aster family having flat-topped clusters of small tubular flowers, usually purple or red.

i·ron-willed (ī′ərn wild′) *adj.* having a firm will.

i·ron·wood (ī′ərn wůd′) *n.* **1** any of various trees having hard, heavy wood. **2** the wood itself.

i·ron·work (ī′ərn wėrk′) *n.* things made of iron.

i·ron·work·er (ī′ərn wėr′kər) *n.* **1** a person who makes things of iron. **2** a person whose work is building the framework of bridges, skyscrapers, etc.

i·ron·works (ī′ərn wėrks′) *n.pl. or sing.* a place where iron is made or fashioned into iron articles.

i·ro·ny (ī′rə nē) *n.* **-nies. 1** a method of expression in which the intended meaning is the opposite of, or different from that expressed: *Calling their small bungalow a mansion is irony.* **2** an event contrary to what would naturally be expected: *It was the irony of fate that the great cancer doctor himself died of cancer.* **3** an ironical statement or expression; ironical quality. [< L *ironia* < Gk. *eirōneia* dissimulation < *eirōn* dissembler]

☛ **Irony,** sarcasm, satire are often confused. *Irony,* applying to a kind of humor or way of expressing wit, emphasizes deliberately saying the opposite of what one means, depending on tone of voice or writing to show the real meaning: *the thrill of sitting stil for two hours at a time. Sarcasm* applies only to cruel, biting, contemptuous remarks that may be stated ironically or directly, but are always intended to hurt and ridicule: *When children call a boy "Four Eyes" because he wears glasses, they are using sarcasm. Satire* is the formal use of irony, sarcasm, and other kinds of humor to expose, criticize, or attack follies or vices.

Ir·o·quoi·an (ir′ə kwoi′ən) *n.* **1** a family of N. American Indian languages, including Huron, Mohawk, Oneida, Onondaga, Cayuga, Seneca, Tuscarora, and Cherokee. **2** an Indian belonging to an Iroquoian tribe; an Iroquois. —*adj.* **1** of or having to do with Iroquoian languages. **2** of or having to do with Iroquois Indians or their languages.

Ir·o·quois (ir′ə kwo′) *n.sing. or pl.* **1** a powerful group of N. American Indian tribes called the Five Nations (later, the Six Nations) living mostly in Quebec, Ontario, and New York State. **2** a member of any of the Iroquois tribes.

ir·ra·di·ance (i rā′dē əns) *n.* radiance; shine.

ir·ra·di·ant (i rā′dē ənt) *adj.* irradiating; radiant; shining.

ir·ra·di·ate (i rā′dē āt′) *v.* **-at·ed, -at·ing. 1** shine upon; make bright; illuminate. **2** shine. **3** radiate; give out. **4** treat with ultra-violet rays. [< L *irradiare* < *in-* + *radius* ray] —**ir·ra′di·a·tor,** *n.*

ir·ra·di·a·tion (i rā′dē ā′shən) *n.* **1** the act or process of irradiating. **2** the state or condition of being irradiated. **3** a stream of light; ray. **4** enlightenment of the mind or spirit.

ir·ra·tion·al (i rash′ən əl or i rash′nəl) *adj.* **1** not rational; unreasonable: *It is irrational to be afraid of the number 13.* **2** unable to think and reason clearly. **3** in mathematics: **a** that cannot be expressed by a whole number or a common fraction. $\sqrt{3}$ is an irrational number. **b** of functions, that cannot be expressed as the ratio of two algebraic polynomials in its variables. [< L *irrationalis*] —**ir·ra′tion·al·ly,** *adv.* —**Syn. 1** illogical.

ir·ra·tion·al·i·ty (i rash′ən al′ə tē) *n.* **-ties. 1** a being irrational. **2** something irrational; absurdity.

ir·re·claim·a·ble (ir′i klām′ə bəl) *adj.* that cannot be reclaimed. —**ir′re·claim′a·bly,** *adv.*

ir·rec·on·cil·a·ble (i rek′ən sīl′ə bəl or i rek′ən sīl′ə bəl) *adj.* that cannot be reconciled; that cannot be made to agree; opposed. —*n.* a person who persists in opposing. —**ir·rec′on·cil′a·bly,** *adv.*

ir·re·cov·er·a·ble (ir′i kuv′ər ə bəl or ir′i kuv′rə bəl) *adj.* **1** that cannot be regained or got back: *Wasted time is irrecoverable.* **2** that cannot be remedied: *irrecoverable sorrow.* —**ir′re·cov′er·a·bly,** *adv.* —**Syn. 1** irretrievable.

ir·re·deem·a·ble (ir′i dēm′ə bəl) *adj.* **1** that cannot be bought back. **2** that cannot be exchanged for coin: *irredeemable paper money.* **3** beyond remedy; hopeless. —**ir′re·deem′a·bly,** *adv.*

Ir·re·den·tist (ir′i den′tist) *n.* a member of an Italian political party that became important in 1878. The Irredentists advocated that Italy should gain control of neighboring regions with Italian populations that were under foreign rule. [< Ital. *irredentista* < (*Italia*) *irredenta* unredeemed (Italy), ult. < L *in-* not + *redemptus,* pp. of *redimere* redeem]

ir·re·duc·i·ble (ir′i dūs′ə bəl or ir′i düs′ə bəl) *adj.* that cannot be reduced. —**ir′re·duc′i·bly,** *adv.*

ir·ref·ra·ga·ble (i ref′rə gə bəl) *adj.* that cannot be refuted; unanswerable; undeniable. [< LL *irrefragabilis* < L *in-* not + *refragari* oppose] —**ir·ref′ra·ga·bly,** *adv.*

ir·ref·u·ta·ble (i ref′yů tə bəl or ir′i fūt′ə bəl) *adj.* that cannot be refuted or disproved. —**ir·ref′u·ta·bly,** *adv.* —**Syn.** undeniable, unanswerable.

ir·reg·u·lar (i reg′yů lər) *adj.* **1** not regular; not according to rule; out of the usual order or natural way: *irregular breathing.* **2** not even; not smooth; not straight; without symmetry: *irregular features, an irregular pattern.* **3** not according to law or morals: *irregular behavior.* **4** not in the regular army. **5** in grammar, not inflected in the usual way. *Be* is an irregular verb.
—*n.* a soldier not in the regular army. —**ir·reg′u·lar·ly,** *adv.*

Syn. *adj.* **1 Irregular, abnormal** = out of the usual or natural order or way. **Irregular** = not according to rule or the accepted standard, pattern, way, etc. for the kind of thing or person described: *He has irregular habits.* **Abnormal** = departing from what is regarded as normal, average, or typical, and may describe people or things either above or below normal or showing little relation to the normal: *Seven feet is an abnormal height for a man.* **2** uneven, variable. **3** lawless.

ir·reg·u·lar·i·ty (i reg′yů lar′ə tē) *n.* **-ties. 1** a lack of regularity; being irregular. **2** something irregular.

ir·rel·e·vance (i rel′ə vəns) *n.* **1** the condition of being irrelevant. **2** something irrelevant.

ir·rel·e·van·cy (i rel′ə vən sē) *n.* irrelevance.

ir·rel·e·vant (i rel′ə vənt) *adj.* not to the point; off the subject: *A question about economics is irrelevant in a music lesson.* —**ir·rel′e·vant·ly,** *adv.*

ir·re·li·gion (ir′i lij′ən) *n.* **1** lack of religion. **2** hostility to religion; disregard of religion.

ir·re·li·gious (ir′i lij′əs) *adj.* **1** not religious; indifferent to religion. **2** contrary to religious principles; impious. [< L *irreligiosus*] —**ir′re·li′gious·ly,** *adv.* —**ir′re·li′gious·ness,** *n.*

ir·re·me·di·a·ble (ir′i mē′dē ə bəl) *adj.* that cannot be remedied; incurable. —**ir′re·me′di·a·bly,** *adv.*

ir·re·mov·a·ble (ir′i müv′ə bəl) *adj.* that cannot be removed. —**ir′re·mov′a·bly,** *adv.*

ir·rep·a·ra·ble (i rep′ə rə bəl) *adj.* that cannot be repaired or made good. —**ir·rep′a·ra·bly,** *adv.*

ir·re·place·a·ble (ir′i plās′ə bəl) *adj.* not replaceable; impossible to replace with another.

ir·re·press·i·bil·i·ty (ir′i pres′ə bil′ə tē) *n.* the condition of being irrepressible.

ir·re·press·i·ble (ir′i pres′ə bəl) *adj.* that cannot be repressed or restrained.

ir·re·press·i·bly (ir′i pres′ə blē) *adv.* in an irrepressible manner; uncontrollably.

ir·re·proach·a·ble (ir′i prōch′ə bəl) *adj.* free from blame; faultless. —**ir′re·proach′a·bly,** *adv.*

ir·re·sist·i·ble (ir′i zis′tə bəl) *adj.* that cannot be resisted; too great to be withstood. —**ir′re·sist′i·bly,** *adv.*

ir·res·o·lute (i rez′ə lüt′) *adj.* not resolute; unable to make up one's mind; not sure of what one wants; hesitating: *Irresolute persons make poor leaders.* —**ir·res′o·lute·ly,** *adv.* —**ir·res′o·lute·ness,** *n.* —**Syn.** doubtful, vacillating.

ir·res·o·lu·tion (i rez′ə lü′shən) *n.* lack of resolution; being irresolute; hesitation.

ir·re·spec·tive (ir′i spek′tiv) *adj.* regardless: *Any person, irrespective of age, may join the club.* —**ir′re·spec′tive·ly,** *adv.*

ir·re·spon·si·bil·i·ty (ir′i spon′sə bil′ə tē) *n.* lack of responsibility; being irresponsible.

ir·re·spon·si·ble (ir′i spon′sə bəl) *adj.* **1** not responsible; that cannot be called to account: *A dictator is an irresponsible ruler.* **2** without a sense of responsibility. —**ir′re·spon′si·bly,** *adv.*

ir·re·trace·a·ble (ir′ i trās′ə bəl) *adj.* that cannot be retraced.

ir·re·triev·a·ble (ir′i trēv′ə bəl) *adj.* that cannot be retrieved or recovered; that cannot be recalled or restored to its former condition. —**ir′re·triev′a·bly,** *adv.*

ir·rev·er·ence (i rev′ər əns) *n.* **1** lack of reverence; disrespect. **2** an act showing irreverence.

ir·rev·er·ent (i rev′ər ənt) *adj.* not reverent; disrespectful. [< L *irreverens, -entis*] —**ir·rev′er·ent·ly,** *adv.*

ir·re·vers·i·ble (ir′i vėr′sə bəl) *adj.* not capable of being reversed. —**ir′re·vers′i·bly,** *adv.*

ir·rev·o·ca·bil·i·ty (i rev′ə kə bil′ə tē) *n.* the state of being irrevocable.

ir·rev·o·ca·ble (i rev′ə kə bəl) *adj.* not to be recalled, withdrawn, or annulled: *an irrevocable decision.* —**ir·rev′o·ca·bly,** *adv.*

ir·ri·ga·ble (ir′ə gə bəl) *adj.* that can be irrigated.

ir·ri·gate (ir′ə gāt′) *v.* **-gat·ed, -gat·ing. 1** supply land with water by means of ditches, sprinklers, etc. **2** supply a wound, cavity in the body, etc. with a continuous flow of some liquid. [< L *irrigare* < *in-* + *rigare* wet] —**ir′ri·ga′tor,** *n.*

ir·ri·ga·tion (ir′ə gā′shən) *n.* **1** an irrigating. **2** the state of being irrigated.

ir·ri·ta·bil·i·ty (ir′ə tə bil′ə tē) *n.* **-ties. 1** a being irritable; impatience. **2** in medicine, an unnatural sensitiveness (of an organ or part of the body). **3** in biology, the property that living plant or animal tissue has of responding to a stimulus.

ir·ri·ta·ble (ir′ə tə bəl) *adj.* **1** easily made angry; impatient. **2** of an organ or part of the body, unnaturally sensitive or sore: *A baby's skin is often quite irritable.* **3** in biology, able to respond to stimuli. [< L *irritabilis*] —**ir′ri·ta·ble·ness,** *n.* —**ir′ri·ta·bly,** *adv.*

Syn. 1 Irritable, irascible = easily made angry. **Irritable** = easily annoyed or angered, especially by little things, and suggests having an impatient or excitable temperament or being in a nervous condition: *She has been so irritable lately that I think she must be ill.* **Irascible** = having a quick temper, being by nature or disposition liable to become angry at the slightest excuse: *Irascible people should not have positions which require them to meet the public.*

ir·ri·tant (ir′ə tənt) *n.* a thing that causes irritation: *A mustard plaster is an irritant.* —*adj.* causing irritation. [< L *irritans, -antis,* ppr. of *irritare* enrage, provoke]

hat, āge, cãre, fär; let, ēqual, tėrm; it, īce
hot, ōpen, ôrder; oil, out; cup, pu̇t, rüle, ūse
əbove, takən, pencəl, lemən, circəs
ch, child; ng, long; sh, ship
th, thin; ᴛʜ, then; zh, measure

ir·ri·tate (ir′ə tāt′) *v.* **-tat·ed, -tat·ing. 1** arouse to impatience or anger; annoy; provoke; vex: *The boy's foolish questions irritated his father. Flies irritate horses.* **2** make unnaturally sensitive or sore: *A tight collar irritates the neck.* **3** in medicine, bring (an organ or part) to an excessively sensitive condition. **4** in biology, stimulate (an organ, muscle, tissue, etc.) to perform some characteristic action or function: *A muscle contracts when it is irritated by an electric shock.* [< L *irritare* enrage, provoke] —**ir′ri·tat′ing·ly,** *adv.* —**ir′ri·ta′tor,** *n.*

Syn. 1 Irritate, exasperate, provoke = excite to impatience or anger. **Irritate** suggests annoying a person until he loses patience or flares up in anger: *Her untidiness irritates me.* **Exasperate** = make extremely annoyed or angry by irritating beyond endurance: *Her constant cheating exasperates me.* **Provoke** = do, or keep doing, something displeasing or disturbing to make a person lose patience and become very much annoyed, vexed, or angry: *Her constant interruptions provoke me.*

ir·ri·ta·tion (ir′ə tā′shən) *n.* **1** the act or process of irritating; annoyance; vexation. **2** an irritated condition.

ir·ri·ta·tive (ir′ə tā′tiv) *adj.* **1** producing or causing irritation; irritating. **2** accompanying or caused by irritation: *an irritative fever.*

ir·rup·tion (i rup′shən) *n.* a breaking or bursting in; violent invasion. [< L *irruptio, -onis* < *irrumpere* < *in-* in + *rumpere* break]

ir·rup·tive (i rup′tiv) *adj.* bursting in; rushing in or upon anything. —**ir·rup′tive·ly,** *adv.*

is (iz) *v.* **1** 3rd pers. sing., present indicative of **be. 2 as is,** as it is now; in its present condition. [OE]

Is. 1 Isaiah. **2** Island. **3** Isle.

Isa. Isaiah.

Is·car·i·ot (is kar′ē ət) *n.* **1** the surname of Judas, the disciple who betrayed Jesus for thirty pieces of silver. Matthew 26:14-50. **2** any traitor.

is·chi·um (is′kē əm) *n.* **is·chi·a** (is′kē ə). in anatomy, the lowest bone of the three bones forming either half of the pelvis. [< NL < Gk. *ischion*]

-ise *suffix.* variant of **-ize.** ☛ See **-ize** for usage note.

I·seult (i sült′) *n.* in medieval legend: **1** an Irish princess, wife of King Mark of Cornwall. She was loved by Tristram. **2** the daughter of the king of Brittany, whom Tristram married after his love for the Irish Iseult was discovered. Also, **Isolde, Isolt.**

-ish *suffix.* **1** somewhat, as in *oldish, sweetish.* **2** resembling; like, as in *a childish person.* **3** like that of; having the characteristics of, as in *a childish idea.* **4** of or having to do with; belonging to, as in *British, Spanish, Turkish.* **5** tending to; inclined to, as in *bookish, thievish.* **6** near, but usually somewhat past, as in *fortyish.* [OE *-isc*]

Ish·ma·el (ish′mē əl) *n.* **1** in the Bible, a son of Abraham. Because of Sarah's jealousy, he was driven out into the wilderness. Gen. 16:12. **2** any outcast; someone who is at odds with society.

Ish·ma·el·ite (ish′mē əl īt′) *n.* **1** a descendant of Ishmael. **2** an outcast.

i·sin·glass (ī′zing glas′) *n.* **1** a kind of gelatin obtained from air bladders of sturgeon, cod, and similar fishes, used for making glue, clearing liquors, etc. **2** mica, a mineral that divides into thin semitransparent layers. [alteration of MDu. *huysenblas* sturgeon bladder; influenced by *glass*]

I·sis (ī′sis) *n.* in Egyptian mythology, the goddess of fertility, represented as wearing on her head cow's horns enclosing a solar disk.

isl. 1 island. **2** isle.

Is·lam (is′ləm or is läm′) *n.* **1** the Moslem religion. **2** Moslems as a group. **3** Moslem countries; the Moslem part of the world.

Is·lam·ic (is lam′ik or is läm′ik) *adj.* Moslem.

Is·lam·ism (is′ləm iz′əm) *n.* the Moslem religion.

Is·lam·ite (is′ləm īt′) *n. adj.* a Moslem.

is·land (ī′lənd) *n.* **1** a body of land surrounded by water. **2** something resembling this. **3** a superstructure, especially of a battleship or aircraft carrier. **4 a** a piece of woodland surrounded by prairie. **b** an elevated piece of land surrounded by marshes, etc. **5** in anatomy, a group of cells different in structure or function from those around it. —*v.* make into an island. [OE *īgland* < *īg* island + *land* land; spelling influenced by *isle*] —**is′land·like′**, *adj.*

is·land·er (ī′lən dər) *n.* a native or inhabitant of an island.

isle (īl) *n.* **1** a small island. **2** an island. [ME < OF < L *insula*]

is·let (ī′lit) *n.* a little island. [< earlier F *islette*, dim. of *isle* isle]

ism (iz′əm) *n. Informal.* a distinctive doctrine, theory, system, or practice: *Capitalism, socialism, communism, and fascism are well-known isms.* [see -ISM]

-ism *suffix.* **1** an action; practice, as in *baptism, criticism.* **2** a doctrine; system; principle, as in *communism, socialism.* **3** a quality; characteristic; state; condition, as in *heroism, paganism.* **4** an illustration; case; instance, as in *colloquialism, witticism.* **5** an unhealthy condition caused by, as in *alcoholism, morphinism.* [< Gk. *-ismos, -isma*]

I.S.M. Imperial Service Medal.

is·n't (iz′ənt) is not.

iso- *combining form.* equal; alike, as in *isosceles, isometric, isothermal, isotope.* [< Gk. *iso-* < *isos* equal]

I.S.O. Imperial Service Order.

i·so·bar (ī′sə bär′) *n.* **1** a line on a weather map connecting places having the same average atmospheric pressure (after allowance for height above sea level). **2** in physics and chemistry, one of two or more kinds of atoms that have the same atomic weight, but in most cases different atomic numbers. [< Gk. *isobarēs* < *isos* equal + *baros* weight]

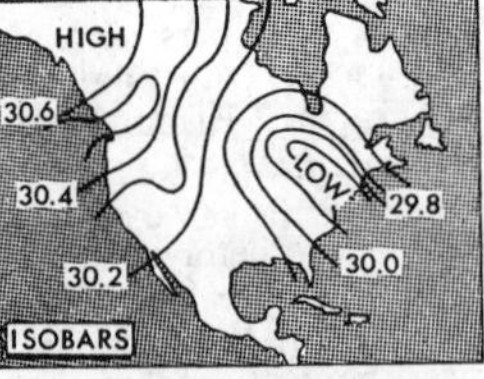

Isobars (the dark lines) showing atmospheric pressure in inches. The location and movements of areas of high and low pressure are used in forecasting weather.

i·so·bar·ic (ī′sə bar′ik) *adj.* **1** of or containing isobars. **2** having or indicating equal atmospheric pressure.

i·soch·ro·nal (ī sok′rə nəl) *adj.* **1** equal or uniform in time. **2** performed or happening in equal periods of time. **3** characterized by motions or vibrations of equal duration. [< Gk. *isochronos* < *isos* equal + *chronos* time] —**i·soch′ro·nal·ly**, *adv.*

i·soch·ro·nous (ī sok′rə nəs) *adj.* isochronal. —**i·soch′ro·nous·ly**, *adv.*

i·so·gloss (ī′sə glos′) *n.* in linguistic geography, a line on a map to separate two adjacent areas in each of which different variants of a pronunciation, grammatical form, or word are current.

i·so·gon·ic (ī′sə gon′ik) *adj.* having equal angles; having to do with equal angles. [< Gk. *isogōnios* < *isos* equal + *gōnia* angle]

i·so·late (ī′ sə lāt′ or, *esp.U.S.*, is′ə lāt′) *v.* **-lat·ed, -lat·ing,** *adj.* —*v.* **1** place apart; separate from others: *People with contagious diseases should be isolated.* **2** in chemistry, obtain (a substance) in a pure or uncombined form: *A chemist can isolate the oxygen from the hydrogen in water.*
—*adj.* isolated; placed apart. An **isolate adjective** is one that stands alone after a linking verb. *Example*: That man is *clever.* [< *isolated* < F *isolé* < Ital. *isolato*, pp. of *isolare* < L *insulare* < *insula* island] —**Syn. 1** segregate, detach.

i·so·la·tion (ī′sə lā′shən or, *esp.U.S.*, is′ə lā′shən) *n.* **1** the act or process of setting apart: *The warden's isolation of the most troublesome prisoners reduced unrest in the jail.* **2** the act or fact of being set apart. **3** the state of being separated from other persons or things: *Robinson Crusoe lived in isolation for years.* —**Syn. 2** See **solitude.**

i·so·la·tion·ism (ī′sə lā′shən iz′əm or, *esp.U.S.*, is′ə lā′shən iz′əm) *n.* the principles or practice of isolationists.

i·so·la·tion·ist (ī′sə lā′shən ist or, *esp.U.S.*, is′ə lā′shən ist) *n.* **1** one who objects to his country's participation in international affairs. **2** in Canada and the United States, a person who favors keeping his country out of European affairs, wars, etc.

I·sol·de (i sōl′də, i sōld′, or i zôl′də) *n.* Iseult.

I·solt (i sōlt′) *n.* Iseult.

i·so·mer (ī′sə mər) *n.* an isomeric compound. [< Gk. *isomerēs* < *isos* equal + *meros* part]

i·so·mer·ic (ī′sə mer′ik) *adj.* **1** in chemistry, composed of the same elements in the same proportions by weight, and (in the usual, restricted sense of the term) having the same molecular weight, but differing in one or more properties because of the difference in arrangement of atoms. **2** of the nuclei of atoms, differing in energy and behavior, but having the same atomic number and mass number.

i·som·er·ous (ī som′ər əs) *adj.* **1** having an equal number of parts, markings, etc. **2** of a flower, having the same number of members in each whorl.

i·so·met·ric (ī′sə met′rik) *adj.* having to do with equality of measure; having equality of measure. A crystal is isometric if it has three equal axes at right angles to one another. Isometric exercises are done without perceptible movement of body parts. [< Gk. *isometros* < *isos* equal + *metron* measure] —**i′so·met′ri·cal·ly**, *adv.*

i·so·met·ri·cal (ī′sə met′rə kəl) *adj.* isometric.

i·so·morph (ī′sə môrf′) *n.* **1** an isomorphic organism or substance. **2** in linguistic geography, an isogloss setting off different morphological features.

i·so·mor·phic (ī′sə môr′fik) *adj.* **1** in biology, having similar appearance or structure, but different ancestry. **2** isomorphous. [< *iso-* + Gk. *morphē* form]

i·so·mor·phous (ī′sə môr′fəs) *adj.* in chemistry, crystallizing in the same form or related forms. Isomorphous is used especially of substances of analogous chemical composition.

i·so·ni·a·zid (ī′sō nī′ə zid) *n.* a drug chemically related to nicotinic acid, used in the treatment of tuberculosis. [< *isoni(cotinic acid hydr)azid(e).* See ISO-.]

i·so·pod (ī′sə pod′) *n.* a crustacean that has a flat, ovoid body and, usually, seven pairs of similar legs. [< NL *Isopoda*, pl. < Gk. *isos* equal + *pous, podos* foot]

i·so·prene (ī′sə prēn′) *n.* in chemistry, a volatile liquid hydrocarbon used in synthetic rubber and turpentine. *Formula*: C_3H_8 [< *iso-* + propyl + *-ene*, as in *benzene*, etc.]

i·sos·ce·les (ī sos′ə lēz′) *adj.* of a triangle, having two sides equal. [< LL < Gk. *isoskelēs* < *isos* equal + *skelos* leg]

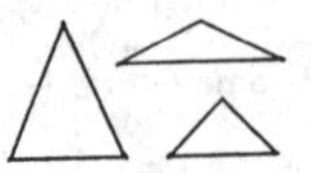
Isosceles triangles

i·so·therm (ī′sə thėrm′) *n.* a line on a weather map connecting places having the same average temperature. [< *iso-* + Gk. *thermē* heat]

i·so·ther·mal (ī′sə thėr′məl) *adj.* **1** indicating equality of temperatures. **2** having to do with isotherms.

i·so·ton·ic (ī′sə ton′ic) *adj.* **1** in physiology and chemistry, having the same osmotic pressure. **2** in physiology, having to do with muscle contractions caused by minor, but constant, tension. **3** in music, characterized by equal tones. [< Gk.]

i·so·tope (ī′sə tōp′) *n.* any of two or more forms of a chemical element that have the same atomic number and chemical properties, but different atomic weights and radio-active behavior: *Chlorine, whose atomic weight is 35.5, is a mixture of two isotopes, one having an atomic weight of 37, the other, 35. Heavy hydrogen (deuterium) is an isotope of hydrogen.* [< *iso-* + Gk. *topos* place]

i·so·trop·ic (ī′sə trop′ik) *adj.* in physics, having the same properties, such as elasticity or conduction, in all directions. [< *iso-* + Gk. *tropos* turn, way]

i·sot·ro·pous (ī sot′rə pəs) *adj.* isotropic.

Is·ra·el (iz′rē əl or iz′rāl) *n.* **1** in the Bible, a name given to Jacob after he had wrestled with the angel. Gen. 32:28. **2** the name given to his descendants; the Jews; the Hebrews.

Is·rae·li (iz rā′lē) *n.* **-lis,** *adj.* —*n.* a citizen or inhabitant of modern Israel, a republic comprising a portion of Palestine. —*adj.* of or having to do with modern Israel.

Israeli pound 1 a unit of money in Israel. See table at **money. 2** a note or coin worth one Israeli pound.

Is·ra·el·ite (iz′rē əl īt′) *n.* a Jew; Hebrew; a descendant of Israel. —*adj.* of or having to do with Israel or the Jews.

Is·ra·el·it·ish (iz′rē əl īt′ish) *adj.* Jewish.

Is·sei (ēs′sā′) *n.* **-sei.** a first-generation Japanese living in Canada or the United States. A second-generation Japanese living in Canada or the United States is a Nisei. [< Japanese *is-sei* first generation < *ichi* one + *sei* generation]

is·su·ance (ish′ü əns) *n.* an issuing; issue.

is·sue (ish′ü) *v.* **-sued, -su·ing,** *n.* —*v.* **1** send out; put forth: *The government issues money and stamps.* **2** come out; go out; proceed: *Smoke issues from the chimney.* **3** be published. **4** put into public circulation; publish. **5** distribute (supplies, etc.) to a person or persons. **6** send forth; discharge; emit: *The chimney issues smoke from the fireplace.* **7** emerge. **8** result or end (*in*): *The game issued in a tie.* **9** result (*from*). **10** be born; be descended; be derived. [< n.]
—*n.* **1** something sent out; quantity (of bonds, stamps, copies of a magazine, etc.) sent out at one time. **2** a sending out; a putting forth. **3** a coming forth; a flowing out; a discharge: *A nosebleed is an issue of blood from the nose.* **4** a way out; outlet; exit. **5** that which comes out. **6** a profit; production. **7** the result; outcome: *the issue of the battle.* **8** a point to be debated; problem: *political issues.* **9** a child or children; offspring. **10 at issue,** in question; to be considered or decided. **11 face the issue,** admit the facts and do what must be done. **12 join issue,** take opposite sides in an argument. **13 make an issue (of),** provoke argument or discussion (of). **14 take issue,** disagree. [ME < OF *issue* < *eissir* go out < L *exire* < *ex-* out + *ire* go] —**is′su·a·ble,** *adj.* —**is′su·er,** *n.*
Syn. *v.* **2, 5 Issue, emerge, emanate** = come out. **Issue** = go or come out, usually through an opening, from a source or place where it has been confined, and often suggests flowing out in a moving mass like water: *Pus issued from the wound.* **Emerge** emphasizes coming into sight from a place where it has been hidden or covered up: *The train emerged from the tunnel.* **Emanate,** used only of things without physical body, means "flow out from a source": *Heat emanates from fire.* **4** print. -*n.* **3** outflow.

-ist *suffix.* **1** a person who does or makes, as in *theorist, tourist.* **2** one who knows about or has skill with, as in *biologist, flutist.* **3** one engaged in or busy with, as in *horticulturist, machinist.* **4** one who believes in; an adherent of, as in *abolitionist, idealist.* [< Gk. *-istēs*]

isth·mi·an (is′mē ən) *adj.* **1** of or having to do with an isthmus. **2 Isthmian, a** of or having to do with the Isthmus of Panama. **b** of or having to do with the Isthmus of Corinth in Greece. The **Isthmian games** were national festivals of ancient Greece.

isth·mus (is′məs) *n.* **-mus·es.** a narrow strip of land, having water on either side, connecting two large bodies of land. [< L < Gk. *isthmos*]

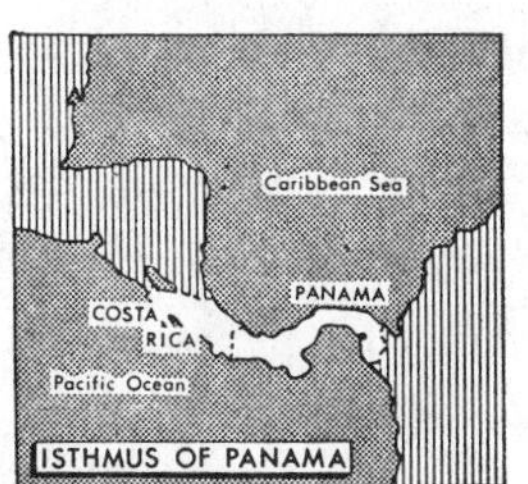

ISTHMUS OF PANAMA

is·tle (is′tlē) *n.* a fibre of certain tropical American plants, used in making bags, carpets, cordage, nets, etc. [< Mexican *ixtli*]

it (it) *pron. nom.* **it;** *poss.* **its** or (*Obsolete or dialect*) **it;** *obj.* **it;** *pl. nom.* **they;** *poss.* **theirs;** *obj.* **them.** **1** the thing, part, animal, or, sometimes, baby already spoken about and identified. **2** the subject of an impersonal verb: *It rains.* **3** an apparent subject of a clause when the logical subject comes later: *It is hard to believe that he is dead.* **4** the antecedent to any relative pronoun when separated by the predicate: *It was a blue car that passed.* **5** an object without definite force or

hat, āge, cãre, fär; let, ēqual, tėrm; it, īce
hot, ōpen, ôrder; oil, out; cup, pu̇t, rüle, ūse
əbove, takən, pencəl, lemən, circəs
ch, child; ng, long; sh, ship
th, thin; ᴛʜ, then; zh, measure

reference: *He lorded it over us.*
—*n.* **1** in games, the player who must catch, find, guess, etc. **2** something neither male nor female: *If it's not a he or a she, it must be an it.* [OE *hit*]

it. italic; italics.

It. 1 Italy. **2** Italian.

ital. italic; italics.

Ital. 1 Italy. **2** Italian.

I·tal·ian (i tal′yən) *adj.* of Italy, a country in S. Europe, its people, or their language. —*n.* **1** a person born in or living in Italy. **2** a citizen of Italy. **3** the language of Italy.

I·tal·ian·ate (*adj.* i tal′yə nāt′ or i tal′yə nit; *v.* i tal′yə nāt′) *adj. v.* **-at·ed, -at·ing.** —*adj.* of Italian style, manner, or form. —*v.* Italianize.

I·tal·ian·ize (i tal′yən īz′) *v.* **-ized, -iz·ing.** make Italian. —**I·tal′ian·i·za′tion,** *n.*

i·tal·ic (i tal′ik) *adj.* **1** of or in type whose letters slant to the right: *This sentence is in italic type.* **2 Italic,** of ancient Italy, its people, or their languages. —*n.* **1** an italic type, letter, or number. **2** Often, **italics,** *pl.* type whose letters slant to the right. [< L *Italicus* < *Italia* Italy < Gk.]
☛ **italics.** In manuscript, both longhand and typewritten, italics are shown by single underlining.

i·tal·i·cize (i tal′ə sīz′) *v.* **-cized, -ciz·ing. 1** print in type in which the letters slant to the right: *This sentence is italicized.* **2** underline with a single line to indicate italics. **3** use italics.

itch (ich) *n.* **1** a tickly, prickling feeling in the skin that makes one want to scratch. **2 the itch,** a contagious disease of the skin caused by a tiny mite, and accompanied by an itchy feeling. **3** a restless, uneasy feeling, longing, or desire for anything: *an itch to get away and explore.* [OE *gicce*]
—*v.* **1** cause an itching feeling: *Mosquito bites itch.* **2** have an itching feeling. **3** have an uneasy desire: *He itched to know our secret.* [OE *gyccan*]

itch·y (ich′ē) *adj.* **itch·i·er, itch·i·est.** itching; like the itch. —**itch′i·ness,** *n.*

-ite[1] *suffix.* **1** a native or inhabitant of, as in *Israelite.* **2** a person associated with, as in *laborite.* **3** a mineral species, or a rock substance, as in *hematite.* **4** especially in the names of commercially manufactured products, resembling; derived from; having the property of, as in *dynamite, ebonite.* [< F *-ite* (< L *-ita, ites*) or < L (< Gk. *-itēs*) or directly < Gk. *-itēs*]

-ite[2] *suffix.* a salt of, as in *phosphite, sulphite, nitrite.* [< F *-ite,* arbitrarily created var. of *-ate*[2]]

i·tem (ī′təm) *n.* **1** a separate thing or article: *This list contains twelve items.* **2** a piece of news; a bit of information: *There were several interesting items in today's paper.* —*adv.* also; likewise (in introducing each item of an enumeration). [< L *item,* adv., likewise]
Syn. *n.* **1 Item, detail, particular** = a separate thing that is part of a whole. **Item** applies to a separate thing included in a list, account, or total, or to an article listed: *An itemized account should list every item.* **Detail** applies to a separate thing that is part of something larger put together or done: *His report gave all the details.* **Particular** emphasizes the singleness or extreme smallness of a detail, item, point, circumstance, etc.: *Nobody wants to hear all the particulars of your troubles.*

i·tem·ize (ī′təm īz′) *v.* **-ized, -iz·ing.** give each item of; list by items: *itemize the cost of a trip.* —**i′tem·i·za′tion,** *n.*

it·er·ate (it′ər āt′) *v.* **-at·ed, -at·ing.** repeat. [< L *iterare* < *iterum* again] —**it′er·a′tion,** *n.*

it·er·a·tive (it′ər ə tiv or it′ər ā′ tiv) *adj.* repeating; full of repetitions.

i·tin·er·a·cy (ī tin′ər ə sē or i tin′ər ə sē) *n.* itinerancy.

i·tin·er·an·cy (ī tin′ər ən sē or i tin′ər ən sē) *n.* **1** a travelling from place to place. **2** a body of itinerant preachers or judges. **3** official work requiring much travel from place to place, or frequent changes of residence.

i·tin·er·ant (ī tin′ər ənt or i tin′ər ənt) *adj.* travelling from place to place. —*n.* a person who travels from place to place. [< LL *itinerans, -antis,* ppr. of *itinerari* travel < L *iter, itineris* journey < *ire* go] —**i·tin′er·ant·ly,** *adv.*

i·tin·er·ar·y (ī tin′ər er′ē or i tin′ər er′ē) *n.* **-ar·ies,** *adj.* —*n.* **1** a route of travel; a plan of travel. **2** a record of travel. **3** a guidebook for travellers. —*adj.* **1** of travelling or routes of travel. **2** itinerant.

i·tin·er·ate (ī tin′ər āt′ or i tin′ər āt′) *v.* **-at·ed, -at·ing.** travel from place to place. [< L *itinerari.* See ITINERANT.

-itious *combining form.* of or having the nature of: *fictitious = having the nature of fiction.*

-itis *suffix.* an inflammation of; inflammatory disease of, as in *appendicitis, bronchitis, tonsillitis.* [< Gk. *-itis,* fem. of *-itēs.* Cf. -ITE[1].]

ITO International Trade Organization.

it's (its) **1** it is. **2** it has.

its (its) *pron. adj.* of it; belonging to it: *The dog wagged its tail.*

it·self (it self′) *pron.* **1** the emphatic form of **it**: *The land itself is worth more than the old house.* **2** the reflexive form of **it**: *The horse tripped and hurt itself.*

-ity *suffix.* the condition or quality of being —— as in *absurdity, brutality, cordiality, activity, hostility, sincerity.* [< F *-ité* < L *itas, -itatis*]

IU or **I.U.** in biochemistry, international unit or units.

I've (īv) I have.

-ive *suffix.* **1** of or having to do with, as in *interrogative, inductive.* **2** tending to; likely to, as in *active, appreciative, imitative.* [< F *-ive* (fem. of *-if* < L *-ivus*) or directly < L *-ivus*]

i·vied (ī′vēd) *adj.* covered or overgrown with ivy.

i·vo·ry (īv′rē or ī′və rē) *n.* **-ries,** *adj.* —*n.* **1** a hard, white substance composing the tusks of elephants, walruses, etc. Ivory is used for piano keys, billiard balls, ornaments, etc. **2** a substance like ivory. **3** a creamy white. **4 ivories,** *pl. Slang.* **a** piano keys. **b** dice. **c** billiard balls. **d** teeth.
—*adj.* **1** made of ivory. **2** of or like ivory. **3** creamy-white. [ME < AF *ivorie* < L *eboreus* of ivory < *ebur* ivory < Egyptian]

ivory black a fine black coloring matter made by burning ivory.

ivory nut the nutlike seed of a tropical palm tree that is white and very hard when dry.

ivory palm the palm tree that ivory nuts grow on.

ivory tower a condition or attitude of withdrawal from the world of practical affairs into a world of ideas and dreams.

i·vy (ī′vē) *n.* **i·vies. 1** a climbing plant having smooth, shiny, evergreen leaves; English ivy. **2** any of various other climbing plants that resemble the English ivy, such as **American ivy, Boston ivy, Japanese ivy, poison ivy.** [OE *ifig*]

iv·y-league (ī′vē lēg′) *adj.* characteristic of or having to do with the Ivy League, the colleges belonging to it, their faculties, or their students.

Ivy League 1 a group of eight old and prestigious universities of eastern U.S., including Harvard, Yale, and Princeton. **2** behavior, customs, etc. associated with the students of these colleges. [originally, an athletic association composed of the eight colleges]

i·wis (i wis′) *adv. Archaic.* certainly; indeed. [OE *gewis*]

Ix·i·on (iks ī′ən) *n.* in Greek legend, the father of the Centaurs, who made love to Hera and was punished in Hades by being bound to a fiery wheel.

I·yar or **Iy·yar** (ē′yär) *n.* in the Hebrew calendar, the second month of the ecclesiastical year and the eighth month of the civil year.

-ize *suffix.* **1** make, as in *legalize, centralize.* **2** become, as in *crystallize, materialize.* **3** engage in; be busy with; use, as in *apologize, theorize.* **4** treat with, as in *circularize, macadamize.* **5** other meanings, as in *alphabetize, colonize, criticize, memorize.* Also, **-ise.** [< F *iser* (< L *-izare*) or < L (< Gk. *-izein*) or directly < Gk. *-izein*]

☞ **-ize, -ise.** English has many verbs ending in the sound (īz), some of which are spelled *-ise* and some *-ize*, and on many usage is divided. Canadian usage prefers *-ize* in words that contain the Gk. suffix, such as: *apologize, characterize, realize, revolutionize, visualize.* In words such as the following, derived from Old French, *-ise* is the usual spelling: *advertise, chastise, devise, exercise, supervise, surmise.* The form *-ize* is used in forming new words.

iz·zard (iz′ərd) *n.* **1** *Archaic or dialect.* the letter Z. **2 from A to izzard,** from beginning to end; completely. [< *ezed,* variant of *zed,* ? < F *et zed* and Z]

J or **j** (jā) *n.* **J's** or **j's.** **1** the tenth letter of the English alphabet. **2** any speech sound represented by this letter. **3** the tenth of a series, designated alphabetically.

j in physics, joule.

J January.

J or **J.** **1** Judge. **2** Justice. **3** Journal.

Ja. January.

JA or **J.A.** Judge Advocate.

jab (jab) *n. v.* **jabbed, jab·bing.** —*n.* **1** a thrust (*at*) with something pointed; poke. **2** in boxing, a blow in which the arm is extended straight from the shoulder. —*v.* **1** thrust with something pointed; poke. **2** in boxing, hit with a jab. [var. of *job.* v., ME *jobbe(n)*; probably imitative]

jab·ber (jab′ər) *v.* talk very fast in a confused, senseless way; chatter. —*n.* very fast, confused, or senseless talk; chatter. [probably imitative] —**jab′ber·er,** *n.* —**Syn.** *v.* babble.

ja·bot (zha bō′, zhab′ō, or jab′ō) *n.* a ruffle or frill of lace, worn at the throat or down the front of a woman's dress, or, formerly, on a man's shirt. [< F *jabot,* originally, maw of a bird]

jac·a·ran·da (jak′ə ran′də) *n.* **1** any of several tropical American trees having hard scented wood of fine texture and showy blue flowers. **2** the wood of any of these trees. [< Pg.]

ja·cinth (jā′sinth or jas′inth) *n.* a reddish-orange gem, a kind of zircon. [ME < OF *jacinte* < L *hyacinthus* hyacinth < Gk. *hyakinthos,* a kind of flower. Doublet of HYACINTH.]

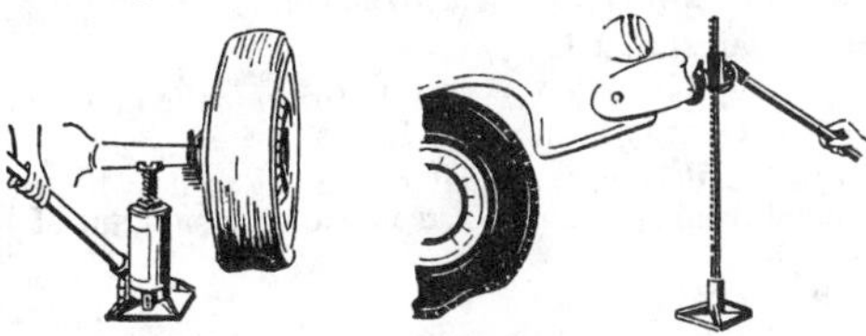

Two types of jack (def. 3) for automobiles

jack (jak) *n.* **1** a man; boy; fellow. **2** Also, **Jack.** a sailor. **3** a device for raising heavy weights a short distance. **4** a playing card with a picture of a court page on it; knave. **5** a jackstone; in a child's game, a pebble or piece of metal tossed up and caught. **6 jacks,** *pl.* jackstones. **7** in lawn bowling, a small ball for players to aim at. **8** a small flag used on a ship to show nationality or to serve as a signal. **9** a device to turn roasting meat. **10** a male donkey. **11** a jack-rabbit. **12** an electrical device to receive a plug. **13** a jacklight. **14** a jackfish. **15 every man jack,** everyone.
—*v.* **1** lift or push up with a jack. **2** hunt or fish using a jacklight, especially when it is illegal. **3 jack up, a** lift with a jack. **b** *Informal.* raise (prices, wages, etc.). **c** *Informal.* remind (someone) of his duty. [ME *Jakke* < OF *Jaques,* a popular name for the French peasant < LL *Jacobus* Jacob]

jack·al (jak′əl, jak′ol, or jak′ôl) *n.* **1** a wild dog of Asia and Africa. It was formerly supposed to hunt prey for the lion and eat what the lion left. **2** a person who does drudgery for another. [< Turkish *chakal* < Persian *shagal*]

jack·a·napes (jak′ə nāps′) *n.* a pert, presumptuous fellow. [var. of ME *Jack Napes,* a name applied to William, Duke of Suffolk, whose badge was a clog and chain, such as was used for tame apes; probably originally the name for a tame ape]

jack·ass (jak′as′) *n.* **1** a male donkey. **2** a very stupid person; fool.

jack·boot (jak′büt′) *n.* a large, strong boot reaching above the knee.

jack·daw (jak′do′ or -dô′) *n.* a small European bird resembling a crow.

jack·et (jak′it) *n.* **1** a short coat. **2** an outer covering. The paper cover for a book, the casing around a steam pipe, and the skin of a potato are jackets. —*v.* put a jacket on; cover with a jacket. [ME < OF *jaquette,* dim. of *jaque* peasant's tunic < *Jaques.* See JACK.] —**jack′et·less,** *adj.*

hat, āge, cãre, fär; let, ēqual, tėrm; it, īce
hot, ōpen, ôrder; oil, out; cup, pu̇t, rüle, ūse
əbove, takən, pencəl, lemən, circəs
ch, child; ng, long; sh, ship
th, thin; ᴛʜ, then; zh, measure

jack·fish (jak′fish′) *n.* **-fish** or **-fish·es.** pike.

Jack Frost frost or freezing cold weather personified.

jack-in-a-box (jak′in ə boks′) *n.* jack-in-the-box.

jack-in-the-box (jak′in ᴛʜə boks′) *n.* a toy figure that springs up from a box when the lid is unfastened.

jack-in-the-pul·pit (jak′in ᴛʜə pu̇l′pit) *n.* a plant having a greenish, petal-like sheath arched over the flower stalk.

Jack Ketch (kech) a public executioner; hangman. [< John *Ketch,* a British executioner, died 1686]

jack-knife (jak′nīf′) *n.* **-knives,** *v.* **-knifed, -knif·ing.** —*n.* **1** a large, strong pocketknife. **2** in swimming, a kind of dive in which the diver touches his feet with his hands before entering the water. —*v.* **1** double up like a jack-knife. **2** in swimming, perform a jack-knife dive. **3** of railway cars, trailers, etc., double up at the connecting hitch when the vehicle is suddenly stopped or thrown off course. Also, **jackknife.**

jack·lad·der (jak′lad′ər) *n.* **1** in nautical use, a Jacob's ladder. **2** in lumbering, a slanting trough having an endless chain by means of which logs are moved from the water to the mill.

jack·light (jak′līt′) *n.* a light used for hunting or fishing at night. Fish or game are attracted by the jacklight so that they may be easily caught. —*v.* hunt or fish using a jacklight, especially when it is illegal; jack. —**jack′light′er,** *n.*

jack·light·ing (jak′līt′ing) *n.* the act or practice, often illegal, of hunting or fishing with a jacklight.

jack of all trades a person who can do many different kinds of work fairly well.

jack-o'-lan·tern (jak′ə lan′tərn) *n.* **1** a pumpkin hollowed out and cut to look like a face, used as a lantern at Halloween. **2** a will-o'-the-wisp (def. 1).

jack pine any one of several kinds of North American pine.

jack pot or **jack·pot** (jak′pot′) *n.* **1** any cumulative pool, as a large prize, that is competed for regularly and is increased as contestants fail to gain it. **2** any large gain. **3** in poker, the stakes that accumulate in a game until some player wins with a pair of jacks or something better. **4 hit the jackpot, a** win a jackpot. **b** have a stroke of very good luck.

jack-rab·bit (jak′rab′it) *n.* a large hare of western North America, having very long legs and ears.

jack·screw (jak′skrü′) *n.* a kind of jack for lifting heavy weights short distances, operated by a screw.

jack·stone (jak′stōn′) *n.* **1** in a child's game, a pebble or piece of metal tossed up and caught. **2 jackstones,** *pl.* a child's game in which pebbles or pieces of metal are tossed up and caught or picked up in various ways; jacks.

jack·straw (jak′stro′ or -strô′) *n.* **1** a straw, strip of wood, bone, etc. used in a game. **2 jackstraws,** *pl.* a game played with a set of these thrown down in a confused pile and picked up one at a time without moving any of the rest of the pile.

☛ **Jackstraws,** the game, is plural in form and singular in use: *Jackstraws is played by children.*

Jack Tar or **jack tar** a sailor.

Ja·cob (jā′kəb) *n.* in the Bible, the son of Isaac and younger twin brother of Esau. From Jacob's 12 sons the 12 tribes of Israel traced their descent. Gen. 25-50.

Jac·o·be·an (jak′ə bē′ən) *adj.* **1** of King James I of England (1566-1625). **2** of the early 17th century, especially the period of his reign, from 1603 to 1625. Jacobean architecture is late English Gothic with a large admixture of Italian forms. [< NL *Jacobaeus* < LL *Jacobus* James]

Jac·o·bin (jak′ə bin) *n.* **1** in France, a member of a radical political organization formed at Versailles in 1789, later spreading throughout France, and abolished in 1796. **2** an extreme radical in politics. **3** a Dominican friar.

[< F < Med.L *Jacobinus* of James < LL *Jacobus* James, from the Dominican convent near the Church of St. James of Compostella, where the Paris organization held its meetings]

Jac·o·bin·ism (jak′ə bin iz′əm) *n.* **1** the principles of the French Jacobins. **2** extreme radicalism in politics.

Jac·o·bite (jak′ə bīt′) *n.* in England, a supporter of James II (1633-1701) and his descendants in their claims to the throne after the Revolution in 1688. [< LL *Jacobus* James]

Jacob's ladder 1 in the Bible, a ladder leading to heaven seen by Jacob in a dream. Gen. 28:12. **2** in nautical use, a rope ladder with wooden or metal rungs.

Ja·cob's-lad·der (jā′kəbz lad′ər) *n.* a common garden plant with ladderlike leaves.

jac·quard or **Jac·quard** (jə kärd′) *adj.* of or indicating a pattern or a fabric woven on a Jacquard loom.

Jacquard loom a loom that can produce more elaborate designs in woven fabrics than the limited patterns obtainable from a standard loom. [< Joseph *Jacquard* (1752-1834), a French weaver who invented it]

Jacque·mi·not (jak′mə nō′) *n.* a deep-red variety of rose. [< Jean Francois *Jacqueminot* (1787-1865), a French general]

Jac·que·rie (zhäk rē′) *n.* **1** a revolt of the peasants of N. France against the nobles in 1358. **2** Also, **jacquerie.** any revolt of peasants. [< F *Jacquerie* peasants < *Jacques.* See JACK.]

jade[1] (jād) *n.* **1** either of two hard minerals, nephrite or jadeite, occurring in a wide variety of colors, especially green and white. **2** a piece of this stone, or a gem, ornament, etc. made from it. **3** green. —*adj.* green. [< F < Sp. (*piedra de*) *ijada* (stone of) colic (jade being supposed to cure this), ult. < L *ilia* flanks]

jade[2] (jād) *n. v.* **jad·ed, jad·ing.** —*n.* **1** an inferior or worn-out horse. **2** (*used contemptuously or playfully*) a woman. —*v.* **1** wear out; tire; weary. **2** dull by continual use; surfeit; satiate. [origin uncertain; cf. ON *jalda* mare]

jad·ed (jād′id) *adj.* **1** worn out; tired; weary: *a jaded horse, a jaded appearance.* **2** dulled from continual use; surfeited; satiated: *a jaded appetite.* —**jad′ed·ly,** *adv.* —**jad′ed·ness,** *n.*

jade·ite (jād′īt) *n.* a mineral, a silicate of sodium-aluminum that is harder and more valuable than nephrite, the other variety of jade.

jae·ger or **jä·ger** (yā′gər or jā′gər) *n.* a sea bird resembling a gull, that pursues weaker birds and makes them disgorge their prey. [< G *Jäger,* literally, hunter]

Jaf·fa (jaf′ə) *n.* a type of orange from Jaffa, a seaport of Israel.

jag[1] (jag) *n. v.* **jagged, jag·ging.** —*n.* a sharp point sticking out; pointed projection. —*v.* **1** make notches in. **2** cut or tear unevenly. [origin uncertain]

jag[2] (jag) *n.* **1** a load: *a jag of fish.* **2** *Slang.* a state of intoxication. **3** *Slang.* a period of uncontrolled indulgence.

JAG or **J.A.G.** Judge Advocate General.

jag·ged (jag′id) *adj.* with sharp points sticking out; notched; unevenly cut or torn. —**jag′ged·ly,** *adv.* —**jag′ged·ness,** *n.*

jag·uar (jag′wär or jag′ū är′) *n.* a fierce animal of the cat family, similar to a leopard but more heavily built. It lives in forests in the warmer parts of America. [< Tupi-Guarani *jaguara*]

Jah·ve or **Jah·veh** (yä′vā) *n.* Yahweh.

jail (jāl) *n.* **1** a prison. **2** a prison for people awaiting trial or being punished for minor offences. **3 break jail,** escape from jail. —*v.* put in jail; keep in jail. Also, *Brit.* **gaol.** [ME < OF *jaiole,* ult. < L *cavea* cage] —**jail′-like′,** *adj.*

jail·bird (jāl′bėrd′) *n. Slang.* **1** a prisoner in jail. **2** a person who has been in jail many times.

jail·break (jāl′brāk′) *n. Informal.* an escape from prison.

jail·er or **jail·or** (jāl′ər) *n.* **1** a keeper of a jail. **2** a person who keeps someone or something confined. Also, *Brit.* **gaoler.**

Jain (jān or jīn) *n.* a member or adherent of Jainism. —*adj.* of or having to do with the Jains or their religion. [< Hind. *Jaina* < *Jina* victorious]

Jain·ism (jā′niz əm or jī′niz əm) *n.* a religion of India founded about 500 B.C. and having Hindu and Buddhist elements. Its beliefs include non-violence, asceticism, and the transmigration of souls.

jal·ap (jal′əp) *n.* **1** a powder made from the dried roots of a Mexican plant, used as a purgative. **2** the plant itself. **3** the roots. [< Sp. *jalapa* < *Jalapa,* a city in Mexico]

ja·lop·y (jə lop′ē) *n.* **-lop·ies.** *Informal.* an old automobile in decrepit condition. [origin uncertain]

jal·ou·sie (zhal′ü zē′) *n.* a window shade or shutter made of horizontal slats set at an angle. [< F *jalousie,* literally, jealousy < *jaloux* jealous, from enabling one to see through the shutter without being seen]

jam[1] (jam) *v.* **jammed, jam·ming,** *n.* —*v.* **1** press; squeeze; hold; stick: *The ship was jammed between two rocks.* **2** crush; bruise: *Her fingers were jammed in the door.* **3** push; shove: *He jammed his fist into my face.* **4** fill up; block up: *The river was jammed with logs.* **5** stick fast or get caught so as not to work properly: *The window has jammed.* **6** cause to stick or catch. **7** make (radio signals, etc.) unintelligible by sending out others of approximately the same frequency.
—*n.* **1** a mass of people or things crowded together so that they cannot move freely: *a traffic jam.* **2** a jamming. **3** a being jammed. **4** *Informal.* a difficulty or tight spot. [? imitative] —**Syn.** *v.* **1** wedge, pack. **3** force, thrust.

jam[2] (jam) *n.* fruit boiled with sugar until thick. [? special use of *jam*[1]] —**jam′like′,** *adj.*

Jam. 1 Jamaica. **2** James.

Ja·mai·ca (jə mā′kə) *n.* a kind of rum made in Jamaica, an island country in the West Indies.

Ja·mai·can (jə mā′kən) *adj.* of, having to do with, or obtained from Jamaica. —*n.* a native or inhabitant of Jamaica.

jamb or **jambe** (jam) *n.* **1** the upright piece forming the side of a doorway, window, fireplace, etc. **2** a piece of armor for the calf of the leg. [ME < OF *jambe,* originally, leg < LL *gamba* hock < Gk. *kampē* a bending]

jam·bo·ree (jam′bə rē′) *n.* **1** *Slang.* a noisy party; lively entertainment. **2** a large rally or gathering of Boy Scouts. [coined from *jam*[1] after *corroboree, shivaree*]

jam-packed (jam′pakt′) *adj. Informal.* filled to capacity; packed tightly.

jam session *Slang.* a gathering at which jazz musicians improvise freely on popular compositions.

Jan. January.

jan·gle (jang′gəl) *v.* **-gled, -gling,** *n.* —*v.* **1** make harsh sounds. **2** cause to sound harshly: *The boys jangled cowbells.* **3** quarrel; dispute. —*n.* **1** a harsh sound. **2** quarrel; dispute. [ME < OF *jangler*] —**jan′gler,** *n.*

Jan·is·sar·y or **jan·is·sar·y** (jan′ə ser′ē) *n.* **-sar·ies.** Janizary.

jan·i·tor (jan′ə tər) *n.* **1** a person hired to take care of a building, offices, etc.; caretaker. **2** a doorkeeper. [< L *janitor* doorkeeper < *janus* arched passageway]

jan·i·tress (jan′ə tris) *n.* a woman janitor.

Jan·i·zar·y or **jan·i·zar·y** (jan′ə zer′ē) *n.* **-zar·ies. 1** in Turkey, a soldier in the Sultan's guard. Janizaries formed the crack fighting force of the Turkish army from the 14th century until 1826. **2** any Turkish soldier. Also, **Janissary** or **janissary.** [< F *janissaire* < Ital. *giannizzero* < Turkish *yeñicheri* < *yeñi* new + *cheri* soldiery]

Jan·sen·ism (jan′sə niz′əm) *n.* the doctrine of a Dutch theologian, Cornelius Jansen (1585-1638), who held that the human will is not free to do good and that salvation is limited to God's chosen few.

Jan·sen·ist (jan′sə nist) *n.* a believer in, or follower of, Jansenism.

Jan·u·ar·y (jan′yə wer′ē or jan′ū er′ē) *n.* **-ar·ies.** the first month of the year. It has 31 days. [< L *Januarius* < *Janus* Janus]

Ja·nus (jā′nəs) *n.* in Roman mythology, the god of gates and doors, and of beginnings and endings, represented as having two faces, one looking forward and the other looking backward.

Ja·nus-faced (jā′nəs fāst′) *adj.* two-faced; double-dealing; deceitful.

Jap (jap) *adj. n. Derogatory.* Japanese.

Jap. 1 Japan. 2 Japanese.

ja·pan (jə pan′) *n. v.* **-panned, -pan·ning.** —*n.* 1 a hard, glossy varnish. Black japan is used on wood or metal. 2 articles varnished and decorated in the Japanese manner. 3 a liquid used to make paint dry faster.
—*v.* put japan on. [< *Japan*]

Japan current a current of warm water in the Pacific Ocean, flowing north from the Philippine Sea, past S.E. Japan, and then into the N. Pacific Ocean.

Jap·a·nese (jap′ə nēz′) *adj. n.* **-nese.** —*adj.* of or having to do with Japan, an island empire, east of Asia, its people, or their language.
—*n.* 1 a person born or living in Japan. 2 a citizen of Japan. 3 the language of Japan.

Japanese beetle a small, green-and-brown beetle that eats fruits, leaves, and grasses. It was accidentally brought from Japan to North America, where it has done much damage to crops.

Japanese quince japonica

jape (jāp) *n. v.* **japed, jap·ing.** 1 joke; jest. 2 trick. [ME; origin uncertain] —**jap′er,** *n.*

ja·pon·i·ca (jə pon′ə kə) *n.* 1 a camellia. 2 a shrub having showy red, pink, or white flowers; flowering quince. [< NL *japonica,* originally fem. adj., Japanese]

jar[1] (jär) *n.* 1 a deep container made of glass, earthenware, etc. with a wide mouth. 2 the amount that it holds. 3 a jar and its contents. [< F *jarre,* ult. < Arabic *jarrah*]

jar[2] (jär) *v.* **jarred, jar·ring,** *n.* —*v.* 1 shake; rattle: *The heavy footsteps jarred my desk so that I had trouble writing.* 2 make a harsh, discordant noise. 3 have a harsh, unpleasant effect on; shock: *The children's screams jar my nerves.* 4 clash; quarrel: *Our opinions jar.*
—*n.* 1 a shake; rattle. 2 a harsh, discordant noise. 3 a harsh, unpleasant effect; shock. 4 a clash; quarrel. [probably imitative] —**Syn.** *v.* 2 scrape, grate.

jar[3] (jär) *n.* 1 a turn; a turning. 2 **on the jar,** ajar; slightly open. [OE *cierr*]

jar·di·niere (jär′də nēr′) *n.* an ornamental pot or stand for flowers or plants. [< F *jardinière* < *jardin* garden]

jar·gon (jär′gən) *n.* 1 confused, meaningless talk or writing. 2 language that is not understood. 3 the language of a particular group, profession, etc.: *the jargon of sailors.* 4 a mixture of languages. 5 chatter.
—*v.* 1 talk jargon. 2 chatter. [ME < OF; probably ult. imitative] —**Syn.** *n.* 3 lingo, cant, argot, slang.

☛ **Jargon** is commonly used to refer to any confused or unintelligible speech or writing: *He spoke such a jargon I couldn't make head or tail of what he said.* Among linguists, *jargon* is a technical word for a dialect composed of the mixture of two or more languages, such as the Chinook jargon of the Pacific Northwest and the Chinese-English jargon, known as pidgin English.

jarl (yärl) *n.* in ancient Scandinavia, a chief or nobleman. [< ON. Related to EARL.]

Jas. James.

jas·mine or **jas·min** (jas′mən or jaz′mən) *n.* 1 a shrub or vine having clusters of fragrant flowers. There are yellow, white, and red jasmines. 2 the essential oil or resin obtained from this plant and used in making perfume. Also, **jessamine.** [< F *jasmin* < Arabic < Persian *yasmin*]

Ja·son (jā′sən) *n.* in Greek legend, the Greek hero who led the expedition of the Argonauts and won the Golden Fleece.

jas·per (jas′pər) *n.* 1 an opaque variety of quartz, usually red or brown. 2 a piece of this stone, or a gem made from it. 3 a green precious stone. [ME < OF *jaspre* < L < Gk. *iaspis* < Semitic]

ja·to (jā′tō) *n.* in aeronautics, a unit consisting of one or more jet engines, used to provide auxiliary propulsion for speeding up the take-off of an airplane. [< *j*et *a*ssisted *t*ake-*o*ff]

hat, āge, cãre, fär; let, ēqual, tėrm; it, īce
hot, ōpen, ôrder; oil, out; cup, pu̇t, rüle, ūse
əbove, takən, pencəl, lemən, circəs
ch, child; ng, long; sh, ship
th, thin; ᴛʜ, then; zh, measure

jaun·dice (jon′dis or jôn′dis) *n. v.* **-diced, -dic·ing.** —*n.* 1 a disease of the liver, characterized by yellowness of the skin, eyes, and body fluids, and disturbed vision. 2 a disturbed or unnaturally sour mental outlook, due to envy, jealousy, etc. —*v.* 1 cause jaundice in. 2 prejudice the mind and judgment of by envy, discontent, etc.; sour the temper of. [ME < OF *jaunisse* < *jaune* yellow < L *galbinus* greenish-yellow]

jaunt (jont or jônt) *n.* a short pleasure trip or excursion. —*v.* take a short pleasure trip or excursion. [origin uncertain]

jaunting car a light cart having two seats back to back, formerly used in Ireland.

jaun·ty (jon′tē or jôn′tē) *adj.* **-ti·er, -ti·est.** 1 easy and lively; sprightly; carefree: *The happy boy walked with jaunty steps.* 2 smart; stylish: *She wore a jaunty little hat.* [formerly *janty* < F *gentil* noble, gentle < L *gentilis.* Doublet of GENTEEL, GENTILE, GENTLE.] —**jaun′ti·ly,** *adv.* —**jaun′ti·ness,** *n.* —**Syn.** 1 airy, gay.

Ja·va (jä′və or jav′ə) *n.* 1 a kind of coffee obtained from Java, a large island southeast of Asia, and nearby islands. 2 *Slang.* coffee.

Java man a very early form of man inferred from fossil remains found in Java.

Jav·a·nese (jav′ə nēz′) *adj. n.* **-nese.** —*adj.* of or having to do with Java, an island southeast of Asia, its people, or their language. —*n.* 1 a native of Java. 2 the language of Java.

jave·lin (jav′lən or jav′ə lin) *n.* a light spear thrown by hand. [< F *javeline*]

Ja·vel water (jə vel′) a solution of sodium or potassium hypochlorite, used as a bleach and disinfectant. [*Javel,* < F *Javelle,* a former town now included in Paris]

jaw (jo or jô) *n.* 1 in anatomy, either of the two bones, or sets of bones, that form the framework of the mouth. The lower jaw is movable. 2 the lower part of the face. 3 **jaws,** *pl.* **a** the mouth with its jawbones and teeth. **b** a narrow entrance to a valley, mountain pass, channel, etc. 4 either of the parts in a tool or machine that grip and hold. A vise has jaws. 5 *Slang.* talk; gossip.
—*v. Slang.* 1 talk; gossip. 2 find fault; scold. [? related to CHEW; influenced by F *joue* cheek] —**jaw′less,** *adj.*

jaw·bone (jo′bōn′ or jô′-) *n.* 1 the bone of either jaw. 2 the bone of the lower jaw.

jaw·break·er (jo′brāk′ər or jô′-) *n. Slang.* 1 a big, hard piece of candy. 2 a word that is hard to pronounce. 3 a machine for crushing ore.

jay (jā) *n.* 1 a noisy North American bird having blue feathers; bluejay. 2 a noisy European bird with a crest. 3 a Canada jay. 4 any of various birds related to these. 5 *Informal.* an impertinent or foolish chatterer. 6 *Slang.* a silly, stupid person. [ME < OF < LL *gaius*]

jay·walk (jā′wok′ or -wôk′) *v. Informal.* walk across a street without paying attention to traffic rules. [< *jay* a stupid person + *walk*] —**jay′walk′er,** *n.*

jazz (jaz) *n.* 1 a type of music characterized by inventive melodic and harmonic patterns, syncopation, long-drawn wavering or wailing sounds, etc. 2 *Slang.* liveliness. 3 *Slang.* worthless nonsense.
—*adj.* of or like jazz: *a jazz band.*
—*v.* 1 play or arrange (music) as jazz. 2 *Slang.* make lively. [of American Negro origin] —**jazz′er,** *n.*

jaz·zy (jaz′ē) *adj. Informal.* 1 having to do with jazz. 2 wildly excited or animated. 3 flashy; loud; too fancy: *jazzy clothes.*

J.C. 1 Jesus Christ. 2 Julius Caesar.

J.C.C. Junior Chamber of Commerce.

J.C.D. 1 Doctor of Canon Law. (for L *Juris Canonici*

Doctor) 2 Doctor of Civil Law. (for L *Juris Civilis Doctor*)

JCS Joint Chiefs of Staff.

jct. or **jctn.** junction.

J.D. Doctor of Laws. (for L *Jurum Doctor*)

Je. June.

jeal·ous (jel′əs) *adj.* **1** fearful that a person one loves may love someone else better or may prefer someone else. One may be jealous of the person loved or of the rival. **2** full of envy; envious: *He is jealous of John or of John's marks.* **3** requiring complete loyalty or faithfulness: "*The Lord thy God is a jealous God.*" **4** watchful in keeping or guarding something; careful: *Quebec is jealous of its rights within Confederation.* **5** close; watchful; suspicious: *The dog was a jealous guardian of the child.* [ME < OF *gelos* < LL *zelosus* < L *zelus* zeal < Gk. *zēlos*. Related to ZEAL.] —**jeal′ous·ly,** *adv.* —**jeal′ous·ness,** *n.* —**Syn. 2** grudging, resentful.

jeal·ous·y (jel′əs ē) *n.* **-ous·ies.** a jealous condition or feeling.

jean (jēn) *n.* **1** a strong, twilled cotton cloth, used for overalls, etc. **2 jeans,** *pl.* **a** pants made of a strong, twilled cotton cloth: *The cowboy wore blue jeans under his chaps.* **b** overalls. [probably < F *Gênes* Genoa, Italy]

Jean Baptiste (zhäN bä tēst′) *Cdn. Slang.* a French-Canadian. [< Saint *Jean Baptiste* St. John Baptist, patron saint]

jeep (jēp) *n.* a small, but powerful, general-purpose automobile or truck, with a four-wheel drive. Jeeps are used in the armed forces and by farmers. [? alteration of G.P. = General Purpose, military designation of the vehicle]

jeer (jēr) *v.* make fun rudely or unkindly; mock; scoff. —*n.* a jeering remark; rude, sarcastic comment. [origin uncertain] —**jeer′er,** *n.* —**Syn.** *v.* See **scoff.**

jeer·ing·ly (jēr′ing lē) *adv.* in a jeering manner; with derision.

Je·ho·vah (ji hō′və) *n.* one of the names of God in the Old Testament. [erroneous modern representation of Hebrew *Yahweh* (originally written without vowels as JHVH), interpreted as meaning "he that is," "the self-existent"]

Jehovah's Witnesses a Christian sect founded by Charles T. Russell in Pennsylvania in the 1870's. Some of their tenets are that organized religion is evil, that personal religious conviction is beyond civil authority, and that the end of the world is near.

je·hu (jē′hū or jā′hū) *n. Informal.* a fast driver. [< *Jehu* (842-815 B.C.), King of Israel, II Kings 9:20, with reference to his furious driving]

je·june (ji jün′) *adj.* **1** lacking nourishing qualities. **2** flat and uninteresting. [< L *jejunus*, originally, hungry] —**je·june′ly,** *adv.* —**je·june′ness,** *n.*

je·ju·num (ji jü′nəm) *n.* in anatomy, the middle portion of the small intestine, between the duodenum and the ileum. [< NL < L *jejunum*, neut., empty]

Jek·yll (jek′əl or jē′kəl) *n.* **1 Dr.,** the chief character in R. L. Stevenson's story *Dr. Jekyll and Mr. Hyde.* He discovered a drug that changed him into a brutal person (Mr. Hyde) and another that changed him back to himself. **2 Jekyll and Hyde,** a dual personality, part good or pleasant and part evil or unpleasant.

jell (jel) *v.* **1** set; become jelly. **2** *Informal.* take definite form; become fixed: *Our plans have jelled.* —*n.* a jelly. [< *jelly*]

jel·lied (jel′ēd) *adj.* **1** turned into jelly; having the consistency of jelly. **2** spread with jelly. **3** prepared in or covered with jelly: *jellied eels.*

jel·ly (jel′ē) *n.* **-lies,** *v.* **-lied, -ly·ing.** —*n.* **1** a food, liquid when hot, but rather firm and partly transparent when cold. Jelly can be made by boiling fruit juice and sugar together, by cooking bones and meat juice, or by using some stiffening preparation like gelatin. **2** a jelly-like substance: *petroleum jelly.* —*v.* **1** become jelly; turn into jelly. **2** prepare in or cover with jelly. [ME < OF *gelee*, originally, frost < L *gelata*, originally fem. pp. of *gelare* congeal] —**jel′ly-like′,** *adj.*

jel·ly·bean (jel′ē bēn′) *n.* a small, bean-shaped jellied candy, coated in different colors.

jel·ly·fish (jel′ē fish′) *n.* **-fish** or **-fishes. 1** any of a group of invertebrate sea animals with a body formed of a mass of jelly-like tissue that is often transparent. Most jellyfish have long, trailing tentacles that may bear stinging hairs or feelers. **2** *Informal.* a person of weak will or character.

jel·ly·roll (jel′ē rōl′) *n.* a thin layer of sponge cake spread with jelly and rolled up while still warm.

je ne sais quoi (zhən sā kwä′) *French.* an indefinable something (literally, I don't know what).

jen·net (jen′it) *n.* **1** a breed of small Spanish horses. **2** a horse of this breed. **3** a female donkey. Also, **genet.** [< F *genet* < Sp. *jinete* mounted soldier < Arabic *Zenāta*, a Berber tribe noted for its cavalry]

jen·ny (jen′ē) *n.* **-nies. 1** a spinning jenny. **2** the female of certain animals and birds. [originally a proper name, dim. of *Jane*, fem. of *John*]

jeop·ard (jep′ərd) *v.* jeopardize.

jeop·ard·ize (jep′ər dīz′) *v.* **-ized, -iz·ing.** risk; endanger; imperil: *Soldiers jeopardize their lives in war.*

jeop·ard·y (jep′ər dē) *n.* **1** risk; danger; peril: *His life was in jeopardy when the tree fell.* **2** in law, the peril of the defendant when put on trial for a crime. [ME < OF *jeu parti* an even or divided game, ult. < L *jocus* play + *pars, partis* part]

Jeph·thah (jef′thə) *n.* in the Bible, a judge of Israel who sacrificed his only daughter to fulfil a rash vow. Judges 11:30-40.

Jer. 1 Jeremiah. **2** Jersey. **3** Jerusalem.

jer·bo·a (jər bō′ə) *n.* a small, mouselike mammal of Asia and N. Africa, having long hind legs for jumping. [< NL < Arabic *yarbu'*]

jer·e·mi·ad (jer′ə mī′ad) *n.* a mournful complaint; lamentation. [< F *jérémiade* < *Jérémie* Jeremiah, the reputed author of *Lamentations* in the Bible]

Jer·e·mi·ah (jer′ə mī′ə) *n.* a Hebrew prophet who denounced and lamented the evils of his time.

Jer·e·mi·as (jer′ə mī′əs) *n.* in the Douay Bible, Jeremiah.

Jer·i·cho (jer′ə kō′) *n.* **-chos. 1** an ancient city in Palestine. According to the Bible, the walls of Jericho fell down at the noise made by the trumpets of Joshua's attacking army. **2** an out-of-the-way place.

jerk[1] (jėrk) *n.* **1** a sudden, sharp pull, twist, or start. **2** a pull or twist of the muscles that one cannot control; twitch. **3** *Slang.* an unsophisticated or stupid person. —*v.* **1** pull or twist suddenly. **2** throw with a movement that stops suddenly. **3** move with a jerk: *The old wagon jerked along.* **4** speak or say abruptly. [probably imitative] —**Syn.** *v.* **1** See **pull.**

jerk[2] (jėrk) *v.* preserve (meat) by cutting it into long thin slices and drying it in the sun. The early settlers in America used to jerk beef. [< Sp. *charquear* < *charqui* jerked meat < *Quechua* (Indian lang. of Peru)]

jer·kin (jėr′kən) *n.* a short coat or jacket, with or without sleeves. Men wore tight leather jerkins in the 16th and 17th centuries. [origin uncertain]

A jerkin

jerk·wa·ter (jėrk′wot′ər or -wô′tər) *Informal.* —*n.* a train on a branch railway. —*adj.* **1** not on the main line. **2** insignificant. [supposedly from small localities where train crews had to "jerk" water from streams with a bucket]

jerk·y[1] (jėr′kē) *adj.* **jerk·i·er, jerk·i·est.** with sudden starts and stops; with jerks. —**jerk′i·ly,** *adv.* —**jerk′i·ness,** *n.*

jerk·y[2] (jėr′kē) *n.* strips of dried beef. [< Sp. *charquí.* See JERK[2].]

jer·o·bo·am (jer′ə bō′əm) *n.* **1 a** a wine bottle holding one gallon. **b** this amount. **2 a** any large container or bottle for alcoholic beverages. **b** its contents. [< *Jeroboam*, a king of ancient Israel]

jer·ry or **Jer·ry** (jer′ē) *n. Slang.* **1** a German soldier. **2** a German. [probably dim. of *German*]

jer·ry-built (jer′ē bilt′) *adj.* built quickly and cheaply of poor materials; flimsy. [? alteration of an earlier *jury-built*; cf. *jury-rigged* rigged for temporary service. See JURY².]

jer·ry-can (jeʹrē kanʹ) *n. Slang.* a four-gallon gasoline container of rectangular shape. It was devised by the Germans during World War II. [< *jerry* + *can*]

jer·sey (jėrʹzē) *n.* **-seys. 1** a close-fitting sweater that is pulled on over the head. **2** a woman's close-fitting knitted undergarment. **3** a machine-knitted cloth. [< *Jersey*]

Jer·sey (jėrʹzē) *n.* **-seys. 1** a breed of small, fawn-colored, dairy cattle that give very rich milk. **2** an animal of this breed. [< *Jersey*, one of the Channel Islands, where this breed of cattle originated]

Jerusalem artichoke (jə rüʹsə ləm) **1** a kind of sunflower whose root is edible. **2** the root of this plant. [<*Jerusalem*, as an alteration of Ital. *girasole* sunflower]

jess (jes) *n.* a short strap fastened around a falcon's leg. A leash could be attached to it. —*v.* put the jesses on. [ME < OF *ges*, ult. < L *jacere* to throw]

jes·sa·mine (jesʹə min) *n.* jasmine.

Jes·se (jesʹē) *n.* in the Bible, the father of David, ancestor of Christ. 1 Sam. 16. Jesse is often depicted as the root of a tree which bears as its fruit David and other royal ancestors of Christ, with the infant Jesus and His Mother on the highest branch.

jest (jest) *n.* **1** a joke. **2** the act of poking fun; mockery. **3** something intended to be mocked or laughed at. **4 in jest,** in fun; not seriously.
—*v.* **1** joke. **2** poke fun (*at*); make fun. [< OF *geste*, originally, story, exploit < L *gesta*, neut. pl., exploits < *gestus*, pp. of *gerere* accomplish] **—jestʹing·ly,** *adv.*
—Syn. *v.* **1** See **joke.**

jest·er (jesʹtər) *n.* a person who jests. In the Middle Ages kings often had jesters to amuse them.

Je·su (jēʹzü or jēʹzü, jēʹsü or jēʹsü) *n. Poetic.* Jesus.

Jes·u·it (jezʹü it or jezhʹü it) *n.* **1** in the Roman Catholic Church, a member of a religious order called the Society of Jesus, founded by Saint Ignatius Loyola in 1534. Some of the first explorers of America were Jesuits. **2** *Derogatory.* a crafty or scheming person, especially in debate or argument. [< NL *Jesuita* < LL *Jesus* Jesus]

Jes·u·it·ic (jezʹü itʹik or jezhʹü itʹik) *adj.* **1** of or having to do with the Jesuits. **2 jesuitic,** *Derogatory.* scheming; using subtle reasoning.

Jes·u·it·ism (jezʹü ə tizʹəm or jezhʹu ə tizʹəm) *n.* **1** the religious order of the Jesuits, or their principles and practices. **2 jesuitism,** *Derogatory.* subtle distinctions; duplicity.

Je·sus (jēʹzəs) *n.* Jesus of Nazareth, the founder of the Christian religion.

Jesus Christ Jesus.

jet¹ (jet) *n. v.* **jet·ted, jet·ting.** —*n.* **1** a stream of water, steam, gas, or any liquid, sent with force, especially from a small opening: *A fountain sends up a jet of water.* **2** a spout or nozzle for sending out a jet. **3** a jet plane. —*v.* **1** gush out; shoot forth in a jet or forceful stream. **2** fly by jet plane. [< F *jet* < *jeter* throw]

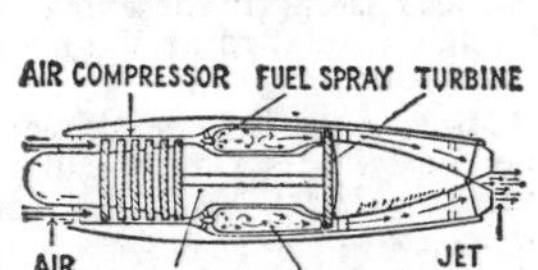

A diagram of a jet airplane engine. The air is sucked in through the front of the engine, compressed, and mixed with fuel. This mixture is burned in the burners, giving off gas which passes out through the rear of the engine, pushing the airplane forward.

jet² (jet) *n.* **1** a hard, black mineral, glossy when polished, used for making beads, buttons, etc. It is a kind of lignite. **2** a deep glossy black. —*adj.* **1** made of jet. **2** deep glossy-black. [ME < OF *jaiet* < L < Gk. *gagatēs* < *Gagas*, a town in Lycia, Asia Minor]

jet-black (jetʹblakʹ) *adj.* very black.

jet engine an engine using jet propulsion.

jet·lin·er (jetʹlīnʹər) *n.* a jet-propelled air liner. See **airplane** for picture.

jet plane an airplane that is driven by jet propulsion. See **airplane** for diagram.

jet·port (jetʹpôrtʹ) *n.* an airport for jet planes.

jet-prop (jetʹpropʹ) *adj.* equipped with turboprop engines. —*n.* an aircraft thus equipped.

hat, āge, cãre, fär; let, ēqual, tėrm; it, īce
hot, ōpen, ôrder; oil, out; cup, pu̇t, rüle, ūse
əbove, takən, pencəl, lemən, circəs
ch, child; ng, long; sh, ship
th, thin; ᴛʜ, then; zh, measure

jet-pro·pelled (jetʹprə peldʹ) *adj.* **1** propelled in a given direction by means of a jet of air, gas, etc. that is forced in the opposite direction. **2** moving very fast and energetically.

jet propulsion propulsion in a given direction by a jet of air, gas, etc. forced in the opposite direction.

jet·sam (jetʹsəm) *n.* **1** goods thrown overboard to lighten a ship in distress. **2** such goods washed ashore. **3** anything tossed aside as useless. [var. of *jetson*, a var. of *jettison*. Doublet of JETTISON.]

jet set a section of society consisting of wealthy people noted for their lavish entertaining and their international travelling, especially to fashionable places and events.

jet stream a current of air travelling at very high speed (up to 350 miles per hour or more) from west to east at high altitudes (six to eight miles). Jet streams are often used by airplane pilots to gain extra speed when travelling in an easterly direction.

jet·ti·son (jetʹə sən or jetʹə zən) *v.* **1** throw (goods) overboard to lighten a ship, aircraft, etc. in distress. **2** throw away; discard. [< n.] —*n.* **1** the act of throwing (goods) overboard to lighten a ship, aircraft, etc. in distress. **2** the goods thrown overboard; jetsam. [< OF *getaison* < L *jactatio, -onis* < *jactare* toss < *jacere* throw. Doublet of JETSAM.]

jet·ty (jetʹē) *n.* **-ties. 1** a structure built out into the water to protect a harbor or influence the current; breakwater. **2** a landing place; pier or dock. [< OF *jetee* (something) thrown out < *jeter* throw, ult. < L *jacere*]

Jew (jü) *n.* **1** a person descended from one of the ancient Hebrew tribes of Israel. **2** a person whose religion is Judaism; Hebrew. —*adj.* Jewish. [ME < OF *giu, jueu* < L *Judaeus* < Gk. *Ioudaios* < Hebrew *y'hudi* belonging to the tribe of Judah]

jew·el (jüʹəl) *n. v.* **-elled** or **-eled, -el·ling** or **-el·ing.**
—*n.* **1** a precious stone; gem. **2** a valuable ornament to be worn, set with precious stones. **3** a person or thing that is very precious. **4** a gem or some substitute used as a bearing in a watch. —*v.* set or adorn with jewels or with things like jewels: *The sky is jewelled with stars.* [ME < AF *juel* trinket, plaything < Med.L *jocalis* < L *jocus* joke, game] **—jewʹel-likeʹ,** *adj.*

jewel case a box or case to hold jewellery.

jew·el·er (jüʹəl ər or jüʹlər) *n.* jeweller.

jew·el·ler or **jew·el·er** (jüʹəl ər or jüʹlər) *n.* a person who makes, sells, or repairs jewels, jewelled ornaments, watches, etc.

jew·el·ler·y or **jew·el·ry** (jüʹəl rē or jülʹrē) *n.* jewels and ornaments set with gems.

jew·el·ry (jüʹəl rē or jülʹrē) *n.* jewellery.

jew·el·weed (jüʹəl wēdʹ) *n.* a plant having yellow or orange-yellow flowers.

Jew·ess (jüʹis) *n.* a Jewish woman or girl.

jew·fish (jüʹfishʹ) *n.* **-fish** or **-fish·es. 1** a giant sea bass. **2** any of various other large fishes of warm seas.

Jew·ish (jüʹish) *adj.* **1** of the Jews; belonging to the Jews; characteristic of the Jews. **2** Yiddish. —*n.* Yiddish. **—Jewʹish·ness,** *n.*

Jewish calendar the Hebrew calendar, which dates the Creation at 3761 B.C. and divides the year into 12 months of 29 or 30 days each, allowing for an extra month of 29 days every second or third year. The ecclesiastical year begins in March or April, and the civil year in September or October.

Jew·ry (jüʹrē) *n.* **-ries. 1** Jews as a group; the Jewish people. **2** *Obsolete.* a district where Jews live; ghetto.

jews'-harp or **jew's-harp** (jüzʹhärpʹ) *n.* a simple musical instrument, held between the teeth and played by striking with a finger the free end of a piece of metal.

Jez·e·bel (jez′ə bəl) *n.* **1** in the Bible, the depraved and wicked wife of Ahab, King of Israel. II Kings 9:7-10, 30-37. **2** any shameless, immoral woman.

J.H.S. Junior High School.

jib[1] (jib) *n.* **1** a triangular sail in front of the foremast. **2 cut of one's jib,** *Informal.* one's outward appearance. [? < *jib*[2]]

JIB
A jib on a yacht

jib[2] (jib) *v.* **jibbed, jib·bing.** jibe[1].

jib[3] (jib) *n. v.* **jibbed, jib·bing.** —*v.* move sidewise or backward instead of forward; refuse to go ahead. —*n.* a horse or other animal that jibs. [origin uncertain] —**jib′ber,** *n.*

jib[4] (jib) *n.* the projecting arm of a crane or derrick. [probably < *gibbet*]

JIB BOOM
BOWSPRIT
FORWARD PART OF SHIP

jib boom a spar extending out from a ship's bowsprit.

jibe[1] (jīb) *v.* **jibed, jib·ing. 1** shift (a sail) from one side of a ship to the other when sailing before the wind. **2** change the course of a ship so that the sails shift in this way. Also, **jib.** [< Du. *gijben,* var. of *gijpen*]

jibe[2] (jīb) *v.* **jibed, jib·ing,** *n.* gibe. —**jib′er,** *n.*

jibe[3] (jīb) *v.* **jibed, jib·ing.** *Informal.* be in harmony; agree. [origin uncertain]

jif·fy (jif′ē) *n.* **jif·fies.** *Informal.* a very short time; moment. [origin unknown]

jig[1] (jig) *n. v.* **jigged, jig·ging.** —*n.* **1** a lively dance, often in triple time. **2** the music for such a dance. **3 The jig is up.** *Slang.* It's all over; there's no more chance. **4 in jig time,** quickly; rapidly. [< v.]
—*v.* **1** dance a jig. **2** move jerkily; jerk up and down or back and forth. **3** sing or play (music) as a jig or in the style of a jig. [< OF *giguer* dance < *gigue* fiddle < Gmc.]

jig[2] (jig) *n. v.* **jigged, jig·ging.** —*n.* **1** fish-hook, or set of fish-hooks, loaded with a bright metal or having a spoon-shaped piece of bone attached, for drawing through the water. **2** any of various mechanical contrivances or devices; especially, a guide in using a drill, file, etc.
—*v.* **1** jerk up and down; move jerkily. **2** fish with a jig. [origin uncertain]

jig·ger[1] (jig′ər) *n.* **1** a small set of ropes and pulleys used on a ship. **2** a small sail. **3** a jigger mast. **4** a machine with a jerky motion. **5** *Informal.* some device, article, or part that one cannot name more precisely; gadget; contraption. **6** a jig used in fishing. **7** a small container that usually holds $1\frac{1}{2}$ ounces, used to measure liquor. **8** the amount that a jigger can hold. **9** a jigger and its contents. **10** in golf, an iron-headed club resembling a mashie and a midiron. **11** a device used for setting a gill net under the ice on lakes and rivers. [< *jig*[2]]

jig·ger[2] (jig′ər) *n.* **1** a small flea; chigoe. **2** a chigger. [alteration of *chigoe*]

jigger mast a mast in the stern of a ship.

jig·ger·y-pok·er·y (jig′ər ē pōk′ər ē) *n.* **-ies.** *Slang.* humbug; fraud; bunk.

jig·gle (jig′əl) *v.* **-gled, -gling,** *n.* —*v.* shake or jerk slightly. —*n.* a slight shake; light jerk. [< *jig*[1]]

jig·saw (jig′so′ or -sô′) *n.* a narrow saw mounted in a frame and worked with an up-and-down motion, used to cut curves or irregular lines.

jigsaw puzzle a picture sawed into irregular pieces that can be fitted together again.

jig time 1 the lively tempo of a jig. **2 in jig time,** *Informal.* in a hurry; fast.

jill or **Jill** (jil) *n. Archaic.* **1** a woman; girl. **2** a sweetheart; wife.

jilt (jilt) *v.* cast off (a lover or sweetheart) after giving encouragement. —*n.* a woman who casts off a lover after encouraging him. [origin uncertain] —**jilt′er,** *n.*

Jim Crow (jim′ krō′) *Esp.U.S.* **1** *Slang.* a derogatory name for a Negro. **2** discrimination against Negroes. [originally a name in a Negro minstrel song (c. 1835)]

jim·jams (jim′jamz′) *n. Slang.* **1** delirium tremens. **2** jitters; a creepy, uneasy feeling. [coined word]

jim·my (jim′ē) *n.* **-mies,** *v.* **-mied, -my·ing.** —*n.* a short crowbar used especially by burglars to force windows, doors, etc. open. —*v.* force open with a jimmy. [apparently a special use of *Jimmy,* familiar form of *James*]

jim·son weed or **Jim·son weed** (jim′sən) a tall, coarse, bad-smelling weed having white flowers and poisonous, narcotic leaves. [*jimson,* alteration of *Jamestown,* Va.]

jin·gle (jing′gəl) *n. v.* **-gled, -gling.** —*n.* **1** a sound like that of little bells, or of coins or keys striking together. **2** a verse or a piece of music that has a jingling sound: *Mother Goose rhymes are jingles. Radio and television advertising uses many jingles.*
—*v.* **1** make a jingling sound: *The sleigh bells jingle as we ride.* **2** cause to jingle: *jingle one's money.* **3** make jingling verses. **4** be full of simple rhymes and repetitions. [imitative] —**jing′ler,** *n.*

jin·gly (jing′glē) *adj.* like a jingle.

jin·go (jing′gō) *n.* **-goes,** *adj.* —*n.* a person who favors an aggressive foreign policy that might lead to war with other nations; chauvinist. —*adj.* of jingoes; like that of jingoes. [< *by Jingo,* a phrase in the refrain of a music-hall song, which became the "theme song" of Disraeli's supporters in 1878; *jingo,* a magician's term; origin uncertain]

jin·go·ism (jing′gō iz′əm) *n.* the attitude of mind, policy, or practices of jingoes; chauvinism.

jin·go·is·tic (jing′gō is′tik) *adj.* of jingoes; like that of jingoes.

jin·ker (jing′kər) *n. Cdn.* in Newfoundland: **1** an imaginary creature to whom bad luck is attributed; gremlin. **2** a person blamed for bad luck; Jonah. [origin uncertain]

jinn (jin) *n. 1,* pl. of **jinni;** *2, sing., pl.* **jinns.** in Moslem mythology: **1** spirits that can appear in human or animal form and do good or harm to people. **2** one of these spirits; jinni. Also, **djinn.** [< Arabic *jinn,* pl. of *jinni*]

jin·ni or **jin·nee** (ji nē′) *n.* **jinn.** one of the jinn.

jin·rik·i·sha or **jin·rick·sha** (jin rik′shə or jin rik′sho) *n.* a small, two-wheeled, hooded carriage pulled by one or more men, used in Japan, China, etc. Also, **rickshaw, ricksha.** [< Japanese *jinrikisha* < *jin* man + *riki* power + *sha* vehicle]

jinx (jingks) *Slang.* —*n.* a person or thing that brings bad luck. —*v.* bring bad luck to. [< L *iynx,* bird used in magic < Gk.]

jit·ney (jit′nē) *n.* **-neys.** *Slang.* **1** an automobile that carries passengers for a small fare. It usually travels along a regular route. **2** a five-cent piece; nickel. [origin uncertain]

jit·ter (jit′ər) *v. Informal.* be nervous; act or speak nervously. [< ? var. of E dial. *chitter* shiver, tremble, var. of *chatter*]

jit·ter·bug (jit′ər bug′) *n. v.* **-bugged, -bug·ging.** *Informal.* —*n.* **1** a person who is enthusiastic about swing music and excited by it to lively dance movements and gestures. **2** a frenzied dance with lively movement. —*v.* dance in such a way. [< *jitter,* v. (see JITTERS) + *bug*]

jit·ters (jit′ərz) *n.pl. Slang.* extreme nervousness.

jit·ter·y (jit′ər ē) *adj. Informal.* nervous. —**jit′ter·i·ness,** *n.*

jiu·jit·su or **jiu·jut·su** (jü jit′sü) *n.* jujitsu.

jive (jīv) *n. v.* **jived, jiv·ing.** *Slang.* —*n.* **1** a kind of lively jazz; swing music. **2** dancing to jive music. **3** the talk of swing enthusiasts. **4** the latest slang.
—*v.* **1** dance to this kind of music. **2** play jive music. [origin uncertain]

Jno. 1 Jonathan. **2** John.

jo (jō) *n.* **joes.** *Scottish.* sweetheart. Also, **joe.** [var. of *joy*]

job (job) *n. adj. v.* **jobbed, job·bing.** —*n.* **1** a piece of work: *Dick had the job of painting the boat.* **2** a definite piece of work undertaken for a fixed price: *If you want your house painted, Mr. Jones will do the job for $300.* **3** *Informal.* work; employment: *Mary's brother is hunting for a job.* **4** anything one has to do; a duty: *I'm not going*

to wash the dishes; that's your job. **5** *Informal.* an affair; matter. **6 on the job,** *Slang.* attending to one's work or duty. **7** a piece of public or official business managed dishonestly for private gain.
—*adj.* done by the job; hired for a particular piece of work.
—*v.* **1** buy (goods) from manufacturers in large quantities and sell to retailers in smaller lots. **2** let out (work) to different contractors, workmen, etc. **3** manage a public matter for private gain in a dishonest way. **4** work at odd jobs. [origin uncertain] —**job′less,** *adj.* —**Syn. 3** See **position.**

Job (jōb) *n.* **1** in the Bible, a man who endured many troubles and still kept his faith in God. **2** any patient, enduring man. **3 Job's comforter, a** a person who increases the misery of the person he pretends to comfort. Job 16:2. **b** a boil. Job 2:7. **4 patience of Job,** great self-control despite trouble or irritation.

job·ber (job′ər) *n.* **1** a person who buys goods from manufacturers in large quantities and sells to retailers in smaller quantities. **2** a person who manages public business dishonestly for private gain. **3** a person who works by the job; pieceworker.

job·hold·er (job′hōl′dər) *n.* a person regularly employed.

job·less (job′lis) *adj.* lacking a job; unemployed.
—*n.* **the jobless,** *pl.* people without jobs; the unemployed. —**job′less·ness,** *n.*

job lot a quantity of goods bought or sold together, often containing several different kinds of things.

jock·ey (jok′ē) *n.* **-eys,** *v.* **-eyed, -ey·ing.** —*n.* a boy or man whose occupation is riding horses in races.
—*v.* **1** ride (a horse) in a race. **2** trick; cheat: *Swindlers jockeyed Mr. Smith into buying some worthless land.* **3** manoeuvre to get advantage: *The crews were jockeying their boats to get into the best position for the race.* [originally a proper name, dim. of *Jock,* Scottish var. of *Jack*]

jo·cose (jō kōs′) *adj.* jesting; humorous; playful. [< L *jocosus* < *jocus* jest] —**jo·cose′ly,** *adv.* —**jo·cose′ness,** *n.*

jo·cos·i·ty (jō kos′ə tē) *n.* **-ties. 1** a jocose quality. **2** a joking. **3** a joke.

joc·u·lar (jok′yů lər) *adj.* funny; joking. [< L *jocularis* < *joculus,* dim. of *jocus* jest] —**joc′u·lar·ly,** *adv.*

joc·u·lar·i·ty (jok′yů lar′ə tē) *n.* **-ties. 1** a jocular quality. **2** jocular talk or behavior. **3** a jocular remark or act.

joc·und (jok′ənd or jō′kənd) *adj.* cheerful; merry; gay. [< L *jocundus,* var. (influenced by *jocus* jest) of *jucundus* pleasant < *juvare* please] —**joc′und·ly,** *adv.*

jo·cun·di·ty (jō kun′də tē) *n.* **-ties. 1** cheerfulness; merriment; gaiety. **2** a jocund remark, act, etc.

jodh·purs (jod′pərz) *n.pl.* breeches for horseback riding, loose above the knees and fitting closely below. [< *Jodhpur,* India]

joe[1] (jō) *n. Scottish.* jo.

joe[2] or **Joe** *Slang. n.* fellow: *a good joe.*

joe-pye weed (jō′pī′) a tall weed of the aster family having pink or purple flowers. [origin uncertain]

jog[1] (jog) *v.* **jogged, jog·ging,** *n.* —*v.* **1** shake with a push or jerk: *I jogged his elbow to get his attention.* **2** stir up or stimulate (one's own or another person's memory). **3** move up and down with a jerking or shaking motion: *The old horse jogged along, and jogged me up and down on his back.* **4** get along; carry on; go (on) in a steady or humdrum fashion: *He is not very enterprising but just jogs along.* **5** go forward heavily and slowly.
6 run at a slow, steady rate, especially for physical conditioning.
—*n.* **1** a shake, push, or nudge. **2** a hint or reminder: *Give your memory a jog.* **3** a slow walk or trot: *The riders went at a jog along the path.* [blend of *jot* jolt, and *shog* shake] —**jog′ger,** *n.*

jog[2] (jog) *n. Informal.* a part that sticks out or in; the unevenness in a line or a surface: *a jog in a wall.* [var. of *jag*]

jog·gle[1] (jog′əl) *v.* **-gled, -gling,** *n.* —*v.* shake slightly. —*n.* a slight shake. [< *jog*[1]]

jog·gle[2] (jog′əl) *n. v.* **-gled, -gling.** —*n.* **1** a projection on one of two joining surfaces, or a notch on the other, to

hat, āge, cãre, fär; let, ēqual, tėrm; it, īce
hot, ōpen, ôrder; oil, out; cup, pů̇t, rüle, ūse
əbove, takən, pencəl, lemən, circəs
ch, child; ng, long; sh, ship
th, thin; ᴛʜ, then; zh, measure

prevent slipping. **2** a joint made in this way.
—*v.* join or fasten with a joggle. [? < *jog*[2]]

jog trot 1 a slow, regular trot. **2** a routine or humdrum way of doing things.

John Bull 1 a personification of England and its people. **2** a supposedly typical Englishman, often represented as stout and red-faced, in top hat and high boots.

John Doe a fictitious name used in legal forms, documents, proceedings, etc. to represent an unspecified person.

John Do·ry (dô′rē) *pl.* **John Do·rys.** an edible sea fish that has a high, flat body, spiny fins, and a large, black, yellow-ringed spot on each side. [< *John* + *dory*[2]]

John Han·cock (han′kok) *Esp.U.S. Slang.* a person's signature. [< signature of *John Hancock,* first signer of the Declaration of Independence]

John Henry *Slang.* a person's signature: *Put your John Henry at the bottom of this form.*

john·ny·cake (jon′ē kāk′) *n.* corn bread in the form of a flat cake. [origin uncertain]

Johnny Canuck *Cdn. Informal.* **1** a Canadian, especially one belonging to the armed services. **2** a personification of Canada.

John·ny-jump-up (jon′ē jump′up′) *n.* **1** a popular name for the wild pansy. **2** any of various North American violets.

John·son·ese (jon′sən ēz′) *n.* a pompous, learned literary style, resembling that of Samuel Johnson (1709-1784), an English author, lexicographer, and literary leader.

John·so·ni·an (jon sō′nē ən) *adj.* **1** of Samuel Johnson or his writings. **2** having a literary style like that of Samuel Johnson; pompous and ponderous. See **Johnsonese.**

John the Baptist in the Bible, the man who foretold the coming of Christ and later baptized Him. Matt. 3.

joie de vi·vre (zhwä′ də vē′vrə) *French.* joy of living; enjoyment of life.

join (join) *v.* **1** bring or put together; connect; fasten: *join hands.* **2** come together; meet: *The two roads join here.* **3** meet and unite with: *The brook joins the river.* **4** make or become one; combine; unite: *join in marriage.* **5** take part (*in*) with others: *join in song.* **6** become a member (of): *join a church.* **7** come into the company of: *I'll join you later.* **8** return to or take one's place in: *After a few days on shore the sailor joined his ship.* **9** adjoin: *His farm joins mine.* **10 join battle,** begin to fight. **11 join up,** enlist in the armed services.
—*n.* **1** a place or line of joining; seam. **2** a joining or being joined. [ME < OF *joindre* < L *jungere*]
Syn. *v.* **1** link, couple. **4 Join, combine, unite** = put or come together so as to form one thing. **Join** emphasizes bringing or coming together, and does not suggest how firm or lasting the association may be: *The two clubs joined forces during the campaign.* **Combine** emphasizes mixing or blending into one, for a common purpose: *He combines business with pleasure.* **Unite** emphasizes the oneness of the result and the loss of separate or divided purposes, interests, etc.: *His family united to help him.*

join·er (join′ər) *n.* **1** a person or thing that joins. **2** a skilled woodworker and furniture maker. **3** *Informal.* a person who joins many clubs, societies, etc.

join·er·y (join′ər ē) *n.* **1** the skill or trade of a joiner. **2** woodwork or furniture made by a joiner.

joint (joint) *n.* **1** the place at which two things or parts are joined together. **2** the way parts are joined: *a perfect joint.* **3** in biology, the parts where two bones move on one another, and the way those parts are put together. **4** one of the parts of which a jointed thing is made up: *the middle joint of the finger.* **5 out of joint,** a out

Finger joints: J, joints; K, knuckles and their joints.

of place at the joint. **b** out of order; in bad condition. **6** in botany, the part of the stem from which a leaf or branch grows. **7** a piece of meat cut for cooking. **8** *Slang.* **a** a cheap, low place for eating, drinking, or entertainment, formerly for the illegal sale of liquor. **b** any place, building, etc. —*v.* **1** connect by a joint or joints. **2** divide at the joints: *Please joint this chicken before sending it.* —*adj.* **1** owned together; owned by, held by, or done by two or more persons: *By our joint efforts we managed to push the car back on the road.* **2** sharing: *My brother and I are joint owners of this dog.* [ME < OF *joint* < *joindre.* See JOIN.] —**joint′er,** *n.*

joint·ly (joint′lē) *adv.* together; in common: *The two boys owned the newsstand jointly.*

joint-stock company a company or firm whose capital is owned in shares by stockholders, any of whom can sell some or all of his shares without the consent of the others.

join·ture (join′chər *n.* in law, the property given to a woman at the time of her marriage. [< F < L *junctura* a joining < *jungere* join. Doublet of JUNCTURE.]

joist (joist) *n.* one of the parallel pieces of timber to which the boards of a floor or ceiling are fastened. —*v.* provide with or lay across joists. [ME < OF *giste*, ult. < L *jacere* lie]

joke (jōk) *n. v.* **joked, jok·ing.** —*n.* **1** something said or done to make somebody laugh; a remark that is clever and amusing; something amusing: *This time the joke was on me.* **2** a person or thing laughed at. **3** something that is not in earnest or actually meant. **4 crack a joke,** tell a joke; say something funny. **5 no joke,** a serious matter. —*v.* **1** make jokes; say or do something as a joke. **2** laugh at; make fun of; tease. [< L *jocus*] —**jok′ing·ly,** *adv.*

Syn. *n.* **1 Joke, jest** = something said or done to cause amusement or laughter. **Joke** applies to anything said or done in fun and intended to cause laughter. **Jest,** more formal, applies chiefly to language, and suggests playful and merry joking, teasing, or poking fun: *Many a truth has been spoken in jest.*

jok·er (jōk′ər) *n.* **1** a person who jokes. **2** in some games, an extra playing card. **3** a trick for getting the better of someone. **4** *Informal.* an obscure phrase or sentence in a law, contract, etc. inserted to defeat its original purpose. **5** *Slang.* **a** a bad-mannered or awkward fellow; clown. **b** a fellow.

jol·li·fi·ca·tion (jol′ə fə kā′shən) *n.* gay entertainment; merrymaking.

jol·li·ty (jol′ə tē) *n.* **-ties.** fun; merriment; festivity; gaiety.

jol·ly (jol′ē) *adj.* **-li·er, -li·est,** *adv. v.* **-lied, -ly·ing.** —*adj.* **1** full of fun; merry. **2** *Brit. Informal.* pleasant; agreeable; delightful. —*adv. Brit. Informal.* extremely; very. —*v. Informal.* **1** flatter (a person) to make him feel good or agreeable. **2** tease playfully; banter. [ME < OF *joli,* ? < Gmc.] —**jol′li·ly,** *adv.* —**jol′li·ness,** *n.* —**Syn.** *adj.* **1** gay, joyful, mirthful, jovial.

jolly boat a small boat carried on a ship.

Jolly Rog·er (roj′ər) a pirates' black flag with a skull and crossbones on it.

jolt (jōlt) *v.* move with a shock or jerk; jar; shake up: *The wagon jolted us when the wheels went over a rock.* —*n.* **1** a jar; jerk: *He put his brakes on suddenly and the car stopped with a jolt.* **2** a sudden surprise or shock: *The loss of so much money gave him a severe jolt.* [origin uncertain] —**jolt′er,** *n.*

jolt·y (jōl′tē) *adj.* jolting.

Jo·nah (jō′nə) *n.* **1** in the Bible, a Hebrew prophet who disobeyed God and was thrown overboard during a storm. He was swallowed by a large fish and later cast up on land. **2** any person whose presence is supposed to bring bad luck. Also, in the Douay Bible, **Jonas.**

Jo·nas (jō′nəs) *n.* in the Douay Bible, Jonah.

Jon·a·than (jon′ə thən) *n.* **1** in the Bible, David's devoted friend, the son of Saul. 1 Sam. 19:1-10. See **David. 2** a bright-red apple that has a fine flavor and ripens in the late autumn.

jon·gleur (jong′glər; *French,* zhôɴ glœr′) *n.* in the Middle Ages, a wandering minstrel or entertainer. [< F < OF *jogleor* juggler; influenced by *jangleor* chatterer. Doublet of JUGGLER.]

jon·quil (jong′kwəl) *n.* **1** a plant having yellow or white flowers and long, slender leaves. It is a kind of narcissus that resembles a daffodil. **2** the flower. [< F < Sp. *junquillo,* dim. of *junco* reed < L *juncus*]

Jordan almond a large almond of high quality.

jo·rum (jô′rəm) *n.* **1** a large drinking bowl. **2** the amount that a jorum can hold. **3** a jorum and its contents. [? < *Joram* (II Sam. 8:10), who brought David drinking vessels of silver]

josh (josh) *Slang.* —*v.* make good-natured fun of; tease playfully. —*n.* banter; raillery. [origin uncertain] —**josh′er,** *n.*

Josh. Joshua.

Josh·u·a (josh′ủ ə or josh′ū ə) *n.* in the Bible, the successor of Moses, who led the children of Israel into the Promised Land. Also, in the Douay Bible, **Josue.**

joss (jos) *n.* an image of a Chinese god; a Chinese idol. [pidgin English form of Pg. *deos* god < L *deus*]

joss house a Chinese temple.

joss stick a slender stick of dried, fragrant paste, burned by the Chinese as incense.

jos·tle (jos′əl) *v.* **-tled, -tling,** *n.* —*v.* crowd, strike, or push against; elbow roughly: *We were jostled by the impatient crowd at the entrance to the circus.* —*n.* a jostling; push; knock. [< *joust*] —**jos′tler,** *n.*

Jos·u·e (jos′ū ē) *n.* in the Douay Bible, Joshua.

jot (jot) *n. v.* **jot·ted, jot·ting.** —*n.* a little bit; a very small amount: *I do not care a jot.* —*v.* write briefly or in haste: *The clerk jotted down the order.* [< L < Gk. *iōta* iota, the smallest letter in the Greek alphabet. Doublet of IOTA.] —**jot′ter,** *n.*

Jo·tun, Jo·tunn, or **Jö·tunn** (yô′tủn) *n.* in Norse mythology, a giant.

Jo·tun·heim, Jo·tunn·heim, or **Jö·tunn·heim** (yô′tủn hām′) *n.* in Norse mythology, the home of the giants.

joual (zhwäl) *n. Cdn.* uneducated or dialectal Canadian French. [< Cdn.F < dial. pronunciation of F *cheval* horse]

joule (joul or jül) *n.* in physics, a unit of work or energy, equal to ten million ergs. *Abbrev.:* J or j [< James Prescott *Joule* (1818-1889), an English physicist]

jounce (jouns) *v.* **jounced, jounc·ing,** *n.* bounce; bump; jolt. [ME; origin uncertain]

jour·nal (jėr′nəl) *n.* **1** a daily record. **2** an account of what happens or of what one thinks, feels, or notices, such as a diary, a ship's log, or the written account of what happens at each meeting of a society or town meeting. **3** a book for keeping such a record. **4** a newspaper; magazine. **5** in bookkeeping, **a** a book in which every item of business is written down so that the item can be entered under the proper account. **b** a daybook. **6** the part of a shaft or axle that turns on a bearing. [ME < OF < LL *diurnalis.* Doublet of DIURNAL.]

jour·nal·ese (jėr′nəl ēz′) *n.* a careless or loose style of writing such as is sometimes found in newspapers, magazines, etc.

jour·nal·ism (jėr′nəl iz′əm) *n.* **1** the work of writing for, editing, managing, or producing a newspaper or magazine. **2** newspapers and magazines as a group.

jour·nal·ist (jėr′nəl ist) *n.* a person engaged in journalism: *Editors and reporters are journalists.*

jour·nal·is·tic (jėr′nəl is′tik) *adj.* of or like journalism or journalists. —**jour′nal·is′tic·ally,** *adv.*

jour·ney (jėr′nē) *n.* **-neys,** *v.* **-neyed, -ney·ing.** —*n.* **1** travel; trip: *a journey around the world.* **2** a distance travelled: *The city is a day's journey from here.* —*v.* take a trip; travel. [ME < OF *journee,* originally, a day, ult. < L *diurnus* of one day < *dies* day] —**Syn.** *n.* excursion, tour, voyage, jaunt. See **trip.**

jour·ney·man (jėr′nē mən) *n.* **-men** (-mən). **1** a workman who knows his trade. **2** an apprentice who has completed his training.

joust (joust, just, or jüst) *n.* **1** a combat between two knights on horseback, armed with lances. **2 jousts,** *pl.* a tournament. [< OF *jouste* < *jouster.* See v.]
—*v.* fight with lances on horseback. Knights used to joust with each other for sport. [ME < OF *jouster* < VL *juxtare* be next to < L *juxta* beside]
—joust′er, *n.*

Jove (jōv) *n.* **1** in Roman mythology, Jupiter. **2** *Poetic.* the planet Jupiter. **3 by Jove,** an exclamation of surprise, pleasure, etc.

jo·vi·al (jō′vē əl) *adj.* good-hearted and full of fun; good-humored and merry. [< L *Jovialis* pertaining to Jupiter (those born under the planet's sign being supposedly cheerful)] **—jo′vi·al·ly,** *adv.* **—jo′vi·al·ness,** *n.*

jo·vi·al·i·ty (jō′vē al′ə tē) *n.* jollity; merriment.

Jo·vi·an (jō′vē ən) *adj.* **1** of or like the god Jove. **2** of the planet Jupiter.

jowl[1] (joul or jōl) *n.* **1** the part under the jaw; jaw. **2** the cheek. [OE *ceafl,* influenced by F *joue* cheek]

jowl[2] (joul) *n.* a fold of flesh hanging from the jaw. [? related to OE *ceole* throat]

joy (joi) *n.* **1** a strong feeling of pleasure; gladness; happiness. **2** something that causes gladness or happiness: "*A thing of beauty is a joy forever.*" **3** an expression of happiness; outward rejoicing. [ME < OF *joie* < L *gaudia,* pl. of *gaudium* joy < *gaudere* rejoice]
—Syn. *n.* **1** delight, rapture, bliss. See **pleasure.**

joy·ance (joi′əns) *n. Archaic.* joy; gladness; gaiety.

joy·ful (joi′fəl) *adj.* **1** glad; happy: *a joyful heart.* **2** causing joy: *joyful news.* **3** showing joy: *a joyful look.* **—joy′ful·ly,** *adv.* **—joy′ful·ness,** *n.*

joy·less (joi′lis) *adj.* **1** without joy; sad; dismal. **2** not causing joy: *a joyless prospect.* **—joy′less·ly,** *adv.* **—joy′less·ness,** *n.*

joy·ous (joi′əs) *adj.* joyful; glad; gay. **—joy′ous·ly,** *adv.* **—joy′ous·ness,** *n.*

joy ride *Informal.* a ride in an automobile for pleasure, especially when the car is driven recklessly or is used without the owner's permission.

joy-ride (joi′rīd′) *v.* **-rode, -rid·den, -rid·ing.** *Informal.* take a joy ride. **—joy′-rid′er,** *n.*

J.P. Justice of the Peace.

Jr. or **jr.** Junior.

Ju·bal (jü′bəl) *n.* in the Bible, the inventor of musical instruments. Gen. 4:21.

ju·bi·lance (jü′bə ləns) *n.* a rejoicing; great joy.

ju·bi·lant (jü′bə lənt) *adj.* **1** rejoicing; exulting. **2** expressing or showing joy. [< L *jubilans, -antis,* ppr. of *jubilare* shout with joy < *jubilum* wild shout]
—ju′bi·lant·ly, *adv.* **—Syn. 1** joyful, exultant.

Ju·bi·la·te (jü′bə lā′tē or jü′bə lä′tē) *n.* the 100th Psalm in the Protestant Bible or the 99th Psalm in the Roman Catholic Bible. [< L *jubilate* shout ye, the first word of the psalm < *jubilare* shout with joy. See JUBILANT.]

ju·bi·la·tion (jü′bə lā′shən) *n.* **1** a rejoicing. **2** a joyful celebration.

ju·bi·lee (jü′bə lē′) *n.* **1** a time of rejoicing or great joy. **2** rejoicing; great joy. **3** a 25th or 50th anniversary. **4** in the Roman Catholic Church, a year in which punishment for sin is remitted, after repentance and the performance of certain acts. [ME < OF *jubile* < LL *jubilaeus,* adj. < Gk. *iōbēlaios* < Hebrew *yobel* trumpet; originally, ram's horn, ram]

Jud. **1** Judges. **2** Judith.

Ju·dae·o-Chris·tian (jü dā′ō kris′chən or jü dē′ō-) *adj.* common to Christianity and Judaism; both Jewish and Christian: *the Judaeo-Christian heritage.* Also, **Judeo-Christian.** [< L *Judaeus* < Gk. *Ioudaios* Jew + E *Christian*]

Ju·dah (jü′də) *n.* **1** the son of Jacob and ancestor of the tribe of Judah. Gen. 29:35. **2** the most powerful of the twelve tribes of Israel.

Ju·da·ic (jü dā′ik) *adj.* of the Jews; Jewish.

Ju·da·ism (jü′dā iz′əm) *n.* **1** the religion of the Jews, one of the great religions of the world. **2** the following of Jewish rules and customs.

hat, āge, cãre, fär; let, ēqual, tėrm; it, īce
hot, ōpen, ôrder; oil, out; cup, pu̇t, rüle, ūse
əbove, takən, pencəl, lemən, circəs
ch, child; ng, long; sh, ship
th, thin; ᴛʜ, then; zh, measure

Ju·da·ist (jü′dē ist) *n.* **1** a follower of Judaism. **2** in the early Christian church, a Jewish convert who advocated retaining Jewish rites and customs.

Ju·da·ize (jü′dā īz′) *v.* **-ized, -iz·ing.** conform to Jewish usages or ideas.

Ju·das (jü′dəs) *n.* **1** in the Bible, the disciple who betrayed Jesus Christ for thirty pieces of silver; Judas Iscariot. Matthew 26:14-50. **2** any treacherous betrayer of friendship; traitor.

Judas tree a tree that has red, pink, or purplish flowers before the leaves come out. [< *Judas,* Christ's apostle, believed to have hanged himself on this tree]

Ju·de·an (jü dē′ən) *adj.* **1** of Judea, the southern part of Palestine when it was a province of the Roman Empire. **2** of the Jews. —*n.* **1** a native or inhabitant of Judea. **2** a Jew. [< L *Judaeus.* See JEW.]

Judg. Judges.

judge (juj) *n. v.* **judged, judg·ing.** —*n.* **1** a government official appointed or elected to hear and decide cases in a law court. In Canada all judges are appointed. **2** a person chosen to settle a dispute or decide who wins. **3** a person who can decide how good a thing is: *a good judge of cattle*; *a poor judge of poetry.* **4** a ruler in ancient Israel before the time of the kings.
—*v.* **1** hear and decide in a law court. **2** settle (a dispute); decide who wins (a race, contest, etc.). **3** make up one's mind (about); form an opinion or estimate (of): *judge the merits of a book.* **4** think; suppose; conclude: *I judged that you had forgotten to come.* **5** criticize; condemn: *Who can judge another?* [ME < OF *juge* < L *judex* < *jus* law + root of *dicere* say] **—judg′er,** *n.* **—Syn.** *v.* **4** deem, regard.

judge advocate an officer appointed to superintend the proceedings of a court-martial, to advise the court on matters of law, and to elicit facts material to the defence.

Judge Advocate General the senior legal officer in the army or air force. *Abbrev.*: J.A.G.

judge·ment (juj′mənt) *n.* judgment.

judge·ship (juj′ship) *n.* the position, duties, or term of office of a judge.

judg·ment or **judge·ment** (juj′mənt) *n.* **1** the act of judging. **2** in law: **a** a decision, decree, or sentence given by a judge or court. **b** a debt arising from a judge's decision. **c** the official certificate recording such a decision. **3** an opinion: *In his judgment the plant was unsatisfactory.* **4** the ability to form opinions; good sense. **5** criticism; condemnation. **6** a misfortune considered as a punishment from God: *The neighbors considered his broken leg a judgment on him for his evil deeds.* **7 the Judgment,** judgment day. **—Syn. 3** estimation, belief.

judgment day the day of God's final judgment of mankind at the end of the world.

ju·di·ca·to·ry (jü′də kə tô′rē) *adj. n.* **-to·ries.** —*adj.* of the administration of justice. —*n.* **1** the administration of justice. **2** a court of justice. [< LL *judicatorius* < L *judex, -dicis* judge]

ju·di·ca·ture (jü′də kə chər or jü′də kə chür′) *n.* **1** the administration of justice. **2** the position, duties, or authority of a judge. **3** the extent of jurisdiction of a judge or court. **4** a group of judges. **5** a court of justice. [< Med.L *judicatura,* ult. < L *judex, -dicis* judge]

ju·di·cial (jü dish′əl) *adj.* **1** of or having to do with courts, judges, or the administration of justice. **2** ordered, permitted, or enforced by a judge or a court. **3** of or suitable for a judge; impartial; fair: *Before making a decision, a judicial mind considers fairly both sides of a dispute.* [ME < L *judicialis* < *judicium* judgment < *judex, -dicis* judge] **—ju·di′cial·ly,** *adv.*

ju·di·ci·ar·y (jü dish′ē er′ē) *n.* **-ar·ies,** *adj.* —*n.* **1** the branch of government that administers justice; system of courts of justice of a country. 2 judges as a group. *—adj.* of or having to do with courts, judges, or the administration of justice.

ju·di·cious (jü dish′əs) *adj.* having, using, or showing good judgment; wise; sensible: *A judicious historian selects and considers facts carefully and critically.* [< F *judicieux* < L *judicium* judgment < *judex, -dicis* judge] **—ju·di′cious·ly,** *adv.* **—Syn.** prudent, astute.

ju·do (jü′dō) *n.* jujitsu.

Ju·dy (jü′dē) *n.* the wife of Punch in the puppet show of *Punch and Judy.*

jug (jug) *n. v.* **jugged, jug·ging.** *—n.* **1** a container for liquids. A jug usually has a handle and either a spout or a narrow neck. **2** the amount that a jug can hold. **3** a jug and its contents. **4** *Slang.* a jail.
—v. Slang. jail. [probably originally proper name, alteration of *Joan,* fem. of *John*]

Jug·ger·naut (jug′ər not′ or jug′ər nôt′) *n.* **1** an idol of the Hindu god Krishna, pulled around on a huge car. Devotees of the god are said to have thrown themselves under the wheels to be crushed to death. **2 juggernaut, a** a frightening, invisible machine, force, etc. that destroys anything in its path. **b** something to which a person blindly devotes himself or is cruelly sacrificed. [< Hind. *Jagannath* < Skt. *Jagannatha* < *jagat* world + *natha* lord]

jug·gle (jug′əl) *v.* **-gled, -gling,** *n.* *—v.* **1** do tricks that require skill of hand or eye. **2** do such tricks with: *He can juggle three balls, keeping them in the air at the same time.* **3** rearrange or change figures so as to deceive or cheat: *The bookkeeper juggled the company's accounts to hide his thefts.* **4** deceive; trick; cheat: *He juggled his brother out of his inheritance.* **5** weigh or balance mentally.
—n. **1** a juggling. **2** a trick; deception; fraud. [ME < OF *jogler* < L *joculari* joke < *joculus,* dim. of *jocus* jest]

jug·gler (jug′lər) *n.* **1** a person who can do juggling tricks. **2** a person who uses tricks, deception, or fraud. [ME < OF *jogleor* < L *joculator* joker, ult. < *jocus* jest. Doublet of JONGLEUR.]

jug·gler·y (jug′lər ē) *n.* **-gler·ies. 1** the skill or tricks of a juggler; sleight of hand. **2** trickery; deception; fraud.

Ju·go·slav or **Ju·go-Slav** (ū′gō slav′ or -släv′) *n. adj.* Yugoslav.

Ju·go·slavic (ū′gō slav′ik or -slä′vik) *adj.* Yugoslavic.

jug·u·lar (jug′yu̇ lər or jü′gyu̇ lər) *adj.* **1** of the neck or throat. **2** of the jugular vein. *—n.* the jugular vein. [< NL *jugularis* < L *jugulum* collarbone, dim. of *jugum* yoke]

jugular vein one of the two large veins on either side of the neck that return blood from the head to the heart.

juice (jüs) *n.* **1** the liquid in fruits, vegetables, and meats. **2** a liquid in the body. The gastric juices of the stomach help to digest food. **3** *Slang.* electricity. **4** *Slang.* gasoline. [ME < OF < L *jus* broth] **—juice′less,** *adj.*

juic·i·ness (jüs′ē nis) *n.* the state or quality of being juicy.

juic·y (jüs′ē) *adj.* **juic·i·er, juic·i·est. 1** full of juice; having much juice. **2** full of interest; lively. **—juic′i·ly,** *adv.*

ju·jit·su (jü jit′sü) *n.* a Japanese method of wrestling or fighting without weapons that uses the strength and weight of an opponent to his disadvantage. Also, **jiujitsu, jiujutsu, jujutsu.** [< Japanese *jūjutsu* < *jū* soft + *jutsu* art]

ju·jube (jü′jüb) *n.* **1** a lozenge or small tablet of gummy candy. **2** an edible datelike fruit of a shrub or tree, used to flavor this candy. **3** the shrub or tree that bears this fruit. [< F *jujube* or < Med.L *jujuba* < LL *zizyphum* < Gk. *zizyphon*]

ju·jut·su (jü jit′sü) *n.* jujitsu.

juke box (jük) *Informal.* an automatic phonograph that plays a record when money is deposited in the slot. [< Gullah *juke* disorderly, wicked]

Jul. July.

ju·lep (jü′ləp) *n.* a drink made of whisky or brandy, sugar, crushed ice, and fresh mint. [< F < Arabic < Pers. *gulab,* originally, rose water]

Jul·ian (jül′yən) *adj.* of Julius Caesar.

Julian calendar a calendar in which the average length of a year was 365¼ days. It was introduced by Julius Caesar in 46 B.C.

ju·li·enne (jü′lē en′) *adj.* cut in thin strips or small pieces. Julienne potatoes are cut in thin strips and fried. *—n.* a clear soup containing vegetables cut into thin strips or small pieces. [< F]

Ju·li·et (jü′lē et′ or jü′lē ət) *n.* the heroine of Shakespeare's play *Romeo and Juliet.*

Ju·ly (ju̇ lī′) *n.* **-lies.** the seventh month of the year. It has 31 days. [OE *Julius* < L *Julius,* after *Julius* Caesar]

jum·ble (jum′bəl) *v.* **-bled, -bling,** *n.* *—v.* mix; confuse: *He jumbled up everything in the drawer when he was hunting for his socks.* *—n.* a confused mixture. [? imitative] **—Syn.** *n.* medley, hodge-podge, muddle, mess.

jum·bo (jum′bō) *n.* **-bos,** *adj.* *Informal.* *—n.* a big, clumsy person, animal, or thing; something unusually large of its kind. *—adj.* very big. [< *Jumbo,* an elephant exhibited by P. T. Barnum (1810-1891), U.S. showman]

jump (jump) *v.* **1** spring from the ground; leap; bound: *jump up and down.* **2** leap over: *jump a stream.* **3** cause to jump: *jump a horse over a fence.* **4** give a sudden start or jerk: *You made me jump.* **5** rise suddenly: *Prices jumped.* **6** in checkers, pass over and capture (an opponent's piece). **7** pounce upon; attack: *The robbers jumped the shopkeeper.* **8** *Slang.* evade by running away: *jump bail.* **9** *Slang.* get aboard (a train) by jumping. **10 jump a claim,** seize a piece of land claimed by another. **11 jump at,** accept eagerly and quickly. **12 jump on,** *Slang.* blame; scold; criticize. **13 jump the track,** of a train, leave the rails suddenly.
—n. **1** a spring from the ground; leap; bound. **2** the thing to be jumped over. **3** the distance jumped. **4** a contest in jumping. **5** a sudden nervous start or jerk. **6** a sudden rise. **7** in checkers, a move made to capture an opponent's piece. **8** a sudden and abrupt transition from one thing to another. **9 jumps,** *Informal.* a nervous condition characterized by sudden starts or jerks. **10 get** or **have the jump on,** *Slang.* get or have an advantage over. **11 on the jump,** *Informal.* rushing around; always busy. [probably imitative]
Syn. *v.* **1, 2 Jump, leap** = spring into or through the air. **Jump** emphasizes springing from the ground or other surface or point: *He jumped from the roof. He jumped across the puddle.* **Leap** emphasizes springing high into or through the air, or to a point, and suggests more grace, lightness, or liveliness than *jump*: *I love to watch a dancer leap. He leaped lightly to the opposite bank of the stream.*

jump area the locality assigned for the landing of parachute troops, usually behind enemy lines.

jump·er[1] (jump′ər) *n.* **1** a person or thing that jumps. **2** a simply constructed sleigh on low wooden runners. [< *jump,* v.]

jump·er[2] (jump′ər) *n.* **1** a loose jacket. Workmen and sailors often wear jumpers to protect their clothes. **2** a loose blouse reaching to the hips. **3** a one-piece, sleeveless dress worn over a blouse. **4 jumpers,** *pl.* rompers. [< *jump* short coat, ? alteration of F *juppe,* ult. < Arabic *jubbah* long open coat]

jump fire a forest fire started by burning material carried ahead by wind from another blaze.

jumping bean a seed of a Mexican plant containing a larva whose movements cause the seed to jump.

jumping jack a toy man or animal that can be made to jump by pulling a string.

jumping pound buffalo jump.

jump·master (jump′mas′tər) *n.* the officer who controls the dropping of parachute troops and their equipment from an aircraft.

jump-off (jump′of′) *n.* **1** the start of a race. **2** the beginning of an attack. **3** a play-off. *—adj.* beginning; starting: *a jump-off place for northern exploration parties.*

jump seat 1 a collapsible extra seat in an automobile, hinged to the floor between the front and back seats. **2** any similar seat in an airplane, elevator, etc.

jump·y (jump′ē) *adj.* **jump·i·er, jump·i·est. 1** moving by jumps; making sudden, sharp jerks. **2** easily excited or frightened; nervous. **—jump′i·ly,** *adv.* **—jump′i·ness,** *n.*

Jun. 1 June. 2 Junior.

Junc. Junction.

jun·co (jung′kō) *n.* **-cos.** any of several small North American finches often seen in flocks during the winter; snowbird. [< Sp. < L *juncus* reed]

junc·tion (jungk′shən) *n.* 1 a joining. 2 a being joined. 3 a place where things join. 4 a place where railway lines meet or cross: *Moncton is an important junction.* [< L *junctio, -onis* < *jungere* join]

junc·ture (jungk′chər) *n.* 1 a point of time. 2 a state of affairs. 3 a crisis. 4 a joint. 5 a joining. 6 a being joined. 7 **at this juncture,** when affairs are (or were) in this state. [< L *junctura* a joining < *jungere* join. Doublet of JOINTURE.]

June (jün) *n.* the sixth month of the year. It has 30 days. [< L *Junius,* originally a Roman gens name]

June beetle June bug.

June bug a large, brown beetle of North America that appears in June.

jun·gle (jung′gəl) *n.* 1 wild land, usually in a tropical country, thickly overgrown with bushes, vines, trees, etc. 2 a tangled mass. 3 a slum area of a city, usually associated with the activity of hoodlums. 4 *Slang.* a camp for tramps. [< Hind. *jangal* < Skt. *jangal* desert, forest]

jungle fowl any of several wild birds of India and Asia that are much like domestic fowl.

jun·ior (jün′yər) *adj.* 1 the younger: *John Parker, Junior, is the son of John Parker, Senior.* 2 of lower position, rank, or standing; of more recent appointment: *a junior officer, a junior partner.* 3 of or having to do with students in grades 4 to 6. 4 of or for young people: *a junior tennis match, junior coats.* 5 of later date.
—*n.* 1 a younger person. 2 a person of lower position, rank, or standing; a person of more recent appointment. *Abbrev.:* Jr. [< L *junior,* comparative of *juvenis* young]

junior college a college giving only the first year or the first two years of a university-degree program.

junior high school a school consisting of grades 7, 8, and 9; any school intermediate between elementary school and high school.

ju·ni·per (jü′nə pər) *n.* 1 any of several evergreen trees and shrubs of the pine family, having small berry-like cones. The red cedar is a kind of juniper. 2 the soft, fragrant wood of any of these trees. [< L *juniperus*]

junk[1] (jungk) *n.* 1 old metal, paper, rags, etc. 2 *Slang.* rubbish; trash. 3 a hard salted meat eaten by sailors. 4 old rope used for making mats, oakum, etc. 5 *Slang.* a narcotic drug, such as heroin or morphine; dope.
—*v. Slang.* throw away or discard as junk. [origin uncertain]

A Chinese junk

junk[2] (jungk) *n.* a Chinese sailing ship. [< Pg. *junco,* probably ult. < Javanese *jong*]

junk·er (junk′ər) *n.* a worn-out automobile, usually one sold for scrap.

Jun·ker or **jun·ker** (yůng′kər) *n.* a member of the aristocratic, formerly privileged class in Prussia. [< G]

jun·ket (jung′kit) *n.* 1 curdled milk, sweetened and flavored. 2 a feast; picnic. 3 a pleasure trip. 4 *Informal.* an unnecessary trip taken by an official at the expense of his government or the firm he works for. —*v.* 1 feast; picnic. 2 go on a pleasure trip. [< dial. OF *jonquette* basket < *jonc* reed < L *juncus*] —**jun′ket·er,** *n.*

junk·ie (jung′kē) *n. Slang.* 1 a person who is addicted to narcotics. 2 a dealer in junk.

junk·man (jungk′man′) *n.* **-men** (-mən′). a man who buys and sells old metal, paper, rags, etc.

Ju·no (jü′nō) *n.* **-nos.** 1 in Roman mythology, the goddess of marriage and childbirth, wife of Jupiter and queen of the gods, identified with the Greek goddess Hera. 2 any stately, majestic woman.

Ju·no·esque or **ju·no·esque** (jü′nō esk′) *adj.* in the manner of Juno; stately and majestic.

jun·ta (jun′tə) *n.* 1 a group of persons forming a government, especially as the result of a revolution:

hat, āge, cãre, fär; let, ēqual, tėrm; it, īce
hot, ōpen, ôrder; oil, out; cup, půt, rüle, ūse
əbove, takən, pencəl, lemən, circəs
ch, child; ng, long; sh, ship
th, thin; ᴛʜ, then; zh, measure

The country was ruled by a military junta. 2 a junto. 3 especially in Spanish or Latin-American countries, a legislative or administrative council. [< Sp. *junta,* ult. < L *jungere* join]

jun·to (jun′tō) *n.* **-tos.** a political faction; a group of plotters or partisans. [alteration of *junta*]

Ju·pi·ter (jü′pə tər) *n.* 1 in Roman mythology, the ruler of the gods and men, identified with the Greek god Zeus. 2 the largest planet.

ju·ral (jür′əl) *adj.* 1 of law; legal. 2 having to do with rights and obligations. [< L *jus, juris* law]

Ju·ras·sic (jů ras′ik) *n.* in geology: 1 the middle period of the Mesozoic era, beginning approximately 170 million years ago, when birds first appeared. 2 the rocks formed during this period. See the chart under **geology.**
—*adj.* of or having to do with the period when birds first appeared or the rocks formed during it. [< F *jurassique,* after the *Jura* Mountains in France and Switzerland]

ju·rid·i·cal (jů rid′ə kəl) *adj.* 1 having to do with the administration of justice. 2 of law; legal. [< L *juridicus,* ult. < *jus, juris* law + *dicere* say] —**ju·rid′i·cal·ly,** *adv.*

ju·ris·con·sult (jür′is kən sult′ or -kon′sult) *n.* a jurist. [< L *jurisconsultus,* ult. < *jus, juris* law + *consulere* consult]

ju·ris·dic·tion (jür′is dik′shən) *n.* 1 the right or power of administering law or justice. 2 authority; power; control. 3 the extent of authority: *The judge ruled that the case was not within his jurisdiction.* 4 the territory over which authority extends. [< L *jurisdictio, -onis,* ult. < *jus, juris* law + *dicere* say]

ju·ris·dic·tion·al (jür′is dik′shə nəl) *adj.* of or having to do with jurisdiction.

ju·ris·pru·dence (jür′is prü′dəns) *n.* 1 the science or philosophy of law. 2 a system of laws. 3 a branch of law. Medical jurisprudence deals with the application of medical knowledge to certain questions of law. [< L *jurisprudentia* < *jus, juris* law + *prudentia* prudence]

ju·rist (jür′ist) *n.* 1 an expert in law. 2 a learned writer on law. 3 a civil lawyer. [< Med.L *jurista* < L *jus, juris* law]

ju·ris·tic (jů ris′tik) *adj.* of or having to do with jurists or jurisprudence; relating to law. —**ju·ris′ti·cal·ly,** *adv.*

ju·ror (jür′ər) *n.* a member of a jury. [ME < AF *jurour* < L *jurator* a swearer < *jurare* swear]

ju·ry[1] (jür′ē) *n.* **ju·ries.** 1 a group of persons selected to hear evidence in a law court and sworn to give a decision in accordance with the evidence presented to it. A **trial jury,** or **petit jury,** decides whether the accused in a trial is guilty or not guilty. A **grand jury** investigates accusations of crime to decide whether a trial is justified. 2 a group of persons chosen to give a judgment or to decide a contest and award prizes. [ME < AF *jurie* < *jurer* swear < L *jurare*]

ju·ry[2] (jür′ē) *adj.* for temporary use on a ship; makeshift. [probably ult. < OF *ajurie, adjutorie* help < L *adjutare* < *ad-* to + *juvare* aid]

ju·ry·man (jür′ē mən) *n.* **-men** (-mən). a member of a jury; juror.

just[1] (just) *adj.* 1 right; fair: *a just price.* 2 righteous: *a just life.* 3 deserved; merited: *a just reward.* 4 having good grounds; well-founded: *just anger.* 5 lawful: *a just claim.* 6 in accordance with standards or requirements; proper: *just proportions.* 7 true; correct: *a just description.* 8 exact: *just weights.*
—*adv.* 1 exactly: *just a pound.* 2 almost exactly: *I saw him just now.* 3 a very short while ago: *He has just gone.* 4 barely: *The shot just missed the mark.* 5 only; merely: *He is just an ordinary man.* 6 *Informal.* quite; truly; positively: *The weather is just glorious.* 7 **just now,** a exactly at this moment; at present. b only a very short time ago. [< L *justus* upright < *jus* right, law]

—**just′ness,** *n.* —**Syn.** *adj.* **1** impartial, equitable. See **fair.** **2** upright, honest. **3** due, rightful, legitimate. **6** fitting. **8** precise.

just[2] (just) *v. n.* joust.

jus·tice (jus′tis) *n.* **1** just conduct; fair dealing: *have a sense of justice.* **2** a being just; fairness; rightness; correctness: *uphold the justice of our cause.* **3** rightfulness; lawfulness; well-founded reason: *He complained with justice of the bad treatment he had received.* **4** just treatment; deserved reward or punishment. **5** the exercise of power and authority to maintain what is just and right. **6** the administration of law; trial and judgment by process of law. **7** a judge. **8** a justice of the peace. **9 bring a person to justice,** do what is necessary in order that a person shall be legally punished for his crime or crimes. **10 do justice to, a** treat fairly. **b** see the good points of. **c** show proper appreciation for: *He did justice to the dinner.* **11 do oneself justice,** do as well as one really can do. [ME < OF < L *justitia* < *justus* just, upright. See JUST[1].]

justice of the peace a local magistrate who tries minor cases, administers oaths, performs civil marriages, etc. *Abbrev.*: J.P.

jus·tice·ship (jus′tis ship′) *n.* the position, duties, or term of office of a justice.

jus·ti·fi·a·bil·i·ty (jus′tə fī′ə bil′ə tē) *n.* the state or quality of being justifiable.

jus·ti·fi·a·ble (jus′tə fī′ə bəl) *adj.* capable of being justified; that can be shown to be just and right; defensible. —**jus′ti·fi′a·bly,** *adv.*

jus·ti·fi·ca·tion (jus′tə fə kā′shən) *n.* **1** a justifying. **2** a being justified. **3** the fact or circumstance that justifies; good reason. **4** in printing, the spacing out of lines of type to make them the proper length and to give even margins. **5** in theology, a freeing or being freed from the guilt or penalty of sin.

jus·ti·fy (jus′tə fī′) *v.* **-fied, -fy·ing. 1** show to be just or right; give a good reason for: *The fine quality of the cloth justifies its high price.* **2** clear of blame or guilt. **3** in printing, make (lines of type) the right length by proper spacing. **4** in law, show a satisfactory reason or excuse for something done. [< MF *justifier* < LL *justificare* < L *justus* just + *facere* make] —**jus′ti·fi′er,** *n.* —**Syn. 1** uphold, defend. **2** exonerate.

just·ly (just′lē) *adv.* **1** in a just manner. **2** rightly.

jut (jut) *v.* **jut·ted, jut·ting,** *n.* —*v.* stick out; project: *The pier juts out from the shore into the water.* —*n.* the part that sticks out; projection. [var. of *jet*[1]]

jute (jüt) *n.* **1** a strong fibre used for making coarse sacks, burlap, rope, etc. Jute is obtained from certain tropical plants. **2** any of these plants. [< Bengali *jhoṭo* < Skt. *jaṭa* mat of hair]

Jute (jüt) *n.* a member of an early Germanic tribe. Some of the Jutes invaded and settled in S.E. England in the fifth century A.D.

ju·ve·nes·cence (jü′və nes′əns) *n.* a renewal of youth; youthfulness.

ju·ve·nes·cent (jü′və nes′ənt) *adj.* growing young again; youthful. [< L *juvenescens, -entis,* ppr. of *juvenescere* grow young again < *juvenis* young]

ju·ve·nile (jü′və nīl′ or jü′və nəl) *adj.* **1** young; youthful. **2** of or for young people: *juvenile books, juvenile delinquency.* —*n.* **1** a young person. **2** a book for young people. **3** an actor or actress who plays youthful parts. [< L *juvenilis* < *juvenis* young] —**Syn.** *adj.* **1** immature, undeveloped. See **young.**

juvenile court a law court where cases involving boys and girls are heard. In Canada, the maximum age at which offenders are tried in juvenile courts varies in the different provinces but is usually either sixteen or eighteen.

ju·ve·nil·i·ty (jü′və nil′ə tē) *n.* a juvenile quality, condition, or manner.

jux·ta·pose (juks′tə pōz′ or juks′tə pōz′) *v.* **-posed, -pos·ing.** put close together; place side by side. [< F *juxtaposer* < L *juxta* beside + F *poser* place. See POSE[1].]

jux·ta·po·si·tion (juks′tə pə zish′ən) *n.* **1** a putting close together; a placing side by side. **2** a position close together or side by side.

Jy. July.

K or **k** (kā) *n.* **K's** or **k's. 1** the eleventh letter of the English alphabet. **2** any speech sound represented by this letter. **3** one (usually the eleventh) of a series designated alphabetically.

k in electricity, capacity.

k. 1 kilogram. **2** kopeck. **3** karat. **4** kilowatt. **5** krona. **6** krone.

K 1 potassium. (for L *Kalium*) **2** in physics, Kelvin temperature scale. **3** Koruna.

K. 1 King; Kings. **2** Knight.

Ka (kä) *n.* in the religion of ancient Egypt, the soul said to dwell in a man's body, and, after death, in his tomb or statue. [< Egyptian]

Kaa·ba (kä′bə) *n.* the most sacred Moslem shrine, a small structure within the Great Mosque at Mecca. It contains a black stone, supposedly given to Abraham by the angel of Gabriel, toward which Moslems face when praying. Also, **Caaba.** [< Arabic *ka'bah*, literally, a square building]

Kab·loo·na or **kab·loo·na** (kab lü′nə) *n. Cdn.* a white man; European. Also, *Kadloona.* [< Eskimo *kabluna(k)* one having big eyebrows]

kad·dish (kä′dish) *n.* in Judaism, a portion of the daily prayer said in the synagogue, also used as a public or official prayer of mourning for a dead relative. [< Aramaic *quaddish* holy]

Kad·loo·na (kad lü′nə) *n.* Kabloona.

Kaf·fir (kaf′ər) *n.* **1** in South Africa, a member of a group of Negroid tribes; a South African Bantu. **2** Kafiri. **3 kaffir,** kaffir corn. [< Arabic *kafir* unbeliever]

kaf·fir corn (kaf′ər) a sorghum grown for grain and forage in dry regions. Kaffir corn has a stout, short-jointed, leafy stalk.

Kaf·ir (kaf′ər) *n.* **1** a member of a people native to Kafiristan in N.E. Afghanistan. **2** Kafiri. **3** Kaffir. [see KAFFIR]

Ka·fi·ri (ka fēr′ē) *n.* the Indo-European language of the Kafirs (def. 1).

kaf·ir corn (kaf′ər) kaffir corn.

kaf·tan (kaf′tən or käf tän′) *n.* caftan.

kai·ak (kī′ak) *n.* kayak.

kail (kāl) *n.* kale.

Kai·ser or **kai·ser** (kī′zər) *n.* **1** the title of the emperors of Germany, 1871-1918. **2** the title of the emperors of Austria, 1804-1918. **3** the title of the emperors of the Holy Roman Empire from A.D. 962 to 1806. **4 kaiser,** emperor. [< G < L *Caesar*]

kale (kāl) *n.* **1** any of various kinds of cabbage that have loose leaves instead of a compact head. Kale resembles spinach. **2** *Slang.* money; cash. [var. of *cole*]

ka·lei·do·scope (kə lī′də skōp′) *n.* **1** a tube containing bits of colored glass and two or more mirrors. As it is turned, it reflects continually changing patterns. **2** anything that changes continually; a continually changing pattern. [< Gk. *kalos* pretty + *eidos* shape + E *-scope*]

ka·lei·do·scop·ic (kə lī′də skop′ik) *adj.* of or like a kaleidoscope; continually changing.

kal·ends (kal′əndz) *n.pl.* calends.

Ka·le·va·la (kä′lä vä′lä) *n.* the national epic poem of Finland, a collection of heroic songs and poems compiled from oral tradition. [< Finnish *Kalevala*, literally, home of a hero]

kal·mi·a (kal′mē ə) *n.* the mountain laurel, or any similar evergreen shrub having clusters of cup-shaped flowers. [< NL, after Peter *Kalm* (1715-1779), a Swedish botanist]

Kal·muck or **Kal·muk** (kal′muk) *n.* **1** a member of a group of Mongol tribes living in W. China and S.E. Soviet Union. **2** their language. [< Turkic *kalmuk*, part of a nomad Tartar tribe remaining at home]

kal·so·mine (kal′sə mīn′ or kal′sə min) *n. v.* **-mined, -min·ing.** calcimine.

kame (kām) *n.* **1** in geology, a small hill or ridge deposited by retreating glaciers. **2** *Scottish.* a comb. [northern E dial. var. of *combe*]

ka·mik (kä′mik) *n. Cdn.* a soft knee-length boot of sealskin or cariboo hide, worn in eastern arctic regions; mukluk. Also, **kumik.** [< Eskimo]

hat, āge, cãre, fär; let, ēqual, tėrm; it, īce
hot, ōpen, ôrder; oil, out; cup, pu̇t, rüle, ūse
əbove, takən, pencəl, lemən, circəs
ch, child; ng, long; sh, ship
th, thin; ᴛʜ, then; zh, measure

ka·mi·ka·ze (kä′mē kä′zē) *n.* in World War II, a Japanese pilot who dived an airplane loaded with explosives into the target he sought to destroy. [< Japanese *kamikaze*, literally, divine wind]

Kam·loops trout (kam′lüps) *Cdn.* a kind of rainbow trout native to the upper Columbia and Fraser River system. [< *Kamloops*, B.C.]

Kan. Kansas.

Ka·nak·a (kə nak′ə or kan′ə kə) *n.* **1** a native of Hawaii. **2** a South Sea islander. [< Hawaiian *kanaka* man]

kan·ga·roo (kang′gə rü′) *n.* **-roos** or (*esp. collectively*) **-roo.** a mammal of Australia and New Guinea having small forelegs and very strong hind legs, which give it great leaping power. The female kangaroo has a pouch in front in which she carries her young. [probably < an Australian native language] **—kan′ga·roo′-like′,** *adj.*

kangaroo court *Informal.* an unauthorized or irregular court in which the law is deliberately disregarded or misinterpreted. A mock court held by convicts in prison is called a kangaroo court.

Kans. Kansas.

Kant·i·an (kan′tē ən) *adj.* of or having to do with Immanuel Kant (1724-1804), a German philosopher, or his system of philosophy. —*n.* a follower of Kant.

ka·o·lin or **ka·o·line** (kā′ə lin) *n.* a fine white clay, used in making porcelain. [< F < Chinese *Kao-ling*, a mountain in China]

ka·pok (kā′pok or kap′ək) *n.* the silky fibres around the seeds of a tropical tree, used for stuffing pillows, life preservers, and mattresses. [< Malay]

kap·pa (kap′ə) *n.* the tenth letter (Κ, κ) of the Greek alphabet.

kar·a·kul (kar′ə kəl) *n.* **1** a variety of Russian or Asiatic sheep. **2** fur with flat, loose curls; caracul. **3** a coat or other garment made of this fur. [< *Kara Kul*, a lake in Turkestan]

kar·at (kar′ət) *n.* carat. *Abbrev.*: k.

ka·ra·te (kə rä′tē) *n.* a Japanese system of self-defence without weapons, using studied hand and foot strokes capable of crippling or killing. [< Japanese; literally, empty-handed]

kar·ma (kär′mə) *n.* **1** in Buddhism and Hinduism, the totality of a person's thoughts, actions, etc. that are supposed to affect or determine his fate in his next incarnation. **2** destiny; fate. [< Skt. *karma* deed, action, fate]

kart (kärt) *n.* go-kart. —*v.* take part in a go-kart race. **—kart′er,** *n.*

ka·tab·o·lism (kə tab′ə liz′əm) *n.* catabolism.

ka·ty·did (kā′tē did′) *n.* a large, green insect resembling a grasshopper. [imitative of the insect's sound]

kau·ri (kou′rē) *n.* **-ris. 1** a tall pine tree that grows in New Zealand. **2** the wood of this tree. **3** a resin that is obtained from it, used in varnish. [< Maori]

kau·ry (kou′rē) *n.* **-ries.** kauri.

kay·ak or **kai·ak** (kī′ak) *n.* **1** an Eskimo canoe made of skins stretched over a light frame of wood or bone, completely enclosed except for a space left for one person. See **canoe** for picture. **2** a similar craft of other material: *Kayak racing is an exciting sport.* [< Eskimo]

ka·zoo (kə zü′) *n.* a toy musical instrument made of a tube sealed off at one end with a membrane or piece of paper that produces a buzzing or vibration when one hums into the tube. [imitative]

K.B. 1 Knight of the (Order of the) Bath. **2** Knight Bachelor. **3** King's Bench.

K.B.E. Knight Commander of the (Order of the) British Empire.

kc. kilocycle; kilocycles.

K.C. 1 Knight(s) of Columbus. 2 King's Counsel.

K.C.B. Knight Commander of the (Order of the) Bath.

K.C.M.G. Knight Commander of (the Order of) St. Michael and St. George.

K.C.V.O. Knight Commander of the (Royal) Victorian Order.

ke·a (kā′ə or kē′ə) *n.* a large, greenish parrot of New Zealand that kills sheep to feed upon their fat. [< Maori]

Kech·ua (kech′wä) *n.* Quechua.

Kech·uan (kech′wən) *adj.* Quechuan.

kedge (kej) *v.* **kedged, kedg·ing,** *n.* —*v.* move (a ship, etc.) by pulling on a rope attached to an anchor that has been dropped some distance away. —*n.* a small anchor used in kedging a boat, etc. [origin uncertain]

kedg·er·ee (kej′ə rē′) *n.* 1 an Indian dish of rice, boiled with split peas, onions, eggs, butter, and spices. 2 a European dish made of fish, boiled rice, eggs, and spices, served hot. [< Hind. *khichri*]

keel (kēl) *n.* 1 the main timber or steel piece that extends the whole length of the bottom of a ship or boat. 2 *Poetic.* a ship. 3 the part in an airplane or airship resembling a ship's keel. 4 **on an even keel, a** horizontal. **b** steady; properly balanced: *His business affairs are on an even keel again.* —*v.* 1 turn upside down; upset. 2 **keel over, a** turn over or upside down; upset. **b** fall over suddenly. **c** *Informal.* faint. [ME < ON *kjölr*]

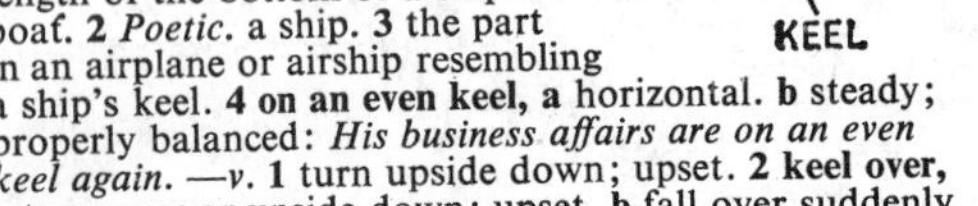

keel·haul (kēl′hol′ or -hôl′) *v.* haul (a person) under the keel of a ship as a punishment. [< Du. *kielhalen* < *kiel* keel + *halen* haul]

keel·son (kel′sən or kēl′sən) *n.* a beam or line of timbers or iron plates fastened along the top of a ship's keel to strengthen it. Also, **kelson.** [ME ? < Scand.; cf. Swedish *kölsvin*]

keen[1] (kēn) *adj.* 1 sharp enough to cut well: *a keen blade.* 2 sharp; piercing; cutting: *a keen wind, keen hunger, keen wit, keen pain.* 3 strong; vivid: *keen competition.* 4 able to do its work quickly and accurately: *a keen mind, a keen sense of smell.* 5 *Informal.* full of enthusiasm; eager: *Tom is keen about sailing.* [OE *cēne*] —**keen′ly,** *adv.* —**Syn. 2** acute, penetrating, biting, bitter. **4** See **sharp. 5** ardent, earnest. See **eager.**

keen[2] (kēn) *n.* a wailing lament for the dead. —*v.* wail; lament. [< Irish *caoine*] —**keen′er,** *n.*

keen·ness (kēn′nis) *n.* 1 a keen or cutting quality; sharpness: *the keenness of an axe, the keenness of the cold wind, the keenness of a man's appetite.* 2 an interest in; enthusiasm for: *His keenness for sports was easy to see.*

keep (kēp) *v.* **kept, keep·ing,** *n.* —*v.* 1 have for a long time or forever: *You may keep this book.* 2 have and not let go; hold; detain: *They were kept in prison. He was kept in hospital for ten days.* 3 not reveal or divulge: *keep a secret.* 4 have and take care of: *My uncle keeps chickens.* 5 take care of and protect: *May God keep you.* 6 have in one's service; employ: *keep a servant.* 7 have and hold; retain: *to keep a thing in mind.* 8 hold back or restrain; prevent: *What is keeping her from coming?* 9 restrain oneself (from); refrain: *The little boy couldn't keep from crying when he fell down.* 10 maintain in good condition; maintain: *keep a garden. She likes keeping house.* 11 be preserved; stay in good condition: *The butter kept in the icebox.* 12 make regular entries or records in: *keep books, keep a diary.* 13 record (transactions, events, etc.) regularly: *No record of this conversation was kept.* 14 stay the same; continue to be; remain: *keep awake. Keep along this road for two miles.* 15 cause to continue in some stated place, condition, etc.: *keep a light burning.* 16 observe; celebrate: *keep Christmas as a holiday.* 17 be faithful to: *keep a promise.* 18 provide for; support: *He is not able to keep himself, much less a family.* 19 have habitually for sale: *That store keeps canned goods.*
keep in with, *Informal.* keep acquaintance or friendship with.
keep on, continue; go.
keep time, go correctly; move at the proper rate.
keep up, a continue; prevent from ending. **b** maintain in good condition. **c** not fall behind.
keep up with, a not fall behind; go or move as fast as. **b** live or do as well as: *She tried hard to keep up with her wealthy neighbors.* **c** stay up to date with: *He keeps up with the news. Try to keep up with your reading.*
—*n.* 1 board and lodging: *He works for his keep.* 2 the strongest part of a castle or fort. 3 **for keeps, a** for the winner to keep his winnings. **b** *Informal.* forever. [OE *cēpan* observe]
Syn. *v.* **2 Keep, retain, withhold** = hold in one's possession. **Keep** is the general word meaning "have and not let go from one's possession, control, or care": *They were kept in prison.* **Retain,** more formal, emphasizes continuing to keep, especially against efforts to take away or make one let go: *My mother retains her youthful looks.* **Withhold** = keep or hold back, and suggests some check or obstacle to letting go or, often, refusing to let go: *Fear made him withhold the truth.* **5** shield, guard. **9** detain, restrain. **16** commemorate. **17** fulfil. -*n.* **1** maintenance, support. **2** stronghold.

keep·er (kēp′ər) *n.* 1 a person or thing that keeps. 2 a guard; watchman. 3 a guardian; protector: *Am I my brother's keeper?* 4 *Brit.* a gamekeeper. 5 a person who owns or carries on some establishment or business: *the keeper of an inn.* 6 any mechanical device for keeping something in its place, as a clasp, catch, or loop. 7 a link set across the poles of a magnet to preserve its magnetism when not in use. 8 a food or other produce that keeps (well or ill). 9 *Informal.* a fish large enough to be legally caught and kept.

keep·ing (kēp′ing) *n.* 1 care; charge; maintenance: *The keeping of the orphaned children was paid for by their uncle.* 2 celebration; observance: *the keeping of Thanksgiving Day.* 3 agreement; harmony: *His action was not in keeping with his word.* 4 being kept for future use; preservation. —**Syn. 1** support. **2** commemoration.

keep·sake (kēp′sāk′) *n.* something kept in memory of the giver: *My friend gave me his picture as a keepsake.* —**Syn.** remembrance, souvenir, memento.

Kees·hond (kās′ hond or kēs′ hond) *n.* 1 a breed of dog developed in the Netherlands, having a gray coat tipped with black, and closely related to the Chow and the Pomeranian. 2 a dog of this breed. [< Du. *keeshond* < *kees* terrier + *hond* dog, hound]

Kee·wa·tin (kē wā′tən) in geology: —*adj.* of or having to do with the earliest period of the Archeozoic era. —*n.* 1 the oldest period of the Archeozoic era. See **geology** for chart. 2 the rocks or rock formations of this period. [< *Keewatin,* a district of the Northwest Territories]

keg (keg) *n.* 1 a small barrel, usually holding less than 10 gallons. 2 100 pounds of nails. 3 a keg and its contents. 4 as much as a keg can hold. [ME < ON *kaggi*]

kelp (kelp) *n.* 1 a large, tough, brown seaweed. 2 ashes of seaweed. Kelp contains iodine. [earlier also *kilpe,* ME *culp(e)*; origin unknown]

kel·pie or **kel·py** (kel′pē) *n.* **-pies.** in Scottish folklore, a water spirit, usually in the form of a horse, supposed to drown people or be an omen of death by drowning. [origin uncertain]

kel·son (kel′sən) *n.* keelson.

Kelt (kelt) *n.* Celt.

Kelt·ic (kel′tik) *adj. n.* Celtic.

kel·vin (kel′vin) *adj.* relating to or having a temperature scale on which absolute zero is 0°, the equivalent of −273.16°C, and the intervals are the same as on the Celsius scale. [after William Thomson *Kelvin* (1824-1907), a physicist and mathematician]

ken (ken) *n. v.* **kenned** or **kent** (kent), **ken·ning.** —*n.* 1 the range of sight. 2 the range of knowledge: *What happens on Mars is beyond our ken.* [< v.] —*v. Scottish.* know. [OE *cennan* make declaration < *cann* know, can[1]]

Ken. Kentucky.

ken·nel (ken′əl) *n. v.* **-nelled** or **-neled, -nel·ling** or **-nel·ing.** —*n.* 1 a house for a dog or dogs. 2 Often, **kennels,** *pl.* **a** a place where dogs are bred. **b** a place where dogs may be lodged and cared for. 3 a pack of dogs. —*v.* 1 put or keep in a kennel. 2 take shelter or lodge in a kennel. [< AF, ult. < L *canis* dog]

ke·no (kē′nō) *n.* a gambling game resembling lotto and bingo in which the players cover numbers on their cards.

Kent·ish (ken′tish) *adj.* of Kent, a county in S.E. England, or its people. —*n.* an Old English dialect spoken in the early English kingdom of Kent.

kep·i (kep′ē) *n.* **kep·is.** a cap with a round, flat top, worn by French soldiers. [< F *képi*, ult. < G *Kappe* cap]

kept (kept) *v.* pt. and pp. of **keep.**

ker·a·tin (ker′ə tin) *n.* in biochemistry, a complex protein, the chief constituent of horn, nails, hair, feathers, etc. [< Gk. *keras, -atos* horn]

kerb (kėrb) *n. Brit.* curb (of a pavement).

ker·chief (kėr′chif) *n.* **1** a square piece of cloth worn over the head or around the neck. **2** a handkerchief. [ME < OF *couvrechief* < *couvrir* cover (< L *cooperire*) + *chief* head < L *caput*]

kerf (kėrf) *n.* **1** a cut made by an axe, saw, etc. **2** a piece cut off. [OE *cyrf* < *ceorfan* carve]

Ker·man (kėr män′) *n.* Kirman.

ker·mess (kėr′mis) *n.* kermis.

ker·mis (kėr′mis) *n.* **1** in the Netherlands, Belgium, etc., a fair with games and merrymaking. **2** any fair or entertainment, usually to raise money for charity. Also, **kirmess.** [< Du. *kermis* < *kerk* church + *mis* Mass]

kern[1] or **kerne** (kėrn) *n.* **1** *Archaic.* **a** an Irish or Scottish foot soldier carrying light weapons. **b** a troop of such soldiers. **2** an Irish peasant. [< Irish *ceithern* troop of soldiers]

kern[2] (kėrn) *n.* in printing, the part of a letter that projects beyond the body of the piece of type. [< F *carne* edge < L *cardo, -dinis* hinge]

ker·nel (kėr′nəl) *n.* **1** the softer part inside the hard shell of a nut or inside the stone of a fruit. **2** a grain or seed like wheat or corn. **3** the central or most important part: *the kernel of an argument.* [OE *cyrnel* < *corn* seed, grain]

ker·o·sene (ker′ə sēn′ or ker′ə sēn′) *n. Cdn.* a thin oil, a mixture of hydrocarbons, usually produced by distilling petroleum; coal oil. It is used in lamps, stoves, some types of engines, etc. [< Gk. *kēros* wax]

Ker·ry (ker′ē) *n.* **-ries. 1** a breed of small, black dairy cattle. **2** an animal of this breed. [< *Kerry*, a county in S.W. Irish Republic, where this breed originated]

ker·sey (kėr′zē) *n.* **-seys. 1** a coarse, ribbed, woollen cloth with a cotton warp. **2 kerseys,** *pl.* trousers made of kersey. [probably < *Kersey*, a village in Suffolk, England]

kes·trel (kes′trəl) *n.* a small European falcon. [probably < OF *cresserelle* < L *crista* crest]

ket·a (kit′ə or ket′ə) *n.* **ket·a.** a species of Pacific salmon; chum or dog salmon. [origin uncertain]

ketch (kech) *n.* **1** a fore-and-aft-rigged sailing ship with a large mainmast toward the bow and a smaller mast toward the stern. **2** formerly, a sturdy sailing vessel with two masts. [? < *catch*]

ketch·up (kech′əp) *n.* a sauce for use with meat, fish, etc. Tomato ketchup is made of tomatoes, onions, salt, sugar, and spices. Also, **catchup, catsup.** [< Malay *kechap* sauce, probably < Chinese *kôe-chiap* brine of pickled fish]

ket·tle (ket′əl) *n.* **1** a metal container for boiling liquids, cooking fruit, etc. **2** a teakettle. **3 kettle of fish,** *Informal.* an awkward state of affairs; mess; muddle. [OE *cetel* < L *catillus*, dim. of *catinus* vessel]

ket·tle·drum (ket′əl drum′) *n.* a drum consisting of a hollow brass or copper hemisphere and a parchment top that can be tuned by adjusting the tension by means of the screws round the circumference. See **drum** for picture.

ke·tu·bah or **Ke·tu·bah** (kə tü′bə) *n.* in Judaism, the marriage contract signed by a couple before the wedding, listing their obligations under Jewish law. [< Hebrew *kethubhah* a writing, written document]

Ke·ween·aw·an (kē′wə no′ən or kē′wə nô′ən) *adj.* of or having to do with the latest period of the Proterozoic era, between the Cambrian and the Huronian; Algonquian.
—*n.* **1** the latest period of the Proterozoic era, between the Cambrian and the Huronian; Algonquian. **2** the copper-bearing rocks or rock formations of this period. See **geology** for chart. [< *Keweenaw*, a promontory on Lake Superior where these rocks are found]

kew·pie doll (kū′pē) **1** a plastic or celluloid doll resembling a fat cherub with tiny wings and a slick topknot. **2 Kewpie Doll,** a trademark for a doll of this type. [? dim. of *Cupid*]

hat, āge, cãre, fär; let, ēqual, tėrm; it, īce
hot, ōpen, ôrder; oil, out; cup, pu̇t, rüle, ūse
əbove, takən, pencəl, lemən, circəs
ch, child; ng, long; sh, ship
th, thin; ᴛʜ, then; zh, measure

key[1] (kē) *n.* **keys,** *adj. v.* **keyed, key·ing.** —*n.* **1** an instrument that locks and unlocks; something that turns or opens: *a key to a door.* **2** something that explains or answers: *the key to a puzzle. The key to an arithmetic book gives the answers to all the problems.* **3** a place that commands or gives control of a sea, a district, etc. because of its position: *Gibraltar is the key to the Mediterranean.* **4** an important or essential person, thing, etc. **5** a pin, bolt, wedge, or other piece put in a hole or space to hold parts together. **6** a device to turn a bolt or nut, etc. Watches used to be wound with keys. **7** one of a set of levers pressed in playing a piano, in typewriting, and in operating other instruments or machines. **8** in music, a scale or system of notes related to one another in a special way and based on a particular note: *This song is written in the key of B flat.* **9** a tone of voice; style of thought or expression: *The poet wrote in a melancholy key.* **10** in botany, a key fruit.
—*adj.* controlling; very important: *the key industries of a nation.*
—*v.* **1** in music, regulate the pitch of: *key a piano up to concert pitch.* **2** adjust (a speech, etc.) as if to a particular key: *He wrote a letter keyed to a tone of defiance.* **3** fasten or adjust with a key. **4** lock. **5** provide with a key or keys. **6 key up,** raise the courage or nerve of (to the point of doing something): *The coach keyed up the team for the big game.* [OE *cǣg*] —**key′less,** *adj.*

key[2] (kē) *n.* **keys.** a low island; reef. There are keys south of Florida. [< Sp. *cayo* < Taino (an Arawakan language) *cayo*, or *caya* small island; influenced by *key*[1]]

key block a large conical block of snow, dropped into place at the centre of an igloo dome, serving to lock the structure firmly together.

key·board (kē′bôrd′) *n.* in a piano, organ, typewriter, calculating machine, etc., a set of keys.

keyed (kēd) *adj.* **1** having keys: *a keyed flute or trombone.* **2** set or pitched in a particular key. **3** fastened or strengthened with a key. **4** constructed with a keystone.

key fruit in botany, a dry, winged fruit. The seeds of elm, ash, maple, etc. are contained in key fruits.

key·hole (kē′hōl′) *n.* an opening in a lock through which a key is inserted to turn the lock.

key·note (kē′nōt′) *n. v.* **-not·ed, -not·ing.** —*n.* **1** in music, the note on which a scale or system of tones is based. **2** the main idea; guiding principle: *World peace was the keynote of his speech.* —*v.* give the keynote speech of (a conference, political campaign, etc.)

keynote speech a speech, as at a political gathering, that presents the principal issues in which those present are interested.

key signature in music, one or more sharps or flats placed after the clef at the beginning of each staff to indicate the key.

key·stone (kē′stōn′) *n.* **1** in architecture, the middle stone at the top of an arch, holding the other stones or pieces in place. **2** the part on which other associated parts depend; essential principle.

KEYSTONE

kg. kilogram; kilograms.

K.G. Knight (of the Order) of the Garter.

khak·i (kär′kē, kä′kē, or kak′ē) *adj. n.* **khak·is.** —*adj.* dull yellowish-brown. —*n.* **1** a dull, yellowish brown. **2** a stout twilled cloth of this color, used for soldiers' uniforms. **3** a uniform or uniforms made of this cloth: *Khakis will be worn for drill.* [< Hind. *khaki*, originally, dust-colored < Persian *khak* dust]

kha·lif (kā′lif or kal′if) *n.* caliph.

khan[1] (kän or kan) *n.* **1** the title of a ruler among Tartar or Mongol tribes, or of the emperor of China during the Middle Ages. **2** a title of dignity in Iran, Afghanistan, India, etc. [ME < MF < Turkish]

khan[2] (kän or kan) *n.* in Turkey and nearby countries, an inn without furnishings. [Arabic < Persian]

khan·ate (kän′āt or kan′āt) *n.* **1** the territory ruled by a khan. **2** the position or authority of a khan.

khe·dive (kə dēv′) *n.* the title of the Turkish viceroys who ruled Egypt between 1867 and 1914. [< F < Persian *khidiv* ruler]

kib·butz (ki bütz′) *n.* **kib·butz·im** (ki bü tsēm′). *Hebrew.* a communal settlement or farm co-operative in Israel.

kibe (kīb) *n.* a chapped or ulcerated sore, inflammation, or swelling on the heel caused by exposure to cold. [ME; cf. Welsh *cibwst* chilblains, kibes]

kib·itz (kib′its) *v. Slang.* look on as an outsider and offer unwanted advice. [< *kibitzer*]

kib·itz·er (kib′it sər) *n. Slang.* **1** a person watching a card game. **2** a person who watches a card game and insists on making suggestions to the players. **3** a person who gives unwanted advice; meddler. [< Yiddish]

ki·bosh (kī′bosh or ki bosh′) *n. Slang.* **1** humbug; nonsense. **2 put the kibosh on,** finish off; squelch: *The boss put the kibosh on overlong coffee breaks.* [origin uncertain; probably < Yiddish]

kick (kik) *v.* **1** strike out with the foot or hoof: *That horse kicks when anyone comes near him.* **2** strike with the foot or hoof: *The horse kicked the boy.* **3** drive, force, or move by kicking: *kick a ball.* **4** win by a kick: *kick a goal in football.* **5** spring back when fired: *This shotgun kicks.* **6** *Informal.* complain; object; grumble. **7** *Slang.* overcome; break; make oneself free of (a habit, addiction, etc.).
kick about or **around,** *Informal.* **a** be in danger of being damaged; lie about. **b** go about aimlessly. **c** consider; toy with.
kick back, *Informal.* **a** spring back suddenly and unexpectedly. **b** *Slang.* return (a stolen item) to its owner. **c** *Slang.* return (a portion of money received as a fee), often as the result of coercion or a previous arrangement.
kick in, *Slang.* **a** die. **b** pay what is due or expected.
kick off, **a** in football, put a ball in play with a kick. **b** *Slang.* begin. **c** *Slang.* die.
kick out, *Informal.* expel or turn out with a kick or in an ignominious fashion.
kick up, *Slang.* start; cause.
—*n.* **1** the act of kicking. **2** the recoil of a gun. **3** *Slang.* a complaint; cause for complaint; objection. **4** *Slang.* excitement; thrill: *He gets a kick out of gambling. He does it for kicks.* **5** *Slang.* the power of a drink, drug, etc. to intoxicate. **6** *Slang.* a period of intense interest or activity (in something): *She is on a classical music kick.* [origin uncertain]

kick·back (kik′bak′) *n. Informal.* **1** an amount or portion returned, especially as a fee to keep one's job. If you were paid $350 a month and paid back $50 a month to your employer, the $50 would be a kickback. **2** *Slang.* a returning of stolen goods. **3** a sudden violent or vigorous reaction, usually unexpected.

kick·er (kik′ər) *n.* **1** a person, animal, or thing that kicks. **2** *Informal.* an outboard motor.

kick·off (kik′of′) *n.* **1** in football, soccer, rugger, etc., the start of a game: *The kickoff is scheduled for 2.00 p.m.* **2** *Informal.* the start of any activity.

kick·shaw (kik′sho′ or kik′shô′) *n.* **1** a fancy article of food; delicacy. **2** a trifle; trinket. [alteration of F *quelque chose* something]

kid[1] (kid) *n.* **1** a young goat. **2** its flesh, used as food. **3** its skin, used as fur. **4** the leather made from the skin of young goats, used for gloves and shoes. **5 kids,** *pl.* gloves or shoes made of kid. **6** *Informal.* a child or young person: *The kids went to the circus.* [ME < ON *kith*]

kid[2] (kid) *v.* **kid·ded, kid·ding.** *Slang.* **1** tease playfully; talk jokingly; banter. **2** humbug; fool. [? < *kid*[1] in sense of "treat as a child"] —**kid′der,** *n.*

kid-glove (kid′ gluv′) *adj.* **1** wearing kid gloves. **2** *Informal.* careful; considerate; gentle: *This job requires a kid-glove approach.* Also, **kid-gloved.**

kid gloves 1 smooth gloves made of soft kidskin. **2 handle with kid gloves,** treat with special care or consideration.

kid·nap (kid′nap) *v.* **-napped** or **-naped, -nap·ping** or **-nap·ing.** carry off (a child) by force; seize and hold (a person) against his will by force or by fraud: *The banker's son was kidnapped and held for ransom. The gang planned to kidnap the movie star.* [< *kid*[1] child + *nap* snatch away] —**kid′nap·per** or **kid′nap·er,** *n.*

kid·ney (kid′nē) *n.* **-neys. 1** in vertebrates, one of the pair of organs in the body that separate waste matter and water from the blood and pass them off through the bladder as urine. **2** the kidney or kidneys of an animal, cooked for food. **3** nature; kind; sort. [ME < *kidenei* < *kiden-*, of uncertain meaning and origin + *ey* egg] —**kid′ney-like′,** *adj.*

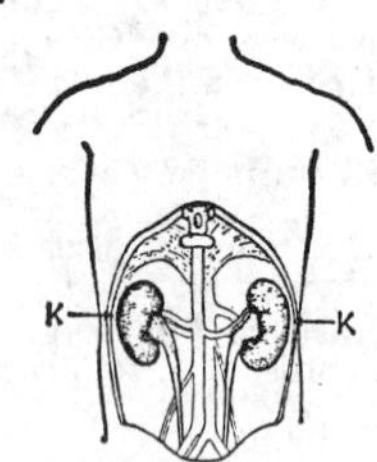

K, the kidneys of a human being

kidney bean 1 a kidney-shaped bean. **2** the plant that it grows on.

kid·skin (kid′skin′) *n.* the leather made from the skin of young goats, used for gloves and shoes.

Ki·ku·yu (kik′ə yü′ or ki kü′yü) *n.* **-yu** or **-yus. 1** one of the principal Negro tribes in Kenya. **2** a member of this tribe. **3** the Bantu language of this tribe.

kill (kil) *v.* **1** put to death; cause the death of: *The blow from the axe killed him.* **2** cause death: *"Thou shalt not kill."* **3** put an end to; destroy: *kill odors, kill faith, kill rumors.* **4** cancel (a word, paragraph, item, etc.). **5** defeat or veto (a legislative bill). **6** destroy or neutralize the active qualities of: *kill land in farming.* **7** spoil the effect of: *One color may kill another near it.* **8** use up (time). **9** in hockey, overcome the disadvantage of (a penalty) by thwarting the opposing team's attempts to score while the penalized player is off the ice: *Toronto managed to kill the penalty and were then able to score the winning goal.* **10** stop; cut off the fuel supply or electrical current of: *He killed the engine.* **11** *Informal.* overcome completely: *It was funny enough to kill anybody.* **12** in tennis, etc., hit (a ball) so hard that it cannot be returned. **13 kill off,** wipe out, exterminate.
—*n.* **1** the act of killing. **2** the animal killed. **3** in tennis, etc., a ball hit so hard as to be unreturnable. [ME *kyllen, cullen*; probably related to QUELL]
Syn. *v.* **1 Kill, murder, slay** = cause death. **Kill** is the general word, meaning "put to death or in any way cause the death of a person, animal, or plant": *Overwork killed him. Lack of water kills flowers.* **Murder** emphasizes wicked and cold-blooded killing, and means "kill a person unlawfully, usually deliberately": *He murdered his rich uncle.* **Slay,** chiefly literary or journalistic, means "kill with violence, in battle or by murdering": *All the captives were slain.*

kill·dee (kil′dē′) *n.* **-dee** or **-dees.** killdeer.

kill·deer (kil′dēr′) *n.* **-deers** or (*esp. collectively*) **-deer.** a small wading bird that has a loud, shrill cry. It is the largest and commonest plover of N. America. [imitative of its call]

kill·er (kil′ər) *n.* **1** a person, animal, or thing that kills. **2** *Slang.* a criminal who recklessly or wantonly kills others. **3** *Slang.* anything that is very difficult: *That climb is a killer.* **4** a killer whale.

killer whale a dolphin that kills and eats large fish, seals, and even whales.

kill·ing (kil′ing) *adj.* **1** deadly; destructive; fatal: *a killing frost.* **2** overpowering; exhausting: *They rode at a killing pace.* **3** *Informal.* extremely funny.
—*n. Informal.* a sudden great financial success: *He made a killing in stocks.* —**kill′ing·ly,** *adv.*

kill-joy (kil′joi′) *n.* a person who spoils other people's fun.

kiln (kiln or kil) *n.* **1** a furnace or oven for burning, baking, or drying something. Limestone is burned in a kiln to make lime. Bricks are baked in a kiln. See picture on the next page. **2** a building containing a furnace for drying grain, hops, etc. or for making malt. —*v.* bake, dry, or burn in a kiln. [OE *cyln, cylen* < L *culina* kitchen]

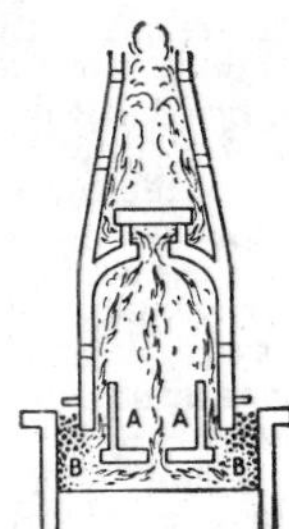

A diagram of an open-fire pottery kiln: A, the chamber for pottery; B, coal.

ki·lo (kē′lō or kil′ō) *n.* **ki·los.** **1** a kilogram. **2** kilometre. [< F]

kilo- *combining form.* one thousand, as in *kilogram, kilometre, kilowatt.* [< F < Gk. *chilioi*]

kilo. **1** kilogram. **2** kilometre. **3** kilowatt.

kil·o·cal·o·rie (kil′ə kal′ə rē) *n.* a large calorie. See **calorie.**

kil·o·cy·cle (kil′ə sī′kəl) *n.* **1** 1,000 cycles. **2** 1,000 cycles per second. Radio frequencies are expressed in kilocycles. *Abbrev.*: kc.

kil·o·gram or **kil·o·gramme** (kil′ə gram′) *n.* 1,000 grams, equal to 2.2046 pounds avoirdupois. *Abbrev.*: k., kg., or kilo. [< F *kilogramme*]

kil·o·gram-me·tre or **kil·o·gram-me·ter** (kil′ə gram mē′tər) *n.* a unit used in measuring work, equal to 7.2334 foot-pounds, the amount of work done in lifting one kilogram one metre.

kil·o·li·tre or **kil·o·li·ter** (kil′ə lē′tər) *n.* 1,000 litres, or one cubic metre, equal to 220.02 imperial gallons, or 1.308 cubic yards. [< F *kilolitre*]

kil·o·me·tre or **kil·o·me·ter** (kil′ə mē′tər or kə lom′ə tər) *n.* 1,000 metres, equal to 3,280.8 feet. *Abbrev.*: kilo. or km. [< F *kilomètre*]

kil·o·met·ric (kil′ə met′rik) *adj.* **1** of a kilometre. **2** measured in kilometres.

kil·o·ton (kil′ə tun′) *n.* a measure of atomic power equivalent to the energy released by one thousand tons of high explosive, specifically TNT. [< *kilo-* + *ton* (of explosive energy of TNT)]

kil·o·watt (kil′ə wot′) *n.* 1,000 watts. *Abbrev.*: k., kilo, or kw.

kil·o·watt-hour (kil′ə wot′our′) *n.* a unit of electrical energy equal to the work done by one kilowatt acting for one hour.

kilt (kilt) *n.* **1** a pleated, knee-length skirt, often worn by both men and women in the Scottish Highlands, in Ireland, and by soldiers in Scottish and Irish regiments, including those in Canada. **2** a similar garment worn by women and girls. [< v.] —*v. Scottish.* tuck up; fasten up. [probably < Scand.; cf. Danish *kilte* tuck (up)] —**kilt′like′,** *adj.*

kil·ter (kil′tər) *n. Informal.* good condition; order: *Our radio is out of kilter.* [origin uncertain]

ki·mo·no (kə mō′nə or kə mō′nō) *n.* **-nos.** **1** a loose outer garment held in place by a sash, worn by Japanese men and women. **2** a loose dressing gown. [< Japanese]

kin (kin) *n.* **1** one's family or relatives; kindred. **2** family relationship; connection by birth or marriage: *What kin is she to you?* **3 near of kin,** closely related. **4 of kin,** related. **5 next of kin,** nearest living relative: *His next of kin is his father.* —*adj.* related. [OE *cynn*; cf. *cennan* beget] —**kin′less,** *adj.*

-kin *suffix.* little, as in *lambkin.* [ME; cf. MDu. *-kijn, -ken*]

ki·nase (kī′nās or kin′ās) *n.* in biochemistry, an enzyme able to activate the inactive form of another enzyme. [< *kin*etic + dia*stase*]

kind[1] (kīnd) *adj.* **1** friendly; doing good: *kind words.* **2** gentle: *Be kind to animals.* **3** showing or characterized by kindness: *a kind master.* [OE (*ge*)*cynde* natural < (*ge*)*cynd* nature, kind[2]]

Syn. 1 Kind, kindly, gracious = having or showing a generous, sympathetic, considerate nature. **Kind** emphasizes a tendency to take a friendly interest in the welfare of others: *The kind old man helped the student get a summer job.* **Kindly,** often used interchangeably with *kind,* emphasizes showing a kind nature, especially by doing kind things: *He gave me some kindly advice.* **Gracious** means kindly and courteous in manner, especially toward younger people or those of lower social position: *The famous singer is a very gracious lady.* **2** tender.

kind[2] (kīnd) *n.* **1** a class; sort, variety: *many kinds of candy. A spaniel is one kind of dog.* **2** a natural group; race. **3 after one's** or **its kind,** *Archaic.* according to one's or its own nature. **4 in kind, a** in goods or produce, not

hat, āge, cãre, fär; let, ēqual, tėrm; it, īce
hot, ōpen, ôrder; oil, out; cup, pu̇t, rüle, ūse
əbove, takən, pencəl, lemən, circəs
ch, child; ng, long; sh, ship
th, thin; ᴛʜ, then; zh, measure

in money. **b** in something of the same sort. **c** in characteristic quality: *There is a difference in kind, not merely in degree, between a hound and a terrier.* **5 kind of,** *Informal.* nearly; almost; somewhat; rather. **6 of a kind, a** of the same kind; alike. **b** of a poor or mediocre quality: *Two boxes and a plank make a table of a kind.* [OE (*ge*)*cynd*]

Syn. 1 Kind, sort = a group of people or things alike in some way. **Kind** applies particularly to a group of the same nature or character, having enough closely similar essential qualities in their make-up to put them together as a class or division in some system of classification: *What kind of cake do you like best?* **Sort,** often interchangeable with *kind,* is usually vaguer, and sometimes carries a suggestion of contempt: *a girl of that sort. That sort of action disgusts me.*

☛ **kind, sort.** *Kind* and *sort* are both singular nouns in form: *This kind of apple is likely to be wormy. That sort of behavior is out of place here.* In informal spoken English the plural idea implied in these words often results in constructions like *those kind of books* and *these sort of ideas,* but it is wise to avoid such constructions in writing.

kin·der·gar·ten (kin′dər gär′tən or kin′də gär′tən) *n.* **1** the year of school that comes before grade 1. **2** a school for younger children; nursery school. [< G *Kindergarten* < *Kinder* children + *Garten* garden]

☛ **Kindergarten** preserves the spelling of its German origin and is ordinarily pronounced with *t* and not *d* in the final syllable.

kind-heart·ed (kīnd′här′tid) *adj.* having or showing a kind heart; kindly; sympathetic. —**kind′-heart′ed·ly,** *adv.* —**kind′-heart′ed·ness,** *n.*

kin·dle (kin′dəl) *v.* **-dled, -dling.** **1** set on fire; light. **2** catch fire; begin to burn: *This damp wood will never kindle.* **3** arouse; stir up: *His cruelty kindled our anger.* **4** become stirred up or aroused. **5** light up; brighten: *The boy's face kindled as he told about the circus.* [ME < ON *kynda* kindle] —**kin′dler,** *n.*

Syn. 1 Kindle, ignite = set on fire. **Kindle** = cause something like wood to burn by setting fire to it, and often suggests trouble in getting a fire going: *He kindled a fire in the fireplace.* **Ignite** emphasizes causing something inflammable (like dry wood and grass, cleaning fluids, gas, oil, etc.) to burst into flame by putting a spark, tiny flame, or great heat to or near it: *Firemen tried to keep flying sparks from igniting the shingles.*

kind·li·ness (kīnd′lē nis) *n.* **1** a kindly feeling or quality. **2** a kindly act.

kin·dling (kin′dling) *n.* small pieces of wood for starting a fire.

kind·ly (kīnd′lē) *adj.* **-li·er, -li·est,** *adv.* —*adj.* **1** kind; friendly: *kindly faces.* **2** pleasant; agreeable: *a kindly shower.* —*adj.* **1** in a kind or friendly way. **2** pleasantly; agreeably: *He does not take kindly to criticism.* [OE (*ge*)*cyndelīc*] —**Syn.** *adj.* **1** See **kind**[1].

kind·ness (kīnd′nis) *n.* **1** the quality of being kind; kind nature. **2** kind treatment. **3** a kind act: *He showed me many kindnesses.*

kin·dred (kin′drid) *n.* **1** one's family or relatives. **2** family relationship; connection by birth or marriage. **3** a likeness; resemblance. —*adj.* **1** related: *kindred tribes.* **2** like; similar: *We are studying about dew, frost, and kindred facts of nature.* [ME < *kyn* family (OE *cynn*) + *rede,* OE *rǣden* condition] —**Syn.** *adj.* **1** cognate, allied.

kine (kīn) *n.pl. Archaic or dialect.* cows; cattle. [earlier *kyen,* double plural < OE *cȳ,* pl. of *cū* cow + plural suffix *-en*]

kin·e·mat·ic (kin′ə mat′ik) *adj.* having to do with pure motion or with kinematics.

kin·e·mat·ics (kin′ə mat′iks) *n.* the branch of physics that deals with the characteristics of different kinds of pure motion, that is, without reference to mass or to the causes of the motion. [< Gk. *kinēma, -atos* motion < *kineein* move]

kin·e·mat·o·graph (kin′ə mat′ə graf′) *n.* cinematograph.

kin·e·ma·tog·ra·phy (kin′ə mə tog′rə fē) *n.* cinematography.

kin·e·scope (kin′ə skōp′) *n.* **1** a record on film of a television show or other entertainment that may be rebroadcast. **2** in television, a cathode-ray tube that has a screen at one end on which images are reproduced. **3 Kinescope,** *Trademark.* a trade name for such a tube.

ki·ne·sic (ki nē′sik or kī nē′sik) *adj.* of or having to do with kinesics.

ki·nes·ics (ki nē′siks or kī nē′siks) *n.* the study of communication by means of gestures, facial expressions, etc., especially as they accompany speech. [< Gk. *kinēsis* motion + E *-ics*]

ki·ne·sis (ki nē′sis or kī nē′sis) *n.* an involuntary reaction or movement, resulting from an external stimulus. [< Gk. *kinēsis* motion]

kin·es·the·sia (kin′əs thē′zhə) *n.* the sensation of movement in the muscles and joints. [< NL < Gk. *kineein* move + *-aisthesia* perception]

kin·es·thet·ic (kin′əs thet′ik) *adj.* having to do with sensations from the muscles and joints.

ki·net·ic (ki net′ik or kī net′ik) *adj.* **1** of motion. **2** caused by motion. [< Gk. *kinētikos* < *kineein* move]

ki·net·ics (ki net′iks or kī net′iks) *n.* the branch of physics that deals with the effects of forces in causing or changing the motion of objects.

kinetic theory in physics, the theory that the constituent particles of matter are in constant motion, and that the temperature of a substance is proportional to the velocity of the particles. Pressure, elasticity, diffusion, and other properties of gases are also explained in terms of molecular activity.

kin·folk (kin′fōk′) *n.pl. Dialect.* kinsfolk.

king (king) *n.* **1** the male ruler of a nation; a male sovereign, with either absolute or limited power. **2** *Informal.* a man supreme in a certain sphere: *a baseball king.* **3** something best in its class. **4** in chess, the chief piece. **5** in checkers, a piece that has moved entirely across the board. **6** a playing card bearing a picture of a king. **7** a king or chinook salmon. **8 king of beasts,** the lion. **9 king of birds,** the eagle. [OE *cyning*] **—king′less,** *adj.*

king·bird (king′bėrd′) *n.* a quarrelsome bird of the flycatcher family.

king·bolt (king′bōlt′) *n.* a vertical bolt connecting the body of a wagon, etc. with the front axle, or the body of a railway car with a set of wheels.

King Charles spaniel **1** a breed of black and tan toy spaniel. **2** a dog of this breed.

king crab horseshoe crab.

king·craft (king′kraft′) *n.* the art of ruling; royal statesmanship.

king·dom (king′dəm) *n.* **1** a country that is governed by a king or a queen. **2** a realm; domain; province: *The mind is the kingdom of thought.* **3** one of the three divisions of the natural world; the animal kingdom, the vegetable kingdom, or the mineral kingdom. [OE *cyningdōm*]

king·fish (king′fish′) *n.* **-fish** or **-fish·es. 1** any of several large food fishes of the Atlantic or Pacific coastal waters. **2** *Informal.* a person having uncontested control in a group or community.

king·fish·er (king′fish′ər) *n.* a bright-colored bird having a large head and a strong beak. The North American kingfishers eat fish; some of the European kinds eat insects.

King James Version an English translation of the Bible published in 1611, during the reign of James I; Authorized Version.

king·let (king′lit) *n.* **1** a petty king; a ruler over a small country. **2** any of various small, greenish songbirds.

king·ly (king′lē) *adj.* **-li·er, -li·est,** *adv.* *—adj.* **1** of a king or kings; of royal rank. **2** fit for a king: *a kingly crown.* **3** like a royal king; noble. *—adv.* as a king does. **—king′li·ness,** *n.* **—Syn.** *adj.* **1** See **royal. 3** regal.

king·mak·er (king′māk′ər) *n.* **1** a person who makes or establishes a king. **2** a person of consequence who can influence or dictate the choice of candidates for political office.

king-of-arms (king′əv ärms′) *n. Brit.* in heraldry, an official responsible for the investigation of rights and titles, the granting of coats of arms, etc.

king·pin (king′pin′) *n.* **1** in bowling games, the pin in front or in the centre. **2** *Informal.* the most important person or thing. **3** a kingbolt.

king post a vertical post between the apex of a triangular roof truss and a tie beam.

KING POST
TIE BEAM
A king post truss

king salmon chinook salmon.

king's counsel or **King's Counsel** a lawyer or barrister who may serve as counsel to the Crown. *Abbrev.*: K.C.

King's Domain *Cdn.* formerly, a vast tract of land lying north of the Lower St. Lawrence and originally belonging to the French kings. [< translation of F *Domaine du Roi*]

King's English the English that is recognized as correct and standard in Britain.

king's evil scrofula, a disease that was supposed to be cured by the touch of a king.

King's highway in Canada, a main road whose maintenance is the responsibility of the provincial government.

king·ship (king′ship) *n.* **1** the position, rank, or dignity of a king. **2** the rule of a king; government by a king.

king-size (king′sīz′) *adj. Informal.* unusually large or long for its kind: *a king-size cigarette.*

king-sized (king′ sīzd′) *adj.* extra large.

King's Post *Cdn.* formerly, one of a number of fur-trading and fishing posts in Quebec, most of them in the region known as the King's Domain.

king's ransom a very large amount of money.

king truss a truss framed with a king post.

kink (kingk) *n.* **1** a twist or curl in thread, rope, hair, etc. **2** a pain or stiffness in the muscles of the neck, back, etc.; crick. **3** *Informal.* a mental twist; queer idea; odd notion; eccentricity; whim: *The old man had many kinks.* **4** a hindrance; difficulty; obstruction.
—v. form a kink; make kinks in. [probably < Du. *kink* twist]

kin·ka·jou (king′kə jü′) *n.* a yellowish-brown mammal of Central and South America. It resembles a raccoon, but has a long prehensile tail. [< F *quincajou* < Tupi-Guarani]

kink·y (kingk′ē) *adj.* **kink·i·er, kink·i·est.** full of kinks; twisted; curly. **—kink′i·ly,** *adv.* **—kink′i·ness,** *n.*

kin·ni·kin·nick (kin′ə kə nik′) *n.* **1** a mixture of various ingredients, such as bearberry, sumac, or dogwood leaves, used by American Indians for smoking. **2** a plant, especially the bearberry, from which the mixture is made. Also, **kinnikinnic.** [< Algonquian *kinikinic* that which is mixed]

kins·folk (kinz′fōk′) *n.pl.* one's family; relatives; kin. Also, *Dialect.* **kinfolk.**

kins·folks (kinz′fōks) *n.pl.* kinsfolk.

kin·ship (kin′ship) *n.* **1** a family relationship. **2** a relationship. **3** a resemblance.

kins·man (kinz′mən) *n.* **-men** (-mən). a male relative.

Kins·men (kins′mən) *n.pl. Cdn.* a national service-club organization of men in business and the professions, founded in 1920 at Hamilton, Ontario.

kins·wom·an (kinz′wům′ən) *n.* **-wom·en.** a female relative.

ki·osk (kē osk′ or kī′osk *for 1*; kē osk′ *for 2*) *n.* **1** a small building, usually with one or more sides open, used as a newsstand, bus shelter, telephone booth, etc. **2** in Turkey, Persia, etc., a light, open summerhouse. [< F < Turkish *kiushk* pavilion]

kip[1] (kip) *n.* the hide of a young or undersized animal. [origin uncertain]

kip[2] (kip) *n. v.* **kipped, kip·ping.** *Slang.* *—n.* **1** a sleeping place; bed. **2** a sleep. *—v.* go to bed. [cf. Danish *kippe* low alehouse]

kip[3] (kip) *n.* **1** a unit of money in Laos. See table at **money. 2** a coin worth one kip. [< Thai]

kip·per (kip′ər) *n.* **1** a herring, salmon, etc. that has been salted and dried or smoked. **2** the male salmon or sea trout during or after the spawning season. **3** *Slang.* **a** a person, especially a child. **b** an Englishman. —*v.* salt and dry or smoke (herring, salmon, etc.). [OE *cypera* male salmon]

Kir·ghiz (kir gēz′) *n.* **-ghiz** or **-ghiz·es. 1** a Mongolian people widely scattered over the western part of central Asia. **2** a member of this people. **3** their language.

kirk (kėrk) *n.* **1** *Scottish.* a church. **2 the Kirk,** the national church of Scotland; the Presbyterian Church of Scotland. [ME < ON *kirkja,* ult. < Gk. *kyriakon* (*doma*). See CHURCH.]

Kir·man (kėr män′) *n.* a type of Oriental rug having elaborate designs in soft, rich colors. Also, **Kerman.** [< *Kerman,* in Persia, where the rugs are made]

kir·mess (kėr′mis) *n.* kermis.

kirsch (kirsh) *n.* a clear, sweet brandy made from fermented wild black cherries, originally from Germany and Alsace. [< F < G *Kirschwasser* cherry water]

kir·tle (kėr′təl) *n. Archaic.* **1** a skirt or dress. **2** a man's short coat. [OE *cyrtel,* probably < L *curtus* short]

Kis·lev or **Kis·lew** (kis′lef) *n.* in the Hebrew calendar, the ninth month of the ecclesiastical year, and the third month of the civil year.

kis·met (kiz′met or kis′met) *n.* fate; destiny. [< Turkish < Arabic *qisma*(*t*) < *qasama* divide]

kiss (kis) *v.* **1** touch with the lips as a sign of love, greeting, or respect. **2** touch gently: *A soft wind kissed the treetops.* **3** put, bring, take, etc. by kissing: *He kissed away her tears.*
—*n.* **1** a touch with the lips. **2** a gentle touch. **3** a piece of candy containing coconut, nuts, or the like and wrapped in a twist of paper. **4** a fancy cake made of white of egg and powdered sugar. [OE *cyssan*]
—kiss′a·ble, *adj.*

kiss·er (kis′ər) *n.* **1** a person who kisses. **2** *Slang.* the face or mouth.

kit[1] (kit) *n.* **1** the equipment that a serviceman carries with him. **2** any person's equipment packed for travelling. **3** an outfit of tools: *a shoemaker's kit.* **4** a bag, case, knapsack, etc. for carrying such equipment or such an outfit. **5** the parts of any article to be assembled by the buyer: *He has bought a hi-fi kit.* **6** *Informal.* a lot; set; collection. **7** a small wooden tub or pail. [probably < MDu. *kitte*]

kit[2] (kit) *n. v.* **kit·ted, kit·ting.** —*n.* **1** the young of certain fur-bearing wild animals. **2** a kitten. —*v.* give birth to kits.

Kit·a·mat (kit′ə mat′) *n.* **-mat** or **-mats.** Kitimat.

kitch·en (kich′ən) *n.* **1** a room where food is cooked. **2** the cooking department. **3** an outfit for cooking. [OE *cycene* < L *coquina* < *coquus* a cook]

kitch·en·ette (kich′ə net′) *n.* **1** a very small, compactly arranged kitchen. **2** a part of a room fitted up as a kitchen. Also, **kitchenet.**

kitchen garden a garden where vegetables and fruit for a household are grown.

kitch·en·maid (kich′ən mād′) *n.* a woman servant who helps in the kitchen.

kitchen midden a mound of shells, bones, and other refuse that accumulated at a site of prehistoric human habitation. [translation of Danish *kjökken-mödding* < *kjökken* kitchen + *mödding* dunghill]

kitchen police *Esp.U.S.* **1** an army duty of helping the cook prepare and serve the food, wash the dishes, and clean up the kitchen. **2** soldiers assigned to this duty, often as punishment for slight offences. *Abbrev.*: K.P.

kitch·en·ware (kich′ən wãr′) *n.* kitchen utensils. Pots, kettles, and pans are kitchenware.

kite (kīt) *n. v.* **kit·ed, kit·ing.** —*n.* **1** a light wooden frame covered with paper or cloth. Kites are flown in the air on the end of a long string. **2** a hawk having long pointed wings. **3** any of the very high and light sails of a ship. **4** a type of aircraft pulled by a towline and supported by the force of air currents. **5** a person who preys upon others; rapacious person; sharper. **6** *Commercial slang.* a fictitious cheque, bill of exchange, etc. representing no actual transaction, used to raise money or to sustain credit. **7** *Slang.* any airplane that was used in World War II.
—*v.* **1** *Informal.* fly like a kite; move rapidly and easily. **2** *Commercial slang.* obtain money or credit by a kite. [OE *cȳta*]

hat, āge, cãre, fär; let, ēqual, tėrm; it, īce
hot, ōpen, ôrder; oil, out; cup, pu̇t, rüle, ūse
əbove, takən, pencəl, lemən, circəs
ch, child; ng, long; sh, ship
th, thin; ᴛʜ, then; zh, measure

kith (kith) *n.* **1 kith and kin,** friends and relatives. **2** friends. [OE *cȳththe* acquaintance < *cunnan* know]

Kit·i·mat (kit′ə mat′) *n.* **-mat** or **-mats. 1** a Wakashan tribe of Indians living near the Douglas Channel, B.C. **2** a member of this tribe. Also, **Kitamat.**

kit·ten (kit′ən) *n.* **1** a young cat. **2** the young of certain other small animals, such as rabbits. **3 have a kitten** or **kittens,** *Slang.* be emotionally upset about something. [ME < AF var. of OF *cheton* < LL *cattus* cat]

kit·ten·ish (kit′ən ish) *adj.* **1** like a kitten. **2** coquettish.

kit·ti·wake (kit′ē wāk′) *n.* a kind of sea gull of the Atlantic and Pacific coasts, whose hind toe is very short. [imitative of its call]

kit·ty[1] (kit′ē) *n.* **-ties. 1** a kitten. **2** a pet name for a cat. [ult. < *kitten*]

kit·ty[2] (kit′ē) *n.* **-ties. 1** in poker, the stakes. **2** in certain games, the money pooled by the players for some special purpose: *The kitty goes to the winner.* **3** in certain card games, a number of cards that may be used by the person making the highest bid. [origin uncertain]

kit·ty-cor·ner (kit′ē kôr′nər) *adj.* diagonal; diagonally opposite: *The barn is kitty-corner from the house.* —*adv.* diagonally. Also, **kitty-cornered.** [< *catty-corner,* var. of *cater-corner* < F *quatre* four + E *corner*]

Ki·wa·ni·an (ki wä′nē ən) *n.* a member of a Kiwanis Club. —*adj.* of or having to do with Kiwanis Clubs.

Ki·wa·nis (ki wä′nis) *n.* an international group of clubs of business and professional men, organized for civic service and higher ideals in business and professional life. The first Kiwanis Club was founded at Detroit in 1915.

ki·wi (kē′wē) *n.* **-wis.** a bird of New Zealand that cannot fly; apteryx. [< Maori]

KKK Ku Klux Klan.

kl. kilolitre; kilolitres.

Klan (klan) *n.* Ku Klux Klan.

Klans·man (klanz′mən) *n.* **-men** (-mən). a member of the Ku Klux Klan.

klep·to·ma·ni·a (klep′tə mā′nē ə) *n.* an uncontrollable impulse to steal. [< NL < Gk. *kleptēs* thief + *mania* madness]

klep·to·ma·ni·ac (klep′tə mā′nē ak′) *n.* a person who has uncontrollable impulses to steal.

klieg light (klēg) a bright, hot arc light used in taking motion pictures. [after Anton (1872-1927) *Kliegl* and his brother John (1869-1959), the inventors]

Klon·dike or **klon·dike** (klon′dīk) *n.* a variety of solitaire, or patience. [< *Klondike,* Y.T., where the game was first played]

Klon·di·ker (klon′dī kər) *n. Cdn.* a person who took part in the Klondike gold rush to the Yukon, 1897-1899.

klys·tron (klīs′tron) *n.* in electronics, a vacuum tube for generating an ultra-high-frequency current, using several resonators to bunch the electrons by advancing and retarding them. [? Gk. *klystēr* pipe syringe + *electron*]

A Boy Scout carrying a knapsack

km. 1 kilometre; kilometres. **2** kingdom.

kn. kronen.

knack (nak) *n.* **1** a special skill; power to do something easily. **2** a trick; habit. [origin uncertain] **—Syn. 1** aptitude, facility.

knap·sack (nap′sak′) *n.* a canvas or leather bag for carrying clothes, equipment, etc. on the back. [< LG *Knapsack* < *knappen* eat + *Sack* sack[1]]

knap·weed (nap′wēd′) *n.* a perennial weed having light-purple flowers. [OE *cnæp* knob + *weed*]

knave (nāv) *n.* **1** a dishonest person; rogue; rascal. **2** the jack, a playing card with a picture of a servant or soldier on it. **3** *Archaic.* a male servant; a man of humble birth or position. [OE *cnafa* boy] —**Syn. 1** scoundrel.

knav·er·y (nāv′ər ē or nāv′rē) *n.* **-er·ies. 1** behavior characteristic of a knave. **2** a tricky, dishonest act.

knav·ish (nāv′ish) *adj.* tricky; dishonest. —**knav′ish·ly,** *adv.* —**knav′ish·ness,** *n.* —**Syn.** rascally, villainous, fraudulent.

knead (nēd) *v.* **1** mix (dough, clay, etc.) by pressing and squeezing, usually with one's hands: *A baker kneads dough.* **2** press and squeeze with the hands; massage: *Stiffness in the muscles may be taken away by kneading.* **3** make or shape by kneading. [OE *cnedan*] —**knead′er,** *n.*

knee (nē) *n. v.* **kneed, knee·ing.** —*n.* **1** the joint between the thigh and the lower leg. See **shin** for picture. **2** any joint corresponding to the human knee or elbow. **3** anything like a bent knee in shape or position. **4** the part of a garment covering the knee. **5 bring to one's knees,** force to yield. **6 on the knees of the gods,** beyond human control. —*v.* strike with the knee. [OE *cnēo*]

knee breeches breeches reaching to or just below the knees.

knee·cap (nē′kap′) *n.* **1** the flat, movable bone at the front of the knee; patella. See **skeleton** for picture. **2** a covering to protect the knee.

-kneed *combining form.* having a —— knee or knees: *knock-kneed = having knock-knees.*

knee-deep (nē′dēp′) *adj.* so deep as to reach the knees.

knee-high (nē′hī′) *adj.* so high as to reach the knees.

kneel (nēl) *v.* **knelt** or **kneeled, kneel·ing. 1** go down on one's knee or knees: *She knelt down to pull a weed from the flower bed.* **2** remain in this position: *They knelt in prayer for half an hour.* [OE *cnēowlian* < *cnēo* knee]

kneel·er (nēl′ər) *n.* **1** one who kneels. **2** a stool to kneel on.

knee·pad (nē′pad′) *n.* a pad worn around the knee for protection.

knee·pan (nē′pan′) *n.* the kneecap; patella.

knell (nel) *n.* **1** the sound of a bell rung slowly after a death or at a funeral. **2** a warning sign of death, failure, etc.: *Their refusal rang the knell of our hopes.* **3** a mournful sound. [ME *knell, knyll* < OE *cnyll*]
—*v.* **1** ring slowly. **2** give a warning sign of death, failure, etc. **3** make a mournful sound. [ME *knelle(n), knylle(n)* < OE *cnyllan*]

knelt (nelt) *v.* a pt. and a pp. of **kneel.**

knew (nū or nü) *v.* pt. of **know.**

Knick·er·bock·er (nik′ər bok′ər) *n. U.S.* **1** a person descended from the early Dutch settlers of New York. **2** a person living in New York. [< Diedrich *Knickerbocker*, fictitious author of Washington Irving's *Knickerbocker's History of New York*, 1809]

knick·er·bock·ers (nik′ər bok′ərz) *n.pl.* knickers.

knick·ers (nik′ərz) *n.pl.* short, loose-fitting trousers gathered in at, or just below, the knee. [short for *knickerbockers* < *Knickerbocker* (said to be due to the costume shown in illustrations in Washington Irving's *Knickerbocker's History of New York*)]

knick-knack (nik′nak′) *n.* a pleasing trifle; ornament; trinket. Also, **nick-nack.** [varied reduplication of *knack*]

knife (nīf) *n.* **knives,** *v.* **knifed, knif·ing.** —*n.* **1** a flat piece of steel, silver, etc. with a sharp edge, fastened in a handle and used as a cutting tool. **2** any weapon having a short blade with a sharp edge and point, as a dagger. **3** a cutting blade in a tool or machine: *The knives of a lawn mower cut grass.* **4 under the knife,** *Informal.* undergoing a surgical operation.
—*v.* **1** cut or stab with a knife. **2** pierce or cut as with a knife: *The wind knifed through his thin jacket.* **3** *Slang.* try to defeat in an underhand way. [OE *cnīf*] —**knife′like′,** *adj.*

knife edge 1 the edge of a knife. **2** anything very sharp. **3** a wedge on the fine edge of which a scale, beam, pendulum, etc. is hung.

knight (nīt) *n.* **1** in the Middle Ages, a man raised to an honorable military rank and pledged to do good deeds. After serving as a page and a squire, a man was made a knight by the king or a lord. **2** in modern times, a man raised to an honorable rank because of personal achievement or because he has won distinction in some way. A knight has the title *Sir* before his name. **3** a man devoted to the service or protection of a lady. **4** in chess, a piece usually shaped like a horse's head. **5** a member or holder of a rank or degree in any order or society that bears the official title of *Knights*: *Knights of Columbus.* —*v.* raise to the rank of knight. [OE *cniht* boy]

knight bachelor See **bachelor.**

knight banneret See **banneret.**

knight-er·rant (nīt′ər′ənt) *n.* **knights-er·rant.** a knight travelling in search of adventure.

knight-er·rant·ry (nīt′er′ən trē) *n.* **knight-er·rant·ries. 1** conduct or action characteristic of a knight-errant. **2** quixotic conduct or action.

knight·hood (nīt′hu̇d) *n.* **1** the rank or dignity of a knight. **2** the profession or occupation of a knight. **3** the character or qualities of a knight. **4** knights as a group or class: *All the knighthood of France came to the aid of the king.*

knight·ly (nīt′lē) *adj.* of, like, or having to do with a knight; brave; generous; courteous; chivalrous. —*adv.* as a knight should do; bravely; generously; courteously. —**knight′li·ness,** *n.*

Knights Hospitalers or **Hospitallers,** see **Hospitaler.**

Knights of Columbus a fraternal society of Roman Catholic men pledged to increase the religious and civic usefulness of its members and to encourage benevolence. It was founded in 1882.

Knight Templar *pl.* **Knights Templars** *for 1*; **Knights Templar** *for 2.* **1** Templar (def. 1). **2** a member of an order of Masons in the United States.

knit (nit) *v.* **knit·ted** or **knit, knit·ting. 1** make (cloth or an article of clothing) by looping yarn or thread together with long needles. **2** make an article or fabric by looping yarn or thread together: *She knits all day.* **3** form (cloth or an article of clothing) by looping stitches, not by weaving: *Jersey is cloth knitted by machine.* **4** join closely and firmly together. **5** grow together; be joined closely and firmly: *A broken bone knits.* **6** draw (the brows) together in wrinkles. [OE *cnyttan* < *cnotta* knot[1]] —**knit′ter,** *n.*

knit·ting (nit′ing) *n.* knitted work.

knitting needle one of a pair of long needles used in knitting.

knives (nīvz) *n.* pl. of **knife.**

knob (nob) *n.* **1** a rounded lump. **2** the handle of a door, drawer, etc. **3** a rounded hill or mountain. [cf. MLG *knobbe*] —**knob′like′,** *adj.* —**Syn. 1** knot, protuberance.

knobbed (nobd) *adj.* having a knob or knobs.

knob·by (nob′ē) *adj.* **-bi·er, -bi·est. 1** covered with knobs. **2** rounded like a knob. —**knob′bi·ness,** *n.*

knock (nok) *v.* **1** hit; strike a blow with the fist, knuckles, or anything hard: *He knocked him on the head.* **2** hit and cause to fall: *Bill ran against another boy and knocked him down.* **3** hit with a noise: *knock on a door.* **4** make a noise, especially a rattling or pounding noise: *The engine is knocking.* **5** *Slang.* criticize; find fault.
knock about, *Informal.* **a** wander from place to place. **b** hit repeatedly.
knock around, knock about.
knock down, a sell (an article) to the highest bidder at an auction. **b** take apart. **c** strike down.
knock off, *Informal.* **a** take off; deduct: *knock off 10 cents from the price.* **b** stop work. **c** accomplish hastily; do quickly: *He knocked off a new poem in just a few minutes.*
knock out, a hit so hard as to make helpless or unconscious. **b** drive out of the contest; vanquish.
knock together, make or put together hastily.
knock up, a tire out; exhaust. **b** *Slang.* make pregnant. **c** *Esp.Brit.* get (someone) out of bed by knocking at the door.
—*n.* **1** a hit. **2** a hit with a noise. **3** the act of knocking. **4** the sound of knocking: *She did not hear the knock at*

the door. **5** a pounding or rattling sound in an engine: *We learned that the knock was caused by inferior gasoline.* **6** a severe criticism. [OE *cnocian*] —**Syn.** *v.* **1** strike, rap, beat. **3** rap.

knock·a·bout (nok′ə bout′) *n.* **1** a small, easily handled sailboat equipped with one mast, a mainsail, and a jib, but no bowsprit. **2** *Brit.* slapstick; horseplay.
—*adj.* **1** suitable for rough use. **2** noisy; boisterous: *a knockabout farce.*

knock·er (nok′ər) *n.* **1** a person or thing that knocks. **2** a knob, ring, etc. fastened on a door for use in knocking.

knock-knee (nok′nē′) *n.* **1** an inward curving of the legs, so that the knees tend to knock together in walking. **2 knock-knees,** *pl.* knees that curve in this way.

knock-kneed (nok′nēd′) *adj.* having legs curved inward so that the knees tend to knock together in walking.

knock·out (nok′out′) *n.* **1** the act of rendering unconscious or helpless by a punch: *The boxer won the fight by a knockout.* **2** the condition of being knocked out. **3** a blow that knocks out. **4** *Slang.* a person or thing considered outstanding: *The party was a knockout.*
—*adj.* **1** *Slang.* that knocks out: *a knockout blow.* **2** that puts something out of operation or diminishes: *a knockout competition.*

knoll (nōl) *n.* a small, rounded hill; mound. [OE *cnoll*]

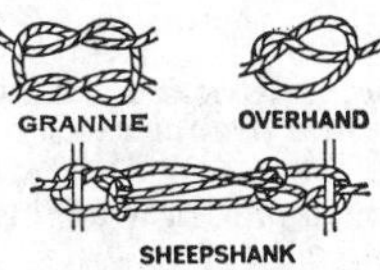

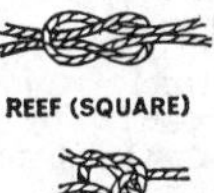

REEF (SQUARE)

SLIP

SHEEPSHANK

SHEET BEND

Some common knots

knot¹ (not) *n. v.* **knot·ted, knot·ting.** —*n.* **1** a fastening made by tying or twining together pieces of rope, cord, string, etc. **2** an accidental tying or twisting of rope, cord, string, etc., usually drawn tight; tangle. **3** a bow of ribbon, etc. worn as an ornament. **4** a group; cluster: *A knot of people stood talking outside the door.* **5** a hard mass of wood formed where a branch grows out from a tree, which shows as a roundish, cross-grained piece in a board. **6** a hard lump. A knot sometimes forms in a tired muscle. **7** in botany, a joint where leaves grow out on the stem of a plant. **8** a unit of speed used for ships and aircraft; one nautical mile per hour: *The ship averaged 12 knots.* **9** a nautical mile, about 6,080 feet. **10** a difficulty; problem. **11** something that unites closely or intricately.
—*v.* **1** tie or twine together in a knot. **2** tangle in knots. **3** make knots for (a fringe). **4** make (a fringe) by tying knots. **5** form into a hard lump. **6** unite closely or intricately. [OE *cnotta*] —**knot′ter,** *n.* —**knot′less,** *adj.*
—**Syn.** *n.* **3** company. **5** knob. **9** puzzle, perplexity. **10** bond, tie, link. –*v.* **2** snarl. **6** bind.

knot² (not) *n.* a small sandpiper, having a reddish breast, that breeds in the Canadian Arctic. [origin uncertain]

knot·grass (not′gras′) *n.* a weed whose stems have large joints.

knot·hole (not′hōl′) *n.* a hole in a board where a knot has fallen out.

knot·ted (not′id) *adj.* having a knot or knots; knotty.

knot·ty (not′ē) *adj.* **-ti·er, -ti·est. 1** full of knots: *knotty wood.* **2** difficult; puzzling: *a knotty problem.*
—**knot′ti·ly,** *adv.* —**knot′ti·ness,** *n.*

knout (nout) *n.* in Russia, a whip formerly used to inflict punishment. —*v.* flog with a knout. [< F < Russian *knut* < Scand.]

know (nō) *v.* **knew, known, know·ing,** *n.* —*v.* **1** be sure of; have true information about: *He knows the facts of the case.* **2** have firmly in the mind or memory: *know a lesson.* **3** be aware of; have seen or heard; have information about: *know a person's name.* **4** be sure or certain because of experience or knowledge: *He does not have to guess, he knows.* **5** be acquainted with; be familiar with: *I know her.* **6** have an understanding of; have experience with; be skilled in: *He knows literature.* **7** recognize; identify: *You would hardly know him since his illness.* **8** be able to tell apart from others; distinguish: *You will know his house by the red roof.*

hat, āge, cãre, fär; let, ēqual, tėrm; it, īce
hot, ōpen, ôrder; oil, out; cup, pu̇t, rüle, ūse
əbove, takən, pencəl, lemən, circəs
ch, child; ng, long; sh, ship
th, thin; ᴛʜ, then; zh, measure

9 know what's what, *Informal.* be well informed.
—*n.* **in the know,** *Informal.* having inside information. [OE *cnāwan*] —**know′er,** *n.*

Syn. *v.* **1 Know, understand** = be sure of the truth of something. **Know** emphasizes having a fact or idea firmly in mind or being well acquainted with a subject, and usually suggests seeing clearly some part of the meaning: *He knows more about Mexico than does anyone else in Canada.* **Understand** emphasizes having a thorough grasp of both facts and meaning, seeing clearly and fully not only the nature and all the implications of a fact or idea, but also its wider relationships: *He understands the workings of the stock market.*

know·a·ble (nō′ə bəl) *adj.* capable of being known.

know-all (nō′ol′ or -ôl′) *n. Slang.* know-it-all.

know-how (nō′hou′) *n. Informal.* the ability to do something; the knowledge required to get something done.

know·ing (nō′ing) *adj.* **1** having knowledge; well-informed. **2** clever; shrewd. **3** suggesting shrewd or secret understanding of matters: *His only answer was a knowing look.* —**Syn. 2** sharp, cunning.

know·ing·ly (nō′ing lē) *adv.* **1** in a knowing way. **2** with knowledge; if one knew it; on purpose: *He would not knowingly hurt anyone.*

know-it-all (nō′it ol′ or -ôl′) *n. Slang.* a person having pretensions to knowing everything.

knowl·edge (nol′ij) *n.* **1** what one knows: *His knowledge of the subject is limited.* **2** all that is known or can be learned. **3** the fact of knowing: *The knowledge of our victory caused great joy.* **4** the act of knowing. [ME *knawlechen* acknowledge, confess, ult. < OE *cnāwan* know]

Syn. 1 Knowledge, information = what a person knows. **Knowledge** applies to all that one knows and understands of facts and general truths and principles, whether gained from books and teachers or by personal experience and observation: *His knowledge of the subject is limited.* **Information** applies to things one has learned through having been told by people or books or through observation, and often suggests isolated or unrelated facts: *She has acquired much information about trips to Europe.*

knowl·edge·a·ble (nol′ij ə bəl) *adj. Informal.* well-informed, especially about a particular subject.
—**knowl′edge·a·bly,** *adv.*

known (nōn) *v.* pp. of **know.**

know-noth·ing (nō′nuth′ing) *n.* an ignorant person.

knuck·le (nuk′əl) *n. v.* **-led, -ling.** —*n.* **1** a finger joint; any of the joints between the fingers and the rest of the hand. See **joint** for picture. **2** the rounded protuberance formed when a joint is bent. **3** the knee or hock joint of an animal used as food: *boiled pigs' knuckles.* **4 knuckles,** *pl.* knuckle-duster.
—*v.* **1** put the knuckles on the ground in playing marbles. **2 knuckle down, a** *Informal.* submit; yield. **b** *Informal.* apply oneself earnestly; work hard. **3 knuckle under,** *Informal.* submit; yield: *He refused to knuckle under to his enemies.* [ME < MDu., dim. of *knoke* bone]

knuckle ball in baseball, a slow pitch thrown from the knuckles and the heel of the palm.

knuck·le·bone (nuk′əl bōn′) *n.* **1** in man, any of the finger or toe bones that forms a knuckle; the rounded end of any of these bones. **2** in animals: **a** a leg bone having a ball-like knob at the joint end; the knob itself. **b** a bone, as in a sheep, corresponding to the human finger or toe bone. **c** a piece of meat including a bone of either such kind.

knuck·le·dust·er (nuk′əl dus′tər) *n.* a piece of metal worn over the knuckles as a weapon.

knuck·le·head (nuk′əl hed′) *n. Slang.* a thoughtless or slow-witted person.

knurl (nėrl) *n.* **1** a knot; knob. **2** a small ridge, such as on the edge of a coin or round nut. [apparently dim. of *knur* knot, ME *knor(re)*; cf. MDu. *knorre*]

knurl·y (nėr′lē) *adj.* **knurl·i·er, knurl·i·est.** gnarled.

K.O. (kā′ ō′) *v.* **K.O.'d, K.O.'ing,** *n. Slang.* —*v.* knock out. —*n.* a knockout. [*k*nock + *o*ut]

ko·a·la (kō ä′ lə) *n.* a gray, furry mammal of Australia that resembles a small bear and carries its young in a pouch. Koalas live in trees and eat eucalyptus leaves. [< native Australian]

ko·bold (kō′ bold or kō′ bōld) *n.* in German folklore: **1** a sprite or goblin. **2** a gnome in mines or caves. [< G]

Ko·di·ak bear (kō′ dē ak′) a large dark-brown or yellowish-brown bear, found on Kodiak Island. It is the largest known species of bear, sometimes reaching a height of over 10 feet.

K. of C. Knight(s) of Columbus.

Kog·mol·ik (kog mō′ lik) *n.* **-ik** or **-iks,** *adj. Cdn.* —*n.* **1** an Eskimo of a number of tribes living to the east of Mackenzie Delta in the Coronation Gulf area. **2** their language. —*adj.* **kogmolik,** *Slang.* commonplace; inferior in style or quality: *a kogmolik knot.*

Koh·i·noor (kō′ ə nür′) *n.* a very large and famous diamond from India that has been one of the British crown jewels since 1849. [< Persian *kohi nur,* literally, mountain of light]

kohl·ra·bi (kōl′ rä′ bē) *n.* **-bies.** a kind of cabbage that has a turniplike edible stem. [< G < Ital. *cavoli rape,* pl. See COLE, RAPE[2].]

Koi·ne (koi nā′) *n.* **1** the common literary language of the Greeks during the Hellenistic period, based on the dialect of Attica. It is the dialect used in the New Testament. **2** Often, **koine.** a dialect or language that has become the common tongue of several peoples over a wide area. [< Gk. *koinē* (*dialektos*) common (language)]

ko·ka·nee (kō′ kə nē′) *n. Cdn.* a small landlocked sockeye salmon common in British Columbia lakes and rivers. [? < *Kokanee* Creek, B.C.]

ko·la (kō′ lə) *n.* **1** a kola nut. **2** a stimulant or tonic made from kola nuts. **3** the tree on which these nuts grow. [< native African]

kola nut a bitter, brownish nut of a tropical tree, containing about 3 per cent of caffeine.

ko·lin·sky (kə lin′ ski) *n.* **-skies. 1** any of several Asian minks. **2** its tawny fur. **3** a coat or other garment made of this fur. [< Russian *kolinski,* adj. < *Kola,* a region of the Soviet Union]

ko·ma·tik (kō′ mə tik′) *n. Cdn.* in the North, a sled, especially a wooden sled used by the Eskimos. [< Eskimo]

Kom·so·mol (kom′ sə mol′) *n.* **1** a Soviet youth organization for people between the ages of 14 and 23. **2** a member of this organization. [< Russian abbrev. of *Kommunisticheskij Sojuz Molodezhi* Communist League of Youth]

koo·doo (kü′ dü) *n.* **-doos.** kudu.

kook (kük) *n. Slang.* a queer or peculiar person. [? < *cuckoo*]

kook·a·bur·ra (ku̇k′ ə bėr′ ə) *n.* a bird of Australia and New Zealand; a laughing jackass. [< native Australian]

kook·y or **kook·ie** (kü′ kē) *adj. Slang.* queer; peculiar.

koo·le·tah (kü′ lə tä′) *n.* kuletuk.

koo·li·tak (kü′ lə täk′) *n.* kuletuk.

Koo·ten·ay (kü′ tə nā′) *n.* **Koo·ten·ay** or **Koo·ten·ays. 1** a tribe of Indians living near Kootenay Lake in S.E. British Columbia. **2** a member of this tribe. **3** the unique language of this tribe.

ko·peck or **ko·pek** (kō′ pek) *n.* **1** a unit of money in the Soviet Union, worth 1/100 of a ruble. **2** a coin worth one kopeck. [<Russian *kopejka,* orig. dim. of *kop'e* spear (kopecks minted from 1535-1719 bore a figure of Ivan IV with a lance)]

Ko·ran (kô rän′ or kô ran′) *n.* the sacred book of the Moslems, consisting of reports of revelations to the prophet Mohammed. [< Arabic *quran* recitation < *qara'a* read]

Kor·a·tron (kôr′ ə tron′) *n. Trademark.* a resin finish that is heat-cured into a fabric after cutting and imparts permanent crease and shape to a garment.

Ko·re·an (kə rē′ ən or kô rē′ ən) *adj.* of or having to do with Korea, a peninsula in E. Asia, its people, or their language. —*n.* **1** a native or inhabitant of Korea. **2** the language of Korea.

ko·ru·na (kô′ rü nä′) *n.* **1** a unit of money in Czechoslovakia. See table at **money. 2** a coin worth one koruna. [< Czech < L *corona* crown]

ko·sher (kō′ shər) *adj.* **1** right or clean according to Jewish ritualistic law. Kosher meat is from an animal killed by a rabbi according to a prescribed ritual. **2** dealing in products that meet the requirements of Jewish law: *a kosher butcher, supermarket, etc.* **3** *Slang.* all right; fine; legitimate: *It's not kosher to change the rules once the game has started.*
—*v.* prepare (food) according to the Jewish law.
—*n. Informal.* **1** food thus prepared. **2** a shop selling such food. [< Hebrew *kasher* proper]

ko·tow (kō′ tou′) *v.* kowtow.

kou·mis or **kou·miss** or **kou·myss** (kü′ mis) *n.* kumiss.

kow·tow (kou′ tou′) *v.* **1** kneel and touch the ground with the forehead to show deep respect, submission, or worship. **2** show slavish respect or obedience (*to*). —*n.* the act of kowtowing. [< Chinese *k'o-t'ou,* literally, knock (the) head] —**kow′tow′er,** *n.*

K.P. *Esp.U.S.* kitchen police. This abbreviation is sometimes used to mean menial work.

Kr krypton.

K.R. King's Regulations.

kraal (kräl) *n.* in South Africa: **1** a native village protected by a fence. **2** a pen for cattle or sheep. [< Afrikaans < Pg. *curral* corral]

kraft (kraft) *n.* a tough, brown wrapping paper made from chemically treated wood pulp. [< G *Kraft* strength]

kraut or **Kraut** (krout) *n. Derogatory slang.* a German. [< Sauer*kraut,* food commonly associated with Germans]

Krem·lin (krem′ lən) *n.* the citadel of Moscow. The chief offices of the Soviet government are in the Kremlin. [< F < Russian *kreml* citadel < Tartar]

kris (krēs) *n.* a dagger with a wavy blade, used by the Malays. Also, **creese.** [< Malay]

Krish·na (krish′ nə) *n.* one of the most important Hindu gods, one of the incarnations of Vishnu. [< Sanskrit]

Kriss Krin·gle (kris′ kring′ gəl) Santa Claus. [< G dial. *Christkindl* Christ child, Christmas gift]

kro·na (krō′ nə) *n.* **-nor** (-nôr). **1** a unit of money in Iceland and Sweden. See table at **money. 2** a coin worth one krona. [ult. < L *corona* crown]

kro·ne[1] (krō′ nə) *n.* **-ner** (-nər). **1** a unit of money in Denmark and Norway. See table at **money. 2** a coin worth one krone. [ult. < L *corona* crown]

kro·ne[2] (krō′ nə) *n.* **-nen** (-nən). **1** a former German gold coin, worth about $2.38. **2** a former Austrian silver coin, worth about 20 cents. [< G *Krone* < L *corona* crown]

krul·ler (krul′ ər) *n.* cruller.

kryp·ton (krip′ ton) *n.* a rare, inert, gaseous chemical element. *Symbol*: Kr; *at.no.* 36; *at.wt.* 83.80. [< NL < Gk. *krypton,* neut. adj., hidden]

Kt. Knight.

K.T. 1 Knight Templar. **2** Knight of the (Order of the) Thistle.

kud·lik (küd′ lik) *n. Cdn.* a dishlike soapstone lamp that burns caribou or seal oil, used by Eskimos. [< Eskimo *gudlik*]

ku·dos (kū′ dos or kü′ dos) *n. Informal.* prestige; glory; fame. [< Gk. *kydos*]

ku·du (kü′ dü) *n.* a large, grayish-brown African antelope having white stripes. Also, **koodoo.** [< Hottentot]

Ku Klux Klan (kū′ kluks′ klan′ or kü′-) *n. U.S.* **1** a secret society of white people formed in the S. United States after the Civil War to regain and maintain their control. **2** a secret society founded in the U.S. in 1915, opposed to Negroes, Jews, Catholics, and foreigners. *Abbrev.*: KKK [probably < Gk. *kyklos* circle + E *clan*]

ku·lak (kü läk′) *n.* **1** in Russia, formerly, a well-to-do peasant, farmer, or trader who opposed collectivization. **2** a Russian peasant who owns and tills his land for his own profit. [< Russian *kulak,* literally, fist; hence, tight-fisted]

hat, āge, cãre, fär; let, ēqual, tėrm; it, īce
hot, ōpen, ôrder; oil, out; cup, pu̇t, rüle, ūse
əbove, takən, pencəl, lemən, circəs
ch, child; ng, long; sh, ship
th, thin; ᴛʜ, then; zh, measure

ku·le·tuk (kü′lə tuk′) *n. Cdn.* a hooded, close-fitting jacket made of skin, often trimmed with fur; parka. Also, **koolitah, koolitak.**

ku·mik (kü′mik) *n.* kamik.

ku·miss (kü′mis) *n.* **1** fermented mare's or camel's milk used as a drink by Asiatic nomads. **2** a drink made from cow's milk, used in special diets. **3** an intoxicating liquor distilled from Asian kumiss (def. 1). Also, **koumis, koumiss,** or **koumyss.** [< Russian *kumys* < Tatar *kumiz*]

küm·mel (kim′əl) *n.* a liqueur flavored with caraway seeds, anise, etc. [< G]

kum·mer·bund (kum′ər bund′) *n.* cummerbund.

kum·quat (kum′kwot) *n.* **1** a yellow fruit resembling a small orange. **2** the tree that it grows on. Also, **cumquat.** [< Chinese (Cantonese dial.)]

Kuo·min·tang (kwō′min tang′ or kwō′min täng′) *n.* a Chinese nationalist party organized in 1912.

Kurd (kėrd or kürd) *n.* a member of a nomadic and warlike Moslem people living chiefly in Kurdistan, a region in S.W. Asia, divided between Turkey, Iran, and Iraq.

Kur·dish (kėr′dish or kür′dish) *adj.* of or having to do with the Kurds or their language. *—n.* the language of the Kurds; a dialect of Iranian.

ku·rus (kə rush′) *n.* **kurus. 1** a unit of money in Turkey, worth 1/100 of a lira. **2** a coin worth one kurus. [< Turkish]

kv. kilovolt; kilovolts.

K.V.A., KVA, or **kva** kilovolt-ampere; kilovolt-amperes.

kw. kilowatt; kilowatts.

kwa·cha (kwä′chä) *n.* **1** a unit of money in Malawi and Zambia. See table at **money. 2** a coin or note worth one kwacha. [native term; literally, dawn]

Kwa·ki·u·tl (kwä′kē ü′təl or kwä kū′təl) *n.* **Kwa·ki·u·tl** or **Kwa·ki·u·tls. 1** a Wakashan tribe of Indians living on the shores of Queen Charlotte Sound and on N. Vancouver Island. **2** a member of this tribe. **3** the language of this tribe.

KWH, kwh, or **kw-hr** kilowatt hour.

Ky. Kentucky.

kyat (kyät) *n.* **1** a unit of money in Burma. See table at **money. 2** a coin worth one kyat. [< Burmese]

L or **l** (el) *n.* **L's** or **l's. 1** the twelfth letter of the English alphabet. **2** any speech sound represented by this letter. **3** one (usually twelfth) of a series designated alphabetically. **4** anything shaped like L.

l. or **l** **1** litre. **2** line. **3** league. **4** length. **5** lira; lire. **6** leaf. **7** left. **8** book (for L *liber*).

L **1** Latin. **2** in physics, length. **3** longitude. **4** pound (sterling). **5** Libra. **6** large. **7** the land element of the Canadian Forces. **8** the Roman numeral for 50.

L. **1** Latin. **2** low. **3** licentiate. **4** lake.

£ pound (or pounds) sterling.

la[1] (lä) *n.* in music, a syllable used for the sixth tone of an eight-tone scale. See **do**[2] for diagram. [see GAMUT]

la[2] (lä) *interj. Archaic.* an exclamation of surprise.

La lanthanum.

La. Louisiana.

L.A. **1** Legislative Assembly. **2** Los Angeles.

lab (lab) *n. Informal.* laboratory.

Lab. **1** Labrador. **2** *Brit.* **a** Labour (Party). **b** Labourite.

la·bel (lā′bəl) *n. v.* **-belled** or **-beled, -bel·ling** or **-bel·ing.** *—n.* **1** a slip of paper or other material attached to anything and marked to show what or whose it is, or where it is to go. **2** a short phrase used to describe some person, thing, or idea: *"Land of Opportunity" is a label often given to Canada.*
—v. **1** put or write a label on: *The bottle is labelled "Poison."* **2** put in a class; call; name: *He hesitated to label the man a liar.* **3** infuse or treat (a substance) with a radio-active chemical or isotope so that its course or activity can be noted. [ME < OF < Gmc.] **—la′bel·ler** or **la′bel·er,** *n.*

la·bel·lum (lə bel′əm) *n.* **-bel·la** (-bel′ə). in botany, the middle petal of an orchid, usually different in shape and color from the other two and suggestive of a lip. [< L *labellum*, dim. of *labium* lip]

la·bi·al (lā′bē əl) *adj.* **1** of the lips. **2** in phonetics, articulated by closing, nearly closing, or rounding the lips. **3** in music, having tones produced by the impact of an air current on the edge of a lip, as a flute or an organ flue pipe. *—n.* **1** in phonetics, a sound articulated with the lips. **2** in music, a flue pipe, as distinguished from a reed pipe. [< Med.L *labialis* < L *labium* lip]

la·bi·ate (lā′bē āt′ or lā′bē it) *adj.* having one or more liplike parts. [< NL *labiatus* < L *labium* lip]

la·bile (lā′bīl or lā′bəl) *adj.* liable to change; unstable. [< L *labilis* < *labi* fall]

la·bil·i·ty (lə bil′ə tē) *n.* **-ties.** the state of being labile.

labio- *combining form.* made with the lips and ——: *labio-dental = made with the lips and teeth.*

la·bi·o·den·tal (lā′bē ō den′təl) in phonetics: *—adj.* articulated with the lower lip and upper teeth; articulated with the lips and teeth. *—n.* a sound articulated in this way. The sounds (f) and (v) are labiodentals.

la·bi·um (lā′bē əm) *n.* **-bi·a** (-bē ə). **1** a lip or liplike part. **2** in botany, a portion of the corolla of certain flowers, especially the lower part, shaped to suggest a lip. [< L]

la·bor or **la·bour** (lā′bər) *n.* **1** work; toil. **2** a piece of work; task. **3** work done by skilled and unskilled workers who are not clerks, managers, professional workers, or owners. **4** in economics, the work of human beings that produces goods or services. *Land, labor,* and *capital* are the three principal factors of production. **5** skilled and unskilled workers as a group: *Labor favors a seven-hour day.* **6** the process of childbirth.
—v. **1** work; toil. **2** do work; work hard. **3** elaborate with effort or in detail: *The speaker labored the point so much that we lost interest.* **4** move slowly and heavily: *The ship labored in the high waves.* **5** be burdened, troubled, or distressed: *labor under a misapprehension.* **6** be in childbirth. [ME < OF < L *labor*] **—Syn.** *n.* **1** See **work.**

lab·o·ra·to·ry (lab′rə tô′rē or lə bô′rə trē) *n.* **-ries. 1** a place where scientific work is done; a room or building fitted with apparatus for conducting scientific investigations, experiments, tests, etc. **2** a place fitted up for manufacturing chemicals, medicines, explosives, etc. **3** any place, not a classroom or library, equipped for systematic study: *a language laboratory.* [< Med.L *laboratorium* < L *laborare* to work < *labor* work]

Labor Day or **Labour Day** the first Monday in September, a legal holiday in Canada and the United States in honor of labor and laborers.

la·bored or **la·boured** (lā′bərd) *adj.* done with effort; forced; not easy or natural. —**la′bored·ly** or **la′boured·ly,** *adv.* —**Syn.** See **elaborate.**

la·bor·er or **la·bour·er** (lā′bər ər) *n.* **1** a worker. **2** a person who does work requiring strength rather than skill or training.

la·bo·ri·ous (lə bô′rē əs) *adj.* **1** requiring much work; requiring hard work: *Climbing a mountain is laborious.* **2** hard-working; industrious: *Bees and ants are laborious insects.* **3** showing signs of effort; not easy. [< L *laboriosus* < *labor* labor] —**la·bo′ri·ous·ly,** *adv.* —**la·bo′ri·ous·ness,** *n.*

la·bor·ite or **la·bour·ite** (lā′bər īt′) *n.* a member of a labor party.

labor party or **labour party** **1** any political party organized to protect and promote the interests of workers. **2** See **labour party.**

Labor Progressive Party *Cdn.* formerly, the official name of the Communist party in Canada.

la·bor-sav·ing or **la·bour-sav·ing** (lā′bər sāv′ing) *adj.* that takes the place of or lessens labor.

labor union or **labour union** an association of workers to protect and promote their common interests, and for dealing collectively with employers.

la·bour (lā′bər) *n. v.* labor.

la·bour·ite (lā′bər īt′) *n.* **1** a laborite. **2 Labourite,** in Great Britain, a member of the Labour Party.

labour party **1** a labor party. **2 Labour Party,** in Great Britain, a political party that claims especially to protect and advance the interests of working people. It was founded by the trade unions.

Lab·ra·dor Current (lab′rə dôr′) the cold arctic current that flows southward past Labrador and Newfoundland, where it joins the Gulf Stream.

lab·ra·dor·ite (lab′rə dôr īt′ or lab′rə dôr′ īt) *n.* **1** a kind of feldspar that gleams with brilliant colors. **2** a piece of this stone, or a gem made from it. [< *Labrador,* where it is found + *-ite*]

Labrador retriever **1** a breed of medium-sized hunting dog, having a thick, water-resistant coat that is black, chocolate, or yellow. It is used as a retriever on both land and water. **2** a dog of this breed. [< *Labrador,* where the breed was originated]

Labrador tea **1** any of a group of small evergreen shrubs growing in arctic and subarctic swamplands. **2** a kind of tea brewed from its leaves.

la·bret (lā′bret) *n.* an ornament of bone, shell, wood, etc. stuck into or through the lower lip to stretch it, worn by various primitive peoples. [< *labrum* + *-et*]

la·brum (lā′brəm or lab′rəm) *n.* **la·bra** (lā′brə or lab′rə). **1** a lip or liplike part. **2** in anatomy, a ring of cartilage surrounding a bony socket.

la·bur·num (lə bėr′nəm) *n.* a small tree or shrub having hanging clusters of yellow flowers. [< L]

lab·y·rinth (lab′ə rinth′ or lab′rinth) *n.* **1** a place through which it is hard to find one's way; maze. **2** a confusing, complicated arrangement. **3** a confusing, complicated state of affairs. **4 Labyrinth,** in Greek mythology, the maze built by Daedalus for King Minos of Crete. The Minotaur was kept there. **5** in anatomy, the inner ear. [< L < Gk. *labyrinthos*]

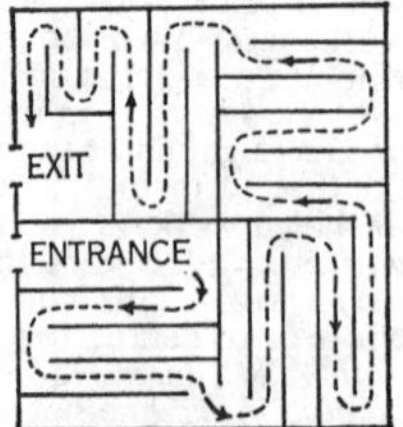

A diagram of a labyrinth (def. 1) designed to puzzle a person or animal trying to find their way through.

lab·y·rin·thine (lab′ə rin′thən or lab′ə rin′thēn′) *adj.* **1** of a labyrinth; forming a labyrinth. **2** intricate; confusing; complicated.

lac (lak) *n.* a resinous substance deposited on trees in S. Asia by certain insects. Lac is used in making sealing wax, varnish, red dye, etc. [< Hind. *lakh* < Skt. *laksha*]

L.A.C. Leading Aircraftman.

lace (lās) *n. v.* **laced, lac·ing.** —*n.* **1 a** a delicate netlike fabric having ornamental designs of threads applied by hand or machine. **b** any of several kinds of fabrics having a similar appearance. **2** a cord, string, leather strip, etc. for pulling or holding together. **3** gold or silver braid used for trimming. Some uniforms have lace on them. —*v.* **1** trim with lace. **2** put laces through; pull or hold together with a lace or laces. **3** be laced: *These shoes lace easily.* **4** adorn or trim with narrow braid: *His uniform was laced with gold.* **5** interlace; intertwine. **6** mark with streaks; streak: *a white petunia laced with purple.* **7** *Informal.* lash; beat; thrash. **8** add a dash of brandy, whisky, etc. to (a beverage, especially coffee). **9** squeeze in the waist by a tight corset. **10 lace into, a** attack. **b** criticize severely. [ME < OF *laz* < L *laqueus* noose. Doublet of LASSO.] —**lace′like′,** *adj.*

Lac·e·dae·mo·ni·an (las′ə dē mō′nē ən) *adj. n.* Spartan.

lac·er·ate (*v.* las′ər āt′; *adj.* las′ə rāt′ or las′ər it) *v.* **-at·ed, -at·ing,** *adj.* —*v.* **1** tear roughly; mangle: *The bear's claws lacerated his flesh.* **2** wound; hurt (the feelings, etc.). —*adj.* **1** deeply or irregularly indented as if torn: *lacerate leaves.* **2** torn; jagged. [< L *lacerare* < *lacer* mangled]

lac·er·a·tion (las′ər ā′shən) *n.* **1** a lacerating. **2** a rough tear; mangled place; wound.

lace·wing (lās′wing′) *n.* an insect that has four lacelike wings.

lace·work (lās′wėrk′) *n.* **1** lace. **2** openwork like lace.

lach·es (lach′iz) *n.* in law, failure to do a thing at the right time; inexcusable negligence. [ME < OF *laschesse,* ult. < L *laxus* loose]

Lach·e·sis (lak′ə sis) *n.* in Greek mythology, one of the three Fates. Lachesis measures off the thread of human life.

lach·ry·mal (lak′rə məl) *adj.* **1** of tears; producing tears. **2** for tears. **3** in anatomy, of, having to do with, or situated near the glands (lachrymal glands) that secrete tears, or the ducts leading from them. —*n.* **lachrymals,** *pl.* in anatomy, the glands that produce tears. Also, **lacrimal.** [< Med.L *lachrymalis* < L *lacrima* tear]

lach·ry·ma·to·ry (lak′rə mə tô′rə) *adj. n.* **-ries.** —*adj.* **1** of tears; producing tears. **2** for tears. —*n.* a small vase with a narrow neck found in ancient Roman tombs and once believed to be used to hold the tears of mourning friends.

lach·ry·mose (lak′rə mōs′) *adj.* tearful; mournful. [< L *lacrimosus* < *lacrima* tear] —**lach′ry·mose·ly,** *adv.*

lac·ing (lās′ing) *n.* **1** a cord, string, etc. for pulling or holding something together. **2** gold or silver braid used for trimming. **3** *Informal.* a lashing; beating; thrashing.

lack (lak) *v.* **1** have less than enough; need: *A desert lacks water.* **2** be without: *A homeless person lacks a home.* **3** be absent or missing. —*n.* **1** a shortage; not having enough: *Lack of rest made her tired.* **2** the fact or condition of being without: *Lack of a fire made him cold.* **3** the thing needed: *If you are cold, your lack is heat.* **4 supply the lack,** supply what is needed. [cf. MDu. *lac,* MLG *lak*]

Syn. *v.* **1, 2 Lack, want, need** = be without something. **Lack** = be completely without or without enough of something, good or bad: *A coward lacks courage.* **Want** = lack something worth having, desired, or, especially, necessary for completeness: *That dress wants a belt.* **Need** = lack something required for a purpose or that cannot be done without: *He does not have the tools he needs. She needs more sleep.* -*n.* **1** deficiency.

lack·a·dai·si·cal (lak′ə dā′zə kəl) *adj.* languid; listless; dreamy; weakly sentimental. [< *lackaday*] —**lack′a·dai′si·cal·ly,** *adv.* —**lack′a·dai′si·cal·ness,** *n.*

lack·a·day (lak′ə dā′) *interj. Archaic.* alas. [var. of *alack a day!*]

lack·ey (lak′ē) *n.* **-eys,** *v.* **-eyed, -ey·ing.** —*n.* **1** a male servant; footman. **2** a slavish follower. —*v.* **1** wait on. **2** be slavish to. [< F *laquais* < Sp. *lacayo* foot soldier]

lack·ing (lak′ing) *adj.* **1** not having enough; deficient: *A weak person is lacking in strength.* **2** absent; not present: *Water is lacking because the pipe is broken.* —*prep.* without; not having: *Lacking anything better, use what you have.*

lack·lus·tre or **lack·lus·ter** (lak′lus′tər) *adj.* not shining or bright; dull.

la·con·ic (lə kon′ik) *adj.* using few words; brief in speech or expression; concise. [< L < Gk. *lakōnikos* Spartan; Spartans were noted for the brevity, or terseness, of their speech]

la·con·i·cal·ly (lə kon′ik lē) *adv.* in few words; briefly; concisely.

lac·o·nism (lak′ə niz′əm) *n.* **1** laconic brevity. **2** a laconic speech or expression.

lac·quer (lak′ər) *n.* **1** a varnish consisting of shellac dissolved in alcohol, used for coating brass and other metals. **2** a varnish made from the resin of a sumac tree of S.E. Asia. It gives a very high polish on wood. **3** wooden articles coated with such varnish. **4** a dressing for the hair, made from gum or resin. **5** a nail polish. —*v.* coat with lacquer. [< F < Pg. *laca* lac[1]] —**lac′quer·er,** *n.*

lac·ri·mal (lak′rə məl) *adj. n.* lachrymal.

la·crosse (lə kros′) *n. Cdn.* a game played, as a rule, on a field by two teams of 12 players equipped with lacrosse sticks, by means of which an India rubber ball is carried and passed from player to player in an attempt to score a goal. [< Cdn.F *la crosse,* the racket used in the game]

lacrosse stick an L-shaped stick strung with leather thongs that form a kind of pouch for carrying the ball in the game of lacrosse.

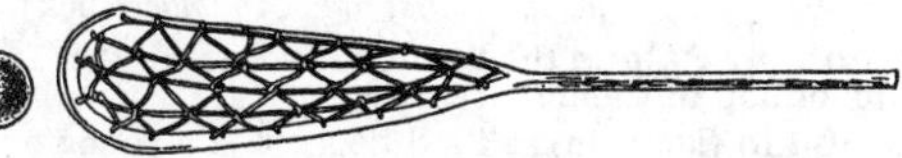

A lacrosse stick and ball

lac·tate[1] (lak′tāt) *n.* any salt of lactic acid. [< *lact(ic acid)* + *-ate*[2]]

lac·tate[2] (lak′tāt) *v.* **-tat·ed, -tat·ing. 1** secrete milk. **2** give suck. **3** convert into milk; cause to resemble milk. [< L *lactare* suckle, with E *-ate*[1]]

lac·ta·tion (lak tā′shən) *n.* **1** the act of suckling a baby. **2** the time during which a mother gives milk. **3** the secretion or formation of milk.

lac·te·al (lak′tē əl) *adj.* **1** of milk; like milk; milky. **2** carrying chyle, a milky liquid formed from digested food. —*n.* in anatomy, any of the tiny vessels that carry chyle from the small intestine to be mixed with the blood in the thoracic duct. [< L *lacteus* < *lac* milk]

lac·te·ous (lak′tē əs) *adj.* milky.

lac·tic (lak′tik) *adj.* of milk; from milk. [< L *lac, lactis* milk]

lactic acid a colorless, odorless acid formed in sour milk, in the fermentation of vegetable juices, etc. *Formula:* $C_3H_6O_3$

lac·to·fla·vin (lak′tō flā′vən) *n.* riboflavin.

lac·tom·e·ter (lak tom′ə tər) *n.* an instrument for testing the purity or richness of milk. [< *lacto-* milk (< L *lac*) + *-meter*]

lac·tose (lak′tōs) *n.* a white, odorless crystalline sugar present in milk; milk sugar. *Formula:* $C_{12}H_{22}O_{11}$ [< L *lac, lactis* milk]

la·cu·na (lə kū′nə) *n.* **-nas, -nae** (-nē or -nī). **1** an empty space; gap; blank: *There were several lacunas in her letter where words had been erased.* **2** in biology, a tiny cavity in bones or tissues. [< L *lacuna* hole < *lacus* cistern, lake. Doublet of LAGOON.]

la·cus·trine (lə kus′trin) *adj.* **1** of lakes. **2** in or on lakes: *Some prehistoric peoples built lacustrine dwellings.* [< L *lacustris,* adj. of *lacus* lake + E *-ine*[1]]

lac·y (lās′ē) *adj.* **lac·i·er, lac·i·est. 1** of lace. **2** like lace; having an open pattern. —**lac′i·ly,** *adv.* —**lac′i·ness,** *n.*

lad (lad) *n.* **1** a boy; young man. **2** *Informal.* a man. [ME *ladde*]

lad·der (lad′ər) *n.* **1** a set of rungs or steps fastened to two long sidepieces, for use in climbing. **2** a means of climbing higher. **3** an ascending series of little pools built to enable fish to swim upstream past a dam or falls; fishway. **4** anything resembling or suggesting a ladder: *This company has an elaborate promotion ladder.* **5** a run in a knitted garment.
—*v.* of knitted garments, especially stockings, develop ladders as the result of the breaking of a thread. [OE *hlǣder*] —**lad′der·like′,** *adj.*

hat, āge, cãre, fär; let, ēqual, tėrm; it, īce
hot, ōpen, ôrder; oil, out; cup, pu̇t, rüle, ūse
əbove, takən, pencəl, lemən, circəs
ch, child; ng, long; sh, ship
th, thin; ᴛʜ, then; zh, measure

lad·die (lad′ē) *n. Scottish.* **1** a young boy. **2** a man.

lade (lād) *v.* **lad·ed, lad·en** or **lad·ed, lad·ing. 1** put a burden on; load. **2** dip; scoop; ladle. **3** take on cargo. [OE *hladan*]

lad·en (lād′ən) *adj.* loaded; burdened. —*v.* a pp. of **lade.**

lad·ing (lād′ing) *n.* **1** the act of loading. **2** a load; freight; cargo.

la·dle (lā′dəl) *n. v.* **-dled, -dling.** —*n.* a large, cup-shaped spoon with a long handle, for dipping out liquids.
—*v.* **1** dip out. **2** carry in a ladle. [OE *hlædel* < *hladan* lade] —**la′dler,** *n.*

A ladle

la·dy (lā′dē) *n.* **-dies. 1** a woman who has the rights or authority of a lord; a mistress of a household. **2** a noblewoman; a woman who has the title of Lady. **3** a woman of refinement and courtesy. **4** a woman of high social position. **5 Lady,** in the United Kingdom, a title given to women of certain ranks of nobility: **a** a marchioness, countess, viscountess, or baroness. **b** a daughter of a duke, marquis, or earl. **c** the wife of a man having a courtesy title of Lord. **d** the wife or widow of a knight or baronet. **6** any woman. **7** a woman whom a man loves or is devoted to. **8** a wife. **9 Our Lady,** the Virgin Mary. [OE *hlǣfdīge,* literally, loaf-kneader] —**Syn. 3, 4** See **female.**

☛ **lady.** In formal English *lady* is used to mean a well-bred woman; a woman of high social position. Though *lady* is often used in everyday speech to refer to any woman, no matter what her social position or background (*lady cab driver, lady clerk*), the term is usually considered too affected. *Woman* would be more appropriate in such cases. ☛ See **man** for another usage note.

la·dy·bird (lā′dē bėrd′) *n.* ladybug.

la·dy·bug (lā′dē bug′) *n.* a small, round beetle having an orange shell covered with black spots. Ladybugs eat aphids and other destructive insects.

Lady Day March 25, the day the angel told Mary that she would be the mother of Jesus; Annunciation Day.

la·dy·fin·ger (lā′dē fing′gər) *n.* a small sponge cake that resembles a finger in size and shape.

la·dy-in-wait·ing (lā′dē in wāt′ing) *n.* **la·dies-in-wait·ing.** a lady who is an attendant of a queen or princess.

la·dy-kill·er (lā′dē kil′ər) *n. Slang.* a man supposed to be dangerously fascinating to women.

la·dy·like (lā′dē līk′) *adj.* **1** like a lady. **2** suitable for a lady. —**Syn. 1** refined, well-bred.

la·dy·love (lā′dē luv′) *n.* a woman who is loved by a man; sweetheart.

la·dy·ship (lā′dē ship′) *n.* **1** the rank or position of a lady. **2** Often, **Ladyship.** in the United Kingdom, a title used in speaking to or of a woman having the rank of Lady: "*your Ladyship,*" "*her Ladyship.*"

la·dy-slip·per (lā′dē slip′ər) *n.* a lady's-slipper.

la·dy's-slip·per (lā′dēz slip′ər) *n.* a wild orchid whose flower resembles a slipper.

lag[1] (lag) *v.* **lagged, lag·ging,** *n.* —*v.* **1** move too slowly; fall behind: *The child lagged because he was tired.* **2** in physics, (of an electric current) fall behind (the voltage) in speed or response to alternations. **3** in economic statistics, follow changes in another variable by a regular interval: *Changes in employment tend to lag changes in*

wholesale prices.
—*n.* **1** a lagging. **2** the amount by which a person or thing lags. **3** in physics, the retardation, or amount of retardation, in any current or movement. **4** the last or hindmost one (in a race, game, sequence of any kind). [origin unknown] —**lag′ger,** *n.* —**Syn.** *v.* See **linger.**

lag[2] (lag) *n. v.* **lagged, lag·ging.** —*n.* **1** a strip of material used in encasing or insulating a drum, boiler, etc. **2** a barrel stave or slat. —*v.* cover with insulating material. [? < Scand; cf. Old Icelandic *lögg* barrel rim < Swedish *lagg* stave]

la·ger (lä′gər) *n.* a light beer which is slowly fermented at a low temperature and stored from six weeks to six months before being used. [short for *lager beer,* half translation of G *Lagerbier* < *Lager* bed, storehouse + *Bier* beer]

lag·gard (lag′ərd) *n.* a person who moves too slowly or falls behind; backward person. —*adj.* slow; falling behind; backward. —**lag′gard·ly,** *adv.* —**lag′gard·ness,** *n.*

lag·ging (lag′ing) *n.* **1** a lag[2] (def. 1) or lags. **2** the act of lagging. **3** planking or framing to prevent cave-ins of earthwork, or to support an arch in construction.

la·goon (lə gün′) *n.* **1** a pond or small lake connected with a larger body of water. **2** shallow water separated from the sea by low sandbanks. **3** the water within a ring-shaped coral island. [< Ital. *laguna* < L *lacuna* pond, hole. Doublet of LACUNA.]

la·ic (lā′ik) *adj.* lay; secular. —*n.* a layman. [< LL *laicus* < Gk. *laikos* < *laos* people. Doublet of LAY[2].]

laid (lād) *v.* pt. and pp. of **lay**[1]. —*adj.* **1 laid up, a** stored up; put away for future use. **b** *Informal.* forced by illness to stay indoors or in bed. **c** of ships, dismantled and put in dock. **2** marked with close parallel lines or watermarks: *laid paper.*

lain (lān) *v.* pp. of **lie**[2].

lair (lãr) *n.* the den or resting place of a wild animal. [OE *leger* < *licgan* lie[2]]

laird (lãrd) *n. Scottish.* an owner of land, especially of a landed estate. [Scottish var. of *lord*]

lais·sez faire or **lais·ser faire** (les′ā fãr′) **1** the principle of letting people do as they please. **2** the absence of governmental regulation and interference in trade, business, industry, etc. [< F *laissez faire* allow to do]

lais·sez-faire (les′ā fãr′) *adj.* of or based on laissez faire.

la·i·ty (lā′ə tē) *n.* **-ties.** laymen; the people as distinguished from the clergy or from a professional class: *Doctors use many words that the laity do not understand.* [< *lay*[3] + *-ity*]

lake[1] (lāk) *n.* **1** a large body of water usually surrounded by land. **2** a wide place in a river. [< L *lacus*]

lake[2] (lāk) *n.* **1** a deep-red or purplish-red coloring matter. **2** an insoluble colored compound formed from animal, vegetable, or coal tar coloring matters and metallic oxides. **3** a pool of liquid, as of oil, tar, etc. [< F *laque,* ult. < Persian *lak*]

lake dweller in prehistoric times, a person who lived in a house built on piles over a lake.

lake dwelling in prehistoric times, a house built on piles over a lake.

lake·front (lāk′frunt′) *n.* the land fronting on a lake.

Lake·head (lāk′hed′) *n.* the city of Thunder Bay, Ontario, and the surrounding region, on the northwest shore of Lake Superior. Also, **lakehead.**

lak·er (lāk′ər) *n.* **1** a person living or working on a lake. **2** a lake boat, especially one operating on the Great Lakes. **3** a lake fish, especially a lake trout.

lake trout a large dark trout with gray or yellowish spots, found in cold lakes of Canada and the northern United States. It may weigh up to 100 pounds when full-grown.

lam (lam) *n. Slang.* **on the lam, a** escaping. **b** in hiding. [origin unknown]

lam. laminated.

la·ma (lä′mə or lam′ə) *n.* in Tibet and Mongolia, a Buddhist priest or monk. [< Tibetan *blama*]

La·ma·ism (lä′mə iz′əm or lam′ə iz′əm) *n.* the religious system of the lamas in Tibet and Mongolia, a form of Buddhism.

La·marck·i·an (lə mär′kē ən) *adj.* of Jean de Lamarck, 1744-1829, a French biologist, or of Lamarckism. —*n.* a person who supports Lamarckism.

La·marck·ism (lə mär′kiz əm) *n.* the evolutionary theory of Jean de Lamarck (1744-1829), a French scientist who held that characteristics acquired by parents tend to be inherited by their descendants.

la·ma·ser·y (lä′mə ser′ē or lam′ə ser′ē) *n.* **-ser·ies.** in Tibet and Mongolia, a building, or group of buildings, where lamas live, work, and worship.

lamb (lam) *n.* **1** a young sheep. **2** the meat from a lamb. **3** lambskin. **4 the Lamb,** Jesus Christ. John 1:29 and 36. **5** a young, dear, or innocent person. **6** *Slang.* **a** a person who is easily cheated. **b** an inexperienced speculator. **7** *Informal.* Persian lamb. **8 like a lamb, a** meekly; timidly. **b** easily fooled. —*v.* give birth to a lamb or lambs. [OE] —**lamb′like′,** *adj.*

lam·baste (lam bāst′) *v.* **-bast·ed, -bast·ing.** *Slang.* **1** beat; thrash. **2** scold roughly; denounce. [? < *lam* beat, thrash (cf. ON *lemja* and E *lame*) + *baste*[3]]

lamb·da (lam′də) *n.* the 11th letter of the Greek alphabet (Λ, λ).

lam·ben·cy (lam′bən sē) *n.* a lambent quality or condition.

lam·bent (lam′bənt) *adj.* **1** moving lightly over a surface: *a lambent flame.* **2** playing lightly and brilliantly over a subject: *a lambent wit.* **3** softly bright: *Moonlight is lambent.* [< L *lambens, -entis,* ppr. of *lambere* lick]

Lambeth Palace the London residence of the Archbishop of Canterbury.

lamb·kin (lam′kin) *n.* **1** a little lamb. **2** a young or dear person.

Lamb of God Christ. John 1: 29 and 36.

lam·bre·quin (lam′brə kin or lam′bər kin) *n.* a drapery covering the top of a window or door, or hanging from a shelf. [< F]

lamb·skin (lam′skin′) *n.* **1** the skin of a lamb, especially with the wool on it. **2** leather made from the skin of a lamb. **3** parchment.

lambs·quar·ter (lamz′ kwôr′tər) *n.* an edible weed of the same family as spinach, used in salad or as a potherb. Also, **lamb's quarter.**

lame (lām) *adj.* **lam·er, lam·est,** *v.* **lamed, lam·ing.** —*adj.* **1** not able to walk properly; having an injured leg or foot; crippled. **2** stiff and sore: *His arm is lame from playing ball.* **3** poor; weak; unsatisfactory: *Sleeping too long is a lame excuse for being late.* —*v.* **1** make lame; cripple: *The accident lamed him for life.* **2** become lame; go lame. [OE *lama*] —**lame′ly,** *adv.* —**lame′ness,** *n.* —**Syn.** *adj.* **1** disabled, halt.

la·mé (la mā′ or lä mā′) *n.* a rich fabric made, wholly or partly, of metal threads. [< F *lamé,* literally, laminated < *lame* metal leaf]

lame duck 1 *U.S.* an elected representative or group that has been defeated for re-election and is serving the last part of the current term. **2** *Informal.* a disabled or helpless person or thing.

la·mel·la (lə mel′ə) *n.* **-mel·las, -mel·lae** (-mel′ē or -mel′ī). a thin plate, scale, or layer, especially of flesh or bone. [< L *lamella,* dim. of *lamina* thin plate]

la·mel·lar (lə mel′ər or lam′ə lər) *adj.* having, consisting of, or arranged in lamellas. —**la·mel′lar·ly,** *adv.*

lam·el·late (lam′ə lāt′, lam′ə lit, lə mel′āt, or lə mel′it) *adj.* lamellar.

la·ment (lə ment′) *v.* **1** express grief for; mourn for: *lament the dead.* **2** express grief; mourn; weep: *Why does she lament?* **3** regret: *We lamented his absence.*
—*n.* **1** an expression of grief; wail. **2** a poem, song, or tune that expresses grief. **3** a regret. [< L *lamentari* < *lamentum* a wailing] —**la·ment′er,** *n.* —**la·ment′ing·ly,** *adv.* —**Syn.** *v.* **1** bewail, deplore. **2** grieve, wail.

lam·en·ta·ble (lam′ən tə bəl) *adj.* **1** to be regretted or pitied: *a lamentable accident, a lamentable failure.*

2 sorrowful; mournful. —**lam′en·ta·bly,** *adv.*

lam·en·ta·tion (lam′ən tā′shən) *n.* **1** loud grief; mourning; wailing; cries of sorrow. **2 Lamentations,** a book of the Old Testament, said to have been written by Jeremiah.

lam·i·na (lam′ə nə) *n.* **-nae** (-nē′ or -nī′) or **-nas. 1** a thin plate, scale, or layer. **2** in botany, the flat, wide part of a leaf. [< L]

lam·i·nar (lam′ə nər) *adj.* having, consisting of, or arranged in thin layers, plates, or scales.

lam·i·nate (*v.* lam′ə nāt′; *adj. n.* lam′ə nāt′ or lam′ə nit) *v.* **-nat·ed, -nat·ing,** *adj. n.* —*v.* **1** split into thin layers. **2** make by putting layer on layer. **3** beat or roll (metal) into a thin plate. **4** cover with thin plates. —*adj.* laminated; laminar. —*n.* a laminated plastic.

lam·i·na·tion (lam′ə nā′shən) *n.* **1** the process of laminating. **2** the state of being laminated. **3** a laminated structure; an arrangement in thin layers. **4** a thin layer.

Lam·mas (lam′əs) *n.* **1** in the Roman Catholic Church, August 1, a religious feast commemorating the imprisonment and miraculous escape of Saint Peter. Acts 12:4-10. **2** August 1, the day of a harvest festival formerly held in England. Also, **Lammas Day.** [OE *hlāfmæsse* < *hlāf* bread, loaf + *mæsse* mass (because of the consecration of loaves made from the year's first grain)]

lamp (lamp) *n.* **1** a device consisting of a container of oil or alcohol and a wick that, when lighted, provides light: *a coal-oil lamp.* **2** a similar device for providing heat: *a spirit lamp.* **3** a device for providing light by gas or electricity: *a gas lamp, a street lamp, a floor lamp.* **4** a device for providing healthful rays: *a sun lamp.* **5** an electric light bulb. **6** *Slang.* the eye. [ME < OF < L < Gk. *lampas* < *lampein* shine]

lamp·black (lamp′blak′) *n.* a fine, black soot consisting of almost pure carbon that is deposited when oil, gas, etc. burn incompletely. Lampblack is used as a coloring agent in paint and ink.

lamp·light (lamp′līt′) *n.* the light from a lamp.

lamp·light·er (lamp′līt′ər) *n.* **1** a person who lights street lamps. **2** a torch, twisted paper, etc. used to light lamps.

lam·poon (lam pün′) *n.* a piece of writing that attacks and ridicules a person in a malicious or abusive way. —*v.* attack in a lampoon. [< F *lampon* drinking song < *lampons* let us drink] —**lam·poon′er,** *n.*

lam·poon·ist (lam pün′ist) *n.* a person who writes lampoons.

lamp·post (lamp′pōst′) *n.* a post used to support a street lamp.

lam·prey (lam′prē or lam′prā) *n.* **-preys.** an eel-like fish having a large round mouth with horny teeth and no jaws. Some species of lamprey live parasitically on the blood of fish they attach themselves to. [ME < OF *lampreie* < Med.L *lampreda* < LL *naupreda*; form influenced by L *lambere* lick. Doublet of LIMPET.]

Lan·cas·ter (lang′kəs tər) *n.* the English royal house from 1399 to 1461. Its emblem was a red rose.

Lan·cas·tri·an (lang kas′trē ən) *adj.* of the English royal house of Lancaster. —*n.* a supporter or member of the house of Lancaster.

lance (lans) *n. v.* **lanced, lanc·ing.** —*n.* **1** a long wooden spear with a sharp iron or steel head: *In the Middle Ages knights were often armed with lances.* **2** a soldier armed with a lance. **3** any instrument like a soldier's lance. **4** a lancet.
—*v.* **1** pierce with a lance. **2** cut open with a lancet: *The dentist lanced the gum so that the new tooth could come through.* [< F < L *lancea* light Spanish spear]

lance-bom·bar·dier (lans′bom′bə dēr′) *n.* in the artillery, a non-commissioned officer of the lowest rank, junior to a bombardier. *Abbrev.:* L/Bdr.

lance-corporal (lans′kôr′pə rəl) *n.* in the army, a non-commissioned officer of the lowest rank, junior to a corporal. *Abbrev.:* L/Cpl.

Lan·ce·lot (lan′sə lot′) *n.* in Arthurian legend, the bravest of King Arthur's knights. His love for Guinevere led to the break-up of the Round Table.

hat, āge, cãre, fär; let, ēqual, tėrm; it, īce
hot, ōpen, ôrder; oil, out; cup, pu̇t, rüle, ūse
əbove, takən, pencəl, lemən, circəs
ch, child; ng, long; sh, ship
th, thin; ᴛʜ, then; zh, measure

lan·ce·o·late (lan′sē ə lāt′ or lan′sē ə lit) *adj.* shaped like the head of a lance: *a lanceolate leaf.* [< L *lanceolatus* < *lanceola,* dim. of *lancea* lance]

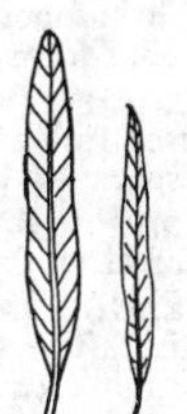
Lanceolate leaves

lanc·er (lan′sər) *n.* a mounted soldier armed with a lance.

lanc·ers (lan′sərz) *n.pl.* **1** a form of square dance. **2** the music for this dance.

lance-sergeant (lans′sär′jənt) *n.* a corporal appointed to act temporarily as sergeant. *Abbrev.:* L/Sgt.

lan·cet (lan′sit) *n.* **1** a small, sharp-pointed surgical knife, usually having two sharp edges. Doctors use lancets for opening boils, abscesses, etc. **2** a narrow, sharply pointed arch or window. [ME < OF *lancette,* dim. of *lance* lance < L *lancea*]

lance·wood (lans′wu̇d′) *n.* **1** a tough, straight-grained, springy wood, used for fishing rods, carriage shafts, cabinetwork, etc. **2** the tropical American tree that yields this wood.

land (land) *n.* **1** the solid part of the earth's surface: *dry land.* **2** ground; soil: *This is good land for a garden.* **3** landed property; real estate. **4** in economics, anything furnished by nature without the help of man, as soil, mineral deposits, water, wildlife. *Land, labor,* and *capital* are the three principal factors of production. **5** a country; region: *mountainous land.* **6** the people of a country: nation. **7 how the land lies,** what the state of affairs is.
—*v.* **1** come to land; bring to land: *The ship landed at the pier. The pilot landed the airplane in a field.* **2** put on land; set ashore: *The ship landed its passengers.* **3** go ashore: *The passengers landed.* **4** *Cdn.* enter or be permitted to enter Canada as an immigrant. **5** arrive; cause to arrive: *The thief landed in jail. His careless driving landed him in jail.* **6** *Informal.* catch; get: *land a job, land a fish.* **7** *Slang.* get (a blow) home: *I landed one on his chin.* [OE] —**land′er,** *n.* —**Syn.** *n.* **2** earth.

lan·dau (land′o, lan′dô, or lan′dou) *n.* **1** a four-wheeled carriage with two seats that face each other and a top made in two parts that can be folded back. **2** an automobile with a similar top and seats. [< *Landau,* a town in West Germany, where this type of carriage was first made]

lan·dau·let or **lan·dau·lette** (lan′do let′ or lan′dô let′) *n.* **1** a small landau. **2** an automobile with a folding top.

land breeze a breeze blowing from the land toward the sea.

land·ed (lan′did) *adj.* **1** owning land: *landed gentry.* **2** consisting of land. Landed property is real estate.

landed immigrant *Cdn.* a person admitted to Canada as a settler and potential Canadian citizen.

land·fall (land′fol′ or -fôl′) *n.* **1** an approach to land from the sea or air; landing. **2** the sighting of land. **3** the place where land is sighted or reached from the sea: *The explorer's landfall was near the mouth of the St. Lawrence.*

land·fill (land′fil′) *n.* the disposal of waste by burying it under a shallow layer of ground.

land·form (land′fôrm′) *n.* the natural physical features of the land.

land grant a grant of land; a gift of land by the government for colleges, railways, etc.

land·grave (land′grāv′) *n.* **1** in the Middle Ages, a German count having authority over a considerable territory or over other counts. **2** in modern times, the title of certain German princes. [< G *Landgraf* < *Land* land + *Graf* count]

land·hold·er (land′hōl′dər) *n.* a person who owns or occupies land.

land·hold·ing (land′hōl′ding) *adj.* that owns or occupies land. —*n.* an owning or occupying of land.

land·ing (lan′ding) *n.* **1** a coming to land; a coming ashore: *The army made a landing in France.* **2** a bringing to land. **3** a place where persons or goods are landed from a ship: *the steamboat landing.* **4** a platform between flights of stairs. **5** the floor at the head or foot of a staircase. **6** in lumbering, a place where logs are gathered before being transported to a sawmill.

landing craft any of various kinds of boats or ships used for landing troops or equipment on a shore, especially during an assault.

landing field a field large enough and smooth enough for aircraft to land on and take off from safely.

landing gear the wheels, pontoons, etc. under an aircraft. When on land or water, an aircraft rests on its landing gear.

landing mat a 12-by-3-foot mat of meshed steel that can be joined to others to furnish a landing surface for aircraft.

landing net a net attached to a handle, for taking fish from the water after they are caught.

landing place 1 a place to land people or goods. **2** a platform at the end of a flight of stairs.

landing stage a floating platform used for loading and unloading people and goods.

landing strip a long, narrow runway for airplanes to take off from and land on.

land·la·dy (land′lā′dē) *n.* **-dies. 1** a woman who owns buildings or land that she rents to others. **2** a woman who keeps a boarding house, lodging house, or inn.

land·less (land′lis) *adj.* without land; owning no land. **—land′less·ness,** *n.*

land·line (land′līn) *n.* a telegraph or similar cable running under or on the ground.

land·locked (land′lokt′) *adj.* **1** shut in, or nearly shut in, by land: *a landlocked harbor.* **2** living in waters shut off from the sea: *landlocked salmon.*

land·lord (land′lôrd′) *n.* **1** a person who owns buildings or land that he rents to others. **2** the keeper of a boarding house, lodging house, or inn.

land·lub·ber (land′lub′ər) *n.* a person not used to being on ships; a person clumsy on ships.

land·mark (land′märk′) *n.* **1** something familiar or easily seen, used as a guide. **2** an important fact or event; happening that stands out above others: *The printing press, the telephone, the telegraph, and the radio are landmarks in the progress of communications.* **3** a stone or other object that marks the boundary of a piece of land.

land mine a container filled with explosives or chemicals, placed on the ground or lightly covered, and usually set off by the weight of vehicles or troops passing over it.

land office a government office that takes care of the business connected with public lands, and records sales, transfers, etc.

Land of Promise in the Bible, the country promised by God to Abraham and his descendants; Canaan. Gen. 15:18; 17:8.

Land of the Little Sticks a region of stunted trees at the southern limits of the Barren Ground in N. Canada.

land·own·er (land′ōn′ər) *n.* a person who owns land.

land·own·er·ship (land′ōn′ər ship′) *n.* the state of being a landowner.

land-poor (land′pür′) *adj.* **1** owning much land but needing ready money. **2** poor because of taxes, etc. on one's land.

land·scape (land′skāp′ or lan′skāp′) *n. v.* **-scaped, -scap·ing.** *—n.* **1** a view of scenery on land. **2** a picture, often a painting, showing a land scene. *—v.* make (land) more pleasant to look at by arranging trees, shrubs, flowers, and lawns: *The builder agreed to landscape the lot around the new house.* [< Du. *landschap* < *land* land + *-schap* -ship) **—land′scap′er,** *n.*

landscape gardener a person whose business is landscape gardening.

landscape gardening the arrangement of trees, shrubs, flowers, and lawns to give a pleasing appearance to grounds, parks, etc.

land·shark (land′shärk) *n.* a person who buys up land illegally or unfairly to make large profits on its resale.

land·slide (land′slīd′) *n.* **1** a sliding down of a mass of soil or rock on a steep slope. **2** the mass that slides down. **3** an overwhelming majority of votes for one political party or candidate.

lands·man (landz′mən) *n.* **-men** (-mən). **1** a man who lives or works on land. **2** an inexperienced seaman.

land·ward (land′wərd) *adv. adj.* toward the land.

land·wards (land′wərdz) *adv.* landward.

land wind a wind blowing from the land toward the sea.

lane (lān) *n.* **1** a narrow way between hedges, walls, or fences; a narrow country road. **2** any narrow way. A highway is often marked off in lanes for separate lines of traffic. **3** an alley between buildings. **4** a course or route used by ships or aircraft going in the same direction. **5** one of the narrow alleys on a track, marked by chalked lines, especially one in which a runner must stay during sprint or hurdle races. **6** a bowling alley (def. 1). [OE *lanu*]

lang. language.

lang syne (lang′ sīn′) *Scottish.* long since; long ago.

lan·guage (lang′gwij) *n.* **1** human speech, spoken or written. **2** the distinct form of speech common to a people, nation, or group of peoples: *the French language.* **3** a form, style, or kind of: *bad language, Shakespeare's language, the language of chemistry.* **4** the wording or words: *in the language of the Lord's Prayer.* **5** any means of expressing thoughts or feelings: *A dog's language is made up of barks, looks, and actions.* **6** the study of language or languages; linguistics. **7** a set of assumptions or attitudes, often held by a group: *He just doesn't speak my language.* [ME < OF *langage* < *langue* tongue < L *lingua*]

Syn. 2 Language, dialect, idiom = the forms and patterns of speech of a particular group of people. **Language** applies to the body of words, forms, and patterns of sounds and structures making up the speech of a people, nation, or group of peoples: *French Canadians speak the French language.* **Dialect** applies to a socially or regionally restricted variety of a language: *The dialect of the English language spoken in Nova Scotia sounds strange to a westerner.* **Idiom** applies to a particular language's characteristic manner of using words and putting them together in phrases and sentences: *Foreign students find the correct use of prepositions a difficult feature of English idiom.*

language arts the part of the school curriculum directly concerned with the study of language, especially that part devoted to reading, speaking, listening, and writing.

language laboratory in an educational institution, a room equipped with tape-recorders, record-players, etc. that enable students to practise hearing and speaking a language they are studying.

langue d'oc (läNG dôk′) *French.* the group of dialects spoken in S. France in the Middle Ages. One of these dialects developed into modern Provençal. [< OF; the two major OF dialect groups were named for the respective words for "yes": *oc* and *oïl* (see next entry)]

langue d'o·ïl (läNG dô ēl′) *French.* the group of dialects spoken in N. France in the Middle Ages. One of these dialects developed into modern standard French. [see LANGUE D'OC]

lan·guid (lang′gwid) *adj.* **1** drooping; weak; weary; without energy: *A hot, sticky day makes a person feel languid.* **2** without interest or enthusiasm; indifferent. **3** sluggish; dull; not brisk or lively. [< L *languidus* < *languere* be faint] **—lan′guid·ly,** *adv.* **—lan′guid·ness,** *n.* **—Syn. 1** feeble, fatigued, exhausted. **2** apathetic, listless.

lan·guish (lang′gwish) *v.* **1** become weak or weary; lose energy; droop: *The flowers languished from lack of water.* **2** suffer under any unfavorable conditions: *He languished in prison for twenty years.* **3** grow dull, slack, or less intense: *His vigilance never languished.* **4** long or pine (*for*): *She languished for home.* **5** assume a soft, tender look for effect. [< F *languiss-*, a stem of *languir* < L *languere*] **—lan′guish·er,** *n.* **—Syn. 1** wither, fade.

lan·guish·ing (lang′gwish ing) *adj.* **1** drooping; pining; longing. **2** tender; sentimental; loving. **3** lasting; lingering. **—lan′guish·ing·ly,** *adv.*

lan·guish·ment (lang′gwish mənt) *n.* **1** a languishing; drooping, pining condition. **2** a languishing look or manner.

lan·guor (lang′ gər) *n.* 1 a lack of energy; weakness; weariness: *A long illness causes languor.* 2 a lack of interest or enthusiasm; indifference. 3 softness or tenderness of mood. 4 quietness; stillness: *the languor of a summer afternoon.* 5 lack of activity; sluggishness. [< L] —**Syn. 1** feebleness, fatigue. **2** apathy.

lan·guor·ous (lang′ gər əs) *adj.* 1 languid. 2 causing languor. —**lan′guor·ous·ly,** *adv.*

lan·gur (lung gür′) *n.* a large, slender, long-tailed monkey of S. Asia. [< Hind.]

lan·iard (lan′ yərd) *n.* lanyard.

lank (langk) *adj.* 1 long and thin; slender; lean: *a lank boy.* 2 straight and flat; not curly or wavy: *lank hair.* [OE *hlanc*] —**lank′ly,** *adv.* —**lank′ness,** *n.*

lank·i·ly (langk′ ə lē) *adv.* in a lanky condition or form.

lank·y (langk′ ē) *adj.* **lank·i·er, lank·i·est.** awkwardly long and thin; tall and ungraceful. —**lank′i·ness,** *n.*

lan·o·lin (lan′ ə lin) *n.* fat or grease obtained from wool, used in cosmetics, ointments, etc. [< L *lana* wool + *oleum* oil]

lan·o·line (lan′ ə lin or lan′ ə lēn′) *n.* lanolin.

lan·tern (lan′ tərn) *n.* 1 a case to protect a light from wind, rain, etc. It has sides of glass or some other material through which the light can shine. 2 the room at the top of a lighthouse where the light is. 3 an upright structure on a roof or dome, for letting in light and air or for decoration. 4 a magic lantern. [ME < OF < L *lanterna*]

lan·tern-jawed (lan′ tərn jod′ or -jôd′) *adj.* having hollow cheeks and long, thin jaws.

lantern slide a small, thin sheet of glass with a picture on it that is shown on a screen by a projector.

lan·tha·nide (lan′ thə nīd′) *n.* in chemistry, an element of the series having the atomic numbers 58 through 71.

lan·than·um (lan′ thə nəm) *n.* a soft, white, metallic element that tarnishes easily, found in rare-earth minerals. *Symbol*: La; *at.no.* 57; *at.wt.* 138.91. [< NL < Gk. *lanthanein* escape notice]

lan·yard (lan′ yərd) *n.* 1 a short rope or cord used on ships to fasten rigging. Sailors sometimes use a lanyard to hang a knife around their necks. 2 a cord with a small hook at one end, used in firing certain kinds of cannon. Also, **laniard.** [< *lanyer* (< F *lanière* thong) + *yard*[2]]

La·oc·o·ön (lā ok′ ō on′ or lā ok′ ə won′) *n.* in Greek legend, a priest of Apollo at Troy. He warned the Trojans against the wooden horse and was killed together with his two sons by two serpents sent by Athena.

La·od·i·ce·an (lā od′ ə sē′ ən) *n.* 1 a lukewarm or indifferent Christian. 2 a lukewarm or indifferent person.

La·o·tian (lā ō′ shən or lä ō′ shən) *adj.* of or having to do with Laos, a country in S.E. Asia. —*n.* a native or inhabitant of Laos.

Lao-Tse or **Lao-Tze** (lou′ tsē′) *n.* 604?-531? B.C., a Chinese philosopher and the founder of Taoism.

lap[1] (lap) *n.* 1 the front part from the waist to the knees of a person sitting down, with the clothing that covers it. 2 the place where anything rests or is cared for. 3 a loosely hanging edge of clothing; flap. [OE *læppa*]

lap[2] (lap) *v.* **lapped, lap·ping,** *n.* —*v.* 1 place or be placed together, one partly over or beside another: *Shingles lap on a roof.* 2 extend beyond a limit: *The reign of Queen Elizabeth I (from 1558 to 1603) lapped over into the seventeenth century.* 3 wind or wrap (*around*); fold (*over* or *about*): *He lapped the blanket around him.* 4 be wound or wrapped around something; be folded. 5 enwrap; wrap up (*in*): *He lapped himself in a warm blanket.* 6 surround; envelop. 7 in a race, get a lap or more ahead of (other racers).
—*n.* 1 a lapping over. 2 the amount of lapping over. 3 the part that laps over. 4 one time around a race track. 5 a part of any course travelled: *The last lap of our all-day hike was the toughest.* [< *lap*[1]]

lap[3] (lap) *v.* **lapped, lap·ping,** *n.* —*v.* 1 drink by lifting up with the tongue: *Cats and dogs lap water.* 2 move or beat gently with a lapping sound; splash gently: *Little waves lapped against the boat.* 3 **lap up, a** drink by lapping. **b** *Informal.* consume or absorb eagerly: *The advanced students lapped up the new math course.*
—*n.* 1 the act of lapping. 2 the sound of lapping: *the lap of the waves against my boat.* [OE *lapian*] —**lap′per,** *n.*

hat, āge, cãre, fär; let, ēqual, tėrm; it, īce
hot, ōpen, ôrder; oil, out; cup, pu̇t, rüle, ūse
əbove, takən, pencəl, lemən, circəs
ch, child; ng, long; sh, ship
th, thin; ŦH, then; zh, measure

lap·board (lap′ bôrd′) *n.* a thin, flat board held on the lap and used as a table.

lap dog a small pet dog.

la·pel (lə pel′) *n.* the part of the front of a coat folded back just below the collar. [dim. form of *lap*[1] + diminutive suffix *-el*]

Lapels

lap·ful (lap′ fu̇l) *n.* **-fuls.** as much as a lap can hold.

lap·i·dar·y (lap′ ə der′ ē) *n.* **-dar·ies,** *adj.* —*n.* a person who cuts, polishes, or engraves precious stones.
—*adj.* 1 of or having to do with cutting or engraving precious stones. 2 engraved on stone. 3 characteristic of stone inscriptions; monumental; stately; grandiose: *lapidary language.* [< L *lapidarius* < *lapis, -idis* stone]

lap·in (lap′ ən; *French,* lä paN′) *n.* 1 a rabbit. 2 rabbit fur. 3 a coat or other garment of this fur. [< F]

lap·is laz·u·li (lap′ is laz′ ū lī or laz′ ū lē) 1 a deep-blue, opaque semiprecious stone containing sodium, aluminum, sulphur, and silicon in a mixture of minerals. 2 a piece of this stone or a gem made from it. 3 deep blue. [< Med.L < L *lapis* stone + Med.L *lazuli,* gen. of *lazulum* lapis lazuli < Arabic < Persian *lajward.* Cf. AZURE.]

Lap·land·er (lap′ lan dər) *n.* Lapp (def. 1).

Lap·land long·spur (lap′ land lông′ spėr′ or long′-) a variety of finch that nests in the Arctic and winters in the United States.

Lapp (lap) *n.* 1 a member of a people having certain Mongoloid characteristics and living in Lapland, a region of N. Scandinavia and N.W. Soviet Union. The Lapps are small and have short, broad heads. 2 the Finno-Ugric language of the Lapps. [< Swedish]

lap·pet (lap′ it) *n.* 1 a small flap or fold. 2 a loose fold of flesh or membrane. 3 the lobe of the ear. [< *lap*[1]]

lap robe a blanket, fur robe, etc. used to keep the lap and legs warm when riding in an automobile, carriage, etc.

lapse (laps) *n. v.* **lapsed, laps·ing.** —*n.* 1 a slight mistake or error. A slip of the tongue, pen, or memory is a lapse. 2 a slipping or falling away from what is right: *a moral lapse.* 3 a slipping back; sinking down; slipping into a lower condition: *a lapse into savage ways.* 4 a slipping by; a passing away: *A minute is a short lapse of time.* 5 the ending of a right or privilege because it was not renewed, not used, or otherwise neglected.
—*v.* 1 make a slight mistake or error. 2 slip or fall away from what is right. 3 slip back; sink down: *The house lapsed into ruin.* 4 slip by; pass away: *The boy's interest soon lapsed.* 5 of a right or privilege, end because it was not renewed, not used, etc. If a legal claim is not enforced, it lapses after a certain number of years. [< L *lapsus* fall < *labi* to slip] —**Syn.** *n.* **1** slip, fault.

lap·strake (lap′ strāk′) *adj.* of boats, made of boards or metal plates that overlap one another; clinker-built. —*n.* a boat that is clinker-built. Also, **lapstreak.**

lap·streak (lap′ strēk′) *adj. n.* lapstrake.

lap·sus lin·guae (lap′ səs ling′ gwē or ling′ gwī) *Latin.* a slip of the tongue.

lap·wing (lap′ wing′) *n.* a crested plover of Europe, Asia, and N. Africa that has a slow, irregular flight and a peculiar wailing cry. [OE *hlēapewince* < *hlēapan* leap + *-wince* (related to WINK)]

lar·board (lär′ bərd or -bôrd) *n.* the side of a ship to the left of a person looking from the stern toward the bow; port. —*adj.* on this side of a ship. [ME *ladeborde,* originally, the loading side; influenced by *starboard*]

lar·ce·nous (lär′ sə nəs) *adj.* 1 of or like larceny;

characterized by larceny. 2 thievish; guilty of larceny.

lar·ce·ny (lär′sə nē) *n.* **-nies.** 1 theft. 2 in law, the unlawful taking, carrying away, and using of the personal property belonging to another person. [< AF *larcin* < L *latrocinium* < *latro* bandit]

larch (lärch) *n.* 1 a tree of the pine family having small woody cones and needles that fall off in the autumn. 2 its strong, tough wood. [< G *Lärche,* ult. < L *larix, -icis*]

lard (lärd) *n.* the fat of pigs melted down and made clear. It is used in cooking. —*v.* 1 insert strips of bacon or salt pork in (meat or poultry) before cooking. 2 put lard on; grease. 3 give variety to; enrich: *lard a long speech with stories.* [ME < OF < L *lardum*] —**lard′like′,** *adj.*

lar·der (lär′dər) *n.* 1 a pantry; place where food is kept. 2 a stock of food. [ME < OF *lardier* < *lard* lard < L *lardum*]

lar·es (lär′ēz) *n.pl.* in ancient Rome, the guardian spirits of the house. [< L, pl. of *lar*]

lares and penates 1 in ancient Rome, the household gods, the lares protecting the home from outside damage, the penates protecting the interior. 2 the cherished possessions of a household. [< L]

large (lärj) *adj.* **larg·er, larg·est,** *n.* —*adj.* 1 of great size, amount, or number; big: *a large crowd, a large sum of money, a large animal.* 2 of great scope or range; extensive; broad: *a man of large experience.* 3 on a great scale: *a large employer of labor.*
—*n.* 1 **at large, a** at liberty; free. **b** fully; in detail. **c** as a whole; altogether. **d** representing a whole area, business, group, etc.: *the firm's representative at large.* 2 **in large** or **in the large,** on a big scale. [ME < OF < L *largus* copious] —**large′ness,** *n.* —**Syn.** *adj.* 1 huge, great, vast, enormous. See **great.**

large-heart·ed (lärj′här′tid) *adj.* generous; liberal.

large intestine the lower part of the intestines, between the small intestine and the anus.

large·ly (lärj′lē) *adv.* 1 in great quantity; much. 2 to a great extent; mainly; for the most part.

large-scale (lärj′skāl′) *adj.* 1 wide; extensive; involving many persons or things: *a large-scale disaster.* 2 made or drawn to a large scale.

lar·gesse or **lar·gess** (lär′jis or lär jes′; *French,* lär zhes′) *n.* 1 generous giving. 2 a generous gift or gifts. [ME < OF *largesse* < *large* < L *largus* copious]

lar·ghet·to (lär get′ō) *adj. adv. n.* **-ghet·tos.** in music: —*adj.* rather slow; not so slow as largo, but usually slower than andante. —*adv.* rather slowly. —*n.* a passage or composition in rather slow time. [< Ital. *larghetto,* dim. of *largo*]

larg·ish (lär′jish) *adj.* rather large.

lar·go (lär′gō) *adj. adv. n.* **-gos.** in music: —*adj.* slow and dignified; stately. —*adv.* in largo tempo. —*n.* a slow, stately passage or piece of music. [< Ital. *largo* large, slow < L *largus* large]

lar·i·at (lar′ē ət) *n.* 1 a long rope with a running noose at one end; lasso. 2 a rope for fastening horses, mules, etc. to a stake while they are grazing. [< Sp. *la reata* the rope]

lark[1] (lärk) *n.* 1 a small songbird of Europe, Asia, and N. Africa, having brown feathers and long hind claws. One kind, the skylark, sings while soaring in the air. 2 a meadow lark, titlark, or any of several similar songbirds. [OE *lāwerce*]

lark[2] (lärk) *Informal.* —*n.* a merry adventure; frolic; prank. —*v.* have fun; play pranks. [origin uncertain]

lark·spur (lärk′spėr) *n.* a plant whose flowers have a petal-like sepal shaped like a spur. Most larkspurs have clusters of blue flowers on tall stalks. [< *lark*[1] + *spur*]

lar·ri·gan (lar′ə gən) *n. Cdn.* an oiled leather moccasin, usually having a flexible sole. [origin unknown]

lar·rup (lar′əp) *v.* **-ruped, -rup·ing.** *Informal.* beat; thrash. [origin uncertain] —**lar′rup·er,** *n.*

lar·va (lär′və) *n.* **-vae.** 1 the early form of an insect from the time it leaves the egg until it becomes a pupa. A caterpillar is the larva of a butterfly or moth. A grub is the larva of a beetle. Maggots are the larvae of flies. 2 an immature form of certain animals that is different in structure from the adult form. A tadpole is the larva of a frog or toad. [< L *larva* ghost]

lar·vae (lär′vē, lär′vī, or lär′və) *n.* pl. of **larva.**

lar·val (lär′vəl) *adj.* 1 of or having to do with a larva or larvae. 2 characteristic of larvae. 3 in the form of a larva. 4 of a disease, latent; undeveloped.

la·ryn·gal (lə ring′gəl) *adj. n.* laryngeal.

la·ryn·ge·al (lə rin′jē əl) *adj.* 1 of or having to do with the larynx. 2 in or produced in the larynx. 3 used on the larynx. —*n.* a laryngeal sound. [< NL *laryngeus*]

lar·yn·gi·tis (lar′ən jī′tis) *n.* inflammation of the larynx. A person with laryngitis has a very sore throat and finds it difficult and even painful to talk. [< NL *laryngitis* < *laryng-* larynx (< Gk. *larynx, -yngos*) + *-itis*]

la·ryn·go·scope (lə ring′gə skōp′) *n.* an instrument equipped with mirrors for examining the larynx. [< *laryngo-* larynx + *-scope*]

la·ryn·go·scop·ic (lə ring′gə skop′ik) *adj.* having to do with laryngoscopy or a laryngoscope.

lar·yn·gos·co·py (lar′ing gos′kə pē) *n.* the examination of the larynx by means of a laryngoscope.

lar·ynx (lar′ingks) *n.* **la·ryn·ges** (lə rin′jēz) or **lar·ynx·es.** 1 in anatomy, the cavity at the upper end of the windpipe, containing the vocal bands and acting as a speech organ. 2 in zoology: **a** a similar organ in other mammals, or a corresponding structure in other animals. **b** in birds, either of two cavities, one at the top and one at the bottom of the windpipe. [< Gk.]

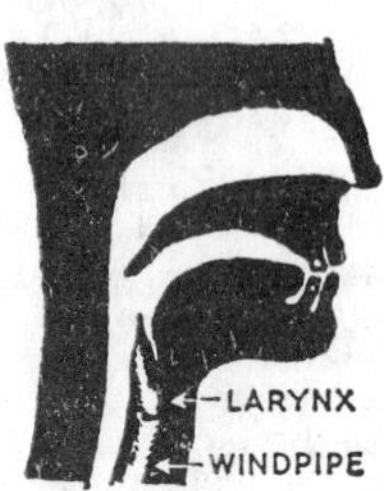

la·sa·gna (lə zän′yə) *n.* a dish of noodles stuffed with chopped meat, cheese, and tomato sauce. [< Ital.]

las·car (las′kər) *n.* an East Indian sailor. [< Pg. *laschar,* probably < Persian *lashkar* army < Arabic *al'askar*]

las·civ·i·ous (lə siv′ē əs) *adj.* 1 feeling lust. 2 showing lust. 3 causing lust. [ME < LL *lasciviosus* < L *lascivia* playfulness < *lascivus* playful] —**las·civ′i·ous·ly,** *adv.* —**las·civ′i·ous·ness,** *n.*

la·ser (lā′zər) *n.* in physics, a device for amplifying light waves, producing an intense, narrow beam of light; an optical maser. Laser beams can cut through metal and have many potential uses in surgery, communications, etc. [*l*ight *a*mplification by *s*timulated *e*mission of *r*adiation]

lash[1] (lash) *n.* 1 a whip, especially the rope, thong, etc. that is attached to the handle. 2 a stroke or blow with a whip, etc. 3 a sudden, swift movement. 4 anything that hurts like a blow from a whip. 5 an eyelash.
—*v.* 1 beat or drive with a whip, etc. 2 wave or beat back and forth: *The lion lashed his tail. The wind lashes the sails.* 3 rush violently; pour: *The rain lashed against the windows.* 4 hit out: *The horse lashed at him with its hoofs.* 5 hurt with angry words, scold severely: *The captain lashed the crew with his tongue.* 6 **lash out, a** hit out; attack; strike. **b** attack severely in words; scold vigorously. **c** break forth into violent action, excess, or extravagance. [ME *lasche;* origin uncertain] —**lash′er,** *n.* —**Syn.** *v.* 1 flog, scourge. 5 berate, scold.

lash[2] (lash) *v.* tie or fasten with a rope, cord, etc. [? ult. < OF *lache* lace]

lash·ing[1] (lash′ing) *n.* 1 a whipping, especially as a punishment. 2 a severe attack in words; sharp scolding. 3 **lashings,** *pl.* abundance; great plenty. [< *lash*[1]]

lash·ing[2] (lash′ing) *n.* rope, cord, etc. used in tying or fastening. [< *lash*[2]]

lass (las) *n.* 1 a girl, especially a young girl; young woman. 2 a sweetheart. [ME *lasse;* origin uncertain]

las·sie (las′ē) *n. Esp.Scottish.* 1 a young girl. 2 a sweetheart.

las·si·tude (las′ə tūd′ or las′ə tüd′) *n.* lack of energy; weakness; weariness. [< L *lassitudo* < *lassus* tired]

las·so (la sü′ or, *esp.U.S.,* las′ō) *n.* **-sos** or **-soes,** *v.* **-soed, -so·ing.** —*n.* a long rope with a running noose at one end; lariat. —*v.* catch with a lasso. [< Sp. *lazo* < L *laqueus* noose. Doublet of LACE.]

last[1] (last) *adj.* 1 coming after all others; being at the end; final: *the last page of the book.* 2 next before a specified point of time: *last night, last week, last year.* 3 previous; the one before this one: *The last caller was a woman.* 4 most unlikely; least suitable: *That is the last thing one would expect.* 5 very great; extreme: *a paper of last importance.* 6 that remains: *He spent his last dollar.* —*adv.* 1 after all others; at the end; finally: *He arrived last.* 2 on the latest or most recent occasion: *When did you last see him?*
—*n.* 1 a person or thing that is last: *the last in the row.* 2 the end: *faithful to the last.* 3 **at last,** at the end; after a long time; finally: *So you have come home at last!* 4 **breathe one's last,** die. 5 **see the last of,** not see again. [OE *latost, lætest,* superlative of *læt* late]
Syn. *adj.* 1 **Last, final, ultimate** = coming after all others. **Last** = coming after all others in a series or succession of things, events, or people. **Final** emphasizes the idea of bringing to a definite end or completing a series of events or a set of actions: *The last day of school each year is the final one for the graduating seniors.* **Ultimate** = the last possible that can ever be reached either by going forward or by tracing backward: *The ultimate cause of some diseases is unknown.*

last[2] (last) *v.* 1 go on; hold out; continue to be; endure: *The storm lasted three days.* 2 continue in good condition, force, etc.: *I hope these shoes last a year.* 3 be enough (for): *while our money lasts.* [OE *lǣstan* < *lǣst* track. Related to LAST[3].] —**Syn.** 1 persist, abide. See **continue.**

last[3] (last) *n.* 1 a block shaped like a person's foot, on which shoes and boots are formed or repaired: *a shoemaker's last.* 2 **stick to one's last,** pay attention to one's own work; mind one's own business. —*v.* form (shoes and boots) on a last. [OE *lǣste* < *lǣst* track]

last-ditch (last′ dich′) *adj.* 1 serving as a last resort or line of defence: *a last-ditch move.* 2 resisting to the last extremity: *last-ditch survivors of the attack.*

last·ing (las′ting) *adj.* that lasts a long time; that lasts; that will last; permanent; durable. —**last′ing·ly,** *adv.*
Syn. Lasting, enduring, permanent = existing or continuing for a long time or forever. **Lasting** emphasizes going on and on indefinitely, long past what would be normal or expected: *The experience had a lasting effect on him.* **Enduring** emphasizes the idea of being able to withstand the attacks of time and circumstance: *All the world hoped for enduring peace.* **Permanent** emphasizes staying in the same state or position, without changing or being likely to change: *What is your permanent address?*

Last Judgment God's final judgment of all mankind at the end of the world.

last·ly (last′lē) *adv.* finally; in the last place; in conclusion.

last offices prayers for a dead person.

last post in the armed services, the bugle call that gives the hour of retiring. It is blown also at military funerals, Remembrance Day ceremonies, etc.

last quarter the period between the second half moon and the new moon; the phase of the moon represented by the half moon after full moon.

last rites religious rites performed for a dying person or at a funeral.

last sleep death.

last straw the last of a series of troublesome things resulting in a collapse, outburst, etc.

Last Supper the supper of Jesus and His disciples on the evening before He was crucified.

last word 1 the last thing said; the last say on a subject. 2 *Informal.* the latest thing; most up-to-date style. 3 *Informal.* something that cannot be improved.

lat (lät) *n.* a unit of money in Latvia; Latvian coin worth about 20 cents in ordinary times. [< *Lat*(*vija*) Latvia]

lat. latitude.

Lat. 1 Latin. 2 Latvia.

latch (lach) *n.* 1 a catch for fastening a door, gate, or window. It consists of a movable piece of metal or wood that fits into a notch, opening, etc. 2 **on the latch,** not locked; fastened only with a latch. [< v.] —*v.* fasten with a latch. [OE *læccan* grasp]

A latch on a door

hat, āge, cãre, fär; let, ēqual, tėrm; it, īce
hot, ōpen, ôrder; oil, out; cup, pu̇t, rüle, ūse
əbove, takən, pencəl, lemən, circəs
ch, child; ng, long; sh, ship
th, thin; ᴛʜ, then; zh, measure

latch·et (lach′it) *n. Archaic.* a strap or lace for fastening a shoe or sandal. [< dial. OF *lachet,* ult. < *laz* lace. See LACE.]

latch·key (lach′kē′) *n.* a key used to draw back or unfasten the latch of a door.

latch·string (lach′string′) *n.* a string used to unfasten the latch of a door.

late (lāt) *adj.* **lat·er** or **lat·ter, lat·est** or **last,** *adv.* **lat·er, lat·est** or **last.** —*adj.* 1 happening, coming, etc. after the usual or proper time: *We had a late dinner last night.* 2 happening, coming, etc. at an advanced time: *success late in life.* 3 recent: *The late storm did much damage.* 4 recently dead: *The late John Smith was a fine man.* 5 gone out of or retired from office: *The late Prime Minister is still working actively.* 6 **of late,** lately; a short time ago; recently.
—*adv.* 1 after the usual or proper time: *He worked late.* 2 at an advanced time: *It rained late in the afternoon.* 3 recently. 4 recently but no longer: *John Smith, late of Victoria.* [OE *læt*] —**late′ness,** *n.*
Syn. *adj.* 1 **Late, tardy** = happening or coming after the usual or proper time. **Late,** describing people or things, emphasizes the idea of being after the usual, right, proper, expected time: *He was late for school this morning.* **Tardy** = not prompt, not on time, and emphasizes lateness and slowness in coming, getting somewhere, or doing something: *Please accept my tardy thanks.* ☛ See **first** for usage note.

la·teen (la tēn′) *adj.* having a lateen sail. [< F *voile latine* Latin sail]

la·teen-rigged (la tēn′rigd′) *adj.* having a lateen sail.

lateen sail a triangular sail held up by a long yard on a short mast.

A boat with lateen sails

Late Greek the Greek language from about A.D. 300 to 700.

Late Latin the Latin language from about A.D. 300 to 700.

late·ly (lāt′lē) *adv.* a short time ago; recently.

la·ten·cy (lā′tən sē) *n.* a latent condition or quality.

la·tent (lā′tənt) *adj.* 1 present but not active; hidden; concealed: *latent powers, latent ability.* 2 of infection, present in an undeveloped stage only; not yet manifest: *a test to reveal latent tuberculosis.* 3 in botany, dormant or undeveloped, as buds that are not externally visible until stimulated to grow. [< L *latens, -entis,* ppr. of *latere* lie hidden] —**la′tent·ly,** *adv.*
Syn. Latent, potential = existing as a possibility or fact, but not now showing itself plainly. **Latent** = actually existing as a fact, but lying hidden, not active or plainly to be seen at the present time: *The power of a grain of wheat to grow into a plant remains latent if it is not planted.* **Potential** = existing as a possibility and capable of coming into actual existence or activity if nothing happens to stop development: *That boy has great potential ability in science.*

lat·er·al (lat′ər əl) *adj.* 1 of the side; at the side; from the side; toward the side. A lateral branch of a family is a branch not in the direct line of descent. 2 in phonetics, articulated so that the breath passes out on one or both sides of the tongue, as in pronouncing the English (l) in *law* or *all.*
—*n.* 1 a lateral part or outgrowth. 2 in phonetics, a lateral sound, such as (l) in *law* or *all.* 3 in mining: **a** a drift other than the main drift. **b** a connecting tunnel between main haulage ways. 4 in football, a lateral pass. [< L *lateralis* < *latus, -teris* side]

lat·er·al·ly (lat′ər əl ē) *adv.* 1 in a lateral direction; at the side; sideways. 2 from a lateral branch.

lateral pass in football, a throwing of a ball from one player to another in a direction almost parallel with the goal line.

la·tex (lā′teks) *n.* **lat·i·ces** (lat′ə sēz′) or **la·tex·es**

(lā′tək siz). a milky liquid in certain plants, such as milkweeds, poppies, and plants yielding rubber. [< L *latex* liquid]

lath (lath) *n.* **laths** (laᴛʜz or laths) *v.* —*n.* **1** one of the thin, narrow strips of wood used to form a support for plaster or to make a lattice. **2** a sheet of plasterboard or latticed metal, used as a support for plaster. **3** a lining made of laths; laths. The walls of a frame house are usually built with lath and plaster. —*v.* cover or line with laths. [ME *laththe*]

lathe (lāᴛʜ) *n.* a machine for holding articles of wood, metal, etc. and turning them against a cutting tool used to shape them. [cf. Danish *(dreje)lad* (turning) lathe]

lath·er[1] (laᴛʜ′ər) *n.* **1** the foam made from soap and water. **2** the foam formed in sweating. —*v.* **1** put lather on. **2** form a lather. **3** become covered with the foam formed in sweating. **4** *Informal.* beat; flog. [OE *lēathor*]

lath·er[2] (lath′ər) *n.* a workman who puts laths on walls, ceilings, etc. [< *lath*]

lath·ing (lath′ing) *n.* **1** laths collectively. **2** the work of putting laths on walls, etc.

lath·work (lath′wėrk′) *n.* lathing.

lat·i·go (lat′ə gō′) *n.* in the West, a tough leather strap on a saddle for tightening and fastening the cinch. [< Sp.]

Lat·in (lat′ən) *n.* **1** the language of the ancient Romans, considered classical in the form it acquired during the 2nd and 1st centuries B.C. **2** a member of any of the peoples whose languages come from Latin. The Italians, French, Spanish, Portuguese, and Romanians are Latins. **3** a native or inhabitant of Latium or of ancient Rome. **4** a Roman Catholic.
—*adj.* **1** of Latin; in Latin. **2** of the Latin peoples. **3** of Latium or its people; ancient Roman. **4** Roman Catholic. [< L *Latinus* of Latium]

Latin Church that part of the Roman Catholic Church which uses Latin in its worship.

Latin cross a cross in which the upright is longer than the crossbeam. See **cross** for picture.

Lat·in·ism (lat′ən iz′əm) *n.* **1** a Latin idiom or expression. **2** conformity to Latin models.

Lat·in·ist (lat′ən ist) *n.* a person with much knowledge of the Latin language; Latin scholar.

La·tin·i·ty (lə tin′ə tē) *n.* the use of Latin idioms or expressions.

Lat·in·ize (lat′ən īz′) *v.* **-ized, -iz·ing. 1** translate into Latin. **2** make like Latin. **3** cause to conform to the ideas, customs, etc. of the Latins or the Latin Church.
—**Lat′in·i·za′tion,** *n.*

Latin Quarter a district in Paris, on the south bank of the Seine River, a traditional resort of artists. [translation of F *Quartier Latin*]

lat·ish (lāt′ish) *adj. adv.* rather late.

lat·i·tude (lat′ə tūd′ or lat′ə tüd′) *n.* **1** the distance north or south of the equator, measured in degrees. **2** a place or region having a certain latitude: *Polar bears live in the cold latitudes.* **3** room to act; scope; freedom from narrow rules: *An artist is allowed more latitude than a bricklayer.* **4** in photography, the range between the shortest and the longest exposures that produce good negatives on a given film. **5** transverse dimension; extent as measured from side to side; width of a surface, as opposed to length. [< L *latitudo* < *latus* wide]

Circles of latitude

lat·i·tu·di·nal (lat′ə tū′də nəl or lat′ə tü′də nəl) *adj.* of or relating to latitude. —**lat·i·tu′di·nal·ly,** *adv.*

lat·i·tu·di·nar·i·an (lat′ə tū′də nãr′ē ən or lat′ə tü′də nãr′ē ən) *adj.* allowing others their own beliefs; not insisting on strict adherence to established principles, especially in religious views. —*n.* a person who cares little about creeds, forms of worship, or methods of church government.

la·trine (lə trēn) *n.* a toilet in a camp, factory, etc.; privy. [< F < L *latrina,* originally, washroom < *lavare* wash]

lat·ter (lat′ər) *adj.* **1** second of two: *In "Jack and Jill," Jill is the latter.* **2** later; more recent; nearer the end: *Friday comes in the latter part of the week.* [OE *lætra* later]

lat·ter-day (lat′ər dā′) *adj.* of recent or modern times: *latter-day religions.*

Latter-day Saint a Mormon.

lat·ter·ly (lat′ər lē) *adv.* lately; recently.

lat·tice (lat′is) *n. v.* **-ticed, -tic·ing.** —*n.* **1** a structure of crossed wooden or metal strips with open spaces between them. **2** a window, gate, etc. having a lattice. **3** any pattern or decoration resembling a lattice.
—*v.* **1** form into a lattice; make like a lattice. **2** furnish with a lattice. [ME < OF *lattis* < *latte* lath < Gmc.]
—**lat′tice·like′,** *adj.*

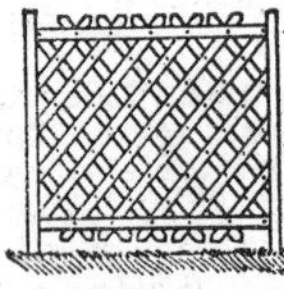
A lattice

lat·tice·work (lat′is wėrk′) *n.* **1** a lattice. **2** lattices.

Lat·vi·an (lat′vē ən) *adj.* of or having to do with Latvia, a republic in the N.W. Soviet Union, its people, or their language. —*n.* **1** a native or inhabitant of Latvia. **2** the Baltic language of Latvia; Lettish.

laud (lod or lôd) *v.* praise. [ME < L *laudare* < *laus, laudis,* n., praise] —*n.* **1** praise. **2** a song or hymn of praise. **3 lauds** or **Lauds,** *pl.* **a** a morning church service with psalms of praise to God. **b** in the Roman Catholic Church, a prescribed devotional service for priests and religious, forming, with matins, the first of the seven canonical hours. [ME < OF *laude* < L *laus, laudis* praise] —**laud′er,** *n.*

laud·a·bil·i·ty (lod′ə bil′ə tē or lôd′-) *n.* praiseworthiness.

laud·a·ble (lod′ə bəl or lôd′-) *adj.* worthy of praise; commendable: *Selflessness is laudable.* —**laud′a·bly,** *adv.* —**Syn.** praiseworthy.

lau·da·num (lo′də nəm or lô′də nəm) *n.* a solution of opium in alcohol, used to lessen pain. [< NL < Med.L *laudanum,* var. of L *ladanum* < Gk. *lādanon* mastic]

lau·da·tion (lo dā′shən or lô dā′shən) *n.* praise.

laud·a·to·ry (lod′ə tô′rē or lôd′-) *adj.* expressing praise.

laugh (laf) *v.* **1** make the sounds and movements of the face and body that show mirth, amusement, scorn, etc. **2** express with laughter: *laugh a reply.* **3** drive by or with laughing: *laugh one's tears away.* **4** suggest the feeling of joy; be lively. **5 laugh at, a** make fun of. **b** disregard or make light of: *He laughed at danger.* **6 laugh off,** pass off, dismiss, or free oneself from (something) with a laugh; get out of by laughing. **7 laugh on the other side** or **wrong side of one's mouth,** *Informal.* be annoyed; be made sorry. **8 laugh up one's sleeve,** laugh secretly or to oneself. —*n.* the act or sound of laughing. [OE *hliehhan*] —**laugh′er,** *n.* —**Syn.** *v.* **1** chuckle, chortle, giggle.

laugh·a·ble (laf′ə bəl) *adj.* such as to cause laughter; amusing; ridiculous. —**laugh′a·ble·ness,** *n.* —**laugh′a·bly,** *adv.* —**Syn.** comical, humorous. See **funny.**

laugh·ing (laf′ing) *adj.* **1** that laughs or seems to laugh: *the laughing brook.* **2** accompanied by laughter. **3 no laughing matter,** a matter that is serious. —*n.* laughter. —**laugh′ing·ly,** *adv.*

laughing gas nitrous oxide, a colorless gas that makes one insensible to pain. This gas makes some people laugh and become excited. *Formula:* N_2O

laughing jackass an Australian bird having a harsh, cackling voice.

laugh·ing·stock (laf′ing stok′) *n.* an object of ridicule; a person or thing that is made fun of.

laugh·ter (laf′tər) *n.* **1** the action of laughing. **2** the sound of laughing: *Laughter filled the room.* [OE *hleahtor*]

launch[1] (lonch or lônch) *n.* **1** a motorboat used for pleasure trips. **2** the largest boat carried by a warship. [< Sp., Pg. *lancha* < *lanchar* launch[2]]

launch[2] (lonch or lônch) *v.* **1** cause to slide into the water; set afloat: *A new ship is launched from the supports on which it has been built.* **2** push out or put forth on the water or into the air: *launch a plane from an aircraft carrier.* **3** start; set going; set out: *His friends launched him in business by lending him the necessary capital.* **4** throw; hurl; send out: *An angry person launches threats against enemies. A bow launches arrows into the air.* **5** burst; plunge: *The leader of the opposition launched into a violent attack on the government.* **6 launch out,** begin; start.
—*n.* a launching or being launched. [ME < AF *launcher,* var. of *lancer* use a lance < *lance* lance < L *lancea*] —**launch′er,** *n.*

launching pad a surface on which a rocket or missile is prepared for launching and from which it is shot into the air.

laun·der (lon′dər or lôn′dər) *v.* **1** wash and iron (clothes, etc.). **2** be able to be washed; stand washing. [ME *lander* one who washes linen < OF *lavandier* washer < VL *lavandarius* < L *lavanda* (things) to be washed < *lavare* wash] —**laun′der·er,** *n.*

laun·dress (lon′dris or lôn′dris) *n.* a woman whose work is washing and ironing clothes, etc.

laun·dro·mat (lon′drə mat′ or lôn′drə mat′) *n.* a self-service laundry having automatic washing machines and dryers, especially one having coin-operated machines. [< *Laundromat,* a trademark]

laun·dry (lon′drē or lôn′drē) *n.* **-dries. 1** a room or building where clothes, etc. are washed and ironed. **2** clothes, etc. washed or to be washed. **3** the washing and ironing of clothes.

laun·dry·man (lon′drē mən or lôn′drē-) *n.* **-men** (-mən). **1** a man who works in a laundry. **2** a man who collects and delivers laundry.

laun·dry·wom·an (lon′drē wům′ən or lôn′drē-) *n.* **-wom·en.** laundress.

lau·re·ate (lô′rē it) *adj.* **1** crowned with a laurel wreath as a mark of honor. **2** honored; distinguished.
—*n.* the poet laureate. [< L *laureatus* < *laurea* laurel wreath < *laurus* laurel]

lau·re·ate·ship (lô′rē it ship′) *n.* **1** the position of poet laureate. **2** the time during which a poet is poet laureate.

lau·rel (lô′rəl) *n.* **1** a small evergreen tree having smooth, shiny leaves; bay tree. **2** the leaves. The ancient Greeks and Romans crowned victors with wreaths of laurel. **3** any tree or shrub of the same family as the bay tree. **4** a North American evergreen shrub, the mountain laurel. **5** Usually, **laurels,** *pl.* **a** honor; fame. **b** victory. **6 look to one's laurels,** guard one's reputation or record from rivals. **7 rest on one's laurels,** be satisfied with honors already won. [ME < OF *lorier, laurier* < *lor* < L *laurus*]

lau·relled or **lau·reled** (lô′rəld) *adj.* **1** crowned with a laurel wreath. **2** honored.

Lau·ren·tian (lôr en′shən) *adj.* **1** of or having to do with the St. Lawrence River and adjoining lands. **2** in geology, of or having to do with intrusive granites found in the oldest pre-Cambrian rocks of the Canadian Shield. **3** of or having to do with the Laurentian Mountains; Laurentide. **4** of or having to do with Quebec. [< *Laurentius,* L form of *Lawrence* + *-ian*]

Laurentian Shield the Canadian Shield.

Lau·ren·tide (lô′ren tīd′) *adj. Cdn.* of or having to do with the Laurentians, the range of low mountains lying between Hudson Bay and the St. Lawrence River. [< Cdn.F]

la·va (lav′ə or lä′və) *n.* **1** the molten rock flowing from a volcano or fissure in the earth. **2** the rock formed by the cooling of this molten material. Some lavas are hard and glassy; others are light and porous. [< dial. Ital. *lava* stream, ult. < L *lavare* wash]

lava bed a layer or surface of lava.

la·va·bo (lə vä′ bō or lə vā′bō) *n.* **1** Also, **Lavabo.** in the Roman Catholic church: **a** the ritual washing of the celebrant's hands during the Mass, before the consecration. **b** the portion of Psalm 25 said during this rite. **2** a washbasin and a tank with a spigot that are fastened to a wall. **3** a small, ornamental basin on a wall, used as a planter. [< L *lavabo* I will wash, the first word of Ps. 25:6 in the Douay version]

hat, āge, cãre, fär; let, ēqual, tėrm; it, īce
hot, ōpen, ôrder; oil, out; cup, pu̇t, rüle, ūse
əbove, takən, pencəl, lemən, circəs
ch, child; ng, long; sh, ship
th, thin; ᴛʜ, then; zh, measure

lava field a large area of cooled lava.

lav·a·liere, lav·a·lier, or **lav·al·lière** (lav′ə lēr′; *French,* lä vä lyãr′) *n.* an ornament hanging from a small chain, worn around the neck by women. [< F *lavallière* < Louise, Duchesse de *La Vallière* (1644-1710), a mistress of Louis XIV of France]

lav·a·to·ry (lav′ə trē or lav′ə tô′rē) *n.* **-ries. 1** a room where a person can wash his hands and face. **2** a bowl or basin to wash in. **3** a toilet or rest room. [ME < LL *lavatorium* < L *lavare* wash. Doublet of LAVER.]

lave (lāv) *v.* **laved, lav·ing.** *Poetic.* **1** wash; bathe. **2** wash or flow against: *The stream laves its banks.* [OE *lafian* < L *lavare*]

lav·en·der (lav′ən dər) *n.* **1** a pale purple. **2** a small shrub having spikes of fragrant pale-purple flowers, yielding an oil much used in perfumes. **3** the dried flowers, leaves, and stalks of the lavender plant, used to perfume or preserve linens, cloths, etc. —*adj.* pale-purple. [ME < AF < Med.L *lavendula*]

la·ver (lā′vər) *n. Archaic.* a bowl or basin to wash in. [ME < OF *laveoir* < LL *lavatorium* a place for washing < L *lavare* wash. Doublet of LAVATORY.]

lav·ish (lav′ish) *adj.* **1** very free or too free in giving or spending; prodigal: *A rich person can afford to be lavish with his money.* **2** very abundant; more than enough; given or spent too freely: *many lavish gifts.* —*v.* give or spend very freely or too freely: *It is a mistake to lavish kindness on ungrateful people.* [ult. < OF *lavasse* flood < *laver* wash < L *lavare*] —**lav′ish·er,** *n.* —**lav′ish·ly,** *adv.* —**lav′ish·ness,** *n.* —**Syn.** *adj.* **1** extravagant. **2** See **profuse.**

law (lo or lô) *n.* **1** a body of rules recognized by a country, province, state, municipality, or community as binding on its members: *English law is different from French law.* **2** one of these rules: *Good citizens obey the laws.* **3** the controlling influence of these rules, or the condition of society brought about by their observance: *maintain law and order.* **4** law as a system: *courts of law.* **5** the department of knowledge or study concerned with these rules; jurisprudence: *study law.* **6** a body of such rules concerned with a particular subject or derived from a particular source: *commercial law, criminal law.* **7** the legal profession: *enter the law.* **8** legal action. **9** any statute passed by the legislative body of a province, state, or nation: *a Federal law.* **10** any rule or principle that must be obeyed: *the laws of hospitality, a law of grammar.* **11 a** legal authorities. **b** *Informal.* a policeman or detective. **12** a statement of a relation or sequence of phenomena invariable under the same conditions: *the law of gravitation, Mendel's law, Ohm's law.* **13** a divine rule or commandment. **14** a mathematical rule on which the construction of a curve, a series, etc. depends.
go to law, appeal to law courts; take legal action.
lay down the law, a give orders that must be obeyed. **b** give a scolding.
read law, study to be a lawyer.
take the law into one's own hands, take steps to gain one's rights or avenge a wrong without going to court.
the Law, a the books of the Old Testament that contain the Mosaic law. **b** the Old Testament. [OE *lagu* < Scand.; cf. ON *lög*]
Syn. 2 Law, statute = a rule or regulation recognized by a community as governing the action or procedure of its members. **Law** is the general word applying to any such rule or regulation, written or unwritten, laid down by the highest authority, passed by action of a lawmaking body such as Parliament, a provincial legislature, or a city council, or recognized as custom and enforced by the courts. **Statute** applies to a formally written law passed by a legislative body.

L.A.W. Leading Aircraftwoman.

law·a·bid·ing (lo′ə bīd′ing or lô′-) *adj.* obedient to the law; peaceful and orderly.

law·break·er (lo′brāk′ər or lô′-) *n.* a person who breaks the law.

law·break·ing (lo′brāk′ing or lô′-) *n.* a breaking of the law. —*adj.* breaking the law.

law court a place where justice is administered; a court of law.

law·ful (lo′fəl or lô′-) *adj.* **1** according to law; done as the law directs: *lawful arrest.* **2** allowed by law; rightful: *lawful demands.* —**law′ful·ly,** *adv.* —**law′ful·ness,** *n.*
Syn. 1, 2 Lawful, legal, legitimate = according to law. **Lawful** = in agreement with or not against the laws of the community, the laws of a church, or moral law: *To some people gambling is not lawful.* **Legal** = authorized by or according to the actual terms of the legislative acts and other laws of a community enforced by the courts: *Divorce is legal in most provinces.* **Legititimate** = rightful according to law, recognized authority, or established standards: *Sickness is a legitimate reason for a child's being absent from school.*

law·giv·er (lo′giv′ər or lô′-) *n.* a man who prepares and puts into effect a system of laws for a people; lawmaker.

law·less (lo′lis or lô′-) *adj.* **1** paying no attention to the law; breaking the law. **2** hard to control; unruly. **3** having no laws: *In pioneer days much of the West was lawless.* —**law′less·ly,** *adv.* —**law′less·ness,** *n.* —**Syn.** **2** uncontrolled, ungovernable, unbridled.

law·mak·er (lo′māk′ər or lô′-) *n.* a person who helps to make laws; a member of a parliament, legislature, or congress; legislator.

law·mak·ing (lo′māk′ing or lô′-) *adj.* that makes laws; legislative. —*n.* the making of laws; legislation.

lawn[1] (lon or lôn) *n.* land covered with grass kept closely cut, especially near or around a house. [ME < OF *launde* wooded ground < Celtic]

lawn[2] (lon or lôn) *n.* a thin, sheer cotton or linen cloth. [? ult. < *Laon* a city in France]

lawn mower a machine with revolving blades for cutting the grass on a lawn.

lawn tennis an outdoor game in which a ball is hit back and forth over a low net.

law of Moses the first five books of the Old Testament: Genesis, Exodus, Leviticus, Numbers, and Deuteronomy.

law of the Medes and Persians a law that cannot be changed.

law·ren·ci·um (lô ren′sē əm) *n.* a short-lived artificial radio-active element produced from Californium. *Symbol*: Lw; *at.no.* 103; *at.wt.* 257; *half-life* 8 seconds. [after Ernest O. *Lawrence*, 1901-1958, an American physicist]

law·suit (lo′süt′ or lô′-) *n.* a case in a law court; application to a court for justice: *Injustices are often remedied by lawsuits.*

law·yer (loi′yər, lo′yər, or lô′yər) *n.* a person whose profession is giving advice about the laws or acting for others in a law court.

lax (laks) *adj.* **1** not firm or tight; loose; slack. **2** not strict; careless. **3** loose in morals. **4** not exact; vague. [< L *laxus*] —**lax′ly,** *adv.* —**lax′ness,** *n.* —**Syn. 1** relaxed, flabby. **2** negligent, remiss.

lax·a·tive (lak′sə tiv) *n.* a medicine that makes the bowels move. —*adj.* making the bowels move. [< L *laxativus* loosening, ult. < *laxus* loose]

lax·i·ty (lak′sə tē) *n.* a lax condition or quality. [< F *laxité* < L *laxitas* < *laxus* loose]

lay[1] (lā) *v.* **laid, lay·ing,** *n.* —*v.* **1** bring down; beat down: *A storm laid the crops.* **2** put down; keep down: *Lay your hat on the table.* **3** make quiet or make disappear: *lay a ghost. A shower has laid the dust.* **4** smooth down: *lay the nap of cloth.* **5** place in a laying-down position or a position of rest: *Lay the baby down gently.* **6** place, set or cause to be in a particular situation or condition; place; put; set: *She lays great emphasis on good manners. The scene of the story is laid in Montreal.* **7** place in proper position or in orderly fashion: *lay bricks.* **8** devise; arrange: *lay plans.* **9** put down as a bet; wager: *I lay five dollars that he will not come.* **10** impose a burden, penalty, etc.: *lay a tax on property.* **11** present; bring forward: *lay claim to an estate.* **12** impute; attribute: *The theft was laid to him.* **13** produce (an egg or eggs) from the body: *Birds, fish, and reptiles lay eggs.* **14** of hens, produce an egg or eggs: *All the hens are laying well. This hen hasn't laid yet this morning.* **15** apply oneself vigorously: *The men laid to their oars.* **16** in nautical use, take up a specified position: *The men lay aft.*
lay about, hit out on all sides.
lay a course, in nautical use, lie or sail in a certain direction without being obliged to tack.
lay aside, away, or **by, a** put away for future use; save. **b** put away from one's person, from consideration, etc.; put on one side.
lay down, a declare; state. **b** give; sacrifice. **c** *Slang.* quit; resign. **d** store away for future use. **e** bet. **f** survey; draw in on a chart or map.
lay for, *Informal.* lie in wait for.
lay in, provide; save; put aside for the future.
lay into, a *Informal.* beat; thrash. **b** *Slang.* scold.
lay low, humble; bring down.
lay off, a put aside. **b** *Slang.* stop for a time; take a rest. **c.** stop teasing or interfering with; desist. **d** put out of work. **e** mark off.
lay on, a apply. **b** supply. **c** strike; inflict.
lay oneself or **one open,** expose oneself or another (*to*): *He lays himself open to ridicule by his many boasts.*
lay oneself out, *Informal.* make a big effort; take great pains.
lay open, a make bare; expose. **b** make an opening in; wound.
lay out, a spread out. **b** prepare (a dead body) for burial. **c** arrange; plan. **d** mark off: *They laid out a tennis court.* **e** *Slang.* spend. **f** *Slang.* knock unconscious; put out of the fight.
lay over, a *Informal.* break a journey; stay for a time: *We shall lay over in Vancouver for a few days and then start driving to California.* **b** *Slang.* be better than; surpass; excel.
lay to, a blame on; accuse of. **b** of ships, head into the wind and stand still.
lay up, a put away for future use; save. **b** cause to stay in bed or indoors because of illness or injury: *He was laid up with flu for a week.* **c** put (a ship) in dock.
—*n.* **1** the way or position in which a thing is laid or lies: *the lay of the ground.* **2** the amount and direction of the twist given to the strands or other components of a rope. **3** a share of the profits or of the catch of a whaling or fishing vessel. **4** a lease to work a gold claim for a share of the proceeds. **5** terms of employment or sharing. **6 lay of the land, a** the nature of the place; position of hills, water, woods, etc.: *Spies were sent to find out the lay of the land.* **b** the existing situation; condition of things. [OE *lecgan*, causative of *licgan* lie[2]]
☛ **lay, lie.** In uneducated English the work of these two verbs is generally done by one (*lay, lay* or *laid, laid*). In standard speech and writing they are kept distinct: *lie* (to recline, intransitive) *lay, lain*; *lay* (to place, transitive), *laid, laid*. You *lie* down for a rest or *lie* down on the job. A farm *lies* in a valley. You *lay* a floor, *lay* a book on the table, *lay* a bet, *lay* out clothes.

lay[2] (lā) *v.* pt. of **lie**[2].

lay[3] (lā) *adj.* **1** of ordinary people; not of the clergy. A lay sermon is one preached by a person who is not a clergyman. **2** of ordinary people; not of lawyers, doctors, or those learned in the profession in question: *The lay mind understands little of the cause of disease.* [ME < OF *lai* < L *laicus.* Doublet of LAIC.]

lay[4] (lā) *n.* **1** a short poem to be sung; poem. **2** a song; tune. [ME < OF *lai* origin uncertain]

lay·er (lā′ər) *n.* **1** one that lays. **2** one thickness or fold. A cake is often made of two or more layers put together. **3** a branch of a plant bent down and covered with earth so that it will take root and form a new plant. —*v.* form (new plants) by layers; spread by layers.

lay·ette (lā et′) *n.* a set of clothes, bedding, etc. for a newborn baby. [< F *layette* < *laie* chest]

lay figure 1 a jointed model of a human body. Lay figures are used by artists and for window displays. **2** an unimportant person; puppet. [earlier *layman* < Du. *leeman* < *lee* limb + *man* man]

lay·man (lā′mən) *n.* **-men** (-mən). a person outside of any particular profession, especially one not belonging to the clergy. [< *lay*[3] + *man*]

lay·off (lā′of′) *n.* **1** a temporary dismissal of workmen: *Because of a shortage of steel, there was a layoff at the plant.* **2** the time during which the workmen are temporarily out of work.

lay·out (lā′out′) *n.* **1** the act of laying out. **2** an arrangement; plan: *This map shows the layout of the camp.* **3** a plan or design for an advertisement, book, etc. **4** a thing laid or spread out; display. **5** an outfit; supply; set.

lay·o·ver (lā′ ō′vər) *n.* a stopping for a time in a place.

laz·ar (laz′ər or lā′zər) *n. Archaic.* **1** a leper. **2** a poor, sick person. [ME < Med.L *lazarus* < *Lazarus*, the beggar]

laz·a·ret or **laz·a·rette** (laz′ə ret′) *n.* lazaretto.

laz·a·ret·to (laz′ə ret′ō) *n.* **-tos. 1** a hospital for people having contagious or loathsome diseases; pesthouse. **2** a building or ship used for quarantine purposes. **3** a place in some merchant ships, near the stern, in which supplies are kept. [< Ital. *lazzaretto*, blend of *lazzaro* lazar, and the name of a hospital, Santa Maria di *Nazaret*, Venice, Italy]

Laz·a·rus (laz′ə rəs) *n.* **1** in the Bible: **a** the brother of Mary and Martha, whom Jesus raised from the dead. John 11: 1-44. **b** a beggar who suffered on earth but went to heaven. Luke 16: 19-25. **2** any diseased beggar, especially a leper.

laze (lāz) *v.* **lazed, laz·ing. 1** be lazy or idle. **2** pass (time) lazily. [< *lazy*]

la·zi·ness (lā′zē nis) *n.* dislike of work; unwillingness to work or be active; the state of being lazy.

la·zy (lā′zē) *adj.* **la·zi·er, la·zi·est. 1** not willing to work or be active. **2** characterized by, suggestive of, or conducive to idleness: *a lazy mood, a lazy summer day.* **3** moving slowly; not very active. [? < MLG *lasich* weak, feeble] **—la′zi·ly,** *adv.* **—Syn. 1** See **idle.**

la·zy·bones (lā′zē bōnz′) *n.pl. or sing. Informal.* a lazy person.

lazy Susan a revolving tray for holding different kinds of food, condiments, etc., placed on a table or used for storage in a cupboard.

lb. *pl.* **lbs.** pound. (for L *libra*)

L/Bdr. Lance-Bombardier.

l.c. lower case; in small letters, not capital letters.

L.C. 1 Lower Canada. **2** Library of Congress.

L.C.D., l.c.d., or **lcd** least (or lowest) common denominator.

L.Cdr. Lieutenant Commander.

L.C.M., l.c.m., or **lcm** least (or lowest) common multiple.

L/Cpl. Lance-Corporal.

Ld. 1 Lord. **2** Limited.

-le *suffix.* **1** small; little, as in *follicle.* **2** again and again, as in *grapple, sparkle.* [def. 1, OE *-el*; def. 2, ME *-elen*, OE *-lian*]

lea (lē) *n.* a grassy field; meadow; pasture. [OE *lēah*]

leach (lēch) *v.* **1** run (water, etc.) through slowly; filter. **2** dissolve out by running water through slowly: *Potash is leached from wood ashes.* **3** dissolve out soluble parts from (ashes, etc.) by running water through slowly. **4** lose soluble parts when water passes through. **—*n.*** a container for use in leaching. [OE *leccan* wet] **—leach′er,** *n.*

lead[1] (lēd) *v.* **led, lead·ing,** *n.* **—*v.* 1** show the way by going along with or in front of; guide: *The star led the three Wise Men to Bethlehem.* **2** conduct by the hand, a rope, etc.: *lead a horse.* **3** act as guide: *You lead, I will follow.* **4** provide a way to a certain condition; be a means of proceeding to or effecting a certain result: *Hard work leads to success.* **5** conduct or bring (water, steam, a rope, a wire, etc.) in a particular channel or course. **6** pass or spend (life, time, etc.): *He leads a quiet life in the country.* **7** afford passage or way: *This road leads to the city.* **8** influence; induce: *Such actions led us to distrust him.* **9** be led; submit to being led: *This horse leads easily.* **10** *Archaic.* take or bring: *We led them away prisoners.* **11** go or be at the head of: *The elephants led the parade.* **12** go or be first; have first place: *In algebra he is way down in the class, but in history he leads.* **13** be chief of; command; direct: *A general leads an army.* **14** be chief; direct; act as leader. **15** begin or open: *She led the dance.* **16** in card games: **a** begin with (card or suit named). **b** make first play at cards. **17** in boxing, direct a blow at an opponent. **18** in curling, throw first on a team. **19 lead off,** begin; start. **20 lead up to,** prepare the way for.
—*n.* 1 guidance; direction; example; precedence. **2** the first or foremost place; a position in advance: *take the lead.* **3** the distance, number of points, etc. that one is ahead: *He had a lead of 3 yards at the halfway mark.* **4** in card games: **a** the right of playing first. **b** the card or suit so played. **5** something that leads. **6** in the theatre, motion pictures, etc.: **a** the principal part in a play, film, etc. **b** the person who plays such a part. **7** a string, strap, etc. for leading a dog or other animal. **8** a guiding indication. **9** in mining, a lode. **10** an open channel through an ice field. **11** a conductor conveying electricity. **12** in boxing, a blow directed at an opponent. **13** the opening paragraph in a newspaper article. **14** the main front-page story in a magazine, newspaper, etc. **15** in curling, the man on a team who throws first in each end, usually the least experienced player. [OE *lǣdan*]
—Syn. *v.* 1 conduct. See **guide. 8** persuade, entice. **14** head.

☞ **lead, led.** *Lead* and *led* illustrate the confusion that English suffers because of representing one sound by different symbols. *Lead* (lēd), the present tense of the verb, gives no trouble; but *led*, the past tense, is often incorrectly spelled with *ea* by analogy with *read* (rēd), *read* (red): *Please lead the horse away. The culprit was led into the office.*

lead[2] (led) *n.* **1** a heavy, easily melted, bluish-gray, metallic chemical element. It is used to make pipes, in alloys, etc. *Symbol*: Pb; *at.no.* 82; *at.wt.* 207.19. **2** something made of this metal or one of its alloys. **3** a weight on a line used to find the depth of water; plummet. **4** bullets; shot. **5** a long, thin piece of graphite as used in pencils. **6** in printing, a metal strip for widening the space between lines. **7 leads,** *pl.* **a** strips of lead used to cover roofs. **b** the frames of lead in which panes of glass are set.
—*adj.* made of lead: *lead pipe.*
—*v.* 1 in printing, insert leads between the lines of (print). **2** cover, frame, or weight with lead. **3** use a weighted line to find out the depth of water. **4** glaze (pottery) with glaze containing lead. [OE *lēad*]

lead dog (lēd′) the dog that leads a team of huskies; leader.

lead·en (led′ən) *adj.* **1** made of lead: *a leaden coffin.* **2** heavy; hard to lift or move: *The tired runner could hardly lift his leaden legs.* **3** oppressive: *leaden air.* **4** dull; gloomy. **5** bluish-gray: *leaden clouds.*

lead·er (lēd′ər) *n.* **1** a person or thing that leads: *an orchestra leader.* **2** a person who is well fitted to lead. **3** the horse harnessed at the front of a team. **4** the dog that leads a dog-sled team: *The leader was a powerful husky.* **5** an important or leading article or editorial in a magazine, newspaper, etc. **6** a short length of nylon, wire, etc. used to attach the lure to a fishing line. **7** an article offered at a low price to attract customers. **8 leaders,** *pl.* a row of dots or dashes to guide the eye across a printed page. **—lead′er·less,** *adj.*

lead·er·ship (lēd′ər ship′) *n.* **1** the state or position of being a leader. **2** the qualities of a leader. **3** the ability to lead: *Leadership is a great asset to an officer.*

lead·ing[1] (lēd′ing) *n.* the act of someone or something that leads; guidance; direction. **—*adj.* 1** guiding; directing. **2** most important; chief; principal: *the leading lady in a play.* [< *lead*[1]] **—Syn. *adj.* 2** main, foremost.

lead·ing[2] (led′ing) *n.* **1** a covering or frame of lead. **2** the metal strips for widening the space between lines of type. [< *lead*[2]]

Leading Aircraftman in the air force, a man senior to an aircraftman and junior to a corporal. *Abbrev.*: L.A.C.

Leading Aircraftwoman or **Airwoman** in the air force, a woman senior to an aircraftwoman and junior to a corporal. *Abbrev.*: L.A.W.

leading article (lēd′ing) an important editorial or article in a newspaper, magazine, etc.

leading question (lēd′ing) a question so worded that it suggests the answer desired or makes the desired answer unavoidable.

hat, āge, cãre, fär; let, ēqual, tėrm; it, īce
hot, ōpen, ôrder; oil, out; cup, pu̇t, rüle, ūse
əbove, takən, pencəl, lemən, circəs
ch, child; ng, long; sh, ship
th, thin; ᴛʜ, then; zh, measure

Leading Seaman in the navy, a man senior to an able seaman and junior to a petty officer. *Abbrev.*: L.S.

leading strings (lēd′ing) **1** strings for supporting a child when learning to walk. **2** close guidance; too close guidance: *A boy of eighteen should not be kept in leading strings by his mother.*

lead pencil (led) an ordinary pencil having a graphite core for writing.

leaf (lēf) *n.* **leaves,** *v.* —*n.* **1** one of the thin, flat green parts that grow on the stem of a tree or other plant. **2** the petal of a flower. **3** a sheet of paper. Each side of a leaf is called a page. **4** a very thin sheet of metal, etc.: *gold leaf.* **5** a flat, movable piece in the top of a table. **6** the sliding, hinged, or movable part of a door, shutter, etc. **7 take a leaf from someone's book,** *Informal.* follow someone's example; copy someone's conduct. **8 turn over a new leaf,** start all over again; try to do or be better in the future.
—*v.* **1** put forth leaves: *The trees begin to leaf in the spring.* **2** turn the pages of. [OE *lēaf*] —**leaf′like′,** *adj.*

leaf·age (lēf′ij) *n.* leaves; foliage.

leaf bud a bud producing a stem having leaves only.

leaf·hop·per (lēf′hop′ər) *n.* any of several small homopterous insects that suck plant juices.

leaf·less (lēf′lis) *adj.* having no leaves. —**leaf′less·ness,** *n.*

leaf·let (lēf′lit) *n.* **1** a small or young leaf. **2** in botany, one of the separate blades or divisions of a compound leaf. **3** a small, flat or folded sheet of printed matter: *advertising leaflets.*

leaf·stalk (lēf′stok′ or -stôk′) *n.* the stalk by which a leaf is attached to a stem; petiole.

leaf·y (lēf′ē) *adj.* **leaf·i·er, leaf·i·est.** having many leaves; covered with leaves. —**leaf′i·ness,** *n.*

league[1] (lēg) *n. v.* **leagued, lea·guing.** —*n.* **1** an association of persons, parties, or countries formed to help one another. **2** the persons, parties, or countries associated in a league. **3** a group of teams that play a schedule of games against each other: *a hockey league, a bowling league.* **4 in league,** associated by agreement; associated. **5 the League,** the League of Nations.
—*v.* associate in a league; form a league. [< F *ligue* < Ital. *liga*, var. of *lega* < *legare* < L *ligare* bind]
—**Syn.** *n.* **1** union, federation, society.

league[2] (lēg) *n.* a measure of distance, usually about three miles. [ME < LL *leuga* < Celtic]

League of Nations an association of many countries, formed in 1919 to promote peace and co-operation among nations. It was dissolved in April, 1946.

lea·guer[1] (lē′gər) *Archaic.* —*v.* besiege. [< n.]
—*n.* **1** a siege. **2** the camp of a besieging army. [< Du. *leger* camp]

lea·guer[2] (lē′gər) *n.* a member of a league. [< *league*[1]]

leak (lēk) *n.* **1** a hole or crack, caused either by accident or by wear and tear, that lets something in or out: *a leak in a boat, a roof, a tire, etc.* **2** a leakage. **3** a means of escape, loss, etc. **4** the escape or loss itself: *a news leak.* **5** in electricity: **a** an escape of current from a conductor, especially as a result of poor insulation. **b** the point where such escape occurs.
—*v.* **1** go in or out through a hole or crack. **2** let something in that should be kept out; let something out that should be kept in: *His boat leaks. Her teakettle leaks.* **3** let (something) pass in or out: *That pipe leaks gas.* **4** become known gradually: *The secret leaked out.* **5** come in or go out in a secret or stealthy way: *Spies somehow leaked into the city.* **6** pass (away) by gradual waste: *The natural resources of our country are leaking away through misuse.* **7** *Informal.* make known: *Someone leaked the information to the press.* [< ON *leka*]

leak·age (lēk′ij) *n.* **1** a leaking; an entering or escaping. **2** that which leaks in or out. **3** the amount that leaks in or out: *The leakage was estimated at ten gallons an hour.* **4** in electricity, a leak. **5** *Informal.* a disclosure: *Sometimes leakages of secret information happen in newspaper stories.*

leak·y (lēk′ē) *adj.* **leak·i·er, leak·i·est.** leaking; having a leak or leaks. —**leak′i·ness,** *n.*

leal (lēl) *adj. Archaic or Scottish.* loyal. [ME < OF *leial* < L *legalis* legal < *lex* law. Doublet of LEGAL, LOYAL.]

lean[1] (lēn) *v.* **leaned** or **leant, lean·ing,** *n.* —*v.* **1** stand slanting, not upright; bend: *A small tree leans over in the wind.* **2** rest in a sloping or slanting position: *Lean against me.* **3** set or put in a leaning position: *Lean the picture against the wall till I am ready for it.* **4** depend; rely: *lean on a friend's advice.* **5** bend or turn a little: *lean toward mercy.* **6 lean over backward,** *Informal.* go to extremes in one direction so as to more than balance a tendency in the opposite direction. —*n.* the act of leaning; inclination. [OE *hlinian*] —**Syn.** *v.* **1** slant, incline, slope.

lean[2] (lēn) *adj.* **1** with little or no fat: *a lean horse.* **2** producing little; scant: *a lean harvest, a lean diet.* —*n.* meat having little fat. [OE *hlǣne*] —**lean′ness,** *n.* —**lean′ly,** *adv.* —**Syn.** *adj.* **1** spare, skinny, gaunt. See **thin. 2** meagre, barren.

Le·an·der (lē an′dər) *n.* in Greek legend, a lover who swam the Hellespont to visit his sweetheart, Hero, every night until he was finally drowned. See **Hero.**

lean·ing (lēn′ing) *n.* a tendency; inclination. —**Syn.** proneness, bias, bent.

Leaning Tower of Pisa a famous tower at Pisa, Italy, whose foundations have slipped so that it leans to one side.

leant (lent) *v.* a pt. and a pp. of **lean**[1].

lean-to (lēn′tü′) *n.* **-tos,** *adj.* —*n.* **1** a building attached to another, toward which its roof or supports are slanted. **2** a crude shelter built against a tree or post. It is usually open on one side. **3** a similar shelter made by leaning logs or poles against a bank or rock face and covering them with boards, sods, etc.
—*adj.* having supports pitched against or leaning on an adjoining wall or building: *a lean-to roof.*

A lean-to on a barn

leap (lēp) *n. v.* **leaped** or **leapt, leap·ing.** —*n.* **1** a jump or spring. **2** something to be jumped. **3** the distance covered by a jump. **4 by leaps and bounds,** very fast and very much; swiftly and effectively. **5 leap in the dark,** an action taken without knowing what its results will be.
—*v.* **1** jump: *A frog leaps.* **2** fly, shoot, or flash quickly: *The sword leaps from the scabbard. Water, flame, or light leaps up.* **3** jump over: *leap a fence.* **4** cause to leap. [OE *hlȳp*, n., *hlēapan*, v.] —**Syn.** *v.* **1** spring, bound. See **jump. 2** vault.

leap·frog (lēp′frog′) *n. v.* **-frogged, -frog·ging.** —*n.* a game in which one player jumps over another who is bending down. —*v.* **1** leap or jump as in the game of leapfrog. **2** skip over; side-step; avoid.

leapt (lept or lēpt) *v.* a pt. and a pp. of **leap.**

leap year a year having 366 days, the extra day being February 29. The number of any leap year can be exactly divided by 4, except for century years, which must be divisible by 400; thus 1960 and 2000 are leap years, whereas 1900 and 1961 are not.

learn (lėrn) *v.* **learned** or **learnt, learn·ing. 1** gain knowledge of (a subject) or skill in (an art, trade, etc.) by study, instruction, or experience: *learn French.* **2** acquire knowledge, skill, etc.: *He learns easily.* **3** memorize: *He learnt the poem in five minutes.* **4** find out; come to know: *He tried to learn the details of the train wreck.* **5** become informed; hear. [OE *leornian*] —**learn′a·ble,** *adj.*

☛ **learn, teach.** Substandard English often uses *learn* in the sense of *teach*: *He learned me how to play chess.* Educated usage keeps the distinction: *I learned how to play chess from him. He taught me how to play chess.*

learn·ed (lėr′nid) *adj.* having, showing, or requiring much knowledge; scholarly: *a learned man, a learned book.* —**learn′ed·ly,** *adv.* —**Syn.** educated, erudite.

learned borrowing a word or expression borrowed from a language at the scholarly, technical, or scientific level. *Flora* and *fauna* are learned borrowings from Latin.

learn·er (lėr′nər) *n.* **1** a person who is learning. **2** a beginner.

learn·ing (lėr′ning) *n.* **1** the gaining of knowledge or skill. **2** the possession of knowledge gained by study;

scholarship. 3 knowledge. —**Syn. 2** education.

learnt (lėrnt) *v.* a pt. and a pp. of **learn.**

lear·y (lēr′ē) *adj.* leery.

lease (lēs) *n. v.* **leased, leas·ing.** —*n.* **1** a contract, usually in the form of a written agreement, giving the right to use property for a certain length of time, usually by paying rent. **2** the length of time for which such an agreement is made. **3** the property held by a lease. **4 new lease on life,** the chance to live a longer, better, or happier life.
—*v.* **1** give a lease on. **2** take a lease on. **3** be leased.
[< AF *les* < *lesser* let, let go < L *laxare* loosen < *laxus* loose]

lease·hold (lēs′hōld′) *n.* **1** a holding by a lease. **2** real estate held by a lease. —**lease′hold′er,** *n.*

leash (lēsh) *n.* **1** a strap, chain, etc. for holding a dog or other animal in check. **2 hold in leash,** control; restrain. **3** a group of three animals: *a leash of hounds.* —*v.* fasten or hold in with a leash; control. [ME < OF *laisse* < L *laxa,* fem., loose]

least (lēst) *adj.* less than any other; smallest; slightest: *The least bit of dirt in a watch may make it stop.*
—*n.* **1** the least amount or degree: *That is the least you can do.* **2 at least** or **at the least, a** at the lowest estimate. **b** at any rate; in any case. **3 not in the least,** not at all.
—*adv.* to the least extent, amount, or degree: *He liked that book least of all.* [OE *lǣst*]

least common denominator the lowest common multiple of all the denominators of a group of fractions. 20 is the least common denominator of 1/2, 3/4, 4/5. *Abbrev.:* L.C.D., l.c.d., or lcd

least common multiple the least quantity that contains two or more given quantities exactly. The least common multiple of 3 and 4 and 6 is 12. *Abbrev.:* L.C.M., l.c.m., or lcm

least·ways (lēst′wāz′) *adv. Informal.* leastwise.

least·wise (lēst′wīz′) *adv. Informal.* at least; at any rate.

leath·er (leᴛʜ′ər) *n.* **1** a material made from the skin of animals by removing the hair and then tanning the skin. **2** an article made of leather. —*adj.* made of leather: *leather gloves.* —*v.* **1** furnish or cover with leather. **2** *Informal.* beat with a strap; thrash. [OE *lether*]

leath·er·ette (leᴛʜ′ər et′) *n.* imitation leather.

leath·ern (leᴛʜ′ərn) *adj.* **1** made of leather. **2** like leather.

leath·er·neck (leᴛʜ′ər nek′) *n. U.S. Slang.* a United States marine.

leath·er·y (leᴛʜ′ər ē) *adj.* like leather in appearance, texture, or toughness. —**leath′er·i·ness,** *n.*

leave[1] (lēv) *v.* **left, leav·ing. 1** go away: *We leave tonight.* **2** go away from: *He left the house.* **3** stop living in, belonging to, or working at or for: *leave the country, leave the club.* **4** go without taking; let remain: *I left a book on the table.* **5** go away and let remain in a particular condition: *leave a window open.* **6** let remain when one dies; bequeath: *He left a large fortune.* **7** give to be kept; deposit; give: *I left my suitcase in the station while I walked around the town.* **8** let (a person, etc.) alone to do something; let be: *Leave me to settle the matter.* **9** let remain for someone to do: *Leave the matter to me.* **10** let remain uneaten, unused, unremoved, etc.: *There is some coal left.* **11 leave off,** stop. **12 leave out,** fail to do, say, or put in; omit. [OE *lǣfan*] —**leav′er,** *n.* —**Syn. 1, 2** depart. See **go.** ☛ See **let**[1] for usage note.

leave[2] (lēv) *n.* **1** permission; consent: *They gave him leave to go.* **2** permission to be absent from duty. **3** the length of time that such permission lasts. **4 on leave,** absent from duty with permission. **5 take leave of,** say good-bye to. [OE *lēaf*] —**Syn. 1** authorization, liberty.

leave[3] (lēv) *v.* **leaved, leav·ing.** put forth leaves: *Trees begin to leave in the spring.* [var. of *leaf*]

leav·en (lev′ən) *n.* **1** any substance, such as yeast, that will cause fermentation and make dough rise. **2** a small amount of fermenting dough kept for this purpose. **3** an influence that, spreading silently and strongly, changes conditions or opinions. **4** a tempering or modifying element; a tinge or admixture: *mix a leaven of charity in one's judgments.*
—*v.* **1** raise with a leaven; make (dough) light or lighter. **2** spread through and transform. **3** blend or temper with some modifying element: *Hope leavened our despair.* [ME < OF *levain* < L *levamen* a lifting < *levare* raise]

hat, āge, cãre, fär; let, ēqual, tėrm; it, īce
hot, ōpen, ôrder; oil, out; cup, pu̇t, rüle, ūse
əbove, takən, pencəl, lemən, circəs
ch, child; ng, long; sh, ship
th, thin; ᴛʜ, then; zh, measure

leav·en·ing (lev′ən ing) *n.* a thing that leavens.

leave of absence 1 permission to be absent from duty. **2** the length of time that absence from duty is permitted.

leaves (lēvz) *n.* **1** pl. of **leaf. 2** pl. of **leave**[2]**.**

leave-tak·ing (lēv′tāk′ing) *n.* the act of taking leave; saying good-bye.

leav·ings (lēv′ingz) *n.pl.* leftovers; remnants.

Leb·a·nese (leb′ə nēz′) *adj.* of or having to do with Lebanon, a country at the eastern end of the Mediterranean, or its people. —*n.* a native or inhabitant of Lebanon.

Le·bens·raum or **le·bens·raum** (lā′bəns roum′) *n. German.* **1** the territory that a nation supposedly must possess in order to be economically self-sufficient. **2** the space, freedom, etc. required for existence, activity, or expansion. [literally, living space]

lech·er (lech′ər) *n.* a man who indulges in lechery. [ME < OF *lecheor* licker < *lechier* lick < Gmc.]

lech·er·ous (lech′ər əs) *adj.* lewd; lustful.

lech·er·y (lech′ər ē) *n.* lewdness; gross indulgence of lust.

lec·tern (lek′tərn) *n.* **1** a reading desk in a church, especially the desk from which the lessons are read at daily prayer. **2** any reading desk or stand. [ME < OF *lettrun, leitrun* < Med.L *lectrum* < L *legere* read]

lec·ture (lek′chər) *n. v.* **-tured, -tur·ing.** —*n.* **1 a** a speech or planned talk on a chosen subject, usually for the purpose of instruction. **b** such a speech or talk written down or printed. **2** a scolding. —*v.* **1** give a lecture. **2** instruct or entertain by a lecture. **3** scold; reprove. [ME < LL *lectura* < L *legere* read]

lec·tur·er (lek′chər ər) *n.* **1** a person who gives a lecture or lectures. **2** a teacher of junior rank at some universities.

led (led) *v.* pt. and pp. of **lead**[1]**.** ☛ See **lead**[1] for usage note.

Le·da (lē′də) *n.* in Greek mythology, the mother of Clytemnestra. Leda was visited by Zeus in the form of a swan and by him became the mother of Castor and Pollux and of Helen of Troy.

ledge (lej) *n.* **1** a narrow shelf: *a window ledge.* **2** a shelf or ridge of rock. **3** a layer or mass of metal-bearing rock. [ME < *legge(n)* lay[1]]

ledg·er (lej′ər) *n.* a book of accounts in which a business keeps a record of all money transactions. [ME < *legge(n)* lay[1]]

ledger line in music, a line added above or below the staff for notes that are too high or too low to be put on the staff.

lee (lē) *n.* **1** shelter. **2** the side or part sheltered from the wind. **3** the side away from the wind. **4** the direction toward which the wind is blowing.
—*adj.* **1** sheltered from the wind. **2** on the side away from the wind. **3** in the direction toward which the wind is blowing. [OE *hlēo*]

lee·board (lē′bôrd′) *n.* a large, flat board lowered into the water on the lee side of a sailboat to keep the boat from drifting sideways.

leech[1] (lēch) *n.* **1** a worm living in ponds and streams that sucks the blood of animals. Doctors formerly used leeches to suck blood from sick people. **2** a person who persistently tries to get what he can out of others. **3** *Archaic.* a doctor. —*v. Archaic.* cure; heal. [OE *lǣce*]

leech[2] (lēch) *n.* the edge of a sail not fastened to a rope or spar. [origin uncertain]

leek (lēk) *n.* a vegetable resembling an onion, but having larger leaves, an elongated bulb, and a milder flavor: *The leek is the emblem of Wales.* [OE *lēac*]

leer (lēr) *n.* a sly, sidelong look; evil glance. —*v.* give a sly, sidelong look; glance evilly. [? OE *hlēor* cheek, from idea of looking over one's cheek, looking askance] **—leer′ing·ly,** *adv.*

leer·y (lēr′ē) *adj. Informal.* **1** wary; suspicious. **2** afraid. **3** sly; cunning and knowing. Also, **leary. —leer′i·ly,** *adv.* **—leer′i·ness,** *n.*

lees (lēz) *n.pl.* dregs; sediment. [< F *lie* < Celtic]

lee shore the shore toward which the wind is blowing.

lee·ward (lē′wərd or lü′ərd) *adj. adv.* **1** on the side away from the wind. **2** in the direction toward which the wind is blowing. *—n.* the side away from the wind.

lee·way (lē′wā′) *n.* **1** the side movement of a ship to leeward, out of its course. **2** extra space at the side; more time, money, etc. than is needed; a margin of safety. **3** convenient room or scope for action.

left[1] (left) *adj.* **1** belonging to the side of the body that is toward the west when one faces north; belonging to the side of the body where the heart is normally located; having this relation to the front of any object: *the left wing of an army.* **2** situated nearer the observer's or speaker's left hand than his right. **3** in politics, of or having to do with a person, party, etc. that advocates or favors social or economic reform; liberal; radical.
—adv. on or to the left side: *turn left.*
—n. **1** the left side or hand. **2** in politics: **a** a person, party, etc. that advocates or favors social or economic reform; liberal; radical. **b** the part of a lawmaking body, consisting of the radical or liberal parties, that sits on the left of the presiding officer. **c** all the people and parties that favor reform. **3** in boxing, a blow struck with the left hand. [dial. OE *left* (for *lyft*) weak]

left[2] (left) *v.* pt. and pp. of **leave**[1].

left face a turn to the left.

left-hand (left′hand′) *adj.* **1** on or to the left. **2** of, for, or with the left hand.

left-hand·ed (left′han′did) *adj.* **1** using the left hand more easily and readily than the right. **2** done with the left hand. **3** made to be used with the left hand. **4** turning from right to left: *a left-handed screw.* **5** clumsy; awkward. **6** doubtful; insincere: *a left-handed compliment.* **—left′-hand′ed·ly,** *adv.* **—left′-hand′ed·ness,** *n.*

left-hand·er (left′han′dər) *n.* **1** a left-handed person. **2** a stroke or blow with the left hand.

left·ist (lef′tist) *n.* in politics: **1** a person who supports or favors the left. **2** a member of an organization of the left. *—adj. Informal.* having radical ideas.

left·o·ver (left′ō′vər) *n.* anything that is left. Scraps of food from a meal are leftovers. *—adj.* that is left; remaining.

left wing 1 the people advocating or favoring reform, especially the radical members of a political organization. **2** in hockey, lacrosse, etc.: **a** the playing position to the left of centre on a forward line. **b** a left winger.

left winger in hockey, lacrosse, etc., the player who occupies the position to the left of centre.

leg (leg) *n. v.* **legged, leg·ging.** *—n.* **1** one of the limbs on which human beings and animals support themselves and walk. **2** the part of a garment that covers a leg. **3** anything shaped or used like a leg: *a table leg.* **4** one of the distinct portions or stages of any course: *the last leg of a trip.* **5** the side of a triangle that is not the base or hypotenuse. **6** in cricket: **a** that part of the field to the left of and behind a right-handed batsman as he faces the bowler. **b** the fielder placed there.
give a leg up, *Informal.* help.
have not a leg to stand on, *Informal.* have no defence or reason.
on one's last legs, *Informal.* about to fall, collapse, die, etc.
pull one's leg, *Informal.* fool, trick, or make fun of one.
shake a leg, *Slang.* **a** hurry up. **b** dance.
stretch one's legs, *Informal.* take a walk.
—v. Informal. walk; run: *We could not get a ride, so we had to leg it.* [ME < ON *leggr*] **—leg′less,** *adj.*

Leg. or **leg. 1** legislature. **2** legislative. **3** legal. **4** legate. **5** legato.

leg·a·cy (leg′ə sē) *n.* **-cies. 1** the money or other property left to a person by a will. **2** something that has been handed down from an ancestor or predecessor. [ME < OF *legacie* < Med.L *legatia* < L *legatum* bequest, ult. < *lex, legis* covenant]

le·gal (lē′gəl) *adj.* **1** of law: *legal knowledge.* **2** of lawyers. **3** according to law; lawful. [< L *legalis* < *lex, legis* law. Doublet of LEAL, LOYAL.] **—Syn. 3** See **lawful.**

le·gal·ism (lē′gəl iz′əm) *n.* strict adherence to law or prescription.

le·gal·ist (lē′gəl ist) *n.* a person who adheres strictly to laws or rules.

le·gal·is·tic (lē′gəl is′tik) *adj.* adhering strictly to law or prescription.

le·gal·i·ty (li gal′ə tē) *n.* **-ties.** accordance with law; lawfulness.

le·gal·ize (lē′gəl īz′) *v.* **-ized, -iz·ing.** make legal; authorize by law; sanction. **—le′gal·i·za′tion,** *n.*

le·gal·ly (lē′gəl ē) *adv.* **1** in a legal manner. **2** according to law.

legal tender money that must, by law, be accepted in payment of debts.

leg·ate (leg′it) *n.* **1** a representative of the Pope. **2** an ambassador; representative; messenger. [< L *legatus,* originally, provided with a contract < *lex, legis* contract]

leg·a·tee (leg′ə tē′) *n.* a person to whom a legacy is left.

le·ga·tion (li gā′shən) *n.* **1** the diplomatic representative of a country and his staff of assistants. A legation ranks next below an embassy. **2** the official residence, offices, etc. of such a representative in a foreign country. **3** the office, position, or dignity of a legate. [ME < L *legatio, -onis,* ult. < *legare* dispatch < *legatus.* See LEGATE.]

le·ga·to (li gä′tō) in music: *—adj.* smooth and connected; without breaks between successive tones. *Legato* is the opposite of *staccato.* *—adv.* in a legato manner. *—n.* a legato passage, style, or performance. [< Ital. *legato* bound]

leg·end (lej′ənd) *n.* **1** a story coming down from the past, which has been widely accepted as true: *The stories about King Arthur and his Knights of the Round Table are legends, not history.* **2** such stories considered collectively. **3** the inscription on a coin or medal. **4** the words, etc. accompanying a picture, map, or diagram; caption. [ME < OF *legende* < Med.L < L *legenda* (things) to be read < *legere* read]

☛ **legend, myth.** *Legend* applies particularly to a story associated with some period in the history of a people or nation, often containing an element of fact but sometimes wholly untrue. Legends are intended to glorify a hero, saint, object, etc. and tell marvellous deeds he or it supposedly performed. *Myth* applies particularly to a story connected with the religion of a primitive civilization. Myths are told about gods or superhuman beings and are invented to explain certain beliefs or some aspect of nature.

leg·end·ar·y (lej′ən der′ē) *adj.* of a legend or legends; like a legend; not historical. **—leg′end·ar′i·ly,** *adv.*

leg·er·de·main (lej′ər də mān′) *n.* **1** sleight of hand; conjuring tricks; jugglery: *A common trick of legerdemain is to take rabbits from an apparently empty hat.* **2** trickery. [< F *léger de main* quick of hand]

-legged (legd or leg′id) *combining form.* having —— leg(s): *two-legged, bandy-legged.*

leg·gings (leg′ingz) *n.pl.* extra outer coverings of cloth or leather for the legs, for use out of doors; gaiters.

Leggings

leg·gy (leg′ē) *adj.* **1** having long legs. **2** having awkwardly long legs. **—leg′gi·ness,** *n.*

Leg·horn (leg′hôrn or leg′ərn) *n.* **1** a breed of rather small chickens. **2** a chicken of this breed. **3 leghorn, a** a hat made of flat, yellow, braided straw. **b** the braided straw from which such a hat is made. [< *Leghorn,* a seaport in W. Italy]

leg·i·bil·i·ty (lej′ə bil′ə tē) *n.* a legible condition or quality; clearness of print or writing.

leg·i·ble (lej′ə bəl) *adj.* **1** that can be read. **2** easy to read; plain and clear: *Her handwriting is both beautiful and legible.* [< LL *legibilis* < L *legere* read] **—leg′i·ble·ness,** *n.*

leg·i·bly (lej′ə blē) *adv.* clearly.

le·gion (lē′jən) *n.* **1** a large body of soldiers; army. **2** in the ancient Roman army, a body of soldiers consisting of 3,000 to 6,000 foot soldiers and 300 to 700 cavalrymen. **3** a great many; a very large number. **4 Legion,** Royal Canadian Legion. [ME < OF < L *legio, -onis* < *legere* choose]

le·gion·ar·y (lē′jən er′ē) *adj. n.* **-ar·ies.** —*adj.* of or belonging to a legion. —*n.* a soldier of a legion.

le·gion·naire (lē′jən ãr′) *n.* **1** a member of the Royal Canadian Legion. **2** formerly, a member of the French Foreign Legion. **3** a soldier of a legion. [< F]

Legion of Honor or **Honour** an honorary society founded by Napoleon in 1802, in which membership is given as a reward for great services to France.

leg·is·late (lej′is lāt′) *v.* **-lat·ed, -lat·ing. 1** make laws: *Parliament legislates for Canada.* **2** force by legislation: *The council legislated him out of office.* [< *legislator*]

leg·is·la·tion (lej′is lā′shən) *n.* **1** the making of laws. **2** the laws made.

leg·is·la·tive (lej′is lā′tiv) *adj.* **1** having to do with making laws: *legislative reforms.* **2** having the duty and power of making laws: *Parliament is a legislative body.* **3** ordered by law. —**leg′is·la′tive·ly,** *adv.*

Legislative Assembly in Canada, the group of representatives elected to the legislature of a province.

Legislative Council formerly in Quebec, the upper chamber of the legislature, composed of 24 members appointed for life by the Lieutenant-Governor in Council: *The Legislative Council in Quebec was abolished in 1968.*

leg·is·la·tor (lej′is lā′tər) *n.* a lawmaker; a member of a legislative body. [< L *legis lator* proposer of a law]

leg·is·la·ture (lej′is lā′chər) *n.* **1** a group of persons having the duty and power to make laws for a country, province, or state: *Each Canadian province has a legislature.* **2** the place where the legislators meet.

le·git (lə jit′) *adj. Slang.* legitimate.

le·git·i·ma·cy (lə jit′ə mə sē) *n.* the quality or state of being legitimate or lawful.

le·git·i·mate (*adj.* lə jit′ə mit; *v.* lə jit′ə māt′) *adj. v.* **-mat·ed, -mat·ing.** —*adj.* **1** rightful; lawful: *The Prince of Wales is the legitimate heir to the throne of England.* **2** allowed; acceptable: *Sickness is a legitimate reason for staying home from school.* **3** conforming to accepted standards: *a legitimate work of art.* **4** born of parents who are married. **5** resting on, or ruling by, the principle of hereditary right: *the legitimate title to a throne, a legitimate sovereign.* **6** logical: *a legitimate conclusion.* —*v.* make or declare lawful. [< Med.L *legitimatus* < L *legitimus* lawful < *lex, legis* law] —**le·git′i·mate·ly,** *adv.* —**Syn.** *adj.* **1** See **lawful.**

legitimate stage drama acted on the stage as opposed to motion pictures, vaudeville, burlesque, etc.

le·git·i·mist (lə jit′ə mist) *n.* a supporter of legitimate authority, especially of claims to rule based on direct descent.

le·git·i·mize (lə jit′ə mīz′) *v.* **-mized, -miz·ing.** make or declare to be legitimate. —**le·git′i·mi·za′tion,** *n.*

leg·man (leg′man′) *n.* **-men** (-men′). **1** a reporter who collects information at the scene of an event. **2** anyone who collects information, delivers messages, or does similar work.

leg-of-mut·ton (leg′əv mut′ən) *adj.* having the shape of a leg of mutton; wide at one end and narrow at the other.

leg·ume (leg′ūm or li gūm′) *n.* **1** a plant having a number of seeds in a pod, such as beans, peas, etc. **2** the seed pod of such a plant. **3** in botany, a dry, several-seeded fruit, characteristic of plants of the pea family. [< F < L *legumen*]

le·gu·mi·nous (li gū′mə nəs) *adj.* **1** of or bearing legumes. **2** of the same group of plants as beans and peas.

lei (lā) *n.* **leis.** a wreath of flowers, leaves, etc. [< Hawaiian]

A girl wearing a lei

Leices·ter (les′tər) *n.* **1** a breed of sheep having long wool. **2** a sheep of this breed. [*Leicester,* a county in England, where this breed originated]

hat, āge, cãre, fär; let, ēqual, tėrm; it, īce
hot, ōpen, ôrder; oil, out; cup, pu̇t, rüle, ūse
əbove, takən, pencəl, lemən, circəs
ch, child; ng, long; sh, ship
th, thin; ᴛʜ, then; zh, measure

leis·ter (lēs′tər or lis′tər) *n.* a spear having two or more barbed prongs, used in fishing. —*v.* spear with a leister. [< ON *liόstr* < *liόsta* strike]

leis·ure (lezh′ər or lē′zhər) *n.* **1** the time free from required work, in which a person may rest, amuse himself, and do the things he likes to do. **2 at leisure, a** free; not busy. **b** without hurry; taking plenty of time. **3 at one's leisure,** when one has free time; at one's convenience. —*adj.* **1** free; not busy: *leisure hours.* **2** having leisure. [ME < OF *leisir* < L *licere* be allowed]

leis·ured (lezh′ərd or lē′zhərd) *adj.* **1** having leisure. **2** leisurely.

leis·ure·ly (lezh′ər lē or lē′zhər lē) *adj. adv.* without hurry; taking plenty of time. —**leis′ure·li·ness,** *n.* —**Syn.** *adj.* See **slow.**

leit·mo·tif or **leit·mo·tiv** (līt′mō tēf′) *n.* **1** in music, a short theme or passage in a composition, repeated throughout the work and associated with a certain person, situation, or idea. **2** any repeating theme or subject. [< G *Leitmotiv* leading motive]

lek (lek) *n.* **1** a unit of money in Albania. See table at **money. 2** a coin worth one lek. [< Albanian]

lem·an (lem′ən) *n. Archaic.* **1** a sweetheart. **2** a lover or mistress. [ME *leofman* < OE *lēof* dear + *mann* man]

lem·ming (lem′ing) *n.* a small, mouselike arctic animal, having a short tail and furry feet. [< Norwegian]

lem·on (lem′ən) *n.* **1** an acid-tasting, light-yellow citrus fruit growing in warm climates. **2** a thorny tree that bears this fruit. **3** a pale yellow. **4** *Slang.* a thing or person that is considered inferior or disagreeable: *The last car I bought was a lemon.* **5** a soft drink flavored with lemon juice. —*adj.* pale-yellow. [ME < OF *limon* < Arabic *laimun* < Persian *limun*]

lem·on·ade (lem′ən ād′) *n.* a soft drink made of lemon juice, sugar, and water. [< F *limonade*]

lem·pi·ra (lem pē′rā) *n.* **1** a unit of money in Honduras. See table at **money. 2** a coin worth one lempira. [< Am.Sp.]

le·mur (lē′mər) *n.* an animal resembling a monkey but having a foxlike face and woolly fur, found mainly in Madagascar. [< L *lemures,* pl., spectres, ghosts; with reference to their nocturnal habits]

lend (lend) *v.* **lent, lend·ing. 1** let another have or use for a time: *Will you lend me your bicycle for an hour?* **2** give the use of (money) for a fixed or specified amount of payment: *Banks lend money and charge interest.* **3** make a loan or loans. **4** give; contribute or add: *The beautiful graduation gowns lent charm to the girls.* **5 lend itself** or **oneself to,** help or be suitable for; make oneself available for: *Don't lend yourself to foolish schemes.* **6 lend a hand,** help: *She lent a hand with the dishes.* [OE *lǣnan* < *lǣn* loan] —**lend′er,** *n.* ☛ See **loan** for usage note.

lend-lease (lend′lēs′) *n. v.* **-leased, -leas·ing.** —*n.* a system of making a loan of equipment in return for some service or material. —*v.* lend under this system.

length (length) *n.* **1** how long a thing is; a thing's measurement from end to end; the longest way a thing can be measured: *the length of your arm.* **2** the distance a thing extends: *The length of a race is the distance run.* **3** the extent in time: *the length of an hour.* **4** a long stretch or extent. **5** a piece or portion of cloth, pipe, rope, etc. of given length: *a length of rope.* **6** the distance from end to end of a boat, horse, etc., considered as a unit of measurement in racing: *The gray horse finished the race two lengths ahead of the brown one.* **7 at full length,** with the body stretched out flat. **8 at length, a** at last; finally. **b** with all the details; fully. **9 go to any length,** do everything possible. **10 keep at arm's length,** discourage from being too familiar. [OE *length* < *lang* long[1]]

length·en (leng′thən) *v.* **1** make longer. **2** become or grow longer.
Syn. 1, 2 Lengthen, extend, prolong = make or become longer.

Lengthen = make or become longer in space or time: *There is no way to lengthen a day.* **Extend** suggests stretching out beyond the present point or limits: *We had to extend the table for our Thanksgiving dinner.* **Prolong** = lengthen in time beyond a normal, proper, or desirable limit: *She decided to prolong her visit.*

length·ways (length′wāz′) *adv. adj.* lengthwise.

length·wise (length′wīz′) *adv. adj.* in the direction of the length.

length·y (leng′thē) *adj.* **length·i·er, length·i·est.** long; too long. —**length′i·ly,** *adv.* —**length′i·ness,** *n.*

len·ien·cy (lē′nē ən sē or lēn′yən sē) *n.* mildness; gentleness; mercy. Also, **lenience.**

len·ient (lē′nē ənt or lēn′yənt) *adj.* mild or gentle; merciful: *a lenient punishment.* [< L *leniens, -entis,* ppr. of *lenire* soften < *lenis* mild] —**len′ient·ly,** *adv.* —**Syn.** compassionate, tolerant, forbearing.

len·i·tive (len′ə tiv) *adj.* **1** softening; soothing; mitigating. **2** mildly laxative. —*n.* **1** anything that soothes or softens; palliative. **2** a mild laxative. [< Med.L *lenitivus* < L *lenitus,* pp. of *lenire* soften]

len·i·ty (len′ə tē) *n.* **-ties.** mildness; gentleness; mercifulness. [< L *lenitas* < *lenis* mild]

lens (lenz) *n.* **lens·es. 1** a piece of glass, or something like glass, that brings closer together or sends wider apart the rays of light passing through it. The lens of a camera forms images; the lenses of a telescope make things look larger and nearer. **2** a combination of two or more of these pieces, especially as used in a camera. **3** in anatomy, a clear, oval structure in the eye directly behind the iris, that directs light rays upon the retina. **4** a device that focusses sound waves, streams of electrons, etc. [< L *lens, lentis* lentil (which has a biconvex shape)]

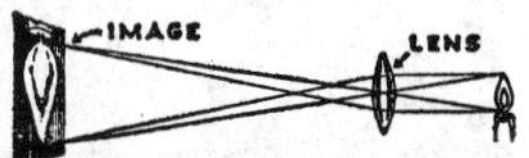

A lens. The light from the candle's flame passes through the lens and is bent so that an upside-down image of this flame is produced on the card behind the lens.

lent (lent) *v.* pt. and pp. of *lend.*

Lent (lent) *n.* in the Christian church, the forty days before Easter, kept as a time for fasting and repenting of sins. [OE *lencten* spring < W.Gmc. **lang* -long[1] (with reference to lengthening days)]

len·ta·men·te (len′tə men′tā) *adv.* in music, slowly. [< Ital.]

len·tan·do (len tän′dō) *adj.* in music, slowing down. [< Ital.]

Lent·en or **lent·en** (len′tən) *adj.* of Lent; during Lent; suitable for Lent. [originally noun; OE *lencten.* See LENT.]

len·ti·cel (len′tə səl) *n.* a ventilating pore in the bark of woody plants. [< F *lenticelle,* dim. of L *lens, lentis* lentil, because of its shape]

len·til (len′təl) *n.* **1** a plant whose pods contain two seeds shaped like double-convex lenses, growing mostly in S. Europe and Asia. **2** the edible seed of this plant. [< F *lentille* < L *lenticula,* dim. of *lens, lentis* lentil]

len·to (len′tō) in music: —*adj.* slow. —*adv.* slowly. —*n.* a slow movement or passage. [< Ital.]

l'en·voi or **l'en·voy** (len′voi or lon vwä′) *n.* **1** a short stanza ending a poem. **2** a postscript to a prose work, giving a moral, dedication, etc. [< F *l'envoi,* literally, the sending. Cf. ENVOY[2].]

Le·o (lē′ō) *n.* **1** in astronomy, a northern constellation supposed to have the shape of a lion. **2** in astrology, the fifth sign of the zodiac; the Lion. The sun enters Leo about July 22. [< L]

le·on·e (lē ō′nē) *n.* **1** a unit of money in Sierra Leone. See table at **money. 2** a coin worth one leone.

Le·o·nid (lē′ə nid) *n.* one of a shower of meteors occurring annually about November 14. The Leonids seem to come from the constellation Leo.

le·o·nine (lē′ə nīn′) *adj.* of or like a lion. [< L *leoninus* < *leo* lion]

leop·ard (lep′ərd) *n.* **1** a fierce mammal of the cat family, native to Africa and Asia, that has a dull-yellowish skin spotted with black. **2** any of various mammals closely related to the leopard, such as the jaguar, ocelot, or snow leopard. **3** the fur of a leopard. **4** a coat or other garment made of this fur. [ME < OF < L < Gk. *leopardos* < *leōn* lion + *pardos* leopard]

leop·ard·ess (lep′ər dis) *n.* a female leopard.

le·o·tard (lē′ə tärd′) *n.* **1** a one-piece, close-fitting garment worn by dancers, acrobats, etc. **2 leotards,** *pl.* tights. [< Jules *Léotard,* 19th-century French gymnast]

lep·er (lep′ər) *n.* a person who has leprosy. [ME < OF < L < Gk. *lepra* leprosy. See LEPROUS.]

lep·i·dop·ter·ous (lep′ə dop′tər əs) *adj.* belonging to the group of insects including butterflies and moths. The larvae are wormlike; the adults have four broad wings more or less covered with small scales. [< NL *Lepidoptera,* pl. < Gk. *lepis, -idos* scale + *pteron* wing]

lep·re·chaun (lep′rə kon′ or lep′rə kôn′) *n.* in Irish folklore, a sprite or goblin resembling a little old man. [< Irish *lupracán*]

lep·ro·sy (lep′rə sē) *n.* a chronic, mildly infectious, bacterial disease, characterized by ulcers and white, scaly scabs. Leprosy attacks the nerves, causing weakening and wasting of muscles, and may lead to tuberculosis or other diseases. [< *leprous*]

lep·rous (lep′rəs) *adj.* **1** having leprosy. **2** of or like leprosy. **3** scaly or scurfy. **4** causing leprosy. [< L *leprosus* < *lepra* leprosy < Gk. *lepra* < *lepein* to peel] —**lep′rous·ly,** *adv.*

lep·ton (lep′ton) *n.* **-ta** (-tə). **1** a unit of money in Greece, worth 1/100 of a drachma. **2** a coin worth one lepton. [< Gk.]

Les·bi·an (lez′bē ən) *n.* **1** a homosexual woman. **2** a native or inhabitant of the Greek island of Lesbos. —*adj.* **1** having to do with homosexuality in women. **2** of or having to do with the island of Lesbos. [< *Lesbos,* the home of the supposedly homosexual Greek poetess *Sappho,* who lived about 600 B.C.]

Les·bi·an·ism (lez′bē ə niz′əm) *n.* homosexuality in women.

lèse-ma·jes·té (lez′mä zhes tā′) *n. French.* lese-majesty.

lese-maj·es·ty (lēz′maj′is tē) *n.* a crime or offence against the sovereign power in a state; treason. [< F *lèse-majesté* < L *laesa majestas* injured majesty]

le·sion (lē′zhən) *n.* **1** an injury; hurt. **2** in medicine, a diseased condition often causing a change in the structure of an organ or tissue. [< L *laesio, -onis* injury < *laedere* to strike]

less (les) *adj.* **1** smaller; not so much: *of less width, eat less meat.* **2** lower in age, rank, or importance: *no less a person than the Prince of Wales.*
—*n.* a smaller amount or quantity: *He refused to take less than $5.*
—*adv.* to a smaller extent or degree: *less important.*
—*prep.* lacking; without; minus: *a year less two days.* [OE *lǣs(sa)*]

☛ **less, lesser.** Both are used as comparative (of *little*), *less* more usually referring to size or quantity: *less time, less food*; *lesser,* a formal word, referring to value or importance: *a lesser writer.*
☛ See **fewer** for another usage note.

-less *suffix.* **1** without; that has no: *homeless = without a home.* **2** that does not: *ceaseless = that does not cease.* **3** that cannot be ——ed: *countless = that cannot be counted.* [OE *-lēas,* suffixal use of *lēas* free from]
☛ **-less** is freely added to almost any noun and many verbs to form adjectives with the above meanings.

les·see (les ē′) *n.* a person to whom a lease is granted.

L. ès Sc. Licentiate in Sciences. (for F *Licencié ès Sciences*)

less·en (les′ən) *v.* **1** grow less. **2** make less; decrease. **3** represent as less; minimize; belittle. —**Syn. 1, 2** diminish, shrink.

less·er (les′ər) *adj.* **1** less; smaller. **2** the less important of two. ☛ See **less** for usage note.

les·son (les′ən) *n.* **1** something learned or studied. **2** a unit of learning or teaching; what is to be studied or practised at one time: *a music lesson.* **3** an instructive experience, serving to encourage or warn. **4** a selection from the Bible or other sacred writings, read as part of a religious service. **5** a rebuke; lecture.
—*v.* **1** give a lesson to. **2** rebuke; lecture. [ME < OF *lecon* < L *lectio, -onis* reading < *legere* read]

les·sor (les′ ôr or les ôr′) *n.* a person who grants a lease.

lest (lest) *conj.* **1** for fear that: *Be careful lest you fall from that tree.* **2** that: *I was afraid lest he should come too late to save us.* [ME *leste* < OE *thȳ lǣs the* by so much the less that]

let[1] (let) *v.* **let, let·ting. 1** allow; permit: *Let the dog have a bone.* **2** allow to pass, go, or come: *Let all passengers board ship.* **3** allow to run out: *Doctors used to let blood from people to lessen a fever.* **4** rent; hire out: *let a boat by the hour.* **5** be rented: *That house lets for $80 a month.* **6** *Let* is used in giving suggestions or giving commands: "*Let's go home*" *means* "*I suggest that we go home.*" **7** suppose; assume: *Let the two lines be parallel.*
let down, a lower. **b** slow up. **c** disappoint. **d** humiliate.
let go, a allow to escape; set at liberty; release one's hold of: *let go a rope or an anchor. Let me go.* **b** give up; abandon; cease to regard or consider: *He let go all thought of winning a prize.* **c** cease to restrain; allow to follow a course unchecked: *let oneself go.*
let in, admit; permit to enter.
let in for, open the way to; cause (trouble, unpleasantness, etc.): *He let his friends in for a lot of questioning when he left town so suddenly.*
let loose, allow to go free; liberate; release from restraint.
let off, a allow to go free; release: *let off steam.* **b** free from: *The teacher would not let us off homework.* **c** fire; explode: *let off a detonation.* **d** discharge; allow to get off.
let on, *Informal.* **a** allow to be known; reveal one's knowledge of. **b** pretend; make believe.
let out, a permit to go out. **b** make (garments) larger. **c** rent (a house, apartment, etc.). **d** *Informal.* dismiss or be dismissed. **e** make known; disclose.
let up, *Informal.* stop; pause. [OE *lǣtan*]
☞ **let, leave.** A common uneducated and regional idiom is the use of *leave* where formal and informal English use *let,* for example, *Leave me go* instead of *Let me go.*

let[2] (let) *v.* **let·ted** or **let, let·ting,** *n.* —*v. Archaic.* prevent; hinder; obstruct. —*n.* **1** *Archaic.* a prevention; hindrance; obstruction. **2 without let or hindrance,** with nothing to prevent, hinder, or obstruct. **3** in tennis and similar games, interference with the ball. When this fault occurs, the ball or point must be played over again. [OE *lettan* < *læt* late]

-let *suffix.* **1** little, as in *booklet, streamlet, wavelet.* **2** a thing worn as a band on, as an *anklet, armlet, wristlet.* **3** other meanings, as in *couplet, gauntlet, ringlet.* [< OF *-elet* < *-el* (< L *-ellus,* dim. suffix or < L *-ale,* neut.) + *-et* < VL *-ittus,* dim. suffix, ? < Celtic]

let·down (let′doun′) *n.* **1** a slowing up. **2** *Informal.* a disappointment. **3** a humiliation.

le·thal (lē′thəl) *adj.* causing death; deadly: *lethal weapons, a lethal dose.* [< L *let(h)alis* < *letum* death] —**le′thal·ly,** *adv.*

le·thar·gic (lə thär′jik) *adj.* **1** unnaturally drowsy; sluggish; dull: *A hot, humid day often makes us feel lethargic.* **2** producing lethargy. —**le·thar′gi·cal·ly,** *adv.*

leth·ar·gy (leth′ər jē) *n.* **-gies. 1** drowsy dullness; lack of energy; sluggish inactivity. **2** in medicine, a condition characterized by unnatural drowsiness or prolonged sleep. [< L < Gk. *lēthargia* < *lēthargos* forgetful < *lēthē* forgetfulness + *argos* lazy] —**Syn. 1** torpor, apathy, stupor.

Le·the (lē′thē) *n.* **1** in Greek mythology, a river in Hades. By drinking its water, the dead could forget the past. **2** forgetfulness; oblivion. [< L < Gk. *lēthē* oblivion]

Le·the·an (lē thē′ən) *adj.* **1** having to do with Lethe or its water. **2** causing forgetfulness.

let's (lets) let us.

Lett (let) *n.* **1** a member of a group of people living in Latvia, Lithuania, Estonia, and other Baltic regions. **2** their Baltic language; Lettish.

let·ter (let′ər) *n.* **1** a symbol or sign (on paper, etc.) that stands for any one of the sounds that make up words. **2** a written or printed message. **3** an official document granting some right or privilege. **4** the exact wording; actual terms: *He kept the letter of the law but not the spirit.* **5 to the letter,** very exactly; just as one has been told. **6 letters,** *pl.* **a** literature. **b** a knowledge of literature; literary culture. **c** the profession of an author. **7** in printing: **a** a bit of metal type bearing a letter; type face. **b** a particular style of type.

hat, āge, cãre, fär; let, ēqual, tėrm; it, īce
hot, ōpen, ôrder; oil, out; cup, pu̇t, rüle, ūse
əbove, takən, pencəl, lemən, circəs
ch, child; ng, long; sh, ship
th, thin; ᴛʜ, then; zh, measure

—*v.* **1** mark with letters. **2** inscribe (something) in letters. **3** make letters. [ME < OF < L *littera*] —**let′ter·er,** *n.*
Syn. *n.* **2 Letter, epistle** = a written message. **Letter** is the general word applying to a written, typed, or printed message, either personal, business, or official: *Put a stamp on that letter before you mail it.* **Epistle,** chiefly literary, applies to a long letter written in formal or elegant language, intended to teach or advise: *This year we are studying the epistles of some famous poets.*

letter carrier a person who collects or delivers mail; postman; mailman.

let·tered (let′ərd) *adj.* **1** marked with letters. **2** able to read and write; educated. **3** knowing literature; having literary culture.

let·ter·gram (let′ər gram′) *n.* a type of telegram in which up to 50 words are allowed at reduced rates, because it is transmitted outside regular business hours.

let·ter·head (let′ər hed′) *n.* **1** words printed at the top of a sheet of paper, usually a name and address. **2** a sheet of paper so printed.

let·ter·ing (let′ər ing) *n.* **1** letters drawn, painted, stamped, etc. **2** a marking with letters; making letters.

letter of credit a document issued by a bank, allowing the person named in it to draw money up to a certain amount from other specified banks.

let·ter-per·fect (let′ər pėr′fikt) *adj.* **1** knowing one's part or lesson perfectly. **2** correct in every detail.

letter press 1 a machine for making copies of letters. **2** printing from type, or from relief plates, as distinguished from offset, lithography, photogravure, etc.

let·ter·press (let′ər pres′) *n.* printed words, as distinguished from illustrations, etc.

letter rate the postage rate for first-class mail.

letters of marque or **letters of marque and reprisal** an official document giving a person permission from a government to capture the merchant ships of an enemy.

letters patent an official document giving a person or a corporation authority from a government to do some act or to have some right.

Let·tish (let′ish) *adj.* of or having to do with the Letts or their language. —*n.* the Baltic language of the Letts; Latvian.

let·tre de ca·chet (let′rə də kä shā′) *French.* formerly, a letter under the seal of the King of France, especially one ordering someone to be sent to prison or exile.

let·tuce (let′is) *n.* **1** the large, crisp, green leaves of a garden plant much used in salad. **2** the plant. [ME < OF *laitues,* pl. < L *lactuca* lettuce < *lac, lactis* milk; with reference to the milky juice of the plant]

let·up (let′up′) *n. Informal.* a stop; pause.

leu (lē′ü) *n.* **lei** (lā). **1** a unit of money in Romania. See table at **money. 2** a coin worth one leu. [< Romanian]

leu·co·cyte (lü′kə sīt′) *n.* in physiology, one of the tiny, white or colorless cells in the blood that destroy disease germs; a white blood corpuscle. [< Gk. *leukos* white + E *-cyte*]

leu·ke·mi·a (lü kē′mē ə or lü kēm′yə) *n.* a cancerous disease of the blood, usually fatal, characterized by a large excess of white corpuscles in the blood. [< NL < Gk. *leukos* white + *-aimia* blood < *haima*]

lev (lef) *n.* **1** a unit of money in Bulgaria. See table at **money. 2** a coin worth one lev. [< Bulgarian]

Lev. Leviticus.

Le·van·tine (lə van′tin, lev′ən tīn′, or lev′ən tēn′) *adj.* of the Levant, countries on the Mediterranean Sea, east of Italy. —*n.* a person or ship of the Levant.

lev·ee[1] (lev′ē) *n.* a bank built to keep a river from overflowing: *Many citizens manned the levees during the flood.* [< F *levée* < *lever* raise < L *levare*]

lev·ee[2] or **lev·ée** (lev′ē or le vē′) *n.* **1** a formal reception: *The regiment holds a levee on New Year's Day. He received an invitation to the Governor General's levee.* **2** *Archaic.* a rising from bed; a reception held while rising. French kings used to hold levees in the morning while they were getting up and dressing. [< F *levé, lever* a rising < *lever* raise. See LEVEE[1].]

lev·el (lev′əl) *adj. n. v.* **-elled** or **-eled, -el·ling** or **-el·ing.** —*adj.* **1** having the same height everywhere; flat; even: *a level floor.* **2** of equal height, importance, etc.: *The table is level with the edge of the window.* **3** even; uniform; steady: *a calm and level tone.* **4** *Informal.* well-balanced; sensible. **5 one's level best,** *Informal.* one's very best; as well as one can do. [< n.]

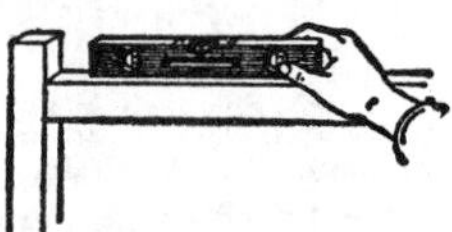

A level in use (def. 2). It has a glass tube containing a liquid with an air bubble in it. If the surface is level, the bubble stays at the centre; if not, the bubble moves to the higher side.

—*n.* **1** something that is level. **2** an instrument for showing whether a surface is level. **3** the measuring of differences in height with such an instrument. **4** a level position or condition. **5** height: *The flood rose to a level of 60 feet.* **6** a position or standard from a social, moral, or intellectual point of view. **7** a horizontal passage in a mine: *The explosion occurred on the third level near the working face.* **8 find one's** or **its level,** arrive at the natural or proper level. **9 on the level,** *Informal.* in a fair straightforward manner.
—*v.* **1** make level; put on the same level. **2** bring to a level. **3** lay low; bring (something) to the level of the ground. **4** raise and hold level for shooting; aim: *The soldier levelled his rifle.* **5** aim or direct (words, intentions, etc.). **6** remove or reduce (differences, etc.); make uniform. **7 level off, a** come to an equilibrium; even off; steady; come to the end of a rise or decline in something. **b** in aeronautics, return to a horizontal position in flight, as in landing or after a climb or dive. **8 level out,** level off. **9 level with,** *Slang.* be honest with; tell the truth.
[ME < OF *livel* < VL *libellum* < L *libella,* dim. of *libra* balance] —**lev′el·ler** or **lev′el·er,** *n.* —**lev′el·ly,** *adv.* —**lev′el·ness,** *n.*
Syn. *adj.* **1 Level, even, smooth** = flat or having a flat surface. **Level** = not sloping and having no noticeably high or low places on the surface: *We built our house on level ground.* **Even** = having a uniformly flat, but not necessarily level, surface, with no irregular places: *The top of that card table is not even.* **Smooth** = perfectly even, without a trace of roughness to be seen or felt: *We sandpapered the shelves until they were smooth.*

level crossing a place where a railway track crosses a street or another railway track on the same level; railway crossing.

lev·el-head·ed (lev′əl hed′id) *adj.* having good common sense or good judgment; sensible. —**lev′el-head′ed·ly,** *adv.*

le·ver (lē′vər or lev′ər) *n.* **1** a bar for raising or moving a weight at one end by pushing down at the other end. The bar or lever must be supported at a point in between the ends. See **fulcrum** for picture. **2** any bar working on an axis or support: *a brake lever.* **3** any means of exerting control: *He used his knowledge of the crime as a lever to gain secret information.* —*v.* **1** move with a lever. **2** use a lever. [ME < OF *leveor* < *lever* raise < L *levare*]

lev·er·age (lē′vər ij or lev′ər ij) *n.* **1** the action of a lever. **2** the advantage or power gained by using a lever. **3** increased power of action.

lev·er·et (lev′ər it) *n.* a young hare. [< AF *leveret,* dim. of OF *lievre* < L*l epus, -poris* hare]

le·vi·a·than (lə vī′ə thən) *n.* **1** in the Bible, a huge sea animal. **2** a huge ship. **3** any great and powerful person or thing. [< LL < Hebrew *livyathan* dragon]

le·vis (lē′vīz) *n.pl.* **1** tight-fitting, heavy trousers of blue denim reinforced at strain points with copper rivets or extra stitching. **2 Levis,** *Trademark.* a name for this kind of trousers reinforced with copper rivets. [originally, *Levi's* < *Levi* Strauss and Company, an early manufacturer of overalls]

lev·i·tate (lev′ə tāt′) *v.* **-tat·ed, -tat·ing.** **1** rise or float in the air. **2** cause to rise or float in the air. [< L *levitas* lightness (see LEVITY), modelled after *gravitate*]

lev·i·ta·tion (lev′ə tā′shən) *n.* **1** a levitating. **2** the act or process of rising, or raising (a body), from the ground by spiritualistic means.

Le·vite (lē′vīt) *n.* a member of the tribe of Levi, from which assistants to the Jewish priests were chosen.

Le·vit·i·cal (lə vit′ə kəl) *adj.* **1** of the Levites. **2** of Leviticus or the law contained in it.

Le·vit·i·cus (lə vit′ə kəs) *n.* the third book of the Old Testament, containing the laws for the priests and Levites and the ritual for Jewish rites and ceremonies. [< LL *Leviticus* (*liber*) (The Book) of the Levites < Gk. *Leuitikos* < *Leuitēs* Levite]

lev·i·ty (lev′ə tē) *n.* **-ties.** lightness of mind, character, or behavior; lack of proper seriousness or earnestness. [< L *levitas* < *levis* light] —**Syn.** flippancy, frivolity.

lev·u·lose (lev′yù lōs′) *n.* a form of sugar in honey, fruits, etc.; fruit sugar. *Formula*: $C_6H_{12}O_6$ [< L *laevus* left; under polarized light its plane of polarization is turned to the left]

lev·y (lev′ē) *v.* **lev·ied, lev·y·ing,** *n.* **lev·ies.** —*v.* **1** order to be paid: *The government levies taxes to pay its expenses.* **2** collect (men) for an army: *levy troops in time of war.* **3** seize by law for unpaid debts. **4 levy war on,** make war on; start a way against. [< n.]
—*n.* **1** money collected by authority or force. **2** the men collected for an army. **3** a levying. [< F *levée* < *lever* raise. See LEVEE[1].]

lewd (lüd) *adj.* not decent; lustful. [OE *lǣwede* laic] —**lewd′ly,** *adv.* —**lewd′ness,** *n.* —**Syn.** lecherous.

lew·is·ite (lü′is īt′) *n.* a colorless, oily liquid, used in chemical warfare as a poison gas. It causes severe blistering of the skin and lungs. *Formula*: $C_2H_2AsCl_3$ [< *lewis* (W. Lee Lewis, 1878-1943, an American chemist) + *-ite*[1]]

lex (leks) *n.* **le·ges** (leg′ās or lej′ās). *Latin.* law.

lex·i·cal (lek′sə kəl) *adj.* of or having to do with the basic meaning of a word.

lex·i·cog·ra·pher (lek′sə kog′rə fər) *n.* a person who compiles dictionaries. [< Gk. *lexikographos* < *lexikon* wordbook + *graphein* write]

lex·i·co·graph·ic (lek′sə kə graf′ik) *adj.* lexicographical.

lex·i·co·graph·i·cal (lek′sə kə graf′ə kəl) *adj.* of or having to do with lexicography. —**lex′i·co·graph′i·cal·ly,** *adv.*

lex·i·cog·ra·phy (lek′sə kog′rə fē) *n.* the science or practice of compiling dictionaries.

lex·i·col·o·gist (lek′sə kol′ə jist) *n.* an expert in lexicology.

lex·i·col·o·gy (lek′sə kol′ə jē) *n.* the study of the history, form, and meaning of words. [< Gk. *lexikon* word + E *-logy*]

lex·i·con (lek′sə kən or lek′sə kon′) *n.* **1** a dictionary, especially of Greek, Latin, or Hebrew. **2** the vocabulary belonging to a certain subject, group, or activity. **3** in linguistics, the inventory, or total stock, of morphemes in a language. [< Gk. *lexikon* (*biblion*) wordbook < *lexis* word < *legein* say]

Leyden jar a device for accumulating frictional electricity, consisting essentially of a glass jar lined inside and outside, for most of its height, with tin foil. [< *Leyden, Leiden,* Netherlands]

LF, l.f., or **lf** low frequency.

lg. or **lge.** large.

l.g. left guard.

LG Low German.

LGk. Late Greek.

l.h. or **L.H.** left hand.

Lha·sa ap·so (lä′sə ap′sō) **1** a Tibetan breed of small watchdog having a heavy, usually light brown, coat and much hair over the eyes. **2** a dog of this breed. [< *Lhasa,* the capital of Tibet + Tibetan *apso* watchdog]

Li lithium.

L.I. Long Island.

li·a·bil·i·ty (lī′ə bil′ə tē) *n.* **-ties.** **1** the state of being susceptible: *liability to disease.* **2** the state of being under obligation: *liability for a debt.* **3** debt. **4** something to one's disadvantage: *Poor handwriting is a liability in getting a job.*

li·a·ble (lī′ə bəl or, *for def. 1*, lī′bəl) *adj.* **1** likely; unpleasantly likely: *Glass is liable to break. One is liable to slip on ice.* **2** in danger of having, doing, etc.: *We are all liable to diseases.* **3** responsible; bound by law to pay: *The Post Office Department is not liable for damage to a parcel sent by mail unless it is insured.* **4** under obligation; subject: *Citizens are liable to jury duty.* [< F *lier* bind < L *ligare*] —**Syn. 1** apt. **3** accountable, answerable. ☛ See **likely** for usage note.

li·aise (lē āz′) *v.* **-aised, -ais·ing.** act as liaison officer or establish liaison (*with*): *An envoy liaises with a foreign government.* [back formation from *liaison*]
☛ Many people consider **liaise** to be jargon, unacceptable in good usage.

li·ai·son (lē ā′zon, lē′ā zon′, or lē′ə zon′) *n.* **1** communication between parts of an armed force to secure proper co-operation. **2** similar communication between civilian bodies, such as government departments, companies, or schools. **3** an unlawful intimacy between a man and a woman. **4** in speaking French, the pronouncing of a usually silent final consonant joining it syllabically to a following word that begins with a vowel or mute *h.* [< F < L *ligatio, -onis* < *ligare* bind]

liaison officer 1 an officer in the armed services whose duty is to secure proper co-operation between parts of an armed force. **2** a similar official in a government department, company, etc.

li·a·na (lē ä′nə or lē an′ə) *n.* a climbing tropical vine having a woody stem. Giant lianas wind around the trunks and climb from tree to tree in jungles. [< F *liane*, earlier *liorne*]

li·ane (lē än′) *n.* liana.

li·ar (lī′ər) *n.* a person who tells lies; a person who says what is not true.

li·ard (lē′ərd, lē är′, or lē ärd′) *n. Cdn.* especially in the North, the balsam poplar; tacamahac. [< Cdn.F < OF *liard* gray]

lib. 1 librarian. **2** library. **3** book (for L *liber*).

Lib. 1 Liberal. **2** Liberia.

li·ba·tion (lī bā′shən) *n.* **1** a pouring out of wine, water, etc. as an offering to a god. **2** the wine, water, etc. offered in this way. [< L *libatio, -onis* < *libare* pour out]

li·bel (lī′bəl) *n. v.* **-belled** or **-beled, -bel·ling** or **-bel·ing.** —*n.* **1** in law: **a** a written or printed statement tending to damage a person's reputation. **b** the crime of writing or printing a libel. **2** any false or damaging statement about a person. —*v.* **1** write or print a libel about. **2** make false or damaging statements about. [< L *libellus*, dim. of *liber* book]

li·bel·ler or **li·bel·er** (lī′bəl ər) *n.* a person who libels another.

li·bel·lous or **li·bel·ous** (lī′bəl əs) *adj.* **1** containing a libel. **2** spreading libels: *a libellous tongue.* —**li′bel·lous·ly,** *adv.*

lib·er·al (lib′ər əl or lib′rəl) *adj.* **1** generous: *a liberal donation.* **2** plentiful; abundant: *He put in a liberal supply of coal for the winter.* **3** broad-minded; not narrow in one's ideas: *a liberal thinker.* **4** favoring progress and reforms. **5** Often, **Liberal, a** of or belonging to a political party that advocates moderate reforms. **b** of Liberals or their party. **6** giving the general thought, not a word-for-word rendering: *a liberal translation.*
—*n.* **1** a person favorable to progress and reforms. **2** Often, **Liberal. a** a member of a political liberal party. **b** in Canada, a member of the Liberal Party, one of the principal political groups; a person who supports the views and principles of this party. [< L *liberalis* befitting free men < *liber* free] —**lib′er·al·ly,** *adv.* —**lib′er·al·ness,** *n.* —**Syn.** *adj.* **1** bountiful. **2** ample, large. **3** tolerant.

liberal arts subjects such as literature, languages, history, and philosophy as distinct from technical or professional subjects.

liberal education an education in the liberal arts, especially as distinct from a technical or professional education.

lib·er·al·ism (lib′ər əl iz′əm or lib′rəl iz′əm) *n.* **1** liberal principles and ideas; belief in progress and reforms. **2** Often, **Liberalism.** the principles and practices of a political liberal party.

hat, āge, cãre, fär; let, ēqual, tėrm; it, īce
hot, ōpen, ôrder; oil, out; cup, pu̇t, rüle, ūse
əbove, takən, pencəl, lemən, circəs
ch, child; ng, long; sh, ship
th, thin; ᴛʜ, then; zh, measure

lib·er·al·ist (lib′ər əl ist or lib′rəl ist) *n.* a person who holds liberal principles and ideas; a believer in progress and reforms.

lib·er·al·i·ty (lib′ər al′ə tē) *n.* **-ties. 1** generosity. **2** a gift. **3** broad-mindedness.

lib·er·al·ize (lib′ər əl īz′ or lib′rəl īz′) *v.* **-ized, -iz·ing.** make or become liberal. —**lib′er·ali·za′tion,** *n.* —**lib′er·al·iz′er,** *n.*

liberal party 1 Liberal Party, one of the principal political parties of Canada. **2** a political party in certain other countries, usually one having moderately progressive policies.

lib·er·ate (lib′ər āt′) *v.* **-at·ed, -at·ing. 1** set free. **2** in chemistry, set free from combination: *liberate a gas.* [< L *liberare* < *liber* free] —**lib′er·a′tor,** *n.* —**Syn.** emancipate, release.

lib·er·a·tion (lib′ər ā′shən) *n.* **1** the act or process of setting free. **2** the process of being set free. **3** the state of being free.

Li·be·ri·an (lī bēr′ē ən) *adj.* of or having to do with Liberia, a country in W. Africa, or its people. —*n.* a native or inhabitant of Liberia.

lib·er·tar·i·an (lib′ər tãr′ē ən) *n.* **1** one who advocates full civil liberty in thought and action. **2** one who advocates freedom of the will. —*adj.* **1** of or having to do with civil liberty. **2** having to do with or advocating freedom of the will.

lib·er·tar·i·an·ism (lib′ər tãr′ē ə niz′əm) *n.* the doctrine or principles of libertarians.

lib·er·tine (lib′ər tēn′) *n.* **1** a person without moral restraints; a rake. **2** a freedman in ancient Rome. —*adj.* without moral restraints; dissolute; licentious. [< L *libertinus* freedman < *libertus* made free < *liber* free]

lib·er·tin·ism (lib′ər tēn iz′əm or lib′ər tin iz′əm) *n.* the behavior of a libertine.

lib·er·ty (lib′ər tē) *n.* **-ties. 1** freedom: *The prisoner yearned for liberty.* **2** the right or power to do as one pleases; power or opportunity to do something: *liberty of speech or action.* **3** the leave granted to a sailor to go ashore. **4** the right of being in, using, etc.: *We give our dog the liberty of the yard.* **5** a privilege or right granted by a government. **6** too great freedom; setting aside rules and manners. **7 at liberty, a** free. **b** allowed; permitted. **c** not busy. **8 take liberties,** be too familiar: *The soldiers soon gave up trying to take liberties with their new sergeant.* [ME < OF < L *libertas* < *liber* free] —**Syn. 1** emancipation. See **freedom.**

Liberty Ship a cargo ship carrying about 10,000 gross tons, built in large numbers by the United States during the second World War.

li·bid·i·nous (lə bid′ə nəs) *adj.* lustful; lewd. [< L *libidinosus* < *libido.* See LIBIDO.] —**li·bid′i·nous·ly,** *adv.* —**li·bid′i·nous·ness,** *n.*

li·bi·do (lə bē′dō) *n.* **1** sexual desire or instinct. **2** instinct generally; the vital impulse; the force motivating mental life. [< L *libido* desire < *libere* be pleasing]

Li·bra (lī′brə) *n.* **1** in astronomy, a southern constellation that was thought of as arranged in the shape of a pair of scales. **2** in astrology, the seventh sign of the zodiac; Scales. The sun enters Libra about September 23. See **zodiac** for diagram. [< L *libra* a balance]

li·brar·i·an (lī brãr′ē ən) *n.* **1** a person in charge of a library or part of a library. **2** a person trained for work in a library.

li·brar·y (lī′brer′ē or lī′brə rē) *n.* **-brar·ies. 1** a collection of books: *He borrowed a book from the teacher's library.* **2** a room or building where a collection of books is kept. **3** a circulating library; any library that lends books: *He goes to the library every Saturday.* [< L *librarium* bookcase < *liber* book]

li·bret·tist (lə bret′ist) *n.* the writer of a libretto.

li·bret·to (lə bret′ō) *n.* **-tos. 1** the words of an opera or other long musical composition. **2** a book containing these words. [< Ital. *libretto,* dim. of *libro* book]

Lib·y·an (lib′ē ən or lib′yən) *adj.* of or having to do with Libya, a country in N. Africa, or its people. *—n.* **1** a native or inhabitant of Libya. **2** the Berber language, or the ancient Hamitic language group to which Berber belongs.

lice (līs) *n.* pl. of **louse.**

li·cence or **li·cense** (lī′səns) *n.* **1** permission given by law to do something. **2** the paper, card, plate, etc. showing such permission: *The barber hung his licence on the wall.* **3** the fact or condition of being permitted to do something. **4** freedom of action, speech, thought, etc. that is permitted or conceded. Poetic licence is the freedom from rules that is permitted in poetry and art. **5** too much liberty; disregard of what is right and proper; abuse of liberty. [ME < OF *licence* < L *licentia* < *licere* be allowed]

li·cense or **li·cence** (lī′səns) *v.* **-censed** or **-cenced, -cens·ing** or **-cenc·ing. 1** permit by law: *A doctor is licensed to practise medicine.* **2** give authority to do something: *Who licensed you to wear my tie?* **—li′cens·er** or **li′cenc·er,** *n.*

li·cen·see (lī′sən sē′) *n.* a person to whom a licence is given.

li·cen·ti·ate (lī sen′shē it, lī sen′shē āt′, or, *esp. for def. 2,* lə sen′shē it) *n.* **1** a person who has a licence or permit to practise an art or profession. **2** in some European and French-Canadian universities, an academic degree ranking below the doctorate.

li·cen·tious (lī sen′shəs) *adj.* **1** disregarding commonly accepted rules or principles. **2** lawless; immoral. **3** lewd. [< L *licentiosus* < *licentia.* See LICENSE.] **—li·cen′tious·ly,** *adv.* **—li·cen′tious·ness,** *n.* **—Syn. 3** lustful, lascivious, sensual, wanton.

li·chee (lē′chē) *n.* litchi.

li·chen (lī′kən) *n.* a flowerless plant that resembles moss and grows in patches on trees, rocks, etc. A lichen consists of a fungus and an alga growing together so that they look like one plant. [< L < Gk. *leichēn,* originally, what eats around itself < *leichein* lick]

li·chen·ous (lī′kən əs) *adj.* of, like, or abounding in lichens.

lich gate (lich) a roofed gate to a churchyard. Also, **lych gate.** [*lich,* OE *līc* body, corpse]

A lich gate

lic·it (lis′it) *adj.* lawful; permitted. [< L *licitus* < *licere* be allowed] **—lic′it·ly,** *adv.* **—lic′it·ness,** *n.*

lick (lik) *v.* **1** pass the tongue over. **2** lap up with the tongue. **3** make or bring by using the tongue: *The cat licked the plate clean.* **4** pass about or play over as a tongue would: *The flames were licking the roof.* **5** *Informal.* beat; thrash. **6** *Informal.* defeat in a fight, etc.; conquer. **7 lick into shape,** *Informal.* make presentable or usable.
—n. **1** a stroke of the tongue over something. **2** a place where natural salt is found and where animals go to lick it up. **3** *Informal.* a blow. **4** a small quantity: *She didn't do a lick of work.* **5** *Informal.* a brief stroke of activity or effort: *a lick and a promise.* **6** *Informal.* speed. [OE *liccian*]

lick·er·ish (lik′ər ish) *adj.* **1** fond of choice food. **2** greedy. **3** lecherous. [ME *lickerous* < an AF var. of OF *lecheros* lecherous < *lecheor.* See LECHER.]

lick·spit·tle (lik′spit′əl) *n.* a contemptible flatterer; parasite.

lic·o·rice (lik′ə rish, lik′rish, or lik′ə ris) *n.* **1** a sweet, black, gummy extract obtained from the roots of a European plant, used as a flavoring. **2** a plant that yields this. **3** its root. **4** candy flavored with this extract. Also, **liquorice.** [ME < AF *lycorys* < LL *liquiritia* < L *glycyrrhiza* < Gk. *glykyrrhiza* < *glykys* sweet + *rhiza* root]

lic·tor (lik′tər) *n.* in ancient Rome, an attendant on a public official, who punished offenders at the official's orders. [< L *lictor,* related to *ligare* bind]

lid (lid) *n.* **1** a movable cover; top: *the lid of a box.* **2** the cover of skin that is moved in opening and shutting the eye; eyelid. **3** *Slang.* a hat; cap. **4** *Informal.* a restraint; check; curb: *put the lid on gambling.* **5 flip one's lid,** *Slang.* get very excited. [OE *hlid*]

L.I.D. Local Improvement District.

lid·less (lid′lis) *adj.* **1** having no lid. **2** having no eyelids. **3** *Poetic.* watchful.

lie[1] (lī) *n. v.* **lied, ly·ing.** *—n.* **1** a false statement, known to be false by the person who makes it. **2** something intended to give a false impression. **3** a false statement. **4 give the lie to, a** call a liar; accuse of lying. **b** show to be false.
—v. **1** tell lies. **2** get, bring, put, etc. by lying: *lie oneself out of a difficulty.* **3** make a false statement. [OE *lyge,* n., *lēogan,* v.]
Syn. *n.* **1 Lie, falsehood, fib** = an untruthful statement. **Lie** applies to an untruthful statement deliberately made with knowledge that it is untruthful and with the purpose of deceiving, sometimes of hurting, others: *Saying that his friend had stolen the money was a lie.* **Falsehood** = an untruthful statement made for a purpose, but can apply to one made when the truth would be undesirable or impossible: *Not wishing to hurt his sister's feelings, he told a falsehood and said he didn't know.* **Fib** = a lie or excusable falsehood about something unimportant: *Many children tell fibs.*

lie[2] (lī) *v.* **lay, lain, ly·ing,** *n.* *—v.* **1** have one's body in a flat position along the ground or on some other surface: *lie on the grass.* **2** assume such a position: *lie down on the couch.* **3** be in a horizontal or flat position: *The book was lying on the table.* **4** be kept or stay in a given position, state, etc.: *lie idle.* **5** be; be placed: *The ship lies to the south of us.* **6** exist; be; have its place; belong: *The cure lies in education.* **7** be in the grave; be buried: *His body lies in Halifax.* **8** *Archaic.* spend the night; lodge. **9 lie in,** be confined in child-birth. **10 lie off,** of a ship, etc., stay not far from. **11 lie over,** be left waiting until a later time. **12 lie to,** of a ship, etc., come almost to a stop, facing the wind: *During the storm, the ship lay to.* **13 take (a thing) lying down,** yield to (something); not to stand up to.
—n. **1** the manner, position, or direction in which something lies. **2** the place where an animal is accustomed to lie or lurk. **3** in golf, the position of the ball after a drive, in regard to obstacles on the ground or accessibility to the green. [OE *licgan*] **—Syn.** *v.* **1** recline, repose. ☛ See **lay** for usage note.

lie·der·kranz (lē′dər kränts′) *n.* **1** a smooth cheese with a strong odor. **2 Liederkranz,** a trademark for this cheese. [< G *Liederkranz* garland of songs]

lief (lēf) *adv. Archaic.* willingly: *I'd as lief stay here.* Also, **lieve.** [OE *lēof* dear]

liege (lēj) *Archaic. —n.* in the Middle Ages: **1** a lord having a right to the homage and loyal service of his vassals. **2** a vassal obliged to give homage and loyal service to his lord. *—adj.* **1** having a right to the homage and loyal service of vassals. **2** obliged to give homage and loyal service to a lord. [ME < OF < LL *leticus* < *letus* freedman, ult. < Gmc.]

liege lord a feudal lord.

liege·man (lēj′mən) *n.* **-men (-mən). 1** a vassal. **2** a faithful follower.

lien (lēn or lē′ən) *n.* a legal claim on the property of another in settlement of a debt: *The garage owner has a lien upon my car until I pay his bill.* [< F < L *ligamen* bond < *ligare* bind]

lie of the land 1 the natural features of a landscape. **2** the condition in which things are.

lieu (lü) *n.* **1** *Archaic.* place; stead. **2 in lieu of,** in place of; instead of. [< F < L *locus*]

Lieut. Lieutenant.

lieu·ten·an·cy (lef′ten′ən sē) *n.* **-cies.** the rank, commission, or authority of a lieutenant.

lieu·ten·ant (lef ten′ənt; *esp.U.S.,* lü ten′ənt) *n.* **1** a person who acts for someone senior to him in authority: *He was one of the gang leader's lieutenants.* **2** in the army, a commissioned officer senior to a second lieutenant and junior to a captain. **3** in the navy, a commissioned officer senior to a sub-lieutenant and junior to a lieutenant-commander. *Abbrev.:* Lieut. or Lt. [< F *lieutenant* < *lieu* a place (< L *locus*) + *tenant*, ppr. of *tenir* hold < L *tenere*]

lieutenant-colonel (lef ten′ənt kėr′nəl) *n.* in the army, a commissioned officer senior to a major and junior to a colonel. *Abbrev.*: Lt.Col.

lieutenant commander in the navy, a commissioned officer senior to a lieutenant and junior to a commander. *Abbrev.*: L.Cdr. or Lt.Cdr.

lieutenant-general (lef ten′ənt jen′ər əl or -jen′rəl) *n.* in the army, a commissioned officer senior to a major-general and junior to a general. *Abbrev.*: Lt.Gen.

lieutenant-governor (lef ten′ənt guv′ər nər) *n.* the official head of a provincial government, appointed by the Governor General in Council, for a term of five years; representative of the Crown in a province. *Abbrev.*: Lt.Gov.

lieve (lēv) *adv. Archaic.* lief.

life (līf) *n.* **lives. 1** the state of living or being alive; quality that human beings, animals, and plants have and that rocks, dirt, and metals lack. **2** the time of being alive: *a short life.* **3** the time of existence or action of inanimate things: *a machine's life, the life of a lease.* **4** a living being; person: *Five lives were lost in the fire.* **5** living things considered together: *The desert island had almost no animal or vegetable life.* **6** a way of living: *a dull life.* **7** an account of a person's life: *a life of Mackenzie King.* **8** spirit; vigor: *Put more life into your work.* **9** a source of activity or liveliness. **10** a period of existence in the world of affairs or society. **11** the living form or model, especially as represented in art: *The portrait was painted from life.*
as large or **as big as life, a** as big as the living person or thing. **b** in person.
for dear life, to save or as if to save one's life: *He ran for dear life.*
for life, a during the rest of one's life. **b** to save one's life.
for the life of me, *Informal.* if my life depended on it.
from life, using a living model.
see life, *Informal.* get experience, especially of the exciting features of human activities.
take life, kill.
take one's own life, kill oneself.
to the life, like the model; exactly; perfectly.
true to life, true to reality; as in real life. [OE *līf*]
—**Syn. 1** being, existence. **7** biography. **8** animation, liveliness, vivacity.

life belt a life preserver made like a belt.

life·blood (līf′blud′) *n.* **1** blood necessary to life. **2** a source of strength and energy.

life·boat (līf′bōt′) *n.* **1** a strong boat specially built for saving lives at sea or along the coast. **2** a boat carried on davits on a ship for use by the passengers in an emergency.

life buoy a life preserver (def. 1).

life·guard (līf′gärd′) *n.* a person who is trained in lifesaving and who is responsible for the safety of swimmers and bathers at a public pool or beach.

Life Guards two British cavalry regiments whose duty it is to guard the king and queen of England.

life insurance 1 a system by which a person pays a small sum regularly in order to have a large sum paid to his family or heirs at his death. **2** the sum paid by the insurance company at death. **3** the payments made to the insurance company. **4** a combination of life insurance and endowment insurance.

life jacket a sleeveless jacket having a filling of kapok, cork, or compressed air and designed to save a person from drowning.

life·less (līf′lis) *adj.* **1** not living; without life: *a lifeless planet.* **2** dead: *lifeless bodies on the battlefield.* **3** dull: *a lifeless performance.* —**life′less·ly,** *adv.* —**life′less·ness,** *n.* —**Syn. 1** inanimate. **2** See **dead. 3** sluggish, torpid.

life·like (līf′līk′) *adj.* like life; looking as if alive; like the real thing: *a lifelike portrait.* —**life′like′ness,** *n.*

life line 1 a rope for saving life, such as one thrown to a ship from the shore. **2** a line across a deck or passageway of a ship to grab to prevent falling or being washed overboard. **3** a diver's signalling line. **4** anything that maintains or helps to maintain something that cannot exist by itself.

hat, āge, cãre, fär; let, ēqual, tėrm; it, īce
hot, ōpen, ôrder; oil, out; cup, pu̇t, rüle, ūse
əbove, takən, pencəl, lemən, circəs
ch, child; ng, long; sh, ship
th, thin; ᴛʜ, then; zh, measure

life·long (līf′long′) *adj.* lasting all one's life: *a lifelong companion.*

life net a strong net or sheet of canvas, used to catch people jumping from burning buildings.

life peer *Brit.* a peer whose title is not hereditary.

life preserver 1 a wide belt, jacket, or circular tube, made of a substance that will keep a person afloat in the water; something to keep a person afloat until rescued. **2** *Esp.Brit.* a short stick with a heavy head, used for self-defence.

lif·er (līf′ər) *n. Slang.* a convict in prison for life.

life·sav·er (līf′sāv′ər) *n.* **1** a person who saves people from drowning. **2** a lifeguard. **3** *Informal.* a person or thing that saves someone from trouble, discomfort, embarrassment, etc.

life·sav·ing (līf′sāv′ing) *adj.* **1** saving people's lives; keeping people from drowning: *lifesaving work.* **2** designed or used to save people's lives: *lifesaving classes, lifesaving equipment.* —*n.* the act of saving people's lives.

life-size (līf′sīz′) *adj.* having the same size as the living person, animal, etc.: *a life-size statue.*

life·time (līf′tīm′) *n.* **1** the time of being alive; time during which a life lasts. **2** the time during which something is enforced, functions efficiently, etc. —*adj.* for life.

life·work (līf′wėrk′) *n.* work that takes or lasts a whole lifetime; main work in life.

lift (lift) *v.* **1** raise; take up; raise into a higher position: *lift a chair.* **2** hold up; display on high. **3** raise in rank, condition, estimation, etc.; elevate; exalt. **4** rise and go; go away: *The darkness lifts.* **5** go up; allow (itself, etc.) to be raised: *This window will not lift.* **6** pull or tug upward. **7** send up loudly: *lift a voice or cry.* **8** rise to view above the horizon. **9** tighten the skin and erase the wrinkles of (a person's face) through surgery. **10** take up out of the ground, as crops, treasure, etc. **11** *Informal.* pick or take up; steal: *lift things from a store.* **12** pay off: *lift a mortgage.*
—*n.* **1** an elevating influence. **2** the act of lifting. **3** the distance through which a thing is lifted. **4** a helping hand: *I gave him a lift with the heavy box.* **5** a ride given to a pedestrian or hiker: *He often gave the neighbor's boy a lift to school.* **6** *Esp.Brit.* an elevator. **7** one of the layers of leather in the heel of a shoe. **8** a rise in ground. **9** elevated carriage (of the head, neck, eyes, etc.): *a haughty lift of the chin.* **10** an improvement in spirits: *The promotion gave him a lift.* **11** a cable or rope with seats or attachments for holding on to, to raise a skier to the top of a slope. **12** in aeronautics, **a** the force exerted on an airfoil by a flow of air over and around it acting perpendicular to the direction of flight. **b** the upward tendency of an airship or balloon caused by the gas it contains. [ME < ON *lypta* to raise; akin to *lopt* air. See LOFT.] —**Syn.** *v.* **1** See **raise.**

lift·er (lif′tər) *n.* **1** a person or thing that lifts. **2** a thing used for lifting.

lift lock a canal or river lock in which one or more water-filled compartments are hydraulically raised and lowered.

lift·off (lift′of′) *n.* of rockets, etc., a launching or firing; the act or moment of rising from the launching pad.

lift pump a pump that lifts a liquid without forcing it out under pressure.

lig·a·ment (lig′ə mənt) *n.* **1** in anatomy, a band of strong tissue that connects bones or holds parts of the body in place. **2** a tie; bond. [ME < L *ligamentum* < *ligare* bind]

li·gate (lī′gāt) *v.* **-gat·ed, -gat·ing.** bind; tie up: *ligate a bleeding artery.* [< L *ligare*] —**li·ga′tion,** *n.*

lig·a·ture (lig′ə chər or lig′ə chür′) *n. v.* **-tured, -tur·ing.** —*n.* **1** anything used to bind or tie up; bandage, cord, etc. 2 in surgery, a thread, string, etc. used to tie up a bleeding artery or vein. 3 a binding or tying up. 4 in music, a slur or a group of notes connected by a slur. 5 in printing, two or three letters joined. *Æ* and *ffl* are ligatures. —*v.* bind or tie up with a ligature. [ME < LL *ligatura* < L *ligare* bind]

A ligature (def. 4)

light[1] (līt) *n. adj. v.* **light·ed** or **lit, light·ing.** —*n.* **1** that by which we see; the form of radiant energy that acts on the retina of the eye. **2** anything that gives light. The sun, a lamp, or a lighthouse is called a light. **3** a supply of light: *The tall building to the south of us cuts off our light.* **4** brightness; clearness; the amount or degree of illumination: *a strong or dim light.* **5** a bright part: *light and shade.* **6** daytime. **7** dawn. **8** something by which to let light in, such as a window or a windowpane. **9** something with which to start something else burning. **10** knowledge; information; illumination of mind: *We need more light on this subject.* **11** public knowledge; open view. **12** the aspect in which a thing is viewed: *He put the matter in the right light.* **13** a shining figure; model; example: *The actor was a leading light in the theatre.* **14** favor; approval.
according to one's lights, following one's own ideas, intelligence, and conscience in the best way that one knows.
bring to light, reveal; expose.
come to light, be revealed or exposed.
in the light of, a by considering. **b** from the standpoint of.
see the light, or **see the light of day, a** be born. **b** be made public. **c** get the right idea.
shed or **throw light on,** explain; make clear.
strike a light, make a light.
—*adj.* **1** having light. **2** bright; clear: *It is as light as day.* **3** pale in color; whitish: *light hair, light blue.*
—*v.* **1** cause to give light: *She lighted the lamp.* **2** give light to; provide with light: *The room is lighted by six windows.* **3** make or become bright: *Her face was lighted by a smile.* **4** become light: *The sky lights up at sunset.* **5** show (a person) the way by means of a light: *Here is a candle to light you to bed.* **6** set fire to: *She lighted the candles.* **7** take fire. [OE *lēoht*] —**Syn.** *n.* **4** radiance, luminosity.

☛ **lighted, lit.** Both forms are in good use as the past tense and past participle of *light. Lighted* is probably the form generally used as the adjective and past participle: *She carried a lighted lamp. He had lighted a fire. Lit* is perhaps more common as the past tense: *He lit a cigarette.*

light[2] (līt) *adj.* **1** easy to carry; not heavy: *a light load.* **2** of little weight for its size: *a light metal.* **3** of less than usual weight: *light clothing.* **4** less than usual in amount, force, or strength: *a light blow, a light sleep.* **5** easy to do or bear; not hard or severe: *light punishment, a light task.* **6** not looking heavy; graceful; delicate: *a light bridge, light carving.* **7** moving easily; nimble: *light on one's feet.* **8** happy; gay; cheerfully careless: *a light laugh.* **9** not serious enough; fickle: *a light mind, light of purpose.* **10** aiming to entertain; not serious: *light reading.* **11** not important: *light losses.* **12** careless in morals. **13** not dense: *a light fog.* **14** porous, sandy: *a light soil.* **15** containing little alcohol: *a light wine.* **16** built small and without much weight; adapted for light loads and for swift movement: *a light truck.* **17** lightly armed or equipped: *light cavalry, in light marching order.* **18 light in the head, a** dizzy. **b** silly; foolish. **c** crazy; out of one's head. **19 make light of,** treat as of little importance.
—*adv.* lightly. [OE *lēoht, līht*] —**Syn.** *adj.* **7** agile, active. **8** buoyant. **11** slight, trivial, unimportant.

light[3] (līt) *v.* **light·ed** or **lit, light·ing. 1** come down to the ground; alight: *He lighted from his horse.* **2** come down from flight: *A bird lighted on the branch.* **3** come by chance: *His eye lighted upon a familiar face in the crowd.* **4** fall suddenly: *The blow lit on his head.* **5 light into,** *Slang.* **a** attack. **b** scold. **6 light out,** *Slang.* leave suddenly; go away quickly. [OE *līhtan* < *līht* light[2]]

light-armed (līt′ärmd′) *adj.* equipped with light weapons.

light·en[1] (līt′ən) *v.* **1** make light; grow light: *The sky lightens before the dawn.* **2** brighten: *Her face lightened.* **3** flash with lightning. [ME *lighten* < *light*[1]]

light·en[2] (līt′ən) *v.* **1** reduce the load of (a ship, etc.); have the load reduced. **2** make or become less of a burden: *lighten taxes.* **3** make or become more cheerful. [ME *lighten* < *light*[2]]

light·er[1] (līt′ər) *n.* a thing or person that starts something burning. [ME *lighter* < *light*[1], v.]

light·er[2] (līt′ər) *n.* a flat-bottomed barge used for loading and unloading ships. —*v.* carry (goods) in a flat-bottomed barge. [< *light*[2] or ? < Du. *lichter*]

light·er·age (līt′ər ij) *n.* **1** the loading, unloading, or carrying of goods in a lighter. **2** the charge for this.

light·face (līt′fās′) *n.* in printing, the type normally used in the body of a work; opposed to *boldface.* The definitions and illustrative phrases and sentences in this dictionary are printed in lightface.

light-fin·gered (līt′fing′gərd) *adj.* **1** thievish; skilful at picking pockets. **2** having nimble fingers.

light-foot (līt′fu̇t′) *adj. Poetic.* light-footed.

light-foot·ed (līt′fu̇t′id) *adj.* stepping lightly. —**light-foot′ed·ly,** *adv.* —**light′foot′ed·ness,** *n.*

light-head·ed (līt′hed′id) *adj.* **1** dizzy. **2** delirious. **3** frivolous; flighty. —**light′-head′ed·ly,** *adv.* —**light′-head′ed·ness,** *n.*

light-heart·ed (līt′här′tid) *adj.* carefree; cheerful; gay. —**light′-heart′ed·ly,** *adv.* —**light′-heart′ed·ness,** *n.*

light heavyweight a boxer who weighs between 161 and 175 pounds.

light horse cavalry that carries light weapons and equipment.

light-horse·man (līt′hôrs′mən) *n.* **-men** (-mən). a cavalryman who carries light weapons and equipment.

light·house (līt′hous′) *n.* a tower or framework with a bright light that shines far over the water. Lighthouses are usually located at dangerous places to warn and guide ships.

light infantry infantry that carries light arms and equipment.

light·ing (līt′ing) *n.* **1** the giving of light; providing with light. **2** the way in which lights are arranged. **3** a starting to burn.

light·ly (līt′lē) *adv.* **1** with little weight, force, etc.: *rest lightly on a thing.* **2** to a small degree or extent: *lightly clad.* **3** in an airy way: *flags floating lightly.* **4** quickly; easily: *jump lightly aside.* **5** cheerfully: *take bad news lightly.* **6** indifferently; slightingly: *speak lightly of a person.* **7** thoughtlessly; carelessly: *behave lightly.*

light meter 1 a device for measuring the intensity of light. **2** a device for measuring and recording the amount of electricity used.

light-mind·ed (līt′mīn′did) *adj.* empty-headed; thoughtless; frivolous. —**light′-mind′ed·ly,** *adv.* —**light′-mind′ed·ness,** *n.*

light·ness[1] (līt′nis) *n.* **1** brightness; clearness. **2** paleness; whitishness. **3** the amount of light: *The lightness of the sky showed that the rain was really over.* [OE *līhtnes* < *lēoht* light[1]]

light·ness[2] (līt′nis) *n.* **1** the state of being light or of not being heavy: *The lightness of this load is a relief after the weight of the one I have been carrying.* **2** the state of not being hard or severe. **3** gracefulness; delicacy. **4** the state of being gay or cheerful: *lightness of spirits.* **5** a lack of proper seriousness: *Such lightness of conduct is not to be permitted in church.* [< *light*[2]]

light·ning (līt′ning) *n.* a discharge or flash of electricity in the sky. —*adj.* like lightning; very fast or sudden: *lightning calculations.* [< *lighten*[1]]

lightning bug firefly.

lightning rod a metal rod fixed on a building or ship to conduct lightning into the earth or water to prevent fire.

lights (līts) *n.pl.* the lungs of sheep, pigs, etc. [so called because of their light weight]

light·ship (līt′ship′) *n.* a ship with a bright light that shines far over the water, anchored at a dangerous place to warn and guide ships.

light·some (līt′səm) *adj.* **1** nimble; lively. **2** happy; gay; cheerful. **3** frivolous.

light·weight (līt′wāt′) *n.* 1 a person or thing of less than average weight. 2 a boxer who weighs less than 135 pounds and more than 125 pounds. 3 *Informal.* a person who has little intelligence or importance. —*adj.* light in weight.

light-year (līt′yēr′) *n.* the distance that light travels in one year; about 6,000,000,000,000 miles.

lig·ne·ous (lig′nē əs) *adj.* of or like wood; woody. [< L *ligneus* < *lignum* wood]

lig·nite (lig′nīt) *n.* a dark-brown kind of coal in which the texture of the original wood can be seen. [< F < L *lignum* wood]

lig·num vi·tae (lig′nəm vī′tē or vē′tī) 1 an extremely heavy and hard wood, used for making pulleys, rulers, etc. 2 the tropical tree from which it comes. [< L *lignum vitae* wood of life; from its supposed medicinal value]

Li·gu·ri·an (li gū′rē ən) *adj.* of Liguria, a district in N.W. Italy, or its people. —*n.* a native or inhabitant of Liguria.

lik·a·ble (līk′ə bəl) *adj.* having qualities that win good will or friendship; popular: *a likable person.* —**lik′a·ble·ness,** *n.* —**lik′a·bly,** *adv.*

like[1] (līk) *adj. Poetic.* **lik·er, lik·est,** *prep. adv. n. conj. v.* **liked, lik·ing.** —*adj.* 1 similar; similar to; resembling something or each other: *Our house is like theirs.* 2 characteristic of: *Isn't that just like a boy?* 3 giving promise or indicative of: *It looks like rain.* 4 in the right state or frame of mind for: *I feel like working.* 5 *Archaic.* likely: *The king is sick and like to die.* 6 **had like,** *Dialect.* came near; was about (*to*): *He had like to have killed himself.* 7 **nothing like,** not nearly. 8 **something like,** about; almost.
—*prep.* 1 similar; similar to; resembling something or each other: *She sings like a bird.* 2 characteristic of. 3 in the right state or frame of mind for. 4 in like manner with; similarly to: *She works like a beaver.*
—*adv.* 1 *Informal.* probably: *Like enough it will rain.* 2 in like manner. 3 *Archaic.* to a like extent or degree. 4 similarly to.
—*n.* 1 a person or thing like another; match; counterpart or equal. 2 **and the like, a** and so forth: *He studied music, painting, and the like.* **b** and similar things; and other things of the same class: *At the zoo we saw tigers, lions, bears, and the like.*
—*conj. Informal.* like as; as.
—*v.* 1 *Obsolete.* compare. 2 *Dialect.* come near.
[OE (*ge*)*līc*]
☛ **like, as.** In written English *as* and *as if* are used to introduce clauses of comparison: *He still writes as he used to when he was a child. Act as if you were accustomed to being here.* In informal English *like* is often used in clauses of comparison: *He writes like he used to when he was a child.* In standard usage *like* is used in phrase comparison: *She swims like a fish.* Although historically both *like* and *as* are justified, custom has made *as* the preferred form when introducing clauses in formal writing.

like[2] (līk) *v.* **liked, lik·ing,** *n.* —*v.* 1 be pleased with; have affection for; be satisfied with. 2 wish for; wish. —*n.* a liking; preference. [OE *līcian* to please]
☛ **Like, love** are not interchangeable. *Like* = find pleasure or satisfaction in something or someone, or have friendly feelings for a person, but does not suggest strong feelings or emotion: *I like books. Boys like to play. Love* emphasizes strong feelings and deep attachment, and is used to express the emotion of love: *She loves her mother. He loves music.* But *love* is often used informally instead of *like* in an intensified sense.

-like *suffix.* 1 like: *wolflike* = *like a wolf.* 2 like that of; characteristic of: *childlike* = *like that of a child.* 3 suited to; fit or proper for: *businesslike* = *suited to business.* [< *like*[1], adj.]
☛ **-like** is a living suffix that can be freely added to nouns to form adjectives.

like·a·ble (līk′ə bəl) *adj.* likable. —**like′a·ble·ness,** *n.* —**like′a·bly,** *adv.*

like·li·hood (līk′lē hůd′) *n.* probability: *Is there any likelihood of rain this afternoon?*

like·ly (līk′lē) *adj.* **-li·er, -li·est,** *adv.* —*adj.* 1 probable: *Flooding is one likely result of the heavy rain.* 2 to be expected: *It is likely to be hot in August.* 3 suitable: *Is there a likely place to fish?* 4 promising: *a likely boy.* —*adv.* probably: *I shall very likely be at home all day.* [< ON *likligr*]
☛ **likely, apt, liable.** The principal meanings of these words are: *likely*: expected, probably; *liable*: possible (of an unpleasant event); responsible (as for damages); *apt*: tending toward, naturally fit. *Likely* is the most commonly needed of the three, and informally both *apt* and (in some localities) *liable* are used in the ordinary sense of *likely*: *It's likely* (or, *apt*; or, locally, *liable*) *to rain when the wind is southwest.*

hat, āge, cãre, fär; let, ēqual, tėrm; it, īce
hot, ōpen, ôrder; oil, out; cup, půt, rüle, ūse
əbove, takən, pencəl, lemən, circəs
ch, child; ng, long; sh, ship
th, thin; ᴛʜ, then; zh, measure

lik·en (līk′ən) *v.* compare; represent as like.

like·ness (līk′nis) *n.* 1 a resemblance; a being alike: *a boy's likeness to his father.* 2 something that is like; a copy; picture, snapshot, etc.: *The great artist painted a likeness of the queen.* 3 the appearance; shape: *The magician made the princess assume the likeness of a swan.*

like·wise (līk′wīz′) *adv.* 1 the same: *Go and do likewise.* 2 also; moreover; too: *Mary must go home now, and Nell likewise.*

lik·ing (līk′ing) *n.* 1 a preference or taste: *He had a liking for apples.* 2 a fondness or kindly feeling: *She had a liking for chlldren.* 3 taste; pleasure: *food to your liking.* [OE *līcung* < *līcian* to please]

li·lac (lī′lək or lī′lok) *n.* 1 a shrub having clusters of tiny fragrant flowers, usually pale pinkish-purple or white. 2 the cluster of flowers. 3 a pale pinkish purple. —*adj.* pale pinkish-purple. [< F < Sp. < Arabic < Persian *lilak* < *nil* indigo < Skt. *nila*]

Lil·ith (lil′ith or lī′lith) *n.* 1 in early Semitic legend, a female demon or vampire, believed to live in deserted places and to prey on children. 2 in medieval Jewish folklore, the first wife of Adam, ousted by Eve.

Lil·li·put (lil′ə put′) *n.* an imaginary island described in Swift's *Gulliver's Travels.* Its tiny people are represented as being about six inches tall.

Lil·li·pu·tian (lil′ə pū′shən) *adj.* 1 of or suitable for Lilliput. 2 very small; tiny; petty. —*n.* 1 an inhabitant of Lilliput. 2 a very small person; dwarf.

lilt (lilt) *v.* sing or play (a tune) in a light, tripping manner. —*n.* 1 a lively song or tune with a swing. 2 a lively, gay tone of voice: *He has an Irish lilt.* 3 a lively, springy movement. [ME *lulte,* ult. origin uncertain]

lil·y (lil′ē) *n.* **lil·ies,** *adj.* —*n.* 1 a plant that grows from a bulb, having large, bell-shaped flowers. The lily is the floral emblem of Quebec. 2 the flower of any lily plant: *The tiger, or prairie, lily is the floral emblem of Saskatchewan.* 3 the bulb. 4 any of various related or similar plants, such as the calla lily or water lily. 5 the design on the royal coat of arms of France, also appearing on the arms and flag of Quebec; fleur-de-lis.
—*adj.* like a lily; white; pale; pure; lovely; delicate. [OE *lilie* < L *lilium* (akin to Gk. *leirion*)] —**lil′y-like′,** *adj.*

lily family a group of herbs, shrubs, and trees that usually have flowers with six parts, grow from rootstocks or bulbs, and have stemless leaves. Tulips, hyacinths, onions, asparagus, and smilax belong to the lily family.

lil·y-liv·ered (lil′ē liv′ərd) *adj.* cowardly.

lily of the valley *pl.* **lilies of the valley.** a plant having tiny, fragrant, bell-shaped, white flowers arranged up and down a single stem.

Li·ma bean (lī′mə) 1 a broad, flat bean used for food. 2 the plant that it grows on.

limb (lim) *n.* 1 a leg, arm, or wing: *The rickety old wooden bridge is a danger to life and limb.* 2 a large branch of a tree; bough: *They sawed off the dead limb.* 3 the part that projects: *the four limbs of a cross.* 4 a person or thing thought of as a branch or offshoot: *I call that rascal a limb of Satan.* 5 a mischievous child; scamp. 6 **go out on a limb,** *Informal.* risk one's own safety and comfort; expose oneself to attack, criticism, etc. 7 **limb from limb,** completely apart; entirely to pieces. [OE *lim*] —**limb′less,** *adj.* —**Syn.** *n.* 2 See **branch.** 3 arm, shoot.

lim·ber[1] (lim′bər) *adj.* bending easily; flexible: *A pianist should have limber fingers.* —*v.* make or become supple or more easily flexed: *Tom is stiff when he begins to skate, but limbers up easily.* [? < *limp*[2] or *limb*] —**lim′ber·ness,** *n.* —**Syn.** *adj.* See **flexible.**

lim·ber[2] (lim′bər) *n.* the detachable front part of the carriage of a field gun. [? < F *limonière* wagon with shafts < *limon* shaft]

lim·bo[1] (lim′bō) *n.* **1** Often, **Limbo.** in the Roman Catholic Church, a place for those who have not received the grace of Christ while living, and yet have not deserved the punishment of willful and impenitent sinners. **2** a place for people and things forgotten, cast aside, or out of date: *The belief that the earth is flat belongs to the limbo of outworn ideas.* **3** a prison; jail; confinement. [< L (*in*) *limbo* on the edge]

lim·bo[2] (lim′bō) *n.* a West Indian dance in which the dancers pass under a bar which is placed at successively lower levels.

limb of the law a policeman, lawyer, or judge.

Lim·burg·er (lim′bėr gər) *n.* a soft cheese having a strong smell. [< *Limbourg*, a province of Belgium]

lime[1] (līm) *n. v.* **limed, lim·ing.** —*n.* **1** a white substance obtained by burning limestone, shells, bones, etc.; calcium oxide, quicklime. Lime is used to make mortar and on fields to improve soil. *Formula*: CaO **2** birdlime.
—*v.* **1** put lime on. **2** smear (branches, etc.) with birdlime. **3** catch (birds) with birdlime. [OE *līm*]

lime[2] (līm) *n.* **1** a greenish-yellow citrus fruit that resembles a lemon, but is smaller and sourer. **2** the tree this fruit grows on. **3** a soft drink flavored with lime juice. [< F < Sp. < Arabic *lima*. Akin to LEMON.]

lime[3] (līm) *n.* the linden tree. [var. of earlier *line* < OE *lind*]

lime·ade (līm′ād) *n.* a soft drink made of lime juice, sugar, and water.

lime·kiln (līm′kiln′ or -kil′) *n.* a furnace for making lime by burning limestone, shells, etc.

lime·light (līm′līt′) *n.* **1** in a theatre, a strong light thrown upon the stage to light up certain persons or objects and draw attention to them. **2** the centre of public attention and interest.

lim·er·ick (lim′ər ik′ or lim′rik) *n.* a kind of humorous verse of five lines. *Example*:

"There was a young lady from Lynn
Who was so exceedingly thin
That when she essayed
To drink lemonade
She slid down the straw and fell in."

[apparently from a song about *Limerick*, Irish Republic]

lime·stone (līm′stōn′) *n.* a rock consisting mostly of calcium carbonate, used for building and for making lime. Marble is a kind of limestone.

lime·wa·ter (līm′wot′ər or -wô′tər) *n.* a solution of slaked lime in water, used to counteract an acid condition.

lim·ey or **Lim·ey** (lī′mē) *Slang.* —*n.* **1** an Englishman. **2** an English sailor or soldier. **3** an English ship. —*adj.* English. [< *limejuicer*, from the former use of lime juice on British ships to prevent scurvy]

lim·it (lim′it) *n.* **1** the farthest edge or boundary; where something ends or must end: *Keep within the limits of the school grounds.* **2** in mathematics, a value toward which terms of a sequence, values of a function, etc. approach indefinitely near. **3** in betting games, the agreed maximum amount of any bet or raise. **4** *Cdn.* in lumbering, a concession; timber limit. **5 limits, a** bounds. **b** territories or regions. **6** the maximum quantity of fish or game that the law allows one to take in a specified period. **7 the limit,** as much as, or more than, one can stand.
—*v.* set a limit to; restrict: *We must limit our expenditure to $10. Her food was limited to bread and water.* [ME < OF < L *limes, limitis* boundary] —**lim′it·a·ble,** *adj.* —**lim′it·er,** *n.* —**Syn.** *n.* **1** border, bound —*v.* **1** restrain, check.

lim·i·ta·tion (lim′ə tā′shən) *n.* **1** a limiting. **2** a limited condition. **3** anything that limits; limiting rule or circumstance; restriction. **4** a period of time, set by law, after which a claim cannot be enforced.

lim·i·ta·tive (lim′ə tā′tiv) *adj.* limiting; restrictive.

lim·it·ed (lim′ə tid) *adj.* **1** kept within limits; restricted. **2** of business organizations, restricted as to the amount of debt that any individual member is liable for. **3** travelling rapidly and making only a few stops: *a limited train, bus, etc.* —*n.* a train, bus, etc. that travels rapidly and makes only a few stops.

lim·it·ed-ac·cess (lim′ə tid ak′ses) *adj.* of highways, having access roads at relatively few points.

limited company a corporation in which the liability of stockholders is limited to a specified amount.

limited monarchy a monarchy in which the ruler's powers are limited by law.

lim·it·less (lim′it lis) *adj.* without limits; boundless; infinite. —**lim′it·less·ly,** *adv.* —**lim′it·less·ness,** *n.* —**Syn.** illimitable, unlimited.

limn (lim) *v.* **1** paint (a picture). **2** portray in words. [ME *lymne(n)*, var. of *lumine(n)* < OF *luminer* < L *luminare* light up, make bright < *lumen* light] —**lim′ner,** *n.*

Li·moges (li mōzh′) *n.* **1** a kind of fine porcelain. **2** something made of this porcelain. [< *Limoges*, France, where this porcelain is made]

li·mo·nite (lī′mə nīt′) *n.* a kind of iron ore, varying in color from dark brown to yellow. *Formula*: $2Fe_2O_3 \cdot 3H_2O$ [< Gk. *leimōn* meadow]

lim·ou·sine (lim′ə zēn′ or lim′ə zēn′) *n.* a closed automobile, seating from three to five passengers, with a partition between them and the driver. [< F *limousine* < *Limousin*, former province of France]

limp[1] (limp) *n.* a lame step or walk. —*v.* **1** walk with a limp: *After falling down the stairs, he limped for several days.* **2** proceed in a halting or labored manner: *The new project limped along, for no one seemed very interested in it.* [cf. OE *lemphealt* lame] —**limp′er,** *n.*

limp[2] (limp) *adj.* lacking stiffness or firmness: *A starched collar soon gets limp in hot weather.* [origin uncertain; cf. ON *limpa* weakness] —**limp′ly,** *adv.* —**limp′ness,** *n.*
Syn. Limp, flabby = lacking firmness, both literally and as used figuratively to describe character, principles, etc. **Limp** = lacking, or having lost, stiffness or, figuratively, firmness and strength, and suggests drooping or hanging loosely: *Hot weather always makes me feel limp. He has a limp handshake.* **Flabby** = lacking firmness and hardness or, figuratively, forcefulness, energy, or strength, and suggests being soft and weak, flapping or shaking easily: *She is so fat her flesh is flabby.*

lim·pet (lim′pit) *n.* a small shellfish that sticks to rocks, used for bait and sometimes for food. [OE *lempedu* < Med.L *lampreda* lamprey. Doublet of LAMPREY.]

lim·pid (lim′pid) *adj.* clear; transparent: *limpid water, limpid eyes.* [< L *limpidus*] —**lim′pid·ly,** *adv.* —**lim′pid·ness,** *n.*

lim·pid·i·ty (lim pid′ə tē) *n.* a limpid quality or condition.

lim·y (līm′ē) *adj.* **lim·i·er, lim·i·est. 1** of, containing, or resembling lime. **2** smeared with birdlime.

lin·age (līn′ij) *n.* lineage[2].

linch·pin (linch′pin′) *n.* a pin inserted through a hole in the end of an axle to keep the wheel on. [< *linch-*, OE *lynis* linchpin + *pin*]

Lin·coln (ling′kən) *n.* **1** a breed of sheep having long wool. **2** a sheep of this breed. [< *Lincolnshire*, a county in E. England, where this breed originated]

lin·den (lin′dən) *n.* a shade tree having heart-shaped leaves and clusters of small, fragrant yellowish flowers. [OE *linden*, originally adj. < *lind* linden, lime[3]]

line[1] (līn) *n.* **lined, lin·ing.** —*n.* **1** a piece of rope, cord, or wire. **2** a cord for measuring, making level, etc. **3** a cord with a hook for catching fish. **4** a long, narrow mark: *Draw two lines along the margin.* **5** anything like such a mark: *the lines in your face.* **6** a straight line: *The lower edges of the two pictures are about on a line.* **7** in mathematics, the path or track a point may be imagined to leave as it moves. **8** in drawing, the use of lines: *clearness of line in an artist's work.* **9 lines,** *pl.* **a** an outline; contour: *a ship of fine lines.* **b** the plan of construction: *two books written on the same lines.* **c** poetry; verses. **d** the words that an actor speaks in a play. **e** one's fate or fortune: *His demotion was hard lines.* **f** reins. **g** *Informal.* a marriage certificate. **10** an edge;

limit; boundary: *That hedge marks our property line.* **11** a row of persons or things: *a line of trees.* **12** a row of words on a page or in a column: *a column of 40 lines.* **13** a short letter; note: *Drop me a line.* **14** a connected series of persons or things following one another in time: *The Stuarts were a line of English kings.* **15** family or lineage: *of noble line.* **16** a course; track; direction: *the line of march of an army.* **17** a course of action, conduct, or thought: *a line of policy.* **18** in military use: **a** the front. **b lines,** *pl.* a double row (front and rear rank) of soldiers. **c** troops or ships arranged abreast. **d** an arrangement of an army or fleet for battle. **19** in a telephone, telegraph, etc. system: **a** a wire or wires connecting points or stations. **b** the system itself. **20** any rope, wire, pipe, hose, etc. running from one point to another. **21** a single track of railway. **22 a** one branch of a system of transportation: *the main line of a railway.* **b** a whole system of transportation or conveyance: *the Cunard Line.* **23** a branch of business; kind of activity: *the dry-goods line.* **24** a kind or brand of goods: *a good line of hardware.* **25** *Slang.* an exaggerated story, intended to impress or deceive. **26** a single row of words in poetry. **27** in music, one of the horizontal lines that make a staff. **28** 1/12 of an inch. **29** *Cdn.* in Ontario, a concession road.
all along the line, at every point; everywhere.
bring into line, cause to agree or conform.
come or **get into line,** agree; conform.
get or **have a line on,** *Informal.* get or have information about.
in line, a in alignment. **b** in agreement. **c** ready. **d** in order; in succession: *next in line.*
on a line, even; level.
on the line, in between; neither one thing nor the other.
out of line, a in disagreement. **b** behaving improperly.
read between the lines, get more from the words than they say; find a hidden meaning.
the line, a the equator. **b** the border between two countries, especially that between Canada and the United States: *south of the line.* **c** the regular armed services; the soldiers, ships, or aircraft that do all the fighting.
—*v.* **1** mark with lines on paper, etc. **2** cover with lines: *a face lined by age.* **3** arrange in line. **4** arrange a line along; form a line along: *Cars lined the road for a mile.* **5** take a position in a line; form a line; range. **6** in baseball, hit a liner. **7 line up,** form a line; form into a line: *Cars were lined up along the road for a mile.* [fusion of OE *līne* line, rope and F *ligne* line, both < L *linea* line, linen thread < *linum* flax] —**Syn.** *n.* **4** stroke, scratch, streak, dash. **11** rank. **16** route, way.

line[2] (līn) *v.* **lined, lin·ing. 1** put a layer inside (something). **2** fill: *line one's pockets with money.* **3** serve as a lining for. [OE *līn* flax]

lin·e·age[1] (lin′ē ij) *n.* **1** one's descent in a direct line from an ancestor. **2** one's family or race. [ME < OF *lignage* < *ligne* line < L *linea*] —**Syn. 1** ancestry. **2** stock, extraction.

line·age[2] (līn′ij) *n.* **1** the orderly arrangement of lines. **2** the quantity of printed or written matter estimated in lines. **3** in advertising, the charge or rate of charge for a line. Also, **linage.**

lin·e·al (lin′ē əl) *adj.* **1** in the direct line of descent: *A grandson is a lineal descendant of his grandfather.* **2** having to do with such descent; hereditary. **3** linear. [ME < OF < LL *linealis* < L *linea* line[1]]

lin·e·al·ly (lin′ē əl ē) *adv.* in the direct line of descent.

lin·e·a·ment (lin′ē ə mənt) *n.* **1** a part or feature; distinctive characteristic. **2** a part or feature of a face with attention to its outline. [< L *lineamentum* < *linea* line[1]]

lin·e·ar (lin′ē ər) *adj.* **1** of a line or lines. **2** made of lines; making use of lines. **3** in a line or lines. **4** of length. **5** like a line; long and narrow. [< L *linearis* < *linea* line[1]] —**lin′e·ar·ly,** *adv.*

linear accelerator an accelerator in which charged particles are driven in straight lines through vacuum tubes by means of impulses from electric fields.

linear measure 1 measure of length. **2** a system for measuring length.

12 inches = 1 foot
3 feet = 1 yard
5½ yards = 1 rod
40 rods = 1 furlong
8 furlongs (1,760 yards or 5,280 feet) = 1 mile

hat, āge, cãre, fär; let, ēqual, tėrm; it, īce
hot, ōpen, ôrder; oil, out; cup, pu̇t, rüle, ūse
əbove, takən, pencəl, lemən, circəs
ch, child; ng, long; sh, ship
th, thin; ᴛʜ, then; zh, measure

line·back·er (līn′bak′ər) *n.* in football, a defensive player whose playing position is just behind the line of scrimmage.

line·man (līn′mən) *n.* **-men** (-mən). **1** a man who sets up or repairs telegraph, telephone, or electric wires. **2** in football, a centre, guard, tackle, or end. **3** in hockey, any person playing in the forward line. **4** a man who inspects railway tracks. **5** in surveying, the man who carries the line.

lin·en (lin′ən) *n.* **1** a thread made from flax. **2** cloth made from linen thread. **3** articles made of linen or some substitute. Tablecloths, serviettes, sheets, towels, shirts, collars, and handkerchiefs are all called linen. **4 wash one's dirty linen in public,** mention publicly one's quarrels or difficulties. —*adj.* made of linen. [OE *līnen,* adj. < *līn* flax]

line of battle soldiers or ships in battle formation.

line of duty 1 service or duty, especially military duty. **2 in the line of duty,** in the course of doing one's duty, especially military duty.

line of fire the path of a bullet, shell, etc.

line of force in physics, a line in a field of electrical or magnetic force, the line that indicates the direction in which the force is acting.

lin·er[1] (līn′ər) *n.* **1** a ship or airplane belonging to a transportation line or system. **2** a person or thing that makes lines. **3** in baseball, a ball hit so that it travels not far above the ground.

lin·er[2] (līn′ər) *n.* something used to line something else; a lining: *a diaper liner, a hat liner.*

lines·man (līnz′mən) *n.* **-men** (-mən). **1** a lineman. **2** in certain games, a person who watches the lines that mark out the field, rink, court, etc. and assists the umpire or referee.

line-up or **line·up** (līn′up′) *n.* **1** the formation of persons or things into a line: *a police line-up.* **2** in sports: **a** the players named to represent a team in a given game. **b** arrangement of players before a play begins. **3** any alignment of persons or groups for a common purpose.

ling (ling) *n.* **ling** or **lings. 1** a fish of N. Europe and Greenland, used for food. **2** a freshwater fish of North America. [ME *lenge* < OE *lang* long[1]]

-ling *suffix.* **1** little; unimportant, as in *duckling.* **2** one that is, as in *underling.* **3** one belonging to or concerned with, as in *earthling, hireling.* [OE]

lin·ger (ling′gər) *v.* **1** stay on; go slowly, as if unwilling to leave: *She lingered as long as she could at the party. The tune lingers in my mind.* **2** be slow or late in doing or beginning anything; hesitate; delay; dawdle: *He lingered too long on the way home.* **3** continue alive, in spite of weakness, sickness, or other adverse conditions. **4 linger over,** dwell on with pleasure: *She lingered over her memories of the dance.* [frequentative of earlier *leng* delay, OE *lengan* < *lang* long[1]] —**lin′ger·er,** *n.* —**lin′ger·ing·ly,** *adv.*
Syn. Linger, loiter, lag = delay in starting or along the way. **Linger** emphasizes delay in starting, and suggests slowness in going because unwilling to leave: *She lingered quite a while after the others had left.* **Loiter** emphasizes stopping and lingering along the way, and suggests moving slowly and aimlessly: *Mary loitered downtown, looking into all the shopwindows.* **Lag** = linger or fall behind others or in one's work, and suggests failing to keep up the necessary speed or pace: *The child lagged because he was tired.*

lin·ge·rie (lan′zhə rē′ or lon′zhə rā′) *n.* women's undergarments, nightgowns, etc. [< F *lingerie* < *linge* linen]

lin·go (ling′gō) *n.* **-goes.** *Derogatory.* **1** language. **2** any speech regarded as outlandish or queer: *Writers about baseball use their own lingo.* [blend of Provençal *lengo* and Ital. *lingua,* both < L *lingua* tongue]

lin·gua fran·ca (ling′gwə frang′kə) **1** a hybrid language, consisting largely of Italian, used by the Latin peoples in dealing with Arabs, Turks, Greeks, etc. **2** any hybrid language similarly used. [< Ital. *lingua franca* Frankish language]

lin·gual (ling′gwəl) *adj.* **1** of the tongue: *a lingual defect.* **2** in phonetics, articulated with the aid of the tongue. —*n.* in phonetics, a sound articulated with the aid of the tongue. The sounds generally represented by *d* and *t* are linguals. [< Med.L *lingualis* < L *lingua* tongue]

lin·guist (ling′gwist) *n.* **1** a person skilled in a number of languages besides his own. **2** an expert in linguistics. **3** a philologist. [< L *lingua* tongue + E *-ist*]

lin·guis·tic (ling gwis′tik) *adj.* having to do with language or the study of languages. —**lin·guis′ti·cal·ly,** *adv.*

lin·guis·tics (ling gwis′tiks) *n.* the science of language; the descriptive, historical, and comparative study of languages.

lin·i·ment (lin′ə mənt) *n.* a liquid for rubbing on the skin to relieve soreness, sprains, bruises, etc. [< LL *linimentum* < *linere* anoint]

lin·ing (līn′ing) *n.* **1** a layer of material covering the inner surface of something: *the lining of a coat, the lining of a stove.* **2** the material used to line. [< *line*²]

link¹ (lingk) *n.* **1** one ring or loop of a chain. **2** anything that joins as a link joins: *Father lost a cuff link.* **3** a fact or thought that connects others: *a link in a chain of evidence.* **4** a link of a surveying chain used as a measure; 7.92 inches. **5** in chemistry, a bond. —*v.* join as a link does; unite or connect. [ME < ON **hlenkr.* Akin to LANK.]

link² (lingk) *n.* a torch. [origin uncertain]

link·age (lingk′ij) *n.* **1** a linking. **2** the state of being linked. **3** an arrangement or system of links. **4** in biology, the association of two or more genes or their characteristics on the same chromosome so that they are transmitted together.

linking verb in grammar, a verb that links a subject to a predicate adjective or noun without expressing any action. *Example*: John *is* a boy.

☛ Many verbs with full meanings of their own (such as *taste, feel, act, look*) can also be used as linking verbs: *The butter tastes rancid. She felt sad. He acts old. This looks excellent.*

links (lingks) *n.pl.* a golf course. [OE *hlinc* rising ground]

☛ **Links,** meaning a golf course, although plural in form is used as singular or plural: *Do you know of a links where we can play tomorrow? These links are always crowded.*

Lin·ne·an or **Lin·nae·an** (lə nē′ən) *adj.* of Carolus Linnaeus, 1707-1778, a Swedish botanist. The **Linnean system** of naming animals and plants uses two words, the first for the genus and the second for the species.

lin·net (lin′it) *n.* a small songbird of Europe, Asia, and Africa. [< OF *linette* < *lin* flax < L *linum*; it feeds on flaxseed]

li·no·le·um (lə nō′lē əm) *n.* **1** a floor covering made by putting a hard surface of ground cork mixed with oxidized linseed oil on a canvas back. **2** any similar floor covering. [< L *linum* flax + *oleum* oil]

li·no·type (lī′nə tīp′) *n.* a typesetting machine that is operated like a typewriter and that casts each line of type in one piece. [originally *line o' type* line of type]

lin·seed (lin′sēd′) *n.* the seed of flax. [OE *līnsǣd* flaxseed]

linseed oil a yellowish oil pressed from linseed, used in making paints, printing inks, linoleum, etc.

lin·sey (lin′zē) *n.* **-seys.** linsey-woolsey.

lin·sey-wool·sey (lin′zē wůl′zē) *n.* **-wool·seys.** a strong, coarse fabric made of linen and wool or of cotton and wool. [ME *linsey* a linen fabric (< *lin-*, OE *līn* linen) + E *wool*, with a rhyming ending]

lin·stock (lin′stok) *n.* formerly, a stick used to hold a fuse or match in firing a cannon. [< Du. *lontstok* < *lont* match + *stok* stock]

lint (lint) *n.* **1** a soft down or fleecy material obtained by scraping linen. **2** tiny bits of thread or shreds of fabric. [ME *linnet*, probably ult. < L *linum* or OE *līn* flax]

lin·tel (lin′təl) *n.* a horizontal beam or stone over a door, window, etc. to support the structure above it. [ME < OF *lintel*, ult. < L *limes, limitis* boundary]

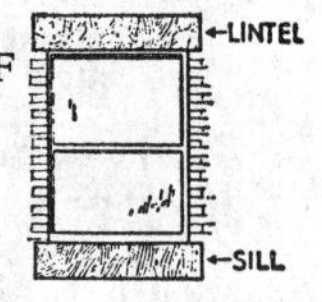

li·on (lī′ən) *n.* **1** a large, strong, tawny, carnivorous mammal of the cat family, found in Africa and S. Asia. The male has a full, flowing mane of coarse hair. **2** a very brave or strong person. **3** a famous person. **4 a** the lion as the national emblem of the U.K. **b** the British nation itself. **5 Lion,** in astrology, the fifth sign of the zodiac; Leo. **6 beard the lion in his den,** defy a person in his own home, office, etc. **7 put one's head in the lion's mouth,** put oneself in a dangerous position. **8 twist the lion's tail,** say or do something intended to excite the resentment of some government or other authority, especially the government or people of the U.K. [ME < AF < L *leo* < Gk. *leōn*] —**li′on·like′,** *adj.*

li·on·ess (lī′ən is) *n.* a female lion.

li·on-heart·ed (lī′ən här′tid) *adj.* brave.

li·on·ize (lī′ən īz′) *v.* **-ized, -iz·ing.** treat as very important. —**li′on·i·za′tion,** *n.* —**li′on·iz′er,** *n.*

lion's share the biggest or best part.

lip (lip) *n. v.* **lipped, lip·ping,** *adj.* —*n.* **1** either of the two fleshy, movable edges of the mouth. **2 lips,** *pl.* the mouth. **3** a folding or bent-out edge of any opening: *the lip of a pitcher.* **4** in music: **a** the mouthpiece of a musical instrument. **b** the shaping of the lips in order to play a wind instrument. **5** *Slang.* impudent talk. **6** in botany: **a** either of the two parts of a labiate corolla or calyx, the upper lip being closest to the axis of the inflorescence and the lower lip farthest away from the axis. **b** in an orchid, the labellum. **7 hang on the lips of,** listen to with great attentiveness and admiration. **8 keep a stiff upper lip,** be brave or firm; show no fear or discouragement.
—*v.* **1** touch with the lips. **2** use the lips in playing a musical wind instrument. **3** murmur. **4** hit a golf ball so that it touches the hole but does not drop in.
—*adj.* not heartfelt or deep, but just on the surface: *pay lip service.* [OE *lippa*] —**lip′like′,** *adj.* —**Syn.** *adj.* superficial.

li·pase (lī′pās or lip′ās) *n.* an enzyme occurring in the pancreatic juice, certain seeds, etc., capable of changing fats into fatty acids and glycerin. [< Gk. *lipos* fat]

lipped (lipt) *adj.* **1** having a lip, or lips. **2** in botany, labiate.

-lipped *combining form.* having —— lips: *thick-lipped = having thick lips.*

lip-read (lip′rēd′) *v.* **-read, -read·ing.** understand speech by watching the movements of the speaker's lips. —**lip′-read′er,** *n.*

lip reading the process of understanding speech by watching the movements of the speaker's lips.

lip-serv·ice (lip′sėr′vis) *n.* service expressed in words only; pretended loyalty or devotion; insincerity.

lip·stick (lip′stik′) *n.* **1** a small stick of rouge, etc. used for coloring the lips. **2** the rouge itself: *There was some lipstick on the rim of the cup.* **3** a similar preparation in liquid form.

liq. **1** liquid. **2** liquor.

liq·ue·fac·tion (lik′wə fak′shən) *n.* **1** the process of changing into a liquid. **2** a liquefied condition.

liq·ue·fy (lik′wə fī′) *v.* **-fied, -fy·ing.** change into a liquid. [< L *liquefacere* < *liquere* be fluid + *facere* make] —**liq′ue·fi′a·ble,** *adj.* —**liq′ue·fi′er,** *n.*

li·ques·cence (li kwes′əns) *n.* a liquescent condition.

li·ques·cent (li kwes′ənt) *adj.* become liquid. [< L *liquescens, -entis,* ppr. of *liquescere* become liquid]

li·queur (li kůr′ or li kėr′) *n.* a strong, sweet, highly flavored alcoholic liquor. [< F < L *liquor.* Doublet of LIQUOR.]

liq·uid (lik′wid) *n.* **1** a substance that is neither a solid nor a gas; a substance that flows freely like water. **2** in phonetics, the sound of *l* or *r.*
—*adj.* **1** in the form of a liquid; melted: *liquid soap.* **2** clear and bright like water. **3** clear and smooth-flowing in sound: *the liquid notes of a bird.* **4** easily turned into cash: *Canada Savings Bonds are a liquid investment.*

[ME < L *liquidus* < *liquere* be fluid]
Syn. *n.* **1 Liquid, fluid** = a substance that flows. **Liquid** applies to a substance that is neither a solid nor a gas, but flows freely like water: *Milk and oil are liquids; oxygen is not.* **Fluid** applies to anything that flows in any way, either a liquid or a gas: *Milk, water, and oxygen are fluids.*

liquid air the intensely cold, transparent liquid formed when air is very greatly compressed and then cooled.

liq·ui·date (lik′wə dāt′) *v.* **-dat·ed, -dat·ing. 1** pay (a debt). **2** settle the accounts of (a business, etc.); clear up the affairs of (a bankrupt). **3** get rid of (an undesirable person or thing): *The Russian revolution liquidated the nobility.* **4** convert into cash. **5** in law, determine and apportion by agreement or litigation the amount of (indebtedness or damages). **6** kill ruthlessly; exterminate. [< Med.L *liquidare* < L *liquidus.* See LIQUID.] **—liq′ui·da′tion,** *n.* **—liq′ui·da′tor,** *n.*

liquid fire flaming oil or a flaming chemical usually hurled from flame throwers, used against fortified emplacements, tanks, etc.

li·quid·i·ty (li kwid′ə tē) *n.* the state or quality of being liquid.

liquid measure 1 the measurement of liquids. **2** a system for measuring liquids.

4 gills = 1 pint
2 pints = 1 quart
4 quarts = 1 gallon
35 imperial gallons = 1 barrel
52½ imperial gallons = 1 hogshead

liq·uor (lik′ər) *n.* **1** an alcoholic drink, especially brandy, gin, rum, and whisky. **2** any liquid: *Pickles are put up in salty liquor.* [< L. Doublet of LIQUEUR.]

liq·uo·rice (lik′ə rish, lik′rish, or lik′ə ris) *n.* licorice.

li·ra (lēr′ə) *n.* **li·re** (lēr′ā) or **li·ras. 1** a unit of money in Italy and Turkey. See table at **money. 2** a coin or note worth a lira. [< Ital. < L *libra,* a unit of weight]

lisle (līl) *n.* a fine, strong, linen or cotton thread, used for making stockings, gloves, etc. *—adj.* made of lisle. [< F *Lisle,* the former name of *Lille,* a town in N. France]

lisp (lisp) *v.* **1** say the sound (th) for (s) or (ᴛʜ) for (z) in speaking certain words, for example, to say *thing* for *sing.* **2** speak imperfectly: *Babies are said to lisp.* *—n.* the act, habit, or sound of lisping. [ult. < OE *wlisp,* adj., lisping] **—lisp′er,** *n.*

lis·some or **lis·som** (lis′əm) *adj.* **1** lithe; limber; supple. **2** nimble; active. [var. of *lithesome*]

list[1] (list) *n.* **1** a series of names, numbers, words, or other items: *a shopping list.* **2** list price.
—v. **1** make a list of; enter in a list. **2** enlist. [< F *liste* < Gmc.]
Syn. *n.* **List, catalogue, roll** = a series of names or items. **List** is the general word applying to a series of names, figures, etc.: *This is the list of the people who are going to the picnic.* **Catalogue** applies to a complete list arranged alphabetically or according to some other system, often with short descriptions of the items: *Has the new mail-order catalogue come?* **Roll** applies to a list of the names of all members of a group: *His name is on the honor roll.*

list[2] (list) *n.* **1** the woven edge of cloth, where the material is a little different; selvage. **2** a cheap fabric made out of such edges. *—v.* put list around the edges of. [OE *līste*]

list[3] (list) *n.* a tipping to one side; tilt: *the list of a ship.* *—v.* tip to one side; tilt: *The damaged schooner was listing badly to starboard.* [extended use of *list* inclination, desire < *list*[4]]

list[4] (list) *v. Archaic.* **1** be pleasing to; please: *It lists me not to speak.* **2** like; wish: *The wind bloweth where it listeth.* [OE *lystan* < *lust* pleasure]

list[5] (list) *v. Archaic and poetic.* **1** listen. **2** listen to. [OE *hlystan* < *hlyst* hearing. Related to LISTEN.]

lis·ten (lis′ən) *v.* **1** try to hear; attend closely for the purpose of hearing. **2** give heed (to advice, temptation, etc.); pay attention. **3 listen in, a** listen to others talking on a telephone. **b** listen to the radio. [OE *hlysna.* Related to LIST[5].] **—lis′ten·er,** *n.* **—Syn. 1** See **hear.**

list·er (lis′tər) *n.* a plough that throws the dirt to both sides of the furrow. [< *list*[2]]

list·less (list′lis) *adj.* seeming too tired to care about anything; not interested in things, not caring to be active: *a listless gesture.* [< *list* a desire < *list*[4]] **—list′less·ly,** *adv.* **—list′less·ness,** *n.* **—Syn.** indifferent, languid.

hat, āge, cãre, fär; let, ēqual, tėrm; it, īce
hot, ōpen, ôrder; oil, out; cup, pu̇t, rüle, ūse
əbove, takən, pencəl, lemən, circəs
ch, child; ng, long; sh, ship
th, thin; ᴛʜ, then; zh, measure

list price the price given in a catalogue or list. Discounts are figured from it.

lists (lists) *n.pl.* **1** in the Middle Ages: **a** a place where knights fought in tournaments. **b** the barriers enclosing such a field. **2** any place or scene of combat. **3 enter the lists,** join in a contest; take part in a fight, argument, etc. [blend of *list*[2] and OF *lice* place of combat < Gmc.]

lit (lit) *v.* a pt. and a pp. of **light**[1] and **light**[3].

lit. 1 litre; litres. **2** literature. **3** literal. **4** literally.

lit·a·ny (lit′ə nē) *n.* **-nies. 1** a series of prayers by the clergyman with responses by the congregation. **2** a repeated series. [ME < OF < LL *litania* < Gk. *litaneia* litany, an entreating < *litesthai* entreat]

Lit.B. Bachelor of Letters or of Literature. (for L *Literarum Baccalaureus*)

li·tchi (lē′chē) *n.* **-tchis. 1** a nut-shaped fruit having a hard, rough skin. **2** the tree that this fruit grows on. Also, **lichee.** [< Chinese]

Lit.D. Doctor of Letters or of Literature. (for L *Literarum Doctor*)

-lite *combining form.* stone; stony: *Chrysolite = gold-colored stone.* [< F *-lite* < earlier *-lithe* < Gk. *lithos* stone]

li·ter (lē′tər) *n.* litre.

lit·er·a·cy (lit′ər ə sē) *n.* the ability to read and write.

lit·er·al (lit′ər əl or lit′rəl) *adj.* **1** following the exact words of the original: *a literal translation.* **2** taking words in their usual meaning, without exaggeration or imagination; matter-of-fact: *the literal meaning of a word, a literal type of mind.* **3** true to fact: *a literal account.* **4** of the letters of the alphabet; expressed by letters. [ME < LL *lit(t)eralis* < L *lit(t)era* letter]

lit·er·al·ism (lit′ər əl iz′əm or lit′rəl iz′əm) *n.* a keeping to the literal meaning in translation or interpretation.

lit·er·al·ist (lit′ər əl ist or lit′rəl ist) *n.* **1** a person who adheres to the exact literal meaning. **2** a person who represents or portrays without idealizing.

lit·er·al·ly (lit′ər əl ē or lit′rəl ē) *adv.* **1** word for word: *translate literally.* **2** in a literal sense; without exaggeration: *Is this literally true? I am literally penniless.*

lit·er·ar·y (lit′ər er′ē) *adj.* **1** having to do with literature. **2** knowing much about literature. **3** engaged in literature as a profession.

lit·er·ate (lit′ər it) *adj.* **1** able to read and write. **2** acquainted with literature; educated. *—n.* **1** a person who can read and write. **2** an educated person. [ME < L *lit(t)eratus* < *lit(t)era* letter]

lit·e·ra·ti (lit′ə rä′tē or lit′ə rā′tī) *n.pl.* scholarly or literary people. [< L *lit(t)erati,* pl., literally, lettered]

lit·e·ra·tim (lit′ə rā′tim) *adv.* letter for letter; exactly as written. [< Med.L *lit(t)eratim* < L *lit(t)era* letter]

lit·er·a·ture (lit′ər ə chər, lit′rə chər, or lit′ər ə chür′) *n.* **1** the writings of a period or of a country, especially those kept alive by their beauty of style or thought: *Shakespeare is a great name in English literature.* **2** all the books and articles on a subject: *the literature of stamp collecting.* **3** the profession of a writer. **4** the study of literature: *I shall take literature and mathematics this spring.* **5** leaflets and pamphlets informing people about a product, a candidate for election, etc.: *campaign literature.* [ME < L *lit(t)eratura* writing < *lit(t)era* letter] **—Syn. 1** belles-lettres.

lith·arge (lith′ärj or li thärj′) *n.* a yellow oxide of lead, used in making glass, glazes for pottery, and driers for paints and varnishes. *Formula:* PbO [ME < OF *litarge* < L < Gk. *lithargyros* < *lithos* stone + *argyros* silver]

lithe (līᴛʜ) *adj.* bending easily; supple. [OE *lithe* mild] **—lithe′ly,** *adv.* **—lithe′ness,** *n.*

lithe·some (līᴛʜ′səm) *adj.* lithe.

lith·i·a (lith′ē ə) *n.* a white oxide of lithium. *Formula:* Li_2O [< NL < Gk. *lithos* stone]

lith·ic (lith′ik) *adj.* **1** consisting of stone or rock. **2** in medicine, of or having to do with stone or stony concretions formed within the body, especially in the bladder. [< Gk. *lithikos* < *lithos* stone]

lith·i·um (lith′ē əm) *n.* a soft, silver-white, metallic chemical element similar to sodium. Lithium is the lightest of all the metals. *Symbol:* Li; *at.no.* 3; *at.wt.* 6.939. [< NL < Gk. *lithos* stone]

lith·o·graph (lith′ə graf′) *n.* a picture, print, etc. made from a flat, specially prepared stone or a metal plate. —*v.* print from a stone or plate. [< Gk. *lithos* stone + E *-graph*]

li·thog·ra·pher (li thog′rə fər) *n.* a person who lithographs or practises lithography.

lith·o·graph·ic (lith′ə graf′ik) *adj.* **1** of a lithograph. **2** of or made by lithography. —**lith′o·graph′i·cal·ly,** *adv.*

li·thog·ra·phy (li thog′rə fē) *n.* the art or process of making lithographs.

lith·o·pone (lith′ə pōn′) *n.* a white pigment, made of zinc and barium, used in paint, rubber, plastic wood, waterproofing, etc. [< Gk. *lithos* stone + ?< L *ponere* place]

lith·o·sphere (lith′ə sfēr′) *n.* the crust of the earth. [< Gk. *lithos* stone + E *sphere*]

Lith·u·a·ni·an (lith′ů ā′nē ən) *adj.* of or having to do with Lithuania, a republic in the W. Soviet Union, its people, or their language. —*n.* **1** a native or inhabitant of Lithuania. **2** the Baltic language of Lithuania.

lit·i·ga·ble (lit′ə gə bəl) *adj.* capable of being made the subject of a suit in a law court.

lit·i·gant (lit′ə gənt) *n.* a person engaged in a lawsuit. —*adj.* engaging in a lawsuit.

lit·i·gate (lit′ə gāt′) *v.* **-gat·ed, -gat·ing. 1** engage in a lawsuit. **2** contest in a lawsuit. [< L *litigare* < *lis, litis* lawsuit + *agere* drive] —**lit′i·ga′tor,** *n.*

lit·i·ga·tion (lit′ə gā′shən) *n.* **1** the act of carrying on a lawsuit. **2** a going to law. **3** a lawsuit.

li·ti·gious (lə tij′əs) *adj.* **1** having the habit of going to law. **2** offering material for a lawsuit; that can be disputed in a court of law. **3** of lawsuits. [< L *litigiosus* < *litigium* dispute < *litigare.* See LITIGATE.] —**li·ti′gious·ly,** *adv.* —**li·ti′gious·ness,** *n.*

lit·mus (lit′məs) *n.* a blue coloring matter, obtained from certain plants. [ME < ON *litmose* dyer's herb < *litr* color + *mosi* moss]

litmus paper paper treated with litmus. It turns red when put into acid and back to blue when put into alkali.

li·to·tes (lī′tə tēz′ or lit′ə tēz′) *n.* a form of understatement in which something is said by denying its opposite. *Examples:* The palace was no small bungalow. He had plenty to eat and not a little to drink. [< Gk. *litotēs* < *litos* simple, plain]

li·tre (lē′tər) *n.* in the metric system, a measure of capacity equal to 1.7598 imperial pints. *Abbrev.:* l., l, or lit. Also, **liter.** [< F *litre* < *litron,* an obs. French measure of capacity < Med.L *litra* < Gk. *litra,* a unit of weight]

Litt.B. Bachelor of Letters or of Literature. (for L *Litterarum Baccalaureus*]

Litt.D. Doctor of Letters or of Literature. (for L *Litterarum Doctor*)

lit·ter (lit′ər) *n.* **1** scattered rubbish; things scattered about or left in disorder. **2** disorder; untidiness. **3** the young animals produced at one time: *a litter of puppies.* **4** straw, hay, etc. used as bedding for animals. **5** a stretcher for carrying a sick or wounded person. **6** a framework to be carried on men's shoulders or by beasts of burden, with a couch usually enclosed by curtains. —*v.* **1** leave (odds and ends) lying around; scatter (things) about. **2** make disorder or untidy: *He littered the yard with bottles and cans.* **3** give birth to (young animals). **4** make a bed for (an animal) with straw, hay, etc. [ME < AF *litere* < Med.L *lectaria* < L *lectus* bed]

lit·té·ra·teur or **lit·te·ra·teur** (lit′ə rə tėr′) *n.* a literary man; a writer or critic of literature. [< F]

lit·ter·bug (lit′ər bug′) *n.* one who leaves papers, trash, etc. around in public places.

lit·tle (lit′əl) *adj.* **less** or **less·er, least;** or **lit·tler, lit·tlest;** *adv.* **less, least;** *n.* —*adj.* **1** not great or big; small: *A grain of sand is little. The little dog barked loudly.* **2** not much; small in number, amount, degree, or importance: *little money, little hope, a little army.* **3** short; brief: *She took a little walk.* **4** mean in thought; narrow-minded: *little opinions.*
—*adv.* **1** in a small amount or degree; to a small extent; slightly: *They live in a little-known town. He travels little.* **2** not at all: *He little knows what will happen.*
—*n.* **1** a small amount, quantity, or degree: *add a little.* **2** a short time or distance: *move a little to the left.* **3 in little,** on a small scale. **4 little by little,** slowly; gradually; by a small amount at a time. **5 make little of,** treat or represent as of little importance: *She made little of her troubles.* **6 not a little,** much; very: *He was not a little upset by the accident.* **7 think little of, a** not value much; consider as unimportant or worthless. **b** not hesitate about. [OE *lȳtel*] —**lit′tle·ness,** *n.*
Syn. *adj.* **1, 2 Little, small, diminutive** = not large or great. **Little** = not big or great in size, quantity, degree, importance, etc., and can be used to express attitudes toward what is described: *He is a funny little boy.* **Small,** often used interchangeably with *little,* particularly means "not large," and often suggests being below average, especially in size, number, or measure: *He is small for his age.* **Diminutive** = very small in size: *Her feet are diminutive.*

Little Assembly *Informal.* the interim committee of the United Nations General Assembly.

Little Bear Little Dipper.

Little Dipper in astronomy, a group of stars in the constellation of Ursa Minor (the Little Bear).

little magazine or **review** a small magazine devoted to printing experimental writing, criticism, etc.

little people the fairies.

little theatre 1 a small theatre, especially one that presents experimental plays. **2** an amateur theatre group. **3** such theatres or groups considered collectively.

lit·to·ral (lit′ə rəl) *adj.* **1** of a shore. **2** on the shore. —*n.* the region along the shore. [ult. < L *litoralis* < *litus, litoris* shore]

li·tur·gic (lə tėr′jik) *adj.* liturgical.

li·tur·gi·cal (lə tėr′jə kəl) *adj.* of or having to do with liturgy. —**li·tur′gi·cal·ly,** *adv.*

lit·ur·gy (lit′ər jē) *n.* **-gies.** a form of public worship, especially the Eucharistic service. Different churches use different liturgies. [< LL *liturgia* < Gk. *leitourgia* public worship, ult. < *leitos* public + *ergon* work]

liv·a·ble (liv′ə bəl) *adj.* **1** fit to live in. **2** easy to live with. **3** worth living; endurable.

live[1] (liv) *v.* **lived, liv·ing. 1** have life; be alive; exist: *All creatures have an equal right to live.* **2** remain alive; last; endure: *He managed to live through the war.* **3** keep up life: *live on one's income.* **4** feed or subsist: *The Chinese live largely on rice.* **5** pass (life): *live in peace, live a life of ease.* **6** dwell: *My aunt lives in Victoria.* **7** carry out or show in life: *live one's ideals.* **8** have a rich and full life. **9 live** (something) **down,** live so worthily that (some fault or sin) is overlooked or forgotten. **10 live it up,** *Slang.* enjoy life to the full. **11 live out,** stay alive through; last through. **12 live up to,** act according to; do (what is expected or promised). [OE *lifian, libban*] —**Syn. 6** reside, sojourn, lodge, abide.

live[2] (līv) *adj.* **1** having life; alive: *a live dog.* **2** burning or glowing: *live coals.* **3** full of energy or activity: *a live person.* **4** *Informal.* up-to-date: *live ideas.* **5** of present interest: *a live question.* **6** moving or imparting motion: *live wheels, a live axle.* **7** still in use or to be used: *live steam.* **8** carrying an electric current; charged electrically: *a live wire.* **9** of telephones, microphones, etc., not shut off; operating or functioning. **10** loaded: *a live cartridge.* **11** in the native state; not mined or quarried: *live metal.* **12** not recorded on tape or film: *a live television show.* —*adv.* with the actual performance or event shown; as it takes place: *The game will be broadcast live.* [var. of *alive*]

live·a·ble (liv′ə bəl) *adj.* livable.

-lived (līvd or livd) *combining form.* having a —— life or lives: *Short-lived* = *having a short life.*

live·li·hood (līv′lē hu̇d′) *n.* a means of living, that is, of obtaining the money necessary to buy food, clothing, and shelter; a means of supporting oneself and one's family: *He sold newspapers for a livelihood.* [OE *līf(ge)lād* (see LIFE, LOAD), influenced by obs. *livelihood* liveliness] —**Syn.** See **living.**

live·long (liv′long′ or līv′-) *adj.* the whole length of; whole; entire: *She is busy the livelong day.*

live·ly (līv′lē) *adj.* **-li·er, -li·est,** *adv.* —*adj.* **1** full of life; active; vigorous; spirited. **2** exciting. **3** bright; vivid. **4** cheerful; gay: *a lively conversation.* **5** bounding back quickly: *a lively baseball.* —*adv.* in a lively manner. [OE *līflīc* living] —**live′li·ness,** *n.* —**Syn.** *adj.* **1** brisk, energetic, animated, vivacious. **4** blithe, buoyant.

liv·en (līv′ən) *v.* make or become more lively; brighten.

live oak (līv) **1** an evergreen oak of the southern United States. **2** its wood, used in shipbuilding, etc.

liv·er[1] (liv′ər) *n.* **1** in vertebrates, a large, reddish-brown organ that secretes bile and helps in the absorption of food. A person's liver was once thought to be the source of his emotions. **2** an animal's liver used as food. [OE *lifer*]

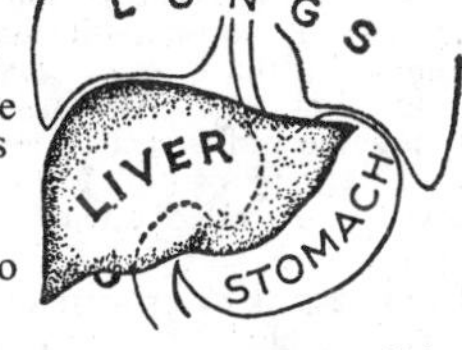

The liver of a human being

liv·er[2] (liv′ər) *n.* a person who lives. [< *live*[1]]

liv·ere (liv′yər) *n.* liveyere.

liv·er·ied (liv′ər ēd or liv′rēd) *adj.* clothed in a livery.

liv·er·ish (liv′ər ish) *adj. Informal.* having a sour or peevish disposition, one of the supposed symptoms of liver trouble; irritable.

liv·er·wort (liv′ər wėrt′) *n.* **1** any of various plants that grow mostly on damp ground, the trunks of trees, etc. Liverworts resemble mosses. **2** a hepatica.

liv·er·wurst (liv′ər wėrst′ or -wu̇rst′) *n.* a sausage consisting largely of liver. [< G *Leberwurst* liver sausage]

liv·er·y (liv′ər ē or liv′rē) *n.* **-er·ies. 1** any special uniform provided for the servants of a household, or adopted by any group or profession. **2** any characteristic dress, garb, or outward appearance. **3** the feeding, stabling, and care of horses for pay; the hiring out of horses and carriages. **4** the keeping of cars, boats, bicycles, etc. for hire. **5** a livery stable. [ME < AF *livere* < *livrer* dispense < L *liberare* liberate; originally, provisions dispensed to servants]

liv·er·y·man (liv′ər ē mən or liv′rē-) *n.* **-men** (-mən). **1** a person who works in or keeps a livery stable. **2** a person wearing livery.

livery stable a stable engaged in the livery business.

lives (līvz) *n.* pl. of **life.**

live·stock (līv′stok′) *n.* farm animals. Cows, horses, sheep, and pigs are livestock.

live wire 1 a wire in which an electric current is flowing. **2** *Informal.* an energetic, wide-awake person.

live·yere (liv′yər) *n. Cdn.* **1** in Newfoundland, a permanent resident, as opposed to those who are on the island or in Labrador for the fishing or sealing season only. **2** a permanent resident of the north shore of the Gulf of St. Lawrence. Also, **livere, livier.** [< *livier,* formerly, a type of manorial worker having certain property rights < AF *livere.* Cf. LIVERY.]

liv·id (liv′id) *adj.* **1** having a dull-bluish or leaden color: *His face turned livid with shock.* **2** discolored by a bruise. **3** excited with rage; flushed with anger. [< L *lividus* < *livere* be bluish] —**liv′id·ly,** *adv.* —**liv′id·ness,** *n.*

liv·ier (liv′yər) *n.* liveyere.

liv·ing (liv′ing) *adj.* **1** having life; being alive: *a living plant.* **2** full of life; vigorous; strong; active: *a living faith.* **3** in actual existence; still in use: *a living language.* **4** true to life; vivid; lifelike: *a living picture.* **5** of life; for living in: *living conditions.* **6** sufficient to live on: *a living wage.* —*n.* **1** the act or condition of one that lives. **2** a means of obtaining what is needed to support life; livelihood. **3** a manner of life: *right living.* **4** a position in the church, including the income attached to it; benefice.

hat, āge, cãre, fär; let, ēqual, tėrm; it, īce
hot, ōpen, ôrder; oil, out; cup, pu̇t, rüle, ūse
əbove, takən, pencəl, lemən, circəs
ch, child; ng, long; sh, ship
th, thin; ᴛʜ, then; zh, measure

Syn. *adj.* **2** lively. —*n.* **2 Living, livelihood, support** = a person's means of providing shelter, food, etc. for himself. **Living** is the general word, and suggests nothing more: *He always had to work hard for his living.* **Livelihood** often applies to the work a person does to earn enough to live on or to the pay he gets: *Mowing lawns is his only livelihood.* **Support** applies to the providing of a means of living: *They depend on his father for their support.*

living quarters a place to live.

living room a room in a house, usually used for leisure time and for entertaining.

living wage sufficient pay to buy the necessities of life.

li·vre (lē′vər) *n.* a former French silver coin. [< F < L *libra,* a unit of weight]

liz·ard (liz′ərd) *n.* any of a large group of reptiles, most of which are small and have long, scaly bodies with four legs and a long tail. Chameleons, horned toads, and glass snakes are lizards. Some lizards without limbs look much like snakes, but have movable eyelids. [ME < OF *lesard* < L *lacertus*] —**liz′ard·like′,** *adj.*

ll. lines.

LL Late Latin.

lla·ma (lä′mə or lam′ə) *n.* **-mas** or (*esp. collectively*) **-ma. 1** a cud-chewing, woolly-haired South American mammal resembling a camel, but smaller and without a hump. Llamas are used as beasts of burden. **2** its wool. [< Sp. < Quechua (Indian lang. of Peru)]

lla·no (lä′nō or lan′ō) *n.* **-nos.** a broad, treeless plain. [< Sp. < L *planus* level]

LL.B. Bachelor of Laws. (for L *Legum Baccalaureus*)

LL.D. Doctor of Laws. (for L *Legum Doctor*)

Lloyd's (loidz) *n.* in London, England, an association of businessmen dealing in many kinds of insurance, especially marine insurance.

lo (lō) *interj.* look! see! behold! [OE *lā*]

loach (lōch) *n.* a small European fresh-water fish. [ME < OF *loche,* ?< Celtic]

load (lōd) *n.* **1** what one is carrying; burden: *The cart has a load of hay.* **2** the quantity that can be or usually is carried; such quantity taken as a unit of measure or weight. **3** something that weighs down, oppresses, or impedes: *a load of debt, a load of anxiety, a load of guilt.* **4 loads,** *pl. Informal.* a great quantity or number. **5** in mechanics, the weight supported by a structure or part. **6** the external resistance overcome by an engine, dynamo, or the like, under a given condition, measured by the power required. **7** one charge of powder and shot for a gun. **8** *Slang.* enough liquor to make one drunk. —*v.* **1** place on or in something for conveyance: *load grain.* **2** put a load in or on: *load a car, ship, horse, basket, etc.* **3** take on a load. **4** burden; oppress. **5** supply amply or in excess: *They loaded her with compliments.* **6** add weight to: *load dice.* **7** put a charge in (a gun). [OE *lād* course, carrying; cf. *lode*] —**load′er,** *n.*

Syn. *n.* **1 Load, burden** = what one is carrying. **Load,** the general word, applies literally to whatever is carried by a person or animal or in a vehicle, boat, or plane, and figuratively to something that weighs heavily on the mind or spirit: *That is a heavy load of groceries.* **Burden** = something borne, and now except in a few phrases is used only figuratively, applying to sorrow, care, duty, or work: *She had too heavy a burden and became sick.*

load·ed (lōd′id) *adj.* **1** carrying a load. **2** with a charge in it. **3** weighted, especially with lead: *a loaded stick or whip.* **4** *Slang.* drunk. **5** *Slang.* having plenty of money; rich. **6** *Informal.* full of hidden meanings or implications: *a loaded question.*

load·star (lōd′stär′) *n.* lodestar.

load·stone (lōd′stōn′) *n.* **1** a stone that attracts iron as a magnet does; a kind of magnetite. **2** something that attracts: *Gold was the loadstone that drew men to the Yukon.* Also, **lodestone.** [< *load* + *stone*]

loaf[1] (lōf) *n.* **loaves. 1** bread that is shaped and baked as one piece. **2** a rather large cake, often baked in the shape of a loaf of bread. **3** food shaped like a loaf of bread. Veal loaf is veal chopped and mixed with egg and then baked. **4** formerly, a cone-shaped mass of sugar. [OE *hlāf*]

loaf[2] (lōf) *v.* spend time idly; do nothing: *I can loaf all day Saturday.* [origin uncertain; cf. G dial. *lofen* run about, idle]

loaf·er (lōf′ər) *n.* **1** one who loafs. **2** Usually **loafers,** *pl.* a shoe resembling a moccasin, but with sole and heel stitched to the upper.

loam (lōm) *n.* **1** rich, fertile earth; loose, crumbly soil in which much humus is mixed with clay and sand. **2** a mixture of clay, sand, and straw used to make moulds for large metal castings, and also to plaster walls, stop holes, etc. —*v.* cover or fill with loam. [OE *lām*]

loam·y (lōm′ē) *adj.* of or like loam.

loan (lōn) *n.* **1** the giving of something to someone on condition that it be returned: *She asked for a loan of his pen.* **2** money lent: *The man went to his bank for a loan.* **3** anything lent. —*v.* make a loan; lend. [ME < ON *lán*] —**loan′er,** *n.*

☞ **loan, lend.** In formal usage *loan* is a noun and *lend* a verb. But in informal usage *loan* is both a verb and a noun: *I loaned* (or *lent*) *him my tuxedo. He asked me for a loan of five dollars.*

loan shark *Informal.* a person who lends money at an extremely high or unlawful rate of interest.

loan·word (lōn′ wėrd′) *n.* a word borrowed from another language, especially a foreign word that has been Anglicized. *Examples*: khaki (from Hindi), intelligentsia (from Russian).

loath (lōth) *adj.* **1** unwilling; reluctant: *The little girl was loath to leave her mother.* **2 nothing loath,** *Archaic.* willing; willingly. Also, **loth.** [OE *lāth* hostile] —**Syn. 1** See **reluctant.**

loathe (lōᴛʜ) *v.* **loathed, loath·ing.** feel strong dislike and disgust for; abhor; hate. [OE *lāthian* hate < *lāth* hostile] —**Syn.** abominate, detest.

loath·ing (lōᴛʜ′ing) *n.* strong dislike and disgust; intense aversion.

loath·ly[1] (lōᴛʜ′lē) *adj.* loathsome. [OE *lāthlīc* < *lāth* hostile, odious]

loath·ly[2] (lōth′lē; *older* lōᴛʜ′lē) *adv. Rare.* unwillingly; reluctantly. [OE *lāthlīce* < *lāth* hostile]

loath·some (lōᴛʜ′səm) *adj.* disgusting; sickening: *a loathsome odor.* —**loath′some·ly,** *adv.* —**loath′some·ness,** *n.* —**Syn.** abominable, detestable, repulsive.

loaves (lōvz) *n.* pl. of **loaf**[1].

lob (lob) *n. v.* **lobbed, lob·bing.** —*n.* **1** in tennis, a ball hit high to the back of the opponent's court. **2** a slow underarm throw. [< v.] —*v.* **1** in tennis, hit (a ball) high to the back of an opponent's court. **2** throw (a ball) with a slow underarm movement. [ME *lobbe(n)* move clumsily]

lo·bar (lō′bər) *adj.* of or having to do with a lobe or lobes.

lo·bate (lō′bāt) *adj.* having a lobe or lobes; having the form of a lobe. The liver is lobate.

lo·ba·tion (lō bā′shən) *n.* **1** a lobate formation. **2** a lobe.

lob·by (lob′ē) *n.* **-bies,** *v.* **-bied, -by·ing.** —*n.* **1** an entrance hall; vestibule or waiting room: *a theatre lobby. A hotel lobby usually has chairs and couches to sit on.* **2** a room or hall outside a legislative chamber: *the lobby of the House of Commons.* **3** a person or group that tries to influence legislators.

—*v.* **1** try to influence legislators to vote in a certain way. **2** get or try to get (a bill) passed by lobbying. [< Med.L *lobia* covered walk < Gmc. See LODGE.]

lob·by·ist (lob′ē ist) *n.* a person who tries to influence legislators.

lobe (lōb) *n.* a rounded projecting part. The lobe of the ear is the lower rounded end. [< F < LL < Gk. *lobos*]

lobed (lōbd) *adj.* having a lobe or lobes.

lo·bel·ia (lō bēl′ē ə or lō bēl′yə) *n.* any of various plants, both wild and cultivated, having blue, red, yellow, or white flowers. [< NL; after Matthias de *Lobel* (1538-1616), a Flemish botanist]

lo·bot·o·my (lō bot′ə mē) *n.* in surgery, an operation that involves cutting into or across a lobe of the brain, used in treating some mental disorders.

lob·ster (lob′stər) *n.* an edible crustacean having two big claws in front and eight legs. [OE *loppestre* < L *locusta* locust; influenced by OE < *loppe* spider]

lob·ster·man (lob′stər mən) *n.* a man who catches lobsters.

lobster pot a trap for lobsters.

lob·stick (lob′stik′) *n.Cdn.* in the North, a tall, prominently situated spruce or pine trimmed of all but its topmost branches, originally used by the Indians as a talisman and landmark. The voyageurs often trimmed a lobstick as a memorial to an honored fellow traveller or a respected superior. Also, **lopstick.**

lob·ule (lob′ūl) *n.* **1** a small lobe. **2** a part of a lobe.

lo·cal (lō′kəl) *adj.* **1** having to do with a certain place or places: *the local doctor, local self-government, local news.* **2** restricted to one part of the body: *a local pain, local disease, local application of a remedy.* **3** making all, or almost all, stops: *a local train.*

—*n.* **1** a train, bus, etc. that makes all, or almost all, stops. **2** a local inhabitant. **3** a branch or chapter of a labor union, fraternity, etc. **4** a newspaper item of interest to a particular place. **5** a person, team, etc. from a given locality. **6** a telephone extension. [< L *localis* < *locus* place]

local color or **colour** the customs, peculiarities, etc. of a certain place or period, used in stories and plays to make them seem more real.

lo·cale (lō kal′) *n.* location, site, or place, especially with reference to events or circumstances connected with it. [< F *local* local]

local government **1** the system of administration of local affairs in a township, city, etc. by its own people through their elected representatives. **2** the group, or council, elected for this purpose.

local government district in the Prairie Provinces, a district administered by provincial officials because it is too thinly populated to have a municipal government of its own.

local improvement district local government district.

lo·cal·ism (lō′kəl iz′əm) *n.* **1** a local practice, custom, etc. **2** a word or expression, etc. peculiar to a certain area: *"Outport," meaning an outlying fishing village, is a Newfoundland localism.* **3** provincialism. **4** attachment to a certain place.

lo·cal·i·ty (lō kal′ə tē) *n.* **-ties. 1** a place; region. **2** places and things considered as related to others in a region. A sense of locality enables one to find one's way.

lo·cal·ize (lō′kəl īz′) *v.* **-ized, -iz·ing.** make local; fix in, assign, or limit to a particular place or locality: *The infection seemed to be localized in the foot.* —**lo′cal·i·za′tion,** *n.* —**lo′cal·iz′er,** *n.*

lo·cal·ly (lō′kəl ē) *adv.* **1** in a local manner or respect; with regard to place: *be separated locally.* **2** in a particular place or in particular places; not everywhere: *Outbreaks of the disease occurred locally.*

local option the right of choice exercised by a minor political division, such as a county or city, especially as to whether the sale of liquor shall be permitted within its limits.

Lo·car·no Pact (lō kär′nō) a group of treaties and agreements made in 1925 to guarantee boundaries and maintain peace in western and central Europe between Germany and Great Britain, France, Belgium, Italy, Czechoslovakia, and Poland.

lo·cate (lō′kāt or lō kāt′) *v.* **-cat·ed, -cat·ing. 1** establish in a place: *He located his new store on Bay Street.* **2** establish oneself in a place: *Early settlers located where there was water.* **3** find out the exact position of: *The general tried to locate the enemy's camp.* **4** state or show the position of: *locate Regina on the map.* **5 be located,** be situated. [< L *locare* < *locus* place] —**lo′ca·tor,** *n.*

lo·ca·tion (lō kā′shən) *n.* **1** a locating. **2** a being located. **3** a position; place. **4** a plot of ground marked out by boundaries; lot: *a mining location.* **5** a place outside of the studio used in making all or part of a motion picture: *shoot a film on location.* —**Syn. 3** locality.

loc·a·tive (lok′ə tiv) in grammar: —*adj.* indicating place.

—*n.* 1 the case used to indicate place in which something is, takes place, etc. 2 a word in this case. [< L *locatus*, pp. of *locare*. See LOCATE.]

loc. cit. in the place cited. (for L *loco citato*)

loch (lok or loH) *n. Scottish.* 1 a lake: *Loch Lomond.* 2 an arm of the sea partly shut in by land. [< Scots Gaelic]

Loch·in·var (lok′ən vär′) *n.* the hero of a poem by Scott, who boldly carries off his sweetheart just as she is about to be married to another man.

lo·ci (lō′sī or lō′sē, lō′kī or lō′kē) *n.* pl. of **locus.**

lock[1] (lok) *n.* 1 a means of fastening doors, boxes, etc., usually needing a key of special shape to open it. 2 the part of a canal, dock, etc. in which the level of the water can be changed by letting water in or out in order to raise or lower ships. 3 the part of a gun by which the charge is fired. 4 a device to keep a wheel from turning. A lock is used when a vehicle is going downhill. 5 an airtight chamber admitting to a compartment in which there is compressed air. 6 in wrestling, a kind of hold. 7 **lock, stock, and barrel,** *Informal.* completely; entirely. 8 **under lock and key,** locked up; in a place that is locked.

Locks in a canal (def. 2). They enable ships to go where there were formerly waterfalls, or to go around a dam. If the ship enters from below, the gates are closed, the water level is raised (by means of pipes) to equal the level above the lock, then the upper gates are opened. If the ship enters from above, the process is reversed.

—*v.* 1 fasten with a lock. 2 shut (something in or out or up). 3 hold fast: *The ship was locked in ice. The secret was locked in her heart.* 4 join, fit, jam, or link together: *The girls locked arms.* 5 become locked: *Two cars locked together in passing.* 6 fasten (a wheel) to keep from turning. 7 in printing, fasten (type, blocks, etc. in a chase) for printing or plating. 8 go or pass by means of a lock; move (a ship) by means of a lock. 9 **lock out,** refuse to give work to workers until they accept the employer's terms. [OE *loc*] —**Syn.** *n.* 1 bolt.

lock[2] (lok) *n.* 1 a curl of hair. 2 **locks,** *pl.* the hair of the head: *The child has curly locks.* 3 a tuft of hair, wool, etc. [OE *locc*]

lock·age (lok′ij) *n.* 1 the construction, use, or operation of locks in canals or streams. 2 the passing of ships through a lock. 3 the walls, gates, etc. forming a lock. 4 the amount of elevation and descent affected by a lock or locks. 5 the toll paid for passage through a lock.

lock·er (lok′ər) *n.* 1 a person or thing that locks. 2 a chest, drawer, closet, or cupboard that can be locked. 3 a refrigerated compartment for storing frozen foods.

lock·et (lok′it) *n.* a small ornamental case of gold, silver, etc. for holding a picture of someone or a lock of hair. It is usually worn around the neck on a necklace. [< F *loquet* latch, dim. of OF *loc* < Gmc.]

lock·jaw (lok′jo′ or -jô′) *n.* a form of blood poisoning in which the jaws become firmly closed; tetanus.

lock·out (lok′out′) *n.* the closure of a factory, office, etc. or the refusal of work by an employer in order to make his employees agree to terms.

lock·smith (lok′smith′) *n.* a man who makes or repairs locks and keys.

lock step a way of marching in step very close together.

lock stitch a sewing-machine stitch in which two threads are fastened together at short intervals.

lock·up (lok′up′) *n. Informal.* jail.

lo·co (lō′kō) *n.* **-cos,** *v.* **-coed, -co·ing,** *adj.* —*n.* 1 the locoweed. 2 the disease caused by eating this weed. —*v.* poison with this weed. —*adj. Slang.* crazy. [< Sp. *loco* insane]

lo·co·mo·tion (lō′kə mō′shən) *n.* the act or power of moving from place to place. Walking and flying are common forms of locomotion. [< L *loco* from a place + E *motion*]

lo·co·mo·tive (lō′kə mō′tiv) *n.* 1 a railway engine. 2 any engine that goes from place to place on its own power. —*adj.* 1 moving from place to place: *locomotive bacteria.* 2 having to do with the power to move from place to place.

hat, āge, cãre, fär; let, ēqual, tėrm; it, īce
hot, ōpen, ôrder; oil, out; cup, pu̇t, rüle, ūse
əbove, takən, pencəl, lemən, circəs
ch, child; ng, long; sh, ship
th, thin; ᴛʜ, then; zh, measure

lo·co·mo·tor (lō′kə mō′tər) *n.* a person, animal, or thing that is capable of locomotion. —*adj.* of or having to do with locomotion.

locomotor ataxia a degenerative disease of the spinal cord, marked by loss of control over walking and certain other movements.

lo·co·weed (lō′kō wēd′) *n.* a plant of W. North America that affects the brains of animals that feed on it. Also, **loco.**

lo·cum te·nens (lō′kəm tē′nənz) a person temporarily holding the place or office of another; deputy; substitute. [< Med.L < L *locum*, accus. of *locus* place < *tenens*, ppr. of *tenere* hold]

lo·cus (lō′kəs) *n.* **lo·ci.** 1 a place. 2 in mathematics, a curve, surface, or other figure that contains all the points, and only those points, that satisfy a given condition. The locus of a point 1 ft. distant from a given point is the surface of a sphere. [< L]

lo·cust (lō′kəst) *n.* 1 any of the grasshoppers having short antennae. Certain kinds of locust migrate in great swarms, destroying crops. 2 a cicada. 3 **a** a tree having small, rounded leaflets and clusters of sweet-smelling, white flowers. **b** its wood, hard and resisting decay. 4 **a** a tree native to the region of S.W. Asia. **b** the fruit of this tree, a long, flat pod containing a number of hard seeds: *John the Baptist existed for a time on locusts and honey.* [< L *locusta*]

lo·cu·tion (lō kū′shən) *n.* 1 style of speech. 2 form of expression. [< L *locutio, -onis* < *loqui* speak]

lode (lōd) *n.* a vein of metal ore: *The miners struck a rich lode of copper.* [OE *lād* course, carrying. Cf. LOAD.]

lode mining hardrock mining.

lode·star (lōd′stär′) *n.* 1 a star that serves as a guide in navigation. 2 the polestar; North Star. 3 a guiding principle. Also, **loadstar.** [< *load* + *star*]

lode·stone (lōd′stōn′) *n.* loadstone.

lodge (loj) *v.* **lodged, lodg·ing,** *n.* —*v.* 1 live in a place for a time. 2 provide with a place to live in or sleep in for a time. 3 live in a rented room in another's house. 4 rent a room or rooms to. 5 get caught or stay in a place: *The kite lodged in the top of a tree.* 6 put or send into a place: *The hunter lodged a bullet in the lion's heart.* 7 put for safekeeping: *lodge money in a bank.* 8 put before some authority: *We lodged a complaint with the police.* 9 put (power, authority, etc.) in a person or thing. 10 of wind or rain, beat down (crops); lay flat. [ME < OF *logier* < *loge.* See n.]
—*n.* 1 a place to live in; an inn, hotel, or motel, usually of an expensive nature. 2 a small or temporary house; house: *My uncle rents a fishing lodge every summer.* 3 **a** a branch of a society. **b** the place where such a group meets. 4 the den of a beaver or otter. 5 a North American Indian dwelling. 6 a North American Indian household. [ME < OF *loge* arbor, covered walk < OHG **laubja.* Doublet of LOBBY, LOGE, LOGGIA.] —**Syn.** *v.* 1 dwell, reside.

lodge·ment (loj′mənt) *n.* lodgment.

lodge·pole pine (loj′pōl′) a slim, straight pine common in British Columbia and the Rocky Mountain region.

lodg·er (loj′ər) *n.* a person who lives in a rented room in another's house.

lodg·ing (loj′ing) *n.* 1 a place to live in for a time. 2 **lodgings,** *pl.* a rented room or rooms in a house, not in a hotel.

lodging house a house in which rooms are rented.

lodg·ment or **lodge·ment** (loj′mənt) *n.* 1 a lodging. 2 a being lodged. 3 something lodged or deposited. 4 in military use: **a** a position gained; foothold. **b** an entrenchment built temporarily on a position gained from the enemy.

lo·ess (lō′is or lœs) *n.* a yellowish-brown loam, usually deposited by the wind. [< G *Löss*]

loft (loft) *n.* **1** an attic. **2** a room under the roof of a barn. **3** a gallery in a church or hall. **4** in golf: **a** the backward slope of the face of a club. **b** a stroke that drives a ball upward.
—*v.* in golf, hit (a ball) high up into the air. [OE < ON *lopt* air, sky, loft]

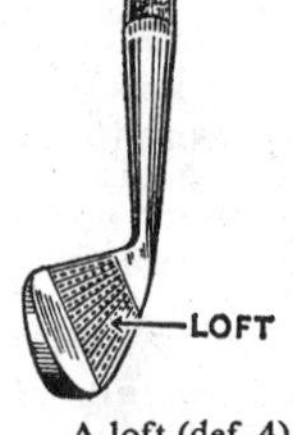

A loft (def. 4)

loft·y (lof′tē) *adj.* **loft·i·er, loft·i·est.** **1** very high: *lofty mountains.* **2** exalted; dignified; grand: *lofty aims.* **3** proud; haughty: *He had a lofty contempt for others.* —**loft′i·ly,** *adv.* —**loft′i·ness,** *n.*
—**Syn. 1** tall. See **high. 2** sublime, stately. **3** arrogant.

log (log) *n. v.* **logged, log·ging.** —*n.* **1** a length of wood just as it comes from the tree. **2** the daily record of a ship's voyage. **3** the record of an airplane trip, performance of an engine, etc. **4** a float for measuring the speed of a ship.
—*v.* **1** cut down trees, cut them into logs, and get them out of the forest. **2** cut (trees) into logs. **3** cut down trees on (land). **4** enter in a ship's log. **5** enter the name and offence of (a sailor) in a ship's log. **6 log off,** in lumbering, clear (land) of trees. [ME *logge*; origin uncertain]
—**log′like′,** *adj.*

log or **log.** logarithm.

lo·gan (lō′gən) *n. Cdn.* pokelogan.

lo·gan·ber·ry (lō′gən ber′ē) *n.* **-ries.** a large, purplish-red fruit of a bramble developed from a cross between a blackberry and a red raspberry. [< J. H. *Logan* (1841-1928), an American jurist and horticulturist, its first grower]

log·a·rithm (log′ə riᴛʜ′əm) *n.* **1** in mathematics, an exponent of the power to which a fixed number (usually 10) must be raised in order to produce a given number. If the fixed number is 10, the logarithm of 1,000 is 3; the logarithm of 10,000 is 4; the logarithm of 100,000 is 5. **2** one of a system of such exponents used to shorten calculations in mathematics. [< NL *logarithmus* < Gk. *logos* proportion + *arithmos* number]

log·a·rith·mic (log′ə riᴛʜ′mik) *adj.* of or having to do with a logarithm or logarithms.

log·a·rith·mi·cal (log′ə riᴛʜ′mə kəl) *adj.* logarithmic.

log·book (log′bůk′) *n.* **1** a book in which a daily record of a ship's voyage is kept. **2** a book for records of an airplane's trip. **3** a journal of travel.

loge (loj or lōzh) *n.* **1** a box in a theatre or opera house. **2** a balcony or mezzanine in a theatre, especially the front part of such a balcony. [< F. See LODGE.]

log·ger (log′ər) *n.* **1** a person whose work is logging; lumberjack. **2** a machine for loading or hauling logs.

log·ger·head (log′ər hed′) *n.* **1** a stupid person. **2** a large-headed marine turtle of the Atlantic Ocean. **3 at loggerheads,** disputing; in disagreement. [< *logger*, var. of *log* + *head*]

log·gia (loj′ə; *Italian.* lôd′jä) *n.* **log·gias** (lōj′əz) or (*Italian*) **log·gie** (lôd′jā). a gallery or arcade open to the air on at least one side. [< Ital. < F *loge.* See LODGE.]

log·ging (log′ing) *n.* the work of cutting down trees, cutting them into logs, and removing them from the forest.

log·ic (loj′ik) *n.* **1** the science of formal reasoning and inference. **2** a book on logic. **3** reasoning; the use of argument. **4** reason; sound sense: *There is much logic in what he says.* [ME < OF *logique* < LL < Gk. *logikē* (*technē*) reasoning (art) < *logos* word]

log·i·cal (loj′ə kəl) *adj.* **1** having to do with logic; according to the principles of logic. **2** reasonable; reasonably expected. **3** reasoning correctly. —**log′i·cal·ly,** *adv.* —**log′i·cal·ness,** *n.* —**Syn. 2** consistent. **3** rational, sound.

lo·gi·cian (lō jish′ən) *n.* an expert in logic.

lo·gis·tic (lō jis′tik) *adj.* of or having to do with logistics.

lo·gis·ti·cal (lō jis′tə kəl) *adj.* logistic.

lo·gis·tics (lō jis′tiks) *n.* the art of planning and carrying out military movement, evacuation, and supply. [< F *logistique*, ult. < *loger* lodge]

log·jam (log′jam′) *n. v.* **-jammed, -jam·ming.** —*n.* **1** an accumulation of floating logs jammed together in the water. **2** any deadlock or blockage. —*v.* delay, block, or obstruct.

log·o·type (log′ə tīp′) *n.* in printing, a word or several frequently used letters cast in one piece but not connected, such as *Ltd., Co.,* etc.

log·roll (log′rōl′) *v. Informal.* **1** take part in logrolling. **2** *Esp.U.S.* get (a bill) passed by logrolling. —**log′roll′er,** *n.*

log·roll·ing (log′rōl′ing) *n.* **1** the act of rolling logs, especially by treading on them. **2** *Esp.U.S.* the giving of political aid in return for a like favor.

log·wood (log′wůd′) *n.* **1** the heavy, brownish-red wood of a tropical American tree, used in dyeing. **2** the tree.

lo·gy (lō′gē) *adj.* **-gi·er, -gi·est.** *Informal.* heavy; sluggish; dull. [cf. Du. *log*]

-logy *combining form.* **1** an account, doctrine, or science of, as in *biology, theology.* **2** speaking; discussion, as in *eulogy.* **3** special meanings, as in *analogy, anthology.* [< Gk. *-logia*, in a few cases < *logos* word, discourse, but usually < *-logos* treating of < *legein* speak (of), mention]

loin (loin) *n.* **1** Usually, **loins,** *pl.* the part of the body between the ribs and the hips. The loins are on both sides of the backbone. **2** a piece of meat from this part: *a loin of pork.* See **pork** for diagram. **3 gird up one's loins,** get ready for action. [ME < OF *loigne*, ult. < L *lumbus*]

loin·cloth (loin′kloth′) *n.* a piece of cloth fastened around the waist and covering the thighs. The loincloth is worn by people of warm countries.

loi·ter (loi′tər) *v.* **1** linger idly; stop and play along the way. **2** spend (time) idly: *loiter the hours away.* [ME < MDu. *loteren* be loose] —**loi′ter·er,** *n.* —**Syn. 1** delay, tarry, lag, dawdle. See **linger.**

Lo·ki (lō′kē) *n.* in Norse mythology, the god of destruction and mischief. He caused the death of Balder.

L.O.L. Loyal Orange Association (or Lodge).

loll (lol) *v.* **1** recline or lean in a lazy manner: *loll on a chesterfield.* **2** hang out loosely or droop: *A dog's tongue lolls out in hot weather.* **3** allow to hang out or droop: *A dog lolls out his tongue.* —*n.* a lolling. [ME *lolle*(*n*)]

Lol·lard (lol′ərd) *n.* a follower of John Wycliffe, 1320?-1384, an English religious reformer. The Lollards advocated certain religious, political, and economic reforms, and were persecuted as heretics. [< MDu. *lollaerd* mumbler < *lollen* mumble]

Lol·lard·ism (lol′ər dism) *n.* Lollardry.

Lol·lard·ry (lol′ər drē) *n.* **1** the principles and beliefs of the Lollards. **2** support for these principles and beliefs. Also, **Lollardy.**

Lol·lard·y (lol′ər dē) *n.* Lollardry.

lol·li·pop or **lol·ly·pop** (lol′ē pop′) *n.* a piece of hard candy, usually on the end of a small stick. [< dial. *lolly* tongue + *pop*]

Lom·bard (lom′bärd or lom′bərd, lum′bärd or lum′bərd) *n.* **1** a member of a Germanic tribe that in the sixth century A.D. conquered the part of N. Italy since known as Lombardy. **2** a native or inhabitant of Lombardy. [< Ital. *Lombardo* < LL *Langobardus* < Gmc.; original meaning, long beard]

Lombard Street 1 in London, a street famous as a financial centre. **2** the London money market or financiers as a group.

Lom·bard·y poplar (lom′bər dē or lum′bər dē) a tall, slender variety of poplar whose branches curve upward.

lon. longitude.

Lon·don·er (lun′dən ər) *n.* a native or inhabitant of London, England.

lone (lōn) *adj.* **1** alone; solitary. **2** lonesome; lonely: *a lone life.* **3** *Humorous.* single or widowed. **4** standing apart; isolated: *a lone house.* [var. of *alone*

lone·ly (lōn′lē) *adj.* **-li·er, -li·est. 1** feeling oneself alone and longing for company or friends: *She was lonely when among strangers.* **2** used by only a few people: *a lonely road.* **3** alone: *a lonely tree.* —**lone′li·ness,** *n.* —**Syn. 1** lonesome. **2** secluded. **3** solitary.

lon·er (lōn′ər) *n. Informal.* a person who prefers to live or be alone.

lone·some (lōn′səm) *adj.* **-som·er, -som·est. 1** feeling lonely. **2** making one feel lonely. **3** unfrequented; desolate: *a lonesome road.* **4** solitary: *One lonesome pine stood there.* —**lone′some·ly** *adv.* —**lone′some·ness,** *n.*

lone wolf *Informal.* **1** a person who chooses to work alone, or who forms his opinions by himself. **2** a wolf that hunts or lives alone.

long[1] (long) *adj.* **long·er** (long′gər), **long·est** (long′gist), *adv. n.* —*adj.* **1** measuring much, or more than usual, from end to end in space or time: *a long distance, a long speech.* **2** continuing too long; lengthy; tedious: *long hours of waiting.* **3** beyond the normal extension in space, duration, quantity, etc.: *a long dozen, a long ton.* **4** having a specified length in space or time: *five feet long, two hours long.* **5** thin and narrow: *a long pole.* **6** far-reaching; extending to a great distance in space or time: *a long memory, a long look into the future.* **7** of vowels or syllables, taking a relatively long time to pronounce. **8** involving considerable risk, liability to error, etc.: *a long chance.* **9** well supplied (with some commodity or stock). **10** depending on a rise in prices for profit. **11 in the long run,** over a long period of time; eventually: *The system will work out fairly well in the long run.*
—*adv.* **1** throughout the whole length of: *all night long.* **2** for a long time: *a reform long advocated.* **3** at a point of time far distant from the time indicated: *long before, long since.* **4 as long as,** provided that. **5 so long as,** provided that.
—*n.* **1** a long time: *for long.* **2** a long sound. **3 before long,** soon; in a short time. **4 the long and the short of it,** the sum total (of something); substance; upshot. [OE *lang*] —**Syn.** *adj.* **1** extended, prolonged.

long[2] (long) *v.* wish very much; have a strong desire. [OE *langian* < *lang* long[1]] —**Syn.** yearn, crave.

long. longitude.

long·boat (long′bōt′) *n.* the largest and strongest boat carried by a sailing ship.

long·bow (long′bō′) *n.* **1** a bow drawn by hand and discharging a long, feathered arrow; distinguished from *crossbow.* **2 draw the longbow,** tell exaggerated stories.

long·cloth (long′kloth′) *n.* a kind of fine, soft cotton cloth.

long-dis·tance (long′dis′təns) *adj.* **1** of or having to do with telephone service to another town, city, etc. **2** for or over great distances: *a long-distance moving van.* —*n.* an operator or exchange that takes care of long-distance calls.

long dozen thirteen.

long-drawn (long′dron′ or -drôn′) *adj.* lasting a long time; prolonged to great length.

lon·gev·i·ty (lon jev′ə tē) *n.* long life. [< L *longaevitas* < *longaevus* long-lived < *longus* long + *aevum* age]

long·hand (long′hand′) *n.* ordinary writing, not shorthand or typewriting.

long-head·ed (long′hed′id) *adj.* **1** having a long head. **2** shrewd; far-sighted.

long·horn (long′hôrn′) *n.* **1** a breed of cattle that has very long horns. **2** an animal of this breed.

long house a communal dwelling of certain North American Indian tribes, especially of the Iroquois.

long·ing (long′ing) *n.* an earnest desire. —*adj.* having or showing earnest desire. —**long′ing·ly,** *adv.* —**Syn.** *n.* craving, yearning, pining. See **desire.**

long·ish (long′ish) *adj.* rather long.

lon·gi·tude (lon′jə tūd′ or lon′jə tüd′, long′gə tūd′ or long′gə tüd′) *n.* **1** a distance east or west on the earth's surface, measured in degrees from a certain meridian. Usually the meridian through Greenwich, England, is used. See diagram in the next column.

hat, āge, cãre, fär; let, ēqual, tėrm; it, īce
hot, ōpen, ôrder; oil, out; cup, pu̇t, rüle, ūse
əbove, takən, pencəl, lemən, circəs
ch, child; ng, long; sh, ship
th, thin; ᴛʜ, then; zh, measure

2 *Humorous.* length. [ME < L *longitudo* length < *longus* long]

lon·gi·tu·di·nal (lon′jə tū′də nəl or lon′jə tü′də nəl, long′gə tū′də nəl or long′gə tü′də nəl) *adj.* **1** of length; in length: *The longitudinal measurements were inaccurate.* **2** running lengthwise: *longitudinal stripes.* **3** of longitude.

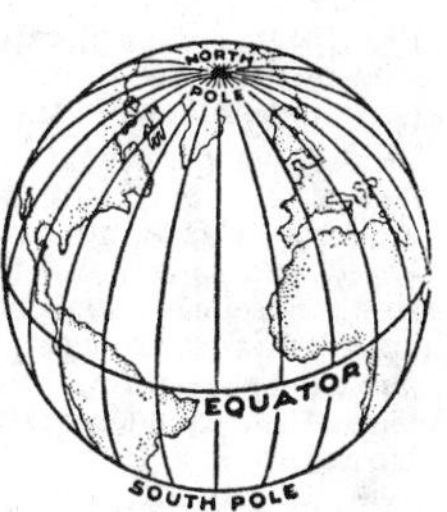

Circles of longitude

lon·gi·tu·di·nal·ly (lon′jə-tū′də nəl ē or lon′jə tü′də nəl ē, long′gə tū′də nəl ē or long′gə-tü′də nəl ē) *adv.* **1** lengthwise. **2** according to longitude.

long johns (jonz) *Informal.* men's ankle-length underwear; long underwear.

long·line (long′līn′) *n.* a fishing line, sometimes several miles long, that has many baited hooks, used for deep-sea fishing.

long·lin·er (long′līn′ər) *n.* a fishing vessel that uses longlines.

long-lived (long′livd′ or -līvd′) *adj.* living or lasting a long time.

long measure linear measure.

Long Parliament in England, the Parliament that assembled in 1640, was expelled by Cromwell in 1653, reassembled in 1659, and was dissolved in 1660.

long-play·ing (long′plā′ing) *adj.* of a phonograph record, for playing at a speed slower than 78 r.p.m., especially at 33⅓ r.p.m.

long-range (long′rānj′) *adj.* **1** looking ahead; future: *long-range plans.* **2** capable of covering a great distance: *long-range missiles.*

long·shore (long′shôr′) *adj.* **1** of or having to do with longshoremen or the waterfront. **2** employed or found along the shore.

long·shore·man (long′shôr′mən) *n.* **-men** (-mən). a man whose work is loading and unloading ships. [for *alongshoreman*]

long shot *Informal.* **1** something that is very unlikely to happen. **2** someone who is very unlikely to succeed. **3** in betting, a horse, team, etc. backed against heavy odds and with almost no chance of winning. **4** a scene or picture photographed from a considerable distance. **5 not by a long shot,** not at all; hardly.

long-sight·ed (long′sīt′id) *adj.* **1** far-sighted; focussing at more than the right distance. **2** having foresight; wise. —**long′-sight′ed·ly,** *adv.* —**long′-sight′ed·ness,** *n.*

long-stand·ing (long′stan′ding) *adj.* having lasted for a long time: *a long-standing feud.*

long-suf·fer·ing (long′suf′ər ing or -suf′ring) *adj.* enduring trouble, pain, or injury long and patiently. —*n.* long and patient endurance of trouble, pain, or injury.

long suit 1 in card games, the suit in which one has most cards. **2** a strong point.

long-term (long′tėrm′) *adj.* **1** lasting or intended for a long time: *our long-term plans and ambitions.* **2** falling due in several years: *a long-term loan.*

long ton the British ton, 2,240 pounds.

long-tongued (long′tungd′) *adj.* **1** having a long tongue. **2** talking much or too much.

long·ways (long′wāz′) *adv.* lengthwise; in the direction of the length.

long-wind·ed (long′win′did) *adj.* **1** capable of long effort without getting out of breath: *A long-distance runner must be long-winded.* **2** talking or writing at great lengths; tiresome: *a long-winded speaker.*
—**long′-wind′ed·ly,** *adv.* —**long′-wind′ed·ness,** *n.*

long·wise (long′wīz′) *adv.* lengthwise.

loo (lü) *n.* a kind of card game in which forfeits are paid into a pool. [short for *lanterloo* < F *lanturelu,* a meaningless word in the refrain of an old French song]

look (lůk) *v.* **1** see; try to see; direct the eyes: *He looked this way.* **2** direct a look at: *look one in the eyes.* **3** glance or gaze in a certain way: *look questioningly or kindly at a person.* **4** search: *I looked everywhere for my socks.* **5** appear equal to: *He doesn't look his age.* **6** seem; appear: *She looks pale.* **7** face; have a view: *Our house looks upon a garden.* **8** express or suggest by looks.
look after, attend to; take care of.
look alive, hurry.
look at, examine, pay attention.
look back, recollect; think about the past.
look daggers, look angrily.
look down on, despise; scorn.
look for, seek or search for; expect.
look forward to, expect with pleasure; be eager for.
look in, make a short visit.
look into, examine; inspect.
look on, a watch without taking part. **b** regard; consider.
look oneself, seem like oneself; seem well.
look out, be careful; watch out.
look over, examine, inspect: *look over papers.*
look through, a direct the eyes through. **b** search: *I looked through the drawer to see if I could find my keys.*
look to, a attend to; take care of. **b** turn to for help.
look up, a find; refer to. **b** *Informal.* call on; visit. **c** *Informal.* get better; improve.
look up to, respect; admire.
—*n.* **1** the act of looking. **2** a search. **3** appearance; aspect. **4 looks,** *pl.* **a** personal appearance: *Good looks means a good appearance.* **b** *Informal.* general appearance: *the look of a situation.* [OE *lōcian*] —**Syn.** *v.* **1** gaze, stare, observe, glance.
☛ **look.** When used as a verb of complete meaning (use the eyes, gaze), *look* is modified by an adverb: *look searchingly, look sharp.* As a linking verb, equivalent to *seem* or *appear, look* is followed by an adjective that modifies the subject: *He looks well (healthy, tired, etc.).*

look·er (lůk′ər) *n.* **1** a person who looks. **2** *Slang.* a person who is good-looking; attractive person.

look·er-on (lůk′ər on′) *n.* **look·ers-on.** a person who watches without taking part; spectator.

looking glass mirror.

look·out (lůk′out′) *n.* **1** a careful watch: *Be on the lookout for trouble.* **2** a person or group that keeps such a watch. **3** a place from which to watch, as for forest fires. **4** what is seen ahead; outlook. **5** *Informal.* something to be cared for or worried about: *That is his lookout.*

look-see (lůk′sē) *n. Slang.* a quick search or survey. [< pidgin English]

loom[1] (lüm) *n.* a machine for weaving cloth. —*v.* weave on a loom. [OE *(ge)lōma* implement]

loom[2] (lüm) *v.* **1** appear indistinctly: *A large iceberg loomed through the fog. A shadow loomed up in front of us.* **2** appear in a vague, unusually large, or threatening shape: *War loomed ahead.* [origin uncertain]

loon[1] (lün) *n.* a large web-footed diving bird that has a loud, wild cry. [earlier *loom* < ON *lómr*]

loon[2] (lün) *n.* a worthless or stupid person. [cf. MDu. *loen* stupid fellow]

loon·y (lün′ē) *adj.* **loon·i·er, loon·i·est,** *n.* **loon·ies.** *Slang.* —*adj.* crazy. —*n.* a crazy person; lunatic. [var. of *luny* < *lunatic*] —**loon′i·ness,** *n.*

loop (lüp) *n.* **1** the shape of a curved string, ribbon, bent wire, etc. that crosses itself. In handwriting, *b* and *g* and *h* and *l* often have loops. **2** anything shaped like this. **3** a fastening or ornament formed of cord, etc. bent and crossed. **4** a complete vertical turn or revolution, especially one made by an airplane.
—*v.* **1** make a loop of. **2** make loops in. **3** fasten with a loop: *He looped the sail to the mast with rope.* **4** encircle with a loop. **5** form a loop or loops. **6 loop the loop,** turn over and over; make a loop in the air. [ME *loupe,* ? < Celtic]

loop·hole (lüp′hōl′) *n.* **1** a small opening in a wall to shoot through, look through, or let in light and air. **2** a means of escape, evasion, or excuse: *The lawyer found a loophole in the law to save his client.* [? < MDu. *lupen* peer]

loose (lüs) *adj.* **loos·er, loos·est,** *v.* **loosed, loos·ing,** *adv. n.* —*adj.* **1** not fastened: *a loose thread.* **2** not tight: *loose clothing.* **3** not firmly set or fastened in: *a loose tooth.* **4** not bound together: *loose papers.* **5** not put up in a box, can, etc.: *loose coffee.* **6** free; not shut in or up: *We let the dog loose at night.* **7** not pressed close together: *loose earth, cloth with a loose weave.* **8** not strict, close, or exact: *a loose translation from another language, loose thinking.* **9** moving too freely: *a loose tongue.* **10** careless about morals or conduct: *a loose woman.* **11** *Informal.* not tense; relaxed. **12** *Informal.* not employed; not appropriated: *loose hours, loose funds.* **13** of a chemical element, free; uncombined.
—*v.* **1** set free; let go: *They loosed the prisoners.* **2** shoot (an arrow, gun, etc.). **3** make loose; untie; unfasten. **4** relax.
—*adv.* **1** in a loose manner. **2 break loose, a** separate from anything; break a connection or relation. **b** run away; free oneself. **c** *Slang.* go on a spree. **3 cast loose,** unfasten; separate. **4 cut loose,** break loose. **5 let loose,** set free; release; let go. **6 set** or **turn loose,** set free; release; let go.
—*n.* **on the loose,** *Informal.* **a** free; without restraint. **b** on a spree. **c** absent without leave. [ME < ON *lauss*] —**loose′ly,** *adv.* —**loose′ness,** *n.* —**Syn.** *adj.* **1** unbound, unfastened, untied. **8** vague, indefinite, careless. **10** wanton, immoral.

loose-joint·ed (lüs′join′tid) *adj.* **1** having loose joints; loosely built. **2** able to move very freely.

loose-leaf (lüs′lēf′) *adj.* having pages or sheets that can be taken out and replaced.

loos·en (lüs′ən) *v.* **1** make loose or looser; untie; unfasten: *The doctor loosened the stricken man's collar.* **2** become loose or looser. —**loos′en·er,** *n.*

loose·strife (lüs′strīf′) *n.* **1** a tall, downy weed, having purple flowers. **2** any of various plants characterized by a straight calyx, from 4 to 8 petals, and a pod included in the tube of the calyx. [literal translation of L *lysimachia* < Gk. *Lysimachos* (as if < *lyein* to loose + *machē* battle), the supposed discoverer]

loose-tongued (lüs′ tungd′) *adj.* talking too much; irresponsible in speech.

loot (lüt) *n.* **1** spoils; plunder; booty: *loot taken by soldiers from a captured town.* **2** *Slang.* money or other capital: *That's a lot of loot to spend for a record player!* —*v.* plunder; rob: *The jewellery store was looted by burglars.* [< Hind. *lūt*] —**loot′er,** *n.* —**Syn.** *n.* See **plunder.** –*v.* pillage, sack, rifle.

lop[1] (lop) *v.* **lopped, lop·ping. 1** cut; cut off. **2** cut branches, twigs, etc. from. [origin uncertain]

lop[2] (lop) *v.* **lopped, lop·ping. 1** hang loosely; droop. **2** flop. [origin uncertain]

lope (lōp) *v.* **loped, lop·ing,** *n.* —*v.* run with a long, easy stride: *The horse loped along the trail.* —*n.* a long, easy stride. [ME < ON *hlaupa* leap] —**lop′er,** *n.*

lop-eared (lop′ērd′) *adj.* having ears that hang loosely or droop.

lop·sid·ed (lop′sīd′id) *adj.* larger or heavier on one side than the other; unevenly balanced; leaning to one side. —**lop′sid′ed·ly,** *adv.* —**lop′sid′ed·ness,** *n.*

lop·stick (lop′stik′) *n.* lobstick.

lo·qua·cious (lō kwā′shəs or lə kwā′shəs) *adj.* talking much; fond of talking. —**lo·qua′cious·ly,** *adv.* —**Syn.** See **talkative.**

lo·quac·i·ty (lō kwas′ə tē or lə kwas′ə tē) *n.* an inclination to talk a great deal; talkativeness. [< L *loquacitas* < *loquax* talkative < *loqui* talk] —**Syn.** garrulity, volubility.

lo·quat (lō′kwot or lō′kwat) *n.* **1** a small evergreen tree having small, yellow, edible, plumlike fruit, native to China and Japan. **2** the fruit of this tree. [< Chinese]

lo·ran (lô′rən) *n.* a device by which a navigator can

determine his geographical position by utilizing signals sent out from two or more radio stations. [*long range navigation*]

lord (lôrd) *n.* **1** an owner, ruler, or master; one who has the power. **2** a feudal superior. **3 the Lord, a** God. **b** Christ. **4** in the United Kingdom, a peer of the realm; person entitled by courtesy to the title of lord. **5 Lord, a** in the United Kingdom, a titled nobleman or peer of the realm belonging to the House of Lords. **b** a title used in speaking to or of noblemen of certain ranks: *Lord Beaverbrook was born in Ontario.* **c** a title given by courtesy to men holding certain positions: *Lord Chief Justice.* **6 the Lords,** the House of Lords; the upper house of the British Parliament. **7** *Archaic.* a husband.
—*v.* **1** rule; domineer; behave like a lord. **2** raise to the rank of lord. **3 lord it over,** domineer over. [OE *hlāford* < *hlāf* loaf + *weard* keeper, ward]

Lord Chamberlain in Great Britain, a government officer and the official in charge of the royal household.

Lord Chancellor or **Lord High Chancellor** in the United Kingdom, the highest-ranking official of state, with the exception of the royal princes and the Archbishop of Canterbury. He is chairman of the House of Lords, keeper of the Great Seal, and a cabinet member by political appointment.

lord·ling (lôrd′ling) *n.* a little or unimportant lord.

lord·ly (lôrd′lē) *adj.* **-li·er, -li·est,** *adv.* —*adj.* **1** like a lord; suitable for a lord; grand; magnificent. **2** haughty; insolent; scornful. —*adv.* in a lordly manner.
—**lord′li·ness,** *n.* —**Syn.** *adj.* **1** noble, aristocratic. **2** arrogant, proud, overbearing.

Lord Mayor in England, the title of the mayors of London and of some other large cities.

lor·do·sis (lôr dō′sis) *n.* **-ses** (-sēz). in physiology, a curvature of the spine. [< Gk. *lordos* bent back + E *-osis*]

Lord's Day Sunday.

Lord's Day Alliance of Canada a national organization of Anglican, Baptist, Methodist, and Presbyterian churches founded in 1888 for preserving Sunday as a day of rest.

lord·ship (lôrd′ship) *n.* **1** the rank or position of a lord. **2** Often, **Lordship,** *Brit.* a title used in speaking to or of a lord: *your Lordship, his Lordship.* **3** rule; ownership.

Lord's Prayer in the Bible, a prayer given by Jesus to His disciples. Matt. 6:9-13.

Lord's Supper 1 Jesus' last supper with His disciples. **2** the religious service in memory of this; Holy Communion.

lore (lôr) *n.* **1** the facts and stories about a certain subject. **2** learning; knowledge. [OE *lār.* Related to LEARN.]

Lor·e·lei (lôr′ə lī′) *n.* in German legend, a siren of the Rhine whose beauty and singing distracted sailors and caused them to wreck their ships. [< G]

lor·gnette (lôr nyet′) *n.* **1** eyeglasses mounted on a handle. **2** an opera glass. [< F *lorgnette* < *lorgner* look sidelong at, eye < OF *lorgne* squinting]

A woman using a lorgnette (def. 1)

lo·ris (lôr′is) *n.* **1** one of two small, slow-moving, tail-less, nocturnal lemurs of southern Asia: the **slender loris** and the **slow loris.** **2** a larger-limbed lemur of India and Malaya. [< F *loris,* ? < Du. *loeris* booby]

lorn (lôrn) *adj.* **1** forsaken; forlorn. **2** *Archaic.* lost; ruined. [OE *-loren,* pp. of *-lēosan* lose. Related to FORLORN.]

lor·ry (lôr′ē) *n.* **-ries. 1** a long, flat wagon without sides. **2** *Brit.* a motor truck. [cf. dial. E *lurry* pull, lug]

lo·ry (lô′rē) *n.* **-ries.** a small, bright-colored parrot of Australia and nearby islands. [< Malay *luri*]

lose (lüz) *v.* **lost, los·ing. 1** not have any longer; have taken away from one by accident, carelessness, gambling, parting, death, etc.: *lose one's life.* **2** be unable to find: *lose a book.* **3** fail to keep, preserve, or maintain; cease to have: *lose patience, lose all fear.* **4** fail to follow with eye, hearing, mind, etc.: *lose words here and there in a speech.* **5** fail to have, get, catch, etc.: *lose a sale.*

hat, āge, cãre, fär; let, ēqual, tėrm; it, īce
hot, ōpen, ôrder; oil, out; cup, pu̇t, rüle, ūse
əbove, takən, pencəl, lemən, circəs
ch, child; ng, long; sh, ship
th, thin; ᴛʜ, then; zh, measure

6 fail to win: *lose the prize.* **7** be defeated: *Our team lost.* **8** bring to destruction; ruin: *The ship and its crew were lost.* **9** let pass without use or profit; waste: *lose an opportunity, lost time. The hint was not lost on him.* **10** suffer loss: *lose on a contract.* **11** cause the loss of: *Delay lost the battle.* **12** cause to lose: *That one act lost him his job.* **13 lose oneself, a** let oneself go astray; become bewildered. **b** become absorbed. **14 lose out,** fail; be unsuccessful. [OE *losian* be lost < *los* destruction]
—**los′er,** *n.*

los·ings (lüz′ingz) *n.pl.* losses.

loss (los) *n.* **1** a losing or being lost. **2** the person or thing lost. **3** the amount lost. **4** the harm or disadvantage caused by losing something. **5** a defeat: *Our team had two losses and one tie out of ten games played.* **6** in military use, the losing of soldiers by death, capture, or wounding. **7** in insurance, the occurrence of death, property damage, or other contingency against which a person is insured under circumstances that make the insurer liable under the contract. **8** in electricity, the reduction in power, measured by the difference between the power input and power output, in an electric circuit, device, system, etc., corresponding to the transformation of electric energy into heat. **9 at a loss,** puzzled; uncertain; in difficulty; unable to think of the appropriate thing to do or say: *He was at a loss for words.* **10 at a loss to,** unable to. [OE *los*]

loss leader in business, an article sold at a loss in order to attract customers.

lost (lost) *v.* pt. and pp. of **lose.** —*adj.* **1** no longer possessed or retained: *lost friends.* **2** no longer to be found; missing: *lost articles.* **3** attended with defeat: *a lost battle.* **4** not used to good purpose; wasted: *lost time.* **5** having gone astray. **6** destroyed or ruined. **7** bewildered. **8 lost in,** completely absorbed or interested in. **9 lost to, a** no longer possible or open to: *The chance of promotion was lost to him.* **b** no longer belonging to: *After that incident, her son was lost to her.* **c** insensible to: *He was lost to all sense of duty.* —**Syn.** *adj.* **2** astray.

lost cause an undertaking already defeated or one certain to be defeated.

lost sheep a person who has strayed from the right sort of conduct or religious belief.

lot (lot) *n. v.* **lot·ted, lot·ting,** *adv.* —*n.* **1** an object used to decide something by chance: *We drew lots to decide who should be captain.* **2** such a method of deciding: *divide property by lot.* **3** a choice made in this way: *The lot fell to me.* **4** what one gets by lot; share or portion. **5** one's fate; fortune: *a happy lot.* **6** a plot of ground. **7** a place where motion pictures are made. **8** a distinct portion or parcel of anything. **9** a number of persons or things considered as a group; a collection: *a fine lot of boys.* **10** Often, **lots,** *pl. Informal.* a great many; a great deal: *a lot of books, lots of money.* **11** *Informal.* a person of a certain kind: *He is a bad lot.* **12 cast** or **draw lots,** use lots to decide something. **13 cast** or **throw in one's lot with,** share the fate of; become a partner with.
—*v.* divide into lots.
—*adv.* a great deal; much: *I feel a lot better.* [OE *hlot*]
—**Syn.** *n.* **4** allotment, part, parcel. **5** destiny, doom.

☞ **lot, lots of.** Formal English avoids using *lots* and *lots of* in the informal sense of "a considerable quantity or number." Informal: *He tried lots of different shots, but lost.* Formal: *He tried a variety of* (or *a great many different*) *shots, but lost.*

Lot (lot) *n.* in the Bible, a righteous man who was allowed to escape from Sodom before God destroyed it. His wife looked back and was changed into a pillar of salt. Gen. 19:1-26. [< Hebrew]

loth (lōth) *adj.* loath.

Lo·thar·i·o (lō thãr′ē ō′) *n.* **-thar·i·os.** a man who makes love to many women; rake; libertine. [< *Lothario,* a character in Nicholas Rowe's *The Fair Penitent*]

lo·tion (lō′shən) *n.* a liquid containing medicine, used on the skin to soothe, heal, or cleanse. [< L *lotio, -onis* a washing, ult. < *lavere* wash]

lo·tos (lō′təs) *n.* lotus.

lot·ter·y (lot′ər ē) *n.* **-ter·ies. 1** a scheme for distributing prizes by lot or chance. In a lottery a large number of tickets are sold, only some of which win prizes. **2** a distribution by chance of success, fortune, happiness, etc.: *the lottery of life.* [< Ital. *lotteria* < *lotto* lot. See LOTTO.]

lottery wheel a revolving drum used for shuffling lottery tickets.

lot·to (lot′ō) *n.* a game played by drawing numbered disks from a bag or box and covering the corresponding numbers on cards. [< Ital. *lotto* lot, ult. < Gmc. Akin to LOT.]

lo·tus (lō′təs) *n.* **1** a water lily having showy flowers and large, usually floating leaves, that grows in Egypt and Asia. **2** a plant having red, pink, or white flowers, of the same family as the pea. **3** a plant whose fruit was supposed to cause a dreamy and contented forgetfulness in those who ate it. [< L < Gk. *lōtos*]

lo·tus-eat·er (lō′təs ēt′ər) *n.* a person who leads a life of dreamy, indolent ease.

loud (loud) *adj.* **1** making a noise; not quiet or soft: *a loud voice.* **2** resounding; noisy: *loud music.* **3** clamorous; insistent: *He was loud in his demands.* **4** *Informal.* showy or flashy: *loud clothes.* **5** *Informal.* obtrusive; somewhat vulgar.
—*adv.* in a loud manner. [OE *hlūd*] **—loud′ly,** *adv.* **—loud′ness,** *n.*

Syn. *adj.* **1 Loud, noisy** = making much or intense sound. **Loud** emphasizes the idea of being not quiet, low, or soft, and suggests strength or intensity of sound, but does not necessarily suggest making much noise: *The speaker's voice was not loud enough to be heard in the back of the room.* **Noisy** = disagreeably loud or harsh, and emphasizes continued loudness or continual sounds and noises: *The people next door are noisy.* **2** deafening.

loud·hail·er (loud′hāl′ər) *n.* a type of electrically operated megaphone.

loud·ish (loud′ish) *adj.* rather loud.

loud·mouth (loud′mouth′) *n. Slang.* a loudmouthed person.

loud·mouthed (loud′mouᴛʜd′ or -moutht′) *adj.* offensively noisy; given to talking too loudly.

loud·speak·er (loud′spēk′ər) *n.* a device for amplifying the sound of a speaker's voice, music, etc.

lough (loʜ) *n. Irish.* **1** a lake. **2** an arm of the sea. [< Irish Gaelic *loch*]

lou·is d'or (lü′ē dôr′) **1** an old French gold coin, worth from about $4 to about $4.60. **2** a later French gold coin worth 20 francs. [< F *louis d'or* gold louis]

Lou·i·si·an·a Purchase (lu̇ ē′zē an′ə) an extensive region that the United States bought from France in 1803. It extended from the Mississippi River to the Rocky Mountains and from Canada to the Gulf of Mexico.

Lou·is Quatorze (lü′ē kä tôrz′) in architecture, art, decoration, furniture, etc.: **1** a style developed in France during the reign of King Louis XIV (1643-1715). **2** of or having to do with this style. **3** something, especially a piece of furniture, in this style. [< F *Louis Quatorze* Louis the Fourteenth]

Lou·is Quinze (lü′ē kaɴz) in architecture, art, decoration, furniture, etc.: **1** a style developed in France during the reign of King Louis XV (1715-1774). **2** of or having to do with this style. **3** something, especially a piece of furniture, in this style. [< F *Louis Quinze* Louis the Fifteenth]

Lou·is Seize (lü′ē sez) in architecture, art, decoration, furniture, etc.: **1** a style developed in France during the reign of King Louis XVI (1774-1792). **2** of or having to do with this style. **3** something, especially a piece of furniture, in this style. [< F *Louis Seize* Louis the Sixteenth]

lounge (lounj) *v.* **lounged, loung·ing,** *n.* **—***v.* **1** stand, stroll, sit, or lie at ease and lazily. **2** pass time indolently; idle at one's ease. —*n.* **1** the act or state of lounging. **2** a comfortable and informal room in which one can lounge, smoke, and be at ease. **3** a couch; chesterfield. [< 15th-century Scottish dial.; ? < *lungis* laggard] **—loung′er,** *n.*

loupe (lüp) *n.* an eyepiece fitted with a magnifying glass for use by jewellers, watchmakers, etc. [< F]

lour (lour) *v. n.* lower².

louse (lous) *n.* **lice,** *v.* **loused, lous·ing.** **—***n.* **1** a small, wingless insect that infests the hair or skin of people and animals, causing great irritation. **2** any of various other insects that are parasitic on animals or plants. **3** a mean, contemptible person. —*v.* **louse up,** *Slang.* spoil; get (something) all confused or in a mess: *louse up a song, joke, or deal.* [OE *lūs*]

louse·wort (lous′wėrt′) *n.* any of a group of plants of the figwort family, found in marshy fields and believed to breed lice in livestock that feed on them.

lous·y (louz′ē) *adj.* **lous·i·er, lous·i·est. 1** infested with lice. **2** bad; poor; of low quality. **3** *Slang.* dirty; disgusting. **4** *Slang.* well-supplied (*with*): *lousy with money.* **—lous′i·ly,** *adv.* **—lous′i·ness,** *n.*

lout (lout) *n.* an awkward, stupid fellow; boor. [< ON *lútr* bent down, stooping]

lout·ish (lout′ish) *adj.* awkward and stupid; boorish. **—lout′ish·ly,** *adv.* **—lout′ish·ness,** *n.*

lou·ver or **lou·vre** (lü′vər) *n.* **1** a window or other opening covered with louver boards. **2** a ventilating slit. [ME < OF *lover*]

louver boards or **louvre boards** horizontal strips of wood set slanting in a window or other opening, so as to keep out rain, but provide ventilation.

lou·vered or **lou·vred** (lü′vərd) *adj.* **1** made or fitted with louvers. **2** arranged like louvers.

lou·vre (lü′vər) *n.* louver.

lov·a·ble (luv′ə bəl) *adj.* deserving love; endearing. **—lov′a·ble·ness,** *n.* **—lov′a·bly,** *adv.* **—Syn.** likable, winning, pleasing, amiable.

love (luv) *n. v.* **loved, lov·ing.** **—***n.* **1** strong devotion to or passionate affection for another person or persons. **2** an instance of such feeling. **3** this feeling as a subject for books, or as a personified influence. **4 Love, a** Venus. **b** Cupid. **5** a loved one; sweetheart. **6** a warm liking; fond or tender feeling. **7** a strong liking: *a love of books.* **8** *Informal.* something charming or delightful. **9** Godly affection, devotion, and brotherhood. **10** in tennis and certain other games, no score.
fall in love, begin to love; come to feel love.
for love, a for nothing; without pay. **b** for pleasure; not for money.
for the love of, for the sake of; because of:
in love, feeling love.
make love, a behave like lovers; do as lovers do; woo. **b** have sexual intercourse.
not for love or money, not on any terms.
—*v.* **1** be in love with. **2** be in love; fall in love. **3** make love to. **4** *Informal.* like very much; take great pleasure in: *Most children love ice cream.* **5** be fond of; hold dear. **6** have affection: *He can hate but cannot love.* [OE *lufu,* n., *lufian,* v.]

Syn. *n.* **6 Love, affection** = a feeling of warm liking and tender attachment. **Love,** an emotion, emphasizes strength, depth, sincerity, and warmth of feeling, suggesting also tenderness, as for a child or parent, devotion and loyalty, as to friends or family, reverence, as for God, passion, as for man or woman or belief, etc.: *Every person needs to give and receive love.* **Affection** applies to a less strong feeling, suggesting tenderness and warm fondness: *I like my teacher, but feel no affection for her.* ☛ See **like** for usage note.

love apple formerly, the tomato.

love·bird (luv′bėrd′) *n.* **1** a small parrot that shows great affection for its mate. **2** *Informal.* a person in love.

love feast 1 a meal eaten together by the early Christians as a symbol of brotherly love. **2** a religious ceremony imitating this. **3** a banquet or other gathering to promote good feeling.

love-in-i·dle·ness (luv′in ī′dəl nis) *n.* wild pansy.

love knot an ornamental knot or bow of ribbon as a token of love.

love·less (luv′lis) *adj.* **1** not loving. **2** not loved.

love-lies-bleed·ing (luv′līz blēd′ing) *n.* a kind of amaranth having spikes of crimson flowers.

love·li·ness (luv′lē nis) *n.* beauty.

love·lock (luv′lok′) *n.* **1** any conspicuous lock of hair, especially a curl worn on the forehead. **2** formerly, a long, flowing lock dressed separately from the rest of the hair, worn by courtiers.

love·lorn (luv′lôrn′) *adj.* suffering because of love; forsaken by the person whom one loves.

love·ly (luv′lē) *adj.* **-li·er, -li·est. 1** beautiful in mind or character; beautiful. **2** *Informal.* very pleasing; delightful. **—Syn. 1** See **beautiful.**

love match a marriage for love, not for money or social position.

lov·er (luv′ər) *n.* **1** a person who loves. **2** a man who is in love with a woman. **3 lovers,** *pl.* a man and a woman who are in love with each other. **4** a person who loves illicitly; paramour. **5** a person having a strong liking: *a lover of books.* **—lov′er·like′,** *adj.* **—Syn. 2** suitor, admirer, beau.

love seat a seat or small sofa for two persons.

love·sick (luv′sik′) *adj.* languishing because of love.

lov·ing (luv′ing) *adj.* feeling or showing love; affectionate; fond. **—lov′ing·ly,** *adv.*

loving cup a large cup with handles, passed around for all to drink from.

lov·ing-kind·ness (luv′ing kīnd′nis) *n.* kindness coming from love: *the loving-kindness of God.*

low[1] (lō) *adj.* **1** not high or tall: *low walls.* **2** rising but slightly from a surface: *low relief.* **3** of less than ordinary height, depth, or quantity: *The well is getting low.* **4** near the ground, floor, or base: *a low shelf.* **5** lying or being below the general level: *low ground.* **6** small in amount, degree, force, value, etc.: *a low price.* **7** not loud; soft: *a low whisper.* **8** not advanced in civilization, organization, etc.; inferior: *a low organism.* **9** lacking in dignity or elevation: *low thoughts.* **10** humble: *low birth.* **11** affording little strength; feeble; weak: *a low state of health.* **12** unfavorable; poor: *I have a low opinion of his abilities.* **13** depressed or dejected: *low spirits.* **14** mean or base; coarse; vulgar; degraded: *low company.* **15** near the horizon: *a low sun.* **16** near the equator: *low latitudes.* **17** prostrate or dead: *lay one low.* **18** deep: *a low bow.* **19** in music, not high in the scale: *a low note.* **20** of speech sounds, pronounced with the tongue far from the palate. **21** relatively recent. **22** in the Anglican Church, maintaining Low-Church practices. *—adv.* **1** near the ground, floor, or base: *fly low.* **2** in, at, or to a low portion, point, degree, condition, price, etc.: *The sun sank low. Supplies are running low.* **3** at low pitch; softly: *speak low.* **4** humbly; meanly. **5** near the horizon. **6** near the equator. **7** lately. **8 lay low, a** knock down. **b** kill. **9 lie low,** *Informal.* stay hidden; keep still. *—n.* **1** that which is low. **2** in automobiles and similar machines, an arrangement of the gears used for the lowest speed. **3** in meteorology, an area of low barometric pressure. [ME < ON *lágr*] **—low′ness,** *n.* **—Syn.** *adj.* **6** moderate. **10** obscure, lowly. **14** See **base**[2].

low[2] (lō) *v.* make the sound of a cow mooing; moo. *—n.* the sound a cow makes; mooing. [OE *hlōwan*]

low·born (lō′bôrn′) *adj.* of humble birth.

low·boy (lō′boi′) *n.* a low chest of drawers.

A lowboy

low·bred (lō′bred′) *adj.* coarse; vulgar.

low·brow (lō′brou′) *Informal.* *—n.* a person lacking in appreciation of intellectual or artistic things. *—adj.* **1** being a lowbrow; incapable of culture. **2** fit for lowbrows.

Low-Church (lō′chėrch′) *adj.* of a party in the Anglican Church, laying little stress on church authority and ceremonies; more like Protestant denominations, and less like the Roman Catholic Church.

low comedy broadly humorous comedy.

Low Countries the Netherlands, Belgium, and Luxemburg.

low-coun·try (lō′kun′trē) *adj.* of or having to do with the Low Countries (Netherlands, Belgium, and Luxemburg).

low-down (lō′doun′) *adj. Informal.* low; mean; contemptible: *a low-down trick.*

low·down (lō′doun′) *n. Slang.* the actual facts or truth.

hat, āge, cãre, fär; let, ēqual, tėrm; it, īce
hot, ōpen, ôrder; oil, out; cup, pu̇t, rüle, ūse
əbove, takən, pencəl, lemən, circəs
ch, child; ng, long; sh, ship
th, thin; ᴛʜ, then; zh, measure

low·er[1] (lō′ər) *v.* **1** let down or haul down: *lower the flag.* **2** make lower: *lower the volume of a radio.* **3** sink; become lower: *The sun lowered slowly.* **4** in music, depress in pitch. **5** bring down in rank, station, or estimation; degrade; dishonor. *—adj. adv.* the comparative of **low.** [< *low*[1]] **—Syn.** *v.* **2** decrease, diminish. **3** descend, fall.

low·er[2] (lou′ər) *v.* **1** look dark and threatening. **2** frown; scowl. *—n.* **1** a dark and threatening look. **2** a frown; scowl. Also, **lour.** [ME *loure(n)*]

Lower Canada 1 a traditional name for the province of Quebec. **2** until 1841, the official name of the region between the Ottawa River and New Brunswick, now included in the province of Quebec. Lower Canada was lower down the St. Lawrence River than Upper Canada. *Abbrev.:* L.C.

lower case in printing, small letters, not capital.

low·er-case (lō′ər kās′) *adj.* in printing, in small letters, not capitals. *Abbrev.:* l.c.

Lower Chamber or **lower chamber** Lower House.

Lower House or **lower house** the more representative branch of a legislature that has two branches. The members of the Lower House of a legislature are usually elected.

low·er·ing (lou′ər ing) *adj.* **1** dark and threatening: *a lowering sky.* **2** frowning; scowling. **—low′er·ing·ly,** *adv.*

Lower Lakes the most southerly of the Great Lakes, Lakes Erie and Ontario.

low·er·most (lō′ər mōst) *adj.* lowest.

lower regions hell; Hades.

lower world 1 hell; Hades. **2** earth.

lowest common denominator 1 in mathematics, the least common denominator. *Abbrev.:* L.C.D., l.c.d., or lcd. **2** the level of the feelings, tastes, or opinions supposedly common to the majority of people.

low-fre·quen·cy (lō′ frē′kwən sē) *adj.* in electronics, of or having to do with a frequency that ranges from 30 to 300 kilocycles per second: *a low-frequency radio station. Abbrev.:* LF, l.f., or lf.

Low German 1 the Germanic speech of the Low Countries (Dutch, Flemish, etc.) and especially of N. Germany. **2** the group of west Germanic dialects from which English, Flemish, Dutch, Frisian, etc. are derived.

low-key (lō′kē′) *adj.* played down; restrained: *a low-key attack on government policy.*

low·land (lō′lənd) *n.* **1** land that is lower and flatter than the neighboring country. **2 Lowlands,** *pl.* a low, flat region in S. and E. Scotland. *—adj.* of or in the lowlands.

Low·land·er (lō′lən dər) *n.* a native of the lowlands of Scotland.

Low Latin Latin as spoken in the Middle Ages.

low·life (lō′līf′) *Slang. —n.* **1** a debased or vile person; a criminal. **2** immoral people or surroundings. *—adj.* **1** resembling a lowlife; debased; immoral. **2** crude; cheap.

low·lin·er (lō′līn′ər) *n.* in a Maritime fishing fleet: **1** the boat making the smallest catch within a specified time. **2** the captain of such a boat.

low·ly (lō′lē) *adj.* **-li·er, -li·est,** *adv. —adj.* **1** low in rank, station, position, or development: *a lowly corporal, a lowly occupation.* **2** modest in feeling, behavior, or condition; humble; meek: *He held a lowly opinion of himself. —adv.* humbly; meekly. **—low′li·ness,** *n.* **—Syn.** *adj.* **1** inferior. **2** unassuming. See **humble.**

Low Mass a simplified form of High Mass, conducted by one priest assisted by altar boys. There is no chanting in Low Mass.

low-mind·ed (lō′mīn′did) *adj.* mean; vulgar.

low-necked (lō′nekt′) *adj.* of a dress, etc., cut low so as to show the neck, part of the bosom, and shoulders or back.

low-pitched (lō′picht′) *adj.* 1 of low tone or sound; deep. 2 having little slope.

low-pres·sure (lō′presh′ər) *adj.* having or using less than the usual pressure.

low relief sculpture in which the figures stand out slightly from the background; bas-relief.

low-spir·it·ed (lō′spir′ə tid) *adj.* sad; depressed. —**low′-spir′it·ed·ly,** *adv.* —**low′-spir′it·ed·ness,** *n.*

low spirits sadness; depression.

low tide 1 the lowest level of the tide. 2 the time when the tide is lowest. 3 the lowest point.

low water 1 the lowest level of water. 2 low tide.

low-water mark (lō′wo′tər or -wô′tər) 1 a mark showing low water. 2 the lowest point.

lox[1] (loks) *n.* thinly sliced smoked salmon. [< Yiddish *laks* < MHG *lacs* salmon]

lox[2] or **LOX** (loks) *n.* liquid oxygen. [< *l*iquid *ox*ygen]

loy·al (loi′əl) *adj.* 1 faithful to love, promise, or duty. 2 faithful to one's king, government, or country: *a loyal citizen.* [< F *loyal* < L *legalis* legal < *lex, legis* law. Doublet of LEAL, LEGAL.] —**loy′al·ly,** *adv.* —**Syn. 1, 2** true, constant. See **faithful.**

loy·al·ist (loi′əl ist) *n.* 1 a person who supports his king or the existing government, especially in time of revolt. 2 **Loyalist, a** a United Empire Loyalist. **b** any American who remained loyal to Great Britain during the American Revolution. 3 **Loyalist,** in Spain, a person loyal to the Republic during the civil war (1936-1939).

Loyal Orange Association a Protestant organization, named after William, Prince of Orange, who became King William III of England.

loy·al·ty (loi′əl tē) *n.* **-ties.** loyal feeling or behavior; faithfulness. —**Syn.** fidelity, allegiance.

loz·enge (loz′inj) *n.* 1 a small tablet of medicine or a piece of candy: *Cough drops are sometimes called lozenges.* 2 a design or figure shaped like this ◇. [ME < OF *losenge,* ult. < LL *lausa* slab < Celtic]

LP a long-playing phonograph record, usually having 33⅓ revolutions per minute. [< a trademark]

L.P.P. Labour Progressive Party, the former name of the Communist Party in Canada.

L.S. Leading Seaman.

LSD Lysergic acid diethylamide.

L.S.D. or **l.s.d.** pounds, shillings, and pence.

L/Sgt. Lance-Sergeant.

Lt. Lieutenant.

Lt.Cdr. Lieutenant Commander.

Lt.Col. Lieutenant-Colonel.

Ltd. limited.

Lt.Gen. Lieutenant-General.

Lt.Gov. Lieutenant-Governor.

Lu lutecium.

lub·ber (lub′ər) *n.* 1 a big, clumsy, stupid fellow. 2 a clumsy sailor. [ME *lober*] —**Syn. 1** dolt, bumpkin.

lub·ber·ly (lub′ər lē) *adj.* 1 loutish; clumsy; stupid. 2 awkward in the work of a sailor.—*adv.* in a lubberly manner.

lu·bri·cant (lü′brə kənt) *n.* 1 oil, grease, etc. for putting on parts of machines that slide or move against one another, to make them work smoothly and easily. 2 a lubricating jelly. —*adj.* lubricating.

lu·bri·cate (lü′brə kāt′) *v.* **-cat·ed, -cat·ing.** 1 put a lubricant on. 2 make slippery or smooth. [< L *lubricare* < *lubricus* slippery] —**lu′bri·ca′tion,** *n.*

lu·bri·ca·tor (lü′brə kā′tər) *n.* 1 a person or thing that lubricates. 2 a device for lubricating machinery.

lu·bric·i·ty (lü bris′ə tē) *n.* **-ties.** 1 oily smoothness; slipperiness. 2 shiftiness. 3 lewdness. [< LL *lubricitas* < L *lubricus* slippery, slimy]

lu·cent (lü′sənt) *adj. Archaic.* 1 shining; luminous. 2 letting the light through; clear. [< L *lucens, -entis,* ppr. of *lucere* shine] —**lu′cent·ly,** *adv.*

lu·cerne (lü sėrn′) *n.* alfalfa. [< F *luzerne* < Provençal *luzerno,* ult. < L *lux, lucis* light]

lu·cid (lü′sid) *adj.* 1 easy to understand: *a lucid explanation.* 2 shining; bright. 3 sane: *Some insane persons have lucid intervals.* 4 clear; transparent: *a lucid stream.* [< L *lucidus* < *lux, lucis* light] —**lu′cid·ly,** *adv.*

lu·cid·i·ty (lü sid′ə tē) *n.* a lucid quality or condition.

Lu·ci·fer (lü′sə fər) *n.* 1 the chief rebel angel said to have been cast out of heaven; Satan. 2 the planet Venus when it is the morning star. 3 **lucifer,** a match that lights by friction. [< L *lucifer* the morning star, literally, bringing light < *lux, lucis* light + *ferre* bring]

Lu·cite (lü′sīt) *n. Trademark.* a clear plastic compound used for airplane windows, ornaments, etc. [< L *lux, lucis* light]

luck (luk) *n.* 1 that which seems to happen or come to one by chance; chance. 2 good fortune: *Lots of luck to you. He thinks a horseshoe brings luck.* 3 **down on one's luck,** *Informal.* having bad luck; unlucky. 4 **in luck,** having good luck; lucky. 5 **out of luck,** having bad luck; unlucky. 6 **try one's luck,** see what one can do. 7 **worse luck,** unfortunately. [ME < MDu. (*ghe*)*luc,* MLG (*ge*)*lucke*]

luck·i·ly (luk′ə lē) *adv.* by good luck; fortunately.

luck·less (luk′lis) *adj.* having or bringing bad luck; unlucky. —**luck′less·ly,** *adv.* —**luck′less·ness,** *n.*

luck·y (luk′ē) *adj.* **luck·i·er, luck·i·est.** having or bringing good luck. —**luck′i·ness,** *n.* —**Syn.** happy. See **fortunate.**

lu·cra·tive (lü′krə tiv) *adj.* bringing in money; profitable. [ME < L *lucrativus* < *lucrari* to gain < *lucrum* gain] —**lu′cra·tive·ly,** *adv.* —**lu′cra·tive·ness,** *n.* —**Syn.** gainful, remunerative.

lu·cre (lü′kər) *n. Derogatory.* money: *filthy lucre.* [ME < L *lucrum*]

lu·cu·bra·tion (lü′kyů brā′shən) *n.* 1 study carried on late at night. 2 laborious study. 3 a learned or carefully written production, especially one that is labored and dull. [< L *lucubratio, -onis* < *lucubrare* work at night]

Lu·cul·li·an (lü kul′ē ən) *adj.* rich; luxurious; magnificent. [< *Lucullus* (110?-57? B.C.), a wealthy Roman famous for his luxurious banquets]

lu·di·crous (lü′də krəs) *adj.* amusingly absurd; ridiculous. [< L *ludicrus* < *ludus* sport] —**lu′di·crous·ly,** *adv.* —**lu′di·crous·ness,** *n.* —**Syn.** laughable, droll, comical.

luff (luf) *v.* 1 turn the bow of a ship toward the wind. 2 **luff the helm,** move the helm so that the bow of the ship turns toward the wind. [< n.] —*n.* 1 the act of turning the bow of a ship toward the wind. 2 the forward edge of a fore-and-aft sail. [ME; cf. Du. *loef*]

Luft·waf·fe (lůft′wof′ə; *German,* lůft′väf′ə) *n.* the German air force, especially under the Nazis in World War II.

lug[1] (lug) *v.* **lugged, lug·ging.** 1 pull along or carry with effort; drag. 2 of a ship, carry (sail) beyond the limit of safety in a strong wind. [ME; cf. Swedish *lugga* pull by the hair]

lug[2] (lug) *n.* 1 *Esp.Scottish.* an ear. 2 a projecting part used to hold or grip something. 3 a flange or stud projecting from the outer surface of a wheel to increase traction on soft ground: *Tractors having lugs should stay off paved highways.* 4 *Slang.* a clumsy or stupid person. [origin uncertain; cf. Swedish *lugg* forelock]

lug[3] (lug) *n.* lugsail. [? < *lug*[2]]

lug[4] (lug) *n.* lugworm. [origin uncertain; cf. Du. *log* slow, heavy]

luge (lüzh) *n.* a kind of sleigh used principally in Switzerland. [< Swiss dial.]

lu·ger or **Lu·ger** (lü′gər) *n.* an automatic pistol first made in Germany. [< George *Luger,* a 19th-century German engineer]

lug·gage (lug′ij) *n.* baggage. See **baggage** for usage note. [< *lug*[1]]

lug·ger (lug′ər) *n.* a boat with lugsails.

A lugger

lugs (lugz) *n.pl.* a cloth flap in certain kinds of caps, pulled down as protection for the ears in cold weather. [< *lug*[2]]

lug·sail (lug′sāl′ or lug′səl) *n.* a four-cornered sail held by a yard that slants across the mast.

lu·gu·bri·ous (lü gü′brē əs) *adj.* sad; mournful. [< L *lugubris* < *lugere* mourn] —**lu·gu′bri·ous·ly,** *adv.* —**lu·gu′bri·ous·ness,** *n.* —**Syn.** dismal, doleful, melancholy.

lug·worm (lug′wėrm′) *n.* a kind of worm that burrows in sand along the seashore. [< *lug*[4]]

luke·warm (lük′wôrm′) *adj.* **1** neither hot nor cold. **2** showing little enthusiasm; half-hearted: *a lukewarm greeting.* [expansion of dial. *luke* lukewarm < dial. *lew;* cf. OE *hlēo* shelter (warm place)] —**luke′warm′ly,** *adv.* —**luke′warm′ness,** *n.* —**Syn. 1** tepid. **2** indifferent, unconcerned.

lull (lul) *v.* **1** hush to sleep: *The mother lulled the crying baby.* **2** quiet: *lull one's suspicions.* **3** become calm or more nearly calm: *The wind lulled.* —*n.* **1** a period of less noise or violence; brief calm: *a lull in a storm.* **2** something that lulls. **3** a period of reduced activity: *a lull in trade.* [ME *lulle(n)*]

lul·la·by (lul′ə bī′) *n.* **-bies. 1** a song to put a baby to sleep. **2** any soothing song. **3** a quiet, soothing instrumental composition. [< *lull* + *by* as in *good-bye*]

lum·ba·go (lum bā′gō) *n.* a sickness causing pain in the muscles of the small of the back and in the loins. It is often caused by a slipping of the cartilage disk between adjacent vertebrae. [< LL < L *lumbus* loin]

lum·bar (lum′bər or lum′bär) *adj.* of the loin or loins: *the lumbar region.* —*n.* a lumbar vertebra, artery, nerve, etc. [< NL *lumbaris* < L *lumbus* loin]

lum·ber[1] (lum′bər) *n.* **1** timber, logs, beams, boards, etc. roughly cut and prepared for use. **2** household articles no longer in use; old furniture, etc. that takes up room. —*v.* **1** cut and prepare lumber. **2** fill up or obstruct by taking space that is wanted for something else. [original meaning "useless goods," ? < *lombard* pawnshop]

lum·ber[2] (lum′bər) *v.* move along heavily and noisily. [ME *lomeren* < Scand.; cf. Swedish dial. *loma* walk heavily] —**lum′ber·ing·ly,** *adv.*

lum·ber·ing (lum′bər ing or lum′bring) *n.* the business of cutting and preparing timber for use.

lum·ber·jack (lum′bər jak′) *n.* **1** a man whose work is cutting down trees and getting out the logs to the mills; logger. **2** *Cdn.* a Canada jay.

lum·ber·man (lum′bər mən) *n.* **-men** (-mən). **1** a lumberjack. **2** a man whose work is cutting and preparing timber for use. **3** a man whose business is buying and selling timber or lumber.

lum·ber·yard (lum′bər yärd′) *n.* a place where lumber is stored and sold.

lu·men (lü′mən) *n.* **1** in physics, a unit for measuring luminous flux. Today, light bulbs are rated by lumens instead of by candle power. **2** the inner space or passage in a blood vessel or within a cell wall. [< L]

lu·mi·nar·y (lü′mə ner′ē) *n.* **-nar·ies. 1** the sun, moon, or other light-giving body. **2** a distinguished person, especially one who enlightens. [ME < Med.L *luminarium* < L *lumen, -minis* light]

lu·mi·nes·cence (lü′mə nes′əns) *n.* an emission of light occurring at a temperature below that of incandescent bodies. Luminescence includes phosphorescence and fluorescence. [< L *lumen, luminis* light + E *-escence* a beginning to be < L *-escentia*]

lu·mi·nes·cent (lü′mə nes′ənt) *adj.* giving out light without being much heated.

lu·mi·nif·er·ous (lü′mə nif′ər əs) *adj.* producing or transmitting light. [< L *lumen, luminis* light + E *-ferous*]

lu·mi·nos·i·ty (lü′mə nos′ə tē) *n.* **-ties. 1** a luminous quality or condition. **2** something luminous.

lu·mi·nous (lü′mə nəs) *adj.* **1** shining by its own light: *The sun and stars are luminous.* **2** full of light; bright. **3** treated with some substance that glows in the dark: *The numbers on some watches are luminous.* **4** easily understood; clear; enlightening. [ME < L *luminosus* < *lumen* light] —**lu′mi·nous·ly,** *adv.* —**lu′mi·nous·ness,** *n.*

luminous flux the rate of flow of light, or luminous energy, measured in lumens.

lum·mox (lum′əks) *n. Informal.* an awkward, stupid person. [origin uncertain]

lump[1] (lump) *n.* **1** a solid mass of no particular shape: *a lump of coal.* **2** a cube or oblong piece of sugar. **3** a swelling; bump: *a lump on the head.* **4** a lot; mass. **5** *Informal.* a dull or stupid person. **6** a heavy, sturdy person; a fat person. **7 in a lump,** as a whole or in one amount.
—*v.* **1** make lumps of, on, or in. **2** form into a lump or lumps. **3** put together; deal with in a mass or as a whole: *We will lump all our expenses.*
—*adj.* **1** in lumps; in a lump. **2 a lump sum, a** an amount of money that covers the entire cost of something when given in payment: *He paid for the car in a lump sum rather than by instalments.* **b** an amount of money that covers the cost of a number of items. [ME < Scand.; cf. Danish *lump(e)*]

hat, āge, cãre, fär; let, ēqual, tėrm; it, īce
hot, ōpen, ôrder; oil, out; cup, put, rüle, ūse
əbove, takən, pencəl, lemən, circəs
ch, child; ng, long; sh, ship
th, thin; ᴛʜ, then; zh, measure

lump[2] (lump) *v. Informal.* put up with; endure: *If you don't like it, you can lump it.* [origin uncertain]

lump·ish (lump′ish) *adj.* **1** like a lump; heavy and clumsy. **2** stolid; stupid.

lump sugar small blocks of sugar shaped like cubes, dominoes, etc.

lump·y (lump′ē) *adj.* **lump·i·er, lump·i·est. 1** full of lumps: *lumpy gravy.* **2** covered with lumps: *lumpy ground.* **3** heavy and clumsy: *a lumpy animal.* **4** rough: *lumpy water.* —**lump′i·ly,** *adv.* —**lump′i·ness,** *n.*

Lu·na (lü′nə) *n.* **1** in Roman mythology, the goddess of the moon. **2** the moon. [< L *luna* moon]

lu·na·cy (lü′nə sē) *n.* **-cies. 1** insanity. **2** extreme folly. [< *lunatic*]

luna moth or **Luna Moth** a large North American moth having light-green wings with crescent-shaped spots.

lu·nar (lü′nər) *adj.* **1** of the moon. **2** like the moon. [< L *lunaris* < *luna* moon]

lunar month the interval between one new moon and the next, about 29½ days.

lu·nate (lü′nāt) *adj.* crescent-shaped. [< L *lunatus* < *luna* moon]

lu·na·tic (lü′nə tik′) *n.* **1** an insane person. **2** an extremely foolish person. —*adj.* **1** insane. **2** for insane people. **3** extremely foolish. [ME < LL *lunaticus* < L *luna* moon]

lunatic fringe *Informal.* those whose zeal in some cause, movement, etc. goes beyond reasonable limits.

lunch (lunch) *n.* **1** a light meal between breakfast and dinner, or breakfast and supper: *We usually have lunch at noon.* **2** a light meal eaten at any time: *We had a lunch at bedtime.* —*v.* eat lunch. [shortened form of *luncheon*] —**lunch′er,** *n.*

lunch·eon (lun′chən) *n.* **1** a lunch. **2** a formal lunch. —*v.* lunch. [< dial. *luncheon* hunk, large lump of food < dial. *lunch* lump, formed after obs. synonym *nuncheon*]

lunch·eon·ette (lun′chən et′) *n.* a restaurant that serves lunches.

lunch-room (lunch′rüm′ or -rům′) *n.* **1** a public dining room; restaurant. **2** a room in a plant, school, etc. where employees, teachers, or students may eat the lunches they have brought. Also, **lunch room.**

lune (lün) *n.* **1** anything shaped like a crescent or a half moon. **2** in geometry, a crescent-shaped plane figure bounded by two arcs of circles; a figure formed on a sphere by two arcs of circles that enclose a space. [< F < L *luna* moon]

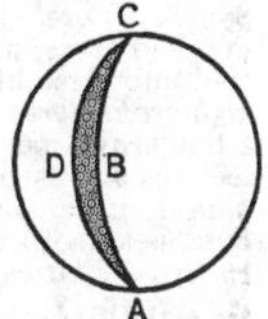

ABCD is a lune (def. 2)

lu·nette (lü net′) *n.* **1** in architecture: **a** a crescent-shaped opening or space in a vaulted ceiling, dome, wall, etc. **b** a painting, piece of sculpture, etc. that fills this space. **c** an arched or rounded opening, window, etc. **2** a projecting part of a rampart, shaped like an arch. See picture on the next page. [< F *lunette,* dim. of *lune* moon < L *luna*]

lung (lung) *n.* **1** in vertebrates, one of the pair of breathing organs by means of which the blood receives oxygen and is relieved of carbon dioxide. **2** a similar organ in certain invertebrates, such as snails and spiders. **3** a mechanical device for supplying respiration. [OE *lungen*]

A lunette (def. 2)

lunge[1] (lunj) *n. v.* **lunged, lung·ing.** —*n.* any sudden forward movement; thrust: *The catcher made a lunge toward the ball.* —*v.* move suddenly forward; thrust. [ult. < F *allonger*, ult. < L *ad-* toward + *longus* long] —**lung′er,** *n.*

TRACHEA OR WINDPIPE
BRONCHI
LUNGS

The lungs of a human being

lunge[2] (lunj) *n. v.* **lunged, lung·ing.** —*n.* **1** a long rope used for training or exercising a horse. **2** the training of a horse with such a rope. **3** a ring or circular exercise track for training horses. —*v.* train, exercise, or move (a horse tied with a lunge) around a circular track. [< F *longe* cord, halter < OF *loigne*]

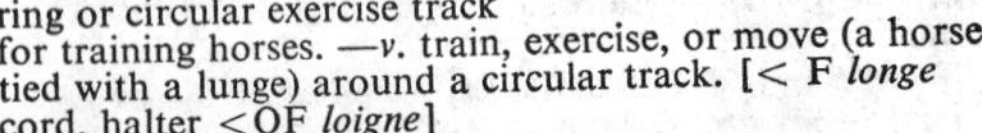

lunge[3] or **'lunge** (lunj) *n. Informal.* muskellunge.

lung·fish (lung′fish′) *n.* **-fish** or **fish·es.** a fish that can obtain oxygen by gulping air through the mouth as well as by passing water through its gills. Lungfish are found in Australia, Africa, and S. America.

lung·wort (lung′wėrt′) *n.* a European plant of the same family as borage, having blue flowers and spotted leaves.

lun·ker (lung′kər) *n. Informal.* anything considered large for its kind, especially a game fish. [origin uncertain]

Lu·per·ca·li·a (lü′pər kā′lē ə) *n.* in ancient Rome, a fertility festival celebrated on February 15. [< *Lupercus*, a rural god]

lu·pin or **lu·pine**[1] (lü′pən) *n.* any of several plants of the same family as peas and beans, that have long spikes of flowers, radiating clusters of grayish, hairy leaflets and flat pods with bean-shaped seeds. [< L *lupinus, lupinum.* See LUPINE[2].]

lu·pine[2] (lü′pīn) *adj.* **1** wolflike; fierce. **2** related to the wolf. [ME < L *lupinus* < *lupus* wolf]

lu·pus (lü′pəs) *n.* a skin disease caused by the tubercle bacillus. [< L *lupus* wolf]

lurch[1] (lėrch) *n.* a sudden leaning or roll to one side: *The car gave a lurch and overturned.* —*v.* lean or roll suddenly to one side. [origin uncertain] —**Syn.** *v.* pitch, stagger, sway, lunge.

lurch[2] (lėrch) *n.* **1** in certain games, a condition in which one player scores nothing or is badly beaten. **2 leave in the lurch,** leave in a helpless condition or difficult situation. [< F *lourche*, the name of a game]

lurch·er (lėr′chər) *n.* **1** a prowler; petty thief; poacher. **2** a mongrel hunting dog much used by poachers.

lure (lür) *n. v.* **lured, lur·ing.** —*n.* **1** an attraction: *the lure of the sea.* **2** a decoy; bait. —*v.* **1** lead away or into something by arousing desire; attract; tempt. **2** attract with a bait. [ME < OF *luerre* < Gmc.] —**lur′er,** *n.*
Syn. *v.* **1 Lure, allure, entice** = attract or tempt. **Lure,** commonly in a bad sense, means "tempt by arousing desire and usually to lead into something bad or not to one's advantage": *The hope of high profits lured him into questionable dealings.* **Allure,** seldom in a bad sense, means "tempt by appealing to the senses and feelings and by offering pleasure or advantage": *The Caribbean allures many tourists.* **Entice,** in a good or bad sense, means "tempt by appealing to hopes and desires and by using persuasion": *We enticed the kitten down from the tree.*

lu·rid (lür′id) *adj.* **1** lighted up with a red or fiery glare: *The sky was lurid with the flames of the burning city.* **2** glaring in brightness or color: *a lurid red.* **3** terrible; sensational; startling: *lurid crimes.* [< L *luridus*]

lurk (lėrk) *v.* **1** stay about without arousing attention; wait out of sight. **2** be hidden. [apparently < *lour* lower[2]] —**lurk′er,** *n.* —**lurk′ing·ly,** *adv.*
Syn. **1 Lurk, skulk** = keep out of sight or move in a secret or furtive way. **Lurk** = lie hidden and waiting or move about so as to keep from arousing attention, and often but not always suggests an evil purpose: *A tiger was lurking in the jungle.* **Skulk** suggests sneakiness and fear, cowardice, or shame: *The cattle thieves skulked in the woods until the posse had passed.*

lus·cious (lush′əs) *adj.* **1** delicious; richly sweet: *a luscious peach.* **2** very pleasing to taste, smell, hear, see, or feel. [ME; ? var. of *delicious*] —**lus′cious·ly,** *adv.* —**lus′cious·ness,** *n.* —**Syn. 1** See **delicious. 2** savory.

lush[1] (lush) *adj.* **1** tender and juicy; growing thick and green: *Lush grass grows along the river banks.* **2** characterized by abundant growth. **3** abundant. **4** very rich; too ornamented; extravagant: *lush description.* [< OF *lasche* lax] —**lush′ly,** *adv.* —**lush′ness,** *n.*

lush[2] (lush) *Slang.* —*n.* **1** one who drinks too much alcoholic liquor. **2** formerly, alcoholic drink; liquor. —*v.* **1** drink liquor, especially to excess. **2** provide with liquor. [? < *lush*[1]]

lust (lust) *n.* **1** strong, passionate desire. **2** sexual desire or appetite, especially when excessive. —*v.* have a strong, passionate desire: *A miser lusts after gold.* [OE *lust* pleasure]

lus·ter (lus′tər) *n.* lustre.

lus·ter·ware (lus′tər wãr′) *n.* lustreware.

lust·ful (lust′fəl) *adj.* **1** full of lust. **2** *Archaic.* lusty. —**lust′ful·ly,** *adv.* —**lust′ful·ness,** *n.* —**Syn. 1** lecherous, lascivious.

lus·tral (lus′trəl) *adj.* **1** of or used in ceremonial purification. **2** occurring every five years.

lus·trate (lus′trāt) *v.* **-trat·ed, -trat·ing.** purify by a propitiatory offering; purify by any ceremonial method. [< L *lustrare* brighten, clean < *lustrum* lustrum]

lus·tra·tion (lus trā′shən) *n.* a ceremonial washing or purification.

lus·tre or **lus·ter** (lus′tər) *n.* **1** a bright shine on the surface: *the lustre of pearls.* **2** brightness: *Her eyes lost their lustre.* **3** fame; glory; brilliance. **4** a kind of china or pottery that has a lustrous metallic, often iridescent surface. **5** a thin fabric of cotton and wool that has a lustrous surface.
—*v.* finish or shine with a lustre or gloss. [< F < Ital. *lustro* < *lustrare* < L *lustrare* illuminate] —**Syn. 1** sheen, gloss. See **polish.**

lus·tre·ware or **lus·ter·ware** (lus′tər wãr′) *n.* a kind of earthenware or china that has a lustrous, often iridescent glaze.

lus·trous (lus′trəs) *adj.* having lustre; shining; glossy: *lustrous satin.* —**lus′trous·ly,** *adv.*

lus·trum (lus′trəm) *n.* **-trums, -tra** (-trə). **1** in ancient Rome, a ceremonial purification, performed every five years. **2** a period of five years. [< L]

lust·y (lus′tē) *adj.* **lust·i·er, lust·i·est.** strong and healthy; full of vigor. —**lust′i·ly,** *adv.* —**lust′i·ness,** *n.* —**Syn.** robust, sturdy, vigorous, hearty.

lute (lüt) *n.* a stringed musical instrument, formerly much used, having a long neck and a hollow resonant body, played with the fingers of one hand or with a plectrum. [ME < OF < Provençal *laut* < Arabic *al'ud* the lute]

A lute

lu·te·ti·um (lü tē′shē əm) *n.* a rare metallic chemical element. *Symbol:* Lu; *at.no.* 71; *at.wt.* 174.97. Also, **lutecium.** [< NL < L *Lutetia* Paris]

Lu·ther·an (lü′thər ən or lüth′rən) *adj.* having to do with Martin Luther, 1483-1546, the leader of the Protestant Reformation in Germany, or the Church that was named for him. —*n.* a member of the Lutheran Church.

Lu·ther·an·ism (lü′thər ən iz′əm or lüth′rən iz′əm) *n.* the doctrine, organization, and manner of worship of the Lutheran Church.

lux (luks) *n.* **lux·es** or **lu·ces.** the international unit of illumination, equal to one lumen per square metre. [< L *lūx* light[1]]

lux·ate (luk′sāt) *v.* **-at·ed, -at·ing.** dislocate; put out of joint. [< L *luxare* dislocate] —**lux·a′tion,** *n.*

lux·u·ri·ance (lug zhür′ē əns or luk shür′ē əns) *n.* luxuriant growth or productiveness; rich abundance. —**Syn.** richness, profusion.

lux·u·ri·ant (lug zhür′ē ənt or luk shür′ē ənt) *adj.* **1** growing in a vigorous and healthy way; thick and lush: *In spring the grass on our lawn is luxuriant. She has a luxuriant head of hair.* **2** producing abundantly. **3** rich in ornament. [< L *luxurians, -antis,* ppr. of *luxuriare.* See LUXURIATE.] —**lux·u′ri·ant·ly,** *adv.*

lux·u·ri·ate (lug zhür′ē āt′ or luk shür′ē āt′) *v.* **-at·ed, -at·ing. 1** indulge in luxury. **2** take great delight. **3** grow very abundantly. [< L *luxuriare* < *luxuria* luxury < *luxus* excess]

lux·u·ri·ous (lug zhür′ē əs or luk shür′ē əs) *adj.* **1** fond of luxury; tending toward luxury; self-indulgent. **2** giving luxury; very comfortable and beautiful. —**lux·u′ri·ous·ly,** *adv.* —**lux·u′ri·ous·ness,** *n.*

lux·u·ry (luk′shə rē or lug′zhə rē) *n.* **-ries. 1** an abundance of the comforts and beauties of life beyond what is really necessary. **2** the use of the best and most costly food, clothes, houses, furniture, and amusements. **3** anything that one enjoys, usually something choice and costly. **4** something pleasant but not necessary. [< L *luxuria* < *luxus* excess]

Lw lawrencium.

LXX Septuagint.

-ly[1] *adverb-forming suffix.* **1** in a —— manner: *cheerfully = in a cheerful manner.* **2** in —— ways or respects: *financially = in financial respects.* **3** to a —— degree or extent: *greatly = to a great degree.* **4** in, to, or from a —— direction: *northwardly = to or from the north.* **5** in a —— place: *thirdly = in the third place.* **6** at a —— time: *recently = at a recent time.* [OE *-līce* < *-līc* -ly[2]]

-ly[2] *adjective-forming suffix.* **1** like a ——: *a ghostly form = a form like a ghost.* **2** like that of a ——; characteristic of a ——: *A brotherly kiss = a kiss like that of a brother.* **3** suited to a ——; fit or proper for a ——: *womanly kindness = kindness suited to a woman.* **4** of each or every ——; occurring once per ——: *daily = of every day.* **5** being a ——; that is a ——: *a heavenly home = a home that is a heaven.* [OE *-līc,* representing *līc* body]

ly·cée (lē sā′) *n.* in France, a secondary school maintained by the government. [< F < L *Lyceum.* Doublet of LYCEUM.]

ly·ce·um (lī sē′əm or lī′sē əm) *n.* **1** a lecture hall; a place where lectures are given. **2 Lyceum,** an ancient outdoor grove and gymnasium near Athens, where Aristotle taught. [< L *Lyceum* < Gk. *Lykeion* (def. 2), from the nearby temple of Apollo, *Lykeios.* Doublet of LYCÉE.]

lych gate (lich) lich gate.

ly·co·po·di·um (lī′kə pō′dē əm) *n.* **1** any of a group of evergreen plants, including some creepers, that resemble mosses. Club moss is a lycopodium. **2** a fine yellow powder made from the spores of certain lycopodiums. [< NL < Gk. *lykos* wolf + *pous, podos* foot]

lydd·ite (lid′īt) *n.* a high explosive, consisting chiefly of picric acid. [< *Lydd,* a town in S.E. England]

Lyd·i·an (lid′ē ən) *adj.* **1** of Lydia, in ancient times, a country in W. Asia Minor, its people, or their language. **2** soft; gentle; effeminate. —*n.* **1** an inhabitant of Lydia. **2** the language of Lydia.

lye (lī) *n.* any strong alkaline solution. Lye is used in making soap and in cleaning. Sodium hydroxide and potassium hydroxide are kinds of lye. [OE *lēag*]

ly·ing[1] (lī′ing) *n.* the telling of a lie; habit of telling lies. —*adj.* false; untruthful: *a lying report.* —*v.* ppr. of **lie**[1].

ly·ing[2] (lī′ing) *v.* ppr. of **lie**[2].

ly·ing-in (lī′ing in′) *n.* confinement in childbirth.

lymph (limf) *n.* in physiology, a nearly colorless liquid in the tissues of the body, resembling blood without the red corpuscles. [< L *lympha* clear water]

lym·phat·ic (lim fat′ik) *adj.* **1** of lymph; carrying lymph. **2** sluggish; lacking energy. —*n.* a vessel that contains or carries lymph.

hat, āge, cãre, fär; let, ēqual, tėrm; it, īce
hot, ōpen, ôrder; oil, out; cup, pu̇t, rüle, ūse
əbove, takən, pencəl, lemən, circəs
ch, child; ng, long; sh, ship
th, thin; ŦH, then; zh, measure

lymph gland or **lymphatic gland** in physiology, any of the glandlike bodies occurring in the course of the lymphatic vessels, and supposed to be a source of leucocytes.

lym·pho·cyte (lim′fə sīt′) *n.* in physiology, one of the colorless cells of lymph. [< L *lympha* clear water + E *-cyte* hollow body (< Gk. *kytos*)]

lymph·oid (lim′foid) *adj.* **1** of, having to do with, or resembling lymph or lymphocytes. **2** of, having to do with, or resembling lymphoid tissue.

lynch (linch) *v.* kill or put to death, usually by hanging, without a proper trial: *The angry mob lynched an innocent man.* [see LYNCH LAW] —**lynch′er,** *n.*

lynch law the act of putting an accused person to death without a proper trial. [originally *Lynch's law* < William *Lynch* (1742-1820), a Virginia magistrate]

lynx (lingks) *n.* **lynx·es** or (*esp. collectively*) **lynx.** a wildcat having a short tail, rather long legs, and tufted ears. [< L < Gk.] —**lynx′like′,** *adj.*

lynx-eyed (lingks′īd′) *adj.* having sharp eyes; sharp-sighted.

ly·on·naise (lī′ə nāz′) *adj.* fried with pieces of onions: *lyonnaise potatoes.* [< F *lyonnaise* < *Lyon* Lyons, a city in E. France]

Ly·ra (lī′rə) *n.* a small northern constellation that was once thought of as arranged in the shape of a lyre. It contains the star Vega.

ly·rate (lī′rāt) *adj.* shaped like a lyre.

lyre (līr) *n.* an ancient stringed musical instrument resembling a small harp. [ME < L < Gk. *lyra*]

A lyre

lyre·bird (līr′bėrd′) *n.* an Australian bird, the male of which has a long tail that is lyre-shaped when spread.

lyr·ic (lir′ik) *n.* **1** a short poem expressing personal emotion. Love poems, patriotic songs, laments, and hymns are all lyrics. **2** *Informal.* the words for a song. —*adj.* **1** having to do with lyric poems: *a lyric poet.* **2** characterized by a spontaneous expression of feeling. **3** of or suitable for singing. **4** in music, having a light, melodic singing voice. [< L *lyricus* < Gk. *lyrikos* of a lyre]

lyr·i·cal (lir′ə kəl) *adj.* **1** emotional; poetic. **2** lyric. —**lyr′i·cal·ly,** *adv.*

lyr·i·cism (lir′ə siz′əm) *n.* **1** a lyric style, quality, or form of expression: *Keats' lyricism.* **2** high-flown sentiments; exuberance.

lyr·i·cist (lir′ə sist) *n.* **1** a writer of lyrics or of popular songs. **2** a lyric poet.

ly·ser·gic acid (lī sėr′jik) in chemistry, a crystalline compound produced synthetically or as an extract from ergot. *Formula:* $C_{16}H_{16}N_2O_2$

lysergic acid di·eth·yl·am·ide (dī eth′ə lam′īd) a drug that can produce hallucinations and schizophrenic symptoms. *Formula:* $C_{20}H_{25}N_3O$ *Abbrev.:* LSD

ly·sin (lī′sən) *n.* in biochemistry, any of a class of substances that are developed in blood serum, and that are capable of causing the dissolution or destruction of bacteria, blood corpuscles, and other cellular elements. [< Gk. *lysis* a loosening]

Ly·sol (lī′sōl or lī′sol) *n. Trademark.* a brown, oily liquid containing cresols and soap, used as a disinfectant and antiseptic. [< Gk. *lysis* a loosening + L *oleum* oil]

M or **m** (em) *n.* **M's** or **m's.** **1** the thirteenth letter of the English alphabet. **2** any speech sound represented by this letter. **3** one (usually thirteenth) of a series designated alphabetically. **4** in printing, an em, the unit for measuring the length of line.

m. **1** minute. **2** midnight. **3** metre. **4** married. **5** masculine. **6** mile. **7** in German money, mark. **8** minim. **9** month. **10** manual. **11** mill.

M the Roman numeral for 1,000.

M. **1** Monday. **2** Midnight. **3** Monsieur. **4** Master. **5** Mass. **6** Noon (for L *meridies*).

ma (mo, mä, or ma) *n. Informal.* mamma; mother.

Ma masurium.

MA in psychology, mental age.

M.A. Master of Arts (for L *Magister Artium*).

ma'am (mam or mäm) *n. Informal.* madam.

ma·ca·ber (mə kä′bər) *adj.* macabre.

ma·ca·bre (mə kä′brə or mə kä′bər) *adj.* gruesome; horrible; ghastly. [< F]

ma·ca·co (mə kā′kō) *n.* **-cos.** a black, short-tailed lemur of Asia and Africa. [< Pg. < native African]

mac·ad·am (mə kad′əm) *n.* **1** small, broken stones, generally mixed with tar or asphalt as a binding agent. In the making of roads, layers of macadam are rolled until solid and smooth. **2** a road surfaced with macadam. [after John L. *McAdam* (1756-1836), a Scottish engineer]

mac·ad·am·ize (mə kad′əm īz′) *v.* **-ized, -iz·ing.** surface a road with macadam. **—mac·ad′am·i·za′tion,** *n.*

ma·caque (mə käk′) *n.* any of several kinds of monkeys of Asia, the East Indies, and Africa. [< F < Pg. < native African]

mac·a·ro·ni (mak′ə rō′nē) *n.* **-nis** or **-nies.** flour paste that has been dried, usually in the form of hollow tubes, to be cooked for food. [< earlier Ital. *maccaroni*, pl., ult. < LGk. *makaria* barley broth]

mac·a·roon (mak′ə rün′) *n.* a very sweet cookie made of whites of eggs, sugar, and coconut, corn flakes, or ground almonds. [< F < Ital. *maccarone*, sing. of *maccaroni.* See MACARONI.]

ma·caw (mə kô′) *n.* any of several large parrots of South and Central America, characterized by long tails, brilliant feathers, and harsh voices. [< Pg. *macao* < Brazilian]

Macc. Maccabees.

Mac·ca·bees (mak′ə bēz′) *n.pl.* **1** a family of Jewish patriots who led successful revolts against Syria in the second century B.C. **2** two books of the Old Testament Apocrypha telling about these revolts.

mace[1] (mās) *n.* **1** a staff used as a symbol of authority. **2** the bearer of a mace. **3** in the Middle Ages, a war club having a heavy metal head. [ME < OF < VL *mattea* < L *matteola* kind of hammer]

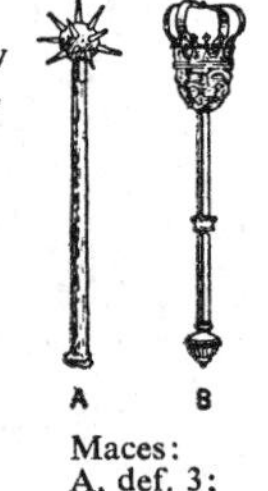

Maces: A, def. 3; B, def. 1.

mace[2] (mās) *n.* a spice made from the dried outer covering of nutmegs. [ME < OF *macis* < L *macir* reddish rind of an Indian root < Gk. *makir*]

mac·é·doine (mas′ə dwän′ or mas′ā dwän′) *n.* a mixture of vegetables or fruits, sometimes in jelly. [< F *macédoine* Macedonian]

mac·er·ate (mas′ər āt′) *v.* **-at·ed, -at·ing.** **1** soften by soaking for some time. Flowers are macerated to extract their perfume. **2** break up or soften (food) by the digestive process. **3** cause to grow thin. **4** become thin; waste away. [< L *macerare* soften] **—mac′er·a′tion,** *n.*

Mach (mok or mak) *n.* Mach number.

ma·chet·e (mə shet′ē or mə shet′; *Spanish,* mä chā′tā) *n.* a large, heavy knife, used as a tool and weapon in South America, Central America, and the West Indies. [< Sp., ult. < L *mactare* kill]

Mach·i·a·vel·li·an or **Mach·i·a·vel·i·an** (mak′ē ə vel′ē ən) *adj.* **1** of or having to do with Niccolo Machiavelli, 1469-1527, an Italian statesman and writer who wrote *The Prince*, a detailed study of how force, deceit, and other unscrupulous methods were used to gain and hold power. **2** of or having to do with the crafty political methods described by Machiavelli. **3** characterized by subtle or unscrupulous cunning; crafty; wily; astute. —*n.* a person who uses such crafty political methods as were described by Machiavelli.

ma·chic·o·lat·ed (mə chik′ə lāt′id) *adj.* having machicolations.

ma·chic·o·la·tion (mə chik′ə lā′shən) *n.* in architecture: **1** an opening in the floor of a projecting gallery or parapet, or in the roof of an entrance, through which missiles, hot liquids, etc. might be cast upon attackers. Machicolations were much used in medieval fortified structures. **2** a projecting gallery or parapet with such openings. [< Med.L *machicolatio, -onis* < OF < Provençal *machacol* projection, balcony < *macar* crush (< Gmc.) + *col* neck < L *collum*]

mach·i·nate (mak′ə nāt′ or mash′ə nāt′) *v.* **-nat·ed, -nat·ing.** contrive or devise artfully or with evil purpose; plot; intrigue. [< L *machinari* < *machina.* See MACHINE.] **—mach′i·na′tor,** *n.*

mach·i·na·tion (mak′ə nā′shən or mash′ə nā′shən) *n.* **1** evil or artful plotting; scheming against authority. **2** Usually, **machinations,** *pl.* an evil plot; secret or cunning scheme.

ma·chine (mə shēn′) *n. v.* **-chined, -chin·ing.** —*n.* **1** an arrangement of fixed and moving parts designed for doing work, each part having some special job to do: *Sewing machines and washing machines make housework easier.* **2** a device for applying power or changing its direction. Levers and pulleys are simple machines. **3** an automobile. **4** an airplane. **5** a person or group that acts without thinking. **6** a group of people controlling a political organization.
—*v.* make or finish with a machine. [< F < L *machina* < Gk. *machana,* dial. var. of *mēchanē* device, means] **—ma·chin′er,** *n.* **—ma·chine′like′,** *adj.*

machine gun a gun that uses small-arms ammunition automatically and can keep up a rapid fire of bullets.

ma·chine-gun (mə shēn′gun′) *v.* **-gunned, -gun·ing.** fire at with a machine gun.

ma·chine-made (mə shēn′mād′) *adj.* made by machinery, not by hand.

ma·chin·er·y (mə shēn′ər ē or mə shēn′rē) *n.* **-er·ies.** **1** machines: *There is a lot of machinery in a shoe factory.* **2** the parts or works of a machine: *Machinery is oiled to keep it running smoothly.* **3** any combination of persons or things by which something is kept going or something is done: *Policemen, judges, courts, and prisons are the legal machinery of a state.*

machine shop a workshop where men make or repair machines or parts of machines.

machine tool a power-driven tool or machine used to form metal into desired shapes by cutting, hammering, squeezing, etc.

ma·chin·ist (mə shēn′ist) *n.* **1** a skilled worker who uses machine tools. **2** a person who runs a machine. **3** a man who makes and repairs machinery.

Mach·me·ter (mok′mē′tər or mak′-) *n.* a device that indicates the speed of an aircraft relative to the speed of sound.

Mach number a number representing the ratio of the speed of an object to the speed of sound in the same medium. Mach number 1 equals the speed of sound; thus Mach number 2 is twice the speed of sound, and Mach number 0.5 is half the speed of sound. [after Ernst *Mach,* 1838-1916, an Austrian physicist]

Mach One in aeronautics, the speed of sound (about 1,087 feet per second in dry air at 32° F.).

mac·in·tosh (mak′ən tosh′) *n.* mackintosh.

mack·er·el (mak′ər əl or mak′rəl) *n.* **-el** or **-els.** a salt-water fish in the N. Atlantic Ocean, much used for food. [ME < AF *makerel*]

mackerel sky sky spotted with small, white fleecy clouds.

mack·i·naw (mak′ə no′ or mak′ə nô′) *n.* **1** a kind of short coat made of heavy woollen cloth. **2** a kind of thick blanket that often has bars of color, used in the North and West by Indians, trappers, etc. **3** a large, heavy, flat-bottomed boat, formerly used in the region of the Upper Great Lakes. [< Cdn.F *Mackinac* < *Michilimackinac* Mackinac Island < Algonquian (Ojibwa) *mitchimakinak* large turtle]

mack·in·tosh (mak′ən tosh′) *n.* **1** a raincoat. **2** waterproof cloth. Also, **macintosh.** [< Charles *Macintosh* (1766-1843), the inventor]

mac·ra·mé (mak′rə mā′) *n.* a coarse lace or fringe, made by knotting thread or cord in patterns. [apparently < Turkish *maqrama* napkin < Arabic]

mac·ro·cosm (mak′rə koz′əm) *n.* the universe. [< F < Med.L *macrocosmus* < Gk. *makros* great + *kosmos* world]

ma·cron (mak′ron or mā′kron) *n.* a short, horizontal line (¯) placed over a vowel letter to identify a sound differing from that represented by the same letter without such a mark. *Example*: (mak′ron or māk′ron). [< Gk. *makron*, neut. adj., long]

mad (mad) *adj.* **mad·der, mad·dest. 1** out of one's mind; crazy; insane. **2** much excited; wild. **3 like mad,** furiously; very hard, fast, etc. **4** foolish; unwise. **5** very gay: *a mad party.* **6** blindly and unreasonably fond. **7** *Informal.* very angry. **8** having rabies or hydrophobia. A mad dog foams at the mouth and may bite people. **9 mad as a hatter,** completely crazy. **10 mad as a March hare,** completely crazy. [OE (*ge*)*mæded*] **—Syn. 1** See **crazy.**

mad·am (mad′əm) *n.* **mad·ams** or (*for def. 1*) **mes·dames** (mā däm′). **1** a polite title used in speaking to or of a lady. **2** a woman who runs a brothel. [ME < OF *ma dame* my lady]

mad·ame (mad′əm; *French,* mä däm′) *n.* **mes·dames** (me däm′). **1** a French title for a married woman; Mrs. **2** a title often used by women singers, artists, etc. *Abbrev.*: Mme. [< F]

mad·cap (mad′kap′) *n.* a very impulsive person. *—adj.* impulsive; hasty; wild.

mad·den (mad′ən) *v.* **1** make crazy. **2** make very angry or excited; irritate greatly.

mad·der (mad′ər) *n.* **1** a vine having small yellowish flowers. **2** its red root. **3** a red dye made from these roots. **4** red; crimson. [OE *mædere*]

mad·ding (mad′ing) *adj.* **1** mad; acting as if mad: *the madding crowd.* **2** making mad.

made (mād) *v.* pt and pp. of **make.** *—adj.* **1** built; formed. **2** specially prepared. **3** artificially produced: *made land.* **4** invented. **5** *Informal.* certain of success; successful.

Ma·dei·ra or **ma·dei·ra** (mə dēr′ə) *n.* a kind of wine made on the island of Madeira.

mad·e·moi·selle (mad′ə mə zel′; *French,* mäd mwä zel′) *n.* **mes·de·moi·selles** (med mwä zel′). a French title for an unmarried woman; Miss. *Abbrev.*: Mlle.

made-to-meas·ure (mād′ tə mezh′ər) *adj.* of clothing, made to the buyer's own measurements.

made-to-or·der (mād′tə ôr′dər) *adj.* made according to the buyer's wishes.

made-up (mād′up′) *adj.* **1** put together. **2** invented; untrue. **3** painted, powdered, etc. with cosmetics: *made-up lips.*

mad·house (mad′hous′) *n.* **1** an asylum for the mentally ill. **2** a place of uproar and confusion: *The arena was a madhouse after the home team won the championship game.*

Mad·i·son Avenue (mad′ə sən) **1** in New York City, a street where most of the major U.S. advertising agencies have their offices. **2** the U.S. advertising industry, its techniques, language, influence, etc.

mad·ly (mad′lē) *adv.* **1** insanely. **2** furiously. **3** foolishly.

mad·man (mad′man′ or mad′mən) *n.* **-men** (-men′ or -mən). **1** an insane man; a crazy person. **2** a person whose behavior is so foolish or unconventional as to appear irrational.

mad·ness (mad′nis) *n.* **1** a being crazy; the loss of one's mind. **2** a great rage; fury. **3** folly.

Ma·don·na (mə don′ə) *n.* **1** Mary, the mother of Jesus. **2** a picture or statue of her. [< Ital. *madonna* my lady]

mad·ras (mad′rəs or mə dras′) *n.* a closely woven cotton cloth, used for shirts, dresses, etc. [< *Madras,* a city and state in India]

hat, āge, cãre, fär; let, ēqual, tėrm; it, īce
hot, ōpen, ôrder; oil, out; cup, pu̇t, rüle, ūse
əbove, takən, pencəl, lemən, circəs
ch, child; ng, long; sh, ship
th, thin; ᴛʜ, then; zh, measure

mad·re·pore (mad′rə pôr′) *n.* a tropical genus of stony corals that often form reefs. [< F < Ital. *madrepora* < *madre* mother (< L *mater*) + *poro,* ult. < Gk. *poros,* kind of stone]

mad·ri·gal (mad′rə gəl) *n.* **1** a short poem, often about love, that can be set to music. **2** a song with parts for several voices, sung without instrumental accompaniment. **3** any song. [< Ital. < LL *matricale* original, chief < *matrix* womb]

mad·ri·lene or **mad·ri·lène** (mad′rə lən or mad′rə len′) *n.* a consommé flavored with tomato, usually served cold. [< F *madrilène* of Madrid, Spain < Sp. *madrileño*]

mad·wom·an (mad′wu̇m′ən) *n.* **-women. 1** a woman who is insane. **2** a woman whose behavior is so foolish or unconventional as to appear irrational.

Mae·ce·nas (mī sē′nəs or mi sē′nas) *n.* a generous patron of literature or art. [< *Maecenas* (74?-8 B.C.), a Roman statesman and patron of literature]

mael·strom (māl′strəm) *n.* **1** a great or turbulent whirlpool. **2** a violent confusion of feelings, ideas, or conditions. **3 Maelstrom,** a dangerous whirlpool off N.W. Norway. [< earlier Du. *maelstrom* < *malen* grind + *stroom* stream]

mae·nad (mē′nad) *n.* **1** in Greek and Roman mythology, a woman attendant of Dionysus or Bacchus. **2** a woman extremely excited or in a frenzy. Also, **menad.** [< L *maenas, -adis* < Gk. *mainas, -adis*]

ma·es·to·so (mä′es tō′sō) in music: *—adj. adv.* stately; with dignity. *—n.* a stately movement or passage; a composition to be played or sung in this way. [< Ital.]

maes·tro (mīs′trō; *Italian,* mä es′trō) *n.* **-tros** or (*Italian*) **ma·es·tri** (mä es′trē). **1** a great composer, teacher, or conductor of music. **2** a master of any art. [< Ital. < L *magister* master]

Mae West (mā′ west′) an inflatable vest worn as a life preserver by an aviator in flying over water. [< *Mae West,* born 1892, an American actress]

Ma·fi·a (mä′fē ä) *n.* a world-wide secret organization of criminal elements engaged in illicit activities such as racketeering and gambling. Also, **mafia.** [< Ital.]

mag. 1 magazine. **2** magnet. **3** magnetism. **4** in astronomy, magnitude.

mag·a·zine (mag′ə zēn′ or mag′ə zēn′) *n.* **1** a publication appearing regularly and containing stories, articles, etc. by various writers. Most magazines are published either weekly or monthly. **2** a room in a fort or warship for storing gunpowder and other explosives. **3** a building for storing gunpowder, guns, food, or other military supplies. **4** a place for cartridges in a repeating rifle or revolver. **5** a place for film in a camera, for fuel in a stove, etc. [< F < Ital. *magazzino,* ult. < Arabic *makhzan* storehouse]

MAGAZINE
The magazine of a rifle

Mag·da·lene (mag′də lēn′) *n.* **1** in the Bible, a woman from whom Jesus cast out seven devils. Luke 8:2. She is commonly supposed to be the repentant sinner forgiven by Jesus. Luke 7:37-50. **2 magdalene,** any woman who has reformed from a sinful life, especially a repentant prostitute.

mage (māj) *n. Archaic.* magician. [< OF < L *magus.* See MAGI.]

ma·gen·ta (mə jen′tə) *n.* **1** a purplish-red dye. **2** a purplish-red. *—adj.* purplish-red. [< dye named after Battle of *Magenta,* Italy, 1859, because it was discovered in that year]

mag·got (mag′ət) *n.* a legless larva of any of various kinds of flies, often living in decaying matter. [ME *magot*; origin uncertain]

Mag·i (mā′jī or maj′ī) *n.* pl. of **Magus. 1** in the Bible, the Three Wise Men who, according to the New Testament, brought gifts to the infant Jesus. Matt. 2:1 and 2: 7-12. **2** priests of ancient Persia. [< L *magi,* pl. of *magus* < Gk. *magos* < OPersian]

mag·ic (maj′ik) *n.* **1** the pretended or supposed art of making things happen by secret charms and sayings: *The fairy's magic changed the brothers into swans.* **2** something that produces results as if by magic; mysterious influence; unexplained power: *the magic of music.* **3** sleight of hand.
—*adj.* **1** done by magic or as if by magic. **2** magical. [ME < OF *magique,* ult. < Gk. *magikos* < *magos* astrologer < OPersian] —**Syn.** *n.* **1** sorcery, necromancy, witchcraft.

mag·i·cal (maj′ə kəl) *adj.* **1** of magic; used in magic; done by magic. **2** like magic; mysterious; unexplained. —**mag′i·cal·ly,** *adv.*

magic eye any of several electronic monitoring devices, used for checking the functioning of machinery for activating mechanisms, for operating traffic signals, etc.

ma·gi·cian (mə jish′ən) *n.* **1** a person skilled in the use of magic. **2** a person skilled in sleight of hand. [ME < OF *magicien*] —**Syn. 1** sorcerer, necromancer. **2** conjurer.

magic lantern a device with a lamp and lenses for throwing a picture upon a screen, in magnified form, from a glass slide.

Ma·gi·not line (mazh′ə nō′) an elaborate system of defences built by France against Germany after the first World War. [after André *Maginot* (1877-1932), a French minister of war]

mag·is·te·ri·al (maj′is tēr′ē əl) *adj.* **1** of a magistrate; suited to a magistrate: *A judge has magisterial rank.* **2** showing authority: *The captain spoke with a magisterial voice.* **3** imperious; domineering; overbearing. [< Med.L *magisterialis,* ult. < L *magister* master] —**mag′is·te′ri·al·ly,** *adv.* —**Syn. 2** authoritative. **3** dictatorial, haughty, arrogant.

mag·is·tra·cy (maj′is trə sē) *n.* **-cies. 1** the position, rank, or duties of a magistrate. **2** magistrates as a group. **3** a district under a magistrate.

mag·is·trate (maj′is trāt′ or maj′is trit) *n.* a judge in a police or lower court. [< L *magistratus,* ult. < *magister* master]

magistrate's court a court that deals with minor offences.

mag·ma (mag′mə) *n.* **-ma·ta** (-mə tə) or **-mas. 1** any soft, pastelike mixture of mineral or organic substances. **2** in geology, the mixture of gas and molten rock material beneath the earth's crust from which igneous rock is formed. Volcanic lava is magma from which the gas has escaped. **3** in pharmacy, a suspension of insoluble or almost insoluble material in a small volume of water. [< L *magma* dregs of an unguent < Gk. *magma* an unguent, ult. < *massein* knead, mould]

Mag·na Char·ta or **Car·ta** (mag′nə kär′tə) **1** the great charter, guaranteeing personal and political liberties, forcibly secured from King John of England by the barons at Runnymede on June 15, 1215. **2** any fundamental constitution guaranteeing civil and political rights. [< Med.L *magna charta* great charter]

mag·na cum lau·de (mag′nə kům′ lou′dā or kum lô′dā) with high honors. [< L *magna cum laude* with great praise]

mag·na·nim·i·ty (mag′nə nim′ə tē) *n.* **-ties. 1** the quality of being magnanimous. **2** a magnanimous act.

mag·nan·i·mous (mag nan′ə məs) *adj.* **1** noble in soul or mind; generous in forgiving; free from mean or petty feelings or acts. **2** showing or arising from a generous spirit: *a magnanimous attitude toward a conquered enemy.* [< L *magnanimus* < *magnus* great + *animus* spirit] —**mag·nan′i·mous·ly,** *adv.* —**mag·nan′i mous·ness,** *n.* —**Syn. 1** highminded, unselfish.

mag·nate (mag′nāt) *n.* **1** a great man; an important person. **2** a prominent or distinguished person in any field: *a railroad magnate, a baseball magnate.* [< LL *magnas, -atis* < L *magnus* great]

mag·ne·sia (mag nē′zhə, mag nē′zē ə, or mag nē′shə) *n.* **1** a white, tasteless powder, used as a laxative, etc.; magnesium oxide. *Formula*: MgO **2** magnesium. [ME < Med.L < Gk. *hē Magnēsia lithos* the Magnesian stone (from *Magnesia,* in Thessaly)]

mag·ne·site (mag′nə sīt′) *n.* a mineral, carbonate of magnesium, occurring in white crystalline or granular masses, used industrially in making steel, etc. *Formula*: $MgCO_3$ [< *magnes*ium + *-ite*]

mag·ne·si·um (mag nē′zē əm, mag nē′zhē əm or mag nē′shē əm) *n.* a light, silver-white metallic chemical element that burns with a dazzling white light. Magnesium is used in metal alloys, fireworks, etc. *Symbol*: Mg; *at.no.* 12; *at.wt.* 24.312. [< NL < *magnesia.* See MAGNESIA.]

mag·net (mag′nit) *n.* **1** a mass or piece of iron, steel, etc. that has the property, or power, of attracting iron and some other metals to it. **2** an artificially magnetized piece of iron, steel, etc.: *a horseshoe magnet.* **3** anything that attracts: *The rabbits in our back yard were a magnet that attracted all the children in the neighborhood.* [ME < OF *magnete* < L < Gk. *hē Magnētis lithos* the magnet. Related to MAGNESIA.]

mag·net·ic (mag net′ik) *adj.* **1** having the properties of a magnet. **2** of or having to do with magnetism; producing magnetism. **3** of or having to do with the earth's magnetism: *the magnetic meridian.* **4** capable of being magnetized or of being attracted by a magnet. **5** attractive: *a magnetic personality.* —**mag·net′i·cal·ly,** *adv.*

magnetic field 1 the space around a magnet, magnetic body (as the earth), or an electric current in which the magnetic force of the magnet or current is felt. **2** the magnetic forces present in such a space.

magnetic mine an underwater mine that is exploded by the action of the metal parts of an approaching ship upon a magnetic needle.

magnetic needle a slender bar of magnetized steel. When mounted so that it turns easily, it points approximately north and south toward the earth's Magnetic Poles.

magnetic pole 1 one of the two poles of a magnet. **2 Magnetic Pole,** one of the two points on the earth's surface toward which a magnetic needle points. The **North Magnetic Pole** is approximately in 71° North latitude and 95° West longitude. The **South Magnetic Pole** is approximately in 72° South latitude and 154° East longitude.

The North Magnetic Pole

magnetic tape 1 a thin ribbon of plastic, metal, or paper, treated usually with iron oxide. It records sounds by responding to electromagnetic impulses. **2** in television, a tape used to record both sound and image.

mag·net·ism (mag′nə tiz′əm) *n.* **1** the properties of a magnet; manifestation of magnetic properties. **2** the branch of physics dealing with magnets and magnetic properties. **3** the power to attract or charm: *His magnetism was shown by the number of his friends and admirers.*

mag·net·ite (mag′nə tīt′) *n.* an important iron ore that is strongly magnetic; black iron oxide. *Formula*: Fe_3O_4

mag·net·ize (mag′nə tīz′) *v.* **-ized, -iz·ing. 1** give the properties of a magnet to. An electric current in a coil around a bar of iron will magnetize the bar. **2** attract or influence (a person). —**mag′net·iz′a·ble,** *adj.* —**mag′net·i·za′tion,** *n.* —**mag′net·iz′er,** *n.*

mag·ne·to (mag nē′tō) *n.* **-tos.** a small machine for producing electricity. In some gasoline engines, a magneto supplies an electric spark to explode the vapor. [< *magneto*electric machine]

mag·ne·to·e·lec·tric (mag nē′tō i lek′trik) *adj.* of electricity produced by magnets.

mag·ne·tom·e·ter (mag′nə tom′ə tər) *n.* an instrument used to measure magnetic forces.

mag·nif·ic (mag nif′ik) *adj. Archaic.* **1** magnificent. **2** pompous. [< L *magnificus* < *magnus* great + *facere* make]

mag·nif·i·cal (mag nif′ə kəl) *adj. Archaic.* magnific.

Mag·nif·i·cat (mag nif′ə kat′) *n.* **1** a hymn of the Virgin Mary beginning "My soul doth magnify the Lord." Luke 1:46-55. **2** the music for this hymn. [< L *magnificat* magnifies]

mag·ni·fi·ca·tion (mag′nə fə kā′shən) *n.* **1** the act of magnifying. **2** a magnified condition. **3** the power to magnify. **4** a magnified copy, model, or picture.

mag·nif·i·cence (mag nif′ə səns) *n.* richness of material, color, and ornament; grand beauty; splendor. [< OF < L *magnificentia* < *magnificus* noble. See MAGNIFIC.] —**Syn.** grandeur, sumptuousness.

mag·nif·i·cent (mag nif′ə sənt) *adj.* **1** richly colored or decorated; splendid; grand; stately: *a magnificent royal palace, a magnificent ceremony.* **2** impressive; noble; exalted: *magnificent words, magnificent ideas.* **3** extraordinarily fine; superb: *a magnificent view of the mountains, a magnificent opportunity.* [< OF *magnificent* < *magnificence* < L *magnificentia.* See MAGNIFICENCE.] —**mag·nif′i·cent·ly,** *adv.*
Syn. Magnificent, splendid, superb = impressive in dignity and beauty, brilliance, or excellence. **Magnificent** emphasizes impressive beauty and costly richness or stateliness of things like natural scenery, jewels, buildings, etc., and noble greatness of ideas: *Westminster Abbey is magnificent.* **Splendid** emphasizes impressive brilliance or shining brightness in appearance or character of things, people, or deeds: *He had a splendid record in the army.* **Superb** denotes the highest possible excellence, magnificence, splendor, richness, etc.: *We have a superb view of the ocean.*

mag·nif·i·co (mag nif′ə kō′) *n.* **-coes. 1** a Venetian nobleman. **2** an important person. [< Ital.]

mag·ni·fi·er (mag′nə fī′ər) *n.* **1** one that magnifies. **2** a lens that magnifies things; magnifying glass.

mag·ni·fy (mag′nə fī′) *v.* **-fied, -fy·ing. 1** cause to look larger than the real size; increase the apparent size of an object. **2** make too much of; go beyond the truth in telling. **3** *Archaic.* praise highly. [< L *magnificare* esteem greatly, ult. < *magnus* great + *facere* make] —**Syn. 1** enlarge, amplify. **2** exaggerate, overstate.

magnifying glass a lens or combination of lenses that causes things to look larger than they would to the naked eye.

mag·nil·o·quence (mag nil′ə kwəns) *n.* **1** a high-flown, lofty style of speaking or writing; the use of big and unusual words, elaborate phrases, etc. **2** boastfulness. [< L *magnus* great + *loquens,* ppr. of *loqui* speak]

mag·nil·o·quent (mag nil′ə kwənt) *adj.* **1** using big and unusual words; in high-flown language. **2** boastful. [< *magniloquence*] —**mag·nil′o·quent·ly,** *adv.*

mag·ni·tude (mag′nə tūd′ or mag′nə tüd′) *n.* **1** size. **2** importance. **3** in astronomy, the degree of brightness of a star. Stars of the first magnitude are the brightest. **4** in geometry, the measure or extent of a particular line, area, volume, or angle. **5** in mathematics, a number given to a quantity so that it may be compared with similar quantities. **6** the measurement of the force of an earthquake, expressed on a scale of 0 to 10. [< L *magnitudo* < *magnus* large]

mag·no·lia (mag nōl′ē ə or mag nōl′yə) *n.* **1** a tree having large, white, pink, or purplish flowers that come out in the spring. **2** the flower of this tree. [< NL < Pierre *Magnol* (1638-1715), a French botanist]

mag·num (mag′nəm) *n.* **1** a bottle that holds two quarts of alcoholic liquor. **2** the amount that it holds. [< L *magnum,* neut. adj., great]

mag·num o·pus (mag′nəm ō′pəs) **1** a great work of literature, music, or art. **2** a person's greatest work. [< L]

mag·pie (mag′pī) *n.* **1** a noisy, black-and-white bird having a long tail and short wings, and related to the jays. **2** a person who chatters. [< *Mag,* for *Margaret* + *pie*[2]]

Ma·gus (mā′gəs) *n.* **Ma·gi.** one of the Magi.

Mag·yar (mag′yär; *Hungarian,* mod′yor) *n.* **1** a member of the largest ethnic group living in Hungary. **2** their language; Hungarian. It is closely related to Finnish. —*adj.* of the Magyars or their language; Hungarian. [< Hungarian]

Ma·ha·bha·ra·ta (mə hä′bä′rə tə) *n.* one of the two great Hindu epics, believed to have been written before 500 B.C. The other is the Ramayana. [< Skt.]

hat, āge, cãre, fär; let, ēqual, tėrm; it, īce
hot, ōpen, ôrder; oil, out; cup, pu̇t, rüle, ūse
əbove, takən, pencəl, lemən, circəs
ch, child; ng, long; sh, ship
th, thin; ᴛʜ, then; zh, measure

ma·ha·ra·jah or **ma·ha·ra·ja** (mä′hə rä′jə) *n.* **1** formerly, the title of certain ruling princes in India. **2** a person holding this title. [< Skt. *maharaja* < *maha-* great + *raja* rajah]

ma·ha·ra·ni or **ma·ha·ra·nee** (mä′hə rä′nē) *n.* **1** the wife of a maharajah. **2** a woman holding in her own right a rank equal to that of a maharajah. [< Hind. *maharani* < Skt. *maha-* great + *rajni* queen]

ma·hat·ma (mə hat′mə or mə hät′mə) *n.* in India, a wise and holy person who has extraordinary powers. [< Skt. *mahatman* < *maha-* great + *atman* soul]

Mah·di (mä′dē) *n.* **-dis.** in the Moslem religion: **1** the leader expected to come and establish a reign of righteousness. **2** a person claiming to be this leader. [< Arabic *mahdiy* one who is guided aright < *hada* lead aright]

mah-jong or **mah-jongg** (mä′jong′ or mä′zhong′) *n.* a game of Chinese origin played with 144 domino-like pieces. Each player tries to form winning combinations by drawing or discarding. [< Chinese *ma chiang,* the name of the game, literally, sparrows]

ma·hog·a·ny (mə hog′ə nē) *n.* **-nies,** *adj.* —*n.* **1** the hard reddish-brown wood of a large evergreen tree growing in the West Indies and tropical America. Because mahogany takes a high polish, it is used in making furniture. **2** the tree itself. **3** a dark reddish brown. —*adj.* **1** made of mahogany. **2** dark reddish-brown. [< obs. Sp. *mahogani,* probably of West Indian origin]

Ma·hom·et (mə hom′it) *n.* Mohammed.

Ma·hom·et·an (mə hom′ə tən) *adj. n.* Mohammedan; Moslem.

Ma·hom·et·an·ism (mə hom′ə tən iz′əm) *n.* Mohammedanism.

ma·hout (mə hout′) *n.* in India and the East Indies, the keeper and driver of an elephant. [< Hind. *mahaut*]

maid (mād) *n.* **1** a young unmarried woman; girl. **2** a woman servant: *a kitchen maid.* **3 the Maid,** Joan of Arc (1412-1431), a French heroine who led armies against invading England. [shortened from *maiden*]

maid·en (mād′ən) *n.* a young unmarried woman; girl. —*adj.* **1** of a girl or maid. **2** unmarried; virgin: *a maiden aunt.* **3** new; fresh; untried; unused: *maiden ground.* **4** first: *a ship's maiden voyage.* [OE *mægden*]

maid·en·hair (mād′ən hãr′) *n.* a fern having very slender stalks and delicate, finely divided fronds.

maid·en·head (mā′dən hed′) *n.* **1** the hymen. **2** *Archaic.* maidenhood; virginity.

maid·en·hood (mād′ən hu̇d′) *n.* **1** the condition of being a maiden. **2** the time when one is a maiden.

maid·en·ly (mād′ən lē) *adj.* **1** of a maiden. **2** like a maiden; gentle; modest. **3** suited to a maiden: *maidenly reserve.* —**maid′en·li·ness,** *n.*

maiden name a woman's surname before her marriage: *Mrs. Brown's maiden name was Smith.*

maid-in-waiting (mād′in wāt′ing) *n.* **maids-in-waiting.** an unmarried noblewoman who attends a queen or princess.

maid of all work a woman servant who does all kinds of housework.

maid of honor or **honour 1** an unmarried woman who is the chief attendant of the bride at a wedding. **2** an unmarried noblewoman who attends a queen or princess.

Maid of Orleans the Maid (def. 3).

maid·serv·ant (mād′sėr′vənt) *n.* a woman servant.

mail[1] (māl) *n.* **1** letters, postcards, papers, parcels, etc. sent or to be sent by post. **2** the system by which such mail is sent, managed by the Post Office Department. **3** all that comes by one post or delivery. **4** a train, boat, etc.

that carries mail. —*v.* post; send by mail; put in a mailbox: *He mailed the letter for his mother.* —*adj.* of mail. [ME < OF *male* wallet < Gmc.]

mail² (māl) *n.* **1** armor made of metal rings, or small loops of chain, linked together. **2** armor; protective covering. **3** the protective shell of certain animals, such as the tortoise or lobster. —*v.* cover or protect with mail. [ME < OF *maille* < L *macula* a mesh in network]

mail·box (māl′boks′) *n.* **1** a public box from which mail is collected; postbox. **2** a private box to which mail is delivered.

mail coach formerly, a stagecoach that carried mail.

mailed (māld) *adj.* covered or protected with mail.

mailed fist military force; aggression, especially by one nation against another. —**mailed′-fist′,** *adj.*

mail·er (mā′lər) *n.* **1** a person who mails. **2** a mailing machine. **3** a boat for carrying mail. **4** a container in which to mail things. Cylindrical mailers are often used for maps, photographs, etc. **5** a mail-order form.

mail·lot (mä yō′) *n. French.* **1** a bathing suit, especially a one-piece bathing suit. **2** a one-piece, tightly fitting garment worn by dancers, gymnasts, etc.

mail·man (māl′man′) *n.* **-men** (-men′). a man who carries or delivers mail; postman.

mail order an order for goods sent by mail.

mail-or·der (māl′ôr′dər) *adj.* of or having to do with mail orders or a mail-order business. —*v.* send (tickets, merchandise, etc.) to fill orders received by mail.

mail-order house a business that receives orders and sends goods by mail.

maim (mām) *v.* cause permanent damage to or loss of a limb or other part of the body; cripple; disable: *Automobile accidents maim thousands of people each year.* [var. of *mayhem*] —**maim′er,** *n.*

main (mān) *adj.* **1** most important; largest: *the main street of a town.* **2 by main force** or **strength,** by using full strength.
—*n.* **1** a large pipe for water, gas, etc. **2** *Poetic.* the open sea; ocean. **3** *Archaic.* the mainland. **4 in the main,** for the most part; chiefly; mostly. **5 with might and main,** with all one's force. [OE *mægen* power] —**Syn.** *adj.* **1** principal, leading, chief.

main clause in grammar, a clause that can stand by itself as a sentence; independent clause.

main drag *Slang.* the chief thoroughfare of a town or city.

main·land (mān′land′ or mān′lənd) *n.* the principal part of a continent or land mass, apart from peninsulas and outlying islands.

main·land·er (mān′land′ər or mān′lənd ər) *n.* a person who lives on the mainland.

main·lin·er (mān′līn′ər) *n.* a railway train, airplane, boat, etc. that follows the principal route.

main·ly (mān′lē) *adv.* for the most part; chiefly; mostly.

main·mast (mān′mast′ or mān′məst) *n.* the principal mast of a ship.

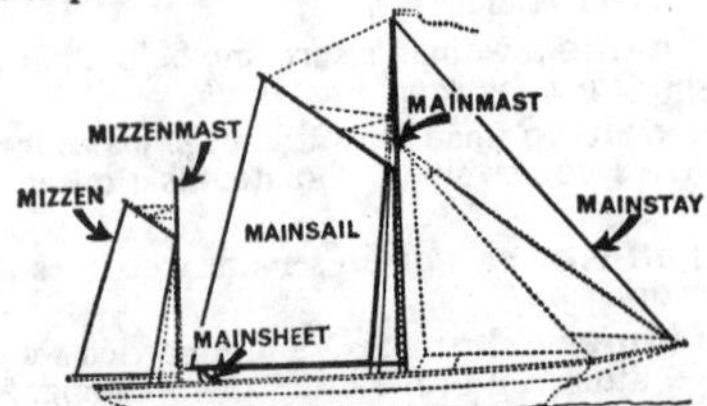

main·sail (mān′sāl′ or mān′səl) *n.* the largest sail of a ship.

main·sheet (mān′shēt′) *n.* a rope that controls the angle at which the mainsail is set.

main·spring (mān′spring′) *n.* **1** the principal spring in a clock, watch, etc. **2** the main cause, motive, or influence.

main·stay (mān′stā′) *n.* **1** a rope supporting the mainmast. **2** the main support: *Loyal friends are a person's mainstay in time of trouble.*

main·stream (mān′strēm′) *n.* the chief course of development of an institution, movement, art form, etc.

main·tain (mān tān′) *v.* **1** keep; keep up; carry on: *maintain a business. Policemen maintain order. Maintain your hold.* **2** bear the expenses of; provide for: *maintain a family.* **3** support; uphold: *maintain an opinion.* **4** keep in good repair: *He employs a mechanic to maintain his fleet of trucks.* **5** declare to be true: *He maintained that he was innocent.* **6** affirm; assert against opposition: *He maintains his innocence.* [ME < OF *maintenir* < L *manu tenere* hold by the hand] —**main·tain′a·ble,** *adj.* —**main·tain′er,** *n.* —**Syn. 1** continue, preserve. **3** defend. See **support. 5** assert, contend.

main·te·nance (mān′tə nəns) *n.* **1** a maintaining: *Maintenance of quiet is necessary in a hospital.* **2** a being maintained; support: *A government collects taxes to pay for its maintenance.* **3** a keeping in good repair: *The army devotes much time to the maintenance of its equipment.* **4** enough to support life; means of living: *His small farm provides a maintenance, but not much more.*

main·top (mān′top′) *n.* a platform on the mainmast.

main·top·gal·lant (mān′top′gal′ənt or mān′tə gal′ənt) *n.* a mast, sail, or yard above the maintopmast.

main·top·mast (mān′top′mast′ or -top′məst) *n.* the second section of the mainmast above the deck.

main·top·sail (mān′top′sāl′ or -top′səl) *n.* the sail above the mainsail.

main yard the beam or pole fastened across the mainmast, used to support the mainsail.

mai·son·ette or **mai·son·nette** (mā′zə net′) *n.* an apartment, especially one that occupies more than one floor. [< F, dim. of *maison* house]

maî·tre d'hô·tel (me′trə dō tel′) **1** a butler; steward. **2** a hotel manager. **3** a headwaiter. **4** served with a sauce of melted butter, chopped parsley, and lemon juice. [< F]

maize (māz) *n.* **1** a kind of grain that grows on large ears; corn; Indian corn. **2** the plant that it grows on. **3** the color of ripe corn; yellow. [< Sp. *maíz,* of West Indian origin]

Maj. Major.

ma·jes·tic (mə jes′tik) *adj.* grand; noble; dignified; stately. —**Syn.** regal, august, imposing.

ma·jes·ti·cal (mə jes′tə kəl) *adj.* majestic. —**ma·jes′ti·cal·ly,** *adv.*

maj·es·ty (maj′is tē) *n.* **-ties. 1** grandeur; nobility; dignity; stateliness: *We were much impressed by the majesty of the coronation ceremony.* **2** the supreme power or authority: *Policemen and judges uphold the majesty of the law.* **3 Majesty,** a title used in speaking to or of a king, queen, emperor, empress, etc.: *Your Majesty, His Majesty, Her Majesty.* [ME < OF < L *majestas*]

Maj.Gen. Major-General.

ma·jol·i·ca (mə jol′ə kə or mə yol′ə kə) *n.* **1** a kind of enamelled Italian pottery richly decorated in color. **2** something made of this pottery. [< Ital. < *Maiolica* Majorca]

ma·jor (mā′jər) *adj.* **1** larger; greater; more important: *Take the major share of the profits.* **2** of the first rank or order: *E. J. Pratt is a major poet.* **3** of legal age. **4** of, having to do with, or designating a student's principal subject or course of study. **5** in music: **a** of an interval, greater by a half step than the minor; having the difference of pitch which is found between the tonic and the second, third, sixth, or seventh tone (or step) of a major scale: *a major second, third, sixth, seventh.* **b** of a scale, key, or mode, in which the interval between the tonic and the third step is a major third (two whole steps): *C major scale or key.* **c** of a chord, especially a triad, containing a major third (two whole steps) between the root and the second tone or note.
—*n.* **1** in the army, a commissioned officer senior to a captain and junior to a lieutenant-colonel. *Abbrev.:* Maj. **2** a person of the legal age of responsibility. **3** the subject or course of study to which a student gives most of his time and attention. **4** in music, a major interval, key,

scale, chord, etc.: *The scale of C major has neither sharps nor flats.* **5** a major penalty. **6 the majors,** *pl.* the major leagues.
—*v.* of a student, take courses (in) as one's principal subject: *Susan majored in mathematics.* [< L *major,* comparative of *magnus* great. Doublet of MAYOR.]

ma·jor-do·mo (mā′jər dō′mō) *n.* **-mos. 1** a man in charge of a royal or noble household. **2** a butler; steward. [< Sp. or Ital. < Med.L *major domus* chief of the household]

ma·jor·ette (mā′jə ret′) *n.* a girl who is a drum major.

major-general (mā′jər jen′ə rəl or -jen′rəl) *n.* in the army, a commissioned officer senior to a brigadier and junior to a lieutenant-general. *Abbrev.*: Maj.Gen.

ma·jor·i·ty (mə jôr′ə tē) *n.* **-ties. 1** the larger number; greater part; more than half. **2** a larger number of votes than all the rest. If Smith received 12,000 votes, Adams 7,000, and White 3,000, Smith had a majority of 2,000 and a plurality of 5,000. **3** the legal age of responsibility. A person who is 21 years old or over has reached his majority and may manage his own affairs. **4** in the army, the rank or position of a major.

major league 1 in baseball, either of the two chief leagues of American professional teams. **2** in hockey, the National Hockey League.

major penalty in hockey, a five-minute penalty awarded for certain serious infractions of the rules, including fighting and instances of highsticking, slashing, etc. that draw blood.

major scale in music, a scale having eight notes, with half steps instead of whole steps after the third and seventh notes.

make (māk) *v.* **made, mak·ing,** *n.* —*v.* **1** bring into being; put together; build; form; shape: *make a new dress, make a boat, make jelly.* **2** have the qualities needed for: *Wood makes a good fire.* **3** cause; bring about: *make trouble, make a noise.* **4** cause to; force to: *He made me go.* **5** cause to be or become; cause oneself to be: *make a room warm, make a fool of oneself.* **6** turn out to be; become: *He will make a good legislator.* **7** get ready for use; arrange: *make a bed.* **8** get; obtain; acquire, earn: *make a fortune, make one's living.* **9** do; perform: *make an attempt, make a mistake.* **10** amount to; add up to; count as: *Two and two make four.* **11** think of as; figure to be: *I make the distance across the room 15 feet.* **12** reach; arrive at: *The ship made port.* **13** go; travel: *Some airplanes can make 200 miles an hour.* **14** cause the success of: *One big deal made the young businessman.* **15** *Informal.* get on; get a place on: *He made the football team.* **16** in card games: **a** win (a trick or hand). **b** state (the trump, or bid). **c** win a trick with (a card). **d** shuffle (the cards). **17** in electricity, close (a circuit). **18** in sports and games, score; have a score of.
make after, follow; chase; pursue.
make as if, pretend that; act as if.
make away with, a get rid of. **b** kill. **c** steal.
make believe, pretend: *The girl liked to make believe she was a queen.*
make fast, attach firmly.
make for, a go toward. **b** rush at; attack. **c** help bring about; favor.
make fun of, mock; ridicule.
make it, *Informal.* succeed.
make like, *Informal.* **a** imitate; act the part of. **b** perform the services of: *make like a cook.*
make off, run away.
make off with, steal; take without permission: *He made off with some apples.*
make or break, cause to succeed or fail.
make out, a write out. **b** show to be; prove. **c** try to prove; declare to be. **d** understand. **e** see with difficulty; distinguish: *I can barely make out three ships near the horizon.* **f** *Informal.* get along; manage.
make over, a alter; make different. **b** hand over; transfer ownership of.
make time, go with speed.
make up, a put together. **b** invent. **c** make satisfactory. **d** pay for. **e** become friends again after a quarrel. **f** put paint, powder, etc. on the face. **g** arrange (type, pictures, etc.) in the pages of a book, paper, or magazine. **h** complete; fill out: *We need two more eggs to make up a dozen.* **i** go to form or produce: *Girls make up most of that class.*

hat, āge, cãre, fär; let, ēqual, tėrm; it, īce
hot, ōpen, ôrder; oil, out; cup, pu̇t, rüle, ūse
əbove, takən, pencəl, lemən, circəs
ch, child; ng, long; sh, ship
th, thin; ᴛʜ, then; zh, measure

make up for, give or do in place of: *make up for lost time.*
make up one's mind, decide.
make up to, try to get the friendship of; flatter.
—*n.* **1** the way in which a thing is made; style; fashion: *Do you like the make of that coat?* **2** a kind; brand: *What make of car is this?* **3** the nature; character. **4** the act of making. **5** the amount made. **6 on the make,** *Informal.* trying for success, profit, etc. [OE *macian*]
Syn. *v.* **1 Make, construct, fashion** = put together or give form to something. **Make** is the general word, meaning "bring something into existence by forming or shaping it or putting it together": *She made a cake.* **Construct** means "put parts together in proper order, or build," and suggests a plan or design: *They constructed a bridge.* **Fashion** means "give a definite form, shape, or figure to something," and usually suggests that the maker is inventive or resourceful: *He fashions beautiful totems out of argillite.*

make-be·lieve (māk′bi lēv′) *n.* **1** pretence. **2** a pretender. —*adj.* pretended.

mak·er (māk′ər) *n.* **1** one that makes. **2 Maker,** God.

make-read·y (māk′red′ē) *n.* in printing, the preparation of a form for the press by levelling and adjusting type, plates, etc. to ensure a clear and even impression.

make·shift (māk′shift′) *n.* something used for a time in place of the proper thing; temporary substitute: *When the electric lights went out, we used candles as a makeshift.* —*adj.* **1** used for a time instead of the proper thing: *The boys made a makeshift tent.* **2** characterized by makeshifts: *makeshift endeavors.*

make-up (māk′up′) *n.* **1** the way of being put together. **2** one's nature or disposition: *a nervous make-up.* **3** the way in which an actor is dressed and painted to look his part. **4** the paint, powder, wigs, etc. used by actors taking part in a play: *His make-up was so effective that we didn't recognize him.* **5** the powder, rouge, lipstick, etc. used by women: *Her skilful use of make-up added to her charm.* **6** in printing, the arrangement of type, pictures, etc. in a book, paper, or magazine.

make·weight (māk′wāt′) *n.* anything added to make up for some lack.

make-work (māk′wėrk′) *n.* **1** the finding of unnecessary jobs; featherbedding. **2** the providing of work for unemployed people. —*adj.* **1** of or used for unnecessary work. **2** planned so as to provide work.

mak·ing (māk′ing) *n.* **1** the cause of a person's success; means of advancement: *Early hardships were the making of him.* **2** the material needed. **3** the qualities needed: *I see in him the making of a hero.* **4** something made. **5** the amount made at one time. **6 makings,** *pl. Informal.* **a** the tobacco and papers used in making one's own cigarettes. **b** a cigarette made with such materials. **7 in the making,** in the process of being made; not yet fully developed.

mal- *combining form.* bad or badly; poor or poorly, as in *malnutrition, maltreat.* [< F *mal-* < L *male* badly < *malus* bad]

Mal. 1 Malachi. **2** Malay. **3** Malayan. **4** Malta.

M.A.L. *Cdn.French.* Membre de l'Assemblée législative (Member of the Legislative Assembly).

Malacca cane (mə lak′ə) a light walking stick made of rattan. [< *Malacca,* a state of Malaya]

mal·a·chite (mal′ə kīt′) *n.* a green mineral, a basic carbonate of copper, used for ornamental articles. *Formula*: $Cu_2(OH)_2CO_3$ [< F < Gk. *malachē* mallow (from the similarity of color)]

mal·ad·just·ed (mal′ə jus′tid) *adj.* badly adjusted; not in a healthy relation with one's environment.

mal·ad·just·ment (mal′ə just′mənt) *n.* poor or unsatisfactory adjustment.

mal·ad·min·is·ter (mal′əd min′is tər) *v.* administer badly; manage inefficiently or dishonestly.

mal·a·droit (mal′ə droit′) *adj.* unskilful; awkward; clumsy. [< F] **—mal′a·droit′ly,** *adv.* **—mal′a·droit′ness,** *n.*

mal·a·dy (mal′ə dē) *n.* **-dies.** a sickness, illness, or disease. [ME < OF *maladie* < *malade* ill < L *male habitus* doing poorly]

Mal·a·ga (mal′ə gə) *n.* **1** a kind of large, oval, white grape. **2** a kind of white wine. [< *Málaga*, a city and province in S. Spain]

Mal·a·gas·y (mal′ə gas′ē) *n.* **-gas·y** or **-gas·ies,** *adj.* —*n.* **1** a native of the Malagasy Republic (Madagascar). **2** the Malay-Polynesian language of Malagasy. —*adj.* of or having to do with Malagasy, its people, or their language.

ma·laise (ma lāz′) *n.* vague bodily discomfort. [< F *malaise* < *mal-* ill + *aise* ease]

Mal·a·mute (mal′ə mūt′ or mal′ə müt′) *n.* Malemute.

mal·a·pert (mal′ə pėrt′) *adj. Archaic.* too bold; pert; saucy. [ME < OF *malapert* < *mal* badly + *apert* adroit, expert]

Mal·a·prop (mal′ə prop′) *n.* **Mrs.,** in Richard Brinsley Sheridan's play *The Rivals*, a woman noted for her ridiculous misuse of words. [< F *mal à propos*. See MALAPROPOS.]

mal·a·prop·ism (mal′ə prop iz′əm) *n.* **1** a ridiculous misuse of words. **2** a misused word. [after Mrs. *Malaprop*]

☛ A malapropism is a confusion of two words somewhat similar in sound but different in meaning, as *arduous love* for *ardent love*. Malapropisms are often unconscious, but are sometimes intentionally used for humorous effect.

mal·ap·ro·pos (mal′ap rə pō′) *adv. adj.* at the wrong time or place. [< F *mal à propos*]

ma·lar·i·a (mə lãr′ē ə) *n.* **1** a disease characterized by periodic chills followed by fever and sweating. Malaria is caused by microscopic parasitic animals in the red blood corpuscles, and is transmitted by the bite of anopheles mosquitoes that have bitten infected persons.
2 unwholesome or poisonous air, especially that of marshes. [< Ital. *malaria* < *mala aria* bad air]

ma·lar·i·al (mə lãr′ē əl) *adj.* **1** having malaria. **2** of or like malaria. **3** causing, or helping to cause, malaria: *a malarial swamp.*

ma·lar·key or **ma·lar·ky** (mə lär′kē) *n. Slang.* sheer nonsense. [origin uncertain]

ma·la·thi·on (mal′ə thī′ən) *n.* a very powerful insecticide recognizable by its pungent, unpleasant odor. *Formula*: $C_{10}H_{19}O_6PS_2$

Ma·lay (mə lā′ or mā′lā) *n.* **1** a brown-skinned people living in the Malay Peninsula and nearby islands. **2** a member of this people. **3** their language. —*adj.* of the Malays, their country, or their language.

Mal·a·ya·lam (mal′ə yä′ləm) *n.* a Dravidian language, spoken on the southwestern coast of India.

Ma·lay·an (mə lā′ən) *n. adj.* Malay.

Ma·lay·sian (mə lā′zhən or mə lā′shən) *adj.* of or having to do with Malaysia, its people, or their languages. —*n.* a native or inhabitant of Malaysia.

mal·con·tent (mal′kən tent′) *adj.* discontented; rebellious. —*n.* a discontented person; a rebellious person.

mal de mer (mäl də mãr′) *French.* seasickness.

male (māl) *n.* **1** a man or boy. **2** an animal belonging to the sex that fathers young. **3** in botany, a plant having stamens and no pistils.
—*adj.* **1** of or having to do with men or boys. **2** belonging to the sex that fathers young. **3** in botany, able to fertilize the female. The same plant may have both male and female flowers. **4** designating a part of a machine, connection, etc. that fits into a corresponding part: *a male plug.* **5** composed of men or boys: *a male choir.* [ME < OF *male, masle* < L *masculus*, dim. of *mas* male]
Syn. *adj.* **1 Male, masculine, manly** = having to do with men or the sex to which they belong. **Male,** describing plants, animals, or human beings, suggests only sex: *We have a male avocado tree.* **Masculine** describes things and suggests qualities (especially strength, vigor, etc.) belonging to or characteristic of men and boys as distinguished from women and girls: *He is a big, masculine man.* **Manly** suggests the finer qualities of a man, such as courage and honor: *He is an upright, manly youth.*

Mal·e·cite (mal′ə sēt′ or mal′ə sīt′) *n.* **-cite** or **-cites.** a member of the Abenaki group of Algonquian Indians. The Malecite lived in Western New Brunswick and the adjoining parts of Quebec and Maine.

mal·e·dic·tion (mal′ə dik′shən) *n.* a speaking of evil to or against a person; a curse. [ME < L *maledictio, -onis* < *maledicere* < *male* ill + *dicere* speak. Doublet of MALISON.]

mal·e·fac·tion (mal′ə fak′shən) *n.* a crime; an evil deed.

mal·e·fac·tor (mal′ə fak′tər) *n.* a criminal; an evildoer. [ME < L *malefactor* < *malefacere* < *male* badly + *facere* do]

ma·lef·i·cence (mə lef′ə səns) *n.* harm; evil. [< L *maleficentia* < *maleficus* wicked < *male* badly + *facere* do]

ma·lef·i·cent (mə lef′ə sənt) *adj.* harmful; evil. [< *maleficence*]

Mal·e·mute (mal′ə mūt′ or mal′ə müt′) *n.* **1** a group of Eskimos living on the Bering Sea coast. **2** a member of this group. **3** a breed of hardy, strong dog, native to Alaska, used for pulling sleds. **4** a dog of this breed. [< Eskimo *Mahle*, the name of a tribe + *mut* village]

ma·lev·o·lence (mə lev′ə ləns) *n.* the wish that evil may happen to others; ill will; spite.

ma·lev·o·lent (mə lev′ə lənt) *adj.* wishing evil to happen to others; showing ill will; spiteful. [< L *malevolens, -entis*, ult. < *male* ill + *velle* wish] —**ma lev′o·lent·ly,** *adv.*

mal·fea·sance (mal fē′zəns) *n.* misconduct by a public official; violation of a public trust or duty: *A judge is guilty of malfeasance if he accepts a bribe.* [< F *malfaisance*, ult. < *mal-* badly + *faire* do]

mal·for·ma·tion (mal′fôr mā′shən) *n.* a distorted or abnormal shape; faulty structure.

mal·formed (mal fôrmd′) *adj.* badly shaped; having a faulty structure.

mal·func·tion (mal′fungk′shən) *n.* **1** a failure to function; a breakdown. **2** in medicine, a disorder or failure of part of the body: *an intestinal malfunction.* —*v.* function poorly; perform badly.

mal·ic acid (mal′ik or mā′lik) an acid found in apples and numerous other fruits. *Formula*: $C_4H_6O_5$ [< F *malique* < L *malum* apple < Doric Gk. *malon*]

mal·ice (mal′is) *n.* **1** active ill will; a wish to hurt others; spite. **2** in law, intent to commit an act which will result in harm to another person without justification. [ME < OF < L *malitia* < *malus* evil] —**Syn.** spitefulness, grudge, rancor. See **spite.**

ma·li·cious (mə lish′əs) *adj.* showing active ill will; wishing to hurt others; spiteful: *malicious gossip.* —**ma·li′cious·ly,** *adv.* —**ma·li′cious·ness,** *n.*

ma·lign (mə līn′) *v.* speak evil of; slander: *You malign a generous person if you call him stingy.* [ME < OF *malignier* < LL *malignare* < L *malignus.* See adj.] —*adj.* **1** evil; injurious: *Gambling often has a malign influence.* **2** hateful; malicious. **3** very harmful; threatening to be fatal. [ME < OF < L *malignus* < *malus* evil + *gen-* birth, nature] —**ma·lign′er,** *n.*

ma·lig·nance (mə lig′nəns) *n.* malignancy.

ma·lig·nan·cy (mə lig′nən sē) *n.* a malignant condition, quality, or tendency.

ma·lig·nant (mə lig′nənt) *adj.* **1** extremely evil, hateful, or malicious. **2** extremely harmful. **3** extremely infectious; dangerous; capable of causing death: *Cancer is a malignant growth.* [< LL *malignans, -antis* acting from malice < *malignus.* See MALIGN.] —**ma·lig′nant·ly,** *adv.*

ma·lig·ni·ty (mə lig′nə tē) *n.* **-ties. 1** great malice; extreme hate. **2** great harmfulness; dangerous quality; deadliness. **3** a malignant act. —**Syn. 1** enmity.

ma·lines or **ma·line** (mə lēn′) *n.* **1** Mechlin lace. **2** a thin, stiff, silk net used in dressmaking. [< F *malines*, after *Malines* (or Mechlin), a town in Belgium]

ma·lin·ger (mə ling′gər) *v.* pretend to be sick in order to escape work or duty; shirk. [< F *malingre* sickly < OF *mal-* badly (< L *male*) + *heingre* sick (< Gmc.)]

mal·i·son (mal′ə zən or mal′ə sən) *n. Archaic.* a malediction; curse. [ME < OF *maleison* < L *maledictio.* Doublet of MALEDICTION.]

mall (mol or môl) *n.* **1** a shaded walk; a public walk or promenade. **2** a walk lined with stores; a place to walk in a shopping centre. **3** a shopping centre; plaza. [ME

< OF *ma(i)l* mallet < L *malleus* hammer; originally, a mallet used in pall-mall (an old game); later, the game itself; then, a lane or alley in which the game was played]

mal·lard (mal′ərd) *n.* **-lards** or (*esp. collectively*) **-lard.** a kind of wild duck. The male has a greenish-black head and a white band around his neck. [ME < OF *mallart*, probably < Gmc.]

mal·le·a·bil·i·ty (mal′ē ə bil′ə tē) *n.* a malleable quality or condition.

mal·le·a·ble (mal′ē ə bəl) *adj.* **1** capable of being hammered or pressed into various shapes without being broken. Gold, silver, copper, and tin are malleable; they can be beaten into thin sheets. **2** adaptable; yielding: *a malleable person.* [ME < OF < L *malleare* to hammer < *malleus*, n.] **—mal′le·a·ble·ness,** *n.* **—mal′le·a·bly,** *adv.*

mal·let (mal′it) *n.* **1** a hammer having a head of wood, rubber, or other fairly soft material. **2** a long-handled wooden mallet used to play croquet or polo. [ME < OF *maillet*, dim. of *mail* < L *malleus* hammer]

mal·le·us (mal′ē əs) *n.* **mal·le·i** (mal′ē ī). in anatomy, the outermost of three small bones in the middle ear, shaped like a hammer. See **ear** for picture. [< L *malleus* hammer]

mal·low (mal′ō) *n.* **1** an ornamental plant having purple, pink, or white flowers, and hairy leaves and stems. **2** in botany, any of a family of plants, most of which have mucilaginous juice, and flowers shaped like those of the hollyhock. Mallows, hollyhock, cotton, etc. belong to this family. [OE *mealwe* < L *malva*. Doublet of MAUVE.]

malm·sey (mom′zē or mäm′zē) *n.* a kind of strong, sweet wine. [ME < Med.L *malmasia*, from *Monembasia*, a town in Greece]

mal·nu·tri·tion (mal′nū trish′ən or -nü trish′ən) *n.* poor nourishment; lack of nourishment. Improper food can cause malnutrition.

mal·oc·clu·sion (mal′ə klü′zhən) *n.* in dentistry, failure of the upper and lower teeth to meet or close properly.

mal·o·dor·ous (mal′ō′dər əs) *adj.* smelling bad. **—mal·o′dor·ous·ly,** *adv.* **—mal·o′dor·ous·ness,** *n.* **—Syn.** unsavory, fetid.

mal·peque (mal pēk′ or mal pek′) *n.* a variety of oyster, found in Malpeque Bay, Prince Edward Island.

mal·prac·tice (mal′prak′tis) *n.* **1** criminal neglect or unprofessional treatment of a patient by a doctor. **2** wrong practice or conduct in any official or professional position.

malt (molt or môlt) *n.* **1** barley or other grain soaked in water until it sprouts and tastes sweet. Malt is used in brewing and distilling alcoholic liquors. **2** *Informal.* beer or ale. *—v.* **1** change or be changed into malt. **2** prepare with malt. [OE *mealt*]

Mal·tese (mol tēz′ or môl tēz′) *n.* **-tese,** *adj.* *—n.* **1** a native of Malta, an island in the Mediterranean, south of Sicily. **2** the native language of Malta. It is a North Arabic dialect with many Italian loan words. *—adj.* of Malta, its people, or their language.

Maltese cat **1** a breed of short-haired, bluish-gray cat. **2** a cat of this breed.

Maltese cross a kind of cross. See the picture.

malt extract a sugary substance obtained by soaking malt in water.

A Maltese cross

Mal·thu·sian (mal thü′zhən or mal thü′zē ən) *adj.* of or having to do with Malthus or his theory that the world's population tends to increase faster than the food supply. *—n.* a believer in his theory. [< Thomas Robert *Malthus* (1766-1834), an English economist]

malt·ose (mol′tōs or môl′tōs) *n.* a white, crystalline sugar made by the action of diastase on starch. *Formula*: $C_{12}H_{22}O_{11} \cdot H_2O$

mal·treat (mal trēt′) *v.* treat roughly or cruelly; abuse: *Only vicious persons maltreat animals.*

mal·treat·ment (mal trēt′mənt) *n.* rough or cruel treatment; abuse.

malt·ster (molt′stər or môlt′stər) *n.* a person who makes or sells malt.

malt sugar maltose.

mal·ver·sa·tion (mal′vər sā′shən) *n.* corrupt conduct in a position of trust. [< F *malversation* < *malverser*

hat, āge, cãre, fär; let, ēqual, tėrm; it, īce
hot, ōpen, ôrder; oil, out; cup, pu̇t, rüle, ūse
əbove, takən, pencəl, lemən, circəs
ch, child; ng, long; sh, ship
th, thin; ᴛʜ, then; zh, measure

peculate < L *maleversari* behave badly]

ma·ma (mo′mə or mä′mə; *esp.Brit.*, mə mä′) *n.* mother.

mam·ba (mam′bə) *n.* any of several long and venomous snakes found in central and southern Africa.

mam·bo (mom′bō, mäm′bō, or mam′bō) *n.* **1** a ballroom dance of Caribbean origin. **2** the music for such a dance. [< Haitian Creole]

Mam·e·luke (mam′ə lük′) *n.* **1** a member of a military group that ruled Egypt from about 1250 to 1517 and had great power until 1811. The Mamelukes were originally slaves. **2 mameluke,** in Moslem countries, a slave. [< Arabic *mamluk* slave]

mam·ma[1] (mo′mə or mä′mə; *esp.Brit.*, mə mä′) *n.* mother. [reduplication of an infantile sound]

mam·ma[2] (mam′ə) *n.* **mam·mae** (mam′ē or mam′ī). in female mammals, a milk-giving gland. [< L *mamma* breast]

mam·mal (mam′əl) *n.* any of a class of vertebrate animals of which the females have milk-giving glands (mammae) to feed their young. Human beings, horses, dogs, lions, rats, and whales are all mammals. [< NL *mammalia*, pl., ult. < L *mamma* breast]

mam·ma·li·an (ma mā′lē ən or ma māl′yən) *adj.* of mammals. *—n.* a mammal.

mam·mal·o·gist (ma mal′ə jist) *n.* an expert in mammalogy.

mam·mal·o·gy (ma mal′ə jē) *n.* the branch of zoology that deals with the study of mammals. [< *mammal*ia + *-logy*]

mam·ma·ry (mam′ə rē) *adj.* of the mammae. The mammary glands secrete milk.

Mam·mon or **mam·mon** (mam′ən) *n.* **1** wealth thought of as an idol or god. **2** riches thought of as an evil; greed for wealth. [< L *mammona* < Gk. *mammōnas* < Aramaic *mamon* riches]

mam·moth (mam′əth) *n.* an extinct member of the elephant family. Mammoths, which were extremely large, were covered with hair and had long, curved tusks. *—adj.* huge; gigantic. [< earlier Russian *mammot*] **—Syn.** *adj.* colossal, immense.

mam·my (mam′ē) *n.* **-mies. 1** a child's word for "mother." **2** *U.S.* a Negro woman who takes care of white children, or is a servant in a white household.

man (man) *n.* **men** (men), *v.* **manned, man·ning.** *—n.* **1** an adult male person. **2** a person; human being: *Death comes to all men.* **3** the human race: *Man has existed for thousands of years.* **4** men as a group; the average man: *The man of today is better educated than his ancestors.* **5** a male follower, servant, or employee. **6** a member of the armed services, especially one who is not an officer. **7** a male member of a team, organization, etc. **8** a husband or lover. **9** in chess, checkers, etc., one of the pieces used. **10** a person characterized by manly qualities: *He was every inch a man.* **11 act the man,** be courageous. **12 as a man,** from a human point of view. **13 as one man,** with complete agreement; unanimously. **14 be one's own man, a** be free to do as one pleases. **b** have complete control of oneself. **15 man and boy,** from boyhood on; as a youth and as an adult. **16 to a man,** without an exception; all. *—v.* **1** supply with men: *Sailors man a ship.* **2** serve or operate; get ready to operate: *Man the guns.* **3** make (oneself) strong in anticipation; brace: *The captive manned himself to endure torture.*
—interj. Informal. an exclamation of surprise, joy, excitement, etc., or for effect: *Man, what a player!* [OE *mann*] **—man′less,** *adj.* **—Syn.** *n.* **2** individual, being, mortal. **3** humanity, mankind. **5** valet, attendant.

☛ **man, gentleman.** *Man* is now generally preferred to the more pretentious *gentleman*, unless a note of special courtesy or respect is desired.

Man. Manitoba.

man about town a man who spends much of his time

in clubs, theatres, etc.

man·a·cle (man′ə kəl) *n. v.* **-cled, -cling.** —*n.* **1** Usually, **manacles,** *pl.* a handcuff; fetter for the hands. See **handcuff** for picture. **2** a restraint. —*v.* **1** put manacles on: *The pirates manacled their prisoners.* **2** restrain. [ME < OF < L *manicula,* dim. of *manicae* sleeves, manacles < *manus* hand]

man·age (man′ij) *v.* **-aged, -ag·ing. 1** control; conduct; handle; direct: *manage a business, manage a horse.* **2** conduct affairs. **3** succeed in accomplishing; contrive; arrange: *I finally managed to get the job done.* **4** get along: *manage on one's income.* **5** make use of. **6** get one's way with (a person) by craft or flattery. [< Ital. *maneggiare* < *mano* hand < L *manus*]
Syn. *v.* **1 Manage, conduct, direct** = guide or handle with authority. **Manage** emphasizes the idea of skilful handling of people and details so as to get results: *He manages a large department store.* **Conduct** emphasizes the idea of supervising the action of a group working together for something: *The Scouts are conducting a safety drive.* **Direct** emphasizes the idea of guiding the affairs or actions of a group by giving advice and instructions to be followed: *A lawyer directed our anti-noise campaign.*

man·age·a·bil·i·ty (man′ij ə bil′ə tē) *n.* the condition or quality of being manageable.

man·age·a·ble (man′ij ə bəl) *adj.* that can be managed. —**man′age·a·ble·ness,** *n.* —**man′age·a·bly,** *adv.*

man·age·ment (man′ij mənt) *n.* **1** control; handling; direction: *Bad management caused the failure.* **2** the persons that manage a business or an institution: *The management of the store decided to use red wrapping paper at Christmas time.* —**Syn. 1** guidance, regulation. **2** administration.

management consultant a specialist or expert who can be hired to examine the operations of a company and advise on planning, organization, and other management problems.

man·ag·er (man′ij ər) *n.* **1** a person who manages: *a bank manager, an advertising manager.* **2** a person skilled in managing (affairs, time, money, etc.): *Mrs. Jones is not much of a manager, but the family gets along somehow.* —**Syn. 1** director, executive, administrator.

man·a·ge·ri·al (man′ə jēr′ē əl) *adj.* of a manager; having to do with management. —**man′a·ge′ri·al·ly,** *adv.*

ma·ña·na (mä nyä′nä) *n. adv.* tomorrow; some time. [< Sp.]

man-at-arms (man′ət ärmz′) *n.* **men-at-arms** (men′-). **1** a soldier. **2** a heavily armed soldier on horseback.

man·a·tee (man′ə tē′) *n.* a large sea mammal having two flippers and a flat, oval tail, living in warm shallow water near coasts; sea cow. [< Sp. *manatí* < Carib lang.]

man·chet (man′chit) *n. Archaic.* **1** bread made of the finest white flour. **2** a small loaf or roll of such bread. [origin uncertain]

Man·chu (man′chü) *n.* **1** a member of a Mongoloid people living in Manchuria, who conquered China in 1644 and ruled it until 1912. **2** their language. —*adj.* of the Manchus, their country, or their language.

Man·chu·ri·an (man chür′ē ən) *adj.* of or having to do with Manchuria, an eastern Asian region that includes several Chinese provinces. —*n.* a native or inhabitant of Manchuria.

man·ci·ple (man′sə pəl) *n.* in England, a person who buys provisions for a college or other institution; steward. [ME < OF < L *manicipium* office of purchaser < *manceps* buyer, ult. < *manu capere* take in hand]

man·da·mus (man dā′məs) *n.* in law, a written order from a higher court to a lower court, an official, a city, a corporation, etc. directing that a certain thing be done. [< L *mandamus* we order]

man·da·rin (man′də rin) *n.* **1** under the Chinese empire, an official of high rank. **2** a senior civil servant thought to exercise considerable power. **3 Mandarin, a** formerly, the northern dialect of China, the language of the court, government officials, and other educated people under the Empire. **b** the main dialect of modern China, the variety spoken in Peking being the standard form of Chinese. **3** Also, **Mandarin orange, a** a kind of small, sweet, spicy orange having a very loose reddish-yellow peel. **b** the tree or shrub this fruit grows on. [< Chinese Pidgin English < Pg. *mandar* order (< L *mandare*), blended with Malay *mantri* < Hind. < Skt. *mantrin* adviser]

man·da·tar·y (man′də ter′ē) *n.* **-tar·ies. 1** a nation to which a mandate over another country has been given. **2** in law, a person to whom a mandate is given.

man·date (*n.* man′dāt or man′dit; *v.* man′dāt) *n. v.* **-dat·ed, -dat·ing.** —*n.* **1** a command; order. **2** in law, an order from a higher court or official to a lower one. **3** the will of voters expressed to their representative. **4** a commission given to one nation by a group of nations to administer the government and affairs of a territory, etc. **5** a mandated territory, etc.
—*v.* put (a territory, etc.) under the administration of another nation. [< L *mandatum,* n. use of neut. pp. of *mandare* order] —**Syn.** *n.* **1** edict, behest, injunction.

MANDIBLES
MAXILLAE

Mandibles (def. 3)

man·da·to·ry (man′də tô′rē) *adj. n.* **-ries.** —*adj.* **1** of, like, or having to do with a mandate; giving a command or order. **2** required by a command or order. —*n.* mandatary.

man·di·ble (man′də bəl) *n.* **1** a jaw, especially the lower jaw. **2** either part of a bird's beak. **3** in insects, an organ for seizing and biting. [< LL *mandibula* < L *mandere* chew]

man·do·lin (man′də lin′ or man′də lin′) *n.* a musical instrument with a pear-shaped body, having metal strings, played with a plectrum. [< F < Ital. *mandolino,* dim. of *mandola,* ult. < Gk. *pandoura* three-stringed instrument]

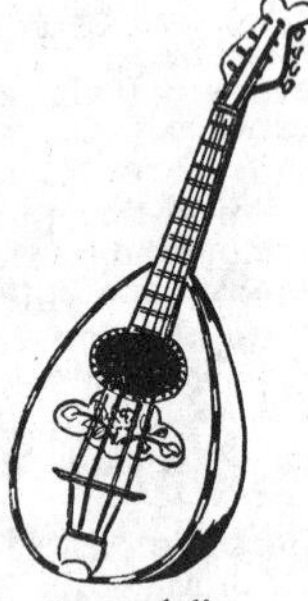

A mandolin

man·drag·o·ra (man drag′ə rə) *n.* mandrake. [ME < L < Gk. *mandragoras*]

man·drake (man′drāk) *n.* **1** a plant having a very short stem and a thick root, used in medicine. **2** the May apple. [by popular etymology < *mandragora*]

man·drel or **man·dril** (man′drəl) *n.* **1** the spindle or bar of a lathe that supports the material being turned. **2** a rod or core around which metal is shaped. [< F *mandrin*]

man·drill (man′drəl) *n.* a large, fierce baboon of W. Africa. The face of the male mandrill is marked with blue and scarlet. [< *man* + *drill* baboon (< native African)]

mane (mān) *n.* the long, heavy hair on the back of the neck of a horse, lion, etc. [OE *manu*]

ma·nège (mə nezh′ or mə nāzh′) *n.* **1** the art of training or riding horses; horsemanship. **2** the movements of a trained horse. **3** a riding school. [< F < Ital. *maneggio* < *maneggiare* manage]

ma·nes or **Ma·nes** (mā′nēz) *n.pl.* **1** in the ancient Roman religion, the deified souls of dead ancestors, together with the gods of the lower world. **2** the spirit or shade of a particular person. [< L]

ma·neu·ver (mə nü′vər) *n. v.* manoeuvre.

ma·neu·ver·a·bil·i·ty (mə nü′vrə bil′ə tē or mə nü′və rə bil′ə tē′) *n.* manoeuvrability.

man Friday a faithful servant. [< *Friday,* Robinson Crusoe's servant]

man·ful (man′fəl) *adj.* manly; brave; resolute. —**man′ful·ly,** *adv.* —**man′ful·ness,** *n.*

man·ga·nese (mang′gə nēz′ or mang′gə nēs′) *n.* a hard, brittle, grayish-white metallic element. Substances containing manganese are used in making steel, glass, paints, and medicines. *Symbol:* Mn; *at.no.* 25; *at.wt.* 54.9380. [< F < Ital. *manganese,* alteration of Med.L *magnesia.* See MAGNESIA.]

mange (mānj) *n.* an itchy skin disease of dogs, horses, cattle, etc., in which tiny skin sores form and the hair falls off in patches. [ME < OF *mangue* or *mangeue* the itch < *mangier* eat < L *manducare, mandere* chew]

man·gel (mang′gəl) *n.* a large, coarse variety of beet, used as a food for cattle. [shortened form of *mangel-wurzel*]

man·gel-wur·zel (mang′gəl wėr′zəl) *n.* mangel. [<G *Mangelwurzel*, var. of *Mangoldwurzel* beet root]

man·ger (mān′jər) *n.* a box or trough in which hay can be placed for horses or cows to eat. [ME < OF *mangeoire*, ult. < L *manducare* eat]

man·gle[1] (mang′gəl) *v.* **-gled, -gling. 1** cut or tear (the flesh) roughly. **2** do or play badly; ruin. [< AF *mangler*, ? < OF *mahaignier* < *mahaigne* injury. Cf. MAYHEM.] **—Syn. 1** lacerate, mutilate.

man·gle[2] (mang′gəl) *n. v.* **-gled, -gling.** *—n.* **1** a machine with rollers for pressing and smoothing cloth. **2** a wringer. *—v.* press with a mangle; put through a mangle. [< Du. *mangel* < MDu. *mange* < LL *manganum* contrivance < Gk.]

man·go (mang′gō) *n.* **-goes** or **-gos. 1** a tart, juicy tropical fruit having a thick, yellowish-red rind. Mangoes are eaten when ripe or pickled when green. **2** the tropical tree that mangoes grow on. [< Pg. < Malay < Tamil *mankay*]

man·gold (mang′gold) *n.* a mangel.

man·go·nel (mang′gə nəl) *n.* formerly, a machine used in war for throwing large stones, etc. [ME < OF < VL *manganellum*, dim. of LL *manganum* device, contrivance < Gk. *manganon*]

man·go·steen (mang′gə stēn′) *n.* **1** a juicy, edible fruit with a thick, reddish-brown rind. **2** the tree of the East Indies that this fruit grows on. [< Malay *mangustan*]

man·grove (mang′grōv) *n.* a tropical tree that sends down many branches that take root and form new trunks. Mangroves grow in swamps along the banks of rivers. [< Sp. *mangle* < Malay *manggi-manggi*; influenced by *grove*]

Mangroves (10 to 20 ft. high)

man·gy (mān′jē) *adj* **-gi·er, -gi·est. 1** having the mange; with the hair falling out: *a mangy dog.* **2** shabby and dirty: *a mangy house.* **3** *Informal.* mean; contemptible. **—man′gi·ness,** *n.*

man·han·dle (man′han′dəl) *v.* **-dled, -dling. 1** treat roughly; pull or push about. **2** move by human strength without mechanical appliances.

Man·hat·tan (man hat′ən) *n.* a cocktail made of vermouth, rye whisky, and bitters.

man·hole (man′hōl′) *n.* a hole through which a workman may enter a sewer, steam boiler, etc.

man·hood (man′hůd) *n.* **1** the condition or time of being a man. **2** courage; manliness. **3** men as a group: *the manhood of Canada.* **—Syn. 2** virility, bravery.

man-hour (man′our′) *n.* an hour of work done by one man, used as a time unit in industry.

man·hunt (man′hunt′) *n.* an organized hunt for a criminal, escaped convict, etc.

ma·ni·a (mā′nē ə) *n.* **1** a form or phase of mental disorder, extremes of joy or rage, uncontrolled and often violent activity, extravagant and irregular speech, etc., often followed by depression, as in manic-depressive psychosis. **2** an excessive and abnormal fondness; craze. [< L < Gk. *mania* madness]

ma·ni·ac (mā′nē ak′) *n.* **1** a person affected by mania (def. 1). **2** a person having a mania (def. 2). *—adj.* insane, raving.

ma·ni·a·cal (mə nī′ə kəl) *adj.* **1** insane; raving. **2** of or characteristic of mania or a maniac. **—ma·ni′a·cal·ly,** *adv.*

ma·nic (man′ik or mā′nik) *adj.* **1** of or like mania. **2** suffering from mania.

man·ic-de·pres·sive (man′ik di pres′iv) *adj.* having alternating attacks of mania and depression: *manic-depressive psychosis.* *—n.* a person who has such attacks.

man·i·cure (man′ə kūr′) *v.* **-cured, -cur·ing,** *n.* *—v.* care for the fingernails and hands; trim, clean, and polish the fingernails. *—n.* **1** the care of the hands and fingernails. **2** a treatment for the hands and fingernails: *She went to the beauty parlor for a manicure.* **3** a manicurist. [< F < L *manus* hand + *cura* care]

hat, āge, cãre, fär; let, ēqual, tėrm; it, īce
hot, ōpen, ôrder; oil, out; cup, půt, rüle, ūse
əbove, takən, pencəl, lemən, circəs
ch, child; ng, long; sh, ship
th, thin; ᴛʜ, then; zh, measure

man·i·cur·ist (man′ə kūr′ist) *n.* a person whose work is manicuring.

man·i·fest (man′ə fest′) *adj.* apparent to the eye or to mind; plain; clear: *His guilt was manifest.*
—v. **1** show plainly; reveal; display. **2** prove; put beyond doubt. **3 a** record (an item) in a ship's manifest. **b** present the manifest of (a ship's cargo).
—n. **1** a list of a ship's cargo. **2** a list of passengers, freight, etc. on an airplane flight. **3** a bill of lading. [< L *manifestus* palpable, near at hand; ult. < *manus* hand] **—man′i·fest′ly,** *adv.* **—man′i·fest·ness,** *n.* **—Syn.** *adj.* obvious, evident, unmistakable. *—v.* **1** exhibit, disclose.

man·i·fes·ta·tion (man′ə fes tā′shən) *n.* **1** a manifesting. **2** a being manifested. **3** something that manifests: *A brave deed is a manifestation of courage.* **4** a public demonstration. **5** an occurrence or occasion in which a spiritualistic materialization is supposed to be demonstrated: *No manifestation occurred at the first séance.*

man·i·fes·to (man′ə fes′tō) *n.* **·toes.** a public declaration of intentions, purposes, or motives by an important person or group; proclamation. [< Ital.]

man·i·fold (man′ə fōld′) *adj.* **1** of many kinds; many and various. **2** having many parts or forms. **3** doing many things at the same time.
—n. **1** a pipe with several openings for connection with other pipes. **2** a pipe in an internal-combustion engine, connecting the cylinders with a main inlet or outlet. **3** one of many copies.
—v. **1** make many copies of. **2** make manifold; multiply. [OE *manigfeald*] **—Syn.** *adj.* **1** varied.

man·i·kin (man′ə kin) *n.* **1** a little man; dwarf. **2** a mannequin. Also, **mannikin.** [< Du. *manneken*, dim. of *man* man]

ma·nil·a or **ma·nil·la** (mə nil′ə) *n.* **1** Manila hemp. **2** Manila paper. **3** Manila rope. [< *Manila*, the capital of Philippines]

Manila hemp a strong fibre made from the leaves of a Philippine banana plant, used for making ropes and fabrics.

Manila paper a strong, brown or brownish-yellow wrapping paper.

Manila rope a strong rope made from Manila hemp.

man in the street the average person.

man·i·oc (man′ē ok′ or mā′nē ok′) *n.* cassava. [< Sp., Pg. < Tupi-Guarani *manioca*]

ma·nip·u·late (mə nip′yů lāt′) *v.* **·lat·ed, -lat·ing. 1** handle or treat skilfully; handle: *The driver of an automobile manipulates levers and pedals.* **2** manage by clever use of personal influence, especially unfair influence: *He so manipulated the ball team that he was elected captain.* **3** change for one's own purpose or advantage: *The book-keeper manipulated the company's accounts to conceal his theft.* [back formation < *manipulation*] **—ma·nip′u·la′tor,** *n.*

ma·nip·u·la·tion (mə nip′yů lā′shən) *n.* **1** skilful handling or treatment. **2** clever use of influence. **3** a change made for one's own purpose or advantage. [< F, ult. < L *manipulus* handful < *manus* hand + root of *plere* to fill]

ma·nip·u·la·tive (mə nip′yů lə tiv or mə nip′yů lā′tiv) *adj.* **1** of or having to do with manipulation. **2** done by manipulation.

man·i·to (man′ə tō′) *n.* **-tos.** manitou.

Man·i·to·ba maple (man′ə tō′bə) a variety of maple tree common in western Canada; box elder.

Man·i·to·ban (man′ə tō′bən) *adj.* of or having to do with Manitoba or its people. *—n.* a native or permanent resident of Manitoba.

man·i·tou or **man·i·tu** (man′ə tü′) *n.* the spirit worshipped by Algonquian Indians as a force of nature. The Manitou is the Great Spirit. [< Algonquian]

man·kind (man′kīnd′ *for 1*; man′kīnd′ *for 2*) *n.* **1** the human race; all human beings. 2 men collectively, as opposed to womankind.

man·like (man′līk′) *adj.* 1 like a man. 2 suitable for a man.

man·ly (man′lē) *adj.* **-li·er, -li·est.** 1 like a man; as a man should be; strong, frank, brave, noble, independent, and honorable. 2 suitable for a man; masculine. **—man′li·ness,** *n.* **—Syn. 1** See **male.**

man·na (man′ə) *n.* 1 in the Bible, the food that miraculously fell from heaven to the Israelites when they were starving in the wilderness. Exod. 16:14-36. 2 food for the soul. 3 a much-needed thing that is unexpectedly supplied. [ME < LL < Gk. < Hebrew *man*]

man·ne·quin (man′ə kin) *n.* 1 a model of a human figure, on which to shape or display clothes, used by tailors, stores, etc. 2 a woman whose work is wearing new clothes to show them to potential customers; model. Also, **manikin.** [< F < Du. *manneken.* See MANIKIN.]

man·ner (man′ər) *n.* 1 the way something happens or is done: *The trouble arose in a curious manner.* 2 a way of acting or behaving: *a kind manner.* 3 **manners,** *pl.* **a** ways of behaving: *good manners, bad manners.* **b** polite ways of behaving. **c** customs; ways of living: *a comedy of manners.* 4 kind or kinds: *We saw all manner of birds in the forest. What manner of person was he?* 5 **by all manner of means,** most certainly. 6 **by no manner of means,** not at all; under no circumstances. 7 **in a manner of speaking,** as one might say. 8 **to the manner born,** accustomed since birth to some way or condition. [ME < AF *manere* < L *manuaria,* fem. of *manuarius* belonging to the hand, ult. < *manus* hand] **—Syn. 1** mode, fashion. See **way.** 2 bearing, demeanoı, deportment.

man·nered (man′ərd) *adj.* 1 having manners of a certain kind: *a well-mannered child.* 2 affected; artificial; having many mannerisms.

man·ner·ism (man′ər iz′əm) *n.* 1 too much use of some manner in speaking, writing, or behaving. 2 an odd little trick; a queer habit; a peculiar way of acting. 3 **Mannerism,** in art and architecture, a style developed in Europe during the late 16th century, marked by the use of distortion and exaggeration as a conscious revolt against the classical principles of the Renaissance. **—Syn. 1** affectation. 2 peculiarity.

man·ner·ist (man′ər ist) *n.* 1 an artist, musician, or anyone given to mannerisms. 2 Often, **Mannerist.** an artist whose work is characterized by Mannerism.

man·ner·less (man′ər lis) *adj.* having bad manners.

man·ner·ly (man′ər lē) *adj.* having or showing good manners; polite. *—adv.* politely. **—man′ner·li·ness,** *n.* **—Syn.** *adj.* courteous, civil, well-behaved.

man·ni·kin (man′ə kin) *n.* manikin.

man·nish (man′ish) *adj.* 1 peculiar to a man: *a mannish way of holding a baby.* 2 imitating a man: *a mannish style of dress.* **—man′nish·ly,** *adv.* **—man′nish·ness,** *n.*

ma·noeu·vra·bil·i·ty or **ma·neu·ver·a·bil·i·ty** (mə nü′vrə bil′ə tē or mə nü′və rə bil′ə tē′) *n.* the quality of being manoeuverable.

ma·noeu·vre (mə nü′vər) *n. v.* **-vred** or **-vring.** *—n.* 1 a planned movement of troops or warships: *The army practises warfare by holding manoeuvres.* 2 a skilful plan; clever trick: *His superior manoeuvres won the game.* *—v.* 1 perform manoeuvres. 2 cause to perform manoeuvres. 3 plan skilfully; use clever tricks: *A scheming person is always manoeuvring for some advantage.* 4 force by skilful plans; get by clever tricks: *She manoeuvred her mother into letting her have a party.* Also, **maneuver.** [< F *manoeuvre,* ult. < L *manu operare* work by hand] **—ma·noeu′vra·ble** or **ma·noeu′ver·a·ble,** *adj.*

Man of Galilee Jesus.

man of God 1 a holy man; saint; prophet. 2 a clergyman.

man of letters 1 a writer. 2 a person who has a wide knowledge of literature.

man of straw an imaginary person whose arguments can easily be proved wrong.

man of the world a man who has a wide knowledge of people and customs, and is tolerant of both.

man-of-war (man′əv wôr′) *n.* **men-of-war.** a warship of a type used in former times.

ma·nom·e·ter (mə nom′ə tər) *n.* 1 an instrument for measuring the pressure of gases or vapors. 2 an instrument for measuring blood pressure. [< F < Gk. *manos* thin + *metron* measure]

man·o·met·ric (man′ə met′rik) *adj.* 1 having to do with a manometer. 2 having to do with the measurement of gas pressures.

man on horseback a military leader whose influence over the people threatens the government.

man·or (man′ər) *n.* 1 in the Middle Ages, a feudal estate, part of which was set aside for the lord and the rest divided among his peasants. If the lord sold his manor, the peasants or serfs were sold with it. 2 a large holding of land. 3 a large house on an estate, especially a manor house. [ME < AF *maner* < L *manere* stay]

manor house the house of the owner of a manor.

ma·no·ri·al (mə nô′rē əl) *adj.* 1 of a manor. 2 forming a manor.

man·pow·er (man′pou′ər) *n.* 1 the power supplied by the physical work of men. 2 strength thought of in terms of the number of men needed or available. Also, **man power.**

man·sard (man′särd) *n.* 1 a roof with two slopes on each side. 2 the storey under such a roof. [after François *Mansard* (1598-1666), a French architect]

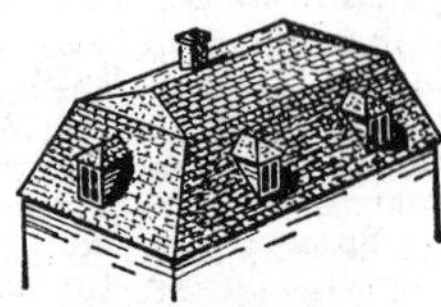

A mansard roof

manse (mans) *n.* a minister's house; parsonage. [ME < Med.L *mansa* dwelling, n. use of fem. pp. of L *manere* stay]

man·serv·ant (man′sėr′vənt) *n.* **men·serv·ants.** a male servant.

man·sion (man′shən) *n.* a large house; stately residence. [ME < OF < L *mansio, -onis* < *manere* stay]

man-sized (man′sīzd′) *adj.* 1 suited to a man; large: *a man-sized meal.* 2 *Informal.* requiring the strength, skill, judgment, etc. of a mature man: *a man-sized problem.*

man·slaugh·ter (man′slo′tər or -slô′tər) *n.* 1 the killing of a human being. 2 in law, the unpremeditated killing of a human being, as under sudden provocation: *The charge against the prisoner was changed from murder to manslaughter.*

man·tel (man′təl) *n.* 1 a shelf above a fireplace, with its supports. 2 the shelf. *—adj.* made to rest on such a shelf or similar surface: *a mantel radio.* [var. of *mantle*]

man·tel·et (man′təl et′ or mant′lit) *n.* 1 a short mantle or cape. 2 formerly, a large movable shelter, shield, or screen, used in war to protect soldiers firing a gun.

man·tel·piece (man′təl pēs′) *n.* a mantel (def. 2).

man·til·la (man til′ə or man tē′yə; *Spanish,* män tēl′yə) *n.* 1 a lace or silk veil or scarf covering the hair and falling down over the shoulders, worn especially by Spanish and Spanish-American women. 2 a short mantle or cape. [< Sp. < L *mantellum* mantle]

man·tis (man′tis) *n.* an insect that holds its forelegs doubled up as if praying. [< NL use of Gk. *mantis* prophet (from its praying posture)]

man·tis·sa (man tis′ə) *n.* in mathematics, the decimal part of a logarithm. In the logarithm 2.95424, the characteristic is 2 and the mantissa is .95424. [< L *mantissa* addition < Etruscan]

man·tle (man′təl) *n. v.* **-tled, -tling.** *—n.* 1 a loose cloak without sleeves. 2 anything that covers like a mantle: *The hill was wreathed in a mantle of snow.* 3 a lacelike tube around a flame that gets so hot that it glows and gives light. 4 that part of the earth between the outer crust and the core, about 1,800 miles thick. See **core** for diagram. *—v.* 1 cover with a mantle. 2 cover; conceal. 3 redden: *Her cheek mantled.* 4 become covered with a coating or scum: *The pond has mantled.* [OE *mentel* < L *mantellum* and < OF *mantel* < L *mantellum*]

man-to-man (man′tə man′) *adj.* 1 honest; sincere;

straightforward. **2** in certain sports, referring to a defence system in which players do not guard zones but cover individual opponents. *—adv.* honestly; sincerely.

man·tu·a (man′chü ə) *n.* **1** a loose gown or cloak formerly worn by women. **2** a mantle. [< *Mantua,* a town in Italy]

man·u·al (man′ū əl) *adj.* of the hands; done with the hands: *manual labor.* *—n.* **1** a small book that helps its readers to understand or use something; handbook. **2** in an organ, a keyboard played with the hands. [< L *manualis* < *manus* hand]

man·u·al·ly (man′ū əl ē) *adv.* **1** by hand; with the hands. **2** with respect to hand work.

manual training training in work done with the hands; practice in various arts and crafts, especially in making things out of wood.

man·u·fac·to·ry (man′yů fak′tə rē) *n.* **-ries.** a factory.

man·u·fac·ture (man′yů fak′chər) *v.* **-tured, -tur·ing,** *n.* *—v.* **1** make by hand or by machine: *This factory manufactures outboard motors.* **2** make into something useful: *Iron is manufactured into steel.* **3** invent; make up: *The dishonest lawyer manufactured evidence.* [< n.] *—n.* **1** the act of manufacturing. **2** the thing manufactured. [< F < Med.L *manufactura* < L *manu facere* make by hand]

man·u·fac·tur·er (man′yů fak′chər ər) *n.* a person whose business is manufacturing; owner of a factory.

man·u·mis·sion (man′yů mish′ən) *n.* **1** a freeing from slavery. **2** a being freed from slavery. [< L *manumissio, -onis*]

man·u·mit (man′yů mit′) *v.* **-mit·ted, -mit·ting.** set free from slavery. [< L *manu mittere* release from control]

ma·nure (mə nür′ or mə nūr′) *n. v.* **-nured, -nur·ing.** *—n.* any substance put in or on the soil as fertilizer: *The cleanings from a stable are a kind of manure.* [< v.] *—v.* put manure in or on. [ME < AF *maynoverer* work with the hands < OF *manuevre* hand-work (in F *manoeuvre*). See MANOEUVRE.] **—ma·nur′er,** *n.*

man·u·script (man′yů skript′) *n.* **1** a book or paper written by hand or with a typewriter. **2** handwritten or typewritten condition: *His last book was three years in manuscript.* **3** a book, document, etc. written by hand before the introduction of printing.*—adj.* written by hand or with a typewriter. *Abbrev.*: MS., MS, ms., or ms [< Med.L < L *manu scriptus* written by hand]

Manx (mangks) *adj.* of the Isle of Man, its people, or their language. *—n.* **1** the people of the Isle of Man. **2** their Celtic language.

☛ **Manx,** meaning the people of the Isle of Man, is plural in use: *The Manx are hard-working people. Manx,* meaning the language of these people, is singular in use: *Manx is now extinct.*

Manx cat **1** a breed of medium-sized cat that is tail-less and has a thick undercoat and a longer-haired outer coat. **2** a cat of this breed.

Manx·man (mangks′mən) *n.* **-men** (-mən). a native of the Isle of Man.

man·y (men′ē) *adj.* **more, most,** *n.* *—adj.* a large number of; numerous: *many people, many years ago.* *—n.* **1** a large number of people or things: *There were many at the fair.* **2 a good many,** a fairly large number. **3 a great many,** a very large number. **4 one too many for,** more than a match for. **5 the many, a** most people. **b** the common people. [OE *manig*]

Syn. *adj.* **Many, innumerable** = consisting of a large number. **Many** is the general word: *Were many people there?* **Innumerable** means more than can be counted, or so many that counting would be very hard: *The sands of the desert are innumerable.*

man·y·plies (men′ē plīz′) *n.* the third stomach of a cow or other ruminant; omasum. [< *many* + *plies,* pl. of *ply,* n.]

man·y-sid·ed (men′ē sīd′id) *adj.* **1** having many sides. **2** having many interests or abilities.

man·za·ni·ta (man′zə nē′tə) *n.* **1** any of various evergreen shrubs or trees of the heath family that grows in western North America, such as the bearberry. **2** the fruit of any of these plants. [< Sp. *manzanita,* dim. of *manzana* apple]

Ma·o·ri (mou′rē or mä′ō rē) *n.* **-ris,** *adj.* *—n.* **1** the native brown-skinned people of New Zealand. **2** a member of this people. **3** their language. *—adj.* of or having to do with the Maoris or their Polynesian language.

map (map) *n. v.* **mapped, map·ping.** *—n.* **1** a drawing

hat, āge, cãre, fär; let, ēqual, tėrm; it, īce
hot, ōpen, ôrder; oil, out; cup, pût, rüle, ūse
əbove, takən, pencəl, lemən, circəs
ch, child; ng, long; sh, ship
th, thin; ᴛʜ, then; zh, measure

representing the earth's surface or part of it, usually showing countries, cities, rivers, seas, lakes, and mountains. **2** a drawing representing part of the sky, showing the position of the stars. **3** a maplike drawing of anything: *a highway map, a road map.* **4 off the map,** *Informal.* of no importance; of no account. **5 put on the map,** *Informal.* give prominence to; make well-known. *—v.* **1** make a map of; show on a map. **2** plan; arrange in detail: *map out the week's work.* [< Med.L *mappa mundi* map of the world (< L *mappa* napkin)]

Syn. *n.* **1 Map, chart** = a drawing representing a surface or area. **Map** applies particularly to a representation of some part of the earth's surface or an area of land, showing relative geographical positions, shape, size, etc. of certain places or features: *A map of a city shows streets and parks.* **Chart,** as contrasted with *map,* applies to a map used especially in sea or air navigation, showing deep and shallow places, islands, channels, etc. in a body of water, or air currents, air lanes, etc.: *The reef that the ship struck is marked on the chart.*

ma·ple (mā′pəl) *n.* **1** a tree grown for its shade, its wood, or its sap. There are many kinds of maples, but all have dry fruits with two wings and opposite leaves without stipules. **2** its hard, light-colored wood. **3** a flavoring made from maple sugar or maple syrup: *She liked maple ice cream.* [OE *mapeltrēow* maple tree] **—ma′ple-like′,** *adj.*

maple leaf **1** a leaf of the maple tree. **2** this leaf as a Canadian emblem. A red maple leaf on a white background is in the centre of the Canadian flag. The song "The Maple Leaf Forever" was written in 1867 by Alexander Muir.

maple sugar sugar made from the sap of the sugar maple.

maple syrup syrup made from the sap of the sugar maple.

Ma·quis (mä kē′) *n.* **Maquis. 1** the French underground resistance movement against the Germans in World War II. **2** a member of, or a guerrilla fighter in, this movement. **3** an underground resistance movement in Algeria. *—adj.* of or having to do with the Maquis or their tactics. [< F < *maquis* bushy land < Ital. *macchia* thicket; with reference to the cover bandits take in bushy regions]

mar (mär) *v.* **marred, mar·ring.** spoil the beauty of; damage; injure. [OE *merran* waste] **—Syn.** disfigure.

mar. **1** married. **2** marine. **3** maritime.

Mar. March.

mar·a·bou (mar′ə bü′) *n.* **1** a kind of large stork common in Africa and Asia. **2** a furlike trimming made from its soft, downy feathers. [< F]

ma·ra·ca (mə rä′kə or mə rak′ə) *n.* a percussion instrument resembling a rattle, consisting of a gourd or gourd-shaped body containing seeds or pebbles and attached to a handle, usually played in pairs. [< Pg.]

mar·a·schi·no (mar′ə shē′nō or mar′ə skē′nō) *n.* a strong, sweet alcoholic drink made from a kind of small black cherry. [< Ital. *maraschino* < *marasca* shortened form of *amarasca* a sour cherry, ult. < L *amarus* sour]

maraschino cherries cherries preserved in a syrup flavored with maraschino.

mar·a·thon (mar′ə thon′ or mer′ə thon′) *n.* **1** a foot race of 26 miles, 385 yards. It was introduced in 1896 with the revival of the Olympic games, in memory of the runner who carried the news to Athens that the Athenians had defeated the Persians in the battle of Marathon (490 B.C.). **2** any long race or contest.

ma·raud (mə rod′ or mə rôd′) *v.* go about in search of plunder; make raids for booty. [< F *marauder* < *maraud* rascal] **—ma·raud′er,** *n.*

mar·ble (mär′bəl) *n. adj. v.* **-bled, -bling.** *—n.* **1** a hard limestone, white or colored, capable of taking a beautiful polish. **2** a small ball of clay, glass, stone, etc. used in games. **3 marbles,** *pl.* **a** a game played with these marbles. **b** a collection of marble sculptures. **4 lose one's marbles,** *Slang.* go crazy; become insane.

—*adj.* **1** made of marble. **2** like marble; white, hard, cold, or unfeeling.
—*v.* color in imitation of the patterns in marble: *Binders marble the edges of some books.* [ME < OF *marbre* < L *marmor* < Gk. *marmaros* gleaming stone] —**mar′ble-like′**, *adj.*
☛ Marbles, the game (def. 3a), is plural in form and singular in use: *Marbles is played by many boys.*

mar·ca·site (mär′kə sīt′) *n.* **1** a native iron disulphide, white iron pyrites, similar to and of the same composition as ordinary pyrites: *Marcasite is often used in jewellery. Formula*: FeS_2 **2** a piece of jewellery made from this material. [< Med.L *marcasita* < Arabic *marqashita* < Aramaic]

mar·cel (mär sel′) *n. v.* **-celled, -cel·ling.** —*n.* a series of regular waves put in the hair. —*v.* put a series of regular waves in (the hair). [after *Marcel*, a French hairdresser of the 19th century]

march[1] (märch) *v.* **1** walk as soldiers do, in time and with steps of the same length. **2** walk or proceed steadily. **3** cause to march or go: *The policeman marched the thief off to jail.* **4** advance; progress.
—*n.* **1** the movement of troops: *The army is prepared for the march.* **2** the act or fact of marching. **3** in music: **a** a composition to march to, having a regular, strongly accented metre, usually in 4/4 time. **b** any composition or part of a composition having similar characteristics: *He enjoyed listening to marches.* **4** the distance marched. **5** a long, hard walk. **6** advance; progress: *History records the march of events.* **7 on the march,** moving forward; advancing. **8 steal a march on,** gain an advantage over without being noticed. [< F *marcher*, earlier, to trample, ult. < LL *marcus* hammer < L *marculus* small hammer] —**march′er**, *n.*

march[2] (märch) *n.* **1** the land along the border of a country; frontier. **2 the Marches,** *pl.* the districts along the border between England and Scotland, or between England and Wales. [ME < OF *marche* < Gmc.]

March (märch) *n.* the third month of the year. It has 31 days. [ME < OF *marche* < L *Martius* (month) of Mars]

mar·chion·ess (mär′shən is or mär′shən es′) *n.* **1** the wife or widow of a marquis. **2** a woman with a rank equal to that of a marquis. [< Med.L *marchionissa* < *marchio* marquis < *marcha, marca* march[2] < Gmc.]

march·pane (märch′pān′) *n.* marzipan.

march·past (märch′past′) *n.* a display, especially a military parade, in which troops, etc. march past a reviewing stand.

Mar·di gras (mär′dē grä′) the last day before Lent; Shrove Tuesday. [< F *mardi gras* fat (that is, meat-eating) Tuesday]

mare (mãr) *n.* a female horse, donkey, etc. [OE *mere*]

mare's-nest (mãrz′nest′) *n.* **1** something supposed to be a great discovery that turns out to be a mistake or joke. **2** *Informal.* a situation that is disordered or confused.

mare's-tail (mãrz′tāl′) *n.* **1** a water plant having many circles of narrow, hairlike leaves around the stems. **2** horse-tail, the plant. **3** a high, white, filmy cloud, shaped somewhat like a horse's tail.

mar·ga·rin (mär′jə rin) *n.* margarine.

mar·ga·rine (mär′jə rin or mär′jə rēn′) *n.* a compound of vegetable oils, used for cooking or as a spread, often as a substitute for butter; oleomargarine. [< F]

marge[1] (märj) *n. Poetic.* an edge; border. [< F]

marge[2] (märj) *n. Informal.* margarine.

mar·gin (mär′jən) *n.* **1** an edge; border: *the margin of a lake.* **2** the blank space around the writing or printing on a page. **3** the space left at the left-hand side, or sometimes on both sides, by a person writing or typing. **4** an extra amount; amount beyond what is necessary; difference: *We allow a margin of 15 minutes when we want to catch a train.* **5** the difference between the cost and selling price of stocks, etc. **6** in finance: **a** the money or security deposited with a broker to protect him from loss on contracts undertaken for the real buyer or seller. **b** the amount of such a deposit. **c** the transaction itself, financed by both the broker and his customer: *When you buy on margin, you put up only part of the total cost and the broker lends you the remainder.* **d** the customer's profit or loss in such a transaction. **7** the point at which an economic activity yields just enough return to cover its costs and below which the activity will result in a loss. **8** a condition beyond which something ceases to exist or be possible; limit: *the margin of subsistence, the margin of consciousness.*
—*v.* **1** provide with a margin. **2** in finance: **a** deposit a margin upon (stock, etc.). **b** secure by a margin. [ME < L *margo, -ginis* edge]

mar·gin·al (mär′jə nəl) *adj.* **1** written or printed in a margin. **2** of a margin. **3** on or near the margin. Marginal land is barely fit for farming. **4** relatively slight: *of marginal importance.* **5** existing or occurring on the fringes of anything established; only partly taken in: *a marginal culture.* **6 a** barely producing or capable of producing goods, crops, etc. at a rate necessary to cover the costs of production. **b** of, having to do with, or obtained from goods that are so produced and marketed. **7** in sociology, only partially assimilated in a social group.

mar·gin·al·ly (mär′jə nəl ē) *adv.* in the margin.

mar·grave (mär′grāv) *n.* **1** the title of certain princes of the Holy Roman Empire. **2** a German nobleman whose rank corresponds to that of a marquis. **3** formerly, a German military governor of a border province. [< MDu. *markgrave* count of the marches]

mar·gra·vine (mär′grə vēn′) *n.* the wife or widow of a margrave.

mar·gue·rite (mär′gə rēt′) *n.* a kind of daisy having white petals and a yellow centre. [< F < L < Gk. *margaritēs* pearl]

mar·i·gold (mar′ə gōld′ or mer′ə gōld′) *n.* **1** a plant of the aster family having yellow, orange, or red flowers. **2** the flower of this plant. [< (the Virgin) *Mary* + *gold*]

mar·i·jua·na or **mar·i·hua·na** (mar′ə wä′nə) *n.* **1** a kind of hemp. **2** a narcotic made from its dried leaves and flowers. [< Mexican Sp. *mariguana, marihuana*]

ma·rim·ba (mə rim′bə) *n.* a musical instrument resembling a xylophone. [< Bantu]

ma·ri·na (mə rē′nə) *n.* a place on a waterfront where boats may be moored and where fuel and equipment may be bought: *It is often possible to buy boats and motors at a marina.* [< Ital. *marina* shore, coast < L *marina.* See MARINE.]

mar·i·nade (*n.* mar′ə nād′; *v.* mar′ə nād′) *n. v.* **-nad·ed, -nad·ing.** —*n.* **1** a spiced vinegar or wine in which meat, fish, etc. are soaked to gain added flavor before being cooked. **2** meat or fish soaked in such vinegar or wine. —*v.* marinate. [< F *marinade* < *mariner* marinate]

mar·i·nate (mar′ə nāt′) *v.* **-nat·ed, -nat·ing.** **1** soak in brine or marinade. **2** soak in oil and vinegar. [< F *mariner* < *marin* marine]

ma·rine (mə rēn′) *adj.* **1** of the sea; found in the sea; produced by the sea: *Whales are marine animals.* **2** of or having to do with shipping; maritime: *marine law.* **3** of or having to do with a navy; naval: *marine power.* **4** for use at sea, on a ship, etc.: *marine supplies, a marine engine.* **5** in nautical use: **a** of or having to do with ships, sailors, etc.: *marine lore.* **b** of or having to do with navigation at sea: *a marine compass.*
—*n.* **1** shipping; a fleet: *our merchant marine.* **2** a soldier formerly serving only at sea, now also participating in land and air action: *Canada has no marines.* **3** a picture showing a sea scene. [< F < L *marina*, fem. < *mare* sea]

mar·i·ner (mar′ə nər) *n.* a sailor; seaman; one who navigates a ship. [ME < AF *mariner* < OF *marin* < L *marinus* < *mare* sea]

A marionette. One set of strings moves his legs, the other his arms, head, and body. The operator stays out of sight of the audience, behind or above the stage.

mar·i·o·nette (mar′ē ə net′ or mer′ē ə net′) *n.* a small doll or puppet made to imitate a person or animal and moved by strings or the hands. A marionette show is often given on a miniature stage. [< F *marionette*, ult. < *Marie* Mary]

Mar·i·po·sa lily (mar′ə pō′sə or mar′ə pō′zə) **1** a plant having tuliplike flowers and growing in western North America. 2 the flower of this plant. [< Sp. *mariposa* butterfly]

mar·i·tal (mar′ə təl) *adj.* 1 of or having to do with marriage: *A man and woman take marital vows when they marry.* 2 of or having to do with a husband: *Providing for one's wife is a marital obligation.* [< L *maritalis* < *maritus* married man] —**mar′i·tal·ly,** *adv.*

mar·i·time (mar′ə tīm′ or mer′ə tīm′) *adj.* 1 on or near the sea: *Halifax is a maritime city.* 2 living near the sea: *Many maritime peoples are fishermen.* 3 of the sea; having to do with shipping and sailing: *Ships and sailors are governed by maritime law.* 4 **Maritime,** of or having to do with the Maritime Provinces. [< L *maritimus* < *mare* sea] —**Syn. 3** nautical.

Maritime Provinces the provinces on the eastern seaboard of Canada, especially New Brunswick, Nova Scotia, and Prince Edward Island.

Mar·i·tim·er (mar′ə tīm′ər or mer′ə tīm′ər) *n.* a person born in or living in the Maritime Provinces.

Mar·i·times (mar′ə tīmz′ or mer′ə tīmz′) *n.* the Maritime Provinces.

mar·jo·ram (mär′jə rəm) *n.* a fragrant plant of the same family as mint. [ME < OF *majorane* < Med.L *majorana, majoraca,* ? < L *amaracus* < Gk.]

mark[1] (märk) *n.* 1 a trace or impression made by some object on the surface of another. A line, dot, spot, stain, or scar is a mark. 2 a line, dot, etc. to show position. The line where a race starts is the mark. 3 something that shows what or whose a thing is; sign; indication. 4 a written or printed stroke or sign: *punctuation marks.* 5 a grade or rating. 6 a cross made by a person who cannot write his name. 7 something to be aimed at; target; goal. 8 what is usual, proper, or expected; standard: *A tired person does not feel up to the mark.* 9 influence; impression: *A great man leaves his mark on whatever he does.* 10 a tag with a mark on it: *Remove the price mark from your new suit.* 11 *Informal.* a person who is an easy prey for pickpockets, tricksters, etc.; sucker; gull. 12 *Archaic.* a border or frontier. 13 in the Middle Ages, a tract of land held in common by a community.
beside the mark, a not hitting the thing aimed at. **b** not to the point; not relevant.
hit the mark, a succeed in doing what one tried to do. **b** be exactly right.
make one's mark, succeed; become famous.
miss the mark, a fail to do what one tried to do. **b** be not exactly right.
of mark, important; famous.
wide of the mark, a missing the thing aimed at by a considerable margin. **b** irrelevant.
—*v.* 1 give grades to; rate. 2 make a mark or marks; put a mark or marks on. 3 trace or form by marks or as if by marks. 4 show by a mark or marks. 5 show clearly; manifest: *A frown marked her displeasure.* 6 distinguish; set off: *Many important inventions mark the last 150 years.* 7 pay attention to; notice; observe: *Mark well my words; his plan will fail.* 8 keep (the score); record. 9 put a price mark on; tag.
mark down, a write down; note down. **b** mark for sale at a lower price.
mark off or **out,** make lines, etc. to show the position of or to separate.
mark out for, set aside for; select for.
mark time, a move the feet as in marching, but remaining in the same spot. **b** suspend progress temporarily. **c** go through the motions without accomplishing anything.
mark up, a make marks on: *Don't mark up the desks.* **b** mark for sale at a higher price. [OE *mearc*]
Syn. *n.* **3 Mark, sign, token** = an indication of something not visible or readily apparent. **Mark** particularly suggests an indication of the character of the thing: *Generosity is often a mark of greatness.* **Sign** is the general word, applying to any indication, mark, or token, such as of a quality, idea, mental or physical state, etc.: *We could see no sign of life.* **Token** applies especially to something that stands as a reminder or promise of something else, such as of a feeling, event, etc.: *This gift is a token of my love.* -*v.* 7 note, heed, regard, consider.

mark[2] (märk) *n.* 1 a unit of money in Germany. The mark of West Germany (*Deutsche mark*) is worth 30 cents. The mark of East Germany is worth about 45 cents. 2 a coin or note worth one mark. [< G]

marked (märkt) *adj.* 1 having a mark or marks on it. 2 very noticeable; very clear; easily recognized: *There is a marked difference between a grape and an orange.*

hat, āge, cãre, fär; let, ēqual, tėrm; it, īce
hot, ōpen, ôrder; oil, out; cup, pu̇t, rüle, ūse
əbove, takən, pencəl, lemən, circəs
ch, child; ng, long; sh, ship
th, thin; ᴛʜ, then; zh, measure

mark·ed·ly (mär′kid lē) *adv.* in a marked manner or degree; conspicuously; noticeably; plainly.

marked man a person watched as an object of suspicion, hatred, or vengeance.

mark·er (mär′kər) *n.* 1 a person or thing that marks. 2 in games, a person or thing that keeps the score. 3 a bookmark.

mar·ket (mär′kit) *n.* 1 a meeting of people for buying and selling. 2 the people so gathered. 3 a space or building in which provisions, cattle, etc. are shown for sale. 4 a store for the sale of provisions: *a meat market.* 5 trade, especially as regards a particular article: *the cotton market.* 6 the opportunity to buy or sell: *lose one's market.* 7 the demand (for goods): *There was not enough cheese to supply the market.* 8 the price offered: *a falling market.* 9 a region where goods can be sold: *Africa is a new market for many products.* 10 **be in the market for,** be a possible buyer of. 11 **play the market,** speculate on the stock exchange. 12 **price out of the market,** lose business by setting a price above that of competitors or above what buyers will pay: *The firm priced itself out of the market.* 13 **the market,** the stock market.
—*v.* 1 buy or sell in a market. 2 sell: *He cannot market the goods he makes.* 3 carry or send to market. [ME < ONF < L *mercatus* trade, ult. < *merx, mercis* merchandise] —**mar′ket·er,** *n.*

mar·ket·a·bil·i·ty (mär′kit ə bil′ə tē) *n.* the quality of being marketable.

mar·ket·a·ble (mär′kit ə bəl) *adj.* that can be sold.

market place 1 a place where a market is held. 2 the world of business and commerce.

market price the price that an article brings when sold; current price.

market value market price.

mark·ing (mär′king) *n.* 1 a mark or marks. 2 the arrangement of marks. 3 the act of grading students' work: *The teacher had a lot of marking to do.*

mark·ka (märk′kä) *n.* **-kaa** (-kä). 1 a unit of money in Finland. See table at **money.** 2 a coin worth one markka. [< Finnish]

marks·man (märks′mən) *n.* **-men** (-mən). a person who shoots; person who shoots well.

marks·man·ship (märks′mən ship′) *n.* skill in shooting.

mark·up (märk′up′) *n.* 1 an increase in the price of an article. 2 the amount of this increase. 3 the percentage or amount added to the cost to take care of profit and overhead when establishing the selling price of a commodity; the difference between the cost price and the selling price.

marl (märl) *n.* 1 soil containing clay and calcium carbonate, used in making cement and as a fertilizer. 2 *Poetic.* earth. [ME < OF *marle* < Med.L *margila* < L *marga,* probably < Celtic]

mar·lin (mär′lən) *n.* a large sea fish resembling a sailfish. [short for *marlinespike*]

mar·line (mär′lən) *n.* a small cord that sailors wind around the ends of a rope to keep it from fraying. [< Du. *marlijn* < *marren* tie + *lijn* line]

mar·line·spike or **mar·lin·spike** (mär′lən spīk′) *n.* a pointed iron implement used by sailors to separate strands of rope in splicing, etc.

mar·ma·lade (mär′mə lād′) *n.* a preserve resembling jam, made of oranges or other fruit. The peel is usually sliced and boiled with the fruit. [< F < Pg. *marmelada* < *marmelo* quince < L < Gk. *melimēlon* < *meli* honey + *mēlon* apple]

mar·mo·re·al (mär mô′rē əl) *adj.* **1** of marble. **2** like marble; cold; smooth; white. [< L *marmoreus* < *marmor* marble]

mar·mo·set (mär′mə set′ or mär′mə zet′) *n.* a very small, Central or South American monkey having soft, thick fur. [< OF *marmouset* grotesque figurine < *merme* under age < L *minimus* very small, influenced by Gk. *mormotos* fearful]

mar·mot (mär′mət) *n.* a rodent having a thick body and a bushy tail. Groundhogs or woodchucks, and prairie dogs are marmots. [< F *marmotte* < *marmottaine* < Med.L *mus* (*muris*) *montanus* mouse of the mountains]

mar·o·cain (mar′ə kān′) *n.* a crepelike dress fabric of silk woven with cotton or wool. [< F *marocain* relating to Morocco < *Maroc* Morocco]

ma·roon[1] (mə rün′) *n. adj.* dark brownish-red. [< F < Ital. *marrone* chestnut]

ma·roon[2] (mə rün′) *v.* **1** put (a person) ashore in a lonely place and leave him there: *Pirates used to maroon people on desert islands.* **2** leave in a lonely, helpless position. [< n.] —*n.* **1** a descendant of escaped Negro slaves living in the West Indies and Surinam. **2** an escaped Negro slave, an ancestor of these people. **3** a person who is marooned. [< F *marron*, ? < Sp. *cimarron* wild < *cimarra* bushes] —**ma·roon′er,** *n.*

mar·plot (mär′plot′) *n.* a person who spoils some plan by meddling or blundering.

marque (märk) *n.* the official permission from a government to capture enemy merchant ships. [< F < Provençal *marca* reprisal < *marcar* seize as a pledge, ult. < Gmc.]

mar·quee (mär kē′) *n.* **1** a large tent, often one put up for some outdoor entertainment. **2** a rooflike shelter over an entrance. [< F *marquise* (misunderstood as plural) < OF (*tente*) *marquise* a large tent for officers, literally, for a marquis]

mar·quess (mär′kwis) *n. Esp.Brit.* marquis.

mar·que·try (mär′kə trē) *n.* **-tries.** decoration made with thin pieces of wood, ivory, metal, etc. fitted together to form a design on furniture. [< F *marqueterie* < *marqueter* inlay < *marque* mark[1] < Gmc.]

mar·quis (mär′kwis) *n.* a nobleman ranking below a duke and above an earl or count. [ME < OF *marquis*, *marchis* < *marche* march[2] < Gmc.]

mar·quis·ate (mär′kwiz it) *n.* the position or rank of marquis.

mar·quise (mär kēz′) *n.* **1** the wife or widow of a marquis. **2** a woman equal in rank to that of a marquis. **3** a gem of a pointed oval shape, or a ring set with such a stone. **4** a marquee (def. 2). [< F *marquise*, fem. of *marquis*]

mar·qui·sette (mär′kə zet′ or mär′kwə zet′) *n.* a very thin fabric with square meshes, made of cotton, silk, rayon, nylon, etc. and often used for window draperies. [< F *marquisette*, dim. of *marquise* marquise]

mar·riage (mar′ij) *n.* **1** the state or condition of living together as husband and wife; married life: *We wished the bride and groom a happy marriage.* **2** the ceremony of being married; a marrying: a wedding. **3** a close union: *the marriage of words and melody.* [ME < OF *mariage* < *marier.* See MARRY[1].]

Syn. 1, 2 Marriage, matrimony, wedding = the state of being married or the act of marrying. **Marriage** is the general and common word applying to the institution, the legal and spiritual relation, the state of being married, or, less often, the ceremony. **Matrimony** is the formal and religious word, and applies especially to the spiritual relation or the religious ceremony (sacrament). **Wedding** is the common word for the ceremony or celebration.

mar·riage·a·bil·i·ty (mar′ij ə bil′ə tē) *n.* the state of being marriageable.

mar·riage·a·ble (mar′ij ə bəl) *adj.* fit for marriage; old enough to marry.

marriage portion a dowry.

mar·ried (mar′id) *adj.* **1** living together as husband and wife. **2** having a husband or wife. **3** of marriage; of husbands and wives. **4** closely united: *The painter was married to his art.*

married quarters housing provided for married members of the armed services.

mar·row[1] (mar′ō) *n.* **1** the soft tissue that fills the cavities of most bones. **2** the inmost or essential part: *He was chilled to the marrow.* [OE *mearg*]

mar·row[2] (mar′ō) *n.* an oblong vegetable of the squash family; vegetable marrow. Some marrows have a light-yellow skin when ripe.

mar·row·bone (mar′ō bōn′) *n.* **1** a bone containing marrow. **2 marrowbones,** *pl.* **a** knees. **b** crossbones.

mar·row·fat (mar′ō fat′) *n.* a kind of pea that has a large seed.

mar·ry[1] (mar′ē) *v.* **-ried, -ry·ing. 1** join as husband and wife: *The minister married them.* **2** take as husband or wife: *John planned to marry Grace.* **3** become married; take a husband or wife: *She married late in life.* **4** give in marriage: *He married his daughter to a young lawyer.* **5** unite closely. [ME < OF *marier* < L *maritare* < *maritus* husband, formed after *marita* woman with husband < *mas, mari-* a male]

mar·ry[2] (mar′ē) *interj. Archaic.* an exclamation showing surprise, indignation, etc. [< (the Virgin) *Mary*]

Mars (märz) *n.* **1** in Roman mythology, the god of war, son of Jupiter and Juno, identified with the Greek god Ares. **2** war. **3** in astronomy, the planet next beyond the earth and the fourth in order from the sun.

Mar·seil·laise (mär′sə lāz′) *n.* the national anthem of France, written in 1792 during the French Revolution. [< *Marseilles*, France; because first sung by a group of men from Marseilles]

mar·seilles (mär sālz′) *n.* a thick cotton cloth woven in figures or stripes, used for bedspreads, etc. [< *Marseilles*]

marsh (märsh) *n.* low land covered at times by water; soft, wet land; swamp. [OE *mersc* < *mere* lake] —**Syn.** bog.

mar·shal (mär′shəl) *n. v.* **-shalled** or **-shaled, -shal·ling** or **-shal·ing.** —*n.* **1** any of various kinds of officer: *a fire marshal.* **2** in certain armies, an officer of a high, or the highest, rank: *a field marshal.* **3** a person who arranges the order of march in a parade: *a parade marshal.* **4** a person in charge of events or ceremonies.
—*v.* **1** arrange in order: *He marshalled his facts well.* **2** conduct with ceremony: *We were marshalled before the king.* **3** arrange in military order; prepare for war. [ME < OF *mareschal* < LL *mariscalcus* groom < Gmc., literally, horse servant] —**mar′shal·ler** or **mar′shal·er,** *n.*

marsh gas a gas formed by the decomposition of organic substances in marshes; methane.

marsh·land (märsh′land′ or märsh′lənd) *n.* marshy land.

marsh mallow a plant having pink flowers and growing in marshy places.

marsh·mal·low (märsh′mal′ō or märsh′mel′ō) *n.* a soft, usually white, spongy candy, covered with powdered sugar. [OE *merscmealwe*; originally made from the root of the marsh mallow]

marsh marigold the cowslip.

marsh·y (mär′shē) *adj.* **marsh·i·er, marsh·i·est. 1** soft and wet like a marsh. **2** having many marshes. **3** of marshes. —**marsh′i·ness,** *n.*

mar·su·pi·al (mär sü′pē əl) *n.* a mammal that carries its young in a pouch. Kangaroos and opossums are marsupials. —*adj.* **1** of marsupials. **2** having a pouch for carrying the young.

mar·su·pi·um (mär sü′pē əm) *n.* **-pi·a** (-pē ə). a pouch or fold of skin on the abdomen of a female marsupial for carrying the young. [< L < Gk. *marsupion*, dim. of *marsipos* pouch]

mart (märt) *n.* a market; a centre of trade. [< Du. *markt* market]

Mar·tel·lo tower (mär tel′ō) a fort like a round tower, formerly built on coasts for defence against invasion. Also, **martello tower.** [< alteration (influenced by Ital. *martello* hammer) of Cape *Mortella*, Corsica, where such a tower was built]

mar·ten (mär′tən) *n.* **-tens** or (*esp. collectively*) **-ten. 1** a slender, carnivorous mammal like a weasel, but larger. **2** its valuable fur. **3** a coat or other garment made of this fur. [ME < Du. *martren* < OF *martrine*, ult. < Gmc.]

Mar·tha (mär′thə) *n.* **1** in the Bible, the sister of Lazarus and Mary. Luke 10: 38-42. **2** a practical woman who leads a busy, active life.

mar·tial (mär′shəl) *adj.* **1** of war; suitable for war: *martial music.* **2** fond of fighting; warlike; brave: *a man of martial spirit.* [ME < L *Martialis* < *Mars, Martis* Mars] **—mar′tial·ly,** *adv.* **—Syn. 1, 2 See military.**

martial law temporary rule by the army or militia with special military courts instead of by the usual civil authorities. Martial law is declared during a time of trouble or war.

Mar·tian (mär′shən) *adj.* of the planet Mars. *—n.* a supposed inhabitant of the planet Mars. [< L *Martius* of Mars]

mar·tin (mär′tən) *n.* a swallow having a short beak and a forked or square tail. [< F *Martin,* the bird being supposed to migrate at Martinmas]

mar·ti·net (mär′tə net′ or mär′tə net′) *n.* a person who enforces very strict discipline. [after Jean *Martinet,* a 17th-century French general]

mar·tin·gale (mär′tən gāl′) *n.* **1** the strap of a horse's harness that prevents the horse from rising on its hind legs or throwing back its head. **2** a rope or spar that steadies the jib boom on a ship. [< F *martingale,* ? ult. < *Martigues,* name of a town]

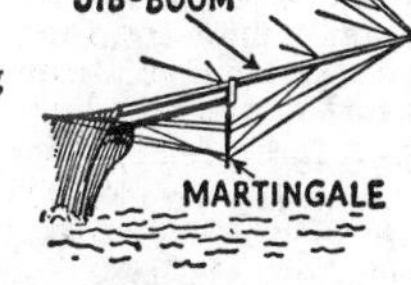

mar·ti·ni (mär tē′nē) *n.* a cocktail made of gin and dry vermouth. [< *Martini* and Rossi, vermouth and wine makers]

Mar·tin·mas (mär′tən məs) *n.* November 11, a Christian church festival in honor of Saint Martin.

mar·tyr (mär′tər) *n.* **1** a person who chooses to die or suffer rather than renounce his faith; a person who is put to death or made to suffer greatly for his religion or other beliefs. Many of the early Christians were martyrs. **2** a person who suffers great pain or anguish. **3** a person who puts on a false appearance of suffering in order to attract sympathy or attention.
—v. **1** put (a person) to death or torture because of his religion or other beliefs. **2** cause to suffer greatly; torture. [OE < L < Gk. *martyr* witness] **—mar′tyr·like′,** *adj.*

mar·tyr·dom (mär′tər dəm) *n.* **1** the death or suffering of a martyr. **2** great suffering; torment.

mar·vel (mär′vəl) *n. v.* **-velled** or **-veled, -vel·ling** or **-vel·ing.** *—n.* something wonderful; astonishing thing: *the marvels of science.* *—v.* be filled with wonder; be astonished: *She marvelled at the beautiful sunset.* [ME < OF *merveillier* < VL < L *mirabilia* wonders, ult. < *mirus* strange]

mar·vel·lous or **mar·vel·ous** (mär′vəl əs) *adj.* **1** wonderful; extraordinary. **2** improbable. **3** *Informal.* excellent; splendid; fine: *a marvellous time.*
—mar′vel·lous·ly or **mar′vel·ous·ly,** *adv.*
—mar′vel·lous·ness or **mar′vel·ous·ness,** *n.* **—Syn. 1** See **wonderful.**

Marx·i·an (märk′sē ən) *adj.* of or having to do with Karl Marx (1818-1883), a German writer on economics, or his theories. *—n.* a follower of Marx; believer in his theories.

Marx·ism (märk′siz əm) *n.* the political and economic theories of Karl Marx and Friedrich Engels, who interpreted history as a continuing economic class struggle and believed that the eventual result would be the establishment of a classless society and communal ownership of all natural and industrial resources.

Marx·ist (märk′sist) *n.* a follower or disciple of Karl Marx; a believer in Marxism. *—adj.* Marxian.

Mar·y (mãr′ē) *n.* in the Bible, the mother of Jesus. Matt. 1:18-25.

Mary Magdalene See **Magdalene.**

mar·zi·pan (mär′zə pan′) *n.* a confection of ground almonds and sugar, moulded into various forms. Also, **marchpane.** [< G < Ital. *marzapane,* a medieval coin < Arabic]

Ma·sai (mä sī′) *n.* **Ma·sai** or **Ma·sais. 1** a tribe of tall hunting and cattle-raising natives of East Africa. **2** a member of this tribe.

masc. masculine.

hat, āge, cãre, fär; let, ēqual, tėrm; it, īce
hot, ōpen, ôrder; oil, out; cup, pu̇t, rüle, ūse
əbove, takən, pencəl, lemən, circəs
ch, child; ng, long; sh, ship
th, thin; ᴛʜ, then; zh, measure

M.A.Sc. Master of Applied Science.

mas·car·a (mas kar′ə) *n.* a cosmetic preparation for darkening the eyelashes. [< Sp. *máscara* mask, Ital. *maschera.* See MASK.]

mas·cot (mas′kot) *n.* an animal, person, or thing supposed to bring good luck. [< F *mascotte* < Provençal *mascotto,* dim. of *masco* witch < Gmc.]

mas·cu·line (mas′kyu̇ lin) *adj.* **1** of men; male. **2** like a man; manly; strong; vigorous. **3** having qualities suited to a man; mannish. **4** in grammar, of the gender to which male names normally belong. *Actor, king, ram,* and *bull* are masculine nouns.
—n. in grammar: **1** the masculine gender. **2** a word or form in the masculine gender. [< L *masculinus,* ult. < *mas* male] **—mas′cu·line·ly,** *adv.* **—Syn.** *adj.* **1, 2** See **male.**

masculine rhyme a rhyme in which the final syllables are stressed, as in *disdain* and *complain.*

mas·cu·lin·i·ty (mas′kyu̇ lin′ə tē) *n.* a masculine quality or condition.

ma·ser (mā′zər) *n.* in physics, a device for amplifying microwaves. Masers have many uses in microwave radiation, radio-astronomy, etc. [*m*icrowave *a*mplification by *s*timulated *e*mission of *r*adiation]

mash (mash) *n.* **1** a soft mixture; soft mass. **2** a warm mixture of bran or meal and water for horses and cattle. **3** any of various mixtures of ground grain, often supplemented with proteins, antibiotics, etc., used as feed for poultry, livestock, etc. **4** crushed malt or meal soaked in hot water for making beer. **5** a similar preparation of rye, corn, barley, etc., used to make whisky.
—v. **1** beat into a soft mass; crush to a uniform mass. **2** mix (crushed malt or meal) with hot water in brewing. [OE *māsc-*] **—mash′er,** *n.*

mash·ie or **mash·y** (mash′ē) *n.* **mash·ies.** in golf, a club with a short, sloping face made of steel. [cf. F *massue* a club]

mashie niblick in golf, a club with a face that slopes more than that of a mashie, but less than that of a niblick.

mask (mask) *n.* **1** a covering to hide or protect the face. **2** a false face worn for amusement, especially at a carnival, a masquerade, Halloween, etc. **3** a masked person. **4** anything that hides or disguises: *He hid his evil plans under a mask of friendship.* **5** a clay, wax, or plaster likeness of a person's face. **6** the hollow figure of a human head worn by Greek and Roman actors to identify the character represented and increase the volume of the voice. **7** masque. **8** a carved or moulded face or head, usually grotesque, used as an architectural ornament. **9** a piece of fine gauze worn over the mouth and nose of surgeons, nurses, etc. during operations.
—v. **1** cover (the face) with a mask. **2** hide; disguise: *A smile masked his disappointment.* [< F *masque* < Ital. *maschera* < Arabic *maskhara*ʻ buffoon < *sakhira* to ridicule] **—mask′er,** *n.*

masked ball a dance at which masks are worn.

mas·kin·onge (mas′kə nonj′) *n. Cdn.* **mas·kin·onge.** muskellunge.

mas·och·ism (mas′ə kiz′əm or maz′ə kiz′əm) *n.* **1** a condition in which abnormal sexual pleasure results from being beaten, dominated, etc.; opposed to *sadism.* **2** a tendency to experience pleasure from being mistreated, dominated, etc. [< Leopold Von Sacher-*Masoch,* (1836-1895), an Austrian novelist who described the condition in his books]

mas·o·chist (mas′ə kist or maz′ə kist) *n.* a person who is characterized by masochism. **—mas′o·chis′tic,** *adj.*

ma·son (mā′sən) *n.* **1** a man whose work is building with stone or brick. **2** Often, **Mason.** a member of the worldwide secret society of Freemasons. [ME < OF *masson* < LL *machio, -onis,* probably < Gmc.]

Ma·son·ic or **ma·son·ic** (mə son′ik) *adj.* of Masons or Masonry; having to do with the Freemasons or Freemasonry.

ma·son·ry (mā′sən rē) *n.* **-ries. 1** the work done by a mason; stonework; brickwork. **2** the trade or skill of a mason. **3** Often, **Masonry. a** the principles or doctrines of Freemasons. **b** the members of the society of Freemasons.

masque (mask) *n.* **1** an amateur dramatic entertainment in which fine costumes, scenery, music, and dancing are more important than the story. Masques were often given in England in the 16th and 17th centuries, at court and at the homes of nobles. **2** the play written for such an entertainment. **3** a masked ball; masquerade. [< F *masque.* See MASK.]

mas·quer·ade (mas′kər ād′) *n. v.* **-ad·ed, -ad·ing.** —*n.* **1** a party or dance at which masks and fancy costumes are worn. **2** the costume and mask worn at such a party or dance. **3** a false pretence; disguise. **4** a going about or acting under false pretences.
—*v.* **1** take part in a masquerade. **2** disguise oneself; go about under false pretences: *The king masqueraded as a beggar to find out if his people really liked him.* [< F < Ital. *mascherata* < *maschera.* See MASK.]
—**mas′quer·ad′er,** *n.*

mass[1] (mas) *n.* **1** a lump: *a mass of dough.* **2** a large quantity together: *a mass of flowers.* **3** the majority; greater part. **4** bulk; size. **5** in physics, a measure of the quantity of matter a body contains. **6** mass number; the integer closest to the atomic weight of an isotope. **7** an expanse of color, light, shade, etc. in a painting. **8** in pharmacy, a thick, pasty preparation from which pills are made. **9 in the mass,** as a whole; without distinguishing parts or individuals. **10 the masses,** the common people; the working classes; the lower classes.
—*v.* form or collect into a mass; assemble.
—*adj.* **1** on a large scale: *mass buying.* **2** of or by many people: *a mass protest.* **3** of or having to do with the masses: *mass culture.* [ME < OF < L *massa* kneaded dough < Gk. *maza* barley bread < *massein* knead]
—**Syn.** *n.* **2** aggregate, accumulation. -*v.* gather.

Mass or **mass**[2] (mas) *n.* **1** the central service of worship in the Roman Catholic Church and in some other Christian churches; Holy Eucharist as a sacrifice. The ritual of the Mass consists of various prayers and ceremonies. **2** a piece of music written for or suggested by certain parts of the Mass. [OE *mæsse* < LL *missa* < L *mittere* send away]

Mass. Massachusetts.

mas·sa·cre (mas′ə kər) *n. v.* **-cred, -cring.** —*n.* a wholesale, pitiless slaughter of people or animals.
—*v.* kill (many people or animals) needlessly or cruelly; slaughter in large numbers. [< F *massacre,* in OF *macecle* shambles, ult. origin uncertain]

mas·sage (mə säzh′ or mə säj′) *n. v.* **-saged, -sag·ing.** —*n.* a rubbing and kneading of the body to stimulate the circulation of the blood and make the muscles and joints more supple: *A thorough massage relaxes tired muscles.*
—*v.* give a massage to. [< F *massage,* ult. < *masse* mass]

mas·sa·sau·ga (mas′ə so′gə or mas′ə sô′gə) *n.* a small, deadly rattlesnake, found in the Great Lakes region and to the south and west. [< *Missisauga* River, Ontario, < Algonquian (Ojibwa) < *misi* great + *sauk* river mouth]

mas·seur (mas ėr′; *French,* mä sœr′) *n.* a man whose work is massaging. [< F]

mas·seuse (ma sėz′; *French,* mä sœz′) *n.* a woman whose work is massaging.

mas·sif (mas′if; *French,* mä sēf′) *n.* in geology: **1** a main part or mass of a mountain range, surrounded by depressions. **2** a large block of the earth's crust that has shifted as a unit and is bounded by faults. [< F]

mas·sive (mas′iv) *adj.* **1** big and heavy; large and solid; bulky: *a massive building, a massive wrestler.* **2** giving the impression of being large and broad: *a massive forehead.* **3** imposing; impressive. **4** in or by great numbers; broad in scope; extensive: *a massive assault, massive retaliation.* **5** of gold, silver, plate, etc., solid rather than hollow. **6 a** affecting a large area of bodily tissue: *a massive tumor.* **b** much larger or more than usual: *a massive dose.* **7** in mineralogy, not definitely crystalline. **8** in geology, without definite structural divisions.
—**mas′sive·ly,** *adv.* —**mas′sive·ness,** *n.*

mass medium *pl.* **media.** any of the modern means of communication that reach a vast audience, such as television, radio, motion pictures, and the press.

mass meeting a large public gathering of people to hear or discuss some matter of common interest.

mass number the whole number that most closely indicates the mass of an isotope, equal to the sum of the protons and neutrons in the nucleus.

mass-pro·duce (mas′prə dūs′ or -prə düs′) *v.* **-duced, -duc·ing.** make or manufacture anything by mass production. —**mass′-pro·duc′er,** *n.*

mass production the making of goods in large quantities by machinery.

mast[1] (mast) *n.* **1** on a ship, a long pole of wood or steel set upright to support the sails and rigging. **2 before the mast,** serving as an ordinary seaman. **3** any upright pole: *a flag mast, a TV mast.* [OE *mæst*] —**mast′less,** *adj.* —**mast′like′,** *adj.*

mast[2] (mast) *n.* acorns, chestnuts, beechnuts, etc. that have accumulated on the ground. Pigs eat mast. [OE *mæst*]

mas·ta·ba (mas′tə bə) *n.* an ancient Egyptian tomb, oblong in shape, with sloping sides and flat top, set over a mummy chamber or burial pit. [< Arabic *mastabah*]

mas·ter (mas′tər) *n.* **1** a person who has power or authority; one in control; employer; owner. **2** the man at the head of a household. **3** the captain of a merchant ship. **4** a male teacher, especially in private schools. **5** a great artist. **6** a picture or painting by a great artist: *an old master.* **7** a person who knows all about his work; expert. **8** a skilled craftsman, especially one authorized to teach and employ apprentices and able to work independently. **9 the Master,** Jesus. **10** a title of respect for a boy: *Master James Smith.* **11** a victor. **12** a court officer appointed to assist the judge. **13** an initial recording, mould, stencil, etc. used for making duplications.
—*adj.* **1** of a master; by a master. **2** main; controlling: *a master plan.*
—*v.* **1** become master of; conquer; control. **2** become expert in; become skilful at. [< OF *maistre,* OE *mægester* < L *magister*; cf. *magis* more] —**Syn.** *n.* **1** chief, ruler, commander, manager, director. -*v.* **1** overcome, subjugate, subdue.

mas·ter-at-arms (mas′tər ət ärmz′) *n.* **mas·ters-at-arms.** in the navy, a police officer who keeps order on a ship and takes charge of prisoners.

master builder 1 a person skilled in planning buildings; architect. **2** a person who directs the construction of buildings; contractor.

mas·ter·dom (mas′tər dəm) *n.* mastery; control.

mas·ter·ful (mas′tər fəl) *adj.* **1** fond of power or authority; domineering. **2** expert; skilful.
—**mas′ter·ful·ly,** *adv.* —**Syn. 1** imperious, lordly.

master key a key that opens all the different locks in a building or apartment block.

mas·ter·ly (mas′tər lē) *adj.* expert; skilful. —*adv.* expertly; skilfully. —**mas′ter·li·ness,** *n.* —**Syn.** *adj.* proficient, finished, excellent.

mas·ter·mind (mas′tər mīnd′) *n.* a person who plans and directs a complex project, usually from behind the scenes. —*v.* plan and direct a complex project.

Master of Arts 1 a degree given by a college or university to a person who has completed an advanced course of study, or as an honor. *Abbrev.*: M.A. **2** a person who has this degree.

master of ceremonies a person in charge of a ceremony or entertainment who announces the successive events and makes sure that they take place in the proper order. *Abbrev.*: M.C.

Master of Science 1 a degree given by a college or university to a person who has completed an advanced course of study in science, or as an honor. *Abbrev.*: M.Sc. **2** a person who has this degree.

mas·ter·piece (mas′tər pēs′) *n.* **1** anything done or made with wonderful skill; a perfect piece of art or workmanship. **2** a person's greatest work.

mas·ter·ship (mas′tər ship′) *n.* **1** the position of a

hat, āge, cãre, fär; let, ēqual, tėrm; it, īce
hot, ōpen, ôrder; oil, out; cup, pu̇t, rüle, ūse
əbove, takən, pencəl, lemən, circəs
ch, child; ng, long; sh, ship
th, thin; ᴛʜ, then; zh, measure

master. **2** the position of a teacher in a school. **3** power; rule; control. **4** great skill; expert knowledge.

master stroke a very skilful act or achievement.

mas·ter·y (mas′tər ē or mas′trē) *n.* **-ter·ies. 1** power such as a master has; rule; control. **2** the upper hand; victory. **3** great skill; expert knowledge. —**Syn. 1** command, sway. **2** triumph. **3** grasp.

mast·head (mast′hed′) *n.* **1** the top of a ship's mast. A crow's-nest near the masthead of the lower mast is used as a lookout. **2** the part of a newspaper or magazine that gives the title, the names of the owners and editors, and the publication address.

mas·tic (mas′tik) *n.* **1** a yellowish resin used in making varnish, chewing gum, and incense, and as an astringent. **2** any of various cements or mortars. [ME < OF < L < Gk. *mastichē*]

mas·ti·cate (mas′tə kāt′) *v.* **-cat·ed, -cat·ing. 1** chew. **2** crush or knead (rubber, etc.) to a pulp. [< LL *masticare* < Gk. *mastichaein* gnash the teeth] —**mas′ti·ca′tion,** *n.*

mas·ti·ca·tor (mas′tə kā′tər) *n.* **1** an animal or organ that chews. **2** a machine for cutting things into small pieces.

mas·ti·ca·to·ry (mas′tə kə tô′rē) *adj. n.* **-ries.** —*adj.* of chewing; used in chewing. —*n.* a substance chewed to increase the flow of saliva.

mas·tiff (mas′tif) *n.* **1** a breed of large, strong dog having a short, thick coat, drooping ears, and hanging lips. **2** a dog of this breed. [ME < OF *mastin*, ult. < L *mansuetus* tame; influenced by OF *mestif* mongrel]

mas·to·don (mas′tə don′) *n.* an extinct animal that resembled an elephant. [< NL < Gk. *mastos* breast + *odōn* tooth; from the nipple-like projections on its molars]

mas·toid (mas′toid) *n.* the projection of bone behind the ear. [< Gk. *mastoeidēs* < *mastos* breast + *eidos* form]

mas·toid·i·tis (mas′toid ī′tis) *n.* inflammation of the mastoid.

mas·tur·bate (mas′tər bāt′) *v.* **-bat·ed, -bat·ing.** engage in masturbation. [< L *masturbari*] —**mas′tur·ba′tor,** *n.*

mas·tur·ba·tion (mas′tər bā′shən) *n.* the manipulation of the genitals to induce sexual excitement.

ma·su·ri·um (mə sür′ē əm) *n.* a chemical element first reported in 1925, now known as technetium. *Symbol*: Ma [< *Masuria*, a region in Poland]

mat[1] (mat) *n. v.* **mat·ted, mat·ting.** —*n.* **1** a piece of coarse fabric like a rug, made of woven grass, straw, rope, etc. **2** a piece of material to put under a dish, vase, lamp, etc. **3** a large, thick pad on the floor of a ring, etc. to protect wrestlers or gymnasts. **4** anything packed or tangled thickly together: *a mat of weeds, a mat of hair.* —*v.* **1** cover with mats. **2** weave together as a mat. **3** be tangled or twisted together into a matlike condition: *The swimmer's wet hair was matted.* [OE *matt* < LL *matta*]

mat[2] (mat) *n. v.* **mat·ted, mat·ting.** —*n.* a border for a picture, usually between the picture and the frame. —*v.* put a mat around. [< F *mat*, originally adj., dull, dead. See MAT[3].]

mat[3] (mat) *adj. n. v.* **mat·ted, mat·ting.** —*adj.* dull; not shiny. —*n.* a dull surface or finish. —*v.* give a dull finish to. [< F *mat* < *mater* subdue, checkmate]

mat[4] (mat) *n.* matrix.

mat. 1 matinee. **2** matins. **3** maturity.

mat·a·dor (mat′ə dôr′) *n.* the man who kills the bull in bullfights. [< Sp. *matador* < *matar* kill < Arabic *mat*]

match[1] (mach) *n.* **1** a short, slender piece of wood or pasteboard tipped with a mixture that takes fire when rubbed on a rough or specially prepared surface. **2** a cord prepared to burn at a uniform rate, for firing guns and cannon. [ME < OF *mesche*, probably ult. < Gk. *myxa* lamp wick, influenced by VL *muccare* snuff < L *muccus* mucus]

match[2] (mach) *n.* **1** a person or thing equal to another. **2** a person or thing like another. **3** two persons or things that are alike and thus go well together. **4** a game; contest: *a boxing match, a tennis match.* **5** a marriage. **6** a person considered as a possible husband or wife. —*v.* **1** be equal to; be a match for. **2** be alike; go well together. **3** be the same as. **4** find one like; get a match for. **5** make like; fit together. **6** put in opposition; oppose. **7** marry. [OE *(ge)mæcca* companion] —**match′er,** *n.* —**Syn.** *n.* **4** competition, tournament, tourney.

match·book (mach′bu̇k′) *n.* a small paper folder to hold safety matches, having a striking surface on the cover.

match·box (mach′boks′) *n.* a stiff cardboard box for matches, usually having a striking surface on one side.

match·less (mach′lis) *adj.* so great or wonderful that it cannot be equalled. —**match′less·ly,** *adv.* —**match′less·ness,** *n.* —**Syn.** unequalled, unparalleled, unrivalled.

match·lock (mach′lok′) *n.* an old type of gun fired by lighting the powder with a wick or cord.

match·mak·er[1] (mach′māk′ər) *n.* **1** a person who arranges, or tries to arrange, marriages for others. **2** a person who arranges contests, prize fights, races, etc. [*match*[2] + *maker*]

match·mak·er[2] (mach′māk′ər) *n.* a person who makes matches for lighting. [*match*[1] + *maker*]

match·mak·ing[1] (mach′māk′ing) *n.* **1** the practice of trying to arrange marriages. **2** the business of arranging contests, prize fights, races, etc. —*adj.* having to do with matchmakers or matchmaking.

match·mak·ing[2] (mach′māk′ing) *n.* the business of making matches for lighting. —*adj.* of or having to do with matchmakers or matchmaking.

match play 1 in golf, a form of competition in which the game is won by the winner of the greatest number of holes rather than by the player or side taking the fewest strokes. **2** a play in any match, as in tennis or hardball.

match point in tennis, etc., the final point needed to win a game.

match·stick (mach′stik′) *n.* a small, thin stick of wood from which a match is made.

match·wood (mach′wu̇d′) *n.* **1** wood for making matches. **2** splinters; tiny pieces.

mate[1] (māt) *n. v.* **mat·ed, mat·ing.** —*n.* **1** one of a pair. **2** a husband or wife. **3** either of two animals (male and female) that have come together to produce young. **4** a ship's officer next below the captain. On large ships there is usually more than one mate: a first mate, a second mate, and sometimes, a third mate. **5** an assistant. **6** a companion; fellow worker. —*v.* **1** join in a pair. **2** especially of animals and birds, unite or come together as a pair (male and female) to produce young. **3** marry. [apparently < MLG *mate* messmate. Akin to MEAT.] —**Syn.** *n.* **6** comrade, crony.

mate[2] (māt) *n. v.* **mat·ed, mat·ing,** *interj.* in chess: —*n.* a checkmate. —*v.* checkmate; defeat. —*interj.* checkmate. [ME < OF *mater* checkmate < *mat* checkmated, defeated < Arabic]

ma·té or **ma·te**[3] (mä′tā or mat′ā) *n.* **1** a kind of tea made from the dried leaves of a South American plant. **2** the plant. **3** its leaves. [< Sp. < Quechua (Indian lang. of Peru) *mati* calabash dish]

ma·ter (mā′tər) *n. Brit. Informal.* mother. [< L]

ma·te·ri·al (mə tēr′ē əl) *n.* **1** what a thing is made from; substance of anything manufactured or built: *building materials.* **2** cloth: *I bought 4 yards of material for a dress.* **3** anything serving as crude or raw matter for working upon or developing: *His files contain enough notes, facts, ideas, and other material for a score of books.* —*adj.* **1** having to do with whatever occupies space; of matter; physical. **2** of the body: *Food and shelter are material comforts.* **3** caring more for things of this world than for intellectual or spiritual needs. **4** that matters; important: *Hard work is a material factor in success.* [ME < OF < LL *materialis* < *materia* timber, matter < *mater* trunk (of a tree). Doublet of MATÉRIEL.] —**Syn.** *n.* See **substance.** *-adj.* **2** bodily. **4** essential.

ma·te·ri·al·ism (mə tēr′ē əl iz′əm) *n.* **1** the belief that all action, thought, and feeling can be explained by the movements and changes of matter. **2** a tendency to care more for the things of this world than for intellectual or spiritual needs.

ma·te·ri·al·ist (mə tēr′ē əl ist) *n.* **1** a believer in materialism. **2** a person who cares more for the things of this world than for intellectual or spiritual needs.

ma·te·ri·al·is·tic (mə tēr′ē əl is′tik) *adj.* of materialism; of materialists. —**ma·te′ri·al·is′ti·cal·ly,** *adv.*

ma·te·ri·al·ize (mə tēr′ē əl īz′) *v.* **-ized, -iz·ing.** **1** become an actual fact; be realized: *Our plans were good, but they did not materialize.* **2** give material form to: *An inventor materializes his ideas by building a model.* **3** appear in bodily form: *A spirit materialized from the smoke of the magician's fire.* **4** cause to appear in bodily form. —**ma·te′ri·al·i·za′tion,** *n.*

ma·te·ri·al·ly (mə tēr′ē əl ē) *adv.* **1** with regard to material things; physically: *The nation got better materially but worse spiritually.* **2** considerably; greatly. **3** in matter or substance; not in form.

ma·te·ri·a med·i·ca (mə tēr′ē ə med′ə kə) **1** drugs or other substances used in medicine. **2** the branch of medical science dealing with these drugs and substances. [< NL *materia medica* medical material]

ma·té·ri·el (mə tēr′ē el′) *n.* everything used by an army, organization, undertaking, etc.; equipment. [< F *matériel* material < L *materialis.* Doublet of MATERIAL.]

ma·ter·nal (mə tėr′nəl) *adj.* **1** of or like a mother; motherly. **2** related on the mother's side of the family: *maternal grandparents.* **3** received or inherited from a mother. [< F *maternel* < L *maternus* < *mater* mother] —**ma·ter′nal·ly,** *adv.*

ma·ter·ni·ty (mə tėr′nə tē) *n.* **1** motherhood; being a mother. **2** motherliness; qualities of a mother. *—adj.* for an expectant mother: *a maternity dress.*

maternity hospital a hospital providing facilities for childbirth and care for the mothers and their new-born babies.

math (math) *n. Informal.* mathematics.

math. mathematics.

math·e·mat·i·cal (math′ə mat′ə kəl or math mat′ə kəl) *adj.* **1** of mathematics; having to do with mathematics. **2** exact; accurate.

math·e·mat·i·cal·ly (math′ə mat′ik lē or math mat′ik lē) *adv.* **1** according to mathematics. **2** exactly; accurately; in a mathematical manner.

math·e·ma·ti·cian (math′ə mə tish′ən or math′mə tish′ən) *n.* a person skilled in mathematics.

math·e·mat·ics (math′ə mat′iks or math mat′iks) *n.* the science dealing with the measurement, properties, and relationships of quantities. Mathematics includes arithmetic, algebra, geometry, calculus, etc. [pl. of *mathematic* < L *mathematicus* < Gk. *mathēmatikos,* ult. < *manthanein* learn]

mat·i·née or **mat·i·nee** (mat′ə nā′ or mat′ə nā′) *n.* a performance held in the afternoon, especially a dramatic or musical one. [< F *matinée* < *matin* morning]

ma·tins (mat′ənz) *n.pl.* **1** in the Roman Catholic Church, the first of the seven canonical hours in the breviary. **2** in the Anglican and certain other churches, morning service; morning prayers. **3** Also, **matin.** *Poetic.* morning song. [ME < OF < LL *matutinus* of or in the morning < *Matuta* dawn goddess]

ma·tri·arch (mā′trē ärk′) *n.* **1** a mother who is the ruler of a family or tribe. **2** a venerable old woman. [< *matri-* (< L *mater, matris* mother) + patri*arch*]

ma·tri·ar·chal (mā′trē är′kəl) *adj.* **1** of a matriarch or matriarchy. **2** suitable for a matriarch.

ma·tri·ar·chy (mā′trē är′kē) *n.* **-chies.** a form of social organization in which the mother is the ruler of a family or tribe and in which descent is traced through the mother.

matric. or **matric** matriculation.

ma·tri·ces (mā′trə sēz′ or mat′rə sēz′) *n.* pl. of **matrix.**

ma·tri·cid·al (mā′trə sīd′əl or mat′rə sīd′əl) *adj.* killing or tending to kill one's mother.

ma·tri·cide[1] (mā′trə sīd′ or mat′rə sīd′) *n.* the act of killing one's mother. [< L *matricidium* < *mater* mother + *-cidium* act of killing]

ma·tri·cide[2] (mā′trə sīd′ or mat′rə sīd′) *n.* a person who kills his mother. [< L *matricida* < *mater* mother + *-cida* killer]

ma·tric·u·late (mə trik′yů lāt′) *v.* **-lat·ed, -lat·ing.** **1** enrol as a student in a college or university. **2** enrol as a candidate for a degree. [< LL *matricula,* dim. of L *matrix, -icis* register] —**ma·tric′u·la·tor,** *n.*

ma·tric·u·la·tion (mə trik′yů lā′shən) *n.* **1** an examination held at the end of secondary school or as a university entrance requirement. **2** the act of matriculating. **3** the fact or state of having matriculated.

mat·ri·mo·ni·al (mat′rə mō′nē əl) *adj.* of marriage; having to do with marriage.

mat·ri·mo·ni·al·ly (mat′rə mō′nē əl ē) *adv.* **1** according to the custom or laws of matrimony. **2** with regard to matrimony. **3** by matrimony.

mat·ri·mo·ny (mat′rə mō′nē) *n.* **-nies. 1** married life. **2** the act of marrying; the rite or ceremony of marriage. **3** the relation between married persons. [< L *matrimonium* < *mater* mother] —**Syn. 2, 3** See **marriage.**

ma·trix (mā′triks or mat′riks) *n.* **ma·tri·ces** or **ma·trix·es. 1** that which gives origin or form to something enclosed within it. A mould for a casting or the rock in which gems are embedded is called a matrix. **2** in printing, a mould for casting faces of type. **3** the womb. [< L *matrix* womb]

ma·tron (mā′trən) *n.* **1** a married woman or widow. **2** a woman who manages the household affairs or supervises the inmates of a school, hospital, or other institution. **3** a woman who is placed in charge of female prisoners in a jail, penitentiary, etc. [ME < OF < L *matrona* < *mater* mother]

ma·tron·ly (mā′trən lē) *adj.* like a matron; suitable for a matron; dignified. —**ma′tron·li·ness,** *n.*

matron of honor or **honour** a married woman who is the chief attendant of the bride at a wedding.

Matt. Matthew.

mat·ted[1] (mat′id) *adj.* formed into a mat; entangled in a thick mass: *a matted growth of shrubs.* [< *mat*[1]]

mat·ted[2] (mat′id) *adj.* having a dull finish. [< *mat*[3]]

mat·ter (mat′ər) *n.* **1** the material of which something is made or composed; substance. **2** the substance of the material world; the opposite of mind or spirit. Matter occupies space. **3** a concern; occasion: *business matters, a matter of life and death.* **4** what is said or written, thought of apart from the way in which it is said or written; content: *There was very little matter of interest in his speech.* **5** grounds; occasion; cause: *a matter for complaint.* **6** an instance or case; a thing: *a matter of fact, a matter of record, a matter of business.* **7** an amount; quantity: *a matter of 20 miles.* **8** importance; significance. **9** mail: *Letters are first-class matter.* **10** a substance secreted by a living body, especially pus. **11** things written or printed: *reading matter.* **12** in printing: **a** something to be printed; copy. **b** type that has been composed. **13 as a matter of fact,** actually; in reality. **14 for that matter,** so far as that is concerned. **15 matter of course,** something to be expected. **16 matter of opinion,** a debatable assertion or belief. **17 no matter, a** it is not important. **b** regardless of. **18 What is the matter?** What is the trouble?
—*v.* **1** be of importance. **2** form pus; discharge pus; suppurate. [ME < AF *matere* < L *materia,* originally, timber] —**Syn.** *n.* **1** stuff. See **substance. 4** topic, subject. **8** moment, concern.

mat·ter-of-fact (mat′ər əv fakt′) *adj.* dealing with facts; not fanciful; unimaginative: *a matter-of-fact report.*

mat·ting (mat′ing) *n.* fabric of grass, straw, hemp, or other fibre, for covering floors, for mats, for wrapping material, etc.

mat·tock (mat′ək) *n.* a tool like a pickaxe, but having a flat blade on one side or flat blades on both sides, used for

A mattock

loosening soil and cutting roots. [OE *mattuc*]

mat·tress (mat′ris) *n.* a covering of strong cloth filled with foam rubber, hair, cotton, etc. used on a bed or as a bed. A spring mattress contains wire springs. [ME < OF < Ital. *materasso* < Arabic *almaṭraḥ* cushion]

mat·u·rate (mach′ů rāt′) *v.* **-rat·ed, -rat·ing. 1** discharge pus; suppurate. **2** ripen; mature. [< L *maturare* < *maturus* ripe]

mat·u·ra·tion (mach′ů rā′shən) *n.* **1** a discharge of pus; suppuration. **2** a ripening; a maturing. **3** in biology, the final stages in the preparation of germ cells for fertilization.

ma·ture (mə chür′ or mə tūr′) *adj. v.* **-tured, -tur·ing.** —*adj.* **1** ripe; full-grown: *Grain is harvested when it is mature.* **2** fully developed in body and mind: *a mature person.* **3** brought by time, treatment, etc. to the condition of full excellence: *mature wine, mature cheese.* **4** characteristic of full development: *a mature appearance, mature wisdom.* **5** fully worked out; carefully thought out; fully developed: *mature plans.* **6** due; payable. —*v.* **1** come to full growth; ripen. **2** bring to full growth. **3** work out carefully. **4** fall due: *This note to the bank matured yesterday.* [< L *maturus* ripe] **—ma·ture′ly,** *adv.* **—ma·ture′ness,** *n.* **—ma·tur′er,** *n.*

ma·tu·ri·ty (mə chür′ə tē or mə tūr′ə tē) *n.* **1** a state of ripeness; full growth. **2** a being completed or ready: *When their plans reached maturity, they were able to begin.* **3** a falling due; the time a debt is payable.

ma·tu·ti·nal (mə tū′tə nəl or mə tü′tə nəl) *adj.* occurring in the morning; early in the day; having to do with the morning. [< LL *matutinalis* < *matutinus* of or in the morning. See MATINS.]

matz·o (mät′sō) *n.* **matz·oth** (mät′sōth) or **matz·os** (mät′sōs). a thin piece of unleavened bread, eaten by Jews especially during the Passover. [< Hebrew *matstsōth,* pl. of *matstsāh,* a cake of unleavened bread]

maud·lin (mod′lən or môd′lən) *adj.* **1** sentimental in a weak, silly way: *Sympathy for criminals is often maudlin.* **2** sentimental and tearful because of drunkenness or excitement. [alteration of Mary *Magdalene,* often painted as weeping]

mau·ger (mo′gər or mô′gər) *prep. Archaic.* maugre.

mau·gre (mo′gər or mô′gər) *prep. Archaic.* in spite of; notwithstanding. [ME < OF *maugre,* originally n., ill will < L *malus* bad + *gratus* pleasing]

maul (mol or môl) *n.* a very heavy hammer or mallet. —*v.* beat and pull about; handle roughly: *The lion mauled its keeper badly.* [var. of *mall*]

Mau Mau (mou′ mou′) a secret society consisting chiefly of Kikuyu tribesmen sworn to expel Europeans from Kenya by violent means, active approximately between 1952 and 1956.

maun·der (mon′dər or môn′dər) *v.* **1** talk in a rambling, foolish way: *People who maunder talk much but say little.* **2** move or act in an aimless, confused manner: *The injured man maundered about in a daze.* [origin uncertain] **—maun′der·er,** *n.*

Maun·dy Thursday (mon′dē or môn′di) the Thursday before Easter. [*Maundy,* ME < OF *mande* < L *mandatum* a command]

Mau·ser (mou′zər) *n. Trademark.* a kind of powerful repeating rifle or pistol. [after Paul *Mauser* (1838-1914), a German inventor]

mau·so·le·um (mo′sə lē′əm or mô′sə lē′əm, mo′zə lē′əm or mô′zə lē′əm) *n.* **-le·ums, -le·a** (-lē′ə). **1 Mausoleum,** at Halicarnassus, the magnificent tomb of King Mausolos of Caria, in ancient times a kingdom in S.W. Asia Minor. The tomb was one of the seven wonders of the ancient world. **2** a large, magnificent tomb. [< L < Gk. *Mausōleion*]

mauve (mōv, mov, or môv) *n. adj.* delicate, pale-purple. [< F < L *malva* mallow. Doublet of MALLOW.]

mav·er·ick (mav′ər ik) *n.* **1** a calf or other animal not marked with an owner's brand. **2** *Esp.U.S. Informal.* one who refuses to affiliate with a regular political party. **3** *Informal.* any person or organization that is unconventional or unwilling to conform; a rebel. [probably after Samuel *Maverick* (1803-1870), a Texan who did not brand his cattle]

ma·vis (mā′vis) *n.* the European song thrush. [ME < OF *mauvis* < Celtic]

hat, āge, cãre, fär; let, ēqual, tėrm; it, īce
hot, ōpen, ôrder; oil, out; cup, pů̇t, rüle, ūse
əbove, takən, pencəl, lemən, circəs
ch, child; ng, long; sh, ship
th, thin; ᴛʜ, then; zh, measure

ma·vour·neen or **ma·vour·nin** (mə vür′nēn) *n. Irish.* my darling. [< Irish *mo mhuirnín*]

maw (mo or mô) *n.* **1** the mouth, throat, or stomach of animals or birds. **2** anything thought of as resembling this in appetite: *Nations continue to pour wealth into the maw of war.* [OE *maga*]

mawk·ish (mok′ish or môk′ish) *adj.* **1** sickening. **2** sickly sentimental; weakly emotional. [originally, maggoty < *mawk* maggot < ON *mathkr*] **—mawk′ish·ly,** *adv.* **—mawk′ish·ness,** *n.*

max. maximum.

max·i- *combining form.* large; great; long: *a maxi-skirt.*

max·il·la (mak sil′ə) *n.* **max·il·lae** (mak sil′ē or mak sil′ī). **1** in vertebrates, the jaw; jawbone; upper jawbone. **2** either of a pair of appendages just behind the mandibles of insects, crabs, etc. See **mandible** for picture. [< L *maxilla* jaw]

max·il·lar·y (mak′sə ler′ē) *adj. n.* **-lar·ies.** —*adj.* of or having to do with the jaw or jawbone. —*n.* the maxilla.

max·im (mak′səm) *n.* a short rule of conduct; proverb; statement of a general truth: *"Look before you leap" is a maxim.* [ME < OF < LL *maxima* (*propositio*) axiom, literally, greatest proposition]

max·i·ma (mak′sə mə) *n.* a pl. of **maximum.**

max·i·mize (mak′sə mīz′) *v.* **-mized, -miz·ing.** increase or intensify as much as possible; make as great as possible. [< *maximum* + *-ize*] **—max′i·mi·za′tion,** *n.*

max·i·mum (mak′sə məm) *n.* **-mums** or **ma,** *adj.* —*n.* the largest or highest amount; greatest possible amount. —*adj.* largest; highest; greatest possible: *The maximum score on the test is 100.* [< L *maximum,* neut. adj., superlative of *magnus* great]

may (mā) *auxiliary v.* **might.** *May* is used to express: **1** possibility, opportunity, or permission: *You may enter.* **2** a wish or prayer: *May you be very happy.* **3** contingency, especially in clauses, expressing condition, concession, purpose, result, etc.: *I write that you may know my plans.* **4** ability or power (more commonly *can*). [OE *mæg*]
☛ See **can** for usage note.

May (mā) *n.* the fifth month of the year. It has 31 days. [< L *Maius*]

ma·ya (mä′yə) *n.* in Hindu philosophy, illusory nature of the sense world, often personified as a woman. [< Skt.]

Ma·ya (mä′yə) *n.* **1** a tribe of Indians living in Central America. The Mayas had achieved a high degree of civilization when America was discovered. **2** a member of this tribe. **3** their language.

Ma·yan (mä′yən) *adj.* of or having to do with the Mayas or their language. —*n.* **1** one of the Mayas. **2** the language of the Mayas.

May apple 1 a North American plant having a large, white flower. **2** its edible, yellowish, egg-shaped fruit.

may·be (mā′bē) *adv.* possibly; perhaps; it may be so.
☛ **maybe, may be.** *Maybe* is an adverb meaning "perhaps"; *may be* is a verb form: *Maybe you'll have better luck next time. He may be the next mayor.*

May Day May 1. It is often celebrated by crowning the May queen and dancing around the Maypole. In some places, labor parades and meetings are held on May Day.

May·day (mā′dā′) *n.* an international signal of distress, used in emergencies by ships and aircraft. [< F *m'aidez* help me]

May·fair (mā′fãr′) *n.* **1** a fashionable section of London. **2** fashionable London society.

may·flow·er (mā′flou′ər) *n.* **1** a plant or tree that flowers in May; trailing arbutus; hawthorn or cowslip. **2 Mayflower,** the ship on which the Pilgrims came to America in 1620.

May fly 1 a slender insect, having the forewings much larger than the hind wings, that dies soon after reaching the adult stage; ephemerid. 2 an artificial fishing fly made in imitation of this insect.

may·hap (mā′hap′ or mā′hap) *adv. Archaic.* perhaps. [for *it may hap*]

may·hem (mā′hem or mā′əm) *n.* 1 in law, the crime of maiming a person or injuring him so that he is less able to defend himself. 2 confusion and willful violence. [< AF *mahaym* maim; origin uncertain]

May·ing (mā′ing) *n.* the celebration of May Day; taking part in May festivities.

may·n't (mā′ənt or mānt) may not. ☞ See **can't** for usage note.

may·on·naise (mā′ə nāz′) *n.* a salad dressing made of egg yolks, olive oil, vinegar or lemon juice, and seasoning, beaten together until thick. [< F *mayonnaise*, ult. < *Mahón*, a seaport in Minorca, captured by the Duc de Richelieu, whose chef introduced the *Mahonnaise* after his master's victory]

may·or (mā′ər or mãr) *n.* the chief elected official of a city, town, or village. [ME < OF *maire, maor* < L *major.* Doublet of MAJOR.]

may·or·al·ty (mā′ər əl tē or mãr′əl tē) *n.* **-ties.** 1 the position of mayor. 2 a mayor's term of office.

May·pole or **may·pole** (mā′pōl′) *n.* a high pole decorated with flowers or ribbons, around which merrymakers dance on May Day.

May queen a girl crowned with flowers and honored as queen on May Day.

mayst (māst) *v. Archaic.* 2nd pers. sing. present tense of **may.** "Thou mayst" means "you may" (sing.).

May·time (mā′tīm′) *n.* the month of May.

maze (māz) *n.* 1 a network of paths through which it is hard to find one's way. See **labyrinth** for diagram. 2 any complicated arrangement, as of streets, buildings, etc. 3 a state of confusion; muddled condition. [var. of *amaze*] —**Syn.** 3 bewilderment, perplexity.

ma·zu·ma (mə zü′mə) *n. Slang.* money. [< Yiddish < Hebrew *mazumon*]

ma·zur·ka or **ma·zour·ka** (mə zėr′kə or mə zür′kə) *n.* 1 a lively Polish dance. 2 the music for this dance, in 3/4 or 6/8 time. [< Polish *mazurka*, a woman of *Mazovia*, a province of Poland]

maz·y (māz′ē) *adj.* **maz·i·er, maz·i·est.** like a maze, intricate. —**maz′i·ly,** *adv.* —**maz′i·ness,** *n.*

M.B.E. Member of (the Order of) the British Empire.

M.C. 1 Military Cross. 2 Member of Congress. 3 Master of Ceremonies. 4 Medical Corps.

McCar·thy·ism (mə kär′thē iz′əm) *n.* 1 the act or practice of making sensational public accusations of political disloyalty or corruption, usually with little evidence. 2 the practice of holding public investigations, supposedly to reveal Communist sympathy or activity. [< Senator Joseph R. *McCarthy*, 1909-1957, chairman of the U.S. Senate Permanent Investigations Committee]

Mc·Coy (mə koi′) *n.* **the real McCoy,** a genuine person or thing. [origin uncertain]

Mc·In·tosh (mak′ən tosh′) *n.* a bright-red winter apple having crisp, white flesh. [< John *McIntosh* (1777-?), an Ontario farmer, who discovered the tree producing this apple in 1811]

McIntosh Red McIntosh apple.

Md mendelevium.

Md. Maryland.

M.D. 1 Doctor of Medicine. (for L *Medicinae Doctor*) 2 Municipal District.

MDB or **M.D.B.** Maritime Development Board.

M.D.S. Master of Dental Surgery.

mdse. merchandise.

MDT, M.D.T., or **m.d.t.** Mountain Daylight Time.

M. du C. Médaille du Canada.

me (mē; *unstressed,* mi) *pron.* the objective form of I: *The dog bit me. Give me a bandage.* [OE *mē*]

Me methyl.

Me. Maine.

ME or **M.E.** Middle English.

M.E. 1 Master of Engineering. 2 Mechanical Engineer. 3 Mining Engineer. 4 Methodist Episcopal.

mead[1] (mēd) *n. Poetic.* meadow. [OE *mǣd*]

mead[2] (mēd) *n.* an alcoholic drink made from fermented honey. [OE *medu*]

mead·ow (med′ō) *n.* 1 a piece of grassy land; a field where hay is grown. 2 low, wet, grassy land near a stream. [OE *mǣdwe*, oblique case of *mǣd* mead[1]]

meadow lark a North American songbird, about the size of a robin, having a black crescent on a yellow breast.

mead·ow·sweet (med′ō swēt′) *n.* a shrub of the rose family having dense clusters of small, fragrant, pink or white flowers.

mead·ow·y (med′ō ē) *adj.* 1 like a meadow. 2 of meadows.

mea·gre or **mea·ger** (mē′gər) *adj.* 1 poor; scanty: *a meagre meal.* 2 thin; lean: *a meagre face.* 3 without fullness or richness; deficient in quality or quantity. [ME < OF *maigre* < L *macer* thin] —**mea′gre·ly** or **mea′ger·ly,** *adv.* —**mea′gre·ness** or **mea′ger·ness,** *n.* —**Syn.** 1 sparse. See **scanty.**

meal[1] (mēl) *n.* 1 breakfast, lunch, dinner, supper, or tea. 2 the food served or eaten at any one time. [OE *mǣl*]

meal[2] (mēl) *n.* 1 ground grain, especially corn meal. 2 anything ground to a powder. [OE *melu*]

meal ticket 1 a ticket authorizing a person to obtain a meal. 2 *Slang.* someone or something that provides a living for another or others.

meal·time (mēl′tīm′) *n.* the usual time for eating a meal.

meal·y (mēl′ē) *adj.* **meal·i·er, meal·i·est.** 1 like meal; dry and powdery. 2 of meal. 3 covered with meal. 4 pale. 5 mealy-mouthed. —**meal′i·ness,** *n.*

meal·y-mouthed (mēl′ē mouᴛʜd′ or -moutht′) *adj.* unwilling to tell the truth in plain words; using soft, insincere words.

mean[1] (mēn) *v.* **meant, mean·ing.** 1 refer to; signify; denote: *What does this word mean?* 2 indicate or intend to express. "*Keep out; that means you.*" 3 convey; communicate: *What is that look supposed to mean?* 4 have as a purpose; have in mind; intend: *I do not mean to go.* 5 have intentions of some kind; be minded or disposed: *She means well.* 6 design for a definite purpose; destine: *Fate meant us for each other. He was meant for a soldier.* 7 **mean well by,** have kindly feelings toward. [OE *mænan*] —**Syn.** 4 design, purpose. See **intend.**

mean[2] (mēn) *adj.* 1 low in quality or grade; poor. 2 low in social position or rank; humble: *A peasant is of mean birth.* 3 of little importance or value: *the meanest flower.* 4 of poor appearance; shabby: *a mean house.* 5 small-minded; ignoble: *mean thoughts.* 6 stingy: *mean about money.* 7 *Informal.* humiliated; ashamed: *feel mean.* 8 *Informal.* hard to manage; troublesome; bad-tempered: *a mean horse.* 9 selfish and ill-tempered; vicious; cruel. 10 *Informal.* in poor physical condition; unwell: *I feel mean today.* 11 *Slang.* expert; effected with skill. 12 **no mean,** very good. [OE (*ge*)*mæne* common] —**mean′ly,** *adv.* —**Syn.** 2 common, plebeian. 3 insignificant, paltry, petty. 5 base, contemptible, despicable.

mean[3] (mēn) *adj.* 1 halfway between two extremes. 2 intermediate in kind, quality, or degree. 3 in mathematics, having a value intermediate between the values of other quantities: *a mean diameter.*
—*n.* 1 **means,** *pl.* a what a thing is done by; agency; method or methods: *by fair means.* b wealth: *a man of means.* 2 a condition, quality, or course of action halfway between two extremes: *a happy mean between extravagance and stinginess.* 3 in mathematics: a a quantity having a value intermediate between the values of other quantities, especially the average obtained by dividing the sum of several quantities by their number. b either the second or third term of a proportion of four terms. 4 **by all means,** certainly; without fail. 5 **by any means,** in any possible way; at any cost. 6 **by means of,** by the use of; through; with. 7 **by no means,** certainly not; not at all; under no circumstances. 8 **means to an end,** a way of getting or doing something. [ME < OF *meien* < L *medianus*

middle < *medius*] —**Syn.** *adj.* **2** medium, average.
—*n.* **1 a** device, instrumentality, expedient, shift, way. **b** resources, funds, income, property.

☛ **Means** meaning "what a thing is done by," is plural in form and singular or plural in use: *A means of communication is lacking. The means of helping others are never lacking.* **Means** meaning "wealth," is plural in form and in use: *His means permit him to live comfortably.*

me·an·der (mē an′dər) *v.* **1** follow a winding course: *A brook meanders through the meadow.* **2** wander aimlessly: *We meandered through the park.* [< n.] —*n.* **1** a winding course. **2** an aimless wandering. [< L < Gk. *Maiandros,* the name of a winding river in Asia Minor]

mean·ing (mēn′ing) *n.* what is meant or intended; significance. —*adj.* that means something; expressive: *a meaning look.* —**mean′ing·ly,** *adv.*
Syn. *n.* **Meaning, sense, purport** = what is expressed or meant to be. **Meaning** is the general word applying to the idea expressed or intended by a word, statement, gesture, action, painting, etc.: *The meaning of the sentence is clear.* **Sense** applies to the meaning of something said, especially to a particular meaning of a word: *In other senses this word is not a synonym of "meaning."* **Purport,** formal, means "the main idea or general drift of a longer statement": *That was the purport of the president's address.*

mean·ing·ful (mēn′ing fəl) *adj.* full of meaning; having much meaning; significant. —**mean′ing·ful·ly,** *adv.* —**mean′ing·ful·ness,** *n.*

mean·ing·less (mēn′ing lis) *adj.* without meaning; not making sense; not significant. —**mean′ing·less·ly,** *adv.* —**mean′ing·less·ness,** *n.*

mean·ness (mēn′nis) *n.* **1** a being mean in grade or quality; poorness. **2** a being selfish in small things; stinginess. **3** a mean act.

meant (ment) *v.* pt. and pp. of **mean**[1].

mean·time (mēn′tīm′) *n.* the time between. —*adv.* **1** in the time between. **2** at the same time.

mean·while (mēn′hwīl′ or -wīl′) *n. adv.* meantime.

mea·sles (mē′zəlz) *n.pl. or sing.* **1** an infectious disease characterized by a bad cold, fever, and a breaking out of small, red spots on the skin. **2** a similar but much less severe disease, properly called **German measles. 3** a disease of pigs and cattle caused by the larvae of tapeworms. [ME *meseles,* pl. of *mesel* spot characteristic of measles; akin to MDu. *masel*]

☛ **Measles** is plural in form but generally used with a singular verb: *Measles is a children's disease.*

mea·sly (mē′zlē) *adj.* **-sli·er, -sli·est. 1** of or like measles. **2** having measles. **3** *Slang.* scanty; meagre; worthless.

meas·ur·a·ble (mezh′ər ə bəl) *adj.* capable of being measured.

meas·ur·a·bly (mezh′ər ə blē) *adv.* to an amount or degree that can be measured; perceptibly.

meas·ure (mezh′ər) *v.* **-ured, -ur·ing.** *n.* —*v.* **1** find out the extent, size, quantity, capacity, etc. of (something); estimate by some standard: *measure a room.* **2** be of specified measure: *This brick measures 2 × 4 × 8 inches.* **3** get or take by measuring: *measure out a bushel of potatoes.* **4** take measurements; find out sizes or amounts. **5** admit of measurement. **6** serve as a measure of. **7** assess; estimate: *One measures a man's character by his actions.* **8** adjust (*to*): *He measured his expenses to his income.* **9** *Poetic.* travel over; traverse. **10 measure one's length,** fall, be thrown, or lie flat on the ground. **11 measure out, a** distribute by measuring. **b** distribute carefully. **12 measure swords, a** fight with swords. **b** take part in a duel, battle, debate, etc. **13 measure up,** have the necessary qualifications. [ME < OF *mesurer* < L *mensurare* < *mensura.* See n.]
—*n.* **1** the act or process of finding extent, size, quantity, capacity, etc. of something, especially by comparison with a standard. **2** the size, dimensions, quantity, etc. thus ascertained: *His waist measure is 30 inches.* **3** an instrument for measuring: *a pint measure.* **4** a system of measuring: *dry measure.* **5** a unit or standard of measuring. Inch, quart, pound, and hour are common measures. **6** any standard of comparison, estimation, or judgment. **7** a quantity or degree that should not be exceeded; reasonable limit: *angry beyond measure.* **8** quantity; extent; degree; proportion: *Accidents can in great measure be prevented. The measure of his courage was remarkable.* **9** rhythm, as in poetry or music: *the stately measures of blank verse.* **10** a metrical unit; foot of poetry. **11** in music: **a** a unit of rhythm, consisting of one strong beat and a number of weak beats. **b** the notes contained between two bar lines; bar. **12** a dance or dance movement. **13** a course of action; procedure: *take measures to relieve suffering.* **14** a legislative enactment. **15** in mathematics, a quantity contained in another a certain number of times without remainder. **16** a definite quantity measured out: *drink a measure.*

Measures (def. 11)

hat, āge, cãre, fär; let, ēqual, tėrm; it, īce
hot, ōpen, ôrder; oil, out; cup, pu̇t, rüle, ūse
əbove, takən, pencəl, lemən, circəs
ch, child; ng, long; sh, ship
th, thin; ᴛʜ, then; zh, measure

beyond measure, greatly; exceedingly.
for good measure, as something extra; as something not necessarily expected.
full measure, all it should be.
in a measure, to some degree; partly.
take measures, do something; act.
take one's measure, judge one's character or one's abilities.
tread a measure, *Archaic.* dance. [ME < OF *mesure* < L *mensura,* n., < *mensus,* pp. of *metiri* to measure]
—**meas′ur·er,** *n.*

meas·ured (mezh′ərd) *adj.* **1** regular; uniform. **2** rhythmical. **3** written in poetry, not in prose. **4** deliberate and restrained, not hasty or careless. —**meas′ured·ly,** *adv.*

meas·ure·less (mezh′ər lis) *adj.* too great to be measured; unlimited; vast. —**meas′ure·less·ly,** *adv.* —**meas′ure·less·ness,** *n.*

meas·ure·ment (mezh′ər mənt) *n.* **1** a way of measuring; way of finding the size, quantity, or amount: *Clocks give us a measurement of time.* **2** the act or fact of measuring: *The measurement of length with the help of a yardstick is easy.* **3** the size or amount found by measuring. **4** a system of measuring or of measures.

measuring worm the larva of any geometrid moth. It moves by bringing the rear end of its body forward, forming a loop, and then advancing the front end.

meat (mēt) *n.* **1** animal flesh used as food. Fish and poultry are not usually called meat. **2** food of any kind: *meat and drink.* **3** the part of anything that can be eaten: *the meat of a nut.* **4** a meal: *Say grace before meat.* **5** the essential part or parts; substance; food for thought: *the meat of an argument, the meat of a book.* **6** *Slang.* something a person finds easy and pleasant: *Something to do with electronics would be more his meat than a job in commerce.* [OE *mete*] —**meat′less,** *adj.*

meat packing the business of slaughtering animals and preparing their meat for transportation and sale.

me·a·tus (mē ā′təs) *n.* **-tus·es** or **-tus.** in anatomy, a passage, duct, or opening. [< L *meatus* path < *meare* pass]

meat·y (mēt′ē) *adj.* **meat·i·er, meat·i·est. 1** of meat; having the flavor of meat. **2** like meat. **3** full of meat. **4** full of substance; giving food for thought: *The speech was very meaty; it contained many valuable ideas.*

Mec·ca or **mec·ca** (mek′ə) *n.* **1** a place that many people visit. **2** a place that a person longs to visit. **3** the goal of one's desires or ambitions. Also, **Mekka.** [< *Mecca,* a capital of Saudi Arabia, the birthplace of Mohammed and holy city of the Moslems]

me·chan·ic (mə kan′ik) *n.* **1** a worker skilled with tools. **2** a worker who repairs machinery. [ME < L < Gk. *mēchanikos* < *mēchanē* machine]

me·chan·i·cal (mə kan′ə kəl) *adj.* **1** having to do with machinery. **2** made or worked by machinery. **3** like a machine; like that of a machine; automatic; without expression: *Her singing is very mechanical.* **4** of, having to do with, or in accordance with, the science of mechanics.

mechanical drawing drawing done with the help of rulers, scales, compasses, etc.

me·chan·i·cal·ly (mə kan′ik lē) *adv.* **1** by machinery. **2** in a mechanical manner. **3** in mechanical respects.

4 toward mechanics (def. 2): *He is mechanically inclined.*

mech·a·ni·cian (mek′ə nish′ən) *n.* a worker skilled in making and repairing machines.

me·chan·ics (mə kan′iks) *n.* **1** the branch of physics dealing with the action of forces on bodies and with motion. Mechanics includes kinetics, statics, and kinematics. **2** knowledge about machinery. **3** the mechanical part; technique: *the mechanics of playing the piano.*

mech·a·nism (mek′ə niz′əm) *n.* **1** the means or way by which something is done; machinery: *Committees are a useful mechanism for getting things done.* **2** the system of parts working together as the parts of a machine do: *The bones and muscles are parts of the mechanism of the body.* **3** a machine or its working parts: *the mechanism of a watch. An automobile engine is a complex mechanism.* **4** a mechanical part; technique. **5** in psychology: **a** the arrangements in the mind or brain that determine thought, feeling, or action in regular and predictable ways. **b** a response unconsciously selected to protect oneself or find satisfaction for an unfulfilled desire: *a defence mechanism.* **6** the theory that everything in the universe is produced by mechanical or material forces.

mech·a·nist (mek′ə nist) *n.* **1** a person who believes that all the changes in the universe are the effects of physical and chemical forces. **2** a mechanician.

mech·a·nis·tic (mek′ə nis′tik) *adj.* of or having to do with mechanists, mechanism, mechanics, or mechanical theories. —**mech′a·nis′ti·cal·ly,** *adv.*

mech·a·ni·za·tion (mek′ə nə zā′shən or mek′ə nī zā′shən) *n.* **1** the act or process of mechanizing. **2** the state of being mechanized.

mech·a·nize (mek′ə nīz′) *v.* **-nized, -niz·ing.** **1** make mechanical. **2** do by machinery, rather than by hand: *Much housework can be mechanized.* **3** replace men or animals by machinery (in a business, etc.). **4** equip (a military unit) with armored vehicles, tanks, and other machines.

Mech·lin (mek′lən) *n.* a fine lace with the pattern clearly outlined by a distinct thread. [< *Mechlin,* a city in N. Belgium, where this lace is made]

med. **1** medical. **2** medieval. **3** medium.

Med. Medieval.

M.Ed. Master of Education.

med·al (med′əl) *n.* a small, flat piece of metal stamped with a figure and an inscription: *The captain won a medal for bravery. She won the gold medal for having the highest marks in the school. A medal was struck to commemorate the coronation.* [< F < Ital. *medaglia,* ult. < L *metallum* metal]

med·al·ist (med′əl ist) *n.* **1** a person who designs or makes medals. **2** a person who has won a medal. Also, **medallist.**

me·dal·lion (mə dal′yən) *n.* **1** a large medal. **2** a design, ornament, etc. shaped like a medal. [< F < Ital. *medaglione* large medal]

med·al·list (med′əl ist) *n.* medalist.

med·dle (med′əl) *v.* **-dled, -dling.** busy oneself with other people's things or affairs without being asked or needed. [ME < OF *medler,* ult. < L *miscere* mix] —**med′dler,** *n.*

Syn. Meddle, tamper, interfere = concern oneself unnecessarily or unduly with someone or something. **Meddle** emphasizes busying oneself, without right or permission, with something not one's own affair or strictly the affair of another: *That old busybody is always meddling in someone's business.* **Tamper** emphasizes meddling in order to alter or experiment with a thing or improperly influence a person: *Don't tamper with electrical appliances.* **Interfere** suggests meddling in a way that disturbs or hinders: *She interferes when we scold the children.*

med·dle·some (med′əl səm) *adj.* fond of meddling in other people's affairs; meddling. —**med′dle·some·ly.** *adv.* —**med′dle·some·ness,** *n.* —**Syn.** interfering.

Mede (mēd) *n.* a native or inhabitant of Media, in ancient times a country in S.W. Asia, south of the Caspian Sea.

Me·de·a (mə dē′ə) *n.* in Greek mythology, a sorceress who helped Jason get the Golden Fleece. They were married but she was later deserted by him. Medea then killed their children as well as her rival, burned her palace, and fled to Athens.

Med.Gk. Medieval Greek.

me·di·a (mē′dē ə) *n.* pl. of **medium.** *Newspapers, magazines, billboards, television, and radio are advertising media.*

me·di·ae·val (mē′dē ē′vəl or med′ē ē′vəl) *adj.* medieval.

me·di·al (mē′dē əl) *adj.* **1** in the middle. **2** having to do with a mathematical mean or average. **3** average; ordinary. [< LL *medialis* < L *medius* middle]

me·di·al·ly (mē′dē əl ē) *adv.* in the middle; in a medial position.

me·di·an (mē′dē ən) *adj.* **1** of, having to do with, or in the middle; middle. **2** having to do with or designating the plane that divides something into two equal parts. **3** of a median; having as many above as below a certain number: *The median age of the population was found to be 21* (*that is, there were as many persons above 21 as below it*), *while the average age was found to be 25.* —*n.* **1** the middle number of a series: *The median of 1, 3, 4, 8, 9 is 4.* **2** a measurement so chosen that half the numbers in the series are above it and half are below it: *The median of 1, 3, 4, 8, 9, 10 is 6.* **3** a line or point in the middle. **4** on a highway, a central strip of grass or pavement separating the lanes used by traffic proceeding in opposite directions. [< L *medianus* < *medius* middle]

Me·di·an (mē′dē ən) *adj.* of Media, an ancient country in S.W. Asia, south of the Caspian Sea, or the Medes. —*n.* a Mede.

me·di·ant (mē′dē ənt) *n.* in music, the third tone of a scale, half-way from the tonic or keynote to the dominant. [< Ital. *mediante* < LL *medians, -antis,* pres. part. of *mediari.* See MEDIATE.]

me·di·ate (*v.* mē′dē āt′; *adj.* mē′dē it) *v.* **-at·ed, -at·ing,** *adj.* —*v.* **1** be a go-between; act in order to bring about an agreement between persons or sides. **2** effect by intervening; settle by intervening. **3** be a connecting link between: *Canada is often said to mediate between the United States and Great Britain.* **4** be the medium for effecting (a result), for conveying (a gift), or for communicating (knowledge). —*adj.* **1** connected, but not directly; connected through some other person or thing. **2** intermediate. [< LL *mediari* be in the middle, intervene < L *medius* middle] —**me′di·a·tor,** *n.*

me·di·a·tion (mē′dē ā′shən) *n.* a mediating; effecting an agreement; friendly interference.

me·di·a·to·ry (mē′dē ə tô′rē) *adj.* mediating; having to do with mediation.

med·ic[1] (med′ik) *n. Informal.* **1** a physician. **2** a medical student. **3** a member of the medical branch of any of the armed services. [< L *medicus* physician]

med·ic[2] (med′ik) *n.* a plant like clover having purple or yellow flowers. Alfalfa is a kind of medic. [< L *medica* < Gk. (*poa*) *Mēdikē* Median (herb)]

med·i·ca·ble (med′ə kə bəl) *adj.* capable of being cured or relieved by medical treatment.

med·i·cal (med′ə kəl) *adj.* of or having to do with the science or practice of medicine: *medical advice, medical schools, medical treatment.* —*n. Informal.* **1** a medical student; a doctor. **2** a medical examination. [< F < LL *medicalis* < L *medicus* doctor] —**med′i·cal·ly,** *adv.*

me·dic·a·ment (mə dik′ə mənt or med′ə kə mənt) *n.* a substance used to cure or heal; medicine. [< L *medicamentum,* ult. < *medicus* healing]

med·i·care (med′ə kãr′) *n.* a government-sponsored scheme of health insurance, usually covering hospital costs, doctors' fees, and other medical expenses. [< *medical* + *care*]

med·i·cate (med′ə kāt′) *v.* **-cat·ed, -cat·ing.** **1** treat with medicine. **2** put medicine on or in. [< L *medicare* < *medicus* healing]

med·i·cat·ed (med′ə kāt′id) *adj.* containing medicine: *medicated gauze.*

med·i·ca·tion (med′ə kā′shən) *n.* **1** treatment with medicine. **2** putting medicine on or in: *The doctor was responsible for the medication of the wound.*

Med·i·ci (med′ə chē) *n.* a rich, famous, and powerful

family of Florence, Italy, during the 15th and 16th centuries.

me·dic·i·nal (mə dis′ə nəl) *adj.* having value as medicine; healing; helping; relieving.

me·dic·i·nal·ly (mə dis′ə nəl ē) *adv.* as medicine.

med·i·cine (med′ə sən or med′sən) *n.* **1** any substance, drug, or means used to cure disease or improve health. **2** the science of curing disease or improving health; skill in healing; doctor's art; treatment of diseases or sickness: *The young man decided to study medicine.* **3** the profession of medicine. **4** the magic power that savages believe certain men have over disease, evil spirits, and other things. **5** any object or ceremony, such as a spell, charm, or fetish, supposed by the North American Indians or other primitive peoples to have magical power or influence. **6 take one's medicine,** do what one must; do something one dislikes to do. [< L *medicina* < *medicus* doctor]

medicine ball a large, heavy leather ball tossed from one person to another for exercise.

medicine man a man believed by North American Indians and other primitive peoples to have magic power over diseases, evil spirits, and other things.

med·i·co (med′ə kō′) *n.* **-cos.** *Informal.* **1** a doctor. **2** a medical student. [< Ital. *medico* or Sp. *médico* physician, learned borrowing from L *medicus.* See MEDIC.]

me·di·e·val or **me·di·ae·val** (mē′dē ē′vəl or med′ē ē′vəl) *adj.* **1** belonging to or having to do with the Middle Ages, the period from about A.D. 500 to about 1450: *medieval customs.* **2** like that of the Middle Ages. [< L *medium* middle + *aevum* age] **—me′di·e′val·ly,** *adv.*

me·di·e·val·ism or **me·di·ae·val·ism** (mē′dē ē′vəl iz′əm or med′ē ē′vəl iz′əm) *n.* **1** the spirit, ideals, and customs of the Middle Ages; medieval thought, religion, and art. **2** devotion to medieval ideals; adoption of medieval customs. **3** a medieval belief or custom.

me·di·e·val·ist or **me·di·ae·val·ist** (mē′dē ē′vəl ist or med′ē ē′vəl ist) *n.* **1** a person who knows much about the Middle Ages. **2** a person who is in sympathy with medieval ideals, customs, etc.

Medieval Latin or **Mediaeval Latin** the Latin language from about A.D. 700 to about 1500.

me·di·o·cre (mē′dē ō′kər or mē′dē ō′ kər) *adj.* neither good nor bad; average; ordinary: *a mediocre cake, a mediocre student.* [< F < L *mediocris,* originally, middling < *medius* middle] **—Syn.** medium, commonplace, indifferent.

me·di·oc·ri·ty (mē′dē ok′rə tē) *n.* **-ties. 1** mediocre quality. **2** mediocre ability or accomplishment. **3** a mediocre person. [< L *mediocritas*]

med·i·tate (med′ə tāt′) *v.* **-tat·ed, -tat·ing. 1** think; reflect: *Monks meditate on holy things.* **2** think about; consider; plan; intend. [< L *meditari*] **—Syn. 2** ponder. See **think.**

med·i·ta·tion (med′ə tā′shən) *n.* **1** continued thought; reflection. **2** contemplation on sacred or solemn subjects, especially as a devotional exercise. **3** a contemplative or devotional writing or talk. **—Syn.** contemplation.

med·i·ta·tive (med′ə tā′tiv) *adj.* **1** fond of meditating. **2** expressing meditation. **—med′i·ta′tive·ly,** *adv.* **—med′i·ta′tive·ness,** *n.*

Med·i·ter·ra·ne·an (med′ə tə rā′nē ən or med′ə tə rān′yən) *adj.* of or having to do with the Mediterranean Sea or the lands around it. [< L *mediterraneus* < *medius* middle + *terra* land]

me·di·um (mē′dē əm) *adj. n.* **-di·ums** or **-di·a** (except for def. 6). *—adj.* having a middle position; moderate. *—n.* **1** that which is in the middle; neither one extreme nor the other; middle condition. **2** a substance or agent through which anything acts; a means: *Radio is a medium of communication.* **3** a means of artistic expression: *The sculptor did some carving in stone, but his favorite medium was wood.* **4** a substance in which something can live; environment: *Water is the medium in which fish live.* **5 a** a nutritive substance, either liquid or solid, such as agar-agar or gelatin, in or upon which bacteria, fungi, and other micro-organisms are grown for study. **b** a substance used for displaying, preserving, etc. organic specimens. **6** a liquid with which paints are mixed. **7** a person through whom spirits of the dead can supposedly communicate with the living. [< L *medium* neut. adj., middle]

hat, āge, cãre, fär; let, ēqual, tėrm; it, īce
hot, ōpen, ôrder; oil, out; cup, pu̇t, rüle, ūse
əbove, takən, pencəl, lemən, circəs
ch, child; ng, long; sh, ship
th, thin; TH, then; zh, measure

me·di·um-sized (mē′dē əm sīzd′) *adj.* neither large nor small of its kind.

Med.L. Medieval Latin.

med·lar (med′lər) *n.* **1** a fruit that looks like a small, brown apple. It is eaten when partly decayed. **2** the small, bushy tree of the rose family that the fruit grows on. [ME < OF *meslier* (the tree) < *mesle* (its fruit), ult. < L < Gk. *mespilon*]

med·ley (med′lē) *n.* **-leys,** *adj. —n.* **1** a mixture of things that ordinarily do not belong together. **2** in music, a vocal or instrumental composition made up of tunes, usually familiar, or excerpts from other pieces. *—adj.* made up of parts that are not alike; mixed. [ME < OF *meslee* < *mesler* mix, ult. < L *miscere.* Doublet of MELEE.]

Médoc or **Me·doc** (mā dok′) *n.* a red wine, a type of claret. [< *Médoc,* a district in S.W. France, where it is made]

me·dul·la (mə dul′ə) *n.* **me·dul·lae** (-ē or -ī). **1** in anatomy: **a** the medulla oblongata. **b** the marrow of bones. **c** the inner substance of an organ or structure. **2** in botany, the pith. [< L *medulla* marrow]

medulla ob·lon·ga·ta (ob′long gä′tə or ob′long gā′tə) in anatomy, the lowest part of the brain, at the top end of the spinal cord. See **brain** for diagram. [< NL *medulla oblongata* prolonged medulla]

med·ul·lar·y (med′ə ler′ē or mə dul′ər ē) *adj.* of, having to do with, or like medulla or the medulla oblongata.

me·du·sa (mə dū′sə or mə dü′sə, mə dū′zə or mə dü′zə) *n.* **-sas, -sae** (-sē or -sī, -zē or -zī). a jellyfish. [< *Medusa*]

Me·du·sa (mə dū′sə or mə dü′sə, mə dū′zə or mə dü′zə) *n.* **-sas.** in Greek legend, a horrible monster, one of the three Gorgons. She had snakes for hair, and anyone who looked upon her was turned to stone. She was killed by Perseus. **—Me·du′sa-like′,** *adj.*

meed (mēd) *n. Poetic.* what one deserves; reward. [OE *mēd*]

meek (mēk) *adj.* **1** patient; not easily angered; mild. **2** submitting tamely when ordered about or injured by others: *The boy was meek as a lamb when he was reproved.* [ME < ON *miukr* soft] **—meek′ly,** *adv.* **—meek′ness,** *n.* **—Syn. 1** forbearing. See **gentle. 2** submissive, yielding, docile. See **humble.**

meer·schaum (mēr′shəm, mēr′shom, or mēr′shôm) *n.* **1** a very soft, light magnesium silicate used to make tobacco pipes. *Formula:* $H_4Mg_2Si_3O_{10}$ **2** a tobacco pipe made of this material. [< G *Meerschaum* sea foam]

meet[1] (mēt) *v.* **met, meet·ing,** *n. —v.* **1** come face to face; come face to face with: *Their cars met on the narrow road.* **2** come together; come into contact or connection with: *Sword met sword in battle.* **3** join: *where two streets meet.* **4** be united; join in harmony: *His is a nature in which courage and caution meet.* **5** come into company with; be together: *The hosts met their guests at the restaurant.* **6** keep an appointment with: *Meet me at 1:00.* **7** be introduced to; become acquainted: *Have you met my sister?* **8** be present at the arrival of: *meet a boat.* **9** satisfy; comply with: *meet obligations, objections, etc.* **10** pay: *meet bills, debts, etc.* **11** fight with; oppose; deal with. **12** fight. **13** face directly: *He met her glance with a smile.* **14** experience: *He met open scorn before he won fame.* **15** assemble: *Parliament will meet next month.* **16 meet the eye** or **the ear,** be seen or heard. **17 meet up with,** meet. **18 meet with, a** come across. **b** get: *The plan met with approval.* **c** talk with. *—n.* **1** a meeting; a gathering; competition: *a racing meet, an athletic meet.* **2** the people at a meeting. **3** the place of meeting. [OE *mētan*] **—Syn.** *v.* **1** confront, encounter. **9** settle, fulfil.

meet[2] (mēt) *adj. Archaic.* suitable; proper; fitting: *It is meet that you should help your friends.* [OE (*ge*)*mǣte*]

meet·ing (mēt′ing) *n.* **1** a coming together: *He looked forward to a meeting with his sister.* **2** a gathering or assembly for business discussion, social purposes, etc. **3** an assembly of people for worship. **4** a place where things meet; junction.
Syn. 2 Meeting, assembly, gathering = a coming together of a group of people. **Meeting** applies especially to the coming together of a body of people to discuss or arrange business or action: *The club held a meeting.* **Assembly,** more formal, emphasizes coming or calling together for a common purpose, such as social pleasure, religious worship, or, particularly, joining in deliberation or action: *The principal called an assembly.* **Gathering** suggests less formal or organized coming together of a number of people: *There was a large gathering at her house.*

meeting house **1** a building used for worship by Quakers. **2** any place of worship; church. **3** a building used for public meetings.

meet·ly (mēt′lē) *adv.* suitably; properly.

meg. **1** megacycle. **2** megohm.

mega- *combining form.* **1** large: *megacephalic* = *large-headed.* **2** one million: *megacycle* = *one million cycles*; *megaton* = *one million tons.* Also, **meg-** before vowels. [< Gk. *megas* great]

meg·a·ce·phal·ic (meg′ə sə fal′ik) *adj.* large-headed; having a skull with a cranial capacity above the average. [< *mega-* + Gk. *kephalē* head + E *-ic*]

meg·a·cy·cle (meg′ə sī′kəl) *n.* in radio, a million cycles. *Abbrev.*: meg. [< *mega-* one million times (< Gk. *megas* great) + *cycle*]

meg·a·death (meg′ə deth′) *n.* the death of one million persons. [< *mega-* one million times (< Gk. *megas* great) + *death*]

meg·a·lith (meg′ə lith′) *n.* a stone of great size, especially in ancient constructive work or in monuments left by primitive people. [< Gk. *megas* great + *lithos* stone]

megalo- *combining form.* great; large. [< Gk. *megas, -galou*]

meg·a·lo·ma·ni·a (meg′ə lō mā′nē ə) *n.* a mental illness characterized by delusions of greatness, wealth, etc. [< Gk. *megas, megalou* great + *mania* madness]

meg·a·lo·ma·ni·ac (meg′ə lō mā′nē ak′) *n.* a person who suffers from megalomania.

meg·a·lop·o·lis (meg′ə lop′ə lis) *n.* a city of great or overpowering size, especially one thought of as a centre of the power, wealth, and influence of a country. [< Gk. *mega, megalou* great + *polis* city]

meg·a·phone (meg′ə fōn′) *n.* a large, funnel-shaped horn used to increase the loudness of the voice or the distance at which it can be heard. [< Gk. *megas* great + *phōnē* sound]

meg·a·ton (meg′ə tun′) *n.* a measure of atomic power equivalent to the energy released by one million tons of high explosive, specifically TNT. [< *mega-* one million times (< Gk. *megas* great) + (*1000-kilo*)*ton*]

A cheer leader using a megaphone

meg·ohm (meg′ōm′) *n.* a million ohms. *Abbrev.*: meg. [< *mega-* one million times (< Gk. *megas* great) + *ohm*]

me·grim (mē′grim) *n.* **1** migraine. **2** a whim; fancy. **3 megrims,** *pl.* morbid low spirits. [var. of *migraine*; influenced by *grim*]

mei·o·sis (mī ō′sis) *n.* **-ses** (-sēz). **1** in biology, a process of cell division by which the number of chromosomes in each cell is halved to allow for subsequent doubling by fertilization. **2** litotes. [< NL *meiosis* < Gk. *meiōsis* a lessening < *meioein* lessen < *meiōn* less]

mei·ot·ic (mī ot′ik) *adj.* of or having to do with meiosis.

Meis·sen (mī′sən) *n.* a kind of porcelain. [< *Meissen,* a city in East Germany, where it is made]

Meis·ter·sing·er (mīs′tər sing′ər; *German,* mīs′tər zing′ər) *n.* a member of one of the guilds, chiefly of workingmen, established in the principal German cities in the 14th, 15th, and 16th centuries for the cultivation of poetry and music.

Mek·ka (mek′ə) *n.* Mecca.

mel·a·mine (mel′ə mēn′ or mel′ə min) *n.* a hard plastic used for buttons, fabric finishes, etc. and especially for unbreakable dishes and dinnerware. [< *mel*am, a chemical compound + *amine*]

mel·an·cho·li·a (mel′ən kō′lē ə) *n.* a mental disorder characterized by great depression of spirits and gloomy fears. [< LL < Gk. *melancholia* < *melas* black + *cholē* bile]

mel·an·chol·ic (mel′ən kol′ik) *adj.* **1** melancholy; gloomy. **2** suffering from melancholia.

mel·an·chol·y (mel′ən kol′ē) *n.* **-chol·ies,** *adj.* —*n.* **1** sadness; low spirits; a tendency to be sad. **2** sober thoughtfulness; pensiveness. **3** black bile, the one of the four humors of ancient physiology believed to cause low spirits.
—*adj.* **1** sad; gloomy. **2** causing sadness; depressing: *a melancholy scene.* **3** expressive of sadness: *a melancholy smile.* **4** lamentable; deplorable: *a melancholy fact.* **5** soberly thoughtful; pensive. —**Syn.** *n.* **1** depression, dejection. *-adj.* **1** depressed, despondent, downcast.

Mel·a·ne·sian (mel′ə nē′zhən or mel′ə nē′shən) *n.* **1** a member of any of the dark-skinned peoples living in Melanesia, a group of islands in the Pacific Ocean, northeast of Australia. **2** the languages of Melanesia. —*adj.* of Melanesia or its people, or their languages.

mé·lange (mā läNzh′) *n.* a mixture; medley. [< F *mélange* < *mêler* mix]

Mel·ba toast (mel′bə) very thin, crisp toast.

meld (meld) *v.* in canasta, pinochle, etc. announce and show (cards for a score). —*n.* **1** the act of melding. **2** the cards that can be melded. [< G *melden* announce]

Mel·e·a·ger (mel′ē ā′jər) *n.* in Greek legend, the hero who killed the Calydonian boar. He was one of the Argonauts.

me·lee or **mê·lée** (mel′ā, mā′lā, or mā lā′; *French,* me lā′) *n.* **1** a confused fight; hand-to-hand fight among a number of fighters. **2** any similar state of hectic confusion. [< F *mêlée* (in OF *meslee*). Doublet of MEDLEY.]

mel·i·nite (mel′ə nīt′) *n.* a powerful explosive containing picric acid. [< F < Gk. *mēlinos* quince-yellow < *mēlon* quince]

mel·io·rate (mēl′yə rāt′ or mē′lē ə rāt′) *v.* **-rat·ed, -rat·ing.** improve. [< LL *meliorare* < L *melior* better] —**mel′io·ra′tion,** *n.* —**mel′io·ra′tor,** *n.*

mel·io·ra·tive (mēl′yə rā′tiv or mē′lē ə rā′tiv) *adj.* tending to improve.

mel·lif·lu·ence (mə lif′lü əns) *n.* a sweet sound; smooth flow.

mel·lif·lu·ent (mə lif′lü ənt) *adj.* mellifluous. —**mel·lif′lu·ent·ly,** *adv.*

mel·lif·lu·ous (mə lif′lü əs) *adj.* sweetly or smoothly flowing: *a mellifluous speech.* [< LL *mellifluus* < L *mel* honey + *fluere* to flow] —**mel·lif′lu·ous·ly,** *adv.* —**mel·lif′lu·ous·ness,** *n.*

mel·low (mel′ō) *adj.* **1** soft and full-flavored from ripeness; sweet and juicy: *a mellow apple.* **2** fully matured: *mellow wine.* **3** soft and rich: *a violin with a mellow tone, a mellow light in a picture, mellow color.* **4** rich; loamy: *mellow soil.* **5** softened and made wise by age and experience. **6** affected by liquor or drinking; slightly tipsy.
—*v.* make or become mellow. [var. of OE *mearu* soft, tender] —**mel′low·ly,** *adv.* —**mel′low·ness,** *n.*

me·lo·de·on (mə lō′dē ən) *n.* a small reed organ in which air is sucked inward by a bellows. [pseudo-Gk. form of earlier *melodium* < *melody*]

me·lod·ic (mə lod′ik) *adj.* **1** having to do with melody. **2** melodious. —**me·lod′i·cal·ly,** *adv.*

me·lo·di·ous (mə lō′dē əs) *adj.* **1** sweet-sounding; pleasing to the ear; musical: *a melodious voice.* **2** producing melody: *a melodious bird.* —**me·lo′di·ous·ly,** *adv.* —**me·lo′di·ous·ness,** *n.* —**Syn. 1** melodic, tuneful, harmonious.

mel·o·dist (mel′ə dist) *n.* a composer or singer of melodies.

hat, āge, cãre, fär; let, ēqual, tėrm; it, īce
hot, ōpen, ôrder; oil, out; cup, pu̇t, rüle, ūse
əbove, takən, pencəl, lemən, circəs
ch, child; ng, long; sh, ship
th, thin; ᴛʜ, then; zh, measure

mel·o·dra·ma (mel′ə dram′ə or -drä′mə) *n.* **1** a sensational drama with exaggerated appeal to the emotions and, usually, a happy ending. **2** any sensational writing, speech, or action with exaggerated appeal to the emotions. [< F < Gk. *melos* music + *drama* drama]

mel·o·dra·mat·ic (mel′ə drə mat′ik) *adj.* of, like, or suitable for melodrama; sensational and exaggerated. —**mel′o·dra·mat′i·cal·ly,** *adv.* —**Syn.** See **dramatic.**

mel·o·dy (mel′ə dē) *n.* **-dies. 1** any agreeable succession of sounds. **2** musical quality: *The melody of good speech.* **3** in music: **a** a succession of single tones, arranged in a rhythmical pattern; tune. **b** the main tune in a harmonized composition; air. **4** a poem to be sung to music. [ME < OF < LL < Gk. *melōidia,* ult. < *melos* song + *ōidē* song] —**Syn. 3** theme.

mel·on (mel′ən) *n.* **1** a large, juicy fruit that grows on a vine. Watermelons, cantaloupes or muskmelons, and honeydew melons are common kinds of melon. **2** a deep-pink color. **3 cut** or **split a melon,** *Slang.* divide extra profits among those considered to have a claim on them. [ME < OF < LL *melo, -onis,* short for L *melopepo* < Gk. *mēlopepōn* < *mēlon* apple + *pepōn* gourd] —**mel′on·like′,** *adj.*

Mel·pom·e·ne (mel pom′ə nē′) *n.* in Greek mythology, the Muse of tragedy.

melt (melt) *v.* **melt·ed, melt·ed** or **mol·ten, melt·ing,** *n.* —*v.* **1** change or be changed from solid to liquid: *Great heat melts iron. The ice melted quickly.* **2** dissolve: *Sugar melts in water.* **3** disappear or cause to disappear gradually: *As the sun came out, the clouds melted away.* **4** blend or merge gradually: *In the rainbow, the green melts into blue, the blue into violet. At the horizon the sea melted into the sky.* **5** waste away; dwindle: *His wealth melted away.* **6** soften: *Pity for his wounded enemy melted his heart.*
—*n.* **1** the act or process of melting. **2** the state of being melted. **3** a melted metal. **4** a quantity of metal melted at one operation or over a specified period, especially a single charge in smelting. [OE *meltan*] —**melt′er,** *n.*
Syn. 1 Melt, dissolve, thaw = change from a solid state. **Melt** suggests a gradual change caused by heat, by which a solid softens, loses shape, and finally becomes liquid: *The warm air melted the butter.* **Dissolve** emphasizes a breaking up of a solid into its smallest parts, caused by putting it in a liquid that reduces it and of which it becomes a part: *Dissolve some salt in a glass of water.* **Thaw,** used only of frozen things, means "change to the unfrozen state": *She thawed the frozen fruit.* **6** mollify.

melting point the degree of temperature at which a solid substance melts.

melting pot 1 a pot or other vessel to melt something in. **2** a country or city thought of as a place in which various races or sorts of people are assimilated. North America is often called a melting pot.

mel·ton (mel′tən) *n.* a smooth, heavy woollen cloth. Overcoats are often made of melton. [< *Melton* (*Mowbray*), a town in central England]

melt·wa·ter (melt′wo′tər or -wô′tər) *n.* water from melting glaciers or snows.

mem·ber (mem′bər) *n.* **1** a person belonging to a group: *a member of our club.* **2** a person elected to a legislative body: *a Member of Parliament, a Member of the Legislative Assembly.* **3** a constituent part of a whole: *a member of an equation.* **4** a part of the human body or of an animal or plant: *The legs and arms are members of the body.* [ME < OF < L *membrum* limb, part] —**Syn. 3** component. **4** organ, limb.

Member of Parliament in Canada, a title given to each of the representatives elected to the Federal Parliament in Ottawa. *Abbrev.:* M.P. or MP

Member of Provincial Parliament in Ontario, a member of the Legislative Assembly. *Abbrev.:* M.P.P. or MPP

Member of the Legislative Assembly a title given to each of the representatives elected to the legislatures of most Canadian provinces. *Abbrev.:* M.L.A. or MLA

mem·ber·ship (mem′bər ship′) *n.* **1** the fact or state of being a member. **2** the members. **3** the number of members.

mem·brane (mem′brān) *n.* **1** a thin, soft sheet or layer of animal tissue, lining or covering some part of the body. **2** a similar layer of vegetable tissue. [< L *membrana* < *membrum* member]

mem·bra·nous (mem′brə nəs or mem brā′nəs) *adj.* **1** of or like membrane. **2** characterized by the formation of a membrane. In **membranous croup,** a membrane forms in the throat and hinders breathing.

me·men·to (mə men′tō) *n.* **-tos** or **-toes. 1** something serving as a reminder, warning, or remembrance: *These post cards are mementos of our trip abroad.* **2 Memento,** in the Roman Catholic Church, either of two prayers beginning "Memento" ("Remember") in the canon of the Mass, in which the living and the dead respectively are commemorated. [< L *memento* remember!]

Mem·non (mem′non) *n.* **1** in Greek legend, an Ethiopian king killed by Achilles. **2** a huge statue of an Egyptian king at Thebes, Egypt.

mem·o (mem′ō) *n.* **mem·os.** *Informal.* a memorandum.

mem·oir (mem′wär or mem′wôr) *n.* **1** a biography. **2** a report of a scientific or scholarly study. **3 memoirs,** *pl.* **a** a record of facts and events written from personal knowledge or special information. **b** a record of a person's own experiences; autobiography. [< F *mémoire* < L *memoria.* Doublet of MEMORY.]

mem·o·ra·bil·i·a (mem′ə rə bil′ē ə) *n.pl.* things or events worth remembering. [< L *memorabilia,* pl. of *memorabilis.* See MEMORABLE.]

mem·o·ra·ble (mem′ə rə bəl) *adj.* worth remembering; not to be forgotten; notable. [< L *memorabilis,* ult. < *memor* mindful] —**mem′o·ra·bly,** *adv.* —**Syn.** remarkable, extraordinary.

mem·o·ran·da (mem′ə ran′də) *n.* a pl. of **memorandum.**

mem·o·ran·dum (mem′ə ran′dəm) *n.* **-dums** or **-da. 1** a short written statement for future use; a note to aid the memory. **2** an informal letter, note, or report. **3** in diplomacy, a summary of facts and arguments on some issue or arrangement that concerns two or more governments. [< L *memorandum* (thing) to be remembered]

me·mo·ri·al (mə mô′rē əl) *n.* **1** something that is a reminder of some important event or person, such as a statue, an arch or column, a book, or a holiday. **2** a statement sent to a government or person in authority, usually giving facts and asking that some wrong be corrected. —*adj.* helping to keep something fresh in people's memories: *memorial services.* [ME < OF < L *memorialis* < *memoria.* See MEMORY.]

me·mo·ri·al·ize (mə mô′rē əl īz′) *v.* **-ized, -iz·ing. 1** preserve the memory of; commemorate. **2** submit a memorial to; petition. —**me·mo′ri·al·iz′er,** *n.*

mem·o·rize (mem′ə rīz′) *v.* **-rized, -riz·ing.** commit to memory; learn by heart. —**mem′o·ri·za′tion,** *n.* —**mem′o·riz′er,** *n.*

mem·o·ry (mem′ə rē or mem′rē) *n.* **-ries. 1** the ability to remember. **2** the act of remembering. **3** all that a person remembers. **4** a person, thing, or event that is remembered. **5** the length of time during which the past is remembered: *This has been the hottest summer within living memory.* **6** reputation after death. **7 in memory of,** as a help in remembering; as a remembrance of: *On November 11 we observe a two-minute silence in memory of those who died fighting for their country.* [ME < OF < L *memoria* < *memor* mindful. Doublet of MEMOIR.]
Syn. 2 Memory, recollection = the act or fact of remembering. **Memory** emphasizes the ability to keep in the mind or call back something once learned, experienced, or otherwise known: *That vacation lives in her memory.* **Recollection,** applying to the act or to what is remembered, emphasizes calling back to mind, often with effort, something not thought of for a long time or forgotten: *I have little recollection of my childhood.*

mem·sa·hib (mem′sä′ib) *n.* in India: **1** a lady. **2** formerly, a European lady, especially the wife of a British colonial official. [< Hind. *mem-sahib* < *mem* (< E *ma'am*) + *sahib* sir]

men (men) *n.* pl. of **man. 1** more than one man. **2** human beings; people in general.

men·ace (men′is) *n. v.* **-aced, -ac·ing.** —*n.* a threat: *In dry weather forest fires are a menace.* —*v.* threaten: *Floods menaced the valley with destruction.* [ME < OF < L *minaciae* (pl.), ult. < *minae* projecting points, threats] —**men′ac·ing·ly,** *adv.* —**Syn.** *v.* See **threaten.**

me·nad (mē′nad) *n.* maenad.

mé·nage or **me·nage** (mā näzh′) *n.* **1** a household; domestic establishment. **2** housekeeping; management of a household. [< F]

me·nag·er·ie (mə naj′ər ē or mə nazh′ər ē) *n.* **1** a collection of wild animals kept in cages for exhibition. **2** the place where such animals are kept. [< F *ménagerie,* literally, management of a household]

mend (mend) *v.* **1** put in good condition again; make whole; repair: *mend a flat tire.* **2** set right; improve: *He should mend his manners.* **3** get back one's health. —*n.* **1** a place that has been mended. **2** a mending; improvement. **3 on the mend, a** improving. **b** getting well. [var. of *amend*] —**mend′er,** *n.*

Syn. *v.* **1 Mend, repair, patch** = put in good or usable condition again. **Mend** = make whole again something that has been broken, torn, or worn, but is now seldom used of large things: *She mended the broken vase with cement.* **Repair** = make right again something damaged, run down, decayed, weakened, etc.: *He repaired the electric toaster.* **Patch** = mend by putting a piece (or amount) of material on or in a hole, tear, or worn place: *His mother patched his torn trousers.* **2** correct, rectify, better.

men·da·cious (men dā′shəs) *adj.* **1** lying; untruthful. **2** false; untrue. [< L *mendax, -acis* lying] —**men·da′cious·ly,** *adv.* —**men·da′cious·ness,** *n.*

men·dac·i·ty (men das′ə tē) *n.* **-ties. 1** the habit of telling lies; untruthfulness. **2** a lie.

men·de·le·vi·um (men′də lā′vē əm) *n.* a rare, radioactive, synthetic chemical element, produced as a by-product of nuclear fission. *Symbol:* Md; *at.no.* 101; *at.wt.* 256 (most stable isotope). [after Dmitri Ivanovich *Mendeleev* (1834-1907), a Russian chemist]

Men·de·li·an (men dē′lē ən) *adj.* **1** of or having to do with Gregor Johann Mendel, 1822-1884, an Austrian monk and biologist. His investigations of heredity laid the foundations for the science of genetics. **2** inherited in accordance with Mendel's Law.

Mendel's law (men′dəlz) a law governing the inheritance of many characteristics in plants and animals, according to which there occurs, in the second and later generations of hybrids, every possible combination of the characteristics of the original parent animals or plants, each combination in a definite proportion of individuals.

men·di·can·cy (men′də kən sē) *n.* the act of begging; the state of being a beggar.

men·di·cant (men′də kənt) *adj.* begging: *mendicant friars.* —*n.* **1** a beggar. **2** a mendicant friar. [< L *mendicans, -antis* < *mendicus* beggar]

Men·e·la·us (men′ə lā′əs) *n.* in Greek legend, a king of Sparta, husband of Helen, and brother of Agamemnon.

men·folk (men′fōk′) *n.pl.* men.

men·ha·den (men hā′dən) *n.* **-den.** a sea fish common along the eastern coast of the United States, used for making oil and fertilizer. [< Algonquian]

me·ni·al (mē′nē əl or mēn′yəl) *adj.* suited to or belonging to a servant; low; mean. —*n.* **1** a servant who does the humblest and most unpleasant tasks. **2** a low, mean, or servile person; flunky. [ME < *meynie* household < OF *mesnie* < VL *mansionata* < L *mansio* habitation < *manere* remain] —**me′ni·al·ly,** *adv.*

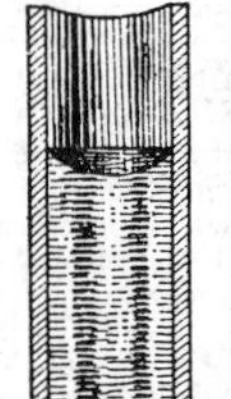

The meniscus of a column of liquid: A, concave; B, convex.

me·nin·ges (mə nin′jēz) *n.* pl. of **me·ninx** (mē′ningks). in anatomy, the three membranes that surround the brain and spinal cord. [< NL (pl.) < Gk. *mēninx, -ingos*]

men·in·gi·tis (men′in jī′tis) *n.* a serious disease in which the meninges are inflamed. [< NL < Gk. *mēninx, -ingos* membrane + *-itis*]

me·nis·cus (mə nis′kəs) *n.* **-nis·cus·es, -nis·ci** (-nis′ī or -nis′ē). **1** in physics, the curved upper surface of a column of liquid. See picture in the previous column. **2** in optics, a lens that is convex on one side and concave on the other. **3** a crescent; crescent-shaped body. [< NL < Gk. *mēniskos,* dim. of *mēnē* moon]

A meniscus lens

Men·non·ite (men′ən īt′) *n.* **1** a member of a Christian church opposed to infant baptism, taking oaths, holding public office, and military service. **2** a member of the Mennonite ethnic group. [after *Menno* Simons (1492-1559), a Dutch leader of the Mennonites]

me·nom·i·nee (mə nom′ə nē) *n. Cdn.* wild rice. [< Cree]

men·o·pause (men′ə poz′ or -pôz′) *n.* in women, the final cessation of the menses, occurring normally between the ages of 45 and 50. [< NL < Gk. *mēn* month + *pausis* pause]

Me·nor·ah or **me·nor·ah** (mə nôr′ə) *n.* **1** in the Jewish religion, a candelabrum used in temple services, and at home celebrations during Hanukkah. **2** a Jewish fraternal and cultural society. [< Hebrew *manorah*]

men·ses (men′sēz) *n.pl.* a discharge of blood from the uterus that normally occurs every four weeks between puberty and the menopause. [< L *menses,* pl. of *mensis* month]

Men·she·vik or **men·she·vik** (men′shə vik′) *n.* **-viks** or **-vi·ki** (-vē′kē), *adj.* —*n.* in Russia, a member of the conservative wing of the Social Democratic Party opposed to the more radical Bolsheviks from 1903 to 1917. —*adj.* of or having to do with the Mensheviks or Menshevism. [< Russian *Menshevik* < *menshe* less; because it was at one time the minority wing. Opposed to BOLSHEVIK.]

men·stru·al (men′strü əl) *adj.* **1** having to do with the menses. **2** monthly.

men·stru·ate (men′strü āt′) *v.* **-at·ed, -at·ing.** of women, have a discharge of blood from the uterus, normally at intervals of four weeks. [< LL *menstruare,* ult. < *mensis* month]

men·stru·a·tion (men′strü ā′shən) *n.* the act or period of menstruating.

men·stru·um (men′strü əm) *n.* **-stru·ums, -stru·a** (-strü ə). *Archaic.* a liquid that dissolves solids; a solvent. [< Med.L *menstruum,* neut. of L *menstruus* monthly]

men·su·ra·bil·i·ty (men′shə rə bil′ə tē or men′sə rə bil′ə tē) *n.* the property of being mensurable.

men·su·ra·ble (men′shə rə bəl or men′sə rə bəl) *adj.* measurable. [< LL *mensurabilis* < L *mensurare.* See MEASURE, V.]

men·su·ra·tion (men′shə rā′shən or men′sə rā′shən) *n.* **1** the act, art, or process of measuring. **2** the branch of mathematics that deals with finding lengths, areas, and volumes. [< LL *mensuratio, -onis,* ult. < L *mensura.* See MEASURE.]

mens·wear (menz′wār′) *n.* **1** men's clothing. **2** cloth suitable for making men's clothing. —*adj.* of or made from this kind of cloth: *menswear terylene.*

-ment *suffix forming nouns from verbs or the stems of verbs.* **1** the act or state or fact of ——ing, as in *enjoyment, management.* **2** the state or condition or fact of being ——ed, as in *amazement, astonishment.* **3** the product or result of ——ing, as in *pavement.* **4** a means or instrument for ——ing, as in *inducement.* **5** two or more of these meanings, as in *improvement, measurement, settlement.* [< F < L *-mentum*]

men·tal (men′təl) *adj.* **1** of the mind: *a mental test, a mental disease.* **2** for the mind; done by the mind: *mental arithmetic.* **3 a** having a mental disease or weakness: *a mental patient.* **b** for people who are mentally ill: *a mental hospital.* [< LL *mentalis* < L *mens, mentis* mind]

mental age in psychology, an estimate of the level of mental development as measured against the chronological age at which this development is reached by the average person.

men·tal·i·ty (men tal′ə tē) *n.* **-ties. 1** mental capacity; mind: *An idiot has a very low mentality.* **2** attitude or outlook: *the Eastern mentality.*

men·tal·ly (men′təl ē) *adv.* **1** in the mind; with the mind. **2** with regard to the mind.

mental reservation an unexpressed qualification of a statement.

mental telepathy extrasensory perception.

men·thol (men′thol) *n.* a white crystalline substance obtained from oil of peppermint, used in medicine. *Formula*: $C_{10}H_{20}O$ [< G < L *menta* mint + *oleum* oil]

men·tho·lat·ed (men′thə lāt′id) *adj.* containing menthol.

men·tion (men′shən) *v.* **1** speak about; refer to. **2 not to mention,** not even considering; besides. [< n.] —*n.* **1** a short statement (about); reference (to). **2 make mention of,** speak of; refer to. [ME < OF < L *mentio, -onis*] —**men′tion·a·ble,** *adj.*

men·tor (men′tər) *n.* a wise and trusted adviser. [< *Mentor*, a faithful friend of Ulysses. He was the teacher and adviser of Ulysses' son.]

men·u (men′ū) *n.* **1** a list of the food served at a meal; bill of fare. **2** the food served. [< F *menu* small, detailed < L *minutus* made small. Doublet of MINUTE[2].]

me·ow (mē ou′) *n.* the sound made by a cat. —*v.* make the sound of a cat. Also, **miaow, miaou.** [imitative]

Meph·i·stoph·e·les (mef′ə stof′ə lēz′) *n.* **1** in the Faust legend, the devil. **2** a powerful evil spirit; a crafty devil.

Meph·is·to·phe·li·an (mef′is tə fē′lē ən) *adj.* **1** like Mephistopheles; wicked and crafty; sardonic; scoffing. **2** of or having to do with Mephistopheles.

me·phit·ic (mi fit′ik) *adj.* **1** having a nasty smell. **2** noxious; poisonous; pestilential. [< LL *mephiticus* < *mephitis* stench]

me·phi·tis (mi fī′tis) *n.* **1** a foul or nasty smell. **2** a poisonous or nasty vapor arising from the earth. [< L < Gk.]

mer·can·tile (mėr′kən tīl′) *adj.* **1** of or having to do with merchants or trade; commercial: *a successful mercantile venture.* **2** engaged in trade or commerce: *a mercantile firm.* **3** of or having to do with mercantilism. [< F < Ital. *mercantile* < *mercante* merchant]

mercantile system mercantilism.

mer·can·til·ism (mėr′kən tīl iz′əm) *n.* a theory or system of political economy that stressed the holding of gold and other precious metals, a greater volume of exports than imports, and the exploitation of colonies. Mercantilism replaced feudalism.

mer·can·til·ist (mėr′kən tīl′ist) *n.* a person who favors mercantilism.

Mer·ca·tor's projection (mėr kā′tərz) a method of drawing maps with straight instead of curved lines for latitude and longitude. [after Gerhardus *Mercator* (1512-1594), a Flemish map maker]

mer·ce·nar·y (mėr′sə ne′rē) *adj. n.* **-nar·ies.** —*adj.* **1** working for money only; acting with money as the sole motive. **2** done only for money or gain. —*n.* a soldier serving for pay in a foreign army. [ME < L *mercenarius* < *merces* wages] —**mer′ce·nar′i·ly,** *adv.* —**mer′ce·nar′i·ness,** *n.* —**Syn.** *adj.* **1** hireling, grasping. -*n.* hireling.

mer·cer·ize (mėr′sər īz′) *v.* **-ized, -iz·ing.** treat (cotton thread or cloth) with a chemical solution that strengthens it, makes it hold dyes better, and gives it a silky lustre. [after John *Mercer* (1791-1866), a British calico printer, who patented the process in 1850]

mer·chan·dise (*n.* mėr′chən dīs′ or mėr′chən dīz′; *v.* mėr′chən dīz′) *n. v.* **-dised, -dis·ing.** —*n.* goods for sale; wares; articles bought and sold. —*v.* **1** buy and sell; trade. **2** strive for increased sales or greater acceptance of goods, services, etc. by attractive display, advertising, etc. [ME < OF *marchandise* < *marchand* merchant] —**mer′chan·dis′er,** *n.*

hat, āge, cãre, fär; let, ēqual, tėrm; it, īce
hot, ōpen, ôrder; oil, out; cup, pu̇t, rüle, ūse
əbove, takən, pencəl, lemən, circəs
ch, child; ng, long; sh, ship
th, thin; ᴛʜ, then; zh, measure

mer·chant (mėr′chənt) *n.* **1** a person who buys and sells commodities for profit. **2** a storekeeper. —*adj.* trading; having to do with trade: *merchant ships.* [ME < OF *marchant*, ult. < L *merx, mercis* wares]

mer·chant·a·ble (mėr′chən tə bəl) *adj.* marketable. [ME < obs. v. *merchant* + *-able*]

mer·chant·man (mėr′chənt mən) *n.* **-men** (-mən). a ship used in commerce.

merchant marine 1 ships used in commerce. **2** the sailors who work on such ships, thought of as a group: *John's brother is in the merchant marine.*

merchant vessel a ship used in commerce.

Mer·cian (mėr′sē ən, mėr′shē ən, or mėr′shən) *adj.* of Mercia, in ancient times an Anglo-Saxon kingdom in central England, its people, or their dialect. —*n.* **1** a native or inhabitant of Mercia. **2** the dialect of Anglo-Saxon spoken in Mercia.

mer·ci·ful (mėr′si fəl) *adj.* having mercy; showing or feeling mercy; full of mercy. —**mer′ci·ful·ly,** *adv.* —**mer′ci·ful·ness,** *n.* —**Syn.** compassionate, clement, kind, lenient.

mer·ci·less (mėr′si lis) *adj.* without mercy; having no mercy; showing no mercy: *The soldiers' cruelty was merciless.* —**mer′ci·less·ly,** *adv.* —**mer′ci·less·ness,** *n.* —**Syn.** relentless, implacable, pitiless, ruthless.

mer·cu·ri·al (mər kūr′ē əl) *adj.* **1** sprightly; quick. **2** changeable; fickle. **3** caused by the use of mercury: *mercurial poisoning.* **4** containing mercury: *a mercurial ointment.* —*n.* a drug containing mercury. —**mer·cu′ri·al·ly,** *adv.*

mer·cu·ric (mər kūr′ik) *adj.* of compounds, containing mercury with a valence of two.

Mer·cu·ro·chrome (mər kūr′ə krōm′) *n. Trademark.* a red liquid containing mercury, used as an antiseptic. *Formula*: $C_{20}H_8Br_2HgNa_2O_6$ [< *mercury* + *chrome*]

mer·cu·rous (mər kūr′əs or mėr′kyu̇ rəs) *adj.* of compounds, containing mercury with a valence of one.

mer·cu·ry (mėr′kyu̇ rē) *n.* **-ries. 1** a heavy, silver-white metallic chemical element that is liquid at ordinary temperatures. *Symbol*: Hg; *at.no.* 80; *at.wt.* 200.59. **2** the column of mercury in a thermometer or barometer. **3 Mercury, a** in Roman mythology, the messenger of the gods, the god of commerce, skill of hands, quickness of wit, and eloquence, identified with the Greek god Hermes. **b** in astronomy, the smallest planet in the solar system and nearest to the sun. [< L *Mercurius* Mercury]

mer·cy (mėr′sē) *n.* **-cies. 1** more kindness than justice requires; kindness beyond what can be claimed or expected. **2** kindly treatment; pity. **3** something to be thankful for; blessing. **4 at the mercy of,** in the power of. [ME < OF *merci* < L *merces* reward]
Syn. 1 Mercy, clemency = kindness or mildness shown to an enemy, an offender, etc. **Mercy** = compassion shown by refraining from punishing severely those deserving severity or from treating harshly enemies and others in one's power: *The guard showed mercy to the prisoners.* **Clemency** suggests showing mercy because of mildness of disposition rather than from sympathy: *That judge's clemency is well known.*

mercy flight *Cdn.* especially in the North, an aircraft flight to fetch a seriously ill or injured person to hospital for treatment.

mercy seat 1 in the Bible, the gold covering on the Ark of the Covenant, regarded as the resting place of God. **2** the throne of God.

mere[1] (mēr) *adj. superl.* **mer·est.** nothing else than; only; simple: *The cut was a mere scratch.* [< L *merus* pure] —**Syn.** bare, sheer.

mere[2] (mēr) *n. Poetic or dialect.* lake; pond. [OE]

mere·ly (mēr′lē) *adv.* simply; only; and nothing more; and that is all.

me·ren·gue (mə reng′gā′) *n.* a gay West Indian dance having fast, limping side steps. [< Sp.]

mer·e·tri·cious (mer′ə trish′əs) *adj.* attractive in a showy way; alluring by false charms: *A wooden building painted to look like marble is meretricious.* [< L *meretricius* < *meretrix, -tricis* prostitute < *mereri* earn] **—mer′e·tri′cious·ly,** *adv.* **—mer′e·tri′cious·ness,** *n.*

mer·gan·ser (mər gan′sər) *n.* **-sers** or (*esp. collectively*) **-ser.** any of several kinds of large North American ducks that have long, slender bills. The male has a crested head. [< NL *merganser* < *mergus* diver + *anser* goose]

merge (mėrj) *v.* **merged, merg·ing. 1** swallow up; absorb; combine and absorb; combine: *The steel combines merged various small businesses.* **2** become swallowed up or absorbed in something else: *The twilight merges into darkness.* [< L *mergere* dip] **—Syn. 1** consolidate, fuse.

merg·er (mėr′jər) *n.* **1** a merging; absorption; combination: *One big company was formed by the merger of four small ones.* **2** a person or thing that merges.

me·rid·i·an (mə rid′ē ən) *n.* **1** an imaginary circle passing through any place on the earth's surface and through the North and South Poles. **2** the half of such a circle from pole to pole. All the places on the same meridian have the same longitude. **3** the highest point that the sun or a star reaches in the sky. **4** the highest point: *The meridian of life is the prime of life.* **5** one of a series of north-south lines used as a basis of land surveys.
—adj. highest; greatest. [ME < OF < L *meridianus,* ult. < *medius* middle + *dies* day]

NORTH POLE
SOUTH POLE
Meridians of longitude

me·rid·i·o·nal (mə rid′ē ə nəl) *adj.* **1** southern; southerly; characteristic of the south or people living there, especially of southern France. **2** of, having to do with, or resembling a meridian. **3** along a meridian; in a north-south direction: *a meridional flow of air, a meridional chain of weather stations.* *—n.* an inhabitant of the south, especially the south of France. [< LL *meridionalis* < L *meridies* noon, south < *medius* middle + *dies* day; patterned after *septentrionalis* northern]
—me·rid′i·o·nally, *adv.*

me·ringue (mə rang′) *n.* **1** a mixture made of egg whites beaten stiff and sweetened with sugar. Meringue is often spread on pies, puddings, etc. and lightly browned in the oven. **2** a tart shell made of this mixture and filled with fruit, whipped cream, etc. [< F]

me·ri·no (mə rē′nō) *n.* **-nos,** *adj.* *—n.* **1** a breed of sheep, originating in Spain, having long, fine wool. **2** a sheep of this breed. **3** the wool of this sheep. **4** a soft woollen yarn made from it. **5** a thin, soft woollen cloth made from this yarn or some substitute.
—adj. made of this wool, yarn, or cloth. [< Sp.]

mer·it (mer′it) *n.* **1** goodness; worth; value. **2** anything that deserves praise or reward. **3 on its merits,** without prejudice; on the actual facts or qualities, whether good or bad: *The judge will consider the case on its merits.*
—v. deserve. [< F < L *meritum* earned]
Syn. *n.* **1 Merit, worth** = the goodness or value of someone or something. **Merit** emphasizes the idea of something earned, and suggests an excellence in accomplishment or quality that deserves praise: *The merits of your plan outweigh the defects.* **Worth** emphasizes inherent excellence or value, apart from any connections or conditions affecting its usefulness, value, or importance: *The worth of the new drugs is certain, although all their uses are not yet known.*

mer·i·to·ri·ous (mer′ə tô′rē əs) *adj.* deserving reward or praise; having merit; worthy. **—mer′i·to′ri·ous·ly,** *adv.* **—mer′i·to′ri·ous·ness,** *n.*

merle or **merl** (mėrl) *n. Poetic.* the common European blackbird. [< F < L *merula*]

mer·lin (mėr′lən) *n.* a kind of small falcon. [ME < AF *merilun* < OF *esmeril* < Gmc.]

Mer·lin (mėr′lən) *n.* in Arthurian legend, the magician who was adviser to King Arthur.

mer·lon (mėr′lən) *n.* the solid part between two openings in a battlement. See picture in the next column. [< F < Ital. *merlone*]

EMBRASURES
MERLONS

mer·maid (mėr′mād′) *n.* in fairy tales, a maiden having the form of a fish from the waist down. [< *mere*[2] + *maid*]

mer·man (mėr′man′ or mėr′mən) *n.* **-men** (-men′ or -mən). in fairy tales, a man having the shape of a fish from the waist down.

Mer·o·vin·gi·an (mer′ə vin′jē ən) *adj.* designating or having to do with the Frankish line of kings who reigned in France from about A.D. 500 to 751. *—n.* one of these kings.

mer·ri·ment (mer′ē mənt) *n.* laughter and gaiety; fun; mirth; merry enjoyment.

mer·ry (mer′ē) *adj.* **-ri·er, -ri·est. 1** laughing and gay; full of fun. **2** gay; joyful: *a merry holiday.* **3** *Archaic.* pleasant; delightful. **4 make merry,** laugh and be gay; have fun. [OE *myrge*] **—mer′ri·ly,** *adv.* **—mer′ri·ness,** *n.* **—Syn. 1** jolly, jovial. See **gay.**

mer·ry-an·drew (mer′ē an′drü) *n.* a clown; buffoon.

mer·ry-go-round (mer′ē gō round′) *n.* **1** a set of model animals and seats on a circular platform that is driven round and round by machinery. **2** any whirl or rapid round: *The holidays were a merry-go-round of parties.*

mer·ry·mak·er (mer′ē māk′ər) *n.* a person who is being merry; a person engaged in merrymaking.

mer·ry·mak·ing (mer′ē māk′ing) *n.* **1** laughter and gaiety; fun. **2** a gay festival; merry entertainment. *—adj.* gay and full of fun; engaged in merrymaking.

mer·ry·thought (mer′ē thot′ or -thôt′) *n.* a wishbone.

me·sa (mā′sə) *n. U.S.* a small, high plateau with steep sides. [< Sp. < L *mensa* table]

A mesa

mé·sal·li·ance (mā zal′ē əns; *French,* mā zä lyäɴs′) *n. French.* a misalliance; marriage with a person of lower social position.

mes·cal (mes kal′) *n.* **1** an alcoholic drink made from the fermented juice of an agave plant. **2** the plant itself. **3** a small cactus whose buttonlike tops are dried and chewed as a stimulant by some North American Indians. [< Sp. < Nahuatl *mexcalli* liquor]

mes·cal·in (mes′kə lin) *n.* mescaline.

mes·cal·ine (mes′kəl ēn′ or mes′kəl in) *n.* a narcotic drug that produces hallucinations and is chemically related to LSD, derived from mescal (def. 3). *Formula:* $C_{11}H_{17}NO_3$

mes·dames (me däm′) *n.* pl. of **madame.**

mes·de·moi·selles (med mwä zel′) *n.* pl. of **mademoiselle.**

me·seems (mi sēmz′) *v.* **-seemed.** *Archaic.* it seems to me.

mes·en·ter·y (mes′ən ter′ē) *n.* **-ter·ies.** in anatomy, a membrane that enfolds and supports an internal organ, attaching it to the body wall or to another organ. [< Med.L < Gk. *mesenterion* < *mesos* middle + *enteron* intestine]

mesh (mesh) *n.* **1** one of the open spaces of a net, sieve, or screen: *This net has half-inch meshes.* **2** the cord, wire, etc. used in a net, screen, etc. **3** the engagement of gear teeth. **4 in mesh,** in gear; fitted together. **5 meshes,** *pl.* **a** network. **b** snares.
—v. **1** catch or be caught in a net. **2** engage or become engaged. The teeth of the small gear mesh with the teeth of a larger one. See **engage** for picture. [cf. OE *mǣscre* net]

mes·mer·ic (mes mer′ik or mez mer′ik) *adj.* hypnotic. **—mes·mer′i·cal·ly,** *adv.*

mes·mer·ism (mes′mər iz′əm or mez′mər iz′əm) *n.* hypnotism. [after Franz Anton *Mesmer* (1734-1815), an Austrian physician who popularized it]

mes·mer·ist (mes′mər ist or mez′mər ist) *n.* a hypnotist.

mes·mer·ize (mes′mər īz′ or mez′mər īz′) *v.* **-ized, -iz·ing.** hypnotize. —**mes′mer·iz′er,** *n.*

mes·o·carp (mes′ə kärp′) *n.* in botany, the middle layer of the pericarp, such as the fleshy part of a peach or plum. [< Gk. *mesos* middle + *karpos* fruit]

mes·o·derm (mes′ə derm′) *n.* in biology, the middle layer of cells in an embryo. [< Gk. *mesos* middle + *derma* skin]

mes·o·lith·ic or **Mes·o·lith·ic** (mes′ə lith′ik) *adj.* in anthropology, of or relating to the period in the Stone Age between the neolithic and the paleolithic periods. [< Gk. *mesos* middle + *lithos* stone + E *-ic*]

mes·on (mes′on) *n.* a highly unstable particle found in the nucleus of an atom, having either a positive or negative charge and a very short lifetime (about a millionth of a second or less). Theoretically, mesons exert nuclear forces of attraction. [< Gk. *meson,* neut. of adj. *mesos* middle]

Mes·o·po·ta·mi·a (mes′ə pə tā′mē ə or mes′ə pə tām′yə) *n.* an ancient country in S.W. Asia, between the Tigris and Euphrates rivers. —**Mes′o·po·ta′mi·an,** *adj. n.*

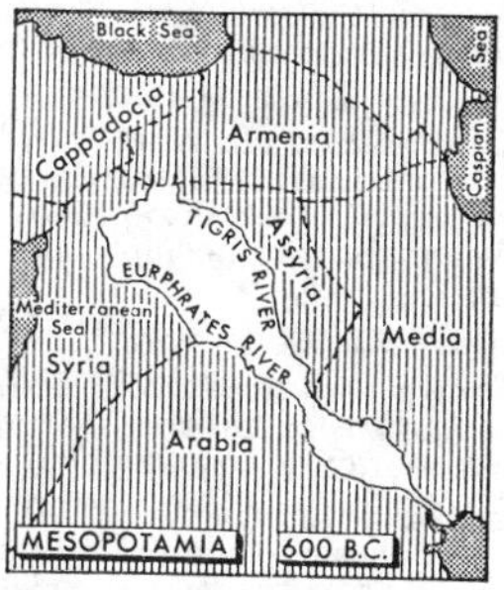

mes·o·tron (mes′ə tron′) *n.* a meson. [< *meson* + *electron*]

Mes·o·zo·ic (mes′ə zō′ik) in geology: —*n.* **1** the era before the present era, beginning approximately 200 million years ago; the age of reptiles. See the chart under **geology. 2** the rocks formed in this era. —*adj.* of or having to do with this era or the rocks formed during it. [< Gk. *mesos* middle + *zōē* life]

mes·quite (mes kēt′ or mes′kēt) *n.* a deep-rooted shrublike tree that often grows in dense clumps or thickets. Cattle eat mesquite pods. [< Sp. *mezquite* < Nahuatl *mizquitl*]

mess (mes) *n.* **1** a dirty or untidy mass or group of things; a dirty or untidy condition: *There was a mess of dirty dishes in the sink.* **2** a state of confusion or difficulty: *The company's records were in a mess.* **3** an unpleasant or unsuccessful affair or state of affairs. **4** a group of people who eat together regularly, especially such a group in the armed services. **5** a meal for such a group: *The officers are at mess now.* **6** in the armed services: **a** an organization for social purposes: *He was secretary of the sergeants' mess.* **b** the dining-room, lounge, etc. used by members of such an organization. **7** a portion of food; portion of soft food: *a mess of porridge, a mess of fish.* **8** food that does not look or taste good.
—*v.* **1** take one's meals (*with*). **2 mess about** or **mess around,** be busy without really accomplishing anything. **3 mess up** or **make a mess of, a** make dirty or untidy: *The clay made a mess of her shoes.* **b** spoil the appearance of; disfigure: *He messed up his book by scribbling on the pages.* **c** do badly at; make a failure of: *She made a mess of her final examinations.* [ME < OF *mes* < LL *missus* (course) put (i.e., on the dinner table), pp. of *mittere* send]

mes·sage (mes′ij) *n.* **1** information or instructions sent from one person to another. **2** an official speech or writing: *On Christmas Day we listened to the Queen's message to the Commonwealth.* **3** a lesson or moral implied in a work or works of fiction, a motion picture, play, etc.: *Films with a message sometimes run the risk of spoiling good plots.* **4** inspired words: *the message of a prophet.* **5** the business entrusted to a messenger; mission; errand: *His message completed, he went on his way.* [ME < OF, ult. < L *missus,* pp. of *mittere* send] —**Syn. 1** communication, letter, note, dispatch.

mes·sa·line (mes′ə lēn′ or mes′ə lēn′) *n.* a thin, soft silk cloth with a surface like satin. [< F]

mes·sen·ger (mes′ən jər) *n.* **1** a person who carries a message or goes on an errand. **2** a sign that something is coming; forerunner: *Dawn is the messenger of day.* **3** a government official employed to carry dispatches; courier. [ME *messanger,* earlier *messager* < OF *messagier* < *message.* See MESSAGE.]

hat, āge, cãre, fär; let, ēqual, tėrm; it, īce
hot, ōpen, ôrder; oil, out; cup, pu̇t, rüle, ūse
əbove, takən, pencəl, lemən, circəs
ch, child; ng, long; sh, ship
th, thin; ᴛʜ, then; zh, measure

mess hall in the armed services, a place where a group of people eat together regularly.

Mes·si·ah (mə sī′ə) *n.* **1** the expected deliverer of the Jewish people. **2** in Christian use, Jesus. **3** Often, **messiah.** any person hailed as or thought of as a savior, liberator, or deliverer. [var. of LL *Messias* < Gk. < Hebrew *mashiaḥ* anointed]

Mes·si·an·ic (mes′ē an′ik) *adj.* **1** of the Messiah. **2** Also, **messianic.** of a savior; characteristic of a Messiah or believers in a Messiah.

mes·sieurs (mes′ərz; *French,* mā syœ′) *n.* pl. of **monsieur.** gentlemen. See **Messrs.** for usage note.

mess·man (mes′mən) *n.* **-men** (-mən). a waiter on a ship.

mess·mate (mes′māt′) *n.* especially in the armed services, one of a group of people who eat together regularly.

Messrs. (mes′ərz) *n.* Messieurs.
☛ Messrs. is used as the plural of *Mr.* (*Messrs. Diefenbaker and Pearson*) and sometimes, though rarely now in Canadian usage, in addressing firms (*Messrs. Brown, Hubbell, and Company*).

mess·y (mes′ē) *adj.* **mess·i·er, mess·i·est. 1** untidy; in disorder; dirty. **2** badly done. —**mess′i·ness,** *n.*

mes·ti·zo (mes tē′zō) *n.* **-zos** or **-zoes.** a person of mixed blood, especially the child of a Spaniard and an American Indian. [< Sp., ult. < L *mixtus* mixed]

met (met) *v.* pt. and pp. of **meet**[1].

met. 1 metaphor. **2** metaphysics. **3** meteorological. **4** metronome. **5** metropolitan.

meta- *prefix.* **1** behind, beyond, or after, as in *metaphysics.* **2** change of state or place, as in *metamorphosis.* **3** between or among, as in *metatarsal.* **4** transposed or reciprocal, as in *metathesis.* **5** similar in chemical composition, as in *metaphosphate.* [< Gk. *meta* with, after]

met·a·bol·ic (met′ə bol′ik) *adj.* having to do with metabolism. —**met′a·bol′i·cal·ly,** *adv.*

me·tab·o·lism (mə tab′ə liz′əm) *n.* the processes of building up food into living matter and using living matter so that it is broken down into simpler substances or waste matter, giving off energy. [< Gk. *metabolē* change < *meta-* into a different position + *bolē* a throwing]

met·a·car·pal (met′ə kär′pəl) in anatomy: —*adj.* of or having to do with the metacarpus. —*n.* a bone of the metacarpus.

met·a·car·pus (met′ə kär′pəs) *n.* **-pi** (-pī or -pē). in anatomy: **1** the part of a hand between the wrist and the fingers. **2** the part of a forefoot between the carpus and the phalanges. [< NL, ult. < Gk. *meta-* after + *karpos* wrist]

met·al (met′əl) *n. v.* **-alled** or **-aled, -al·ling** or **-al·ing.**
—*n.* **1** a substance such as gold, silver, iron, copper, lead, tin, aluminum, steel, bronze, and brass. **2** in chemistry, any element that can form a salt by replacing the hydrogen of an acid, or any mixture of such elements. **3** broken stone, cinders, etc. used for roads and roadbeds. **4** the melted material that becomes glass or pottery. **5** material; substance: *Cowards are not made of the same metal as heroes.* **6** in printing: **a** type metal. **b** the state of being set or composed in type. **7** the aggregate number, mass, or power of the guns of a warship.
—*v.* furnish, cover, or fit with metal.
—*adj.* made of metal. [ME < OF < L < Gk. *metallon,* originally, mine]

metal fatigue the deterioration and breakdown of metal as a result of slight but constant stress, such as continual tapping, vibration, etc.

me·tal·lic (mə tal′ik) *adj.* **1** of, containing, or consisting of metal. **2** like metal; characteristic of metal; that suggests metal: *a metallic lustre, a metallic voice.* **3** resembling the sound produced when metal is struck. **4** in chemistry, having the form or outward characteristics of a metal (usually said of a metal when occurring uncombined with other substances). —**me·tal′li·cal·ly,** *adv.*

met·al·lif·er·ous (met′əl if′ər əs) *adj.* containing or yielding metal: metalliferous rocks. [< L *metallifer* < *metallum* metal + *ferre* to bear]

met·al·lur·gic (met′əl ėr′jik or mə tal′ər jik) *adj.* metallurgical.

met·al·lur·gi·cal (met′əl ėr′jə kəl) *adj.* of or having to do with metallurgy.

met·al·lur·gist (met′əl ėr′jist or mət al′ər jist) *n.* a person who is trained in metallurgy.

met·al·lur·gy (met′əl ėr′jē or mə tal′ər jē) *n.* the science or art of working with metals. It includes the separation and refining of metals from their ores, the production of alloys, and the shaping and treatment of metals by heat, rolling, etc. [< NL *metallurgia,* ult. < Gk. *metallon* metal + *ergon* work]

met·al·work (met′əl wėrk′) *n.* **1** things made out of metal. **2** the act of making things out of metal.

met·al·work·er (met′əl wėr′kər) *n.* a person who makes things out of metal.

met·al·work·ing (met′əl wėr′king) *n.* the process of making things out of metal.

met·a·mor·phic (met′ə môr′fik) *adj.* **1** characterized by change of form; having to do with change of form. **2** of rocks, having undergone structural change caused by pressure, heat, chemical action, etc.

met·a·mor·phism (met′ə môr′fiz əm) *n.* **1** a change of form. **2** in geology, a change in the structure of a rock caused by pressure, heat, etc.

met·a·mor·phose (met′ə môr′fōz or met′ə môr′fōs) *v.* **-phosed, -phos·ing. 1** change in form; transform: *The witch metamorphosed people into animals.* **2** change the form or structure of by metamorphosis or metamorphism. **3** undergo metamorphosis or metamorphism.

met·a·mor·pho·sis (met′ə môr′fə sis or met′ə môr fō′sis) *n.* **-ses** (-sēz′). **1** a change of form. Tadpoles become frogs by metamorphosis; they lose their tails and grow legs. **2** the changed form. **3** a noticeable or complete change of character, appearance, or condition. **4** a marked change in the form, and usually the habits, of an animal in its development after the embryonic stage. **5** the structural or functional modification of a plant organ or structure during the course of its development. [< L < Gk. *metamorphōsis,* ult. < *meta-* over + *morphē* form]

met·a·phor (met′ə fər or met′ə fôr′) *n.* **1** an implied comparison between two different things; a figure of speech in which a word or phrase that ordinarily means one thing is used of another thing in order to suggest a likeness between the two: "*A copper sky*" *and* "*a heart of stone*" *are metaphors.* **2 mix metaphors,** confuse two or more metaphors in the same expression. [< F < L < Gk. *metaphora* transfer, ult. < *meta-* over + *pherein* carry]

☛ **Metaphors and similes both make comparisons.** The difference between them is largely one of phrasing: where the *metaphor* implies the likeness, *a simile* says specifically that one resembles the other, using the words *like* or *as.*

met·a·phor·i·cal (met′ə fôr′ə kəl) *adj.* using metaphors; figurative. —**met′a·phor′i·cal·ly,** *adv.*

met·a·phys·i·cal (met′ə fiz′ə kəl) *adj.* **1** of metaphysics; about the real nature of things. **2** highly abstract; hard to understand. **3** concerned with abstract thought or subjects: *a metaphysical mind.* **4** of or having to do with a group of English poets of the 1600's whose verse is characterized by abstruse conceits and the use of unexpected or elaborate imagery. —**met′a·phys′i·cal·ly,** *adv.*

met·a·phy·si·cian (met′ə fə zish′ən) *n.* a person skilled in or familiar with metaphysics.

met·a·phys·ics (met′ə fiz′iks) *n.* **1** the branch of philosophy that tries to explain reality and knowledge; philosophical study of the real nature of the universe. **2** the more abstruse or speculative divisions of philosophy, thought of as a unit. **3** *Informal.* any process of reasoning thought of as abstruse or extremely subtle. [ME < Med.L *metaphysica* < Med.Gk. (*ta*) *metaphysika* for Gk. *ta meta ta physika* those (works) after the Physics; with reference to the philosophical works of Aristotle]

me·tas·ta·sis (mə tas′tə sis) *n.* **-ses** (-sēs′). **1** in medicine, the growth or spread of cells, especially of the diseased cells of a tumor or cancer, from one organ or part of the body to another. **2** in physics, a change in nuclear structure resulting from the emission of an alpha particle. **3** *Rare.* metabolism. **4** in rhetoric, a change of theme or subject. [< LL < Gk. *metastasis* removal, ult. < *meta-* + *histanai* place]

met·a·tar·sal (met′ə tär′səl) in anatomy: —*adj.* of the metatarsus. —*n.* a bone of the metatarsus.

met·a·tar·sus (met′ə tär′səs) *n.* **-si** (-sī or -sē). **1** in anatomy, the part of a foot between the ankle and the toes. **2** in zoology, the part (or bony part) of a hind foot between the tarsus and the phalanges. [< NL < Gk. *meta-* after + *tarsos* flat of the foot]

me·tath·e·sis (mə tath′ə sis) *n.* **-ses** (-sēz′). **1** the transposition of sounds, syllables, or letters in a word. **2** in chemistry, the interchange of atoms between two molecules. **3** a transposition; reversal. [< LL < Gk. *metathesis* transposition, ult. < *meta-* over + *tithenai* set]

met·a·zo·a (met′ə zō′ə) *n.* pl. of **metazoon.**

Met·a·zo·a (met′ə zō′ə) *n.* in zoology, a large division of animals comprising the metazoans. [< NL, ult. < Gk. *meta-* after + *zōion* animal]

met·a·zo·an (met′ə zō′ən) *n.* in zoology, any of a large division that includes all animals except the protozoans, having the body composed of many cells developed from a single cell. —*adj.* of or having to do with the metazoans. [< *Metazoa*]

met·a·zo·on (met′ə zō′on or -zō′ən) *n.* **-zo·a** (-zō′ə). metazoan.

mete[1] (mēt) *v.* **met·ed, met·ing. 1** give to each a share of; distribute; allot. **2** *Poetic.* measure. [OE *metan*]

mete[2] (mēt) *n.* **1** a boundary. **2** a boundary stone. [ME < OF < L *meta*]

met·em·psy·cho·sis (met′əm sī kō′sis or mə temp′sə kō′sis) *n.* **-ses** (-sēz). the passing of the soul at death into a new body. Some Oriental philosophies, such as Hinduism and Buddhism, teach that by metempsychosis a person's soul lives again in an animal's body. [< L < Gk. *metempsychosis* < *meta-* over + *empsychoein* animate, ult. < *en* in + *psychē* soul]

me·te·or (mē′tē ər) *n.* a mass of stone or metal that comes toward the earth from outer space at enormous speed; shooting star. Meteors become so hot from hurtling through the air that they glow and usually burn up. [ME < Med.L < Gk. *meteōron* (thing) in the air, ult. < *aeirein* lift]

me·te·or·ic (mē′tē ôr′ik) *adj.* **1** of meteors. **2** flashing like a meteor; brilliant and soon ended; swift. **3** of the atmosphere: *Wind and rain are meteoric phenomena.*

me·te·or·ite (mē′tē ər īt′) *n.* a mass of stone or metal that has fallen to the earth from outer space; fallen meteor.

me·te·o·ri·tic (mē′tē ə rit′ik) *adj.* of or having to do with meteorites: *meteoritic craters.*

me·te·or·o·log·ic (mē′tē ər ə loj′ik) *adj.* meteorological.

me·te·or·o·log·i·cal (mē′tē ər ə loj′ə kəl) *adj.* **1** of or having to do with the atmosphere and weather. **2** of or having to do with meteorology.

me·te·or·o·log·i·cal·ly (mē′tē ər ə loj′ik lē) *adv.* in meteorological respects; by meteorology; according to meteorology.

me·te·or·ol·o·gist (mē′tē ər ol′ə jist) *n.* a person trained in meteorology.

me·te·or·ol·o·gy (mē′tē ər ol′ə jē) *n.* the science of the atmosphere and atmospheric conditions, especially as they relate to the weather. [< Gk. *meteōrologia* < *meteōron* (thing) in the air + *-logos* treating of]

me·ter[1] (mē′tər) *n.* metre.

me·ter[2] (mē′tər) *n.* **1** a device for measuring. **2** a device for measuring and recording the amount of gas, water, electricity, etc. used. —*v.* measure with a meter. [< *-meter*]

-meter *combining form.* **1** a device for measuring, as in *speedometer, thermometer.* **2** having —— feet, as in *tetrameter, hexameter.* [< NL *-metrum* < Gk. *metron* measure]

Meth. Methodist.

meth·ane (meth′ān) *n.* a colorless, odorless, inflammable gas, the simplest of the hydrocarbons. Methane comes from marshes, petroleum wells, volcanoes, and coal mines. *Formula*: CH_4 [< *methyl*]

me·theg·lin (mə theg′lin) *n.* an alcoholic drink made from fermented honey and water; a kind of mead. [< Welsh *meddyglyn*]

me·thinks (mi thingks′) *v.* **-thought.** *Archaic.* it seems to me. [OE *mē thyncth* it seems to me]

meth·od (meth′əd) *n.* **1** a way of doing something. **2** a system in doing things; order in thinking. **3 method in one's madness,** system and sense underlying apparent folly. [< L < Gk. *methodos,* originally, pursuit < *meta-* after + *hodos* a travelling] —**Syn. 1** mode, manner. See **way.**

me·thod·ic (mə thod′ik) *adj.* methodical.

me·thod·i·cal (mə thod′ə kəl) *adj.* according to a method; systematic; orderly. —**me·thod′i·cal·ly,** *adv.* —**me·thod′i·cal·ness,** *n.* —**Syn.** See **orderly.**

Meth·od·ism (meth′əd iz′əm) *n.* the doctrine, organization, and manner of worship of the Methodist Church.

Meth·od·ist (meth′əd ist) *n.* a member of a Christian church that had its origin in the teachings and work of John Wesley, 1703-1791, an English clergyman, and his brother Charles, 1707-1788. —*adj.* of or having to do with the Methodists or Methodism.

meth·od·ize (meth′əd īz′) *v.* **-ized, -iz·ing.** reduce to a method; arrange with method. —**me′thod·iz′er,** *n.*

meth·od·ol·o·gist (meth′ə dol′ə jist′) *n.* an expert in methodology.

meth·od·ol·ogy (meth′ə dol′ə jē) *n.* **1** the analysis or the science of method. **2** the systematic procedures or methods used in any field, arrived at by applying the principles of logic to this field. **3** the branch of logic that deals with such methods. **4** methods of teaching; principles and practices of instruction. [< NL *methodologia* < Gk. *methodos* method + *-logia* science]

me·thought (mē thot′ or -thôt′) *v.* pt. of **methinks.** *Archaic.* it seemed to me.

Me·thu·se·lah (mə thü′zə lə) *n.* **1** in the Bible, a man said to have lived 969 years. Gen. 5:27. **2** a very old man.

meth·yl (meth′əl) *n.* a univalent, hydrocarbon radical that occurs in many organic compounds. *Formula*: CH_3 [< F *méthyle,* ult. < Gk. *methy* wine + *hylē* wood]

methyl alcohol a colorless, poisonous, inflammable liquid obtained from the distillation of wood or from the catalytic treatment of carbon monoxide and hydrogen. It is widely used as a fuel, as a solvent, etc. *Formula*: CH_3OH

meth·yl·ene (meth′ə lēn′) *n.* **1** in commercial use, methyl alcohol. **2** in chemistry, a bivalent organic radical derived from methane. *Formula*: CH_2

me·tic·u·lous (mə tik′yù ləs) *adj.* extremely or excessively careful about small details. [< L *meticulosus* < *metus* fear] —**me·tic′u·lous·ly,** *adv.*

mé·tier (mā tyā′) *n.* **1** a trade; profession. **2** the kind of work for which one has special ability. [< F < L *ministerium.* Doublet of MINISTRY.]

Mé·tis or **Me·tis** (mā tēs′ or mā tē′; *often,* mē′təs) *n.* **-tis.** *Cdn.* a person of mixed white (especially French) and North American Indian ancestry; half-breed. [< Cdn.F *métis* half-breed]

Mé·tisse (mā tēs′) *n. Cdn. Rare.* a female Métis. [< Cdn.F]

me·ton·y·my (mə ton′ə mē) *n.* the use of the name of one thing for that of another which it naturally suggests. *Example*: The pen (power of literature) is mightier than the sword (military force). [< LL < Gk. *metonymia,* literally, change of name < *meta-* over + dial. *onyma* name]

hat, āge, cãre, fär; let, ēqual, tėrm; it, īce
hot, ōpen, ôrder; oil, out; cup, pùt, rüle, ūse
əbove, takən, pencəl, lemən, circəs
ch, child; ng, long; sh, ship
th, thin; ᴛʜ, then; zh, measure

met·o·pe (met′ə pē′ or met′ōp) *n.* in Doric architecture, one of the square spaces, either decorated or plain, between triglyphs in a frieze. [< L < Gk. *metopē* < *meta-* between + *opē* opening]

me·tre[1] or **me·ter**[1] (mē′tər) *n.* **1** in verse, the rhythmical pattern resulting from the arrangement of stressed and unstressed syllables in regularly recurring groups (feet). **2** in music: **a** a unit for measuring the rhythmical pattern of a composition, determined by the division of each bar into the same number of beats, the first of which is always the strongest, and a uniform arrangement of strong and weak beats. **b** any such rhythmical pattern. [OE *meter* < L *metrum* poetic metre < Gk. *metron* measure, metre]

me·tre[2] or **me·ter**[2] (mē′tər) *n.* in the metric system, a measure of length equal to 39.37 inches. [< F *mètre* < L < Gk. *metron* measure]

-metre *combining form.* metre; 39.37 inches, as in *kilometre, millimetre.*

met·ric (met′rik) *adj.* **1** of or having to do with the metre or the system of measurement based on it. **2** metrical. [(def. 1) < F *métrique* < *mètre* < L < Gk. *metron* measure; (def. 2) < L *metricus* < Gk. *metrikos* < *metron* measure, metre]

met·ri·cal (met′rə kəl) *adj.* **1** of or having to do with metre; having a regular arrangement of stresses; written in verse, not in prose: *a metrical translation of Homer.* **2** of, having to do with, or used in, measurement.

met·ri·cal·ly (met′rik lē) *adv.* in metre; according to metre.

met·ri·ca·tion (met′rə kā′shən) *n.* the process of converting to the metric system of weights and measures.

metric system a decimal system of measurement that uses the metre (39.37 in.) as its unit of length. The gram (.0022046 pound) is the unit of mass or weight, and the litre (61.024 cubic inches or 1 cubic decimetre) is the unit of volume. A cubic centimetre of water weighs approximately one gram. The measures of length and weight are:

1 millimetre = 1/1000 metre	1 milligram = 1/1000 gram
1 centimetre = 1/100 metre	1 centigram = 1/100 gram
1 decimetre = 1/10 metre	1 decigram = 1/10 gram
1 decametre = 10 metres	1 decagram = 10 grams
1 hectometre = 100 metres	1 hectogram = 100 grams
1 kilometre = 1,000 metres	1 kilogram = 1,000 grams

metric ton a measure of weight equal to 1,000 kilograms or 2,204.62 avoirdupois pounds.

met·ro (met′rō) *n. Informal.* **1** a metropolitan (adj., def. 3) government. **2** a metropolitan area.

me·trol·o·gy (mə trol′ə jē) *n.* **1** the science of weights and measures. **2** a system of weights and measures. [< Gk. *metron* measure + E *-logy*]

met·ro·nome (met′rə nōm′) *n.* a timing device having a pendulum that can be adjusted to tick at different speeds. A metronome is mainly used by persons practising musical instruments to help them keep time. [< Gk. *metron* measure + *-nomos* regulating < *nemein* regulate]

A metronome

met·ro·nom·ic (met′rə nom′ik) *adj.* of or like a metronome.

me·trop·o·lis (mə trop′ə lis) *n.* **1** the most important city of a country or region: *London is the metropolis of England.* **2** a large city; important centre: *Montreal is a busy metropolis.* **3** the chief diocese of a church, or ecclesiastical, province; the see of a metropolitan bishop. [< LL < Gk. *mētropolis* < *mētēr* mother + *polis* city]

met·ro·pol·i·tan (met′rə pol′ə tən) *adj.* 1 of a large city; belonging to large cities: *metropolitan newspapers.* 2 constituting a metropolis: *a metropolitan centre.* 3 denoting a form of municipal government consisting of a type of federation of several municipalities within a metropolitan area. 4 of or having to do with the chief diocese of a church or province. 5 constituting the mother city or the mainland territory of the parent state: *metropolitan France.*
—*n.* 1 a person who lives in a large city and knows its ways. 2 a the chief bishop of a church province, having authority over the bishops (suffragans) within the territory. b in the Western Church, an archbishop presiding over a province. c in the Greek Church, a prelate ranking above an archbishop and below a patriarch.

metropolitan area the area or region including a large city and its suburbs.

-metry *combining form.* the process or art of measuring, as in *biometry.* [< Gk. *-metria* < *metron* measure]

met·tle (met′əl) *n.* 1 disposition or temperament. 2 spirit; courage. 3 **on one's mettle,** ready to do one's best. [var. of *metal*]

met·tle·some (met′əl səm) *adj.* full of mettle; spirited; courageous. —**Syn.** ardent, fiery.

me·tump (mə tump′) *n.* tumpline. [? < Abenaki]

Mev (mev) *n.* a million electron volts.

mew[1] (mū) *n.* the sound made by a cat. —*v.* make the sound of a cat or one like it. [imitative]

mew[2] (mū) *n.* a sea gull; gull. [OE *mǣw*]

mew[3] (mū) *n.* 1 a cage in which hawks are kept, especially while moulting. 2 a place of retirement or concealment; secret place; den.—*v.* 1 cage (a hawk), especially at moulting time. 2 shut up in a cage; conceal; confine. 3 *Archaic.* change (feathers, etc.); moult. [ME < OF *mue* < *muer* molt < L *mutare*]

mewl (mūl) *v.* cry like a baby; whimper. [imitative]

mews (mūz) *n. Esp.Brit.* 1 stables built around a court or alley. 2 such stables converted into dwellings: *an apartment in a mews.* [originally pl. of *mew*[3]]

Mex. 1 Mexico. 2 Mexican.

Mex·i·can (mek′sə kən) *adj.* of or having to do with Mexico, a country in North America, or its people.
—*n.* 1 a person born in or living in Mexico. 2 a citizen of Mexico.

mez·za·nine (mez′ə nēn′) *n.* 1 a partial storey between two main floors of a building. It is usually just above the ground floor. 2 in a theatre, the first balcony, or its front section. [< F < Ital. *mezzanino* < *mezzano* middle < L *medianus.* See MEDIAN.]

mez·zo (met′sō or mez′ō) *adj.* 1 in music, middle; medium; half. 2 *Informal.* mezzo-soprano. —*n. Informal.* mezzo-soprano. [< Ital. < L *medius* middle]

mez·zo·for·te (met′sō fôr′tā or mez′ō-) *adj. adv.* in music, moderately loud; half as loud as forte. [< Ital.]

mez·zo-so·pran·o (met′sō sə pran′ō or mez′ō-) *n.* **-pran·os,** *adj.* —*n.* 1 a voice between soprano and contralto. 2 a singer having such a voice. —*adj.* of or for a mezzo-soprano; that can sing a mezzo-soprano part.

mez·zo·tint (met′sō tint′ or mez′ō-) *n.* 1 an engraving on copper or steel made by polishing and scraping away parts of a roughened surface. 2 a print made from such an engraving. 3 this method of engraving pictures.
—*v.* engrave in mezzotint. [< Ital. *mezzotinto* half-tint]

mf. or **mf** in music, moderately loud. (for Ital. *mezzo forte*)

M.F. Master of Forestry.

mfg. manufacturing.

mfr. manufacturer.

Mg magnesium.

mg. milligram; milligrams.

Mgr. 1 Manager. 2 Monsignor. 3 Monseigneur.

MHG or **M.H.G.** Middle High German.

mho (mō) *n.* the unit of electrical conductance equal to that of a body whose resistance is one ohm. [*ohm* spelled backwards]

mi (mē) *n.* in music, a syllable used for the third tone of an eight-tone scale. See **do**[2] for diagram. [see GAMUT]

mi. 1 mile; miles. 2 mill; mills.

M.I.5 *Brit.* the branch of Military Intelligence dealing with security and counter-espionage in the United Kingdom.

mi·aow or **mi·aou** (mē ou′) *n. v.* meow.

mi·as·ma (mī az′mə or mē az′mə) *n.* **-mas, -ma·ta** (-mə tə). 1 a poisonous vapor rising from the earth and infecting the air. The miasma of swamps was formerly supposed to cause disease. 2 an atmosphere or influence that infects or corrupts: *a miasma of evil thoughts.* [< NL < Gk. *miasma* pollution < *miainein* pollute]

mi·ca (mī′kə) *n.* a mineral that divides into thin, partly transparent layers; isinglass. Mica is used in electric fuses, etc. where the heat might break glass. [< L *mica* grain, crumb]

mice (mīs) *n.* pl. of **mouse.**

Mich. 1 Michigan. 2 Michaelmas.

Mich·ael·mas (mik′əl məs) *n. Esp.Brit.* September 29, a Christian festival in honor of the archangel Michael.

mick·ey (mik′ē) *n. Slang.* 1 a Mickey Finn. 2 *Cdn.* a half bottle of liquor or wine. 3 the detonator of a bomb.

Mickey Finn or **mickey finn** (mik′ē fin′) *Slang.* 1 a pill, etc. put into an alcoholic drink in order to drug it. 2 a drink so drugged.

mick·le (mik′əl) *adj. adv. n. Archaic or dialect.* much. [OE *micel*]

Mic·mac (mik′mak′) *n.* 1 a tribe of Algonquian Indians that formerly lived in Newfoundland, New Brunswick, and Nova Scotia. 2 a member of this tribe. [< Algonquian *migmac,* literally, allies]

micro- *combining form.* 1 small; very small, as in *micro-organism.* 2 abnormally small, as in *microcephalic.* 3 one millionth of a ——, as in *microfarad.* 4 done with or involving the use of a microscope, as in *microbiology.* [< Gk. *mikros* small]

mi·cro·bar·o·graph (mī′krō bar′ə graf′) *n.* an instrument for recording very minor fluctuations in atmospheric pressure.

mi·crobe (mī′krōb) *n.* 1 a microscopic organism, usually of vegetable nature; germ. 2 a bacterium, especially one causing disease. [< F < Gk. *mikros* small + *bios* life]

mi·cro·bi·ol·o·gy (mī′krō bī ol′ə jē) *n.* the biology of micro-organisms.

mi·cro·chem·is·try (mī′krō kem′əs trē) *n.* the branch of chemistry dealing with minute samples or quantities.

mi·cro·cir·cuit (mī′krō sėr′kit) *n.* in electronics, a circuit composed of miniaturized elements.

mi·cro·coc·cus (mī′krō kok′əs) *n.* **-coc·ci** (-kok′sī or -kok′sē). a spherical or egg-shaped bacterium. Certain micrococci cause disease; others produce fermentation.

mi·cro·cop·y (mī′krō kop′ē) *n.* **-cop·ies,** *v.* **-cop·ied, cop·y·ing.** —*n.* a copy made on microfilm. —*v.* make a copy of on microfilm.

mi·cro·cosm (mī′krō koz′əm) *n.* 1 a little world; universe in miniature. 2 man thought of as a miniature representation of the universe. [< F < LL *microcosmus* < LGk. *mikros kosmos* little world]

mi·cro·far·ad (mī′krō far′əd or -far′ad) *n.* in electricity, a unit of capacity; one millionth of a farad.

mi·cro·fiche (mī′krə fēsh′) *n.* **-fich·es, -fiche** (-fēsh′). a single piece of microfilm, usually 4×6 in. [< *micro-* + F *fiche* card]

mi·cro·film (mī′krō film′) *n.* 1 a film for making very small photographs of pages of a book, newspapers, etc. to preserve them in a very small space. 2 a photograph made on such film. —*v.* photograph on microfilm.

mi·cro·groove (mī′krō grüv′) *n.* a narrow groove used on long-playing phonograph records.

mi·crom·e·ter (mī krom′ə tər) *n.* an instrument for measuring very small distances, angles, objects, etc.

hat, āge, cãre, fär; let, ēqual, tėrm; it, īce
hot, ōpen, ôrder; oil, out; cup, pu̇t, rüle, ūse
əbove, takən, pencəl, lemən, circəs
ch, child; ng, long; sh, ship
th, thin; ᴛʜ, then; zh, measure

Certain kinds are used with a microscope or telescope. [< F *micromètre*]

micrometer calliper or **caliper** a calliper having an adjusting screw with a fine thread, and so capable of making very accurate measurements.

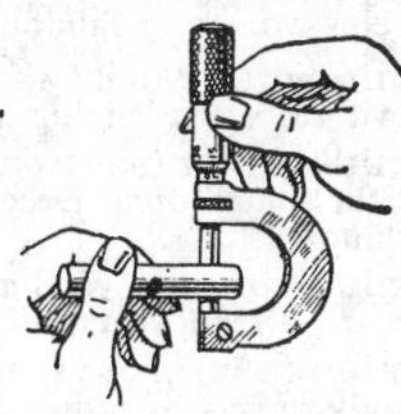

A micrometer combined with callipers. The scale is just below the thumb of the upper hand.

mi·cron (mī′kron) *n.* **mi·crons, mi·cra** (mī′krə). one millionth of a metre. *Symbol:* μ [< NL < Gk. *micron,* neut. adj., small]

Mi·cro·ne·sian (mī′krō nē′zhən) *adj.* of or having to do with Micronesia, one of the three main island groups in the Pacific (including the Marianas and the Marshall Islands), its inhabitants, languages, etc. —*n.* **1** a native of Micronesia, of mixed Polynesian, Melanesian, and Malay ancestry. **2** any of the languages spoken in Micronesia.

mi·cro-or·gan·ism (mī′krō ôr′gən iz′əm) *n.* an animal or vegetable organism too small to be seen except with a microscope. Bacteria are micro-organisms.

mi·cro·phone (mī′krə fōn′) *n.* an instrument for magnifying small sounds or for transmitting sounds. Microphones that are used in radio broadcasting change sound waves into variations of an electric current.

mi·cro·phy·sics (mī′krō fiz′iks) *n.* the branch of physics dealing with the structure of molecules, atoms, electrons, and other minute particles of matter.

mi·cro·scope (mī′krə skōp′) *n.* an instrument with a lens or combination of lenses for making small things look larger. [< NL *microscopium* < Gk. *mikros* small + *-skopion* means of viewing < *skopeein* look at]

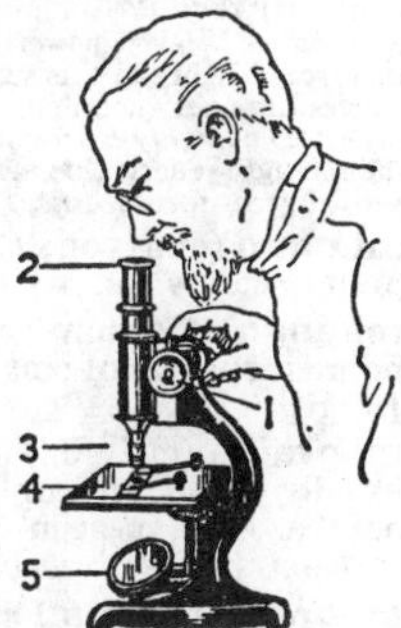

A microscope. 1, screws to adjust focus. 2, eyepiece. 3, objective. 4, platform to hold objects. 5, mirror. There are magnifying lenses in the eyepiece and objective. The mirror reflects light up through the platform, which has an opening in it or is made of glass.

mi·cro·scop·ic (mī′krə skop′ik) *adj.* **1** that cannot be seen without using a microscope; tiny. **2** like a microscope; suggesting a microscope: *a microscopic eye for mistakes.* **3** of or having to do with a microscope; with a microscope.

mi·cro·scop·i·cal (mī′krə skop′ə kəl) *adj.* microscopic.

mi·cro·scop·i·cal·ly (mī′krə skop′ik lē) *adv.* **1** by the use of a microscope. **2** as if with a microscope; in great detail.

mi·cros·co·pist (mī kros′kə pist or mī′krə skō′pist) *n.* a person trained in the use of the microscope.

mi·cros·co·py (mī kros′kə pē or mī′krə skō′pə) *n.* the use of a microscope; microscopic investigation.

mi·cro·spore (mī′krə spôr′) *n.* **1** in botany, a small spore from which a male gametophyte develops. **2** in seed plants, a pollen grain.

mi·cro·wave (mī′krō wāv′) *n.* a high-frequency electromagnetic wave having a very short length, usually ranging from .03937 of an inch to one foot.

mid[1] (mid) *adj.* in the middle of; middle. [OE *midd*]

mid[2] or **'mid** (mid) *prep. Poetic.* amid. [var. of *amid*]

mid- *combining form.* middle; mid; the middle point or part of: *midair = the middle part of the air.*

mid. middle.

mid·air or **mid-air** (mid′ãr′) *n.* **1** the sky; air: *The parachute floated in midair.* **2** uncertainty; doubt: *With the contract still in midair, the board recessed.* —*adj.* in midair: *a midair collision of two jets.*

Mi·das (mī′dəs) *n.* **1** in Greek legend, a king of Phrygia whose touch turned everything to gold. Unable to eat or drink, he begged that his gift be removed, and he was permitted to wash it away. **2** a man of great moneymaking ability. **3 the Midas touch,** the ability to make money easily. —**Mi′das-like′,** *adj.*

mid·brain (mid′brān′) *n.* the middle part of the brain.

mid·chan·nel (mid′chan′əl) *n.* the middle part of a channel.

mid·con·ti·nent (mid′kon′tə nənt) *n.* the middle part of a continent.

mid·day (mid′dā′) *n.* the middle of the day; noon. —*adj.* of midday. [OE *middæg*]

mid·den (mid′ən) *n.* **1** a kitchen midden. **2** *Dialect.* a dunghill; refuse heap. [apparently < Scand.; cf. Danish *mödding,* alteration of *mög dynge* muck heap]

mid·dle (mid′əl) *adj.* **1** halfway between; in the centre; at the same distance from either end or side; *the middle house in the row.* **2** in between; medium: *a man of middle size.* **3** intermediate. **4** between old and modern: *Middle English.*
—*n.* **1** the point or part that is the same distance from each end or side or other limit; central part. **2** the middle part of a person's body; waist. [OE *middel*]
Syn. *n.* **1 Middle, centre** = a point or part halfway between certain limits. **Middle** most commonly applies to the part more or less the same distance from each end, side, or other limit of a thing or between the beginning and end of a period of action: *He came in the middle of the day.* **Centre** applies to the point in the exact middle of something having a definite outline or shape, as of a circle, sphere, square, or to something thought of as the point from, to, or around which everything moves: *Ottawa is the centre of our government.*

middle age the time of life between youth and old age.

mid·dle-aged (mid′əl ājd′) *adj.* between youth and old age.

Middle Ages the period of European history between ancient and modern times, from about A.D. 500 (or from A.D. 476, the date of the fall of Rome) to about A.D. 1450.

middle C in music, the note on the first added line below the treble staff and the first above the bass staff.

middle class people between the aristocracy or the very wealthy and the working class.

mid·dle-class (mid′əl klas′) *adj.* of or characteristic of the middle class; bourgeois.

middle distance 1 the area between the foreground and the background, as in a photograph or painting. **2** in track, any race from 440 yards up to, and often including, the mile.

middle ear a cavity between the eardrum and the inner ear; tympanum. In man it contains three bones: the malleus, incus, and stapes.

Middle East the region between the E. Mediterranean and India. The term has no exact geographical limits, but is usually taken to include the Near East.

Middle English 1 the period in the development of the English language between Old English and Modern English, lasting from about 1100 to about 1500. **2** the language of this period. Chaucer wrote in Middle English.

Middle French the French language from 1400 to 1600.

Middle High German the High German language from 1100 to 1450.

Middle Low German the Low German language from 1100 to 1450.

mid·dle·man (mid′əl man′) *n.* **-men** (men′). a trader or merchant who buys goods from the producer and sells them to a retailer or directly to the consumer.

mid·dle·most (mid′əl mōst′) *adj.* in the exact middle; nearest the middle; midmost.

mid·dle-of-the-road (mid′əl əv ᴛʜə rōd′) *adj.* not extreme; moderate. —**mid′dle-of-the-road′er,** *n.*

middle term in logic, a term in the major and minor

premises of a syllogism but not in the conclusion.

mid·dle·weight (mid′əl wāt′) *n.* **1** one of average weight. **2** a boxer or wrestler who weighs more than 147 pounds and less than 160 pounds.

mid·dling (mid′ling) *adj.* medium in size, quality, grade, etc. *—adv. Informal or dialect.* moderately; fairly. *—n.* **middlings,** *pl.* **a** products of medium size, quality, grade, or price. **b** coarse particles of ground wheat mixed with bran. [< *middle*]

mid·dy (mid′ē) *n.* **-dies. 1** a middy blouse. **2** *Informal.* a midshipman.

middy blouse a loose blouse similar to those worn by sailors.

Mid·gard (mid′gärd′) *n.* in Norse mythology, the earth.

midge (mij) *n.* **1** a kind of very small insect; gnat. **2** a very small person. [OE *mycg*]

midg·et (mij′it) *n.* **1** a very small person; dwarf. **2** anything much smaller than the usual size for its type or kind. *—adj.* **1** much smaller than the usual size for its type or kind: *a midget submarine.* **2** in sports: **a** of or for very young or very small players. **b** bantam. [< *midge*] —**Syn.** See **dwarf.**

Mi·di (mē dē′) *n.* the south, especially the south of France.

Mid·i·an·ite (mid′ē ən īt′) *n.* in the Bible, a member of a wandering tribe of Arabs that fought against the Israelites.

mid·i·ron (mid′ī′ərn) *n.* in golf, a club with a steel or iron head having a face of medium slope.

mid·land (mid′lənd) *n.* the middle part of a country; the interior. *—adj.* in or of the midland.

mid·most (mid′mōst′) *adj.* in the exact middle; nearest the middle.

mid·night (mid′nīt′) *n.* twelve o'clock at night; the middle of the night. *—adj.* **1** of or like midnight. **2 burn the midnight oil,** study or work late at night.

midnight sun the sun seen at midnight in the arctic and antarctic regions during summer.

mid·rib (mid′rib′) *n.* the central vein of a leaf.

mid·riff (mid′rif) *n.* **1** the muscular wall separating the chest cavity from the abdomen; diaphragm. **2** the middle portion of the human body. [OE *midhrif* < *midd* mid + *hrif* belly]

mid·ship (mid′ship′) *adj.* in or of the middle of a ship.

mid·ship·man (mid′ship′mən) *n.* **-men** (-mən). **1** a junior officer training for a commission in the navy. **2** formerly, a boy who assisted the officers of a ship.

mid·ships (mid′ships′) *adv.* amidships.

midst[1] (midst) *n.* **1** the middle. **2 in the midst of,** in the middle of; among; surrounded by. [OE *tō middes* in the middle; and < *mid* + *-est*]

midst[2] or **'midst** (midst) *prep.* amidst; amid.

mid·stream (mid′strēm′) *n.* the middle of a stream.

mid·sum·mer (mid′sum′ər) *n.* **1** the middle of summer. **2** the time around June 21. *—adj.* in the middle of summer.

mid·town (mid′toun′) *n.* the most central location in a city or town. *—adj.* of or located in midtown.

mid-Vic·to·ri·an (mid′vik tô′rē ən) *adj.* **1** in Great Britain, of or having to do with the middle period of Queen Victoria's reign, from about 1850 to 1890. **2** like this period; old-fashioned; strict in morals. *—n.* **1** a person who lived during the middle period of Queen Victoria's reign. **2** a person with old-fashioned ideas and tastes, and strict in morals.

mid·way (mid′wā′) *adv. adj.* halfway; in the middle. *—n.* **1** a middle way or course. **2** at a fair or exhibition, the area where the side shows, rides, and other amusements are located. [OE *midweg*]

mid·week (mid′wēk′) *n.* the middle of the week. *—adj.* in the middle of the week.

mid·wife (mid′wīf′) *n.* **-wives** (-wīvz′). a woman who helps women in childbirth. [OE *mid* with + *wīf* woman]

mid·wife·ry (mid′wīf′ə rē or -wīf′rē, mid′wif′ə rē or -wif′rē) *n.* the helping of women in childbirth.

mid·win·ter (mid′win′tər) *n.* **1** the middle of winter. **2** the time around December 21. *—adj.* in the middle of winter.

mid·year (mid′yēr′) *adj.* happening in the middle of the year. *—n.* **midyears,** *pl. Informal.* midyear examinations.

mien (mēn) *n.* one's manner of holding the head and body; a way of acting and looking: *The colonel had the mien of a soldier.* [probably < *demean*; influenced by F *mine* expression < Celtic] —**Syn.** bearing, demeanor, appearance.

miff (mif) *Informal. —n.* a peevish fit; petty quarrel. *—v.* be offended; have a petty quarrel. [origin uncertain]

MIG or **Mig** (mig) *n.* a Russian-designed jet fighter plane. [< Artem *Mi*koyan and Mikhail *G*urevish, Russian airplane designers of the 1900's]

might[1] (mīt) *v.* pt. of **may.** [OE *mihte*] ☛ See **could** for usage note.

might[2] (mīt) *n.* **1** great power; strength. **2 with might and main,** with all one's strength. [OE *miht*]

might·i·ly (mīt′ə lē) *adv.* **1** in a mighty manner; powerfully; vigorously. **2** very much; greatly.

might·i·ness (mīt′ē nis) *n.* power; strength.

might·y (mīt′ē) *adj.* **might·i·er, might·i·est,** *adv. —adj.* **1** showing strength or power; powerful; strong: *a mighty ruler, mighty force.* **2** very great: *a mighty famine.* **3** very proud: *high and mighty. —adv. Informal.* very; extremely: *a mighty cold day.*

Syn. *adj.* **1 Mighty, powerful** = having or showing great strength or force. **Mighty** in this sense is now used chiefly for effect, suggesting overwhelming strength or force or a power above all other: *The mighty battleship steamed into port.* **Powerful** = having the strength, energy, or authority to do great things or having shown great force: *A heavy truck needs a powerful engine.*

mi·gnon (min′yon; *French,* mē nyoɴ′) *adj.* small and pretty; dainty. [< F]

mi·gnon·ette (min′yən et′) *n.* a plant having long, pointed clusters of small, fragrant, greenish-white flowers. [< F]

mi·graine (mī′grān) *n.* a severe, recurrent headache, usually on one side only and often accompanied by nausea. Also, **megrim.** [< F < LL < Gk. *hemikrania* < *hemi-* half + *kranion* skull]

mi·grant (mī′grənt) *n.* a person, animal, bird, or plant that migrates. *—adj.* migrating.

mi·grate (mī′grāt or mī grāt′) *v.* **-grat·ed, -grat·ing. 1** move from one place to settle in another. **2** go from one region to another with the change in the seasons. Many birds migrate to warmer countries in the winter. [< L *migrare*]

mi·gra·tion (mī grā′shən) *n.* **1** a migrating. **2** a number of people or animals migrating together. **3 a** a movement of one or more atoms from one place to another within the molecule. **b** the movement of ions between the two electrodes during electrolysis.

mi·gra·to·ry (mī′grə tô′rē) *adj.* **1** migrating; that migrates. **2** of migration. **3** wandering.

mi·ka·do or **Mi·ka·do** (mə kä′dō) *n.* **-dos.** the title of the emperor of Japan. [< Japanese *mikado* < *mi* august, honorable + *kado* door, gate]

mike (mīk) *n. Informal.* microphone.

mil[1] (mil) *n.* a unit of length, .001 of an inch, used in measuring the diameter of wires. [< L *mille* thousand]

mil[2] (mil) *n.* **1** a unit of money in Cyprus and Malta, worth 1/1000 of a pound. **2** a coin worth one mil. [< L *mille* thousand]

mil. 1 military. **2** militia. **3** mileage. **4** million.

mi·la·dy or **mi·la·di** (mi lā′dē) *n.* **-dies. 1** my lady. **2** an English lady.

mil·age (mīl′ij) *n.* mileage.

Mi·lan or **mi·lan** (mi lan′ or mil′ən) *n.* a finely woven straw used for hats. [< *Milan,* Italy, where it is made]

milch (milch) *adj.* giving milk; kept for the milk it gives: *a milch cow.* [OE *-milce* milking < *mioluc* milk]

mild (mīld) *adj.* **1** gentle; kind: *a mild old gentleman.*

2 warm; temperate; moderate; not harsh or severe: *a mild climate, a mild winter.* 3 soft or sweet to the senses; not sharp, sour, bitter, or strong in taste: *mild cheese, a mild cigar.* [OE *milde*] —**mild′ly,** *adv.* —**mild′ness,** *n.*
—**Syn. 1** tender, lenient, merciful. See **gentle. 2** clement, pleasant, bland.

mil·dew (mil′dū or -dü) *n.* a kind of fungus that appears on plants or on paper, clothes, leather, etc. during damp weather or in humid climatic conditions.
—*v.* cover or become covered with mildew. [OE *mildēaw* honeydew]

mile (mīl) *n.* **1** a unit of measure equal to 5,280 feet (a statute mile). **2** an international unit of linear measure for sea and air navigation, equal to 6,076.103 feet (international nautical mile). *Abbrev.*: mi. [OE *mīl* < L *milia* (*passuum*), pl. of *mille* (*passus*) a thousand (paces)]

mile·age (mīl′ij) *n.* **1** the miles covered or travelled: *The mileage on our speedometer last year was 10,000.* **2** the length, extent, or distance in miles. The mileage of a railway is its total number of miles of roadbed. **3** an allowance for travelling expenses at so much a mile. **4** *Informal.* value; benefit: *The firm got little mileage from its new advertising campaign.* Also, **milage.**

mile·post (mīl′pōst′) *n.* a post set up to show the distance in miles to a certain place.

mile·stone (mīl′stōn′) *n.* **1** a stone set up to show the distance in miles to a certain place. **2** an important event: *The invention of printing was a milestone in the progress of education.*

mil·foil (mil′foil) *n.* yarrow. [ME < OF < L *millefolium* < *mille* thousand + *folium* leaf]

mi·lieu (mē lü′; *French,* mē lyœ′) *n.* surroundings; environment. [< F]

mil·i·tan·cy (mil′ə tən sē) *n.* warlike behavior or tendency; militant spirit or policy.

mil·i·tant (mil′ə tənt) *adj.* **1** aggressive; fighting; warlike. **2** active in serving a cause or in spreading a belief: *a militant churchman.* —*n.* **1** a warlike or aggressive person. **2** a person active in serving a cause or in spreading a belief. [< L *militans, -antis* serving as a soldier, ult. < *miles* soldier] —**mil′i·tant·ly,** *adv.*

mil·i·ta·rism (mil′ə tə riz′əm) *n.* **1** the policy of making military organization and power very strong. **2** the political condition in which the military interest is predominant in government or administration. **3** military spirit and ideals.

mil·i·ta·rist (mil′ə tə rist) *n.* **1** a person who believes in a powerful military organization. **2** an expert in warfare and military matters.

mil·i·ta·ris·tic (mil′ə tə ris′tik) *adj.* of or having to do with militarists or militarism. —**mil′i·ta·ris′ti·cal·ly,** *adv.*

mil·i·ta·rize (mil′ə tə rīz′) *v.* **-rized, -riz·ing. 1** make the military organization of (a country) very powerful. **2** fill with military spirit and ideals. —**mil′i·ta·ri·za′tion,** *n.*

mil·i·tar·y (mil′ə ter′ē) *adj.* **1** of or having to do with soldiers or war. **2** done by soldiers. **3** fit for soldiers. **4** suitable for war; warlike. **5** belonging to the army.
—*n.* the army; soldiers. [< L *militaris* < *miles* soldier]
—**mil′i·tar′i·ly,** *adv.*
Syn. *adj.* **1 Military, martial, warlike** = having to do with war. **Military** emphasizes the idea of war as a serious business, and describes anything having to do with affairs of war or the armed services (especially the army): *He has a military bearing.* **Martial** emphasizes the glory and pomp or the gallantry of fighting men: *Troops paraded in martial array.* **Warlike** suggests a fighting nature, and especially describes acts, feelings, words, etc. threatening or fit for war: *The Iroquois were a warlike people.*

Military Cross an award for bravery for officers of the army up to the rank of captain. *Abbrev.*: M.C.

military law a system of regulations governing the armed forces and others in military service.
☛ Military law is not to be confused with *martial law,* which replaces *civil law* in times of emergency and applies to civilians as well as military personnel.

military police soldiers who act as police in an army. *Abbrev.*: M.P. or MP.

Military Regime in Canada, the period of military rule between 1759 and 1764.

mil·i·tate (mil′ə tāt′) *v.* **-tat·ed, -tat·ing.** act; work; operate (*against* or *in favor of*): *Bad weather militated against the success of the picnic.* [< L *militare* serve as a soldier < *miles* soldier]

hat, āge, cãre, fär; let, ēqual, tėrm; it, īce
hot, ōpen, ôrder; oil, out; cup, pu̇t, rüle, ūse
əbove, takən, pencəl, lemən, circəs
ch, child; ng, long; sh, ship
th, thin; ᴛʜ, then; zh, measure

mi·li·tia (mə lish′ə) *n.* an organization made up of citizens who are not regular soldiers but who undergo training for emergency duty or national defence; the reserve army. [< L *militia* < *miles* soldier]

mi·li·tia·man (mə lish′ə mən) *n.* **-men** (-mən). a soldier in the militia.

Mil·i·um (mil′ē əm) *n. Trademark.* a fabric or material sprayed with a metal solution and used as insulation in clothing, draperies, etc.

milk (milk) *n.* **1** the white liquid secreted by female mammals for the nourishment of their young. **2** any kind of liquid resembling this: *the milk of a coconut.* **3 cry over spilt milk,** waste sorrow or regret on what has happened and cannot be remedied.
—*v.* **1** draw milk from; strip of milk: *He used to milk twenty cows a day.* **2** yield or produce milk. **3** extract as if by milking; drain contents, strength, information, wealth, etc. from: *The dishonest treasurer milked the club treasury.* **4** draw juice, poison, etc. from: *milk a snake.* [OE *mioluc*]

milk bar a store or counter specializing in dairy products such as ice-cream, milk shakes, yogurt, etc.

milk·er (mil′kər) *n.* **1** a person who milks. **2** a machine that milks. **3** a cow, goat, etc. that gives milk.

milk·ing (mil′king) *n.* the amount of milk obtained at one time.

milk leg a painful swelling of the leg caused by clots in the veins.

milk·maid (milk′mād′) *n.* a woman who milks cows.

milk·man (milk′man′) *n.* **-men** (men′). a man who sells or delivers milk.

milk of human kindness natural sympathy and affection.

milk of magnesia a milky-white medicine in water, used as a laxative and antacid. *Formula*: $Mg(OH)_2$

milk shake a drink made of milk, flavoring, and, usually, ice cream, whipped together until foamy.

milk snake a small, harmless, gray snake.

milk·sop (milk′sop′) *n.* an unmanly fellow; coward.

milk sugar lactose.

milk tooth one of the first set of teeth; a temporary tooth of a young child or animal.

milk·weed (milk′wēd′) *n.* a weed having white juice that looks like milk.

milk-white (milk′hwīt′ or -wīt′) *adj.* white as milk.

milk·y (mil′kē) *adj.* **milk·i·er, milk·i·est. 1** like milk; white as milk; whitish. **2** of milk; containing milk. **3** mild; weak; timid. —**milk′i·ness,** *n.*

Milky Way 1 a broad band of faint light that stretches across the sky at night. It is made up of countless stars, too far away to be seen separately without a telescope. **2** the galaxy in which the earth, the sun, etc. are included.

mill[1] (mil) *n.* **1** a machine for grinding grain into flour or meal. **2** a building containing such a machine. **3** any machine for crushing or grinding: *a coffee mill.* **4** a building where manufacturing is done: *Cotton cloth is made in a cotton mill.* **5** *Slang.* a fight with the fists. **6 go through the mill,** *Informal.* **a** get a thorough training or experience. **b** learn by hard or painful experience. **7 put through the mill,** *Informal.* **a** test; examine; try out. **b** teach by hard or painful experience.
—*v.* **1** grind (grain) into flour or meal. **2** grind into powder or pulp. **3** manufacture. **4** cut a series of fine notches or ridges on the edge of (a coin): *A dime is milled.* **5** move or cause to move around in confusion: *The frightened cattle began to mill. The crowd was still milling around.* **6** *Slang.* fight with the fists; box. [OE *mylen* < LL *molinum* < L *mola* millstone]

mill[2] (mil) *n.* $.001, or 1/10 of a cent. Mills are used in accounting, but not as coins. [short for L *millesimum* one thousandth < *mille* thousand]

mill·dam (mil′dam′) *n.* **1** a dam built in a stream to supply water power for a mill. **2** a pond made by such a dam.

mil·len·ni·al (mə len′ē əl) *adj.* **1** of a thousand years. **2** like that of the millennium; fit for the millennium.

mil·len·ni·um (mə len′ē əm) *n.* **mil·len·ni·ums, mil·len·ni·a** (mə len′ē ə). **1** a period of a thousand years: *The world is many millenniums old.* **2** the period of a thousand years during which, according to the Bible, Christ is expected to reign on earth. Rev. 20:1-7. **3** a period of righteousness and happiness. [< NL < L *mille* thousand + *annus* year]

mil·le·pede (mil′ə pēd′) *n.* millipede.

mil·le·pore (mil′ə pôr′) *n.* a kind of coral that has very small openings on its surface. [< NL *millepora* < L *mille* thousand + *porus* pore]

mill·er (mil′ər) *n.* **1** a person who owns or runs a mill, especially a flour mill. **2** a moth whose wings look as if they were powdered with flour.

mil·les·i·mal (mə les′ə məl) *adj.* **1** thousandth. **2** consisting of thousandth parts. —*n.* a thousandth part. [< L *millesimus* thousandth part < *mille* thousand]

mil·let (mil′it) *n.* **1** a very small grain used for food in Asia and Africa. **2** the plant that it grows on. In North America and Europe, millet is used for hay. [< F, ult. < L *milium*]

milli- *combining form.* one thousandth of a ——, as in *milliampere, millimetre.* [< L *mille*]

mil·li·am·pere (mil ē am′ pēr) *n.* one thousandth of an ampere.

mil·liard (mil′yərd or mil′yärd) *n.* a thousand million; 1,000,000,000. [< F < L *mille* thousand]

mil·li·bar (mil′ə bär′) *n.* a unit of atmospheric pressure equal to one thousandth of a bar.

mil·lieme (mēl yem′) *n.* **1** a unit of money in Tunisia, worth 1/1000 of a dinar. **2** a unit of money in Libya, worth 1/1000 of a pound. **3** a coin worth one millieme. [< F]

mil·li·gram or **mil·li·gramme** (mil′ə gram′) *n.* one thousandth of a gram, equal to .0154 of a grain, or about two millionths of a pound. *Abbrev.*: mg. or mg

mil·li·li·tre or **mil·li·li·ter** (mil′ə lē′tər) *n.* one thousandth of a litre, equal to 1.000027 cubic centimetres or .061 cubic inch.

mil·li·me·tre or **mil·li·me·ter** (mil′ə mē′tər) *n.* one thousandth of a metre, or .03937 inch. *Abbrev.*: mm.

mil·li·ner (mil′ə nər) *n.* a person who makes, trims, or sells women's hats. [var. of *Milaner*, a dealer in goods from Milan, Italy, famous for straw]

mil·li·ner·y (mil′ə ner′ē or mil′ə nər ē) *n.* **1** women's hats. **2** the business of making, trimming, or selling women's hats.

mill·ing (mil′ing) *n.* **1** the business or process of grinding grain in a mill. **2** manufacturing. **3** the business or process of cutting notches or ridges on the edge of a coin. **4** such notches or ridges.

mil·lion (mil′yən) *n. adj.* **1** one thousand thousand; 1,000,000. **2** a very large number; very many. [ME < OF < Ital. *milione*, ult. < L *mille* thousand]

mil·lion·aire (mil′yən ãr′) *n.* **1** a person who has a million or more dollars, pounds, francs, etc. or its equivalent in property. **2** a very wealthy person. [< F]

mil·lion·fold (mil′yən fōld′) *adv. adj.* a million times as much or as many.

mil·lionth (mil′yənth) *adj. n.* **1** last in a series of a million. **2** one of a million equal parts.

mil·li·pede (mil′ə pēd′) *n.* a small, wormlike, arthropod that has two pairs of legs apiece for most of its segments. Also, **millepede.** [< L *millepeda* < *mille* thousand + *pes, pedis* foot]

mill·pond (mil′pond′) *n.* a pond supplying water to drive a mill wheel.

mill·race (mil′rās′) *n.* **1** a current of water that drives a mill wheel. **2** the channel in which it flows to the mill.

mill rate a rate used for calculating and levying municipal taxes. A mill rate of 5.6 means that a property owner pays a tax of 5.6 mills per dollar of the assessed value of his property.

mill·stone (mil′stōn′) *n.* **1** either of a pair of round, flat stones used for grinding corn, wheat, etc. **2** a heavy burden. **3** anything that grinds or crushes.

mill·stream (mil′strēm′) *n.* the stream in a millrace.

mill wheel a wheel that is turned by water and supplies power for a mill.

mill·work (mil′wėrk′) *n.* **1** doors, windows, mouldings, etc. made in a planing mill. **2** the work done in a mill.

mill·wright (mil′rīt′) *n.* **1** a person who designs, builds, or sets up mills or machinery for mills. **2** a mechanic who sets up and takes care of the machinery in a factory, etc.

mi·lord (mi lôrd′) *n.* **1** my lord. **2** an English gentleman.

milque·toast (milk′tōst′) *n.* an extremely timid person. [< Mr. *Milquetoast*, a comic-strip character]

milt (milt) *n.* **1** the sperm cells of male fishes together with the milky fluid containing them. **2** the reproductive gland in male fishes. [for older *milk*; influenced by *milt* spleen (OE *milte*), and perhaps by Du. *milt* milt of fish, spleen]

Mil·ton·ic (mil ton′ik) *adj.* **1** of or having to do with John Milton (1608-1674), an English poet. **2** resembling Milton's literary style; solemn and majestic.

mime (mīm) *n. v.* **mimed, mim·ing.** —*n.* **1** a jester; clown; mimic. **2** in ancient Greece and Rome: **a** a coarse farce using funny actions and gestures. **b** an actor in such a farce. **3** an actor who uses gestures and movements but not words. **4** pantomime: *the art of mime.*
—*v.* **1** imitate; mimic. **2** act in a mime; act without using words. [< L < Gk. *mimos*] —**mim′er,** *n.*

mim·e·o·graph (mim′ē ə graf′) *n.* a machine for making copies of written or typewritten materials by means of stencils. —*v.* make (copies) with a mimeograph. [< *Mimeograph*, a trademark < Gk. *mimeesthai* imitate + E *-graph*]

mi·me·sis (mi mē′sis or mī mē′sis) *n.* **1** mimicry or imitation. **2** in biology, protective coloring or markings in plants, animals, etc., imitating the surroundings. **3** in art and literature, the imitation or representation of reality. **4** the assuming of the symptoms of one disease by another disease. [< Gk. *mimēsis* < *mimeisthai* imitate < *mimos* mine]

mi·met·ic (mi met′ik or mī met′ik) *adj.* **1** imitative: *mimetic gestures.* **2** mimic or make-believe. **3** having to do with or exhibiting mimicry. [< Gk. *mimetikos* < *mimeesthai* imitate]

mim·ic (mim′ik) *v.* **-icked, -ick·ing,** *n. adj.* —*v.* **1** make fun of by imitating. **2** copy closely; imitate: *A parrot can mimic a person's voice.* **3** represent imitatively, as by drawing; simulate. **4** of things, be an imitation of. **5** resemble closely: *Some insects mimic leaves.* [< n.]
—*n.* a person or thing that imitates. [< adj.]
—*adj.* **1** not real, but imitated or pretended for some purpose: *a mimic battle.* **2** imitative. [< L *mimicus* < Gk. *mimikos* < *mimos* mime]

mim·ic·ry (mim′ik rē) *n.* **-ries.** a mimicking.

mi·mo·sa (mi mō′sə or mi mō′zə) *n.* a tree, shrub, or plant growing in tropical or warm regions, and usually having fernlike leaves, and heads or spikes of small flowers. The acacia and sensitive plant are mimosas. [< NL *mimosa* < L *mimus* mime < Gk. *mimos*; from mimicry of animal reactions]

min. **1** minute; minutes. **2** minimum.

mi·na (mī′nə) *n.* **mi·nae** (mī′nē or mī′nī) or **mi·nas.** a unit of weight and value used by the ancient Greeks, Egyptians, and others. [< L < Gk. *mna* < Semitic; cf. Babylonian *manū*]

mi·na·cious (mi nā′shəs) *adj.* menacing; threatening. [< L *minax, minacis,* ult. < *minae* projecting points, threats] —**mi·na′cious·ly,** *adv.* —**mi·na′cious·ness,** *n.*

min·a·ret (min′ə ret′ or min′ə ret′) *n.* a slender, high tower of a Moslem mosque,

A minaret

having one or more projecting balconies, from which a muezzin or crier calls the people to prayer. [< F or Sp. < Arabic *manārat* lighthouse]

min·a·to·ry (min′ə tô′rē) *adj.* menacing; threatening. [< LL *minatorius* < L *minari* threaten, ult. < *minae* projecting points, threats]

mince (mins) *v.* **minced, minc·ing,** *n.* —*v.* **1** chop up into very small pieces. **2** speak or do in an affectedly polite or elegant manner. **3** minimize in representation; soften or moderate (words, etc.) as in stating unpleasant facts: *The judge, in addressing the jury, spoke bluntly, mincing no words.* **4 not to mince matters,** to speak plainly and frankly. **5** walk with dainty, short steps. —*n.* **1** meat cut up into very small pieces. **2** mincemeat. [ME < OF *mincier*, ult. < L *minutus* small]

mince·meat (mins′mēt′) *n.* **1** a mixture of chopped meat, apples, suet, raisins, currants, spices etc., used as a filling for pies. **2 make mincemeat of,** reduce as if into little pieces; cut down; defeat overwhelmingly: *Our team made mincemeat of the rest of the league.*

mince pie a pie filled with mincemeat.

minc·ing (min′sing) *adj.* **1** too polite; too nice. **2** walking with dainty, short steps. —**minc′ing·ly,** *adv.*

mind (mīnd) *n.* **1** that which thinks, feels, and wills. **2** the intellect. **3** a person who has intelligence. **4** the intellectual powers or capacities of a body of persons: *the popular mind.* **5** reason; sanity: *be out of one's mind.* **6** mental or physical activity in general, as opposed to matter. **7** a conscious or intelligent agency or being: *the doctrine of a mind creating the universe.* **8** a way of thinking and feeling: *change one's mind.* **9** one's desire, purpose, intention, or will. **10** remembrance or recollection; memory: *Keep the rules in mind.*

bear in mind, keep one's attention on; remember.

be in (or **of**) **two** (**many** etc.) **minds,** vacillate between two (many, etc.) intentions.

be of one mind, agree.

call to mind, a recall. **b** remember.

have a mind of one's own, have definite or decided opinions, inclinations, or purposes.

have a mind to, intend to; think of favorably: *I have a mind to watch hockey tonight.*

have half a mind, be somewhat inclined.

have in mind, a remember. **b** think of; consider. **c** intend; plan.

keep in mind, remember.

know one's mind, know what one really thinks, wishes, or intends.

make up one's mind, decide; resolve.

on one's mind, in one's thoughts; troubling one.

pass out of mind, be forgotten.

put in mind, remind.

set one's mind on, want very much.

speak one's mind, give one's frank opinion.

take one's mind off, distract one's attention from; divert from (something unpleasant).

to one's mind, in one's opinion; to one's way of thinking.

—*v.* **1** bear in mind; give heed to: *Mind my words!* **2** take notice; observe. **3** be careful concerning: *Mind the step.* **4** be careful. **5** look after; take care of; tend: *Mind the baby.* **6** obey: *Mind your father and mother.* **7** feel concern about; object to: *We mind parting from a friend.* **8** feel concern; object: *Do you mind?* **9** *Archaic or dialect.* remember. **10** *Archaic or dialect.* remind. [OE (*ge*)*mynd*] —**mind′er,** *n.*

Syn. *n.* **1, 2 Mind, intellect** = the part of a human being that enables him to know, think, and act effectively. **Mind** in general usage is the inclusive word, meaning the part that knows, thinks, feels, wills, remembers, etc., thought of as distinct from the body: *To develop properly, the mind needs training and exercise.* **Intellect** applies to the knowing and thinking powers of the mind, as distinct from the powers of feeling and will: *Many motion pictures appeal to the feelings rather than the intellect.*

mind·ed (mīn′did) *adj.* **1** having a certain kind of mind: *high-minded, strong-minded.* **2** inclined; disposed: *I am minded to stay home today.*

mind·ful (mīnd′fəl) *adj.* **1** having in mind: *Mindful of your advice, I went slowly.* **2** taking thought; careful: *We had to be mindful of every step we took on the slippery sidewalk.* —**mind′ful·ly,** *adv.* —**mind′ful·ness,** *n.* —**Syn. 1** aware, cognizant. **2** heedful, attentive.

mind·less (mīnd′lis) *adj.* **1** without intelligence; stupid. **2** not taking thought; careless. —**mind′less·ly,** *adv.*

mind reader a person who can guess the thoughts of others.

hat, āge, cãre, fär; let, ēqual, tėrm; it, īce
hot, ōpen, ôrder; oil, out; cup, pu̇t, rüle, ūse
əbove, takən, pencəl, lemən, circəs
ch, child; ng, long; sh, ship
th, thin; ᴛʜ, then; zh, measure

mind's eye the imagination.

mine[1] (mīn) *pron.* **1** belonging to me: *This book is mine.* **2** the one or ones belonging to me: *Your shoes are black; mine are brown.* **3 of mine,** that belongs to me. —*adj. Archaic.* my (used only before a vowel or *h*, or after a noun): *mine eyes, mine heart, sister mine.* [OE *mīn*]

☛ See note at **my.**

mine[2] (mīn) *n. v.* **mined, min·ing.** —*n.* **1** a large hole or space dug in or under the earth to get out something valuable: *a coal mine, a gold mine.* **2** a rich or plentiful source: *a mine of information.* **3** an underground passage in which an explosive is placed to blow up the enemy's forts, etc. **4** a container holding an explosive charge that is put under water and exploded by propeller vibrations (**acoustic** or **sonic mine**), or by magnetic attraction (**magnetic mine**), or laid on the ground or shallowly buried and exploded by contact with a vehicle, etc. (**land mine**).
—*v.* **1** dig a mine; make a hole, space, passage, etc. below the earth. **2** dig into (the earth, a hill, etc.) for coal, ore, etc. **3** get (metal, etc.) from a mine. **4** dig in; make (passages, etc.) by digging. **5** put explosive mines in or under; lay explosive mines. **6** destroy secretly; ruin slowly; undermine. [< F < Celtic]

mine field 1 an area throughout which explosive mines have been laid. **2** the pattern of mines in such an area.

min·er (mī′nər) *n.* a person who mines, especially one who works in a mine.

min·er·al (min′ər əl or min′rəl) *n.* **1** a substance obtained by mining. Coal is a mineral. **2** any substance that is neither plant nor animal. —*adj.* **1** of minerals. **2** like a mineral. **3** containing minerals: *mineral water.* [ME < OF *mineral*, ult. < *mine* mine[2] < Celtic]

min·er·al·ize (min′ər əl īz′ or min′rəl īz′) *v.* **-ized, -iz·ing. 1** convert into mineral substance; transform (metal) into an ore. **2** impregnate or supply with mineral substances. **3** search for minerals. —**min′er·al·i·za′tion,** *n.*

min·er·a·log·i·cal (min′ər ə loj′ə kəl) *adj.* of mineralogy. —**min·er·a·log·i·cal·ly,** *adv.*

min·er·al·o·gist (min′ər ol′ə jist or min′ər al′ə jist) *n.* a person who is skilled in mineralogy.

min·er·al·o·gy (min′ər ol′ə jē or min′ər al′ə jē) *n.* the science of minerals.

mineral oil 1 an oil obtained from the earth. Petroleum is a mineral oil. **2** any oil derived from a mineral substance, as from coal. **3** a colorless, odorless, tasteless oil obtained from petroleum, used as a laxative.

mineral right a right both to the mineral deposits in a given piece of land and to the royalties accruing from their extraction.

mineral water water containing mineral salts or gases. People drink various mineral waters for their health.

Mi·ner·va (mə nėr′və) *n.* in Roman mythology, the goddess of wisdom, the arts, and defensive war, identified with the Greek goddess Athena.

min·e·stro·ne (min′ə strō′nē) *n.* a thick soup containing vegetables, vermicelli, etc. [< Ital.]

mine sweeper a ship used for dragging a harbor, the sea, etc. in order to remove mines laid by an enemy.

Ming (ming) *n.* **1** a kind of fine porcelain. **2** something made of this porcelain. [< *Ming*, a dynasty that ruled China 1368-1644, when this porcelain was made]

min·gle (ming′gəl) *v.* **-gled, -gling. 1** mix: *The two rivers join and mingle their waters.* **2** associate: *mingle with important people.* [ME *mengele(n)* < OE *mengan* mix] —**min′gler,** *n.* —**Syn. 1** blend, fuse, combine.

min·i (min′ē) *n. Informal.* something small for its kind. [< *miniature*]

mini- *combining form.* small for its kind; miniature, as in *minibus, minidress.*

min·i·a·ture (min′ə chər or min′ē ə chər) *n.* **1** anything represented on a small scale: *In the museum there is a miniature of the ship "Victory."* **2** a very small painting, usually a portrait. **3 in miniature,** on a small scale; reduced in size. *—adj.* done or made on a very small scale; tiny: *She had miniature furniture for her doll house.* [< Ital. *miniatura* < Med.L *miniare* illuminate (a manuscript) < L *miniare* paint red < *minium* red lead; confused with L *minutus* small]

miniature camera a camera using narrow film (35 mm. or smaller).

min·i·a·tur·ize (min′ə chə rīz′ or min′ē ə chə rīz′) *v.* **-ized, -iz·ing.** reduce to a very small size: *miniaturized electronic devices.* **—min′i·a·tur·i·za′tion,** *n.*

min·i·fy (min′ə fī′) *v.* **-fied, -fy·ing.** make small or less important. [< L *minor*, neuter of *minus* less + E *-fy*]

min·im (min′əm) *n.* **1** the smallest liquid measure, one sixtieth of a dram, or about one drop. **2** in music, a half note. **3** a very small amount. **4** something very small or insignificant. [< L *minimus* smallest]

min·i·ma (min′ə mə) *n.* a pl. of **minimum.**

min·i·mal (min′ə məl) *adj.* least possible; very small; having to do with a minimum.

min·i·mize (min′ə mīz′) *v.* **-mized, -miz·ing. 1** reduce to the least possible amount or degree: *The polar explorers took every precaution to minimize the dangers of their trip.* **2** state at the lowest possible estimate; make the least of: *An ungrateful person minimizes the help others have given him.* **—min′i·mi·za′tion,** *n.* **—min′i·miz′er,** *n.*

min·i·mum (min′ə məm) *n.* **-mums** or **-ma,** *adj.* *—n.* **1** the least or smallest quantity possible or permitted: *Eight hours' sleep is the minimum that children should have.* **2** in mathematics, a value of a variable less than or equal to any values close to it. *—adj.* **1** least possible: *Twenty-one is the minimum age for voting in Ontario.* **2** basic; lowest: *a minimum rate.* [< L *minimum* smallest (thing)]

☛ Minimum has two plurals: *minimums* and *minima*. The first is more common in informal English.

minimum wage the wage agreed upon or fixed by law as the lowest payable to certain employees.

min·ing (mīn′ing) *n.* **1** the act or practice of working mines for ore, coal, etc. **2** the business of digging coal or ore from mines. **3** the act of laying explosive mines. *—adj.* of, about, or having to do with mining for ore: *a mining school.*

min·ion (min′yən) *n.* **1** a person willing to do whatever he is ordered, especially a servile or obsequious follower. **2** *Derogatory.* a darling; favorite. **3** a mistress; paramour. **4** in printing, a size of type; 7-point. [< F *mignon* dainty]

min·is·cule (min′ə skūl′) *adj.* minuscule.

min·is·ter (min′is tər) *n.* **1** a clergyman serving a church; spiritual guide; pastor. **2** a member of the Cabinet who is in charge of a government department: *the Minister of Labor.* **3** a person sent to a foreign country to represent his own government; a diplomat ranking below an ambassador: *the British Minister to France.* **4** a person or thing employed in carrying out (purpose, will, etc.): *The storm which killed the murderer seemed the minister of God's vengeance.* **5** *Archaic.* a servant. *—v.* **1** act as a servant or nurse; be of service: *She ministers to the sick.* **2** be helpful; give aid: contribute. **3** *Archaic.* furnish; supply. [< L *minister* servant < *minus* less; patterned after *magister* master] **—Syn.** *v.* **1** serve, attend. **2** help, assist.

min·is·te·ri·al (min′is tēr′ē əl) *adj.* **1** of or having to do with a minister. **2** of or having to do with the ministry. **3** suitable for a clergyman. **4** executive; administrative. **5** acting as an agent; subordinate; helping. **—min′is·te′ri·al·ly,** *adv.*

minister plenipotentiary *pl.* **ministers plenipotentiary.** a plenipotentiary.

minister without portfolio a cabinet minister who is not connected with any particular cabinet post or department.

min·is·trant (min′is trənt) *adj.* ministering. *—n.* one who ministers. [< L *ministrans, -antis,* ppr. of *ministrare* < *minister* servant]

min·is·tra·tion (min′is trā′shən) *n.* **1** service as a minister of a church. **2** help; aid: *give ministration to the poor.*

min·is·try (min′is trē) *n.* **-tries. 1** the office, duties, or time of service of a minister. **2** the ministers of a church. **3** the ministers of a government. **4** in the United Kingdom, Europe, Canada, etc.: **a** a government department under a minister. **b** the offices of such a department. **6** a ministering or serving. [< L *ministerium* office, service < *minister.* See MINISTER. Doublet of METIER.]

min·i·ver (min′ə vər) *n.* a fur or combination of furs formerly much used for lining and trimming garments. Miniver included spotted white and gray fur, white fur symmetrically adorned with bits of dark fur, plain white fur, and winter ermine. [ME < OF *menu vair* small vair (a type of fur used in the 14th century and the animal from which it was obtained); *menu* < L *minutus* made small (see MINUTE²); *vair* < L *varius* variegated]

mink (mingk) *n.* **mink** or **minks. 1** a weasel-like mammal that normally lives near water. **2** its valuable fur. **3** a coat or other garment made of this fur. [apparently < Scand.; cf. Swedish *mänk*] **—mink′like′,** *adj.*

Minn. Minnesota.

min·ne·sing·er or **Min·ne·sing·er** (min′ə sing′ər) *n.* a German lyrical poet and singer in the 12th, 13th, and 14th centuries. [< G *Minnesinger* love singer]

min·now (min′ō) *n.* **1** a very small fresh-water fish. **2** any very tiny fish. [ME *minwe*; cf. OE *myne*]

Mi·no·an (mi nō′ən) *adj.* of or having to do with the civilization of Crete from about 3400 to about 1200 B.C. [< *Minos*]

mi·nor (mī′nər) *adj.* **1** smaller; lesser; less important: *a minor fault, a minor poet.* **2** under legal age. **3** in music: **a** less by a half step than the corresponding major interval. **b** noting a scale, mode, or key whose third tone is minor in relation to the fundamental tone. **c** of a chord. especially a triad, containing a minor third between the root and the second tone or note.
—n. **1** a person under the legal age of responsibility (usually 21 years). You cannot vote while you are still a minor. **2** a subject or course of study to which a student gives much time and attention, but less than to his major subject. **3** in music, a minor interval, key, scale, chord, etc. **4** a minor penalty. **5 the minors,** *pl.* the minor leagues.
—v. **minor in,** have or take as a minor subject of study. [< L *minor* lesser] **—Syn.** *adj.* **1** subordinate, secondary, lower, inferior.

Mi·nor·ca (mə nôr′kə) *n.* **1** a breed of chickens having black or white feathers. **2** a chicken of this breed. [< *Minorca*, one of the Balearic Islands]

mi·nor·i·ty (mə nôr′ə tē or mī nôr′ə tē) *n.* **-ties,** *adj.* *—n.* **1** a smaller number or part; less than half: *The minority must often accept what the majority decides to do.* **2** the condition or time of being under the legal age of responsibility. *—adj.* **1** of or constituting a minority: *a minority vote, group, etc.* **2** belonging to a minority: *a minority opinion.*

minor league any professional sports league or association, as in baseball or hockey, other than the major leagues.

mi·nor-league (mī′nər lēg′) *adj.* **1** of or having to do with minor leagues. **2** *Informal.* inferior; second rate; not top quality.

minor penalty in hockey, a two-minute penalty awarded for certain infractions of the rules, such as highsticking, hooking, slashing, tripping, etc. The referee may award a major penalty for many such infractions, especially when the offended player is injured.

minor scale in music, a scale having eight notes with half steps instead of whole steps after the 2nd and 5th notes.

Mi·nos (mī′nəs or mī′nos) *n.* in Greek legend: **1** a king and lawgiver of Crete who became a judge in Hades. **2** his grandson, who built the Labyrinth at Crete to house the Minotaur.

Min·o·taur (min′ə tôr′) *n.* in Greek legend, a monster with a bull's head and a man's body, kept in the Labyrinth of Crete and fed with human flesh. The Minotaur was killed by Theseus. [< L < Gk. *Minotauros* < *Minos*

Minos + *tauros* bull]

min·ster (min′stər) *n. Esp.Brit.* **1** the church of a monastery. **2** a large or important church; cathedral. [OE *mynster* < LL *monasterium.* Doublet of MONASTERY.]

min·strel (min′strəl) *n.* **1** in the Middle Ages, a singer or musician who went about and sang or recited poems, often of his own making. **2** formerly, a singer or musician in the household of a lord. **3** a member of a company of theatrical performers, usually white men made up as Negroes, who entertain with songs, dancing, and jokes. [ME < OF < LL *ministerialis* < L *ministerium.* See MINISTRY.]

min·strel·sy (min′strəl sē) *n.* **-sies. 1** the art or practice of a minstrel. **2** a collection of songs and ballads. **3** a company of minstrels.

mint[1] (mint) *n.* **1** an aromatic plant used for flavoring: *Mint is often used with roast lamb.* **2** a piece of candy flavored with mint. [OE *minte* < L *menta* < Gk. *minthē*]

mint[2] (mint) *n.* **1** a place where money is coined by public authority: *The Royal Canadian Mint.* **2** a large amount: *A million dollars is a mint of money.* **3** a place where anything is made or fabricated.
—v. **1** coin (money). **2** make or fabricate; originate.
—adj. **1** of a stamp or coin, in the condition of issue. **2** without a blemish; as good as new: *a car in mint condition.* [OE *mynet* coin < L *moneta* mint, money. Doublet of MONEY.] **—min′ter,** *n.*

mint·age (min′tij) *n.* **1** a minting; coinage. **2** the product of minting; output of a mint. **3** a charge for coining; cost of coining. **4** a stamp or character impressed.

min·u·end (min′ū end′) *n.* a number or quantity from which another is to be subtracted. In 100 − 23 = 77, the minuend is 100. [< L *minuendus* be made smaller < *minus* less]

min·u·et (min′ū et′) *n.* **1** a slow, stately dance that originated in France in the 17th century. **2** the music for such a dance. [< F *menuet,* dim. of *menu* small]

mi·nus (mī′nəs) *prep.* **1** less; decreased by: *5 minus 2 leaves 3.* **2** *Informal.* lacking: *a book minus its cover.*
—adj. **1** less than: *A mark of B minus is not so high as B.* **2** showing subtractions; *The minus sign is —.* **3** less than zero: *If you have no money and owe someone three cents, you have minus three cents.* *—n.* the sign (−) meaning that the quantity following it is to be subtracted. [< L *minus* less]

mi·nus·cule (mi nus′kūl or min′ə skūl′) *adj.* **1** Also, **miniscule.** minute; very small. **2** in paleography, of or written in small letters, or in minuscules. *—n.* **1** a lowercase letter. **2** in paleography: **a** the small, cursive script developed from the uncial, about A.D. 600-800. **b** a small letter, neither capital nor uncial. [< F *minuscule,* learned borrowing from L *minuscula* (*littera*) slightly smaller (letters) < *minus* less]

min·ute[1] (min′it) *n.* **1** sixty seconds; one sixtieth of an hour. **2** a short time: instant: *I'll be there in a minute.* **3** a point of time: *Come here this minute.* **4** one sixtieth of a degree. 10°10′ means ten degrees and ten minutes. *Abbrev.*: m. or min. **5 minutes,** *pl.* a written summary; the official record of the proceedings of a society, board, committee, etc. **6 up to the minute,** up-to-date. [ME < OF < LL *minuta* small part < L *minuta,* fem. of *minutus,* adj. See MINUTE[2].]
Syn. 2, 3 Minute, moment, instant = a point or extremely short period of time. **Minute** usually suggests a measurable, although very short, amount of time: *May I rest a minute?* **Moment** is more vague, suggesting a very brief period that is noticeable but not measurable or definite: *I'll be with you in a moment.* **Instant,** often used interchangeably with *moment,* is more definite and particularly suggests a point of time, a period too brief to be noticed: *Come this instant!*

mi·nute[2] (mī nūt′ or mī nüt′) *adj.* **1** very small. **2** going into or concerned with very small details: *a minute observer, minute instructions.* **3** unimportant, petty. [ME < L *minutus* made small < *minus* less. Doublet of MENU.] **—Syn. 1** tiny, diminutive, little. **2** detailed, particular.

minute hand (min′it) on a watch or clock, the hand that indicates minutes. It moves round the dial once in each hour.

mi·nute·ly (mī nūt′lē or mī nüt′lē) *adv.* in minute manner, form, degree, or detail.

hat, āge, cãre, fär; let, ēqual, tėrm; it, īce
hot, ōpen, ôrder; oil, out; cup, put, rüle, ūse
əbove, takən, pencəl, lemən, circəs
ch, child; ng, long; sh, ship
th, thin; ᴛʜ, then; zh, measure

mi·nute·ness (mī nūt′nis or mī nüt′nis) *n.* **1** extreme smallness. **2** attention to very small details.

mi·nu·ti·ae (mi nū′shē ē′ or mi nü′shē ē′, mi nū′shē ī′ or mi nü′shē ī′) *n.pl.* very small matters; trifling details. [< L *minutiae* trifles, pl. of *minutia* smallness < *minutus.* See MINUTE[2].]

minx (mingks) *n.* a pert girl. [? < LG *minsk,* impudent woman; cf. G *Mensch* person]

Mi·o·cene (mī′ə sēn′) in geology: *—n.* **1** a period of the Cenozoic era, beginning approximately 30 million years ago. **2** the rocks formed in this period. See the chart under **geology.** *—adj.* of or having to do with this period or the rocks formed during it. [< Gk. *meiōn* less + *kainos* new]

mir (mēr) *n.* in Imperial Russia, a self-governing farming community. [< Russian]

Mi·ra (mī′rə) *n.* a first magnitude star in the constellation Cetus, the first variable star discovered. [< NL *Mira* < L *mira* wonderful]

mir·a·cle (mir′ə kəl) *n.* **1** a wonderful happening that is contrary to or independent of the known laws of nature: *It would be a miracle if the sun stood still in the heavens for an hour.* **2** something marvellous; a wonder. **3** a remarkable example: *A mother must be a miracle of patience to answer all the questions that children ask.* **4** a miracle play. [ME < OF < L *miraculum,* ult. < *mirus* wonderful]

miracle play a play based on Bible stories or on legends of the saints, especially popular during the Middle Ages.

mi·rac·u·lous (mə rak′yů ləs) *adj.* **1** contrary to or independent of the known laws of nature. **2** wonderful; marvellous: *miraculous good fortune.* **3** having the power to produce a miracle. [< Med.L *miraculosus* < L *miraculum.* See MIRACLE.] **—mi·rac′u·lous·ly,** *adv.* **—mi·rac′u·lous·ness,** *n.* **—Syn. 1** supernatural. **2** extraordinary.

mi·rage (mə räzh′) *n.* **1** a misleading appearance, usually in the desert or at sea, resulting from a reflection of some distant scene in such a way as to give the impression that it is near. Often the objects reflected are inverted. Travellers on the desert sometimes see a mirage of palm trees and water. **2** an illusion; thing that does not exist. [< F *mirage* < *mirer* look at carefully, *se mirer* look at oneself in a mirror, see reflected < L *mirare,* var. of *mirari* wonder (at), admire]

mire (mīr) *n. v.* **mired, mir·ing.** *—n.* **1** soft, deep mud; slush. **2** a bog; swamp.
—v. **1** cause to get stuck in mire: *He mired his horses and had to go for help.* **2** stick in mire. **3** soil with mud or mire. **4** involve in difficulties. [ME < ON *mýrr*]

mirk (mėrk) *n.* murk.

mir·ror (mir′ər) *n.* **1** a looking glass; a surface that reflects light. **2** whatever reflects or gives a true description: *This book is a mirror of Laurier's life.* **3** a model; example; pattern: *That knight was a mirror of chivalry.* *—v.* **1** reflect as a mirror does: *The still water mirrored the trees along the bank.* **2** give a true description or picture of: *The book mirrored colonial life in Canada.* [ME < OF *mirour,* ult. < L *mirari* wonder, admire] **—mir′ror·like′,** *adj.*

mirth (mėrth) *n.* merry fun; a being joyous or gay; laughter: *His sides shook with mirth.* [OE *myrgth* < *myrge* merry] **—Syn.** merriment, gaiety, jollity, **glee,** hilarity.

mirth·ful (mėrth′fəl) *adj.* merry; gay; laughing. **—mirth′ful·ly,** *adv.* **—mirth′ful·ness,** *n.*

mirth·less (mėrth′lis) *adj.* without mirth; joyless; gloomy. **—mirth′less·ly,** *adv.* **—mirth′less·ness,** *n.*

mir·y (mīr′ē) *adj.* **mir·i·er, mir·i·est. 1** muddy; swampy. **2** dirty; filthy. **—mir′i·ness,** *n.*

mis- *prefix.* **1** bad, as in *misformation, misgovernment.* **2** badly, as in *misbehave, mismanage.* **3** wrong, as in *mispronunciation, misvaluation.* **4** wrongly, as in *misunderstand, mislabel.* [OE *mis(s)-*, or in borrowed words < OF *mes-* < OHG *missi-, missa-*]

mis·ad·ven·ture (mis′əd ven′chər) *n.* an unfortunate accident; an instance of bad luck; mishap.

mis·al·li·ance (mis′ə lī′əns) *n.* an unsuitable alliance or association, especially in marriage.

mis·an·thrope (mis′ən thrōp′ or miz′ən thrōp′) *n.* a hater of mankind; person who dislikes or distrusts human beings. [< Gk. *misanthrōpos* < *miseein* hate + *anthrōpos* man]

mis·an·throp·ic (mis′ən throp′ik) *adj.* of or like a misanthrope. **—mis·an·throp′i·cal·ly,** *adv.*

mis·an·throp·ist (mis an′thrə pist) *n.* a misanthrope.

mis·an·thro·py (mis an′thrə pē) *n.* a hatred, dislike, or distrust of human beings.

mis·ap·pli·ca·tion (mis′ap lə kā′shən) *n.* a wrong application; misapplying or being misapplied.

mis·ap·plied (mis′ə plīd′) *adj.* put to a wrong use; applied wrongly.

mis·ap·ply (mis′ə plī′) *v.* **-plied, -ply·ing.** apply wrongly; make a wrong application or use of.

mis·ap·pre·hend (mis′ap ri hend′) *v.* misunderstand.

mis·ap·pre·hen·sion (mis′ap ri hen′shən) *n.* a misunderstanding; wrong idea.

mis·ap·pro·pri·ate (mis′ə prō′prē āt′) *v.* **-at·ed, -at·ing.** **1** put to a wrong use. **2** use dishonestly as one's own: *The treasurer had misappropriated the club funds.*

mis·ap·pro·pri·a·tion (mis′ə prō′prē ā′shən) *n.* **1** a dishonest use of something as one's own. **2** any act of putting something to a wrong use.

mis·be·came (mis′bi kām′) *v.* pt. of **misbecome.**

mis·be·come (mis′bi kum′) *v.* **-came, -come, -com·ing.** be unbecoming to; be unfit for.

mis·be·got·ten (mis′bi got′ən) *adj.* begotten unlawfully; illegitimate.

mis·be·have (mis′bi hāv′) *v.* **-haved, -hav·ing.** behave badly.

mis·be·hav·ior or **mis·be·hav·iour** (mis′bi hāv′yər) *n.* bad behavior.

mis·be·lief (mis′bi lēf′) *n.* **1** a wrong or erroneous belief. **2** a belief in a religion that is not the regularly accepted one.

mis·be·liev·er (mis′bi lēv′ər) *n.* **1** one who holds a wrong or erroneous belief. **2** a person who believes in a religion that is not the regularly accepted one.

mis·brand (mis brand′) *v.* brand or mark incorrectly.

misc. **1** miscellaneous. **2** miscellany.

mis·cal·cu·late (mis kal′kyù lāt′) *v.* **-lated, -lat·ing.** calculate wrongly. **—mis′cal·cu·la′tion,** *n.* **—mis·cal′cu·la′tor,** *n.*

mis·call (mis kol′ or -kôl′) *v.* call by a wrong name.

mis·car·riage (mis kar′ij) *n.* **1** a failure: *The jury was biassed, and the trial resulted in a miscarriage of justice.* **2** a failure to arrive: *the miscarriage of a letter.* **3** the birth of a baby before it is able to live.

mis·car·ry (mis kar′ē) *v.* **-ried, -ry·ing.** **1** go wrong: *John's plans miscarried, and he could not come.* **2** fail to arrive. **3** have a miscarriage.

mis·cast (mis kast′) *v.* put a person in an unsuitable role: *The actor was quite miscast as the villain.*

mis·ce·ge·na·tion (mis′ə jə nā′shən) *n.* an interbreeding between different races. [< L *miscere* mix + *genus* race]

mis·cel·la·ne·ous (mis ə lā′nē əs) *adj.* **1** not all of one kind or nature: *He had a miscellaneous collection of stones, butterflies, marbles, stamps, and many other things.* **2** many-sided: *a miscellaneous writer.* **3** of many kinds: *miscellaneous talents.* [< L *miscellaneus* < *miscellus* mixed, ult. < *miscere* mix] **—mis′cel·la′ne·ous·ly,** *adv.* **—mis′cel·la′ne·ous·ness,** *n.*

Syn. 1 Miscellaneous, indiscriminate = including various things or kinds, without plan or order in selection. **Miscellaneous,** describing a group or mass, emphasizes the idea of mixing, and means "of varied nature, usually gathered together without special order, plan, or care in selection": *A person's miscellaneous expenses include stamps and haircuts.* **Indiscriminate,** applying chiefly to actions, feelings, methods, purposes, etc., emphasizes lack of selection or judgment in selection, and means "including all, good and bad, deserving and undeserving, etc. without distinction": *Indiscriminate buying is wasteful.*

mis·cel·la·ny (mis′ə lā′nē or mis el′ə nē) *n.* **-nies. 1** a miscellaneous collection; mixture. **2 miscellanies,** *pl.* a collection of miscellaneous articles in one book. [< L *miscellanea,* neut. pl. of *miscellaneus.* See MISCELLANEOUS.]

mis·chance (mis chans′) *n.* misfortune; bad luck.

mis·chief (mis′chif) *n.* **1** injury, usually done by some person; harm. **2** conduct that causes harm or trouble, often without meaning it. **3** a person who does harm or causes damage, often just in fun. **4** merry teasing; lighthearted merriment: *Her eyes were full of mischief.* [ME < OF *meschief,* ult. < *mes-* bad (see MIS-) + *chever* come to an end < *chief* head < L *caput*] **—Syn. 1** damage, hurt.

mis·chief-mak·er (mis′chif māk′ər) *n.* a person who makes mischief by tale-bearing, inciting quarrels, gossiping, etc.

mis·chief-mak·ing (mis′chif māk′ing) *adj.* stirring up trouble. *—n.* the act or practice of stirring up trouble.

mis·chie·vous (mis′chə vəs) *adj.* **1** harmful: *a mischievous belief.* **2** full of mischief; naughty. **3** full of pranks and teasing fun. **—mis′chie·vous·ly,** *adv.* **—mis′chie·vous·ness,** *n.* **—Syn. 1** hurtful, injurious. **3** playful, teasing, roguish.

mis·ci·ble (mis′ə bəl) *adj.* capable of being mixed. [< L *miscere* mix]

mis·con·ceive (mis′kən sēv′) *v.* **-ceived, -ceiv·ing.** have wrong idea about; misunderstand.

mis·con·cep·tion (mis′kən sep′shən) *n.* a mistaken idea or notion; incorrect conception.

mis·con·duct (*n.* mis kon′dukt; *v.* mis′kən dukt′) *n.* **1** bad behavior. **2** bad management: *Misconduct of the business resulted in a loss.* **3** in hockey, a ten-minute penalty awarded for improper behavior, such as insulting the referee or using foul or abusive language. **4** in law: **a** adultery. **b** malfeasance. *—v.* **1** behave badly. **2** manage badly.

mis·con·struc·tion (mis′kən struk′shən) *n.* a mistaken meaning; misunderstanding: *What you said was open to misconstruction.*

mis·con·strue (mis′kən strü′) *v.* **-strued, -stru·ing.** take in an incorrect sense; misunderstand.

mis·count (*v.* mis kount′; *n.* mis′kount′) *v.* count incorrectly. *—n.* an incorrect count.

mis·cre·ant (mis′krē ənt) *adj.* **1** morally base; depraved. **2** *Archaic.* unbelieving; heretical. *—n.* **1** a villain. **2** *Archaic.* an unbeliever; heretic. [ME < OF *mescreant* < *mes-* wrongly (see MIS-) + *creant,* ppr. of *creire* believe < L *credere*] **—Syn.** *adj.* **1** vile, detestable.

mis·cue (mis kū′) *n. v.* **-cued, -cu·ing.** *—n.* in billiards, pool, etc., a bad stroke that does not hit the ball squarely. *—v.* **1** in billiards, pool, etc., make a miscue. **2** in the theatre, miss one's cue; respond to a wrong cue.

mis·date (mis dāt′) *v.* **-dat·ed, -dat·ing,** *n.* *—v.* date incorrectly; assign or affix an incorrect date to. *—n.* a wrong date.

mis·deal (*v.* mis dēl′; *n.* mis′dēl′) *v.* **-dealt, -deal·ing,** *n.* in card games: *—v.* deal incorrectly *—n.* an incorrect deal.

mis·dealt (mis delt′) *v.* pt. and pp. of **misdeal.**

mis·deed (mis dēd′ or mis′dēd′) *n.* a bad or wicked act. **—Syn.** misdemeanor, offence.

mis·de·mean (mis′di mēn′) *v.* behave badly.

mis·de·mean·or or **mis·de·mean·our** (mis′di mēn′ər) *n.* **1** a breaking of the law, not so serious as a felony. Disturbing the peace and breaking traffic laws are misdemeanors. **2** a wrong deed. **3** bad behavior.

mis·did (mis did′) *v.* pt. of **misdo.**

mis·di·rect (mis′də rekt′ or -dī rekt′) *v.* direct incorrectly.

mis·di·rec·tion (mis′də rek′shən or -dī rek′shən) *n.* an incorrect direction.

mis·do (mis dü′) *v.* **-did, -done, -do·ing.** do wrongly. [OE *misdōn*] **—mis·do′er,** *n.*

mis·do·ing (mis dü′ing) *n.* wrongdoing.

mis·done (mis dun′) *v.* pp. of **misdo.**

mis·doubt (mis dout′) *Archaic.* —*v.* **1** have doubts about; suspect; distrust. **2** fear. —*n.* suspicion; distrust; doubt.

mis·em·ploy (mis′əm ploi′) *v.* use wrongly or improperly. —**mis′em·ploy′ment,** *n.*

mi·ser (mī′zər) *n.* a person who loves money for its own sake; one who lives poorly in order to save money and keep it. A miser dislikes spending money, except to gain more money. [< L *miser* wretched] —**Syn.** skinflint, niggard.

mis·er·a·ble (miz′ər ə bəl or miz′rə bəl) *adj.* **1** unhappy: *A sick child is often miserable.* **2** causing trouble or unhappiness: *a miserable cold.* **3** poor; mean; wretched: *They live in miserable surroundings.* **4** pitiable; deplorable; sorry: *a miserable failure, miserable sinners.* [< L *miserabilis,* ult. < *miser* wretched] —**mis′er·a·ble·ness,** *n.* —**mis′er·a·bly,** *adv.* —**Syn. 1** See **wretched. 3** deplorable, pitiable, sordid.

Mis·e·re·re (miz′ə rãr′ē or miz′ə rēr′ē) *n.* **1** in the Revised and Authorized versions of the Bible, the 51st Psalm; in the Douay version of the Bible, the 50th Psalm. **2** the music for it. **3 miserere,** a speech, prayer, etc. for mercy. [< L *miserere* have pity, the first word of this psalm in the Vulgate]

mi·ser·ly (mī′zər lē) *adj.* of, like, or suited to a miser; stingy. —**mi′ser·li·ness,** *n.* —**Syn.** niggardly, close.

mis·er·y (miz′ər ē or miz′rē) *n.* **-er·ies. 1** a miserable, unhappy state of mind. **2** poor, mean, miserable circumstances: *the misery of poverty.* **3** *Informal.* a wretched or miserable person: *He's an old misery.* [< L *miseria* < *miser* wretched] —**Syn. 1** wretchedness, distress, woe.

mis·fea·sance (mis fē′zəns) *n.* **1** in law, the wrongful performance of a lawful act; wrongful and injurious exercise of lawful authority. **2** any wrong done. [ME < OF *mesfaisance* < *mes-* wrong (see MIS-) + *faire* do < L *facere*]

mis·fire (mis fīr′) *v.* **-fired, -fir·ing,** *n.* —*v.* **1** fail to discharge or go off: *The pistol misfired.* **2** fail to start; fail to ignite at the proper moment: *The old engine misfired.* **3** go wrong; fail. —*n.* a failure to discharge or start.

mis·fit (*n.* mis′fit′; *v.* mis fit′) *n. v.* **-fit·ted, -fit·ting.** —*n.* **1** a bad fit. **2** a person who is not suited to his job. **3** a person who does not get along with other people. —*v.* fit badly.

mis·for·tune (mis fôr′chən) *n.* **1** bad luck. **2** a piece of bad luck; unlucky accident.
Syn. 1, 2 Misfortune, adversity, mishap = bad luck. **Misfortune** applies to either an unfortunate condition, ordinarily not one's own fault, or a particular turning of affairs against one, or an unlucky happening: *She had the misfortune to break her arm.* **Adversity** applies chiefly to a condition of great and continued misfortune, marked by serious accidents, hardships, and distress: *Displaced persons have experienced adversity.* **Mishap** applies to a minor accident or unlucky incident: *Breaking a dish is a mishap.*

mis·give (mis giv′) *v.* **-gave, -giv·en, -giv·ing.** cause to feel doubt, suspicion, or anxiety.

mis·giv·en (mis giv′ən) *v.* pp. of **misgive.**

mis·giv·ing (mis giv′ing) *n.* a feeling of doubt, suspicion, or anxiety: *We start off through the storm with some misgivings.* —**Syn.** foreboding, apprehension.

mis·gov·ern (mis guv′ərn) *v.* govern or manage badly. —**mis·gov′ern·ment,** *n.* —**mis·gov′er·nor,** *n.*

mis·guid·ance (mis gīd′əns) *n.* bad or wrong guidance.

mis·guide (mis gīd′) *v.* **-guid·ed, -guid·ing.** lead into mistakes or wrongdoing; mislead.

mis·guid·ed (mis gīd′id) *adj.* misled; led into mistakes or wrongdoing: *The misguided boy joined a gang of hoodlums.*

mis·han·dle (mis han′dəl) *v.* **-dled, -dling.** handle badly; maltreat.

mis·hap (mis′hap or mis hap′) *n.* an unlucky accident. —**Syn.** See **misfortune.**

Mish·na or **Mish·nah** (mish′nə) *n.* the collection of the interpretations and discussions of the law of Moses by the Jewish rabbis, completed in A.D. 200; the oral law of the Hebrews. The Mishna is a part of the Talmud. [< post-Biblical Hebrew *mishnah* instruction < *shanah* teach, learn < Hebrew *shanah* repeat]

hat, āge, cãre, fär; let, ēqual, tėrm; it, īce
hot, ōpen, ôrder; oil, out; cup, put, rüle, ūse
əbove, takən, pencəl, lemən, circəs
ch, child; ng, long; sh, ship
th, thin; ᴛʜ, then; zh, measure

mis·in·form (mis′in fôrm′) *v.* give incorrect or misleading information to. —**mis·in·form′er,** *n.*

mis·in·for·ma·tion (mis′in fər mā′shən) *n.* incorrect, inaccurate, or misleading information.

mis·in·ter·pret (mis′in tėr′prit) *v.* interpret incorrectly; explain incorrectly; misunderstand. —**Syn.** misconstrue.

mis·in·ter·pre·ta·tion (mis′in tėr′prə tā′shən) *n.* an incorrect interpretation; an incorrect explanation; misunderstanding.

mis·judge (mis juj′) *v.* **-judged, -judg·ing. 1** judge incorrectly: *The archer misjudged the distance to the target and his arrow fell short.* **2** judge unjustly: *The teacher soon discovered that she had misjudged the girl's character.*

mis·judg·ment or **mis·judge·ment** (mis juj′mənt) *n.* a wrong or unjust judgment.

mis·laid (mis lād′) *v.* pt. and pp. of **mislay.**

mis·lay (mis lā′) *v.* **-laid, -lay·ing. 1** put in the wrong place. **2** put in a place and then forget where it is: *Mother is always mislaying her glasses.*

mis·lead (mis lēd′) *v.* **-led, -lead·ing. 1** lead astray; cause to go in the wrong direction: *Our guide misled us in the woods, and we got lost.* **2** cause to do wrong; lead into wrongdoing: *Bad companions often mislead young people.* **3** lead to think what is not so; deceive: *His lies misled me.* —**mis·lead′er,** *n.* —**Syn. 1** misguide, misdirect. **3** delude, beguile, dupe.

mis·lead·ing (mis lēd′ing) *adj.* **1** causing wrong conclusions: *The detectives found that the false clue was misleading.* **2** causing mistakes or wrongdoing; deceiving: *Bad advice can be misleading.* —**mis·lead′ing·ly,** *adv.*

mis·led (mis led′) *v.* pt. and pp. of **mislead.**

mis·like (mis līk′) *v.* **-liked, -lik·ing. 1** dislike. **2** displease.

mis·man·age (mis man′ij) *v.* **-aged, -ag·ing.** manage badly. —**mis·man′a·ger,** *n.*

mis·man·age·ment (mis man′ij mənt) *n.* bad management.

mis·match (mis mach′) *v.* match badly or unsuitably. —*n.* a bad or unsuitable match.

mis·mate (mis māt′) *v.* **-mat·ed, -mat·ing.** mate unsuitably.

mis·name (mis nām′) *v.* **-named, -nam·ing.** call by an incorrect name.

mis·no·mer (mis nō′mər) *n.* **1** a name that describes wrongly: "*Lightning*" *is a misnomer for that slow, old horse.* **2** an error in naming. [ME < AF < OF *mesnommer* < *mes-* wrongly (see MIS-) + *nommer* to name < L *nominare*]

mi·sog·a·mist (mi sog′ə mist) *n.* a person who hates marriage.

mi·sog·a·my (mi sog′ə mē) *n.* a hatred of marriage. [< Gk. *misos* hatred + *gamos* marriage; formed on the pattern of *misogyny, misanthrope,* etc.]

mi·sog·y·nist (mi soj′ə nist) *n.* a hater of women.

mi·sog·y·nous (mi soj′ə nəs) *adj.* hating women.

mi·sog·y·ny (mi soj′ə nē) *n.* a hatred of women. [< Gk. *misogynia* < *misogynēs* woman-hater < *misos* hatred + *gynē* woman]

mis·place (mis plās′) *v.* **-placed, -plac·ing. 1** put in the wrong place. **2** *Informal.* put in a place and then forget where it is. **3 misplace one's trust, love,** etc., place one's trust, love, etc. in the wrong person or thing. —**mis·place′ment,** *n.*

mis·play (mis plā′) *n.* an incorrect play. —*v.* play incorrectly.

mis·print (*n.* mis′print′; *v.* mis print′) *n.* a mistake in printing. —*v.* print incorrectly.

mis·pri·sion (mis prizh′ən) *n.* **1** a wrongful action or omission, especially by a public official. **2** in law, the failure of an individual to give to the proper authorities information which he knows may lead to the apprehension of a felon: *misprision of treason.* [ME < AF < OF *mesprision* < *mesprendre* mistake, act wrongly < *mes-* wrongly (see MIS-) + *prendre* take < L *prehendere*]

mis·prize (mis prīz′) *v.* **-prized, -priz·ing.** despise; undervalue; slight. [ME < OF *mesprisier* < *mes-* *wrongly* (see MIS-) + *prisier*, var. of *preisier* praise, ult. < L *pretium* price]

mis·pro·nounce (mis′prə nouns′) *v.* **-nounced, -nounc·ing.** pronounce incorrectly.

mis·pro·nun·ci·a·tion (mis′prə nun′sē ā′shən) *n.* an incorrect pronunciation.

mis·quo·ta·tion (mis′kwō tā′shən) *n.* an incorrect quotation.

mis·quote (mis kwōt′) *v.* **-quot·ed, -quot·ing.** quote incorrectly.

mis·read (mis rēd′) *v.* **-read** (-red′), **-read·ing. 1** read incorrectly. **2** misunderstanding; interpret incorrectly: *She misread the recipe and spoiled the cake.*

mis·rep·re·sent (mis′rep ri zent′) *v.* represent falsely; give a mistaken idea of: *He misrepresented the facts of the case.*

mis·rep·re·sen·ta·tion (mis′rep ri zen tā′shən) *n.* **1** a false representation: *He obtained the position by misrepresentation.* **2** an incorrect story or explanation.

mis·rule (mis rül′) *n. v.* **-ruled, -rul·ing. —***n.* **1** bad or unwise rule. **2** disorder. —*v.* rule badly.

miss[1] (mis) *v.* **1** fail to hit: *He fired twice, but both shots missed.* **2** fail to find, get, meet, attend, use, catch, hear, read, do, solve, etc.: *miss a train.* **3** let slip by; not seize: *I missed my chance.* **4** escape or avoid: *barely miss being hit.* **5** notice the absence of: *I did not miss my purse till I got home.* **6** feel keenly the absence of: *He missed his mother when she went away.* **7** fail to work properly; misfire: *The car was missing on two cylinders.* **8 miss fire,** misfire. —*n.* **1** a failure to hit, attain, etc. **2 A miss is as good as a mile,** A close miss is no better than a wide miss. [OE *missan*]

miss[2] (mis) *n.* **miss·es. 1** a girl; a young woman. **2 Miss,** a title put before a girl's or unmarried woman's name: *Miss Brown, the Misses Brown, the Miss Browns.* [short for *mistress*]

Miss. Mississippi.

mis·sal (mis′əl) *n.* **1** in the Roman Catholic Church, a book containing the prayers, etc. for celebrating Mass throughout the year. **2** any book of devotions, prayers, etc. [< Med.L *missale* < LL *missa* Mass]

mis·say (mis sā′) *v.* **-said, -say·ing.** *Archaic.* **1** speak ill of; slander. **2** say wrongly. **3** speak wrongly.

mis·shape (mis shāp′) *v.* **-shaped, -shaped** or **-shap·en, -shap·ing.** shape badly; deform; make in the wrong shape.

mis·shap·en (mis shāp′ən) *adj.* badly shaped; deformed. —*v.* a pp. of **misshape.**

mis·sile (mis′īl or mis′əl) *n.* **1** an object that is thrown, hurled, or shot, such as a stone, bullet, arrow, or lance. **2** a self-propelled bomb or rocket. [< L *missilis*, ult. < *mittere* send]

mis·sile·man (mis′əl mən) *n.* **-men** (-mən). *Esp.U.S.* a person who works with missiles and rockets.

miss·ing (mis′ing) *adj.* **1** lacking or wanting: *It was a good cake but something was missing.* **2** lost; gone; out of its usual place: *The missing ring was found under the dresser. One of the books was missing.* **3** absent: *Two children were missing from school today.* **—Syn.** lost.

mis·sion (mish′ən) *n.* **1** a sending or being sent on some special work; errand. An operation by one or more aircraft against the enemy is called a mission. **2** a group sent on some special business: *He was one of a mission sent by our government to France.* **3** the business on which a mission is sent. **4** the station or headquarters of a religious mission. **5** a program or course of religious services for converting unbelievers or stimulating faith and zeal. **6 missions,** *pl.* an organized effort to spread the Christian religion. **7** the district assigned to a priest or pastor from a neighboring parish. **8** a place where persons may go for aid, such as food, clothing, shelter, or counsel. **9** one's business or purpose in life; calling: *It seemed to be her mission to care for her brother's children.* [< L *missio, -onis* < *mittere* send] **—Syn. 2** commission, delegation. **3** message, charge, duty, trust.

mis·sion·ar·y (mish′ən er′ē) *n.* **-ar·ies,** *adj.* **—***n.* **1** a person sent on a religious mission: *The missionary went to India to convert people to Christianity.* **2** a person who works to advance some cause or idea. —*adj.* of or having to do with missions or missionaries.

mission furniture heavy, plain, dark furniture.

mis·sis or **mis·sus** (mis′iz or mis′əz) *n.* the spoken form of **Mrs.**

miss·ish (mis′ish) *adj.* prim; prudish; affected.

Mis·sis·sip·pi·an (mis′ə sip′ē ən) *adj.* **1** of or having to do with Mississippi or the Mississippi River. **2** in geology, having to do with or designating the early Carboniferous period of the Paleozoic era in North America. See the chart under **geology.** —*n.* **1** a native or inhabitant of Mississippi. **2** in geology, the Mississipian period or rock system.

mis·sive (mis′iv) *n.* a written message; letter. [< Med.L *missivus*, ult. < L *mittere* send]

mis·speak (mis spēk′) *v.* **-spoke, -spo·ken, -speak·ing.** speak, utter, or pronounce wrongly or incorrectly.

mis·spell (mis spel′) *v.* **-spelled** or **spelt, -spell·ing.** spell incorrectly.

mis·spell·ing (mis spel′ing) *n.* an incorrect spelling.

mis·spelt (mis spelt′) *v.* a pt. and a pp. of **misspell.**

mis·spend (mis spend′) *v.* **-spent, -spend·ing.** spend foolishly or wrongly; waste.

mis·spent (mis spent′) *v.* pt. and pp. of **misspend.**

mis·spoke (mis spōk′) *v.* pt. of **misspeak.**

mis·spo·ken (mis spō′kən) *v.* pp. of **misspeak.**

mis·state (mis stāt′) *v.* **-stat·ed, -stat·ing.** make incorrect or misleading statements about. **—Syn.** misrepresent, distort, falsify.

mis·state·ment (mis stāt′mənt) *n.* a wrong or erroneous statement.

mis·step (mis step′ or mis′step′) *n.* **1** a wrong step. **2** an error or slip in conduct.

miss·y (mis′ē) *n.* **missies.** *Informal.* little miss; miss.

mist (mist) *n.* **1** a cloud of very fine drops of water in the air; fog. **2** anything that dims, blurs, or obscures: *A mist of prejudice marred his judgment.* **3** a haze before the eyes due to illness or tears.
—*v.* **1** come down in mist; rain in very fine drops. **2** become covered with mist; become dim: *The windows are misting.* **3** cover with a mist; put a mist before; make dim: *Tears misted her eyes.* **4 mist over** or **mist up,** become covered with mist. [OE] **—Syn.** *n.* **1** haze.

mis·tak·a·ble (mis tāk′ə bəl) *adj.* that may be mistaken or misunderstood.

mis·take (mis tāk′) *n. v.* **-took, -tak·en, -tak·ing. —***n.* **1** an error; blunder; misunderstanding: *I used your towel by mistake.* **2 and no mistake,** without a doubt; surely. [< v.] **—***v.* **1** misunderstand (what is seen or heard). **2** take wrongly; take to be some other person or thing. **3** make a mistake. [ME < ON *mistaka*] **—Syn.** *n.* **1** fault, oversight, slip. See **error.**

mis·tak·en (mis tāk′ən) *adj.* **1** wrong in opinion; having made a mistake: *A mistaken person should admit his error.* **2** wrong; wrongly judged; misplaced: *It was a mistaken kindness to give that boy more candy.* —*v.* pp. of **mistake.**

mis·tak·en·ly (mis tāk′ən lē) *adv.* by mistake; wrongly.

mis·ter (mis′tər) *n.* **1 Mister,** Mr., a title put before a man's name or the name of his office: *Mr. Smith, Mr. Speaker.* **2** *Informal.* sir: *Good morning, mister.* [var. of *master*]

mis·time (mis tīm′) *v.* **-timed, -tim·ing. 1** say or do at the wrong time. **2** misstate the time of.

mis·tle·toe (mis′əl tō′) *n.* **1** a plant having small, waxy, white berries and yellow flowers, which grows as a parasite on certain trees. **2** a sprig of mistletoe, often used as a Christmas decoration. [OE *misteltān* < *mistel* mistletoe + *tān* twig]

mis·took (mis tu̇k′) *v.* pt. of **mistake.**

mis·tral (mis′trəl or mis träl′) *n.* a cold, dry, northerly wind common in S. France and neighboring regions. [< F < Provençal *mistral,* originally, dominant < L *magistralis* < *magister* master]

mis·trans·late (mis′trans lāt′ or mis trans′lāt, mis′tranz lāt′ or mis tranz′lāt) *v.* **-lat·ed, -lat·ing.** translate incorrectly.

mis·trans·la·tion (mis′trans lā′shən or -tranz lā′shən) *n.* an incorrect translation.

mis·treat (mis trēt′) *v.* treat badly.

mis·treat·ment (mis trēt′mənt) *n.* ill treatment.

mis·tress (mis′tris) *n.* **1** the woman who is at the head of a household. **2** a woman or nation that is in control or can rule. **3** a woman who has a thorough knowledge or mastery. **4** a woman teaching in a school, or at the head of a school, or giving lessons in a special subject: *the dancing mistress.* **5** *Poetic.* a woman loved and courted by a man. **6** a woman who improperly occupies the place of a wife. **7 Mistress,** a title of courtesy for a married woman, usually abbreviated in writing to "Mrs." and pronounced (mis′iz). **8** *Archaic or dialect.* Mrs., Madam, or Miss. [ME < OF *maistresse* < *maistre.* See MASTER.]

mis·tri·al (mis trī′əl) *n.* **1** a trial that is void in law because of some error in the proceedings. **2** *Informal.* an inconclusive trial.

mis·trust (mis trust′) *v.* feel no confidence in; doubt. —*n.* a lack of trust or confidence. —**mis·trust′er,** *n.* —**Syn.** *v.* suspect, distrust. –*n.* doubt, suspicion.

mis·trust·ful (mis trust′fəl) *adj.* lacking confidence; distrustful; doubting; suspicious. —**mis·trust′ful·ly,** *adv.*

mist·y (mis′tē) *adj.* **mist·i·er, mist·i·est. 1** of mist. **2** characterized by mist; covered with mist. **3** not clearly seen or outlined. **4** as if seen through a mist; vague; indistinct: *a misty idea.* [OE *mistig*] —**mist′i·ly,** *adv.* —**mist′i·ness,** *n.*

mis·un·der·stand (mis′un dər stand′) *v.* **-stood, -stand·ing. 1** understand wrongly. **2** take in a wrong sense; give the wrong meaning to. —**Syn. 1** misapprehend, misconceive. **2** misinterpret.

mis·un·der·stand·ing (mis′un dər stan′ding) *n.* **1** a failure to understand; a mistake as to meaning; wrong understanding. **2** a disagreement: *After their misunderstanding, they scarcely spoke to each other for months.*

mis·un·der·stood (mis′un dər stůd′) *v.* pt. and pp. of **misunderstand.** —*adj.* not understood; not properly appreciated.

mis·us·age (mis ūs′ij or -ūz′ij) *n.* **1** a wrong or improper usage. **2** ill usage; bad treatment.

mis·use (*v.* mis ūz′; *n.* mis ūs′) *v.* **-used, -us·ing,** *n.* —*v.* **1** use for the wrong purpose. **2** abuse; ill-treat: *He misuses his horses by giving them loads that are too heavy.* —*n.* a wrong use. —**Syn.** *v.* **1** misapply. **2** maltreat.

mite[1] (mīt) *n.* any of various tiny animals that belong to the same class as spiders and live in foods, on plants, or on other animals. [OE *mīte*]

mite[2] (mīt) *n.* **1** anything very small; little bit: *Though poor, she gave her mite to charity.* **2** a coin of slight value. **3** a very small child. —*adv. Informal.* little; a bit. [< MDu. *mite,* ult. identical with *mite*[1]]

mi·ter (mī′tər) *n. v.* mitre.

mi·tered (mī′tərd) *adj.* mitred.

Mith·ra·ic (mith rā′ik) *adj.* of or having to do with Mithras or his cult.

Mith·ras (mith′ras) *n.* in ancient Persian mythology, the god of light, truth, and justice, often taken as representing the sun. He became the subject of an extensive cult during the late Roman Empire.

mit·i·gate (mit′ə gāt′) *v.* **-gat·ed, -gat·ing.** make or become mild; make or become milder; soften. Anger, grief, pain, punishments, heat, cold, and many other conditions may be mitigated. [< L *mitigare* < *mitis* gentle] —**mit′i·ga′tor,** *n.*

mit·i·ga·tion (mit′ə gā′shən) *n.* **1** a mitigating. **2** a being mitigated. **3** something that mitigates: *The breeze was a welcome mitigation of the heat.*

mit·i·ga·tive (mit′ə gā′tiv) *adj.* tending to mitigate. —*n.* something that mitigates.

hat, āge, cãre, fär; let, ēqual, tėrm; it, īce
hot, ōpen, ôrder; oil, out; cup, pu̇t, rüle, ūse
əbove, takən, pencəl, lemən, circəs
ch, child; ng, long; sh, ship
th, thin; ᴛʜ, then; zh, measure

mi·to·sis (mi tō′sis or mī tō′sis) *n.* in biology, a method of cell division in which the chromatin of the nucleus forms into a thread that separates into segments or chromosomes, each of which in turn separates longitudinally into two parts. [< NL < Gk. *mitos* thread]

mi·tot·ic (mi tot′ik or mī tot′ik) *adj.* of mitosis.

mi·tre or **mi·ter** (mī′tər) *n. v.* **mi·tred, mi·tring.** —*n.* **1** a tall, pointed, folded cap worn by bishops during sacred ceremonies. **2** the official head-dress of the ancient Jewish high priest. **3** a kind of joint or corner where two pieces of wood are fitted together at right angles with the ends cut slanting, as at the corners of a picture frame. **4** the bevel on either of the pieces in a mitre joint. **5** in sewing, a corner or angle joining made by a diagonal seam.
—*v.* **1** bestow a mitre on; make a bishop. **2** join with a mitre joint; prepare (ends of wood) for joining in a mitre joint. **3** sew together in a mitre. [ME < OF < L < Gk. *mitra* headband]

A mitre (def. 1)

mi·tred (mī′tərd) *adj.* **1** having a mitre joint. **2** wearing a bishop's mitre.

mitre joint a right-angled joint made by cutting the ends of two pieces of wood on equal slants.

MITRE JOINT

mitt (mit) *n.* **1** a mitten. **2** a kind of long glove without fingers, or with very short fingers. **3** in baseball, a glove with a big pad over the palm and fingers. **4** *Slang.* a hand. [short for *mitten*]

mit·ten (mit′ən) *n.* **1** a kind of winter glove covering the four fingers together and the thumb separately. **2** a mitt (def. 2). **3 get the mitten,** *Archaic or informal.* be refused as a lover. **4 give the mitten to,** *Archaic or informal.* refuse as a lover. [< F *mitaine* half glove, ult. < L *medius* middle]

mix (miks) *v.* **mixed** or **mixt, mix·ing,** *n.* —*v.* **1** put together; stir well together: *mix ingredients to make a cake.* **2** prepare by putting different things together: *mix a cake.* **3** join: *mix business and pleasure.* **4** be mixed: *Milk and water mix.* **5** get along together; make friends easily: *She found it difficult to mix with strangers. He doesn't mix very well.* **6 mix up, a** confuse: *I was so mixed up that I lost my way.* **b** involve; concern: *He did not want to be mixed up in the affair.*
—*n.* **1** a mixture. **2** *Informal.* a mixed condition; mess. **3** an already mixed preparation: *a cake mix.* **4** ginger ale, soda water, etc. to mix with alcoholic drinks. [< *mixt* mixed < F < L *mixtus,* pp. of *miscere* mix]
Syn. *v.* **1 Mix, blend** = put two or more things together. **Mix** emphasizes forming a mass or compound in which the parts or ingredients are well scattered or spread into one another: *Mix the dry ingredients before adding a liquid.* **Blend** = mix thoroughly and smoothly together, or one thing little by little into the other, so that the parts lose their separate and distinct existence and the whole has the qualities of both (or all): *Blend the flour into the melted butter.* **5** fraternize.

mixed (mikst) *adj.* **1** put together or formed by mixing; composed of different parts or elements; of different kinds combined: *mixed candies, mixed emotions.* **2** of different classes, kinds, etc.; not exclusive: *mixed company.* **3** of or for persons of both sexes: *a mixed chorus.* **4** *Informal.* mentally confused.

mixed farming the practice of combining the production of grain, livestock, dairy products, etc. on the same farm.

mixed number a number consisting of a whole number and a fraction, such as $1\frac{1}{2}$, $16\frac{2}{3}$, and $25\frac{9}{10}$.

mixed train a train composed of both freight and passenger cars.

mix·er (mik′sər) *n.* **1** a thing that mixes: *a bread mixer.*

2 a person who mixes. 3 a person who gets along well with others, making friends easily: *She is a good mixer.* 4 a mix (def. 4).

mix·ture (miks′chər) *n.* 1 a mixing. 2 a being mixed. 3 what has been mixed. 4 in chemistry, two or more substances that are mixed together, but retain their individual chemical properties. [< L *mixtura* < *miscere* mix] —**Syn.** 1 blending, fusing. 3 blend.

mix-up (miks′up′) *n. Informal.* 1 confusion; mess. 2 a confused fight.

Miz·pah (miz′pə) *n.* a word used to recall this prayer: "The Lord watch between me and thee, when we are absent one from another." Gen. 31:49. [< Hebrew *mitspeh* outlook-point, watchtower]

miz·zen (miz′ən) *n.* 1 a fore-and-aft sail on the mizzenmast. 2 a mizzenmast. See **mainsail** for picture. [< F < Ital. *mezzana* < L *medianus* in the middle < *medius* middle]

miz·zen·mast (miz′ən mast′ or miz′ən məst) *n.* the mast nearest the stern in a two-masted or three-masted ship. See **mainsail** for picture.

mk. mark.

mkt. market.

M.L.A. Member of the Legislative Assembly.

MLG or **M.L.G.** Middle Low German.

Mlle. or **Mlle** *pl.* **Mlles.** or **Mlles** Mademoiselle.

M.L.S. Master of Library Science.

mm. millimetre; millimetres.

MM. or **MM** Messieurs.

M.M. Military Medal.

Mme. or **Mme** *pl.* **Mmes.** or **Mmes** Madame.

Mn manganese.

mne·mon·ic (ni mon′ik) *adj.* 1 aiding the memory. 2 intended to aid memory. 3 of or having to do with memory. —*n.* a device to aid the memory. —**mne·mon′i·cal·ly,** *adv.* [< Gk. *mnēmonikos* < *mnamnasthai* remember]

Mne·mos·y·ne (ni mos′ə nē′) *n.* in Greek mythology, the goddess of memory and mother of the Muses.

mo. month; months.

Mo molybdenum.

Mo. Missouri.

M.O. 1 Money Order. 2 Medical Officer.

mo·a (mō′ə) *n.* an extinct bird of New Zealand, that resembled an ostrich. [< Maori]

Mo·ab (mō′ab) *n.* an ancient kingdom in Syria.

Mo·ab·ite (mō′əb īt′) *n.* an inhabitant of Moab. —*adj.* of or having to do with Moab or its people.

moan (mōn) *n.* 1 a long, low sound of suffering. 2 any similar sound: *the moan of the wind.* 3 complaint; lamentation. 4 an instance of this: *Her moan was only that she had not been invited.*
—*v.* 1 make moans. 2 utter with a moan. 3 complain about; complain: *He was always moaning about his luck.* 4 grieve; grieve for: *He moaned the loss of his friends.* [ME *man*; cf. OE *mǣnan* complain] —**moan′ing·ly,** *adv.* —**Syn.** *v.* 1 wail. See **groan.** 3, 4 lament, bewail.

moat (mōt) *n.* 1 a deep, wide ditch dug around a castle or town as a protection against enemies. Moats were usually kept filled with water. 2 a similar ditch used to separate areas in a zoo. —*v.* surround with a moat. [ME < OF *mote* mound]

mob (mob) *n. v.* **mobbed, mob·bing.** —*n.* 1 a large number of people, usually crowded closely together. 2 the common mass of people. 3 a lawless crowd, easily moved to act without thinking. 4 *Slang.* a gang of criminals. 5 **the mob,** a the common mass of people, thought of as lacking taste, culture, etc.; the masses. b the lawless part of the populace; the rabble. c *Slang.* the dominant group in the underworld of a city, state, etc.: *The metropolis had been ruled by the mob for years.*
—*v.* 1 crowd around in curiosity, eagerness, anger, etc. 2 attack with violence, as a mob does. [shortened form of L *mobile vulgus* fickle common people]

mob·cap (mob′kap′) *n.* a large, loose cap, fitting down over the ears, formerly worn indoors by women. [< obs. *mob* muffle the head]

mo·bile[1] (mō′bīl, mō′bəl, or mō′bēl) *adj.* 1 capable of being moved easily; moving easily; movable: *A car is a mobile machine.* 2 easily changed or altered; quick to change from one position to another: *mobile features, a mobile mind.* [< L *mobilis* movable < *movere* move]

mo·bile[2] (mō′bīl or mō′bēl) *n.* pieces of metal, wood, paper, etc. suspended on wires or threads and balanced to move in a slight breeze, used decoratively. [< *mobile*[1]]

mobile home a large, well-equipped house trailer.

mo·bil·i·ty (mō bil′ə tē) *n.* **-ties.** a being mobile; ability or readiness to move or be moved.

mo·bi·li·za·tion (mō′bə lə zā′shən or mō′bə lī zā′shən) *n.* 1 a mobilizing; calling troops, ships, etc. into active military service. 2 a being mobilized.

mo·bi·lize (mō′bə līz′) *v.* **-lized, -liz·ing.** 1 call (troops, warships, etc.) into active military service; organize for war. 2 assemble and prepare for war: *The troops mobilized quickly.* 3 put into action or active use: *mobilize the wealth of a country.* [< F *mobiliser* < *mobile* mobile] —**mo′bi·liz′a·ble,** *adj.* —**mo′bi·liz′er,** *n.*

mob·ster (mob′stər) *n. Slang.* a member of a gang of criminals.

moc·ca·sin (mok′ə sən) *n.* 1 a soft shoe, often made from the skin of a deer, having the sides and sole formed of one piece of leather: *Moccasins were worn and made by North American Indians.* 2 a shoe or slipper of similar style. [< Algonquian]

moccasin dance *Cdn.* a dance, often held outdoors or in a rink, for which moccasins are worn.

moccasin flower a pink or white orchid shaped like a slipper.

moccasin telegraph *Cdn. Informal.* 1 grapevine (def. 2). 2 formerly, the sending of messages by Indian runner.

Mo·cha (mō′kə) *n.* 1 a choice variety of coffee originally coming from the Arabian peninsula. 2 a flavoring made from coffee or chocolate and coffee. 3 a kind of soft leather used for gloves. Also, **mocha.** —*adj.* **mocha,** flavored with coffee, or with chocolate and coffee: *a mocha cake.* [< *Mocha,* a port in S.W. Yemen]

mock (mok) *v.* 1 laugh at; make fun of. 2 make fun of by copying or imitating. 3 imitate; copy. 4 scoff. 5 make light of; pay no attention to. 6 deceive; disappoint. —*adj.* not real; copying; sham; imitation: *a mock battle.* —*n.* 1 an action or speech that mocks. 2 a person or thing scorned or deserving scorn. 3 **make mock of,** ridicule. [ME < OF *mocquer*] —**mock′er,** *n.* —**Syn.** *v.* 1 deride, taunt, gibe. See **ridicule.** 3 mimic, ape. 6 delude, fool. *-adj.* feigned, pretended, counterfeit.

mock·er·y (mok′ər ē) *n.* **-er·ies.** 1 a making fun; ridicule. 2 a person or thing to be made fun of. 3 a bad copy or imitation. 4 a disregarding; a setting at naught: *The unfair trial was a mockery of justice.* 5 **make mockery of,** ridicule.

mock-he·ro·ic (mok′hi rō′ik) *adj.* imitating or burlesquing what is heroic. Pope's *Rape of the Lock* is a mock-heroic poem. —*n.* an imitation or burlesque of what is heroic.

mock·ing (mok′ing) *adj.* that mocks; deriding; mimicking; deluding. —**mock′ing·ly,** *adv.*

mock·ing·bird (mok′ing bėrd′) *n.* a songbird of the southern United States, Central America, and South America that imitates the notes of other birds.

mock orange the syringa.

mock turtle soup a soup made in imitation of green turtle soup.

mock-up (mok′up′) *n.* a full-sized model of an airplane, machine, etc. used for teaching or experimental purposes.

mo·dal (mō′dəl) *adj.* of or having to do with mode, grammatical mood, manner, or form. [< Med.L *modalis* < L *modus* measure]

modal auxiliary in grammar, a word such as *may, can, must, would,* and *should,* that indicates the grammatical mood of the verb with which it is used.

mo·dal·i·ty (mō dal′ə tē) *n.* 1 the fact, state, or

quality of being modal; form. 2 mode; method. 3 in medicine, a therapeutic method or apparatus, especially physiotherapy or electrotherapy. 4 in logic, a proposition having some qualification, such as contingency, necessity, possibility, or impossibility.

mode[1] (mōd) *n.* 1 the manner or way in which a thing is done. 2 the form of a verb that shows whether the act or state is thought of as a fact, command, etc.; mood: *the indicative mode, the imperative mode.* 3 in music: **a** any of various arrangements of the tones of an octave. **b** either of the two classes of keys in music: *major and minor modes.* **c** any of various Greek or medieval scales, each having a different pattern of intervals: *The keyboard of the modern piano represents the Dorian mode.* 4 in logic: **a** the form of a proposition with reference to the necessity, contingency, possibility, or impossibility of its content. **b** any of the various forms of valid syllogisms, depending on the quantity and quality of their constituent propositions. 5 the actual mineral composition of a rock, stated quantitatively in percentages by weight. [< L *modus* measure] —**Syn.** 1 method.

mode[2] (mōd) *n.* the style, fashion, or custom that prevails; the way most people are behaving, talking, dressing, etc. [< F < L *modus* mode[1]] —**Syn.** vogue.

Mod.E. Modern English.

mod·el (mod′əl) *n. v.* **-elled** or **-eled, -el·ling** or **-el·ing.** *adj.* —*n.* 1 a small copy: *a model of a ship.* 2 a figure, object, etc. in clay, wax, etc. that is to be copied in marble, bronze, etc.: *a model for a statue.* 3 the way in which a thing is made; design or style. 4 a thing or person to be imitated: *The boy wrote so well that the teacher used his composition as a model for the class.* 5 a person, especially a woman, who poses for artists, photographers, etc. 6 a person, especially a woman, employed to put on clothes in order to display them to customers.
—*v.* 1 make; shape; fashion; design; plan: *model a bird's nest in clay.* 2 make models; design: *model in clay.* 3 follow as a model; form (something) after a particular model: *He modelled himself on his father.* 4 be a model. 5 display clothes by wearing them: *That girl usually models evening gowns.*
—*adj.* 1 used or serving as a model. 2 just right or perfect, especially in conduct: *a model child.* [< F < Ital. *modello,* dim. of *modo* mode[1]]
Syn. *n.* 4 **Model, example, pattern** = someone or something to be copied or followed. **Model** applies to a person or thing thought especially worth copying or imitating: *The famous surgeon is his model.* **Example** applies to a person, his conduct, or actions likely for some reason to be imitated: *He follows his father's example.* **Pattern** applies particularly to a fine example or model set up as worth imitating or following as closely as a worker follows designs in making something: *Her book gives a pattern for behavior.*

mod·el·ling or **mod·el·ing** (mod′əl ing) *n.* 1 the act or art of one who models or is modelled. 2 the production of designs in some plastic material, for reproduction in a more durable material. 3 the representation of solid form, as in sculpture. 4 the bringing of surfaces into proper relief, as in carving. 5 the rendering of the appearance of relief, as in painting.

mod·er·ate (*adj., n.* mod′ər it; *v.* mod′ər āt′) *adj. n. v.* **-at·ed, -at·ing.** —*adj.* 1 kept or keeping within proper bounds; not extreme: *moderate expenses, moderate styles.* 2 not violent; calm: *moderate in speech or opinion.* 3 fair; medium; not very large or good: *a moderate profit.*
—*n.* a person who holds moderate opinions.
—*v.* 1 make less violent. 2 become less extreme or violent. 3 act as moderator; preside (over). [< L *moderatus,* pp. of *moderare* regulate < *modus* measure] —**mod′er·ate·ly,** *adv.*
Syn. *adj.* 1, 2 **Moderate, temperate** mean "not extreme in any way," and are often interchangeable. But **moderate** emphasizes freedom from excess, not going beyond or above the proper, right, or reasonable limit: *He is a moderate eater.* **Temperate** emphasizes restraint, holding back within limits, especially with regard to the feelings or appetites: *He feels things deeply, but is always temperate in speech.* -*v.* 1, 2 diminish, lessen.

mod·er·a·tion (mod′ər ā′shən) *n.* 1 freedom from excess; proper restraint; temperance. 2 a moderating or moving away from an extreme: *The rain brought moderation to the uncomfortably hot weather.* 3 calmness; lack of violence. 4 **in moderation,** within limits; not going to extremes.

mod·e·ra·to (mod′ə rä′tō) in music: —*adj. adv.* in moderate time. —*n.* a moderate movement or passage; a composition to be played or sung at this tempo. [< Ital.]

hat, āge, cãre, fär; let, ēqual, tėrm; it, īce
hot, ōpen, ôrder; oil, out; cup, pu̇t, rüle, ūse
əbove, takən, pencəl, lemən, circəs
ch, child; ng, long; sh, ship
th, thin; ᴛʜ, then; zh, measure

mod·er·a·tor (mod′ər ā′tər) *n.* 1 a presiding officer; chairman. 2 an arbitrator; mediator. 3 in certain churches, the chief elected officer. 4 material used in a reactor to slow down nuclear fission.

mod·ern (mod′ərn) *adj.* 1 of the present time; of times not long past: *Television is a modern invention.* 2 up-to-date; not old-fashioned. —*n.* 1 a person of modern times. 2 a person who has modern ideas and tastes. [< LL *modernus* < L *modo* just now (originally, with measure, ablative of *modus* measure)] —**mod′ern·ly,** *adv.* —**mod′ern·ness,** *n.* —**Syn.** *adj.* 1 See **new.**

Modern English 1 the period in the development of the English language from about 1500 to the present. 2 the language of this period.

mod·ern·ism (mod′ər niz′əm) *n.* 1 modern attitudes or methods; sympathy with what is modern. 2 the tendency to interpret the teachings of the Bible or the Christian church in accordance with modern scientific theories. 3 a modern word or phrase.

mod·ern·ist (mod′ər nist) *n.* 1 a person who holds modern views or uses modern methods. 2 a person who interprets religious teachings in a modern way.

mod·ern·is·tic (mod′ər nis′tik) *adj.* 1 modern. 2 having to do with modernism or modernists.

mo·der·ni·ty (mə dėr′nə tē or mō dėr′nə tē) *n.* **-ties.** 1 a being modern. 2 something modern.

mod·ern·ize (mod′ər nīz′) *v.* **-ized, -iz·ing.** 1 make modern; bring up to present ways or standards. 2 become modern. —**mod′ern·i·za′tion,** *n.* —**mod′ern·iz′er,** *n.*

mod·est (mod′ist) *adj.* 1 not thinking too highly of oneself; not vain; humble. 2 bashful; not bold; shy; held back by a sense of what is fit and proper. 3 not calling attention to one's body; decent. 4 not too great; not asking too much: *a modest request.* 5 not gaudy; humble in appearance; quiet: *a modest little house.* [< L *modestus* in due measure < *modus* measure] —**mod′est·ly,** *adv.*
Syn. 1 unpretentious, unassuming. 2 diffident. **Modest, demure** = not bold or pushing oneself forward in the presence of others. **Modest** emphasizes a sense of fit and proper behavior and a lack of conceit that hold a person back from calling attention to himself: *I like a modest girl, one who is neither shy nor loud.* **Demure** now chiefly suggests an unnatural modesty or pretended shyness thought to be attractive and put on for effect: *She sipped her soda and looked demure.*

mod·es·ty (mod′is tē) *n.* **-ties.** 1 freedom from vanity; a being modest or humble. 2 shyness; bashfulness. 3 the fact or condition of being decent. —**Syn.** 1 humility. 2 diffidence.

mod·i·cum (mod′ə·kəm) *n.* a small or moderate quantity. [< L *modicum,* neut., moderate < *modus* measure]

mod·i·fi·ca·tion (mod′ə fə kā′shən) *n.* 1 a partial alteration or change: *The teacher recommended six modifications in my essay.* 2 a modifying or being modified; a toning down: *The modification of his anger made him able to think clearly again.* 3 a limitation of meaning. 4 a modified form or variety: *The most recent modification of the long-range missile performs flawlessly.* 5 in biology, a change in an organism resulting from external influences, and not inheritable.

mod·i·fi·er (mod′ə fī′ər) *n.* 1 in grammar, a word or group of words that limits the meaning of another word or group of words. In "a very tight coat," the adjective *tight* is a modifier of *coat,* and the adverb *very* is a modifier of *tight.* 2 a person or thing that modifies.

mod·i·fy (mod′ə fī′) *v.* **-fied, -fy·ing.** 1 change somewhat: *modify the terms of a lease.* 2 make less; tone down; make less severe or strong: *modify one's demands.* 3 limit the meaning of; qualify. Adverbs modify verbs, adjectives, and other adverbs. [< L *modificare* limit

< *modus* measure + *facere* make] —**mod′i·fi′a·ble,** *adj.* —**Syn. 1** alter. **2** temper.

mod·ish (mōd′ish) *adj.* fashionable; stylish. —**mod′ish·ly,** *adv.* —**mod′ish·ness,** *n.*

mo·diste (mō dēst′) *n.* a maker of or dealer in women's gowns, hats, etc.; dressmaker. [< F]

Mo·dred (mō′dred) *n.* in Arthurian legend, King Arthur's nephew and one of his knights. He was a traitor and led the rebellion against Arthur. Also, **Mordred.**

mod·u·lar (moj′ù lər) *adj.* **1** of or having to do with a module or a modulus. **2** constructed in standard pieces or units flexible enough to be interchanged. **3** of or having to do with building materials, furniture, etc. that can be interchanged.

mod·u·late (moj′ù lāt′) *v.* **-lat·ed, -lat·ing. 1** regulate; adjust; vary; soften; tone down. **2** alter (the voice) for expression. **3** in music, change from one key or note to another. **4** vary the frequency of (electrical waves). **5** change (a radio current) by adding sound waves to it. [< L *modulari,* ult. < *modus* measure]

mod·u·la·tion (moj′ù lā′shən) *n.* **1** a modulating or being modulated. **2** in music, a change from one key to another. **3** in electronics, a varying of high-frequency waves.

mod·u·la·tor (moj′ù lā′tər) *n.* **1** a person or thing that modulates. **2** a device for changing a radio current by adding sound waves to it.

mod·ule (moj′ül) *n.* **1** a standard or unit for measuring. **2** the size of some part taken as a unit of measure. **3** a standard piece or component. [< L *modulus,* dim. of *modus* measure. Doublet of MOULD[1].]

mod·u·lus (moj′ù ləs) *n.* **-li** (-lī′ or -lē′). in science, a quantity expressing the measure of some function, property, or the like, especially under conditions where the measure is unity.

mo·dus o·pe·ran·di (mō′dəs op′ə ran′dī or op′ə ran′dē) *Latin.* a method or manner of working.

mo·dus vi·ven·di (mō′dəs vi ven′dī or vi ven′dē) *Latin.* a mode of living; a way of getting along; a temporary arrangement while waiting for a final settlement.

Mo·gul (mō′gul or mō gul′) *n.* **1** a Mongolian. **2** one of the Mongol conquerors of India in the 16th century or one of their descendants. **3 mogul,** an important person, especially a tycoon. [< Arabic and Persian *Mugul* < the native name *Mongol*]

M.O.H. Medical Officer of Health.

mo·hair (mō′hăr) *n.* **1** cloth made from the long, silky hair of the Angora goat. **2** a similar cloth made of wool and cotton or rayon. **3** the hair of the Angora goat. [ult. < Arabic *mukhayyar*; conformed to *hair*]

Mo·ham·med (mō ham′id) *n.* A.D. 570?-632, a prophet and the founder of Islam, one of the world's great religions. His words are preserved in the Koran. Also, **Mahomet, Muhammad.**

Mo·ham·med·an (mō ham′ə dən) *adj. n.* Moslem. Also, **Mahometan.**

Mo·ham·med·an·ism (mō ham′ə dən iz′əm) *n.* the religion of the Moslems. Also, **Mahometanism.**

Mo·hawk (mō′hok or mō′hôk) *n.* **-hawk** or **-hawks. 1** a tribe of North American Indians belonging to the Five Nations confederacy, now living mainly in Ontario and Quebec. **2** a member of this tribe. **3** the Iroquoian language of this tribe.

Mo·hi·can (mō hē′kən) *n.* **1** a tribe of North American Indians formerly living in the upper Hudson valley and in Connecticut. **2** a member of this tribe. [< Algonquian word for "wolf"]

Mo·hole (mō′hōl′) *n.* a drilling project for geological study of the earth's crust down to the Mohorovicic discontinuity. [< *Mo*horovicic + *hole.* See MOHOROVICIC DISCONTINUITY.]

Mo·hor·o·vic·ic discontinuity (mə hôr′ə vis′ik or mə hôr′ə vich′ik) in geology, a rock layer separating the earth's crust and its mantle at a depth of about 6 miles under ocean beds and 20 miles on land. [after Andrija *Mohorovicic,* a Yugoslavian geologist who discovered it in 1909]

moi·dore (moi′dôr) *n.* a former gold coin of Portugal, worth about $6.50. [< Pg. *moeda d'ouro* coin of gold]

moi·e·ty (moi′ə tē) *n.* **-ties. 1** half. **2** an indefinite part: *Only a moiety of high-school graduates go to college.* [ME < OF < LL *medietas* half < L *medietas* the middle < *medius* middle]

moil (moil) *v.* work hard; drudge. —*n.* **1** hard work; drudgery. **2** trouble; confusion. [ME < OF *moillier* moisten < L *mollis* soft]

moiré or **moire** (mwä rā′, mwär, or mô rā′) *n.* a fabric, usually silk or rayon, having a wavelike pattern; watered fabric. —*adj.* having a wavelike pattern; watered: *moiré silk.* [< F *moire,* alteration of E *mohair*]

moist (moist) *adj.* **1** slightly wet; damp. **2** rainy. [ME < OF *moiste* < LL *muccidus* mouldy, musty < L *mucus* mucus] —**moist′ly,** *adv.* —**moist′ness,** *n.* —**Syn. 1** humid, dank. See **damp.**

moist·en (moi′sən) *v.* **1** make moist: *moisten the lips.* **2** become moist.

mois·ture (mois′chər) *n.* a slight wetness; water or other liquid spread in very small drops in the air or on a surface.

mo·lar[1] (mō′lər) *n.* a tooth with a broad surface for grinding. A person's back teeth are molars. See **tooth** for diagram. —*adj.* **1** adapted for grinding. **2** of the molar teeth. [< L *molaris* < *mola* mill]

mo·lar[2] (mō′lər) *adj.* in physics, of mass, acting on or by means of large masses of matter. [< L *moles* mass]

mo·las·ses (mə las′iz) *n.* a sweet syrup obtained in making sugar from sugar cane. [< Pg. < LL *mellaceum* must < *mel* honey]

mold (mōld) *n. v.* mould.

mold·board (mōld′bôrd′) *n.* mouldboard.

mold·er (mōl′dər) *v. n.* moulder.

mold·ing (mōl′ding) *n.* moulding.

mold·y (mōl′dē) *adj.* **mold·i·er, mold·i·est.** mouldy. —**mold′i·ness,** *n.*

mole[1] (mōl) *n.* a congenital spot on the skin, usually brown. [OE *māl*]

mole[2] (mōl) *n.* **1** a small mammal that lives underground most of the time. Moles have velvety fur and small, weak eyes. **2** a person who works in obscurity, especially one who works patiently and painstakingly. [ME *molle*] —**mole′like′,** *adj.*

mole[3] (mōl) *n.* **1** a barrier built of stone to break the force of the waves; breakwater. **2** a harbor formed by a mole. [< L *moles* mass]

mo·lec·u·lar (mə lek′yù lər) *adj.* having to do with, caused by, or consisting of molecules.

mol·e·cule (mol′ə kūl′) *n.* **1** in chemistry: **a** the smallest particle into which a substance can be divided without chemical change. A molecule of an element consists of one or more atoms. A molecule of a compound consists of two or more atoms. **b** the amount of a substance whose weight is equal to the molecular weight of the substance; gram molecule. **2** a very small particle. [< NL *molecula,* dim. of L *moles* mass]

mole·hill (mōl′hil′) *n.* **1** a small mound or ridge of earth raised up by moles burrowing under the ground. **2** something insignificant. **3 make a mountain (out) of a molehill,** give great importance to something which is really insignificant.

mole·skin (mōl′skin′) *n.* **1** the skin of the mole used as fur. **2** a strong cotton fabric used for sportsmen's and laborers' clothing. **3 moleskins,** *pl.* trousers made of this fabric.

mo·lest (mə lest′) *v.* **1** meddle with and injure; disturb. **2** interfere with improperly or indecently. [< OF < L *molestare* < *molestus* troublesome < *moles* burden] —**mo·lest′er,** *n.* —**Syn.** harass, harry.

mo·les·ta·tion (mō′les tā′shən or mol′es ta′shən) *n.* a molesting or being molested; annoying interference.

moll (mol) *n. Slang.* **1** a female companion of a criminal or vagrant. **2** a prostitute. [short for *Molly,* familiar var. of *Mary*]

mol·li·fy (mol′ə fī′) *v.* **-fied, -fy·ing.** soften; appease;

mitigate: *mollify a person.* [< F < LL *mollificare* < *mollis* soft + *facere* make] —**mol′li·fi·ca′tion,** *n.* —**mol′li·fi′er,** *n.*

mol·lusc or **mol·lusk** (mol′əsk) *n.* any of a large group of invertebrates having unsegmented, soft bodies usually covered with a hard shell. Snails, mussels, oysters, and clams are molluscs. [< F < L *molluscus* soft (of a nutshell)]

mol·ly·cod·dle (mol′ə kod′əl) *n. v.* **-dled, -dling.** —*n.* a boy or man accustomed to being fussed over and pampered; milksop. —*v.* coddle; pamper. [< *Molly* (familiar var. of *Mary*) + *coddle*] —**mol′ly·cod′dler,** *n.*

Mo·loch (mō′lok) *n.* **1** a Semitic deity whose worship demanded the sacrifice of children by their parents. **2** anything thought of as requiring frightful sacrifice: *War is a Moloch.*

molt (mōlt) *v. n.* moult.

mol·ten (mōl′tən) *adj.* **1** melted. **2** *Archaic.* made by melting and casting: *a molten image.* —*v.* a pp. of **melt.**

mo·ly (mō′lē) *n.* **mo·lies. 1** a fabulous herb with a milk-white flower and a black root, having magic properties. Hermes gave Odysseus moly to counteract the spells of Circe. **2** wild garlic. [< L < Gk.]

mo·lyb·de·nite (mə lib′də nīt′ or mol′ib dē′nīt′) *n.* a soft native sulphide of molybdenum that resembles graphite. It is the chief ore of molybdenum. *Formula:* MoS_2

mol·yb·de·nous (mə lib′də nəs or mol′ib dē′nəs) *adj.* **1** of molybdenum. **2** containing molybdenum that has a valence of two.

mo·lyb·de·num (mə lib′də nəm or mol′ib dē′nəm) *n.* a heavy, silver-white, metallic chemical element of the chromium group. Molybdenum occurs only in combination and is used to harden steel. *Symbol:* Mo; *at.no* 42, *at.wt.* 95.94. [< NL < L *molybdaena* < Gk. *molybdaina* < *molybdos* lead]

mom (mom) *n. Informal.* mother.

mo·ment (mō′mənt) *n.* **1** a very short space of time; instant: *In a moment, all was changed.* **2** a present or other particular point of time: *We both arrived at the same moment.* **3** a definite state, period, or turning point in a course of events. **4** a period of temporary excellence or distinction: *He has his moments.* **5** importance or significance: *a matter of moment.* **6** in physics, the tendency to cause rotation around a point or axis. [< L *momentum* < *movere* move. Doublet of MOMENTUM.] —**Syn. 1** second. See **minute. 5** consequence, significance.

mo·men·ta (mō men′tə) *n.* a pl. of **momentum.**

mo·men·tar·i·ly (mō′mən ter′ə lē or mō′mən tãr′ə lē) *adv.* **1** for a moment: *hesitate momentarily.* **2** at every moment; from moment to moment: *The danger was momentarily increasing.* **3** at any moment: *We expect him to arrive momentarily.*

mo·men·tar·y (mō′mən ter′ē) *adj.* lasting only a moment —**mo′men·tar′i·ness,** *n.* —**Syn.** fleeting, transitory, temporary.

mo·ment·ly (mō′mənt lē) *adv.* **1** every moment; from moment to moment. **2** at any moment. **3** for a moment.

mo·men·tous (mō men′təs) *adj.* very important: *Choosing between peace and war is a momentous decision.* —**mo·men′tous·ness,** *n.* —**Syn.** weighty, serious, critical.

mo·men·tous·ly (mō men′təs lē) *adv.* with important effect or influence.

mo·men·tum (mō men′təm) *n.* **-tum** or **-ta** (-tə). **1** the force with which a body moves, the product of its mass and its velocity: *A falling object gains momentum as it falls.* **2** the impetus resulting from movement. [< L *momentum* moving power. Doublet of MOMENT.] —**Syn. 2** impulse, force.

mom·ism (mom′iz əm) *n.* an excessively sentimental worship of motherhood. [< *mom* + *-ism* (coined by Philip Wylie, a U.S. author, born 1902)]

Mo·mus (mō′məs) *n.* **1** in Greek mythology, the god of mockery, who was banished from heaven for his ridicule and criticism of the gods. **2** any critical person; fault-finder.

mon. 1 monetary. **2** monastery.

Mon. Monday.

mon·ad (mon′ad or mō′nad) *n.* **1** a unit. **2** a very simple single-celled animal or plant. **3** in chemistry, an atom, element, or radical having a valence of one. **4** in philosophy, an entity thought of as being an ultimate unit. [< LL < Gk. *monas, -ados* unit < *monos* alone]

hat, āge, cãre, fär; let, ēqual, tėrm; it, īce
hot, ōpen, ôrder; oil, out; cup, pu̇t, rüle, ūse
əbove, takən, pencəl, lemən, circəs
ch, child; ng, long; sh, ship
th, thin; ᴛʜ, then; zh, measure

mo·nad·nock (mə nad′nok) *n.* an isolated hill or mass of rock left by erosion in a peneplain. [after Mount *Monadnock* in New Hampshire]

mo·nan·drous (mə nan′drəs) *adj.* **1** having only one husband at a time. **2** of a flower, having only one stamen. **3** of a plant, having monandrous flowers. [< Gk. *monandros* < *monos* single + *anēr, andros* husband]

mon·arch (mon′ərk) *n.* **1** a king, queen, emperor, etc.; ruler. **2** a person or thing similar to a monarch. **3** a large orange-and-black butterfly. [< LL < Gk. *monarchēs* < *monos* alone + *archein* rule]

mo·nar·chal (mə när′kəl) *adj.* **1** of or having to do with a monarch. **2** characteristic of a monarch. **3** suitable for a monarch. —**mo·nar′chal·ly,** *adv.*

mo·nar·chi·al (mə när′kē əl) *adj.* monarchal.

mo·nar·chic (mə när′kik) *adj.* monarchical.

mo·nar·chi·cal (mə när′kə kəl) *adj.* **1** of a monarch or monarchy. **3** favoring a monarchy. —**mo·nar′chi·cal·ly,** *adv.*

mon·ar·chism (mon′ər kiz′əm) *n.* **1** the principles of monarchy. **2** the advocacy of monarchical principles.

mon·ar·chist (mon′ər kist) *n.* a person who supports or favors government by a monarch.

mon·ar·chy (mon′ər kē) *n.* **-chies. 1** government by or under a monarch. **2** a nation governed or headed by a monarch. [ME < LL < Gk. *monarchia* < *monos* alone + *archein* rule]

mon·as·te·ri·al (mon′əs tēr′ē əl) *adj.* **1** of a monastery. **2** characteristic of a monastery.

mon·as·ter·y (mon′əs ter′ē) *n.* **-ter·ies. 1** a building where monks or nuns live a contemplative life according to fixed rules and under religious vows. **2** the monks or nuns who live in such a building. [ME < LL *monasterium* < Gk. *monastērion,* ult. < *monos* alone. Doublet of MINSTER.]

mo·nas·tic (mə nas′tik) *adj.* **1** of or having to do with monks or nuns: *monastic vows.* **2** of or having to do with monasteries. **3** like that of monks or nuns. —*n.* a monk. [< LL *monasticus* < LGk. *monastikos,* ult. < *monos* alone] —**mo·nas′ti·cal·ly,** *adv.*

mo·nas·ti·cal (mə nas′tə kəl) *adj.* monastic.

mo·nas·ti·cism (mə nas′tə siz′əm) *n.* the system or condition of living according to fixed rules and under religious vows, usually in a monastery or convent.

mon·au·ral (mon ô′rəl) *adj.* **1** of or having to do with one ear. **2** in sound reproduction, having only one channel of sound.

Mon·day (mun′dē or -dā) *n.* the second day of the week, following Sunday. [OE *mōn(an)dæg* the moon's day, translation of LL *lunae dies*]

Mo·nel metal (mō nel′) *Trademark.* an alloy containing 67 per cent nickel and 28 per cent copper, made from ore having the metals in this proportion. [< Ambrose *Monel,* an American manufacturer]

mon·e·tar·y (mon′ə ter′ē or mun′ə ter′ē) *adj.* **1** of the money of a country: *The monetary unit in Canada is the dollar.* **2** of money: *a monetary reward.* [< LL *monetarius* < *moneta.* See MONEY.] —**mon′e·tar′i·ly,** *adv.* —**Syn. 2** See **financial.**

mon·e·ti·za·tion (mon′ə tə zā′shən or mun′ə tə zā′shen, mon′ə tī zā′shən or mun′ə tī zā′shən) *n.* a monetizing.

mon·e·tize (mon′ə tīz′ or mun′ə tīz′) *v.* **-tized, -tiz·ing. 1** legalize as money. **2** coin into money.

mon·ey (mun′ē) *n.* **-eys** or **-ies. 1** current coin; gold, silver, or other metal made into coins; bank notes, etc. representing gold or silver; any medium of exchange. **2** a particular form or denomination of money. **3** a sum of money used for a particular purpose or belonging to a particular person. **4** wealth: *He is a man of money.* **5 moneys** or **monies, a** sums of money: *The treasurer was responsible for the moneys entrusted to him.* **b** more than one kind of money: *He had a collection of the moneys issued by different countries.* **6** any object or material serving as a medium of exchange and a measure of value, as cheques drawn on a bank, or nuggets or the dust of a precious metal. **7 for my money,** *Informal.* for my choice; in my opinion; as I see it. **8 make money, a** get money. **b** become rich. [ME < OF *moneie* < L *moneta* mint, money < *Juno Moneta,* in whose temple money was coined. Doublet of MINT[2].] —**mon′ey·less,** *adj.*

☛ **money.** Exact sums of money are usually written in figures: *72 cents; $4.98; $5; $168.75; $42,810.* Round sums are more likely to be written in words: *two hundred dollars, a million and a half dollars.* In factual books or articles involving frequent references to sums of money, however, figures are often used throughout.

mon·ey·bag (mun′ē bag′) *n.* **1** a bag for money. **2 moneybags** *pl. Informal.* **a** wealth; riches. **b** a wealthy or avaricious person.

☛ **Moneybags,** meaning "wealth," is plural in form and use. When *moneybags* means a wealthy person, it is plural in form and singular in use: *Old moneybags is finally giving a little to charity.*

mon·ey·chang·er (mun′ē chān′jər) *n.* a person whose business is to exchange money, usually that of one country for that of another.

mon·eyed (mun′ēd) *adj.* **1** having money; wealthy: *a moneyed family.* **2** consisting of or representing money or people having money: *moneyed resources, moneyed interests.* Also, **monied.**

mon·ey·lend·er (mun′ē len′dər) *n.* a person whose business is lending money at interest.

mon·ey-mak·er (mun′ē māk′ər) *n.* **1** a person who is clever at making money; one who is paid well. **2** a product that yields large profits.

mon·ey-mak·ing (mun′ē māk′ing) *n.* the gaining or accumulating of wealth. —*adj.* **1** engaged in gaining wealth. **2** yielding large profits; lucrative.

money of account a monetary denomination used in reckoning, especially one not issued as a coin. In Canada, the mill is a money of account but not a coin. The nickel is a coin, but not a money of account.

money order an order for the payment of money. One can buy a money order at a post office or at a bank and send it to a person in another city, who can collect the money at a post office or bank there.

-monger (mung′gər or mong′gər) *combining form.* **1** a dealer in ——; a person who sells ——: *Fishmonger = a dealer in fish.* **2** a person who exploits ——; a person who spreads or busies himself with ——: *Scandalmonger = a person who spreads scandal.* [OE *mangere,* ult. < L *mango* trader < Gk.]

Mon·gol (mong′gəl, mong′gol, or mong′gōl) *n.* **1** a member of an Asiatic people now inhabiting Mongolia, a region including part of northern China and the Mongolian People's Republic, and nearby parts of China and Siberia. **2** a Mongolian. —*adj.* **1** of this people. **2** Mongolian.

Mon·go·li·an (mong gō′lē ən) *n.* **1** a member of the yellow-skinned race living mainly in Asia, having slanting eyes, prominent cheekbones, a short, broad nose, and straight, black hair. The Chinese are Mongolians. **2** their language or languages. **3** a person suffering from mongolism.
—*adj.* **1** of Mongolia, the Mongolians, or their languages. **2** displaying characteristics of mongolism.

mon·gol·ism (mong′gəl iz′əm) *n.* the condition of being a mongoloid.

mon·gol·oid (mong′gəl oid′) *n.* a person born with 47 chromosomes instead of 46, usually having slanting eyes and a broad, flat face: *Mongoloids never progress beyond the level of a child in their ability to learn.*
—*adj.* having the characteristics of a mongoloid: *a mongoloid child.*

Mon·gol·oid (mong′gəl oid′) *adj.* resembling the Mongols; having characteristics of the Mongolian race. —*n.* a person of Mongolian race.

mon·goose or **mon·goos** (mong′güs) *n.* **-goos·es.** a slender, ferretlike carnivorous mammal of India, used for destroying rats, and noted for its ability to kill certain poisonous snakes. [< Marathi (lang. of W. India) *mangus*]

mon·grel (mong′grəl or mung′grəl) *n.* an animal or plant of mixed breed, especially a dog. —*adj.* of mixed breed, race, origin, nature, etc.: *He spoke a mongrel type of speech that was half French and half Indian.* [cf. OE *gemang* mixture]

mon·ies (mun′ēz) *n.pl.* moneys.

mon·i·ker or **mon·ick·er** (mon′ə kər) *n. Informal.* **1** a person's name, nickname, or signature. **2** any identifying mark or sign, such as initials, used by a tramp. [origin uncertain]

mon·ism (mon′iz əm or mō′niz əm) *n.* in philosophy: **1** the doctrine that the universe can be explained by one substance or principle. **2** the doctrine that reality is an indivisible, universal organism. [< NL < Gk. *monos* single]

mon·ist (mon′ist or mō′nist) *n.* a person who believes in monism.

mo·nis·tic (mō nis′tik) *adj.* of or having to do with monism.

mo·ni·tion (mō nish′ən) *n.* **1** an admonition; warning. **2** an official or legal notice: *The bishop sent a monition to three clergymen.* [< L *monitio, -onis* < *monere* warn]

mon·i·tor (mon′ə tər) *n.* **1** in schools, a pupil with special duties, such as helping to keep order and taking attendance. **2** a person who gives advice or warning. **3** something that reminds or gives warning. **4** a large lizard of Africa, Australia, and S. Asia. **5** a receiver used for checking radio or television transmissions, etc.
—*v.* **1** check (a radio or television transmission, etc.) by listening in with a receiver. **2** in physics, test the intensity of radiations, especially of radiations produced by radio-activity. **3** check in order to control something. [< L *monitor* < *monere* admonish]

mon·i·to·ri·al (mon′ə tô′rē əl) *adj.* **1** of or having to do with a monitor. **2** using monitors. **3** serving to admonish or warn. —**mon′i·to′ri·al·ly,** *adv.*

mon·i·tor·ship (mon′ə tər ship′) *n.* the office, work, or period of service of a monitor.

mon·i·to·ry (mon′ə tô′rē) *adj. n.* **-ries.** —*adj.* admonishing; warning. —*n.* a letter containing admonition.

monk (mungk) *n.* **1** in the Christian church, a man who gives up all worldly things, takes the vows of poverty, chastity, and obedience, and, usually, lives in a monastery. **2** in other religions, especially Buddhism and Islam, a man who gives up everything else for religion and enters a monastery to live. [OE *munuc* < LL < LGk. < Gk. *monachos* individual < *monos* alone]

☛ **monk, friar.** Though the terms *monk* and *friar* are often used as synonyms, a *monk* specifically is a member of an order living a cloistered life; a *friar* is a member of a mendicant order.

mon·key (mung′kē) *n.* **-keys,** *v.* **-keyed, -key·ing.** —*n.* **1** an animal of the highest order of mammals, including the large apes, chimpanzees, etc. Monkeys resemble and, of all mammals, are most closely related to man. **2** an animal of this order, such as the capuchin monkey and the baboon. **3** a person, especially a child, who is full of mischief. —*v. Informal.* play; fool; trifle: *Don't monkey with the TV set.* [probably < MLG *Moneke,* son of Martin the Ape in the story of Reynard] —**mon′key·like′,** *adj.*

monkey jacket a short, close-fitting jacket, formerly much worn by sailors.

mon·key·shine (mung′kē shīn′) *n. Slang.* a mischievous trick; a clownish joke.

monkey wrench a wrench with a movable jaw that can be adjusted to fit different sizes of nuts. See **wrench** for diagram.

monk·ish (mungk′ish) *adj.* **1** of or having to do with monks. **2** like a monk; characteristic of a monk. **3** like monks or their way of life. —**monk′ish·ly,** *adv.* —**monk′ish·ness,** *n.*

monks·hood (mungks′hůd′) *n.* a kind of aconite, so called from its hooded flowers.

mono- *combining form.* one; single, as in *monogamy, monosyllable, monotone.* [< Gk. *monos* single]

MONEY: major currencies of the world

Currency unit	Country	Lesser unit	Canadian par value
afghani	Afghanistan	100 puls	.013
baht (or tical)	Thailand	100 satang	.047
balboa	Panama	100 centesimos	.995
bolivar	Venezuela	100 centimos	.224
cedi	Ghana	100 pesawa	.547
colon	Costa Rica	100 centimos	.148
	El Salvador	100 centavos	.393
cordoba	Nicaragua	100 centavos	.140
cruzeiro	Brazil	100 centavos	.164
Deutsche mark	West Germany	100 pfennig	.306
dinar	Algeria	100 centimes	2.03
	Bahrain	1000 fils	2.110
	Iraq	1000 fils	2.786
	Jordan	1000 fils	2.80
	Kuwait	1000 fils	2.80
	Tunisia	1000 millimes	1.95
	Yugoslavia	100 paras	.057
dirham	Morocco	100 francs	.19
dollar	Australia	100 cents	1.173
	Bahamas	100 cents	1.026
	Bermuda	100 cents	.974
	Canada	100 cents	1.00
	Ethiopia	100 cents	.403
	Guyana	100 cents	.448
	Hong Kong	100 cents	.174
	Jamaica	100 cents	1.169
	Liberia	100 cents	1.00
	Malaysia	100 cents	.359
	New Zealand	100 cents	1.19
	Rhodesia	10 shillings	2.77
	Singapore	100 cents	.359
	Trinidad and Tobago	100 cents	.487
	United States	100 cents	.995
	West Indies (Leeward Islands)	100 cents	.487
drachma	Greece	100 lepta	.033
East African shilling	Kenya	100 cents	.131
	Tanzania	100 cents	.131
	Uganda	100 cents	.140
escudo	Chile	100 centesimos	.022
	Portugal	100 centavos	.035
Finnmark	Finland	See markka	
florin	Netherlands	See guilder	
	Surinam		
forint	Hungary	100 fillér	.093
franc	Belgium	100 centimes	.022
	Burundi	100 centimes	.011
	France	100 centimes	.195
	Luxembourg	100 centimes	.022
	Rwanda	100 centimes	.010
	Switzerland	100 centimes	.258
franc (CFA)	Cameroon	100 centimes	.004
	Central African Republic	100 centimes	.004
	Chad	100 centimes	.004
	Congo Republic (Brazzaville)	100 centimes	.004
	Dahomey	100 centimes	.004
	Gabon	100 centimes	.004
	Guinea	100 centimes	.004
	Ivory Coast	100 centimes	.004
	Malagasy	100 centimes	.004
	Mali	100 centimes	.004
	Mauritania	100 centimes	.004
	Niger	100 centimes	.004
	Senegal	100 centimes	.004
	Togo	100 centimes	.004
	Upper Volta	100 centimes	.004
gourde	Haiti	100 centimes	.199
guarani	Paraquay	100 centimos	.008
guilder (or florin)	Netherlands	100 cents	.304
	Surinam	100 cents	.528
Israeli pound (or lira)	Israel	100 agorot	.238
kip	Laos	100 at	.004
koruna (crown)	Czechoslovakia	100 heller	.137
krona	Iceland	100 aurar	.012
	Sweden	100 öre	.209
krone	Denmark	100 öre	.142
	Norway	100 öre	.148
kwacha	Malawi	100 tambala	1.20
	Zambia	100 ngwee	1.40
kyat	Burma	100 pyas	.178
lek	Albania	100 qintars	.20
lempira	Honduras	100 centavos	.497
leone	Sierra Leone	100 cents	1.204
leu	Romania	100 bani	.163
lev	Bulgaria	100 stotinki	.921
lira	Israel	See Israeli pound	
	Italy	100 centesimi	.002
	Turkey (formerly pound)	100 piastres	.066
mark	East Germany	100 pfennig	.450
markka (or Finnmark)	Finland	100 pennia	.238
peseta	Spain	100 centimos	.016
peso	Argentina	100 centavos	.100
	Bolivia	100 centavos	.050
	Colombia	100 centavos	.044
	Cuba	100 centavos	1.00
	Dominican Republic	100 centavos	.995
	Mexico	100 centavos	.078
	Phillipines	100 centavos	.153
	Uruguay	100 centesimos	.001
piastre	South Vietnam	100 cents	.003
pound	Cyprus	1000 mils	2.304
	Egypt (UAR)	100 piastres	2.28
	Gambia	20 shillings	2.40
	Ireland	100 new pence	2.338
	Lebanon	100 piastres	.327
	Libya	1000 milliemes	2.81
	Malta	100 cents	2.40
	Nigeria	20 shillings	2.78
	Sudan	100 piastres	2.87
	Syria	100 piastres	.236
	United Kingdom	100 new pence	2.338
quetzal	Guatemala	100 centavos	.983
rand	Lesotho	100 cents	1.40
	South Africa	100 cents	1.271
rial	Iran	100 dinars	.014
	Saudi Arabia	See riyal	
riel	Cambodia	100 sen	.018
riyal or rial	Saudi Arabia	20 qurshes	.233
	Yemen	40 bugshahs	9.09
ruble	U.S.S.R.	100 kopecks	1.18
rupee	Ceylon	100 cents	.148
	India	100 paise	.127
	Pakistan	100 paise	.869
rupiah	Indonesia	100 sen	.002
schilling	Austria	100 groschen	.042
sol	Peru	100 centavos	.023
sucre	Ecuador	100 centavos	.039
tical	Thailand	See baht	
won	Korea (north)	100 chon	.385
	Korea (south)	100 chon	.003
yen	Japan	100 sen	.003
yuan	China, People's Republic	100 fen or 10 chiao	.441
zaire	Zaire	100 likuta	1.99
zloty	Poland	100 groszy	.050

mon·o·ba·sic (mon′ō bā′sik) *adj.* of an acid, having but one atom of hydrogen replaceable by an atom or radical of a base in forming salts.

mon·o·chord (mon′ə kôrd′) *n.* **1** a sounding board with a single string, used for measuring musical intervals. **2** a harmonious combination of sounds. **3** harmony; agreement.

mon·o·chro·mat·ic (mon′ə krō mat′ik) *adj.* **1** of one color only. **2** of light, consisting of one wave length. **3** producing such light.

mon·o·chrome (mon′ə krōm′) *n.* a painting, drawing, print, etc. in a single color or shades of a single color. [< Gk. *monochrōmos* < *monos* single + *chrōma* color]

mon·o·cle (mon′ə kəl) *n.* an eyeglass for one eye. [< F < LL *monoculus* one-eyed < Gk. *monos* single + L *oculus* eye]

A monocle. It rests on the cheekbone and is held in place by the eyebrow muscle.

mon·o·cled (mon′ə kəld) *adj.* wearing a monocle.

mon·o·cot·y·le·don (mon′ə kot′ə lē′dən) *n.* in botany, a plant having only one cotyledon.

mo·noc·u·lar (mə nok′yu̇ lər) *adj.* **1** having only one eye. **2** having to do with or intended for use by one eye only.

mon·o·cul·ture (mon′ə kul′chər) *n.* the use of land for the cultivation of a single product to the exclusion of any other.

mon·o·dy (mon′ə dē) *n.* **-dies. 1** a mournful song. **2** a plaintive poem in which one person laments another's death. **3** in music: **a** a style of composition that has only one predominating melody or part. **b** a composition written in such a style. [< LL < Gk. *monōidia,* ult. < *monos* single + *aeidein* sing]

mo·noe·cious or **mo·ne·cious** (mə nē′shəs) *adj.* **1** in botany, having the stamens and the pistils in separate flowers on the same plant. **2** in zoology, having both male and female organs in the same individual; hermaphroditic. [< NL *Monoecia,* pl., class name < Gk. *monos* single + *oikos* house]

mo·nog·a·mist (mə nog′ə mist) *n.* a person who practises or believes in monogamy.

mo·nog·a·mous (mə nog′ə məs) *adj.* **1** practising or advocating monogamy. **2** of or having to do with monogamy.

mo·nog·a·my (mə nog′ə mē) *n.* **1** the practice or condition of being married to only one person at a time. **2** in zoology, the habit of having only one mate. [< L < Gk. *monogamia* < *monos* single + *gamos* marriage]

mon·o·gram (mon′ə gram′) *n.* a person's initials combined in one design. Monograms are often used on note paper, table linen, clothing, jewellery, etc. [< LL *monograma* < L.Gk. *monogrammon,* neut., consisting of a single letter < Gk. *monos* single + *gramma* letter]

A monogram

mon·o·graph (mon′ə graf′) *n.* a book or article written on a particular subject. —*v.* write a monograph on; treat in a monograph.

mon·o·graph·ic (mon′ə graf′ik) *adj.* **1** having to do with or like a monograph. **2** of or having to do with a monogram. —**mon′o·graph′i·cal·ly,** *adv.*

mo·nog·y·nous (mə noj′ə nəs) *adj.* **1** having one wife at a time. **2** in botany: **a** of a flower, having one pistil. **b** of a plant, having such flowers.

mo·nog·y·ny (mə noj′ə nē) *n.* the practice or state of having one wife at a time. [< *mono-* + Gk. *gynē* woman + E *-y*[3]]

mon·o·lith (mon′ə lith′) *n.* **1** a single large block of stone. **2** a monument, column, statue, etc. formed of a single large block of stone. **3** a nation, political party, culture, etc. that is single, uniform, undifferentiated, and massive, and consequently rigid and unyielding in its attitudes and policies. [< L < Gk. *monolithos* < *monos* single + *lithos* stone]

mon·o·lith·ic (mon′ə lith′ik) *adj.* **1** of a monolith; being a monolith. **2** massively uniform, as when individuals are absolutely subservient to the state: *a monolithic society, a monolithic state.*

mon·o·log (mon′ə log′) *n.* monologue.

mon·o·logue (mon′ə log′) *n.* **1** a long speech by one person in a group. **2** an entertainment by a single speaker. **3** a play for a single actor. **4** a part of a play in which a single actor speaks alone. Also, **monolog.** [< F < LGk. *monologos* < *monos* single + *logos* speech, discourse]

mon·o·logu·ist (mon′ə log′ist) *n.* **1** one who talks or acts in monologue, or delivers monologues. **2** one who monopolizes conversation. Also, **monologist.**

mon·o·ma·ni·a (mon′ə mā′nē ə) *n.* **1** a form of mental disorder restricted to one idea or emotion only. **2** a dominant or obsessive interest or tendency.

mon·o·ma·ni·ac (mon′ə mā′nē ak′) *n.* a person affected with monomania.

mon·o·ma·ni·a·cal (mon′ə mə nī′ə kəl) *adj.* of, having to do with, or characterized by monomania.

mon·o·me·tal·lic (mon′ō mə tal′ik) *adj.* **1** using one metal only. **2** having to do with monometallism.

mon·o·met·al·lism (mon′ō met′əl iz′əm) *n.* the use of one metal only as the standard of money values.

mo·no·mi·al (mō nō′mē əl) *adj.* consisting of a single word or term. —*n.* **1** a name consisting of a single word. **2** an expression consisting of a single term. z, a^3b^4, and $\frac{m_1m_2}{d^2}$ are monomials. [< *mono-* + *-nomial,* modelled after *binomial*]

mon·o·nu·cle·o·sis (mon′ə nū′klē ō′sis or -nü′klē ō′sis) *n.* a bodily condition characterized by abnormal increase of the leucocytes.

mon·o·pho·nic (mon′ə fon′ik) *adj.* **1** monaural. **2** in music, having a single melody, with no accompaniment.

mon·oph·thong (mon′əf thong′ or mon′ə thong′) *n.* **1** a single vowel sound. **2** a letter representing a single vowel sound.

mon·o·plane (mon′ə plān′) *n.* an airplane having one set of wings: *Most modern planes are monoplanes.*

mo·nop·o·list (mə nop′ə list) *n.* **1** a person who has a monopoly. **2** a person who favors monopoly.

mo·nop·o·lis·tic (mə nop′ə lis′tik) *adj.* **1** that monopolizes. **2** of or having to do with monopolies or monopolists. —**mo·nop′o·lis′ti·cal·ly,** *adv.*

mo·nop·o·lize (mə nop′ə līz′) *v.* **-lized, -liz·ing. 1** have or get exclusive possession or control of. **2** occupy wholly; keep entirely to oneself. —**mo·nop′o·liz′er,** *n.*

mo·nop·o·ly (mə nop′ə lē) *n.* **-lies. 1** the exclusive control of a commodity or service: *The only milk company in town has a monopoly on milk sales.* **2** such control granted by a government: *An inventor has a monopoly on his invention for a certain number of years.* **3** a control that, though not exclusive, enables the person or company to fix prices. **4** a commercial product or service that is exclusively controlled or nearly so. **5** a person or company that has a monopoly of some commodity or service. **6** the exclusive possession or control of something. [< L < Gk. *monopōlion* < *monos* single + *pōleein* sell]

mon·o·rail (mon′ə rāl′) *n.* **1** a single rail serving as a complete track. **2** a railway on which cars run on a single rail.

mon·o·so·di·um glu·ta·mate (mon′ə sō′dē əm glü′tə māt′) a white, crystalline powder made from various vegetable proteins and used for seasoning foods. *Formula:* $C_5H_8NNaO_4$

mon·o·syl·lab·ic (mon′ə sə lab′ik) *adj.* **1** having only one syllable. **2** consisting of a word or words of one syllable each.

mon·o·syl·la·ble (mon′ə sil′ə bəl) *n.* a word of one syllable. *Yes* and *no* are monosyllables.

mon·o·the·ism (mon′ə thē′iz əm) *n.* the doctrine or belief that there is only one God. [< *mono-* + Gk. *theos* god]

mon·o·the·ist (mon′ə thē′ist) *n.* a believer in only one God.

mon·o·the·is·tic (mon′ə thē is′tik) *adj.* **1** believing in only one God. **2** having to do with belief in only one God.

mon·o·tone (mon′ə tōn′) *n.* 1 sameness of tone, of style of writing, of color, etc. 2 a person who sings or speaks in a monotone. *—adj.* continuing on one tone; of one tone, style, or color.

mo·not·o·nous (mə not′ə nəs) *adj.* 1 continuing in the same tone: *She spoke in a monotonous voice.* 2 not varying; without change: *monotonous meals.* 3 wearying because of its sameness: *monotonous work.*
—mo·not′o·nous·ly, *adv.* **—Syn. 1** singsong. **2** unvarying, uniform. **3** tedious, humdrum.

mo·not·o·ny (mə not′ə nē) *n.* 1 sameness of tone or pitch. 2 a lack of variety. 3 a wearisome sameness. [< Gk. *monotonia,* ult. < *monos* single + *tonos* tone]

mon·o·treme (mon′ə trēm′) *n.* in zoology, one of the lowest order of mammals. Duckbills and echidnas are monotremes. [< *mono-* + Gk. *trēma* hole]

mon·o·type (mon′ə tīp′) *n. v.* **-typed, -typ·ing.** *—n.* 1 Monotype, *Trademark.* a set of two machines (keyboard machine and casting machine) for setting and making type in separate letters. 2 the sole type of its group. A single species constituting a genus is a monotype. 3 a a print from a metal plate on which a picture has been painted in color with oil or printing ink, which is transferred to paper by a rubbing process. b the method of producing such a print.
—v. set with a Monotype machine.

mon·o·va·lent (mon′ə vā′lənt) *adj.* in chemistry, having a valence of one.

mon·ox·ide (mon ok′sīd or -ok′sid) *n.* an oxide containing one oxygen atom in each molecule.

Monroe Doctrine the doctrine that European nations should not interfere with American nations or try to acquire more territory in America. [< James *Monroe* (1758-1831), President of the United States from 1817 to 1825]

Mon·sei·gneur or **mon·sei·gneur** (môɴ se nyœr′) *n.* **Mes·sei·gneurs** or **mes·sei·gneurs** (mā se nyœr′). *French.* 1 a title of honor given to princes, bishops, and other persons of importance. 2 a person bearing this title. [< F < *mon* my + *seigneur* lord]

mon·sieur (mə syœ′) *n.* **mes·sieurs** (mā syœ′). *French.* Mr.; sir. [< F *monsieur,* earlier *mon sieur* my lord]

Mon·si·gnor or **mon·si·gnor** (mon sēn′yər; *Italian,* mōn′sē nyōr′) *n.* **Mon·si·gnors** or **mon·si·gnors**; *Italian,* **Mon·si·gno·ri** or **mon·si·gno·ri** (mōn′sē nyō′rē) in the Roman Catholic Church: 1 a title given to certain dignitaries. 2 a person having this title. [< Ital. *monsignor,* half-translation of F *monseigneur* monseigneur]

mon·soon (mon sün′) *n.* 1 a seasonal wind of the Indian Ocean and S. Asia, blowing from the southwest from April to October and from the northeast during the rest of the year. 2 a rainy season during which this wind blows from the southwest. [< Du. < Pg. < Arabic *mausim* season]

mon·ster (mon′stər) *n.* 1 any animal or plant that is out of the usual course of nature: *A two-headed calf is a monster.* 2 an imaginary creature having parts of different animals: *Mermaids and centaurs are monsters.* 3 an imaginary animal of strange and horrible appearance: *The story was about monsters from Mars.* 4 a huge creature or thing. 5 a person who is extremely evil or cruel: *The man in charge of the slaves was a monster.* 6 something unnatural and horrible. *—adj.* huge. [ME < OF *monstre* < L *monstrum* divine warning < *monstrare* show]
—mon′ster·like′, *adj.* **—Syn.** *n.* **2** giant.

mon·strance (mon′strəns) *n.* in the Roman Catholic Church, a receptacle in which the consecrated Host is shown for adoration or is carried in procession. [< Med.L *monstrantia* < L *monstrare* show]

mon·stros·i·ty (mon stros′ə tē) *n.* **-ties.** 1 a monster. 2 the state or character of being monstrous.

mon·strous (mon′strəs) *adj.* 1 huge; enormous. 2 wrongly formed or shaped; like a monster. 3 so wrong or absurd as to be almost unheard of. 4 shocking; horrible; dreadful.
—adv. Informal. very; extremely. **—mon′strous·ly,** *adv.* **—mon′strous·ness,** *n.* **—Syn.** *adj.* **1** colossal, prodigious, stupendous. **4** atrocious.

Mont. 1 Montreal. 2 Montana.

mon·tage (mon täzh′) *n.* 1 the combination of several distinct pictures to make a composite picture. 2 a composite picture so made. 3 in motion pictures, television, etc., any combining or blending of pictures or their elements, at once or in succession, to suggest mental processes. 4 any combining or blending of different elements: *His latest novel is a montage of biography, history, and fiction.* [< F *montage* < *monter* mount]

hat, āge, cãre, fär; let, ēqual, tėrm; it, īce
hot, ōpen, ôrder; oil, out; cup, pu̇t, rüle, ūse
əbove, takən, pencəl, lemən, circəs
ch, child; ng, long; sh, ship
th, thin; ᴛʜ, then; zh, measure

Mon·ta·gnais (mon′tə nyā′) *n.* **-gnais** (-nyā′ or -nyāz′) or **-gnaises** (-nyāz′). 1 an Indian tribe of N. Quebec. 2 a member of this tribe. 3 the Cree dialect spoken by this tribe. 4 Chipewyan. [< F < *montagne* mountain]

mon·te (mon′tē) *n.* a Spanish gambling game played with cards. [< Sp. *monte* mountain, i.e., of cards]

Mon·te·ne·grin (mon′tə nē′grin) *adj.* of or having to do with Montenegro a former kingdom in S. Europe (now part of Yugoslavia) or its people. *—n.* a native or inhabitant of Montenegro.

month (munth) *n.* 1 one of the 12 parts into which the year is divided. 2 the time from any day of one month to the corresponding day of the next month. 3 in astronomy: a the time it takes the moon to make one complete revolution around the earth; lunar month. b the time from one new moon to the next, about 29.53 days; synodical month. c one twelfth of a solar year, about 30.41 days; solar month. d a sidereal month. [OE *mōnath.* Related to MOON.]

☛ months. In reference matter and informal writing, the names of months with more than four letters are abbreviated in dates: *Jan. 21, 1951,* but *June 30, 1950.* When only the month or month and year are given, abbreviations would be rare: *January, 1950. Every January he tries again.* In formal writing, the names of the months are not abbreviated.

month·ly (munth′lē) *adj. adv. n.* **-lies.** *—adj.* 1 of a month; for a month. 2 done, happening, payable, etc. once a month. *—adv.* once a month; every month. *—n.* a magazine published once a month.

Mont·re·al canoe (mont′rē ol′ or mun′trē ol′) *Cdn.* formerly, the largest canoe of the fur trade, used especially on the Great Lakes and the St. Lawrence River. It was up to 40 ft. long and could carry a cargo of four or five tons. Also, **canot du maître.**

mon·u·ment (mon′yu̇ mənt) *n.* 1 something set up to preserve the memory of a person or an event. A monument may be a building, pillar, arch, statue, tomb, or stone. 2 anything that keeps alive the memory of a person or an event. 3 an enduring or prominent instance: *The professor's publications were monuments of learning.* 4 something set up to mark a boundary. [< L *monumentum* < *monere* remind]

mon·u·men·tal (mon′yu̇ men′təl) *adj.* 1 of a monument. 2 serving as a monument. 3 like a monument. 4 weighty and lasting; important: *The British North America Act is a monumental document.* 5 very great: *monumental ignorance.* **—mon′u·men′tal·ly,** *adv.*

moo (mü) *n.* **moos,** *v.* **mooed, moo·ing.** *—n.* the sound made by a cow. *—v.* make the sound of a cow or one like it.

mooch (müch) *v. Slang.* 1 sneak; skulk; rove about. 2 steal. 3 beg; get (something) at another person's expense. 4 in fishing, drift with light tackle for big fish. [origin uncertain] **—mooch′er,** *n.*

mood[1] (müd) *n.* 1 a state of mind or feeling. 2 **moods,** *pl.* fits of depression or bad temper. [OE *mōd* spirit]
Syn. 1 **Mood, humor** = a person's state of mind or feeling at a particular time. **Mood** applies to a way of thinking and feeling determined by some emotion or desire and influencing everything a person says and does while in this frame of mind: *He is in no mood to study just now.* **Humor** applies to a state of mind and spirits caused by a person's disposition or the way he feels physically, and especially suggests changing suddenly without apparent reason: *He is in good humor now.*

mood[2] (müd) *n.* in grammar, the form of a verb that shows whether the act or state is thought of as a fact, a command, etc.: *the indicative mood, the imperative mood.* Also, **mode.** [alteration of *mode*; influenced by *mood*[1]]

mood·y (müd′ē) *adj.* **mood·i·er, mood·i·est. 1** likely to have changes of mood. **2** often having gloomy moods. **3** sunk in sadness; gloomy; sullen. **4** expressive of a mood, especially a bad mood. —**mood′i·ly,** *adv.* —**mood′i·ness,** *n.* —**Syn. 3** melancholy, sad.

moon (mün) *n.* **1** a heavenly body that revolves around the earth once in approximately 28 days. The moon looks bright because it reflects the sun's light. **2** the moon at a certain period of time: **new moon** (visible as a slender crescent), **half moon** (visible as a half circle), **full moon** (visible as a circle), **old moon** (waning). **3** a lunar month; month. **4** moonlight. **5** something shaped like the moon in any of its appearances. **6** a satellite of any planet: *the moons of Jupiter.* **7** an artificial earth satellite. —*v.* wander about or gaze idly or listlessly. [OE *mōna*] —**moon′less,** *adj.* —**moon′like′,** *adj.*

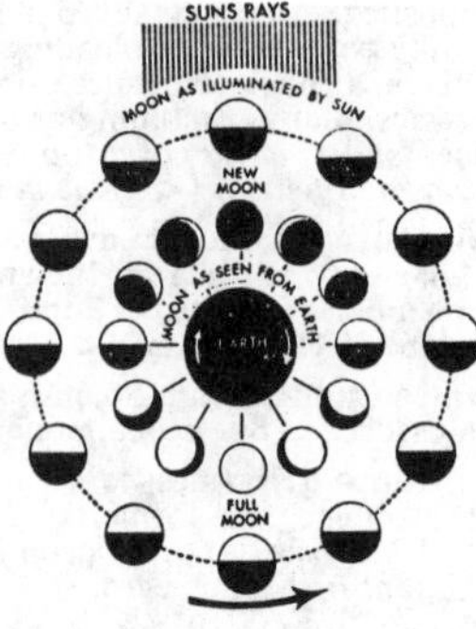

The phases of the moon

moon·beam (mün′bēm′) *n.* a ray of moonlight.

moon·calf (mün′kaf′) *n.* an idiot; a born fool.

moon eye (mün′ī′) *n.* **-eye** or **-eyes.** one of a group of fresh-water fish that also includes the goldeye.

moon·light (mün′līt′) *n.* the light of the moon. —*adj.* **1** having the light of the moon. **2** while the moon is shining; by night. —*v. Informal.* work at a second job, usually at night, in order to supplement the wages earned at a regular job. —**moon′light′er,** *n.*

moon·lit (mün′lit′) *adj.* lighted by the moon.

moon·quake (mün′kwāk′) *n.* an agitation of the surface of the moon, of the same kind as an earthquake.

moon·shine (mün′shīn′) *n.* **1** moonlight. **2** empty talk; empty show; nonsense. **3** *Informal.* intoxicating liquor made unlawfully, or smuggled.

moon·shin·er (mün′shīn′ər) *n. Informal.* **1** a person who makes intoxicating liquor contrary to law. **2** a person who follows an unlawful trade at night.

moon·stone (mün′stōn′) *n.* **1** a whitish variety of feldspar having a pearly lustre. **2** a piece of this stone, or a gem made from it.

moon·struck (mün′struk′) *adj.* dazed; crazed.

moon·y (mün′ē) *adj.* **moon·i·er, moon·i·est. 1** of the moon. **2** like the moon; crescent-shaped. **3** dreamy; listless.

moor[1] (mür) *v.* **1** put or keep (a ship, etc.) in place by means of ropes or chains fastened to the shore or to anchors. **2** moor a ship. **3** be made secure by ropes, anchors, etc. [ME *more(n)*; cf. OE *mærels* mooring rope]

moor[2] (mür) *n. Brit.* open waste land, usually hilly or high up and having low plant growth. [OE *mōr*]

Moor (mür) *n.* a member of a people related to the Arabs, living in N.W. Africa. In the eighth century A.D. the Moors invaded and conquered Spain. They were finally driven out in 1492. [ME < OF *More, Maure* < L < Gk. *Mauros*]

moor·age (mür′ij) *n.* **1** a mooring or being moored. **2** a place for mooring. **3** the charge for its use.

moor cock the male red grouse.

moor·fowl (mür′foul′) *n.* the red grouse.

moor hen 1 a female red grouse. **2** any of various wading birds, such as the gallinule, rail, and coot.

moor·ing (mür′ing) *n.* **1** the act of tying up or securing a ship, etc. **2** a place where a ship is or may be tied up. **3 moorings,** the ropes, cables, anchors, etc. by which a ship is made fast.

mooring mast the mast to which an airship is moored.

Moor·ish (mür′ish) *adj.* **1** of or having to do with the Moors. **2** in architecture, painting, etc., in the style of the Moors.

moor·land (mür′land′ or mür′lənd) *n. Brit.* land covered with heather; moor.

moose (müs) *n.* **moose. 1** a large ruminant mammal related to the deer family, living in the Northern Hemisphere throughout the world. The male has a heavy build, large head, and broad antlers. **2** the European elk. [< Algonquian]

moose·bird (müs′bėrd′) *n. Cdn.* Canada jay.

moose·milk (müs′milk′) *n. Cdn. Slang.* **1** a drink made of rum or other liquor and milk. **2** in the North, home-distilled liquor.

moose pasture *Cdn. Slang.* mining claims that are considered worthless.

moose-yard (müs′yärd′) *n. Cdn.* a space in the woods where moose in winter tread down the snow, remaining there for protection and warmth, feeding on tender shoots and saplings.

moot (müt) *adj.* debatable; doubtful: *a moot point.* [< n.] —*v.* **1** argue. **2** bring forward (a point, subject, case, etc.) for discussion. [def. 1 < n.; def. 2 < OE *mōtian* < *(ge)mōt* meeting] —*n.* an assembly. [OE *(ge)mōt* meeting]

moot court a mock court held in a law school to give students practice.

mop[1] (mop) *n. v.* **mopped, mop·ping.** —*n.* **1** a bundle of coarse yarn, rags, etc. fastened at the end of a stick, for cleaning floors, dishes, etc. **2** a thick head of hair like a mop.
—*v.* **1** wash or wipe up; clean with a mop. **2** wipe. **3 mop up, a** finish. **b** in military use, clear out or rid (an area, town, etc.) of scattered or remaining enemy troops. [probably < OF *mappe* < L *mappa* napkin] —**mop′per,** *n.*

mop[2] (mop) *v.* **mopped, mop·ping,** *n.* —*v.* **1** grimace. **2 mop and mow,** make faces. —*n.* a grimace. [cf. Du. *moppen* to pout]

mope (mōp) *v.* **moped, mop·ing,** *n.* —*v.* be indifferent and silent; be gloomy and sad. —*n.* a person who mopes. [? related to MOP[2]] —**mop′er,** *n.*

mop·ish (mōp′ish) *adj.* inclined to mope; sad and listless.

mop·pet (mop′it) *n. Informal.* child. [< obs. *mop* doll]

mop-up (mop′up′) *n. Informal.* **1** a finishing off or a wiping out; a clean up. **2** in battle, the finishing off of an action in an area by the killing or capture of enemy troops.

mo·quette (mō ket′) *n.* a thick, velvety carpet. [< F]

mo·raine (mə rān′) *n.* a mass of rocks, dirt, etc. deposited at the side or end of a glacier, or along its course. A moraine often takes the form of a ridge. [< F]

mor·al (môr′əl) *adj.* **1** good in character or conduct; virtuous according to civilized standards of right and wrong; right; just: *a moral act, a moral man.* **2** capable of understanding right and wrong: *A little baby is not a moral being.* **3** having to do with character or with the difference between right and wrong: *a moral question.* **4** based on the principles of right conduct rather than on law or custom. **5** teaching a good lesson; having a good influence: *a moral book.* **6** depending upon considerations of what generally occurs; resting upon grounds of probability: *moral evidence, moral arguments.*
—*n.* **1** the lesson, inner meaning, or teaching of a fable, a story, or an event: *The moral of the story was* "*Look before you leap.*" **2 morals,** *pl.* **a** one's behavior in matters of right and wrong. **b** character. **c** one's principles in regard to conduct. [ME < L *moralis* < *mos, moris* custom (pl., manners)]

Syn. *adj.* **1 Moral, ethical** = in agreement with a standard of what is right and good in character or conduct. **Moral** = right and good according to the customary rules and accepted standards of society: *He leads a moral life.* **Ethical** particularly suggests agreement with principles of right conduct or good living expressed in a system or code, especially of the branch of philosophy dealing with moral conduct or of a profession or business: *It is not considered ethical for doctors to advertise.*

☛ **moral, morale.** A common error is to write *moral* (concerning right conduct) when *morale* (mental condition as regards courage, confidence, enthusiasm, etc.) is the word intended.

moral certainty a probability so great that it might just as well be a certainty.

mo·rale (mə ral′ or mə räl′) *n.* the moral or mental condition or attitude of a person or group of persons as regards courage, confidence, enthusiasm, etc.: *The morale of the army was low after their defeat in battle.* [< F *moral*, mistakenly spelt *morale* in English to keep the pronunciation] ☛ See **moral** for usage note.

mor·al·ist (môr′əl ist) *n.* **1** a person who thinks much about moral duties, sees the moral side of things, and leads a moral life. **2** a person who teaches, studies, or writes about morals.

mor·al·is·tic (môr′əl is′tik) *adj.* **1** moralizing; teaching the difference between right and wrong. **2** of or having to do with a moralist or moral teaching. —**mo′ral·is′ti·cal·ly,** *adv.*

mo·ral·i·ty (mə ral′ə tē) *n.* **-ties. 1** the right or wrong of an action. **2** the doing of right; virtue. **3** a system of morals; a set of rules or principles of conduct. **4** moral instruction; a moral lesson or precept. **5** a morality play.

morality play a form of drama popular during the 15th and 16th centuries, in which vices and virtues are personified.

mor·al·ize (môr′əl īz′) *v.* **-ized, -iz·ing. 1** think, talk, or write about questions of right and wrong. **2** point out the lesson or inner meaning of. **3** improve the morals of. —**mor′al·i·za′tion,** *n.* —**mor′al·iz′er,** *n.*

mor·al·ly (môr′əl ē) *adv.* **1** in a moral manner. **2** in morals; as to morals. **3** from a moral point of view; ethically. **4** practically.

moral philosophy ethics.

Moral Rearmament a twentieth-century religious movement to reform the world through the improvement of personal morals and character; Buchmanism.

moral support approval but not active or tangible help.

moral victory a defeat that has the effect on the mind that a victory would have.

mo·rass (mə ras′) *n.* **1** a piece of low, marshy ground; swamp. **2** a difficult situation; a puzzling mess. [< Du. *moeras* < OF *marais* < Gmc.]

mor·a·to·ri·um (môr′ə tô′rē əm) *n.* **-ri·ums, -ri·a** (-rē ə). **1** a legal authorization to delay payments of money due. **2** the period during which such authorization is in effect. **3** a voluntary or negotiated temporary cessation of action on any issue. [< NL < L *morari* delay < *mora* a delay]

Mo·ra·vi·an (mô rā′vē ən) *adj.* **1** having to do with Moravia, a region in central Czechoslovakia, or its Slavic inhabitants. **2** of or having to do with the Protestant church founded by John Huss. —*n.* **1** a native or inhabitant of Moravia. **2** a member of the Moravian church.

mo·ray (mô′rā or mô rā′) *n.* a fierce, often brilliantly colored, tropical eel. [< Pg. *moreia* < L *murena*, var. of *muraena* < Gk.]

mor·bid (môr′bid) *adj.* **1** unhealthy; not wholesome: *A liking for horrors is morbid.* **2** caused by disease; characteristic of disease; diseased: *Cancer is a morbid growth.* **3** horrible; gruesome; grisly: *the morbid details of a murder.* [< L *morbidus* < *morbus* disease] —**mor′bid·ly,** *adv.* —**mor′bid·ness,** *n.*

mor·bid·i·ty (môr bid′ə tē) *n.* **1** a morbid state or quality. **2** the proportion of sickness in a certain group or locality: *Morbidity statistics show that tuberculosis is on the decline in Canada.*

mor·dan·cy (môr′dən sē) *n.* a mordant quality.

mor·dant (môr′dənt) *adj.* **1** biting; cutting; sarcastic: *Their mordant criticisms hurt his feelings.* **2** in dyeing, that fixes colors. —*n.* **1** a substance that fixes colors. **2** an acid that eats into metal. [< OF *mordant*, ppr. of *mordre* bite < L *mordere*]

Mor·dred (môr′dred) *n.* Modred.

more (môr) *adj.* (*used as comparative of* **much** *and* **many,** *with the superlative* **most**) *n. adv.* —*adj.* **1** greater in number, quantity, amount, degree, or importance: *more men, more help.* **2** further; additional: *Take more time.* —*n.* **1** a greater number, quantity, amount, or degree: *The more they have, the more they want.* **2** an additional amount: *Tell me more.*
—*adv.* **1** in or to a greater extent or degree: *It hurts more to beg than to borrow.* **2** in addition; further; longer; again: *Sing once more.* **3 be no more,** be dead. **4 more or less, a** rather; somewhat: *Most people are more or less selfish.* **b** nearly; approximately: *The distance is five miles, more or less.* [OE *māra*]

hat, āge, cãre, fär; let, ēqual, tėrm; it, īce
hot, ōpen, ôrder; oil, out; cup, pu̇t, rüle, ūse
əbove, takən, pencəl, lemən, circəs
ch, child; ng, long; sh, ship
th, thin; ᴛʜ, then; zh, measure

☛ **More** and **most** are often used before adjectives and adverbs to form comparatives and superlatives. *More* and *most* are put before all adjectives and adverbs of three syllables or more, and before many of two syllables. They may also be used with those of one syllable, so that for many comparatives and superlatives there are two forms: *empty; emptier, more empty; emptiest, most empty.*

mo·reen (mə rēn′) *n.* a heavy fabric of wool, or wool and cotton, usually with a watered finish. [? related to MOIRÉ]

mo·rel (mə rel′) *n.* a small, edible mushroom. [< F *morille* < Gmc.]

more·o·ver (môr ō′vər) *adv.* also; besides; in addition to that: *His power is absolute and, moreover, hereditary.* —**Syn.** furthermore, also.

mores (mô′rēz or mô′rāz) *n.pl.* customs prevailing among a people or a social group that are accepted as right and obligatory; traditional rules; ways; manners. [< L *mores* manners]

Mo·resque (mə resk′) *adj.* Moorish; in the Moorish style.

mor·ga·nat·ic (môr′gə nat′ik) *adj.* designating or having to do with a form of marriage in which a man of high rank marries a woman of lower rank with an agreement that neither she nor her children shall have any claim to his rank or property. [< NL *morganaticus* < Med.L (*matrimonium ad*) *morganaticam* (marriage with) morning gift, ult. < OHG *morgangeba* < *morgan* morning + *geban* give; the "morning gift" to the bride on the day after the wedding was her only share in her husband's goods and rights]

Mor·gan le Fay (môr′gən lə fā′) in Arthurian legend, a fairy and King Arthur's half sister, usually represented as trying to harm him at every opportunity.

morgue (môrg) *n.* **1** a place, often within a hospital or police station, where bodies of unknown persons found dead are kept for identification or removal for burial. **2** that part of a hospital where autopsies are performed. **3** in a newspaper office, the reference library. [< F]

mor·i·bund (môr′ə bund′) *adj.* dying. [< L *moribundus*, ult. < *mori* die]

mo·ri·on (mô′rē on′) *n.* a helmet without a visor, shaped like a hat, worn especially by Spanish foot soldiers in the 1500's and 1600's. [< F < Sp. *morrion* < *morra* crown of head]

MORION

Mor·mon (môr′mən) *n.* **1** a member of the Church of Jesus Christ of Latter-day Saints, founded in 1830 by Joseph Smith. **2 The Book of Mormon,** a sacred book of the Church of Jesus Christ of Latter-day Saints. —*adj.* of or having to do with the Mormons or their religion. [< the name of the narrator of "The Book of Mormon"]

Mor·mon·ism (môr′mən iz′əm) *n.* the religious system of the Mormons.

morn (môrn) *n. Poetic.* morning. [OE *morgen*]

morn·ing (môr′ning) *n.* **1** the early part of the day, ending at noon. **2** the first or early part of anything: *the morning of life.* —*adj.* of or in the morning. [ME *morwening* < *morwen* morn (OE *morgen*) + *-ing*; patterned on *evening*] —**Syn.** *n.* **2** dawn.

morning coat a cutaway.

morn·ing-glo·ry (môr′ning glô′rē) *n.* **-ries.** a vine having heart-shaped leaves and funnel-shaped blue, lavender, pink, or white flowers.

morning star a planet, especially Venus, seen in the eastern sky before sunrise.

Mo·ro (mô′rō) *n.* **Mo·ros. 1** a member of any of various tribes of Moslem Malays in the S. Philippine Islands. **2** the language of these people. [< Sp. *Moro* a Moor]

Mo·roc·can (mə rok′ən) *adj.* of or having to do with

Morocco, a country in northwest Africa, or its people. —*n.* a native or inhabitant of Morocco.

mo·roc·co (mə rok′ō) *n.* **-cos. 1** a fine leather made from goatskins, used in binding books. **2** a leather imitating this. [< *Morocco*, a country in N.W. Africa, where it was first made]

mo·ron (mô′ron) *n.* **1** a person having an intelligence quotient of 50 to 70. A moron is less mentally deficient than an imbecile or idiot, and is capable of doing routine jobs. **2** *Informal.* a stupid or annoyingly ignorant person; dullard; dunce. [< Gk. *mōron*, neut. of *mōros* foolish, dull]

mo·rose (mə rōs′) *adj.* gloomy; sullen; ill-humored: *He has a morose expression.* [< L *morosus*, originally, set in one's ways < *mos, moris* habit] **—mo·rose′ly,** *adv.* **—mo·rose′ness,** *n.* **—Syn.** moody, surly, gruff.

mor·pheme (môr′fēm′) *n.* in linguistics, the smallest meaningful element of a language or dialect, such as *un-*, *-ing*, *do*, *make*, or *snow*. Simple words, bases, and affixes are morphemes.

Mor·phe·us (môr′fē əs or môr′fūs) *n.* in Greek mythology, the god of dreams; popularly, the god of sleep. [ME < L *Morpheus* fashioner or moulder < Gk. *morphē* form, shape, in allusion to the forms seen in dreams]

mor·phi·a (môr′fē ə) *n.* morphine.

mor·phine (môr′fēn) *n.* a bitter, white, crystalline drug made from opium, used to dull pain and to cause sleep. [< F < G *Morphin* < *Morpheus* Morpheus]

mor·phin·ism (môr′fin iz′əm) *n.* **1** a morbid condition caused by habitual use of morphine. **2** the morphine habit.

mor·pho·log·ic (môr′fə loj′ik) *adj.* morphological.

mor·pho·log·i·cal (môr′fə loj′ə kəl) *adj.* of or having to do with morphology; relating to form; structural. **—mor′pho·log′i·cal·ly,** *adv.*

mor·phol·o·gy (môr fol′ə jē) *n.* **1** the branch of biology that deals with the forms and structure of animals and plants. **2** the form and structure of an organism or of one of its parts. **3** the branch of the science of language that deals with forms of words as affected by inflection, derivation, etc. **4** the study of forms in any science, as in physical geography or geology. [< Gk. *morphē* form + E *-logy*]

mor·ris (môr′is) *n.* a morris dance.

Morris chair or **morris chair** an armchair with an adjustable back. [after William *Morris* (1834-1896), an English poet and painter, who invented it]

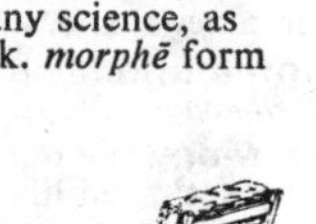
A morris chair. The back rests against a bar which can be moved to any of the grooves in the extensions of the arms.

morris dance 1 an old English dance performed by people in fancy costumes. **2** the music for such a dance. [*morris*, earlier *morys* Moorish]

mor·row (môr′ō) *n.* **1** the following day or time: *We expected her on the morrow.* **2 good morrow,** *Archaic.* good morning. [ME *morwe*, var. of *morwen* morn, OE *morgen*]

Morse (môrs) *adj.* having to do with or designating the Morse code, or a telegraph system using it. —*n.* the Morse code. [< Samuel F. B. *Morse* (1791-1872), American inventor of the telegraph]

Morse code a system by which letters, numbers, etc. are expressed by dots, dashes, and spaces, used in telegraphy, signalling, etc.

mor·sel (môr′səl) *n.* **1** a small bite; mouthful. **2** a piece; fragment. **3** a dish of food; tidbit: *a dainty morsel.* **4** something to be enjoyed, disposed of, or endured: *find a person a tough morsel. This decision was a bitter morsel.* [ME < OF *morsel*, dim. of *mors* a bite, ult. < L *morsum*, pp. of *mordere* bite]

mort (môrt) *n.* in hunting, a note sounded on a horn at the death of a deer. [< F *mort* death < L *mors, mortis*]

mor·tal (môr′təl) *adj.* **1** sure to die sometime. **2** of man; of mortals. **3** of death. **4** causing death of the soul: *mortal sin.* **5** causing death: *a mortal wound, a mortal illness.* **6** to the death: *a mortal enemy, a mortal battle.* **7** very great; deadly: *mortal terror.* —*n.* **1** a being that is sure to die sometime. All living creatures are mortals. **2** a man; human being. [< L *mortalis* < *mors, mortis* death] **—Syn.** *adj.* **2** human. **5** lethal. See **fatal.**

mor·tal·i·ty (môr tal′ə tē) *n.* **1** mortal nature; the state of being sure to die sometime. **2** a loss of life on a large scale: *The mortality from automobile accidents is very serious.* **3** the death rate; number of deaths per thousand cases of a disease, or per thousand persons in the population.

mor·tal·ly (môr′təl ē) *adv.* **1** in a mortal manner. **2** fatally; so as to cause death: *mortally wounded.* **3** very greatly; bitterly; grievously: *mortally offended.*

mortal sin in Roman Catholic theology, a sin so serious that it causes the death of the soul.

mor·tar[1] (môr′tər) *n.* a mixture of lime, sand, and water, or of cement, sand, and water, used for holding bricks or stones together. —*v.* plaster with mortar; fix with mortar. [ME < OF *mortier* < L *mortarium*]

mor·tar[2] (môr′tər) *n.* **1** a bowl of very hard material, in which substances may be pounded to a powder. **2** a very short artillery piece for shooting shells or fireworks at high angles. [ME < OF *mortier* < L *mortarium*]

A mortar and pestle

mor·tar·board (môr′tər bôrd′) *n.* **1** a flat, square board used by masons to hold mortar. **2** a cap having a close-fitting crown topped by a stiff, flat, cloth-covered square piece with a tassel attached to the centre, worn by teachers and students in some schools and colleges on certain occasions.

mort·gage (môr′gij) *n. v.* **-gaged, -gag·ing.** —*n.* **1** a claim on property, given to a person who has loaned money in case the money is not repaid when due. **2** a document that gives such a claim. —*v.* **1** give a lender a claim to (one's property) in case a debt is not paid when due. **2** put under some obligation; pledge: *Faust mortgaged his soul to the devil.* [ME < OF *mortgage* < *mort* dead (< L *mortuus*) + *gage* pledge, gage[1] < Gmc.]

mort·ga·gee (môr′gi jē′) *n.* one to whom property is mortgaged.

mort·gag·er or **mort·ga·gor** (môr′gi jər) *n.* one who mortgages his property.

mor·tice (môr′tis) *n. v.* **-ticed, -tic·ing.** mortise.

mor·ti·cian (môr tish′ən) *n. Esp.U.S.* an undertaker. [< *mort*uary + *-ician*, probably on analogy with *physician*]

mor·ti·fi·ca·tion (môr′tə fə kā′shən) *n.* **1** extreme embarrassment; shame: *The boy was overcome with mortification when he spilled milk on his host's suit.* **2** the cause of such feelings. **3** a mortifying or being mortified: *the mortification of the body by fasting.* **4** the death of one part of the body while the rest is alive; gangrene: *His leg had to be amputated because mortification had set in.* **—Syn. 1** chagrin, embarrassment.

mor·ti·fy (môr′tə fī′) *v.* **-fied, -fy·ing. 1** make ashamed; humiliate: *A mother is mortified when her child behaves badly.* **2** overcome (bodily desires and feelings) by pain and self-denial: *The saint mortified his body.* **3** die; decay: *The injured foot has mortified and must be cut off.* [ME < OF *mortifier* < L *mortificare* kill < *mors, mortis* death + *facere* make] **—mor′ti·fi′er,** *n.* **—Syn. 1** chagrin, embarrass. See **ashamed.**

mor·tise (môr′tis) *n. v.* **-tised, -tis·ing.** —*n.* a hole in one piece of wood cut to receive a projection on another piece, called the tenon, so as to form a joint (**mortise and tenon joint**). —*v.* fasten by a mortise: *Good furniture is mortised together, not nailed.* [ME < OF *morteise* < Arabic *murtazz* fastened]

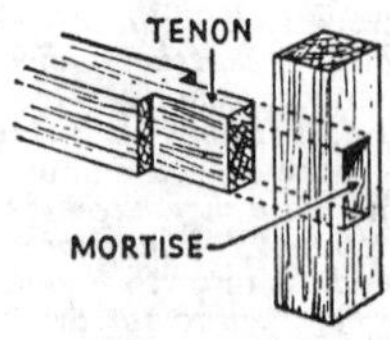

A mortise and tenon joint

mort·main (môrt′mān) *n.* in law,

an inalienable possession; the condition of lands or tenements held without right to sell them or give them away. [ME < OF *mortemain*, translation of Med.L *mortua manus* dead hand; with reference to corporations as not being persons]

mor·tu·a·ry (môr′chü er′ē) *n.* **-ries,** *adj.* —*n.* **1** that part of a funeral parlor or of a cemetery where bodies of dead people await burial. **2** a morgue. —*adj.* of death or burial. [ME < AF < Med.L *mortuarium*, ult. < L *mors, mortis* death]

mos. months.

mo·sa·ic (mō zā′ik) *n.* **1** a type of ornamental work consisting of small pieces of stone, glass, wood, etc. of various colors inlaid to form a picture or design. **2** a picture or design made of mosaic. Mosaics are used in floors, ceilings, and walls of buildings, for table tops, and on pottery items such as ash trays. **3** the process of making mosaics. **4** anything like a mosaic. —*adj.* of, formed by, having to do with, or resembling a mosaic. [< F *mosaïque* < Italian < Med.L *mosaicus*, var. of *musaicus* of the Muses, artistic]

A mosaic design

Mo·sa·ic (mō zā′ik) *adj.* of Moses or of writings ascribed to him.

Mosaic law 1 the ancient law of the Hebrews, ascribed to Moses. **2** the part of the Bible where these laws are stated.

Mo·selle (mō zel′) *n.* a kind of white wine made in the valley of the Moselle River.

Mo·ses (mō′ziz or mō′zis) *n.* in the Bible, the great leader and lawgiver who led the Israelites out of captivity in Egypt toward the Promised Land, and who received the Ten Commandments from God on Mount Sinai.

mo·sey (mō′zē) *v.* **-seyed, -sey·ing.** *Slang.* **1** shuffle along. **2** saunter; amble. [origin uncertain]

Mos·lem (moz′ləm or mos′ləm) *n.* **-lems** or **-lem,** *adj.* —*n.* a follower of Mohammed; a believer in the religion founded by him. —*adj.* of or having to do with Mohammed or the religion founded by him. Also, **Muslem, Muslim.** [< Arabic *muslim* one who submits < *aslama* submit. Related to SALAAM.]

mosque (mosk) *n.* a Moslem place of worship. [< F < Ital. < Arabic *masjid* < *sajada* prostrate oneself]

mos·qui·to (məs kē′tō) *n.* **-toes** or **-tos.** a small, slender insect. The female gives a bite or sting that itches. [< Sp. *mosquito*, dim. of *mosca* < L *musca* fly]

moss (mos) *n.* **1** any of various very small, soft, green or brown plants that grow close together like a carpet on the ground, on rocks, on trees, etc. **2** any of various similar plants. [OE *mos* bog] —**moss′like′,** *adj.*

moss agate a variety of agate that has brown, black, or green mosslike markings.

moss·back (mos′bak′) *n. Slang.* a person whose ideas are out of date.

moss-bag (mos′bag′) *n. Cdn.* a kind of bag of leather or cloth used by certain Indian tribes to carry a baby on journeys. Packed with dry moss, which serves as a diaper, it is laced up in front and usually carried strapped to a cradle board. See **cradle board** for picture.

moss rose a cultivated rose having a mosslike growth on the calyx and stem.

moss·y (mos′ē) *adj.* **moss·i·er, moss·i·est. 1** covered with moss: *a mossy bank.* **2** like moss: *mossy green.* —**moss′i·ness,** *n.*

most (mōst) *adj.* (*used as superlative of* **much** *and* **many,** *with the comparative* **more**) *n. adv.* —*adj.* **1** the greatest quantity, amount, measure, degree, or number of: *The winner gets the most money.* **2** almost all: *Most children like candy.* **3 for the most part,** mainly; usually.
—*n.* **1** the greatest quantity, amount, degree, or number: *He did most of the work.* **2 at most** or **at the most,** not more than. **3 make the most of,** make the best use of.
—*adv.* **1** in or to the greatest extent or degree: *Which hurt most?* **2** *Informal.* almost; nearly. [OE *māst*]
most, almost. *Most* is the common informal shortening of *almost*: *A drop in prices will appeal to most everybody.* It is sometimes used in writing conversation and in informal style, but is ordinarily out of place in written English. ☛ See **more** for another usage note.

hat, āge, cãre, fär; let, ēqual, tėrm; it, īce
hot, ōpen, ôrder; oil, out; cup, pu̇t, rüle, ūse
əbove, takən, pencəl, lemən, circəs
ch, child; ng, long; sh, ship
th, thin; ᴛʜ, then; zh, measure

-most a suffix forming superlatives as in *foremost, inmost, topmost, uttermost.* [ME < OF *-mest*; influenced by *most*]

most·ly (mōst′lē) *adv.* almost all; for the most part; mainly; chiefly.

mot (mō) *n.* a clever or witty remark. [< F < L *muttum* grunt, word. Doublet of MOTTO.]

mote[1] (mōt) *n.* a speck of dust. [OE *mot*]

mote[2] (mōt) *v. Archaic.* may; might. [OE *mōtan.* Related to MUST[1].]

mo·tel (mō tel′) *n.* a roadside hotel or a group of furnished cottages or cabins providing accommodation for motorists. Most motels have units that can be entered directly from the parking area. [< *mo*tor + ho*tel*]

mo·tet (mō tet′) *n.* in music, a polyphonic composition having a sacred theme, usually sung unaccompanied. [ME < OF *motet*, dim. of *mot* word]

moth (moth) *n.* **moths** (moᴛʜz or moths). **1** a small, winged insect that lays eggs in cloth, fur, etc. Its larvae eat holes in carpets and clothes. **2** a broad-winged insect very much like a butterfly, but flying mostly at night. [OE *moththe*]

moth ball a small ball made of naphthalene, camphor, or some other strong-smelling substance, used for putting in garments or in clothes closets to keep moths away.

moth-eat·en (moth′ēt′ən) *adj.* **1** eaten by moths; having holes made by moths. **2** worn-out; out-of-date.

moth·er[1] (muᴛʜ′ər) *n.* **1** a female parent. **2** the cause; source: *Necessity is the mother of invention.* **3** the head of a female religious community. **4** a woman exercising control and responsibility like that of a mother. **5** a familiar name for an old woman.
—*v.* **1** be mother of; act as mother to. **2** acknowledge oneself mother of or assume as one's own.
—*adj.* **1** that is a mother. **2** like a mother. **3** of a mother. **4** native. [OE *mōdor*] —**moth′er·less,** *adj.*

moth·er[2] (muᴛʜ′ər) *n.* a stringy, sticky substance, consisting of bacteria that is formed in vinegar or on the surface of liquids that are turning to vinegar. [special use of *mother*[1]]

Mother Car·ey's chicken (kãr′ēz) **1** the stormy petrel. **2** any of various other petrels.

mother church a church from which or by which others have been formed.

mother country 1 the country where a person was born. **2** a country in relation to its colonies or its natives.

Mother Goose 1 the imaginary author of a book of fairy tales by Charles Perrault, 1628-1703, a French author, published in 1697. **2** the imaginary author of English nursery rhymes, actually of folk origin and first published in book form by John Newbury, 1713-1767. Mother Goose is a traditional character of nursery tales in Europe.

moth·er·hood (muᴛʜ′ər hu̇d′) *n.* **1** the state of being a mother. **2** the qualities of a mother. **3** mothers.

Mother Hub·bard (hub′ərd) **1** the subject of a well-known Mother Goose nursery rhyme beginning "Old Mother Hubbard went to the cupboard." **2** a full, loose gown for women.

moth·er-in-law (muᴛʜ′ər in lo′ or -lô′) *n.* **moth·ers-in-law.** the mother of one's husband or wife.

moth·er·land (muᴛʜ′ər land′) *n.* **1** one's native country. **2** the land of one's ancestors.

mother lode the main vein of ore in an area or mine.

moth·er·ly (muᴛʜ′ər lē) *adj.* **1** of a mother. **2** like a mother; like a mother's; kindly. —**moth′er·li·ness,** *n.*

moth·er-of-pearl (muᴛʜ′ər əv pėrl′) *n.* the hard, rainbow-colored lining of certain shells. It is used for buttons and ornaments.

Mother's Day the second Sunday of May, set apart in Canada and the United States in honor of mothers.

mother superior a woman who is in charge of a convent of nuns.

mother tongue 1 one's native language. 2 a language to which other languages owe their origin.

mother wit natural intelligence; common sense.

moth·proof (moth′prüf′) *adj.* repellent or resistant to moths. —*v.* make repellent or resistant to moths.

moth·y (moth′ē) *adj.* **moth·i·er, moth·i·est.** containing moths; moth-eaten.

mo·tif (mō tēf′) *n.* 1 in art or literature, a subject for development or treatment; dominant, usually recurring idea or feature; theme: *The Cinderella motif is found in the literature of many countries.* 2 a distinctive, often repeated figure in a decorative design. 3 in music: **a** the shortest intelligible melodic or rhythmic fragment of a theme or subject. **b** a subject. **c** a leitmotif. [< F < Med.L *motivus* moving. Doublet of MOTIVE.]

mo·tile (mō′tīl or mō′təl) *adj.* in biology, able to move by itself. [< L *motus* moved + E *-ile*, capable of (< L *-ilis*)]

mo·til·i·ty (mō til′ə tē) *n.* a motile quality.

mo·tion (mō′shən) *n.* 1 the condition or state of moving; a movement or a change of position or place: *He swayed with the motion of the moving train. Everything is either in motion or at rest.* 2 a formal suggestion made in a meeting or law court: *The motion to adjourn was carried.* 3 **in motion,** moving; going. 4 in law, an application made to a court or judge for an order, ruling, etc. 5 in music: **a** the melodic progression of a single part or voice from one pitch to another. **b** the progression of two or more parts or voices with relation to each other.
—*v.* 1 make a movement, as of the hand or head, to show one's meaning. 2 show (a person) what to do by such a motion: *He motioned me out.* [< L *motio, -onis* < *movere* move]
Syn. *n.* 1 **Motion, movement** = change of place, position, or condition. **Motion** = the state of not being at rest or the process of moving, especially as thought of apart from any particular thing or when the kind of action is not stressed: *We study the laws of motion.* **Movement,** usually applying to the motion of someone or something, emphasizes a definite moving in a particular direction and regular way: *the movement of the earth.* –*v.* 1 gesticulate.

mo·tion·less (mō′shən lis) *adj.* not moving. —**mo′tion·less·ly,** *adv.* —**mo′tion·less·ness,** *n.* —**Syn.** inert, stationary, still, quiet.

motion picture 1 a series of pictures on a continuous strip of film, projected on a screen in such rapid succession that the viewer gets the impression that the persons and things pictured are moving. 2 a story or drama told by this means; moving picture or movie.

mo·ti·vate (mō′tə vāt′) *v.* **-vat·ed, -vat·ing.** provide with a motive; act upon as a motive.

mo·ti·va·tion (mō′tə vā′shən) *n.* the act or process of furnishing with an incentive or inducement to action.

mo·ti·va·tion·al (mō′tə vā′shə nəl) *adj.* 1 of or having to do with motivation: *Advertisers use the techniques of motivational research to find out why people buy or do not buy a product.* 2 motivating.

mo·tive (mō′tiv) *n.* 1 the thought or feeling that makes one act: *His motive in going away was a wish to travel.* 2 a motif. —*adj.* that makes something move. [< Med.L *motivus* moving, impelling < L *motus*, pp. of *movere* move. Doublet of MOTIF.] —**Syn.** *n.* 1 incentive. See **reason.**

motive power 1 power used to impart motion; source of mechanical energy: *The motive power of trains is usually steam or electricity.* 2 all the locomotives of a railway collectively.

mot juste (mō zhʏst′) *French.* a word or phrase that exactly fits the situation.

mot·ley (mot′lē) *n.* **-leys,** *adj.* —*n.* 1 a suit of more than one color worn by clowns. 2 a mixture of things that are different. —*adj.* 1 of different colors like a clown's suit. 2 made up of units not alike: *a motley collection.* [ME *motteley*, apparently < AF **motelé* < OE *mot* mote[1]]

mo·tor (mō′tər) *n.* 1 an engine that makes a machine go: *an electric motor.* 2 a dynamo. 3 an internal-combustion engine. 4 an automobile. 5 that which causes motion.
—*adj.* 1 powered by a motor. 2 of, by, or by means of automobiles: *a motor tour.* 3 causing or having to do with motion or action; functioning like a motor. 4 **a** of nerves, conveying or imparting an impulse from the central nervous system to a muscle which results or tends to result in motion. **b** of muscles, impulses, nerve centres, etc., concerned in motion. **c** designating the effect of stimuli from the central nervous system causing motion or action. 5 in psychology, of, having to do with, or involving muscular or glandular activity: *a motor response.*
—*v.* travel by automobile. [< L *motor* mover < *movere* move] —**mo′tor·less,** *adj.*

motor area the part of the brain that is believed to control muscular movement.

mo·tor·boat (mō′tər bōt′) *n.* a boat that is propelled by a motor.

mo·tor·bus (mō′tər bus′) *n.* a bus powered by a motor.

mo·tor·cade (mō′tər kād′) *n.* a procession or long line of automobiles.

motor car an automobile.

motor coach motor bus.

motor court a group of small buildings providing accommodation for motorists.

mo·tor·cy·cle (mō′tər sī′kəl) *n., v.* **-cy·cled, -cy·cling.** —*n.* a motor-propelled, two-wheeled vehicle. —*v.* travel by motorcycle.

mo·tor·cy·clist (mō′tər sī′klist) *n.* a person who rides a motorcycle.

motor generator an apparatus consisting of a combination of motor and dynamo, used to reduce voltage, etc.

motor hotel or **inn** a hotel for accommodating motorists, somewhat more elaborate than a motel and usually consisting of several floors of rooms and suites.

mo·tor·ist (mō′tər ist) *n.* a person who travels by automobile, especially one who does so a great deal.

mo·tor·ize (mō′tər īz′) *v.* **-ized, -iz·ing.** 1 furnish with a motor. 2 supply with motor-driven vehicles in place of horses and horse-drawn vehicles. 3 equip (infantry) with motor-driven transport vehicles, especially trucks. —**mo′tor·i·za′tion,** *n.*

motor lodge motor inn.

mo·tor·man (mo′tər mən) *n.* **-men** (-mən). 1 a man who operates an electric streetcar or train. 2 a man who operates a motor.

motor truck a truck with an engine and chassis made for carrying heavy loads.

mot·tle (mot′əl) *v.* **-tled, -tling,** *n.* —*v.* mark with spots or streaks of different colors. —*n.* a mottled coloring or pattern. [apparently < AF **moteler* speckle < OE *mot* speck, mote[1]. Related to MOTLEY.]

mot·to (mot′ō) *n.* **-toes** or **-tos.** 1 a brief sentence adopted as a rule of conduct: "*Think before you speak*" *is a good motto.* 2 a sentence, word, or phrase written or engraved on some object. [< Ital. < L *muttum* grunt, word. Doublet of MOT.] —**Syn.** 1 proverb, adage, saying.

moue (mü) *n.* a grimace; pout. [< F]

mou·fle (mu′fəl) *n. Cdn.* the thick, edible upper part of the snout of the moose. Also, **muffle.** [< Cdn.F < F *mufle* flabby face]

mouf·lon or **mouf·flon** (müf′lon) *n.* 1 a wild sheep of the mountainous regions of Sardinia, Corsica, etc. 2 its wool, used for fur. [< F < Corsican Ital. < LL *mufro*]

mou·jik (mü zhik′ or mü′zhik) *n.* muzhik.

mou·lage (mü läzh′) *n.* 1 the making of a cast or mould of a footprint or other evidence connected with criminal investigation. 2 the mould itself. 3 a rubber or wax model of a body injury used in physiotherapy. [< F]

mould[1] or **mold** (mōld) *n.* 1 a hollow shape in which anything is formed or cast: *Molten metal is poured into a mould to harden into shape.* 2 the shape or form which is given by a mould. 3 the model according to which anything is shaped. 4 something shaped in a mould: *a mould of pudding.* 5 the nature or character of anything. 6 the shape or frame on or about which something is made.

—*v.* **1** form; shape: *We mould statues out of clay.* **2** make or form into shape: *We mould wax into candles. Our characters are moulded by our conduct.* [ME < OF *modle* < L *modulus.* Doublet of MODULE.]

mould[2] or **mold** (mōld) *n.* a greenish or grayish fungoid growth, resembling wool or fur, that appears on food and other animal or vegetable substances. Mould is caused by the presence of microbes which flourish in warm, moist surroundings. —*v.* **1** become covered with mould: *The boots moulded in the cellar.* **2** cover with mould. [ME *moul,* earlier *muwle(n),* probably influenced by *mould*[3]]

mould[3] or **mold** (mōld) *n.* **1** soft, rich, crumbly soil; earth mixed with decaying leaves, manure, etc.: *Many wild flowers grow in the forest mould.* **2** *Archaic.* ground; earth. [OE *molde*]

mould·board or **mold·board** (mōld′bôrd′) *n.* a curved metal plate on a plough, that turns over the earth from the furrow.

mould·er[1] or **mold·er** (mōl′dər) *v.* turn into dust by natural decay; crumble; waste away. [probably < *mould*[3]]

mould·er[2] or **mold·er** (mōl′dər) *n.* a person or thing that moulds; a person who shapes something. [< *mould*[1]]

mould·ing or **mold·ing** (mōl′ding) *n.* **1** the act of shaping: *the moulding of dishes from clay.* **2** something moulded. **3** a shaped strip of wood, such as that often found around the upper walls of a room. Mouldings may be simply ornamental, or they may be used to support pictures, to cover electric wires, etc.

moulding board or **molding board** a board used for kneading bread, rolling cookies, etc.

mould·y or **mold·y** (mōl′dē) *adj.* **mould·i·er** or **mold·i·er, mould·i·est** or **mold·i·est. 1** covered with mould. **2** musty; stale: *a mouldy smell.* —**mould′i·ness** or **mold′i·ness,** *n.*

mou·lin (mü laN′) *n.* in geology, a nearly vertical cavity in a glacier, worn by water falling through a crevice. [< F *moulin,* literally, mill; from the noise sometimes made by the rushing water]

moult or **molt** (mōlt) *v.* **1** shed the feathers, skin, etc. before a new growth. Birds and snakes moult. **2** shed (feathers, etc.): *We saw the snake moult its skin.* —*n.* **1** the act or process of moulting. **2** the time of moulting. [ME *mout* < OE *mūtian* (as in *bemūtian* exchange for) < L *mutare* change]

mound (mound) *n.* **1** a bank or heap of earth or stones. **2** a small hill. **3** in baseball, the slightly elevated ground from which a pitcher pitches. —*v.* **1** enclose with a mound. **2** heap up. [OE *mund* protection; meaning influenced by *mount*[2]]

Mound Builders people who lived in North America long ago, from the Great Lakes region to Florida. They built mounds of earth to bury their dead or for defence.

mount[1] (mount) *v.* **1** go up; ascend: *mount stairs.* **2** move or proceed upwards: *A flush mounted to her brow.* **3** rise; increase; rise in amount: *The cost of living mounts steadily.* **4** get up on: *mount a platform.* **5** get on a horse; get up on something: *mount and ride away.* **6** put on a horse; furnish with a horse: *Many policemen in this city are mounted.* **7** put in proper position or order for use: *mount specimens on slides.* **8** fix in a setting, backing, support, etc.: *mount a picture on cardboard.* **9** have or carry (guns) as a fortress or ship does. **10** provide (a play) with scenery and costumes. **11** go on (guard) as a sentry or watch does. **12** set or place upon an elevation: *a small house mounted on poles.*
—*n.* **1** a horse provided for riding. **2** a setting; backing; support. **3** an act or occasion of riding a horse, especially in a race. **4** the act or manner of mounting. [ME < OF *monter* < L *mons, montis* mountain] —**mount′a·ble,** *adj.* —**Syn.** *v.* **1** See **climb.**

mount[2] (mount) *n.* a mountain or high hill. *Mount* is often used before the names of mountains: *Mount Robson, Mount Everest, Mount Olympus.* [OE *munt* < L *mons, montis*]

moun·tain (moun′tən) *n.* **1** a very high hill: *the Rocky Mountains.* **2 mountains,** *pl.* a series of such hills. **3** something resembling a high hill: *a mountain of rubbish.* **4** a huge amount: *a mountain of difficulties.* —*adj.* **1** of or having to do with mountains. **2** living, growing, or found on mountains. **3** resembling or suggesting a mountain. [ME < OF *montaigne* < *mont* < L *mons, montis*] —**Syn.** *n.* **1** elevation, peak.

hat, āge, cãre, fär; let, ēqual, tėrm; it, īce
hot, ōpen, ôrder; oil, out; cup, pu̇t, rüle, ūse
əbove, takən, pencəl, lemən, circəs
ch, child; ng, long; sh, ship
th, thin; ᴛʜ, then; zh, measure

mountain ash any of several trees of the rose family having pinnate leaves, white flowers, and bright-red berries; the rowan.

mountain badger hoary marmot.

mountain cat 1 a cougar. **2** a bobcat.

mountain chain a connected series of mountains.

moun·tain·eer (moun′tə nēr′) *n.* **1** a person who lives in the mountains. **2** a person skilled in mountain climbing. **3 Mountaineer,** a Montagnais. —*v.* climb mountains.

mountain goat the white antelope of the Rockies.

mountain laurel an evergreen shrub having glossy leaves and pale-pink or white flowers.

mountain lion a cougar.

moun·tain·ous (moun′tə nəs) *adj.* **1** covered with mountain ranges: *mountainous country.* **2** huge: *a mountainous wave.*

mountain range a row of mountains; series of mountains.

mountain sickness sickness caused by the rarefied air at high altitudes. The common symptoms are difficulty in breathing, headache, and nausea.

moun·tain·top (moun′tən top′) *n.* the top or summit of a mountain.

moun·te·bank (moun′tə bangk′) *n.* **1** a person who sells quack medicines in public, appealing to his audience by tricks, stories, jokes, etc. **2** anybody who tries to deceive people by tricks, stories, and jokes. [< Ital. *montambanco* for *monta in banco* mount-on-bench]

mount·ed (moun′tid) *adj.* **1** on horseback. **2** in a position for use: *a mounted telescope.* **3** on a support; in a setting: *a mounted jewel.*

Mount·ie or **mount·ie** (moun′tē) *n.* **-ies.** *Cdn. Informal.* a member of the Royal Canadian Mounted Police, maintained by the government of Canada.

mount·ing (moun′ting) *n.* a support, setting, or the like. The mounting of a photograph is the paper or cardboard on which it is pasted.

mourn (môrn) *v.* **1** grieve. **2** feel or show sorrow over. [OE *murnan*] —**Syn. 1** lament, sorrow.

mourn·er (môr′nər) *n.* **1** a person who mourns, especially at a funeral. **2** a sinner who repents and seeks salvation at a religious revival meeting.

mourners' bench a front seat reserved for repenting sinners at a religious revival meeting.

mourn·ful (môrn′fəl) *adj.* **1** sad; sorrowful. **2** gloomy; dreary. —**mourn′ful·ly,** *adv.* —**mourn′ful·ness,** *n.* —**Syn. 1** doleful, dolorous, melancholy.

mourn·ing (môr′ning) *n.* **1** the act of sorrowing; lamentation. **2 a** the wearing of black or some other color (white in the Orient), to show sorrow for a person's death. **b** the period during which black, etc. is worn. **3** the draping of buildings, the flying of flags at half-mast, etc. as outward signs of such sorrow. **4** clothes, decorations, draperies, etc. worn or displayed to show such sorrow: *The widow was dressed in mourning.* —*adj.* of or having to do with mourning; used in mourning. —**mourn′ing·ly,** *adv.*

mourning dove a wild dove of North America that makes a mournful sound.

mouse (*n.* mous; *v. sometimes,* mouz) *n.* **mice,** *v.* **moused, mous·ing.** —*n.* **1** a small, gray rodent that is found throughout the world. **2** a shy, timid person. —*v.* **1** hunt for mice; catch mice for food. **2** search as a cat does; move about as if searching. [OE *mūs*] —**mouse′like,** *adj.*

mous·er (mou′sər or mouz′ər) *n.* **1** an animal that catches mice. **2** a person that prowls about and pries into matters.

mouse·trap (mous′trap′) *n.* a trap for catching mice.

mous·ey (mous′ē) *adj.* **mous·i·er, mous·i·est. 1** resembling or suggesting a mouse in color, odor, behavior, etc.: *She had mousey hair.* **2** quiet as a mouse. **3** infested with mice. Also, **mousy.**

mous·ing (mouz′ing) *n.* several turns of small rope, etc. uniting the shank and point of a hook.

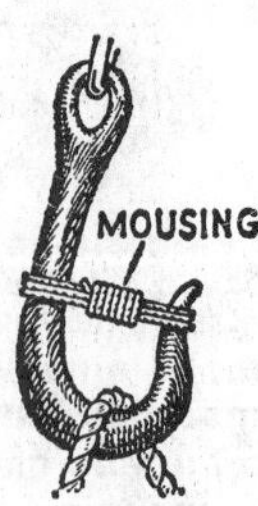

Mousing used to keep a loop from slipping off a hook

mousse (müs) *n.* **1** a dessert normally made with whipped cream or gelatin, frozen without stirring: *chocolate mousse.* **2** a meat or fish purée lightened with gelatin or whipped cream or both. [< F *mousse* moss < Gmc.]

mousse·line (müs lēn′) *n. French.* muslin.

mousse·line de soie (müs lēn′ də swä′) *French.* a thin silk fabric.

mous·tache (mus′tash or məs tash′) *n.* mustache.

mous·y (mous′ē) *adj.* **mous·i·er, mous·i·est.** mousey.

mouth (*n.* mouth; *v.* mouтн) *n.* **mouths** (mouтнz) *v.* —*n.* **1** the opening through which a person or an animal takes in food; space in the head containing the tongue and teeth. **2** an opening suggesting a mouth: *the mouth of a cave.* **3** a part of a river or the like where its waters are emptied into some other body of water: *the mouth of the Ottawa River.* **4** a grimace. **5** a person or an animal requiring food or support: *He has seven mouths to feed in his family.* **6 a** the mouth as the source of spoken words. **b** utterance of words, speech: *get news by mouth, give mouth to one's thoughts.* **7 down in the mouth,** *Informal.* in low spirits; discouraged. **8 from the horse's mouth,** from the original source; from a well-informed source; from the person in charge. **9 laugh on the other side** or **wrong side of one's mouth,** *Informal.* be annoyed; be made sorry. **10 shoot off one's mouth,** or **shoot one's mouth off,** *Slang.* talk freely and indiscreetly.
—*v.* **1** seize or rub with the mouth. **2** utter (words) in an affected or pompous way. **3** speak oratorically. **4** make grimaces. **5** accustom (a horse) to the bit and bridle. [OE *mūth*] —**mouth′like′** *adj.*

mouthed (mouтнd or moutht) *adj.* having a mouth or opening.

-mouthed *combining form.* having a —— mouth: *small-mouthed* = *having a small mouth.*

mouth·er (mouтн′ər) *n. Informal.* a long-winded talker.

mouth·ful (mouth′fůl) *n.* **-fuls. 1** the amount that the mouth can easily hold. **2** what is taken into the mouth at one time. **3** a small amount. **4** *Slang.* an important or significant statement: *You said a mouthful.*

mouth·less (mouth′lis) *adj.* having no mouth or opening.

mouth organ 1 a harmonica. **2** a Panpipe.

mouth·piece (mouth′pēs′) *n.* **1** the part of a telephone, musical instrument, etc. that is placed in or against a person's mouth. **2** the part of a bit that goes in a horse's mouth. **3** a piece placed at the mouth of something or forming its mouth. **4** a person, newspaper, etc. that speaks for others.

mouth·wash (mouth′wosh′) *n.* an antiseptic liquid for cleaning the mouth and teeth.

mouth-wa·ter·ing (mouth′wo′tər ing or -wô′tər ing) *adj.* making the mouth water; tempting; appetizing.

mouth·y (mouтн′ē or mouth′ē) *adj.* **mouth·i·er, mouth·i·est.** loud-mouthed; ranting; bombastic. —**mouth′i·ly,** *adv.* —**mouth′i·ness,** *n.*

mou·ton (mü′ton) *n.* Also, **mouton lamb.** fur made from sheepskin that is pressed and dyed to look like beaver or seal. —*adj.* made of mouton: *mouton coats.* [< F]

mov·a·bil·i·ty (müv′ə bil′ə tē) *n.* the state or quality of being movable. Also, **moveability.**

mov·a·ble (müv′ə bəl) *adj.* **1** that can be moved. **2** that can be carried from place to place as personal possessions can. **3** changing from one date to another in different years: *Easter is a movable holy day.* —*n.* **1** a piece of furniture that is not a fixture but can be moved to another house. **2** a thing that can be moved, removed, or set in motion. **3** Usually, **movables,** *pl.* in law, personal property. —**mov′a·ble·ness,** *adj.* —**mov′a·bly,** *adv.*

move (müv) *v.* **moved, mov·ing,** *n.* —*v.* **1** change the place or position of: *Do not move your hand.* **2** change place or position: *The child moved in his sleep.* **3** change one's abode: *We move to the country next week.* **4** in a game, make a move; be moved: *The chess player moved a pawn.* **5** put or keep in motion: *The wind moves the leaves.* **6** of the bowels, empty or cause to be emptied: *Castor oil moves the bowels.* **7** act: *God moves in a mysterious way.* **8** impel; rouse; excite: *What moved you to do this?* **9** effect with emotion; excite to tender feeling: *The sad story moved her to tears.* **10** make a formal request, application, or proposal; propose: *Mr. Chairman, I move that we adjourn.* **11** sell or be sold: *These pink dresses are moving slowly.* **12** make progress: *The train moved slowly.* **13** exist; be active: *She moved in the best society.* **14** turn; swing; operate: *Most doors move on a hinge.* **15** carry oneself: *move with dignity and grace.* **16** *Informal.* start off; depart: *It's time to be moving.* **17 move in,** move oneself, one's family, one's belongings, etc. into a new place to live or work. **18 move out,** move oneself, one's family, one's belongings, etc. out of a place where one has lived or worked.
—*n.* **1** in a game: **a** the right or time to move. **b** the moving of a piece. **2** the act of moving; movement. **3** an action taken to bring about some result. **4 get a move on,** *Slang.* **a** make haste; hurry up. **b** begin to move. **5 on the move,** moving about; travelling. [ME < AF < L *movere*]
Syn. *v.* **1** shift, remove, transfer. **8 Move, actuate** = rouse a person to action or to act in a certain way. **Move,** the general word, does not suggest whether the thing that rouses is an outside force or influence or an inner urge or personal motive: *Praise moved him to work harder.* **Actuate,** a formal word, always implies a powerful inner force, like a strong feeling, desire, principle, etc.: *He was actuated by desire for praise.* **9** influence. **12** See **advance.**

move·a·ble (müv′ə bəl) *adj.* movable.

move·ment (müv′mənt) *n.* **1** the act or fact of moving. **2** a change in the placing of troops or ships. **3** the moving parts of a machine; a special group of parts that move on each other. The movement of a watch consists of many little wheels. **4** in music: **a** the kind of rhythm of a composition: *a waltz movement.* **b** its speed. **c** one division of a long composition: *the second movement of a symphony.* **5** in literature and the arts, the suggestion of action or progress. **6** the efforts and results of a group of people working together to bring about some one thing: *the movement for peace.* **7** a notable change in the price of something. **8 a** an emptying of the bowels. **b** the matter discharged by it. —**Syn. 1** move, action, stir. See **motion.**

mov·er (müv′ər) *n.* **1** a person or thing that moves. **2** a person whose occupation is moving furniture, etc. from one house, etc. to another.

mov·ie (müv′ē) *n. Informal.* a motion picture.

mov·ing (müv′ing) *adj.* **1** that moves. **2** causing motion; actuating. **3** touching; pathetic. *a moving story.* —**mov′ing·ly,** *adv.*

moving picture a motion picture.

mow[1] (mō) *v.* **mowed, mowed** or **mown, mow·ing. 1** cut down with a machine or scythe. **2** cut down the grass or grain from. **3** cut down grass, etc.: *The men are mowing today.* **4** destroy at a sweep or in large numbers, as if by mowing: *The machine guns mowed down our men like grass.* [OE *māwan*] —**mow′er,** *n.*

mow[2] (mou or mō) *n.* **1** the place in a barn where hay, alfalfa, grain, or straw is piled or stored. **2** a pile of hay, grain, etc. in a barn. [OE *mūga*]

mow[3] (mō or mou) *v. n.* grimace. [ME < OF *moue*]

mow·ing (mō′ing) *n.* **1** the act or process of cutting grass with a scythe or machine. **2** meadowland. **3** the hay mowed at one time.

mown (mōn) *v.* a pp. of **mow**[1].

mox·ie (mok′sē) *n. Slang.* **1** courage; bravery; nerve. **2** know-how; skill; experience. [< earlier *Moxie,* a trademark for a soft drink (because the drink supposedly gave courage)]

Moz·za·rel·la or **moz·za·rel·la** (moz′ə rel′ə or mot′sə rel′ə) *n.* a soft Italian cheese, used especially in the making of pizza. [< Ital.]

MP or **M.P. 1** Member of Parliament. **2** Military Police. **3** Mounted Police. **4** Metropolitan Police.

mph or **m.p.h.** miles per hour.

MPP or **M.P.P.** Member of the Provincial Parliament.

Mr. or **Mr** (mis′tər) *pl.* **Messrs.** Mister.
☛ **Mr.** is written out only when it represents informal usage

and when it is used without a name: "*They're only five cents for two, mister.*"

Mrs. or **Mrs** (mis′iz) *pl.* **Mmes.** a contracted form of mistress; title put in front of a married woman's name: *Mrs. Jackson.*
☛ Mrs. is written out only in representing informal usage and is then spelled *missis* (or *missus*): *Mrs. Dorothy Adams, Mrs. Adams. "Where's the missis?"*

MS., MS, ms., or **ms** manuscript.

M.S. 1 Master of Surgery. 2 Master of Science.

M.Sc. Master of Science.

Msgr. 1 Monsignor. 2 Monseigneur.

m'sieur (mə syœ′) *n. French.* monsieur.

M.S.M. Meritorious Service Medal.

MSS., MSS, mss., or **mss** manuscripts.

MST, M.S.T., or **m.s.t.** Mountain Standard Time.

M.S.W. Master of Social Work.

Mt. *pl.* Mts. 1 Mount. 2 Mountain.

mtg. 1 meeting. 2 mortgage.

mtge. mortgage.

Mtl. Montreal.

Mtn. *pl.* Mtns. Mountain.

Mt.Rev. Most Reverend.

mu (mū) *n.* the 12th letter of the Greek alphabet (M, μ).

much (much) *adj.* **more, most,** *adv.* **more, most,** *n.*
—*adj.* in great quantity, amount, or degree: *much money, much time.*
—*adv.* **1** to a great extent or degree: *much pleased.* **2** nearly; about: *This is much the same as the others.*
—*n.* **1** a great deal: *Much of this is not true.* **2** a great, important, or notable thing or matter: *The rain did not amount to much.* **3 make much of,** treat, represent, or consider as of great importance. **4 much of a size, height, etc.,** nearly the same size, height, etc. **5 not much of a,** not a very good: *This is not much of a game.* **6 too much for,** more than a match for; more than one can cope with, stand, or bear: *The work is too much for him. Their team was too much for ours.* [var. of OE *micel*]

much·ness (much′nis) *n.* **1** greatness; magnitude. **2 much of a muchness,** much alike; nearly equivalent.

mu·ci·lage (mū′sə lij) *n.* **1** a gummy substance used to make things stick together. **2** in plants, a substance like glue or gelatin. [< F < LL *mucilago* musty juice < L *mucus* mucus]

mu·ci·lag·i·nous (mū′sə laj′ə nəs) *adj.* **1** sticky; gummy. **2** containing mucilage.

muck (muk) *n.* **1** dirt; filth. **2** anything filthy, dirty, or disgusting. **3** moist farmyard manure. **4 a** well-decomposed peat, used as manure. **b** a heavy soil containing a high percentage of this. **5** in mining, unwanted earth, rock, etc. that is dug out or otherwise removed. **6** *Informal.* mess; untidy condition.
—*v.* **1** soil or make dirty. **2** put muck on. **3** in mining, remove unwanted earth, rock, etc. **4 muck about** or **around,** *Slang.* waste time; putter; go about aimlessly. **5 muck out,** clean out (a stable, mine, etc.). [ME < ON *myki* cow dung]

muck·er (muk′ər) *n.* **1** *Slang.* a vulgar, ill-bred person. **2** in mining, etc., one who removes muck.

muck·rake (muk′rāk′) *v.* **-raked, -ra·king.** hunt for and expose corruption. —**muck′rak′er,** *n.*

muck·y (muk′ē) *adj.* **muck·i·er, muck·i·est. 1** of muck; like muck. **2** filthy; dirty.

mu·cous (mū′kəs) *adj.* **1** of or like mucus. **2** containing or secreting mucus. [< L *mucosus* < *mucus* mucus]

mucous membrane the tissue that lines the nose, throat, and other cavities of the body that are open to the air.

mu·cus (mū′kəs) *n.* a slimy substance that moistens the mucous membranes. A cold in the head causes a discharge of mucus. [< F]

mud (mud) *n.* **1** soft, sticky, wet earth. **2** slander; libel; defamation. **3** any place, situation, etc. that is mean or degrading. **4 clear as mud,** incomprehensible; obscure. [ME *mudde*] —**Syn.** mire, slime, ooze.

mud·dle (mud′əl) *v.* **-dled, -dling,** *n.* —*v.* **1** mix up; cause confusion or disorder in. **2** make confused or stupid or slightly drunk. **3** make (water, etc.) muddy. **4** waste or squander (money, time, etc.) stupidly. **5** think or act in a confused, blundering way. **6 muddle through,** manage somehow; succeed in one's object in spite of lack of skill and foresight.
—*n.* **1** a mess; disorder; confusion. **2 make a muddle of,** bungle. [< *mud*] —**mud′dle·ment,** *n.*

mud·dle-head·ed (mud′əl hed′id) *adj.* stupid; confused.

mud·dler (mud′lər) *n.* **1** one who muddles or muddles through. **2** a thin plastic or metal stick for stirring drinks or other liquids.

mud·dy (mud′ē) *adj.* **-di·er, -di·est,** *v.* **-died, -dy·ing.**
—*adj.* **1** of or like mud. **2** having much mud; covered with mud. **3** clouded with mud or as if with mud; dull; not pure: *muddy water, a muddy color.* **4** confused; not clear.
—*v.* **1** make muddy. **2** become muddy. —**mud′di·ly,** *adv.* —**mud′di·ness,** *n.* —**Syn.** *adj.* **3** turbid, cloudy.

mud·guard (mud′gärd′) *n.* a guard or shield so placed as to protect riders or passengers from the mud thrown up by the moving wheels of a vehicle.

mud hen a water bird that resembles a large chicken and lives in marshes.

mud puppy an aquatic salamander.

mud room in a school or other building, a room near the entrance in which overshoes, rubbers, etc. are deposited before entering.

mud·sill (mud′sil′) *n.* the lowest sill of a structure, usually one placed in or on the ground.

mud turtle any of various fresh-water turtles of North America.

mu·ez·zin (mū ez′ən) *n.* a crier who, at certain hours, calls Moslems to prayer. [< Arabic *mu'adhdhin* < *adhana* proclaim]

muff (muf) *n.* **1** a cylindrical covering of fur or other material for keeping both hands warm. One hand is put in at each end. **2** a clumsy failure to catch and hold a ball that comes into one's hands. **3** awkward handling; bungling.
—*v.* **1** fail to catch and hold (a ball) when it comes into one's hands. **2** handle awkwardly; bungle: *Through sloppy play the team muffed its chance to win the game.* [< Du. *mof* < F *moufle* mitten < OF *moufle* thick glove (cf. Med.L *muffula*), probably < Gmc. Related to MUFFLE.]

A muff (def. 1)

muf·fin (muf′ən) *n.* **1** a small, cupshaped bread made of wheat flour, bran, or corn meal, etc., eaten with butter. **2** *Esp.Brit.* a round, flat, spongy cake, usually eaten toasted and with butter. [origin uncertain]

muf·fle[1] (muf′əl) *v.* **-fled, -fling.** *n.* —*v.* **1** wrap or cover up in order to keep warm and dry. **2** wrap oneself in garments, etc. **3** wrap up the head of (a person) in order to keep him from speaking. **4** wrap in something in order to soften or stop the sound. **5** dull or deaden (a sound).
—*n.* **1** a muffled sound. **2** something that muffles. [ME < OF *mofler* stuff (cf. OF *enmouflé,* pp., wrapped up) < *moufle* thick glove. Related to MUFF.]

muf·fle[2] (muf′əl) *n.* moufle.

muf·fler (muf′lər) *n.* **1** a wrap or scarf worn around the neck for warmth. **2** anything used to deaden sound. An automobile engine has a muffler attached to the exhaust pipe.

muf·ti (muf′tē) *n.* **1** ordinary clothes, not a uniform: *The retired general appeared in mufti.* **2** a Moslem official who assists a judge by formal exposition of the religious law. **3** in Turkey, the official head of the state religion, or one of his deputies. [< Arabic *mufti* judge (apparently because of the informal costume traditional for the stage role of a *mufti*)]

mug (mug) *n. v.* **mugged, mug·ging.** —*n.* **1** a heavy earthenware or metal drinking cup with a handle. **2** the

amount a mug holds. 3 *Slang.* the face. 4 *Slang.* the mouth. 5 *Slang.* a ruffian; hoodlum; petty criminal.
—*v.* *Slang.* 1 attack (a person) from behind by locking the forearm around the neck and choking. 2 make a photograph of (a person's face) for police purposes. 3 *Slang.* exaggerate one's facial expressions, as in acting. [cf. Norwegian *mugge*; defs. 3 and 4 derive from the common shape of mugs in earlier times]

mug·gy (mug′ē) *adj.* **-gi·er, -gi·est.** warm and humid; damp and close. [< dial. *mug* drizzle < Scand.; cf. ON *mugga* fine rain] **—mug′gi·ness,** *n.*

mug-up (mug′up′) *n.* a light meal, especially one taken at a break in a journey.

mug·wump (mug′wump′) *n.* *U.S.* an independent in politics. [< Algonquian *mukquomp* great man]

Mu·ham·mad (mů ham′əd) *n.* Mohammed.

mu·jik (mü zhik′ or mü′zhik) *n.* muzhik.

muk·luk (muk′luk) *n.* *Cdn.* 1 a high, waterproof boot, often made of sealskin, worn by Eskimos and others in the North. 2 *Informal.* any boot. [< Eskimo *muklok* bearded seal, a large seal]

muk·tuk (muk′tuk′) *n.* *Cdn.* the thin outer skin of the belugâ or white whale, or of the narwhal, used as food by the Eskimos. [< Eskimo]

mu·lat·to (mə lat′ō or mū lat′ō) *n.* **-toes.** 1 a person having one white and one Negro parent. 2 a person having both white and Negro ancestors. [< Sp. and Pg. *mulato* < *mulo* mule < L; from the mule's hybrid origin]

mul·ber·ry (mul′ber′ē or mul′bər ē) *n.* **-ries.** 1 any of various trees such as the **American mulberry** that yields a berry-like fruit or the **white mulberry** whose leaves are used for feeding silkworms. 2 the berry-like fruit of any of these trees. 3 a dark purplish red. [OE *mōrberie* < L *morum* mulberry + OE *berie* berry]

mulch (mulch) *n.* straw, leaves, loose earth, etc. spread on the ground around trees or plants. Mulch is used to protect the roots from cold or heat, to prevent evaporation of moisture from the soil, or to keep the fruit clean.
—*v.* cover with straw, leaves, etc. [OE *mylsc* mellow]

mulct (mulkt) *v.* 1 deprive of something by fraud or deceit: *He was mulcted of his money by a shrewd trick.* 2 punish by a fine. —*n.* a fine; penalty. [< L *mulctare,* erroneous var. of *multare* < *multa* a fine]

mule[1] (mūl) *n.* 1 the offspring of the ass and horse, especially of a male ass and a mare. It has the form and size of a horse, but the large ears, small hoofs, and tufted tail of an ass. 2 *Informal.* a stupid or stubborn person. 3 a kind of spinning machine. [ME < OF < L *mulus*]

mule[2] (mūl) *n.* a loose slipper, worn by women, covering only the toes and part of the instep, and leaving the rest of the foot and the heel uncovered. [< F < Du. *muil* < L *mulleus* shoe of red leather]

mule deer a deer of W. North America that has very long ears and a white tail with a black tip.

mule skinner *Informal.* a person who drives mules; muleteer.

mu·le·teer (mū′lə tēr′) *n.* a driver of mules. [< F *muletier* < *mulet,* dim. of OF *mul* mule < L *mulus*]

mul·ish (mūl′ish) *adj.* like a mule; stubborn; obstinate. **—mul′ish·ly,** *adv.* **—mul′ish·ness,** *n.*

mull[1] (mul) *v.* *Informal.* think (about) without making much progress: *He mulled over his problems.* [origin uncertain]

mull[2] (mul) *v.* make (wine, beer, etc.) into a warm drink, with sugar, spices, etc. [origin uncertain]

mull[3] (mul) *n.* a thin, soft muslin. [for *mulmul* < Hind., Persian *malmal*]

mul·lah (mul′ə or můl′ə) *n.* in Moslem countries, a title of respect for one who is learned in the sacred law. [< Turkish, Persian, Hind. *mulla* < Arabic *maula*]

mul·lein or **mul·len** (mul′ən) *n.* a weed having coarse, woolly leaves and spikes of yellow flowers. [ME < AF *moleine*]

mul·let (mul′it) *n.* **-let** or **-lets.** a kind of edible fish. There are red mullet and gray mullet. [ME < OF *mulet* < L *mullus* red mullet < Gk. *myllos*]

mul·li·gan (mul′ə gən) *n.* *Slang.* a stew of meat or, sometimes, fish and vegetables. [origin uncertain]

mul·li·ga·taw·ny (mul′ə gə to′nē or mul′ə gə tô′nē) *n.* a soup made of chicken or meat stock and flavored with curry. [< Tamil *milagu-tanni* pepper water]

mul·lion (mul′yən) *n.* 1 a vertical bar between the panes of a window, the panels in the wall of a room, or the like. 2 a radiating bar in a round window. [alteration of ME *muniall, monial* < OF *moi(e)nel,* earlier *meienel* in the middle < *meien* in the middle < L *medianus* < *medius*]

M, a mullion (def. 1)

mul·lioned (mul′yənd) *adj.* having mullions.

multi- *combining form.* 1 having many or several, as in *multiform.* 2 many or several times, as in *multimillionaire.* [< L *multi-* < *multus* much, many]

mul·ti·cel·lu·lar (mul′tē sel′yů lər) *adj.* having more than one cell.

mul·ti·col·ored or **mul·ti·col·oured** (mul′tē kul′ərd) *adj.* having many colors.

mul·ti·far·i·ous (mul′tə fãr′ē əs) *adj.* 1 having many different parts, elements, forms, etc. 2 many and various. [< L *multifarius*] **—mul′ti·far′i·ous·ly,** *adv.* **—mul′ti·far′i·ous·ness,** *n.*

mul·ti·fold (mul′tə fōld′) *adj.* manifold.

mul·ti·form (mul′tə fôrm′) *adj.* having many different shapes, forms, or kinds.

Mul·ti·graph (mul′tə graf′) *n.* *Trademark.* a machine for printing circulars, letters, etc. that has type like a typewriter's. —*v.* **multigraph,** make copies (of) by means of a Multigraph.

mul·ti·lat·er·al (mul′tē lat′ər əl) *adj.* 1 having many sides; many-sided. 2 involving two or more nations. **—mul′ti·lat′er·al·ly,** *adv.*

mul·ti·mil·lion·aire (mul′tē mil′yen ãr′) *n.* a person who has several millions in cash or its equivalent in property.

mul·tip·a·rous (mul tip′ə rəs) *adj.* producing many, or more than one, at a birth. [< NL *multiparus* < L *multus* much, many + *parere* bring forth]

mul·ti·ple (mul′tə pəl) *adj.* of, having, or involving many parts, elements, relations, etc.: *a man of multiple interests.* —*n.* a number that contains another number a certain number of times without a remainder: *12 is a multiple of 3.* [< F < LL *multiplus* manifold]

multiple sclerosis a disease that cripples and can destroy vital parts of the nervous system.

mul·ti·plex (mul′tə pleks′) *adj.* manifold; multiple. **Multiplex telegraphy** is a system by which it is possible to send more than two messages in opposite directions over the same wire at the same time. [< L *multiplex* < *multus* much + *-plex* -fold]

mul·ti·pli·cand (mul′tə plə kand′) *n.* in mathematics, the number or quantity to be multiplied by another. In 5 times 497, the multiplicand is 497. [< L *multiplicandus,* gerundive of *multiplicare.* See MULTIPLY.]

mul·ti·pli·ca·tion (mul′tə plə kā′shən) *n.* 1 the act or process of multiplying. 2 the state of being multiplied.

mul·ti·plic·i·ty (mul′tə plis′ə tē) *n.* **-ties.** 1 a manifold variety. 2 a great many: *a multiplicity of interests.* [< LL *multiplicitas* < L *multiplex.* See MULTIPLEX.]

mul·ti·pli·er (mul′tə plī′ər) *n.* 1 in mathematics, the number by which another number is to be multiplied. In 5 times 83, the multiplier is 5. 2 one that multiplies.

mul·ti·ply (mul′tə plī′) *v.* **-plied, -ply·ing.** 1 increase in number or amount: *As we climbed up the mountain, the dangers and difficulties multiplied.* 2 take (a number or quantity) a given number of times. To multiply 16 by 3 means to take 16 three times, making a total of 48. 3 increase by procreation. 4 produce (animals or plants) by propagation. [ME < OF *multiplier* < L *multiplicare* < *multiplex.* See MULTIPLEX.]

mul·ti·stage (mul′tē stāj′) *adj.* 1 of a rocket or missile, having several sections, each of which lifts the rocket or missile to a greater height before burning out and dropping off. **2** having a number of stages in the completion of a process: *a multistage automatic washer.*

mul·ti·tude (mul′tə tūd′ or mul′tə tüd′) *n.* **1** a great many; crowd. **2 the multitude,** the common people. [< L *multitudo* < *multus* much] —**Syn. 1** host, throng, horde, legion, army, swarm.

mul·ti·tu·di·nous (mul′tə tū′də nəs or mul′tə tü′də nəs) *adj.* **1** forming a multitude; very numerous. **2** including many parts, elements, items, or features. —**mul′ti·tu′di·nous·ly,** *adv.* —**mul′ti·tu′di·nous·ness,** *n.*

mul·ti·va·lence (mul′tə vā′ləns or mul tiv′ə ləns) *n.* a multivalent quality.

mul·ti·va·lent (mul′tə vā′lənt or mul tiv′ə lənt) *adj.* in chemistry: **1** having a valence of three or more. **2** having more than one degree of valence.

mum[1] (mum) *adj.* silent; saying nothing. —*interj.* be silent! say nothing! [ME; ? imitative]
mum's the word, keep silent.

mum[2] (mům) *n. Informal.* mother.

mum[3] (mum) *v.* **mummed, mum·ming. 1** be a mummer; act or play in a mask or disguise. **2** masquerade. **3** *Archaic.* act in a dumb show. [perhaps back formation < *mommyng* mummer's play. See MUMMER.]

mum[4] (mum) *n. Informal.* a chrysanthemum.

mum·ble (mum′bəl) *v.* **-bled, -bling,** *n.* —*v.* **1** speak indistinctly, as a person does when he moves his lips only slightly. **2** chew as a person does who has no teeth. —*n.* a mumbling. [ME *momele(n),* ? < *mum*[1]] —**mum′bler,** *n.* —**mum′bling·ly,** *adv.* —**Syn.** *v.* **1** See **murmur.**

Mum·bo Jum·bo or **mum·bo jum·bo** (mum′bō jum′bō) **1** the guardian genius of a native African village in western Sudan, represented by a masked medicine man who fends off evil and keeps the women in subjection. **2** foolish or meaningless incantation; ritualistic or ceremonial nonsense. **3** a bogey; object foolishly worshipped or feared. [? < a West African language]

mum·mer (mum′ər) *n.* **1** a person who wears a mask, fancy costume, or disguise for fun. **2** an actor. **3** an actor in one of the rural plays traditionally performed in England and elsewhere at Christmas. [ME < OF *momeur* < *momer* mask oneself]

mum·mer·y (mum′ər ē) *n.* **-mer·ies. 1** a performance of mummers. **2** any useless or silly show or ceremony. [< OF *mommerie*]

mum·mi·fy (mum′ə fī′) *v.* **-fied, -fy·ing. 1** make (a dead body) into a mummy; make like a mummy. **2** dry or shrivel up. —**mum′mi·fi·ca′tion,** *n.*

mum·my[1] (mum′ē) *n.* **-mies. 1** a dead body preserved from decay by the ancient Egyptian or some other method. Egyptian mummies have lasted more than 3,000 years. **2** a dead human or animal body dried and preserved by nature. **3** a withered or shrunken living being. [< F *momie* < Med.L *mumia* < Arabic *mumiya* mummy < *mum* wax]

mum·my[2] (mum′ē) *n.* **-mies.** *Informal.* mother.

An Egyptian mummy and coffin. The body was treated with chemicals, then wrapped in linen.

mumps (mumps) *n.pl.* a contagious virus disease marked by swelling of the face and difficulty in swallowing. [pl. of obs. *mump* grimace]
☛ Mumps is plural in form and singular in use: *Mumps is generally a children's disease.*

munch (munch) *v.* chew vigorously and steadily; chew noisily: *A horse munches its oats.* [apparently imitative]

mun·dane (mun′dān or mun dān′) *adj.* **1** of this world, not of heaven; earthly. **2** ordinary; everyday; humdrum: *mundane matters of business.* **3** of the universe; of the world. [< F < L *mundanus* < *mundus* world]

Mu·nich (mū′nik) *n.* an instance of appeasement which ultimately or immediately involves yielding to an aggressor at the expense of a principle or ally, and hence brings shame to the appeaser. [< *Munich* Pact, an agreement signed September 29, 1938, by Germany, France, Great Britain, and Italy]

mu·nic·i·pal (mū nis′ə pəl) *adj.* **1** of or having to do with the affairs of a city, town, or other municipality. **2** run by a municipality: *municipal affairs.* **3** having local self-government: *a municipal district.* [< L *municipalis,* ult. < *munia* official duties + *capere* take on]

hat, āge, cãre, fär; let, ēqual, tėrm; it, īce
hot, ōpen, ôrder; oil, out; cup, pu̇t, rüle, ūse
əbove, takən, pencəl, lemən, circəs
ch, child; ng, long; sh, ship
th, thin; ᴛʜ, then; zh, measure

mu·nic·i·pal·i·ty (mū nis′ə pal′ə tē) *n.* **-ties.** a city, town, county, district, township, or other area having local self-government.

mu·nic·i·pal·ly (mū nis′ip lē) *adv.* by a city or town; with regard to a city or town or to municipal affairs.

mu·nif·i·cence (mū nif′ə səns) *n.* **1** very great generosity. **2** ample measure; bountiful quality: *the munificence of a gift.* [< L *munificentia* < *munificus* generous, ult. < *munus* gift + *facere* make]

mu·nif·i·cent (mū nif′ə sənt) *adj.* **1** extremely generous. **2** characterized by great generosity: *a munificent reward.* [< *munificence*] —**mu·nif′i·cent·ly,** *adv.* —**Syn.** bountiful, bounteous, lavish, liberal.

mu·ni·ment (mū′nə mənt) *n.* **1** a defence; protection. **2 muniments,** *pl.* in law, a document, such as a title deed or charter, by which rights or privileges are defended or maintained. [< Med.L *munimentum* document, title deed < L *munimentum* defence, fortification < *munire* fortify < *moenia* walls]

mu·ni·tion (mū nish′ən) *n.* **munitions,** *pl.* material used in war. Munitions are military supplies, such as guns, powder, or bombs. —*adj.* having to do with military supplies. A munition plant is a factory for making munitions. —*v.* provide with military supplies: *munition a fort.* [< L *munitio, -onis* < *munire* fortify < *moenia* walls]

mu·ral (mūr′əl) *adj.* **1** on a wall. A mural painting is painted on a wall of a building. **2** of a wall; having to do with walls; like a wall. —*n.* a picture painted on a wall. [< F < L *muralis* < *murus* wall]

mu·ral·ist (mūr′ə list) *n.* a designer or painter of murals.

mur·der (mėr′dər) *n.* **1** the intentional and unlawful killing of a human being. **2** an instance of such a crime: *The detective solved the murder.* **3** *Informal.* a novel, story, etc. in which the plot is based on a murder and the discovery of the murderer. **4** *Slang.* anything exceedingly difficult or unpleasant: *That job was murder.* **5 murder will out, a** murder cannot be hidden. **b** any great wrong will be found out.
—*v.* **1** kill a human being intentionally and unlawfully: *Cain murdered his brother.* **2** do something very badly; spoil; ruin: *She murdered the song every time she tried to sing it.* [var. of *murther*] —**Syn.** *v.* **1** slay. See **kill.**

mur·der·er (mėr′dər ər) *n.* one who is guilty of murder.

mur·der·ess (mėr′dər is) *n.* a woman guilty of murder.

mur·der·ous (mėr′dər əs) *adj.* **1** able to kill: *a murderous blow.* **2** ready to murder: *a murderous villain.* **3** causing murder: *a murderous plot.* **4** characterized by or involving murder, death, or bloodshed; bloody: *a murderous riot.* —**mur′der·ous·ly,** *adv.*

mu·ri·ate (mūr′ē āt′) *n.* a chloride, especially potassium chloride, used for fertilizer. [< F *muriate* < L *muria* brine]

mu·ri·at·ic acid (mūr′ē at′ik) hydrochloric acid. [< L *muriaticus* < *muria* brine]

murk (mėrk) *n.* darkness; gloom. —*adj. Poetic.* dark; gloomy. Also, **mirk.** [OE *mirce*]

murk·y (mėr′kē) *adj.* **murk·i·er, murk·i·est.** dark; gloomy. —**murk′i·ly,** *adv.* —**murk′i·ness,** *n.*

mur·mur (mėr′mər) *n.* **1** a soft, low, indistinct sound that rises and falls a little but goes on without breaks: *the murmur of a stream, of little waves, or of voices in another room.* **2** a sound in the heart or lungs, especially an abnormal sound due to a leaky valve in the heart. **3** a softly spoken word or speech. **4** a complaint made under

the breath, not aloud.
—*v.* **1** make a soft, low, indistinct sound. **2** utter in a murmur. **3** complain under the breath; grumble. [< L] **—mur′mur·er,** *n.* **—mur′mur·ing·ly,** *adv.*

Syn. *n.* **1** hum, babble. *–v.* **2 Murmur, mumble, mutter** = speak indistinctly. **Murmur** = speak too softly to be clearly heard or plainly understood: *He murmured his thanks.* **Mumble** = speak with the lips partly closed, so that the sounds are not properly formed or articulated: *This boy mumbles half the time.* **Mutter** = mumble in a low voice, as if not wanting to be heard, and especially suggests complaining or anger: *He muttered some rude remarks.*

Murphy bed a bed that folds away or slides into a closet.

mur·rain (mėr′ən) *n.* **1** an infectious disease of cattle. **2** *Archaic.* a pestilence; plague. [ME < OF *morine,* ult. < L *mori* die]

murre (mėr) *n.* **1** any of various sea birds of the guillemot family. **2** razor-billed auk. [origin uncertain]

mur·ther (mėr′ᴛʜər) *n. v. Dialect.* murder. [OE *morthor*] **—mur′ther·er,** *n.*

mus. **1** music. **2** museum.

Mus.B. Bachelor of Music. (for L *Musicae Baccalaureus*)

mus·cat (mus′kat or mus′kət) *n.* **1** a light-colored grape with the flavor or odor of musk. **2** muscatel wine. [< F < Provençal *muscat* having the fragrance of musk < *musc* musk < LL *muscus.* See MUSK.]

mus·ca·tel (mus′kə tel′) *n.* **1** a strong, sweet wine made from muscat grapes. **2** the muscat grape. [< MF, dim. of *muscat* < Provençal. See MUSCAT.]

mus·cle (mus′əl) *n. v.* **-cled, -cling.** *—n.* **1** in anatomy: **a** a fibrous or cellular tissue that can contract or relax in order to produce movement. **b** an organ composed of such tissue. **2** strength. **3 not move a muscle,** keep perfectly still. *—v.* **muscle in,** *Slang.* force oneself into a situation where one is not wanted. [< F < L *musculus,* dim. of *mus* mouse; from the appearance of certain muscles] **—Syn.** *n.* **2** brawn, sinew.

mus·cle-bound (mus′əl bound′) *adj.* having some of the muscles stiff or tight, usually as a result of too much or too little exercise.

mus·cle·man (mus′əl man′) *n.* **-men** (-men′). **1** *Informal.* a brawny, muscular man. **2** *Slang.* a ruffian; strong-arm man.

Mus·co·vite (mus′kə vīt′) *n.* **1** a native or inhabitant of Muscovy; Russian. **2** a native or inhabitant of Moscow. **3 muscovite,** a light-colored variety of mica. *—adj.* **1** of or having to do with Muscovy; Russian. **2** of or having to do with Moscow.

Mus·co·vy (mus′kə vē) *n. Archaic.* **1** originally, the principality of Moscow. **2** Russia.

Muscovy duck **1** a breed of large, crested, greenish-black ducks, originally native from Mexico to South America, but now widely domesticated. **2** a duck of this breed. [for *musk duck*]

mus·cu·lar (mus′kyů lər) *adj.* **1** of the muscles; influencing the muscles: *a muscular strain.* **2** having well-developed muscles; strong: *a muscular arm.* **3** consisting of muscle. **—Syn. 2** sinewy, brawny, powerful. **—mus′cu·lar·ly,** *adv.*

muscular dystrophy a disease characterized by progressive degeneration of the muscles and nerves.

mus·cu·lar·i·ty (mus′kyů lar′ə tē) *n.* muscular development or strength.

mus·cu·la·ture (mus′kyů lə chər or mus′kyů lə chůr′) *n.* a system or arrangement of muscles. [< F]

muse (mūz) *v.* **mused, mus·ing. 1** think in a dreamy way; think; meditate. **2** look thoughtfully. **3** say thoughtfully. [ME < OF *muser* loiter] **—mus′er,** *n.* **—Syn. 1** ponder, reflect, ruminate.

Muse (mūz) *n.* **1** in Greek mythology, one of the nine goddesses of the fine arts and sciences. The best-known of the Muses are Calliope, Clio, Melpomene, Terpsichore, and Thalia. **2 muse,** the spirit that inspires a poet or composer. [ME < OF < L *Musa* < Gk. *Mousa*]

mu·sette (mū zet′) *n.* **1 a** a gentle pastoral air written for a bagpipe, or imitating the effect of a bagpipe. **b** a dance for this air. **2** a kind of bagpipe. **3** a musette bag. [< F < OF *musette* < *muse* bagpipe < *muser* play the musette]

musette bag a small bag carried by means of a shoulder strap, used by soldiers and hikers to carry food, belongings, etc.

mu·se·um (mū zē′əm) *n.* the building or rooms where a collection of objects illustrating science, art, ancient life, or other subjects is kept. [< L < Gk. *mouseion* seat of the Muses < *Mousa* Muse]

mush¹ (mush) *n.* **1** *Esp.U.S.* corn meal boiled in water. **2** any soft, thick mass. **3** *Informal.* weak sentiment; sentimentality; silly talk. [var. of *mash*; cf. Du. *moes*]

mush² (mush) *n.* **1** a command to advance given to sled dogs. **2** a journey made by dogsled, especially while driving the team from behind the sled. *—v.* **1** urge sled dogs onward by shouting commands: *He mushed his dog team through the blinding storm.* **2** follow a dogsled on foot: *For six days he mushed across the barren lands.* [< F *marche* (*donc*), a command to horses < *marcher* go, walk] **—mush′er,** *n.*

mush·mel·on (mush′mel′ən) *n.* muskmelon; cantaloupe.

mush·room (mush′rüm or -rům) *n.* **1** a small fungus, often umbrella-shaped, that grows very fast. Some mushrooms are edible; some are poisonous. **2** anything shaped or growing like a mushroom. *—adj.* **1** of or like a mushroom. **2** made of or with mushrooms: *mushroom soup.* **3** of very rapid growth. *—v.* **1** grow very fast: *The little town mushroomed into a city.* **2** flatten at one end. A bullet sometimes mushrooms when it hits a very hard object. [ME < OF *mousseron* < LL *mussirio, -onis*]

Mushroom stalks (2 to 5 in. high)

mushroom cloud a rapidly rising mushroom-shaped cloud of radio-active matter that follows a nuclear explosion.

mush·y (mush′ē) *adj.* **mush·i·er, mush·i·est. 1** like mush; pulpy. **2** *Informal.* weakly sentimental. **—mush′i·ly,** *adv.* **—mush′i·ness,** *n.*

mu·sic (mū′zik) *n.* **1** the art of organizing sounds of varying pitch and volume into rhythmical patterns for vocal or instrumental reproduction. **2** such an organization of sounds; a musical composition or compositions. **3** the science or principles governing this art. **4** a succession of pleasant sounds: *the music of the wind.* **5 a** signs or symbols used to write or print music. **b** written or printed music using these signs or symbols. **6** responsiveness to, or appreciation of, musical sounds. **7 face the music,** *Informal.* meet difficulties or punishment resulting from one's actions. **8 set to music,** provide (the words of a song) with music. [ME < OF *musique* < L *musica* < Gk. *mousikē* (*technē*) art of the Muse < *Mousa* Muse]

mu·si·cal (mū′zə kəl) *adj.* **1** of or having to do with music. **2** capable of producing music; intended for playing music: *musical instruments.* **3** like music; melodious and pleasant. **4** set to music or accompanied by music. **5** fond of music. **6** skilled in music; talented as a musician. *—n.* **1** a stage entertainment or motion picture in which a story is told through music, singing, and dancing. **2** *Informal.* musicale.

musical chairs an elimination game in which players march to music around chairs numbering always one less than the players. When the music stops, everyone rushes to sit down and the person left standing is eliminated.

musical comedy a gay and amusing play in which plot and characterization are less important than singing, dancing, and costumes.

mu·si·cale (mū′zə kal′) *n.* a social gathering to enjoy music. [< F *musicale,* short for *soirée musicale* musical evening]

musical instrument **1** any stringed, wind, or percussion instrument, as a violin, trumpet, or drum, employed, or designed to be employed in producing music or musical sounds. **2** an electronic instrument used to produce, not reproduce, musical sounds.

mu·si·cal·i·ty (mū′zə kal′ə tē) *n.* **1** ability or skill in playing, conducting, or composing music. **2** musical quality.

mu·si·cal·ly (mū′zik lē) *adv.* **1** in a musical manner.

2 in music: *She is well educated musically.*

music box a box or case containing apparatus for producing music mechanically.

music drama 1 a type of opera in which words and music are intimately linked, the music's prime purpose being to indicate dramatic development, character, mood, etc.: *Wagner's "Lohengrin" is a music drama.* 2 any opera.

music hall 1 a hall for musical entertainments. 2 *Esp. Brit.* a theatre for vaudeville.

mu·si·cian (mū zish′ən) *n.* 1 a person skilled in music. 2 a person who sings, plays a musical instrument, or conducts a band or orchestra, especially one who earns a living in this way. 3 a composer of music.

mu·si·co·log·i·cal (mū′zə kə loj′ə kəl) *adj.* of or having to do with musicology.

mu·si·col·o·gist (mū′zə kol′ə jist) *n.* a specialist in musicology.

mu·si·col·o·gy (mū′zə kol′ə jē) *n.* the study of the forms, principles, literature, and history of music.

mus·ing (mūz′ing) *adj.* dreamy; meditative; absorbed in thought.

musk (musk) *n.* 1 a a substance with a strong and lasting odor, used in making perfumes. Musk is found in a special gland in the male musk deer. b a strong-smelling substance found in the glands of other animals, as the mink and muskrat. 2 an artificial imitation of this substance. 3 the odor of musk. 4 the musk deer or any animal like it, or one that has a musky smell. 5 any plant whose leaves or flowers smell like musk, such as the musk rose. [ME < OF < LL *muscus* < LGk. *moschos* < Persian *mushk* < Skt. *mushka* testicle]

musk deer a small, hornless deer of central Asia, the male of which has a gland containing musk.

mus·keg (mus′keg) *n. Cdn.* 1 a swamp or marsh. 2 an area of bog composed of decaying plant life, especially moss: *There are vast regions of muskeg in northern Alberta.* [< Algonquian; cf. Cree *muskak* swamp]

mus·kel·lunge (mus′kə lunj′) *n.* **-lunge.** a very large freshwater fish of the pike family: *The muskellunge is highly valued as a food and game fish.* [< Algonquian (Ojibwa) *mashkinonge* great pike]

mus·ket (mus′kit) *n.* formerly, a kind of gun. Soldiers used muskets before rifles were invented. [< F *mousquet* < Ital. *moschetto*, originally, a kind of hawk < *mosca* fly < L *musca*]

mus·ket·eer (mus′kə tēr′) *n.* a soldier armed with a musket.

mus·ket·ry (mus′kit rē) *n.* 1 muskets. 2 the act of shooting with muskets or rifles. 3 soldiers armed with muskets.

mus·kie (mus′kē) *n. Cdn. Informal.* muskellunge.

musk·mel·on (musk′mel′ən) *n.* 1 a kind of sweet, edible, juicy melon; cantaloupe. 2 the plant it grows on.

musk-ox (musk′oks′) *n.* **-ox** or **-ox·en.** an arctic mammal having a shaggy coat and a strong, musky smell. The musk-ox looks like a sheep in some ways and like an ox in others.

musk·rat (musk′rat′) *n.* **-rats** or (*esp. collectively*) **-rat.** 1 a water rodent of North America, having a musky odor and resembling a rat, but larger. 2 its valuable dark-brown fur. 3 a coat or other garment made of this fur.

musk·y (mus′kē) *adj.* **musk·i·er, musk·i·est.** of musk; like musk; like that of musk: *a musky odor.*

Mus·lem or **Mus·lim** (muz′ləm or mus′ləm) *n. adj.* Moslem.

mus·lin (muz′lən) *n.* 1 a thin, fine cotton cloth, used for dresses, curtains, etc. 2 a heavier cotton cloth, used for sheets, undergarments, etc. —*adj.* made of muslin. [< F < Ital. *mussolina* < *Mussolo* Mosul, a city in Iraq]

Mus.M. Master of Music. (for L *Musicae Magister*)

mus·pike (mus′pīk′) *n. Cdn.* a hybrid game fish crossbred from muskellunge and pike.

mus·quash (mus′kwosh) *n.* **-quash.** muskrat.

muss (mus) *Informal.* —*v.* 1 put into disorder; rumple. 2 smear or soil; mess: *muss up one's hands.* —*n.* disorder; a mess. [var. of *mess*]

hat, āge, cãre, fär; let, ēqual, tėrm; it, īce
hot, ōpen, ôrder; oil, out; cup, put, rüle, ūse
əbove, takən, pencəl, lemən, circəs
ch, child; ng, long; sh, ship
th, thin; ᴛʜ, then; zh, measure

mus·sel (mus′əl) *n.* 1 an edible salt-water mollusc that looks like a small clam, having black, hinged shells. 2 a freshwater mollusc whose shells are used in making buttons. 3 any mollusc of the same family as these. [OE *muscle, musle* < L *musculus* mussel, muscle. See MUSCLE.]

Mus·sul·man (mus′əl mən) *n.* **-mans.** Moslem. [< Persian *musulmān*, adj., Mohammedan < *muslim* a Moslem < Arabic *muslim.* See MOSLEM.]

muss·y (mus′ē) *adj.* **muss·i·er, muss·i·est.** *Informal.* untidy; messy; rumpled. —**muss′i·ly,** *adv.*

must[1] (must; *unstressed,* məst) *auxiliary verb.* **must,** *n. adj.* —*aux. v.* 1 be obliged to; be forced to: *Man must eat to live.* 2 ought to; should: *I must go home soon.* 3 be certain to: *I must seem very rude.* 4 be supposed or expected to: *You must have that book.* 5 *Must* is sometimes, when motion is implied, used with its verb omitted: *We must to horse. We must away.*
—*n.* something necessary; obligation: *This rule is a must.*
—*adj. Informal.* demanding attention or doing; necessary: *a must item, must legislation.* [OE *mōste,* pt. of *mōtan* mote[2]]

must[2] (must) *n.* the unfermented juice of the grape; new wine. [OE < L (*vinum*) *mustum* fresh (wine)]

must[3] (must) *n.* a musty condition; mould. —*v.* make musty; become musty. [< *musty*]

mus·tache (mus′tash or məs tash′) *n.* 1 the hair that grows on the upper lip, especially when groomed and not shaved smooth. 2 the hair growing on any person's upper lip. 3 the hairs or bristles growing near the mouth of an animal. Also, **moustache.** [< F < Ital. < Med.L *mustacia* < Gk. *mystax* upper lip, mustache]

mus·ta·chio (məs tä′shō or məs tä′shē ō′) *n.* **-chios.** mustache.

mus·tang (mus′tang) *n.* the small, wild or half-wild horse of the North American plains. [< Sp. *mestengo* untamed]

mus·tard (mus′tərd) *n.* 1 a yellow powder or paste used as seasoning to give food a pungent taste. 2 the plant from whose seeds it is made. 3 a dark-yellow color. [ME < OF *moustarde,* ult. < L *mustum* must[2]]

mustard gas a poison gas that causes burns, blindness, and death. *Formula:* $(ClCH_2CH_2)_2S$

mustard plaster a poultice made of mustard and water, or of mustard, flour, and water.

mustard seed the seed of the mustard plant.

mus·ter (mus′tər) *v.* 1 assemble; gather together; collect: *muster soldiers.* 2 summon: *muster up courage.* 3 **muster in,** enlist. 4 **muster out,** discharge.
—*n.* 1 an assembly; collection. 2 a bringing together of men or troops for review or service. 3 the list of those mustered. 4 the number mustered. 5 **pass muster,** be inspected and approved; come up to the required standards. [ME < OF *mostrer* < L *monstrare* show < *monstrum* portent] —**Syn.** *v.* 1 convene, marshal, array.

must·n't (mus′ənt) must not.

mus·ty (mus′tē) *adj.* **-ti·er, -ti·est.** 1 having a smell or taste suggesting mould or damp; mouldy: *a musty room, musty crackers.* 2 stale; out-of-date: *musty laws.* 3 lacking vigor; dull: *a musty old fellow.* [? < *moisty* < *moist* + -y[1]] —**mus′ti·ly,** *adv.* —**mus′ti·ness,** *n.*

mu·ta·bil·i·ty (mū′tə bil′ə tē) *n.* 1 a tendency to change. 2 fickleness.

mu·ta·ble (mū′tə bəl) *adj.* 1 liable to change: *mutable customs.* 2 fickle: *a mutable person.* [< L *mutabilis* < *mutare* change] —**Syn.** 1 changeable, variable.

mu·tant (mū′tənt) *n.* a new variety of plant or animal resulting from mutation.

mu·tate (mū′tāt or mū tāt′) *v.* **-tat·ed, -tat·ing.** 1 change.

2 produce mutations. 3 change by umlaut.

mu·ta·tion (mū tā′shən) *n.* 1 a change; alteration. 2 in biology: a a new feature that appears suddenly in animals or plants and can be inherited. b a new variety of animal or plant formed in this way. 3 an umlaut. [< L *mutatio, -onis* < *mutare* change]

mu·ta·tis mu·tan·dis (mū tā′tis mū tan′dis) *Latin.* with the necessary changes.

mute (mūt) *adj. n. v.* **mut·ed, mut·ing.** —*adj.* 1 not making any sound; silent. 2 unable to speak; dumb. 3 of alphabetical letters, not pronounced. The *e* in *mute* is mute.
—*n.* 1 a person who cannot speak. 2 a clip or some other device put on a musical instrument to soften the sound. 3 a silent letter.
—*v.* put a clip or some other device on (a musical instrument) to soften the sound. [< L *mutus*] —**mute′ly,** *adv.* —**mute′ness,** *n.* —**Syn.** *adj.* 1, 2 See **dumb.**

mu·ti·late (mū′tə lāt′) *v.* **-lat·ed, -lat·ing.** 1 cut, tear, or break off a part of; injure seriously by cutting, tearing, or breaking off some part: *The victims of the accident were badly mutilated; some lost arms, some lost legs.* 2 make (a story, song, etc.) imperfect by removing parts. [< L *mutilare* < *mutilus* maimed] —**mu′ti·la′tor,** *n.* —**Syn.** 1 maim, mangle, disfigure.

mu·ti·la·tion (mū′tə lā′shən) *n.* 1 the art or process of mutilating. 2 the state of being mutilated.

mu·ti·neer (mū′tə nēr′) *n.* a person who takes part in a mutiny. [< MF *mutinier*]

mu·ti·nous (mū′tə nəs) *adj.* rebellious. —**mu′ti·nous·ly,** *adv.* —**Syn.** riotous, insubordinate.

mu·ti·ny (mū′tə nē) *n.* **-nies,** *v.* **-nied, -ny·ing.** —*n.* an open rebellion against lawful authority, especially by sailors or soldiers against their officers. —*v.* take part in a mutiny; rebel. [< obs. *mutine* revolt < OF *mutiner* < *mutin* rebellious, ult. < L *movere* move] —**Syn.** *n.* insurrection, revolt, uprising. -*v.* revolt.

mutt (mut) *n. Slang.* 1 a dog, especially a mongrel. 2 a stupid person. [origin uncertain]

mut·ter (mut′ər) *v.* 1 speak softly and indistinctly with lips partly closed. 2 complain; grumble —*n.* 1 the act of muttering. 2 muttered words. [ME *mutere(n)*; probably imitative] —**mut′ter·er,** *n.* —**Syn.** *v.* 1 See **murmur.**

mut·ton (mut′ən) *n.* the meat from a sheep. [ME < OF *moton* < Med.L *multo, -onis* ram < Celtic]

mutton chop 1 a small piece of mutton, usually from the ribs or loin, for broiling or frying. 2 a patch of whiskers on each side of the face, shaped somewhat like a chop.

Mutton chop (def. 2)

mu·tu·al (mū′chü əl) *adj.* 1 done, said, felt, etc. by each toward the other; given and received: *mutual promises, mutual dislike.* 2 each to the other: *mutual enemies.* 3 *Informal.* belonging to each of several: *our mutual friend.* 4 of or having to do with mutual insurance: *a mutual company.* —*n.* 1 a mutual insurance company. 2 a mutual fund. [< L *mutuus* reciprocal] —**mu′tu·al·ly,** *adv.* —**Syn.** *adj.* 1 reciprocal. ☛ See **common** for usage note.

mutual fund a financial organization that invests the pooled capital of its members in diversified securities.

mutual insurance or **plan** a system of insurance by which the policyholders own the company and share the gains and losses of a common fund.

mu·tu·al·i·ty (mū′chü al′ə tē) *n.* the state or quality of being mutual.

mu·u·mu·u (mü′mü′; *Hawaiian,* mü′ü mü′ü) *n.* a woman's long, loose, flowing gown that is gathered at the neckline. [< Hawaiian]

Mu·zak (mū′zak) *n. Trademark.* music that is transmitted by telephone or FM radio, used by restaurants, offices, public areas, etc.

mu·zhik (mü zhik′ or mü′zhik) *n.* a Russian peasant. Also, **moujik, mujik.** [< Russian]

muz·zle (muz′əl) *n. v.* **-zled, -zling.** —*n.* 1 the nose, mouth, and jaws of a four-footed animal. 2 a cover of straps or wires for putting over an animal's head to keep it from biting or eating. 3 the open front end of a gun, pistol, rifle, etc. 4 **put a muzzle on,** prevent persons, newspapers, etc. from expressing free opinions.
—*v.* 1 put a muzzle (def. 2) on. 2 compel to keep silent about something; prevent from expressing views: *The government muzzled the newspapers during the recent rebellion.* [ME < OF *musel* < *muse* muzzle] —**muz′zler,** *n.*

muz·zle·load·er (muz′əl lōd′ər) *n.* a muzzleloading gun.

muz·zle·load·ing (muz′əl lōd′ing) *adj.* of firearms, loaded by putting gunpowder in through the open front end of the barrel and ramming it down.

MVD the Ministry of Internal Affairs of the Soviet Union; the secret police, formerly called OGPU and, later, NKVD.

M.V.O. Member of the (Royal) Victorian Order.

my (mī) *adj.* of me; belonging to me: *my house.* —*interj. Informal.* an exclamation of surprise. [OE *mīn*]
☛ **My, mine** are the possessive forms of *I. My* is always followed by a noun: *This is my hat. Mine* stands alone: *This hat is mine.*

my·ce·li·um (mī sē′lē əm) *n.* **-li·a** (-lē ə). the main part of a fungus, consisting of interwoven fibres. [< NL < Gk. *mykēs* mushroom]

My·ce·nae (mī sē′nē) *n.* in ancient times, a city in Greece.

My·ce·nae·an (mī′sə nē′ən) *adj.* of or having to do with Mycenae or the civilization that flourished there.

my·col·o·gy (mī kol′ə jē) *n.* the branch of botany that deals with fungi. [< Gk. *mykēs* fungus + E *-logy*]

my·na or **my·nah** (mī′nə) *n.* any of various Asiatic starlings. They can mimic human speech and are often trained and kept as pets. [< Hind. *maina*]

my·o·pi·a (mī ō′pē ə) *n.* 1 near-sightedness. 2 shortsightedness: *intellectual myopia.* [< NL < Gk. *myōps,* ult. < *myein* shut + *ōps* eye]

my·op·ic (mī op′ik) *adj.* near-sighted.

myr·i·ad (mir′ē əd) *n.* 1 ten thousand. 2 an extremely large number: *There are myriads of stars.* —*adj.* 1 ten thousand. 2 countless. [< LL < Gk. *myrias, -ados* ten thousand, myriad]

myr·i·a·pod (mir′ē ə pod′) *n.* an arthropod having a wormlike body with many segments and many legs. Centipedes and millipedes are myriapods. [< Gk. *myrias* myriad + *pous, podos* foot]

Myr·mi·don (mėr′mə don′) *n.* 1 in Greek mythology, a member of a warlike people of ancient Thessaly who accompanied Achilles, their king, to the Trojan War. 2 **myrmidon,** a an obedient and unquestioning follower. b a policeman; bailiff.

myrrh (mėr) *n.* a fragrant, gummy substance with a bitter taste, used in medicines, perfumes, and incense. It is obtained from a shrub that grows in Arabia and E. Africa. [OE *myrre* < L *myrrha* < Gk. *myrra,* ult. < Semitic]

myr·tle (mėr′təl) *n.* 1 an evergreen shrub of S. Europe having shiny leaves, fragrant, white flowers, and black berries. 2 a low, creeping evergreen vine having blue flowers; periwinkle. [ME < OF *mirtile,* dim. of L *myrtus* < Gk. *myrtos*]

my·self (mī self′) *pron.* **ourselves.** 1 the emphatic form of **me** or **I**: *I myself will go.* 2 the reflexive form of **me**: *I hurt myself.* 3 my real or true self; my normal self: *I am not myself today.*

My·si·a (mish′ē ə) *n.* in ancient times, a country in Asia Minor.

mys·te·ri·ous (mis tēr′ē əs) *adj.* 1 full of mystery; hard to explain or understand; secret; hidden. 2 suggesting mystery. —**mys·te′ri·ous·ly,** *adv.* —**mys·te′ri·ous·ness,** *n.*
Syn. 1 **Mysterious, inscrutable** = hard to explain or understand. **Mysterious** describes a person, thing, or situation about which there is something secret, hidden, or unknown that arouses curiosity, conjecture, or wonder: *She had a mysterious telephone call.* **Inscrutable** describes a thing that is so mysterious or such a riddle that it is impossible to make out its meaning, or a person who keeps his feelings, thoughts, and intentions completely hidden: *His mother began to cry, but his father's face was inscrutable.*

mys·ter·y[1] (mis′tər ē or mis′trē) *n.* **-ter·ies.** 1 a secret; something that is hidden or unknown. 2 secrecy;

obscurity. **3** a novel, story, etc. in which suspense is derived from calculated development of a crime, or crimes, with the solution comprising the dénouement: *a writer of mysteries.* **4** something that is not explained or understood. **5** a religious idea or doctrine that human reason cannot understand. **6** a secret religious rite to which only initiated persons are admitted. **7** a mystery play. **8 a** a sacramental rite of the Christian religion. **b** the Eucharist; Communion; Mass. [ME < L < Gk. *mystērion* < *mystēs* an initiate < *myein* close (i.e., the lips or eyes)] —**Syn. 1** enigma.

mys·ter·y[2] (mis′tər ē or mis′trē) *n.* **-ter·ies.** *Archaic.* **1** a craft; trade. **2** an association of craftsmen or merchants; guild. [< Med.L *misterium* for L *ministerium* ministry; form influenced by *mystery*[1]]

mystery play a play based on the Bible, so called because such plays were performed by members of a "mystery" or medieval guild.

mys·tic (mis′tik) *adj.* **1** mystical. **2** having to do with the ancient religious mysteries or other occult rites: *mystic arts.* **3** of or having to do with mystics or mysticism. **4** of hidden meaning or nature; enigmatical; mysterious. —*n.* a person who believes that truth or God can be known through spiritual insight. [< L < Gk. *mystikos* < *mystēs* an initiate. See MYSTERY[1].]

mys·ti·cal (mis′tə kəl) *adj.* **1** having some secret meaning; beyond human understanding; mysterious. **2** spiritually symbolic: *The lamb and the dove are mystical symbols of the Christian religion.* **3** of or concerned with mystics or mysticism. **4** of or having to do with secret rites open only to the initiated. —**mys′ti·cal·ly,** *adv.* —**mys′ti·cal·ness,** *n.*

mys·ti·cism (mis′tə siz′əm) *n.* **1** the beliefs or mode of thought of mystics. **2** the doctrine that truth or God may be known through spiritual insight, independent of the mind.

mys·ti·fi·ca·tion (mis′tə fə kā′shən) *n.* **1** a mystifying or being mystified; bewilderment; perplexity. **2** something that mystifies or is designed to mystify.

mys·ti·fy (mis′tə fī′) *v.* **-fied, -fy·ing. 1** bewilder purposely; puzzle; perplex: *The magician's tricks mystified the audience.* **2** make mysterious; involve in mystery. [< F *mystifier* < *mystique* mystic (< L *mysticus*; see MYSTIC) + *-fier* < L *-ficare* make < *-ficus* making < *facere* make] —**mys′ti·fi′er,** *n.* —**Syn. 1** confuse, nonplus.

mys·tique (mis tēk′) *n.* **1** a mystical or peculiar way of interpreting reality, especially one associated with a cult or doctrine and acting as a guide to action. **2** an atmosphere of mystery associated with a particular person, institution, profession, etc. **3** any highly specialized skill or technique admired by the layman.

myth (mith) *n.* **1** a legend or story about events in some supernatural world often attempting to account for something in nature. The myth of Proserpina is the ancient Greek explanation of summer and winter. **2** any invented story. **3** an imaginary person or thing: *Her wealthy uncle was a myth invented to impress the other girls.* [< NL < LL < Gk. *mythos* word, story]
☛ See **legend** for usage note.

myth. mythology.

myth·ic (mith′ik) *adj.* mythical.

myth·i·cal (mith′ə kəl) *adj.* **1** of myths; like a myth; in myths. **2** not real; made-up; imaginary. —**myth′i·cal·ly,** *adv.* —**Syn. 2** fictitious.

myth·o·log·i·cal (mith′ə loj′ə kəl) *adj.* of or having to do with mythology.

myth·o·log·i·cal·ly (mith′ə loj′ik lē) *adv.* according to mythology.

my·thol·o·gist (mi thol′ə jist) *n.* **1** a writer of myths. **2** a person who knows much about mythology.

my·thol·o·gy (mi thol′ə jē) *n.* **-gies. 1** a body of myths relating to a particular country or person: *Greek mythology.* **2** myths collectively: *Mythology is an aspect of religion.* **3** the study of myths. **4** a book of myths; treatise on myths. [< LL < Gk. *mythologia* < *mythos* word, story + *logos* word, discourse]

myx·o·ma·to·sis (mik′sō mə tō′sis) *n.* a usually fatal disease of rabbits, sometimes induced by inoculation with the virus. [< Gk. *myxa* mucus + E *-oma* + *-osis*]

hat, āge, cãre, fär; let, ēqual, tėrm; it, īce
hot, ōpen, ôrder; oil, out; cup, pu̇t, rüle, ūse
əbove, takən, pencəl, lemən, circəs
ch, child; ng, long; sh, ship
th, thin; TH, then; zh, measure

N or **n** (en) *n.* **N's** or **n's. 1** the fourteenth letter of the English alphabet. **2** any speech sound represented by this letter. **3** one (usually fourteenth) of a series designated alphabetically. **4** in printing, an en; half the width of an em. **5** in mathematics, an indefinite number. See **nth.**

n in algebra, an indefinite number.

n. 1 born. (for L *natus*) **2** name. **3** noun. **4** neuter. **5** north. **6** northern. **7** nominative. **8** new. **9** number. **10** in chemistry, normal. **11** net. **12** nephew. **13** noon.

N 1 nitrogen. **2** North. **3** Northern.

N. 1 North. **2** Northern. **3** New. **4** Noon. **5** November. **6** Nationalist. **7** Norse. **8** Navy.

Na sodium. (for L *natrium*)

N.A. 1 North America. **2** not applicable.

NAACP in the United States, National Association for the Advancement of Colored People.

nab (nab) *v.* **nabbed, nab·bing.** *Slang.* **1** catch or seize suddenly; grab. **2** arrest: *The police soon nabbed the thief.* [earlier *nap*, probably < Scand.; cf. Swedish *nappa* catch, snatch]

na·bob (nā′bob) *n.* **1** a nawab (def. 1 a). **2** a very rich man, especially one who lives on a lavish scale. **3** any important person. [< Hind. *nabab*, colloquial var. of *nav(v)ab*. See NAWAB.]

na·celle (nə sel′) *n.* of an aircraft, an enclosed part containing an engine or passengers. [< F < L *navicella*, double dim. of *navis* ship]

na·cre (nā′kər) *n.* mother-of-pearl. [< F < OItal. *naccara* drum < Arabic < *naqir* hollowed]

na·dir (nā′dər) *n.* **1** the point in the heavens directly beneath the place where one stands; point opposite the zenith. **2** the lowest point. [ME < OF < Arabic *nadir* opposite (i.e., to the zenith)]

ZENITH
180°
OBSERVER ON EARTH
NADIR

nae (nā) *adj. adv. Scottish.* no.

nag[1] (nag) *v.* **nagged, nag·ging. 1** irritate or annoy by peevish complaints; scold. **2** find fault with (a person) all the time. [< Scand.; cf. Icelandic *nagga* grumble. Akin to GNAW.] —**nag′ger,** *n.* —**Syn.** torment.

nag[2] (nag) *n.* **1** *Informal.* a horse, especially an inferior horse. **2** a small riding horse. [ME; cf. Du. *negge*]

Nah. Nahum.

Na·hua·tl (nä′wä təl) *n.* any of a group of languages spoken by the Aztecs, Toltecs, and other American Indian tribes of central Mexico and parts of Central America. —*adj.* of or having to do with this group of languages.

nai·ad (nī′ad or nā′ad) *n.* **-ads, -a·des** (-ə dēz′). **1** Also, **Naiad.** in Greek and Roman mythology, a nymph guarding a stream or spring. **2** a girl swimmer. [< L < Gk. *Naias, -ados* (related to *naein* flow)]

nail (nāl) *n.* **1** a slender piece of metal to be hammered into or through wood to hold separate pieces together or to be used as a peg. **2** a thin, horny plate on the upper side of the end of a finger or toe. **3 hard as nails, a** tough; physically fit. **b** without pity; merciless. **4 hit the nail on the head,** *Informal.* guess or understand correctly; say or do something just right. **5 on the nail,** *Informal.* at once; immediately; without delay.
—*v.* **1** fasten with a nail or nails. **2** *Informal.* hold or keep fixed. **3** *Informal.* catch; seize. **4** *Informal.* secure by prompt action; catch; seize. **5** *Informal.* detect and expose (a lie, etc.). [OE *nægel*] —**nail′er,** *n.*

nail·set (nāl′set′) *n.* a tool for driving nails beneath the surface.

nain·sook (nān′su̇k or nan′su̇k) *n.* a soft cotton cloth. [< Hind. *nainsukh* < *nain* eye + *sukh* pleasure]

na·ïve or **na·ive** (nī ēv′; *French,* nä ēv′) *adj.* simple in nature; like a child; artless; not sophisticated: *For a grown man he had a very naïve attitude toward the problem.* [< F *naïve*, fem. of *naïf* < L *nativus*. Doublet of NATIVE.] —**na·ïve′ly** or **na·ive′ly,** *adv.* —**Syn.** unaffected, artless, unsophisticated, natural, open, sincere.

na·ïve·te or **na·ive·te** (nī ēv′ tā or nī ēv′ə tā′; *French,* nä ēv′ tā′) *n.* **1** the quality of being naïve; unspoiled freshness. **2** a naïve action, remark, etc. [< F]

na·ked (nā′kid) *adj.* **1** with no clothes on; bare. **2** not covered; stripped: *naked fields.* **3** not protected; exposed: *a naked sword.* **4** without addition of anything else; plain: *the naked truth.* **5 naked eye,** the eye not helped by any glass, telescope, or microscope. [OE *nacod*] —**na′ked·ly,** *adv.* —**na′ked·ness,** *n.* —**Syn. 1** nude, unclothed, undressed. See **bare. 2** uncovered. **3** unprotected. **4** simple.

N.Am. North America.

nam·a·ble (nām′ə bəl) *adj.* that can be named.

nam·ay·cush (nam′ā kůsh′) *n.* **-cush.** *Cdn. Rare.* lake trout. [< Algonquian]

nam·by-pam·by (nam′bē pam′bē) *adj. n.* **-bies.** —*adj.* weakly simple or sentimental; insipid: *Valentines are often namby-pamby.* —*n.* **1** namby-pamby talk or writing. **2** a namby-pamby person. [alteration of *Nam*, short for *Ambrose* Philips, (1674-1749), a British poet ridiculed by Alexander Pope]

name (nām) *n. v.* **named, nam·ing.** —*n.* **1** the word or words by which a person, animal, place, or thing is spoken of or to. **2** a word or words applied descriptively; an appellation, title, or epithet: *the name of a friend.* **3** the persons grouped under one name; family; clan; tribe. **4** reputation; fame: *This honest man is proud of his good name.* **5 call names,** call bad names; swear at; curse. **6 in name only,** supposed to be, but not really so. **7 in the name of, a** with appeal to the name of. **b** on the authority of; acting for: *He bought the car in the name of his wife.* **8 know only by name,** know only by hearing about. **9 to one's name,** belonging to one.
—*v.* **1** give a name to: *name a newborn baby.* **2** call by name; mention by name: *Three persons were named in the report.* **3** give the right name for: *Can you name these flowers?* **4** mention; speak of; state: *name several reasons.* **5** specify or fix: *name a price.* **6** choose for some duty or office; nominate: *John was named captain of the team.* [OE *nama*] —**nam′er,** *n.*

Syn. *n.* **2 Name, title** = what someone or something is called. **Name** is used of a descriptive or characterizing word or phrase applied to a person or thing because of certain qualities or acts or to express an attitude toward him (or it): "*Gastown*" *was an old name for Vancouver.* **Title** is used of a descriptive or characterizing name given to a book, song, play, etc. or to a person as a sign of honor, rank, office, occupation: *His title is Secretary.* **4** renown, note. *-v.* **1** denominate, entitle, call. **2** designate. **6** appoint, select.

name-call·ing (nām′kol′ing or -kôl′ing) *n.* the act or fact of giving a bad name to a person; slandering; defamation.

name day 1 the feast day of the saint whose name one bears. **2** the day on which a child is named; baptismal day.

name-drop·ping (nām′drop′ing) *n.* the act or habit of mentioning the names of famous people frequently in familiar or casual conversation, so as to convey the impression that one has met them or is familiar with them. —**name′-drop′per,** *n.*

name·less (nām′lis) *adj.* **1** having no name: *a nameless grave.* **2** that cannot be named or described: *a strange, nameless longing.* **3** not fit to be mentioned: *nameless crimes.* **4** not named: *a book by a nameless author.* **5** unknown to fame; obscure. —**name′less·ly,** *adv.* —**name′less·ness,** *n.*

name·ly (nām′lē) *adv.* that is to say: *The railway connects two cities, namely, Toronto and Montreal.*

name·sake (nām′sāk′) *n.* a person having the same name as another; especially, one named after another. [for *name's sake*]

nan·keen or **nan·kin** (nan kēn′) *n.* **1** a firm, yellow or buff cloth. **2 nankeens,** *pl.* trousers made of nankeen. [alteration of *Nanking*, China]

nan·ny (nan′ē) *n.* **-nies.** *Informal.* **1** a woman hired to look after the children of a family. **2** a nanny goat.

nan·ny goat *Informal.* a female goat.

nano- *combining form.* **1** exceedingly small. **2** in technical use, one billionth of, as in nanosecond. [< Gk. *nanos* dwarf]

na·no·sec·ond (nā′nə sek′ənd or nan′ə-) *n.* a billionth of a second. [< *nano-* + *second*]

Nantes (nants; *French,* näNt) *n.* **Edict of,** an edict issued in 1598 by Henry IV of France securing for the French Protestants full civil rights, liberty of conscience, partial freedom of public worship, and the temporary possession of certain fortified cities. This edict was revoked in 1685. [< *Nantes*, France, where the edict was signed]

Na·o·mi (nā′ō′mē or nā′ō mē) *n.* in the Bible, Ruth's mother-in-law, from whom Ruth refused to part.

nap[1] (nap) *n. v.* **napped, nap·ping.** —*n.* a short sleep. [< v.] —*v.* **1** take a short sleep. **2 catch napping,** find off guard; take unprepared: *The test caught me napping.* [OE *hnappian* sleep lightly]

nap[2] (nap) *n.* the soft, short, woolly threads or hairs on the surface of cloth: *the nap on velvet or flannelette.* [ME *noppe* < MDu. or MLG] —**nap′less,** *adj.*

na·palm (nā′pom′, nā′päm′, or nap′om) *n.* **1** a chemical substance used to thicken gasoline for use in certain military weapons, especially incendiary bombs. **2** the thickened gasoline. [< *na*phthenic and *palm*itic acids, used in its manufacture]

nape (nāp) *n.* the back of the neck. [ME; origin uncertain]

na·per·y (nā′pər ē or nāp′rē) *n.* tablecloths, serviettes, and doilies. [ME < OF *naperie* < *nape* < L *mappa* napkin]

naph·tha (nap′thə or naf′thə) *n.* an inflammable liquid distilled from petroleum, coal tar, etc., used as fuel and to remove spots from clothing. [< L < Gk. *naphtha*, originally, an inflammable liquid issuing from the earth < Iranian]

naph·tha·lene or **naph·tha·line** (naf′thə lēn′ or nap′thə lēn′) *n.* a white crystalline hydrocarbon, usually distilled from coal tar, used in making moth balls, dyes, disinfectants, etc. *Formula:* $C_{10}H_8$ [< *naphtha*]

naph·tha·lin (naf′thə lin or nap′thə lin) *n.* naphthalene.

naph·thol (naf′thol or naf′thôl, nap′thol or nap′thôl) *n.* a colorless crystalline substance obtained from naphthalene, used in making dyes, as an antiseptic, etc. [< *naphtha*]

nap·kin (nap′kin) *n.* **1** a piece of cloth used at meals for protecting the clothing or for wiping the lips or fingers; serviette. **2** any similar piece of cloth or paper, such as a small towel. **3** a baby's diaper. [ME *napekyn*, dim. of OF *nape* cloth. See NAPERY.]

na·po·le·on (nə pō′lē ən or nə pōl′yən) *n.* **1** formerly, a French gold coin worth 20 francs, or about $3.86. **2** a kind of pastry with a cream or jam filling. [< *Napoleon* Bonaparte (1769-1821), Emperor of the French]

Na·po·le·on·ic (nə pō′lə on′ik) *adj.* of, having to do with, or resembling, Napoleon Bonaparte, 1769-1821, Emperor of the French.

nap·pie or **nap·py** (nap′ē) *n.* **-pies. 1** a small dish used for serving fruit; a fruit dish. **2** *Informal.* a baby's diaper or napkin.

nar·cis·sism (när sis′iz əm) *n.* excessive absorption in one's own personal comfort, importance, etc.; self-love.

nar·cis·sist (när sis′ist) *n.* a person who indulges in narcissism.

nar·cis·sis·tic (när′si sis′tik) *adj.* of or having to do with narcissism.

nar·cis·sus (när sis′əs) *n.* **-cis·sus·es, -cis·si** (-sis′ī or -sis′ē). **1** a spring plant having yellow or white flowers and long, slender leaves. The narcissus grows from a bulb. **2** the flower. [< L < Gk. *narkissos*; associated (from the sedative effect of the plant) with *narkē* numbness]

Nar·cis·sus (när sis′əs) *n.* in Greek mythology, a beautiful youth who was caused to fall in love with his own reflection in the water of a spring. He pined away and was changed into the narcissus flower.

nar·co·sis (när kō′sis) *n.* **1** stupor; insensibility. **2** the action or effect of narcotics. [< NL < Gk. *narkōsis* < *narkoein* benumb. See NARCOTIC.]

nar·cot·ic (när kot′ik) *n.* **1** a drug that produces

drowsiness, sleep, dullness, or an insensible condition, and lessens pain by dulling the nerves. Opium is a powerful narcotic. **2** a person addicted to the use of narcotics; drug addict. **3** anything that numbs, soothes, or dulls.
—*adj.* **1** having the properties and effects of a narcotic. **2** of or having to do with narcotics or their use. **3** having to do with or intended for use in the treatment of drug addicts. [ME < Med.L < Gk. *narkōtikos* < *narkoein* benumb < *narkē* numbness] —**Syn.** *n.* **1** opiate, anodyne.

nard (närd) *n.* spikenard. [ME < L < Gk. *nardos* < Phoenician < Skt.]

nar·es (nãr′ēz) *n.* pl. of **nar·is** (nãr′is). the nostrils; nasal passages. [< L *nares*, pl.]

nar·ghi·le or **nar·gi·le** (när′gə lē′) *n.* an Oriental tobacco pipe in which the smoke is drawn through water. See **hookah** for picture. [ult. < Persian *nargileh* < *nargil* coconut, the original material used in making the pipe]

nar·rate (na rāt′ or nar′āt) *v.* **-rat·ed, -rat·ing. 1** tell (a story, etc.) of. **2** tell stories, etc. [< L *narrare* relate] —**nar·ra′tor,** *n.* —**Syn. 1** relate, recount, repeat. See **describe.**

nar·ra·tion (na rā′shən) *n.* **1** the act of telling. **2** the form of composition that relates an event or a story. Novels, short stories, histories, and biographies are forms of narration. **3** a story; account. —**Syn. 3** See **narrative.**

nar·ra·tive (nar′ə tiv) *n.* **1** a story. **2** the art of narration; storytelling. —*adj.* that narrates: "*David*" *by Earle Birney is a narrative poem.*
Syn. *n.* **1** tale, anecdote. **Narrative, narration** = something told as a story. **Narrative** chiefly applies to what is told, a story or an account of real events or experiences told like a story in connected and interesting form: *The account of his trip through the Near East made an interesting narrative.* **Narration** chiefly applies to the act of telling a story or relating an experience or a series of events, and emphasizes the way in which the narrative is put together and presented: *His narration of their trip was interesting.*

nar·row (nar′ō) *adj.* **1** not wide; having little width; of less than the specified, understood, or usual width: *narrow cloth.* **2** limited in extent, space, amount, range, scope, opportunity, etc.: *He had only a narrow circle of friends.* **3** with little margin: *a narrow escape.* **4** lacking breadth of view or sympathy; not liberal; prejudiced: *a narrow mind.* **5** close; careful; minute: *a narrow scrutiny.* **6** with barely enough to live on: *live in narrow circumstances.* **7** in phonetics: **a** pronounced with a narrowed opening of the vocal organs; tense. **b** indicating minute details of pronunciation: *a narrow phonetic transcription.*
—*n.* **narrows,** *pl.* the narrow part of a river, strait, sound, valley, pass, etc.
—*v.* make or become narrower; decrease in breadth, extent, etc.; limit. [OE *nearu*] —**nar′row·ly,** *adv.* —**nar′row·ness,** *n.* —**Syn.** *adj.* **2** confined, strait, restricted. **4** illiberal, bigoted. **5** detailed, scrupulous. **6** scanty, meagre, impoverished.

nar·row-gauge (nar′ō gāj′) *adj.* **1** having railway tracks less than 56½ inches apart. **2** narrow-minded.

nar·row-mind·ed (nar′ō mīn′did) *adj.* lacking breadth of view or sympathy; prejudiced. —**nar′row-mind′ed·ly,** *adv.* —**nar′row·mind′ed·ness,** *n.* —**Syn.** illiberal, intolerant.

narrow squeak *Informal.* a narrow escape.

nar·thex (när′theks) *n.* **1** a portico or vestibule in ancient churches. **2** a vestibule leading into the nave of a church. [< Gk.]

nar·whal (när′hwəl or när′wəl) *n.* a kind of arctic whale whose body is about 16 feet long. The male has a long tusk extending forward from the upper jaw. [< Danish or Swedish *narhval* < *nár* corpse + *hval* whale]

na·sal (nā′zəl) *adj.* **1** of, in, or from the nose: *nasal catarrh, a nasal discharge.* **2** speaking or spoken through the nose: *His voice had a nasal quality.* **3** in phonetics, requiring the nose passage to be open. The letters *m, n,* and *ng* represent nasal sounds. —*n.* in phonetics, a sound that is made by expelling air through the nose. The sounds of (m), (n), and (ng) are nasals. [< L *nasus* nose] —**na′sal·ly,** *adv.*

na·sal·i·ty (nā zal′ə tē) *n.* a nasal quality.

na·sal·ize (nā′zəl īz′) *v.* **-ized, -iz·ing.** utter or speak with a nasal resonance or quality. —**na′sal·i·za′tion,** *n.*

nas·cent (nas′ənt or nā′sənt) *adj.* **1** in the process of coming into existence; just beginning to exist, grow, or develop. **2** in chemistry: **a** having to do with the state or condition of an element at the instant it is set free from a combination. **b** of an element, being in a free or uncombined state: *nascent chlorine.* [< L *nascens, -entis,* ppr. of *nasci* be born]

hat, āge, cãre, fär; let, ēqual, tėrm; it, īce
hot, ōpen, ôrder; oil, out; cup, pu̇t, rüle, ūse
əbove, takən, pencəl, lemən, circəs
ch, child; ng, long; sh, ship
th, thin; ᴛʜ, then; zh, measure

Nas·ka·pi (nas′kə pē′) *n.* **Nas·ka·pi** or **Nas·ka·pis. 1** a group of Indians living in northern Quebec and the interior of Labrador. **2** a member of this group. **3** the Algonquian dialect of this people.

na·stur·tium (nə stėr′shəm) *n.* **1** a plant having yellow, orange, pink, and red flowers, and sharp-tasting seeds and leaves. **2** the flower. [< L *nasturtium* < *nasus* nose + *torquere* twist; from its pungent odor]

nas·ty (nas′tē) *adj.* **-ti·er, -ti·est. 1** disgustingly dirty; filthy: *a nasty room.* **2** morally filthy; vile: *a nasty word, a nasty mind.* **3** offensive to smell or taste; nauseous: *a nasty medicine.* **4 a** very unpleasant: *nasty weather.* **b** obnoxious; objectionable. **5** ill-natured; disagreeable (to another): *a nasty temper.* **6** rather serious; bad: *a nasty accident.* [ME; cf. Du. *nestig*] —**nas′ti·ly,** *adv.* —**nas′ti·ness,** *n.* —**Syn. 1** foul, squalid. **2** obscene, ribald, indecent. **3** disagreeable, repulsive.

nat. 1 national. **2** native. **3** natural. **4** naturalist.

na·tal (nā′təl) *adj.* **1** of one's birth: *One's natal day is one's birthday.* **2** *Poetic.* native. [ME < L *natalis,* ult. < *nasci* be born. Doublet of NOËL.]

na·tal·i·ty (nā tal′ə tē) *n.* birth rate.

na·tant (nā′tənt) *adj.* swimming; floating; represented as swimming. [< L *natans, -antis,* ppr. of *natare* float, swim, ult. < *nare* float]

na·ta·to·ri·al (nā′tə tô′rē əl) *adj.* having to do with, adapted for, or characterized by swimming: *Ducks are natatorial birds.* [< LL *natatorialis,* ult. < L *natare* swim. See NATANT.]

na·ta·to·ri·um (nā′tə tô′rē əm) *n.* **-ri·ums, -ri·a** (-rē ə). a swimming pool, especially an indoor one. [< LL]

na·ta·to·ry (nā′tə tô′rē) *adj.* natatorial.

nathe·less (nāth′lis or nath′lis) *Archaic.* —*adv.* nevertheless. —*prep.* notwithstanding. [OE *nā thȳ lǣs*]

na·tion (nā′shən) *n.* **1** a group of people occupying the same country, united under the same government, and, usually, speaking the same language: *the English nation.* **2** a people, race, or tribe; those having the same descent, history, and, as a rule, language: *the Scottish nation.* **3** such a group considered as a political unity: *the French-Canadian nation.* **4** a North American Indian tribe, especially one belonging to a confederacy. **5 the nation,** the country: *There was cold weather throughout the nation over the weekend.* [< L *natio, -onis* stock, race, ult. < *nasci* be born] —**Syn. 1** See **people.**

na·tion·al (nash′nəl or nash′ən əl) *adj.* **1** of a nation; affecting or belonging to a whole nation: *national laws, a national disaster.* **2** strongly upholding one's own nation; patriotic. **3** extending throughout the nation; having chapters, branches, or members in every part of the nation. —*n.* a citizen of a nation.

National Assembly in Quebec, the group of representatives elected to the legislature; legislative assembly.

na·tion·al·ism (nash′nəl iz′əm or nash′ən əl iz′əm) *n.* **1** patriotic feelings or efforts. **2** the desire and plans for national independence. **3** the desire of a people to preserve its own language, religion, traditions, etc. **4** a form of socialism that advocates government ownership and control of all major industries.

na·tion·al·ist (nash′nəl ist or nash′ən əl ist) *n.* an upholder of nationalism; a person who believes in nationalism. —*adj.* nationalistic.

na·tion·al·is·tic (nash′nəl is′tik or nash′ən əl is′tik) *adj.* of nationalism or nationalists. —**na′tion·al·is′ti·cal·ly,** *adv.*

na·tion·al·i·ty (nash nal′ə tē or nash′ən al′ə tē) *n.* **-ties. 1** the fact of belonging to a nation: *His passport showed* *that his nationality was Canadian.* **2** the condition of being a nation; the fact of having national existence; nationhood.

na·tion·al·ize (nash′nəl īz′ or nash′ən əl īz′) *v.* **-ized, -iz·ing. 1** make national. **2** bring (land, industries, railways, etc.) under the control or ownership of a nation. **3** make into a nation. **—na′tion·al·i·za′tion,** *n.*

na·tion·al·ly (nash′nəl ē or nash′ən əl ē) *adv.* **1** in a national manner; as a nation. **2** throughout the nation: *The Prime Minister's speech was broadcast nationally.*

national park land kept by the federal government for people to enjoy because of its beautiful scenery, historical interest, etc.

National Socialist Party the political party, led by Adolf Hitler, that controlled Germany from 1933 to 1945.

na·tion·hood (nā′shən hůd′) *n.* the condition or state of being a nation; the fact of having national existence: *A country's nationhood is sometimes threatened by civil wars.*

na·tion-wide (nā′shən wīd′) *adj.* extending throughout the nation: *a nation-wide election.*

na·tive (nā′tiv) *n.* **1** a person born in a certain place or country: *He is a native of Montreal.* **2** one of the original inhabitants of a place, as contrasted with conquerors, settlers, visitors, etc.; especially, a member of a less civilized race: *The natives were quite suspicious of strangers.* **3** *Derogatory.* a member of a less civilized race, usually not white. **4** an animal or plant living in the place where it originated. [< Med.L *nativus* a native < L *nativus.* See NATIVE, adj.]
—*adj.* **1** born in a certain place or country: *He is a native son of Winnipeg.* **2** belonging to one because of his birth: *one's native land.* **3** belonging to one because of his country or the nation to which he belongs: *one's native language.* **4** born in a person; natural: *native ability, native courtesy.* **5** of or having to do with the original inhabitants: *native customs, native huts.* **6** originating, grown, or produced in a certain place: *The Manitoba maple is native to Canada.* **7** found pure in nature: *native copper.* **8** found in nature; not produced: *Native salt is refined for use.* **9 go native,** live as the less civilized natives do. [< L *nativus* innate, ult. < *nasci* be born. Doublet of NAÏVE.] **—na′tive·ly,** *adv.* **—na′tive·ness,** *n.*
Syn. *adj.* **4 Native, natural** = belonging to someone or something by birth or nature. **Native** emphasizes the idea of being born in a person, as contrasted with being acquired: *He has native artistic talent.* **Natural** emphasizes being part of the nature of a person, animal, or thing, belonging by birth or because of essential character: *Sugar has natural sweetness.* **5** aboriginal. **6** indigenous.

na·tive-born (nā′tiv bôrn′) *adj.* born in the place or country indicated: *a native-born Canadian.*

na·tiv·i·ty (nə tiv′ə tē or nā tiv′ə tē) *n.* **-ties. 1** birth. **2** a horoscope. **3 the Nativity, a** the birth of Christ. **b** a picture showing the new-born infant Jesus, usually with his parents and often with animals and shepherds grouped around the manger. **c** Christmas; December 25. [ME < OF *nativite* < LL *nativitas*]

natl. national.

NATO (nā′tō) North Atlantic Treaty Organization.

na·tron (nā′tron) *n.* native sodium carbonate. *Formula*: $Na_2CO_3 \cdot 10H_2O$ [< F < Sp. < Arabic *natrun* < Gk. *nitron* < Semitic. Doublet of NITRE.]

nat·ter (nat′ər) *v.* **1** mutter discontentedly; fret. **2** prate; chatter. [< earlier *gnatter*; origin uncertain]

nat·ty (nat′ē) *adj.* **-ti·er, -ti·est.** trim and tidy; neatly smart in dress or appearance: *a natty uniform, a natty young officer.* [origin uncertain] **—nat′ti·ly,** *adv.* **—nat′ti·ness,** *n.*

nat·u·ral (nach′rəl or nach′ə rəl) *adj.* **1** produced by nature; based on some state of things in nature: *Scenery has natural beauty.* **2** not artificial: *Coal and oil are natural products.* **3** instinctive; inborn: *natural ability.* **4** coming in the ordinary course of events; normal: *a natural death.* **5** in accordance with the nature of things or the circumstances of the case: *a natural response.* **6** instinctively felt to be right and fair: *natural law, natural rights.* **7** like nature; true to nature: *The picture looked natural.* **8** free from affectation or restraint: *a natural manner.* **9** of or having to do with nature: *the natural sciences.* **10** concerned with natural science. **11** based on what is learned from nature: *natural religion.* **12** in music: **a** neither sharp nor flat; without sharps and flats. **b** neither sharped nor flatted: *C natural.* **c** having the pitch affected by the natural sign. **d** produced without the aid of valves or keys, as in brass instruments. **13** by birth, but not legally recognized; illegitimate: *a natural son.* **14** in mathematics, having 1 as the base of the system (applied to a function or number belonging or referred to such a system).
—*n.* **1** that which is natural. **2** in music: **a** a natural tone or note. **b** a sign (♮) used to cancel the effect of a preceding sharp or flat. **c** a white key on keyboard instruments. **3** *Archaic.* a half-witted person. **4** *Informal.* an expert by nature. **5** *Informal.* a sure success. [ME < L *naturalis* < *natura.* See NATURE.] **—nat′u·ral·ness,** *n.*
—Syn. *adj.* **3** innate, inherent. See **native. 4** regular, usual. **8** simple, ingenuous, artless, unaffected.

natural gas a combustible gas formed naturally in the earth, consisting of methane, hydrogen, and other gases.

natural history the study of animals, plants, minerals, and other things in nature.

nat·u·ral·ism (nach′rəl iz′əm or nach′ə rəl iz′əm) *n.* **1** in art and literature, a style characterized by a scientific and objective portrayal of nature, life, etc. **2** the principles of certain 19th-century writers, especially in France, who strove for a type of realism that stressed the unpleasant and sordid aspects of life. **3** action based on natural instincts. **4** in philosophy, a view of the world which takes account only of natural elements and forces, excluding the supernatural or spiritual. **5** the doctrine that all religious truth is derived from the study of nature.

nat·u·ral·ist (nach′rəl ist or nach′ə rəl ist) *n.* **1** a person who makes a study of animals and plants. **2** a writer or artist who represents life exactly as it is; extreme realist.

nat·u·ral·is·tic (nach′rəl is′tik or nach′ə rəl is′tik) *adj.* **1** of natural history or naturalists. **2** of naturalism, especially in art and literature. **3** of or in accordance with nature.

nat·u·ral·ize (nach′rəl īz′ or nach′ə rəl īz′) *v.* **-ized, -iz·ing. 1** grant the rights of citizenship to persons native to other countries; admit (a foreigner) to citizenship: *The government naturalizes many New Canadians every year.* **2** adopt (a foreign word or custom): *"Chauffeur" is a French word that has been naturalized in English.* **3** introduce and make at home in another country: *The English sparrow has become naturalized in most of Canada.* **4** make natural; free from conventional characteristics. **5** regard or explain as natural rather than supernatural. **6** become like a native. **—nat′u·ral·i·za′tion,** *n.*

natural law 1 a law, or the laws, of nature. **2** a rule of conduct supposedly based on reason inherent in nature.

nat·u·ral·ly (nach′rəl ē or nach′ə rəl ē) *adv.* **1** in a natural way: *speak naturally.* **2** by nature: *a naturally obedient child.* **3** as might be expected; of course.

natural magnet a piece of magnetite; loadstone.

natural number a whole number, as 1, 2, or 3.

natural philosophy physics.

natural resource a kind of material that is supplied by nature and is useful or necessary to man: *Minerals and water power are natural resources.*

natural science the science of nature. Zoology, botany, and geology are natural sciences.

natural selection the process by which animals and plants best adapted to their environment tend to survive.

natural sign a natural (n. def. 2b).

natural year the astronomical year.

na·ture (nā′chər) *n.* **1** the world; all things except those made by man. **2** the sum total of the forces at work throughout the universe: *the laws of nature.* **3 Nature,** the personification of all natural facts and forces. **4** the instincts or inherent tendencies directing conduct: *It is against nature for a mother to kill her child.* **5** reality: *true to nature.* **6** a primitive, wild condition; condition of human beings before social organization. **7** the qualities that a person or thing is born with; character; way or manner: *It is the nature of birds to fly.* **8** sort; kind. **9** a person of a particular character: *She is a gentle nature.* **10** physical being; vital powers: *food sufficient to sustain nature.* **11** moral nature unaffected by grace. **12 by nature,** because of the essential character of the person or thing. **13 of** or **in the nature of,** having the nature of; being a kind of. [ME < OF < L *natura* birth, character, ult. < *nasci* be born] **—Syn. 1** universe, cosmos. **8** type.

hat, āge, cãre, fär; let, ēqual, tėrm; it, īce
hot, ōpen, ôrder; oil, out; cup, pu̇t, rüle, ūse
əbove, takən, pencəl, lemən, circəs
ch, child; ng, long; sh, ship
th, thin; ᴛʜ, then; zh, measure

-natured *combining form.* having the nature of: *bad-natured = having a bad nature.*

nature study the study of animals, plants, and other things and events in nature.

naught (not or nôt) *n.* nothing: *All his work went for naught.* [OE *nāwiht* < *nā* no + *wiht* wight]

naugh·ty (not′ē or nô′tē) *adj.* **-ti·er, -ti·est. 1** bad; not obedient. **2** improper. [< *naught* wickedness] **—naugh′ti·ly,** *adv.* **—naugh′ti·ness,** *n.*

nau·se·a (no′zē ə or nô′zē ə, no′shə or nô′shə) *n.* **1** the feeling that one has when about to vomit. **2** seasickness. **3** extreme disgust; loathing. [< L < Gk. *nausia* < *naus* ship. Doublet of NOISE.]

nau·se·ate (no′zē āt′ or nô′zē āt′, no′sē āt′ or nô′sē āt′) *v.* **-at·ed, -at·ing. 1** cause nausea in; make sick. **2** feel nausea; become sick. **3** cause to feel loathing. [< L *nauseare*]

nau·se·ous (no′zē əs or nô′zē əs, no′shəs or nô′shəs) *adj.* **1** causing nausea; sickening. **2** disgusting; loathsome. [< L *nauseosus*] **—nau′seous·ly,** *adv.*

naut. nautical.

nautch (noch or nôch) *n.* in India, an entertainment consisting of dancing by professional dancing girls. [< Hind. *nach* dance]

nau·ti·cal (no′tə kəl or nô′tə kəl) *adj.* of or having to do with ships, sailors, or navigation. [< L < Gk. *nautikos,* ult. < *naus* ship] **—nau′ti·cal·ly,** *adv.* **—Syn.** maritime.

nautical measure the system of measurement used in navigation.

nautical mile a unit of distance used in air and sea navigation, equal to a sixtieth of a degree of the earth's equator. It is about 6,080 feet.

nau·ti·lus (no′tə ləs or nô′tə ləs) *n.* **-lus·es, -li** (-lī′ or -lē′). either of two kinds of cephalopod. The **pearly nautilus** has a spiral shell, pearly inside. The **paper nautilus,** related to the octopus, has sail-like arms and a very thin shell. [< L < Gk. *nautilos,* originally, sailor, ult. < *naus* ship]

nav. **1** naval. **2** navigation.

Nav·a·ho or **Nav·a·jo** (nav′ə hō′) *n.* **-ho** or **-hos, -jo** or **-jos. 1** a tribe of American Indians living in New Mexico, Arizona, and Utah. **2** a member of this tribe. **3** the language of this tribe.

na·val (nā′vəl) *adj.* **1** of, having to do with, or for warships or the navy: *a naval officer, naval supplies.* **2** having a navy: *the naval powers.* [< L *navalis* < *navis* ship] **—na′val·ly,** *adv.*

naval stores materials, such as tar, resin, turpentine, etc. that are used for building and repairing wooden ships.

nave[1] (nāv) *n.* the main part of a church between the side aisles. The nave extends from the main entrance to the transepts. See **apse** for diagram. [< Med.L < L *navis* ship]

nave[2] (nāv) *n.* the central part of a wheel; hub. [OE *nafu*]

na·vel (nā′vəl) *n.* **1** the mark or scar, usually a puckered depression, in the middle of the surface of the abdomen where the umbilical cord was attached during prenatal development. **2** the centre; middle: *Some people say that "Mexico" means "the navel of the world."* [OE *nafela.* Related to NAVE[2].]

navel orange a seedless orange having a small growth that resembles a navel in shape and contains a small secondary fruit.

nav·i·ga·bil·i·ty (nav′ə gə bil′ə tē) *n.* the state or quality of being navigable.

nav·i·ga·ble (nav′ə gə bəl) *adj.* **1** that ships can travel on: *The St. Lawrence River is deep enough to be navigable.* **2** seaworthy. **3** that can be steered.

nav·i·gate (nav′ə gāt′) *v.* **-gat·ed, -gat·ing. 1** sail, manage, or steer (a ship, aircraft, etc.). **2** sail on or over (a sea or river): *Many ships navigate the St. Lawrence Seaway each year.* **3** travel by water; sail. **4** convey (goods) by water. **5** sail through (the air) in an aircraft, etc. **6** plot the position and course of a ship, aircraft, etc. [< L *navigare* < *navis* ship + *agere* drive]

nav·i·ga·tion (nav′ə gā′shən) *n.* **1** the act or process of navigating. **2** the art or science of plotting the position and course of a ship, aircraft, etc.

nav·i·ga·tion·al (nav′ə gā′shə nəl) *adj.* of, having to do with, or used in navigation.

nav·i·ga·tor (nav′ə gā′tər) *n.* **1** a person skilled in the science of navigating ships or aircraft: *The ship took on a special navigator to guide her through the dangerous waters. He served as a navigator in the R.C.A.F.* **2** a person who sails the seas, especially an explorer. **3** one who plots the position and course of a ship, aircraft, etc. [< L]

nav·vy (nav′ē) *n.* **-vies.** *Brit.* an unskilled laborer who works on canals, railways, roads, etc. [< *navigator*]

na·vy (nā′vē) *n.* **-vies. 1** all the ships of war of a country, with their officers and men. **2** in Canada, the sea element. **3** the officers and men of a navy. **4** *Archaic or poetic.* a fleet of ships. **5** a dark blue. [ME < OF *navie,* ult. < L *navis* ship]

navy bean the common white bean, dried for keeping until used for food.

navy blue a dark blue.

na·wab (nə wob′) *n.* **1** in India: **a** a native ruler under the Mogul empire. **b** a title given to important Moslems. **2** a nabob (def. 2). [< Hind. *nav(v)ab* < Arabic *nuwwab,* pl. of *nā'ib* deputy]

nay (nā) *adv.* **1** *Archaic.* no. **2** not only that, but also: *We are willing, nay, eager to go.* —*n.* **1** no; a denial or refusal. **2** a negative vote or voter. [ME < ON *nei* < *ne* not + *ei* ever]

Naz·a·rene (naz′ə rēn′ or naz′ə rēn′) *n.* **1** a native or inhabitant of Nazareth, the boyhood home of Jesus. **2 the Nazarene,** Jesus. **3** an early Christian. —*adj.* of or having to do with the Nazarenes or with Nazareth.

Naz·a·rite (naz′ə rīt′) *n.* **1** among the ancient Hebrews, a Jew who had taken certain strict religious vows. Num. 6. **2** a native of Nazareth. Also, **Nazirite.**

Na·zi (nat′sē or nä′tsē) *n.* **Na·zis,** *adj.* —*n.* **1** a member or supporter of the National Socialist Party in Germany, organized under the leadership of Adolf Hitler. **2** Often, **nazi.** a believer in similar doctrines in any country; fascist. —*adj.* of or having to do with the Nazis. [< G *Nazi,* short for *Nationalsozialist* National Socialist]

☛ Nazi was a political nickname for the National Socialist Party in Germany and is capitalized like *Conservative* or *Liberal.* The type of party represented by the Nazis is usually referred to as *fascist* or *totalitarian.*

Na·zi·fy or **na·zi·fy** (nat′sə fī′ or nä′tsə fī′) *v.* **-fied, -fy·ing. 1** place under control of the Nazis. **2** indoctrinate with Nazi views. **—Na′zi·fi·ca′tion, na′zi·fi·ca′tion,** *n.*

Na·zi·ism (nat′sē iz′əm or nä′tsē iz′əm) *n.* the doctrines of the Nazis, including totalitarian government and state control of industry, but opposed to communism.

Na·zism (nat′siz əm or nä′tsiz əm) *n.* Naziism.

Nb niobium.

N.B. New Brunswick.

N.B. or **n.b.** nota bene.

☛ N.B., the abbreviation of the Latin *nota bene,* meaning "note well," is occasionally found in formal announcements: *N.B. Members are to pay their dues not later than Monday, May 5.*

NBC in the United States, National Broadcasting Company.

N.C. North Carolina.

N.C.O. non-commissioned officer.

n.d. **1** no date. **2** not dated.

Nd neodymium.

N.Dak. or **N.D.** North Dakota.

NDP or **N.D.P.** New Democratic Party.

NDT, N.D.T., or **n.d.t.** Newfoundland Daylight Time.

Ne neon.

N.E., NE, or **n.e.** 1 northeast. 2 northeastern.

Ne·an·der·thal (nē an′dər täl′, nē an′dər thol′, or nē an′dər thôl′) *adj.* of or having to do with Neanderthal man.

Neanderthal man an extinct people widespread in Europe, N. Africa, and parts of Asia in the early Stone Age. [< *Neanderthal*, a valley in W. Germany, where evidence of this people was found]

neap (nēp) *adj.* designating those tides which attain the least height. —*n.* a neap tide. [OE *nēp*]

Ne·a·pol·i·tan (nē′ə pol′ə tən) *adj.* **1** of or having to do with Naples, a city in Italy. **2** having layers of different colors and flavors: *Neapolitan ice cream.* —*n.* a native of Naples. [< L *Neapolitanus* < *Neapolis* Naples < Gk.]

neap tide the tide that occurs when the difference in height between high and low tide is least; lowest level of high tide. Neap tide comes twice a month.

near (nēr) *adv.* **1** close; not far: *Christmas is near.* **2** closely: *tribes near allied.* **3** *Informal.* all but; almost: *The war lasted near a year.* **4 come near doing,** almost do. **5 near at hand, a** within easy reach. **b** not far in the future.
—*adj.* **1** close by; not distant; less distant: *The post office is quite near.* **2** intimate; familiar: *a near friend.* **3** closely related: *a near relative.* **4** approximating or resembling closely: *near silk, near beer.* **5** left (opposed to *off* or *right*): *The near horse and the off horse make a team.* **6** short; direct: *Go by the nearest route.* **7** stingy. **8** by a close margin: *a near escape.*
—*prep.* close to in space, time, condition, etc.: *Our house is near the river.*
—*v.* come or draw near; approach: *The ship neared the land.* [OE *nēar*, comparative of *nēah* nigh] —**near′ness,** *n.*
—**Syn.** *adj.* **1** close, nigh.

near·by (nēr′bī′; *adj. preceding a noun,* nēr′bī′) *adj. adv.* near; close at hand.

Near East 1 *Canada and U.S.* the Balkans and the countries of S.W. Asia. **2** *Brit.* the Balkans.

near·ly (nēr′lē) *adv.* **1** almost: *I nearly missed the train.* **2** closely: *a matter that concerns you very nearly.*

near-miss (nēr′mis′) *n.* **1** a narrow escape from danger. **2** anything approaching, but not quite fulfilling, excellence or perfection.

near-sight·ed (nēr′sīt′id) *adj.* not able to see far; seeing distinctly at a short distance only: *Near-sighted people usually wear glasses.* —**near′-sight′ed·ly,** *adv.* —**near′-sight′ed·ness,** *n.*

neat[1] (nēt) *adj.* **1** clean and in order: *a neat desk, a neat room, a neat dress.* **2** able and willing to keep things in order: *a neat child.* **3** well-formed; in proportion: *a neat design.* **4** skilful; clever: *a neat trick.* **5** without anything mixed in it; straight: *He took a drink of brandy neat.* [< F *net* < L *nitidus* gleaming < *nitere* shine]
—**neat′ly,** *adv.* —**neat′ness,** *n.*
Syn. 1 **Neat, tidy, trim** = in good order. **Neat** emphasizes cleanness and absence of disorder or litter: *Her clothes are always neat.* **Tidy** emphasizes orderliness and showing painstaking care in having a place for everything and everything in its place: *She keeps her room tidy.* **Trim** adds the idea of being pleasing in appearance, sometimes suggesting smartness, sometimes good proportion, clean lines, and compactness: *That is a trim sailing boat.* **4** deft, adroit. **5** undiluted, pure, clear.

neat[2] (nēt) *n.pl. or sing. Archaic.* cattle; oxen. [OE *nēat*]

neat·en (nēt′ən) *v.* make neat; tidy up.

neath or **'neath** (nēth) *prep. Poetic.* beneath.

neat·herd (nēt′hėrd′) *n. Archaic.* a cowherd.

neat's-foot oil (nēts′fůt′) an oil obtained from the feet and shinbones of cattle by boiling. Neat's-foot oil is used to soften leather.

neb (neb) *n. Scottish.* **1** a bill; beak. **2** a person's mouth or nose. **3** an animal's snout. **4** the tip of anything; nib. [OE *nebb*]

Nebr. or **Neb.** Nebraska.

neb·u·la (neb′yů lə) *n.* **-lae** (-lē′ or -lī′) or **-las. 1** in astronomy, a bright spot like a small, bright cloud, visible in the sky at night. A nebula may be either a mass of luminous gas or a cluster of stars very far away from our sun and its planets. **2** a cloudlike spot on the cornea of the eye. **3** cloudiness of the urine. [< L *nebula* mist]

neb·u·lar (neb′yů lər) *adj.* of or concerning a nebula or nebulae.

nebular hypothesis the theory that the solar system developed from a luminous mass of gas.

neb·u·los·i·ty (neb′yů los′ə tē) *n.* **-ties. 1** a cloudlike quality; mistiness; nebulous state. **2** cloudlike matter; nebula.

neb·u·lous (neb′yů ləs) *adj.* **1** hazy; vague; confused. **2** cloudlike. **3** of or like a nebula or nebulae. [< L *nebulosus* < *nebula* mist] —**neb′u·lous·ly,** *adv.* —**neb′u·lous·ness,** *n.*

nec·es·sar·i·ly (nes′ə ser′ə lē or nes′ə săr′ə lē) *adv.* **1** as a necessity: *Leaves are not necessarily green.* **2** as a necessary result: *War necessarily causes misery and waste.*

nec·es·sar·y (nes′ə ser′ē) *adj. n.* **-sar·ies.** —*adj.* that must be, be had, or be done; inevitable; required; indispensable: *Death is a necessary end.*
—*n.* **1** something essential; something that cannot be done without: *Food, clothing, and shelter are necessaries of life.* **2 necessaries,** *pl.* in law, the things, as food, shelter, clothing, etc., required to support a dependent or similar person in a way suitable to his station in life. **3 the necessary,** money: *Have you the necessary?* [< L *necessarius* < *necesse* unavoidable, ult. < *ne-* not + *cedere* withdraw]
Syn. *adj.* **Necessary, indispensable, essential** = needed or required. **Necessary** applies to whatever is needed but not absolutely required: *Work is a necessary part of life.* **Indispensable** implies that, without the thing referred to, the intended result or purpose cannot be achieved: *Work is an indispensable part of success.* **Essential** implies that the existence or proper functioning of something depends upon the thing referred to: *Work is essential to happiness.*

ne·ces·si·tate (nə ses′ə tāt′) *v.* **-tat·ed, -tat·ing. 1** make necessary: *His broken leg necessitated an operation.* **2** *Archaic.* compel; force. —**Syn. 1** require, demand.

ne·ces·si·tous (nə ses′ə təs) *adj.* very poor; needy. —**ne·ces′si·tous·ly,** *adv.* —**ne·ces′si·tous·ness,** *n.*

ne·ces·si·ty (nə ses′ə tē) *n.* **-ties. 1** the fact of being necessary; extreme need: *We understand the necessity of eating.* **2** the quality of being necessary. **3** anything that cannot be done without: *Water is a necessity.* **4** that which forces one to act in a certain way: *Necessity often drives people to do disagreeable things.* **5** that which is inevitable: *Night follows day as a necessity.* **6** need; poverty: *This poor family is in great necessity.* **7 of necessity,** because it must be. [< L *necessitas* < *necesse.* See NECESSARY.] —**Syn. 1** exigency. See **need. 3** essential, requisite.
☛ **necessity.** The idiom is *necessity of* or *for* doing something (not *to* do something): *Most athletes can see the necessity of* (or *for*) *training.*

neck (nek) *n.* **1** the part of the body that connects the head with the shoulders. **2** the part of a garment that fits the neck. **3** any narrow part like a neck. **4** a narrow strip of land. **5** the slender part of a bottle, flask, retort, or other container. **6** in architecture, the lowest part of the capital of a column. **7** the long slender part of a violin or similar instrument, extending from the body to the head; finger board. **8** the part of a tooth between the crown and the root. **9** a slender or constricted part of a bone or organ. **10** in racing, the length of the neck of a horse or other animal as a measure.
get it in the neck, *Slang.* receive a severe scolding, defeat, etc.
neck and neck, a abreast. **b** in a race or contest, running equal or even.
neck of the woods, *Slang.* a part of the country: *There are few good roads in this neck of the woods.*
neck or nothing, venturing all.
stick (one's) neck out, *Informal.* put oneself in a dangerous or vulnerable position by foolish or zealous action.
win by a neck, a win a horse race by the length of a head and neck. **b** win by a close margin.
—*v. Slang.* embrace; hug; kiss and caress. [OE *hnecca*]

neck·band (nek′band′) *n.* **1** a band worn around the neck. **2** the part of a shirt, blouse, etc. to which the collar is attached. **3** the part of a garment that fits the neck.

neck·cloth (nek′kloth′) *n.* a cloth worn round the neck cravat.

hat, āge, cãre, fär; let, ēqual, tėrm; it, īce
hot, ōpen, ôrder; oil, out; cup, pu̇t, rüle, ūse
əbove, takən, pencəl, lemən, circəs
ch, child; ng, long; sh, ship
th, thin; ᴛʜ, then; zh, measure

neck·er·chief (nek′ər chif) *n.* a cloth worn round the neck.

neck·lace (nek′lis) *n.* a string of jewels, gold, silver, beads, etc. worn around the neck as an ornament.

neck·line (nek′līn′) *n.* the line or shape of the neck of a garment.

neck·piece (nek′pēs′) *n.* a fur scarf.

neck·tie (nek′tī′) *n.* a narrow band of cloth worn around the neck and tied in front; tie.

neck·wear (nek′wãr′) *n.* collars, ties, and other articles that are worn around the neck.

ne·crol·o·gy (ne krol′ə jē) *n.* **-gies. 1** a list of persons who have died. **2** a notice of a person's death. [< Med.L *necrologia* < Gk. *nekros* dead body + *logos* count, reckoning]

nec·ro·man·cer (nek′rə man′sər) *n.* **1** a person who is supposed to foretell the future by communicating with the dead. **2** a magician; sorcerer; wizard.

nec·ro·man·cy (nek′rə man′sē) *n.* **1** a supposed foretelling of the future by communicating with the dead. **2** magic; enchantment; sorcery. [ME < OF < Med.L *nigromantia* < L *necromantia* < Gk. *nekromanteia* < *nekros* dead body + *manteia* divination; confusion with L *niger* "black" led to interpretation as "black art"]

ne·crop·o·lis (ne krop′ə lis) *n.* **-lis·es.** a cemetery. [< NL < Gk. *nekropolis* < *nekros* dead body + *polis* city]

ne·cro·sis (ne krō′sis) *n.* **-ses** (-sēz). **1** the death or decay of body tissues. It may result from a degenerative disease, stoppage of the oxygen supply, infection, or destructive burning or freezing. **2** a disease of plants characterized by small black spots of decayed tissue. [< NL < Gk. *necrosis*, ult. < *nekros* dead body]

nec·tar (nek′tər) *n.* **1** in Greek mythology: **a** the drink of the gods. **b** the food of the gods. **2** any delicious drink. **3** a sweet liquid found in many flowers. Bees gather nectar and make it into honey. [< L < Gk. *nektar*] **—nec′tar·like′,** *adj.*

nec·tar·ine (nek′tər ēn′ or nek′tər ēn′) *n.* a kind of peach having no down on its skin. [< *nectar*]

nec·ta·ry (nek′tə rē) *n.* **-ries.** the part of a flower that secretes nectar.

née or **nee** (nā) *adj.* born. [< F *née*, fem. pp. of *naître* be born < L *nasci*]

☛ Née may be placed after the name of a married woman to show her maiden name: *Mrs. Smith, née Adams.*

need (nēd) *n.* **1** a lack of a useful or desired thing: *a need of grammar.* **2** a useful or desired thing that is lacking: *In the desert their need was water.* **3** necessity: *There is no need to hurry.* **4** a situation or time of difficulty: *a friend in need.* **5** extreme poverty. **6 have need to,** must; should; have to; ought to. **7 if need be,** if it has to be.
—*v.* **1** have need of; want; require: *need money.* **2** be necessary. **3** must; should; have to; ought to: *He need not go. Need she go?* **4** be in want: *Give to those that need.* [OE *nēd*] **—need′er,** *n.*
Syn. *n.* **1 Need, necessity** = lack of something required or desired. **Need** suggests pressing want, lack or absence of something required for the welfare or success of a person or thing or of something useful or satisfying: *She is in need of a rest.* **Necessity** emphasizes the idea of something that cannot be avoided or done without, an urgent need or demand, but expresses a more objective attitude and less appeal to the emotions than *need* sometimes does: *She realizes the necessity of getting enough sleep.* **5** want, destitution, indigence. -*v.* **1** See **lack.**

need·ful (nēd′fəl) *adj.* needed; necessary. **—need′ful·ly,** *adv.* **—Syn.** requisite, required, indispensable.

nee·dle (nē′dəl) *n. v.* **-dled, -dling.** —*n.* **1** a slender piece of steel for sewing, having a sharp point at one end and at the other a hole or eye for passing thread through. **2** a slender rod used in knitting. **3** a rod with a hook at one end used in crocheting, etc. **4** a thin steel pointer on a compass or on electrical machinery. **5** a slender steel tube with a sharp point at the end of a hypodermic syringe used for injecting something below the skin, withdrawing blood, etc. **6** an instrument resembling a needle, used in etching and engraving. **7** a phonograph needle. **8** any of various small objects resembling a needle in sharpness: *needles of broken glass, ice, etc.* **9** a slender, needle-shaped rod that controls the opening of a valve. **10** the needle-shaped leaf of the fir, pine, spruce, or larch. **11** a pillar; obelisk: *Cleopatra's needle.* **12** in mineralogy and chemistry, a crystal or spicule like a needle in shape. **13** in geology, a pinnacle of rock tapering to a point.
—*v. Informal.* vex by repeated sharp prods, gibes, etc.; goad or incite. [OE *nǣdl*]

nee·dle·ful (nē′dəl fu̇l′) *n.* **-fuls.** a suitable length of thread for using at one time with a needle.

needle point 1 embroidery made on a coarse, stiff canvas cloth and used to cover chairs, footstools, etc. **2** lace made entirely with a needle instead of a bobbin.

nee·dle-point (nē′dəl point′) *adj.* having to do with needle point.

need·ler (nēd′lər) *n. Informal.* a person who nags or irritates others; heckler.

need·less (nēd′lis) *adj.* not needed; unnecessary. **—need′less·ly,** *adv.* **—need′less·ness,** *n.*

needle valve a valve whose very small opening is controlled by a slender, needle-shaped rod.

nee·dle·wom·an (nē′dəl wu̇m′ən) *n.* **-wom·en. 1** a woman who is a skilful sewer. **2** a woman who earns her living by sewing.

nee·dle·work (nē′dəl wėrk′) *n.* work done with a needle; sewing; embroidery.

need·n't (nēd′ənt) need not.

needs (nēdz) *adv.* because of necessity; necessarily: *A soldier needs must go where duty calls.* [OE *nēdes*, originally gen. of *nēd* need]

need·y (nēd′ē) *adj.* **need·i·er, need·i·est.** very poor; not having enough to live on. **—need′i·ness,** *n.* **—Syn.** indigent, destitute, penniless.

ne'er (nãr) *adv. Poetic.* never.

ne'er-do-well (nãr′dü wel′) *n.* a worthless fellow; good-for-nothing person. —*adj.* worthless; good-for-nothing.

ne·far·i·ous (ni fãr′ē əs) *adj.* very wicked; villainous. [< L *nefarius*, ult. < *ne-* not + *fas* right, originally, (divine) decree < *fari* speak] **—ne·far′i·ous·ly,** *adv.* **—ne·far′i·ous·ness,** *n.* **—Syn.** heinous, atrocious, infamous.

ne·gate (ni gāt′) *v.* **-gat·ed, -gat·ing.** deny; nullify. [< L *negare* say no]

ne·ga·tion (ni gā′shən) *n.* **1** a denying; denial: *Shaking the head is a sign of negation.* **2** the absence or opposite of some positive thing or quality: *Darkness is the negation of light.* [< L *negatio, -onis* < *negare* say no]

neg·a·tive (neg′ə tiv) *adj. n. v.* **-tived, -tiv·ing.** —*adj.* **1** saying no: *His answer was negative.* **2** not positive; consisting in the lack of the opposite: *Not being unkind is only negative kindness.* **3** in mathematics and physics: **a** counting down from zero; minus: *Three below zero is a negative quantity.* **b** measured or proceeding in the opposite direction to that considered as positive. **4 a** of the kind of electricity produced on resin when it is rubbed with silk, or that present in a charged body which has an excess of electrons. **b** characterized by the presence or production of such electricity. **5** in photography, showing the lights and shadows reversed: *the negative image on a photographic plate.* **6** in chemistry, having a tendency to gain electrons, and thus to become charged with negative electricity, as an element or radical. **7** showing an absence of the germs, symptoms, etc. of an illness. **8** in psychology, resisting suggestions; very unco-operative.
—*n.* **1** a word or statement that says no or denies. **2** in a debate or argument, the side that says no or denies. **3** a negative quality or characteristic. **4** a minus quantity, sign, etc. **5** the kind of electricity produced on resin when it is rubbed with silk. **6** the negative element in an electric cell. See **electrode** for diagram. **7** in photography, an image in which the lights and shadows are reversed and from which prints can be made. **8** the right of veto. **9 in the negative, a** in favor of denying (a request, suggestion, etc.). **b** saying no; denying.

—*v.* **1** say no to; deny; vote against. **2** disprove. **3** make useless; counteract; neutralize. [< L *negativus* < *negare* say no] —**neg′a·tive·ly,** *adv.*

neg·a·tiv·ism (neg′ə tiv iz′əm) *n.* **1** a tendency to say or do the opposite of what is suggested. **2** in psychology, a type of behavior marked by resistance to suggestion.

neg·lect (ni glekt′) *v.* **1** give too little care or attention to: *neglect one's health.* **2** leave undone; not attend to: *The maid neglected her work.* **3** omit; fail: *Don't neglect to water the plants.* —*n.* **1** the act of neglecting; disregard. **2** a want of attention to what should be done. **3** a being neglected. [< L *neglectus,* pp. of *negligere, neglegere,* var. of *neclegere* < *nec* not (< *ne-* not + *que* and) + *legere* pick up] —**neg·lect′er,** *n.*
Syn. *v.* **1** See **slight. 2** disregard, ignore. —*n.* **1 Neglect, negligence** = lack of proper care or attention. **Neglect** applies especially to the act or fact of giving too little care or attention to one's duty or work or leaving it undone: *That car has been ruined by neglect.* **Negligence** applies especially to the quality of being inclined to neglect, possessed by a person or group or shown by inattentiveness to work or duty or carelessness in doing it: *Many accidents in industry are caused by the negligence of workers.*

neg·lect·ful (ni glekt′fəl) *adj.* careless; negligent. —**neg·lect′ful·ly,** *adv.*

né·gli·gé (nā glē zhā′) *n. French.* negligee.

neg·li·gee (neg′lə zhā′ or neg′lə zhā) *n.* **1** a woman's loose dressing gown of a light fabric, usually trimmed with lace, ruffles, etc. **2** easy, informal dress or attire. [< F *négligée,* fem. pp. of *négliger* neglect]

neg·li·gence (neg′lə jəns) *n.* **1** a lack of proper care or attention; neglect: *Because of the owner's negligence the house was in great need of repair.* **2** carelessness; indifference. [< L *negligentia* < *negligere.* See NEGLECT.] —**Syn. 1** remissness, inattention. See **neglect. 2** heedlessness.

neg·li·gent (neg′lə jənt) *adj.* **1** neglectful; given to neglect; showing neglect. **2** careless; indifferent: *His negligent behavior resulted in an accident.* [< L *negligens, -entis,* ppr. of *negligere.* See NEGLECT.] —**neg′li·gent·ly,** *adv.* —**Syn. 1** remiss, derelict. **2** heedless.

neg·li·gi·ble (neg′lə jə bəl) *adj.* that can be disregarded: *In buying a suit, a difference of fifty cents in prices is negligible.*

ne·go·tia·bil·i·ty (ni gō′shə bil′ə tē or ni gō′shē ə bil′ə tē) *n.* a being negotiable.

ne·go·tia·ble (ni gō′shə bəl or ni gō′shē ə bəl) *adj.* **1** capable of being negotiated or sold; whose ownership can be transferred. **2** that can be got past or over.

ne·go·ti·ate (ni gō′shē āt′) *v.* **-at·ed, -at·ing. 1** talk over and arrange terms: *The colonists negotiated for peace with the Indians.* **2** arrange for: *They finally negotiated a peace treaty.* **3** sell. **4** *Informal.* get past or over: *The car negotiated the sharp curve by slowing down.* [< L *negotiare* < *negotium* business < *neg-* not + *otium* ease] —**ne·go′ti·a′tor,** *n.* —**Syn. 1** parley, confer, consult.

ne·go·ti·a·tion (ni gō′shē ā′shən) *n.* a negotiating; arrangement: *Negotiations for the new school are finished.*

Ne·gress (nē′gris′) *n. Often derogatory.* a Negro girl or woman.

Ne·gri·to (ni grē′tō) *n.* **-tos** or **-toes. 1** certain dwarfish Negroid people of Central Africa and of S.E. Asia, especially of the Philippine Islands and East Indies. **2** a member of these peoples. [< Sp. *negrito,* dim. of *negro* Negro]

Ne·gro (nē′grō) *n.* **-groes,** *adj.* —*n.* **1** a person belonging to any of the black peoples of Africa. **2** a colored person having some black ancestors. —*adj.* of or having to do with Negroes. [< Sp. < L *niger* black]

Ne·groid (nē′groid) *adj.* resembling Negroes; akin to the Negro race; of a Negro type. —*n.* a person of a Negroid race.

ne·gus (nē′gəs) *n.* a drink made of wine, hot water, sugar, lemon, and nutmeg. [after Colonel Francis *Negus* (died 1732), its inventor]

Ne·gus (nē′gəs) *n.* the ruler of Ethiopia. [< Amharic]

Neh. Nehemiah.

neigh (nā) *n.* the sound that a horse makes. [< v.] —*v.* make the sound that a horse makes or one like it. [OE *hnǣgan*]

neigh·bor or **neigh·bour** (nā′bər) *n.* **1** one who lives near another. **2** a person or thing that is near another. **3** a fellow human being. —*v.* **1** live or be near to. **2** adjoin; border on. **3** be friendly with. —*adj.* living or situated near to another. [OE *nēahgebūr* < *nēah* nigh + *gebūr* dweller, countryman] —**neigh′bor·less** or **neigh′bour·less,** *adj.*

neigh·bor·hood or **neigh·bour·hood** (nā′bər hůd′) *n.* **1** the region near some place or thing. **2** a place; district: *Is your new house in an attractive neighborhood?* **3** the people of a place or district: *The whole neighborhood came to the big party.* **4** neighborly feeling or conduct. **5** nearness. **6 in the neighborhood of,** *Informal.* somewhere near; about: *The car cost in the neighborhood of $2,500.* —*adj.* of or having to do with a neighborhood: *a neighborhood newspaper.* —**Syn.** *n.* **1** vicinity; environs. **2** locality.

neigh·bor·ing or **neigh·bour·ing** (nā′bər ing or nā′bring) *adj.* living or being near; bordering; adjoining; near.

neigh·bor·ly or **neigh·bour·ly** (nā′bər lē) *adj.* kindly; friendly; sociable. —**neigh′bor·li·ness** or **neigh′bour·li·ness,** *n.*

neigh·bour (nā′bər) *n. v. adj.* neighbor.

nei·ther (nē′ᴛʜər or nī′ᴛʜər) *conj.* **1** not either: *Neither you nor I will go.* **2** nor yet: *"They toil not, neither do they spin."* —*adj.* not either: *Neither statement is true.* —*pron.* not either: *Neither of the statements is true.* [ME *neither* < *ne* not + *either*]

nel·son (nel′sən) *n.* either of two holds in wrestling. See **half nelson** and **full nelson.** [origin uncertain]

nem·a·tode (nem′ə tōd′) *adj.* of or belonging to a class of worms characterized by an elongated, unsegmented, cylindrical body. —*n.* a worm of this class. Hookworms, pinworms, and trichinae are nematodes. [< NL *Nematoda,* pl., ult. < Gk. *nēma, -atos* thread < *neein* spin]

Ne·me·an games (ni mē′ən or nē′mē ən) in ancient Greece, a Panhellenic festival held every two years in Nemea.

Nemean lion the lion killed by Hercules as one of his twelve tasks.

ne·mer·te·an or **ne·mer·ti·an** (ni mėr′tē ən) *n.* any of a class of brightly colored marine worms having a flat, unsegmented body and a long, extensible proboscis. —*adj.* of or having to do with, the nemerteans. [< NL *Nemertea,* the class name < Gk. *Nēmertēs* a sea nymph + E *-an, -ian*]

Nem·e·sis (nem′ə sis) *n.* **-ses** (-sēz′). **1** in Greek mythology, the goddess of vengeance. **2 nemesis, a** just punishment for evil deeds. **b** a person who punishes another for evil deeds. [< Gk. *Nemesis* < *nemein* give what is due]

neo- *combining form.* new; recent, as in *Neozoic.* [< Gk. *neos*]

Ne·o·cene (nē′ə sēn′) in geology: —*n.* **1** the later division of the Tertiary system, comprising the Miocene and Pliocene periods. **2** the rocks formed during this division. —*adj.* of or having to do with this division or the rocks formed during it. [*neo-* + Gk. *kainos* recent]

ne·o·class·ic (nē′ō klas′ik) *adj.* of or having to do with neoclassicism.

ne·o·clas·si·cism (nē′ō klas′ə siz′əm) *n.* **1** in the visual arts, the revival of classical ideals of form, proportion, and restraint. **2** in literature, a similar style or movement, especially that which prevailed in 18th-century England. **3** in music, a 20th-century movement marked by a return to the style of classical composers such as Johann Sebastian Bach.

ne·o·clas·si·cist (nē′ō klas′ə sist) *n.* a follower of neoclassicism.

ne·o·dym·i·um (nē′ō dim′ē əm) *n.* a rare-earth metallic chemical element found in certain rare minerals. *Symbol:* Nd; *at.no.* 60; *at.wt.* 144.24. [< *neo-* + *didymium*]

ne·o·fas·cism (nē′ō fash′iz əm) *n.* any movement to restore the former beliefs or principles of fascism.

ne·o·fas·cist (nē′ō fash′ist) *n.* **1** a member of a political party favoring neofascism. **2** a person who supports or favors neofascism. —*adj.* of or having to do with neofascists.

ne·o·lith·ic (nē′ə lith′ ik) *adj.* of the later Stone Age, when polished stone weapons and tools were first made and used, marked also by the appearance of settled agriculture and of accompanying social development: *neolithic man.* [< *neo-* + Gk. *lithos* stone]

ne·ol·o·gism (ni ol′ə jiz′əm) *n.* **1** the use of new words or new meanings for old words. **2** a new word; new meaning for an old word. [< F < Gk. *neos* new + *logos* word]

ne·o·my·cin (nē′ō mī′sən) *n.* an antibiotic drug obtained from the soil. [< *neo-* + Gk. *mykēs* fungus]

ne·on (nē′on) *n.* an inert chemical element that is a colorless, odorless gas, forming a very small part of the air. Tubes containing neon are used in electric signs and television sets. *Symbol*: Ne; *at.no.* 10; *at.wt.* 20.183. [< NL < Gk. *neon*, neut., new]

ne·o-Na·zi (nē′ō nat′sē or -nä′tsē) *n.* **1** a member of a political party favoring neo-Naziism. **2** a person who supports or favors neo-Naziism. —*adj.* of or having to do with neo-Naziism or neo-Nazis.

ne·o-Na·zi·ism (nē′ō nat′sē iz′əm or -nä′tsē iz′əm) *n.* a movement to restore the principles and beliefs of Naziism.

ne·o-Na·zism (nē′ō nat′siz əm or -nä′tsiz əm) *n.* neo-Naziism.

ne·o·phyte (nē′ə fīt′) *n.* **1** a new convert; one recently admitted to a religious body. **2** a beginner; novice. [< L < Gk. *neophytos* < *neos* new + *phyein* to plant]

ne·o·prene (nē′ə prēn′) *n.* a synthetic rubber made from chloroprene.

Ne·o·zo·ic (nē′ə zō′ik) *adj.* in geology, noting or having to do with the period from the end of the Mesozoic to the present; Cenozoic. [< *neo-* + Gk. *zōē* life]

Nep·al·ese (nep′ə lēz′) *n.* a native or inhabitant of Nepal, a country lying between India and China. —*adj.* of or having to do with Nepal or its people.

ne·pen·the (ni pen′thē) *n.* **1** a drug supposed to bring forgetfulness of sorrow or trouble. **2** anything that brings forgetfulness. [< L < Gk. *nēpenthēs* < *nē-* not + *penthos* grief]

neph·ew (nef′ū; *esp.Brit.* nev′ū) *n.* **1** the son of one's brother or sister. **2** the son of one's brother-in-law or sister-in-law. [ME < OF *neveu* < L *nepos*]

neph·rite (nef′rīt) *n.* a silicate of calcium and either magnesium or iron, one of the two varieties of jade. It is not as hard or as valuable as jadeite, the other variety of jade. [< G *Nephrit* < Gk. *nephros* kidney (from its supposed value in curing kidney disease)]

ne·phrit·ic (ni frit′ik) *adj.* **1** of, having to do with, or affected with kidney disease. **2** used against kidney disease. **3** of or having to do with a kidney, or kidneys.

ne·phri·tis (ni frī′tis) *n.* inflammation of the kidneys, especially Bright's disease. [< LL < Gk. *nephritis* < *nephros* kidney]

ne plus ul·tra (nē′ or nā′ plus′ ul′trə) *Latin.* highest or furthest point attainable; height of excellence or achievement; culmination.

nep·o·tism (nep′ə tiz′əm) *n.* the showing of too much favor by one in power to his relatives, especially by giving them desirable appointments. [< F < Ital. *nepotismo* < *nepote* nephew]

Nep·tune (nep′tūn or nep′tün) *n.* **1** in Roman mythology, the god of the sea, identified with the Greek god Poseidon. **2** the fourth largest planet in the solar system and the eighth in distance from the sun. It is too far from the earth to be seen with the naked eye.

nep·tu·ni·um (nep tū′nē əm or nep tü′nē əm) *n.* a radio-active chemical element obtained by bombardment of uranium with neutrons, used in certain types of atomic bombs. *Symbol*: Np; *at.no.* 93; *at.wt.* 237 (most stable isotope). [< *Neptune*]

Ne·re·id or **ne·re·id** (nēr′ē id) *n.* in Greek mythology, any of the fifty daughters of Nereus. The Nereids were sea nymphs who attended Poseidon.

Ne·reus (nēr′üs or nēr′ē əs) *n.* in Greek mythology, a sea god, father of the Nereids.

ner·ka (nėr′kə) *n.* sockeye. [? a native name]

ner·va·tion (nėr vā′shən) *n.* in biology, the arrangement of veins or ribs in a leaf or an insect's wing.

hat, āge, cãre, fär; let, ēqual, tėrm; it, īce
hot, ōpen, ôrder; oil, out; cup, pu̇t, rüle, ūse
əbove, takən, pencəl, lemən, circəs
ch, child; ng, long; sh, ship
th, thin; ᴛʜ, then; zh, measure

nerve (nėrv) *n. v.* **nerved, nerv·ing.** —*n.* **1** in physiology, a fibre or bundle of fibres connecting the brain or spinal cord with the eyes, ears, muscles, glands, etc. **2** mental strength; courage. **3** strength; vigor; energy. **4** *Informal.* rude boldness; impudence. **5** in biology: **a** a vein of a leaf. **b** one of the thicker lines in an insect's wing. **6 get on one's nerves,** annoy or irritate one. **7 nerves,** *pl.* **a** nervousness. **b** an attack of nervousness. **8 strain every nerve,** exert oneself to the utmost.
—*v.* arouse strength or courage in: *The soldiers nerved themselves for the battle.* [< L *nervus* sinew, tendon]

nerve cell **1** a neurone; cell that conducts impulses. **2** the cell body of a neurone, excluding its fibres.

nerve centre or **center** **1** a group of nerve cells closely connected with one another and acting together in the performance of some function. **2 a** any place that is the centre of activity or a source of direction. **b** the person or persons who control such a place.

nerve fibre or **fiber** any of the threadlike fibres that constitute the chief part of nerves. The long processes of certain neurones become a nerve fibre.

nerve gas a gas containing invisible particles that penetrate the skin and attack the central nervous system, causing extreme weakness or death. Nerve gas is used in warfare.

nerve·less (nėrv′lis) *adj.* **1** without strength or vigor; feeble; weak. **2** without courage or firmness. **3** without nerves. —**nerve′less·ly,** *adv.*

nerve-wrack·ing or **nerve-rack·ing** (nėrv′rak′ing) *adj.* trying to the limit of endurance; exasperating.

nerv·ous (nėr′vəs) *adj.* **1** of the nerves: *The brain is a part of the nervous system of the body.* **2** having delicate or easily excited nerves. **3** having or proceeding from nerves that are out of order: *a nervous patient, a nervous tapping of the fingers.* **4** deriving from a tense or quickened condition of the nerves: *nervous energy.* **5** restless; uneasy; timid. **6** having nerves. **7** strong; vigorous. [< L *nervosus* sinewy < *nervus* sinew, tendon] —**nerv′ous·ly,** *adv.* —**nerv′ous·ness,** *n.* —**Syn. 2** high-strung, excitable.

nervous breakdown any mental or emotional disorder that requires treatment.

nervous system the system of nerves and nerve cells in a person or animal. Man's central nervous system includes the brain and spinal cord.

ner·vure (nėr′vūr) *n.* in biology: **1** a vein of a leaf. **2** a rib of an insect's wing. [< F]

nerv·y (nėr′vē) *adj.* **nerv·i·er, nerv·iest. 1** *Slang.* rude and bold. **2** requiring courage or firmness. **3** strong; vigorous. **4** nervous.

NES or **N.E.S.** National Employment Service.

nes·cience (nesh′əns or nesh′ē əns) *n.* ignorance. [< LL *nescientia*, ult. < L *ne-* not + *scire* know]

ness (nes) *n.* a cape or promontory. [ME *nasse* < OE *næs*, akin to OE *nosu* nose]

-ness *suffix.* **1** the quality, state, or condition of being ——: *preparedness* = *the state of being prepared.* **2** —— action; —— behavior: *carefulness* (*in some uses*) = *careful action*; *careful behavior.* [OE *-nes*(*s*)]
☛ **-ness** is a living suffix and can be freely used to form new words.

Nes·sus (nes′əs) *n.* in Greek legend, a centaur shot by Hercules with a poisoned arrow. Hercules was himself fatally poisoned by a shirt steeped in the blood of Nessus.

nest (nest) *n.* **1** a structure or place used by birds for laying eggs and rearing young. **2** a place used by insects, fish, turtles, rabbits, etc. for depositing eggs or young. **3** a snug abode, retreat, or resting place. **4** a place where evil or harmful persons gather; a den: *a nest of thieves.* **5** the birds, animals, or insects living in a nest. **6** a set or series (often from large to small) such that each fits within another: *a nest of drinking cups.* **7** *Informal.* a base for guided missiles.

—*v.* 1 build or have a nest. 2 settle or place in, or as if in, a nest. [OE]

nest egg 1 a natural or artificial egg left in a nest to induce a hen to continue laying eggs there. 2 something, usually a sum of money, as the beginning of a fund or as a reserve: *When he got married, he had already saved quite a nest egg.*

nes·tle (nes′əl) *v.* **-tled, -tling.** 1 settle oneself comfortably or cosily: *She nestled down into the big chair.* 2 be settled comfortably or cosily; be sheltered: *The little house nestled among the trees.* 3 press close in affection or for comfort: *nestle up to one's mother, nestle a baby in one's arms.* 4 make or have a nest; settle in a nest. [OE *nestlian* < *nest* nest] —**nes′tler,** *n.*

nest·ling (nest′ling) *n.* 1 a bird too young to leave the nest. 2 a young child.

Nes·tor (nes′tər) *n.* 1 in Greek legend, a king of Pylos who led the Greeks to Troy. He was famed for his great age, eloquence, and wisdom. 2 any wise old man.

net[1] (net) *n. v.* **net·ted, net·ting.** —*n.* 1 an open fabric made of string, cord, thread, or hair, knotted together in such a way as to leave holes regularly arranged. 2 a piece of net used for some special purpose: *a fish net, a hair net, a tennis net.* 3 anything like a net; a set of things that cross each other. 4 a lacelike cloth. 5 a trap or snare. 6 in tennis, etc., a ball that hits the net.
—*v.* 1 catch in a net: *net a fish.* 2 cover, confine, or protect with a net. 3 make into a net. 4 make with net. 5 in tennis, etc., hit (a ball) into the net. [OE *nett*]
—**Syn.** *n.* 1 mesh, network, reticulation.

net[2] (net) *adj. n. v.* **net·ted, net·ting.** —*adj.* remaining after deductions; free from deductions. A net gain or profit is the actual gain after all working expenses have been paid. The net weight of a glass jar of candy is the weight of the candy itself. The net price of a book is the real price, from which no discount can be made. —*n.* the net weight, profit, price, etc. —*v.* gain: *The sale netted me a good profit.* [< F. See NEAT[1].]

neth·er (neᴛʜ′ər) *adj.* lower: *nether garments, nether regions.* [OE *neothera*]

Neth·er·land·er (neᴛʜ′ər lan′dər) *n.* a native or inhabitant of the Netherlands, a small country in Europe, west of Germany and north of Belgium.

neth·er·most (neᴛʜ′ər mōst′) *adj.* lowest.

net·ting (net′ing) *n.* a netted or meshed material: *mosquito netting, wire netting for window screens.*

net·tle (net′əl) *n. v.* **-tled, -tling.** —*n.* a kind of plant whose leaves have sharp hairs that sting the skin when touched. —*v.* sting the mind of; irritate; provoke; vex: *Father was nettled by the boy's frequent interruptions.* [OE *netele*] —**net′tle-like′,** *adj.* —**Syn.** *v.* exasperate, incense.

net·work (net′wėrk′) *n.* 1 a netting; net. 2 any netlike combination of things: *a network of vines, a network of highways.* 3 a group of radio or television stations that usually carry the same programs: *the French network of the CBC.*

neu·ral (nūr′əl or nür′əl) *adj.* of or having to do with a nerve, neurone, or nervous system. [< Gk. *neuron* nerve]

neu·ral·gia (nū ral′jə or nü ral′jə) *n.* pain, usually sharp, along the course of a nerve. [< NL < Gk. *neuron* nerve + *algos* pain]

neu·ral·gic (nū ral′jik or nü ral′jik) *adj.* of or having to do with neuralgia.

neu·ras·the·ni·a (nūr′əs thē′nē ə or nür′əs thē′nē ə) *n.* 1 nervous exhaustion or weakness. 2 a neurosis accompanied by local digestive or circulatory upset of uncertain origin, and characterized by extreme fatigue and chronic depression. [< NL < Gk. *neuron* nerve + *astheneia* weakness]

neu·ras·then·ic (nūr′əs then′ik or nür′əs then′ik) *adj.* having to do with or suffering from neurasthenia.
—*n.* a person suffering from neurasthenia.

neu·ri·tis (nū rī′tis or nü rī′tis) *n.* inflammation of a nerve or nerves. [< NL < Gk. *neuron* nerve + *-itis*]

neu·rol·o·gist (nū rol′ə jist or nü rol′ə jist) *n.* a person trained in neurology.

neu·rol·o·gy (nū rol′ə jē or nü rol′ə jē) *n.* the study of the nervous system and its diseases. [< Gk. *neuron* nerve + E *-logy*]

neu·ron (nūr′on or nür′on) *n.* neurone.

neu·rone (nūr′ōn or nür′ōn) *n.* in physiology, one of the conducting cells of which the brain, spinal cord, and nerves are composed. A neurone consists of a cell body containing the nucleus, and processes or fibres, some of which may be very long. [< Gk. *neuron* nerve]

neu·ro·phys·i·ol·o·gy (nūr′ō fiz ē ol′ə jē or nür′ō-) *n.* the branch of physiology dealing with the nervous system.

neu·ro·psy·chi·a·try (nūr′ō sī kī′ə trē or nür′ō-) *n.* the branch of medicine dealing with neurology and psychiatry.

neu·ro·sis (nū rō′sis or nü rō′sis) *n.* **-ses** (-sēz). any of certain mental diseases or disorders, less severe than psychosis. [< NL < Gk. *neuron* nerve]

neu·ro·sur·ge·ry (nūr′ō sėr′jə rē or nür′ō-) *n.* surgery of the nervous system, especially of the brain.

neu·rot·ic (nū rot′ik or nü rot′ik) *adj.* 1 suffering from a neurosis. 2 too nervous. —*n.* a person with a neurosis. —**neu·rot′i·cal·ly,** *adv.* —**neu·rot′i·cism** (-ə siz′əm), *n.*

neut. neuter.

neu·ter (nū′tər or nü′tər) *adj.* 1 in grammar, neither masculine nor feminine. *It* is a neuter pronoun. 2 **a** in zoology, having no sex organs or having sex organs that are not fully developed: *Worker bees are neuter.* **b** in botany, having neither stamens nor pistils; functionally asexual. 3 being on neither side; neutral. —*n.* 1 in grammar: **a** a neuter word or form. **b** the neuter gender. 2 in biology, an animal, plant, or insect that is neuter. [< L *neuter* < *ne-* not + *uter* either]

neu·tral (nū′trəl or nü′trəl) *adj.* 1 on neither side in a quarrel or war: *Switzerland was neutral during the last two wars in Europe.* 2 of or belonging to a neutral country or neutral zone: *a neutral port.* 3 being neither one thing nor the other; indefinite. 4 having little or no color; grayish. 5 in chemistry, neither acid not alkaline. 6 of electricity, neither positive nor negative. 7 in biology, not developed in sex.
—*n.* 1 a neutral person or country; one not taking part in a quarrel or war. 2 the position of gears when they do not transmit motion from the engine to the wheels or other working parts. [< L *neutralis* < *neuter.* See NEUTER.] —**neu′tral·ly,** *adv.*

neu·tral·ist (nū′trəl ist or nü′trəl ist) *n.* a person who practises or advocates neutrality, especially in international affairs. —*adj.* practising or advocating neutrality: *India is a neutralist country.* —**neu′tral·ism,** *n.*

neu·tral·i·ty (nū tral′ə tē or nü tral′ə tē) *n.* a being neutral; the attitude or policy of a nation that does not take part directly or indirectly in a war between other nations; neutral character or status. —**Syn.** impartiality.

neu·tral·ize (nū′trəl īz′ or nü′trəl īz′) *v.* **-ized, -iz·ing.** 1 make neutral. 2 keep war out of. 3 make of no effect by some opposite force; counterbalance. Alkalis neutralize acids. —**neu′tral·i·za′tion,** *n.* —**neu′tral·iz′er,** *n.* —**Syn.** 3 counteract, offset.

neutral vowel schwa.

neu·tri·no (nū trē′nō or nü trē′nō) *n.* an atomic particle having no electric charge and no mass when in a state of rest.

neu·tron (nū′tron or nü′tron) *n.* a particle that is neutral electrically and has about the same mass as a proton. [< *neutral* neither positively nor negatively charged + *-on* (after *electron, proton*)]

Nev. Nevada.

né·vé (nā′vā′) *n.* 1 granular snow that is compacted and partly converted into ice, found at the surface on the upper part of a glacier. 2 a field of this snow. [< F, ult. < L *nix, nivis* snow]

nev·er (nev′ər) *adv.* 1 not ever; at no time: *He has never seen a more perfect copy.* 2 in no case; not at all; to no extent or degree: *never the wiser.* 3 **never mind, a** pay no attention to; forget about: *Never mind the noise. Never mind your coats.* **b** it doesn't matter; forget it. 4 **never so, a** not even so. **b** no matter how. [OE *nǣfre* < *ne* not + *ǣfre* ever]

nev·er·more (nev′ər môr′) *adv.* never again.

nev·er-nev·er (nev′ər nev′ər) *adj. Informal.* **1** illusory; imaginary. **2** ideal; not easily visualized; implausible. —*n.* Also, **never never.** *Brit. Slang.* instalment buying.

nev·er·the·less (nev′ər ᴛʜə les′) *adv.* however; none the less; for all that; in spite of it: *She was very tired; nevertheless, she kept on working.* —**Syn.** but, still.

new (nū or nü) *adj.* **1** never having existed before; now first made, thought out, known or heard of, felt, or discovered: *a new invention.* **2** lately grown, come, or made; not old: *a new bud.* **3** now first used; not worn or used up: *a new path.* **4** beginning again: *The new moon is the moon when seen as a thin crescent.* **5** as if new; fresh: *go on with new courage. After taking a shower he felt a new man.* **6** different; changed: *He is a new man now.* **7** not familiar: *a new country to me.* **8** not yet accustomed: *new to the work.* **9** later; modern; recent: *new dances.* **10** just come; having just reached the position: *a new arrival, a new president.* **11** being the later or latest of two or more things of the same kind: *New France, New Testament.* **12** further; additional; more: *He sought new information on the subject.*
—*adv.* **1** newly; recently or lately; freshly: *new-mown hay.* **2** again; anew. [OE *nīwe*] —**new′ness,** *n.*
Syn. *adj.* **1 New, novel, modern** = having only now or recently come into existence or knowledge. **New** describes something now existing, made, seen, or known for the first time: *They own a new house.* **Novel** adds and emphasizes the idea of being unusual, strikingly different, or strange, not of the ordinary kind: *Their house has a novel dining room.* **Modern** describes people and things belonging to or characteristic of the present time, or recent times, and sometimes suggests being up-to-date, not old-fashioned: *The architecture is modern.* **3** fresh, unused. **7** unfamiliar, strange.

new·born (nū′bôrn′ or nü′-) *adj.* **1** recently or only just born: *a newborn baby.* **2** ready to start a new life; born again.

New Caledonia an early name for that part of British Columbia lying between the Rocky Mountains and the Coast Range.

New Canadian **1** a person who has recently arrived in Canada from another country with the intention of becoming a Canadian citizen. **2** a person originally from another country who has recently become a Canadian citizen.

New·cas·tle (nū′kas′əl or nü′-) *n.* **carry coal to Newcastle, a** waste one's time, effort, etc. **b** bring something to a place where it is not needed (as coal to Newcastle, England, where it is plentiful).

new·com·er (nū′kum′ər or nü′-) *n.* a person who has just come or who came not long ago.

New Deal in the United States, the policies and measures advocated in the 1930's by President Franklin D. Roosevelt as a means of improving economic and social welfare.

New Democratic Party a Canadian political party, founded in 1961.

new·el (nū′əl or nü′əl) *n.* **1** the post at the top or bottom of a stairway that supports the railing. **2** the central post of a winding stairway. [ME < OF *nouel,* ult. < L *nux* nut; influenced by OF *noel* bud, ult. < L *nodus* knot]

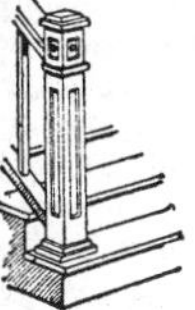
A newel

New Englander a native or inhabitant of New England, the northeastern part of the United States.

new·fan·gled (nū′fang′gəld or nü′-) *adj.* **1** lately come into fashion; of a new kind. **2** fond of novelty. [ME *newefangle* < *newe* new + *fange(n)* take]

new-fash·ioned (nū′fash′ənd or nü′-) *adj.* of a new fashion; lately come into style.

New·found·land (nū′found′lənd or nü′-) *n.* **1** a breed of very large, intelligent dog resembling a spaniel but much larger, having a shaggy, usually black, coat. **2** a dog of this breed. [< *Newfoundland,* where this powerful swimming dog was originally trained to rescue people from drowning]

New France the name of the territory in North America belonging to France from 1609 to 1763. Among other regions, it included Quebec, Acadia, and the Louisiana Territory.

New·gate (nū′gāt or nü′-) *n.* formerly, a famous prison in London. It was demolished in 1902.

hat, āge, cãre, fär; let, ēqual, tėrm; it, īce
hot, ōpen, ôrder; oil, out; cup, pu̇t, rüle, ūse
əbove, takən, pencəl, lemən, circəs
ch, child; ng, long; sh, ship
th, thin; ᴛʜ, then; zh, measure

New Jerusalem heaven.

New Latin the Latin language after 1500, especially as used for scientific terms. *Abbrev.*: NL or N.L.

new·ly (nū′lē or nü′-) *adv.* **1** lately; recently: *newly wedded.* **2** again; freshly: *a newly revived scandal.* **3** in a new way.

new·ly·wed (nū′lē wed′ or nü′lē-) *n.* a newly married person.

new moon the moon when seen as a thin crescent with the hollow side on the left.

new penny *n.* **new pence.** a British bronze coin of the decimal system officially introduced in 1971, worth about 2½ cents. 100 new pence = one pound.

news (nūz or nüz) *n.* **1** something told as having just happened; information about something that has just happened or will soon happen. **2** a report of a current happening or happenings in a newspaper, on television, radio, etc. **3 break the news,** make something known; tell something. [ME *newes,* pl. of *newe* that which is new, adj. used as n.] —**Syn. 1** tidings, advices, intelligence, information.
☛ **news.** Though plural in form, *news* is used as a singular: *The news from the various districts is sent to a central office.*

news·boy (nūz′boi′ or nüz′-) *n.* a boy or man who sells or delivers newspapers.

news·cast (nūz′kast′ or nüz′-) *n.* a radio or television program devoted to current events, news bulletins, etc. —*v.* broadcast (news). —**news′cast′er,** *n.*

news·hound (nūz′hound′ or nüz′-) *n. Informal.* a news reporter.

news·let·ter (nūz′let′ər or nüz′-) *n.* a written or printed letter presenting an informal or confidential coverage of the news.

news magazine (nūz′mag′ə zēn′ or nüz′-) a magazine, usually one published weekly, that reports, comments on, and interprets the news and current events.

news·man (nūz′man′ or nüz′-) *n.* **-men** (-men′). **1** a man who sells or delivers newspapers. **2** a newspaperman or newscaster.

news·mon·ger (nūz′mung′gər or nüz′-, nūz′mong′gər or nüz′-) *n.* a person who gathers and spreads news.

news·pa·per (nūz′pā′pər or nüz′-) *n.* **1** a publication consisting of folded sheets of paper usually printed daily or weekly and containing news stories and pictures, advertisements, and other reading matter of general interest. **2** the paper used; newsprint. **3** the company or organization that publishes a newspaper: *The newspaper sent a reporter to the scene of the accident.*

news·pa·per·man (nūz′pā′pər man′ or nüz′-) *n.* **-men** (-men′). a newspaper reporter, editor, etc.

news·print (nūz′print′ or nüz′-) *n.* a soft, cheap, coarse paper made from wood pulp, the kind on which newspapers are usually printed.

news·reel (nūz′rēl′ or nüz′-) *n.* a motion picture showing current events.

news·room (nūz′rüm′ or nüz′-, nūz′ru̇m or nüz′-) *n.* a room or section of a newspaper office or radio or television station where news is collected and edited for publication or broadcasting.

news·stand (nūz′stand′ or nüz′-) *n.* a place where newspapers and magazines are sold.

New Style the method of reckoning time according to the Gregorian calendar, adopted in England, and generally throughout the English-speaking world, in 1752. See **Old Style.**

news·wor·thy (nūz′wėr′ᴛʜē or nüz′-) *adj.* of sufficient importance or interest to be reported and published or broadcast.

news·y (nūz′ē or nüz′ē) *adj.* **news·i·er, news·i·est,** *n.* **news·ies.** *Informal.* —*adj.* full of news. —*n.* a newsboy or newsman.

newt (nüt or nüt) *n.* any of various small salamanders that live in water part of the time. [OE *efete*; ME *an ewt* taken as *a newt*]

New Testament the part of the Bible that contains the life and teachings of Christ recorded by His followers, together with their own experiences and teachings.

new·ton (nü′tən or nü′ tən) *n.* a measure of force, equal to 100,000 dynes. *Symbol*: N [after Sir Isaac *Newton*. See NEWTONIAN.]

New·to·ni·an (nü tō′nē ən or nü tō′nē ən) *adj.* of or by Sir Isaac Newton, 1642-1727, the English scientist and mathematician who discovered the law of gravitation.

New World the Western Hemisphere.

new-world (nü′wėrld′ or nü′-) *adj.* of or having to do with the Western Hemisphere.

new year 1 the year approaching or newly begun. 2 **New Year** or **New Year's,** January 1; the first day or days of the year.

New Year's Day January 1, usually observed as a legal holiday.

New Zea·land·er (zē′lən dər) a native or inhabitant of New Zealand, a British dominion in the S. Pacific.

next (nekst) *adj.* **1** nearest in position: *Who is the girl next to you?* **2** nearest in succession of time or order: *We'll catch the next train. The next day after Sunday is Monday.*
—adv. **1** in the next place: *I am going to do my arithmetic problems next.* **2 next door to, a** in or at the house next to. **b** almost; very close to: *Cheating is an act next door to crime.* **3 next to, a** nearest to. **b** almost; nearly.
—prep. nearest to: *We live in the house next the church.* [OE *nēhst*, superlative of *nēah* nigh]

next-door (nekst′dôr′) *adj.* in or at the next house.

next of kin the nearest blood relative or relatives.

nex·us (nek′səs) *n.* **nex·us. 1** a connection; link. **2** a connected series. [< L *nexus*, ult. < *nectere* bind]

Nez Per·cé (nez′pėrs′; *French*, nā per sā′) *n.* **Nez Per·cés** (nez′ pėr′siz; *French*, nā per sā′). **1** an American Indian tribe that formerly lived in Idaho, Oregon, and Washington. **2** a member of this tribe. **3** the language of this tribe. [< F *nez percé*, literally, pierced nose]

Nez Percé horse appaloosa.

N.F. 1 Newfoundland. 2 Norman-French. 3 New France.

NFB or **N.F.B.** National Film Board.

Nfld. Newfoundland.

N.G. or **n.g.** no good.

N.H. New Hampshire.

NHL or **N.H.L.** National Hockey League.

Ni nickel.

N.I. Northern Ireland.

ni·a·cin (nī′ə sin) *n.* nicotinic acid. [< trademark < *ni(cotinic) ac(id)*]

nib (nib) *n.* **1** the point of a pen; either of its parts. **2** the tip; point. **3** a bird's bill. [var. of *neb*]

nib·ble (nib′əl) *v.* **-bled, -bling,** *n.* —*v.* **1** eat away with quick, small bites, as a rabbit or a mouse does. **2** bite gently or lightly: *A fish nibbles at the bait.* **3** eat little or lightly. **4** take apart or attack, as if by taking small bites: *critics nibbling at a new play.* —*n.* a nibbling; small bite. [cf. LG *nibbelen*] **—nib′bler,** *n.*

Ni·be·lung (nē′bə lu̇ng′) *n.* **-lungs** or **-lung·en** (-lu̇ng′ən). in German legend, any of a northern race of dwarfs. Siegfried and his followers captured their treasure.

Ni·be·lung·en·lied (nē′bə lu̇ng′ən lēd′; *German*, nē′bə lu̇ng′ən lēt′) *n.* a German epic given its present form in S. Germany during the first half of the 13th century. [< G, literally, Lay of the Nibelungs]

nib·lick (nib′lik) *n.* in golf, a club with a short, flat, iron head having a slanting face, used when the ball is in a hole, close behind a bunker, etc. [origin uncertain]

nibs (nibz) *n. Informal.* (used with a possessive pronoun) a humorous title of pretended respect for someone who is, or supposes himself to be, of importance: *How is his nibs today?* [origin uncertain]

Nic·a·ra·guan (nik′ə rä′gwən or nik′ə rag′wən) *adj.* of or having to do with Nicaragua, a republic of Central America, or its people. —*n.* a native or inhabitant of Nicaragua.

nice (nīs) *adj.* **nic·er, nic·est. 1** pleasing; agreeable; satisfactory: *a nice face.* **2** thoughtful; kind: *He was nice to us.* **3** exact; precise; discriminating: *a nice ear for music.* **4** minute; fine; subtle: *a nice distinction.* **5** delicately skilful; requiring care, skill, or tact: *a nice problem.* **6** exacting; particular; hard to please; fastidious; dainty: *nice in his eating.* **7** proper; suitable. **8** scrupulous: *too nice to be a crook.* **9** *Archaic.* modest; reserved. **10** refined; cultured: *nice manners.* [ME < OF *nice* silly < L *nescius* ignorant < *ne-* not + *scire* know] **—nice′ly,** *adv.* **—nice′ness,** *n.* **—Syn. 1** gratifying, enjoyable. **3** accurate. **6** delicate. **7** fitting, seemly.

Ni·cene (nī sēn′ or nī′sēn) *adj.* of or having to do with Nicaea, an ancient town in Asia Minor.

Nicene Council either of two general ecclesiastical councils that met at Nicaea, the first in A.D. 325 to deal with the Arian heresy, the second in A.D. 787 to consider the question of images.

Nicene Creed a formal statement of the chief tenets of Christian belief, based on that adopted by the first Nicene Council, and generally accepted throughout western Christendom.

ni·ce·ty (nī′sə tē) *n.* **-ties. 1** exactness; accuracy; delicacy: *Television sets require nicety of adjustment.* **2** a fine point; small distinction; detail. **3** the quality of being very particular; daintiness; refinement. **4** something dainty or refined. **5 to a nicety,** just right: *cakes browned to a nicety.* [ME < OF *nicete* < *nice.* See NICE.]

niche (nich) *n.* **1** a recess or hollow in a wall for a statue, vase, etc. **2** a suitable place or position; place for which a person is suited: *John will find his niche in the world.* [< F *niche*, ult. < L *nidus* nest] **—Syn. 1** nook, cavity.

A vase in a niche

Nich·o·las (nik′ə ləs or nik′ləs) *n.* **Saint. 1** the patron saint of young people, sailors, travellers, and Russians. He was a bishop in Asia Minor in the fourth century A.D. **2** Santa Claus.

nick (nik) *n.* **1** a place where a small bit has been cut or broken out; notch; groove: *He cut nicks in a stick to keep count of his score.* **2 in the nick of time,** just in time; barely in time. —*v.* **1** make a nick or nicks in. **2** cut into or through. **3** hit, guess, catch, etc. exactly. [origin uncertain] **—Syn.** *n.* **1** dent, indentation.

nick·el (nik′əl) *n. v.* **-elled** or **-eled, -el·ling** or **-el·ing.** —*n.* **1** a hard, metallic chemical element that looks like silver and iron, much used as an alloy. *Symbol*: Ni; *at.no.* 28; *at.wt.* 58.71. **2** a coin made of or containing nickel; a five-cent piece. —*v.* cover or coat with nickel. [< Swedish < G *Kupfernickel*, literally, copper devil; the ore resembles copper but yields none]

nick·el·o·de·on (nik′əl ō′dē ən) *n.* **1** in the early days of motion pictures, a place of amusement with motion-picture exhibitions, etc., to which the price of admission was five cents. **2** a juke box. [< *nickel* + *odeon*, var. of *odeum* < L < Gk. *oideion* music hall < *ōidē* song]

nickel plate a thin coating of nickel deposited on a metal object to prevent rust, improve the appearance, etc.

nick·el-plate (nik′əl plāt′) *v.* **-plat·ed, -plat·ing.** coat with nickel.

nickel silver an alloy of copper, zinc, and nickel; German silver.

nick-nack (nik′nak′) *n.* knick-knack.

nick·name (nik′nām′) *n. v.* **-named, -nam·ing.** —*n.* a name added to a person's real name or used instead of it: *Roy's nickname was "Buzz."* —*v.* give a nickname to: *They nicknamed the short boy "Shorty."* [ME *ekename* < *eke* an addition, OE *ēaca* + *name* name, OE *nama*; *an ekename* taken as *a nekename*]

nic·o·tine (nik′ə tēn′) *n.* a poisonous alkaloid contained in the leaves of tobacco. [< F; after Jacques *Nicot* (1530-1600), a French ambassador to Portugal, who introduced tobacco into France about 1560]

nic·o·tin·ic acid (nik′ə tin′ik) one of a group of vitamins that is found in lean meat, live wheat germ, milk, eggs, yeast, etc. Persons who lack nicotinic acid often suffer from pellagra.

niece (nēs) *n.* **1** the daughter of one's brother or sister. **2** the daughter of one's brother-in-law or sister-in-law. [ME < OF *niece*, ult. < L *neptis* granddaughter]

nif·ty (nif′tē) *adj.* **-ti·er, -ti·est.** *Slang.* attractive; stylish. [origin uncertain]

Ni·ge·ri·an (nī jēr′ē ən) *adj.* of or having to do with Nigeria, a country in W. Africa, or its people. —*n.* a native or inhabitant of Nigeria.

nig·gard (nig′ərd) *n.* a stingy person. —*adj.* stingy. [ME < earlier *nig* < Scand. + E pejorative suffix *-ard*, as in *drunkard*; cf. ON *hnöggr* stingy]

nig·gard·ly (nig′ərd lē) *adj.* **1** stingy. **2** meanly small or scanty: *a niggardly gift.* —*adv.* stingily. —**nig′gard·li·ness,** *n.* —**Syn.** *adj.* **1** miserly, illiberal, stinting.

nig·ger (nig′ər) *n.* **1** *Usually derogatory.* a member of a dark-skinned race, especially a Negro. **2** *Slang.* any person discriminated against or treated as a second-class citizen. [< *neger* < *nègre* < Sp. *negro.* See NEGRO.]

nig·gle (nig′əl) *v.* **-gled, -gling.** be concerned with petty or trifling things or details. [apparently < Scand.; cf. dial. Norwegian *nigla*] —**nig′gler,** *n.*

nigh (nī) *adv. adj.* **nigh·er, nigh·est** or **next,** *prep.* —*adv.* **1** near. **2** nearly. —*adj. prep. Archaic or dialect.* near. [OE *nēah*]

night (nīt) *n.* **1** the period of darkness between evening and morning; the time between sunset and sunrise. **2** the darkness of night; the dark. **3** the darkness of ignorance, sin, sorrow, old age, death, etc. **4** evening; nightfall. **5 make a night of it,** celebrate until very late at night. [OE *niht*]

night blindness a condition of the eyes in which the sight is normal in the day or in a strong light, but is abnormally poor or wholly gone at night or in a dim light.

night·cap (nīt′kap′) *n.* **1** a cap for wearing in bed: *Nightcaps are not much worn these days.* **2** a drink taken just before going to bed. **3** *Informal.* the last event in a sports program, especially the second baseball game of a double-header.

night club a place for dancing, eating, and entertainment, open only at night.

night·crawl·er (nīt′krol′ər or -krôl′ər) *n. Esp.U.S.* dew-worm.

night·dress (nīt′dres′) *n.* nightgown.

night·fall (nīt′fol′ or -fôl′) *n.* the coming of night.

night·gown (nīt′goun′) *n.* a loose garment to be worn in bed.

night·hawk (nīt′hok′ or -hôk′) *n.* **1** any of several birds of the goatsucker family, related to the whip-poor-will. **2** *Informal.* a person who stays up late at night.

night·in·gale (nīt′ən gāl′ or nīt′ing gāl′) *n.* **1** a small, reddish-brown bird of Europe. The male sings sweetly at night as well as in the daytime. **2** a person who sings or speaks with a melodious voice. [for *nightgale*, OE *nihtegale* < *niht* night + *galan* sing]

night·jar (nīt′jär′) *n.* a European bird that flies and feeds mostly at night; goatsucker.

night latch a latch unfastened by a key from the outside or by a knob from the inside.

night letter a telegram sent overnight at a cheap rate.

night light a small lamp that provides a dim light, used in a bedroom or sickroom.

night·light·er (nīt′līt′ər) *n.* a person who hunts game, often deer, illegally by means of a bright light; jacklighter.

night·light·ing (nīt′līt′ing) *n.* the practice of hunting game, often deer, illegally by means of a bright light; jack-lighting.

night·long (nīt′long′) *adj.* lasting all night. —*adv.* through the whole night.

night·ly (nīt′lē) *adj.* **1** done, happening, or appearing every night. **2** done, happening, or appearing at night. —*adv.* **1** every night: *Performances are given nightly except on Sunday.* **2** at night; by night.

night·mare (nīt′mãr′) *n.* **1** a very distressing dream.

hat, āge, cãre, fär; let, ēqual, tėrm; it, īce
hot, ōpen, ôrder; oil, out; cup, pu̇t, rüle, ūse
əbove, takən, pencəl, lemən, circəs
ch, child; ng, long; sh, ship
th, thin; ᴛʜ, then; zh, measure

2 a very distressing experience: *The week of the dust storm was a nightmare.* **3** a horrible fear or a feeling of dread. **4** a sight, object, or person such as might be seen in a nightmare. [ME < OE *niht* night + *mare* monster oppressing men during sleep]

night·mar·ish (nīt′mãr′ish) *adj.* like a nightmare; strange and horrifying; causing fear. —**night′mar′ish·ly,** *adv.*

night owl *Informal.* a person who often stays up late.

night school a school held in the evening for persons who work during the day.

night·shade (nīt′shād′) *n.* any of various plants somewhat like the potato and the tomato. The **black nightshade** has white flowers and black, poisonous berries. The **deadly nightshade,** or belladonna, has red berries. [OE *nihtscada*]

night·shirt (nīt′shėrt′) *n.* a long, loose shirt to be worn in bed.

night·time (nīt′tīm′) *n.* the time between evening and morning.

night watch **1** a watch or guard kept during the night. **2** the person or persons keeping such a watch. **3** a period or division of the night.

ni·hil (nī′hil) *n. Latin.* nothing.

ni·hil·ism (nī′ə liz′əm) *n.* **1** the entire rejection of the usual beliefs in religion, morals, government, laws, etc. **2** in philosophy, the denial of all existence. **3** in Russia, the beliefs of a revolutionary party, which found nothing good in the old order of things and wished to clear it away to make place for a better state of society. **4** the use of violent methods against a ruler. [< L *nihil* nothing]

Ni·hil·ism (nī′ə liz′əm) *n.* the beliefs of a 19th-century Russian revolutionary party, that advocated the removal of the old society by violence and terror.

ni·hil·ist (nī′ə list) *n.* **1** a person who believes in some form of nihilism. **2** a terrorist.

Ni·hil·ist (nī′ə list) *n.* a member of the Russian revolutionary party that advocated Nihilism.

ni·hil·is·tic (nī′ə lis′tik) *adj.* of nihilists or nihilism.

Ni·ke (nī′kē or nē′kā) *n.* in Greek mythology, the goddess of victory, usually represented with outspread wings.

nil (nil) *n.* nothing. [< L *nil*, a shortened form of *nihil*]

nim·ble (nim′bəl) *adj.* **-bler, -blest. 1** active and sure-footed; light and quick; quick-moving: *Goats are nimble in climbing among the rocks.* **2** quick to understand and to reply; clever: *a nimble mind.* [ME *nymel* < OE *niman* take] —**nim′ble·ness,** *n.* —**nim′bly,** *adv.* —**Syn. 1** agile, lively, spry, brisk.

nim·bo·stra·tus (nim′bō strā′təs or -strat′əs) *n.* **-ti** (-tī or -tē). in meteorology, a low, dark-gray layer of rain or snow cloud; nimbus. [< L *nimbus* + E *stratus*]

nim·bus (nim′bəs) *n.* **-bus·es, -bi** (-bī or -bē). **1** a light disk or other radiance about the head of a divine or sacred person in a picture. **2** a bright cloud surrounding a god, person, or thing. **3** a rain cloud. [< L *nimbus* cloud]

Nim·rod (nim′rod) *n.* **1** in the Bible, a king who was a great builder and a mighty hunter. Gen. 10: 8-9. **2** any enthusiastic hunter.

nin·com·poop (nin′kəm püp′ or ning′kəm püp′) *n.* a fool; simpleton.

nine (nīn) *n.* **1** one more than eight; 9. **2** a set of nine persons or things. **3** a playing card, etc. having nine spots. **4** a team of nine players: *a baseball nine.* **5 the Nine,** the Muses. —*adj.* being one more than eight. [OE *nigon*]

nine days' wonder anything that causes a short period of excitement and great interest.

nine-eight (nīn′āt′) *adj.* in music, indicating or having nine eighth notes in a bar or measure.

nine·fold (nīn′fōld′) *adj.* 1 nine times as much or as many. 2 having nine parts. —*adv.* nine times as much or as many.

nine·pin (nīn′pin′) *n.* 1 **nine pins,** a game in which nine large wooden pins are set up to be bowled down with a ball. 2 one of the pins used in this game.

nine·teen (nīn′tēn′) *n. adj.* nine more than ten; 19. [OE *nigontēne*]

nine·teenth (nīn′tēnth′) *adj.* next after the 18th; last in a series of 19. —*n.* 1 the next after the 18th; last in a series of 19. 2 one of 19 equal parts.

nine·ti·eth (nīn′tē ith) *adj.* next after the 89th; last in a series of 90. —*n.* 1 the next after the 89th; last in a series of 90. 2 one of 90 equal parts.

nine·ty (nīn′tē) *n.* **-ties,** *adj.* nine times ten; 90. [OE *nigontig*]

Nin·e·veh (nin′ə və) *n.* an ancient city of Assyria. Its ruins are on the Tigris River, opposite Mosul in N. Iraq.

nin·ny (nin′ē) *n.* **-nies.** a fool.

ninth (nīnth) *adj.* next after the eighth; last in a series of nine. —*n.* 1 the next after the eighth; last in a series of nine. 2 one of nine equal parts.

Ni·o·be (nī′ō bē or nī′ə bē) *n.* in Greek mythology, a mother whose fourteen beautiful children were slain because she boasted about them. Turned by Zeus into a stone fountain, she weeps forever for her children.

ni·o·bi·um (nī ō′bē əm) *n.* a rare, steel-gray, metallic chemical element that resembles tantalum in chemical properties. *Symbol*: Nb; *at.no.* 41; *at.wt.* 92.906. Formerly, **columbium.** [< NL; after *Niobe*]

nip[1] (nip) *v.* **nipped, nip·ping,** *n.* —*v.* 1 squeeze tight and suddenly. 2 take off by biting, pinching, or snipping. 3 injure or spoil as by frost or wind: *plants nipped by frost.* 4 have a sharp, biting effect on: *Cold winds nip your ears and nose.* 5 **nip in the bud,** stop at the very beginning.
—*n.* 1 a tight squeeze or pinch; sudden bite. 2 an injury caused by frost or wind. 3 sharp coldness; chill: *There is a nip in the air on a frosty morning.* 4 a small bit. 5 **nip and tuck,** *Informal.* in a race or contest, so evenly matched that the issue remains in doubt till the end. [ME *nyppen*; cf. Du. *nijpen*]

nip[2] (nip) *n. v.* **nipped, nip·ping.** —*n.* a small drink: *a nip of brandy.* —*v.* drink nips. [for *nipperkin* a small vessel; origin uncertain]

nip·per (nip′ər) *n.* 1 one that nips. 2 a big claw of a lobster or crab. 3 Usually, **nippers,** *pl.* pincers, forceps, pliers, or any tool that nips. 4 *Informal.* a small boy.

nip·ple (nip′əl) *n.* 1 in mammals, the small projection on a breast or udder, through which a baby gets its mother's milk. 2 the rubber cap or mouthpiece of a baby's bottle. 3 anything shaped or used like a nipple. [earlier *neble,* probably dim. of *neb* peak, tip]

Nip·pon·ese (nip′ə nēz′) *adj. n.* **-ese.** Japanese.

nip·py (nip′ē) *adj.* **-pi·er, -pi·est.** biting; sharp.

nir·va·na or **Nir·va·na** (nėr vä′nə or nėr van′ə) *n.* 1 in Buddhism, heavenly peace; perfect happiness reached by complete absorption of oneself into the supreme universal spirit. 2 in Hinduism, freedom of the soul; reunion with the universal soul reached by the suppression of individual existence. 3 blessed oblivion. [< Skt. *nirvāna* extinction < *nis-* out + *vā-* blow]

Ni·san (nē sän′ or nis′ən) *n.* in the Hebrew calendar, the first month of the ecclesiastical year, and the seventh month of the civil year.

Ni·sei (nē′sā′) *n.* **-sei.** a native-born Canadian or United States citizen whose parents were Japanese immigrants. [< Japanese *nisei* second generation < *ni* two + *sei* generation]

Nis·sen hut (nis′ən) a prefabricated shelter for soldiers, semicylindrical in shape, made of corrugated iron, with a concrete floor. [after Lt.Col. Peter N. *Nissen* (1871-1930), who designed it]

nit (nit) *n.* 1 the egg of a louse or similar insect. 2 a very young louse or similar insect. [OE *hnitu*]

nitch·ie (nich′ē) *n. Cdn.* 1 in Indian use, a friend (especially of another Indian). 2 *Derogatory slang.* an Indian. 3 *Rare.* a small Indian pony; cayuse. [< Algonquian]

ni·ter (nī′tər) *n.* nitre.

ni·ton (nī′ton) *n.* an early name of radon. *Symbol*: Nt [< NL < L *nitere* shine]

ni·trate (nī′trāt) *n. v.* **-trat·ed, -trat·ing.** —*n.* 1 a salt or ester of nitric acid. 2 potassium nitrate, or sodium nitrate, used as a fertilizer. —*v.* treat with nitric acid or a nitrate. —**ni·tra′tion,** *n.*

ni·tre or **ni·ter** (nī′tər) *n.* 1 potassium nitrate, obtained from potash, used in making gunpowder; saltpetre. *Formula*: KNO_3 2 sodium nitrate or Chile saltpetre, used as a fertilizer. *Formula*: $NaNO_3$ [< F < L *nitrum* < Gk. *nitron* < Semitic. Doublet of NATRON.]

ni·tric (nī′trik) *adj.* of or containing nitrogen. [< F *nitrique*]

nitric acid a clear, colorless liquid that eats into flesh, clothing, metal, and other substances. Nitric acid is used in making dyes, explosives, etc., and in etching, metallurgy, etc. *Formula*: HNO_3

ni·tride (nī′trīd or nī′trid) *n.* a compound of nitrogen with a more electropositive element or radical, such as phosphorus, boron, or a metal.

ni·tri·fy (nī′trə fī′) *v.* **-fied, -fy·ing.** 1 oxidize (ammonia compounds, etc.) to nitrites or nitrates, especially by bacterial action. 2 impregnate (soil, etc.) with nitrates. [< F *nitrifier*] —**ni′tri·fi·ca′tion,** *n.*

ni·trite (nī′trīt) *n.* a salt or ester of nitrous acid.

ni·tro·ben·zene (nī′trō ben′zēn or -ben zēn′) *n.* a poisonous, yellowish liquid obtained from benzene by the action of nitric acid, used as a reagent in making perfumes. *Formula*: $C_6H_5NO_2$

ni·tro·gen (nī′trə jən) *n.* a colorless, odorless, tasteless gaseous chemical element that forms about four-fifths of the earth's atmosphere by volume. *Symbol*: N; *at.no.* 7; *at.wt.* 14.0067. [< F *nitrogène* < Gk. *nitron* native sodium carbonate + *-genēs* born, produced]

ni·trog·e·nous (nī troj′ə nəs) *adj.* of or containing nitrogen or a compound of nitrogen.

ni·tro·glyc·er·in or **ni·tro·glyc·er·ine** (nī trə glis′ər in) *n.* an oily, explosive liquid made by treating glycerin with nitric and sulphuric acids. Nitroglycerin is used in dynamite. *Formula*: $C_3H_5(NO_3)_3$

ni·trous (nī′trəs) *adj.* 1 of nitrogen; containing nitrogen. 2 of nitre. [< L *nitrosus* < *nitrum.* See NITRE.]

nitrous oxide a colorless gas that causes laughing and inability to feel pain; laughing gas. It is sometimes used as an anesthetic by dentists. *Formula*: N_2O

nit·wit (nit′wit′) *n. Slang.* a very stupid person. [< *nit* + *wit*]

nix[1] (niks) *n. interj. Slang.* nothing; no. [< G *nix,* dial. var. of *nichts* nothing]

nix[2] (niks) *n.* **nix·es.** in German legend, a water fairy. [< colloquial Du. or G]

nix·ie (nik′sē) *n.* in German legend, a female water fairy. [< G *Nixe*]

Ni·zam (ni zäm′ or ni zam′, nī zäm′ or nī zam′) *n.* in India, formerly, the title of the ruler of Hyderabad. [< Urdu and Turkish *nizām* < Arabic *nizām* order, arrangement]

N.J. New Jersey.

NKVD formerly, the secret police of the Soviet Union, now the MVD.

NL or **N.L.** New Latin.

N.Mex. New Mexico.

NNE, N.N.E., or **n.n.e.** north northeast, a direction halfway between north and northeast.

NNW, N.N.W., or **n.n.w.** north northwest, a direction halfway between north and northwest.

no (nō) *n.* **noes,** *adj. adv.* —*n.* 1 a word used to deny, refuse, or disagree. 2 a denial; refusal. 3 a negative vote or voter: *The noes have it.* [< adv.]
—*adj.* not any; not a: *He has no friends.* [var. of *none*]
—*adv.* 1 a word used to deny, refuse, or disagree: *Will you come with us? No.* 2 not in any degree; not at all:

He is no better. **3** not, chiefly in phrases like *whether or no.* [OE *nā* < *ne* not + *ā* ever] ☛ See yes for usage note.

No nobelium.

No. or **no. 1** north. **2** northern. **3** number.
☛ No. The abbreviation *No.* for *number* (from the Latin *numero* by number) is usually written with a capital. It is appropriate chiefly in business and technical English.

no-ac·count (nō′ə kount′) *Informal.* —*adj.* no good; worthless. —*n.* a good-for-nothing person; a person of no importance at all.

No·ah (nō′ə) *n.* in the Bible, a man who was told by God to build an ark to save himself, his family, and a pair of each kind of animal from the Flood. Gen. 5:28-9:29.

Noah's Ark the ark built by Noah.

nob (nob) *n. Slang.* **1** the head. **2** a person of wealth or social importance. [? var. of *knob*]

nob·by (nob′ē) *adj.* **-bi·er, -bi·est.** *Slang.* **1** smart; fashionable; elegant. **2** first-rate.

no·be·li·um (nō bē′lē əm) *n.* an artificial radio-active element. *Symbol*: No; *at.no.* 102; *at.wt.* 254 (most stable isotope); *half life* 10 min. [< Alfred B. *Nobel,* who established the Nobel prizes]

No·bel prize (nō bel′) one of five money prizes, averaging $40,000 each, established by Alfred Bernhard Nobel (1833-1896), a Swedish manufacturer and the inventor of dynamite, to be given annually to those persons or organizations who have done most in physics, chemistry, medicine, literature, and the promotion of peace. The prizes were first awarded in 1901.

no·bil·i·ty (nō bil′ə tē) *n.* **-ties. 1** people of noble rank. Earls, marquises, and counts belong to the nobility. **2** noble birth; noble rank. **3** noble character. [ME < OF < L *nobilitas*] —**Syn. 1** peerage. **3** greatness.

no·ble (nō′bəl) *adj.* **-bler, -blest,** *n.* —*adj.* **1** high and great by birth, rank, or title. **2** high and great in character; showing greatness of mind; good: *a noble knight, a noble deed.* **3** excellent; fine; splendid; magnificent: *Niagara Falls is a noble sight.* **4** of metals, precious or valuable: *Silver is a noble metal.* **5** chemically inert, as helium, neon, etc.
—*n.* **1** a person high and great by birth, rank, or title. **2** an old English coin. [< F < L *nobilis* renowned] —**no′ble·ness,** *n.* —**Syn.** *adj.* **1** aristocratic, high-born, patrician. **2** honorable, worthy. **3** imposing, stately. See **grand.**

no·ble·man (nō′bəl mən) *n.* **-men** (-mən). a man of noble rank, title, or birth.

no·blesse o·blige (nô bles′ ô blēzh′) *French.* persons of noble rank should behave nobly.

no·ble·wom·an (nō′bəl wům′ən) *n.* **-wom·en.** a woman of noble birth or rank.

no·bly (nō′blē) *adv.* in a noble manner; splendidly; as a noble person would do.

no·bod·y (nō′bud′ē, nō′bod′ē or nō′bə dē) *pron. n.* **-bod·ies.** —*pron.* no one; no person. —*n.* a person of no importance.
☛ **Nobody, nothing, nowhere** are written as single words. *Nobody* and *nothing* are singular, though *nobody* is informally treated as a collective: *Nothing is further from the truth. Nobody thinks that his own dog is a nuisance.* Informal: *Nobody thinks their own dog is a nuisance.*

nock (nok) *n.* a notch on a bow or arrow for the bow-string. —*v.* **1** make such a notch. **2** fit (an arrow) to the bowstring for shooting. [ME *nocke*]

noc·tur·nal (nok tėr′nəl) *adj.* **1** of the night; in the night: *Stars are a nocturnal sight.* **2** active in the night: *The owl is a nocturnal bird.* **3** closed by day, open by night: *a nocturnal flower.* [< LL *nocturnalis,* ult. < L *nox* night]

noc·tur·nal·ly (nok tėr′nəl ē) *adv.* **1** at night. **2** every night.

noc·turne (nok′tėrn) *n.* **1** in music, a dreamy or pensive composition. **2** a painting of a night scene. [< F]

nod (nod) *v.* **nod·ded, nod·ding,** *n.* —*v.* **1** bow (the head) slightly and raise it again quickly. **2** show agreement by nodding. **3** express by bowing the head: *nod consent.* **4** let the head fall forward and bob about when sleepy or falling asleep. **5** be sleepy; become careless and dull. **6** droop, bend, or sway back and forth: *Trees nod in the wind.*

hat, āge, cãre, fär; let, ēqual, tėrm; it, īce
hot, ōpen, ôrder; oil, out; cup, půt, rüle, ūse
əbove, takən, pencəl, lemən, circəs
ch, child; ng, long; sh, ship
th, thin; ᴛʜ, then; zh, measure

—*n.* **1** a nodding of the head. **2 get** or **give the nod,** *Informal.* **a** receive or give approval. **b** receive or give a victory or decision to. [ME *nodden*; origin uncertain]

nod·al (nōd′əl) *adj.* having to do with nodes; like a node.

nod·ding (nod′ing) *adj.* casual; slight: *a nodding acquaintance.*

nod·dle (nod′əl) *n. Informal.* the head. [ME *nodel, nodul*; origin uncertain]

nod·dy (nod′ē) *n.* **-dies.** a fool. [origin uncertain]

node (nōd) *n.* **1** a knot; knob; swelling. **2** in botany, a joint in a stem; part of a stem that normally bears a leaf or leaves. **3** in physics, a point, line, or plane in a vibrating body at which there is comparatively no vibration. **4** a central point in any system. **5** a knotlike swelling or mass of specialized tissue on the body or an organ: *a lymph node.* **6** a knot or complication in the plot or character development of a story, play, etc. [< L *nodus* knot]

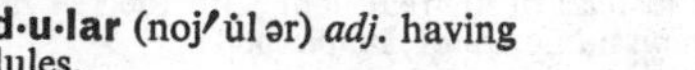

Nodes (def. 2)

nod·u·lar (noj′ůl ər) *adj.* having nodules.

nod·ule (noj′ül) *n.* **1** a small knot, knob, or swelling. **2** a small, rounded mass or lump: *nodules of pure gold.* **3** in botany, a small tuber. [< L *nodulus,* dim. of *nodus* knot]

no·ël (nō el′) *n.* **1** a Christmas song; carol. **2** an expression of joy used in Christmas songs. **3 Noël,** Christmas. [< F < L *natalis* natal (i.e. the natal day of Christ) < *nasci* be born. Doublet of NATAL.]

nog·gin (nog′ən) *n.* **1** a small mug. **2** a small drink; ¼ pint. **3** *Informal.* a person's head. [origin uncertain]

no-hit·ter (nō′hit′ər) *n.* in baseball, a game in which the pitcher prevents the opposing team from gaining any base hits.

no-holds-barred (nō′hōldz′bärd′) *adj. Informal.* **1** without rules or restrictions; unrestrainedly violent: *a no-holds-barred fight.* **2** complete; utmost: *a no-holds-barred effort.*

no·how (nō′hou′) *adv. Informal.* in no way; not at all.

noil (noil) *n.* **1** a short fibre combed out during the preparation of wool, cotton, or silk yarn. **2** the waste material composed of these fibres. [origin unknown]

noise (noiz) *n. v.* **noised, nois·ing.** —*n.* **1** a sound that is not musical or pleasant. **2** a sound. **3** a din of voices and movements; loud shouting; outcry; clamor. **4 a** in physics, a group of sound waves which are not periodic and which are produced by irregular vibrations; sound of no single fundamental frequency but many nonharmonic frequency components of varying amplitudes randomly placed. **b** any undesired or unintended disturbance in a radio or television signal. **5 big noise,** *Informal.* an important person.
—*v. Archaic.* spread the news of; tell: *It was noised abroad that the king was dying.* [ME < OF *noise* < L *nausea.* Doublet of NAUSEA.]
Syn. *n.* **1 Noise, din, uproar** = disagreeably loud, confused, or harsh and clashing sound. **Noise** applies to any disagreeably unmusical or loud sound made by one or more people or things: *The noise kept me awake.* **Din** applies to a prolonged and deafening confusion of clanging or piercing noises: *The din of machines and factory whistles hurt my ears.* **Uproar** applies especially to the tumult, shouting, and loud noises of a crowd: *You should have heard the uproar when officials called back the touchdown.* **2** See **sound**[1]. **3** babble, uproar, hubbub, tumult.

noise·less (noiz′lis) *adj.* making no noise; making little noise: *a noiseless typewriter.* —**noise′less·ly,** *adv.* —**noise′less·ness,** *n.*

noise·mak·er (noiz′māk′ər) *n.* **1** a person who makes too much noise. **2** something that makes noise, especially a horn, rattle, etc. used to make noise at a party, a game, etc.

noi·some (noi′səm) *adj.* **1** offensive; disgusting; smelling bad: *a noisome slum.* **2** harmful; injurious: *a noisome pestilence.* [< *noy* (var. of *annoy*) + *-some*[1]] **—noi′some·ly,** *adv.* **—noi′some·ness,** *n.*

nois·y (noiz′ē) *adj.* **nois·i·er, nois·i·est. 1** making much noise: *a noisy boy.* **2** full of noise: *a noisy street.* **3** accompanied by much noise: *a noisy quarrel.* **—nois′i·ly,** *adv.* **—nois′i·ness,** *n.* **—Syn. 1** shouting, clamorous, brawling, blatant. See **loud.**

nom. nominative.

no·mad (nō′mad) *n.* **1** a member of a tribe that moves from place to place to have pasture for its cattle or to be near its own food supply: *Many Arabs and Eskimos are nomads.* **2** a wanderer. *—adj.* **1** wandering from place to place to find pasture. **2** wandering. [< L < Gk. *nomas, -ados,* ult. < *nemein* to pasture]

no·mad·ic (nō mad′ik) *adj.* of nomads or their life; wandering; roving. **—no·mad′i·cal·ly,** *adv.*

no·mad·ism (nō′mad iz′əm) *n.* the way that nomads live.

no man's land 1 in war, the land between opposing lines of trenches. **2** a tract of land to which no one has a recognized or established claim.

nom de guerre (nom′də gãr′; *French,* nôɴ də gãr′) *French.* an assumed name under which to pursue a profession, undertaking, or the like.

nom de plume (nom′ də plüm′) a pen name; name used by a writer instead of his real name. [formed in E from F words: *nom* name, *de* of, *plume* pen]

no·men·cla·ture (nō′mən klā′chər or nō men′klə chər) *n.* a set or system of names or terms: *the nomenclature of music.* [< L *nomenclatura* < *nomen* name + *calare* to call]

nom·i·nal (nom′ə nəl) *adj.* **1** being so in name only; not real: *The president is the nominal head of the club, but the secretary really runs its affairs.* **2** so small that it is not worth considering; unimportant compared with the real value: *We paid a nominal rent for the cottage—$5 a month.* **3 a** giving the name or names: *a nominal roll of the pupils in our room.* **b** mentioning specifically by name: *a nominal appeal.* **c** assigned to a person by name: *a nominal share of stock.* **4** in grammar: **a** of, as, or like a name or a noun. *Day* is the nominal root of *daily, daybreak,* and *Sunday.* **b** of a word or phrase, used or functioning as a noun or nouns. *Rich* and *poor* in the phrase *the rich and the poor* are nominal adjectives. **5** of, having to do with, or consisting in a name or names. [< L *nominalis* < *nomen, -inis* name]

nom·i·nal·ly (nom′ə nəl ē) *adv.* **1** in name; as a matter of form; in a nominal way only. **2** by name.

nom·i·nate (nom′ə nāt′) *v.* **-nat·ed, -nat·ing. 1** name as candidate for an office: *Mr. Smith was nominated to be a candidate for Parliament.* **2** appoint to an office or duty: *The Prime Minister nominated him Secretary of State.* [< L *nominare,* ult. < *nomen* name] **—nom′i·na′tor,** *n.* **—Syn. 1** designate.

nom·i·na·tion (nom′ə nā′shən) *n.* **1** the naming of someone as a candidate for an office. **2** a selection for office or duty; appointment to office or duty. **3** a being nominated.

nom·i·na·tive (nom′ə nə tiv, nom′nə tiv, or nom′ə nā′tiv) *adj.* **1** of certain pronouns, having that form which is employed as the subject of a verb. *I, he, she, we, who,* and *they* are in the nominative case. **2** of nouns and their equivalent, used as the subject of a verb: *Nouns do not have a special form to show nominative case; most personal pronouns do.* *—n.* in grammar: **1** the nominative case. **2** a word in that case. *Who* and *I* are nominatives. *Abbrev.*: nom. [< L *nominativus*]

nom·i·nee (nom′ə nē′) *n.* a person who is nominated.

non- *prefix.* not; not a; opposite of; lack of; failure of, as in *non-conformity, non-acceptance, non-payment.* [< L *non* not < OL *ne-* not + *oinom* one]

If an adjective formed with *non-* is not defined in this dictionary, its meaning will be clear if *not* is put in place of the *non.* If a noun formed with *non-* is not defined, its meaning will be clear if *not, not a, the opposite of,* or *the absence of* is put in place of the *non. Non-* is a living prefix and may be used with any noun, adjective, or adverb; but if there is a commonly used word of the same meaning formed with *un-, in-,* or *dis-,* that word is usually preferable. Most of the words that have *non-* as the preferred usage, or as a respectable rival of *un-,* are listed below, or as regular entries.

non′-ab·sorb′ent
non′-ad·ja′cent
non′-ag·gres′sive
non′-al·co·hol′ic
non′-a·quat′ic
non′-as·sess′a·ble
non′-as·sim′i·la′tion
non′-be·liev′er
non′-bel·lig′er·ent
non-break′a·ble
non-Cath′o·lic
non-Chris′tian
non-civ′i·lized′
non-cler′i·cal
non′-col·laps′i·ble
non′-col·le′giate
non-com′bat
non′-com·bus′ti·ble
non′-com·mer′cial
non′-com·mu′ni·ca·ble
non′-com·pet′i·tive
non′-com·pul′sion
non′-con·du′cive
non′-con·form′ing
non′-con·sec′u·tive
non′-con·sent′
non′-con·serv′a·tive
non′-con·sti·tu′tion·al
non′-con·ta′gious
non′-con·tem′po·rar′y
non′-con·tin′u·ance
non′-con·tin′u·ous
non-con′tra·band′
non′-con·tra·dic′to·ry
non′-co-op′er·a·tive
non′-cor·ro′sive
non-crit′i·cal
non-crys′tal·line
non-cu′mu·la·tive
non′-de·cep′tive
non′-de·cid′u·ous
non′-dem·o·crat′ic
non′-de·struc′tive
non-dir′i·gi·ble
non′-dis·crim′i·na′tion
non′-dis·pos′al
non′-dis·tinc′tive
non′-di·ver′gent
non′-di·vis′i·ble
non′-dog·mat′ic
non′-dra·mat′ic
non-earn′ing
non-ed′i·ble
non-ed′u·ca·ble
non′-ed·u·ca′tion·al
non′-e·mo′tion·al
non′-en·force′ment
non-Eng′lish
non′-e·quiv′a·lent
non-eth′i·cal
non′-Eu·clid′e·an
non′-ex·change′a·ble
non′-ex·clu′sive
non′-ex·ist′ent
non′-ex·ist′ing
non′-ex·plo′sive
non′-ex·port′a·ble
non′-ex·tend′ed
non-ex′tra·dit′a·ble
non-fac′tu·al
non-fad′ing
non-fed′er·al
non-fed′er·at′ed
non-fer′rous
non-fes′tive
non-fic′tion·al
non-fis′cal
non-fis′sion·a·ble
non-freez′ing
non-func′tion·al
non-gas′e·ous
non-hab′it·a·ble
non′-he·red′i·tar′y
non-her′it·a·ble
non′-his·tor′ic
non-hu′man
non-hu′mor·ous
non′-i·den′ti·cal
non′-i·den′ti·ty
non′-id·i·o·mat′ic
non′-im·mu′ni·ty
non′-im·por·ta′tion
non′-im·preg′nat·ed
non′-in·clu′sive
non′-in·dict′a·ble
non′-in·dict′ment
non′-in·dus′tri·al
non′-in·fec′tion
non′-in·fec′tious
non′-in·flect′ed
non′-in·form′a·tive
non′-in·her′ent
non′-in·her′it·a·ble
non-in′ter·course′
non′-in·ter·fer′ence
non′-in·ter·sect′ing
non′-in·tox′i·cant
non′-in·tox′i·cat′ing
non-ir′ri·ga·ble
non-ir′ri·tant
non-ir′ri·tat′ing
non-Jew′ish
non-le′gal
non-lit′er·ar′y
non-mar′ry·ing
non-mar′tial
non′-me·chan′i·cal
non′-me·dic′i·nal
non′-me·lo′di·ous
non-melt′ing
non-mem′ber
non-mi′gra·to′ry
non-mil′i·tant
non-mil′i·tar′y
non-min′er·al
non-nav′i·ga·ble
non′-ne·go′tia·ble
non-neu′tral
non-nu′cle·ar
non′-nu·tri′tious
non′-o·be′di·ence
non′-ob·lig′a·to′ry
non′-ob·serv′ance
non-o′dor·ous
non′-of·fi′cial
non-orth′o·dox′
non′-pa·rish′ion·er
non′-par·lia·men′ta·ry
non′-par·o′chi·al
non′-par·tic′i·pa′tion
non-pay′ing
non-per′ma·nent
non-per′me·a·ble
non′-per·pen·dic′u·lar
non′-per·sist′ence
non′-phil·o·soph′i·cal
non′-po·et′ic
non-poi′son·ous
non′-po·lit′i·cal
non-po′rous
non-pred′a·to′ry
non′-pre·dic′ta·ble
non′-pre·hen′sile
non′-pre·scrip′tive
non′-pro·duc′ing
non′-pro·fes′sion·al
non′-prof·it·eer′ing
non′-pro·gres′sive
non′-pro·tec′tive
non-Prot′es·tant
non-pun′ish·a·ble
non-ra′cial
non′-re·al′i·ty
non′-re·cip′ro·cal
non′-rec·og·ni′tion
non′-re·cur′rent
non′-re·fill′a·ble
non′-re·fu′el·ling
non-reg′i·ment′ed
non′-re·li′gious
non′-re·mu′ner·a·tive
non′-re·new′a·ble
non′-res·i·den′tial
non′-re·strict′ed
non′-re·turn′a·ble
non′-re·vers′i·ble
non-rhym′ing
non-rhyth′mic
non-rig′id
non-ru′ral
non-Rus′sian
non-sal′a·ble
non-sal′a·ried
non′-sci·en·tif′ic
non-sea′son·al
non-sec′tion·al
non′-se·lec′tive
non-sen′si·tive
non-shar′ing
non-shat′ter
non-shrink′a·ble
non-sink′a·ble
non-smok′ing
non-so′cial

non-spe′cial·ized′
non-spir′i·tu·al
non-stain′a·ble
non-stand′ard·ized′
non-strik′er
non-strik′ing
non′-sub·mis′sive
non′-sub·scrib′er
non′-suc·ces′sive
non′-sup·port′er
non′-sup·port′ing
non′-sus·tain′ing
non′-sym·met′ri·cal
non-sym′pa·thiz′er
non′-sys·tem·at′ic
non-tax′a·ble
non-teach′a·ble
non-tech′ni·cal
non′-ter·ri·to′ri·al
non-tox′ic
non′-trans·fer′a·ble
non-trib′u·tar′y
non-typ′i·cal
non-us′er
non-ver′ti·cal
non-vet′er·an
non′-vi·o·la′tion
non-vis′u·al
non′-vo·cal′ic
non′-vo·ca′tion·al
non-vol′a·tile′
non-vol′un·tar′y
non-vot′ing
non-work′er
non-work′ing
non-yield′ing

non·ac·cept·ance (non′ak sep′təns) *n.* a failure or refusal to accept.

non·age (non′ij or nō′nij) *n.* **1** a being under the legal age of responsibility; minority. **2** an early stage; period before maturity. [ME < AF *nonnage* < *non-* not (< L) + *age* age < VL *aetaticum* < L *aetas*]

non·a·ge·nar·i·an (non′ə jə nãr′ē ən or nō′nə jə nãr′ē ən) *n.* a person who is 90 years old or between 90 and 100 years old. —*adj.* 90 years old or between 90 and 100 years old. [< L *nonagenarius* of ninety]

non·ag·gres·sion (non′ə gresh′ən) *n.* absence of aggression: *a pact of non-aggression.*

non·a·gon (non′ə gon′) *n.* a plane figure having nine angles and nine sides. [< L *nonus* ninth + Gk. *gōnia* angle]

A nonagon

non·ap·pear·ance (non′ə pēr′əns) *n.* the fact of not appearing; failure to appear.

non·at·tend·ance (non′ə ten′dəns) *n.* failure to be present.

non-capital murder murder that is not punishable by death.

nonce (nons) *n.* **1** the one or particular occasion or purpose. **2 for the nonce,** for the present time or occasion. —*adj.* serving a single occasion: *a nonce word, nonce use.* [ME (*for then*) *ones* (for the) once, taken as (*for the*) *nones*]

nonce word a word formed and used for a single occasion.

non·cha·lance (non′shə lons′ or non′shə ləns) *n.* cool unconcern; indifference: *Eleanor received the prize with pretended nonchalance.*

non·cha·lant (non′shə lont′ or non′shə lənt) *adj.* without enthusiasm; coolly unconcerned; indifferent: *She remained quite nonchalant during all the excitement.* [< F *nonchalant* < *non-* not (< L) + *chaloir* be warm < L *calere*] —**non′cha·lant·ly,** *adv.*

non-com (non′kom′) *n. Informal.* a non-commissioned officer.

non-com. non-commissioned officer.

non-com·bat·ant (non′kəm bat′ənt or non kom′bə tənt) *n.* **1** a person in the armed services who is not a fighter. Surgeons, nurses, chaplains, etc. are non-combatants even though with the army. **2** a civilian in wartime. —*adj.* **1** not fighting. **2** having civilian status in wartime.

non-com·mis·sioned (non′kə mish′ənd) *adj.* without a commission; not commissioned. Corporals and sergeants are non-commissioned officers.

non-com·mit·tal (non′kə mit′əl) *adj.* not committing oneself; not saying yes or no. *I will think it over* is a noncommittal answer. —**non′com·mit′tal·ly,** *adv.*

non-com·pli·ance (non′kəm plī′əns) *n.* the fact of not complying; failure to comply.

non com·pos men·tis (non′ kom′pəs men′tis) *Latin.* mentally unable to manage one's affairs; not of sound mind.

non-con·duct·ing (non′kən duk′ting) *adj.* not conducting; that is a non-conductor. Asbestos is a non-conducting material used in heat insulation.

non-con·duc·tor (non′kən duk′tər) *n.* a substance that does not readily conduct heat, electricity, etc. Rubber is a non-conductor of electricity.

non·con·form·ance (non′kən fôr′məns) *n.* the fact of not conforming; failure to conform.

hat, āge, cãre, fär; let, ēqual, tėrm; it, īce
hot, ōpen, ôrder; oil, out; cup, pu̇t, rüle, ūse
əbove, takən, pencəl, lemən, circəs
ch, child; ng, long; sh, ship
th, thin; ᴛʜ, then; zh, measure

non·con·form·ist (non′kən fôr′mist) *n.* **1** a person who refuses to conform to an established church. **2** a person who refuses to conform to accepted practices, conventions, etc.: *Some nonconformists are rejected by society; others achieve distinction as artists, inventors, or philosophers.* **3** Usually, **Nonconformist.** in England, a Protestant who is not a member of the Church of England.

non·con·form·i·ty (non′kən fôr′mə tē) *n.* **1** a lack of conformity; failure or refusal to conform. **2** a failure or refusal to conform to an established church. **3** Usually, **Noncomformity.** in England, the principles or practices of Protestants who do not belong to the Church of England.

non-co-op·er·a·tion (non′kō op′ər ā′shən) *n.* **1** a failure or refusal to co-operate. **2** a refusal to co-operate with a government for political reasons.

non-de·liv·er·y (non′di liv′ər ē or -di liv′rē) *n.* failure to deliver.

non·de·script (non′də skript′) *adj.* not easily classified; not of any one particular kind: *eyes of nondescript shade, neither brown, blue, nor gray.* —*n.* a nondescript person or thing. [< *non-* + L *descriptus* described]

none[1] (nun) *pron.* **1** not any: *We have none of that paper left.* **2** no one; not one: *None of these is a typical case.* **3** no persons or things: *None have arrived.* **4** no part; nothing: *She has none of her mother's beauty.* —*adv.* **1** to no extent; in no way; not at all: *Our supply is none too great.* **2 none the less,** nevertheless. [OE *nān* < *ne* not + *ān* one]

☛ **none, no one.** *None* is a single word, but *no one* is often used instead of *none,* for emphasis. *None* may be either singular or plural, and now is more common with the plural: *As only ten jurors have been chosen so far, none of the witnesses were called* (or *was called.*) *She tried on ten hats, but none of them were attractive. I read three books on the subject, no one of which was helpful.*

none[2] (nōn) *n.* sing. of **nones**[2].

non·en·ti·ty (non en′tə tē) *n.* **-ties. 1** a person or thing of little or no importance. **2** something that does not exist.

nones[1] (nōnz) *n.pl.* in the ancient Roman calendar, the ninth day before the ides, counting both days, this being the 7th of March, May, July, and October, and the 5th of the other months. [< L *nonae,* originally fem. pl. of *nonus* ninth]

nones[2] (nōnz) *n.pl.* **1** the first of the seven canonical hours. **2** the service or services for it. [pl. of *none*[2], OE *nōn* < L *nona.* Doublet of NOON.]

non-es·sen·tial (non′ə sen′shəl) *adj.* not essential; not necessary. —*n.* a person or thing not essential.

none·such (nun′such′) *n.* a person or thing without equal or parallel; paragon. Also, **nonsuch.**

non-ex·ist·ence (non′eg zis′təns) *n.* **1** the condition of not existing. **2** something that has no existence.

non-fic·tion (non fik′shən) *n.* prose literature that is not a novel, short story, or other form of writing based on imaginary people and events. Biographies and histories are non-fiction.

non-fig·ur·a·tive (non′fig′ər ə tiv or -fig′yər ə tiv) *adj.* **1** in painting, sculpture, etc., non-objective; having abstract as opposed to traditional or recognizable forms. **2** not figurative; literal: *a non-figurative use of a word.*

non-ful·fil·ment or **non-ful·fill·ment** (non′fu̇l fil′mənt) *n.* a failure to fulfil; failure to be fulfilled.

non-in·ter·ven·tion (non′in tər ven′shən) *n.* **1** a failure or refusal to intervene. **2** the systematic avoidance of any interference by a nation in the affairs of other nations or of its own states, etc.

non-ju·ror (non jür′ər) *n.* **1** one who refuses to take a required oath. **2 Non-juror,** in England, one of those clergymen of the Church of England who in 1689 refused to swear allegiance to William and Mary.

non-liv·ing (non′liv′ing) *adj.* not living.

non-met·al (non′met′əl) *n.* any chemical element not having the character of a metal. Carbon and nitrogen are non-metals.

non-me·tal·lic (non′mə tal′ik) *adj.* not like a metal. Carbon, oxygen, sulphur, and nitrogen are non-metallic chemical elements.

non-mor·al (non môr′əl) *adj.* having no relation to morality; neither moral nor immoral.

non-op·er·at·ing (non op′ə rā′ting) *adj.* of or having to do with railway workers, such as ticket agents, etc., not directly concerned with the operation of trains: *a non-operating union.*

non·pa·reil (non′pə rel′) *adj.* having no equal. —*n.* **1** a person or thing having no equal. **2** a kind of apple. **3** in printing, a size of type; 6-point. This sentence is in nonpareil. [< F *nonpareil* < *non-* not (< L) + *pareil* equal, ult. < L *par*]

non-par·ti·san or **non-par·ti·zan** (non pär′tə zən or -par′tə zan′) *adj.* **1** not partisan. **2** not supporting, or controlled by, any of the regular political parties.

non-pay·ment (non pā′mənt) *n.* a failure to pay; condition of not being paid.

non-per·form·ance (non′pər fôr′məns) *n.* the fact of not performing; failure to perform.

non·plus (non plus′ or non′plus) *v.* **-plussed** or **-plused, -plus·sing** or **-plus·ing,** *n.* —*v.* puzzle completely; make unable to say or do anything: *We were nonplussed to see two roads leading off to the left where we had expected only one.* —*n.* a state of being nonplussed. [< L *non plus* no further] —**Syn.** *v.* confound, confuse, mystify, embarrass. -*n.* confusion, embarrassment.

non-pro·duc·tive (non′prə duk′tiv) *adj.* **1** not productive. **2** not directly connected with production. —**non′-pro·duc′tive·ness,** *n.*

non-prof·it (non prof′it) *adj.* not for profit; without profit.

non-rep·re·sen·ta·tion·al (non′rep ri zen tā′shə nəl) *adj.* not intended to represent or resemble natural objects; abstract: *non-representational art.*

non-res·i·dence (non rez′ə dəns) *n.* a being non-resident.

non-res·i·dent (non rez′ə dənt) *adj.* **1** not residing in a particular place. **2** not residing where official duties require one to reside. —*n.* a non-resident person.

non-re·sist·ance (non′ri zis′təns) *n.* the fact or condition of not resisting; lack of resistance.

non-re·sist·ant (non′ri zis′tənt) *adj.* not resisting; passively obedient. —*n.* one who does not resist authority or force; one who maintains that violence should never be resisted by force.

non-re·stric·tive (non′ri strik′tiv) *adj.* **1** in grammar, adding descriptive detail. Modifiers which do not limit the meaning of a noun but add a descriptive detail are non-restrictive modifiers. **2** that does not restrict.

non-sched·uled (non′skej′üld or -shej′üld) *adj.* not according to a set plan, program, or schedule: *a non-scheduled flight, a non-scheduled stop.*

non-sec·tar·i·an (non′sek tãr′ē ən) *adj.* not connected with any religious denomination.

non·sense (non′sens or non′səns) *n.* words, ideas, or acts without meaning; foolish talk or doings; a plan or suggestion that is foolish. [< *non-* + *sense*] —**Syn.** foolishness, absurdity.

non·sen·si·cal (non sen′sə kəl) *adj.* foolish; absurd. —**non·sen′si·cal·ly,** *adv.* —**Syn.** senseless, silly, preposterous.

non-sep·a·ra·tist (non′sep′rə tist) *n.* in Quebec, a person who is against the separation of the province from Confederation.

non seq. non sequitur.

non se·qui·tur (non sek′wə tər) an inference or conclusion that does not follow from the premises. [< L *non sequitur* it does not follow]

non-skid (non′skid′) *adj.* made so as to prevent skidding: *non-skid tires.*

non-stand·ard (non′stan′dərd) *adj.* **1** not conforming to regulations, accepted specifications, etc. **2** outside the generally accepted pattern; different from what is held to be normal.

non-stop (*adj.* non′stop′; *adv.* non′stop′) *adj. adv.* without stopping.

non·such (nun′such′) *n.* nonesuch.

non·suit (non′süt′) *n.* in law, a judgment given against a person beginning a lawsuit who neglects to prosecute, or who fails to show a legal case, or who fails to bring sufficient evidence. —*v.* stop by a nonsuit.

non-sup·port (non′sə pôrt′) *n.* **1** a lack of support. **2** in law, the failure to provide for someone for whom one is legally responsible.

non-treat·y (non′trē′tē) *adj. Cdn.* of Indians, not under the terms of a treaty with the Canadian government but living, usually, on a reserve.

non trop·po (nōn trō′pō) in music, not too much. [< Ital.]

non-un·ion (non ūn′yən) *adj.* **1** not belonging to a trade union. **2** not following trade-union rules. **3** not recognizing or favoring trade unions. **4** manufactured by other than union labor.

non-un·ion·ism (non ūn′yən iz′əm) *n.* the theories or practices of those opposed to trade unions.

non-un·ion·ist (non ūn′yən ist) *n.* **1** a person who is opposed to trade unions. **2** a person who does not belong to a trade union.

non-vi·o·lence (non′vī′ə ləns) *n.* **1** the absence of violence. **2** passive non-co-operation with authority, as opposed to mob violence, used as a means of influencing political or social events.

non-vot·er (non vōt′ər) *n.* a person who does not vote or does not have the right to vote.

non-white (non′hwīt′ or -wīt′) *n.* **1** a person who is not Caucasian. **2** in South Africa, a person who is not of European origin. —*adj.* **1** not Caucasian. **2** of or having to do with non-whites.

non-wo·ven (non′wō′vən) *n.* a fabric made by a method other than weaving. —*adj.* **1** made by a method other than weaving. **2** made of a non-woven fabric: *non-woven raincoats and aprons.*

noo·dle¹ (nü′dəl) *n.* a mixture of flour and water, or flour and eggs, like macaroni, but made in flat strips. [< G *Nudel*]

noo·dle² (nü′dəl) *n.* **1** a very stupid person; fool. **2** *Slang.* the head. [origin uncertain]

nook (nůk) *n* **1** a cosy little corner. **2** a hidden spot; sheltered place. [ME *noke*] —**Syn. 1** recess, niche.

noon (nün) *n.* twelve o'clock in the daytime; the middle of the day. —*adj.* of noon. [OE *nōn* < L *nona* (*hora*) ninth (hour), 3 p.m.; the meaning shifted with a change in time of church service. Doublet of NONE² (see NONES²).]

noon·day (nün′dā′) *n. adj.* noon.

no one or **no-one** (nō′wun′ or nō′wən) no person; nobody. ☛ See **none** for usage note.

noon hour noon; the time around noon. —**noon′-hour′,** *adj.*

noon·ing (nün′ing) *n.* **1** a rest or time for rest at noon. **2** a meal at noon. **3** noon.

noon·tide (nün′tīd′) *n.* noon.

noon·time (nün′tīm′) *n.* noon.

noose (nüs) *n. v.* **noosed, noos·ing.** —*n.* **1** a loop with a slip knot that tightens as the string or rope is pulled. Nooses are used especially in lassos and snares. **2** a snare. —*v.* **1** make a noose with; tie a noose in. **2** catch with a noose. **3** snare. [probably < OF *nos* < Provençal *nous* < L *nodus* knot]

A noose

Noot·ka (nüt′kə) *n.* **1** a tribe of North American Indians living on Vancouver Island. **2** a member of this tribe. **3** the Wakashan language of this tribe.

Nootka cypress yellow cedar. [< *Nootka* Sound, Vancouver Island, B.C.]

Nootka fir Douglas fir.

nor (nôr; *unstressed,* nər) *conj.* and not; or not; neither; and not either. *Nor* is used: **1** with a preceding *neither* or negative: *Not a boy nor a girl stirred.* **2** *Poetic.* with preceding *neither* or *not* left out: "*Great brother, thou nor I have made the world.*" **3** *Poetic.* instead of *neither* as correlative to a following *nor*: "*Drake nor Devil nor Spaniard feared.*" [OE (unstressed) *nā(hwæ)ther* < *ne* not + *ā(hwæ)ther* either]

Nor. 1 North. 2 Norway. 3 Norwegian. 4 Norman.

Norad (nôr′ad) North American Air Defence (Command).

Nor·dic (nôr′dik) *adj.* designating, belonging to, or having to do with a type of people characterized by tall stature, blond hair, blue eyes, and long heads. *—n.* a member of the Nordic people. Many Scandinavians are Nordics. [< F *nordique* < *nord* north < Gmc.]

Nor·folk jacket (nôr′fək) a loose-fitting, single-breasted jacket with a belt and box pleats in front and back.

norm (nôrm) *n.* the standard for a certain group; type; model; pattern: *In mathematics this class is above the norm for the senior year.* [< L *norma* a rule, pattern]

nor·mal (nôr′məl) *adj.* **1** of the usual standard; regular; usual: *The normal temperature of the human body is 98.6 degrees. Sane people are normal; insane people are not.* **2** in geometry, being at right angles; perpendicular. **3** in chemistry: **a** of an acidic or basic solution, containing the equivalent of one gram of hydrogen ion per litre. **b** of or denoting an aliphatic hydrocarbon or hydrocarbon derivative. **c** not found in association, as molecules.
—n. **1** the usual state or level: *two pounds above normal.* **2** in geometry, a line or plane that is at right angles to another. [< L *normalis* < *norma* a rule, pattern] **—Syn.** *adj.* **1** natural, typical.

nor·mal·cy (nôr′məl sē) *n.* a normal condition.

nor·mal·i·ty (nôr mal′ə tē) *n.* a normal condition.

nor·mal·ize (nôr′məl īz′) *v.* **-ized, -iz·ing.** make normal. **—nor′mal·i·za′tion,** *n.* **—nor′mal·iz′er,** *n.*

nor·mal·ly (nôr′məl ē) *adv.* in the normal way; regularly; if things are normal.

normal school a school where people are trained to be elementary-school teachers. [after F *école normale*]

Nor·man (nôr′mən) *n.* **1** a native or inhabitant of Normandy in France. **2** a member of the people descended from the native French and from the Scandinavians who settled in Normandy in the tenth century A.D. **3** one of the Scandinavian ancestors of these people; a Northman. **4** Norman-French. *—adj.* **1** of the Normans or Normandy. **2** Norman-French. [< OF *Normans,* pl. of *Normant* < Gmc.]

Norman Conquest the conquest of England by the Normans in 1066, under the leadership of William the Conqueror.

Nor·man-French (nôr′mən french′) *n.* **1** a dialect of the French language spoken by the Normans who conquered England in 1066. **2** a later form of this dialect, surviving in certain English legal phrases; law French. *—adj.* of or having to do with this dialect or those who spoke it; Anglo-French; Anglo-Norman.

Norn (nôrn) *n.* in Norse mythology, one of the three goddesses of fate, who rule over gods and men.

Norse (nôrs) *adj.* **1** of or having to do with ancient Scandinavia, its people, or their language. **2** of or having to do with Norway, a country in N. Europe, or its people. *—n.* **1** the people of ancient Scandinavia; Norsemen; Northmen. **2** Norwegians. **3** the language of the ancient Scandinavians, often called Old Norse. **4** the language of Norway. [< Du. *Noorsch* Norwegian]
☛ **Norse,** meaning the people of ancient Scandinavia and Norwegians, is singular in form and plural in use: *The Norse are a hardy people.* When *Norse* means the language, it is singular in form and use.

Norse·man (nôrs′mən) *n.* **-men** (-mən). a member of a tall, blond people that lived in ancient Scandinavia; Northman. The Vikings were Norsemen.

north (nôrth) *n.* **1** the direction to which a compass needle points; direction to the right as one faces the setting sun. **2** Also, **North.** the part of any country toward the north. **3 the North,** in Canada, the northern parts of the provinces from Quebec westward and the territory lying north of these provinces. **4 the North,** in the United States, the northern part of the country; states north of Maryland, the Ohio River, and Missouri.
—adj. **1** toward the north. **2** from the north. **3** in the north; northern: *North China.*
—adv. toward the north: *Their trip north was long but uneventful.* [OE]

hat, āge, cãre, fär; let, ēqual, tėrm; it, īce
hot, ōpen, ôrder; oil, out; cup, pu̇t, rüle, ūse
əbove, takən, pencəl, lemən, circəs
ch, child; ng, long; sh, ship
th, thin; ᴛʜ, then; zh, measure

North American **1** of or having to do with North America. **2** a native or inhabitant of North America.

north·bound (nôrth′bound′) *adj.* going toward the north.

North canoe *Cdn.* formerly, a canoe used by the fur brigades on the rivers of the north and northwest. It was about 25 feet long and carried three or four passengers and over a ton of cargo.

North Country **1** the northern parts of North America. **2** northern England.

north·east (nôrth′ēst′) *adj.* **1** halfway between north and east. **2** lying toward or situated in the northeast. **3** of, at, in, toward, or from the northeast: *a northeast wind.* **4** directed toward the northeast. *—n.* **1** a northeast direction. **2** a place that is in the northeast part or direction. *—adv.* **1** toward the northeast. **2** from the northeast. **3** in the northeast.

north·east·er (nôrth′ēs′tər) *n.* a wind or storm from the northeast.

north·east·er·ly (nôrth′ēs′tər lē) *adj. adv.* **1** toward the northeast. **2** from the northeast.

north·east·ern (nôrth′ēs′tərn) *adj.* of, at, in, to, toward, or from the northeast.

north·east·ward (nôrth′ēst′wərd) *adv. adj.* **1** toward the northeast. **2** northeast. *—n.* the northeast.

north·east·ward·ly (nôrth′ēst′wərd lē) *adj.* **1** toward the northeast. **2** of winds, from the northeast. *—adv.* toward the northeast.

north·east·wards (nôrth′ēst′wərdz) *adv.* northeastward.

north·er (nôr′ᴛʜər) *n.* a wind or storm from the north.

north·er·ly (nôr′ᴛʜər lē) *adj.* **1** toward the north. **2** from the north: *a northerly wind.* **3** of the north. *—adv.* **1** toward the north. **2** from the north.

north·ern (nôr′ᴛʜərn) *adj.* **1** toward the north. **2** from the north: *a northern breeze.* **3** of or in the north; of or in the northern part of the country: *He has travelled in northern countries. Churchill is a northern port.* [OE *northerne*]

north·ern·er (nôr′ᴛʜər nər) *n.* a native or inhabitant of the north.

northern lights the aurora borealis; streams and bands of light appearing in the sky in northern regions.

north·ern·most (nôr′ᴛʜərn mōst′) *adj.* farthest north.

northern service officer *Cdn.* a federal government officer in charge of a district in the far North.

north·ing (nôr′thing or nôr′ᴛʜing) *n.* the distance measured in a northerly direction.

north·land (nôrth′lənd *for 1*; nôrth′land′ *for 2*) *n.* **1** land in the north; the northern part of a country. **2 Northland, a** the northern regions of the world. **b** the northern regions of Canada: *The Yukon is a fast-growing part of Canada's Northland.* **c** a peninsula containing Norway and Sweden. [OE]

north·land·er (nôrth′lən dər) *n.* an inhabitant of the northland.

North·man (nôrth′mən) *n.* **-men** (-mən). **1** a Norseman. **2** a native or inhabitant of northern Europe.

North Pole the northern end of the earth's axis.

North Star the bright star almost directly above the North Pole.

North·um·bri·an (nôr thum′brē ən) *adj.* **1** of or having to do with Northumbria, an ancient kingdom in N. England, its people, or their dialect. **2** of or having to do with Northumberland, its people, or their dialect.
—n. **1** a native or inhabitant of Northumbria. **2** a dialect

of Old English spoken in Northumbria. **3** a native or inhabitant of Northumberland. **4** the Northumberland dialect.

north·ward (nôrth′wərd) *adv.* toward the north: *Rocks lay northward of the ship's course.* —*adj.* toward the north; north: *the northward slope of a hill.* —*n.* the north.

north·ward·ly (nôrth′wərd lē) *adj.* **1** toward the north. **2** of winds, from the north. —*adv.* toward the north.

north·wards (nôrth′wərdz) *adv.* northward.

north·west (nôrth′west′) *adj.* **1** halfway between north and west. **2** lying toward or situated in the northwest. **3** of, at, in, to, toward, or from the northwest: *a northwest wind.* **4** directed toward the northwest. —*n.* **1** a northwest direction. **2** a place that is in the northwest part or direction. **3 Northwest,** the general region of Canada north and west of the Great Lakes. —*adv.* **1** toward the northwest. **2** from the northwest. **3** in the northwest.

North West Company a loosely organized group of companies and individuals formed in Montreal during the late eighteenth century to promote the fur trade in Canada. It was absorbed by the Hudson's Bay Company in 1821.

north·west·er (nôrth′wes′tər) *n.* a wind or storm from the northwest.

North-west·er (nôrth′west′ər) *n. Cdn.* formerly, a wintering partner or employee of the North West Company.

north·west·er·ly (nôrth′wes′tər lē) *adj. adv.* **1** toward the northwest. **2** of winds, from the northwest.

north·west·ern (nôrth′wes′tərn) *adj.* of, at, in, to, toward, or from the northwest.

North West Mounted Police a former name of the Royal Canadian Mounted Police. *Abbrev.*: NWMP or N.W.M.P.

Northwest Passage a route for ships from the Atlantic to the Pacific along the northern coast of North America.

Northwest Rebellions the two uprisings in 1869 and 1885 against the coming of agricultural settlement to the old Northwest. The uprisings were the result of the fear of the Métis that they would lose their hunting rights.

north·west·ward (nôrth′west′wərd) *adj. adv.* **1** toward the northwest. **2** northwest. —*n.* the northwest.

north·west·ward·ly (nôrth′west′wərd lē) *adj.* **1** toward the northwest. **2** of winds, from the northwest. —*adv.* toward the northwest.

north·west·wards (nôrth′west′wərdz) *adv.* northwestward.

Nor·we·gian (nôr wē′jən) *adj.* of or having to do with Norway, a country in N. Europe, its people, or their language. —*n.* **1** a native or inhabitant of Norway. **2** the language of Norway; Norse.

nor'west·er (nôr wes′tər) *n.* a heavy, waterproof oilskin coat worn by seamen.

Nor'West·er (nôr′west′ər) *n. Cdn.* North-wester.

Nos. or **nos.** numbers.

nose (nōz) *n. v.* **nosed, nos·ing.** —*n.* **1** the part of the face or head just above the mouth, serving as the opening for breathing and as the organ of smell. **2** the sense of smell: *a dog with a good nose.* **3** a faculty for perceiving or detecting: *A reporter must have a nose for news.* **4** a part that stands out. The bow of a ship or airplane is often called the nose.
count noses, find out how many people are present.
follow one's nose, a go straight ahead. b be guided by one's instinct. c be guided by one's sense of smell.
lead by the nose, have complete control over.
look down one's nose at, *Informal.* feel contempt for.
on the nose, a exactly. b solidly.
pay through the nose, pay a great deal too much.
poke one's nose into, pry into; meddle in.
put someone's nose out of joint, *Informal.* a take one's place in another's favor. b destroy one's hopes, plans, etc.
thumb one's nose, put one's thumb to one's nose in scorn.
turn up one's nose at, treat with contempt or scorn.
under one's nose, in plain sight; very easy to notice.
—*v.* **1** discover by smelling; smell out. **2** smell; sniff. **3** rub with the nose. **4** push with the nose or forward end. **5** push (one's way): *The little boat nosed carefully between the rocks.* **6** search (*for*); pry (*into*). **7 nose out,** find out by looking around quietly or secretly. [OE *nosu*]

nose bag a bag containing food, to be hung on a horse's head.

nose·band (nōz′band′) *n.* the part of a bridle that goes over the animal's nose.

nose·bleed (nōz′blēd′) *n.* a bleeding from the nose.

nose cone the separable front section of a missile, made to carry the payload and to withstand the intense heat encountered in re-entering the earth's atmosphere.

nose-dive (nōz′dīv′) *n. v.* **-dived, -div·ing.** —*n.* **1** a swift plunge straight downward by an aircraft. **2** a sudden, sharp drop. —*v.* **1** of an aircraft, plunge swiftly downward. **2** take a sharp, sudden drop: *The price of gasoline nose-dived overnight.*

nose·gay (nōz′gā′) *n.* a bunch of flowers; bouquet. [< *nose* + *gay*, obs. n., something gay or pretty]

nose·guard (nōz′gärd′) *n.* the part of a football helmet that covers and protects the nose.

nose·piece (nōz′pēs′) *n.* **1** the part of a helmet that covers and protects the nose. **2** a noseband for an animal.

nos·ey or **nos·y** (nōz′ē) *adj.* **nos·i·er, nos·i·est.** *Informal.* prying, inquisitive.

Nosey Park·er (pärk′ər) a person showing a persistent and offensive curiosity about things which do not concern him or her. Also, **Nosy Parker.**

nos·tal·gia (nos tal′jə or nos tal′jē ə) *n.* **1** homesickness. **2** a painful or wistful yearning for anything far removed in space or time. [< NL < Gk. *nostos* homecoming + *algos* pain]

nos·tal·gic (nos tal′jik) *adj.* feeling or showing nostalgia; homesick. —**nos·tal′gi·cal·ly,** *adv.*

nos·tril (nos′trəl) *n.* either of the two external openings in the nose. Air is breathed into the lungs through the nostrils. [OE *nosthyrl* < *nosu* nose + *thyrel* hole]

nos·trum (nos′trəm) *n.* **1** a medicine made by the person who is selling it; a quack remedy; a patent medicine. **2** a pet scheme for producing wonderful results; cure-all. [< L *nostrum* ours; because usually prepared by the person recommending it]

nos·y (nōz′ē) *adj.* **nos·i·er, nos·i·est.** nosey.

Nosy Parker Nosey Parker.

not (not) *adv.* a word used to make a negative statement: *That is not true.* [unstressed var. of *nought*]

no·ta be·ne (nō′tə bē′nē or ben′ē) *Latin.* note well; observe what follows; take notice. *Abbrev.*: N.B. or n.b.

no·ta·bil·i·ty (nō′tə bil′ə tē) *n.* **-ties. 1** the quality of being notable; distinction. **2** a prominent person.

no·ta·ble (nō′tə bəl) *adj.* **1** worthy of notice; striking; remarkable: *a notable event, a notable man, a notable book, a notable painter.* **2** that can be noted or perceived; perceptible; appreciable: *a notable quantity.* —*n.* an important or famous person: *Many notables attended the Governor General's levee.* [ME < OF < L *notabilis* < *notare* note < *nota* a mark] —**no′ta·ble·ness,** *n.*
—**Syn.** *adj.* memorable, conspicuous, famous.

no·ta·bly (nō′tə blē) *adv.* in a notable manner; to a notable degree.

no·tar·i·al (nō tãr′ē əl) *adj.* **1** of or having to do with a notary public. **2** made or done by a notary public.

no·ta·rize (nō′tə rīz′) *v.* **-rized, -riz·ing.** certify (a contract, deed, will, etc.).

no·ta·ry (nō′tə rē) *n.* **-ries. 1** notary public. **2** in Quebec, a lawyer who has the same training as a barrister but who is not permitted to plead in court. [< L *notarius* clerk, ult. < *nota* note]

notary public a person who is authorized to certify deeds and contracts, to record the fact that a certain person swears that something is true, and to attend to certain other legal matters. *Abbrev.*: N.P.

no·ta·tion (nō tā′shən) *n.* **1** a set of signs or symbols used to represent numbers, quantities, or other values: *In arithmetic we use the Arabic notation (1, 2, 3, 4, etc.).* **2** the representing of numbers, quantities, or other values

hat, āge, cãre, fär; let, ēqual, tėrm; it, īce
hot, ōpen, ôrder; oil, out; cup, pu̇t, rüle, ūse
əbove, takən, pencəl, lemən, circəs
ch, child; ng, long; sh, ship
th, thin; ᴛʜ, then; zh, measure

by symbols or signs: *Music and chemistry have special systems of notation.* **3** a note to assist memory; record; jotting. **4** the act of noting. [< L *notatio, -onis* < *notare* to note < *nota* a mark]

notch (noch) *n.* **1** a V-shaped nick or cut made in an edge or on a curving surface: *The Indians cut notches on a stick to keep count of numbers.* **2** a deep, narrow pass or gap between mountains. **3** in Newfoundland, an entrance to a harbor. **4** a grade; step; degree. —*v.* **1** make a notch or notches in. **2** record by notches; score; tally. [< MF *oche* < OF *oschier* notch; *an och* taken as *a noch*] —**Syn.** *n.* **1** dent, indentation.

Notches on a stick

note (nōt) *n. v.* **not·ed, not·ing.** —*n.* **1** a short sentence, phrase, or single word written down to remind one of something: *Her notes helped her remember what the speaker said.* **2** notice; heed; observation. **3** a comment, remark, or piece of information added concerning a word or passage in a book. **4** a brief letter. **5** a letter from one government to another; diplomatic or official communication in writing. **6** a single sound of definite pitch made by a musical instrument or voice. **7** in music: **a** a written sign to show the pitch and length of a sound. **b** a black or white key of a piano or other keyboard instrument. **8** a bird's song or call. **9** a song; melody; tune. **10** a significant sound or way of expression: *a note of anxiety in her voice.* **11** a sign, token, or proof of genuineness; characteristic or distinguishing feature. **12** distinction, importance, or consequence. **13** in business, a written promise to pay a certain sum of money at a certain time. **14** a certificate of a government or bank that may be used as money.
compare notes, exchange ideas or opinions.
make a note of, write down as something to be remembered.
of note, a that is important, great, or notable: *a writer of note.* **b** of being noticed: *worthy of note.*
strike the right note, say or do something suitable.
take note of, take notice of; give attention to; observe.
take notes, write down things to be remembered.
—*v.* **1** write down as a thing to be remembered. **2** observe carefully; give attention to; take notice of: *Now note what I do next.* **3** mention specially. **4** indicate, signify, or denote. [ME < OF < L *nota* mark] —**note′less,** *adj.* —**not′er,** *n.* —**Syn.** *n.* **11** mark, symbol, character. **12** repute, significance. –*v.* **1** record. **2** regard, perceive.

A B C D

Notes in music: A, whole note; B, half note; C, quarter note; D, eighth note.

note·book (nōt′bu̇k′) *n.* a book in which to write notes of things to be learned or remembered.

not·ed (nōt′id) *adj.* **1** especially noticed; conspicuous; well-known; celebrated; famous: *Samson was noted for his strength. Shakespeare is a noted English author.* **2** observed or noticed: *His absence from class was noted.* —**Syn.** renowned, distinguished. See **famous.**

note·paper (nōt′pā′pər) *n.* paper used for writing letters.

note·wor·thy (nōt′wėr′ᴛʜē) *adj.* worthy of notice; remarkable: *noteworthy achievement.* —**note′wor′thi·ness,** *n.*

noth·ing (nuth′ing) *n.* **1** not anything; no thing: *Nothing arrived by mail.* **2** something that does not exist: *create a world out of nothing.* **3** a thing of no importance or value; person of no importance: *People regard him as a nothing.* **4** zero; nought. **5 make nothing of, a** be unable to understand. **b** fail to use or do. **c** treat as unimportant or worthless. **6 nothing less than,** just the same as. **7 think nothing of, a** consider as easy to do. **b** treat as unimportant or worthless. —*adv.* not at all: *be nothing wiser than before.* [< *no* + *thing*] ☛ See **nobody** for usage note.

noth·ing·ness (nuth′ing nis) *n.* **1** a being nothing; non-existence. **2** a being of no value; worthlessness. **3** an unimportant or worthless thing. **4** unconsciousness.

no·tice (nō′tis) *n. v.* **-ticed, -tic·ing.** —*n.* **1** observation; heed; attention: *escape one's notice.* **2** advance information; warning: *The whistle blew to give notice that the boat was about to leave.* **3** a written or printed sign; paper posted in a public place. **4** a warning or announcement that one will end an agreement with another at a certain time: *The servant gave notice.* **5** a paragraph or article about something: *The new book got a favorable notice.* **6 serve notice,** give warning; inform; announce. **7 take notice,** give attention; observe; see. —*v.* **1** take notice of; give attention to; perceive: *I noticed a big difference at once.* **2** mention; refer to. [< F < L *notitia* < *notus* known] —**Syn.** *n.* **1** regard, note. **2** notification. **3** bulletin, placard. –*v.* **1** see, mark, note, heed.

no·tice·a·ble (nō′tis ə bəl) *adj.* **1** easily seen or noticed: *The class has made noticeable improvement.* **2** worth noticing. —**Syn. 1** discernible, observable, conspicuous.

no·tice·a·bly (nō′tis ə blē) *adv.* to a noticeable degree: *It is noticeably cooler in the shade.*

no·ti·fi·ca·tion (nō′tə fə kā′shən) *n.* **1** a notifying. **2** a notice: *Have you received a notification of the meeting?*

no·ti·fy (nō′tə fī′) *v.* **-fied, -fy·ing.** give notice to; let know; inform; announce to: *Our teacher notified us that there would be a test on Monday.* [ME < OF < L *notificare* < *notus* known + *facere* make] —**no′ti·fi′er,** *n.* —**Syn.** apprise, acquaint. See **inform.**

no·tion (nō′shən) *n.* **1** an idea; understanding: *He has no notion of what I mean.* **2** an opinion; view; belief: *It is a common notion that red hair means a quick temper.* **3** intention: *He has no notion of risking his money.* **4** a foolish idea or opinion. **5 notions,** *pl.* small useful articles, such as pins, needles, thread, tape, etc. [< L *notio, -onis,* ult. < *noscere* know] —**Syn. 1** concept, impression. See **idea.**

no·tion·al (nō′shən əl) *adj.* **1** having to do with ideas or opinions. **2** in one's imagination or thought only; not real.

no·to·chord (nō′tə kôrd′) *n.* **1** a rodlike structure that is the primitive cartilaginous backbone of the lowest vertebrates. **2** a similar structure in the embryos of higher vertebrates. [< Gk. *nōton* back + E *chord*[2]]

no·to·ri·e·ty (nō′tə rī′ə tē) *n.* **-ties. 1** a being famous for something bad; ill fame: *A crime or scandal brings much notoriety to those involved in it.* **2** the state of being widely known. **3** a well-known person.

no·to·ri·ous (nō tô′rē əs) *adj.* **1** well-known because of something unfavorable or unpleasant; having a bad reputation: *The notorious thief was sent to prison for his many crimes.* **2** well-known. [< Med.L *notorius* < L *notus* known] —**no·to′ri·ous·ly,** *adv.* —**no·to′ri·ous·ness,** *n.*
☛ **Notorious** = well-known for unsavory reasons: *a notorious cheat.* **Famous** = well-known for accomplishments or excellence: *a famous writer or aviator.*

No·tre Dame (nō′trə däm′) **1** *French.* Our Lady, the Virgin Mary. **2** in Paris, France, a famous cathedral.

no-trump (nō′trump′) *adj.* without any trumps. —*n.* in bridge and certain other games: **1** a declaration to play with no suit as trumps. **2** a hand that is so played.

not·with·stand·ing (not′with stan′ding or -wiᴛʜ-) *prep.* in spite of: *He bought it notwithstanding the high price.* —*conj.* in spite of the fact that: *Notwithstanding there was a need for haste, he still delayed.* —*adv.* in spite of it; nevertheless: *It is raining; but I shall go, notwithstanding.*

nou·gat (nü′gət or nü′gä) *n.* a kind of soft candy containing nuts. [< F < Provençal *noga,* ult. < L *nux, nucis* nut]

nought (not or nôt) *n.* **1** zero; 0. **2** naught; nothing. —*adv. Archaic.* in no way; not at all. [see NAUGHT]

noughts and crosses (nots′ ən kros′iz or nôts′-) tick-tack-toe.

noun (noun) *n.* a word used as the name of a person, place, thing, quality, event, etc. Words like *John, table, school, kindness, skill,* and *party* are nouns. —*adj.* used as a noun. [ME < AF *nom* < L *nomen* name]
☛ **forms of nouns.** Nouns may be single words or compound

words written solid or as two words or hyphenated: *ceremony, bookcase, high school, go-getter.* Most nouns change their form to make the plural, most of them adding *-s* or *-es*: *boys, kindnesses, manufacturers.* Nouns change their form for case only in the genitive or possessive, typically by adding *'s* or *s'*: *boy's, Harriet's, Dickens'.* A very few nouns in English may have different forms for male and female sex: *usher—usherette, executor—executrix, actor—actress.*

nour·ish (nėr′ish) *v.* **1** make grow, or keep alive and well, with food; feed: *Milk nourishes a baby.* **2** maintain; foster: *nourish a hope.* [ME < OF *noriss-*, a stem of *norir* < L *nutrire* feed] **—nour′ish·er,** *n.* **—Syn. 1** nurture. **2** support, encourage.

nour·ish·ment (nėr′ish mənt) *n.* **1** food. **2** the act of nourishing or the condition of being nourished.

nou·veau riche (nü vō rēsh′) *pl.* **nou·veaux riches** (nü vō rēsh′). *French.* one who has recently become rich; often, one who makes a vulgar display of his wealth.

Nov. November.

no·va (nō′və) *n.* **no·vae** (nō′vē or nō′vī), **no·vas.** in astronomy, a star that suddenly becomes brighter and then gradually fades away.

No·va Sco·tian (nō′və skō′shən) *n.* a native or inhabitant of Nova Scotia. *—adj.* of or concerning Nova Scotia.

nov·el[1] (nov′əl) *adj.* of a new kind or nature; strange; new: *Red snow is a novel idea to us.* [ME < OF < L *novellus*, dim of *novus* new] **—Syn.** unfamiliar. See **new.**

nov·el[2] (nov′əl) *n.* **1** a fictional story with characters and a plot, long enough to fill one or more volumes. **2 the novel,** the branch of literature having to do with such works: *He is studying the novel.* [< Ital. *novella* < L *novella* new things, neut. pl. of *novellus* (see NOVEL[1]); intermediate meaning probably "a composition showing originality"]

Syn. Novel, romance = a long fictitious story. **Novel** applies particularly to a long work of prose fiction dealing with characters, situations, and scenes that represent those of real life and setting forth the action in the form of a plot. **Romance** applies especially to a story, often a novel in form, presenting characters and situations not likely to be found in real life and emphasizing exciting or amazing adventures, love, etc., usually set in distant or unfamiliar times or places.

nov·el·ette (nov′əl et′) *n.* a short novel.

nov·el·ist (nov′əl ist) *n.* a writer of novels.

nov·el·is·tic (nov′əl is′tik) *adj.* of or like novels.

no·vel·la (nō vel′ə; *Italian,* nō vel′lä) *n.* **no·vel·las, no·vel·le** (*Italian,* nō vel′lā). a short story with a simple plot. [< Ital.]

nov·el·ty (nov′əl tē) *n.* **-ties. 1** newness; novel character: *After the novelty of washing dishes wore off, Mary lost interest* **2** a new or unusual thing: *Staying up late was a novelty to the children.* **3 novelties,** *pl.* small, unusual articles; toys, cheap jewellery, etc. [ME < OF *novelte* < L *novellitas* < *novellus.* See NOVEL[1].] **—Syn. 1** recentness, freshness.

No·vem·ber (nō vem′bər) *n.* the 11th month of the year. It has 30 days. [< L *November* < *novem* nine; from the order of the early Roman calendar]

no·ve·na (nō vē′nə) *n.* **-nas, -nae** (-nē or -nī). in the Roman Catholic Church, a religious exercise consisting of prayers or services on nine days, or nine corresponding days in consecutive months: *a novena of nine first Fridays.* [< Med.L *novena*, ult. < L *novem* nine]

nov·ice (nov′is) *n.* **1** one who is new to what he is doing; beginner. **2** a person who is received into a religious order or community on probation before taking final vows. Before becoming a monk or a nun, a person is a novice. [ME < OF < L *novicius* < *novus* new] **—Syn. 1** tyro, apprentice.

no·vi·ti·ate or **no·vi·ci·ate** (nō vish′ē it or nō vish′ē āt′) *n.* **1** a period of probation before taking final vows in a religious order or community. **2** a novice. **3** a house or rooms occupied by religious novices. **4** the state or period of being a beginner in anything. [< Med.L *novitiatus*, ult. < *novus* new]

no·vo·caine or **no·vo·cain** (nō′və kān′) *n.* **1** an alkaloid compound, used as a local anesthetic. **2 Novocain,** a trademark for this compound. [< L *novus* new + E (*co*)*caine*]

now (nou) *adv.* **1** at the present time: *He is here now.* **2** by this time: *She must have reached the city now.* **3** at once: *Do it now!* **4** then; next: *If passed, the bill now goes to the Senate.* **5** at the time referred to: *The clock now struck three.* **6** a little while ago: *I saw him just now.* **7** under the present circumstances; as things are; as it is: *I would believe almost anything now.* **8** *Now* is also used to introduce, emphasize, lessen the severity of a sentence, or sometimes just to fill in: *Now what do you mean? Oh, come now!* **9 now and again,** from time to time; once in a while. **10 now and then,** from time to time; once in a while.
—n. the present; this time.
—conj. since; inasmuch as: *Now I am older, I have changed my mind.*
—interj. be careful! please! [OE *nū*]

now·a·days (nou′ə dāz′) *adv.* at the present day; in these times. *—n.* the present day; these times.

no·way (nō′ wā′) *adv.* nowise.

no·ways (nō′ wāz′) *adv.* noway.

no·where (nō′ hwãr′ or nō′ wãr′) *adv.* in no place; at no place; to no place. [OE *nāhwǣr*] ☛ See **nobody** for usage note.

no·wise (nō′ wīz′) *adv.* in no way; not at all.

nox·ious (nok′shəs) *adj.* **1** extremely harmful; poisonous: *Fumes from the exhaust of an automobile are noxious.* **2** morally hurtful; corrupting. [< L *noxius* < *noxa* hurt < *nocere* hurt] **—nox′ious·ly,** *adv.* **—nox′ious·ness,** *n.* **—Syn.** hurtful, unhealthful, deadly.

noz·zle (noz′əl) *n.* **1** a tip put on a hose, pipe, etc. so that the flow of gas or liquid can be controlled: *He adjusted the nozzle so that the water came out in a fine spray.* **2** *Slang.* the nose. [dim. of *nose*]

Np neptunium.

N.P. Notary Public.

n.p.t. normal pressure and temperature.

nr. near.

NRC or **N.R.C.** National Research Council.

Ns in meteorology, nimbo-stratus.

N.S. 1 Nova Scotia. **2** New Style.

NSF or **nsf** not sufficient funds.

N.S.O. or **NSO** northern service officer.

NST, N.S.T., or **n.s.t.** Newfoundland Standard Time.

N.S.W. New South Wales.

Nt niton.

N.T. New Testament.

nth (enth) *adj.* **1** last in the series 1, 2, 3, 4 . . . n; being of the indefinitely large or small amount denoted by *n.* **2 to the nth degree** or **power, a** to any degree or power. **b** *Informal.* to the utmost: *He was dressed to the nth degree for the occasion.*

nt.wt. net weight.

nu (nū or nü) *n.* the 13th letter (Ν, ν) of the Greek alphabet, pronounced like English *n.*

nu·ance (nū äns′ or nü äns′, nū′äns or nü′äns) *n.* **1** a shade of expression, meaning, feeling, etc. **2** a shade of color or tone. [< F]

nub (nub) *n.* **1** a knob; protuberance. **2** a lump or small piece. **3** *Informal.* the point or gist of anything. [apparently var. of *knob*]

Nu·bi·an (nū′bē ən or nü′bē ən) *adj.* of or having to do with Nubia, a region in N.E. Africa, its people, or their language. *—n.* **1** one of the negroid natives of Nubia. **2** the language spoken by these people.

nub·bin (nub′ən) *n.* **1** a small lump or piece. **2** a small or imperfect ear of corn. **3** an undeveloped fruit. [dim. of *nub*]

nu·bile (nū′bīl or nü′bīl, nū′bəl or nü′bəl) *adj.* old enough to be married; marriageable. [< L *nubilis* < *nubere* take a husband]

nu·cle·ar (nū′klē ər or nü′klē ər) *adj.* **1** forming a nucleus. **2** of or having to do with a nucleus, as of a cell or an atom or the particles contained within the nucleus: *nuclear disintegration, a nuclear charge.* **3** having the character or position of a nucleus; like a nucleus. **4 a** of or having to do with atomic energy: *nuclear age, nuclear processes.* **b** used in atomic energy; using atomic energy: *nuclear materials, a nuclear submarine.* **c** of or having to do with nuclear weapons or their use: *nuclear disarmament.*

nuclear club the countries that have developed atomic weapons, thought of as belonging to a group: *China joined the nuclear club in 1965.*

nuclear fission fission (def. 3).

nuclear fuel a fissile substance that will sustain a chain reaction.

nuclear fusion fusion (def. 4).

nuclear physics the branch of physics that is concerned with atoms and their nuclear structure.

nuclear reactor reactor.

nu·cle·ate (*v.* nū′klē āt′ or nü′klē āt′; *adj.* nū′klē it or nü′klē it, nū′klē āt′ or nü′klē āt′) *v.* **-at·ed, -at·ing,** *adj.* —*v.* form into a nucleus or around a nucleus. —*adj.* having a nucleus. [< LL *nucleare* become full of kernels < L *nucleus* kernel] —**nu′cle·a′tion,** *n.*

nu·cle·i (nū′klē ī′ or nü′klē ī′) *n.* pl. of **nucleus.**

nu·cle·o·lus (nū klē′ə ləs or nü klē′ə ləs) *n.* **-li** (-lī′ or -lē′). in biology, a small structure, usually round, found within the nucleus in most cells. [< LL *nucleolus,* dim. of L *nucleus* kernel]

nu·cle·on (nū′klē on′ or nü′klē on′) *n.* one of the atomic particles that make up the nucleus of an atom, such as a neutron or proton.

nu·cle·on·ics (nū′klē on′iks or nü′klē on′iks) *n.* the study and science of the behavior and characteristics of nucleons.

nu·cle·us (nū′klē əs or nü′klē əs) *n.* **-cle·i** or **-cle·us·es.** **1** a beginning to which additions are to be made. **2** a central part or thing around which other parts or things are collected. **3** in physics, a proton, or group of protons and neutrons (sometimes including alpha particles), forming the central part of an atom and carrying a positive charge. **4** in chemistry, the basic arrangement of atoms in a particular compound. **5** in biology, an active body lying within the protoplasm of a cell of an animal or a plant, without which the cell cannot grow and divide. **6** in astronomy, the dense, central part of a comet's head. **7** in meteorology, a particle of dust, etc., upon which water vapor condenses so as to form a drop. [<L *nucleus* < *nux, nucis* nut] —**Syn. 2** centre, core, heart.

nude (nūd or nüd) *adj.* naked; unclothed; bare. —*n.* **1** in painting, sculpture, or photography, a naked figure. **2 the nude, a** the naked figure. **b** a naked condition. [< L *nudus*] —**nude′ness,** *n.* —**Syn.** *adj.* See **bare.**

nudge (nuj) *v.* **nudged, nudg·ing,** *n.* —*v.* **1** push slightly; jog with the elbow to attract attention. **2** prod; stimulate: *nudge one's memory, nudge a person into action.* **3** approach closely: *She is nudging forty.* —*n.* a slight push or jog. [origin uncertain]

nud·ism (nūd′iz əm or nüd′iz əm) *n.* the cult or practice of going naked, especially for the sake of one's health.

nud·ist (nūd′ist or nüd′ist) *n.* a person who practises nudism. —*adj.* of nudism or nudists.

nu·di·ty (nū′də tē or nü′də tē) *n.* **-ties. 1** nakedness. **2** something naked.

nu·ga·to·ry (nū′gə tô′rē or nü′gə tô′rē) *adj.* **1** trifling; worthless. **2** of no force; invalid. **3** ineffective; useless. [< L *nugatorius* < *nugari* trifle < *nugae* trifles]

nug·get (nug′it) *n.* **1** a lump. **2** a lump of native gold. **3** anything valuable. [? < *nug* lump]

nui·sance (nū′səns or nü′səns) *n.* a thing or person that annoys, troubles, offends, or is disagreeable: *Flies are a nuisance.* [ME < OF *nuisance* < *nuire* harm < L *nocere*] —**Syn.** annoyance, plague, trouble, inconvenience.

nuisance ground in the West, a garbage dump; a place where worn-out and useless material is thrown.

nuisance tax a tax that is annoying because it is collected in very small amounts from the consumer.

null (nul) *adj.* **1** not binding; of no effect; as if not existing: *A promise obtained by force is legally null.* **2** unimportant; useless; meaningless; valueless. **3** not any; zero. **4 null and void,** without force or effect; worthless. [< L *nullus* < *ne-* not + *ullus* any]

hat, āge, cãre, fär; let, ēqual, tėrm; it, īce
hot, ōpen, ôrder; oil, out; cup, pu̇t, rüle, ūse
əbove, takən, pencəl, lemən, circəs
ch, child; ng, long; sh, ship
th, thin; ᴛʜ, then; zh, measure

nul·li·fy (nul′ə fī′) *v.* **-fied, -fy·ing. 1** make not binding; render void: *nullify a law.* **2** make unimportant, useless, or meaningless; destroy; cancel: *The difficulties of the plan nullify its advantages.* [< L *nullificare* < *nullus* not any + *facere* make] —**nul′li·fi·ca′tion,** *n.* —**nul′li·fi′er,** *n.* —**Syn. 1** annul, repeal.

nul·li·ty (nul′ə tē) *n.* **-ties. 1** futility; nothingness. **2** a mere nothing. **3** something that is null, such as a nullified law or agreement. [< Med.L *nullitas* < L *nullus* not any]

Num. Numbers.

numb (num) *adj.* having lost the power of feeling or moving: *My fingers are numb with cold.* —*v.* **1** make numb. **2** dull the feelings of: *numbed with grief.* [ult. < OE *numen* taken, seized] —**numb′ly,** *adv.* —**numb′ness,** *n.* —**Syn.** *adj.* deadened, insensible, benumbed.

num·ber (num′bər) *n.* **1** a word or symbol used in counting; numeral. Two, fourteen, twenty-six, second, fourteenth, twenty-sixth, 2, 14, and 26 are all numbers. **2** the amount of units; sum; total: *The number of your fingers is ten.* **3** a quantity: *a number of reasons.* **4** a collection or company: *the number of saints.* **5** the particular number that indicates the place of a person or object in a series, and is a means of identifying it: *an apartment number, a licence number.* **6** one of a numbered series; a single part of a program, etc.: *The program consisted of four musical numbers.* **7** a song or other piece of music: *She sings many old numbers.* **8** a single issue of a periodical. **9** *Informal.* any thing or person thought of as standing apart from a collection or company: *That dress is the most fashionable number in the store.* **10** in grammar: **a** the property or feature of words that indicates whether they refer to one, or more than one, person or thing. *Boy, ox,* and *this* are in the singular number; *boys, oxen,* and *these* are in the plural number. **b** the form or group of forms indicating this. **11 a number of,** several; many. **12 beyond number,** too many to count. **13 numbers,** *pl.* **a** arithmetic. **b** many: *Numbers were turned away.* **c** numerical preponderance; a being more: *win a battle by force of numbers.* **d** *Archaic.* poetry. **e** a group of musical notes or measures. **14 Numbers,** the fourth book of the Old Testament. It tells about the counting of the Israelites after they left Egypt. **15 one's number is up,** *Informal.* one is doomed. **16 without number,** too many to be counted.
—*v.* **1** mark with a number; assign a number to; distinguish with a number: *The pages of this book are numbered.* **2** be able to show; have: *This city numbers a million inhabitants.* **3** amount to: *a crew numbering 20 men.* **4** reckon as one of a class or collection: *numbered among his followers.* **5** fix the number of; limit: *His days in office are numbered.* **6** count. [ME < OF *nombre* < L *numerus*] —**num′ber·er,** *n.*

Syn. *n.* **2 Number, sum** = the total of two or more persons, things, or units taken together. **Number** applies to the total reached by counting the persons or things in a group or collection: *Only twelve came, a smaller number than usual.* **Sum** applies to the total reached by adding figures or things: *The sum of two and two is four.*

☛ **Number** is a collective noun, requiring a singular or plural verb according as the total or the individual units are meant: *A number of tickets have already been sold. The number of tickets sold is astonishing.* See **amount** for another usage note.

☛ **numbers.** Usage varies in writing numbers that are parts of consecutive sentences. In general, newspapers and informal writing have figures for numbers over ten, words for smaller numbers; rather conservative magazine and book styles have figures for numbers over 100 except when they can be written in two words: Informal: *four, ten, 15, 92, 114.* Formal: *four, ten, fifteen, ninety-two, 114.* But practice is not consistent.

num·ber·less (num′bər lis) *adj.* **1** very numerous; too many to count: *There are numberless fish in the sea.* **2** without a number. —**Syn. 1** countless, myriad, infinite.

number one 1 *Informal.* oneself: *He worries too much about number one.* **2** the first or best in a series.

numb·skull (num′skul′) *n.* numskull.

nu·mer·a·ble (nū′mər ə bəl or nü′mər ə bəl) *adj.* that can be counted.

nu·mer·al (nū′mər əl or nü′mər əl) *n.* a figure, letter, or word standing for a number; group of figures, letters, or words standing for a number. 1, 5, 10, 50, 100, and 1,000 are Arabic numerals. I, V, X, L, C, and M are Roman numerals. —*adj.* of numbers; standing for a number. [< LL *numeralis* < L *numerus* number]

nu·mer·ate (nū′mər āt′ or nü′mər āt′) *v.* **-at·ed, -at·ing.** 1 number; count; enumerate. 2 read (an expression in numbers). [< L *numerare* < *numerus* number]

nu·mer·a·tion (nū′mər ā′shən or nü′mər ā′shən) *n.* 1 a numbering; a counting; a calculating. 2 a reading of numbers expressed in figures.

nu·mer·a·tor (nū′mər ā′tər or nü′mər ā′tər) *n.* 1 in a fraction, the number above the line that shows how many parts are taken: *In* $\frac{3}{8}$, *3 is the numerator and 8 is the denominator.* 2 a person or thing that makes a count, takes a census, etc. [< LL *numerator* (def. 2)]

nu·mer·ic (nū mer′ik or nü mer′ik) *adj.* numerical.

nu·mer·i·cal (nū mer′ə kəl or nü mer′ə kəl) *adj.* 1 of a number; having to do with numbers; in numbers; by numbers. 2 shown by numbers, not by letters: *10 is a numerical quantity; bx is a literal or algebraic quantity.* 3 of a mathematical quantity, designating the value in figures without considering the sign: *The numerical value of +4 is less than that of −7, though its algebraic value is more.*

nu·mer·i·cal·ly (nū mer′ik lē or nü mer′ik lē) *adv.* by numbers; in a numerical manner; in numerical respects; so far as numbers are concerned.

nu·mer·ol·o·gist (nū′mə rol′ə jist or nü′mə rol′ə jist) *n.* a person who practises numerology.

nu·mer·ol·o·gy (nū′mə rol′ə jē or nü′mə rol′ə jē) *n.* a system of foretelling the future, based on the supposedly mystic influence of numbers.

nu·mer·ous (nū′mər əs or nü′mər əs) *adj.* 1 very many. 2 in great numbers: *He has a numerous acquaintance among politicians.* [< L *numerosus*] —**nu′mer·ous·ly,** *adv.* —**nu′mer·ous·ness,** *n.* —**Syn. 1** manifold, innumerable.

Nu·mid·i·an (nū mid′ē ən) *adj.* of or having to do with Numidia, an ancient country in N. Africa, its people, or their language. —*n.* 1 a native or inhabitant of Numidia. 2 the Hamitic language of Numidia.

nu·mis·mat·ic (nū′miz mat′ik or nü′miz mat′ik) *adj.* 1 of numismatics or numismatists. 2 of coins and medals.

nu·mis·mat·ics (nū′miz mat′iks or nü′miz mat′iks) *n.* the study of coins and medals. [< F < L *numisma* coin < Gk. *nomisma* < *nomizein* have in use]

nu·mis·ma·tist (nū miz′mə tist or nü miz′mə tist) *n.* one who knows much about numismatics.

num·skull (num′skul′) *n. Informal.* a stupid person; blockhead. [for *numb skull*]

nun (nun) *n.* a woman who lives under religious vows, usually in a convent. Nuns teach, take care of sick people, etc. [OE *nunne* < LL *nonna,* fem. of *nonnus* monk]

nu·na·tak (nü′nə tak′) *n. Cdn.* the peak of a mountain rising above the surrounding glacial ice. [< Eskimo]

Nunc Di·mit·tis (nungk′dē mit′is) the canticle of Simeon, beginning "Lord, now lettest thou thy servant depart in peace." Luke 2:29-32. [< L *Nunc dimittis* now dost thou dismiss, the first words as given in the Vulgate]

nun·ci·o (nun′shē ō′) *n.* **-ci·os.** an ambassador from the Pope to a government. [< Ital. < L *nuntius* messenger]

nun·ner·y (nun′ər ē) *n.* **-ner·ies.** a building or buildings where nuns live; convent.

nun·ny bag (nun′ē) *Cdn.* in Newfoundland, a kind of haversack, often made of sealskin.

nun's veiling a thin, plain-woven, woollen fabric, used mainly for women's dresses.

nup·tial (nup′shəl) *adj.* of marriage or weddings. —*n.* **nuptials,** *pl.* a wedding; the wedding ceremony. [< L *nuptialis,* ult. < *nubere* take a husband]

nurse (nėrs) *n. v.* **nursed, nurs·ing.** —*n.* 1 a person who takes care of the sick, the injured, or the old, or is trained to do this. 2 a woman who cares for and brings up the young children or babies of another person. 3 one who feeds and protects.
—*v.* 1 be a nurse; act as a nurse; work as a nurse. 2 act as a nurse for; wait on or try to cure (the sick); take care of (sick, injured, or old people). 3 cure or try to cure by care: *She nursed a bad cold by going to bed.* 4 take care of and bring up (another's baby or young child). 5 nourish; protect; make grow: *nurse a plant, nurse a fire.* 6 use or treat with special care: *He nursed his sore arm by using it very little.* 7 hold closely; clasp fondly. 8 give milk to (a baby). 9 of a baby, suck milk. [ME < OF *nurrice* < L *nutricia* < *nutrire* feed, nourish]

nurse·ling (nėrs′ling) *n.* nursling.

nurse·maid (nėrs′mād′) *n.* a maid employed to care for children.

nurs·er·y (nėr′sər ē or nėrs′rē) *n.* **-er·ies.** 1 a room set apart for the use of children and babies. 2 a piece of ground or place where young trees and plants are raised for transplanting or sale. 3 a place or condition that helps something to grow and develop: *Slums are often nurseries of disease.* 4 a nursery school.

nurs·er·y·maid (nėr′sər ē mād′ or nėrs′rē-) *n.* a nursemaid.

nurs·er·y·man (nėr′sər ē mən or nėrs′rē-) *n.* **-men** (-mən). a man who grows or sells young trees and plants.

nursery rhyme a little poem for children.

nursery school a school for children over three years and, usually, under five.

nursing station *Cdn.* in the North, a small hospital for emergency cases, served by nurses and visited periodically by a doctor.

nurs·ling (nėrs′ling) *n.* 1 a baby that is being nursed. 2 any person or thing that is having tender care.

nur·ture (nėr′chər) *v.* **-tured, -tur·ing,** *n.* —*v.* 1 raise; rear; bring up; care for; foster; train: *She nurtured the child as if he had been her own.* 2 nourish. [< n.] —*n.* 1 the act or process of raising or rearing; a bringing up; training; education. 2 nourishment. [ME < OF *nourture* < LL *nutritura* a nursing, suckling < L *nutrire* nurse] —**nur′tur·er,** *n.*

nut (nut) *n. v.* **nut·ted, nut·ting,** *adj.* —*n.* 1 a dry fruit or seed with a hard, woody, or leathery shell and a kernel inside that is sometimes good to eat. 2 the kernel of a nut. 3 a small block, usually of metal, that screws on to a bolt to hold the bolt in place. 4 a piece at the upper end of a violin, cello, etc. over which the strings pass. 5 *Slang.* the head. 6 *Slang.* a queer or crazy person. 7 **hard nut to crack,** *Informal.* a difficult question, problem, or undertaking. —*v.* gather nuts. —*adj.* **nuts,** *Slang.* queer; crazy. [OE *hnutu*] —**nut′like′,** *adj.*

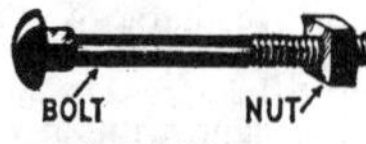

A bolt with nut screwed on

nut·crack·er (nut′krak′ər) *n.* 1 an instrument for cracking the shells of nuts. 2 any of several birds of the same family as the crow, that feed on nuts.

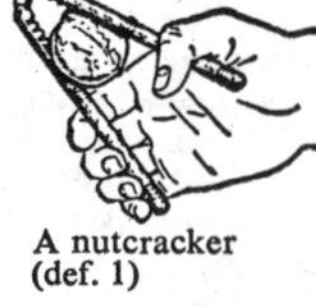
A nutcracker (def. 1)

nut·gall (nut′gol′ or -gôl′) *n.* a lump or ball that swells up on an oak tree where it has been injured by an insect; gall.

nut·hatch (nut′hach′) *n.* a small, sharp-beaked bird that feeds on small nuts, seeds, and insects. [ME *notehache,* literally, nut hacker]

nut·house (nut′hous′) *n. Slang.* a mental hospital.

nut·let (nut′lit) *n.* 1 a small nut. 2 the stone of a peach, plum, cherry, etc.

nut·meat (nut′mēt′) *n.* the kernel of a nut.

nut·meg (nut′meg) *n.* 1 a hard, spicy seed about as big as a marble, obtained from the fruit of an East Indian tree. Nutmeg is grated and used for flavoring food. 2 the tree. [ME; half-translation of OF **nois mugue,* var. of *nois muguete,* originally, nut smelling like musk (*nois* < L *nux*; *mugue,* ult. < LL *muscus*)]

nu·tri·a (nū′trē ə or nü′trē ə) *n.* 1 the coypu, an aquatic rodent native to South America but now widely bred for its fur. 2 its valuable beaverlike fur. 3 a coat or other garment made of this fur. [< Sp. < L *lutra*]

nu·tri·ent (nū′trē ənt or nü′trē ənt) *adj.* nourishing. —*n.* a nourishing substance. [< L *nutriens, -entis,* ppr. of *nutrire* nourish]

nu·tri·ment (nū′trə mənt or nü′trə mənt) *n.*

nourishment; food. [< L *nutrimentum* < *nutrire* nourish]

nu·tri·tion (nū trish′ən or nü trish′ən) *n.* **1** food; nourishment: *A balanced diet gives good nutrition.* **2** the series of processes by which food is changed to living tissues.

nu·tri·tion·al (nū trish′ən əl or nü trish′ən əl) *adj.* having to do with nutrition. **—nu·tri′tion·al·ly,** *adv.*

nu·tri·tion·ist (nū trish′ə nist or nü trish′ə nist) *n.* an expert in the processes of nutrition.

nu·tri·tious (nū trish′əs or nü trish′əs) *adj.* valuable as food; nourishing. [< L *nutritius, nutricius* < *nutrix* nurse < *nutrire* nourish] **—nu·tri′tious·ly,** *adv.* **—nu·tri′tious·ness,** *n.*

nu·tri·tive (nū′trə tiv or nü′trə tiv) *adj.* **1** having to do with foods and the use of foods. Digestion is part of the nutritive process. **2** nutritious. **—nu′tri·tive·ness,** *n.*

nut·shell (nut′shel′) *n.* **1** the shell of a nut. **2** something extremely small in size or scanty in amount. **3 in a nutshell,** in very brief form; in a few words.

nut·ting (nut′ing) *n.* the act of looking for nuts; gathering nuts.

nut·ty (nut′ē) *adj.* **-ti·er, -ti·est. 1** containing many nuts: *nutty cake.* **2** like nuts; tasting like nuts. **3** *Slang.* queer; crazy. **4** *Slang.* very interested or enthusiastic. **—nut′ti·ly,** *adv.* **—nut′ti·ness,** *n.*

nux vom·i·ca (nuks′vom′ə kə) **1** a drug containing strychnine, made from the seed of a tree growing in the East Indies. **2** the seed. **3** the tree. [< Med.L *nux vomica* vomiting nut < L *nux* nut + *vomere* vomit]

nuz·zle (nuz′əl) *v.* **-zled, -zling. 1** poke or rub with the nose; press the nose against: *The calf nuzzles his mother.* **2** nestle; snuggle; cuddle. **3** burrow or dig with the nose. [< *nose*; influenced by *nestle*]

NW, N.W., or **n.w. 1** northwest. **2** northwestern.

NWMP or **N.W.M.P.** North West Mounted Police.

N.W.T. Northwest Territories.

N.Y. New York (State).

ny·lon (nī′lon) *n.* **1** an extremely strong, durable, elastic substance, used to make clothing, stockings, bristles, etc. **2 nylons,** *pl.* stockings made of nylon. *—adj.* made of nylon. [< *Nylon,* a trademark]

nymph (nimf) *n.* **1** in Greek and Roman mythology, one of the lesser goddesses of nature, thought of as living in seas, rivers, springs, hills, woods, or trees. **2** *Poetic.* a beautiful or graceful young woman. **3** an insect in the stage of development between larva and adult insect. It has no wings. [ME < OF < L < Gk. *nymphē*] **—nymph′like′,** *adj.*

nym·pho·ma·ni·a (nim′fə mā′nē ə) *n.* in psychiatry, excessive, uncontrollable sexual desire in a woman. [< Gk. *nymphē* nymph, bride + E *mania*]

nym·pho·ma·ni·ac (nim′fə mā′nē ak′) *adj.* **1** of or characterized by nymphomania. **2** suffering from nymphomania. *—n.* a woman who suffers from nymphomania.

N.Z. New Zealand.

hat, āge, cãre, fär; let, ēqual, tėrm; it, īce
hot, ōpen, ôrder; oil, out; cup, pu̇t, rüle, ūse
əbove, takən, pencəl, lemən, circəs
ch, child; ng, long; sh, ship
th, thin; ᴛʜ, then; zh, measure

O or **o** (ō) *n.* **O's** or **o's. 1** the fifteenth letter of the English alphabet. **2** any speech sound represented by this letter. **3** one (usually fifteenth) of a series arranged alphabetically. **4** zero. **5** anything shaped like this letter.

o' (ə or ō) *prep.* **1** of: *man-o'-war.* **2** on.

O or **Oh** (ō) *interj.* oh!

o- form of *ob-* before *m,* as in *omit.*

o ohm.

o. 1 octavo. **2** in baseball, out.

O 1 oxygen. **2** one of the four main blood groups.

O. 1 Ohio. **2** Ocean. **3** October. **4** Octavo.

oaf (ōf) *n.* **oafs. 1** a very stupid child or man. **2** a deformed child. **3** a clumsy person. [< ON *álfr* elf]

oaf·ish (ōf′ish) *adj.* extremely stupid; clumsy. **—oaf′ish·ly,** *adv.* **—oaf′ish·ness,** *n.*

oak (ōk) *n.* **1** a large tree having hard, durable wood and nuts called acorns. **2** its wood: *The ship had timbers of oak.* **3** a tree or shrub resembling or suggesting an oak. *—adj.* **1** of an oak: *oak leaves,* **2** made of oak: *an oak table.* [OE *āc*] **—oak′like′** *adj.*

oak apple a lump or ball on an oak leaf or stem resulting from injury by an insect.

oak·en (ōk′ən) *adj.* made of oak wood: *the old oaken bucket.*

oak gall oak apple.

Oak·ley (ōk′lē) *n. Slang.* See **Annie Oakley.**

oa·kum (ō′kəm) *n.* a loose fibre obtained by untwisting and picking apart old ropes, used for stopping up the seams or cracks in ships. [OE *ācumba* offcombings]

oar (ôr) *n.* **1** a long pole fashioned so as to have a handgrip at one end and a broad, flat blade at the other: *Oars are used for rowing a boat. Sometimes an oar is used in steering a boat.* **2 put one's oar in,** meddle; interfere. **3 rest on one's oars,** stop working or trying and take a rest. **4** a person who rows. *—v.* row. [OE *ār*]

oar·lock (ôr′lok′) *n.* a notch or U-shaped support in which the oar rests in rowing; rowlock. [OE *ārloc*]

oars·man (ôrz′mən) *n.* **-men** (-mən). **1** a man who rows. **2** a man who rows well.

OAS 1 Organization of American States. **2** Secret Army Organization. (for F *Organisation de l'Armée Secrète*)

o·a·ses (ō ā′sēz or ō′ə sēz′) *n.* pl. of **oasis.**

o·a·sis (ō ā′sis or ō′ə sis) *n.* **-ses. 1** a fertile spot in the desert: *Water is always available at an oasis.* **2** any fertile spot in a barren land; any pleasant place in a desolate region. [< L < Gk. *oasis,* apparently < Egyptian]

oat (ōt) *n.* **1** Usually, **oats,** *pl.* a tall cereal grass whose grain is used in making oatmeal and as a food for horses. **2 oats,** *pl.* the grain of the oat plant. **3 feel one's oats,** *Slang.* **a** be lively or frisky. **b** feel pleased or important and show it. **4 sow one's wild oats,** do the things that wild young people do before settling down. **5** *Poetic.* a musical pipe made of an oat straw. [OE *āte*]

oat·cake (ōt′kāk′) *n.* a thin cake made of oatmeal.

oat·en (ōt′ən) *adj.* made of oats, oat straw, or oatmeal.

oath (ōth) *n.* **oaths** (ōᴛʜz or ōths) **1** a solemn promise to perform an undertaking or a statement that something is true, which God or some holy person or thing is called on to witness. **2** the name of God or some holy person or thing used as an exclamation to add force or to express anger. **3** a curse; swear word. **4 take oath,** make an oath; promise or state solemnly. *—v.* swear. [OE *āth*] **—Syn. 1** vow. **2** pledge. **3** expletive, malediction.

oat·meal (ōt′mēl′) *n.* **1** oats made into meal; ground oats; rolled oats. **2** porridge made from oatmeal.

ob- *prefix.* **1** against; in the way; opposing; hindering, as in *obstruct.* **2** inversely; contrary to the usual position, as in *oblate.* **3** toward; to, as in *obvert.* **4** on; over, as in *obscure.* Also: **o-,** before *m;* **oc-,** before *c;* **of-,** before *f;*

op-, before *p*; **os-**, in some cases before *c* and *t*. [< L]

ob. 1 died. (for L *obiit*) 2 oboe.

ob·bli·ga·to (ob′lə gä′tō) *adj. n.* **-tos.** in music: *—adj.* accompanying a solo, but having a distinct character and independent importance. *—n.* an obbligato part or accompaniment. Also, **obligato.** [< Ital. *obbligato*, literally, obliged]

ob·du·ra·cy (ob′dyů rə sē) *n.* a being obdurate.

ob·du·rate (ob′dyů rit) *adj.* **1** stubborn; unyielding: *an obdurate refusal.* **2** hardened in feelings or heart; not repentant: *an obdurate criminal.* [< L *obduratus*, pp. of *obdurare* < *ob-* against + *durare* harden] **—ob′du·rate·ly,** *adv.* **—ob′du·rate·ness,** *n.* **—Syn. 1** obstinate, unbending, inexorable. **2** callous, impenitent.

O.B.E. Officer (of the Order) of the British Empire.

o·be·di·ence (ō bē′dē əns or ō bē′dyəns) *n.* the act or habit of doing what one is told; submission to authority or law: *Soldiers act in obedience to the orders of their officers.* **—Syn.** compliance, subservience.

o·be·di·ent (ō bē′dē ənt) *adj.* doing what one is told; willing to obey. [< F < L *oboediens, -entis*, ppr. of *oboedire* obey] **—o·be′di·ent·ly,** *adv.*

Syn. **Obedient, compliant, docile** = acting as another asks or commands. **Obedient** emphasizes being willing to follow instructions and carry out orders of someone whose authority or control one acknowledges: *The obedient dog came at his master's whistle.* **Compliant** emphasizes bending easily, sometimes too easily, to another's will and being ready to do whatever he wishes or commands: *Compliant people are not good leaders.* **Docile** emphasizes having a submissive disposition, especially a willingness to be taught: *Janet always rides a docile horse.*

o·bei·sance (ō bā′səns or ō bē′səns) *n.* **1** a movement of the body expressing deep respect; deep bow: *The men made obeisance to the king.* **2** deference; homage. [ME < OF *obeisance* obedience < *obeir* obey < L *oboedire.* See OBEY.]

ob·e·lisk (ob′ə lisk′) *n.* **1** a tapering, four-sided shaft of stone with a top shaped like a pyramid. **2** something resembling such a shaft. **3** in printing, a dagger (†). [< L *obeliscus* < Gk. *obeliskos*, dim. of *obelos* a spit]

An obelisk

O·ber·on (ō′bər on′) *n.* in medieval folklore, the king of the fairies and husband of Titania. He is one of the chief characters in Shakespeare's *A Midsummer Night's Dream.*

o·bese (ō bēs′) *adj.* extremely fat. [< L *obesus* < *ob-* in addition + *edere* eat] **—o·bese′ly,** *adv.* **—o·bese′ness,** *n.*

o·bes·i·ty (ō bēs′ə tē or ō bes′ə tē) *n.* extreme fatness.

o·bey (ō bā′) *v.* **1** do what one is told: *The child obeyed and stayed home.* **2** follow the orders of: *Obey your father.* **3** yield to (authority, law, or control); comply with: *obey the laws.* **4** yield to the control of: *A car obeys the driver.* [< F *obeir* < L *oboedire* < *ob-* to + *audire* give ear] **—o·bey′er,** *n.*

ob·fus·cate (ob′fus kāt′ or ob fus′kāt) *v.* **-cat·ed, -cat·ing. 1** confuse; stupefy: *A man's mind may be obfuscated by liquor.* **2** darken; obscure. [< L *obfuscare* < *ob-* + *fuscus* dark] **—ob′fus·ca′tion,** *n.* **—ob·fus′ca·tor,** *n.*

o·bi (ō′bē) *n.* a long, broad sash worn by Japanese women and children. [< Japanese]

ob·i·ter dic·tum (ob′ə tər or ō′bə tər dik′təm) *pl.* **ob·i·ter dic·ta** (dik′tə). **1** an incidental remark. **2** in law, an incidental opinion given by a judge. [< L *obiter dictum* said by the way]

o·bit·u·ar·y (ō bich′ü er′ē) *n.* **-ar·ies,** *adj.* *—n.* a notice of death, often with a brief account of the person's life. *—adj.* of a death; recording a death. [< Med.L *obituarius*, ult. < L *obire* (*mortem*) meet (death) < *ob-* up to + *ire* go]

obj. 1 object. **2** objective. **3** objection.

ob·ject (*n.* ob′jikt or ob′jekt; *v.* əb jekt′) *n.* **1** anything that can be seen or touched; thing; article. **2** a person or thing toward which feeling, thought, or action is directed: *an object of charity.* **3** a person or thing that is absurd, funny, or foolish. **4** something aimed at; end; purpose. **5** in grammar, a word or group of words toward which the action of the verb is directed or to which a preposition expresses some relation. In "He threw the ball to his brother," *ball* is the object of *threw*, and *brother* is the object of *to.* **6 a** anything that can be presented to the mind: *objects of thought.* **b** a thing with reference to the impression it makes on the mind: *an object of pity.* *—v.* **1** make objections; be opposed; feel dislike: *I made my suggestion, but John objected. Many people object to loud noise.* **2** give a reason against; bring forward in opposition; oppose: *Mother objected that the weather was too wet to play outdoors.* [< Med.L *objectum* thing presented to the mind or thought, neut. of L *objectus*, pp. of *obicere* throw before, put in the way of < *ob-* against + *jacere* throw] **—ob·ject′ing·ly,** *adv.* **—ob·jec′tor,** *n.* **—Syn.** *n.* **1** article. **4** goal, aim.

object glass in a telescope, microscope, etc., the lens or combination of lenses that first receives light rays from the object and forms the image viewed through the eyepiece.

ob·jec·ti·fy (əb jek′tə fī′) *v.* **-fied, -fy·ing.** make objective; externalize: *Experiments in chemistry objectify the teaching. Kind acts objectify kindness.*

ob·jec·tion (əb jek′shən) *n.* **1** something said in objecting; reason or argument against something: *One of his objections to the plan was that it would cost too much.* **2** a feeling of disapproval or dislike: *A lazy person has strong objections to working.* **3** the act of objecting: *What is the basis for your objection?* **4** a ground or cause of objecting. **—Syn. 2** opposition.

ob·jec·tion·a·ble (əb jek′shən ə bəl) *adj.* **1** likely to be objected to. **2** unpleasant; disagreeable. **—ob·jec′tion·a·bly,** *adv.* **—Syn. 2** undesirable, offensive.

ob·jec·tive (əb jek′tiv) *n.* **1** something aimed at: *My objective this summer will be learning to play tennis better.* **2** something real and observable. **3** in grammar, the objective case. **4** a word in that case. *Whom* and *me* are objectives. **5** the lens or lenses nearest to the thing seen through a telescope, microscope, etc. **6** an objective test. *—adj.* **1** being the object of endeavor. **2** existing outside the mind as an actual object and not merely in the mind as an idea; real. Actions are objective; ideas are subjective. **3** about outward things, not about the thoughts and feelings of the speaker, writer, painter, etc.; giving facts as they are without a bias toward either side; impersonal: *A scientist must be objective in his experiments.* **4** in grammar, used as the object of a verb or of a preposition. In "John hit me," *me* is in the objective case. **5 a** of a work of art, representing or resembling natural objects; not abstract. **b** in perspective, that is, or belongs to, the object of which the delineation is required: *an objective point.* **—ob·jec′tive·ly,** *adv.* **—ob·jec′tive·ness,** *n.* **—Syn.** *n.* **1** object, aim, goal.

objective test a test in which one has to fill in blanks, mark statements as true or false, or choose from a number of possible answers provided.

ob·jec·tiv·i·ty (ob′jek tiv′ə tē) *n.* the state or quality of being objective; intentness on objects external to the mind; external reality.

object lesson 1 instruction conveyed by means of material objects. **2** a practical illustration of a principle: *Most street accidents are object lessons in the dangers of carelessness.*

ob·jet d'art (ôb zhe där′) *pl.* **ob·jets d'art** (ôb zhe där′). *French.* a small picture, vase, etc. of some artistic value.

ob·jur·gate (ob′jər gāt′ or əb jėr′gāt) *v.* **-gat·ed, -gat·ing.** reproach vehemently; upbraid violently; berate. [< L *objurgare* < *ob-* against + *jurgare* scold] **—ob′jur·ga′tion,** *n.* **—ob′jur·ga′tor,** *n.* **—Syn.** vituperate.

ob·jur·ga·to·ry (əb jėr′gə tô′rē) *adj.* vehemently reproachful; upbraiding; berating.

ob·late[1] (ob′lāt or ob lāt′) *adj.* flattened at the poles. The earth is an oblate spheroid. [< NL *oblatus* < L *ob-* inversely + (*pro*)*latus* prolate] **—ob′late·ly,** *adv.* **—ob′late·ness,** *n.*

ob·late[2] (ob′lāt or ō′blāt′) *n.* in the Roman Catholic Church, a member of any of various secular institutes devoted to religious work. *—adj.* dedicated to religious work. [< Med.L *oblatus*, noun use of pp. of L *offerre* offer]

ob·la·tion (ob lā′shən) *n.* **1** an offering to God or a god. **2 a** the offering of bread and wine in the Communion service. **b** the Communion service. [< LL *oblatio, -onis* < *ob-* up to + *latus,* pp. of *ferre* bring]

ob·li·gate (ob′lə gāt′) *v.* **-gat·ed, -gat·ing.** bind morally or legally; pledge: *A witness in court is obligated to tell the truth.* [< L *obligare* < *ob-* to + *ligare* bind. Doublet of OBLIGE.]

ob·li·ga·tion (ob′lə gā′shən) *n.* **1** a duty under the law; duty due to a promise or contract; duty on account of social relationship or kindness received: *A wife's first obligation is to her husband and children.* **2** the binding power (of a law, promise, sense of duty, etc.): *The one who did the damage is under obligation to pay for it.* **3** a binding legal agreement; bond; contract: *The firm was not able to meet its obligations.* **4** a being in debt for a favor, service, or the like. **5** a service; favor; benefit: *An independent person likes to repay all obligations.* —**Syn. 1** responsibility. See **duty.**

ob·li·ga·to (ob′lə gä′tō) *adj. n.* **-tos.** obbligato.

ob·lig·a·to·ry (əb lig′ə tô′rē or ob′lə gə tô′rē) *adj.* binding morally or legally; required: *Attendance at school is obligatory.* [< LL *obligatorius*]

o·blige (ə blīj′) *v.* **o·bliged, o·blig·ing. 1** bind by a promise, contract, duty, etc.; compel; force: *The law obliges parents to send their children to school.* **2** put under a debt of thanks for some favor; do a favor: *She obliged us with a song.* [ME < OF *obliger* < L *obligare.* Doublet of OBLIGATE.] —**o·blig′er,** *n.* —**Syn. 1** constrain. **2** accommodate.

ob·li·gee (ob′lə jē′) *n.* **1** in law, one to whom another is bound by contract; person to whom a bond is given. **2** one under obligation to another.

o·blig·ing (ə blīj′ing) *adj.* willing to do favors; helpful. —**o·blig′ing·ly,** *adv.* —**o·blig′ing·ness,** *n.*

ob·lique (əb lēk′) *adj. v.* **-liqued, -liqu·ing.** —*adj.* **1** not straight up and down; not straight across; slanting. In the diagram, AB, CD, EF, and GH are oblique lines. An oblique angle is any angle that is not a right angle. **2** not straightforward; indirect: *She made an oblique reference to her illness.* **3** not upright and moral; underhanded: *oblique dealings.* **4** of a solid figure, not having the axis perpendicular to the plane of the base. **5** in grammar, of or in an oblique case. **6** in botany, having unequal sides: *an oblique leaf.*
—*v.* advance in an oblique manner; slant. [< L *obliquus*]

oblique angle any angle that is not a right angle.

oblique case in grammar, any case of a noun, pronoun, or adjective except the nominative and vocative.

ob·liq·ui·ty (əb lik′wə tē) *n.* **-ties. 1** indirectness or crookedness of thought or behavior, especially conduct that is not upright and moral. **2** a being oblique.

ob·lit·er·ate (əb lit′ər āt′) *v.* **-at·ed, -at·ing.** remove all traces of; blot out; destroy: *Heavy rain obliterated the footprints.* [< L *oblit(t)erare* < *ob literas* (*scribere*) (draw) across the letters] —**ob·lit′er·a′tion,** *n.* —**ob·lit′er·a′tor,** *n.* —**Syn.** efface, expunge, erase.

ob·liv·i·on (əb liv′ē ən) *n.* **1** the condition of being entirely forgotten: *Many ancient cities have long since passed into oblivion.* **2** the condition of being unaware of what is going on; forgetfulness. [< L *oblivio, -onis* < *oblivisci* forget, originally, even off, smooth out + *ob-* + *levis* smooth]

ob·liv·i·ous (əb liv′ē əs) *adj.* **1** forgetful; not mindful; unaware: *The book was so interesting that I was oblivious of my surroundings.* **2** bringing or causing forgetfulness. [< L *obliviosus*] —**ob·liv′i·ous·ly,** *adv.* —**ob·liv′i·ous·ness,** *n.* —**Syn. 1** unmindful, heedless.

ob·long (ob′long) *adj.* **1** longer than broad: *an oblong loaf of bread.* See **elongate** for picture. **2** rectangular but not square. —*n.* a rectangle that is not a square. [< L *oblongus* < *ob-* + *longus* long]

An oblong

ob·lo·quy (ob′lə kwē) *n.* **-quies. 1** public reproach; abuse; blame. **2** disgrace; shame. [< LL *obloquium,* ult. < L *ob-* against + *loqui* speak] —**Syn. 1** censure.

hat, āge, cãre, fär; let, ēqual, tėrm; it, īce
hot, ōpen, ôrder; oil, out; cup, pu̇t, rüle, ūse
əbove, takən, pencəl, lemən, circəs
ch, child; ng, long; sh, ship
th, thin; ᴛʜ, then; zh, measure

ob·nox·ious (əb nok′shəs) *adj.* very disagreeable; offensive; hateful: *His disgusting table manners made him obnoxious to us.* [< L *obnoxiosus,* ult. < *ob-* + *noxa* injury] —**ob·nox′ious·ly,** *adv.* —**ob·nox′ious·ness,** *n.* —**Syn.** objectionable. See **hateful.**

An oboe

o·boe (ō′bō) *n.* **1** a wooden musical wind instrument in which a thin, poignant tone is produced by a double reed. **2** a reed stop in an organ that produces a penetrating tone like that of the oboe. [< Ital. < F *hautbois* hautboy]

o·bo·ist (ō′bō ist) *n.* a player of the oboe.

obs. 1 obsolete. **2** observation. **3** observatory.

ob·scene (əb sēn′ or ob sēn′) *adj.* offending modesty or decency; impure; filthy; vile. [< L *obscenus*] —**ob·scene′ly,** *adv.* —**Syn.** indecent, gross, lewd, ribald.

ob·scen·i·ty (əb sen′ə tē or əb sēn′ə tē) *n.* **-ties. 1** an obscene quality. **2** obscene language or behavior; an obscene word or act.

ob·scur·ant·ism (əb skūr′ən tiz′əm or ob′skyə ran′tiz əm) *n.* **1** opposition to progress and the spread of knowledge and enlightenment. **2** in art or literature, a quality or style that is complex and obscure: *the obscurantism of modern poetry.* [< L *obscurans, -antis,* ppr. of *obscurare* to obscure < *obscurus* obscure]

ob·scur·ant·ist (əb skūr′ən tist) *n.* a person who is opposed to progress and the spread of knowledge. —*adj.* of obscurantists or obscurantism.

ob·scu·ra·tion (ob′skyů rā′shən) *n.* **1** an obscuring. **2** the state of being obscured.

ob·scure (əb skūr′) *adj.* **-scur·er, -scur·est,** *v.* **-scured, -scur·ing.** —*adj.* **1** not clearly expressed: *an obscure passage in a book.* **2** not expressing meaning clearly: *an obscure style of writing.* **3** not well known; attracting no notice: *an obscure little village, an obscure poet, an obscure position in the government.* **4** not easily discovered; hidden: *an obscure path, an obscure meaning.* **5** not distinct; not clear: *an obscure form, obscure sounds, an obscure view.* **6** dark; dim: *an obscure corner.* **7** indefinite: *an obscure brown, an obscure vowel.*
—*v.* hide from view; make obscure; dim; darken: *Clouds obscure the sun.* [ME < OF < L *obscurus* < *ob-* over + *scur-* cover] —**ob·scure′ly,** *adv.* —**ob·scure′ness,** *n.* —**ob·scur′er,** *n.*
Syn. *adj.* **1 Obscure, vague, ambiguous** = not clearly expressed or understood. **Obscure** suggests that the meaning of something is hidden from the understanding, because it is not clearly or plainly expressed or the reader lacks the knowledge necessary for understanding: *Much legal language is obscure.* **Vague** = not definite, too general in meaning or statement or not clearly and completely thought out: *No one can be sure what a vague statement means.* **Ambiguous** = so expressed that either of two meanings is possible: *"She kissed her when she left" is an ambiguous statement.* **3** unknown, undistinguished, humble. **4** secluded. **6** dusky, murky, gloomy. -*v.* eclipse, conceal.

ob·scu·ri·ty (əb skūr′ə tē) *n.* **-ties. 1** a lack of clearness; difficulty in being understood: *The obscurity of the passage makes several interpretations possible.* **2** something obscure; something hard to understand; point of passage not clearly expressed; doubtful or vague meaning. **3** the state or condition of being unknown: *The Premier rose from obscurity to fame.* **4** a little-known person or place. **5** a lack of light; dimness. —**Syn. 1** ambiguity, vagueness. **5** darkness, shade.

ob·se·quies (ob′sə kwēz) *n.pl.* funeral rites or ceremonies; stately funeral. [ME < OF < Med.L *obsequiae,* pl., for L *exsequiae* < *ex-* out + *sequi* follow]

ob·se·qui·ous (əb sē′kwē əs) *adj.* polite or obedient from hope of gain or from fear; servile; fawning: *Obsequious courtiers greeted the king.* [< L *obsequiosus,* ult. < *ob-*

after + *sequi* follow] **—ob·se′qui·ous·ly,** *adv.* **—ob·se′qui·ous·ness,** *n.* **—Syn.** slavish.

ob·serv·a·ble (əb zėr′və bəl) *adj.* **1** that can be or is noticed; noticeable; easily seen. **2** that can be or is observed: *Lent is observable by most churches.*

ob·serv·a·bly (əb zėr′və blē) *adv.* so as to be observed; to an observable degree.

ob·serv·ance (əb zėr′vəns) *n.* **1** the act of observing or keeping laws or customs: *the observance of the Sabbath.* **2** an act performed as a sign of worship or respect; a religious ceremony. **3** a rule or custom to be observed. **4** *Archaic.* respectful attention or service. **5** an observation. **—Syn. 1** celebration. **2** rite. ☛ See **observation** for usage note.

ob·serv·ant (əb zėr′vənt) *adj.* **1** quick to notice; watchful; observing: *If you are observant in the fields and woods, you will find many flowers that others fail to notice.* **2** careful in observing (a law, rule, custom, etc.): *observant of the traffic rules.* [< L *observans, -antis,* ppr. of *observare.* See OBSERVE.] **—ob·serv′ant·ly,** *adv.* **—Syn. 1** heedful, regardful, attentive.

ob·ser·va·tion (ob′zər vā′shən) *n.* **1** the act, habit, or power of seeing and noting: *His keen observation helped him to become a good scientist.* **2** the fact of being seen; being seen; notice: *The tramp escaped observation.* **3** something seen and noted. **4** the act of watching for some special purpose; study: *The observation of nature is important in science.* **5** a remark; comment. **6** *Obsolete or rare.* an observance.

☛ **Observation, observance** are sometimes confused because both are related to the verb *observe.* **Observation,** connected with the meaning "watch closely," applies especially to the act or power of noticing things or watching closely, or to being watched or noticed: *An observatory is a building designed for the observation of the stars.* **Observance,** connected with the meaning "keep," applies to the act of keeping and following customs or duties, or to a rule, rite, etc. kept or celebrated: *You go to church for the observance of religious duties.* **Observation** sometimes means "*observance,*" but this meaning is obsolete or rare.

ob·ser·va·tion·al (ob′zər vā′shən əl) *adj.* of, having to do with, or founded on observation, especially as contrasted with experiment.

observation car a railway passenger car having large windows, a glass dome, or an open platform at one end, to enable passengers to view the scenery easily.

ob·serv·a·to·ry (əb zėr′və tô′rē) *n.* **-ries. 1** a place or building equipped with a telescope, etc. for observing the stars and other heavenly bodies. **2** a place or building for observing facts or happenings of nature. **3** a high place or building giving a wide view.

ob·serve (əb zėrv′) *v.* **-served, -serv·ing. 1** see and note; notice: *I observed nothing queer in his behavior.* **2** examine for some special purpose; study: *An astronomer observes the stars.* **3** remark; comment: "*Foul weather,*" *the captain observed.* **4** keep; follow in practice: *observe silence, observe a rule.* **5** show regard for; celebrate: *observe the Sabbath.* [ME < OF < L *observare* < *ob-* over + *servare* watch, keep] **—ob·serv′er,** *n.* **—Syn. 1** perceive. See **see. 2** survey, watch. **3** mention.

ob·serv·ing (əb zėr′ving) *adj.* observant.

ob·sess (əb ses′) *v.* fill the mind of; keep the attention of; haunt: *The fear that someone might steal his money obsessed him.* [< L *obsessus,* pp. of *obsidere* < *ob-* by + *sedere* sit]

ob·ses·sion (əb sesh′ən) *n.* **1** an obsessing or being obsessed; the influence of a feeling, idea, or impulse that a person cannot escape. **2** the feeling, idea, or impulse itself. **3** in psychiatry, a compelling or fixed idea or feeling, usually irrational, over which a person has little conscious control; compulsion.

ob·ses·sive (əb ses′iv) *adj.* of, having to do with, or causing obsession. **—ob·ses′sive·ly,** *adv.*

ob·sid·i·an (ob sid′ē ən) *n.* a hard, dark, glassy rock that is formed when lava cools; volcanic glass. [< L *obsidianus,* mistaken reading for *obsianus;* after *Obsius,* its discoverer]

ob·so·les·cence (ob′sə les′əns) *n.* the condition or state of passing out of use; getting out of date; a becoming obsolete.

ob·so·les·cent (ob′sə les′ənt) *adj.* **1** passing out of use; tending to become out of date: *Horse carriages are obsolescent.* **2** in biology, gradually disappearing; imperfectly or slightly developed: *obsolescent organs.* [< L *obsolescens, -entis,* ppr. of *obsolescere* fall into disuse, ult. < *ob-* + *solere* be usual, be customary]

ob·so·lete (ob′sə lēt′) *adj.* **1** no longer in use. "Eft," meaning "again," is an obsolete word. **2** out-of-date: *We still use this machine though it is obsolete.* [< L *obsoletus,* pp. of *obsolescere.* See OBSOLESCENT.] **—ob′so·lete·ly,** *adv.* **—ob′so·lete·ness,** *n.*

ob·sta·cle (ob′stə kəl) *n.* something that stands in the way or stops progress: *Blindness is an obstacle in most occupations.* [ME < OF < L *obstaculum* < *ob-* in the way of + *stare* stand]

Syn. Obstacle, obstruction, hindrance = something that gets in the way of action or progress. **Obstacle** = an object, condition, etc. that stands in the way and must be moved or overcome before someone or something can continue toward a goal: *A tree fallen across the road was an obstacle to our car.* **Obstruction** applies especially to something that blocks a passage: *The enemy built obstructions in the road.* **Hindrance** applies to a person or thing that holds back or makes progress difficult: *Noise is a hindrance to studying.*

ob·stet·ric (ob stet′rik) *adj.* having to do with the care of women in childbirth.

ob·stet·ri·cal (ob stet′rə kəl) *adj.* obstetric; of or having to do with obstetrics. **—ob·stet′ri·cal·ly,** *adv.*

ob·ste·tri·cian (ob′stə trish′ən) *n.* a doctor who specializes in obstetrics.

ob·stet·rics (ob stet′riks) *n.* the branch of medicine and surgery concerned with caring for and treating women before, in, and after childbirth. [< L *obstetrica,* fem. *obstetrix, -tricis* midwife < *ob-* by + *stare* stand]

ob·sti·na·cy (ob′stə nə sē) *n.* **-cies. 1** stubbornness; a being obstinate. **2** an obstinate act.

ob·sti·nate (ob′stə nit) *adj.* **1** not giving in; stubborn: *The obstinate girl would go her own way, in spite of all warnings.* **2** hard to control or treat: *an obstinate cough.* [ME < L *obstinatus,* pp. of *obstinare,* ult. < *ob-* by + *stare* stand] **—ob′sti·nate·ly,** *adv.*

Syn. 1 Obstinate, stubborn = fixed in purpose or opinion. **Obstinate** suggests persistent holding to a purpose, opinion, or way of doing something and sometimes being unreasonable or contrary: *The obstinate man refused to obey orders.* **Stubborn,** often interchangeable with *obstinate,* but more often describing animals and things, especially suggests a quality of character that makes a person resist attempts to change his mind or an animal or thing hard to handle: *He is stubborn as a mule.* **2** persistent; intractable.

ob·strep·er·ous (əb strep′ər əs) *adj.* **1** noisy; boisterous. **2** unruly; disorderly. [< L *obstreperus* < *ob-* against + *strepere* make a noise] **—ob·strep′er·ous·ly,** *adv.* **—ob·strep′er·ous·ness,** *n.* **—Syn. 1** clamorous, vociferous.

ob·struct (əb strukt′) *v.* **1** make hard to pass through; block up: *Fallen trees obstruct the road.* **2** be in the way of; hinder: *Trees obstruct our view of the ocean.* [< L *obstructus,* pp. of *obstruere* < *ob-* in the way of + *struere* pile] **—ob·struct′er,** *n.* **—Syn. 1** close, choke, clog. **2** impede.

ob·struc·tion (əb struk′shən) *n.* **1** anything that obstructs; something in the way: *The soldiers had to get over such obstructions as ditches and barbed wire. Ignorance is an obstruction to progress.* **2** a blocking; a hindering: *the obstruction of progress by prejudices.* **—Syn. 1** See **obstacle.**

ob·struc·tion·ism (əb struk′shən iz′əm) *n.* the hindering of the progress of business in a meeting, legislature, etc.

ob·struc·tion·ist (əb struk′shən ist) *n.* one who hinders (progress, legislation, reform, etc.).

ob·struc·tive (əb struk′tiv) *adj.* tending or serving to obstruct; blocking; hindering. **—ob·struct′ive·ly,** *adv.* **—ob·struct′ive·ness,** *n.*

ob·tain (əb tān′) *v.* **1** get or procure through diligence or effort; come to have: *He worked hard to obtain the prize. We study to obtain knowledge.* **2** be in use; be customary: *Different rules obtain in different schools.* [ME < OF < L *obtinere* < *ob-* to + *tenere* hold] **—ob·tain′a·ble,** *adj.* **—ob·tain′er,** *n.* **—Syn. 1** secure, gain. See **get.**

ob·trude (əb trüd′) *v.* **-trud·ed, -trud·ing. 1** put forward unasked and unwanted; force: *Don't obtrude your opinions on others.* **2** come unasked and unwanted; force oneself; intrude. 3 push out; thrust forward: *A turtle obtrudes its head from its shell.* [< L *obtrudere* < *ob-* toward + *trudere* thrust] **—ob·trud′er,** *n.*

ob·tru·sion (əb trü′zhən) *n.* 1 an obtruding. 2 something obtruded. [< LL *obtrusio, -onis* < L *obtrudere.* See OBTRUDE.]

ob·tru·sive (əb trü′siv) *adj.* inclined to obtrude; intrusive. **—ob·tru′sive·ly,** *adv.* **—ob·tru′sive·ness,** *n.* **—Syn.** meddlesome, officious.

ob·tuse (əb tūs′ or əb tüs′) *adj.* 1 not sharp or acute; blunt. 2 having more than 90° of angle but less than 180°. See **angle** for diagram. 3 slow in understanding; stupid: *He was too obtuse to take the hint.* 4 not sensitive; dull: *One's hearing often becomes obtuse in old age.* [< L *obtusus,* pp. of *obtundere* < *ob-* on + *tundere* beat] **—ob·tuse′ly,** *adv.* **—ob·tuse′ness,** *n.*

obtuse angle an angle greater than a right angle.

ob·verse (*n.* ob′vėrs; *adj.* ob vėrs′ or ob′vėrs) *n.* 1 the side of a coin, medal, etc. that has the principal design. 2 the face of anything that is meant to be turned toward the observer; front. 3 a counterpart. 4 in logic, a proposition derived through obversion; the negative (or affirmative) counterpart of a given affirmative (or negative) proposition. [< adj.]
—adj. 1 turned toward the observer. 2 being a counterpart to something else. 3 having the base narrower than the top or tip: *an obverse leaf.* [< L *obversus,* pp. of *obvertere* < *ob-* toward + *vertere* to turn]
—ob·verse′ly, *adv.*

ob·vert (ob vėrt′) *v.* 1 turn (something) toward an object. 2 in logic, change (a proposition) to the denial of its opposite. [< L *obvertere.* See OBSERVE.]

ob·vi·ate (ob′vē āt′) *v.* **-at·ed, -at·ing.** meet and dispose of; clear out of the way; remove: *obviate a difficulty, obviate danger, obviate objections.* [< LL *obviare* < *obvius* in the way. See OBVIOUS.] **—ob′vi·a′tion,** *n.* **—ob′vi·a′tor,** *n.*

ob·vi·ous (ob′vē əs) *adj.* easily seen or understood; clear to the eye or mind; not to be doubted; plain: *It is obvious that two and two make four.* [< L *obvius* < *obviam* in the way < *ob* across + *via* way] **—ob′vi·ous·ly,** *adv.* **—ob′vi·ous·ness,** *n.*
Syn. Obvious, apparent, evident = plain to see, easy to understand. **Obvious** suggests standing out so prominently that the eye or mind cannot miss it: *His exhaustion was obvious when he fell asleep standing up.* **Apparent** = plainly to be seen as soon as one looks (with eye or mind) toward it: *A dent in the fender is apparent.* **Evident** = plainly to be seen because all the apparent facts point to it: *When he did not drive the car home, it was evident that he had had an accident.*

oc- a form of **ob-** before *c,* as in *occasion.*

O.C. Officer in Charge; Officer Commanding.

oc·a·ri·na (ok′ə rē′nə) *n.* a musical instrument shaped like a sweet potato, with finger holes and whistle-like mouthpiece. [probably dim. of Ital. *oca* goose; with reference to the shape]

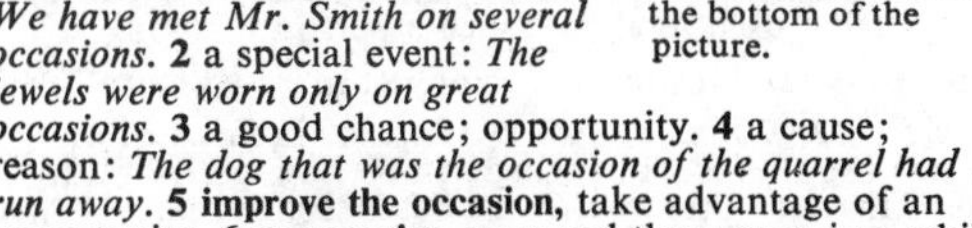

An ocarina. The mouthpiece is at the bottom of the picture.

oc·ca·sion (ə kā′zhən or ō kā′zhən) *n.* 1 a particular time: *We have met Mr. Smith on several occasions.* 2 a special event: *The jewels were worn only on great occasions.* 3 a good chance; opportunity. 4 a cause; reason: *The dog that was the occasion of the quarrel had run away.* 5 **improve the occasion,** take advantage of an opportunity. 6 **on occasion,** now and then; once in a while. *—v.* cause; bring about: *His queer behavior occasioned talk.* [< L *occasio, -onis,* ult. < *ob-* in the way of + *cadere* fall]

oc·ca·sion·al (ə kā′zhən əl or ə kāzh′nəl) *adj.* 1 happening or coming now and then, or once in a while: *an occasional thunderstorm.* 2 caused by or used for some special time or event: *occasional poetry.* 3 for use once in a while, not forming part of a set: *occasional chairs.*

oc·ca·sion·al·ly (ə kā′zhən əl ē or ə kāzh′nəl ē) *adv.* at times; now and then.

Oc·ci·dent (ok′sə dənt) *n.* 1 the countries in Europe and America; the West; opposed to *Orient.* 2 **occident,** the west. [< L *occidens, -entis,* ppr. of *occidere* fall towards, go down < *ob-* towards + *cadere* fall; with reference to the setting sun]

hat, āge, cãre, fär; let, ēqual, tėrm; it, īce
hot, ōpen, ôrder; oil, out; cup, pu̇t, rüle, ūse
əbove, takən, pencəl, lemən, circəs
ch, child; ng, long; sh, ship
th, thin; ᴛʜ, then; zh, measure

Oc·ci·den·tal (ok′sə den′təl) *adj.* 1 Western; of the Occident. 2 **occidental,** western. *—n.* a native of the West. Europeans are Occidentals.

oc·cip·i·tal (ok sip′ə təl) *adj.* of or having to do with the back part of the head or skull. *—n.* the occipital bone. [< Med.L *occipitalis* < L *occiput.* See OCCIPUT.]

occipital bone in anatomy, the compound bone forming the lower back part of the skull.

oc·ci·put (ok′sə pət) *n.* **oc·cip·i·ta** (ok sip′ə tə). in anatomy, the back part of the head or skull. [< L *occiput* < *occipitium* < *ob-* behind + *caput* head]

oc·clude (o klüd′) *v.* **-clud·ed, -clud·ing.** 1 stop up (a passage, pores, etc.); close. 2 shut in, out, or off. 3 in chemistry, absorb and retain (gases). Platinum occludes hydrogen. 4 in dentistry, meet closely. The teeth in the upper jaw and those in the lower jaw should occlude. [< L *occludere* < *ob-* up + *claudere* close]

oc·clu·sion (o klü′zhən) *n.* an occluding or being occluded. [< L *occlusus,* pp. of *occludere.* See OCCLUDE.]

oc·cult (o kult′ or ok′ult) *adj.* 1 beyond the bounds of ordinary knowledge; mysterious. 2 outside the laws of the natural world; magical: *Astrology and alchemy are occult sciences.* *—n.* **the occult,** the occult sciences. [< L *occultus* hidden, pp. of *occulere* < *ob-* up + *celare* cover] **—Syn. 1** secret, hidden, mystic.

oc·cul·ta·tion (ok′ul tā′shən) *n.* 1 a hiding of one heavenly body by another passing between it and the observer: *the occultation of a star by the moon.* 2 a disappearance from view or notice.

oc·cult·ism (o kul′tiz əm or ok′ul tiz′əm) *n.* 1 a belief in occult powers. 2 the study or use of occult sciences.

oc·cu·pan·cy (ok′yu̇ pən sē) *n.* the act or fact of occupying; holding (land, houses, a pew, etc.) by being in possession.

oc·cu·pant (ok′yu̇ pənt) *n.* 1 a person who occupies. 2 the person in actual possession of a house, office, etc. [< L *occupans, -antis,* ppr. of *occupare.* See OCCUPY.]

oc·cu·pa·tion (ok′yu̇ pā′shən) *n.* 1 one's business; employment; trade: *Teaching is a teacher's occupation.* 2 a being occupied; possession; occupying: *the occupation of a town by the enemy.* [< L *occupatio, -onis* < *occupare.* See OCCUPY.]
Syn. 1 Occupation, business, employment = work a person does regularly or to earn his living. **Occupation** = work of any kind one does regularly or for which he is trained, whether or not he is working at the moment or is paid: *By occupation she is a housewife.* **Business** = work done for profit, often for oneself, especially in commerce, banking, merchandising, etc.: *My business is real estate.* **Employment** = work done for another, for which one is paid: *He has no employment.*

oc·cu·pa·tion·al (ok′yu̇ pā′shən əl or ok′yu̇ pāsh′nəl) *adj.* of or having to do with occupation, especially of or having to do with trades, callings, etc.: *occupational diseases.*

occupational therapy the treatment of persons having physical disabilities through specific types of exercises, work, etc. to promote rehabilitation.

oc·cu·py (ok′yu̇ pī′) *v.* **-pied, -py·ing.** 1 take up; fill: *The building occupies an entire block.* 2 keep busy; engage; employ: *Sports often occupy a boy's attention.* 3 take possession of: *The enemy occupied our fort.* 4 keep possession of; hold: *The judge occupies an important position.* 5 live in: *The owner and his family occupy the house.* [ME < OF < L *occupare* seize < *ob-* onto + *cap-* grasp] **—oc′cu·pi′er,** *n.* **—Syn. 2** absorb. 4 possess.

oc·cur (ə kėr′) *v.* **-curred, -cur·ring.** 1 take place; happen: *Storms often occur in winter.* 2 be found; exist: *"E" occurs in English more than any other letter.* 3 come to mind; suggest itself: *Did it occur to you to close the window?* [< L *occurrere* < *ob-* in the way of + *currere* run]

oc·cur·rence (ə kėr′əns) *n.* 1 an occurring: *The occurrence of storms delayed our trip.* 2 event: *an* *unexpected occurrence.* —**Syn. 2** incident, happening. **See event.**

o·cean (ō′shən) *n.* **1** the great body of salt water that covers almost three fourths of the earth's surface. **2** any of its four main divisions—the Atlantic, Pacific, Indian, and Arctic oceans. **3** a vast expanse or quantity: *oceans of trouble.* [< L *oceanus* < Gk. *ōkeanos*] —**Syn. 1** sea, main, deep.

ocean bed the bottom of the ocean.

o·ce·an·ic (ō′shē an′ik) *adj.* **1** of the ocean. **2** living in the ocean. **3** like the ocean; wide; vast.

O·ce·a·nid (ō sē′ə nid) *n.* in Greek mythology, a sea nymph; daughter of Oceanus, the ocean god.

o·cean·o·graph·ic (ō′shə nə graf′ik) *adj.* of or having to do with oceanography.

o·cean·og·ra·phy (ō′shən og′rə fē) *n.* the branch of physical geography dealing with oceans and ocean life.

O·ce·a·nus (ō sē′ə nəs) *n.* in Greek mythology, the god of the great stream that was supposed to surround all the land.

o·cel·lus (ō sel′əs) *n.* **o·cel·li** (ō sel′ī or ō sel′ē). **1** a little eye; one of the single-lens eyes, usually three in number, situated between the compound eyes of insects and some other animals. **2** an eye-like spot or marking. There are ocelli on peacock feathers. [< L *ocellus,* dim. of *oculus* eye]

o·ce·lot (ō′sə lot′ or os′ə lot′) *n.* a spotted wildcat resembling a leopard, found from Texas through South America. [< F < Mexican *ocelotl*]

o·chre or **o·cher** (ō′kər) *n.* **1** any of various earths ranging in coloring from pale yellow to orange, brown, and red, used as pigments. **2** a pale brownish yellow. —*adj.* pale brownish-yellow. [ME < OF *ocre* < L < Gk. *ōchra* < *ōchros* pale yellow]

o'clock (ə klok′) of the clock; by the clock.

oct- *combining form.* the form of *octo-* or *octa-* before vowels, as in *octet.*

Oct. October.

octa- *combining form.* a variant of *octo-,* as in *octagon.*

oc·ta·gon (ok′tə gon′ or ok′tə gən) *n.* a plane figure having eight angles and eight sides. [< Gk. *oktagōnos* < *oktō* eight + *gōnia* angle]

An octagon

oc·tag·o·nal (ok tag′ə nəl) *adj.* having eight angles and eight sides.

oc·ta·he·dral (ok′tə hē′drəl) *adj.* having eight plane faces.

oc·ta·he·dron (ok′tə hē′drən) *n.* **-drons, -dra** (-drə). a solid figure having eight plane faces or sides. [< Gk. *oktaedron,* neut. of *oktaedros* < *oktō* eight + *hedra* seat, base]

oc·tane (ok′tān) *n.* a colorless, liquid hydrocarbon that occurs in petroleum. Good gasoline contains much octane. *Formula:* C_8H_{18} [< *oct-* eight (< Gk. *oktō*) + *-ane,* chemical suffix < L *-anus,* adj. suffix]

octane number the number indicating the quality of a motor fuel, based on its antiknock properties.

oc·tave (ok′tiv or ok′tāv) *n.* **1** in music: **a** the interval between a note and another note having twice or half as many vibrations per second. From middle C to the C above it is an octave. **b** the eighth note above or below a given tone, having twice or half as many vibrations per second. **c** the series of notes or of keys of an instrument, filling the interval between a note and its octave. **d** the combination of a note and its octave. **2** a group of eight. **3** in poetry: **a** an eight-line stanza. **b** the first eight lines of a sonnet; octet. **4** in ecclesiastical use: **a** a festival and the week after it. **b** the last day of such a week. [< L *octavus* eighth < *octo* eight]

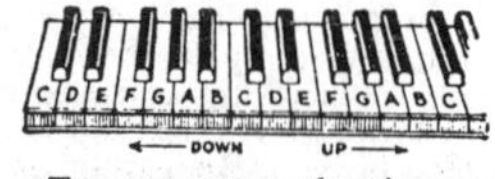

Two octaves on the piano (def. 1c)

oc·ta·vo (ok tā′vō or ok tav′ō) *n.* **-vos. 1** the page size of a book in which each leaf is one eighth of a whole sheet of paper. **2** a book having this size, usually about 6 by 9½ inches. [< Med.L *in octavo* in an eighth]

oc·tet or **oc·tette** (ok tet′) *n.* **1** a musical composition for eight voices or instruments. **2** eight singers or players. **3** in poetry: **a** the first eight lines of a sonnet. **b** an eight-line stanza; octave. **4** any group of eight. [< *oct-* eight + *-et,* patterned on *duet,* etc.]

oc·til·lion (ok til′yən) *n.* **1** in Canada, the United States, and France, 1 followed by 27 zeros. **2** in Great Britain and Germany, 1 followed by 48 zeros. [< F < L *octo* eight + F *million* million]

octo- or **oct-** or **octa-** *combining form.* eight, as in *octopus* and *octagon.* [< Gk. *oktō*]

Oc·to·ber (ok tō′bər) *n.* the tenth month of the year. October has 31 days. [< L *October* < *octo* eight; from the order of the Roman calendar]

oc·to·ge·nar·i·an (ok′tə jə när′ē ən) *n.* a person who is 80 years old or between 80 and 90 years old. —*adj.* 80 years old or between 80 and 90 years old. [< L *octogenarius* containing eighty]

oc·to·pus (ok′tə pəs) *n.* **1** a sea mollusc having a soft body and eight arms with suckers on them. **2** any person or thing like an octopus. **3** a powerful, grasping organization with far-reaching influence. [< NL < Gk. *oktopous* < *oktō* eight + *pous* foot]

oc·to·roon (ok′tə rün′) *n.* a person having one eighth Negro blood or ancestry. [< *octo-* eight + quad*roon*]

oc·u·lar (ok′yù lər) *adj.* **1** of or having to do with the eye: *an ocular muscle.* **2** like an eye. **3** received by actual sight; seen. —*n.* the eyepiece of a telescope, microscope, etc. [< LL *ocularis* of the eyes < L *oculus* eye]

oc·u·list (ok′yù list) *n.* a doctor skilled in the examination and treatment of the eyes. [< F *oculiste*]

O.D. Officer of the Day.

o·da·lisque or **o·da·lisk** (ō′də lisk′) *n.* a female slave in an Oriental harem. [< F < Turkish *odaliq* < *odah* room in a harem; influenced by suffix *-isque* -ish]

odd (od) *adj.* **1** left over: *Pay the bill with this money and keep the odd change.* **2** being one of a pair or set of which the rest is missing: *an odd stocking.* **3** extra; occasional; casual: *odd jobs, odd moments, odd players.* **4** with some extra: *six hundred odd.* **5 a** leaving a remainder of 1 when divided by 2: *Seven is an odd number.* **b** of such a number: *the odd symphonies of Beethoven.* **6** strange; peculiar; queer: *It is odd that I cannot remember his name.* **7** out-of-the-way; secluded. [ME < ON *odda-*] —**odd′ness,** *n.* —**Syn. 2** unmatched, unmated, single. **6** freakish, uncommon. See **strange.**

odd·ball (od′bol′ or -bôl′) *Slang.* —*n.* a person whose behavior is eccentric or unconventional. —*adj.* eccentric; unconventional.

odd·i·ty (od′ə tē) *n.* **-ties. 1** strangeness; queerness; peculiarity. **2** a strange, queer, or peculiar person or thing. —**Syn. 1** singularity. **2** freak, curiosity.

odd·ly (od′lē) *adv.* queerly; strangely.

odd-man-out (od′man′out′) *n.* **1** one who does not fit into a group. **2** one who is left out of a group. **3 a** a person chosen by lot to do something special. **b** a method of selection used to choose such a person.

odd·ment (od′mənt) *n.* a thing left over; an extra bit.

odds (odz) *n.pl. or sing.* **1** a difference in favor of one as against another; advantage. In betting, odds of 3 to 1 mean that 3 will be paid if the bet is lost for every 1 that is received if the bet is won. **2** in games, an extra allowance given to the weaker side. **3** things that are odd, uneven, or unequal. **4** difference: *It makes no odds when he goes.* **5 at odds,** quarrelling; disagreeing: *The two boys had been at odds for months.* **6 odds and ends,** things left over; extra bits; odd pieces; scraps; remnants. **7 The odds are,** the chances are; the probability is.

ode (ōd) *n.* a lyric poem full of noble feeling expressed with dignity, often addressed to some person or thing: *Ode to a Nightingale.* [< F < LL *ode* < Gk. *ōidē,* ult. < *aeidein* sing]

O·din (ō′dən) *n.* in Norse mythology, the chief deity and god of wisdom, culture, war, and the dead, corresponding to the Anglo-Saxon god *Woden.*

o·di·ous (ō′dē əs) *adj.* very displeasing; hateful; offensive: *odious behavior.* [ME < OF < L *odiosus*

hat, āge, cãre, fär; let, ēqual, tėrm; it, īce
hot, ōpen, ôrder; oil, out; cup, pu̇t, rüle, ūse
əbove, takən, pencəl, lemən, circəs
ch, child; ng, long; sh, ship
th, thin; ᴛʜ, then; zh, measure

< *odium* hate] —**o′di·ous·ly,** *adv.* —**o′di·ous·ness,** *n.*
—**Syn.** detestable, abominable, abhorrent, repulsive. See **hateful.**

o·di·um (ō′dē əm) *n.* **1** hatred; dislike. **2** reproach; blame. [< L *odium* < *odisse* hate] —**Syn. 1** detestation. **2** disfavor, disgrace.

o·dom·e·ter (ō dom′ə tər) *n.* an instrument for measuring the distance a vehicle travels by counting the number of wheel revolutions. [< F *odomètre* < Gk. *hodometron* < *hodos* way + *metron* a measure]

o·don·tol·o·gy (ō′don tol′ə jē) *n.* the branch of anatomy dealing with the structure, development, and diseases of the teeth; dentistry. [< Gk. *odous, -ontos* tooth + E *-logy*]

o·dor or **o·dour** (ō′dər) *n.* **1** a smell. **2** reputation. **3** a fragrance; perfume. **4** a taste or quality characteristic or suggestive of something: *There is no odor of impropriety about the case.* **5 be in bad odor,** have a bad reputation or inferior standing. [ME < AF < L] —**o′dor·less** or **o′dour·less,** *adj.* —**Syn. 1** scent. See **smell. 3** aroma.

o·dor·if·er·ous (ō′dər if′ər əs) *adj.* giving forth an odor; fragrant. [ME < L *odorifer* < *odor* odor + *ferre* bear] —**o′dor·if′er·ous·ly,** *adv.* —**o′dor·if′er·ous·ness,** *n.*

o·dor·ous (ō′dər əs) *adj.* giving forth an odor; having an odor; sweet-smelling; fragrant: *Spices are odorous.* [< L *odorous*] —**o′dor·ous·ly,** *adv.* —**o′dor·ous·ness,** *n.*

o·dour (ō′dər) *n.* odor.

O·dys·se·us (ō dis′ē əs) *n.* the Greek name of Ulysses.

Od·ys·sey (od′ə sē) *n.* **-seys. 1** a long Greek epic poem by Homer, describing the ten years of wandering of Ulysses after the Trojan War and his final return home. **2** Also, **odyssey.** any long series of wanderings and adventures.

OE or **O.E.** Old English (Anglo-Saxon).

oec·u·men·i·cal (ek′yu̇ men′ə kəl) *adj.* ecumenical.

Oed·i·pus (ē′də pəs or ed′ə pəs) *n.* in Greek legend, a king of Thebes who unknowingly killed his father and married his mother. When he learned what he had done, he blinded himself and passed the rest of his life wandering miserably.

o'er (ôr) *prep. adv. Poetic.* over.

oe·soph·a·gus (ē sof′ə gəs) *n.* **-gi** (-jī′ or -jē′). esophagus.

of (uv or ov; *unstressed,* əv) *prep.* **1** belonging to; associated with; forming a part of: *the children of a family.* **2** made from: *a house of bricks.* **3** that has; containing; with: *a house of six rooms.* **4** that has as a quality: *a look of pity.* **5** that is the same as; that is; named: *the city of Vancouver.* **6** away from; from: *north of Brandon.* **7** having to do with; in regard to; concerning; about: *think well of someone.* **8** that has as a purpose: *the hour of prayer.* **9** by: *the writings of Shakespeare.* **10** as a result of having or using; through: *die of grief.* **11** out of: *She came of a noble family.* **12** among: *a mind of the finest.* **13** during: *of late years.* **14** in telling time, before: *ten minutes of six.* **15** in; as to: *She is sixteen years of age.* **16** *Of* connects nouns and adjectives having the meaning of a verb with what would be the object of the verb: *The eating of fruit, a hall smelling of onions.* [OE (unstressed) *of.* Cf. OFF.]

☛ **of, off.** In informal speech *of* is frequently used in doubling prepositions: *inside of, off of, outside of. Inside of* and *outside of* also are used in informal writing, but not *off of,* which should be reduced to *off: He stepped off* [*of*] *the sidewalk.*

of- the form of **ob-** before *f,* as in *offer.*

OF or **O.F.** Old French.

off (of) *prep.* **1** not in the usual or correct position on; not in the usual or correct condition of; not on: *A button is off his coat.* **2** from; away from: *miles off the main road.* **3** seaward from: *The ship anchored off Victoria.*
—*adv.* **1** from the usual or correct position, condition, etc.: *He took off his hat.* **2** away: *go off on a journey.* **3** distant in time: *Christmas is only five weeks off.* **4** so as to stop or lessen: *Turn the water off. The game was called off.* **5** without work: *an afternoon off.* **6** in full; wholly: *Pay off the debt.* **7** on one's way: *The train started and we were off on our trip.* **8 be off,** go away; leave quickly. **9 off and on,** at some times and not at others; now and then.
—*adj.* **1** not connected; stopped: *The electricity is off.* **2** without work: *He pursues his hobby during off hours.* **3** in a specified condition in regard to money, property, etc.: *How well off are the Smiths?* **4** not very good; not up to average: *Bad weather made last summer an off season for fruit.* **5** deteriorated in quality, etc.: *The milk seems to be off.* **6** possible but not likely: *I came on the off chance that I would find you.* **7** on one's way. **8** more distant; farther: *the off side of a wall.* **9** on the right-hand side: *The nigh horse and the off horse make a team.* **10** seaward.
—*interj.* **1** go away! stay away! **2 off with, a** take off. **b** cut off: *Off with his head!* **c** away with!
—*n.* in cricket, the side opposite to the batsman. [OE (stressed) *of.* Cf. OF.] ☛ See **of** for usage note.

off. 1 office. **2** officer. **3** official.

of·fal (of′əl) *n.* **1** the waste parts of an animal killed for food. **2** garbage; refuse. [< *off* + *fall*]

off-and-on (of′ən on′) *Informal.* —*adj.* intermittent; uncertain. —*adv.* intermittently.

off-bal·ance (of′bal′əns) *adj.* unsteady; unprepared. —*adv.* unsteadily; by surprise.

off·beat (of′bēt′) *n.* in music, a beat that has relatively little stress. —*adj.* **1** in music, of or having to do with offbeats. **2** *Informal.* unconventional; not usual; odd.

off·cast (of′kast′) *adj.* rejected; cast off. —*n.* a person or thing that is cast off or rejected.

off-col·or or **off-col·our** (of′kul′ər) *adj.* **1** defective in color. **2** somewhat improper: *an off-color joke.* **3** not well: *She was feeling off-color yesterday.*

of·fence or **of·fense** (ə fens′ or ō fens′) *n.* **1** a breaking of the law; sin. Offences against the law are punished by fines or imprisonment. **2** a cause of wrongdoing. **3** the condition of being offended; hurt feelings; anger: *He tried not to cause offence.* **4** the act of offending or hurting someone's feelings: *No offence was intended.* **5** the act of attacking: *The army proved weak in offence.* **6** an attacking team or force. **7 give offence,** offend. **8 take offence,** be offended. [ME *offens* < OF < L *offensum* offence, annoyance; and ME *offense* < OF < L *offensa* hurt, injury, wrong; both L nouns < L *offendere.* See OFFEND.] —**Syn. 1** misdemeanor, transgression. See **crime. 3** resentment, displeasure.

of·fence·less or **of·fense·less** (ə fens′lis) *adj.* **1** without offence; incapable of offence or attack. **2** not offending; inoffensive.

of·fend (ə fend′) *v.* **1** hurt the feelings of; make angry; displease. **2** give offence; cause displeasure. **3** sin; do wrong. [ME < OF < L *offendere* < *ob-* against + *-fendere* strike] —**Syn. 1** affront, provoke.

of·fend·er (ə fen′dər) *n.* **1** a person who offends. **2** a person who does wrong or breaks a law.

of·fense (ə fens′ or ō fens′) *n.* offence.

of·fen·sive (ə fen′siv) *adj.* **1** giving offence; irritating; annoying: "*Shut up*" *is an offensive retort.* **2** unpleasant; disagreeable; disgusting: *Bad eggs have an offensive odor.* **3** ready to attack; attacking: *an offensive army.* **4** used for attack; having to do with attack: *offensive weapons, an offensive war for conquest.*
—*n.* **1** the position or attitude of attack: *The army took the offensive.* **2** an attack: *Our hockey team has a strong offensive.* —**of·fen′sive·ly,** *adv.* —**of·fen′sive·ness,** *n.*
—**Syn.** *adj.* **2** displeasing; distasteful. **3** aggressive.

of·fer (of′ər) *v.* **1 a** hold out to be taken or refused; present: *He offered us his help.* **b** present for sale: *offer suits at reduced prices.* **2** be willing if another approves: *He offered to help us.* **3** bring forth for consideration; propose: *She offered a few ideas to improve the plan.* **4** present in worship: *offer prayers.* **5** give; show: *The enemy offered resistance to our soldiers' attack.* **6** present itself; occur: *I will come if the opportunity offers.* **7** show intention; attempt; try: *He did not offer to hit back.* **8** present to sight or notice. **9** bid as a price: *He offered twenty dollars for our old stove.*
—*n.* **1** the act of offering: *an offer of money, an offer to*

sing, an offer of marriage, an offer of $10,000 for a house. **2** a thing that is offered. **3** in law, a proposal from one person to another which, if accepted, will become a contract. **4** an attempt or show of intention. [OE *offrian* < L *offerre* < *ob-* to + *ferre* bring]
Syn. *v.* **1 Offer, proffer, tender** = hold out something to someone to be accepted. **Offer** is the common word meaning "hold out" something to be taken or refused as one chooses or pleases: *She offered him coffee.* **Proffer** is the literary word, usually suggesting volunteering or offering with warmth, courtesy, or earnest sincerity: *He refused the proffered hospitality.* **Tender** is a formal word meaning "offer formally" something like services, not objects: *He tendered his apologies.* 3 advance, suggest. 7 endeavor.

of·fer·ing (of′ər ing or of′ring) *n.* **1** the giving of something as an act of worship. **2** a contribution. **3** the act of one that offers.

of·fer·to·ry (of′ər tô′rē) *n.* **-ries. 1** a collection, usually of money, at a religious service. **2** the verses said or the music sung or played while the offering is received. **3 a** in the Roman Catholic Church, the part of the Mass at which bread and wine are offered to God. **b** in the Anglican Church, a similar offering of bread and wine to God. **c** the prayers said or sung at this time. [< LL *offertorium* place to which offerings were brought]

off·hand (*adv.* of′hand′; *adj.* of′hand′) *adv.* without previous thought or preparation: *The carpenter could not tell offhand how much the work would cost.*
—*adj.* **1** done or made on the spur of the moment without previous thought or planning: *His offhand remarks were often very funny.* **2** casual; informal. **3** impolite; without due courtesy: *The boy's offhand ways angered his father.*
—**Syn.** *adj.* **1** unpremeditated, unstudied, impromptu, extemporaneous. **2** unceremonious.

off·hand·ed (of′han′did) *adj.* offhand. —**off′hand′ed·ly,** *adv.* —**off′hand′ed·ness,** *n.*

of·fice (of′is) *n.* **1** a place where the work of managing a business is done, as distinct from a workshop or factory; a room or rooms in which clerical work is done. **2** the place where a doctor, lawyer, etc. sees his patients or clients. **3** a place where particular services are made available to the public: *The post office is downtown.* **4** a position, especially in the public service: *The M.P. was appointed to the office of Minister of Defence.* **5** the duty of one's position; task; job; work: *A teacher's office is teaching.* **6** the staff of persons carrying on work in an office. **7** an administrative department of a governmental organization. **8** an act of kindness or unkindness; attention; service; injury: *Through the good offices of a friend, he was able to get a job.* **9** a religious ceremony or prayer: *the communion office, last offices.* **10 offices,** *pl.* the parts of a house devoted to household work, such as kitchen, pantry, laundry, etc., often also stables and buildings. [ME < OF < L *officium* service < *opus* work + *facere* do] —**Syn. 4** post, situation. **5** function, charge.

office boy a boy whose work is doing odd jobs in an office.

of·fice·hold·er (of′is hōl′dər) *n.* a person who holds a public office; government official.

of·fi·cer (of′ə sər) *n.* **1** a person who commands others in the navy, army, or air force. **2** the captain of a ship or any of his chief assistants. **3** a person who holds an office in the government, the church, the public service, etc.: *a health officer, a police officer.* **4** a person appointed or elected to an administrative position in a company, club, society, etc. **5** in some societies, any member above the lowest rank.
—*v.* **1** provide with officers. **2** direct; conduct; manage. [ME < AF *officer,* OF *officier* < Med.L *officiarius* < L *officium* service] —**of′fi·cer·less,** *adj.*

officer of the day in the armed services, an officer who has charge, for the time being, of the guards, prisoners, barracks, etc. *Abbrev.:* O.D.

office seeker a person who tries to obtain a public office.

of·fi·cial (ə fish′əl or ō fish′əl) *n.* **1** a person who holds a public position or who is in charge of some public work or duty: *Postmasters are government officials.* **2** a person holding office; officer: *bank officials.*
—*adj.* **1** of or having to do with an office: *Policemen wear an official uniform.* **2** having authority: *An official record is kept of the proceedings of Parliament.* **3** being an official: *Each province has its own official representatives in Parliament.* **4** suitable for a person in office: *the official dignity of a judge.* **5** holding office. [< LL *officialis* < *officium* service]

of·fi·cial·dom (ə fish′əl dəm or ō fish′əl-) *n.* **1** the position or domain of officials. **2** officials collectively.

of·fi·cial·ism (ə fish′əl iz′əm or ō fish′əl-) *n.* **1** official methods or systems. **2** an excessive attention to official routine.

of·fi·cial·ly (ə fish′əl ē or ō fish′əl ē) *adv.* in an official manner; as an official.

of·fi·ci·ate (ə fish′ē āt′ or ō fish′ē āt′) *v.* **-at·ed, -at·ing. 1** perform the duties of any office or position: *The president officiates as chairman at all club meetings.* **2** perform the duties of a priest, minister, or rabbi: *The bishop officiated at the cathedral.* **3** do anything as a ritual or ceremony: *officiate in carving the Thanksgiving turkey.* [< Med.L *officiare* < L *officium* service]

of·fic·i·nal (ə fis′ə nəl or ō fis′ə nəl) *adj.* **1** kept in stock by druggists. **2** recognized by the pharmacopoeia.
—*n.* a drug that is kept in stock. [< Med.L *officinalis* < L *officina* shop, storeroom, ult. < *opus* work + *facere* do]

of·fi·cious (ə fish′əs or ō fish′əs) *adj.* too ready to offer services or advice; minding other people's business; fond of meddling. [< L *officiosus* dutiful < *officium* service] —**of·fi′cious·ly,** *adv.* —**of·fi′cious·ness,** *n.* —**Syn.** meddlesome, intrusive.

off·ing (of′ing) *n.* **1** the more distant part of the sea as seen from the shore. **2** a position at a distance from the shore. **3 in the offing, a** just visible from the shore. **b** within sight. **c** not far off. **d** due to come, happen, etc. soon but at a time as yet unspecified: *There is a general election in the offing.*

off·ish (of′ish) *adj. Informal.* inclined to keep aloof; distant and reserved in manner. —**off′ish·ness,** *n.*

off-key (of′kē′) *adj.* **1** in music, not in the correct musical key; inharmonious. **2** *Informal.* improper; ill-timed.

off·print (of′print′) *n.* a separate reprint or reproduction of a story, article, etc. from a journal, book, etc.; printed excerpt. —*v.* reprint separately as an excerpt.

off·scour·ings (of′skour′ingz) *n.pl.* **1** filth; refuse. **2** low, worthless people.

off-screen (of′skrēn′) *adj.* **1** not seen on a movie or television screen: *an off-screen commentary.* **2** not engaged in acting for movies or television. —*adv.* so as not to be seen on a movie or television screen.

off-sea·son (of′sē′zən) *n.* the slack or slow season of a business, sport, etc. —*adj.* in or for the off-season: *Off-season hotel rates are usually low.*

off·set (*v.* of′set′; *n.* of′set′) *v.* **-set, -set·ting,** *n.* —*v.* **1** make up for; counterbalance; compensate for: *The better roads offset the greater distance.* **2** balance (one thing) by another as an equivalent: *We offset the greater distance by the better roads.* **3** set off or balance: *We offset the better roads against the greater distance.* **4** form an offset. **5** in printing, make an offset.
—*n.* **1** something that makes up for something else; compensation. **2** in botany, a short side shoot from a main stem or root that starts a new plant. **3** any offshoot. **4** in printing: **a** the process in which an inked impression is first made on a rubber roller and then on the paper, instead of directly on the paper. **b** an impression made by such a process. **5** in surveying, a short distance measured perpendicularly from a main line. **6** in architecture, a ledge formed on a wall by lessening its thickness above. **7** an abrupt bend in a pipe or bar to carry it past some obstruction. —**Syn.** *v.* **1** counterbalance, neutralize.

off·shoot (of′shüt′) *n.* **1** in botany, a shoot or branch growing out from the main stem of a plant, tree, etc. **2** anything coming, or thought of as coming, from a main part, stock, race, etc.

off·shore (of′shôr′) *adj.* **1** off or away from the shore: *an offshore wind.* **2** done or working away from the shore: *offshore fisheries.* —*adv.* toward the water; from the shore: *The wind was blowing offshore.*

off·side or **off-side** (of′sīd′) *adj.* away from one's own or the proper side; being on the wrong side.

hat, āge, cãre, fär; let, ēqual, tėrm; it, īce
hot, ōpen, ôrder; oil, out; cup, pùt, rüle, ūse
əbove, takən, pencəl, lemən, circəs
ch, child; ng, long; sh, ship
th, thin; ᴛʜ, then; zh, measure

off·spring (of′spring′) *n.* **1** what is born from or grows out of something; child or children; descendant. **2** a result; effect. [OE *ofspring*] —**Syn. 1** progeny, issue.

off-stage (of′stāj′) *adj.* away from the part of the stage that the audience can see.

off-street (of′strēt′) *adj.* away from the street: *More off-street parking will ease downtown traffic congestion.*

off-the-cuff (of′ᴛʜə kuf′) *Informal.* —*adj.* not prepared beforehand; impromptu: *The minister's speech was off-the-cuff, not a formal statement.* —*adv.* extemporaneously; on the spur of the moment.

off-the-rec·ord (of′ᴛʜə rek′ərd) *adj.* **1** not to be written in the minutes or proceedings (of a meeting, conference, etc.). **2** not for publication or release as news. —*adv.* so as to be off-the-record.

off-track (of′trak′) *adj.* **1** not conducted at a race track: *off-track betting.* **2** out of the way; off the beaten track.

off-white (of′hwīt′ or -wīt′) *n.* a very pale beige or light gray, almost white. —*adj.* almost white.

off-year (of′yēr′) *n.* a year of lower returns or of poor conditions in business, farming, etc.

oft (oft) *adv. Archaic.* often. [OE]

of·ten (of′ən or of′tən) *adv.* in many cases; many times; frequently: *Blame is often misdirected. He comes here often.* [ME *often* oft, the form of *ofte* before a vowel]

Syn. Often, frequently = many times or in many instances, and are mostly interchangeable. But **often** suggests only that something happens or occurs a number of times or in a considerable proportion of the total number of instances: *We often see him.* **Frequently** emphasizes happening or occurring again and again, regularly or at short intervals: *We saw him frequently last week.*

of·ten·times (of′ən tīmz′ or of′tən-) *adv.* often.

oft·times (oft′tīmz′) *adv. Poetic.* often.

o·gee (ō jē′ or ō′jē) *n.* **1** an S-shaped curve or line. **2** in architecture, a moulding with such a curve. **3** an ogee arch. [< F *ogive*]

An ogee arch

ogee arch a form of pointed arch, each side of which has the curve of an ogee.

o·give (ō′jīv or ō jīv′) *n.* **1** in architecture: **a** a pointed arch. **b** a diagonal rib across a vault. **2** in statistics, a distribution graph or curve showing cumulative frequencies. [< MF; origin uncertain]

o·gle (ō′gəl) *v.* **o·gled, o·gling,** *n.* —*v.* **1** look at with desire; make eyes at. **2** look with desire; make eyes. —*n.* an ogling look. [< Du. *oogelen* < *oog* eye] —**o′gler,** *n.*

Og·pu (og′pü) *n.* in the Soviet Union, the official organization of secret police from 1922 to 1935. [Abbrev. of Russian for "Unified State Political Administration"]

o·gre (ō′gər) *n.* **1** in folklore and fairy tales, a giant or monster that supposedly eats people. **2** a man like such a monster in appearance or character. [< F]

o·gre·ish (ō′gər ish) *adj.* like an ogre.

o·gress (ō′gris) *n.* a female ogre.

oh or **Oh** (ō) *interj.* **1** a word used before names in addressing persons: *Oh Mary, look!* **2** an expression of surprise, joy, grief, pain, and other feelings. Also, **O.**

OHG or **O.H.G.** Old High German.

ohm (ōm) *n.* a unit of electrical resistance. One ohm is the resistance of a conductor through which one volt can send a current of one ampere. *Abbrev.*: o [after Georg Simon *Ohm* (1787-1854), a German physicist]

ohm·ic (ōm′ik) *adj.* of or having to do with the ohm.

OHMS or **O.H.M.S.** On Her (or His) Majesty's Service.

o·ho or **O·ho** (ō hō′) *interj.* an exclamation expressing a taunt, surprise, or exultation.

-oid *suffix.* **1** like; like that of, as in *Mongoloid, amoeboid.* **2** thing like a, as in *spheroid, alkaloid.* [< Gk. *-oeidēs* < *eidos* form]

oil (oil) *n.* **1** any of several kinds of thick, fatty or greasy liquids that are lighter than water, that burn easily, and that dissolve in alcohol, but not in water. Mineral oils are used for fuel; animal and vegetable oils are used in cooking, medicine, and in many other ways. Essential or volatile oils, such as oil of peppermint, are distilled from plants, leaves, flowers, etc. and are thin and evaporate very quickly. **2** mineral oil; petroleum. **3** olive oil. **4** any substance that resembles oil in some respect. Sulphuric acid is called oil of vitriol. **5** oil paint. **6** an oil painting. **7 pour oil on troubled waters,** make things calm and peaceful. **8 strike oil, a** find oil by boring a hole in the earth. **b** find something very profitable.
—*v.* **1** become oil: *Butter oils when heated.* **2** put oil on or in. **3** make smooth or oily. **4** seek to persuade by bribery, flattery, etc. [ME < ONF *olie* < L *oleum* < Gk. *elaion*]

oil burner 1 a furnace, ship, etc. that uses oil for fuel. **2** the part of such a furnace in which the fuel oil is atomized, mixed with air, and burnt.

oil cake a mass of linseed, cottonseed, etc. from which the oil has been pressed. Oil cakes are used as a food for cattle and sheep or as a fertilizer.

oil·cloth (oil′kloth′) *n.* **1** a waterproof fabric consisting of a heavy cotton cloth treated on one side with a coating of oil or paint. **2** oilskin.

oil color or **colour 1** paint made by mixing pigment with oil. **2** a painting done in such colors.

oil·er (oil′ər) *n.* **1** a person or thing that oils. **2** a can with a long spout used in oiling machinery. **3** an oil tanker. **4 oilers,** *pl.* oilskin or other waterproof clothing.

oil field an area where petroleum has been found.

oil of turpentine a colorless, inflammable, volatile oil made from turpentine, used in mixing paints.

oil of vitriol sulphuric acid.

oil paint paint made by mixing pigment with oil.

oil painting 1 a picture painted with oil colors. **2** the art of painting with oil colors.

oil·pa·per (oil′pā′pər) *n.* paper treated with oil to make it transparent and waterproof.

oil sand any rock, especially sandstone, that contains large deposits of oil.

oil·skin (oil′skin′) *n.* **1** cloth treated with oil to make it waterproof. **2** Usually, **oilskins,** *pl.* a coat and trousers made of this cloth.

oil·stone (oil′stōn′) *n.* a fine-grained stone used for sharpening tools, the rubbing surface of which is oiled.

oil tanker a ship having special tanks to transport oil.

oil well a well drilled in the earth to get oil.

oil·y (oil′ē) *adj.* **oil·i·er, oil·i·est. 1** of oil. **2** containing oil. **3** covered or soaked with oil. **4** like oil; smooth; slippery. **5** too smooth; suspiciously or disagreeably smooth: *an oily smile, an oily manner.* —**oil′i·ness,** *n.*

oint·ment (oint′mənt) *n.* a substance made from oil or fat, often containing medicine, used on the skin to heal or to make it soft and white. Cold cream and salve are ointments. [ME < OF *oignement,* ult. < L *unguere* anoint; form influenced by *anoint*] —**Syn.** unguent, salve, balm.

O·jib·wa or **O·jib·way** (ō jib′wā) *n.* **-wa** or **-was. 1** an Indian tribe inhabiting the region around Lake Superior and westward, formerly occupying an area stretching from the Ottawa Valley to the prairies. **2** a member of this tribe. **3** the Algonquian language of this tribe.

O.K. or **OK** (ō′kā′) *adj. adv. v.* **O.K.'d** or **OK'd, O.K.'ing** or **OK'ing,** *n.* **O.K.'s** or **OK's.** *Informal.* —*adj. adv.* all right; correct; approved. —*v.* endorse; approve.
—*n.* approval. [probably from the "O.K. Club," a Democratic club of New York City formed in 1840 by supporters of Martin Van Buren; so called in allusion to "Old Kinderhook," Van Buren having been born at Kinderhook, N.Y.]

O.ka (ō′kə) *n. Cdn.* a cheese, cured with brine, made by Trappist monks in Oka, Quebec.

o·ka·pi (ō kä′pē) *n.* **-pis** or **-pi.** an African mammal resembling the giraffe, but smaller and with a much shorter neck. [< an African lang.]

o·kay (ō′kā′) *adj. adv. v. n. Informal.* O.K.

O·kie (ō′kē) *n. U.S. Informal.* a migratory farm worker, originally one of many from Oklahoma who wandered in search of work during the depression of the 1930's.

Okla. Oklahoma.

o·kra (ō′krə) *n.* **1** a plant cultivated for its sticky pods, which are used in soups and as a vegetable. **2** the pods of the okra plant. **3** a stew or soup made with okra pods; gumbo. [< West African lang.]

-ol *combining form.* containing, derived from, or like an alcohol or phenol. [< alcoh*ol*]

old (ōld) *adj.* **old·er** or **eld·er, old·est** or **eld·est,** *n.* —*adj.* **1** having existed long; aged: *an old wall.* **2** of age; in age: *The baby is one year old.* **3** not new; made long ago; ancient: *an old excuse, an old tomb.* **4** much worn by age or use: *old clothes.* **5** looking or seeming old; mature: *old for her years.* **6** having much experience: *be old in wrongdoing.* **7** former: *An old student came back to visit his teacher.* **8** earlier or earliest: *Old English.* **9** familiar; dear: *good old fellow.* **10** *Informal.* good; fine: *We had a high old time at the party.*
—*n.* time long ago: *the heroes of old.* [OE *ald*]
—**old′ness,** *n.*

Syn. *adj.* **1 Old, elderly, ancient** = having existed a long time. **Old,** describing people, animals, or things, means not young or new, but near the end of life or having been in existence, use, or a particular relation, a long or relatively long time: *We are old friends.* **Elderly,** describing people, means past middle age and getting old: *He is an elderly man, about sixty.* **Ancient** = having come into existence or use, or having existed or happened, in the distant past: *Jerusalem is an ancient city.* **4** dilapidated, decayed, shabby, outworn. **6** experienced, practised. ☛ See **elder** for usage note.

old age the years of life from about 65 on.

Old Bai·ley (bā′lē) in London, England, the chief court for trying criminal cases.

Old Country the country an emigrant comes from, most frequently used of Great Britain or Ireland.

old·en (ōl′dən) *adj. Poetic.* of old; old; ancient.

Old English **1** the period in the history of the English language before 1100. **2** the language of this period; Anglo-Saxon. **3** in printing, a kind of black-letter type. This is Old English.

Old English sheep dog **1** a breed of English work dog, having a long, shaggy, blue or grizzly gray coat and docked tail. **2** a dog of this breed.

old fashioned a cocktail made of whisky, sugar, and bitters with a slice of orange and a cherry, mixed with soda and served cold.

old-fash·ioned (ōld′fash′ənd) *adj.* **1** of an old fashion; out of date in style, construction, etc.: *an old-fashioned dress.* **2** keeping to old ways, ideas, etc.: *an old-fashioned housekeeper.*

old-fo·gey or **old-fo·gy** (ōld′fō′gē) *adj.* out-of-date; behind the times.

old-fo·gey·ish or **old-fo·gy·ish** (ōld′fō′gē ish) *adj.* old-fogey.

Old French the French language from about A.D. 800 to about 1400.

Old Guard **1** the imperial guard of Napoleon I. It made the last French charge at Waterloo. **2** Usually, **old guard.** the conservative members of a country, community, organization, etc.

old hand an expert; a very skilled or experienced person.

Old Har·ry (har′ē) the Devil.

old hat **1** *Informal.* well-known; familiar. **2** old-fashioned; out-of-date.

Old High German the form of the German language that was spoken in S. Germany from about A.D. 800 to 1100. Modern standard German is descended from Old High German.

Old Icelandic Old Norse (def. 2).

old·ish (ōld′ish) *adj.* somewhat old.

Old Latin the Latin language before the second century B.C.

old-line (ōld′līn′) *adj.* **1** keeping to old ideas and ways; conservative. **2** having a long history; established.

old maid **1** a woman who has not married and seems unlikely to do so. **2** a prim, fussy person: *What an old maid he is!* **3** a very simple card game. —**Syn. 1** spinster.

old-maid·ish (ōld′mād′ish) *adj.* like, suggesting, or befitting an old maid; prim; fussy.

Old Man of the Sea **1** in *The Arabian Nights,* a horrible old man who clung to the back of Sinbad. **2** any person or thing that is hard to get rid of.

old master **1** any great painter who lived before 1700. **2** a painting by such a painter.

old moon the moon when seen as a thin crescent with the hollow side on the right.

Old Nick (nik) the Devil.

Old Norse **1** Scandinavian speech from the Viking period to about 1300. **2** the Icelandic language in the Middle Ages.

Old Saxon the form of Low German spoken by the Saxons in N.W. Germany from about A.D. 800 to about 1100.

old school any group of people who have old-fashioned or conservative ideas.

old·ster (ōld′stər) *n. Informal.* an old or older person.

Old Style **1** a method of reckoning time according to the calendar used until 1582, when the date was moved ahead 10 days. In Great Britain the Old Style calendar was used until 1752, when all dates were moved ahead 11 days. **2** **old style,** in printing, a kind of type. This sentence is printed in old style.

Old Testament the earlier part of the Bible, which contains the religious and social laws of the Hebrews, a record of their history, their important literature, and writings of their prophets.

old-time (ōld′tīm′) *adj.* of former times; like old times.

old-tim·er (ōld′tīm′ər) *n. Informal.* **1** a person who has long been a resident, member, worker, etc. **2** a person who favors old ideas and ways.

old wives' tale a foolish story; silly belief.

old-wom·an·ish (ōld′wu̇m′ən ish) *adj.* like, suggesting, or befitting an old woman; fussy.

old-world (ōld′wėrld′) *adj.* **1** of or having to do with the ancient world: *an old-world mammoth.* **2** belonging to or characteristic of a former period: *old-world courtesy.* **3** Also, **Old-World.** of or having to do with the Eastern Hemisphere, or the Old World: *Old-World folk songs.*

Old World Europe, Asia, and Africa.

o·le·ag·i·nous (ō′lē aj′ə nəs) *adj.* oily. [< L *oleaginus* of the olive < *olea* olive, alteration of *oliva.* See OLIVE.]

o·le·an·der (ō′lē an′dər) *n.* a poisonous evergreen shrub having fragrant red, pink, or white flowers. [< Med.L]

o·le·ate (ō′lē āt′) *n.* a salt of oleic acid.

o·le·ic acid (ō lē′ik or ō′lē ik) an oily liquid obtained by hydrolyzing various animal and vegetable oils and fats. *Formula:* $C_{17}H_{33}COOH$ [*oleic* < L *oleum* oil]

o·le·in (ō′lē in) *n.* an ester of oleic acid and glycerin. Lard, olive oil, and cottonseed oil are mostly olein. [< L *oleum* oil]

o·le·o (ō′lē ō) *n.* oleomargarine.

o·le·o·mar·ga·rin (ō′lē ō mär′jə rin) *n.* oleomargarine.

o·le·o·mar·ga·rine (ō′lē ō mär′jə rin or ō′lē ō mär′jə-rēn′) *n.* a substitute for butter made from animal fats and vegetable oils; margarine. [< L *oleum* oil + E *margarine*]

o·le·o·res·in (ō′lē ō rez′ən) *n.* a natural or prepared solution of resin in oil. [< L *oleum* oil + E *resin*]

ol·fac·tion (ol fak′shən) *n.* **1** the act of smelling. **2** the sense of smell. [< L *olfactus,* pp. of *olfacere* smell at < *olere* emit a smell + *facere* make]

ol·fac·to·ry (ol fak′tə rē) *adj. n.* **-ries.** —*adj.* having to do with smelling; of smell. The nose is an olfactory organ. —*n.* an olfactory organ.

ol·i·garch (ol′ə gärk′) *n.* one of a small number of persons holding the ruling power in a state.

ol·i·gar·chic (ol′ə gär′kik) *adj.* of an oligarchy or oligarchs; having to do with rule by a few.

ol·i·gar·chi·cal (ol′ə gär′kə kəl) *adj.* oligarchic.

ol·i·gar·chy (ol′ə gär′kē) *n.* **-chies.** **1** a form of government in which a few people have the power. **2** a country or state having such a government. Ancient Sparta was really an oligarchy, though it had two kings. **3** the ruling few. [< Gk. *oligarchia*, ult. < *oligos* few + *archos* leader]

Ol·i·go·cene (ol′ə gō sēn′) in geology: —*n.* **1** an early period of the Cenozoic era, beginning approximately 40 million years ago. **2** the rocks formed in this period. See the chart under **geology.** —*adj.* in geology, of or having to do with this period or rocks formed during it. [< Gk. *oligos* small, little + *kainos* new, recent]

ol·ive (ol′iv) *n.* **1** a kind of evergreen tree having gray-green leaves that grows in S. Europe and other warm regions. **2** the fruit of this tree. Olives are eaten green or ripe. Olive oil is pressed from olives. **3** the wood of the olive tree. **4** a wreath of olive leaves; olive branch. **5** a yellowish green: *The uniform was made of olive cloth.* **6** a yellowish brown: *The man had an olive complexion.* —*adj.* **1** yellowish-green. **2** yellowish-brown. [ME < OF < L *oliva* < Gk. **elaiwa*, dial. var. of *elaia*]

olive branch 1 a branch of the olive tree as an emblem of peace. **2** anything offered as a sign of peace. **3** a child.

olive drab a dark greenish-yellow.

olive oil oil pressed from olives, used as food and in medicine.

Ol·i·ver (ol′ə vər) *n.* one of Charlemagne's heroic followers and the close friend of Roland, with whom he engaged in a fight which neither of them could win. See **Roland.**

ol·i·vine (ol′ə vēn′ or ol′ə vēn′) *n.* chrysolite, especially when greenish. [< *olive*; from the color]

ol·o·gy (ol′ə jē) *n.* **-gies.** any science or branch of knowledge. [< connective *-o-* + *-logy*]

O·lym·pi·a (ō lim′pē ə) *n.* in ancient Greece, a plain where games were held every four years in honor of Zeus.

O·lym·pi·ad or **o·lym·pi·ad** (ō lim′pē ad′) *n.* **1** in ancient times, a period of four years reckoned from one celebration of the Olympic games to the next, by which Greeks computed time from 776 B.C. **2** the celebration of the modern Olympic games. [< L < Gk. *Olympias, -ados*, ult. < *Olympus*, a mountain in N.E. Greece]

O·lym·pi·an (ō lim′pē ən) *adj.* **1** having to do with Olympia or with Mount Olympus. **2** like a god; heavenly. **3** rather too gracious; magnificent; superior: *Olympian calm, Olympian manners.* —*n.* **1** any of the major Greek gods. **2** a contender in the Olympic games.

Olympian games Olympic games.

O·lym·pic (ō lim′pik) *adj.* **1** of or having to do with Olympia in ancient Greece: *the Olympic games.* **2** of or having to do with Mount Olympus. —*n.* **Olympics,** *pl.* the Olympic games.

Olympic games 1 in ancient times, contests in athletics, poetry, and music, held every four years by the Greeks in honor of Zeus. **2** in modern times, athletic contests imitating the athletic contests of these games. They were revived in 1896 and are held once every four years in a different country, and athletes from many nations compete in them.

O·lym·pus (ō lim′pəs) *n.* heaven. [< Mount *Olympus*, in Greece, regarded as the home of the ancient Greek deities]

O.M. Order of Merit.

-oma *combining form.* a tumor or growth, as in *carcinoma.* [< Gk. noun suffix *-ōma, -ōmatos*]

o·ma·sum (ō mā′səm) *n.* -sa (-sə). the third stomach of a cow or other ruminant. The omasum receives the food when it is swallowed the second time. [< L]

om·buds·man (om budz′mən) *n.* **-men** (-mən). a government official appointed to receive and investigate citizens' grievances against the government. The office of ombudsman originated in the Scandinavian countries. [< Swedish]

o·meg·a (ō meg′ə, ō mē′gə, or ō′mig ə) *n.* **1** the last of any series; end. **2** the last letter of the Greek alphabet. (Ω or ω). [< LGk. *o mega* big *o*]

om·e·lette or **om·e·let** (om′ə lit or om′lit) *n.* eggs beaten with milk or water, fried or baked, and usually folded for serving: *Omelettes are sometimes filled with chopped meat, mushrooms, etc.*

hat, āge, cãre, fär; let, ēqual, térm; it, īce
hot, ōpen, ôrder; oil, out; cup, pu̇t, rüle, ūse
əbove, takən, pencəl, lemən, circəs
ch, child; ng, long; sh, ship
th, thin; ᴛʜ, then; zh, measure

o·men (ō′mən) *n.* **1** a sign of what is to happen; object or event that is believed to mean good or bad fortune: *Spilling salt is said to be an omen of misfortune.* **2** prophetic meaning: *Some people consider a black cat a creature of ill omen.* —*v.* be a sign of; presage. [< L] —**Syn.** *n.* **1** augury, portent, presage. See **sign.**

O.M.I. Oblates of Mary Immaculate.

om·i·cron (ō′mə kron′ or om′ə kron′) *n.* the 15th letter of the Greek alphabet (O or *o*). [< Gk. *o micron* small *o*]

om·i·nous (om′ə nəs) *adj.* of bad omen; unfavorable; threatening: *The watchdog gave an ominous growl.* [< L *ominosus* < *omen* omen] —**om′i·nous·ly,** *adv.* —**om′i·nous·ness,** *n.* —**Syn.** inauspicious, foreboding.

o·mis·sion (ō mish′ən) *n.* **1** an omitting or being omitted. **2** anything omitted: *He said he'd take care of any omissions.* [< LL *omissio, -onis* < L *omittere.* See OMIT.]

o·mit (ō mit′) *v.* **o·mit·ted, o·mit·ting. 1** leave out: *You have omitted a letter in this word.* **2** fail to do; neglect: *Mary omitted to make her bed.* [< L *omittere* < *ob-* by + *mittere* let go] —**Syn. 2** overlook, ignore, skip.

om·ni·bus (om′nə bus′ or om′nə bəs) *n.* **-bus·es,** *adj.* —*n.* **1** a large passenger vehicle having seats inside and sometimes also on the roof; bus. **2** a volume of works by a single author, or of similar works by several authors: *a Hemingway omnibus, a science-fiction omnibus.* —*adj.* covering many things at once: *an omnibus law.* [< L *omnibus* for all]

om·ni·far·i·ous (om′nə fãr′ē əs) *adj.* of all forms, varieties, or kinds. [< LL *omnifarius,* < L *omnis* all + *fas, faris,* originally, pronouncement < *fari* speak]

om·nip·o·tence (om nip′ə təns) *n.* complete power; unlimited power: *the omnipotence of God.*

om·nip·o·tent (om nip′ə tənt) *adj.* having all power; almighty: *an omnipotent ruler.* —*n.* **the Omnipotent,** God. [< L *omnipotens, -entis* < *omnis* all + *potens* being able] —**om nip′o·tent·ly,** *adv.*

om·ni·pres·ence (om′nə prez′əns) *n.* presence everywhere at the same time: *God's omnipresence.*

om·ni·pres·ent (om′nə prez′ənt) *adj.* present everywhere at the same time. [< Med.L *omnipraesens, -entis* < L *omnis* all + *praesens* present]

om·nis·cience (om nis′ē əns or om nish′əns) *n.* knowledge of everything; complete or infinite knowledge. [< Med.L *omniscientia* < L *omnis* all + *scientia* knowledge]

om·nis·cient (om nis′ē ənt or om nish′ənt) *adj.* knowing everything; having complete or infinite knowledge. —**om·nis′cient·ly,** *adv.*

om·ni·um·gath·er·um (om′nē əm gaᴛʜ′ər əm) *n.* a miscellaneous collection; a confused mixture. [< L *omnium* of all + *gatherum,* pseudo-Latin form from E *gather*]

om·niv·o·rous (om niv′ə rəs) *adj.* **1** eating every kind of food. **2** eating both animal and vegetable food: *Man is an omnivorous animal.* **3** taking in everything; fond of all kinds: *An omnivorous reader reads all kinds of books.* [< L *omnivorus* < *omnis* all + *vorare* eat greedily] —**om·niv′o·rous·ly,** *adv.* —**om·niv′o·rous·ness,** *n.*

on (on) *prep.* **1** above and supported by: *The book is on the table.* **2** touching so as to cover, be around, etc.: *Put the ring on her finger.* **3** close to; along the edge of: *a house on the shore. He lives on the next street.* **4** in the direction of; toward: *The workers marched on the capital.* **5** against; upon: *the picture on the wall.* **6** by means of; by the use of: *This news is on good authority.* **7** in the condition of; in the process of; in the way of: *on half pay, on purpose, on duty.* **8** at the time of; during: *They greeted us on our arrival.* **9** in relation to; in connection with; concerning: *a book on animals.* **10** for the purpose of: *He went on an errand.* **11** in addition to: *Defeat on*

defeat discouraged them. **12** among: *on the committee.* —*adv.* **1** on something: *The walls are up, and the roof is on.* **2** to something: *Hold on, or you may fall.* **3** toward something: *Some played; the others looked on.* **4** farther: *March on.* **5** in or into a condition, process, manner, action, etc.: *Turn the gas on.* **6** from a time; forward: *later on, from that day on.* **7 and so on,** and more of the same. **8 on and on,** without stopping.
—*adj.* taking place: *The race is on.* [OE]

ON or **O.N.** Old Norse.

once (wuns) *adv.* **1** one time: *He comes once a day.* **2** at some one time in the past; formerly: *a once powerful nation.* **3** even a single time; ever: *if the facts once become known.*
once and again, repeatedly.
once and for all, finally; once for all.
once for all, finally or decisively.
once in a while, now and then.
once or twice, a few times.
once over, a single time over.
once upon a time, long ago; once.
—*n.* **1** a single occasion: *Once is enough.* **2 all at once,** suddenly. **3 at once, a** immediately. **b** at one and the same time. **4 for once,** for one time at least.
—*conj.* **1** when; whenever; as soon as: *Once you cross the river, you are safe.* **2** if; if ever: *Once he hesitates, he is lost.* —*adj.* former: *a once friend.* [OE *ānes* < *ān* one]

once-o·ver (wuns′ō′vər) *n. Informal.* a short, quick look.

on·com·ing (on′kum′ing) *adj.* approaching: *oncoming winter.* —*n.* approach: *the oncoming of the storm.*

one (wun) *n.* **1** the first and lowest whole number; 1. **2** a single person or thing: *I gave him the one he wanted.* **3** a playing card, die, domino, etc. having one spot. **4 at one,** in agreement or harmony. **5 make one, a** form or be one of a number, assembly, or party. **b** join together; unite in marriage. **6 one and all,** everyone. **7 one by one,** one after another. **8 one up on,** *Informal.* an advantage over.
—*adj.* **1** being a single unit or individual: *one apple.* **2** some: *One day he will be sorry. I saw him one day last week.* **3** the same: *They held one opinion.* **4** joined together; united: *They replied in one voice.* **5** a certain: *One John Smith was elected.* **6 all one,** all the same. **7 one or two,** a few.
—*pron.* **1** some person or thing: *One of the poems was selected for the book.* **2** any person or thing: *One must work hard to achieve success.* **3** the same person or thing: *Dr. Jekyll and Mr. Hyde were one and the same.* **4 one or two.** a few. [OE (*stressed*) ān. Cf. A[1], AN[1].]

☛ **one.** The use of the impersonal pronoun *one* is characteristically formal, especially if it must be repeated. Informal: *You can't be too careful, can you?* Formal: *One can't be too careful, can one?* This repetition of *one* sounds stilted when *you* would be more natural.

one another one the other: *They struck at one another. They were in one another's way.*

☛ **one another, each other.** As a reciprocal pronoun, **one another** is usually used with reference to more than two, **each other** with reference to two: *The members of the team support one another. The two hate each other.*

one-celled (wun′seld′) *adj.* having only one cell.

one-horse (wun′hôrs′) *adj.* **1** drawn or worked by a single horse: *a one-horse sleigh.* **2** using or having only a single horse: *a one-horse farmer.* **3** *Informal.* of little scope, capacity, or importance; minor: *a one-horse town.*

O·nei·da (ō nī′də) *n.* **1** a tribe of North American Indians belonging to the Five Nations confederacy, living mainly in New York State, and later in S.W. Ontario and Wisconsin. **2** a member of this tribe. **3** the Iroquoian language of this tribe.

one-man (wun′man′) *adj.* **1** of or by only one person: *one-man rule, a one-man art show.* **2** made for or to be used by one man: *a one-man space ship.* **3** showing loyalty to or affection for one person only: *one-man dog.*

one·ness (wun′nis) *n.* **1** the quality of being one in number or the only one of its kind; singleness. **2** the quality of being the same in kind; sameness. **3** the fact of forming one whole; unity. **4** agreement in mind, feeling, or purpose; harmony.

on·er·ous (on′ər əs or ō′nər əs) *adj.* burdensome; oppressive: *Overtime work is well paid, but it is often onerous.* [< L *onerosus* < *onus* burden] —**on′er·ous·ly,** *adv.* —**on′er·ous·ness,** *n.* —**Syn.** heavy, weighty, arduous.

one·self (wun self′) *pron.* **1** one's own self: *One should not praise oneself.* **2 be oneself, a** have full control of one's mind or body. **b** act naturally.

one-sid·ed (wun′sīd′id) *adj.* **1** seeing only one side of a question; partial; unfair; prejudiced. **2** uneven; unequal: *If one team is much better than the other, a game is one-sided.* **3** having but one side. **4** on only one side. **5** having one side larger or more developed than the other.

one's self oneself.

one-step (wun′step′) *n. v.* **-stepped, -step·ping.** —*n.* **1** a dance much like a quick walk. **2** the music for such a dance. —*v.* dance the one-step.

one-time (wun′tīm′) *adj.* of the past; former.

one-track (wun′trak′) *adj.* **1** having only one track. **2** *Informal.* understanding or preoccupied with only one thing at a time: *one-track mind.*

one-up·man·ship (wun′up′mən ship′) *n. Informal.* the art or practice of outdoing one's opponents, especially by giving the appearance of being better informed, more experienced, etc.

one-way (wun′wā′) *adj.* moving or allowing movement in only one direction: *one-way traffic.*

one-world·er (wun′wėrl′dər) *n.* one who favors internationalism.

on·ion (un′yən) *n.* **1** a bulblike root, eaten raw and used in cooking. Onions taste and smell strong and sharp. **2** the plant it grows on. [< F *oignon* < L *unio, -onis* onion, kind of pearl] —**on′ion·like′,** *adj.*

on·ion·skin (un′yən skin′) *n.* a thin, glossy, translucent paper.

on·look·er (on′lůk′ər) *n.* a person who watches without taking part; spectator.

on·look·ing (on′lůk′ing) *adj. n.* watching; seeing; noticing.

on·ly (ōn′lē) *adj.* **1** by itself or themselves; sole, single, or few of the kind or class: *an only son.* **2** best; finest: *He is the only writer for my taste.*
—*adv.* **1** merely; just: *He sold only two.* **2** and no one else; and nothing more; and that is all: *Only he remained. I did it only through friendship.* **3 if only,** I wish: *If only wars would cease!* **4 only too,** very: *She was only too glad to help us.*
—*conj.* except that; but: *I would have gone, only you objected.* [OE *ānlīc*] —**Syn.** *adj.* **1** solitary, unique. See **single.**

on·o·mat·o·poe·ia (on′ə mat′ə pē′ə) *n.* **1** the formation of a name or word by imitating the sound associated with the thing designated, as in *buzz, hum, cuckoo, slap, splash.* **2** a word or passage so formed. **3** the adaptation of the sound to the sense for rhetorical effect, as in "the murmurous haunt of flies on summer eves." [< L < Gk. *onomatopoiia* < *onoma, -matos* word, name + *-poios* making]

on·o·mat·o·poe·ic (on′ə mat′ə pē′ik) *adj.* having to do with or like onomatopoeia; imitative in sound; echoic.

on·o·mat·o·po·et·ic (on′ə mat′ə pō et′ik) *adj.* onomatopoeic.

On·on·da·ga (on′ən do′gə or on′ən dä′gə) *n.* **1** a tribe of North American Indians belonging to the Five Nations confederacy, living mainly in New York State. **2** a member of this tribe. **3** the Iroquoian language of the tribe. [< Iroquois *Ononta' gé,* a place name meaning "on top of the hill"]

on·rush (on′rush′) *n.* a violent forward movement: *He was knocked down by the onrush of water.*

on·set (on′set′) *n.* **1** an attack: *The onset of the enemy took us by surprise.* **2** the beginning: *the onset of a disease.* —**Syn. 1** assault, onslaught. **2** commencement.

on·shore (on′shôr′) *adv. adj.* **1** toward the land. **2** on the land.

on·side (on′sīd′) *adj. adv.* in a position allowed by the rules of a game.

on-site (on′sīt′) *adj.* on the spot; at the actual location: *an on-site inspection.*

on·slaught (on′slot′ or on′slôt′) *n.* a vigorous attack:

The Indians made an onslaught on the settlers' fort.

Ont. Ontario.

On·tar·i·an (on tãr′ē ən) *n.* a native or permanent resident of Ontario. *—adj.* of or concerning Ontario.

On·tar·i·o·an (on tãr′ē ō′ən) *n.* Ontarian.

on·to (on′tü; *before consonants often* on′tə) *prep.* **1** on to; to a position on: *throw a ball onto the roof, get onto a horse, a boat driven onto the rocks.* **2** *Slang.* familiar with; aware of; experienced in: *get onto a new job.*

☛ **onto, on to.** When *on* is an adverb and *to* a preposition in a separate locution, they should of course be written as two words: *The rest of us drove on to the city.* When the words are combined to make a compound preposition, they are usually written solid: *The team trotted onto the floor. They looked out onto the park.*

onto- *combining form.* being, existence, as in *ontogenesis.* [< Gk. *ōn, ontos* ppr. of *einai* to be]

on·to·gen·e·sis (on′tə jen′ə sis) *n.* the growth processes of an organism, ontogeny. [< *onto-* + Gk. *-geneia* origin < *-genēs* born, produced]

on·to·ge·net·ic (on′tō jə net′ik) *adj.* of or having to do with ontogenesis.

on·tog·e·ny (on toj′ə nē) *n.* in biology, the development of an individual organism. [< Gk. *ōn, ontos* being + *-geneia* origin < *-genēs* born, produced]

on·to·log·i·cal (on′tə loj′ə kəl) *adj.* of or having to do with ontology.

on·tol·o·gy (on tol′ə jē) *n.* the part of philosophy that deals with the nature of reality. [< NL *ontologia* < Gk. *ōn, ontos* being + *-logos* treating of]

o·nus (ō′nəs) *n.* a burden; responsibility: *The onus of housekeeping fell upon the daughters.* [< L]

on·ward (on′wərd) *adv.* toward the front; further on; on; forward: *The army marched onward. —adj.* on; further on; toward the front; forward: *An onward movement began.* **—Syn.** *adv.* forth. See **forward.**

on·wards (on′wərdz) *adv.* onward.

on·yx (on′iks) *n.* **1** a semiprecious variety of quartz with layers of different colors and shades. **2** a piece of this stone, or a gem made from it. [< L < Gk. *onyx* nail, claw]

oo·li·chan (ü′lə kən) *n.* **oo·li·chan** or **oo·li·chans.** a small fish of the smelt family found on the Pacific coast; candlefish. Also, **eu′la·chon.** [< Chinook jargon]

o·o·lite or **o·ö·lite** (ō′ə līt′) *n.* a rock, usually limestone, composed of rounded concretions resembling the roe of fish. [< F *oölithe* < Gk. *ōon* egg + *lithos* stone]

oo·long (ü′long) *n.* a black tea consisting of leaves that were partially fermented before they were dried. [< Chinese *wu-lung* black dragon]

oo·loo (ü′lü) *n. Cdn.* a crescent-shaped, bone-handled knife used by Eskimo women. Also, **ulu.** [< Eskimo]

oo·mi·ak (ü′mē ak) *n.* a large, flat-bottomed Eskimo boat made of skins covering a wooden frame and propelled by paddles. Oomiaks are used for freight and are usually worked by women. Also, **umiak.** [< Eskimo]

An oomiak

ooze[1] (üz) *v.* **oozed, ooz·ing,** *n. —v.* **1** pass slowly through small openings; leak slowly and quietly: *Blood oozed from his scraped knee. The mud oozed into his boots.* **2** disappear or drain away: *His courage oozed away as he waited.* **3** give out slowly: *The cut oozed blood.* [< n.] *—n.* **1** a slow flow. **2** something that oozes. [OE *wōs* juice]

ooze[2] (üz) *n.* a soft mud or slime, especially that at the bottom of a pond, lake, river, or on the ocean bottom. [OE *wāse* mud]

oo·zy[1] (ü′zē) *adj.* oozing. [< *ooze*[1]] **—oo′zi·ly,** *adv.*

oo·zy[2] (ü′zē) *adj.* containing ooze; muddy and soft; slimy. [< *ooze*[2]] **—oo′zi·ly,** *adv.*

op- the form of **ob-** before *p,* as in *oppress.*

op. 1 opus; opera. **2** opposite. **3** operation.

o.p. out of print.

hat, āge, cãre, fär; let, ēqual, tėrm; it, īce
hot, ōpen, ôrder; oil, out; cup, pu̇t, rüle, ūse
əbove, takən, pencəl, lemən, circəs
ch, child; ng, long; sh, ship
th, thin; ŦH, then; zh, measure

O.P. 1 Order of Preachers (Dominican). **2** observation post.

o·pac·i·ty (ō pas′ə tē) *n.* **-ties. 1** the state or quality of being opaque; darkness; being impervious to light. **2** the state or quality of being impervious to sound. **3** obscurity of meaning. **4** something opaque. [< L *opacitas* < *opacus* dark]

o·pal (ō′pəl) *n.* **1** a mineral, an amorphous form of silica, found in many varieties and colors, certain of which have a peculiar rainbow play of colors and are valued for gems. **2** a piece of this stone, or a gem made from it. [< L *opalus* < Gk. *opallios* < Skt. *upala* precious stone]

o·pal·esce (ō′pəl es′) *v.* **-esced, -esc·ing.** exhibit a play of colors like that of the opal. [< *opal* + *-esce* begin to be, become (< L *-escere*)]

o·pal·es·cence (ō′pəl es′əns) *n.* the exhibition of a play of colors like an opal's.

o·pal·es·cent (ō′pəl es′ənt) *adj.* showing opalescence.

o·pal·ine (ō′pəl īn′ or ō′pəl in) *adj.* of or like opal.

o·paque (ō pāk′) *adj.* **1** not letting light through; not transparent: *A brick wall is opaque.* **2** not shining; dark; dull. **3** obscure; hard to understand. **4** stupid. *—n.* something opaque. [< L *opacus* dark, shady] **—o·paque′ly,** *adv.* **—o·paque′ness,** *n.*

op art (op) a style of drawing and painting that creates optical illusions of motion and depth by means of complex geometrical designs. [shortened from *optical art,* on analogy with *pop art*]

op.cit. in the book, passage, etc. previously referred to. [for L *opere citato*]

ope (ōp) *v.* **oped, op·ing,** *adj. Poetic.* open.

o·pen (ō′pən) *adj.* **1** not shut; not closed; letting (anyone or anything) in or out: *an open drawer. Open windows let in the fresh air.* **2** not having its door, gate, lid, etc. closed: *an open box, an open house.* **3** not closed in: *an open field.* **4** unfilled; not taken: *a position still open, have an hour open.* **5** that may be entered, used, shared, competed for, etc. by all: *an open meeting, an open market.* **6** ready for business or for admission of the public: *The exhibition is now open. This store stays open till 9:30 p.m.* **7** accessible or available: *the only course still open.* **8** without prohibition or restriction: *open season for hunting.* **9** *Informal.* allowing saloons, gambling, etc.: *an open town.* **10** undecided; not settled: *an open question.* **11** having no cover, roof, etc.; letting in air freely: *an open car.* **12** not covered or protected; exposed: *open to temptation.* **13** not obstructed: *an open view.* **14** unprejudiced; ready to consider new ideas: *an open mind.* **15** exposed to general view, knowledge, etc.; not secret: *open disregard of rules.* **16** having spaces or holes: *open ranks, cloth of open texture.* **17** in music: **a** of an organ pipe, not closed at the upper end. **b** of a string on a violin, cello, etc., not stopped by the finger. **c** of a note, produced by such a pipe or string, or without aid of slide, key, etc. **18** in phonetics, uttered with relatively wide opening between the tongue and the roof of the mouth. **19** unreserved, candid, or frank: *an open face.* **20** that is spread out; expanded: *an open flower, an open newspaper.* **21** generous; liberal: *Give with an open hand.* **22** free from frost: *an open winter.* **23** free from ice: *open water on the lake.* **24** of an electric circuit, not complete or closed. **25** of a city, town, etc., unfortified; protected from enemy attack under international law: *In World War II Rome was declared an open city.* **26 open to, a** ready to take; willing to consider. **b** liable to. **c** to be had or used by. *—n.* **1** an open or clear space; opening. **2 the open, a** the open country, air, sea, etc. **b** public view or knowledge. *—v.* **1** afford access (into, to, etc.); have an opening. **2** become open or more open; become accessible: *The valley opens wide lower down.* **3** cause to be open or more open; make accessible: *Open a path through the woods.* **4** clear of obstructions; make (a passage, etc.) clear. **5** make or become accessible to knowledge, sympathy, etc.; enlighten or become enlightened: *open a person's eyes.* **6** lay bare; expose to view; uncover; disclose; reveal; divulge. **7** come to view. **8** expand, extend, or spread out; make or become less compact: *The ranks opened.* **9** establish or set going: *He opened a new store.* **10** begin; start: *School opens today.* **11** cut into: *open a wound.* **12** come apart, especially so as to allow passage or show the contents: *The wound opened. The clouds opened and the sun shone through.* **13** in law, make the first statement of (a case) to the court or jury. **14 open up, a** make or become open. **b** unfold; spread out. **c** begin; start; develop: *The early settlers opened up the West.* [OE. Related to UP.] —**o′pen·er,** *n.* —**o′pen·ly,** *adv.* —**Syn.** *adj.* **1** unclosed, ajar, unlocked. **4** unoccupied, free. **10** unsettled, debatable. **12** uncovered, unprotected. **15** public. **16** perforated, porous. **19** straightforward.

open air the out-of-doors.

o·pen-air (ō′pən ãr′) *adj.* outdoor.

open door free and equal chance for all countries to do business in another country.

o·pen-end (ō′pən end′) *adj.* **1** allowing for change or revision: *an open-end mortgage.* **2** of or having to do with investment groups that issue or recall shares on demand, since the capital is open, not fixed.

o·pen-end·ed (ō′pən end′id) *adj.* **1** open to change, revision, or adjustment. **2** not closed at either end: *an open-ended container.* **3** permitting free discussion; open to differing interpretations: *an open-ended question.*

o·pen-eyed (ō′pən īd′) *adj.* **1** having eyes wide open as in wonder. **2** having the eyes open; watchful or vigilant; observant. **3** done or experienced with the eyes open.

o·pen-face (ō′pən fās′) *adj.* of a sandwich, made without the top slice of bread.

o·pen-faced (ō′pən fāst′) *adj.* **1** open-face. **2** not having the face or surface covered. **3** of a watch, having no cover over the dial. **4 a** having a frank and honest face. **b** honest; ingenuous.

o·pen-hand·ed (ō′pən han′did) *adj.* generous; liberal. —**o′pen-hand′ed·ly,** *adv.* —**o′pen-hand′ed·ness,** *n.*

o·pen-heart·ed (ō′pən här′tid) *adj.* **1** candid; frank; unreserved. **2** kindly; generous. —**o′pen-heart′ed·ly,** *adv.* —**o′pen-heart′ed·ness,** *n.*

o·pen-hearth (ō′pən härth′) *adj.* having an open hearth; using a furnace with an open hearth.

open-hearth process a process of making steel in a furnace in which the flame is directed onto the raw material, the impurities becoming oxidized.

open house 1 a social event held by individuals, families, clubs, etc.: *The Browns held an open house last night.* **2** an occasion when a school, university, factory, etc. is opened for inspection by the public: *We saw an electronic computer at the university's open house.* **3** a house that is open to all friends who wish to visit. **4 keep open house,** offer food, or food and lodging, to all visitors.

o·pen·ing (ō′pən ing or ōp′ning) *n.* **1** an open or clear space; gap; hole: *an opening in a wall, an opening in the forest.* **2** the first part; beginning: *the opening of a lecture.* **3** a formal beginning. **4** a job, place, or position that is open or vacant. **5** a favorable chance or opportunity. **6** in law, the statement of the case made by the lawyer to the court or jury before adducing evidence. —**Syn. 1** aperture, fissure, orifice. **2** start, commencement, introduction. **4** vacancy.

open letter a letter addressed to a particular person but published in a newspaper, magazine, etc.

o·pen-mind·ed (ō′pən mīn′did) *adj.* having or showing a mind open to new arguments or ideas. —**o′pen-mind′ed·ly,** *adv.* —**o′pen-mind′ed·ness,** *n.*

o·pen-mouthed (ō′pən mouᴛʜd′ or -moutht′) *adj.* **1** having the mouth open. **2** gaping with surprise or astonishment. **3** greedy, ravenous, or rapacious. **4** vociferous or clamorous: *open-mouthed hounds.* **5** having a wide mouth: *an open-mouthed pitcher.*

o·pen·ness (ō′pən nis) *n.* **1** a being open. **2** a lack of secrecy. **3** frankness. **4** a willingness to consider new ideas or arguments.

o·pen-pit (ō′pən pit′) *adj.* worked on from the exposed surface, or slightly below the surface; not underground: *open-pit mining.*

open question something undecided or uncertain.

open secret a supposed secret that is actually known to everyone.

open ses·a·me (ses′ə mē) **1** in the *Arabian Nights,* the magic words that opened the door of the robbers' den in the story of Ali Baba. **2** any password at which doors or barriers fly open.

open shop a factory, shop, or other establishment that will employ both union and non-union workers.

open water 1 water free of obstructions. **2** *Cdn.* especially in the North: **a** the time when rivers and lakes become free of ice; break up: *At open water he got twenty beaver and two otter.* **b** the period during which rivers and lakes are free of ice; the time between break-up and freeze-up: *We have good hunting here during open water.*

o·pen·work (ō′pən wėrk′) *n.* ornamental work that shows openings.

op·er·a[1] (op′ər ə or op′rə) *n.* **1** a kind of drama set to music, performed by a group of singers usually to an orchestral accompaniment. In an opera, the words are usually sung, rather than spoken. **2** the art of creating or performing operas: *the history of opera.* **3** a performance of an opera. **4** the music of an opera. **5** a company that performs opera. **6** a theatre where operas are performed. [< Ital. *opera,* for *opera in musica* a (dramatic) work to music; *opera* < L *opera* effort (related to OPUS a work)]

op·er·a[2] (op′ər ə) *n.* pl. of **opus.**

op·er·a·ble (op′ər ə bəl or op′rə bəl) *adj.* **1** fit for, or admitting of, a surgical operation. **2** fit or able to be operated.

o·pé·ra bouffe (op′ər ə büf′ or op′rə büf′; *French,* ô pā rä büf′) **1** comic opera; light opera. **2** an absurd situation; ridiculous arrangement. [< F *opéra bouffe* comic opera]

opera glasses a small binocular telescope for use at the opera and in theatres. Opera glasses are like field glasses, but smaller.

Opera glasses

opera hat a tall collapsible hat, worn with formal clothes by men.

opera house 1 a theatre where operas are performed. **2** any theatre.

op·er·and (op′ə rand′) *n.* in mathematics, any symbol or quantity that is subject to an operation. [< L *operandum,* gerundive of *operari.* See OPERATE.]

op·er·ate (op′ər āt′) *v.* **-at·ed, -at·ing. 1** be at work; run: *The machinery operates night and day.* **2** keep at work; drive: *Who operates this elevator?* **3** direct the working of as owner or manager; manage: *That company operates factories in seven countries.* **4** produce an effect; work; act: *Several causes operated to bring on the war.* **5** go into action; become effective: *The medicine operated quickly.* **6** in medicine, treat the body, especially using instruments, to remedy an injury, disease, etc.: *The doctor operated on the injured man.* **7** carry on military movements. **8** buy and sell stocks and bonds: *operate in stocks or grain futures.* [< L *operare* < *opus* a work, or *opera* effort] —**Syn. 1** perform, function.

op·er·at·ic (op′ər at′ik) *adj.* of, like, or having to do with the opera: *operatic music.* —**op′er·at′i·cal·ly,** *adv.*

op·er·a·tion (op′ər ā′shən) *n.* **1** working: *The operation of a railway requires many men.* **2** the way a thing works: *the operation of a machine.* **3** an action; activity: *the operation of brushing one's teeth.* **4 in operation, a** running; working; in action. **b** in use or effect. **5** in medicine, a treatment, especially one using instruments, given to the body to remedy an injury, disease, etc. **6** movements of soldiers, ships, supplies, etc. for military purposes. **7** in mathematics, something done to a number or quantity. Addition, subtraction, multiplication, and division are the four commonest operations in arithmetic. **8** a commercial transaction, especially one that is speculative and on a large scale: *operations in stocks or wheat.*

op·er·a·tion·al (op′ə rā′shə nəl or op′ər āsh′nəl) *adj.* **1** of or having to do with any kind of operation. **2** of equipment, in working order. **3** of a military operation, ready or equipped to perform a certain mission. —**op′er·a′tion·al·ly,** *adv.*

hat, āge, cãre, fär; let, ēqual, tėrm; it, īce
hot, ōpen, ôrder; oil, out; cup, pu̇t, rüle, ūse
əbove, takən, pencəl, lemən, circəs
ch, child; ng, long; sh, ship
th, thin; ᴛʜ, then; zh, measure

op·er·a·tive (op′ər ə tiv, op′ər ā′tiv, or op′rə tiv) *adj.* **1** operating; effective: *the laws operative in a community.* **2** having to do with work or productiveness: *operative departments of a manufacturing establishment.* **3** of or concerned with surgical operations: *The disease requires operative measures.* —*n. Informal.* **1** a worker; laborer. **2** a detective.

op·er·a·tor (op′ər ā′tər) *n.* **1** a person who operates. **2** a skilled worker who operates a machine, telephone switchboard, telegraph, etc. **3** a person who runs a factory, mine, etc. **4** *Informal.* a shrewd individual who manoeuvres people and events for his own purposes. **5** a person who speculates in stocks or a commodity. **6** a doctor who performs surgical operations; surgeon.

o·per·cu·lum (ō pėr′kyu̇ ləm) *n.* **-la** (-lə) or **-lums.** in biology, any lidlike part or organ; any flap covering an opening. [< L *operculum* < *operire* cover]

op·er·et·ta (op′ər et′ə) *n.* **-tas.** a short, amusing opera. [< Ital. *operetta,* dim. of *opera* opera]

o·phid·i·an (ō fid′ē ən) *n.* a snake. —*adj.* **1** like a snake. **2** of or having to do with snakes. [< NL *Ophidia* an order of reptiles < Gk. *ophidion,* dim. of *ophis* serpent]

O·phir (ō′fər) *n.* in the Bible, a place from which Solomon obtained gold. I Kings 9:28.

oph·thal·mi·a (of thal′mē ə) *n.* an acute infection of the eye or the membrane around the eye, which may sometimes cause blindness. [< LL < Gk. *ophthalmia* < *ophthalmos* eye; cf. *ōps* eye, *thalamos* chamber]

oph·thal·mic (of thal′mik) *adj.* **1** of or having to do with the eye. **2** having to do with or affected with ophthalmia.

oph·thal·mol·o·gist (of′thal mol′ə jist) *n.* a physician whose specialty is ophthalmology.

oph·thal·mol·o·gy (of′thal mol′ə jē) *n.* the science that deals with the structure, functions, and diseases of the eye. [< Gk. *ophthalmos* eye + E *-logy*]

oph·thal·mo·scope (of thal′mə skōp′) *n.* an instrument for examining the interior of the eye or the retina. [< Gk. *ophthalmos* eye + E *-scope*]

o·pi·ate (ō′pē it or ō′pē āt′) *n.* **1** any powerful drug containing opium or a derivative of opium (such as morphine) and used especially to dull pain or to bring sleep. **2** anything that quiets. —*adj.* **1** containing opium. **2** bringing sleep or ease. [< Med.L *opiatus* < L *opium* opium]

o·pine (ō pīn′) *v.* **o·pined, o·pin·ing.** *In humorous use.* hold or express an opinion; think. [< F < L *opinari*] —**o·pin′er,** *n.*

o·pin·ion (ə pin′yən or ō pin′yən) *n.* **1** what one thinks; belief not so strong as knowledge; judgment. **2** an impression; estimate: *Everyone has a poor opinion of a coward.* **3** a formal judgment made by an expert; professional advice. **4** in law, a statement by a judge or jury of the reasons for the decision of the court. [< L *opinio, -onis*]
Syn. 1 Opinion, view = what a person thinks about something. **Opinion** is the general word applying to what one thinks or believes about something, but particularly suggests a carefully thought out conclusion based on facts, but without the certainty of knowledge: *I try to learn the facts and form my own opinions.* **View** applies to a particular way of looking at something, and especially suggests a personal opinion affected by personal leanings or feelings: *His views are conservative.*

o·pin·ion·at·ed (ə pin′yən āt′id) *adj.* obstinate or conceited with regard to one's opinions; dogmatic.

o·pin·ion·a·tive (ə pin′yən ā′tiv) *adj.* opinionated. —**o·pin′ion·a·tive·ly,** *adv.* —**o·pin′ion·a′tive·ness,** *n.*

o·pi·um (ō′pē əm) *n.* a bitter, milky substance derived from a kind of poppy. Opium is a powerful drug that causes sleep and eases pain. [ME < L < Gk. *opion,* dim. of *opos* vegetable juice]

o·pos·sum (ə pos′əm) *n.* a small mammal that lives most of the time in trees, common in the S. United States and found in S. Ontario; possum. When caught or frightened, it becomes unconscious and appears to be dead. [< Algonquian word meaning "white animal"]

op·po·nent (ə pō′nənt) *n.* a person who is on the other side in a fight, game, or discussion; a person fighting, struggling, or speaking against another. —*adj.* opposing. [< L *opponens, -entis* < *ob-* against + *ponere* place]
Syn. *n.* **Opponent, antagonist, adversary** = someone against a person or thing. **Opponent** applies to someone on the other side in an argument, game, or other contest, or against a proposed plan, law, etc. but does not suggest personal ill will: *He defeated his opponent in the election.* **Antagonist,** more formal, suggests active, personal, and unfriendly opposition, often in a fight for power or control: *Hamlet and his uncle were antagonists.* **Adversary** now usually means a definitely hostile antagonist actively blocking or openly fighting another: *Gamblers found a formidable adversary in the new chief of police.*

op·por·tune (op′ər tūn′ or op′ər tün′) *adj.* fortunate; well-chosen; suitable; favorable: *You have come at a most opportune moment.* [< L *opportunus* favorable (of wind) < *ob portum* (*ferens*) (bringing) to port] —**op′por·tune′ly,** *adv.* —**op′por·tune′ness,** *n.* —**Syn.** See **timely.**

op·por·tun·ism (op′ər tūn′iz əm or op′ər tün′iz əm) *n.* the policy or practice of adapting thought and action to particular circumstances rather than to general principles.

op·por·tun·ist (op′ər tūn′ist or op′ər tün′ist) *n.* a person influenced more by particular circumstances than by general principles.

op·por·tu·ni·ty (op′ər tū′nə tē or op′ər tü′nə tē) *n.* **-ties.** a good chance; favorable time; convenient occasion.

op·pos·a·ble (ə pōz′ə bəl) *adj.* **1** capable of being opposed. **2** capable of being placed opposite something else. The human thumb is opposable to the fingers.

op·pose (ə pōz′) *v.* **-posed, -pos·ing. 1** be against; be in the way of; act, fight, or struggle against; try to hinder; resist: *The enemy opposed the advance of our army. Many people oppose the death penalty.* **2** set up against; place in the way of: *Let us oppose good nature to anger.* **3** put in contrast: *Love is opposed to hate.* **4** put in front of; cause to face: *oppose one's finger to one's thumb.* [ME < OF *opposer* < *op-* (< L *ob-*) against + *poser* put (see POSE[1])] —**op·pos′er,** *n.*
Syn. 1 Oppose, resist, withstand = act or stand against someone or something. **Oppose** = set oneself against a person or thing, especially an idea, plan, etc. but does not suggest the nature, purpose, form, or effectiveness of the action or stand taken: *We opposed the plan because of the cost.* **Resist** = make a stand and actively strive against an attack or force of some kind: *The bank messenger resisted the attempt to rob him.* **Withstand** emphasizes holding firm against attack: *The bridge withstood the flood.*

op·po·site (op′ə zit or op′sit) *adj.* **1** placed against; face to face; back to back: *The house straight across the street is opposite to ours.* **2** as different as can be; just contrary: *Sour is opposite to sweet.* **3** in botany, situated on diametrically opposed sides of an axis: *opposite leaves.* —*n.* a thing or person that is opposite: *Black is the opposite of white.*
—*prep.* opposite to: *opposite the church.* [< L *oppositus,* pp. of *opponere* < *ob-* against + *ponere* place] —**op′po·site·ly,** *adv.* —**op′po·site·ness,** *n.*
Syn. *adj.* **2 Opposite, contrary** = completely different (from each other). **Opposite** particularly suggests two things thought of as standing one at each end of a diameter, so far apart in position, nature, meaning, etc. that they can never be brought together: *"True" and "false" have opposite meanings.* **Contrary** particularly suggests two things going in opposite directions, or set against each other, often in strong disagreement or conflict: *Your statement is contrary to the facts.*

op·po·si·tion (op′ə zish′ən) *n.* **1** action against; resistance: *The mob offered opposition to the police.* **2** contrast: *His views were in opposition to mine.* **3** the political party or parties not in power: *In parliament, the party having the second largest number of elected members is called the official opposition.* **4** a placing opposite. **5** an opposite direction or position. **6** in astronomy, the position of two heavenly bodies when their longitude differs by 180 degrees. [< L *oppositio, -onis* < *opponere.* See OPPOSITE.]

op·press (ə pres′ or ō pres′) *v.* **1** govern harshly; keep down unjustly or by cruelty: *A good ruler will not oppress the poor.* **2** weigh down; lie heavily on; burden: *A sense of trouble ahead oppressed my spirits.* [< Med.L *oppressare,* ult. < L *ob-* against + *premere* press] —**Syn. 2** overburden, crush.

op·pres·sion (ə presh′ən or ō presh′ən) *n.* **1** an

oppressing; a burdening: *The oppression of the people by the nobles caused the war.* **2** a being oppressed or burdened: *They fought against oppression.* **3** cruel or unjust treatment. **4** a heavy, weary feeling. —**Syn. 3** tyranny, persecution, despotism. **4** weariness, lassitude, depression.

op·pres·sive (ə pres′iv or ō pres′iv) *adj.* **1** harsh; severe; unjust. **2** hard to bear; burdensome. —**op·pres′sive·ly,** *adv.* —**op·pres′sive·ness,** *n.*

op·pres·sor (ə pres′ər or ō pres′ər) *n.* a person who is cruel or unjust to people under him.

op·pro·bri·ous (ə prō′brē əs) *adj.* expressing scorn, reproach, or abuse: *Coward, liar, and thief are opprobrious names.* [< LL *opprobriosus*] —**op·pro′bri·ous·ly,** *adv.*

op·pro·bri·um (ə prō′brē əm) *n.* disgrace or reproach caused by shameful conduct; infamy; scorn; abuse. [< L *opprobrium,* ult. + *ob-* at + *probrum* infamy, reproach]

op·so·nin (op′sə nin) *n.* a substance in the blood serum that weakens microbes so that the white blood corpuscles can destroy them more easily. [< L *opsonium* relish (meat, fish) < Gk. *opsonion* pay, originally, relish-money < *opson* relish + *ōnos* price]

opt (opt) *v.* **1 opt for,** choose; decide on: *We will opt for the first alternative.* **2 opt out,** decide to leave, choose to drop out or keep out: *Several countries wanted to opt out of the alliance.* [< L *optare* choose, desire]

opt. 1 optative. **2** optical. **3** optics. **4** optional.

op·ta·tive (op′tə tiv) in grammar: —*adj.* **1** expressing a wish: "*Oh! that I had wings to fly!*" *is an optative expression.* **2 a** in Greek and certain other languages, having to do with the verbal mood that expresses desire, wish, etc. **b** having to do with distinctive verb forms with such meaning or function.—*n.* **1** the optative mood. **2** a verb in the optative mood. [< LL *optativus* < L *optare* wish]

op·tic (op′tik) *adj.* of the eye; of the sense of sight. —*n. Informal.* the eye. [< Med.L *opticus* < Gk. *optikos* < *op-* see]

op·ti·cal (op′tə kəl) *adj.* **1** of the eye; visual: *Being near-sighted is an optical defect.* **2** made to assist sight: *A telescope is an optical instrument.* **3** of vision and light in relation to each other. **4** of or having to do with optics. —**op′ti·cal·ly,** *adv.*

op·ti·cian (op tish′ən) *n.* a maker or seller of eyeglasses and other optical instruments. [< F *opticien*]

optic nerve a nerve that goes from the eye to the brain. See **eye** for diagram.

op·tics (op′tiks) *n.* the science that deals with light and vision.

op·ti·mal (op′tə məl) *adj.* most favorable.

op·ti·mism (op′tə miz′əm) *n.* **1** a tendency to look on the bright side of things. **2** a belief that everything will turn out for the best. **3** in philosophy, the doctrine that the existing world is the best of all possible worlds. [< NL *optimismus* < L *optimus* best]

op·ti·mist (op′tə mist) *n.* **1** a person who looks on the bright side of things. **2** a person who believes that everything in life will turn out for the best. **3** a person who believes in the doctrine of optimism.

op·ti·mis·tic (op′tə mis′tik) *adj.* **1** inclined to look on the bright side of things. **2** hoping for the best. **3** having to do with optimism. —**op′ti·mis′ti·cal·ly,** *adv.*

op·ti·mum (op′tə məm) *n.* **-mums, -ma** (-mə). the best or most favorable point, degree, amount, etc. for the purpose. [< L]

op·tion (op′shən) *n.* **1** the right or freedom to choose. **2** a choosing; choice: *Our option was to take Latin instead of German.* **3** the thing chosen: *John's option was German.* **4** the right to buy something at a certain price within a certain time: *The man paid $500 for an option on the land.* —*v.* obtain or grant an option in reference to (something). [< L *optio, -onis*] —**Syn. 2** preference.

op·tion·al (op′shən əl) *adj.* left to one's choice; not required. —**op′tion·al·ly,** *adv.*

op·tom·e·trist (op tom′ə trist) *n.* a person skilled in examining the eyes and prescribing the kind of glasses needed.

op·tom·e·try (op tom′ə trē) *n.* the measurement of powers of sight; the practice or art of testing eyesight. [< Gk. *optos* seen + E *-metry*]

op·u·lence (op′yů ləns) *n.* **1** wealth; riches. **2** abundance; plenty.

op·u·lent (op′yů lənt) *adj.* **1** wealthy; rich. **2** abundant; plentiful. [< L *opulens, -entis* < *ops* power, resources] —**Syn. 1** affluent. **2** profuse.

o·pus (ō′pəs) *n.* **op·er·a** or **o·pus·es.** a literary work or musical composition: *The violinist played his own opus, No. 16.* [< L]

☛ **opera, opuses.** Because the Latin plural is identical with *opera,* "musical drama," it is now generally replaced, except in learned use, by *opuses.*

or[1] (ôr; *unstressed,* ər) *conj.* **1** a word used to express a choice, alternative, difference, etc.: *You can go or stay. Is it sweet or sour?* **2** and if not; otherwise: *Either eat this or go hungry. Hurry, or you will be late.* **3** that is; being the same as: *This is the end or last part.* [OE (unstressed) *ā(hwæ)ther* < *ā* ever + *hwæther* either, whether]

or[2] (ôr) *prep. conj. Archaic.* before; ere. [OE *ār* early, confused with OE *ǣr* ere]

or[3] (ôr) *n.* in heraldry, gold or yellow. [< F < L *aurum* gold]

-or *suffix.* **1** a person or thing that ——s, as in *actor, accelerator, orator, survivor, sailor.* **2** an act, state, condition, quality, characteristic, etc., especially in words from Latin, as in *error, horror, labor, terror.* [< L]

☛ **-or, -our.** In Canada usage varies, although most newspapers, magazines, etc. prefer *-or* in such words as *color, honor,* and *neighbor.* In the United States preference for *-or* is virtually universal. However, *Saviour* (referring to Jesus Christ) and *glamour* are considered exceptions, both in U.S. and Canadian usage. But even in British usage, which prefers *-our* spellings, derivatives ending in *-ation, -ary, -ific,* and *-ous* are spelled with *-or-*. Thus, *honorific, honorary, humorous, odoriferous* are so spelled on both sides of the Atlantic.

o.r. owner's risk.

OR or **O.R. 1** operating room. **2** orderly room.

or·a·cle (ôr′ə kəl) *n.* **1** in ancient times: **a** an answer given by a god through a priest or priestess to some question. **b** the place where the god gave answers. A famous oracle was at Delphi. **c** the priest, priestess, or other means by which the god's answer was given. **2** a very wise person. **3** something regarded as a reliable and sure guide. [ME < OF < L *oraculum* < *orare,* originally, recite solemnly]

o·rac·u·lar (ô rak′yů lər) *adj.* **1** of or like an oracle. **2** with a hidden meaning that is difficult to make out. **3** very wise. —**o·rac′u·lar·ly,** *adv.*

o·ral (ô′rəl) *adj.* **1** spoken; using speech. **2** of the mouth. **3** taken by mouth: *oral medicine.* [< L *os, oris* mouth]

☛ **oral, verbal.** Strictly, *oral* means "spoken," and *verbal,* used as an adjective, means "in words"; but *verbal* has been used so long with the same sense as *oral* that there is no longer a distinction between the two: *He gave an oral report. They had only a verbal agreement.*

o·ral·ly (ô′rəl ē) *adv.* **1** by or through spoken words: *The speech was delivered orally.* **2** by the mouth: *The medicine was taken orally.*

-orama *combining form.* variant of *-rama.*

or·ange (ôr′inj) *n.* **1** a round, reddish-yellow, juicy, edible fruit that grows in warm climates. **2** the tree it grows on. The orange has fragrant white blossoms. **3** any fruit or tree that suggests an orange. **4** a reddish yellow. **5** a soft drink flavored with orange juice. —*adj.* **1** of or like an orange. **2** reddish-yellow. [ME < OF *orenge* < Sp. *naranja* < Arabic < Persian *narang*; in OF blended with the word *or* meaning "gold"] —**or′ange·like′,** *adj.*

Or·ange (ôr′inj) *n.* a princely family of Europe that ruled the former principality of Orange in W. Europe, now a part of S.E. France. William III of England was of this family, and so is the present royal family of the Netherlands.

or·ange·ade (ôr′inj ād′) *n.* a drink made of orange juice, sugar, and water.

Orange Association the Loyal Orange Association.

Or·ange·ism (ôr′inj iz′əm) *n.* the principles and practices of the Loyal Orange Association.

Or·ange·man (ôr′inj mən) *n.* **-men** (-mən). **1** a member of a secret society, formed in the north of Ireland in 1795, to uphold the Protestant religion and Protestant control in Ireland. **2** a member of the Loyal Orange Association.

Orange Order the Loyal Orange Association.

orange pekoe a black tea that comes from Ceylon or India.

o·rang-ou·tang (ô rang′ü tang′) *n.* orang-utan.

o·rang-u·tan (ô rang′ü tan′) *n.* a large ape of the forests of Borneo and Sumatra, having very long arms and long, reddish-brown hair. Orang-utans live much of the time in trees and eat fruits and leaves. [< Malay *orangutan* < *orang* man + *utan* wild]

o·rate (ô rāt′ or ô′rāt) *v.* **o·rat·ed, o·rat·ing.** *Informal.* make an oration; talk in a grand manner. [< *oration*]

o·ra·tion (ô rā′shən) *n.* **1** a formal public speech delivered on a special occasion. **2** a speech given in an overly formal or affected style. [< L *oratio, -onis* < *orare* speak formally. Doublet of ORISON.] —**Syn.** address. See **speech.**

or·a·tor (ôr′ə tər) *n.* **1** a person who makes an oration. **2** a person who can speak very well in public.

or·a·tor·i·cal (ôr′ə tôr′ə kəl) *adj.* **1** of oratory; having to do with orators or oratory: *an oratorical contest.* **2** characteristic of orators or oratory: *an oratorical manner.* —**or′a·tor′i·cal·ly,** *adv.*

or·a·to·ri·o (ôr′ə tô′rē ō′) *n.* **-ri·os. 1** a musical drama performed without action, costumes, or scenery, for solo voices, chorus, and orchestra. Oratorios are usually based on Biblical or historical themes. **2** the art of creating or performing oratorios. **3** a performance of an oratorio. **4** the music of an oratorio. [< Ital. *oratorio,* originally, place of prayer < LL *oratorium.* Doublet of ORATORY[2].]

or·a·to·ry[1] (ôr′ə tô′rē) *n.* **1** skill in public speaking; fine speaking. **2** the art of public speaking. [< L (*ars*) *oratoria* oratorical (art), ult. < *orare* plead, speak formally] —**Syn. 1** eloquence.

or·a·to·ry[2] (ôr′ə tô′rē) *n.* **-ries.** a small chapel; a room set apart for prayer. [< LL *oratorium* < *orare* pray. Doublet of ORATORIO.]

orb (ôrb) *n.* **1** a sphere; globe. **2** a jewelled sphere, symbol of royal power. **3** the sun, moon, a planet or star. **4** *Esp.Poetic.* the eyeball or eye. —*v.* **1** form into a circle or sphere. **2** *Poetic.* encircle; enclose. [< L *orbis* circle] —**Syn.** *n.* **1** ball.

or·bic·u·lar (ôr bik′yů lər) *adj.* like a circle or sphere; rounded. [< LL *orbicularis* < L *orbiculus,* dim. of *orbis* circle]

or·bic·u·late (ôr bik′yů lit or ôr bik′yů lāt′) *adj.* orbicular. [< L *orbiculatus* < *orbiculus.* See ORBICULAR.]

An orbicular leaf

or·bit (ôr′bit) *n.* **1** the path of the earth or any one of the planets about the sun. **2** the path of any heavenly body about another heavenly body. See **aphelion** for diagram. **3** the path of a man-made satellite. **4** the regular course of life or experience. **5** the bony cavity or socket in which the eyeball is set. [< L *orbita* wheel track < *orbis* wheel, circle]
—*v.* **1** go round in an orbit: *Many artificial satellites are orbiting the earth.* **2** send round in an orbit: *The Russians are about to orbit a new satellite.* **3** of a satellite, etc., arrive in its orbit; achieve orbital velocity.

or·bit·al (ôr′bə təl) *adj.* of an orbit.

or·chard (ôr′chərd) *n.* **1** a piece of ground on which fruit trees are grown. **2** the trees in an orchard. [OE *ortgeard* < *ort-* (apparently < L *hortus* garden) + *geard* yard[1]]

or·ches·tra (ôr′kis trə) *n.* **1** a relatively large group of musicians organized to rehearse and play together. An orchestra is usually distinguished from a band by its having violins and other stringed instruments: *a symphony orchestra, a dance orchestra.* **2** the violins, cellos, clarinets, and other instruments played together by the musicians in an orchestra. **3** of a theatre: **a** the part just in front of the stage, where the musicians sit to play. **b** the main floor, especially the part near the front. [< L < Gk. *orchēstra* the space where the chorus of dancers performed, ult. < *orcheesthai* dance]

or·ches·tral (ôr kes′trəl) *adj.* of or having to do with an orchestra; composed for or performed by an orchestra. —**or·ches′tral·ly,** *adv.*

or·ches·trate (ôr′kis trāt′) *v.* **-trat·ed, -trat·ing.** compose or arrange (music) for performance by an orchestra.

hat, āge, cãre, fär; let, ēqual, tėrm; it, īce
hot, ōpen, ôrder; oil, out; cup, půt, rüle, ūse
əbove, takən, pencəl, lemən, circəs
ch, child; ng, long; sh, ship
th, thin; ŦH, then; zh, measure

or·ches·tra·tion (ôr′kis trā′shən) *n.* **1** an arrangement of music for an orchestra. **2** the art of creating such an arrangement.

or·chid (ôr′kid) *n.* **1** a plant having beautiful, unusually shaped flowers that are formed of three petal-like sepals and three petals, one petal being very different from the other two. **2** its flower. **3** a light purple. —*adj.* light-purple. [< NL *orchideae,* ult. < L < Gk. *orchis* testicle; from shape of root]

or·dain (ôr dān′) *v.* **1** order; fix; decide; appoint; establish as a law. **2** officially appoint or consecrate as a clergyman. [ME < OF < L *ordinare* < *ordo, -inis* order] —**or·dain′er,** *n.* —**Syn. 1** decree, prescribe.

or·deal (ôr dēl′ or ôr′dēl) *n.* **1** a severe test or experience. **2** in early times, an effort to decide the guilt or innocence of an accused person by making him do something dangerous such as putting his hand in a fire or taking poison. It was supposed that an innocent person would not be harmed by such an ordeal. [OE *ordǣl* judgment] —**Syn. 1** trial.

or·der (ôr′dər) *n.* **1** the way one thing follows another: *in order of size, in alphabetical order.* **2** a condition in which every part or piece is in its right place: *put a room in order.* **3** a condition; state: *My affairs are in good order.* **4** the way the world works; way things happen: *the order of nature.* **5** the state or condition of things in which the law is obeyed and there is no disturbance: *keep order.* **6** the principles and rules by which a meeting is run. **7** a telling what to do; command: *The orders of the captain must be obeyed.* **8** the direction of a court or judge made in writing and not included in a judgment. **9** a paper saying that money is to be given or paid, or something handed over: *a postal money order.* **10** a statement or list of things telling a store or tradesman what you wish sent. **11** a kind or sort: *have ability of a high order.* **12** in biology, a group in the classifying of plants and animals that is below or smaller than a class, but larger than a family. The rose family, the bean family, and several others belong to one order. **13** a social rank, grade, or class: *all orders of society.* **14** a rank or position in the church: *the order of bishops.* **15** ordination. **16** a group of people banded together for some purpose or united by something they share in common: *the Franciscan order, the Imperial Order Daughters of the Empire.* **17** a society to which one is admitted as an honor: *the Order of the Golden Fleece.* **18** a modern fraternal organization: *the Order of Freemasons.* **19** a badge worn by those belonging to an honorary order. **20** any one of the classical styles of columns and architecture: *the Doric, Ionic, and Corinthian orders.* **21** the regular form of worship for a given occasion. **22** a portion or serving of food served in a restaurant, etc.: *I'd like one order of chips, please.*

Doric

Ionic

Corinthian

The Greek orders of architecture (def. 20)

by order, according to an order given by the proper person: *by order of the Premier.*
call to order, ask to be quiet and start work.
in holy orders, being a clergyman.
in order, a in the right arrangement or condition. **b** working properly. **c** allowed by the rules of a meeting, etc.
in order that, so that; with the purpose that.
in order to, as a means to; with a view to; for the purpose of: *She worked hard in order to win the prize.*
in short order, quickly.
made to order, made to fit a certain person or place.
on order, ordered but not yet received.
on the order of, resembling; similar to.
out of order, a in a wrong arrangement or condition.

b not working properly. **c** against the rules of a meeting.
take holy orders, become a clergyman.
to order, according to the buyer's wishes.
—*v.* **1** put in order; arrange: *order one's affairs.* **2** tell what to do; give an order; command; bid: *He ordered that the prisoners be handcuffed.* **3** give order, directions, etc.: *Please order for me.* **4** give (a store, etc.) an order for: *He ordered a new car from the dealer.* **5** decide; will: *The gods ordered it otherwise.* **6** invest with clerical rank or authority. **7 order about** or **around,** send here and there; tell to do this and that. [ME < OF *ordre* < L *ordo, -inis* row, rank] —**Syn.** *n.* **1** sequence, succession. -*v.* **1** regulate. **2** direct, instruct. See **command.**

order in council a regulation made by a federal or provincial cabinet under the authority of the Governor General or the Lieutenant-Governor.

or·der·ly (ôr′dər lē) *adj. n.* **-lies.** —*adj.* **1** in order; with regular arrangements, method, or system: *an orderly arrangement of dishes on shelves, an orderly mind.* **2** keeping order; well-behaved or regulated: *an orderly class.* **3** concerned with carrying out orders; being on duty. —*n.* **1** in the army, a non-commissioned officer or private soldier who attends a superior officer to carry orders, etc. **2** a hospital attendant who keeps things clean and in order. —**or′der·li·ness,** *n.*
Syn. *adj.* **1 Orderly, methodical, systematic** = following a plan of arrangement or action. **Orderly** suggests lack of confusion and arrangement of details or things in proper relation to each other according to some rule or scheme: *The chairs are in orderly rows.* **Methodical** suggests an orderly way of doing something, following step by step a plan carefully worked out in advance or regularly followed: *Police made a methodical search for the weapon.* **Systematic** adds to *methodical* and emphasizes the idea of thoroughness and completeness: *The committee began a systematic investigation of crime.*

orderly officer officer of the day.

or·di·nal (ôr′də nəl) *adj.* **1** showing order or position in a series. **2** in biology, having to do with an order of animals or plants. —*n.* **1** an ordinal number. **2** a book of special forms for certain church ceremonies. [ME < LL *ordinalis* < L *ordo, -inis* order]

ordinal number a number that shows order or position in a series. *First, second, third,* etc. are ordinal numbers; *one, two, three,* etc. are cardinal numbers. ☛ See **cardinal number** for usage note.

or·di·nance (ôr′də nəns) *n.* **1** a rule or law made by authority; decree: *Some cities have ordinances forbidding the use of soft coal.* **2** an established religious ceremony. [ME < OF *ordenance,* ult. < L *ordinare* arrange, regulate. See ORDAIN.] —**Syn. 1** canon, regulation.

or·di·nar·i·ly (ôr′də ner′ə lē or ôr′də ner′ə lē) *adv.* **1** usually; regularly. **2** to the usual extent.

or·di·nar·y (ôr′də ner′ē) *adj. n.* **-nar·ies.** —*adj.* **1** usual; regular; customary: *Jack's ordinary supper consists of bread and milk.* **2** somewhat below the average: *The speech was ordinary and tiresome.*
—*n.* **1 out of the ordinary,** unusual; not regular or customary. **2** *Archaic.* **a** a meal served at a fixed price. **b** an inn; dining room of an inn. **3** a person who has authority in his own right, especially a bishop or a judge. **4** a form for saying Mass. **5** in heraldry, a bearing of the earliest, simplest, and commonest kind, usually bound by straight lines. **6 in ordinary,** in regular service: *physician in ordinary to the king.* [< L *ordinarius* < *ordo, -inis* row, rank] —**Syn.** *adj.* **1** normal, habitual, wonted. See **common. 2** mediocre, inferior.

or·di·nate (ôr′də nit or ôr′də nāt′) *n.* a vertical line drawn on a graph to define a point in a system of co-ordinates. [< L *ordinatus,* pp. of *ordinare.* See ORDAIN.]

An ordinate: P, any point; PM and NO, the ordinate of P; YY, the axis of the ordinate

or·di·na·tion (ôr′də nā′shən) *n.* **1** the act or ceremony of admitting a person to the ministry of a church. **2** the state of being admitted as a minister in a church. [< L *ordinatio, -onis* < *ordinare.* See ORDAIN.]

ord·nance (ôrd′nəns) *n.* **1** artillery; big guns or cannon. **2** military weapons and equipment of all kinds. [var. of *ordinance*]

Or·do·vi·cian (ôr′də vish′ən) in geology: —*n.* **1** an early period of the Paleozoic era, beginning approximately 445 million years ago. **2** the rocks formed in this period. See the chart under **geology.**
—*adj.* of or having to do with an early Paleozoic period or the rocks formed during it. [< L *Ordovices* an ancient Celtic tribe in Wales where this rock abounds]

or·dure (ôr′jər or ôr′dyůr) *n.* **1** filth; dung. **2** vile language. [ME < OF *ordure* < *ord* filthy < L *horridus* horrid]

ore (ôr) *n.* rock, sand, or dirt containing some metal. [OE *ār* brass]

ö·re (œ′rə) *n.* **1** a unit of money in Norway and Denmark, worth 1/100 of a krone. **2** a unit of money in Sweden, worth 1/100 of a krona. **3** a coin worth one öre. [< Danish, Norwegian, Swedish, ult. < L *aureus* a gold coin]

Ore. Oregon.

O·re·ad or **o·re·ad** (ô′rē ad′) *n.* in Greek mythology, a mountain nymph. [< L *Oreas, -adis* < Gk. *Oreias* < *oros* mountain]

ore·bod·y (ôr′bod′ē) *n.* **-bod·ies.** a vein or bed of ore.

Oreg. Oregon.

o·reg·a·no (ə reg′ə nō′ or ôr′ə gä′nō) *n.* a type of mint having fragrant leaves that are used in seasoning. [< Sp. *orégano* < L < Gk. *origanon* wild marjoram]

O·res·tes (ô res′tēz) *n.* in Greek mythology, the son of Agamemnon and Clytemnestra, who killed his mother because she had murdered his father. He was pursued by the Furies for his crime.

or·gan (ôr′gən) *n.* **1** a musical instrument having a keyboard and pedals that regulate the flow of air through pipes of different lengths, thus producing different tones. Organs are found in most churches. **2** any of various other musical instruments with organlike tones, such as the electric organ, reed organ, mouth organ, or accordion. **3** any part of an animal or plant that is composed of various tissues organized to perform some particular function. An eye, lung, stomach, root, stamen, or pistil is an organ. **4** a means of action; instrument: *A court is an organ of government.* **5** a means of giving information or expressing opinions; newspaper or magazine that speaks for and gives the views of a political party or some other organization. [ME < OF < L < Gk. *organon* instrument < *ergon* work]

or·gan·dy or **or·gan·die** (ôr′gən dē) *n.* **-dies.** a fine, thin, stiff muslin, used for dresses, curtains, etc. [< F *organdi*]

organ grinder a person who plays a hand organ by turning a crank.

or·gan·ic (ôr gan′ik) *adj.* **1** of the bodily organs; vital; affecting the structure of an organ: *an organic disease.* **2** produced by animal or plant activities: *Starch is an organic compound.* **3** having organs, or an organized physical structure, as plants and animals have; not of the mineral kingdom. **4** made up of related parts, but being a unit; co-ordinated: *Canada is an organic whole made up of ten provinces.* **5** that is part of the structure or constitution of a person or thing; fundamental: *The British North America Act is the organic law of Canada.* **6** of carbon; containing carbon: *organic compounds.* [< L *organicus* < Gk. *organikos* < *organon* instrument] —**Syn. 4** organized. **5** inherent, innate, constitutional.

or·gan·i·cal·ly (ôr gan′ik lē) *adv.* **1** in an organic manner. **2** by or with animal or plant organs. **3** in organization. **4** as part of an organization.

organic chemistry the branch of chemistry that deals with compounds of carbon. Organic chemistry teaches us about foods and fuels.

or·gan·ism (ôr′gən iz′əm) *n.* **1** a living body having organs or an organized structure; an individual animal or plant. **2** a very tiny animal or plant. **3** a whole made up of related parts that work together. Human society, or any community, may be spoken of as a social organism.

or·gan·ist (ôr′gən ist) *n.* a person who plays an organ.

or·gan·i·za·tion (ôr′gən ə zā′shən or ôr′gən ī zā′shən) *n.* **1** a group of persons united for some purpose. Churches, clubs, and political parties are organizations. **2** the act of organizing; the grouping and arranging of parts to form a whole: *The organization of a big picnic takes time and thought.* **3** the way in which a thing's parts are arranged to work together: *The organization of the human body is very complicated.* 4 something made up of related parts, each having a special duty: *A tree is an organization of roots, trunk, branches, leaves, and fruit.* —**or′gan·i·za′tion·al,** *adj.* —**or′gan·i·za′tion·al·ly,** *adv.*

or·gan·ize (ôr′gən īz′) *v.* **-ized, -iz·ing. 1** put into working order, get together and arrange: *The explorer organized an expedition to the North Pole.* **2** combine in a company, society, party, labor union, etc. **3** furnish with organs. [ME < LL *organizare* < L *organum* < Gk. *organon.* See ORGAN.] —**or′gan·iz′a·ble,** *adj.* —**or′gan·iz′er,** *n.* —**Syn. 1** systematize, form.

organized labor or **labour** workers who belong to labor unions.

or·gan·za (ôr gan′zə) *n.* a crisp, sheer, silky fabric of silk, rayon, nylon, etc., used in making dresses. [probably < *Lorganza,* a trade name]

or·gasm (ôr′gaz əm) *n.* **1** the climax or culmination of sexual excitement. **2** an instance of frenzied excitement or behavior. [NL *orgasmus* < Gk. *orgasmos* < *orgaein* swell]

or·gi·as·tic (ôr′jē as′tik) *adj.* of, having to do with, or of the nature of orgies; wild; frenzied. [< Gk. *orgiastikos,* ult. < *orgia* secret rites] —**or′gi·as′ti·cal·ly,** *adv.*

or·gy (ôr′jē) *n.* **-gies. 1** a wild, drunken revel. **2 a** a period of uncontrolled indulgence. **b** a period within which controls are lacking or ineffective: *an orgy of bloodshed or crime.* **3 orgies,** *pl.* secret rites or ceremonies in the worship of certain Greek and Roman gods, especially Dionysus, the god of wine, celebrated with drinking, wild dancing, and singing. [< L < Gk. *orgia* secret rites]

o·ri·el (ô′rē əl) *n.* a bay window projecting from the outer face of a wall. [ME < OF *oriol* porch]

An oriel

o·ri·ent (*n. adj.* ô′rē ənt; *v.* ô′ri ent) *n.* **1 Orient,** the East; countries in Asia. China and Japan are important nations of the Orient. **2** *Poetic.* the east. —*adj.* **1** *Poetic.* eastern. **2** bright; shining. **3** rising. —*v.* orientate. [< L *oriens, -entis,* ppr. of *oriri* rise with reference to the rising sun] ☛ See **orientate** for usage note.

O·ri·en·tal (ô′rē en′təl) *adj.* **1** Eastern; of the Orient. **2 oriental,** eastern: *oriental music.* —*n.* a native of the East. Turks, Arabs, Iranians, Hindus, and Chinese are Orientals.

O·ri·en·tal·ism or **o·ri·en·tal·ism** (ô′rē en′təl iz′əm) *n.* **1** Oriental character or characteristics; an Oriental peculiarity. **2** a knowledge of Oriental languages, literature, etc.

O·ri·en·tal·ist or **o·ri·en·tal·ist** (ô′rē en′təl ist) *n.* a person skilled in Oriental languages, literature, history, etc.

o·ri·en·tate (ô′rē en tāt′) *v.* **-tat·ed, -tat·ing. 1** put facing east. **2** place so that it faces in any indicated direction: *The building is orientated north and south.* **3** find the direction of. **4** place in the proper position. **5 orientate oneself,** get in the right relationship with one's surroundings; adjust oneself to a situation.

☛ **orientate, orient.** Though **orientate** has been considered the preferred form in British and Canadian use, **orient,** which is the common form in the United States, seems to be gaining in popularity among educated speakers of the language.

o·ri·en·ta·tion (ô′rē en tā′shən) *n.* **1** an orienting. **2** a being oriented. **3** a finding out of the actual facts or conditions and putting oneself in the right relation to them. **4** the ability of many birds and other animals to find their way back to their usual habitat after going to another point distant from it. **5** a general point of view toward a topic or object.

or·i·fice (ôr′ə fis) *n.* a mouth; opening; hole: *the orifice of a tube or pipe.* [< F < L *orificium* < *os, oris* mouth + *facere* make]

or·i·flamme (ôr′ə flam′) *n.* **1** the red banner carried as a military ensign by the early kings of France. **2** any banner used as an ensign or standard. **3** anything that is bright, colorful, or showy. [ME < OF *orieflambe*; ult. < L *aurum* gold + *flamma* flame]

orig. 1 origin. **2** originally.

hat, āge, cãre, fär; let, ēqual, tėrm; it, īce
hot, ōpen, ôrder; oil, out; cup, pu̇t, rüle, ūse
əbove, takən, pencəl, lemən, circəs
ch, child; ng, long; sh, ship
th, thin; ᴛʜ, then; zh, measure

or·i·ga·mi (ôr′i gä′mē) *n.* a kind of paper sculpture developed by the Japanese in which paper is folded to make birds, flowers, etc. [< Japanese]

or·i·gin (ôr′ə jin) *n.* **1** the thing from which anything comes; source; beginning. **2** parentage; ancestry; birth: *The general was a man of humble origin.* **3** the act or fact of rising or springing from a particular source; derivation: *these and other reports of like origin.* [< L *origo, -ginis* < *oriri* rise] —**Syn. 1** root.

o·rig·i·nal (ə rij′ə nəl) *adj.* **1** belonging to the beginning; first; earliest: *the original settlers.* **2** new; fresh; novel: *plan an original game for the party.* **3** able to do, make, or think something new; inventive. **4** not copied, imitated, or translated from something else.
—*n.* **1** anything from which something else is copied, imitated, or translated. **2** the language in which a book was first written. **3** an unusual person; queer person. **4** the origin; source. —**Syn.** *adj.* **1** initial. **3** creative, ingenious.

o·rig·i·nal·i·ty (ə rij′ə nal′ə tē) *n.* **1** the ability to do, make, or think up something new. **2** freshness; novelty. **3** a being original.

o·rig·i·nal·ly (ə rij′ə nəl ē) *adv.* **1** by origin: *The family was originally Irish.* **2** at first; in the first place: *a house originally small.* **3** in an original manner.

original sin 1 in Christian theology, a depravity, or tendency to evil, held to be innate in mankind and transmitted from Adam in consequence of his sin. **2** in Roman Catholic theology, the privation of sanctifying grace in consequence of Adam's sin.

o·rig·i·nate (ə rij′ə nāt′) *v.* **-nat·ed, -nat·ing. 1** cause to be; invent. **2** come into being; begin; arise. —**o·rig′i·na′tor,** *n.*

o·rig·i·na·tion (ə rij′ə nā′shən) *n.* **1** an originating. **2** origin.

o·rig·i·na·tive (ə rij′ə nə tiv or ə rij′ə nā′tiv) *adj.* inventive; creative.

o·ri·ole (ô′rē əl or ô′rē ōl′) *n.* **1** any of several North American birds having yellow- or orange-and-black feathers. **2** any of several European birds having yellow-and-black feathers. [< NL *oriolus* < OF, ult. < L *aurum* gold]

O·ri·on (ô rī′ən) *n.* a constellation near the equator of the heavens, thought by the ancients to suggest a man with a belt around his waist and a sword by his side.

or·i·son (ôr′ə zən) *n.* *Archaic or poetic.* a prayer. [ME < OF < LL *oratio, -onis* prayer < L *oratio* speech < *orare* pray. Doublet of ORATION.]

Or·lon (ôr′lon) *n.* *Trademark.* a light-weight synthetic fibre that resists sun, water, and chemicals, used for clothing, curtains, sails, awnings, etc.

or·mo·lu (ôr′mə lü′) *n.* an alloy of copper and zinc, used to imitate gold. Ormolu is used in decorating furniture, clocks, etc. [< F *or moulu* ground gold]

or·na·ment (*n.* ôr′nə mənt; *v.* ôr′nə ment′) *n.* **1** something pretty; something to add beauty: *Jewellery and vases are ornaments.* **2** the use of ornaments. **3** a person or act that adds beauty, grace, or honor. **4** things used in church services, such as the organ, bells, silver plate, etc. **5** in music, an additional note or notes introduced as an embellishment but not essential to the harmony or melody. —*v.* add beauty to; make more pleasing or attractive; decorate. [ME < OF < L *ornamentum* < *ornare* adorn] —**Syn.** *n.* **1** adornment, decoration. -*v.* See **decorate.**

or·na·men·tal (ôr′nə men′təl) *adj.* **1** of or having to do with ornament: *ornamental purposes.* **2** for ornament; used as an ornament: *ornamental plants.* **3** decorative: *ornamental vases.* —**or′na·men′tal·ly,** *adv.*

or·na·men·ta·tion (ôr′nə men tā′shən) *n.* **1** the act of ornamenting or the condition of being ornamented. **2** decorations; ornaments.

or·nate (ôr nāt′) *adj.* **1** much adorned; much ornamented: *She liked ornate furniture.* **2** characterized by the use of elaborate figures of speech, flowery language, etc.: *an ornate style of writing.* [< L *ornatus*, pp. of *ornare* adorn] —**or·nate′ly,** *adv.* —**or·nate′ness,** *n.* —**Syn.** elaborate, showy.

or·ner·y (ôr′nər ē) *adj. Informal or dialect.* **1** inferior. **2** homely. **3** mean in disposition. **4** low; vile. [contraction of *ordinary*] —**or′ner·i·ness,** *n.*

or·ni·tho·log·i·cal (ôr′nə thə loj′ə kəl) *adj.* dealing with birds.

or·ni·thol·o·gist (ôr′nə thol′ə jist) *n.* a person who studies birds or who knows much about birds.

or·ni·thol·o·gy (ôr′nə thol′ə jē) *n.* **1** the branch of zoology that deals with birds. **2** a book on this subject. [< NL *ornithologia* < Gk. *ornis, -nithos* bird + *-logos* treating of]

o·ro·tund (ô′rə tund′) *adj.* **1** strong, full, rich, and clear in voice or speech. **2** pompous; bombastic. [alteration of L *ore rotundo*, literally, with round mouth]

or·phan (ôr′fən) *n.* a child whose parents are dead; child whose father or mother is dead. —*adj.* **1** of or for orphans: *an orphan asylum.* **2** without a father or mother or both. —*v.* make an orphan of. [< LL < Gk. *orphanos* bereaved]

or·phan·age (ôr′fən ij) *n.* **1** a home for orphans. **2** the condition of being an orphan.

Or·phe·an (ôr fē′ən) *adj.* **1** of or having to do with Orpheus. **2** like the music of Orpheus.

Or·phe·us (ôr′fē əs or ôr′fyůs) *n.* in Greek mythology, the son of Calliope and Apollo, who played his lyre so sweetly that animals and even trees and rocks followed him. With his music he charmed Pluto into releasing his wife Eurydice from Hades, but he lost her again when he disobeyed Pluto's order not to look back at her before reaching Earth.

Or·phic (ôr′fik) *adj.* **1** of or having to do with Orpheus. **2** having to do with religious or philosophical cults ascribed to Orpheus as founder. **3** Also, **orphic.** mystic; oracular. **4** melodious; entrancing.

Or·ping·ton (ôr′ping tən) *n.* **1** a breed of large buff, white, or black chickens. **2** a chicken of this breed. [< *Orpington*, a town in Kent, England]

or·rer·y (ôr′ər ē) *n.* **-rer·ies.** a device with balls representing various planets, that are moved by clockwork to illustrate motions of the solar system. [after Charles Boyle, Earl of *Orrery* (1676-1731), who first had such a device made]

or·ris (ôr′is) *n.* **1** orrisroot. **2** the plant that it grows on; a kind of iris. [apparently an alteration of *iris*]

or·ris·root (ôr′is rüt′) *n.* a fragrant rootstock of a variety of iris, used in making perfume, toothpaste, etc.

ortho- *combining form.* **1** straight, as in *orthopterous.* **2** correct; accepted, as in *orthodox.* **3** correcting irregularities in; corrective, as in *orthodontia.* [< Gk. *orthos* straight]

or·tho·don·tia (ôr′thə don′shə or ôr′thə don′shē ə) *n.* the branch of dentistry that deals with straightening and adjusting teeth. [< NL < Gk. *orthos* straight + *odōn, odontos* tooth]

or·tho·don·tist (ôr′thə don′tist) *n.* a dentist who specializes in orthodontia.

or·tho·dox (ôr′thə doks′) *adj.* **1** generally accepted, especially in religion. **2** having generally accepted views or opinions, especially in religion. **3** approved by convention; usual; customary: *The orthodox Christmas dinner is turkey and plum pudding.* [< LL < Gk. *orthodoxos* < *orthos* correct + *doxa* opinion < *dokeein* think]

Or·tho·dox (ôr′thə doks′) *adj.* **1** of or having to do with the Eastern Church or any of various national churches conforming to its doctrines. **2** of or having to do with the branch of Judaism adhering most closely to ancient customs and traditions. **3** of or having to do with the branch of Quakers adhering most closely to the original traditions of the Society of Friends.

Orthodox Church a group of Christian churches in E. Europe and W. Asia that do not recognize the Pope as the supreme head of the Church.

or·tho·dox·y (ôr′thə dok′sē) *n.* **-dox·ies.** the holding of correct or generally accepted beliefs; orthodox practice, especially in religion; a being orthodox.

or·tho·ep·ic (ôr thō ep′ik) *adj.* **1** relating to correct pronunciation. **2** describing the relationship between spelling and pronunciation: *orthoepic rules.*

or·tho·e·pist (ôr thō′ə pist or ôr′thō ə pist) *n.* a person who knows much about the pronunciation of words.

or·tho·e·py (ôr thō′ə pē or ôr′thō ə pē) *n.* **1** correct pronunciation. **2** the part of grammar that deals with pronunciation; phonology. [< Gk. *orthoepeia* < *orthos* correct + *epos* utterance]

or·tho·gen·e·sis (ôr′thō jen′ə sis) *n.* the alleged development of one species into another in a definite line, which is predetermined by the constitution that outward circumstances have given to each organism.

or·thog·o·nal (ôr thog′ə nəl) *adj.* rectangular; having to do with or involving right angles. [< obs. *orthogon* a right-angled triangle < L < Gk. *orthogōnios* < *orthos* right + *gōnia* angle]

or·thog·ra·pher (ôr thog′rə fər) *n.* **1** a person who knows much about spelling. **2** a person who spells correctly.

or·tho·graph·ic (ôr′thə graf′ik) *adj.* **1** having to do with orthography. **2** correct in spelling.

or·tho·graph·i·cal (ôr′thə graf′ə kəl) *adj.* orthographic. —**or′tho·graph′i·cal·ly,** *adv.*

or·thog·ra·phy (ôr thog′rə fē) *n.* **-phies.** **1** correct spelling; spelling considered as right or wrong. **2** the art of spelling; the study of spelling. **3** a drawing in a kind of projection in which the object is projected on a plane by lines perpendicular to the plane. [< L < Gk. *orthographia* < *orthos* correct + *graphein* write]

or·tho·pae·dic (ôr′thə pē′dik) *adj.* orthopedic.

or·tho·pe·dic (ôr′thə pē′dik) *adj.* of or having to do with orthopedics.

or·tho·pe·dics (ôr′thə pē′diks) *n.* the branch of surgery that deals with deformities and diseases of bones and joints, especially in children. [< Gk. *orthos* correct + *paideia* rearing of children < *pais, paidos* child]

or·tho·pe·dist (ôr′thə pē′dist) *n.* a surgeon who specializes in orthopedics.

Or·thop·ter·a (ôr thop′tər ə) *n.pl.* an order of insects (including crickets, grasshoppers, cockroaches, etc.) having longitudinally folded, membranous hind wings, covered by hard narrow outer wings. [< NL < Gk. *orthos* straight + *pteron* wing]

or·thop·ter·ous (ôr thop′tər əs) *adj.* of or belonging to the Orthoptera.

or·to·lan (ôr′tə lən) *n.* **1** a small European bunting whose meat is regarded as a specially delicate food. **2** in North America, any of various small, edible birds, such as the bobolink. [< F < Provençal < L *hortulanus* of gardens < *hortus* garden]

-ory *suffix.* **1** ——ing, as in *compensatory, contradictory.* **2** of or having to do with ——; of or having to do with ——ion, as in *advisory, auditory.* **3** characterized by ——ion, as in *adulatory.* **4** serving to ——, as in *expiatory.* **5** tending to ——; inclined to ——, as in *conciliatory.* **6** a place for ——ing; establishment for ——ing, as in *depository.* **7** other meanings, as in *conservatory, desultory.* [< L *-orius, -orium*]

o·ryx (ô′riks) *n.* **o·ryx·es** (ô′rik siz) or (*esp. collectively*) **o·ryx.** an African antelope having long, nearly straight horns. [ME < L < Gk. *oryx* antelope, pickaxe; with reference to pointed horns]

os[1] (os) *n.* **os·sa** (os′ə). *Latin.* bone.

os[2] (os) *n.* **o·ra** (ô′rə). *Latin.* a mouth; opening.

os- a form of **ob-** (from the form *obs-*) in some cases before *c* and *t*, as in *oscine, ostensible.*

Os osmium.

O.S. Old Style.

O.S.A. Order of St. Augustine.

Osage orange (ō′sāj) **1** a tree having glossy leaves and fruit resembling an orange. **2** the inedible fruit of this tree.

os·car (os′kər) *n.* a small statuette awarded annually by the American Academy of Motion Picture Arts and Sciences for the best performances, production, photography, etc. during the year. [supposedly from the remark, "He reminds me of my Uncle Oscar," made by the secretary of the Academy upon seeing one of the statuettes]

os·cil·late (os′ə lāt′) *v.* **-lat·ed, -lat·ing. 1** swing to and fro like a pendulum; move to and fro between two points. **2** cause to swing to and fro. **3** vary between opinions, purposes, etc. **4** in physics, cause an electric current to alternate at a high frequency; produce oscillations. [< L *oscillare*]

os·cil·la·tion (os′ə lā′shən) *n.* **1** the fact or process of oscillating. **2** a single swing of a vibrating body. **3** in physics: **a** a single forward and backward surge of a charge of electricity. **b** a rapid change in electromotive force. **c** a single complete cycle of an electric wave.

os·cil·la·tor (os′ə lā′tər) *n.* **1** a person or thing that oscillates. **2** a device producing the oscillations that give rise to electric waves. The vacuum tube of a radio transmitting apparatus is an oscillator.

os·cil·la·to·ry (os′ə lə tô′rē) *adj.* oscillating.

os·cil·lo·graph (os′ə lə graf′ or ə sil′ə graf′) *n.* an instrument for recording oscillations.

os·cil·lo·scope (ə sil′ə skōp′) *n.* an electronic instrument for representing wave oscillations on the screen of a cathode-ray tube. Tuning pianos and checking motors can be done with very great accuracy by means of oscilloscopes.

os·cine (os′in or os′īn) *adj.* of or belonging to a large group of perching birds, including thrushes and sparrows, that have well-developed vocal organs. —*n.* a bird of this group. [< L *oscines*, pl., < *ob-* to + *canere* sing]

os·cu·late (os′kyů lāt′) *v.* **-lat·ed, -lat·ing. 1** kiss. **2** come into close contact. **3** in geometry: **a** have three or more points coincident with: *A plane or a circle is said to osculate a curve when it has three coincident points in common with the curve.* **b** of two curves, surfaces, etc., osculate each other. [< L *osculari* < *osculum* little mouth, kiss, dim. of *os* mouth]

os·cu·la·tion (os′kyů lā′shən) *n.* **1** the act of kissing. **2** a kiss. **3** in geometry, a contact between two curves, surfaces, etc. at three or more common points.

os·cu·la·to·ry (os′kyů lə tô′rē) *adj.* **1** kissing. **2** coming into close contact.

-ose[1] *suffix.* **1** full of; having much or many, as in *verbose.* **2** inclined to; fond of, as in *jocose.* **3** like, as in *schistose.* [< L *-osus*]

-ose[2] *suffix.* used to form chemical terms, especially names of sugars and other carbohydrates, as in *fructose, lactose,* and of protein derivatives, as in *proteose.* [< F *-ose* in *glucose*]

o·sier (ō′zhər) *n.* **1** *Esp.Brit.* a kind of willow tree. **2** *Esp.Brit.* a tough, flexible branch or twig of this tree. Osiers are woven into baskets. **3** a kind of North American dogwood. —*adj.* made of osiers. [< F]

O·si·ris (ō sī′ris) *n.* the chief god of ancient Egypt, husband of Isis, ruler of the underworld, and judge of the dead. He represented good and productivity, and was identified with the Sun and the Nile.

-osis *combining form.* **1** denoting an act, process, state, or condition, as in *osmosis.* **2** in medicine, denoting an abnormal or diseased condition, as in *neurosis.* [< L < Gk.]

Os·man·li (oz man′lē or os man′lē) *n.* **-lis,** *adj.* —*n.* **1** an Ottoman. **2** the language of the Ottoman Turks. —*adj.* Ottoman. [< Turkish *Osmanli* belonging to *Osman*, Arabic *Othman.* See OTTOMAN.]

os·mi·um (oz′mē əm) *n.* a hard, heavy, grayish, metallic chemical element, used for electric-light filaments, etc. *Symbol*: Os; *at.no.* 76; *at.wt.* 190.2. [< NL < Gk. *osmē* smell, odor; from the odor of one of the osmium oxides]

os·mo·sis (oz mō′sis or os mō′sis) *n.* **1** the tendency of two fluids that are separated by something porous to go through it and become mixed. **2** the diffusion or spreading of fluids through a membrane or partition till they are mixed. **3** a gradual, often unconscious, absorbing or understanding of facts, theories, ideas, etc. [latinized var. of *osmose* < Gk. *ōsmos* a thrust]

hat, āge, cãre, fär; let, ēqual, tėrm; it, īce
hot, ōpen, ôrder; oil, out; cup, pů t, rüle, ūse
əbove, takən, pencəl, lemən, circəs
ch, child; ng, long; sh, ship
th, thin; ᴛʜ, then; zh, measure

os·mot·ic (oz mot′ik or os mot′ik) *adj.* of or having to do with osmosis.

os·prey (os′prē or os′prā) *n.* **-preys. 1** a large fish-eating hawk with white underparts and dark-brown back and wings. **2** an ornamental feather, used for trimming hats, etc. [ult. < L *ossifraga* < *os* bone + *frangere* break]

Os·sa (os′ə) *n.* **Mount,** a mountain in N.E. Greece. In Greek legend, when the giants made war on the gods, they piled Mount Ossa on Mount Olympus and Mount Pelion upon Mount Ossa in an attempt to reach heaven.

os·se·ous (os′ē əs) *adj.* **1** bony. **2** containing bones. [< L *osseus* < *os, ossis* bone]

Os·si·an (os′ē ən or ō shēn′) *n.* in Irish legend, a Gaelic warrior and poet of about the 3rd century A.D.

os·si·fi·ca·tion (os′ə fə kā′shən) *n.* **1** the fact or process of changing into bone. **2** a being changed into bone. **3** the part that is ossified. **4** the fact or process of becoming hard, fixed, hard-hearted, or very conservative.

os·si·fy (os′ə fī′) *v.* **-fied, -fy·ing. 1** change into bone; become bone: *The soft parts of a baby's skull ossify as the baby grows older.* **2** harden like bone; make or become fixed, hard-hearted, or very conservative. [< L *os, ossis* bone + E *-(i)fy*]

os·su·ary (os′ū er′ē or osh′ü er′ē) *n.* **-ar·ies.** an urn, vault, or other place to hold the bones of the dead. [< LL *ossuarium*, neuter of *ossuarius* of bones]

os·ten·si·ble (os ten′sə bəl) *adj.* apparent; pretended; professed: *Her ostensible purpose was to borrow sugar, but she really wanted to see the new furniture.* [< F < L *ostendere* show < *os-* < *obs-* toward + *tendere* stretch]

os·ten·si·bly (os ten′sə blē) *adv.* apparently; on the face of it; as openly stated or shown.

os·ten·ta·tion (os′tən tā′shən or os′ten tā′shən) *n.* a showing off; display intended to impress others. [< L *ostentatio, -onis*, ult. < *ob-* toward + *tendere* stretch] —**Syn.** parade, pomp.

os·ten·ta·tious (os′tən tā′shəs or os′ten tā′shəs) *adj.* **1** done for display; intended to attract notice. **2** showing off; liking to attract notice: *an ostentatious prince.* —**os′ten·ta′tious·ly,** *adv.* —**Syn. 1** showy, spectacular, pretentious, gaudy.

osteo- *combining form.* bone, as in *osteoarthritis.* [< Gk. *osteon* bone]

os·te·o·ar·thri·tis (os′tē ō är thrī′tis) *n.* arthritis caused by joint and cartilage degeneration.

os·te·ol·o·gy (os′tē ol′ə jē) *n.* **1** the branch of anatomy that deals with bones. **2** the bony structure or system of bones of an animal or major part of an animal, as the head, trunk, etc. [< Gk. *osteon* bone + E *-logy*]

os·te·o·my·e·li·tis (os′tē ō mī′ə lī′tis) *n.* inflammation of the bone, or bone marrow. [< *osteo-* + Gk. *myelos* marrow + E *-itis*]

os·te·o·path (os′tē ə path′) *n.* a person who treats disease by manipulating the bones and muscles. [< *osteopathy*]

os·te·o·path·ic (os′tē ə path′ik) *adj.* of osteopathy or osteopaths.

os·te·op·a·thist (os′tē op′ə thist) *n.* osteopath.

os·te·op·a·thy (os′tē op′ə thē) *n.* a system of medicine that considers diseases as structural abnormalities in the body and treats them by manipulation of the bones and other affected parts. [< Gk. *osteon* bone + E *-pathy*]

os·ti·na·to (os′tə nä′tō) *n.* **-tos.** in music, a phrase repeated over and over in the same voice or pitch. [< Ital. *ostinato*, literally, obstinate < L *obstinatus*]

ost·ler (os′lər) *n.* hostler.

os·tra·cism (os′trə siz′əm) *n.* **1** banishment from one's native country. **2** the act or state of being shut out from society, from favor, from privileges, or from association with one's fellows.

os·tra·cize (os′trə sīz′) *v.* **-cized, -ciz·ing. 1** banish. In ancient Greece, a dangerous or unpopular citizen was ostracized by public vote. **2** shut out from society, from favor, from privileges, etc. [< Gk. *ostrakizein* < *ostrakon* tile, potsherd, originally used in balloting]

os·trich (os′trich) *n.* **1** a large bird of Africa and the Near East, that can run swiftly but cannot fly. Ostriches have two toes on each foot and are the largest of existing birds. They have large feathers or plumes which are often used as ornaments. **2** a person who avoids facing reality or an approaching danger, from the ostrich's supposed habit of burying its head in the sand to avoid oncoming danger. [ME < OF < LL *avis struthio* < L *avis* bird, LL *struthio* < Gk. *strouthiōn* < *strouthos* ostrich]

Os·tro·goth (os′trə goth′) *n.* a member of the eastern division of Goths that overran the Roman Empire and controlled Italy from A.D. 493 to 555. [< LL *Ostrogothi,* earlier *Austrogothi* < Gmc.; probably originally "the splendid Goths," but later taken as "the eastern Goths"]

O.T. Old Testament.

oth·er (uᴛʜ′ər) *adj.* **1** remaining: *John is here, but the other boys are at school.* **2** additional or further: *I have no other books with me.* **3** not the same as one or more already mentioned: *Come some other day.* **4** different: *I would not have him other than he is.* **5 every other,** every second; alternate: *She buys cream every other day.* **6 the other day (night,** etc.), recently.
—pron. **1** the other one; not the same ones: *Each praises the other.* **2** another person or thing: *There are others to be considered.* **3 of all others,** more than all others.
—adv. otherwise; differently: *I can't do other than to go.* [OE *ōther*]

oth·er·wise (uᴛʜ′ər wīz′) *adv.* **1** in a different way; differently: *I could not do otherwise.* **2** in other ways: *He is noisy, but otherwise a very nice boy.* **3** under other circumstances; in a different condition: *He reminded me of what I should otherwise have forgotten.* *—adj.* different: *It might have been otherwise.* *—conj.* or else; if not: *Come at once; otherwise you will be too late.* [< *other* + *wise*²]

other world the world to come; life after death.

oth·er·world·ly (uᴛʜ′ər wėrld′lē) *adj.* **1** of or devoted to another world, such as the world of mind or imagination, or the world to come. **2** supernatural; weird. **—oth′er·world′li·ness,** *n.*

o·ti·ose (ō′shē ōs′ or ō′tē ōs′) *adj.* **1** lazy; idle. **2** ineffective; futile. **3** superfluous; useless. [< L *otiosus* < *otium* leisure]

o·to·log·i·cal (ō′tə loj′ə kəl) *adj.* of or having to do with otology.

o·tol·o·gist (ō tol′ə jist) *n.* a doctor who specializes in otology.

o·tol·o·gy (ō tol′ə jē) *n.* the branch of medicine dealing with the ear and its diseases, including their diagnosis and treatment. [< Gk. *ous, ōtos* ear + E *-logy*]

ot·ta·va ri·ma (ō tä′və rē′mə) a stanza of eight lines with the lines according to the rhyme scheme *a b a b a b c c.* In Italian each line normally has eleven syllables; in English, ten. [< Ital. *ottava rima* octave rhyme]

Ot·ta·wa (ot′ə wo′ or ot′ə wə) *n.* **1** a tribe of North American Indians who formerly lived near Lake Superior and later near Lake Huron. **2** a member of this tribe. **3** the Algonquian language of this tribe.

ot·ter (ot′ər) *n.* **-ters** or (*esp. collectively*) **-ter. 1** any of several mammals related to the mink and weasel, that are good swimmers and have webbed toes with claws. **2** the dark brown fur of any otter. Otter is short, thick, and glossy, resembling seal or beaver. **3** a coat or other garment made of this fur. [OE *oter*]

Ot·to·man (ot′ə mən) *n.* **-mans,** *adj.* *—n.* **1** a Turk. **2 ottoman, a** a low, cushioned seat, usually without back or arms. **b** a cushioned footstool. **3** a heavy, corded fabric of silk or rayon, often with a cotton woof. *—adj.* **1** Turkish. **2** of or having to do with the Turkish dynasty founded by Osman I about 1300 or the Ottoman Empire. [< F < Ital. *Ottomano* < Arabic *Othmani* belonging to *Othman,* the name of the founder of the empire]

Ottoman Empire a former empire of the Turks in S.E. Europe, S.W. Asia, and N. Africa; Turkish Empire.

oua·na·niche (wä′nə nēsh′) *n. Cdn.* a kind of Atlantic salmon that remains all its life in fresh water, native to Lake St. John and certain other lakes in Quebec and Ontario. [< Cdn.F < Algonquian (Montagnais *wananish* little salmon)]

ou·bli·ette (ü′blē et′) *n.* **1** a secret dungeon with an opening only at the top. **2** a deep pit in the floor of a dungeon. [< F *oubliette* < *oublier* forget]

ouch (ouch) *interj.* an exclamation expressing sudden pain.

ought[1] (ot or ôt) *auxiliary verb.* **1** have a duty; be obliged: *You ought to obey your parents.* **2** be right or suitable: *It ought to be allowed.* **3** be wise: *I ought to go before it rains.* **4** be expected: *At your age you ought to know better.* **5** be very likely: *The fastest one ought to win the race.* [OE *āhte* (infinitive, *āgan* owe)] **—Syn. 1** must, should.
☛ **ought.** *Had ought* and *hadn't ought* are redundant substandard expressions avoided in general English. Substandard: *He had ought to dress more carefully.* General: *He ought to dress more carefully.*

ought[2] (ot or ôt) *n. adv.* aught; anything.

ought[3] (ot or ôt) *n. Informal.* nought; zero; the cipher 0. [var. of *nought, a nought* taken as *an ought*]

Oui·ja (wē′jə) *n. Trademark.* a device consisting of a small board on legs that rests on a larger board marked with words, letters of the alphabet, or other characters. The person wishing an answer to questions rests his fingers lightly on the small board which may then move and touch letters or words. Ouijas are used at spiritualistic meetings and as games. [< F *oui* yes + G *ja* yes]

ounce[1] (ouns) *n.* **1** a unit of weight, $\frac{1}{16}$ of a pound in avoirdupois, and $\frac{1}{12}$ of a pound in troy weight. **2** a measure for liquids; fluid ounce. 20 ounces = 1 imperial pint. **3** a little bit; very small amount: *He hadn't an ounce of strength left.* [ME < OF *unce* < L *uncia* twelfth part. Doublet of INCH.]

ounce[2] (ouns) *n.* a grayish wild cat having black spots, that resembles a leopard; snow leopard. It is found in the mountains of central Asia. [ME < OF *once* for *lonce* < L *lynx* lynx < Gk.]

our (our or är) *adj.* of us; belonging to us: *our coats.* [OE *ūre*]
☛ **Our, ours** are the possessive forms of *we. Our* is always followed by a noun: *This is our car. Ours* stands alone: *This car is ours.*

Our Lady the Virgin Mary.

ours (ourz or ärz) *pron.* **1** of us; belonging to us: *This garden is ours.* **2** the one or ones belonging to us: *Ours is a large house.*
☛ See note at our.

our·self (our self′ or är self′) *pron.* myself.
☛ **Ourself** is used by an author, judge, etc.: "*We shall ourself reward the victor," said the queen.*

our·selves (our selvz′ or är selvz′) *pron.pl.* **1** the emphatic form of **we** or **us**: *We did it ourselves.* **2** the reflexive form of **us**: *We hurt ourselves.* **3** our real or true selves: *We weren't ourselves when we said that.*

-ous *suffix.* **1** having; having much; full of, as in *joyous, perilous.* **2** characterized by, as in *blasphemous, parsimonious, zealous.* **3** having the nature of, as in *murderous, idolatrous.* **4** of or having to do with, as in *monogamous.* **5** like, as in *thunderous.* **6** committing or practising, as in *bigamous.* **7** inclined to, as in *amorous.* **8** in chemistry, implying a larger proportion of the element indicated by the word than *-ic* implies. *Stannous* means containing tin in larger proportions than a corresponding *stannic* compound. [ME < OF < L *-osus*; often used to represent L *-us,* adj. (e.g., *omnivorus* omnivorous) or Gk. *-os,* adj. (e.g., *anonymos* anonymous)]

ou·sel (ü′zəl) *n.* ouzel.

oust (oust) *v.* force out; drive out. [< AF *ouster* (cf. F *ôter*) < L *obstare* block, hinder < *ob-* in the way of + *stare* stand. Related to OBSTACLE.] **—Syn.** evict, expel.

oust·er (ous′tər) *n.* **1** an ousting, especially an illegal forcing of a person out of his property. **2** one who ousts.

out (out) *adv.* **1** away; forth: *rush out.* **2** not in or at a place, position, state, etc.: *That dress is out of fashion. The miners are going out on strike.* **3** into the open air: *He*

hat, āge, cãre, fär; let, ēqual, tėrm; it, īce
hot, ōpen, ôrder; oil, out; cup, pu̇t, rüle, ūse
əbove, takən, pencəl, lemən, circəs
ch, child; ng, long; sh, ship
th, thin; ᴛʜ, then; zh, measure

went out at noon. 4 to or at an end: *fight it out.* 5 from the usual place, condition, position, etc.: *Put the light out. The boy turned his pockets out.* 6 completely; effectively: *fit out.* 7 so as to project or extend: *stand out.* 8 into or in existence, activity, or outward manifestation: *Fever broke out. Flowers are out.* 9 aloud; loudly: *Speak out.* 10 to others: *Give out the books.* 11 from a number, stock, store, source, cause, material, etc.: *She picked out a new coat.* 12 in the wrong: *be out in one's calculations.* 13 from a state of composure, satisfaction, or harmony: *feel put out.* 14 at a money loss: *be out ten dollars.* 15 in baseball, etc., not in play; no longer at bat or on base. 16 **out and away**, by far. 17 **out and out**, thoroughly. 18 **out of**, a from within: *He came out of the house.* b not within; away from; outside of; beyond: *The boat has gone out of sight.* c without; not having: *We are out of coffee.* d so as to take away: *She was cheated out of her money.* e from: *My dress is made out of silk.* f from among: *We picked our puppy out of that litter.* g because of: *I went only out of curiosity.*
—*adj.* 1 not in possession or control: *The Liberals are out, the Conservatives in.* 2 not in use, action, fashion, etc.: *The fire is out. Full skirts are out this season.* 3 without money, supplies, etc.: *"Have you any cigarettes left?" "No, I'm right out."* 4 in baseball, not having its inning: *the out side.* 5 external; exterior; outer; outlying: *an out island.* 6 not usual: *an out size.* 7 **out for**, looking for; trying to get. 8 **out to**, eagerly trying to.
—*n.* 1 one who is out. 2 something wrong. 3 that which is omitted. 4 in baseball, a being out or putting out. 5 **at outs** or **on the outs**, quarrelling; disagreeing. —*prep.* 1 from out; forth from: *He went out the door.* 2 *Informal.* out along: *Drive out Main Street.*
—*v.* 1 go or come out: *Murder will out.* 2 put out: *Please out the fire.*
—*interj. Archaic.* an exclamation of indignation, reproach, etc.: *Out upon you!* [OE *ūt*]

out- *prefix.* 1 outward; forth; away, as in *outburst, outgoing.* 2 outside; at a distance, as in *outbuilding, outfield, outlying.* 3 more than; longer than, as in *outbid, outlive, outnumber.* 4 better than, as in *outdo, outrun.*

out·age (out′ij) *n.* 1 a time of interrupted service, especially a suspension of gas, electric, or water power. 2 an interruption or failure in service, function, or use.

out-and-out (out′ənd out′) *adj.* thorough.

out·back (out′bak′) *n.* 1 in Australia, the unsettled part of the interior; back country. 2 any similarly unsettled area.

out·bid (out bid′) *v.* **-bid, -bid** or **-bid·den, -bid·ding.** bid higher than (someone else).

out·board (out′bôrd′) *adj. adv.* 1 outside the hull of a ship or boat. 2 away from the middle of a ship or boat. —*n.* 1 a boat equipped with an outboard motor. 2 the motor itself.

outboard motor a portable gasoline motor attached to the stern of a boat or canoe.

out·bound (out′bound′) *adj.* outward bound.

out·brave (out brāv′) *v.* **-braved, -brav·ing.** 1 face bravely. 2 be braver than.

out·break (out′brāk′) *n.* 1 a breaking out: *outbreaks of anger.* 2 a riot; public disturbance. —**Syn.** 1 outburst.

out·build (out bild′) *v.* **-built, -build·ing.** build more or better than.

out·build·ing (out′bil′ding) *n.* a shed or building built near a main building: *Barns are outbuildings on a farm.*

out·burst (out′bėrst′) *n.* a bursting forth: *an outburst of laughter, anger, smoke, etc.*

out·cast (out′kast′) *n.* a person or animal cast out from home and friends: *Criminals are outcasts of society.* —*adj.* being an outcast; homeless; friendless.

out·class (out klas′) *v.* be of higher class than; be much better than.

out·come (out′kum′) *n.* a result; consequence. —**Syn.** upshot, issue.

out·crop (*n.* out′krop′; *v.* out krop′) *n. v.* **-cropped, -crop·ping.** —*n.* 1 a coming to the surface of the earth: *the outcrop of a vein of coal.* 2 the part that comes to the surface: *The outcrop that we found proved to be very rich in gold.* —*v.* come to the surface; appear.

out·cry (out′krī′) *n.* **-cries.** 1 a crying out; sudden cry or scream. 2 a great noise or clamor. 3 *Archaic.* an auction. —**Syn.** 1 shout. 2 uproar.

out·curve (out′kėrv′) *n.* in baseball, a ball that curves away from the batter.

out·dat·ed (out dāt′id) *adj.* out-of-date; old-fashioned; obsolete: *The coal-oil lamp is outdated.*

out·did (out did′) *v.* pt. of **outdo.**

out·dis·tance (out dis′təns) *v.* **-tanced, -tanc·ing.** leave behind; outstrip.

out·do (out dü′) *v.* **-did, -done, -do·ing.** do more or better than; surpass. —**Syn.** exceed. See **excel.**

out·done (out dun′) *v.* pp. of **outdo.**

out·door (out′dôr′) *adj.* done, used, or living outdoors: *outdoor games.*

out·doors (out′dôrz′) *adv.* out in the open air; not indoors or in the house. —*n.* the world outside of houses; the open air.

out·er (out′ər) *adj.* farther out; outside: *The rocket was shot into outer space.* —**Syn.** outward, exterior, external.

out·er·most (out′ər mōst′) *adj.* farthest out.

outer space 1 space immediately beyond the earth's atmosphere: *The moon is in outer space.* 2 space between the planets or between the stars. —**out′er·space′,** *adj.*

out·face (out fās′) *v.* **-faced, -fac·ing.** 1 face boldly; defy. 2 stare at (a person) until he stops staring back; browbeat; abash.

out·field (out′fēld′) *n.* in baseball: 1 the part of the field beyond the diamond or infield. 2 the three players in the outfield.

out·field·er (out′fēl′dər) *n.* in baseball, a player stationed in the outfield.

out·fit (out′fit) *n. v.* **-fit·ted, -fit·ting.** —*n.* 1 all the articles necessary for any undertaking or purpose: *a sailor's outfit, the outfit for a camping trip, a bride's outfit.* 2 a group working together. 3 a regiment, a squadron, a ship's company, etc.: *His father was in the same outfit as mine during the war.* 4 the land, cattle, buildings, etc. of a ranch. —*v.* furnish with everything necessary for any purpose; equip. —**out′fit′ter,** *n.* —**Syn.** *n.* 1 equipment, gear.

out·flank (out flangk′) *v.* 1 go or extend beyond the flank of (an opposing army, etc.); turn the flank of. 2 get the better of; circumvent.

out·flow (out′flō′) *n.* 1 a flowing out: *the outflow from a waterpipe, an outflow of sympathy.* 2 that which flows out.

out·gen·er·al (out jen′ər əl or -jen′rəl) *v.* **-alled** or **-aled, -al·ling** or **-al·ing.** be a better general than; get the better of by superior strategy.

out·go (out′gō′) *n.* **-goes.** what goes out; what is paid out; an amount that is spent.

out·go·ing (out′gō′ing) *n.* 1 a going out. 2 that which goes out. —*adj.* 1 a departing; outward bound. b retiring or defeated: *an outgoing legislator.* 2 inclined to offer one's time, ideas, etc. without much urging; very friendly and helpful to others; sociable: *a very outgoing person.*

out·grow (out grō′) *v.* **-grew, -grown, -grow·ing.** 1 grow too large for. 2 grow beyond or away from; get rid of by growing older: *outgrow early friends, outgrow a babyish habit.* 3 grow faster or taller than. 4 grow out; project.

out·growth (out′grōth′) *n.* 1 a natural development, product, or result: *This big store is an outgrowth of the little shop started ten years ago.* 2 an offshoot; something that has grown out of something else: *A corn is an outgrowth on a toe.* 3 a growing out or forth: *the outgrowth of new leaves in the spring.*

out·guess (out ges′) *v.* be too clever for; get the better of.

out·house (out′hous′) *n.* 1 a separate building used in connection with a main building. 2 an outdoor toilet.

out·ing (out′ing) *n.* a short pleasure trip; walk or airing; holiday spent outdoors away from home.

out·ing flannel a cotton cloth woven to look like flannel.

out·land (out′land) *adj.* **1** *Archaic.* foreign. **2** outlying: *outland districts.* —*n.* **1** *Archaic.* a foreign land. **2** outlying land: *the outland of an estate.*

out·land·er (out′lan′dər) *n.* **1** a foreigner; alien. **2** *Informal.* an outsider; stranger.

out·land·ish (out lan′dish) *adj.* **1** not familiar; queer; strange or ridiculous. **2** looking or sounding as if it belonged to a foreign country. —**out land′ish·ly,** *adv.* —**out·land′ish·ness,** *n.* —**Syn. 1** odd, bizarre.

out·last (out last′) *v.* last longer than.

out·law (out′lo′ or -lô′) *n.* **1** a person outside the protection of the law; exile; outcast. **2** a lawless person; criminal. **3** an unbroken horse.
—*v.* **1** make or declare (a person) an outlaw. **2** make or declare illegal: *A group of nations agreed to outlaw war.* **3** deprive of legal force. An outlawed debt is one that cannot be collected because it has been due too long. [OE *ūtlaga* < ON *útlagi*] —**Syn.** *n.* **2** bandit, highwayman, desperado.

out·law·ry (out′lô′rē) *n.* **-ries. 1** the condition of being outlawed. In the early Middle Ages outlawry was used as a punishment in England. **2** the condition of being an outlaw.

out·lay (*n.* out′lā′; *v.* out lā′) *n. v.* **-laid, -lay·ing.** —*n.* **1** a spending; expense; a laying out of money: *a large outlay for clothing.* **2** the amount spent. —*v.* expend: *outlay money in improvements.*

out·let (out′let′ or out′lət) *n.* **1** a means or place of letting out or getting out; way out: *the outlet of a lake, an outlet for one's energies.* **2 a** a market for a product. **b** a store selling the products of a particular manufacturer: *The shoe manufacturer had several outlets.* **3** a place in a wall, etc. for inserting an electric plug. —**Syn. 1** vent, opening, exit.

out·li·er (out′lī′ər) *n.* **1** a person, place, or thing that is detached from the main body or system. **2** in geology, a formation surrounded by older strata and exposed because of erosion, denudation, etc.

out·line (out′līn′) *n. v.* **-lined, -lin·ing.** —*n.* **1** the line that shows the shape of an object; line that bounds a figure: *We saw the outlines of the mountains against the evening sky.* **2** a drawing or style of drawing that gives only outer lines. **3** a general plan; rough draft: *Make an outline before trying to write a composition.* **4 in outline, a** with only the outline shown. **b** with only the main features.
—*v.* **1** draw the outer line of. **2** indicate or define the outline of: *hills outlined against the sky.* **3** give a plan of; sketch: *She outlined their trip abroad.* —**out′lin′er,** *n.*
Syn. *n.* **1 Outline, contour, profile** = the line or lines showing the shape of something. **Outline** applies to the line marking the outer limits or edge of an object, figure, or shape: *We could see the outline of a man.* **Contour** emphasizes the shape shown by the outline: *The contours of his face are rugged.* **Profile** applies to the side view of something seen in outline, especially against a background: *You would stand up straight if you could see your profile when you slouch.*

out·live (out liv′) *v.* **-lived, -liv·ing.** live or last longer than: *The idea was good once, but it has outlived its usefulness.* —**Syn.** survive, outlast.

out·look (out′lůk′) *n.* **1** what one sees on looking out; view: *The room has a pleasant outlook.* **2** what seems likely to happen; prospect: *Because of the black clouds, the outlook for our picnic is not very good.* **3** a way of thinking about things; attitude of mind; point of view: *a gloomy outlook on life.* **4** a lookout; tower or other high place to watch from. —**Syn. 1** scene.

out·ly·ing (out′lī′ing) *adj.* lying outside the boundary; far from the centre; remote: *the outlying settlements of the frontier.* —**Syn.** distant, isolated.

out·ma·noeu·vre or **out·ma·neu·ver** (out′mə nü′vər) *v.* **-vred** or **-vered, -vring** or **-ver·ing.** outdo in manoeuvring; get the better of by manoeuvring.

out·mode (out mōd′) *v.* **-mod·ed, -mod·ing.** make out of date or out of fashion.

out·mod·ed (out mōd′id) *adj.* out-of-date.

out·num·ber (out num′bər) *v.* be more than; exceed in number: *They outnumbered us three to one.*

out-of-bounds (out′ əv boundz′) *adj. adv.* **1** in sports, outside the boundary line. **2** outside the established limits of use or entry.

out-of-date (out′əv dāt′) *adj.* old-fashioned; not in present use.

out-of-door (out′əv dôr′) *adj.* outdoor.

out-of-doors (out′əv dôrz′) *adj.* outdoor. —*n. adv.* outdoors.

out-of-the-way (out′əv ᴛʜə wā′) *adj.* **1** remote; unfrequented; secluded: *an out-of-the-way cottage.* **2** seldom met with; unusual: *out-of-the-way details.*

out-of-town (out′ əv toun′) *adj.* of, having to do with, or situated on land outside a city or town.

out·pace (out′pās′) *v.* **-paced, -pac·ing. 1** run faster than. **2** outdo; excel.

out·pa·tient (out′pā′shənt) *n.* a patient receiving treatment at a hospital but not staying there.

out·play (out plā′) *v.* play better than.

out·point (out point′) *v.* **1** score more points than. **2** sail closer to the wind than.

out·port (out′pôrt′) *n. Cdn.* any one of the isolated fishing villages along the coasts of Newfoundland.

out·post (out′pōst′) *n.* **1** a guard, or small number of soldiers, placed at some distance from an army or camp to prevent surprise attack. **2** the place where such guards are stationed. **3** a settlement or village in an outlying place: *a frontier outpost.* **4** anything thought of as an outpost or advance guard: *Missionaries and traders have been outposts of civilization.*

out·pour (*n.* out′pôr′; *v.* out pôr′) *n.* **1** a pouring out. **2** an uncontrolled expression of thoughts or feelings. —*v.* pour out.

out·pour·ing (out′pôr′ing) *n.* **1** anything that is poured out. **2** an uncontrolled expression of thoughts or feelings.

out·put (out′půt′) *n.* **1** the amount produced; product or yield: *the daily output of automobiles.* **2** a putting forth: *a sudden output of effort.* **3** information produced from the storage unit of a computer.

out·rage (out′rāj′) *n. v.* **-raged, -rag·ing.** —*n.* **1** an act showing no regard for the rights or feelings of others. **2** an overturning of the rights of others by force; act of violence; offence; insult. —*v.* **1** offend greatly; do violence to; insult. **2** break (the law, a rule of morality, etc.) openly; treat as nothing at all. [ME < OF *outrage,* ult. < L *ultra* beyond] —**Syn.** *n.* affront, indignity.

out·ra·geous (out rā′jəs) *adj.* shocking; very offensive or insulting. —**out·ra′geous·ly,** *adv.* —**out·ra′geous·ness,** *n.* —**Syn.** villainous, heinous.

out·ran (out ran′) *v.* pt. of **outrun.**

out·rank (out rangk′) *v.* rank higher than.

ou·tré (ü trā′) *adj.* passing the bounds of what is usual and considered proper; eccentric; bizarre. [< F *outré,* pp. of *outrer* exaggerate, ult. < L *ultra* beyond]

out·reach (out rēch′) *v.* **1** reach beyond. **2** reach out; extend; stretch out.

out·ride (out rīd′) *v.* **-rode, -rid·den, -rid·ing. 1** ride faster or better than. **2** of ships, last through (a storm).

out·rid·er (out′rīd′ər) *n.* a servant or attendant riding on a horse before or beside a carriage or wagon, etc.: *A chuckwagon team consists of a driver and his outriders.*

out·rig·ger (out′rig′ər) *n.* **1** a framework ending in a float, extending outward from the side of a canoe to prevent upsetting. **2** a bracket extending outward from either side of a boat to hold a rowlock. **3** a boat equipped with such brackets. **4** a projecting spar, framework, or part: *an outrigger from a ship's mast to extend a sail, an outrigger from an airplane to support the rudder.*

An outrigger (def. 1)

out·right (out′rīt′) *adv.* **1** altogether; entirely; not gradually: *sell a thing outright.* **2** openly; without restraint: *I laughed outright.* **3** at once; on the spot: *kill a person outright.* —*adj.* **1** complete; thorough: *an outright loss.* **2** downright; straightforward; direct: *an outright refusal.* **3** entire; total.

out·run (out run′) *v.* **-ran, -run, -run·ning. 1** run faster than. **2** leave behind; go beyond; pass the limits of: *I am afraid your story outruns the facts.*

out·sell (out sel′) *v.* **-sold, -sell·ing. 1** outdo in selling; sell more than. **2** sell for more than.

out·set (out′set′) *n.* a setting out; start; a beginning: *At the outset, it looked like a nice day.*

out·shine (out shīn′) *v.* **-shone, -shin·ing. 1** shine more brightly than. **2** be more brilliant or excellent than; surpass.

out·shoot (*v.* out shüt′; *n.* out′shüt′) *v.* **-shot, -shoot·ing,** *n.* —*v.* **1** shoot better or farther than. **2** shoot forth. —*n.* **1** a projection. **2** an offshoot.

out·side (out′sīd′; *prep. also,* out′sīd′) *n.* **1** the side or surface that is out; outer part. **2** the external appearance. **3** a space or position without. **4** *Cdn.* the settled parts of Canada: *In the North, people refer to the rest of Canada as the outside.* **5 at the outside,** *Informal.* at the utmost limit. **6 outside in,** so that what should be outside is inside; with the outside not showing.
—*adj.* **1** on the outside; of or nearer the outside: *the outside leaves.* **2** not belonging to a certain group, set, district, etc.: *Outside people tried to get control of the business.* **3** being, acting, done, or originating without or beyond a wall, boundary, etc.: *Outside noises disturbed the class.* **4** *Informal.* highest; largest; reaching the utmost limit: *an outside estimate.* **5** slight; small: *He had only an outside chance of winning the race.* **6** covering the greater distance in making a turn or following a circular course: *The righthand wheels are the outside wheels in a turn to the left.*
—*adv.* **1** on or to the outside. **2** outdoors.
—*prep.* **1** *Informal.* with the exception: *Outside John, none of us liked the play.* **2** out of; beyond the limits of: *Stay outside the house.* —**Syn.** *n.* **1** exterior.

out·sid·er (out′sīd′ər) *n.* **1** a person who is outside. **2** a person not belonging to a particular group, set, company, party, district, etc. **3** a person unconnected or unacquainted with the matter in question. **4** a person, horse, etc. supposed to have no chance of winning a race. **5** *Cdn.* a person who does not live in the North: *The people of Whitehorse, Y.T., call the people of Edmonton outsiders.*

out·size (out′sīz′) *adj.* larger than the usual size. —*n.* an article of clothing, etc. larger than the usual size.

out·skirts (out′skėrts′) *n.pl.* the outer parts or edges of a town, district, etc.; outlying parts.

out·smart (out smärt′) *v. Informal.* outdo in cleverness.

out·spo·ken (out′spō′kən) *adj.* frank; not reserved: *an outspoken person, outspoken criticism.* —**out′spo′ken·ly,** *adv.* —**out′spo′ken·ness,** *n.* —**Syn.** blunt. See **frank.**

out·spread (*adj.* out′spred′; *v.* out spred′) *adj. v.* **-spread, -spreading.** —*adj.* spread out; extended: *an eagle with outspread wings.* —*v.* spread out; extend.

out·stand·ing (out stan′ding) *adj.* **1** standing out from others; well-known; important. **2** unpaid: *outstanding debts.* **3** needing attention; *outstanding letters.* **4** projecting. —**out·stand′ing·ly,** *adv.*

out·stay (out stā′) *v.* stay longer than.

out·stretched (out′strecht′) *adj.* stretched out; extended: *He welcomed his old friend with outstretched arms.*

out·strip (out strip′) *v.* **-stripped, -strip·ping. 1** go faster than; leave behind in a race. **2** do better than; excel.

out·talk (out tok′ or -tôk′) *v.* talk better, faster, longer, or louder than; get the better of by talking.

out·vote (out vōt′) *v.* **-vot·ed, -vot·ing.** defeat in voting; cast more votes than.

out·ward (out′wərd) *adj.* **1** going toward the outside; turned toward the outside: *an outward motion, an outward glance.* **2** outer: *to all outward appearances.* **3** that can be seen; plain to see: *We were all amazed when that outward reformation took place.* **4** seeming; on the surface: *the outward man.*
—*adv.* **1** toward the outside; away. **2** away from the dock, station, etc.: *That ship is outward bound.* **3** on the outside. [OE *ūtweard*] —**Syn.** *adj.* **2** external, exterior, superficial.

hat, āge, cãre, fär; let, ēqual, tėrm; it, īce
hot, ōpen, ôrder; oil, out; cup, pu̇t, rüle, ūse
əbove, takən, pencəl, lemən, circəs
ch, child; ng, long; sh, ship
th, thin; ᴛʜ, then; zh, measure

out·ward·ly (out′wərd lē) *adv.* **1** on the outside or outer surface. **2** toward the outside. **3** as regards appearance or outward manifestation.

out·wards (out′wərdz) *adv.* outward.

out·wash (out′wash′) *n.* in geology, rock fragments or other glacial debris carried beyond the glacier by meltwater.

out·wear (out wãr′) *v.* **-wore, -worn, -wear·ing. 1** wear longer than. **2** wear out. **3** outgrow.

out·weigh (out wā′) *v.* **1** weigh more than. **2** exceed in value, importance, influence, etc.: *The advantages of the plan outweigh its disadvantages.*

out·wit (out wit′) *v.* **-wit·ted, -wit·ting.** get the better of by being more intelligent; be too clever for: *The prisoner outwitted his guards and escaped.*

out·work (*n.* out′wėrk′; *v.* out wėrk′) *n.* a part of the fortifications of a place lying outside the main ones; a less important defence: *the outworks of a castle.* —*v.* surpass in working; work harder or faster than.

out·worn (*adj.* out′wôrn′; *v.* out wôrn′) *adj.* **1** worn out. **2** out-of-date. —*v.* pp. of **outwear.**

ou·zel (ü′zəl) *n.* **1** a European thrush that has a white ring or bar on the chest, and is usually called the **ring ouzel. 2** a thrush of Europe and Asia that is often called the blackbird. **3** any of several songbirds, related to the thrushes and wrens, that often wade into deep water. Also, **ousel.** [OE *ōsle*]

o·va (ō′və) *n.* pl. of **ovum.**

o·val (ō′vəl) *adj.* **1** egg-shaped. **2** shaped like an ellipse. —*n.* something having an oval shape. [ME < NL *ovalis* < L *ovum* egg]

An oval

o·val·ly (ō′vəl ē) *adv.* in an oval form.

o·var·i·an (ō vãr′ē ən) *adj.* of or having to do with an ovary.

o·va·ry (ō′və rē) *n.* **-ries. 1** the organ of a female in which eggs are produced. **2** the part of a plant enclosing the young seeds. See **pistil** for drawing. [< NL *ovarium* < L *ovum* egg]

o·vate (ō′vāt) *adj.* egg-shaped: *an ovate leaf.* [< L *ovatus* < *ovum* egg]

o·va·tion (ō vā′shən) *n.* an enthusiastic public welcome; burst of loud clapping or cheering. [< L *ovatio, -onis* < *ovare* rejoice]

ov·en (uv′ən) *n.* **1** a space in a stove or near a fireplace, for baking food. **2** a small furnace for heating or drying. [OE *ofen*]

An ovate leaf

ov·en·bird (uv′ən bėrd′) *n.* any of various birds that build nests with dome-shaped roofs. The ovenbird of North America is a warbler that has an olive-green back and black-spotted white breast.

ov·en·proof (uv′ən prüf′) *adj.* able to stand the heat of an oven without cracking.

ov·en·ware (uv′ən wãr′) *n.* dishes made to be ovenproof.

o·ver (ō′vər) *prep.* **1** above in place or position: *the roof over one's head.* **2** above in authority, power, etc.: *We have a captain over us.* **3** on; upon: *a blanket lying over a bed.* **4** at all or various places on: *A blush came over her face. Farms were scattered over the valley.* **5** above and to the other side of; across: *leap over a wall.* **6** on the other side of: *lands over the sea.* **7** out and down from: *He fell over the edge of the cliff.* **8** more than; beyond: *It costs over ten dollars.* **9** here and there on or in; round about; all through: *We shall travel over Europe.* **10** from end to end of; along: *We drove over the new highway.* **11** during; in the course of: *over many years.* **12** in reference to; concerning; about: *He is troubled over his health.* **13** while engaged on or concerned with: *fall*

asleep over one's work. **14** until the end of: *stay over the weekend.*
—*adv.* **1** above: *The cliff hung over.* **2** so as to cover the surface, or affect the whole surface: *Cover the tar over with sand until it has hardened.* **3** from side to side; to the other side; across any intervening space: *Go over to the store for me.* **4** from one to another: *Hand the money over.* **5** on the other side; at some distance: *over in Europe, over by the hill.* **6** down; out and down: *She went too near the edge and fell over. When he lost his balance, he fell over.* **7** so as to bring the upper side or end down or under: *turn over a page.* **8** again; in repetition: *ten times over. Do that homework over.* **9** too (used chiefly in compounds), as in *overnice.* **10** through a region, area, etc.: *travel all over.* **11** from beginning to end: *read a newspaper over.* **12** throughout or beyond a period of time: *Please stay over till Monday.* **13** in excess or addition: *receive the full sum and something over.* **14 over again,** once more. **15 over against, a** opposite to; in front of. **b** so as to bring out a difference. **16 over and above,** besides; in addition to. **17 over and over,** again and again.
—*adj.* **1** upper; higher up: *the over crust of a pie.* **2** higher in authority, station, etc. (used chiefly in compounds), as in *overlord.* **3** surplus; extra (used chiefly in compounds), as in *pay for overtime.* **4** too much; too great (used chiefly in compounds), as in *overuse of drugs.* **5** at an end: *The play is over.*
—*n.* **1** the amount in excess. **2** in cricket: **a** the number of balls (usually six) delivered between successive changes of bowlers. **b** the part of the game between such changes. [OE *ofer*]

Syn. *prep.* **1, 2. Over, above** express a relation in which one thing is thought of as being higher than another. **Over,** the opposite of *under*, suggests being directly higher or in the position or space immediately higher up: *Carry the umbrella over your head. A sergeant is over a corporal.* **Above,** opposed to *below* and *beneath*, suggests being on or at or rising to a higher level, but seldom suggests being straight up or a direct connection: *The plane flew above the clouds. An admiral is above a sergeant.*

☛ **over with.** Used in informal speech and writing to mean "over" or "finished." Spoken: *I'd like to get this over with today.* More formal: *I'd like to get this finished today.*

over- *prefix.* **1** too; too much; too long, etc., as in *overcrowded, overfull, overburden, overpay, oversleep.* **2** extra, as in *oversize, overtime.* **3** over, as in *overflow, overlord, overseas, overthrow.*

If an adjective beginning with *over* is not specially defined in this dictionary, its meaning may be learned by putting *too* in place of *over.* Some such words are:

o'ver·a·bun'dant
o'ver·am·bi'tious
o'ver·anx'ious
o'ver·bold'
o'ver·bus'y
o'ver·ca'pa·ble
o'ver·care'ful
o'ver·cau'tious
o'ver·child'ish
o'ver·con'fi·dent
o'ver·con·ser'va·tive
o'ver·crit'i·cal
o'ver·cu'ri·ous
o'ver·del'i·cate
o'ver·dig'ni·fied'
o'ver·ea'ger
o'ver·e·mo'tion·al
o'ver·en·thu'si·as'tic
o'ver·ex·cit'a·ble
o'ver·fa·mil'i·ar
o'ver·fond'
o'ver·fre'quent
o'ver·full'
o'ver·gen'er·ous
o'ver·great'
o'ver·greed'y
o'ver·hast'y
o'ver·jeal'ous
o'ver·long'
o'ver·mer'ry
o'ver·mod'est
o'ver·mourn'ful
o'ver·neg'li·gent
o'ver·nerv'ous
o'ver·o·be'di·ent
o'ver·plump'
o'ver·pop'u·lous
o'ver·pow'er·ful
o'ver·proud'
o'ver·rash'
o'ver·re·li'gious
o'ver·ripe'
o'ver·scep'ti·cal
o'ver·scru'pu·lous
o'ver·sen'si·tive
o'ver·se'ri·ous
o'ver·strict'
o'ver·stu'di·ous
o'ver·sub'tle
o'ver·suf·fi'cient
o'ver·sus·pi'cious
o'ver·sweet'
o'ver·talk'a·tive
o'ver·tech'ni·cal
o'ver·vi'o·lent
o'ver·word'y
o'ver·zeal'ous

If a noun beginning with *over* is not specially defined in this dictionary, its meaning may be learned by putting *too much* or *excessive* in place of *over.* Some such words are:

o'ver·a·bun'dance
o'ver·ac·tiv'i·ty
o'ver·anx·i'e·ty
o'ver·cau'tion
o'ver·con'fid·ence
o'ver·ex·er'tion
o'ver·ex·pan'sion
o'ver·in·dul'gence
o'ver·pay'ment
o'ver·pop'u·la'tion
o'ver·sim·plic'i·ty
o'ver·spec'ul·a'tion
o'ver·strain'
o'ver·stud'y
o'ver·val'u·a'tion

If a verb beginning with *over* is not specially defined in this dictionary, its meaning may be learned by putting *too much* in place of *over.* Some such words are:

o'ver·buy'
o'ver·cook'
o'ver·eat'
o'ver·em'pha·size'
o'ver·ex'er·cise'
o'ver·ex·ert'
o'ver·ex·pand'
o'ver·ex·pose'
o'ver·feed'
o'ver·heat'
o'ver·in·dulge'
o'ver·pay'
o'ver·pop'u·late'
o'ver·praise'
o'ver·prize'
o'ver·pro·vide'
o'ver·sim'pli·fy'
o'ver·stim'u·lat'ed
o'ver·strain'
o'ver·stud'y
o'ver·tire'
o'ver·val'ue
o'ver·wor'ry

☛ **over-** is a living prefix and may be used freely to form new words. Such words usually do not require a hyphen after the prefix.

o·ver·act (ō'vər akt') *v.* act to excess; overdo in acting; act (a part) in an exaggerated manner.

o·ver·ac·tive (ō'vər ak'tiv) *adj.* too active; active to excess. —**o'ver·ac'tive·ly,** *adv.*

o·ver·all (ō'vər ol' or -ôl') *adj.* **1** from one end to the other. **2** including everything: *an overall estimate.*

o·ver·alls (ō'vər olz' or -ôlz') *n.pl.* loose trousers worn over clothes to keep them clean. Overalls usually have a part that covers the chest.

o·ver·arch (ō'vər ärch') *v.* **1** arch over; span with or like an arch: *The street was overarched by elm trees.* **2** curve like an arch.

o·ver·arm (ō'vər ärm') *adj.* with the arm raised above the shoulder; overhand: *an overarm stroke, an overarm throw.*

o·ver·awe (ō'vər o' or -ô') *v.* **-awed, -aw·ing.** overcome or restrain with awe: *Seeing an airplane overawed the savages.* —**Syn.** intimidate, cow.

o·ver·bal·ance (ō'vər bal'əns) *v.* **-anced, -anc·ing. 1** be greater than in weight, importance, value, etc.: *The gains overbalanced the losses.* **2** cause to lose balance. **3** lose balance: *He overbalanced and fell from the wall.*

o·ver·bear (ō'vər bãr') *v.* **-bore, -borne, -bear·ing. 1** overcome by weight or force; oppress; master: *He overbore all my objections.* **2** bear down by weight or force; overthrow; upset.

o·ver·bear·ing (ō'vər bãr'ing) *adj.* inclined to dictate; forcing others to one's own will; domineering. —**o'ver·bear'ing·ly,** *adv.* —**Syn.** dictatorial, imperious, arrogant. See **proud.**

o·ver·bid (ō'vər bid') *v.* **-bid, -bid** or **-bid·den, -bid·ding. 1** bid more than the value of (a thing). **2** bid higher than (a person).

o·ver·blown (ō'vər blōn') *adj.* **1** more than full-blown: *an overblown flower.* **2** blown over.

o·ver·board (ō'vər bôrd') *adv.* **1** from a ship into the water. **2 throw overboard, a** throw into the water. **b** *Informal.* get rid of; give up; abandon; discard.

o·ver·bore (ō'vər bôr') *v.* pt. of **overbear.**

o·ver·borne (ō'vər bôrn') *v.* pp. of **overbear.**

o·ver·bur·den (*v.* ō'vər bėr'dən; *n.* ō'vər bėr'dən) *v.* overload. —*n.* **1** too great a burden; something that overloads. **2** in geology: **a** rock, clay, etc. that overlays and hides a deposit of ore. **b** soil, gravel, or other material that overlays bedrock.

o·ver·came (ō'vər kām') *v.* pt. of **overcome.**

o·ver·cap·i·tal·ize (ō'vər kap'ə təl īz') *v.* **-ized, -iz·ing.** fix or estimate the capital of (a company, enterprise, etc.) at too high an amount. —**o'ver·cap'i·tal·i·za'tion,** *n.*

o·ver·cast (ō'vər kast') *adj. v.* **-cast, -cast·ing.** —*adj.* **1** cloudy; dark; gloomy: *The sky was overcast before the storm.* **2** sad; gloomy: *His face was overcast.* **3** sewed with overcast stitches. —*v.* **1** cover or be covered with clouds or darkness. **2** sew over and through (the edges of a seam) with long stitches to prevent ravelling.

o·ver·charge (*v.* ō'vər chärj'; *n.* ō'vər chärj') *v.* **-charged, -charg·ing,** *n.* —*v.* **1** charge too high a price: *The grocer overcharged you for the eggs.* **2** load too heavily; fill too full: *The overcharged musket burst.* —*n.* **1** a charge that is too great. **2** too heavy or too full a load.

o·ver·cloud (ō'vər kloud') *v.* **1** cloud over; become clouded over; darken. 2 make or become gloomy.

o·ver·coat (ō′vər kōt′) *n.* a coat worn over the regular clothing.

o·ver·come (ō′vər kum′) *v.* **-came, -come, -com·ing.** 1 get the better of; win the victory over; conquer; defeat: *overcome an enemy, one's faults, all difficulties.* 2 make weak or helpless: *overcome by weariness.* 3 confuse: *The girl was so overcome by the noise and the lights that she couldn't speak.* [OE *ofercuman*] —**Syn. 1** overpower, vanquish, master. See **defeat.**

o·ver·crowd (ō′vər kroud′) *v.* crowd too much.

o·ver·de·vel·op (ō′vər di vel′əp) *v.* develop too much or too long. If a photograph is overdeveloped, it will be too dark.

o·ver·do (ō′vər dü′) *v.* **-did, -done, -do·ing.** 1 do too much: *She overdoes exercise.* 2 exaggerate: *The funny scenes in the play were overdone.* 3 cook too much. 4 exhaust; tire. [OE *oferdōn*] —**Syn. 4** fatigue.

o·ver·dose (*n.* ō′vər dōs′; *v.* ō′vər dōs′) *n. v.* **-dosed, -dos·ing.** —*n.* too big a dose. —*v.* give too large a dose to.

o·ver·draft (ō′vər draft′) *n.* 1 an overdrawing of an account, especially, a bank account. 2 the amount of the excess.

o·ver·draw (ō′vər drô′) *v.* **-drew, -drawn, -draw·ing.** 1 draw from (a bank account, allowance, etc.) more than one has a right to. 2 exaggerate: *The characters in the book were greatly overdrawn.*

o·ver·dress (*v.* ō′vər dres′; *n.* ō′vər dres′) *v.* dress or adorn excessively. —*n.* a dress worn over the main dress.

o·ver·drive (ō′vər drīv′) *n.* an arrangement of gears whereby less power produces more speed in high gear.

o·ver·due (ō′vər dū′ or -dü′) *adj.* more than due; due some time ago but not yet arrived, paid, etc.: *The train is overdue. This bill is overdue.*

o·ver·es·ti·mate (*v.* ō′vər es′tə māt′; *n.* ō′vər es′tə mit) *v.* **-mat·ed, -mat·ing,** *n.* —*v.* estimate at too high a value, amount, rate, etc. —*n.* an estimate that is too high. —**o′ver·es′ti·ma′tion,** *n.*

o·ver·ex·po·sure (ō′vər eks pō′zhər) *n.* too much or too long an exposure.

o·ver·fill (ō′vər fil′) *v.* fill too full; fill so as to cause overflowing.

o·ver·flight (ō′vər flīt′) *n.* the act or fact of flying over an area, especially the territory of another country.

o·ver·flow (*v.* ō′vər flō′; *n.* ō′vər flō′) *v.* **-flowed, -flown, -flow·ing,** *n.* —*v.* 1 flow over the bounds: *Rivers often overflow in the spring.* 2 cover; flood: *The river overflowed my garden.* 3 have the contents flowing over: *My cup is overflowing.* 4 flow over the top of: *The milk is overflowing the cup.* 5 extend out beyond; be too many for: *The crowd overflowed the little parlor and filled the hall.* 6 be very abundant: *an overflowing harvest, overflowing kindness.*
—*n.* 1 an overflowing; excess: *The overflow from the glass ran into the sink.* 2 an outlet or container for overflowing liquid. [OE *oferflōwan*] —**Syn.** *v.* **2** inundate, overrun.

o·ver·grow (ō′vər grō′) *v.* **-grew, -grown, -grow·ing.** 1 grow over: *The wall is overgrown with vines.* 2 grow too fast; become too big. 3 outgrow.

o·ver·grown (ō′vər grōn′) *adj.* grown too big: *an overgrown boy.* —*v.* pp. of **overgrow.**

o·ver·growth (ō′vər grōth′) *n.* 1 too great or too rapid growth. 2 growth overspreading or covering something.

o·ver·hand (ō′vər hand′) *adj. adv.* 1 with the hand raised above the shoulder: *an overhand throw, pitch overhand.* 2 with the knuckles upward. 3 over and over; with stitches passing successively over an edge. See **knot** for diagram.

o·ver·hang (*v.* ō′vər hang′; *n.* ō′vər hang′) *v.* **-hung, -hang·ing,** *n.* —*v.* 1 hang over; project over: *Trees overhang the street to form an arch of branches.* 2 hang over so as to darken, sadden, or threaten. —*n.* 1 something that projects: *The overhang of the roof shaded the flower bed beneath.* 2 the extent of projecting.

o·ver·haul (*v.* ō′vər hol′ or -hôl′; *n.* ō′vər hol′ or -hôl′) *v.* 1 examine thoroughly so as to make any repairs or changes that are needed. 2 gain upon; overtake. —*n.* a thorough examination to find and make necessary repairs.

hat, āge, çãre, fär; let, ēqual, tėrm; it, īce
hot, ōpen, ôrder; oil, out; cup, pu̇t, rüle, ūse
əbove, takən, pencəl, lemən, circəs
ch, child; ng, long; sh, ship
th, thin; ᴛʜ, then; zh, measure

o·ver·haul·ing (ō′vər hol′ing or -hôl′ing) *n.* a thorough examination to find and make any needed repairs or changes.

o·ver·head (*adv.* ō′vər hed′; *adj. n.* ō′vər hed′) *adv.* in the sky; on the floor above; on high; above: *the stars shone overhead.* —*adj.* 1 being, working, or passing overhead: *overhead wires.* 2 applying to one and all; general. —*n.* general expenses or charges, such as rent, lighting, heating, taxes, repairs.

o·ver·hear (ō′vər hēr′) *v.* **-heard, -hear·ing.** hear when one is not supposed to hear: *They spoke so loudly that I could not help overhearing what they said.* [OE *oferhīeran*]

o·ver·hung (*adj.* ō′vər hung′; *v.* ō′vər hung′) *adj.* 1 hung from above: *an overhung door.* 2 of the upper jaw, projecting beyond the lower jaw. —*v.* pt. and pp. of **overhang.**

o·ver·joy (ō′vər joi′) *v.* make extremely joyful.

o·ver·kill (ō′vər kil′) *n.* a capacity for destruction in excess of that required to destroy a target or enemy.

o·ver·lad·en (ō′vər lād′ən) *adj.* overloaded.

o·ver·laid (ō′vər lād′) *v.* pt. and pp. of **overlay**[1].

o·ver·lain (ō′vər lān′) *v.* pp. of **overlie.**

o·ver·land (ō′vər land′ or ō′vər lənd) *adv. adj.* on land; by land: *travel overland from Halifax to Montreal.*

O·ver·land·er (ō′vər land′ər) *n. Cdn.* a person who went from E. Canada to the Cariboo gold rush in 1862; Argonaut (def. 3).

o·ver·lap (*v.* ō′vər lap′; *n.* ō′vər lap′) *v.* **-lapped, -lap·ping,** *n.* —*v.* lap over; cover and extend beyond: *Shingles are laid to overlap each other.* —*n.* 1 a lapping over. 2 the amount by which one thing laps over another. 3 the part that overlaps.

o·ver·lay[1] (*v.* ō′vər lā′; *n.* ō′vər lā′) *v.* **-laid, -lay·ing,** *n.* —*v.* 1 lay or place (one thing) over or upon another. 2 cover, overspread, or surmount with something; especially, finish with a layer or applied decoration of something: *wood overlaid with gold.* 3 weigh down. —*n.* 1 something laid over something else; layer or decoration; covering. 2 a sheet of transparent material having marks on it, that is keyed to a design, chart, or map over which it is placed to give additional information.

o·ver·lay[2] (ō′vər lā′) *v.* pt. of **overlie.**

o·ver·leap (ō′vər lēp′) *v.* leap over; pass beyond.

o·ver·lie (ō′vər lī′) *v.* **-lay, -lain, -ly·ing.** 1 lie over; lie upon. 2 smother by lying on.

o·ver·load (*v.* ō′vər lōd′; *n.* ō′vər lōd′) *v.* load too heavily. —*n.* too great a load.

o·ver·look (ō′vər lu̇k′) *v.* 1 fail to see: *Here are the letters you overlooked.* 2 pay no attention to; excuse: *I will overlook your bad behavior this time.* 3 have a view of from above; be higher than: *This high window overlooks half the city.* 4 manage; look after and direct. 5 look over; watch: *She did not know that she was being overlooked by the woman next door.* —**o′ver·look′er,** *n.* —**Syn. 1** disregard, ignore, neglect. See **slight. 2** forgive, condone.

o·ver·lord (ō′vər lôrd′) *n.* a person who is lord over another lord or other lords: *The duke was the overlord of barons and knights who held land from him.*

o·ver·ly (ō′vər lē) *adv.* overmuch; excessively; too.

o·ver·mas·ter (ō′vər mas′tər) *v.* overcome; overpower.

o·ver·match (ō′vər mach′) *v.* be more than a match for; surpass.

o·ver·much (ō′vər much′) *adj. adv. n.* too much.

o·ver·nice (ō′vər nīs′) *adj.* too fastidious.

o·ver·night (*adv.* ō′vər nīt′; *adj. n.* ō′vər nīt′) *adv.* 1 during one night: *stay overnight.* 2 on the night before: *Preparations were made overnight for an early start.* —*adj.* 1 done, occurring, etc. during the night: *an* *overnight stop.* **2** for the night: *An overnight bag contains articles needed for one night's stay.* **3** of or having to do with the night before. —*n.* the previous evening.

overnight bag a bag used to carry articles needed for a night's stay.

o·ver·pass (*v.* ō′vər pas′; *n.* ō′vər pas') *v.* **-passed** or **-past, -pass·ing,** *n.* —*v.* **1** pass over (a region, bounds, etc.). **2** go beyond; exceed; surpass. **3** overlook; disregard. —*n.* a bridge over a road, railway, canal, etc.

o·ver·play (ō'vər plā′) *v.* **1** play (a part, etc.) in an exaggerated manner. **2** seek to obtain too much or too great an advantage from; exploit too vigorously. **3** play better than; surpass; defeat. **4** in golf, hit (the ball) past the green.

o·ver·plus (ō′vər plus') *n.* a surplus; too great an amount.

o·ver·pow·er (ō'vər pou′ər) *v.* **1** overcome; master; overwhelm: *overpower one's enemies.* **2** be so much greater than, that nothing else is felt: *Sudden anger overpowered every other feeling.* —**o'ver·pow′er·ing·ly,** *adv.* —**Syn. 1** conquer, vanquish, defeat, overthrow.

o·ver·price (ō'vər prīs′) *v.* **-priced, -pric·ing.** price too high; price (something) higher than its real value.

o·ver·print (*v.* ō'vər print′; *n.* ō′vər print') *v.* **1** print additional matter, revisions, etc. on sheets already printed. **2** in photography, print a positive darker than desired. —*n.* **1** anything overprinted. **2** any design or mark printed across a stamp to change its use, value, etc. **3** a postage stamp printed in this way.

o·ver·pro·duce (ō'vər prə dūs′ or -prə düs′) *v.* **-duced, -duc·ing. 1** produce more than necessary. **2** produce more than can be sold profitably.

o·ver·pro·duc·tion (ō'vər prə duk′shən) *n.* **1** production of more than is needed. **2** production of more than can be sold at a profit.

o·ver·proof (ō'vər prüf′) *adj.* higher than 100 proof; containing more alcohol than proof spirit contains.

o·ver·rate (ō'vər rāt′) *v.* **-rat·ed, -rat·ing.** rate or estimate too highly.

o·ver·reach (ō'vər rēch′) *v.* **1** reach over or beyond. **2** reach too far. **3** get the better of by cunning: *overreach a man in a bargain.* **4** cheat. **5 overreach oneself, a** fail or miss by trying for too much. **b** fail by being too crafty or tricky. —**Syn. 4** defraud, swindle, dupe.

o·ver·ride (ō'vər rīd′) *v.* **-rode, -rid·den, -rid·ing. 1** act in spite of: *override advice or objections.* **2** prevail over: *The new rule overrides all previous ones.* **3** ride over; trample on. **4** ride over (a region, place, etc.). **5** tire out by riding; ride too much. [OE *oferrīdan*]

o·ver·rule (ō'vər rül′) *v.* **-ruled, -rul·ing. 1** rule or decide against (a plea, argument, objection, etc.); set aside. **2** prevail over; be stronger than. —**o'ver·rul′ing·ly,** *adv.* —**Syn. 1** override, reject.

o·ver·run (*v.* ō'vər run′; *n.* ō′vər run') *v.* **-ran, -run, -run·ning,** *n.* —*v.* **1** spread over and spoil or harm in some way: *Weeds had overrun the old garden.* **2** spread over: *Vines overran the wall.* **3** run or go beyond; exceed: *The speaker overran the time set for him.* **4** in printing: **a** carry over (words or lines of type) into another line or page to provide for addition or removal of other matter. **b** remake (columns, pages, etc.) by carrying over words, lines, etc. —*n.* **1** an overrunning. **2** the amount overrunning or carried over, as a balance or surplus; an excess. —**Syn. 1** invade, ravage, infest.

o·ver·saw (ō'vər so′ or -sô′) *v.* pt. of **oversee.**

o·ver·sea (*adv.* ō'vər sē′; *adj.* ō′vər sē') *adv. adj.* overseas.

o·ver·seas (*adv.* ō'vər sēz′; *adj.* ō′vər sēz') *adv.* **1** across the sea; beyond the sea; abroad. **2** of the armed services, serving across the sea: *My father was overseas during the war.* —*adj.* **1** done, used, or serving overseas. **2** of countries across the sea; foreign: *overseas trade.*

o·ver·see (ō'vər sē′) *v.* **-saw, -seen, -see·ing.** look after and direct (work or workers); superintend; manage. [OE *oferseōn*] —**Syn.** supervise, inspect.

o·ver·se·er (ō′vər sē'ər) *n.* **1** one who oversees, superintends, or looks after the work of others. **2** *Cdn.* in certain provinces, the head of a township council; reeve.

o·ver·sell (ō'vər sel′) *v.* **-sold, -sell·ing. 1** sell to excess; sell more of than can be delivered. **2** *Informal.* urge (a person) to buy something too aggressively or too long, often at the risk of losing a sale.

o·ver·set (*v.* ō'vər set′; *n.* ō′vər set') *v.* **-set, -set·ting,** *n.* —*v.* **1** upset; overturn. **2** overthrow. —*n.* an overthrow

o·ver·sew (ō'vər sō′ or ō'vər sō′) *v.* **-sewed** or **-sewn, -sew·ing.** sew overhand with close stitches.

o·ver·sexed (ō'vər sekst′) *adj.* having excessive sexual desire or capacity.

o·ver·shad·ow (ō'vər shad′ō) *v.* **1** be more important than: *The boy overshadowed his brother as a hockey player.* **2** cast a shadow over.

o·ver·shoe (ō′vər shü') *n.* a shoe of rubber, nylon, felt, etc., having a rubber sole and worn over another shoe to keep the foot dry and warm.

o·ver·shoot (ō'vər shüt′) *v.* **-shot, -shoot·ing. 1** shoot over, higher than, or beyond. **2** go over, higher than, or beyond. **3** go too far.

o·ver·shot (*adj.* ō′vər shot'; *v.* ō'vər shot′) *adj.* **1** having the upper jaw projecting beyond the lower. **2** driven by water flowing over from above. —*v.* pt. and pp. of **overshoot.**

An overshot water wheel (cross section). The force of the falling water and the weight of the water-filled buckets make the wheel turn. Its axle is connected to machinery.

o·ver·sight (ō′vər sīt') *n.* **1** a failure to notice or think of something. **2** watchful care. —**Syn. 1** overlooking, inadvertence, omission, slip. **2** supervision, superintendence, charge.

o·ver·size (ō′vər sīz') *adj.* too big. —*n.* **1** a size larger than the proper or usual size. **2** something larger than is necessary.

o·ver·skirt (ō′vər skėrt') *n.* **1** an outer skirt. **2** a separate skirt over the main skirt.

o·ver·sleep (ō'vər slēp′) *v.* **-slept, -sleep·ing.** sleep beyond a certain hour; sleep in; sleep too long.

o·ver·spread (ō'vər spred′) *v.* **-spread, -spread·ing.** spread over: *A smile overspread his broad face.*

o·ver·state (ō'vər stāt′) *v.* **-stat·ed, -stat·ing.** state too strongly; exaggerate. —**o'ver·state′ment,** *n.*

o·ver·stay (ō'vər stā′) *v.* stay beyond the time of.

o·ver·step (ō'vər step′) *v.* **-stepped, -step·ping.** go beyond; exceed.

o·ver·stock (*v.* ō'vər stok′; *n.* ō′vər stok') *v.* supply with more than is needed. —*n.* too great a stock or supply.

o·ver·strung (ō′vər strung′) *adj.* too nervous or sensitive.

o·ver·stuff (ō'vər stuf′) *v.* **1** stuff too full. **2** make (upholstered furniture) soft and comfortable by thick padding.

o·ver·sub·scribe (ō'vər səb skrīb′) *v.* **-scribed, -scrib·ing.** subscribe or subscribe for in excess of what is available or required.

o·ver·sub·scrip·tion (ō'vər səb skrip′shən) *n.* an oversubscribing.

o·ver·sup·ply (*v.* ō′vər sə plī′; *n.* ō′vər sə plī') *v.* **-plied, -ply·ing,** *n.* **-plies.** —*v.* supply in excess. —*n.* an excessive supply.

o·vert (ō′vėrt or ō vėrt′) *adj.* open; evident; not hidden; public: *Hitting someone is an overt act.* [ME < OF *overt,* pp. of *ovrir* open < L *aperire*] —**o′vert·ly,** *adv.* —**Syn.** plain, manifest, apparent.

o·ver·take (ō'vər tāk′) *v.* **-took, -tak·en, -tak·ing. 1** come up with and pass: *The blue car overtook ours.* **2** come upon suddenly: *A storm overtook the children.*

o·ver·task (ō'vər task′) *v.* give too long or too hard tasks to.

o·ver·tax (ō'vər taks′) *v.* **1** tax too heavily. **2** put too heavy a burden on. —**o'ver·tax·a′tion,** *n.*

o·ver·threw (ō'vər thrü′) *v.* pp. of **overthrow.**

hat, āge, cãre, fär; let, ēqual, tėrm; it, īce
hot, ōpen, ôrder; oil, out; cup, pu̇t, rüle, ūse
əbove, takən, pencəl, lemən, circəs
ch, child; ng, long; sh, ship
th, thin; ᴛʜ, then; zh, measure

o·ver·throw (*v.* ō′vər thrō′; *n.* ō′vər thrō′) *v.* **-threw, -thrown, -throw·ing,** *n.* —*v.* **1** take away the power of; defeat: *overthrow a government.* **2** put an end to; destroy: *overthrow slavery.* **3** overturn; upset; knock down. —*n.* **1** a defeat; upset: *the overthrow of one's plans.* **2** a ball thrown past the place for which it is intended. —**Syn.** *v.* **1** rout, conquer, vanquish, overcome. –*n.* **1** destruction.

o·ver·thrown (ō′vər thrōn′) *v.* pp. of **overthrow.**

o·ver·thrust (ō′vər thrust′) *n.* in geology, a fault in which rocks of an older, lower stratum are pushed on top of those of a newer, originally higher stratum.

o·ver·time (*n. adv. adj.* ō′vər tīm′; *v.* ō′vər tīm′) *n. adv. adj. v.* **-timed, -tim·ing.** —*n.* **1** extra time; time beyond the regular hours. **2** wages for this period: *pay overtime.* **3** in games, a period or periods beyond the normal game time. —*adv. adj.* **1** beyond the regular hours: *He worked overtime.* **2** beyond the allotted or permitted time: *overtime parking.* —*v.* give too much time to: *overtime a camera exposure.*

o·ver·tone (ō′vər tōn′) *n.* **1** in music, a tone heard along with the main or fundamental tone and whose rate of vibration is an integral multiple of the main tone; harmonic. **2** a hint or suggestion of something felt, believed, etc.: *an overtone of anger.*

o·ver·took (ō′vər tu̇k′) *v.* pt. of **overtake.**

o·ver·top (ō′vər top′) *v.* **-topped, -top·ping. 1** rise above; be higher than. **2** surpass; excel.

o·ver·train (ō′vər trān′) *v.* especially of athletes, subject to or undergo excessive training.

o·ver·trump (ō′vər trump′) *v.* play a higher trump; play a higher trump than.

o·ver·ture (ō′vər chür′ or ō′vər chər) *n.* **1** a proposal; offer: *The enemy is making overtures for peace.* **2** in music: **a** a musical composition played by the orchestra as an introduction to an opera, oratorio, etc. **b** an independent composition for orchestra. [ME < OF < L *apertura* opening. Doublet of APERTURE.] —**Syn. 1** proposition. **2** prelude.

o·ver·turn (*v.* ō′vər tėrn′; *n.* ō′vər tėrn′) *v.* **1** turn upside down. **2** upset; fall down; fall over: *The boat overturned.* **3** make fall down; overthrow; destroy the power of: *The rebels overturned the government.* —*n.* an overturning. —**Syn.** *v.* **1** invert. **2** capsize. See **upset.**

o·ver·view (ō′vər vū′) *n.* an overall examination or survey.

o·ver·watch (ō′vər woch′) *v.* **1** watch over. **2** make weary by watching.

o·ver·ween·ing (o′vər wēn′ing) *adj.* thinking too much of oneself; conceited; self-confident; presumptuous. [ppr. of *overween* < *over-* + *ween* expect (OE *wēnan*)] —**o′ver·ween′ing·ly,** *adv.*

o·ver·weigh (ō′vər wā′) *v.* **1** be greater than in weight, importance, etc.; outweigh. **2** oppress.

o·ver·weight (*adj. n.* ō′vər wāt′; *v.* ō′vər wāt′) *adj.* having too much weight: *a boy overweight for his age.* —*n.* **1** too much weight. **2** extra weight: *The butcher gave us overweight on this roast.* —*v.* overburden.

o·ver·whelm (ō′vər hwelm′ or -welm′) *v.* **1** overcome completely; crush: *overwhelm with grief.* **2** cover completely as a flood would: *A great wave overwhelmed the boat.* [< *over-* + ME *whelmen* turn upside down < Gmc.; cf. ON *hvelfa* overturn]

o·ver·whelm·ing (ō′vər hwel′ming or -wel′ming) *adj.* too many, too great, or too much to be resisted; overpowering: *an overwhelming majority of votes.* —**o′ver·whelm′ing·ly,** *adv.*

o·ver·work (*n.* ō′vər wėrk′; *v.* ō′vər wėrk′) *n. v.* **-worked** or **-wrought, -work·ing.** —*n.* **1** too much or too hard work. **2** extra work. —*v.* **1** work or cause to work too hard or too long. **2** *Informal.* use to excess: *overwork a pose of childlike innocence.* **3** work too much upon (a book, speech, etc.); elaborate too much. **4** figure or decorate the surface of.

o·ver·wrap (ō′vər rap′) *n.* a second, outside wrapper of transparent paper, cellophane, etc.

o·ver·wrought (ō′vər rot′ or -rôt′) *adj.* **1** wearied; excited: *overwrought nerves.* **2** decorated all over: *an overwrought platter.* **3** too elaborate. —*v.* a pt. and a pp. of **overwork.**

o·vi·duct (ō′və dukt′) *n.* the tube through which the ovum or egg passes from the ovary. [< NL *oviductus* < L *ovum* egg + *ductus* duct]

o·vi·form (ō′və fôrm′) *adj.* egg-shaped. [< L *ovum* egg + E *-form*]

o·vine (ō′vīn or ō′vin) *adj.* of, like, or having to do with sheep. [< LL *ovinus* < *ovis* sheep]

o·vip·a·rous (ō vip′ə rəs) *adj.* producing eggs that are hatched after leaving the body. Birds are oviparous. [< L *oviparus* < *ovum* egg + *parere* bring forth]

o·vi·pos·i·tor (ō′və poz′ə tər) *n.* in certain insects, an organ at the end of the abdomen, by which eggs are deposited. [< L *ovum* egg + *positor* placer < *ponere* place]

o·void (ō′void) *adj.* egg-shaped. —*n.* an egg-shaped object. [< L *ovum* egg]

o·vu·lar (ō′vyu̇ lər) *adj.* of an ovule; being an ovule.

o·vu·la·tion (ō′vu̇ lā′shən) *n.* **1** the period when an ovum or female germ cell is produced or formed. **2** the discharge of ova from the ovary. [ult. < NL *ovulum*, dim. of *ovum* egg]

o·vule (ō′vūl) *n.* **1** a little ovum. **2** the part of a plant that develops into a seed. [< NL *ovulum*, dim. of L *ovum* egg]

o·vum (ō′vəm) *n.* **o·va.** a female germ cell; egg. [< L *ovum* egg]

owe (ō) *v.* **owed, ow·ing. 1** have to pay; be in debt for: *I owe the grocer $10.* **2** be in debt: *He is always owing for something.* **3** be obliged or indebted for. **4** have or cherish toward another: *owe a grudge.* [OE *āgan*]

ow·ing (ō′ing) *adj.* **1** that owes: *a man owing money.* **2** due; owed; *pay what is owing.* **3 owing to,** an account of; because of; due to; as a result of.

owl (oul) *n.* a bird having a big head, big eyes, and a short, hooked beak. Owls hunt mice and small birds at night. Some kinds have tufts of feathers on their heads, called "horns" or "ears." [OE *ūle*] —**owl′-like′,** *adj.*

owl·et (oul′it) *n.* **1** a young owl. **2** a small owl.

owl·ish (oul′ish) *adj.* **1** like an owl; like an owl's. **2** trying to look wise. —**owl′ish·ly,** *adv.*

own (ōn) *adj.* **1** of oneself or itself; belonging to oneself or itself: *We have our own troubles. The house is her own.* **2** in closest relationship: *Own brothers have the same parents.*
—*n.* **1** the one or ones belonging to oneself or itself. **2 come into one's own, a** get what belongs to one. **b** get the success or credit that one deserves. **3 hold one's own,** keep one's position; not be forced back. **4 of one's own,** belonging to oneself. **5 on one's own,** *Informal.* on one's own account, responsibility, resources, etc.
—*v.* **1** possess: *He owns much land.* **2** acknowledge; admit, confess: *He owned his guilt. She owns to many faults.* **3** acknowledge as one's own: *His father will not own him.* **own up,** confess: *If nobody owns up, everybody will be punished.* [OE *āgen*, originally pp. of *āgan* owe] —**Syn.** *v.* **1** hold. See **have. 2** concede, grant.

own·er (ōn′ər) *n.* one who owns: *the owner of the dog.* —**own′er·less,** *adj.*

own·er·ship (ōn′ər ship′) *n.* the state of being an owner; the possessing (of something); right of possession.

ox (oks) *n.* **ox·en. 1** the full-grown male of cattle, that has been castrated and is used as a draft animal or for beef. **2** any of a group of mammals having horns and cloven hoofs, including domestic cattle, buffalo, bison, etc. [OE *oxa*] —**ox′like′** *adj.*

ox·a·late (ok′sə lāt′) *n.* a salt of oxalic acid.

ox·al·ic acid (oks al′ik) a poisonous organic acid that occurs in many plants. It is used for bleaching, removing stains, making dyes, etc. *Formula*: $C_2H_2O_4 \cdot 2H_2O$ [< F < L *oxalis* sorrel[2] < Gk. *oxalis* < *oxys* sour]

ox·a·lis (ok′sə lis) *n.* any of several plants having acid juice, usually having leaves composed of three heart-shaped leaflets, and white, yellow, or pink flowers; wood sorrel. [< L < Gk. *oxalis* < *oxys* sour]

ox·blood (oks′blud′) *n.* a deep red.

ox·bow (oks′bō′) *n.* **1** a U-shaped piece of wood placed under and around the neck of an ox, with the upper ends inserted in the bar of the yoke. **2** a U-shaped bend in a river. **3** the land contained within such a bend.

OXBOWS

oxbow lake a small pond or lake which originally formed an oxbow but which became a separated body of water when the river straightened its course.

ox·cart (oks′kärt′) *n.* a cart drawn by an ox or oxen.

ox·en (ok′sən) *n.* pl. of **ox.**

ox·eye (oks′ī′) *n.* **1** the common North American daisy. **2** any of several plants like it.

ox-eyed (oks′īd′) *adj.* having large full eyes like those of an ox.

ox·ford (oks′fərd) *n.* **1** a kind of low shoe. **2** a very dark gray. [< *Oxford,* a city in S. England]

Ox·ford (oks′fərd) *n.* **1** the very old and famous university located in Oxford, England. **2** an oxford.

Oxford gray a very dark gray.

Oxford movement **1** a movement in the Church of England, favoring High-Church principles, which originated at Oxford University about 1833. **2** a modern religious movement that stresses public confession of one's faults and direct guidance by God.

ox·heart (oks′härt′) *n.* a large, heart-shaped cherry.

ox·id (ok′sid) *n.* oxide.

ox·i·da·tion (ok′sə dā′shən) *n.* **1** an oxidizing; the combining of oxygen with another element to form one or more new substances. **2** the process or state of being oxidized.

ox·ide (ok′sīd or ok′sid) *n.* a compound of oxygen with another element or radical. [< F *oxide* (now *oxyde*) < *ox(ygène)* oxygen + *(ac)ide* acid]

ox·i·dize (ok′sə dīz′) *v.* **-dized, -diz·ing. 1** combine with oxygen. When a substance burns or rusts, it is oxidized. **2** rust. **3** lose or cause to lose hydrogen. **4** change to a higher positive valence. **—ox′i·diz′er,** *n.*

ox·lip (oks′lip′) *n.* a primrose that has clusters of pale-yellow flowers. [OE *oxanslyppe* < *oxan* ox's + *slyppe* slime]

Oxon. **1** Oxford. **2** Oxonian. **3** Oxfordshire.

Ox·o·ni·an (oks ō′nē ən) *adj.* of or having to do with Oxford University or Oxford, England. *—n.* **1** a member or graduate of Oxford University. **2** a native or inhabitant of Oxford, England. [< Med.L *Oxonia* Oxford]

ox·tail (oks′tāl′) *n.* the tail of a cow, ox, or steer, skinned and cut up to make soup.

oxy-[1] *combining form.* **1** pointed, as in *oxymoron.* **2** acid, as in *oxygen.* [< Gk. *oxys* sharp, acid]

oxy-[2] *combining form.* in chemistry: **1** oxygen, or containing oxygen or one of its compounds, as in *oxygenated.* **2** a product of oxidation, as in *oxysulphide.* [< *oxy*gen]

ox·y·a·cet·y·lene (ok′sē ə set′ə lēn′) *adj.* of, having to do with, or using a mixture of oxygen and acetylene.

oxyacetylene torch a tool with a very hot flame for welding or cutting metals. It uses a mixture of oxygen and acetylene.

ox·y·gen (ok′sə jən) *n.* a colorless, odorless, gaseous chemical element that forms about one fifth of the air and occurs in a combined form in many substances. Animals and plants cannot live, and fire will not burn, without oxygen. *Symbol:* O; *at.no.* 8; *at.wt.* 16.00 [< F *oxygène,* intended as "acidifying (principle)" < Gk. *oxys* sharp + *-genēs* born]

ox·y·gen·ate (ok′sə jən āt′) *v.* **-at·ed, -at·ing. 1** treat or combine with oxygen. **2** oxidize. **—ox′y·gen·a′tion,** *n.*

ox·y·gen·ize (ok′sə jən īz′) *v.* **-ized, -iz·ing.** treat with oxygen; combine with oxygen. **—ox′y·gen·iz′a·ble,** *adj.*

oxygen mask a device worn over the nose and mouth by aviators at very high altitudes, through which supplementary oxygen is supplied from an attached container.

oxygen tent a small tent that can be filled with oxygen, used in treating some diseases.

ox·y·hy·dro·gen (ok′sē hī′drə jən) *adj.* of, having to do with, or using a mixture of oxygen and hydrogen.

oxyhydrogen torch a tool with a very hot flame for welding or cutting metals. It uses a mixture of oxygen and hydrogen.

ox·y·mor·on (ok′sē môr′on) *n.* **-mor′a** (-môr′ə). a figure of speech in which contradictory words or connotations are placed together. *Example:* Avoid accidents by making haste slowly. [< Gk. *oxymōron,* neuter of *oxymōros* pointedly stupid, foolish < *oxys* sharp + *mōros* stupid]

O·yez or **O·yes** (ō′yes or ō′yez) *interj. n.* Hear! Attend! A cry uttered, usually three times, by a public or court crier to command silence and attention before a proclamation, etc. is made. [ME < AF *oyez* hear ye! < *oyer* hear, var. of *oïr* < L *audire*]

oys·ter (ois′tər) *n.* **1** a kind of mollusc much used as food, having a rough, irregular shell in two halves. Oysters are found in shallow water along seacoasts. Some kinds of oysters yield pearls. **2** an oyster-shaped bit of dark meat in the back of a fowl. **3** *Informal.* a very reserved or uncommunicative person. **4** something from which to take or derive advantage. [ME < OF *oistre* < L < Gk. *ostreon*]

oyster bed a place where oysters breed or are cultivated.

oyster catcher any of various large shore birds of the plover family, having black and white coloring and red, chisel-like bills for opening shellfish.

oyster crab a small crab that lives within the shell of a live oyster, but without harm to its host.

oyster cracker a small, round or hexagonal, salted cracker eaten with oysters, soups, etc.

oyster farm a place where oysters are raised for the market.

oyster plant salsify, a parsniplike vegetable.

oz. ounce; ounces.

o·zone (ō′zōn) *n.* **1** a form of oxygen with a peculiar odor, produced by electricity and present in the air, especially after a thunderstorm. *Formula:* O_3 **2** *Informal.* pure air that is refreshing. [< F *ozone* < Gk. *ozein* smell + F *-one,* chemical suffix]

o·zo·nif·er·ous (ō′zə nif′ər əs) *adj.* containing ozone.

hat, āge, cãre, fär; let, ēqual, tėrm; it, īce
hot, ōpen, ôrder; oil, out; cup, pu̇t, rüle, ūse
əbove, takən, pencəl, lemən, circəs
ch, child; ng, long; sh, ship
th, thin; ᴛʜ, then; zh, measure

P or **p** (pē) *n.* **P's** or **p's. 1** the sixteenth letter of the English alphabet. **2** any speech sound represented by this letter. **3** one (usually sixteenth) of a series designated alphabetically. **4 mind one's p's and q's,** be careful about details.

p or **p. 1** in music, piano. **2** in baseball, pitcher.

p. 1 page. **2** participle. **3** part. **4** past. **5** penny. **6** pressure. **7** peso. **8** peseta. **9** pint. **10** population.

P phosphorus.

P. 1 Pastor. **2** President. **3** Priest. **4** Prince. **5** Father. (for F *père*; L *pater*)

pa (po, pä, or pa) *n. Informal.* papa; father.

Pa protactinium.

Pa. Pennsylvania.

p.a. 1 participial adjective. **2** per annum.

P.A. 1 public address (system). **2** press agent. **3** power of attorney. **4** private account. **5** purchasing agent.

pab·u·lum (pab′yu̇ ləm) *n.* **1** food. **2** intellectual or spiritual nourishment; food for the mind. [< L *pabulum* fodder]

Pac. Pacific.

pace (pās) *n. v.* **paced, pac·ing.** —*n.* **1** rate of movement; speed: *a fast pace in walking.* **2** a step. **3** the length of a step in walking; about 2½ feet. **4** a way of stepping. The walk, trot, and canter are some of the paces of a horse. **5** a particular pace of some horses in which the feet on the same side are lifted and put down together. **6 keep pace with,** keep up with; go as fast as. **7 put one through his paces,** try one out; find out what one can do. **8 set the pace, a** set speed for others to keep up with. **b** be an example or model for others to follow.
—*v.* **1** set the pace for: *A motorboat will pace the boys training for the rowing match.* **2** walk over with regular steps: *pace the floor.* **3** walk with regular steps. **4** measure by paces: *We paced off the distance.* **5** train (a horse) to a certain step, especially to lift and put down the feet on the same side together. **6** of a horse, move at a pace. [ME < OF < L *passus* step] —**Syn.** *n.* **4** gait.

pace·mak·er (pās′māk′ər) *n.* **1** a person, animal, or thing that sets the pace. **2** a node of specialized tissue near the top of the wall of the right auricle of the heart where the impulse that results in the heartbeat begins. **3** an electrical device applied to the wall of the heart when the natural pacemaker does not function, to maintain or restore the rhythm of the heartbeat.

pac·er (pās′ər) *n.* **1** one that paces. **2** a horse that lifts and puts down the feet on the same side together. **3** a pacemaker.

pa·cha (pə shä′, pash′ə, or pä′shə) *n.* pasha.

pa·chi·si (pə chē′ zē) *n.* parcheesi.

pach·y·derm (pak′ə dėrm′) *n.* **1** a thick-skinned mammal having hoofs. The elephant, hippopotamus, and rhinoceros are pachyderms. **2** a thick-skinned person; one who is not sensitive to criticism or ridicule. [< F < Gk. *pachydermos* < *pachys* thick + *derma* skin]

pa·cif·ic (pə sif′ik) *adj.* **1** tending to make peace; making peace. **2** loving peace; not warlike: *a pacific nation.* **3** peaceful; calm; quiet: *a pacific nature.* [< L *pacificus,* ult. < *pax, pacis* peace + *facere* make]
—**pa·cif′i·cal·ly,** *adv.* —**Syn. 1** peaceable, conciliatory. **3** placid, tranquil.

Pa·cif·ic (pə sif′ik) *adj.* **1** of the Pacific Ocean. **2** on or near the Pacific Ocean.

pac·i·fi·ca·tion (pas′ə fə kā′shən) *n.* a pacifying or being pacified.

pa·cif·i·ca·to·ry (pə sif′ə kə tô′rē) *adj.* tending to make peace; conciliatory.

pac·i·fi·er (pas′ə fī′ər) *n.* **1** a person or thing that pacifies. **2** a rubber nipple or ring given to a baby to suck.

pac·i·fism (pas′ə fiz′əm) *n.* the principle or policy of establishing and maintaining universal peace; settlement of all differences between nations by peaceful means; opposition to war.

pac·i·fist (pas′ə fist) *n.* a person who is opposed to war and favors settling all disputes between nations by peaceful means.

pac·i·fis·tic (pas′ə fis′tik) *adj.* of pacifism or pacifists.

pac·i·fy (pas′ə fī′) *v.* **-fied, -fy·ing. 1** make calm; quiet down: *Can't you pacify that screaming baby?* **2** bring peace to: *Soldiers were sent to pacify the country.* [< L *pacificare* < *pax, pacis* peace + *facere* make] —**Syn. 1** See **appease.**

pack[1] (pak) *n.* **1** a bundle of things wrapped up or tied together for carrying. **2** the amount packed: *This year's pack of fish is larger than last year's.* **3** a set; lot; a number of things together: *a pack of thieves, a pack of nonsense, a pack of lies.* **4** a number of animals hunting together; a number of dogs kept together for hunting. **5** a complete set of playing cards, usually 52. **6** a large area of floating pieces of ice pushed together. **7** something put on the body or skin as a treatment. A cloth soaked in hot or cold water is often used as a pack. **8** a company or troop of Wolf Cubs or Brownies.
—*v.* **1** put together in a bundle, box, bale, etc.: *Pack your clothes in this bag.* **2** put things together in a bundle, box, bale, etc.: *Are you ready to pack?* **3** fill with things; put one's things into: *Pack your trunk.* **4** fit together closely; admit of storing and shipping: *These goods pack well.* **5** press or crowd closely together: *A hundred men were packed into one small room.* **6** press together; make firm: *The heavy trucks packed the snow on the highway.* **7** fill (a space) with all that it will hold: *pack a small theatre with a large audience.* **8** become packed; crowd together. **9** become relatively compact: *The Navaho Indians found that mud will pack easily to make bricks.* **10** put into a container to be sold or stored: *Meat, fish, and vegetables are often packed in cans.* **11** make tight with something that water, steam, air, etc. cannot leak through. **12** load (an animal) with a pack; burden. **13** *Informal.* carry: *pack a gun.* **14** carry in a pack: *pack supplies up a mountain.* **15** cover, surround, or protect with closely applied materials; treat with a therapeutic pack: *The dentist packed my gum after he extracted my tooth.* **16** *Informal.* **a** possess as a characteristic or power: *That mule packs a knockout punch in its hind feet.* **b** be capable of administering. **17 pack off,** send away: *The child was packed off to bed.* **18 pack up,** *Informal.* **a** stop working; cease operating; fail: *One of the aircraft's engines packed up.* **b** die. **19 send packing,** send away in a hurry. [ME< MLG *packe*] —**Syn.** *n.* **1** parcel, bale, package. –*v.* **5** cram.

pack[2] (pak) *v.* arrange unfairly. To pack a jury or a convention is to fill it unfairly with those who will favor one side. [? akin to PACT; partly associated with *pack*[1]]

pack·age (pak′ij) *n. v.* **-aged, -ag·ing.** —*n.* **1** a bundle of things packed or wrapped together; a box with things packed in it; parcel. **2 a** a box, can, bottle, jar, case, or other receptacle for packing goods, especially one designed for a particular commodity and printed with matter intended both to identify it and to attract buyers. **b** such a package with its contents, as offered for sale. **3** a group of related items or elements, such as goods, services, laws, articles of agreement in a negotiation, etc., offered, provided, sold, accepted, or rejected as a unit, often as an indivisible unit: *Our Montreal package includes transportation, hotel, and meals for a week.*
—*v.* **1** put in a package. **2** make a package or packages out of: *wrap and package Christmas presents.*
—**pack′ag·er,** *n.*

package deal a bargain, sale, or business deal in which a number of items are presented as a single offer.

pack animal an animal used for carrying loads or packs.

pack-board (pak′bôrd′) *n.* a light wooden or metal frame, covered usually with canvas and strapped to the back for carrying heavy loads.

pack·er (pak′ər) *n.* **1** a person or thing that packs. **2 a** person or company that packs meat, fruit, vegetables, etc. to be sold at wholesale or to wholesalers: *a meat packer.* **3** a person who transports goods by means of pack animals. **4** a fishing vessel equipped as a mobile cannery.

pack·et (pak′it) *n.* **1** a small package; parcel. **2** a packet boat. [< AF *pacquet*, dim. of ME *pakke* pack]

packet boat a boat that carries mail, passengers, and goods regularly on a fixed route, usually along a river or the coast.

pack horse a horse used to carry packs of goods.

pack ice ice pushed by wind or current into a solid mass.

pack·ing (pak′ing) *n.* **1** material used to pack or to make watertight, steamtight, etc.: *the packing around the valves of a radiator.* **2** the business of preparing and packing meat, fish, fruit, vegetables, etc. to be sold.

packing house a place where meat, fruit, vegetables, etc. are prepared and packed to be sold.

pack mule a mule used for carrying loads.

pack rat a large, bushy-tailed North American rat that carries away and hides food, clothing, tools, etc. and often leaves something else as if in exchange.

pack·sad·dle (pak′sad′əl) *n.* a saddle specially adapted for supporting the load on a pack animal.

pack strap tumpline.

pack·thread (pak′thred′) *n.* a strong thread or twine for sewing or tying up packages.

pack train a line or group of animals carrying loads.

pack·y (pak′ē) *adj.* of snow, of such consistency that it packs and binds together easily.

pact (pakt) *n.* an agreement; compact: *The two nations signed a peace pact.* [< L *pactum*, originally, pp. of *pacisci* covenant] —**Syn.** covenant, treaty.

pad[1] (pad) *n. v.* **pad·ded, pad·ding.** —*n.* **1** a soft mass used for comfort, protection, or stuffing; cushion. **2** a soft, stuffed saddle. **3** one of the cushionlike parts on the bottom side of the feet of dogs, foxes, and some other animals. **4** the foot of such animals as dogs, foxes, and wolves. **5** the large floating leaf of a water lily. **6** a number of sheets of paper fastened along an edge or edges; tablet. **7** a cloth soaked with ink to use with a rubber stamp; stamp pad. **8** the launching platform for a rocket or missile; launching pad: *The man-made satellite rose from the pad at midnight.* **9** *Slang.* a place where a person sleeps, as a bed, a room, an apartment, etc.
—*v.* **1** fill with something soft; stuff. **2** make (a written paper or speech) longer by using unnecessary words just to fill space: *Don't pad your compositions.* **3** increase the amount of (a bill, expense account, etc.) by false entries. [origin uncertain]

pad[2] (pad) *v.* **pad·ded, pad·ding,** *n.* —*v.* **1** walk; tramp; trudge. **2** walk or trot softly. —*n.* **1** a dull sound, as of footsteps on the ground. **2** a slow horse for riding on a road. [< Du. or LG. Akin to PATH.]

pad·ded cell (pad′id) in a mental institution, a room having padded walls to prevent a violent patient from injuring himself.

pad·ding (pad′ing) *n.* **1** material used to pad with, such as hair, cotton, or straw. **2** unnecessary words used just to fill space in making a speech or a written paper longer.

pad·dle[1] (pad′əl) *n. v.* **-dled, -dling.** —*n.* **1** a short oar with a broad blade at one end or both ends, used without resting it against the boat. **2** the act of paddling; a turn at the paddle. **3** one of the broad boards fixed around a water wheel or a paddle wheel to push, or be pushed by, the water. **4** a paddle-shaped piece of wood used for stirring, for mixing, for beating clothes, etc.
—*v.* **1** move (a boat or canoe) with a paddle or paddles. **2** use a paddle to move a canoe, etc. **3** row gently. **4** *Informal.* beat with a paddle or something similar; spank. [origin uncertain] —**pad′dler,** *n.*

A man using a paddle (def. 1)

pad·dle[2] (pad′əl) *v.* **-dled, -dling. 1** move the hands or feet about in water. **2** wade in water without shoes and stockings: *Children love to paddle at the beach.* [apparently < *pad*[2]] —**pad′dler,** *n.*

pad·dle·fish (pad′əl fish′) *n.* **-fish** or **-fish·es.** a large fish whose long, flat snout resembles a canoe paddle.

paddle wheel a wheel that propels a ship through the water by means of an arrangement of paddles.

A paddle wheel on a stern-wheeler

pad·dle·wheel·er (pad′əl hwēl′ər or -wēl′ər) *n.* a boat or ship having one or more paddle wheels.

pad·dock (pad′ək) *n.* **1** a small field near a stable or house, used as a pasture. **2** a pen for horses at a race track. [var. of *parrock*, OE *pearroc* enclosed space, fence < Med.L *parricus* enclosure. Doublet of PARK.]

pad·dy (pad′ē) *n.* **-dies. 1** rice. **2** rice in the husk, uncut or gathered. **3** a field of rice. [< Malay *padi*]

Pad·dy (pad′ē) *n.* **-dies.** a nickname for an Irishman.

paddy wagon *Slang.* a patrol wagon.

pad·i (pad′ē) *n.* **pad·is.** paddy.

pad·lock (pad′lok′) *n.* a lock that can be put on and removed. It hangs by a curved bar, hinged at one end and, when locked, snapped shut at the other. —*v.* fasten with such a lock.

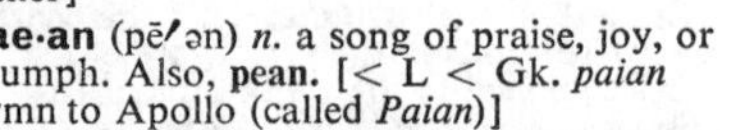

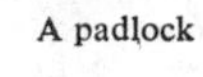
A padlock

pa·dre (pä′drā) *n.* **1** father. It is used as a name for a priest. **2** in the armed services, a chaplain. **3** a chaplain at certain universities. [< Ital., Sp., Pg. < L *pater* father]

pae·an (pē′ən) *n.* a song of praise, joy, or triumph. Also, **pean.** [< L < Gk. *paian* hymn to Apollo (called *Paian*)]

pa·gan (pā′gən) *n.* **1** a person who is not a Christian, Jew, or Moslem; heathen. The ancient Greeks and Romans were pagans. **2** a person who has no religion. —*adj.* **1** having to do with pagans; not Christian, Jewish, or Moslem: *pagan customs.* **2** not religious. [< L *paganus* rustic (at a time when Christianity was accepted by the urban population), in LL, heathen < *pagus* village] —**Syn.** *n.* **1** See **heathen.**

pa·gan·dom (pā′gən dəm) *n.* the pagan world; pagans collectively; all pagans.

pa·gan·ism (pā′gən iz′əm) *n.* **1** a pagan attitude toward religion or morality. **2** the beliefs and practices of pagans. **3** the condition of being a pagan.

page[1] (pāj) *n. v.* **paged, pag·ing.** —*n.* **1** one side of a leaf or sheet of paper: *a page in this book.* **2** the print or writing on one side of a leaf. **3** a record: *the pages of history.* **4** a happening or time considered as part of history: *The building of the transcontinental railway is a stirring page in the history of Canada.* —*v.* number the pages of. [< F < L *pagina* < *pangere* fasten]

page[2] (pāj) *n. v.* **paged, pag·ing.** —*n.* **1** a servant, often a boy, who runs errands, carries hand luggage, etc. for guests at hotels, etc. **2** a boy who carries messages, books, etc. for members of the House of Commons, the Senate, or a legislative assembly. **3** a young man who attends a person of rank. **4** in former times, a young man preparing to be a knight.
—*v.* try to get a message to someone in a hotel, club, etc. by having a page move about calling the wanted person's name; try to gain someone's attention by having his name called out over a public address system.
[ME < OF < Ital. *paggio*, ult. < Gk. *paidion* lad, dim. of *pais, paidos* child]

pag·eant (paj′ənt) *n.* **1** an elaborate spectacle; procession in costume; pomp; display: *The coronation of the new king was a splendid pageant.* **2** a public entertainment that represents scenes from history, legend, or the like. 3 empty show, not reality. [ME *pagent, pagen* < Med.L *pagina* movable scaffold fixed with planks, serving as a stage < L *pangere* fix]

pag·eant·ry (paj′ənt rē) *n.* **-ries.** 1 a splendid show; gorgeous display; pomp. 2 mere show; empty display.

page·boy (pāj′boi′) *n.* 1 page[2]. 2 a woman's hair style, often shoulder-length, in which the hair in the back and sides is turned under at the ends in a smooth roll.

pag·i·na·tion (paj′ə nā′shən) *n.* 1 the act of numbering the pages of books, etc. 2 the figures with which pages are numbered. 3 the number of pages in a book, etc.

pa·go·da (pə gō′də) *n.* a temple with many stories forming a tower. Pagodas are found in India, China, and Japan. [< Pg. *pagode* < Tamil *pagavadi* < Skt. *bhagavati* of a goddess < *bhagavat* a deity]

A pagoda

paid (pād) *adj.* 1 receiving money; hired. 2 no longer owed; settled. 3 cashed.
—*v.* pt. and pp. of **pay**[1].

☛ **paid, payed.** *Paid* is the spelling of the past tense and past participle of *pay*[1] (He *paid* his bills) in all senses except "let out" (They *payed out* the rope), and occasionally in that sense also.

pail (pāl) *n.* 1 a round container for carrying liquids, etc.; bucket. 2 the amount a pail holds. 3 a pail and its contents. [OE *pægel* and < OF *paielle*, both < Med.L *pagella* a measure, dim. of L *pagina*, originally, something fixed]

pail·ful (pāl′fůl) *n.* **-fuls.** the amount that fills a pail.

pail·lasse (pal′ē as′ or pal′yas) *n.* a mattress filled with straw. [< F *paillasse* < *paille* straw < L *palea*]

pain (pān) *n.* 1 a feeling of being hurt; suffering. 2 a single or localized feeling of hurt: *a sharp pain in one's back.* 3 **on** or **under pain of,** with the punishment or penalty of (unless a certain thing is done). 4 **pain in the neck,** *Slang.* a very troublesome or irritating thing or person. 5 **pains,** *pl.* **a** a trouble to do something; effort; care. **b** sufferings of childbirth.
—*v.* cause to suffer; give pain. [ME < OF *peine* < L *poena* penalty < Gk. *poinē*]

Syn. *n.* 1 **Pain, ache** mean a feeling of being hurt, bodily or mentally. **Pain** particularly suggests a sharp hurt, but of any degree from a sudden jab in one spot to a very severe and sometimes long-lasting hurt of the whole body or, figuratively, a sorrow that causes severe mental suffering: *I have a pain in my side.* **Ache** means a steady, usually dull hurt, and used figuratively suggests longing for something: *I have an earache.* –*v.* hurt, afflict, torture.

pained (pānd) *adj.* 1 distressed, grieved, mentally hurt, etc. 2 showing pain: *a pained face.*

pain·ful (pān′fəl) *adj.* 1 causing pain; unpleasant; hurting: *a painful illness, a painful duty.* 2 difficult. —**pain′ful·ly,** *adv.* —**pain′ful·ness,** *n.*

pain·kill·er (pān′kil′ər) *n.* anything, especially a drug, that relieves pain.

pain·less (pān′lis) *adj.* without pain; causing no pain. —**pain′less·ly,** *adv.* —**pain′less·ness,** *n.*

pains·tak·ing (pānz′tāk′ing) *adj.* very careful. —**pains′tak′ing·ly,** *adv.* —**Syn.** particular, scrupulous.

paint (pānt) *n.* 1 **a** a mixture of a solid coloring matter and liquid that can be applied to a surface so as to form a thin colored coating. **b** the solid coloring matter alone; pigment: *a box of paints.* 2 any cosmetic that colors or tints. [< v.]
—*v.* 1 cover or decorate with paint: *paint a house.* 2 use paint. 3 represent (an object, etc.) in colors. 4 make pictures. 5 picture vividly in words. 6 put on like paint: *The doctor painted iodine on the cut.* 7 use cosmetics to color or tint. 8 **paint black,** represent as evil or wicked: *not so black as he is painted.* [ME < OF *peint*, pp. of *peindre* paint < L *pingere*]

paint·brush (pānt′brush′) *n.* a brush for applying paint.

paint·er[1] (pān′tər) *n.* 1 a person who paints pictures; artist. 2 a person who paints houses, woodwork, etc. [< OF *peintour*, ult. < L *pictor* < *pingere* to paint]

paint·er[2] (pān′tər) *n.* a rope, usually fastened to the bow of a boat, for tying it to a ship, pier, etc. [probably < OF *pentoir* hanging cordage, ult. < L *pendere* hang]

paint·ing (pān′ting) *n.* 1 something painted; picture. 2 the act of one that paints. 3 the art of representation, decoration, and creating beauty with paints.

hat, āge, cãre, fär; let, ēqual, tėrm; it, īce
hot, ōpen, ôrder; oil, out; cup, pu̇t, rüle, ūse
əbove, takən, pencəl, lemən, circəs
ch, child; ng, long; sh, ship
th, thin; ᴛʜ, then; zh, measure

pair (pãr) *n.* **pairs** or (*sometimes after a numeral*) **pair,** *v.* —*n.* 1 a set of two; two that go together: *a pair of shoes, a pair of horses.* 2 a single thing consisting of two parts that cannot be used separately: *a pair of scissors, a pair of trousers.* 3 two people who are married or are engaged to be married. 4 two partners in a dance. 5 two animals that are mated. 6 in cards: **a** two cards of the same value in different suits, viewed as a unit in one's hand: *a pair of sixes, jacks, etc.* **b** in games using a multiple deck, two identical cards. 7 in a legislative body: **a** two members on opposite sides who arrange not to vote on a certain question. **b** the arrangement thus made.
—*v.* 1 arrange or be arranged in pairs. 2 join in love and marriage. 3 mate. 4 agree with a member of the opposite party in a legislative body that both shall abstain from voting on a certain question or for a certain time. 5 **pair off,** arrange in pairs; form into pairs. [< F *paire* < L *paria*, neut. pl., equals]

Syn. *n.* 1 **Pair, couple** = two of the same kind. **Pair** applies to two things that belong together, either because they go together to make a set or because they are used together and each is needed to make the other useful or because they are so well matched they seem to belong together: *I bought a new pair of gloves.* **Couple** applies to any two of the same kind: *I bought a couple of shirts.*

☛ **pair.** In informal usage the plural of *pair* is often *pair* when it comes after a number: *six pair of socks.* In other positions *pairs* is the usual plural.

pai·sa (pī′sä) *n.* **pai·se** (pī sā′). 1 a unit of money in India and Pakistan, worth 1/100 of a rupee. 2 a coin worth one paisa. [< Hind.]

pais·ley (pāz′lē) *n.* **-leys,** *adj.* —*n.* 1 an elaborate, colorful fabric design of curving lines and figures: *silk paisley.* 2 something made of fabric having such a design. —*adj.* made of fabric having a paisley design; having a design like paisley. [< *Paisley*, a city in Scotland, where woollen shawls having this design were first made]

pa·ja·mas (pə jam′əz or pə jä′məz) *n.pl.* pyjamas.

pal (pal) *n. v.* **palled, pal·ling.** *Informal.* —*n.* a comrade; mate; partner; chum; accomplice. —*v.* associate as pals. [< Romany *pal* brother, var. of *pral* or *plal*, ult. < Skt. *bhratr* brother]

pal·ace (pal′is) *n.* 1 a large and impressive house for a king, queen, bishop, or some other exalted personage to live in. 2 a very fine house or building. 3 a gaudy or pretentious place of entertainment: *an old movie palace.* [ME < OF *palais* < L *Palatium* Palatine Hill, the site of the Roman emperor's palace] —**Syn.** 1 castle.

pal·a·din (pal′ə din) *n.* 1 one of the twelve knights in attendance on Charlemagne. 2 a knightly defender. [< F < Ital. *paladino*]

pa·laes·tra (pə les′trə) *n.* 1 in ancient Greece, a public place for physical exercise and training. 2 a wrestling school. [< L < Gk. *palaistra* < *palaiein* wrestle]

pal·an·quin or **pal·an·keen** (pal′ən kēn′) *n.* a covered couch carried by poles resting on men's shoulders. [< Pg. *palanquim*; cf. Skt. *palyanka* couch]

pal·at·a·ble (pal′ə tə bəl) *adj.* agreeable to the taste; pleasing. —**pal′at·a·bly,** *adv.*

pal·a·tal (pal′ə təl) *adj.* 1 of or having to do with the palate. 2 of speech sounds, made with the tongue near or in contact with the hard palate. The (y) in *yet* is palatal. —*n.* a palatal sound. [< F < L *palatum* palate]

pal·a·tal·ize (pal′ə təl īz′) *v.* **-ized, -iz·ing.** change into a palatal sound; pronounce (a speech sound) with the tongue near or in contact with the hard palate. —**pal′a·tal·i·za′tion,** *n.*

pal·ate (pal′it) *n.* 1 the roof of the mouth. The bony part in front is the **hard palate**; the fleshy part at the back is the **soft palate.** 2 the sense of taste: *The new flavor pleased his palate.* 3 a liking. [< L *palatum*]

pa·la·tial (pə lā′shəl) *adj.* like a palace; fit for a palace; magnificent. [< L *palatium* palace] —**pa·la′tial·ly,** *adv.*

pa·lat·i·nate (pə lat′ə nāt′ or pə lat′ə nit) *n.* a region under the rule of a count palatine. See **palatine,** def. 1.

pal·a·tine (pal′ə tīn′ or pal′ə tin) *adj.* **1** having royal rights in his own territory. A count palatine was subject only to the emperor or king. **2** of a lord who has royal rights in his own territory. **3** palatial. **4 Palatine,** of the Palatinate, a region in West Germany, west of the Rhine. —*n.* **1** a lord having royal rights in his own territory. **2 Palatine,** a native or inhabitant of the Palatinate. **3 Palatine,** the Palatine Hill. [< L *palatinus,* adj., < *palatium* palace]

Palatine Hill one of the seven hills on which the city of Rome was built.

pa·lav·er (pə lav′ər or pə lä′vər) *n.* **1** a parley or conference, especially between travellers or explorers and natives. **2** empty or idle talk. **3** smooth, persuading talk; fluent talk; flattery. —*v.* **1** talk. **2** talk fluently or flatteringly. [< Pg. *palavra* < L *parabola* story, parable. Doublet of PARABLE, PAROLE.]

pale[1] (pāl) *adj.* **pal·er, pal·est,** *v.* **paled, pal·ing.** —*adj.* **1** without much color; whitish. **2** not bright; dim. **3** lacking vigor; feeble; faint: *a pale policy.* —*v.* turn pale; cause to turn pale. [ME < OF < L *pallidus* < *pallere* be pale. Doublet of PALLID.] —**pale′ly,** *adv.* —**pale′ness,** *n.*

Syn. *adj.* **1 Pale, pallid, wan** = with little or no color. **Pale,** describing the face of a person, means "without much natural or healthy color," and describing things, "without much brilliance or depth": *She is pale and tired-looking. The walls are pale green.* **Pallid,** chiefly describing the face, suggests having all color drained away as by sickness or weakness: *Her pallid face shows her suffering.* **Wan** emphasizes the idea of a faintness and whiteness coming from a weakened or unhealthy condition: *The starved refugees looked wan.*

pale[2] (pāl) *n. v.* **paled, pal·ing.** —*n.* **1** a long, narrow board pointed at the top, used for fences. **2** a boundary: *outside the pale of civilized society.* **3** in heraldry, a broad vertical stripe in the middle of an escutcheon. **4 the English Pale,** in French history, the territory of Calais. **5 the Pale,** that part of eastern Ireland (varying in extent at different times) over which English jurisdiction was established. —*v.* enclose with pales. [ME < OF *pal* < L *palus.* Doublet of POLE[1].]

A fence made of pales

pale- *combining form.* the form of **paleo-** usually used before vowels, as in *paleontology.*

pale·face (pāl′fās′) *n.* a white person. The North American Indians are said to have called white people palefaces.

paleo- *combining form.* **1** old; ancient: *paleography = ancient writing.* **2** of a relatively early time division: *Paleocene = the earliest epoch of the Tertiary period.* [< Gk. *palaio-* < *palaios* ancient]

Pa·le·o·cene (pā′lē ə sēn′ or pal′ē ə-) in geology: —*n.* the oldest epoch of the Tertiary period, before the Eocene. See the chart under **geology.** —*adj.* of or having to do with this epoch, its strata, etc. [< *paleo-* + Gk. *kainos* new]

pa·le·og·ra·pher (pā′lē og′rə fər or pal′ē og′rə fər) *n.* a person skilled in paleography.

pa·le·o·graph·ic (pā′lē ə graf′ik or pal′ē ə-) *adj.* of or having to do with paleography.

pa·le·og·ra·phy (pā′lē og′rə fē or pal′ē og′rə fē) *n.* **1** ancient writing or ancient forms of writing. **2** the study of ancient writings to determine their dates, origins, meaning, etc. [< Gk. *palaios* ancient + E *-graphy*]

pa·le·o·lith·ic (pā′lē ə lith′ik or pal′ē ə-) *adj.* of or having to do with the earlier part of the Stone Age. Paleolithic tools were crudely chipped out of stone. [< Gk. *palaios* ancient + *lithos* stone]

pa·le·on·tol·o·gist (pā′lē on tol′ə jist or pal′ē on tol′ə jist) *n.* a person skilled in paleontology.

pa·le·on·tol·o·gy (pā′lē on tol′ə jē or pal′ē on tol′ə jē) *n.* the science that deals with the forms of life existing long ago, as represented by fossil animals and plants. [< Gk. *palaios* ancient + *ōn, ontos* being + E *-logy*]

Pa·le·o·zo·ic (pā′lē ə zō′ik or pal′ē ə-) *n.* in geology: **1** an era whose fossils represent the early forms of life, beginning approximately 550,000,000 years ago; the age of fishes. See **geology** for chart. **2** the rocks formed during this era. —*adj.* of this era or these rocks. [< Gk. *palaios* ancient + *zōē* life]

pal·ette (pal′it) *n.* **1** a thin board, usually oval or oblong, with a thumb hole at one end, used by painters to lay and mix colors on. **2** a set of colors on this board. **3** the selection of colors used by a particular artist: *use a wide palette.* [< F *palette* < L *pala* spade]

An artist's palette (def. 1)

pal·frey (pol′frē or pôl′frē) *n.* **-freys.** *Archaic.* a gentle riding horse, especially one used by ladies. [ME < OF *palefrey* < LL *paraveredus* < Gk. *para-* beside + L *veredus* light horse < Celtic]

pal·imp·sest (pal′imp sest′) *n.* a piece of parchment or other writing material from which one writing has been erased to make room for another; a manuscript with one text written over another. [< L < Gk. *palimpsestos* scraped again, ult. < *palin* again + *psaein* rub smooth]

pal·in·drome (pal′in drōm′) *n.* a word, phrase, or sentence which reads the same backward as forward. The sentence "Madam, I'm Adam" is a palindrome. [< Gk. *palindromos* a running back < *pálin* again, back + *drómos* a running, related to *drameîn* run]

pal·ing (pāl′ing) *n.* **1** a fence of pales. **2** pales collectively, as fencing material. **3** a pale in a fence.

pal·i·sade (pal′ə sād′) *n. v.* **-sad·ed, -sad·ing.** —*n.* **1** a long, strong wooden stake pointed at the top end. **2** a fence of stakes set firmly in the ground to enclose or defend. **3** Usually, **palisades,** *pl.* a line of high, steep cliffs. —*v.* furnish or surround with a palisade. [< F *palissade* < Provençal *palissada* < L *palus* stake]

pall[1] (pol or pôl) *n.* **1** a heavy cloth of black, purple, or white velvet spread over a coffin, a hearse, or a tomb. **2** a dark, gloomy covering: *A pall of smoke shut out the sun from the city.* [OE *pæll* < L *pallium* cloak]

pall[2] (pol or pôl) *v.* **1** become distasteful or very tiresome because there has been too much of it. **2** cloy. [var. of *appall*]

pal·la·di·um[1] (pə lā′dē əm) *n.* a rare, silver-white metallic chemical element, harder than platinum. *Symbol:* Pd; *at.no.* 46; *at.wt.* 106.40. [< NL; after the asteroid *Pallas*]

pal·la·di·um[2] (pə lā′dē əm) *n.* **-di·a** (-dē ə). **1** anything regarded as an important safeguard. **2 Palladium,** in Troy, the statue of Pallas Athena, on which the safety of the city was supposed to depend. [< L < Gk. *palladion,* dim. of *Pallas*]

Pal·las (pal′əs) *n.* a title of the Greek goddess Athena.

pall·bear·er (pol′bãr′ər or pôl′-) *n.* one of the men who walk beside or carry the coffin at a funeral.

pal·let[1] (pal′it) *n.* a bed of straw; inferior bed. [ME < OF *paillet* < *paille* straw < L *palea*]

pal·let[2] (pal′it) *n.* **1** a flat blade used by potters and others. **2** a painter's palette. **3** in mechanics, a projection on a pawl. **4** a frame on which goods can be stacked and transported from place to place in a factory, warehouse, etc. [var. of *palette*]

pal·li·ate (pal′ē āt′) *v.* **-at·ed, -at·ing. 1** lessen without curing; mitigate: *palliate a disease.* **2** make appear less serious; excuse: *palliate a fault.* [< L *palliare* cover with a cloak < *pallium* clock] —**pal′li·a′tion,** *n.*

pal·li·a·tive (pal′ē ə tiv or pal′ē ā′tiv) *adj.* useful to lessen or soften; mitigating; excusing. —*n.* something that lessens, softens, mitigates, or excuses.

pal·lid (pal′id) *adj.* lacking color; pale: *a pallid face.* [< L *pallidus.* Doublet of PALE[1].] —**Syn.** See **pale.**

pal·lor (pal′ər) *n.* a lack of color from fear, illness, death, etc.; paleness. [< L]

palm[1] (pom or päm) *n.* **1** the inside of the hand between the wrist and the fingers. **2** a similar part of the forefoot of a four-footed animal. **3** the part of a glove covering the palm. **4** the width of a hand; 3 to 4 inches. **5 grease the palm of,** bribe. **6 have an itching palm,** be greedy for money. —*v.* **1** conceal in the hand. **2** pass or get accepted (something not good). **3** touch or stroke with the palm or hand; handle. **4 palm off,** pass off or get accepted by tricks, fraud, or false representation. [ME < OF < L *palma*]

palm[2] (pom or päm) *n.* **1** any of many kinds of trees growing in warm climates. Most palms are tall and have a bunch of large leaves at the top. **2** a branch or leaf of a palm tree as a symbol of victory or triumph. **3** a victory; triumph. **4 bear** or **carry off the palm,** be the victor; win. **5 yield the palm to,** admit defeat by. [OE < L *palma* palm tree, from the spreading shape of the leaves. See PALM[1].]

pal·mate (pal′māt) *adj.* **1** shaped like a hand with the fingers spread out: *a palmate leaf.* **2** in zoology, web-footed; having the front toes joined by a web; webbed. [< L *palmatus* < *palma* palm (of the hand)]

A palmate leaf

pal·ma·tion (pal mā′shən) *n.* a palmate formation or structure; one division of a palmate structure.

palm·er[1] (pom′ər or päm′ər) *n.* **1** a pilgrim returning from the Holy Land bringing a palm branch as a token. **2** a pilgrim. [ME < AF < Med.L *palmarius* < L *palma* palm[2]]

palm·er[2] (pom′ər or päm′ər) *n.* a person who palms or conceals something. [< *palm*[1]]

palmer worm any of various caterpillars destructive to fruit trees. [< *palmer*[1]; so named from its wandering habits]

pal·met·to (pal met′ō) *n.* **-tos** or **-toes. 1** any of several kinds of palm trees having fan-shaped leaves, abundant on the southeastern coast of the United States. **2** the leaves of any of these trees, used in making baskets. [< Sp. *palmito,* dim. of *palma* palm]

palm·ist (pom′ist or päm′ist) *n.* a person who claims to tell fortunes by examining the palm of the hand.

palm·is·try (pom′is trē or päm′is trē) *n.* the supposed art of telling a person's fortune from the lines and marks in the palm of his hand. [ME *pawmestry, palmestrie* < *paume, palme* palm (of the hand) + a word element of uncertain origin]

palm leaf a leaf of a palm tree, used for making hats, baskets, fans, etc.

palm oil a yellow fat from the fruit of a palm tree, used to make soap and candles.

Palm Sunday the Sunday before Easter Sunday.

palm·y (pom′ē or päm′ē) *adj.* **palm·i·er, palm·i·est. 1** abounding in palm trees. **2** flourishing; prosperous.

pal·o·mi·no (pal′ə mē′nō) *n.* **-nos. 1** a breed of cream-colored horses of Arabian stock. The mane and tail are usually lighter colored than the body. **2** a horse of this breed. **3** a golden-tan or cream color. [< Sp.]

pa·loo·ka (pə lü′kə) *n. Slang.* **1** a poor or inferior boxer. **2** a stupid lout, especially a muscular one. [coined word]

Palouse horse an Appaloosa.

palp (palp) *n.* palpus. [< F *palpe*]

pal·pa·bil·i·ty (pal′pə bil′ə tē) *n.* the state or quality of being palpable.

pal·pa·ble (pal′pə bəl) *adj.* **1** readily seen or heard and recognized; obvious: *a palpable error.* **2** that can be touched or felt: *a palpable hit.* [ME < LL *palpabilis* < L *palpare* feel] —**Syn. 1** perceptible, plain, evident, manifest. **2** tangible.

pal·pa·bly (pal′pə blē) *adv.* **1** plainly; obviously. **2** to the touch.

pal·pate[1] (pal′pāt) *v.* **-pat·ed, -pat·ing.** examine or feel with the hands, especially for purposes of medical diagnosis. [< L *palpatus,* pp. of *palpare* feel, pat] —**pal·pa·tion,** *n.*

pal·pate[2] (pal′pāt) *adj.* having a palpus or palpi.

pal·pi (pal′pī or pal′pē) *n.* pl. of **palpus.**

pal·pi·tate (pal′pə tāt′) *v.* **-tat·ed, -tat·ing. 1** beat very rapidly: *Your heart palpitates when you are excited.* **2** quiver; tremble: *His body palpitated with terror.* [< L *palpitare* throb < *palpare* pat]

pal·pi·ta·tion (pal′pə tā′shən) *n.* **1** very rapid beating of the heart. **2** a quivering; trembling.

hat, āge, cãre, fär; let, ēqual, tėrm; it, īce
hot, ōpen, ôrder; oil, out; cup, pu̇t, rüle, ūse
əbove, takən, pencəl, lemən, circəs
ch, child; ng, long; sh, ship
th, thin; ᴛʜ, then; zh, measure

pal·pus (pal′pəs) *n.* **pal·pi.** the jointed feeler attached to the mouth of insects, spiders, lobsters, etc. Palpi are organs of touch or taste. [< L]

PALPI

pal·sied (pol′zēd or pôl′zēd) *adj.* **1** having the palsy; paralysed. **2** shaking; trembling.

pal·sy (pol′zē or pôl′zē) *n.* **-sies,** *v.* **-sied, -sy·ing.** —*n.* loss of the power to feel, to move, or to control motion in any part of the body; paralysis. —*v.* paralyse. [ME *palesie* < OF *paralysie* < L < Gk. *paralysis.* Doublet of PARALYSIS.]

pal·ter (pol′tər or pôl′tər) *v.* **1** talk or act insincerely; trifle deceitfully. **2** act carelessly; trifle: *Do not palter with a decision involving life and death.* **3** deal crookedly; use tricks and dodges in bargaining. [origin uncertain]

pal·try (pol′trē or pôl′trē) *adj.* **-tri·er, -tri·est. 1** almost worthless; trifling. **2** petty; mean. [? < dial. *palt* trash] —**pal′tri·ly,** *adv.* —**pal′tri·ness,** *n.* —**Syn. 1** insignificant.

pam·pas (*n.* pam′pəz; *adj.* pam′pəs) *n.pl.* **1** the vast, treeless plains of South America, especially those in Argentina. **2 Pampas,** a highly productive region of Argentina.
—*adj.* of the pampas: *pampas grass.* [< Sp. *pampas,* pl., < Peruvian *pampa* a plain]

pam·per (pam′pər) *v.* indulge too much; allow too many privileges to: *pamper a child, pamper one's appetite.* [ME *pampere(n)*] —**pam′per·er,** *n.* —**Syn.** spoil, humor.

pam·phlet (pam′flit) *n.* **1** a booklet in paper covers. It often deals with a question of current interest. **2** any printed booklet with a few pages: *an advertising pamphlet.* [ME < Anglo-L *panfletus,* for *Pamphilet,* the popular name for the 12th-century poem, "Pamphilus, seu de Amore"]

pam·phlet·eer (pam′flit ēr′) *n.* a writer of pamphlets. —*v.* write and issue pamphlets.

pan[1] (pan) *n. v.* **panned, pan·ning.** —*n.* **1** a dish for cooking and other household uses, usually broad, shallow, and coverless. **2** anything like this. Gold and other metals are sometimes obtained by washing ore in pans. The dishes on a pair of scales are called pans. **3** in old-fashioned guns, the hollow part of the lock that held a little gunpowder to set the gun off. **4** hard subsoil. **5** a flat cake of drifting ice, often having upturned edges. **6** *Slang.* the human face. **7** *Slang.* in baseball, the home plate. **8** *Slang.* a severely critical review of a play, motion picture, etc.
—*v.* **1** cook in a pan. **2** wash in a pan: *pan gold.* **3** wash (gravel, sand, etc.) in a pan to get gold. **4** yield gold. **5** *Informal.* criticize severely. **6 pan out,** *Informal.* turn out. [OE *panne*]

pan[2] (pan) *v.* **panned, pan·ning.** in motion pictures or television, move a camera so as to take in a whole scene, follow a moving character or object, etc. [< *pan*orama]

Pan (pan) *n.* in Greek mythology, the god of forests, pastures, flocks, and shepherds, represented as a man having the horns, ears, and legs of a goat and playing upon a reed pipe, or Panpipe.

pan- *combining form.* all, as in *Pan-American, Pan-Christian, pandemonium.* [< Gk. *pan,* neut. of *pas* all]

pan·a·ce·a (pan′ə sē′ə) *n.* a remedy for all diseases or ills; cure-all. [< L < Gk. *panakeia,* ult. < *pan-* all + *akos* cure]

pa·nache (pə nash′ or pə näsh′) *n.* **1** an ornamental plume or bunch of feathers, especially on a helmet. **2** swagger; verve. [< F *panache* < MF *penache* < Ital. *pennaccio,* var. of *pennachio* < *penna* feather < L]

Pan-Af·ri·can (pan af′rə kən) *adj.* of or for all African peoples: *Pan-African freedom.*

Pan-Af·ri·can·ism (pan af′rə kə niz′əm) *n.* **1** the theory of or movement towards a political union of all African peoples. 2 belief in or support of such a theory or movement.

pan·a·ma (pan′ə mä′) *n.* **1** a fine hat woven from the young leaves of a palmlike plant of Central and South America. **2** the leaves from which the hat is made.

Pan·a·ma·ni·an (pan′ə mā′nē ən or pan′ə mä′nē ən) *adj.* of or having to do with Panama, a country in Central America. —*n.* a native or inhabitant of Panama.

Pan-A·mer·i·can (pan′ə mer′ə kən) *adj.* **1** of all Americans. **2** including all the countries of North, Central, and South America.

Pan-A·mer·i·can·ism (pan′ə mer′ə kən iz′əm) *n.* the principle or policy that all the countries in South America, Central America, and North America should co-operate for the improvement of their welfare.

Pan American Union a permanent body and the central office of the Organization of American States.

pan·broil (pan′broil′) *v.* cook with little or no fat in a heavy frying pan over high heat.

pan·cake (pan′kāk′) *n. v.* **-caked, -cak·ing.** —*n.* **1** a thin, flat cake of batter, fried in a pan or on a griddle. **2** a quick, almost flat landing made by an airplane. —*v.* of an airplane, make such a landing.

Pancake Day Shrove Tuesday.

pan·chro·mat·ic (pan′krō mat′ik) *adj.* sensitive to light of all colors: *a panchromatic photographic film.*

pan·cre·as (pan′krē əs) *n.* a gland near the stomach that discharges into the intestine a secretion that helps digestion. The pancreas of animals, when used for food, is called sweetbread. [< NL < Gk. *pankreas* < *pan-* all + *kreas* flesh]

pan·cre·at·ic (pan′krē at′ik) *adj.* of the pancreas. The pancreatic juice aids digestion.

pan·da (pan′də) *n.* **1** the giant panda, a bearlike mammal of Tibet, mostly white with black legs. **2** the lesser panda, a reddish-brown mammal resembling a raccoon, found in the Himalayas. [origin uncertain]

pan·dect (pan′dekt) *n.* **1** a complete body of laws. **2** a comprehensive digest. **3 Pandects,** *pl.* a digest of Roman civil law in 50 books, made by order of Justinian in the sixth century A.D. [< L < Gk. *pandektēs* < *pan-* all + *dechesthai* receive]

pan·de·mo·ni·um (pan′də mō′nē əm) *n.* **1** the abode of all the demons. **2** a place of wild disorder or lawless confusion. **3** wild uproar or lawlessness. **4 Pandemonium,** in Milton's *Paradise Lost*, the capital of Hell. [< NL < Gk. *pan-* all + *daimōn* demon; coined by Milton]

pan·der (pan′dər) *n.* a person who helps other people indulge low desires, passions, or vices. —*v.* act as a pander; supply material or opportunity for vices: *The newspaper pandered to people's liking for sensational stories.* [from the name of a character in a story told by Boccaccio and Chaucer]

Pan·do·ra (pan dô′rə) *n.* in Greek mythology, the first woman, created by the gods to punish mankind for having learned the use of fire. Curiosity led her to open a box **(Pandora's box)** and thus let out all sorts of ills into the world; only Hope remained at the bottom.

pan·dow·dy (pan dou′dē) *n.* **-dies.** *Esp.U.S.* a deep apple pie with top crust only; brown betty. [origin uncertain]

pane (pān) *n.* a single sheet of glass in a window, a door, or a sash. [ME < OF *pan* < L *pannus* piece of cloth]

pan·e·gyr·ic (pan′ə jir′ik or pan′ə jīr′ik) *n.* **1** something written or spoken in praise of a person or thing. **2** enthusiastic or extravagant praise. [< L < Gk. *panēgyrikos* < *pan-* all + *agyris* assembly]

pan·e·gyr·ist (pan′ə jir′ist or pan′ə jīr′ist) *n.* a person who praises enthusiastically or extravagantly.

pan·el (pan′əl) *n. v.* **-elled** or **-eled, -el·ling** or **-el·ing.** —*n.* **1** a strip or surface that is different in some way from what is around it. A panel is often sunk below or raised above the rest, and used for a decoration. Panels may be in a door or other woodwork, on large pieces of furniture, or made as parts of a dress. **2** a long, narrow picture, photograph, or design. **3** a list of persons called as jurors; the members of a jury. **4** a group of selected persons formed to discuss questions of general interest. **5** a group of persons who ask questions in certain guessing games and other entertainments on radio and television shows. **6 a** one section of a switchboard. **b** the whole, or a section, of an instrument board containing the controls and indicators used in operating an automobile, aircraft, or complex mechanism such as a computer. **7** a panel truck.
—*v.* arrange in panels; furnish or decorate with panels. [ME < OF *panel* piece < VL *pannellus* < L *pannus* piece of cloth]

panel discussion the discussion of a particular issue by a selected group of people, usually experts.

pan·el·ing (pan′əl ing) *n.* panelling.

pan·el·ist or **pan·el·list** (pan′əl ist) *n.* one of a group of persons making up a panel.

pan·el·ling or **pan·el·ing** (pan′əl ing) *n.* panels collectively.

panel truck a small, fully enclosed truck.

pang (pang) *n.* **1** a sudden, short, sharp pain or feeling: *the pangs of a toothache.* **2** a sudden feeling of regret or pity, etc.: *a pang of remorse.* [origin uncertain]

pan·go·lin (pang gō′lən) *n.* a scaly, toothless mammal of tropical Asia and Africa that rolls itself into a ball when in danger; scaly anteater. [< Malay *peng-goling* roller]

pan·han·dle[1] (pan′han′dəl) *n.* **1** the handle of a pan. **2** a narrow strip of land projecting like a handle: *the Alaska Panhandle.*

pan·han·dle[2] (pan′han′dəl) *v.* **-dled, -dling.** *Informal.* beg, especially in the streets. [? < *panhandler* < *pan* receptacle used for collecting money + *handler*] —**pan′han′dler,** *n.*

Pan·hel·len·ic or **pan·hel·len·ic** (pan′hə len′ik) *adj.* **1** having to do with all members of the Greek people. **2** of or having to do with all college fraternities and sororities.

pan·ic (pan′ik) *n. adj. v.* **-icked, -ick·ing.** —*n.* **1** fear spreading through a multitude of people so that they lose control of themselves; unreasoning fear: *When the theatre caught fire, there was a panic.* **2** *Slang.* a very amusing person or thing: *His costume is a panic.*
—*adj.* caused by panic; showing panic.
—*v.* **1** lose control of oneself through fear. **2** cause panic in. **3** *Slang.* amuse greatly. [< F < L *panicus* < Gk. *panikos* of god Pan (who caused fear)]

pan·ick·y (pan′ik ē) *adj.* **1** caused by panic. **2** showing panic. **3** like panic. **4** liable to lose self-control and have a panic.

pan·i·cle (pan′ə kəl) *n.* a loose, diversely branching flower cluster; compound raceme: *a panicle of oats.* [< L *panicula*, dim. of *panus* a swelling, thread wound on a bobbin, ear of millet; cf. Gk. *pēnos* web]

A panicle

pan·ic-strick·en (pan′ik strik′ən) *adj.* frightened out of one's wits; demoralized by fear.

pa·nic·u·late (pə nik′yù lāt′) *adj.* in botany, growing in a panicle; arranged in panicles.

Pan·ja·bi (pun jä′bē) *n.* an Indo-European language spoken in the Punjab, derived from Sanskrit. Also, **Punjabi.**

pan·jan·drum (pan jan′drəm) *n.* a mock title for an official of imaginary or exaggerated importance or power. [coined by Samuel Foote, 1720-1777, an English dramatist]

pan·ni·er (pan′ē ər) *n.* **1** a basket, especially one of a pair of considerable size to be slung across the shoulders or across the back of a beast of burden. **2** formerly, a frame to stretch out the skirt of a woman's dress at the hips. **3** puffed drapery about the hips. [ME < OF < L *panarium* bread basket < *panis* bread]

Panniers

pan·ni·kin (pan′ə kin) *n.* **1** a small pan. **2** a metal cup or mug.

pa·no·cha (pə nō′chə) *n.* **1** a coarse dark-brown sugar from Mexico. **2** penuche. [< Mexican Sp.]

pan·o·plied (pan′ə plēd) *adj.* completely armed, equipped, covered, or arrayed.

pan·o·ply (pan′ə plē) *n.* **-plies. 1** a complete suit of armor. **2** complete equipment or covering: *the panoply of war.* [< Gk. *panoplia* < *pan-* all + *hopla* arms]

pan·o·ram·a (pan′ə ram′ə) *n.* **1** a wide, unbroken view of a surrounding region. **2** a complete survey of some subject: *a panorama of history.* **3** a picture of a landscape or other scene, often shown as if seen from a central point; a picture unrolled a part at a time and made to pass continuously before the spectators. **4** a continuously passing or changing scene: *the panorama of city life.* [< *pan-* + Gk. *horama* view]

pan·o·ram·ic (pan′ə ram′ik) *adj.* of or like a panorama: *a panoramic view.* —**pan′o·ram′i·cal·ly,** *adv.*

Pan·pipe (pan′pīp′) *n.* an early musical instrument made of reeds or tubes of different lengths, fastened together in the order of their length. The reeds or tubes were closed at one end; the player blew across their tops.

A Panpipe

Pan's pipes Panpipe.

pan·sy (pan′zē) *n.* **-sies,** *adj.* —*n.* **1** a variety of violet having large flowers with flat, velvety petals usually of several colors. **2** the flower. **3** *Slang.* **a** a homosexual man or boy. **b** an effeminate man or boy. —*adj. Slang.* **1** homosexual. **2** effeminate. [< F *pensée* thought < *penser* think. Related to PENSIVE.]

pant (pant) *v.* **1** breathe hard and quickly. **2** speak with short, quick breaths: *"Come quickly! Come quickly!" panted Joe.* **3** long eagerly. **4** throb violently. —*n.* **1** a short, quick breath. **2** the puff of an engine. **3** a throb. [ME < OF *pantoisier* < VL *phantasiare* be oppressed with nightmare, ult. < L < Gk. *phantasia* appearance, image] —**Syn.** *v.* **1** gasp, puff.

pan·ta·lets or **pan·ta·lettes** (pan′tə lets′) *n.pl.* **1** long drawers extending to the ankles, formerly worn by women and girls. **2** a pair of trimmed pieces for attaching to the legs of drawers. [dim. < *pantaloon*]

pan·ta·loon (pan′tə lün′) *n.* **1** a clown. **2 Pantaloon,** in traditional Italian comedy and in pantomime, a thin, foolish old man wearing pantaloons and slippers with stockings attached. **3 pantaloons,** *pl. Archaic.* close-fitting trousers. [< F < Ital. *Pantalone,* a comic character in early Italian comedies; originally a Venetian < *Pantaleone* the patron saint of Venice]

pan·the·ism (pan′thē iz′əm) *n.* **1** the belief that God and the universe are identical. **2** the worship of all the gods.

pan·the·ist (pan′thē ist) *n.* a person who believes in pantheism.

pan·the·is·tic (pan′thē is′tik) *adj.* of or having to do with pantheism or pantheists.

pan·the·is·ti·cal·ly (pan′thē is′tik lē) *adv.* according to pantheism; from a pantheist's point of view.

Pan·the·on (pan′thē on′ or pan thē′ən) *n.* **1** in Rome, a temple for all the gods, built about 27 B.C. and later used as a Christian church. **2** in Paris, a public building containing tombs or memorials of famous French people. **3 pantheon, a** a temple dedicated to all the gods. **b** a public building containing tombs or memorials of the illustrious dead of a nation. **c** all the deities of a people. [ME < L < Gk. *pantheion* < *pan-* all + *theos* god]

pan·ther (pan′thər) *n.* **-thers** or (*esp. collectively*) **-ther. 1** a puma; mountain lion. **2** a leopard. **3** a jaguar. [ME < OF < L *panthera* < Gk. *panthēr*]

pan·ties (pan tēz) *n.pl.* **1** short pants worn as an undergarment by girls and women. **2** pants worn by babies. —*adj.* **pantie,** of or to do with panties. [dim. of *pants*]

pan·to·graph (pan′tə graf′) *n.* an instrument for copying plans, drawings, etc. on any scale desired. [< Gk. *pas, pantos* all + E *-graph*]

hat, āge, cãre, fär; let, ēqual, tėrm; it, īce
hot, ōpen, ôrder; oil, out; cup, pu̇t, rüle, ūse
əbove, takən, pencəl, lemən, circəs
ch, child; ng, long; sh, ship
th, thin; ᴛʜ, then; zh, measure

pan·to·mime (pan′tə mīm′) *n. v.* **-mimed, -mim·ing.** —*n.* **1** a play without words, in which the actors express themselves by gestures. **2** gestures without words. —*v.* express by gestures. [< L < Gk. *pantomimos* < *pas, pantos* all + *mimos* mimic]

pan·to·mim·ic (pan′tə mim′ik) *adj.* of, in, or like pantomime.

pan·to·mim·ist (pan′tə mīm′ist) *n.* an actor in a pantomime.

pan·try (pan′trē) *n.* **-tries.** a small room in which food, dishes, silverware, table linen, etc. are kept. [ME < OF *paneterie,* ult. < L *panis* bread]

pants (pants) *n.pl. Informal.* **1** trousers. **2** panties. —*adj.* **pant,** of or having to do with pants. [short for *pantaloons*]

☛ **pants, trousers.** In formal usage the word for men's breeches is *trousers*; on the other levels the word is *pants.*

pan·ty (pan′tē) *n.* sing. of *panties.* —*adj.* of or having to do with panties.

pan·ty·hose (pan′tē hōz′) *n.* a garment combining panties (def. 1) and stockings.

pan·ty·waist (pan′tē wāst′) *n.* **1** a child's garment consisting of short pants and shirt buttoned together. **2** *Slang.* a sissy (def. 2).

pan·zer (pan′zər) *adj.* armored; mechanized and armored. A panzer division consists largely of tanks. [< G *Panzer* armor]

pap (pap) *n.* **1** soft food for infants or invalids. **2** ideas or facts watered down to a characterless consistency, considered as innocuous and as unsuitable for adults as baby food. [cf. LG *pappe*]

pa·pa (po′pə or pä′pə) *n.* father; daddy. [< F]

pa·pa·cy (pā′pə sē) *n.* **-cies. 1** the position, rank, or authority of the Pope. **2** the time during which a pope rules. **3** all the popes. **4** government by the Pope. [< Med.L *papatia* < LL *papa* pope. See POPE.]

pa·pal (pā′pəl) *adj.* **1** of or having to do with the Pope: *a papal letter.* **2** of or having to do with the papacy. **3** of or having to do with the Roman Catholic Church: *papal ritual.* [< Med.L *papalis* < LL *papa* pope. See POPE.]

pa·paw (po′po or pô′pô) *n.* **1** a small North American tree bearing oblong, yellowish, edible fruit having many beanlike seeds. **2** this fruit. **3** papaya. Also, **pawpaw.** [< Sp. *papaya.* See PAPAYA.]

pa·pa·ya (pə pä′yə) *n.* **1** a tropical American tree having a straight, palmlike trunk with a tuft of large leaves at the top and edible, melonlike fruit with yellowish pulp. **2** the fruit. [< Sp. *papaya* (def. 2) < *papayo* (def. 1) < Carib]

pa·per (pā′pər) *n.* **1** a material in the form of thin sheets made from wood pulp, rags, etc. and used for writing, printing, wrapping packages, etc. **2** a piece or sheet of paper. **3** a piece or sheet of paper with writing or printing on it; document: *Important papers were stolen.* **4** a wrapper, container, or sheet of paper containing something. **5** a newspaper. **6** an article; essay: *Professor Smith read a paper on the teaching of English.* **7** a written examination. **8** a written promise to pay money; note. **9** paper money. **10** wallpaper. **11 on paper, a** in writing or print. **b** in theory. **12 papers,** *pl.* documents telling who or what one is.
—*adj.* **1** made of paper: *paper dolls.* **2** having to do with or used with paper: *a paper clip.* **3** like paper; thin: *almonds with paper shells.* **4** of, consisting of, or carried on by means of letters to newspapers, pamphlets, or books: *paper warfare.* **5** existing only on paper: *When he tried to sell, his paper profits disappeared.*
—*v.* **1** cover with paper, especially wallpaper. **2** *Slang.* fill (a place of entertainment) with an audience admitted mostly by free passes: *To get a crowd at the concert they had to paper the house.* [ME < AF *papir* < L < Gk. *papyros.* Doublet of PAPYRUS.] —**pa′per·er,** *n.*

pa·per·back (pā′pər bak′) *n.* a book with a paper cover, especially one that is small and inexpensive.

paper birch a large North American birch having a strong, white bark formerly used by the Indians in making canoes and tents; white birch.

pa·per·boy (pā′pər boi′) *n.* a boy who sells or delivers newspapers; newsboy.

paper hanger a person whose business is to cover walls with wallpaper.

paper knife a knife with a blade of metal, wood, ivory, etc. used to open letters and cut the pages of books.

pa·per·mak·er (pā′pər māk′ər) *n.* a person who makes or manufactures paper.

pa·per·mak·ing (pā′pər māk′ing) *n.* the science, process, or business of making paper.

paper money money made of paper, not metal. A dollar bill is paper money.

paper nautilus a sea mollusc having eight arms, resembling an octopus. The female has a very thin, delicate shell in which the young develop.

paper profits profits existing on paper but not yet realized.

pa·per·weight (pā′pər wāt′) *n.* a small, heavy object put on papers to keep them from being scattered.

pa·per·work (pā′pər wėrk′) *n.* **1** work done on or with paper, as writing, other office or clerical work, etc. **2** the written work of a student. **3** a structure or part of a structure made of paper.

pa·per·y (pā′pər ē) *adj.* thin like paper.

pap·e·terie (pap′ə trē; *French,* päp trē′) *n.* a set of stationery, such as note paper and envelopes, in a box or other package. [< F]

pa·pier-mâ·ché (pā′pər ma shā′; *French,* pä pyā mä shā′) *n.* a paper pulp mixed with some stiffener and moulded when moist, and which becomes hard and strong when dry. —*adj.* made of papier-mâché. [< F *papier mâché* chewed paper]

pa·pil·la (pə pil′ə) *n.* **-pil·lae. 1** a small, nipple-like projection. **2** a small vascular process at the root of a hair or feather. **3** one of certain small protuberances concerned with the senses of touch, taste, or smell: *the papillae on the tongue.* [< L *papilla* nipple]

pa·pil·lae (pə pil′ē or pə pil′ī) *n.* pl. of **papilla.**

pap·il·lar·y (pap′ə ler′ē) *adj.* **1** of or like a papilla. **2** having papillae.

pap·il·lose (pap′ə lōs′) *adj.* having many papillae.

pa·pist (pā′pist) *n. adj. Usually, derogatory.* a Roman Catholic. [< NL < LL *papa* pope. See POPE.]

pa·poose (pa püs′) *n.* a North American Indian baby. Also, **pappoose.** [< Algonquian *papeisses* < *peisses* child]

pap·pus (pap′əs) *n.* **pap·pi** (pap′ī or pap′ē). in botany, an appendage to a seed, often made of down or bristles. Dandelion and thistle seeds have pappi. [< NL < Gk. *pappos*]

pap·py (pap′ē) *adj.* like pap; soft; mushy.

pap·ri·ka (pa prē′kə or pap′rə kə) *n.* a kind of red pepper less hot than the ordinary kind. [< Hungarian]

Pap·u·an (pap′ū ən) *adj.* of or having to do with Papua, or New Guinea, an island north of Australia, or with the negroid people living in Papua. —*n.* **1** a native or inhabitant of Papua. **2** any of the Papuan languages or dialects.

pa·py·rus (pə pī′rəs) *n.* **-ri** (-rī or -rē). **1** a tall water plant from which the ancient Egyptians, Greeks, and Romans made a kind of paper to write on. **2** a writing material made from the pith of the papyrus plant. **3** an ancient record written on papyrus. [< L < Gk. *papyros.* Doublet of PAPER.]

par (pär) *n.* **1** equality; an equal level: *The gains and losses are about on a par. He is quite on a par with his brother in intelligence.* **2** an average or normal amount, degree, or condition: *A sick person feels below par.* **3** the value of a bond, a note, a share of stock, etc. that is printed on it; face value: *That stock is selling above par.* **4** the established normal value of the money of one country in terms of the money of another country. **5** in golf, the number of strokes set as an expert score for any one hole. The sum of the par scores for each hole is par for the course. —*adj.* **1** average; normal. **2** of or at par. [< L *par* equal. Doublet of PEER[1].]

par- the form of **para-** before vowels and *h,* as in *parenthesis, parhelion.*

par. 1 paragraph. **2** parallel. **3** parenthesis. **4** parish.

pa·ra (pä rä′) *n.* **1** a unit of money in Yugoslavia, worth 1/100 of a dinar. **2** a coin worth one para. [< Turkish]

para-[1] *prefix.* **1** beside; near, as in *paragraph, parathyroid.* **2** disordered condition, as in *paranoia.* Also, **par-** before vowels and *h.* [< Gk. *para-* < *para,* prep.]

para-[2] *combining form.* **1** a defence against; protection from: *parachute = a device that protects against falls; parasol = a device that protects from the sun.* **2** that uses a parachute: *paratrooper = a soldier that uses a parachute.* [< F < Ital. < *para,* imperative of *parare* ward off, defend against < L *parare* prepare against]

para. paragraph.

Para. Paraguay.

par·a·ble (par′ə bəl) *n.* a short story used to teach some truth or moral lesson: *Jesus often taught in parables.* [< L *parabola* < Gk. *parabolē* comparison < *para-* alongside + *bolē* a throwing. Doublet of PALAVER, PAROLE.] ☛ See **allegory** for usage note.

pa·rab·o·la (pə rab′ə lə) *n.* **-las.** in geometry, a plane curve formed by the intersection of a cone with a plane parallel to a side of the cone. See **conic section** for diagram. [< NL < Gk. *parabolē* juxtaposition. See PARABLE.]

par·a·bol·ic[1] (par′ə bol′ik) *adj.* having to do with or resembling a parabola.

par·a·bol·ic[2] (par′ə bol′ik) *adj.* of, having to do with, or expressed in a parable.

A man descending by parachute. It is fastened on by means of a harness and can be folded into a pack that is worn on the back or chest.

par·a·chute (par′ə shüt′) *n. v.* **-chut·ed, -chut·ing.** —*n.* an umbrella-like apparatus made of nylon, silk, etc. and used in descending through the air from a great height. —*v.* **1** come down by, or as if by, a parachute. **2** convey by a parachute. [< F *parachute* < *para-* (< Ital. *para* guard against, ult. < L *parare* prepare) + *chute* a fall]

par·a·chut·ist (par′ə shüt′ist) *n.* a person who uses a parachute; person skilled in making descents with a parachute.

pa·rade (pə rād′) *n. v.* **-rad·ed, -rad·ing.** —*n.* **1** a march for display; procession: *The circus had a parade.* **2** a group of people walking for display or pleasure. **3** a place where people walk for display or pleasure. **4** a great show or display: *A modest man will not make a parade of his wealth.* **5** a military display or review of troops. **6** a parade ground or parade square.
—*v.* **1** march through with display: *The performers and animals paraded the streets.* **2** march in procession; walk proudly as if in a parade. **3** make a great show of. **4** come together in military order for review or inspection. **5** assemble (troops) for review. [< F < Sp. *parada,* ult. < L *parare* prepare] —**pa·rad′er,** *n.* —**Syn.** *v.* **3** display, flaunt.

parade ground the area where troops parade, drill, etc.

parade square parade ground.

par·a·digm (par′ə dīm′ or par′ə dim′) *n.* **1** a pattern; example. **2** in grammar, an example of a noun, verb, pronoun, etc. in all its inflections. [< L < Gk. *paradeigma* pattern, ult. < *para-* side by side + *deiknunai* to show]

par·a·dise (par′ə dīs′) *n.* **1** heaven. **2** a place or condition of great happiness. **3** a place of great beauty. **4** Also, **Paradise.** the Garden of Eden. [ME < OF < L *paradisus* < Gk. *paradeisos* < OPersian *pairidaeza* park < *pairi* around + *daeza* wall]

par·a·dox (par′ə doks′) *n.* **1** a statement that may be true but seems to say two opposite things: *"More haste, less speed" and "The child is father to the man" are paradoxes.* **2** a statement that is false because it says two opposite things. **3** a person or thing that seems to be full of contradictions. **4** any inconsistent or contradictory fact, action, or condition. [< L < Gk. *paradoxos* < *para-* contrary to + *doxa* opinion] ☛ See **epigram** for usage note.

par·a·dox·i·cal (par′ə dok′sə kəl) *adj.* **1** of paradoxes; involving a paradox. **2** having the habit of using paradoxes. —**par′a·dox′i·cal·ly,** *adv.*

par·af·fin (par′ə fin) *n.* **1 a** a white, tasteless substance like wax, used for making candles, for sealing jars, etc. It is obtained chiefly from crude petroleum. **b** any of various other mixtures of hydrocarbons. **2** in chemistry, any hydrocarbon of the methane series. —*v.* treat with paraffin. [< G < L *parum* not very < *affinis* related; from its small affinity for other substances]

par·af·fine (par′ə fin) *n. v.* **-fined, -fin·ing.** paraffin.

par·a·gon (par′ə gon′) *n.* **1** a model of excellence or perfection. **2** a flawless diamond weighing 100 carats or more. [< OF < Ital. *paragone* touchstone < Med.Gk. *parakonē* whetstone]

par·a·graph (par′ə graf′) *n.* **1** a group of sentences that belong together; a distinct part of a chapter, letter, or composition. It is customary to begin a paragraph on a new line and to indent this line. **2** a separate note or item of news in a newspaper. **3** a sign (¶) used to show where a paragraph begins or should begin. It is used mostly in correcting written work. —*v.* **1** divide into paragraphs. **2** write paragraphs about. [< LL < Gk. *paragraphos* line (in the margin) marking a break in sense < *para-* beside + *graphein* write] —**par′a·graph′er,** *n.*

Par·a·guay·an (par′ə gwā′ən or par′ə gwī′ən) *adj.* of or having to do with Paraguay, a country in central South America, or its inhabitants. —*n.* a native or inhabitant of Paraguay.

par·a·keet (par′ə kēt′) *n.* any of various small parrots, most of which have slender bodies and long tails. Also, **parrakeet, paroquet.** [< OF *paroquet*, apparently alteration of *perrot* parrot < *Perrot*, dim. of *Pierre* Peter]

par·al·lac·tic (par′ə lak′tik) *adj.* of or having to do with a parallax.

par·al·lax (par′ə laks′) *n.* the change or amount of change in the direction in which an object is seen or photographed, caused by a change in the position of the observer or camera. Seen from A, star S is in direction AS. Seen from B, it is in direction BS. The parallax is the difference between these two directions, or the angle ASB. [< Gk. *parallaxis* deviation, ult. < *para-* + *allassein* to change]

A parallax

par·al·lel (par′ə lel′) *adj. n. v.* **-lelled** or **-leled, -lel·ling** or **-lel·ing.** —*adj.* **1** at or being the same distance apart everywhere, like the two rails of a railway track. See **parallelogram** for diagram. **2** similar; corresponding: *parallel points in the characters of different men.*
—*n.* **1** a parallel line or surface. **2** in geography: **a** any of the imaginary circles around the earth parallel to the equator, marking degrees of latitude: *The 49th parallel marks much of the boundary between Canada and the United States.* **b** the markings on a map that represent these circles. **3** something like or similar to another: *Her experience was an interesting parallel to ours.* **4** a comparison to show likeness: *Draw a parallel between this winter and last winter.* **5** in electricity, an arrangement of the wiring of batteries, lights, etc. in which all the positive poles or terminals are joined to one conductor, and all the negative to the other.
—*v.* **1** be at the same distance from throughout the length: *The street parallels the railway.* **2** cause to be or run parallel to. **3** be like; be similar to: *Your story closely parallels what he told me.* **4** find a case which is similar or parallel to: *Can you parallel that for friendliness?* **5** compare in order to show likeness. [< L < Gk. *parallēlos* < *para allēlōn* beside one another]
—**Syn.** *adj.* **2** analogous, like.

par·al·lel·e·pi·ped (par′ə lel′ə pī′pid) *n.* a prism whose six sides are parallelograms. [< Gk. *parallēlepipedon* body with parallel surfaces < *parallēlos* parallel + *epipedon* a plane surface]

par·al·lel·ism (par′ə lel iz′əm) *n.* **1** the quality or state of being parallel. **2** a likeness; correspondence; agreement.

hat, āge, cãre, fär; let, ēqual, tėrm; it, īce
hot, ōpen, ôrder; oil, out; cup, pu̇t, rüle, ūse
əbove, takən, pencəl, lemən, circəs
ch, child; ng, long; sh, ship
th, thin; ᴛʜ, then; zh, measure

par·al·lel·o·gram (par′ə lel′ə gram′) *n.* **1** in geometry, a four-sided figure whose opposite sides are parallel and equal. **2** something having this shape. [< Gk. *parallēlogrammon*, neut. < *parallēlos* parallel + *grammē* line]

Parallel lines　　Parallelograms

par·a·lyse or **par·a·lyze** (par′ə līz′) *v.* **-lysed** or **-lyzed, -lys·ing** or **-lyz·ing. 1** affect with a lessening or loss of the power of motion or feeling: *His left arm was paralysed.* **2** make powerless or helplessly inactive; cripple; stun; deaden: *Fear paralysed my mind.*

pa·ral·y·sis (pə ral′ə sis) *n.* **-ses** (-sēz′). **1** a lessening or loss of the power of motion or sensation in any part of the body. **2** a condition of powerlessness or helpless inactivity; crippling: *The war caused a paralysis of trade.* [< L < Gk. *paralysis*, ult. < *para-* from beside + *lyein* to loose. Doublet of PALSY.]

par·a·lyt·ic (par′ə lit′ik) *adj.* of paralysis; having paralysis. —*n.* a person who has paralysis.

par·a·lyze (par′ə līz′) *v.* paralyse.

par·a·me·ci·um (par′ə mē′shē əm or par′ə mē′sē əm) *n.* **-ci·a** (-shē ə or -sē ə). a one-celled animal shaped like a slender slipper, that is covered with cilia and has a groove along one side leading into an open mouth. Paramecia are free-swimming ciliates that usually live in stagnant water. [< NL < Gk. *paramēkēs* oblong < *para-* on one side + *mēkos* length]

pa·ram·e·ter (pə ram′ə tər) *n.* **1** in mathematics, a quantity that is constant in a particular calculation or case but varies in other cases. **2** a factor: *parameters of space and time.* [< NL *parametrum* < Gk. *para-* beside + *métron* meter]

par·a·mount (par′ə mount′) *adj.* chief in importance; above others; supreme: *Truth is of paramount importance.* —*n.* an overlord; supreme ruler. [< AF *paramont* above < *par* by (< L *per*) + *amont* up < L *ad montem* to the mountain] —**Syn.** See **dominant.**

par·amour (par′ə mür′) *n.* **1** a person who takes the place of a husband or wife illegally. **2** *Archaic.* a lover. [ME < OF *paramour* < *par amour* by love < L *per amorem*]

par·a·noi·a (par′ə noi′ə) *n.* a mental disorder, often chronic, characterized by elaborate delusions of persecution or grandeur. [< NL < Gk. *paranoia*, ult. < *para-* amiss + *nous* mind]

par·a·noi·ac (par′ə noi′ak) *n.* a person afflicted with paranoia. —*adj.* of or like paranoia.

par·a·pet (par′ə pet′ or par′ə pit) *n.* **1** a low wall or mound of stone, earth, etc. to protect soldiers. See **rampart** for picture. **2** a low wall at the edge of a balcony, roof, bridge, etc. [< Ital. *parapetto* < *para* defend (< L *parare* prepare) + *petto* breast < L *pectus*]

par·a·pher·nal·ia (par′ə fə nā′lē ə or par′ə fər nāl′yə) *n.pl.* **1** personal belongings. **2** equipment; outfit. [< Med.L *paraphernalia*, ult. < Gk. *parapherna* < *para-* besides + *phernē* dowry]
☛ **Paraphernalia,** meaning "personal belongings," is plural in form and use: *My paraphernalia are ready to be shipped.* When the meaning is "equipment," *paraphernalia* is sometimes singular in use: *Military paraphernalia includes guns, rifles, ammunition, etc.*

par·a·phrase (par′ə frāz′) *v.* **-phrased, -phras·ing,** *n.* —*v.* state the meaning of (a passage) in other and different words. [< n.] —*n.* an expression of the meaning of a passage in other words. [< F < L < Gk. *paraphrasis* < *para-* alongside of + *phrazein* say]

par·a·ple·gi·a (par′ə plē′jē ə) *n.* paralysis of the legs and the lower part of the trunk. [< NL < Gk. *paraplēgia* paralysis of one side of the body]

par·a·ple·gic (par′ə plē′jik or par′ə plej′ik) *n.* a person afflicted with paraplegia. —*adj.* having to do with, or afflicted with, paraplegia.

par·a·site (par′ə sīt′) *n.* **1** an animal or plant that lives on, with, or in another, from which it gets its food. Lice and tapeworms are parasites. Mistletoe is a parasite on oak trees. **2** a person who lives on others without making any useful and fitting return. **3** in ancient Greece and Rome, a person who ate at the table or at the expense of another, earning meals by flattery or wit. [< L < Gk. *parasitos* < *para-* alongside of + *sitos* food]

par·a·sit·ic (par′ə sit′ik) *adj.* of or like a parasite; living on others. —**par′a·sit′i·cal·ly,** *adv.*

par·a·sit·i·cal (par′ə sit′ə kəl) *adj.* parasitic.

par·a·sol (par′ə sol′ or par′ə sôl′) *n.* a light umbrella used as a protection from the sun. [< F < Ital. *parasole* < *para* ward off + *sole* sun]

par·a·thy·roid (par′ə thī′roid) *adj.* **1** near the thyroid gland. **2** of, having to do with, or caused by the parathyroid glands. —*n.* one of the parathyroid glands. [< *para-*¹ + *thyroid*]

parathyroid glands small glands near the thyroid glands. Their secretion, which enables the body to use calcium, is necessary for life.

par·a·troop·er (par′ə trüp′ər) *n.* a soldier trained to use a parachute for descent from an aircraft into a battle area. [< *para*chute + *trooper*]

par·a·troops (par′ə trüps′) *n.pl.* troops moved by air and landed by parachutes in a battle area.

par·a·ty·phoid (par′ə tī′foid) *n.* a type of infectious disease having symptoms resembling those of typhoid fever. [< *para*¹- + *typhoid*]

par·boil (pär′boil′) *v.* **1** boil till partly cooked. **2** overheat. [< F < LL *perbullire* < *per-* thoroughly + *bullire* boil; *par-* confused with *part*]

Par·cae (pär′sē or pär′kī) *n.pl.* in Roman mythology, the Fates.

par·cel (pär′səl) *n. v.* **-celled** or **-celed, -cel·ling** or **-cel·ing.** —*n.* **1** a bundle of things wrapped or packed together; package. **2** a container with things packed in it. **3** a piece: *a parcel of land.* **4** a group; lot; pack. —*v.* **1** make a parcel of. **2 parcel out,** divide into, or distribute in, portions. [ME < OF *parcelle,* ult. < L *particula,* dim. of *pars, partis* part] —**Syn.** *n.* **1** See **bundle.**

parcel post the branch of the postal service that carries parcels.

parch (pärch) *v.* **1** make hot and dry or thirsty. **2** become dry, hot, or thirsty. **3** dry by heating; roast slightly: *Corn is sometimes parched.* [ME *parchen, perchen*; origin uncertain] —**Syn. 3** scorch, sear, singe, char.

par·chee·si or **par·che·si** (pär chē′zē or pär chē′zə) *n.* a game resembling backgammon, played by moving pieces according to throws of dice. [< Hind. *pachisi* < *pachis* twenty-five (highest throw)]

parch·ment (pärch′mənt) *n.* **1** the skin of sheep, goats, etc. prepared for use as a writing material. **2** a manuscript or document written on parchment. **3** a kind of paper that looks like parchment. [ME < OF *parchemin* < VL *particaminum,* blending of *parthica* (*pellis*) Parthian (leather) and *pergamina* of Pergamum, a city in Greece, whence it came]

pard¹ (pärd) *n. Archaic.* leopard; panther. [ME < OF < L < Gk. *pardos*]

pard² (pärd) *n. Slang.* a partner; friend; companion. [for *partner*]

par·don (pär′dən) *n.* **1** forgiveness. **2** an excuse. **3** a setting free from punishment. **4** a legal document setting a person free from punishment. **5** a papal indulgence. [ME < OF *pardon* < *pardonner* to pardon. See v.] —*v.* **1** forgive. **2** excuse: *She pardoned his bad manners.* **3** set free from punishment: *The Governor General pardoned the criminal.* [ME < OF *pardonner* < LL *perdonare* < L *per-* thoroughly + *donum* gift] —**Syn.** *n.* **1** absolution, amnesty. -*v.* **1** acquit, absolve. See **excuse.** ☞ See **excuse** for usage note.

par·don·a·ble (pär′dən ə bəl or pärd′nə bəl) *adj.* that can be pardoned; excusable. —**par′don·a·bly,** *adv.*

par·don·er (pär′dən ər or pärd′nər) *n.* **1** a person who pardons. **2** in the Middle Ages, an ecclesiastical official charged with the granting of indulgences.

pare (pãr) *v.* **pared, par·ing. 1** cut, trim, or shave off the outer part of; peel: *pare an apple.* **2** cut away (an outer layer, part, etc.): *pare a layer from a corn.* **3** cut away little by little: *pare down expenses.* [ME < OF < L *parare* make ready. Doublet of PARRY.] —**Syn. 1** skin.

par·e·gor·ic (par′ə gôr′ik) *n.* a soothing medicine containing camphor and a little opium. —*adj.* soothing. [< LL < Gk. *parēgorikos* soothing, ult. < *para-* at the side of + *-agoros* speaking]

paren. parenthesis.

pa·ren·chy·ma (pə reng′kə mə) *n.* **1** in botany, the fundamental tissue in plants, composed of living, unspecialized cells from which all other cells are formed. Most of the tissue in the softer parts of leaves, the pulp of fruits, the pith of stems, etc. is parenchyma. **2** in biology, the essential tissue of an animal organ, as distinguished from its connective or supporting tissue. [< Gk. *parenchyma* < *para-* beside + *en-* in + *chyma* what is poured]

par·ent (pãr′ənt) *n.* **1** a father or mother. **2** any animal or plant that produces offspring or seed. **3** a source; cause: *Envy is the parent of hate.* [ME < OF < L *parens, -entis,* originally active pp. of *parere* bring forth]

par·ent·age (pãr′ən tij) *n.* **1** descent from parents; family line; ancestry. **2** the state of being a parent.

pa·ren·tal (pə ren′təl) *adj.* of or having to do with a parent; like a parent's. —**pa·ren′tal·ly,** *adv.*

parent element in physics, an element that yields an isotope or daughter element through radio-active decay or nuclear bombardment.

pa·ren·the·ses (pə ren′thə sēz′) *n.* pl. of **parenthesis.**

pa·ren·the·sis (pə ren′thə sis) *n.* **-ses. 1** a word, phrase, sentence, etc. inserted within a sentence to explain or qualify something. **2** either or both of two curved lines ( ) used to set off such an expression. [< L < Gk. *parenthesis,* ult. < *para-* beside + *en-* in + *thesis* a placing]

pa·ren·the·size (pə ren′thə sīz′) *v.* **-sized, -siz·ing.** insert as or in a parenthesis; put between the marks of parenthesis; put many parentheses in.

par·en·thet·ic (par′ən thet′ik) *adj.* **1** qualifying; explanatory. **2** put in parentheses. **3** using parentheses. —**par′en·thet′i·cal·ly,** *adv.*

par·en·thet·i·cal (par′ən thet′ə kəl) *adj.* parenthetic.

par·ent·hood (pãr′ənt hůd′) *n.* the state of being a parent.

pa·re·sis (pə rē′sis or par′ə sis) *n.* **1** an incomplete paralysis that affects the ability to move, but does not affect ability to feel. **2** a disease of the brain that gradually causes general paralysis. [< NL < Gk. *paresis* a letting go, ult. < *para-* by + *hienai* let go]

pa·ret·ic (pə ret′ik or pə rē′tik) *adj.* of or having to do with paresis; caused by paresis. —*n.* a person having paresis.

par ex·cel·lence (pär ek sə läns′; *French,* pä rek se läns′) *French.* beyond comparison; above all others of the same sort.

par·fait (pär fā′; *French,* pär fe′) *n.* **1** ice cream with syrup or crushed fruit and whipped cream, served in a tall glass. **2** a rich ice cream, containing eggs and whipped cream, frozen unstirred. [< F *parfait* perfect]

par·fleche (pär′flesh or pär flesh′) *n. Cdn.* **1** rawhide made from buffalo skin that has been soaked in lye to remove the hair and then dried in the sun. **2** an article, such as a shield or bag, made from this rawhide. [< Cdn. F *parflèche,* apparently < F *parer* to parry, ward off + *flèche* arrow]

par·he·li·on (pär hē lē ən or pär hēl′yən) *n.* **-he·li·a** (-hē′lē ə or -hēl′yə). a bright circular spot on a solar halo. [< L < Gk. *parēlion* < *para-* beside + *hēlios* sun]

pa·ri·ah (pə rī′ə) *n.* **1** an outcast. **2** Usually, **Pariah.** in S. India and Burma, a member of a low caste. [< Tamil *paraiyar,* pl. or *paraiyan* drummer; because this caste provided the drummers at festivals]

pa·ri·e·tal (pə rī′ə təl) *adj.* the wall of the body or one of its cavities. —*n.* in anatomy, either of two bones that form part of the sides and top of the skull. [< LL *parietalis* < L *paries, -etis* wall]

par·i·mu·tu·el (par′ē mū′chü əl) *n.* **1** a system of betting on horse races in which those who have bet on the winning horses divide the money lost by the losers. **2** a machine for recording such bets. [< F *pari-mutuel* mutual wager; *pari* < *parier* bet < L *pariare* make equal < *par* equal]

par·ing (pãr′ing) *n.* a part pared off; skin; rind.

par·i pas·su (par′ē pas′ü or pãr′ī pas′ū) *Latin.* at an equal rate of progress; side by side; equally.

Par·is (par′is) *n.* in Greek legend, a son of Priam, king of Troy. His abduction of Helen, the wife of King Menelaus of Sparta, caused the Trojan war.

Paris green a poisonous, emerald-green powder used as a pigment and in making sprays for killing insects. It is a compound of copper, arsenic, and acetic acid.

par·ish (par′ish) *n.* **1** a district that has its own church and clergyman. **2** the people of a parish. **3** the members of the congregation of a particular church. **4** in New Brunswick, a political unit similar to a township. **5** in Quebec, a civil district, a municipality similar to a township and related to a religious parish. **6** in Great Britain, a civil district. [ME < OF *paroisse* < LL *parochia* < Gk. *paroikia,* ult. < *para-* near + *oikos* dwelling]

pa·rish·ion·er (pə rish′ən ər or pə rish′nər) *n.* a member of a parish. [earlier *parishion* < OF *paroissien*]

Pa·ri·sian (pə rizh′ən or pə rē′zyən) *adj.* of or having to do with Paris, the capital of France, or its people. —*n.* a native or inhabitant of Paris.

par·i·ty (par′ə tē) *n.* **1** equality; similarity or close correspondence with regard to state, position, condition, value, quality, degree, etc. **2** an equality between the market prices received by a farmer for his commodities and the prices that he has to pay for labor, taxes, etc. [< L *paritas* < *par* equal]

park (pärk) *n.* **1** land set apart for the pleasure of the public: *Many cities have beautiful parks.* **2** land set apart for wild animals. **3** the grounds around a fine house. **4** a place to leave an automobile, etc. for a time. **5** a space where army vehicles, supplies, and artillery are put when an army camps.
—*v.* **1** leave (an automobile, etc.) for a time in a certain place. **2** arrange (army vehicles, artillery, etc.) in a park. **3** *Informal.* place, put, or leave. [ME < OF *parc* < Med.L *parricus* enclosure. Doublet of PADDOCK.]

par·ka (pär′kə) *n.* **1** a fur jacket with a hood, worn in the North. **2** a long woollen shirt or jacket with a hood: *Parkas are popular as winter wear in many parts of Canada.* **3** a hood. [< Aleut.]

parking meter a device containing a coin-operated clock mechanism for indicating the time that an automobile may remain in a parking area.

park·land (pärk′land′) *n.* **1** *Cdn.* the region between the foothills of the Rockies and the prairie. **2** *Cdn.* the wooded region between the Barrens and the prairie. **3** land kept free from buildings, factories, etc. and maintained as a public park: *Parklands are intended to preserve the scenic beauty of the countryside.*

park ranger an official who patrols and helps maintain a national or provincial park.

park·way (pärk′wā′) *n.* a broad road through an area kept up as a park, made attractive by grass, trees, flowers, etc.: *There is a beautiful parkway running through Ottawa.*

par·lance (pär′ləns) *n.* a way of speaking; talk; language. [< OF *parlance* < *parler* speak. See PARLEY.]

par·lay (pär′lā or pär′lē) *v.* **1** risk (an original bet and its winnings) on another bet. **2** build up by taking risks: *He parlayed a few hundred dollars into a fortune.* [alteration of *paroli* < F < Ital. *paroli* grand cast at dice]

par·ley (pär′lē) *n.* **-leys,** *v.* **-leyed, -ley·ing.** —*n.* **1** a conference; informal talk. **2** an informal discussion with an enemy about terms of surrender, exchange of prisoners, etc. —*v.* discuss terms, especially with an enemy. [< F *parlée* < a pp. of *parler* speak, ult. < L *parabola* parable]

par·lia·ment (pär′lə mənt) *n.* **1** the highest lawmaking body in certain countries. **2 Parliament, a** the national

hat, āge, cãre, fär; let, ēqual, tėrm; it, īce
hot, ōpen, ôrder; oil, out; cup, pu̇t, rüle, ūse
əbove, takən, pencəl, lemən, circəs
ch, child; ng, long; sh, ship
th, thin; ᴛʜ, then; zh, measure

lawmaking body of Canada, consisting of the Senate and the House of Commons. **b** the national lawmaking body of the U.K., consisting of the House of Lords and the House of Commons. **c** the lawmaking body of a country or colony having the British system of government. [ME < OF *parlement* < *parler* speak. See PARLEY.]

par·lia·men·tar·i·an (pär′lə men tãr′ē ən) *n.* **1** one skilled in parliamentary procedure or debate. **2 Parliamentarian,** a person who supported Parliament against Charles I of England.

par·lia·men·ta·ry (pär′lə men′tə rē or pär′lə men′trē) *adj.* **1** of a parliament. **2** according to the rules and customs of a parliament or other lawmaking body: *Our debating society functions in accordance with the rules of parliamentary procedure.* **3** done by a parliament. **4** having a parliament.

parliamentary secretary a member of the House of Commons appointed to assist a Cabinet Minister in his parliamentary work.

par·lor or **par·lour** (pär′lər) *n.* **1** a room for receiving or entertaining guests; sitting room or living room. **2** a decorated room in which some kind of business is carried on; shop: *a beauty parlor.* **3** a place where refreshments of various kinds are sold: *an ice-cream parlor, a beer parlor.* [ME < AF *parlur* < *parler* speak. See PARLEY.]

parlor car or **parlour car** a railway passenger car for day travel, more luxurious and more expensive than ordinary cars.

par·lour (pär′lər) *n.* parlor.

par·lous (pär′ləs) *Archaic or dialect.* —*adj.* **1** perilous. **2** very clever; shrewd. —*adv.* extremely. [var. of *perilous*]

Par·me·san (pär′mə zan′) *n.* a hard, dry Italian cheese made from skim milk. [< *Parma,* Italy]

Par·nas·sus (pär nas′əs) *n.* **1** the fabled mountain of poets, of which the summit is supposed to be their goal. **2** a collection of poems or belles lettres. **3 try to climb Parnassus,** try to write poetry. [< Mount *Parnassus,* in S. Greece, in ancient times sacred to Apollo and the Muses]

pa·ro·chi·al (pə rō′kē əl) *adj.* **1** of or in a parish: *a parochial school.* **2** narrow; limited: *a parochial viewpoint.* [ME < OF < LL *parochialis* < *parochia* parish. See PARISH.] **—pa·ro′chi·al·ly,** *adv.*

pa·ro·chi·al·ism (pə rō′kē əl iz′əm) *n.* a parochial character or tendency; narrowness of interests or views.

parochial school a local school maintained by a church.

par·o·dist (par′ə dist) *n.* a writer of parodies.

par·o·dy (par′ə dē) *n.* **-dies,** *v.* **-died, -dy·ing.** —*n.* **1** a humorous imitation of a serious writing. A parody follows the form of the original, but changes its sense to nonsense, thus making fun of the characteristics of the original. **2** a poor imitation. **3** a musical composition making fun of another. —*v.* **1** make fun of by imitating; make a parody on. **2** imitate poorly. [< L < Gk. *parōidia* < *para-* beside + *ōidē* song]

pa·role (pə rōl′) *n. v.* **-roled, -rol·ing.** —*n.* **1** a conditional release from prison or jail before the full term is served: *The prisoner was released on parole.* **2** conditional freedom allowed in place of imprisonment. **3** word of honor: *The prisoner of war gave his parole not to try to escape.* —*v.* put on parole; release on parole. [< F *parole* word < L *parabola* parable. Doublet of PARABLE, PALAVER.]

par·o·quet (par′ə ket′) *n.* parakeet.

pa·rot·id (pə rot′id) *adj.* in anatomy, near the ear. The **parotid glands,** one in front of each ear, supply saliva to the mouth through the **parotid ducts.** —*n.* in anatomy, a parotid gland. [< L < Gk. *parōtis, -idos* < *para-* beside + *ous, ōtos* ear]

par·ox·ysm (par′ək siz′əm) *n.* **1** a severe, sudden attack: *a paroxysm of coughing.* **2** a fit; convulsion: *a paroxysm of rage.* [< Med.L < Gk. *paroxysmos,* ult. < *para-* + *oxynein* render acute]

par·ox·ys·mal (par′ək siz′məl) *adj.* of, like, or having paroxysms. —**par′ox·ys′mal·ly,** *adv.*

par·quet (pär kā′ or pär ket′) *n. v.* **-quet·ted** or **-quet·ed, -quet·ting** or **-quet·ing.** —*n.* **1** an inlaid wooden flooring. **2 a** the main floor of a theatre. **b** the part of the main floor of a theatre from the orchestra to the parquet circle. —*v.* make or put down (an inlaid wooden floor). [< F *parquet,* dim. of *parc* park]

parquet circle the part of the main floor of a theatre that is under the balcony.

par·quet·ry (pär′kit rē) *n.* **-ries.** a mosaic of wood used for floors, wainscotting, etc.

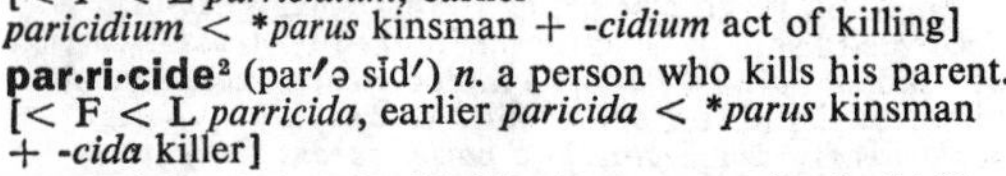
Parquetry

parr (pär) *n.* **parr** or **parrs.** a young salmon before it leaves fresh water and enters the sea. [< Scottish dial.]

par·ra·keet (par′ə kēt′) *n.* parakeet.

par·ri·cid·al (par′ə sīd′əl) *adj.* of or having to do with parricide.

par·ri·cide[1] (par′ə sīd′) *n.* the crime of killing one's parent or parents. [< F < L *parricidium,* earlier *paricidium* < **parus* kinsman + *-cidium* act of killing]

par·ri·cide[2] (par′ə sīd′) *n.* a person who kills his parent. [< F < L *parricida,* earlier *paricida* < **parus* kinsman + *-cida* killer]

par·rot (par′ət) *n.* **1** a bird having a stout, hooked bill and, often, bright-colored feathers. Some parrots can imitate sounds and repeat words and sentences. **2** a person who repeats words or acts without understanding them. —*v.* repeat without understanding. [< F *Perrot,* dim. of *Pierre* Peter] —**par′rot·like′,** *adj.*

par·ry (par′ē) *v.* **-ried, -ry·ing,** *n.* **-ries.** —*v.* ward off; turn aside; evade (a thrust, stroke, weapon, question, etc.) —*n.* the act of parrying; avoiding. [< F *parez,* imperative of *parer* < Ital. *parare* ward off < L *parare* prepare. Doublet of PARE.]

parse (pärs or pärz) *v.* **parsed, pars·ing. 1** analyse (a sentence) grammatically, describing the function of each part. **2** describe (a word) grammatically, telling what part of speech it is, its form, and its use in a sentence. [< L *pars* (*orationis*) part (of speech)]

Par·see or **Par·si** (pär′sē or pär sē′) *n.* in India, a member of a Zoroastrian sect, descended from Persians who first settled there early in the eighth century A.D. [< Persian and Hind. *Parsi* a Persian]

Par·si·fal (pär′sə fəl or pär′sə fäl′) *n.* Parzifal.

par·si·mo·ni·ous (pär′sə mō′nē əs) *adj.* too economical; stingy. —**par′si·mo′ni·ous·ly,** *adv.* —**par′si·mo′ni·ous·ness,** *n.* —**Syn.** frugal, stinting, miserly.

par·si·mo·ny (pär′sə mō′nē) *n.* extreme economy; stinginess. [< L *parsimonia* < *parcere* spare]

pars·ley (pärs′lē) *n.* **-leys.** a garden plant having finely divided, fragrant leaves, used to flavor food and to garnish platters of meat, etc. [OE *petersilie,* also < OF *peresil*; both < VL *petrosilium* < L < Gk. *petroselinon* < *petros* rock + *selinon* parsley]

pars·nip (pärs′nip) *n.* **1** a vegetable that is the long, tapering, whitish root of a plant belonging to the same family as the carrot. **2** the plant. [ME < OF *pasnaie* < L *pastinaca* (cf. *pastinare* dig); form influenced by ME *nep* turnip]

par·son (pär′sən) *n.* **1** a minister in charge of a parish. **2** any clergyman; minister. [< Med.L *persona* parson < L *persona* person, character. Doublet of PERSON.]

par·son·age (pär′sən ij) *n.* the house provided for a minister by his church.

part (pärt) *n.* **1** something less than the whole: *What part of the chicken do you like best?* **2** each of several equal quantities into which a whole may be divided: *A dime is a tenth part of a dollar.* **3** a thing that helps to make up a whole: *spare parts. A radio has many parts.* **4** a share: *Everyone must do his part.* **5** a side in a dispute or contest: *He always takes his brother's part.* **6** a character in a play; the words spoken by a character: *Jane spoke the part of the fairy in our play.* **7** a role played by a person in real life. **8** a dividing line left in combing one's hair. **9** in music: **a** one of the voices or instruments. The four parts in singing are soprano, alto, tenor, and bass. **b** the music for one voice or instrument.
for one's part, as far as one is concerned.
for the most part, mostly: *The attempts were for the most part unsuccessful.*
in good part, in a friendly or gracious way.
in part, in some measure or degree; to some extent; partly.
on the part of one or **on one's part, a** as far as one is concerned. **b** by one.
parts, a ability; talent: *a man of parts.* **b** regions; districts; places: *He has travelled much in foreign parts.*
part and parcel, a necessary part.
take part, take or have a share. [< L *pars, partis*]
—*v.* **1** divide into two or more pieces. **2** force apart; divide: *The policeman on horseback parted the crowd.* **3** go apart; separate: *The friends parted in anger.* **4** comb (the hair) away from a dividing line. **5 part from,** go away from; leave. **6 part with,** give up; let go.
—*adj.* less than the whole: *part-time.*
—*adv.* in some measure or degree; partly. [ME < OF < L *partire* < *pars, partis,* n.]
Syn. *n.* **1 Part, portion, piece** = something less than the whole. **Part** is the general word and means an element, fraction, or member of a whole, considered apart from the rest: *Save part of the roast for tomorrow night.* **Portion** means a part thought of not so much in relation to the whole from which it is taken as an amount or quantity making up a section or share: *Give a portion of each day to recreation.* **Piece** means a separate part, often thought of as complete in itself: *He ate a big piece of cake.* –*v.* **1** sever, sunder.
☛ **on the part of** is often a rather clumsy substitute for *by, among, for,* and the like: *In recent years there has been a noticeable feeling on the part of* (*among*) *students that education is all-important.*

part. 1 participle. **2** particular.

par·take (pär tāk′) *v.* **-took, -tak·en, -tak·ing. 1** eat or drink some; take some: *We are eating lunch. Will you partake?* **2** take or have a share. **3 partake of, a** have a share in. **b** have to some extent the nature or character of: *Her graciousness partakes of condescension.* [< *partaker,* for *part-taker*] —**par·tak′er,** *n.* —**Syn. 2** See **share.**

par·tak·en (pär tāk′ən) *v.* pp. of **partake.**

par·terre (pär tãr′) *n.* **1** the part of the main floor of a theatre under the balcony. **2** an ornamental arrangement of flower beds. [< F *parterre* < *par terre* on the ground]

par·the·no·gen·e·sis (pär′thə nō jen′ə sis) *n.* in biology, reproduction without any male element. [< Gk. *parthenos* virgin + E *genesis*]

Par·the·non (pär′thə non′ or pär′thə nən) *n.* in Athens, the temple of Athena on the Acropolis, regarded as the finest example of Doric architecture. [< L < Gk. *Parthenon* < *hē parthenos* the Virgin, i.e., Athena]

Par·thi·a (pär′thē ə) *n.* an ancient country in Asia southeast of the Caspian Sea, now a part of N.E. Iran. —**Par′thi·an,** *n. adj.*

Par·thi·an shot (pär′thē ən) a sharp parting remark or action. Parthian archers used to aim at their enemies while fleeing or pretending to flee.

par·tial (pär′shəl) *adj.* **1** not complete; not total: *a partial loss.* **2** inclined to favor one side more than another; favoring unfairly: *A father should not be partial to any one of his children.* **3** favorably inclined: *He is partial to sports.* [< LL *partialis* < L *pars, partis* part] —**Syn. 1** incomplete, imperfect. **2** biassed, prejudiced.

par·ti·al·i·ty (pär′shē al′ə tē or pär shal′ə tē) *n.* **-ties. 1** a favoring of one more than another or others; favorable prejudice; a being partial. **2** a particular liking; fondness: *Children often have a partiality for candy.* —**Syn. 1** bias, favoritism. **2** preference, bent.

par·tial·ly (pär′shəl ē) *adv.* **1** in part; not generally or totally; partly. **2** in a partial manner; with undue bias. —**Syn. 1** See **partly.**

par·tic·i·pant (pär tis′ə pənt) *n.* one who shares or participates. —*adj.* participating.

par·tic·i·pate (pär tis′ə pāt′) *v.* **-pat·ed, -pat·ing.** have a share; take part: *The teacher participated in the children's games.* [< L *participare,* ult. < *pars, partis* part + *capere* take] —**par·tic′i·pa′tor,** *n.* —**par·tic′i·pa·to′ry,** *adj.* —**Syn.** See **share.**

hat, āge, cãre, fär; let, ēqual, tėrm; it, īce
hot, ōpen, ôrder; oil, out; cup, pu̇t, rüle, ūse
əbove, takən, pencəl, lemən, circəs
ch, child; ng, long; sh, ship
th, thin; ᴛʜ, then; zh, measure

par·tic·i·pa·tion (pär tis′ə pā′shən) *n.* a participating; a taking part.

par·ti·cip·i·al (pär′tə sip′ē əl) *adj.* of or having to do with a participle; as, a **participial adjective** (a *masked* man, a *becoming* dress), a **participial noun** (for *cutting* ice, the fatigue of *marching*). —**par′ti·cip′i·al·ly,** *adv.*

par·ti·ci·ple (pär′tə sip′əl) *n.* a form of a verb used as an adjective. [ME < OF *participle,* var. of *participe* < L *participium* a sharing. Related to PARTICIPATE.]
☛ A **participle** retains the attributes of a verb, such as tense, voice, power to take an object, and modification by adverbs. *Examples*: the girl *writing* sentences at the blackboard, the recently *stolen* silver, John *having missed* the boat. In these phrases, *writing* is a present participle; *stolen* is a past participle; *having missed* is a perfect participle.

par·ti·cle (pär′tə kəl) *n.* **1** a very small bit: *I had a particle of dust in my eye.* **2** a prefix or suffix. **3** in physics: **a** a minute mass of matter that while still having inertia and attraction is treated as a point without length, breadth, or thickness. **b** one of the fundamental units of matter, as the electron, neutron, photon, or proton; elementary particle. **4** a preposition, conjunction, article, or interjection. *In, if, an,* and *ah* are particles. [< L *particula,* dim. of *pars, partis* part]

par·ti-col·ored or **par·ti-col·oured** (pär′tē kul′ərd) *adj.* **1** colored differently in different parts. **2** diversified: *a parti-colored story.* Also, **party-colored** or **party-coloured.** [*parti-* < F *parti* divided, pp. of *partir* < L *partire* < *pars, partis* a part]

par·tic·u·lar (pər tik′yu̇ lər) *adj.* **1** apart from others; considered separately; single: *That particular chair is already sold.* **2** belonging to some one person, thing, group, occasion, etc.: *A particular characteristic of a skunk is his smell.* **3** different from others; unusual; special: *a particular friend.* **4** hard to please; wanting everything to be just right; very careful: *She is very particular; nothing but the best will do.* **5** giving details; full of details: *a particular account of the game.*
—*n.* **1** an individual part; item; point: *The work is complete in every particular.* **2 in particular,** especially. [ME < OF < L *particularis* < *particula.* See PARTICLE.]
Syn. *adj.* **1** See **special. 2** individual, distinctive. **4** precise, exacting, fastidious. **5** detailed, minute. *-n.* **1** See **item.**

par·tic·u·lar·i·ty (pər tik′yu̇ lar′ə tē) *n.* **-ties. 1** a detailed quality; minuteness. **2** special carefulness. **3** attentiveness to details. **4** a particular feature or trait. **5** the quality of being hard to please. **6** the quality or fact of being particular.

par·tic·u·lar·ize (pər tik′yu̇ lər īz′) *v.* **-ized, -iz·ing. 1** mention particularly or individually; treat in detail. **2** mention individuals; give details. —**par·tic′u·lar·iz′er,** *n.* —**par·tic′u·lar·i·za′tion,** *n.*

par·tic·u·lar·ly (pər tik′yu̇ lər lē) *adv.* **1** in a high degree; especially. **2** in a particular manner. **3** in detail; minutely. —**Syn. 1** principally, mainly. See **especially.**

part·ing (pär′ting) *n.* **1** a departure; going away; taking leave. **2** a division; separation. **3** a place of division or separation: *Her hair is arranged with a side parting.*
—*adj.* **1** given, taken, spoken, done, etc. on going away: *a parting request, a parting shot.* **2** departing. **3** dividing; separating. [< *part,* v.]

Parti Quebecois (pär tē′ kā bek wä′) a Quebec political party, founded in 1968.

Par·ti rouge (pär′tē rüzh′) *French.* the name of a radical French-Canadian political party of the mid-nineteenth century, inspired by Louis Joseph Papineau, that supported universal suffrage, called for the abolition of the seigniorial system, and opposed political action by the Church.

par·ti·san (pär′tə zan′ or pär′tə zən) *n.* **1** a strong supporter of a person, party, or cause; one whose support is based on feeling rather than on reasoning. **2** a member of light, irregular troops; guerrilla. —*adj.* of or like a partisan. [< F < Ital. *partigiano* < *parte* part] —**Syn.** *n.* **1** follower, adherent, disciple.

par·ti·san·ship (pär′tə zən ship′) *n.* **1** strong loyalty to a party or cause. **2** the act of taking sides.

par·ti·tion (pär tish′ən) *n.* **1** a division into parts: *the partition of a man's wealth when he dies.* **2** a portion; part. **3** something that separates, such as a wall between rooms, a membrane, etc. —*v.* **1** divide into parts: *partition an empire among three brothers, partition a house into rooms.* **2** separate by a partition. [< L *partitio, -onis* < *partire.* See PART, v.] —**Syn.** *n.* **1** apportionment.

par·ti·tive (pär′tə tiv) *n.* a word or phrase referring to a part of a collective whole. *Some, few,* and *any* are partitives. —*adj.* expressing a part of a collective whole: *a partitive adjective.* —**par′ti·tive·ly,** *adv.*

par·ti·zan (par′tə zan′ or pär′tə zən) *n. adj.* partisan.

part·ly (pärt′lē) *adv.* in part; in some measure or degree.
Syn. Partly, partially = in part or to a certain extent, not wholly or totally. **Partly** = not wholly or entirely what is described or stated, with all parts included or in all ways or respects, but only in part or in some measure or degree: *He is partly to blame.* **Partially** = not totally or generally, with no exceptions and nothing held back, but affecting only one part or to only a limited extent: *He is partially paralyzed.*

part·ner (pärt′nər) *n.* **1** one who shares: *My sister was the partner of my sorrows.* **2** a member of a company or firm who shares the risk and profits of the business. **3** a wife or husband. **4** a companion in a dance. **5** in games such as cards or tennis, a player on the same team or side. [var. of *parcener* < AF *parconier* < *parçon* partition < L *partitio, -onis;* influenced by *part.* See PARTITION.] —**Syn. 1** sharer, partaker.

part·ner·ship (pärt′nər ship′) *n.* **1** the state or condition of being a partner; joint interest; association: *a business partnership, the partnership of marriage.* **2** a company or firm with two or more members who share in the risk and profits of the business.

part of speech one of the following groups into which words are divided: noun, pronoun, adjective, verb, adverb, preposition, conjunction, and interjection.
☛ **parts of speech.** One of the fundamental facts of English grammar is that a word may function as more than one part of speech: In *spell the word,* we use *word* as a noun, in *Write a word picture, word* is an adjective, and in *How will I word the message?, word* is a verb.

par·took (pär tu̇k′) *v.* pt. of **partake.**

par·tridge (pär′trij) *n.* **-tridg·es** or (*esp. collectively*) **-tridge. 1** any of several kinds of game birds belonging to the same group as the quail, pheasant, and grouse. **2** in North America, the ruffed grouse or the quail. [ME < OF *perdriz* < L < Gk. *perdix*]

par·tridge·ber·ry (pär′trij ber′ē) *n.* **-ries. 1** a North American trailing plant having evergreen leaves, fragrant white flowers, and scarlet berries. **2** the berry.

part song a song with parts in simple harmony for two or more voices, especially one meant to be sung without an accompaniment.

part time part of the time.

part-time (pärt′tīm′) *adj.* for part of the usual time: *He works about ten hours a week at a part-time job.*

par·tu·ri·ent (pär tür′ē ənt or pär tūr′ē ənt) *adj.* **1** bringing forth young; about to give birth to young. **2** having to do with childbirth. **3** ready to bring forth or produce a discovery, idea, principle, etc.

par·tu·ri·tion (pär′tyu̇ rish′ən, pär′tu̇ rish′ən, or pär′chu̇ rish′ən) *n.* childbirth. [< L *parturitio, -onis* < *parturire* be in labor, ult. < *parere* bear]

par·ty (pär′tē) *n.* **-ties,** *adj.* —*n.* **1** a group of people doing something together: *a sewing party, a dinner party, a scouting party of three soldiers.* **2** a gathering for pleasure: *On her birthday she had a party and invited her friends.* **3** a group of people wanting the same kind of government or action: *the Liberal, Conservative, or New Democratic Party.* **4** one who takes part in, aids, or knows about: *He was a party to our plot.* **5** each of the persons or sides in a contract, lawsuit, etc. **6** *Informal.* a person. **7** any one of two or more persons or families using the same telephone line. —*adj.* of or having to do with a party. [ME < OF *partie* < a pp. of *partir* divide < L *partire* < *pars, partis* part] —**Syn.** *n.* **1** band.
☛ See **person** for usage note.

par·ty-col·ored or **par·ty-col·oured** (pär′tē kul′ərd) *adj.* parti-colored.

party line 1 a telephone line by which two or more

subscribers are connected with the exchange by one circuit. **2** a boundary line between adjoining premises. **3** the officially adopted policies of a political party, especially of the Communist Party.

party liner one who follows the official policy of a political party, especially of the Communist Party.

party wall in law, a wall dividing adjoining properties. Each owner has certain rights in it.

par value the value of a stock, bond, note, etc. printed on it; face value.

par·ve·nu (pär′və nū′ or pär′və nü′) *n.* **1** a person who has risen above his class. **2** one who has risen to a higher place that he is fit for; upstart. [< F *parvenu*, pp. of *parvenir* arrive < L *pervenire* < *per-* through + *venire* come]

Par·zi·fal (pär′tsi fäl′) *n.* in German legend, a knight who successfully sought the Holy Grail. As **Parsifal,** he is the hero of a music drama by Wagner.

pas (pä) *n. French.* **1** in dancing, a step or movement. **2** a kind of dance.

pas·cal (pas kal′) *n.* a measure of pressure equal to one newton per square metre. *Symbol*: Pa [after Blaise *Pascal* (1623–62), a French mathematician]

pas·chal (pas′kəl) *adj.* **1** of or having to do with the Passover. **2** of or having to do with Easter; used in Easter celebrations. [ME < OF < LL *paschalis* < L *pascha* < Gk. < Hebrew *pesah* Passover]

pa·sha (pash′ə, po sha′, or pä′shə) *n.* in Turkey, a former title of rank. Also, **pacha.** [< Turkish *pasha*, var. of *basha* < *bash* head]

pasque·flow·er (pask′flou′ər) *n.* any of several anemones that bloom early in the spring. [*pasque* < OF *pasque* Easter < L < Gk. < Hebrew *pesah* Passover]

pas·quin·ade (pas′kwə nād′) *n. v.* **-ad·ed, -ad·ing.** —*n.* a publicly posted satirical writing; lampoon. —*v.* attack by lampoons. [< F < Ital. *pasquinata* < *Pasquino*, the name of a statue on which lampoons were posted]

pass (pas) *v.* **passed, passed** or (*Archaic*) **past, pass·ing,** *n.* —*v.* **1** go by; move past: *The parade passed. We passed the big truck.* **2** move on; go: *The salesman passed from house to house.* **3** go from one to another: *His estate passed to his children.* **4** cause to go from one to another; hand around: *The old coin was passed around for everyone to see.* **5** get through or by: *We passed the dangerous section of the road successfully.* **6** go across or over: *The horse passed the stream.* **7** put or direct (a rope, string, etc.): *He passed a rope around his waist for support.* **8** disappear; go away; depart: *The time for action has already passed.* **9** cause to go, move onward, or proceed: *pass troops in review.* **10** discharge from the body. **11** be successful in (an examination, a course, etc.): *Jim passed Latin.* **12** cause or allow to go through something; sanction or approve: *pass accounts as correct.* **13** ratify or enact: *pass a bill or law.* **14** be approved by (a law-making body, etc.): *The new law passed the city council.* **15** go beyond; exceed; surpass: *His strange story passes belief.* **16** come to an end; die: *King Arthur passed in peace.* **17** use; spend: *We passed the days pleasantly.* **18** change: *Water passes from a liquid to a solid state when it freezes.* **19** take place; happen: *Tell me all that passed.* **20** go about; circulate: *Money passes from person to person.* **21** be accepted (*for* or *as*): *Use silk or a material that will pass for silk.* **22** cause to be accepted: *The inspector passed the item after examining it.* **23** express; pronounce: *A judge passes sentence on guilty persons.* **24** give a judgment or opinion: *The judges passed on each contestant.* **25** go without notice: *He was rude, but let that pass.* **26** let go without action. **27** leave out; omit. **28** in football, hockey, etc. transfer (the ball, etc.). **29** in cardplaying, give up a chance to play a hand, refuse to play a hand, or refuse to bid. **30** thrust. **31** in fencing, make a thrust. **32** promise: *pass one's word.*
bring to pass, accomplish; cause to be.
come to pass, take place; happen.
pass away, a come to an end. **b** die.
pass by, fail to notice; overlook; disregard.
pass off, a go away. **b** take place; be done. **c** get accepted; pretend to be.
pass on, a pass from one person to another. **b** die.
pass out, a *Informal.* faint; lose consciousness. **b** hand out or circulate: *The teacher passed out the report cards.*
pass over, a fail to notice; overlook; disregard. **b** die. **c** ignore the claims of (a person) to promotion, a post, honor, etc.
pass up, a give up; renounce. **b** fail to take advantage of.
—*n.* **1** the act of passing; passage. **2** success in an examination, etc.; passing an examination but without honors. **3** permission or licence to pass; free ticket: *No one can get into the fort without a pass.* **4** state; condition: *Things have come to a strange pass when children give orders to their parents.* **5** a motion of the hands. **6** a sleight-of-hand motion; manipulation; trick. **7** a narrow road, path, way, channel, etc.; a narrow passage through mountains. **8** in football, hockey, etc., a transference of a ball, puck, etc. **9** in fencing, a thrust. **10** a refusal of the opportunity to bet, bid, raise, double, etc. in playing cards. **11** *Informal.* an attempt to kiss or otherwise flirt. [ME < OF *passer*, ult. < L *passus* step]
—**pass′er,** *n.* —**Syn.** *v.* **2** proceed, advance. **13** sanction, confirm. **15** transcend.

pass. 1 passive. **2** passenger.

pass·a·ble (pas′ə bəl) *adj.* **1** fairly good; moderate: *a passable knowledge of geography.* **2** that can be passed: *a passable river.* **3** current; valid: *passable coin.* **4** that may be enacted: *a passable bill.* [< F *passable* < *passer* to pass] —**Syn. 1** tolerable, mediocre, middling.

pass·a·bly (pas′ə blē) *adv.* fairly; moderately.

pas·sage (pas′ij) *n.* **1** a hall or way through a building; passageway. **2** a means of passing; way through: *ask for passage through a crowd.* **3** right, liberty, or leave to pass: *The guard refused us passage.* **4** a passing: *the passage of time.* **5** a piece from a speech or writing: *a passage from the Bible.* **6** a going across; voyage: *We had a stormy passage across the Atlantic.* **7** a ticket that entitles the holder to transportation, especially by boat: *secure a passage for Europe.* **8** a making into law by a favoring vote of a legislature: *the passage of a bill.* **9** what passes between persons. **10** an exchange of blows. **11** in music, a phrase or other division of a composition. [ME < OF *passage* < *passer* pass. See PASS.] —**Syn. 1** corridor.

passage of arms an exchange of blows; quarrel.

pas·sage·way (pas′ij wā′) *n.* a way along which one can pass; passage. Halls and alleys are passageways.

pas·sant (pas′ənt) *adj.* in heraldry, walking and looking towards the right side: *a lion passant.* [ME < OF *passant* walking, ppr. of *passer*. See PASS.]

pass·book (pas′bu̇k′) *n.* a book in which a bank keeps an account of what a person puts in and takes out.

pas·sé (pa sā′; *French*, pä sā′) *adj.* **1** past. **2** past its usefulness; out of date. [< F *passé* passed]

pas·sen·ger (pas′ən jər) *n.* a traveller in a train, bus, aircraft, boat, etc., usually one who pays a fare. [ME < OF *passagier* < *passage*. See PASSAGE.]

passenger pigeon a kind of wild pigeon of North America, now extinct, that flew great distances in very large flocks.

passe par·tout (pas′ pär tü′) **1** a frame for a picture, consisting of strips of gummed paper that fasten the glass to the backing. **2** paper prepared for this purpose. **3** something that passes or allows one to pass everywhere. [< F *passe partout* pass everywhere]

pass·er-by (pas′ər bī′) *n.* **pass·ers-by.** one that passes by.

pas·ser·ine (pas′ər īn′ or pas′ər in) *adj.* belonging to or having to do with the very large group of perching birds including more than half of all birds. —*n.* a bird that perches. [< L *passerinus* < *passer* sparrow]

pas·sim (pas′im) *adv. Latin.* here and there; in various places.

☛ **Passim is used in footnotes in referring to material found in several places in some book or books.**

pass·ing (pas′ing) *adj.* **1** that passes. **2** transient; fleeting. **3** cursory; incidental: *a passing fancy.* **4** that is now happening. **5** allowing one to pass an examination or test: *75 will be a passing mark.*
—*n.* **1** the act of one that passes; a going by; a departure. **2** a means or place of passing. **3 in passing, a** as one proceeds or passes. **b** by the way; incidentally: *In passing, I'd like to compliment you on your excellent work.*
—*adv. Archaic.* surpassingly; very: *passing strange.*
—**Syn.** *adj.* **2** transitory.

hat, āge, cãre, fär; let, ēqual, tėrm; it, īce
hot, ōpen, ôrder; oil, out; cup, pu̇t, rüle, ūse
əbove, takən, pencəl, lemən, circəs
ch, child; ng, long; sh, ship
th, thin; ᴛʜ, then; zh, measure

pas·sion (pash′ən) *n.* **1** very strong feeling: *Hate and fear are passions.* **2** a violent anger; rage: *He flew into a passion.* **3** intense love or sexual desire. **4** a very strong liking: *Anne has a passion for music.* **5** the object of a passion: *Music is her passion.* **6** *Archaic.* suffering. **7** Often, **Passion. a** the sufferings of Jesus on the cross or after the Last Supper. **b** the story of these sufferings in the Bible. **c** a musical setting of this story. **d** a representation in art of the sufferings of Christ. [ME < OF < L *passio, -onis,* ult. < *pati* suffer] —**Syn. 1** emotion. See **feeling.**

pas·sion·ate (pash′ən it) *adj.* **1** having or showing strong feelings: *The Fathers of Confederation were passionate believers in unity.* **2** easily moved to anger. **3** resulting from strong feeling: *He made a passionate speech.* **4** having or showing a very strong love, as a man for a woman: *a passionate lover.* [< Med.L *passionatus* < L *passio, -onis.* See PASSION.]
—**pas′sion·ate·ly,** *adv.* —**pas′sion·ate·ness,** *n.* —**Syn. 2** quick-tempered, irascible, fiery.

pas·sion·flow·er (pash′ən flou′ər) *n.* **1** a plant having showy flowers supposed to suggest the crown of thorns, the wounds, the nails, etc. of Christ's crucifixion. **2** the flower.

pas·sion·less (pash′ən lis) *adj.* without passion; calm.

Passion Play or **passion play** a play representing the sufferings and death of Christ. A Passion Play is given every ten years at Oberammergau, West Germany.

Passion Sunday the second Sunday before Easter Sunday. It is the fifth Sunday in Lent.

Passion Week the second week before Easter; the fifth week in Lent, between Passion Sunday and Palm Sunday.

pas·sive (pas′iv) *adj.* **1** not acting in return; being acted on without itself acting: *a passive disposition.* **2** not resisting: *The passive obedience of a slave.* **3** in grammar, showing the subject as acted on. In "The window was broken by John," *was broken* is in the passive voice. **4** not readily entering into chemical combination; inert; inactive. **5** of or having to do with an abnormal condition of the body that causes reduced vitality and imperfect muscular reaction.
—*n.* in grammar, the passive voice. [< L *passivus,* ult. < *pati* suffer] —**pas′sive·ness,** *n.* —**Syn.** *adj.* **1** impassive. **2** submissive.

pas·sive·ly (pas′iv lē) *adv.* **1** in a passive manner. **2** as a passive verb. **3** in the passive voice.

pas·siv·i·ty (pa siv′ə tē) *n.* the state of being passive; lack of action; non-resistance.

pass·key (pas′kē′) *n.* **-keys. 1** a key for opening several locks; master key. **2** a private key.

Pass·o·ver (pas′ō′vər) *n.* the annual feast of the Jews in memory of the sparing of the Hebrews in Egypt, when God killed the first-born children of the Egyptians. Exod. 12. [from the *passing over* of the destroying angel]

pass·port (pas′pôrt) *n.* **1** a paper or book giving official permission to travel in certain foreign countries, under the protection of one's own government. **2** anything that gives one admission or acceptance: *An interest in gardening was a passport to my aunt's favor.* [< F *passeport* < *passer* pass + *port* harbor]

pass·word (pas′wėrd′) *n.* a secret word that allows a person speaking it to pass a guard.

past (past) *adj.* **1** gone by; ended: *Our troubles are past.* **2** just gone by: *The past year was full of trouble.* **3** having served a term in office: *a past president.* **4** indicating time gone by, or former action or state: *the past tense, a past participle.*
—*n.* **1** time gone by; time before; what has happened: *Life began far back in the past.* **2** a past life or history: *Our country has a glorious past.* **3** one's past life, especially if hidden or unknown: *He was a man with a past; no one knew that he had been in prison.* **4** the past tense or a verb form in it.
—*prep.* **1** beyond; farther on than: *It went past the mark.* **2** later than; after: *It is past noon.* **3** beyond in number, amount, or degree. **4** beyond the ability, range, scope, etc. of: *absurd fancies that are past belief.*
—*adv.* so as to pass by or beyond: *The cars go past once an hour.*
—*v. Archaic.* a pp. of **pass.** —**Syn.** *adj.* **2** bygone, preceding, foregoing.

pas·ta (pas′tə or päs′tə) *n.* **1** a type of flour paste used in foods such as spaghetti and ravioli. **2** such foods in general. [< Ital.]

past absolute the past tense; preterite.

paste (pāst) *n. v.* **past·ed, past·ing.** —*n.* **1** a mixture, such as flour and water boiled together, that will stick paper together. **2** dough for pastry. **3** a soft, dough-like mixture. Fish paste is pounded fish, highly seasoned. Pottery is made from a paste of clay and water. **4 a** a hard, glassy material used in making imitations of precious stones. **b** an artificial gem made of this. **5** a soft, jellylike candy. **6** a mixture of meal, fish, etc. used for spreading on sandwiches: *liver paste, chicken paste.*
—*v.* **1** stick with paste. **2** cover by pasting. **3** *Slang.* hit with a hard, sharp blow. [ME < OF < LL *pasta* < Gk. *pasta* porridge < *passein* sprinkle]

paste·board (pāst′bôrd′) *n.* **1** a stiff material made of sheets of paper pasted together or of paper pulp pressed and dried. **2** *Slang.* a playing card.

pas·tel (pas tel′ or pas′tel) *n.* **1** a kind of crayon used in drawing, especially when made from a dried paste of pigments mixed with clay and resin or gum. **2** the paste used in making such crayons. **3** a drawing made with such crayons. **4** the art of drawing with pastels. **5** a soft, pale shade of some color. **6** a short and slight prose sketch.
—*adj.* soft and pale: *pastel pink, pastel shades.* [< F < Ital. *pastello* < LL < Gk. *pasta.* See PASTE.]

past·er (pās′tər) *n.* **1** a slip to paste on or over something. **2** a person or thing that pastes.

pas·tern (pas′tərn) *n.* the part of a horse's foot between the fetlock and the hoof. [ME < OF *pasturon,* dim. of *pasture* tether for a horse, ult. < L *pastor* shepherd. See PASTOR.]

FETLOCK
PASTERN
HOOF

pas·teur·i·za·tion (pas′chər ə zā′shən or pas′chər ī zā′shən, pas′tər ə zā′shən or pas′tər ī zā′shən) *n.* **1** the process of pasteurizing. **2** the fact or state of being pasteurized.

pas·teur·ize (pas′chər īz′ or pas′tər īz′) *v.* **-ized, -iz·ing.** heat (milk, etc.) hot enough and long enough (for example, at 145° F. for 30 minutes) to destroy harmful bacteria. [after Louis *Pasteur* (1822-1895), a French chemist]

pas·til (pas′təl) *n.* pastille.

pas·tille (pas tēl′) *n.* **1** a flavored or medicated lozenge. **2** a small roll or cone of aromatic paste, burnt as a disinfectant, incense, etc. **3** pastel for crayons. **4** a crayon made from pastel. [< F < L *pastillus* roll, aromatic lozenge, dim. of *panis* bread]

pas·time (pas′tīm′) *n.* a pleasant way of passing time; a form of amusement; recreation. Games and sports are pastimes. [< *pass* + *time*] —**Syn.** diversion.

past master 1 one who has filled the office of master in a society, lodge, etc. **2** a person who has much experience in any profession, art, etc.

pas·tor (pas′tər) *n.* a minister in charge of a church; spiritual guide. [< L *pastor* shepherd, ult. < *pascere* feed]

pas·tor·al (pas′tər əl) *adj.* **1** of or having to do with shepherds or country life. **2** simple or naturally beautiful like the country: *a pastoral scene.* **3** of a pastor or his duties. —*n.* **1** a pastoral play, poem, or picture. **2** a letter from a bishop to his clergy or to the people of his church district. [< L *pastoralis* < *pastor.* See PASTOR.]
—**pas′tor·al·ly,** *adv.* —**Syn.** *adj.* **1** rustic, country, bucolic. See **rural.**

pas·tor·ate (pas′tər it) *n.* **1** the position or duties of a pastor. **2** the term of service of a pastor. **3** pastors as a group.

past participle a participle that indicates time gone by, or a former action or state. *Played* and *thrown* are past participles in "She has played all day," "The ball should have been thrown to me." *Abbrev.*: pp. ☛ See **participle** for usage note.

past perfect 1 a verb form employing the preterite of the verb *have* with a past participle and showing that an event was completed before a given past time. In "He had learned to read before he went to school," *had learned* is the past perfect of *learn. Past perfect* and *pluperfect* mean the same. 2 the past perfect tense or a verb form in this tense.

pas·tra·mi (pəs trä′mē) *n.* a smoked and well-seasoned cut of beef, especially a shoulder cut. [< Yiddish]

pas·try (pās′trē) *n.* **-tries.** 1 food made of baked flour paste, made rich with lard, butter, or a vegetable shortening. 2 pies, tarts, and other foods wholly or partly made of rich flour paste. 3 a pie, tart, etc. of this kind. [< *paste* + *-ry*]

past tense 1 a tense expressing time gone by, or a former action or state. 2 a verb form in the past tense.

pas·tur·age (pas′chər ij) *n.* 1 the growing grass and other plants for cattle, sheep, or horses to feed on. 2 pasture land. 3 a pasturing. 4 the right to pasture cattle, etc. on certain land. [< OF *pasturage*, ult. < *pasture.* See PASTURE.]

pas·ture (pas′chər) *n. v.* **-tured, -tur·ing.** —*n.* 1 a grassy field or hillside; grasslands on which cattle, sheep or horses can feed. 2 grass and other growing plants. —*v.* 1 put (cattle, sheep, etc.) out to pasture. 2 of cattle, sheep, etc., feed on (growing grass, etc.). [ME < OF *pasture* < LL *pastura*, ult. < L *pascere* feed]

past·y[1] (pās′tē) *adj.* **past·i·er, past·i·est.** 1 like paste. 2 pale. 3 flabby. [< *paste*] —**past′i·ness,** *n.*

pas·ty[2] (pas′tē) *n.* **-ties.** pie filled with game, fish, etc.: *a venison pasty.* [ME < OF *pastee* < *paste* paste < LL *pasta.* See PASTE. Doublet of PATTY.]

pat[1] (pat) *v.* **pat·ted, pat·ting,** *n.* —*v.* 1 strike or tap lightly with something flat: *She patted the dough into a flat cake.* 2 tap lightly with the hand as a sign of sympathy, approval, or affection: *pat a dog.* 3 walk or run with a patting sound. 4 **pat on the back,** praise; compliment. —*n.* 1 a light stroke or tap with the hand or with something flat. 2 the sound made by patting. 3 a small mass, especially of butter. 4 **pat on the back,** a compliment. [? imitative]

pat[2] (pat) *adj.* apt; suitable; to the point: *a pat reply.* —*adv.* 1 aptly; exactly; suitably. 2 **have pat** or **know pat,** *Informal.* have perfectly; know thoroughly. 3 **stand pat,** *Informal.* keep the same position; hold to things as they are and refuse to change. [probably special use of *pat*[1]]

Pat·a·go·ni·an (pat′ə gō′nē ən or pat′ə gōn′yən) *adj.* of or having to do with Patagonia, a region in the extreme south of South America, or its people. —*n.* 1 a native or inhabitant of Patagonia. 2 a member of a tribe of very tall Indians living in Patagonia.

patch (pach) *n.* 1 a piece put on to mend a hole or a tear. 2 a piece of cloth, etc. put over a wound or a sore. 3 a protective pad over an injured eye to protect it. 4 formerly, a small bit of black cloth that ladies wore on their faces to show off their fair skin. 5 a small, uneven spot: *a patch of brown on the skin.* 6 a piece of ground: *a garden patch.* 7 a scrap or bit of cloth left over. —*v.* 1 protect or adorn with a patch or patches; put patches on; mend. 2 mend clothes with patches. 3 piece together; make hastily. 4 **patch up, a** put an end to; settle: *patch up a quarrel.* **b** make right hastily or for a time. **c** put together hastily or poorly. [ME *pacche*, ? var. of *pece* piece. See PIECE.] —**patch′er,** *n.* —**Syn.** *v.* 1 See **mend.**

patch logging a system of logging by which only patches of trees in a stand are cut down, the surrounding trees being left intact to ensure natural reseeding of the cutover patch.

patch·ou·li or **patch·ou·ly** (pach′ů lē or pə chü′lē) *n.* 1 a penetrating perfume derived from an East Indian plant. 2 the plant itself. [< Tamil]

patch·work (pach′wėrk′) *n.* 1 pieces of cloth of various colors or shapes sewed together. 2 anything like this: *From the airplane, we saw a patchwork of fields and woods.* —*adj.* made in this way: *a patchwork quilt.*

patch·y (pach′ē) *adj.* **patch·i·er, patch·i·est.** 1 abounding in or characterized by patches. 2 occurring in, forming, or resembling patches. —**patch′i·ly,** *adv.* —**patch′i·ness,** *n.*

pate (pāt) *n.* 1 the top of the head; head: *a bald pate.* 2 brains. [ME; origin uncertain]

pâ·té (pä tā′) *n. French.* 1 a pastry case filled with chicken, sweetbreads, oysters, etc.; patty. 2 a meat paste, usually highly seasoned.

pâ·té de foie gras (pä tā′ də fwä grä′) *French.* a patty or paste made with livers of specially fattened geese.

pa·tel·la (pə tel′ə) *n.* **-tel·las, -tel·lae** (-tel′ē or -tel′ī). 1 in anatomy, the kneecap. See **skeleton** for diagram. 2 in archaeology, a small pan or shallow vessel. 3 in botany and zoology, a panlike or cuplike formation. [< L *patella*, dim. of *patina* pan. See PATEN.]

pa·tel·lar (pə tel′ər) *adj.* having to do with the kneecap.

pat·en (pat′ən) *n.* 1 the plate on which the bread is placed at the celebration of the Eucharist or Mass. 2 a plate or flat piece of metal. [ME < OF < L *patena* or *patina* pan, dish < Gk. *patanē*]

pa·ten·cy (pā′tən sē or pat′ən sē) *n.* a being patent; obviousness.

pat·ent (*n. adj. 1, v.* pat′ənt or pā′tənt; *adj. 2, 3* pā′tənt) *n.* 1 a right given by a government to a person by which he is the only one allowed to make, use, or sell a new invention for a certain number of years. 2 an invention that is protected by a patent. 3 an official document from a government giving a right or privilege. —*adj.* 1 given or protected by a patent. 2 evident; plain: *It is patent that cats dislike dogs.* 3 open. —*v.* get a patent for. [< L *patens, -entis*, ppr. of *patere* lie open] —**pat′ent·a·ble,** *adj.*

pat·ent·ee (pat′ən tē′) *n.* 1 a person to whom a patent is granted. 2 a person licensed to use another's patent.

pat·ent leather (pat′ənt) leather with a very glossy, smooth surface, usually black, made by a process formerly patented.

pa·tent·ly (pā′tənt lē or pat′ənt lē) *adv.* 1 plainly; clearly; obviously. 2 openly.

patent medicine 1 medicine that is patented. 2 medicine that some company owns and sells.

Patent Office a government office that issues patents.

pa·ter (pā′tər) *n. Brit. Informal.* father. [< L]

pa·ter·fa·mil·i·as (pat′ər fə mil′ē əs or pā′tər-) *n.* a father or head of a family. [< L *paterfamilias* < *pater* father + OL *familias*, gen., of a family]

pa·ter·nal (pə tėr′nəl) *adj.* 1 of or like a father; fatherly. 2 related on the father's side of the family: *a paternal aunt.* 3 received or inherited from one's father: *Mary's blue eyes were a paternal inheritance.* [< LL *paternalis*, ult. < L *pater* father] —**pa·ter′nal·ly,** *adv.*

pa·ter·nal·ism (pə tėr′nəl iz′əm) *n.* the principle or practice of managing the affairs of a country or group of people as a father manages the affairs of his children.

pa·ter·nal·is·tic (pə tėr′nəl is′tik) *adj.* having to do with or characterized by paternalism.

pa·ter·ni·ty (pə tėr′nə tē) *n.* 1 the fact or state of being a father; fatherhood. 2 paternal origin. [< LL *paternitas* < L *paternus* fatherly < *pater* father]

pat·er·nos·ter (pat′ər nos′tər or pā′tər-) *n.* 1 the Lord's Prayer, especially in Latin. 2 one of the beads of a rosary on which the Lord's Prayer is said. [< L *pater noster* our father]

path (path) *n.* **paths** (paᴛʜz). 1 a track made by people or animals walking. It is usually too narrow for automobiles or wagons. 2 a walk through a garden or park. 3 a line along which a person or thing moves; route; track: *The moon has a regular path through the sky.* 4 a way of acting or behaving. [OE *pæth*] —**path′less,** *n.* —**Syn. 1** walk, trail, lane. 3 course.

pa·thet·ic (pə thet′ik) *adj.* 1 pitiful; arousing pity. 2 of the emotions. [< LL < Gk. *pathētikos*, ult. < *pathein* suffer] —**pa·thet′i·cal·ly,** *adv.* —**Syn. 1** pitiable, moving, touching, affecting.

pa·thet·i·cal (pə thet′ə kəl) *adj.* pathetic.

pathetic fallacy the attribution of human emotions

and characteristics to nature or inanimate things, especially as a figure of speech.

path·find·er (path′fīn′dər) *n.* one who finds a path or way, as through a wilderness.

patho- *combining form.* disease, as in *pathology.* [< Gk. *pathos* disease, suffering]

path·o·gen·ic (path′ə jen′ik) *adj.* having to do with pathogeny; producing disease. [< Gk. *pathos* disease + *gen-* produce]

pa·thog·e·ny (pa thoj′ə nē) *n.* the production of disease.

path·o·log·ic (path′ə loj′ik) *adj.* pathological.

path·o·log·i·cal (path′ə loj′ə kəl) *adj.* **1** of pathology; dealing with diseases or concerned with diseases: *pathological studies.* **2** due to disease or accompanying disease: *a pathological condition of the blood cells.* —**path′o·log′i·cal·ly,** *adv.*

pa·thol·o·gist (pa thol′ə jist) *n.* a person skilled in pathology.

pa·thol·o·gy (pa thol′ə jē) *n.* **-gies. 1** the study of the causes and nature of diseases. **2** unhealthy conditions and processes caused by a disease.

pa·thos (pā′thos) *n.* the quality in speech, writing, music, events, or a scene that arouses a feeling of pity or sadness. [< Gk. *pathos* suffering, feeling]

path·way (path′wā′) *n.* a path.

-pathy *combining form.* **1** a feeling, as in *telepathy.* **2** a disease, as in *neuropathy.* **3** the treatment of disease, as in *osteopathy.* [< Gk. *-patheia*]

pa·tience (pā′shəns) *n.* **1** willingness to put up with waiting, pain, trouble, etc.; calm endurance without complaining or losing self-control. **2** long, hard work; steady effort. **3** a card game played by one person; solitaire. [ME < OF < L *patientia* < *patiens, -entis.* See PATIENT.]

Syn. 1 Patience, forbearance, fortitude = power to endure, without complaining, something unpleasant or painful. **Patience** = calmness and self-control in enduring suffering or trouble, waiting, or doing something requiring steady effort: *Teachers need patience.* **Forbearance** = uncommon patience and self-control in keeping oneself from doing or saying something when greatly tried or provoked: *I admire their forbearance.* **Fortitude** sometimes suggests patience, but emphasizes strength and firmness of character and means calm courage in facing danger or enduring suffering: *With fortitude the disabled veteran learned a new trade.*

pa·tient (pā′shənt) *adj.* **1** willing to put up with waiting, pain, trouble, etc.; enduring calmly without complaining or losing self-control. **2** with steady effort or long, hard work. —*n.* a person who is being treated by a doctor, dentist, etc. [ME < OF < L *patiens, -entis* suffering] —**pa′tient·ly,** *adv.*

pat·i·na (pat′ə nə) *n.* **1** a film or incrustation, usually green, on the surface of old bronze. **2** a film or coloring produced in the course of time on wood, stone, or other substance. **3** a surface appearance added to or assumed by anything: *the patina of soft, supple leather, the patina of success.* [< Ital. *patina,* ? < L *patina* dish, pan]

pat·i·o (pat′ē ō) *n.* **-i·os. 1** an inner court or yard open to the sky. **2** a terrace of cement or flat stones, used for outdoor eating, lounging, etc. [< Sp.]

pat·ois (pat′wä; *French,* pä twä′) *n.* **pat·ois** (pat′wäz; *French,* pä twä′). any dialect spoken by the common people of a district. [< F *patois* < OF *patoier* handle clumsily < *pate* paw < Gmc.]

pa·tri·arch (pā′trē ärk′) *n.* **1** the father and ruler of a family or tribe. In the Bible, Abraham, Isaac, and Jacob are patriarchs. **2** a person thought of as the father or founder of something. **3** a venerable old man. **4** in the early Christian church, a bishop of the highest rank. **5** in modern times, a high-ranking bishop in certain churches, especially the Roman Catholic Church and the Eastern Church. [< L < Gk. *patriarchēs* < *patria* family + *archos* leader]

pa·tri·ar·chal (pā′trē är′kəl) *adj.* **1** suitable to a patriarch; having to do with a patriarch. **2** under the rule of a patriarch: *patriarchal life, a partriarchal church.*

pa·tri·ar·chate (pā′trē är′kit) *n.* **1** the position, dignity, or authority of a church patriarch. **2** a church district under a patriach's authority. **3** patriarchy.

pa·tri·ar·chy (pā′trē är′kē) *n.* **-chies. 1** a form of social organization in which the father is head of the family and in which descent is reckoned in the male line, the children belonging to the father's clan. **2** a family community, or tribe governed by a patriarch or the eldest male.

hat, āge, cãre, fär; let, ēqual, tėrm; it, īce
hot, ōpen, ôrder; oil, out; cup, pu̇t, rüle, ūse
əbove, takən, pencəl, lemən, circəs
ch, child; ng, long; sh, ship
th, thin; ŦH, then; zh, measure

pa·tri·cian (pə trish′ən) *n.* **1** in ancient Rome, a member of the nobility. **2** a noble; aristocrat. —*adj.* **1** of the patricians. **2** of high social rank; aristocratic. **3** suitable for an aristocrat. [< L *patricius,* adj. < *patres* senators (literally, fathers) of Rome]

pat·ri·cide[1] (pat′rə sīd′) *n.* the crime of killing one's father. [< LL *patricidium* < L *pater* father + *-cidium* act of killing]

pat·ri·cide[2] (pat′rə sīd′) *n.* one who kills his father. [< Med.L *patricida* < L *pater* father + *-cida* killer]

pat·ri·mo·ni·al (pat′rə mō′nē əl) *adj.* having to do with a patrimony; inherited from one's father or ancestors.

pat·ri·mo·ny (pat′rə mō′nē) *n.* **-nies. 1** property inherited from one's father or ancestors. **2** property belonging to a church, monastery, or convent. **3** any heritage. [ME < OF < L *patrimonium* < *pater* father]

pa·tri·ot (pā′trē ət or pat′rē ət) *n.* a person who loves and loyally supports his country. [< LL < Gk. *patriōtēs,* ult. < *patris* fatherland]

pa·tri·ot·ic (pā′trē ot′ik or pat′rē ot′ik) *adj.* **1** loving one's country. **2** showing love and loyal support of one's own country. —**pa′tri·ot′i·cal·ly,** *adv.*

pa·tri·ot·ism (pā′trē ət iz′əm or pat′rē ət iz′əm) *n.* love and loyal support of one's country.

pa·tris·tic (pə tris′tik) *adj.* having to do with the early leaders, or fathers, of the Christian church or with their writings.

pa·trol (pə trōl′) *v.* **-trolled, -trol·ling,** *n.* —*v.* **1** go the rounds as a watchman or a policeman does. **2** go around (a town, camp, etc.) to watch or guard.
—*n.* **1** the men who patrol: *The patrol was changed at midnight.* **2** a going of the rounds to watch or guard. **3** a group of soldiers, ships, or aircraft, sent out to find out all they can about the enemy. **4** one of the subdivisions of a troop of Boy Scouts or Girl Guides: *There are eight people in a patrol, including a patrol leader and a second.* [< F *patrouiller* paddle in mud]

patrol leader **1** the person in charge of a military patrol. **2** the person in charge of a patrol of Boy Scouts or Girl Guides.

pa·trol·man (pə trōl′mən) *n.* **-men** (-mən). **1** a man who patrols. **2** a policeman who patrols a certain district.

patrol wagon a closed van or truck used by the police for carrying prisoners.

pa·tron (pā′trən) *n.* **1** one who buys regularly at a given store or goes regularly to a given restaurant, hotel, etc. **2** a person who gives his approval and support to some person, art, cause, or undertaking. **3** a guardian saint or god; protector. **4** in ancient Rome, an influential man who took certain persons under his protection. —*adj.* guarding; protecting: *a patron saint.* [ME < OF < L *patronus* < *pater* father. Doublet of PADRONE, PATROON.] —**Syn.** *n.* **2** sponsor.

pa·tron·age (pā′trən ij or pat′rə nij) *n.* **1** the regular business given to a store, hotel, etc. by customers. **2** the favor, encouragement, or support given by a patron. **3** favor, kindness, etc. given in a haughty, condescending way: *an air of patronage.* **4** the power to give jobs or favors: *the patronage of a premier, mayor, or reeve.* **5** political jobs or favors.

pa·tron·ess (pā′trən is or pat′rən is) *n.* **1** a woman patron. **2** a woman who helps a charitable entertainment or other function with her name, money, or presence.

pa·tron·ize (pā′trən īz′ or pat′rən īz′) *v.* **-ized, -iz·ing. 1** be a regular customer of; give regular business to. **2** act as a patron toward; support or protect: *patronize the ballet.* **3** treat in a haughty, condescending way: *We dislike anyone patronizing us.* —**pa′tron·iz′er,** *n.* —**pa′tron·iz′ing·ly,** *adv.*

patron saint a saint regarded as the special guardian of a person, church, city, etc.

pat·ro·nym·ic (pat′rə nim′ik) *n.* a name derived from the name of a father or ancestor: *Williamson, meaning "son of William," is a patronymic.* [< LL < Gk. *patrōnymikos* < *patēr* father + dial. *onyma* name]

pa·troon (pə trün′) *n. U.S.* a landowner who had certain privileges under the former Dutch governments of New York and New Jersey. A patroon usually owned a large amount of land. [< Du. < L *patronus.* Doublet of PADRONE, PATRON.]

pat·ten (pat′ən) *n.* **1** a wooden overshoe with a thick sole. **2** a kind of wooden sandal or overshoe, mounted on an iron ring, to raise the foot above wet ground. [ME < OF *patin* < *pate* paw < Gmc.]

A patten (def. 2)

pat·ter[1] (pat′ər) *v.* **1** make rapid taps: *The rain patters on a windowpane. Bare feet pattered along the hard floor.* **2** move with a rapid tapping sound: *patter across the room.* —*n.* a series of quick taps or the sound they make. [< *pat*[1]]

pat·ter[2] (pat′ər) *n.* **1** rapid and easy talk: *a magician's patter.* **2** the talk of a class or group: *the patter of beggars and thieves.* **3** rapid speech, usually for comic effect, introduced into a song. —*v.* talk or say rapidly and easily, without much thought: *patter a prayer.* [var. of *pater* in *paternoster*]

pat·tern (pat′ərn) *n.* **1** an arrangement of forms and colors; design: *the patterns of wallpaper, rugs, cloth, and jewellery.* **2** a model or guide for something to be made: *She used a paper pattern in cutting out her new dress.* **3** a fine example; model to be followed. **4** form; shape; configuration: *a large, deep cup with a bowl-like pattern.* **5** the arrangement and use of content in particular forms, styles, etc. in a work of literature, music, etc.: *the regular, easily recognized pattern of a Haydn symphony.* **6** in sociology, the customs, structure, values, etc. of a society arranged to reveal a form that can be studied and compared with other groups.
—*v.* **1** make according to a pattern: *She patterned herself after her mother.* **2** work or decorate with a pattern. [ME < OF *patron* pattern, patron < L *patronus* (see PATRON); with reference to a client's copying his patron]
—**Syn.** *n.* **1** motif. **2** See **model. 3** ideal.

pat·ty (pat′ē) *n.* **-ties. 1** a hollow form of pastry filled with chicken, oysters, etc. **2** a small, round, flat piece of food or candy. [< F *pâté* < OF *pastee.* Doublet of PASTY[2].]

patty pan a small pan for baking little cakes, patties, etc.

pau·ci·ty (po′sə tē or pô′sə tē) *n.* **1** a small number; fewness. **2** a small amount; scarcity; lack. [< L *paucitas* < *paucus* few]

Paul·ine (pol′īn or pôl′īn) *adj.* **1** of, having to do with, or written by the Apostle Paul. **2** of his doctrines or writings, especially the epistles attributed to him in the New Testament.

paunch (ponch or pônch) *n.* **1** the belly; stomach. **2** a large, protruding belly. **3** the first stomach of a cud-chewing animal. [ME < ONF *panche* < L *pantex, -ticis*]

paunch·y (pon′chē or pôn′chē) *adj.* having a big paunch. —**paunch′i·ness,** *n.*

pau·per (po′pər or pô′pər) *n.* **1** a very poor person. **2** a person supported by charity or by public welfare. [< L *pauper* poor. Doublet of POOR.]

pau·per·ism (po′pər iz′əm or pô′pər iz′əm) *n.* poverty.

pau·per·ize (po′pər īz′ or pô′pər īz′) *v.* **-ized, -iz·ing.** make a pauper of. —**pau′per·i·za′tion,** *n.* —**pau′per·iz·er,** *n.*

pause (poz or pôz) *v.* **paused, paus·ing,** *n.* —*v.* **1** stop for a time; wait. **2** dwell; linger: *pause upon a word.* [partly < n., partly < LL *pausare* < L *pausa.* See n.]
—*n.* **1** a moment of silence; stop; rest. **2** a brief stop in speaking or reading. **3** any punctuation mark indicating such a stop. **4** in music: **a** a sign (◡ or ⌒) above or below a note, meaning that it is to be held for a longer time. **b** a rest. [ME < OF < L *pausa* < Gk. *pausis* < *pauein* to stop] —**paus′er,** *n.* —**Syn.** *v.* **1** See **stop.**

pave (pāv) *v.* **paved, pav·ing. 1** cover (a street, sidewalk, etc.) with a pavement. **2** make smooth or easy; prepare: *He paved the way for me by doing careful work.* [ME < OF *paver,* ult. < L *pavire* beat, tread down] —**pav′er,** *n.*

pave·ment (pāv′mənt) *n.* **1** a covering or surface for streets, sidewalks, etc. made of stones, bricks, wood, asphalt, etc. **2** the material used for paving. **3** a paved road, etc. [ME < OF *pavement,* ult. < L *pavimentum* a beaten-down floor < *pavire* beat, tread down]

pa·vil·ion (pə vil′yən) *n.* **1** a building, usually open-sided, used for shelter, pleasure, etc.: *a bathing pavilion.* **2** a large tent raised on posts; tent. **3** a part of a building higher and more decorated than the rest. **4** one of a group of buildings forming a hospital. —*v.* furnish with a pavilion; enclose or shelter in a pavilion. [ME < OF < L *papilio, -onis* tent, butterfly]

pav·ing (pāv′ing) *n.* **1** the material for pavement. **2** pavement.

paw (po or pô) *n.* **1** the foot of an animal having claws. Cats and dogs have paws. **2** *Informal.* the hand.
—*v.* **1** touch or strike with the paws or feet: *The cat pawed the mouse.* **2** scrape with paws, hoofs, or feet: *The horse pawed the ground, eager to be going again.* **3** *Informal.* handle awkwardly, roughly, or in too familiar a manner. [ME < OF *powe* < Gmc.]

pawl (pol or pôl) *n.* a pivoted bar arranged to catch in the teeth of a ratchet wheel or the like so as to prevent movement backward or to impart motion. [origin uncertain]

A, pawls; B, a ratchet wheel. When the handle is raised, one pawl pushes the wheel forward; the other keeps it from slipping back.

pawn[1] (pon or pôn) *v.* give (something) as security that borrowed money will be repaid: *He pawned his watch to buy food until he could get work.* [< n.]
—*n.* **1** something left as security. **2 in pawn,** in another's possession as security. **3** a pledge. [ME < OF *pan*]

pawn[2] (pon or pôn) *n.* **1** in chess, one of the 16 pieces of lowest value. **2** an unimportant person or thing used by someone for his own purposes. [ME < AF *paon,* var. of OF *peon* < LL *pedo, pedonis* foot soldier < L *pes, pedis* foot. Doublet of PEON.]

pawn·bro·ker (pon′brō′kər or pôn′-) *n.* a man who lends money at interest on articles that are left with him as security for the loan.

pawn·shop (pon′shop′ or pôn′-) *n.* a pawnbroker's shop.

paw·paw (po′po or pô′pô) *n.* papaw.

pax vo·bis·cum (paks′ vō bis′kəm) *Latin.* peace be with you.

pay[1] (pā) *v.* **paid** or (*obsolete except for def. 12*) **payed, pay·ing,** *n. adj.* —*v.* **1** give (a person) what is due for goods, services, work, etc. **2** give (money, etc.) that is due. **3** give money; give what is owed. **4** give money for: *Pay your way.* **5** hand over (money owed); hand over the amount of: *pay a debt.* **6** give; offer: *pay attention, pay compliments.* **7** be profitable to; be worth while to: *It pays me to keep that stock. It wouldn't pay me to take that job.* **8** yield as a return: *That stock pays me four per cent.* **9** be profitable: *It pays to be polite.* **10** reward or punish: *He paid them for their insults by causing them trouble.* **11** suffer; undergo: *The one who does wrong must pay the penalty.* **12** let out (a rope, etc.). **13** in nautical use, fall off to leeward. **14 pay as you go,** pay or discharge obligations as they are incurred. **15 pay back, a** return borrowed money. **b** give the same treatment as received. **c** take revenge on: *I'll pay you back yet!* **16 pay off, a** give all the money that is owed; pay in full. **b** get even with; get revenge on. **c** *Informal.* pay money for so-called protection, but actually as a tribute to racketeers, etc. **17 pay up,** pay; pay in full.
—*n.* **1** money or equivalent given for goods, services, or work; wages; salary. **2 in the pay of,** paid by and working for. **3** a source of payment. **4** a reward; punishment: *Dislike is the pay for being mean.* **5** the act of paying; payment, especially of wages: *rate of pay.*

6 the condition of being paid, or receiving wages: *workers in a person's pay or employment.*
—*adj.* **1** containing a device for receiving money for use: *a pay telephone.* **2** containing enough metal, oil, etc. to be worth mining, drilling, etc.: *a pay lode.* [ME < OF *paier* < L *pacare* pacify < *pax, pacis* peace]
Syn. *v.* **1 Pay, compensate, remunerate** = give someone money or its equivalent in return for something. **Pay** is the common word and means "give someone money due for goods, work, or services": *He paid the doctor.* **Compensate** suggests making up for time spent, thing lost, service given, etc.: *The railway compensated the farmer for his cow.* **Remunerate** suggests giving a reward in return for services, trouble, etc. and, like *compensate*, is used especially as being more polite than *pay* and as not suggesting crudely that money is expected or due: *The club remunerated the lecturer.* –*n.* **1** compensation, remuneration. ☛ See **paid** for usage note.

pay² (pā) *v.* **payed, pay·ing.** cover (a ship's bottom, seams, rope, etc.) with tar, pitch, or another waterproof substance. [ME < OF *peier* < L *picare* < *pix, picis* pitch]

pay·a·ble (pā′ə bəl) *adj.* **1** required to be paid; due. **2** that may be paid. —**Syn. 1** owing, unpaid.

pay·day (pā′dā′) *n.* a day on which wages are paid.

pay dirt 1 earth, ore, etc. containing enough metal to be worth mining. **2** *Informal.* something that yields a profit or beneficial result.

pay·ee (pā ē′) *n.* a person to whom money is paid or is to be paid.

pay·er (pā′ər) *n.* one who pays; one who is to pay.

pay·load (pā′lōd′) *n.* **1** the part of a vehicle's load that produces revenue. **2** the warhead, instruments, etc. carried by a missile or rocket.

pay·mas·ter (pā′mas′tər) *n.* a person whose job is to pay wages.

pay·ment (pā′mənt) *n.* **1** the act or fact of paying. **2** the amount paid. **3** pay: *My child's good health is payment enough for me.* **4** reward or punishment. —**Syn. 1** compensation, remuneration, settlement.

pay·nim or **Pay·nim** (pā′nim) *n. adj. Archaic.* **1** pagan; heathen. **2** Moslem; Saracen. [ME < OF *paienisme* < LL *paganismus* < L *paganus* rustic. See PAGAN.]

pay-off (pā′of′) *n.* **1** a paying of wages. **2** the time of such payment. **3 a** returns for an enterprise, specific action, etc. **b** *Informal.* a dividing of the returns from some undertaking among those having an interest in it. **4** *Slang.* the climax (of a story, situation, etc.).

pay phone a coin-operated telephone.

pay roll 1 a list of persons to be paid and the amounts that each one is to receive. **2** the total amount to be paid to them.

payt. payment.

Pb lead. (for L *plumbum*)

PBX Private Branch (Telephone) Exchange.

pc. 1 piece. **2** price.

p.c. 1 per cent. **2** post card. **3** petty cash.

P.C. 1 Police Constable. **2** Progressive Conservative. **3** Privy Council. **4** Privy Councillor. **5** Past Commander.

pct. percent.

pd. paid.

p.d. 1 per diem. **2** potential difference.

Pd palladium.

P.D. 1 Police Department. **2** per diem. **3** Postal District.

PDT, P.D.T., or **p.d.t.** Pacific Daylight Time.

P.E. 1 Protestant Episcopal. **2** Petroleum Engineer.

pea (pē) *n.* **peas** or (*Archaic*) **pease,** *adj.* —*n.* **1** the round seed in the pod of a leguminous plant, used as a vegetable. **2** the plant itself. **3** any seed or plant like a pea. **4 as like as two peas,** exactly alike. —*adj.* of the size of a pea: *pea coal.* [< *pease*, originally sing., later taken as a pl.]

peace (pēs) *n.* **1** freedom from war or strife of any kind. **2** public quiet, order, and security. **3** an agreement between contending parties to end war: *the Peace of Paris.* **4** quiet; calm; stillness: *peace of mind.* **5 at peace, a** not in a state of war. **b** not at strife or at variance. **c** in a state of quietness; quiet; peaceful. **6 hold** or **keep one's peace,** be silent. **7 keep the peace,** refrain, or prevent others, from disturbing the (public) peace; maintain

hat, āge, cãre, fär; let, ēqual, tėrm; it, īce
hot, ōpen, ôrder; oil, out; cup, pu̇t, rüle, ūse
əbove, takən, pencəl, lemən, circəs
ch, child; ng, long; sh, ship
th, thin; ᴛʜ, then; zh, measure

public order. **8 make peace, a** effect a reconciliation between persons or parties at variance. **b** conclude peace with a nation at the close of a war.
—*interj.* keep still! stay quiet! be silent! [ME < OF *pais* < L *pax, pacis*] —**Syn.** *n.* **1** harmony, concord, amity. **4** tranquillity, serenity.

peace·a·ble (pēs′ə bəl) *adj.* **1** liking peace; keeping peace. **2** peaceful. —**peace′a·ble·ness,** *n.* —**peace′a·bly,** *adv.* —**Syn. 1** pacific, amicable, friendly.
☛ **Peaceable, peaceful** are often confused. **Peaceable** means "loving peace and avoiding quarrelling and strife," and describes only people and their actions, thoughts, feelings, speech, etc. as they show this quality of character: *Peaceable people keep out of quarrels.* **Peaceful** means "full of peace and quiet and free from disturbance and strife," and describes a country, period, scene, condition, state of mind, life, face, etc. but almost never a person or his actions or the activities of his mind or feelings: *These are not peaceful days in which we live.*

peace·ful (pēs′fəl) *adj.* **1** full of peace; quiet, calm. **2** liking peace; keeping peace. **3** of or having to do with peace. —**peace′ful·ly,** *adv.* —**peace′ful·ness,** *n.*
Syn. 1 Peaceful, placid, serene = quiet and calm. **Peaceful** suggests a state of deep inner quiet, coming from release or freedom from everything that disturbs or excites: *It was peaceful in the mountains.* **Placid** suggests contentment and absence of excitement, especially associated with a disposition or nature that stays even and calm in the midst of excitement: *Placid cows grazed beside the highway.* **Serene** suggests a state of peacefulness and calmness that is above all disturbance: *She is always cool, gracious, and serene.* ☛ See **peaceable** for usage note.

peace·mak·er (pēs′māk′ər) *n.* a person who makes peace.

peace offering 1 an offering made to obtain peace. **2** in old Jewish custom, an offering of thanksgiving to God.

peace officer a policeman or constable.

peace pipe a pipe smoked by North American Indians as a token or pledge of peace; calumet.

Peace River Block a settled region in northern British Columbia and Alberta, lying in the fertile valley of the Peace River. It is often called the Peace River Country.

peace·time (pēs′tīm′) *n.* a time of peace. —*adj.* of or having to do with a time of peace.

peach¹ (pēch) *n.* **1** a juicy, roundish fruit having a soft, pinkish-yellow, fuzzy skin and a rough stone or pit. Peaches are grown in temperate climates. **2** the tree that it grows on. **3** any fruit or tree like a peach. **4** a yellowish pink. **5** *Slang.* a person or thing especially admired or liked.
—*adj.* yellowish-pink. [ME < OF *pesche*, ult. < L *Persicum* (*malum*) Persian apple < Gk.]

peach² (pēch) *v. Slang.* give secret information; turn informer. [ME, var. of *appeach* < AF var. of OF *empechier* hinder < LL *impedicare* < L *in-* on + *pedica* shackle. Cf. IMPEACH.]

peach·y (pēch′ē) *adj.* **peach·i·er, peach·i·est. 1** like a peach; like that of a peach. **2** *Slang.* fine; wonderful. —**peach′i·ness,** *n.*

pea·cock (pē′kok′) *n.* **-cocks** or (*esp. collectively*) **-cock,** *v.* —*n.* **1** a bird having beautiful green, blue, and gold feathers. The tail feathers, which have spots like eyes, can be spread out and held upright like a fan. **2** any male peacock, especially as contrasted with the peahen. **3** a person who is vain and fond of showing off. —*v.* strut like a peacock. [ult. < OE *pēa* (< L *pavo* peafowl) + *cock¹*]

peacock blue greenish blue.

pea·fowl (pē′foul′) *n.* a peacock or peahen.

pea green light green.

pea·hen (pē′hen′) *n.* the female of the peacock.

pea jacket a short coat of thick woollen cloth worn by sailors. [< Du. *pij-jekker* < *pij* a coarse woollen cloth + *jekker* jacket]

peak (pēk) *n.* **1** the pointed top of a mountain or hill. **2** a mountain that stands alone. **3** the highest point. **4** any pointed end or top: *the peak of a beard, the peak of a roof.* **5** the front part or the brim of a cap. **6** the narrow part of a ship's hold at the bow or the stern. **7** the upper rear corner of a sail. **8** a promontory or point of land; headland. **9** an advancing or retreating point formed by the hair on the forehead.
—*adj.* of or having to do with a peak: *peak output.*
—*v.* raise straight up; tilt up. [var. of *pick*[2]] —**Syn.** *n.* **3** summit, pinnacle.

peaked[1] (pēkt or pēk′id) *adj.* having a peak; pointed: *a peaked hat.*

peak·ed[2] (pēk′id) *adj.* sickly in appearance; wan; thin. [< *peak*, v., look sick; origin uncertain]

peal (pēl) *n.* **1** a loud, long sound: *a peal of thunder, peals of laughter.* **2** the loud ringing of bells. **3** a set of bells; chimes. —*v.* sound out in a peal; ring: *The bells pealed forth their message of Christmas joy.* [ME *pele*]

pe·an (pē′ən) *n.* paean.

pea·nut (pē′nut′) *n.* **1** a plant of the same family as the pea, whose pods ripen underground and contain large edible seeds. **2** one of these pods containing seeds. **3** one of these seeds. **4** a small or unimportant person. **5 peanuts,** *Slang.* something of little or no value; a relatively small amount of money.

peanut butter a spread made from peanuts, used as a filling for sandwiches, etc.

pear (pãr) *n.* **1** a sweet, juicy, edible fruit rounded at one end and smaller toward the stem end. **2** the tree that it grows on. **3** any fruit or plant like a pear. [OE *pere* < LL *pira* < L *pirum*]

pearl (pėrl) *n.* **1** a white or nearly white gem that has a soft shine like satin. Pearls are formed inside the shell of a kind of oyster, and in other similar shellfish. **2** a similar gem made artificially. **3** anything that looks like a pearl, such as a dewdrop or a tear. **4** a very fine one of its kind. **5** a very pale, clear, bluish-gray. **6** mother-of-pearl. **7** in printing, a size of type; 5 point. **8 cast pearls before swine,** give something very fine to a person who cannot appreciate it.
—*adj.* **1** very pale, clear bluish-gray. **2** formed into small, round pieces: *pearl tapioca.*
—*v.* **1** hunt or dive for pearls. **2** adorn or set with or as with pearls, or with mother-of-pearl. **3** make pearly in color or lustre. **4** convert or reduce to small, round pieces. [ME < OF *perle* < VL *perla*]

pearl·ash (pėrl′ash′) *n.* potassium carbonate, usually made by refining potash.

pearl gray or **grey** a soft, pale, bluish-gray.

pearl nautilus any of several sea molluscs that resemble squids. The shell has a pearly lining and is coiled in a flat spiral composed of a series of chambers.

pearl·y (pėr′lē) *adj.* **pearl·i·er, pearl·i·est. 1** like a pearl; having the color or lustre of pearls: *pearly teeth.* **2** like mother-of-pearl. **3** adorned with or containing many pearls. —**pearl′i·ness,** *n.*

peas·ant (pez′ənt) *n.* in Europe, a person who lives in the country and works on the land, especially a farm laborer or tenant farmer. —*adj.* of peasants: *peasant labor.* [ME < AF var. of OF *paysant* < *pays* country, ult. < L *pagus* district]

peas·ant·ry (pez′ənt rē) *n.* peasants collectively.

peas·cod (pēz′kod′) *n.* peasecod.

pease (pēz) *n. Archaic.* a pl. of **pea.** [OE *pise* < LL *pisa* < L *pisum* < Gk. *pison*]

pease·cod (pēz′kod′) *n.* the pod of a pea.

pea·shoot·er (pē′shü′tər) *n.* a toy blowgun through which to blow peas and other small objects.

pea soup 1 a thick soup made from dried peas, meat, and other vegetables and, in Canada, associated especially with Quebec. **2** peasouper.

pea·soup·er (pē′süp′ər) *n.* **1** *Cdn. Slang.* a French Canadian. **2** *Informal.* a thick, heavy fog. Also, **peasoup.**

peat (pēt) *n.* a kind of turf, used as fuel after being dried. Peat is made of partly rotted moss and other vegetation. [ME *pete* < Anglo-L *peta*; origin uncertain]

pea·vey (pē′vē) *n.* **-veys.** a strong stick tipped with an iron or steel point and having a hinged hook near the tip. Lumbermen use peaveys in managing logs. [after Joseph *Peavey*, the inventor]

A man using a peavey to move a log

pea·vy (pē′vē) *n.* **-vies.** peavey.

peb·ble (peb′əl) *n. v.* **-bled, -bling.** —*n.* **1** a small stone, usually worn smooth and round by being rolled about by water. **2** a rough, uneven surface on leather, paper, etc. —*v.* **1** prepare (leather) so that it has a grained surface. **2** pelt with pebbles. [OE *pæbbel* (in place names)] —**peb′ble-like′,** *adj.*

peb·bly (peb′lē) *adj.* having many pebbles; covered with pebbles.

pe·can (pē′kan or pi kan′) *n.* **1** an olive-shaped, edible nut with a smooth, thin shell, that grows on a kind of hickory tree common in the S. United States. **2** the tree that it grows on. [< Algonquian *pakan* hard-shelled nut]

pec·ca·dil·lo (pek′ə dil′ō) *n.* **-loes** or **-los.** a slight sin or fault. [< Sp. *pecadillo*, dim. of *pecado* sin < L *peccatum*]

pec·ca·ry (pek′ə rē) *n.* **-ries** or (*esp. collectively*) **-ry.** a kind of wild pig found in South America and as far north as Texas. [< Carib *pakira*]

peck[1] (pek) *n.* **1** a unit of dry measure, eight quarts or one fourth of a bushel. **2** a container, for measuring, holding just a peck. **3** a great deal: *a peck of trouble.* [ME *pec*; origin uncertain]

peck[2] (pek) *v.* **1** strike and pick with the beak or with something pointed like a beak. **2** make by striking with the beak or with something pointed: *Woodpeckers peck holes in trees.* **3** aim with a beak; make a pecking motion. **4** strike at and pick up with the beak: *A hen pecks corn.* **5** *Informal.* eat only a little, bit by bit. **6** *Informal.* kiss lightly and hurriedly. **7** find fault. **8 peck at, a** try to peck. **b** *Informal.* eat only a little, bit by bit. **c** keep criticizing.
—*n.* **1** a stroke made with the beak. **2** a hole or mark make by pecking. **3** *Informal.* a light kiss given in a hasty manner. [akin to *pick*[1]]

peck·er (pek′ər) *n.* **1** a person or thing that pecks. **2** a woodpecker. **3** *Esp.Brit. Slang.* courage: *Keep your pecker up!*

pecking order 1 an order of superiority established in flocks of chickens, etc., each bird enjoying the right of dominating those weaker than itself. **2** any similar hierarchy or order of precedence in human society.

pec·ten (pek′tən) *n.* a comblike part; especially, a membrane in the eyes of birds and reptiles that has parallel folds suggesting the teeth of a comb. [< L *pecten* < *pectere* to comb]

pec·tin (pek′tən) *n.* a substance that occurs in ripe fruits and is used to stiffen fruit jelly. [< Gk. *pēktos* congealing, curdling < *pēgnynai* make stiff]

pec·to·ral (pek′tə rəl) *adj.* **1** of, in, or on the breast or chest. **2** good for diseases of the lungs. —*n.* a medicine for the lungs. [< L *pectoralis* < *pectus* chest]

pec·u·late (pek′yů lāt′) *v.* **-lat·ed, -lat·ing.** steal (money or goods entrusted to one); embezzle. [< L *peculari* embezzle < *peculium* property < *pecu* money, cattle] —**pec′u·la′tion,** *n.* —**pec′u·la′tor,** *n.*

pe·cul·iar (pi kūl′yər) *adj.* **1** strange; odd; unusual. **2** belonging to one person or thing and not to any other; special: *This book has a peculiar value. Some minerals are peculiar to the Canadian Shield.* [< L *peculiaris* of one's own < *peculium* property. See PECULATE.] —**pe·cul′iar·ly,** *adv.* —**Syn. 1** eccentric, queer, singular. See **strange. 2** particular, distinctive.

pe·cu·li·ar·i·ty (pi kū′lē ar′ə tē) *n.* **-ties. 1** a being peculiar; strangeness; oddness; unusualness. **2** some thing or feature that is strange or odd. **3** a peculiar or characteristic quality. **4** a distinguishing quality or feature. —**Syn. 1** eccentricity. **3** idiosyncrasy.

pe·cu·ni·ar·y (pi kū′nē er′ē) *adj.* of or having to do with money; in the form of money. [< L *pecuniarius* < *pecunia* money < *pecu* money, cattle]

ped·a·gog (ped′ə gog′) *n.* pedagogue.

ped·a·gog·ic (ped′ə goj′ik or ped′ə gō′jik) *adj.* of teachers or teaching; of pedagogy. —**ped′a·gog′i·cal·ly,** *adv.*

ped·a·gog·i·cal (ped′ə goj′ə kəl or ped′ə gō′ jə kəl) *adj.* pedagogic.

ped·a·gogue (ped′ə gog′) *n.* **1** a teacher. **2** a narrow-minded teacher. [ME < OF < L < Gk. *paidagōgos* < *pais, paidos* boy + *agōgos* leader]

ped·a·go·gy (ped′ə goj′ē or ped′ə gō′jē) *n.* **1** teaching. **2** the science or art of teaching.

ped·al (*n. v.* ped′əl; *adj.* ped′əl or pē′dəl) *n. v.* **-alled** or **-aled, -al·ling** or **-al·ing,** *adj.* —*n.* a lever worked by the foot; the part on which the foot is placed to move any kind of machinery. Organs and pianos have pedals for changing the tone. The two pedals of a bicycle, pushed down one after the other, make it go.
—*v.* **1** work or use the pedals of; move by pedals: *pedal a bicycle up a hill.* **2** work pedals.
—*adj.* of or having to do with the foot or feet. [< F < Ital. < L *pedale* (thing) of the foot < *pes* foot]

ped·ant (ped′ənt) *n.* **1** a person who displays his knowledge in an unnecessary or tiresome way. **2** a dull, narrow-minded teacher or scholar. [< Ital. *pedante,* ult. < Gk. *paideuein* educate < *pais, paidos* boy]

pe·dan·tic (pi dan′tik) *adj.* **1** displaying one's knowledge more than is necessary. **2** tediously learned; scholarly in a dull and narrow way. —**pe·dan′ti·cal·ly,** *adv.*

ped·ant·ry (ped′ənt rē) *n.* **-ries. 1** an unnecessary or tiresome display of knowledge. **2** overemphasis on book learning. **3** a pedantic form or expression.

ped·ate (ped′āt) *adj.* **1** having feet. **2** footlike. **3** having divisions like toes: *a pedate leaf.* [< L *pedatus* < *pes, pedis* foot]

ped·dle (ped′əl) *v.* **-dled, -dling. 1** carry from place to place and sell. **2** sell or deal out in small quantities: *peddle candy, peddle gossip.* **3** travel about with things to sell. [apparently < *peddler*]

ped·dler (ped′lər) *n.* a man who travels about selling things that he carries in a pack, in a cart, or on a truck. Also, **pedlar.** [ME *pedlere* < *pedder* < *ped* basket]

ped·es·tal (ped′is təl) *n.* **1** the base on which a column or a statue stands. **2** the base of a tall vase, lamp, etc. **3** a base; support; foundation. **4 place on a pedestal,** accord an important place to; idolize. [< F < Ital. *piedestallo* < *pie* foot (< L *pes, pedis*) + *di* of + *stallo* stall¹ (< Gmc.)]

pe·des·tri·an (pə des′trē ən) *n.* a person who goes on foot; walker. —*adj.* **1** going on foot; walking. **2** without imagination; dull; slow: *a pedestrian style in writing.* [< L *pedester, -tris* on foot < *pes, pedis* foot]

pe·des·tri·an·ism (pə des′trē ən iz′əm) *n.* walking.

pe·di·at·ric (pē′dē at′rik) *adj.* of or having to do with pediatrics.

pe·di·a·tri·cian (pē′dē ə trish′ən or ped′ē ə trish′ən) *n.* a doctor who specializes in pediatrics.

pe·di·at·rics (pē′dē at′riks or ped′ē at′riks) *n.* the branch of medicine dealing with children's diseases and the care of babies and children. [pl. of *pediatric* < Gk. *pais, paidos* child + *iatreia* medical treatment < *iaesthai* heal]

ped·i·cel (ped′ə səl) *n.* a small stalk or stalklike part. [< NL *pedicellus,* ult. < L *pes, pedis* foot]

PEDICEL
PEDUNCLE

ped·i·gree (ped′ə grē′) *n.* **1** the list of ancestors of a person or animal; family tree. **2** ancestry; line of descent. **3** derivation, as from a source: *the pedigree of a word.* **4** distinguished or noble descent: *a man of pedigree.* —*adj.* of unmixed breed: *a pedigree cat.* [apparently < F *pied de grue* foot of a crane; from appearance of 3-branched mark used in genealogies]

ped·i·greed (ped′ə grēd′) *adj.* having a known pedigree.

ped·i·ment (ped′ə mənt) *n.* **1** in architecture, a broad, triangular part on the front of a building, especially over a portico or door. A pediment is like a gable. **2** a similar decorative part inside a building. [earlier *periment, peremint,* probably alteration of *pyramid*]

A pediment

hat, āge, cãre, fär; let, ēqual, tėrm; it, īce
hot, ōpen, ôrder; oil, out; cup, pu̇t, rüle, ūse
əbove, takən, pencəl, lemən, circəs
ch, child; ng, long; sh, ship
th, thin; ᴛʜ, then; zh, measure

ped·lar (ped′lər) *n.* peddler.

pe·dom·e·ter (pi dom′ə tər) *n.* an instrument for recording the number of steps taken and thus measuring the distance travelled. [< F *pédomètre* < L *pes, pedis* foot + Gk. *metron* measure]

pe·dun·cle (pi dung′kəl) *n.* a stalk; stem; a stalklike part (of a flower, fruit cluster, or animal body). See **pedicel** for picture. [< NL *pedunculus,* dim. of L *pes, pedis* foot]

pe·dun·cu·lar (pi dung′kyu̇ lər) *adj.* of or having to do with a peduncle.

pe·dun·cu·late (pi dung′kyu̇ lit or pi dung′kyu̇ lāt′) *adj.* having a peduncle; growing on a peduncle.

peek (pēk) *v.* look quickly and slyly; peep. —*n.* a quick, sly look. [ME *piken;* origin uncertain]

peel¹ (pēl) *n.* the rind or outer covering of certain fruit or vegetables. [< v.]
—*v.* **1** strip skin, rind, or bark from. **2** strip: *The Indians peeled the bark from trees to make canoes.* **3** come off: *When I was sunburnt, my skin peeled.* **4** *Informal.* remove clothing, entirely or in part; strip. [var. of obs. *pill;* ME *pele(n)* < OE *pilian* and OF *peler,* both < L *pilare* strip of hair < *pilus* body hair] —**peel′er,** *n.*
—**Syn.** *n.* skin, bark, husk.

peel² (pēl) *n.* a long-handled shovel used to put bread, pies, etc. into an oven or take them out. [ME < OF *pele* < L *pala* spade]

peel·ing (pēl′ing) *n.* a part peeled off or pared off.

peep¹ (pēp) *v.* **1** look through a small or narrow hole or crack. **2** look when no one knows it. **3** look out, as if peeping. **4** come partly out. —*n.* **1** a look through a hole or crack. **2** a small hole or crack to look through. **3** a secret look. **4** the first looking or coming out: *at the peep of day.* [? var. of *peek*] —**Syn.** *v.* **1** peer, peek.

peep² (pēp) *n.* a short, sharp sound made by a young bird or chicken. —*v.* **1** make this sound or one like it: *The bird peeped.* **2** speak in a thin, weak voice. [imitative]

peep·er (pēp′ər) *n.* **1** one that peeps. **2** any of certain frogs that make peeping noises. **3** *Informal.* an eye.

peep·hole (pēp′hōl′) *n.* a hole through which one may peep.

peep show an exhibition of objects or pictures viewed through a small opening, usually fitted with a magnifying glass.

peer¹ (pēr) *n.* **1** a person of the same rank, ability, etc. as another; equal. **2** a man who has a title or who is high and great by birth. Dukes, marquises, earls, counts, viscounts, and barons are peers. [ME < OF *per* < L *par* equal. Doublet of PAR.]

peer² (pēr) *v.* **1** look closely to see clearly, as a near-sighted person does: *She peered at the tag to read the price.* **2** come out slightly; peep out: *The sun was peering from behind a cloud.* **3** *Poetic.* appear. [apparently a var. of *appear*]

peer·age (pēr′ij) *n.* **1** the rank or dignity of a peer. **2** the peers of a country. **3** a book giving a list of the peers of a country.

peer·ess (pēr′is) *n.* **1** the wife or widow of a peer. **2** a woman having the rank of a peer in her own right.

peer·less (pēr′lis) *adj.* without an equal; matchless: *He was a peerless leader.* —**peer′less·ly,** *adv.* —**peer′less·ness,** *n.* —**Syn.** unequalled.

peeve (pēv) *v.* **peeved, peev·ing,** *n. Informal.* —*v.* make peevish. —*n.* an annoyance.

pee·vish (pē′vish) *adj.* cross; fretful; complaining. [ME *pevysh;* origin uncertain] —**pee′vish·ly,** *adv.* —**pee′vish·ness,** *n.* —**Syn.** petulant, pettish, irritable.

pee·wee (pē′wē) *n.* in boys' or girls' sports, a player aged between 8 and 12. Also, **pewee.**

peg (peg) *n. v.* **pegged, peg·ging.** —*n.* **1** a pin or small bolt of wood, metal, etc. used to fasten parts together, to hang things on, to stop a hole, to make fast a rope or string, to mark the score in a game, etc. **2** a step; degree. **3 take (someone) down a peg,** lower the pride of; humble. **4** a small drink of alcoholic liquor.
—*v.* **1** fasten or hold with pegs. **2** mark with pegs. **3** work hard. **4** keep the price of (a stock, bond, etc.) from going up or down. **5** *Informal.* aim; throw. [apparently < MDu. *pegge*]

Peg·a·sus (peg′ə səs) *n.* **1** in Greek mythology, a horse with wings, the steed of the Muses. **2** poetic genius; the means by which poets soar in the realms of poetry. **3** in astronomy, a northern constellation.

peg leg 1 a wooden leg. **2** *Informal.* a person who has a wooden leg.

peg top 1 a wooden top spinning on a metal peg. **2 peg tops,** *pl.* trousers gradually narrowing to the ankles.

P.E.I. Prince Edward Island.

peign·oir (pān wär′ or pān′wär) *n.* **1** a woman's dressing gown. **2** a negligee. [< F *peignoir* < *peigner* < L *pectinare* comb < *pecten* a comb]

pe·jo·ra·tive (pi jôr′ə tiv′) *adj.* tending to make worse; disparaging; depreciatory. —*n.* a pejorative word, suffix, or phrase. [< L *pejoratus* < *pejor* worse]

Pe·kin (pē′kin′) *n.* **1** a breed of large white ducks, originally from China, raised primarily for their meat. **2** a duck of this breed. [< F *Pékin* Peiping, the capital of China]

Pe·kin·ese (pē′kən ēz′) *n.* **-ese,** *adj.* Pekingese.

Pe·king·ese (pē′king ēz′) *n.* **1** a breed of small dog having long, silky hair and a pug nose. **2** a dog of this breed. **3** a native or inhabitant of Peiping. —*adj.* of or having to do with Peiping, China, or its people. [< *Peking* Peiping, the capital of China]

pe·koe (pē′kō) *n.* a kind of black tea. [< Chinese *pek-ho* white down; because the leaves are picked young with the "down" still on them]

pel·age (pel′ij) *n.* the hair, fur, wool, or other soft covering of a mammal. [< F < OF *peil* hair < L *pilus*]

pe·lag·ic (pə laj′ik) *adj.* of the ocean or the open sea. [< L < Gk. *pelagikos* < *pelagos* sea]

pelf (pelf) *n.* money or riches, thought of as bad or degrading. [ME < OF *pelfre* spoils]

pel·i·can (pel′ə kən) *n.* a large fish-eating water bird having a huge bill with a pouch on the underside for storing food. [< LL < Gk. *pelekan,* ? ult. < *pelekys* axe]

pe·lisse (pə lēs′) *n.* **1** a coat lined or trimmed with fur. **2** a woman's long cloak. [< F *pelisse,* ult. < LL *pelliceus* of fur < *pellis* skin]

pel·lag·ra (pə lag′rə or pə lā′grə) *n.* a disease marked by eruption on the skin, a nervous condition, and sometimes insanity. It is caused by lack of vitamin B in the diet. [< Ital. < L *pellis* skin; apparently patterned after *podagra* gout in the feet (< Gk.)]

pel·let (pel′it) *n.* **1** a little ball of mud, paper, food, medicine, etc.; pill. **2** a bullet. [ME < OF *pelote* < L *pila* ball]

pel·li·cle (pel′ə kəl) *n.* a very thin skin; membrane. [< L *pellicula,* dim. of *pellis* skin]

pell-mell or **pell·mell** (pel′mel′) *adv.* **1** in a rushing, tumbling mass or crowd. **2** in headlong haste. —*adj.* headlong; tumultuous. —*n.* violent disorder or confusion. [< F *pêle-mêle,* latter element apparently < *mêler* mix]

pel·lu·cid (pə lü′sid) *adj.* **1** transparent; clear: *a pellucid stream.* **2** clearly expressed; easy to understand: *pellucid language.* [< L *pellucidus,* ult. < *per-* through + *lucere* to shine] —**pel·lu′cid·ly,** *adv.* —**pel·lu′cid·ness,** *n.*

Pel·o·pon·ne·sian (pel′ə pə nē′shən or pel′ə pə nē′zhən) *adj.* of or having to do with the Peloponnesus, a peninsula in S. Greece, or its people. —*n.* a native or inhabitant of the Peloponnesus.

Pel·o·pon·ne·sus (pel′ə pə nē′səs) *n.* a peninsula that constitutes the southern part of Greece.

pe·lo·ta (pe lô′tə) *n.* a game of Basque or Spanish origin played on a walled court with a hard ball that is struck with a curved wicker racket fastened to a glove on the hand. [< Sp. *pelota* < *pella* ball < L *pila*]

pelt[1] (pelt) *v.* **1** throw things at; attack; assail: *The boys were pelting the dog with stones.* **2** beat heavily: *The rain came pelting down.* **3** throw: *The clouds pelted rain upon us.* **4** hurry.
—*n.* **1** a pelting. **2** speed: *The horse is coming at full pelt.* [ME *pelten,* ? var. of *pulten* hasten, thrust < L *pultare* strike]

pelt[2] (pelt) *n.* **1** the skin of a sheep, goat, or small fur-bearing animal, before it is tanned. **2** the skin. [probably < *peltry*] —**Syn. 1** See **skin.**

pelt·ry (pel′trē) *n.* **-ries. 1** pelts; skins; furs. **2** a pelt. [< AF var. of OF *peleterie* < *pel* skin < L *pellis*]

pel·vic (pel′vik) *adj.* of or having to do with the pelvis.

pel·vis (pel′vis) *n.* **-ves** (-vēz). **1** in anatomy, the basin-shaped cavity formed by the hipbones and the end of the backbone. See **skeleton** for diagram. **2** a corresponding cavity of any vertebrate. **3** bones forming this cavity. [< L *pelvis* basin]

pem·bi·na (pem′bə nə or pem bē′nə) *n. Cdn.* a type of cranberry. [< Cdn.F *pimbina* < ? Cree]

pembina cart *Cdn.* formerly, a simple two-wheeled cart used by the early settlers of the Canadian West. [? < *Pembina* (now Cavalier), a town in North Dakota, probably after *pembina* growing in its valleys]

pem·mi·can (pem′ə kən) *n.* dried, lean meat pounded into a paste with melted fat: *Pemmican was the usual food of the voyageurs.* [< Algonquian (Cree) *pimikan* < *pimikew* he makes grease]

pen[1] (pen) *n. v.* **penned, pen·ning.** —*n.* **1** a small metal instrument with a split point used with a holder, for writing with ink. **2** a tool to use in writing with ink; pen and holder together. **3** a ball-point pen. **4** style of writing; writing. —*v.* write. [ME < OF < L *penna* feather] —**pen′like′,** *adj.*

pen[2] (pen) *n. v.* **penned** or **pent, pen·ning.** —*n.* **1 a** a small, closed yard for cows, sheep, pigs, chickens, etc. **b** any of various enclosures for keeping something, as a portable playpen for a baby, or a place to keep a dog in a kennel. **2** the number of animals in a pen, or required to fill a pen. **3** a dock or slip, often protected by a concrete superstructure, for docking and reconditioning submarines. —*v.* **1** shut in a pen. **2** shut in; confine closely. [OE *penn*] —**pen′like′,** *adj.*

pen[3] (pen) *n. Slang.* penitentiary.

Pen. or **pen.** peninsula.

pe·nal (pē′nəl) *adj.* **1** of, having to do with, or given as punishment: *penal laws, penal labor.* **2** liable to be punished: *Robbery is a penal offence.* [ME < L *poenalis* < *poena* punishment < Gk. *poinē* penalty]

pe·nal·ize (pē′nəl īz′ or pen′əl īz′) *v.* **-ized, -iz·ing. 1** declare punishable by law or by rule; set a penalty for: *Speeding on city streets is penalized. Fouls are penalized in many games.* **2** inflict a penalty on; punish: *Our team was penalized five yards.*

pen·al·ty (pen′əl tē) *n.* **-ties. 1** a punishment: *The minimum penalty for speeding is a fine of ten dollars.* **2** in games, a disadvantage imposed on a side or player for breaking rules. **3** a disadvantage attached to some act or condition: *the penalties of old age.* **4** a handicap.

penalty box in hockey, a special bench where players awarded penalties spend their time off the ice.

pen·al·ty-kill·er (pen′əl tē kil′ər) *n.* in hockey, a player put on the ice when his team is shorthanded, to check the opposing forwards closely and to control the puck as much as possible in order to prevent any scoring by the opposite side.

pen·al·ty-kill·ing (pen′əl tē kil′ing) *n.* in hockey, the preventing of the opposite side from scoring while one's own team is shorthanded.

pen·ance (pen′əns) *n.* **1** a punishment borne to show sorrow for sin, to make up for a wrong done, and to obtain pardon from the church for sin. **2** in the Roman Catholic Church, the sacrament that includes contrition, confession, satisfaction, and absolution. **3 do penance,**

perform some act, or undergo some penalty, in satisfaction for sin. [ME < OF *pen(e)ance* < L *paenitentia* penitence. Doublet of PENITENCE.]

pe·na·tes or **Pe·na·tes** (pə nā′tēz) *n.pl.* in ancient Rome, the gods of the household. [< L *penates* < *penus* interior of the house]

pence (pens) *n. Brit.* a pl. of **penny.**

pen·chant (pen′chənt) *n.* a strong taste or liking; inclination: *a penchant for taking long walks.* [< F *penchant,* ppr. of *pencher* incline, ult. < L *pendere* hang]

pen·cil (pen′səl) *n. v.* **-cilled** or **-ciled, -cil·ling** or **-cil·ing.** —*n.* **1** a pointed tool to write or draw with, usually made of wood and having a long, thin piece of graphite or crayon in the centre. **2** an object of like shape. **3** a stick of coloring matter. **4** an artist's paintbrush. **5** a set of lines, light rays, or the like, coming to a point or extending in different directions from a point. **6** the skill or style of an artist.
—*v.* **1** mark or write with a pencil. **2** draw or sketch with a pencil: *pencil an outline of a house.* [ME < OF *pincel,* ult. < L *penicillus* (painter's brush), double dim. of *penis,* originally, tail]

pend (pend) *v.* remain undecided or unsettled. [< L *pendere* hang]

pend·ant (pen′dənt) *n.* **1** a hanging ornament, such as a locket. **2** an ornament hanging down from ceiling or roof. **3** an attachment by which something is suspended. —*adj.* pendent. [ME < OF *pendant,* ppr. of *pendre* hang, ult. < L *pendere*]

pend·ent (pen′dənt) *adj.* **1** hanging: *the pendent branches of a willow.* **2** overhanging. **3** pending. —*n.* a pendant. [ME < L *pendens, -entis,* ppr. of *pendere* hang] —**Syn.** *adj.* **1** suspended.

pend·ing (pen′ding) *adj.* waiting to be decided or settled: *The agreement was pending.* —*prep.* **1** while waiting for; until: *Pending his return, let us get everything ready.* **2** during: *pending the investigation.*

pen·drag·on or **Pen·drag·on** (pen drag′ən) *n.* the chief leader, a title of ancient British chiefs. [< Welsh *pendragon* < *pen* chief + *dragon* war leader, dragon]

pen·du·lous (pen′jü ləs or pen′dyü ləs) *adj.* **1** hanging loosely: *The oriole builds a pendulous nest.* **2** swinging. [< L *pendulus* < *pendere* hang] —**pen′du·lous·ly,** *adv.* —**pen′du·lous·ness,** *n.*

pen·du·lum (pen′jü ləm or pen′dyü ləm) *n.* a weight so hung from a fixed point that it is free to swing to and fro. The movement of the works of a tall clock is often timed by a pendulum. [< NL *pendulum,* neut. < L *pendulus.* See PENDULOUS.]

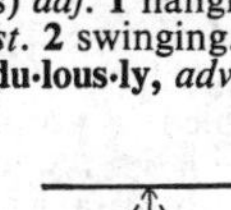
A pendulum. The dotted lines show motion.

Pe·nel·o·pe (pə nel′ə pē′) *n.* in Greek legend, the faithful wife of Odysseus. She waited twenty years for his return from the Trojan War in spite of the entreaties of her many suitors. She told them she would remarry when she had finished the weaving on which she was working, but each night she undid the work she had done during the day.

pe·ne·plain (pē′nə plān′) *n.* a formerly mountainous or hilly area reduced nearly to a plain by erosion. [< L *paene* almost + E *plain*]

pen·e·tra·bil·i·ty (pen′ə trə bil′ə tē) *n.* the capability of being penetrated.

pen·e·tra·ble (pen′ə trə bəl) *adj.* that can be penetrated. [< L *penetrabilis*]

pen·e·trate (pen′ə trāt′) *v.* **-trat·ed, -trat·ing. 1** pass into or through: *A bullet can penetrate a wooden wall.* **2** pierce through: *Our eyes could not penetrate the darkness.* **3** make a way: *Even where the trees were thickest, the sunshine penetrated.* **4** soak through; spread through: *The smell penetrated the whole house.* **5** see into; understand: *I could not penetrate the mystery.* **6** affect or impress very much. [< L *penetrare,* ult. < *penitus* inmost]
Syn. 1 Penetrate, pierce = go into or through something. **Penetrate** = go deeply into something, or into it and out the other side, and suggests the driving force or keenness of what goes in: *The bullet penetrated the board.* **Pierce** = stab through the surface, or pass right through, with a sharp-pointed object or something sharp and cutting, as a knife: *The dagger pierced his side.* **4** permeate, pervade. **5** discern, comprehend.

hat, āge, cãre, fär; let, ēqual, tėrm; it, īce
hot, ōpen, ôrder; oil, out; cup, pu̇t, rüle, ūse
əbove, takən, pencəl, lemən, circəs
ch, child; ng, long; sh, ship
th, thin; ꟈH, then; zh, measure

pen·e·trat·ing (pen′ə trāt′ing) *adj.* **1** sharp; piercing. **2** having an acute mind; understanding thoroughly. —**pen′e·trat′ing·ly,** *adv.*

pen·e·tra·tion (pen′ə trā′shən) *n.* **1** the act or power of penetrating. **2** the act of entering a country and gaining influence there. **3** sharpness of intellect; insight. —**Syn. 3** acumen, shrewdness, discernment. See **insight.**

pen·e·tra·tive (pen′ə trā′tiv) *adj.* penetrating; piercing; keen. —**pen′e·tra′tive·ly,** *adv.* —**pen′e·tra′tive·ness,** *n.*

P.Eng. Professional Engineer.

pen·guin (pen′gwin or peng′gwin) *n.* a sea bird, native to cold waters of the southern hemisphere, having wings like flippers which it uses for diving and swimming, not for flying. [?< Breton *penguin* white head; cf. Welsh *pen* head + *gwyn* white]

pen·hold·er (pen′hōl′dər) *n.* **1** the handle by which a pen is held in writing. **2** a stand or rack for a pen or pens.

pen·i·cil·lin (pen′ə sil′ən) *n.* a very powerful antibiotic drug made from a penicillium mould and used to destroy or check certain kinds of bacteria. [< *penicillium*]

pen·i·cil·li·um (pen′ə sil′ē əm) *n.* **-cil·li·ums** or **-cil·li·a** (-sil′ē ə). any of a certain kind of fungi. The mould on cheese is a penicillium. [< L *penicillus* small brush or tail, double dim. of *penis* tail]

pen·in·su·la (pən in′sə lə or pən in′syu̇ lə) *n.* a piece of land almost surrounded by water, or extending far out into the water. Nova Scotia is a peninsula. [< L *paeninsula* < *paene* almost + *insula* island]

pen·in·su·lar (pən in′sə lər or pən in′syu̇ lər) *adj.* **1** like a peninsula. **2** in or of a peninsula.

pe·nis (pē′nis) *n.* **-nis·es** (-nis iz) or **-nes** (-nēz). the male sexual organ. [< L *penis* penis, originally, tail]

pen·i·tence (pen′ə təns) *n.* sorrow for sinning or doing wrong; repentance. [ME < OF *penitence* < L *paenitentia* < *paenitere* repent. Doublet of PENANCE.]

pen·i·tent (pen′ə tənt) *adj.* sorry for sinning or doing wrong; repenting. —*n.* **1** a person who is sorry for sin or wrongdoing. **2** a person who confesses and does penance for his sins under the direction of the church.
—**pen′i·tent·ly,** *adv.* —**Syn.** *adj.* repentant, contrite, remorseful.

pen·i·ten·tial (pen′ə ten′shəl) *adj.* **1** of, showing, or having to do with penitence: *The penitential psalms express remorse for sin.* **2** of or having to do with penance. —*n.* **1** a person performing or undergoing penance; penitent. **2** a book or code of the church canons on penance, its imposition, etc.

pen·i·ten·tia·ry (pen′ə ten′shə rē) *n.* **-ries,** *adj.* —*n.* a prison, especially a federal prison for persons convicted of serious crimes. —*adj.* **1** making one liable to punishment in a prison: *a penitentiary offence.* **2** used for punishment, discipline, and reformation: *penitentiary measures.* **3** of penance; penitential.

pen·knife (pen′nīf′) *n.* **-knives.** a small pocketknife.

pen·man (pen′mən) *n.* **-men** (-mən). **1** a person whose handwriting is good. **2** a person who writes; author.

pen·man·ship (pen′mən ship′) *n.* **1** skill in writing with pen, pencil, etc. **2** a style of handwriting.

Penn. or **Penna.** Pennsylvania.

pen name a name used by a writer instead of his real name. —**Syn.** pseudonym; nom de plume.

pen·nant (pen′ənt) *n.* **1** a flag, usually long and narrow, used on ships for signalling, as a school banner, etc. **2** any flag taken as an emblem of superiority or success, especially in an athletic contest. [blend of *pendant* and *pennon*]

A pennant

pen·nate (pen′āt) *adj.* having wings; having feathers. [< L *pennatus* < *penna* feather, wing]

pen·ni (pen′ē) *n.* **pen·ni·a** (pen′ē ə). **1** a unit of money in Finland, worth 1/100 of a markka. **2** a coin worth one penni. [< Finnish < G *pfennig* penny]

pen·ni·less (pen′i lis) *adj.* without a cent; having no money; very poor. —**Syn.** destitute, indigent. See **poor.**

pen·non (pen′ən) *n.* **1** a long, triangular flag, originally carried on the lance of a knight. **2** any flag or banner. [ME < OF *penon,* ult. < L *penna* feather]

Penn·syl·va·ni·a Dutch (pen′səl vā′nē ə) **1** the descendants of 17th- and 18th-century immigrants to S.E. Pennsylvania from S. Germany and Switzerland. **2** people of this stock who settled in Upper Canada after the American Revolution. **3** the German dialect spoken by the Pennsylvania Dutch.

Penn·syl·va·ni·an (pen′səl vā′nē ən) *adj.* **1** of or having to do with the state of Pennsylvania. **2** in geology, of or having to do with the later Carboniferous period of the Paleozoic era in North America. See the chart under **geology.** —*n.* **1** a native or inhabitant of Pennsylvania. **2** in geology, the Pennsylvanian period or rock system.

pen·ny (pen′ē) *n.* **pen·nies** or *esp.Brit.* (*collectively for 2*) **pence. 1** a cent; copper coin of Canada and the United States. **2** a former British bronze coin equal to one twelfth of a shilling, or about one cent. **3** a new penny. **4** a sum of money. **5 a pretty penny,** *Informal.* a large sum of money. **6 turn an honest penny,** earn money honestly. [OE *pen(d)ing, penig*; cf. ON *penning* and G *Pfennig* < OHG *pfenning*]

pen·ny·roy·al (pen′ē roi′əl) *n.* **1** a plant of the same family as the mint. **2** a fragrant oil made from this plant. [apparently alteration of earlier *puliall royal*; *puliall* < OF *pouliol* < VL dim. of L *puleium* pennyroyal]

pen·ny·weight (pen′ē wāt′) *n.* in troy weight, 24 grains or 1/20 of an ounce.

pen·ny-wise (pen′ē wīz′) *adj.* **1** thrifty in regard to small sums. **2 penny-wise and pound-foolish,** thrifty in small expenses and wasteful in big ones.

pen·ny·worth (pen′ē wėrth′) *n.* **1** as much as can be bought for a penny. **2** a small amount.

pe·nol·o·gy (pē nol′ə jē) *n.* the science of the reforming and punishing of criminals and the managing of prisons. [< Gk. *poinē* punishment + E *-logy*]

pen·sile (pen′sīl or pen′səl) *adj.* **1** hanging; pendent. **2** of birds, building a hanging nest. [< L *pensilis* < *pendere* hang]

pen·sion[1] (pen′shən) *n.* a regular payment to a person that is not wages. Pensions are often paid because of long service, special merit, injuries, etc. —*v.* **1** give a pension to. **2 pension off,** retire from service with a pension. [ME < OF < L *pensio, -onis* < *pendere* weight, pay]

pen·sion[2] (päN syôN′) *n. French.* **1** a boarding house. **2** accommodation; board and lodging. **3** payment for board and lodging. **4** a boarding school. [< OF *pension* rent, payment. See PENSION[1].]

pen·sion·er (pen′shən ər) *n.* **1** a person who receives a pension. **2** a hireling; dependent.

pen·sive (pen′siv) *adj.* **1** thoughtful in a serious or sad way. **2** melancholy. [ME < OF *pensif* < *penser* think < L *pensare* weight, ponder < *pendere* weigh] —**pen′sive·ly,** *adv.* —**pen′sive·ness,** *n.* —**Syn. 1** meditative, reflective. **2** sober, grave, sad.

pen·stock (pen′stok′) *n.* **1** a channel for carrying water to a water wheel. **2** a gate for controlling the flow of water, etc. [< *pen*[2] + *stock,* in the sense of "trough"]

pent (pent) *adj.* closely confined; penned; shut: *We were pent in the house all winter.* —*v.* a pt. and a pp. of **pen**[2].

penta- *combining form.* five: *pentatonic* = *five-toned.* Also, **pent-** before vowels. [< Gk. *penta-* < *pente* five]

pen·ta·gon (pen′tə gon′) *n.* **1** a figure having five sides and five angles. **2 the Pentagon,** in the United States: **a** a building that is the headquarters of the Department of Defense, just outside Washington, D.C. **b** the Department of Defense, its policies, etc. [< LL < Gk. *pentagōnon* < *pente* five + *gōnia* angle]

A pentagon

pen·tag·o·nal (pen tag′ə nəl) *adj.* having five sides and five angles.

pen·ta·he·dron (pen′tə hē′drən) *n.* **-drons, -dra** (-drə). a solid figure having five faces. [< Gk. *pente* five + *hedra* base]

pen·tam·e·ter (pen tam′ə tər) *n.* verse having five feet or measures in each line. *Example:*

A lit | tle learn | ing is | a dan | g'rous thing.

—*adj.* consisting of five feet or measures. [< L < Gk. *pentametros* < *pente* five + *metron* meter]

pen·tane (pen′tān) *n.* any of three hydrocarbons of the methane series. *Formula*: C_5H_{12} [< Gk. *pente* five]

Pen·ta·teuch (pen′tə tūk′ or pen′tə tük′) *n.* the first five books of the Old Testament. Genesis, Exodus, Leviticus, Numbers, and Deuteronomy make up the Pentateuch. [< L < Gk. *pentateuchos* < *pente* five + *teuchos* vessel, book]

pen·tath·lon (pen tath′lən) *n.* an athletic contest consisting of five different events, in which the person having the highest total score wins. [< Gk. *pentathlon* < *pente* five + *athlon* contest]

pen·ta·ton·ic (pen′tə ton′ik) *adj.* in music, having five tones in the scale: *pentatonic scale.*

Pen·te·cost (pen′tə kost′) *n.* **1** the seventh Sunday after Easter, a Christian festival in memory of the descent of the Holy Ghost upon the Apostles. Acts 2. Also called **Whitsunday. 2** a Jewish religious holiday, observed about seven weeks after the Passover, celebrating the harvest and also the giving of the law to Moses. [OE < LL *pentecoste* < Gk. *pentēkostē* (*hēmera*) fiftieth (day)]

Pen·te·cos·tal or **pen·te·cos·tal** (pen′tə kos′təl) *adj.* of or having to do with Pentecost.

pent·house (pent′hous′) *n.* **1** an apartment or house built on the top of a building. **2** a sloping roof projecting from a building. **3** a shed with a sloping roof attached to a building. [ME *pentis* < OF *apentis,* ult. < L *appendere* append < *ad-* on + *pendere* hang]

pent-up (pent′up′) *adj.* shut up; closely confined: *pent-up feelings.*

pe·nu·che or **pe·nu·chi** (pə nü′chē) *n.* a candy or fudge made of brown sugar, butter, milk, and nuts. [< Mexican Sp. *panocha* brown or raw sugar]

pe·nult (pē′nult, pen′ult, or pi nult′) *n.* the next to the last syllable in a word. [< L *paenultima* (*syllaba*) next-to-last (syllable) < *paene* almost + *ultimus* last]

pe·nul·ti·mate (pi nul′tə mit) *adj.* **1** next to the last. **2** of or having to do with the penult. —*n.* the penult.

pe·num·bra (pi num′brə) *n.* **-brae** (-brē or -brī) or **-bras. 1** the partial shadow outside of the complete shadow formed by the sun, moon, etc. during an eclipse. See **eclipse** for diagram. **2** the grayish outer part of a sunspot. [< NL *penumbra* < L *paene* almost + *umbra* shadow]

pe·nu·ri·ous (pi nūr′ē əs or pi nür′ē əs) *adj.* mean about spending or giving money; stingy. —**pe·nu′ri·ous·ly,** *adv.* —**pe·nu′ri·ous·ness,** *n.*

pen·u·ry (pen′yů rē) *n.* great poverty. [< L *penuria*]

pe·on (pē′on or pē′ən) *n.* in Latin America, a person doing work that requires little skill. [< Sp. < LL *pedo, -onis* foot soldier. Doublet of PAWN[2].]

pe·on·age (pē′ən ij) *n.* the condition or service of a peon.

pe·o·ny (pē′ə nē) *n.* **-nies. 1** a perennial garden plant having large, showy flowers. **2** its flower. [ult. < Gk. *paiōnia* < *Paiōn* physician of the gods; from the plant's use in medicine]

peo·ple (pē′pəl) *n.* **-ple** or (*for def. 2*) **-ples,** *v.* **-pled, -pling.** —*n.* **1** men, women, and children; persons. **2** a race; nation. **3** the body of citizens of a state; the public. **4** the persons of a place, class, or group: *city people, Prairie people.* **5** the common people; the lower classes. **6** persons in relation to a superior: *A king rules over his people.* **7** *Informal.* family; relatives.
—*v.* **1** fill with people; populate: *Canada was very largely peopled by Europeans.* **2** stock with animals, etc. [ME < AF < L *populus*]

Syn. *n.* **2 People, race, nation** = a group of persons thought of as a unit larger than a family or community. **People** emphasizes cultural and social unity, applying to a group united by a common culture, common ideas, and a feeling of unity arising from common responsibilities and interests: *The Letts are a people, not* *a nation*. Race emphasizes biological unity, having common descent and common physical characteristics: *The Japanese belong to the Mongolian race.* Nation emphasizes political unity, applying to a group united under one government: *Norwegians are a people and a nation, not a race.* 3 inhabitants, population.

pep (pep) *n. v.* **pepped, pep·ping.** *Slang.* —*n.* spirit; energy; vim or enthusiasm. —*v.* **pep up,** fill or inspire with energy, etc.; put new life into. [short for *pepper*]

pep·lum (pep′ləm) *n.* **-lums** or (*esp. for def. 2*) **-la** (-lə). 1 a piece of draped, gathered, or pleated material attached over the waist of a skirt, jacket, etc. and usually extending to the hips. 2 in ancient Greece, a full garment worn by women. [< L < Gk. *peplos*]

PEPLUM

pep·per (pep′ər) *n.* 1 a seasoning with a hot taste, used for soups, meats, vegetables, etc. See **black pepper, cayenne, red pepper, white pepper.** 2 a plant bearing berries from which pepper is made. 3 any of several hollow, green or red vegetables with many seeds. They are eaten raw or cooked or pickled. 4 the plant bearing any such vegetable. 5 a small container for pepper. —*v.* 1 season or sprinkle with pepper. 2 sprinkle thickly: *His face is peppered with freckles.* 3 hit with small objects sent thick and fast: *We peppered the enemy with shot.* [OE *pipor* < L *piper* < Gk. *peperi*]

pep·per-and-salt (pep′ər ən solt′ or -sôlt′) *adj.* black and white finely mixed: *a pepper-and-salt coat.*

pep·per·box (pep′ər boks′) *n.* a container with holes in the top for sprinkling pepper on food.

pep·per·corn (pep′ər kôrn′) *n.* a dried berry of the pepper plant. [OE *piporcorn*]

pepper cress a kind of cress having a small oval leaf and a sharp taste, used in salads.

pep·per·grass (pep′ər gras′) *n.* 1 a kind of cress having a peppery taste. 2 pepper cress.

pep·per·mint (pep′ər mint′) *n.* 1 an herb grown for its oil, used in medicine and in candy. 2 the oil of this herb. 3 candy flavored with peppermint oil.

pep·pery (pep′ər ē) *adj.* 1 full of pepper; like pepper. 2 hot; sharp. 3 having a hot temper; easily made angry. —**pep′per·i·ness,** *n.*

pep·py (pep′ē) *adj.* **-pi·er, -pi·est.** *Slang.* full of pep; energetic; lively. —**pep′pi·ness,** *n.*

pep rally *Informal.* a meeting organized to stimulate support and enthusiasm for a team, cause, campaign, etc.

pep·sin (pep′sən) *n.* 1 an enzyme in the gastric juice of the stomach that helps to digest meat, eggs, cheese, and other proteins. 2 a medicine containing this enzyme, used to help digestion. [< Gk. *pepsis* digestion]

pep talk *Informal.* a short speech or talk organized to arouse enthusiasm or urge to action.

pep·tic (pep′tik) *adj.* 1 promoting digestion; digestive. 2 able to digest. 3 of or having to do with pepsin. —*n.* a substance promoting digestion. [< L < Gk. *peptikos* < *peptos* cooked, digested]

peptic ulcer an ulcer of the stomach or duodenum resulting from the digestive action of gastric juices.

pep·tone (pep′tōn) *n.* any of a class of diffusible and soluble substances into which meat, eggs, cheese, and other proteins are changed by pepsin or trypsin. [< G *Pepton* < Gk. *pepton*, neut. of *peptos* cooked, digested]

per (pər; *stressed,* pėr) *prep.* 1 for each: *a pound of candy per child, ten cents per pound.* 2 through; by means of: *I send this per my son.* [< L]

☛ **Per,** the Latin for *through, by, by the, among,* is found chiefly in business or technical English: *per capita, per cent, $28 per week, revolutions per minute.* The English equivalent is usually more appropriate in general English: *$28 a week, eight hours a day.*

per- *prefix.* 1 through; throughout. 2 thoroughly; utterly; very. 3 in chemistry, the maximum or a large amount of, as in *peroxide.* [< L]

per. 1 person. 2 period.

per·ad·ven·ture (pėr′əd ven′chər) *adv. Archaic.* perhaps: *Peradventure he will come today.* —*n.* chance; doubt. [ME < OF *par aventure* < *par* by (< L *per*) + *aventure* adventure < L *adventura* (*res*) (thing) about to happen < *advenire* arrive]

per·am·bu·late (pər am′byů lāt′) *v.* **-lat·ed, -lat·ing.** 1 walk through. 2 walk about. 3 walk through and examine. [< L *perambulare* < *per-* through + *ambulare* walk] —**per·am′bu·la′tion,** *n.*

hat, āge, cãre, fär; let, ēqual, tėrm; it, īce
hot, ōpen, ôrder; oil, out; cup, pùt, rüle, ūse
əbove, takən, pencəl, lemən, circəs
ch, child; ng, long; sh, ship
th, thin; ᴛʜ, then; zh, measure

per·am·bu·la·tor (pər am′byů lā′tər) *n.* 1 a small carriage in which a baby is pushed about. 2 a person who perambulates.

per an·num (pər an′əm) yearly; for each year: *Her salary was $5,000 per annum.* [< L]

per·cale (pər kāl′ or pər kal′) *n.* a closely woven cotton cloth with a smooth finish. [< F < Persian]

per cap·i·ta (pər kap′ə tə) for each person: *$40 for eight men is $5 per capita.* [< L *per capita* by heads]

per·ceive (pər sēv′) *v.* **-ceived, -ceiv·ing.** 1 be aware of through the senses; see, hear, taste, smell, or feel. 2 take in with the mind; observe: *I perceived that I could not make him change his mind.* [ME < OF *perceivre* < L *percipere* < *per-* fully + *capere* grasp] —**per·ceiv′er,** *n.* —**Syn. 1, 2** See **see.**

per cent or **per·cent** (pər sent′) *n.* 1 hundredths; parts in each hundred. Five per cent (5%) of 40 is the same as 5/100 × 40. *Abbrev.*: p.c. or pct. 2 for each hundred; in each hundred: *seven per cent of all the students failed.* [for LL *per centum*]

☛ **Per cent** may be written as either two words or one and is not followed by a period. Informally it is used in place of *percentage*: *A large per cent of the apple crop was ruined.*

per·cent·age (pər sen′tij) *n.* 1 the rate or proportion of each hundred; part of each hundred: *What percentage of children were absent?* 2 a part; proportion: *A large percentage of schoolbooks now have pictures.* 3 an allowance, commission, discount, rate of interest, etc. figured by per cent. 4 *Slang.* advantage or profit.

per·cen·tile (pər sen′tīl or pər sen′təl) *n.* any value in a series of points on a scale arrived at by dividing a group into a hundred equal parts in order of magnitude: *A student at the fiftieth percentile is at a point halfway between the top and the bottom of his group.*

per centum 1 by the hundred. 2 for or in every hundred.

per·cept (pėr′sept) *n.* 1 that which is perceived. 2 understanding that is the result of perceiving. [< L *perceptum*, pp. neut. of *percipere* perceive. See PERCEIVE.]

per·cep·ti·bil·i·ty (pər sep′tə bil′ə tē) *n.* the fact, quality, or state of being perceptible.

per·cep·ti·ble (pər sep′tə bəl) *adj.* that can be perceived. —**Syn.** palpable.

per·cep·ti·bly (pər sep′tə blē) *adv.* in a perceptible way or amount; to a perceptible degree.

per·cep·tion (pər sep′shən) *n.* 1 the act of perceiving: *His perception of the change came in a flash.* 2 the power of perceiving: *a keen perception.* 3 a percept. [< L *perceptio, -onis* < *percipere* perceive. See PERCEIVE.] —**Syn. 1** insight, apprehension, discernment, comprehension.

per·cep·tive (pər sep′tiv) *adj.* 1 having to do with perception. 2 having the power of perceiving. —**per·cep′tive·ly,** *adv.* —**per·cep′tive·ness,** *n.*

per·cep·tu·al (pər sep′chü əl) *adj.* of or having to do with perception.

perch[1] (pėrch) *n.* 1 a bar, branch, or anything else on which a bird can come to rest. 2 a rather high place or position. 3 a measure of length; rod; 5½ yards. 4 a measure of area; square rod; 30¼ square yards. —*v.* 1 alight and rest; sit. 2 sit rather high: *He perched on a stool.* 3 place high up: *a village perched on a hill.* [ME < OF *perche* < L *pertica* pole] —**perch′er,** *n.*

perch[2] (pėrch) *n.* **perch** or **perch·es.** 1 a kind of small fresh-water fish, used for food. 2 a similar salt-water fish. [ME < OF *perche* < L < Gk. *perkē*]

per·chance (pər chans′) *adv. Archaic or poetic.* perhaps. [ME < AF *par chance* < *par* by (< L *per*) + *chance* < L *cadentia* a falling < *cadere* fall]

Per·che·ron (pėr′chə ron′ or pėr′shə ron′) *n.* 1 a breed of large and strong horses. 2 a horse of this breed. [< F *Percheron* < *Le Perche*, a district in France]

per·cip·i·ence (pər sip′ē əns) *n.* perception.

per·cip·i·ent (pər sip′ē ənt) *adj.* **1** perceiving. **2** having perception. —*n.* one that perceives. [< L *percipiens, -entis,* ppr. of *percipere.* See PERCEIVE.]

per·co·late (pėr′kə lāt′) *v.* **-lat·ed, -lat·ing. 1** drip or drain through small holes or spaces. **2** filter through; permeate: *Water percolates sand.* **3** make coffee in a percolator. **4** of coffee, bubble up and drip through in a percolator. [< L *percolare,* ult. < *per-* through + *colum* strainer] —**per′co·la′tion,** *n.*

per·co·la·tor (pėr′kə lā′tər) *n.* **1** a kind of coffee pot in which boiling water continually bubbles up through a tube and drips down through ground coffee. **2** anything that percolates.

per·cus·sion (pər kush′ən) *n.* **1** the striking of one body against another with force; stroke; blow. **2** the shock made by the striking of one object against another with force. **3** in medicine, the tapping of a part of the body by a doctor. **4** in music, the section of an orchestra or band composed of percussion instruments. [< L *percussio, -onis* < *per-* (intensive) + *quatere* strike, beat]

percussion cap a small cap containing powder that explodes when struck by the hammer of a gun.

percussion instrument a musical instrument played by striking it, such as a drum or cymbal.

per di·em (pər dē′əm or dī′əm) *Latin.* **1** per day; for each day. **2** an allowance of so much every day. [< L *per diem* per day]

per·di·tion (pər dish′ən) *n.* **1** the loss of one's soul and the joys of heaven. **2** hell. **3** utter loss. [< L *perditio, -onis* < *perdere* destroy < *per-* (intensive) + *dare* give]

per·e·grin (per′ə grin) *n. adj.* peregrine.

per·e·gri·nate (per′e grə nāt′) *v.* **-nat·ed, -nat·ing.** travel; journey. [< L *peregrinari* < *peregrinus.* See PEREGRINE.] —**per′e·gri·na′tion,** *n.* —**per′e·gri·na′tor,** *n.*

per·e·grine (per′ə grin or per′ə grēn′) *n.* a large falcon, formerly much used in Europe for hawking. —*adj.* **1** not native; foreign. **2** outlandish; strange. **3** journeying as a pilgrim; travelling abroad; migratory. [< L *peregrinus* from foreign parts, ult. < *per-* outside + *ager* (*Romanus*) the (Roman) territory. Doublet of PILGRIM.]

per·emp·to·ry (pər emp′tə rē or per′əmp tô′rē) *adj.* **1** imperious; positive: *a peremptory teacher.* **2** allowing no denial or refusal: *a peremptory command.* **3** leaving no choice; decisive; final; absolute: *a peremptory decree.* [< L *peremptorius* deadly, that puts an end to, ult. < *per-* (intensive) + *emere,* originally, take] —**per·emp′to·ri·ly,** *adv.* —**per·emp′to·ri·ness,** *n.* —**Syn. 1** arbitrary, dogmatic.

per·en·ni·al (pər en′ē əl) *adj.* **1** lasting through the whole year: *a perennial stream.* **2** lasting for a very long time; enduring: *the perennial beauty of the hills.* **3** having underground parts that live more than two years: *perennial garden plants.* —*n.* a perennial plant. Roses are perennials. [< L *perennis* lasting < *per-* through + *annus* year] —**per·en′ni·al·ly,** *adv.* —**Syn.** *adj.* **2** abiding.

perf. 1 perfect. **2** perforated.

per·fect (*adj. n.* pėr′fikt; *v.* pər fekt′) *adj.* **1** without defect; faultless: *Perfect work is the result when attention is given to detail.* **2** completely skilled; expert: *a perfect golfer.* **3** having all its parts; complete: *The set was perfect; nothing was missing or broken.* **4** entire; utter: *He was a perfect stranger to us.* **5** in grammar, showing an action or state thought of as being completed. There are three perfect tenses: **perfect, past perfect,** and **future perfect. 6** in botany, having both stamens and pistils. **7** in music, having to do with the intervals or original consonances of unison, a fourth, fifth, and octave, as contrasted with the major intervals of a third and sixth. —*v.* **1** remove all faults from; make perfect; improve; add the finishing touches to: *The artist was perfecting his picture. We will perfect our plan as it is tried out.* **2** complete.
—*n.* in grammar: **1** the perfect tense. **2** a verb form in this tense. *Have eaten* is the perfect of *eat.* [ME < OF < L *perfectus* completed, pp. of *perficere* < *per-* thoroughly + *facere* make, do] —**per·fect′er,** *n.* —**per′fect·ness,** *n.*

per·fect·i·bil·i·ty (pər fek′tə bil′ə tē) *n.* the capability of becoming, or being made, perfect.

per·fect·i·ble (pər fek′tə bəl) *adj.* capable of becoming, or being made, perfect.

per·fec·tion (pər fek′shən) *n.* **1** a perfect condition; faultlessness; highest excellence. **2** a perfect person or thing. **3** a making complete or perfect: *The perfection of our plans will take another week.* **4 to perfection,** perfectly.

per·fec·tion·ist (pər fek′shən ist) *n.* **1** a person who is not content with anything that is not perfect or nearly perfect. **2** a person who believes it possible to lead a sinless life.

per·fect·ly (pėr′fikt lē) *adv.* in a perfect manner or degree; completely or thoroughly; fully; faultlessly; with utmost exactness; entirely.

perfect number a number that is equal to the sum of its factors. Six is a perfect number because its factors, 1, 2, and 3, add up to six.

per·fec·to (pər fek′tō) *n.* **-tos.** a thick cigar that tapers at both ends. [< Sp. *perfecto* perfect]

perfect participle a participle, preceded by a form of the verb *have,* expressing action completed before the time of speaking or acting. In "Having written the letter, she mailed it," *having written* is a perfect participle. ☛ See **participle** for usage note.

per·fer·vid (pėr fėr′vid) *adj.* very fervid.

per·fid·i·ous (pər fid′ē əs) *adj.* deliberately faithless; treacherous. [< L *perfidiosus* < *perfidia.* See PERFIDY.] —**per·fid′i·ous·ly,** *adv.* —**per·fid′i·ous·ness,** *n.*

per·fi·dy (pėr′fə dē) *n.* **-dies.** a breaking faith; base treachery; being false to a trust. [<L *perfidia,* ult. < *per-* + *fides* faith]

per·fo·li·ate (pər fō′lē it or -fō′lē āt′) *adj.* in botany, having the stem apparently passing through the leaf: *a perfoliate leaf.* [< NL *perfoliatus* < L *per-* through + *folium* leaf]

per·fo·rate (*v.* pėr′fə rāt′; *adj.* pėr′fə rit or pėr′fə rāt′) *v.* **-rat·ed, -rat·ing.** *adj.* —*v.* **1** make a hole or holes through: *His bullets perforated the target.* **2** make a row or rows of holes through: *Sheets of postage stamps are perforated.* —*adj.* pierced. [< L *perforare* < *per-* through + *forare* bore]

per·for·a·tion (pėr′fə rā′shən) *n.* **1** a hole bored or punched through something: *the perforations in a saltcellar.* **2** a perforating. **3** a being perforated.

per·fo·ra·tor (pėr′fə rā′tər) *n.* **1** one that perforates. **2** an instrument or machine for perforating.

per·force (pər fôrs′) *adv.* by necessity; necessarily. [< F *par* by + *force*]

per·form (pər fôrm′) *v.* **1** do; carry out: *Perform your duties well.* **2** put into effect; fulfil: *Perform your promise.* **3** go through; render: *perform a piece of music.* **4** act, play, sing, or do tricks in public. [< AF *perfourmer,* var. of OF *parfournir* < *par-* completely + *-fournir* furnish, finish; influenced by *forme* form]
Syn. 1 See **do. 2 Perform, execute, discharge** = carry out or put into effect. **Perform** = carry out a process, usually one that is long or that requires effort, attention, or skill: *The surgeon performed an operation.* **Execute** = put into effect a plan or proposal or carry out an order: *The nurse executed the doctor's orders.* **Discharge** = carry out an obligation or duty, by performing or executing the acts or steps necessary to relieve oneself of the responsibility: *She gave a large party to discharge all her social obligations.*

per·form·ance (pər fôr′məns) *n.* **1** a performing: *in the performance of one's regular duties.* **2** the thing performed; act; deed. **3** the giving of a play, concert, circus, or other show: *The evening performance is at 8 o'clock.*

per·form·er (pər fôr′mər) *n.* a person who performs, especially one who performs for the entertainment of others; player.

per·fume (*n.* pėr′fūm or pər fūm′; *v.* pər fūm′) *n. v.* **-fumed, -fum·ing.** —*n.* **1** a liquid having the sweet smell of flowers. **2** a sweet smell. [< F *parfum* < *parfumer* scent. See v.] —*v.* **1** fill with sweet odor: *Flowers perfumed the air.* **2** put a sweet-smelling liquid on. [< F *parfumer* < OItal. < L *per-* through + *fumare* smoke] —**Syn.** *n.* **2** fragrance, scent.

per·fum·er (pər fūm′ər) *n.* **1** a maker or seller of perfumes. **2** a person or thing that perfumes.

per·fum·er·y (pər fūm′ər ē or pər fūm′rē) *n.* **-er·ies.** **1** a perfume. **2** perfumes collectively. **3** the business of making or selling perfumes.

per·func·to·ry (pər fungk′tə rē) *adj.* **1** done merely for the sake of getting rid of the duty; mechanical; indifferent: *The little boy gave his face a perfunctory washing.* **2** acting in a perfunctory way: *The new nurse was perfunctory; she did not really care about her work.* [< LL *perfunctorius,* ult. < L *perfungi* perform < *per-* to the end + *fungi* execute] **—per·func′to·ri·ly,** *adv.* **—per·func′to·ri·ness,** *n.* **—Syn. 1** careless, superficial.

per·fuse (pər fūz′) *v.* **-fused, -fus·ing. 1** overspread (something) with a vapor, fluid, color, etc.; permeate; suffuse. **2** cause (something) to flow through or spread over. [< L *perfusus,* pp. of *perfundere* pour out < *per-* (intensive) + *fundere* pour out] **—per·fu′sion,** *n.*

per·go·la (pėr′gə lə) *n.* an arbor made of a trellis supported by posts. [< Ital. < L *pergula,* probably dim. of **perga* timber work]

per·haps (pər haps′ or pər aps′) *adv.* maybe; possibly. [ME *per happes* by chances (pl. of *hap* chance)]

pe·ri (pēr′ē) *n.* **pe·ris.** in Persian mythology, a beautiful fairy shut out from paradise until forgiven. [< Persian]

peri- *prefix.* **1** around; surrounding, as in *periscope, periphery.* **2** near, as in *perigee, perihelion.* [< Gk.]

per·i·anth (per′ē anth′) *n.* in botany, the envelope of a flower, including the calyx and the corolla. [< NL < Gk. *peri-* around + *anthos* flower]

per·i·car·di·ac (per′ə kär′dē ak′) *adj.* pericardial.

per·i·car·di·al (per′ə kär′dē əl) *adj.* **1** around the heart. **2** of or having to do with the pericardium.

per·i·car·di·tis (per′ə kär dī′tis) *n.* in medicine, an inflammation of the pericardium.

per·i·car·di·um (per′ə kär′dē əm) *n.* **-di·a** (-dē ə). in anatomy, the membranous sac enclosing the heart. [< Gk. *pericardion* < *peri-* around + *kardia* heart]

per·i·carp (per′ə kärp′) *n.* in botany, the walls of a ripened ovary or fruit, sometimes consisting of three layers, the epicarp, mesocarp, and endocarp; seed vessel. [< NL < Gk. *perikarpion* < *peri-* around + *karpos* fruit]

Per·i·cle·an (per′ə klē′ən) *adj.* of or having to do with Pericles or with the period of his leadership.

per·i·cra·ni·um (per′ə krā′nē əm) *n.* **-ni·a** (-nē ə). in anatomy, the membrane covering the bones of the skull. [< Gk. *perikranion* < *peri-* around + *kranion* skull]

per·i·gee (per′ə jē′) *n.* in astronomy, the point in the orbit of a heavenly body where it comes closest to the earth. See **apogee** for diagram. [< F < NL < Gk. *perigeion* < *peri-* near + *gē* earth]

per·i·he·li·on (per′ə hē′lē ən or per′ə hēl′yən) *n.* **-he·li·a** (-hē′lē ə or -hēl′yə). in astronomy, the point in its orbit where a heavenly body comes closest to the sun. See **aphelion** for diagram. [< NL < Gk. *peri-* near + *hēlios* sun]

per·il (per′əl) *n. v.* **-illed** or **-iled, -il·ling** or **-il·ing.** —*n.* a chance of harm; danger. —*v.* put in danger; expose to risk. [ME < OF < L *periculum*] **—Syn.** *n.* jeopardy, hazard, risk. See **danger.**

per·il·ous (per′ə ləs) *adj.* dangerous. [< AF *perillous* < L *periculosus*] **—per′il·ous·ly,** *adv.* **—per′il·ous·ness,** *n.* **—Syn.** hazardous, risky, unsafe.

pe·rim·e·ter (pə rim′ə tər) *n.* **1** the outer boundary of a surface or figure. **2** the distance around such a boundary. The perimeter of a square equals four times the length of one side. [< L < Gk. *perimetros* < *peri-* around + *metron* measure]

per·i·ne·al (per′ə nē′əl) *adj.* of or having to do with the perineum.

per·i·ne·um (per′ə nē′əm) *n.* **-ne·a** (-nē′ə). in anatomy: **1** the region of the body between the thighs. **2** the region included in the opening of the pelvis. [< LL < Gk. *perinaion*]

pe·ri·od (pēr′ē əd) *n.* **1** a span of time, having certain features or conditions: *He visited us for a short period.* **2** a portion of time marked off by events that happen again and again; time after which the same things begin to happen again. A month, from new moon to new moon, is a period. **3** in geology, a subdivision of an era. **4** the portion of a game during which there is actual play: *There are three twenty-minute periods in a hockey game.* **5** one of the portions of time into which a school day is divided. **6** the time needed for a disease to run its course. **7** a dot (.) marking the end of sentences or showing an abbreviation. *Examples*: Mr., Dec. **8** the pause at the end of a sentence. **9** a complete sentence: *The orator spoke in stately periods.* **10** an end; termination; final stage. **11** the time of menstruating; menstruation. **12** in physics, the interval of time between the recurrence of like phases in a vibration or other periodic motion or phenomenon.
—*adj.* characteristic of a certain period of time: *period furniture.*
—*interj. Informal.* that's it! that's final! *The discussion is over, period!* [< L < Gk. *periodos* a going around, cycle < *peri-* around + *hodos* a going] **—Syn.** *n.* **1** term, interval.

☛ **Period.** A period coming at the end of a quotation is generally placed inside the quotation marks: "*The longer you put it off,*" *he said,* "*the harder it's going to be.*"

pe·ri·od·ic (pēr′ē od′ik) *adj.* **1** occurring, appearing, or done again and again at regular intervals: *periodic attacks of malaria.* **2** happening every now and then: *a periodic fit of clearing up one's desk.* **3** having to do with a period. **4** expressed in formal sentences whose meanings are not complete without the final words.

pe·ri·od·i·cal (pēr′ē od′ə kəl) *n.* a magazine that appears regularly. —*adj.* **1** of or having to do with periodicals. **2** published at regular intervals, less often than daily. **3** periodic.

pe·ri·od·i·cal·ly (pēr′ē od′ik lē) *adv.* **1** at regular intervals. **2** every now and then.

pe·ri·o·dic·i·ty (pēr′ē ə dis′ə tē) *n.* **-ties.** a periodic character; tendency to happen at regular intervals.

periodic law in chemistry, the law stating that when the elements are arranged in the order of their atomic numbers, the properties of the elements recur at regular intervals.

periodic table in chemistry, a table in which the elements, arranged in the order of their atomic weights, are shown in related groups. See table on the next page.

per·i·os·te·um (per′ē os′tē əm) *n.* **-te·a** (-tē ə). in anatomy, the dense fibrous membrane covering the surface of bones except at the joints. [< NL < LL < Gk. *periosteon* < *peri-* around + *osteon* bone]

per·i·pa·tet·ic (per′ə pə tet′ik) *adj.* **1** walking about; travelling from place to place. **2 Peripatetic,** having to do with the philosophy of Aristotle, who taught while walking. —*n.* **1** a person who wanders or travels about from place to place. **2 Peripatetic,** a disciple of Aristotle. [< L < Gk. *peripatētikos* < *peri-* around + *pateein* walk; with reference to Aristotle's manner of teaching]

pe·riph·er·al (pə rif′ər əl) *adj.* **1** having to do with, situated in, or forming an outside boundary. **2 a** of the surface or outer part of a body; external. **b** perceived or perceiving near the outer edges of the retina: *peripheral vision.* **—pe·riph′er·al·ly,** *adv.* **—Syn.** marginal.

pe·riph·er·y (pə rif′ər ē) *n.* **-er·ies.** an outside boundary. The periphery of a circle is called the circumference. [< LL < Gk. *periphereia* < *peri-* around + *pherein* carry]

per·i·phrase (per′ə frāz′) *n. v.* **-phrased, -phras·ing.** —*n.* a roundabout way of speaking or writing; circumlocution: "*The wife of your father's brother*" *is a periphrase for* "*your aunt.*" —*v.* express in a roundabout way.

pe·riph·ra·sis (pə rif′rə sis) *n.* **-ses** (-sēz′). periphrase. [< L < Gk. *periphrasis,* ult. < *peri-* around + *phrazein* speak]

per·i·phras·tic (per′ə fras′tik) *adj.* **1** expressed in a roundabout way. **2** in grammar, formed by using auxiliaries or particles rather than inflection. *Examples:*

hat, āge, cãre, fär; let, ēqual, tėrm; it, īce
hot, ōpen, ôrder; oil, out; cup, pu̇t, rüle, ūse
əbove, takən, pencəl, lemən, circəs
ch, child; ng, long; sh, ship
th, thin; ᴛʜ, then; zh, measure

PERIODIC TABLE OF THE ELEMENTS

Information about each element is given in the following order: atomic number, name, chemical symbol, atomic weight. The atomic weights are those based on the standard carbon-12 = 12. A figure in parentheses indicates the mass number of the most stable isotope.

1 Hydrogen H 1.00797																1 Hydrogen H 1.00797	2 Helium He 4.0026
3 Lithium Li 6.939	4 Beryllium Be 9.0122											5 Boron B 10.811	6 Carbon C 12.01115	Nitrogen N 14.0067	8 Oxgyen O 15.9994	9 Fluorine F 18.9984	10 Neon Ne 20.183
11 Sodium Na 22.9898	12 Magnesium Mg 24.312											13 Aluminum Al 26.9815	14 Silicon Si 28.086	15 Phosphorus P 30.9738	16 Sulphur S 32.064	17 Chlorine Cl 35.453	18 Argon Ar 39.948
19 Potassium K 39.102	20 Calcium Ca 40.08	21 Scandium Sc 44.956	22 Titanium Ti 47.90	23 Vanadium V 50.942	24 Chromium Cr 51.996	25 Manganese Mn 54.9380	26 Iron Fe 55.847	27 Cobalt Co 58.9332	28 Nickel Ni 58.71	29 Copper Cu 63.54	30 Zinc Zn 65.37	31 Gallium Ga 69.72	32 Germanium Ge 72.59	33 Arsenic As 74.9216	34 Selenium Se 78.96	35 Bromine Br 79.909	36 Krypton Kr 83.80
37 Rubidium Rb 85.47	38 Strontium Sr 87.62	39 Yttrium Y 88.905	40 Zirconium Zr 91.22	41 Niobium Nb 92.906	42 Molybden- Mo um 95.94	43 Technetium Tc (99)	44 Ruthenium Ru 101.07	45 Rhodium Rh 102.905	46 Palladium Pd 106.4	47 Silver Ag 107.870	48 Cadmium Cd 112.40	49 Indium In 114.82	50 Tin Sn 118.69	51 Antimony Sb 121.75	52 Tellurium Te 127.60	53 Iodine I 126.9044	54 Xenon Xe 131.30
55 Cesium Cs 132.905	56 Barium Ba 137.34	57 Lanthanum La 138.91	72 Hafnium Hf 178.49	73 Tantalum Ta 180.948	74 Tungsten W 183.85	75 Rhenium Re 186.2	76 Osmium Os 190.2	77 Iridium Ir 192.2	78 Platinum Pt 195.09	79 Gold Au 196.967	80 Mercury Hg 200.59	81 Thallium Tl 204.37	82 Lead Pb 207.19	83 Bismuth Bi 208.980	84 Polonium Po (210)	85 Astatine At (210)	86 Radon Rn (222)
87 Francium Fr (223)	88 Radium Ra (226)	89 Actinium Ac (227)															
		Lanthanide series	58 Cerium Ce 140.12	59 Praseodym- Pr ium 140.907	60 Neodymium Nd 144.24	61 Promethium Pm (147)	62 Samarium Sm 150.35	63 Europium Eu 151.96	64 Gadolinium Gd 157.25	65 Terbium Tb 158.924	66 Dysprosium Dy 162.50	67 Holmium Ho 164.930	68 Erbium Er 167.26	69 Thulium Tm 168.934	70 Ytterbium Yb 173.04	71 Lutecium Lu 174.97	
		Actinide series	90 Thorium Th 232.038	91 Protoactin- Pa ium (231)	92 Uranium U 238.03	93 Neptunium Np (237)	94 Plutonium Pu (242)	95 Americium Am (243)	96 Curium Cm (247)	97 Berkelium Bk (249)	98 Californium Cf (251)	99 Einsteinium Es (254)	100 Fermium Fm (253)	101 Mendelev- Md ium (256)	102 Nobelium No (254)	103 Lawrencium Lw (257)	

of John rather than *John's* (periphrastic genitive); *did run* rather than *ran* (periphrastic conjugation). —**per'i·phras'ti·cal·ly,** *adv.*

per·i·scope (per'ə skōp') *n.* **1** an instrument that allows those in a submarine or trench to obtain a view of the surface. It is a tube with an arrangement of prisms or mirrors that reflect light rays down the tube. **2** an arrangement of mirrors used for seeing round corners, looking over the heads of people in a crowd, etc. [< Gk. *peri-* around + E *-scope*]

A periscope on a submarine. It can be turned in any direction, and also raised and lowered.

per·i·scop·ic (per'ə skop'ik) *adj.* **1** giving distinct vision obliquely as well as in a direct line. **2** of or having to do with periscopes.

per·ish (per'ish) *v.* **1** be destroyed; die: *The buildings perished in the flames. Many soldiers perished in the battle.* **2** decay; become spoiled: *Fruit perishes quickly in hot weather.* [ME < OF *periss-*, a stem of *perir* < L *perire* < *per-* (intensive) + *ire* go]—**Syn.** See **die.**

per·ish·a·ble (per'ish ə bəl) *adj.* liable to spoil or decay: *Fresh fruit is perishable.* —*n.* Usually, **perishables,** *pl.* something perishable. —**per'ish·a·ble·ness,** *n.*

per·i·stal·sis (per'ə stal'sis) *n.* **-ses** (-sēz). in physiology, a movement in the wall of a hollow organ by which it propels its contents onward, especially the wavelike circular contractions of the alimentary canal. [< NL < Gk. *peristalsis,* ult. < *peri-* around + *stellein* wrap]

per·i·stal·tic (per'ə stal'tik) *adj.* of or having to do with peristalsis.

per·i·style (per'ə stīl') *n.* **1** a row of columns surrounding a building, court, etc. **2** a space or court so enclosed. [< F < L < Gk. *peristylon* < *peri* around + *stylos* pillar]

per·i·to·ne·al (pər'ə tə nē'əl) *adj.* of the peritoneum.

per·i·to·ne·um or **per·i·to·nae·um** (per'ə tə nē'əm) *n.* **-ne·a** or **-nae·a** (-nē'ə). in anatomy, a membrane that lines the walls of the abdomen and covers the organs in it. [< LL < Gk. *peritonaion,* neut. adj., stretched over, ult. < *peri-* around + *teinein* stretch]

per·i·to·ni·tis (per'ə tə nī'tis) *n.* inflammation of the peritoneum. [< NL < LL *peritonaeum* peritoneum + Gk. *-itis*]

per·i·wig (per'ə wig') *n.* a wig. [earlier *perewyke* < F *perruque.* Cf. PERUKE.]

per·i·win·kle[1] (per'ə wing'kəl) *n.* **1** a low, trailing evergreen plant having blue flowers. The North American periwinkle is called myrtle. **2** a light blue. [< L *pervinca*; influenced by *periwinkle*[2]]

per·i·win·kle[2] (per'ə wing'kəl) *n.* a sea snail having a thick, cone-shaped, spiral shell, used for food in Europe. [OE *pinewincle*; *pine-* ? < L *pina* mussel < Gk. *pinē*]

per·jure (pėr'jər) *v.* **-jured, -jur·ing,** *n.* —*v.* make (oneself) guilty of perjury; swear falsely; lie when on oath; swear that something is true which one knows to be false: *The witness perjured himself at the trial.* —**per'jur·er,** *n.* [ME < AF < L *perjurare* < *per-* to destruction + *jurare* swear < *jus, juris* right (n.)]

per·jured (pėr'jərd) *adj.* **1** guilty of perjury: *a perjured witness.* **2** characterized by or involving perjury: *perjured evidence.*

per·ju·ry (pėr'jər ē) *n.* **-ries.** the act of swearing that something is true which one knows to be false. [ME < AF *perjurie* < L *perjurium* < *perjurare.* See PERJURE.]

perk[1] (pėrk) *v.* **1** move, lift the head, or act briskly or saucily. **2** raise smartly or briskly: *The sparrow perked up his tail.* **3** make trim or smart: *She is all perked out in her Sunday clothes.* **4** put oneself forward briskly or assertively. **5 perk up,** brighten up; become lively and vigorous. [ME *perke(n)* ? < OF *perquer* perch]

perk[2] (pėrk) *v. Informal.* **1** percolate. **2** be in a state of activity; go well: *To keep the economy perking is difficult under inflation.* [short for *percolate*]

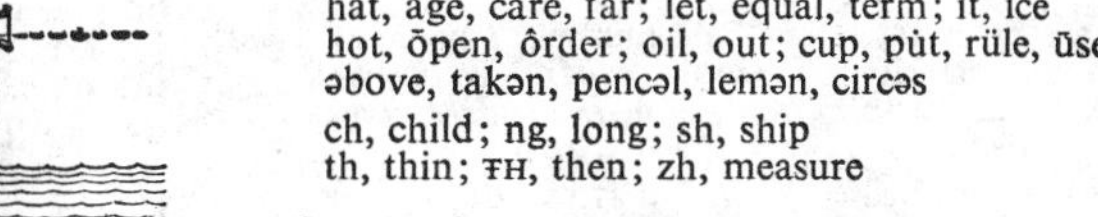
hat, āge, cãre, fär; let, ēqual, tėrm; it, īce
hot, ōpen, ôrder; oil, out; cup, pu̇t, rüle, ūse
əbove, takən, pencəl, lemən, circəs
ch, child; ng, long; sh, ship
th, thin; ᴛʜ, then; zh, measure

perk·y (pėr'kē) *adj.* **perk·i·er, perk·i·est.** smart; brisk; saucy; pert. —**perk·i·ly,** *adv.* —**perk'i·ness,** *n.*

perm (pėrm) *n. Informal.* a permanent wave.

per·ma·frost (pėr'mə frost') *n.* ground or subsoil that is permanently frozen.

per·ma·nence (pėr'mə nəns) *n.* the state or condition of being permanent; lasting quality or condition.

per·ma·nen·cy (pėr'mə nən sē) *n.* **-cies. 1** permanence. **2** a permanent person, thing, or position.

per·ma·nent (pėr'mə nənt) *adj.* lasting; intended to last; not for a short time only: *a permanent filling in a tooth. After doing odd jobs for a week, he got a permanent position as office boy.* —*n. Informal.* a permanent wave. [< L *permanens, -entis* staying to the end, ppr. of *permanere* < *per-* through + *manere* stay] —**per'ma·nent·ly,** *adv.* —**Syn.** *adj.* enduring. See **lasting.**

permanent married quarters a government housing development for married members of the armed services.

permanent wave 1 a process of tightly winding the hair on rollers and applying chemicals or chemicals and heat in order to prepare the hair to keep a long-lasting curl or wave. **2** the curl or wave set in the hair after this process.

per·man·ga·nate (pər mang'gə nāt') *n.* a salt of an acid containing manganese. A solution of potassium permanganate is used as an antiseptic.

per·me·a·bil·i·ty (pėr'mē ə bil'ə tē) *n.* a being permeable.

per·me·a·ble (pėr'mē ə bəl) *adj.* that can be permeated: *A sponge is permeable by water.* [< LL *permeabilis* < L *permeare.* See PERMEATE.]

per·me·ate (pėr'mē āt') *v.* **-at·ed, -at·ing. 1** spread through the whole of; pass through; soak through: *Smoke permeated the house.* **2** penetrate: *Water will easily permeate a cotton dress.* [< L *permeare* < *per-* through + *meare* pass]

per·me·a·tion (pėr'mē ā'shən) *n.* a permeating; penetration; diffusion through; saturation.

Per·mi·an (pėr'mē ən) in geology: —*n.* **1** a late period of the Paleozoic era, beginning approximately 235 million years ago. **2** the rocks formed in this period. See the chart under **geology.** —*adj.* of or having to do with this period or the rocks formed during it. [< *Perm,* a former province in E. Russia where such rocks are found]

per·mis·si·ble (pər mis'ə bəl) *adj.* that may be permitted; allowable. —**per·mis'si·bly,** *adv.*

per·mis·sion (pər mish'ən) *n.* consent; leave; permitting: *He asked the teacher's permission to go early.* [< L *permissio, -onis* < *permittere.* See PERMIT.] —**Syn.** sufferance, authorization, sanction.

per·mis·sive (pər mis'iv) *adj.* **1** permitting; allowing. **2** permitted; allowed. **3** not strict in discipline; tolerant; lenient: *permissive parents.* —**per·mis'sive·ness,** *n.*

per·mit (*v.* pər mit'; *n.* pėr'mit or pər mit') *v.* **-mit·ted, -mit·ting,** *n.* —*v.* **1** allow (a person, etc.) to do something: *Permit me to explain.* **2** let (something) be done or occur: *The law permits smoking in this store.* —*n.* **1** a formal written order giving permission to do something: *a permit to fish or hunt.* **2** permission. [< L *permittere* < *per-* through + *mittere* let go]

Syn. *v.* **1 Permit, allow** = let someone or something do something. **Permit** emphasizes the idea of expressing willingness or giving consent: *His parents permitted him to have a car when he was seventeen.* **Allow** = not to forbid or prevent, without necessarily giving permission or approval: *That teacher allows too much noise in the room.*

per·mu·ta·tion (pėr'myu̇ tā'shən) *n.* **1** an alteration. **2** in mathematics: **a** a changing of the order of a set of things; arranging in different orders. **b** such an arrangement or group. The permutations of *a, b,* and *c* are *abc, acb, bac, bca, cab, cba.* [< L *permutatio, -onis* < *permutare* < *per-* across + *mutare* change]

per·mute (pər mūt′) *v.* **-mut·ed, -mut·ing. 1** change; alter. **2** in mathematics, change the order of (numbers, letters, etc.); subject to permutation. [< L *permutare.* See PERMUTATION.]

per·ni·cious (pər nish′əs) *adj.* **1** that will destroy or ruin; causing great harm or damage; injurious: *pernicious habits.* **2** fatal. [< L *perniciosus,* ult. < *per-* + *nex, necis* death] **—per·ni′cious·ly,** *adv.* **—per·ni′cious·ness,** *n.* **—Syn. 1** injurious, noxious.

pernicious anemia a severe disease in which the number of red corpuscles in the blood keeps decreasing.

per·nick·e·ty (pər nik′ə tē) *adj. Informal.* **1** fastidious; fussy. **2** requiring precise and careful handling. [origin uncertain]

per·o·gy (pə rog′ē) *n.* a Slavic dish of a dumpling or turnover with a filling of meat, vegetables, cheese, or fruit. [< Old Slavic *pir* feast + *og*]

per·o·rate (per′ə rāt′) *v.* **-rat·ed, -rat·ing. 1** make a formal conclusion to a speech. **2** speak at length; make a speech. [< L *perorare.* See PERORATION.]

per·o·ra·tion (per′ə rā′shən) *n.* the last part of an oration or discussion, summing up what has been said. [< L *peroratio, -onis* < *perorare* < *per-* to a finish + *orare* speak formally]

per·ox·id (pər ok′sid) *n.* peroxide.

per·ox·ide (pər ok′sīd) *n. v.* **-id·ed, -id·ing. —*n.* 1** in chemistry, an oxide of a given element or radical that contains the greatest, or an unusual, amount of oxygen. **2** hydrogen peroxide. **—*v.*** bleach (hair) by applying hydrogen peroxide.

per·pen·dic·u·lar (pėr′pən dik′yů lər) *adj.* **1** upright; standing straight up. **2** in geometry, at right angles. See the diagrams. **3** Also, **Perpendicular.** of or having to do with a type of Gothic architecture developed in England toward the end of the 14th century and characterized by a marked emphasis on vertical lines. **—*n.* 1** a perpendicular line or plane. **2** a perpendicular position. [< L *perpendicularis* < *perpendiculum* plumb line, ult. < *per-* + *pendere* hang]

per·pe·trate (pėr′pə trāt′) *v.* **-trat·ed, -trat·ing.** do or commit (crime, fraud, or anything bad or foolish). [< L *perpetrare* < *per-* (intensive) + *patrare* perform] **—per′pe·tra′tion,** *n.* **—per′pe·tra′tor,** *n.*

per·pet·u·al (pər pech′ü əl) *adj.* **1** lasting forever; eternal: *the perpetual hills.* **2** lasting throughout life: *a perpetual income.* **3** continuous; never ceasing: *a perpetual stream of visitors; perpetual motion.* **4** in horticulture, being in bloom more or less continuously throughout the year or the season. [< L *perpetualis* < *perpetuus* < *perpes, -etis* continuous < *per-* to the end + *petere* seek] **—Syn. 1** permanent, everlasting, enduring.

per·pet·u·al·ly (pər pech′ü əl ē) *adv.* forever.

per·pet·u·ate (pər pech′ü āt′) *v.* **-at·ed, -at·ing.** make perpetual; keep from being forgotten: *The Brock Monument was built to perpetuate the memory of a great man.* [< L *perpetuare* < *perpetuus.* See PERPETUAL.] **—per·pet′u·a′tion,** *n.* **—per·pet′u·a′tor,** *n.*

per·pe·tu·i·ty (pėr′pə tū′ə tē or pėr′pə tü′ə tē) *n.* **-ties. 1** a being perpetual; existence forever. **2** a perpetual possession, tenure, or position. **3** in law: **a** of an estate, the quality or condition of being inalienable perpetually or longer than the legal time limit. **b** the estate so restricted. **4** a perpetual annuity. **5 in perpetuity,** forever. [< F < L *perpetuitas* < *perpetuus.* See PERPETUAL.]

per·plex (pər pleks′) *v.* **1** trouble with doubt; puzzle; bewilder. **2** make difficult to understand or settle; confuse: *This further perplexes the problem.* [originally adj., < L *perplexus* confused, ult. < *per-* completely + *plectere* intertwine] **—per·plex′ing·ly,** *adv.* **—Syn. 1** See **puzzle.**

per·plex·i·ty (pər plek′sə tē) *n.* **-ties. 1** a perplexed condition; confusion; the state of being puzzled or not knowing what to do or how to act. **2** something that perplexes. **—Syn. 1** bewilderment.

per·qui·site (pėr′kwə zit) *n.* **1** anything received for work besides the regular pay: *The maid had the old dresses of her mistress as a perquisite.* **2** any privilege, benefit, or advantage expected or due: *the perquisites of trade.* [< Med.L *perquisitum* (thing) gained, ult. < L *per-* thoroughly + *quaerere* seek]

per se (pėr sē′ or pėr sā′) *Latin.* by itself; in itself; intrinsically.

per·se·cute (pėr′sə kūt′) *v.* **-cut·ed, -cut·ing. 1** treat badly; do harm to again and again; oppress. **2** punish for religious reasons. **3** annoy: *persecuted by silly questions.* [< *persecution*] **—per′se·cu′tor,** *n.* **—Syn. 1** wrong, torment. **3** harass, worry, vex.

per·se·cu·tion (pėr′sə kū′shən) *n.* **1** a persecuting. **2** a being persecuted. [< L *persecutio, -onis,* ult. < *per-* perseveringly + *sequi* follow]

Per·seph·o·ne (pər sef′ə nē′) *n.* in Greek mythology, Proserpina.

Per·se·us (pėr′sē əs or pėr′sūs) *n.* **1** in Greek mythology, a Greek hero who slew Medusa and rescued Andromeda from a sea monster. **2** in astronomy, a northern constellation near Cassiopeia.

per·se·ver·ance (pėr′sə vēr′əns) *n.* a sticking to a purpose or an aim; never giving up what one has set out to do. **—Syn.** tenacity, diligence. See **persistence.**

per·se·vere (pėr′sə vēr′) *v.* **-vered, -ver·ing.** continue steadily in doing something hard; persist. [< F < L *perseverare* < *per-* very + *severus* strict] **—per′se·ver′ing·ly,** *adv.*

Per·sian (pėr′zhən) *adj.* of or having to do with Persia (or Iran), a country in southwestern Asia, its people, or their language. **—*n.* 1** a native or inhabitant of Persia (or Iran). **2** the language of Persia (or Iran).

Persian cat 1 a breed of cat having a chunky build and long, glossy hair. **2** a cat of this breed.

Persian lamb 1 a very curly fur from karakul lambs raised in Iran and some parts of central Asia. **2** a coat or other garment made from this fur.

per·si·flage (pėr′sə fläzh′) *n.* light, joking talk. [< F *persiflage* < *persifler* banter, apparently < *per-* (< L) + *siffler* whistle, hiss < L *sibilare*]

per·sim·mon (pər sim′ən) *n.* **1** a North American plumlike fruit, containing one to ten seeds, that is bitter when green, but sweet and tasty when ripe. **2** the hardwood tree that bears this fruit. [< Algonquian]

per·sist (pər sist′ or pər zist′) *v.* **1** continue firmly: *She persisted till she had solved the difficult problem.* **2** refuse to stop or be changed. **3** last; stay; endure: *On the tops of very high mountains snow persists throughout the year.* **4** say again and again; maintain. [< *persistere* < *per-* to the end + *sistere* stand] **—Syn. 1** persevere.

per·sist·ence (pər sis′təns or pər zis′təns) *n.* **1** the quality or state of being persistent. **2** the continuing existence: *the persistence of a cough.*

Syn. 1 Persistence, perseverance = a holding fast to a purpose or course of action. **Persistence,** having a good or bad sense according to one's attitude toward what is done, emphasizes holding stubbornly or obstinately to one's purpose and continuing firmly and often annoyingly against disapproval, opposition, advice, etc.: *By persistence many people won religious freedom.* **Perseverance,** always in a good sense, emphasizes refusing to be discouraged by obstacles or difficulties, but continuing steadily with courage and patience: *Perseverance leads to success.*

per·sist·en·cy (pər sis′tən sē or pər zis′tən sē) *n.* persistence.

per·sist·ent (pər sis′tənt or pər zis′tənt) *adj.* **1** persisting; having lasting qualities, especially in the face of dislike, disapproval, or difficulties: *a persistent worker, a persistent beggar.* **2** lasting; going on; continuing: *a persistent headache that lasted for three days.* **3** in botany, continuing without withering, as a calyx which remains after the corolla has withered; permanent. **4** in zoology, permanent; not lost or altered during development: *persistent horns.* **—per·sist′ent·ly,** *adv.* **—Syn. 1** persevering, untiring, insistent.

per·son (pėr′sən) *n.* **1** a man, woman or child; human being. **2** a human body; bodily appearance: *He has a fine person.* **3 in person, a** in one's own individual character. **b** really present, not merely thought of. **4** in grammar: **a** a change in a pronoun or verb to show the person speaking **(first person),** the person spoken to **(second person),** or the person or thing spoken of **(third person).**

I and *we* are used for the first person; *you*, for the second person; *he, she, it*, and *they*, for the third person. **b** a form of a pronoun or verb giving such indication. *Comes* is third person singular of *come*. **5** in Christianity, any of the three modes of being in the Trinity (Father, Son, and Holy Ghost). **6** in law, a human being, or an entity such as a corporation, a partnership, or occasionally a collection of property, as the estate of a dead person, recognized by the law as capable of having legal rights and duties. [ME < OF < L *persona* character, mask worn by actor. Doublet of PARSON.]

☛ **person, individual, party. Person** is the ordinary word for referring to a human being. **Individual** has the same meaning (though it is applied to single objects and animals as well) but emphasizes the person's singleness, aloneness, and is slightly heavy or pretentious unless that emphasis is needed. **Party** is legal or substandard.

per·son·a·ble (pėr′sən ə bəl) *adj.* having a pleasing appearance; good-looking; attractive.

per·son·age (pėr′sən ij) *n.* **1** a person of importance. **2** a person. **3** a character in a book, play, etc. [< OF]

per·so·na gra·ta (pər sō′nə grä′tə, grat′ə, or grā′tə) *Latin.* an acceptable person.

per·son·al (pėr′sən əl or pėrs′nəl) *adj.* **1** individual; private: *a personal letter.* **2** done in person; directly by oneself, not through others or by letter: *a personal visit.* **3** of the body or bodily appearance: *personal beauty.* **4** about or against a person or persons: *personal abuse.* **5** inclined to make remarks to or ask questions of others: *Don't be too personal.* **6** in grammar, showing person. *I, we, thou, you, he, she, it*, and *they* are **personal pronouns.** **7** in law, of or having to do with possessions that can be moved, not land or buildings. —*n.* a short paragraph in a newspaper about a particular person or persons. [< LL *personalis*]

personal equation individual tendencies for which allowance should be made.

per·son·al·i·ty (pėr′sə nal′ə tē) *n.* **-ties. 1** the personal or individual quality that makes one person be different or act differently from another: *A baby two weeks old does not have much personality.* **2** the qualities of a person: *The boy is developing a fine personality.* **3** a remark made about or against some person: *Personalities are not in good taste in general conversation.* **4** a person; personage. **5** the quality or state of being a person, not a thing. —**Syn. 1** See **character.**

per·son·al·ize (pėr′sən əl īz′) *v.* **-ized, -iz·ing. 1** make personal. **2** personify. —**per′son·al·i·za′tion,** *n.*

per·son·al·ly (pėr′sən əl ē or pėrs′nəl ē) *adv.* **1** in person; not by the aid of others: *The hostess personally saw to the comforts of her guests.* **2** as far as oneself is concerned. **3** as a person: *We like him personally, but dislike his way of living.*

personal property property that is not land, buildings, mines, or forests; movable possessions.

per·son·al·ty (pėr′sən əl tē) *n.* **-ties.** in law, personal property.

per·so·na non gra·ta (pər sō′nə non grät′ə, grat′ə, or grā′tə) *Latin.* a person who is not acceptable.

per·son·ate (pėr′sən āt′) *v.* **-at·ed, -at·ing. 1** act the part of (a character in a play, etc.). **2** act; play a part. **3** in law, pretend to be (someone else), usually for purposes of fraud. [< obs. *personate*, adj., feigned < L *personatus* < *persona* a mask] —**per′son·a′tor,** *n.*

per·son·a·tion (pėr′sən ā′shən) *n.* **1** a personating. **2** a personifying.

per·son·i·fi·ca·tion (pər son′ə fə kā′shən) *n.* **1** a striking example; type: *A miser is the personification of greed.* **2** a representing as a person, such as speaking of the sun as *he* and the moon as *she.* **3** a person or creature imagined as representing a thing or idea: *Satan is the personification of evil.* **4** a figure of speech in which a lifeless thing or quality is spoken of as if alive.

per·son·i·fy (pər son′ə fī′) *v.* **-fied, -fy·ing. 1** be a type of; embody: *Satan personifies evil.* **2** regard or represent as a person. We often personify the sun and moon, referring to the sun as *he* and the moon as *she.*

per·son·nel (pėr′sə nel′) *n.* persons employed in any work, business, or service. [< F *personnel* personal; adj. used as n.]

per·spec·tive (pər spek′tiv) *n.* **1 a** the art of picturing objects on a flat surface so as to give the appearance of distance. **b** a drawing or picture in perspective. **2** the effect of distance on the appearance of objects. **3** the effect of the distance of events upon the mind: *Many happenings of last year seem less important when viewed in perspective.* **4** a view of things or facts in which they are in the right relations. **5** a view in front; distant view. —*adj.* drawn so as to show the proper perspective. [< Med.L *perspectiva (ars)* (science) of optics, ult. < L *per-* through + *specere* look]

hat, āge, cãre, fär; let, ēqual, tėrm; it, īce
hot, ōpen, ôrder; oil, out; cup, pu̇t, rüle, ūse
əbove, takən, pencəl, lemən, circəs
ch, child; ng, long; sh, ship
th, thin; ᴛʜ, then; zh, measure

per·spi·ca·cious (pėr′spə kā′shəs) *adj.* keen in observing and understanding; discerning: *a perspicacious judgment.* [< L *perspicax, -acis* sharp-sighted, ult. < *per-* through + *specere* to look] —**per′spi·ca′cious·ly,** *adv.* —**Syn.** shrewd, acute.

per·spi·cac·i·ty (pėr′spə kas′ə tē) *n.* keen perception; discernment; wisdom and understanding in dealing with people or with facts.

per·spi·cu·i·ty (pėr′spə kū′ə tē) *n.* clearness in expression; ease in being understood. —**Syn.** lucidity, plainness.

per·spic·u·ous (pər spik′ū əs) *adj.* clear; easily understood: *a perspicuous style.* [< L *perspicuus*, ult. < *per-* through + *specere* look] —**per·spic′u·ous·ly,** *adv.* —**per·spic′u·ous·ness,** *n.*

per·spi·ra·tion (pėr′spə rā′shən) *n.* **1** sweat. **2** a sweating or perspiring. —**Syn. 1** See **sweat.**

per·spire (pər spīr′) *v.* **-spired, -spir·ing.** sweat. [< L *perspirare* < *per-* through + *spirare* breathe]

per·suade (pər swād′) *v.* **-suad·ed, -suad·ing. 1** win over to do or believe; make willing or sure by urging, arguing, etc. **2** convince: *I am persuaded that death does not end all.* [< L *persuadere* < *per-* strongly + *suadere* urge] —**per·suad′er,** *n.*

Syn. 1 Persuade, convince = get someone to do or believe something. **Persuade** emphasizes winning a person over to a desired belief or action by strong urging, arguing, advising, and appealing to his feelings as well as to his mind: *I knew I should study, but he persuaded me to go to the movies.* **Convince** emphasizes overcoming a person's objections or disbelief by proof or arguments appealing to his reason and understanding: *I have convinced her that she needs a vacation, but cannot persuade her to take one.*

per·sua·si·ble (pər swā′sə bəl) *adj.* that can be persuaded; open to persuasion.

per·sua·sion (pər swā′zhən) *n.* **1** a persuading: *All our persuasion was of no use; she would not come.* **2** the power of persuading. **3** a firm belief: *He and his brother were of different political persuasions.* **4 a** a religious belief; creed: *All Christians are not of the same persuasion.* **b** a body of persons holding a particular religious belief; sect; denomination. **5** *Humorous.* kind; sort. [ME < L *persuasio, -onis* < *persuadere.* See PERSUADE.] —**Syn. 3** conviction.

per·sua·sive (pər swā′siv or pər swā′ziv) *adj.* able, intended, or fitted to persuade: *The salesman had a very persuasive way of talking.* —**per·sua′sive·ly,** *adv.* —**per·sua′sive·ness,** *n.* —**Syn.** winning, moving.

pert (pėrt) *adj.* **1** too forward or free in speech or action; saucy; bold. **2** *Informal.* lively; in good health or spirits. [for *apert*, ME < OF *apert* open < L *apertus*; influenced by OF *aspert* expert] —**pert′ly,** *adv.* —**pert′ness,** *n.* **Syn. 1** impudent, impertinent.

per·tain (pər tān′) *v.* **1** belong or be connected as a part, possession, etc.: *We own the house and the land pertaining to it.* **2** refer; be related: *"Pertaining to school" means "having to do with school."* **3** be appropriate: *We had turkey and everything else that pertains to Thanksgiving Day.* [ME < OF < L *pertinere* < *per-* across + *tenere* reach]

per·thite (pėr′thīt) *n.* a type of feldspar. [< *Perth*, Ontario, where it occurs]

per·ti·na·cious (pėr′tə nā′shəs) *adj.* **1** holding firmly to a purpose, action, or opinion; very persistent: *A bulldog is a very pertinacious fighter.* **2** stubborn to excess;

obstinate. 3 obstinately or persistently continuing; not yielding to treatment: *a pertinacious cough.* [< L *pertinacia* firmness < *per-* very + *tenax, -acis* tenacious] **—per′ti·na′cious·ly,** *adv.* **—per′ti·na′cious·ness,** *n.* **—Syn. 1** determined, dogged, stubborn.

per·ti·nac·i·ty (pėr′tə nas′ə tē) *n.* great persistence; holding firmly to a purpose, action, or opinion.

per·ti·nence (pėr′tə nəns) *n.* a being to the point; fitness; relevance: *The pertinence of the boy's replies showed that he was not stupid.*

per·ti·nen·cy (pėr′tə nən sē) *n.* pertinence.

per·ti·nent (pėr′tə nənt) *adj.* having to do with what is being considered; relating to the matter in hand; to the point. [< L *pertinens, -entis,* ppr. of *pertinere* pertain. See PERTAIN.] **—per′ti·nent·ly,** *adv.*
Syn. Pertinent, relevant = relating to the matter in hand. **Pertinent** = directly to the point of the matter, belonging properly and fittingly to what is being considered and helping to explain or solve it: *He asked for all the pertinent information about the events leading up to this situation.* **Relevant** = having some bearing on the problem or enough connection with it to have some meaning or importance: *Even incidents seeming unimportant in themselves might be relevant.*

per·turb (pər tėrb′) *v.* disturb greatly; make uneasy or troubled: *The doctor was much perturbed by his patient's relapse.* [< L *perturbare* < *per-* thoroughly + *turbare* confuse] **—per·turb′er,** *n.* **—Syn.** excite, agitate, trouble, distress.

per·tur·ba·tion (pėr′tər bā′shən) *n.* **1** a perturbing. **2** a perturbed condition. **3** a thing, act, or event that causes this condition.

pe·ruke (pə rük′) *n.* a wig. Men in the 17th and 18th centuries wore perukes. [< F *perruque*]

pe·rus·al (pə rüz′əl) *n.* a perusing; reading: *the perusal of a letter.*

pe·ruse (pə rüz′) *v.* **-rused, -rus·ing. 1** read thoroughly and carefully. **2** read. **3** examine, inspect, or consider in detail. [originally, use up, < L *per-* to the end + E *use*]

Pe·ru·vi·an (pə rü′vē ən) *adj.* of or having to do with Peru, a country on the western coast of South America, or its people. *—n.* a native or inhabitant of Peru.

Peruvian bark a bark from which quinine is obtained; cinchona.

per·vade (pər vād′) *v.* **-vad·ed, -vad·ing. 1** go or spread throughout; be throughout: *The odor of pines pervades the air.* **2** be found throughout (the body of a work, etc.), so as to characterize, flavor unmistakably, etc.: *The author's anger at injustice pervades the whole novel.* [< L *pervadere* < *per-* through + *vadere* go] **—per·vad′er,** *n.* **Syn. 1** penetrate, permeate, impregnate.

per·va·sion (pər vā′zhən) *n.* a pervading or being pervaded; permeation.

per·va·sive (pər vā′siv or pər vā′ziv) *adj.* **1** tending to pervade. **2** having power to pervade. **—per·va′sive·ly,** *adv.* **—per·va′sive·ness,** *n.*

per·verse (pər vėrs′) *adj.* **1** contrary and willful; stubborn: *The perverse child did just what we told him not to do.* **2** persistent in wrong. **3** wicked. **4** not correct; wrong: *perverse reasoning.* [< L *perversus* turned away, pp. of *pervertere.* See PERVERT.] **—per·verse′ly,** *adv.* **—per·verse′ness,** *n.* **—Syn. 1** obstinate, wayward.

per·ver·sion (pər vėr′zhən or pər vėr′shən) *n.* **1** a turning or being turned to what is wrong; change to what is unnatural, abnormal, or wrong: *A tendency to eat sand is a perversion of appetite.* **2** a perverted form.

per·ver·si·ty (pər vėr′sə tē) *n.* **-ties. 1** the quality of being perverse. **2** a perverse character or conduct.

per·vert (*v.* pər vėrt′; *n.* pėr′vėrt) *v.* **1** lead or turn from the right way or from the truth: *Reading comic books often perverts our taste for good books.* **2** give a wrong meaning to: *His enemies perverted his friendly remark and made it into an insult.* **3** use for wrong purposes or in a wrong way: *A clever criminal perverts his talents.* **4** change from what is natural or normal, now especially what is generally accepted or defined by law as natural or normal in sexual behavior.
—n. a perverted person, now especially one who practises sexual perversion. [< L *pervertere* < *per-* (intensive) + *vertere* turn] **—per·vert′er,** *n.* **—Syn.** *v.* **1** corrupt, debase, deprave. **2** misinterpret, distort, falsify.

per·vi·ous (pėr′vē əs) *adj.* **1** giving passage or entrance: *Sand is easily pervious to water.* **2** open to influence, argument, etc. [< L *pervius* < *per-* through + *via* way] **—per′vi·ous·ness,** *n.*

pe·sa·wa (pə sä′wə) *n.* **1** a unit of money in Ghana, worth 1/100 of a cedi. **2** a coin worth one pesawa.

pe·se·ta (pə sā′tə) *n.* **1** a unit of money in Spain. See table at **money. 2** a coin worth one peseta. [< Sp., dim. of *peso*]

pes·ky (pes′kē) *adj.* **-ki·er, -ki·est.** *Informal.* troublesome; annoying. [? alteration of *pesty* < *pest*]

pe·so (pā′sō) *n.* **-sos. 1** a unit of money in Mexico, Cuba, the Philippines, Bolivia, Colombia, Argentina, Uruguay, and the Dominican Republic. See table at **money. 2** a note or coin worth one peso. [< Sp. < L *pensum,* pp. of *pendere* weigh]

pes·si·mism (pes′ə miz′əm) *n.* **1** a tendency to look on the dark side of things or to see difficulties and disadvantages. **2** a belief that things naturally tend to evil, or that life is not worth while. [< L *pessimus* worst + *-ism*]

pes·si·mist (pes′ə mist) *n.* **1** a person inclined to see all the difficulties and disadvantages or to look on the dark side of things. **2** a person who thinks that life holds more evil than good, and so is not worth living.

pes·si·mis·tic (pes′ə mis′tik) *adj.* **1** disposed to take a gloomy view of things and to see the dark side of life. **2** believing that life holds more evil than good, and so is not worth while. **—pes′si·mis′ti·cal·ly,** *adv.* **—Syn. 1** See **cynical.**

pest (pest) *n.* **1** any thing or person that causes trouble, injuries, or destruction; nuisance: *Mosquitoes are pests.* **2** *Archaic.* pestilence. [< L *pestis* plague] **—Syn. 1** annoyance.

pes·ter (pes′tər) *v.* annoy; trouble; vex: *Flies pester us.* [apparently < OF *empestrer* hobble (an animal); influenced by *pest*] **—pes′ter·er,** *n.* **—Syn.** See **tease.**

pest·house (pest′hous′) *n. Archaic.* a hospital for persons ill with highly infectious and dangerous diseases.

pes·ti·cide (pes′tə sīd′) *n.* any chemical agent or other substance used to destroy plant or animal pests. [< L *pestis* plague, pest + E *-cide;* probably patterned on *insecticide*]

pes·tif·er·ous (pes tif′ər əs) *adj.* **1** bringing disease or infection. **2** bringing moral evil: *the pestiferous influence of a bad example.* **3** *Informal.* troublesome; annoying. [< L *pestiferus* < *pestis* plague + *ferre* bring]

pes·ti·lence (pes′tə ləns) *n.* a disease that spreads rapidly, causing many deaths. Smallpox, yellow fever, and cholera are pestilences. **—Syn.** epidemic, pest.

pes·ti·lent (pes′tə lənt) *adj.* **1** often causing death: *a pestilent disease.* **2** harmful to morals; destroying peace: *a pestilent den of vice, the pestilent effects of war.* **3** troublesome; annoying. [< L *pestilens, -entis* < *pestis* pest] **—pes′ti·lent·ly,** *adv.*

pes·ti·len·tial (pes′tə len′shəl) *adj.* **1** like a pestilence; having to do with pestilences. **2** carrying infection. **3** harmful; dangerous. **—pes′ti·len′tial·ly,** *adv.*

pes·tle (pes′əl) *n. v.* **-tled, -tling.** *—n.* **1** a tool for pounding or crushing substances into a powder in a mortar. See **mortar** for picture. **2** any of various mechanical appliances for pounding, stamping, pressing, etc., as a vertically moving or pounding part in a machine. *—v.* pound or crush with a pestle. [ME < OF *pestel* < L *pistillum,* ult. < *pinsere* pound. Doublet of PISTIL.]

pet[1] (pet) *n. adj. v.* **pet·ted, pet·ting.** *—n.* **1** an animal kept as a favorite and treated with affection. **2** a darling; a favorite.
—adj. **1** treated as a pet. **2** showing affection: *a pet name.* **3** darling; favorite. **4** *Informal.* particular; special: *a pet aversion, a pet theory, a pet phrase.*
—v. **1** treat as a pet. **2** stroke; pat; touch lovingly and gently. **3** yield to the wishes of; indulge. [< Scots Gaelic *peata*] **—Syn.** *v.* coddle, pamper.

pet[2] (pet) *n.* a fit of peevishness; fretful discontent. [origin uncertain]

pet·al (pet′əl) *n.* one of the parts of a flower that are usually colored; one of the leaves of a corolla. A daisy has many petals. See **sepal** for picture. [< NL < Gk. *petalon* leaf, originally neut. adj., outspread]

-pet·alled or **-pet·aled** (pet′əld) *combining form.* having —— petals: *six-petalled* = *having six petals.*

pe·tard (pi tärd′) *n.* **1** an explosive device formerly used in warfare to break doors or gates. **2 hoist with** (or **on**) **one's own petard,** injured or destroyed by one's own scheme or device for the ruin of others. [< F *pétard* < *péter* break wind, ult. < L *pedere*]

pet·cock (pet′kok′) *n.* a small tap for draining a pipe or cylinder, releasing pressure, etc. [< obs. *pet* < F *péter* break wind + *cock*[1]]

A petcock

pe·ter (pē′tər) *v. Informal.* **peter out,** gradually come to an end; fail; give out. [origin unknown]

Pe·ter·bor·ough or **Pe·ter·bor·o** (pē′tər bėr′ə) *n. Cdn.* a type of canoe made from wood or birchbark, formerly manufactured at Peterborough, Ontario.

Pe·ter·head or **pe·ter·head** (pē′tər hed′) *n. Cdn.* a decked launch or large whaleboat equipped with a sail and a small motor, much used by Eskimos and others in the Eastern Arctic. Also, **Peterhead boat.** [< *Peterhead*, Scotland, where early boats of this type were made]

pet·i·o·late (pet′ē ə lāt′) *adj.* having a petiole.

pet·i·ole (pet′ē ōl′) *n.* **1** in botany, the slender stalk by which a leaf is attached to the stem. **2** in zoology, a stalklike part. A petiole connects the thorax and abdomen of a wasp. [< L *petiolus*, dim. of *pes, pedis* foot]

PETIOLE
STEM

pet·it (pet′ē) *adj. Used now only in legal phrases.* small; petty; minor: *petit larceny.* [< F *petit* < VL stem *pit-* little. Doublet of PETTY.]

petit bourgeois (pə tē bür zhwä′) *pl.* **petits bourgeois** (pə tē bür zhwä′). *French.* **1** a member of the lower middle class. **2** the lower middle class.

pe·tite (pə tēt′) *adj.* little; of small size; tiny, especially with reference to a woman or girl. [< F *petite*, fem. of *petit* little]

pet·it four (pet′ē fôr′) *pl.* **pet·its fours** (pet′ē fôrz′). a small fancy cake with decorative frosting. [< F *petit four* little oven]

pe·ti·tion (pə tish′ən) *n.* **1** a formal request to a superior or to one in authority for some privilege, right, benefit, etc.: *The people signed a petition asking the city council for a new sidewalk.* **2** in law, a written application for an order of court for some action by a judge. **3** a prayer. **4** that which is requested or prayed for. **5** the act of formally asking or humbly requesting.
—*v.* **1** ask earnestly; make a petition to: *They petitioned the mayor to use his influence with the city council.* **2** pray. [< L *petitio, -onis* < *petere* seek] —**pe·ti′tion·er,** *n.* —**Syn.** *n.* **1** suit, entreaty, supplication. -*v.* **1** entreat, beg.

pe·ti·tion·ar·y (pə tish′ən er′ē) *adj.* of a petition.

petit jury a group of persons sworn, in a court of law, to deliver a verdict on the basis of evidence presented to them; trial jury. Opposed to **grand jury.**

petit larceny petty larceny.

pe·tit mal (pə tē mal′ or -mäl′) a mild type of epilepsy. [< F]

pet·it point (pet′ē point′) **1** an embroidery stitch used in fine, decorative needlework. **2** a tapestry made in this stitch. [< F *petit* small + *point* stitch]

pet·rel (pet′rəl) *n.* any of various sea birds, especially a small black-and-white bird having long, pointed wings. [apparently dim. of St. *Peter*, who walked on the sea]

Petri dish or **petri dish** (pā′trē or pē′trē) a round, shallow, glass container used in laboratories to hold bacteria cultures. [< Julius *Petri*, 1852-1922, a German bacteriologist, who invented it]

pet·ri·fac·tion (pet′rə fak′shən) *n.* **1** the process of petrifying. **2** the condition or quality of being petrified. **3** something petrified.

pet·ri·fi·ca·tion (pet′rə fə kā′shən) *n.* petrifaction.

hat, āge, cãre, fär; let, ēqual, tėrm; it, īce
hot, ōpen, ôrder; oil, out; cup, pủt, rüle, ūse
əbove, takən, pencəl, lemən, circəs
ch, child; ng, long; sh, ship
th, thin; ᴛʜ, then; zh, measure

Petrified Forest an ancient forest in Arizona whose trees have turned to stone.

pet·ri·fy (pet′rə fī′) *v.* **-fied, -fy·ing. 1** replace normal organic cells with a mineral such as silica; turn into stone; become stone. **2** harden; stiffen; deaden. **3** paralyse with fear, horror, or surprise: *The bird was petrified as the snake came near.* [< F *pétrifier*, ult. < L *petra* stone < Gk.] —**Syn. 1** fossilize.

petro- *combining form.* **1** rock: *petroglyph* = *a rock carving.* **2** petroleum: *petrochemical* = *a chemical made of or from petroleum.* [< Gk. *petra* rock]

pet·ro·chem·i·cal (pet′rō kem′ə kəl) *n.* a chemical made or derived from petroleum. —*adj.* of or having to do with petrochemicals or petrochemistry.

pet·ro·glyph (pet′rə glif′) *n.* a carving or inscription on rock. [< F *petroglyphe* < Gk. *petra* rock + *glyphē* a carving]

pet·ro·graph (pet′rə graf′) *n.* a painting or inscription on rock.

pe·trog·ra·phy (pi trog′rə fē) *n.* the branch of geology that deals with the description and classification of rocks. [< Gk. *petra* rock, *petros* stone + E *-graphy*]

pet·rol (pet′rəl) *n. Esp.Brit.* gasoline. [< F < Med.L *petroleum.* Doublet of PETROLEUM.]

pet·ro·la·tum (pet′rə lā′təm) *n.* **1** a salve or ointment made from petroleum. **2** mineral oil. [< NL < E *petrol*]

pe·tro·le·um (pə trō′lē əm) *n.* an oily, dark-colored, inflammable liquid consisting mainly of a mixture of various hydrocarbons, found in the earth. Gasoline, kerosene, and paraffin are made from petroleum. [< Med.L < Gk. *petra* rock, *petros* stone + L *oleum* oil. Doublet of PETROL.]

pe·trol·o·gy (pi trol′ə jē) *n.* the branch of geology that deals with rocks, including their origin, structure, changes, etc. [< Gk. *petra* rock, *petros* stone + E *-logy*]

pet·ti·coat (pet′ē kōt′) *n.* **1** an underskirt, often stiffened and trimmed with lace, flounces, etc. **2** a skirt. **3** *Slang.* a woman; girl. —*adj.* female; feminine: *petticoat government.* [originally, *petty coat* little coat]

pet·ti·fog·ger (pet′ē fog′ər) *n.* **1** an inferior lawyer who uses petty, mean, cheating methods. **2** any inferior person who uses petty, mean, cheating methods. [apparently < *petty* + *fogger* (origin unknown)]

pet·ti·fog·ging (pet′ē fog′ing) *adj.* tricky. —*n.* trickery.

pet·tish (pet′ish) *adj.* peevish; cross: *a pettish reply, a pettish child.* [< *pet*[2]] —**pet′tish·ly,** *adv.* —**pet′tish·ness,** *n.*

pet·ty (pet′ē) *adj.* **-ti·er, -ti·est. 1** having little importance or value; small: *She insisted on telling me all her petty troubles.* **2** mean; narrow-minded. **3** lower; subordinate. [ME < OF *petit* < VL stem *pit-* little. Doublet of PETIT.] —**pet′ti·ly,** *adv.* —**pet′ti·ness,** *n.* —**Syn. 1** trifling, trivial, slight, paltry, insignificant. **3** minor.

petty cash 1 small sums of money spent or received. **2** a sum of money kept on hand to pay small expenses.

petty jury petit jury.

petty larceny a theft in which the value of the property taken is less than a certain amount.

petty officer in the navy, a noncommissioned officer senior to a leading seaman and junior to a chief petty officer. *Abbrev.*: P.O.

pet·u·lance (pech′ủ ləns) *n.* the quality or state of being irritated by trifles; peevishness; bad humor.

pet·u·lan·cy (pech′ủ lən sē) *n.* petulance.

pet·u·lant (pech′ủ lənt) *adj.* peevish; subject to little fits of bad temper; irritable over trifles. [< L *petulans, -antis*, ult. < *petere* seek, aim at] —**pet′u·lant·ly,** *adv.*

Pe·tun (pə tün′) *n.* **1** an extinct North American Indian people who lived between Lakes Huron and Ontario, noted for their tobacco cultivation and trade. **2** a member of this people. 3 the Iroquoian dialect of this people. [< Cdn.F < MF *petun* tobacco]

pe·tu·ni·a (pə tū′nē ə, pə tūn′yə or pə tü′nē ə) *n.* **1** a plant having funnel-shaped flowers of white, pink, and various shades of purple. **2** the flower. [< NL < F *petun* tobacco < South Am.Ind.]

pew (pū) *n.* in a church, a bench for people to sit on, fastened to the floor and provided with a back. In some churches the pews are separated by partitions. [ME < OF *puie* < L *podia*, pl. of *podium* elevated place, balcony. See PODIUM.]

pe·wee (pē′wē) *n.* **1** a small North American bird having an olive-colored or gray back. **2** peewee. [imitative]

pe·wit (pē′wit or pū′it) *n.* **1** the lapwing. **2** the European black-headed gull. [imitative]

pew·ter (pū′tər) *n.* **1** an alloy of tin with lead, copper, or other metals. **2** a dish, etc. made of this alloy. —*adj.* made of pewter. [ME < OF *peutre*]

pey·o·te (pā ō′tē; *Spanish*, pā yō′tā) *n.* **1** any of various cactuses, especially mescal. **2** a hallucinogenic drug found in the small pods, or buttons, of the mescal, used as a stimulant by various American Indians; mescaline. [< Mexican Sp. *peyote* < Nahuatl *peyotl*, literally, a caterpillar; from the mescal's soft, furry centre]

pf. 1 pfennig. **2** preferred.

Pfc. *U.S.* private first class.

pfd. preferred.

pfen·nig (pfen′ig) *n.* **pfen·nigs, pfen·ni·ge** (pfen′i gə). **1** a unit of money in West Germany, worth 1/100 of a Deutsche mark. **2** a unit of money in East Germany, worth 1/100 of a mark. **3** a coin worth one pfennig. [< G]

pfg. pfennig.

pg. page

Pg. 1 Portugal. **2** Portuguese.

pH in chemistry, a symbol used to express acid or alkaline content, used in testing water and soils, for various applications in industry, etc. A pH of 14 denotes high alkaline content, and a pH of 0 indicates high acidity; pH 7 is taken as neutral. [< *p*otential of *H*ydrogen]

Ph phenyl.

Pha·ë·thon (fā′ə thon′ or fā′ə tən) *n.* in Greek mythology, the son of Helios, who tried for one day to drive the sun, his father's chariot. He so nearly set the earth on fire that Zeus had to strike him dead with a thunderbolt.

pha·e·ton (fā′ə tən) *n.* **1** a light, four-wheeled carriage with or without a top. **2** an open automobile of the touring-car type. [< F *phaéton*, after *Phaëthon*, son of Helios]

-phage *combining form.* eating; devouring, as in *bacteriophage.* [< Gk. *phagein* eat]

phag·o·cyte (fag′ə sīt′) *n.* in physiology, a white blood corpuscle, or leucocyte, capable of absorbing and destroying waste or harmful material, such as disease microbes. [< Gk. *-phagos* -eating + E *-cyte* cell (< Gk. *kytos* hollow container)]

pha·lan·ger (fə lan′jər) *n.* a small, tree-climbing marsupial of the Australian region. [< NL < Gk. *phalangion* spiderweb < *phalanx, -angos* spider; with reference to webbed toes]

pha·lanx (fal′angks or fā′langks) *n.* **pha·lanx·es** or **pha·lan·ges** (fə lan′jēz). **1** in ancient Greece, a special battle formation of infantry fighting in close ranks with their shields joined and long spears overlapping each other. **2** a compact or closely massed body of persons, animals, or things. **3** a number of persons united for a common purpose. **4** in anatomy and zoology, any bone in the fingers or toes. [< L < Gk.]

phal·a·rope (fal′ə rōp′) *n.* **phal·a·rope.** any of three species of small birds that are good swimmers. The male phalarope rears the young. [< F < NL, ult. < Gk. *phalaros* white-crested + *pous, podos* foot]

phal·lic (fal′ik) *adj.* of or having to do with a phallus; symbolic of male generative power. [< Gk. *phallikós* < *phallós* penis, phallus]

phal·lus (fal′əs) *n.* **phal·li** (fal′ī). **1** an image or model of the penis, symbolizing the generative power of nature. **2** the penis. [< L *phallus* < Gk. *phallós* penis, phallus]

phan·tasm (fan′taz əm) *n.* **1** a thing seen only in one's imagination; unreal fancy: *the phantasms of a dream.* **2** a supposed appearance of an absent person, living or dead. **3** a deceiving likeness (of something). [< L < Gk. *phantasma* image, ult. < *phainein* show. Doublet of PHANTOM.]

phan·tas·ma·go·ri·a (fan taz′mə gô′rē ə) *n.* **1** a shifting scene of real things, illusions, imaginary fancies, deceptions, and the like: *the phantasmagoria of a dream.* **2** a display of optical illusions in which figures increase or decrease in size, fade away, and pass into each other. [< Gk. *phantasma* image + ? *agora* assembly]

phan·tas·mal (fan taz′məl) *adj.* of a phantasm; unreal; imaginary.

phan·ta·sy (fan′tə sē or fan′tə zē) *n.* **-sies.** fantasy.

phan·tom (fan′təm) *n.* **1** an image of the mind: *phantoms of a dream.* **2** a vague, dim, or shadowy appearance; ghost. **3** a mere show; appearance without material substance. —*adj.* like a ghost; unreal: *a phantom ship.* [ME < OF *fantosme* < VL < Gk. *phantasma* image. Doublet of PHANTASM.] —**Syn.** *n.* **2** apparition, spectre.

Phar·aoh (fãr′ō) *n.* a title given to the kings of ancient Egypt.

Phar·i·sa·ic (far′ə sā′ik) *adj.* **1** of or having to do with the Pharisees. **2 pharisaic, a** making an outward show of religion or morals without the real spirit. **b** thinking oneself more moral than others; hypocritical.

phar·i·sa·i·cal (far′ə sā′ə kəl) *adj.* pharisaic. —**phar′i·sa′i·cal·ly,** *adv.*

Phar·i·sa·ism (far′ə sā iz′əm) *n.* **1** the doctrine and practice of the Pharisees. **2 pharisaism, a** rigid observance of the external forms of religion without genuine piety. **b** self-righteousness; hypocrisy.

Phar·i·see (far′ə sē′ or fer′ə sē′) *n.* **1** in ancient times, a member of a Jewish sect that was very strict in keeping to tradition and the laws of its religion. **2 pharisee, a** a person who makes a show of religion rather than following its spirit. **b** a person who considers himself much better than other men. [OE *farisē* < L *pharisaeus* < Gk. *pharisaios* < Aramaic *perishaiya* separated]

phar·i·see·ism (far′ə sē iz′əm) *n.* pharisaism.

phar·ma·ceu·tic (fãr′mə sü′tik) *adj.* pharmaceutical. [< LL < Gk. *pharmakeutikos*, ult. < *pharmakon* drug, poison]

phar·ma·ceu·ti·cal (fãr′mə sü′tə kəl) *adj.* having to do with pharmacy. —*n.* a medicinal drug.

phar·ma·ceu·tics (fãr′mə sü′tiks) *n.* pharmacy (def. 1).

phar·ma·cist (fãr′mə sist) *n.* a chemist who prepares drugs, medicines, etc.; druggist.

phar·ma·col·o·gist (fãr′mə kol′ə jist) *n.* a person who is skilled in the science of drugs.

phar·ma·col·o·gy (fãr′mə kol′ə jē) *n.* the science of drugs, their preparation, uses, and effects. [< Gk. *pharmakon* drug + E *-logy*]

phar·ma·co·poe·ia (fãr′mə kə pē′ə) *n.* **1** a book containing an official list and description of drugs and medicines. **2** a stock or collection of drugs. [< Gk. *pharmakopoiia* < *pharmakon* drug + *poieein* make]

phar·ma·cy (fãr′mə sē) *n.* **-cies. 1** the preparation and dispensing of drugs and medicines; occupation of a druggist. **2** a drugstore. **3** the department of a hospital where drugs, medicines, etc. are prepared. [< LL < Gk. *pharmakeia*, ult. < *pharmakon* drug]

Phar·os (fãr′os) *n.* a small peninsula in N. Egypt. In ancient times, it was an island with a famous lighthouse.

pha·ryn·gal (fə ring′gəl) *adj.* pharyngeal.

pha·ryn·ge·al (fə rin′jē əl or far′in jē′əl) *adj.* **1** of or having to do with or connected with the pharynx. **2** in phonetics, articulated in the pharynx. —*n.* a sound articulated in the pharynx. Also, **pharyngal.**

phar·yn·gi·tis (far′in jī′tis) *n.* an inflammation of the mucous membrane of the pharynx. [< NL < Gk. *pharynx, -yngos* pharynx + *-itis*]

phar·ynx (far′ingks) *n.* **phar·ynx·es** or **pha·ryn·ges** (fə rin′jēs). in anatomy, the tube or cavity that connects the mouth with the esophagus. In mammals, the pharynx contains the opening from the mouth, the opening of the esophagus, of the larynx, and of the passages from the nose. [< NL < Gk.]

phase (fāz) *n.* **1** one of the changing states or stages of development of a person or thing: *The pupa is a phase in the life cycle of the moth.* **2** one side, part, or view (of a subject): *What phase of mathematics are you studying now?* **3** in astronomy, the apparent shape of the moon or of a planet at a given time. The new moon, first quarter, full moon, and last quarter are four phases of the moon. **4** in physics, a particular stage or point in a recurring sequence of movements or changes, considered in relation to a starting point of normal position: *The current in all parts of a series circuit is in the same phase.* **5** one of the states, especially of coloration, of fur, plumage, etc., characteristic of certain animals at certain seasons or ages; color phase: *Ermine is the fur of a weasel in its winter phase.* **6** in biology, one of the distinct stages in meiosis or mitosis.
—*v.* **1** plan an enterprise or project in orderly stages: *a phased withdrawal of troops.* **2. phase in,** bring about an innovation or reform of existing conditions in orderly stages. **3 phase out,** eliminate an old system, order, etc. gradually, in planned stages. [< NL < Gk. *phasis* appearance < *phainein* show]

Ph.B. Bachelor of Philosophy. (for L *Philosophiae Baccalaureus*)

Ph.D. Doctor of Philosophy. (for L *Philosophiae Doctor*)

pheas·ant (fez′ənt) *n.* **-ants** or (*esp. collectively*) **-ant.** a game bird having a long tail and brilliant feathers. Wild pheasants live in many parts of Europe and America. [ME < AF < Provençal *faisan* < L < Gk. *phasianos*, literally, Phasian; with reference to the river Phasis in Colchis]

phe·nac·e·tin (fə nas′ə tin) *n.* a white crystalline powder used to relieve fever and pain. *Formula*: $C_{10}H_{13}NO_2$ [< Gk. *phainein* show + E *acet(ic)*]

Phe·ni·cia (fə nish′ə) *n.* Phoenicia.

phe·nix (fē′niks) *n.* phoenix.

phe·no·bar·bi·tal (fē′nō bär′bə tol′ or -bär′bə tôl′) *n.* a white powder, used as a hypnotic or sedative.

phe·nol (fē′nol or fē′nōl) *n.* carbolic acid. [< Gk. *phainein* show + E *-ol*, chemical suffix (shortened form of *alcohol*)]

phe·nol·ic (fə nol′ik) *adj.* of, like, or pertaining to phenol. —*n.* in chemistry, any of a group of synthetic plastics or resins, used in varnishes, coatings, etc.

phe·nol·phthal·ein (fē′nōl thal′ēn or fē′nōl fthal′ēn) *n.* a white powder used in testing acidity, making dyes, medicines, etc. Its solution is red when basic, colorless when acid. *Formula*: $C_{20}H_{14}O_4$

phe·nom·e·na (fə nom′ə nə) *n.* pl. of **phenomenon.**

phe·nom·e·nal (fə nom′ə nəl) *adj.* **1** of or having to do with a phenomenon or phenomena. **2** having the nature of a phenomenon. **3** extraordinary: *a phenomenal memory.* —**phe·nom′e·nal·ly,** *adv.*

phe·nom·e·non (fə nom′ə non′ or fə nom′ə nən) *n.* **-na** or (*esp. for def. 2*) **-nons. 1** a fact, event, or circumstance that can be observed: *Lightning is an electrical phenomenon. Fever and inflammation are phenomena of disease.* **2** something or someone extraordinary or remarkable. [< L < Gk. *phainomenon*, neut. ppr. of *phainesthai* appear]

phen·yl (fen′əl or fē′nəl) *n.* in chemistry, a univalent radical derived from benzene, that forms the basis of phenol, aniline, and other aromatic compounds. *Formula*: C_6H_5 *Abbrev.*: Ph

phew (fū) *interj.* an exclamation of disgust, impatience, etc.

phi (fī or fē) *n.* the 21st letter of the Greek alphabet (Φ, φ).

phi·al (fī′əl) *n.* a small bottle; vial. [ME < OF < LL < L *phiala* < Gk. *phialē* a broad flat vessel]

Phi Be·ta Kap·pa (fī′bā′tə kap′ə or bē′tə) an honorary society composed of college students and graduates who have ranked high in scholarship.

hat, āge, cãre, fär; let, ēqual, tėrm; it, īce
hot, ōpen, ôrder; oil, out; cup, pu̇t, rüle, ūse
əbove, takən, pencəl, lemən, circəs
ch, child; ng, long; sh, ship
th, thin; ᴛʜ, then; zh, measure

Phil. 1 Philip. **2** Philippians. **3** Philippine.

phi·lan·der (fə lan′dər) *v.* of a man, make love without serious intentions; flirt. [originally n., < Gk. *philandros* < *philos* loving + *anēr, andros* man; apparently taken as "lover"] —**phi·lan′der·er,** *n.*

phil·an·throp·ic (fil′ən throp′ik) *adj.* **1** having to do with or characterized by philanthropy. **2** charitable; benevolent; kindly.

phil·an·throp·i·cal (fil′ən throp′ə kəl) *adj.* philanthropic. —**phil′an·throp′i·cal·ly,** *adv.*

phi·lan·thro·pist (fə lan′thrə pist) *n.* a person who shows his love for mankind by practical kindness and helpfulness to humanity.

phi·lan·thro·py (fə lan′thrə pē) *n.* **-pies. 1** love of mankind shown by practical kindness and helpfulness to humanity: *The Red Cross appeals to philanthropy.* **2** a thing that benefits humanity: *A hospital is a useful philanthropy.* [< LL < Gk. *philanthrōpia*, ult. < *philos* loving + *anthrōpos* man] —**Syn. 1** benevolence, charity.

phil·a·tel·ic (fil′ə tel′ik) *adj.* of or having to do with philately.

phi·lat·e·list (fə lat′ə list) *n.* a collector of postage stamps, postmarks, cancellations, etc.

phi·lat·e·ly (fə lat′ə lē) *n.* the collecting, arranging, and study of postage stamps, postmarks, cancellations, etc. [< F *philatélie*, ult. < Gk. *philos* loving + *ateleia* exemption from tax; the stamp indicated the tax was paid]

-phile *combining form.* a lover of —— ; a person who is fond of —— : *discophile = a person who is fond of records, or disks.* Also, **phil-.** [< F *-phile*, ult. < Gk. *philos* loving]

phil·har·mon·ic (fil′här mon′ik or fil′ər mon′ik) *adj.* **1** devoted to music; loving music. A musical club is often called a philharmonic society. **2** given by a philharmonic society: *a philharmonic concert.* —*n.* **1** a philharmonic society or concert. **2 Philharmonic,** a symphony orchestra: *the London Philharmonic.* [< F *philharmonique*, ult. < Gk. *philos* loving + *harmonia* music]

Phi·lip·pic (fə lip′ik) *n.* **1** any of several orations by Demosthenes denouncing King Philip II of Macedonia and arousing the Athenians to resist Philip's growing power. **2** any of several orations by the Roman statesman, Cicero, denouncing Mark Antony. **3 philippic,** a bitter attack in words. [< L < Gk. *Philippikos* having to do with *Phillipos* Philip]

Phil·ip·pine (fil′ə pēn′) *adj.* of or having to do with the Philippines, a group of islands in the W. Pacific, or its inhabitants. Also, **Filipine, Filipino.**

Phi·lis·ti·a (fə lis′tē ə) *n.* **1** in ancient times, the land of the Philistines. **2** a place inhabited or frequented by people with uncultured tastes.

Phi·lis·tine (fə lis′tən, fil′əs tīn′ or fil′əs tēn′) *n.* **1** in ancient times, one of the warlike people in S.W. Palestine who repeatedly attacked the Israelites. **2** a person having commonplace ideas and tastes; one who is indifferent to or contemptuous of poetry, music, the fine arts, etc. —*adj.* **1** of the Philistines. **2** lacking culture; commonplace. [< LL *Philistini*, pl. < Gk. *Philistinoi* < Hebrew]

Phi·lis·tin·ism (fə lis′tən iz′əm or fil′əs tin iz′əm) *n.* the character or views of uncultured persons.

phil·o·den·dron (fil′ə den′drən) *n.* **1** any of the tropical American plants of the arum family, often grown as house plants for their thick, glossy leaves. **2** any of certain similar or related plants. [< NL *Philodendron* the genus name < Gk. *philodendron*, neut. of *philodendros* < *philos* fond of + *dendron* tree, because it clings to trees]

phil·o·log·i·cal (fil′ə loj′ə kəl) *adj.* having to do with philology.

phi·lol·o·gist (fə lol′ə jist) *n.* a person skilled in philology.

phi·lol·o·gy (fə lol′ə jē) *n.* **1** the science of language, especially historical and comparative linguistics. **2** the study of literary and other records. [< L < Gk. *philologia*, ult. < *philos* loving + *logos* word, speech, story]

phil·o·mel or **Phil·o·mel** (fil′ə mel′) *n. Poetic.* the nightingale. [< L < Gk. *Philomela*, a woman's name]

Phil·o·me·la (fil′ə mē′lə) *n.* **1** in Greek mythology, a princess who was turned into a nightingale and continued to lament the tragedy of her life. **2** *Poetic.* the nightingale.

phi·los·o·pher (fə los′ə fər) *n.* **1** a person who studies widely in philosophy. **2** a person who has a system of philosophy. **3** a person who shows the calmness of philosophy under hard conditions, accepting life and making the best of it. [ME < AF < L < Gk. *philosophos* lover of wisdom < *philos* loving + *sophos* wise]

philosophers' stone formerly, a substance believed to have the power to change base metals into gold or silver.

phil·o·soph·ic (fil′ə sof′ik) *adj.* **1** of philosophy. **2** knowing much about philosophy. **3** devoted to philosophy. **4** wise; calm; reasonable.

phil·o·soph·i·cal (fil′ə sof′ə kəl) *adj.* philosophic; like a philosopher. **—phil′o·soph′i·cal·ly,** *adv.*

phi·los·o·phize (fə los′ə fīz′) *v.* **-phized, -phiz·ing.** think or reason as a philosopher does; try to understand and explain things: *philosophize about life, death, mind, matter, God, etc.* **—phi·los′o·phiz′er,** *n.*

phi·los·o·phy (fə los′ə fē) *n.* **-phies. 1** the study of the truth or principles underlying all knowledge; study of the most general causes and principles of the universe. **2** an explanation or theory of the universe. **3** a system for guiding life, such as a body of principles of conduct, religious beliefs, or traditions. **4** the broad general principles of a particular subject: *the philosophy of history.* **5** a reasonable attitude; calmness; the practice of accepting things as they are and making the best of them. [< L < Gk. *philosophia* love of wisdom, ult. < *philos* loving + *sophos* wise]

phil·tre or **phil·ter** (fil′tər) *n.* **1** a drug or potion used to make a person fall in love. **2** a magic drink. [< F < L < Gk. *philtron* love charm, ult. < *philos* loving]

phle·bi·tis (fli bī′tis) *n.* the inflammation of a vein. [< NL < Gk. *phleps, phlebos* vein + *-itis*]

phle·bot·o·mist (fli bot′ə mist) *n.* a person who treats patients by phlebotomy.

phle·bot·o·my (fli bot′ə mē) *n.* the opening of a vein to let blood; bleeding. [ME < OF < LL < Gk. *phlebotomia*, ult. < *phleps, phlebos* vein + *-tomos* cutting]

phlegm (flem) *n.* **1** the thick discharge from the nose and throat that accompanies a cold. **2** the one of the four humors of ancient physiology believed to cause sluggishness. **3** a sluggish disposition or temperament; indifference. **4** coolness; calmness. [ME < OF < LL < Gk. *phlegma* clammy humor (resulting from heat) < *phlegein* burn]

phleg·mat·ic (fleg mat′ik) *adj.* **1** sluggish; indifferent. **2** cool; calm: *John is phlegmatic; he never seems to get excited about anything.* [< LL < Gk. *phlegmatikos* < *phlegma.* See PHLEGM.]

phleg·mat·i·cal (fleg mat′ə kəl) *adj.* phlegmatic. **—phleg·mat′i·cal·ly,** *adv.*

phlo·em or **phlo·ëm** (flō′em) *n.* in botany, the tissue in a plant or tree through which the sap containing food materials passes from one part to another; bast. [< G < Gk. *phloos* bark]

phlo·gis·ton (flō jis′tən) *n.* a supposed element causing inflammability, once thought to exist in all things that burn. [< NL < Gk. *phlogiston*, neut. adj., inflammable, ult. < *phlox, phlogos* flame]

phlox (floks) *n.* **1** a plant having clusters of showy flowers in various colors. **2** the flower. [< L < Gk. *phlox*, a kind of plant, literally, flame]

Phm.B. Bachelor of Pharmacy.

-phobe *combining form.* a person who has hatred or fear toward ——: *Anglophobe = a person who hates or fears the English or England.* [< F *phobe*, learned borrowing < L *phobus* < Gk. *phobos* panic, fear]

pho·bi·a (fō′bē ə) *n.* **1** a morbid or insane fear. **2** *Informal.* any marked dislike or aversion.

-phobia *combining form.* hatred or fear of ——: *hydrophobia = hatred or fear of water.* [< Gk. *phobia* < *phobos.* See -PHOBE.]

phoe·be (fē′bē) *n.* a small North American bird having a grayish-olive back, a yellowish breast, and a low crest on the head. [imitative, but spelling adapted to that of *Phoebe*]

Phoe·be (fē′bē) *n.* **1** in Greek mythology, the goddess of the moon. She was also called Artemis by the Greeks and Diana by the Romans. **2** *Poetic.* the moon.

Phoe·bus (fē′bəs) *n.* **1** Apollo, the Greek god of the sun. **2** *Poetic.* the sun.

Phoe·ni·cia (fə nish′ə) *n.* an ancient country in W. Syria, on the Mediterranean Sea, famous for its traders. Also, **Phenicia.**

Phoe·ni·cian (fə nish′ən) *adj.* of or having to do with Phoenicia, its people, or their language. *—n.* **1** one of the people of Phoenicia. **2** the language of Phoenicia.

phoe·nix (fē′niks) *n.* a mythical bird, the only one of its kind, said to live 500 or 600 years, to burn itself on a funeral pile, and to rise again from the ashes, fresh and beautiful, for another long life. Also, **phenix.** [ME < OF < L < Gk. *phoinix*, probably < Egyptian *bonū, bennu* heron]

phone[1] (fōn) *n. v.* **phoned, phon·ing.** *Informal.* telephone. [short for *telephone*]

phone[2] (fōn) *n.* in phonetics, a speech sound. [< Gk.]

-phone *combining form.* sound: *telephone = sound from far.* [< Gk. *phōnē* sound]

pho·neme (fō′nēm) *n.* in linguistics, one of a set of sounds used to distinguish the words of a language one from another. The words *cat* and *bat* are distinguished by their initial phonemes /k/ and /b/. A phoneme comprises several slightly different sounds (allophones), the differences between which cannot be used to distinguish one word from another. The *p* in *pin* and the *p* in *spin*, though differing slightly in pronunciation, belong to the one phoneme /p/. [< Gk. *phōnēma* a sound]

pho·net·ic (fə net′ik) *adj.* **1** of or having to do with speech sounds: *phonetic laws.* **2 a** representing the sounds of speech. In this dictionary the phonetic symbol (ə) stands for the vowel sound in the second syllable of *taken, pencil, lemon, circus.* **b** of a system of spelling, having each sound represented by one letter and each letter representing one sound: *a phonetic alphabet.* [<NL < Gk. *phōnētikos*, ult. < *phōnē* sound]

pho·net·i·cal·ly (fə net′ik lē) *adv.* in a phonetic manner; as regards the sound and not the spelling of words.

pho·ne·ti·cian (fō′nə tish′ən) *n.* a person skilled in phonetics.

pho·net·ics (fə net′iks) *n.* the science dealing with speech sounds and the art of pronunciation.

phon·ic (fon′ik or fō′nik) *adj.* **1** of sound. **2** of speech sounds; phonetic. **3** voiced. [< Gk. *phōnē* sound]

phon·ics (fon′iks or fō′niks) *n.* a way of teaching reading and spelling by means of elementary phonetics.

phono- *combining form.* sound; sounds: *phonology = the study of (speech) sounds.* [< Gk.]

pho·no·gram (fō′nə gram′) *n.* a character or symbol representing a single speech sound, syllable, or word. [< Gk. *phōnē* sound + E *-gram*]

pho·no·graph (fō′nə graf′) *n.* an instrument that reproduces recorded sounds; record player. [< Gk. *phōnē* sound + E *-graph*]

pho·no·graph·ic (fō′nə graf′ik) *adj.* **1** of a phonograph. **2** of phonography. **—pho′no·graph′i·cal·ly,** *adv.*

pho·nog·ra·phy (fō nog′rə fē) *n.* **1** the art of writing according to sound; phonetic spelling. **2** phonetic shorthand.

pho·nol·o·gist (fō nol′ə jist) *n.* an expert in phonology.

pho·nol·o·gy (fō nol′ə jē) *n.* **1** the system of sounds used in a language. **2** the study of the sounds of a language, their history and changes. [< Gk. *phōnē* sound + E *-logy*]

pho·ny (fō′ nē) *adj.* **-ni·er, -ni·est,** *n.* **-nies.** *Slang.* —*adj.* not genuine; counterfeit; fake. —*n.* a fake; pretender. [< *fawney*, a gilt brass ring used by swindlers < Irish Gaelic *fáinne* ring] —**pho′ ni·ness,** *n.*

phoo·ey (fü′ ē) *interj. Slang.* an exclamation of contempt or distaste; bah. [< Yiddish < G *pfui*]

-phore *combining form.* a thing that carries: *semaphore = a device that carries signals.* [< Gk. *-phoros* < *pherein* to bear, carry]

phos·gene (fos′ jēn) *n.* a colorless, poisonous gas, a compound of carbon monoxide and chlorine; carbonyl chloride. *Formula*: $COCl_2$ [< Gk. *phōs* light + *-genēs* born, produced]

phos·phate (fos′ fāt) *n.* **1** a salt or ester of an acid containing phosphorus. Bread contains phosphates. **2** a fertilizer containing such salts. **3** a drink made of carbonated water flavored with fruit syrup, and containing a little phosphoric acid. [< F *phosphate* < *phosphore* phosphorus]

phos·phide (fos′ fīd or fos′ fid) *n.* a compound of phosphorus with a basic element or radical.

phos·phite (fos′ fīt) *n.* a salt of phosphorous acid.

Phos·phor (fos′ fər) *n. Poetic.* the morning star, especially Venus.

phos·pho·rate (fos′ fə rāt′) *v.* **-rat·ed, -rat·ing.** combine or impregnate with phosphorus.

phos·pho·resce (fos′ fə res′) *v.* **-resced, -resc·ing.** be luminous without noticeable heat.

phos·pho·res·cence (fos′ fə res′ əns) *n.* **1** a giving out light without burning or by very slow burning that seems not to give out heat. **2** such light. **3** the property of a substance that causes this. **4** in physics, light given off by a substance as a result of the absorption of certain rays, as X rays or ultraviolet rays, and continuing for a period of time after the substance has ceased to be exposed to these rays.

phos·pho·res·cent (fos′ fə res′ ənt) *adj.* showing phosphorescence.

phos·phor·ic (fos fôr′ ik) *adj.* having to do with or containing phosphorus, especially in its higher valence.

phosphoric acid a colorless, odorless acid containing phosphorus. *Formula*: H_3PO_4

phos·pho·rous (fos′ fə rəs) *adj.* having to do with or containing phosphorus, especially in its lower valence.

phosphorous acid a colorless, unstable acid. *Formula*: H_3PO_3

phos·pho·rus (fos′ fə rəs) *n.* a solid, non-metallic chemical element existing in two forms: one yellow, poisonous, inflammable, and luminous in the dark; the other red, non-poisonous, and less inflammable. *Symbol*: P; *at.no.* 15; *at.wt.* 30.9738. [< L < Gk. *phōsphoros* the morning star < *phōs* light + *pherein* bring]

phos·phu·ret·ted or **phos·phu·ret·ed** (fos′ fyù ret′ id) *adj.* combined with phosphorus.

phot. **1** photograph. **2** photographic. **3** photography.

pho·to (fō′ tō) *n.* **-tos.** *Informal.* photograph.

photo- *combining form.* **1** light, as in *photometry.* **2** photographic or photograph, as in *photo-engraving.* [< Gk. *phōs, phōtos* light]

pho·to·chem·i·cal (fō′ tə kem′ ə kəl) *adj.* of or having to do with the chemical action of light.

pho·to·cop·y (fō′ tə kop′ ē) *n.* **-cop·ies,** *v.* **-cop·ied, -cop·y·ing.** —*n.* a photographic reproduction of a document or other printed matter. —*v.* make a photocopy.

pho·to-e·lec·tric (fō′ tō i lek′ trik) *adj.* **1** having to do with the electricity or electrical effects produced by light. **2** of or having to do with an apparatus for taking photographs by electric light.

photo-electric cell a cell or vacuum tube that produces variations in an electric current in accordance with variations in the light falling upon it: *Photo-electric cells can be used to open doors automatically.*

pho·to-en·grave (fō′ tō en grāv′) *v.* **-graved, -grav·ing.** produce by photo-engraving. —**pho′ to-en·grav′ er,** *n.*

pho·to-en·grav·ing (fō′ tō en grāv′ ing) *n.* **1** a process by which plates to print from are produced with the aid of photography. **2** a plate so produced. **3** a picture printed from it.

hat, āge, cãre, fär; let, ēqual, tėrm; it, īce
hot, ōpen, ôrder; oil, out; cup, pùt, rüle, ūse
əbove, takən, pencəl, lemən, circəs
ch, child; ng, long; sh, ship
th, thin; ᴛʜ, then; zh, measure

photo finish **1** in racing, a finish so close that a photograph is required to decide the winner. **2** any contest decided by a narrow margin of victory.

pho·to·flash lamp (fō′ tə flash′) in photography, a flash bulb.

pho·to·flood lamp (fō′ tə flud′) an electric lamp that gives very bright, sustained light for taking pictures.

pho·to·gen·ic (fō′ tə jen′ ik) *adj.* **1** photographing very well, especially in motion pictures: *a photogenic face.* **2** in biology, phosphorescent; luminescent. Certain bacteria are photogenic. [< *photo-* + Gk. *gen-* producing, produced (by)] —**pho′ to·gen′ i·cal·ly,** *adv.*

pho·to·gram·me·trist (fō′ tə gram′ ə trist) *n.* an expert in photogrammetry.

pho·to·gram·me·try (fō′ tə gram′ ə trē) *n.* the technique of making maps or surveys with the help of photographs, especially of aerial photographs. [< *photogram*, obs. var. of *photograph* + *-metry*; probably influenced by G *Photogrammetrie*]

pho·to·graph (fō′ tə graf′) *n.* a picture made with a camera. A photograph is made by the action of the light rays from the thing pictured coming through the lens of the camera onto a film spread over the surface of glass, paper, celluloid, or metal. —*v.* **1** take a photograph of. **2** take photographs. **3** look (clear, natural, etc.) in a photograph: *She does not photograph well.*

pho·tog·ra·pher (fə tog′ rə fər) *n.* **1** a person who takes photographs. **2** a person whose business is taking photographs.

pho·to·graph·ic (fō′ tə graf′ ik) *adj.* **1** of or like photography: *photographic accuracy.* **2** used in or produced by photography: *photographic plates, a photographic record of a trip.* —**pho′ to·graph′ i·cal·ly,** *adv.*

pho·tog·ra·phy (fə tog′ rə fē) *n.* the taking of photographs.

pho·to·gra·vure (fō′ tə grə vūr′ or -grā′ vūr) *n.* **1** photo-engraving. **2** a picture printed from a metal plate on which a photograph has been engraved.

pho·to·me·chan·i·cal (fō′ tə mə kan′ ə kəl) *adj.* relating to or designating any of various methods, such as photo-engraving or phototype, of making printing plates with the aid of photography.

pho·tom·e·ter (fō tom′ ə tər) *n.* an instrument for measuring the intensity of light or the relative illuminating power of different lights.

pho·to·met·ric (fō′ tə met′ rik) *adj.* having to do with photometry or a photometer. —**pho′ to·met′ ri·cal·ly,** *adv.*

pho·tom·e·try (fō tom′ ə trē) *n.* **1** the branch of physics dealing with the measurement of the intensity of light. **2** the measurement of the intensity of light, especially by means of a photometer.

pho·to·mi·cro·graph (fō′ tə mī′ krə graf′) *n.* a photograph taken through a microscope.

pho·ton (fō′ ton) *n.* in physics, a quantum or unit particle of light, having a momentum equal to its energy and moving with the velocity of light. [< *photo* electr*on*]

pho·to·play (fō′ tə plā′) *n.* a motion picture.

pho·to·re·con·nais·sance (fō′ tə rə kon′ ə səns) *n.* reconnaissance made by aerial photographs.

pho·to·sen·si·tive (fō′ tə sen′ sə tiv) *adj.* sensitive to light; easily stimulated by light or other radiant energy.

pho·to·sphere (fō′ tə sfēr′) *n.* **1** the layer of ionized gases forming the intensely luminous surface of the sun or any star as seen from the earth. **2** a sphere of light, radiance, or glory.

pho·to·stat (fō′ tə stat′) *n.* **1** **Photostat,** *Trademark.* a special camera for making copies of maps, drawings, pages of books, etc. directly on specially prepared paper. **2** a photograph made with it. —*v.* make a photostat of.

[< *photo-* light + Gk. *-statēs* that brings to a stop]

pho·to·syn·the·sis (fō′tə sin′thə sis) *n.* the process by which plant cells make sugar from carbon dioxide and water in the presence of chlorophyl and light. [< NL]

pho·to·te·leg·ra·phy (fō′tə tə leg′rə fē) *n.* **1** telegraphy by means of light, as with a heliograph. **2** the electric transmission of facsimiles of photographs.

pho·tot·rop·ism (fō tot′rə piz′əm) *n.* in botany, a tendency to turn in response to light. [< *photo-* + Gk. *-tropos* turning]

pho·to·type (fō′tə tīp′) *n.* **1** a block on which a photograph is reproduced so that it can be printed. **2** the process used in making such a block. **3** a picture printed from such a block.

phrase (frāz) *n. v.* **phrased, phras·ing.** —*n.* **1** a combination of words: *He spoke in simple phrases so that the children understood him.* **2** a short, often used expression: "*Call up*" *is the common phrase for* "*make a telephone call to.*" **3** a short, striking expression. *Examples*: From sea to sea. Atoms for peace. A war to end wars. **4** in grammar, a group of words not containing a subject and predicate and used as a single word. *Examples*: in the house; coming by the church; to eat too fast. **5** in music, a short part of a composition, usually containing four measures.
—*v.* **1** express in a particular way: *She phrased her excuse politely.* **2** in music, mark off or bring out the phrases of (a composition). [< L < Gk. *phrasis* <*phrazein* express]

phrase·book (frās′bu̇k′) *n.* a collection of idioms and everyday phrases used in a language, with their translations.

phra·se·o·log·i·cal (frā′zē ə loj′ə kəl) *adj.* **1** of or having to do with phraseology. **2** characterized by a special phraseology, or by the choice of particular words, expressions, etc.

phra·se·ol·o·gy (frā′zē ol′ə jē) *n.* **-gies.** the selection and arrangement of words; the particular way in which a person expresses himself in language. —**Syn.** See **diction.**

phras·ing (frāz′ing) *n.* **1 a** the style of wording or verbal expression; phraseology. **b** the grouping of spoken words by pauses. **2** in music: **a** a grouping or dividing into phrases. **b** the playing of phrases. **c** the style in which the composition is phrased.

phra·try (frā′trē) *n.* **-tries. 1** in ancient Athens, each of the subdivisions of a tribe. **2** a similar tribal division among primitive races. [ME < Gk. *phratria* < *phratēr* clansman, brother]

phre·net·ic (fri net′ik) *adj.* **1** frenzied; fanatic. **2** insane. [ME < OF < L < Gk. *phrenetikos* < *phrenitis* disease of the mind < *phrēn* mind. Doublet of FRANTIC.] —**phre·net′i·cal·ly,** *adv.*

phren·o·log·i·cal (fren′ə loj′ə kəl) *adj.* of or having to do with phrenology.

phre·nol·o·gist (fri nol′ə jist) *n.* a person who professes to tell a person's character from the shape of his skull.

phre·nol·o·gy (fri nol′ə jē) *n.* a theory that the shape of the skull shows what sort of mind and character a person has; practice of reading character from the shape of the skull. [< Gk. *phrēn* mind + E *-logy*]

Phryg·i·a (frij′ē ə) *n.* an ancient country in the central and northwestern part of Asia Minor.

Phryg·i·an (frij′ē ən) *adj.* of or having to do with Phrygia, an ancient country in west central Asia Minor, its people, or their language. —*n.* **1** a native or inhabitant of Phrygia. **2** the Indo-European language of the ancient Phrygians.

phthis·ic (tiz′ik) *n. Archaic.* phthisis.

phthis·i·cal (tiz′ə kəl) *adj.* having to do with, having the nature of, or affected by phthisis.

phthi·sis (thī′sis) *n.* tuberculosis of the lungs; consumption. [< L < Gk. *phthisis* < *phthinein* waste away]

phy·lac·ter·y (fə lak′tər ē) *n.* **-ter·ies. 1** either of two small leather cases containing texts from the Jewish law, worn by orthodox Jews during prayer to remind them to keep the law. **2** a reminder. **3** a charm worn as a protection. [ME < LL < Gk. *phylaktērion* safeguard, ult. < *phylax, phylakos* watchman]

phy·le (fī′lē) *n.* **-lae** (-lē or -lī). in ancient Greece: **1** a clan or tribe. **2** in Athens, a large political sub-division. [< Gk.]

phy·lo·gen·e·sis (fī′lō jen′ə sis) *n.* phylogeny.

phy·lo·ge·net·ic (fī′lō jə net′ik) *adj.* of or having to do with phylogeny. —**phy′lo·ge·net′i·cal·ly,** *adv.*

phy·lo·gen·ic (fī′lō jen′ik) *adj.* of or having to do with phylogeny.

phy·log·e·ny (fī loj′ə nē) *n.* **-nies. 1** racial history. **2** the origin and development of anything, especially of an animal or plant. [< G < Gk. *phylon* race + *-geneia* origin]

phyl·lox·e·ra (fil′ək sēr′ə or fə lok′sə rə) *n.* a kind of plant louse that destroys grapevines. [< NL < Gk. *phyllon* leaf + *xēros* dry]

phy·lum (fī′ləm) *n.* **-la** (-lə). in biology, a primary division of the animal or vegetable kingdom, usually equivalent to a subkingdom. [< NL < Gk. *phylon* race, stock]

phys·ic (fiz′ik) *n. v.* **-icked, -ick·ing.** —*n.* **1** medicine, expecially one that moves the bowels. **2** the art of healing; science and practice of medicine. —*v.* **1** move the bowels of. **2** give medicine to. **3** act like a medicine on; cure. [ME < OF *fisique* < L < Gk. *physikē* (*epistēmē*) (knowledge) of nature, ult. < *phyein* produce]

phys·i·cal (fiz′ə kəl) *adj.* **1** of the body: *physical exercise.* **2** of matter; material: *The tide is a physical force.* **3** according to the laws of nature: *It is a physical impossibility to stop the earth's movement around the sun.* **4** of the science of physics. —**phys′i·cal·ly,** *adv.*

physical chemistry the branch of chemistry that deals with the physical properties of substances and their relations to chemical composition and changes.

physical education instruction in how to exercise and take care of the body.

physical geography the study of land forms, climate, winds, and all other features of the earth.

physical science 1 physics. **2** physics, chemistry, geology, astronomy, and other sciences dealing with inanimate matter.

physical training the practice of doing exercises of various kinds so as to keep the body in good condition.

phy·si·cian (fə zish′ən) *n.* a doctor of medicine. [ME < OF *fisicien* < L *physica.* See PHYSIC.]

phys·i·cist (fiz′ə sist) *n.* a person trained in physics.

phys·ics (fiz′iks) *n.* **1** the science that deals with the properties and interrelationships of matter and energy, excluding chemical and biological change. Physics studies mechanics, heat, light, sound, electricity, magnetism, radiation, and atomic structure. **2** a textbook or handbook dealing with this subject. [pl. of *physic* (= Gk. *ta physika* the natural things)]

physio- *combining form.* of or having to do with physical form or function, as in *physiography.* Also, **physi-** before vowels. [< Gk. *physis* nature]

phys·i·og·no·my (fiz′ē og′nə mē or fiz′ē on′ə mē) *n.* **-mies. 1** the kind of features or type of face one has; one's face. **2** the art of estimating character from the features of the face or the form of the body. **3** the general aspect or looks of a countryside, a situation, etc. [ME < OF < LL < Gk. *physiognōmonia* < *physis* nature + *gnōmōn* judge < *gnōnai* recognize]

phys·i·og·ra·pher (fiz′ē og′rə fər) *n.* a person skilled in physiography.

phys·i·o·graph·ic (fiz′ē ə graf′ik) *adj.* of or having to do with physiography.

phys·i·og·ra·phy (fiz′ē og′rə fē) *n.* physical geography.

phys·i·o·log·i·cal (fiz′ē ə loj′ə kəl) *adj.* **1** having to do with physiology: *Digestion is a physiological process.* **2** having to do with the normal or healthy functioning of an organism: *Food and sleep are physiological needs.* —**phys′i·o·log′i·cal·ly,** *adv.*

hat, āge, cãre, fär; let, ēqual, tėrm; it, īce
hot, ōpen, ôrder; oil, out; cup, pu̇t, rüle, ūse
əbove, takən, pencəl, lemən, circəs
ch, child; ng, long; sh, ship
th, thin; TH, then; zh, measure

phys·i·ol·o·gist (fiz′ē ol′ə jist) *n.* an expert in physiology.

phys·i·ol·o·gy (fiz′ē ol′ə jē) *n.* **1** the science dealing with the normal functions of living things or their organs: *animal physiology, plant physiology.* **2** all the functions and activities of a living thing or of one of its organs. [< L < Gk. *physiologia* < *physis* nature + *-logos* treating of]

phy·si·o·ther·a·pist (fiz′ē ō ther′ə pist) *n.* an expert in physiotherapy.

phys·i·o·ther·a·py (fiz′ē ō ther′ə pē) *n.* the treatment of diseases and defects by physical remedies, such as massage or electricity (rather than by drugs).

phy·sique (fə zēk)′) *n.* the body; bodily structure, organization, or development: *a man of strong physique.* [< F *physique* physical]

-phyte *combining form.* a growth; plant, as in *epiphyte.* [< Gk. *phyton*]

phyto- *combining form.* a plant; plants: *phytology = the science of plants.* Also, **phyt-** before vowels. [< Gk. *phyton* plant]

phy·to·bi·ol·o·gy (fī′tō bī ol′ə jē) *n.* the branch of biology that deals with plants.

phy·to·chem·is·try (fī′tō kem′is trē) *n.* the chemistry of plants.

phy·to·gen·e·sis (fī′tō jen′ə sis) *n.* the science of the evolution and development of plants.

phy·to·ge·net·ic (fī′tō jə net′ik) *adj.* **1** of or having to do with phytogenesis. **2** of plant or vegetable origin.

phy·tog·e·ny (fī toj′ə nē) *n.* phytogenesis.

phy·to·ge·og·ra·phy (fī′tō jē og′rə fē) *n.* the science that deals with the geographical distribution of plant life.

pi[1] (pī) *n.* **pis. 1** the ratio of the circumference of any circle to its diameter, usually written as π (= 3.141592+). **2** the 16th letter of the Greek alphabet (Π, π). [def. 1, use of Gk. letter to mean Gk. *periphereia* periphery. See PERIPHERY.]

pi[2] (pī) *n. v.* **pied, pi·ing.** —*n.* **1** printing types all mixed up. **2** any confused mixture. —*v.* mix up (type). Also **pie.** [extended use of *pie*[1]]

P.I. Philippine Islands.

pi·a ma·ter (pī′ə mā′tər) in anatomy, the innermost of three membranes enveloping the brain and spinal cord. [< Med.L *pia mater* pious mother, a wrong translation of Arabic *umm raqiqah* thin or tender mother]

pi·a·nis·si·mo (pē′ə nis′ə mō′) in music: —*adj.* very soft. —*adv.* very softly. —*n.* a very soft movement or passage; composition to be played or sung very softly. *Abbrev.*: pp. [< Ital. *pianissimo*, superlative of *piano* soft. See PIANO[2].]

pi·an·ist (pē an′ist or pē′ə nist) *n.* a person who plays the piano.

pi·an·o[1] (pē an′ō) *n.* **-an·os.** a large, stringed musical instrument that is played by hammers operated from a manual keyboard. [for *pianoforte*]

pi·a·no[2] (pē ä′nō) in music: —*adj.* soft. —*adv.* softly. —*n.* a soft movement or passage; composition to be played or sung softly. *Abbrev.*: p. [< Ital. *piano* < L *planus* plain, flat. Doublet of PLAIN[1] and PLAN.]

pi·an·o·for·te (pē an′ə fôr′tē or pē an′ə fôrt′) *n.* piano[1]. [< Ital. *pianoforte* < *piano* soft + *forte* loud]

pi·as·tre or **pi·as·ter** (pē as′tər) *n.* **1** a unit of money in South Vietnam. See table at **money. 2** a unit of money equalling 1/100 of the standard of currency in certain other countries. **3** a coin worth one piaster. [< Ital. *piastra* metal plate < L]

pi·az·za (pē az′ə) *n.* **1** a large porch or veranda along one or more sides of a house. **2** in Italy, an open public square. [< Ital. *piazza* < L < Gk. *plateia (hodos)* broad (way). Doublet of PLACE and PLAZA.]

pi·broch (pē′brok) *n.* music, usually warlike or sad, played on the bagpipe. [< Scots Gaelic *piobaireachd* pipe music, ult. < *piob* pipe]

pi·ca (pī′kə) *n.* **1** in printing, a size of type, 12 point.
This sentence is in pica.
2 this size of type used as a measure; about 1/6 inch. **3** a size of typewriter type, larger than elite, corresponding to 12-point printing type. There are 10 pica characters to the inch. [< Anglo-L *pica*, the name of a book of rules concerning holy days, supposed (? erroneously) to be printed in pica]

pic·a·dor (pik′ə dôr′) *n.* one of the horsemen who begin a bullfight by irritating the bull with pricks of their lances. [< Sp. *picador* < *picar* pierce]

pic·a·resque (pik′ə resk′) *adj.* dealing with wandering rogues and their adventures: *a picaresque novel.* [< Sp. *picaresco* < *picaro* rogue]

pic·a·roon (pik′ə rün′) *n.* **1** a rogue; thief; brigand. **2** a pirate. **3** a piratical or privateering ship. —*v.* act or cruise as a brigand or pirate. [< Sp. *picarón* < *picaro* rogue]

pic·a·yune (pik′ə ūn′) *adj.* small; petty; mean. [< Louisiana F *picaillon* coin worth 5 cents < Provençal *picaioun* coin]

pic·ca·lil·li (pik′ə lil′ē) *n.* a relish made of chopped pickles, onions, tomatoes, etc. and hot spices. [origin uncertain; ? < *pickle*]

pic·co·lo (pik′ə lō′) *n.* **-los.** a small, shrill flute, pitched an octave higher than the ordinary flute. [< Ital. *piccolo* small]

pick[1] (pik) *v.* **1** choose; select: *I picked a winning horse at the races.* **2** pull away with the fingers; gather: *We pick fruit and flowers.* **3** pierce, dig into, or break up with something pointed: *pick ground, rocks, etc.* **4** use something pointed to remove things from: *pick one's teeth, pick a bone.* **5 a** open with a pointed instrument, wire, etc., or by manipulation of the mechanism: *pick a lock or safe.* **b** steal the contents of: *pick a pocket or purse.* **6** prepare for use by removing feathers, waste parts, etc.: *pick a chicken.* **7** pull apart: *The stuffing in the pillow has matted and needs to be picked.* **8** use the fingers on with a plucking motion: *play the banjo by picking its strings.* **9** seek and find occasion for; seek and find: *pick a quarrel, pick flaws.* **10 a** take up (seeds, small pieces of food, etc.) with the bill or teeth, as a bird or squirrel does. **b** eat (food) in small pieces, slowly, or without appetite.
pick a lock, open a lock with a pointed instrument, wire, etc.
pick a person's brains, find out and turn to one's own advantage, or use as one's own, the ideas, skills, etc. of another.
pick a pocket, steal from a person's pocket.
pick at, a pull on with the fingers, etc. **b** eat only a little at a time. **c** *Informal.* find fault with; nag.
pick off, a shoot one at a time. **b** in baseball, catch (a runner) off base and throw him out.
pick on, a *Informal.* find fault with. **b** *Informal.* annoy; tease. **c** bully; take advantage of. **d** select.
pick one's way or steps, move with great care and caution over treacherous ground, a difficult situation, etc.
pick out, a choose; select. **b** distinguish a thing from surroundings. **c** make out the sense or meaning. **d** select the notes of (a tune) one by one, especially laboriously, on a keyboard, etc., and so play it. **e** embellish, especially by lines or spots of contrasting color following outlines, etc. **f** remove or extract by picking.
pick over, a look over carefully. **b** prepare for use.
pick up, a take up. **b** summon courage, etc. **c** get by chance: *pick up a bargain.* **d** give (a person) fresh energy, courage, etc.: *A good dinner will pick you up.* **e** acquire (a particular skill); become skilful at; master: *He picked up the trumpet after just a few lessons.* **f** learn without being taught: *He picks up games easily.* **g** take up into a vehicle or ship. **h** get and take along with one: *pick up a coat at the cleaners.* **i** *Informal.* improve. **j** regain; find again. **k** succeed in seeing, hearing, etc.: *pick up a radio program from Paris.* **l** go faster; increase in speed. **m** *Informal.* become acquainted with without being introduced. **n** tidy up; put in order.
—*n.* **1** a choice or selection. **2** the best or most desirable

part. 3 the amount of a crop gathered at one time. 4 something held in the fingers and used to pull on the strings of a musical instrument. [ME *picke(n)*; cf. OE *pīcung* pricking]

pick[2] (pik) *n.* **1** a heavy, sharp-pointed tool for breaking earth, rock, etc.; pickaxe. **2** a sharp-pointed tool. Ice is broken into pieces with a pick. [ME *picke*, var. of *pike* pike[2], OE *pīc*]

pick·a·back (pik′ə bak′) *adv.* on the back or shoulders; piggyback.

pick·a·nin·ny (pik′ə nin′ē) *n.* **-nies.** *U.S. Usually, derogatory.* **1** a small Negro child. **2** any small child. [< Pg. *pequenino* very small]

pick·axe or **pick·ax** (pik′aks′) *n.* a heavy tool with a sharp point for breaking up dirt, rocks, etc.; pick. [alteration of ME *picois* < OF *picois* (cf. OF *pic* pike[1])]

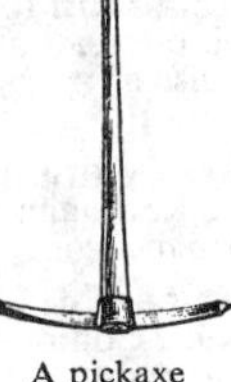
A pickaxe

picked (pikt) *adj.* **1** with waste parts removed and ready for use. **2** specially chosen or selected for merit.

pick·er (pik′ər) *n.* **1** a person who gathers, picks, or collects. **2** a tool for picking anything. **3 a** a machine for separating and cleaning the fibres of cotton, wool, etc. **b** a person who runs such a machine.

pick·er·el (pik′ər əl or pik′rəl) *n.* **-el** or **-els.** a kind of large fresh-water fish having a long, narrow, pointed head. It is a kind of pike. [dim. of *pike*[3]]

pick·er·el·weed (pik′ər əl wēd′ or pik′rəl-) *n.* a plant having blue flowers and heart-shaped leaves, growing in shallow water.

pick·et (pik′it) *n.* **1** a pointed stake or peg driven into the ground to make a fence, to tie a horse to, etc. **2** a small body of troops, or a single man, posted at some place to watch for the enemy and guard against surprise. **3** a person stationed by a labor union near a factory, store, etc. where there is a strike. Pickets try to prevent employees from working or customers from buying. —*v.* **1** enclose with pickets; fence. **2** tie to a picket. **3** station as pickets. **4** station pickets at or near: *picket a factory during a strike.* **5** act as a picket. [< F *piquet*, dim. of *pic* a pick. See PIKE[1].] —**pick′et·er,** *n.* —**Syn.** *n.* **2** sentry, sentinel.

picket fence a fence made of pickets.

picket ship a ship using radar for ocean patrol.

pick·ings (pik′ingz) *n.pl.* **1** the amount picked. **2** things left over; scraps. **3** things stolen or received dishonestly.

pick·le (pik′əl) *n. v.* **-led, -ling.** —*n.* **1** salt water, vinegar, or some other liquid in which meat and vegetables can be preserved. **2** a cucumber preserved in pickle. **3** any other vegetable preserved in pickle. **4** *Informal.* trouble; difficulty. **5** an acid bath for cleaning metal casting, etc. —*v.* **1** preserve in pickle: *to pickle beets.* **2** clean with acid. [< MDu. *pekel*]

pick·pock·et (pik′pok′it) *n.* a person who steals from people's pockets.

pick-up (pik′up′) *n.* **1** a picking up. **2** *Slang.* a getting better; improvement. **3** a going faster; increase in speed; acceleration. **4** *Informal.* an acquaintance made without an introduction, especially an acquaintance of the opposite sex. **5** something obtained or secured without planning and as chance offers, such as a bargain or a hurried meal. **6** a catching or hitting of a ball very soon after it has bounced on the ground. **7** in radio: **a** the reception of sound waves and their conversion into electrical waves for broadcasting. **b** an apparatus for such reception. **c** the place where it occurs. **d** the electrical system for connecting to the broadcasting station or studio a program originating outside. **8** in television: **a** the reception of images and their conversion into electric waves for broadcasting. **b** an apparatus that does this. **9** on a record player or phonograph, a device equipped with a needle, for transforming into electrical current the sound impulses communicated to the needle by the undulations in the grooves of a record. **10** a small truck for collecting and delivering light loads. **11** anything that is picked up.
—*adj.* **1** obtained, chosen, assembled, etc. without planning and from whatever is on hand: *a pick-up meal. We soon chose a pick-up team from among those present.* **2** of or for collecting and delivering: *a pick-up schooner.*

Pick·wick·i·an (pik wik′ē ən) *adj.* **1** of, having to do with, or characteristic of Samuel Pickwick, the kindly, genial hero of Dickens' *Pickwick Papers*, or his club. **2** given a special meaning for the occasion: *words used in a Pickwickian sense.*

pick·y (pik′ē) *adj.* **pick·i·er, pick·i·est.** *Informal.* too fussy or particular; inclined to find fault with trifles.

pic·nic (pik′nik) *n. v.* **-nicked, -nick·ing.** —*n.* **1** a pleasure trip with a meal in the open air. **2** *Slang.* a pleasant time or experience; very easy job. —*v.* **1** go on a picnic. **2** eat in picnic style. [< F *piquenique*]

picnic ham a smoked shoulder of pork, cut to resemble a ham.

pic·nick·er (pik′nik ər) *n.* a person who picnics.

pi·cot (pē′kō) *n.* one of a number of fancy loops in embroidery, tatting, etc. or along the edge of lace, ribbon, etc. —*v.* trim with picots. [< F *picot*, dim. of *pic* a pick. See PIKE[1].]

pic·ric acid (pik′rik) a yellow, intensely bitter acid used as a dye and in explosives. *Formula*: $C_6H_3N_3O_7$ [< Gk. *pikros* bitter]

Pict (pikt) *n.* a member of a people of disputed origin, formerly living in Scotland, especially N. Scotland. [< LL *Picti*, pl.]

Pict·ish (pik′tish) *adj.* of or having to do with the Picts.

pic·to·graph (pik′tə graf′) *n.* a picture used as a sign or symbol. [< L *pictus* painted + E *-graph*]

pic·to·graph·ic (pik′tə graf′ik) *adj.* of pictographs. —**pic′to·graph′ical·ly,** *adv.*

Pictographs for "weeping" and "forest"

pic·to·ri·al (pik tô′rē əl) *adj.* **1** having to do with pictures; expressed in pictures. **2** making a picture for the mind; vivid. **3** illustrated by pictures: *a pictorial history.* **4** having to do with painters or painting. —*n.* a magazine in which pictures are an important feature. [< L *pictorius* < *pictor* painter] —**pic·to′ri·al·ly,** *adv.*

pic·ture (pik′chər) *n. v.* **-tured, -tur·ing.** —*n.* **1** a drawing, painting, portrait, or photograph; a print of any of these. **2** a scene. **3** a mental image; a visualized conception; idea: *have a clear picture of the problem.* **4** something beautiful: *She was a picture in her new dress.* **5** image; likeness: *He is the picture of his father.* **6** an example; embodiment: *She was a picture of despair.* **7** a vivid description. **8** a motion picture. **9** an image on a television screen. **10** *Informal.* state of affairs; condition; situation: *the employment picture.*
—*v.* **1** draw, paint, etc.; make into a picture. **2** form a picture of in the mind; imagine: *It is hard to picture life a hundred years ago.* **3** show by words; describe vividly: *The speaker pictured the suffering of the poor.* [ME < L *pictura*, ult. < *pingere* to paint]

picture hat a woman's hat having a very wide brim, originally often trimmed with ostrich feathers.

pic·tur·esque (pik′chər esk′) *adj.* **1** quaint or interesting enough to be used as the subject of a picture: *a picturesque old mill.* **2** making a picture for the mind; vivid. [< F *pittoresque* < Ital. *pittoresco* in the style of a painter < *pittore* painter < L *pictor*; influenced by *picture*] —**pic′tur·esque′ly,** *adv.* —**pic′tur·esque′ness,** *n.*

picture tube a cathode ray tube that produces a transmitted picture on a television screen.

picture writing **1** the recording of events or expressing of ideas by pictures. **2** pictures used to record events or express ideas.

pid·dle (pid′əl) *v.* **-dled, -dling.** **1** do anything in a trifling or ineffective way. **2** urinate. —*n. Informal.* urine. [origin uncertain] —**pid′dler,** *n.*

pid·dling (pid′ling) *adj.* trifling; petty.

pid·gin (pij′ən) *n.* a mixed jargon, combining simplified grammatical forms and vocabulary from two different languages, used for trade or communication between different peoples or groups. [< *pidgin English*]

pidgin English one of several forms of English, with simplified grammatical structure and vocabulary, used in W. Africa, Australia, Melanesia, and formerly in China, as a trade or communication jargon. [*pidgin*, Chinese alteration of *business*]

pie[1] (pī) *n.* **1** a food consisting of fruit, meat, etc. set in a shell of pastry, fine crumbs, etc. and sometimes covered with pastry, and baked or chilled. **2** a layer cake with a filling of whipped cream, jelly, etc.: *Boston cream pie.* **3** something that may be divided into portions. **4** *Slang.* something that is desirable: *as easy as pie.* [ME *pye;* origin uncertain]

pie[2] (pī) *n.* magpie. [ME < OF < L *pica*]

pie[3] (pī) *n. v.* **pied, pie·ing.** pi[2]. [? extended use of *pie*[1]]

pie·bald (pī′bold′ or -bôld′) *adj.* spotted in two colors, especially black and white. —*n.* a spotted animal, especially a horse. [apparently < *pie*[2] + *bald;* with reference to dark color of magpie]

piece (pēs) *n. v.* **pieced, piec·ing.** —*n.* **1** one of the parts into which a thing is divided or broken; bit: *The cup broke in pieces.* **2** a portion; part; small quantity: *a piece of land, a piece of bread.* **3** a single part or member of a set or class: *This set of china has 144 pieces.* **4** a coin: *A nickel is a five-cent piece.* **5** an example; instance: *Sleeping with the light on is a piece of nonsense.* **6** in art, music, etc., a single composition: *a new piece at the theatre.* **7** a gun; cannon. **8** the quantity in which goods are made: *She bought the whole piece of muslin.* **9** in checkers, chess, etc., a figure, disk, block, etc. used in playing. **10** a snack between meals. **11** formerly, a package weighing about 90 pounds, the standard load carried by the fur brigades. **12 go to pieces, a** break into fragments; break up. **b** become shattered; break down physically or mentally; collapse. **13 of a piece,** of the same kind; in keeping. **14 piece of one's mind,** *Informal.* **a** a candid opinion. **b** a scolding. **15 speak one's piece,** voice one's opinions.
—*v.* **1** make or repair by adding or joining pieces. **2** join the pieces of. **3** eat between meals: *The child was always piecing.* [ME *pece* < OF < Med.L *petia* fragment < Celtic] —**piec′er,** *n.* —**Syn.** *n.* **1** fragment, scrap. **2** See **part.**

pièce de ré·sis·tance (pyes′ də rā zis tᴏɴs′; *French,* pyes də rā zēs täɴs′) *French.* **1** the chief dish of a meal. **2** the most important or outstanding item in any collection or series.

piece·meal (pēs′mēl′) *adv.* **1** piece by piece; a little at a time: *work done piecemeal.* **2** piece from piece; to pieces; into fragments. —*adj.* done piece by piece. [ME *pecemele* < *pece* piece + *-mele* < OE *mæl* part, measure]

piece of eight in former times, a Spanish dollar.

piece·work (pēs′wėrk′) *n.* work paid for by the amount done, not by the time it takes.

piece·work·er (pēs′wėr′kər) *n.* a person who does piecework.

pie crust pastry used for the bottom or top of a pie.

pie·crust (pī′krust′) *adj.* having a fluted edge like that of a pie crust: *a piecrust table.*

pied (pīd) *adj.* **1** having patches of two or more colors; many-colored. **2** spotted. **3** wearing a costume of two or more colors. [< *pie*[2]; with reference to magpie's plumage]

Pie·gan (pē′gan) *v.* **-gan** or **-gans. 1** one of the three North American Indian tribes that made up the Blackfeet union. **2** a member of this tribe.

pie in the sky *Slang.* something pleasant but unattainable; an impractical ideal.

pier (pēr) *n.* **1** a structure supported on columns extending into the water, used as a walk or a landing place. **2** a breakwater. **3** one of the solid supports on which the arches of a bridge rest; any solid support of masonry. **4** the solid part of a wall between windows, doors, etc. [< Med.L *pera*]

pierce (pērs) *v.* **pierced, pierc·ing. 1** go into; go through: *A tunnel pierces the mountain.* **2** make a hole in; bore into or through: *A nail pierced the tire of our car.* **3** force a way; force a way through or into: *A sharp cry pierced the air.* **4** make a way through with the eye or mind: *pierce a disguise, pierce a mystery.* **5** affect sharply: *a heart pierced with grief.* [< OF *percier,* ult. < L *pertusus*

hat, āge, cãre, fär; let, ēqual, tėrm; it, īce
hot, ōpen, ôrder; oil, out; cup, pu̇t, rüle, ūse
əbove, takən, pencəl, lemən, circəs
ch, child; ng, long; sh, ship
th, thin; ᴛʜ, then; zh, measure

pierced, pp. of *pertundere* < *per-* through + *tundere* beat] —**Syn. 1** See **penetrate. 2** prick, perforate.

pierc·ing (pēr′sing) *adj.* that pierces; penetrating; sharp; keen. —**pierc′ing·ly,** *adv.* —**pierc′ing·ness,** *n.*

pier glass a tall mirror, as originally used to fill the space, or pier, between two windows.

Pi·e·ri·an (pī ēr′ē ən) *adj.* of or having to do with the Muses. [< *Pieria,* in ancient Thessaly, supposed home of the Muses]

Pierian spring the supposed fountain of knowledge and poetic inspiration.

Pi·er·rot (pē′ər ō′; *French,* pye rō′) *n.* a clown who is a traditional character in French pantomime. He has his face whitened and wears white pantaloons and, usually, a white jacket with big buttons. [< F *Pierrot,* dim. of *Pierre* Peter]

Pierrot

pie·tà or **Pie·tà** (pyā tä′) *n.* in art, a representation of the Virgin holding the dead Christ in her arms. [< Ital. *pietà* piety, pity < L *pietas*]

pi·e·tism (pī′ə tiz′əm) *n.* **1** deep piety. **2** pretended piety. **3 Pietism,** a 17th-century movement for reviving piety in the Lutheran Church. [< G *Pietismus* (def. 3)]

pi·e·tist (pī′ə tist) *n.* **1** one conspicuous for pietism. **2 Pietist,** an adherent of Pietism.

pi·e·tis·tic (pī′ə tis′tik) *adj.* conspicuous for pietism; very pious.

pi·e·ty (pī′ə tē) *n.* **-ties. 1** the condition of being pious or of having reverence for God; devotion to religion; holiness; goodness. **2** a dutiful regard for one's parents. **3** a pious act, remark, belief, etc. [ME < OF *piete* < L *pietas* < *pius* pious. Doublet of ᴘɪᴛʏ.]

pif·fle (pif′əl) *n. Informal.* silly talk; nonsense. [? related to OE *pyffan* puff]

pif·fling (pif′ling) *adj. Informal.* insignificant; trifling, piddling.

pig (pig) *n.* **1** a cloven-hoofed mammal having a long snout, especially one that is domesticated and raised for its meat. **2** a young swine. **3** pork. **4** *Informal.* a person who seems or acts like a pig; one who is greedy, dirty, dull, sullen, or stubborn. **5** an oblong mass of metal that has been run into a mould while hot. **6 buy a pig in a poke,** buy something without seeing or knowing its real nature or value.
—*v.* **1** give birth to pigs; farrow. **2** Also, **pig it.** lodge or crowd together like pigs; live in poor or crowded conditions. [OE *picg* (in *picg-bred* mast[2], literally, pig-bread); origin uncertain]

pi·geon (pij′ən) *n.* **1** a kind of bird having a plump body, strong wings, and short legs; a dove. **2** *Slang.* a person who is easily tricked. [ME < OF *pijon* < VL < LL *pipio, -onis* squab; named from the sound (cf. L *pipiare* cheep)]

pigeon hawk a pigeon-sized falcon which breeds in northern North America, related to the merlin.

pi·geon·hole (pij′ən hōl′) *n. v.* **-holed, -hol·ing.** —*n.* **1** a small place built, usually as one of a series, for a pigeon to nest in. **2** one of a set of boxlike compartments for holding papers and other articles in a desk, a cabinet, etc. —*v.* **1** put in a pigeonhole; put away. **2** classify and lay aside in memory where one can refer to it. **3** put aside with the idea of dismissing, forgetting, or neglecting: *The city council pigeonholed the request for a new park.*

pi·geon-toed (pij′ən tōd′) *adj.* having the toes or feet turned inward.

pig·ger·y (pig′ər ē) *n.* **-ger·ies.** *Esp.Brit.* a place where pigs are kept.

pig·gish (pig′ish) *adj.* like a pig; greedy; filthy. —**pig′gish·ly,** *adv.* —**pig′gish·ness,** *n.*

pig·gy (pig′ē) *n.* **-gies.** a little pig.

pig·gy·back (pig′ē bak′) *n.* **1** a carrying or being carried on the back or shoulders: *He gave the child a piggyback.* **2** the act or process of transporting loaded truck trailers on flatcars.
—*adv.* **1** on the back or shoulders. **2** by piggyback (n. def. 2).
—*v.* carry by piggyback.

piggy bank 1 a small container designed in the likeness of a pig and having a slot in the top for coins. **2** any coin bank.

pig-head·ed (pig′hed′id) *adj.* stupidly obstinate or stubborn. —**pig′-head·ed·ness,** *n.*

pig iron crude iron as it first comes from the blast furnace or smelter, usually cast into oblong masses called pigs.

pig latin a children's jargon in which the syllable *-ay* (ā) is added to the end of a word, any initial consonant being placed immediately before this ending. *Examples*: oodgay = good, offay = off, ordway = word.

pig·let (pig′lit) *n.* a little pig; baby pig.

pig·ment (pig′mənt) *n.* **1** a coloring matter, especially a powder or some easily pulverized dry substance, that, when mixed with oil, water, or other liquid vehicle, constitutes a paint. **2** in biology, any organic substance occurring in and coloring any part of an animal or plant; the natural coloring matter of a cell or tissue. [ME < L *pigmentum,* ult. < *pingere* paint. Doublet of PIMENTO.]

pig·men·tar·y (pig′mən ter′ē) *adj.* of or containing pigment.

pig·men·ta·tion (pig′mən tā′shən) *n.* **1** a deposit of pigment in the tissue of a living animal or plant, causing coloration or discoloration. **2** the coloration of an animal or plant.

pig·my (pig′mē) *n.* **-mies,** *adj.* pygmy.

pig·nut (pig′nut′) *n.* **1** the nut of the brown hickory of North America. **2** the tree itself. **3** the tuber of a certain European plant, a kind of earthnut.

pig·pen (pig′pen′) *n.* **1** a pen where pigs are kept. **2** a filthy place.

pig·skin (pig′skin′) *n.* **1** the skin of a pig. **2** leather made from it. **3** *Informal.* a football.

pig·sty (pig′stī′) *n.* **-sties.** a pigpen.

pig·tail (pig′tāl′) *n.* **1** a braid of hair hanging from the back of the head. **2** a twist of tobacco.

pig·weed (pig′wēd′) *n.* **1** a coarse weed having narrow, notched leaves. **2** green amaranth.

pi·ka (pī′kə) *n.* any of various small, virtually tail-less, short-eared, rabbitlike animals found in mountainous regions of Asia and North America, especially in the Rockies. [< Tungus (Siberia) *piika,* probably imitative of its cry]

pike[1] (pīk) *n.* a long wooden shaft with a sharp-pointed metal head; spear. Foot soldiers used to carry pikes. [< F *pique* < *piquer* pierce < *pic* a pick < Gmc.]

pike[2] (pīk) *n.* a sharp point; spike. [OE *pīc* pick]

pike[3] (pīk) *n.* a large, slender fresh-water fish having a long, narrow, pointed head and spiny fins. [apparently < *pike*[2] + *fish* (because of the shape of its snout)]

pike[4] (pīk) *n.* turnpike.

pike·man (pīk′mən) *n.* **-men** (-mən). a soldier armed with a pike.

pike-perch (pīk′pėrch′) *n.* walleyed pike; doré.

pike-pole or **pike·pole** (pīk′pōl′) *n.* a long pole with a pike, or spike, at one end, especially one used by lumbermen to direct floating logs.

pik·er (pīk′ər) *n. Slang.* a person who does things in a small or cheap way. [origin uncertain]

pike·staff (pīk′staf′) *n.* **-staves** (-stāvz′). **1** the staff or shaft of a pike or spear. **2** a staff with a metal point or spike, used by travellers.

pi·laf or **pi·laff** (pi läf′) *n.* pilau.

pi·las·ter (pə las′tər) *n.* a rectangular pillar, especially when it forms part of a wall from which it projects slightly. [< F < Ital. *pilastro* < L *pila* pillar]

A pilaster

pi·lau or **pi·law** (pi lo′ or pi lô′) *n.* an Oriental food consisting of rice boiled with mutton, fowl, etc. and flavored with spices, raisins, etc. [< Persian *pilaw*]

pil·chard (pil′chərd) *n.* **1** a sardine. **2** a small sea fish resembling a sardine. [origin uncertain]

pile[1] (pīl) *n. v.* **piled, pil·ing.** —*n.* **1** many things lying one upon another in a more or less orderly way: *pile of wood.* **2** a heap; mass like a hill or mound: *pile of dirt.* **3** a heap of wood on which a dead body or sacrifice is burned. **4** a large structure or mass of buildings. **5** *Informal.* a large amount or number: *a pile of work, a pile of dishes.* **6** *Informal.* a large amount of money; fortune. **7** in nuclear physics, a reactor. **8** in electricity: **a** a series of plates of different metals, arranged alternately with cloth or paper wet with acid between them, for producing an electric current. **b** any similar arrangement for producing an electric current; battery.
—*v.* **1** make into a pile; heap evenly; heap up. **2** gather or rise in piles. **3** cover with large amounts. **4** go in a confused, rushing crowd. [ME < OF < L *pila* pillar]
—**pil′er,** *n.* —**Syn.** *n.* **1** heap, stack.

pile[2] (pīl) *n. v.* **piled, pil·ing.** —*n.* a heavy beam driven into the earth, often under water, to help support a bridge, wharf, building, etc. —*v.* furnish with piles; drive piles into. [OE *pīl* stake < L *pilum* javelin]

pile[3] (pīl) *n.* **1** a soft, thick nap on velvet, plush, and many carpets. **2** a soft, fine hair or down. [< L *pilus* hair]

piled (pīld) *adj.* having a soft, thick nap.

pile driver a machine for driving down piles or stakes, usually a tall framework in which a heavy weight is raised to a height and then allowed to fall upon the pile.

piles (pīlz) *n.pl.* a swelling of blood vessels at the anus; often painful; hemorrhoids. [ME *pyle,* sing., ? < L *pila* ball]

pil·fer (pil′fər) *v.* steal in small quantities; steal. [ME < OF *pelfrer* rob] —**pil′fer·er,** *n.* —**Syn.** filch. See **steal.**

pil·grim (pil′grəm) *n.* **1** a person who goes on a journey to a sacred or holy place as an act of religious devotion. **2** a traveller; wanderer. **3 Pilgrim,** one of the English Puritan settlers who founded Plymouth Colony (in what is now Massachusetts) in 1620. [ME < AF **pelegrim,* var. of OF *pelerin* < Med.L *peregrinus* pilgrim < L *peregrinus* foreigner. Doublet of PEREGRINE.]

pil·grim·age (pil′grə mij) *n.* **1** a pilgrim's journey; journey to some sacred place as an act of religious devotion. **2** a long journey. **3** life thought of as a journey. [ME < OF *pelerinage* < *peleriner* go as a pilgrim]

pil·ing (pīl′ing) *n.* **1** piles or heavy beams driven into the ground, etc. **2** a structure made of piles.

pill (pil) *n.* **1** medicine made up into a tiny ball to be swallowed whole. **2** a very small ball of anything. **3** something unpleasant that has to be endured: *Our defeat was a bitter pill.* **4** *Slang.* a ball, especially a baseball or golf ball. **5** *Slang.* an unpleasant person. [< MDu. or MLG < L *pilula,* dim. of *pila* ball]

pil·lage (pil′ij) *v.* **-laged, -lag·ing,** *n.* —*v.* rob with violence; plunder: *Pirates pillaged the towns along the coast.* —*n.* plunder; robbery. [ME < OF *pillage* < *piller* plunder < VL *pileare* flay] —**pil′lag·er,** *n.* —**Syn.** *v.* sack, strip.

pil·lar (pil′ər) *n.* **1** a slender, upright structure; column. Pillars are usually made of stone, wood, or metal and used as supports or ornaments for a building. **2** anything slender and upright like a pillar. **3** an important support or supporter: *He is a pillar of the church.* **4 from pillar to post,** from one thing or place to another without any definite purpose. **5 pillar of society,** an influential and dependable member of the community. [ME < OF *piler,* ult. < L *pila* pillar, pile[1]]

Pillars around a building

pil·lared (pil′ərd) *adj.* **1** having pillars. **2** formed into pillars.

Pillars of Hercules two high points of land at the eastern end of the Strait of Gibraltar, one on either side of the strait. The point on the European side is the Rock of Gibraltar and the one on the African side is Jebel Musa.

pill·box (pil′boks′) *n.* **1** a box, usually shallow and often round, for holding pills. **2** a small, low fortress with very thick walls and roof, having machine guns, anti-tank weapons, etc. **3** a brimless hat, fashioned like a shallow cylinder.

pil·lion (pil′yən) *n.* a pad attached behind a saddle on a horse or motorcycle for a person to sit on. [< Scots Gaelic *pillin* or *pillean*, dim. of *pell* cushion < L *pellis* skin]

pil·lo·ry (pil′ə rē) *n.* **-ries,** *v.* **-ried, -ry·ing.** —*n.* a frame of wood with holes through which a person's head and hands were put. In former times, the pillory was used as a punishment, being set up in a public place where the crowd could make fun of the offender. —*v.* **1** put in the pillory. **2** expose to public ridicule, contempt, or abuse. [< OF *pellori* < Provençal *espilori*; origin uncertain]

A man in a pillory

pil·low (pil′ō) *n.* **1** a bag or case filled with feathers, down, or some other soft material, usually used to support the head when resting or sleeping. **2** anything used for a similar purpose. **3** a pad on which a kind of lace is made. **4** a supporting piece or part, such as the block on which the inner end of a bowsprit rests. —*v.* **1** rest on a pillow. **2** be a pillow for. [OE *pyle, pylu*, ult. < L *pulvinus*] —**pil′low·like′,** *adj.*

pil·low·case (pil′ō kās′) *n.* a removable cotton or linen cover for a pillow.

pil·low·slip (pil′ō slip′) *n.* pillowcase.

pi·lose (pī′lōs) *adj.* covered with soft hair; hairy. [< L *pilosus* < *pilus* hair]

pi·lot (pī′lət) *n.* **1** a person who operates the controls of an aircraft in flight. **2** one whose business is steering ships in or out of a harbor or through dangerous waters. A ship takes on a pilot before coming into a strange harbor. **3** one who steers a ship. **4** a guide; leader. **5** a device that controls the action of one part of a machine, motor, etc. **6** a pilot film, project, etc.
—*v.* **1** act as the pilot of; steer. **2** guide; lead: *The manager piloted us through the big factory.*
—*adj.* **1** of or having to do with a pilot or pilots: *a pilot launch.* **2** that acts as a pilot or in any way as a guide: *a pilot star.* **3 a** that guides, controls, or indicates the operation of another, usually a larger and more complex, part. **b** that serves as an advance, preliminary, or experimental version of some action, operation, etc. to be carried out on a larger or more elaborate scale: *a pilot run of a new process.* [< F < Ital. *pilota*]

pi·lot·age (pī′lət ij) *n.* **1** a piloting. **2** a pilot's art or duties. **3** the fee paid for a pilot's service.

pilot biscuit or **bread** a ship biscuit; large, flat cracker.

pilot film in television, a filmed program designed to be shown as a sample of a new series to sell the series to a network or sponsor.

pilot fish a small, bluish fish found in warm seas, often accompanying sharks.

pilot house an enclosed place on the deck of a ship, sheltering the steering wheel and helmsman.

pilot light a small light kept burning all the time and used to light a main light whenever desired. Gas stoves often have pilot lights.

pilot officer in the air force, a commissioned officer senior to a warrant officer and junior to a flying officer. *Abbrev.*: P.O.

pilot plant in manufacturing, engineering, etc., a small plant established for initial or experimental production.

pilot study a preliminary study undertaken to provide a limited, tentative analysis of a problem, situation, proposal, etc. as a basis for further inquiry.

pilot whale a blackfish (def. 2).

hat, āge, cãre, fär; let, ēqual, tėrm; it, īce
hot, ōpen, ôrder; oil, out; cup, pu̇t, rüle, ūse
əbove, takən, pencəl, lemən, circəs
ch, child; ng, long; sh, ship
th, thin; ᴛʜ, then; zh, measure

Pil·sen·er (pil′sə nər or pil′snər) *n.* a pale lager beer. [< G *Pilsener* < *Pilsen*, a city in Czechoslovakia]

Pilt·down man (pilt′doun′) a supposed type of prehistoric man of which fossil remains found at Piltdown, Sussex, were thought to be the most ancient yet discovered in England; they are now generally considered to have been a hoax.

pi·men·to (pə men′tō) *n.* **-tos. 1** a kind of sweet pepper, used as a vegetable, relish, and stuffing for green olives. **2** allspice. **3** the tree that allspice grows on. [< Sp. *pimienta* pepper, *pimiento* capsicum < Med.L *pigmentum* spice < LL *pigmentum* vegetable juice < L *pigmentum* pigment. Doublet of PIGMENT.]

pi·mien·to (pi myen′tō) *n.* **-tos.** a sweet pepper. [< Sp. *pimiento.* See PIMENTO.]

pim·o·la (pim ō′lə) *n.* an olive stuffed with red sweet pepper. [? < *pimento*]

pimp (pimp) *n. v.* pander.

pim·per·nel (pim′pər nel′) *n.* **1** a small scarlet, purple, or white flower that closes in cloudy or rainy weather. **2** the plant that it grows on. [ME < OF *pimprenele*, ult. < VL *piperinus* of peppercorns < L *piper* pepper]

pim·ple (pim′pəl) *n.* a small, inflamed swelling of the skin. [cf. OE *piplian* grow pimply]

pim·pled (pim′pəld) *adj.* having pimples.

pim·ply (pim′plē) *adj.* **-pli·er, -pli·est.** having pimples.

pin (pin) *n. v.* **pinned, pin·ning.** —*n.* **1** a short, slender piece of wire with a point at one end and a head at the other, used for fastening things together. **2** a kind of badge with a pin or clasp to fasten it to the clothing. **3** an ornament that has a pin or clasp; brooch. **4** any of various fastenings consisting essentially or in part of a pointed penetrating bar: *a safety pin.* **5** a peg made of wood or metal, used to fasten things together, hold something, hang things on, etc.: *a clothes pin.* **6** a belaying pin. **7** a peg that holds an oar in place. **8** in a stringed musical instrument, a peg to which a string is fastened. **9** in the game of ninepins, tenpins, etc., any of the bottle-shaped pieces of wood used as targets. **10** in golf, a stick for the flag marking a hole on a course. **11** something small or worthless. **12 on pins and needles,** very anxious or uneasy. **13 pins,** *Informal.* legs.
—*v.* **1** fasten with a pin or pins; put a pin through. **2** fasten or attach firmly to or on; tack; fasten as if with pins. **3** hold fast in one position: *When the tree fell, it pinned his shoulder to the ground.* **4** bind to an undertaking or pledge. **5 pin down, a** hold or bind to an undertaking or pledge. **b** fix firmly; determine with accuracy; establish. [OE *pinn* peg] —**pin′like′,** *adj.*

pin·a·fore (pin′ə fôr′) *n.* **1** an apron that covers most of the dress. **2** a light, sleeveless dress. [< *pin*, v. + *afore*]

pin·ball (pin′bol′ or -bôl′) *n.* a game in which a ball rolls down a board, which is studded with pins or pegs, into numbered compartments.

pinball machine a gambling device used for playing pinball.

pince-nez (pans′nā′ or pins′nā′; *French,* pᴀɴs nā′) *n.* eyeglasses kept in place by a spring that pinches the nose. [< F *pince-nez* pinch-nose]

Pince-nez

pin·cers (pin′sərz) *n.pl. or sing.* **1** a tool for gripping and holding tight, made like scissors but with jaws instead of blades. **2** a large claw of crabs, lobsters, etc. that can be used to pinch or nip; pair of claws. **3** in military use, an operation in which the enemy is surrounded and crushed by the meeting of columns driven on each side of him.

Pincers (def. 1)

—*adj.* **pincer,** of or having to do with pincers. [ME < AF < OF *pynceours* < *pincier* to pinch]

pinch (pinch) *v.* **1** squeeze between two hard edges; squeeze with thumb and forefinger. **2** squeeze or press so as to hurt; get squeezed. **3** cause sharp discomfort or distress to. **4** cause to shrink or become thin: *a face pinched by hunger.* **5** limit closely; stint: *to be pinched for space.* **6** be stingy. **7** be stingy with: *The miser knew how to pinch pennies.* **8** *Slang.* arrest. **9** *Slang.* steal; pilfer.
—*n.* **1** a squeeze between two hard edges; squeeze with thumb and forefinger. **2** sharp pressure that hurts; squeeze. **3** as much as can be taken up with the tips of finger and thumb: *a pinch of salt.* **4** sharp discomfort or distress: *the pinch of hunger.* **5** a time of special need; emergency. **6** *Slang.* an arrest. **7** *Slang.* a stealing. [ME < ONF < OF *pincier*] —**pinch′er,** *n.* —**Syn.** *v.* **1** nip, tweak. **3** afflict. -*n.* **3** bit. **5** hardship, strait.

pinch·beck (pinch′bek) *n.* **1** an alloy of zinc and copper, used in imitation of gold. **2** something not genuine; an imitation. —*adj.* **1** made of pinchbeck. **2** not genuine; sham. [after Christopher *Pinchbeck* (1670?-1732), the inventor]

pin cherry a wild cherry having light-red, sour-tasting fruit.

pinch·ers (pin′chərz) *n.pl. or sing.* pincers.

pinch-hit (pinch′hit′) *v.* **-hit, -hit·ting. 1** in baseball, bat for another player when a hit is badly needed. **2** take another's place in an emergency. —**pinch′hit′ter,** *n.*

pinch·pen·ny (pinch′pen′ē) *adj. n.* **-nies.** *Informal.* —*adj.* too thrifty; overfrugal; mean with money. —*n.* a niggardly or miserly person.

pin curl a curl kept in place by a hairpin or clip.

pin·cush·ion (pin′kůsh′ən) *n.* a small cushion to stick pins in for use as needed.

Pin·dar·ic (pin dar′ik) *adj.* of, having to do with, or in the style of Pindar, 522?-443? B.C., a Greek lyric poet.

pin·dling (pin′dling) *adj. Informal.* puny; sickly. [? euphemistic var. of *piddling*]

pine[1] (pīn) *n.* **1** any of a group of evergreen trees that have cones, and clusters of needle-shaped leaves that grow out from temporary scale-like leaves. Pines are valuable as a source of timber, turpentine, resin, tar, etc. **2** the wood of any of these trees. [OE *pīn* < L *pinus*] —**pine′like′,** *adj.*

pine[2] (pīn) *v.* **pined, pin·ing. 1** long eagerly; yearn. **2** waste away with pain, hunger, grief, or desire. [OE *pīnian* < *pīn*, n., torture < L *poena* penalty < Gk. *poinē*]

pin·e·al (pin′ē əl) *adj.* **1** resembling a pine cone in shape. **2** having to do with the pineal body. [< F < L *pinea* pine cone < *pinus* pine]

pineal body or **pineal gland** a small body of unknown function, present in the brain of all vertebrates having a cranium.

pine·ap·ple (pīn′ap′əl) *n.* **1** a large, edible, tropical fruit resembling a large pine cone. **2** the plant the pineapple grows on. **3** *Slang.* a hand grenade or bomb.

pine drops (pīn′ drops′) *n.* **-drops.** a purplish, leafless plant of North America that has clusters of white or red flowers and is a parasite on the roots of pine trees.

pine family a large group of trees and shrubs that have resinous sap, including the fir, cedar, spruce, hemlock, and cypress.

pine needle the very slender leaf of a pine tree.

pin·er·y (pīn′ər ē) *n.* **-er·ies. 1** a forest or plantation of pine trees. **2** a place where pineapples are grown.

pine·y (pīn′ē) *adj.* **pin·i·er, pin·i·est.** piny.

pin·feath·er (pin′feᴛʜ′ər) *n.* an undeveloped feather that looks like a small stub.

pin·fold (pin′fōld′) *n.* a place where stray animals are kept. —*v.* confine in a pinfold. [< *pind* enclose, OE *pyndan* + *fold*[2]]

ping (ping) *n.* a sound like that of a rifle bullet whistling through the air or striking an object. —*v.* produce a ping. [imitative]

pin·go (ping′gō) *n.* **ping·os** or **ping·oes.** *Cdn.* in the arctic, a mound or small hill caused by the heaving of ice under great pressure. A pingo may be covered with soil and vegetation on the outside but the core is of solid ice. [< Eskimo]

ping-pong (ping′pong′) *n.* table tennis. [< *Ping-pong*, a trademark]

pin·head (pin′hed′) *n.* **1** the head of a pin. **2** something very small or worthless. **3** *Slang.* a person of little intelligence; nitwit.

pin·hole (pin′hōl′) *n.* **1** a hole made by a pin. **2** a hole for a pin or peg to go in.

pin·ion[1] (pin′yən) *n.* **1** the last joint of a bird's wing. **2** *Poetic.* a bird's wing. **3** any one of the stiff flying feathers of a bird's wing. —*v.* **1** cut off or tie the pinions of (a bird) to prevent flying. **2** bind; bind the arms of; bind (to something): *pinion a man's arms.* [ME < OF *pignon*, ult. < L *pinna* feather]

pin·ion[2] (pin′yən) *n.* a small gear with teeth that fit into those of a larger gear or rack. See **differential** for diagram. [< F *pignon* < OF *pignon* battlement, ult. < L *pinna* pinnacle]

pink[1] (pingk) *n.* **1** the color obtained by mixing red with white; light or pale red. **2** Also, **Pink.** *Informal.* a person with somewhat radical political opinions. **3** the highest degree or condition: *in the pink of health.* **4** a plant having spicy-smelling flowers of various colors, mostly white, pink, and red. A carnation is a variety of pink. **5** the flower of this plant.
—*adj.* **1** pale-red. **2** *Informal.* moderately radical. **3** *Informal.* over-refined; exquisite; smart: *a pink tea.* [origin uncertain]

pink[2] (pingk) *v.* **1** prick or pierce with a sword, spear, or dagger. **2** cut the edge of (cloth) in small notches or scallops. **3** ornament with small, round holes. **4** adorn. [ME *pynke(n)* < OE *pynca* point]

pink[3] (pingk) *n.* a flat-bottomed, narrow-sterned sailing vessel with bulging sides. Also, **pinkie.** [apparently < MDu. *pincke* small ship, fishing boat]

pink·eye (pingk′ī′) *n.* an acute, contagious disease characterized by inflammation and soreness of the membrane that lines the eyelids and covers the eyeball.

pink·ie[1] (pingk′ē) *n. Informal.* the smallest finger.

pink·ie[2] (pingk′ē) *n.* pink[3].

pink·ish (pingk′ish) *adj.* somewhat pink.

pink salmon the smallest species of Pacific salmon.

pin money 1 an allowance of money made by a man to his wife or daughter for her own use. **2** a small amount of money used to buy extra things for one's own use.

pin·na (pin′ə) *n.* **pin·nae** (pin′ē or pin′ī) or **pin·nas. 1** in zoology: **a** feather, wing, or winglike part. **b** a fin; flipper. **2** in anatomy, the auricle of the ear; external ear. **3** in botany, one of the primary divisions of a pinnate leaf; leaflet. [< L]

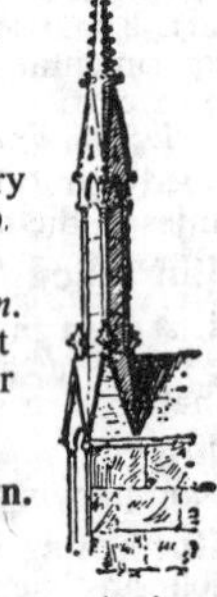
A pinnacle

pin·nace (pin′is) *n.* **1** a ship's boat. **2** a very small schooner. [< F < Ital. *pinaccia* or Sp. *pinaza*, ult. < L *pinus* pine[1]]

pin·na·cle (pin′ə kəl) *n. v.* **-cled, -cling.** —*n.* **1** a high peak or point of rock. **2** the highest point: *at the pinnacle of his fame.* **3** a slender turret or spire. —*v.* **1** put on a pinnacle. **2** furnish with pinnacles. [ME < OF < L *pinnaculum*, dim. of *pinna* wing, point] —**Syn.** *n.* **2** apex, top, zenith, acme.

pin·nate (pin′āt or pin′it) *adj.* **1** like a feather. **2** of a leaf, having leaflets on each side of a stalk. [< L *pinnatus* < *pinna* feather] —**pin′nate·ly,** *adv.*

pinnate grouse a prairie chicken.

pi·noch·le or **pi·noc·le** (pē′nuk′əl or pē′nok′əl) *n.* **1** a game played with 48 cards, in which points are scored according to the value of certain combinations of cards. **2** a combination of the jack of diamonds and the queen of spades in this game. [origin uncertain]

A pinnate leaf

pi·ñon (pin′yən or pēn′yōn) *n.* **1** a pine, especially of the Rocky Mountain region, producing large, edible, nutlike seeds. 2 its seed. [< Sp. *piñón* < *piña* pine cone]

pin·point (pin′point′) *v.* aim at accurately; determine precisely. *—adj.* 1 of the size of a pinpoint; very small. 2 extremely accurate or precise: *pinpoint bombing.* *—n.* 1 the point of a pin. 2 something very small.

pin·scher (pin′shər) *n.* Doberman pinscher.

pin·stripe (pin′strīp′) *n.* 1 a fine stripe. 2 cloth having fine stripes. 3 a garment made of such cloth.

pint (pīnt) *n.* 1 a unit of measure equal to half a quart. *Abbrev.*: p., pt. 2 a container holding a pint. 3 the amount that a pint can hold. [< F < MDu. *pinte* plug]

pin·tail (pin′tāl′) *n.* any of various birds that have long feathers in the centre of the tail.

pin·tle (pin′təl) *n.* a pin or bolt, especially one upon which something turns, as in a hinge. [OE *pintel* penis]

pin·to (pin′tō) *adj. n.* **-tos.** *—adj.* spotted in two colors; piebald. *—n.* a pinto horse. [< Sp. *pinto* painted]

pint-sized (pīnt′sīzd′) *adj. Informal.* smaller than usual for its kind; very small: *a pint-sized tractor.*

pin-up (pin′up′) *n.* 1 a picture of a person considered to be highly attractive, pinned up on a wall by an admirer. 2 a person considered as a suitable subject for a pin-up. *—adj.* very attractive.

pin·wheel (pin′hwēl′ or -wēl′) *n.* 1 a kind of firework that revolves when lighted. 2 a toy made of a paper wheel fastened to a stick by a pin so that it revolves in the wind.

pin·worm (pin′wėrm′) *n.* a small, threadlike worm infesting the rectum, especially of children.

pin·y (pīn′ē) *adj.* **pin·i·er, pin·i·est.** 1 abounding in or covered with pine trees; *piny mountains.* 2 having to do with or suggesting pine trees: *a piny fragrance.* Also, **piney.**

pi·o·neer (pī′ə nēr′) *n.* 1 a person who settled in a region that has not been occupied before, except perhaps by primitive tribes. 2 a person who goes first or does something first, thus preparing the way for others. 3 in military use, one of a group of soldiers whose job it is to go in advance of other troops, preparing camps, roads, trenches, etc.; engineer. *—v.* prepare or open up for others; take the lead in doing. [< F *pionnier* < OF *peon* foot soldier < LL *pedo, pedonis,* < L *pes, pedis* foot. Related to PAWN², PEON.]

pi·ous (pī′əs) *adj.* 1 having or showing reverence for God; religious. 2 done or used from real or pretended religious motives. 3 *Archaic.* dutiful to parents. [< L *pius*] *—***pi′ous·ly,** *adv.* *—***pi′ous·ness,** *n.*

Syn. 1 **Pious, devout** = religious. **Pious** emphasizes showing religion or reverence for God by carefully observing religious duties and practices, such as going to church, and sometimes suggests that more religion is shown than felt: *She is pious enough to go to church in the morning but she gossips all afternoon.* **Devout** emphasizes feeling true reverence that usually is expressed in prayer or devotion to religious observances, but may not be shown at all: *He is a devout Christian and a good man.*

pip¹ (pip) *n.* 1 the seed of an apple, orange, etc. 2 *Slang.* a person or thing that is very attractive, admirable, or extraordinary: *Wait till you meet her—she's really a pip!* [short for *pippin*]

pip² (pip) *n.* 1 a contagious disease of birds, characterized by the secretion of thick mucus in the mouth and throat. 2 *Informal.* a slight illness. 3 **give one the pip,** *Informal.* make one sick; disgust one; irritate one: *That man's nasty way of talking gives me the pip.* [ME < MDu. < VL *pippita* < L *pituita* phlegm]

pip³ (pip) *n.* 1 one of the spots on playing cards, dominoes, or dice. 2 in the army, one of the stars of rank worn on the shoulders of certain officers: *A captain wears three pips, a lieutenant two.* [earlier *peep*; origin uncertain]

pip⁴ (pip) *v.* **pipped, pip·ping.** 1 peep; chirp. 2 of a young bird, break through (the shell). [? var. of *peep*]

pipe (pīp) *n. v.* **piped, pip·ing.** *—n.* 1 a tube through which a liquid or gas flows. 2 a tube with a bowl of clay, wood, etc. at one end, for smoking. 3 a quantity of tobacco a pipe will hold. 4 a musical wind instrument with a single tube into which the player blows. 5 **pipes,** *pl.* a a set of musical tubes: *the pipes of Pan.* b a bagpipe. 6 any one of the tubes in an organ. 7 a shrill sound, voice, or song. 8 a boatswain's whistle. 9 a cask for wine.

hat, āge, cãre, fär; let, ēqual, tėrm; it, īce
hot, ōpen, ôrder; oil, out; cup, pu̇t, rüle, ūse
əbove, takən, pencəl, lemən, circəs
ch, child; ng, long; sh, ship
th, thin; ᴛʜ, then; zh, measure

10 anything shaped like a tube. 11 *Cdn.* formerly, in the fur trade: a a rest period on a journey, originally one in which to smoke a pipe. b a spell of travelling between rest periods. [OE *pipe* < VL *pipa* < L *pipare* chirp; (def. 9) < OF]
—v. 1 carry by means of a pipe or pipes. 2 transmit (a recording, television program, conversation, etc.) by means of radio-frequency, telephone, or other types of transmission lines. 3 supply with pipes. 4 play on a pipe. 5 make a shrill noise; sing or speak in a shrill voice. 6 sing; utter. 7 give orders, signals, etc. with a boatswain's whistle. 8 summon by a pipe: *All hands were piped on deck.* 9 trim (a dress, etc.) with piping (def. 5). 10 **pipe down,** *Slang.* be quiet; shut up. 11 **pipe up,** a begin to play (music). b *Slang.* speak. [< L *pipare* chirp] *—***pipe′like′,** *adj.*

pipe clay a fine white clay used for making tobacco pipes, whitening shoes, etc.

pipe dream *Informal.* an impractical idea.

pipe·ful (pīp′fu̇l) *n.* **-fuls.** the quantity sufficient to fill the bowl of a pipe.

pipe·line (pīp′līn′) *n. v.* **-lined, -lin·ing.** *—n.* 1 a line of pipes for carrying gas, oil, or other liquids. 2 a source of information, usually secret. 3 a flow of materials through a series of productive processes. *—v.* 1 carry by a pipeline. 2 provide with a pipeline.

pipe organ an organ with pipes of different lengths sounded by air blown through them.

pip·er (pīp′ər) *n.* 1 a person who plays on a pipe or bagpipe. 2 **pay the piper,** pay for one's pleasure; bear the consequences.

pi·pette (pi pet′ or pī pet′) *n.* a slender pipe or tube for transferring or measuring liquids. [< F *pipette,* dim. of *pipe* pipe]

pipe wrench an adjustable wrench for gripping and turning pipes, used by plumbers, etc.

pip·ing (pīp′ing) *n.* 1 pipes. 2 the material for pipes. 3 a shrill sound. 4 the music of pipes. 5 a narrow band of material, sometimes containing a cord, used for trimming along edges and seams: *The dress was trimmed with black satin piping.* 6 ornamental lines of icing, frosting, meringue, etc. *—adj.* 1 shrill. 2 **piping hot,** very hot.

pip·it (pip′it) *n.* a small bird resembling a lark, that sings while flying: *One kind of pipit nests on the northern barrens.* [imitative]

pip·kin (pip′kin) *n.* a small earthen pot. [? dim. of *pipe* (def. 9)]

pip·pin (pip′ən) *n.* any of several kinds of apple, such as **Grimes' golden pippin,** the **Newtown pippin,** the **white pippin.** [ME < OF *pepin*]

pip·sis·se·wa (pip sis′ə wə) *n.* a small plant whose evergreen leaves are used in medicine as a tonic, astringent, etc. [< Algonquian]

pip·squeak (pip′skwēk′) *n. Slang.* 1 an insignificant person or thing. 2 a petty, officious person. [name given to a small German high-speed shell of World War I, so named because of its sound in flight]

pi·quan·cy (pē′kən sē) *n.* a piquant quality.

pi·quant (pē′kənt) *adj.* 1 stimulating to the mind; interest, etc.: *a piquant bit of news.* 2 charming; interesting. 3 pleasantly sharp; stimulating to the taste: *a piquant sauce.* [< F *piquant* pricking, stinging] *—***pi′quant·ly,** *adv.*

pique (pēk) *n. v.* **piqued, pi·quing.** *—n.* a feeling of anger at being slighted; wounded pride: *She left the party in a pique.* [< F *pique* < *piquer,* v. See v.] *—v.* 1 cause a feeling of anger in; wound the pride of: *It piqued her that they should have a secret she did not share.* 2 arouse; stir up: *The curiosity of the boys was piqued by the locked trunk.* 3 **pique oneself on** or **upon,** feel proud about. [< F *piquer* prick, sting < *pic* a pick (< Gmc.)]

pi·qué (pē kā′) *n.* a cotton, silk, or rayon fabric with narrow ribs or raised stripes. [< F *piqué* quilted, pp. of *piquer* stitch, prick]

pi·quet (pi ket′) *n.* a complicated card game for two people, played with a deck of 32 cards. [< F]

pi·ra·cy (pī′rə sē) *n.* **-cies. 1** robbery on the sea. **2** the act of publishing, reproducing, or using a book, play, musical composition, etc. without permission. **3** *Informal.* the charging of excessively high prices: *The price of the dress was sheer piracy.* [ME < Med.L < Gk. *peirateia*]

pi·ra·gua (pə rä′gwə or pə rag′wə) *n.* pirogue.

pi·ra·nha (pi rän′yə) *n.* **-nha** or **-nhas.** any of several small fresh-water South American fish so voracious that schools of them will attack and consume men and other large mammals. [< Portuguese *piranha* < Tupi (Brazil) *pira nya,* toothed fish]

pi·rate (pī′rit) *n. v.* **-rat·ed, -rat·ing.** —*n.* **1** one who attacks and robs ships; a robber on the sea. **2** a ship used by pirates. **3** a person who publishes, reproduces, or uses a book, play, musical composition, etc. without permission. —*v.* **1** be a pirate; plunder; rob. **2** publish, reproduce, or use without permission. [ME < L < Gk. *peiratēs* < *peiraein* attack] —**pi′rate·like′,** *adj.*

pi·rat·i·cal (pī rat′ə kəl) *adj.* of pirates; like pirates; like piracy. —**pi·rat′i·cal·ly,** *adv.*

pi·rogue (pə rōg′) *n.* **1** a canoe hollowed from the trunk of a tree; dugout. **2** any canoe. **3** a two-masted, flat-bottomed sailing barge. [< F; probably < Carib. dial.]

pir·ou·ette (pir′ü et′) *n. v.* **-et·ted, -et·ting.** —*n.* a whirling about on one foot or on the toes, as in dancing. —*v.* whirl in this way. [< F *pirouette* spinning top]

pis·ca·to·ri·al (pis′kə tô′rē əl) *adj.* of or having to do with fishermen or fishing. [< L *piscatorius,* ult. < *piscis* fish]

pis·ca·to·ry (pis′kə tô′rē) *adj.* piscatorial.

Pis·ces (pis′ēz or pis′kēz) *n.pl.* **1** in astronomy, a northern constellation that was considered to have the shape of a fish. **2** in astrology, the 12th sign of the zodiac; the Fishes. The sun enters Pisces about February 21. See **zodiac** for diagram. **3** in zoology, a class that includes all true fishes. [< L *pisces,* pl. of *piscis* fish]

pis·cine (pis′īn or pis′in) *adj.* of, having to do with, or characteristic of a fish or fishes. [< L *piscis* fish + E *-ine*[1]]

pish (pish or psh) *interj. n.* a sound made to express contempt or impatience. —*v.* make such a sound.

pis·mire (pis′mīr′) *n. Archaic.* an ant. [ME *pissemire* < *pisse* urine (with reference to the formic acid discharged by ants, popularly regarded as urine) + *mire* ant < Scand.; cf. Norwegian *myre*]

pis·ta·chi·o (pis tash′ē ō′ or pis tä′shē ō) *n.* **-chi·os.** **1** a greenish nut having a flavor that suggests almond. **2** a small tree that it grows on. **3** the flavor of the nut. **4** a light green. [< Ital. < L *pistachium* < Gk. *pistakion* < *pistakē* the tree < OPersian]

pis·ta·reen (pis′tə rēn′) *n.* formerly, a Spanish coin, worth about 20 cents, used as currency in the West Indies, the United States, and Canada during the eighteenth and early nineteenth centuries. —*adj.* petty; trifling. [apparently < modification of Sp. *peseta* peseta]

pis·til (pis′təl) *n.* in botany, the part of a flower that produces seeds, consisting, when complete, of an ovary, a style, and a stigma. [< NL *pistillum* < L *pistillum* pestle. Doublet of PESTLE.]

pis·til·late (pis′tə lit or pis′tə lāt′) *adj.* **1** having a pistil or pistils. **2** having a pistil or pistils but no stamens.

pis·tol (pis′təl) *n.* a small, short gun capable of being held and fired with one hand: *A revolver is a kind of pistol.* [< F *pistole* < G < Czech *pišťala*]

pis·tole (pis tōl′) *n.* **1** a former gold coin of Spain worth about $4.00. **2** any of various other old European gold coins of about the same value. [< F *pistole* coin, pistol. See PISTOL.]

pis·ton (pis′tən) *n.* **1** a short cylinder, or a flat, round piece of wood or metal, fitting closely inside a tube or hollow cylinder in which it is moved back and forth by some force (often the pressure of steam). A piston receives or transmits motion by means of a rod (**piston rod**) that is attached to it. **2** in a musical wind instrument, a sliding valve that, when pressed by the fingers, lowers the pitch. [< F < Ital. *pistone* < *pistare* pound, ult. < L *pistus,* pp. of *pinsere* pound]

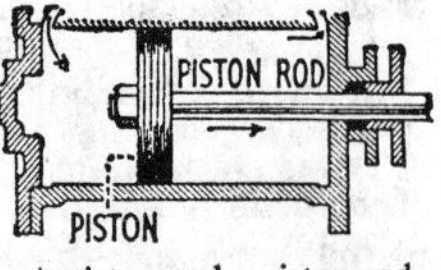

A piston and a piston rod. The upper arrows show where steam or gas enters and leaves the cylinder.

piston ring a metal ring, split so it can expand, put around a piston to insure a tight fit.

piston rod a rod that moves, or is moved by, a piston.

pit[1] (pit) *n. v.* **pit·ted, pit·ting.** —*n.* **1** a natural hole in the ground. **2** a hole dug deep in the earth such as a mine or the shaft of a mine. **3** a hollow on the surface of anything; hole. **4** a little hole or scar, such as is left by smallpox. **5** a covered hole used as a trap for wild animals. **6** an unsuspected danger. **7** *Brit.* **a** the rear part of the main floor of a theatre, where the seats are cheap. **b** the people who sit there. **8** the part of the floor of an exchange devoted to a special business: *the wheat pit.* **9** a place where dogs or cocks were made to fight. **10** a large grave for many bodies. **11** hell, or part of it. **12 pits,** in automobile racing, an area beside the track for the repair, refuelling, inspection, etc. of participating cars. —*v.* **1** mark with small pits or scars. **2** set to fight or compete; match: *The little man pitted his brains against the big man's strength.* [OE *pytt,* ult. < L *puteus* well] —**Syn.** *n.* **2** excavation. **6** snare, pitfall.

pit[2] (pit) *n. v.* **pit·ted, pit·ting.** —*n.* the hard seed of a cherry, peach, plum, date, etc.; stone. —*v.* remove pits from (fruit). [< Du. *pit* kernel]

pit·a·pat (pit′ə pat′) *adv.* with a quick succession of beats or taps. —*n.* the movement or sound of something going pitapat.

pitch[1] (pich) *v.* **1** throw; fling; hurl; toss: *The men were pitching horseshoes.* **2** pick up and fling (hay, straw, etc.) in a mass with a pitchfork onto a vehicle, into a barn, etc. **3 a** in baseball, throw the ball for the batter to hit. **b** in golf, loft (a ball) so that it alights with little roll. **4** *Slang.* sell or try to sell (a product, service, etc.) often by high-pressure means. **5** erect; set up: *pitch a tent, pitch camp.* **6** take up a position; settle. **7** fix firmly, in or as in the ground. **8** fall or plunge forward: *The man lost his balance and pitched down the cliff.* **9** of a boat or ship, plunge with the bow rising and then falling: *The ship pitched about in the storm.* **10** set at a certain point, degree, or level. **11** in music, determine the key of (a tune, instrument, etc.). **12** slope. **13** in card games: **a** indicate one's choice of trump by an opening lead of (a card of the suit chosen). **b** settle (the trump suit) thus. **14 pitch in,** *Informal.* **a** work vigorously. **b** help with work. **15 pitch into,** *Informal.* attack, usually with the fists. **16 pitch on** or **upon,** choose; select.
—*n.* **1** a throw; fling; hurl; toss. **2** a point; position; degree: *The poor man has reached the lowest pitch of bad fortune.* **3** the degree of highness or lowness of a sound. **4** in music: **a** the exact number of vibrations producing a particular tone. **b** a particular standard of pitch: *concert pitch.* **5** height. **6** the act or manner of pitching. **7** that which is pitched. **8** *Slang.* **a** a talk, argument, offer, plan, etc. used to persuade, as in selling, or to promote an idea, product, etc. **b** a television or radio commercial. **9 a** a place of pitching or encamping or taking up a position. **b** a spot in a street or market place where a peddler, street performer, etc. regularly stations himself; stand. **10** the amount of slope. **11** the distance between the successive teeth of a cogwheel. **12** the distance between two things in a machine. **13** the piece of ground on which certain games are played: *a cricket pitch, a horseshoe pitch.* **14** the movement of the longitudinal axis of an aircraft up or down from the horizontal plane. **15** a plunge forward or headlong; lurch. **16** a downward plunging of the fore part of a ship in a rough sea. **17** the act of pitching on or choosing a place to live in, etc. **18 make a pitch for,** *Informal.* make a persuasive request for; make a bid for. [ME *picche(n)*] —**Syn.** *v.* **1** cast, heave.

hat, āge, cãre, fär; let, ēqual, tėrm; it, īce
hot, ōpen, ôrder; oil, out; cup, pu̇t, rüle, ūse
əbove, takən, pencəl, lemən, circəs
ch, child; ng, long; sh, ship
th, thin; ᴛʜ, then; zh, measure

pitch[2] (pich) *n.* **1** a black, sticky substance made from tar or turpentine, used to cover the seams of ships, to cover roofs, to make pavements, etc. **2** the resin from certain evergreen trees. *—v.* cover with pitch. [OE *pic* < L *pix, picis*]

pitch·blende (pich′blend′) *n.* a mineral consisting largely of uranium oxide, occurring in black, pitchlike masses. It is a source of radium, uranium, and actinium. [half-translation of G *Pechblende*]

pitch-dark (pich′därk′) *adj.* very dark.

pitched battle a battle with troops drawn up in battle array.

pitch·er[1] (pich′ər) *n.* **1** a container for holding and pouring liquids, with a lip on one side and a handle on the other. **2** the amount that a pitcher holds. [ME < OF *pichier*]

pitch·er[2] (pich′ər) *n.* in baseball, the player who throws the ball to the batter. [< *pitch*[1]]

pitch·er·ful (pich′ər fu̇l) *n.* **-fuls.** the quantity sufficient to fill a pitcher.

pitcher plant a bog plant having leaves resembling a pitcher in shape.

pitch·fork (pich′fôrk′) *n.* a large fork with a long handle, for lifting and throwing hay or straw. *—v.* lift and throw with a pitchfork.

pitch·man (pich′man′) *n.* **-men** (-men′). **1** *Informal.* a man who sells articles such as small toys on the street or at carnivals. **2** *Slang.* a high-pressure promoter or salesman: *a television pitchman.*

pitch pine a pine tree from which pitch or turpentine is obtained.

pitch pipe a small musical pipe having a fixed tone or tones, used to give the pitch for singing or for tuning an instrument.

pitch·y (pich′ē) *adj.* **pitch·i·er, pitch·i·est. 1** full of pitch. **2** like pitch; sticky. **3** black.

pit·e·ous (pit′ē əs) *adj.* to be pitied; moving the heart; deserving pity. [ME < OF *pitos* < Med.L *pietosus* pitiful < L *pietas* pity; influenced in form by ME *pite* pity] **—pit′e·ous·ly,** *adv.* **—pit′e·ous·ness,** *n.* **—Syn.** See **pitiful.**

pit·fall (pit′fol′ or -fôl′) *n.* **1** a hidden pit to catch animals in. **2** any trap or hidden danger.

pith (pith) *n.* **1** the central, spongy tissue in the stems of certain plants. **2** a similar soft tissue: *the pith of an orange.* **3** an important or essential part: *the pith of a speech.* **4** strength; energy. [OE *pitha*] **—Syn. 3** essence, gist. **4** vigor, force.

Pith·e·can·thro·pus (pith′ə kan thrō′pəs or pith′ə kan′thrə pəs) *n.* **-pi** (-pī or -pē). a type of extinct, prehistoric ape man, whose existence is assumed from remains found in Java in 1891 and 1892. [< NL < Gk. *pithēkos* ape + *anthrōpos* man]

pith helmet a sun hat shaped like a helmet, originally made from the dried pith of Bengal spongewood.

pith·y (pith′ē) *adj.* **pith·i·er, pith·i·est. 1** full of substance, meaning, force, or vigor: *pithy phrases, a pithy speaker.* **2** of or like pith. **3** having much pith: *a pithy orange.* **—pith′i·ly,** *adv.* **—pith′i·ness,** *n.* **Syn. 1** pointed.

pit·i·a·ble (pit′ē ə bəl) *adj.* **1** to be pitied; moving the heart; deserving pity. **2** deserving contempt; mean; to be scorned. **—pit′i·a·ble·ness,** *n.* **—pit′i·a·bly,** *adv.* **—Syn. 1** lamentable, deplorable. See **pitiful.**

pit·i·ful (pit′ē fəl) *adj.* **1** to be pitied; moving the heart; deserving pity. **2** feeling or showing pity: *He watched the crippled children with a pitiful expression on his face.* **3** deserving contempt; mean; to be scorned: *His half-hearted attempts to help were pitiful.* **—pit′i·ful·ly,** *adv.*
Syn. 1 Pitiful, piteous, pitiable = arousing pity or to be pitied. **Pitiful** emphasizes the effect on others, that of arousing pity, made by someone or something felt to be touching or pathetic: *The deserted children were pitiful.* **Piteous** emphasizes the quality in the thing itself that makes it appeal for pity and move the heart: *Their sad faces were piteous.* **Pitiable** emphasizes arousing sorrow or regret, often mixed with contempt, for what deserves or needs to be pitied: *Their bodies and clothes were in a pitiable condition.* **2** compassionate, merciful.

pit·i·less (pit′ē lis) *adj.* without pity or mercy. **—pit′i·less·ly,** *adv.* **—pit′i·less·ness,** *n.* **—Syn.** merciless. See **cruel.**

pi·ton (pē′ton or pi ton′; *French,* pē tôɴ′) *n.* **1** an iron spike with a ring at one end, used in mountain climbing. It can be driven into a crack in rock or ice and used to secure a rope or as a step. **2** a sharply pointed mountain or rock peak. [< F *piton* point, peak]

pit·tance (pit′əns) *n.* **1** a small allowance of money. **2** a small amount or share. [ME < OF *pitance,* ult. < L *pietas* piety]

pit·ter-pat·ter (pit′ər pat′ər) *n.* a rapid succession of light beats or taps, as of rain. *—adv.* with a rapid succession of beats or taps.

pi·tu·i·tar·y (pə tū′ə ter′ē or pə tü′ə ter′ē) *adj.* **1** having to do with the pituitary gland. **2** of, having to do with, or secreting mucus. *—n.* **1** the pituitary gland. **2** medicine made from an extract of this gland. [< L *pituitarius* < *pituita* phlegm]

pituitary body pituitary gland.

pituitary gland in anatomy, a small, oval endocrine gland situated beneath the brain. It secretes hormones that promote growth, stimulate other glands, etc.

pit·y (pit′ē) *n.* **pit·ies,** *v.* **pit·ied, pit·y·ing.** *—n.* **1** sympathy; sorrow for another's suffering or distress; a feeling for the sorrows of others. **2** a cause for pity or regret; something to be sorry for: *It is a pity to be kept in the house in good weather.* **3 have** or **take pity on,** show pity for. *—v.* feel pity for. [ME < OF *pite* < L *pietas.* Doublet of PIETY.] **—pit′y·ing·ly,** *adv.*
Syn. *n.* **1 Pity, compassion, sympathy** = a feeling for the sorrows or suffering of others. **Pity** = a feeling of sorrow for someone who is suffering or in sorrow or distress, and often felt to be weak or unfortunate: *Nobody wants pity from his friends.* **Compassion** adds the idea of tenderness and a strong desire to help or protect: *He had compassion on the sobbing child.* **Sympathy** = a feeling with another in his sorrow and sharing and understanding it: *He expects sympathy from his brother.*

piv·ot (piv′ət) *n.* **1** a shaft, pin, or point on which something turns. **2** that on which something turns, hinges, or depends; central point. **3** in hockey, the centre player of a forward line. *—v.* **1** mount on, attach by, or provide with a pivot. **2** turn on a pivot. [< F]

piv·ot·al (piv′ə təl) *adj.* of, having to do with, or serving as a pivot; being that on which something turns, hinges, or depends; very important.

pix·ie or **pix·y** (pik′sē) *n.* **pix·ies.** a fairy or elf. [origin uncertain]

pizza (pēt′sə) *n.* an open pie, usually made of a layer of bread dough covered with a savory mixture of tomatoes, cheese, olives, etc. and baked. [< Ital.]

pizza pie pizza.

piz·zi·ca·to (pit′sə kä′tō) *adj. adv. n.* **-ti** (-tē). in music: *—adj.* played by plucking the strings of a musical instrument with the finger instead of using the bow. *—adv.* in a pizzicato manner. *—n.* a note or passage so played. [< Ital. *pizzicato* picked]

pk. 1 peck. **2** peak. **3** park. **4** pack.

pkg. package.

pl. 1 plural. **2** place. **3** plate.

pla·ca·ble (plak′ə bəl or plā′kə bəl) *adj.* forgiving; easily quieted; mild. [ME < OF < L *placabilis* < *placare* placate] **—pla′ca·ble·ness,** *n.* **—pla′ca·bly,** *adv.*

plac·ard (*n.* plak′ärd; *v.* plə kärd′ or plak′ärd) *n.* a notice to be posted in a public place; poster. *—v.* **1** put placards on or in: *The circus placarded the city with advertisements.* **2** give notice of with placards. **3** post as a placard. [< F *placard* < *plaque* plaque]

pla·cate (plak′āt, plā′kāt, or plə kāt′) *v.* **-cat·ed, -cat·ing.** soothe or satisfy the anger of; make peaceful: *to placate a person one has offended.* [< L *placare*] **—pla′cat·er,** *n.* **—pla′cat·ing·ly,** *adv.*

place (plās) *n. v.* **placed, plac·ing.** *—n.* **1** the space occupied by a person or thing. **2** a particular portion of space or of the earth's surface, of a definite or indefinite size, but of definite position; location. **3** a city, town, village, district, etc. **4** a building or spot used for a certain purpose. A church is a place of worship. A store or office is a place of business. **5** a house; house and grounds; dwelling. **6** a part or spot in something: *The dentist filled the decayed place in the tooth.* **7** a particular page or other point in a book or other writing: *mark one's place.* **8** reasonable ground or occasion. **9** the proper or natural position: *books in place on shelves.* **10** a rank; position; way of life: *A master and a slave have very different places in life.* **11** a position in time: *The performance went too slowly in several places.* **12** a space or seat for a person: *Keep a place for me if you reach the bus first.* **13** a situation; post or office; official employment or position. **14** duty; business: *It is not my place to find fault.* **15** a step or point in order of proceeding: *In the first place, the room is too small; in the second place, it is too dirty.* **16** in mathematics, the position of a figure in a number: *in the third decimal place.* **17** a position among the leaders at the finish of a race: *John won first place.* **18** a ranking position, especially one of the first three, at the end of a race. **19** the second position at the end of a horse race. **20** a short street or court. **21** an open space or square in a city, town, etc.

give place, a make room. **b** yield; give in.

go places, *Slang.* advance rapidly toward success; achieve success.

in place, a on the proper or usual place; in the original place. **b** fitting, appropriate, or timely.

in place of, instead of.

know one's place, act according to one's position in life.

out of place, a not in the proper or usual place. **b** inappropriate or ill-timed.

take place, happen; occur.

—*v.* **1** put (in a spot, position, condition, or relation). **2** put in the proper order or position; arrange: dispose. **3** give the place, position, or condition of; identify: *I remember his name, but I cannot place him.* **4** determine the date of; assign to an age, etc. **5** appoint (a person) to a post or office; find a situation, etc. for. **6** attribute or ascribe. **7** entrust to an appropriate person, firm, etc. for action, treatment, disposal, etc. **8** be among the three leaders at the finish of a race or competition, usually the second. **9** produce (sounds of song or speech) with emphasis upon resonance assisted by the body organs involved; pitch. [ME < OF < VL *plattia* < L < Gk. *plateia* (*hodos*) broad (way) < *platys* broad. Doublet of PLAZA and PIAZZA.] —**Syn.** *n.* **12** room. –*v.* **1** locate, set. See **put.**

pla·ce·bo (plə sē′bō) *n.* **-bos** or **-boes. 1** in the Roman Catholic Church, the vespers of the office for the dead. **2** in medicine, a pill, etc. containing no drug but given to humor or satisfy a patient, or to serve as a control in an experiment to test a new drug. **3** something said only to flatter or mollify. [< L *placebo* I shall please, the opening word of the church service]

place in the sun a favorable position; as favorable a position as any occupied by others.

place mat a small piece of linen, plastic, paper, straw, etc. put under a person's plate or place setting.

place·ment (plās′mənt) *n.* **1** a placing or being placed; location; arrangement. **2** the finding of work or a job for a person. **3** in football: **a** a placing of the ball on the ground for a placement kick. **b** a placement kick.

placement kick in football, a kick given to a ball after it has been placed on the ground.

place name a name of a place, city, area, country, etc.; any geographical name. Athens, Asia, Niagara Falls, Arctic Ocean are place names.

pla·cen·ta (plə sen′tə) *n.* **-tae** (-tē or -tī) or **-tas. 1** the organ by which the fetus is attached to the wall of the womb and nourished. **2** the part of the ovary of flowering plants that bears the ovules. [< NL < L *placenta* flat cake < Gk. *plakounta*, accus. < *plax*, *plakos* flat surface]

pla·cen·tal (plə sen′təl) *adj.* **1** of or having to do with the placenta. **2** having a placenta.

plac·er[1] (plās′ər) *n.* a person or thing that places.

plac·er[2] (plas′ər) *n.* a place where gold or other minerals can be washed out of loose sand or gravel. [< Am.Sp. *placer* sandbank. Akin to PLAZA.]

placer mining the process of washing loose sand or gravel for gold or other minerals: *Placer mining was a common practice in the Klondike.*

place setting the dishes or cutlery required to set one place at a table.

plac·id (plas′id) *adj.* calm; peaceful; quiet: *a placid lake.* [< L *placidus* < *placere* please] —**plac′id·ly,** *adv.* —**plac′id·ness,** *n.* —**Syn.** See **peaceful.**

pla·cid·i·ty (plə sid′ə tē) *n.* calmness; peace.

plack·et (plak′it) *n.* an opening or slit at the top of a skirt, the side of a dress, etc. to make it easy to put on. [? var. of *placard*]

pla·gia·rism (plā′jə riz′əm) *n.* **1** the act of plagiarizing. **2** an idea, expression, plot, etc. taken from another and used as one's own. [< L *plagiarius* kidnapper, ult. < *plaga* net]

pla·gia·rist (plā′jə rist) *n.* a person who plagiarizes.

pla·gia·rize (plā′jə rīz′) *v.* **-rized, -riz·ing.** take and use as one's own (the thoughts, writings, inventions, etc. of another); especially, to take and use a passage, plot, etc. from the work of another writer. —**pla′gia·riz′er,** *n.*

plague (plāg) *n. v.* **plagued, pla·guing.** —*n.* **1** a very dangerous disease that spreads rapidly and often causes death. It occurs in several forms, one of which is bubonic plague. The plague is common in Asia and has several times swept through Europe. **2** a punishment thought to be sent from God. **3** anything or anyone that torments, vexes, annoys, troubles, offends, or is disagreeable. —*v.* **1** cause to suffer from a plague. **2** vex; annoy; bother: *Stop plaguing me for money.* [ME < L *plaga* blow, pestilence < dial. Gk. *plaga* blow] —**Syn.** *v.* **2** trouble, worry, pester. See **tease.**

pla·guey (plā′gē) *adj. Informal.* plaguy.

pla·guy (plā′gē) *adj. Informal.* troublesome; annoying.

plaice (plās) *n.* **plaice** or **plaic·es. 1** a European flatfish that is important for food. **2** any of various North American flatfishes or flounders. [ME < OF < LL *platessa* flatfish < Gk. *platys* flat]

plaid (plad) *n.* **1** any cloth with a pattern of checks or crisscross stripes. **2** a pattern of this kind. **3** a long piece of woollen cloth, usually having a tartan pattern, worn about the shoulders by the Scottish Highlanders. —*adj.* having a pattern of checks or crisscross stripes: *a plaid dress.* [< Scots Gaelic *plaide*]

plaid·ed (plad′id) *adj.* **1** made of plaid; having a plaid pattern. **2** wearing a plaid.

plain[1] (plān) *adj.* **1** easy to understand; easily seen or heard; clear: *The meaning is plain.* **2** that is clearly what the name expresses; unmistakable; downright; absolute: *plain foolishness.* **3** not intricate; uncomplicated: *plain sewing.* **4** straightforward; direct: *give a plain answer to a question.* **5** without ornament or decoration; simple: *a plain dress.* **6** without figured pattern, varied weave, or variegated color: *a plain-blue dress.* **7** not rich or highly seasoned: *plain food.* **8** common; ordinary; simple in manner: *a plain man of the people.* **9** not pretty: *a plain girl.* **10** not very hard; easy. **11** frank; honest; sincere: *plain speech.* **12** flat; level; smooth; plane. —*adv.* in a plain manner; clearly: *Speak it plain.* —*n.* **1** a flat stretch of land; prairie. **2 plains,** *pl.* prairies. [ME < OF < L *planus* flat. Doublet of PIANO[2], PLAN.] —**plain′ly,** *adv.* —**plain′ness,** *n.* —**Syn.** *adj.* **1** apparent, manifest, evident, obvious. **11** unaffected, candid, straightforward.

plain[2] (plān) *v. Archaic and dialect.* complain. [ME < OF, ult. < L *plangere* lament]

plain-clothes man (plān′klōz′ or -klōTHz′) a policeman or detective wearing ordinary clothes, not a uniform, when on duty.

plain sailing 1 sailing on a smooth, easy course. **2** easy, clear action.

Plains Cree one of the two main groups of the Cree tribe of North American Indians. The Plains Cree migrated to the prairies from the eastern woodlands.

plains·man (plānz′mən) *n.* **-men** (-mən). a man who lives on the plains.

Plains of Abraham See **Abraham, Plains of.**

plain song vocal music used in the Christian church from the earliest times. Plain song is sung in unison. It is rhythmical, although the beats are not regular.

plain-spo·ken (plān′spō′kən) *adj.* plain or frank in speech.

plaint (plānt) *n.* **1** a complaint. **2** *Archaic.* a lament. [ME < OF < L *planctus* lamentation < *plangere* lament]

plain·tiff (plān′tif) *n.* in law, a person who begins a lawsuit: *The plaintiff accused the defendant of fraud.* [ME < OF *plaintif* complaining. See PLAINTIVE.]

plain·tive (plān′tiv) *adj.* mournful; sad. [ME < OF *plaintif*, ult. < L *planctus* complaint] **—plain′tive·ly,** *adv.* **—plain′tive·ness,** *n.* **—Syn.** doleful, sorrowful.

plais·ter (plās′tər) *n. v Obs.* plaster.

plait (plāt or plat *for 1*; plāt or plēt *for 2*) *n. v.* **1** braid. **2** pleat. [ME < OF *pleit*, ult. < L *plicare* fold]

plan (plan) *n. v.* **planned, plan·ning.** *—n.* **1** a way of making or doing something that has been worked out beforehand; scheme of arrangement. **2** a drawing or diagram to show how a garden, a floor of a house, a park, etc. is arranged. *—v.* **1** think out beforehand how (something) is to be made or done; design, scheme, or devise: *to plan a trip.* **2** make plans. **3** make a drawing or diagram of. [< F *plan*, literally, a plane < L *planus*; with reference to a sketch on a flat surface. Doublet of PLAIN[1], PIANO[2].]

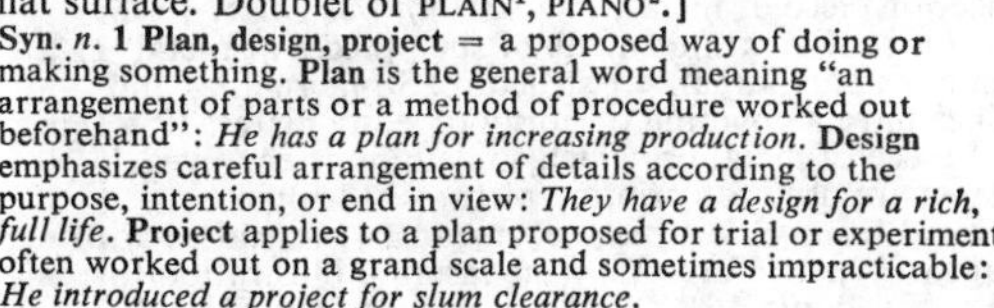

A plan (def. 2)

Syn. *n.* **1 Plan, design, project** = a proposed way of doing or making something. **Plan** is the general word meaning "an arrangement of parts or a method of procedure worked out beforehand": *He has a plan for increasing production.* **Design** emphasizes careful arrangement of details according to the purpose, intention, or end in view: *They have a design for a rich, full life.* **Project** applies to a plan proposed for trial or experiment, often worked out on a grand scale and sometimes impracticable: *He introduced a project for slum clearance.*

pla·nar·i·an (plə nãr′ē ən) *n.* in zoology, any of a group of fresh-water flatworms having three-branched intestines, flattened bodies, and the power of growing again when cut apart. *—adj.* of or belonging to the planarians. [< NL *Planaria* < L *planus* flat; level + E *-an*]

plan·chette (plan shet′) *n.* a small board supported on two casters and having a vertical pencil. The pencil is supposed to write words, sentences, etc. involuntarily when a person rests his fingers lightly on the board. [< F *planchette*, dim. of *planche* plank]

plane[1] (plān) *n. adj. v.* **planed, plan·ing.** *—n.* **1** any flat or level surface. **2** a level; grade: *Try to keep your work on a high plane.* **3** a thin, flat or curved supporting surface of an airplane. **4** an airplane. **5** in geometry, a surface such that if any two points on it are joined by a straight line, the line will be contained wholly in the surface. *—adj.* **1** flat; level. **2** being wholly in a plane: *a plane figure.* **3** of or having to do with such figures: *plane geometry.* *—v.* **1** travel in an airplane. **2** glide as an airplane does. **3** rise slightly out of the water while moving. [< L *planum* level place]

plane[2] (plān) *n. v.* **planed, plan·ing.** *—n.* **1** a carpenter's tool with a blade for smoothing or removing wood. **2** a machine for smoothing or removing metal. *—v.* **1** smooth with a plane. **2** remove with a plane. [< F *plane*, ult. < LL *plana*]

A carpenter's plane in use. The blade is fastened at a slant between the two handles. It is lowered or raised to shave more or less wood at each stroke.

plane[3] (plān) *n.* plane tree.

plan·er (plān′ər) *n.* a person or thing that planes, especially a machine for planing wood or for finishing flat surfaces on metal.

plan·et (plan′it) *n.* **1** in astronomy, one of the heavenly bodies (except comets and meteors) that move around the sun. Mercury, Venus, the Earth, Mars, Jupiter, Saturn, Uranus, Neptune, and

hat, āge, cãre, fär; let, ēqual, tėrm; it, īce
hot, ōpen, ôrder; oil, out; cup, pu̇t, rüle, ūse
əbove, takən, pencəl, lemən, circəs
ch, child; ng, long; sh, ship
th, thin; ᴛʜ, then; zh, measure

Pluto are planets. **2** in astrology, a heavenly body supposed to influence people's lives. [< LL < Gk. *planētēs* < *planaesthai* wander]

plan·e·tar·i·um (plan′ə tãr′ē əm) *n.* **-i·a** (-ē ə) or **-i·ums. 1** an apparatus that shows the movements of the sun, moon, planets, and stars by projecting lights on the inside of a dome. **2** a room or building with such an apparatus. [< NL]

plan·e·tar·y (plan′ə ter′ē) *adj.* **1** of a planet; having to do with planets. **2** wandering; erratic. **3** terrestrial; mundane. **4** having to do with a form of transmission for varying the speed in automobiles.

plan·e·tes·i·mal (plan′ə tes′ə məl) *adj.* of or having to do with minute bodies in space that, according to a certain hypothesis, move in planetary orbits and gradually unite to form the planets of a given planetary system. [< *planet*, modelled on *infinitesimal*]

plan·et·oid (plan′ə toid′) *n.* a minor planet; asteroid.

plane tree a tall, spreading tree having broad leaves and bark that scales off in irregular patches. The North American plane tree is also called the buttonwood or sycamore. [ME < OF < L < Gk. *platanos* < *platys* broad]

plank (plangk) *n.* **1** a long, flat piece of sawed timber thicker than a board. **2** an article or feature of the platform of a political party, etc. **3** a flat timber forming part of the outer side of a ship's hull. **4** anything that supports or saves in time of need (with allusion to the use of a plank to save a ship-wrecked man from drowning). **5 walk the plank,** be forced to walk off a plank extending from a ship's side over the water. Pirates used to make their prisoners do this. *—v.* **1** cover or furnish with planks. **2** cook on a board. Steak is sometimes planked. **3** *Informal.* put or set with force: *He planked it on the table. He planked down the package.* **4** *Informal.* pay at once: *She planked out her money.* [ME < ONF < L *planca*]

plank·ing (plangk′ing) *n.* **1** the act of laying or covering with planks. **2** planks collectively.

plank·ton (plangk′tən) *n.* the small animal and plant organisms that float or drift in water, especially on or near the surface. [< F < Gk. *plankton*, neut., wandering, verbal adj. to *plazesthai* wander]

plan·ner (plan′ər) *n.* a person who plans.

pla·no-con·cave (plā′nō kon′kāv) *adj.* flat on one side and concave on the other. [< L *planus* flat + E *concave*]

pla·no-con·vex (plā′nō kon′veks) *adj.* flat on one side and convex on the other. [< L *planus* flat + E *convex*]

plant (plant) *n.* **1** a living thing that is not an animal. Trees, shrubs, herbs, fungi, algae, etc. are plants. **2** a living thing that has leaves, roots, and a soft stem, and is small in contrast with a tree or shrub. **3** a young growth ready to be set out in another place. **4** the buildings, machinery, etc. used in manufacturing: *There is an aluminum plant in Kingston.* **5** the workmen employed at a plant: *The whole plant is on strike.* **6** the complete apparatus used for a specific mechanical operation or process: *the heating plant on a ship.* **7** buildings, equipment, etc. for any purpose: *a college plant.* **8** *Slang.* a scheme to trap, trick, mislead, or deceive. **9** *Slang.* a person or thing so placed or a plan so devised as to trap, trick, lure, or deceive criminals or wrongdoers. **10** a person, supposedly a member of the audience, who assists a performer on the stage: *a magician's plant.* *—v.* **1** put or set in the ground to grow. **2** furnish; stock; put seed in. **3** deposit (young fish, spawn, oysters) in a river, lake, etc. **4** set firmly; put; place. **5** post; station: *plant guards at an entrance.* **6** establish or set up (a colony, city, etc.). **7** implant (principles, doctrines, etc.). **8** *Slang.* hide (something stolen, etc.). **9** *Slang.* deliver (a blow, etc.) with a definite aim. **10** *Slang.* place (a person or thing) as a plant, trap, or trick. [OE *plante* < L *planta* sprout]

Plan·tag·e·net (plan taj′ə nit) *n.* a member of the royal family that ruled England from 1154 to 1485. The English kings from Henry II through Richard III were Plantagenets.

plan·tain[1] (plan′tən) *n.* **1** a kind of large banana. **2** the plant that it grows on. [< Sp. *plántano*]

plan·tain[2] (plan′tən) *n.* a common weed having large, spreading leaves close to the ground and long, slender spikes carrying flowers and seeds. [ME < OF < L *plantago, -ginis* < *planta* sole of the foot; from its flat leaves]

plan·ta·tion (plan tā′shən) *n.* **1** a large farm or estate, especially in a tropical or semitropical country, on which cotton, tobacco, sugar, etc. are grown. The work on a plantation is done by laborers who live there. **2** a large group of trees or other plants that have been planted. **3** a colony. [< L *plantatio, -onis* a planting < *planta* sprout]

plant·er (plan′tər) *n.* **1** a man who owns or runs a plantation. **2** a machine for planting. **3** a person who plants. **4** an enclosure in which flowers are planted at the side of a building. **5** a box, often on legs, that is used for growing plants in the house. **6** in Newfoundland, a small trader; a person who hires others to fish for him, advancing their supplies and taking a share of the catch. **7** an early settler; colonist.

plan·ti·grade (plan′tə grād′) *adj.* walking on the whole sole of the foot. A bear is a plantigrade animal. [< L *planta* sole + *gradi* walk]

plant louse an aphid.

plaque (plak) *n.* **1** an ornamental tablet of metal, porcelain, etc. **2** a platelike ornament or badge. [< F < Du. *plak* flat board]

plash (plash) *v. n.* splash.

plasm (plaz′əm) *n.* plasma.

plas·ma (plaz′mə) *n.* **1** the liquid part of blood or lymph, as distinguished from the corpuscles. **2** the watery part of milk, as distinguished from the globules of fat. **3** in physics, a highly ionized gas, consisting of almost equal numbers of free electrons and positive ions. **4** protoplasm. **5** a green, faintly translucent variety of quartz. [< LL < Gk. *plasma* something formed or moulded < *plassein* mould]

plas·ter (plas′tər) *n.* **1** a soft mixture of lime, sand, and water that hardens in drying, used for covering walls or ceilings. **2** plaster of Paris. **3** in medicine, a preparation consisting of a pastelike substance spread on cloth, that will stick to the body and protect cuts, relieve pain, etc.
—*v.* **1** cover with plaster. **2** spread with anything thickly. **3** make smooth and flat: *He plastered his hair down.* **4** apply a plaster to. **5** apply like a plaster. [OE < Med.L *plastrum* < L *emplastrum* < Gk. *emplastron* < *en-* on + *plassein* mould] **—plas′ter·like′,** *adj.*

plas·ter·board (plas′tər bôrd′) *n.* a thin board made of plaster between sheets of heavy paper: *Plasterboard is much used in building walls and partitions.*

plaster cast **1** a mould made with plaster of Paris. **2** a mould made from a bandage of gauze and plaster of Paris to hold a broken or dislocated bone in place.

plas·ter·er (plas′tər ər) *n.* a person who plasters walls, etc.

plas·ter·ing (plas′tər ing) *n.* a covering of plaster on walls, etc.

plaster of Paris (par′is) a mixture of powdered gypsum and water, which hardens quickly and is used for making moulds, cheap statuary, casts, etc.

plas·tic (plas′tik) *adj.* **1** made of plastic: *plastic cups.* **2** moulding or giving shape to material. **3** concerned with moulding or modelling: *Sculpture is a plastic art.* **4** easily moulded or shaped: *Clay, wax, and plaster are plastic substances.* **5** easily influenced; impressionable.
—*n.* any of various substances that harden and retain their shape after being moulded or shaped when softened by heat, pressure, etc. Glass, celluloid, Bakelite, vulcanite, and nylon are all plastics. [< L *plasticus* < Gk. *plastikos,* ult. < *plassein* form, shape]

Plas·ti·cine (plas′ti sēn′) *n. Trademark.* a substance used for modelling, especially by children.

plas·tic·i·ty (plas tis′ə tē) *n.* plastic quality.

plas·tics (plas′tiks) *n. adj.* —*n.* **1** the branch of chemistry that deals with the study and use of materials, such as glass or nylon, that can be shaped or moulded when hot, becoming hard when cooled. **2** the whole range of such materials: *Plastics are important in modern industry.* —*adj.* of or having to do with such materials.

plastic surgery surgery that restores, remedies, or improves the outer appearance of the body.

plas·tron (plas′trən) *n.* **1** a metal breastplate worn under a coat of mail. **2** a leather guard worn over the chest of a fencer. **3** an ornamental, detachable front of a woman's bodice. **4** the ventral part of the shell of a turtle or tortoise. [< F < Ital. *piastrone* < *piastra* plate of metal < Med.L *plastrum* plaster. See PLASTER.]

plat[1] (plat) *n. v.* **plat·ted, plat·ting.** —*n.* **1** a map; chart; plan. **2** a small piece of ground; plot. —*v.* map; chart; plan. [ME < OF < VL < Gk. *platys* broad, flat; meaning of def. 2 from *plot*]

plat[2] (plat) *n. v.* **plat·ted, plat·ting.** braid; plait. [var. of *plait*]

plate (plāt) *n. v.* **plat·ed, plat·ing.** —*n.* **1** a dish, usually round, that is almost flat. **2** the contents of such a dish. **3** a plateful. **4** something having the shape of a plate. A plate is passed in church to receive the collection. **5** a part of a meal, served on or in a separate dish; course. **6** the dishes and food served to one person at a meal. **7** dishes or utensils of silver or gold. **8** dishes and utensils covered with a thin layer of silver or gold. **9** a thin, flat sheet or piece of metal: *The warship was covered with steel plates.* **10** armor made of such pieces of metal. **11** a platelike part, organ, or structure. Some reptiles and fishes have a covering of horny or bony plates. **12** a thin, flat piece of metal on which something is engraved. Plates are used for printing pictures. **13** something printed from such a piece of metal. **14** a metal copy of a page of type. **15** any full-page inserted illustration forming part of a book. **16** a thin sheet of glass coated with chemicals that are sensitive to light. Plates are sometimes used in taking photographs. **17** in baseball: **a** the place where the batter stands to hit a pitched ball; home base. **b** the place where the pitcher stands; slab. **18** in dentistry, a piece of metal, plastic, or other firm material shaped to the mouth, with false teeth set into it. **19** a thin cut of beef from the lower end of the ribs. See **beef** for diagram. **20** the part of a vacuum tube to which the electrons flow. **21** timber laid horizontally to receive the ends of other timbers. **22** *Esp. Brit.* **a** a gold or silver cup or other prize given to the winner of a race, especially a horse race. **b** a contest in which the prize is (or was originally) such an object.
—*v.* **1** cover with a thin layer of silver, gold, or other metal. **2** cover with metal plates for protection. **3** make a plate from (type) for printing. [ME < OF *plate,* ult. < VL *plattus* flat < Gk. *platys*]

pla·teau (pla tō′) *n.* **-teaus** or **-teaux** (-tōz′). **1** a plain in the mountains or at a height above the sea level; a large, high plain. **2** a level, especially the level at which something is stabilized for a period. **3** in psychology, a temporary halt in the learning progress of an individual, depicted by a level stretch on the curve or chart showing the rate of learning. [< F < OF *platel,* dim. of *plat* flat < VL *plattus.* See PLATE.]

PLATEAUS
PLAIN
SEA LEVEL
MOUNTAINS

plate·ful (plāt′fůl) *n.* **-fuls.** as much as a plate will hold.

plate glass thick and very clear glass used for large windowpanes, mirrors, etc.

plate·let (plāt′lit) *n.* one of many small, colorless disks that float in the blood plasma.

plat·en (plat′ən) *n.* **1** in a printing press, a flat metal plate that presses the paper against the inked type. **2** in a typewriter, the roller against which the paper rests. [< F *platine* < *plat* flat < VL *plattus.* See PLATE.]

plat·form (plat′fôrm) *n.* **1** a raised, level surface. There usually is a platform beside the track at a railway station. A hall usually has a platform for speakers. **2** a plan of

hat, āge, cãre, fär; let, ēqual, tėrm; it, īce
hot, ōpen, ôrder; oil, out; cup, pu̇t, rüle, ūse
ə bove, takən, pencəl, lemən, circəs
ch, child; ng, long; sh, ship
th, thin; ᴛʜ, then; zh, measure

action or statement of principles of a group. A political party is said to have a platform. **3** an extra layer in a sole of a shoe, to give additional thickness. [< F *plateforme* flat form]

plat·ing (plāt′ing) *n.* **1** a thin layer of silver, gold, or other metal. **2** a covering of metal plates.

plat·i·num (plat′ə nəm) *n.* **1** a heavy, precious, metallic chemical element that looks like silver or white gold and does not tarnish or melt easily. It is used as a catalyst, in jewellery, etc. *Symbol*: Pt; *at.no.* 78; *at.wt.* 195.09. **2** a light-gray color, less bright than silver and having a faint bluish tinge. [< NL *platinum*, ult. < Sp. *plata* silver]

platinum blond **1** the color of whitish silver. **2** having this color. **3** a person having hair of this color. ☛ See **blond** for usage note.

platinum blonde a woman or girl having hair the color of whitish silver. ☛ See **blond** for usage note.

plat·i·tude (plat′ə tūd′ or plat′ə tüd′) *n.* **1** a dull or commonplace remark, especially one given out solemnly as if it were fresh and important: "*Better late than never*" *is a platitude.* **2** flatness; triteness; dullness. [< F *platitude* < *plat* flat]

plat·i·tu·di·nous (plat′ə tū′də nəs or plat′ə tü′də nəs) *adj.* characterized by platitudes; using platitudes; being a platitude. **—plat′i·tu′di·nous·ly,** *adv.* **—plat′i·tu′di·nous·ness,** *n.*

Pla·ton·ic (plə ton′ik) *adj.* **1** of or having to do with Plato, 427?-347? B.C., a Greek philosopher, or his philosophy. **2** Also, **Platonic. a** designating love or affection, especially for one of the opposite sex, of a purely spiritual character, and free from sensual desire. **b** feeling or professing such love. **3** idealistic; not practical: *The League of Nations seemed a Platonic scheme to many people.* **—pla·ton′i·cal·ly,** *adv.*

Pla·to·nism (plā′tə niz′əm) *n.* **1** the philosophy or doctrines of Plato or his followers. **2** a Platonic doctrine or saying. **3** the doctrine or practice of Platonic love.

Pla·to·nist (plā′tə nist) *n.* a follower of Plato; person who believes in Plato's philosophy.

pla·toon (plə tün′) *n.* **1** in the army, a group of soldiers acting as a unit. A platoon is smaller than a company and larger than a section. **2** a small group of people. **3** in football, either of two divisions of a team, one of which is specially trained for offence and one for defence. [< F *peloton* group, little ball, dim. of *pelote* ball. Related to PELLET.]

plat·ter (plat′ər) *n.* a large, shallow dish used for holding or serving food, especially meat and fish. [ME < AF *plater* < OF *plat* plate < VL *plattus* flat. See PLATE.]

plat·y·pus (plat′ə pəs) *n.* **-pus·es, -pi** (-pī′). the duckbill. [< NL < Gk. *platypous* < *platys* flat + *pous* foot]

plau·dit (plo′dit or plô′dit) *n.* Usually, **plaudits,** *pl.* a round of applause; enthusiastic expression of approval or praise. [alteration of L *plaudite* applaud!]

plau·si·bil·i·ty (plo′zə bil′ə tē or plô′zə bil′ə tē) *n.* the appearance of being true or reasonable; a plausible quality.

plau·si·ble (plo′zə bəl or plô′zə bəl) *adj.* **1** appearing true, reasonable, or fair. **2** apparently worthy of confidence but often not really so: *a plausible liar.* [< L *plausibilis* deserving applause, pleasing < *plaudere* applaud] **—plau′si·bly,** *adv.*

play (plā) *n.* **1** something done to amuse oneself; fun; sport; recreation. **2** a turn, move, or act in a game: *It is your play next. The centre made a brilliant play.* **3** the act of carrying on a game. **4 in play, a** in active use in a game. **b** as a joke. **5** a way of carrying on a game. **6 a** a story written for or presented as a dramatic performance; drama. **b** a stage, radio, television, etc. performance of such a story. **7** action: *foul play.* **8** a light, quick movement or change: *the play of sunlight on leaves, the play of color in an opal.* **9** freedom for action, movement, etc. **10** operation; working. **11** gambling. **12** the act of lightly or briskly wielding or plying (used especially in combinations): *sword play.* [OE *plega*]
—*v.* **1** have fun; do something in sport; take part in a game. **2** do in sport. **3** do; perform: *He played a mean trick.* **4** take part in (a game): *play tag.* **5** take part in a game against. **6** put in the game; cause to play in a game: *Each coach played his best goalie.* **7** act on a stage, or as if on a stage; act a part. **8** act the part of (a character in a play, etc.). **9** give theatrical performances in: *to play the larger cities.* **10** act in a specified way: *to play sick.* **11** make believe; play in fun: *to play cowboys.* **12** make music. **13** produce (music) on an instrument. **14** perform on (a musical instrument). **15** move lightly or quickly: *A breeze played on the water.* **16** cause to act, move, or work; direct (on, over, along): *to play a hose on a burning building.* **17** put into action in a game: *Play your ten of hearts.* **18** operate with continued or repeated action: *A fountain played in the garden.* **19** allow (a hooked fish) to exhaust itself by pulling on the line. **20** act carelessly; do foolish things: *Don't play with matches.* **21** gamble; bet. **22** bet on: *He plays the horses.*
played out, a exhausted. **b** finished; done with.
play into the hands of, act so as to give the advantage to.
play off, a hold a competition in which players or teams are pitted against each other to decide the championship. **b** play an extra game or round to settle a tie.
play on or **upon,** take advantage of; make use of.
play out, play (drama, etc.) to the end; bring to end.
play up to, *Slang.* try to get the favor of; flatter. [OE *plegan* to exercise]
Syn. *n.* **1 Play, sport, game** = activity or exercise of mind or body engaged in for recreation or fun. **Play** is the general word: *Play is as necessary as work.* **Sport** applies to any form of athletics or an outdoor pastime, whether it requires much or little activity or is merely watched for pleasure: *Fencing, swimming, fishing, and horse racing are his favorite sports.* **Game** applies especially to an activity in the form of a contest, mental or physical, played by certain rules: *Tennis and chess are games.* –*v.* **1** frolic, revel.

play·a·ble (plā′ə bəl) *adj.* **1** that can be played. **2** fit to be played on.

play-act (plā′akt′) *v.* **1** pretend; make believe. **2** perform in a play.

play·back (plā′bak′) *n.* a replaying of a tape recording or video tape, especially when it has just been made.

play·bill (plā′bil′) *n.* **1** a handbill or placard announcing a play. **2** the program of a play.

play·boy (plā′boi′) *n. Slang.* a man, usually wealthy, whose chief interest is in having a good time.

play·down (plā′doun′) *n.* playoff.

play·er (plā′ər) *n.* **1** a person who plays: *a baseball player.* **2** an actor in a theatre. **3** a person who plays a musical instrument; musician. **4** a device that plays: *a record player.*

player piano a piano that has machinery for playing pieces automatically.

play·fel·low (plā′fel′ō) *n.* playmate.

play·ful (plā′fəl) *adj.* **1** full of fun; fond of playing. **2** joking; not serious. **—play′ful·ly,** *adv.* **—play′ful·ness,** *n.* **—Syn. 1** sportive, frolicsome. **2** humorous, jocular, bantering, jesting.

play·go·er (plā′gō′ər) *n.* a person who goes often to the theatre.

play·ground (plā′ground′) *n.* a place for outdoor play, usually having swings, slides, etc.

play·house (plā′hous′) *n.* **1** a small house for a child to play in. **2** a child's toy house; doll house. **3** a theatre. [OE *pleghūs*]

playing card a card used in playing games like bridge, poker, hearts, euchre, and pinochle; one of a set of 52 cards including 4 suits (spades, hearts, diamonds, and clubs) of 13 cards each.

play·mate (plā′māt′) *n.* one who plays with another.

play·off (plā′of′) *n.* **1** an extra game or round played off to settle a tie. **2** one of a series of games played by the top teams in a league to determine the winner of the championship, of a special trophy, etc.

play on words pun.

play pen a small, portable enclosure for very young children to play in.

play·thing (plā′thing′) *n.* a thing to play with; toy.

play·time (plā′tīm′) *n.* time for playing.

play·wright (plā′rīt′) *n.* a writer of plays; dramatist.

pla·za (plaz′ə or plä′zə) *n.* **1** a public square in a city or town. **2** a shopping centre. [< Sp. *plaza* < L < Gk. *plateia* (*hodos*) broad (way). Doublet of PLACE and PIAZZA.]

plea (plē) *n.* **1** a request; appeal; entreaty: *a plea for pity.* **2** an excuse; defence: *The man's plea was that he did not see the signal.* **3** in law: **a** the answer made by a defendant to a charge against him in a court. **b** an argument or allegation of fact made in support of one side in a lawsuit. **c** a plea which alleges some new fact on the basis of which the suit should be dismissed, delayed, or barred, but does not answer the charge; special plea. [ME < OF *plaid* < L *placitum* (that) which pleases]

pleach (plēch) *v.* interweave (growing branches, vines, etc.); entwine. [ME < OF *plechier,* ult. < L *plectere* weave]

plead (plēd) *v.* **plead·ed** or **pled** (pled), **plead·ing. 1** offer reasons for or against; argue. **2** ask earnestly; make an earnest appeal. **3** offer as an excuse: *The woman who stole pleaded poverty.* **4** in law: **a** speak for or against in a court: *He had a good lawyer to plead his case.* **b** conduct a case in a court. **c** answer to a charge in a court: *The prisoner pleaded guilty.* [ME < OF *plaidier* < VL *placitare,* ult. < L *placere* please] **—plead′ing·ly,** *adv.* **—Syn. 2** entreat, supplicate, implore, beseech.

plead·er (plēd′ər) *n.* a person who pleads, especially in a law court.

plead·ings (plēd′ingz) *n.pl.* in law, the claim made by the plaintiff and the defendant's answer to it in a court.

pleas·ance (plez′əns) *n.* **1** a pleasant place, usually with trees, fountains, and flowers. **2** *Archaic.* a pleasure. [ME < OF *plaisance* < *plaisant* pleasing. See PLEASANT.]

pleas·ant (plez′ənt) *adj.* **1** pleasing; agreeable; giving pleasure. **2** easy to get along with; friendly. **3** fair; not stormy. [ME < OF *plaisant,* ppr. of *plaisir* please < L *placere*] **—pleas′ant·ly,** *adv.* **—pleas′ant·ness,** *n.*

Syn. 1 Pleasant, pleasing, agreeable = giving pleasure or satisfaction to the mind, feelings, or senses. **Pleasant** emphasizes that the person or thing described has certain qualities that give pleasure: *We spent a pleasant evening.* **Pleasing** emphasizes the effect on the one knowing or experiencing what is described: *It was pleasing to me because I wanted to see them.* **Agreeable** = pleasing because to a person's own taste or liking: *I think this cough medicine has an agreeable flavor.* **2** congenial, amiable.

pleas·ant·ry (plez′ənt rē) *n.* **-ries. 1** a good-natured joke; witty remark: *He meant it as a pleasantry.* **2** lively, good-humored talk: *There was an air of pleasantry in the room.* **—Syn. 1** witticism, jest. **2** drollery, banter, raillery.

please (plēz) *v.* **pleased, pleas·ing. 1** be agreeable to: *Toys please children.* **2** be agreeable: *Such a fine meal cannot fail to please.* **3** wish; think fit: *Do what you please.* **4** be the will of. **5** may it please you (now used merely as a polite addition to requests or commands): *Come here, please.* **6 be pleased, a** be moved to pleasure. **b** be disposed; like; choose. **7 if you please,** if you like; with your permission. **8 please God,** if it is God's will. [ME < OF *plaisir* < L *placere*] **—Syn. 1** gratify, content, suit.

☛ **Pleased** is followed by *with,* not *at*: *His boss was very much pleased with his work.*

pleas·ing (plēz′ing) *adj.* giving pleasure; pleasant. **—pleas′ing·ly,** *adv.* **—Syn.** See **pleasant.**

pleas·ur·a·ble (plezh′ər ə bəl) *adj.* pleasant; agreeable. **—pleas′ur·a·bly,** *adv.*

pleas·ure (plezh′ər) *n.* **1** a feeling of being pleased; enjoyment; delight. **2** something that pleases; cause of joy or delight. **3** worldly or frivolous enjoyment. **4** one's will, desire, or choice: *What is your pleasure in this matter?* **5 at one's pleasure,** as or when one pleases; at will; at discretion. **6 during one's pleasure,** while one pleases. **7 take pleasure,** be pleased; delight: *He takes his pleasure in hunting and fishing.* [ME < OF *plaisir,* nominal use of infinitive. See PLEASE.]

Syn. 1 Pleasure, delight, joy = a feeling of satisfaction and happiness coming from having, experiencing, or expecting something good or to one's liking. **Pleasure** is the general word applying to this feeling whether or not it is shown in any way: *The compliment gave her pleasure.* **Delight** = great pleasure, usually shown or expressed in a lively way: *The child clapped her hands in delight.* **Joy** applies to a strong emotion of intense delight and shining happiness, expressing itself in gladness or rejoicing: *Success brought him joy.*

pleat (plēt) *n.* a flat, usually narrow, fold made in cloth by doubling it on itself and stitching or pressing it in place. *—v.* fold or arrange in pleats. [var. of *plait*] **—pleat′er,** *n.*

ple·be·ian (pli bē′ən) *n.* **1** in ancient Rome, one of the common people. **2** a common, vulgar person. *—adj.* **1** of the common people. **2** common; vulgar. [< L *plebeius* < *plebs* the common people]

ple·be·ian·ism (pli bē′ən iz′əm) *n.* plebeian character or ways.

pleb·i·scite (pleb′ə sīt′ or pleb′ə sit′) *n.* a direct vote by the qualified voters of a country, province, municipality, etc. on some question. [< L *plebiscitum* < *plebs* the common people + *scitum* decree]

plebs (plebz) *n.* **ple·bes** (plē′bēz). in ancient Rome, the common people. [< L]

plec·trum (plek′trəm) *n.* **-trums, -tra** (-trə). a small piece of ivory, horn, metal, etc. used for plucking the strings of a mandolin, lyre, zither, etc. [< L *plectrum* < Gk. *plēktron* < *plēssein* strike]

pled (pled) *v. Informal.* a pt. and a pp. of **plead.**

pledge (plej) *n. v.* **pledged, pledg·ing.** *—n.* **1** a solemn promise. **2** something that secures or makes safe; security: *The knight left a jewel as pledge for the borrowed horse.* **3** the condition of being held as security. **4** a person who has promised to join an organization but is serving a probationary period before being granted membership. **5** something given to show favor or love or as a promise of something to come; sign; token. **6** the drinking of a health or toast. **7 take the pledge,** *Informal.* promise not to drink alcoholic liquor.
—v. **1** promise solemnly. **2** cause to promise solemnly; bind by a promise. **3** give as security. **4** drink a health to; drink in honor of (someone) and wish (him) well. [ME < OF *plege* < Med.L *plebium* < Gmc. Akin to PLIGHT[2].] **—pledg′er,** *n.* **—Syn.** *n.* **1** covenant, vow. **2** surety, guarantee.

pledg·ee (plej ē′) *n.* a person with whom something is deposited as a pledge.

Plei·ad (plē′ad or plī′ad) *n.* any of the Pleiades.

Ple·ia·des (plē′ə dēz′ or plī′ə dēz′) *n.pl.* **1** a group of hundreds of stars in the constellation Taurus, commonly spoken of as seven, though only six can normally be seen with the naked eye. **2** in Greek mythology, seven of the daughters of Atlas, who were transformed by the gods into this group of stars. [< L *Pleiades,* pl. of *Pleias* < Gk.]

Plei·o·cene (plī′ə sēn′) *n. adj.* Pliocene.

Pleis·to·cene (plīs′tə sēn′) in geology: *—n.* **1** the period before the present period, beginning approximately one million years ago; ice age. **2** the deposits of gravel, etc. made in this period. See **geology** for chart. *—adj.* of or having to do with this period or these deposits. [< Gk. *pleistos* most + *kainos* recent]

ple·na·ry (plē′nə rē or plen′ə rē) *adj.* **1** full; complete; entire; absolute. **2** attended by all of its qualified members. [< LL *plenarius* < L *plenus* full] **—ple′na·ri·ly,** *adv.*

plen·i·po·ten·ti·ar·y (plen′ə pə ten′shē er′ē or -pə ten′shə rē) *n.* **-ar·ies,** *adj. —n.* a diplomatic agent having full power or authority. *—adj.* having or giving full power and authority. [< Med.L, ult. < L *plenus* full + *potens, -entis* powerful]

plen·i·tude (plen′ə tūd′ or plen′ə tüd′) *n.* fullness; completeness; abundance. [ME < OF < *plenitudo* < *plenus* full]

plen·te·ous (plen′tē əs) *adj.* plentiful. **—plen′te·ous·ly,** *adv.* **—plen′te·ous·ness,** *n.*

plen·ti·ful (plen′tē fəl) *adj.* more than enough; ample; abundant: *Ten gallons of gasoline is a plentiful supply for a seventy-mile trip.* **—plen′ti·ful·ly,** *adv.* **—plen′ti·ful·ness,** *n.* **—Syn.** bountiful, copious, profuse.

plen·ty (plen′tē) *n.* **-ties,** *adj. adv.* —*n.* **1** a full supply; all that one needs; large enough number or quantity: *There is plenty of time.* **2** the quality or condition of being plentiful; abundance: *years of peace and plenty.* —*adj.* enough; plentiful; abundant: *Six potatoes will be plenty.* —*adv. Informal.* quite; fully: *plenty good enough.* [ME < OF < L *plenitas* fullness < *plenus* full] —**Syn.** *n.* **1** profusion, copiousness.

ple·o·nasm (plē′ə naz′əm) *n.* **1** the use of more words than are necessary to express an idea. *Examples*: both of the two, the two twins. **2** the unnecessary word, phrase, or expression. [< LL < Gk. *pleonasmos,* ult. < *pleon* more]

ple·o·nas·tic (plē′ə nas′tik) *adj.* using more words than are needed; superfluous; redundant. —**ple·o·nas′ti·cal·ly,** *adv.*

ple·si·o·saur (plē′sē ə sôr′) *n.* a large sea reptile, now extinct, that had a long neck and flippers instead of legs. [< NL *plesiosaurus* < Gk. *plēsios* near + *sauros* lizard]

pleth·o·ra (pleth′ə rə) *n.* **1** excessive fullness; too much; superabundance. **2** a disease caused by excess of red corpuscles in the blood or increase in the quantity of blood. [< NL < Gk. *plēthorē* < *plēthein* be full]

ple·thor·ic (ple thôr′ik or pleth′ə rik) *adj.* **1** too full; inflated. **2** having too much blood or too many red corpuscles in the blood.

pleu·ra (plür′ə) *n.* **pleu·rae** (plür′ē or plür′ī). in mammals, a thin membrane covering the lungs and folded back to make a lining for the thorax or chest cavity. [< NL < Gk. *pleura* rib]

pleu·ral (plür′əl) *adj.* of the pleura.

pleu·ri·sy (plür′ə sē) *n.* inflammation of the pleura. [ME < OF *pleurisie* < LL *pleurisis,* for L *pleuritis* < Gk. *pleuritis* < *pleura* rib]

pleu·rit·ic (plü rit′ik) *adj.* **1** having pleurisy. **2** of pleurisy. **3** causing pleurisy.

Plex·i·glas (plek′sə glas′) *n. Trademark.* a light, transparent thermoplastic, often used in place of glass. [*pl*astic + flex*i*ble + gla*s*s]

plex·us (plek′səs) *n.* **-us·es** or **-us. 1** a network of nerves, blood vessels, etc. The **solar plexus** is a collection of nerves behind the stomach. **2** any complicated network. [< L *plexus* < *plectere* twine, braid]

pli·a·bil·i·ty (plī′ə bil′ə tē) *n.* the state or quality of being pliable..

pli·a·ble (plī′ə bəl) *adj.* **1** easily bent; flexible; supple: *Willow twigs are pliable.* **2** easily influenced; yielding: *He is too pliable to be a good leader.* [< F *pliable* < *plier* bend]

pli·an·cy (plī′ən sē) *n.* the state or quality of being easily bent or influenced.

pli·ant (plī′ənt) *adj.* **1** bending easily; flexible; supple. **2** easily influenced; yielding. [ME < OF *pliant* bending, ppr. of *plier.* See PLY[2].] —**pli′ant·ly,** *adv.* —**Syn. 1** pliable, limber. See **flexible.**

pli·cate (plī′kāt) *adj.* folded like a fan. [< L *plicatus* folded]

pli·ers (plī′ərz) *n.pl. or sing.* small pincers with long jaws, used for bending wire, holding small objects, etc. [< *ply*[1]]

Pliers

plight[1] (plīt) *n.* a condition or state, usually bad. [ME < AF *plit,* originally, manner of folding, ult. < L *plicare* fold; confused with *plight*[2]] —**Syn.** dilemma, scrape, fix. See **predicament.**

plight[2] (plīt) *v.* **1** pledge; promise. **2 plight one's troth, a** promise to be faithful. **b** promise to marry. [< n.] —*n.* a solemn promise; pledge. [OE *pliht* danger]

Plimsoll mark or **line** (plim′səl) a mark or line painted on a ship's hull to show how deeply it may be loaded. This mark is required by law on British merchant ships and also on most other merchant ships. [< Samuel *Plimsoll,* 1824-1898, a member of Parliament, who had the law on overloading passed]

plink (plingk) *v.* **1** play on a musical or other instrument so as to produce a tinkling sound. **2** aim or throw at a target casually. —*n.* a tinkling sound.

hat, āge, cãre, fär; let, ēqual, tėrm; it, īce
hot, ōpen, ôrder; oil, out; cup, pu̇t, rüle, ūse
əbove, takən, pencəl, lemən, circəs
ch, child; ng, long; sh, ship
th, thin; ᴛʜ, then; zh, measure

plinth (plinth) *n.* **1** in architecture, the lower, square part of the base of a column. **2** a square base of a pedestal. [< L < Gk. *plinthos*]

PLINTH

Pli·o·cene (plī′ə sēn′) in geology: —*n.* **1** a period beginning approximately 12 million years ago. **2** the rocks formed in this period. See **geology** for chart. —*adj.* of or having to do with this period or the rocks formed during it. Also, **Pleiocene.** [< Gk. *pleiōn* more + *kainos* recent]

plod (plod) *v.* **plod·ded, plod·ding. 1** walk heavily; trudge. **2** walk slowly or heavily along: *We plodded the mountain path.* **3** proceed in a slow or dull way; work patiently with effort: *He plods away at his lessons until he learns them.* [? imitative] —**plod·der,** *n.* —**Syn. 1** See **walk.**

plop (plop) *n. v.* **plopped, plop·ping,** *adv.* —*n.* **1** a sound like that of a flat object striking water without a splash. **2** a falling with a plop. —*v.* **1** make a sound like that of a flat object striking water without a splash. **2** fall or cause to fall with such a sound. —*adv.* with a plop. [imitative]

plo·sive (plō′siv or plō′ziv) *adj. n.* in phonetics, explosive.

plot (plot) *n. v.* **plot·ted, plot·ting.** —*n.* **1** a secret plan, especially to do something wrong: *Two men formed a plot to rob the bank.* **2** the plan or main story of a play, novel, poem, etc. **3** a small piece of ground: *a garden plot.* **4** a map; diagram.
—*v.* **1** plan secretly with others; plan. **2** divide (land) into plots. **3** make a map or diagram of. **4** mark the position of (something) on a map or diagram: *The admiral plotted the position of all the ships in the fleet.* **5** in mathematics: **a** determine the location of a point by means of its co-ordinates; mark a point on graph paper. **b** make a curve by connecting points marked out on a graph. **c** represent (an equation, etc.) by means of a curve drawn through points on a graph. [OE *plot* patch of ground; meaning influenced by *complot* a joint plot (< F)] —**plot′less,** *adj.* —**plot′ter,** *n.*
Syn. *n.* **1** intrigue, conspiracy. –*v.* **1 Plot, conspire, scheme** = plan secretly. **Plot** = form secretly, alone or together with others, a carefully designed plan, usually harmful or treacherous, against a person, group, or country: *Enemy agents plotted to blow up the plant.* **Conspire** emphasizes the combining of one person or group with another, usually secretly, to carry out an illegal act, especially treachery or treason: *They conspired to overthrow the government.* **Scheme** suggests careful planning, often in a crafty or underhand way, to gain one's own ends: *He schemed to become president.*

plough or **plow** (plou) *n.* **1** a big, heavy farm implement for cutting the soil and turning it over. **2** a machine for removing snow; snowplough.
—*v.* **1** turn over (soil) with a plough. **2** use a plough. **3** move as a plough does; advance slowly and with effort. **4** remove with a plough or as if with a plough: *plough up old roots.* **5** furrow: *plough a field, wrinkles ploughed in one's face by time.* **6** cut the surface of (water). **7** *Esp.Brit. Informal.* reject (a candidate) or be rejected in an examination. **8 plough back,** reinvest (profits) in the same business. **9 plough into,** *Informal.* **a** hit hard or at speed and travel into: *The car went out of control and ploughed into the building.* **b** undertake (a job, project, etc.) with energy and determination.
10 plough under, a plough into the ground to make manure. **b** defeat; destroy; overwhelm. [OE *plōg*] —**plough′er** or **plow′er,** *n.*

plough·boy or **plow·boy** (plou′boi′) *n.* **1** boy who guides the horses drawing a plough. **2** a country boy.

plough·man or **plow·man** (plou′mən) *n.* **-men** (-mən). **1** man who guides a plough. **2** a farm worker.

plough·share or **plow·share** (plou′shãr′) *n.* the blade of a plough, the part that cuts the soil.

plov·er (pluv′ər or plō′vər) *n.* a shore bird having a

short tail, long, pointed wings, and a short bill. [ME < AF *plover,* ult. < L *pluvia* rain]

plow (plou) *n. v.* plough.

plow·boy (plou′boi′) *n.* ploughboy.

plow·man (plou′mən) *n.* **-men** (-mən). ploughman.

plow·share (plou′shãr′) *n.* ploughshare.

ploy (ploi) *n.* **1** *Informal.* an action or words by which advantage over another may be gained: *He won the game by a clever ploy.* **2** *Brit. Informal.* a sporting or amusing action or proceeding. [? < *employ,* n., in obs. meaning of "use"]

pluck (pluk) *v.* **1** pull off; pick: *She plucked flowers in the garden.* **2** pull at; pull; tug; jerk. **3** pull on (the strings of a musical instrument). **4** pull off the feathers or hair from: *pluck a chicken.* **5** *Slang.* rob; swindle. **6** *Brit. Informal.* reject (a candidate) in an examination. **7 pluck up,** gather up (courage, etc.).
—*n.* **1** the act of picking or pulling. **2** courage. **3** the heart, liver, and lungs of an animal killed for food. [OE *pluccian*] —**Syn.** *v.* **2** tweak. -*n.* **2** resolution, stamina, spirit.

pluck·y (pluk′ē) *adj.* **pluck·i·er, pluck·i·est.** having or showing courage. —**pluck′i·ly,** *adv.* —**pluck′i·ness,** *n.*

plug (plug) *n. v.* **plugged, plug·ging.** —*n.* **1** a piece of wood or some other substance used to stop up a hole. **2** a device to make an electrical connection. **3** a place where a hose can be attached; hydrant. **4** a cake of pressed tobacco; piece of this cut off for chewing. **5** a spark plug. **6** *Informal.* an advertisement, especially one put in a radio or television program. **7** *Informal.* a worn-out or inferior horse. **8** a lure for catching fish. **9** in geology, a cylindrical mass of igneous rock formed in the crater of an extinct volcano.
—*v.* **1** stop up or fill with a plug. **2** *Slang.* hit; shoot. **3** *Informal.* work steadily; plod. **4** *Informal.* work steadily for by advertisements or publicity: *plug a new product.* **5 plug in,** make an electrical connection by inserting a plug. [< MDu. *plugge*] —**plug′ger,** *n.*

plug hat *Informal.* a man's tall silk hat.

plug-in (plug′in′) *adj.* able to operate simply by being plugged into an electric outlet. —*n.* a socket or outlet where a plug-in device may be connected.

plug-ug·ly (plug′ug′lē) *n.* **-lies.** *Slang.* a ruffian.

plum (plum) *n.* **1** a roundish, juicy fruit having a smooth skin and a stone or pit. There are purple, red, green, and yellow plums. **2** a tree that it grows on. **3** a raisin in a pudding, cake, etc. **4** a sugarplum. **5** something very good or desirable: *His new job is quite a plum.* **6** a dark, bluish purple. —*adj.* dark bluish-purple. [OE *plūme* < VL *pruna* < L *prunum* < Gk. *proumnon.* Doublet of PRUNE.]

plum·age (plüm′ij) *n.* the feathers of a bird: *A parrot has bright plumage.* [ME < OF *plumage* < *plume* plume. See PLUME.]

plumb (plum) *n.* **1** a small weight used on the end of a line to find the depth of water or to see if a wall is vertical. **2 out of plumb** or **off plumb,** not vertical. —*adj.* **1** vertical. **2** *Informal.* complete; thorough. —*adv.* **1** vertically. **2** *Informal.* completely; thoroughly. —*v.* **1** test or adjust by a plumb line; test; sound: *Our line was not long enough to plumb the depths of the lake.* **2** get to the bottom of: *No one could plumb the mystery.* [ME < OF *plomb* < L *plumbum* lead]

A plumb being used to test the vertical line of a wall

plum·ba·go (plum bā′gō) *n.* graphite. [< L *plumbago* lead ore < *plumbum* lead]

plumb bob weight at the end of a plumb line.

plumb·er (plum′ər) *n.* a man whose work is putting in and repairing water pipes and fixtures in buildings. [ME < OF *plummier* < L *plumbarius,* ult. < L *plumbum* lead]

plumb·ing (plum′ing) *n.* **1** the work or trade of a plumber. **2** the water pipes and fixtures in a building or part of a building: *the bathroom plumbing.*

plumb line the line with a plumb at the end, used to find the depth of water or to test the straightness of a wall.

plume (plüm) *n. v.* **plumed, plum·ing.** —*n.* **1** a large, long feather; feather. **2** a feather, bunch of feathers, or tuft of hair worn as an ornament on a hat, helmet, etc. **3** something resembling a plume. **4** the hollow cylinder of spray thrown up by an underwater atomic explosion. —*v.* **1** furnish with plumes. **2** smooth or arrange the feathers of: *The eagle plumed its wing.* **3 plume oneself on,** be proud of; show pride concerning. [ME < OF < L *pluma*]

plum·met (plum′it) *n.* a weight fastened to a line; plumb. —*v.* plunge; drop. [ME < OF *plommet* < *plomb* lead. See PLUMB.]

plu·mose (plü′mōs) *adj.* **1** having feathers or plumes; feathered. **2** feathery; like a plume. [< L *plumosus* < *pluma* feather]

plump[1] (plump) *adj.* rounded out; attractively fat. —*v.* make plump; become plump. [cf. MDu. *plomp,* MLG *plump* blunt, thick] —**plump′ness,** *n.*

plump[2] (plump) *v.* **1** fall or drop heavily or suddenly: *All out of breath, she plumped down on a chair.* **2 a** drop, let fall, etc.: *plump down one's bags at the station.* **b** pay at once and in one lot: *plump down $10.* **3** *Informal.* burst or plunge: *plump out of a room, plump into the water.* **4 plump for,** give one's complete support to; support wholeheartedly, unanimously, etc.: *plump for lower taxes.* —*n.* **1** *Informal.* a sudden plunge; heavy fall. **2** *Informal.* the sound made by a plunge or fall. —*adv.* **1** heavily or suddenly: *He ran plump into me.* **2** directly; bluntly. —*adj.* direct; downright; blunt. [cf. Du. *plompen,* LG *plumpen,* and *plump*[1]]

plum pudding a rich boiled or steamed pudding containing raisins, currants, spices, etc.

plu·mule (plü′mūl) *n.* **1** a small, soft feather. **2** the bud of a plant still in the seed. [< L *plumula,* dim. of *pluma* feather]

PLUMULE

A plumule (def. 2)

plum·y (plüm′ē) *adj.* **1** having plumes or feathers. **2** adorned with a plume or plumes. **3** like a plume.

plun·der (plun′dər) *v.* rob by force; rob. —*n.* **1** things taken in plundering; booty; loot: *They carried off the plunder in their ships.* **2** the act of robbing by force. [< G *plündern* < *Plunder* household goods] —**plun′der·er,** *n.*

Syn. *v.* loot, sack. -*n.* **1 Plunder, booty, loot** = things taken by force. **Plunder** applies to things carried off by invading soldiers during a war or by bandits and other robbers: *The soldiers returned home with their plunder.* **Booty** applies particularly to things carried off and shared later by a band of robbers: *The bandits fought over their booty.* **Loot** applies particularly to things carried off from bodies and buildings in a city destroyed in war or the scene of a fire, wreck, etc., but is used also of anything taken by robbery or other crime: *Much loot was sold after the great earthquake.*

plunge (plunj) *v.* **plunged, plung·ing,** *n.* —*v.* **1** throw or thrust with force into a liquid, place, or condition. **2** throw oneself (into water, danger, a fight, etc.). **3** rush; dash. **4** pitch or lurch suddenly and violently. **5** *Slang.* gamble heavily. —*n.* **1** the act of plunging. **2** a dive into the water. **3** a place for diving. **4** a swim. [ME < OF *plungier,* ult. < L *plumbum* lead] —**Syn.** *v.* **1** immerse, submerge. See **dip. 2** leap, dive.

plung·er (plun′jər) *n.* **1** a person or thing that plunges. **2** a part of a machine that acts with a plunging motion. See the picture under **piston,** which is a kind of plunger, and the picture under **cam. 3** a rubber suction cup on a long stick, used for unplugging stopped-up drains, toilets, etc. **4** a reckless speculator.

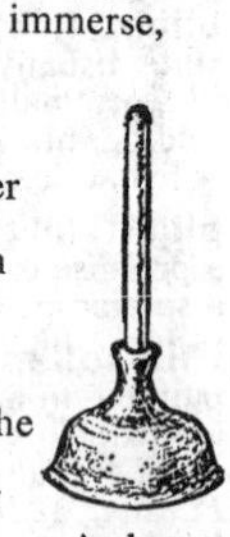

A plunger (def. 3)

plunk (plungk) *v.* **1** pluck (a banjo, guitar, etc.). **2** make a sudden twanging sound like the plucking of a stringed musical instrument; twang. **3** throw, push, put, drop, etc., heavily or suddenly. **4 plunk down,** hand over payment: *He plunked down four thousand dollars for the car.* **5 plunk for,** *Informal.* plump for. —*n. Informal.* the act or sound of plunking. —*adv.* with a plunk. [imitative]

plu·per·fect (plü′pėr′fikt) *n. adj.* past perfect. [short for L *plus quam perfectum* more than perfect]

plupf. pluperfect.

plur. **1** plural. **2** plurality.

plu·ral (plür′əl) *adj.* **1** more than one. **2** in grammar, indicating or implying more than one. —*n.* in grammar, a form of a word to show that it means more than one or refers to more than one. The plural of *book* is *books*; of *man*, *men*; of *is*, *are*; of *I*, *we*; of *this*, *these*. [ME < L *pluralis* < *plus* more]

plu·ral·ism (plür′ə liz′əm) *n.* **1** the state or quality of being plural. **2** in some philosophical systems, the belief that there is more than one principle or entity in ultimate being. **3** in some churches, the practice or system in which one person holds two or more offices at the same time.

plu·ral·i·ty (plü ral′ə tē) *n.* **-ties.** **1** in an election, the difference between the largest number of votes and the next largest. **2** the greatest number; the majority. **3** a large number; multitude. **4** the state or fact of being plural.

plu·ral·ly (plür′əl ē) *adv.* in the plural number; so as to express or imply more than one.

plus (plus) *prep.* **1** added to: *Three plus two equals five.* **2** and also: *The work of an engineer requires intelligence plus experience.*
—*adj.* **1** and more: *His mark was B plus.* **2** showing addition: *the plus sign.* **3** positive; positively electrified. **4 be plus,** *Informal.* have in addition: *We are plus a puppy.*
—*n.* **1** the plus sign (+). **2** an added quantity. **3** a positive quantity. [< L *plus* more]

plus fours loose-fitting baggy trousers gathered below the knee.

plush (plush) *n.* a silk, rayon, etc. fabric resembling velvet but thicker and softer. —*adj. Slang.* luxurious; stylish: *a plush office.* [< MF *pluche*, ult. < L *pilus* hair]

Plu·to (plü′tō) *n.* **1** in Greek and Roman mythology, the god of the lower world. He was also called Hades by the Greeks and Dis by the Romans. **2** the planet that is farthest from the sun.

plu·toc·ra·cy (plü tok′rə sē) *n.* **-cies.** **1** a system of government in which the rich rule. **2** a ruling class of wealthy people. [< Gk. *ploutokratia* < *ploutos* wealth + *kratos* power]

plu·to·crat (plü′tə krat′) *n.* **1** a person who has power or influence because of his wealth. **2** a wealthy person.

plu·to·crat·ic (plü′tə krat′ik) *adj.* **1** having power and influence because of wealth. **2** of or having to do with plutocrats or plutocracy. —**plu′to·crat′i·cal·ly,** *adv.*

Plu·to·ni·an (plü tō′nē ən) *adj.* of or having to do with Pluto or the lower world.

Plu·ton·ic (plü ton′ik) *adj.* **1** Plutonian; infernal. **2** of or having to do with the theory that the present condition of the earth's crust is mainly due to igneous action. **3 plutonic,** of or having to do with a class of igneous rocks that have solidified far below the earth's surface.

plu·to·ni·um (plü tō′nē əm) *n.* a radio-active chemical element derived from neptunium, important in atomic fission. *Symbol*: Pu; *at.no.* 94; *at.wt.* 242 (most stable isotope). [< L *plutonium*, neut. < *Pluto*, *-onis* Pluto]

plu·vi·al (plü′vē əl) *adj.* **1** of or having to do with rain. **2** caused by rain. [< L *pluvialis* < *pluvia* rain]

plu·vi·om·e·ter (plü′vē om′ə tər) *n.* an instrument for measuring the amount of rainfall. [< L *pluvia* rain + E *-meter*]

plu·vi·ous (plü′vē əs) *adj.* rainy; of rain.

ply[1] (plī) *v.* **plied, ply·ing.** **1** work with; use: *The dressmaker plies her needle.* **2** keep up work on; work steadily at or on: *We plied the water with our oars.* **3** work busily or steadily. **4** urge again and again: *The enemy plied our messenger with questions to make him tell his errand.* **5** supply with in a pressing manner: *ply a person with food or drink.* **6** go back and forth regularly between certain places: *A bus plies between the station and the hotel.* **7** go back and forth regularly on: *Boats ply the river.* **8** travel; go; move. [ult. var. of *apply*]

ply[2] (plī) *n.* **plies.** a thickness; layer; fold; twist. Three-ply rope is made up of three twists. [< F *pli* < OF *plier* < L *plicare* fold]

hat, āge, cãre, fär; let, ēqual, tėrm; it, īce
hot, ōpen, ôrder; oil, out; cup, pu̇t, rüle, ūse
əbove, takən, pencəl, lemən, circəs
ch, child; ng, long; sh, ship
th, thin; ᴛʜ, then; zh, measure

Ply·mouth Brethren (plim′əth) a Protestant religious sect that recognizes no formal creed or ministerial orders. It originated about 1830 in Plymouth, England.

Ply·mouth Rock (plim′əth) **1** a North American breed of gray-and-black chickens. **2** a chicken of this breed. [< the rock at Plymouth, Massachusetts, on which the Pilgrims are said to have landed in 1620]

ply·wood (plī′wu̇d′) *n.* a board or boards made of several thin layers of wood glued together.

p.m. **1** post meridiem. **2** post mortem.

Pm promethium.

P.M. (pē′em′) **1** Prime Minister. **2** post meridiem. **3** Postmaster. **4** Provost Marshal. **5** Police Magistrate. **6** Paymaster.

PMQ's permanent married quarters.

P/N or **p/n** promissory note.

pneu·mat·ic (nū mat′ik or nü mat′ik) *adj.* **1** filled with air; containing air: *a pneumatic tire.* **2** worked by air pressure: *a pneumatic drill.* **3** having to do with air and other gases. [< L < Gk. *pneumatikos* < *pneuma*, *-atos* wind] —**pneu·mat′i·cal·ly,** *adv.*

pneu·mat·ics (nū mat′iks or nü mat′iks) *n.* the branch of physics that deals with the pressure, elasticity, weight, etc. of air and other gases.

pneu·mo·nia (nū mōn′yə or nü mōn′yə, nū mō′nē ə or nü mō′nē ə) *n.* a disease in which the lungs are inflamed. [< NL < Gk. *pneumonia* < *pneumōn* lung]

Po polonium.

P.O. **1** Post Office. **2** Petty Officer. **3** Pilot Officer. **4** Personnel Officer.

poach[1] (pōch) *v.* **1** trespass on (another's land), especially to hunt or fish. **2** take (game or fish) illegally. **3** trample (soft ground) into muddy holes. **4** of land, become soft, miry, and full of holes by being trampled. **5** sink into wet, heavy ground in walking. **6 a** mix with water and reduce to a uniform consistency. **b** mix thoroughly (paper pulp) with the bleach liquor. [< MF *pocher* poke out < Gmc. Akin to POKE[1].] —**poach′er,** *n.*

poach[2] (pōch) *v.* **1** cook an egg by breaking it into boiling water. **2** cook an egg in a very small pan over boiling water. **3** cook fish, etc. in liquid that is not quite boiling. [ME < OF *pochier* < *poche* cooking spoon < Celtic] —**poach′er,** *n.*

pock (pok) *n.* a pimple, mark, or pit on the skin, caused by smallpox and certain other diseases.
—*v.* **1** pit, scar, or mark as if with pocks. **2** scatter over (an area) like pocks. [OE *pocc*]

pock·et (pok′it) *n.* **1** a small pouch sewn into clothing, usually for carrying money, a purse, or other small articles. **2** a hollow place; enclosed place. **3** a small bag or pouch. **4** the bag at the corner or side of a pool or billiard table. **5** a hole in the earth containing gold or other ore; single lump of ore: *The miner struck a pocket of silver.* **6** a limited area of a small group of persons or things isolated or otherwise distinguished from a larger area or group surrounding it: *The victorious invaders still encountered pockets of resistance. Pockets of silent onlookers were to be seen in the midst of the cheering crowd.* **7** any current or condition in the air that causes an airplane to drop suddenly. **8 be out of pocket, a** spend or lose money. **b** be a loser. **9 in pocket,** having or gaining money.
—*v.* **1** put in one's pocket. **2** shut in; hem in. **3** hold back; suppress; hide: *He pocketed his pride and said nothing.* **4** take and endure, without doing anything about it: *He pocketed the insult.* **5** take secretly or dishonestly: *Tom pocketed all the profits.* **6** in billiards, etc., drive into a pocket.
—*adj.* **1** meant to be carried in a pocket. **2** small enough to go in a pocket. [ME < AF *pokete*, dim. of *poke* poke[2]]

pock·et·book (pok′it bu̇k′) *n.* **1** a woman's purse. **2** a case for carrying money, papers, etc. in a pocket. **3** a person's supply of money: *This kind of vacation is easy on the pocketbook.* **4** Also, **pocket book.** a book, usually paper-covered and inexpensive, small enough to be carried in the pocket; paperback.

pock·et·ful (pok′it fu̇l) *n.* **-fuls.** as much as a pocket will hold.

pocket gopher any of a group of burrowing rodents having large cheek pouches; gopher. Adult pocket gophers grow up to eight inches long.

pock·et·knife (pok′it nīf′) *n.* **-knives.** a small knife with one or more blades that fold into the handle.

pocket money money for minor personal expenses.

pock·mark (pok′märk′) *n.* pock.

pock·marked (pok′märkt′) *adj.* marked with pocks.

po·co (pō′kō) *adv.* in music, slightly; little. [< Ital. *poco* < L *paucus* little, few]

po·co a po·co (pō′kō ä pō′kō) in music, little by little; gradually. [< Ital.]

pod[1] (pod) *n. v.* **pod·ded, pod·ding.** —*n.* **1** a bivalve shell or case in which plants like beans and peas grow their seeds. **2** any dry, dehiscent pericarp, usually having several seeds, whether of one carpel or of several. **3** a streamlined cover over anything carried externally, especially on the wings or fuselage of an aircraft: *a gun pod or missile pod.* —*v.* **1** produce pods. **2** fill out into a pod. [origin uncertain] —**pod′like′,** *adj.*

A pod of peas

pod[2] (pod) *n.* **1** a small flock of birds. **2** a small herd of whales, seals, etc. [origin unknown]

podg·y (poj′ē) *adj.* **podg·i·er, podg·i·est.** short and fat; pudgy. —**podg′i·ness,** *n.*

po·di·a·try (pə dī′ə trē) *n.* the study and treatment of disorders of the human foot. [< Gk. *poús, podós* foot + *iātreiā* a healing]

po·di·um (pō′dē əm) *n.* **-di·a** (-dē ə). **1** a raised platform. **2** an animal structure that serves as a foot. [< L < Gk. *podion,* dim. of *pous, podos* foot]

pod·zol (pod′zol) *n.* a type of leached, whitish gray soil usually found in moist, sub-polar climates. Also, **podsol.** [< Russian *podzol* < *pod* under + *zola* ashes]

pod·zol·ic (pod zol′ik) *adj.* of or pertaining to podzol soil. Also, **podsolic.**

po·em (pō′əm) *n.* **1** an arrangement of words in lines with a regularly repeated stress; composition in verse. **2** a composition showing great beauty or nobility of language or thought. **3** something beautiful. [< L < Gk. *poēma,* var. of *poiēma* < *poieein* make, compose]

po·e·sy (pō′ə sē or pō′ə zē) *n.* **-sies.** *Archaic.* poetry. [ME < OF *poesie* < L *poesis* < Gk. *poēsis,* var. of *poiēsis* composition]

po·et (pō′it) *n.* **1** a person who writes poetry. **2** a person who has great ability to feel and express beauty. [ME < OF < L *poeta* < Gk. *poētēs* composer, maker]

po·et·as·ter (pō′it as′tər) *n.* a writer of rather poor poetry. [< NL *poetaster* < L *poeta* + *-aster,* denoting inferiority]

po·et·ess (pō′it is) *n.* a woman poet.

po·et·ic (pō et′ik) *adj.* **1** having to do with poems or poets. **2** suitable for poems or poets. *Alas, o'er, plenteous,* and *blithe* are poetic words. **3** showing beautiful or noble language, imagery, or thought. —**po·et′i·cal·ly,** *adv.*

po·et·i·cal (pō et′ə kəl) *adj.* poetic.

poetic justice the ideal justice of poems, plays, etc. with the proper distribution of rewards and punishments.

poetic licence or **license** in poetry, the freedom to vary known facts or accepted rules or conventions, etc. for effect.

po·et·ics (pō et′iks) *n.* the part of literary criticism that deals with the nature and laws of poetry.

poet laureate *pl.* **poets laureate. 1** in Great Britain, a poet appointed by the monarch to write poems in celebration of court and national events. **2** the official poet of any country, state, etc.

po·et·ry (pō′it rē) *n.* **1** poems: *a collection of poetry.* **2** the art of writing poems: *masters of English poetry.* **3** a poetic quality; poetic spirit or feeling. [ME < OF < LL *poetria* < L *poeta* poet. See POET.]

po·gey or **po·gy** (pō′gē) *n. Cdn. Slang.* **1** money or forms of relief given by the government to unemployed persons, especially in times of extreme economic depression; dole. **2 on the pogey,** drawing such relief. **3** the office providing such relief. **4** a hostel supervised by the local relief agency. **5** unemployment insurance. —*adj.* obtained from the relief office: *pogey boots.* [originally, hobo slang for "workhouse"]

pogo stick (pō′gō) a play stick that a person can use to hop from place to place by jumping up and down on the spring-supported footrests near the bottom of the stick, while holding the handle at the top.

po·grom (pō grom′ or pō′grəm) *n.* an organized attack, especially against the Jews. [< Russian *pogrom* devastation]

poign·an·cy (poin′yən sē or poin′ən sē) *n.* a being poignant; sharpness; piercing quality.

poign·ant (poin′yənt or poin′ənt) *adj.* **1** very painful; piercing: *poignant suffering.* **2** keen; intense: *a subject of poignant interest.* **3** sharp to the taste or smell: *poignant sauces.* [ME < OF *poignant,* ppr. of *poindre* prick < L *pungere*] —**poign′ant·ly,** *adv.* —**Syn. 1** severe.

poi·lu (pwä′lü) *n.* a nickname for a French soldier. [< F *poilu,* originally, hairy, ult. < L *pilus* hair]

poin·ci·a·na (poin′sē an′ə) *n.* any of a group of tropical shrubs or small trees of the pea or bean family, having red, yellow, or orange flowers. [< NL *Poinciana,* the genus name < *de Poinci,* a governor of the Antilles in the 1600's, who wrote a natural history of the islands]

poin·set·ti·a (poin set′ē ə) *n.* a plant having a small flower surrounded by large, scarlet leaves resembling petals. [< NL; after Joel R. *Poinsett,* (1779-1851), its discoverer]

point (point) *n.* **1** a sharp end; something having a sharp end: *the point of a needle.* **2** a tiny, round mark; dot: *A period is a point. Use a point to set off decimals.* **3** in mathematics, something that has position but not extension: *Two lines meet or cross at a point.* **4** a particular place or spot: *He drew a circle around a certain point on the map.* **5** a particular time or moment: *At this point he lost interest in the game.* **6** any particular or definite position, condition, or state; degree; stage: *boiling point.* **7** an item; detail: *He answered my questions point by point.* **8** a distinguishing mark or quality: *one's good points.* **9** a physical characteristic or feature of an animal. **10** the main idea or purpose; important or essential thing: *I missed the point of your talk.* **11** force; effectiveness. **12** a particular aim, end, or purpose. **13 a** each of the 32 positions indicating direction marked at the circumference of the card of a compass. **b** the interval between any two adjacent points of a compass; 11 degrees 15 minutes. **14** a piece of land with a sharp end sticking out into the water; cape. **15** a unit of credit, scoring, or measuring; unit of price quotations: *The university accredited him with five points for the semester's work. That stock has gone up a point.* **16** in printing, a unit for measuring type; about 1/72 inch. **17** *Informal.* a hint; suggestion. **18** lace made with a needle. **19** *Brit.* a railway switch. **20** in hockey, a position at the opponents' blueline, taken by an offensive player when the puck is within their defensive zone, especially during a power play. **21** in lacrosse, one of the defencemen playing out in front of the goalie. **22** in hunting, the attitude, usually with muzzle pointing and one foreleg raised, assumed by a pointer or setter on finding game. **23 a** a tungsten or platinum piece, especially in the distributor of an automobile engine, for making or breaking the flow of current. **b** *Esp. Brit.* an outlet; socket.

at the point of, in the act of; very near to.

beside the point, having little or nothing to do with the matter being discussed.

in point of, as regards.

make a point, state an opinion clearly and logically.

make a point of, be particular about: *He always makes a point of being on time.*
on the point of, just about; on the verge of.
strain or **stretch a point,** **a** exceed the reasonable limit. **b** make a special exception.
to the point, pertinent, apt: *His speech was to the point.*
—*v.* **1** sharpen: *to point a pencil.* **2** mark with dots; punctuate. **3** give force to (speech, action, etc.). **4** aim; tend. **5** indicate position or direction, or direct attention with, or as if with, the finger. **6** show with the finger; call attention to. **7** direct a finger, weapon, etc. **8** have a specified direction: *The signboard points north.* **9** of a dog, show the presence of game by standing rigid and looking toward it. **10** fill joints of (brickwork) with mortar or cement. **11** of an abscess, come to a head. **12 point off,** mark off with points or dots. **13 point out,** show or call attention to. **14 point up,** put emphasis on; call or give special attention to. [ME < OF *point* mark, moment and *pointe* sharp point, both ult. < L *pungere* prick] —**Syn.** *n.* **7** particular. **8** trait, characteristic. *-v.* **7** aim, level.

point-blank (*adj.* point′blangk′; *adv.* point′blangk′) *adj.* **1** aimed straight at the mark, without allowing for the bullet, shell, etc. dropping from the original line of flight. **2** close enough for aim to be taken in this way: *He fired the gun from point-blank range.* **3** plain and blunt; direct: *a point-blank question.* —*adv.* **1** straight at the mark. **2** from close range. **3** plainly and bluntly; directly: *One boy gave excuses, but the other refused point-blank.* [apparently < *point*, v. + *blank* the white mark in the centre of a target]

point blanket *Cdn.* a Hudson's Bay Company blanket.

pointe (pwaɴt or point; *French,* pwaɴt) *n.* in ballet: **1** the toe, or the tip of the toe. **2** the reinforced toe of a ballet slipper. [< F]

point·ed (poin′tid) *adj.* **1** having a point or points: *a pointed roof.* **2** sharp; piercing: *a pointed wit.* **3** directed; aimed. **4** emphatic: *He showed pointed attention to the new girl.* —**point′ed·ly,** *adv.* —**point′ed·ness,** *n.*

point·er (poin′tər) *n.* **1** one that points. **2** a long, tapering stick used in pointing things out on a map, blackboard, etc. **3** a hand of a clock, meter, etc. **4** one of several breeds of hunting dog, having short, smooth hair, and trained to show where game is by standing still and looking at the game. **5** a dog of one of these breeds. **6** *Informal.* a hint; suggestion. **7** *Cdn.* a river boat that is pointed at both bow and stern and is of shallow draft, designed for use in logging drives.

poin·til·lism (pwan′tə liz′əm) *n.* in art, the use of tiny points, or dots, of color that blend together when seen from a distance of a few feet. It is a form of impressionism and was developed by the French painter Georges Seurat (1859-1891). [< F *pointillisme* < *pointiller* mark with little dots or points]

point lace lace made with a needle.

point·less (point′lis) *adj.* **1** without a point. **2** without force or meaning. —**point′less·ly,** *adv.*

point man in hockey, a player assigned to play the point.

point of honor or **honour** a matter that affects a person's honor, principles, sense of duty, etc.

point of order a question raised as to whether proceedings are according to the rules.

point-of-pur·chase (point′əv pėr′chəs) *adj.* relating to a type of advertising aimed at a buyer when he is in a store.

point of view **1** a position from which objects are considered. **2** an attitude of mind.

points of the compass the 32 directions marked on a compass. North, south, east, and west are the four main, or cardinal, points of the compass.

point-to-point (point′tə point′) *n.* a steeplechase or cross-country race over a course marked by flags at the main points. —*adj.* made in a direct line from one point or place to another.

poise (poiz) *n. v.* **poised, pois·ing.** —*n.* **1** mental balance, composure, or self-possession: *She has perfect poise and never seems embarrassed.* **2** balance; the manner in which the body is carried: *He admired the major's poise.* [ME < OF *pois* < L *pensum* weight] —*v.* **1** balance: *Poise yourself on your toes.* **2** hold or carry evenly or steadily: *The athlete poised the weight in the air before throwing it.* [ME < OF *peser* weigh < L *pensare*, intensive of *pendere* weigh]

hat, āge, cãre, fär; let, ēqual, tėrm; it, īce
hot, ōpen, ôrder; oil, out; cup, pu̇t, rüle, ūse
əbove, takən, pencəl, lemən, circəs
ch, child; ng, long; sh, ship
th, thin; ᴛʜ, then; zh, measure

poi·son (poi′zən) *n.* **1** a drug or other substance that is very dangerous to health and capable of causing death. Strychnine and opium are poisons. **2** anything dangerous or deadly.
—*v.* **1** kill or harm by poison. **2** put poison in or on. **3** have a dangerous or harmful effect on. **4** turn (someone) against; make someone think badly of someone else.
—*adj.* poisonous. [ME < OF *poison* < L *potio, -onis* potion. Doublet of POTION.] —**poi′son·er,** *n.*

poison ivy a plant having glossy, green compound leaves of three leaflets each, that causes a painful rash on most people if they touch it.

Poison ivy

poison oak **1** a kind of poison ivy. **2** poison sumac.

poi·son·ous (poi′zən əs) *adj.* **1** containing poison; very harmful to health and capable of causing death. **2** having the power to poison. **3** having a dangerous or harmful effect. —**poi′son·ous·ly,** *adv.* —**poi′son·ous·ness,** *n.*

poison sumac a shrub growing in swamps, having leaves composed of seven to thirteen leaflets and bearing white berry-like fruit. It causes a severe rash on most people if they touch it.

poke[1] (pōk) *v.* **poked, pok·ing,** *n.* —*v.* **1** push against with something pointed; jab: *He poked me in the ribs with his elbow.* **2** thrust; push: *The old gossip was always poking her nose into other people's business.* **3** stir a fire with a poker. **4** punch: *He threatened to poke his brother in the nose.* **5** pry. **6** make by poking. **7** go lazily; loiter.
—*n.* **1** a poking; thrust; push. **2** a punch. **3** a slow, lazy person. [ME; cf. MDu., MLG *poken*] —**Syn.** *v.* **1** prod, nudge. **5** search, grope. **7** dawdle.

poke[2] (pōk) *n.* **1** *Dialect.* a bag; sack. **2** *Archaic.* a pocket. [ME; akin to OE *pocca* bag, pocket]

poke[3] (pōk) *n.* a bonnet or hat with a large brim in front. [? n. use of *poke*[1]]

poke[4] (pōk) *n.* pokeweed. [< Algonquian]

poke·ber·ry (pōk′ber′ē) *n.* **-ries.** **1** a berry of the pokeweed. **2** the pokeweed.

poke bonnet a bonnet with a projecting brim.

poke check in hockey, a quick thrust or jab with one's stick at the puck in order to get it away from an opponent.

poke-check (pōk′chek′) *v.* **1** carry out a poke check. **2** administer a poke check to (an opposing player).

poke·lo·gan (pōk′lō′gən) *n.* *Cdn.* a small stagnant backwater in a stream; logan. [< Algonquian]

A poke bonnet

pok·er[1] (pōk′ər) *n.* **1** one that pokes. **2** a metal rod for stirring a fire. [< *poke*[1]]

pok·er[2] (pōk′ər) *n.* a card game in which the players bet on the value of the cards that they hold in their hands. [origin uncertain]

poker face *Informal.* **1** a face or facial expression that does not show one's thoughts or feelings. **2** a person having such a face or facial expression.

poke·weed (pōk′wēd′) *n.* a tall weed of North America having juicy, purple berries and poisonous roots. [*poke*[4] + *weed*]

pok·ey[1] or **pok·y**[1] (pōk′ē) *n.* **-eys** or **-ies.** *Slang.* a jail.

pok·ey[2] or **pok·y**[2] (pōk′ē) *adj.* **pok·i·er, pok·i·est.** **1** puttering; dull; stupid: *a pokey old man.* **2** moving, acting, etc. slowly; slow. **3** small; confined; cramped; mean. **4** shabby; dowdy. [< *poke*[1]] —**pok′i·ly,** *adv.*

pol. 1 political. 2 politics.

Pol. Polish.

Po·lack (pō′lok *for 1*; pō′lak *for 2*) *n.* 1 *Derogatory slang.* a person of Polish descent. 2 *Obsolete.* a a native or inhabitant of Poland. b the king of Poland. [< Polish *Polak*]

Poland China (pō′lənd) 1 a breed of black-and-white pig. 2 a pig of this breed.

po·lar (pō′lər) *adj.* 1 of or near the North or South Pole. It is very cold in the polar regions. 2 having to do with a pole or poles. 3 of the poles of a magnet, electric battery, etc. 4 opposite in character, like the poles of a magnet: *Love and hate are polar feelings or attitudes.* 5 in chemistry, ionizing when dissolved or fused. [< Med.L *polaris* < L *polus* pole. See POLE².]

polar bear a large, white bear living in arctic regions.

polar front the line or region where cold air from the polar regions meets warm air from the tropics, usually producing strong winds and storms.

Po·lar·is (pō lăr′is) *n.* the North Star; polestar.

po·lar·i·scope (pō lar′ə skōp′) *n.* an instrument for showing the polarization of light, or for examining substances in polarized light.

po·lar·i·ty (pō lar′ə tē) *n.* 1 the possession of two opposed poles. A magnet or battery has polarity. 2 a positive or negative polar condition, as in electricity. 3 the possession or exhibition of two opposite or contrasted principles or tendencies.

po·lar·i·za·tion (pō′lər ə zā′shən or pō′lər ī zā′shən) *n.* 1 the production or acquisition of polarity. 2 a process by which gases produced during electrolysis are deposited on one or both electrodes of a cell, giving rise to a reverse electromotive force. 3 in optics, a state, or the production of a state, in which rays of light exhibit different properties in different directions.

po·lar·ize (pō′lər īz′) *v.* **-ized, -iz·ing.** give polarity to; cause polarization in. [< F *polariser*]

pol·der (pol′dər) *n.* an area of low, marshy land reclaimed from the sea or some other body of water and protected by dikes. [< Du.]

pole¹ (pōl) *n. v.* **poled, pol·ing.** —*n.* 1 a long, slender piece of wood, metal, etc.: *a telephone pole, a flagpole, a ski pole.* 2 a measure of length; rod; 5½ yards. 3 a measure of area; square rod; 30¼ square yards. —*v.* make (a boat) go with a pole. [OE *pāl* < L *palus* stake. Doublet of PALE².]

pole² (pōl) *n.* 1 either end of the earth's axis. The North Pole and the South Pole are opposite each other. 2 either of two parts where opposite forces are strongest. A magnet or battery has both a positive pole and a negative pole. 3 either end of the axis of any sphere. 4 either of two opinions, forces, etc. considered as being opposite extremes. 5 **poles apart,** very much different; in strong disagreement: *Their viewpoints on the subject were poles apart.* [ME < L *polus* < Gk. *polos*]

Pole (pōl) *n.* a native or inhabitant of Poland, a country in central Europe.

pole·axe or **pole·ax** (pōl′aks′) *n. v.* **-axed, -ax·ing.** —*n.* an axe with a long handle and a hook or spike opposite the blade. —*v.* fell with or as if with a poleaxe. [ME *pollax* < *pol(le)* poll, head + *ax* axe]

pole·cat (pōl′kat′) *n.* 1 a small, dark-brown carnivorous European mammal having a very disagreeable odor. 2 the North American skunk. 3 *Informal.* a mean or contemptible person. [ME *polcat* < OF *poule* fowl, hen (< VL *pulla,* fem. to L *pullus* young fowl) + ME *cat* cat; so called because it preys on poultry]

po·lem·ic (pə lem′ik) *n.* an argument; dispute; controversy. —*adj.* of controversy or disagreement; of dispute. [< Gk. *polemikos* belligerent < *polemos* war]

po·lem·i·cal (pə lem′ə kəl) *adj.* polemic. —**po·lem′i·cal·ly,** *adv.*

po·lem·ics (pə lem′iks) *n.* the art or practice of disputation or controversy, especially in theology.

pole·star (pōl′stär′) *n.* 1 the North Star, formerly much used as a guide by sailors. 2 a guiding principle; guide. 3 a centre of attraction, interest, or attention.

pole vault a vault over a high, horizontal bar using a long pole.

pole-vault (pōl′volt or -vôlt) *v.* make a pole vault. —**pole′-vault′er,** *n.*

po·lice (pə lēs′) *n. v.* **-liced, -lic·ing.** —*n.* 1 the persons whose duty is keeping order and arresting people who break the law. 2 department of government that keeps order and arrests persons who break the law. —*v.* keep order in: *to police the streets, to police an army camp.* [< F *police* < L < Gk. *politeia* polity. Doublet of POLICY¹, POLITY.]

police court a court that deals only with charges laid by the police: *The man was summoned to the police court and charged with speeding.*

police dog 1 a kind of large, strong dog that looks like a wolf; German shepherd dog. 2 any dog used in police work.

police force the law-enforcing body of a community.

po·lice·man (pə lēs′mən) *n.* **-men** (-mən). 1 a man who is a member of a police force. 2 in hockey, a rugged player responsible for keeping opposing players from treating his team-mates roughly.

police state a country strictly controlled by governmental authority, thus having only a minimum of social, economic, and political liberty.

police village in Ontario, an unincorporated village administered by a board of trustees.

po·lice·wom·an (pə lēs′wům′ən) *n.* **-wom·en.** a woman who is a member of a police force.

po·li·cing (pə lē′sing) *n.* the regulation and control of a community, especially with reference to matters of order, public safety, etc.: *The R.C.M.P. are responsible for policing in many areas.*

pol·i·cy¹ (pol′ə sē) *n.* **-cies.** 1 a plan of action; way of management: *It is a poor policy to promise more than you can give.* 2 practical wisdom; prudence. 3 political skill or shrewdness. [ME < OF *policie* < L < Gk. *politeia* polity. Doublet of POLICE, POLITY.]

pol·i·cy² (pol′ə sē) *n.* **-cies.** a written agreement about insurance. [< F < Ital. *pólizza* < Med.L < Gk. *apodeixis* declaration]

pol·i·cy·hold·er (pol′ə sē hōl′dər) *n.* one who holds an insurance policy.

po·li·o (pō′lē ō′) *n. Informal.* poliomyelitis.

po·li·o·my·e·li·tis (pō′lē ō mī′ə lī′tis or pol′ē ō-) *n.* 1 infantile paralysis. 2 any inflammation of the gray matter of the spinal cord. [< NL < Gk. *polios* gray + *myelos* marrow + *-itis*]

pol·ish (pol′ish) *v.* 1 make smooth and shiny: *polish shoes.* 2 become smooth and shiny. 3 remove by smoothing. 4 put into a better condition; improve. 5 make elegant; refine. 6 **polish off,** *Informal.* get done with; finish. 7 **polish up,** get into a better condition; improve.
—*n.* 1 a substance used to give smoothness or shine: *silver polish.* 2 shininess; smoothness: *The polish of the furniture reflected the lamplight.* 3 a polishing or being polished. 4 culture; elegance; refinement. [ME < OF *poliss-,* a stem of *polir* < L *polire*] —**pol′ish·er,** *n.*
Syn. *v.* 1 burnish, brighten. *-n.* 2 **Polish, lustre, sheen** = the shine of a surface. **Polish** suggests the shine given a surface by rubbing: *Rain spoiled the car's bright polish.* **Lustre** emphasizes shining by reflecting light, often of shifting colors: *Furniture that has been waxed has a lustre.* **Sheen** suggests a more steady gleam or brilliance: *Highly polished metal has a sheen.*

Pol·ish (pōl′ish) *adj.* of or having to do with Poland, its people, or their language. —*n.* the language of Poland.

Po·lit·bu·ro (pə lit′būr′ō or pol′it būr′ō) *n.* formerly, the Communist Party executive committee that examined and controlled policy and matters of state in the Soviet Union, replaced in 1952 by the Presidium.

po·lite (pə līt′) *adj.* 1 having or showing good manners; behaving properly. 2 refined; elegant. [< L *politus* polished] —**po·lite′ly,** *adv.* —**po·lite′ness,** *n.*
Syn. 1 **Polite, civil, courteous** = having the manners necessary in social relations. **Polite** = having and showing good manners at all times, and emphasizes following the rules for behaving properly: *That polite boy gave me his seat.* **Civil** = being just polite enough

not to be rude: *All I expect is a civil answer.* **Courteous** adds to *polite* the idea of showing thoughtful attention to the feelings and wishes of others: *I go to that store because the clerks are courteous.* **2** polished, cultured.

pol·i·tic (pol′ə tik′) *adj.* **1** wise in looking out for one's own interests; prudent: *He thought it politic to put some money in the bank.* **2** scheming; crafty. **3** political: *The state is a body politic.* [ME < OF < L < Gk. *politikos*, ult. < *polis* city-state] **—pol′i·tic·ly,** *adv.* **—Syn. 1** shrewd, astute.

po·lit·i·cal (pə lit′ə kəl) *adj.* **1** of or concerned with politics. **2** having to do with public affairs or government: *Treason is a political offence.* **3** of politicians or their methods. **4** having a definite system of government. **—po·lit′i·cal·ly,** *adv.*

political economy economics.

political science the science of the principles and conduct of government.

pol·i·ti·cian (pol′ə tish′ən) *n.* **1** a person who gives much time to political affairs; a person experienced in politics. **2** a person active in politics chiefly for his own profit or that of his party. **3** a person holding a political office.

Syn. 1 Politician, statesman = someone active or skilled in public or governmental affairs. **Politician** especially suggests ability to deal with people and accomplish things for the good of the people and the country, but often is used slightingly or contemptuously to suggest a man without principles scheming for his own or his party's good: *All office-holders are politicians.* **Statesman,** always in a good sense, emphasizes sound judgment, shrewdness, far-sightedness, and skill in dealing with public problems and managing national affairs: *Churchill was a great statesman.*

pol·i·tick (pol′ə tik′) *v.* engage in political affairs; practise politics; intrigue.

po·lit·i·co (pə lit′ə kō′) *n.* **-cos.** *Often derogatory.* a politician.

pol·i·tics (pol′ə tiks′) *n.sing. or pl.* **1** the management of political affairs: *Mackenzie King was engaged in politics for many years.* **2** political principles or opinions. **3** political methods or manoeuvres. **4** the science and art of government.

☞ Politics may be used as either singular or plural, but should not be both in the same passage: *Politics is a good topic for discussion. His politics were a matter of great concern to his friends.*

pol·i·ty (pol′ə tē) *n.* **-ties. 1** government. **2** a particular form or system of government. **3** a community with a government; state. [< obs. F *politie* < L < Gk. *politeia*, ult. < *polis* city-state. Doublet of POLICE, POLICY[1].]

pol·ka (pōl′kə or pō′kə) *n. v.* **-kaed, -ka·ing.** **—***n.* **1** a kind of lively dance. **2** the music for this dance. **—***v.* dance a polka. [< F < G *Polka*, probably < Slavic]

pol·ka dot (pō′kə) **1** a dot or round spot repeated to form a pattern on cloth. **2** a pattern or fabric with such dots.

poll (pōl) *n.* **1** a voting; collection of votes. **2** the number of votes cast. **3** the results of these votes. **4** a list of persons, especially a list of voters. **5 polls,** *pl.* the place where votes are cast and counted. **6** a survey of public opinion concerning a particular subject. **7** the head, especially the part of it on which the hair grows. **—***v.* **1** receive (as votes): *The mayor polled a record vote.* **2** vote; cast (a vote). **3** take or register the votes of. **4** question or canvass in a public-opinion poll. **5** cut off or cut short the hair, wool, horns, branches, etc. of. [cf. MDu. *pol(le)* top, MLG *pol* head]

pol·lack (pol′ək) *n.* pollock.

pol·len (pol′ən) *n.* a fine, yellowish powder formed on the anthers of flowers. Grains of pollen carried to the pistils of flowers fertilize them. [< L *pollen* mill dust]

pol·li·nate (pol′ə nāt′) *v.* **-nat·ed, -nat·ing.** carry pollen from stamens to pistils of; shed pollen on. Many flowers are pollinated by bees. **—pol′li·na′tion,** *n.*

polling booth in a polling station, a screened or otherwise enclosed space where a voter marks his ballot in privacy.

polling station during an election, a room or building set up as a place where the people living nearby may vote.

pol·li·wog (pol′ē wog′) *n.* a tadpole. [cf. ME *polwigle* < *pol(le)* poll, head + *wigle* wiggle]

pol·lock (pol′ək) *n.* **-lock** or **-locks. 1** a food fish of the cod family, found in the N. Atlantic Ocean, especially off the coast of Nova Scotia. **2** a similar fish found in the N. Pacific. Also, **pollack.**

hat, āge, cãre, fär; let, ēqual, tėrm; it, īce
hot, ōpen, ôrder; oil, out; cup, pút, rüle, ūse
əbove, takən, pencəl, lemən, circəs
ch, child; ng, long; sh, ship
th, thin; ᴛʜ, then; zh, measure

poll·ster (pōl′stər) *n.* one who takes a public-opinion poll.

poll tax a tax on every person, or on every person of a specified class, especially as a prerequisite to the right to vote.

pol·lu·tant (pə lü′tənt) *n.* a medium or agent of pollution.

pol·lute (pə lüt′) *v.* **-lut·ed, -lut·ing.** make dirty; defile: *The water at the bathing beach was polluted by refuse from the factory.* [< L *pollutus*, pp. of *polluere*] **—pol·lut·er,** *n.*

pol·lu·tion (pə lü′shən) *n.* **1** a polluting; defiling. **2** a condition of uncleanness in the air, water, or other aspect of the environment.

Pol·lux (pol′əks) *n.* **1** in Greek and Roman mythology, one of the twin sons of Zeus and Leda. Pollux was immortal; his brother Castor was mortal. **2** one of the two brightest stars in the constellation Gemini. [< L < Gk. *Polydeukēs*]

Pol·ly·an·na (pol′ē an′ə) *n.* one who is always cheerful, or overly cheerful, and always sees good in everything, even in the face of disaster. [after *Pollyanna*, the heroine of stories by Eleanor H. Porter (1868-1920)]

pol·ly·wog (pol′ē wog′) *n.* polliwog.

po·lo (pō′lō) *n.* **1** a game played on a field by men on horseback with long-handled mallets and a wooden ball. **2** water polo. [? ult. < Tibetan *pulu*]

A man playing polo

pol·o·naise (pol′ə nāz′ or pō′lə nāz′) *n.* **1** a slow, stately dance in three-quarter time. **2** the music for such a dance. **3** a woman's overdress with a waist and an open skirt. [< F *polonaise*, fem. adj., literally, Polish]

po·lo·ni·um (pə lō′nē əm) *n.* a radio-active chemical element that occurs in pitchblende. *Symbol:* Po; *at.no.* 84; *at.wt.* 210 (most stable isotope). [< NL < Med.L *Polonia* Poland, the homeland of Marie Curie (1867-1934), who, with her husband, discovered it]

Po·lo·ni·us (pə lō′nē əs) *n.* a pompous old man who is the father of Ophelia in Shakespeare's *Hamlet.*

A woman wearing a polonaise

pol·ter·geist (pol′tər gīst′) *n.* a ghost or spirit supposedly responsible for door slamming, chain rattling, and other inexplicable disturbances. [< G *Poltergeist* noisy ghost]

pol·troon (pol trün′) *n.* a wretched coward. [< F *poltron* < Ital. *poltrone* < *poltro* colt, ult. < L *pullus* young animal]

poly- *combining form.* **1** more than one; many; extensive, as in *polyangular.* **2** polymeric; polymerized, as in *polyethylene, polystyrene.* [< Gk. *poly-* < *polys* much, many]

pol·y·an·drous (pol′ē an′drəs) *adj.* **1** having more than one husband at one time. **2** in botany, having numerous stamens.

pol·y·an·dry (pol′ē an′drē) *n.* **1** the practice or condition of having more than one husband at the same time. **2** in botany, the condition of being polyandrous. [< Gk. *polyandria* < *polys* many + *anēr, andros* man, husband]

pol·y·an·thus (pol′ē an′thəs) *n.* **1** the oxlip. **2** a kind of narcissus bearing clusters of small, yellow or white flowers. [< NL < Gk. *polyanthos* < *polys* many + *anthos* flower]

pol·y·car·pous (pol′i kär′pəs) *adj.* in botany, consisting of many or several carpels. [< *poly-* + Gk. *karpos* fruit]

pol·y·chrome (pol′i krōm′) *adj.* having many or various colors; decorated in many colors. —*n.* **1** a work of art in several colors. **2** a combination of many colors. [< Gk. *polychrōmos* < *polys* many + *chrōma* color]

pol·y·clin·ic (pol′i klin′ik) *n.* a clinic or hospital dealing with many different diseases.

pol·y·es·ter (pol′ē es′tər) *n.* one of a widely varying group of very durable plastics and resins formed by polymerization or condensation. Polyesters are used in the manufacture of trays, fibres, paints, etc.

pol·y·eth·y·lene (pol′ē eth′ə lēn′) *n.* any of various very durable thermoplastics produced by the polymerization of ethylene, used for insulation, packaging, etc. *Formula:* $(C_2H_4)_n$

po·lyg·a·mist (pə lig′ə mist) *n.* a person who practises or favors polygamy.

po·lyg·a·mous (pə lig′ə məs) *adj.* **1** having more than one wife at the same time. **2** in botany, bearing both unisexual and hermaphrodite flowers on the same plant or on different plants of the same species. **3** in zoology: **a** of an animal, having several mates. **b** of a species, characterized by polygamy. —**po·lyg′a·mous·ly,** *adv.*

po·lyg·a·my (pə lig′ə mē) *n.* **1** the practice or condition of having more than one wife at the same time. **2** in zoology, the practice of mating with several individuals of the opposite sex, usually one male with several females. [< Gk. *polygamia* < *polys* many + *gamos* marriage]

pol·y·glot (pol′i glot′) *adj.* **1** knowing several languages. **2** written in several languages. —*n.* **1** a person who knows several languages. **2** a book written in several languages. **3** a mixture or confusion of several languages. [< Gk. *polyglōttos* < *polys* many + *glōtta* tongue]

pol·y·gon (pol′i gon′) *n.* a closed plane figure having straight sides and, usually, more than four sides and angles. [< LL < Gk. < *polys* many + *gōnia* angle]

Polygons

po·lyg·o·nal (pə lig′ə nəl) *adj.* having more than four angles and four sides.

pol·y·graph (pol′i graf′) *n.* **1** a device resembling a pantograph, for drawing or writing two or more copies of the same thing at the same time. **2** a versatile or prolific writer. **3** in medicine, a device for simultaneously recording changes in the normal heartbeat, blood pressure, breathing, etc. It is sometimes used as a lie detector.

pol·y·he·dral (pol′i hē′drəl) *adj.* **1** of or having to do with a polyhedron. **2** having many faces.

pol·y·he·dron (pol′i hē′drən) *n.* **-drons, -dra** (-drə). a solid figure having many faces. [< NL < Gk. *polyedros* < *polys* many + *hedra* seat, side]

pol·y·mer (pol′i mər) *n.* a giant molecule formed by the combining of two or more identical or similar molecules, having the same components as the originals and in the same proportions.

pol·y·mer·ic (pol′i mer′ik) *adj.* having the same elements combined in the same proportions by weight, but differing in molecular weights and chemical properties. Acetylene, C_2H_2, and benzene, C_6H_6, are polymeric compounds. [< Gk. *polymerēs* < *polys* many + *meros* part]

pol·y·mer·i·za·tion (pol′i mər ə zā′shən or pol′i mər ī zā′shən) *n.* in chemistry, the process of forming a polymer or polymeric compound.

pol·y·mer·ize (pol′i mə rīz′ or pə lim′ə rīz′) *v.* **-rized, -riz·ing. 1** form a polymer; make polymeric. **2** undergo polymerization.

pol·y·mor·phic (pol′i môr′fik) *adj.* polymorphous.

pol·y·mor·phism (pol′i môr′fiz əm) *n.* the state or quality of being polymorphous.

pol·y·mor·phous (pol′i môr′fəs) *adj.* having, assuming, or passing through many or various forms, states, etc. [< Gk. *polymorphos* < *polys* many + *morphē* form]

Pol·y·ne·sian (pol′i nē′zhən) *n.* **1** a member of any of the brown peoples that live in Polynesia, a group of islands in the Pacific Ocean, east of Australia. **2** the languages of Polynesia, including Maori, Hawaiian, etc. —*adj.* of or having to do with Polynesia, its people, or their languages.

pol·y·no·mi·al (pol′i nō′mē əl) *n.* in algebra, an expression consisting of two or more terms. ab, x^2y, and $3npq$ are monomials; $ab + x^2y$ and $pq - p^2 + q$ are polynomials. —*adj.* consisting of two or more terms. *Homo sapiens* is a polynomial expression. [< *poly-* + *-nomial,* as in *binomial*]

po·lyn·ya or **po·lyn·ia** (pə lin′yə) *n.* a fairly large area of open water surrounded by pack ice. [< Russian]

pol·yp (pol′ip) *n.* **1** a simple form of water animal, not much more than a saclike stomach with fingerlike tentacles around the edge to gather in food. Polyps often grow in colonies, with their bases connected. Corals and sea anemones are polyps. **2** in medicine, a tumor arising from a mucous or serous surface. [< F < L < Gk. *polypous* < *polys* many + *pous* foot]

pol·y·phon·ic (pol′i fon′ik) *adj.* **1** in music: **a** having two or more voices or parts, each with an independent melody, but all harmonizing; contrapuntal. **b** that can produce two or more sounds at the same time, as a piano. **2** producing many sounds; many-voiced. **3** in phonetics, representing more than one sound, as English *oo* in *food, good.*

po·lyph·o·ny (pə lif′ə nē) *n.* **1** in music, a polyphonic composition; counterpoint. **2** a multiplicity of sounds. **3** in phonetics, the representation of more than one sound by the same letter or symbol. [< Gk. *polyphōnia* < *polys* many + *phōnē* voice]

pol·y·pro·py·lene (pol′i prō′pə lēn′) *n.* a lightweight thermoplastic, similar to, but harder than, polyethylene, used for a wide variety of moulded articles, insulating materials, etc. It is a polymer of propylene. *Formula:* $(C_3H_6)_n$

pol·y·pus (pol′i pəs) *n.* **-pi** (-pī′ or -pē′). polyp.

pol·y·sty·rene (pol′i stī′rēn or -stir′ən) *n.* a clear, colorless plastic, a polymer of styrene, used in a wide variety of articles, appliances, toys, dishes, etc. *Formula:* $(C_8H_8)_n$

pol·y·syl·lab·ic (pol′i sə lab′ik) *adj.* of more than three syllables. —**pol′y·syl·lab′i·cal·ly,** *adv.*

pol·y·syl·la·ble (pol′i sil′ə bəl) *n.* a word of more than three syllables.

pol·y·syn·the·sis (pol′i sin′thə sis) *n.* **-ses** (-sēz′). **1** the synthesis of several elements. **2** in linguistics, the combination of the subject, object, verb, and modifiers into one unit or expression of which the elements have no separate existence as words, as in Eskimo or certain Amerindian languages.

pol·y·syn·thet·ic (pol′i sin thet′ik) *adj.* of or having to do with polysynthesis.

pol·y·tech·nic (pol′i tek′nik) *adj.* having to do with or dealing with many arts or sciences: *a polytechnic school.* —*n.* a technical school. [< F < Gk. *polytechnos* < *polys* many + *technē* art]

pol·y·the·ism (pol′i thē′iz əm) *n.* belief in more gods than one. The religion of the ancient Greeks was polytheism. [< F *polythéisme,* ult. < Gk. *polys* many + *theos* god]

pol·y·the·ist (pol′i thē′ist) *n.* a person who believes in more than one god.

pol·y·the·is·tic (pol′i thē is′tik) *adj.* having to do with or characterized by belief in many gods. —**pol′y·the·is′ti·cal·ly,** *adv.*

pol·y·ton·al (pol′i tōn′əl) *adj.* in music, using or having polytonality. —**pol·y·ton′al·ly,** *adv.*

pol·y·ton·al·i·ty (pol′i tō nal′ə tē) *n.* in music: **1** the use of several keys at the same time. **2** the sounds thus produced.

pol·y·ur·e·thane (pol′ē ūr′ə thān′) *n.* a tough plastic that is highly resistant to weather, acids, fire, etc., used to stiffen sheet metal, to strengthen fractured bones, and as an insulator, filler, binder, etc.

pol·y·vi·nyl (pol′i vī′nəl) *adj.* of or having to do with a group of thermoplastic resins formed by the polymerization of vinyl.

pom·ace (pum′is) *n.* **1** apple pulp or similar fruit pulp before or after the juice has been pressed out. **2** what is left after oil has been pressed out of something. [ult. < Med.L *pomacium* cider < L *pomum* apple]

po·ma·ceous (pə mā′shəs) *adj.* belonging to the same family of plants as the apple. [< NL *pomaceus* < L *pomum* apple]

po·made (pə mād′) *n.* a perfumed ointment for the scalp and hair. [< F < Ital. *pomata* < L *pomum* fruit]

po·man·der (pə man′dər or pō′man dər) *n.* a ball of mixed aromatic substances formerly carried for perfume or as a guard against infection. [var. of earlier *pomeamber* < *pome* + *amber*]

pome (pōm) *n.* an apple or any fruit like it; a fruit consisting of firm, juicy flesh surrounding a core that contains several seeds. Apples, pears, and quinces are pomes. [ME < OF *pome*, ult. < L *pomum* apple]

pome·gran·ate (pom′gran′it or pom′ə gran′it) *n.* **1** a reddish-yellow fruit having a thick skin, red pulp, and many seeds. **2** the tree that this fruit grows on. [ME < OF *pome grenate* < *pome* fruit (ult. < L *pomum*) + *grenate* having grains < L *granata*, fem. < *granum* grain]

Pom·er·a·ni·an (pom′ər ā′nē ən) *adj.* of or having to do with Pomerania, an area on the south coast of the Baltic Sea, or its people. —*n.* **1** a native or inhabitant of Pomerania. **2** a breed of small dog, weighing 3 to 7 pounds, having a sharp nose, pointed ears, and long, thick, silky hair. **3** a dog of this breed.

pom·mel (pum′əl or pom′əl) *n. v.* **-melled** or **-meled, -mel·ling** or **-mel·ing.** —*n.* **1** the part of a saddle that sticks up at the front. See **saddle** for picture. **2** a rounded knob on the hilt of a sword, dagger, etc. —*v.* beat with the fists; strike; beat; pummel. [ME < OF *pomel*, ult. < L *pomum* apple] —**pom′mel·ler** or **pom′mel·er,** *n.*

po·mol·o·gist (pō mol′ə jist) *n.* a person who is skilled in pomology. [< NL *pomologia* < L *pomum* fruit, apple + *-logia* -logy]

po·mol·o·gy (pə mol′ə jē) *n.* the branch of science that deals with fruits and fruit growing. [< NL < L *pomum* fruit + Gk. *-logos* treating of]

pomp (pomp) *n.* **1** a stately display; splendor; magnificence: *The king was crowned with great pomp.* **2** a showy display. [ME < OF < Gk. *pompē* parade] —**Syn.** **1** flourish, grandeur.

pom·pa·dour (pom′pə dôr′) *n.* **1** an arrangement of a woman's hair in which it is puffed high over the forehead. **2** an arrangement of a man's hair in which it is brushed straight up and back from the forehead. [after Jeanne Antoinette Poisson, Marquise de *Pompadour* (1721-1764), a mistress of Louis XV of France]

A woman with a pompadour

pom·pa·no (pom′pə nō′) *n.* **-nos.** a food fish of the West Indies and neighboring coasts of North America. [< Sp.]

Pom·pei·an (pom pā′ən) *adj.* of or having to do with Pompeii or its people.

Pom·peii (pom pā′ē or pom pā′) *n.* a city in ancient Italy, which was buried by an eruption of Mount Vesuvius in A.D. 79. Its ruins have been partly laid bare by excavation.

pom-pom (pom′pom) *n.* an automatic anti-aircraft gun, used especially on shipboard. [imitative]

pom·pom (pom′pom) *n.* **1** an ornamental tuft or ball of feathers, silk, etc. worn on a hat or dress, on the shoes, etc. **2** a ball of wool worn on the front of a certain kind of soldier's hat. **3** a kind of chrysanthemum or dahlia having very small, rounded flowers. [< F *pompon* < *pompe* pomp]

A pompom on a clown's hat

pom·pon (pom′pon) *n.* pompom.

pom·pos·i·ty (pom pos′ə tē) *n.* **-ties. 1** a pompous quality. **2** a show of self-importance.

hat, āge, cãre, fär; let, ēqual, tėrm; it, īce
hot, ōpen, ôrder; oil, out; cup, pu̇t, rüle, ūse
əbove, takən, pencəl, lemən, circəs
ch, child; ng, long; sh, ship
th, thin; ᴛʜ, then; zh, measure

pom·pous (pom′pəs) *adj.* **1** trying to seem magnificent; fond of display; acting proudly; self-important: *The leader of the band bowed in a pompous manner.* **2** splendid; magnificent; stately. [< F *pompeux* < LL *pomposus*] —**pom′pous·ly,** *adv.* —**pom′pous·ness,** *n.* —**Syn.** **1** pretentious, inflated, grandiose.

pon·cho (pon′chō) *n.* **-chos.** a large piece of cloth, often waterproof, with a slit in the middle for the head to go through. Ponchos are worn in South America as cloaks. Waterproof ponchos are used in the army and navy and by hikers and campers. [< Sp. < Araucanian (S.Am.Ind.) *pontho*]

pond (pond) *n.* a body of still water, smaller than a lake. [originally, var. of *pound*[3]]

pon·der (pon′dər) *v.* consider carefully; think over. [ME < OF < L *ponderare* weigh < *pondus, -deris* weight] —**pon′der·er,** *n.* —**pon′der·ing·ly,** *adv.*

pon·der·a·ble (pon′dər ə bəl) *adj.* capable of being weighed; having perceptible weight.

pon·de·ro·sa pine (pon′də rō′sə) **1** a tall pine tree of W. North America. **2** the wood of this tree, much used for lumber. [< L *ponderosus* heavy. See PONDEROUS.]

pon·der·os·i·ty (pon′dər os′ə tē) *n.* the quality of being ponderous.

pon·der·ous (pon′dər əs) *adj.* **1** very heavy. **2** heavy and clumsy. **3** dull; tiresome: *The speaker talked in a ponderous way.* [ME < OF < L *ponderosus* < *pondus, -deris* weight] —**pon′der·ous·ly,** *adv.* —**pon′der·ous·ness,** *n.* —**Syn. 1** weighty, massive. **2** unwieldy, cumbersome.

pond hockey *Cdn.* **1** unorganized hockey played on frozen ponds, streams, etc. **2** *Slang.* poorly played hockey; hockey of a low standard.

pond lily water lily.

pond·weed (pond′wēd′) *n.* any of a large group of water plants that grow in still water. Most pondweeds have oval leaves on the surface of the water and grasslike leaves under water.

pone (pōn) *n.* *Southern U.S.* **1** bread made of corn meal. **2** a loaf or cake of this bread. [< Algonquian]

pon·gee (pon jē′) *n.* a kind of thin, soft silk, usually left in natural brownish-yellow color. [? < dial. Chinese *punchi* home-woven]

pon·iard (pon′yərd) *n.* a dagger. [< F *poignard*, ult. < L *pugnus* fist]

Pon·ti·ac Conspiracy (pon′tē ak′) an Indian uprising against the British in the old Northwest Territory from 1763 to 1766, organized and led by Pontiac, 1720?-1769, a chief of the Ottawa tribe.

pon·ti·fex (pon′tə feks′) *n.* **pon·tif·i·ces. 1** in ancient Rome, a member of the principal college of priests. **2** pontiff. [< L *pontifex* a high priest of Rome, probably < *pons, pontis* bridge + *facere* make. Doublet of PONTIFF.]

pon·tiff (pon′tif) *n.* **1** the Pope. **2** a bishop. **3** a high priest; chief priest. [< F *pontife* < L *pontifex* a high priest of Rome. Doublet of PONTIFEX.]

pon·tif·i·cal (pon tif′ə kəl) *adj.* **1** of or having to do with the Pope; papal. **2** of or having to do with a bishop. **3** characteristic of a pontiff; stately; pompous. —*n.* **pontificals,** *pl.* the vestments and marks of dignity used by cardinals and bishops at certain ecclesiastical functions or ceremonies. —**pon·tif′i·cal·ly,** *adv.*

Pontifical Zouave a member of a force of volunteers from various countries, including Canada, recruited to fight for the Holy See in the 19th century when the independence of the Vatican was threatened by Piedmont.

pon·tif·i·cate (*n.* pon tif′ə kit or pon tif′ə kāt′; *v.* pon tif′ə kāt′) *n. v.* **-cat·ed, -cat·ing.** —*n.* the office or term of office of a pontiff. —*v.* **1** speak pompously. **2** officiate as a pontiff, especially as a bishop.

pon·tif·i·ces (pon tif′ə sēz′) *n.* pl. of **pontifex.**

pon·til (pon′təl) *n.* a steel or iron rod used as a glass blower's tool. Also, **pontil rod.** [< F *pontil* < Ital. *pontello*, diminutive < *punto* < L *punctum*]

pon·toon (pon tün′) *n.* 1 a low, flat-bottomed boat. 2 such a boat, or some other floating structure, used as one of the supports of a temporary bridge. 3 either of the two boat-shaped parts of an airplane, for landing on or taking off from water. [< F *ponton* < L *ponto, -onis* < *pons, pontis* bridge]

A bridge supported by pontoons (def. 2)

pontoon bridge a temporary bridge supported by low, flat-bottomed boats or other floating structures.

Pon·tus (pon′təs) *n.* 1 an ancient name of the Black Sea. 2 in ancient times, a country in N.E. Asia Minor, just south of the Black Sea. It became a Roman province.

po·ny (pō′nē) *n.* **-nies. 1 a** a breed of very small horses, especially those not over 14 hands high. **b** a horse of this breed. 2 *Informal. Esp.U.S.* a translation of a book, which a pupil uses to avoid translating the book himself. 3 *Informal.* **a** a small glass for alcoholic liquor. **b** the amount the glass holds. [< obs. F *poulenet*, ult. < L *pullus* foal]

pony express *U.S.* formerly, a system of carrying mail, etc. by men on fast ponies or horses.

pooch (püch) *n. Slang.* a dog. [origin uncertain]

pood (püd) *n.* a Russian weight equal to about 36 pounds. [< Russian, ult. < L *pondus* weight]

poo·dle (pü′dəl) *n.* 1 a breed of intelligent pet dog having thick hair that is often clipped and shaved in an elaborate manner. Some poodles have wiry, curly hair; others have long, silky hair. 2 a dog of this breed. [< G *Pudel*, short for *Pudelhund* < dial. *pudeln* splash water] **—poo′dle-like′,** *adj.*

poof (püf) *n.* a sound resembling the puff of breath in blowing out a candle. *—interj.* an expression of rejection or contempt. Also, **pouf.** [imitative]

pooh (pü) *interj. n.* an exclamation of contempt.

Pooh-Bah (pü′bä′) *n.* 1 a self-important, pompous person. 2 a person holding many insignificant offices. [< *Pooh-Bah*, a character in Gilbert and Sullivan's *The Mikado*]

pooh-pooh (pü′pü′) *v.* express contempt for; make light of. *—interj.* an exclamation of contempt.

pool[1] (pül) *n.* 1 a small body of still water; a small pond. 2 a still, deep place in a stream: *Trout are often found in the pools of a brook.* 3 a puddle of any spilled liquid. 4 a tank of water to swim or bathe in: *a swimming pool.* [OE *pōl*]

pool[2] (pül) *n.* 1 a game played on a special table with six pockets. The players try to drive balls into the pockets with cues. 2 the things or money put together by different persons for common advantage. 3 a group of people, usually having the same skills, who are drawn upon as needed: *the labor pool.* 4 an arrangement between several companies, groups, etc. to prevent competition by controlling prices. 5 a car pool. 6 the persons who form a pool. 7 **a** a fund raised by a group of persons for purposes of speculation, as in the stock market, commodities, etc. **b** the members of such a group. 8 in some games, etc., the stake played.
—v. 1 put (things or money) together for common advantage: *The three boys pooled their savings for a year to buy a boat.* 2 form a pool. [< F *poule* booty, originally, hen < LL *pulla* chick; meaning influenced by *pool*[1]]

pool·room (pül′rüm′ or -rům′) *n.* a room or place in which the game of pool is played.

pool train or **pooled train** a train that is operated over a line of track by more than one railway company: *A pool train used to run between Toronto and Montreal.*

poop[1] (püp) *n.* 1 a deck at the stern above the ordinary deck, often forming the roof of a cabin. 2 the stern of a ship. *—v.* of a wave, break over the stern of (a ship). [ME < OF < Ital. *poppa* < L *puppis* stern]

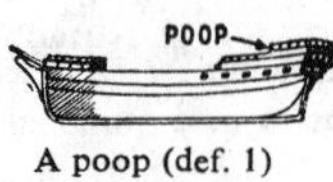

A poop (def. 1)

poop[2] (püp) *v. Slang.* 1 become worn out; be exhausted. 2 **poop out,** become exhausted. [origin unknown]

poor (pür) *adj.* 1 having few things or nothing; needy. 2 not good in quality; lacking something needed: *poor soil, a poor crop, a poor cook, poor health.* 3 scanty. 4 needing pity; unfortunate: *This poor child has hurt himself.* 5 not favorable: *a poor chance for recovery.* *—n.* **the poor,** persons who are needy. [ME < OF *povre* < L *pauper*. Doublet of PAUPER.] **—poor′ness,** *n.*
Syn. *adj.* 1 **Poor, penniless, impoverished** = with little or no money or property. **Poor** has a rather wide range of meaning, from "having no money or property at all and being dependent on charity for the necessities of life," to "having no money to buy comforts or luxuries": *She is a poor widow.* **Penniless** = without any money at all, but sometimes only temporarily: *She found herself penniless in a strange city.* **Impoverished** = reduced to poverty from comfortable circumstances, even wealth: *Many stars of silent movies are now impoverished.*

poor·house (pür′hous′) *n.* a house in which paupers live at public expense.

poor law a law providing for the relief of the poor.

poor·ly (pür′lē) *adv.* in a poor manner; not enough; badly; meanly. *—adj. Informal.* in bad health.

poor-spir·it·ed (pür′spir′ə tid) *adj.* having or showing a poor, cowardly, or abject spirit.

poor white in the S. United States, a member of a group or class of white people characterized by poverty, lack of education, opportunity, etc.

poor-will (pür′wil) *n.* a bird of western North America, resembling the whip-poor-will. [imitative]

pop[1] (pop) *v.* **popped, pop·ping,** *n. adv.* *—v.* 1 make a short, quick, explosive sound. 2 move, go, or come suddenly or unexpectedly. 3 thrust or put suddenly. 4 put (a question) suddenly. 5 *Informal.* shoot. 6 burst open with a pop. 7 heat or roast (popcorn) until it bursts with a pop. 8 bulge: *The surprise made her eyes pop out.* 9 in baseball, hit a short, high ball over the infield. 10 **pop off,** *Slang.* **a** fall asleep. **b** die. **c** state loudly as a complaint. 11 **pop the question,** *Informal.* propose marriage.
—n. 1 a short, quick, explosive sound. 2 a shot from a gun, etc. 3 a non-alcoholic carbonated drink. 4 in baseball, a fly ball that can be easily caught.
—adv. with a pop; suddenly. [imitative]

pop[2] (pop) *Slang.* *—adj.* popular. *—n.* 1 a piece of popular music. 2 pop art.

pop[3] (pop) *n. Informal.* papa; father.

pop. 1 population. 2 popular.

pop art a form of painting and sculpture based on the style of comic strips, advertising posters, etc.

pop·corn (pop′kôrn′) *n.* 1 a kind of Indian corn, the kernels of which burst open and puff out when heated. 2 the white, puffed-out kernels.

Pope or **pope** (pōp) *n.* the supreme head of the Roman Catholic Church: *the Pope, the last three popes.* [OE *pāpa* < LL *papa* pope < L *papa* tutor, bishop < Gk. *pap(p)as* father]

pop·er·y (pōp′ər ē) *n. Derogatory.* the doctrines, customs, and ceremonies of the Roman Catholic Church.

pop·eye (pop′ī′) *n.* a prominent or bulging eye. **—pop′eyed′,** *adj.*

pop·gun (pop′gun′) *n.* a toy gun that shoots with a popping sound.

pop·in·jay (pop′in jā′) *n.* 1 a vain, overtalkative person; conceited, silly person. 2 *Obsolete.* a parrot. [ME < OF *papingay* parrot < Sp.; cf. Arabic *babagha*]

pop·ish (pōp′ish) *adj. Derogatory.* of or having to do with the Roman Catholic Church. **—pop′ish·ly,** *adv.* **—pop′ish·ness,** *n.*

pop·lar (pop′lər) *n.* 1 any of several trees such as the Lombardy poplar, the cottonwood, and the aspen, that grow very rapidly and produce light, soft wood. 2 the wood of such a tree. [ME < OF *poplier* < L *populus*]

poplar bluff in the West, a grove of poplar trees: *The farmhouse nestled in the shady poplar bluff.*

pop·lin (pop′lən) *n.* a ribbed dress fabric, made of silk and wool, cotton and wool, or cotton. [< F < Ital. *papalina*, fem., papal, perhaps from the one-time papal capital Avignon, France, where the fabric was first made]

pop·o·ver (pop′ō′vər) *n.* a very light and hollow muffin.

pop·per (pop′ər) *n.* **1** one that pops. **2** a wire basket or metal pan used for popping popcorn.

pop·pet (pop′it) *n.* **1** a valve that controls the flow of water, gas, etc. by moving straight up and down instead of being hinged. **2 a** one of the small pieces of wood on the gunwale of a boat forming the rowlocks. **b** a timber placed beneath a ship's hull to support the ship in launching. **3** a bead that can be attached to other beads by a snap coupling to form a chain. Poppets are used especially to make necklaces, bracelets, etc. adjustable in length. **4** a small or dainty person, especially a pretty child, girl, etc.; pet. [var. of *puppet*]

pop·py (pop′ē) *n.* **-pies. 1** a kind of plant having showy red, yellow, or white flowers. Opium is made from one kind of poppy. **2** the flower. **3** a bright red. *—adj.* bright-red. [OE *popæg, papig*, ult. < L *papaver*]

pop·py·cock (pop′ē kok′) *n. interj. Informal.* nonsense; bosh.

pop·si·cle (pop′sə kəl) *n.* fruit-flavored ice on a small stick. [< trademark]

pop·u·lace (pop′yů lis) *n.* the common people; masses. [< F < Ital. *popolaccio*, ult. < L *populus* people]

pop·u·lar (pop′yů lər) *adj.* **1** liked by acquaintances or associates. **2** liked by many people; intended for the mass of people: *a popular song.* **3** of the people; by the people; representing the people: *Canada has a popular government.* **4** widespread among many people; common: *It is a popular belief that black cats bring bad luck.* **5** suited to or intended for ordinary people: *popular prices.* [< L *popularis* < *populus* people] **—Syn. 3** See **general. 4** prevailing, current.

popular front or **Popular Front** a coalition of communist, socialist, and moderate political parties against fascism, especially in France.

pop·u·lar·i·ty (pop′yů lar′ə tē) *n.* the fact or condition of being liked generally.

pop·u·lar·ize (pop′yů lər īz′) *v.* **-ized, -iz·ing.** make popular. **—pop′u·lar·i·za′tion,** *n.* **—pop′u·lar·iz′er,** *n.*

pop·u·lar·ly (pop′yů lər lē) *adv.* **1** in a popular manner. **2** by the people; in general.

popular vote the vote of the entire electorate thought of as including all the people.

pop·u·late (pop′yů lāt′) *v.* **-lat·ed, -lat·ing. 1** inhabit: *This city is densely populated.* **2** furnish with inhabitants: *Europeans populated much of the Canadian West.* [< Med.L *populare*, ult. < L *populus* people]

pop·u·la·tion (pop′yů lā′shən) *n.* **1** the people of a city or a country. **2** the number of people. **3** a part of the inhabitants distinguished in any way from the rest: *the Eskimo population.* **4** the act or process of furnishing with inhabitants. **5** in biology: **a** the aggregate of organisms that inhabit a particular locality or region. **b** a (specified) portion of this aggregate: *the deer population of North America.*

pop·u·lous (pop′yů ləs) *adj.* full of people; having many people per square mile. [ME < L *populosus* < *populus* people] **—pop′u·lous·ly,** *adv.* **—pop′u·lous·ness,** *n.*

por·ce·lain (pôr′sə lin or pôrs′lən) *n.* **1** very fine earthenware; china. **2** something made of porcelain. [< F < Ital. *porcellana*, a kind of shell, ult. < L *porcus* hog; from the shell being shaped like a pig's back]

porch (pôrch) *n.* **1** a covered entrance to a building; veranda. **2** a platform at the entrance to a house; stoop. **3** a sun porch. [ME < OF *porche* < L *porticus*. Doublet of PORTICO.]

por·cine (pôr′sīn or pôr′sən) *adj.* **1** of pigs or hogs. **2** like or characteristic of pigs or hogs. [< L *porcinus* < *porcus* pig]

por·cu·pine (pôr′kyů pīn′) *n.* a rodent covered with spines or quills. [ME < OF *porc-espin*, ult. < L *porcus* pig + *spina* thorn]

pore[1] (pôr) *v.* **pored, por·ing. 1** gaze earnestly or steadily. **2** study long and steadily: *He would rather pore over a book than play.* **3** meditate or ponder intently. [origin uncertain] **—por′er,** *n.*

hat, āge, cãre, fär; let, ēqual, tėrm; it, īce
hot, ōpen, ôrder; oil, out; cup, půt, rüle, ūse
əbove, takən, pencəl, lemən, circəs
ch, child; ng, long; sh, ship
th, thin; ᴛʜ, then; zh, measure

pore[2] (pôr) *n.* a very small opening. Sweat comes through the pores in the skin. See **epidermis** for diagram. [ME < OF < L < Gk. *poros*, literally, passage]

por·gy (pôr′gē) *n.* **-gies** or (*esp. collectively*) **-gy.** any of various salt-water food fishes, such as the scup of the eastern coast of the United States and the sea bream of Mediterranean and Atlantic waters.

pork (pôrk) *n.* **1** the meat of a pig used for food. **2** *U.S. Slang.* money from Federal or State appropriations, taxes, licences, etc. spent to confer local benefits for political reasons. [ME < OF < L *porcus* pig]

Pork showing various cuts

pork barrel *Slang. Esp.U.S.* a term used to describe government appropriations for projects that may not be needed but are likely to appeal to certain constituents.

pork·eat·er (pôrk′ēt′ər) *n. Cdn.* formerly, a French Canadian voyageur, especially a greenhorn.

pork·er (pôr′kər) *n.* a pig, especially one fattened to eat.

pork·pie (pork′pī′) *n.* **1** a deep, crusted pie filled with minced pork. **2** a hat having a low, flat crown resembling a pork pie. Also, **pork pie.**

pork·y (pôr′kē) *adj.* **1** of or like pork. **2** fat.

porn (pôrn) *n. Slang.* pornography. Also, **porno.**

por·no·graph·ic (pôr′nə graf′ik) *adj.* obscene.

por·nog·ra·phy (pôr nog′rə fē) *n.* obscene writings or pictures. [ult. < Gk. *pornē* harlot + *-graphos* writing about]

po·ros·i·ty (pô ros′ə tē) *n.* a porous quality or condition.

po·rous (pô′rəs) *adj.* full of pores or tiny holes; permeable by water, air, etc.: *Cloth, blotting paper, and ordinary flowerpots are porous.* **—po′rous·ness,** *n.*

por·phy·ry (pôr′fə rē) *n.* **-ries. 1** in ancient Egypt, a red or purplish rock containing white crystals. **2** any igneous rock in which crystals are scattered through a mass of fine-grained minerals. [< F *porfire*, ult. < Gk. *porphyra* purple dye of shellfish]

por·poise (pôr′pəs) *n.* **-pois·es** or (*esp. collectively*) **-poise.** a sea animal from five to eight feet long, resembling a small whale. [ME < OF *porpeis*, ult. < L *porcus* hog + *piscis* fish]

por·ridge (pôr′ij) *n.* a food made of oatmeal or other cereal boiled in water or milk until thick. [var. of *pottage*]

por·rin·ger (pôr′ən jər) *n.* a small dish from which soup, porridge, etc. can be eaten. [earlier *pottanger*, alteration of *potager* < OF *potager* < *potage*. See POTTAGE.]

port[1] (pôrt) *n.* **1** a harbor; a place where ships and boats can take shelter from storms. **2** a place where ships and boats can load and unload. **3** a city or town with a harbor. Halifax and Vancouver are important Canadian ports. **4** any place where one can find shelter. [OE < L *portus*] **—Syn. 1, 2** See **harbor.**

port[2] (pôrt) *n.* **1** an opening in the side of a ship for letting in light and air; porthole. **2** an opening in a wall or in a ship's side for shooting through. **3** the cover for such an opening. **4** an opening in machinery for steam, air, water, etc. to pass through. **5** in curling and lawn bowling, an opening between stones or woods, large enough for another stone or wood to pass through. [< L *porta* gate]

port[3] (pôrt) *n.* the left side of a ship or aircraft when one is facing the bow or front. See **aft** for picture. *—adj.* on the left side of a ship. *—v.* turn or shift to the left side. [origin uncertain]

port[4] (pôrt) *n.* **1** a way of holding one's head and body;

bearing. **2** the position of a weapon when ported. —*v.* bring, hold, or carry (a rifle or sword) across and close to the body with the barrel or blade near the left shoulder. [< F *port* < *porter* carry < L *portare*]

port[5] (pôrt) *n.* a strong, sweet wine that is dark red or tawny. [< *Oporto,* a city in Portugal]

Port. 1 Portugal. 2 Portuguese.

port·a·ble (pôr′tə bəl) *adj.* capable of being carried; easily carried. —*n.* **1** a portable radio, phonograph, etc. **2** a temporary building on the grounds of an overcrowded school, used as an extra classroom. [< LL *portabilis* < L *portare* carry]

portable pension a pension plan under which, if a person changes his job, his pension contributions and entitlements continue unchanged.

por·tage (pôr′tij) *v.* **-taged, -tag·ing.** —*n.* **1** a carrying of boats, canoes, provisions, etc. overland from one stretch of water to another. **2** a place where such a carrying takes place. **3** the act of carrying. **4** the cost of carrying. **5** an instance of such a carrying: *He made the trip without a single portage.*
—*v.* **1** carry canoes, etc. from one stretch of water to another. **2** make a portage. [ME < OF *portage* < *porter* carry]

por·tal (pôr′təl) *n.* a door, gate, or entrance, usually an imposing one. [< Med.L *portale* < L *porta* gate]

portal-to-portal pay wages paid to an employee for the time he spends moving to and from his actual place of work while on the grounds or premises of the employer.

por·ta·men·to (pôr′tə men′tō; *Italian,* pôr′tä men′tō) *n.* **-ti** (-tē). in music, a smooth, legato movement gliding from one note or pitch to another without a break. [< Ital. *portamento* < L *portare* carry]

port authority a commission appointed to manage a port.

port·cul·lis (pôrt kul′is) *n.* a strong gate or grating of iron sliding up and down in grooves, used to close the gateway of a castle or fortress. [ME < OF *porte coleice* sliding gate, ult. < L *porta* gate + *colare* filter through]

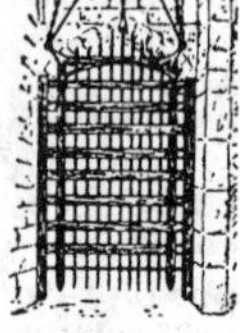
A portcullis

porte-co·chere or **porte-co·chère** (pôrt′kō shãr′) *n.* **1** a porch at the door of a building under which carriages and automobiles stop so that persons getting in or out are sheltered. **2** an entrance for carriages, leading into a courtyard. [< F *porte-cochère* coachgate]

porte-mon·naie (pôrt′mun′ē; *French,* pôrt mô ne′) *n.* a purse; pocketbook. [< F *porte-monnaie* < *porter* carry + *monnaie* (small) change]

por·tend (pôr tend′) *v.* indicate beforehand; be a portent of: *Black clouds portend a storm.* [ME < L *portendere* < *por-* before + *tendere* extend] —**Syn.** foreshadow, betoken, forebode.

por·tent (pôr′tent) *n.* a warning of coming evil; sign; omen. [< L *portentum,* originally neut. pp. of *portendere.* See PORTEND.] —**Syn.** token, presage.

por·ten·tous (pôr ten′təs) *adj.* **1** indicating evil to come; ominous; threatening. **2** amazing; extraordinary. —**por·ten′tous·ly,** *adv.* —**por·ten′tous·ness,** *n.* —**Syn. 1** foreboding. **2** wonderful, marvellous.

por·ter[1] (pôr′tər) *n.* **1** a man employed to carry burdens or baggage. **2** the attendant in a parlor car or sleeping car of a railway train. [ME < OF *porteour,* ult. < L *portare* carry]

por·ter[2] (pôr′tər) *n.* **1** a doorkeeper; gatekeeper. **2** a janitor. [ME < OF *portier* < LL *portarius* < L *porta* gate]

por·ter[3] (pôr′tər) *n.* a heavy, dark-brown beer. [short for *porter's ale* (i.e., ale for a *porter*[1])]

por·ter·house (pôr′tər hous′) *n.* a choice beefsteak containing the tenderloin. [possibly because made popular about 1814 by the keeper of a New York porterhouse (a place where porter and other liquors were sold)]

porterhouse steak porterhouse.

port·fo·li·o (pôrt fō′lē ō′) *n.* **-li·os. 1** a brief case; portable case for loose papers, drawings, etc. **2** the position and duties of the office of a cabinet minister or a minister of state: *The Minister of Defence resigned his portfolio.* **3** holdings in the form of stocks, bonds, etc. [< Ital. *portafoglio,* ult. < L *portare* carry + *folium* sheet, leaf]

port·hole (pôrt′hōl′) *n.* **1** an opening in a ship's side to let in light and air. **2** an opening in a wall or in a ship's side for shooting through.

por·ti·co (pôr′tə kō) *n.* **-coes** or **-cos.** a roof supported by columns, forming a porch or a covered walk. [< Ital. *portico* < L *porticus.* Doublet of PORCH.]

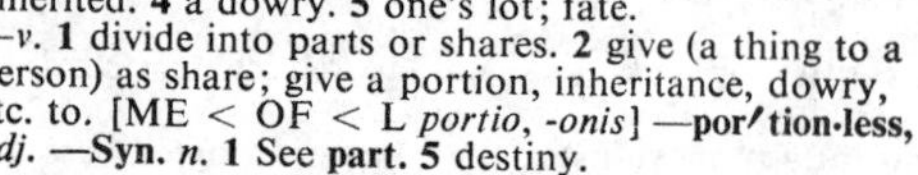
A portico

por·tiere or **por·tière** (pôr tyãr′) *n.* a curtain hung at a doorway. [< F *portière* < *porte* door]

por·tion (pôr′shən) *n.* **1** a part or share. **2** the quantity of food served for one person. **3** the part of an estate that goes to an heir; property inherited. **4** a dowry. **5** one's lot; fate.
—*v.* **1** divide into parts or shares. **2** give (a thing to a person) as share; give a portion, inheritance, dowry, etc. to. [ME < OF < L *portio, -onis*] —**por′tion·less,** *adj.* —**Syn.** *n.* **1** See **part. 5** destiny.

Port·land cement (pôrt′lənd) a kind of cement made by burning limestone and clay in a kiln. [< Isle of *Portland,* a peninsula of southern England]

port·ly (pôrt′lē) *adj.* **-li·er, -li·est. 1** stout; corpulent. **2** stately; dignified. [< *port*[4]] —**port′li·ness,** *n.* —**Syn. 1** See **fat.**

port·man·teau (pôrt man′tō) *n.* **-teaus** or **-teaux** (-tōz). *Esp.Brit.* a travelling bag, especially a stiff, oblong one with two compartments opening like a book. [< F *portmanteau* < *porter* carry + *manteau* mantle]

portmanteau word in linguistics, a word that is made by combining parts of two other words; blend. *Smog* is a portmanteau word made from *smoke* and *fog.*

por·trait (pôr′trit or pôr′trāt) *n.* **1** a picture, especially a painting, of a person. **2** a picture in words; description. [< F *portrait,* originally pp. of *portraire* portray]

por·trait·ist (pôr′trā tist) *n.* a person who paints portraits.

por·trai·ture (pôr′trə chər or pôr′trə chür′) *n.* **1** the act of portraying. **2** the art of making portraits. **3** a portrait or portraits. [ME < OF *portraiture* < *portrait* portrait < *portraire.* See PORTRAY.]

por·tray (pôr trā′) *v.* **1** describe or picture in words: *The book portrays life long ago.* **2** make a picture of. **3** represent on the stage. [ME < OF *portraire* < L *protrahere* < *pro-* forth + *trahere* draw] —**por·tray′er,** *n.* —**Syn. 1** depict. **3** impersonate, act.

por·tray·al (pôr trā′əl) *n.* **1** a portraying by pictures or in words. **2** a picture; description.

Por·tu·guese (pôr′chů gēz′ or pôr′chů gēz′) *n.* **-guese,** *adj.* —*n.* **1** a native or inhabitant of Portugal, a country in S.W. Europe. **2** the language of Portugal. Portuguese is also the chief language of Brazil. —*adj.* of or having to do with Portugal, its people, or their language.

por·tu·lac·a (pôr′chů lak′ə) *n.* a low plant having thick, fleshy leaves and variously colored flowers. [< L *portulaca* purslane]

pose[1] (pōz) *n. v.* **posed, pos·ing.** —*n.* **1** a position of the body; a way of holding the body. **2** an attitude assumed for effect; pretence; affectation: *She takes the pose of being an invalid when really she is well and strong.*
—*v.* **1** hold a position: *He posed an hour for his portrait.* **2** put in a certain position: *The artist posed him before painting his picture.* **3** put on an attitude for effect; make a false pretence: *He posed as a rich man though he owed more than he owned.* **4** put forward for discussion; state: *pose a question.* [< F *poser* < LL *pausare* pause < L *pausa* a pause; in Romance languages influenced by stem *pos-* of L *ponere* place (from meaning "cause to pause, set down"); this influence spread to many compounds, e.g., *compose, dispose, oppose*]

pose[2] (pōz) *v.* **posed, pos·ing.** puzzle completely. [var. of *appose,* var. of *oppose*]

hat, āge, cãre, fär; let, ēqual, tėrm; it, īce
hot, ōpen, ôrder; oil, out; cup, put, rüle, ūse
əbove, takən, pencəl, lemən, circəs
ch, child; ng, long; sh, ship
th, thin; TH, then; zh, measure

Po·sei·don (pə sī′dən) *n.* in Greek mythology, the god of the sea and of horses, identified with the Roman god Neptune. He is usually represented carrying a trident.

pos·er[1] (pōz′ər) *n.* a person who poses. [< *pose*[1]]

pos·er[2] (pōz′ər) *n.* a very puzzling problem. [< *pose*[2]]

po·seur (po′zėr; *French,* pō zœr′) *n.* an affected person; one who poses to impress others. [< F *poseur* < *poser* pose]

posh (posh) *adj. Informal.* well-appointed; stylish; elegant. [origin uncertain]

pos·it (poz′it) *v.* lay down or assume as a fact or principle; affirm. [< L *positus,* pp. of *ponere* set, place]

po·si·tion (pə zish′ən) *n.* **1** a place where a thing or person is: *The house is in a sheltered position. Your careless remark put me in an awkward position.* **2** a way of being placed: *Sit in a more comfortable position.* **3** the proper place. **4** a condition with reference to place or circumstances: *The army manoeuvred for position before attacking.* **5** a job. **6** a rank; standing, especially high standing: *He was raised to the position of captain.* **7** a way of thinking; set of opinions: *What is your position on this question?* **8** the place held by a player on the team: *My position on the hockey team was defence.* —*v.* put in position; place: *The general positioned his soldiers behind the line of trees.* [< L *positio, -onis* < *ponere* set]
Syn. 1 situation, site, location. **5 Position, job, situation** = employment. **Position** is the formal word, but usually suggests white-collar work, in business or a profession: *He has a position in a bank.* **Job** is the informal and colloquial word applying to any kind of employment, but emphasizes the idea of work to do: *He has a job on a ranch this summer.* **Situation** emphasizes the idea of a place to work, and now chiefly means a position or job wanted or applied for: *She desires a situation as housekeeper.* **6** status.

pos·i·tive (poz′ə tiv) *adj.* **1** admitting of no question; without doubt; sure. **2** too sure; too confident: *Her positive manner annoys people.* **3** definite; emphatic. **4** that can be thought of as real and present: *Light is a positive thing; darkness is only the absence of light.* **5** showing that a particular disease, condition, germ, etc. is present. **6** that definitely does something or adds something; practical: *Don't just make criticisms; give us some positive help.* **7** tending in the direction thought of as that of increase or progress: *Motion in the direction that the hands of a clock move is positive.* **8** counting up from zero; plus: *Five above zero is a positive quantity.* **9** of the kind of electricity produced by rubbing glass with silk; lacking electrons. **10** in photography, having the lights and shadows in the same position as in the original. **11** in grammar, of the simple form of an adjective or adverb. **12** in biology, moving or turning toward light, the earth, or any other stimulus. **13** having a tendency to lose electrons and thus become charged with positive electricity, as a chemical element or radical. **14** in philosophy, concerned with or based on matters of experience; not speculative or theoretical; empirical. **15** having no relation to or comparison with other things; absolute; unconditional.
—*n.* **1** a positive degree or quantity. **2** in electricity, the plate in a battery from which the current flows into the wire. See **electrode** for diagram. **3** in photography, a print made from a photographic film or plate. **4** in grammar, the simple form of an adjective or adverb, as distinct from the comparative and superlative. *Fast* is the positive; *faster* is the comparative; *fastest* is the superlative. [ME < OF < L *positivus,* ult. < *ponere* to set] —**pos′i·tive·ly,** *adv.* —**pos′i·tive·ness,** *n.* —**Syn.** *adj.* **1** unquestionable, unmistakable, indisputable.

pos·i·tiv·ism (poz′ə tiv iz′əm) *n.* **1** a philosophical system founded by Auguste Comte, 1798-1857, a French philosopher and sociologist, which deals only with positive facts and phenomena, rejecting abstract speculation. **2** the state or quality of being positive; definiteness; assurance; dogmatism.

pos·i·tron (poz′ə tron′) *n.* in physics, a particle having the same magnitude of mass and charge as an electron, but exhibiting a positive charge; positive electron. [< *positive* + *electron*]

poss. 1 possessive. **2** possession. **3** possibly. **4** possible.

pos·se (pos′ē) *n.* **1** a group of men summoned by a law officer to help him follow and capture a criminal: *Posses were often formed during frontier days in the West.* **2** in western Canada, a troop of horses and riders trained for special exercises and drills, often giving exhibitions at stampedes and rodeos. [< Med.L *posse* power < L *posse* be able]

pos·sess (pə zes′) *v.* **1** own; have: *The general possessed great wisdom.* **2** hold as property; hold; occupy. **3** control; influence strongly. **4** control by an evil spirit: *He fought like one possessed.* **5** maintain; keep: *Possess your soul in patience.* **6** *Archaic.* take; win. [ME < OF *possessier* < *possession* possession < L *possessio* < *possidere* possess]

pos·sessed (pə zest′) *adj.* **1** dominated by passion, or as by an evil spirit; lunatic; demoniac. **2** owning or having as one's own: *He is possessed of great courage.* **3** maintaining poise and calm; unruffled.

pos·ses·sion (pə zesh′ən) *n.* **1** a possessing; holding. **2** ownership. **3** something possessed; property. **4** a territory under the rule of a country: *Greenland is a possession of Denmark.* **5** domination by a particular feeling, idea, etc. **6** self-control. —**Syn. 1** tenure. **3** belonging.

pos·ses·sive (pə zes′iv) *adj.* **1** of possession. **2** showing possession. *My* and *your* are two of the possessive adjectives. **3** desirous of ownership: *a possessive nature.* **4** asserting or claiming ownership: *a possessive manner.* —*n.* in grammar: **1** the possessive case. **2** a word in this case. In "the boy's books," *boy's* is a possessive. —**pos·ses′sive·ly,** *adv.* —**pos·ses′sive·ness,** *n.*

possessive adjective an adjective that shows possession, related to a personal pronoun.

possessive pronoun a pronoun that shows possession.

pos·ses·sor (pə zes′ər) *n.* one that possesses.

pos·set (pos′it) *n.* a hot drink made of milk, alcoholic liquor, and spices. [ME *possot*]

pos·si·bil·i·ty (pos′ə bil′ə tē) *n.* **-ties. 1** the state or quality of being possible: *There is a possibility that the train may be late.* **2** any thing or event that is possible; a person considered as a possible choice: *He would be a good possibility for captain.*

pos·si·ble (pos′ə bəl) *adj. n.* **1** that can be; that can be done; that can happen: *Come if possible.* **2** that can be true or a fact: *It is possible that he went.* **3** that can be done, chosen, etc. properly: *the only possible candidate.* —*n.* **1** a possible candidate, winner, etc. **2** a perfect score: *The marksman scored a possible on one target.* [ME < L *possibilis* < *posse* be able]
Syn. 1 Possible, practicable, feasible = capable of happening or being done. **Possible** = that with suitable conditions and methods something may exist, happen, or be done: *It is possible to cure tuberculosis.* **Practicable** = that under present circumstances or by available means something (a plan, method, invention) can easily or effectively be carried out, done, or used: *The X-ray is a practicable way of discovering unsuspected diseases.* **Feasible** especially suggests something not yet tried, but seeming likely to be practicable: *Would compulsory X-rays, like vaccination, be feasible?*

pos·si·bly (pos′ə blē) *adv.* **1** by any possibility; no matter what happens: *I cannot possibly go.* **2** perhaps: *Possibly you are right.*

pos·sum (pos′əm) *n.* **1** opossum. **2 play possum,** pretend to be dead or asleep. [var. of *opossum*]

post[1] (pōst) *n.* **1** a length of timber, metal, etc. set upright, usually as a support: *the posts of a door or bed, a hitching post.* **2** the post, line, etc. where a race starts or ends.
—*v.* **1** fasten (a notice) up in a place where it can easily be seen. **2** make known by, or as if by, a posted notice; offer publicly: *post a reward.* **3** announce in a posted notice. **4** cover (a wall, etc.) with notices or bills. **5** put up notices warning people to keep out of. [OE < L *postis*]

post[2] (pōst) *n.* **1** a place where a soldier, policeman, etc. is stationed; a place where one is supposed to be when on duty. **2** a place where soldiers are stationed; a military

station; fort. **3** the soldiers occupying a military station. **4** *Esp.U.S.* a local branch of a veterans' organization. **5** a job or position. **6** a trading station, especially in an uncivilized or unsettled country. **7** either of two bugle calls (first post and last post) calling soldiers to their quarters for the night.
—*v.* **1** station at a post; place troops at a particular point: *We posted guards at the door.* **2** in the armed services, appoint to a post. [< F < Ital. < L *positus,* pp. of *ponere* station, place]

post[3] (pōst) *n.* **1** an established system for carrying letters, papers, packages, etc.; the mail: *to send by post.* **2** *Esp.Brit.* a single mail; the letters, etc. thus delivered: *this morning's post.* **3** *Archaic and dialect.* a postman. **4** *Archaic.* a person, vehicle, or ship that carries mail. **5** a post office. **6** a letter box. **7** one of a series of fixed stations along a route for furnishing relays of men and horses for carrying letters, etc. and supplying service to travellers by post horse, post chaise, etc. **8** a size of paper, about 16 × 20 inches.
—*v.* **1** send by post; mail: *to post a letter.* **2** travel with post horses or by post chaise. **3** travel with speed; hasten. **4** rise and fall in the saddle in rhythm with the horse's trot. **5** supply with information up to date; inform. **6** in bookkeeping: **a** transfer (an entry) from journal to ledger. **b** enter (an item) in due place and form. **c** make all requisite entries in (a ledger, etc.).
—*adv.* by post; speedily. [< F < Ital. < L *posita,* fem. pp. of *ponere* place]

post- *prefix.* after, as in *postgraduate, post-mortem, postscript.* [< L *post-* < *post,* prep. adv., after, behind]

post·age (pōs′tij) *n.* the amount paid on anything sent by mail.

postage stamp an official stamp placed on mail to show that postage has been paid.

post·al (pōs′təl) *adj.* having to do with mail and post offices.

postal card a post card.

post-and-lin·tel (pōst′ ən lin′təl) *adj.* in architecture, of or having to do with a type of construction based on the use of vertical supports and horizontal beams rather than vaults and arches.

post bel·lum (pōst bel′əm) *Latin.* after the war.

post box a box into which letters, parcels, etc. are put for collection and delivery by the Post Office.

post·boy (pōst′boi′) *n.* **1** a boy or man who carries mail. **2** a man who rides one of the horses drawing a carriage.

post card 1 a card with a government postage stamp printed on it. **2** any card, especially one with a picture on one side, for sending a message by mail.

post chaise a hired carriage that was used for travelling before there were railways.

post·date (pōst′dāt′) *v.* **-dat·ed, -dat·ing. 1** give (to a letter, cheque, etc.) a later date than the actual date of writing. **2** follow in time.

post·ed (pōs′tid) *adj.* **1** having posts. **2** informed.

post·er (pōs′tər) *n.* **1** a large printed advertisement or notice, often illustrated, put up in some public place. **2** a person who posts notices, etc.

pos·te·ri·or (post tēr′ē ər) *adj.* **1** situated behind; back; rear; hind. **2** later; coming after. —*n. Informal.* the buttocks; rump. [< L *posterior,* comparative of *posterus* subsequent < *post* after]

pos·ter·i·ty (pos ter′ə tē) *n.* **1** the generations of the future: *How many of our achievements will be valued by posterity?* **2** all of a person's descendants. [ME < OF < L *posteritas* < *posterus.* See POSTERIOR.]

pos·tern (pōs′tərn or pos′tərn) *n.* **1** a back door or gate. **2** any small door or gate. —*adj.* **1** of or like a postern. **2** rear; lesser: *The castle had a postern door.* [ME < OF *posterne,* ult. < L *posterus* behind. See POSTERIOR.]

post exchange *Esp.U.S.* a general store at a military post or station that sells food and other goods to members of the armed services and authorized civilians. *Abbrev.*: PX or P.X.

post·grad·u·ate (pōst′graj′ü it) *n.* a student who continues his studies at a level beyond that of a bachelor's degree. —*adj.* **1** taking a course of study at such a level. **2** of or for postgraduates.

post·haste (pōst′hāst′) *adv.* very speedily; in great haste. [< *post*[3] + *haste*]

post horse formerly, a horse hired for use in travelling by relay, each horse being changed for a fresh one after a certain distance.

post·hu·mous (pos′chů məs) *adj.* **1** born after the death of the father: *a posthumous son.* **2** published after the death of the author. **3** happening after death: *posthumous fame.* [< LL *posthumus,* var. of L *postumus* last, originally superlative of *post* after; *h* added by confusion with *humus* earth, in sense of "burial"]

post·hu·mous·ly (pos′chů məs lē) *adv.* after death.

pos·til·ion or **pos·til·lion** (pōs til′yən or pos til′yən) *n.* a man who rides one of the horses drawing a carriage. [< F *postillon*]

post·lude (pōst′lüd) *n.* **1** anything coming at the end. **2** in music: **a** a concluding composition or movement. **b** a composition played at the end of a religious service. [< *post-* + pre*lude*]

post·man (pōst′mən) *n.* **-men** (-mən). a man who carries and delivers mail for the government.

post·mark (pōst′märk′) *n.* an official mark stamped on mail to cancel the postage stamp and record the place and date of mailing. —*v.* stamp with a postmark.

post·mas·ter (pōst′mas′tər) *n.* the person in charge of a post office.

Postmaster General *pl.* **Postmasters General.** the federal cabinet minister responsible for the Post Office.

post·me·rid·i·an (pōst′mə rid′ē ən) *adj.* occurring after noon; of or having to do with the afternoon.

post me·rid·i·em (pōst′ mə rid′ē əm) after noon. *Abbrev.*: P.M. or p.m. [< L *post meridiem* after midday]

post·mis·tress (pōst′mis′tris) *n.* a woman in charge of a post office.

post-mor·tem (pōst′môr′təm) *adj.* after death. —*n.* an examination of a dead body; autopsy. [< L *post mortem* after death]

post·na·tal (pōst nā′təl) *adj.* after birth.

post-o·bit (pōst′ō′bit or -ob′it) *n.* a written agreement signed by a borrower promising to pay a certain sum of money to the lender on the death of a person whose heir the borrower expects to be. —*adj.* effective after a person's death. [< L *post obitum* after death]

post office 1 a place where mail is handled and postage stamps are sold. **2** Often, **Post Office.** the government department in charge of mail. *Abbrev.*: P.O.

post-op·er·a·tive (post op′ər ə tiv or -op′ə rā′tiv) *adj.* after or following a surgical operation.

post·paid (pōst′pād′) *adj.* with the postage paid for.

post·pone (pōs pōn′ or pōst pōn′) *v.* **-poned, -pon·ing.** put off till later; put off to a later time; delay. [< L *postponere* < *post-* after + *ponere* put] —**Syn.** defer. See **delay.**

post·pone·ment (pōs pōn′mənt or pōst pōn′mənt) *n.* a putting off till later; delay: *the postponement of a game.*

post·pran·di·al (pōst′pran′dē əl) *adj.* after-dinner: *postprandial speeches.* [< *post-* + L *prandium* lunch] —**post′pran′di·al·ly,** *adv.*

post·rid·er (pōst′rīd′ər) *n.* formerly, a person, especially one carrying mail, travelling by means of relays of horses. See **post horse.**

post road 1 a road or route over which mail is or was carried. **2** formerly, a road with stations providing horses for use in relays.

post·script (pōst′skript) *n.* **1** an addition to a letter, written after the writer's name has been signed. **2** a supplementary part appended to any composition or literary work. [< L *postscriptum,* originally neut. pp., < *post-* after + *scribere* write]

pos·tu·lant (pos′chů lənt) *n.* **1** a candidate, especially for admission to a religious order. **2** a person who asks or applies for something; petitioner. [< L *postulans, -antis,* ppr. of *postulare* demand]

hat, āge, cãre, fär; let, ēqual, tėrm; it, īce
hot, ōpen, ôrder; oil, out; cup, pu̇t, rüle, ūse
əbove, takən, pencəl, lemən, circəs
ch, child; ng, long; sh, ship
th, thin; ᴛʜ, then; zh, measure

pos·tu·late (*n.* pos′chu̇ lit; *v.* pos′chu̇ lāt′) *n. v.* **-lat·ed, -lat·ing.** —*n.* something taken for granted or assumed as a basis for reasoning; a fundamental principle; necessary condition: *One postulate of geometry is that a straight line may be drawn between any two points.* —*v.* **1** take for granted; assume without proof as a basis of reasoning; require as a fundamental principle or necessary condition. **2** require; demand; claim. [< L *postulatum*, originally pp. neut. of *postulare* demand] —**pos′tu·la′tion,** *n.* —**pos′tu·la′tor,** *n.*

pos·tur·al (pos′chər əl) *adj.* of or having to do with posture.

pos·ture (pos′chər) *n. v.* **-tured, -tur·ing.** —*n.* **1** a position of the body; way of holding the body: *Good posture is important for health.* **2** a condition; situation; state: *In the present posture of public affairs it is difficult to invest money safely.* **3** a mental or spiritual attitude.
—*v.* **1** take a certain posture: *The dancer postured before the mirror, bending and twisting her body.* **2** put in a certain posture. **3** pose for effect. [< F < Ital. < L *positura* < *ponere* place]

post·war (pōst′wôr′) *adj.* after the war.

po·sy (pō′zē) *n.* **-sies. 1** a flower. **2** a bunch of flowers; bouquet. **3** a motto or line of poetry engraved within a ring. [var. of *poesy*]

pot (pot) *n. v.* **pot·ted, pot·ting.** —*n.* **1** a round, deep container made of metal, earthenware, glass, etc.: *a cooking pot, a flower pot, a coffee pot.* **2** a pot and what is in it; the amount a pot can hold. **3** alcoholic liquor. **4** a basket used to catch fish, lobsters, etc. **5** *Informal.* a large sum of money. **6** *Informal.* all the money bet at one time. **7** *Slang.* a potbelly. **8** *Slang.* marijuana. **9 go to pot,** go to ruin: *After losing his job he took to drinking and went to pot.* **10 keep the pot boiling,** *Informal.* **a** make a living. **b** keep things going in a lively way.
—*v.* **1** put into a pot. **2** cook and preserve in a pot. **3** take a pot shot at; shoot. [OE *pott* < VL *pottus* < LL *potus* cup < L *potus* a drinking] —**pot′like′,** *adj.*

pot. potential.

po·ta·ble (pō′tə bəl) *adj.* fit for drinking. —*n.* Usually, **potables,** *pl.* anything drinkable. [< LL *potabilis* < L *potare* to drink]

pot·ash (pot′ash′) *n.* **1** any of several substances, such as sodium carbonate, made from wood ashes and used in soap, fertilizers, etc. **2** any of several potassium salts, such as potassium chloride, mined and processed for use in agriculture and industry. **3** potassium, or a potassium oxide, especially K_2O. **4** potassium hydroxide. [< Du. *potasch*, literally, pot ash]

po·tas·si·um (pə tas′ē əm) *n.* a soft, silver-white metallic chemical element, occurring in nature only in compounds. *Symbol*: K; *at.no.* 19; *at.wt.* 39.102. [< NL < E *potash*]

potassium bromide a white crystalline substance used in medicine, photography, etc. *Formula*: KBr

potassium carbonate a white alkaline compound obtained from wood ash, etc., used for making soap, glass, fertilizer, etc. *Formula*: K_2CO_3

potassium chlorate a colorless crystalline substance used as an oxidizing agent in explosives, matches, etc. *Formula*: $KClO_3$

potassium chloride a white or colorless crystalline salt, used in explosives, fertilizers, etc. *Formula*: KCl

potassium cyanide a very poisonous white crystalline substance used for removing gold from ore, electroplating, killing insects, etc. *Formula*: KCN

potassium hydroxide a very strong alkali; caustic potash. *Formula*: KOH

potassium nitrate a colorless crystalline substance used as an oxidizing agent, in gunpowder, in explosives, etc.; nitre; saltpetre. *Formula*: KNO_3

potassium permanganate a nearly black crystalline compound used as an oxidizing agent, disinfectant, etc. *Formula*: $KMnO_4$

po·ta·tion (pō tā′shən) *n.* **1** the act of drinking. **2** a drink, especially of alcoholic liquor. [ME < OF < L *potatio, -onis* < *potare* to drink]

po·ta·to (pə tā′tō) *n.* **-toes. 1** a starchy tuber of a cultivated plant of the potato family, the vegetable most widely used in Europe and North America (also called **white potato** and **Irish potato**). **2** the plant producing these tubers. **3** a sweet potato. [< Sp. *patata* < *Haitian*]

potato beetle a beetle having black and yellow stripes that damages potato plants.

potato bug potato beetle.

potato chip 1 a crisp, thin, dry slice of potato that has been fried in deep fat: *Potato chips are eaten cold.* **2** a slice of potato, usually oblong, fried in deep fat and eaten while hot: *Potato chips are often called French fries.*

potato family a large group of plants, shrubs, and trees, most of which have alternate leaves, flowers with a five-lobed calyx and a five-lobed corolla, and berries or capsules with many seeds.

pot·bel·lied (pot′bel′ēd) *adj.* **1** having a potbelly. **2** shaped like a potbelly: *a potbellied stove.*

pot·bel·ly (pot′bel′ē) *n.* a distended or protuberant belly.

potbelly stove or **potbellied stove** a squat, bulging stove that burns wood or coal.

pot·boiler (pot′boil′ər) *n. Informal.* a work of literature, art, or music produced merely to make a living.

pot·bound (pot′bound′) *adj.* of plants, having roots that have outgrown the size of the pot and so cannot continue growing without being replanted.

pot·boy (pot′boi′) *n.* a man or boy who works in a tavern, serving customers, washing glasses, etc.

po·ten·cy (pō′tən sē) *n.* **-cies. 1** power; strength: *the potency of an argument, the potency of a drug.* **2** the power to develop. **3** sexual capability. [< L *potentia* < *potens.* See POTENT.]

po·tent (pō′tənt) *adj.* **1** powerful; having great power: *a potent remedy for a disease.* **2** exercising great moral influence: *His good deeds had a potent effect on his comrades.* **3** of males, capable of having sexual intercourse. [< L *potens, -entis*, ppr. of OL **potere* be powerful] —**po′tent·ly,** *adv.* —**Syn. 1** mighty, strong.

po·ten·tate (pō′tən tāt′) *n.* **1** a person having great power: *The Roman emperors were potentates.* **2** a ruler: *the potentates of ancient India.* [ME < LL < L *potentatus* power, dominion < *potens, -entis.* See POTENT.]

po·ten·tial (pə ten′shəl) *adj.* **1** possible as opposed to actual; capable of coming into being or action: *a potential danger.* **2** in grammar, expressing possibility by the use of *may, might, can, could,* etc.: *the potential mood of a verb.*
—*n.* **1** something potential; possibility. **2** in grammar, the potential mood. **3** the amount of electrification of a point with reference to some standard. A current of high potential is used in transmitting electric power over long distances. [< LL *potentialis*, ult. < L *potens, -entis* potent] —**Syn.** *adj.* **1** See **latent.**

potential energy energy that is due to position, not to motion. A tightly coiled spring or a raised weight has potential energy.

po·ten·ti·al·i·ty (pə ten′shē al′ə tē) *n.* **-ties. 1** a potential state or quality; possibility as opposed to actuality; latent power or capacity. **2** something potential; a possibility.

po·ten·tial·ly (pə ten′shəl ē) *adv.* possibly, but not yet actually.

po·ten·ti·ate (pə ten′shē āt′) *v.* **-ated, -ating.** make more active or potent. —**po·ten′ti·a′tion,** *n.*

po·ten·ti·om·e·ter (pə ten′shē om′ə tər) *n.* an instrument for measuring electromotive force. [< *potential* + *-meter*]

pot·head (pot′hed′) *n.* especially in Newfoundland, pilot whale.

poth·er (poᴛʜ′ər) *n.* confusion; disturbance; fuss. —*v.* bother; fuss. [origin uncertain]

pot·herb (pot′ėrb′ or -hėrb′) *n.* **1** any plant whose leaves and stems are boiled as a vegetable, such as spinach. **2** any plant used as seasoning in cooking. Sage and parsley are potherbs.

pot·hole (pot′hōl′) *n.* **1** a deep, round hole, especially one made in rock by stones and gravel being spun around in the current of a river. **2** a hole in the surface of a road. **3** a slough. **4** a dugout (def. 4).

pothole trout *Cdn.* on the Prairies, trout planted in sloughs or dugouts.

pot·hook (pot′hu̇k′) *n.* **1** a hook for hanging a pot or kettle over an open fire. **2** a rod with a hook for lifting hot pots, etc. **3** in writing, an S-shaped stroke, especially one made by children in learning to write.

pot·hunt·er (pot′hun′tər) *n.* **1** a person who shoots anything he comes upon regardless of rules of sport. **2** a person who takes part in contests merely to win prizes. **3** a person who hunts for food or for profit.

po·tion (pō′shən) *n.* a drink, especially one that is used as a medicine or poison, or in magic. [< L *potio, -onis.* Doublet of POISON.]

pot·latch (pot′lach) *n.* **1** a West-Coast Indian gift-giving ceremony and festival. **2** a social gathering where Indians engage in races, games, dancing, etc. **3** *Informal.* a party. [< Chinook Jargon < Nootka *patshatl* gift]

pot·luck (pot′luk′) *n.* **1** whatever food happens to be ready or on hand for a meal. **2 take potluck, a** be a guest and eat whatever food is ready or on hand. **b** accept whatever is available.

pot·pie (pot′pī′) *n.* **1** a baked meat pie. **2** a stew with dumplings.

pot·pour·ri (pō′pü rē′ or pot pür′ē) *n.* **1** a musical or literary medley. **2** a fragrant mixture of dried flower petals and spices. [< F *potpourri,* translation of Sp. *olla podrida* rotten pot < L *olla* pot and VL *putrita,* fem. pp. of *putrire* rot < L *puter* soft, rotten]

pot roast beef browned in a pot and cooked slowly with only a little water.

pot·sherd (pot′shėrd′) *n.* a broken piece of earthenware. [< *pot* + *sherd,* var. of *shard*]

pot shot **1** a shot taken at game just to provide a meal, with little regard to the rules of sport. **2** a quick shot at something from close range without careful aim.

pot·tage (pot′ij) *n.* a thick soup. [ME < OF *potage* < *pot* pot < VL *pottus.* See POT.]

pot·ted (pot′id) *adj.* **1** put into a pot. **2** cooked and preserved in pots or cans. **3** *Slang.* drunk; intoxicated.

pot·ter[1] (pot′ər) *n.* a person who makes pots, dishes, vases, etc. out of clay. [OE *pottere* < *pott.* See POT.]

pot·ter[2] (pot′ər) *v.* putter[1]. [< earlier *pote* poke, OE *potian* push. Related to PUT.] —**pot′ter·er,** *n.*

potter's field a piece of ground used for burying people who have no friends or money. [with reference to the story of Judas. Matt. 27:7]

potter's wheel a rotating horizontal disk upon which clay is moulded into dishes, etc.

A man using a potter's wheel. This kind is operated by means of a treadle, and the momentum of the heavy wheel at the bottom helps keep the upper wheel in motion. Some kinds are operated by electricity.

pot·ter·y (pot′ər ē) *n.* **-ter·ies.** **1** pots, dishes, vases, etc. made from clay and hardened by heat. **2** the art or business of making such things. **3** a place where they are made. [< OF *poterie* < *potier* potter < *pot* pot < VL *pottus.* See POT.]

pot·tle (pot′əl) *n.* **1** a former liquid measure equal to two quarts. **2** a pot or tankard holding two quarts. **3** the liquid in it. **4** alcoholic liquor. [ME < OF *potel,* dim. of *pot* pot < VL *pottus* pot. See POT.]

pouch (pouch) *n.* **1** a bag; sack: *a postman's pouch.* **2** a baglike fold of skin. A kangaroo carries its young in a pouch. —*v.* **1** put into a pouch. **2** form a pouch. [ME < ONF *pouche* < Gmc. Akin to POKE[2].] —**pouch′like′,** *adj.*

pouch·y (pouch′ē) *adj.* like a pouch, or having pouches; baggy.

pouf (püf) *n.* **1** a women's hair style, originating in the 18th century, consisting of high rolls or puffs of hair. **2** any puffed or gathered part of a dress. **3** a cushioned or upholstered, backless chair; ottoman. [< F *pouf* a puff]

pou·lard (pü lard′) *n.* a pullet that has been spayed to improve its eating qualities; a fattened hen. [< MF *poularde* < *poule* hen + *-arde,* a noun suffix]

poult (pōlt) *n.* a young chicken, turkey, pheasant, etc. [ME *poult,* short for *poullet* pullet]

poul·ter·er (pōl′tər ər) *n.* a dealer in poultry. [< obs. *poulter,* of the same meaning < OF *pouletier* < *poulet.* See POULTRY.]

poul·tice (pōl′tis) *n. v.* **-ticed, -tic·ing.** —*n.* a soft, moist mass of mustard, herbs, etc. applied to the body as a medicine. —*v.* put a poultice on. [ult. < L *pultes,* pl. of *puls* mush]

poul·try (pōl′trē) *n.* domestic fowl such as chickens, turkeys, geese, ducks, etc. [ME < OF *pouleterie* < *poulet,* dim. of *poule* hen < VL *pulla,* fem. to L *pullus* young fowl. Related to PULLET.]

pounce[1] (pouns) *v.* **pounced, pounc·ing,** *n.* —*v.* **1** come down with a rush and seize. **2** dash, come, or jump suddenly. —*n.* **1** a sudden swoop or pouncing. **2** a claw or talon of a bird of prey. [ME < *ponson, pounson,* dagger, pointed instrument < MF *poinçon,* ult. < L *punctus,* pp. of *pungere* prick. Related to PUNCHEON, POINT.]

pounce[2] (pouns) *n.* **1** a fine powder formerly used to prevent ink from spreading in writing, or to prepare parchment for writing. **2** a fine powder used for transferring a design through a stencil. —*v.* **1** trace (a design) with pounce rubbed through perforations. **2** sprinkle, smooth, or prepare with pounce. [< F *ponce* < L *pumex, -micis* pumice. Doublet of PUMICE.]

pound[1] (pound) *n.* **pounds** or (*esp. collectively*) **pound.** **1** a unit of weight. 1 pound avoirdupois = 16 ounces. 1 pound troy = 12 ounces. **2** a unit of money in the United Kingdom, Australia, Ireland, New Zealand, and certain other countries of the British Commonwealth. See table at **money.** **3** a unit of money in Egypt, Syria, and certain other countries. See table at **money.** **4** a piece of paper money or a coin worth one pound. **5** a former money of account of Scotland. **6** in the New Testament, a mina (a Semitic money unit). [OE *pund* < L *pondo,* originally, *libra pondo* a pound by weight, ult. < *pendere* to weigh]

pound[2] (pound) *v.* **1** hit hard again and again; hit heavily: *He pounded the door with his fist.* **2** beat hard; throb: *After running fast, you can feel your heart pound.* **3** make into a powder or pulp by pounding. **4** move with a pounding sound: *John pounded down the hill to catch the bus.* **5** produce (sound) by pounding or as if by pounding: *We could hear drums pounding in the distance.* —*n.* **1** the act of pounding. **2** a heavy or forcible blow. **3** the sound of a blow. [OE *pūnian*] —**Syn.** *v.* **1** thump. See **beat.**

pound[3] (pound) *n.* **1** an enclosed place, nowadays usually a building, where stray animals are kept. **2** an enclosure for keeping, confining, or trapping animals. **3** a place of confinement. [OE *pund-*]

pound·age (poun′dij) *n.* a tax, commission, rate, etc. of so much per pound of British money or per pound of weight.

pound·al (poun′dəl) *n.* in physics, the amount of force that, acting for one second on a mass of one pound, gives it a velocity of one foot per second. 1 poundal = 13,825 dynes. [< *pound*[1]]

pound cake **1** a cake made with a pound of sugar and a pound of butter for each pound of flour, and plenty of eggs. **2** a rich, sweet cake.

pound·er[1] (poun′dər) *n.* one that pounds, pulverizes, or beats. [< *pound*[2]]

pound·er[2] (poun′dər) *n.* a person or thing weighing, having, or associated with a specified number of pounds: *That fish is a ten pounder.* [< *pound*[1]]

pound-fool·ish (pound′fül′ish) *adj.* foolish or careless in regard to large sums of money. See **penny-wise.**

pound sterling a unit of money of the United Kingdom.

1 pound = 20 shillings: *The pound sterling is worth about three dollars.*

pour (pôr) *v.* **1** cause to flow in a steady stream: *I poured the milk from the bottle.* **2** flow in a steady stream: *The crowd poured out of the church. The rain poured down.* **3** pour tea or coffee at a formal reception. **4** make known freely or without reserve: *The melancholy poet poured forth his sorrow in a song.* **5 it never rains but it pours,** events of a kind, especially misfortunes, come all together or not at all. **6 pour it on,** *Informal.* **a** to do or express something with great vigor and enthusiasm, especially in advancing one's interest, using persuasion, etc. **b** keep increasing one's score or advantage in a game, even when victory is no longer at issue.
—*n.* **1** a pouring. **2** a heavy rain. [ME *poure(n)*; origin uncertain] **—pour′er,** *n.*

pour·boire (pür bwär′) *n. French.* a small present of money; tip; literally, (money) for drinking.

pout[1] (pout) *v.* **1** thrust or push out the lips, as a displeased or sulky child does. **2** show displeasure. **3** swell out; protrude. —*n.* **1** a pushing out of the lips when displeased or sulky. **2** a fit of sullenness. [ME *poute(n)*]

pout[2] (pout) *n.* **pout** or **pouts.** a kind of fresh-water catfish. [OE *-pūte,* as in *ǣlepūte* eelpout]

pout·er (pout′ər) *n.* **1** a person who pouts. **2 a** a breed of domestic pigeons that puff out their chests. **b** a pigeon of this breed.

pout·y (pout′ē) *adj. Informal.* inclined to pout.

pov·er·ty (pov′ər tē) *n.* **1** the condition of being poor. **2** a lack of what is needed: *The poverty of the soil makes the crops small.* **3** a small amount: *A dull person's talk shows poverty of ideas.* [ME < OF < L *paupertas* < *pauper* poor]

Syn. 1 Poverty, want, destitution = the condition of being in need. **Poverty** emphasizes, more strongly than *poor* does, being in actual need, owning nothing at all or having not enough for all the necessities of life: *Their tattered clothes and broken furniture indicated their poverty.* **Want** emphasizes extreme need, having too little to live on: *Welfare agencies help those in want.* **Destitution** emphasizes complete lack even of food and shelter, and often suggests having been deprived of possessions once had: *The Red Cross relieved the destitution following the floods.*
2 deficiency.

pov·er·ty-strick·en (pov′ər tē strik′ən) *adj.* extremely poor.

P.O.W. or **POW** prisoner of war.

pow·der (pou′dər) *n.* **1** a solid reduced to dust by pounding, crushing, or grinding. **2** some special kind of powder: *face powder.* **3** gunpowder. —*v.* **1** make into powder. **2** become powder. **3** sprinkle or cover with powder. **4** apply powder to (the face, etc.). **5** sprinkle. [ME < OF *poudre* < L *pulvis, -veris* dust]
—pow′der·er, *n.*

powder blue a light blue.

powder flask a flask or case of horn, metal, or leather for carrying gunpowder.

powder horn a powder flask made of an animal's horn.

A powder horn

powder keg 1 a small barrel for holding or storing gunpowder. **2** anything that threatens to explode suddenly: *In August, 1914, Europe was a powder keg.*

powder magazine a place where gunpowder is stored.

powder puff a soft puff or pad for applying powder to the skin.

powder room a small rest room or lavatory, especially one having a dressing table for make-up, etc.

pow·der·y (pou′dər ē) *adj.* **1** of powder. **2** like powder; in the form of powder. **3** easily made into powder. **4** sprinkled or covered with powder.

pow·er (pou′ər) *n.* **1** strength; might; force. **2** the ability to do or act: *I will give you all the help in my power.* **3** a particular ability: *He has great powers of concentration.* **4** control; authority; influence; right: *Parliament has power to declare war.* **5 in power,** having control or authority. **6** any person, thing, body, or nation having authority or influence: *Five powers held a peace conference.* **7** in mechanics, energy or force that can do work: *Running water produces power to run mills.* **8** a simple machine. **9** the capacity for exerting mechanical force, as measured by the rate at which it is exerted or at which the work is done. Power is expressed in foot-pounds per minute, ergs per second, horsepower, watts, etc. **10** in mathematics, the product of a number multiplied by itself: *16 is the 4th power of 2.* **11** the capacity of an instrument to magnify. The higher the power of a telescope or microscope the more details you can see. **12** Often, **powers,** *pl.* deity; divinity. **13** an order of angels. **14 the powers that be,** those who have control or authority.
—*v.* provide with power or energy: *a boat powered by an outboard motor.*
—*adj.* operated by a motor; equipped with its own motor: *power tools, power steering.* [ME *poër,* n. < AF *poër,* var. of OF *poeir,* n. use of infinitive < VL *potere* for L *posse* be able]

Syn. *n.* **1 Power, strength, force** = ability to do something or capacity for something. **Power** is the general word applying to any physical, mental, or moral ability or capacity, whether used or not: *Every normal, healthy person has power to think.* **Strength** = a power within the person or thing, belonging to it as a quality, to do, bear, or resist much: *He has strength of character.* **Force** = active use of power or strength to get something done or bring something about: *We had to use force to get into the house.*
3 faculty. **4** command, sway, dominion.

hat, āge, cãre, fär; let, ēqual, tėrm; it, īce
hot, ōpen, ôrder; oil, out; cup, pu̇t, rüle, ūse
əbove, takən, pencəl, lemən, circəs
ch, child; ng, long; sh, ship
th, thin; ᴛʜ, then; zh, measure

pow·er·boat (pou′ər bōt′) *n.* a motorboat, especially a boat propelled by an engine on board.

power dive in aeronautics, a dive made by an airplane at or near peak power.

po·wer-dive (pou′ər dīv′) *v.* **-dived** or **-dove, -dived, -div·ing.** make a power dive.

power drill a drill worked by a motor, not by hand.

pow·er·ful (pou′ər fəl) *adj.* having great power or force; mighty; strong. **—Syn.** potent. See **mighty.**

pow·er·ful·ly (pou′ər fəl ē or pou′ər flē) *adv.* strongly; with power.

pow·er·house (pou′ər hous′) *n.* **1** a building containing boilers, engines, dynamos, etc. for generating power. **2** *Informal.* a powerful, energetic, or highly effective person, group, machine, etc.

pow·er·less (pou′ər lis) *adj.* without power; helpless. **—pow′er·less·ly,** *adv.* **—pow′er·less·ness,** *n.* **—Syn. weak,** impotent.

power loom a loom worked by steam, electricity, water power, etc., not by hand.

power of attorney a written statement giving one person legal power to act for another. *Abbrev.:* **P.A.**

power plant 1 a building with machinery for generating power. **2** a motor; engine.

power play in hockey, a special combination of players put on the ice when the opposition is shorthanded.

power politics in international affairs, diplomacy that uses the threat of superior military power.

power squadron an association of owners and operators of powerboats, yachts, etc. to promote safe boating, good seamanship, etc.

power station a powerhouse (def. 1).

pow·wow (pou′wou′) *n.* **1** a North American Indian ceremony, usually accompanied by magic, feasting, and dancing, performed for the cure of disease, success in hunting, etc. **2** a council or conference of or with North American Indians. **3** *Informal.* any conference or meeting. —*v.* hold a powwow; confer. [< Algonquian]

pox (poks) *n.* **1** any disease that covers the body or parts of the body with sores, such as chicken pox or smallpox. **2** syphilis. [var. of *pocks,* pl. of *pock.* See POCK.]

poz·zo·lan (pot′sə lən) *n.* pozzuolana.

poz·zo·la·na (pot′sə lä′nə) *n.* pozzuolana.

poz·zuo·la·na (pot′su̇ə lä′nə) *n.* **1** volcanic ash, etc. used by the ancient Romans in making mortar. **2** a cement additive, usually made from shale and containing silica, alumina, etc. [< Ital. *pozzuolana*, n. use of fem. adj. < *Pozzuoli*, a seaport in S. Italy, where it was first found]

pp. 1 pages. 2 past participle. 3 in music, pianissimo. 4 privately printed.

p.p. 1 past participle. 2 postpaid. 3 parcel post.

P.P. 1 Parcel Post. 2 Parish Priest.

ppd. 1 postpaid. 2 prepaid.

ppr. or **p.pr.** present participle.

P.P.S. or **p.p.s.** 1 a second postscript. (for L *post postscriptum*) 2 in the United Kingdom, Parliamentary Private Secretary.

P.Q. Province of Quebec.

pr. 1 pair. 2 price. 3 present. 4 prince. 5 printing. 6 pronoun.

Pr praseodymium.

P.R. 1 Puerto Rico. 2 proportional representation.

P.R. or **PR** public relations.

praam (präm) *n.* pram².

prac·ti·ca·bil·i·ty (prak′tə kə bil′ə tē) *n:* the quality of being practicable; capability of being done, effected, or used.

prac·ti·ca·ble (prak′tə kə bəl) *adj.* **1** that can be done; capable of being put into practice: *a practicable idea.* **2** that can be used: *a practicable road.* [< F *practicable* < *pratiquer* practise; influenced in English by obs. *practic.* See PRACTICAL.] **—prac′ti·ca·bly,** *adv.* **—Syn. 1** feasible. See **possible.**

prac·ti·cal (prak′tə kəl) *adj.* **1** having to do with action or practice rather than thought or theory: *Earning a living is a practical matter.* **2** fit for actual practice: *a practical plan.* **3** useful. **4** having good sense. **5** engaged in actual practice or work: *A practical farmer runs a farm.* **6** being such in effect; virtual: *So many of our soldiers were killed that our victory was a practical defeat.* [< earlier *practic* < LL *practicus* < Gk. *praktikos* < *prassein* do] **—prac′ti·cal·ness,** *n.* **—Syn. 1** See **sensible.**

prac·ti·cal·i·ty (prak′tə kal′ə tē) *n.* **-ties. 1** the quality of being practical; practical usefulness; a practical habit of mind. **2** a practical matter.

practical joke a trick played on a person to have a laugh at him.

practical joker a person who plays practical jokes on others.

prac·ti·cal·ly (prak′tik lē) *adv.* **1** really; in effect: *He practically runs the team.* **2** *Informal.* almost; nearly. **3** in a practical way; in a useful way. **4** by actual practice.

practical nurse a woman whose occupation is to care for the sick, but who has not the hospital training or diploma of a trained nurse.

prac·tice (prak′tis) *n.* **1** an action done many times over in order to gain skill: *Practice makes perfect.* **2** the skill gained by experience or exercise: *He was out of practice at batting.* **3** the action or process of doing or being something: *His plan is good in theory, but not in actual practice.* **4** the usual way; custom: *It is the practice at the factory to blow a whistle at noon.* **5** the working at or following of a profession or occupation: *engaged in the practice of law.* **6** the business of a doctor or lawyer: *Dr. Adams sold his practice.* **7** *Archaic.* a scheme; plot. **8** in law, the established method of conducting legal proceedings. **9** a period set aside for practising: *He went to the hockey practice last night.* Also, **practise.** [ME < *practise,* v. < OF *practiser*, ult. < LL *practicus.* See PRACTICAL.] **—Syn. 1** drill, exercise. **4** habit. See **custom.**

prac·ti·cum (prak′tə kəm) *n.* **-cums** or **-ca** (-kə). in schools and colleges: **1** a course in independent research or in practical work. **2** a practical part of a course, such as laboratory or field work. [< NL (*collegium*) *practicum* practical course < Med.L *practicare* to practise]

prac·tise or **prac·tice** (prak′tis) *v.* **-tised** or **-ticed, -tis·ing** or **-tic·ing. 1** do something again and again so as to learn to do it well: *practise playing the piano.* **2** do as a rule; make a custom of: *Practise what you preach.* **3** follow, observe, or use day after day: *practise moderation.* **4** work at or follow as a profession, act, or occupation: *practise medicine.* **5** practise a profession. **6** give training to; drill. **7** *Archaic.* scheme; plot. **8** take advantage of. [see PRACTICE] **—prac′tis·er** or **prac′tic·er,** *n.* **—Syn. 1** See **exercise. 6** train.

prac·tised or **prac·ticed** (prak′tist) *adj.* **1** experienced; skilled; expert; proficient. **2** acquired or perfected through practice. **—Syn. 1** versed, accomplished.

prac·ti·tion·er (prak tish′ən ər or prak tish′nər) *n.* a person engaged in the practice of an art or profession: *He was a medical practitioner for ten years; later he taught medicine.*

prae·fect (prē′fekt) *n.* prefect.

prae·no·men (prē nō′mən) *n.* **-nom·i·na** (-nom′ə nə). in ancient Rome, the first or personal name of a citizen. [< L *praenomen* < *prae-* before + *nomen* name]

prae·tor (prē′tər or prē′tôr) *n.* in ancient Rome, a magistrate or judge, ranking next below a consul. Also, **pretor.** [< L *praetor*, ult. < *prae-* before + *ire* go]

prae·to·ri·an (prē tô′rē ən) *adj.* in ancient Rome: **1** of or having to do with a praetor. **2** having to do with the bodyguard of a commander or emperor. *—n.* **1** a man having the rank of a praetor. **2** a soldier of the bodyguard of a commander or emperor.

prag·mat·ic (prag mat′ik) *adj.* **1** concerned with practical results or values; of or having to do with pragmatism: *a pragmatic philosophy.* **2** having to do with the affairs of a state or community. **3** busy; active. **4** meddlesome; interfering. **5** conceited; opinionated. **6** matter-of-fact. **7** treating the facts of history systematically, with special reference to their causes and effects. [< L *pragmaticus* < Gk. *pragmatikos* efficient, ult. < *prassein* do]

prag·mat·i·cal (prag mat′ə kəl) *adj.* pragmatic. **—prag·mat′i·cal·ly,** *adv.*

pragmatic sanction any of various imperial decrees issued as fundamental law.

prag·ma·tism (prag′mə tiz′əm) *n.* **1** a philosophy that tests the value and truth of ideas by their practical consequences. **2** a pragmatic quality or condition. **3** officiousness. **4** dogmatism. **5** a matter-of-fact way of viewing things.

prag·ma·tist (prag′mə tist) *n.* a person who believes in pragmatism.

prai·rie (prãr′ē) *n.* **1** a large area of level or rolling land with grass but no or very few trees. **2 the Prairies,** *pl.* **a** the great, almost treeless, plain that covers much of central North America. **b** the part of this plain that covers much of central and southern Manitoba, Saskatchewan, and Alberta. *—adj.* Often, **Prairie.** of or having to do with the Prairies. [< F *prairie*, ult. < L *pratum* meadow]

prairie chicken 1 a grouse found on the Prairies, especially in S. Saskatchewan, but now becoming rare. **2** sharp-tailed grouse.

prairie dog 1 an animal resembling a groundhog but smaller, found on the Great Plains of North America: *In Canada, prairie dogs are found in southern Saskatchewan.* **2** a gopher.

prairie oyster 1 a raw egg swallowed whole or drunk in vinegar, brandy, etc. **2** *Cdn.* a testicle of a bull calf prepared for eating.

Prairie Provinces Manitoba, Saskatchewan, and Alberta.

prairie schooner especially in the United States, a large covered wagon used by pioneers in crossing the plains before the railways were built.

A prairie schooner

prairie wolf coyote.

praise (prãz) *n. v.* **praised, prais·ing.** *—n.* **1** the act of saying that a thing or person is good; words that tell the worth or value of a thing or person. **2** words or song setting forth the glory and goodness of God. **3 damn with faint praise,** praise with so little enthusiasm as to condemn. **4 sing the praise** or **praises of,** praise with enthusiasm. [< v.]
—v. **1** express approval or admiration of. **2** worship in words or song: *praise God.* [ME < OF *preisier*, ult. < L

pretium price] —**prais′er**, *n.*

Syn. *n.* 1 commendation, acclaim. –*v.* **1 Praise, approve, commend** = think or speak well of. **Praise** = express in a hearty or enthusiastic way one's high opinion or admiration of someone or something: *The coach praised the team for its fine playing.* **Approve** = think or express a favorable opinion or admiration: *Everyone approved his idea.* **Commend,** more formal in use, suggests a more formal expression of favorable opinion: *The mayor commended the boys for their quick thinking at the disaster.*

praise·wor·thy (prāz′ wėr′ ᴛʜē) *adj.* worthy of praise; deserving approval. —**praise′wor′thi·ly,** *adv.* —**praise′wor′thi·ness,** *n.*

Pra·krit (prä′krit) *n.* any of the Indo-European vernacular languages or dialects of northern and central India, especially those of the ancient and medieval periods. [< Skt. *prakrta* natural, common, vulgar. Cf. SANSKRIT.]

pra·line (prä′lēn) *n.* a small cake of brown candy made of sugar and nuts, usually pecans or almonds. [< F; invented by the cook of Marshal Duplessis-*Praslin* (1598-1675)]

pram[1] (pram) *n. Esp.Brit.* a perambulator; baby carriage.

pram[2] (pram) *n.* a small flat-bottomed boat having a blunt, square bow. Also, **praam.** [< Du. *praam*]

prance (prans) *v.* **pranced, pranc·ing,** *n.* —*v.* **1** spring about on the hind legs. Horses prance when they feel lively. **2** ride on a horse doing this. **3** move gaily or proudly; swagger. **4** caper; dance. —*n.* a prancing. [ME *prance(n)*, *praunce(n)*; origin uncertain] —**pranc′er,** *n.* —**pranc′ing·ly,** *adv.*

prank[1] (prangk) *n.* a piece of mischief; playful trick: *On April Fool's Day people play pranks on each other.* [origin uncertain]

prank[2] (prangk) *v.* **1** dress in a showy way; adorn. **2** make a show or display. [cf. MLG *prank* showiness]

prank·ish (prangk′ish) *adj.* **1** full of pranks; fond of pranks. **2** like a prank. —**prank′ish·ly,** *adv.* —**prank′ish·ness,** *n.*

prank·ster (prangk′stər) *n.* a person who plays pranks or other practical jokes.

pra·se·o·dym·i·um (prā′zē ō dim′ē əm) *n.* a rare metallic chemical element of the same group as cerium. *Symbol*: Pr; *at.no.* 59; *at.wt.* 140.907. [< NL *praseodymium*, ult. < Gk. *prasios* bluish-green + E *(di)dymium*, a rare element < Gk. *didymos* twin]

prate (prāt) *v.* **prat·ed, prat·ing,** *n.* —*v.* talk a great deal in a foolish way; prattle. —*n.* empty or foolish talk. [cf. MDu., MLG *praten*] —**prat′er,** *n.* —**prat′ing·ly,** *adv.*

prat·fall (prat′fol or -fôl) *n. Slang.* **1** a fall on the rump or backside, as part of a slapstick performance. **2** any laughable or disconcerting blunder. [< earlier *prat* buttocks + *fall*]

prat·tle (prat′əl) *v.* **-tled, -tling,** *n.* —*v.* **1** talk as a child does; tell freely and carelessly. **2** talk or tell in a foolish, empty way. **3** sound like baby talk; babble. —*n.* **1** simple, artless talk. **2** baby talk; foolish, empty talk. **3** sounds like baby talk; babble. [< *prate*] —**prat′tler,** *n.*

prawn (pron or prôn) *n.* any of several edible shellfish resembling shrimp but larger. —*v.* fish for or catch prawns. [ME *prane*; origin uncertain] —**prawn′er,** *n.*

pray (prā) *v.* **1** speak to God in worship; enter into spiritual communion with God; offer worship. **2** make earnest request to God or to any other object of worship: *pray for help, pray for one's family.* **3** ask earnestly: *pray God for help or to help.* **4** ask earnestly for. **5** bring or get by praying. **6** please: *Pray come with me.* [ME < OF *preier* < L *precari* < *prex, precis* prayer] —**pray′er,** *n.* —**Syn.** **3** entreat, implore, beseech, beg.

prayer (prãr) *n.* **1** the act of praying: *She was at prayer.* **2** the thing prayed for: *Our prayers were granted.* **3** the form of words to be used in praying. **4** a form of worship; religious service consisting mainly of prayers. **5** an earnest or humble request. [ME < OF *preiere*, ult. < L *prex, precis* prayer]

prayer book **1** a book of prayers. **2 Prayer Book,** the Book of Common Prayer.

prayer·ful (prãr′fəl) *adj.* having the habit of praying often; devout. —**prayer′ful·ly,** *adv.* —**prayer′ful·ness,** *n.*

prayer meeting a meeting for prayer and worship.

hat, āge, cãre, fär; let, ēqual, tėrm; it, īce
hot, ōpen, ôrder; oil, out; cup, pu̇t, rüle, ūse
əbove, takən, pencəl, lemən, circəs
ch, child; ng, long; sh, ship
th, thin; ᴛʜ, then; zh, measure

prayer wheel a wheel or cylinder inscribed with prayers, each turn of the wheel counting as an uttered prayer, used by the Buddhists of Tibet.

praying mantis mantis.

pre- *prefix.* before in place, time, order, or rank, as in *prepay, prevision, prewar.* [< L *prae-* before]

preach (prēch) *v.* **1** speak publicly on a religious subject. **2** deliver (a sermon). **3** make known by preaching; proclaim: *preach the Gospel.* **4** urge; recommend strongly: *He preached patience and moderation.* **5** give earnest advice, usually in a meddling or tiresome way. [ME < OF *prechier* < L *praedicare* declare, preach. Doublet of PREDICATE.]

preach·er (prēch′ər) *n.* a person who preaches; clergyman; minister.

preach·i·fy (prēch′ə fī′) *v.* **-fied, -fy·ing.** *Informal.* preach or moralize too much.

preach·ing (prēch′ing) *n.* what is preached; a sermon.

preach·ment (prēch′mənt) *n.* **1** a preaching. **2** a long, tiresome sermon or speech.

preach·y (prēch′ē) *adj.* **preach·i·er, preach·i·est.** *Informal.* **1** inclined to preach. **2** suggestive of preaching.

pre·am·ble (prē′am′bəl or prē am′bəl) *n.* **1** a preliminary statement; introduction to a speech or a writing. The reasons for a law and its general purpose are often stated in a preamble. **2** a preliminary or introductory fact or circumstance. [< F < Med.L *praeambulum*, originally neut. adj., walking before, ult. < L *prae-* before + *ambulare* walk]

pre·am·pli·fi·er (prē am′plə fī′ər) *n.* a unit that amplifies very weak signals enabling them to be sent into the main amplifier.

pre·ar·range (prē′ə rānj′) *v.* **-ranged, -rang·ing.** arrange beforehand. —**pre′ar·range′ment,** *n.*

preb·end (preb′ənd) *n.* **1** the salary given to a clergyman connected with a cathedral or a collegiate church. **2** the particular property or church tax from which the money comes for this salary. **3** a prebendary. [ME < OF < LL *praebenda* allowance < L *praebenda* (things) to be furnished < *praebere* furnish < *prae-* before + *habere* hold]

preb·en·dar·y (preb′ən der′ē) *n.* **-dar·ies.** a clergyman who has a prebend.

prec. preceding.

Pre·cam·bri·an or **Pre-Cam·bri·an** (prē′kam′brē ən) in geology: —*n.* **1** the period that preceded the Cambrian, including the Proterozoic and Archeozoic Eras. **2** the rocks formed in this period. —*adj.* of or having to do with this period or the rocks formed during it.

pre·can·cel (prē kan′səl) *v.* **-celled** or **-celed, -cel·ling** or **-cel·ing,** *n.*—*v.* cancel (a postage stamp) before sale. —*n.* a precancelled postage stamp.

pre·car·i·ous (pri kãr′ē əs) *adj.* **1** dependent on the will or pleasure of another. **2** not safe or secure; uncertain; dangerous; risky: *A soldier leads a precarious life.* **3** poorly founded; doubtful; assumed: *a precarious opinion or conclusion.* [< L *precarius*, originally, obtainable by entreaty, ult. < *prex, precis* prayer] —**pre·car′i·ous·ly,** *adv.* —**pre·car′i·ous·ness,** *n.* —**Syn.** **2** perilous, hazardous.

pre·cau·tion (pri ko′shən or -kô′shən) *n.* **1** care taken beforehand: *When handling sharp knives, precaution is needed.* **2** a measure taken beforehand; something done beforehand to ward off evil or to secure good results: *Locking doors is a precaution.* [< LL *praecautio, -onis* < L *praecavere* guard against beforehand < *prae-* before + *cavere* be on one's guard]

pre·cau·tion·ar·y (pri ko′shən er′ē or -kô′shən er′ē) *adj.* of or using precaution.

pre·cede (prē sēd′) *v.* **-ced·ed, -ced·ing.** **1** go before;

come before: *The band preceded the soldiers in the parade.* 2 be higher than in rank or importance: *A major precedes a captain.* [< L *praecedere* < *prae-* before + *cedere* go]

prec·e·dence (pres′ə dəns or pri sēd′əns) *n.* **1** the act or fact of preceding. **2** a higher position or rank; greater importance: *take precedence over all others.* **3** the right to precede others in ceremonies or social affairs; social superiority: *A major takes precedence over a captain.*

prec·e·den·cy (pres′ə dən sē or prē sēd′ən sē) *n.* **-cies.** precedence.

prec·e·dent (*n.* pres′ə dənt or prē′sə dənt; *adj.* prē sēd′ənt or pres′ə dənt) *n.* **1** a case that may serve as an example or reason for a later case. **2** in law, a judicial decision, case, proceeding, etc. that serves as a guide or pattern in future similar or analogous situations. —*adj.* preceding. [< L *praecedens, -entis,* ppr. of *praecedere.* See PRECEDE.]

pre·ced·ing (prē sēd′ing) *adj.* going before; coming before; previous: *the preceding page.* —**Syn.** See **previous.**

pre·cen·tor (pri sen′tər) *n.* a person who leads and directs the singing of a church choir or congregation. [< LL *praecentor,* ult. < L *prae-* before + *canere* sing]

pre·cept (prē′sept) *n.* a rule of action or behavior; maxim: "*If at first you don't succeed, try, try, try again*" *is a familiar precept.* [< L *praeceptum,* originally neut. pp. of *praecipere* enjoin, anticipate < *prae-* before + *capere* take] —**Syn.** teaching, adage, axiom.

pre·cep·tor (pri sep′tər) *n.* an instructor; teacher. [< L *praeceptor* < *praecipere.* See PRECEPT.]

pre·cep·to·ri·al (prē′sep tô′rē əl) *adj.* **1** of a preceptor; like that of a preceptor. **2** using preceptors.

pre·cep·tress (pri sep′tris) *n.* a woman preceptor.

pre·ces·sion (prē sesh′ən) *n.* the act, fact, or condition of going first; precedence. [< LL *praecessio, -onis* < L *praecedere.* See PRECEDE.]

pre·cinct (prē′singkt) *n.* **1** a space within a boundary: *Do not leave the school precincts during school hours.* **2** Often, **precincts,** *pl.* a boundary; limit. **3** *U.S.* a district within certain boundaries, for administration or other purposes: *a police precinct.* [< Med.L *praecinctum,* originally neut. pp. of *praecingere* enclose < *prae-* before + *cingere* gird]

pre·ci·os·i·ty (presh′ē os′ə tē) *n.* **-ties.** too much refinement; affectation. [< F *préciosité* < *précieux* precious]

pre·cious (presh′əs) *adj.* **1** worth much; valuable. Gold, platinum, and silver are often called the precious metals. **2** much loved; dear. **3** too nice; overrefined. **4** *Informal.* very great. **5** of great moral or spiritual worth: *the precious blood of Christ* (I Peter 1:19). —*adv. Informal.* very: *precious little money.* [ME < OF *precios* < L *pretiosus* < *pretium* value] —**pre′cious·ness,** *n.* —**Syn.** *adj.* **1** See **valuable.**

pre·cious·ly (presh′əs lē) *adv.* **1** at great cost. **2** in a valuable manner or degree. **3** extremely. **4** with extreme care in matters of detail.

precious metal a valuable metal such as gold, silver, or platinum.

precious stone a jewel; gem. Diamonds, rubies, and sapphires are precious stones.

prec·i·pice (pres′ə pis) *n.* a very steep cliff; almost vertical slope; the face of a cliff. [< F < L *praecipitium* < *praeceps, -cipitis* steep, literally, headlong < *prae-* first + *caput* head]

pre·cip·i·tance (pri sip′ə təns) *n.* headlong haste; rashness.

pre·cip·i·tan·cy (pri sip′ə tən sē) *n.* precipitance.

pre·cip·i·tant (pri sip′ə tənt) *adj.* **1** very sudden or abrupt. **2** acting in a hasty or rash manner. **3** falling or rushing headlong. —*n.* a substance that causes another substance in solution in a liquid to be deposited in solid form. [< L *praecipitans, -antis,* ppr. of *praecipitare.* See PRECIPITATE.] —**pre·cip′i·tant·ly,** *adv.*

pre·cip·i·tate (*v.* pri sip′ə tāt′; *adj. n.* pri sip′ə tāt′ or pri sip′ə tit) *v.* **-tat·ed, -tat·ing,** *adj. n.* —*v.* **1** hasten the beginning of; bring about suddenly: *to precipitate a war.* **2** throw headlong; hurl: *to precipitate a rock down a cliff.* **3** separate (a substance) out from a solution as a solid. **4 a** condense from vapor in the form of rain, dew, etc. **b** be condensed in this way.
—*adj.* **1** very hurried; sudden: *A cool breeze caused a precipitate drop in the temperature.* **2** with great haste and force; plunging or rushing; hasty; rash: *precipitate actions.*
—*n.* a substance, usually crystalline, separated out from a solution as a solid. [< L *praecipitare* < *praeceps* headlong. See PRECIPICE.] —**pre·cip′i·tate·ly,** *adv.* —**pre·cip′i·ta′tor,** *n.*

pre·cip·i·ta·tion (pri sip′ə tā′shən) *n.* **1** the act or state of precipitating; a throwing down or falling headlong. **2** a hastening or hurrying. **3** a sudden bringing on: *the precipitation of a war without warning.* **4** unwise or rash rapidity; sudden haste. **5 a** the separating out of a substance from a solution as a solid. **b** substance separated out from a solution as a solid. **6 a** the depositing of moisture in the form of rain, dew, or snow. **b** something that is precipitated, such as rain, dew, or snow. **c** the amount that is precipitated.

pre·cip·i·tous (pri sip′ə təs) *adj.* **1** like a precipice; very steep: *precipitous cliffs.* **2** hasty; rash. —**pre·cip′i·tous·ly,** *adv.* —**pre·cip′i·tous·ness,** *n.* —**Syn. 1** See **steep.**

pré·cis (prā′sē or prā sē′) *n.* **-cis.** a summary of an essay, speech, book, etc.; abstract. [< F *précis,* originally adj. < L *praecisus.* See PRECISE.]

pre·cise (pri sīs′) *adj.* **1** exact; accurate; definite: *The precise sum was 34 cents.* **2** careful. **3** strict; scrupulous. [< L *praecisus* abridged, pp. of *praecidere* < *prae-* in front + *caedere* cut] —**pre·cise′ness,** *n.* —**Syn. 1** correct.

pre·cise·ly (pri sīs′lē) *adv.* in a precise manner; exactly.

pre·ci·sion (pri sizh′ən) *n.* accuracy; exactness: *the precision of a machine.* —**Syn.** correctness, preciseness.

pre·clude (pri klüd′) *v.* **-clud·ed, -clud·ing.** shut out; make impossible; prevent. [< L *praecludere* < *prae-* before + *claudere* shut] —**Syn.** exclude, hinder.

pre·clu·sion (pri klü′shən) *n.* the act of precluding or the state of being precluded. [< L *praeclusus,* pp. of *praecludere.* See PRECLUDE.]

pre·clu·sive (pri klü′siv) *adj.* tending or serving to preclude. —**pre·clu′sive·ly,** *adv.*

pre·co·cious (pri kō′shəs) *adj.* **1** developed earlier than usual: *This very precocious child could read well at the age of four.* **2** developed too early. [< L *praecox, -ocis,* ult. < *prae-* before (its time) + *coquere* ripen] —**pre·co′cious·ly,** *adv.* —**pre·co′cious·ness,** *n.*

pre·coc·i·ty (pri kos′ə tē) *n.* precocious development; early maturity.

pre·cog·ni·tion (prē′kog nish′ən) *n.* **1** prior knowledge or cognition; foreknowledge. **2** in Scottish law: **a** a preliminary examination of witnesses, etc. **b** the evidence taken at this examination.

pre·con·ceive (prē′kən sēv′) *v.* **-ceived, -ceiv·ing.** form an idea or opinion of beforehand.

pre·con·cep·tion (prē′kən sep′shən) *n.* an idea or opinion formed beforehand.

pre·con·cert (prē′kən sėrt′) *v.* arrange beforehand.

pre·con·di·tion (prē′kən dish′ən) *n.* something that must be fulfilled before something else can come about; prerequisite. —*v.* prepare or condition in advance.

pre·cur·sor (pri kėr′sər) *n.* a forerunner: *A severe cold may be the precursor of pneumonia.* [< L *praecursor,* ult. < *prae-* before + *currere* run] —**Syn.** predecessor, herald.

pre·cur·so·ry (pri kėr′sə rē) *adj.* indicative of something to follow; introductory.

pred. predicate.

pre·da·cious (pri dā′shəs) *adj.* living by preying; predatory. [< L *praedari* rob < *praeda* prey]

pre·da·tion (prē dā′shən) *n.* **1** the act or fact of preying on other animals. **2** *Obsolete.* the act of pillaging; depredation.

pred·a·to·ry (pred′ə tô′rē) *adj.* **1** of or inclined to plundering or robbery: *Predatory tramps infested the highways.* **2** preying upon other animals. **Hawks and owls**

are predatory birds. 3 inclined to injure or exploit others for the sake of one's own interests, profit, etc. [< L *praedatorius*, ult. < *praeda* prey] —**Syn.** 1 marauding, thieving, rapacious.

pred·e·ces·sor (prē′də ses′ər or pred′ə ses′ər) *n.* **1** a person holding a position or office before another: *Edward VII was the predecessor of George V as King of England.* **2** something that came before another. **3** an ancestor; forefather. [< LL *praedecessor*, ult. < *prae-* before + *decedere* retire < *de-* from + *cedere* withdraw]

pre·des·ti·nate (prē des′tə nāt′) *v.* **-nat·ed, -nat·ing.** **1** decree or ordain beforehand. **2** foreordain by divine purpose. [< L *praedestinare* appoint beforehand < *prae-* before + *destinare* make fast, ult. < *de-* + *stare* stand]

pre·des·ti·na·tion (prē′des tə nā′shən) *n.* **1** an ordaining beforehand; destiny; fate. **2** an action of God in deciding beforehand what shall happen. **3** a doctrine that by God's decree certain souls will be saved and others lost.

pre·des·tine (prē des′tən) *v.* **-tined, -tin·ing.** determine or settle beforehand; foreordain.

pre·de·ter·mine (prē′di tėr′mən) *v.* **-mined, -min·ing.** **1** determine or decide beforehand: *The time for the meeting was predetermined.* **2** direct or impel beforehand (to something). —**pre′de·ter′mi·na′tion,** *n.*

pred·i·ca·ble (pred′ə kə bəl) *adj.* that can be predicated or affirmed. —**pred′i·ca·bly,** *adv.*

pre·dic·a·ment (pri dik′ə mənt) *n.* **1** an unpleasant, difficult, or dangerous situation. **2** any condition, state, or situation. **3** that which can be predicated; attribute. [< LL *praedicamentum* quality, category < L *praedicare.* See PREDICATE.]

Syn. 1 Predicament, plight, dilemma = a difficult situation. **Predicament** = a position or situation in which someone finds himself, that is hard to get out of or presents a problem difficult to solve: *The world is in a dangerous predicament.* **Plight** applies to a state or condition, usually unhappy or unfortunate, often hopeless: *He is worried by the plight of his relatives in enemy-conquered territory.* **Dilemma** = a predicament forcing a choice between two things, both disagreeable: *He is faced with the dilemma of telling the truth or betraying his friend.*

pred·i·cate (*n. adj.* pred′ə kit; *v.* pred′ə kāt′) *n. adj. v.* **-cat·ed, -cat·ing.** —*n.* **1** a word or words expressing what is said about the subject; that part of a sentence containing a verb. *Examples:* Men *work.* The men *dug wells.* The men *are soldiers.* **2** in logic, that which is said of the subject in a proposition.
—*adj.* in grammar, belonging to the predicate. In "Horses are strong," *strong* is a **predicate adjective.**
—*v.* **1** found or base (a statement, action, etc.) on something. **2** declare, assert, or affirm to be real or true: *Most religions predicate life after death.* **3** connote; imply. **4** declare to be an attribute or quality (of some person or thing): *We predicate goodness and mercy of God.* **5** in logic, assert (something) about the subject of a proposition. [< L *praedicatus*, pp. of *praedicare* < *prae-* before + *dicare* make known. Doublet of PREACH.]

☞ **predicate.** A predicate of a clause or sentence is the verb with its modifiers, object, complement, etc. It may be a simple verb of complete meaning (The big bell *tolled*), a verb and adverbial modifier (The sun *went behind the cloud*), a transitive verb and its modifiers and object (He *finally landed the big fish*), a linking verb and its complement (The oldest member of a family *is usually the first to go*).

pred·i·ca·tion (pred′ə kā′shən) *n.* **1** the act of predicating; affirming; assertion. **2** in logic, the assertion of something about the subject of a proposition.

pred·i·ca·tive (pred′ə kā′tiv or pri dik′ə tiv) *adj.* **1** predicating; expressing predication. **2** acting as a predicate. —**pred′i·ca′tive·ly,** *adv.*

pre·dict (pri dikt′) *v.* tell beforehand; prophesy: *The weather bureau predicts rain for tomorrow.* [< L *praedictus*, pp. of *praedicere* < *prae-* before + *dicere* say] —**pre·dict′a·ble,** *adj.* —**pre·dict′a·bly,** *adv.* —**pre·dic′tor,** *n.* —**Syn.** foretell, presage.

pre·dic·tion (pri dik′shən) *n.* **1** the act of predicting. **2** something predicted; prophecy: *The weather prediction was for a storm.*

pre·dic·tive (pri dik′tiv) *adj.* foretelling; prophetic.

pre·di·gest (prē′də jest′ or -dī jest′) *v.* **1** digest beforehand. **2** treat (food) by an artificial process, similar to digestion, in order to make it more digestible.

pre·di·lec·tion (prē′də lek′shən or pred′ə lek′shən) *n.* a liking; preference. [< F *prédilection*, ult. < L *prae-* before + *diligere* choose] —**Syn.** partiality, predisposition.

hat, āge, cãre, fär; let, ēqual, tėrm; it, īce
hot, ōpen, ôrder; oil, out; cup, pu̇t, rüle, ūse
əbove, takən, pencəl, lemən, circəs
ch, child; ng, long; sh, ship
th, thin; ᴛʜ, then; zh, measure

pre·dis·pose (prē′dis pōz′) *v.* **-posed, -pos·ing.** **1** give an inclination or tendency to; make liable or susceptible: *A cold predisposes a person to other diseases.* **2** put into a favorable or suitable frame of mind, emotional condition, etc.: *He is predisposed to be generous to his friends.* **3** dispose of, give away, or bequeath before the usual or specified time.

pre·dis·po·si·tion (prē′dis pə zish′ən) *n.* a previous inclination or tendency; susceptibility or liability: *a predisposition to look on the dark side of things.*

pre·dom·i·nance (pri dom′ə nəns) *n.* the state or quality of being predominant.

pre·dom·i·nant (pri dom′ə nənt) *adj.* **1** having more power, authority, or influence than others; superior. **2** prevailing; most noticeable. —**pre·dom′i·nant·ly,** *adv.* **Syn. 1** controlling, ruling. See **dominant.**

pre·dom·i·nate (pri dom′ə nāt′) *v.* **-nat·ed, -nat·ing.** be greater in power, strength, influence, or numbers. —**pre·dom′i·nat′ing·ly,** *adv.* —**pre·dom′i·na′tor,** *n.*

pre·dom·i·na·tion (pri dom′ə nā′shən) *n.* the act of predominating; superior power or influence; prevalence.

pre-Dor·set (prē dôr′sit) *n.* an Eskimo culture of N.E. Canada and N. Greenland, earlier than the Dorset and dating from about 2000 B.C.

pre-em·i·nence (prē em′ə nəns) *n.* excellence; superiority: *the pre-eminence of Edison among the inventors of his day.*

pre-em·i·nent (prē em′ə nənt) *adj.* standing out above all others; superior to others. [< L *praeeminens, -entis*, ppr. of *praeeminere* < *prae-* before + *eminere* stand out] —**pre-em′i·nent·ly,** *adv.*

pre-empt (prē empt′) *v.* **1** secure before someone else can; acquire or take possession of beforehand: *The cat pre-empted the comfortable chair.* **2** settle on (land) with the right to buy it before others. [< *pre-emption*] —**pre-emp′tor,** *n.*

pre-emp·tion (prē emp′shən) *n.* the act or right of buying before others or in preference to others. [< *pre-* + L *emptio, -onis* buying < *emere* to buy]

pre-emp·tive (prē emp′tiv) *adj.* having to do with pre-emption; having pre-emption.

preen (prēn) *v.* **1** of birds, smooth or arrange (the feathers) with the beak. **2** dress (oneself) carefully. **3** pride (oneself). [? var. of *prune* preen, dress carefully, influenced by ME *preonen* prick with a pin < OE *prēon* pin]

pre-ex·ist (prē′eg zist′) *v.* exist beforehand, or before something else.

pre-ex·ist·ence (prē′eg zis′təns) *n.* a previous existence.

pre-ex·ist·ent (prē′eg zis′tənt) *adj.* existing previously.

pref. 1 preface. 2 prefix. 3 preferred.

pre·fab (prē fab′) *n. v.* **-fabbed, -fab·bing.** —*n.* a prefabricated house. —*v.* prefabricate.

pre·fab·ri·cate (prē fab′rə kāt′) *v.* **-cat·ed, -cat·ing.** **1** make all standardized parts of (a house, etc.). The erection of a prefabricated house requires merely the assembling of the various sections. **2** put together or prepare in advance. —**pre′fab·ri·ca′tion,** *n.*

pref·ace (pref′is) *n. v.* **-aced, -ac·ing.** —*n.* an introduction to a book, writing, or speech: *This book has a preface written by the author.* —*v.* **1** introduce by written or spoken remarks; give a preface to. **2** be a preface to; begin. [ME < OF *preface*, ult. < L *praefatio* < *prae-* before + *fari* speak] —**Syn.** *n.* See **introduction.**

pref·a·to·ry (pref′ə tô′rē) *adj.* of or like a preface; given as a preface; introductory; preliminary.

pre·fect (prē′fekt) *n.* **1** in ancient Rome, etc., a title of various military and civil officers. **2** in France, the chief administrative official of a department. **3** in some schools, a senior student who has some authority over other students; monitor. Also, **praefect.** [< L *praefectus*, originally pp. of *praeficere* put in charge < *prae-* in front + *facere* make]

pre·fec·ture (prē′fek chər) *n.* the office, jurisdiction, territory, or official residence of a prefect. [< L *praefectura*]

pre·fer (pri fėr′) *v.* **-ferred, -fer·ring. 1** like better; choose rather: *I will come later, if you prefer.* **2** put forward; present: *prefer a claim to property. The constable preferred charges of speeding against the driver.* **3** promote; advance. [ME < OF < L *praeferre* < *prae-* before + *ferre* carry] —**pre·fer′rer,** *n.*

☞ **prefer.** The idiom is with *to*: *I prefer chemistry to physics. She preferred dressing formally to wearing sports clothes.*

pref·er·a·ble (pref′ər ə bəl or pref′rə bəl) *adj.* to be preferred; more desirable.

pref·er·a·bly (pref′ər ə blē or pref′rə blē) *adv.* by choice: *He wants a secretary, preferably one who is a college graduate.*

pref·er·ence (pref′ər əns or pref′rəns) *n.* **1** the act or attitude of liking better: *My preference is for beef rather than lamb.* **2** something preferred; first choice: *Her preference in reading is novels.* **3** in international trade, a granting of certain concessions, especially lower import tariffs, to another country or countries. —**Syn. 1** selection, election. See **choice.**

pref·er·en·tial (pref′ər en′shəl) *adj.* of, giving, or receiving preference. —**pref′er·en′tial·ly,** *adv.*

preferential shop a shop giving preference to union members in hiring, promotion, etc.

preferential voting a system of voting whereby the voter can indicate an order in the choice of candidates, as first, second, third, etc. so that in case no one candidate gets a clear majority, the election may be determined by totalling the points for first choice, second choice, etc.

pre·fer·ment (pri fėr′mənt) *n.* **1** advancement; promotion: *Captain White seeks preferment in the army.* **2** a position or office giving social or financial advancement, especially one in the church.

preferred stock stock on which dividends must be paid before any can be paid on the common stock.

pre·fig·ur·a·tion (prē′fig ər ā′shən or -fig yər ā′shən) *n.* **1** a prefiguring; representation beforehand by a figure or type. **2** that in which something is prefigured; prototype.

pre·fig·ure (prē fig′ər or -fig′yər) *v.* **-ured, -ur·ing. 1** represent beforehand by a figure or type: *In one painting of Christ, His shadow resembles that of a cross, prefiguring the Crucifixion.* **2** imagine to oneself beforehand. [ME < LL *praefigurare* < L *prae-* before + *figurare* form, shape < *figura* a form] —**pre·fig′ure·ment,** *n.*

pre·fix (*n.* prē′fiks; *v.* prē′fiks or prē fiks′) *n.* a syllable, syllables, or word put at the beginning of a word to change its meaning or to form a new word, as in *pre*paid, *under*line, *dis*appear, *un*like. —*v.* put before: *We prefix "Mr." to a man's name.* [< L *praefixum*, neut. of *praefixus*, pp. of *praefigere* < *prae-* in front + *figere* fix]

preg·na·ble (preg′nə bəl) *adj.* open to attack; assailable. [ME < OF *prenable* < *prendre* < L *prendere*, shortened form of *prehendere* seize, take]

preg·nan·cy (preg′nən sē) *n.* **-cies. 1** the condition of having an embryo or embryos developing in the uterus. **2** the time this condition lasts. **3** the quality of being pregnant: *the pregnancy of his remarks.*

preg·nant (preg′nənt) *adj.* **1** having an embryo or embryos developing in the uterus; being with child or young. **2** filled; loaded. **3** fertile; rich; abounding: *His speech was pregnant with emotion.* **4** filled with meaning; very significant: *a pregnant remark.* [ME < L *praegnans, -antis* < *prae-* before + *gen-* bear] —**preg′nant·ly,** *adv.*

pre·heat (prē hēt′) *v.* heat before using.

pre·hen·sile (pri hens′īl or pri hen′səl) *adj.* adapted for seizing, grasping, or holding on. Many monkeys have prehensile tails. [< F *préhensile*, ult. < L *prehendere* grasp]

pre·his·tor·ic (prē′his tôr′ik) *adj.* of or belonging to periods before recorded history: *Some prehistoric people lived in caves.*

pre·his·tor·i·cal (prē′his tôr′ə kəl) *adj.* prehistoric.

pre·his·tor·i·cal·ly (prē′his tôr′ik lē) *adv.* before recorded history.

pre·his·to·ry or **pre-his·to·ry** (prē his′tə rē or -his′trē) *n.* **1** the history of mankind before the period of written history, learned from anthropology, archaeology, geology, paleontology, etc. **2** a history or account of the background of a situation or event.

pre·judge (prē juj′) *v.* **-judged, -judg·ing.** judge beforehand; judge without knowing all the facts. —**pre·judg′ment** or **pre·judge′ment,** *n.*

prej·u·dice (prej′ə dis) *n. v.* **-diced, -dic·ing.** —*n.* **1** an opinion formed without taking time and care to judge fairly: *a prejudice against doctors.* **2** harm; injury: *I will do nothing to the prejudice of my cousin in this matter.* —*v.* **1** cause a prejudice in; fill with prejudice: *One unfortunate experience prejudiced him against all lawyers.* **2** damage; harm; injure. [ME < OF < L *praejudicium* < *prae-* before + *judicium* judgment]

Syn. *n.* **1 Prejudice, bias** = an opinion or judgment without a good basis. **Prejudice** applies to an opinion, usually unfavorable, formed beforehand with no basis except personal feelings: *She has a prejudice against modern furniture.* **Bias** applies to an opinion or judgment slanted against or in favor of someone or something, based on personal liking or a fixed idea: *He often does foolish things because of his bias in favor of the underdog.*

prej·u·diced (prej′ə dist) *adj.* having an emphatic opinion without good reasons: *She is so prejudiced in favor of living in the country that she will not even try the city.*

prej·u·di·cial (prej′ə dish′əl) *adj.* causing prejudice or disadvantage; hurtful. —**Syn.** detrimental, damaging.

prej·u·di·cial·ly (prej′ə dish′əl ē) *adv.* in a prejudiced manner; with prejudice.

prel·a·cy (prel′ə sē) *n.* **-cies. 1** the position or rank of a prelate. **2** prelates. **3** church government by prelates.

prel·ate (prel′it) *n.* a clergyman of high rank, such as a bishop. [< Med.L < L *praelatus* one preferred, originally pp. to L *praeferre* prefer. See PREFER.]

prelim. preliminary.

pre·lim·i·nar·y (pri lim′ə ner′ē) *adj. n.* **-nar·ies.** —*adj.* coming before the main business; leading to something more important: *After the preliminary exercises of prayer and song, the principal made a speech.* —*n* a preliminary step; something preparatory: *A physical examination is a preliminary to joining the army.* [< NL *praeliminaris*, ult. < L *prae-* before + *limen, -minis* threshold] —**pre·lim′i·nar′i·ly,** *adv.* —**Syn.** *adj.* prefatory, introductory.

prel·ude (prel′ūd or prē′lüd) *n. v.* **-ud·ed, -ud·ing.** —*n.* **1** anything serving as an introduction. **2** in music: **a** a composition, or part of it, that introduces another composition or part. **b** an independent instrumental composition, usually short. **c** a composition played at the beginning of a church service. —*v.* **1** be a prelude or introduction to. **2** introduce with a prelude. [< F < Med.L *praeludium*, ult. < L *prae-* before + *ludere* play]

pre·mar·i·tal (prē mar′ə təl) *adj.* before marriage; prior to marriage.

pre·ma·ture (prē′mə chür′ or prem′ə chür′) *adj.* before the proper time; too soon. [< L *praematurus* < *prae-* before + *maturus* ripe]

pre·ma·ture·ly (prē′mə chür′lē) *adv.* before the proper time.

pre·med·i·cal (prē med′ə kəl) *adj.* preparing for the study of medicine: *a premedical student.*

pre·med·i·tate (prē med′ə tāt′) *v.* **-tat·ed, -tat·ing.** consider or plan beforehand: *The murder was premeditated. The general premeditated his plan before giving the order to attack.* [< L *praemeditari* < *prae-* before + *meditari* meditate]

pre·med·i·ta·tion (prē′med ə tā′shən) *n.* a previous deliberation or planning.

pre·mier (prē′mēr, prē′myər, or pri mēr′) *n.* **1** the prime minister of a province: *The ten premiers attended a conference with the Prime Minister in Ottawa.* **2** the chief officer of a government. —*adj.* **1** first in rank or quality:

a premier performance. **2** first in time; earliest. [< F *premier* first < L *primarius* primary < *primus* first]

premier danseur (prə myā′ däɴ sœr′) *French.* the principal male dancer in a ballet or ballet company.

pre·mière (pri mēr′; *French,* prə myãr′) *n.* **1** a first public performance. **2** the leading woman (in a play, etc.). [< F *première,* originally fem. of *premier.* See PREMIER.]

pre·mière dan·seuse (prə myãr′ däɴ sœz′) *French.* the principal female dancer in a ballet or ballet company.

pre·mier·ship (prē′myər ship′ or pri mēr′ship) *n.* **1** the rank or office of a prime minister or premier. **2** the state of being first in any rank.

prem·ise (*n.* prem′is; *v.* pri mīz′) *n. v.* **pre·mised, pre·mis·ing.** —*n.* **1** in logic, a statement assumed to be true and used to draw a conclusion. *Example*: Major premise: Children should go to school. Minor premise: He is a child. Conclusion: He should go to school. **2 premises,** *pl.* **a** a house or building with its grounds. **b** in law, things mentioned previously, such as the names of the parties concerned, a description of the property, the price, etc. **c** in law, the property forming the subject of a document. —*v.* set forth as an introduction or explanation; mention beforehand. [< Med.L *praemissa,* originally fem. pp., "put before," ult. < L *prae-* before + *mittere* send]

pre·mi·um (prē′mē əm) *n.* **1** a reward; prize: *Some magazines give premiums to salesmen who obtain new subscriptions.* **2** something more than the ordinary price or wages. **3** the amount of money paid for insurance: *He pays premiums on his life insurance four times a year.* **4** something given away or offered at a reduced price to purchasers of a product, service, etc. **5** the excess value of one form of money over another of the same nominal value. **6** unusual or unfair value: *Giving money to beggars may put a premium on idleness.* **7 at a premium, a** at more than the usual value or price. **b** very valuable; much wanted. —*adj.* of a higher grade or quality. [< L *praemium* reward < *prae-* before + *emere,* originally, take]

pre·mo·lar (prē mō′lər) *n.* one of the permanent teeth in front of the molars; bicuspid. See **tooth** for diagram. —*adj.* of the premolars.

pre·mo·ni·tion (prē′mə nish′ən or prem′ə nish′ən) *n.* a forewarning. [< obs. F < L *praemonitio, -onis,* ult. < *prae-* before + *monere* warn]

pre·mon·i·to·ry (pri mon′ə tô′rē) *adj.* giving warning beforehand.

pre·na·tal (prē nā′təl) *adj.* previous to birth.

pren·tice (pren′tis) *Archaic.* —*n.* an apprentice. —*adj.* of or like an apprentice; inexperienced; unskilled.

pre·oc·cu·pa·tion (prē ok′yů pā′shən) *n.* **1** the act of preoccupying. **2** absorption; the state of being preoccupied.

pre·oc·cu·py (prē ok′yů pī′) *v.* **-pied, -py·ing. 1** take up all the attention of: *The question of getting to Vancouver preoccupied her mind.* **2** occupy beforehand; take possession of before others: *Our favorite seats had been preoccupied.*

pre·or·dain (prē′ôr dān′) *v.* decide or settle beforehand; foreordain.

pre·or·di·na·tion (prē′ôr də nā′shən) *n.* the act of preordaining or the state of being preordained.

prep (prep) *adj. Informal.* preparatory.

prep. 1 preposition. **2** preparatory.

pre·pack·age (prē pak′ij) *v.* **-aged, -ag·ing.** package before sale according to certain weights, grades, prices, etc.

pre·paid (prē pād′) *v.* pt. and pp. of **prepay.**

prep·a·ra·tion (prep′ə rā′shən) *n.* **1** the act of preparing. **2** the state of being prepared. **3** anything done to prepare for something: *He made careful preparations for his holidays.* **4** a medicine, food, or other substance made by a special process: *The preparation included camphor.*

pre·par·a·tive (pri par′ə tiv) *adj.* preparatory. —*n.* something that helps to prepare.

pre·par·a·to·ry (pri par′ə tô′rē) *adj.* **1** of or for preparation; preparing: *Preparatory schools fit students for college.* **2** as an introduction; preliminary.

hat, āge, cãre, fär; let, ēqual, tėrm; it, īce
hot, ōpen, ôrder; oil, out; cup, pu̇t, rüle, ūse
əbove, takən, pencəl, lemən, circəs
ch, child; ng, long; sh, ship
th, thin; ᴛʜ, then; zh, measure

pre·pare (pri pãr′) *v.* **-pared, -par·ing. 1** make ready; get ready: *prepare a meal.* **2** make by a special process. [< L *praeparare* < *prae-* before + *parare* make ready] —**pre·par′er,** *n.* —**Syn. 2** devise, contrive.

pre·par·ed·ness (pri pãr′id nis or pri pãrd′nis) *n.* **1** the state or quality of being prepared; readiness. **2** the possession of adequate military forces and defences to meet threats or outbreaks of war.

pre·pay (prē pā′) *v.* **-paid, -pay·ing. 1** pay in advance. **2** pay for in advance. —**pre·pay′ment,** *n.*

pre·pense (pri pens′) *adj.* planned beforehand. [ME, ult. < OF *purpenser* meditate (with prefix *pre-* substituted) < *pur-* (< L *pro-* before) + *penser* think. See PENSIVE.]

pre·pon·der·ance (pri pon′dər əns) *n.* **1** a greater number; greater weight; greater power or influence: *In July hot days have the preponderance.* **2** the condition of being the chief or most important element: *the preponderance of oaks in these woods.*

pre·pon·der·ant (pri pon′dər ənt) *adj.* **1** weighing more; being stronger or more numerous; having more power or influence. **2** chief; most important: *Greed is a miser's preponderant characteristic.* —**pre·pon′der·ant·ly,** *adv.*

pre·pon·der·ate (pri pon′dər āt′) *v.* **-at·ed, -at·ing. 1** be greater than something else in weight, power, force, influence, number, amount, etc.: *Oaks and maples preponderate in our eastern woods.* **2** be chief; be most important. **3** be greater than; outweigh. [< L *praeponderare* outweigh, ult. < *prae-* before + *pondus, -deris* weight]

prep·o·si·tion (prep′ə zish′ən) *n.* a word that shows certain relations between other words. *With, for, by,* and *in* are prepositions in the sentence "A man *with* rugs *for* sale walked *by* our house *in* the morning." [< L *praepositio, -onis,* ult. < *prae-* before + *ponere* place]

☛ **preposition at end of sentence.** Under certain conditions, it is normal English structure for a preposition to stand at the end of the clause or sentence it belongs to, as in *What did you do it for?* Efforts to avoid this in favor of a more formal style often result in awkwardness: *This is the sort of writing up with which I will not put.*

prep·o·si·tion·al (prep′ə zish′ən əl) *adj.* **1** having to do with a preposition. **2** having the nature or function of a preposition. —**prep′o·si′tion·al·ly,** *adv.*

pre·pos·sess (prē′pə zes′) *v.* **1** fill with a favorable feeling or opinion: *We were prepossessed by the boy's modest behavior.* **2** fill with a feeling or opinion.

pre·pos·sess·ing (prē′pə zes′ing) *adj.* making a favorable first impression; attractive; pleasing.

pre·pos·ses·sion (prē′pə zesh′ən) *n.* bias; prejudice; a favorable feeling or opinion formed beforehand.

pre·pos·ter·ous (pri pos′tər əs or pri pos′trəs) *adj.* contrary to nature, reason, or common sense; absurd; senseless: *It would be preposterous to shovel coal with a teaspoon.* [< L *praeposterus* in reverse order, ult. < *prae-* before + *post* after] —**pre·pos′ter·ous·ly,** *adv.* —**pre·pos′ter·ous·ness,** *n.* —**Syn.** See **ridiculous.**

pre·puce (prē′pūs) *n.* the foreskin. [< F < L *praeputium*]

Pre-Raph·a·el·ite (prē′raf′ē əl īt′ or -rā′fē əl īt) *n.* **1** any Italian painter preceding Raphael (1483-1520), a famous Italian painter. **2** one of a group of English artists and poets formed in 1848, including Millais and Dante Gabriel Rossetti, who aimed to work in the spirit that prevailed before the time of Raphael. **3** any modern artist having similar aims or methods.

pre·req·ui·site (prē rek′wə zit) *n.* something required beforehand: *The completion of a high-school course is the usual prerequisite to college work.* —*adj.* required beforehand.

pre·rog·a·tive (pri rog′ə tiv) *n.* a right or privilege that nobody else has: *The government has the prerogative of* *coining money.* —*adj.* having or exercising a prerogative. [< L *praerogativa*, originally fem. adj., asked to vote first, ult. < *prae-* before + *rogare* ask] —**Syn.** *n.* See **privilege.**

pres. present.

Pres. **1** President. **2** Presbyterian.

pres·age (*n.* pres′ij; *v.* pri sāj′) *n. v.* **pre·saged, pre·sag·ing.** —*n.* **1** a sign felt as a warning; omen. **2** a feeling that something is about to happen. —*v.* **1** give warning of; predict: *Some people think that a circle around the moon presages a storm.* **2** have or give a prophetic impression (of). [ME < OF < L *praesagium*, ult. < *prae-* before + *sagus* prophetic] —**pre·sag′er,** *n.*

Presb. Presbyterian.

pres·by·ter (prez′bə tər or pres′bə tər) *n.* **1** an elder in the early Christian church. **2** in the Presbyterian Church, a minister or a lay elder. **3** in Anglican churches, a minister or a priest. [< L *presbyter* elder < Gk. *presbyteros*, comparative of *presbys* old. Doublet of PRIEST.]

Pres·by·te·ri·an (prez′bə tēr′ē ən or pres′bə tēr′ē ən) *adj.* **1** concerned with or of a Protestant denomination or church governed by elected presbyters or elders, all of equal rank. **2** of the Presbyterian Church. —*n.* a member of the Presbyterian Church.

Pres·by·te·ri·an·ism (prez′bə tēr′ē ən iz′əm or pres′bə tēr′ē ən iz′əm) *n.* **1** the system of church government by elders, all (including ministers) of equal rank. **2** the beliefs of Presbyterian churches.

pres·by·ter·y (prez′bə ter′ē or pres′bə ter′ē) *n.* **-ter·ies.** **1** in the Presbyterian Church, the United Church of Canada, etc.: **a** a meeting or court of all the ministers and certain of the elders within a district. **b** a district under the jurisdiction of such a meeting or court. **2** a part of a church set aside for the clergy.

pre·school (prē′skül′) *adj.* before the age of going to regular school.

pre·sci·ence (prē′shē əns or presh′ē əns) *n.* a knowledge of things before they exist or happen; foreknowledge; foresight. [< LL *praescientia* < L *praesciens*, ppr. of *praescire* foreknow < *prae-* before + *scire* know]

pre·sci·ent (prē′shē ənt or presh′ē ənt) *adj.* knowing beforehand; forseeing. —**pre′sci·ent·ly,** *adv.*

pre·scribe (pri skrīb′) *v.* **-scribed, -scrib·ing.** **1** order; direct: *Good citizens do what the laws prescribe.* **2** order as a remedy or treatment: *The doctor prescribed quinine.* **3** give medical advice. **4** in law: **a** make or become invalid or outlawed because of the passage of time. **b** claim a right or title to something by virtue of long use and enjoyment of it. [< L *praescribere* < *prae-* before + *scribere* write] —**Syn. 1** command, assign, set.

pre·script (*n.* prē′skript; *adj.* pri skript′ or prē′skript) *n.* rule; order; direction. —*adj.* prescribed. [< L *praescriptum*, neut. of *praescriptus*, ppr. of *praescribere.* See PRESCRIBE.]

pre·scrip·tion (pri skrip′shən) *n.* **1** an order; direction. **2** a written direction for preparing and using a medicine. **3** the medicine itself. **4** in law: **a** the possession or use of a thing long enough to give one a right or title to it. **b** the right or title thus established.

pre·scrip·tive (pri skrip′tiv) *adj.* **1** prescribing. **2** depending on legal prescription. **3** established by long use or custom. —**pre·script′ive·ly,** *adv.* —**pre·script′ive·ness,** *n.*

pres·ence (prez′əns) *n.* **1** the fact or condition of being present in a place: *I knew of his presence in the other room.* **2** the place where a person is: *The messenger was admitted to my presence.* **3** a formal attendance upon a person of very high rank: *The knight retired from the royal presence.* **4** appearance; bearing: *a man of noble presence.* **5** something present, especially a ghost, spirit, etc. **6 in the presence of,** in the sight or company of. **7 saving your presence,** with an apology for doing or saying this in your presence. [ME < OF < L *praesentia* < *praesens* present. See PRESENT[1].]

presence chamber the room in which a king or some very important person receives guests.

presence of mind the ability to think calmly and quickly when taken by surprise.

pres·ent[1] (prez′ənt) *adj.* **1** being in the place or thing in question; at hand, not absent: *Every member of the class was present.* **2** at this time; being or occurring now: *present prices.* **3** in grammar, denoting action now going on or a state now existing. *Go* is a present tense; *went* is a past tense.
—*n.* **1** the present time: *At present people need courage.* **2** in grammar, the present tense or a verb form in that tense. **3 by these presents,** by these words; by this document. [ME < OF < L *praesens, -entis* < *prae-* before + *esse* be] —**Syn.** *adj.* **2** See **current.**

pre·sent[2] (*v.* pri zent′; *n.* prez′ənt) *v.* **1** give: *They presented flowers to their teacher.* **2** offer; offer formally: *The servant presented the sandwiches to each guest.* **3** bring before the mind; offer for consideration: *He presented reasons for his action.* **4** offer to view or notice: *The new City Hall presents a fine appearance.* **5** bring before the public: *Our school presented a play.* **6** set forth in words. **7** hand in; send in: *The grocer presented his bill.* **8** introduce (one person to another); introduce formally: *Miss Smith, may I present Mr. Brown?* **9** bring before a person of high rank: *She was presented to the Governor General.* **10** direct; point; turn: *The soldier presented his face to the enemy.* **11 present arms,** salute by bringing a rifle, etc. to a vertical position in front of one's body. **12 present with,** furnish with (something as a gift).
—*n.* something given; gift. [ME < OF < L *praesentare* < *praesens, -entis* present. See PRESENT[1].] —**Syn.** *v.* **1** See **give. 8** See **introduce.** *-n.* See **gift.**

pre·sent·a·ble (pri zen′tə bəl) *adj.* **1** fit to be seen. **2** suitable in appearance, dress, manners, etc. for being introduced into society or company. **3** suitable to be offered or given. —**pre·sent′a·bly,** *adv.*

pres·en·ta·tion (prez′ən tā′shən) *n.* **1** a giving: *the presentation of a gift.* **2** a gift. **3** a proposal for consideration. **4** an offering to be seen; showing: *the presentation of a play.* **5** a formal introduction, especially to somebody of high rank: *the presentation of a lady to the Queen.* **6** a function at which a gift is presented: *A presentation was held when the manager retired.*

pres·ent-day (prez′ənt dā′) *adj.* of the present time.

pre·sen·ti·ment (pri zen′tə mənt) *n.* a feeling or impression that something is about to happen; vague sense of approaching misfortune; foreboding. [< MF *presentiment*, ult. < L *prae-* before + *sentire* sense]

pres·ent·ly (prez′ənt lē) *adv.* **1** before long; soon: *The clock will strike presently.* **2** at once. **3** at present; now: *The Prime Minister is presently in Ottawa.* —**Syn. 1** See **immediately.**

pre·sent·ment (pri zent′mənt) *n.* **1** a bringing forward; offering to be considered. **2** a showing; offering to be seen. **3** a representation on the stage or by a portrait. **4** a statement by a grand jury of an offence from their own knowledge. [ME < OF *presentement* < *presenter* < L *praesentare.* See PRESENT[2].]

present participle a participle that expresses time that is now. In "Singing merrily, we turn our steps toward home," *singing* is a present participle. *Abbrev.*: ppr. or p.pr. ☛ See **participle** for usage note.

present tense a tense that expresses time that is now.

pres·er·va·tion (prez′ər vā′shən) *n.* **1** the act of preserving; keeping safe. **2** the state of being preserved; being kept safe.

pre·serv·a·tive (pri zėr′və tiv) *n.* any substance that will prevent decay or injury. Paint is a preservative for wood surfaces. Salt is a preservative for meat. —*adj.* that preserves.

pre·serve (pri zėrv′) *v.* **-served, -serv·ing,** *n.* —*v.* **1** keep from harm or change; keep safe; protect. **2** keep up; maintain. **3** keep from spoiling: *Ice helps to preserve food.* **4** prepare (food) to keep it from spoiling. Boiling with sugar, salting, smoking, and pickling are different ways of preserving food.
—*n.* **1** Usually, **preserves,** *pl.* fruit cooked with sugar and sealed from the air. **2** a place where wild animals or fish are protected; provincial park. [ME < OF < LL *praeservare* < L *prae-* before + *servare* keep] —**pre·serv′a·ble,** *adj.* —**Syn.** *v.* **1** save, shield, guard.

pre·serv·er (pri zėr′vər) *n.* a person or thing that

hat, āge, cãre, fär; let, ēqual, tėrm; it, īce
hot, ōpen, ôrder; oil, out; cup, pu̇t, rüle, ūse
əbove, takən, pencəl, lemən, circəs
ch, child; ng, long; sh, ship
th, thin; ꜰʜ, then; zh, measure

preserves or protects from danger: *a life preserver.*

pre·set (prē set′) *v.* **-set, -set·ting.** set beforehand.

pre·side (pri zīd′) *v.* **-sid·ed, -sid·ing. 1** hold the place of authority; have charge of a meeting. **2** have authority; have control: *Father usually presides over the family.* [< L *praesidere* < *prae-* before + *sedere* sit] **—pre·sid′er,** *n.*

pres·i·den·cy (prez′ə dən sē) *n.* **-cies. 1** the office of president. **2** the time during which a president is in office. **3 Presidency,** the office or time of office of a President.

pres·i·dent (prez′ə dənt) *n.* **1** the chief officer of a company, college, society, club, etc. **2 President,** the highest executive officer of the United States. **3** Often, **President.** the highest executive officer of a republic. [< L *praesidens, -entis* presiding, ppr. of *praesidere.* See PRESIDE.]

pres·i·dent-e·lect (prez′ə dənt i lekt′) *n.* a president elected but not yet inaugurated.

pres·i·den·tial (prez′ə den′shəl) *adj.* of, having to do with, or belonging to a president or presidency. **—pres′i·den′tial·ly,** *adv.*

pre·sid·i·um (pri sid′ē əm) *n.* in the Soviet Union: **1** a governmental administrative committee. **2 Presidium,** the chief executive and policy-making committee. [< L *praesidium* a presiding over < *praesidere.* See PRESIDE.]

press[1] (pres) *v.* **1** use force or weight steadily against; push with steady force: *Press the button to ring the bell.* **2** squeeze; squeeze out. **3** use force steadily. **4** clasp; hug. **5** make smooth; flatten: *Press clothes with an iron.* **6** put a crease in: *My mother pressed my trousers.* **7** push forward; keep pushing: *The boy pressed on in spite of the wind.* **8** move by pushing steadily (up, down, against, etc.). **9** urge onward; cause to hurry. **10** crowd; throng. **11** urge (a person); keep asking; entreat: *Because it was so stormy, we pressed our guest to stay all night.* **12** lay stress upon; insist on. **13** constrain; compel; force. **14** urge for acceptance. **15** harass; oppress; trouble. **16** weigh heavily upon (the mind, a person, etc.). **17** demand prompt action; be urgent.
—n. **1** a pressing; pressure; push. **2** a pressed condition. **3** any of various instruments or machines for exerting pressure. **4** a machine for printing; printing press. **5** an establishment for printing books, etc. **6** the process or art of printing. **7 go to press,** begin to be printed. **8** newspapers and periodicals and those who write for them. **9** a notice given in newspapers or magazines: *The star actress got a good press for her performance.* **10** a crowd; throng. **11** a pressing forward or together; crowding. **12** urgency; hurry. **13** a cupboard for clothes, books, etc. **14** a crease. [ME < OF < L *pressare,* ult. < *premere* press] **—press′er,** *n.*

press[2] (pres) *v.* **1** force into service, usually naval or military. **2** seize and use. *—n.* **1** an impressment into service, usually naval or military. **2** an order for such impressment. [obs. *prest* < OF *prester* furnish, ult. < L *praesto* ready]

press agent an agent in charge of publicity for a person, organization, etc.

press box at a sports stadium, arena, race track, etc. an enclosed space set aside for reporters.

press conference a meeting for the giving of information to reporters by a person or group. Some press conferences are called to announce specific items of news, others to provide opportunities for reporters to question particular individuals.

press gang in former times, a group of men whose job it was to obtain men, often by force, for service in the navy or army.

press·ing (pres′ing) *adj.* requiring immediate action or attention; urgent. *—n.* the act of pressing or creasing with an iron: *That dress needs a good pressing.* **—press′ing·ly,** *adv.*

press·man (pres′mən) *n.* **-men** (-mən). a man who operates or has charge of a press, especially a printing press.

pres·sure (presh′ər) *n.* **1** the continued action of a weight or force: *The pressure of the wind filled the sails of the boat.* **2** the force per unit of area: *There is a pressure of 20 pounds to the inch in this tire.* **3** a state of trouble or strain: *the pressure of poverty.* **4** a compelling force or influence: *He changed his mind under pressure from others.* **5** the need for prompt or decisive action; urgency: *the pressure of business.* **6** electromotive force.
—v. force or urge by exerting pressure: *The opposition pressured the government into debating the matter.* [ME < OF < L *pressura,* ult. < *premere* press]

pressure cooker an airtight apparatus for cooking with steam under pressure.

pressure group any business, professional, or labor group that attempts to further its interests in the federal or provincial legislatures or elsewhere.

pressure ice ridges of ice formed by vast areas of sea ice pressing against each other.

pres·sur·ize (presh′ər īz′) *v.* **-ized, -iz·ing. 1** keep the atmospheric pressure inside of (the cabin of an airplane) at a normal level in spite of the altitude. **2** place under high pressure.

press·work (pres′wėrk′) *n.* **1** the working or management of a printing press. **2** the work done by a printing press.

Pres·ter John (pres′tər) a legendary Christian priest and king of the Middle Ages, said to have ruled a kingdom somewhere in Asia or Africa.

pres·ti·dig·i·ta·tion (pres′tə dij′ə tā′shən) *n.* sleight of hand. [< F]

pres·ti·dig·i·ta·tor (pres′tə dij′ə tā′tər) *n.* a man skilled in sleight of hand. [< F < L *praestigiator* juggler; form influenced by F *preste* quick and L *digitus* finger]

pres·tige (pres tēzh′ or pres tēj′) *n.* reputation, influence, or distinction based on what is known of one's abilities, achievements, opportunities, associations, etc. [< F *prestige* magic spell, ult. < L *praestigiae* tricks]

pres·ti·gious (pres tij′əs) *adj.* having or conferring prestige. **—pres·ti′gious·ly,** *adv.*

pres·tis·si·mo (pres tis′ə mō′) in music: *—adv.* very quickly. *—adj.* very quick.*—n.* a very quick movement or passage; composition to be played or sung at this tempo. [< Ital. *prestissimo,* superlative of *presto* quick, quickly]

pres·to (pres′tō) *adv. adj. n.* **-tos.** *—adv.* quickly. *—adj.* quick. *—n.* a quick movement or passage; composition to be played or sung at this tempo. [< Ital. *presto,* ult. < L *praesto,* adv., ready]

pre·sum·a·ble (pri züm′ə bəl or pri zūm′ə bəl) *adj.* that can be presumed or taken for granted; probable; likely.

pre·sum·a·bly (pri züm′ə blē or pri zūm′ə blē) *adv.* as may reasonably be supposed; probably.

pre·sume (pri züm′ or pri zūm′) *v.* **-sumed, -sum·ing. 1** take for granted without proving; suppose: *The law presumes innocence until guilt is proved.* **2** take upon oneself; venture; dare: *May I presume to tell you what to do?* **3** take an unfair advantage (used with *on* or *upon*): *Don't presume on a person's good nature by borrowing from him every week.* [ME < OF < L *praesumere* take for granted < *prae-* before + *sumere* take] **—pre·sum′er,** *n.* **—pre·sum′ing·ly,** *adv.*

pre·sum·ed·ly (pri züm′id lē or pri züm′id lē) *adv.* as is or may be supposed.

pre·sump·tion (pri zump′shən) *n.* **1** the act of presuming. **2** something taken for granted; a conclusion based on good evidence: *Since he had the stolen jewels, the presumption was that he was the thief.* **3** a cause or reason for presuming; probability. **4** unpleasant boldness: *It is presumption to ask for a four-day week.* [ME < OF < L *praesumptio, -onis* < *praesumere.* See PRESUME.] **—Syn. 4** forwardness, effrontery.

pre·sump·tive (pri zump′tiv) *adj.* **1** based on likelihood; presumed: *heir presumptive.* **2** giving ground for presumption or belief: *The man's running away was regarded as presumptive evidence of his guilt.*

pre·sump·tive·ly (pri zump′tiv lē) *adv.* by presumption; presumably.

pre·sump·tu·ous (pri zump′chü əs) *adj.* acting without permission or right; too bold; forward. [ME < OF < LL *praesumptuosus* < L *praesumptio* audacity (< *praesumere.* See PRESUME.), but modelled on *sumptuosus* expensive < *sumptus* expense] **—pre·sump′tu·ous·ly,** *adv.* **—pre·sump′tu·ous·ness,** *n.* **—Syn.** overbold, impudent, arrogant.

pre·sup·pose (prē′sə pōz′) *v.* **-posed, -pos·ing. 1** take for granted in advance; assume beforehand: *Let us presuppose that he wants more money.* **2** require as a necessary condition; imply: *A fight presupposes fighters.*

pre·sup·po·si·tion (prē′sup ə zish′ən) *n.* **1** the act of presupposing. **2** a thing presupposed.

pret. preterite.

pre·tence or **pre·tense** (pri tens′ or prē′tens) *n.* **1** a false appearance: *Under pretence of picking up the handkerchief, she took the money.* **2** a false claim: *The girls made a pretence of knowing the answer.* **3** a claim. **4** a pretending; make-belief: *His anger was all pretence.* **5** a showing off; display: *Her manner is free from pretence.* **6** anything done to show off. [ME < AF *pretense,* ult. < L *praetendere.* See PRETEND.] **—Syn. 5** ostentation.

pre·tend (pri tend′) *v.* **1** make believe. **2** claim falsely: *She pretends to like you, but talks about you behind your back.* **3** claim falsely to have: *She pretended illness.* **4** claim: *I don't pretend to be a musician.* **5** lay claim: *James Stuart pretended to the English throne.* **6** venture; attempt; presume: *I cannot pretend to judge between them.* [ME < OF < L *praetendere* < *prae-* before + *tendere* stretch]
Syn. 2, 3 Pretend, affect, assume = claim falsely to have or be something. **Pretend** = make out that one has or feels something and try to act as if he did: *She pretended ignorance of the whole affair.* **Affect** = put on some characteristic or feeling, for some intended effect: *When she applied for a job, she affected simplicity.* **Assume** = put on the appearance of feeling something, to cover up one's real feelings: *She assumed a look of sorrow.*

pre·tend·ed (pri ten′did) *adj.* claimed falsely; asserted falsely. **—pre·tend′ed·ly,** *adv.*

pre·tend·er (pri ten′dər) *n.* **1** a person who pretends. **2** a person who makes claims to a throne without just right.

pre·tense (pri tens′ or prē′tens) *n.* pretence.

pre·ten·sion (pri ten′shən) *n.* **1** a claim: *The young prince has pretensions to the throne.* **2** a putting forward of a claim. **3** a pretentious display.

pre·ten·tious (pri ten′shəs) *adj.* **1** making claims to excellence or importance: *a pretentious person, book, or speech.* **2** doing things for show or to make a fine appearance; showy: *a pretentious style of entertaining guests.* [< F *prétentieux,* ult. < L *praetendere.* See PRETEND.] **—pre·ten′tious·ly,** *adv.* **—pre·ten′tious·ness,** *n.*

pret·er·ite or **pret·er·it** (pret′ər it) *n.* a verb form that expresses occurrence in the past; the past tense. *Obeyed* is the preterite of *obey*; *spoke,* of *speak*; and *saw,* of *see.* *—adj.* expressing past time. [ME < OF < L *praeteritus,* ult. < *praeter-* past + *ire* go]

pre·ter·mit (prē′tər mit′) *v.* **-mit·ted, -mit·ting. 1** leave out; omit. **2** let pass without notice. [< L *praetermittere* < *praeter-* past + *mittere* let go]

pre·ter·nat·u·ral (prē′tər nach′ə rəl or -nach′rəl) *adj.* **1** out of the ordinary course of nature; abnormal. **2** due to something above or beyond nature; supernatural. [< Med.L *praeternaturalis,* ult. < L *praeter-* beyond + *natura* nature] **—pre′ter·nat′u·ral·ly,** *adv.*

pre·text (prē′tekst) *n.* a false reason concealing the real reason; pretence; excuse: *He used his sore finger as a pretext for not going to school.* [< L *praetextus,* ult. < *prae-* in front + *texere* weave]

pre·tor (prē′tər or prē′tôr) *n.* praetor.

pret·ti·fy (prit′ə fī′) *v.* **-fied, -fy·ing.** make artificially pretty.

pret·ty (prit′ē) *adj.* **-ti·er, -ti·est,** *n.* **-ties,** *adv. v.* *—adj.* **1** attractive or pleasing. **2** not at all pleasing: *a pretty mess.* **3** too dainty or delicate. **4** *Archaic.* brave; bold; fine. **5** *Informal.* considerable in amount or extent. **6 sitting pretty,** *Slang.* well off.
—n. a pretty person or thing.
—adv. fairly; rather: *It is pretty late.*
—v. **pretty up,** *Informal.* make pretty. [OE *prættig* cunning < *prætt* trick] **—pret′ti·ly,** *adv.* **—pret′ti·ness,** *n.*

pretty penny *Informal.* a large sum of money.

pret·zel (pret′səl) *n.* a hard biscuit made in the shape of a knot and salted on the outside. [< G *Brezel* < Med.L *bracellus* bracelet, ult. < Gk. *brachion* arm]

pre·vail (pri vāl′) *v.* **1** exist in many places; be in general use: *That custom still prevails.* **2** be the most usual or strongest: *Sadness prevailed in our minds.* **3** be the stronger; win the victory; succeed: *The knights prevailed against their foe.* **4** be effective. **5 prevail on, upon,** or **with,** persuade. [< L *praevalere* < *prae-* before + *valere* have power]

pre·vail·ing (pri vāl′ing) *adj.* **1** that prevails; having superior force or influence; victorious. **2** in general use; most common. **—pre·vail′ing·ly,** *adv.* **—Syn. 2** See **current.**

prev·a·lence (prev′ə ləns) *n.* widespread occurrence; general use: *the prevalence of complaints about the weather.*

prev·a·lent (prev′ə lənt) *adj.* **1** widespread; general; common: *Colds are prevalent in the winter.* **2** predominant; victorious. [< L *praevalens, -entis,* ppr. of *praevalere* prevail. See PREVAIL.] **—Syn.** usual, ordinary, prevailing.

pre·var·i·cate (pri var′ə kāt′) *v.* **-cat·ed, -cat·ing.** turn aside from the truth in speech or act; lie. [< L *praevaricari* make a sham accusation, ult. < *prae-* before + *varicus* straddling < *varus* crooked] **—pre·var′i·ca′tor,** *n.*

pre·var·i·ca·tion (pri var′ə kā′shən) *n.* the act of prevaricating; departure from the truth.

pre·vent (pri vent′) *v.* **1** keep (*from*): *Illness prevented him from doing his work.* **2** keep from happening: *Rain prevented the game.* **3** hinder. [< L *praeventus,* pp. of *praevenire* < *prae-* before + *venire* come] **—pre·vent′er,** *n.*
Syn. Prevent, hinder, impede = get in the way of action or progress. **Prevent** = keep a person or thing from doing something or making progress, acting or setting up an obstacle to stop him or it: *Business prevented his going.* **Hinder** = hold back, so that making, starting, going ahead, or finishing is late, difficult, or impossible: *An unbalanced diet hinders growth.* **Impede** = slow up movement and progress by putting something binding, fouling, etc. on or in the way: *Mud impedes the advance of troops.*

pre·vent·a·ble (pri ven′tə bəl) *adj.* that can be prevented.

pre·vent·a·tive (pri ven′tə tiv) *adj. n.* preventive.

pre·vent·i·ble (pri ven′tə bəl) *adj.* preventable.

pre·ven·tion (pri ven′shən) *n.* **1** a preventing: *the prevention of fire.* **2** something that prevents.

pre·ven·tive (pri ven′tiv) *adj.* that prevents: *preventive measures against disease.* *—n.* something that prevents: *Vaccination is a preventive against smallpox.* **—pre·ven′tive·ly,** *adv.* **—pre·ven′tive·ness,** *n.*

preventive war an aggressive war waged against another nation, supposedly started in anticipation of attack by that nation.

pre·view (prē′vū′) *n.* **1** a previous view, inspection, survey, etc. **2** the advance showing of scenes from a play, motion picture, etc. *—v.* view beforehand.

pre·vi·ous (prē′vē əs) *adj.* **1** coming or going before; that came before; earlier. **2** *Informal.* quick. **3 previous to,** before: *Previous to her departure she gave a party.* **4** premature: *His remarks were considered previous.* [< L *praevius* leading the way < *prae-* before + *via* road]
Syn. 1 Previous, preceding, prior = coming before something. **Previous** = earlier in time, made or done sometime earlier or being the last one before the present: *I cannot go, for I have a previous engagement* (made before). **Preceding** = coming immediately before in order of time or in place: *Check the preceding statement.* **Prior** adds to *previous* the idea of coming first in order of importance: *I have a prior engagement* (one that has first call).

pre·vi·ous·ly (prē′vē əs lē) *adv.* at a previous time: *I had not met him previously.*

previous question the question whether a vote shall be taken on the main question without further debate.

pre·vi·sion (prē vizh′ən) *n.* **1** foresight; foreknowledge.

2 a prophetic vision or perception: *prevision of trouble.*

pre·vi·sion·al (prē vizh′ən əl) *adj.* foreseeing; forecasting; of or having to do with prevision.

pre·war (prē′wôr′) *adj.* before the war.

prex·y (prek′sē) *n. Slang.* president, especially of a college or university.

prey (prā) *n.* **1** an animal hunted or seized for food, especially by another animal: *Mice and birds are the prey of cats.* **2** a person or thing injured; victim: *be a prey to fear or disease.* **3 birds of prey** and **beasts of prey,** birds and animals, such as hawks and lions, that hunt and kill other animals for food. —*v.* **prey on** or **upon, a** hunt or kill for food: *Cats prey on mice.* **b** be a strain upon; injure; irritate. **c** rob; plunder. **d** hunt. [ME < OF < L *praeda*]

price (prīs) *n. v.* **priced, pric·ing.** —*n.* **1** the amount for which a thing is sold or can be bought; cost to the buyer. **2** a reward offered for the capture of a person alive or dead. **3** what must be given, done, undergone, etc. to obtain a thing: *We paid a heavy price for the victory, for we lost ten thousand soldiers.* **4** value; worth. **5 at any price,** at any cost, no matter how great. **6 beyond** or **without price,** so valuable that it cannot be bought.
—*v.* **1** put a price on; set the price of. **2** *Informal.* ask the price of; find out the price of: *price a rug.* [ME < OF *pris* < L *pretium*]
Syn. *n.* **1 Price, charge, cost** = the amount asked or paid for something. **Price** = the amount of money for which something is sold, but especially suggests what the seller asks for things: *The price of meat is high now.* **Charge** = the amount asked, especially for services: *There is no charge for delivery.* **Cost** = the amount paid for goods or services or whatever is given or spent, such as effort, to get anything: *The cost of the house was high.*

price·less (prīs′lis) *adj.* beyond price; extremely valuable: *a priceless painting.* —**price′less·ness,** *n.*

price support a system by which the government guarantees a given price to the farmer for his produce.

price tag 1 a ticket or tag on merchandise showing its price. **2** *Informal.* an estimated value, price, or cost.

price war a system in which sellers try to capture the market by repeatedly undercutting the prices of competitors.

prick (prik) *n.* **1** a sharp point. **2** a little hole or mark made by a sharp point. **3** a pricking. **4** a sharp pain. **5 kick against the pricks,** make useless resistance that only hurts oneself.
—*v.* **1** make a little hole in with a sharp point. **2** mark with a sharp point. **3** cause sharp pain to. **4** cause or feel a sharp pain. **5** raise or erect: *The dog pricked his ears at the sound of footsteps.* **6** *Archaic.* spur; urge on. **7** *Archaic.* ride fast. **8 prick up,** point upward. **9 prick up the ears, a** point the ears upward. **b** give sudden attention. **c** listen carefully. [OE *prica* point] —**prick′er,** *n.* —**Syn.** *v.* **1** puncture, pierce. **4** sting.

prick·le (prik′əl) *n. v.* **-led, -ling.** —*n.* **1** a small, sharp point; thorn; spine. **2** a prickly or smarting sensation.
—*v.* **1** feel a prickly or smarting sensation. **2** cause such a sensation in. [OE *pricel* < *prica* point]

prick·ly (prik′lē) *adj.* **-li·er, -li·est. 1** having many sharp points like thorns: *a prickly rosebush, the prickly porcupine.* **2** sharp and stinging; itching: *Heat sometimes causes a prickly rash on the skin.* **3** hard to deal with; likely to raise problems, controversy, etc.: *a prickly question.* **4** quick to take offence; easily angered: *He is a prickly individual.* —**prick′li·ness,** *n.*

prickly heat a red, itching rash on the skin caused by inflammation of the sweat glands.

prickly pear 1 a pear-shaped, edible fruit of a certain kind of cactus. **2** the plant that it grows on.

pride (prīd) *n. v.* **prid·ed, prid·ing.** —*n.* **1** a high opinion of one's own worth or possessions. **2** pleasure or satisfaction in something concerned with oneself. **3** something that one is proud of. **4** too high an opinion of oneself. **5** an acting as if better than others; scorn of others. **6** the best part; most flourishing period: *in the pride of manhood.* **7** of lions, a group. —*v.* **pride oneself on,** be proud of. [OE *prȳde* < *prūd* proud]
Syn. *n.* **1 Pride, conceit** = a high opinion of oneself. **Pride** = a feeling of pleased satisfaction with what one is, has, or has done, and suggests either proper self-respect and personal dignity because of real worth or excessive self-love and arrogance because of imagined superiority: *A man without pride deserves contempt.*

hat, āge, cãre, fär; let, ēqual, tėrm; it, īce
hot, ōpen, ôrder; oil, out; cup, pu̇t, rüle, ūse
əbove, takən, pencəl, lemən, circəs
ch, child; ng, long; sh, ship
th, thin; ᴛʜ, then; zh, measure

Conceit = much too high an opinion of one's own abilities and accomplishments, and often suggests an unpleasantly assertive manner: *Conceit makes the criminal think he is too clever to be caught.* **4** vanity, arrogance.

pride·ful (prīd′fəl) *adj.* proud. —**pride′ful·ly,** *adv.*

prie-dieu (prē dyœ′) *n. French.* a small desk for a prayer book, etc. with a piece on which to kneel. [< F *prie-dieu,* literally, pray God]

pries (prīz) *n.* pl. of **pry**[2].

priest (prēst) *n.* **1** a special servant of a god: *a priest of Apollo.* **2** a clergyman or minister of certain Christian churches. **3** a clergyman authorized to administer the sacraments and pronounce absolution. **4** a minister of any religion: *a Buddhist priest.* [OE *prēost,* ult. < L *presbyter.* Doublet of PRESBYTER.]

priest·ess (prēs′tis) *n.* a woman priest: *a priestess of the goddess Diana.*

priest·hood (prēst′hu̇d) *n.* **1** the position or rank of priest. **2** priests as a group.

priest·ly (prēst′lē) *adj.* **-li·er, -li·est. 1** of or having to do with a priest: *priestly duties.* **2** like a priest; suitable to a priest. —**priest′li·ness,** *n.*

prig (prig) *n.* a person who is too affected in speech and manners, and prides himself on being better than others. [origin uncertain]

prig·ger·y (prig′ər ē) *n.* **-ger·ies.** the conduct or character of a prig.

prig·gish (prig′ish) *adj.* too particular about doing right in things that show outwardly; priding oneself on being better than others. —**prig′gish·ly,** *adv.* —**prig′gish·ness,** *n.*

prim (prim) *adj.* **prim·mer, prim·mest.** stiffly precise, neat, proper, or formal. [< MF *prim* fine, delicate < L *primus* first. Doublet of PRIME[1], adj.] —**prim′ly,** *adv.* —**prim′ness,** *n.*

pri·ma·cy (prī′mə sē) *n.* **-cies. 1** the condition of being first in order, rank, importance, etc. **2** the position or rank of a primate (def. 1). **3** in the Roman Catholic Church, the supreme power of the Pope. [ME < OF < Med.L *primatia* < L *primas, -atis* of first rank. See PRIMATE.]

pri·ma don·na (prē′mə don′ə) *pl.* **pri·ma don·nas. 1** the principal woman singer in an opera. **2** a temperamental person. [< Ital. *prima donna* first lady]

prim. 1 primitive. **2** primary.

pri·ma fa·ci·e (prī′mə fā′shē ē or fā′shē; *Latin,* prē′mä fä′kē ā) at first view; before investigation. [< L *prima facie,* abl. of *prima facies* first appearance]

pri·mal (prī′məl) *adj.* **1** of early times; first; primeval. **2** chief; fundamental. [< Med.L *primalis* < L *primus* first] —**pri′mal·ly,** *adv.*

pri·ma·ri·ly (prī′mer′ə lē, prī′mə rə lē, or prī mãr′ə lē) *adv.* **1** chiefly; principally: *Napoleon was primarily a general.* **2** at first; originally.

pri·ma·ry (prī′mer′ē or prī′mə rē) *adj. n.* **-ries.** —*adj.* **1** first in time; first in order. **2** from which others have come; original; fundamental. **3** first in importance; chief. **4** in electricity, of or having to do with the inducing circuit, coil, or current in an induction coil or the like. **5** of or having to do with one of the large flight feathers growing on the distal section of a bird's wing. **6** utilizing the crude products of nature as raw materials: *a primary industry.* **7** in education, of or having to do with grades 1, 2, and 3: *primary teachers.*
—*n.* **1** anything that is first in order, rank, or importance. **2** a primary color. **3** a primary coil or circuit. **4** *U.S.* primary election. **5** a primary feather. [ME < L *primarius* first in rank < *primus* first] —**Syn.** *adj.* **1** See **elementary. 3** principal, prime.

primary accent primary stress.

primary colors or **colours** the pigments or colors that are, or are thought to be, fundamental. Red, yellow, and blue are the primary colors in pigments. In psychology, yellow, blue, green, and red are called primary colors.

primary election *U.S.* an election to choose candidates for office from a certain political party.

primary school the first three or four grades of the elementary school.

primary stress **1** the strongest stress or accent in the pronunciation of a word. **2** a mark, such as (ʹ) used to show where this stress falls.

pri·mate (prīʹmit or prīʹmāt) *n.* **1** an archbishop or bishop ranking above all other bishops in a country or church province. **2** any of the highest order of mammals, including human beings, apes, and monkeys. [ME < OF < L *primas, -atis* of first rank < *primus* first]

prime[1] (prīm) *adj.* **1** first in rank; chief: *His prime object was to lower the tax rate.* **2** first in time or order; fundamental. **3** first in quality; first-rate; excellent: *prime ribs of beef.* **4** in mathematics: **a** that cannot be divided without a remainder by any whole number except itself and 1. Seven is a prime number. **b** having no common divisor but 1. 2 is prime to 9. [< L *primus* first. Doublet of PRIM.]
—*n.* **1** the best time; best condition: *A man of forty is in the prime of life.* **2** the best part. **3** the first part; beginning. **4** springtime. **5** early manhood or womanhood; youth. **6** the second of the seven canonical hours, or the service for it, originally fixed for the first hour of the day (beginning at 6 a.m.). **7** a prime number. **8 a** one of the sixty minutes in a degree. **b** the mark (ʹ) indicating such a part. **9** in music: **a** the tonic, or keynote. **b** the interval between two tones of the same or different quality but identical pitch; unison. **c** a tone sung or played in unison with another. [OE *prīm* (def. 6), ult. < L *primus* first]
—**primeʹness,** *n.*

prime[2] (prīm) *v.* **primed, prim·ing. 1** prepare by putting something in or on. **2** supply a gun with powder. **3** cover (a surface) with a first coat of paint or oil so that paint will not soak in. **4** equip (a person) with information, words, etc. **5** pour water into (a pump) to start action. [probably < *prime*[1]]

prime meridian the meridian from which the longitude east and west is measured. It passes through Greenwich, England, and its longitude is 0°.

prime minister in certain governments, the chief minister, usually the leader of the majority party in parliament; head of the cabinet: *The Prime Minister of Canada is the first minister of the federal government at Ottawa. Abbrev.*: P.M.

prime number a number that cannot be divided without a remainder by any whole number except itself and 1. *Examples*: 2, 3, 5, 7, 11, 13.

prim·er[1] (primʹər) *n.* **1** a first book in reading. **2** a beginner's book. **3 great primer,** 18-point type. **4 long primer,** 10-point type. [ME < Med.L *primarius* < L *primarius* first in rank. See PRIMARY.]

prim·er[2] (prīmʹər) *n.* **1** a person or thing that primes. **2** a cap or cylinder containing a little gunpowder, used for firing a charge of dynamite, etc. **3** a first coat of paint, etc. [< *prime*[2]]

pri·me·val (prī mēʹvəl) *adj.* **1** of or having to do with the first age or ages, especially of the world: *In its primeval state the earth was a fiery, glowing ball.* **2** ancient: *primeval forests untouched by the axe.* [< L *primaevus* early in life < *primus* first + *aevum* age] —**pri·meʹval·ly,** *adv.*

prim·ing (prīmʹing) *n.* **1** powder or other material used to set fire to an explosive. **2** a first coat of paint, sizing, etc.

prim·i·tive (primʹə tiv) *adj.* **1** of early times; of long ago: *Primitive people often lived in caves.* **2** first of the kind: *primitive Christians.* **3** very simple; such as people had early in human history; crude: *A primitive way of making fire is by rubbing two sticks together.* **4** original; primary. **5** in biology: **a** primordial. **b** representing or related to an ancient group or species. **6** old-fashioned: *The farmer drove a primitive buggy.*
—*n.* **1** an artist belonging to an early period, especially before the Renaissance. **2** an artist who imitates early painters, or who paints with directness and simplicity. **3** a picture by such an artist. **4** a person living in a primitive society or in primitive times. **5** an algebraic or geometrical expression from which another is derived. **6** a word from which another is derived. [ME < OF < L *primitivus*, ult. < *primus* first] —**primʹi·tive·ly,** *adv.* —**primʹi·tive·ness,** *n.*

pri·mo·gen·i·tor (prīʹmə jenʹə tər) *n.* **1** an ancestor; forefather. **2** the earliest ancestor. [< LL *primogenitor* < L *primus* first + *genitor* begetter]

pri·mo·gen·i·ture (prīʹmə jenʹə chər or prīʹmə jenʹə chürʹ) *n.* **1** the state, condition, or fact of being the first-born of the children of the same parents. **2** the right or principle of inheritance or succession by the first-born, especially the inheritance of a family estate by the eldest son. [< Med.L *primogenitura*, ult. < L *primus* first + *gignere* beget]

pri·mor·di·al (prī môrʹdē əl) *adj.* **1** existing at the very beginning; primitive. **2** in biology, formed first in the course of development: *primordial leaves.* **3** original; elementary: *primordial laws.* [ME < LL *primordialis* < L *primordium* beginning]

pri·mor·di·al·ly (prī môrʹdē əl ē) *adv.* under original conditions; at the beginning.

primp (primp) *v.* **1** dress (oneself) for show; prink. **2** dress carefully. [apparently var. of *prim*, v. < *prim*, adj.]

prim·rose (primʹrōzʹ) *n.* **1** any of a large group of plants having flowers of various colors. The common primrose of Europe is pale yellow. **2** the flower of one of these plants. **3** a pale yellow. —*adj.* **1** pale-yellow. **2** of or like a primrose; gay; pleasant. [< Med.L *prima rosa* first rose]

primrose path a pleasant way; path of pleasure.

pri·mus (prīʹməs) *n.* a portable stove that burns vaporized oil. [< trademark]

prin. **1** principally. **2** principle.

prince (prins) *n.* **1** a male member of a royal family; especially, in Great Britain, a son or grandson of a king or queen. **2** a sovereign. **3** a ruler of a small state subordinate to a king or emperor. **4** in certain countries, a high-ranking member of the nobility. **5** the greatest or best of a group; chief. [ME < OF < L *princeps* chief < *primus* first + *capere* take]

Prince Albert a man's long, double-breasted coat.

prince consort a prince who is the husband of a queen or empress ruling in her own right.

prince·dom (prinsʹdəm) *n.* **1** the territory ruled by a prince. **2** the position, rank, or dignity of a prince.

prince·ling (prinsʹling) *n.* a young, little, or petty prince.

prince·ly (prinsʹlē) *adj.* **-li·er, -li·est. 1** of a prince or his rank; royal. **2** like a prince; noble. **3** fit for a prince; magnificent: *He earns a princely salary.* —**princeʹli·ness,** *n.* —**Syn. 3** sumptuous.

Prince of Darkness the Devil; Satan.

prince of the blood a prince of a royal family.

Prince of Wales in the United Kingdom, a title conferred on the eldest son, or heir apparent, of the sovereign.

prince royal the oldest son of a king or queen.

prin·cess (prinʹsis or prinʹses) *n.* **1** a daughter of a king or queen or of a king's or queen's son. **2** the wife or widow of a prince. **3** a woman having the same rank as a prince. [< F *princesse*, fem. of *prince* prince]

prin·cesse or **prin·cess** (prin sesʹ, prinʹses, or prinʹsis) *adj.* of women's one-piece dresses, having an unbroken line from the shoulder to the hem, a fitted top, and a gently flaring skirt. [< F *princesse* princess]

princess royal the oldest daughter of a king or queen.

prin·ci·pal (prinʹsə pəl) *adj.* most important; main; chief: *St. John's is the principal city of Newfoundland.*
—*n.* **1** a chief person; one who gives orders. **2** the head, or one of the heads, of a school, college, etc. **3** a sum of money on which interest is paid. **4** the money or property from which income is received. **5** a person who hires another person to act for him. **6** a person directly responsible for a crime. **7** a person responsible for the

payment of a debt that another person has endorsed or guaranteed. **8** a sum of money that has been borrowed, as opposed to the interest payable on it. **9** a person who employs an agent. [< L *principalis* < *princeps* chief. See PRINCE.] —**Syn.** *adj.* cardinal, foremost, prime, leading.
☛ **principal, principle.** Do not confuse these two words of entirely different meaning. *Principal* as an adjective means "chief," and as a noun, "chief person." Associate this word with the head or chief person of a school—the principal. The noun *principal,* the sum of money on which interest is paid, was once *the principal sum. Principle* is used only as a noun, meaning a basic truth (*the principles of democracy*), or a rule of conduct (*Good character depends upon high principles*).

prin·ci·pal·i·ty (prin′sə pal′ə tē) *n.* **-ties. 1** a small state or country ruled by a prince. **2** a country from which a prince gets his title. **3** a supreme power.

prin·ci·pal·ly (prin′sə plē or prin′sə pəl ē) *adv.* for the most part; above all; chiefly. —**Syn.** See **especially.**

principal parts the main parts of a verb, from which the rest can be derived. In English the principal parts are the present infinitive, past tense or preterite, and past participle. *Examples*: go, went, gone; do, did, done; drive, drove, driven; push, pushed, pushed.

prin·ci·pal·ship (prin′sə pəl ship′) *n.* the position or office of a principal.

prin·ci·pate (prin′sə pāt′) *n.* **1** a chief place or authority. **2** a principality. [ME < L *principatus* < *princeps* chief. See PRINCE.]

prin·ci·ple (prin′sə pəl) *n.* **1** a truth that is a foundation for other truths: *the principles of democratic government.* **2** a fundamental belief: *religious principles.* **3** a rule of action or conduct: *I make it a principle to save some money each week.* **4** uprightness; honor: *Joseph Howe was a man of principle.* **5** a rule of science explaining how things act: *the principle by which a machine works.* **6** the method of operation. **7** a source; origin; first cause or force. **8** one of the elements that compose a substance, especially one that gives some special quality or effect: *the bitter principle in a drug.* **9 in principle,** as regards the general truth or rule. **10 on principle, a** according to a certain principle. **b** for reasons of right conduct. [ME < OF < L *principium* < *princeps* chief. See PRINCE.]
☛ See **principal** for usage note.

prink (pringk) *v.* **1** dress (oneself) for show. **2** fuss over one's appearance. [origin uncertain] —**prink′er,** *n.*

print (print) *v.* **1** use type, blocks, plates, etc. and ink or dye to stamp (words, pictures, or designs) on paper or some other surface. **2** stamp letters, words, or designs on with type, etc. **3** cause to be printed; publish. **4** produce books, newspapers, etc. by printing press. **5** make (words or letters) the way they look in print instead of in writing. **6** make with such letters: *Print your name clearly.* **7** stamp with designs, patterns, pictures, etc.: *Machines print wallpaper, cloth, etc.* **8** stamp; produce (marks or figures) by pressure; impress. **9** fix: *The scene is printed on my memory.* **10** take an impression from type, etc. **11** produce a photograph by transmission of light through (a negative). [< n.]
—*n.* **1** printed words, letters, etc.: *This book has clear print.* **2** a printed condition. **3 in print, a** in printed form. **b** of books, etc., still available for purchase from the publisher. **4 out of print,** no longer sold by the publisher. **5** a printed publication; newspaper or magazine. **6** an edition or impression of a book, etc. made at one time. **7** a picture or design printed from a block or plate. **8** cloth with a pattern printed on it. **9** a mark made by pressing or stamping: *the print of a foot.* **10** something that prints; stamp; die. **11** something that has been marked or shaped by pressing or stamping. **12** a photograph produced from a negative. [ME < OF *priente,* ult. < L *premere* press]

print·a·ble (prin′tə bəl) *adj.* **1** capable of being printed. **2** capable of being printed from. **3** fit to be printed.

print·er (prin′tər) *n.* a person whose business or work is printing or setting type.

printer's devil formerly, a young helper or errand boy in a printing shop.

print·ing (prin′ting) *n.* **1** the producing of books, newspapers, etc. by stamping in ink from plates or movable types. **2** printed words, letters, etc. **3** all the copies printed at one time. **4** letters made like those in print.

hat, āge, cãre, fär; let, ēqual, tėrm; it, īce
hot, ōpen, ôrder; oil, out; cup, pu̇t, rüle, ūse
əbove, takən, pencəl, lemən, circəs
ch, child; ng, long; sh, ship
th, thin; ᴛʜ, then; zh, measure

printing press a machine for printing from types, plates, etc.

print-out (print′out′) *n.* **1** the printed output of an electronic computer. **2** the act of producing such an output.

pri·or[1] (prī′ər) *adj.* **1** coming before; earlier: *I can't go with you because I have a prior engagement.* **2 prior to,** coming before in time, order, or importance; earlier than; before. [< L] —**Syn. 1** See **previous.**

pri·or[2] (prī′ər) *n.* the head of a priory or monastery for men. Priors usually rank below abbots. [OE < Med.L *prior,* n. use of L *prior* prior[1]]

pri·or·ess (prī′ər is) *n.* the head of a convent or priory for women. Prioresses usually rank below abbesses.

pri·or·i·ty (prī ôr′ə tē) *n.* **-ties. 1** the fact of being earlier in time. **2** a coming before in order or importance: *Fire engines and ambulances have priority over other traffic.* **3** a governmental rating giving right of way to persons or things important in national defence, essential affairs of state, etc. in order of importance. **4** a preferential position allotted to any project, research, development, etc., giving it first claim to the necessary resources.

pri·o·ry (prī′ə rē) *n.* **-ries.** a monastery, convent, etc. governed by a prior or prioress. A priory is often, but not necessarily, dependent on an abbey. [ME < AF < Med.L *prioria* < *prior.* See PRIOR[2].]

prise (prīz) *v.* **prised, pris·ing.** prize[4].

prism (priz′əm) *n.* **1** a solid whose bases or ends have the same size and shape and are parallel to one another, and each of whose sides has two pairs of parallel edges. A six-sided pencil before it is sharpened has the shape of one kind of prism. **2** a transparent prism, usually with three-sided ends, that separates white light passing through it into the colors of the rainbow. [< LL < Gk. *prisma* < *priein* to saw]

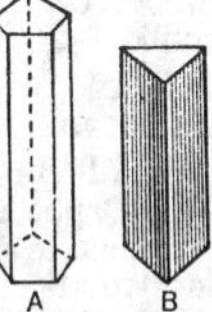

Prisms: A, def. 1; B, def. 2.

pris·mat·ic (priz mat′ik) *adj.* **1** of or like a prism. **2** formed by a transparent prism. **3** varied in color.

pris·mat·i·cal·ly (priz mat′ik lē) *adv.* by, or as if by, a prism.

prismatic colors colors formed when white light is passed through a prism; red, orange, yellow, green, blue, indigo, and violet; the colors of the rainbow.

pris·on (priz′ən) *n.* **1** a public building in which criminals are confined. **2** any place where a person is shut up against his will. —*v.* imprison. [ME < OF < L *pre-hensio, -onis* arrest < *prehendere* seize] —**pris′on·like′,** *adj.*

pris·on·er (priz′ən ər or priz′nər) *n.* **1** a person who is kept shut up against his will or who is not free to move. **2** a person arrested and held for trial. **3 prisoner of war,** a person taken by the enemy in war.

pris·sy (pris′ē) *adj.* **-si·er, -si·est. 1** too precise and fussy. **2** too easily shocked; overnice. [blend of *prim* and *sissy*]

pris·tine (pris′tēn, pris′tən, or pris′tīn) *adj.* as it was in its earliest time or state; original; primitive: *The colors of the paintings inside the pyramid had kept their pristine freshness.* [< L *pristinus*]

prith·ee (priᴛʜ′ē) *interj. Archaic.* I pray thee.

pri·va·cy (prī′və sē) *n.* **-cies. 1** the condition of being private; the state of being away from others. **2** an absence of publicity; secrecy: *He told me in strict privacy.*

pri·vate (prī′vit) *adj.* **1** not for the public; for just a few special people or for one: *a private car, a private house, a private letter.* **2** not public; individual; personal: *the private life of a king, my private opinion.* **3** secret; confidential: *a private drawer.* **4** secluded: *some private corner.* **5** having no public office: *a private citizen.*
—*n.* **1** in the army, a soldier of the lowest rank. **2 in**

private, **a** not publicly. **b** secretly. [ME < L *privatus* apart from the state, originally pp. of *privare* set apart, deprive < *privus* one's own. Doublet of PRIVY.] **—pri′vate·ly,** *adv.* **—pri′vate·ness,** *n.* **—Syn.** *adj.* **4** isolated, solitary.

private enterprise **1** the production and sale of goods, etc. by industries under private control and ownership rather than under government control or ownership. **2** a business operating under this system.

pri·va·teer (prī′və tēr′) *n.* **1** an armed ship owned by private persons and holding a government commission to attack and capture enemy ships. **2** the commander or one of the crew of a privateer. —*v.* cruise as a privateer.

pri·va·teers·man (prī′və tērz′mən) *n.* **-men** (-mən). an officer or sailor of a privateer.

private eye *Slang.* a person who is not a member of a public police force but engages in detective work on behalf of private individuals or corporations.

private member in Parliament, a member who is not in the cabinet or one of the leaders of the Opposition party; back-bencher.

private school a school that is under private or corporate management and is not part of the government-supported school system of a province, state, or country.

pri·va·tion (prī vā′shən) *n.* **1** the lack of the comforts or of the necessities of life: *Many children died because of privation during the war.* **2** the state of being deprived; loss; absence. [ME < L *privatio, -onis* < *privare* deprive. See PRIVATE.] **—Syn. 1** need, destitution.

priv·a·tive (priv′ə tiv) in grammar: —*adj.* expressing deprivation or denial of something. *Un-* is a privative prefix. *Unwise* means *not wise.* —*n.* a privative prefix or suffix. [< L *privativus* < *privare* deprive. See PRIVATE.]

priv·et (priv′it) *n.* any of several shrubs having small leaves, much used for hedges. [origin uncertain]

priv·i·lege (priv′ə lij or priv′lij) *n. v.* **-leged, -leg·ing.** —*n.* a special right, advantage, or favor. —*v.* give a privilege to. [ME < L *privilegium* law applying to one individual < *privus* individual + *lex* law]

Syn. *n.* **Privilege, prerogative** = a special right. **Privilege** = a special right given to a person as a favor or due him because of his position, age, sex, citizenship, etc. that often gives him an advantage over others: *Alumni have the privilege of buying football tickets at special rates.* **Prerogative** = a privilege or legal right belonging to a person by birth, office, position, etc., which always places him before or above others: *Changing her mind is often jokingly called a woman's prerogative.*

priv·i·ly (priv′ə lē) *adv.* in a private manner; secretly.

priv·y (priv′ē) *adj. n.* **priv·ies.** —*adj.* **1** private. **2** *Archaic.* secret; hidden. **3 privy to,** having secret or private knowledge of. —*n.* a small outhouse used as a toilet. [ME < OF *prive* < L *privatus.* Doublet of PRIVATE.]

privy council a group of personal advisers to a ruler.

Privy Council **1** in Canada, a body of advisers to the Governor General, that includes the ministers of the federal cabinet. **2** in the United Kingdom, a body of advisers to the Queen, including members of the cabinet and certain commonwealth leaders. *Abbrev.*: P.C.

Privy Councillor a member of the Privy Council: *Privy Councillors hold office for life. Abbrev.*: P.C.

privy seal in the United Kingdom, the seal affixed to grants, etc. that are afterwards to receive the great seal, and to documents that do not require the great seal.

prize[1] (prīz) *n.* **1** a reward won in a contest or competition: *Prizes will be given for the three best stories.* **2** a reward worth working for. —*adj.* **1** given as a prize. **2** that has won a prize. **3** worthy of a prize. [alteration of ME *pris* < OF *pris* (see PRICE) under the influence of *prise.* See PRIZE[2].] **—Syn.** *n.* **1** award, premium.

prize[2] (prīz) *n.* a thing or person that is taken or captured, especially an enemy's ship and its cargo taken at sea. [ME *prise* < OF *prise* seizure, alteration (under the influence of pp. *pris* seized) < VL *presa* < stem of L *prensus,* pp. of *pre(he)ndere* seize]

prize[3] (prīz) *v.* **prized, priz·ing.** **1** value highly: *She prizes her best china.* **2** estimate the value of. [ME < OF *prisier,* var. of *preisier* praise. See PRAISE.]

prize[4] (prīz) *v.* **prized, priz·ing.** raise or move by force; pry. Also, **prise.** [< obs. *prize* lever < OF *prise* a taking hold, grasp. See PRIZE[2].]

prize court an international court that makes decisions concerning ships and other property captured at sea during a war.

prize fight a boxing match fought for money.

prize fighter a person who fights boxing matches for money.

prize fighting the fighting of boxing matches for money.

prize money **1** money obtained by the sale of ships and other property captured at sea in the course of a war, sometimes divided among those who made the capture. **2** in races, contests, etc., the money offered as a prize.

prize ring **1** a square space enclosed by ropes, used for prize fights. **2** prize fighting.

pro[1] (prō) *adv. n.* **pros.** —*adv.* in favor of; for. —*n.* **1** reason in favor of. The pros and cons of a question are the arguments for and against it. **2** a person who votes for or favors something. **3** a vote in favor of something. [abstracted from *pro and con,* or independent use of *pro-*[1]]

pro[2] (prō) *n.* **pros,** *adj. Informal.* **1** a professional. **2** a prostitute.

pro-[1] *prefix.* **1** forward, as in *proceed, project.* **2** forth; out, as in *prolong, proclaim.* **3** on the side of; in favor of; in behalf of, as in *pro-British.* **4** in place of; acting as, as in *pronoun, proconsul.* [< L *pro,* prep.]

pro-[2] *prefix.* before; in front of, as in *prologue, proscenium.* [< Gk. *pro,* prep.]

pro·a (prō′ə) *n.* a swift Malay sailing boat built with one side flat and balanced by an outrigger. [< Malay *prau*]

prob·a·bil·i·ty (prob′ə bil′ə tē) *n.* **-ties.** **1** the quality or fact of being likely or probable; chance: *There is a probability that school will close a week earlier than usual.* **2 in all probability,** probably. **3** something likely to happen: *A storm is one of the probabilities for tomorrow.* **4** the ratio $\frac{p}{p+q}$, where p is the probable number of occurrences and q is the probable number of non-occurrences.

prob·a·ble (prob′ə bəl) *adj.* **1** likely to happen: *Cooler weather is probable after this shower.* **2** likely to be true: *Something he ate is the probable cause of his pain.* [ME < OF < L *probabilis* < *probare.* See PROVE.]

prob·a·bly (prob′ə blē) *adv.* more likely than not.

pro·bate (prō′bāt) *n. adj. v.* **-bat·ed, -bat·ing.** in law: —*n.* **1** the official proving of a will as genuine. **2** a true copy of a will with a certificate that it has been proved genuine. —*adj.* of or concerned with the probating of wills: *a probate court.* —*v.* prove by legal process the genuineness of (a will). [ME < L *probatum,* originally neut. pp. of *probare* make good < *probus* good]

pro·ba·tion (prō bā′shən) *n.* **1** a trial or testing of conduct, character, qualifications, etc.: *After a period of probation the novice became a nun.* **2** the time of trial or testing. **3** the system of letting young offenders against the law, or first offenders, go free without receiving the punishment which they are sentenced to unless there is a further offence. **4** the time that a first offender against the law is kept under supervision by a probation officer.

pro·ba·tion·al (prō bā′shən əl) *adj.* probationary.

pro·ba·tion·ar·y (prō bā′shən er′ē) *adj.* **1** of or having to do with probation. **2** on probation.

pro·ba·tion·er (prō bā′shən ər) *n.* a person who is on probation.

probation officer an officer appointed by a court of law to supervise offenders who have been placed on probation.

pro·ba·tive (prō′bə tiv) *adj.* **1** giving proof or evidence. **2** for a trial or test.

probe (prōb) *v.* **probed, prob·ing,** *n.* —*v.* **1** search into; examine thoroughly; investigate: *probe one's thoughts or feelings to find out why one acted as one did.* **2** search; penetrate: *probe into the causes of crime.* **3** examine with a probe. [< n.]
—*n.* **1** a thorough examination; investigation. **2** an investigation, usually by a legislative body, in an effort to discover evidences of law violation. **3** a slender instrument with a rounded end for exploring the depth or direction of a wound, a cavity in the body, etc. **4** an

instrument, often electronic, used to test or explore. **5** a rocket, unmanned artificial satellite, etc. used to test conditions in outer space and radio information back to earth. [< LL *proba*, n., < L *probare* prove. Doublet of PROOF.] **—prob′er,** *n.* **—prob′ing·ly,** *adv.*

pro·bie (prō′bē) *n. Informal.* a nursing student who is on probation; a probationer.

pro·bi·ty (prō′bə tē) *n.* uprightness; honesty; high principle. [< L *probitas* < *probus* righteous]

prob·lem (prob′ləm) *n.* **1** a question, especially a difficult question. **2** a matter of doubt or difficulty. **3** something to be worked out: *a problem in algebra.* *—adj.* that causes difficulty: *a problem child.* [ME < OF < L < Gk. *problēma* < *proballein* propose < *pro-* forward + *ballein* throw]

prob·lem·at·ic (prob′ləm at′ik) *adj.* having the nature of a problem; doubtful; uncertain; questionable.

prob·lem·at·i·cal (prob′ləm at′ə kəl) *adj.* problematic. **—prob′lem·at′i·cal·ly,** *adv.*

pro bo·no pu·bli·co (prō′ bō′nō pub′lə kō) *Latin.* for the public welfare.

pro·bos·cis (prō bos′is) *n.* **-bos·cis·es. 1** an elephant's trunk. **2** a long, flexible snout. **3** the mouth parts of some insects, developed to great length for sucking: *the proboscis of a fly or a mosquito.* **4** *Humorous.* a person's nose. [< L < Gk. *proboskis*]

The head of a type of monkey that has a proboscis

proc. 1 proceedings. **2** procedure. **3** process.

pro·ce·dur·al (prə sē′jər əl) *adj.* of or having to do with procedure. **—pro·ce′dur·al·ly,** *adv.*

pro·ce·dure (prə sē′jər) *n.* **1** a way of proceeding; a method of doing things. **2** the customary manners or ways of conducting business: *parliamentary procedure, legal procedure.* [< F *procédure* < *procéder* proceed]

pro·ceed (*v.* prə sēd′ or prō sēd′; *n.* prō′sēd) *v.* **1** go on after having stopped; move forward: *Please proceed with your story.* **2** be carried on; take place: *The trial may proceed.* **3** carry on any activity: *He proceeded to light his pipe.* **4** come forth; issue; go out: *Heat proceeds from fire.* **5** advance to a higher status: *He proceeded to Office Manager.* **6** begin and carry on an action at law.
—n. Usually, **proceeds,** *pl.* money obtained from a sale, etc.: *The proceeds from the school play will be used to buy a new curtain for the stage.* [ME < OF < L *procedere* < *pro-* forward + *cedere* move] **—pro·ceed′er,** *n.* **—Syn.** *v.* **1** progress. See **advance. 4** emanate.

pro·ceed·ing (prə sēd′ing) *n.* **1** action; conduct; what is done. **2 proceedings,** *pl.* **a** the action in a case in a law court. **b** a record of what was done at the meetings of a society, club, etc.; minutes. **—Syn. 1** performance.

pro·cess (prō′ses or pros′es) *n.* **1** a set of actions or changes in a special order: *By what process or processes is cloth made from wool?* **2** a part that grows out or sticks out: *the process of a bone.* **3** a written command or summons to appear in a law court. **4** the proceedings in a legal case or action. **5 in process, a** in the course or condition: *In process of time the house will be finished.* **b** in the course or condition of being done: *The author has just finished one book and has another in process.*
—v. **1** treat or prepare by some special method. **2** start legal action against.
—adj. treated or prepared by some special method. [ME < OF < L *processus* progress < *procedure.* See PROCEED.] **—pro′ces·sor,** *n.* **—Syn.** *n.* **1** procedure, operation.

process cheese or **processed cheese** a blend of cheddar or other natural cheeses and flavorings, powdered milk, emulsifier, etc.

pro·ces·sion (prə sesh′ən) *n.* **1** something that moves forward; persons marching or riding: *A funeral procession filled the street.* **2** an orderly moving forward: *We formed lines to march in procession onto the platform.*

pro·ces·sion·al (prə sesh′ən əl) *adj.* **1** of a procession. **2** used or sung in a procession. *—n.* **1** processional music: *The choir and clergy marched into the church singing the processional.* **2** a book containing hymns, etc., for use in religious processions.

hat, āge, cãre, fär; let, ēqual, tėrm; it, īce
hot, ōpen, ôrder; oil, out; cup, pu̇t, rüle, ūse
əbove, takən, pencəl, lemən, circəs
ch, child; ng, long; sh, ship
th, thin; ᴛʜ, then; zh, measure

pro·claim (prə klām′) *v.* **1** make known publicly and officially; declare publicly: *War was proclaimed. The people proclaimed him king.* **2 a** declare (a person) an outlaw; denounce. **b** subject (a place) to legal restrictions. [ME < L *proclamare* < *pro-* forth + *clamare* shout] **—Syn. 1** publish. See **announce.**

proc·la·ma·tion (prok′lə mā′shən) *n.* an official announcement; a public declaration: *A proclamation was issued to announce the forthcoming election.*
Syn. Proclamation, edict = a notice or order issued by authority. **Proclamation** = an official public announcement by an executive or administrative officer, such as a president, premier, mayor: *The Prime Minister issued a proclamation declaring martial law in the disaster area.* **Edict** = a public order or law proclaimed by the highest authority, usually a decree of a ruler or court with supreme or absolute authority: *The dictator issued an edict seizing the mines.*

pro·cliv·i·ty (prō kliv′ə tē) *n.* **-ties.** a tendency; inclination. [< L *proclivitas,* ult. < *pro-* forward + *clivus* slope] **—Syn.** bias, bent.

pro·con·sul (prō kon′səl) *n.* **1** in ancient Rome, the governor or military commander of a province, with duties and powers like those of a consul. **2** the governor of a British or French colony. **3 Proconsul,** a manlike ape of the Miocene period, that lived in Africa approximately 25,000,000 years ago and is considered by some anthropologists to be an ancestor of man. [ME < L *proconsul,* from the phrase *pro consule* in place of a consul]

pro·con·su·lar (prō kon′sə lər) *adj.* of, having to do with, or governed by a proconsul.

pro·con·su·late (prō kon′sə lit) *n.* the position or term of a proconsul.

pro·con·sul·ship (prō kon′səl ship′) *n.* proconsulate.

pro·cras·ti·nate (prō kras′tə nāt′) *v.* **-nat·ed, -nat·ing.** put things off until later; delay; delay repeatedly. [< L *procrastinare,* ult. < *pro-* forward + *cras* tomorrow] **—pro·cras′ti·na′tor,** *n.* **—Syn.** defer, postpone.

pro·cras·ti·na·tion (prō kras′tə nā′shən) *n.* the act or habit of putting things off till later; delay.

pro·cre·ate (prō′krē āt′) *v.* **-at·ed, -at·ing. 1** become father to; beget. **2** produce offspring. **3** bring into being; produce. [< L *procreare* < *pro-* forth + *creare* create] **—pro′cre·a′tor,** *n.*

pro·cre·a·tion (prō′krē ā′shən) *n.* **1** a begetting; a becoming a father. **2** a production.

pro·cre·a·tive (prō′krē ā′tiv) *adj.* **1** begetting; bringing into being. **2** concerned with or having to do with procreation. **—pro′cre·a′tive·ness,** *n.*

Pro·crus·te·an (prō krus′tē ən) *adj.* **1** of or having to do with Procrustes or his bed. **2** tending to produce conformity by violent or arbitrary means.

Pro·crus·tes (prō krus′tēz) *n.* in Greek legend, a robber who either stretched his victims or cut off their legs to make them fit the length of his bed.

proc·tor (prok′tər) *n.* **1** in a university or school: **a** an official who keeps order. **b** a person who supervises students during an examination. **c** a prefect or monitor. **2** a person employed to manage another's case in a law court. *—v.* serve as a proctor at an examination. [short for *procurator*]

proc·to·ri·al (prok tô′rē əl) *adj.* of or having to do with a proctor.

proc·tor·ship (prok′tər ship′) *n.* the position of a proctor.

pro·cum·bent (prō kum′bənt) *adj.* **1** lying face down; prone; prostrate. **2** of a plant or stem, lying along the ground but not sending down roots. [< L *procumbens, -entis,* ppr. of *procumbere* lean forward]

proc·u·ra·tor (prok′yů rā′tər) *n.* **1** a person employed to manage the affairs of another; a person authorized to act for another; agent. **2** in ancient Rome, a financial agent or administrator of a province. [< L *procurator* < *procurare.* See PROCURE.]

pro·cure (prə kūr′) *v.* **-cured, -cur·ing. 1** obtain by care or effort; get: *A friend procured a position in the bank for my big brother.* **2** bring about; cause: *procure a person's death.* **3** obtain women to gratify the lust of others. [ME < OF < L *procurare* manage, ult. < *pro-* before + *cura* care] **—pro·cur′a·ble,** *adj.* **—pro·cur′er,** *n.* **—Syn. 1** acquire, gain, win, secure.

pro·cure·ment (prə kūr′mənt) *n.* a procuring.

pro·cur·ess (prə kūr′is) *n.* a female keeper of a brothel; bawd.

Pro·cy·on (prō′sē on) *n.* a star of the first magnitude in the constellation Canis Minor. [< L < Gk. *Prokyon* < *pro-* before + *kyon* dog; because it rises before the Dog Star, Sirius]

prod (prod) *v.* **prod·ded, prod·ding,** *n.* **—***v.* **1** poke or jab with something pointed: *prod an animal with a stick.* **2** stir up; urge on: *prod a lazy boy to action by threats and entreaties.* **—***n.* **1** poke or thrust. **2** a sharp-pointed stick; goad. **3** something that prods; reminder. [OE *prod-*, as in *prodbor* borer] **—prod′der,** *n.*

prod. 1 product. **2** produced.

prod·i·gal (prod′ə gəl) *adj.* **1** spending too much; wasting money or other resources; wasteful: *Canada has been prodigal of its forests.* **2** abundant; lavish. **—***n.* a person who is wasteful or extravagant; spendthrift. [< MF, back-formation from *prodigalite* < LL *prodigalitas.* See PRODIGALITY.] **—prod′i·gal·ly,** *adv.* **—Syn.** *adj.* **1** extravagant.

prod·i·gal·i·ty (prod′ə gal′ə tē) *n.* **-ties. 1** wasteful or reckless extravagance. **2** rich abundance; profuseness. [< LL *prodigalitas* (modelled on L *liberalitas* < *liber*) < L *prodigus* wasteful < *prodigere* drive forth, squander < *prod-* (var. of *pro-*) forth + *agere* drive]

pro·di·gious (prə dij′əs) *adj.* **1** very great; huge; vast: *The ocean contains a prodigious amount of water.* **2** wonderful; marvellous. [< L *prodigiosus* < *prodigium* prodigy, omen] **—pro·di′gious·ly,** *adv.* **—pro·di′gious·ness,** *n.*

prod·i·gy (prod′ə jē) *n.* **-gies. 1** a marvel; wonder. An infant prodigy is a child remarkably brilliant in some respect. **2** a marvellous example: *The warriors performed prodigies of valor.* **3** *Rare.* a wonderful sign or omen. [< L *prodigium* omen]

pro·duce (*v.* prə dūs′ or prə düs′; *n. adj.* prod′ūs or prō′düs) *v.* **-duced, -duc·ing,** *n. adj.* **—***v.* **1** make; bring into existence: *This factory produces stoves.* **2** bring about; cause: *Hard work produces success.* **3** bring forth or yield offspring, crops, products, dividends, interest, etc. **4** bring forth; supply; create: *Hens produce eggs.* **5** bring forward; show; present: *Produce your proof.* **6** bring (a play, etc.) before the public. **7** extend; continue (a line or plane).
—*n.* **1** what is produced; yield: *Vegetables are a garden's produce.* **2** fruit and vegetables.
—*adj.* of fruit and vegetables: *He owns a produce market.* [ME < L *producere* < *pro-* forth + *ducere* bring] **—Syn.** *v.* **1** manufacture. **2** effect. **4** yield.

pro·duc·er (prə dūs′ər or prə düs′ər) *n.* **1** one who produces. **2** a person who grows or makes things that are to be used or consumed by others. **3** a person who has general charge of the production of motion pictures, plays, or radio or television programs. ☛ For def. 3, see **director** for usage note.

pro·duc·i·ble (prə dūs′ə bəl or prə düs′ə bəl) *adj.* capable of being produced.

prod·uct (prod′əkt) *n.* **1** that which is produced; result of work or of growth: *factory products, farm products.* **2** a number or quantity resulting from multiplying: *The product of 5 and 8 is 40.* **3** in chemistry, a substance obtained from another substance through chemical change. [ME < L *productus*, pp. of *producere.* See PRODUCE.]

pro·duc·tion (prə duk′shən) *n.* **1** the act of producing; creation; manufacture: *His business is the production of automobiles.* **2** something that is produced: *The school play was a fine production.* **3** the amount produced.

production line in a factory, a row of machines and equipment along which workers oversee the various stages of production; assembly line.

production model an article in regular production; a standard or standardized product.

production number a part of a musical play, motion picture, television show, etc. that is given spectacular presentation with elaborate scenery, costumes, dances, etc.: *The first act ended with a colorful production number.*

pro·duc·tive (prə duk′tiv) *adj.* **1** capable of producing or bringing forth: *fields now productive only of weeds, hasty words that are productive of quarrels.* **2** producing food or other articles of commerce: *Farming is productive labor.* **3** producing abundantly; fertile: *a productive farm, writer, etc.* **—pro·duc′tive·ly,** *adv.* **—pro·duc′tive·ness,** *n.* **—Syn. 3** See **fertile.**

pro·duc·tiv·i·ty (prō′duk tiv′ə tē or prod′ək tiv′ə tē) *n.* the power to produce; productiveness.

pro·em (prō′em) *n.* an introduction; preface. [ME < OF < L < Gk. *prooimion* < *pro-* before + *oimē* song]

prof (prof) *n. Informal.* professor.

Prof. *pl.* **Profs.** professor.

prof·a·na·tion (prof′ə nā′shən) *n.* the act of showing contempt or disregard toward something holy; mistreatment of something sacred. **—Syn.** desecration, defilement.

pro·fan·a·to·ry (prə fan′ə tô′rē) *adj.* profaning.

pro·fane (prə fān′ or prō fān′) *adj. v.* **-faned, -fan·ing. —***adj.* **1** not sacred; worldly: *profane literature.* **2** with contempt or disregard for God or holy things: *profane language.* **—***v.* **1** treat (holy things) with contempt or disregard: *Soldiers profaned the church by stabling horses there.* **2** put to wrong or unworthy use. [ME < OF < L *profanus* not sacred < *pro-* in front (outside) of + *fanum* shrine] **—pro·fane′ly,** *adv.* **—pro·fane′ness,** *n.*

pro·fan·i·ty (prə fan′ə tē) *n.* **-ties. 1** the use of profane language; swearing. **2** the quality of being profane; lack of reverence.

pro·fess (prə fes′) *v.* **1** lay claim to; claim: *He professed the greatest respect for the law. I don't profess to be an expert.* **2** declare openly: *He professed his loyalty to his country.* **3** declare one's belief in: *Christians profess Christ and the Christian religion.* **4** have as one's profession or business: *profess law.* **5** receive or admit into a religious order. [< *professed*] **—Syn. 1** assume, pretend. **2** own, aver, acknowledge.

pro·fessed (prə fest′) *adj.* **1** alleged; pretended. **2** avowed or acknowledged; openly declared. **3** having taken the vows of, or been received into, a religious order. [ME < L *professus*, pp. of *profiteri* < *pro-* forth + *fateri* confess]

pro·fess·ed·ly (prə fes′id lē) *adv.* **1** avowedly. **2** ostensibly.

pro·fes·sion (prə fesh′ən) *n.* **1** an occupation requiring higher education and a specialized training, especially law, medicine, teaching, or the ministry. **2** the people engaged in such an occupation. **3** the act of professing; open declaration: *a profession of friendship.* **4** a declaration of belief in a religion. **5** the religion or faith professed. **6** the act of taking vows and entering a religious order.

pro·fes·sion·al (prə fesh′ən əl or prə fesh′nəl) *adj.* **1** of or having to do with a profession; appropriate to a profession: *professional skill, a professional manner.* **2** engaged in a profession: *A lawyer or a doctor is a professional man.* **3** making a business or trade of something that others do for pleasure: *a professional ballplayer.* **4** undertaken or engaged in by professionals rather than amateurs: *a professional ball game.* **5** making a business of something not properly to be regarded as a business: *a professional politician.* **—***n.* a person who makes a business or trade of something that others do for pleasure.

pro·fes·sion·al·ism (prə fesh′ən əl iz′əm or prə fesh′nəl iz′əm) *n.* **1** professional character, spirit, or methods. **2** the standing, practice, or methods of a professional, as distinguished from those of an amateur.

pro·fes·sion·al·ize (prə fesh′ən əl īz′ or

prə fesh′nəl īz′) *v.* **-ized, -iz·ing.** make or become professional.

pro·fes·sion·al·ly (prə fesh′ən əl ē or prə fesh′nəl ē) *adv.* in a professional manner; in professional matters; because of one's profession.

pro·fes·sor (prə fes′ər) *n.* **1** a teacher of the highest rank in a college or university. **2** *Informal.* any teacher at a college or university. **3** a person who professes. **4** a person who declares his belief in a religion. [ME < L *professor* < *profiteri* profess. See PROFESSED.]

pro·fes·sor·ate (prə fes′ər it) *n.* **1** the office or term of service of a professor. **2** a group of professors.

pro·fes·so·ri·al (prof′ə sô′rē əl or prō′fə sô′rē əl) *adj.* of, having to do with, or characteristic of a professor. **—pro′fes·so′ri·al·ly,** *adv.*

pro·fes·sor·ship (prə fes′ər ship′) *n.* the position or rank of a professor.

prof·fer (prof′ər) *v.* offer; offer for acceptance: *We proffered regrets at having to leave so early.* —*n.* an offer made: *His proffer of advice was accepted.* [ME < AF < *pro-* forth (< L *pro-*) + *offrir* offer < L *offerre*] **—Syn.** *v.* tender. See **offer.**

pro·fi·cien·cy (prə fish′ən sē) *n.* **-cies.** the quality or condition of being proficient; knowledge; skill; expertness.

pro·fi·cient (prə fish′ənt) *adj.* advanced in any art, science, or subject; skilled; expert: *She was very proficient in music.* —*n.* an expert. [< L *proficiens, -entis* making progress, ppr. of *proficere* < *pro-* forward + *facere* make] **—pro·fi′cient·ly,** *adv.* **—Syn.** *adj.* versed, qualified, adept, competent. See **expert.**

pro·file (prō′fīl) *n. v.* **-filed, -fil·ing.** —*n.* **1** a side view. **2** an outline. **3** a drawing of a transverse vertical section of a building, bridge, etc. **4** a concise description of a person's abilities, character, or career. —*v.* draw a profile of. [< Ital. *profilo* < *profilare* draw in outline < L *pro-* forth + *filum* thread] **—Syn.** *n.* **2** See **outline.**

prof·it (prof′it) *n.* **1** Often, **profits,** *pl.* the gain from a business; what is left when the cost of goods and of carrying on the business is subtracted from the amount of money taken in. **2** advantage; benefit: *What profit is there in worrying?*
—*v.* **1** make a gain from a business; make a profit. **2** get advantage; gain; benefit: *A wise person profits by his mistakes.* **3** be an advantage or benefit (to). [ME < OF < L *profectus* advance < *proficere.* See PROFICIENT.] **—prof′it·er,** *n.* **—prof′it·less,** *adj.* **—Syn.** *n.* **1** revenue, returns, proceeds. **2** See **advantage.**

prof·it·a·ble (prof′ə tə bəl) *adj.* **1** yielding a financial profit. **2** giving a gain or benefit; useful: *We spent a profitable afternoon in the library.* **—prof′it·a·ble·ness,** *n.* **—prof′it·a·bly,** *adv.*

prof·it·eer (prof′ə tēr′) *n.* a person who makes an unfair profit by taking advantage of public necessity. —*v.* seek or make excessive profits by taking advantage of public necessity.

profit sharing the sharing of profits between employer and employees. **—prof′it-shar′ing,** *adj.*

prof·li·ga·cy (prof′lə gə sē) *n.* **1** great wickedness; vice. **2** reckless extravagance.

prof·li·gate (prof′lə git) *adj.* **1** very wicked; shamelessly bad. **2** recklessly extravagant. —*n.* a person who is very wicked or extravagant. [<L *profligatus,* pp. of *profligare,* intensive of *profligere* ruin < *pro-* down + *fligere* strike, dash] **—prof′li·gate·ly,** *adv.*

pro·found (prə found′) *adj.* **1** very deep: *a profound sigh, a profound sleep.* **2** deeply felt; very great: *profound despair, profound sympathy.* **3** going far deeper than what is easily understood; having or showing great knowledge or understanding: *a profound book, a profound thinker.* **4** low; carried far down; going far down: *a profound bow.* [ME < OF < L *profundus* < *pro-* towards + *fundus* bottom] **—pro·found′ly,** *adv.* **—pro·found′ness,** *n.* **—Syn. 3** abstruse, recondite.

pro·fun·di·ty (prə fun′də tē) *n.* **-ties. 1** the state or quality of being profound; great depth. **2** a very deep thing or place. [< LL *profunditas* < L *profundus.* See PROFOUND.]

pro·fuse (prə fūs′) *adj.* **1** very abundant: *profuse thanks.* **2** spending or giving freely; lavish; extravagant: *He was so profuse with his money that he is now poor.* [ME < L *profusus* poured forth, pp. of *profundere* < *pro-* forth + *fundere* pour] **—pro·fuse′ly,** *adv.* **—pro·fuse′ness,** *n.*

hat, āge, cãre, fär; let, ēqual, tėrm; it, īce
hot, ōpen, ôrder; oil, out; cup, pu̇t, rüle, ūse
əbove, takən, pencəl, lemən, circəs
ch, child; ng, long; sh, ship
th, thin; ᴛʜ, then; zh, measure

Syn. 1, 2 Profuse, lavish = occurring, spending, or given freely. **Profuse** suggests a quantity that is more than enough, poured out in streams, sometimes too freely: *They were profuse in their praise.* **Lavish** suggests pouring out in a flood, showing no attempt to limit the amount or be saving, but implies generosity or liberality more than extravagance: *It was a lavish display of gifts.*

pro·fu·sion (prə fū′zhən) *n.* **1** a great abundance: *There was a profusion of gulls on the breakwater.* **2** extravagance; lavishness.

Prog. Progressive.

pro·gen·i·tor (prō jen′ə tər) *n.* an ancestor in the direct line; forefather. [< L *progenitor* < *pro-* forth + *gignere* beget]

pro·gen·i·ture (prō jen′ə chər) *n.* **1** a begetting; birth. **2** offspring.

prog·e·ny (proj′ə nē) *n.* **-nies.** children; offspring; descendants. [ME < OF < L *progenies,* ult. < *pro-* forth + *gignere* beget]

prog·na·thous (prog′nə thəs or prog nā′thəs) *adj.* of a skull or a person, having the jaws protruding beyond the upper part of the face. [< *pro-*[2] forward + Gk. *gnathos* jaw]

prog·no·sis (prog nō′sis) *n.* **-ses** (-sēz). **1** a forecast of the probable course of a disease. **2** an estimate of what will probably happen. [< LL < Gk. *prognōsis,* ult. < *pro-* before + *gignōskein* recognize]

prog·nos·tic (prog nos′tik) *adj.* indicating something in the future. —*n.* **1** an indication; sign. **2** a forecast; prediction. [< Med.L < Gk. *prognōstikos* foretelling, ult. < *pro-* before + *gignōskein* recognize]

prog·nos·ti·cate (prog nos′tə kāt′) *v.* **-cat·ed, -cat·ing.** predict from facts; forecast.,**—prog·nos′ti·ca′tion,** *n.* **—prog·nos′ti·ca′tor,** *n.*

pro·gram or **pro·gramme** (prō′gram or prō′grəm) *n. v.* **-grammed, -gram·ming.** —*n.* **1** a list of items or events; list of performers, players, etc.: *a theatre program.* **2** the items composing an entertainment: *The entire program was delightful.* **3** a plan of what is to be done: *a school program, a business program, a government program.* **4 a** a set of instructions fed into a computer outlining the steps to be performed by the machine in a specific operation. **b** a set of instructions arranged for any automatic machine to follow. **5** in education, a unit of subject matter arranged in a series of small steps for programmed learning.
—*v.* **1** arrange or enter in a program. **2** draw up a program or plan for. **3** prepare a set of instructions for (a computer or other automatic machine). **4** in education, arrange in a series of small steps for programmed learning. [< LL < Gk. *programma* proclamation, ult. < *pro-* forth + *graphein* write] **—pro′gram·mer,** *n.*

pro·gram·mat·ic (prō′grə mat′ik) *adj.* **1** of or having to do with a program. **2** of or having to do with program music.

programmed learning a method of study by which a person works step by step through a series of problems, checking the correctness of his response to each step before proceeding to the next.

program music or **programme music** music that portrays or suggests a particular event, story, atmosphere, etc.

prog·ress (*n.* prō′gres or prog′res; *v.* prə gres′) *n.* **1** an advance; growth; development; improvement: *the progress of science.* **2** a moving forward; going ahead: *make rapid progress on a journey.*
—*v.* **1** get better; advance; develop: *We progress in learning step by step.* **2** move forward; go ahead: *The building of the city hall has progressed a great deal this week.* [< L *progressus,* ult. < *pro-* forward + *gradi* walk] **—Syn.** *v.* **1** improve, grow.

pro·gres·sion (prə gresh′ən) *n.* **1** a moving forward; going ahead: *Creeping is a slow method of progression.* **2** in mathematics, a succession of quantities in which there is always the same relation between each quantity and the one succeeding it. 2, 4, 6, 8, 10 are in **arithmetical progression.** 2, 4, 8, 16 are in **geometrical progression.** **3** in music: **a** a moving from one tone or chord to another. **b** a sequence of tones, chords, etc.

pro·gres·sive (prə gres′iv) *adj.* **1** making progress; advancing to something better; improving: *a progressive nation.* **2** favoring progress; wanting improvement or reform in government, business, etc. **3** moving forward; going ahead. **4** going from one to the next; involving shifts of players or guests from one table to another. **5** of, following, or based on the theories and practices of progressive education: *a progressive school.* **6** in grammar, showing the action as going on. *Is reading, was reading,* and *has been reading* are progressive forms of *read.* **7** increasing in proportion to the increase of something else: *A progressive income tax increases as a person's earnings increase.* —*n.* a person who favors improvement and reform in government, business, etc.: *He is a progressive in his beliefs.* —**pro·gres′sive·ly,** *adv.* —**pro·gres′sive·ness,** *n.*

Progressive Conservative **1** a member of the Progressive Conservative Party. **2** a person who supports the policies of this party.

Progressive Conservative Party one of the principal political parties of Canada.

pro·hib·it (prō hib′it) *v.* **1** forbid by law or authority: *Picking flowers in this park is prohibited.* **2** prevent: *The high price prohibits my buying the bicycle.* [ME < L *prohibitus,* pp. of *prohibere* < *pro-* away + *habere* keep] —**pro·hib′i·tor,** *n.* —**Syn. 1** See **forbid.**

☛ **Prohibited** is followed by *from,* not *against*: *We are prohibited from smoking on school grounds.* The noun *prohibition* is followed by *against*: *The prohibition against smoking in laboratories is strictly enforced.*

pro·hi·bi·tion (prō′ə bish′ən) *n.* **1** the act of prohibiting or forbidding. **2** a law or order that prohibits. **3** a law or laws against making or selling alcoholic liquors. **4** the time during which such a law, or laws, is enforced.
☛ See **prohibit** for usage note.

pro·hi·bi·tion·ist (prō′ə bish′ən ist) *n.* one who favors laws against the manufacture and sale of alcoholic liquors.

pro·hib·i·tive (prō hib′ə tiv) *adj.* **1** prohibiting; preventing. **2** preventing or discouraging purchase: *The cost of the house was prohibitive.*

pro·hib·i·to·ry (prō hib′ə tô′rē) *adj.* prohibitive.

proj·ect (*n.* prō′jekt or proj′ekt; *v.* prə jekt′) *n.* **1** a plan; scheme: *Flying in a heavy machine was once thought an impossible project.* **2** an undertaking; enterprise. [< v.]
—*v.* **1** plan; scheme. **2** stick out: *The rocky point projects far into the water.* **3** cause to stick out or protrude. **4** throw or cast forward: *A catapult projects stones.* **5** cause to fall on a surface: *Motion pictures are projected on the screen. The tree projects a shadow on the grass.* **6** draw lines through (a point, line, figure, etc.) and reproduce it on a surface. **7** in psychology, treat as objective and external (what is essentially subjective). [< L *projectus,* pp. of *proicere, projicere* < *pro-* forward + *jacere* to throw] —**Syn.** *n.* **1** See **plan.** -*v.* **1** devise, contrive. **2** protrude.

pro·jec·tile (prə jek′tīl or prə jek′təl) *n.* any object that is thrown, hurled, or shot, as a rocket, stone, or bullet. —*adj.* **1** capable of being thrown, hurled, or shot. **2** forcing forward; impelling: *a projectile force.* **3** that can be thrust forward: *the projectile jaws of a fish.*

pro·jec·tion (prə jek′shən) *n.* **1** a part that projects or sticks out: *rocky projections on the face of a cliff.* **2** a sticking out. **3** a throwing or casting forward: *the projection of a shell from a field gun.* **4** in geometry, the projecting of a figure, etc. upon a surface. **5** a representation, upon a flat surface, of all or part of the surface of the earth. **6** a forming of projects or plans. **7** in psychology and psychiatry, the treating of what is essentially subjective as objective and external.

pro·jec·tion·ist (prə jek′shən ist) *n.* a person who operates a motion-picture projector or a television camera.

pro·jec·tor (prə jek′tər) *n.* **1** an apparatus for projecting a picture on a screen. **2** a person who forms projects; schemer.

prol. prologue.

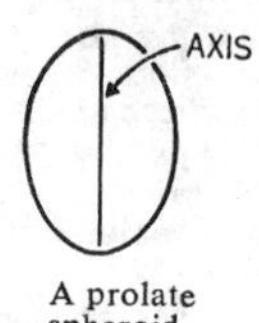

A prolate spheroid

pro·late (prō′lāt) *adj.* elongated in the direction of the polar diameter. A prolate spheroid is generated by the revolution of an ellipse about its longer axis. [< L *prolatus,* pp. to *proferre* extend, bring forward < *pro-* forth + *ferre* bring]

pro·le·tar·i·an (prō′lə tãr′ē ən) *adj.* of or belonging to the proletariat. —*n.* a person belonging to the proletariat. [< L *proletarius* furnishing the state only with children < *proles* offspring < *pro-* forth + *alescere* grow]

pro·le·tar·i·at (prō′lə tãr′ē ət) *n.* **1** the lowest class in economic and social status. The proletariat includes unskilled laborers, casual laborers, and tramps. **2** the laboring class. [< F *prolétariat*]

pro·lif·er·ate (prə lif′ə rāt′) *v.* **-at·ed, -at·ing.** **1** grow, reproduce, or propagate rapidly and abundantly, as in cell division, budding, etc. **2** spread; multiply: *Today in the suburbs, housing projects proliferate.*

pro·lif·er·a·tion (prə lif′ə rā′shən) *n.* **1** rapid reproduction or propagation. **2** a spreading; multiplication.

pro·lif·er·ous (prə lif′ər əs) *adj.* growing or spreading rapidly.

pro·lif·ic (prə lif′ik) *adj.* **1** producing offspring abundantly: *prolific animals.* **2** producing much: *a prolific garden, imagination, or writer.* [< Med.L *prolificus* < L *proles* offspring + *facere* make] —**pro·lif′i·cal·ly,** *adv.*

pro·lif·i·ca·cy (prə lif′ə kə sē) *n.* the quality or state of being prolific.

pro·lix (prō liks′ or prō′liks) *adj.* using too many words; too long; tedious. [ME < L *prolixus* stretched out < *pro-* forth + **lixus* having trickled, flowed (cf. *lixa* water)] —**pro·lix′ness,** *n.* —**Syn.** wordy, verbose.

pro·lix·i·ty (prō lik′sə tē) *n.* too great length; tedious length of speech or writing.

pro·log (prō′log) *n.* prologue.

pro·logue (prō′log) *n.* **1** a speech or poem addressed to the audience by one of the actors at the beginning of a play, opera, etc. **2** an introduction to a novel, poem, or other literary work. **3** any introductory act or event. [ME < OF < L < Gk. *prologos* < *pro-* before + *logos* speech]

pro·long (prə long′) *v.* make longer; draw out. [ME < LL *prolongare* < *pro-* forth + *longus* long] —**pro·long′er,** *n.* —**Syn.** stretch, protract. See **lengthen.**

pro·lon·ga·tion (prō′long gā′shən) *n.* **1** an extension; lengthening in time or space: *the prolongation of one's school days by graduate study.* **2** an added part.

prom (prom) *n. Informal.* a dance or ball given by a college or high-school class. [short for *promenade*]

prom·e·nade (prom′ə nād′ or prom′ə näd′) *n. v.* **-nad·ed, -nad·ing.** —*n.* **1** walk for pleasure or display: *The Easter promenade is well known as a fashion show.* **2** a public place for such a walk. **3** a dance; ball. **4** a march of all the guests at the opening of a formal dance. **5** a square-dancing figure in which a couple or, usually, all the couples of a set march once around the square, circle, etc.
—*v.* **1** walk about or up and down for pleasure or for display: *He promenaded back and forth on the ship's deck.* **2** walk through. **3** take on a promenade. [< F *promenade* < *promener* take for a walk] —**prom′e·nad′er,** *n.*

promenade deck an enclosed upper deck on a ship.

Pro·me·the·an (prə mē′thē ən) *adj.* of, having to do with, or suggestive of Prometheus.

Pro·me·the·us (prə mē′thē əs or prə mē′thūs) *n.* in Greek mythology, one of the Titans. He stole fire from heaven and taught men its use. Zeus punished him by chaining him to a rock.

pro·me·thi·um (prə mē′thē əm) *n.* a rare metallic chemical element. *Symbol*: Pm; *at.no.* 61; *at.wt.* 147 (most stable isotope). Formerly, **illinium.** [< *Prometheus*]

prom·i·nence (prom′ə nəns) *n.* **1** the quality or fact of being prominent, distinguished, or conspicuous: *the prominence of athletics in some schools.* **2** something that juts out or projects, especially upward. A hill is a prominence.

prom·i·nent (prom′ə nənt) *adj.* **1** well-known; important: *a prominent citizen.* **2** easy to see: *A single tree in a field is prominent.* **3** standing out; projecting: *Some insects have prominent eyes.* [< L *prominens, -entis,* ppr. of *prominere* project < *pro-* forward + *men-* jut] **—prom′i·nent·ly,** *adv.*

Syn. 1 leading. See **eminent. 2 Prominent, conspicuous** = attracting attention and easily seen. **Prominent** describes something that so stands out above its surroundings or from its background that it attracts attention and is easy to see: *He put her picture in a prominent position on his desk.* **Conspicuous** describes something so plain that it is impossible not to see it, or so unusual, odd, loud, colorful, etc. that it attracts attention: *Bright sweaters are conspicuous in an office.*

prom·is·cu·i·ty (prom′is kū′ə tē) *n.* the fact, state, or condition of being promiscuous.

pro·mis·cu·ous (prə mis′kū əs) *adj.* **1** mixed and in disorder: *a promiscuous heap of clothing on your closet floor.* **2** making no distinctions; lacking discrimination, especially in sexual relations: *promiscuous behavior.* [< L *promiscuus* < *pro* for + *miscere* mix] **—pro·mis′cu·ous·ly,** *adv.* **—pro·mis′cu·ous·ness,** *n.* **—Syn. 1** miscellaneous.

prom·ise (prom′is) *n. v.* **-ised, -is·ing.** **—*n.* 1** the words that bind a person to do or not to do something. **2** an indication of what may be expected: *The clouds give promise of rain.* **3** an indication of future excellence; something that gives hope of success: *a young scholar who shows promise.*
—*v.* 1 make a promise of (something) to (a person, etc.). **2** give one's word; make a promise. **3** give indication of; give hope of; give ground for expectation: *The rainbow promises fair weather tomorrow.* [< L *promissum,* originally neut. pp. of *promittere* promise < *pro-* before + *mittere* put] **—prom′is·er,** *n.* **—Syn. *n.* 1** vow, pledge, covenant.

Promised Land 1 in the Bible, the country promised by God to Abraham and his descendants; Canaan. Gen. 15:18; 17:1-8. **2** heaven. **3 promised land,** a place or condition of expected happiness: *Canada is a promised land for many immigrants.*

prom·is·ing (prom′is ing) *adj.* likely to turn out well: *a promising student.* **—prom′is·ingly,** *adv.*

prom·is·so·ry (prom′ə sô′rē) *adj.* containing a promise.

promissory note a written promise to pay a stated sum of money to a certain person at a certain time. *Abbrev.*: P/N or p/n

prom·on·to·ry (prom′ən tô′rē) *n.* **-ries. 1** a high point of land extending from the coast into the water; headland. **2** in anatomy, a part that bulges out. [< Med.L *promontorium,* var. of L *promunturium* < *pro-* forward + *mons, montis* mountain]

pro·mote (prə mōt′) *v.* **-mot·ed, -mot·ing. 1** raise in rank, condition, or importance: *Those who pass the test will be promoted to the next higher grade.* **2** help to grow or develop; help to success: *The United Nations has done much to promote peace.* **3** help to organize; start: *Several bankers promoted the new company.* **4** further the sale of (an article) by advertising. [< L *promotus,* pp. of *promovere* < *pro-* forward + *movere* move]

Syn. 1 advance, elevate, exalt. **2 Promote, further** = help something move toward a desired end. **Promote** emphasizes causing a movement, cause, scheme, undertaking to move forward by giving open and active support and encouragement and helping it grow and develop: *The scholarships promote better understanding of the West Indies.* **Further** emphasizes helping a cause, project, etc. to keep going ahead: *Getting a scholarship will further his education.*

pro·mot·er (prə mōt′ər) *n.* **1** a person or thing that promotes. **2** one who organizes new companies and secures capital for them.

pro·mo·tion (prə mō′shən) *n.* **1** advancement or an advance in rank or importance: *The clerk was given a promotion and an increase in salary.* **2** helping to grow or develop; helping along to success: *The doctors were busy in the promotion of a health campaign.* **3** the act of helping to organize or get started: *It took much time and money for the promotion of the new company.*

hat, āge, cãre, fär; let, ēqual, tėrm; it, īce
hot, ōpen, ôrder; oil, out; cup, pu̇t, rüle, ūse
əbove, takən, pencəl, lemən, circəs
ch, child; ng, long; sh, ship
th, thin; ᴛʜ, then; zh, measure

pro·mo·tion·al (prə mō′shə nəl) *adj.* of, having to do with, or used in the promotion of a product, enterprise, etc.; pertaining to publicity. **—pro·mo·tion·al·ly,** *adv.*

prompt (prompt) *adj.* **1** on time; quick: *Be prompt to obey.* **2** done at once; made without delay: *I expect a prompt answer.* **3** of a prompter; used in prompting: *a prompt box on a stage.*
—*v.* 1 cause (someone) to do something: *His curiosity prompted him to ask questions.* **2** give rise to; suggest; inspire: *A kind thought prompted the gift.* **3** remind (a learner, speaker, actor, etc.) of the words or actions needed.
—*n.* 1 an act of prompting. **2** something that prompts. **3** in commerce: **a** a limit of time allowed for payment of goods purchased. **b** the contract determining this limit of time. [ME < L *promptus,* originally pp. of *promere* bring forth < *pro-* forward + *emere,* originally, take. Doublet of PRONTO.] **—prompt′ly,** *adv.* **—prompt′ness,** *n.*
—Syn. *adj.* **1** punctual. See **ready. 2** immediate, swift.
-*v.* 1 incite, impel, induce.

prompt·er (promp′tər) *n.* a person who supplies actors, speakers, etc. with their lines from off the stage when they forget them.

promp·ti·tude (promp′tə tūd′ or promp′tə tüd′) *n.* promptness; readiness in acting or deciding.

pro·mul·gate (prom′əl gāt′ or prō mul′gāt) *v.* **-gat·ed, -gat·ing. 1** proclaim formally; announce officially: *The king promulgated a decree.* **2** spread far and wide: *Schools try to promulgate knowledge and good habits.* [< L *promulgare* < *pro-* forth + **mulgare,* intensive of *mulgere,* originally, press]

pro·mul·ga·tion (prō′mul gā′shən or prom′əl gā′shən) *n.* **1** the act of promulgating. **2** the state of being promulgated.

pro·mul·ga·tor (prō mul′gā tər or prom′əl gā′tər) *n.* one that promulgates.

pron. 1 pronoun. **2** pronunciation.

prone (prōn) *adj.* **1** inclined; liable: *We are prone to think evil of people we dislike.* **2** lying face down. **3** lying flat. [ME < L *pronus* < *pro-* forward]

prone·ness (prōn′nis) *n.* **1** an inclination; tendency; preference. **2** a prone position.

prong (prong) *n.* **1** one of the pointed ends of a fork, antler, etc. **2** a branch or fork of a small stream. **—*v.*** pierce or stab with a prong. [ME *prange*; origin uncertain]

pronged (prongd) *adj.* having prongs.

prong·horn (prong′hôrn′) *n.* **-horns** or (*esp. collectively*) **-horn.** a mammal like an antelope, found on the plains of W. North America.

pro·nom·i·nal (prō nom′ə nəl) *adj.* of or having to do with pronouns; having the nature of a pronoun. [< LL *pronominalis* < L *pronomen.* See PRONOUN.]

pro·nom·i·nal·ly (prō nom′ə nəl ē) *adv.* like a pronoun.

pro·noun (prō′noun) *n.* a word used to indicate without naming; word used instead of a noun. *Examples*: I, we, you, he, it, they, who, whose, which, this, mine, whatever. [< F *pronom* < L *pronomen* < *pro-* in place of + *nomen* noun]

pro·nounce (prə nouns′) *v.* **-nounced, -nounc·ing. 1** make the sounds of; speak: *Pronounce your words clearly.* **2** pronounce words. **3** give an opinion or decision: *Only an expert should pronounce on this case.* **4** declare (a person or thing) to be: *The doctor pronounced her cured.* **5** declare formally or solemnly: *The judge pronounced sentence on the criminal.* [ME < OF < L *pronuntiare,* ult. < *pro-* forth + *nuntius* messenger] **—pro·nounce′a·ble,** *adj.* **—pro·nounc′er,** *n.*

pro·nounced (prə nounst′) *adj.* strongly marked; decided: *She held pronounced opinions on gambling.*

pro·nounc·ed·ly (prə noun′sid lē) *adv.* in a pronounced manner; to a pronounced degree.

pro·nounce·ment (prə nouns′mənt) *n.* **1** a formal statement; declaration. **2** an opinion; decision.

pron·to (pron′tō) *adv. Informal.* promptly; quickly; right away. [< Sp. *pronto* < L *promptus* prompt. Doublet of PROMPT.]

pro·nun·ci·a·men·to (prə nun′sē ə men′tō) *n.* **-tos.** a formal announcement; proclamation. [< Sp. *pronunciamiento* < *pronunciar* pronounce]

pro·nun·ci·a·tion (prə nun′sē ā′shən) *n.* **1** the way of pronouncing. Most dictionaries give the pronunciation of each entry word. **2** a pronouncing. [< L *pronuntiatio, -onis* < *pronuntiare.* See PRONOUNCE.]

proof (prüf) *n.* **1** a way or means of showing beyond doubt the truth of something. **2** the establishment of the truth of anything. **3** the act of testing; trial. **4** the condition of having been tested and approved. **5** in printing, a trial impression from type. A book is first printed in proof so that errors can be corrected. **6** a trial print of an etching, photographic negative, etc. **7 a** the standard strength of alcoholic liquors, considered as 100; in Canada, 57.10% by volume of alcohol at 60° F. **b** strength with reference to this standard: *What proof is this brandy?*
—*adj.* **1** of tested value against something: *Now we know that we are proof against being taken by surprise.* **2** of an alcoholic liquor, of standard strength: *proof spirit.*
[ME < OF *prueve* < LL *proba* < L *probare* prove. Doublet of PROBE.] —**Syn.** *n.* **1** See **evidence. 2** confirmation, corroboration. **3** experiment.

-proof *suffix.* protected against; safe from, as in *fireproof, waterproof, bombproof.*

proof·read (prüf′rēd′) *v.* **-read** (-red′), **-read·ing.** read (printers' proofs, etc.) and mark errors to be corrected.

prop[1] (prop) *v.* **propped, prop·ping,** *n.* —*v.* **1** hold up by placing a support under or against: *Prop the clothesline with a stick.* **2** support; sustain: *He was propped up in bed with pillows.* —*n.* a thing or person used to support another: *A son should be the prop of his father's old age.* [cf. MDu. *proppe*] —**Syn.** *n.* support, brace, stay.

prop[2] (prop) *n. Informal.* **1** any article, such as a table or a weapon, used in staging a play. **2 props,** a property man. [short for *(stage) property*]

prop[3] (prop) *n. Slang.* a propeller (def. 1). [short for *propeller*]

prop. 1 proprietor. **2** properly. **3** proposition.

prop·a·gan·da (prop′ə gan′də) *n.* **1** systematic efforts to spread opinions or beliefs, especially by distortion and deception: *The Nazis were experts in propaganda.* **2** any plan or method for spreading opinions or beliefs. **3** the opinions or beliefs thus spread. [< NL *congregatio de propaganda fide* congregation for propagating the faith]

prop·a·gan·dism (prop′ə gan′diz əm) *n.* the use of propaganda.

prop·a·gan·dist (prop′ə gan′dist) *n.* a person who gives time or effort to the spreading of some opinion, belief, or principle. —*adj.* of propaganda or propagandists.

prop·a·gan·dize (prop′ə gan′dīz) *v.* **-dized, -diz·ing. 1** propagate or spread (doctrines, etc.) by propaganda. **2** carry on propaganda.

prop·a·gate (prop′ə gāt′) *v.* **-gat·ed, -gat·ing. 1** produce offspring. **2** reproduce. **3** increase in number: *Trees propagate themselves by seeds.* **4** cause to increase in number by the production of young. **5** spread (news, knowledge, etc.): *Don't propagate unkind reports.* **6** pass on; send further: *Sound is propagated by vibrations.*
[< L *propagare,* originally, plant slips < *pro-* widely + **pagare,* frequentative of *pangere* make fast]
—**prop′a·ga′tor,** *n.* —**Syn. 3** multiply. **5** extend, diffuse.

prop·a·ga·tion (prop′ə gā′shən) *n.* **1** the breeding of plants or animals: *Our propagation of poppies is by seed, and of roses by cuttings.* **2** the act of spreading or getting more widely believed; making more widely known: *the propagation of the principles of science.* **3** a passing on; sending further; spreading or extending: *the propagation of the shock of an earthquake.*

pro·pane (prō′pān) *n.* a heavy, colorless hydrocarbon gas of the methane series, found in petroleum and used for fuel, refrigeration, etc. *Formula:* C_3H_6 [*propyl* + *methane*]

pro pat·ri·a (prō′ pat′rē ə or pā′trē ə) *Latin.* for one's country or native land.

pro·pel (prə pel′) *v.* **-pelled, -pel·ling.** drive forward; force ahead: *propel a boat by oars, a person propelled by ambition.* [ME < L *propellere* < *pro-* forward + *pellere* push] —**pro·pel′la·ble,** *adj.*

pro·pel·lant (prə pel′ənt) *n.* **1** something that propels, such as the fuel of a missile or the explosive charge of a shell. **2** a person who propels.

pro·pel·lent (prə pel′ənt) *adj.* propelling; driving forward. —*n.* a propellant.

pro·pel·ler (prə pel′ər) *n.* **1** a device consisting of a revolving hub with blades, for propelling boats, airships, and airplanes. **2** a person or thing that propels.

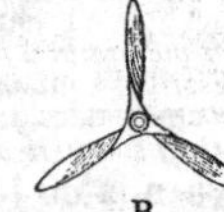

A, a ship's propeller; B, an airplane propeller.

pro·pen·si·ty (prə pen′sə tē) *n.* **-ties.** a natural inclination or bent; inclination: *Most boys have a propensity for playing with machinery.* [< L *propensus* inclined, ult. < *pro-* forward + *pendere* hang]

prop·er (prop′ər) *adj.* **1** correct; right; fitting: *Night is the proper time to sleep, and bed the proper place.* **2** strictly so called; in the strict sense of the word: *The population of Vancouver proper does not include that of the suburbs.* **3** decent; respectable: *proper conduct.* **4** in grammar, referring to a particular person, place, institution, etc.: "*John Smith,*" "*Canada,*" *and* "*The Royal Military College*" *are all proper names.* **5** *Informal.* complete; thorough; fine; excellent. **6** *Archaic.* good-looking; handsome. **7** belonging exclusively or distinctively: *qualities proper to a substance.* **8** in heraldry, represented in its natural colors: *an eagle proper.*
[ME < OF < L *proprius*] —**Syn. 1** suitable, becoming, appropriate. **3** seemly.

☛ **proper adjectives.** Proper nouns used as adjectives and adjectives directly derived from proper names and still referring to the place or person are capitalized. After proper adjectives lose the reference to their origins, they become simple adjectives and are not capitalized: *the French language, Roman ruins* (but *roman type*).

proper fraction a fraction less than 1. 2/3, 1/8, 3/4, and 199/200 are proper fractions.

prop·er·ly (prop′ər lē) *adv.* **1** in a proper, correct, or fitting manner: *eat properly.* **2** rightly; justly: *be properly indignant at the offer of a bribe.* **3** strictly: *Properly speaking, a whale is not a fish.*

proper noun a noun naming a particular person or thing. *John* and *Calgary* are proper nouns.

prop·er·tied (prop′ər tēd) *adj.* owning property.

prop·er·ty (prop′ər tē) *n.* **-ties. 1** any thing or things owned; possession or possessions. **2** possessions; wealth: *a man of property.* **3** a piece of land or real estate: *He owns some property out West.* **4** the owning of land, etc.; the people who own land, etc.: *the demands of property.* **5** a quality or power belonging specially to something: *Soap has the property of removing dirt.* **6 properties,** *pl.* the furniture, weapons, etc. used in staging a play, opera, etc. [ME < OF *propriete* < L *proprietas* < *proprius* one's own]

Syn. 1 Property, goods, effects = what someone owns. **Property** = whatever someone legally owns, including land, buildings, animals, money, stocks, documents, objects, and rights: *Landed property is taxable.* **Goods** = movable personal property, as distinguished from land, buildings, etc. and applies chiefly to things of use in the house or on the land, such as furniture, furnishings, and implements, but never to money or papers, etc.: *Professional movers packed our goods.* **Effects** = personal possessions, including goods, clothing, jewellery, personal belongings, and papers: *I packed our other effects.* **5** See **quality.**

proph·e·cy (prof′ə sē) *n.* **-cies. 1** a telling of what will happen; the foretelling of future events. **2** something told about the future. **3** a divinely inspired utterance, revelation, writing, etc. [ME < OF < L < Gk. *prophēteia* < *prophētēs.* See PROPHET.]

proph·e·sy (prof′ə sī′) *v.* **-sied, -sy·ing. 1** tell what will happen. **2** foretell; predict: *The sailor prophesied a severe storm.* **3** speak when or as if divinely inspired: *Daniel* *prophesied the destruction of Babylon.* **4** utter in prophecy. **—proph′e·si′er,** *n.*

proph·et (prof′it) *n.* **1** a person who tells what will happen. **2** a person who preaches what he thinks has been revealed to him. **3 the Prophet, a** Mohammed. **b** Joseph Smith, the founder of the Mormon religion. **4 the Prophets,** books of the Old Testament written by prophets. [ME < OF < L < Gk. *prophētēs,* ult. < *pro-* before + *phanai* speak]

proph·et·ess (prof′it is) *n.* a woman prophet.

pro·phet·ic (prə fet′ik) *adj.* **1** belonging to a prophet; such as a prophet has: *prophetic power.* **2** containing prophecy: *a prophetic saying.* **3** giving warning of what is to happen; foretelling. **—pro·phet′i·cal·ly,** *adv.*

pro·phy·lac·tic (prō′fə lak′tik or prof′ə lak′tik) *adj.* **1** protecting from disease. **2** protective; preservative; precautionary. *—n.* **1** a medicine or treatment that protects against disease. **2** a precaution. [< Gk. *prophylaktikos,* ult. < *pro-* before + *phylassein* guard < *phylax, -akos* a guard] **—pro′phy·lac′ti·cal·ly,** *adv.*

pro·phy·lax·is (prō′fə lak′sis or prof′ə lak′sis) *n.* **1** protection from disease. **2** treatment to prevent disease. [< NL < Gk. *pro-* before + *phylaxis* protection]

pro·pin·qui·ty (prō ping′kwə tē) *n.* **1** nearness in place, especially personal nearness. **2** nearness of blood; kinship. [< L *propinquitas,* ult. < *prope* near]

pro·pi·ti·ate (prə pish′ē āt′) *v.* **-at·ed, -at·ing.** prevent or reduce the anger of; win the favor of; appease or conciliate. [< L *propitiare,* ult. < *propitius* propitious. See PROPITIOUS.] **—pro·pi′ti·a′tor,** *n.*

pro·pi·ti·a·tion (prə pish′ē ā′shən) *n.* **1** the act of propitiating. **2** something that propitiates.

pro·pi·ti·a·to·ry (prə pish′ē ə tô′rē) *adj.* intended to propitiate; making propitiation; conciliatory: *a propitiatory offering.*

pro·pi·tious (prə pish′əs) *adj.* **1** favorable: *It seemed propitious weather for our trip.* **2** favorably inclined; gracious. [< L *propitius,* originally, falling forward < *pro-* forward + *petere* go toward] **—pro·pi′tious·ly,** *adv.* **—pro·pi′tious·ness,** *n.* **—Syn. 1** auspicious, promising.

pro·po·nent (prə pō′nənt) *n.* **1** one who makes a proposal or proposition. **2** a favorer; supporter. [< L *proponens, -entis,* ppr. of *proponere* set forth. See PROPOUND.]

pro·por·tion (prə pôr′shən) *n.* **1** the relation in size, number, amount, or degree of one thing compared to another: *Each man's pay will be in proportion to his work.* **2** a proper relation between parts: *His short legs were not in proportion to his long body.* **3 proportions,** *pl.* **a** size; extent. **b** dimensions. **4** a part; share: *A large proportion of British Columbia is mountainous.* **5** in mathematics: **a** an equality of ratios. *Examples*: 4 is to 2 as 10 is to 5. **b** a method of finding the fourth term of such a proportion when three are known.
—v. **1** fit one thing to another so that they go together: *The designs in that rug are well proportioned.* **2** adjust in proper proportion or relation. [< L *proportio, -onis* < phrase *pro portione* in relation to the part] **—pro·por′tion·er,** *n.* **—pro·por′tion·ment,** *n.*

pro·por·tion·a·ble (prə pôr′shən ə bəl) *adj.* being in due proportion; proportional.

pro·por·tion·al (prə pôr′shən əl) *adj.* in the proper proportion; corresponding: *The increase in price is proportional to the improvement in the car. —n.* in mathematics, one of the terms of a proportion.

pro·por·tion·al·ly (prə pôr′shən əl ē) *adv.* in proportion.

proportional representation an electoral system in which the number of seats that each party or group is given is proportional to its share of the total number of votes cast.

pro·por·tion·ate (prə pôr′shən it) *adj.* in the proper proportion; proportioned; proportional: *The money obtained by the bazaar was really not proportionate to the effort we put into it.*

pro·por·tion·ate·ly (prə pôr′shən it lē) *adv.* in proportion.

pro·por·tioned (prə pôr′shənd) *adj.* adjusted in proportion.

hat, āge, cãre, fär; let, ēqual, tėrm; it, īce
hot, ōpen, ôrder; oil, out; cup, pu̇t, rüle, ūse
əbove, takən, pencəl, lemən, circəs
ch, child; ng, long; sh, ship
th, thin; ᴛʜ, then; zh, measure

pro·pos·al (prə pōz′əl) *n.* **1** what is proposed; plan; scheme; suggestion: *The club will now hear this member's proposal.* **2** an offer of marriage. **3** the act of proposing: *Proposal is easier than performance.*
Syn. 1 Proposal, proposition = something put forward for consideration. **Proposal** = a suggestion, offer, plan, terms put forward for consideration and acceptance or action, but emphasizes the idea of offering for acceptance or refusal or suggesting for consideration: *The young people made a proposal to the City Council.* **Proposition,** sometimes confused with *proposal* but interchangeable with it only in business use, emphasizes what is put forward as a proposal and how it is set forth, the statement of the terms, plan, scheme: *The Council approved the idea, but not the proposition set forth.*

pro·pose (prə pōz′) *v.* **-posed, -pos·ing. 1** put forward for consideration, discussion, acceptance, etc.; suggest. **2** present (the name of someone) for office, membership, etc. **3** present as a toast to be drunk. **4** intend; plan: *She proposes to save half of all she earns.* **5** make an offer of marriage. [< F *proposer* < *pro-* forth (< L) + *poser* (see POSE[1])] **—pro·pos′er,** *n.* **—Syn. 1** offer.

prop·o·si·tion (prop′ə zish′ən) *n.* **1** what is offered to be considered; a proposal: *The tailor made a proposition to buy out his rival's business.* **2** an assertion; statement. *Example*: The earth is round. **3** a statement that is to be proved true, as in a debate. *Example*: "*Resolved.* That our school should have a bank." **4** a problem to be solved: *a proposition in geometry.* **5** *Informal.* a business enterprise; an undertaking. **6** *Informal.* a person or thing to be dealt with. **7** *Informal.* an improper or immodest proposal.
—v. Informal. propose a scheme, plan, or action to, often an improper one. [< L *propositio, -onis* a setting forth < *proponere* < *pro-* forth + *ponere* put, place] **—Syn. 1** See **proposal.**
☛ **Proposition** is originally a business word for *offer, plan, proposal* and is inappropriate in general usage. "I have a proposition for you" = "I have a plan . . . ."

pro·pound (prə pound′) *v.* put forward; propose: *propound a theory, a question, or a riddle.* [earlier *propone* < L *proponere* < *pro-* before + *ponere* set] **—pro·pound′er,** *n.*

pro·prae·tor or **pro·pre·tor** (prō prē′tər or prō prē′tôr) *n.* in ancient Rome, an officer who, after having served as praetor, was sent to govern a province. [< L]

pro·pri·e·tar·y (prə prī′ə ter′ē) *adj. n.* **-tar·ies.** *—adj.* **1** belonging to a proprietor. **2** holding property. **3** owned by a private person or company; belonging to or controlled by a private person as property. A proprietary medicine is a patent medicine, that is, one which can be made and sold only by some one person or certain persons.
—n. **1** an owner. **2** a group of owners. **3** ownership; the holding of property. **4** in former times, the holder or group of holders of a grant from a king of England. **5** a proprietary medicine. [< LL *proprietarius* < L *proprietas* ownership. See PROPRIETY.]

pro·pri·e·tor (prə prī′ə tər) *n.* an owner or manager. [alteration of *proprietary*]

pro·pri·e·tor·ship (prə prī′ə tər ship′) *n.* ownership.

pro·pri·e·tress (prə prī′ə tris) *n.* a woman owner or manager.

pro·pri·e·ty (prə prī′ə tē) *n.* **-ties. 1** the quality of being proper; fitness. **2** proper behavior: *Propriety demands that a boy tip his hat to a lady whom he knows.* **3 proprieties,** *pl.* the conventional standards or requirements of proper behavior. [< L *proprietas* appropriateness, peculiar nature (translation by Cicero of Gk. *idiōtēs*) < *proprius* one's own, proper (= Gk. *idios*)] **—Syn. 1** aptness, suitability. **2** etiquette, decorum, decency.

pro·pul·sion (prə pul′shən) *n.* **1** the act or process of driving forward or onward. **2** a propelling force or impulse: *jet propulsion.* [< F]

pro·pul·sive (prə pul′siv) *adj.* propelling; driving forward or onward.

prop·y·lae·um (prop′ə lē′əm) *n.* an elaborate or imposing gateway, entrance, or vestibule to a temple or other building. [< L *propylaeum* < Gk. *propylaion* entrance]

pro·py·lene (prō′pə lēn′) *n.* a colorless hydrocarbon gas obtained from propane, similar in type and structure to ethylene. *Formula*: C_3H_6

pro ra·ta (prō′ rä′tə or rā′tə) in proportion; according to the share, interest, etc. of each. [< L *pro rata* (*parte*) according to the portion figured (for each); *rata* < *ratus*, pp. of *reri* count, figure]

pro·rate (prō rāt′ or prō′rāt′) *v.* **-rat·ed, -rat·ing.** distribute or assess proportionally: *We prorated the money according to the number of days each had worked.* [< *pro rata*]

pro·ro·ga·tion (prō′rə gā′shən) *n.* the discontinuance of the meetings of a lawmaking body without dissolving it.

pro·rogue (prō rōg′) *v.* **-rogued, -rogu·ing.** discontinue the regular meetings of (a lawmaking body) for a time. [< F < L *prorogare* defer < *pro-* forward + *rogare* ask for]

pro·sa·ic (prō zā′ik) *adj.* like prose; matter-of-fact; ordinary; not exciting. [< Med.L *prosaicus* < L *prosa*. See PROSE.] **—pro·sa′i·cal·ly,** *adv.* **—Syn.** commonplace, humdrum, dull, tedious.

pro·sce·ni·um (prō sē′nē əm) *n.* **-ni·a** (-nē ə). **1** the part of the stage in front of the curtain. **2** the curtain and the framework that holds it. **3** the stage of an ancient theatre, or of a modern theatre having no curtain. [< L *proscaenium* < Gk. *proskēnion* < *pro-* in front of + *skēnē* stage, originally, tent]

pro·scribe (prō skrīb′) *v.* **-scribed, -scrib·ing. 1** prohibit as wrong or dangerous; condemn: *In earlier days, the church proscribed dancing and cardplaying.* **2** put outside of the protection of the law; outlaw. **3** forbid to come into a certain place; banish. [< L *proscribere* < *pro-* openly, publicly + *scribere* write] **—pro·scrib′er,** *n.* **—Syn. 1** forbid, interdict. **3** exile.

pro·scrip·tion (prō skrip′shən) *n.* **1** the act of proscribing. **2** the state of being proscribed. [< L *proscriptio, -onis* < *proscribere.* See PROSCRIBE.]

pro·scrip·tive (prō skrip′tiv) *adj.* proscribing; tending to proscribe. **—pro·scrip′tive·ly,** *adv.*

prose (prōz) *n. adj. v.* **prosed, pros·ing. —***n.* **1** the ordinary form of spoken or written language; plain language not arranged in verses. **2** dull, ordinary talk. —*adj.* **1** of prose; in prose. **2** lacking imagination; matter-of-fact; commonplace. —*v.* talk or write in a dull, commonplace way. [< F < L *prosa* (*oratio*) straight (speech), ult. < *pro-* forward + *vertere* turn]

pros·e·cute (pros′ə kūt′) *v.* **-cut·ed, -cut·ing. 1** in law: **a** bring before a court: *Reckless drivers will be prosecuted.* **b** bring a case before a court. **2** carry out; follow up: *He prosecuted an inquiry into reasons for the company's failure.* **3** carry on (a business or occupation). [ME < L *prosecutus*, pp. of *prosequi* pursue < *pro-* forth + *sequi* follow. Related to PURSUE.]

pros·e·cu·tion (pros′ə kū′shən) *n.* **1** in civil law: **a** the carrying on of a lawsuit: *He abandoned his prosecution of the case for damages.* **b** in criminal law, the side that institutes criminal proceedings against another. The prosecution makes charges against the defence. **2** a carrying out; following up: *In prosecution of his plan, he stored away a supply of food.*

pros·e·cu·tor (pros′ə kū′tər) *n.* **1** in criminal law: **a** a lawyer in charge of the government's side of a case against an accused person. **b** in civil law, a person who starts legal proceedings against another person. **2** a person who prosecutes.

pros·e·lyte (pros′ə līt′) *n. v.* **-lyt·ed, -lyt·ing. —***n.* a person who has been converted from one opinion, religious belief, etc. to another. —*v.* convert from one opinion, religious belief, etc. to another. [ME < LL < Gk. *prosēlytos* having arrived < *pros-* over + *ely-* come] **—pros′e·lyt′er,** *n.*

pros·e·lyt·ism (pros′ə līt iz′əm or pros′ə lə tiz′əm) *n.* the act or fact of proselyting.

pros·e·lyt·ize (pros′ə lə tīz′ or pros′ə lī tīz′) *v.* **-ized, -iz·ing.** make converts; proselyte.

Pro·ser·pi·na (prō sėr′pə nə) *n.* in Roman mythology, the daughter of Jupiter and Ceres. Pluto carried her off to make her queen of the underworld, but allowed her to spend part of each year on earth. Her coming brings spring and summer; her departure, fall and winter. The Greeks called her Persephone. Also, **Proserpine.**

Pro·ser·pi·ne (pros′ər pīn′ or prō sėr′pə nē′) *n.* Proserpina.

pro·sit (prō′sit) *interj.* To your health! [< L *prosit* may it benefit]

pros·o·dist (pros′ə dist) *n.* a person skilled in the technique of versification.

pros·o·dy (pros′ə dē) *n.* the science of poetic metres and versification. [< L < Gk. *prosōidia* all the features (accent, modulation, etc.) that characterize speech < *pros* in addition to + *ōidē* song, poem]

pros·pect (pros′pekt) *n.* **1** anything expected or looked forward to. **2** the act of looking forward; expectation: *The prospect of a vacation is pleasant.* **3** the outlook for the future. **4 in prospect,** expected; looked forward to. **5** a person who may be a customer, candidate, etc.; prospective customer: *The salesman had several prospects in mind.* **6** a view; scene: *The prospect from the mountain was grand.* —*v.* search: *prospect for gold, prospect a region for silver.* [< L *prospectus*, ult. < *pro-* forward + *specere* look] **—Syn.** *n.* **2** anticipation.

pro·spec·tive (prə spek′tiv) *adj.* **1** probable; expected: *a prospective client.* **2** looking forward to the future: *a prospective suggestion.*

pro·spec·tive·ly (prə spek′tiv lē) *adv.* in prospect or expectation; in the future.

pros·pec·tor (pros′pek tər or prə spek′tər) *n.* a person who explores or examines a region for gold, silver, oil, etc.

pro·spec·tus (prə spek′təs) *n.* a printed statement describing and advertising something. [< L *prospectus.* See PROSPECT.]

pros·per (pros′pər) *v.* **1** be successful; have good fortune; flourish. **2** make successful. [ME < OF < L *prosperare* < *prosperus* prosperous]

pros·per·i·ty (pros per′ə tē) *n.* **-ties.** a prosperous condition; good fortune; success.

pros·per·ous (pros′pər əs) *adj.* **1** successful; thriving; doing well; fortunate. **2** favorable; helpful: *prosperous weather for growing wheat.* [< L *prosperus* < *pro-* according to + *spes* hope] **—pros′per·ous·ly,** *adv.* **—pros′per·ous·ness,** *n.* **—Syn. 1** flourishing, rich, wealthy.

pros·tate (pros′tāt) in anatomy: —*n.* a large gland surrounding the male urethra in front of the bladder. —*adj.* designating or having to do with this gland. [< Med.L < Gk. *prostatēs* one standing in front, ult. < *pro-* before + *stenai* stand]

pros·the·sis (pros′thə sis) *n.* **-the·ses** (-thē′sēz). **1** the addition of a false tooth, artificial leg, etc. to the body. **2** the part itself. [< LL < Gk. *prosthesis* addition, ult. < *pros* to + *tithenai* put]

pros·thet·ics (pros thet′iks) *n.* the branch of dentistry or surgery pertaining to prosthesis.

pros·ti·tute (pros′tə tūt′ or pros′tə tüt′) *n. v.* **-tut·ed, -tut·ing. —***n.* **1** a woman who engages in sexual intercourse for pay. **2** a person who does unworthy things for money, position, or other personal advantage. —*v.* put to an unworthy use. [< L *prostitutus*, pp. of *prostituere* prostitute < *pro-* publicly + *statuere* cause to stand]

pros·ti·tu·tion (pros′tə tū′shən or pros′tə tü′shən) *n.* **1** the act or business of engaging in sexual intercourse for pay. **2** the use of one's honor, talents, etc. in an unworthy way.

pros·trate (pros′trāt) *v.* **-trat·ed, -trat·ing,** *adj.* —*v.* **1** lay down flat; cast down: *The captives prostrated themselves before the conqueror.* **2** make very weak or helpless; exhaust: *Sickness often prostrates people.* —*adj.* **1** lying flat, with the face downward. **2** lying flat. **3** helpless; overcome: *a prostrate enemy.* [< L *prostratus*, pp. of *prosternere* < *pro-* forth + *sternere* strew] **—Syn.** *adj.* **1, 2** prone.

pros·tra·tion (pros trā′shən) *n.* **1** the act of prostrating; bowing down low or lying face down in submission, respect, or worship. **2** the state or condition of being very much worn out in body or mind; exhaustion; dejection.

pros·y (prōz′ē) *adj.* **pros·i·er, pros·i·est.** like prose; commonplace; dull; tiresome. —**pros′i·ly,** *adv.* —**pros′i·ness,** *n.*

Prot. Protestant.

prot·ac·tin·i·um (prōt′ak tin′ē əm) *n.* a rare radioactive metallic chemical element. *Symbol*: Pa; *at.no.* 91; *at.wt.* 231 (most stable isotope). Formerly, **protoactinium.** [< *proto-* (< Gk. *protos* first) + *actinium*]

pro·tag·o·nist (prō tag′ə nist) *n.* **1** the main character in a play, story, or novel. **2** a person who takes a leading part; an active supporter. [< Gk. *prōtagōnistēs* < *prōtos* first + *agōnistēs* actor < *agōn* contest < *agein* do]

pro·te·an (prō′tē ən or prō tē′ən) *adj.* readily assuming different forms or characters; exceedingly variable. [< *Proteus*]

pro·tect (prə tekt′) *v.* **1** shield from harm or danger; shelter; defend; guard. **2** guard (home industry) by taxing competing foreign goods that are imported into the country. [< L *protectus*, pp. of *protegere* < *pro-* in front + *tegere* to cover] —**Syn. 1** secure. See **guard.**

pro·tect·ing·ly (prə tek′ting lē) *adv.* so as to protect.

pro·tec·tion (prə tek′shən) *n.* **1** the act of protecting; condition of being kept from harm; defence: *We have policemen for our protection.* **2** a thing or person that prevents damage: *An apron offers protection for a person doing dirty work.* **3** the system of taxing imported foreign goods so that people are more likely to buy goods made in their own country; the opposite of free trade. **4** something that assures safe passage through a region; a passport. **5** *Informal.* the payment of money to racketeers or gangsters as a form of tribute in order not to be molested. —**Syn. 1** guard, security. **2** shield, safeguard, bulwark.

pro·tec·tion·ism (prə tek′shən iz′əm) *n.* in economics, the system or theory of protection.

pro·tec·tion·ist (prə tek′shən ist) *n.* a person who favors protectionism. —*adj.* of protectionism or protectionists.

pro·tec·tive (prə tek′tiv) *adj.* **1** being a defence; protecting: *the hard protective covering of a turtle.* **2** preventing injury to those around: *a protective device on a machine.* **3** guarding against the competition of foreign-made goods by putting a high tax or duty on them: *a protective tariff.* —**pro·tec′tive·ly,** *adv.* —**pro·tec′tive·ness,** *n.*

protective coloring or **colouring** a coloring some animals have that makes them hard to distinguish from their surroundings, and so hides them from their enemies.

protective mimicry a close resemblance of an animal to its surroundings or to some different animal, that prevents its enemies from attacking it.

pro·tec·tor (prə tek′tər) *n.* **1** a person or thing that protects; defender. **2** the head of a kingdom when the king or queen cannot rule.

pro·tec·tor·ate (prə tek′tər it) *n.* **1** a weak country under the protection and partial control of a strong country. Parts of Africa are European protectorates. **2** such protection and control. **3** the position or term of a protector. **4** government by a protector. **5 Protectorate,** the period (1653-1659) during which Oliver and Richard Cromwell were Lord Protectors of England.

pro·tec·tress (prə tek′tris) *n.* a woman protector.

pro·té·gé (prō′tə zhā′) *n.* a person under the patronage or protection of another. [< F *protégé*, pp. of *protéger* < L *protegere.* See PROTECT.]

pro·té·gée (prō′tə zhā′) *n.* a woman protégé.

pro·te·id (prō′tē id) *n. adj.* protein.

pro·te·in (prō′tēn or prō′tē in) *n.* a complex compound containing nitrogen that is a necessary part of the cells of animals and plants. Meat, milk, cheese, eggs, and beans contain protein. [< L < Gk. *prōteios* of the first quality]

pro tem. pro tempore.

pro tem·po·re (prō′tem′pə rē) *Latin.* for the time being; temporarily.

hat, āge, cãre, fär; let, ēqual, tėrm; it, īce
hot, ōpen, ôrder; oil, out; cup, pu̇t, rüle, ūse
əbove, takən, pencəl, lemən, circəs
ch, child; ng, long; sh, ship
th, thin; ᴛʜ, then; zh, measure

Prot·er·o·zo·ic (prot′ər ə zō′ik) in geology: —*n.* **1** a very early era, beginning approximately 1200 million years ago. **2** the rocks formed in this era. See **geology** for chart. —*adj.* of or having to do with this era or the rocks formed during it. [< Gk. *proteros* prior + *zōē* life]

pro·test (*n.* prō′test; *v.* prə test′) *n.* **1** a statement that denies or objects strongly: *They yielded only after protest.* **2** a solemn declaration: *The accused man was judged guilty in spite of his protest of innocence.* **3 under protest,** unwillingly; though objecting. **4** a written statement by a notary public that a bill, note, cheque, etc. has been presented to someone who has refused to pay it or accept it. **5** in sports, an objection to a player or a play as illegal.
—*v.* **1** make objections; object: *The boys protested against having girls in the game.* **2** object to: *protest a decision.* **3** declare solemnly; assert: *The accused man protested his innocence.* **4** state that (a cheque, note, bill, etc.) has not been paid. [ME < OF *protest* < *protester* protest < L *protestari*, ult. < *pro-* forth + *testis* witness]

Prot·es·tant (prot′is tənt) *n.* **1** a member of any of certain Christian churches that have developed after the break with the Roman Catholic Church in the sixteenth century. Baptists, Presbyterians, and United Church members are all Protestants. **2 protestant,** a person who protests. —*adj.* **1** of Protestants or their religion. **2 protestant,** protesting. [< L *protestans, -antis*, ppr. of *protestari.* See PROTEST.]

Protestant Episcopal Church in the United States, a Protestant church having principles and beliefs similar to those of the Anglican Church of Canada.

Prot·es·tant·ism (prot′is tənt iz′əm) *n.* **1** the religion of Protestants. **2** their principles and beliefs. **3** Protestants or Protestant churches as a group.

prot·es·ta·tion (prot′is tā′shən) *n.* **1** a solemn declaration; protesting: *make a protestation of one's innocence.* **2** a protest.

Pro·te·us (prō′tē əs or prō′tūs) *n.* in Greek mythology, a sea god who had the power of assuming many different forms.

pro·thal·li·um (prō thal′ē əm) *n.* **-thal·li·a** (-thal′ē ə). **1** the gametophyte of ferns, etc. **2** the analogous rudimentary gametophyte of seed-bearing plants. [< NL *prothallium*, ult. < Gk. *pro-* before + *thallos* sprout]

pro·tho·rax (prō thôr′aks) *n.* **-tho·rax·es** or **-tho·rac·es** (-thôr′ə sēz′). the anterior segment of an insect's thorax, bearing the first pair of legs. [< F *prothorax* < NL < Gk. *pro-* + *thorax* chest, throat]

pro·to·ac·tin·i·um (prō′tō ak tin′ē əm) *n.* the former name of **protactinium.**

pro·to·col (prō′tə kol′) *n.* **1** a first draft or record from which a document, especially a treaty, is prepared. **2** the rules of etiquette of the diplomatic corps. **3** the rules for any procedure. [< OF < Med.L *protocollum* < Gk. *prōtokollon* a first leaf (with date and contents) glued onto a papyrus roll < *prōtos* first + *kolla* glue]

pro·ton (prō′ton) *n.* a tiny particle carrying one unit of positive electricity. All atoms are built up of electrons and protons. [< Gk. *prōton*, neut. adj., first]

pro·to·plasm (prō′tə plaz′əm) *n.* living matter; the substance that is the physical basis of life; the living substance of all plant and animal cells. Protoplasm is a colorless matter somewhat like soft jelly or white of egg. [< G *Protoplasma* < Gk. *prōtos* first + *plasma* something moulded < *plassein* mould]

pro·to·plas·mic (prō′tə plaz′mik) *adj.* of or having to do with protoplasm.

pro·to·type (prō′tə tīp′) *n.* the first or primary type of anything; the original or model: *A modern ship has its prototype in the hollowed log used by savages.* [< NL < Gk. *prōtotypon*, originally neut. of *prōtotypos* original, primitive < *prōtos* first + *typos* type, model]

Pro·to·zo·a (prō′tə zō′ə) *n.pl.* protozoans. [< NL *Protozoa*, pl., < Gk. *prōtos* first + *zōion* animal]

pro·to·zo·an (prō′tə zō′ən) *n.* a microscopic animal that consists of a single cell. —*adj.* belonging or having to do with the single-celled animals.

pro·tract (prō trakt′) *v.* **1** draw out; lengthen in time: *protract a visit.* **2** slide out; thrust out; extend. **3** draw by means of a scale and protractor. [< L *protractus*, pp. of *protrahere* < *pro-* forward + *trahere* drag]

pro·trac·tile (prō trak′tīl or -trak′təl) *adj.* capable of being lengthened out, or of being thrust forth. The turtle has a protractile head.

pro·trac·tion (prō trak′shən) *n.* **1** the act of drawing out; extension. **2** a drawing that has exactly the same proportions as the thing it represents.

pro·trac·tor (prō trak′tər) *n.* **1** an instrument for drawing or measuring angles. **2** a person or thing that protracts.

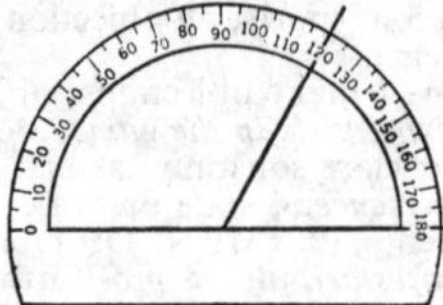

A protractor measuring a 120-degree angle. It may **be made of metal,** plastic, **etc.**

pro·trude (prō trüd′ or prə trüd′) *v.* **-trud·ed, -trud·ing. 1** thrust forth; stick out: *The saucy child protruded her tongue.* **2** be thrust forth; project: *Her teeth protrude too far.* [< L *protrudere* < *pro-* forward + *trudere* thrust]

pro·trud·ent (prō trüd′ənt) *adj.* protruding.

pro·tru·sion (prō trü′zhən) *n.* **1** the act of protruding or the state of being protruded. **2** something that sticks out; projection. [< L *protrusus*, pp. of *protrudere*. See PROTRUDE.]

pro·tru·sive (prō trü′siv) *adj.* sticking out; projecting. —**pro·tru′sive·ly,** *adv.*

pro·tu·ber·ance (prō tū′bər əns or prō tü′bər əns) *n.* a part that sticks out; bulge; swelling.

pro·tu·ber·ant (prō tū′bər ənt or prō tü′bər ənt) *adj.* bulging out; sticking out; prominent. [< LL *protuberans, -antis* bulging, ppr. of *protuberare*, ult. < *pro-* forward + *tuber* lump] —**pro·tu′ber·ant·ly,** *adv.*

proud (proud) *adj.* **1** thinking well of oneself. **2** feeling or showing pleasure or satisfaction. **3** having a becoming sense of what is due to oneself, one's position, or character. **4** thinking too well of oneself; haughty; arrogant: *He was too proud to share a taxi with a stranger.* **5** such as to make a person proud; highly honorable, creditable, or gratifying: *a proud moment.* **6** proceeding from pride; due to pride: *a proud smile.* **7** imposing; stately; majestic; magnificent: *proud cities.* **8** of persons, of exalted rank or station: *proud nobles.* **9** full of spirit or mettle: *a proud war horse.* **10 do one proud,** *Informal.* make proud; do very well; gratify highly. **11 proud of,** thinking well of; being well satisfied with; proud because of. [OE *prūd* < OF *prod, prud* valiant < LL *prode* of use < L *prodesse* be useful] —**proud′ly,** *adv.* —**proud′ness,** *n.*

Syn. 1 Proud, overbearing, supercilious = having or showing a high opinion of oneself. **Proud** may mean either holding oneself above anything low, mean, or contemptible or thinking oneself better than others, but usually also suggests a haughty or conceited manner or appearance: *He has a strong, proud face.* **Overbearing** suggests being rudely dictatorial or haughtily insulting in behavior and speech: *Promoted too quickly, the conceited youth became overbearing.* **Supercilious** suggests conceit, but emphasizes a coolly scornful attitude: *With a supercilious smile he refused our invitation.*

proud flesh the formation of too many grainlike particles of flesh during the healing of a wound or sore.

prov. 1 province. **2** provincial. **3** provisional. **4** provost.

Prov. 1 Proverbs. **2** Provence. **3** Province. **4** Provost.

prove (prüv) *v.* **proved, proved** or **prov·en, prov·ing. 1** establish as true; make certain. **2** establish the genuineness or validity of, especially of a will. **3** be found to be: *This book proved interesting.* **4** try out; test; subject to some testing process: *prove a new gun.* [ME < OF *prover* < L *probare* < *probus* worthy] —**prov′a·ble,** *adj.* —**Syn. 1** corroborate, verify, confirm.

prov·en (prüv′ən) *v.* a pp. of **prove.**

Pro·ven·çal (prov′ən sal′; *French,* prô väN säl′) *n.* **1** a native or inhabitant of Provence, a region in S.E. France. **2** the language of Provence. —*adj.* of or having to do with Provence, its people, or their language.

prov·en·der (prov′ən dər) *n.* **1** dry food for animals, such as hay or corn. **2** *Informal.* food. [ME < OF *provendre* < VL *probenda* < L *praebenda.* See PREBEND.]

prov·erb (prov′ėrb) *n.* **1** a short saying expressing a general truth, accepted and used for a long time. **2** an enigmatic statement. **3** a well-known example: *He is a proverb for carelessness.* **4 Proverbs,** a book of the Old Testament made up of sayings of the wise men of Israel, including Solomon. [ME < OF < L *proverbium* < *pro-* forth + *verbum* word, originally, a speaking] ☛ See **epigram** for usage note.

pro·ver·bi·al (prə vėr′bē əl) *adj.* **1** of proverbs; expressed in a proverb; like a proverb: *proverbial brevity, proverbial wisdom, a proverbial saying.* **2** that has become a proverb: *the proverbial stitch in time.* **3** well-known: *the proverbial loyalty of dogs.* —**pro·ver′bi·al·ly,** *adv.*

pro·vide (prə vīd′) *v.* **-vid·ed, -vid·ing. 1** supply; furnish: *Sheep provide us with wool.* **2** supply means of support; arrange to supply means of support: *A father provides for his family.* **3** take care for the future: *provide against accident, provide for old age.* **4** state as a condition beforehand: *Our club's rules provide that dues must be paid monthly.* **5** get ready; prepare. [< L *providere* < *pro-* ahead + *videre* see. Doublet of PURVEY.] —**pro·vid′er,** *n.*

pro·vid·ed (prə vīd′id) *conj.* on the condition that; if: *She will go provided her friends can go also.*

prov·i·dence (prov′ə dəns) *n.* **1** God's care and help. **2** an instance of God's care and help. **3** care for the future; good management. **4 Providence,** God.

prov·i·dent (prov′ə dənt) *adj.* **1** having or showing foresight; careful in providing for the future: *Provident men lay aside money for their families.* **2** economical; frugal. [ME < L *providens, -entis,* ppr. of *providere.* See PROVIDE.] —**prov′i·dent·ly,** *adv.* —**Syn. 1** prudent.

prov·i·den·tial (prov′ə den′shəl) *adj.* **1** fortunate: *Our delay seemed providential, for the train we had planned to take was wrecked.* **2** of or proceeding from divine power or influence. —**prov′i·den′tial·ly,** *adv.*

pro·vid·ing (prə vīd′ing) *conj.* on the condition that: *I shall go providing it doesn't rain.*

prov·ince (prov′əns) *n.* **1** in Canada, one of the ten main political divisions: *Newfoundland became the tenth province on April 1, 1949.* **2** in certain other countries, a main political or economic division. **3** a part of a country outside the capital or the largest cities. **4** proper work or activity: *Teaching spelling is not within the province of a college.* **5** division; department: *the province of science, the province of literature.* **6** in ancient Rome, a territory outside Italy, ruled by a Roman governor. **7** a large church district governed by an archbishop. [ME < OF < L *provincia*]

pro·vin·cial (prə vin′shəl) *adj.* **1** of a province. **2** belonging or peculiar to some particular province or provinces rather than to the whole country; local: *provincial English, provincial customs.* **3** having the manners, speech, dress, point of view, etc. of people living in a province. **4** lacking refinement or polish; narrow: *a provincial point of view.*
—*n.* **1** a person born or living in a province. **2** a provincial person. **3** *Cdn.* a member of the provincial police. —**pro·vin′cial·ly,** *adv.*

pro·vin·cial·ise (prə vin′shə līz′) *v.* **-ised, -is·ing.** provincialize.

pro·vin·cial·ism (prə vin′shəl iz′əm) *n.* **1** provincial manners, habits of thought, etc. **2** narrow-mindedness. **3** a word, expression, or way of pronunciation peculiar to a district of a country; localism.

pro·vin·ci·al·i·ty (prə vin′shē al′ə tē) *n.* **-ties. 1** a provincial quality or character. **2** a provincial characteristic or trait.

pro·vin·cial·ize (prə vin′shə līz′) *v.* **-ized, -iz·ing. 1** bring under the authority of a province. **2** give a provincial status or name to; make provincial. Also, **provincialise.**

provincial judge, a magistrate.

provincial park *Cdn.* a tract of land established by a

provincial government as a preserve for wild life and as a holiday area: *Algonquin Park in Ontario is a well-known provincial park.*

provincial parliament *Cdn.* the legislative assembly of a province.

provincial police in Ontario and Quebec, a police force maintained by the provincial government.

pro·vi·sion (prə vizh′ən) *n.* **1** a statement making a condition: *A provision of the lease is that the rent must be paid promptly.* **2** a taking care for the future. **3** care taken for the future; an arrangement made beforehand: *There is a provision for making the building larger if necessary.* **4** that which is made ready; supply; stock, especially of food; food. **5 make provision,** take care for the future; make arrangement beforehand. **6 provisions,** *pl.* a supply of food and drinks. —*v.* supply with provisions. [ME < OF < L *provisio, -onis* < *providere.* See PROVIDE.] —**Syn.** *n.* **6** See **food.**

pro·vi·sion·al (prə vizh′ən əl) *adj.* for the time being; temporary: *a provisional agreement, a provisional government.* —*n.* a postage stamp issued for use until the regular issue is available.

pro·vi·sion·al·ly (prə vizh′ə nəl ē) *adv.* **1** for the time being; temporarily. **2** conditionally.

pro·vi·so (prə vī′zō) *n.* **-sos** or **-soes.** a sentence or part of a sentence in a contract, or other agreement, that states a condition; condition: *He was admitted to the advanced course with the proviso that he was to be put back if he failed.* [< L *proviso* it being provided < *providere.* See PROVIDE.]

pro·vi·so·ry (prə vī′zə rē) *adj.* **1** containing a proviso; conditional. **2** provisional.

pro·vo·ca·teur (prô vô kä tœr′) *n. French.* one who stirs up trouble or provokes violence.

prov·o·ca·tion (prov′ə kā′shən) *n.* **1** the act of provoking. **2** something that stirs one up; a cause of anger: *Their insulting remarks were a provocation.* [ME < OF < L *provocatio, -onis* < *provocare.* See PROVOKE.]

pro·voc·a·tive (prə vok′ə tiv) *adj.* **1** irritating; vexing. **2** tending or serving to call forth action, thought, laughter, anger, etc.: *a remark provocative of mirth.* —*n.* something that rouses or irritates. —**pro·voc′a·tive·ly,** *adv.* —**pro·voc′a·tive·ness,** *n.*

pro·voke (prə vōk′) *v.* **-voked, -vok·ing. 1** make angry; vex. **2** stir up; excite: *An insult provokes a person to anger.* **3** call forth; bring about; start into action; cause. [< L *provocare* < *pro-* forth + *vocare* call] —**pro·vok′er,** *n.* —**Syn. 1** exasperate, nettle. See **irritate. 2** rouse, kindle.

pro·vok·ing (prə vōk′ing) *adj.* that provokes; irritating. —**pro·vok′ing·ly,** *adv.*

pro·vo·lo·ne (prō′vō lō′nā) *n. Italian.* a hard, sharp cheese having a smoky flavor.

prov·ost (prov′əst) *n.* **1** a person appointed to superintend, maintain discipline, or preside, such as the head of certain colleges or churches. **2** in Scotland, the chief magistrate of a town. [partly OE *profost,* partly < OF *provost,* both < Med.L *propositus,* used for L *praepositus* placed in charge of, originally pp. of *praeponere* place before < *prae-* at the head of + *ponere* to place]

pro·vost marshal (prō′vō) **1** in the army and air force, an officer acting as head of police in a camp or district, and charged with the maintenance of order, etc. **2** in the navy, an officer charged with the safekeeping of prisoners until their trial by court-martial. *Abbrev.:* P.M.

prow (prou) *n.* **1** the pointed front part of a ship or boat; bow. **2** something like this: *the prow of an airship.* [< F *proue* < Ital. < L < Gk. *prōira*]

prow·ess (prou′is) *n.* **1** bravery; daring. **2** brave or daring acts. **3** unusual skill or ability. [ME < OF *proece* < *prod* valiant. See PROUD.] —**Syn. 1** courage, valor.

prowl (proul) *v.* **1** go about slowly and secretly hunting for something to eat or steal: *Many wild animals prowl at night.* **2** wander; cruise about. —*n.* the act of prowling. [ME *prolle(n)*; origin uncertain] —**prowl′er,** *n.* —**Syn.** *v.* **1** slink.

prowl car a police car that patrols roads and streets and maintains contact with headquarters by radio telephone; squad car; cruiser.

hat, āge, cãre, fär; let, ēqual, tėrm; it, īce
hot, ōpen, ôrder; oil, out; cup, pu̇t, rüle, ūse
əbove, takən, pencəl, lemən, circəs
ch, child; ng, long; sh, ship
th, thin; ᴛʜ, then; zh, measure

prox·i·mal (prok′sə məl) *adj.* situated toward the point of origin or attachment. *Proximal* is opposed to *distal.* [< L *proximus* nearest]

prox·i·mate (prok′sə mit) *adj.* **1** next; nearest. **2** near the exact amount; approximate. [< pp. of Med.L **proximare* bring near < L *proximare* come near < *proximus* nearest]

prox·i·mate·ly (prok′sə mit lē) *adv.* next; very nearly; approximately.

prox·im·i·ty (proks im′ə tē) *n.* nearness; closeness. [< L *proximitas* < *proximus* nearest]

proximity fuse a tiny electronic device set in the nose of a projectile to make the shell explode at a certain distance from the target.

prox·i·mo (prok′sə mō′) *adv.* in or of the coming month: *on the 1st proximo.* [short for L *proximo mense* during next month]

prox·y (prok′sē) *n.* **prox·ies. 1** the action of a deputy or substitute. In marriage by proxy, someone is substituted for the absent bridegroom at the marriage service. **2** an agent; deputy; substitute. **3** a written statement authorizing a proxy to act or vote for a person. **4** the vote so given. [ME *prokecye,* alteration of *procuracy* the office of proctor < Med.L *procuratia,* ult. < L *procurare.* See PROCURE.]

prude (prüd) *n.* a person who is affectedly proper or modest in matters concerning sex; person who puts on extremely proper or modest airs. [< F *prude* < *prudefemme* excellent woman < OF *prou, prod* excellent + *femme* woman]

pru·dence (prü′dəns) *n.* **1** the exercising of careful thought before taking action; good judgment or discretion. **2** good management; economy.

Syn. 1 Prudence, foresight = thought in acting and planning. **Prudence** emphasizes common sense in directing oneself and one's affairs, giving thought to one's actions and their consequences, and usually suggests caution, watchfulness, and saving: *Prudence is wisdom in everyday life.* **Foresight** emphasizes ability to see what is likely to happen, and giving thought to being prepared: *He had the foresight to carry fire insurance.*

pru·dent (prü′dənt) *adj.* planning carefully ahead of time; sensible; discreet: *A prudent man saves part of his wages.* [ME < L *prudens, -entis,* var. of *providens.* See PROVIDENT.] —**pru′dent·ly,** *adv.* —**Syn.** judicious, wise, cautious.

pru·den·tial (prü den′shəl) *adj.* of, marked by, or showing prudence. —**pru·den′tial·ly,** *adv.*

prud·er·y (prüd′ər ē) *n.* **-er·ies. 1** extreme modesty or propriety, especially when not genuine. **2** a prudish act or remark.

prud·ish (prüd′ish) *adj.* like a prude; extremely proper or modest; too modest. —**prud′ish·ly,** *adv.* —**prud′ish·ness,** *n.*

prune[1] (prün) *n.* **1** a kind of dried sweet plum. **2** a plum suitable for drying. **3** *Slang.* a person thought to be unattractive, stupid, or unpleasant. [ME < OF < VL *pruna* < L *prunum* < Gk. *proumnon.* Doublet of PLUM.]

prune[2] (prün) *v.* **pruned, prun·ing. 1** cut out useless or undesirable parts from. **2** cut superfluous or undesirable twigs or branches from (a bush, tree, etc.). **3** cut off or out. [ME < OF *prooignier* < *por-* (< L *pro-*) + *rooignier* clip, originally, round off < L *rotundus* round] —**prun′er,** *n.*

pruning hook an implement with a hooked blade, used for pruning vines, etc.

pru·ri·ence (prür′ē əns) *n.* the state or quality of being prurient.

pru·ri·en·cy (prür′ē ən sē) *n.* prurience.

pru·ri·ent (prür′ē ənt) *adj.* having lustful thoughts or wishes. [< L *pruriens, -entis,* ppr. of *prurire* itch, be wanton] —**pru′ri·ent·ly,** *adv.*

Prus·sian (prush′ən) *adj.* of or having to do with

Prussia, a former state in Europe, and, later, part of Germany, its people, or their language. —*n.* **1** a native or inhabitant of Prussia. **2** the dialect of German spoken in Prussia.

Prussian blue a deep-blue pigment, essentially a cyanogen compound of iron. [so called from its discovery in Berlin, the capital of Prussia, in 1704]

prus·sic acid (prus′ik) a deadly poison that smells like bitter almonds; hydrocyanic acid. [*prussic* < F *prussique* < *Prusse* Prussia]

pry[1] (prī) *v.* **pried, pry·ing,** *n.* **pries.** —*v.* look with curiosity; peep: *She likes to pry into others' affairs.* —*n.* an inquisitive person. [ME *prie(n)*; origin uncertain]

pry[2] (prī) *v.* **pried, pry·ing,** *n.* **pries.** —*v.* **1** raise or move by force. **2** get with much effort: *We finally pried the secret out of him.* [< n.] —*n.* a lever for prying. [< obs. *prize* a lever, taken as a pl. See PRIZE[4].]

pry·ing (prī′ing) *adj.* looking or searching curiously; inquisitive. —**Syn.** See **curious.**

Ps. Psalm; Psalms.

P.S. 1 postscript. (for L *post scriptum*) **2** privy seal. **3** public school. **4** public sale. **5** passenger steamer.

psalm (som or säm) *n.* **1** a sacred song or poem. **2 Psalm,** any of the 150 sacred songs or hymns that together form a book of the Old Testament. **3 Psalms,** a book of the Old Testament consisting of 150 psalms. [OE *psalm, sealm* < LL < Gk. *psalmos,* originally, performance on a stringed instrument < *psallein* pluck]

psalm·book (som′bůk′ or säm′-) *n.* a collection of metrical translations of the Psalms prepared for public worship.

psalm·ist (som′ist or säm′ist) *n.* **1** the author of a psalm or psalms. **2 the Psalmist,** King David.

psalm·o·dy (som′ə dē or säm′ə dē) *n.* **-dies. 1** the act, practice, or art of singing psalms or hymns. **2** psalms or hymns. [ME < LL < Gk. *psalmōidia* < *psalmos* psalm + *ōidē* song]

Psal·ter (sol′tər or sôl′tər) *n.* **1** the Book of Psalms. **2** a version of the Psalms for liturgical or devotional use. **3** a prayer book containing such a version. [ME < OF < L < Gk. *psaltērion.* See PSALTERY.]

psal·ter·y (sol′tər ē or sôl′tər ē) *n.* **-ter·ies.** an ancient musical instrument played by plucking the strings. [OE *saltere* < L < Gk. *psaltērion,* originally, stringed instrument < *psallein* pluck]

pseud. pseudonym.

pseu·do (sü′dō) *adj.* **1** false; sham; pretended. **2** having only the appearance of. [< Gk. *pseudēs* false]

pseu·do·nym (sü′də nim′) *n.* a name used by an author instead of his real name. Ralph Connor is a pseudonym for Charles William Gordon. [< Gk. *pseudonymon* < *pseudēs* false + dial. *onyma* name]

p.s.f. pounds per square foot.

pshaw (sho or shô) *interj. n.* an exclamation expressing impatience, contempt, etc.

psi[1] (sī or psē) *n.* the 23rd letter of the Greek alphabet (Ψ, ψ).

psi[2] (sī or sē) *n.* psychic or psychological processes or phenomena, such as extrasensory perception, telepathy, clairvoyance, etc. [< Gk. *psi,* the first letter of *psychē* soul, life]

psit·ta·co·sis (sit′ə kō′sis) *n.* a contagious disease of parrots and other birds, communicable to people. [< NL < Gk. *psittakos* parrot + *-osis* diseased condition]

PST, P.S.T., or **p.s.t.** Pacific Standard Time.

psych. 1 psychology. **2** psychological.

psy·che (sī′kē) *n.* **1** the human soul or spirit. **2** the mind. [< L < Gk. *psychē* breath, life < *psychein* breathe, blow]

Psy·che (sī′kē) *n.* in Greek and Roman mythology, the human soul or spirit pictured as a beautiful young girl, usually with butterfly wings. Psyche was loved by Cupid, and was made immortal by Jupiter.

psy·che·del·ic (sī′kə del′ik) *adj.* revealing new areas of perception; expanding the consciousness. —*n.* a drug having such an effect. [coined word; lit. "mind-revealing," < Gk. *psychē* + *dēlein* to show + E *-ic*]

psy·chi·at·ric (sī′kē at′rik) *adj.* of or having to do with the treatment of mental diseases. —**psy·chi·at′ri·cal·ly,** *adv.*

psy·chi·a·trist (sī kī′ə trist or si kī′ə trist) *n.* a doctor who treats mental disorders.

psy·chi·a·try (sī kī′ə trē or si kī′ə trē) *n.* the study and treatment of mental disorders. [< *psycho-* + Gk. *iatreia* cure, ult. < *iaesthai* heal]

psy·chic (sī′kik) *adj.* **1** of the soul or mind; mental: *illness due to psychic causes.* **2** outside the known laws of physics; supernatural. A psychic force or influence is believed by spiritualists to explain second sight, telepathy, table moving, tappings, etc. **3** especially susceptible to psychic influences. —*n.* **1** a person supposed to be specially sensitive or responsive to psychic force or spiritual influences; medium. **2** things that are psychic. [< Gk. *psychikos* < *psychē* soul, mind]

psy·chi·cal (sī′kə kəl) *adj.* psychic. —**psy′chi·cal·ly,** *adv.*

psycho- *combining form.* mind, as in *psychoanalysis.* Also, **psych-** before some vowels. [< Gk. *psychē* soul, mind]

psy·cho·an·a·lyse or **psy·cho·an·a·lyze** (sī′ko an′ə līz′) *v.* **-lysed** or **-lyzed, -lys·ing** or **-lyz·ing.** examine by psychoanalysis. —**psy′cho·an′a·lys′er** or **psy′cho·an′a·lyz′er,** *n.*

psy·cho·a·nal·y·sis (sī′kō ə nal′ə sis) *n.* **1** the minute examination of a mind or minds to discover the underlying mental causes producing certain mental and nervous disorders; analysis of mind or personality. **2** the body of theory originated and first developed by Sigmund Freud, 1856-1939, an Austrian neurologist.

psy·cho·an·a·lyst (sī′kō an′ə list) *n.* a person who is skilled in or practises psychoanalysis.

psy·cho·an·a·lyt·ic (sī′kō an′ə lit′ik) *adj.* having to do with or of the nature of psychoanalysis.

psy·cho·an·a·lyt·i·cal (sī′kō an′ə lit′ə kəl) *adj.* psychoanalytic. —**psy′cho·an′a·lyt′i·cal·ly,** *adv.*

psy·cho·an·a·lyze (sī′kō an′ə līz′) *v.* **-lyzed, -lyz·ing.** psychoanalyse. —**psy′cho·an′a·lyz′er,** *n.*

psy·cho·chem·i·cal (sī′kō kem′ə kəl) *adj.* of chemical compounds, capable of modifying people's behavior, attitudes, etc. —*n.* any chemical compound of this nature: *Psychochemicals are used in chemical warfare.*

psy·cho·log·ic (sī′kə loj′ik) *adj.* psychological.

psy·cho·log·i·cal (sī′kə loj′ə kəl) *adj.* **1** of the mind. **2** of or having to do with psychology or psychologists. —**psy′cho·log′i·cal·ly,** *adv.*

psychological moment 1 the moment psychologically most appropriate to achieve a desired end. **2** the critical moment.

psychological warfare systematic efforts to affect morale, loyalty, etc., especially of large national groups.

psy·chol·o·gist (sī kol′ə jist) *n.* a person skilled or trained in psychology.

psy·chol·o·gy (sī kol′ə jē) *n.* **-gies. 1** the study of the mind and the ways of thought. Psychology tries to explain why people act, think, and feel as they do. **2** a textbook or handbook of psychology. **3** the mental states and processes of a person or persons; mental nature and behavior: *Mrs. Jones knew her husband's psychology.* [< NL *psychologia* < Gk. *psychē* soul, mind + *-logos* treating of]

psy·cho·mo·tor (sī′kō mō′tər) *adj.* of or having to do with muscular activity resulting from mental processes.

psy·cho·neu·ro·sis (sī′kō nū rō′sis or -nü rō′sis) *n.* **-ses** (-sēz). a mental disorder with physical symptoms but without apparent organic disease.

psy·cho·path (sī′kə path′) *n.* one who is suffering from mental illness.

psy·cho·path·ic (sī′kə path′ik) *adj.* **1** of or having to do with mental disorders. **2** having a mental disorder. —**psy′cho·path′i·cal·ly,** *adv.*

psy·chop·a·thy (sī kop′ə thē) *n.* **1** mental disorder. **2** mental eccentricity or instability so extreme as to border on insanity.

hat, āge, cãre, fär; let, ēqual, tėrm; it, īce
hot, ōpen, ôrder; oil, out; cup, pu̇t, rüle, ūse
əbove, takən, pencəl, lemən, circəs
ch, child; ng, long; sh, ship
th, thin; ᴛʜ, then; zh, measure

psy·cho·ses (sī kō′sēz) *n.* pl. of **psychosis.**

psy·cho·sis (sī kō′sis) *n.* **-ses.** any severe form of mental disturbance or disease. [< NL < Gk. *psychosis* < *psychē* soul, mind]

psy·cho·so·mat·ic (sī′kō sə mat′ik) *adj.* **1** of or having to do with both mind and body. **2** of or having to do with physical disorders caused by mental or emotional disturbances. **—psy′cho·so·mat′i·cal·ly,** *adv.*

psychosomatic medicine the branch of medicine that deals with the inter-relationships between physical disorders and mental or emotional disturbances.

psy·cho·ther·a·py (sī′kō ther′ə pē) *n.* the treatment of mental or physical disorders by psychological methods.

psy·chot·ic (sī kot′ik) *adj.* of or having to do with psychosis; unstable; insane. *—n.* an unstable or insane person.

psy·chrom·e·ter (sī krom′ə tər) *n.* a type of hygrometer having dry-bulb and wet-bulb thermometers, for measuring humidity. [< Gk. *psychros* cold + E *-meter*]

pt. **1** pint. **2** part. **3** point. **4** past tense. **5** preterite. **6** port.

Pt platinum.

P.T. physical training.

PTA or **P.T.A.** Parent-Teacher Association.

ptar·mi·gan (tär′mə gən) *n.* **-gans** or (*esp. collectively*) **-gan.** any of several kinds of grouse that have feathered feet and are found in mountainous and cold regions. [< Scots Gaelic *tarmachan*, *p* added by mistaken analogy with Gk. word]

PT boat *U.S.* a small, fast motorboat that carries torpedoes, depth bombs, etc. [< *P*atrol *T*orpedo *boat*]

Pte. Private.

pter·i·do·phyte (ter′ə dō fīt′) *n.* any of the highest group of seedless plants having roots, stems, and leaves. Ferns, horsetails, and club mosses are pteridophytes. [< Gk. *pteris, pteridos* fern + E *-phyte*]

pter·o·dac·tyl (ter′ə dak′təl) *n.* an extinct flying reptile that had wings resembling those of a bat. [< Gk. *pteron* wing + *daktylos* finger, toe]

pter·o·saur (ter′ə sôr′) *n.* any of an extinct order of flying reptiles.

P.T.O. or **p.t.o.** please turn (the page) over.

Ptol·e·ma·ic (tol′ə mā′ik) *adj.* **1** of or having to do with Claudius Ptolemy, a Greek mathematician, astronomer, and geographer, who lived in the second century A.D. The **Ptolemaic system** of astronomy taught that the earth was the fixed centre of the universe, around which the heavenly bodies moved. **2** of or having to do with the Ptolemies, who were rulers of Egypt from 323 B.C. to 30 B.C.

Ptol·e·my (tol′ə mē) *n.* any of a certain family of Egyptian rulers who ruled Egypt from 323 to 30 B.C.

pto·maine or **pto·main** (tō′mān or tō mān′) *n.* a basic, nitrogenous, organic substance, often poisonous, produced in decaying matter. Improperly canned foods may contain ptomaines. [< Ital. *ptomaina* < Gk. *ptōma* corpse]

ptomaine poisoning poisoning caused by ptomaines.

pts. **1** pints. **2** parts. **3** points.

pty·a·lin (tī′ə lin) *n.* an enzyme contained in the saliva of man and of certain other animals that converts starch into dextrin and maltose, thus aiding digestion. [< Gk. *ptyalon* saliva < *ptyein* spit]

Pu plutonium.

pub (pub) *n. Informal.* a saloon; tavern; beer parlor. [short for *public house*]

pu·ber·ty (pū′bər tē) *n.* the physical beginning of manhood and womanhood. Puberty comes at about 14 in boys and at about 12 in girls. [< L *pubertas* < *pubes* adult]

pu·bes·cence (pū bes′əns) *n.* **1** arrival at puberty. **2** a soft, downy growth on plants and some insects. **3** the fact of having such a growth.

pu·bes·cent (pū bes′ənt) *adj.* **1** arriving or arrived at puberty. **2** covered with down or fine, short hair: *a pubescent stem or leaf.* [< L *pubescens, -entis* reaching puberty < *pubes* adult]

pu·bic (pū′bik) *adj.* having to do with the pubis.

pu·bis (pū′bis) *n.* **-bes** (-bēz). in anatomy, part of either hipbone that, with the corresponding part of the other, forms the front of the pelvis. [< NL *os pubis* bone of the groin]

pub·lic (pub′lik) *adj.* **1** of, belonging to, or concerning the people as a whole: *public affairs.* **2** done, made, acting, etc. for the people as a whole: *public relief.* **3** open to all the people; serving all the people: *a public park.* **4** of or engaged in the affairs or service of the people: *a public official.* **5** known to many or all; not private: *The fact became public.* **6** international: *public law.*
—n. **1** the people in general; all the people. **2** a particular section of the people: *A popular actor has a large public.* **3 in public,** not in private or secretly; publicly; openly. [< L *publicus*, ult. < *populus* the people; form influenced by *pubes* adult male population]

public address system an arrangement of loudspeakers used to carry speeches, messages, music, etc. to an audience in a large room, in different rooms of one building, or in the open air. *Abbrev.*: P.A. system.

pub·li·can (pub′lə kən) *n.* **1** *Brit.* a keeper of a public house. **2** in ancient Rome, a tax collector. [< L *publicanus* (def. 2) < *publicum* public revenue, originally neut. of *publicus.* See PUBLIC.]

pub·li·ca·tion (pub′lə kā′shən) *n.* **1** a book, newspaper, or magazine; anything that is published. **2** the printing and selling of books, newspapers, magazines, etc. **3** the act of making known; the fact or state of being made known. [< L *publicatio, -onis*, ult. < *publicus.* See PUBLIC.]

public domain **1** lands belonging to the government. **2 in the public domain,** of works, material, etc., available for unrestricted use because unprotected by copyright or patent.

public enemy a person who is a menace to the public.

public funds money provided by the government: *Public funds are used to pay for defence.*

public house **1** *Brit.* a place where alcoholic liquor is sold to be drunk; saloon. **2** an inn; hotel.

pub·li·cist (pub′lə sist) *n.* **1** a person skilled or trained in law or in public affairs. **2** a writer on law, politics, or public affairs.

pub·lic·i·ty (pub lis′ə tē) *n.* **1** the fact of being brought to public notice by special effort, through newspapers, signs, radio, etc. **2** public notice: *the publicity that actors desire.* **3** measures used for getting, or the process of getting, public notice: *a campaign of publicity for a new automobile.* **4** the state of being public; being seen by or known to everybody: *in the publicity of the street.*

pub·li·cize (pub′lə sīz′) *v.* **-cized, -ciz·ing.** give publicity to.

pub·lic·ly (pub′lik lē) *adv.* **1** in a public manner; openly. **2** by the public.

public opinion the opinion of the people in a country, community, etc.

public relations the relations of an organization, institution, etc. with the public and the activities it undertakes to create and keep up a favorable public image of itself. *Abbrev.*: P.R. or PR.

public school **1** in Canada and the United States, a free school maintained by taxes. **2** in the United Kingdom, an endowed private boarding school.

public servant a person who works for the government.

pub·lic-spir·it·ed (pub′lik spir′ə tid) *adj.* having or showing an unselfish desire for the public good.

public utility a company formed or chartered to render services to the public, such as a company furnishing electricity or gas, a railway, a streetcar or bus line, etc.

public works things built by the government at public expense and for public use, such as roads, docks, canals, and waterworks.

pub·lish (pub′lish) *v.* **1** prepare and offer a book, paper, map, piece of music, etc. for sale or distribution. 2 bring out the book or books of: *Some Canadian writers are published abroad before being published in Canada.* 3 come into circulation; be published: *The newspapers here publish every weekday.* 4 make publicly or generally known: *Don't publish the faults of your friends.* [ME < OF *publier,* ult. < L *publicus* (see PUBLIC); modelled after *punish,* etc.] —**pub′lish·a·ble,** *adj.* —**Syn. 4** divulge, reveal, disclose.

pub·lish·er (pub′lish ər) *n.* a person or company whose business is to publish books, newspapers, magazines, etc.

PUC or **P.U.C.** Public Utilities Commission.

puce (pūs) *n. adj.* purplish or dark brown. [< F *puce* a flea < OF *pulce* < L *pulex, -licis*]

puck[1] (puk) *n.* 1 a mischievous spirit; goblin. 2 **Puck,** in English folklore, a mischievous fairy who appears in Shakespeare's play *A Midsummer Night's Dream.* [OE *pūca* goblin]

puck[2] (puk) *n.* a hard, black rubber disk used in hockey. [E dial. var. of *poke*[1]]

puck·a (puk′ə) *adj.* pukka.

puck-car·ri·er (puk′kar′ē ər) *n.* in hockey, the player in possession of the puck.

puck·er (puk′ər) *v.* draw into wrinkles or irregular folds: *pucker one's brow, pucker cloth in sewing. The baby's lips puckered just before he began to cry.* —*n.* an irregular fold; wrinkle: *There are puckers at the shoulders of this ill-fitting coat.* [apparently < *poke*[2]] —**Syn.** *v.* crease, purse.

puck·ish (puk′ish) *adv.* mischievous; impish. —**puck′ish·ly,** *adv.* —**puck′ish·ness,** *n.*

pud·ding (pu̇d′ing) *n.* 1 a soft dessert food, often having a milk base, and flavored and sweetened: *rice pudding.* 2 a cakelike dessert, flavored and sweetened and usually steamed or baked: *plum pudding.* 3 a kind of sausage. 4 anything soft like a pudding. [cf. F *boudin* stuffed sausage, ult. < L *botulus* sausage; cf. also OE *puduc* wart]

pud·dle (pud′əl) *n. v.* **-dled, -dling.** —*n.* 1 a small pool of water, especially dirty water. 2 a small pool of any liquid. 3 wet clay and sand stirred into a paste. —*v.* 1 make wet or muddy. 2 mix up (wet clay and sand) into a thick paste. 3 use a mixture of wet clay and sand to stop water from running through: *Puddle up that hole.* 4 stir (melted iron) with an oxidizing agent to make wrought iron. [ME *puddel,* dim. of OE *pudd* ditch] —**pud′dler,** *n.*

pud·dling (pud′ling) *n.* the act or process of converting pig iron into wrought iron by stirring the molten metal with an oxidizing agent.

pud·dly (pud′lē) *adj.* 1 full of puddles. 2 like a puddle.

pudg·y (puj′ē) *adj.* **pudg·i·er, pudg·i·est.** short and fat or thick. [Scots dial.] —**pudg′i·ly,** *adv.* —**pudg′i·ness,** *n.*

pueb·lo (pweb′lō) *n.* **-los.** 1 an Indian village built of adobe and stone. There were many pueblos in the S.W. United States. 2 **Pueblo, a** a group of tribes of North American Indians that live in pueblos. **b** a member of any of this group. [< Sp. *pueblo* people < L *populus*]

pu·er·ile (pū′ər īl′ or pū′ər əl) *adj.* foolish for a grown person to say or do; childish. [< L *puerilis* < *puer* boy] —**pu′er·ile′ly,** *adv.* —**pu′er·ile′ness,** *n.* —**Syn.** juvenile, immature.

pu·er·il·i·ty (pū′ər il′ə tē) *n.* **-ties.** 1 childishness; foolishness. 2 a foolish act, idea, or statement.

pu·er·per·al (pū ėr′pər əl) *adj.* of or having to do with childbirth. [< NL *puerperalis,* ult. < L *puer* child + *parere* bear]

Puer·to Ri·can (pwer′tə rē′kən) *adj.* of or having to do with Puerto Rico or its inhabitants. —*n.* a native or inhabitant of Puerto Rico.

puff (puf) *v.* 1 blow with short, quick blasts. 2 breathe quickly and with difficulty. 3 give out puffs; move with puffs: *The engine puffed out of the station.* 4 move or come in puffs: *Smoke puffed out of the chimney.* 5 smoke: *puff a cigar.* 6 swell with air or pride: *He puffed out his cheeks.* 7 arrange in soft, round masses. 8 praise in exaggerated language: *They puffed him to the skies.* —*n.* 1 a short, quick blast: *a puff of wind.* 2 a small quantity of air, smoke, etc. blown out in short, quick blasts. 3 a quick, hard breath. 4 the act or process of swelling. 5 a soft, round mass: *a puff of hair.* 6 a small pad for putting powder on the skin, etc. 7 a light pastry filled with whipped cream, jam, etc. 8 extravagant praise. 9 a portion of material gathered and held down at the edges but left full in the middle in dresses, etc. [cf. OE *pyffan*]

puff adder a large and poisonous African snake that puffs up the upper part of its body when excited.

puff·ball (puf′bol′ or -bôl′) *n.* a ball-shaped fungus resembling a mushroom. A ripe puffball gives off a cloud of tiny spores when suddenly broken.

puffed-up (puft′up′) *adj.* 1 bloated; swollen. 2 conceited; vain. 3 inflated with air.

puff·er (puf′ər) *n.* 1 one that puffs. 2 any of various fishes capable of inflating the body, such as the globefish.

puf·fin (puf′ən) *n.* a sea bird of the N. Atlantic that has a high, narrow, furrowed, parti-colored bill. [ME *poffin;* ? ult. < *puff* (from its puffed-up appearance)]

puff pastry a sweet pastry used for pie shells, etc. and made from a light, rich, flaky dough.

puff·y (puf′ē) *adj.* **puff·i·er, puff·i·est.** 1 puffed out; swollen. 2 puffed up; vain. 3 coming in puffs. —**puff′i·ness,** *n.*

pug (pug) *n.* 1 a breed of small, tan dog having a curly tail and turned-up nose. 2 a dog of this breed. 3 a pug nose. [probably a variant of *puck*[1]]

pu·gi·lism (pū′jə liz′əm) *n.* the art of fighting with the fists; boxing. [< L *pugil* boxer]

pu·gi·list (pū′jə list) *n.* a person who fights with the fists; boxer.

pu·gi·lis·tic (pū′jə lis′tik) *adj.* of or having to do with pugilism or pugilists. —**pu·gi·lis′ti·cal·ly,** *adv.*

pug·na·cious (pug nā′shəs) *adj.* having the habit of fighting; fond of fighting; quarrelsome. [< L *pugnax, -acis,* ult. < *pugnus* fist] —**pug·na′cious·ly,** *adv.* —**pug·na′cious·ness,** *n.* —**Syn.** combative.

pug·nac·i·ty (pug nas′ə tē) *n.* a fondness for fighting; quarrelsomeness.

pug nose a short, turned-up nose.

pug-nosed (pug′nōzd′) *adj.* having a pug nose.

pu·is·sance (pū′ə səns or pwis′əns) *n.* power; might; force; strength.

pu·is·sant (pū′ə sənt or pwis′ənt) *adj.* powerful; mighty; strong. [ME < OF *puissant* being powerful, ult. < var. of L *posse* be able] —**pu′is·sant·ly,** *adv.*

puke (pūk) *n. v.* **puked, puk·ing.** *Not now in polite use.* vomit. [origin uncertain]

puk·ka (puk′ə) *adj. Anglo-Indian.* 1 reliable; good. 2 solid; substantial. 3 permanent. Also, **pucka.** [< Hind. *pakka* cooked, ripe]

pul (pül) *n.* 1 a unit of money in Afghanistan, worth 1/100 of an afghani. 2 a coin worth one pul. [< Persian]

pul·chri·tude (pul′krə tūd′ or pul′krə tüd′) *n.* beauty. [ME < L *pulchritudo* < *pulcher* beautiful]

pule (pūl) *v.* **puled, pul·ing.** cry in a thin voice, as a sick child does; whimper; whine. [? imitative]

Pu·lit·zer Prize (pū′lit sər or pu̇l′it sėr) in the United States, any one of various prizes given each year for the best American drama, novel, biography, history, book of verse, editorial, and cartoon. They were established by Joseph Pulitzer (1847-1911), an American journalist, and first awarded in 1917.

pull (pu̇l) *v.* 1 move with the fingers, claws, teeth, etc. in such a way that the thing moved follows the fingers, etc.: *pull a tooth, pull a trigger, pull a sled up a hill.* 2 tug with the fingers, etc.: *He pulled at his tie.* 3 move, usually with effort or force: *The train pulled out of the station.* 4 pick; pluck: *pull flowers.* 5 tear; rip: *The baby pulled the toy to pieces.* 6 stretch too far; strain: *The football player pulled a ligament in his leg.* 7 row: *Pull for the shore.* 8 be provided or rowed with: *The boat pulls eight oars.* 9 drink. 10 suck: *pull at a cigar.* 11 hold back, especially to keep from winning: *pull one's punches in a fight.* 12 *Informal.* perform; carry through: *Don't pull any tricks.* 13 in golf, hit (a ball) so that, in the case of a

hat, āge, cãre, fär; let, ēqual, tėrm; it, īce
hot, ōpen, ôrder; oil, out; cup, pu̇t, rüle, ūse
əbove, takən, pencəl, lemən, circəs
ch, child; ng, long; sh, ship
th, thin; ᴛʜ, then; zh, measure

right-handed player, it curves to the left. **14** in printing, take (an impression or proof).
pull apart, a separate into pieces by pulling. **b** be severely critical of: *pull apart a term paper.*
pull for, *Informal.* give help to.
pull in, a stop; check. **b** *Informal.* arrest: *He was pulled in for speeding.* **c** arrive: *He pulled in this morning.*
pull off, *Slang.* do successfully.
pull oneself together, gather one's faculties, energy, etc.
pull out, withdraw from a venture, undertaking, etc.
pull through, get through a difficult or dangerous situation.
pull together, work in harmony; get on together.
pull up, a tear up; uproot. **b** remove utterly. **c** bring or come to a standstill. **d** move ahead.
—*n.* **1** the act or effort of pulling. **2** a difficult climb, journey, or other effort: *It was a hard pull to get up the hill.* **3** handle, rope, ring, or other thing to pull by. **4** a drink. **5** a suck: *a pull at a cigar.* **6** in golf, a pulling of the ball. **7** *Informal.* influence; advantage. **8** in printing, an impression or proof. [OE *pullian*] **—pull′er,** *n.*
Syn. *v.* **1 Pull, tug, jerk** = draw toward oneself. **Pull** is the general word meaning "draw (or try to draw) toward or after oneself" or in a particular stated or implied direction: *Pull the curtains across.* **Tug** = pull hard and, often, long, but does not always mean causing the thing or person to move: *The dog tugged at the tablecloth.* **Jerk** = pull, push, or twist quickly and suddenly: *She jerked her hand away. He jerked his hat off.*

pul·let (pu̇l′it) *n.* a young hen, usually less than a year old. [ME < OF *poulette,* dim. of *poule* hen < VL *pulla,* fem. of L *pullus* young fowl]

pul·ley (pu̇l′ē) *n.* **-leys. 1** a wheel with a grooved rim in which a rope, belt, or wire can run, making it possible to change the direction of the pull. **2** a set of such wheels used to increase the power applied. **3** a wheel used to transfer power by driving a belt or being driven by a belt that moves some other part of the machine. [ME < OF *poulie,* ult. < Gk. *polos* axle]

A man using a pulley (def. 1). The wheel revolves inside the frame by which it is hung.

Pull·man (pu̇l′mən) *n.* a Pullman car.

Pullman car 1 a railway car with berths or small rooms for passengers to sleep in. **2** a railway car with specially comfortable seats. [after George M. *Pullman* (1831-1897), an American inventor]

pull·o·ver (pu̇l′ō′vər) *n.* a sweater put on by pulling it over the head.

pul·mo·nar·y (pul′mə ner′ē) *adj.* **1** of or having to do with the lungs. Tuberculosis and pneumonia are pulmonary diseases. **2** having lungs. [< L *pulmonarius* < *pulmo* lung]

Pul·mo·tor (pu̇l′mō′tər or pul′mō′tər) *n. Trademark.* a device used to restore natural breathing in persons rescued from suffocation. [< L *pulmo* lung + E *motor*]

pulp (pulp) *n.* **1** the soft part of any fruit or vegetable. **2** of a tooth, the soft inner part containing blood vessels and nerves. **3** any soft, wet mass. Paper is made from wood pulp. **4** *Slang.* a magazine printed on cheap paper, and usually containing matter of a cheap, sensational nature. —*v.* reduce to pulp. [< L *pulpa*] **—pulp′less,** *adj.*

pul·pit (pu̇l′pit) *n.* **1** a platform or raised structure in a church from which the minister preaches. **2** preachers or sermons. [ME < LL *pulpitum* < L *pulpitum* scaffold, platform]

pulp·wood (pulp′wu̇d′) *n.* **1** wood reduced to pulp for making paper. **2** soft wood suitable for making paper.

pulp·y (pul′pē) *adj.* **pulp·i·er, pulp·i·est.** of pulp; like pulp; soft. **—pulp′i·ness,** *n.*

pul·sar (pul′sär) *n.* a radio star that emits pulsed radio waves; a pulsating radio source. [< *pulse* + *ar,* as in *quasar*]

pul·sate (pul′sāt) *v.* **-sat·ed, -sat·ing. 1** beat; throb: *The patient's heart was pulsating rapidly.* **2** vibrate; quiver. [< L *pulsare,* frequentative of *pellere* beat. Doublet of PUSH.]

pul·sa·tion (pul sā′shən) *n.* **1** a beating; throbbing. **2** a beat; throb. **3** a vibration; quiver.

pulse[1] (puls) *n. v.* **pulsed, puls·ing.** —*n.* **1** the beating of the heart; the changing flow of blood in the arteries caused by the beating of the heart. **2** the rate of this beating. **3** any regular, measured beat: *the pulse in music, the pulse of an engine.* **4** feeling; sentiment: *the pulse of the nation.* —*v.* beat; throb; vibrate: *His heart pulsed with excitement.* [< L *pulsus* < *pellere* beat]

pulse[2] (puls) *n.* the edible seeds of peas, beans, lentils, etc. [ME < OF < L *puls* porridge]

pulse·jet (puls′jet′) *n.* a type of jet engine into which the air necessary for the burning of the fuel is admitted in spurts by valves.

pul·ver·ize (pul′vər īz′) *v.* **-ized, -iz·ing. 1** grind to powder or dust. **2** become dust. **3** break to pieces; demolish. [< LL *pulverizare* < L *pulvis, -veris* dust] **—pul′ver·i·za′tion,** *n.* **—pul′ver·iz′er,** *n.*

pu·ma (pū′mə) *n.* a large North American wildcat; cougar. [< Sp. < *Quechua* (S. Am. Ind.)]

pum·ice (pum′is) *n. v.* **-iced, -ic·ing.** —*n.* a light, spongy stone thrown up from volcanoes, used for cleaning, smoothing, and polishing. —*v.* clean, smooth, or polish with pumice. [ME < OF < L *pumex, -micis.* Doublet of POUNCE[2].]

pumice stone pumice.

pum·mel (pum′əl) *v.* **-melled** or **-meled, -mell·ing** or **-mel·ing.** beat; beat with the fists; pommel.

pump[1] (pump) *n.* an apparatus or machine for forcing liquids, air, or gas into or out of things. —*v.* **1** move (liquids, air, etc.) by a pump. **2** blow air into. **3** remove water, etc. from by a pump. **4** work a pump. **5** work as a pump does. **6** move up and down like a pump handle. **7** move by, or as if by, a pump handle: *He pumped my hand.* **8** draw, force, etc. as if from a pump. **9** *Informal.* get information out of; try to get information out of: *Don't let him pump you.* [< F *pompe,* ? < Gmc.]

pump[2] (pump) *n.* a low-cut shoe with no buckles or laces. [origin uncertain]

pum·per·nick·el (pum′pər nik′əl) *n.* a coarse, slightly sour bread made of unsifted rye flour. [< G]

pump·kin (pump′kin) *n.* **1** a large, roundish, orange-yellow fruit of a trailing vine, used for making pies, as a vegetable, and as food for stock. **2** the vine that this fruit grows on. **3** any of certain large squashes. [alteration (with substitution of *-kin*) of earlier *pumpion* < MF *pompon* < L < Gk. *pepōn*]

pump·kin·seed (pump′kin sēd′) *n.* **1** a seed of a pumpkin. **2** any of several North American sunfish.

pun (pun) *n. v.* **punned, pun·ning.** —*n.* a humorous use of a word in which it can be taken as having two or more different meanings; a play on words. *Example:* "We must all hang together, or we shall all hang separately." —*v.* make puns. [? < first syllable of Ital. *puntiglio* verbal quibble] **—pun′ner,** *n.*

punch[1] (punch) *v.* **1** hit with the fist. **2** *Informal.* deliver with force or effectiveness. **3** herd or drive (cattle). —*n.* **1** a quick thrust or blow. **2** *Informal.* vigorous force or effectiveness. [? var. of *pounce*[1]] **—punch′er,** *n.*
—Syn. *v.* **1** strike, poke, cuff.

punch[2] (punch) *v.* **1** pierce, cut, stamp, force, or drive with a punch: *The train conductor punched our tickets.* **2** make (a hole) with a punch or any pointed instrument. —*n.* **1** a tool or apparatus for piercing, perforating, or stamping materials, impressing a design, forcing nails beneath a surface, driving bolts out of holes, etc. **2** a tool for making holes. [short for *puncheon*[1]] **—punch′er,** *n.*
—Syn. *v.* **1** puncture, perforate.

punch[3] (punch) *n.* a drink made of different liquids mixed together. [probably < Hind. *panc* five (< Skt. *pañca*), from the number of ingredients in the drink]

Punch (punch) *n.* **1** a hook-nosed, hump-backed doll in the puppet show *Punch and Judy.* **2 pleased as Punch,** very much pleased. [shortened form of *punchinello*]

Punch-and-Ju·dy show (punch′ən jü′dē) a puppet show in which Punch quarrels violently with his wife Judy.

pun·cheon[1] (pun′chən) *n.* **1** a slab of timber, or a piece of a split log, with the face roughly smoothed. **2** a short, upright piece of wood in the frame of a building. **3** a punching or stamping tool used by goldsmiths, etc. [ME < OF *poinchon, ponson,* ult. < L *pungere* pierce]

pun·cheon[2] (pun′chən) *n.* **1** a large cask for liquor. **2** the amount that it holds. [ME < OF *poinchon*; origin uncertain]

pun·chi·nel·lo (pun′chə nel′ō) *n.* **-los** or **-loes.** a clown. [< dial. Ital. *Pulcinella,* prob. ult. < L *pullus* chick]

punching bag a leather bag filled with air or stuffed, and hung up to be punched with the fists for exercise.

punch line a telling phrase, sentence, etc. that makes the point of a joke, story, or other narrative.

punc·til·i·o (pungk til′ē ō′) *n.* **-i·os. 1** a detail of honor, conduct, ceremony, etc. **2** care in attending to such details. [< Ital. < Sp. *puntillo,* ult. < L *punctum* point]

punc·til·i·ous (pungk til′ē əs) *adj.* **1** very careful and exact: *A nurse should be punctilious in obeying the doctor's orders.* **2** paying strict attention to details of conduct and ceremony. **—punc·til′i·ous·ly,** *adv.* **—punc·til′i·ous·ness,** *n.* **—Syn. 1** particular, meticulous. See **scrupulous. 2** fastidious, ceremonious.

punc·tu·al (pungk′chü əl) *adj.* **1** prompt; on time: *He is punctual to the minute.* **2** being a point; resembling a point. [< Med.L *punctualis* < L *punctus* point]

punc·tu·al·i·ty (pungk′chü al′ə tē) *n.* promptness; being on time.

punc·tu·al·ly (pungk′chü əl ē) *adv.* promptly; on time.

punc·tu·ate (pungk′chü āt′) *v.* **-at·ed, -at·ing. 1** use periods, commas, and other marks to help make the meaning of a sentence clear. **2** put punctuation marks in. **3** interrupt now and then. **4** give point or emphasis to. [< Med.L *punctuare* < L *punctus* point]

punc·tu·a·tion (pungk′chü ā′shən) *n.* **1** the use of periods, commas, and other marks to help make the meaning of a sentence clear. Punctuation does for writing and printing what pauses and changes in the pitch of voice do for speech. **2** punctuation marks.

punctuation marks marks used in writing or printing to help make the meaning of a sentence clear. Periods, commas, question marks, colons, and exclamation marks are punctuation marks.

punc·ture (pungk′chər) *n. v.* **-tured, -tur·ing.** **—***n.* **1** a hole made by something pointed. **2** the act or process of puncturing. **—***v.* **1** make a hole in with something pointed. **2** have or get a puncture. **3** reduce, spoil, or destroy as if by a puncture. [ME < L *punctura* < *pungere* prick] **—Syn.** *v.* **1** pierce, prick, perforate.

pun·dit (pun′dit) *n.* a learned person; expert; authority. [< Hind. < Skt. *pandita* learned]

pun·gen·cy (pun′jən sē) *n.* a pungent quality.

pun·gent (pun′jənt) *adj.* **1** sharply affecting the organs of taste and smell: *a pungent pickle, the pungent smell of burning leaves.* **2** sharp; biting: *pungent criticism.* **3** stimulating to the mind; keen; lively: *a pungent wit.* [< L *pungens, -entis,* ppr. of *pungere* prick] **—pun′gent·ly,** *adv.* **—Syn. 1** piquant, spicy. **2** caustic. **3** poignant.

Pu·nic (pū′nik) *adj.* **1** of or having to do with ancient Carthage or its inhabitants. **2** treacherous; faithless. [< L *Punicus* < *Poenus* Carthaginian (cf. Gk. *Phoinix*)]

pun·ish (pun′ish) *v.* **1** cause pain, loss, or discomfort to because of some fault or offence: *The government punishes criminals.* **2** cause pain, loss, or discomfort for: *The law punishes crimes.* **3** *Informal.* deal with severely, roughly, or greedily. [ME < OF *puniss-,* a stem of *punir* < L *punire* < *poena* penalty] **—pun′ish·er,** *n.*

pun·ish·a·ble (pun′ish ə bəl) *adj.* **1** liable to punishment: *Capital murder is punishable by death.* **2** deserving punishment: *a punishable offence.*

pun·ish·ment (pun′ish mənt) *n.* **1** a punishing; being punished. **2** pain, suffering, or loss. **3** *Informal.* severe or rough treatment.

pu·ni·tive (pū′nə tiv) *adj.* **1** concerned with punishment. **2** inflicting punishment. **—pu′ni·tive·ly,** *adv.* **—pu′ni·tive·ness,** *n.*

pu·ni·to·ry (pū′nə tô′rē) *adj.* punitive.

Pun·ja·bi (pun jä′bē) *n.* **1** a native or inhabitant of the Punjab. **2** Panjabi. **—***adj.* of or having to do with the Punjab or its people.

punk[1] (pungk) *n.* **1** a preparation that burns very slowly. A stick of punk is used to light fireworks. **2** decayed wood used as tinder. [< Am.Ind.]

punk[2] (pungk) *n.* **1** *Slang.* a young hoodlum. **2** *Slang.* a young inexperienced or worthless person. **3** *Obsolete.* a prostitute. **—***adj. Slang.* poor or bad in quality. [origin uncertain]

pun·kah or **pun·ka** (pung′kə) *n.* in India and the East Indies, a fan, especially a large swinging fan hung from the ceiling and kept in motion by a servant or by machinery. [< Hind. *pankha*]

pun·ster (pun′stər) *n.* a person fond of making puns.

punt[1] (punt) *n.* in football, a kick given to a ball before it touches the ground after dropping it from the hands. **—***v.* in football, kick (a ball) before it touches the ground after being dropped from the hands. [origin uncertain]

punt[2] (punt) *n.* a shallow, flat-bottomed boat having square ends, usually moved by pushing with a pole against the bottom of a river, etc. **—***v.* **1** propel (a boat) by pushing with a pole against the bottom of a river, etc. **2** travel in such a boat. [< L *ponto* punt (a kind of ship), pontoon]

punt[3] (punt) *v.* **1** in a card game, bet against the banker. **2** gamble. [< F *ponter* < Sp. *puntar,* ult. < L *punctum* point]

punt·er[1] (pun′tər) *n.* a person who punts a football.

punt·er[2] (pun′tər) *n.* a person who punts a boat.

punt·er[3] (pun′tər) *n.* a person who bets; gambler.

pun·ty (pun′tē) *n.* a steel or iron rod used as a glass blower's tool. [var. of PONTIL]

pu·ny (pū′nē) *adj.* **-ni·er, -ni·est. 1** of less than usual size and strength; weak. **2** petty; not important. [< OF *puisne* later-born < *puis* (ult. < L *postea*) afterwards + *ne* born < L *natus*] **—pu′ni·ly,** *adv.* **—pu′ni·ness,** *n.* **—Syn. 1** undeveloped, stunted, small, feeble. **2** trivial, insignificant.

pup (pup) *n.* **1** a young dog; puppy. **2** a young fox, wolf, seal, etc. **3** a silly, conceited young man. [var. of *puppy*]

pu·pa (pū′pə) *n.* **-pae** (-pē, -pī, or -pā) or **-pas. 1** a stage between the larva and the adult in the development of many insects. **2** the form of an insect in this stage. Most pupae are inactive and some, such as those of many moths, are enclosed in a tough case or cocoon. [special NL use of L *pupa* girl, doll]

pu·pal (pū′pəl) *adj.* of, having to do with, or in the form of the pupa.

pu·pil[1] (pū′pəl) *n.* a person who is learning in school or being taught by someone. [< MF < L *pupillus, pupilla* ward < *pupus* boy, *pupa* girl] **—Syn.** scholar, learner. See **student.**

pu·pil[2] (pū′pəl) *n.* the black spot in the centre of the iris of the eye. The pupil, which is the only place where light can enter the eye, is an opening that expands and contracts, thus controlling the amount of light that strikes the retina. [< L *pupilla,* originally, little doll, dim. of *pupa* girl, doll]

pup·pet (pup′it) *n.* **1** a small doll. **2** a figure made to look like a person and moved by wires, strings, or the hands. **3** anybody who is not independent, who waits to be told how to act, and who does what somebody else says. [earlier *poppet* < OF *poupette* < L *pupa* girl, doll] **—pup′pet·like′,** *adj.*

pup·pet·ry (pup′it rē) *n.* the act of making and manipulating puppets.

pup·py (pup′ē) *n.* **-pies. 1** a young dog. **2** a young fox, wolf, etc. **3** a silly, conceited young man. [probably < F *poupée* doll, ult. < L *pupa*] **—pup′py-like′,** *adj.*

puppy love sentimental love that often exists briefly between adolescent girls and boys.

pur (pėr) *n. v.* **purred, pur·ring.** purr.

pur·blind (pėr′blīnd′) *adj.* **1** nearly blind. **2** slow to discern or understand. [earlier *pur blind* pure blind] **—pur′blind′ness,** *n.*

pur·chase (pėr′chəs) *v.* **-chased, -chas·ing,** *n.* **—***v.* **1** get

by paying a price; buy. 2 get in return for something: *purchase safety at the cost of happiness.*
—*n.* 1 the act of buying. 2 the thing bought. 3 a firm hold to help move something or to keep from slipping: *Wind the rope twice around the tree to get a better purchase.* 4 a device for obtaining such a hold. [ME < AF *purchacer* pursue < *pur-* forth (< L *pro-*) + *chacer* chase[1] < LL *captiare* < L *capere* take]
—pur′chas·er, *n.* **—Syn.** *n.* 1 See **buy.**

pur·dah (pėr′də) *n.* in India: 1 a curtain serving to screen women from the sight of men or strangers. 2 the condition of being kept hidden from men or strangers. [< Hind. < Persian *pardah* veil, curtain]

pure (pūr) *adj.* **pur·er, pur·est,** *n.* —*adj.* 1 not mixed with anything else; unadulterated; genuine: *pure gold.* 2 perfectly clean; spotless: *pure hands.* 3 perfect; correct; without defects: *Does anyone speak pure French?* 4 nothing else than; mere; sheer: *pure accident.* 5 with no evil; without sin; chaste: *a pure mind.* 6 abstract or theoretical (opposed to *applied*): *pure mathematics.* 7 keeping the same qualities, characteristics, etc. from generation to generation; of unmixed descent: *a pure Indian family.*
—*n.* that which is pure. [ME < OF < L *purus*]
—pure′ness, *n.* **—Syn.** *adj.* 1 unalloyed. 2 immaculate. 3 faultless. 4 utter. 5 virtuous.

pure·bred (pūr′bred′) *adj.* denoting an animal or plant whose ancestors are known to have all belonged to one breed and that will itself breed true to type: *a purebred poodle.* —*n.* an animal or plant of this type.

pu·rée (pū rā′ or pūr′ā) *n. v.* **-réed, -ré·ing.** —*n.* 1 food boiled to a pulp and pushed through a sieve. 2 a thick soup. —*v.* make into a purée. [< F *purée* < *purer* strain]

pure·ly (pūr′lē) *adv.* 1 in a pure manner. 2 exclusively; entirely. 3 merely: *He scored the goal purely by chance.* 4 innocently; chastely.

pur·ga·tion (pėr gā′shən) *n.* a purging; cleansing.

pur·ga·tive (pėr′gə tiv) *n.* a medicine that empties the bowels. Castor oil is a purgative. —*adj.* purging. [ME < L *purgativus* < *purgare.* See PURGE.]

pur·ga·to·ri·al (pėr′gə tô′rē əl) *adj.* of, like, or having to do with purgatory.

pur·ga·to·ry (pėr′gə tô′rē) *n.* **-ries.** 1 in Roman Catholic belief, a temporary condition or place in which the souls of those who have died penitent are purified from sin or the effects of sin by punishment. 2 any condition or place of temporary suffering or punishment. [< Med.L *purgatorium,* originally neut. adj., purging < L *purgare.* See PURGE.]

purge (pėrj) *v.* **purged, purg·ing,** *n.* —*v.* 1 wash away all that is not clean from; make clean. 2 become clean. 3 clear of any undesired thing or person, such as air in a water pipe or opponents in a nation. 4 empty (the bowels). 5 clear of defilement or imputed guilt.
—*n.* 1 the act of purging. 2 a medicine that purges. 3 the elimination of undesired persons from a nation or party. [ME < OF < L *purgare* cleanse, ult. < *purus* pure + *agere* drive]

pu·ri·fi·ca·tion (pūr′ə fə kā′shən) *n.* a purifying; being purified.

pu·ri·fy (pūr′ə fī′) *v.* **-fied, -fy·ing.** 1 make pure. 2 become pure. 3 free from whatever is evil: *purify the heart.* 4 free from objectionable characteristics: *purify a language.* 5 clear or purge (of or from). [ME < OF < L *purificare* < *purus* pure + *facere* make] **—pu′ri·fi′er,** *n.*

Pu·rim (pūr′im or pür′im; *Hebrew,* pü rēm′) *n.* a Jewish religious festival, celebrated each year in February or March, commemorating Esther's deliverance of the Jews from being massacred by Haman. Esther 9:20-32. [< Hebrew *purim,* pl. of *pur* lot]

pur·ism (pūr′iz əm) *n.* an insistence on purity and correctness, especially in language or art.

pur·ist (pūr′ist) *n.* 1 a person who is very careful or too careful about purity and correctness, especially in language. A purist dislikes slang and all expressions that are not formally correct. 2 anyone overcareful about principles of purity in art.

pu·ris·tic (pū ris′tik) *adj.* very careful or too careful about purity and correctness, especially in language.

Pu·ri·tan (pūr′ə tən) *n.* 1 during the 16th and 17th centuries, a member of a group in the Church of England who wanted simple forms of worship and stricter morals. 2 **puritan,** a person who is very strict in morals and religion. —*adj.* 1 of the Puritans. 2 **puritan,** very strict in morals and religion. [< LL *puritas* purity + E *-an*]

hat, āge, cãre, fär; let, ēqual, tėrm; it, īce
hot, ōpen, ôrder; oil, out; cup, pu̇t, rüle, ūse
əbove, takən, pencəl, lemən, circəs
ch, child; ng, long; sh, ship
th, thin; ᴛʜ, then; zh, measure

pu·ri·tan·ic (pūr′ə tan′ik) *adj.* puritanical.

pu·ri·tan·i·cal (pūr′ə tan′ə kəl) *adj.* of or like a puritan; very strict or too strict in morals or religion. **—pu′ri·tan′i·cal·ly,** *adv.*

Pu·ri·tan·ism (pūr′ə tən iz′əm) *n.* the principles and practices of the Puritans.

pu·ri·ty (pūr′ə tē) *n.* 1 freedom from dirt or mixture; clearness; cleanness. 2 freedom from evil; innocence. 3 freedom from foreign or inappropriate elements; correctness: *purity of style.* [< LL *puritas* < *purus* pure]

purl[1] (pėrl) *v.* flow with rippling motions and a murmuring sound: *A shallow brook purls.* —*n.* a purling motion or sound. [? < Scand.; cf. Norwegian *purla*]

purl[2] (pėrl) *v.* 1 knit with inverted stitches. 2 border (material) with small loops. 3 *Archaic.* embroider with gold or silver thread. —*n.* 1 an inversion of stitches in knitting, producing a ribbed appearance. 2 a loop or chain of small loops along the edge of lace, braid, ribbon, etc. 3 a thread of twisted gold or silver wire. [< *pirl* twist; origin uncertain]

pur·lieu (pėr′lü) *n.* 1 a piece of land on the border of a forest. 2 one's haunt or resort; one's bounds. 3 any bordering, neighboring, or outlying region or district. [alteration of earlier *puraley* (influenced by F *lieu* place) < AF *puralee* < *poraler* go through < *por-* forth (< L *pro-*) + *aler* go]

pur·lin or **pur·line** (pėr′lən) *n.* a horizontal beam running the length of a roof and supporting the top rafters of the roof. [ME; ? < OF]

pur·loin (pėr loin′) *v.* steal. [ME < AF *purloigner* remove < *pur-* forth (< L *pro-*) + *loin* afar < L *longe*] **—pur·loin′er,** *n.*

pur·ple (pėr′pəl) *n. adj. v.* **-pled, -pling.** —*n.* 1 a color made by mixing red and blue. 2 in ancient times, crimson. 3 purple cloth or clothing, especially as worn by emperors, kings, etc. to indicate high rank. 4 imperial, royal, or high rank. A prince is born to the purple. 5 the rank or position of a cardinal.
—*adj.* 1 of the color of purple. 2 crimson. 3 imperial; royal. 4 brilliant; gorgeous. 5 **turn purple,** become very angry or furious.
—*v.* make or become purple. [OE *purple,* var. of *purpure* < L *purpura* < Gk. *porphyra* a shellfish, or the purple dye from it]

purple martin a large, blue-black swallow of North America.

pur·plish (pėr′plish) *adj.* somewhat purple.

pur·port (*v.* pər pôrt′ or pėr′pôrt; *n.* pėr′pôrt) *v.* 1 claim; profess: *The document purported to be official.* 2 have as its main idea; mean. —*n.* the meaning; main idea. [ME < AF *purporter* < *pur-* forth (< L *pro-*) + *porter* carry < L *portare*] **—Syn.** *n.* sense, gist, signification. See **meaning.**

pur·pose (pėr′pəs) *n. v.* **-posed, -pos·ing.** —*n.* 1 something one intends to get or do; plan; aim; intention: *His purpose was to pass his exams.* 2 an object or end for which a thing is made, done, used, etc. 3 **on purpose,** with a purpose; not by accident. 4 **to good purpose,** with good results. 5 **to little** (or **no**) **purpose,** with few (or no) results. —*v.* plan; aim; intend. [ME < OF *pourpos* < *pourposer* propose < *pour-* (< L *pro-*) + *poser* (see POSE[1])] **—Syn.** *n.* 1 See **intention.**

pur·pose·ful (pėr′pəs fəl) *adj.* having a purpose: *He worked with purposeful movements.* **—pur′pose·ful·ly,** *adv.* **—pur′pose·ful·ness,** *n.*

pur·pose·less (pėr′pəs lis) *adj.* lacking a purpose. **—pur′pose·less·ly,** *adv.* **—pur′pose·less·ness,** *n.*

pur·pose·ly (pėr′pəs lē) *adv.* on purpose; intentionally.

purr (pėr) *n.* a low, murmuring sound such as a cat makes when pleased. —*v.* make a low, murmuring sound. Also, **pur.** [imitative]

purse (pėrs) *n. v.* **pursed, purs·ing.** —*n.* **1** a bag or case used by women for carrying money, make-up, etc.; handbag. **2** a small bag or pouch used for carrying money, especially small change, often carried inside a handbag. **3** money; resources; treasury: *the nation's purse.* **4** a sum of money: *A purse was made up for the victims of the fire.* —*v.* draw together; press into folds or wrinkles. [OE *purs* < LL *bursa* < Gk. *byrsa* hide, skin. Doublet of BOURSE, BURSA.]

purse-proud (pėrs′proud′) *adj.* proud of being rich.

purs·er (pėr′sər) *n.* an officer who keeps the accounts of a ship or airplane, pays wages, and attends to other matters of business.

purse seine a large fishing net held by two boats, one on each side of a school of fish, so arranged that the ends can be pulled like a purse to enclose the fish.

purse strings 1 strings pulled to close a purse. **2 control** or **hold the purse strings,** control the expenditure of money. **3 tighten** (or **loosen**) **the purse strings,** be sparing (or generous) in spending money.

purs·lane (pėrs′lān or pėrs′lən) *n.* **1** a common plant that has small, yellow flowers and small, thick leaves. **2** any of several plants resembling purslane. [ME < OF *porcelaine,* alteration of L *porcilaca,* var. of *portulaca*]

pur·su·ance (pər sü′əns) *n.* a following; carrying out; pursuit: *In pursuance of duty, the soldier risked his life.*

pur·su·ant (pər sü′ənt) *adj.* **1** following; carrying out; according. **2 pursuant to,** following; acting according to; in accordance with.

pur·sue (pər sü′) *v.* **-sued, -su·ing. 1** follow to catch or kill; chase. **2** proceed along; follow in action; follow: *He pursued a wise course, taking no chances.* **3** strive for; try to get; seek: *pursue pleasure.* **4** carry on; keep on with: *She pursued the study of French for four years.* **5** continue to annoy or trouble: *pursue a person with questions.* [ME < AF *pursuer,* ult. < L *prosequi.* See PROSECUTE.] —**pur·su′a·ble,** *adj.* —**pur·su′er,** *n.* —**Syn. 1** hunt, track.

pur·suit (pər süt′) *n.* **1** the act of pursuing; chase. **2** an occupation or pastime.

pursuit plane a fighter aircraft that has high speed and a high rate of climb, and that can be manoeuvred with ease.

pur·sui·vant (pėr′swə vənt) *n.* **1** an assistant to a herald; officer below a herald in rank. **2** a follower; attendant. [ME < OF *poursuivant,* originally ppr. of *poursuivre* pursue, ult. < L *prosequi.* See PURSUE.]

pur·sy (pėr′sē) *adj.* **-si·er, -si·est. 1** shortwinded or puffy. **2** fat. [ME < AF *pursif,* var. of OF *polsif* < *polser* pant] —**pur′si·ness,** *n.*

pu·ru·lence (pūr′ə ləns or pūr′yü ləns) *n.* the formation or discharge of pus; suppuration.

pu·ru·len·cy (pūr′ə lən sē or pūr′yü lən sē) *n.* purulence.

pu·ru·lent (pūr′ə lənt or pūr′yü lənt) *adj.* **1** full of pus; discharging pus; like pus: *a purulent sore.* **2** corrupt; rotten; cheap. [< L *purulentus* < *pus* pus] —**pu′ru·lent·ly,** *adv.*

pur·vey (pėr vā′) *v.* supply (food or provisions); provide; furnish: *purvey meat for an army, purvey for a royal household.* [ME < AF *porveier* < L *providere.* Doublet of PROVIDE.]

pur·vey·ance (pėr vā′əns) *n.* **1** a purveying. **2** provisions; supplies. **3** formerly, in England, the right of the king or queen to supplies, use of horses, and personal service.

pur·vey·or (pėr vā′ər) *n.* **1** a person who supplies provisions. **2** a person who supplies anything. **3** formerly, in England, an officer who provided or exacted food, etc. in accordance with the right of purveyance.

pur·view (pėr′vū) *n.* a range of operation, activity, concern, etc.; scope; extent. [ME < AF *purveu,* originally pp. of *porveier* purvey. See PURVEY.]

pus (pus) *n.* a liquid formed by inflammation of infected tissue in the body, consisting of white blood cells, bacteria, serum, etc. [< L]

push (pu̇sh) *v.* **1** move (something) away by pressing against it: *Push the door; don't pull it.* **2** move up, down, back, forward, etc. by pressing: *Push him outdoors.* **3** thrust: *Trees push their roots down into the ground.* **4** press hard: *push with all one's might.* **5** go forward by force: *push on at a rapid pace.* **6** force (one's way): *We had to push our way through the crowd.* **7** make go forward; urge: *He pushed his plans cleverly.* **8** continue with; follow up: *push a claim.* **9** extend: *Alexander pushed his conquests still farther east.* **10** urge the use, sale, etc. of. **11 push around,** *Informal.* treat roughly or with contempt; bully. **12 push off, a** move from shore: *We pushed off in the boat.* **b** *Informal.* go away; depart.
—*n.* **1** *Informal.* force; energy. **2** the act of pushing. **3** a hard effort; determined advance. [ME < OF < L *pulsare* beat. Doublet of PULSATE.]
Syn. *v.* **1. Push, shove** = move someone or something by pressing against it. **Push** emphasizes pressing against the person or thing in order to move it ahead, aside, etc. away from oneself or something else: *She pushed the drawer shut.* **Shove** emphasizes moving someone or something out of the way by pushing roughly, or something hard to move or heavy by pushing it along with force and effort: *He shoved his way through the crowd. He shoved the piano across the room.*

push·ball (pu̇sh′bol′ or -bôl′) *n.* **1** a game played with a large, heavy ball, usually about six feet in diameter. Two sides of players try to push the ball toward opposite goals. **2** the ball used in this game.

push button a small button or knob pushed to switch an electric current on or off.

push·cart (pu̇sh′kärt′) *n.* a light cart pushed by hand.

push·er (pu̇sh′ər) *n.* **1** a person or thing that pushes. **2** an airplane with propeller behind instead of in front. **3** *Slang.* a person who sells narcotics illegally.

push-o·ver (pu̇sh′ō′vər) *n. Slang.* **1** something very easy to do. **2** a person very easy to beat in a contest. **3** a person easily influenced or swayed or unable to resist a particular appeal.

push-up (pu̇sh′up′) *n.* **1** an exercise in which a person, in a prone position, raises and lowers himself on his hands and toes, the body being held stiff. **2** *Cdn.* a structure of grass and other vegetation pushed by a muskrat into a breathing-hole in the ice to keep it from freezing up; used also by the muskrat as a home or shelter.

push·y (pu̇sh′ē) *adj.* aggressively ambitious; determined.

pu·sil·la·nim·i·ty (pū′sə lə nim′ə tē) *n.* cowardliness; timidity.

pu·sil·lan·i·mous (pū′sə lan′ə məs) *adj.* cowardly; mean-spirited; faint-hearted. [< L *pusillanimus* < *pusillus* little + *animus* courage] —**pu′sil·lan′i·mous·ly,** *adv.* —**Syn.** timorous, spiritless.

puss[1] (pu̇s) *n.* **1** a cat. **2** a hare. **3** a girl. [cf. Du. *poes,* LG *puus, puus-katte*]

puss[2] (pu̇s) *n. Slang.* the face; mouth. [< Irish Gaelic *pus* mouth, lips]

puss·y[1] (pu̇s′ē) *n.* **puss·ies. 1** a cat. **2** a catkin. [dim. of *puss*]

puss·y[2] (pus′ē) *adj.* **-si·er, -si·est.** full of pus. [< *pus* + *-y*[1]]

puss·y·foot (pu̇s′ē fu̇t′) *v. n.* **-foots.** *Informal.* —*v.* **1** move softly and cautiously to avoid being seen. **2** be cautious and timid about revealing one's opinions or committing oneself. —*n.* a person who pussyfoots.

pussy willow a small willow having silky, grayish catkins.

pus·tu·lar (pus′chu̇ lər) *adj.* of, like, or having to do with pustules; characterized by pustules.

pus·tu·late (*v.* pus′chu̇ lāt′; *adj.* pus′chu̇ lit) *v.* **-lat·ed, -lat·ing,** *adj.* —*v.* form or cover with pustules. —*adj.* having pustules. [< L *pustulare* < *pustula* + E *-ate*[1]]

pus·tu·la·tion (pus′chu̇ lā′shən) *n.* the formation of pustules.

pus·tule (pus′chül) *n.* **1** a pimple containing pus. **2** any swelling like a pimple or blister, such as the pustules of chicken pox. [< L *pustula* < *pus* pus]

put (pu̇t) *v.* **put, put·ting,** *n.* —*v.* **1** cause to be in some

place or position; place; lay: *I put sugar in my tea. Put away your toys.* **2** cause to be in some state, condition, position, relation, etc.: *The murderer was put to death. Put your room in order.* **3** express: *The teacher puts things clearly.* **4** propose or submit for answer, consideration, deliberation, etc.: *He put several questions before me.* **5** take one's course; go; turn; proceed: *The ship put out to sea.* **6** throw or cast (a 16-lb. ball, etc.) from the hand placed close to the shoulder. **7** set at a particular place, point, amount, etc. in a scale of estimation; appraise: *He puts the distance at five miles.* **8** apply: *A doctor puts his skill to good use.* **9** impose: *put a tax on gasoline.* **10** assign; attribute: *He put a wrong construction on my action.*
put about, a put (a ship) on the opposite tack. **b** change direction.
put across, *Informal.* **a** carry out successfully. **b** get accepted.
put aside or **by, a** save for future use. **b** set aside; turn away.
put away, a lay by (money, etc.); save for future use. **b** *Slang.* consume (food, drink, etc.). **c** *Slang.* imprison. **d** *Slang.* pawn. **e** *Archaic.* divorce.
put down, a put an end to; suppress. **b** write down. **c** pay as a down payment. **d** preserve. **e** snub; belittle.
put forth, a stretch. **b** send out; sprout: *put forth buds.* **c** exert: *put forth effort.* **d** start, especially to sea.
put in, a *Informal.* spend (time) as specified. **b** enter port. **c** enter a place for safety, supplies, etc. **d** do; accomplish: *He always puts in a good day's work.*
put off, a lay aside; postpone. **b** bid or cause to wait. **c** hold back or stop from. **d** get rid of.
put on, a clothe or adorn oneself with; don: *She put on her new hat.* **b** assume or take on, especially as a pretence: *She put on an air of innocence.* **c** add to; increase: *The driver put on speed.* **d** advance; move ahead: *put on the clock.* **e** present on a stage; produce: *The class put on a play.*
put out, a extinguish (a fire). **b** confuse; embarrass. **c** distract, disturb, or interrupt. **d** destroy (an eye, etc.). **e** cause to be out in a game. **f** publish. **g** offend; provoke.
put over, *Informal.* **a** carry out successfully. **b** impose (something false or deceptive) on a person.
put through, carry out successfully.
put to it, force to a course; put in difficulty.
put up, a offer; give; show. **b** make. **c** build. **d** lay aside. **e** put in its usual place. **f** preserve (fruit, etc.). **g** give lodging or food to. **h** *Informal.* incite: *Who put you up to this?* **i** make available: *He put up the money for the car.* **j** *Informal.* plan beforehand craftily.
put upon, impose upon; take advantage of; victimize.
put up with, bear with patience; tolerate.
—*n.* a throw or cast. [cf. OE *putung* impulse]
Syn. *v.* **1, 2 Put, place, set** = cause someone or something to be in some place, position, condition, relation, etc. **Put** emphasizes the action of moving something into or out of a place or position or bringing it into some condition, state, or relation: *Put your hand in mine.* **Place** emphasizes the idea of a definite spot, condition, etc. more than action: *Place your hands behind your head.* **Set** emphasizes causing to be in a stated or certain position, etc.: *Set the box down over there.*

pu·ta·tive (pū′tə tiv) *adj.* supposed; reputed: *the putative author of a book.* [< L *putativus* < *putare* think] —**pu′ta·tive·ly,** *adv.*

put·down (pu̇t′doun′) *n. Informal.* **1** a slighting or belittling of a person or thing. **2** a comment, reply, etc. intended to snub or belittle.

put-on (pu̇t′on′) *adj.* assumed; affected; pretended. —*n.* **1** a pretension or affectation. **2** *Slang.* a mischievous joke or trick played for fun; practical joke; hoax.

put-put (put′put′) *n. v.* **-put·ted, -put·ting.** —*n.* **1** the series of short, explosive sounds made by a small motor. **2** a small boat or other vehicle run by such a motor. **3** the motor itself. —*v.* move or travel by means of this type of motor.

pu·tre·fac·tion (pū′trə fak′shən) *n.* decay; rotting.

pu·tre·fac·tive (pū′trə fak′tiv) *adj.* **1** causing putrefaction. **2** characterized by or having to do with putrefaction.

pu·tre·fy (pū′trə fī′) *v.* **-fied, -fy·ing.** rot; decay. [ME < OF < L *putrifieri,* ult. < *puter* rotten + *fieri* become]

pu·tres·cence (pū tres′əns) *n.* a putrescent condition.

pu·tres·cent (pū tres′ənt) *adj.* **1** becoming putrid; rotting. **2** having to do with putrefaction. [< L

hat, āge, cãre, fär; let, ēqual, tėrm; it, īce
hot, ōpen, ôrder; oil, out; cup, pu̇t, rüle, ūse
əbove, takən, pencəl, lemən, circəs
ch, child; ng, long; sh, ship
th, thin; ᴛʜ, then; zh, measure

putrescens, -entis, ppr. of *putrescere* grow rotten, ult. < *puter* rotten]

pu·trid (pū′trid) *adj.* **1** rotten; foul. **2** thoroughly corrupt or depraved; extremely bad. **3** gangrenous: *putrid flesh.* [< L *putridus,* ult. < *puter* rotten] —**pu′trid·ly,** *adv.* —**pu′trid·ness,** *n.*

pu·trid·i·ty (pū trid′ə tē) *n.* **1** a putrid condition. **2** putrid matter.

putt (put) in golf: —*v.* strike (a ball) gently and carefully in an effort to make it roll into the hole. —*n.* the stroke itself. [var. of *put*]

put·tee (put′ē or pu tē′) *n.* **1** a long, narrow strip of cloth wound round the leg from ankle to knee, worn by soldiers, sportsmen, etc. **2** a gaiter of cloth or leather reaching from ankle to knee, worn by soldiers, riders, etc. [< Hind. *patti* bandage, strip]

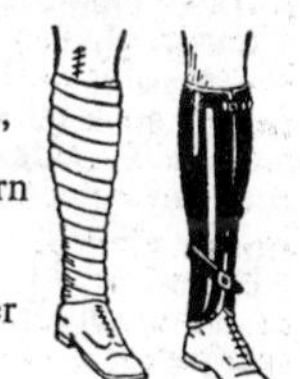

Puttees: A, cloth; B, leather.

put·ter[1] (put′ər) *v.* keep busy in a rather useless way. Also, **potter.** [var. of *potter*[2]] —**put′ter·er,** *n.*

putt·er[2] (put′ər) *n.* **1** a person who putts. **2** in golf, a club with an upright face and a short, rigid shaft, used in putting. [< *putt*]

put·ter[3] (pu̇t′ər) *n.* one that puts. [< *put*]

putt·ing green (put′ing) that part of a golf course within 20 yards of a hole, except the hazards; the smooth turf or sand around a golf hole.

put·ty (put′ē) *n.* **-ties,** *v.* **-tied, -ty·ing.** —*n.* **1** a soft mixture of whiting and linseed oil, used mainly for fastening panes of glass into window frames. **2** a pipe-joint compound. **3** the color of putty, a kind of light gray. —*v.* stop up or cover with putty. [< F *potée,* originally, potful < *pot* pot] —**put′ti·er,** *n.*

put-up (pu̇t′up′) *adj. Informal.* planned beforehand, or deliberately, in a secret or crafty manner: *a put-up job.*

puz·zle (puz′əl) *n. v.* **-zled, -zling.** —*n.* **1** a difficult problem. **2** a problem or task to be done for fun. **3** a puzzled condition.
—*v.* **1** make unable to answer, solve, or understand something; perplex. **2** be perplexed. **3** exercise one's mind on something hard. **4 puzzle out,** find out by thinking or trying hard. **5 puzzle over,** think hard about; try hard to do or work out. [origin uncertain] —**puz′zler,** *n.*
Syn. *n.* **3** bewilderment, quandary. -*v.* **1 Puzzle, perplex, bewilder** = make a person uncertain what to think, say, or do. **Puzzle** suggests a problem having so many parts or sides and being so mixed up or involved that it is hard to understand or solve: *My friend's behavior puzzles me.* **Perplex** adds the idea of troubling with doubt about how to decide or act: *The boy's obstinacy perplexes his parents.* **Bewilder** adds and emphasizes the idea of confusing and causing one to feel lost among all the various possibilities: *City traffic bewilders him.*

puz·zle·ment (puz′əl mənt) *n.* a puzzled condition.

pwt. pennyweight.

PX or **P.X.** Post Exchange.

pya (pyä) *n.* **1** a unit of money in Burma. **2** a coin worth one pya. [< Burmese]

py·e·mi·a or **py·ae·mi·a** (pī ē′mē ə) *n.* a form of blood poisoning caused by bacteria that produce pus. [< NL < Gk. *pyon* pus + *haima* blood]

Pyg·ma·li·on (pig mā′lē ən or pig māl′yən) *n.* in Greek mythology, a sculptor who made a statue of a woman and then fell in love with it. Aphrodite gave the statue life, and it became Galatea.

pyg·my (pig′mē) *n.* **-mies,** *adj.* —*n.* a very small person; dwarf. The pygmies living in Africa and Asia are less than five feet high. —*adj.* very small. Also, **pigmy.** [< L < Gk. *pygmaioi,* originally pl. adj., dwarfish < *pygmē* cubit, fist] —**Syn.** See **dwarf.**

Pyg·my (pig′mē) *n.* **1** one of various Negroid peoples of equatorial Africa five feet or less in height. **2** one of a group of very short people, said to dwell in Asia and Africa. —*adj.* of or having to do with the Pygmies. Also, **Pigmy.**

py·ja·mas or **pa·ja·mas** (pə jam′əz or pə jä′məz) *n.pl.* 1 garments for sleeping or lounging in, consisting of a coat or loose blouse and a pair of loose pants fastened at the waist. 2 loose trousers worn in the Orient, especially by Moslem men and women. —*adj.* **pyjama** or **pajama,** of or having to do with pyjamas. [< Hind. < Persian *paejamah* < *pae* leg + *jamah* garment]

A pylon (def. 3)

py·lon (pī′lon) *n.* 1 a post or tower for guiding pilots in an air race. 2 a tall steel framework used to carry high-tension wires across country. 3 a gateway, particularly of an ancient Egyptian temple. [< Gk. *pylōn* gateway < *pylē* gate]

py·lor·ic (pī lôr′ik) *adj.* of or having to do with the pylorus.

py·lo·rus (pī lô′rəs) *n.* **-ri** (rī or -rē). in anatomy, the opening that leads from the stomach into the intestine. [< LL < Gk. *pylōros*, originally, gatekeeper < *pylē* gate + *-horos* watching (cf. *horaein* see)]

py·or·rhe·a or **py·or·rhoe·a** (pī′ə rē′ə) *n.* a disease of the gums in which pockets of pus form about the teeth, the gums shrink, and the teeth become loose. [< NL < Gk. *pyon* pus + *rhoia* a flow < *rheein* flow]

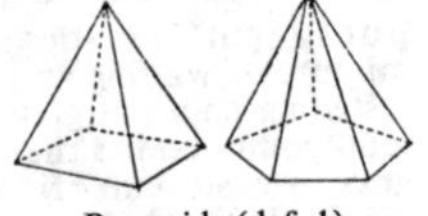
Pyramids (def. 1)

pyr·a·mid (pir′ə mid′) *n.* 1 a solid having triangular sides meeting in a point. 2 any thing or things having the form of a pyramid. 3 a building, often massive, having the form of a pyramid and serving as a temple, tomb, etc. 4 **Pyramids,** *pl.* the huge, massive stone pyramids, serving as royal tombs, built by the ancient Egyptians. —*v.* 1 be or put in the form of a pyramid. 2 raise or increase (costs, wages, etc.) gradually. 3 increase (one's operations) in buying or selling stock on margin by using the profits to buy or sell more. [< L < Gk. *pyramis, -idos* < Egyptian]

One of the huge stone pyramids of Egypt

py·ram·i·dal (pə ram′ə dəl) *adj.* shaped like a pyramid.

pyre (pīr) *n.* 1 a pile of wood on which a dead body is burned as a funeral rite. 2 any large pile or heap of burnable material. [< L < Gk. *pyra* < *pyr* fire]

Pyr·e·ne·an (pir′ə nē′ən) *adj.* of the Pyrenees, a mountain range between France and Spain.

py·re·thrum (pī rē′thrəm) *n.* **-thrums.** 1 any of various chrysanthemums cultivated for their striking red, white, or lilac flowers. 2 the powdered flower heads of certain of these chrysanthemums, used as a medicine or as an insecticide. [< L *pyrethrum* feverfew < Gk. *pyrethron*, probably < *pyr* fire]

py·ret·ic (pī ret′ik) *adj.* 1 of or having to do with fever. 2 producing fever. 3 feverish. [< NL < Gk. *pyretos* fever < *pyr* fire]

Py·rex (pī′reks) *n. Trademark.* a kind of glassware that is highly resistant to heat.

pyr·i·dox·ine (pir′ə dok′sēn or pir′ə dok′sən) *n.* vitamin B_6, essential to human nutrition, found in wheat germ, fish, liver, etc. *Formula*: $C_8H_{11}O_3N$

py·rite (pī′rīt) *n.* an iron ore that has a yellow color and glitters so that it suggests gold; fool's gold. *Formula*: FeS_2 [< L < Gk. *pyritēs* flint < *pyr* fire]

py·ri·tes (pī rī′tēz or pī′rīts) *n.pl.* any of various compounds of sulphur and a metal, especially pyrite.

pyro- *combining form.* fire, as in *pyrography.* [< Gk. *pyr, pyros*]

py·rog·ra·phy (pī rog′rə fē) *n.* the art of burning designs on wood, leather, etc.

py·ro·ma·ni·a (pī′rə mā′nē ə) *n.* an obsessive desire to set things on fire.

py·ro·ma·ni·ac (pī′rə mā′nē ak′) *n.* a person affected with pyromania.

py·ro·ma·ni·a·cal (pī′rō mə nī′ə kəl) *adj.* 1 caused by a pyromaniac. 2 of or having a tendency toward pyromania.

py·ro·tech·nic (pī′rə tek′nik) *adj.* 1 of or having to do with fireworks. 2 resembling fireworks; brilliant; sensational: *pyrotechnic eloquence.*

py·ro·tech·ni·cal (pī′rə tek′nə kəl) *adj.* pyrotechnic.

py·ro·tech·nics (pī′rə tek′niks) *n.* 1 the making of fireworks. 2 use of fireworks. 3 a display of fireworks. 4 a brilliant or sensational display.

py·rox·y·lin (pī rok′sə lin) *n.* any of various substances made by nitrating certain forms of cellulose. Guncotton and the soluble cellulose nitrates used in making celluloid, collodion, etc. are pyroxylins. [< *pyro-* + Gk. *xylon* wood]

Pyr·rhic (pir′ik) *adj.* of or having to do with Pyrrhus, King of Epirus.

Pyrrhic victory a victory won at too great cost, so named after Pyrrhus, who won a battle with an enormous loss of life. [< *Pyrrhus*, king of Epirus in Greece, 300-272 B.C.]

pyr·rho·tite (pir′ə tīt′) *n.* a bronze-colored, slightly magnetic iron sulphide, sometimes containing nickel. *Formula*: FeS [< Gk. *pyrrhotēs* redness < *pyrrhos* fiery red < *pyr* fire (because of its color) + E *-ite*[1]]

Py·thag·o·re·an (pə thag′ə rē′ən) *adj.* of or having to do with Pythagoras, 582?-500? B.C., a Greek philosopher and mathematician, his teachings, or his followers. —*n.* a follower of Pythagoras.

Pyth·i·a (pith′ē ə) *n.* the priestess of Apollo at Delphi, who delivered the divine responses to questions asked of the oracle.

Pyth·i·an (pith′ē ən) *adj.* of or having to do with Apollo or the oracle at Delphi. [< L < Gk. *Pythios* of Delphi (earlier called Pytho), or the Delphic Apollo]

Pythian games in ancient Greece, one of the great Panhellenic festivals, held every four years at Delphi in honor of Apollo.

Pyth·i·as (pith′ē əs) *n.* in Roman legend, a man famous for his devoted friendship with Damon, who pledged his life for him. See **Damon.**

py·thon (pī′thon or pī′thən) *n.* 1 any of several large snakes of the Old World that are related to the boas and kill their prey by crushing. Pythons usually live in trees near water. 2 any large boa. [< L < Gk.]

py·tho·ness (pī′thə nis) *n.* 1 the priestess of Apollo at Delphi, who gave out the answers of the oracle. 2 any prophetess. [earlier *phytoness* < OF < LL *pythonissa* < Gk. *pythōn* familiar spirit < *Pythō*, seat of the Delphic oracle]

pyx (piks) *n.* 1 in ecclesiastical use, a box in which the consecrated Host is kept or carried. 2 in the United Kingdom, a box at the mint in which specimen coins are kept to be tested for weight and purity. [< L < Gk. *pyxis* < *pyxos* boxwood]

A pyxidium

pyx·id·i·um (piks id′ē əm) *n.* **-i·a** (-ē ə). in botany, a seed vessel that bursts open transversely into a top and bottom part, the top part acting as a lid. [< NL < Gk. *pyxidion*, dim. of *pyxis* box. See PYX.]

Q or **q** (kū) *n.* **Q's** or **q's. 1** the seventeenth letter of the English alphabet. **2** any speech sound represented by this letter. **3** one (usually seventeenth) of a series designated alphabetically.

q. 1 quart; quarts. **2** quarterly.

Q. 1 Queen. **2** question; query. **3** quarto. **4** quire. **5** quarterly.

Q.B. Queen's Bench.

Q.C. Queen's Counsel.

Q.E.D. which was to be demonstrated or proved. (for L *quod erat demonstrandum*)

qin·tar (kin tär′) *n.* **1** a unit of money in Albania, worth 1/100 of a lek. **2** a coin worth one qintar. [< Albanian, akin to *quintal*]

qiv·i·ut (kiv′ē u̇t′) *n.* the soft, silky under wool of the arctic muskox, used as a textile fibre. [< Eskimo]

Q.M. or **QM** quartermaster.

Q.M.G. or **QMG** Quartermaster-General.

qr. *pl.* **qrs. 1** quarter. **2** quire. **3** quarterly.

Q.R. Queen's Regulations.

qt. *pl.* **qts. 1** quart; quarts. **2** quantity.

q.t. or **Q.T.** *Slang.* **1** quiet. **2 on the q.t.,** very secretly; quietly.

qto. quarto.

qu. 1 quart. **2** quarterly. **3** question.

qua (kwā or kwä) *adv.* as; in the capacity of: *Qua father, he pitied the boy; qua judge, he condemned him.* [< L *quā*, abl. fem. sing. of rel. pron. *quī* who]

quack[1] (kwak) *n.* **1** the sound a duck makes. **2** any similar sound. —*v.* make the sound of a duck or one like it. [imitative]

quack[2] (kwak) *n.* **1** a person who practises as a doctor but lacks professional training. **2** an ignorant pretender to knowledge or skill of any sort. —*adj.* **1** used by quacks. **2** not genuine: *quack medicine.* [short for *quacksalver*] —**Syn.** *n.* **2** charlatan.

quack·er·y (kwak′ər ē) *n.* **-er·ies.** the practices or methods of a quack.

quack grass a coarse, weedlike kind of grass: *Quack grass is also called couch grass or twitch grass.*

quak·sal·ver (kwak′sal′vər) *n.* a quack doctor. [< earlier Du. *quacksalver* < *quacken* boast of + *salf* salve]

quad[1] (kwod) *n. Esp.Brit. Informal.* a quadrangle of a college.

quad[2] (kwod) *n. Informal.* quadruplet.

quad[3] (kwod) *n.* quadrat.

Quad·ra·ges·i·ma (kwod′rə jes′ə mə) *n.* **1** the first Sunday in Lent. **2** the forty days of Lent. [< L *quadragesima*, fem. adj., fortieth]

quad·ran·gle (kwod′rang′gəl) *n.* **1** a four-sided space or court wholly or nearly surrounded by buildings. **2** the buildings around a quadrangle. **3** a quadrilateral. [< LL *quadrangulum* < L *quadri-* four + *angulus* angle]

quad·ran·gu·lar (kwod rang′gyu̇ lər) *adj.* like a quadrangle; having four corners or angles.

quad·rant (kwod′rənt) *n.* **1** a quarter of a circle or of its circumference. **2** in astronomy, navigation, etc., an instrument used for measuring altitudes. [< L *quadrans, -antis* a fourth]

Quadrants (def. 1)

quad·rat (kwod′rət) *n.* in printing, a piece of metal used for wide spaces in setting type. [var. of *quadrate,* n.]

quad·rate (*adj. n.* kwod′rit or kwod′rāt; *v.* kwod′rāt) *adj. n. v.* **-rat·ed, -rat·ing.** —*adj.* square; rectangular. —*n.* something square or rectangular. —*v.* agree or conform (with). [< L *quadratus* < *quadrus* square, ult. < *quattuor* four]

quad·rat·ic (kwod rat′ik) in algebra: —*adj.* involving a square or squares, but no higher powers. —*n.* a quadratic equation.

quadratic equation an equation involving a square or squares, but no higher powers, of the unknown quantity or quantities. *Example*: $x^2 + 3x + 2 = 12$

quad·rat·ics (kwod rat′iks) *n.* the branch of algebra that deals with quadratic equations.

quad·ra·ture (kwod′rə chür′ or kwod′rə chər) *n.* **1** the act of squaring. **2** the finding of a square equal in area to a given surface bounded by a curve. **3** in astronomy, the position of any planet or star that is 90 degrees away from another. [< L *quadratura* < *quadratus.* See QUADRATE.]

quad·ren·ni·al (kwod ren′ē əl or kwod ren′yəl) *adj.* **1** occurring every four years: *a quadrennial election.* **2** of or for four years. [< L *quadriennium* period of four years < *quadri-* four + *annus* year]

quad·ren·ni·al·ly (kwod ren′ē əl ē) *adv.* once in four years.

quad·ri·lat·er·al (kwod′rə lat′ər əl) *adj.* having four sides and four angles. —*n.* **1** a plane figure having four sides and four angles. **2** something having this form. [< L *quadrilaterus* < *quadri-* four + *latus, -teris* side]

Quadrilaterals

qua·drille (kwə dril′) *n.* **1** a square dance for four couples that has five parts or movements. **2** the music for such a dance. [< F < Sp. *cuadrilla* troop < *cuadro* battle square < L *quadrus* square]

quad·ril·lion (kwod ril′yən) *n. adj.* **1** in Canada, the United States, and France, 1 followed by 15 zeros. **2** in Great Britain and Germany, 1 followed by 24 zeros. [< F *quadrillon* < *quadri-* four (< L) + *million*]

quad·ri·no·mi·al (kwod′rə nō′mē əl) *adj.* consisting of four terms. —*n.* an expression having four terms. *Example*: $a^2 - ab + 4a - b^2$. [< *quadri-* four (< L) + *-nomial*; modelled after *binomial*]

quad·ri·va·lence (kwod′rə vā′ləns or kwod riv′ə ləns) *n.* a quadrivalent quality or condition.

quad·ri·va·len·cy (kwod′rə vā′lən sē or kwod riv′ə lən sē) *n.* quadrivalence.

quad·ri·va·lent (kwod′rə vā′lənt or kwod riv′ə lənt) in chemistry: —*adj.* **1** having a valence of four. **2** having four separate valences. —*n.* a quadrivalent atom or element. —**quad′ri·va′lent·ly,** *adv.*

quad·riv·i·um (kwod riv′ē əm) *n.* in the Middle Ages, arithmetic, geometry, astronomy, and music, the more advanced group of the seven liberal arts; opposed to *trivium.* [< LL < L *quadrivium* crossroads < *quadri-* four + *via* way]

quad·roon (kwod rün′) *n.* a person having one fourth Negro blood; the child of a mulatto and a white person. [< Sp. *cuarterón* < *cuarto* fourth < L *quartus*]

quad·ru·ped (kwod′rə ped′) *n.* an animal, especially a mammal, that has four feet. —*adj.* having four feet. [< L *quadrupes, -pedis* < *quadru-* four + *pes, pedis* foot]

quad·ru·ple (kwod′rə pəl or kwod rü′pəl) *adj. adv. n. v.* **-pled, -pling.** —*adj.* **1** fourfold; consisting of four parts; including four parts or parties. **2** four times; four times as great. **3** in music, having four beats to each measure, with the first and third beats accented. —*adv.* four times; four times as great. —*n.* a number, amount, etc., four times as great as another: *80 is the quadruple of 20.* —*v.* make or become four times as great. [< L *quadruplus* < *quadru-* four + *-plus* fold]

quad·ru·plet (kwod rü′plit or kwod′rə plit) *n.* **1** one of four children born at the same time from the same mother. **2** a group of four.

quad·ru·plex (kwod′ru̇ pleks′) *adj.* **1** fourfold. **2** in telegraphy, of or having to do with a system in which four messages, two in each direction, may be sent over one wire simultaneously. [< L *quadruplex* fourfold < *quadru-* four + *-plex* fold]

quad·ru·pli·cate (*adj. n.* kwod rü′plə kit; *v.* kwod rü′plə kāt′) *adj. v.* **-cat·ed, -cat·ing,** *n.* —*adj.* fourfold; quadruple. —*v.* make fourfold; quadruple.

—*n.* one of four things, especially four copies of a document, exactly alike. [< L *quadruplicatus,* ult. < *quadru-* four + *plicare* to fold]

quad·ru·pli·ca·tion (kwod rü′plə kā′shən) *n.* **1** a quadruplicating. **2** something quadruplicated.

quaes·tor (kwes′tər or kwēs′tər) *n.* in ancient Rome: **1** an official in charge of the public funds; treasurer. **2** a public prosecutor in certain criminal cases. [< L *quaestor* var. of *quaesitor* < *quaerere* inquire]

quaes·tor·ship (kwes′tər ship′ or kwēs′tər-) *n.* the position or term of office of a quaestor.

quaff (kwof or kwaf) *v.* drink in large drafts; drink freely. —*n.* a quaffing. [origin uncertain]

quag (kwag or kwog) *n.* a bog; quagmire.

quag·gy (kwag′ē or kwog′ē) *adj.* **-gier, -gi·est. 1** boggy; soft and marshy; swampy. **2** flabby; soft and wobbly: *quaggy flesh.* [probably < *quag* bog]

quag·mire (kwag′mīr′) *n.* **1** soft, muddy ground; a boggy or miry place. **2** a difficult situation. [< obs. *quag* to shake + *mire*]

qua·hog or **qua·haug** (kwo′hog or kwə hog′) *n.* a roundish, edible North American clam, found on the Atlantic coast of North America; hard clam. [< Algonquian]

quail[1] (kwāl) *n.* **quails** or (*esp. collectively*) **quail.** any of various game birds belonging to the same group as fowls and partridges: *The bobwhite is a kind of quail.* [ME < OF *quaille* < Gmc.]

quail[2] (kwāl) *v.* be afraid; lose courage; shrink back in fear: *The slave quailed at his master's look.* [ME; origin uncertain] —**Syn.** quake, cower, flinch.

quaint (kwānt) *adj.* strange or odd in an interesting, pleasing, or amusing way: *Old photographs seem quaint to us today.* [ME < OF *cointe* pretty < L *cognitus* known] —**quaint′ly,** *adv.* —**quaint′ness,** *n.*

quake (kwāk) *v.* **quaked, quak·ing,** *n.* —*v.* shake; tremble: *She quaked with fear.* —*n.* **1** a shaking; trembling. **2** an earthquake. [OE *cwacian*] —**Syn.** *v.* See **shiver.**

Quak·er (kwāk′ər) *n.* a member of the Society of Friends. Quakers refuse to fight in a war or to take oaths; their clothes, manners, and religious services are very plain and simple. [< *quake,* v.; said to refer to the fact that George Fox, the founder, bade his followers "tremble at the word of the Lord"]

Quak·er·ess (kwāk′ər is) *n.* a Quaker woman or girl.

Quak·er·ism (kwāk′ər iz′əm) *n.* the principles and customs of the Quakers.

qual·i·fi·ca·tion (kwol′ə fə kā′shən) *n.* **1** that which makes a person fit for a job, task, office, etc.: *Good eyesight is a necessary qualification for a marksman.* **2** a modification; limitation; restriction: *The statement was made without any qualification. His pleasure had one qualification; his friends could not enjoy it, too.*

qual·i·fied (kwol′ə fīd′) *adj.* **1** having the desirable or required qualifications; fitted; adapted: *He is fully qualified for his job.* **2** modified; limited; restricted: *His offer was qualified by certain conditions.*

qual·i·fi·er (kwol′ə fī′ər) *n.* **1** a person or thing that qualifies. **2** a word that qualifies another word: *Adjectives and adverbs are qualifiers.*

qual·i·fy (kwol′ə fī′) *v.* **-fied, -fy·ing. 1** make fit or competent: *qualify oneself for a job.* **2** furnish with legal power; make legally capable. **3** become fit; show oneself fit: *Can you qualify for the Boy Scouts?* **4** in sports, gain the right to compete in a race, contest, or tournament. **5** make less strong; change somewhat; limit; modify: *Qualify your statement that dogs are loyal by adding "usually."* **6** in grammar, limit or modify the meaning of: *Adverbs qualify verbs.* [< Med.L *qualificare* < L *qualis* of what sort + *facere* make] —**Syn. 1** prepare, equip. **5** moderate, temper, adapt.

qual·i·ta·tive (kwol′ə tā′tiv) *adj.* concerned with quality or qualities. —**qual′i·ta′tive·ly,** *adv.*

qualitative analysis the process of determining the chemical components of a substance.

qual·i·ty (kwol′ə tē) *n.* **-ties. 1** something special about an object that makes it what it is: *One quality of iron is hardness; one quality of sugar is sweetness.* **2** a characteristic; attribute: *She has many fine qualities.* **3** the kind that anything is: *That is a poor quality of cloth.* **4** nature; disposition; temper: *Trials often test a man's quality.* **5** character; position; relation: *Dr. Smith was present, but in the quality of a friend, not of a physician.* **6** fineness; merit; excellence: *Look for quality rather than quantity.* **7** an accomplishment; attainment. **8** high rank; good or high social position. **9** people of high rank. **10** the character of a sound aside from pitch and volume or intensity. [ME < OF < L *qualitas* < *qualis* of what sort]

Syn. 1 Quality, property = a distinguishing mark or characteristic of a thing. **Quality** is the general word, applying to some feature possessed by a thing that helps to distinguish its special character, either belonging to it by nature or given to it: *Strength is a quality of steel.* **Property** = a quality properly and specially belonging to the nature of a thing or a power always shown by it: *Heaviness is a property of lead.* **2** trait, feature.

qualm (kwom or kwäm) *n.* **1** a sudden disturbing feeling in the mind; uneasiness; misgiving; doubt: *I tried the test with some qualms.* **2** a disturbance or scruple of conscience: *She felt some qualms at staying away from church.* **3** a momentary feeling of faintness or sickness, especially of nausea. [OE *cwealm* pain]

qualm·ish (kwom′ish or kwäm′ish) *adj.* **1** inclined to have qualms. **2** having qualms.

quan·da·ry (kwon′də rē or kwon′drē) *n.* **-ries.** a state of perplexity or uncertainty; dilemma. [origin uncertain] —**Syn.** predicament, difficulty, puzzle.

quan·ti·fy (kwon′tə fī′) *v.* **-fied, -fy·ing. 1** determine the quantity of; count or measure. **2** express the quantity of: *quantify a syllable or verse.* **3** in logic, express explicitly the quantity or extent of, by using such words as *all, some,* or *most.* [< Med.L *quantificare* < L *quantus* how much + *facere* make]

quan·ti·ta·tive (kwon′tə tā′tiv) *adj.* **1** concerned with quantity. **2** that can be measured. —**quan′ti·ta′tive·ly,** *adv.*

quantitative analysis the process of determining the amount or proportion of each chemical component of a substance.

quan·ti·ty (kwon′tə tē) *n.* **-ties. 1** amount: *Equal quantities of nuts and raisins were used in the cake.* **2** a large amount; a large number: *The baker buys flour in quantity. She owns quantities of books.* **3** something that is measurable. **4** in music, the length of a note. **5** in speech or poetry, the length of a vowel sound or syllable. **6** in mathematics: **a** something having magnitude, or size, extent, amount, etc. **b** a figure or symbol representing this. [< L *quantitas* < *quantus* how much]

quan·tum (kwon′təm) *n.* **-ta** (-tə). in physics: **a** the smallest amount of energy capable of existing independently. **b** this amount of energy regarded as a unit. [< L *quantum,* neut. adj., how much]

quantum theory the theory that whenever radiant energy is transferred, the transfer occurs in pulsations or stages rather than continuously, and that the amount of energy transferred during each stage is of a definite quantity.

quar·an·tine (kwôr′ən tēn′) *v.* **-tined, -tin·ing,** *n.* —*v.* keep away from others for a time, especially in order to prevent the spread of an infectious disease: *People with smallpox are quarantined.* [< n.]
—*n.* **1** the state of being quarantined: *The house was in quarantine when the child had scarlet fever.* **2** detention, isolation, and other measures taken to prevent the spread of an infectious disease. **3** a place where people, animals, plants, ships, etc. are held until it is sure that they have no infectious diseases, insect pests, etc. **4** a period of detention or isolation imposed on ships, persons, etc. when liable or suspected to be bringing some infectious disease. **5** isolation, exclusion, and similar measures taken against an undesirable person, group, etc. [< Ital. *quarantina* < *quaranta* forty < L *quadraginta;* with reference to 40 days as the original period of isolation]

quar·rel[1] (kwôr′əl) *n. v.* **-relled** or **-reled, -rel·ling** or **-rel·ing.** —*n.* **1** an angry dispute or disagreement; a breaking off of friendly relations. **2** a cause for a dispute or disagreement; reason for breaking off friendly relations: *A bully likes to pick quarrels.* **3** one's cause or side in a dispute or contest: *The knight took up the poor man's quarrel and fought his oppressor.*

—*v.* **1** dispute or disagree angrily; break off friendly relations. **2** find fault: *It is useless to quarrel with undeniable facts.* [ME < OF < L *querella*, var. of *querela* complaint < *queri* complain] —**quar′rel·ler** or **quar′rel·er,** *n.*

Syn. *n.* **1 Quarrel, feud** = an angry disagreement or unfriendly relation between two people or groups. **Quarrel** particularly applies to a fight in words, an angry disagreement or dispute, soon over or ending in a fist fight or in severed relations: *The children had a quarrel over the division of the candy.* **Feud** = a long-lasting quarrel, marked by violent and sometimes murderous attacks and revenge when between two groups, by bitter hatred and unfriendly acts and verbal attacks when between individuals: *The senator and the columnist carried on a feud.* –*v.* **1** bicker, wrangle, squabble.

quar·rel² (kwôr′əl) *n.* **1** a bolt or arrow used with a crossbow. **2** a small, square, or diamond-shaped pane of glass, used in latticed windows. **3** a stonemason's chisel. [ME < OF < Med.L *quadrellus*, dim. of L *quadrus* square]

quar·rel·some (kwôr′əl səm) *adj.* too ready to quarrel; fond of fighting and disputing. —**quar′rel·some·ly,** *adv.* —**quar′rel·some·ness,** *n.* —**Syn.** choleric, irascible, disputatious.

quar·ry¹ (kwôr′ē) *n.* **-ries,** *v.* **-ried, -ry·ing.** —*n.* a place where stone is dug, cut, or blasted out for use in building. —*v.* **1** obtain from a quarry. **2** dig out by hard work, as if from a quarry. [ME < Med.L *quareia*, ult. < L *quadrus* square] —**quar′ri·er,** *n.*

quar·ry² (kwôr′ē) *n.* **-ries. 1** an animal chased in a hunt; game; prey. **2** anything hunted or eagerly pursued. [ME < OF *cuiree* < *cuir* hide < L *corium*]

quart (kwôrt) *n.* **1** a measure for liquids, equal to one fourth of a gallon: *a quart of milk.* **2** a measure for dry things, equal to one eighth of a peck: *a quart of berries.* **3** a container holding a quart. **4** such a container and its contents. *Abbrev.*: qt. or qu. [ME < OF < L *quarta*, fem. adj., fourth]

quar·tan (kwôr′tən) *adj.* recurring every fourth day, by inclusive counting. —*n.* a fever or ague with two days between attacks. [< F < L (*febris*) *quartana* quartan (fever) < *quartus* fourth]

quar·ter (kwôr′tər) *n.* **1** one fourth; half of a half; one of four equal or corresponding parts. **2** one fourth of a dollar; 25 cents. **3** in Canada and the United States, a silver coin worth 25 cents. **4** one fourth of an hour; 15 minutes; a moment marking this period. **5** one fourth of a year; 3 months. **6** a phase of the moon: *The quarters of the moon are four periods of seven days each.* **7** one fourth of a yard; 9 inches. **8** one fourth of a hundredweight; 25 pounds (sometimes 28 pounds). **9** a region; place. **10** section; district: *The Italian quarter is on the south side of the town.* **11** a certain part of a community, group, etc.: *The bankers' theory was not accepted in other quarters.* **12 at close quarters,** fighting or struggling close together. **13 quarters,** *pl.* **a** a place to live or stay: *officers' quarters.* **b** proper position or station. **14** a point of the compass; direction: *In what quarter is the wind?* **15 a** mercy shown a defeated enemy in sparing his life. **b** kindly or merciful treatment; indulgence. **16** one of four parts into which an animal's carcass is divided. **17** the leg and its adjoining parts. **18** the part of a ship's side near the stern. **19** in heraldry: **a** one of four (or more) parts into which a shield is divided by lines at right angles. **b** the emblem occupying the upper right fourth of a shield. **20** the part of a boot or shoe above the heel and below the top of either side of the foot from the middle of back to vamp. **21** in music, a quarter note: *That tone is held for two quarters.* **22** one of the four fifteen-minute periods into which a rugby-football game is divided. **23** a quarter-back..
—*v.* **1** divide into quarters. **2** give a place to live in: *Soldiers were quartered in houses of the town.* **3** live or stay in a place. **4** cut the body of (a person or animal) into quarters. **5** of the wind, blow on a ship's quarter. **6** place or bear (coats of arms) in quarters of a shield. —*adj.* being one of four equal parts; being equal to only about one fourth of full measure. [ME < OF < L *quartarius* a fourth < *quartus* fourth]

quar·ter·back (kwôr′tər bak′) *n.* **1** in football, the player whose position is immediately behind the centre of the line of scrimmage: *The quarterback usually directs his team's play in the field.* **2** a person who directs any group or activity.

quarter day the day beginning or ending a quarter of the year.

hat, āge, cãre, fär; let, ēqual, tėrm; it, īce
hot, ōpen, ôrder; oil, out; cup, pu̇t, rüle, ūse
əbove, takən, pencəl, lemən, circəs
ch, child; ng, long; sh, ship
th, thin; ᴛʜ, then; zh, measure

quar·ter·deck (kwôr′tər dek′) *n.* **1** on a sailing vessel, the part of the upper deck between the mainmast and the stern, used especially by the officers of a ship. **2** on a steam naval vessel, a deck area designated as the ceremonial post of the commanding officer.

quar·tered (kwôr′tərd) *adj.* **1** divided into quarters. **2** furnished with rooms or lodging. **3** in heraldry, divided or arranged in quarters. **4** quartersawed.

Quartered arms

quarter horse one of a breed of horses originally bred from thoroughbred stock for racing on quarter-mile tracks, now much used in Canada and the United States for working with cattle, playing polo, etc.

quar·ter-hour (kwôr′tər our′) *n.* **1** fifteen minutes. **2** the point one fourth or three fourths of the way through an hour.

quar·ter·ing (kwôr′tər ing) *n.* **1** the act of dividing into fourths. **2** the act of assigning quarters, especially for soldiers. **3** in heraldry: **a** the division of a shield into quarters or parts. **b** one of such parts. **c** the coat of arms on a quartering. —*adj.* of a wind, blowing on a ship's side near the stern.

quar·ter·ly (kwôr′tər lē) *adj. adv. n.* **-lies.** —*adj.* happening, done, etc., four times a year. —*adv.* once each quarter of a year. —*n.* a magazine published four times a year: *Queen's Quarterly.*

quar·ter·mas·ter (kwôr′tər mas′tər) *n.* **1** in the army, an officer who has charge of providing quarters, clothing, fuel, transportation, etc. for troops. **2** in the navy, an officer on a ship who has charge of the steering, the compasses, signals, etc. *Abbrev.*: Q.M. or QM

quar·tern (kwôr′tərn) *n.* **1** a quarter; fourth part. **2** one fourth of a pint; gill. [ME < OF *quarteron* < *quart* fourth < L *quartus*]

quarter note in music, a note equal to one fourth of a whole note.

A quarter note

quarter rest in music, a rest lasting as long as a quarter note.

quar·ter·saw (kwôr′tər so′ or -sô′) *v.* **-sawed, -sawed** or **-sawn, -saw·ing.** saw (a log) lengthwise into quarters and then into boards.

quarter section a piece of land, usually square, containing 160 acres.

quarter sessions 1 in the United Kingdom, a court, held quarterly, that has limited criminal jurisdiction and certain powers. **2** any of various courts held quarterly.

quar·ter·staff (kwôr′tər staf′) *n.* **-staves.** in former times, an English weapon consisting of a stout pole 6 to 8 feet long, tipped with iron.

quar·ter·staves (kwôr′tər stāvz′) *n.* pl. of **quarterstaff.**

quar·tet or **quar·tette** (kwôr tet′) *n.* **1** a group of four musicians (singers or players). **2** a piece of music for four voices or instruments. **3** any group of four. [< F < Ital. *quartetto* < *quarto* fourth < L *quartus*]

quar·to (kwôr′tō) *n.* **-tos,** *adj.* —*n.* **1** the page size (usually about 9 by 12 inches) of a book in which each leaf is one fourth of a whole sheet of paper. **2** a book having this size. —*adj.* having this size. [< Med.L *in quarto* in the fourth (of a sheet)]

quartz (kwôrts) *n.* a very hard mineral composed of silica. Common quartz crystals are colorless and transparent, but amethyst, jasper, and many other colored stones are quartz. *Formula*: SiO_2 [< G *Quarz*]

quartz·ite (kwôrts′īt) *n.* a granular rock consisting mostly of quartz.

qua·sar (kwā′sär or kwā′zär) *n* a quasi-stellar celestial object or body. [< *quas*(i)-(*stell*)*ar*]

quash¹ (kwosh) *v.* put down completely; crush: *quash a revolt.* [ME < OF *quasser* < L *quassare* shatter, intensive of *quatere* to shake]

quash[2] (kwosh) *v.* make void; annul: *The judge quashed the charges against the prisoner.* [ME < OF *quasser* < LL *cassare* < *cassus* null; influenced in OF by *quasser* quash[1]]

qua·si (kwā′sē or kwā′zē, kwo′sē or kwo′zē) *adj.* seeming; not real; halfway: *quasi humor.* —*adv.* seemingly; not really; partly; almost. [< L]

quasi- *prefix.* the form of **quasi** used in combination, as in *quasi-official.*

quas·sia (kwosh′ə) *n.* **1** a bitter drug obtained from the wood of a tropical American tree, used as a tonic and as a substitute for hops. **2** the wood. **3** the tree. [< NL; after *Quassi,* a Surinam slave who first used the bark as a fever remedy]

Qua·ter·na·ry (kwə tėr′nə rē) in geology: —*n.* **1** the period that includes the Pleistocene and Recent. See **geology** for chart. **2** the deposits made in this period. —*adj.* of or having to do with this period or the deposits made during it. [< L *quaternarius,* ult. < *quater* four times]

quat·rain (kwot′rān) *n.* a stanza or poem of four lines. [< F *quatrain* < *quatre* four < L *quattuor*]

quat·re·foil (kat′ər foil′ or kat′rə foil′) *n.* **1** a leaf or flower composed of four leaflets or petals. The four-leaf clover is a quatrefoil. **2** in architecture, an ornament having four lobes. [ME < OF *quatre* four (< L *quattuor*) + *feuil* leaf < L *folium*]

Architectural quatrefoils

qua·ver (kwā′vər) *v.* **1** shake tremulously; tremble: *The old man's voice quavered.* **2** sing or say in trembling tones. **3** trill in singing or in playing on an instrument. —*n.* **1** a shaking or trembling, especially of the voice. **2** a trill in singing or in playing on an instrument. **3** in music, an eighth note. [frequentative of *quave* shake, ME *cwavie(n)*] —**qua′ver·ing·ly,** *adv.*

qua·ver·y (kwā′vər ē) *adj.* quavering.

quay (kē) *n.* a solid landing place where ships load and unload, often built of stone. [ME < OF *kay* < Celtic]

Que. Quebec.

quean (kwēn) *n.* **1** *Archaic.* a bold, impudent girl or woman; hussy. **2** a prostitute. **3** *Scottish.* a girl or young woman. [OE *cwene*]

quea·sy (kwē′zē) *adj.* **-si·er, -si·est. 1** inclined to nausea; easily upset. **2** tending to unsettle the stomach. **3** uneasy; uncomfortable. **4** squeamish; fastidious. [origin uncertain] —**quea′si·ly,** *adv.* —**quea′si·ness,** *n.*

Quebec heater (kwi bek′ or kā bek′) a kind of stove for heating rooms.

Quebec highlander *Cdn. Slang.* a French-Canadian Roman Catholic cleric.

Que·beck·er or **Que·bec·er** (kwi bek′ər or kā bek′ər) *n.* a person born in or living in the province of Quebec.

Que·bec·ois (kā bek wä′) *n.* **Que·bec·ois.** *French.* a person from Quebec.

que·bra·cho (kā brä′chō) *n.* **1** any of several South American trees, the hard wood and the bark of which are used in tanning and dyeing. **2** the wood or bark of any of these trees. [< Sp. *quebracho,* literally, break-axe < *quebrar* break < L *crepare*]

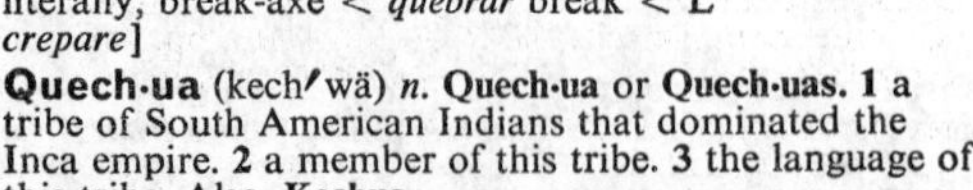

A Quebec heater

Quech·ua (kech′wä) *n.* **Quech·ua** or **Quech·uas. 1** a tribe of South American Indians that dominated the Inca empire. **2** a member of this tribe. **3** the language of this tribe. Also, **Kechua.**

Quech·uan (kech′wən) *adj.* of or having to do with the Quechua or their language. —*n.* Quechua. Also, **Kechuan.**

queen (kwēn) *n.* **1** the wife of a king. **2** a woman ruler. **3** a woman who is very important, very stately, or very beautiful. **4** a fully developed egg-laying female in a colony of bees, ants, etc. There is usually only one queen in a hive of bees. **5** a playing card bearing a picture of a queen. **6** in chess, a piece that can move in any straight or diagonal row. **7** the chief, best, finest, etc.: *the rose, queen of flowers.*
—*v.* **1** be a queen or act like a queen. **2** make a queen of. [OE *cwēn*] —**queen′like′,** *adj.*

Queen Anne 1 a style of English architecture of the early 18th century, characterized by simple design and the use of red brick. **2** a style of upholstered furniture designed in England in the early 18th century.

Queen Anne's lace (anz) the wild carrot. [from its smooth-topped clusters of lacy, white flowers]

Queen City 1 Toronto. **2** Regina.

queen consort the wife of a reigning king.

queen·dom (kwēn′dəm) *n.* **1** the realm of a queen. **2** the position or dignity of a queen.

queen dowager the widow of a king.

queen·ly (kwēn′lē) *adj.* **-li·er, -li·est,** *adv.* —*adj.* **1** of a queen; fit for a queen. **2** like a queen; like a queen's. —*adv.* in a queenly manner; as a queen does. —**queen′li·ness,** *n.*

queen mother the widow of a former king and mother of a reigning king or queen.

queen post one of a pair of timbers extending vertically upward from the tie beam of a roof truss or the like, one on each side of its centre.

queen regent 1 a queen ruling in place of an absent or unfit monarch. **2** a queen ruling in her own right.

Queen's Counsel a lawyer or barrister who may serve as counsel to the crown. *Abbrev.:* Q.C.

Queen's English the English that is recognized as correct and standard in Britain.

Queen's evidence 1 evidence brought forward by the government in a criminal case. **2** testimony given in court by a criminal against his associates in a crime. **3 turn Queen's evidence,** testify in court against one's associates in a crime.

Queen's Highway in Canada, a main road, usually surfaced, that is the responsibility of the provincial government for maintenance, etc.

Queen's Proctor in British law, an officer of the crown having the right to intervene in certain divorce and nullity cases.

queer (kwēr) *adj.* **1** strange; odd; peculiar: *That was a queer remark for her to make.* **2** *Informal.* probably bad; causing doubt or suspicion: *There is something queer about her.* **3** not well; faint; giddy. **4** *Slang.* bad; counterfeit. **5** *Informal.* mentally unbalanced. **6** *Slang.* homosexual.
—*v. Slang.* spoil; ruin.
—*n.* **1** *Informal.* a strange or peculiar person. **2** *Slang.* a homosexual. [< G *quer* oblique] —**queer′ly,** *adv.* —**Syn.** *adj.* **1** singular, curious, unusual.

queer·ness (kwēr′nis) *n.* **1** queer nature or behavior. **2** something strange or odd; a peculiarity.

quell (kwel) *v.* **1** put down (disorder, rebellion, etc.): *quell a riot.* **2** put an end to; overcome: *quell one's fears.* [OE *cwellan* kill]

quench (kwench) *v.* **1** put an end to; stop: *quench a thirst.* **2** drown out; put out: *Water quenched the fire.* **3** cool suddenly by plunging into water or other liquid. Hot steel is quenched to harden it. [OE *cwencan* as in *ācwencan*] —**Syn. 1** allay, slake. **2** extinguish, stifle.

quench·less (kwench′lis) *adj.* that cannot be quenched; inextinguishable.

quern (kwėrn) *n.* **1** a primitive handmill for grinding grain, consisting commonly of two circular stones, the upper one being turned by hand. **2** a small hand mill used to grind pepper or other spices. [OE *cweorn*]

quer·u·lous (kwer′ə ləs or kwer′yů ləs) *adj.* **1** complaining; faultfinding. **2** fretful; peevish. [< L *querulus* < *queri* complain] —**quer′u·lous·ly,** *adv.* —**quer′u·lous·ness,** *n.* —**Syn. 2** petulant.

que·ry (kwēr′ē) *n.* **-ries,** *v.* **-ried, -ry·ing.** —*n.* **1** a question; inquiry. **2** a doubt. **3** a question mark. —*v.* **1** ask; ask about; inquire into. **2** ask questions. **3** express doubt about. [< Med.L *quere* < L *quaere* ask!] —**Syn.** *n.* **1** See **question.**

quest (kwest) *n.* **1** a search; hunt. **2** an expedition of knights: *There are many stories about the quest for the Holy Grail.* **3** the knights in such an expedition. **4** an object sought for. —*v.* search or seek for; hunt. [ME < OF < VL *quaesita* < L *quaerere* seek]

ques·tion (kwes′chən) *n.* **1** something asked; a sentence in interrogative form, addressed to someone to get information; inquiry. **2** a judicial examination or trial; interrogation. **3** a matter of doubt or dispute; controversy: *A question arose about the ownership of the property.* **4** a matter to be talked over, investigated, considered, etc.; problem: *the question of automation.* **5** a proposal to be voted on. **6** the taking of a vote on a proposal.
beside the question, off the subject.
beyond question, without doubt; not to be disputed.
call in question, dispute; challenge.
in question, a under consideration or discussion. **b** in dispute.
out of the question, impossible.
without question, without a doubt; not to be disputed.
—*v.* **1** ask in order to find out; seek information from. **2** ask; inquire. **3** doubt; dispute: *I question the truth of his story.* [ME < OF < L *quaestio, -onis,* ult. < *quaerere* ask] —**ques′tion·er,** *n.* —**ques′tion·ing·ly,** *adv.*
Syn. *n.* **1 Question, query** = something asked. **Question** applies to any request for information: *I have some questions about today's lesson.* **Query** applies particularly to a question raised as a matter of doubt or objection and seeking a specific or authoritative answer: *He put several queries concerning items in the budget.* –*v.* **1 Question, ask, interrogate** = seek information from someone. **Ask** is the general word, and suggests nothing more: *I asked him why he did it.* **Question** = ask a series of questions, sometimes formally and according to some plan: *I questioned the boy until he told all he knew.* **Interrogate** is a formal word meaning "to question formally and methodically": *The intelligence officer interrogated the prisoners.* **3** challenge.

ques·tion·a·ble (kwes′chən ə bəl) *adj.* **1** open to question or dispute; doubtful; uncertain. **2** of doubtful propriety, honesty, morality, respectability, or the like. —**ques′tion·a·bly,** *adv.* —**Syn. 1** debatable, disputable.

question mark a mark (?) put after a question or used to express doubt about something written or printed.

ques·tion·naire (kwes′chən ãr′ or, *esp.Brit.,* kes′chən ãr′) *n.* a list of questions, usually written or printed. [< F]

question time 1 in the House of Commons, a short period several times a week in which ministers answer questions submitted in advance by Members of Parliament. **2** a similar period in any assembly.

quet·zal (ket säl′) *n.* **1** a Central American bird having brilliant golden-green and scarlet plumage. The male has long, flowing tail feathers. **2** a unit of money in Guatemala. See table at **money. 3** a coin worth one quetzal. [< Mexican Sp. < Nahuatl]

queue (kū) *n. v.* **queued, queu·ing.** —*n.* **1** a long line of people, automobiles, etc.; line-up. **2** a braid of hair hanging down the back. —*v.* **1** form or stand in a long line. **2 queue up,** line up. [< F < L *coda,* var. of *cauda* tail]

A queue (def. 2)

quib·ble (kwib′əl) *n. v.* **-bled, -bling.** —*n.* an unfair and petty evasion of the point or truth by using words with a double meaning: *a legal quibble.* —*v.* evade the point or the truth by twisting the meaning of words. [apparently dim. of obs. *quib* quip < L *quibus* (dat. and abl. pl. of *qui* who, which), used in legal jargon] —**quib′bler,** *n.*

quick (kwik) *adj.* **1** fast and sudden; swift: *a quick turn.* **2** begun and ended in a very short time: *a quick visit.* **3** coming soon; prompt: *a quick reply.* **4** not patient; hasty: *a quick temper.* **5** brisk: *a quick fire.* **6** acting quickly; ready; lively: *a quick wit.* **7** understanding or learning quickly: *a child who is quick in school.* **8** readily convertible into cash.
—*n.* **1** the tender, sensitive flesh under a fingernail or toenail. **2** the tender, sensitive part of one's feelings: *Their insults cut him to the quick.* **3** *Archaic.* living persons: *the quick and the dead.*
—*adv.* quickly. [OE *cwic* alive] —**quick′ness,** *n.*
Syn. *adj.* **1 Quick, fast, rapid** = done, happening, moving, or acting with speed. **Quick** especially describes something done or made or happening with speed or without delay: *You made a quick trip.* **Fast** especially describes something moving or acting, and emphasizes the swiftness with which it acts or moves: *I took a fast plane.* **Rapid** emphasizes the speed, the swiftness of the action or movement, or series of movements, performed: *I had to do some rapid planning.* **4** impatient, irascible. **6** nimble, agile.

hat, āge, cãre, fär; let, ēqual, tėrm; it, īce
hot, ōpen, ôrder; oil, out; cup, pu̇t, rüle, ūse
əbove, takən, pencəl, lemən, circəs
ch, child; ng, long; sh, ship
th, thin; ᴛʜ, then; zh, measure

quick bread bread, biscuits, etc. made with a leavening agent that does not require the dough to be left to rise before baking.

quick·en (kwik′ən) *v.* **1** hasten; move more quickly: *Quicken your pace.* **2** stir up; make alive: *He quickened the hot ashes into flames. Reading adventure stories quickened his imagination.* **3** become more active or alive: *His pulse quickened.* **4** of a child in the womb, show life by movements. —**Syn. 1** hurry, expedite, accelerate. **2** rouse, stimulate, animate.

quick-freeze (kwik′frēz′) *v.* **-froze, -fro·zen, -freez·ing.** subject (food) to rapid freezing to prepare it for storing at freezing temperatures.

quick·hatch (kwik′hach′) *n. Cdn.* a wolverine.

quick·ie (kwik′ē) *Slang.* —*n.* **1** a motion picture, novel, etc. produced cheaply and in haste. **2** a short drink of alcoholic liquor. **3** anything done very hastily. —*adj.* **1** fast; quick; requiring little preparation. **2** giving little warning.

quick kick in football, a punt kicked from a running play formation during a down other than the third, the objective being to catch the opposing players out of position and thus to gain ground.

quick·lime (kwik′līm′) *n.* a white, caustic, alkaline substance usually obtained by burning limestone and used for making calcium hydroxide, mortar, and cement; calcium oxide.

quick·ly (kwik′lē) *adv.* rapidly; with haste; very soon.

quick·sand (kwik′sand′) *n.* **1** a soft, wet sand that will not support a person's or animal's weight: *The horse was swallowed by the quicksand.* **2** an expanse of such sand.

quick·set (kwik′set′) *n.* **1** *Esp.Brit.* a plant or cutting, especially of hawthorn, set to grow in a hedge. **2** such plants; a hedge of such plants.

quick·sil·ver (kwik′sil′vər) *n.* mercury. [OE *cwicseolfor,* after L *argentum vivum* living silver]

quick·step (kwik′step′) *n.* **1** a step used in marching in quick time. **2** a lively dance step. **3** music in a brisk march rhythm.

quick-tem·pered (kwik′tem′pərd) *adj.* easily angered.

quick time a fast speed of marching. In quick time, soldiers march four miles an hour.

quick-wit·ted (kwik′wit′id) *adj.* having a quick mind; mentally alert.

quid[1] (kwid) *n.* **1** a piece to be chewed. **2** a bite of chewing tobacco. [OE *cwidu* cud]

quid[2] (kwid) *n.* **quid.** *Brit. Slang.* one pound, or 100 new pence. [origin uncertain]

quid·nunc (kwid′nungk′) *n.* a newsmonger; gossip; inquisitive person. [< L *quid nunc* what now]

quid pro quo (kwid′ prō kwō′) *Latin.* one thing in return for another; compensation.

qui·es·cence (kwī es′əns or kwē′es əns) *n.* an absence of activity; quietness; stillness; motionlessness.

qui·es·cent (kwī es′ənt or kwē′es ənt) *adj.* inactive; quiet; still; motionless. [< L *quiescens, -entis,* ppr. of *quiescere* rest < *quies,* n., rest] —**qui·es′cent·ly,** *adv.*

qui·et (kwī′ət) *adj.* **1** moving very little; still: *a quiet river.* **2** with no or little noise: *quiet footsteps, a quiet room.* **3** saying little. **4** peaceful; gentle; unobtrusive: *a quiet mind, quiet manners.* **5** not showy or bright: *Gray is a quiet color.* **6** not active: *a quiet life in the country.*
—*v.* **1** make quiet: *The mother quieted her frightened child.* **2** become quiet: *The wind quieted down.*
—*n.* **1** a state of rest; stillness; absence of motion or noise. **2** freedom from disturbance; peace.

—*adv.* in a quiet manner. [< L *quietus* resting, pp. of *quiescere* rest < *quies* quiet. Doublet of COY and QUIT, adj.] —**qui′et·er,** *n.* —**qui′et·ly,** *adv.* —**qui′et·ness,** *n.* —**Syn.** *adj.* **1** See **still.**

qui·et·en (kwī′ə tən) *v.* **1** cause to become still or peaceful; make quiet. **2 quieten down,** become quiet.

qui·e·tude (kwī′ə tūd′ or kwī′ə tüd′) *n.* quietness; stillness; calmness. [< LL *quietudo* < L *quietus* quiet]

qui·e·tus (kwī ē′təs) *n.* a final getting rid of anything; finishing stroke; anything that ends or settles: *The arrival of the militia gave the riot its quietus.* [< Med.L *quietus est* he is discharged < L *quietus est* he is at rest. See QUIET.]

quill (kwil) *n.* **1** a large, stiff feather. **2** the hollow stem of a feather. **3** anything made from the hollow stem of a feather, such as a pen, toothpick, or an instrument for plucking strings of a mandolin, etc. **4** a stiff, sharp hair or spine like the end of a feather. A porcupine has quills on its back. [ME *quil*]

A man using a quill (def. 3)

quilt (kwilt) *n.* **1** a bedcover, especially one made of two pieces of cloth with a soft pad between, held in place by lines of stitching. **2** anything resembling a quilt. —*v.* **1** make quilts. **2** stitch together with a soft lining: *quilt a bathrobe.* **3** sew in lines or patterns: *The bedcover was quilted in a flower design.* [ME < OF *cuilte* < L *culcita* cushion] —**quilt·er,** *n.*

quilt·ing (kwil′ting) *n.* **1** quilted work. **2** material for making quilts; a stout fabric woven to appear quilted.

quilting bee a social gathering of women to work on a quilt.

quince (kwins) *n.* **1** a hard, yellowish acid fruit, used for preserves. **2** the tree it grows on. **3** a similar shrub or tree grown for its blossoms. [originally pl. of ME *quyne* < OF *cooin* < L *cotoneum*]

quin·el·la (kwi nel′ə) *n.* a system of betting that two horses in a particular race will occupy the first two places, though either horse may come first.

quin·in (kwin′ən) *n.* quinine.

qui·nine (kwī′nīn or kwi nēn′) *n.* **1** a bitter, colorless crystalline drug made from the bark of the cinchona tree, used in treating colds, malaria, and fevers. **2** any of various compounds of quinine that are used as medicine. [< Sp. *quina* < *Quechua* (S. Am.Ind.) *kina* bark]

quinine water tonic (def. 3).

Quin·qua·ges·i·ma (kwing′kwə jes′ə mə) *n.* the Sunday before the beginning of Lent; Shrove Sunday. [< L *quinquagesima,* fem. adj. fiftieth]

quin·quen·ni·al (kwing kwen′ē əl) *adj.* **1** occurring every five years. **2** of or for five years. —*n.* **1** something that occurs every five years. **2** something lasting five years. [< L *quinquennium* < *quinque* five + *annus* year]

quin·quen·ni·al·ly (kwin kwen′ē ə lē) *adv.* **1** once in five years. **2** during a five-year period.

quin·que·reme (kwing′kwə rēm′) *n.* in former times, a galley with five tiers of oars. [< L *quinqueremis* < *quinque* five + *remus* oar]

quin·sy (kwin′zē) *n.* tonsillitis with pus; a sore throat accompanied by an abscess in the tonsils. [ME < Med.L *quinancia* < Gk. *kynanchē,* originally, dog's collar < *kyon, kynos* dog + *anchein* choke]

quint (kwint) *n. Informal.* quintuplet.

quin·tal (kwin′təl) *n.* **1** a hundredweight. In Canada and the United States, a quintal equals 100 pounds; in the British Isles, 112 pounds. **2** in the metric system, a unit of weight equal to 100 kilograms, or 220.46 pounds avoirdupois. **3** *Cdn.* in Newfoundland: **a** 112 pounds of codfish. **b** a puncheon holding this amount. [ME < Med.L *quintale* < Arabic *qintar* weight of a hundred pounds, probably ult. < L *centenarius* < *centum* hundred]

quin·tes·sence (kwin tes′əns) *n.* **1** pure essence; purest form. **2** the most perfect example of something. [ME < Med.L *quinta essentia* fifth essence]

quin·tes·sen·tial (kwin′tə sen′shəl) *adj.* having the nature of a quintessence; of the purest or most perfect kind.

quin·tet or **quin·tette** (kwin tet′) *n.* **1** a group of five musicians (singers or players). **2** a piece of music for five voices or instruments. **3** any group of five. [< F < Ital. *quintetto* < *quinto* fifth < L *quintus*]

quin·til·lion (kwin til′yən) *n.* **1** in Canada, the United States, and France, 1 followed by 18 zeros. **2** in the British Isles and Germany, 1 followed by 30 zeros. [< L *quintus* fifth + E *million*]

quin·tu·ple (kwin tū′pəl, kwin tü′pəl, or kwin′tə pəl) *adj. v.* **-pled, -pling,** *n.* —*adj.* **1** fivefold; consisting of five parts. **2** five times as great. —*v.* **1** make five times as great. **2** become five times as great. —*n.* a number, amount, etc. five times as great as another. [< F *quintuple* < L *quintus* fifth; patterned on *quadruple*]

quin·tu·plet (kwin tū′plit, kwin tü′plit, or kwin′tə plit) *n.* **1** one of five children born at the same time from the same mother. **2** any group or combination of five. [< *quintuple,* adj.]

quip (kwip) *n. v.* **quipped, quip·ping.** —*n.* **1** a clever or witty saying. **2** a sharp, cutting remark. **3** a quibble. **4** something odd or strange. —*v.* make quips. [for earlier *quippy* < L *quippe* indeed, I dare say]

quire[1] (kwīr) *n.* 24 or 25 sheets of paper of the same size and quality. [ME < OF *quaier,* ult. < L *quaterni* four each]

quire[2] (kwīr) *n. Archaic.* choir.

Quir·i·nal (kwir′ə nəl) *n.* **1** one of the seven hills upon which Rome was built. **2** a palace built on this hill. **3** formerly, the Italian royal court or government, as distinguished from the Vatican (representing the papacy). [< L *Quirinalis* < *Quirinus,* an ancient Roman god of war]

quirk (kwėrk) *n.* **1** a peculiar way of acting. **2** a clever or witty saying. **3** a quibble. **4** a sudden twist or turn: *a quirk in a road, a mental quirk.* **5** in writing, flourish. [origin uncertain]

quirt (kwėrt) *n.* a riding whip with a short, stout handle and a lash of braided leather. [< Sp. *cuarta,* originally, a long whip]

quis·ling (kwiz′ling) *n.* any person who treacherously helps to prepare the way for enemy occupation of his own country. [< Vidkun *Quisling* (1887-1945), a Norwegian puppet ruler for the Nazis]

quit (kwit) *v.* **quit** or **quit·ted, quit·ting,** *adj.* —*v.* **1** stop: *The men quit work when the whistle blew.* **2** stop working. **3** leave: *He quit his room in anger. If he doesn't pay his rent, he will receive notice to quit.* **4** give up; let go. **5** pay back; pay off (a debt). **6** free; clear; rid. **7** *Archaic.* behave or conduct (oneself). —*adj.* free; clear; rid: *I gave him money to be quit of him.* [(v.) ME < OF *quiter* < Med.L *quietare* discharge < L *quietus.* See QUIET; (adj.) ME < OF *quite* < L *quietus.* Doublet of QUIET and COY.]

quitch (kwich) *n.* couch grass. [OE *cwice.* Related to QUICK.]

quitch grass quitch.

quit·claim (kwit′klām′) *n.* **1** the giving up of a claim. **2** a document stating that somebody gives up a claim. —*v.* give up claim to (a possession, etc.). [ME < AF *quiteclamer* < OF *quite* + *clamer.* See QUIT, CLAIM.]

quite (kwīt) *adv.* **1** completely; wholly; entirely: *a hat quite out of fashion.* **2** actually; really; positively: *quite the thing.* **3** *Informal.* to a considerable extent or degree: *quite pretty.* [originally adj., var. of *quit* in sense of "clear"]

☛ **quite.** The formal meaning of *quite* is "entirely, wholly." In informal English, it is generally used with the reduced meaning of "to a considerable extent or degree". Formal: *The fox was quite exhausted when we reached it.* Informal: *He is quite worried. I hiked quite a distance.* A number of convenient phrases with *quite* are good informal usage: *quite a few* people, *quite a little* time, and so on.

quit·rent (kwit′rent′) *n.* under a feudal system, the rent paid in money, instead of services rendered. [< *quit,* adj. + *rent*[1]]

quits (kwits) *adj.* **1** on even terms by repayment or retaliation. **2 be quits with,** get even with; have revenge on. **3 call it quits,** break off or abandon an attempt to do

hat, āge, cãre, fär; let, ēqual, tėrm; it, īce
hot, ōpen, ôrder; oil, out; cup, pu̇t, rüle, ūse
əbove, takən, pencəl, lemən, circəs
ch, child; ng, long; sh, ship
th, thin; ᴛʜ, then; zh, measure

something; stop for a time or permanently. **4 cry quits,** admit that things are now even. [< *quit*, adj.]

quit·tance (kwit′əns) *n.* **1** a release from debt or obligation. **2** the paper certifying a release from debt; a receipt. **3** a repayment. [ME < OF *quitance* < *quiter* quit. See QUIT, v.]

quit·ter (kwit′ər) *n. Informal.* one who gives up easily.

quiv·er[1] (kwiv′ər) *v. n.* shake; shiver; tremble. [cf. OE *cwiferlīce* actively] **—Syn.** *v.* See **shake.**

quiv·er[2] (kwiv′ər) *n.* a case to hold arrows. [ME < AF *quiveir*, probably < Gmc.]

A quiver of arrows

qui vive? (kē′ vēv′) **1** who goes there? **2 on the qui vive,** watchful; alert. [< F *qui vive?*, literally, (long) live who?; expecting such a reply as *Vive le roi!* Long live the king!]

Qui·xo·te (kē hō′tē or kwik′sət; *Spanish,* kē hō′te) *n.* **Don.** See **Don Quixote.**

quix·ot·ic (kwiks ot′ik) *adj.* **1** resembling Don Quixote; extravagantly chivalrous or romantic. **2** visionary; not practical. **—quix·ot′i·cal·ly,** *adv.*

quix·ot·ism (kwik′sət iz′əm) *n.* a quixotic character or behavior.

quiz (kwiz) *v.* **quizzed, quiz·zing,** *n.* **quiz·zes.** *—v.* **1** examine informally by questions; test the knowledge of. **2** make fun of. *—n.* **1** an informal written or oral examination; test. **2** a person who makes fun of others. **3** a practical joke. [origin uncertain] **—quiz′zer,** *n.*

quiz show a radio or television program in which contestants are given prizes for answering questions correctly.

quiz·zi·cal (kwiz′ə kəl) *adj.* **1** odd; queer; comical. **2** that suggests making fun of others; teasing: *a quizzical smile.* **—quiz′zi·cal·ly,** *adv.*

quoin (koin or kwoin) *n.* **1** an external angle of a wall or building. **2** the stone forming an outside angle of a wall; a cornerstone. **3** a wedge-shaped piece of wood, metal, etc. [var. of *coin*]

quoit (kwoit) *n.* **1** a heavy, flattish iron or rope ring thrown to encircle a peg stuck in the ground or to come as close to it as possible. **2 quoits,** *pl.* the game so played. [ME < OF *coite* cushion]

A quoit

☛ **Quoits,** meaning the game, is plural in form and singular in use: *Quoits is often played with horseshoes.*

quon·dam (kwon′dəm) *adj.* that once was; former. [< L *quondam* at one time]

Quon·set hut (kwon′sit) a prefabricated, largely metal building with a semicircular roof. [< *Quonset*, Rhode Island, where such a building was first used at the naval air base]

quo·rum (kwô′rəm) *n.* the number of members of any society or assembly that must be present if the business done is to be legal or binding. [< L *quorum* of whom]

quot. quotation.

quo·ta (kwō′tə) *n.* **1** the share of a total due from or to a particular district, person, etc.: *Each member of the club was given his quota of tickets to sell for the party.* **2** the number of immigrants of any specific nationality who are legally allowed to enter a country in any year. **3** the amount of imports of a specific commodity permitted from a particular country. [< Med.L < L *quota pars* how large a part]

quot·a·ble (kwōt′ə bəl) *adj.* **1** that can be quoted. **2** suitable for quoting.

quo·ta·tion (kwō tā′shən) *n.* **1** somebody's words repeated exactly by another person; a passage quoted from a book, speech, etc.: *From what author does this quotation come?* **2** the practice of quoting: *Quotation is a habit of some preachers.* **3** the stating of the current price of a stock, commodity, etc. **4** the price so stated: *today's quotation on wheat.*

quotation mark one of a pair of marks used to indicate the beginning and end of a quotation. Double quotes (" ") are usually used for a quotation, and single quotes (' ') for a quotation within another quotation.

quote (kwōt) *v.* **quot·ed, quot·ing,** *n.* *—v.* **1** repeat the exact words of; give words or passages from. **2** repeat exactly the words of another or a passage from a book. **3** bring forward as an example or authority: *The judge quoted various cases in support of his opinion.* **4** give (a price): *quote a price on a home.* **5** enclose within quotation marks: *The dialogue in old books is not quoted.* *—n.* **1** a quotation. **2** a quotation mark. [< Med.L *quotare* to number chapters < L *quotus* which (in sequence)] **—quot′er,** *n.*

Syn. *v.* **3 Quote, cite** = bring forward as authority or evidence. Although the distinction is not always kept, **quote** means to bring forward the words of another, either repeated exactly or given in a summary, identifying the speaker: *The Commissioner was quoted as saying action will be taken.* **Cite** = name as evidence or authority, but not to quote, a passage, author, or book, with exact title, page, etc.: *To support his argument he cited Article 68, Chapter 10, of the Charter of the United Nations.*

quoth (kwōth) *v. Archaic.* said. [pt. of *queathe* (OE *cwethan*). Related to BEQUEATH.]

quoth·a (kwōth′ə) *interj. Archaic.* quoth he! indeed! (used ironically or contemptuously in repeating the words of another).

quo·tid·i·an (kwō tid′ē ən) *adj.* reappearing daily; daily. *—n.* a fever or ague that occurs daily. [< L *quotidianus*, var. of *cotidianus* < *cotidie* daily < *quotus* which (in sequence) + *dies* say]

quo·tient (kwō′shənt) *n.* the number obtained by dividing one number by another. In 26 ÷ 2 = 13, 13 is the quotient. [< L *quotiens* how many times]

quo war·ran·to (kwō wə ran′tō) *Latin.* **1** a writ commanding a person to show by what authority he holds a public office, privilege, franchise, etc. **2** the legal proceedings taken against such a person as distinct from a private citizen. [< Med.L *quo warranto* by what warrant]

qursh or **qurush** (ku̇rsh or ku̇r′əsh) *n.* **1** a unit of money in Saudi Arabia, worth 1/20 of a riyal. **2** a coin worth one qursh. [< Arabic *qirsh*]

q.v. which see. (for L *quod vide*)

☛ **q.v.** is used as a reference to another book, article, etc. already mentioned. It is now often replaced in reference works by the English word *see.*

R or **r** (är) *n.* **R's** or **r's. 1** the eighteenth letter of the English alphabet. **2** any speech sound represented by this letter. **3** one (usually eighteenth) of a series designated alphabetically. **4 the three R's,** reading, writing, and arithmetic.

r 1 ratio. **2** radius. **3** in church usage, respond or response. **4** in physics, resistance in ohms.

r. 1 railway. **2** rod. **3** ruble. **4** rupee. **5** road. **6** rare. **7** residence. **8** resides. **9** retired. **10** ratio.

R. 1 River. **2** Republican. **3** railway. **4** railroad. **5** King. (for L *rex*) **6** Queen. (for L *regina*) **7** Royal. **8** Rabbi. **9** Radical. **10** Réaumur. **11** Rector.

Ra (rä) *n.* the Egyptian sun god and supreme deity, typically represented as a hawk-headed man bearing the sun on his head. [< Egyptian *Rā* the sun]

Ra radium.

R.A. 1 Rear Admiral. **2** Royal Academy. **3** Royal Academician. **4** Royal Artillery.

rab·bet (rab′it) *n. v.* **-bet·ed, -bet·ing.** —*n.* **1** a cut, groove, or slot made on the edge or surface of a board, etc. to receive the end or edge of another piece of wood shaped to fit it. **2** a joint so made. —*v.* **1** cut or form a rabbet in. **2** join with a rabbet. [ME < OF *rabat* a beating down < *rabbatre.* See REBATE.]

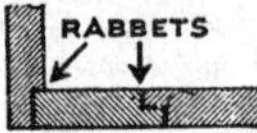

A rabbet

rab·bi (rab′ī) *n.* **-bis.** in the Jewish religion: **1** especially in former times, a teacher or scholar of the law. **2** an ordained religious leader, especially one in charge of a synagogue. [< L < Hebrew *rabbī* my master]

rab·bin·ate (rab′ə nit or rab′ə nāt′) *n.* **1** the position or office of rabbi. **2** rabbis collectively.

Rab·bin·ic (rə bin′ik) *n.* the form of Hebrew used by the medieval rabbis in their writings. —*adj.* **rabbinic,** rabbinical.

rab·bin·i·cal (rə bin′ə kəl) *adj.* of or having to do with rabbis, their learning, writings, etc. —**rab·bin′i·cal·ly,** *adv.*

rab·bit (rab′it) *n.* **1** a burrowing animal about as big as a cat, with soft fur and long ears. **2** its fur. **3** Welsh rabbit. —*v.* hunt or catch rabbits. [ME *rabet*; cf. MDu. *robbe*] —**rab′bit·like′,** *adj.*

rabbit ears 1 *Informal.* a small indoor antenna on a television set, consisting of two adjustable rods meeting at a base. **2** *Slang.* **a** oversensitivity on the part of an umpire, referee, or player to the crowd's reactions at a sports event. **b** an oversensitive umpire, referee, or player.

rab·ble (rab′əl) *n.* **1** a disorderly crowd; mob. **2 the rabble,** in contemptuous use, the lower classes. [cf. Du. *rabbelen* prattle]

rab·ble-rous·er (rab′əl rouz′ər) *n.* a person who tries to incite a mob to acts of violence by arousing passions; demagogue.

rab·ble-rous·ing (rab′əl rouz′ing) *adj.* acting like a rabble-rouser; demagogic. —*n.* the methods or actions of a rabble-rouser; demagoguery.

Rab·e·lai·si·an (rab′ə lā′zē ən or rab′ə lā′zhən) *adj.* of, having to do with, or suggesting François Rabelais, 1495?-1553, a French writer of satire and humor; characterized by broad, coarse humor.

rab·id (rab′id) *adj.* **1** unreasonably extreme; fanatical; violent. **2** furious; raging. **3** having rabies; mad: *a rabid dog.* **4** of rabies. [< L *rabidus* < *rabere* be mad] —**rab′id·ly,** *adv.* —**rab′id·ness,** *n.*

ra·bies (rā′bēz) *n.* a virus disease, often fatal, that makes dogs and certain other animals choke, writhe, and foam at the mouth; hydrophobia. If bitten by a mad dog, a person may get the disease. [< L *rabies* madness < *rabere* be mad]

rac·coon (ra kün′) *n.* **1** a small, brownish, flesh-eating mammal with a bushy, ringed tail. Most of the time raccoons live in trees; they move about at night. **2** its fur. **3** a coat or other garment made of this fur. Also, **racoon.** [< Algonquian]

race[1] (rās) *n. v.* **raced, rac·ing.** —*n.* **1** a contest of speed, as in running, driving, riding, sailing, etc. **2** Often, **races,** *pl.* a series of horse races run at a set time over a regular course. **3** any contest that suggests a race: *a political race.* **4** onward movement: *the race of life.* **5** a strong or fast current of water: *a mill race.* **6** the channel of a stream. **7** a channel leading water to or from a place where its energy is utilized. **8** a track, groove, etc. for a sliding or rolling part of a machine.
—*v.* **1** engage in a contest of speed. **2** try to beat in a contest of speed; run a race with. **3** cause to run in a race. **4** run, move, or go swiftly. **5** cause to run, move, or go swiftly. **6** of a motor, wheel, etc., run too fast when load or resistance is lessened without corresponding lessening of power. [ME < ON *rás*]

race[2] (rās) *n.* **1** one of the major divisions of mankind having certain physical peculiarities in common: *the white race, the yellow race.* **2** a group of persons connected by common descent or origin. **3** a group of animals or plants having the same ancestry: *the race of birds.* **4** especially of people, a group, class, or kind: *the brave race of seamen.* **5** the condition of belonging to a particular stock, or the qualities, etc. due to this: *Ability does not depend on race.* **6** stock of high quality. [< F < Ital. *razza*] —**Syn. 1, 2** See **people.**

race course race track.

race horse a horse for racing.

ra·ceme (rā sēm′ or rə sēm′) *n.* in botany, a simple flower cluster having its flowers on stalks of almost equal length along a stem, the lower flowers blooming first. The lily of the valley, currant, and chokecherry have racemes. See **inflorescence** for picture. [< L *racemus* cluster. Doublet of RAISIN.]

A raceme

rac·er (rās′ər) *n.* **1** a person, animal, boat, automobile, airplane, or bicycle that takes part in races. **2** a harmless North American snake. Racers live on frogs, mice, and insects.

race suicide the extinction of a people that tends to result when, by deliberate limitation of the number of children, the birth rate falls below the death rate.

race track a piece of ground laid out for racing.

ra·chis (rā′kis) *n.* **ra·chis·es, rach·i·des** (rak′ə dēz′ or rā′kə dēz′). **1** in botany, a stalk; shaft. **2** in zoology, the shaft of a bird's feather. **3** in anatomy, a spinal column. [< NL < Gk. *rhachis* backbone]

ra·chit·ic (rə kit′ik) *adj.* having to do with or affected with rachitis.

ra·chi·tis (rə kī′tis) *n.* rickets. [< NL < Gk. *rhachis* backbone + *-itis*]

ra·cial (rā′shəl) *adj.* **1** having to do with a race; characteristic of a race: *racial traits, racial dislikes.* **2** concerning two or more races: *racial problems, racial wars.*

ra·cial·ism (rā′shə liz′əm) *n.* racial prejudice or discrimination; racism.

ra·cial·ly (rā′shəl ē) *adv.* in respect to race.

rac·i·ness (rās′ē nis) *n.* the quality or condition of being racy.

rac·ism (rās′iz əm) *n.* **1** the exaggeration of inherent racial differences. **2** a prejudice in favor of certain races. **3** a political or social policy or system based on racism.

rac·ist (rās′ist) *n.* one who favors or practises racism. —*adj.* of or having to do with racism: *racist policies.*

rack[1] (rak) *n.* **1** a frame with bars, shelves, or pegs to hold, arrange, or keep things on: *a towel rack, a hat rack, a baggage rack.* **2** a frame of bars to hold hay and other food for cattle, etc. **3** a framework set on a wagon for carrying hay, straw, etc. **4** formerly, an instrument used for torturing people by stretching their limbs. The wrists and ankles of victims were bound at each end of a frame to rollers that were rotated in opposite directions. **5** a cause or condition of great suffering in body or mind. **6** a stretch; strain. **7** a bar with pegs or teeth on one edge, into which teeth on the rim of a wheel can fit. **8** in pool, a triangular frame used for arranging the balls. **9 on the rack,** in great pain; suffering very much.

A rack (def. 7). When the wheel turns, the rack moves horizontally.

—*v.* **1** hurt very much: *racked with grief. A toothache racked his jaw.* **2** stretch; strain. **3** torture on the rack. **4 rack one's brains,** think as hard as one can. **5 rack up,** *Informal.* accumulate. [probably < MDu. or MLG *recke*]

rack[2] (rak) *n.* wreck; destruction. [var. of *wrack*[1]]

rack[3] (rak) *n.* **1** a horse's gait in which the forefeet move as in a slow gallop, while the hind feet move as in a trot or pace; single-foot. **2** a pace. —*v.* **1** go at a rack. **2** a pace. [origin uncertain]

rack[4] (rak) *n.* flying, broken clouds driven by the wind. [ME < Scand.; cf. Swedish dial. *rak* wreckage]

rack[5] (rak) *n.* the neck portion of a forequarter of pork, veal, or mutton, sometimes made into a roast. [origin uncertain]

rack·et[1] (rak′it) *n.* **1** a loud noise; loud talk; din. **2** a time of gay parties and much social excitement. **3** *Informal.* a dishonest scheme for getting money from people by threatening violence or damage. **4** *Informal.* any dishonest scheme. **5** *Slang.* an occupation. **6 stand the racket,** hold out against strain or wear and tear.
—*v.* **1** make a racket; move about in a noisy way. **2** live a gay life; take part in social excitement. [formerly British slang (from early 19th century); ? imitative]

rack·et[2] (rak′it) *n.* **1** a light, wide bat made of network stretched on a frame, used for games like tennis. **2 rackets,** *pl.* a game played in a walled court with ball and rackets. **3** raquette. [< F *raquette* < Ital. < Arabic *rāha* palm of the hand]

☛ **Rackets, the game (def. 2), is plural in form and singular in use:** *Rackets is played in a walled court.*

rack·et·eer (rak′ə tēr′) *Informal.* —*n.* a person who extorts money by threatening violence or damage.
—*v.* extort money by threatening violence or damage.

rack·et·eer·ing (rak′ə tēr′ing) *n. Informal.* the business of a racketeer.

rack·et·y (rak′ə tē) *adj.* **1** making a racket; noisy. **2** characterized by revelry or dissipation.

rac·on·teur (rak′on tėr′) *n.* a person clever in telling stories, anecdotes, etc. [< F]

ra·coon (ra kün′) *n.* raccoon.

rac·quet (rak′it) *n.* racket[2].

rac·y (rās′ē) *adj.* **rac·i·er, rac·i·est. 1** vigorous; lively. **2** having an agreeably peculiar taste or flavor. **3** risqué; in doubtful taste, slightly improper: *a racy story.* [< *race*[2], in the sense of particular class or special flavor] —**rac′i·ly,** *adv.* —**Syn. 1** spirited. **2** piquant, spicy.

rad[1] (rad) *n.* a unit of nuclear radiation equal to 100 ergs of energy per gram, for measuring absorbed doses of radiation. [< *rad*iation]

rad[2] (rad) *n. Informal.* radiator.

rad. radical.

ra·dar (rā′där) *n.* **1** an instrument for determining the distance and direction of unseen objects by the reflection of radio waves. **2** this and other instruments and techniques that have developed from it. **3** a process by which the reflection of radio waves is measured. [short for *ra*dio *d*etecting *a*nd *r*anging]

radar fence or **screen** a protective chain of radar posts so placed around an area that their field is continuous.

ra·di·al (rā′dē əl) *adj.* **1** arranged like or in radii or rays. **2** in anatomy, of or near the radius bone.

A radial arrangement

radial engine an internal-combustion engine for an airplane, having radially arranged cylinders.

ra·di·al·ly (rā′dē əl ē) *adv.* like the spokes of a wheel; in rays; like radii or rays.

ra·di·an (rā′dē ən) *n.* an angle at the centre of a circle, that subtends an arc of the circle equal in length to the radius; an angle of 57.2958 degrees. [< *radius*]

ra·di·ance (rā′dē əns) *n.* **1** vivid brightness: *the radiance of the sun, the radiance of a smile.* **2** radiation.

ra·di·an·cy (rā′dē ən sē) *n.* radiance.

ra·di·ant (rā′dē ənt) *adj.* **1** shining; bright; beaming: *a radiant smile.* **2** sending out rays of light or heat: *The sun is a radiant body.* **3** bright with light. **4** sent off in rays from some source; radiated: *We get radiant energy from the sun.* **5** strikingly fine or splendid, as looks, beauty, etc. or the person.
—*n.* in physics, a point or object from which light or heat radiates. [< L *radians, -antis,* ppr. of *radiare* beam < *radius* ray] —**ra′di·ant·ly,** *adv.* —**Syn.** *adj.* **1** See **bright.**

hat, āge, cãre, fär; let, ēqual, tėrm; it, īce
hot, ōpen, ôrder; oil, out; cup, pu̇t, rüle, ūse
əbove, takən, pencəl, lemən, circəs
ch, child; ng, long; sh, ship
th, thin; ᴛʜ, then; zh, measure

radiant energy in physics, a form of energy, consisting of sound, heat, light, or electricity, that is sent out through space.

radiant heating a method of heating a room, building, etc. by means of heating units let into pipes or wires concealed in walls, baseboards, or floors.

ra·di·ate (rā′dē āt′) *v.* **-at·ed, -at·ing,** *adj.* —*v.* **1** give out rays of: *The sun radiates light and heat.* **2** give out rays; shine. **3** issue in rays: *Heat radiates from those hot steam pipes.* **4** give out; send forth: *Her face radiates joy.* **5** spread out from a centre: *Roads radiate from the city in every direction.* —*adj.* **1** having rays: *A daisy is a radiate flower.* **2** radiating from a centre. [ME < L *radiare.* See RADIANT.]

ra·di·a·tion (rā′dē ā′shən) *n.* **1** the act or process of giving out light, heat, or other radiant energy. **2** the energy radiated. **3** a ray or rays. **4** the process of treating disease by radiation from a radio-active material such as radium. **5** *Informal.* the radiators of a central heating system referred to collectively, or their capacity: *The plumbing contractor will figure out how much radiation you need.*

radiation counter any device, such as a Geiger counter, for detecting and counting radiation rays.

radiation sickness a disease resulting from an overdose of radiation from radio-active materials. It is usually characterized by internal bleeding and changes in tissue structure.

ra·di·a·tor (rā′dē ā′tər) *n.* **1** a heating device consisting of a set of pipes through which steam or hot water passes. **2** a device for cooling circulating water. The radiator of an automobile gives off heat very quickly and so cools the water inside it. **3** a person or thing that radiates.

rad·i·cal (rad′ə kəl) *adj.* **1** going to the root; fundamental: *Cruelty is a radical fault. If she wants to reduce, she must make a radical change in her diet.* **2** in politics: **a** advocating or favoring fundamental changes in the social or economic structure; leftist. **b Radical,** of or having to do with certain 20th-century parties, especially in Europe, whose programs range from somewhat leftist to conservative. **3** of or from the root or roots. **4** in botany, arising from the root or the base of the stem; basal. **5** in mathematics, having to do with or forming the root of a number or quantity.
—*n.* **1** in politics: **a** a person who has radical views. **b Radical,** a member of a Radical party. **2** in chemistry, an atom or group of atoms acting as a unit in reactions. Ammonium (NH_4) is a radical in NH_4OH and NH_4Cl. **3** in mathematics, the sign ($\surd$) put before an expression to show that some root of it is to be extracted. **4** in grammar, a root. **5** anything fundamental or basic. [ME < LL *radicalis* < L *radix, -icis* root] —**rad′i·cal·ly,** *adv.* —**rad′i·cal·ness,** *n.*

rad·i·cal·ism (rad′ə kəl iz′əm) *n.* **1** the condition or quality of being radical. **2** in politics, the principles or practices of radicals; extreme views.

rad·i·cle (rad′ə kəl) *n.* in botany: **1** the part of a seed that develops into the main root. **2** a little root. [< L *radicula,* dim. of *radix, -icis* root]

ra·di·i (rā′dē ī′) *n.* a pl. of **radius.**

ra·di·o (rā′dē ō′) *n.* **-di·os,** *adj. v.* **-di·oed, -di·o·ing.** —*n.* **1** a way of sending and receiving words, music, etc. by electric waves, without connecting wires. **2** an apparatus for receiving and making audible the sounds so sent. **3** *Informal.* a message sent by radio. **4** the business of radio broadcasting: *He left the movies and got a job in*

radio. **5** the branch of physics dealing with electromagnetic waves as used in communication.
—*adj*. **1** of, having to do with, used in, or sent by radio. **2** of or having to do with electric frequencies higher than 15,000 per second.
—*v*. transmit or send out by radio. [independent use of *radio-*, abstracted from *radiotelegraphy*, etc.]

radio- *combining form*. **1** radio, as in *radiotelegraphy*. **2** radial, as in *radiosymmetrical* (radially symmetrical). **3** radiant energy, as in *radiograph*. **4** radio-active, as in *radio-isotope* (a radio-active isotope). [< *radius*]

☛ Usage varies as to using a hyphen in combination with *radio-*. In this dictionary a hyphen is used when *radio-* is followed immediately by another vowel: *radio-active*, but *radiotelegraph*.

ra·di·o-ac·tive (rā′dē ō ak′tiv) *adj*. giving off radiant energy in the form of alpha, beta, or gamma rays by the breaking up of atoms. Radium, uranium, and thorium are radio-active metallic elements.

ra·di·o-ac·tiv·i·ty (rā′dē ō ak tiv′ə tē) *n*. **1** the property of being radio-active. **2** the radiation given off.

radio astronomy the branch of astronomy that studies objects in space by analysing radio waves given off by or reflected from them.

radio beacon a radio station for sending special signals so that ships, airplanes, etc. can determine their position.

ra·di·o·bi·o·log·i·cal (rā′dē ō bī′ə loj′ə kəl) *adj*. **1** of or having to do with radiobiology. **2** caused by radiation.

ra·di·o·bi·ol·o·gist (rā′dē ō bī ol′ə jist) *n*. one who is an expert in radiobiology.

ra·di·o·bi·ol·o·gy (rā′dē ō bī ol′ə jē) *n*. the branch of biology that deals with the effects of radiation on living bodies.

ra·di·o·car·bon (rā′dē ō kär′bən) *adj*. having to do with a method of determining the age of a substance, as a fossil, by measuring its radio-active carbon content.

ra·di·o·chem·i·cal (rā′dē ō kem′ə kəl) *adj*. of or having to do with radiochemistry.

ra·di·o·chem·ist (rā′dē ō kem′ist) *n*. one who is an expert in radiochemistry.

ra·di·o·chem·is·try (rā′dē ō kem′is trē) *n*. the branch of chemistry dealing with radio-active phenomena and substances.

ra·di·o-el·e·ment (rā′dē ō el′ə mənt) *n*. a radio-active element.

radio frequency a frequency of electrical vibrations above 15,000 per second. *Abbrev*.: RF, R.F., or r.f.

ra·di·o·gram (rā′dē ō gram′) *n*. **1** a message transmitted by radio. **2** a radiograph.

ra·di·o·graph (rā′dē ō graf′) *n*. a picture produced by X rays or other rays on a photographic plate, commonly called an X-ray picture. —*v*. make a radiograph of.

ra·di·og·ra·phy (rā′dē og′rə fē) *n*. the production of photographs by means of X rays.

ra·di·o-i·so·tope (rā′dē ō ī′sə tōp′) *n*. a radio-active isotope, especially one produced artificially.

ra·di·o·log·i·cal (rā′dē ə loj′ə kəl) *adj*. **1** of or having to do with radiology. **2** of or having to do with the rays from radio-active substances. **—ra′di·o·log′i·cal·ly**, *adv*.

ra·di·ol·o·gist (rā′dē ol′ə jist) *n*. an expert in radiology.

ra·di·ol·o·gy (rā′dē ol′ə jē) *n*. the science that deals with radio-active rays or X rays.

ra·di·o·man (rā′dē ō man′) *n*. **-men** (-men′). **1** a radio operator or technician on an airplane, ship, etc. **2** one who works in radio broadcasting.

ra·di·om·e·ter (rā′dē om′ə tər) *n*. an instrument for indicating the conversion of radiant energy into mechanical force, often consisting of a glass vessel containing vanes that are in a vacuum and rotate when exposed to light.

ra·di·o·phone (rā′dē ō fōn′) *n*. radiotelephone.

ra·di·o·sonde (rā′dē ō sond′) *n*. an instrument for recording and transmitting atmospheric humidity, temperature, pressure, etc., usually carried by a balloon into the stratosphere and then parachuted back to earth. [< *radio* + F *sonde* depth, sounding]

ra·di·o·tel·e·graph (rā′dē ō tel′ə graf′) *n*. a telegraph worked by radio. —*v*. telegraph by radio.

ra·di·o·te·leg·ra·phy (rā′dē ō tə leg′rə fē) *n*. the system of telegraphing by radio.

ra·di·o·tel·e·phone (rā′dē ō tel′ə fōn′) *n*. *v*. **-phoned, -phon·ing.** —*n*. a radio transmitter using voice communication. —*v*. telephone by radio.

ra·di·o·te·leph·o·ny (rā′dē ō tə lef′ə nē) *n*. radio communication by means of voice signals.

radio telescope an apparatus for making observations of bodies in outer space by studying radio waves coming from them or radar waves reflected from them. Some radio telescopes have a large, parabola-shaped antenna made up of a network of wires.

A radio telescope

ra·di·o·ther·a·py (rā′dē ō ther′ə pē) *n*. the treatment of disease by means of radiation.

radio tube a vacuum tube used in a radio set.

rad·ish (rad′ish) *n*. **1** a small, crisp root having a red or white skin, used as a relish and in salads. **2** the plant. [OE *rædic* < L *radix*, *radicis* root. Doublet of RADIX.]

ra·di·um (rā′dē əm) *n*. a radio-active, metallic chemical element found in very small amounts in uranium ores such as pitchblende. Radium is used in treating cancer and in making luminous paint. Radium atoms are constantly breaking up and in this process give off alpha, beta, and gamma rays. *Symbol*: Ra; *at.no*. 88; *at.wt*. 226 (most stable isotope). [< NL < L *radius* ray]

ra·di·us (rā′dē əs) *n*. **-di·i** or **-di·us·es.** **1** any line going straight from the centre to the outside of a circle or a sphere. **2** a circular area measured by the length of its radius: *The explosion could be heard within a radius of ten miles.* **3** in anatomy, that one of the two bones of the forearm that is on the thumb side. See **skeleton** for picture. **4** a corresponding bone in the forelimb of vertebrates other than man. [< L *radius* ray, spoke of a wheel. Doublet of RAY[1].]

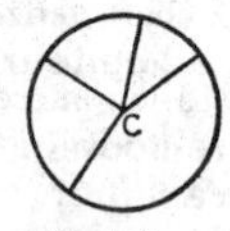

Each line from C (centre) is a radius.

ra·dix (rā′diks) *n*. **rad·i·ces** (rad′ə sēz′ or rā′də sēz′) or **ra·dix·es.** **1** a root; radical; source or origin. **2** in mathematics, a number taken as the base of a system of numbers, logarithms, or the like. The radix of the decimal system is ten. [< L *radix*, *radicis* root. Doublet of RADISH.]

ra·don (rā′don) *n*. a rare, heavy, radio-active, gaseous chemical element that is given off by radium. *Symbol*: Rn; *at.no*. 86; *at.wt*. 222 (most stable isotope). [< *radium*]

R.A.F. or **RAF** in the United Kingdom, Royal Air Force.

raf·fi·a (raf′ē ə) *n*. **1** a fibre from the leafstalks of a kind of palm tree growing in Malagasy, used in making baskets, mats, etc. **2** the palm tree from which this fibre is obtained. [< Malagasy *rafia*]

raf·fish (raf′ish) *adj*. **1** crude; rowdy; vulgar. **2** disreputable; unconventional. **—raf′fish·ly**, *adv*. **—raf′fish·ness**, *n*.

raf·fle (raf′əl) *n*. *v*. **-fled, -fling.** —*n*. a sale in which many people each pay a small sum for a chance of getting an article. —*v*. **1** sell (an article) by a raffle. **2** hold a raffle. [ME *rafle* a dice game < OF *rafle* plundering, stripping, ult. < Du. *rafelen* ravel, pluck]

raft[1] (raft) *n*. **1** logs or boards fastened together to make a floating platform. **2** any floating platform. **3** *Cdn*. in lumbering: **a** pieces of lumber lashed together for floating downstream, as to a mill. **b** formerly, a larger formation of square timber, composed of smaller units called drams, as used on the Great Lakes and the streams of the St. Lawrence River system. **4** a floating ice formation resulting from the piling up of cakes of ice in layers. —*v*. **1** send by raft; carry on a raft. **2** make into a raft. **3** of ice, be piled high, layer upon layer, as a result of pressure. [ME < ON *raptr* log]

hat, āge, cãre, fär; let, ēqual, tėrm; it, īce
hot, ōpen, ôrder; oil, out; cup, pu̇t, rüle, ūse
əbove, takən, pencəl, lemən, circəs
ch, child; ng, long; sh, ship
th, thin; TH, then; zh, measure

raft[2] (raft) *n. Informal.* a large number; abundance. [var. of *raff* heap < *riffraff*]

raft·er[1] (raf′tər) *n.* a supporting beam, often slanting, of a roof. [OE *ræfter*]

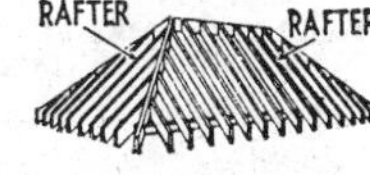

raf·ter[2] (raf′tər) *n.* a person who rafts timber.

rag[1] (rag) *n.* **1** a torn or waste piece of cloth. **2** a small piece of cloth. **3** a small piece of anything of no value. **4 rags,** *pl.* tattered or worn-out clothes. **5** a contemptuous or humorous term for some article of clothing, a flag, a theatre curtain, a piece of paper money, etc. **6** *Informal.* a piece of ragtime music. —*adj.* made from rags. [ME < OE **ragg* < ON *rögg* shaggy tuft] —**rag′like′,** *adj.* —**Syn.** *n.* **4** tatters.

rag[2] (rag) *v.* **ragged, rag·ging.** *Slang.* **1** scold. **2** tease. **3** play jokes on. **4 rag the puck,** in hockey, keep control of the puck by skilful stick-handling and elusive skating, usually as a means of killing time when one's own team is shorthanded. —*n.* a ragging. [origin uncertain]

rag·a·muf·fin (rag′ə muf′ən) *n.* **1** a ragged, disreputable fellow. **2** a dirty, poorly dressed child. [probably < *rag*[1]]

rag·bag (rag′bag′) *n.* **1** a bag containing rags, scraps, etc. **2** a miscellaneous or motley collection.

rage (rāj) *n. v.* **raged, rag·ing.** —*n.* **1** violent anger: *a voice quivering with rage.* **2** a fit of violent anger: *be in a rage.* **3** violence: *the rage of a savage tiger.* **4** a movement, idea, or fashion that is popular for a short time. **5** great enthusiasm.
—*v.* **1** be furious with anger. **2** speak or move with furious anger. **3** act violently; move, proceed, or continue with great violence: *A storm is raging.* [ME < OF < VL *rabia* < L *rabies*]
Syn. *n.* **1 Rage, fury** = violent anger. **Rage** = anger so violent that it causes either complete loss of self-control or a bitter desire to get revenge: *In his rage the child broke his mother's favorite vase.* **Fury** = rage so wild and fierce that it destroys common sense and makes a person like an enraged wild animal, wanting to harm and destroy: *In their fury the hoodlums went through the streets wrecking cars.* **4** vogue.

rag·ged (rag′id) *adj.* **1** worn or torn into rags. **2** wearing torn or badly worn-out clothing: *a ragged beggar.* **3** not straight and tidy; rough: *an Airedale's ragged coat, a ragged garden.* **4** having loose shreds or bits: *a ragged wound.* **5** having rough or sharp points; uneven; jagged: *ragged rocks.* **6** harsh: *a ragged voice.* **7** faulty; imperfect; irregular: *ragged rhyme.* —**rag′ged·ly,** *adv.* —**rag′ged·ness,** *n.* —**Syn. 1** rent, tattered, frayed.

rag·gle-tag·gle (rag′əl tag′əl) *adj. Informal.* ragged; slovenly; down-at-heel.

rag·lan (rag′lən) *n.* a loose-fitting topcoat or overcoat with sleeves cut so as to continue up to the collar. [after Fitzroy James Somerset, Baron *Raglan* (1788-1855), a British field marshal]

rag·man (rag′man′) *n.* **-men** (-men′). a man who gathers, buys, or sells rags.

ra·gout (ra gü′) *n.* a highly seasoned stew of meat and vegetables. [< F *ragoût* < *ragoûter* restore the appetite]

rag·pick·er (rag′pik′ər) *n.* a person who picks up rags and junk, usually to sell them.

rag·time (rag′tīm′) *n. Informal.* **1** in music, a highly syncopated, fast rhythm, usually in 4-4 time. **2** music that has a fast, syncopated rhythm; jazz. [origin uncertain]

rag·weed (rag′wēd′) *n.* any of several coarse weeds of the aster family whose pollen is one of the most common causes of hay fever.

rag·wort (rag′wėrt′) *n.* any of various plants having irregularly lobed leaves and yellow flowers.

rah (rä) *interj. n.* hurrah.

raid (rād) *n.* **1** an attack, especially a sudden attack. **2** a sudden attack by a small force having no intention of holding the territory invaded. **3** an entering and seizing what is inside. **4** a deliberate attempt by speculators to force down prices on stock exchanges.
—*v.* **1** attack suddenly. **2** force a way into; enter and seize what is in: *The police raided the gambling house.* **3** engage in a raid. [northern form of OE *rād* a ride, riding. Cf. ROAD.] —**raid′er,** *n.*

rail[1] (rāl) *n.* **1** a bar of wood or of metal: *stair rails, fence rails.* The steel bars of a railway track are called rails. **2** railway: *ship by rail.* **3** the upper part of the bulwarks of a ship. —*v.* **1** furnish with rails. **2** enclose with bars. **3 rail in,** enclose within a fence. **4 rail off,** separate by a fence. [ME < OF *reille* < L *regula* straight rod. Doublet of RULE.]

rail[2] (rāl) *v.* complain bitterly; use violent and reproachful language: *He railed at his hard luck.* [< F *railler*, ult. < LL *ragere* to scream. Doublet of RALLY[2].] —**rail′er,** *n.* —**Syn.** scold, revile, upbraid.

rail[3] (rāl) *n.* **rails** or (*esp. collectively*) **rail.** any of numerous small birds having short wings, narrow bodies, strong legs, long toes, and a harsh cry. Rails live in marshes and swamps. [< F *râle* < VL *rascla*; probably imitative]

rail·head (rāl′hed′) *n.* **1** the end or terminus of a railway. **2** the farthest point to which the tracks of a railway under construction have been laid; end of steel. **3** a point on a railway that serves as a depot for military supplies, etc.

rail·ing (rāl′ing) *n.* **1** a fence made of rails. **2** a handrail on a staircase, ramp, etc. **3** material for rails. **4** rails collectively.

rail·ler·y (rāl′ər ē) *n.* **-ler·ies. 1** good-humored ridicule; joking; teasing. **2** a bantering remark. [< F *raillerie* < *railler.* See RAIL[2].]

rail·road (rāl′rōd′) *n.* a railway. *Abbrev.*: **R.R.**
—*v.* **1** send by railway; carry on a railway. **2** work on a railway: *He has been railroading all his life.* **3** *Informal.* send along too quickly to be fair; get something done quickly and unfairly: *railroad a man to prison, railroad a bill through a committee.* —**rail′road′er,** *n.*

rail·road·ing (rāl′rōd′ing) *n.* **1** the construction or operation of railways. **2** the act or process of hurrying (a thing or person) along.

rail·way (rāl′wā′) *n.* **1** a road or track with parallel steel rails on which the wheels of locomotives, cars, etc. go. **2** tracks, stations, trains, and other property of a system of transportation that uses rails, together with the people who manage them: *One of Canada's railways is owned by the government.* **3** the company or corporation which owns and operates such a system. *Abbrev.*: Ry.

railway crossing a place where a railway track crosses a street or highway on the same level.

rai·ment (rā′mənt) *n.* clothing; garments. [short for *arraiment* < *array*]

rain (rān) *n.* **1** water falling in drops from the clouds. **2** the fall of such drops. **3** a thick, fast fall of anything: *a rain of bullets.* **4 the rains,** the rainy season; the seasonal rainfalls. —*v.* **1** fall in drops of water. **2** fall like rain: *Sparks rained down from the burning roof.* **3** send like rain: *The children rained confetti on the bride.* **4 rain out,** cancel because of rain. [OE *regn*]

rain·bow (rān′bō′) *n.* **1** a bow or arch of the colors of the spectrum, seen sometimes in the sky after rain, or in mist or spray. The colors are violet, indigo, blue, green, yellow, orange, and red. **2** a rainbow trout. [OE *regnboga*]

rainbow trout a kind of large trout, highly valued as a food and game fish, having along the sides a reddish stripe which is most noticeable at spawning periods.

rain check 1 a ticket for future use, given to the spectators at a baseball game or other outdoor performance stopped by rain. **2** *Informal.* an understanding that an invitation which cannot presently be accepted will be renewed on a future occasion: *May I take a rain check on your invitation to dinner?*

rain·coat (rān′kōt′) *n.* a waterproof coat worn for protection from rain.

rain·drop (rān′drop′) *n.* a drop of rain.

rain·fall (rān′fol′ or -fôl′) *n.* **1** a shower of rain. **2** the amount of water in the form of rain, snow, etc. falling within a given time and area.

rain forest a large, densely wooded region where there is very heavy rainfall throughout the year, usually but not always in tropical climates.

rain gauge an instrument for measuring rainfall.

rain·mak·er (rān′māk′ər) *n.* a person who tries to produce rain, especially one who tries to produce rain by supernatural or artificial means.

rain·mak·ing (rān′māk′ing) *n.* the making of rain artificially, or by supernatural means. One method is to seed a cloud with crystals of silver iodide, which expand with heat, collecting particles of moisture that are released from the cloud as rain.

rain·storm (rān′stôrm′) *n.* a storm with much rain.

rain water water that has fallen as rain.

rain·wear (rān′wãr′) *n.* clothing made to be worn in the rain, such as rubbers, raincoats, etc.

rain·y (rān′ē) *adj.* **rain·i·er, rain·i·est. 1** having rain; having much rain. **2** bringing rain. **3** wet with rain. —**rain′i·ly,** *adv.* —**rain′i·ness,** *n.*

rainy day a time of need in the future: *save for a rainy day.*

raise (rāz) *v.* **raised, rais·ing,** *n.* —*v.* **1** lift up: *raise one's hand.* **2** set upright: *Raise the overturned lamp.* **3** cause to rise: *raise a cloud of dust.* **4** put or take into a higher position; make higher or nobler; elevate: *raise a salesman to manager.* **5** increase in degree, amount, price, pay, etc.: *raise the rent.* **6** make louder or of higher pitch: *I cannot hear you; please raise your voice.* **7** in games, bid or bet more than an opponent. **8** gather together; collect; manage to get: *The leader raised an army.* **9** breed; grow: *The farmer raises crops and cattle.* **10** cause to appear: *raise the ghost of Napoleon.* **11** cause; bring about: *A funny remark raises a laugh.* **12** utter: *raise a shout.* **13** build; create; produce; start; set up: *raise a monument.* **14** rouse; stir up: *The dog raised a rabbit from the underbrush.* **15** bring up; rear: *Parents raise their children.* **16** cause to become light: *Yeast raises bread.* **17** bring back to life: *raise the dead.* **18 a** put an end to: *Our soldiers raised the siege of the fort by driving away the enemy.* **b** break up and remove. **19** come in sight of: *After a long voyage the ship raised land.* **20** falsify the value of (a cheque, note, etc.) by making the sum larger. **21 raise Cain, the devil, mischief,** or **the roof,** *Slang.* make a disturbance; create an uproar or confusion.
—*n.* **1** a raised place. **2** an increase in amount, price, pay, etc. **3** the amount of such an increase. [ME < ON *reisa* < Gmc. causative of *rīsan* rise]
Syn. *v.* **1 Raise, lift, elevate** = move to a higher position. **Raise** = bring something to a high or, especially, vertical position or to move it up from a lower to a higher level: *Raise your right hand.* **Lift** = take something, usually heavy, up from the ground or other low level: *Please lift the table.* **Elevate** chiefly means "to raise to a higher rank or nobler state": *Good reading elevates the mind.* **4** promote, advance, exalt. **8** muster.

rais·er (rāz′ər) *n.* a person who grows or raises things: *a cattle raiser.*

rai·sin (rā′zən) *n.* a sweet dried grape. [ME < OF < L *racemus* grape cluster. Doublet of RACEME.]

rai·son d'être (re zôɴ detr′) *French.* reason for being; justification.

raj (räj) *n.* in India, rule; dominion: *the British raj.* [< Hind. *raj*]

ra·jah (rä′jə) *n.* in Java, Borneo, etc. and formerly in India, a ruler or chief. Also, **raja.** [< Hind. *rājā* < Skt.]

Raj·put (räj′püt) *n.* a member of a Hindu military, land-owning, and ruling caste. [< Hind. *rājput* < Skt. *rājaputra* king's son]

rake[1] (rāk) *n. v.* **raked, rak·ing.** —*n.* a long-handled tool having a bar at one end with teeth in it. A rake is used for smoothing the soil or gathering together loose leaves, hay, or straw.
—*v.* **1** move with a rake: *Rake the leaves off the grass.* **2** use a rake. **3** gather; gather together. **4** search carefully: *He raked the newspapers for descriptions of the accident.* **5** fire guns along the length of (a ship, line of soldiers, etc.). [OE *raca*]

rake[2] (rāk) *n.* a profligate or dissolute person. [short for *rakehell*]

rake[3] (rāk) *n. v.* **raked, rak·ing.** slant; slope. A ship's smokestacks have a slight backward rake. [origin uncertain]

rake·hell (rāk′hel′) *n. Archaic.* a libertine; roué. [< *rake*[1] + *hell*; replacing ME *rakel* rash]

rake-off (rāk′of′) *n. Slang.* a share or portion, often an amount taken or received illicitly.

rak·ish[1] (rāk′ish) *adj.* **1** smart; jaunty; dashing: *a hat set at a rakish angle.* **2** suggesting dash and speed: *He owns a rakish boat.* [< *rake*[3]; influenced in def. 1 by association with *rakish*[2]]

rak·ish[2] (rāk′ish) *adj.* like a rake; immoral; dissolute. [< *rake*[2]] —**Syn.** licentious.

rall. rallentando.

ral·len·tan·do (räl′en tän′dō) in music: —*adj.* slackening; becoming slower. —*adv.* gradually more slowly. —*n.* **1** a gradual decrease in tempo. **2** a passage to be played or sung in this manner. [< Ital. *rallentando* slowing down < *lento* slow]

ral·ly[1] (ral′ē) *v.* **-lied, -ly·ing,** *n.* **-lies.** —*v.* **1** bring together; bring together again; get in order again: *The commander was able to rally the fleeing troops.* **2** pull together; revive: *He rallied all his energy for one last effort.* **3** come together in a body for a common purpose or action. **4** come to help a person, party, or cause: *He rallied to the side of his injured friend.* **5** recover health and strength: *The sick man may rally now.* **6** in tennis, etc., hit the ball back and forth several times.
—*n.* **1** the act of rallying; recovery. **2** a coming together; mass meeting: *a political rally.* **3** in tennis, etc., a hitting of the ball back and forth several times. **4** a meeting of people to take part in a sport: *a cross-country rally, a sportscar rally.* [< F *rallier* < *re-* again + *allier* ally]

ral·ly[2] (ral′ē) *v.* **-lied, -ly·ing.** make fun of; tease. [< F *railler* rail[2]. Doublet of RAIL[2].] —**Syn.** banter.

ram (ram) *n. v.* **rammed, ram·ming.** —*n.* **1** a male sheep. **2** a machine or part of a machine that strikes heavy blows: *a battering ram.* **3** the beak at the bow of a warship, used to break the sides of enemy ships. **4** a ship with such a beak. **5** the plunger of a force pump. **6** a pump in which the force of a descending column of water raises some of the water above its original level. **7 Ram,** in astrology, the first sign of the zodiac; Aries.
—*v.* **1** butt against; strike head on; strike violently: *One ship rammed the other ship.* **2** push hard; drive down or in by heavy blows. [OE *ramm*]

-rama *combining form.* denoting something spectacular or a remarkable display or exhibition, as in *Cinerama.* Also, **-orama.** [formed after *panorama*]

Ram·a·dan (ram′ə dän′) *n.* **1** the ninth month of the Moslem year; during which fasting is rigidly practised daily from dawn until sunset. **2** the fasting itself. [< Arabic *Ramadān*, originally, the hot month]

Ra·ma·ya·na (rä mä′yə nə) *n.* one of the two great epics of India, that tells the story of Rama, a legendary king of N. India, written in Sanskrit early in the Christian era. The other Sanskrit epic is the **Mahabharata.**

ram·ble (ram′bəl) *v.* **-bled, -bling,** *n.* —*v.* **1** wander about: *We rambled here and there through the woods.* **2** talk or write about first one thing and then another with no clear connections. **3** spread irregularly in various directions: *Vines rambled over the wall.* —*n.* a walk for pleasure, with or without any definite route. [var. of ME *romblen*, a frequentative of *romen* roam] —**Syn.** *v.* **1** rove, range, meander. See **roam.**

ram·bler (ram′blər) *n.* **1** a person or thing that rambles. **2** any of various climbing roses.

ram·bunc·tious (ram bungk′shəs) *adj. Informal.* **1** wild and uncontrollable; unruly. **2** noisy and violent; boisterous. [? a mock word formed from *ram* knock around + a var. of *bumptious*]

ram·e·kin or **ram·e·quin** (ram′ə kin) *n.* **1** a small, separately cooked portion of some food, especially one topped with cheese and bread crumbs. **2** a small baking dish holding enough for one portion. [< F *ramequin* < Du.]

ram·ie (ram′ē) *n.* **1** an Asiatic shrub that yields a strong fibre used in making textiles, etc. **2** this fibre. [< Malay *rami* plant]

ram·i·fi·ca·tion (ram′ə fə kā′shən) *n.* **1** a dividing or spreading out into branches or parts. **2** a branch; part. **3** something that springs out like a branch. **4** a result, consequence, extension, etc.: *the ramifications of an idea.*

ram·i·fy (ram′ə fī′) *v.* **-fied, -fy·ing.** divide or spread out into branchlike parts. [< F < Med.L *ramificare* < L *ramus* branch + *facere* make]

ram·jet (ram′jet′) *n.* a type of jet engine in which the fuel is fed into air that is compressed by the forward speed of the airplane, guided missile, etc.

ram·mer (ram′ər) *n.* a person or thing that rams; a device for driving or compacting something.

ra·mose (rā′mōs or rə mōs′) *adj.* having many branches; branching. [< L *ramosus* < *ramus* branch]

ra·mous (rā′məs) *adj.* **1** ramose. **2** of or like a branch.

ramp[1] (ramp) *n.* a sloping way connecting two different levels of a building, road, etc.; slope: *We entered the plane by means of a ramp.* [< F *rampe* < *ramper.* See RAMP[2].]

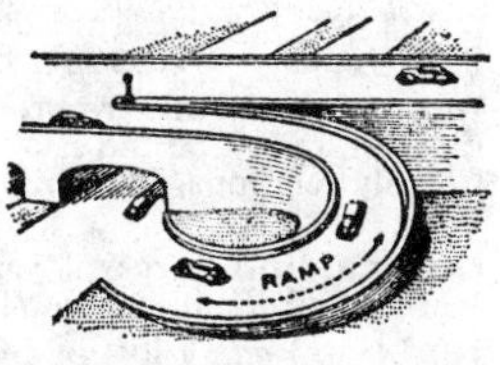

ramp[2] (ramp) *v.* **1** rush wildly about; behave violently. **2** jump or rush with fury. **3** in heraldry, of beasts, rear on their hind feet. [< F *ramper* creep < Gmc.]

ram·page (*n.* ram′pāj; *v.* ram pāj′ or ram′pāj) *n. v.* **-paged, -pag·ing.** —*n.* a spell of violent behavior often accompanied by rushing about wildly; wild outbreak: *The mad elephant went on a rampage and killed its keeper.* —*v.* rush wildly about; behave violently; rage. [? < *ramp*[2]]

ram·pa·geous (ram pā′jəs) *adj.* wild; unruly; boisterous. **—ram·pa′geous·ly,** *adv.* **—ram·pa′geous·ness,** *n.*

ramp·an·cy (ram′pən sē) *n.* the state of being rampant.

ramp·ant (ram′pənt) *adj.* **1** growing without any check: *The vines ran rampant over the fence.* **2** passing beyond restraint or usual limits; unchecked: *Anarchy was rampant after the dictator died.* **3** angry; excited; violent. **4** in heraldry, of beasts, standing up on one hind leg, with the other legs raised. **5** of animals, rearing. [ME < OF *rampant* ramping] **—ramp′ant·ly,** *adv.* **—Syn. 3** furious, raging.

A lion rampant (def. 4)

ram·part (ram′pärt) *n.* **1** a wide bank of earth, often with a wall on top, built around a fort to help defend it. **2** anything that defends; defence; protection. **3** *Cdn.* in the Northwest, a steep, high bank of a river or stream flowing through a gorge or canyon. [< F *rempart* < *remparer* fortify, ult. < L *re-* back + *ante* before + *parare* prepare]

ram·pike (ram′pīk′) *n. Cdn.* the bleached skeleton of a dead tree, especially one killed by fire.

ram·rod (ram′rod′) *n.* **1** a rod for ramming down the charge in a gun that is loaded from the muzzle. **2** a rod for cleaning the barrel of a gun.

ram·shack·le (ram′shak′əl) *adj.* loose and shaky; likely to come apart: *a ramshackle house.* [? ult. < *ransack*] **—Syn.** rickety, dilapidated.

ran (ran) *v.* pt. of **run.**

ranch (ranch) *n.* **1** a large establishment, with a holding of range land, for raising livestock. **2** an establishment for raising fur-bearing animals: *a mink ranch.* **3** a farm: *a fruit ranch.* **4** the persons working or living on a ranch: *The entire ranch was at the party.* **5** a rancherie. **6** on the West coast, an Indian house or dwelling.
—*v.* **1** work on a ranch; operate a ranch. **2** raise fur-bearing animals. [< Sp. *rancho* camp, mess]

ranch·er (ran′chər) *n.* a person who owns, operates, or works on a ranch.

ranch·er·ie (ranch′ər ē) *n.* in British Columbia, a camp or settlement of Indians. [< Sp. *rancheria*]

ranch house 1 the main building on a ranch. **2** on the West coast, a large communal dwelling or house of the Indians. **3** a spacious, one-storey structure modelled on the houses of the Pacific Coast Indians.

hat, āge, cãre, fär; let, ēqual, tėrm; it, īce
hot, ōpen, ôrder; oil, out; cup, pu̇t, rüle, ūse
əbove, takən, pencəl, lemən, circəs
ch, child; ng, long; sh, ship
th, thin; ᴛʜ, then; zh, measure

ranch·man (ranch′mən) *n.* **-men** (-mən). rancher.

ran·cid (ran′sid) *adj.* **1** stale; spoiled: *rancid fat.* **2** tasting or smelling like stale fat or butter. [< L *rancidus* < *rancere* be rank] **—ran′cid·ly,** *adv.* **—ran′cid·ness,** *n.*

ran·cid·i·ty (ran sid′ə tē) *n.* a rancid quality or condition.

ran·cor or **rancour** (rang′kər) *n.* bitter resentment or ill will; extreme hatred or spite. [ME < OF < LL *rancor* rankness < L *rancere* be rank] **—Syn. malice,** animosity.

ran·cor·ous (rang′kər əs) *adj.* spiteful; bitterly malicious. **—ran′cor·ous·ly,** *adv.*

ran·cour (rang′kər) *n.* rancor.

rand (rand) *n.* **1** a unit of money in South Africa. See table at **money. 2** a coin worth one rand. [< Afrikaans < the *Rand,* the gold-mining district in the Transvaal]

ran·dom (ran′dəm) *adj.* by chance; with no plan. —*n.* **at random,** by chance; with no plan or purpose. [ME < OF *randon* rapid rush] **—ran′dom·ly,** *adv.*
Syn. *adj.* **Random, haphazard** = made, done, happening, or coming by chance, not plan. **Random** emphasizes being without definite aim, direction, purpose, or plan. **Haphazard** emphasizes being determined by chance, not by plan or fitness for a purpose or aim: *Because of her haphazard way of choosing clothes, she never looks well dressed.*

ran·dy (ran′dē) *adj. Scottish.* **1** coarse and boisterous in behavior. **2** lustful; lecherous. [origin uncertain]

ra·nee (rä′nē) *n.* **1** the wife of a rajah. **2** a ruling Hindu queen or princess. Also **rani.** [< Hind. *rani* < Skt. *rajni*]

rang (rang) *v.* pt. of **ring**[2].

range (rānj) *n. v.* **ranged, rang·ing,** *adj.* —*n.* **1** the distance between certain limits; extent: *a range of prices from 5 cents to 25 dollars.* **2** the distance a gun, etc. can shoot. **3** the distance from a gun, etc. of an object aimed at. **4** a place to practise shooting. **5** land for grazing. **6** the act of wandering or moving about. **7** a row or line of mountains. **8** a row; line. **9** a line of direction: *The two barns are in direct range with the house.* **10** a rank, class, or order. **11** a district in which certain plants or animals live. **12** a stove for cooking. **13** a row of townships, each six miles square, between two meridians six miles apart. [< v.]
—*v.* **1** vary within certain limits: *prices ranging from $5 to $10.* **2** wander; rove; roam. **3** wander over: *Buffalo once ranged these plains.* **4** put in a row or rows: *Range the books by size.* **5** put in groups or classes. **6** put in a line on someone's side: *Loyal citizens ranged themselves with the king.* **7** run in a line; extend: *a boundary ranging east and west.* **8** be found; occur: *a plant ranging from Canada to Mexico.*
—*adj.* of or on land for grazing. [ME < OF *ranger* array, ult. < *renc* line. See RANK[1].]
Syn. *n.* **1 Range, scope, compass** = the extent of what something can do or take in. **Range** emphasizes the extent (and variety) that can be covered or taken in by something in operation or action, such as the mind, eye, a machine, force, etc.: *The car was out of his range of vision.* **Scope** emphasizes the idea of limits beyond which the understanding, view, application, etc. cannot extend: *Some technical terms are beyond the scope of this dictionary.* **Compass** emphasizes the limits within which something can act or operate: *Geographical names are within its compass.*

range finder an instrument for estimating the range or distance of an object. A range finder indicates the distance between it and its target.

rang·er (rān′jər) *n.* **1** a person or thing that ranges; rover. **2** a person employed to guard a tract of forest. **3** a soldier of certain regiments originally organized for fighting in the North American forests: *the Queen's Rangers.* **4** Also, **Ranger.** a member of the senior branch of the Girl Guides, for girls over 16 years.

rang·ette (rān jet′) *n.* a cooking stove smaller than a range.

rang·y (rān′jē) *adj.* **rang·i·er, rang·i·est. 1** fitted for ranging or moving about. **2** slender and long-limbed: *a rangy horse.* —**rang′i·ness,** *n.*

ra·ni (rä′nē) *n.* ranee.

rank[1] (rangk) *n.* **1** a row or line, especially of soldiers, placed side by side. **2 ranks,** *pl.* **a** the army; soldiers. **b** the rank and file. **3** a position; grade; class: *the rank of colonel.* **4** a high position: *A duke is a man of rank.* **5** an orderly arrangement or array.
—*v.* **1** arrange in a row or line. **2** have a certain place or position in relation to other persons or things: *Bill ranked low in the test.* **3** put in some special order in a list: *Rank the continents in order of size.* **4** be more important than; outrank: *A major ranks a captain.* [ult. < OF *renc* < Gmc.] —**rank′er,** *n.* —**Syn.** *n.* **3** standing, status, station. **4** eminence, distinction.

rank[2] (rangk) *adj.* **1** large and coarse: *rank grass.* **2** growing richly. **3** producing a dense but coarse growth: *rank swamp land.* **4** having a strong, unpleasant smell or taste: *rank meat, rank tobacco.* **5** strongly marked; extreme: *rank ingratitude, rank nonsense.* **6** coarse; not decent. [OE *ranc* proud] —**rank′ly,** *adv.* —**rank′ness,** *n.* —**Syn. 4** rancid. **5** flagrant, absolute. **6** obscene, indecent.

rank and file 1 an army or similar group, excluding its officers or leaders. **2** not the leaders or nobility; ordinary people.

ran·kle (rang′kəl) *v.* **-kled, -kling.** be sore; cause soreness; continue to give pain: *The memory of the insult rankled in his mind.* [ME < OF *draoncler* < Med.L *dracunculus* sore, dim. of L *draco* serpent < Gk. *drakōn*]

ran·sack (ran′sak) *v.* **1** search thoroughly through: *The thief ransacked the house for jewellery.* **2** rob; plunder. [ME < ON *rannsaka,* literally, search a house < *rann* house + *-saka* search] —**ran′sack·er,** *n.* —**Syn. 1** rummage.

ran·som (ran′səm) *n.* **1** the price paid or demanded before a captive is set free: *The robber chief held the travellers as prisoners for ransom.* **2** a ransoming.
—*v.* **1** obtain the release (of a captive) by paying a price. **2** redeem. **3** release upon payment. [ME < OF *ranson* < L *redemptio, -onis.* Doublet of REDEMPTION.]

rant (rant) *v.* **1** speak wildly, extravagantly, violently, or noisily. **2 rant and rave,** scold violently. —*n.* an extravagant, violent, or noisy speech. [< MDu. *ranten*] —**rant′er,** *n.* —**Syn.** *v.* declaim, rave.

rap[1] (rap) *n. v.* **rapped, rap·ping.** —*n.* **1** a quick, light blow; a light, sharp knock. **2** *Slang.* **a** blame; rebuke. **b** conviction; prison sentence. **3** *Slang.* a chat; informal discussion. **4 beat the rap,** *Slang.* escape conviction or prison sentence. **5 take the rap,** *Slang.* pay the penalty; take the blame. —*v.* **1** knock sharply; tap. **2** say sharply: *rap out an answer.* **3** *Slang.* rebuke; criticize; condemn. **4** *Slang.* talk; chat. [imitative] —**rap′per,** *n.*

rap[2] (rap) *n. Informal.* the least bit: *I don't care a rap.* [originally, a counterfeit Irish half-penny]

ra·pa·cious (rə pā′shəs) *adj.* **1** seizing by force; plundering. **2** grasping; greedy. **3** of animals, living by the capture of prey. [< L *rapax, -acis* grasping < *rapere* seize] —**ra·pa′cious·ly,** *adv.* —**ra·pa′cious·ness,** *n.* —**Syn. 2** avaricious. **3** predatory.

ra·pac·i·ty (rə pas′ə tē) *n.* a rapacious spirit, action, or practice; greed.

rape[1] (rāp) *n. v.* **raped, rap·ing.** —*n.* **1** the crime of having sexual intercourse with a woman or girl forcibly and against her will. **2** a seizing and carrying off by force. [< v.] —*v.* **1** seize and carry off by force. **2** force (a woman or girl) to have sexual intercourse against her will. [< L *rapere* seize]

rape[2] (rāp) *n.* a small plant whose leaves are used as food for sheep and hogs. [ME < L *rapa, rapum*]

rape oil an oil made from rape seeds and used as a lubricant.

rap·id (rap′id) *adj.* **1** quick; swift; moving, acting, or doing with speed: *a rapid worker.* **2** going on or forward at a fast rate: *rapid growth.* **3** arranged for brief exposures to light: *a rapid film.* —*n.* Usually, **rapids,** *pl.* a part of a river's course where the water rushes quickly, often over rocks lying near the surface. [< L *rapidus* < *rapere* hurry away] —**rap′id·ly,** *adv.* —**rap′id·ness,** *n.* —**Syn.** *adj.* **1** fleet, speedy. See **quick.**

rap·id-fire (rap′id fīr′) *adj.* **1** firing shots in quick succession. **2** ready and quick; occurring in quick succession.

ra·pid·i·ty (rə pid′ə tē) *n.* quickness; swiftness; speed.

rapid transit fast railway transportation in an urban area, often underground.

ra·pi·er (rā′pē ər) *n.* in fencing, a light sword used for thrusting. [< MF *rapière* < *râpe* grater, rasp; with reference to the perforated guard] —**ra′pi·er·like′,** *adj.*

rap·ine (rap′ēn) *n.* a seizing by force and carrying off; plundering. [< L *rapina*]

rap·port (ra pôrt′; *French,* rä pôr′) *n.* **1** a relation; connection. **2** an agreement; harmony. **3 en rapport** (äɴ rä pôr′), *French.* in close relation, accord, or harmony. [< F *rapport* < *rapporter* bring back]

rap·proche·ment (ra prosh′mᴏɴ; *French,* rä prôsh mäɴ′) *n.* the establishment or renewal of friendly relations. [< F *rapprochement* < *rapprocher* bring near]

rap·scal·lion (rap skal′yən) *n.* a rascal; rogue; scamp. [earlier *rascallion* < *rascal*]

rapt (rapt) *adj.* **1** lost in delight; entranced. **2** so busy thinking of or enjoying one thing as to be unaware of what else is happening. **3** carried away in body or spirit from earth, life, or ordinary affairs. **4** showing that a person is enthralled; caused by a delighted condition: *a rapt smile.* [< L *raptus,* pp. of *rapere* seize] —**rapt′ly,** *adv.* —**rapt′ness,** *n.* —**Syn. 1** enraptured, ecstatic. **2** engrossed, spellbound, absorbed. **3** transported.

rap·to·ri·al (rap tô′rē əl) *adj.* **1** adapted for seizing prey; having a hooked beak and sharp claws suited for seizing prey. **2** belonging to or having to do with an order of birds of prey, such as the eagles, hawks, etc. [ult. < L *raptor* robber < *rapere* seize]

rap·ture (rap′chər) *n.* **1** a strong feeling that absorbs the mind; very great joy. **2** Often, **raptures,** *pl.* an expression of great joy. [< *rapt*]

rap·tur·ous (rap′chər əs) *adj.* full of rapture; expressing or feeling rapture. —**rap′tur·ous·ly,** *adv.*

ra·quet (rä ket′) *n.* raquette.

ra·quette (rä ket′) *n. Cdn.* a snowshoe. [< Cdn.F] Also, **racket** and **raquet.**

rare[1] (rãr) *adj.* **rar·er, rar·est. 1** seldom seen or found: *a rare bird.* **2** not happening often; unusual: *a rare event.* **3** unusually good or great: *Shakespeare had rare powers as a dramatist.* **4** thin; not dense: *The higher you go, the rarer the air becomes.* [< L *rarus*] —**rare′ness,** *n.*
Syn. 1 Rare, scarce = not often or easily found. **Rare** describes something uncommon or unusual at any time because it seldom occurs or only a few specimens exist, and often suggests excellence or value above the ordinary: *The Gutenberg Bible is a rare book.* **Scarce** describes something usually or formerly common or plentiful, but not existing or produced in large enough numbers or quantities at the present time: *Water is becoming scarce in some parts of the country.* **2** infrequent, uncommon.

rare[2] (rãr) *adj.* **rar·er, rar·est.** not cooked much: *a rare steak.* [OE *hrēr*] —**rare′ness,** *n.*

rare·bit (rãr′bit) *n.* Welsh rabbit. [altered < (*Welsh*) *rabbit*]

rare earth any of the oxides of rare-earth elements.

rare-earth (rãr′ėrth′) *adj.* of or having to do with rare earths.

rare-earth element or **metal** any of the rare metallic elements that have atomic numbers from 57 to 71.

rar·e·fac·tion (rãr′ə fak′shən) *n.* **1** the act or process of rarefying. **2** the quality or state of being rarefied.

rar·e·fy (rãr′ə fī′) *v.* **-fied, -fy·ing. 1** make less dense: *The air in the mountains is rarefied.* **2** become less dense. **3** refine; purify. [< L *rarefacere* < *rarus* rare + *facere* make]

rare·ly (rãr′lē) *adv.* **1** seldom; not often. **2** unusually; unusually well: *a rarely carved panel.*
☛ **Rarely ever** is an established informal idiom: *I rarely ever go.* More formal would be: *I rarely go.*

rar·i·ty (rãr′ə tē) *n.* **-ties. 1** something rare: *A man over a hundred years old is a rarity.* **2** the quality of being rare or scarce; scarcity. **3** a lack of density; thinness: *The rarity of mountain air is bad for people with weak hearts.*

hat, āge, cãre, fär; let, ēqual, tėrm; it, īce
hot, ōpen, ôrder; oil, out; cup, pu̇t, rüle, ūse
əbove, takən, pencəl, lemən, circəs
ch, child; ng, long; sh, ship
th, thin; ᴛʜ, then; zh, measure

ras·cal (ras′kəl) *n.* **1** a dishonest person; rogue. **2** a mischievous person or animal. —*adj.* low; mean; dishonest. [ME < OF *rascaille* < *rasque* filth, ult. < L *radere* scratch]

ras·cal·i·ty (ras kal′ə tē) *n.* **-ties.** rascally character, conduct, or act.

ras·cal·ly (ras′kəl ē) *adj.* mean; dishonest; bad.

rase (rāz) *v.* **rased, ras·ing.** raze.

rash[1] (rash) *adj.* too hasty; careless; reckless; taking too much risk. [ME *rasch* quick] —**rash′ly,** *adv.*
Syn. Rash, reckless = acting or speaking without due care or thought. **Rash** emphasizes being in too great a rush, speaking hastily or plunging into action without stopping to think: *You should never make rash promises.* **Reckless** emphasizes being without caution, acting carelessly without paying attention to possible consequences: *The dog was killed by a reckless driver.*

rash[2] (rash) *n.* **1** a breaking out of many small red spots on the skin. Scarlet fever causes a rash. **2** *Informal.* an outbreak: *a rash of investigations, a rash of letters.* [< OF *rasche* scurf, ult. < L *radere* scratch]

rash·er (rash′ər) *n.* a thin slice of bacon or ham for frying or broiling. [origin uncertain]

rash·ness (rash′nis) *n.* unwise boldness; recklessness.

rasp (rasp) *v.* **1** make a harsh, grating sound: *The file rasped on the scythe.* **2** utter with a grating sound: *rasp out a command.* **3** have a harsh or irritating effect (*on*); grate. **4** scrape with a rough instrument. —*n.* **1** a harsh, grating sound: *the rasp of crickets, a rasp in a person's voice.* **2** a coarse file with pointlike teeth. [ME < OF *rasper* < Gmc.] —**rasp′er,** *n.* —**rasp′ing·ly,** *adv.*

A rasp (def. 2)

rasp·ber·ry (raz′ber′ē) *n.* **-ries. 1** a small fruit that grows on brambles. Raspberries are usually red or black, but some kinds are white or yellow. **2** the bramble that it grows on. **3** a reddish purple. **4** *Slang.* a sound of disapproval or derision made with the tongue and lips. —*adj.* **1** made of or flavored with raspberries. **2** reddish-purple. [< earlier *raspis* raspberry (origin uncertain) + *berry*]

rat (rat) *n. interj. v.* **rat·ted, rat·ting.** —*n.* **1** a long-tailed rodent resembling a mouse but larger. Rats are gray, black, brown, or white. **2** *Slang.* a low, mean, disloyal person. **3 smell a rat,** *Informal.* suspect a trick or scheme. **4** formerly, a pad worn to puff out a woman's hair. —*interj.* **rats,** *Slang.* an exclamation used to indicate scornful impatience or disbelief.
—*v.* **1** hunt for rats; catch rats. **2** *Slang.* desert one's associates in a dishonorable manner. **3** *Slang.* turn informer against one's associates. [OE *rætt*]

rat·a·ble (rāt′ə bəl) *adj.* **1** capable of being rated. **2** taxable. Also, **rateable.**

ra·tan (ra tan′) *n.* rattan.

ratch (rach) *n.* ratchet.

ratch·et (rach′it) *n.* **1** a wheel or bar with teeth that strike against a catch fixed so that motion is permitted in one direction but not in the other. **2** the catch. **3** the entire device, wheel and catch or bar and catch. [< F < Ital. *rocchetto,* ult. < Gmc.]

A ratchet (def. 1). The catch is shaped so that the teeth can go past it only in one direction.

ratchet wheel a wheel with teeth and a catch that permits motion in only one direction.

rate[1] (rāt) *n. v.* **rat·ed, rat·ing.** —*n.* **1** a quantity, amount, or degree measured in proportion to something else: *The rate of interest is 6 cents on the dollar. The car was going at the rate of 40 miles an hour.* **2** a price: *We pay the regular rate.* **3** a class; grade; rating. **4** a local tax, often on property. **5 at any rate,** in any case; under any circumstances. **6 at that** or **this rate,** in that or this case; under such circumstances.
—*v.* **1** put a value on: *We rated the house as worth $10,000.* **2** consider; regard: *He was rated as one of the richest men in town.* **3** subject to a certain tax. **4** fix at a certain rate. **5** put in a certain class or grade. **6** be regarded; be classed; rank. **7** *Informal.* be worthy of: *She rates the best seat in the house.* **8** *Informal.* qualify; have value: *You don't rate.* [ME < OF < Med.L *rata (pars)* fixed (amount), pp. of L *reri* reckon] —**rat′er,** *n.* —**Syn.** *n.* **3** rank, order.

rate[2] (rāt) *v.* **rat·ed, rat·ing.** scold. [ME *rate(n)*; ? < OF *rater, areter* scold < L *ad* + *reputare* count. See REPUTE.]

rate·a·ble (rāt′ə bəl) *adj.* ratable.

rate·pay·er (rāt′pā′ər) *n.* a person who pays municipal taxes.

rathe (rāᴛʜ) *adj. adv. Archaic or poetic.* early; growing or blooming early. [OE *hrathe* quickly]

rath·er (raᴛʜ′ər) *adv.* **1** more readily; more willingly: *I would rather go today than tomorrow.* **2** more properly or justly; with better reason: *This is rather for your parents to decide than for you.* **3** more precisely; more truly: *It was late Monday night or, rather, early Tuesday morning.* **4** (with verbs) in some degree: *He rather felt that this was unwise.* **5** to some extent; somewhat; more than a little: *rather good.* **6** on the contrary: *The sick man is no better today; rather he is worse.* **7 had rather,** would more willingly; prefer to. —*interj. Informal.* yes, indeed! certainly! very much so! [OE *hrathor,* comparative of *hrathe* quickly] ☛ See **had** for usage note.

raths·kel·ler (räts′kel′ər) *n.* a restaurant, usually below street level, selling alcoholic drinks. [< G *Ratskeller, Rathskeller* < *Rat(haus)* town hall + *Keller* cellar]

rat·i·fi·ca·tion (rat′ə fə kā′shən) *n.* a confirmation; approval: *the ratification of a treaty by Parliament.*

rat·i·fy (rat′ə fī′) *v.* **-fied, -fy·ing.** confirm; approve: *The two countries will ratify the agreement made by their representatives.* [ME < OF < Med.L *ratificare,* ult. < L *ratus* fixed + *facere* make] —**rat′i·fi′er,** *n.* —**Syn.** sanction, authorize. See **approve.**

rat·ing (rāt′ing) *n.* **1** a class; grade. **2** a position in a class or grade: *the rating of a seaman, the rating of a ship according to tonnage.* **3** in the navy, a sailor of the lowest rank; an ordinary seaman. **4** an amount fixed as a rate or grade: *a rating of 80% in English.* **5** any survey of public taste, especially one taken to establish the popularity of one or more television programs. **6** a level of merit or popularity established by survey. **7** a credit rating.

ra·ti·o (rā′shē ō′ or rā′shō) *n.* **-ti·os. 1** the relative magnitude. "He has sheep and cows in the ratio of 10 to 3" means that he has ten sheep for every three cows, or $3\frac{1}{3}$ times as many sheep as cows. **2** a quotient. The ratio between two quantities is the number of times one contains the other. The ratio of 6 to 10 is 6/10. The ratio of 10 to 6 is 10/6. [< L *ratio* reckoning < *reri* reckon. Doublet of RATION, REASON.]

ra·ti·oc·i·nate (rash′ē os′ə nāt′ or rat′ē os′ə nāt′) *v.* **-nat·ed, -nat·ing.** carry on a process of reasoning; reason. [< L *ratiocinari* < *ratio.* See RATIO.] —**ra′ti·oc′i·na′tion,** *n.* —**ra′ti·oc′i·na·tor,** *n.*

ra·tion (rash′ən or rā′shən) *n.* **1** a fixed allowance of food; daily allowance of food for a person or animal. **2** a portion of anything dealt out: *rations of sugar, of coal, etc.* —*v.* **1** supply with rations: *ration an army.* **2** allow only certain amounts to: *ration citizens when supplies are scarce.* **3** distribute in limited amounts: *ration food to the public in wartime.* [< F < Med.L *ratio, -onis* < L *ratio* reckoning. Doublet of RATIO, REASON.] —**Syn.** *n.* **1** See **food. 2** share, allotment.

ra·tion·al (rash′ən əl or rash′nəl) *adj.* **1** sensible; reasonable; reasoned out: *Angry people seldom act in a rational way.* **2** able to think and reason clearly: *As children grow older, they become more rational.* **3** of reason; based on reasoning. **4** in mathematics: **a** expressible as a whole number or a fraction composed of whole numbers. **b** involving no root that cannot be extracted. [< L *rationalis* < *ratio.* See RATIO.] —**ra′tion·al·ly,** *adv.* —**Syn. 1** sound, wise, judicious, sane. **3** See **reasonable.**

ra·tion·ale (rash′ən al′) *n.* the whys and wherefores; the fundamental reason or logical basis. [< L *rationale,* neut. of *rationalis.* See RATIONAL.]

ra·tion·al·ism (rash′ən əl iz′əm or rash′nəl iz′əm) *n.* **1** the principle or habit of accepting reason as the supreme authority in matters of opinion, belief, or conduct. **2** the philosophical doctrine that reason is in itself a source of knowledge, independent of the senses.

ra·tion·al·ist (rash′ən əl ist or rash′nəl ist) *n.* a person who accepts reason as the supreme authority in matters of opinion, belief, or conduct.

ra·tion·al·is·tic (rash′ən əl is′tik or rash′nəl is′tik) *adj.* of rationalism or rationalists.
—ra·tion′·al·is′ti·cal·ly, *adv.*

ra·tion·al·i·ty (rash′ən al′ə tē or rash′nal′ə tē) *n.* the possession of reason; reasonableness: *Mr. Smith is eccentric, but no one doubts his rationality.*

ra·tion·al·ize (rash′ən əl īz′ or rash′nəl īz′) *v.* **-ized, -iz·ing. 1** make rational or conformable to reason. **2** treat or explain in a rational manner. **3** find (often unconsciously) an explanation or excuse for: *She rationalizes her gluttony by thinking, "I must eat enough to keep up my strength."* **4** find excuses for one's desires.
—rat′tion·al·i·za′tion, *n.* **—ra′tion·al·iz′er,** *n.*

rat·line or **rat·lin** (rat′lən) *n.* one of the small ropes that cross the shrouds of a ship, used as steps for going aloft. [origin uncertain]

R, ratline

RA·TO or **ra·to** (rā′tō) *n.* in aeronautics, a unit of one or more rockets, providing extra power to speed up an aircraft during take-off. [< *r*ocket *a*ssisted *t*ake-*o*ff]

ra·toon (ra tün′) *n.* a new shoot or sprout that grows from the root of a plant already cropped: *ratoons of banana trees.* —*v.* sprout after being cut. Also, rattoon. [< Sp. *retoño* < *retoñar* to sprout]

rat race *Slang.* a frantic confusion or scramble, especially as applied to senseless competition.

rats·bane (rats′bān′) *n.* any poison for rats. [< *rat* + *bane*]

rat·tan (ra tan′) *n.* **1** a kind of palm having a very long stem. **2** the stems of such palm trees, used for wickerwork, canes, etc. **3** a cane or switch made from a piece of such a stem. Also, **ratan.** [ult. < Malay *rotan*]

rat·ter (rat′ər) *n.* **1** an animal, or sometimes, a person that catches rats: *Our terrier is a good ratter.* **2** *Slang.* one who deserts his associates.

rat·tle (rat′əl) *v.* **-tled, -tling,** *n.* —*v.* **1** make a number of short, sharp sounds. **2** cause to rattle. **3** move with short, sharp sounds: *The cart rattled down the street.* **4** talk quickly, on and on. **5** say quickly. **6** *Informal.* confuse; upset: *She was so rattled that she forgot her speech.*
—*n.* **1** a number of short, sharp sounds: *the rattle of empty bottles.* **2** a sound in the throat, occurring in some diseases of the lungs and also often just before death. **3** a racket; uproar. **4** a toy, instrument, etc. that makes a noise when it is shaken. **5** a series of horny pieces at the end of a rattlesnake's tail. [ME *ratele(n)*; probably imitative]

rat·tle·brain (rat′əl brān′) *n.* a giddy, foolish, unthinking person.

rat·tler (rat′lər) *n. Informal.* rattlesnake.

rat·tle·snake (rat′əl snāk′) *n.* a poisonous snake having a thick body and a broad, triangular head, that makes a rattling noise with its tail.

rat·tle·trap (rat′əl trap′) *n.* **1** a rattling, rickety wagon or other vehicle. **2** any shaky, rattling object. **3 rattletraps,** *pl.* odds and ends. —*adj.* rickety; shaky.

rat·tling (rat′ling) *adj.* **1** that rattles. **2** lively; very fast. **3** *Informal.* great; important. —*adv. Informal.* extremely; especially: *a rattling good time.*

rat·toon (ra tün′) *n.* ratoon.

rat·trap (rat′trap′) *n.* **1** a trap to catch rats. **2** a desperate situation.

rat·ty (rat′ē) *adj.* **-ti·er, -ti·est. 1** of rats; like rats. **2** full of rats. **3** *Slang.* poor; shabby. **4** *Slang.* angry; irritable.

rau·cous (ro′kəs or rô′kəs) *adj.* hoarse; harsh-sounding: *the raucous caw of a crow.* [< L *raucus*] **—rau′cous·ly,** *adv.*

rav·age[1] (rav′ij) *v.* **-aged, -ag·ing,** *n.* —*v.* lay waste; damage greatly; destroy: *The forest fire ravaged many miles of country.* —*n.* violence; destruction; great damage: *War causes ravage.* [< F *ravager* < *ravir* ravish]
—rav′ag·er, *n.*

rav·age[2] (rav′ij) *n. Cdn.* a place where a group of moose, deer, or other animals stay for a time feeding on the surrounding vegetation before moving on. [< Cdn.F]

rave (rāv) *v.* **raved, rav·ing,** *n. adj.* —*v.* **1** talk wildly. An excited, angry person raves; so does a madman. **2** talk with too much enthusiasm: *She raved about her food.* **3** howl; roar; rage: *The wind raved about the lighthouse.*
—*n.* **1** a raving; frenzy or great excitement. **2** *Slang.* **a** unrestrained praise. **b** an infatuation, especially such as occurs in adolescence.
—*adj. Informal.* unrestrainedly enthusiastic in praising: *The play got rave notices in the local press.* [ME ? < OF *raver*, var. of *rêver* dream] **—Syn.** *v.* **1** storm, rant.

rav·el (rav′əl) *v.* **-elled** or **-eled, -el·ling** or **-el·ing,** *n.* —*v.* **1** separate the threads of; fray. **2** fray out; separate into threads: *The sweater was ravelled at the elbow.* **3** make plain or clear; unravel. **4** become tangled, involved, or confused. **5** tangle; involve; confuse. —*n.* an unravelled thread or fibre. [probably < MDu. *ravelen*]

rav·el·ling or **rav·el·ing** (rav′əl ing or rav′ling) *n.* something ravelled out; a thread drawn from a woven or knitted fabric.

ra·ven[1] (rā′vən) *n.* a large, black bird, resembling a crow but larger. —*adj.* deep, glossy black: *raven hair.* [OE *hræfn*]

rav·en[2] (rav′ən) *v.* **1** devour greedily. **2** prey on; plunder. —*n.* plunder; rapine. Also, **ravin.** [< OF *raviner* < *ravine* violent rush, robbery. Doublet of RAVINE.]

rav·en·ing (rav′ən ing) *adj.* greedy and hungry.

rav·en·ous (rav′ən əs) *adj.* **1** very hungry. **2** greedy. **3** rapacious. [ME < OF *ravineus* rapacious, violent < *ravine.* See RAVIN.] **—rav′en·ous·ly,** *adv.*
—rav′en·ous·ness, *n.*

rav·in[1] (rav′ən) *n.* rapine. [ME < OF *ravine* robbery < L *rapina* < *rapere* snatch. Doublet of RAVINE.]

rav·in[2] (rav′ən) *n.* raven[2].

ra·vine (rə vēn′) *n.* a long, deep, narrow gorge worn by running water or by the action of glaciers. [< F *ravine* < OF *ravine* violent rush, robbery. Doublet of RAVIN.]

rav·ing (rāv′ing) *adj.* **1** that raves; delirious; frenzied; raging. **2** *Informal.* remarkable; extraordinary.
—*n.* delirious, incoherent talk. **—rav′ing·ly,** *adv.*

rav·i·o·li (rav′ē ō′lē) *n.* small, thin, pieces of dough filled with chopped meat, cheese, etc. cooked in boiling water and served with a highly seasoned tomato sauce. [< Ital. *ravioli*, ult. < L *rapum* beet]

rav·ish (rav′ish) *v.* **1** fill with delight. **2** carry off by force. **3** rape. [ME < OF *raviss-*, a stem of *ravir* < L *rapere* seize] **—rav′ish·er,** *n.* **—Syn. 1** enrapture, entrance, enchant, transport.

rav·ish·ing (rav′ish ing) *adj.* very delightful; enchanting: *jewels of ravishing beauty.* **—rav′ish·ing·ly,** *adv.*

rav·ish·ment (rav′ish mənt) *n.* **1** rapture; ecstasy. **2** the act of carrying off by force. **3** rape.

raw (ro or rô) *adj.* **1** not cooked: *raw oysters.* **2** in the natural state; not manufactured, treated, or prepared: *raw materials, raw hides.* **3** not experienced; not trained: *a raw recruit.* **4** damp and cold: *raw weather.* **5** with the skin off; sore: *a raw spot.* **6** uncivilized; brutal: *the raw frontier.* **7** having a crude quality; not refined in taste: *a raw piece of work, a raw story.* **8** *Slang.* harsh; unfair: *a raw deal.*
—*n.* **1** *Informal.* a state of nakedness. **2** a raw or sore spot on the body. **3 in the raw,** nude. [OE *hrēaw*]
—raw′ly, *adv.* **—raw′ness,** *n.*

Syn. *adj.* **2 Raw, crude** = not processed or prepared for use. **Raw** applies to a material or natural product that has not yet been processed for use or shaped or made into something by treating, tanning, finishing, manufacturing, etc.: *Raw milk is pasteurized to make it ready to drink.* **Crude** applies to a product in a natural state, not freed from impurities or prepared for use or greater usefulness and value by refining, tempering, or treating with chemicals and heat: *Crude rubber is treated with sulphur and heat to make it more elastic and durable.* 3 ignorant, inexperienced.

raw-boned (ro′bōnd′ or rô′-) *adj.* having little flesh on the bones; gaunt.

raw·hide (ro′hīd′ or rô′-) *n. v.* **-hid·ed, -hid·ing.** —*n.* **1** the untanned skin of cattle. **2** a rope or whip made of this skin. **3** *Cdn.* formerly, the dressed but untanned hide of an animal, usually buffalo, used to pack goods in and lashed to rope tugs for hauling over ice and snow.
—*v.* **1** whip with a rawhide. **2** transport by means of a rawhide. —**raw′hid′er,** *n.*

raw material a substance in its natural state; anything that can be manufactured, treated, or prepared to make it more useful or increase its value.

raw milk unpasteurized milk.

ray[1] (rā) *n.* **1** a line or beam of light. **2** a line or stream of heat, electricity, or energy. **3** a thin line like a ray, coming out from a centre. **4** any part like a ray. The petals of a daisy and the arms of a starfish are rays. **5** a slight trace; faint gleam: *Not a ray of hope pierced our gloom.* —*v.* **1** send forth in rays; radiate. **2** treat with rays. [ME < OF *rai* < L *radius.* Doublet of RADIUS.]
—**Syn.** *n.* **1** See **beam.**

ray[2] (rā) *n.* any of several varieties of fishes, related to the sharks, that have broad, flat bodies with very broad pectoral fins. The **electric ray** has organs with which it shocks or kills its prey. [ME < OF < L *raia*]

ray·on (rā′on) *n.* a fibre or fabric made from cellulose treated with chemicals. [< *ray* beam, light]

raze (rāz) *v.* **razed, raz·ing.** tear down; destroy completely. Also, **rase.** [< F *raser* scrape, ult. < L *radere*]

ra·zor (rā′zər) *n.* a device or instrument used for shaving. [ME < OF *rasor* < *raser* scrape, ult. < L *radere.* Related to RAZE.]

ra·zor·back (rā′zər bak′) *n.* **1** a kind of thin, half-wild hog with a ridged back. Razorbacks are common in the southern United States. **2** a finback whale; rorqual. **3** a sharp ridge on a hill, mountain, etc.

ra·zor·bill (rā′zər bil′) *n.* the razor-billed auk.

ra·zor-billed auk (rā′zər bild′) a North Atlantic auk having a sharp-edged bill.

razz (raz) *Slang.* —*v.* **1** laugh at; make fun of. **2** express disapproval of; boo. —*n.* strong disapproval; derision. [< *raspberry*]

raz·zle-daz·zle (raz′əl daz′əl) *adj. v.* **-zled, -zling.** *Slang.* —*n.* **1** confusing or bewildering activity, especially of a spectacular nature. **2** in sports, a deceptive play involving fast movement, crisscrossing, etc. by several players, intended to bewilder the opposing team.
—*adj.* bewildering; flashy. —*v.* bewilder; confuse. [varied reduplication of *dazzle*]

Rb rubidium.

R.C. 1 Roman Catholic. 2 Red Cross.

RCA or **R.C.A.** Royal Canadian Artillery.

RCAF or **R.C.A.F.** Royal Canadian Air Force.

rcd. received.

RCMP or **R.C.M.P.** Royal Canadian Mounted Police.

RCN or **R.C.N.** Royal Canadian Navy.

RCR or **R.C.R.** Royal Canadian Regiment.

RCSC or **R.C.S.C.** Royal Canadian Service Corps.

rd. 1 road. 2 rod; rods.

Rd. Road.

R.D. *U.S.* Rural Delivery.

re[1] (rā or rē) *n.* in music, a syllable used for the second tone of an eight-tone scale. See **do**[2] for diagram. [see GAMUT]

re[2] (rē) *prep.* with reference to; in the matter or case of; about; concerning. [for L *in re* in the matter of]

re- *prefix.* **1** again; anew; once more, as in *reappear, rebuild, reheat, reopen, re-enter.* **2** back, as in *recall, repay, replace.* [< L]

☞ **re-** Usually words formed of the prefix *re-* and another word or word element are not hyphenated: *rearrange, refine, remit.* However, words formed with the prefix *re-* meaning "again" are hyphenated (1) when the word to which it is joined begins with *e*: *re-echo,* (2) when the form with hyphen can have a different meaning from the form without: *reform,* make better—*re-form,* shape again, and (3) (rarely) for emphasis, as in "now *re-seated* in fair comfort," or in informal or humorous compounds: *re-re-married.*

hat, āge, cãre, fär; let, ēqual, tėrm; it, īce
hot, ōpen, ôrder; oil, out; cup, pu̇t, rüle, ūse
əbove, takən, pencəl, lemən, circəs
ch, child; ng, long; sh, ship
th, thin; ᴛʜ, then; zh, measure

The meaning of each of the following words is found by adding *again* or *anew* to the main part. The pronunciation of the main part is not changed.

re′a·dapt′
re′ad·just′
re′ad·just′ment
re′ad·mit′
re′af·firm′
re·an′i·mate′
re′ap·pear′
re′ap·pear′ance
re′ap·ply′
re′ap·point′
re′ap·point′ment
re′ap·por′tion
re′ap·por′tion·ment
re′ap·prais′al
re′ap·praise′
re′as·cend′
re′as·sert′
re′as·sess′
re′as·sign′
re′as·sign′ment
re′as·sume′
re′at·tach′
re′a·wak′en
re′bap·tize′
re·bind′
re·built′
re·cap′i·tal·ize′
re·chris′ten
re·clothe′
re′com·bi·na′tion
re′com·bine′
re′com·mence′
re·con′quer
re·con′quest
re·con′se·crate′
re′con·se·cra′tion
re′con·sid′er
re·con′sti·tute′
re′con·vene′
re·cross′
re·crys′tal·lize′
re·dec′o·rate′
re′dec·o·ra′tion
re′de·fine′
re′de·vel′op
re′dis·cov′er
re′dis·trib′ute
re·dye′
re·ed′it
re·ed′u·cate′
re′-ed·u·ca′tion
re′-em·bark′
re′-el·ect′
re-em′i·grate′
re-em′pha·size′
re′-en·act′
re′-en·act′ment
re′-en·gage′
re′-en·list′
re′-en·list′ment
re-en′ter
re′-es·tab′lish
re′-ex·am′i·na′tion
re′-ex·am′ine
re′-ex·port′
re·fash′ion
re·fas′ten
re·fur′nish
re·gild′
re·group′
re·han′dle
re·heat′
re′ig·nite′
re′im·pose′
re′im·pris′on
re′in·sert′
re·in′te·grate′
re′in·ter′
re′in·tro·duce′
re′in·tro·duc′tion
re′in·vest′
re′in·vest′ment
re′in·vig′or·ate′
re·is′sue
re·kin′dle
re·la′bel
re·light′
re·line′
re·live′
re·load′
re′lo·cate′
re·made′
re·make′
re·mar′riage
re·mar′ry
re·mould′
re·nom′i·nate′
re′nom·i·na′tion
re·num′ber
re′oc·cu·pa′tion
re·oc′cu·py′
re·pack′
re·pa′per
re·pave′
re·plant′
re·play′
re·pop′u·late′
re·pub′lish
re·quick′en
re·read′
re·sad′dle
re·sched′ule
re·seed′
re·sell′
re·set′tle
re·ship′
re·shuf′fle
re·spell′
re·stamp′
re′sur·vey′
re·teach′
re·tell′
re·test′
re·told′
re′trans·late′
re·tri′al
re·try′
re·turf′
re·type′
re′up·hol′ster
re·use′
re·val′u·ate′
re·vict′ual
re·vi′tal·ize′
re·word′
re·work′

Re rhenium.

reach (rēch) *v.* **1** get to; come to; arrive at: *reach the top of a hill, the end of a book, an agreement, etc.* **2** stretch; stretch out: *reach toward a book.* **3** extend in space, time, operation, effect, influence, etc. (*to*): *The power of Rome reached to the ends of the known world.* **4** extend to: *Radio reaches millions.* **5** get or come; function: *farther than the eye can reach.* **6** get in touch with by anything extended, cast, etc.; touch: *The anchor reached bottom.* **7** make a stretch of certain length with the

hand, etc.: *I cannot reach to the top of the wall.* **8** make a stretch in a certain direction: *The man reached for his gun.* **9** get at; influence: *Men are reached by flattery.* **10** amount to; be equal to: *The cost of the war reached billions.* **11** take or pass with the hand: *Please reach me the sugar.* **12** sail on a course with the wind forward of the beam. **13** deliver (a blow, kick, etc.).
—*n.* **1** a stretching out; reaching: *By a long reach, the drowning man grasped the rope.* **2** the extent or distance of reaching: *out of one's reach.* **3** range; power; capacity: *the reach of the mind.* **4** a continuous stretch or extent: *a reach of woodland.* **5** a part of a river between bends. **6** a part of a canal between locks. **7** the distance sailed on one tack. [OE *rǣcan*] —**reach′er,** *n.* —**Syn.** *v.* **1** attain, gain.

re-act (rē akt′) *v.* act over again.

re·act (rē akt′) *v.* **1** act back; have an effect on the one that is acting: *Unkindness often reacts on the unkind person.* **2** act in response: *Dogs react to kindness by showing affection.* **3** act chemically; undergo a reaction. Acids react on metals. **4** return to a previous state, level, etc. **5 react against,** act unfavorably toward somebody or something; adopt an unfavorable attitude toward.

re·act·ance (rē ak′təns) *n.* in electricity, that part of the impedance of an alternating-current circuit which is due to self-induction and capacity.

re·ac·tion (rē ak′shən) *n.* **1** a result that is the opposite of the cause: *Fever is a common reaction from a chill.* **2** in politics, economics, etc., a tendency toward a previous state of affairs. **3 a** an action in response to some influence or force: *Our reaction to a joke is to laugh. The doctor observed carefully his patient's reactions to certain tests.* **b** *Informal.* a response to an idea, plan, etc.; attitude; feeling; opinion: *What was his reaction to the plan?* **4** in chemistry, the action of two substances on each other. Putting an acid and a metal together causes a reaction. **5** the response of a nerve, muscle, or organ to a stimulus. **6** the response of the body to a test for immunization, etc. **7** a process in which the nucleus of an atom becomes transformed; nuclear reaction. **8** a drop in prices following a rise in prices, as on a stock market.

re·ac·tion·ar·y (rē ak′shən er′ē) *adj. n.* **-ar·ies.** —*adj.* having to do with, marked by, or favoring reaction.
—*n.* a person who favors reaction, especially in politics, economics, etc.

re·ac·tor (rē ak′tər) *n.* **1** a special assembly for the production of a limited release of nuclear (atomic) energy, consisting of layers of fissionable material, such as uranium in a controlled chain reaction, spaced with moderators, such as graphite and heavy water, that slow down the speed and number of the neutrons intended for splitting the uranium nuclei; pile. **2** a type of electrical condenser having slow resistance and high inductance. **3** a person or animal that reacts, especially one that reacts positively to a medical test for a disease, allergy, etc.

read[1] (rēd) *v.* **read** (red), **read·ing. 1** distinguish and understand the meaning of symbols such as those used in writing or printing: *read a book. The blind read with their fingers.* **2** learn from writing or printing: *We read of heroes of other days.* **3** speak (printed or written words); say aloud the words one sees, or touches: *Read this story to me.* **4** show by letters, figures, signs, etc.: *The thermometer reads 70 degrees.* **5** give as the word or words in a particular passage: *For "fail," a misprint, read "fall."* **6** study: *read law.* **7** get the meaning of; understand: *read a person's mind. He read her angry look and hurriedly left the room.* **8** give the meaning of; interpret: *A prophet reads the future.* **9** introduce (something not expressed or directly indicated) by one's manner of understanding or interpreting: *read a hostile intent in a friendly letter.* **10** produce a certain impression when read; mean; be in effect when read: *This does not read like a child's composition.* **11** be worded in a certain way: *This line reads differently in the first edition.* **12** admit of being read or interpreted: *A rule that reads two different ways.* **13** bring or put by reading: *He reads himself to sleep.* **14** give (a lecture or a lesson) as a reprimand. **15** of an electronic device, absorb information directly from (written or printed matter) by means of a photo-electric cell. **16 read between the lines,** discover a meaning or implication not stated outright in something. **17 read into,** interpret in a certain way, often attributing more than intended. **18 read out of,** expel from (a political party, etc.). **19 read the water,** *Cdn.* scan the water from one's boat or canoe for signs of danger such as shoals, rapids, and snags.
—*n.* **1** a spell of reading. **2** a piece of reading matter considered in terms of the pleasure it gives: *That novel is a good read.* [OE *rǣdan* guess, read, counsel]

read[2] (red) *adj.* having knowledge gained by reading; informed: *a well-read man.* —*v.* pt. and pp. of **read.** [originally pp. of *read*[1]]

read·a·bil·i·ty (rēd′ə bil′ə tē) *n.* the quality or condition of being readable.

read·a·ble (rēd′ə bəl) *adj.* **1** easy to read; interesting. **2** capable of being read. —**read′a·bly,** *adv.*

re·ad·dress (rē′ə dres′) *v.* **1** put a new address on. **2** speak to again. **3** apply (oneself) anew.

read·er (rēd′ər) *n.* **1** a person who reads. **2** a book for learning and practising reading. **3** a person employed to read manuscripts and estimate their fitness for publication. **4** a proofreader. **5 a** *Esp.Brit.* a senior instructor in certain universities. **b** an assistant who grades and corrects examinations, reads papers, etc. for a professor. **6** a person who reads or recites to entertain an audience. **7** an electronic device that absorbs information directly from written or printed matter through a photo-electric cell or scanner.

read·er·ship (rē′dər ship′) *n.* **1** the reading public or audience of a particular publication or author. **2** the position of a reader.

read·i·ly (red′ə lē) *adv.* **1** quickly: *answer readily.* **2** easily. **3** willingly.

read·i·ness (red′ē nis) *n.* **1** the state of being ready; preparedness. **2** quickness; promptness. **3** ease; facility. **4** willingness.

read·ing (rēd′ing) *n.* **1** the act or process of getting the meaning of writing or printing. **2** a speaking out loud of written or printed words; a public recital. **3** the study of books, etc. **4** written or printed matter read or to be read. **5** a thing shown by letters, figures, or signs: *The reading of the thermometer was 96 degrees.* **6** the interpreting of symbols, designs, plans, etc. **7** the form of a given word or passage in a particular edition of a book: *No two editions have the same reading for that passage.* **8** an interpretation: *Each actor gave the lines a different reading.* **9** the extent to which one has read; literary knowledge.

reading room a special room for reading in a library, club, etc.

read·y (red′ē) *adj.* **read·i·er, read·i·est,** *v.* **read·ied, read·y·ing.** —*adj.* **1** prepared for immediate action or use; prepared: *Dinner is ready. The soldiers are ready for battle.* **2** willing: *The knights were ready to die for their lords.* **3** quick; prompt: *a ready welcome.* **4** quick in thought or action; dexterous: *a ready wit.* **5** apt; likely; liable: *She is too ready to find fault.* **6** immediately available: *ready money.* **7 make ready,** prepare.
—*n.* **at the ready,** ready for action: *guns at the ready.*
—*v.* make ready; prepare. [OE *rǣde* ready]
Syn. *adj.* **2** disposed. **3, 4 Ready, prompt** = quick to understand, observe, or act in response. **Ready,** chiefly describing a person, his mind, hands, instrument, etc., suggests being prepared to act or respond without delay or hesitation and skill or ease in doing: *With ready fingers the surgeons explored the wound.* **Prompt,** more often describing what is done, emphasizes being quick to act when the occasion demands or request is made: *He is prompt to help students.* **5** prone.

read·y-made (red′ē mād′) *adj.* ready for immediate use; made for anybody who will buy; not made to order.

read·y-mix (red′ē miks′) *adj.* ready to cook or use after adding liquid and, sometimes, other ingredients: *ready-mix muffins, ready-mix concrete.*

read·y-to-wear (red′ē tə wär′) *adj.* ready-made.

re·a·gent (rē ā′jənt) *n.* **1** a person, force, etc. that reacts. **2** in chemistry: **a** a substance that takes part in a reaction. Reagents are widely used in medicine, photography, and industry. **b** something that, when added to a substance, causes a reaction that aids in determining the composition of the substance.

re·al[1] (rē′əl or rēl) *adj.* **1** existing as a fact; not imagined or made up; actual; true: *a real experience, the real reason.* **2** genuine: *a real diamond.* **3** in law, of or having to do with immovable property. Lands and houses are called real property. **4** in mathematics, either rational or irrational, not imaginary. **5** in optics, of or having to do with an image formed by actual convergence of rays. **6** in economics, measured by reference to useful goods rather than money: *In a period of rising prices, real incomes fall if money incomes remain steady.* [< LL *realis* < L *res* matter] —**re′al·ness,** *n.*

Syn. 1 Real, actual, true = existing as a fact. **Real** means that what is described is in fact what it seems, is thought, or is said to be, not pretended, imaginary, or made up: *Give your real name.* **Actual** means that what it describes has in reality happened or come into existence, and is not merely capable of happening or existing or existing only in theory: *Name an actual case of bravery.* **True** means "in agreement with what is real or actual, not false": *Tell the true story.* **2** authentic.

☛ **real.** In formal and informal English, *real* is used only as an adjective: *The excursion was a real pleasure for all of us.* In substandard and familiar use, it is also an adverb meaning "really" or "very": *It was real kind of you to come.* Formal and informal: *It was very kind of you to come.*

re·al² (rē′əl; *Spanish,* rä äl′) *n.* **re·als** or (*Spanish*) **re·a·les** (rä ä′lās). formerly, a small Spanish silver coin, worth about 12½ cents. [< Sp. < L *regalis* regal. Doublet of REGAL, ROYAL, RIAL.]

real estate a piece of land, together with the buildings, fences, trees, water, and minerals that belong with it.

re·al·ise (rē′əl īz′) *v.* **-ised, -is·ing.** realize.

re·al·ism (rē′əl iz′əm) *n.* **1** practical tendency: *His realism caused him to dislike fanciful schemes.* **2** in art and literature, a style characterized by picturing nature, life, people, etc. objectively and factually. **3** in philosophy: **a** the doctrine that material objects have a real existence independent of our consciousness of them. **b** the doctrine that general ideas have a real existence independent of the mind.

re·al·ist (rē′əl ist) *n.* **1** a person interested in what is real and practical rather than what is imaginary or theoretical. **2** a writer or artist who represents nature, life, people, etc. objectively and factually. **3** a person who believes in realism.

re·al·is·tic (rē′əl is′tik) *adj.* **1** like the real thing; lifelike. **2** in literature or art, representing nature, life, people, etc. objectively and factually. **3** seeing things as they really are; practical. **4** of or having to do with realists or realism. —**re′al·is′ti·cal·ly,** *adv.*

re·al·i·ty (rē al′ə tē) *n.* **-ties. 1** actual existence; true state of affairs: *Ghosts have no place in reality.* **2** a real thing; an actual fact: *Slaughter and destruction are realities of war.* **3 in reality,** really; actually; in fact: *We thought he was serious, but in reality he was joking.*

re·al·i·za·tion (rē′əl ə zā′shən or rē′əl ī zā′shən) *n.* **1** a clear understanding; full awareness; perception: *The explorers had a realization of the dangers that they must face.* **2** a realizing or being realized: *the realization of your hopes.* **3** an exchange of property for its money value. **4** the obtaining or acquiring (of money, a fortune, etc.).

re·al·ize (rē′əl īz′) *v.* **-ized, -iz·ing. 1** understand clearly; be fully aware of: *She realizes how hard you worked.* **2** make real; bring into actual existence: *Her uncle's present made it possible for her to realize her dream of going to college.* **3** cause to seem real. **4** change (property) into money: *Before going to England to live, he realized all his property in Canada.* **5** obtain as a return or profit: *He realized $10,000 from his investment.* **6** bring as a return or profit. Also, **realise.** —**Syn. 1** comprehend, conceive. **2** achieve.

re·al·ly (rē′əl ē) *adv.* **1** actually; truly; in fact: *things as they really are.* **2** indeed: *Oh, really?*

realm (relm) *n.* **1** a kingdom. **2** a region or sphere in which something rules or prevails. **3** a particular field of something: *the realm of biology.* [ME < OF *realme* < *reial* regal < L *regalis.* See REGAL.]

real·tor (rē′əl tər or rē′əl tôr′) *n.* a member of an organization of persons engaged in the business of buying and selling real estate.

re·al·ty (rē′əl tē) *n.* real estate. [< *real*¹ (def. 3) + *-ty*²]

ream¹ (rēm) *n.* **1** a unit consisting of 500, sometimes 480, sheets of paper of the same size and quality. **2** a very large quantity: *ream upon ream of nonsense.*

hat, āge, cãre, fär; let, ēqual, tėrm; it, īce
hot, ōpen, ôrder; oil, out; cup, pu̇t, rüle, ūse
əbove, takən, pencəl, lemən, circəs
ch, child; ng, long; sh, ship
th, thin; ᴛʜ, then; zh, measure

Abbrev.: rm. [ME < OF *rayme* < Sp. < Arabic *rizmah* bundle]

ream² (rēm) *v.* **1** enlarge or shape (a hole). **2** remove with a reamer. [origin uncertain; perhaps akin to OE *rȳman* enlarge < *rūm* room]

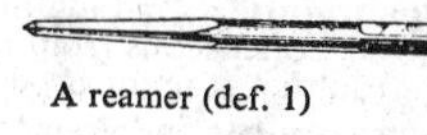
A reamer (def. 1)

ream·er (rēm′ər) *n.* **1** a tool for enlarging or shaping a hole. **2** a utensil for squeezing the juice out of oranges, lemons, etc.

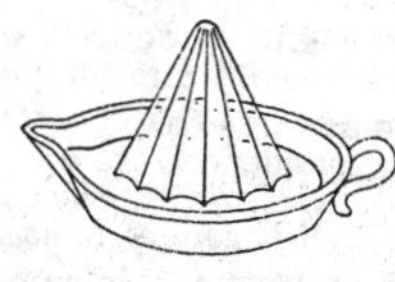
A reamer (def. 2)

reap (rēp) *v.* **1** cut (grain). **2** gather (a crop). **3** cut grain or gather a crop from: *reap fields.* **4** get as a return or reward: *Kind acts reap happy smiles.* **5** get a return. [OE *repan*]

reap·er (rēp′ər) *n.* **1** a person or machine that cuts grain or gathers a crop. **2** a person who reaps.

rear¹ (rēr) *n.* **1** the back part; back. **2** the space or position behind, or at the back of, anything. **3** the last part of an army or fleet. **4** the area most distant from the battlefront. **5 at** or **in the rear of,** behind. **6 bring up the rear,** move onward as the rear part; come last in order. —*adj.* at the back; in the back. [var. of *arrear*]

rear² (rēr) *v.* **1** make grow; help to grow; bring up: *The mother was very careful in rearing her children.* **2** set up; build: *rear a temple.* **3** raise; lift up: *rear one's head.* **4** of an animal, rise on the hind legs; rise: *The horse reared as the fire engine dashed past.* [OE *rǣran* raise, causative of *rīsan* rise] —**Syn. 2** erect. **3** elevate.

Rear Adm. Rear Admiral.

rear admiral in the navy, a commissioned officer senior to a commodore and junior to a vice-admiral. *Abbrev.*: R.A. or Rear Adm.

rear guard that part of an army that protects the rear.

re·arm (rē ärm′) *v.* **1** arm again; arm oneself again. **2** supply with new or better weapons.

re·ar·ma·ment (rē är′mə mənt) *n.* a rearming.

rear·most (rēr′mōst) *adj.* farthest in the rear; last.

re·ar·range (rē′ə rānj′) *v.* **-ranged, -rang·ing. 1** arrange in a new or different way. **2** arrange again. —**re′ar·range′ment,** *n.*

rear·ward (rēr′wərd) *adv. adj.* toward or in the rear.

rea·son (rē′zən) *n.* **1** a cause; motive; ground: *I have my own reasons for doing this.* **2** a justification; explanation: *What is your reason for doing such poor work?* **3** the ability to think and draw conclusions. **4** right thinking; good sense. **5** sanity. **6 bring to reason,** cause to be reasonable. **7 by reason of,** on account of; because of. **8 in reason,** within reasonable and sensible limits. **9 stand to reason,** be reasonable and sensible.
—*v.* **1** think; think logically: *Man can reason.* **2** draw conclusions or inferences from facts or premises. **3** consider; discuss; argue. **4 reason away,** get rid of by reasoning. **5 reason out,** think through and come to a conclusion; think out. [ME < OF *raison* < L *ratio.* Doublet of RATIO, RATION.] —**rea′son·er,** *n.*

Syn. *n.* **1 Reason, cause, motive** = the ground or occasion for an event, action, etc. **Reason** applies to a ground or occasion that explains something that has happened, or one given as explanation, which may or may not be the true cause or motive: *The reason he went to the city was to attend university.* **Cause** applies to a person, thing, incident, or condition that directly brings about an action or happening: *The cause of death was given as poisoning.* **Motive** applies to the feeling or desire that makes a person do what he does: *His motive was to regain his health.*

rea·son·a·ble (rē′zən ə bəl or rēz′nə bəl) *adj.* **1** according to reason; sensible; not foolish. **2** not asking too much; fair; just. **3** not high in price; inexpensive. **4** able to reason. —**rea′son·a·ble·ness,** *n.* —**rea′son·a·bly,** *adv.*

Syn. 1 Reasonable, rational = according to reason. **Reasonable,**

describing people or their actions, words, plans, or procedures, emphasizes showing good judgment and being governed by reason in deciding and choosing: *He took a reasonable view of the dispute and offered a solution that was fair, sensible, and practical.* **Rational** emphasizes having or showing the power to think logically and to draw conclusions that guide in doing or saying what is wise, sensible, or reasonable: *His approach to the problem was rational.*

rea·son·ing (rē′zən ing or rēz′ning) *n.* **1** the process of drawing conclusions from facts. **2** reasons, arguments, etc. resulting from or used in this process.

re·as·sem·ble (rē′ə sem′bəl) *v.* **-bled, -bling.** come or bring together again.

re·as·sur·ance (rē′ə shür′əns) *n.* **1** new or fresh assurance. **2** a restoration of courage or confidence.

re·as·sure (rē′ə shür′) *v.* **-sured, -sur·ing. 1** restore to confidence: *The captain's confidence during the storm reassured the passengers.* **2** assure again or anew. **3** insure again. **—re′as·sur′ing·ly,** *adv.*

Ré·au·mur (rā′ə mūr′; *French,* rā ō mʏr′) *adj.* of, based on, or according to the Réaumur scale for measuring temperature, in which the freezing point of water is 0 degrees and the boiling point is 80 degrees. [< René de *Réaumur,* 1683-1757, a French physicist]

reave (rēv) *v.* **reaved** or **reft, reav·ing.** *Archaic.* deprive by force; strip; rob. [OE *rēafian*]

re·bate (rē′bāt or rē bāt′) *n. v.* **-bat·ed, -bat·ing.** *—n.* the return of part of the money paid; partial refund; discount. [ME < OF *rabat* < *rabattre* beat down. See v.] *—v.* give as a rebate. [ME < OF *rabattre* beat down < *re-* back + *abattre* abate < *a-* (< L *ad-*) + *battre* beat < L *batuere*]

re·bec or **re·beck** (rē′bek) *n.* a musical instrument, resembling a violin, used in the Middle Ages. [< F *rebec,* var. of OF *rebebe,* ult. < Arabic *rabab*]

reb·el (*n. adj.* reb′əl; *v.* ri bel′) *n. adj. v.* **re·belled, re·bel·ling.** *—n.* a person who resists or fights against authority instead of obeying: *The rebels armed themselves against the government.*
—adj. defying law or authority: *a rebel army.* [ME < OF < L *rebellis* < *rebellare* rebel. See v.]
—v. **1** resist or fight against law or authority. **2** feel a great dislike or opposition: *We rebelled at having to stay in on so fine a day.* [ME < OF < L *rebellare,* ult. < *re-* again + *bellum* war. Doublet of REVEL.] **—Syn.** *n.* insurgent. *-v.* **1** revolt, mutiny.

re·bel·lion (ri bel′yən) *n.* **1** the act or state of organized resistance against the authority of a government; a revolt. **2** an act of resistance against any authority; a revolt or fight against any restriction. [< L *rebellio, -onis* < *rebellis* rebel < *rebellare.* See REBEL, v.] **—Syn. 1** insurrection, revolution, sedition. See **revolt.**

re·bel·lious (ri bel′yəs) *adj.* **1** defying authority; acting like a rebel. **2** hard to manage; hard to treat. **—re·bel′lious·ly,** *adv.* **—re·bel′lious·ness,** *n.* **—Syn. 1** mutinous. **2** disobedient.

re·birth (rē′bėrth′ or rē bėrth′) *n.* a new birth; a being born again.

re·born (rē bôrn′) *adj.* born again.

re·bound (*v.* ri bound′; *n.* rē′bound′ or ri bound′) *v.* **1** spring back. **2** resound. *—n.* **1** a springing back. **2** in basketball, a ball that bounds off the backboard when a scoring attempt has been missed. **3 on the rebound,** in a state of shock caused by the abrupt ending of a love affair. [ME < OF *rebondir* < *re-* back (< L) + *bondir* bound, resound, ? < VL *bombitire* < L *bombus* booming sound < Gk. *bombos*] **—Syn.** *v.* **1** recoil.

re·broad·cast (rē brod′kast′ or -brôd′kast′) *v.* **-cast** or **-cast·ed, -cast·ing,** *n.* *—v.* **1** broadcast again or anew. **2** relay by broadcast (messages, speeches, etc. received from a broadcasting station). *—n.* a program, etc. that is rebroadcast.

re·buff (ri buf′) *n.* a blunt or sudden check to a person or animal that makes advances, offers help, makes a request, etc. *—v.* give a rebuff to. [< F < Ital. *ribuffo*] **—Syn.** *v.* check.

re·build (rē′bild′) *v.* **-built, -build·ing.** build again or anew.

re·built (rē′bilt′) *v.* pt. and pp. of **rebuild.**

re·buke (ri būk′) *v.* **-buked, -buk·ing,** *n.* *—v.* express disapproval of; reprove. *—n.* an expression of disapproval; scolding. [ME < ONF *rebuker;* cf. OF *rebuchier* < *re-* back + *buchier* strike] **—re·buk′er,** *n.* **—re·buk′ing·ly,** *adv.* **—Syn.** *v.* reprimand, censure. See **reprove.**

re·bus (rē′bəs) *n.* a representation of a word or phrase by pictures suggesting the syllables or words. A picture of a cat on a log is a rebus for *catalogue.* [< L *rebus* by means of objects]

re·but (ri but′) *v.* **-but·ted, -but·ting.** oppose by evidence on the other side or by argument; try to disprove: *rebut the argument of the other team in a debate.* [ME < OF *reboter* < *re-* back + *boter* butt[3] < Gmc.]

re·but·tal (ri but′əl) *n.* a rebutting.

re·but·ter (ri but′ər) *n.* **1** a person that rebuts. **2** an argument that rebuts.

rec. 1 receipt. **2** recipe. **3** record. **4** recorder.

re·cal·ci·trance (ri kal′sə trəns) *n.* a refusal to submit, conform, or comply.

re·cal·ci·tran·cy (ri kal′sə trən sē) *n.* recalcitrance.

re·cal·ci·trant (ri kal′sə trənt) *adj.* resisting authority or control; disobedient. *—n.* one who is recalcitrant. [< L *recalcitrans, -antis,* ppr. of *recalcitrare* kick back, ult. < *re-* back + *calx, calcis* heel]

re·call (*v.* ri kol′ or -kôl′; *n.* rē′ kol′ or -kôl′, ri kol′ or -kôl′) *v.* **1** call back to mind; remember. **2** call back; order back: *The ambassador was recalled.* **3** bring back: *recalled to life.* **4** take back; withdraw: *The order has been given and cannot be recalled.*
—n. **1** a recalling to mind. **2** a calling back; ordering back. **3** a signal used in calling back men, ships, etc. **4** a taking back; revocation; annulment. **5** the removal of a public official from office by the vote of the people: *There is no longer provision for recall in Canada.* **—Syn.** *v.* **1** recollect. See **remember. 4** revoke, retract.

re·cant (ri kant′) *v.* **1** take back formally or publicly; withdraw or renounce (a statement, opinion, purpose, etc.). **2** renounce an opinion or allegiance: *Though he was tortured to make him change his religion, the prisoner would not recant.* [< L *recantare,* ult. < *re-* back + *canere* sing]

re·can·ta·tion (rē′kan tā′shən) *n.* a recanting.

re·cap[1] (rē′kap′ or rē′ kap′) *v.* **-capped, -cap·ping,** *n.* *—v.* put a strip of rubber or similar material on (a worn surface of an automobile tire), by using heat and pressure to make a firm union. *—n.* a tire repaired in this manner.

re·cap[2] (*v.* rē kap′; *n.* rē′kap) *v.* **-capped, -cap·ping.** recapitulate. *—n. Informal.* a recapitulation.

re·ca·pit·u·late (rē′kə pich′ů lāt′) *v.* **-lat·ed, -lat·ing.** repeat or recite the main points of; tell briefly; sum up. [< L *recapitulare* < *re-* again + *capitulum* chapter, section, dim. of *caput* head]

re·ca·pit·u·la·tion (rē′kə pich′ů lā′shən) *n.* **1** a brief statement of the main points; summary. **2** in music, a repetition, usually in a later movement or section of the initial theme of a composition.

re·cap·ture (rē kap′chər) *v.* **-tured, -tur·ing,** *n.* *—v.* **1** capture again; have again. **2** recall: *The picture album recaptured the days of the horse and buggy.* *—n.* **1** a taking or being taken a second time. **2** the thing that is taken.

re·cast (*v.* rē kast′; *n.* rē′kast′) *v.* **-cast, -cast·ing,** *n.* *—v.* **1** cast again or anew: *recast a bell.* **2** make over; remodel: *recast a sentence.* *—n.* a recasting.

recd. or **rec'd** received.

re·cede (ri sēd′) *v.* **-ced·ed, -ced·ing. 1** go backward; move backward. **2** slope backward: *He has a chin that recedes.* **3** withdraw: *He receded from the agreement.* [< L *recedere* < *re-* back + *cedere* go] **—Syn. 1** retreat, retire.

re·ceipt (ri sēt′) *n.* **1** a written statement that money, a package, a letter, etc. has been received. **2 receipts,** *pl.* money received; the amount or quantity received. **3** a receiving or being received: *On receipt of the news, he went home.* **4** a recipe. *—v.* write on (a bill, etc.) that something has been received or paid for. [ME < ONF < L *recepta,* fem. pp. of *recipere* receive. See RECEIVE.]
☞ **receipt, recipe.** Both words mean "a formula; directions for preparing something to eat." Locally one or the other may be preferred by cooks, but they are interchangeable in meaning.

hat, āge, cãre, fär; let, ēqual, tėrm; it, īce
hot, ōpen, ôrder; oil, out; cup, pu̇t, rüle, ūse
əbove, takən, pencəl, lemən, circəs
ch, child; ng, long; sh, ship
th, thin; ᴛʜ, then; zh, measure

re·ceiv·a·ble (ri sēv′ə bəl) *adj.* **1** fit for acceptance: *Gold is receivable all over the world.* **2** on which payment is to be received. *Bills receivable* is the opposite of *bills payable.* **3** to be received.

re·ceive (ri sēv′) *v.* **-ceived, -ceiv·ing. 1** take (something offered or sent); take into one's hands or possession: *receive gifts.* **2** have (something) bestowed, conferred, etc.: *receive a name.* **3** be given; get: *receive a letter from home.* **4** take, accept, admit, or get something: *Everyone will receive as he deserves.* **5** take; support; bear; hold: *The boat received a heavy load.* **6** take or let into the mind: *receive new ideas.* **7** accept as true or valid: *a theory widely received.* **8** agree to listen to: *receive confession.* **9** experience; suffer; endure: *receive a blow.* **10** let into one's house, society, etc.: *The people of the neighborhood were glad to receive the new couple.* **11** admit to a place; give shelter to: *receive strangers.* **12** admit to a state or condition: *receive a person into the Christian faith.* **13** be at home to friends and visitors: *She receives on Tuesdays.* **14** in radio or television, change electrical waves into sound or picture signals. [ME < ONF < L *recipere* < *re-* back + *capere* take]

Syn. 1 Receive, accept = take what is given, offered, or delivered. **Receive** carries no suggestion of positive action or of activity of the mind or will on the part of the receiver and means nothing more than to take to oneself or take in what is given or given out: *He received a prize.* **Accept** always suggests being willing to take what is offered, or giving one's consent: *She received a gift from him, but refused to accept it.*

re·ceiv·er (ri sēv′ər) *n.* **1** a person who receives. **2** anything that receives. **3** the part of a telephone that receives electrical impulses and converts them into sound. **4** a receiving set for radio, television, telegraph, etc. **5** in law, one appointed to take charge of the property of others. **6** a person who knowingly receives stolen goods or harbors offenders.

re·ceiv·er·ship (ri sēv′ər ship′) *n.* **1** the position of a receiver in charge of the property of others. **2** the condition of being in the control of a receiver.

receiving set 1 an apparatus for receiving sounds sent by radio; a radio or television set. **2** an apparatus for receiving messages sent by telegraph, teletype, etc.

re·cen·cy (rē′sən sē) *n.* the fact or condition of being recent.

re·cent (rē′sənt) *adj.* **1** done or made not long ago: *recent events.* **2** not long past; modern: *a recent period in history.* **3 Recent,** of the Recent geological period. *—n.* **Recent,** the present geological period. See **geology** for chart. [< L *recens, -entis*] **—re′cent·ness,** *n.*

re·cent·ly (rē′sənt lē) *adv.* lately; not long ago.

re·cep·ta·cle (ri sep′tə kəl) *n.* **1** any container or place used to put things in to keep them conveniently. Bags, baskets, and vaults are all receptacles. **2** in botany, the stalklike part of a flower that bears the petals, stamens, and pistils. **3** a wall socket for an electrical plug. [< L *receptaculum,* ult. < *recipere* receive. See RECEIVE.]

re·cep·tion (ri sep′shən) *n.* **1** the act of receiving: *calm reception of bad news.* **2** the fact of being received. **3** a manner of receiving: *a warm reception.* **4** a gathering to receive and welcome people. **5** the quality of the sound or picture signals received by a radio or television set. [< L *receptio, -onis* < *recipere.* See RECEIVE.]

re·cep·tion·ist (ri sep′shən ist) *n.* a person employed to receive callers: *She is a receptionist in a doctor's office.*

re·cep·tive (ri sep′tiv) *adj.* able, quick, or willing to receive ideas, suggestions, or impressions, etc.: *a receptive mind.* **—re·cep′tive·ly,** *adv.* **—re·cep′tive·ness,** *n.*

re·cep·tiv·i·ty (rē′sep tiv′ə tē) *n.* the ability or readiness to receive.

re·cep·tor (ri sep′tər) *n.* in physiology, a cell or group of cells sensitive to stimuli; a sense organ. [< L *receptor* receiver]

re·cess (*n.* rē′ses *for 1,* ri ses′ or rē′ses *for 2 and 3;* *v.* ri ses′) *n.* **1** a time during which work stops: *There will be a short recess before the next meeting.* **2** a part in a wall set back from the rest; alcove; niche. **3** an inner place or part; quiet, secluded place: *the recesses of a cave, the recesses of one's secret thoughts.*
—v. **1** take a recess: *The convention recesses until afternoon.* **2** put in a recess; set back. **3** make a recess in. [< L *recessus* a retreat < *recedere* recede. See RECEDE.] **—Syn.** *n.* **1** intermission.

re·ces·sion[1] (ri sesh′ən) *n.* **1** a going backward; moving backward. **2** a sloping backward. **3** a withdrawal. **4** a period of temporary business decline, shorter and less extreme than a depression. [< L *recessio, -onis* < *recedere* recede. See RECEDE.]

re·ces·sion[2] (ri sesh′ən) *n.* a ceding back to a former owner. [< *re-* + *cession*]

re·ces·sion·al (ri sesh′ən əl) *adj.* **1** sung or played while the clergy and the choir retire from the church at the end of a service. **2** of or having to do with recession. *—n.* a recessional hymn or piece of music.

re·ces·sive (ri ses′iv) *adj.* **1** likely to go back; receding. **2** in biology, of or having to do with a recessive character.

recessive character the one of any pair of opposite characters that is latent in an animal or plant, when both are present in the germ plasm.

Rech·a·bite (rek′ə bīt′) *n.* **1** in the Old Testament, a member of a Jewish family that refused to drink wine. Jer. 35:2-19. **2** a total abstainer from alcohol, especially a member of a fraternal benefit organization affiliated to the Independent Order of Rechabites, founded in England in 1835.

re·cher·ché (rə shãr′shā; *French,* rə sher shā′) *adj.* **1** sought out or devised with care; rare; choice. **2** too studied; far-fetched. [< F *recherché* sought after < *re-* again + *chercher* search]

re·cid·i·vism (rē sid′ə viz′əm) *n.* a tendency to chronic relapse into crime or antisocial behavior. [< L *recidivus* < *recidere* fall back < L *re-* back + *cadere* fall]

re·cid·i·vist (rē sid′ə vist′) *n.* a habitual criminal. *—adj.* of or having to do with recidivism.

rec·i·pe (res′ə pē) *n.* **1** a set of directions for preparing something to eat. **2** a set of directions for preparing anything. **3** a means of reaching some state or condition: *a recipe for happiness.* [< L *recipe* take!, imperative of *recipere* take, receive. See RECEIVE.] ☛ See **receipt** for usage note.

re·cip·i·ent (ri sip′ē ənt) *n.* a person or thing that receives something: *The recipients of the prizes had their names printed in the paper. —adj.* receiving; willing to receive. [< L *recipiens, -entis,* ppr. of *recipere.* See RECEIVE.]

re·cip·ro·cal (ri sip′rə kəl) *adj.* **1** in return: *Although I gave him many presents, I had no reciprocal gifts from him.* **2** mutual: *reciprocal liking, reciprocal distrust.* **3** inversely proportional; inverse. **4** in grammar, expressing mutual action or relation. *Example:* In "The two children like each other," *each other* is a reciprocal pronoun.
—n. **1** a number so related to another that when multiplied together they give 1. The reciprocal of 3 is $\frac{1}{3}$, and the reciprocal of $\frac{1}{3}$ is 3. **2** something that is reciprocal. [< L *reciprocus* returning]

re·cip·ro·cal·ly (ri sip′rə kə lē or ri sip′rə klē) *adv.* in a reciprocal way; each to the other; mutually.

re·cip·ro·cate (ri sip′rə kāt′) *v.* **-cat·ed, -cat·ing. 1** give, do, feel, or show in return: *She loves me, and I reciprocate her love.* **2** move or cause to move with an alternating backward and forward motion. [< L *reciprocare* < *reciprocus* returning] **—re·cip′ro·ca′tion,** *n.* **—re·cip′ro·ca′tor,** *n.*

reciprocating engine an engine in which the piston and piston rod move back and forth in a straight line.

rec·i·proc·i·ty (res′ə pros′ə tē) *n.* **1** a reciprocal state; mutual action. **2** a mutual exchange, especially an exchange of special privileges in regard to trade between two countries.

re·cit·al (ri sīt′əl) *n.* **1** the act of reciting; a telling of facts in detail: *Her recital of her experiences in the hospital bored her hearers.* **2** a story; account. **3** a musical entertainment, given usually by a single performer. **4** a public performance given by a group of pupils (of piano, dance, etc.). **—Syn. 2** narration.

re·ci·tan·do (rā chē tän′dō) *adv.* in music, after the manner of a recitative. [Ital.]

rec·i·ta·tion (res′ə tā′shən) *n.* **1** the act of reciting. **2** a reciting of a prepared lesson by pupils before a teacher. **3** a repeating of something from memory. **4** a piece repeated from memory. [< L *recitatio, -onis* < *recitare.* See RECITE.]

rec·i·ta·tive[1] (res′ə tā′tiv or ri sī′tə tiv) *adj.* of or having to do with recital; reciting: *a recitative account of the event.*

rec·i·ta·tive[2] (res′ə tə tēv′) *n.* in music: **1** a style halfway between speaking and singing. Operas often contain passages of recitative. **2** a passage, part, or composition in this style. [< Ital. *recitativo*]

re·cite (ri sīt′) *v.* **-cit·ed, -cit·ing. 1** say over; repeat: *recite a lesson.* **2** repeat something; say part of a lesson. **3** give an account of in detail: *recite one's adventures.* **4** repeat (a poem, speech, etc.) to entertain an audience. [< L *recitare* < *re-* again + *citare* appeal to] **—re·cit′er,** *n.* **—Syn. 1** rehearse. **3** relate, narrate.

reck (rek) *v. Archaic.* **1** care; heed. **2** be important or interesting; matter. [OE *reccan*]

reck·less (rek′lis) *adj.* rash; heedless; careless: *Reckless of consequences, the boy played truant. Reckless driving causes many automobile accidents.* [OE *recceléas*] **—reck′less·ly,** *adv.* **—reck′less·ness,** *n.* **—Syn.** See **rash.**

reck·on (rek′ən) *v.* **1** find the number or value of; count: *Reckon the cost before you decide.* **2** consider; judge; account: *He is reckoned the best speller in the class.* **3** *Informal.* think; suppose. **4** depend; rely: *You can reckon on our help.* **5** settle; settle account. **6 reckon up,** count up. **7 reckon with,** take into consideration. [OE *(ge)recenian*] **—reck′on·er,** *n.* **—Syn. 1** compute, calculate. **2** regard, deem, esteem.

reck·on·ing (rek′ən ing or rek′ning) *n.* **1** a method of computing; count; calculation: *By my reckoning we are miles from home.* **2** the settlement of an account. **3** a bill, especially at an inn or tavern. **4** the calculation of the position of a ship. **5** the position calculated.

re·claim (ri klām′) *v.* **1** bring back to a useful, good condition: *The farmer reclaimed the swamp by draining it.* **2** demand the return of: *The library sent a notice reclaiming the book.* [ME < OF < L *reclamare* cry out against < *re-* back + *clamare* cry out] **—re·claim′a·ble,** *adj.* **—re·claim′er,** *n.* **—Syn. 1** See **recover.**

rec·la·ma·tion (rek′lə mā′shən) *n.* a reclaiming or being reclaimed; restoration to a useful, good condition: *the reclamation of deserts by irrigation; reclamation of hardened sinners.*

re·cline (ri klīn′) *v.* **-clined, -clin·ing.** lean back; lie down. [< L *reclinare* < *re-* back + *-clinare* lean]

rec·luse (*n.* rek′lüs or ri klüs′; *adj.* ri klüs′) *n.* a person who lives shut up or withdrawn from the world. *—adj.* shut up or apart from the world. [ME < OF < L *reclusus* shut up, pp. of *recludere* < *re-* back + *claudere* shut]

rec·og·ni·tion (rek′əg nish′ən) *n.* **1** a knowing again; recognizing; being recognized: *By a good disguise he escaped recognition.* **2** an acknowledgment: *We insisted on complete recognition of our rights.* **3** notice. **4** a favorable notice; acceptance: *The actor soon won recognition from the public.* **5** a formal acknowledgment conveying acceptance or sanction. [< L *recognitio, -onis*]

rec·og·niz·a·ble (rek′əg nīz′ə bəl) *adj.* capable of being recognized. **—rec′og·niz′a·bly,** *adv.*

re·cog·ni·zance (ri kog′nə zəns) *n.* in law: **1** a bond binding a person to perform some particular act. **2** the sum of money to be forfeited if the act is not performed. [ME < OF *recognoissance* < *reconoistre* recognize. See RECOGNIZE. Doublet of RECONNAISSANCE.]

rec·og·nize (rek′əg nīz′) *v.* **-nized, -niz·ing. 1** know again: *I could scarcely recognize my old friend.* **2** identify: *recognize a person from a description.* **3** acknowledge acquaintance with; greet: *recognize a person on the street.* **4** acknowledge; accept; admit: *He recognized his duty to defend his country.* **5** take notice of: *Anyone who wishes to speak in a public meeting should stand up and wait till the chairman recognizes him.* **6** show appreciation of. **7** acknowledge and agree to deal with: *For some years certain nations did not recognize the new government.* [ME < OF *reconoistre* < L *recognoscere* < *re-* again + *com-* (intensive) + *(g)noscere* learn. Doublet of RECONNOITRE.] **—rec′og·niz′er,** *n.*

re·coil (*v.* ri koil′; *n.* ri koil′ or rē′koil) *v.* **1** draw back; shrink back: *Most people would recoil at seeing a snake in their path.* **2** spring back: *The gun recoiled after I fired.* **3** react: *Revenge often recoils on the avenger.* *—n.* **1** a recoiling. **2** the state of having recoiled: *in recoil from danger.* **3** the distance or force with which a gun, spring, etc. springs back. [ME < OF *reculer,* ult. < L *re-* back + *culus* rump]

re·col·lect (rē′kə lekt′) *v.* **1** collect again. **2** recover control of (oneself). [originally < L *recollectus,* pp. of *recolligere* < *re-* again + *colligere* collect, but later taken as < *re-* + *collect,* and pronounced accordingly]

rec·ol·lect (rek ə lekt′) *v.* call back to mind; remember. [from the same source as *re-collect,* but distinguished in meaning and pronunciation] **—Syn.** See **remember.**

rec·ol·lec·tion (rek′ə lek′shən) *n.* **1** the act or power of recalling to mind. **2** memory; remembrance. **3** something remembered. **—Syn. 2** See **memory.**

rec·om·mend (rek′ə mend′) *v.* **1** speak in favor of; suggest favorably. **2** advise. **3** make pleasing or attractive: *The position of the camp recommends it as a summer home.* **4** hand over for safekeeping. [< Med.L *recommendare* < L *re-* again + *commendare* commend] **—rec′om·mend′er,** *n.*

rec·om·men·da·tion (rek′ə men dā′shən) *n.* **1** a recommending. **2** anything that recommends a person or thing. **3** words of advice or praise. **4** something recommended.

rec·om·men·da·to·ry (rek′ə men′də tô′rē) *adj.* serving to recommend; recommending.

re·com·mit (rē′kə mit′) *v.* **-mit·ted, -mit·ting. 1** commit again. **2** refer again to a committee.

re·com·mit·ment (rē′kə mit′mənt) *n.* **1** a recommitting. **2** the state or fact of being recommitted.

re·com·mit·tal (rē′kə mit′əl) *n.* recommitment.

rec·om·pense (rek′əm pens′) *v.* **-pensed, -pens·ing,** *n.* *—v.* **1** pay (a person); pay back; reward. **2** make a fair return for (an action, anything lost, damage done, hurt received, etc.). *—n.* **1** a payment; reward. **2** a return for anything lost, damaged, etc.; amends. [< LL *recompensare,* ult. < L *re-* back + *com-* with, against + *pendere* weigh out in payment] **—Syn.** *v.* **1** repay, compensate, remunerate, requite.

rec·on·cile (rek′ən sīl′) *v.* **-ciled, -cil·ing. 1** make friends again. **2** settle (a quarrel, disagreement, etc.). **3** make agree; bring into harmony: *It is impossible to reconcile his story with the facts.* **4** make satisfied; make no longer opposed: *It is hard to reconcile oneself to being sick for a long time.* [< L *reconciliare,* ult. < *re-* back + *concilium* bond of union] **—rec′on cil′a·ble,** *adj.* **—rec′on·cil′er,** *n.*

rec·on·cile·ment (rek′ən sīl′mənt) *n.* reconciliation.

rec·on·cil·i·a·tion (rek′ən sil′ē ā′shən) *n.* **1** a reconciling; a bringing together again in friendship. **2** the state of being reconciled; a settlement or adjustment of disagreements, differences, etc.

rec·on·cil·i·a·to·ry (rek′ən sil′ē ə tô′rē) *adj.* tending to reconcile.

rec·on·dite (rek′ən dīt′ or ri kon′dīt) *adj.* **1** hard to understand; profound. **2** little known; obscure. [< L *reconditus,* pp. of *recondere* store away, ult. < *re-* back + *com-* up + *dare* put]

re·con·di·tion (rē′kən dish′ən) *v.* restore to a good or satisfactory condition; put in good condition by repairing, making over, etc.

re·con·nais·sance (ri kon′ə səns) *n.* an examination or survey, especially for military purposes. [< F *reconnaissance* (< OF *recognoissance*). Doublet of RECOGNIZANCE.]

rec·on·noi·tre or **rec·on·noi·ter** (rek′ə noi′tər or rē′kə noi′tər) *v.* **-tred** or **-tered, -tring** or **-ter·ing. 1** approach and examine or observe in order to learn something; make a survey of (the enemy, the enemy's strength or position, a region, etc.) in order to gain information for military purposes. **2** approach a place and make a first survey of it: *It seemed wise to reconnoitre before entering the town.* [< F *reconnoître*, earlier form of *reconnaître* (< OF *reconoistre*). Doublet of RECOGNIZE.] —**rec′on·noi′trer** or **rec′on·noi′ter·er,** *n.*

re·con·struct (rē′kən strukt′) *v.* construct again; rebuild; make over.

re·con·struc·tion (rē′kən struk′shən) *n.* **1** a reconstructing. **2** the thing reconstructed.

re·con·struc·tive (rē′kən struk′tiv) *adj.* tending to reconstruct.

re·cord (*v.* ri kôrd′; *n. adj.* rek′ərd) *v.* **1** set down in writing so as to keep for future use: *Listen to the speaker and record what he says.* **2** put in some permanent form; keep for remembrance: *History is recorded in books.* **3** put on a phonograph disk, or on phonographic tape or wire. **4** tell; indicate: *The thermometer records temperatures.*
—*n.* **1** the thing written or kept. **2** an official written account: *The secretary kept a record of what was done at the meeting.* **3** a disk or cylinder used on a phonograph. **4** the known facts about what a person, animal, ship, etc. has done: *She has a fine record at school.* **5** a criminal record. **6** the best yet done; best amount, rate, speed, etc. yet attained: *He holds the record for the high jump.* **7** a recording or being recorded: *What happened is a matter of record.* **8 break a record,** improve on a record previously set in some athletic event, etc. **9 go on record,** state publicly for the record. **10 off the record,** not to be recorded or quoted. **11 on record,** recorded.
—*adj.* making or affording a record: *a record wheat crop.* [ME < OF < L *recordari* remember, ult. < *re-* back + *cor, cordis* heart, mind]

record club a business organization that regularly supplies selected records to its subscribers.

re·cord·er (ri kôr′dər) *n.* **1** a person whose business is to make and keep records. **2** a machine that records. **3 a** in some cities, etc., a title given to certain judges. **b** in Quebec, a judge of a lower court. **4** a musical wind instrument resembling a flute. **5** a person who records sounds or sound effects for motion pictures or phonograph records.

A recorder

recorder's court magistrate's court.

re·cord·ing (ri kôr′ding) *n.* **1** a sound record made on disk or tape. **2** the original transcription of any sound or combination of sounds.

record player a phonograph.

re-count (rē′kount′) *v.* count again.

re·count[1] (ri kount′) *v.* tell in detail; give an account of: *He recounted all the happenings of the day.* [ME < ONF *reconter* < *re-* again + *conter* relate, count[1]]

re·count[2] (rē′kount′ or rē kount′) *n.* a second count, as of votes.

re·coup (ri küp′) *v.* **1** make up for: *He recouped his losses.* **2** repay. [< F *recouper* < *re-* back + *couper* cut]

re·course (rē′kôrs or ri kôrs′) *n.* **1** an appealing; turning to somebody or something for help or protection: *Our recourse in illness is to a doctor.* **2** a person or thing appealed to or turned to for help or protection: *A child's great recourse in trouble is its mother.* **3** the right to demand compensation from someone. **4 have recourse to,** appeal to; turn to for help. [ME < OF < L *recursus* retreat, ult. < *re-* back + *currere* run]

re-cov·er (rē′kuv′ər) *v.* put a new cover on.

re·cov·er (ri kuv′ər) *v.* **1** get back (something lost, taken away, or stolen). **2** make up for (something lost or damaged): *recover lost time.* **3** bring back to life, health, one's senses, or normal condition. **4** get well; get back to a normal condition. **5** get back to the proper position or condition: *He started to fall but recovered himself.* **6** in law: **a** obtain by judgment in a court. **b** obtain judgment in one's favor in a court. **7** rescue; deliver. **8** regain in usable form; reclaim. Many useful substances are now recovered from materials that used to be thrown away. [ME < OF < L *recuperare*. Doublet of RECUPERATE.]

hat, āge, cãre, fär; let, ēqual, tėrm; it, īce
hot, ōpen, ôrder; oil, out; cup, pu̇t, rüle, ūse
əbove, takən, pencəl, lemən, circəs
ch, child; ng, long; sh, ship
th, thin; ᴛʜ, then; zh, measure

—**re·cov′er·er,** *n.*
Syn. 1 Recover, reclaim, retrieve = get or bring something back. **Recover** = get something back again in one's possession after losing it: *He recovered the stolen furs.* **Reclaim** = bring back into usable or useful condition from a lost state, either something that has gone to waste or been abandoned, or waste land, or someone who has strayed from right living: *Part of his farm is reclaimed swamp.* **Retrieve** = recover by effort or search: *The rescuers retrieved the victims of the mine disaster.*

re·cov·er·y (ri kuv′ər ē or ri kuv′rē) *n.* **-er·ies. 1** a recovering. **2** a coming back to health or normal condition. **3** the getting back of something that was lost, taken away, or stolen. **4** a getting back to a proper position or condition: *He started to fall, but made a quick recovery.* **5** the obtaining of some property or right by the judgment of a law court. **6** the act of locating and repossessing a missile, nose cone, etc. after a flight in space.

recovery room in a hospital, a room in which patients are placed immediately after an operation.

rec·re·an·cy (rek′rē ən sē) *n.* **1** cowardice. **2** unfaithfulness; treason.

rec·re·ant (rek′rē ənt) *adj.* **1** cowardly. **2** disloyal; traitorous. —*n.* **1** a coward. **2** a traitor. [ME < OF *recreant* confessing oneself beaten, ult. < L *re-* back + *credere* believe]

re-cre·ate (rē′krē āt′) *v.* **-at·ed, -at·ing.** create anew.

rec·re·ate (rek′rē āt′) *v.* **-at·ed, -at·ing. 1** refresh with games, pastimes, exercises, etc. **2** take recreation. [ult. < L *recreare* restore < *re-* again + *creare* create]

rec·re·a·tion (rek′rē ā′shən) *n.* any form of play, amusement, or relaxation intended to refresh the body or mind, especially after work. Walking, gardening, and reading are quiet forms of recreation.

rec·re·a·tion·al (rek′rē ā′shən əl) *adj.* of or having to do with recreation.

recreation room a room for recreations such as playing games, lounging, dancing, and other informal activities.

rec·re·a·tive (rek′rē ā′tiv) *adj.* refreshing; restoring.

re·crim·i·nate (ri krim′ə nāt′) *v.* **-nat·ed, -nat·ing.** accuse (someone) in return: *Tom said Harry had lied, and Harry recriminated by saying Tom had lied too.* [< Med.L *recriminare*, ult. < L *re-* back + *crimen* charge]

re·crim·i·na·tion (ri krim′ə nā′shən) *n.* an accusing in return; counter accusation.

re·crim·i·na·tive (ri krim′ə nə tiv or ri krim′ə nā′tiv) *adj.* recriminatory.

re·crim·i·na·to·ry (ri krim′ə nə tô′rē) *adj.* of or involving recrimination.

re·cru·desce (rē′krü des′) *v.* **-desced, -des·cing.** become active again or break out afresh; flare up.

re·cru·des·cence (rē′krü des′əns) *n.* a breaking out afresh; renewed activity: *the recrudescence of an influenza epidemic.* [< L *recrudescere*, ult. < *re-* again + *crudus* raw]

re·cru·des·cent (rē′krü des′ənt) *adj.* breaking out again.

re·cruit (ri krüt′) *n.* **1** a newly enlisted member of the armed services. **2** a new member of any group or class. [< F (obs.) *recrute* < *recruter*. See v.]
—*v.* **1** get people to join one of the armed services. **2** strengthen or supply (armed services) with new men. **3** get (new members). **4** increase or maintain the number of. **5** renew health, strength, or spirits. **6** renew; get a sufficient number or amount of; replenish. [< F *recruter* < *recrue* recruit(ing), new growth < *recrû*, pp. of *recroître* < *re-* again (< L *re-*) + *croître* grow < L *crescere*] —**re·cruit′er,** *n.* —**re·cruit′ment,** *n.*

rect. **1** receipt. **2** rector. **3** rectory.

rec·tal (rek′təl) *adj.* of or having to do with the rectum.

rec·tan·gle (rek′tang′gəl) *n.* a four-sided figure with four right angles. [< F < LL *rectangulum* < L *rectus* right + *angulus* angle]

Rectangles

rec·tan·gu·lar (rek tang′gyů lər) *adj.* 1 shaped like a rectangle. 2 having one or more right angles. 3 placed at right angles. —**rec·tan′gular·ly,** *adv.*

rec·ti·fi·er (rek′tə fī′ər) *n.* 1 a person or thing that makes right, corrects, adjusts, etc. 2 in electricity, a device for changing alternating current into direct current.

rec·ti·fy (rek′tə fī′) *v.* **-fied, -fy·ing.** 1 make right; put right; adjust; remedy: *The storekeeper admitted his mistake and was willing to rectify it.* 2 in electricity, change (an alternating current) into a direct current. 3 purify; refine: *rectify a liquor by distilling it several times.* [< LL *rectificare* < L *rectus* right + *facere* make] —**rec′ti·fi′a·ble,** *adj.* —**rec′ti·fi·ca′tion,** *n.* —**Syn.** 1 correct, amend.

rec·ti·lin·e·ar (rek′tə lin′ē ər) *adj.* 1 forming a straight line. 2 bounded or formed by straight lines. 3 characterized by straight lines. 4 in a straight line; moving in a straight line. [< L *rectus* straight + E *linear*]

rec·ti·tude (rek′tə tūd′ or rek′tə tüd′) *n.* 1 upright conduct or character; honesty; righteousness. 2 correctness. [< LL *rectitudo* < L *rectus* straight]

rec·tor (rek′tər) *n.* 1 in the Anglican Church of Canada or the Church of England, a clergyman who has charge of a parish. 2 in the Roman Catholic Church, a priest who has charge of a congregation or religious house. 3 in some schools, colleges, or universities, the head or principal. [< L *rector* ruler < *regere* to rule]

rec·tor·ate (rek′tər it) *n.* the position, rank, or term of a rector.

rec·to·ry (rek′tə rē or rek′trē) *n.* **-ries.** 1 a rector's house. 2 *Esp.Brit.* a rector's benefice with all its rights, tithes, and lands.

rec·tum (rek′təm) *n.* the lowest part of the large intestine. [< NL *rectum,* for L *intestinum rectum* straight intestine]

re·cum·ben·cy (ri kum′bən sē) *n.* a recumbent position or condition.

re·cum·bent (ri kum′bənt) *adj.* lying down; reclining; leaning. [< L *recumbens, -entis,* ppr. of *recumbere* recline] —**re·cum′bent·ly,** *adv.*

re·cu·per·ate (ri kü′pər āt′ or ri kū′pər āt′) *v.* **-at·ed, -at·ing.** 1 recover from sickness or exhaustion. 2 regain losses: *He worked hard to recuperate the money stolen from him.* 3 restore to health, strength, etc. [< L *recuperare* recover. Doublet of RECOVER.]

re·cu·per·a·tion (ri kü′pər ā′shən or ri kū′pər ā′shən) *n.* recovery from sickness, exhaustion, loss, etc.

re·cu·per·a·tive (ri kü′pər ə tiv or ri kü′pər ā′tiv, ri kū′pər ə tiv or ri kū′pər ā′tiv) *adj.* of recuperation; aiding recuperation.

re·cur (ri kėr′) *v.* **-curred, -cur·ring.** 1 come up again; occur again; be repeated: *A leap year recurs every four years.* 2 return in thought or speech: *Old memories constantly recurred to him. He recurred to the matter of cost.* [< L *recurrere* < *re-* back + *currere* run]

re·cur·rence (ri kėr′əns) *n.* an occurring again; repetition; return: *More care in the future will prevent recurrence of the mistake.*

re·cur·rent (ri kėr′ənt) *adj.* 1 recurring; occurring again; repeated. 2 turned back so as to run in the opposite direction. [< L *recurrens, -entis,* ppr. of *recurrere.* See RECUR.] —**re·cur′rent·ly,** *adv.*

re·curve (rē kėrv′) *v.* **-curved, -curv·ing.** curve back; bend back.

rec·u·san·cy (rek′yů zən sē or ri kū′zən sē) *n.* the act or state of being recusant.

rec·u·sant (rek′yů zənt or ri kū′zənt) *adj.* refusing to submit. —*n.* 1 a person who refuses to submit. 2 formerly, in England, a person, especially a Roman Catholic who refused to attend the services of the established church (the Church of England). [< L *recusans, -antis,* ppr. of *recusare* refuse, ult. < *re-* back + *causa* cause]

red (red) *n. adj.* **red·der, red·dest.** —*n.* 1 the color of blood; the color of the spectrum having the longest light waves, opposite to violet. 2 any shade of that color. 3 a red pigment or dye. 4 red cloth or clothing. 5 a red or reddish person, animal, or thing. 6 **Red,** a radical; revolutionary: *Communists are often referred to as Reds.* 7 *Cdn.* a Liberal. 8 *Informal.* **in the red,** in debt; losing money. 9 **see red,** *Informal.* become very angry. —*adj.* 1 having the color of blood; resembling this color; suggesting this color. 2 sore; inflamed. 3 blushing. 4 radical; revolutionary. 5 of or having to do with Liberals. [OE *rēad*] —**red′ly,** *adv.* —**red′ness,** *n.*

red- form of **re-** in some cases before vowels, as in *redeem.*

re·dac·tion (ri dak′shən) *n.* 1 the preparation of another person's writings for publication; revising; editing. 2 the form or version of a work as prepared by revision or editing. [< L *redactio, -onis* < *redactus,* pp. of *redigere* reduce < *red-* back + *agere* bring]

re·dan (ri dan′) *n.* a fortification with two walls forming an angle that points outward. [< F *redan* a double notching, ult. < L *re-* again + *dens* tooth]

red·bird (red′bėrd′) *n.* 1 a cardinal bird. 2 a scarlet tanager. 3 a European bullfinch.

red-blood·ed (red′blud′id) *adj.* full of life and spirit; vigorous; courageous.

red·breast (red′brest′) *n.* a robin.

red·bud (red′bud′) *n.* a tree that has many small, pink, budlike flowers early in the spring.

red·cap (red′kap′) *n.* a porter at a railway station, bus station, etc., usually wearing a red cap as part of his uniform.

red carpet 1 a carpet, traditionally red, laid out at formal receptions for royalty or other important persons. 2 **roll out the red carpet,** treat royally or preferentially.

red cedar 1 a very tall arbor vitae, of W. North America, found especially on the Pacific Coast and often known as the western red cedar. 2 a kind of juniper having fragrant rose-brown wood that is much used in making moth-proof chests, clothes closets, pencils, etc. 3 the wood of either of these trees.

Red Chamber a name sometimes given to the Canadian Senate because of the color of the rugs, draperies, etc. of the room in which the Senate meets.

red clover a variety of clover that has ball-shaped heads of reddish-purple flowers, cultivated as food for horses, cattle, etc.

red·coat (red′kōt′) *n.* 1 in former times, a British soldier. 2 a member of the R.C.M.P.

Red Cross 1 an international organization, founded in Geneva in 1864, to care for the sick and wounded in war and to relieve suffering caused by floods, fire, diseases, and other calamities. 2 a national society that is a branch of this organization. 3 **red cross,** a red Greek cross on a white ground, the emblem of the Red Cross. 4 the cross of Saint George, England's national emblem.

redd (red) *n.* a depression made on the bed of a river or stream by the female of salmon, trout, etc. for laying eggs in. [origin uncertain]

red deer 1 a deer native to the forests of Europe and Asia, and formerly very numerous in England. 2 the common North American deer in its summer coat.

red·den (red′ən) *v.* 1 make red. 2 become red. 3 blush.

red·dish (red′ish) *adj.* somewhat red.

rede (rēd) *v. Archaic or dialect.* 1 advise. 2 interpret; explain. 3 tell. [OE *rǣdan.* Cf. READ[1].]

re·deem (ri dēm′) *v.* 1 buy back: *The property was redeemed when the loan was paid back.* 2 pay off: *We redeemed the mortgage.* 3 convert (certificates, coupons, etc.) into cash or goods. 4 carry out; make good; fulfill: *We redeem a promise by doing what we said we would.* 5 set free; rescue; save: *redeemed from sin.* 6 make up for; balance: *A very good feature will sometimes redeem several bad ones.* 7 reclaim (land). [< L *redimere* < *red-* back + *emere* buy] —**Syn.** 1 regain. 5 liberate, deliver, release.

re·deem·a·ble (ri dēm′ə bəl) *adj.* 1 capable of being redeemed. 2 that will be redeemed or paid: *bonds redeemable in ten years.*

re·deem·er (ri dēm′ər) *n.* **1** a person who redeems. **2 Redeemer,** Jesus Christ.

re·demp·tion (ri demp′shən) *n.* **1** a redeeming. **2** the state of being redeemed. **3** a deliverance; rescue. **4** deliverance from sin; salvation. [< L *redemptio, -onis* < *redimere* redeem. See REDEEM. Doublet of RANSOM.]

re·demp·tive (ri demp′tiv) *adj.* serving to redeem.

re·demp·to·ry (ri demp′tə rē) *adj.* redemptive.

Red Ensign 1 until 1965, the distinctive flag of Canada. **2** the ensign used by British merchant ships, a red flag with a Union Jack in the upper corner next to the staff.

re·de·ploy (rē di ploi′) *v.* change the position (of troops) from one theatre of war to another. **—re′de·ploy′ment,** *n.*

re·de·vel·op (rē′di vel′əp) *n.* **1** develop again. **2** improve buildings or land. **3** in photography, put through a stronger developer a second time, to intensify the image. **—re′de·vel′op·ment,** *n.*

red·eye (red′ī′) *n. Cdn. Slang.* a drink made of beer and tomato juice.

red fire a chemical that burns with a red light, used in fireworks, signals, etc.

red·fish (red′fish′) *n.* **1** a large rose-colored food fish common in the waters of the East coast. **2** *Cdn.* kokanee.

red flag 1 a symbol of rebellion, revolution, etc. **2** a sign of danger. **3** anything that stirs up anger.

red fox 1 the common reddish fox of Europe. **2** a related fox of North America. **3** the reddish fur of either such fox.

red-hand·ed (red′han′did) *adj.* **1** having hands red with blood. **2** in the very act of crime: *a man caught red-handed in robbery.* **—red′-hand′ed·ly,** *adv.* **—red′-hand′ed·ness,** *n.*

red hat 1 a cardinal's hat. **2** the position or rank of a cardinal.

red·head (red′hed′) *n.* **1** a person having red hair. **2** a duck resembling the canvasback but having a red head.

red·head·ed (red′hed′id) *adj.* **1** having red hair. **2** having a red head.

red herring 1 the common smoked herring. **2** something used to draw attention away from the real issue.

red hot *Informal.* a hot dog.

red-hot (red′hot′) *adj.* **1** red with heat; very hot. **2** very enthusiastic; excited; violent. **3** fresh from the source.

red·in·gote (red′ing gōt′) *n.* **1** formerly, a man's outer coat with long skirts that overlap in front. **2** a somewhat similar coat now worn by women, sometimes forming part of a dress. [< F < E *riding coat*]

A redingote (def. 1)

red·in·te·grate (red in′tə grāt′) *v.* **-grat·ed, -grat·ing. 1** make whole again; restore to a perfect state; renew; re-establish. **2** become whole again; be renewed. [< L *redintegrare,* ult. < *red-* again + *integer* whole] **—red·in′te·gra′tion,** *n.*

re·di·rect (rē′də rekt′ or -dī rekt′) *v.* direct again or anew. *—adj. U.S.* in law, of or having to do with the re-examination of a witness. **—re′di·rec′tion,** *n.*

re·dis·count (rē dis′kount) *v.* discount again. *—n.* **1** a rediscounting. **2** *Informal.* a cheque, note, or draft that has been rediscounted.

re·dis·tri·bu·tion (rē′dis trə bū′shən) *n.* **1** a distribution made again or anew. **2** the revision, made every ten years, of the number of seats in the Canadian House of Commons to which each province is entitled on the basis of its population.

red juniper red cedar (def. 2).

red lead red oxide of lead, used in paint, in making cement for pipes, and in making glass. *Formula:* Pb_3O_4

red-let·ter (red′let′ər) *adj.* **1** marked by red letters. **2** memorable; especially happy.

red light *Informal.* any warning signal or instruction to stop, exercise caution, etc.

red-light (red′līt′) *adj.* **1** of or having to do with a red light. **2** characterized by a concentration of brothels or other places of low repute: *a red-light district.*

hat, āge, cãre, fär; let, ēqual, tėrm; it, īce
hot, ōpen, ôrder; oil, out; cup, pu̇t, rüle, ūse
əbove, takən, pencəl, lemən, circəs
ch, child; ng, long; sh, ship
th, thin; ᴛʜ, then; zh, measure

red line either of two red lines drawn across the ice at each end of a hockey rink as an extension of the goal line.

red man a North American Indian.

red mullet any of a group of reddish fishes valued as food.

re·do (rē dü′) *v.* do again; do over.

red·o·lence (red′ə ləns) *n.* the quality of being redolent.

red·o·lent (red′ə lənt) *adj.* **1** having a pleasant smell; fragrant. **2** smelling strongly; giving off an odor: *a house redolent of fresh paint.* **3** suggesting thoughts or feelings: *"Ivanhoe" is a name redolent of romance.* [< L *redolens, -entis,* ppr. of *redolere* emit scent < *red-* back + *olere* to smell]

re·dou·ble (rē dub′əl) *v.* **-bled, -bling. 1** double again. **2** increase greatly; double: *When he saw land ahead, the swimmer redoubled his speed.* **3** repeat; echo. **4** double back: *The fox redoubled on his trail to escape the hunters.* [< F *redoubler*]

re·doubt (ri dout′) *n.* a small fort standing alone. [< F *redoute* < Ital. < VL *reductus* retreat < L *reducere.* See REDUCE.]

re·doubt·a·ble (ri dout′ə bəl) *adj.* that should be feared or dreaded. [ME < OF *redoutable* < *redouter* dread < *re-* again + *douter* doubt < L *dubitare*] **—re·doubt′a·bly,** *adv.*

re·dound (ri dound′) *v.* come back as a result; contribute: *The number of scholarships we gained redound to the honor of our school.* [ME < OF < L *redundare* overflow, ult. < *red-* back + *unda* wave]

red pepper 1 a plant having a podlike fruit that turns red when ripe. The sweet pepper and cayenne are kinds of red pepper. **2** the ground, dried seeds or fruits of any of these plants, used as a seasoning; cayenne.

red pine 1 a pine tree having long, needle-like leaves and reddish bark, found from the Atlantic coast to Manitoba. **2** the hard wood of this tree, much used in building.

red·poll (red′pōl′) *n.* any of several kinds of small finches. The males have crimson heads.

re·draft (*v.* rē draft′; *n.* rē′draft′) *v.* draft again or anew. *—n.* a second draft.

re·dress (*v.* ri dres′; *n.* rē′dres or ri dres′) *v.* **1** set right; repair; remedy. **2** adjust evenly again. *—n.* a setting right; reparation; relief: *Any man deserves redress if he has been wronged.* [< F *redresser* < *re-* again + *dresser* straighten, arrange]

Red River cart *Cdn.* formerly, a strong, two-wheeled cart pulled by oxen or horses. Red River carts were much used during pioneer days in the West.

A Red River cart

Red River Settlement the colony that was founded on the Red River by Lord Selkirk in 1812. It was made up of Scottish and Irish settlers.

red·skin (red′skin′) *n.* a North American Indian.

red spruce 1 a medium-sized spruce tree having orange-brown twigs and yellow-green leaves, common in Nova Scotia, Prince Edward Island, New Brunswick, and S. Quebec. **2** the soft wood of this tree, used for pulpwood, construction, etc.

red squirrel the common North American squirrel, having reddish fur.

red·start (red′stärt′) *n.* **1** a fly-catching warbler of North America. **2** a small European bird having a reddish tail. [< *red* + *start* tail]

red tape 1 tape having a red color, used for tying up official papers. 2 unnecessarily involved procedures that result in excessive delays, irritation, etc. in dealing with documents, requests, and other business.

red·top (red′top′) *n.* a kind of grass grown for forage and pasture.

re·duce (ri dūs′ or ri düs′) *v.* **-duced, -duc·ing.** 1 make less; make smaller; decrease: *reduce expenses, reduce one's weight.* 2 become less; be made less; become less in weight: *His doctor advised him to reduce.* 3 make lower in degree, intensity, etc.; weaken; dilute. 4 bring down; lower: *Misfortune reduced that poor woman to begging.* 5 bring to a certain state, form, or condition; change: *The teacher soon reduced the noisy class to order.* 6 change to another form: *reduce a statement to writing. If you reduce 3 lb. 7 oz. to ounces, you have 55 ounces.* 7 conquer; subdue: *The army reduced the fort by a sudden attack.* 8 restore to its proper place or normal condition. A doctor can reduce a fracture or dislocation. 9 in chemistry: **a** combine with hydrogen. **b** remove oxygen from. **c** change (a compound) so that the valence of the positive element is lower. 10 in mathematics, simplify (an expression, formula, etc.). 11 smelt: *reduce the ores of silver or copper.* [< L *reducere* < *re-* back + *ducere* bring] —**Syn. 1** lessen, diminish. **3** humble, debase, degrade.

re·duc·er (ri dūs′ər or ri düs′ər) *n.* 1 one that reduces. 2 a threaded cylindrical piece for connecting pipes of different sizes.

re·duc·i·ble (ri dūs′ə bəl or ri düs′ə bəl) *adj.* that can be reduced: *4/8 is reducible to 1/2.*

reducing agent in chemistry, any substance that reduces or removes the oxygen in a compound.

re·duc·ti·o ad ab·sur·dum (ri duk′tē ō or ri duk′shē ō ad′ab sėr′dəm) *Latin.* a reduction to absurdity; a method of proving something false by showing that conclusions to which it leads are absurd.

re·duc·tion (ri duk′shən) *n.* 1 a reducing or being reduced. 2 the amount by which a thing is reduced: *The reduction in cost was $5.* 3 a form of something produced by reducing; copy of something on a smaller scale. 4 in chemistry, a reaction in which each of the atoms affected gains one or more electrons. The atom or group of atoms that lose electrons becomes oxidized. [< L *reductio, -onis* < *reducere.* See REDUCE.]

re·dun·dance (ri dun′dəns) *n.* redundancy.

re·dun·dan·cy (ri dun′dən sē) *n.* **-cies.** 1 more than is needed. 2 a redundant thing, part, or amount. 3 the use of too many words for the same idea.

re·dun·dant (ri dun′dənt) *adj.* 1 extra; not needed. 2 that says the same thing again; using too many words for the same idea; wordy: "*We two both had an apple each*" *is a redundant sentence.* [< L *redundans, -antis,* ppr. of *redundare.* See REDOUND.] —**re·dun′dant·ly,** *adv.*

re·du·pli·cate (*v.* ri dū′plə kāt′ or ri dü′plə kāt′; *adj.* ri dū′plə kit or ri dü′plə kit) *v.* **-cat·ed, -cat·ing,** *adj.* —*v.* double; repeat. —*adj.* doubled or repeated. [< L *reduplicare* < *re-* again + *duplicare* double < *duplex, duplicis* double]

re·du·pli·ca·tion (ri dū′plə kā′shən or ri dü′plə kā′shən) *n.* 1 a reduplicating or being reduplicated; doubling; repetition. 2 something resulting from repeating; a duplicate; copy: *To the prisoner each day seemed a reduplication of the preceding day.*

re·du·pli·ca·tive (ri dū′plə kə tiv or ri dū′plə kā′tiv, ri dü′plə kə tiv or ri dü′plə kā′tiv) *adj.* tending to reduplicate; having to do with or marked by reduplication.

red·wing (red′wing′) *n.* 1 a North American blackbird, the male of which has a scarlet patch on each wing. 2 a European thrush that has reddish color on the under side of the wings.

red-winged blackbird redwing (def. 1).

red·wood (red′wůd′) *n.* 1 an evergreen tree of the western United States that sometimes grows to a height of 300 feet; a sequoia. 2 its brownish-red wood. 3 **a** any of various trees having reddish wood or yielding a red dye. **b** the wood of these trees.

re-echo (rē ek′ō) *v.* **-ech·oed, -ech·o·ing,** *n.* **-ech·oes.** —*v.* echo back. —*n.* the echo of an echo.

reed (rēd) *n.* 1 a kind of tall grass that grows in wet places and has a hollow, jointed stalk. 2 such stalks. 3 a thing made from the stalk of a reed or anything like it. 4 a thin piece of wood or metal in a musical instrument that produces sound when a current of air moves it. 5 a reed instrument. —*adj.* producing tones by means of reeds: *a reed organ.* [OE *hrēod*]

reed·bird (rēd′bėrd′) *n.* bobolink.

reed instrument a musical instrument, the sounds of which are produced by the vibrations of a thin piece of wood or metal. Oboes, clarinets, and saxophones are reed instruments.

reed organ an organ producing tones by means of small metal reeds. Two common forms are the harmonium, in which the air is forced outward through the reeds, and the American organ, in which the air is sucked inward.

reed·y (rēd′ē) *adj.* **reed·i·er, reed·i·est.** 1 full of reeds. 2 made of a reed or reeds. 3 like a reed or reeds. 4 sounding like a reed instrument: *a thin, reedy voice.* —**reed′i·ness,** *n.*

reef[1] (rēf) *n.* 1 a narrow ridge of rocks or sand at or near the surface of the water: *The ship was wrecked on a hidden reef.* 2 a vein or lode in mining. [ult. < ON *rif*]

reef[2] (rēf) *n.* the part of a sail that can be rolled or folded up to reduce its size. —*v.* 1 reduce the size of (a sail) by rolling or folding up a part of it. 2 reduce the length of (a topmast, bowsprit, etc.) by lowering, etc. [ME < ON *rif* rib, reef. Cf. REEF[1].]

A reefed sail

reef·er[1] (rēf′ər) *n.* 1 a person who reefs. 2 a short coat of thick cloth, worn especially by sailors and fishermen. 3 a full-length, usually double-breasted, coat. [< *reef*[2]]

reef·er[2] (rēf′ər) *n. Slang.* a cigarette containing marijuana. [? < *reef*[2], since such cigarettes are rolled by hand]

reef knot square knot. See **knot** for diagram.

reek (rēk) *n.* 1 a strong, unpleasant smell; vapor. 2 the condition of reeking: *in a reek of a sweat.* —*v.* 1 send out vapor or a strong, unpleasant smell. 2 be wet with sweat or blood. 3 be filled with something unpleasant or offensive: *a government reeking with corruption.* 4 give out strongly or unmistakably: *His manner reeks arrogance.* [OE *rēc*]

reel[1] (rēl) *n.* 1 a frame turning on an axis, for winding thread, yarn, a fish line, rope, wire, etc. 2 a spool; roller. 3 something wound on a reel: *two reels of motion-picture film.* 4 a length of motion-picture film on a reel. 5 **off the reel,** *Informal.* quickly and easily. —*v.* 1 wind on a reel. 2 draw with a reel or by winding: *reel in a fish.* 3 **reel off,** say, write, or make in a quick, easy way. [OE *hrēol*]

reel[2] (rēl) *v.* 1 sway, swing, or rock under a blow, shock, etc. 2 sway in standing or walking. 3 be in a whirl; be dizzy. 4 go with swaying or staggering movements. 5 sway; stagger; waver: *Our regiment reeled when the cavalry attacked it.* —*n.* a reeling or staggering movement. [special use of *reel*[1]]

Syn. *v.* **2 Reel, stagger** = stand or move unsteadily. **Reel** particularly suggests dizziness and unsteadiness, a swaying on one's feet and danger of toppling over at any moment: *Sick and faint, he reeled when he tried to cross the room.* **Stagger** particularly suggests being unable to keep one's balance, reeling to one side and the other or walking in a zigzag way: *The boy staggered in with the wood.*

reel[3] (rēl) *n.* 1 a lively dance. Two kinds are the Highland reel and the Virginia reel. 2 the music for a reel. [special use of *reel*[2]]

re-en·try (rē en′trē) *n.* **-tries.** an entering again or returning, especially of a missile or spaceship into the earth's atmosphere.

re-es·tab·lish or **re·ës·tab·lish** (rē′es tab′lish) *v.* establish again; restore. —**re′-es·tab′lish·ment** or **re′ës·tab′lish·ment,** *n.*

reeve[1] (rēv) *n.* 1 *Cdn.* in Ontario and the western provinces, the elected head of a rural municipal council; in Ontario, also the elected head of a village or township council. **2** formerly, a bailiff; steward; overseer. [OE *(ge)rēfa*]

reeve[2] (rēv) *v.* **reeved** or **rove, reev·ing. 1** pass (a rope) through a hole, ring, etc. **2** fasten by placing through or around something. [? < Du. *reven* reef a sail]

reeve·ship (rēv′ship′) *n.* the office or position of reeve.

ref. 1 referee. **2** reference. **3** referred. **4** reformation. **5** refund.

re·face (rē fās′) *v.* **-faced, -fac·ing. 1** mend or repair the face or surface of stone, walls, etc. **2** replace the facing in a garment.

re·fec·tion (ri fek′shən) *n.* **1** refreshment by food or drink. **2** a meal; repast. [< L *refectio, -onis* < *reficere.* See REFECTORY.]

re·fec·to·ry (ri fek′tə rē) *n.* **-ries.** a room for meals, especially in a monastery, convent, or school. [< LL *refectorium,* ult. < L *reficere* refresh < *re-* again + *facere* make]

re·fer (ri fėr′) *v.* **-ferred, -fer·ring. 1** direct attention: *The article often refers us to the dictionary.* **2** relate; apply: *The rule refers only to special cases.* **3** send or direct for information, help, or action: *We referred him to the boss.* **4** turn for information or help: *Writers often refer to a dictionary.* **5** hand over; submit: *Let's refer the dispute to the umpire.* **6** consider as belonging or due; assign: *Many people refer their failures to bad luck instead of to poor work.* [< L *referre* < *re-* back + *ferre* take]

Syn. 1 Refer, allude = speak of something in a way to turn attention to it. **Refer** = make direct and specific mention. **Allude** = mention incidentally or call attention indirectly: *She never referred to the incident, but often alluded to it by hinting.*

ref·er·ee (ref′ər ē′) *n. v.* **-eed, -ee·ing.** —*n.* **1** a judge of play in certain games and sports including hockey, football, and boxing. **2** a person to whom something is referred for decision or settlement. —*v.* act as referee; act as referee in.

ref·er·ence (ref′ər əns) *n.* **1** a referring or being referred. **2** a directing of attention: *This history contains many references to larger histories.* **3** a statement, book, etc. to which attention is directed: *You will find that reference on page 16.* **4** something used for information or help: *A dictionary is a book of reference.* **5** a person who can give information about another person's character or ability. **6** a statement about someone's character or ability: *The boy had excellent references from men for whom he had worked.* **7** relation; respect; regard: *This test is to be taken by all pupils without reference to age or grade.* **8 in** or **with reference to,** about; concerning. **9 make reference to,** mention. —*adj.* used for information or help: *a reference library.*

ref·er·end (ref′ər ənd) *n.* a person or object referred to; referent.

ref·er·en·dum (ref′ər en′dəm) *n.* **-dums, -da** (-də). **1** the process of submitting a law already passed by the law-making body to a direct vote of the citizens for approval or rejection. British Columbia and Alberta have provision for a referendum. **2** the submitting of any matter to a direct vote. [< L *referendum* that which must be referred < *referre.* See REFER.]

ref·er·ent (ref′ər ənt) *n.* **1** a person who is consulted. **2** an idea, person, or thing to which reference is made in an example, statement, etc. —*adj.* containing a reference; referring.

re·fer·ral (ri fer′əl) *n.* **1** a referring or directing to a specific person, place, or group. **2** the person thus referred to.

re·fill (*v.* rē fil′; *n.* rē′fil′) *v.* fill again. —*n.* something to refill a thing. —**re·fill′a·ble,** *adj.*

re·fine (ri fīn′) *v.* **-fined, -fin·ing. 1** make free from impurities. Sugar, oil, and metals are refined before being used. **2** make or become fine, polished, or cultivated. **3** change or remove by polishing, purifying, etc. **4** make very fine, subtle, or exact. **5 refine on** or **upon, a** improve. **b** excel. [< *re-* + *fine* make fine] —**re·fin′er,** *n.*

re·fined (ri fīnd′) *adj.* **1** freed from impurities: *refined sugar.* **2** freed or free from grossness, coarseness, crudeness, vulgarity, etc. **3** having or showing nice feeling, taste, manners, etc.; well-bred. **4** fine; subtle: *refined distinctions.* **5** minutely precise: *refined measurements.* —**Syn. 2** polished, cultured.

hat, āge, cãre, fär; let, ēqual, tėrm; it, īce
hot, ōpen, ôrder; oil, out; cup, půt, rüle, ūse
əbove, takən, pencəl, lemən, circəs
ch, child; ng, long; sh, ship
th, thin; ᴛʜ, then; zh, measure

re·fine·ment (ri fīn′mənt) *n.* **1** fineness of feeling, taste, manners, or language. **2** the act or result of refining. **3** an improvement. **4** a fine point; subtle distinction. **5** an improved, higher, or extreme form of something.

re·fin·er·y (ri fīn′ər ē or ri fīn′rē) *n.* **-er·ies.** an industrial plant for purifying metal, sugar, petroleum, etc.

re·fit (*v.* rē fit′; *n.* rē′fit) *v.* **-fit·ted, -fit·ting,** *n.* —*n.* **1** fit, prepare, or equip for use again: *refit an old ship.* **2** get fresh supplies. —*n.* a fitting, preparing, or equipping for use again: *The ship went to the drydock for a refit.*

re·flect (ri flekt′) *v.* **1** turn back or throw back (light, heat, sound, etc.): *The sidewalks reflect heat on a hot day.* **2** give back an image; give back a likeness or image of: *A mirror reflects your face and body.* **3** reproduce or show like a mirror: *The newspaper reflected the owner's opinions.* **4** think; think carefully: *Take time to reflect before doing important things.* **5** cast blame, reproach, or discredit: *Bad behavior reflects on home training.* **6** serve to cast or bring: *A brave act reflects credit on the person who performs it.* [< L *reflectere* < *re-* back + *flectere* bend] —**Syn. 4** meditate, ponder, deliberate. See **think.**

re·flec·tion (ri flek′shən) *n.* **1** a reflecting or being reflected. **2** something reflected. **3** a likeness; image: *You can see your reflection in a mirror.* **4** thinking; careful thinking: *On reflection, the plan seemed too dangerous.* **5** an idea or remark resulting from careful thinking; idea; remark. **6** a remark, action, etc. that casts blame or discredit. **7** blame; discredit. **8** See **angle of reflection.**

re·flec·tive (ri flek′tiv) *adj.* **1** reflecting: *the reflective surface of polished metal.* **2** thoughtful: *a reflective look.* —**re·flec′tive·ly,** *adv.* —**re·flec′tive·ness,** *n.*

re·flec·tor (ri flek′tər) *n.* any thing, surface, or device that reflects light, heat, sound, etc., especially a piece of glass or metal, usually concave, for reflecting light in a required direction.

re·flex (*adj. n.* rē′fleks; *v.* ri fleks′) *adj.* **1** not voluntary; not controlled by the will; coming as a direct response to a stimulation of some sensory nerve cells. Sneezing is a reflex act. **2** bent back; turned back. **3** of an angle, more than 180 degrees and less than 360 degrees.
—*n.* **1** an involuntary action in direct response to a stimulation of some nerve cells. Sneezing, vomiting, and shivering are reflexes. **2** something reflected; an image; reflection: *A law should be a reflex of the will of the people.* —*v.* bend back; turn back. [< L *reflexus,* pp. of *reflectere.* See REFLECT.]

re·flex·ive (ri flek′siv) in grammar: —*adj.* indicating that an action turns back on the subject. —*n.* a reflexive verb or pronoun. *Example:* In "The boy hurt himself," *hurt* and *himself* are reflexives. —**re·flex′ive·ly,** *adv.*

☛ **reflexive pronouns.** Personal pronouns plus the suffix *-self* or *-selves* (*myself, yourself, himself,* etc.) are called *reflexive pronouns* when they appear in constructions such as: *He shaves himself. She bought herself two hats.* They are called reflexive because the action of the verb is directed toward the subject of the construction. The same words are called **intensive pronouns** when they serve to emphasize, as in *He himself did it.*

ref·lu·ent (ref′lü ənt) *adj.* flowing back; ebbing. [< L *refluens, -entis,* ppr. of *refluere* flow back < *re-* back + *fluere* flow]

re·flux (rē′fluks) *n.* a flowing back; the ebb of a tide. [< *re-* + *flux*]

re·for·est (rē fôr′ist) *v.* replant with trees.

re·for·est·a·tion (rē′fôr is tā′shən) *n.* a replanting or being replanted with trees.

re-form (rē fôrm′) *v.* **1** form again. **2** take a new shape.

re·form (ri fôrm′) *v.* **1** make better: *Prisons should try to reform criminals instead of just punishing them.* **2** improve by removing faults or abuses: *reform a city administration.* **3** become better: *The boy promised to reform if given another chance.* **4** crack and refine (petroleum, gas, etc.). —*n.* improvement, especially one made by removing faults or abuses; a change intended to be an improvement: *The new government put through many needed reforms.* [< L *reformare,* ult. < *re-* again + *forma* form] —**re·form′a·ble,** *adj.*

Re·form (ri fôrm′) *adj.* **1** of or having to do with the liberal branch of Judaism, as contrasted with the Orthodox and Conservative branches. **2** formerly, of or having to do with the Reform Party.

ref·or·ma·tion (ref′ər mā′shən) *n.* **1** a reforming or being reformed; change for the better; improvement. **2 Reformation,** the 16th-century religious movement in Europe that began with the aim of reforms in the Roman Catholic Church and ended with the establishment of certain Protestant churches.

re·form·a·tive (ri fôr′mə tiv) *adj.* tending toward or inducing reform.

re·form·a·to·ry (ri fôr′mə tô′rē) *adj. n.* **-ries.** —*adj.* serving to reform; intended to reform. —*n.* an institution for reforming young offenders against the laws; a prison for young criminals.

Re·formed (ri fôrmd′) *adj.* of or having to do with the Protestant churches, especially the Calvinistic as distinguished from the Lutheran.

re·form·er (ri fôr′mər) *n.* a person who reforms, or tries to reform, some state of affairs, custom, etc.; a supporter of reforms.

Reform Party in the 19th century, the party that opposed Tory rule in Upper Canada and the Maritimes. Joseph Howe was a prominent leader of this party.

reform school reformatory.

re·fract (ri frakt′) *v.* bend (a ray) from a straight course. Water refracts light. See **angle of refraction** for diagram. [< L *refractus,* pp. of *refringere* break up < *re-* back + *frangere* break]

refracting telescope a telescope having one lens that bends light rays to a focus and a second lens that acts as an eyepiece.

re·frac·tion (ri frak′shən) *n.* **1** the turning or bending of a ray of light when it passes obliquely from one medium into another of different density. See **angle of refraction** for diagram. **2** the turning or bending of sound waves, a stream of electrons, etc. when passing from one medium to another of different density.

re·frac·tive (ri frak′tiv) *adj.* refracting; having power to refract; having to do with refraction; caused by refraction. —**re·fract′ive·ly,** *adv.* —**re·fract′ive·ness,** *n.*

re·frac·tor (ri frak′tər) *n.* **1** anything that refracts. **2** a refracting telescope.

re·frac·to·ry (ri frak′tə rē) *adj.* **1** hard to manage; stubborn; obstinate: *Mules are refractory.* **2** not yielding readily to treatment: *He had a refractory cough.* **3** hard to melt, reduce, or work. Some ores are more refractory than others. —*n.* **1** an ore, cement, ceramic material, or similar substance that is hard to melt, reduce, or work. **2** a brick made of refractory material, used for lining furnaces, etc. —**re·frac′to·ri·ly,** *adv.* —**re·frac′to·ri·ness,** *n.*

re·frain[1] (ri frān′) *v.* hold oneself back: *Refrain from crime.* [ME < OF < L *refrenare* < *re-* back + *frenum* bridle]

Syn. Refrain, abstain = keep oneself from (doing) something. **Refrain** emphasizes checking an impulse, and means voluntarily not doing something one feels for a moment like doing or thinks he would like: *He politely refrained from saying what he thought of her hat.* **Abstain** emphasizes holding oneself back by force of will, and means deliberately doing without something one really wants or believes harmful or wrong, especially certain pleasures, food, drink, etc.: *He is abstaining from alcohol.*

re·frain[2] (ri frān′) *n.* **1** a phrase or verse repeated regularly in a song or poem; chorus. **2** the music for a refrain. [ME < OF *refrain,* ult. < VL *refrangere* break off, for L *refringere.* See REFRACT.]

re·fran·gi·bil·i·ty (ri fran′jə bil′ə tē) *n.* **1** the property of being refrangible. **2** the amount of refraction (of light rays, etc.) that is possible.

re·fran·gi·ble (ri fran′jə bəl) *adj.* capable of being refracted: *Rays of light are refrangible.* [< *re-* + L *frangere* to break] —**re·fran′gi·ble·ness,** *n.*

re·fresh (ri fresh′) *v.* make fresh again; renew: *He refreshed his memory by a glance at the book. She refreshed herself with a cup of tea.* [ME < OF *refrescher* < *re-* again + *fresche* fresh < Gmc.] —**Syn.** freshen, renovate, revive, enliven.

re·fresh·er (ri fresh′ər) *adj.* helping to renew knowledge or abilities, or to bring a person needed new knowledge. —*n.* a person or thing that refreshes.

re·fresh·ing (ri fresh′ing) *adj.* **1** that refreshes. **2** welcome as a pleasing change. —**re·fresh′ing·ly,** *adv.*

re·fresh·ment (ri fresh′mənt) *n.* **1** a refreshing or being refreshed. **2** anything that refreshes. **3 refreshments,** *pl.* food or drink: *serve refreshments at a party.*

re·frig·er·ant (ri frij′ər ənt) *adj.* **1** refrigerating; cooling. **2** reducing bodily heat or fever. —*n.* something that cools, etc. Ice is a refrigerant.

re·frig·er·ate (ri frij′ər āt′) *v.* **-at·ed, -at·ing.** make or keep cold or cool. [ult. < L *refrigerare,* ult. < *re-* again + *frigus, -goris* cold]

re·frig·er·a·tion (ri frij′ər ā′shən) *n.* the act or process of cooling or keeping cold.

re·frig·er·a·tor (ri frij′ər ā′tər) *n.* a cabinet, room, etc. for keeping foods, etc. cool. Modern refrigerators usually are run by electricity or gas.

reft (reft) *v.* pt. and pp. of **reave.** deprived by force.

re·fu·el (rē fū′əl) *v.* **-elled** or **-eled, -el·ling** or **-el·ing.** **1** supply with fuel again. **2** take on a fresh supply of fuel.

ref·uge (ref′ūj) *n.* **1** a shelter or protection from danger, trouble, etc. **2** a resort, shift, or expedient in any emergency. [ME < OF < L *refugium* < *re-* back + *fugere* flee] —**Syn. 1** safety, security.

ref·u·gee (ref′yů jē′ or ref′yů jē′) *n.* a person who flees for refuge or safety, especially to a foreign country, in time of persecution, war, etc. [< F *réfugié*]

re·ful·gence (ri ful′jəns) *n.* radiance; brightness.

re·ful·gent (ri ful′jənt) *adj.* shining brightly; radiant; splendid: *a refulgent sunrise.* [< L *refulgens, -entis,* ppr. of *refulgere* < *re-* back + *fulgere* shine] —**re·ful′gent·ly,** *adv.*

re·fund[1] (*v.* ri fund′; *n.* rē′fund) *v.* pay back: *If these shoes do not wear well, the shop will refund your money.* —*n.* **1** the return of money paid. **2** the money paid back. [< L *refundere* < *re-* back + *fundere* pour] —**re·fund′er,** *n.*

re·fund[2] (rē′fund′) *v.* change (a debt, loan, etc.) into a new form. [< *re-* + *fund*]

re·fur·bish (rē fėr′bish) *v.* polish up again; do up anew; brighten; renovate.

re·fus·al (ri fūz′əl) *n.* **1** the act of refusing: *His refusal to play the game provoked the other boys.* **2** the right to refuse or take a thing before it is offered to others: *Give me the refusal of the car till tomorrow.* —**Syn. 1** denial, dissent.

re·fuse[1] (ri fūz′) *v.* **-fused, -fus·ing.** **1** decline to accept; reject: *refuse an offer.* **2** deny (a request, demand, invitation); decline to give or grant: *refuse admittance.* **3** decline (to do something): *refuse to discuss the question.* **4** decline to accept or consent: *She is free to refuse.* [ME < OF *refuser* < L *refusus,* pp. of *refundere.* See REFUND[1].]

Syn. 1 Refuse, decline, reject = not accept something offered. **Refuse** is the blunt term, implying a direct and sometimes an ungracious denial: *He refused to go with me.* **Decline** is more polite, implying a reluctant rather than a direct denial: *He declined my invitation.* **Reject** is more emphatic than *refuse,* implying a very positive and brusque denial: *He rejected my riendly advice.*

ref·use[2] (ref′ūs) *n.* useless stuff; waste; rubbish. —*adj.* rejected as worthless or of little value; discarded. [ME, probably < OF *refuse,* pp. of *refuser.* See REFUSE[1].] —**Syn.** *n.* trash.

ref·u·ta·ble (ref′yů tə bəl or ri fū′tə bəl) *adj.* able to be refuted.

ref·u·ta·tion (ref′yů tā′shən) *n.* disproof of a claim, opinion, or argument.

re·fute (ri fūt′) *v.* **-fut·ed, -fut·ing.** prove (a claim, opinion, or argument) to be false or incorrect. [< L *refutare* < OL *re-* back + *futare* cause to fall] —**re·fut′er,** *n.*

hat, āge, cãre, fär; let, ēqual, tėrm; it, īce
hot, ōpen, ôrder; oil, out; cup, pu̇t, rüle, ūse
əbove, takən, pencəl, lemən, circəs
ch, child; ng, long; sh, ship
th, thin; ᴛʜ, then; zh, measure

reg. 1 register. 2 registered. 3 registrar. 4 registry. 5 regular. 6 regularly. 7 region.

re·gain (ri gān′) *v.* 1 get again; recover: *regain health.* 2 get back to; reach again: *regain the shore.*

re·gal (rē′ gəl) *adj.* 1 belonging to a monarch; royal. 2 kinglike; fit for a monarch; stately; splendid; magnificent. [ME < L *regalis* < *rex, regis* king. Doublet of ROYAL, REAL², RIAL.] **—re′gal·ly,** *adv.* **—Syn. 1** See **royal.**

re·gale¹ (ri gāl′) *v.* **-galed, -gal·ing. 1** entertain agreeably; delight with something pleasing: *The old sailor regaled the boys with sea stories.* 2 entertain with a choice repast; feast. [< F *régaler*, ult. < MDu. *wale* wealth] **—re·gale′ment,** *n.* **—re·gal′er,** *n.*

re·gale² (ri gāl′) *n. Cdn.* formerly: 1 an extra ration, especially of liquor, given to the employees of a fur company for a festive occasion such as Christmas. 2 a party, celebration, etc. held on such an occasion. 3 a ration of liquor given to boatmen at the start or finish of an arduous journey. [< Cdn.F < MF *régale* pleasure, festivity]

re·ga·li·a (ri gā′ lē ə or ri gāl′yə) *n.pl.* 1 the emblems of royalty. Crowns, sceptres, etc. are regalia. 2 the emblems or decorations of any society, order, etc. 3 clothes, especially fine clothes: *in party regalia.* [< L *regalia* royal things, neut. pl. of *regalis.* See REGAL.]

re·gal·i·ty (rē gal′ə tē) *n.* **-ties. 1** royalty; sovereignty; kingship. 2 a right or privilege having to do with a king. 3 a kingdom.

re·gard (ri gärd′) *v.* 1 consider; think of: *He is regarded as the best doctor in town.* 2 show thought or consideration for; care for; respect: *She always regards her parents' wishes.* 3 heed: *None regarded her screams.* 4 look at; look closely at; watch: *He regarded me sternly.* 5 look closely. 6 **as regards,** as for; concerning; relating to: *As regards money, I have enough.*
—n. 1 consideration; thought; care: *Have regard for the feelings of others.* 2 a look; steady look. 3 esteem; favor; good opinion. 4 **regards,** *pl.* good wishes; an expression of esteem. 5 a point; particular matter. 6 **in regard to,** about; concerning; relating to. 7 **without regard to,** not considering. 8 **with regard to,** about; concerning; relating to. [< F *regarder* < *re-* back + *garder* guard] **—Syn.** *v.* 1 deem, hold. 2 esteem. *–n.* 1 See **respect.**

re·gard·ful (ri gärd′fəl) *adj.* 1 heedful; observant; mindful. 2 considerate; respectful. **—re·gard′ful·ly,** *adv.*

re·gard·ing (ri gär′ding) *prep.* with regard to; concerning; about: *a prophecy regarding the future.*

re·gard·less (ri gärd′lis) *adj. adv.* with no heed; careless. **—re·gard′less·ly,** *adv.* **—re·gard′less·ness,** *n.*

re·gat·ta (ri gat′ə) *n.* 1 a boat race. 2 a series of boat races: *the annual regatta of the yacht club.* [< dial. Ital.]

re·gen·cy (rē′jən sē) *n.* **-cies. 1** the position, office, or function of a regent or group of regents: *The Queen Mother held the regency till the young king became of age.* 2 a body of regents. 3 a government consisting of regents. 4 the time during which there is a regency. 5 **Regency, a** in Great Britain, the period from 1811 to 1820 during which George, Prince of Wales, acted as regent for King George III. **b** in architecture and furniture, a style characterized by graceful, elegant lines, developed in England during the Regency. **c** in France, the period from 1715 to 1723 during which Philip, Duke of Orleans, acted as regent for King Louis XV.

re·gen·er·a·cy (ri jen′ər ə sē) *n.* a regenerate state.

re·gen·er·ate (*v.* ri jen′ər āt′; *adj.* ri jen′ər it) *v.* **-at·ed, -at·ing,** *adj.* *—v.* 1 give a new and better spiritual life to. 2 improve the moral condition of; put new life and spirit into. 3 reform. 4 grow again; form (new tissue, a new part, etc.) to replace what is lost. If a young crab loses a claw, it can regenerate a new one. 5 in physics, cause (a substance) to return intermittently to its original state or condition. 6 in electronics, increase the amplification of, by transferring a portion of the power from the output circuit to the input circuit.
—adj. 1 born again spiritually. 2 made over in better form; formed anew morally. [< L *regenerare* make over, ult. < *re-* again + *genus, -neris* birth] **—re·gen′er·a′tor,** *n.*

re·gen·er·a·tion (ri jen′ər ā′shən) *n.* a regenerating or being regenerated.

re·gen·er·a·tive (ri jen′ər ə tiv or ri jen′ər ā′tiv) *adj.* regenerating; tending to regenerate. **—re·gen′er·a′tive·ly,** *adv.*

re·gent (rē′jənt) *n.* 1 a person who rules in place of a sovereign who is absent or unfit: *The Queen will be the regent till her son grows up.* 2 a member of a governing board. Many universities have boards of regents. *—adj.* acting as a regent. [< L *regens, -entis,* ppr. of *regere* rule]

re·gent·ship (rē′jənt ship′) *n.* the position of a regent.

reg·i·cide¹ (rej′ə sīd′) *n.* the crime of killing a monarch. [< L *rex, regis* + E *-cide¹*]

reg·i·cide² (rej′ə sīd′) *n.* a person who kills a monarch. [< L *rex, regis* + E *-cide²*]

re·gime or **ré·gime** (ri zhēm′; *French,* rā zhēm′) *n.* 1 a system of government or rule. 2 a prevailing system; a regular pattern of action, behavior, etc. 3 a system of living; regimen. [< F < L *regimen.* Doublet of REGIMEN.]

reg·i·men (rej′ə mən or rej′ə men′) *n.* 1 a set of rules or habits of diet, exercise, or manner of living intended to improve health, reduce weight, etc. 2 the act of governing; government; rule. 3 in grammar, the influence of one word in determining the case or mood of another; government. [< L *regimen* < *regere* rule. Doublet of REGIME.]

reg·i·ment (*n.* rej′ə mənt; *v.* rej′ə ment′) *n.* 1 in the army, a unit consisting of several companies of soldiers organized into one large group, usually commanded by a colonel. A regiment is larger than a battalion and smaller than a brigade. 2 a large number.
—v. 1 form into a regiment or organized group. 2 assign to a regiment or group. 3 treat in a strict or uniform manner. A totalitarian state regiments its citizens. [< LL *regimentum* rule < L *regere* to rule]

reg·i·men·tal (rej′ə men′təl) *adj.* of a regiment; having to do with a regiment. *—n.* **regimentals,** *pl.* military uniform. **—reg′i·men′tal·ly,** *adv.*

reg·i·men·ta·tion (rej′ə men tā′shən) *n.* 1 a formation into organized or uniform groups. 2 a making uniform. 3 a subjection to control. In time of war there may be regimentation of our work, play, food, and clothing.

re·gion (rē′jən) *n.* 1 any large part of the earth's surface: *the region of the equator.* 2 a place; space; area: *an unhealthful region.* 3 a part of the body: *the region of the heart.* 4 a sphere; domain: *the region of art, the region of imagination.* [< L *regio, -onis* direction < *regere* direct]

re·gion·al (rē′jən əl) *adj.* of or in a particular region: *a regional storm.* **—re′gion·al·ly,** *adv.*

reg·is·ter (rej′is tər) *n.* 1 a list; record: *A register of attendance is kept in our school.* 2 a book in which a list or record is kept: *a hotel register.* 3 anything that records. A cash register shows the amount of money taken in. 4 a registration or registry. 5 a registrar. 6 an opening in a wall or floor with an arrangement to regulate the amount of air or heat that passes through. 7 the range of a voice or an instrument. 8 the set of pipes of an organ stop. 9 in printing, the exact fit or correspondence of lines, columns, colors, etc. 10 the exact adjustment of the focus in a camera. 11 a customs document declaring the nationality of a ship.
—v. 1 write in a list or record: *register the names of the new members.* 2 have one's name written in a list or record: *A person must register before he can vote.* 3 indicate; record: *The thermometer registers 90 degrees.* 4 show (surprise, joy, anger, etc.) by the expression on one's face or by actions. 5 have (a letter, parcel, etc.) recorded in a post office, paying extra postage for special care in delivery. 6 in printing: **a** make (lines, columns, colors, etc.) fit or correspond exactly. **b** fit or correspond exactly. [ME < Med.L *registrum* < L *regestrum,* neut. pp. of *regerere* record < *re-* back + *gerere* carry]

reg·is·tra·ble (rej′is trə bəl) *adj.* that can be registered.

reg·is·trar (rej′is trär′) *n.* **1** an official who keeps a register; an official recorder. **2** in some universities, colleges, etc., the officer in charge of admissions, examinations, and general regulations. [var. of *registrer* < *register*]

reg·is·tra·tion (rej′is trā′shən) *n.* **1** the act of registering. **2** an entry in a register. **3** the number of people registered.

reg·is·try (rej′is trē) *n.* **-tries. 1** a registering; registration. **2** a place where a register is kept; an office of registration. **3** a book in which a list or record is kept.

reg·nant (reg′nənt) *adj.* **1** ruling. **2** exercising sway or influence; predominant. **3** prevalent; widespread. [< L *regnans, -antis,* ppr. of *regnare* rule < *regnum* kingdom]

re·gress (*v.* ri gres′; *n.* rē′gres) *v.* **1** go back; move in a backward direction. **2** return to an earlier or less advanced state. —*n.* a going back; movement backward. [< L *regressus,* pp. of *regredi* < *re-* back + *gradi* go] —**re·gres′sor,** *n.*

re·gres·sion (ri gresh′ən) *n.* **1** the act of going back; backward movement. **2** in psychology, a way of trying to escape difficult problems by casting off responsibility and assuming other characteristics of childhood. **3** in biology, the reversion of offspring toward a more average condition. **4** in statistics, the tendency of one variable that is correlated with another to revert to the general type and not to equal the amount of deviation of the second variable.

re·gret (ri gret′) *n. v.* **-gret·ted, -gret·ting.** —*n.* **1** the feeling of being sorry; sorrow; sense of loss. **2 regrets,** *pl.* a polite reply declining an invitation. —*v.* **1** feel regret about. **2** feel sorry; mourn. [ME < OF *regreter* < Gmc.; cf. ON *gráta* weep] —**re·gret′ter,** *n.*

Syn. *n.* **1 Regret, remorse** = a feeling of sorrow for a fault or wrongdoing. **Regret** suggests a troubled mind and a feeling of being dissatisfied and sorry about something one has or has not done, sometimes something one could not help, and of wishing one had acted differently: *With regret he remembered his forgotten promise.* **Remorse** suggests the mental torment of a gnawing conscience and deep sorrow for a wrong that can never be undone: *The boy was filled with remorse for the worry he had caused his mother.*

re·gret·ful (ri gret′fəl) *adj.* feeling or expressing regret. —**re·gret′ful·ly,** *adv.* —**re·gret′ful·ness,** *n.*

re·gret·ta·ble (ri gret′ə bəl) *adj.* that should be or is regretted. —**re·gret′ta·bly,** *adv.*

Regt. 1 regiment. **2** regent.

reg·u·lar (reg′yů lər) *adj.* **1** fixed by custom or rule; usual; normal: *Six o'clock was his regular hour of rising.* **2** following some rule or principle; according to rule: *A period is the regular ending for a sentence.* **3** coming, acting, or done again and again at the same time: *Saturday is a regular holiday.* **4** steady; habitual: *A regular customer is one who shops frequently at the same store.* **5** even in size, spacing, or speed; well-balanced: *regular features, regular teeth.* **6** symmetrical. **7** having all its angles equal and all its sides equal. **8** in botany, having all the same parts of a flower alike in shape and size. **9** orderly; methodical: *lead a regular life.* **10** properly fitted or trained: *The maid did the cooking while the regular cook was sick.* **11** in grammar, having the usual changes of form to show tense, number, person, etc. **12** *Informal.* a thorough; complete: *a regular bore.* b fine; agreeable; all right: *He's a regular fellow.* **13** permanently organized. The regular army is under the direct control of the federal government. **14** of or belonging to the permanent armed services of a country. **15** belonging to a religious order bound by certain rules. The regular clergy live in religious communities.
—*n.* **1** a member of a regularly paid group of any kind: *The army was made up of regulars and volunteers.* **2** a person who makes the armed services a full-time career. **3** a person belonging to a religious order bound by certain rules. **4** a regular customer, contributor, etc. **5** in sports, a player on the regular team. [ME < OF < L *regularis* < *regula.* See RULE.] —**Syn.** *adj.* **1** typical, standard. **4** constant. See **steady.**

reg·u·lar·i·ty (reg′yů lar′ə tē) *n.* order; system; steadiness; the condition of being regular.

reg·u·lar·ly (reg′yů lər lē) *adv.* **1** in a regular manner. **2** at regular times.

reg·u·late (reg′yů lāt′) *v.* **-lat·ed, -lat·ing. 1** control by rule, principle, or system: *Good schools regulate the behavior of students.* **2** put in condition to work properly. **3** keep at some standard: *This instrument regulates the temperature of the room.* [< LL *regulare* < L *regula.* See RULE.]

reg·u·la·tion (reg′yů lā′shən) *n.* **1** control by rule, principle, or system. **2** a rule; law: *traffic regulations.* —*adj.* **1** according to or required by a regulation; standard: *Soldiers wear a regulation uniform.* **2** usual; ordinary.

reg·u·la·tive (reg′yů lə tiv or reg′yů lā′tiv) *adj.* regulating.

reg·u·la·tor (reg′yů lā′tər) *n.* **1** a person or thing that regulates. **2** a device in a clock or watch to make it go faster or slower. **3** a very accurate clock used as a standard of time.

reg·u·la·to·ry (reg′yů lə tô′rē) *adj.* regulating.

re·gur·gi·tate (rē gėr′jə tāt′) *v.* **-tat·ed, -tat·ing. 1** of liquids, gases, undigested foods, etc., rush, surge, or flow back. **2** throw up: *The baby regurgitated food from his stomach.* [< Med.L *regurgitare,* ult. < L *re-* back + *gurges, -gitis* whirlpool]

re·gur·gi·ta·tion (rē gėr′jə tā′shən) *n.* a regurgitating.

re·ha·bil·i·tate (rē′hə bil′ə tāt′) *v.* **-tat·ed, -tat·ing. 1** restore to a good condition; make over in a new form: *The old house is to be rehabilitated.* **2** restore to former standing, rank, rights, privileges, reputation, etc.: *The former criminal completely rehabilitated himself and was trusted and respected by all.* [< Med.L *rehabilitare,* ult. < L *re-* again + *habilis* fit] —**re′ha·bil′i·ta′tion,** *n.*

re·ha·bil·i·ta·tive (rē′hə bil′ə tə tiv or rē′hə bil′ə tā′tiv) *adj.* of or having to do with rehabilitation.

re·hash (*v.* rē hash′; *n.* rē′hash) *v.* deal with again; work up (old material) into a new form: *The question had been rehashed again and again.* —*n.* **1** a rehashing. **2** something old put into a different form: *That composition is simply a rehash of an article in the encyclopedia.*

re·hears·al (ri hėr′səl) *n.* **1** the act of rehearsing. **2** a performance beforehand for practice or drill.

re·hearse (ri hėrs′) *v.* **-hearsed, -hears·ing. 1** practise (a play, part, etc.) for a public performance. **2** drill or train (a person, etc.) by repetition. **3** tell in detail; repeat: *She rehearsed all the happenings of the day from beginning to end.* [ME < OF *rehercier* < *re-* again + *hercier* harrow, ult. < L *hirpex, hirpicis* rake] —**Syn. 3** narrate, relate, recount.

Reich (rīH) *n. German.* empire, a term applied to the Holy Roman Empire, 962-1806 (**First Reich**); the German Empire, 1871-1918 (**Second Reich**); and Germany under Adolf Hitler, 1933-1945 (**Third Reich**).

reichs·mark (rīHs′märk′) *n.* **-marks** or **-mark.** the unit of money of Germany from 1924 to 1948, originally worth about 40 cents. [< G]

Reichs·tag (rīHs′täk′) *n.* the former elective legislative assembly of the German Empire and Republic. It was established in 1871 but, under Hitler, gradually lost its powers.

reign (rān) *n.* **1** the period of power of a ruler: *Queen Victoria's reign lasted sixty-four years.* **2** the royal power; rule: *The reign of a wise ruler benefits his country.* **3** existence everywhere; prevalence. —*v.* **1** be a ruler: *A king reigns over his kingdom.* **2** exist everywhere; prevail: *On a still night silence reigns.* [ME < OF < L *regnum* < *regere* rule]

Reign of Terror in France, a period of the Revolution from about March, 1793, to July, 1794, during which thousands of people were executed.

re·im·burse (rē′im bėrs′) *v.* **-bursed, -burs·ing.** pay back: *His employer reimbursed him for his travelling expenses.* [< *re-* + obs. *imburse* < Med.L *imbursare* < L *in-* into + LL *bursa* purse; patterned on F *rembourser*] —**re′im·burse′ment,** *n.*

re·im·port (*v.* rē′im pôrt′; *n.* rē im′pôrt) *v.* import something previously exported: *Raw materials are sometimes exported from Canada and later reimported in* *the form of manufactured goods.* —*n.* a reimportation.

re·im·por·ta·tion (rē′im pôr tā′shən) *n.* **1** an importing of something previously exported. **2** the goods reimported.

rein (rān) *n.* **1** a long, narrow strap or line fastened to a bridle or bit, by which to guide and control an animal. A driver or rider of a horse holds the reins in his hands. See **harness** for diagram. **2** a means of control and direction: *taking the reins of government.* **3 draw rein, a** tighten the reins. **b** slow down; stop. **4 give rein to,** let move or act freely, without guidance or control. **5 keep a tight rein on,** keep under close supervision and control. —*v.* **1** check or pull with reins. **2** guide and control: *Rein your tongue.* **3 rein in** or **up,** cause to stop or to go slower. [ME < OF *rene,* ult. < L *retinere* hold back. See RETAIN.]

re·in·car·nate (rē′in kär′nāt) *v.* **-nat·ed, -nat·ing.** give a new body to (a soul).

re·in·car·na·tion (rē′in kär nā′shən) *n.* **1** a rebirth of the soul in a new body. **2** a new incarnation or embodiment.

rein·deer (rān′dēr′) *n.* **-deer.** a kind of large deer with branching horns, living in northern regions: *The caribou is a North American reindeer.* [ME < ON *hreindyri* < *hreinn* reindeer + *dýr* animal]

reindeer moss a gray, tufted, and branched lichen, the main source of winter food for reindeer, caribou, and musk-ox.

re·in·force (rē′in fôrs′) *v.* **-forced, -forc·ing.** **1** strengthen with new force or materials: *reinforce an army or a fleet, reinforce a garment with an extra thickness of cloth, reinforce a wall or a bridge.* **2** strengthen: *reinforce an argument, a plea, an effect, a stock, a supply, etc.* Also, **re-enforce, reënforce.** [< *re-* + *enforce*]

reinforced concrete concrete with metal embedded in it to make the structure stronger.

re·in·force·ment (rē′in fôrs′mənt) *n.* **1** the act of reinforcing. **2** the state of being reinforced. **3** something that reinforces. **4 reinforcements,** *pl.* extra men and equipment, especially additional troops, warships, military aircraft, etc. Also, **re-enforcement, reënforcement.**

re·in·state (rē′in stāt′) *v.* **-stat·ed, -stat·ing.** restore to a former position or condition; establish again. —**re′in·state′ment,** *n.*

re·in·sure (rē′in shür′) *v.* insure again; insure under a contract by which a first insurer relieves himself from the risk and transfers it to another insurer.

reis (rās) *n.pl.* a former Portuguese unit of money. Nine Portuguese reis or eighteen Brazilian reis were worth about one cent. [< Pg.]

re·it·er·ate (rē it′ər āt′) *v.* **-at·ed, -at·ing.** say or do several times; repeat (an action, demand, etc.) again and again: *The boy did not move, though the teacher reiterated her command.* [< L *reiterare,* ult. < *re-* again + *iterum* again] —**re·it′er·a′tion,** *n.* —**Syn.** See **repeat.**

re·ject (*v.* ri jekt′; *n.* rē′jekt) *v.* **1** refuse to take, use, believe, consider, grant, etc.: *He rejected our help. He tried to join the army but was rejected.* **2** throw away as useless or unsatisfactory: *Reject all apples with soft spots.* **3** vomit. —*n.* a rejected person or thing. [< L *rejectus,* pp. of *reicere, rejicere* < *re-* back + *jacere* throw] —**re·ject′er,** *n.* —**Syn.** *v.* **1** decline, rebuff, repulse. See **refuse.**

re·jec·tion (ri jek′shən) *n.* **1** a rejecting. **2** the state of being rejected. **3** the thing rejected.

re·joice (ri jois′) *v.* **-joiced, -joic·ing.** **1** be glad; be filled with joy. **2** make glad; fill with joy. [ME < OF *rejoiss-,* a stem of *rejoïr,* ult. < L *re-* again + *gaudere* be glad] —**re·joic′er,** *n.* —**Syn. 2** cheer, delight.

re·joic·ing (ri jois′ing) *n.* the feeling or expression of joy.

re·join[1] (rē join′) *v.* **1** join again; unite again. **2** join the company of (somebody) again. [< *re-* + *join*]

re·join[2] (ri join′) *v.* answer; reply. [< F *rejoindre* < *re-* back + *joindre* join]

re·join·der (ri join′dər) *n.* an answer to a reply; response. [< F *rejoindre,* infin. used as n.] —**Syn.** retort.

re·ju·ve·nate (ri jü′və nāt′) *v.* **-nat·ed, -nat·ing.** make young or vigorous again; give youthful qualities to. [< *re-* < L *juvenis* young] —**re·ju′ve·na′tion,** *n.* —**re·ju′ve·na′tor,** *n.*

hat, āge, cãre, fär; let, ēqual, tėrm; it, īce
hot, ōpen, ôrder; oil, out; cup, pu̇t, rüle, ūse
əbove, takən, pencəl, lemən, circəs
ch, child; ng, long; sh, ship
th, thin; ᴛʜ, then; zh, measure

rel. **1** relative. **2** relatively. **3** religion. **4** relating.

re-laid (rē lād′) *v.* pt. and pp. of **re-lay.**

re·lapse (ri laps′) *v.* **-lapsed, -laps·ing,** *n.* —*v.* fall or slip back into a former state, way of acting, etc.: *After one cry of surprise, she relapsed into silence.* —*n.* a falling or slipping back into a former state, way of acting, etc.: *He seemed to be getting over his illness but had a relapse.* [< L *relapsus,* pp. of *relabi* < *re-* back + *labi* slip]

re·late (ri lāt′) *v.* **-lat·ed, -lat·ing.** **1** give an account of; tell: *The traveller related his adventures.* **2** connect in thought or meaning: *"Better" and "best" are related to "good."* **3** be connected in any way: *We are interested in what relates to ourselves.* [< L *relatus,* pp. of *referre* < *re-* back + *ferre* bring] —**Syn. 1** recount, recite, narrate. **3** pertain.

re·lat·ed (ri lāt′id) *adj.* **1** connected. **2** belonging to the same family; connected by a common origin: *English and Dutch are closely related languages.* —**re·lat′ed·ness,** *n.* —**Syn. 2** allied, cognate, akin.

re·la·tion (ri lā′shən) *n.* **1** a connection in thought or meaning: *Your answer has no relation to the question.* **2** a connection between persons, groups, countries, etc.: *The relation of mother and child is the closest in the world.* **3** a person who belongs to the same family as another, such as father, brother, aunt, etc.; relative. **4** reference; regard: *We must plan with relation to the future.* **5** the act of telling; account: *We were amused by his relation of his adventures.* **6 in** or **with relation to,** about; concerning; having to do with. [< L *relatio, -onis* < *relatus.* See RELATE.] —**Syn. 2** alliance, relationship, affiliation.

re·la·tion·al (ri lā′shən əl) *adj.* **1** that relates. **2** having to do with relations.

re·la·tion·ship (ri lā′shən ship′) *n.* **1** a connection. **2** the condition of belonging to the same family.

rel·a·tive (rel′ə tiv) *n.* **1** a person who belongs to the same family as another, such as father, brother, aunt, etc. **2** a relative pronoun.
—*adj.* **1** related or compared to each other: *Before ordering our dinner, we considered the relative merits of fried chicken and roast beef.* **2 relative to, a** about; concerning: *a letter relative to my proposal.* **b** in proportion to: *He is strong relative to his size. This subject is little understood relative to its importance.* **3** depending for meaning on a relation to something else: *East is a relative term; for example, Regina is east of Vancouver but west of Toronto.* **4** in grammar, introducing a subordinate clause; referring to another person or thing. *Example*: In "The man who wanted it is gone," *who* is a relative pronoun, and *who wanted it* is a relative clause. [ME < LL *relativus* < L *relatus.* See RELATE.]

☛ **relative clauses.** A relative clause is an adjective clause introduced by a relative pronoun, *that, which,* or *who,* or a relative adverb, *where, when, why*: The ball *that had been lost* was found by the caddy. Mike's plane, *which was lost in the storm,* landed safely in a field. They asked for a student *who would volunteer to play Santa Claus.* That is the place *where he lived.* A relative clause usually stands immediately after the noun it modifies. In the first sentence above, the clause modifies *ball,* in the second *plane,* in the third *student,* and in the fourth *place.* In informal English the relative pronoun is, under certain conditions, often omitted, but it rarely is in formal English. Informal: The ring *he bought* was expensive. Formal: The ring *that he bought* was expensive. See also **restrictive clause.**

☛ **relative pronouns.** The relative pronouns are *that, which* (*of which, whose*), *who* (*whose, whom*), and *as.* They introduce dependent adjective clauses and refer to an antecedent in the main clause: A man *who* was there gave us the details. Our team, *which* scored first, had the advantage. We didn't take the same trail *that* (or *as*) they did. *Who* refers to persons; *which,* to animals or things; and *that,* to persons, animals, or things.

rel·a·tive·ly (rel′ə tiv lē) *adv.* **1** in a relative manner; in relation to something else; comparatively: *a relatively small difference.* **2** relative to.

rel·a·tiv·i·ty (rel′ə tiv′ə tē) *n.* **1** the state or quality of being relative. **2** in physics, the character of being relative rather than absolute, as ascribed to motion or velocity. 3 a theory formulated by Albert Einstein in the equation $E = mc^2$ (energy = mass × the square of the speed of light). The **special theory of relativity** is based on the hypothesis that the speed of light is the same when measured by two observers even though one observer is moving at a constant velocity with respect to the other. The **general theory of relativity** is an extension of the special theory to relate the measurements of observers who are accelerated with respect to each other.

re·la·tor (ri lā′tər) *n.* a person who relates or narrates. [< L]

re·lax (ri laks′) *v.* **1** loosen up; make or become less stiff or firm: *Relax your muscles to rest them.* **2** make or become less strict or severe; lessen in force: *Discipline is relaxed on the last day of school.* **3** relieve or be relieved from work or effort; give or take recreation or amusement: *Take a vacation and relax.* **4** weaken: *Don't relax your efforts because the examinations are over.* [ME < L *relaxare*, ult. < *re-* back + *laxus* loose. Doublet of RELEASE.] —**re·lax′er,** *n.*

re·lax·a·tion (rē′lak sā′shən) *n.* **1** a lessening of tension; loosening: *the relaxation of the muscles.* **2** a lessening of strictness, severity, force, etc.: *the relaxation of discipline.* **3** a relief from work or effort; recreation; amusement. **4** the state or condition of being relaxed.

re·lax·ed·ly (ri lak′sid lē) *adv.* in a relaxed manner.

re·lay (*n.* rē′lā; *v.* ri lā′ or rē′lā) *n.* **1** a fresh supply: *New relays of men were sent to the battle front.* **2 a** a relay race. **b** one part of a relay race. **c relays,** a meeting, or a part of a meeting, at which relay races are run. **3** the act of passing on a ball, puck, etc. from one player to another. **4** an electromagnetic device in which a weak current controls a stronger current. A relay is used in transmitting telegraph or telephone messages over long distances. **5** a device that extends or reinforces the action or effect of an apparatus. **6 a** one of several persons or groups taking on a job, mission, etc. in turn. **b** a system of working, sending messages, etc. by the use of several people or groups acting in turn.
—*v.* **1** take and carry farther: *Messengers will relay your message.* **2** transmit by an electrical relay. **3** receive and then pass to another: *relay a phone message, relay a thrown ball.* [ME < OF *relai* reserve pack of hounds, etc., ult. < *re-* back + *laier* leave < Gmc.]

re·lay (rē lā′) *v.* **-laid, -lay·ing.** lay again.

re·lay race (rē′lā) a race run by teams, the members of each team taking over from one another in succession.

re-lease (rē lēs′) *v.* **-leased, -leas·ing.** lease again.

re·lease (ri lēs′) *v.* **-leased, -leas·ing,** *n.* —*v.* **1** let go; let loose: *The prisoner was released.* **2** set free; relieve: *The nurse is released from duty at seven o'clock.* **3** give up (legal right, claim, etc.); make over to another (property, etc.). **4** permit to be published, shown, sold, etc.
—*n.* **1** a letting go; setting free. **2** freedom; relief. **3** a part that releases other parts of a machine. **4** in law: **a** the legal surrender of right, estate, etc. to another. **b** a document that accomplishes this. **5** an authorization for publication, exhibition, sale, etc. **6** an article, statement, etc. distributed for publication. [ME < OF *relaissier* < L *relaxare*. Doublet of RELAX.] —**re·leas′er,** *n.*
Syn. *v.* **1 Release, free** = set loose from something that holds back or keeps confined. **Release** emphasizes relaxing the hold on the person or thing and letting him go again: *He released the brakes of the truck.* **Free,** more general in meaning and application, emphasizes giving freedom by removing or unfastening whatever is holding: *He freed the bird from the cage.* **2** See **dismiss.**

rel·e·gate (rel′ə gāt′) *v.* **-gat·ed, -gat·ing. 1** send away, usually to a lower position or condition. **2** send into exile; banish. **3** hand over (a matter, task, etc.). [< L *relegare* < *re-* back + *legare* despatch < *legatus* having a commission < *lex, legis* law] —**rel′e·ga′tion,** *n.*

re·lent (ri lent′) *v.* become less strict; be more tender and merciful. [ult. < L *re-* again + *lentus* slow]

re·lent·less (ri lent′lis) *adj.* without pity; unyielding; harsh: *The storm raged with relentless fury.*
—**re·lent′less·ly,** *adv.* —**Syn.** ruthless, implacable.

rel·e·vance (rel′ə vəns) *n.* relevancy.

rel·e·van·cy (rel′ə vən sē) *n.* the condition or act of being relevant.

rel·e·vant (rel′ə vənt) *adj.* bearing upon or connected with the matter in hand; to the point: *relevant questions.* [< L *relevans, -antis* refreshing, ppr. of *relevare*, ult. < *re-* back + *levis* light] —**rel′e·vant·ly,** *adv.* —**Syn.** applicable, appropriate. See **pertinent.**

re·li·a·bil·i·ty (ri lī′ə bil′ə tē) *n.* the quality of being reliable; trustworthiness; dependability.

re·li·a·ble (ri lī′ə bəl) *adj.* worthy of trust; that can be depended on: *reliable sources of news.* —**re·li′a·bly,** *adv.*
Syn. Reliable, trustworthy = worthy of being depended on or trusted. **Reliable** = that the person or thing it describes can safely be believed or trusted, and counted on to do or be what is expected, wanted, or needed: *I have always found this to be a reliable brand of canned goods.* **Trustworthy,** usually describing a person, indicates that he is fully deserving of complete confidence in his truthfulness, honesty, good judgment, justice, etc.: *He is a trustworthy news commentator.*

re·li·ance (ri lī′əns) *n.* **1** trust; dependence: *A child has reliance on his mother.* **2** confidence.

re·li·ant (ri lī′ənt) *adj.* **1** relying; depending. **2** confident. **3** relying on oneself.

rel·ic (rel′ik) *n.* **1** a thing, custom, etc. that remains from the past: *This ruined bridge is a relic of pioneer days.* **2** something belonging to a holy person, kept as a sacred memorial. **3** an object having interest because of its age or its associations with the past; keepsake; souvenir. **4 relics,** *pl.* remains; ruins. [ME < OF *relique* < L *reliquiae*, pl., remains]

rel·ict (rel′ikt) *n.* **1** a widow. **2** a plant or animal surviving from an earlier period. [< Med.L *relicta*, originally fem. pp. of L *relinquere*. See RELINQUISH.]

re·lief (ri lēf′) *n.* **1** the lessening of, or freeing from, a pain, burden, difficulty, etc. **2** something that lessens or frees from pain, burden, difficulty, etc.; aid; help. **3** help, in the form of money or food, given to poor people. **4** something that makes a pleasing change or lessens strain. **5** a release from a post of duty, often by the coming of a substitute: *This nurse is on duty from seven in the morning until seven at night, with only two hours' relief.* **6** a change of persons on duty. **7** a person or persons relieving others from duty: *The sentry was waiting for his relief.* **8** in painting, sculpture, etc., a projection of figures and designs from a flat surface. **9** a figure or design standing out from the surface from which it is cut, shaped, or stamped. **10** the appearance of standing out given to a drawing or painting by use of shadow, shading, color, or line. **11** the different heights of the surface of the earth, moon, etc. **12 in relief,** standing out from a surface. **13** strong, clear manner; distinctness. [ME < AF *relef* < *relever*. See RELIEVE.]

A relief (def. 8, 9)

relief map a map that shows the different heights of a surface by using shading, colors, solid materials, etc.

re·lieve (ri lēv′) *v.* **-lieved, -liev·ing. 1** make less; make easier; reduce the pain or trouble of: *These pills will relieve a headache.* **2** set free: *Your coming relieves me of the bother of writing a long letter.* **3** bring aid to; help: *Soldiers were sent to relieve the fort.* **4** give variety or a pleasing change to: *The black dress was relieved by red trimming.* **5** free (a person on duty) by taking his place. **6** make stand out more clearly. [ME < OF *relever* < L *relevare* lighten. See RELEVANT.] —**re·liev′er,** *n.* —**Syn. 1** mitigate, alleviate.

re·lie·vo (ri lē′vō) *n.* **-vos.** in painting, sculpture, etc., relief. [< Ital. *rilievo*]

re·li·gion (ri lij′ən) *n.* **1** belief in God or gods. **2** the worship of God or gods. **3** a particular system of religious belief and worship: *the Christian religion, the Moslem religion.* **4** a matter of conscience: *She makes a religion of keeping her house neat.* [< L *religio, -onis* respect for what is sacred, probably originally, care (for worship and traditions) < *relegere* go through again < *re-* again + *legere* read]

re·li·gi·os·i·ty (ri lij′ē os′ə tē) *n.* an affectation of religious feelings.

hat, āge, cãre, fär; let, ēqual, tėrm; it, īce
hot, ōpen, ôrder; oil, out; cup, pu̇t, rüle, ūse
əbove, takən, pencəl, lemən, circəs
ch, child; ng, long; sh, ship
th, thin; ᴛʜ, then; zh, measure

re·li·gious (ri lij′əs) *adj.* **1** of religion; connected with religion. **2** much interested in religion; devoted to the worship of God or gods. **3** belonging to an order of monks, nuns, friars, etc. **4** of or connected with such an order. **5** strict; done with care. —*n.* **1** a monk, nun, friar, etc.; member of a religious order. **2** such persons collectively. [ME < OF < L *religiosus* < *religio.* See RELIGION.] —**re·li′gious·ly,** *adv.* —**re·li′gious·ness,** *n.*

re·lin·quish (ri ling′kwish) *v.* give up; let go: *The small dog relinquished his bone to the big dog. She has relinquished all hope of going to Europe this year.* [ME < OF *relinquiss-*, a stem of *relinquir* < L *relinquere* < *re-* behind + *linquere* leave] —**re·lin′quish·er,** *n.* —**Syn.** abandon.

re·lin·quish·ment (ri ling′kwish mənt) *n.* a giving up; abandonment; surrender.

rel·i·quar·y (rel′ə kwer′ē) *n.* **-quar·ies.** a small box or other receptacle for a relic or relics. [< MF *reliquaire* < *relique.* See RELIC.]

rel·ique (rel′ik; *French,* rə lēk′) *n.* relic. [< F]

rel·ish (rel′ish) *n.* **1** a pleasant taste; a good flavor: *Hunger gives relish to simple food.* **2** something to add flavor to food. Olives and pickles are relishes. **3** a kind of pickle made of chopped cucumbers, etc. **4** a slight dash (of something). **5** a liking; appetite; enjoyment: *The hungry boy ate with a great relish. The teacher has no relish for John's jokes.* —*v.* like; enjoy: *A cat relishes cream. He did not relish the prospect of staying after school.* [earlier *reles* < OF *reles* remainder < *relesser, relaissier.* See RELEASE.]

re·luc·tance (ri luk′təns) *n.* **1** a reluctant feeling or action; unwillingness. **2** slowness in action because of unwillingness.

re·luc·tan·cy (ri luk′tən sē) *n.* reluctance.

re·luc·tant (ri luk′tənt) *adj.* **1** unwilling; showing unwillingness. **2** slow to act because unwilling: *He was very reluctant to give his money away.* [< L *reluctans, -antis* struggling against, ppr. of *reluctari,* ult. < *re-* back + *lucta* wrestling] —**re·luc′tant·ly,** *adv.*
Syn. 1 Reluctant, loath = unwilling to do something. **Reluctant** suggests struggling against doing something one finds disagreeable or unpleasant, disapproves of, is afraid of, etc.: *He was reluctant to leave her, but he had no choice.* **Loath** suggests unwillingness because one feels the thing to be done is extremely disagreeable or hateful: *His parents were loath to believe their son would steal.*

re·ly (ri lī′) *v.* **-lied, -ly·ing.** depend; trust: *Rely on your own efforts.* [ME < OF *relier* < L *religare* bind fast < *re-* back + *ligare* bind]
Syn. Rely, depend = have confidence in someone or something. **Rely** = count on, or put one's trust in, someone or something one has reason to believe will never fail to do what is expected or wanted: *He relies on his parents' advice.* **Depend** suggests confidently taking it for granted, with or without reason, that a person or thing will give the help or support expected or needed, and often suggests leaning on others: *She depends on her friends to make her decisions.*

rem (rem) *n.* the unit for measuring the harm caused by radiation on human tissue. It is equal to the effect of one roentgen of X rays. [< *r*oentgen + *e*quivalent + *m*an]

re·main (ri mān′) *v.* **1** continue in a place; stay: *We remained at the lake till September.* **2** continue; last; keep on: *The town remains the same year after year.* **3** be left: *A few apples remain on the trees.* —*n.* **remains,** *pl.* **a** what is left. **b** a dead body. **c** a writer's works not yet published at the time of his death. **d** things left from the past, such as a building, a monument, or parts of an animal or plant: *the remains of an ancient civilization, fossil remains.* [ME < OF *remaindre* < L *remanere* < *re-* back + *manere* stay] —**Syn.** *v.* **1** See **stay.**

re·main·der (ri mān′dər) *n.* **1** the part left over; the rest: *After studying an hour, she spent the remainder of the afternoon in play. If you take 2 from 9, the remainder is 7.* **2** one of the copies of a book left in the publisher's hands after the sale has practically ceased. [ME < OF *remaindre,* infin. used as n. See REMAIN.] —**Syn. 1** residue, remnant, balance, surplus.

re·mand (ri mand′) *v.* **1** send back. **2 a** send back (a prisoner or an accused person) into custody. **b** send back a case to the court it came from for further action there. —*n.* a remanding. [ME < LL *remandare* < L *re-* back + *mandare* order]

re·mark (ri märk′) *v.* **1** say; speak; comment. **2** observe; notice. —*n.* **1** something said in a few words; short statement. **2** the act of noticing; observation. [< F *remarquer* < *re-* again + *marquer* mark] —**Syn.** *v.* **2** note.

re·mark·a·ble (ri mär′kə bəl) *adj.* worthy of notice; unusual. —**re·mark′a·ble·ness,** *n.* —**re·mark′a·bly,** *adv.* —**Syn.** notable, noteworthy, extraordinary, singular.

re·me·di·a·ble (ri mē′dē ə bəl) *adj.* that can be remedied or cured. —**re·me′di·a·bly,** *adv.*

re·me·di·al (ri mē′dē əl) *adj.* acting as a remedy; helping, relieving, or clearing. [< LL *remedialis* < L *remedium.* See REMEDY.]

re·me·di·al·ly (ri mē′dē əl ē) *adv.* so as to remedy.

rem·e·di·less (rem′ə dē lis) *adj.* without remedy; incurable; irreparable.

rem·e·dy (rem′ə dē) *n.* **-dies,** *v.* **-died, -dy·ing.** —*n.* a means of removing or relieving diseases or any undesirable condition; cure. [ME < AF *remedie* < L *remedium.* See v.] —*v.* put right; make right; cure. [ME < L *remediare* < *remedium* < *re-* again + *mederi* heal] —**Syn.** *n.* restorative, corrective. -*v.* See **cure.**

re·mem·ber (ri mem′bər) *v.* **1** have (something) come into the mind again; call to mind; recall. **2** recall something. **3** keep in mind; take care not to forget. **4** have memory: *Dogs remember.* **5** make a gift to; reward; tip: *Grandfather remembered us all in his will.* **6** mention (a person) as sending friendly greetings; recall to the mind of another. [ME < OF *remembrer* < L *rememorari,* ult. < *re-* again + *memor* mindful of]
Syn. 1 Remember, recall, recollect = think of something again by an act of memory. **Remember** emphasizes having something once known or experienced come back into one's mind, sometimes by a conscious effort but often through no act of will: *Do you remember that?* **Recall** emphasizes being able to remember, consciously calling back: *Yes, I recall the incident.* **Recollect,** more formal, particularly suggests a thinking process requiring a conscious or special effort to recall something that has been forgotten: *Now I recollect what he said.*

re·mem·brance (ri mem′brəns) *n.* **1** the power to remember; act of remembering; memory. **2** a state of being remembered. **3** a keepsake; any thing or action that makes one remember a person, place, or event; souvenir. **4 remembrances,** *pl.* greetings.

Remembrance Day November 11, the day set aside to honor the memory of those killed in World Wars I and II.

re·mem·branc·er (ri mem′brən sər) *n.* a person or thing that reminds one; reminder.

re·mind (ri mīnd′) *v.* make (one) think (of something); cause to remember.

re·mind·er (ri mīn′dər) *n.* something to help one remember.

rem·i·nisce (rem′ə nis′) *v.* **-nisced, -nisc·ing.** talk or think about past experiences or events.

rem·i·nis·cence (rem′ə nis′əns) *n.* **1** a remembering; recalling past happenings, etc. **2** Often, **reminiscences,** *pl.* an account of something remembered; recollection: *reminiscences of the war.* **3** something that makes one remember or think of something else. [< L *reminiscentia,* ult. < *reminisci* remember < *re-* again + *men-* think]

rem·i·nis·cent (rem′ə nis′ənt) *adj.* **1** recalling past events, etc.: *reminiscent talk.* **2** awakening memories of something else; suggestive: *a manner reminiscent of a statelier age.* —**rem′i·nis′cent·ly,** *adv.*

re·miss (ri mis′) *adj.* careless; slack; neglectful; negligent: *A policeman who carelessly lets a thief escape is remiss in his duty.* [< L *remissus,* pp. of *remittere* < *re-* back + *mittere* let go] —**re·miss′ness,** *n.* —**Syn.** derelict, thoughtless.

re·mis·si·ble (ri mis′ə bəl) *adj.* that can be remitted.

re·mis·sion (ri mish′ən) *n.* **1** a letting off (from debt, punishment, etc.): *The bankrupt sought remission of his debts.* **2** pardon; forgiveness: *Remission of sins is* *promised to those who repent.* **3** a lessening (of pain, force, labor, etc.).

re·mit (ri mit′) *v.* **-mit·ted, -mit·ting. 1** send money to a person or place: *Enclosed is our bill; please remit.* **2** send (money due). **3** refrain from carrying out; refrain from exacting; cancel: *The king remitted the prisoner's punishment.* **4** pardon; forgive: *power to remit sins.* **5** make less; decrease: *After we had rowed the boat into calm water, we remitted our efforts.* **6** make or become less. **7** send back (a case) to a lower court for further action. [ME < L *remittere* send back, let go. See REMISS.] **—re·mit′ter,** *n.*

re·mit·tal (ri mit′əl) *n.* remission.

re·mit·tance (ri mit′əns) *n.* **1** the act of sending money to someone at a distance. **2** the money that is sent.

remittance man someone who lives abroad on money sent from his relatives at home.

re·mit·tent (ri mit′ənt) *adj.* lessening for a time; lessening at intervals: *a remittent type of fever.* **—re·mit′tent·ly,** *adv.*

rem·nant (rem′nənt) *n.* **1** a small part left. **2** a piece of cloth, ribbon, lace, etc. left after the rest has been used or sold: *She bought a remnant of silk at a bargain.* [ME < OF *remenant,* ppr. of *remenoir* remain < L *remanere.* See REMAIN.] **—Syn. 1** rest, fragment.

re·mod·el (rē mod′əl) *v.* **-elled** or **-eled, -el·ling** or **-el·ing. 1** model again. **2** make over: *The old barn was remodelled into a house.*

re·mon·e·tize (rē mun′ə tīz′ or rē mon′ə tīz′) *v.* **-tized, -tiz·ing.** restore to use as legal tender: *remonetize silver.* **—re·mon′e·ti·za′tion,** *n.*

re·mon·strance (ri mon′strəns) *n.* a protest; complaint. [< Med.L *remonstrantia* < *remonstrare.* See REMONSTRATE.]

re·mon·strant (ri mon′strənt) *adj.* remonstrating; protesting. *—n.* a person who remonstrates.

re·mon·strate (ri mon′strāt or rem′ən strāt′) *v.* **-strat·ed, -strat·ing.** object; protest: *The teacher remonstrated with the boy about his low marks.* [< Med.L *remonstrare* point out, ult. < L *re-* back + *monstrum* sign] **—re·mon′stra·tor,** *n.*

re·mon·stra·tion (rē′mon strā′shən or rem′ən strā′shən) *n.* a remonstrating.

re·mon·stra·tive (ri mon′strə tiv) *adj.* remonstrating.

re·morse (ri môrs′) *n.* deep, painful regret for having done wrong: *Because he felt remorse for his crime, the thief confessed.* [< L *remorsus* tormented, ult. < *re-* back + *mordere* bite] **—Syn.** compunction, contrition. See **regret.**

re·morse·ful (ri môrs′fəl) *adj.* feeling or expressing remorse. **—re·morse′ful·ly,** *adv.* **—re·morse′ful·ness,** *n.*

re·morse·less (ri môrs′lis) *adj.* without remorse; pitiless; cruel. **—re·morse′less·ly,** *adv.* **—re·morse′less·ness,** *n.*

re·mote (ri mōt′) *adj.* **-mot·er, -mot·est. 1** far away; far off: *a remote country.* **2** out of the way; secluded: *a remote village.* **3** distant: *a remote relative.* **4** slight; faint: *I haven't the remotest idea what you mean.* [ME < L *remotus,* pp. of *removere* remove. See REMOVE.] **—re·mote′ly,** *adv.* **—re·mote′ness,** *n.* **—Syn. 1** See **distant.**

remote control 1 control from a distance, usually by electrical connection or radio signal. **2** the device used for operating a remote-control system.

re·mount (*v.* rē mount′; *n.* rē′mount or rē mount′) *v.* **1** mount again. **2** furnish with fresh horses. *—n.* a fresh horse, or a supply of fresh horses, for use.

re·mov·al (ri müv′əl) *n.* **1** a removing; taking away: *We paid ten dollars for garbage removal.* **2** a change of place: *The store announces its removal to larger quarters.* **3** a dismissal from an office or position.

re·move (ri müv′) *v.* **-moved, -mov·ing,** *n.* *—v.* **1** move from a place or position; take off; take away: *Remove your hat.* **2** get rid of; put an end to: *remove all doubt.* **3** kill. **4** dismiss from an office or position: *remove an official for taking bribes.* **5** go away; move away. *—n.* **1** a moving away. **2** a step or degree of distance: *His cruelty was only one remove from crime.* [ME < OF < L *removere* < *re-* back + *movere* move] **—re·mov′a·ble,** *adj.* **—re·mov′er,** *n.* **—Syn.** *v.* **1** dislodge, shift, displace.

re·moved (ri müvd′) *adj.* **1** distant; remote. **2** separated by one or more steps or degrees of relationship.

re·mu·ner·ate (ri mū′nər āt′) *v.* **-at·ed, -at·ing.** pay for work, services, trouble, etc.; reward. [< L *remunerare,* ult. < *re-* back + *munus* gift] **—Syn.** recompense. See **pay.**

re·mu·ner·a·tion (ri mū′nər ā′shən) *n.* a reward; pay; payment.

re·mu·ner·a·tive (ri mū′nər ə tiv or ri mū′nər ā′tiv) *adj.* paying; profitable. **—re·mu′ner·a′tive·ly,** *adv.*

Re·mus (rē′məs) *n.* in Roman mythology, the twin brother of Romulus.

ren·ais·sance (ren′ə säns′, ren′ə säns′, or ri nā′səns) *n.* **1** a revival; new birth. **2 the Renaissance, a** the great revival of art, literature, and learning in Europe during the 14th, 15th, and 16th centuries. **b** the period of time when this revival occurred. **c** in art, architecture, etc., a style developed in this period and characterized by the simplicity, elegance, and proportion of classical Greek and Roman models. [< F *renaissance* < *renaître* be born again, ult. < L *renasci.* See RENASCENT.]

☛ **renaissance.** The word is capitalized when it refers to the period of history: *art of the Renaissance.* It is not capitalized when it refers to a revival: *a renaissance of interest in old-time melodramas.*

re·nal (rē′nəl) *adj.* of or having to do with the kidneys. [< L *renalis* < *ren* kidney]

re·name (rē nām′) *v.* **-named, -nam·ing.** give a new name to; name again.

re·nas·cence (ri nas′əns or ri nā′səns) *n.* **1** a revival; new birth; renewal. **2** a being renascent. **3 the Renascence,** the Renaissance.

re·nas·cent (ri nas′ənt or ri nā′sənt) *adj.* being born again; reviving; springing again into being or vigor. [< L *renascens, -entis,* ppr. of *renasci* < *re-* again + *nasci* be born]

ren·coun·ter (ren koun′tər) *n.* **1** a hostile meeting; conflict; battle; duel. **2** a chance meeting. [< F *rencontre* < *rencontrer* meet < *re-* again + *encontrer* encounter]

rend (rend) *v.* **rent, rend·ing. 1** pull apart violently; tear: *Wolves will rend a lamb.* **2** split: *Lightning rent the tree.* **3** disturb violently: *His mind was rent by doubt.* **4** remove with force or violence. [OE *rendan*] **—Syn. 1** rip.

ren·der (ren′dər) *v.* **1** cause to become; make: *An accident has rendered him helpless.* **2** give; do: *She rendered us a great service by her help.* **3** offer for consideration, approval, payment, etc.; hand in; report: *The treasurer rendered an account of all the money spent.* **4** give in return: *Render thanks for kindness.* **5** pay as due: *The conquered rendered tribute to the conqueror.* **6** bring out the meaning of; represent: *The actor rendered the part of Hamlet well.* **7** play or sing (music). **8** change from one language to another; translate. **9** give up; surrender. **10** melt (fat, etc.); clarify or extract by melting. Fat from pigs is rendered into lard. [ME < OF *rendre* < L *reddere* give as due, pay < *re-* as due + *dare* give; influenced by L *prendere* take]

ren·dez·vous (ron′də vü′; *French,* räN dā vü′) *n.* **-vous** (-vüz′), *v.* **-voused** (-vüd′), **-vous·ing** (-vü′ing). *—n.* **1** an appointment or engagement to meet at a fixed place or time; meeting by agreement. **2** a meeting place; gathering place: *The family had two favorite rendezvous, the library and the garden.* **3** a place agreed on for a meeting at a certain time, especially of ships, troops, or aircraft. *—v.* **1** meet or come together at a rendezvous. **2** bring together at a rendezvous. [< F *rendezvous* < *rendez-vous* betake yourself!]

ren·di·tion (ren dish′ən) *n.* **1** a rendering. **2** the rendering of a dramatic part, music, etc. **3** a translation. [< MF *rendition* < OF *rendre.* See RENDER.]

ren·e·gade (ren′ə gād′) *n.* **1** a deserter from a religious faith, a political party, etc.; traitor. **2** an outlaw. *—adj.* deserting; disloyal; like a traitor. [< Sp. *renegado* < Med.L *renegatus,* pp. of *renegare* deny. See RENEGE.] **—Syn.** *n.* recreant, backslider.

re·nege (ri neg′ or ri nig′) *v.* **-neged, -neg·ing,** *n.* *—v.* **1** in card playing, fail to play a card of the suit that is led, although you have one. It is against the rules of card games to renege. **2** *Informal.* back out; fail to keep a promise. —*n.* in card games, a failure to follow suit when able to do so. [< Med.L *renegare* < L *re-* back + *negare* deny] —**re·neg′er,** *n.*

re·new (ri nū′ or -nü′) *v.* **1** make new again; make like new; restore. **2** make spiritually new. **3** begin again; get again; say, do, or give again: *renew an attack, one's youth, one's vows, one's efforts.* **4** replace by new material or a new thing of the same sort; fill again. **5** give or get for a new period: *We renewed our lease for another year.* **6** renew a lease, note, etc. —**re·new′a·ble,** *adj.* —**re·new′er,** *n.*

Syn. 1 Renew, restore, renovate = put back in a new or former condition. **Renew** = put back in a condition like new something that has lost its freshness, force, or vigor: *He renewed the finish of the table.* **Restore** = put back in its original, former, or normal condition something that has been damaged, worn out, partly ruined, etc.: *That old pioneer fort has been restored.* **Renovate** = put in good condition or make like new by cleaning, repairing, redecorating, etc.: *The store was renovated.*

re·new·al (ri nū′əl or ri nü′əl) *n.* a renewing or being renewed.

re·new·ed·ly (ri nū′id lē or ri nü′id lē) *adv.* anew.

ren·i·form (ren′ə fôrm′ or rē′nə fôrm′) *adj.* kidney-shaped. [< L *ren, renis* kidney + E *-form*]

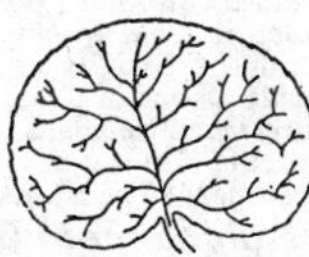
A reniform leaf

ren·net (ren′it) *n.* a substance containing rennin, used for making cheese and junket. [ME *rennet* < *renne(n)* run, OE *rinnan*]

ren·nin (ren′ən) *n.* an enzyme in the gastric juice that coagulates or curdles milk. [< *rennet*]

re·nounce (ri nouns′) *v.* **-nounced, -nounc·ing. 1** declare that one gives up; give up entirely; give up: *He renounced his claim to the money.* **2** make formal surrender. **3** cast off; refuse to recognize as one's own: *He renounced his wicked son.* **4** in card games, play a card of a different suit from that led. [ME < OF *renoncer* < L *renuntiare,* ult. < *re-* back + *nuntius* message] —**re·nounce′ment,** *n.* —**Syn. 1** forego, forsake, relinquish. **3** repudiate.

ren·o·vate (ren′ə vāt′) *v.* **-vat·ed, -vat·ing.** make new again; make like new; restore to good condition: *renovate a garment or a house.* [< L *renovare,* ult. < *re-* again + *novus* new] —**ren′o·va′tor,** *n.* —**Syn.** See **renew.**

ren·o·va·tion (ren′ə vā′shən) *n.* a restoration to good condition; renewal.

re·nown (ri noun′) *n.* fame. [ME < AF *renoun,* ult. < L *re-* repeatedly + *nomen* name] —**Syn.** celebrity, distinction.

re·nowned (ri nound′) *adj.* famed. —**Syn.** See **famous.**

rent[1] (rent) *n.* **1** a payment, especially when made regularly, for the right to occupy or use another's land, buildings, goods, etc. **2** in economics, what is paid for the use of natural resources. **3 for rent,** to be given in return for rent paid.
—*v.* **1** pay for the use of (property): *We rent a house from Mr. Smith.* **2** receive pay for the use of (property): *He rents several other houses.* **3** be leased or let for rent: *This house rents for $150 a month.* [ME < OF *rente,* ult. < L *reddere* render. See RENDER.] —**rent′a·ble,** *adj.* —**rent′er,** *n.*

rent[2] (rent) *n.* a torn place; tear; split. —*adj.* torn; split. —*v.* pt. and pp. of **rend.** [originally v., var. of *rend*]

rent·al (ren′təl) *n.* **1** an amount received or paid as rent: *The monthly rental of her house is $150.* **2** something rented. —*adj.* of or in rent. [< AF]

re·nun·ci·ate (ri nun′sē āt′) *v.* **-at·ed, -at·ing.** give up formally; renounce; disclaim.

re·nun·ci·a·tion (ri nun′sē ā′shən) *n.* a giving up of a right, title, possession, etc.; renouncing. [< L *renuntiatio, -onis* < *renuntiare.* See RENOUNCE.]

re·o·pen (rē ō′pən) *v.* **1** open again. **2** discuss again: *The matter is settled and cannot be reopened.*

re·or·der (rē ôr′dər) *v.* **1** put in order again; rearrange. **2** give a second or repeated order for goods; order again. —*n.* a second or repeated order for goods.

re·or·gan·i·za·tion (rē′ôr gən ə zā′shən or rē′ôr gən ī zā′shən) *n.* **1** a reorganizing. **2** the state of being reorganized.

hat, āge, cãre, fär; let, ēqual, tėrm; it, īce
hot, ōpen, ôrder; oil, out; cup, pu̇t, rüle, ūse
əbove, takən, pencəl, lemən, circəs
ch, child; ng, long; sh, ship
th, thin; ᴛʜ, then; zh, measure

re·or·gan·ize (rē ôr′gən īz′) *v.* **-ized, -iz·ing. 1** organize anew; form again; arrange in a new way: *Classes will be reorganized after the first four weeks.* **2** form a new company to operate (a business in the hands of a receiver). —**re′or′gan·iz′er,** *n.*

rep[1] (rep) *n.* a heavy, ribbed fabric of wool, silk, cotton, etc. Also, **repp.** [< F *reps* < E *ribs*]

rep[2] (rep) *n. Slang.* a representative.

rep. 1 report. **2** reported. **3** reporter. **4** representative.

Rep. 1 Representative. **2** Republican. **3** Republic.

re·paid (ri pād′) *v.* pt. and pp. of **repay.**

re·paint (rē pānt′) *v.* paint again. —*n.* **1** a part of a picture that has been repainted. **2** anything repainted.

re·pair[1] (ri pãr′) *v.* **1** put in good condition again; mend: *He repairs shoes.* **2** make up for: *How can I repair the harm done?*
—*n.* **1** the act or work of repairing: *Repairs on the school building are made during the summer.* **2** an instance or piece of repairing. **3** a condition fit to be used: *Keeping highways in repair is a provincial responsibility.* **4** a condition with respect to repairing: *The house was in bad repair.* [ME < L *reparare* < *re-* again + *parare* prepare] —**re·pair′a·ble,** *adj.* —**re·pair′er,** *n.* —**Syn.** *v.* **1** restore, renovate. See **mend.**

re·pair[2] (ri pãr′) *v.* go (to a place): *After dinner we repaired to the balcony.* [ME < OF *repairer* < LL *repatriare* return to one's own country. Doublet of REPATRIATE.]

re·pair·man (ri pãr′man′ or ri pãr′mən) *n.* **-men** (-men′ or -mən). a man whose work is repairing machines, etc.

rep·a·ra·ble (rep′ə rə bəl) *adj.* that can be repaired or remedied. [< L *reparabilis*] —**rep′a·ra·bly,** *adv.*

rep·a·ra·tion (rep′ə rā′shən) *n.* **1** a giving of satisfaction or compensation for wrong or injury done. **2** a compensation for wrong or injury. **3** Usually, **reparations,** *pl.* compensation demanded from a defeated enemy for the devastation of territory during war. **4** a repairing or being repaired; restoration to good condition. [< LL *reparatio, -onis* < *reparare.* See REPAIR[1].]

rep·ar·tee (rep′ər tē′) *n.* **1** a witty reply or replies. **2** talk characterized by clever and witty replies. **3** cleverness and wit in making replies. [< F *repartie* < *repartir* reply, ult. < L *re-* back + *pars, partis* part]

re·pass (rē pas′) *v.* **1** pass back. **2** pass again.

re·past (ri past′) *n.* **1** a meal; attractive meal; food. **2** a taking of food; eating: *a brief repast.* [ME < OF *repast,* ult. < L *re-* again + *pascere* feed]

re·pa·tri·ate (rē pā′trē āt′ or rē pat′rē āt′) *v.* **-at·ed, -at·ing.** send back or restore to one's own country: *After peace was declared, refugees and prisoners of war were repatriated.* [< LL *repatriare,* ult. < L *re-* back + *patria* native land. Doublet of REPAIR[2].] —**re·pa′tri·a′tion,** *n.*

re·pay (ri pā′) *v.* **-paid, -pay·ing. 1** pay back; give back: *He repaid the money he had borrowed.* **2** make return for: *No thanks can repay such kindness.* **3** make return to: *The boy's success repaid the teacher for her efforts.* [< MF *repaier* < *re-* back (< L) + *paier* pay < L *pacare* pacify < *pax, pacis* peace] —**re·pay′ment,** *n.* —**Syn. 1** refund.

re·pay·a·ble (ri pā′ə bəl) *adj.* that can be repaid; that must be repaid.

re·peal (ri pēl′) *v.* take back; withdraw; do away with: *A law may be repealed by act of Parliament.* —*n.* the act of repealing; withdrawal; abolition: *He voted for the repeal of that law.* [ME < AF *repeler,* alteration of OF *rapeler* < *re-* back + *apeler* call < L *ad-* up + *pellare* call] —**Syn.** *v.* rescind, annul.

re·peat (ri pēt′) *v.* **1** do or make again: *repeat an error.*

2 say again: *repeat a word for emphasis.* 3 say over; recite: *repeat a poem from memory.* 4 say after another says: *Repeat the oath after me.* 5 tell to another or others: *I promised not to repeat the secret.* 6 *U.S.* vote more than once in an election. 7 **repeat oneself,** say what one has already said.
—*n.* 1 a repeating. 2 a thing repeated. 3 in music: **a** a passage to be repeated. **b** a sign indicating this, usually a row of dots. Coming after a double bar line, it indicates the beginning of the passage to be repeated; before a double bar line, it indicates the end of the passage. [< L *repetere* attack again < *re-* again + *petere* aim at]
Syn. *v.* **1, 2 Repeat, reiterate** = do or say again. **Repeat** is the common word meaning "say, do, make, or perform something over again, once or many times": *The Glee Club will repeat the program next week.* **Reiterate,** more formal, means "repeat again and again something said or a statement, objection, accusation, etc. made": *For months we reiterated our requests for better bus service.*

re·peat·ed (ri pēt′id) *adj.* said, done, or made more than once.

re·peat·ed·ly (ri pēt′id lē) *adv.* again and again; more than once.

re·peat·er (ri pēt′ər) *n.* 1 a gun that fires several shots without reloading. 2 a watch or clock that, if a spring is pressed, strikes again the hour it struck last. 3 *U.S.* a person who votes more than once in an election. 4 a student who takes a course again or fails to pass on to the next grade. 5 *Informal.* a person who is repeatedly sent to prison or a reformatory; habitual criminal. 6 **a** a device that amplifies voice sounds in telephonic communication. **b** a similar device for amplifying and relaying radio, telegraph, and radar signals. 7 any person or thing that repeats.

repeating decimal a decimal in which there is an indefinite repetition of the same figure or series of figures. *Examples*: .3333+, .2323+.

repeating rifle a rifle that fires several shots without reloading.

re·pel (ri pel′) *v.* **-pelled, -pel·ling.** 1 force back; drive back; drive away: *They repelled the enemy.* 2 keep off or out; fail to mix with: *Oil and water repel each other. This tent repels moisture.* 3 force apart or away by some inherent force. Particles with similar electric charges repel each other. 4 be displeasing to; cause disgust in. 5 cause dislike; displease. 6 reject. [ME < L *repellere* < *re-* back + *pellere* drive]

re·pel·lent (ri pel′ənt) *adj.* 1 unattractive; disagreeable. 2 repelling; driving back. —*n.* anything that repels: *We sprayed an insect repellent on our arms and legs.*

re·pent (ri pent′) *v.* 1 feel sorrow or remorse for one's sins or errors and seek forgiveness: *He repented after he had done wrong.* 2 feel remorse for; regret: *repent one's choice.* [ME < OF *repentir,* ult. < L *re-* repeatedly + *paenitere* cause to regret] **—re·pent′er,** *n.*

re·pent·ance (ri pen′təns) *n.* 1 sorrow for doing wrong. 2 sorrow; regret. —**Syn. 1** contrition.

re·pent·ant (ri pen′tənt) *adj.* repenting; feeling repentance or regret; sorry for wrongdoing. [< OF *repentant,* ppr. of *repentir.* See REPENT.] **—re·pent′ant·ly,** *adv.*

re·peo·ple (rē pē′pəl) *v.* **-pled, -pling.** 1 fill with people again. 2 restock with animals. [< MF *repeupler* < *re-* again (< L) + *peupler* people, ult. < L *populus* people]

re·per·cus·sion (rē′pər kush′ən) *n.* 1 an indirect influence or reaction from an event. 2 a sound flung back; echo. 3 a springing back; rebound; recoil. [< L *repercussio, -onis,* ult. < *re-* back + *per-* thoroughly + *quatere* beat]

rep·er·toire (rep′ər twär′) *n.* the list of plays, operas, parts, pieces, etc. that a company, an actor, a musician, or a singer is prepared to perform. [< F < LL *repertorium.* Doublet of REPERTORY.]

rep·er·to·ry (rep′ər tô′rē) *n.* **-ries.** 1 a catalogue or list of things; repertoire. 2 a store or stock of things ready for use. 3 a storehouse. [< LL *repertorium* inventory, ult. < *reperire* find, get < *re-* again + *parere* get. Doublet of REPERTOIRE.]

repertory theatre 1 a theatre in which a company of actors, singers, or dancers present a repertoire of productions for a season. 2 a theatre in which one company presents a different production at regular intervals, such as every week, every two weeks, or every month.

rep·e·ti·tion (rep′ə tish′ən) *n.* 1 the act of repeating; doing again; saying again: *Repetition helps learning. Any repetition of the offence will be punished.* 2 the thing repeated. [< L *repetitio, -onis* < *repetere.* See REPEAT.]

rep·e·ti·tious (rep′ə tish′əs) *adj.* full of repetitions; repeating in a tiresome way. **—rep′e·ti′tious·ly,** *adv.* **—rep′e·ti′tious·ness,** *n.*

re·pet·i·tive (ri pet′ə tiv) *adj.* of or characterized by repetition. **—re·pet′i·tive·ly,** *adv.* **—re·pet′i·tive·ness,** *n.*

re·phrase (rē frāz′) *v.* **-phrased, -phras·ing.** phrase again; phrase in a new or different way: *rephrase a speech, rephrase a melody.*

re·pine (ri pīn′) *v.* **-pined, -pin·ing.** be discontented; fret; complain. [< *re-* + *pine*[2]]

re·place (ri plās′) *v.* **-placed, -plac·ing.** 1 fill or take the place of. 2 get another in place of. 3 put back; put in place again. **—re·place′a·ble,** *adj.* **—re·plac′er,** *n.*
Syn. 1 Replace, supersede, supplant = take the place of another. **Replace** = take or fill as substitute or successor the place formerly held by another: *When one of the players on the team was hurt, another replaced him.* **Supersede,** a formal word chiefly used of things, especially suggests causing what is replaced to be put aside as out-of-date, no longer useful, etc.: *Buses are superseding streetcars.* **Supplant** when used of a person especially suggests forcing him out and taking over his place by scheming or treachery: *The dictator supplanted the president.*

re·place·ment (ri plās′mənt) *n.* 1 the act of replacing or the state of being replaced. 2 something or someone that replaces. 3 a person who takes the place of another.

re·play (*v.* rē′plā′; *n.* rē′plā′) *v.* play (a match, etc.) again. —*n.* 1 a match thus played. 2 a repeated, often slow-motion, showing of part of a television sportscast.

re·plen·ish (ri plen′ish) *v.* fill again; provide a new supply for: *Her wardrobe needs replenishing. Please replenish the fire.* [ME < OF *repleniss-,* a stem of *replenir,* ult. < L *re-* again + *plenus* full] **—re·plen′ish·er.** *n.*

re·plen·ish·ment (ri plen′ish mənt) *n.* 1 a replenishing or being replenished. 2 a fresh supply.

re·plete (ri plēt′) *adj.* abundantly supplied; filled. [ME < L *repletus,* pp. of *replere* < OF *re-* again + *plere* fill]

re·ple·tion (ri plē′shən) *n.* fullness; excessive fullness.

re·plev·in (ri plev′ən) *n.* in law: 1 the recovery by a person of goods allegedly taken from him, upon his giving security that the case shall be tried in court and the goods returned if he is defeated. 2 the writ by which the goods are thus recovered. —*v.* recover (goods) by replevin. [ME < AF *replevine,* ult. < OF *re-* again + *plevir* pledge]

rep·li·ca (rep′lə kə) *n.* a copy; reproduction: *The artist made a replica of his picture.* [< Ital. *replica* < *replicare* reproduce < L *replicare* unroll. See REPLY.]

re·ply (ri plī′) *v.* **-plied, -ply·ing,** *n.* **-plies.** —*v.* 1 answer by words or action; answer. 2 give as an answer. —*n.* 1 the act of replying. 2 a response or answer. [ME < OF *replier* < L *replicare* unroll < *re-* back + *plicare* fold] —**Syn.** *v.* **1** See **answer.**

re·port (ri pôrt′) *n.* 1 an account of something seen, heard, read, done, or considered. 2 an account officially expressed, generally in writing. 3 the sound of a shot or an explosion. 4 common talk; rumor: *Report has it that the Smiths are leaving town.* 5 reputation.
—*v.* 1 make a report of; announce. 2 give a formal account of; state officially. 3 take down in writing; write an account of. 4 make a report. 5 act as reporter. 6 repeat (what one has heard, seen, etc.); bring back an account of; describe. 7 present; present oneself: *Report for duty at 9 a.m.* 8 announce as a wrongdoer; denounce: *report one to the police.* [ME < OF *report* < *reporter* < L *reportare* < *re-* back + *portare* carry] —**Syn.** *n.* 1 narrative, description. 4 gossip, hearsay. –*v.* 1 relate, narrate.

re·port·a·ble (ri pôr′tə bəl) *adj.* capable of being reported; worth reporting.

re·port·age (ri pôr′tij or rə pôr täzh′) *n.* a reporting, especially in the style of newspaper reporters.

re·port·er (ri pôr′tər) *n.* 1 a person who reports. 2 a person who gathers news for a newspaper, radio, or television station. **3** a person who takes down reports of law cases: *a court reporter.*

rep·or·to·ri·al (rep′ər tôr′ē əl) *adj.* of or having to do with reporters or reporting.

re·pose[1] (ri pōz′) *n. v.* **-posed, -pos·ing.** **—*n.*** **1** the act of resting or sleeping: *Do not disturb her repose.* **2** quietness; ease: *She has repose of manner.* **3** peace; calmness.
—*v.* **1** lie at rest: *The cat reposed upon the cushion.* **2** lie in a grave. **3** lay to rest. **4** rest from work or toil; take a rest. **5** be supported. **6** depend; rely (on). [< F *repos* < *reposer* < LL *repausare* cause to rest < *re-* again + *pausare* pause]

re·pose[2] (ri pōz′) *v.* **-posed, -pos·ing.** put; place: *We repose complete confidence in his honesty.* [< L *repositus,* pp. of *reponere* < *re-* back + *ponere* place; modelled on verbs ending in *-pose*]

re·pose·ful (ri pōz′fəl) *adj.* calm; quiet. **—re·pose′ful·ly,** *adv.* **—re·pose′ful·ness,** *n.*

re·pos·i·to·ry (ri poz′ə tô′rē) *n.* **-ries. 1** a place or container where things are stored or kept: *The box was the repository for old magazines.* **2** a person to whom something is confided or entrusted. [< L *repositorium* < *reponere* replace. See REPOSE[2].]

re·pos·sess (rē′pə zes′) *v.* possess again; get possession of again.

re·pos·ses·sion (rē′pə zesh′ən) *n.* a repossessing.

re·pous·sé (rə pü sā′) *adj.* **1** raised in relief by hammering on the reverse side. A repoussé design can be made on thin metal. **2** ornamented or made in this manner. **—*n.*** repoussé work. [< F *repoussé* < *re-* back + *pousser* push]

repp (rep) *n.* rep[1].

repr. 1 reprinted. **2** represent. **3** represented.

rep·re·hend (rep′ri hend′) *v.* reprove; rebuke; blame. [ME < L *reprehendere,* originally, pull back < *re-* back + *prehendere* grasp]

rep·re·hen·si·ble (rep′ri hen′sə bəl) *adj.* deserving reproof, rebuke, or blame. **—rep′re·hen′si·bly,** *adv.*

rep·re·hen·sion (rep′ri hen′shən) *n.* reproof; rebuke; blame. [< L *reprehensio, -onis* < *reprehendere.* See REPREHEND.]

rep·re·sent (rep′ri zent′) *v.* **1** stand for; be a sign or symbol of: *The stars on this map represent the cities.* **2** act in place of; speak and act for: *People are elected to represent us in the government.* **3** act the part of: *Each child will represent an animal at the party.* **4** show in a picture, statue, carving, etc.; give a likeness of; portray: *This picture represents the end of the world.* **5** be a type of; be an example of: *A log represents a very simple kind of boat.* **6** describe; set forth: *He represented the plan as safe.* **7** bring before the mind; make one think of: *His fears represented the undertaking as impossible.* [< L *repraesentare* < *re-* back + *praesentare* present[2]]

rep·re·sen·ta·tion (rep′ri zen tā′shən) *n.* **1** the act of representing. **2** the condition or fact of being represented: "*Taxation without representation is tyranny.*" **3** representatives considered as a group. **4** a likeness; picture; model. **5** a performance of a play; presentation. **6** the process of forming mental images or ideas. **7** a protest; complaint. **8** an account; statement.

rep·re·sen·ta·tion·al (rep′ri zen tā′shə nəl) *adj.* **1** in art, of or having to do with a style that attempts to portray people, things, etc. as they are. **2** of or having to do with representation. **—rep′re·sen·ta′tion·al·ly,** *adv.*

rep·re·sent·a·tive (rep′ri zen′tə tiv) *n.* **1** a person appointed to act or speak for others: *He is the club's representative at the convention.* **2 Representative,** in the United States, member of the House of Representatives. **3** an example; type: *The tiger is a representative of the cat family.*
—*adj.* **1** having its citizens represented by chosen persons: *a representative government.* **2** representing: *Images representative of animals were made by the children.* **3** enough like all those of its kind to stand for all the rest: *Oak, birch, and maple are representative North American hardwoods.* **—rep′re·sent′a·tive·ly,** *adv.* **—Syn.** *n.* **1** agent, deputy.

re·press (ri pres′) *v.* **1** prevent from acting; check: *She repressed an impulse to cough.* **2** keep down; put down: *The dictator repressed the revolt.* **3** in psychoanalysis, make the object of repression; force (a painful or undesirable memory or impulse) from the conscious mind into the unconscious mind. [< L *repressus,* pp. of *reprimere* < *re-* back + *premere* press] **—re·press′er,** *n.* **—Syn. 1** curb, restrain. **2** suppress.

hat, āge, cãre, fär; let, ēqual, tėrm; it, īce
hot, ōpen, ôrder; oil, out; cup, pu̇t, rüle, ūse
əbove, takən, pencəl, lemən, circəs
ch, child; ng, long; sh, ship
th, thin; ᴛʜ, then; zh, measure

re·press·i·ble (ri pres′ə bəl) *adj.* that can be repressed.

re·pres·sion (ri presh′ən) *n.* **1** the act of repressing. **2** the state of being repressed. **3** in psychoanalysis, a defence mechanism by which unacceptable or painful impulses, emotions, or memories are put out of the conscious mind, their energy or effect remaining (according to Freudian theory) in the unconscious, where it influences personality and behavior.

re·pres·sive (ri pres′iv) *adj.* tending to repress; having power to repress. **—re·pres′sive·ly,** *adv.* **—re·pres′sive·ness,** *n.*

re·prieve (ri prēv′) *v.* **-prieved, -priev·ing,** *n.* **—*v.*** **1** delay the execution of (a person condemned to death). **2** give relief from any hardship or trouble. **—*n.*** **1** a delay in carrying out a punishment, especially of the death penalty. **2** a temporary relief from any hardship or trouble. [earlier *repry* < F *repris,* pp. of *reprendre* take back < L *reprehendere* (see REPREHEND); influenced by ME *repreve,* var. of *reprove* in sense of "retest"]

rep·ri·mand (rep′rə mand′) *n.* a severe or formal reproof. **—*v.*** reprove severely or formally. [< F *réprimande* < *réprimer* repress < L *reprimere.* See REPRESS.]

re·print (*v.* rē print′; *n.* rē′print′) *v.* print again; print a new impression of. **—*n.*** **1** a reprinting; a new impression of printed work. **2** in philately, a stamp printed from the original plate after the issue has been discontinued.

re·pris·al (ri prīz′əl) *n.* **1** any measure, economic or military, taken in retaliation by one nation against another. **2** any act of retaliation by one person against another. [ME < OF *reprisaille,* ult. < L *reprehendere* reprehend. See REPREHEND.]

re·prise (rə prēz′) *n.* in music, a repetition or return to a previous theme or subject. [< OF *reprise* < *reprendre* take back]

re·proach (ri prōch′) *n.* **1** blame. **2** disgrace. **3** any object of blame, censure, or disapproval. **4** an expression of blame, censure, or disapproval. **—*v.*** **1** blame. **2** disgrace. [< F *reproche* < *reprocher* < VL *repropiare* lay at the door of, ult. < L *re-* again + *prope* near] **—Syn.** *n.* **1** censure. **2** discredit. *-v.* **1** upbraid. See **blame.**

re·proach·ful (ri prōch′fəl) *adj.* full of reproach; expressing reproach. **—re·proach′ful·ly,** *adv.* **—re·proach′ful·ness,** *n.*

re·proach·less (ri prōch′lis) *adj.* without reproach; irreproachable.

rep·ro·bate (rep′rə bāt′) *n. adj. v.* **-bat·ed, -bat·ing. —*n.*** an unprincipled scoundrel. **—*adj.*** morally abandoned; unprincipled: *reprobate acts.* **—*v.*** disapprove; condemn; censure. [< LL *reprobatus,* pp. of *reprobare* reprove < L *re-* dis- + *probare* approve < *probus* good. Doublet of REPROVE.] **—Syn.** *adj.* depraved, corrupt, dissolute, profligate.

rep·ro·ba·tion (rep′rə bā′shən) *n.* disapproval; condemnation; censure.

re·pro·duce (rē′prə dūs′ or rē′prə düs′) *v.* **-duced, -duc·ing. 1** produce again: *A radio reproduces sounds.* **2** make a copy of: *He reproduced the original painting.* **3** produce offspring: *Most plants reproduce by seeds.* **—re′pro·duc′er,** *n.* **—Syn. 3** propagate, generate.

re·pro·duc·i·ble (rē′prə dūs′ə bəl or rē′prə düs′ə bəl) *adj.* that can be reproduced.

re·pro·duc·tion (rē′prə duk′shən) *n.* **1** a reproducing or being reproduced. **2** a copy. **3** the process by which animals and plants produce offspring.

re·pro·duc·tive (rē′prə duk′tiv) *adj.* **1** that reproduces.

2 for or concerned with reproduction. **—re′pro·duc′tive·ly,** *adv.* **—re′pro·duc′tive·ness,** *n.*

re·proof (ri prüf′) *n.* words of blame or disapproval; blame. [ME < OF *reprove* < *reprover*; influenced in form by *proof.* See REPROVE.]

re·prov·a·ble (ri prüv′ə bəl) *adj.* deserving reproof.

re·prov·al (ri prüv′əl) *n.* a reproving or reproof.

re·prove (ri prüv′) *v.* **-proved, -prov·ing.** find fault with; blame: *Reprove the boy for teasing the cat.* [ME < OF *reprover* < LL *reprobare.* Doublet of REPROBATE.] **—re·prov′er,** *n.* **—re·prov′ing·ly,** *adv.*
Syn. Reprove, rebuke = criticize or blame someone for a fault. **Reprove** suggests expressing disapproval or blame directly to the person at fault, usually without scolding and with the purpose or hope of correcting the fault: *The principal reproved the students who had been smoking in the locker room.* **Rebuke** = reprove sharply and sternly, with authority and often in public: *The sergeant rebuked the patrolmen who had been neglecting duty.*

rep·tile (rep′tīl) *n.* **1** a cold-blooded animal that creeps or crawls. Snakes, lizards, turtles, alligators, and crocodiles are reptiles. **2** a low, mean person. *—adj.* **1** of or like a reptile; crawling; creeping. **2** low; mean. [ME < LL *reptile,* originally neut. adj. < L *repere* crawl]

rep·til·i·an (rep til′ē ən) *adj.* **1** of or having to do with reptiles. **2** like a reptile; base; mean. *—n.* a reptile.

re·pub·lic (ri pub′lik) *n.* **1** a nation or state in which the citizens elect representatives to manage the government, the head of which is a president rather than a monarch. **2** any body of persons or things: *the republic of authors and scholars.* [< L *res publica* public interest, state]

re·pub·li·can (ri pub′lə kən) *adj.* **1** of a republic; like that of a republic. **2** favoring a republic. **3 Republican,** *U.S.* of or having to do with the Republican Party. *—n.* **1** a person who favors a republic. **2 Republican,** *U.S.* a member of the Republican Party.

re·pub·li·can·ism (ri pub′lə kən iz′əm) *n.* **1** republican government. **2** republican principles; adherence to republican principles. **3 Republicanism,** *U.S.* the principles or policies of the Republican Party.

Republican Party in the United States, one of the two main political parties.

re·pub·li·ca·tion (rē′pub lə kā′shən) *n.* **1** publication anew. **2** a book, etc. published again.

re·pu·di·ate (ri pū′dē āt′) *v.* **-at·ed, -at·ing. 1** refuse to accept; reject: *repudiate a doctrine.* **2** refuse to acknowledge or pay: *repudiate a debt.* **3** cast off; disown: *repudiate a son.* [< L *repudiare* < *repudium* divorce, probably originally, a spurning < *re-* back, away + *pod-* kick (related to *pes, pedis* foot)] **—re·pu′di·a′tor,** *n.* **—Syn. 1** disclaim.

re·pu·di·a·tion (ri pū′dē ā′shən) *n.* the act of repudiating; fact or condition of being repudiated.

re·pug·nance (ri pug′nəns) *n.* strong dislike, distaste, or aversion.

re·pug·nan·cy (ri pug′nən sē) *n.* repugnance.

re·pug·nant (ri pug′nənt) *adj.* **1** distasteful; disagreeable; offensive: *Work is repugnant to lazy people.* **2** objecting; averse; opposed: *Segregation is repugnant to our idea of equality.* [ME < L *repugnans, -antis,* ppr. of *repugnare* resist < *re-* back + *pugnare* fight] **—re·pug′nant·ly,** *adv.* **—Syn. 1** objectionable.

re·pulse (ri puls′) *v.* **-pulsed, -puls·ing,** *n.* *—v.* **1** drive back; repel. **2** refuse to accept; reject: *She coldly repulsed the plan.* *—n.* **1** a driving back; being driven back: *After the second repulse, the enemy surrendered.* **2** a refusal; rejection. [< L *repulsus,* pp. of *repellere* repel. See REPEL.]

re·pul·sion (ri pul′shən) *n.* **1** a strong dislike or aversion. **2** a repulse; repelling or being repelled.

re·pul·sive (ri pul′siv) *adj.* **1** causing strong dislike or aversion: *Snakes are repulsive to some people.* **2** tending to drive back or repel. **—re·pul′sive·ly,** *adv.* **—re·pul′sive·ness,** *n.*

re·pur·chase (rē pėr′chəs) *v.* **-chased, -chas·ing,** *n.* *—v.* buy again; buy back. *—n.* the act of buying back.

rep·u·ta·ble (rep′yu̇ tə bəl) *adj.* having a good reputation; well thought of; in good repute. **—rep′u·ta·bly,** *adv.* **—Syn.** respectable, estimable.

rep·u·ta·tion (rep′yu̇ tā′shən) *n.* **1** what people think and say the character of a person or thing is; character in the opinion of others: *He had the reputation of being very bright.* **2** a good name; high standing in the opinion of others. **3** fame. **—Syn. 1** name, repute.

re·pute (ri pūt′) *n.* *v.* **-put·ed, -put·ing.** *—n.* **1** reputation. **2** a good reputation. [< v.] *—v.* suppose to be; consider; suppose: *He is reputed the richest man in the city.* [< L *reputare* < *re-* over + *putare* think]

re·put·ed (ri pūt′id) *adj.* accounted or supposed to be such: *the reputed author of a book.*

re·put·ed·ly (ri pūt′id lē) *adv.* by repute; supposedly.

re·quest (ri kwest′) *v.* **1** ask for; ask as a favor: *He requested a loan from the bank.* **2** ask: *He requested her to go with him.* *—n.* **1** the act of asking: *She did it at our request.* **2** what is asked for: *He granted my request.* **3** the state of being asked for or sought after: *She is such a good dancer that she is in great request.* **4 by request,** in response to a request. [ME < OF *requester* < *requeste* < VL *requaesita* < *requaerere* < L *re-* again + *quaerere* ask] **—Syn.** *v.* **1** See **ask. 2** beg, beseech, entreat.

Req·ui·em or **req·ui·em** (rek′wē əm or rē′kwē əm) *n.* **1** a Mass or similar religious service sung for the dead. **2 a** the music for such a service. **b** a musical composition of similar theme and style. **3** any hymn or other composition for the dead. [< L *requiem,* accus. of *requies* rest; the first word of the Mass for the dead]

re·qui·es·cat in pa·ce (rek′wē es′kat in pä′chā) *Latin.* "May he (or she) rest in peace," a wish or prayer for the dead. *Abbrev.:* R.I.P. [< L *requiescat* may he (or she) rest, ult. < *re-* again + *quies* rest; *in pace* in peace < *pax, pacis* peace]

re·quire (ri kwīr′) *v.* **-quired, -quir·ing. 1** have need for; need; want: *We shall require more help.* **2** command; order; demand: *The rules require us all to be present.* [ME < OF < L *requirere* < *re-* again + *quaerere* ask. Related to REQUEST.] **—Syn. 2** See **demand.**

re·quire·ment (ri kwīr′mənt) *n.* **1** a need; something needed: *Patience is a requirement in teaching.* **2** a demand; something demanded: *He has filled all requirements for graduation.*

req·ui·site (rek′wə zit) *adj.* required by circumstances; needed; necessary: *the qualities requisite for a leader, the number of votes requisite for election.* *—n.* the thing needed: *Food and air are requisites for life.* [ME < L *requisitus,* pp. of *requirere.* See REQUIRE.] **—req′ui·site·ly,** *adv.* **—req′ui·site·ness,** *n.* **—Syn.** *adj.* **essential,** indispensable.

req·ui·si·tion (rek′wə zish′ən) *n.* **1** the act of requiring. **2** a demand made, especially a formal written demand: *the requisition of supplies for troops.* **3** the state of being required for use or called into service: *The car was in constant requisition for errands.* **4** an essential condition; requirement.
—v. **1** demand or take by authority: *requisition supplies, horses, or labor.* **2** make demands upon: *The army requisitioned the village for food.*

re·quit·al (ri kwīt′əl) *n.* a repayment; payment; return: *What requital can we make for all his kindness to us?*

re·quite (ri kwīt′) *v.* **-quit·ed, -quit·ing. 1** pay back; make return for: *The Bible tells us to requite evil with good.* **2** make return to: *The knight requited the boy for his warning.* [< *re-* + *quite,* var. of *quit*] **—Syn. 1** repay, reward.

rere·dos (rēr′dos) *n.* a screen or a decorated part of the wall behind an altar. [ME < AF **reredos,* ult. < *rere* rear[1] + *dos* back < L *dossus,* var. of *dorsum*]

re·route (rē rüt′ or -rout′) *v.* **-rout·ed, -rout·ing.** send by a new or different route.

re·run (*v.* rē run′; *n.* rē′run′) *v.* **-ran, -run·ning,** *n.* *—v.* run again. *—n.* **1** a running again. **2** a television program or motion-picture film that is shown again.

re·sale (rē′sāl′ or rē sāl′) *n.* **1** the act of selling again. **2** a selling at retail: *The store has a 20 per cent markup over the wholesale price for resale.*

re·scind (ri sind′) *v.* deprive of force; repeal; cancel:

rescind a law. [< L *rescindere* < *re-* back + *scindere* cut]

re·scis·sion (ri sizh′ən) *n.* a rescinding. [< LL *rescissio, -onis* < L *rescindere.* See RESCIND.]

re·script (rē′skript) *n.* **1** a written answer to a question or petition. **2** an edict; decree; an official announcement. **3** a rewriting. [< L *rescriptum,* originally neut. pp. of *rescribere* write in reply < *re-* back + *scribere* write]

res·cue (res′kū) *v.* **-cued, -cu·ing,** *n.* —*v.* **1** save from danger, capture, harm, etc.; free; deliver. **2** in law, take (a person) forcibly or unlawfully from a jail, the police, etc.; take (property) unlawfully from legal custody.
—*n.* **1** the act of saving or freeing from danger, capture, harm, etc. **2** in law, the forcible or unlawful taking of a person or thing from the care of the law. [ME < OF *rescoure,* ult. < L *re-* back + *ex* out + *quatere* shake] —**res′cu·er,** *n.*
Syn. *v.* **1 Rescue, deliver** = save or free from danger, harm, or restraint. **Rescue** = save, by quick and forceful action, a person from immediate or threatened danger or harm, such as death, injury, attack, capture, confinement, etc.: *Searchers rescued the boys lost in the mountains.* **Deliver** = set someone free from something holding him in captivity or under its power or control, such as prison, slavery, oppression, suffering, temptation, evil, etc.: *Advancing troops delivered the prisoners.*

re·search (ri sėrch′ or rē′sėrch) *n.* a careful hunting for facts or truth; inquiry; investigation: *Medical research has done much to lessen disease.* —*v.* **1** carry out research. **2** inquire into (something) thoroughly; investigate. [< MF *recerche* < *re-* again + *cerche* search]

re·search·er (ri sėr′chər or rē′sėr chər) *n.* a person who carries out research; investigator.

re·seat (rē sēt′) *v.* **1** seat again. **2** provide with a new seat or seats.

re·sec·tion (ri sek′shən) *n.* the removal of an organ, bone, part, etc. by surgery.

re·sem·blance (ri zem′bləns) *n.* a similar appearance; likeness: *Twins often show great resemblance.* [< AF]
Syn. Resemblance, similarity = likeness to another or between two persons or things. **Resemblance** emphasizes looking alike or having some of the same external features or superficial qualities: *There is some resemblance between the accounts of the fire, but all the important details are different.* **Similarity** especially suggests being of the same kind or nature, having some of the same essential qualities and usually a strong resemblance: *The similarity between the two reports suggests that one person wrote both.*

re·sem·ble (ri zem′bəl) *v.* **-bled, -bling.** be like; be similar to; have likeness to in form, figure, or qualities. [ME < OF *resembler,* ult. < L *re-* again + *similis* similar] —**re·sem′bler,** *n.*

re·sent (ri zent′) *v.* feel injured and angry at; feel indignation at: *Our cat seems to resent having anyone sit in its chair.* [< F *ressentir,* ult. < L *re-* back + *sentire* feel] —**re·sent′er,** *n.*

re·sent·ful (ri zent′fəl) *adj.* feeling resentment; injured and angry; showing resentment. —**re·sent′ful·ly,** *adv.* —**re·sent′ful·ness,** *n.*

re·sent·ment (ri zent′mənt) *n.* the feeling that one has at being wronged or insulted; indignation.

res·er·va·tion (rez′ər vā′shən) *n.* **1** a keeping back; hiding in part; something not expressed: *She outwardly approved of the plan with the mental reservation that she would change it to suit herself.* **2** a limiting condition: *The committee accepted the plan with reservations plainly stated.* **3** land set aside for a special purpose; reserve. **4** an arrangement to keep a thing for a person; securing of accommodations, etc.: *We make reservations in advance for rooms at a hotel, seats at a theatre or in a parlor car, etc.* **5** something reserved. **6** in Canada, the provision made for the withholding of royal assent to a bill, federal or provincial, until it has been re-examined.

re·serve (ri zėrv′) *v.* **-served, -serv·ing,** *n. adj.* —*v.* **1** keep back; hold back: *reserve criticism.* **2** set apart: *time reserved for recreation.* **3** save for use later: *Reserve enough money for your fare home.* **4** set aside for the use of a particular person or persons: *Reserve a table.*
—*n.* **1** the actual cash in a bank or assets that can be turned into cash quickly. Banks must keep a reserve of money. **2** in military use: **a** a body of soldiers kept ready to help the main army in battle. **b the reserve,** a section of one of the armed services that in peace time is not on full-time, active duty. **c reserves,** *pl.* members of such a force. **3 a** a tract of land set apart by the government for a special purpose: *a forest reserve.* **b** such a tract set apart, usually by treaty, for the exclusive use of Indians; reservation. **4** a person kept in reserve or available as a substitute: *He is a reserve for the basketball team.* **5** anything kept back for future use. **6** the act of keeping back or holding back. **7** the fact, state, or condition of being kept, set apart, or saved for use later. **8** the act or practice of keeping one's thoughts, feelings, and affairs to oneself; self-restraint; lack of friendliness. **9** an exception or qualification to the acceptance of some idea, belief, etc. **10** a silent or withdrawn manner that keeps people from making friends easily.
—*adj.* kept in reserve; forming a reserve. [ME < OF < L *reservare* < *re-* back + *servare* keep] —**re·serv′er,** *n.* —**Syn.** *v.* **1** retain.

hat, āge, cãre, fär; let, ēqual, tėrm; it, īce
hot, ōpen, ôrder; oil, out; cup, pu̇t, rüle, ūse
əbove, takən, pencəl, lemən, circəs
ch, child; ng, long; sh, ship
th, thin; ᴛʜ, then; zh, measure

reserve army the militia: *Members of the reserve army are not full-time soldiers.*

re·served (ri zėrvd′) *adj.* **1** kept in reserve; kept by special arrangement: *reserved seats.* **2** set apart. **3** self-restrained in action or speech. **4** disposed to keep to oneself. —**Syn. 1** withheld, retained. **3** restrained, reticent.

re·serv·ed·ly (ri zėr′vid lē) *adv.* in a reserved manner.

re·serv·ist (ri zėr′vist) *n.* a member of the reserve.

res·er·voir (rez′ər vwär′ or rez′ər vwôr′) *n.* **1** a place where water is collected and stored for use: *This reservoir supplies the entire city.* **2** anything to hold a liquid: *A fountain pen has an ink reservoir.* **3** a place where anything is collected and stored: *His mind was a reservoir of facts.* **4** a great supply. [< F *réservoir* < *réserver* reserve]

re·set (*v.* rē set′; *n.* rē′set′) *v.* **-set, -set·ting,** *n.* —*v.* set again: *The diamonds were reset in platinum. John's broken arm had to be reset.* —*n.* **1** the act of resetting. **2** the thing reset.

re·set·tle·ment (rē set′əl mənt) *n.* the act or condition of settling again.

re·shape (rē shāp′) *v.* **-shaped, -shap·ing.** shape anew; form into a new or different shape.

re·ship·ment (rē ship′mənt) *n.* **1** a shipping again. **2** that which is shipped again.

re·side (ri zīd′) *v.* **-sid·ed, -sid·ing. 1** live (*in* or *at*) for a long time; dwell. **2** be (*in*); exist (*in*): *Her charm resides in her happy smile.* [< L *residere* < *re-* back + *sedere* sit, settle] —**re·sid′er,** *n.*

res·i·dence (rez′ə dəns) *n.* **1** a place where a person lives; house; home. **2** residing; living; dwelling. **3** a period of residing in a place. **4** a building in which students, nurses, etc. live. **5 in residence, a** living in a place: *The owner of the house is not in residence.* **b** living in an institution while on duty or doing active work: *a doctor in residence.* —**Syn. 1** dwelling, habitation.

res·i·den·cy (rez′ə dən sē) *n.* **-cies. 1** a residence. **2** in India, formerly, the official residence of a representative of the Governor General at a native court. **3** formerly, an administrative division of the Dutch East Indies.

res·i·dent (rez′ə dənt) *n.* **1** a person living in a place, not a visitor. **2** a resident physician, especially one who has completed internship. **3** an official sent to live in a foreign land to represent his country. **4** formerly, a representative of the British Governor General of India at a native court. **5** formerly, the governor of an administrative division of the Dutch East Indies.
—*adj.* **1** staying; dwelling in a place. A resident owner lives on his property. **2** living in a place while on duty or doing active work. **3** not migratory: *English sparrows are resident birds.* [ME < L *residens, -entis,* ppr. of *residere.* See RESIDE.]

res·i·den·tial (rez′ə den′shəl) *adj.* **1** of, having to do with, or fitted for homes or residences: *They live in a good residential district.* **2** having to do with residence: *a residential qualification for schoolteachers.*

re·sid·u·al (ri zij′ü əl) *adj.* **1** of or forming a residue;

remaining; left over. **2** in geology, resulting in the weathering of rock: *residual clay soil, a residual deposit.* —*n.* **1** the amount left over; remainder. **2** a residual quantity. **3** a fee paid to a performer or writer for each rerun of a radio or television broadcast, etc.

re·sid·u·ar·y (ri zij′ü er′ē) *adj.* entitled to the remainder of an estate.

res·i·due (rez′ə dū′ or rez′ə dü′) *n.* **1** what remains after a part is taken; remainder: *The syrup had dried up, leaving a sticky residue.* **2** in law, the part of a testator's estate that is left after all debts, charges, and particular devises and bequests have been satisfied: *Mr. Smith's will directed that the residue of his property should go to his son.* **3** in chemistry, an atom or group of atoms considered as a radical or part of a molecule. [< F < L *residuum,* neut. adj., left over. Doublet of RESIDUUM.]

re·sid·u·um (ri zij′ü əm) *n.* **-sid·u·a** (-zij′ü ə). what is left at the end of any process; residue; remainder. [< L. Doublet of RESIDUE.]

re·sign (ri zīn′) *v.* **1** give up a job, position, etc.: *The minister resigned.* **2** give up (something): *The M.P. resigned his seat in Parliament.* **3 resign oneself,** submit quietly; adapt oneself, often unwillingly. [ME < OF < L *resignare* unseal, ult. < *re-* back + *signum* seal]

☛ Resign is often followed by *from,* though sometimes the object follows without the *from*: *He resigned from the editorship of the magazine.* Or: *He resigned the editorship of the magazine.*

res·ig·na·tion (rez′ig nā′shən) *n.* **1** the act of resigning. **2** a written statement giving notice that one resigns. **3** patient acceptance; quiet submission: *She bore the pain with resignation.* —**Syn. 3** acquiescence, meekness.

re·signed (ri zīnd′) *adj.* showing or feeling resignation; accepting, often unwillingly; submissive. —**Syn.** submissive, acquiescent.

re·sign·ed·ly (ri zīn′id lē) *adv.* in a resigned manner; with resignation.

re·sil·i·ence (ri zil′ē əns or ri zil′yəns) *n.* **1** the power of springing back; elasticity; a resilient quality or nature: *Rubber has resilience.* **2** buoyancy; cheerfulness.

re·sil·i·en·cy (ri zil′ē ən sē or ri zil′yən sē) *n.* resilience.

re·sil·i·ent (ri zil′ē ənt or ri zil′yənt) *adj.* **1** springing back; returning to the original form or position after being bent, compressed, or stretched: *resilient steel, resilient turf.* **2** buoyant; cheerful: *a resilient nature that throws off trouble.* [< L *resiliens, -entis,* ppr. of *resilire* rebound < *re-* back + *salire* jump]

res·in (rez′ən) *n.* **1** a sticky, yellow or brown substance that flows from certain plants and trees, especially the pine and fir. It is used in medicine and varnish. The harder portion of resin remaining after heating is called rosin. **2** any similar substance that is made synthetically. Artificial resins are used in the manufacture of plastics. —*v.* rub, coat, or treat with resin. [< L *resina*]

res·in·ous (rez′ə nəs) *adj.* **1** of resin. **2** like resin. containing resin; full of resin.

re·sist (ri zist′) *v.* **1** act against (something); strive against; oppose: *The window resisted his efforts to open it.* **2** act against something; oppose something: *Do not resist.* **3** strive successfully against; keep from: *I could not resist laughing.* **4** withstand the action or effect of (an acid, storm, etc.). [< L *resistere* < *re-* back + *sistere* make a stand] —**re·sist′er,** *n.* —**Syn. 1** withstand. See **oppose.**

re·sist·ance (ri zis′təns) *n.* **1** the act of resisting: *The bank clerk made no resistance to the robbers.* **2** the power to resist: *She has little resistance to germs and so is often ill.* **3** a thing or act that resists; an opposing force; opposition. An airplane can overcome the resistance of the air and go in the desired direction, while a balloon simply drifts. **4** in electricity, the property of a conductor that opposes the passage of a current and changes electric energy into heat. Copper has a low resistance. **5** a conductor, coil, etc. that offers resistance. **6 Resistance,** an underground movement for guerrilla warfare, sabotage, etc.

resistance coil a coil or wire made of metal that has a high resistance, used especially for measuring resistance, reducing voltage or amperage, and producing heat.

re·sist·ant (ri zis′tənt) *adj.* resisting.

re·sist·i·bil·i·ty (ri zis′tə bil′ə tē) *n.* the quality of being resistible.

re·sist·i·ble (ri zis′tə bəl) *adj.* capable of being resisted.

re·sist·less (ri zist′lis) *adj.* that cannot be resisted: *A resistless impulse made him wander over the earth.*

re·sis·tor (ri zis′tər) *n.* a conducting body or device used in an electric circuit, etc. because of its resistance.

re·sole (rē sōl′) *v.* **-soled, -sol·ing.** put a new sole on (a shoe, etc.).

re·sol·u·ble[1] (ri zol′yů bəl) *adj.* capable of being resolved.

re·sol·u·ble[2] (rē sol′yů bəl) *adj.* capable of being dissolved again.

res·o·lute (rez′ə lüt′) *adj.* **1** determined; firm: *He was resolute in his attempt to climb to the top of the mountain.* **2** bold: *A soldier must be resolute in battle.* **3** indicating firmness, boldness, etc.: *a resolute air.* [< L *resolutus,* pp. of *resolvere* resolve. See RESOLVE.] —**res′o·lute·ly,** *adv.*

res·o·lu·tion (rez′ə lü′shən) *n.* **1** something decided on; thing determined: *He made a resolution to get up early.* **2** an act of resolving or determining. **3** the power of holding firmly to a purpose; determination. **4** a formal expression of opinion: *The club passed a resolution thanking the secretary for his help throughout the year.* **5** a breaking into parts. **6** the act or result of solving; solution.

re·solve (ri zolv′) *v.* **-solved, -solv·ing,** *n.* —*v.* **1** make up one's mind; determine; decide: *He resolved to do better work in the future.* **2** break into parts; break up: *The compound can be made to resolve into its parts.* **3** answer and explain; solve: *His letter resolved all our doubts.* **4** decide by vote: *It was resolved that our community centre have a coffee bar.* **5** present for a decision by voting. **6** change: *The assembly resolved itself into committees.* **7** produce separate images of; make distinguishable by optical instruments, radar, etc:. *resolve a cluster of stars with a high-powered telescope.* —*n.* **1** the thing determined on: *He kept his resolve to do better.* **2** firmness in carrying out a purpose; determination. [< L *resolvere* < *re-* un- + *solvere* loosen] —**re·solv′a·ble** *adj.* —**re·solv′er,** *n.* —**Syn.** *v.* **1** See **decide.**

re·solved (ri zolvd′) *adj.* determined; resolute.

re·solv·ed·ly (ri zol′vid lē) *adv.* in a determined manner; with resolution.

res·o·nance (rez′ə nəns) *n.* **1** a resounding quality; being resonant: *the resonance of an organ.* **2** in physics, a reinforcing and prolonging of sound by reflection or by vibration of other objects. The sounding board of a piano gives it resonance. **3** in electricity, the condition of a circuit adjusted to allow the greatest flow of current at a certain frequency. A radio set must be in resonance to receive music or speech from a radio station.

res·o·nant (rez′ə nənt) *adj.* **1** resounding; continuing to sound; echoing. **2** tending to increase or prolong sounds. **3** of or in resonance. [< L *resonans, -antis,* ppr. of *resonare,* ult. < *re-* back + *sonus* sound] —**res′o·nant·ly,** *adv.*

res·o·nate (rez′ə nāt′) *v.* **-nat·ed, -nat·ing.** resound; exhibit resonance. [< L *resonare.* Doublet of RESOUND.]

res·o·na·tor (rez′ə nā′tər) *n.* **1** something that produces resonance; an appliance for increasing sound by resonance. **2** a device for detecting electromagnetic radiation, as radio broadcasting waves. [< NL]

res·or·cin (rez ôr′sən) *n.* resorcinol. [< *res(in)* + *orcin,* a chemical compound (< NL *orcina*)]

res·or·cin·ol (rez ôr′sə nol′ or rez ôr′sə nōl′) *n.* a colorless crystalline substance that is used in medicine as an antiseptic, and in making dyes, drugs, etc. *Formula*: $C_6H_4(OH)_2$ [< *resorcin* + *-ol*]

re·sort (ri zôrt′) *v.* **1** go; go often: *Many people resort to the beaches in hot weather.* **2** turn for help: *resort to violence.* —*n.* **1** an assembling; going to often: *A park is a place of popular resort in good weather.* **2** a place people go to, usually for relaxation or recreation: *There are many summer resorts in the mountains.* **3** the act of turning for help: *The resort to force is a poor substitute for persuasion.* **4** a person or thing turned to for help. [ME < OF *resortir* < *re-* back + *sortir* go out]

re·sound (ri zound′) *v.* **1** give back sound; echo: *The hills resounded when he shouted.* **2** give back (sound); echo (sound). **3** sound loudly: *Radios resound from every house.* **4** be filled with sound: *The room resounded with the children's shouts.* **5** repeat loudly: *resound a hero's praise.* **6** be much talked about. [< L *resonare*, ult. < *re-* back + *sonus* sound. Doublet of RESONATE.] —**re·sound′ing·ly,** *adv.*

re·source (ri zôrs′ or ri sôrs′) *n.* **1** any supply that will meet a need. We have resources of money, of quick wit, and of strength. **2 resources,** *pl.* the actual and potential wealth of a country; natural resources. **3** any means of getting success or getting out of trouble: *Climbing a tree is a cat's resource when chased by a dog.* **4** skill in meeting difficulties, getting out of trouble, etc. [< F *resource*, ult. < L *re-* again + *surgere* rise]

re·source·ful (ri zôrs′fəl or ri sôrs′-) *adj.* good at thinking of ways to do things; quick-witted. —**re·source′ful·ly,** *adv.* —**re·source′ful·ness,** *n.*

resp. 1 respectively. **2** respondent.

re·spect (ri spekt′) *n.* **1** honor; esteem: *Children should show respect to those who are older and wiser.* **2** consideration; regard: *Show respect for other people's property.* **3 respects,** *pl.* expressions of respect; regards. **4** a point; matter; detail: *The plan is unwise in many respects.* **5** relation; reference. **6 in respect of,** with reference or comparison to. **7 in respect that,** because of the fact that; since. **8 with respect to,** with relation, reference, or regard to (something): *We must plan with respect to the future.* —*v.* **1** feel or show honor or esteem for: *We respect an honest person.* **2** show consideration for: *Respect the ideas and feelings of others.* **3** relate to; refer to; be connected with. [< L *respectus* < *respicere* look back, have regard for < *re-* back + *specere* look] —**re·spect′er,** *n.*
Syn. *n.* **1** reverence, veneration. **2 Respect, regard** = consideration, felt or shown, for someone or something of recognized worth or value. **Respect** emphasizes recognizing or judging the worth or value of someone or something and paying the consideration or honor due: *A soldier may feel respect for an officer he dislikes.* **Regard** emphasizes seeing that a person or thing is entitled to consideration, appreciation, or admiration, and usually suggests a kindly, friendly, or sympathetic feeling: *A person who reads another's mail has no regard for other people's privacy.* **4** particular.

re·spect·a·bil·i·ty (ri spek′tə bil′ə tē) *n.* **-ties. 1** the quality or condition of being respectable. **2** respectable social standing.

re·spect·a·ble (ri spek′tə bəl) *adj.* **1** worthy of respect; having a good reputation: *Respectable citizens obey the laws.* **2** having fair social standing; honest and decent: *His parents were poor, but respectable, people.* **3** fairly good; moderate in size or quality: *John's record in his career was respectable but not brilliant.* **4** good enough to use; fit to be seen. —**re·spect′a·bly,** *adv.*

re·spect·ful (ri spekt′fəl) *adj.* showing respect; polite. —**re·spect′ful·ly,** *adv.* —**re·spect′ful·ness,** *n.*

re·spect·ing (ri spek′ting) *prep.* regarding; about; concerning: *A discussion arose respecting the merits of different automobiles.*

re·spec·tive (ri spek′tiv) *adj.* belonging to each; particular; individual: *The wrestlers returned to their respective corners.*

re·spec·tive·ly (ri spek′tiv lē) *adv.* as regards each one in his turn or in the order mentioned: *Brown, Smyth, and Jones are 27, 43, and 35 years old respectively.*

re·spell (rē′spel′) *v.* spell over again, especially in a phonetic alphabet or in the alphabet or writing system of another language.

res·pi·ra·tion (res′pə rā′shən) *n.* **1** the act of inhaling and exhaling; breathing. **2** in biology, the processes by which an animal, plant, or living cell secures oxygen from the air or water, distributes it, combines it with substances in the tissues, and gives off carbon dioxide.

res·pi·ra·tor (res′pə rā′tər) *n.* **1** a device worn over the nose and mouth to prevent inhaling harmful substances. **2** a device used to help a person breathe.

res·pi·ra·to·ry (res′pə rə tô′rē) *adj.* having to do with or used for breathing. The lungs are respiratory organs.

re·spire (ri spīr′) *v.* **-spired, -spir·ing.** inhale and exhale; breathe. [< L *respirare* < *re-* regularly + *spirare* breathe]

res·pite (res′pit or res′pīt) *n. v.* **-pit·ed, -pit·ing.** —*n.*

hat, āge, cãre, fär; let, ēqual, tėrm; it, īce
hot, ōpen, ôrder; oil, out; cup, pu̇t, rüle, ūse
əbove, takən, pencəl, lemən, circəs
ch, child; ng, long; sh, ship
th, thin; ᴛʜ, then; zh, measure

1 a time of relief and rest; lull: *A thick cloud brought a respite from the glare of the sun.* **2** a putting off; delay, especially in carrying out a sentence of death; reprieve. —*v.* give a respite to. [ME < OF < VL *respectus* delay < LL *respectus* expectation < L *respectare* wait for. Related to RESPECT.]

re·splend·ence (ri splen′dəns) *n.* splendor; great brightness; gorgeous appearance.

re·splend·en·cy (ri splen′dən sē) *n.* resplendence.

re·splend·ent (ri splen′dənt) *adj.* very bright; shining; splendid: *The queen was resplendent with jewels.* [ME < L *resplendens, -entis*, ppr. of *resplendere* glitter < *re-* back + *splendere* shine] —**re·splend′ent·ly,** *adv.*

re·spond (ri spond′) *v.* **1** answer; reply. **2** act in answer; react: *A dog responds to kind treatment by loving its master.* [ME < OF < L *respondere* < *re-* in return + *spondere* promise] —**Syn. 1** See **answer.**

re·spond·ent (ri spon′dənt) *adj.* answering; responding. —*n.* **1** a person who responds. **2** a defendant, especially in a divorce case.

re·sponse (ri spons′) *n.* **1** an answer by word or act. **2** in a religious service, a set of words said or sung by the congregation or choir in answer to the minister. **3** the reaction of body or mind to a stimulus. [< L *responsum*, originally neut. pp. of *respondere* respond. See RESPOND.] —**Syn. 1** rejoinder, reply.

re·spon·si·bil·i·ty (ri spon′sə bil′ə tē) *n.* **-ties. 1** a being responsible; obligation: *A little child does not feel much responsibility.* **2** something for which one is responsible: *Keeping house and caring for the children are her responsibilities.*

re·spon·si·ble (ri spon′sə bəl) *adj.* **1** obliged or expected to account (*for*): *Each pupil is responsible for the care of the books given him. The government is responsible to the people for its proper conduct of the country's affairs.* **2** deserving credit or blame: *The bad weather is responsible for the small attendance.* **3** trustworthy; reliable: *A responsible person should take care of the money.* **4** involving obligation or duties: *The Prime Minister holds a very responsible position.* **5** able to tell right from wrong; able to think and act reasonably: *Insane people are not responsible.* —**re·spon′si·ble·ness,** *n.* —**re·spon′si·bly,** *adv.* —**Syn. 1** accountable, answerable.

re·spon·sive (ri spon′siv) *adj.* **1** making answer; responding: *a responsive glance.* **2** easily moved; responding readily: *have a responsive nature, be responsive to kindness.* **3** using or containing responses: *responsive reading in church in which minister and congregation read in turn.* —**re·spon′sive·ly,** *adv.* —**re·spon′sive·ness,** *n.*

rest[1] (rest) *n.* **1** sleep: *a good night's rest.* **2** ease after work or effort: *Allow an hour for rest.* **3** freedom from anything that tires, troubles, disturbs, or pains; quiet: *The medicine gave the sick man a short rest from pain.* **4** the absence of motion: *The driver brought the car to rest.* **5** a support: *a rest for a billiard cue.* **6** a place of rest: *sailors' rest.* **7** in music: **a** a period of silence, having the same duration as a corresponding note. **b** a mark used to indicate a period of silence. **8** in reading, a pause. **9** death; the grave. **10 at rest, a** asleep. **b** not moving. **c** free from pain, trouble, etc.: *The injured man is now at rest.* **d** dead. **11 lay to rest,** bury. [OE] —*v.* **1** be still; sleep: *Lie down and rest.* **2** be free from work, effort, care, trouble, etc.: *He was able to rest during his holidays.* **3** stop moving; cause to stop moving: *The ball rested at the bottom of the hill.* **4** give rest to; refresh by rest: *Stop and rest your horse.* **5** lie, recline, sit, lean, etc. for rest or ease: *He spent the whole day resting in a chair.* **6** be supported: *The ladder rests against*

Rests (def. 7); W, whole; H, half; Q, quarter; E, eighth; S, sixteenth; T, thirty-second. A whole rest lasts as long as a whole note, a half rest half as long, and so on.

the wall. **7** fix or be fixed: *Our eyes rested on the open book.* **8** be at ease: *Don't let her rest until she promises to visit us.* **9** become inactive; let remain inactive: *Let the matter rest. Rest the matter there.* **10** place for support; lay; lean: *rest one's head in one's hands.* **11** rely (*on*); trust (*in*); depend; be based: *Our hope rests on you.* **12** cause to rely or depend; base: *We rest our hope on you.* **13** be found; be present: *In a democracy, government rests with the people.* **14** be dead; lie in the grave. **15** in law, end voluntarily the introduction of evidence in (a case): *The lawyer rested his case.* **16** of agricultural land, be unused for crops, especially in order to restore fertility. [OE *restan*]

rest² (rest) *n.* what is left; those that are left. —*v.* continue to be: *You may rest assured that I will keep my promise.* [< F *reste,* ult. < L *restare* be left < *re-* back + *stare* stand]

re·state (rē stāt′) *v.* **-stat·ed, -stat·ing. 1** state again or anew. **2** state in a new way.

re·state·ment (rē stāt′ mənt) *n.* **1** a statement made again. **2** a new statement.

res·tau·rant (res′ tə ront or res′ tront) *n.* a place to buy and eat a meal. [< F *restaurant,* originally ppr. of *restaurer* restore]

res·tau·ra·teur (res′ tə rə tėr′) *n.* the owner or manager of a restaurant. [< F]

rest cure a treatment for mental or nervous disorders, consisting of rest and seclusion, a healthful diet, massage, etc.

rest·ful (rest′ fəl) *adj.* **1** full of rest; giving rest. **2** quiet; peaceful. **—rest′ful·ly,** *adv.* **—rest′ful·ness,** *n.*

res·ti·tu·tion (res′ tə tū′ shən or res′ tə tü′ shən) *n.* **1** the giving back of what has been lost or taken away. **2** the act of making good any loss, damage, or injury: *It is only fair that those who do the damage should make restitution.* [< L *restitutio, -onis,* ult. < *re-* again + *statuere* set up] **—Syn. 1** return, restoration. **2** reparation, amends.

res·tive (res′ tiv) *adj.* **1** restless; uneasy. **2** hard to manage. **3** refusing to go ahead; balky. [ME < OF *restif* motionless < *rester* < L *restare.* See REST².] **—res′tive·ly,** *adv.* **—res′tive·ness,** *n.*

rest·less (rest′ lis) *adj.* **1** unable to rest; uneasy: *The dog seemed restless as if he sensed some danger.* **2** without rest or sleep; not restful: *The sick child passed a restless night.* **3** rarely or never still or quiet; always moving. **—rest′less·ly,** *adv.* **—rest′less·ness,** *n.*

re·stock (rē stok′) *v.* supply with a new stock; replenish.

res·to·ra·tion (res′ tə rā′ shən) *n.* **1** the act of restoring or being restored; bringing back to a former condition. **2** something restored. **3 Restoration,** in England: **a** the re-establishment of the monarchy in 1660 under Charles II. **b** the period from 1660 to 1688 during which Charles II and James II reigned.

re·stor·a·tive (ri stôr′ ə tiv) *adj.* capable of restoring; tending to restore health or strength. —*n.* something that restores health and strength.

re·store (ri stôr′) *v.* **-stored, -stor·ing. 1** bring back; establish again: *restore order.* **2** bring back to a former condition or to a normal condition: *The old house has been restored.* **3** give back; put back: *The thief was forced to restore the money to its owner.* [ME < OF < L *restaurare*] **—re·stor′er,** *n.* **—Syn. 2** See **renew.**

re·strain (ri strān′) *v.* **1** hold back; keep down; keep in check; keep within limits: *She could not restrain her curiosity.* **2** keep in prison; confine. [ME < OF *restreindre, restraindre* < L *restringere* restrict. See RESTRICT.] **—re·strain′a·ble,** *adj.* **—re·strain′er,** *n.* **—Syn. 1** detain, repress, curb. See **check.**

re·strain·ed·ly (ri strān′ id lē or ri strānd′ lē) *adv.* in a restrained manner; with restraint.

re·straint (ri strānt′) *n.* **1** a restraining or being restrained. **2** a means of restraining. **3** a tendency to restrain natural feeling; reserve. [ME < OF *restraint(e)* < *restraindre.* See RESTRAIN.] **—Syn. 1** restriction, check, curb.

restraint of trade in business, the limitation or prevention of free competition.

re·strict (ri strikt′) *v.* keep within limits; confine: *Our club membership is restricted to twelve.* [< L *restrictus,* pp. of *restringere* < *re-* back + *stringere* draw tight]

re·stric·tion (ri strik′ shən) *n.* **1** something that restricts; limiting condition or rule: *The restrictions on the use of the new gymnasium are these: no hard-soled boots or shoes; no fighting; no damaging of property.* **2** a restricting or being restricted: *This part is open to the public without restriction.*

re·stric·tive (ri strik′ tiv) *adj.* restricting; limiting: *Some laws are prohibitive; some are only restrictive.* **—re·stric′tive·ly,** *adv.*

restrictive clause in grammar, an adjectival clause that is an essential and inseparable part of the sentence in which it appears.

☛ **A restrictive clause** restricts the noun it modifies in that it identifies or defines the member of the class of things being referred to and is for this reason an inseparable part of the noun construction; such clauses are never set off by commas, nor is there any perceptible pause before or after them in speech. *Example:* The man *who came to dinner* stayed for a month. **A non-restrictive clause** contains nothing more than descriptive detail and for this reason is merely a clause inserted in the main construction; such clauses must be set off from the main clause by commas and there is a perceptible pause, usually accompanied by a change in voice pitch, before and after them in speech. *Example:* The principal of the high school, *who is a most interesting man,* came to our house for dinner last evening.

re·string (rē string′) *v.* **-strung, -string·ing.** put a new string or new strings on.

rest room a room providing toilet facilities in a public building, theatre, store, service station, etc.

re·sult (ri zult′) *n.* **1** that which happens because of something; what is caused: *The result of the fall was a broken leg.* **2** a good or useful result: *We want results, not talk.* **3** in mathematics, a quantity, value, etc. obtained by calculation. **4** an outcome: *the result of a game.* [< v.] —*v.* **1** be a result; follow as a consequence: *Sickness often results from eating too much.* **2** have as a result; end: *Eating too much often results in sickness.* [< L *resultare* rebound, ult. < *re-* back + *salire* spring] **—Syn.** *n.* **1** consequence, outcome. See **effect.**

re·sult·ant (ri zul′ tənt) *adj.* resulting. —*n.* **1** a result. **2** in physics, any force that has the same effect as two or more forces acting together.

re·sume (ri züm′ or ri zūm′) *v.* **-sumed, -sum·ing. 1** begin again; go on: *Resume reading where we left off.* **2** get or take again: *Those standing may resume their seats.* [< L *resumere* < *re-* again + *sumere* take up] **—re·sum′a·ble,** *adj.* **—re·sum′er,** *n.*

rés·u·mé (rez′ ù mā′; *French,* rā zy mā′) *n.* a summary. [< F *résumé,* originally pp. of *résumer* resume]

re·sump·tion (ri zump′ shən) *n.* a resuming: *the resumption of duties after absence.* [ME < LL *resumptio, -onis* < L *resumere.* See RESUME.]

re·sur·face (rē sėr′ fis) *v.* **-faced, -fac·ing.** provide with a new or different surface.

re·surge (ri sėrj′) *v.* **-surged, -surg·ing.** rise again. [< L *resurgere* < *re-* again + *surgere* rise]

re·sur·gence (ri sėr′ jəns) *n.* a rising again.

re·sur·gent (ri sėr′ jənt) *adj.* rising or tending to rise again.

res·ur·rect (rez′ ə rekt′) *v.* **1** raise from the dead; bring back to life. **2** bring back to sight or into use: *resurrect an old custom.* [< *resurrection*]

res·ur·rec·tion (rez′ ə rek′ shən) *n.* **1** a coming to life again; rising from the dead. **2 Resurrection,** the rising of Christ after His death and burial. **3** the state of being alive again after death. **4** a restoration from decay, disuse, etc. [< L *resurrectio, -onis,* ult. < *re-* again + *surgere* rise]

re·sus·ci·tate (ri sus′ ə tāt′) *v.* **-tat·ed, -tat·ing.** bring or come back to life or consciousness; revive. [< L *resuscitare,* ult. < *re-* again + *sub-* up + *citare* rouse < *ciere* stir up] **—re·sus′ci·ta′tion,** *n.*

re·sus·ci·ta·tive (ri sus′ ə tə tiv or ri sus′ ə tā′ tiv) *adj.* helping to resuscitate.

re·sus·ci·ta·tor (ri sus′ ə tā′ tər) *n.* **1** a respirator. **2** one who resuscitates.

hat, āge, cãre, fär; let, ēqual, tėrm; it, īce
hot, ōpen, ôrder; oil, out; cup, pu̇t, rüle, ūse
əbove, takən, pencəl, lemən, circəs
ch, child; ng, long; sh, ship
th, thin; ᴛʜ, then; zh, measure

ret (ret) *v.* **ret·ted, ret·ting.** expose (flax, hemp, etc.) to moisture or soak in water, in order to soften by partial rotting. [< MDu. *reten*]

ret. 1 retain. 2 retired. 3 return.

re·tail (*n. adj. v. 1 and 2* rē′tāl; *v. 3* ri tāl′) *n.* the sale of goods in small quantities at a time: *Our grocer buys at wholesale and sells at retail.*
—*adj.* **1** in small lots or quantities: *The wholesale price of this coat is $40; the retail price is $70.* **2** selling in small quantities: *the retail trade, a retail merchant.*
—*v.* **1** sell in small quantities. **2** be sold in small quantities. **3** tell over again: *She retails everything she hears about her acquaintances.* [ME < OF *retail* scrap, ult. < *re-* back + *taillier* cut, ult. < L *talea* rod]

re·tail·er (rē′tāl ər) *n.* a retail merchant or dealer.

re·tain (ri tān′) *v.* **1** continue to have or hold; keep. **2** keep in mind; remember. **3** employ by payment of a fee: *He retained the best lawyer in the city.* [ME < OF < L *retinere* < *re-* back + *tenere* hold] —**Syn. 1** See **keep.**

re·tain·er[1] (ri tān′ər) *n.* a person who serves a person of rank; vassal; attendant; follower. [< *retain*]

re·tain·er[2] (ri tān′ər) *n.* a fee paid to secure services: *This lawyer receives a retainer before he begins work on a case.* [< F *retenir*, n. use of infin. *retenir* retain]

re·take (*v.* rē tāk′; *n.* rē′tāk′) *v.* **-took, -tak·en, -tak·ing,** *n.* —*v.* **1** take again. **2** take back. —*n.* a retaking: *a retake of a scene in a motion picture.*

re·tal·i·ate (ri tal′ē āt′) *v.* **-at·ed, -at·ing.** repay one injury, etc. with another; return like for like: *If we insult them, they will retaliate.* [< L *retaliare* < *re-* in return + *tal-* pay; influenced by *talis* such]

re·tal·i·a·tion (ri tal′ē ā′shən) *n.* **1** the repaying a wrong, injury, etc. with another; return of like for like. **2** the thing done to retaliate.

re·tal·i·a·tive (ri tal′ē ə tiv or ri tal′ē ā′tiv) *adj.* disposed to retaliate; retaliatory.

re·tal·i·a·to·ry (ri tal′ē ə tô′rē) *adj.* returning like for like, especially one injury for another.

re·tard (ri tärd′) *v.* make slow; delay the progress of; keep back; hinder: *Bad roads retarded the car.* [< L *retardare*, ult. < *re-* back + *tardus* slow] —**re·tard′er,** *n.*

re·tard·ant (ri tärd′ənt) *n.* something, often a chemical, that slows up or delays an effect or an action.
—*adj.* holding back; tending to delay or make slower.

re·tar·da·tion (rē′tär dā′shən) *n.* **1** the act of retarding. **2** the state of being retarded. **3** that which retards; a hindrance.

re·tard·ed (ri tärd′əd) *adj.* **1** held back; hindered. **2** limited or held back in mental development; below a normal level of achievement: *a class for retarded children.*
—*n.* one who is limited in mental development or achievement.

retch (rech) *v.* make efforts to vomit; make movements like those of vomiting. [OE *hrǣcan* clear the throat]

ret'd 1 returned. 2 retired.

re·ten·tion (ri ten′shən) *n.* **1** a retaining. **2** a being retained. **3** the power to retain. **4** the ability to remember. [< L *retentio, -onis* < *retinere* retain. See RETAIN.]

re·ten·tive (ri ten′tiv) *adj.* **1** able to hold or keep. **2** able to remember. —**re·ten′tive·ly,** *adv.* —**re·ten′tive·ness,** *n.*

re·ten·tiv·i·ty (rē′ten tiv′ə tē) *n.* **1** the power to retain; retentiveness. **2** the power of retaining magnetization after the magnetizing force has ceased to operate.

ret·i·cence (ret′ə səns) *n.* a tendency to be silent or say little; reserve in speech.

ret·i·cent (ret′ə sənt) *adj.* disposed to keep silent or say little; not speaking freely; reserved in speech. [< L *reticens, -entis*, ppr. of *reticere* keep silent < *re-* back + *tacere* be silent] —**ret′icently,** *adv.* —**Syn.** reserved, taciturn. See **silent.**

re·tic·u·lar (ri tik′yů lər) *adj.* **1** netlike. **2** intricate; entangled.

re·tic·u·late (*adj.* ri tik′yů lit or ri tik′yů lāt′; *v.* ri tik′yů lāt′) *adj. v.* **-lat·ed, -lat·ing.** —*adj.* netlike; covered with a network. Reticulate leaves have the veins arranged like the threads of a net. —*v.* **1** cover or mark with a network. **2** form a network.

re·tic·u·la·tion (ri tik′yů lā′shən) *n.* **1** a reticulated formation, arrangement, or appearance; network. **2** one of the meshes of a network. [< L *reticulatio, -onis*, ult. < *reticulum*, dim. of *rete* net]

ret·i·cule (ret′ə kūl′) *n.* formerly, a small purse or handbag. [< F < L *reticulum*, dim. of *rete* net. Doublet of RETICULUM.]

re·tic·u·lum (ri tik′yů ləm) *n.* **-la** (-lə). **1** a network; any reticulated system or structure. **2** in zoology, the second stomach of cud-chewing mammals. [< L. Doublet of RETICULE.]

ret·i·na (ret′ə nə) *n.* **-nas, -nae** (-nē′ or -nī′). a membrane at the back of the eyeball, composed of layers of nervous tissue and containing light-sensitive rods and cones. The membrane receives images and passes them on to the optic nerve. See eye for diagram. [< Med.L *retina* < L *retinacula*, pl., band, reins < *retinere* retain. See RETAIN.]

ret·i·nal (ret′ə nəl) *adj.* of or on the retina.

ret·i·nue (ret′ə nū′) *n.* a group of attendants or retainers; following: *The king's retinue accompanied him on the journey.* [ME < OF *retenue*, originally fem. pp. of *retenir* retain < L *retinere*. See RETAIN.]

re·tire (ri tīr′) *v.* **-tired, -tir·ing.** **1** give up an office, occupation, etc.: *The teacher expects to retire at 65.* **2** remove from an office, occupation, etc. **3** go away, especially to be quiet: *She retired to a convent.* **4** withdraw; draw back; send back: *The government retires worn or torn dollar bills from use.* **5** go back; retreat: *The enemy retired before the advance of our troops.* **6** go to bed: *We retire early.* **7** take up and pay off (bonds, loans, etc.). **8** in baseball and cricket, put out (a batter, side, etc.). [< F *retirer* < *re-* back + *tirer* draw] —**Syn. 3** See **depart.**

re·tired (ri tīrd′) *adj.* **1** withdrawn from one's profession or occupation: *a retired sea captain.* **2** reserved; retiring: *a shy, retired nature.* **3** secluded; shut off; hidden: *a retired spot.*

re·tire·ment (ri tīr′mənt) *n.* **1** the act of withdrawing or being withdrawn, especially from one's profession or occupation. **2** the state of being thus withdrawn. **3** a quiet way or place of living: *She lives in retirement, neither making nor receiving visits.*

re·tir·ing (ri tīr′ing) *adj.* shrinking from society or publicity; reserved; shy: *a retiring nature.* —**re·tir′ing·ly,** *adv.*

re·took (rē tůk′) *v.* pt. of **retake.**

re·tort[1] (ri tôrt′) *v.* **1** reply quickly or sharply. **2** return in kind; turn back on: *retort insult for insult or blow for blow.* —*n.* a sharp or witty reply. [< L *retortus*, pp. of *retorquere* throw back < *re-* back + *torquere* twist]

re·tort[2] (ri tôrt′ or rē′tôrt) *n.* a container used for distilling or decomposing substances by heat. [< Med.L *retorta*, originally fem. pp. of L *retorquere*. See RETORT[1].]

A retort; B, receiver; C, flame to heat retort; D, water to keep receiver cool. If impure water is heated in the retort, the water changes to steam and the impurities are left behind. The steam flows into the receiver and condenses into pure water.

re·touch (rē tuch′) *v.* improve (a photographic negative, etc.) by making slight changes.

re·trace (rē trās′) *v.* **-traced, -trac·ing.** trace over again: *Retrace these drawings.* [< *re-* + *trace*]

re·trace (ri trās′) *v.* **-traced, -trac·ing.** go back over: *We retraced our steps to where we started.* [< F *retracer* < *re-* back + *tracer* trace] —**re·trace′a·ble,** *adj.*

re·tract (ri trakt′) *v.* **1** draw back

or in: *The dog snarled and retracted his lips.* **2** withdraw; take back: *retract an offer or an opinion.* [< L *retractare*, ult. < *re-* back + *trahere* draw] —**Syn. 2** revoke, rescind, recall.

re·trac·ta·tion (rē′trak tā′shən) *n.* a retracting of a promise, statement, etc.

re·trac·tile (ri trak′tīl or ri trak′təl) *adj.* capable of being drawn back or in.

re·trac·tion (ri trak′shən) *n.* **1** a drawing or being drawn back or in. **2** a taking back; withdrawal of a promise, statement, etc. **3** retractile power.

re·trac·tive (ri trak′tiv) *adj.* tending or serving to retract.

re·trac·tor (ri trak′tər) *n.* **1** a person or thing that draws back something. **2** in physiology, a muscle that retracts an organ, protruded part, etc. **3** in surgery, an instrument or appliance for drawing and holding back an organ or part.

re·tread (*v.* rē tred′; *n.* rē′tred′) *v.* **-tread·ed, -tread·ing,** *n.* —*v.* put a new tread on. —*n.* a retreaded tire.

re·treat (ri trēt′) *v.* go back; move back; withdraw: *The enemy retreated before the advance of our soldiers.* [< n.]
—*n.* **1** the act of going back or withdrawing: *The army's retreat was orderly.* **2** a signal for retreat: *The drums beat a retreat.* **3** a signal on a bugle or drum, given in the army at sunset. **4** a safe, quiet place; place of rest or refuge. **5** an asylum for mentally ill people and for habitual drunkards. **6** a period of withdrawal from regular life, singly or in a group, devoted to prayer, meditation, and other religious exercises. **7 beat a retreat,** run away; retreat. [ME < OF *retraite*, orig. pp. of *retraire* < L *retrahere* retract < *re-* back + *trahere* draw. Related to RETRACT.] —**Syn.** *n.* **1** withdrawal.

re·trench (ri trench′) *v.* **1** cut down; reduce (expenses, etc.). **2** reduce expenses: *In hard times, we must retrench.* [< MF *retrencher* < *re-* back + *trencher* cut]

re·trench·ment (ri trench′mənt) *n.* **1** a reduction of expenses. **2** a cutting down; cutting off.

ret·ri·bu·tion (ret′rə bū′shən) *n.* **1** a deserved punishment; return for evil done or, sometimes, for good done. **2** the act of punishing or, sometimes, rewarding. [< L *retributio, -onis,* ult. < *re-* back + *tribuere* assign]

re·trib·u·tive (ri trib′yů tiv) *adj.* paying back, especially bringing or inflicting punishment in return for some evil, wrong, etc. —**re·trib′u·tive·ly,** *adv.*

re·trib·u·to·ry (ri trib′yů tô′rē) *adj.* retributive.

re·triev·al (ri trēv′əl) *n.* the act of retrieving.

re·trieve (ri trēv′) *v.* **-trieved, -triev·ing. 1** get again; recover: *retrieve a lost pocketbook.* **2** bring back to a former or better condition; restore: *retrieve one's fortunes.* **3** make good; make amends for; repair: *retrieve a mistake, retrieve a loss or defeat.* **4** find and bring back killed or wounded game: *Some dogs can be trained to retrieve.* [ME < OF *retreuv-*, a stem of *retrouver* < *re-* again + *trouver* find] —**re·triev′a·ble,** *adj.* —**Syn. 1** See **recover.**

re·triev·er (ri trēv′ər) *n.* **1** one of several breeds of dog trained to find killed or wounded game and bring it to a hunter. **2** a dog of any of these breeds. **3** a person or thing that retrieves.

retro- *prefix.* backward; back; behind, as in *retrogress, retro-rocket.* [< L *retro-* < *retro,* adv.]

ret·ro·ac·tive (ret′rō ak′tiv) *adj.* acting back; having an effect on what is past. A retroactive law applies to events that occurred before the law was passed.
—**ret′ro·ac′tive·ly,** *adv.*

ret·ro·cede[1] (ret′rə sēd′) *v.* **-ced·ed, -ced·ing.** go back; recede. [< L *retrocedere* < *retro-* backward + *cedere* go]

ret·ro·cede[2] (ret′rə sēd′) *v.* **-ced·ed, -ced·ing.** cede back (territory, etc.). [< *retro-* + *cede*]

ret·ro·flex (ret′rə fleks′) *adj.* **1** bent backward. **2** having the tip raised and bent backward. **3** made by raising the tip of the tongue and bending it backward: *a retroflex vowel in "hurt."* —*v.* pronounce with the tip of the tongue raised and bent backward. [< L *retroflexus,* pp. of *retroflectere* < *retro-* back + *flectere* bend]

ret·ro·flex·ion (ret′rə flek′shən) *n.* a bending backward.

ret·ro·grade (ret′rə grād′) *adj. v.* **-grad·ed, -grad·ing.** —*adj.* **1** moving backward; retreating. **2** becoming worse. —*v.* **1** move or go backward. **2** fall back toward a worse condition; grow worse; decline. [< L *retrogradus* < *retrogradi,* ult. < *retro-* backward + *gradi* go]

ret·ro·gress (ret′rə gres′ or ret′rə gres′) *v.* **1** move backward; go back. **2** become worse. [< L *retrogressus,* pp. of *retrogradi.* See RETROGRADE.]

ret·ro·gres·sion (ret′rə gresh′ən) *n.* **1** a backward movement. **2** a becoming worse; a falling off; decline.

ret·ro·gres·sive (ret′rə gres′iv) *adj.* **1** moving backward. **2** becoming worse. —**ret′ro·gres′sive·ly,** *adv.*

ret·ro-rock·et (ret′rō rok′it) *n.* on a space ship, artificial satellite, etc., a rocket that fires in a direction opposite to that of the motion of the craft, thus acting as a brake.

ret·ro·spect (ret′rə spekt′) *n.* **1** a survey of past time, events, etc.; thinking about the past. **2 in retrospect,** when looking back. —*v.* think of (something past). [ult. < L *retrospectus* < *retro-* back + *specere* look]

ret·ro·spec·tion (ret′rə spek′shən) *n.* the act of looking back on things past; a survey of past events or experiences.

ret·ro·spec·tive (ret′rə spek′tiv) *adj.* **1** looking back on things past; surveying past events or experiences. **2** applying to the past; retroactive. —*n.* an art exhibition reviewing the work of an artist or group of artists over a number of years. —**ret′ro·spec′tive·ly,** *adv.*

ret·rous·sé (ret′rü sā′) *adj.* turned up: *a retroussé nose.* [< F]

ret·ting (ret′ing) *n.* the process of wetting flax, hemp, etc., and allowing it to decay until the fibres can be easily separated from the woody parts of the stalks. [see RET]

re·turn (ri tėrn′) *v.* **1** go back; come back: *My brother will return this summer.* **2** bring, give, send, hit, put, or pay back: *Return that book to the library.* **3** yield: *The concert returned $50 over expenses.* **4** report or announce officially: *The jury returned a verdict of guilty.* **5** reply: "*No!*" *he returned crossly.* **6** elect to a lawmaking body. **7** in card games, lead (the suit led by one's partner).
—*n.* **1** a going or coming back; happening again. **2** something returned. **3** a bringing back; giving back; sending back; hitting back; putting back: *a poor return for kindness.* **4** Often, **returns,** *pl.* a profit; an amount received. **5 in return,** as a return. **6** a report; account: *election returns.* **7** a reply.
—*adj.* **1** of or having to do with a return: *a return ticket.* **2** sent, given, done, etc. in return: *a return game.* **3** repeated: *a return engagement.* **4** causing or allowing the return of some part of a device to its normal or starting position: *a return spring, a return valve.* [ME < OF *retourner* < *re-* back + *tourner* turn] —**Syn.** *v.* **5** respond, rejoin. –*n.* **1** recurrence.

re·turn·a·ble (ri tėr′nə bəl) *adj.* **1** that can be returned. **2** meant or required to be returned.

returned man *Cdn.* a war veteran.

re·turn·ee (ri tėrn′nē′) *n.* a person who has returned, especially one who has returned to his own country after capture in a war or service abroad.

returning officer an official in charge of the conduct of an election in a constituency. A **deputy returning officer** is in charge of procedures at a polling station.

return trip a trip to a place and back again; a round trip.

re·tuse (ri tūs′ or ri tüs′) *adj.* of a leaf, etc., having an obtuse or rounded apex with a shallow notch. [< L *retusus,* pp. of *retundere* blunt, beat back < *re-* back + *tundere* beat]

A retuse leaf

re·u·ni·fi·ca·tion (rē′ū nə fə kā′shən) *n.* **1** the act or process of reunifying. **2** the state of being reunified.

re·u·ni·fy (rē ū′nə fī′) *v.* **-fied, -fy·ing.** restore unity to; bring back together again.

re·un·ion (rē ūn′yən) *n.* **1** a coming together again: *the reunion of parted friends.* **2** a social gathering of persons who have been separated or who have interests in common: *We have a family reunion every summer.*

re·u·nite (rē′ū nīt′) *v.* **-nit·ed, -nit·ing.** 1 bring together again: *Mother and child were reunited after years of separation.* 2 come together again.

rev (rev) *n. v.* **revved, rev·ving.** *Informal.* —*n.* a revolution (of an engine or motor). —*v.* increase the speed of (an engine or motor).

rev. 1 revenue. 2 reverse. 3 review. 4 revised. 5 revision. 6 revolution.

Rev. 1 Reverend. 2 Revelation.

re·val·ue (rē val′ū) *v.* **-val·ued, -val·u·ing.** value again or anew. —**re′val·u·a′tion,** *n.*

re·vamp (rē vamp′) *v.* patch up; repair.

re·veal (ri vēl′) *v.* 1 make known: *Never reveal my secret.* 2 display; show: *Her smile revealed her even teeth.* [ME < L *revelare*, ult. < *re-* back + *velum* veil] —**re·veal′er,** *n.*

Syn. 1 **Reveal, disclose** = make known something hidden or secret. **Reveal** has a basic sense of uncovering or unveiling, and suggests making known something that has been hidden or screened: *At the new school he revealed an aptitude for science.* **Disclose** has a basic sense of unclosing, and means making known something that has been kept secret, less often to lay open to view something that has been hidden from sight: *She disclosed that she had been married for a month.*

rev·eil·le (rə val′ē) *n.* 1 a signal on a bugle or drum to waken soldiers, sailors, or airmen in the morning. The bugler blows reveille. 2 the time when this signal is sounded. [< F *réveillez(-vous)* awaken!, ult. < L *re-* again + *ex-* up + *vigil* awake]

☛ The pronunciation (rev′ə lē) is American.

rev·el (rev′əl) *v.* **-elled** or **-eled, -el·ling** or **-el·ing,** *n.* —*v.* 1 take great pleasure (*in*): *The children revel in country life.* 2 make merry. —*n.* a noisy good time; merrymaking. [ME < OF *reveler* be disorderly, make merry < L *rebellare*. Doublet of REBEL, v.] —**rev′el·ler** or **rev′el·er,** *n.*

rev·e·la·tion (rev′ə lā′shən) *n.* 1 the act of making known: *The revelation of the thieves' hiding place by one of their own number caused their capture.* 2 the thing made known: *Her true nature was a revelation to me.* 3 in theology, God's disclosure of Himself and of His will to His creatures. 4 **Revelation,** the last book of the New Testament. [ME < LL *revelatio, -onis* < *revelare* reveal. See REVEAL.]

rev·e·la·tor·y (rev′ə lə tôr′ē) *adj.* 1 making known; revealing. 2 concerning religious revelation.

rev·el·ry (rev′əl rē) *n.* **-ries.** boisterous revelling or festivity; wild merrymaking.

re·venge (ri venj′) *n. v.* **-venged, -veng·ing.** —*n.* 1 harm done in return for a wrong; vengeance; returning evil for evil: *a blow struck in revenge.* 2 a desire for vengeance. 3 a chance to win in a return game after losing a game. —*v.* 1 take vengeance. 2 do harm in return for. 3 **be revenged** or **revenge oneself,** get revenge. [ME < MF *revenge* < OF *revengier*, ult. < L *re-* back + *vindicare* avenge < *vindex, -icis* defender]

Syn. **Revenge, avenge.** *Revenge* may be noun or verb, but *avenge* is always a verb. As a verb, *revenge* suggests getting even with someone else, often in a mean or savage way: *The gangsters revenged the murder of one of their gang.* *Avenge* suggests more the morally righteous equalizing of wrongs: *We avenged the insult to our flag.*

re·venge·ful (ri venj′fəl) *adj.* feeling or showing a strong desire for revenge. —**re·venge′ful·ly,** *adv.*

rev·e·nue (rev′ə nū′) *n.* 1 money coming in; income: *The government gets revenue from taxes.* 2 a particular item of income. 3 a source of income. [< F *revenue*, originally fem. pp. of *revenir* < L *re-* back + *venire* come]

revenue stamp a stamp to show that money has been paid to the government as a tax on something.

re·ver·ber·ant (ri vėr′bər ənt) *adj.* reverberating.

re·ver·ber·ate (ri vėr′bər āt′) *v.* **-at·ed, -at·ing.** 1 echo back: *His voice reverberates from the high ceiling.* 2 cast or be cast back; reflect (light or heat). [< L *reverberare* beat back, ult. < *re-* back + *verber* a blow]

re·ver·ber·a·tion (ri vėr′bər ā′shən) *n.* 1 an echoing back of sound; echo. 2 a reflection of light or heat. 3 that which is reverberated.

hat, āge, cãre, fär; let, ēqual, tėrm; it, īce
hot, ōpen, ôrder; oil, out; cup, pu̇t, rüle, ūse
əbove, takən, pencəl, lemən, circəs
ch, child; ng, long; sh, ship
th, thin; ᴛʜ, then; zh, measure

re·ver·ber·a·to·ry (ri vėr′bər ə tô′rē) *adj.* characterized by or produced by reverberations; deflected.

re·vere (ri vēr′) *v.* **-vered, -ver·ing.** love and respect deeply; honor greatly; show reverence for. [< L *revereri* < *re-* back + *vereri* stand in awe of, fear]

Syn. **Revere, reverence** = feel deep respect and honor for someone or something. **Revere** = to regard with deep respect mixed with love someone of very noble character or something associated with such people: *People revered the great philosopher.* **Reverence** = regard with deep respect mixed with wonder, awe, and love something, such as tradition, law, object (seldom a person), considered as almost sacred and not to be violated, injured, or profaned: *We reverence the memory of our heroes.*

rev·er·ence (rev′ər əns or rev′rəns) *n. v.* **-enced, -enc·ing.** —*n.* 1 a feeling of deep respect, mixed with wonder, awe, and love. 2 a deep bow. 3 **Reverence,** a title used in speaking of or to a clergyman. —*v.* regard with reverence; revere. [ME < L *reverentia* < *reverens*. See REVERENT.] —**Syn.** *n.* 1 veneration, adoration. -*v.* See **revere.**

rev·er·end (rev′ər ənd or rev′rənd) *adj.* worthy of great respect. —*n.* 1 **Reverend,** a title for clergymen. 2 *Informal.* a clergyman. [ME < L *reverendus* be respected < *revereri*. See REVERE.]

☛ **Reverend** is not good written usage without the first name or initials of the person to whom it refers. The abbreviation (*Rev.*) is used in newspapers and in more-or-less informal writing: *Reverend James Shaw, Rev. J. T. Shaw.*

rev·er·ent (rev′ər ənt or rev′rənt) *adj.* feeling reverence; showing reverence. [ME < L *reverens, -entis*, ppr. of *revereri* revere. See REVERE.] —**rev′er·ent·ly,** *adv.*

rev·er·en·tial (rev ər en′shəl) *adj.* reverent. —**rev·er·en′tial·ly,** *adv.*

rev·er·ie (rev′ər ē) *n.* 1 dreamy thoughts; dreamy thinking of pleasant things: *He loved to indulge in reveries about the future.* 2 the condition of being lost in dreamy thoughts. 3 a fantastic idea; ridiculous fancy. 4 in music, a composition suggesting a dreamy or musing mood. Also, **revery.** [< F *rêverie* < *rêver* to dream]

re·vers (rə vēr′ or rə vãr′) *n.* **re·vers** (rə vērz′ or rə vãrz′). a part of the front of a garment, especially a coat lapel, that is turned back to show the facing or lining. [< F *revers* reverse]

Revers on a coat

re·ver·sal (ri vėr′səl) *n.* a change to the opposite; a reversing or being reversed.

re·verse (ri vėrs′) *n. adj. v.* **-versed, -vers·ing.** —*n.* 1 the opposite or contrary: *She did the reverse of what I ordered.* 2 **a** the gear or gears that reverse the movement of machinery. **b** the arrangement of such a gear or gears. **c** the position of the control that moves such a gear or gears. 3 movement in an opposite direction; a backward or contrary movement. 4 a change to bad fortune; check; defeat: *He used to be rich, but he met with reverses.* 5 the back: *His name is on the reverse of the medal.*
—*adj.* 1 turned backward; opposite or contrary in position or direction: *the reverse side of a phonograph record.* 2 acting in a manner opposite or contrary to that which is usual. 3 causing an opposite or backward movement.
—*v.* 1 turn the other way; turn inside out; turn upside down. 2 in dancing, turn in a direction opposite to the usual one. 3 change to the opposite; repeal. [ME < L *reversus*, pp. of *revertere* turn around. See REVERT.] —**re·vers′er,** *n.*

Syn. *n.* 3 setback, failure. -*v.* 1 **Reverse, invert** = turn something the other way. **Reverse** is the more general in application, meaning "to turn to the other side or in an opposite position, direction, order, etc.": *In this climate one needs a coat that can be reversed when it begins to rain.* **Invert** = turn upside down: *Invert the glasses to let them drain.*

re·verse·ly (ri vėrs′lē) *adv.* 1 in a reverse position, direction, or order. 2 on the other hand; on the contrary.

re·vers·i·bil·i·ty (ri vėr′sə bil′ə tē) *n.* the fact or quality of being reversible.

re·vers·i·ble (ri vėr′sə bəl) *adj.* **1** that can be reversed; that can reverse. **2** of a fabric, finished on both sides so that either can be used as the right side. —*n.* a garment made so that either side may be worn exposed. —**re·vers′i·bly,** *adv.*

re·ver·sion (ri vėr′zhən or ri vėr′shən) *n.* **1** a return to a former condition, practice, belief, etc.; return. **2** in law: **a** the return of property to the grantor or his heirs. **b** the right to possess a certain property under certain conditions. **3** in biology, a return to certain characteristics that have not been present for two or more generations. [ME < L *reversio, -onis* < *revertere* turn around. See REVERT.]

re·ver·sion·al (ri vėr′zhən əl or ri vėr′shən əl) *adj.* of, having to do with, or involving a reversion.

re·ver·sion·ar·y (ri vėr′zhən er′ē or ri vėr′shən er′ē) *adj.* reversional.

re·vert (ri vėrt′) *v.* **1** go back; return: *If a man dies without heirs, his property reverts to the government.* **2** in biology, return to certain characteristics that have not been present for two or more generations. [ME < OF < L *revertere* < *re-* back + *vertere* turn]

rev·er·y (rev′ər ē) *n.* **-er·ies.** reverie.

re·vet (ri vet′) *v.* **re·vet·ted, re·vet·ting.** face (a wall, embankment, etc.) with masonry or other material. [< F *revêtir* clothe, ult. < L *re-* again + *vestis* garment]

re·vet·ment (ri vet′mənt) *n.* a retaining wall; a facing of stone, brick, cement, etc. [< F *revêtement*]

re·view (ri vū′) *v.* **1** study again; look at again: *He reviewed the scene of the crime.* **2** look back on: *Before falling asleep, Helen reviewed the day's happenings.* **3** examine again; look at with care; examine. A superior court may review decisions of a lower court. **4** inspect formally: *The Admiral reviewed the fleet.* **5** examine to give an account of: *Mr. Brown reviews books for a living.* **6** review books, etc. [< n.]
—*n.* **1** a studying again. **2** a looking back on; survey. **3** a re-examination. **4** an examination; inspection. **5** a critical account of a book, play, etc. giving its merits and faults. **6** a magazine containing articles on subjects of current interest, including accounts of books, etc.: *a law review, a motion-picture review.* **7** a revue. [< F *revue*, originally fem. pp. of *revoir* see again, ult. < L *re-* again + *videre* see]
Syn. *n.* **5 Review, criticism** = an article or account criticizing a book, play, art exhibit, etc. **Review** applies particularly to an account giving some idea of what the book or play, etc. is about, its good and bad points, and the reviewer's critical or personal opinion: *That magazine contains good reviews of the new movies.* **Criticism** applies particularly to an article or essay giving a critical judgment based on deep and thorough study and definite critical standards of what is good and bad in books, music, pictures, etc.: *an anthology of recent Shakespeare criticism.*

re·view·er (ri vū′ər) *n.* **1** a person who reviews. **2** a person who writes articles discussing books, plays, etc.

reviewing stand a raised platform for those reviewing a formal parade of troops, a flypast, etc.

re·vile (ri vīl′) *v.* **-viled, -vil·ing.** call bad names; abuse with words: *The tramp reviled the man who drove him off.* [ME < OF *reviler* despise < *re-* again + *vil* vile < L *vilis* cheap] —**re·vil′er,** *n.*

re·vile·ment (ri vīl′mənt) *n.* **1** the act of reviling. **2** reviling speech.

re·vise (ri vīz′) *v.* **-vised, -vis·ing,** *n.* —*v.* **1** read carefully in order to correct; look over and change; examine and improve. **2** change; alter: *revise one's opinion.* —*n.* **1** the process of revising. **2** a revised form or version. **3** in printing, a proof sheet printed after corrections have been made. [< F *reviser*, ult. < L *re-* again + *videre* see] —**re·vis′er,** *n.*

Revised Standard Version an American Protestant revision of the Bible. The New Testament was published in 1946 and the complete Bible in 1952. *Abbrev.*: RSV or R.S.V.

Revised Version the revised form of the Authorized Version of the Bible. The New Testament was published in 1881 and the Old Testament in 1885. *Abbrev.*: RV or R.V.

re·vi·sion (ri vizh′ən) *n.* **1** the act or work of revising. **2** a revised form: *a revision of a book.*

re·vi·sion·ism (ri vizh′ə niz′əm) *n.* the proposals or beliefs of revisionists.

re·vi·sion·ist (ri vizh′ə nist′) *n.* **1** one who supports or favors revision. **2** a reviser, especially one of those responsible for the Revised Version of the Bible. **3** a communist who believes that the doctrines of Marxism may be interpreted flexibly and revised in the light of national circumstances.

re·vi·so·ry (ri vī′zə rē) *adj.* of or having to do with revision.

re·viv·al (ri vīv′əl) *n.* **1** a bringing or coming back to life or consciousness. **2** a restoration to vigor or health. **3** a bringing or coming back to style, use, activity, etc.: *the revival of a play of years ago.* **4** an awakening or increase of interest in religion. **5** special services or efforts made to awaken or increase interest in religion.

re·viv·al·ist (ri vīv′əl ist) *n.* a person who holds special services to awaken interest in religion.

re·vive (ri vīv′) *v.* **-vived, -viv·ing.** **1** bring back or come back to life or consciousness: *revive a half-drowned person.* **2** bring or come back to a fresh, lively condition: *Flowers revive in water.* **3** make or become fresh; restore: *Hot coffee revived the cold, tired man.* **4** bring back or come back to notice, use, fashion, memory, activity, etc.: *An old play is sometimes revived on the stage.* [< L *revivere* < *re-* again + *vivere* live] —**re·viv′er,** *n.* —**Syn. 3** refresh.

re·viv·i·fy (rē viv′ə fī′) *v.* **-fied, -fy·ing.** restore to life; give new life to. —**re·viv′i·fi·ca′tion,** *n.* —**re·viv′i·fi′er,** *n.*

rev·o·ca·ble (rev′ə kə bəl) *adj.* that can be repealed, cancelled, or withdrawn. —**rev′o·ca·ble·ness,** *n.* —**rev′o·ca·bly,** *adv.*

rev·o·ca·tion (rev′ə kā′shən) *n.* a repeal; cancelling; withdrawal: *the revocation of a law.*

rev·o·ca·to·ry (rev′ə kə tô′rē) *adj.* revoking; recalling; repealing.

re·voke (ri vōk′) *v.* **-voked, -vok·ing,** *n.* —*v.* **1** take back; repeal; cancel; withdraw: *The king revoked his decree.* **2** in cards, fail to follow suit when one can and should; renege. —*n.* in cards, a failure to follow suit when one can and should. [ME < OF < L *revocare* < *re-* back + *vocare* call]

re·volt (ri vōlt′) *n.* the act or state of rebelling: *The town is in revolt.* —*v.* **1** turn away from and fight against a leader; rise against the government's authority: *The people revolted against the dictator.* **2** turn away with disgust: *revolt at a bad smell.* **3** cause to feel disgust. [< F < Ital. *rivolta*, ult. < L *revolvere* revolve. See REVOLVE.] —**re·volt′er,** *n.*
Syn. *n.* **Revolt, insurrection, rebellion** = a rising up in active resistance against authority. **Revolt** emphasizes casting off allegiance and refusing to accept existing conditions or control: *The revolt of the French mob that stormed the Bastille developed into revolution.* **Insurrection** = an armed uprising of a group or section against established authority, often to seize control for their own class or party: *The leader of the insurrection became dictator.* **Rebellion** applies to open armed resistance organized to force the government to do something or to overthrow it: *A rebellion may become civil war.* –*v.* **3** repel, sicken.

re·volt·ing (ri vōl′ting) *adj.* disgusting; repulsive. —**re·volt′ing·ly,** *adv.*

rev·o·lu·tion (rev′ə lü′shən) *n.* **1** a complete, often violent, overthrow of an established government or political system: *The 1917 revolution ended the monarchy in Russia.* **2** a complete change: *The automobile caused a revolution in ways of travelling.* **3** a movement in a circle or curve around some point: *One revolution of the earth around the sun takes a year.* **4** the act or fact of turning round a centre or axis; rotation: *The revolution of the earth causes day and night.* **5** the time or distance of one revolution. **6** a complete cycle or series of events: *The revolution of the four seasons fills a year.* [ME < OF < L *revolutio, -onis* < *revolvere* revolve. See REVOLVE.]

rev·o·lu·tion·ar·y (rev′ə lü′shən er′ē) *adj. n.* **-ar·ies.** —*adj.* **1** of a revolution; connected with a revolution. **2** bringing or causing great changes. —*n.* a revolutionist.

Revolutionary War in the United States, the war from 1775 to 1783 by which the thirteen American colonies won independence from Great Britain.

rev·o·lu·tion·ist (rev′ə lü′shən ist) *n.* a person who advocates, or takes part in, a revolution.

rev·o·lu·tion·ize (rev′ə lü′shən īz′) *v.* **-ized, -iz·ing.**

change completely; produce a very great change in: *The automobile and television have revolutionized country life.*

re·volve (ri volv′) *v.* **-volved, -volv·ing. 1** move in a circle; move in a curve round a point: *The moon revolves around the earth.* **2** turn round a centre or axis; rotate: *The wheels of a moving car revolve.* **3** cause to move round. **4** turn over in the mind; consider from many points of view: *He wishes to revolve the problem before giving an answer.* [ME < L *revolvere* < *re-* back + *volvere* roll] —**re·volv′a·ble,** *adj.* —**Syn. 1** See **turn.**

re·volv·er (ri vol′vər) *n.* **1** a pistol with a revolving cylinder in which the cartridges are contained, that can be fired several times without reloading. **2** a person or thing that revolves.

re·vue (ri vū′) *n.* a theatrical entertainment with singing, dancing, parodies of recent plays, humorous treatments of happenings and fads of the year, etc. [< F. See REVIEW.]

re·vul·sion (ri vul′shən) *n.* **1** a sudden, violent change or reaction. **2** a drawing or being drawn back and away, especially suddenly or violently. [< L *revulsio, -onis,* ult. < *re-* back + *vellere* tear away]

Rev.Ver. Revised Version.

re·ward (ri wôrd′) *n.* **1** a return made for something done. **2** a money payment given or offered for capture of criminals, the return of lost property, etc. —*v.* **1** give a reward to. **2** give a reward for. [ME < ONF *reward* < *rewarder,* dial. var. of *regarder* < *re-* back + *garder* guard. Cf. REGARD.] —**Syn.** *v.* **1** recompense, repay.

re·wire (rē wīr′) *v.* **-wired, -wir·ing. 1** put new wires on or in. **2** telegraph again.

re·write (*v.* rē rīt′, *n.* rē′rīt′) *v.* **-wrote, -writ·ten, -writ·ing.** *n.* —*v.* **1** write again; write in a different form; revise. **2** write (a news story) from material supplied in a form that cannot be used as copy. —*n.* something rewritten, especially for publication.

Reyn·ard (ren′ərd or rā′närd) *n.* **1** a fox that is the main character in a group of medieval fables about animals. **2 reynard,** any fox. [ME < OF *Renart, Renard* < Gmc.]

R.F., r.f., or **r-f** radio frequency.

r.h. 1 right hand. **2** relative humidity.

Rh 1 Rh factor. **2** rhodium.

R.H. 1 Royal Highness. **2** Royal Highlanders.

Rhad·a·man·thine (rad′ə man′thin) *adj.* **1** of or having to do with Rhadamanthus. **2** incorruptibly and sternly just.

Rhad·a·man·thus (rad′ə man′thəs) *n.* in Greek mythology, a son of Zeus and brother of King Minos of Crete. Because he was such a just man during his life, he was made one of the three judges in Hades after his death.

rhap·sod·ic (rap sod′ik) *adj.* rhapsodical.

rhap·sod·i·cal (rap sod′ə kəl) *adj.* of, having to do with, or characteristic of rhapsody; extravagantly enthusiastic; ecstatic. —**rhap·sod′i·cal·ly,** *adv.*

rhap·so·dist (rap′sə dist) *n.* a person who talks or writes with extravagant enthusiasm.

rhap·so·dize (rap′sə dīz′) *v.* **-dized, -diz·ing.** talk or write with extravagant enthusiasm.

rhap·so·dy (rap′sə dē) *n.* **-dies. 1** an utterance or writing marked by extravagant enthusiasm: *She went into rhapsodies over the garden.* **2** in music, an instrumental composition irregular in form: *Liszt's "Hungarian Rhapsodies."* **3** an epic poem, or a part of such a poem, suitable for recitation at one time. [< L < Gk. *rhapsōidia* verse-composition, ult. < *rhaptein* to stitch]

rhe·a (rē′ə) *n.* any of several large birds of South America that resemble the ostrich, but are smaller and have three toes instead of two.

Rhein·gold (rīn′gōld′) *n.* in German and Norse mythology, a magic hoard of gold owned by the Nibelungs and later by Siegfried. Also, **Rhinegold.**

Rhen·ish (ren′ish) *adj.* of the river Rhine or the regions near it. —*n.* Rhine wine. [< L *Rhenus* Rhine]

rhe·ni·um (rē′nē əm) *n.* a rare, hard, grayish metallic chemical element that has chemical properties similar to those of manganese. *Symbol*: Re; *at.no.* 75; *at.wt.* 186.2. [< L *Rhenus* Rhine]

hat, āge, cãre, fär; let, ēqual, tėrm; it, īce
hot, ōpen, ôrder; oil, out; cup, pu̇t, rüle, ūse
əbove, takən, pencəl, lemən, circəs
ch, child; ng, long; sh, ship
th, thin; ᴛʜ, then; zh, measure

rhe·o·stat (rē′ə stat′) *n.* an instrument for regulating the strength of an electric current by introducing different amounts of resistance into the circuit. [< Gk. *rheos* current + *statos* standing still]

rhe·sus (rē′səs) *n.* a small, yellowish-brown monkey with a short tail, found in India. [from a character in the *Iliad*]

Rhe·sus factor (rē′səs) Rh factor.

rhet·o·ric (ret′ə rik) *n.* **1** the art of using words effectively in speaking or writing. **2** a book about this art. **3** language used to persuade or influence others: *The crowd was impressed by the speaker's rhetoric.* **4** mere display in language. [ME < L < Gk. *rhētorikē* (*technē*) art of an orator < *rhētōr* orator]

rhe·tor·i·cal (ri tôr′ə kəl) *adj.* **1** of or having to do with rhetoric. **2** using rhetoric. **3** intended especially for display; artificial. **4** oratorical. —**rhe·tor′i·cal·ly,** *adv.*

rhetorical question a question asked only for effect, not for information, and not expecting an answer.

rhet·o·ri·cian (ret′ə rish′ən) *n.* **1** a person skilled in rhetoric. **2** a person given to display in language.

rheum (rüm) *n.* **1** a watery discharge, such as mucus, tears, or saliva. **2** a cold; catarrh. [ME < OF < L < Gk. *rheuma* a flowing < *rheein* flow]

rheu·mat·ic (rü mat′ik) *adj.* **1** of rheumatism. **2** having rheumatism; liable to have rheumatism. **3** causing rheumatism. **4** caused by rheumatism. —*n.* **1** a person who has rheumatism. **2 rheumatics,** *pl. Informal.* rheumatism. [ME < L < Gk. *rheumatikos* < *rheuma.* See RHEUM.]

rheumatic fever an acute disease occurring usually in children, characterized by fever, swelling, pain in the joints, and inflammation of the heart.

rheu·ma·tism (rü′mə tiz′əm) *n.* a disease characterized by inflammation, swelling, and stiffness of the joints. [< L < Gk. *rheumatismos,* ult. < *rheuma* rheum. See RHEUM.]

rheu·ma·toid (rü′mə toid′) *adj.* **1** resembling or affected by rheumatism: *rheumatoid arthritis.* **2** having rheumatism. —**rheu′ma·toi′dal·ly,** *adv.*

rheumatoid arthritis a persistent disease that produces swelling and inflammation of the joints and is often progressively crippling.

rheum·y (rüm′ē) *adj.* **1** full of rheum. **2** causing rheum; damp and cold.

Rh factor a substance often found in the blood of human beings and the higher mammals. Blood containing this substance (**Rh positive**) does not combine favorably with blood lacking it (**Rh negative**). Also, **Rhesus factor.** [first discovered in the blood of the rhesus monkey]

rhi·nal (rī′nəl) *adj.* of or having to do with the nose; nasal. [< Gk. *rhis, rhinos* nose]

Rhine·gold (rīn′gōld′) *n.* Rheingold.

rhine·stone (rīn′stōn′) *n.* an imitation diamond, made of glass. [translation of F *caillou du Rhin*]

Rhine wine (rīn) a wine produced in the valley of the Rhine. Most Rhine wines are white wines.

rhi·ni·tis (rī nī′tis) *n.* inflammation of the nose or its mucous membrane. [< NL < Gk. *rhis, rhinos* nose + *itis*]

rhi·no (rī′nō) *n.* **-nos.** rhinoceros.

rhi·noc·er·os (rī nos′ər əs) *n.* **-os·es** or (*esp. collectively*) **-os.** a large, thick-skinned mammal of Africa and Asia having one or two upright horns on the snout. [ME < L < Gk. *rhinokerōs,* ult. < *rhis* nose + *keras* horn]

rhi·nol·o·gist (rī nol′ə jist) *n.* an expert in rhinology.

rhi·nol·o·gy (rī nol′ə jē) *n.* the branch of medicine that deals with the nose and its diseases. [< Gk. *rhis, rhinos* nose + E *-logy*]

rhi·zoid (rī′zoid) *adj.* rootlike. —*n.* in mosses, etc., one of the rootlike filaments by which the plant is attached to the substratum. [< Gk. *rhiza* root + *eidos* form]

rhi·zome (rī′zōm) *n.* in botany, a rootlike stem lying along or under the ground, that usually produces roots below and shoots from the upper surface; rootstock. [< Gk. *rhizōma*, ult. < *rhiza* root]

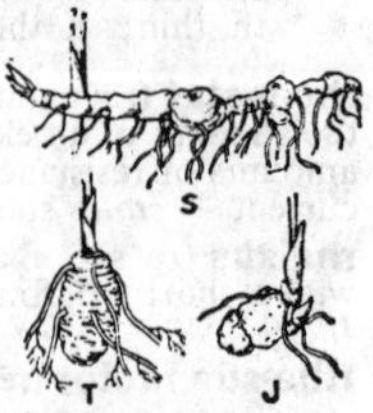

S T J
Forms of rhizome: S, Solomon's-seal; T, trillium; J, jack-in-the-pulpit.

rhi·zo·pod (rī′zə pod′) *n.* in zoology, any of a group of one-celled animals that form temporary projections of protoplasm for moving about and taking in food. Amoebas are rhizopods. [< NL *rhizopoda*, pl. < Gk. *rhiza* root + *pous*, *podos* foot]

rho (rō) *n.* the 17th letter of the Greek alphabet (Ρ, ρ).

Rhode Island Red (rōd) **1** a breed of American chicken that has reddish feathers and a black tail. **2** a chicken of this breed.

Rhodes Scholarship (rōdz) one of a number of scholarships provided for study at Oxford University and awarded annually to candidates **(Rhodes scholar)** from certain Commonwealth countries, South Africa, and the United States. [< Cecil *Rhodes*, 1853-1902, a British colonial statesman]

rho·di·um (rō′dē əm) *n.* a grayish-white metallic chemical element, forming salts that give rose-colored solutions. It is similar to aluminum. *Symbol*: Rh; *at.no.* 45; *at.wt.* 102.905 [< Gk. *rhodon* rose]

rho·do·den·dron (rō′də den′drən) *n.* an evergreen shrub that resembles an azalea. Rhododendrons have beautiful pink, purple, or white flowers. [< NL < Gk. *rhododendron* < *rhodon* rose + *dendron* tree]

rho·dor·a (rō dôr′ə) *n.* any of a group of low-growing rhododendrons common to Canada and New England. Their pink or red flowers appear before or with the leaves. [< NL *Rhodora*, the genus name]

rhomb (rom or romb) *n.* rhombus.

rhom·bic (rom′bik) *adj.* **1** having the form of a rhombus. **2** having a rhombus as base or cross section. **3** bounded by rhombuses. **4** in chemistry, having to do with a system of crystallization characterized by three unequal axes intersecting at right angles.

rhom·boid (rom′boid) *n.* a parallelogram that is not a rectangle. —*adj.* shaped like a rhombus or rhomboid. [< LL < Gk. *rhomboeidēs*]

rhom·boi·dal (rom boi′dəl) *adj.* rhomboid.

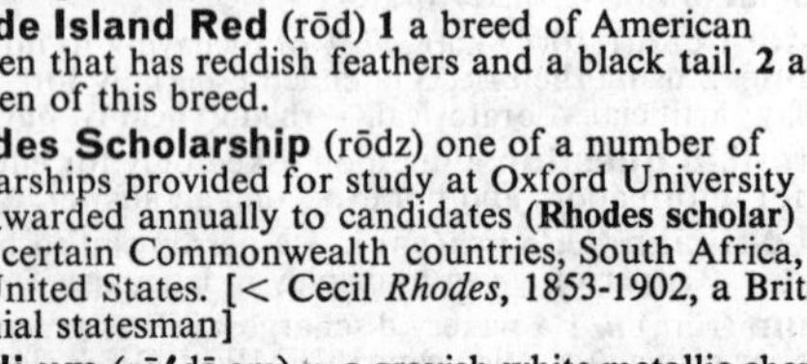

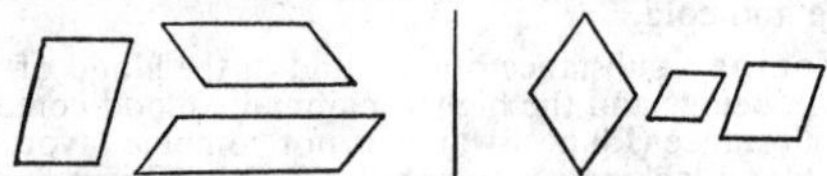

Rhomboids Rhombuses

rhom·bus (rom′bəs) *n.* **-bus·es, -bi** (-bī or -bē). a parallelogram with equal sides, having two obtuse angles and two acute angles; diamond. [< L < Gk. *rhombos*]

rhon·cus (rong′kəs) *n.* **-chi** (-kī or -kē). a coarse rattling or whistling sound resembling a snore, caused by obstruction in the breathing passages. [< L *rhoncus* a snoring, croaking, perhaps related to Gk. *rhenchos* < *renkein* to snore]

rhu·barb (rü′bärb) *n.* **1** a garden plant having very large leaves, whose sour stalks are used for making sauce, pies, etc. **2** the stalks of this plant. **3** the sauce made of the stalks. **4** a purgative medicine made from a kind of rhubarb. **5** *Slang.* a heated dispute, usually marked by scornful comment. [ME < OF < Med.L *rheubarbarum*, ult. < Gk. *rhēon barbaron* foreign rhubarb]

rhumb (rum or rumb) *n.* one of the 32 points of the compass. [ult. (< F, Sp., or Pg.) < L *rhombus* < Gk. *rhombos* rhombus]

rhum·ba (rum′bə) *n. v.* **-baed, -ba·ing.** rumba.

rhyme (rīm) *v.* **rhymed, rhym·ing,** *n.* —*v.* **1** sound alike in the last part: *"Long" and "song" rhyme. "Go to bed" rhymes with "sleepy head."* **2** put or make into rhyme: *rhyme a translation.* **3** make rhymes. **4** use (a word) with another that rhymes with it: *rhyme "love" with "dove."*
—*n.* **1** an agreement in the final sounds of words or lines. **2** a word or line having the same last sound as another: *"Cat" is a rhyme for "mat."* **3** verses or poetry with a regular return of similar sounds. **4 without rhyme or reason,** having no system or sense. Also, **rime.** [ME < OF *rime* < L < Gk. *rhythmos* rhythm. Doublet of RHYTHM.] —**rhym′er,** *n.*

☛ **rhyme, rime.** The simpler spelling seems to be gaining slowly on *rhyme*. It is not only simpler but was the original spelling in English.

rhyme·ster (rīm′stər) *n.* a maker of rather poor rhymes or verse. Also, **rimester.**

rhythm (riŦH′əm) *n.* **1** a movement having a regular repetition of a beat, accent, stress, rise and fall, etc.: *the rhythm of dancing, skating, swimming, the rhythm of the tides, the rhythm of one's heartbeats.* **2** the repetition of an accent; arrangement of beats in a line of poetry: *The rhythms of "The Lord's Prayer," "The Night Before Christmas," and "O Canada" are different.* **3** a grouping by accents or beats: *triple rhythm.* **4** in music, the pattern of movement produced by the combination of accent, metre, and tempo. **5** in biology, a pattern of involuntary behavior, action, etc. occurring regularly and periodically. [< L < Gk. *rhythmos* < *rheein* flow. Doublet of RHYME.]

rhyth·mic (riŦH′mik) *adj.* rhythmical.

rhyth·mi·cal (riŦH′mə kəl) *adj.* having rhythm; of or having to do with rhythm. —**rhyth′mi·cal·ly,** *adv.*

rhythm method a form of birth control involving abstention from sexual intercourse during the estimated period of ovulation.

R.I. **1** Queen and Empress. (for L *Regina et Imperatrix*) **2** King and Emperor. (for L *Rex et Imperator*) **3** Rhode Island.

ri·al (rē′əl) *n.* **1** a unit of money in Iran. See table at **money.** **2** a coin worth one rial. [< Persian < Arabic *riyal* < Sp. *real.* Doublet of REAL², REGAL, ROYAL]

Ri·al·to (ri al′tō) *n.* **1** in Venice: **a** a former business district. **b** a famous bridge that crosses the Grand Canal. **2 rialto,** in business, a place of exchange; market place.

rib (rib) *n. v.* **ribbed, rib·bing.** —*n.* **1** in anatomy, one of the curved bones extending from the backbone and enclosing the upper part of the body. See **skeleton** for diagram. **2** a piece that forms a frame. An umbrella has ribs. **3** in botany, a thick vein of a leaf. **4** in a knitted or woven fabric, a ridge. **5** a cut of meat containing a rib: *a rib of beef.* **6** one of the arches forming the supports for a vault. **7** *Informal.* **a** a joke. **b** a teasing or mocking; a satire on or parody of something. **8 tickle the ribs,** cause laughter, as a joke.
—*v.* **1** furnish or strengthen with ribs. **2** mark with riblike ridges. **3** *Informal.* tease. [OE *ribb*]

rib·ald (rib′əld) *adj.* offensive in speech; coarsely mocking; irreverent; indecent; obscene. [ME < OF *ribauld*, ult. < *riber* to be wanton] —**rib′ald·ly,** *adv.*
—**Syn.** *adj.* indelicate, gross.

rib·ald·ry (rib′əld rē) *n.* ribald language.

rib·band or **rib·and** (rib′ənd) *n. Archaic.* ribbon.

ribbed (ribd) *adj.* having ribs or ridges.

rib·bing (rib′ing) *n.* **1** ribs collectively; a group or arrangement of ribs. **2** *Informal.* a teasing.

rib·bon (rib′ən) *n.* **1** a strip or band of silk, satin, velvet, etc. **2** anything like such a strip: *a typewriter ribbon.* **3** ribbons, torn pieces; shreds: *Her dress was torn to ribbons by the thorns and briars she had come through.* **4** a small badge of cloth worn as a sign of membership in an order, decoration for bravery, etc.: *the ribbon of the Victoria Cross.* [ME < OF *riban* < Gmc.]
—**rib′bon·like′,** *adj.*

ri·bo·fla·vin (rī′bō flā′vən) *n.* a constituent of the vitamin B complex, present in liver, eggs, milk, spinach, etc.; lactoflavin. It is sometimes called vitamin B_2 or G. [< *ribose* + L *flavus* yellow]

ri·bo·nu·cle·ic acid (rī′bō nū klē′ik or -nü klē′ik) in biochemistry, a nucleic acid that helps promote the synthesis of cell proteins. *Abbrev.*: RNA

ri·bose (rī′bōs) *n.* a type of sugar made up of five carbon atoms to the molecule, instead of the six that make up glucose. [< alteration of E *arabinose* (sugar), prepared from gum *arabic*]

rib-tick·ler (rib′tik′lər) *n. Informal.* a joke or funny story.

rice (rīs) *n. v.* **riced, ric·ing.** —*n.* **1** the starchy seeds or grain of a plant grown in warm climates. Rice is an important food in India, China, and Japan. **2** the plant itself. —*v.* reduce to a form like rice: *Potatoes may be riced.* [ME < OF < Ital. *riso*, ult. < Gk. *oryza* < Iranian]

rice paper 1 a thin paper made from the straw of rice. **2** paper made from the pith of certain other plants.

ric·er (rīs′ər) *n.* a utensil for ricing cooked potatoes, etc. by pressing them through small holes.

rich (rich) *adj.* **1** having much money or property: *a rich man.* **2** well supplied; abounding: *Canada is rich in nickel and oil.* **3** abundant: *a rich supply.* **4** producing or yielding abundantly; fertile: *rich soil, a rich mine.* **5** valuable: *a rich harvest.* **6** costly; elegant: *rich dress.* **7** having many desirable elements or qualities. **8** of foods, containing plenty of butter, eggs, flavoring, etc. **9** of colors, sounds, smells, etc., deep; full; vivid. **10** of wine, etc., strong and finely flavored: *a rich, mellow sherry.* **11** of a fuel mixture, containing more fuel than is normally required. **12** *Informal.* very amusing, ridiculous. —*n.* **the rich,** rich people. [OE *rīce* < Celtic] —**rich′ly,** *adv.* —**rich′ness,** *n.*

Syn. *adj.* **1 Rich, wealthy** = having much money or property. **Rich** = having more than enough money, possessions, or resources for all normal needs and desires: *They own the mill in our town and are considered rich.* **Wealthy** = very rich, having a great store of money, property, and valuable possessions or resources: *Wealthy people are often patrons of the arts.* **4** productive, fruitful, fecund. **6** expensive, sumptuous, luxurious.

rich·es (rich′iz) *n.pl.* wealth; abundance of property; much money, land, goods, etc. [ME < OF *richesse*, taken as plural of *riche* rich < Gmc. Akin to RICH.]

Richter scale a scale for measuring the magnitude of earthquakes, ranging from 10 to 0, the smallest earthquake having the magnitude of zero. [after Charles F. *Richter*, American seismologist, born 1900]

rick (rik) *n.* a stack of hay, straw, etc., especially one made so that the rain will run off it. —*v.* form into a rick or ricks. [OE *hrēac*]

rick·ets (rik′its) *n.* a disease of childhood, caused by lack of vitamin D or calcium, that results in softening, and, sometimes, bending of the bones; rachitis. [apparently alteration of *rachitis*, influenced by *wrick* wrench, strain]

rick·et·y (rik′ə tē) *adj.* **1** liable to fall or break down; shaky: *a rickety old chair.* **2** having rickets; suffering from rickets. **3** feeble in the joints. —**rick′et·i·ness,** *n.*

rick·ey (rik′ē) *n.* **1** a drink made of sugar, lime, carbonated water, and gin or some other alcoholic liquor. **2** a similar, non-alcoholic drink.

rick·rack (rik′rak′) *n.* a flat, narrow, zigzag braid used for trimming. [? reduplication of *rack*[1]]

rick·shaw or **rick·sha** (rik′sho or rik′shô) *n.* jinrikisha.

ric·o·chet (rik′ə shā′) *n. v.* **-chet·ted** or **-cheted** (-shād′), **-chet·ting** or **-chet·ing** (-shā′ing). —*n.* the skipping or jumping motion of an object as it goes along a flat surface: *the ricochet of a cannon ball along the ground, the ricochet of a stone thrown along the surface of water.* —*v.* move with a skipping or jumping motion. [< F]

rid[1] (rid) *v.* **rid** or **rid·ded, rid·ding. 1** make free (from): *What will rid a house of rats?* **2 be rid of,** be freed from. **3 get rid of, a** get free from. **b** do away with. [OE *(ge)ryddan* clear land] —**rid′der,** *n.*

rid[2] (rid) *v. Archaic.* a pt. and a pp. of **ride.**

rid·dance (rid′əns) *n.* **1** a clearing away or out; removal. **2 good riddance,** an expression of relief that something or somebody has been removed.

rid·den (rid′ən) *v.* a pp. of **ride.**

rid·dle[1] (rid′əl) *n. v.* **-dled, -dling.** —*n.* **1** a puzzling question, statement, problem, etc. **2** a person or thing that is hard to understand, explain, etc. —*v.* speak in riddles. [OE *rǣdels* < *rǣdan* guess, explain; ME *redels* taken as pl.] —**Syn.** *n.* **1** enigma, puzzle, conundrum.

hat, āge, cãre, fär; let, ēqual, tėrm; it, īce
hot, ōpen, ôrder; oil, out; cup, pu̇t, rüle, ūse
əbove, takən, pencəl, lemən, circəs
ch, child; ng, long; sh, ship
th, thin; ᴛʜ, then; zh, measure

rid·dle[2] (rid′əl) *v.* **-dled, -dling,** *n.* —*v.* **1** make many holes in: *The door of the fort was riddled with bullets.* **2** sift: *riddle gravel.* [< n.] —*n.* a coarse sieve. [OE *hriddel* sieve]

ride (rīd) *v.* **rode** or (*Archaic*) **rid, rid·den** or (*Archaic*) **rid, rid·ing,** *n.* —*v.* **1** sit on a horse or other animal and make it go. **2** sit on a bicycle, etc. and make it go. **3** be carried along as if on horseback; be carried along by anything: *ride on a train.* **4** admit of being ridden: *a horse that rides easily.* **5** ride over, along, or through. **6** be mounted on; be carried on: *The eagle rides the winds.* **7** do or perform: *ride a race.* **8** move on; float; float along: *The ship rode the waves.* **9** *Informal.* make fun of; tease. **10** cause to ride or be carried: *ride a man on a rail as punishment.* **11** control, dominate, or tyrannize over: *be ridden by foolish fears.* **12 let ride,** leave undisturbed or inactive: *Let the matter ride until the next meeting.* **13 ride down, a** knock down. **b** overcome. **c** overtake by riding. **d** exhaust by riding. **14 ride high,** enjoy success; do very well. **15 ride out, a** withstand (a gale, etc.) without damage. **b** endure successfully. **16 ride up,** slide up out of place: *That coat rides up at the back.* —*n.* **1** a trip on the back of a horse, in a carriage, car, train, boat, etc. **2** a path, road, etc. made for riding. **3** a mechanical amusement, such as a merry-go-round, Ferris wheel, etc. **4** a turn on a merry-go-round, Ferris wheel, roller coaster, etc. **5 take for a ride,** *Slang.* **a** murder. **b** cheat. [OE *rīdan*]

Syn. *n.* **1 Ride, drive** = a trip by some means of transportation. **Ride** emphasizes being carried along in or by something, as on horseback, in a boat, train, bus, etc., or in a car if one is going nowhere in particular or is strictly a passenger: *Let's go for a ride in my new car.* **Drive** emphasizes causing to move in a particular direction, and applies only to a trip in a horse-drawn or motor vehicle one controls or operates himself or helps to direct: *Let's take a drive into the country.*

Ri·deau Hall (rē′dō) the official residence of the Governor General of Canada, situated in Ottawa.

rid·er (rid′ər) *n.* **1** a person who rides: *The Calgary Stampede is famous for its riders.* **2** anything added to a record, document, legislative bill, or statement after it was considered to be completed. —**rid′er·less,** *adj.*

ridge (rij) *n. v.* **ridged, ridg·ing.** —*n.* **1** the long and narrow upper part of something: *the ridge of an animal's back.* **2** the line where two sloping surfaces meet: *the ridge of a roof.* **3** a long, narrow chain of hills or mountains. **4** any raised, narrow strip: *the ridges on corduroy cloth, the ridges in ploughed ground.* —*v.* **1** form or make into ridges. **2** cover with ridges; mark with ridges. [OE *hrycg*]

ridge·pole (rij′pōl′) *n.* the horizontal timber along the top of a roof or tent.

ridg·y (rij′ē) *adj.* rising in a ridge or ridges.

rid·i·cule (rid′ə kūl′) *v.* **-culed, -cul·ing,** *n.* —*v.* laugh at; make fun of. [< n.] —*n.* laughter in mockery; words or actions that make fun of somebody or something. [< F < L *ridiculum*, neut. of *ridiculus* ridiculous. See RIDICULOUS.]

Syn. *v.* **Ridicule, deride, mock** = make fun of someone or something and cause him or it to be laughed at. **Ridicule** emphasizes making fun of a person or thing, in either a good-natured or an unkind way, with the intention of making him or it seem little and unimportant: *Boys may ridicule their sisters' friends.* **Deride** emphasizes laughing in contempt and holding up to scorn: *Some people deride patriotic rallies and parades.* **Mock** = ridicule or deride in a scornful way: *The impudent boys mocked the teacher.* —*n.* derision.

ri·dic·u·lous (ri dik′yů ləs) *adj.* deserving ridicule; absurd; laughable. [< L *ridiculus* < *ridere* laugh] —**ri·dic′u·lous·ly,** *adv.* —**ri·dic′u·lous·ness,** *n.*

Syn. Ridiculous, absurd, preposterous = not sensible or reasonable. **Ridiculous** emphasizes the laughable effect produced by something out of keeping with good sense: *His attempts to be the life of the party were ridiculous.* **Absurd** emphasizes the contrast with what is true or sensible: *His belief that he was too clever to be caught in his wrong-doing was absurd.* **Preposterous** adds to *absurd* the idea of being contrary to nature: *The bandit* *made the preposterous suggestion that he would drop his gun if the policeman first dropped his.*

rid·ing (rīd′ing) *n.* **1** *Cdn.* a political division represented by a Member of Parliament or a Member of the Legislative Assembly; constituency. **2** *Brit.* an administrative division: *the West Riding of Yorkshire.* [ME *thriding* < ON *thrithjungr* one third; the *th-* was lost as a result of the previous *-t* or *-th* in the compounds *East Thriding, North Thriding, West Thriding*]

riding boot a high boot worn by riders.

riding crop a short whip with a loop on one end instead of a lash.

riding habit a dress or suit worn by riders.

ri·el (rē el′) *n.* **1** a unit of money in Cambodia. See table at **money.** **2** a coin worth one riel. [origin unknown]

Riel Rebellions (rē el′ or rē′əl) the Northwest Rebellions. [after Louis David *Riel,* 1844-1885, leader of the Métis]

rife (rīf) *adj.* **1** happening often; common; numerous; widespread. **2** full; abounding: *The land was rife with rumors of war.* [OE *rīfe*]

Riff (rif) *n.* **1** a Berber tribe living in the Rif, a mountainous region of N. Morocco. **2** a member of this tribe.

Riff·i·an (rif′ē ən) *adj.* of or having to do with the Rif, a mountainous region of N. Morocco, or its people. *—n.* Riff.

rif·fle (rif′əl) *n. v.* **-fled, -fling.** *—n.* **1** the act of shuffling cards by bending the edges slightly. **2 a** a shoal or other object in a stream causing a ripple or a stretch of choppy water. **b** the ripple itself; a rapid. **3** in placer mining, the slats or bars set diagonally into the bottom of a sluice box to catch the gold particles in gravel, water, etc.
—v. **1** shuffle cards by bending the edges slightly so that the two divisions slide into each other. **2** cause water to run in riffles. **3** leaf through the pages of a book quickly. [? variant of *ripple* or *ruffle*[1]]

riff·raff (rif′raf′) *n.* **1** worthless people. **2** trash. *—adj.* worthless. [ME < OF *rif et raf* every scrap < *rifler* rifle[2] + *raffler* carry off (related to RAFFLE)]

ri·fle[1] (rī′fəl) *n. v.* **-fled, -fling.** *—n.* **1** a gun having spiral grooves in its barrel to spin the bullet as it is fired. **2** such a gun that is fired from the shoulder. *—v.* cut spiral grooves in (a gun). [ult. < F *rifler* scratch, groove, rifle[2]]

ri·fle[2] (rī′fəl) *v.* **-fled, -fling. 1** search and rob; ransack and rob. **2** steal; take away. **3** strip bare: *The boys rifled the apple tree.* [ME < OF *rifler* < Gmc.] **—ri′fler,** *n.*

ri·fle·man (rī′fəl mən) *n.* **-men** (-mən). **1** a soldier armed with a rifle. **2** a man who uses a rifle.

rifle pit a pit or short trench that shelters riflemen firing at an enemy.

rifle range 1 a place for practice in shooting with a rifle. **2** the distance that a rifle will shoot a bullet.

ri·fling (rī′fling) *n.* **1** the act or process of cutting spiral grooves in a gun barrel. **2** the system of spiral grooves in a rifle.

rift (rift) *n. v.* split; cleft; break; crack: *a rift in the clouds.* [ME < Scand.; cf. Danish *rift*]

rig[1] (rig) *v.* **rigged, rig·ging,** *n.* *—v.* **1** equip (a ship) with masts, sails, ropes, etc. **2** move (a shroud, boom, stay, etc.) to its proper place. **3** equip; fit out. **4** *Informal.* dress: *On Halloween the children rig themselves up in queer clothes.* **5** get ready for use. **6** put together in a hurry or by using odds and ends. **7 rig out,** fit out.
—n. **1** on a ship, the arrangement of masts, sails, ropes, etc. A schooner has a fore-and-aft rig; that is, the sails are set lengthwise on the ship. **2** *Informal.* clothes: *John's rig consisted of a silk hat and overalls.* **3** an outfit; equipment: *a drilling rig.* **4** *Informal.* **a** an automobile, truck, etc. **b** a carriage, with its horse or horses. [ME < Scand.; cf. Danish *rigge*]

rig[2] (rig) *n. v.* **rigged, rig·ging.** *—n.* **1** a prank; trick. **2** a fraudulent scheme; swindle. *—v.* **1** arrange dishonestly for one's own advantage: *rig a race.* **2** arrange unfavorably.

-rigged (rigd) *combining form.* having a —— rig: *Full-rigged = having a full rig.*

rig·ger (rig′ər) *n.* **1** a person who rigs. **2** a person who rigs ships, or works with hoisting tackle, etc. **3** *Informal.* a person who manipulates something fraudulently.

rig·ging (rig′ing) *n.* **1** on a ship, the ropes, chains, etc. used to support and work the masts, yards, sails, etc. **2** tackle; equipment.

right (rīt) *adj.* **1** good; just; lawful: *He did the right thing when he told the truth.* **2** correct; true: *the right answer.* **3** proper; fitting: *He always managed to say the right thing at the right time.* **4** favorable: *If the weather is right, we'll go.* **5** healthy; normal: *be in one's right senses.* **6** meant to be seen; most important: *the right side of cloth.* **7** opposite of left; belonging or having to do with the side of anything that is turned east when the main side is turned north. The right bank of a river is the one to the right as one faces downstream. **8** in politics, of or having to do with a person, party, etc. that tends to oppose political and social change. **9** straight: *a right line.* **10** formed by a line drawn to another line or surface by the shortest course: *a right angle, a right cone.* See **angle** for diagram. **11** *Archaic.* rightful; real: *the right owner.*
—adv. **1** in a way that is good, just, or lawful: *He acted right when he told the truth.* **2** correctly; truly: *She guessed right.* **3** properly; well: *It serves you right to lose if you cheat.* **4** favorably: *turn out right.* **5** in a good or suitable condition: *Put things right.* **6** to the right hand: *turn right.* **7** exactly; just; precisely: *Put it right here.* **8** at once; immediately: *Stop playing right now.* **9** (used in some titles) very: *Right Honourable.* **10** *Archaic or informal.* extremely: *I am right glad to see you.* **11** in a straight line; directly: *Look me right in the eye.* **12** completely: *His hat was knocked right off.* **13** yes; very well: *"Come at once," his mother called. "Right," he replied.* **14 right away,** at once; immediately. **15 right off,** at once; immediately.
—n. **1** that which is right: *Do right, not wrong.* **2** a just claim, title, or privilege: *the right to vote.* **3** fair treatment; justice. **4** a blow struck with the right hand. **5** the right side or what is on the right side. **6** in politics: **a** a person, party, etc. that tends to oppose political and social change. **b** the part of a lawmaking body, consisting of conservative or reactionary parties, that sits on the right of the presiding officer. **c** all the people and parties having conservative or reactionary views. **7** in business: **a** the privilege of subscribing for a stock or bond. **b** a certificate granting such a privilege. **8 by right** or **by rights,** justly; properly. **9 in the right,** right. **10 to rights,** *Informal.* in or into proper condition, order, etc.
—v. **1** make correct: *right errors.* **2** do justice to: *right the oppressed.* **3** get or put into proper position: *The ship righted as the wave passed.* **4 right about!** turn in the opposite direction. [OE *riht*] **—right′er,** *n.* **—right′ness,** *n.* **—Syn.** *adj.* **1** equitable, ethical. **2** accurate. **3** fit, seemly, due, appropriate. **4** suitable, propitious. **6** principal, front, upper. *–n.* **2** prerogative. *–v.* **1** rectify, amend. **2** vindicate.

☞ **right.** In the sense of "very," *right* is a localism: *They were right glad to go with us.*

right about-face (rīt′ə bout′fās′) a turn in the opposite direction.

right angle an angle of 90 degrees.

right-an·gled (rīt′ang′gəld) *adj.* containing a right angle or right angles; rectangular.

right·eous (rī′chəs) *adj.* **1** doing right; virtuous; behaving justly. **2** morally right or justifiable: *righteous indignation.* [OE *rihtwīs* < *riht* right + *wīs* way, manner] **—right′eous·ly,** *adv.* **—Syn. 1** upright, just.

right·eous·ness (rī′chəs nis) *n.* upright conduct; virtue; the state or condition of being right and just.

right face a turn to the right.

right·ful (rīt′fəl) *adj.* **1** according to law; by rights: *the rightful owner of this dog.* **2** just and right; proper. **—right′ful·ness,** *n.* **—Syn. 1** lawful. **2** due.

right·ful·ly (rīt′fəl ē) *adv.* **1** according to right, law, or justice. **2** properly; fittingly.

right-hand (rīt′hand′) *adj.* **1** on or to the right. **2** of, for, or with the right hand. **3** most helpful or useful: *one's right-hand man.*

right-hand·ed (rīt′han′did) *adj.* **1** using the right hand more easily and readily than the left. **2** done with the right hand. **3** made to be used with the right hand.

4 turning from left to right: *a right-handed screw.* —**right′-hand′ed·ly,** *adv.*

Right Honourable a title given to all members of the United Kingdom Privy Council. The Prime Minister of Canada has this title. *Abbrev.*: Rt. Hon.

right·ist (rīt′ist) *n.* in politics: **1** a person who supports or favors the right. **2** a member of a conservative or reactionary organization. —*adj. Informal.* having conservative or reactionary ideas.

right·ly (rīt′lē) *adv.* **1** justly; fairly. **2** correctly. **3** properly; suitably. [OE *rihtlīce*]

right-mind·ed (rīt′mīn′did) *adj.* having right opinions or principles. —**right′mind′ed·ly,** *adv.* —**right′-mind′ed·ness,** *n.*

right of way **1** the right to go first; precedence over all others. **2** the right to pass over property belonging to someone else. **3** a strip of land on which a road, railway, power line, etc. is built.

right triangle a triangle, one of whose angles is a right angle.

right whale any of several whales having large heads and long, toothlike whalebones on the sides of the mouth.

right wing **1** the people opposing reform, especially the conservative or reactionary members of a political organization. **2** in hockey, lacrosse, etc.: **a** the playing position to the right of centre on a forward line. **b** the player in this position.

rig·id (rij′id) *adj.* **1** stiff; firm; not bending: *a rigid support.* **2** strict; not changing: *Our club has few rigid rules.* **3** severely exact; rigorous: *a rigid examination.* [< L *rigidus* < *rigere* be stiff] —**rig′id·ly,** *adv.* —**rig′id·ness,** *n.* —**Syn. 1** unyielding, unbending. See **stiff. 3** See **strict.**

ri·gid·i·ty (ri jid′ə tē) *n.* **1** stiffness; firmness. **2** strictness; severity.

rig·ma·role (rig′mə rōl′) *n.* foolish talk; words without meaning; nonsense. [earlier *ragman roll* < *ragman* list, catalogue (origin uncertain) + *roll*]

rig·or or **rig·our** (rig′ər) *n.* **1** strictness; severity; harshness: *the rigor of a long, cold winter.* **2** stiffness; rigidity. **3** a chill caused by illness. [ME < OF < L *rigor* < *rigere* be stiff]

rig·or mor·tis (rig′ər môr′tis) the stiffening of the muscles after death. [< L *rigor mortis* stiffness of death]

rig·o·ro·so (rig ə rō′sō) *adj.* in music, in exact rhythm; in strict timing. [< Ital.]

rig·or·ous (rig′ər əs) *adj.* **1** very severe; harsh; strict: *the rigorous discipline in a prison.* **2** thoroughly logical and scientific; exact: *the rigorous methods of science.* —**rig′or·ous·ly,** *adv.* —**Syn. 1** stern. See **strict.**

rig·our (rig′ər) *n.* rigor.

Rig-Ve·da (rig vā′də or rig vē′də) *n.* the oldest and most important of the sacred books of the Hindus.

rile (rīl) *v.* **riled, ril·ing. 1** make (water, etc.) muddy by stirring up sediment. **2** disturb; irritate; vex. [var. of *roil*]

rill (ril) *n.* a tiny stream; little brook. [cf. Du. *ril* groove, furrow]

rim (rim) *n. v.* **rimmed, rim·ming.** —*n.* an edge, border, or margin on or around anything: *the rim of a wheel, the rim of a cup.* —*v.* **1** form a rim around; put a rim around. **2** surround: *The well was rimmed with grass.* [OE *rima*] —**rim′less,** *adj.*

rime[1] (rīm) *v.* **rimed, rim·ing,** *n.* rhyme. ☛ See **rhyme** for usage note.

rime[2] (rīm) *n. v.* **rimed, rim·ing.** —*n.* white frost; hoarfrost. —*v.* cover with rime. [OE *hrīm*]

rime·ster (rīm′stər) *n.* rhymester.

rim·y (rīm′ē) *adj.* **rim·i·er, rim·i·est.** covered with rime or hoarfrost; frosty.

rind (rīnd) *n.* the firm outer covering (of oranges, melons, cheeses, etc.). The bark of a tree or plant may be called the rind. [OE]

rin·der·pest (rin′dər pest′) *n.* an acute and usually fatal infectious disease of cattle, sheep, etc. [< G *Rinderpest* cattle pest]

hat, āge, cãre, fär; let, ēqual, tėrm; it, īce
hot, ōpen, ôrder; oil, out; cup, pu̇t, rüle, ūse
əbove, takən, pencəl, lemən, circəs
ch, child; ng, long; sh, ship
th, thin; ᴛʜ, then; zh, measure

ring[1] (ring) *n. v.* **ringed, ring·ing.** —*n.* **1** a circle. You can tell the age of a tree by counting the rings in its wood; a new ring grows each year. **2** a thin circle of metal or other material: *a napkin ring, rings on her fingers.* **3** persons or things arranged in a circle. **4** the outer edge or border of a coin, plate, wheel, or anything round. **5** an enclosed space for races, games, circus performances, etc. The ring for a prize fight is square. **6** prize fighting. **7** a competition; rivalry; contest: *in the ring for election to the House.* **8** a group of people combined for a selfish or dishonest purpose: *A ring of corrupt politicians controlled the city.* **9** an enclosed area for the showing and judging of livestock.
—*v.* **1** put a ring around; enclose; form a circle around. **2** toss a horseshoe, ring, etc. around (a certain mark or post). **3** provide with a ring. **4** put a ring in the nose of. **5** form a ring or rings. **6** cut away the bark in a ring around (a tree or branch). [OE *hring*] —**ring′less,** *adj.*

ring[2] (ring) *v.* **rang, rung, ring·ing,** *n.* —*v.* **1** give forth a clear sound, as a bell does. **2** cause to give forth a clear ringing sound: *Ring the bell.* **3** cause a bell to sound: *Did you ring?* **4** make (a sound) by ringing: *The bells rang a joyous peal.* **5** call to church, prayers, etc. by ringing bells. **6** announce or proclaim by ringing; usher; conduct: *Ring out the old year; ring in the new.* **7** proclaim or repeat loudly everywhere: *ring a person's praises.* **8** resound; sound loudly: *The room rang with shouts of laughter.* **9** be filled with report or talk. **10** sound: *His words rang true.* **11** have a sensation as of sounds of bells: *My ears ring.* **12** call on the telephone. **13 ring for,** summon by a bell. **14 ring in,** *Informal.* bring in dishonestly or trickily. **15 ring off,** end a telephone call. **16 ring up, a** record (a specific amount) on a cash register. **b** call on the telephone.
—*n.* **1** the act of ringing. **2** the sound of a bell. **3** a sound like that of a bell. **4** a characteristic sound or quality. **5** a call on the telephone. [OE *hringan*] —**ring′ing·ly,** *adv.*

ring·bolt (ring′bōlt′) *n.* a bolt with a ring fitted in its head.

ringed (ringd) *adj.* **1** having or wearing a ring or rings. **2** marked or decorated with a ring or rings. **3** surrounded by a ring or rings. **4** formed of or with rings; ringlike.

ring·er[1] (ring′ər) *n.* **1** a person or thing that encircles, surrounds with a ring, etc. **2** a quoit, horseshoe, etc. thrown so as to fall over a peg. [< *ring*[1]]

ring·er[2] (ring′ər) *n.* **1** a person or thing that rings; device for ringing a bell. **2** *Slang.* a player who is not an eligible member of the team that he is playing on. **3** *Slang.* a person or thing very much like another. **4 be a (dead) ringer for,** be the image of. [< *ring*[2]]

ring·lead·er (ring′lēd′ər) *n.* a person who leads others in opposition to authority or law. [< the phrase *to lead the ring* to be first]

ring·let (ring′lit) *n.* **1** a little ring. **2** a curl: *She wears her hair in ringlets.*

ring·mas·ter (ring′mas′tər) *n.* a man in charge of the performances in the ring of a circus.

ring-neck (ring′nek′) *n.* **1** a type of green snake that has a yellow ring round its neck. **2** any of various types of birds having a colored ring round the neck, such as the ring-necked duck.

Ring of the Nibelung in German legend, the magic ring made from the Rheingold by the dwarf Alberich, leader of the Nibelungs.

ring·side (ring′sīd′) *n.* **1** a place just outside the ring at a circus, prize fight, etc. **2** a place affording a close view.

ring·worm (ring′wėrm′) *n.* a contagious skin disease, caused by parasites and characterized by ring-shaped patches.

rink (ringk) *n.* **1** a sheet of ice for playing hockey or for pleasure skating. **2** a smooth floor for roller skating. **3** a sheet of ice for curling. **4** a curling team of four players.

5 a building in which there is a rink; arena. [< Scottish < OF *renc* course, rank[1] < Gmc.]

rink rat *Cdn. Slang.* a boy or young man who helps with the chores around a hockey rink, often in return for free skating, free admission to hockey games, etc.

rinse (rins) *v.* **rinsed, rins·ing,** *n.* —*v.* **1** wash with clean water: *Rinse the soap out of your hair.* **2** wash lightly: *Rinse your mouth with water and soda.* —*n.* **1** the act of washing in clean water. **2** a light washing. **3** a preparation to add temporary lustre or color to the hair. [ME < OF *reïncier,* ult. < L *recens* fresh]

ri·ot (rī′ət) *n.* **1** a wild, violent public disturbance; disorder. **2** a loud outburst: *break out in a riot of laughter.* **3** loose living; wild revelling. **4** a bright display: *The garden was a riot of color.* **5** *Informal.* a very amusing person or performance: *He was a riot at the party.* **6 read the riot act, a** give orders for disturbance to cease. **b** reprimand severely. **7 run riot, a** act without restraint. **b** grow wildly or luxuriantly. **c** run wild.
—*v.* **1** behave in a wild, disorderly way. **2** revel. [ME < OF *riote* dispute, ult. < L *rugire* roar] —**ri′ot·er,** *n.* —**Syn.** *n.* **1** outbreak, tumult.

ri·ot·ous (rī′ət əs) *adj.* **1** taking part in a riot. **2** boisterous; disorderly: *He was expelled from school for riotous conduct. Sounds of riotous glee came from the yard.* —**ri′ot·ous·ly,** *adv.* —**Syn. 2** turbulent, tumultuous.

rip[1] (rip) *v.* **ripped, rip·ping,** *n.* —*v.* **1** cut roughly; tear apart; tear off: *Rip the cover off this box.* **2** become torn apart. **3** cut or pull out (the threads in the seams of a garment). **4** saw (wood) along the grain, not across the grain. **5** *Informal.* move fast or violently.
rip into, *Informal.* attack violently.
rip off, *Slang.* take advantage of; cheat.
rip out, *Informal.* speak or say with violence: *He ripped out an angry oath.*
—*n.* **1** a torn place. **2** a seam unstitched in a garment. **3** a tearing. [ME *rippe(n)*] —**Syn.** *v.* **1** rend. See **tear.**

rip[2] (rip) *n.* **1** a stretch of rough water made by cross currents meeting. **2** a swift current made by the tide. [? special use of *rip*[1]]

rip[3] (rip) *n. Informal.* **1** a worthless or dissolute person. **2** a worthless worn-out horse. [? alteration of *rep,* short for *reprobate*]

R.I.P. may he or she (they) rest in peace. (for L *requiescat,* or *requiescant, in pace*)

ri·par·i·an (rə păr′ē ən or rī păr′ē ən) *adj.* of or on the bank of a river, a lake, etc.: *riparian rights, riparian property.* [< L *riparius* < *ripa* riverbank]

rip cord a cord that, when pulled, opens a parachute.

ripe (rīp) *adj.* **rip·er, rip·est. 1** full-grown and ready to be gathered and eaten: *ripe fruit.* **2** resembling ripe fruit in ruddiness and fullness. **3** fully developed and fit to use: *ripe knowledge.* **4** ready to break or be lanced: *a ripe boil.* **5** ready: *ripe for mischief.* **6** far enough along. **7** advanced in years. [OE *rīpe*] —**ripe′ly,** *adv.* —**ripe′ness,** *n.* —**Syn. 1** mellow, mature, matured.

rip·en (rīp′ən) *v.* **1** become ripe. **2** make ripe.

rip-off (rip′of′) *n. Slang.* a making of a profit or other gain by taking advantage of a person or group; a cheating or swindle: *He says selling youth styles for profit is a rip-off.*

ri·poste (rə pōst′) *n. v.* **-post·ed, -post·ing.** —*n.* **1** in fencing, a quick thrust given after parrying a lunge. **2** a quick, sharp reply or return. —*v.* make a riposte; reply; retaliate. [< F < Ital. *risposta* reply, ult. < L *respondere* respond. See RESPOND.]

rip·per (rip′ər) *n.* **1** one that rips. **2** a tool for ripping.

rip·ping (rip′ing) *adj. Brit. Slang.* fine; splendid.

rip·ple (rip′əl) *n. v.* **-pled, -pling.** —*n.* **1** a very little wave: *Throw a stone into still water and watch the ripples spread in rings.* **2** anything that seems like a little wave: *ripples in cardboard.* **3** a sound that reminds one of little waves: *a ripple of laughter in the crowd.* **4** a riffle (def. 2).
—*v.* **1** make a sound like rippling water. **2** form or have little waves. **3** flow with little waves on the surface. **4** make little waves on: *A breeze rippled the quiet waters.* [origin uncertain] —**Syn.** *n.* **1** See **wave.**

rip·ply (rip′lē) *adj.* characterized by ripples; rippling.

rip·rap (rip′rap′) *n. v.* **-rapped, -rap·ping.** —*n.* **1** a wall or foundation of broken stones thrown together irregularly. **2** the broken stones so used. —*v.* build or strengthen with loose, broken stones. [varied reduplication of *rap*[1]]

rip·roar·ing (rip′rôr′ing) *adj. Slang.* hilarious; uproarious.

rip·saw (rip′so′ or -sô′) *n.* a saw for cutting wood along the grain, not across the grain. [< *rip*[1], v. + *saw*[1]]

rip·snort·er (rip′snôrt′ər) *n. Slang.* an extraordinary or violent person or thing: *a ripsnorter of a storm.*

rip·snort·ing (rip′snôrt′ing) *adj. Slang.* loud and boisterous.

rip·tide (rip′tīd′) *n.* a strong current of churning water caused by one tide meeting another.

Rip Van Win·kle (rip′van wing′kəl) **1** the hero of a story by Washington Irving. He falls asleep and wakes 20 years later to find everything changed. **2** someone who is ignorant of present-day conditions.

rise (rīz) *v.* **rose, ris·en, ris·ing,** *n.* —*v.* **1** get up from a lying, sitting, or kneeling position: *rise from a chair.* **2** get up from sleep or rest: *rise at dawn.* **3** go up; come up; ascend: *The kite rises in the air.* **4** extend upward: *The tower rises to a height of 60 feet.* **5** slope upward: *Hills rise in the distance.* **6** cause to rise; cause to rise above the horizon by approaching nearer to it. **7** go higher; increase: *Prices are rising.* **8** advance to a higher level of action, thought, feeling, expression, rank, position, etc.: *He rose from errand boy to president.* **9** become louder or of higher pitch. **10** come above the horizon: *The sun rises in the morning.* **11** start; begin: *The river rises from a spring. Quarrels often rise from trifles.* **12** come into being or action: *The wind rose rapidly.* **13** be built up, erected, or constructed: *Houses are rising on the edge of the town.* **14** become more animated or more cheerful: *His spirits rose.* **15** revolt; rebel: *The slaves rose against their masters.* **16** grow larger and lighter: *Yeast makes dough rise.* **17** come to life again. **18** end a meeting or session; adjourn: *The House rose for the summer.* **19 rise to,** be equal to; be able to deal with: *They rose to the occasion.*
—*n.* **1** an upward movement; ascent: *the rise of a balloon.* **2** the coming of a fish to the surface of the water to seize bait, etc. **3** an upward slope: *The rise of that hill is gradual.* **4** a piece of rising or high ground; hill. **5** the vertical height of a step, slope, arch, etc. **6** an increase. **7** an advance in rank, power, etc. **8** an increase in loudness or in pitch. **9** a coming above the horizon. **10** an origin; beginning. **11 get a rise out of somebody,** cause a person to react in a way expected to some question or situation deliberately put or arranged. **12 give rise to,** start; begin; cause; bring about. [OE *rīsan*] —**Syn.** *v.* **1** arise, stand. **16** swell, increase.
☛ In referring to people, **arise** is formal and poetic; **rise** is rather formal; **get up** is informal.

ris·en (riz′ən) *v.* pp. of **rise.**

ris·er (rīz′ər) *n.* **1** a person or thing that rises: *an early riser.* **2** the vertical part of a step.

ris·i·bil·i·ty (riz′ə bil′ə tē) *n.* **-ties. 1** an ability or inclination to laugh. **2** Often, **risibilities,** *pl.* desire to laugh; sense of humor.

ris·i·ble (riz′ə bəl) *adj.* **1** able or inclined to laugh. **2** of laughter; used in laughter. **3** causing laughter; amusing; funny. [< LL *risibilis,* ult. < L *ridere* laugh]

ris·ing (rīz′ing) *n.* **1** the act of ascending; a coming up. **2** the act of getting up. **3** a rebellion; revolt. —*adj.* that rises.

risk (risk) *n.* **1** a chance of harm or loss; danger. **2** in insurance: **a** a person or thing described with reference to the chance of loss from insuring him or it. **b** an insurance obligation or possible loss. **c** the amount of possible loss. **3** a person or thing that cannot be relied on. **4 run a risk** or **take a risk,** expose oneself to the chance of harm or loss.
—*v.* **1** expose to the chance of harm or loss: *A soldier risks his life.* **2** take the risk of: *They risked getting wet.* [< F *risque* < Ital. *risco* < *risicare* dare, originally, skirt cliffs in sailing < Gk. *rhiza* base, root] —**Syn.** *n.* **1** hazard, peril, jeopardy. –*v.* **1** hazard, endanger, imperil, jeopardize.

hat, āge, cãre, fär; let, ēqual, tėrm; it, īce
hot, ōpen, ôrder; oil, out; cup, pu̇t, rüle, ūse
əbove, takən, pencəl, lemən, circəs
ch, child; ng, long; sh, ship
th, thin; ᴛʜ, then; zh, measure

risk capital capital not covered by collateral and invested in the hope of profit but at the risk of a loss.

risk·y (ris′kē) *adj.* **risk·i·er, risk·i·est. 1** full of risk; dangerous. **2** somewhat improper; risqué. —**risk′i·ly,** *adv.* —**risk′i·ness,** *n.* —**Syn. 1** hazardous, perilous, precarious, unsafe.

ri·sot·to (ri zot′ō; *Italian,* rē sôt′tō) *n.* an Italian dish consisting of rice cooked in oil and chicken broth, served with cut-up chicken, tomato sauce, cheese, and spices. [< Ital.]

ris·qué (ris kā′) *adj.* suggestive of indecency; somewhat improper: *a risqué situation in a play.* [< F *risqué,* pp. of *risquer* to risk]

ris·sole (ris′ōl; *French,* rē sôl′) *n.* a fried ball or cake of meat or fish mixed with bread crumbs, egg, etc. [< F]

rit. or **ritard.** ritardando.

ri·tar·dan·do (rē′tär dän′dō) in music: —*adj.* becoming gradually slower. —*adv.* gradually more slowly. —*n.* a gradual decrease in tempo. *Abbrev.*: rit. or ritard. [< Ital. *ritardando* < *ritardare* retard]

rite (rīt) *n.* **1** a solemn ceremony. Secret societies have their special rites. **2** a particular form or system of ceremonies: *the Latin rite.* [< L *ritus*] —**Syn. 1** See **ceremony.**

rit·u·al (rich′ü əl) *n.* **1** a form or system of rites. The rites of baptism, marriage, and burial are parts of the ritual of the church. **2** a book containing rites or ceremonies. **3** the carrying out of rites. —*adj.* of or having to do with rites; done as a rite: *a ritual dance.* [< L *ritualis* < *ritus* rite]

rit·u·al·ism (rich′ü əl iz′əm) *n.* **1** a fondness for ritual; insistence upon ritual. **2** the study of ritual practices or religious rites.

rit·u·al·ist (rich′ü əl ist) *n.* **1** a person who practises or advocates observance of ritual. **2** a person who studies or knows much about ritual practices or religious rites.

rit·u·al·is·tic (rich′ü əl is′tik) *adj.* **1** having to do with ritual or ritualism. **2** fond of ritual. —**rit′u·al·is′ti·cal·ly,** *adv.*

rit·u·al·ly (rich′ü əl ē) *adv.* with or according to a ritual.

riv. river.

ri·val (rī′vəl) *n. adj. v.* **-valled** or **-valed, -val·ling** or **-val·ing.** —*n.* **1** a person who wants and tries to get the same thing as another; one who tries to equal or do better than another. **2** a thing that will bear comparison with something else; equal; match.
—*adj.* wanting the same thing as another; being a rival: *The rival store tried to get the other's trade.*
—*v.* **1** try to equal or outdo: *The stores rival each other in beautiful window displays.* **2** equal; match: *The sunset rivalled the sunrise in beauty.* [< L *rivalis* using the same stream < *rivus* stream] —**Syn.** *n.* **1** competitor, contestant, antagonist.

ri·val·ry (rī′vəl rē) *n.* **-ries.** the action, position, or relation of a rival or rivals; competition: *There is rivalry among business firms for trade.* —**Syn.** contest.

rive (rīv) *v.* **rived, rived** or **riv·en, riv·ing.** tear apart; split; cleave. [ME < ON *rífa*]

riv·en (riv′ən) *adj.* torn apart; split. —*v.* a pp. of **rive.**

riv·er[1] (riv′ər) *n.* **1** a large natural stream of water. **2** any abundant stream or flow: *rivers of blood.* [ME < OF *rivere* < L *riparius* of a riverbank < *ripa* bank]

riv·er[2] (rīv′ər) *n.* a person or thing that rives. [< *rive*]

river basin land that is drained by a river and its tributaries.

riv·er·head (riv′ər hed′) *n.* the source of a river.

river horse a hippopotamus.

riv·er·ine (riv′ər īn′ or riv′ər ēn′) *adj.* **1** of or having to do with a river. **2** located on or living near a river: *a riverine town.*

riv·er·side (riv′ər sīd′) *n.* the bank of a river. —*adj.* on the bank of a river: *The riverside path is much used.*

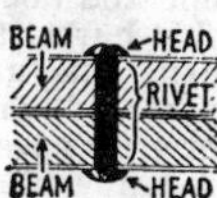

A rivet holding two steel beams together

riv·et (riv′it) *n.* a metal bolt having a head at one end. The other end is passed through holes in the things to be joined and is then hammered into another head. —*v.* **1** fasten with a rivet or rivets. **2** flatten (the end of a bolt) so as to form a head. **3** fasten firmly; fix firmly: *Their eyes were riveted on the speaker.* [ME < OF *rivet* < *river* fix < VL *ripare* come to shore < L *ripa* bank] —**riv′et·er,** *n.*

Riv·i·er·a (riv′ē ãr′ə) *n.* a section of France and Italy along the Mediterranean Sea, famous as a resort area.

riv·u·let (riv′yu̇ lit) *n.* a very small stream. [< Ital. *rivoletto,* ult. < L *rivus* stream]

ri·yal (rē äl′) *n.* **1** a unit of money in Saudi Arabia and Yemen. See table at **money. 2** a coin worth one riyal. [< Arabic *riyal* < Sp. *real*]

rm. *pl.* **rms. 1** room. **2** ream.

R.M. 1 Rural Municipality. **2** Royal Marines.

Rn radon.

R.N. or **RN 1** registered nurse. **2** Royal Navy.

RNA ribonucleic acid.

roach[1] (rōch) *n.* cockroach.

roach[2] (rōch) *n.* **roach** or **roach·es. 1** a European freshwater fish related to the carp. **2** any of various similar fishes, such as the North American sunfish. [ME < OF *roche*]

roach[3] (rōch) *v.* of hair, etc., trim the top so that the part that is left stands upright. —*n.* hair, nap, etc. that has been trimmed short. [origin uncertain]

roach[4] (rōch) *n. Slang.* the butt of a marijuana cigarette.

road (rōd) *n.* **1** a way for passage between places; way made for trucks or automobiles to travel on. **2** a way or course. **3** a railway; railroad. **4** Also, **roads.** a place near the shore where ships can ride at anchor. **5** roadbed.
6 hold the road, drive or travel on a road easily, smoothly, and safely. **7 on the road, a** travelling, especially as a salesman. **b** of a theatre, etc., on tour, as in a theatre company.
8 take to the road, a go on the road; begin to travel.
b formerly, become a highwayman. **9 the road,** the tour of a theatre company, etc. [OE *rād* a riding, journey] —**Syn. 1** roadway, turnpike, thoroughfare. **2** channel, route.

road agent *Esp.U.S.* formerly, a highwayman.

road allowance *Cdn.* land reserved by the government as public property to be used for roads. The road allowance includes the road and a certain amount of land on either side of it.

road·bed (rōd′bed′) *n.* the foundation of a road or of a railway.

road·block (rōd′blok) *n.* **1** a road barricade set up by police to prevent wanted men from escaping: *A roadblock was set up to stop the car thief.* **2** an obstacle placed across a road. **3** any obstacle to progress.

road hog *Informal.* a driver who obstructs traffic by keeping his vehicle in the middle of the road, refusing to let other vehicles pass.

road·house (rōd′hous′) *n.* a restaurant in the country where people can stop for refreshments and, sometimes, entertainment.

road metal broken stone, cinders, etc. used for roads and roadbeds.

road runner a long-tailed bird of the deserts of the S.W. United States that is related to the cuckoo. It usually runs instead of flying.

road show a play, opera, ballet, etc. that travels from city to city.

road·side (rōd′sīd′) *n.* the side of a road. —*adj.* beside a road: *a roadside inn.*

road·stead (rōd′sted) *n.* road (def. 4).

road·ster (rōd′stər) *n.* **1** an open automobile having a single wide seat in front and, often, a rumble seat in the rear. **2** a horse for riding or driving on roads.

road·way (rōd′wā′) *n.* **1** a road. **2** the part of a road used by wheeled vehicles.

road·wor·thy (rōd′wėr′ᴛʜē) *adj.* of vehicles, suitable for use on the road. —**road′wor′thi·ness,** *n.*

roam (rōm) *v.* 1 go about with no special plan or aim; wander: *roam through the fields.* 2 wander over. —*n.* a walk or trip with no special aim; wandering.
—**roam′er,** *n.*

Syn. *v.* 1 **Roam, rove, ramble** = wander. **Roam** = go about here and there as one pleases over a wide area, with no special plan or aim: *The photographer roamed about the world.* **Rove** usually adds the suggestion of a definite purpose, though not of a settled destination: *Submarines roved the ocean.* **Ramble** particularly suggests straying from a regular path or plan and wandering about aimlessly for one's own pleasure: *We rambled through the shopping district.*

roan (rōn) *adj.* yellowish-brown or reddish-brown sprinkled with gray or white. —*n.* 1 a roan horse. 2 a soft, flexible leather made from sheepskin, used in bookbinding. 3 a roan color. [< F < Sp. *roano,* probably < Gmc.]

roar (rôr) *n.* 1 make a loud, deep sound; make a loud noise: *The lion roared.* 2 utter loudly: *roar out an order.* 3 make or put by roaring: *The crowd roared itself hoarse.* 4 laugh loudly. 5 move with a roar: *The train roared past us.* —*n.* a loud, deep sound; loud noise. [OE *rārian*] —**roar′er,** *n.* —**Syn.** *v.* 2 bellow, bawl, howl, yell.

roar·ing (rôr′ing) *adj.* 1 emitting roars; bellowing. 2 riotous; noisy; boisterous. 3 successful; booming: *a roaring business.* —*n.* 1 the act of one that roars. 2 a loud, full cry; bellowing. 3 of horses, a disease characterized by loud breathing. —**roar′ing·ly,** *adv.*

roaring forties the rough, stormy region in the North Atlantic Ocean that lies between 40 degrees and 50 degrees latitude.

roast (rōst) *v.* 1 cook (meat, etc.) by dry heat; cook in an oven, before or over an open fire, or in embers; bake. 2 prepare by heating: *roast coffee, roast a metal ore.* 3 make or become very hot. 4 be baked. 5 *Informal.* **a** make fun of; ridicule. **b** reprove; criticize severely. —*n.* 1 a piece of roasted meat; a piece of meat to be roasted. 2 an informal outdoor meal, at which some food is cooked over an open fire: *a wiener roast.* 3 **rule the roast,** be master. —*adj.* roasted: *roast beef.* [ME < OF *rostir* < Gmc.]

roast·er (rōs′tər) *n.* 1 a pan used in roasting. 2 a chicken, young pig, etc. fit to be roasted. 3 one that roasts.

rob (rob) *v.* **robbed, rob·bing.** 1 take away from by force or threats; steal from: *Bandits robbed the bank.* 2 steal: *They said they would not rob again.* 3 **rob Peter to pay Paul,** take something away from one to pay, satisfy, or advance another. [ME < OF *rober* < Gmc.] —**Syn.** 1 plunder, pillage, loot.

rob·ber (rob′ər) *n.* a person who robs. —**Syn.** See **thief.**

rob·ber·y (rob′ər ē or rob′rē) *n.* **-ber·ies.** an act of robbing; theft. [ME < OF *roberie* < *rober.* See ROB.]

robe (rōb) *n. v.* **robed, rob·ing.** —*n.* 1 a long, loose outer garment. 2 a garment that shows rank, office, etc.: *a judge's robe, the king's robes of state.* 3 a covering or wrap: *Put a robe over you when you go for a ride on a cold day.* 4 formerly, the dressed skin of a buffalo or other animal, used especially for protection against moisture and cold. 5 a bathrobe or dressing gown. —*v.* put a robe on; dress. [ME < OF *robe,* originally, plunder, booty. Cf. ROB.]

rob·in (rob′ən) *n.* 1 a large North American thrush having a reddish breast. 2 a small European bird having a yellowish-red breast. [ME < OF *Robin,* dim. of Robert]

Robin Goodfellow Puck, a mischievous fairy of English folklore.

Robin Hood in English legend, the gay and chivalrous leader of an outlaw band of Sherwood Forest, who robbed the rich to help the poor.

robin's-egg blue greenish blue.

ro·bot (rō′bot or rō′bət) *n.* 1 a machine-made man; a mechanical device that does some of the work of human beings. 2 a person who acts or works in a dull, mechanical way. [invented by Karel Capek (1890-1938), a Czech writer, for his play, *R.U.R.*; suggested by Czech *robota* work, *robotnik* serf]

robot bomb a pilotless jet-propelled airplane that is steered by a mechanical device, and carries a heavy charge of explosives; buzz bomb.

ro·bust (rō bust′ or rō′bust) *adj.* 1 strong and healthy; sturdy: *a robust person, a robust mind.* 2 suited to or requiring bodily strength: *robust exercises.* 3 rough; rude. [< L *robustus,* originally, oaken < *robur* oak] —**ro·bust′ly,** *adv.* —**ro·bust′ness,** *n.* —**Syn.** 1 hardy, stalwart, stout. See **strong.**

ro·bus·tious (rō bus′chəs) *adj. Archaic or humorous.* 1 rough; rude; boisterous. 2 robust; strong; stout.

roc (rok) *n.* in Arabian and other tales, a bird supposed to have enormous size and strength. [< Arabic *rukkh* < Persian]

Ro·chelle salt (rō shel′) a colorless or white crystalline compound, potassium sodium tartrate, used as a laxative. *Formula*: $KNaC_4H_4O_6 \cdot 4H_2O$ [< La *Rochelle,* a city in France]

roch·et (roch′it) *n.* a vestment of linen or lawn resembling a surplice, worn by bishops and abbots. [ME < OF *rochet,* ult. < Gmc.]

rock[1] (rok) *n.* 1 a large mass of stone. 2 any piece of stone; a stone. 3 in geology: **a** the mass of mineral matter of which the earth's crust is made up. **b** a particular layer or kind of such matter. 4 something firm like a rock; support; defence. 5 anything that suggests or acts as a rock. 6 a curling stone. 7 rock candy. 8 *Slang.* a precious stone, especially a diamond. 9 **on the rocks, a** wrecked; ruined. **b** *Informal.* bankrupt. **c** of alcoholic drinks, with ice but without water or mixes: *whisky on the rocks.* 10 **rocks,** *pl. Slang.* money. [ME < OF *roque* < VL *rocca*]

rock[2] (rok) *v.* 1 move backward or forward, or from side to side; sway. 2 move powerfully with emotion. 3 put (to sleep, rest, etc.) with swaying movements. 4 *Informal.* disturb; shake; upset: *The family was rocked by the news.* —*n.* 1 a rocking movement. 2 a dance movement. [OE *roccian*] —**Syn.** *v.* 1 roll. See **swing.**

rock-and-roll (rok′ən rōl′) *n.* 1 in music, a vigorous kind of jazz having a strongly marked, regular beat. 2 a lively style of dancing to such music, characterized by improvisation and exaggerated movements. Also, **rock'n'roll.**

rock bottom the very bottom; lowest level.

rock-bot·tom (rok′bot′əm) *adj.* down to the very bottom; very lowest.

rock-bound (rok′bound′) *adj.* surrounded by rocks; rocky.

rock burst a violent falling in of rocks from the walls of a mine.

rock candy sugar in the form of large, hard crystals.

Rock Cornish hen a small fowl that is a cross between a Cornish chicken and a white Plymouth Rock.

rock crystal a colorless, transparent variety of quartz, often used for jewellery, ornaments, etc.

rock·er (rok′ər) *n.* 1 one of the curved pieces on which a cradle, rocking chair, etc. rocks. 2 a rocking chair. 3 a cradle used in placer mining.

rock·er·y (rok′ər ē) *n.* **rock·er·ies.** an ornamental garden, or part of a garden, consisting of an arrangement of rocks and earth for growing plants and flowers; a rock garden. Rockeries are often built on slopes.

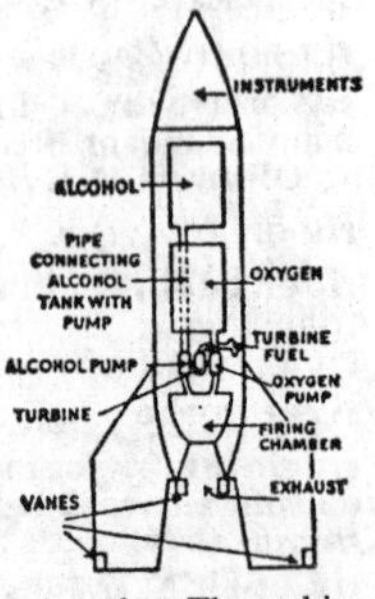

A rocket. The turbine works the pumps, feeding oxygen and fuel into the firing chamber. The exhaust gases from the explosion drive the rocket forward.

rock·et (rok′it) *n.* a projectile consisting of a tube open at one end and filled with some substance that burns rapidly, creating expanding gases that propel the tube and whatever is attached to it at great speed. Rockets are used for fireworks and signalling and for propelling missiles designed for war and in space exploration. —*v.* 1 go like a rocket. 2 fly straight up rapidly. 3 put into orbit with a rocket. [(? < F) < Ital. *rocchetta*, probably dim. of *rocca* distaff (from the similarity in shape) < Gmc.]

rock·et·ry (rok′it rē) *n.* the designing and firing of rockets, missiles, etc.

rock garden a rockery.

rock·hound (rok′hound′) *n. Informal.* a person who collects rocks as a hobby.

rocking chair a chair mounted on rockers, or on springs, so that it can rock back and forth.

rocking horse a toy horse on rockers for children to ride.

rock'n'roll (rok′ ən rōl′) *n.* rock-and-roll.

rock ptarmigan a brown-and-white Arctic ptarmigan, or grouse, that turns white in winter.

rock-ribbed (rok′ribd′) *adj.* **1** having ridges of rock. **2** unyielding.

rock salt common salt obtained from mines; salt in large crystals.

rock·weed (rok′wēd′) *n.* any of various coarse seaweeds growing on rocks near the shore.

rock wool wool-like fibres made from rock or slag and used for insulation and soundproofing.

rock·y[1] (rok′ē) *adj.* **rock·i·er, rock·i·est. 1** full of rocks. **2** made of rock. **3** like rock; hard; firm. [< *rock*[1]]

rock·y[2] (rok′ē) *adj.* **rock·i·er, rock·i·est. 1** likely to rock; shaky: *That table is a bit rocky; put a piece of wood under the short leg.* **2** unpleasantly uncertain. **3** *Informal.* sickish; weak; dizzy. [< *rock*[2]] **—rock′i·ly,** *adv.* **—rock′i·ness,** *n.*

Rocky Mountain goat a goatlike animal of the Rocky Mountains; a mountain goat.

Rocky Mountain sheep the bighorn.

ro·co·co (rō kō′kō or rō′kə kō′) *n.* **1** in architecture and decoration, a style developed in France in the first half of the 18th century, marked by elaborate ornamentation. **2** in literature, a style of florid, ornamental writing. **3** in music, a style characterized by graceful, gay ornamentations. *—adj.* of or having to do with rococo. [< F *rococo,* ? < *rocaille* shellwork < *roc* rock]

rod (rod) *n.* **1** a thin, straight bar of metal or wood. **2** a thin, straight stick, either growing or cut off. **3** anything resembling a rod in shape. **4** a stick used to beat or punish. **5** punishment. **6** a long, light pole. **7** a long, springy, tapered piece of wood, metal, plastic, etc. to which a reel may be attached, used for fishing. **8** a measure of length; 5½ yards or 16½ feet. A square rod is 30¼ square yards or 272¼ square feet. **9** a stick used to measure with. **10** *Slang.* a pistol. **11** a branch of a family or tribe: *the rod of Jesse.* **12** a staff or wand carried as a symbol of one's position. **13** power; authority; tyranny. **14** a divining rod. **15** one of the microscopic sense organs in the retina of the eye that are sensitive to dim light. **16** a cylindrical or rod-shaped bacterium; bacillus. **17 spare the rod,** fail to punish. [OE *rodd*]

rode (rōd) *v.* pt. of **ride.**

ro·dent (rō′dənt) *n.* any of a group of mammals having teeth especially adapted for gnawing wood and similar material. Rats, mice, and squirrels are rodents. *—adj.* **1** gnawing. **2** of or like a rodent. [< L *rodens, -entis,* ppr. of *rodere* gnaw]

ro·de·o (rō′dē ō or rō dā′ō) *n.* **-de·os. 1** a contest or exhibition of skill in roping cattle, riding horses, etc. **2** *Esp.U.S.* the driving together of cattle; roundup. [< Sp. *rodeo* < *rodear* go around]

rod·o·mon·tade (rod′ə mon tād′ or rod′ə mon täd′) *n.* vain boasting; bragging. [< F < Ital. *rodomontata* < *Rodomonte,* a braggart king in a work of Lodovico Ariosto (1474-1533), an Italian poet < dial. *rodare* roll away (ult. < L *rota* wheel) + *monte* mountain < L *mons, montis*]

roe[1] (rō) *n.* fish eggs. [ME *rowe*]

roe[2] (rō) *n.* **roes** or (*esp. collectively*) **roe.** a small deer of Europe and Asia, having forked antlers. [OE *rā*]

roe·buck (rō′buk′) *n.* a male roe deer.

roent·gen (rent′gən) *n.* the unit for measuring the effect of X rays or gamma rays. It is the quantity of radiation required to produce one electrostatic unit of electrical charge in one cubic centimetre of dry air under normal temperature and pressure. [after Wilhelm Konrad *Roentgen* (1845-1923), a German physicist, who discovered X rays]

Roentgen rays X rays.

ro·ga·tion (rō gā′shən) *n.* **1** in Christian churches, a solemn prayer or supplication, especially as chanted on the three days before Ascension Day. **2** in ancient Rome: **a** the proposal of a law by consuls or tribunes to be approved by the people. **b** a law so proposed. [< L *rogatio, -onis* < *rogare* ask]

rog·a·tor·y (rog′ə tôr′ē) *adj.* questioning or asking questions, as in legal investigations: *a rogatory commission.*

rog·er (roj′ər) *interj. Informal.* message received and understood; O.K. [< the signaller's word for the letter *r,* for "received"]

rogue (rōg) *n. v.* **rogued, ro·guing.** *—n.* **1** a tricky, dishonest, or worthless person; rascal. **2** a mischievous person. **3** an animal with a savage nature that lives apart from the herd: *rogue elephant.* **4** in biology, an individual, usually a plant, that varies from the standard. *—v.* **1** eliminate defective plants from. **2** cheat. **3** be a rogue; act like a rogue. [? short for earlier *roger* beggar] **—Syn. 1** knave, scoundrel.

ro·guer·y (rō′gər ē) *n.* **-guer·ies. 1** the conduct of rogues; dishonest trickery. **2** playful mischief. **—Syn. 1** knavery, rascality, fraud. **2** mischievousness, waggery.

rogues' gallery a collection of photographs of known criminals.

ro·guish (rō′gish) *adj.* **1** dishonest; rascally; having to do with or like rogues. **2** playfully mischievous. **—ro′guish·ly,** *adv.* **—ro′guish·ness,** *n.* **—Syn. 1** knavish, tricky, fraudulent. **2** waggish, sportive.

roil (roil) *v.* rile. [< F *rouiller* rust, earlier, make muddy < OF *rouil* mud, rust, ult. < L *robigo* rust]

rois·ter (rois′tər) *v.* be boisterous; revel noisily; swagger. [< MF *ruistre* rude, ult. < L *rus* the country] **—rois′ter·er,** *n.*

Ro·land (rō′lənd) *n.* **1** one of Charlemagne's legendary chiefs, famous for his strength and courage. He and another hero, Oliver, once fought for five days without either gaining the advantage. **2 a Roland for an Oliver,** one thing thought to be a full match for another.

role or **rôle** (rōl) *n.* **1** a performer's part in a play, opera, etc.: *the leading role.* **2** a part played in real life: *He played an important role in the development of art in Canada.* [< F *rôle* the roll (of paper, etc.) on which a part is written]

☛ **role, rôle.** The spelling with the circumflex is still preferred by some people, especially in formal usage.

roll (rōl) *v.* **1** move along by turning over and over: *A ball rolls.* **2** wrap or become wrapped around on itself or on some other thing: *Roll the string into a ball.* **3** move or be moved on wheels: *The car rolled along.* **4** move smoothly; sweep along: *Waves roll in on the beach. The years roll on.* **5** turn around; revolve. **6** of a heavenly body, etc. perform a periodical revolution in an orbit. **7** move from side to side: *The ship rolled in the waves.* **8** turn over, or over and over: *The horse rolled in the dust.* **9** walk with a swaying gait. **10** rise and fall again and again: *rolling country.* **11** *Archaic.* travel; wander; roam. **12** make flat or smooth with a roller; spread out with a rolling pin, etc. **13** put ink on with a roller. **14** make deep, loud sounds: *Thunder rolls.* **15** beat (a drum) with rapid continuous strokes. **16** utter with full, flowing sound: *The organ rolled out the stirring hymn.* **17** utter with a trill: *roll one's r's.* **18** *Informal.* have more than

enough: *be rolling in money.* **19 a** cast dice. **b** turn up (a number) on a dice: *roll a five.* **20** *Slang.* rob (a person who is drunk or helpless), especially by turning him over to search through his pockets. **21 roll back, a** cause (prices, wages, etc.) to return to a lower level. **b** *Informal.* set back; cause to fall behind. **22 roll up,** increase; pile up or become piled up.
—*n.* **1** something rolled up; a cylinder formed by rolling, (often forming a definite measure): *rolls of paper.* **2** a more or less rounded, cylindrical, or rolled-up mass. **3** continued motion up and down, or from side to side. **4** a rapid continuous beating on a drum. **5** a deep, loud sound: *the roll of thunder.* **6** the act of rolling. **7** a motion like that of waves; undulation. **8** a roller; revolving wheel-like tool used by bookbinders. **9** a record; list; list of names: *Call the roll.* **10 a** a small piece of dough which is cut, shaped, and often doubled or rolled over and then baked: *a dinner roll.* **b** a cake rolled up after being spread with something: *jelly roll.* **11** *Slang.* paper money rolled up. **12** *Slang.* money; funds. **13** a part which is rolled or turned over: *the roll in a hem.* **14** a rich or rhythmical flow of words: *the roll of a verse.* **15** a rolling gait; swagger: *walk with a roll.* **16 strike (someone) off the rolls,** expel from membership. [ME < OF *roller,* ult. < L *rota* wheel] —**Syn.** *v.* **2** curl, coil. **3** wheel. **7** rock, sway. –*n.* **1** scroll. **9** roster, register. See **list.**

roll·a·way (rol′ə wā′) *n.* a folding bed having rollers so that it can be easily stored.

roll call **1** the calling of a list of names, as of soldiers, pupils, etc. to find out who are present. **2** the time of day for such a calling.

roll·er (rōl′ər) *n.* **1** anything that rolls; a cylinder on which something is rolled along or rolled up. **2** a cylinder of metal, stone, wood, etc. used for smoothing, pressing, crushing, etc. **3** a long rolled bandage. **4** a long, swelling wave. **5** a person who rolls something. **6** a kind of canary that has a trilling voice. **7** a kind of tumbler pigeon.

roller bearing a bearing in which the shaft turns on rollers to lessen friction.

roller coaster a railway built for amusement, on which small cars roll up and down steep inclines, round sharp corners, etc.

roller skate one of a pair of skates equipped with small wheels, used on floors, roads, sidewalks, etc.

roll·er-skate (rōl′ər skāt′) *v.* **-skat·ed, -skat·ing.** move on roller skates.

rol·lick (rol′ik) *v.* frolic; be merry; enjoy oneself in a free, hearty way. [origin uncertain]

rol·lick·ing (rol′ik ing) *adj.* frolicking; jolly; lively. **—rol′lick·ing·ly,** *adv.*

rol·lick·some (rol′ik səm) *adj.* rollicking.

roll·ing (rōl′ing) *n.* the action, motion, or sound of anything that rolls or is being rolled: *the rolling of a ball, the rolling of thunder.* —*adj.* that rolls. Rolling land rises and falls in gentle slopes. A person with a rolling gait sways from side to side. A rolling collar turns back or folds over.

rolling mill **1** a factory where metal is rolled into sheets and bars. **2** a machine for rolling metal.

rolling pin a cylinder of wood, porcelain, plastic, etc. for rolling out dough.

rolling stock the locomotives and cars of a railway.

roll-top (rōl′top′) *adj.* having a top that rolls back: *a roll-top desk.*

ro·ly-po·ly (rō′lē pō′lē) *adj. n.* **-lies.** —*adj.* short and plump: *a roly-poly child.* —*n.* **1** a short, plump person or animal. **2** a pudding made of jam or fruit spread on a rich dough, rolled up and cooked. [apparently < *roll*]

rom. in printing, roman (type).

Rom. **1** Roman. **2** in the New Testament, Romans. **3** Romance.

Ro·ma·ic (rō mā′ik) *n.* the everyday spoken language of modern Greece. —*adj.* of or having to do with modern Greece or this language.

ro·maine (rō mān′) *n.* a variety of lettuce having long green leaves with crinkly edges, which are joined loosely at the base. [< F *romaine,* fem. adj., Roman]

ro·man (rō mäN′) *n. French.* **1** a romantic novel. **2** a metrical romance of medieval French literature.

Ro·man (rō′mən) *adj.* **1** of or having to do with Rome or its people. **2** of or having to do with the Roman Catholic Church. **3** in architecture, of or having to do with a style developed by the ancient Romans, characterized by massive walls and pillars, rounded arches and vaults, domes, and pediments. **4 roman,** of or in roman type.
—*n.* **1** a native, inhabitant, or citizen of Rome. **2** Also, **roman.** the style of type most used in printing and typewriting. Most of this dictionary is in roman. **3 Romans,** a book of the New Testament, an epistle written by the Apostle Paul to the Christians of Rome. [OE < L *Romanus* < *Roma* Rome]

Roman candle a kind of firework consisting of a tube that shoots out sparks and balls of fire.

Roman Catholic **1** of, having to do with, or belonging to the Christian church that recognizes the Pope as the supreme head. **2** a member of this church.

Roman Catholicism the doctrines, faith, practices, and system of government of the Roman Catholic Church.

ro·mance (*n.* rō mans′ or rō′mans; *v.* rō mans′) *n. v.* **-manced, -manc·ing.** —*n.* **1** a love story. **2** a story of adventure: *"The Arabian Nights" and "Treasure Island" are romances.* **3** a story or poem telling of heroes: *Have you read the romances about King Arthur and his knights?* **4** real events or conditions that are like such stories, full of love, excitement, or noble deeds; the character or quality of such events or conditions. **5** an interest in adventure and love. **6** a love affair. **7** a false or extravagant story: *Nobody believes her romances about the wonderful things that have happened to her.* **8** in music, a short, lyrical composition.
—*v.* **1** make up romances. **2** think or talk in a romantic way. **3** exaggerate; lie. [ME < OF *romanz,* ult. < VL *romanice* in a Romance language < L *Romanus* Roman < *Roma* Rome] —**Syn.** *n.* **1, 2** See **novel.**

Ro·mance (rō mans′ or rō′mans) *adj.* of or having to do with languages that developed from Latin, the language of the Romans. French, Italian, Spanish, Portuguese, Romanian, and Provençal are Romance languages.

ro·manc·er (rō man′sər) *n.* **1** a writer of romance. **2** a person who makes up false or extravagant stories.

Roman Empire the empire of ancient Rome that lasted from 27 B.C. to A.D. 395, when it was divided into the **Eastern Roman Empire** and the **Western Roman Empire.**

Ro·man·esque (rō′mən esk′) *n.* in architecture, a style characterized by massiveness and round arches and vaults, developed in Europe during the early Middle Ages, between the periods of Roman and Gothic architecture. —*adj.* of, in, or having to do with this style of architecture.

Ro·ma·ni·an (rō mā′nē ən) *adj.* of or having to do with Romania, a country in S.E. Europe, its inhabitants, or language.
—*n.* **1** a native inhabitant of Romania. **2** a citizen of Romania. **3** the language of Romania. Also, **Roumanian, Rumanian.**

Ro·man·ic (rō man′ik) *adj.* **1** Romance. **2** Roman. [< L *Romanicus*]

hat, āge, cãre, fär; let, ēqual, tėrm; it, īce
hot, ōpen, ôrder; oil, out; cup, pu̇t, rüle, ūse
əbove, takən, pencəl, lemən, circəs
ch, child; ng, long; sh, ship
th, thin; ᴛʜ, then; zh, measure

Ro·man·ist (rō′mən ist) *n.* **1** *Derogatory.* a member of the Roman Catholic Church. **2** a student of Roman law, institutions, etc.

Ro·man·ize (rō′mən īz′) *v.* **-ized, -iz·ing. 1** make or become Roman in character. **2** make or become Roman Catholic. **3** write or print in or convert to roman characters. **—Ro′man·i·za′tion,** *n.*

Roman law the laws of the ancient Romans. Roman law is the basis of civil law in many countries.

Roman nose a nose having a prominent bridge.

Roman numerals the system of numerals used in ancient Rome, for example XXIII, LVI, and MDCCLX, in which I = 1, V = 5, X = 10, L = 50, C = 100, D = 500, and M = 1000. The values of the numerals are added together, except when one is preceded by another of smaller value; then the smaller is subtracted from the larger. *Example:* XI = 11, but IX = 9.

Ro·ma·no (rō mä′nō) *n.* a hard, sharp Italian cheese having a greenish-black rind. [< Ital.]

Ro·ma·nov or **Ro·ma·noff** (rō′mə nof′ or rō mä′nof) *n.* the royal family of Russia from 1613 to 1917.

Roman rite the system of ceremonies used in the Roman Catholic Church in celebrating the Mass and administering the sacraments.

ro·man·tic (rō man′tik) *adj.* **1** characteristic of romances or romance; appealing to fancy and the imagination: *She likes romantic tales of love and war.* **2** having ideas or feelings suited to romance: *The romantic schoolgirl's mind was full of handsome heroes, jewels, balls, and fine clothes.* **3** suited to a romance: *What a romantic wood! Fairies might live here!* **4** fond of making up fanciful stories. **5** in literature, music, and art, appealing to the emotions and the imagination in subject and style; not classical: "*Jane Eyre*" *and Chopin's music are romantic.* Romantic writing usually tells about the unusual and adventurous aspects of life and uses complete freedom of form and expression. **6** of or having to do with romanticists or romanticism.
—*n.* **1** a romanticist. **2** a romantic person. [< F *romantique* < earlier *romant* a romance, var. of OF *romanz.* See ROMANCE.] **—ro·man′ti·cal·ly,** *adv.* **—Syn. 1** imaginative, fanciful. **2** sentimental.

ro·man·ti·cism (rō man′tə siz′əm) *n.* **1** a romantic spirit or tendency. **2** in art and literature, a style or movement that prevailed in western Europe in the late 18th and early 19th centuries, characterized by a highly imaginative and emotional treatment of life, nature, and the supernatural. **3** in music, a style characterized by melodic inventiveness and rich harmonies.

ro·man·ti·cist (rō man′tə sist) *n.* a follower of romanticism in literature, art, or music. Scott and Wordsworth were romanticists.

ro·man·ti·cize (rō man′tə sīz′) *v.* **-cised, -ciz·ing. 1** make romantic; give a romantic character to. **2** be romantic; act, talk, or write in a romantic manner.

Romantic Movement the tendency toward romanticism in the literature, art, and music of the late 18th century and early 19th century.

Rom·a·ny (rom′ə nē) *n.* **-nies,** *adj.* —*n.* **1** a Gypsy. **2** the language of the Gypsies. —*adj.* belonging or having to do with the Gypsies, their customs, or their language. [< Romany *Romani,* fem. and pl. of *Romano,* adj. < *Rom* gypsy, man, husband]

ro·maunt (rō mont′ or rō mônt′) *n. Archaic.* a romance; a romantic poem or tale. [ME < OF *romaunt,* var. of *romant,* var. of *romanz.* See ROMANCE.]

Rom. Cath. Roman Catholic.

Rome (rōm) *n.* **1** the Roman Catholic Church. **2** the governing authority of the Roman Catholic Church: *The marriage was annulled by Rome.*

Ro·me·o (rō′mē ō′) *n.* **1** the hero of Shakespeare's tragedy *Romeo and Juliet,* who killed himself for love. **2** any young and romantic lover.

romp (romp) *v.* **1** play in a rough, boisterous way; rush, tumble, and punch in play. **2** a run or go rapidly and with little effort, as in racing. **b** win easily. —*n.* **1** a rough, lively play or frolic: *A pillow fight is a romp.* **2** a girl or boy who likes to romp. **3** a swift but effortless victory in which all the others are left behind, as in racing: *win in a romp.* [ult. var. of *ramp,* v.] **—romp′er,** *n.*

romp·ers (romp′ərz) *n.pl.* a loose outer garment, worn by young children.

Rom·u·lus (rom′yu̇ ləs) *n.* in Roman legend, the founder and first king of Rome. As children, he and his brother Remus were nursed by a wolf. Romulus slew Remus for leaping derisively over the walls of his new city of Rome.

ron·deau (ron′dō or ron dō′) *n.* **ron·deaux** (ron′dōz or ron dōz′). a short poem with thirteen (or ten) lines. The opening words are used in two places as a refrain. The poem "In Flanders Fields" is a rondeau. [< MF *rondeau,* var. of *rondel* < OF *rondel.* Doublet of RONDEL.]

ron·del (ron′dəl or ron′del) *n.* a short poem, usually with fourteen lines and two rhymes. The initial couplet is repeated in the middle and at the end. [ME < OF *rondel,* originally dim. of *rond* round < L *rotundus.* Doublet of RONDEAU.]

ron·do (ron′dō or ron dō′) *n.* **-dos.** in music, a composition or movement having one principal theme to which return is made after the introduction of each subordinate theme. [< Ital. < F *rondeau* rondeau]

rood (rüd) *n.* **1** 40 square rods; one fourth of an acre. **2** *Archaic.* the cross on which Christ died. **3** a representation of the cross; crucifix. [OE *rōd*]

roof (rüf) *n.* **roofs** or **rooves. 1** the top covering of a building. **2** something that in form or position resembles the roof of a building: *the roof of a cave, the roof of a car, the roof of the mouth.* **3** a house; home: *live together under the same roof.* —*v.* cover with a roof; form a roof over. [OE *hrōf*]

roof·er (rüf′ər) *n.* a person who makes or repairs roofs.

roof garden 1 a garden on the flat roof of a building. **2** a roof or top storey of a building, ornamented with plants, etc. and used for a restaurant, theatre, etc.

roof·ing (rüf′ing) *n.* material used for roofs. Shingles are a common roofing for houses.

roof·less (rüf′lis) *adj.* **1** having no roof. **2** having no home or shelter.

roof·top (rüf′top′) *n.* the top of the roof.

roof·tree (rüf′trē′) *n.* the horizontal timber along the top of the roof.

rook[1] (ru̇k) *n.* **1** a European crow that often nests in trees near buildings. **2** *Slang.* a person who cheats at cards, dice, etc. —*v. Slang.* cheat. [OE *hrōc*]

rook[2] (ru̇k) *n.* in chess, one of the pieces with which the game is played, also called a castle. [ME < OF *roc,* ult. < Persian *rukh*]

rook·er·y (ru̇k′ər ē) *n.* **-er·ies. 1** a breeding place of rooks; a colony of rooks. **2** a breeding place or colony where other birds or animals are crowded together: *a rookery of seals.* **3** a crowded, dirty, and poor tenement house or group of such houses.

rook·ie (ru̇k′ē) *n. Slang.* **1** an inexperienced recruit. **2** a beginner; novice. **3** in hockey, baseball, etc., a beginner. [? alteration of *recruit*]

room (rüm or ru̇m) *n.* **1** a part of a house, or other building, with walls separating it from the rest of the building of which it is a part. **2 rooms,** *pl.* lodgings. **3** the people in a room. **4** the space occupied by, or available for, something: *There is little room to move in a crowd.* **5** a need: *room for improvement.* **6** opportunity: *room for advancement.* —*v.* **1** occupy a room; lodge. **2** provide with a room. [OE *rūm*]

-roomed *combining form.* having —— rooms: *a six-roomed house.*

room·er (rüm′ər) *n.* a person who lives in a rented room or rooms in another's house.

room·ette (rüm et′) *n.* a small private bedroom on some railway cars.

room·ful (rüm′fu̇l or ru̇m′-) *n.* **-fuls. 1** enough to fill a room. **2** the people or things in a room.

rooming house a house with rooms to rent.

room-mate (rüm′māt′) *n.* a person who shares a room with another or others.

room service in a hotel, lodge, etc., a special service by which one may order food or drink to be brought to one's room.

room·y (rüm′ē) *adj.* **room·i·er, room·i·est.** having plenty of room; large; spacious. **—room′i·ness,** *n.*

roost (rüst) *n.* **1** a bar, pole, or perch on which birds rest or sleep. **2** a place for birds to roost in. **3** a place to rest or stay: *a robber's roost in the mountains.* **4 rule the roost,** *Informal.* be master. —*v.* sit as birds do on a roost; settle for the night. [OE *hrōst*]

roost·er (rüs′tər) *n.* a male chicken; cock.

root[1] (rüt) *n.* **1** the part of a plant that grows downward, usually into the ground, to hold the plant in place, absorb water and mineral foods from the soil, and often to store food material. **2** any underground part of a plant. **3** something like a root in shape, position, use, etc.: *the root of a tooth, the roots of the hair.* **4** a thing from which other things grow and develop; cause; source: *"The love of money is the root of all evil."* **5 take root, a** send out roots and begin to grow. **b** become firmly fixed. **6** the essential part; base. **7** in mathematics: **a** the quantity that produces another quantity when multiplied by itself a certain number of times. 2 is the square root of 4 and the cube root of 8 ($2 \times 2 = 4$, $2 \times 2 \times 2 = 8$). **b** the quantity that satisfies an equation when substituted for an unknown quantity. In the equation $x^2 + 2x - 3 = 0$, 1 and -3 are the roots. **8** a word from which others are derived. *Example: Room* is the root of *roominess, roomer, roommate,* and *roomy.* **9** in music, the fundamental tone of a chord.
—*v.* **1** send out roots and begin to grow; become fixed in the ground: *Some plants root more quickly than others.* **2** fix firmly: *He was rooted to the spot by surprise.* **3** become firmly fixed. **4** pull, tear, or dig *up, out,* etc. by the roots; get completely rid of. [OE *rōt* < ON *rót*; akin to L *radix*] **—root′less,** *adj.*

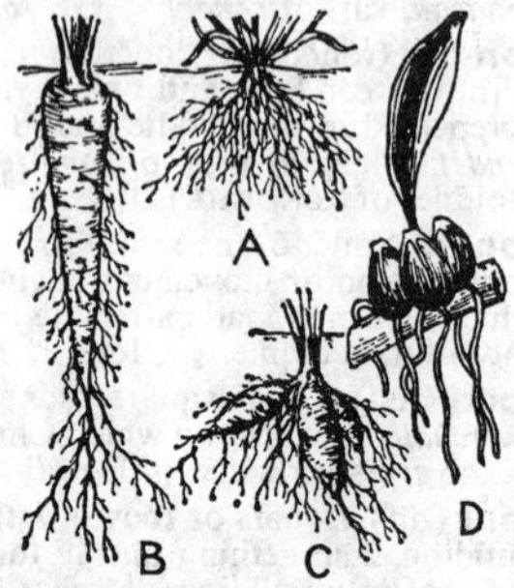

Roots: A, grass; B, carrot; C, sweet potato; D, orchid.

root[2] (rüt) *v.* **1** dig with the snout: *Pigs like to root in gardens.* **2** poke; pry; search. [OE *wrōtan*]

root[3] (rüt) *v. Informal.* cheer or support a contestant, etc. enthusiastically. [probably < earlier *rout* shout, roar < ON *rauta*]

root beer a soft drink flavored with the juice of the roots of certain plants such as sarsaparilla and sassafras.

root·er[1] (rüt′ər) *n.* **1** one who uproots. **2** a person or thing that takes root. **3** a machine that digs or uproots stumps, trees, etc.

root·er[2] (rüt′ər) *n. Informal.* a person who cheers or supports enthusiastically. [< *root*[3]]

root hair a hairlike outgrowth from a root that absorbs water and dissolved minerals from the soil.

root·let (rüt′lit) *n.* a little root; a small branch of a root.

root·stock (rüt′stok′) *n.* rhizome.

root·worm (rüt′wėrm′) *n.* any of various insect larvae or worms that feed on plant roots.

rooves (rüvz) *n.* a pl. of **roof.**

rope (rōp) *n. v.* **roped, rop·ing.** —*n.* **1** a strong, thick line or cord made by twisting smaller cords together. **2** a lasso. **3** a number of things twisted or strung together: *a rope of pearls, a rope of onions.* **4** a cord or noose for hanging a person. **5** death by being hanged. **6** a sticky, stringy mass: *Molasses candy forms a rope.* **7 give one rope,** *Informal.* let him act freely. **8 know the ropes, a** know the various ropes of a ship. **b** *Informal.* know about a business or activity. **9 the end of one's rope,** the end of one's resources, activities, etc.
—*v.* **1** tie, bind, or fasten with a rope. **2** enclose or mark off with a rope. **3** catch (a horse, calf, etc.) with a lasso. **4** form a sticky, stringy mass: *Cook the syrup until it ropes when you lift it with a spoon.* **5 rope in,** *Slang.* get or lead in by tricking. [OE *rāp*]

rope·danc·er (rōp′dan′sər) *n.* a person who dances, walks, etc. on a rope hung high above the floor or ground.

rope·walk (rōp′wok′ or -wôk′) *n.* a place where ropes are made. A ropewalk is usually a long, low shed.

rope·walk·er (rōp′wok′ər or -wôk′ər) *n.* a person who walks on a rope hung high above the floor or ground.

rope·way (rōp′wā′) *n.* an aerial cable along which passengers or freight may be carried.

rop·y (rōp′ē) *adj.* **rop·i·er, rop·i·est. 1** forming sticky threads; stringy. **2** like a rope or ropes. **—rop′i·ly,** *adv.* **—rop′i·ness,** *n.*

roque (rōk) *n.* a form of croquet played on a hard court and modified from ordinary croquet so as to demand greater skill. [abstracted from *croquet*]

Roque·fort (rōk′fərt) *n.* a strongly flavored French cheese made of goats' milk, veined with mould.

ror·qual (rôr′kwəl) *n.* any of the whalebone whales having a dorsal fin; any finback. [< F < Norwegian *röyrkval,* literally, red whale]

Ror·schach test (rôr′shäk) a psychological test that indicates personality traits, based on the subject's interpretation of ten different ink-blot designs. [after Hermann *Rorschach,* 1884-1922, a Swiss psychiatrist]

ro·sa·ceous (rō zā′shəs) *adj.* **1** belonging to the rose family. **2** like a rose. **3** rose-colored. [< L *rosaceus* < *rosa* rose[1]]

ro·sa·ry (rō′zə rē) *n.* **-ries. 1** a string of beads for keeping count in saying a series of prayers. **2** a series of prayers. **3** a rose garden; rose bed. [< Med.L *rosarium* < L *rosarium* rose garden, ult. < *rosa* rose[1]]

rose[1] (rōz) *n. adj. v.* **rosed, ros·ing.** —*n.* **1** a flower that grows on a bush usually having thorny stems. Roses are red, pink, white, or yellow and usually smell very sweet. **2** the bush itself. **3** any of various related or similar plants. or flowers. **4** a pinkish red color. **5** a perfume made from roses. **6** something shaped like a rose or suggesting a rose, such as a rosette, the compass card, the sprinkling nozzle of a water pot, or a gem cut out with faceted top and flat base. **7** a woman of great beauty, loveliness, or excellence. **8 under the rose,** in secret; privately.
—*adj.* pinkish-red.
—*v.* make rosy. [OE < L *rosa*] **—rose′like′,** *adj.*

rose[2] (rōz) *v.* pt. of **rise.**

ro·sé or **Ro·sé** (rō zā′) *n.* a light, pink table wine. [< F]

ro·se·ate (rō′zē it or rō′zē āt′) *adj.* **1** rose-colored; rosy. **2** cheerful; optimistic.

rose·bud (rōz′bud′) *n.* the bud of a rose.

rose bug a bug destructive to roses.

rose·bush (rōz′bůsh′) *n.* a shrub or vine that bears roses.

rose-col·ored or **rose-col·oured** (rōz′kul′ərd) *adj.* **1** pinkish-red. **2** bright; cheerful; optimistic.

rose family a group of many very different trees, shrubs, and plants, including apples, spiraeas, blackberries, and roses. Typical members of the rose family have alternate leaves, five-petalled flowers, and fruits with many seeds.

rose geranium a kind of geranium having fragrant, narrowly divided leaves and small, pinkish flowers.

rose leaf a petal of a rose.

rose mallow a plant having large, rose-colored flowers. The hollyhock and hibiscus are rose mallows.

rose·mar·y (rōz′mãr′ē) *n.* **-mar·ies.** an evergreen shrub whose leaves are much used in cooking and yield a fragrant oil used in making perfume. Rosemary is a symbol of remembrance. [ME < L *ros maris,* literally, dew of the sea; associated with *rose* and *Mary*]

rose of Sharon 1 a shrub having bright flowers; althea.

2 a plant mentioned in the Bible; a kind of St.-John's-wort.

Ro·set·ta stone (rō zet′ə) a slab of black basalt found in 1799 near the mouth of the Nile. A decree carved on it in two kinds of ancient Egyptian writing and in Greek provided the most important key to the understanding of Egyptian hieroglyphics. [< *Rosetta* (< Arabic *Rashid*), a town near one of the mouths of the Nile]

ro·sette (rō zet′) *n.* an ornament, object, or arrangement shaped like a rose. Rosettes are often made of ribbon. Carved or moulded rosettes are used in architecture. [< F *rosette*, dim. of *rose* rose[1]]

rose water water containing oil of roses, used as a perfume and in cooking.

rose window a circular window, usually of stained glass, especially one with a pattern radiating from a centre.

rose·wood (rōz′wu̇d′) *n.* **1** a beautiful reddish wood used in fine furniture. **2** the tropical tree that it comes from.

Rosh Ha·sha·nah or **Ha·sha·na** (rosh′ hə shä′nə) the Jewish New Year (September-early October). [< Hebrew *rōsh* head + *hash-shānāh* the year]

Ro·si·cru·cian (rō′zə krü′shən) *n.* **1** a member of a secret society, especially prominent in the 17th and 18th centuries, that claims to have a special and secret knowledge of nature and religion. **2** a member of any of various similar societies founded later. —*adj.* of or having to do with the Rosicrucians. [< Latinized version of Christian *Rosenkreuz* (1387-1484), the name of the supposed founder of the order]

ros·i·ly (rōz′ə lē) *adv.* **1** with a rosy tinge or color. **2** brightly; cheerfully.

ros·in (roz′ən) *n.* a hard, yellow substance that remains when turpentine is evaporated from pine resin. Rosin is rubbed on violin bows and on the shoes of acrobats, ballet dancers, boxers, etc. to keep them from slipping. —*v.* cover or rub with rosin. [ME var. of *resin*]

Ros·i·nan·te (roz′ə nan′tē) *n.* **1** in Cervantes' *Don Quixote*, the hero's thin and worn-out horse. **2** any very poor, thin, or worn-out horse.

ros·ter (ros′tər) *n.* **1** a list of people's names and the duties assigned to them. **2** any list. [< Du. *rooster*]

ros·tral (ros′trəl) *adj.* of or having to do with a rostrum.

ros·trum (ros′trəm) *n.* **-trums, -tra** (-trə). **1** a platform for public speaking. **2** in ancient times, the beak of a war galley. **3** a beaklike part. [< L *rostrum* beak < *rodere* gnaw; with reference to the speakers' platform in the Roman forum, which was decorated with the beaks of captured war galleys] —**Syn. 1** stage, dais.

ros·y (rōz′ē) *adj.* **ros·i·er, ros·i·est. 1** like a rose; rose-red; pinkish-red. **2** made of roses. **3** bright; cheerful: *a rosy future.* —**ros′i·ness,** *n.*.

rot (rot) *v.* **rot·ted, rot·ting,** *n. interj.* —*v.* **1** decay; spoil. **2** cause to decay. **3** moisten or soak (flax, etc.) in order to soften; ret.
—*n.* **1** the process of rotting; decay. **2** rotten matter. **3** a liver disease of animals, especially of sheep, caused by a liver fluke and marked by anemia, weakness, and swollen jaws. **4** any of various diseases of plants marked by decay and caused by bacteria or fungi, as crown rot. **5** *Slang.* nonsense; rubbish.
—*interj.* nonsense! rubbish! [OE *rotian*] —**Syn.** *v.* **1** decompose, putrefy. See **decay.**

Ro·tar·i·an (rō tãr′ē ən) *n.* a member of a Rotary Club. —*adj.* of, belonging, or having to do with Rotary Clubs.

ro·ta·ry (rō′tə rē) *adj.* **1** turning like a top or a wheel; rotating. **2** having parts that rotate. **3** of an airplane engine, having radially arranged cylinders that revolve around a common fixed crankshaft. **4** of or operating under the rotary system. —*n.* **1** a traffic circle. **2** the rotary system: *All classes are on rotary this year.* [< Med.L *rotarius* < L *rota* wheel]

Rotary Club an association of business and professional men formed with the purpose of serving their community. Rotary Clubs form an international organization.

rotary system in schools, a method of operation under which students move to different rooms (and specialist teachers) for different subjects.

hat, āge, cãre, fär; let, ēqual, tėrm; it, īce
hot, ōpen, ôrder; oil, out; cup, pu̇t, rüle, ūse
əbove, takən, pencəl, lemən, circəs
ch, child; ng, long; sh, ship
th, thin; ᴛʜ, then; zh, measure

ro·tate (rō′tāt or rō tāt′) *v.* **-tat·ed, -tat·ing. 1** move around a centre or axis; turn in a circle; revolve. Wheels, tops, and the earth rotate. **2** change in a regular order; take turns or cause to take turns: *Farmers rotate crops.* [< L *rotare* < *rota* wheel] —**Syn. 1** See **turn.**

ro·ta·tion (rō tā′shən) *n.* **1** the act or process of moving around a centre or axis; turning in a circle; revolving. The earth's rotation causes night and day. **2** a change in a regular order. **3 in rotation,** in turn; in regular succession.

ro·ta·tion·al (rō tā′shən əl) *adj.* of or with rotation.

rotation of crops the varying of the crops grown in the same field to keep the soil from losing its fertility.

ro·ta·tor (rō′tā tər) *n.* **1** a person or thing that rotates. **2** in physiology, a muscle that turns a part of the body. [< L]

ro·ta·to·ry (rō′tə tô′rē) *adj.* **1** rotating; rotary. **2** causing rotation. **3** passing or following from one to another in a regular order.

rote (rōt) *n.* **1** a set, mechanical way of doing things. **2 by rote,** by memory without thought of the meaning. [ME; origin uncertain]

ro·te·none (rō′tə nōn′) *n.* a white crystalline compound obtained from various plant roots, used as an insecticide and fish poison although it is harmless to mammals or birds. *Formula:* $C_{23}H_{22}O_6$ [origin unknown]

rot·gut (rot′gut′) *n. Slang.* raw, cheap alcoholic liquor, especially whisky.

rot·hole (rot′hōl′) *n. Cdn.* a soft place in the ice over a lake, river, etc.

ro·ti·fer (rō′tə fər) *n.* any of a group of complex, microscopic water animals that have one or more rings of cilia on a disk at one end of the body. [< NL *Rotifera*, pl. < *rota* wheel + *ferre* carry]

ro·tis·se·rie (rō tis′ə rē) *n.* **1** a rotating spit used in an oven, under a broiler, or over an open fire, for roasting meat or fowl. **2** a portable oven containing such a device. **3** a shop or restaurant where meats or poultry cooked on a rotisserie are sold. [< F *rotisserie* < *rôtir* to roast]

ro·to·gra·vure (rō′tə grə vūr′ or -grā′vūr) *n.* **1** a process of printing from an engraved copper cylinder on which the pictures, letters, etc. have been depressed instead of raised. **2** a print or section of a newspaper made by this process. [< L *rota* wheel + E *gravure*]

ro·tor (rō′tər) *n.* **1** the rotating part of a machine or apparatus. **2** any of the various combinations of revolving blades by which a helicopter is enabled to fly. [shortened form of *rotator*]

ROTP or **R.O.T.P.** Regular Officers' Training Plan.

rot·ten (rot′ən) *adj.* **1** decayed; spoiled: *a rotten egg.* **2** foul; bad-smelling: *rotten air.* **3** not in good condition; unsound; weak: *rotten ice.* **4** corrupt; dishonest. **5** *Slang.* bad; nasty. [ME < ON *rotinn*] —**rot′ten·ly,** *adv.* —**rot′ten·ness,** *n.* —**Syn. 1** decomposed. **2** putrid, fetid.

rotten borough 1 in England before 1832, a borough that had only a few voters, but kept the privilege of sending a member to Parliament. **2** an electoral district having an insufficient number of voters to justify the representation it has.

ro·tund (rō tund′) *adj.* **1** round; plump. **2** sounding rich and full; full-toned: *a rotund voice.* [< L *rotundus*, ult. < *rota* wheel. Doublet of ROUND.] —**ro·tund′ly,** *adv.*

ro·tun·da (rō tun′də) *n.* **1** a circular building or part of a building, especially one with a dome. **2** a large, circular room with a high ceiling. **3** a large room or area with a high ceiling, such as the lobby of a hotel or the concourse of a railway station. [< L *rotunda*, fem. of *rotundus.* See ROTUND.]

ro·tun·di·ty (rō tun′də tē) *n.* **-ties. 1** roundness; plumpness. **2** something round. **3** rounded fullness of tone.

rou·ble (rü′bəl) *n.* ruble.

rou·é (rü ā′ or rü′ā) *n.* a dissipated man; rake. [< F *roué*, originally pp. of *rouer* break on the wheel < *roue* wheel < L *rota*; first applied to an 18th-century group of profligates]

rouge (rüzh) *n. v.* **rouged, roug·ing.** —*n.* **1** a red powder, paste, or liquid for coloring the cheeks or lips. **2** a red powder, chiefly ferric oxide, used for polishing metal, jewels, etc. **3** in Canadian football, a point scored when a ball kicked into the end zone is not run back into the playing area by the defending team.
—*v.* **1** color with rouge. **2** in Canadian football: **a** score a rouge. **b** tackle (a defending player) in the end zone so as to score a rouge: *Jones rouged Smith on the last play.* [< F *rouge* red]

rouge et noir (rü zhā nwär′) a gambling game played with cards. [< F *rouge et noir* red and black]

rough (ruf) *adj.* **1** not smooth; not level; not even: *rough boards, rough bark.* **2** without polish or fine finish: *rough diamonds.* **3** without luxury and ease: *rough life in camp.* **4** not completed or perfected; done as a first try; without details: *a rough drawing, a rough idea.* **5** coarse and tangled: *a dog with a rough coat of hair.* **6** likely to hurt others; harsh; rude; not gentle: *rough manners.* **7** disorderly; riotous: *a rough crowd.* **8** *Informal.* unpleasant; hard; severe: *He was in for a rough time.* **9** requiring merely strength rather than intelligence or skill: *rough work.* **10** stormy: *rough weather.* **11** violently disturbed or agitated: *a rough sea.* **12** harsh, sharp, or dry to the taste: *rough wines.* **13** in phonetics, pronounced with much breath; aspirated.
—*n.* **1** a coarse, violent person. **2** rough ground. **3** a rough thing or condition. **4** in golf, ground where there is long grass, etc. on a course. **5 in the rough,** not polished or refined; coarse; crude.
—*v.* **1** make rough; roughen. **2** become rough. **3** treat roughly. **4** in hockey, football, etc., intentionally check, tackle, etc. an opponent with unnecessary roughness. **5** shape or sketch roughly. **6 rough it,** live without comforts and conveniences.
—*adv.* roughly. [OE *rūh*] —**Syn.** *adj.* **1** uneven, irregular, broken, jagged. **2** uncultivated, unpolished. **4** approximate, imperfect, incomplete, preliminary. **5** shaggy, bristly. **6** discourteous, impolite, uncivil. **7** boisterous, tumultuous. **8** drastic, rigorous. **10** inclement.

rough·age (ruf′ij) *n.* **1** rough or coarse material. **2** the coarser parts or kinds of food. Bran, fruit skins, and straw are roughage.

rough-and-read·y (ruf′ən red′ē) *adj.* **1** rough and crude, but good enough for the purpose; crude but effective. **2** showing rough vigor rather than refinement.

rough-and-tum·ble (ruf′ən tum′bəl) *adj.* showing confusion and violence; with little regard for rules; unrestrainedly vigorous; boisterous.

rough·cast (ruf′kast′) *n. v.* **-cast, -cast·ing.** —*n.* **1** a coarse plaster for outside surfaces. **2** rough form. —*v.* **1** cover or coat with coarse plaster. **2** make, shape, or prepare in a rough form: *roughcast a story.*

rough-dry (ruf′drī′) *v.* **-dried, -dry·ing.** dry (clothes) after washing without ironing them.

rough·en (ruf′ən) *v.* **1** make rough. **2** become rough.

rough-hew (ruf′hū′) *v.* **-hewed, -hewed** or **-hewn, -hew·ing. 1** hew (timber, stone, etc.) without smoothing or finishing. **2** shape crudely; give crude form to.

rough·house (ruf′hous′) *n. v.* **-housed, -hous·ing.** *Slang.* —*n.* boisterous play; rowdy conduct; disorderly behavior. —*v.* **1** act in a boisterous, disorderly way. **2** disturb by such conduct.

rough·ing (ruf′ing) *n.* in hockey, football, etc., the rough treatment of another player: *a penalty for roughing.*

rough·ly (ruf′lē) *adv.* **1** in a rough manner. **2** approximately.

rough·neck (ruf′nek′) *n.* **1** a rough, coarse, bad-mannered person; a rowdy. **2** *Slang.* a member of an oil-drilling crew.

rough·ness (ruf′nis) *n.* **1** the quality of being rough. **2** rough condition. **3** a rough part.

rough·rid·er (ruf′rīd′ər) *n.* **1** a man used to rough, hard riding. **2** a person who breaks in and rides rough, wild horses.

rough·shod (ruf′shod′) *adj.* **1** having horseshoes equipped with sharp calks to prevent slipping. **2 ride roughshod over,** domineer; show no consideration for; treat roughly.

rou·lade (rü läd′) *n.* **1** in music, a rapid succession of tones sung to a single syllable. **2** a slice of meat rolled about a filling of minced meat and cooked. [< F *roulade* < *rouler* roll]

rou·lette (rü let′) *n.* **1** a gambling game in which the players bet on the turn of a wheel. **2** a small wheel with sharp teeth for making lines of marks, dots, or perforations. [< F *roulette*, ult. < *roue* < L *rota* wheel]

Rou·ma·ni·an (rü mā′nē ən or rü mān′yən) *adj. n.* Romanian.

round (round) *adj.* **1** shaped like a ball, a ring, a cylinder, or the like; having a circular or curved outline or surface. **2** plump: *Her figure was short and round.* **3** by, with, or involving a circular movement: *The waltz is a round dance.* **4** full; complete; large: *a round dozen, a good round sum of money.* **5** plainly expressed; plain-spoken; frank: *The boy's father scolded him in good round terms.* **6** with a full tone: *a mellow, round voice.* **7** vigorous; brisk: *a round trot.* **8** that is in round numbers: *the round sum of one hundred dollars.* **9** rough; approximate: *a round estimate.*
—*n.* **1** anything shaped like a ball, circle, cylinder, etc. The rungs of a ladder are sometimes called rounds. **2** a fixed course ending where it begins: *The watchman makes his rounds of the building every hour.* **3** a movement in a circle or about an axis: *the earth's yearly round.* **4** a series (of duties, events, etc.); routine: *a round of pleasures, a round of duties.* **5** the distance between any limits; range; circuit: *the round of human knowledge.* **6** a section of a game or sport: *a round in a boxing match, a round of cards.* **7** the firing of a number or group of rifles, guns, etc. at the same time. **8** the bullets, powder, etc. for such a shot. **9** a single bullet, artillery shell, etc. **10** an act that a number of people do together: *a round of applause, a round of cheers.* **11** a dance in which the dancers move in a circle. **12** in music, a short song, sung by several persons or groups beginning one after the other: *"Three Blind Mice" is a round.* **13** a form of sculpture in which the figures are apart from any background. **14** a cut of beef just above the hind leg. See **beef** for diagram. **15 go the round,** be passed, told, shown, etc. by many people from one to another. **16 in the round, a** in a form of sculpture in which the figures are apart from any background. **b** in the open; showing all sides or aspects. **17 make** or **go the rounds,** go about from place to place in a certain course or through a certain area. **18 rounds,** the ringing of a set of bells from the highest tone through the major scale to the lowest tone.
—*v.* **1** make or become round: *The carpenter was rounding the corners of a table.* **2** go wholly or partly around: *They rounded the island. The ship rounded Cape Horn.* **3** take a circular course; make a complete or partial circuit: *The car rounded the corner.* **4** turn around; wheel about: *The bear rounded and faced the hunters.* **5** fill (*out*); complete: *round out a paragraph, round out a career.* **6** in phonetics, utter (a vowel) with a small circular opening of the lips: *The rounded vowels include* (ō) *and* (ü). **7 round in,** in nautical use, haul in. **8 round off** or **out, a** make or become round. **b** finish; complete. **9 round on,** turn on to attack, or as if to attack. **10 round to,** in nautical use, come head up to the wind. **11 round up,** draw or drive together.
—*adv.* **1** in a circle; with a whirling motion: *Wheels go round.* **2** on all sides; in every direction: *The travellers were compassed round by dangers.* **3** in circumference: *The pumpkin measures fifty inches round.* **4** by a longer road or way: *We went round by the candy store on our way home.* **5** from one to another: *A report is going round that the stores will close.* **6** through a recurring interval of time: *Summer will soon come round again.* **7** about; around: *He doesn't look fit to be round.* **8** here and there: *I am just looking round.* **9** for all: *There is just enough cake to go round.*
—*prep.* **1** on all sides of: *Bullets whistled round him, but he was not hit.* **2** so as to encircle or surround: *They built a fence round the yard.* **3** so as to make a turn to the

other side of: *He walked round the corner.* **4** in a circuit or course through; to all or various parts of: *We took our cousins round the town.* **5** about; around: *Stand still and look round you.* **6** here and there in: *There are boxes for mail all round the city.* **7 get** or **come round a person, a** outwit him. **b** wheedle him. [ME < OF *roont* (fem. *roonde*) < L *rotundus.* Doublet of ROTUND.] **—round′ness,** *n.* **—Syn.** *adj.* **1** cylindrical, spherical, globular. **2** stout.

☛ **round, around.** In informal usage *round* and *around* are used interchangeably, with a definite tendency to use *round.* In formal English there is some tendency to keep *around* to mean "here and there or in every direction" and *round* for "in a circular motion or in a reverse motion": *I have looked all around. There aren't any around here. He is going round the world. Everyone turned round.*

round·a·bout (round′ə bout′) *adj.* indirect: *a roundabout route, hear in a roundabout way.* —*n.* **1** an indirect way, course, or speech. **2** a short, tight jacket for men or boys. **3** *Brit.* a merry-go-round. **4** *Esp.Brit.* a traffic circle.

round dance 1 a dance performed by couples and characterized by circular or revolving movements. **2** formerly, a dance performed by dancers in a circle.

roun·del (roun′dəl) *n.* **1** a small round ornament, window, panel, tablet, etc. **2** rondel. **3** rondeau. [ME < OF *rondel.* See RONDEL.]

roun·de·lay (roun′də lā′) *n.* **1** a song in which a phrase or a line is repeated again and again. **2** a dance in which the dancers move in a circle. [< MF *rondelet,* dim. of *rondel* (see RONDEL); influenced by *lay*[4]]

Round·head (round′hed′) *n.* in England, a supporter of Oliver Cromwell during the civil wars from 1642 to 1651. The Roundheads wore their hair cut short in contrast to the long curls of their opponents, the Cavaliers.

round·house (round′hous′) *n.* **1** a circular building for storing or repairing locomotives, that is built about a turntable. **2** a cabin on the after part of a ship's deck.

round·ish (roun′dish) *adj.* somewhat round.

round·ly (round′lē) *adv.* **1** in a round manner; in a circle, curve, globe, etc. **2** plainly; bluntly; severely: *scold roundly, refuse roundly.* **3** fully; completely.

round number 1 a whole number without a fraction. **2** a number in even tens, hundreds, thousands, etc. 3,874 in round numbers would be 3,900 or 4,000.

round robin 1 a petition, protest, etc. with the signatures written in a circle, so that it is impossible to tell who signed first. **2** any petition. **3** in hockey, football, etc., a system of scheduling a number of games, in which every competing player or team is matched with every other one.

round-shoul·dered (round′shōl′dərd) *adj.* having the shoulders bent forward.

round steak a cut of beef just above the hind leg.

round table 1 a group of persons assembled for an informal discussion, etc. **2 Round Table, a** the table around which King Arthur and his knights sat. **b** King Arthur and his knights.

round trip a trip to a place and back.

round·up (round′up′) *n.* **1 a** the act of driving or bringing cattle or horses together from long distances. **b** the men and horses that take part in a roundup. **2** any similar gathering: *a roundup of old friends.*

round·worm (round′wėrm′) *n.* any of a group of unsegmented worms that have long, round bodies. The hookworm and trichina are roundworms.

roup (rüp) *n.* **1** either of two diseases of poultry characterized by hoarseness and a discharge of catarrh from the eyes, nostrils, and throat. One form of roup is contagious and is often fatal. **2** hoarseness or huskiness. [origin uncertain]

rouse[1] (rouz) *v.* **roused, rous·ing,** *n.* —*v.* arouse; wake up; stir up: *I was roused by the telephone. He was roused to anger by the insult.* —*n.* **1** a rousing. **2** a signal for rousing or for action. [origin uncertain] **—rous′er,** *n.* **—Syn.** awaken, excite.

rouse[2] (rouz) *n. Archaic.* a drinking party; carouse. [? short for *carouse*]

rous·ing (rouz′ing) *adj.* **1** able to rouse or stir; lively; brisk: *a rousing speech, a rousing response.* **2** *Informal.* extraordinary; exceptional: *a rousing falsehood.* **—rous′ing·ly,** *adv.*

hat, āge, cãre, fär; let, ēqual, tėrm; it, īce
hot, ōpen, ôrder; oil, out; cup, pu̇t, rüle, ūse
əbove, takən, pencəl, lemən, circəs
ch, child; ng, long; sh, ship
th, thin; ᴛʜ, then; zh, measure

roust·a·bout (roust′ə bout′) *n.* an unskilled laborer on wharves, ships, ranches, circuses, etc. [< *roust* move, stir + *about*]

rout[1] (rout) *n.* **1** the flight of a defeated army in disorder. **2** a complete defeat. **3** *Archaic.* a crowd; band. **4** a group of followers. **5** a noisy, disorderly crowd; mob; rabble. **6** a riot; disturbance. **7** *Archaic.* a large evening party. —*v.* **1** put to flight: *Our soldiers routed the enemy.* **2** defeat completely. [ME < OF *route* detachment, ult. < L *rumpere* break]

rout[2] (rout) *v.* **1** dig (*out*); get by searching. **2** put (*out*); force (*out*): *The farmer routed his sons out of bed at five o'clock.* **3** dig with the snout, as pigs do. **4** poke; search; rummage. [var. of *root*[2]]

route (rüt or rout) *n. v.* **rout·ed, rout·ing.** —*n.* **1** a way to go; road. **2** a fixed, regular course or area assigned to a person making deliveries, sales, etc.: *a newspaper route, a milk route.* —*v.* **1** arrange the route for. **2** send by a certain route. [ME < OF < L *rupta* (*via*) (a way) opened up, (a passage) forced < *rumpere* break] **—Syn.** *n.* **1** path.

☛ **route.** The pronunciation (rüt) is the preferred form in Canada but (rout) is in common use, especially with reference to newspaper and delivery routes.

rou·tine (rü tēn′) *n.* **1** a fixed, regular method of doing things; habitual doing of the same things in the same way: *Getting up and going to bed are parts of your daily routine.* **2** an act or skit that is part of some entertainment. —*adj.* using routine: *routine methods, routine workers.* [< F *routine* < *route* route] **—rou·tine′ly,** *adv.*

rove[1] (rōv) *v.* **roved, rov·ing.** wander; wander about; roam: *He loved to rove over the fields and woods.* [origin uncertain] **—Syn.** ramble, range. See **roam.**

rove[2] (rōv) *v.* a pt. and a pp. of **reeve**[2].

rov·er[1] (rōv′ər) *n.* **1** a wanderer or roamer. **2** in lacrosse, a player who holds no special position but who may rove over the entire field. **3 Rover,** a member of the senior branch of the Boy Scouts, for boys over 17 years. [< *rove*[1]]

rov·er[2] (rōv′ər) *n.* **1** a pirate. **2** a pirate ship. [< MDu. *rover* < *roven* rob]

row[1] (rō) *n.* **1** a line of people or things: *a row of potatoes.* **2** a street with a line of buildings on either side. **3 hard row to hoe,** a difficult thing to do. [OE *rāw*] **—Syn. 1** file, series.

row[2] (rō) *v.* **1** use oars to move a boat. **2** move (a boat, etc.) by the use of oars. **3** convey in a rowboat: *We were rowed to the shore.* **4** perform (a race, etc.) by rowing. **5** row against in a race. —*n.* **1** the act of using oars. **2** a trip in a rowboat. [OE *rōwan*] **—row′er,** *n.*

row[3] (rou) *n.* **1** a noisy quarrel; disturbance; clamor. **2** *Informal.* a squabble. —*v.* **1** *Informal.* quarrel noisily; make noise. **2** *Informal.* scold. [origin uncertain]

row·an (rō′ən or rou′ən) *n.* **1** the mountain ash. **2** its red, berry-like fruit. [< Scand.; cf. Norwegian *raun*]

row·boat (rō′bōt′) *n.* a small boat moved by oars.

row·dy (rou′dē) *n.* **-dies,** *adj.* **-di·er, -di·est.** —*n.* a rough, disorderly, quarrelsome person. —*adj.* rough; disorderly; quarrelsome. [probably < *row*[3]] **—row′di·ly,** *adv.* **—row′di·ness,** *n.*

row·dy·ish (rou′dē ish) *adj.* like a rowdy; rough and disorderly; quarrelsome.

row·dy·ism (rou′dē iz′əm) *n.* disorderly, quarrelsome conduct; rough, noisy behavior: *rowdyism at Halloween.*

row·el (rou′əl) *n. v.* **-elled** or **-eled, -el·ling** or **-el·ing.** —*n.* a small wheel having sharp points, attached to the end of a spur. —*v.* use a rowel on. [ME < OF *roel,* ult. < L *rota* wheel]

A rowel on a spur

row house one of several houses built together in a row and constituting one building.

row·lock (rō′lok′) *n.* a notch, metal support, etc. in which the oar rests in rowing; oarlock.

roy·al (roi′əl) *adj.* **1** of or having to do with kings and queens: *the royal family.* **2** belonging to a king or queen: *royal power.* **3** favored or encouraged by a king or queen; serving a king or queen: *the Royal Society of Canada.* **4** from or by a king or queen: *a royal command.* **5** of a kingdom. **6** appropriate for a king or queen; splendid: *a royal welcome.* **7** like a king or queen; noble; majestic. **8** fine; excellent; supreme. **9** rich and bright: *royal blue.*
—*n.* **1** a small mast or sail set above the topgallant. **2** in printing, a size of paper (20 × 25 inches). [ME < OF *roial* < L *regalis.* Doublet of REAL[2], REGAL, RIAL.] —**roy′al·ly,** *adv.*
Syn. *adj.* 1, 2 Royal, regal, kingly = of or belonging to a king or kings. Royal is the most general in application, describing people or things associated with or belonging to a king: *Sherwood Forest is a royal forest.* Regal emphasizes the majesty and stateliness or pomp and magnificence of the office, but is now used chiefly of people or things showing these qualities: *The general has a regal bearing.* Kingly emphasizes the personal character, actions, purposes, or feelings of or worthy of a king: *Tempering justice with mercy is a kingly virtue.* 6 magnificent. 7 august.

royal assent the signature of the Queen or her representative giving approval to a bill that has been passed by Parliament or by a legislative assembly. A bill does not become law until royal assent has been given.

Royal Canadian Air Force formerly, the branch of the armed forces of Canada having to do with land-based aircraft. *Abbrev.*: RCAF or R.C.A.F.

Royal Canadian Legion an organization of Canadian ex-servicemen that sponsors numerous community services and undertakes welfare work for veterans and their families.

Royal Canadian Mounted Police the federal police force of Canada. In some provinces the Royal Canadian Mounted Police act as provincial police. *Abbrev.*: RCMP or R.C.M.P.

Royal Canadian Navy formerly, the branch of the armed forces of Canada having to do with ships of war. *Abbrev.*: RCN or R.C.N.

royal commission 1 any investigation by a person or persons commissioned by the Crown to inquire into some matter on behalf of the federal or a provincial government and to make a report recommending appropriate action. **2** the person or persons so commissioned.

royal flush in poker, a straight flush consisting of the Ace, King, Queen, Jack, and ten of one suit.

roy·al·ism (roi′əl iz′əm) *n.* adherence to a king or to a monarchy.

roy·al·ist (roi′əl ist) *n.* **1** a supporter of a king or of a royal government. **2 Royalist, a** in England, a supporter of Charles I during the civil wars from 1642 to 1651. **b** in the United States, a supporter of George III during the Revolution; loyalist. **c** in France, Spain, etc., a supporter of the monarchy. —*adj.* of or having to do with royalism or royalists.

royal palm a tall palm tree that has a whitish trunk and is often planted for ornament.

roy·al·ty (roi′əl tē) *n.* **-ties. 1** a royal person; royal persons. Kings, queens, princes, and princesses are royalty. **2** the rank or dignity of a king or queen; royal power. **3** kingliness; royal quality; nobility. **4** a royal right or privilege. **5** a share of the receipts or profits paid to an owner of a patent or copyright; payment for the use of any of various rights. [ME < OF *roialte* < *roial.* See ROYAL.]

rpm or **r.p.m.** revolutions per minute.

rps or **r.p.s.** revolutions per second.

R.R. 1 Railroad. **2** Right Reverend. **3** Rural Route.

R.S.F.S.R. Russian Soviet Federated Socialist Republic.

RSV or **R.S.V.** Revised Standard Version.

R.S.V.P. or **r.s.v.p.** please reply. (for F *répondez s'il vous plaît*)

rt. right.

Rt.Hon. Right Honourable.

Rt.Rev. Right Reverend.

Ru ruthenium.

rub (rub) *v.* **rubbed, rub·bing,** *n.* —*v.* **1** move (one thing) back and forth (against another); move (two things) together: *Rub your hands to warm them.* **2** move one's hands or an object over the surface of; push and press along the surface of: *The nurse rubbed my back.* **3** press as it moves: *That door rubs on the floor.* **4** make or bring (to some condition) by sliding the hand or some object over the surface: *rub silver bright, rub the skin off one's back.* **5** clean, smooth, or polish by moving one thing firmly against another. **6** make an image of an engraved or textured surface by rubbing charcoal, graphite, etc. over a piece of paper placed on top of the surface. **7** admit of rubbing. **8** irritate or make sore by rubbing. **9** *Informal.* keep going with difficulty: *Money is scarce, but we shall rub along.* **10 rub down,** rub (the body); massage. **11 rub it in,** *Informal.* keep on mentioning something unpleasant. **12 rub off, a** remove by rubbing. **b** be removed by rubbing. **13 rub off on,** cling to; become part of; take hold of: *Some of his gall has rubbed off on his son.* **14 rub the right way,** please; pacify. **15 rub the wrong way,** annoy; irritate.
—*n.* **1** the act of rubbing. **2** something that rubs or hurts the feelings: *He didn't like her mean rub at his slowness.* **3** a spot or area roughened by rubbing. **4** a difficulty: *The rub came when both boys wanted to sit with the driver.* [ME *rubbe(n)*] —**Syn.** *v.* **8** chafe.

rub·a·boo or **rub·ba·boo** (rub′ə bü′) *n. Cdn.* a soup made by boiling pemmican in water with flour and other ingredients. [< Cdn.F *rababou* < Algonquian]

rub·ber[1] (rub′ər) *n.* **1** an elastic substance obtained from the milky juice of various tropical plants, or by various chemical processes. Rubber will not let air or water through. **2** something made from this or a similar substance. We wear rubbers on our feet when it rains. **3** an eraser. Pencils often have a rubber on one end. **4** a person or thing that rubs. —*adj.* made of rubber.
—*v. Slang.* stretch the neck or turn the head to look at something. [< *rub*] —**rub′ber·like′,** *adj.*

rub·ber[2] (rub′ər) *n.* in bridge and certain other card games: **1** a series of two games out of three, or three games out of five, won by the same side. **2** the deciding game in such a series. [origin uncertain]

rubber band a circular strip of rubber, used to hold things together.

rubber ice *Cdn.* especially in the North, thin, flexible ice on the surface of seas, lakes, etc.

rub·ber·ize (rub′ər īz′) *v.* **-ized, -iz·ing.** cover or treat with rubber.

rub·ber·neck (rub′ər nek′) *Slang.* —*n.* a person who stares and gapes, especially a tourist or sightseer.
—*v.* stare; gape.

rubber plant 1 any plant yielding rubber. **2** an ornamental house plant having oblong, shining, leathery leaves.

rubber stamp 1 a stamp made of rubber, used with ink for printing dates, signatures, etc. **2** *Informal.* a person or group that approves or endorses something without thought or without power to refuse.

rub·ber-stamp (rub′ər stamp′) *v.* **1** print or sign with a rubber stamp. **2** *Informal.* approve or endorse (a policy, bill, etc.) without thought or without power to refuse.

rub·ber·y (rub′ər ē) *adj.* like rubber; elastic; tough.

rub·bing (rub′ing) *n.* **1** the act, fact, or process of rubbing. **2** an image of an engraved or textured surface, such as a brass inscription or rock carving, made by rubbing charcoal, graphite, etc. over a piece of paper placed on top of the surface.

rub·bish (rub′ish) *n.* **1** waste stuff of no use; trash. **2** silly words and thoughts; nonsense. [ME *robys*; origin uncertain] —**Syn. 1** litter, debris, refuse.

rub·ble (rub′əl) *n.* **1** rough, broken stones, bricks, etc. **2** masonry made of this. [ME *robel*; origin uncertain]

rub·down (rub′doun′) *n.* a rubbing of the body; massage.

rube (rüb) *n. Derogatory slang.* a rustic; an unsophisticated person. [< *Reuben,* a traditional rural name]

ru·be·fa·cient (rü′bə fā′shənt) *adj.* producing redness or irritation, especially of the skin: *a rubefacient ointment.* —*n.* a rubefacient medication or substance, such as a mustard plaster. [< L *rubefaciens, -facientis,* pp. of *rubefacere* < *rubeus* red + *facere* to make]

ru·be·o·la (rü bē′ə lə) *n.* **1** measles. **2** German measles. [< NL *rubeola,* dim. of *rubeus* red]

Ru·bi·con (rü′bə kon′) *n.* **1** a point, decision, etc. from which one cannot turn back. **2 cross the Rubicon,** make an important decision from which one cannot turn back. By crossing the Rubicon into the republic in 49 B.C., Julius Caesar started the civil war that made him master of Rome. [< *Rubicon,* a small river in E. Italy, in ancient times forming part of the boundary between the Roman republic and its provinces]

ru·bi·cund (rü′bə kund′) *adj.* reddish; ruddy. [< L *rubicundus* < *rubere* be red]

ru·bi·cun·di·ty (rü′bə kun′də tē) *n.* a rubicund quality or state.

ru·bid·i·um (rü bid′ē əm) *n.* a silver-white metallic chemical element resembling potassium. *Symbol*: Rb; *at.no.* 37; *at.wt.* 85.47. [< NL < L *rubidus* red < *rubere* be red; its spectrum has red lines]

ru·ble (rü′bəl) *n.* **1** a unit of money in the U.S.S.R. See table at **money. 2** a note or coin worth one ruble. Also, **rouble.** [< Russian]

ru·bric (rü′brik) *n.* **1** a title or heading of a chapter, a law, etc. written or printed in red or in special lettering. **2** a direction for the conducting of religious services inserted in a prayer book, ritual, etc. **3** any heading, rule, or guide. [< L *rubrica* red coloring matter < *ruber* red]

ru·bri·cal (rü′brə kəl) *adj.* **1** red; marked with red; printed or written in special lettering. **2** of, having to do with, or according to religious rubrics. —**rub′bri·cal·ly,** *adv.*

ru·bri·cate (rü′brə kāt′) *v.* **-cat·ed, -cat·ing. 1** mark or color with red. **2** furnish with rubrics. **3** regulate by rubrics.

ru·by (rü′bē) *n.* **-bies,** *adj.* —*n.* **1** a clear, hard, red precious stone that is a variety of carborundum. **2** a piece of this stone, or a gem made from it. **3** a deep, glowing red. —*adj.* deep, glowing red: *ruby lips, ruby wine.* [ME < OF *rubi,* ult. (cf. Med.L *rubinus*) < L *rubeus* red] —**ru′by-like′,** *adj.*

ruche (rüsh) *n.* a pleated piece or frill of lace, ribbon, net, etc. used as trimming for women's dresses, blouses, etc. [< F *ruche,* originally, beehive]

ruch·ing (rüsh′ing) *n.* a trimming made of ruches.

ruck (ruk) *n.* a crowd; the great mass of common or inferior people or things. [ME *ruke* heap, stack < Scand.; cf. Norwegian dial. *ruka*]

ruck·sack (ruk′sak′ or ru̇k′sak′) *n.* a kind of knapsack, usually of canvas with two shoulder straps. [< G *Rucksack,* literally, back sack]

ruck·us (ruk′əs) *n. Slang.* a noisy disturbance or uproar. [? blend of *ruction* and *rumpus*]

ruc·tion (ruk′shən) *n. Informal.* a disturbance; quarrel; row. [? alteration of *insurrection*]

rud·der (rud′ər) *n.* **1** a hinged, flat piece of wood or metal at the rear end of a boat or ship, by which it is steered. **2** a similar piece in an airplane, dirigible, etc. hinged vertically (for right-and-left steering). **3** a person or thing that guides or steers. See **airplane** for picture. [OE *rōthor*] —**rud′der·less,** *adj.*

rud·dy (rud′ē) *adj.* **-di·er, -di·est,** *adv.* —*adj.* **1** red. **2** healthy red: *ruddy cheeks.* **3** *Slang.* bloody. —*adv. Slang.* very; surely; extremely. [OE *rudig*] —**rud′di·ly,** *adv.* —**rud′di·ness,** *n.* —**Syn. 1** reddish, rubicund, florid. **2** rosy.

rude (rüd) *adj.* **rud·er, rud·est. 1** impolite; not courteous: *It is rude to stare at people.* **2** roughly made or done; without finish or polish; coarse; crude: *rude tools, a rude cabin.* **3** rough in manner or behavior; violent; harsh: *Rude hands seized the child and threw him into the car.* **4** harsh to the ear; unmusical. **5** not having learned much; uncivilized; rather wild; barbarous. **6** belonging to the poor or to uncultured people; simple; without luxury or elegance. **7** not fully or properly developed. **8** robust;

hat, āge, cãre, fär; let, ēqual, tėrm; it, īce
hot, ōpen, ôrder; oil, out; cup, pu̇t, rüle, ūse
əbove, takən, pencəl, lemən, circəs
ch, child; ng, long; sh, ship
th, thin; ŦH, then; zh, measure

sturdy; vigorous: *rude health, rude strength.* [< L *rudis*] —**rude′ly,** *adv.* —**rude′ness,** *n.* —**Syn. 1** uncivil, discourteous, impertinent, impudent. **2** unwrought, raw, crude. **5** primitive.

ru·di·ment (rü′də mənt) *n.* **1** a part to be learned first; beginning: *the rudiments of grammar.* **2** something in an early stage. **3** in biology, an organ or part incompletely developed in size or structure: *the rudiments of wings on a baby chick.* [< L *rudimentum* < *rudis* rude]

ru·di·men·ta·ry (rü′də men′tə rē or rü′də men′trē) *adj.* **1** to be learned or studied first; elementary. **2** in an early stage of development; undeveloped. —**Syn. 1** See **elementary. 2** embryonic.

rue[1] (rü) *v.* **rued, ru·ing. 1** be sorry for; regret (something). **2** *Archaic.* feel sorrow. [OE *hrēowan*]

rue[2] (rü) *n.* a plant having yellow flowers and leaves that have a strong smell and a bitter taste. [ME < OF < L *ruta,* ? < Gk. *rhytē*]

rue·ful (rü′fəl) *adj.* **1** sorrowful; unhappy; mournful: *a rueful expression.* **2** causing sorrow or pity: *a rueful sight.* —**rue′ful·ly,** *adv.* —**rue′ful·ness,** *n.* —**Syn. 1** doleful, woeful, lugubrious, melancholy.

ruff[1] (ruf) *n.* **1** a deep frill, stiff enough to stand out, worn around the neck by men and women in the 15th century. **2** a collar of specially marked feathers or hairs on the neck of a bird or animal. [akin to RUFFLE[1]]

A man wearing a ruff (def. 1)

ruff[2] (ruf) in card games: —*v.* trump. —*n.* the act of trumping. [< MF *roffle* < OF *roffle, ronfle*; cf. Ital. *ronfa* a card game]

ruffed (ruft) *adj.* having a ruff.

ruffed grouse a North American game bird having a tuft of feathers on each side of the neck. It is in some places called a partridge and in others a pheasant.

ruf·fi·an (ruf′ē ən) *n.* a rough, brutal, or cruel person. —*adj.* rough; brutal; cruel. [< MF] —**Syn.** *n.* bully, rowdy, rough, hoodlum.

ruf·fi·an·ism (ruf′ē ən iz′əm) *n.* brutal conduct; ruffianly conduct or character.

ruf·fi·an·ly (ruf′ē ən lē) *adj.* like a ruffian; violent; lawless.

ruf·fle[1] (ruf′əl) *v.* **-fled, -fling,** *n.* —*v.* **1** make rough or uneven; wrinkle: *A breeze ruffled the lake. The hen ruffled her feathers at the sight of the dog.* **2** gather into a ruffle. **3** trim with ruffles. **4** disturb; annoy: *Nothing can ruffle her calm temper.* **5** become ruffled. **6** shuffle (playing cards).
—*n.* **1** a roughness or unevenness in some surface; wrinkling. **2** a strip of cloth, ribbon, or lace gathered along one edge and used for trimming. Ruffles used to be much worn; men even had shirts with ruffles. **3** a disturbance; annoyance. **4** disorder; confusion. [ME; origin uncertain] —**Syn.** *v.* **1** rumple, roughen. **4** disquiet, discompose.

ruf·fle[2] (ruf′əl) *n. v.* **-fled, -fling.** —*n.* a low, steady beat of a drum. —*v.* beat (a drum) in this way. [? imitative]

A girl wearing a dress with ruffles

ru·fous (rü′fəs) *adj.* reddish or reddish-brown. [< L *rufus*]

rug (rug) *n.* **1** a heavy floor covering. **2** a thick, warm cloth used as covering: *He wrapped his woollen rug around him.* [< Scand.; cf. Norwegian dial. *rugga* coarse covering]

rug·by (rug′bē) *n.* **1** in Canada, a game played by teams of twelve men who carry, pass, or kick an oval ball towards the opposing team's goal; football. **2** rugger. [< *Rugby,* a famous school for boys in Rugby, England]
☞ **rugby, rugger, soccer. Though still heard in Canada, the term**

rugby (or **rugby football**) is gradually being displaced by the American term **football**. As such, it is distinct from **rugger**, played with 15 men a side, and soccer, played with 11 men a side, of whom only the goalie can play the ball with his hands.

rug·ged (rug′id) *adj.* **1** rough; wrinkled; uneven: *rugged ground.* **2** strong; vigorous; sturdy: *The pioneers were rugged people.* **3** strong and irregular: *rugged features.* **4** harsh; stern; severe: *rugged times.* **5** rude; unpolished; unrefined: *rugged manners.* **6** stormy: *rugged weather.* **7** rough or harsh to the ear. [< Scand.; cf. Swedish *rugga* roughen. Cf. RUG.] —**rug′ged·ly,** *adv.*

rug·ger (rug′ər) *n.* a game played by teams of fifteen men who kick or pass an oval ball toward the opposing team's goal. [< *rugby*] ☛ See **rugby** for usage note.

ru·in (rü′ən) *n.* **1 ruins,** *pl.* something left after destruction, decay, or downfall, especially of a building, wall, etc. that has fallen to pieces. **2** very great damage; destruction; overthrow; decay: *His enemies planned the duke's ruin.* **3** a condition of destruction, decay, or downfall: *The house had gone to ruin and neglect.* **4** the cause of destruction, decay, or downfall: *Drink was his ruin.* **5** bankruptcy.
—*v.* **1** bring to ruin; destroy; spoil. **2** be destroyed; come to ruin. **3** make bankrupt. [ME < OF < L *ruina* a collapse < *ruere* collapse]

Syn. *n.* **2 Ruin, destruction** = very great damage or complete loss. **Ruin** emphasizes falling to pieces or falling down, and applies to damage that consists in the falling apart or falling down, partially or completely, of anything, and that impairs or ends its soundness, value, or beauty, whether caused by decay or a destructive force: *Proper care protects property from ruin.* **Destruction** emphasizes breaking to pieces or tearing down, and applies to damage caused by a wrecking or injuring force: *The storm caused widespread destruction.* -*v.* **1** demolish, wreck. See **spoil.**

ru·in·a·tion (rü′ə nā′shən) *n.* ruin; destruction; downfall.

ru·in·ous (rü′ə nəs) *adj.* **1** bringing ruin; causing destruction. **2** fallen into ruins; in ruins. —**ru′in·ous·ly,** *adv.*

rule (rül) *n. v.* **ruled, rul·ing.** —*n.* **1** a statement of what to do and not to do; a law; principle governing conduct, action, arrangement, etc.: *Obey the rules of the game.* **2** in law, an order by a court, based upon a principle of law. **3** a set of rules; code. A religious order lives under a certain rule. **4** control; government: *In a democracy the people have the rule.* **5** a regular method; what usually happens or is done; what is usually true: *Fair weather is the rule in summer.* **6** a straight strip used to measure or as a guide to drawing. **7** a thin, type-high strip of metal, for printing a line or lines. **8 as a rule,** usually.
—*v.* **1** make a rule; decide. **2** make a formal decision: *The judge ruled against them.* **3** exercise the highest authority; control; govern; direct. **4** prevail; be current: *Prices of wheat and corn ruled high all the year.* **5** mark with lines. **6** mark off. **7 rule** (something) **out,** decide that it does not belong in; exclude. [ME < OF *riule* < L *regula* straight stick < *regere* guide. Doublet of RAIL[1].] —**rul′a·ble,** *adj.*

Syn. *n.* **1** regulation, order, precept. **4** direction, authority, dominion, sway. -*v.* **3 Rule, govern** = direct or control by the exercise of authority or power. **Rule** emphasizes complete control over others through supreme or absolute power both to make laws and give commands and to force obedience: *He tries to rule his family as a dictator rules a nation.* **Govern** emphasizes directing and keeping under control by the active use of authority or power, usually for the good of the thing, person, or nation governed: *Parents govern a child until he develops the power to govern himself.*

rule book a book of rules, especially those for some games or sport: *The National Hockey League Rule Book.*

rule of three in mathematics, a method of finding the fourth term in proportion when three are given.

rule of thumb **1** a rule based on experience or practice rather than on scientific knowledge. **2** a rough, practical method of procedure.

rul·er (rül′ər) *n.* **1** a person who rules. **2** a straight strip of wood, metal, etc. used in drawing lines or in measuring.

rul·ing (rül′ing) *n.* **1** a decision of a judge or court. **2** ruled lines. —*adj.* **1** that rules; governing; controlling. **2** predominating; prevalent.

rum[1] (rum) *n.* **1** an alcoholic liquor made from sugar cane, molasses, etc. **2** any alcoholic liquor. [short for *rumbullion* rum; origin uncertain]

rum[2] (rum) *adj. Esp.Brit. Slang.* odd; queer. [origin uncertain]

Rum. **1** Rumania. **2** Rumanian.

Ru·ma·ni·an (rü mā′nē ən or rü mān′yən) *adj.* Romanian.

rum·ba (rum′bə) *n. v.* **-baed, -ba·ing.** **1** a dance in quadruple time, that originated among the Cuban Negroes. **2** the music for such a dance. —*v.* dance a rumba. Also, **rhumba.** [< Sp. *rumba,* probably < African lang.]

rum·ble (rum′bəl) *v.* **-bled, -bling,** *n.* —*v.* **1** make a deep, heavy, continuous sound. **2** move with such a sound. **3** utter with such a sound. —*n.* **1** a deep, heavy, continuous sound: *We hear the far-off rumble of thunder.* **2** *Slang.* a teen-age gang fight. **3** the rear part of an automobile or carriage containing an extra seat or a place for baggage. [ME *romble(n),* ? ult. imitative]

rumble seat in certain old-fashioned types of automobile, an extra, open seat behind and outside the cab, or top.

ru·men (rü′mən) *n.* **ru·mi·na** (rü′mə nə). **1** the first stomach of an animal that chews the cud. **2** the cud of such an animal. [< L *rumen* gullet]

ru·mi·nant (rü′mə nənt) *n.* an animal that chews the cud. Cows, sheep, and camels are ruminants. —*adj.* **1** belonging to the group of ruminants. **2** meditative; reflective. [< L *ruminans, -antis,* ppr. of *ruminare* chew a cud < *rumen* gullet]

ru·mi·nate (rü′mə nāt′) *v.* **-nat·ed, -nat·ing.** **1** chew food for a second time; chew the cud. **2** chew again: *A cow ruminates its food.* **3** ponder; meditate: *He ruminated on the strange events of the past week.* [< L *ruminare* chew the cud < *rumen* gullet] —**ru′mi·nat′ing·ly,** *adv.*

ru·mi·na·tion (rü′mə nā′shən) *n.* **1** the act or process of chewing the cud. **2** meditation; reflection.

ru·mi·na·tive (rü′mə nə tiv or rü′mə nā′tiv) *adj.* meditative; inclined to ruminate. —**ru′mi·na·tive·ly,** *adv.*

rum·mage (rum′ij) *v.* **-maged, -mag·ing,** *n.* —*v.* **1** search thoroughly by moving things about: *I rummaged three drawers before I found my gloves.* **2** search in a disorderly way. **3** pull from among other things; bring to light. [< n.] —*n.* a rummaging search. [< MF *arrumage* < *arrumer* stow cargo < **rum,* var. of *run* hold of a ship < Gmc.] —**rum′mag·er,** *n.* —**Syn.** *v.* **1** See **search.**

rummage sale a sale of odds and ends, old clothing, etc., usually held to raise money for charity.

rum·my[1] (rum′ē) *adj.* **-mi·er, -mi·est.** *Slang.* odd; strange; queer. [< *rum*[2]]

rum·my[2] (rum′ē) *n.* a kind of card game in which points are scored by melding sets of three or four cards of the same rank or sequences of three or more cards of the same suit. [origin uncertain]

ru·mor or **ru·mour** (rü′mər) *n.* **1** a story or statement talked of as news without any proof that it is true. **2** vague, general talk: *Rumor has it that Bill will marry Joan.* —*v.* tell or spread by rumor. [ME < OF < L] —**Syn.** *n.* **1** report.

rump (rump) *n.* **1** the hind part of the body of an animal, where the legs join the back. **2** a cut of beef from this part. See **beef** for diagram. **3** the corresponding part of the human body; buttocks. **4** an unimportant or inferior part; remnant. [ME < Scand.; cf. Danish *rumpe*]

rum·ple (rum′pəl) *v.* **-pled, -pling,** *n.* —*v.* crumple; crush; wrinkle. —*n.* a wrinkle; crease. [cf. MDu. *rompel*] —**Syn.** *v.* pucker, crease, disorder.

rum·pus (rum′pəs) *n. Informal.* **1** a noisy quarrel; disturbance. **2** a noise; uproar. [origin uncertain]

rumpus room a room where children can romp and play; a recreation room.

rum·run·ner (rum′run′ər) *n.* a person or ship that smuggles alcoholic liquor into a country.

run (run) *v.* **ran, run, run·ning,** *n.* —*v.* **1** move the legs quickly; go faster than walking: *A horse can run faster than a man.* **2** go hurriedly; hasten: *Run for help.* **3** flee: *Run for your life.* **4** cause to run; cause to move: *run a horse up and down.* **5 a** perform by, or as by, running:

run errands. **b** carry or take by, or as by, running: *Can you run this book over to the library for me?* **6** go; move; keep going: *This train runs to Calgary.* **7** go on; proceed: *Prices of hats run as high as $50.00.* **8** creep; trail; climb: *Vines run along the sides of the road.* **9** go along (a way, path, etc.): *run the course until the end.* **10** pursue; chase (game, etc.): *run a fox.* **11** pass or cause to pass quickly: *Time runs on.* **12** trace; draw: *Run that report back to its source.* **13** stretch; extend: *Shelves run along the walls.* **14** drive; force; thrust: *He ran a splinter into his hand.* **15** flow; flow with: *The streets ran blood.* **16** discharge fluid, mucus, or pus: *My nose runs.* **17** get; become: *Never run into debt. The well ran dry.* **18** have a specified character, quality, form, size, etc.: *These potatoes run large.* **19** spread: *The color ran when the dress was washed.* **20** continue; last: *a lease to run two years.* **21** have currency or be current; occur: *The story runs that school will close early today.* **22** have legal force. **23** take part in a race or contest. **24 a** be a candidate for election. **b** put up as a candidate. **25** enter (a horse, etc.) in a race. **26** expose oneself to: *run a risk.* **27** move easily, freely, or smoothly; keep operating: *A rope runs in a pulley.* **28** cause to move easily, freely, or smoothly; cause to keep operating: *run a machine.* **29** be worded or expressed: *How does the first verse run?* **30** conduct; maintain; manage: *run a business.* **31** go about, proceed, or grow without restraint: *Children were allowed to run about the streets.* **32** drop stitches, ravel. **33** get past or through: *Enemy ships tried to run the blockade.* **34** smuggle: *run rum.* **35** publish (an advertisement, story, etc.) in a newspaper: *He ran an ad in the evening paper.* **36** soften; become liquid; melt. **37** shape by melting: *run bullets through a mould.* **38** pass to or from the sea; migrate, as for spawning: *The salmon are running.* **39** return often to the mind: *That tune has been running in my head.* **40** make an unbroken sequence of (shots, strokes, etc.) in billiards, pool, etc.

run across, meet by chance.

run away with, do far better than others in.

run down, a cease to go; stop working. **b** pursue till caught or killed; hunt down. **c** knock down by running against. **d** speak disparagingly against. **e** decline or reduce in vigor or health. **f** fall off, diminish, or decrease; deteriorate. **g** in baseball, put a base runner out after trapping him between bases.

run for it, run for safety.

run in, a *Informal.* arrest and put in jail. **b** pay a short visit.

run into, a meet by chance. **b** crash into; collide with.

run off, a cause to be run or played. **b** print; duplicate. **c** run away; flee.

run out, come to an end; become exhausted.

run out of, use up; have no more.

run over, a ride or drive over: *The car ran over some glass.* **b** overflow. **c** go through quickly.

run through, a consume or spend rapidly or recklessly. **b** pierce. **c** review; rehearse: *The teacher ran through the homework assignment a second time.*

run up, *Informal.* **a** make quickly. **b** collect; accumulate: *Don't run up a big bill.*

—n. **1** the act of running: *set out at a run.* **2** a spell or period of causing (a machine, etc.) to operate; the amount of anything produced in such a period: *During a run of eight hours the factory produced a run of 100 cars.* **3** a spell of causing something liquid to run or flow, or the amount that runs: *the run of sap from maple trees.* **4** a trip: *The ship reached port after a six weeks' run.* **5** in baseball or cricket, the unit of score. **6** a continuous spell or course; continuous extent: *a run of bad luck.* **7** a succession of performances: *This play has had a two-year run.* **8** an onward movement; progress; course; trend: *the run of events.* **9** a continuous series or succession of something; succession of demands: *a run on the bank to draw out money.* **10** in music, a rapid succession of tones. **11** a kind or class: *the common run of mankind.* **12** freedom to go over or through, or to use: *The guests were given the run of the house.* **13** a flow or rush of water; small stream. **14** a number of fish moving together, especially a periodic movement to spawning grounds: *a run of salmon.* **15** a way; track; trough; pipe. **16** a stretch or enclosed space for animals: *a chicken run.* **17** a place where stitches have slipped out or become undone: *a run in a stocking.* **18** a landing of smuggled goods. **19** the extreme after part of a ship's bottom. **20 a run for one's money, a** strong competition. **b** satisfaction for one's efforts. **21 in the long run,** on the whole; in the end. **22 on the run, a** hurrying. **b** in retreat or rout. [ME *rinne, renne,* ? < *runnon,* pp. of OE *rinnan* run] —**Syn.** *v.* **1** sprint, gallop. **2** hurry, rush, race, speed.

hat, āge, cãre, fär; let, ēqual, tėrm; it, īce
hot, ōpen, ôrder; oil, out; cup, pu̇t, rüle, ūse
əbove, takən, pencəl, lemən, circəs
ch, child; ng, long; sh, ship
th, thin; ᴛʜ, then; zh, measure

run·a·bout (run′ə bout′) *n.* **1** a light automobile or carriage with a single seat. **2** a small motorboat. **3** a person who runs about from place to place.

run·a·gate (run′ə gāt′) *n. Archaic.* **1** a runaway. **2** a vagabond; wanderer. [< *run* + *agate* away; influenced by ME *renegat* renegade]

run·a·round (run′ə round′) *n.* **1** *Slang.* a series of excuses, evasions, or deceptions: *They gave him the runaround.* **2** in printing, type set narrower than the full width, to permit the insertion of an illustration, etc.

run·a·way (run′ə wā′) *n.* **1** a person, horse, etc. that runs away. **2** a running away; eloping. *—adj.* **1** running with nobody to guide or stop it; out of control. **2** done by runaways. **3** easily won.

run·ci·nate (run′sə nit *or* run′sə nāt′) *adj.* having coarse teethlike notches or lobes pointing backward. [< L *runcina* plane (but taken as "saw") < Gk. *rhykanē*; influenced by L *runcare* clear (of thorns, etc.)]

Runcinate leaves of a dandelion

run-down (run′doun′) *adj.* **1** tired; sick. **2** falling to pieces; partly ruined. **3** that has stopped going or working. *—n.* **1** a brief summary. **2** in baseball, the act of putting a base runner out after trapping him between bases.

rune[1] (rün) *n.* **1** any letter of an ancient Germanic alphabet. **2** a mark that looks like a rune and has some mysterious, magic meaning. [< ON *rún*]

f u th o r k

Runes (def. 1): the first six letters of the English runic alphabet.

rune[2] (rün) *n.* an old Scandinavian poem or song. [< Finnish *runo* < ON *rún*]

rung[1] (rung) *v.* a pt. and a pp. of **ring**[2].

rung[2] (rung) *n.* **1** a rod or bar used as a step of a ladder. **2** a crosspiece set between the legs of a chair or as part of the back or arm of a chair. **3** a spoke of a wheel. **4** a bar of wood resembling a spoke in shape and use. [OE *hrung*]

ru·nic[1] (rü′nik) *adj.* consisting of runes; written in runes; marked with runes. [< *rune*[1]]

ru·nic[2] (rü′nik) *adj.* like a rune. [< *rune*[2]]

run-in (run′in′) *n. Informal.* a sharp disagreement; argument; quarrel.

run·let (run′lit) *n.* a small stream.

run·nel (run′əl) *n.* a small stream or brook. [OE *ryne* < *rinnan* run]

run·ner (run′ər) *n.* **1** a person, animal, or thing that runs; racer. **2** a messenger. **3** a person who runs or works a machine, etc. **4** either of the narrow pieces on which a sleigh or sled slides. **5** the blade of a skate. **6** a long, narrow strip: *We have a runner of carpet in our hall, and runners of linen and lace on our dressers.* **7** a smuggler; person or ship that tries to evade somebody. **8** a slender stem that takes root along the ground, thus producing new plants. Strawberry plants spread by runners. **9** a ravelled place.

A runner of a strawberry plant

run·ner-up (run′ər up′) *n.* the person, player, or team that takes second place in a contest.

run·ning (run′ing) *n.* **1** the act of a person or thing that runs. **2** a flow of liquid; a discharge. **3 be in the running,** have a chance to win. **4 be out of the running,** have no chance to win.
—adj. **1** cursive: *a running hand.* **2** discharging matter: *a running sore.* **3** flowing. **4** liquid. **5** going or carried on

continuously: *a running commentary.* **6** current: *the running month.* **7** repeated continuously: *a running pattern.* **8** following in succession: *for three nights running.* **9** prevalent. **10** moving or proceeding easily or smoothly. **11** moving when pulled or hauled: *a running rope.* **12** slipping or sliding easily: *a running knot or noose.* **13** of plants, creeping or climbing. **14** that is measured in a straight line. **15** of the normal run of a train, bus, etc. **16** performed with or during a run: *a running leap.* **17** in operation; operating.

running board formerly, a metal step along the side of an automobile.

running gear the wheels and axles of an automobile, locomotive, or other vehicle.

running head a heading printed at the top of each page of a book, etc.

running knot a knot so made as to slide along the rope.

running mate *Esp.U.S.* a candidate running jointly with another, but for a less important office, such as a candidate for vice-president.

running noose a noose with a running knot.

running stitch a series of short, even stitches all taken with one passage of the needle.

run-off (run′of′) *n.* **1** something that runs off. **2** the running off of water during the spring thaw. **3** a final, deciding race or contest.

run-of-the-mill (run′ əv ᴛʜə mil′) *adj.* ordinary or commonplace; lacking distinction: *a run-of-the-mill design.*

run-on (run′on′) *adj.* **1** in printing: **a** continued to the end, without a break. **b** of or having to do with copy to be set immediately after the preceding material, without any paragraph break or other indentation. **2** in poetry, continuing to the next line without punctuation. —*n.* **1** in printing, material to be run-on. **2** in a dictionary, a run-on entry.

run-on entry in a dictionary, a derived word that is not defined but is shown at the end of the entry for the word from which it is formed. *Rurally* may be found as a run-on entry under *rural.*

runt (runt) *n.* **1** a stunted animal, person, or plant. **2** an ox or cow of a small breed. [origin uncertain]

runt·y (run′tē) *adj.* **runt·i·er, runt·i·est.** stunted; dwarfish.

run·way (run′ wā′) *n.* **1** a channel, track, groove, trough, etc. along which something moves, slides, etc. **2** the beaten track of deer or other animals. **3** an enclosed place for animals to run in. **4** a strip having a level surface on which planes land and take off.

ru·pee (rü pē′) *n.* **1** a unit of money in India, Pakistan, and Ceylon. See table at **money. 2** a note or coin worth one rupee. [< Hind. *rupiyah* < Skt. *rupya* wrought silver]

Ru·pert's Land (rü′pərts) the name given to the territories granted to the Hudson's Bay Company by Charles II in 1670. Rupert's Land, so named because Prince Rupert was the first governor of the Company, included all the land watered by rivers flowing into Hudson Bay.

ru·pi·ah (rü pē′ə) *n.* **1** a unit of money in Indonesia. See table at **money. 2** a note or coin worth one rupiah. [< Indonesian < Hind. *rupiyah.* See RUPEE.]

rup·ture (rup′chər) *n. v.* **-tured, -tur·ing.** —*n.* **1** a break; breaking: *the rupture of a blood vessel.* **2** a breaking off of friendly relations that threatens to become actual war. **3** the sticking out of some tissue or organ of the body through the wall of the cavity that should hold it in; hernia. —*v.* **1** break; burst; break off. **2** affect with or suffer hernia. [< L *ruptura* < *rumpere* burst]

ru·ral (rür′əl) *adj.* **1** in the country; belonging to the country; like that of the country. **2** of or having to do with agriculture: *rural economy.* [< L *ruralis* < *rus, ruris* country] —**ru′ral·ly,** *adv.*

Syn. Rural, rustic, pastoral = of, relating to, or characteristic of the country. **Rural** expresses an objective attitude toward the country and country life and people as distinguished from towns and cities and city life, but sometimes is used to suggest pleasant country scenes: *Rural life is healthful and quiet.* **Rustic** suggests simplicity, lack of refinement, or roughness and clumsiness, especially in appearance, manners, etc.: *The cottage has a rustic charm.* **Pastoral** has poetic associations, suggesting shepherds, grazing flocks, green pastures, and a simple, peaceful life: *He paints pastoral pictures.*

rural dean *Esp.Brit.* a priest of the highest rank in a district outside the cathedral city. He acts as the local deputy of a bishop or archdeacon.

rural municipality *Cdn.* in certain provinces, a municipal district in a rural area, administered by an elected reeve and council. *Abbrev.*: R.M.

rural route a mail-delivery circuit in the country. *Abbrev.*: R.R.

Rus. 1 Russia. **2** Russian.

ruse (rüz or rüs) *n.* a trick; stratagem. [< F *ruse* < *ruser* dodge] —**Syn.** artifice, dodge, wile. See **stratagem.**

rush[1] (rush) *v.* **1** move with speed or force: *We rushed along.* **2** attack with much speed and force: *They rushed the enemy.* **3** come, go, pass, act, etc. with speed or haste: *He rushes into things without knowing anything about them.* **4** send, push, force, etc. with speed or haste: *Rush this order, please.* **5** urge to hurry: *Don't rush me.* **6** *Informal.* **a** lavish much attention on, especially over a relatively short period: *He rushed the girl all summer.* **b** attempt to persuade to join a fraternity or sorority. **7** advance (a football) by running.
—*n.* **1** the act of rushing: *the rush of the flood.* **2** busy haste; hurry: *the rush of city life.* **3** the effort of many people to go somewhere or get something: *the Christmas rush, the gold rush.* **4** an eager demand; pressure: *A sudden rush of business kept everyone working hard.* **5** in football, an attempt to carry the ball through the opposing line. **6** *Informal.* the lavishing of much attention, especially on a girl. **7 rushes,** the first prints of film shot for a motion picture. **8 with a rush,** suddenly; quickly.
—*adj.* requiring haste: *A rush order must be filled at once.* [originally, force out of place by violent impact; cf. OE *hrȳsc* a blow] —**rush′er,** *n.* —**Syn.** *v.* **1** dash, hurry, speed.

rush[2] (rush) *n.* **1** a plant having pithy or hollow stems, that grows in wet ground. **2** the stem of such a plant, used for making chair seats, baskets, etc. **3** something of little or no value. [OE *rysc*] —**rush′like′,** *adj.*

rush hour the time of day when traffic is heaviest or when trains, buses, etc. are most crowded.

rush seat a seat for a stage show, sports event, etc. that is sold on the day of the performance or event.

rush·y (rush′ē) *adj.* **rush·i·er, rush·i·est. 1** abounding with rushes; covered with rushes. **2** made of rushes.

rus in ur·be (rus′in ėr′bē; *Latin,* rùs′in ür′bā) *Latin.* the country in the city.

rusk (rusk) *n.* **1** a piece of bread or cake toasted in the oven. **2** a kind of light, soft, sweet biscuit. [< Sp., Pg. *rosca* roll]

Russ (rus) *n.sing. or pl.* **1** a Russian. **2** the Russian language. —*adj.* Russian.

Russ. 1 Russia. **2** Russian.

rus·set (rus′it) *adj.* yellowish-brown; reddish-brown. —*n.* **1** a yellowish brown; reddish brown. **2** a coarse, russet-colored cloth. Peasants used to make and wear russet. **3** a kind of apple having a rough, brownish skin. [ME < OF *rousset,* ult. < L *russus* red]

rus·sia (rush′ə) *n.* Russia leather.

Russia leather a fine, smooth leather, often dark-red, produced by careful tanning and dyeing.

Rus·sian (rush′ən) *adj.* of or having to do with Russia, its people, or their language. —*n.* **1** a native or inhabitant of Russia, especially a member of the dominant Slavic peoples of Russia. **2** the language of Russia.

Russian Church a branch of the Eastern Orthodox Church, until 1918 the national church of Russia.

Rus·sian·ize (rush′ən īz′) *v.* **-ized, -iz·ing.** make or become Russian in customs, language, etc.

Russian Revolution the revolution in which Russian workers, sailors, and soldiers, led by Lenin, overthrew the government of the Czar in 1917 and established the Soviet Union.

Russian thistle a large weed having spiny branches. It

develops into a troublesome tumbleweed.

Russian wolfhound borzoi.

rust (rust) *n.* **1** the reddish-brown or orange coating that forms on iron or steel when exposed to air or moisture. **2** any film or coating on any other metal due to oxidization, etc. **3** a harmful growth, habit, influence, or agency. **4** a plant disease that spots leaves and stems. **5** a reddish brown or orange.
—*v.* **1** become covered with rust. **2** coat with rust. **3** spoil by not using. **4** become spoiled by not being used: *Don't let your mind rust during vacation.* **5** have or cause to have the disease rust.
—*adj.* reddish-brown or orange. [OE *rust*, var. of *rūst*]

rus·tic (rus′tik) *adj.* **1** belonging to the country; rural; suitable for the country. **2** simple; plain: *His rustic speech and ways made him uncomfortable in the city school.* **3** rough; awkward. **4** made of branches with the bark still on them: *rustic arches in a garden.* —*n.* a country person. [< L *rusticus* < *rus* country] —**rus′ti·cal·ly,** *adv.* —**Syn.** *adj.* **1** See **rural.**

rus·ti·cate (rus′tə kāt′) *v.* **-cat·ed, -cat·ing. 1** go to the country; stay in the country. **2** send to the country. **3** *Brit.* send (a student) away from a university or college temporarily as a punishment. [< L *rusticari* < *rusticus* rustic. See RUSTIC.]

rus·ti·ca·tion (rus′tə kā′shən) *n.* **1** a rusticating or the state of being rusticated. **2** residence in the country. **3** *Brit.* the temporary dismissal of a student from a university or college as a punishment.

rus·tic·i·ty (rus tis′ə tē) *n.* **-ties. 1** a rustic quality, characteristic, or peculiarity. **2** rural life. **3** awkwardness; ignorance.

rust·i·ly (rus′tə lē) *adv.* in a rusty state; in such a manner as to suggest rustiness.

rus·tle (rus′əl) *n. v.* **-tled, -tling.** —*n.* the sound that leaves make when moved by the wind; a sound like this. [< v.] —*v.* **1** make a light, soft sound of things gently rubbing together. **2** move or stir (something) so that it makes such a sound: *rustle the papers.* **3** *Informal.* steal (cattle, etc.). **4** *Informal.* act, do, or get with energy. [OE *hrūxlian* make noise]

rus·tler (rus′lər) *n.* **1** *Informal.* a cattle thief. **2** an active, energetic person. **3** a person or thing that rustles.

rust·less (rust′lis) *adj.* free from rust; resisting rust.

rust·proof (rust′prüf′) *adj.* resisting rust. —*v.* treat with a preparation that resists rust.

rust·y (rus′tē) *adj.* **rust·i·er, rust·i·est. 1** covered with rust; rusted: *a rusty knife.* **2** made by rust. **3** colored like rust. **4** faded: *a rusty black.* **5** half-forgotten through lack of use. **6** out of practice. —**rust′i·ness,** *n.*

rut[1] (rut) *n. v.* **rut·ted, rut·ting.** —*n.* **1** a track made in the ground by wheels. **2** a fixed or established way of acting. —*v.* make ruts in. [? var. of *route*] —**Syn.** *n.* **1** furrow, groove.

rut[2] (rut) *n. v.* **rut·ted, rut·ting.** —*n.* **1** the sexual excitement of deer, goats, sheep, etc. occurring at regular intervals. **2** the period during which this excitement lasts. —*v.* be in rut. [ME < OF *ruit* < L *rugitus* bellowing < *rūgire* bellow]

ru·ta·ba·ga (rü′tə bā′gə or rü′tə bag′ə) *n.* a kind of large, yellow turnip. [< Swedish (dial.) *rotabagge*, literally, root bag]

ruth (rüth) *n. Archaic.* **1** pity; compassion. **2** sorrow. [ME *rewthe* < *rewen* rue[1] < OE *hrēowan*]

Ruth (rüth) *n.* in the Bible, a Moabite woman famous for her devotion to her mother-in-law, Naomi.

ru·the·ni·um (rü thē′nē əm) *n.* a brittle, gray, metallic chemical element similar to platinum. *Symbol:* Ru; *at.no.* 44; *at.wt.* 101.07. [< NL < Med.L *Ruthenia* Russia; because it was discovered in the Urals]

ruth·less (rüth′lis) *adj.* having no pity; showing no mercy; cruel. —**ruth′less·ly,** *adv.* —**ruth′less·ness,** *n.* —**Syn.** merciless, pitiless, hard-hearted, relentless.

rut·ty (rut′ē) *adj.* **-ti·er, -ti·est.** full of ruts. —**rut′ti·ness,** *n.*

RV or **R.V.** Revised Version.

Rx or **rx 1** in medical prescriptions, take. (for L *recipe*) **2** tens of rupees.

-ry *suffix.* **1** the occupation or work of a ——, as in *dentistry, chemistry.* **2** the act of a ——, as in *mimicry.* **3** the quality, state, or condition of a ——, as in *rivalry.* **4** a group of ——s, considered collectively, as in *peasantry.* [short form of *-ery*]

Ry. railway.

rye (rī) *n.* **1** a hardy annual plant widely grown in cold regions. **2** its seeds or grain. **3** the flour made from them. Peasants in Germany and Russia eat a great deal of almost black rye bread. **4** whisky made from rye. **5** in Canada, a blended whisky made from rye and other grains as well; Canadian whisky. [OE *ryge*]

hat, āge, cãre, fär; let, ēqual, tėrm; it, īce
hot, ōpen, ôrder; oil, out; cup, pu̇t, rüle, ūse
əbove, takən, pencəl, lemən, circəs
ch, child; ng, long; sh, ship
th, thin; ᴛʜ, then; zh, measure

S or **s** (es) *n.* **S's** or **s's. 1** the nineteenth letter of the English alphabet. **2** any speech sound represented by this letter. **3** one (usually nineteenth) of a series designated alphabetically. **4** anything shaped like this letter.

's a shortened form of *us, is,* or *has,* added to the preceding word. *Examples*: Let's eat. He's here. He's just gone.

-s 1 the ending of the third person singular of verbs in the present indicative, as in *asks, lies, sees, tells.* **2** a suffix used to form the plural of most nouns, as in *hats, boys, dogs, houses.* **3** a suffix once used in forming some adverbs, as in *needs, unawares, always*: *I needs must depart.* [OE *-es*]

-'s a suffix used to form the possessive case of nouns in the singular and also of plural nouns not ending in *s,* as in *boy's, man's, child's, men's, children's.* [OE *-(e)s*]

s. 1 shilling; shillings. **2** son. **3** second. **4** singular. **5** south. **6** southern.

S 1 South. **2** sulphur. **3** the sea element of the Canadian Forces.

S. 1 South. **2** Southern. **3** Saint. **4** School. **5** Saturday. **6** Sunday. **7** September. **8** Section. **9** Sea. **10** Senate. **11** Signor.

Sa samarium.

S.A. 1 South America. **2** South Africa. **3** South Australia. **4** Salvation Army.

Sab. Sabbath.

Sab·ba·tar·i·an (sab′ə tãr′ē ən) *n.* **1** a person who observes Saturday as the Sabbath, as most Jews do. **2** a Christian who favors a very strict observance of Sunday. *—adj.* of or to do with the Sabbath or its observance.

Sab·ba·tar·i·an·ism (sab′ə tãr′ē ən iz′əm) *n.* **1** the observance of Saturday as the Sabbath. **2** very strict observance of Sunday.

Sab·bath (sab′əth) *n.* **1** the day of the week set apart for rest and worship. Most Christians observe Sunday as the Sabbath; most Jews observe Saturday as the Sabbath. **2 sabbath,** a period of rest, quiet, etc. *—adj.* of or belonging to the Sabbath. [< L < Gk. *sabbaton* < Hebrew *shabbāth* < *shābath* to rest] **—Syn.** *n.* **1** See **Sunday.**

sab·bat·ic (sə bat′ic) *adj.* sabbatical.

sab·bat·i·cal (sə bat′ə kəl) *adj.* **1** of or suitable for the Sabbath. **2** of or for a rest from work. *—n.* a sabbatical leave. [< Gk. *sabbatikos* < *sabbaton.* See SABBATH.]

sabbatical leave a leave of absence for a year or half year given to teachers, usually in a university and especially once in seven years, for study and travel.

sa·ber (sā′bər) *n. v.* sabre.

Sa·bine (sā′bīn or sab′īn) in ancient times: *—n.* **1** a people that lived in central Italy, conquered by the Romans in the third century B.C. **2** a member of this people. **3** their language. *—adj.* of or belonging to the Sabines or their language. [< L *Sabinus*]

sa·ble (sā′bəl) *n.* **1** a small flesh-eating mammal valued for its dark brown, glossy fur. **2** its fur. Sable is one of the most costly furs. **3 sables,** *pl.* mourning garments. *—adj. Poetic.* black; dark: *a widow's sable garments.* [ME < OF *sable,* ult. < Slavic]

sa·ble·fish (sā′bəl fish′) *n.* **-fish** or **-fish·es.** a large, edible type of black cod, found off the N. Pacific Coast.

sab·ot (sab′ō or sab′ət; *French,* sä bō′) *n.* **1** a shoe hollowed out of a single piece of wood, worn by peasants in France, Belgium, etc. **2** a coarse leather shoe having a thick wooden sole. [< F *sabot* < OF *çabot,* alteration of *çavate* old shoe < Arabic *sabbāt*; influenced by OF *bote* boot]

sab·o·tage (sab′ə täzh′) *n. v.* **-taged, -tag·ing.** *—n.* **1** damage done to work, tools, machinery, etc. by workmen as an attack or threat against an employer. **2** such damage done by civilians of a conquered nation to injure the conquering forces. **3** damage done by enemy agents or sympathizers in an attempt to slow down a nation's war effort. **4** malicious attacking of or secret working against any cause to which co-operation is due. *—v.* damage or destroy deliberately. [< F *sabotage* < *saboter* bungle, walk noisily < *sabot.* See SABOT.]

sab·o·teur (sab′ə tėr′) *n.* a person who practises sabotage. [< F]

sa·bra (sä′brə) *n.* a person born in Israel; native Israeli. [< Hebrew *sābrāh* cactus, thought of as being tough and prickly outside but soft inside]

sa·bre or **sa·ber** (sā′bər) *n. v.* **-bred, -bring.** *—n.* **1** a heavy curved sword having a sharp point and cutting edge, used by cavalry. **2** in fencing, a similar but lighter weapon, used for both thrusting and slashing. *—v.* strike, wound, or kill with a sabre. [< F *sabre,* alteration of *sable,* ult. < Hungarian *száblya* < *szabni* cut]

sabre-toothed tiger or **saber-toothed tiger** an extinct tigerlike mammal having long, curved upper canine teeth.

sac (sak) *n.* a baglike part in an animal or plant, often containing liquids: *the sac of a honeybee.* [< F < L *saccus* sack[1]. See SACK[1].] **—sac′like′,** *adj.*

Sac (sak, sok, or sôk) *n.* Sauk.

SAC *U.S.* Strategic Air Command.

sac·cha·rin (sak′ə rin) *n.* a very sweet, white, crystalline substance obtained from coal tar, used as a substitute for sugar. *Formula*: $C_7H_5NO_3S$

sac·cha·rine (sak′ə rin) *adj.* sugary; very sweet: *a saccharine smile.* *—n.* saccharin. [< Med.L *saccharum* sugar < Gk. *sakcharon,* ult. < Skt. *çarkarā,* originally, gravel, grit] **—sac′cha·rine·ly,** *adv.*

sac·er·do·tal (sas′ər dō′təl) *adj.* of priests or the priesthood; priestly. [< L *sacerdotalis* < *sacerdos, -otis* priest < *sacra* rites + verb stem *dot-* put, set < *dare* give]

sac·er·do·tal·ism (sas′ər dō′təl iz′əm) *n.* a sacerdotal system; the spirit or methods of the priesthood.

sa·chem (sā′chəm) *n.* among certain North American Indians, the chief of a tribe or confederation. [< Algonquian. Related to SAGAMORE.]

sa·chet (sa shā′; *esp.Brit.,* sash′ā) *n.* **1** a small bag or pad containing perfumed powder. **2** perfumed powder. [< F *sachet,* dim. of *sac* sack[1]]

sack[1] (sak) *n.* **1** a large bag made of coarse cloth. Sacks are used for holding grain, flour, potatoes, and coal. **2** the amount that a sack can hold. **3** a sack and its contents. **4** *Esp.U.S.* any bag or what is in it: *a sack of candy.* **5** a loose jacket for a woman, girl, or baby: *a knitted sack for a baby.* **6** formerly, a kind of loose gown worn by women, or a long back piece fastened to the gown at the shoulders and forming a train. **7** *Esp.Brit. Slang.* dismissal from employment. **8 hold the sack,** *Informal.* be left empty-handed. *—v.* **1** put into a sack or sacks. **2** *Esp.Brit. Slang.* dismiss from employment; fire. [OE *sacc* < L *saccus* < Gk. *sakkos* < Hebrew *saq*] **—Syn.** *n.* **1** See **bag.**

sack[2] (sak) *v.* plunder or pillage: *The invaders sacked the town.* [< n.] *—n.* the act or process of plundering. [< F *sac* < Ital. *sacco* < VL *saccare* take by force < Gmc.; influenced by L *saccus* sack[1]] **—sack′er,** *n.* **—Syn.** *v.* devastate.

sack[3] (sak) *n.* dry sherry or other strong, light-colored wine. [< F *(vin) sec* dry (wine) < L *siccus*]

sack·but (sak′but′) *n.* **1** in the Middle Ages, a musical wind instrument resembling the trombone. **2** in ancient times, a stringed instrument. [< F *saquebute* < *saquer* pull + *bouter* push]

sack·cloth (sak′kloth′) *n.* **1** coarse cloth for making sacks. **2** coarse cloth worn as a sign of mourning or penitence.

sack coat a man's loose-fitting suit coat or similar jacket for everyday wear.

sack·ful (sak′fu̇l) *n.* **-fuls.** enough to fill a sack.

sack·ing (sak′ing) *n.* coarse cloth for making sacks, etc.

sacque (sak) *n.* sack[1] (defs. 5, 6). [var. of *sack*[1]]

sac·ra·ment (sak′rə mənt) *n.* **1** in the Christian church, a solemn religious ceremony. Baptism is a sacrament. **2** Often, **Sacrament. a** the Eucharist, or Lord's Supper. **b** the consecrated bread and wine; the bread alone. **3** something especially sacred. **4** a sign; token; symbol. **5** a solemn promise; oath. [< L *sacramentum,* ult. < *sacer* holy]

sac·ra·men·tal (sak′rə men′təl) *adj.* **1** of or having to do with a sacrament; used in a sacrament: *sacramental wine.* **2** especially sacred. —*n.* in the Roman Catholic Church, a ceremony similar to, but not included among, the sacraments. The use of holy water is a sacramental. —**sac′ra·men′tal·ly,** *adv.*

sa·cred (sā′krid) *adj.* **1** belonging to or dedicated to God or a god; holy: *the sacred altar, a sacred building.* **2** connected with religion; religious: *sacred writings, sacred music.* **3** worthy of reverence: *the sacred memory of a dead hero.* **4** dedicated to some person, object, or purpose: *This monument is sacred to the memory of the Unknown Soldier.* **5** that must not be violated or disregarded: *sacred oaths.* [originally pp. of ME *sacre(n)* sanctify < L *sacrare* < *sacer* holy] —**sa′cred·ly,** *adv.* —**sa′cred·ness,** *n.* —**Syn. 1** See **holy.**

Sacred College the College of Cardinals.

sacred cow 1 *Informal.* any person or thing so highly regarded or privileged as to be beyond criticism. **2** a cow held to be sacred, as by Hindus.

sac·ri·fice (sak′rə fīs′) *n. v.* **-ficed, -fic·ing.** —*n.* **1** the act of offering to a god. **2** the thing offered: *The ancient Hebrews killed animals on the altars as sacrifices to God.* **3** the giving up of one thing for another: *Our teacher does not approve of any sacrifice of studies for sports.* **4** the thing given up or set aside. **5** a loss: *He will sell his house at a sacrifice because he needs the money.* **6** in baseball, a bunt or fly that helps the runner to advance although the batter is put out.
—*v.* **1** give or offer to a god. **2** give up: *Many a mother has sacrificed her life for her children.* **3** permit injury or disadvantage to, for the sake of something else: *sacrifice business for pleasure.* **4** offer or make a sacrifice. **5** sell at a loss. **6** in baseball, help (a runner) to advance by a sacrifice. [ME < OF < L *sacrificium,* ult. < *sacra* rites + *facere* perform] —**sac′ri·fic′er,** *n.* —**Syn.** *n.* **1** immolation.

sac·ri·fi·cial (sak′rə fish′əl) *adj.* **1** having to do with, connected with, or used in sacrifice. **2** involving sacrifice or loss to the seller: *a sacrificial sale of summer dresses.* —**sac′ri·fi′cial·ly,** *adv.*

sac·ri·lege (sak′rə lij) *n.* an intentional injury to anything sacred; disrespectful treatment of anyone or anything sacred: *Robbing the church is considered a sacrilege.* [ME < OF < L *sacrilegium* temple robbery < *sacrum* sacred object + *legere* pick up] —**Syn.** profanation.

sac·ri·le·gious (sak′rə lij′əs) *adj.* **1** committing sacrilege; guilty of sacrilege. **2** involving sacrilege: *sacrilegious acts.* —**sac′ri·le′gious·ly,** *adv.* —**Syn.** impious, irreverent.

sac·ris·tan (sak′ris tən) *n.* the person in charge of the sacred vessels, robes, etc. of a church. [ME < Med.L *sacristanus,* ult. < L *sacer* holy. Doublet of SEXTON.]

sac·ris·ty (sak′ris tē) *n.* **-ties.** the place where the sacred vessels, robes, etc. of a church are kept. [< Med.L *sacristia,* ult. < L *sacer* holy]

sac·ro·sanct (sak′rō sangkt′) *adj.* **1** very holy; very sacred. **2** set apart as sacred; consecrated. [< L *sacrosanctus,* ult. < *sacer* sacred + *sancire* consecrate]

sac·ro·sanc·ti·ty (sak′rō sangk′tə tē) *n.* the fact or state of being sacrosanct; an especial sacredness.

sa·crum (sā′krəm or sak′rəm) *n.* **-cra** (-krə) or **-crums.** in anatomy, a bone at the lower end of the spine, formed by the joining of several vertebrae and serving as the back of the pelvis. [< L (*os*) *sacrum* sacred (bone)]

sad (sad) *adj.* **sad·der, sad·dest. 1** not happy; full of sorrow; grieving: *sad looks.* **2** characterized by sorrow; sorrowful: *a sad life, a sad occasion.* **3** causing sorrow; distressing: *a sad disappointment.* **4** expressing sorrow; gloomy; downcast: *sad looks, a sad countenance.* **5** dull in color; dark. **6** *Informal.* shocking; hopeless; pitiable: *a sad mess.* [OE *sæd* sated] —**sad′ly,** *adv.*
Syn. 1 Sad, dejected, depressed = unhappy and low in spirits. **Sad,** the general word, meaning "not glad, cheerful, or happy," particularly suggests feeling sorrowful or mournful, but not the cause or degree of the feeling: *Moonlight makes her sad.* **Dejected** suggests casting down of the spirits by some disappointing, discouraging, or frustrating happening or situation: *She is dejected over his leaving.* **Depressed** suggests sinking into a low-spirited, discouraged, or gloomy state as the result of an experience or physical, mental, or other condition: *He is depressed by his failure.* **2** lamentable, deplorable, grievous.

sad·den (sad′ən) *v.* **1** make sad. **2** become sad.

hat, āge, cãre, fär; let, ēqual, tėrm; it, īce
hot, ōpen, ôrder; oil, out; cup, pu̇t, rüle, ūse
əbove, takən, pencəl, lemən, circəs
ch, child; ng, long; sh, ship
th, thin; ᴛʜ, then; zh, measure

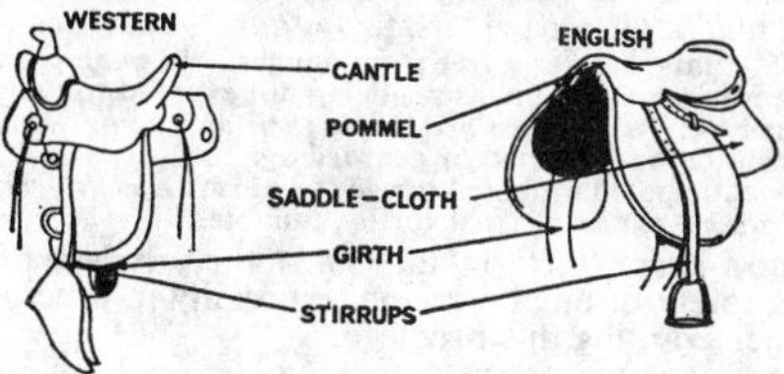

Two types of saddle

sad·dle (sad′əl) *n. v.* **-dled, -dling.** —*n.* **1** a seat for a rider on a horse's back, on a bicycle, etc. **2** the part of a harness that holds the shafts, or to which a checkrein is attached. See **harness** for picture. **3** anything shaped like a saddle. **4** a ridge between two mountain peaks. **5** a piece of meat, especially mutton or venison, consisting of the upper back portion of an animal. **6 in the saddle,** *Informal.* in a position of control.
—*v.* **1** put a saddle on. **2** burden: *He is saddled with a big house that he does not need or want.* **3** put as a burden on. [OE *sadol*]

sad·dle·bag (sad′əl bag′) *n.* one of a pair of bags laid over an animal's back behind the saddle.

sad·dle·bow (sad′əl bō′) *n.* the front part of a saddle, which sticks up.

sad·dle·cloth (sad′əl kloth′) *n.* a cloth put between an animal's back and the saddle. See **saddle** for picture.

saddle horse a horse for riding.

sad·dler (sad′lər) *n.* a person who makes or sells saddles and harness.

sad·dler·y (sad′lər ē) *n.* **-dler·ies. 1** the work of a saddler. **2** the shop of a saddler. **3** saddles, harness, and other equipment for horses.

sad·dle·tree (sad′əl trē′) *n.* the frame of a saddle.

Sad·du·cee (saj′u̇ sē′) *n.* in ancient times, a member of a Jewish sect that accepted the Mosaic law and believed in immortality but denied the resurrection of the dead and the existence of angels. [OE *sadducēas,* pl. < LL < LGk. *Saddoukaios* < Hebrew *Tsaddūq* Zadok, a Hebrew high priest in the time of David]

sad·i·ron (sad′ī′ərn) *n.* a heavy flatiron for pressing clothes. [< *sad,* in obs. or dial. sense of "firm, solid" + *iron*]

sa·dism (sā′diz əm or sad′iz əm) *n.* **1** a condition in which a person gains sexual pleasure from hurting someone else. **2** an unnatural delight in cruelty. [< F; from Comte Donatien de *Sade* (1740-1814), who wrote of this condition]

sa·dist (sā′dist or sad′ist) *n.* one who practises or is affected with sadism.

sa·dis·tic (sə dis′tik) *adj.* of or having to do with sadists or sadism.

sad·ness (sad′nis) *n.* sorrow; grief.

sad sack *Esp.U.S. Slang.* **1** a poor, bewildered soldier who blunders his way through the mazes of army life. **2** any bewildered, blundering person. [from a U.S. comic strip by Sgt. George Baker]

SAE number a number established by the Society of Automotive Engineers to indicate the viscosity of a lubricant, by which SAE 10, SAE 20, etc. indicate increasingly thick oils.

sa·fa·ri (sə fä′rē) *n.* **-ris. 1** an exploring or hunting expedition, especially in E. Africa. **2** any long trip, tour, or expedition. [< Arabic]

safe (sāf) *adj.* **saf·er, saf·est,** *n.* —*adj.* **1** free from harm or danger: *Keep money in a safe place.* **2** not harmed: *He returned from war safe and sound.* **3** out of danger; secure: *We feel safe with the dog in the house.* **4** put beyond power of doing harm: *a criminal safe in prison.* **5** cautious; careful: *a safe guess, a safe move.* **6** that can

be depended on: *a safe guide.* **7** in baseball, (of a batter or base runner) reaching a base or home plate without being out.
—*n.* **1** a steel or iron box for money, jewels, papers, etc. **2** a place made to keep things safe: *a meat safe.* [ME < OF *sauf* < L *salvus*] —**safe′ly,** *adv.* —**safe′ness,** *n.*
Syn. *adj.* **1 Safe, secure** = free from danger. Although often used interchangeably, **safe** emphasizes being not exposed to danger, harm, or risk: *The children are safe in their own yard.* **Secure** emphasizes being protected or guarded against loss, attack, injury, or other anticipated or feared danger or harm: *A child feels secure with his mother.* **6** trustworthy, reliable.

safe-con·duct (sāf′kon′dukt) *n.* **1** the privilege of passing safely through a region, especially in time of war. **2** a paper granting this privilege.

safe-deposit box (sāf′di poz′it) a box for storing valuables, especially in a vault of a bank.

safe·guard (sāf′gärd′) *v.* **1** keep safe; guard against hurt or danger; protect: *Pure food laws safeguard our health.* **2** guard; convoy. [< n.] —*n.* **1** a protection; defence: *Keeping clean is a safeguard against disease.* **2** a guard; convoy. [ME < OF *sauvegarde* < *sauve,* fem. of *sauf* safe (< L *salvus*) + *garde* guard < Gmc.]

safe·keep·ing (sāf′kēp′ing) *n.* a keeping safe; protection; care.

safe·ty (sāf′tē) *n.* **-ties,** *adj.* —*n.* **1** the quality or state of being safe; freedom from harm or danger. **2** freedom from risk or possible damage or hurt; safeness. **3** a device to prevent injury. **4** a device that controls part of the firing mechanism and prevents a gun from being fired. **5** in football, a safety touch. **6** in baseball, a base hit; hit. —*adj.* giving safety; making harm unlikely: *a safety lamp.*

safety belt 1 a seat belt. **2** a strap used by window cleaners, loggers, linemen, etc. to prevent falling.

safety island a marked area or a platform built in a thoroughfare for the convenience of pedestrians boarding and getting off buses, streetcars, etc.: *The city built safety islands at all busy intersections.*

safety lamp 1 a miner's lamp in which the flame is kept from setting fire to explosive gases by a piece of wire gauze. **2** an electric lamp similarly protected.

safety match a match that will ignite only when rubbed on a specially prepared surface.

safety pin a pin bent back on itself to form a spring and having a guard that covers the point in order to prevent accidental unfastening.

safety razor a razor having a replaceable blade that is protected to reduce the risk of the shaver cutting his skin.

safety touch in football, the act of putting a ball down behind one's own goal line after a player on one's own team has made it go there. It counts two points for the other team.

safety valve 1 a valve in a steam boiler, etc. that opens and lets steam or fluid escape when the pressure becomes too great. **2** something that helps a person get rid of anger, nervousness, etc. in a harmless way.

saf·fron (saf′rən) *n.* **1** an orange-yellow coloring matter obtained from a kind of crocus. Saffron is used to color and flavor candy, drinks, etc. **2** an autumn crocus having purple flowers and orange-yellow stigmas. **3** an orange yellow. —*adj.* orange-yellow. [< F *safran,* ult. < Arabic *za'faran*]

S.Afr. 1 South Africa. **2** South African.

sag (sag) *v.* **sagged, sag·ging,** *n.* —*v.* **1** sink under weight or pressure; bend down in the middle. **2** hang down unevenly: *Your dress sags in the back.* **3** become less firm or elastic; yield through weakness, weariness, or lack of effort; droop; sink. **4** decline in price. **5** of a ship, drift from her course. —*n.* **1** the act, state, or degree of sagging. **2** the place where anything sags. [cf. Du. *zakken* sink]

sa·ga (sä′gə) *n.* **1** a type of prose story of heroic deeds written in Iceland or Norway in the Middle Ages. **2** any story of heroic deeds. [< Scand. Akin to SAW[3].]

sa·ga·cious (sə gā′shəs) *adj.* **1** wise in a keen, practical way; shrewd. **2** resulting from or showing wisdom or sagacity. [< L *sagax, -acis*] —**sa·ga′cious·ly,** *adv.* —**sa·ga′cious·ness,** *n.* —**Syn. 1** astute, perspicacious. See **shrewd.**

sa·gac·i·ty (sə gas′ə tē) *n.* **-ties.** keen, sound judgment; mental acuteness; shrewdness. —**Syn.** acumen, perspicacity.

sag·a·more (sag′ə môr′) *n.* among some Algonquian Indian tribes, a chief or great man, usually inferior to a sachem. [earlier *sagamo* < Algonquian. Related to SACHEM.]

sage[1] (sāj) *adj.* **sag·er, sag·est,** *n.* —*adj.* **1** wise: *a sage adviser.* **2** showing wisdom or good judgment: *a sage reply.* **3** wise-looking; grave; solemn: *Owls are sage birds.* —*n.* a very wise man. [ME < OF *sage,* ult. < L *sapere* be wise] —**sage′ly,** *adv.* —**sage′ness,** *n.* —**Syn.** *adj.* **1, 2** judicious, prudent. See **wise.**

sage[2] (sāj) *n.* **1** a plant whose dried leaves are used as seasoning and in medicine. **2** its dried leaves. **3** salvia. **4** sagebrush. [ME < OF *sauge* < L *salvia.* Doublet of SALVIA.]

sage·brush (sāj′brush′) *n.* a grayish-green shrub, common on the dry plains of W. North America.

sage grouse a very large grouse common on the plains of W. North America.

sage hen 1 a sage grouse. **2** a female sage grouse.

Sag·it·tar·i·us (saj′ə tãr′ē əs) *n.* **1** in astronomy, a southern constellation supposed to represent a centaur drawing a bow. **2** in astrology, the ninth sign of the zodiac; the Archer. The sun enters Sagittarius about November 23. See **zodiac** for diagram. [< L *Sagittarius,* literally, the Archer < *sagitta* arrow]

sag·it·tate (saj′ə tāt′) *adj.* shaped like an arrowhead. Calla lilies have sagittate leaves. [< NL *sagittatus* < L *sagitta* arrow]

sa·go (sā′gō) *n.* **-goes. 1** a dry, powdered starch used in making puddings, stiffening textiles, etc. **2** a palm tree **(sago palm)** from whose pith this starch is made. [< Malay *sagu*]

A sagittate leaf

Sa·har·an (sə hãr′ən or sə här′ən) *adj.* of or having to do with the Sahara Desert, or the people inhabiting it. —*n.* a native or inhabitant of the Sahara Desert.

sa·hib (sä′ib or sä′hib) *n.* in India, sir; master. [< Hind. < Arabic *çaḥib* lord]

said (sed) *v.* pt. and pp. of **say.** —*adj.* named or mentioned before: *the said witness.*

sail (sāl) *n.* **1** a piece of cloth spread to the wind to make a ship move through the water. **2** sails. **3** something like a sail, such as the part of an arm of a windmill that catches the wind. **4** ship; ships. **5** a trip on a boat with sails or on any other vessel. **6 in sail,** in a ship with sails. **7 make sail, a** spread out the sails of a ship. **b** begin a trip by water. **8 set sail,** begin a trip by water. **9 take in sail, a** lower or lessen the sails of a ship. **b** lessen one's hopes, ambitions, etc. **10 under sail,** with the sails spread out.
—*v.* **1** travel on water, the driving force being the action of wind on sails. **2** travel on a steamboat, aircraft, etc. **3** move smoothly like a ship with sails: *The hawk sailed by. Mrs. Grand sailed into the room.* **4** to sail upon, over, or through: *sail the seas.* **5** manage a ship or boat: *The boys are learning to sail.* **6** manage or navigate (a ship or boat). **7** begin a trip by water: *We sail at 2 p.m.* **8** travel through the air: *The football sailed over the goal post.* **9 sail into,** *Slang.* **a** attack; beat. **b** criticize; scold. [OE *segl*] —**Syn.** *v.* **1** navigate, cruise.
☛ **Sail** is used collectively when it means sails for a sailing vessel (def. 2): *Our ship had all sail spread.* **Sail** may also mean a ship or ships (def. 4). When it means ships it is used collectively and often with a numeral: *a fleet of thirty sail.*

sail·boat (sāl′bōt′) *n.* a boat that is moved by a sail or sails. See **schooner** and **sloop** for pictures.

sail·cloth (sāl′kloth′) *n.* **1** canvas or other material used for making sails. **2** a similar material used in making clothes, curtains, etc.

sail·er (sāl′ər) *n.* a ship described in terms of its sailing power: *the best sailer in the fleet, a fast sailer.*

sail·fish (sāl′fish′) *n.* **-fish** or **-fishes.** a large saltwater fish related to the swordfish, that has a long, high fin on its back.

sail·ing (sāl′ing) *n.* the act of a person or thing that sails.

sail·or (sāl′ər) *n.* **1** a person whose work is handling a sailboat or other vessel. In these days most sailors are on steamships. **2** a member of a ship's crew, not an officer. **3** one who sails for pleasure; a yachtsman. **4** a person serving in the navy, especially a rating. **5** a flat-brimmed hat modelled after the kind of hat sailors used to wear years ago. **6 a good sailor,** a person who does not get seasick. **7 poor** or **bad sailor,** a person who readily becomes seasick. —*adj.* like that of a sailor: *My middy blouse has a sailor collar.* —**sail′or·like′,** *adj.*

sail·or·ly (sāl′ər lē) *adj.* like a sailor; suitable for a sailor.

sail·plane (sāl′plān′) *n.* a light glider that can stay aloft for a long time supported by air currents.

sain (sān) *v. Archaic.* **1** make the sign of the cross on. **2** protect by prayer, etc. **3** bestow divine favor on. [OE *segnian* < L *signare* mark < *signum* sign]

saint (sānt) *n.* **1** a very holy person; a true Christian. **2** a person who has gone to heaven. **3** in the Roman Catholic Church, a person who has been canonized. **4** a person like a saint. **5** an angel. **6** Also, **Saint. a** in the New Testament, a member of the Christian church. **b** a person belonging to any religious body whose members are called Saints. The Church of Jesus Christ of Latter-Day Saints is the true name of the Mormon Church.
—*v.* **1** make a saint of; canonize. **2** call or consider a saint. —*adj.* holy; sacred. [ME < OF < L *sanctus* consecrated] —**saint′like′,** *adj.*

☛ **Saint.** Entries commonly written in the abbreviated form, such as *St. Elmo's Fire* and *St.-Johns-wort* will be found in their alphabetical places after **St.**

Saint Agnes' Eve (ag′nəs) the night of January 20, when a girl was supposed to see a vision of her future husband if she performed certain ceremonies.

Saint Ber·nard (bər närd′ or bėr′nərd) **1** a breed of big dog, often tan-and-white, having a large head. These intelligent dogs were first bred by the monks of the St. Bernard hospice in the Alps to rescue travellers lost in the snow. **2** a dog of this breed.

saint·ed (sān′tid) *adj.* **1** declared to be a saint. **2** thought of as a saint; gone to heaven. **3** sacred; very holy. **4** saintly.

saint·hood (sānt′hůd) *n.* **1** the character or status of a saint. **2** saints as a group.

Saint-Jean Baptiste Society (saɴ′zhäɴ′bä tēst′) *Cdn.* one of two organizations in the Province of Quebec which are dedicated to the preserving and fostering of French culture in Canada. [< *Saint Jean Baptiste* St. John the Baptist, patron saint of Quebec]

saint·ly (sānt′lē) *adj.* **-li·er, -li·est. 1** like a saint; very holy. **2** very good. —**saint′li·ness,** *n.*

saint·ship (sānt′ship) *n.* sainthood.

Saint Vi·tus's dance (vī′təs iz). See **St. Vitus's dance.**

saith (seth) *v. Archaic.* says.

sake[1] (sāk) *n.* **1** a cause; account; interest. **2** a purpose; end. **3 for the sake of, a** because of; on account of. **b** to help; to please. **4 for your own sake,** on your own account; to help yourself. [OE *sacu* cause at law]

sa·ke[2] (sak′ē or sä′kē) *n.* a fermented, alcoholic beverage made from rice, especially popular in Japan. [< Japanese]

sal (sal) *n.* salt, used especially in druggists' terms, such as *sal ammoniac.* [< L]

sa·laam (sə läm′) *n.* in Moslem countries and India: **1** a greeting that means "Peace." **2** a very low bow, with the palm of the right hand placed on the forehead.
—*v.* **1** greet with a salaam. **2** make a salaam. [< Arabic *salām* peace]

sal·a·bil·i·ty (sāl′ə bil′ə tē) *n.* a salable condition or quality.

sal·a·ble (sāl′ə bəl) *adj.* that can be sold; fit to be sold; easily sold. Also, **saleable.** —**Syn.** marketable, merchantable, purchasable.

sa·la·cious (sə lā′shəs) *adj.* **1** lustful; lewd: *a salacious man.* **2** obscene; indecent: *a salacious novel.* [< L *salax, -acis*] —**sa·la′cious·ly,** *adv.* —**sa·la′cious·ness,** *n.* —**Syn.** lecherous, lascivious.

hat, āge, cãre, fär; let, ēqual, tėrm; it, īce
hot, ōpen, ôrder; oil, out; cup, půt, rüle, ūse
əbove, takən, pencəl, lemən, circəs
ch, child; ng, long; sh, ship
th, thin; ᴛʜ, then; zh, measure

sa·lac·i·ty (sə las′ə tē) *n.* a salacious quality.

sal·ad (sal′əd) *n.* **1** a preparation of raw, fresh vegetables, such as lettuce, tomatoes, and celery, served with a dressing. **2** a similar preparation made from cold meat, fish, eggs, cooked vegetables, or fruits. **3** any green vegetable that can be eaten raw. [ME < OF < Provençal *salada,* ult. < L *sal* salt]

salad days days of youthful inexperience.

salad dressing a sauce to be used in or on a salad.

sal·al (səl al′) *n.* **1** a small shrub native to the Pacific coast. **2** the berry of this shrub. [< Chinook Jargon (*klkwu*)-*shala*]

sal·a·man·der (sal′ə man′dər) *n.* **1** an animal shaped like a lizard, but belonging to the same family as frogs and toads. Salamanders live in damp places. **2** a lizard or reptile formerly supposed to live in fire. **3** a person who likes or can stand a great deal of heat. **4** a spirit or imaginary being that lives in fire. [ME < OF < L < Gk. *salamandra*]

sa·la·mi (sə lä′mē) *n.* a kind of sausage, highly spiced or flavored with garlic. [< Ital. *salami,* pl. of *salame,* ult. < L *sal* salt]

sal ammoniac ammonium chloride.

sal·a·ried (sal′ə rēd or sal′rēd) *adj.* receiving a salary.

sal·a·ry (sal′ə rē or sal′rē) *n.* **-ries.** fixed, periodic payment for regular work: *Teachers, government officials, and clerks receive salaries.* [ME < AF < L *salarium* soldier's allowance for salt < *sal* salt] —**Syn.** stipend.

☛ **salary, wages.** Though these words are synonyms, *salary* generally refers to a fixed compensation for regular work (usually mental or professional) paid at longer intervals than *wages* (usually for manual or mechanical work).

sal·chow (sal′kôv) *n.* in figure skating, a jump that includes a full turn in mid-air. [< Ulrich *Salchow,* a Swedish skating champion]

sale (sāl) *n.* **1** the act of selling; exchange of goods for money: *no sale yet this morning.* **2** the amount sold. **3** the chance to sell; demand; market. **4** a selling at lower prices than usual: *This store is having a sale on suits.* **5** an auction. **6 for sale** or **on sale,** to be sold; available for buying. **7 on sale,** offered at a reduced price. [OE *sala*]

sale·a·ble (sāl′ə bəl) *adj.* salable.

sales·clerk (sālz′klėrk′) *n.* a person whose work is selling in a store.

sales·girl (sālz′gėrl′) *n.* a girl whose work is selling in a store.

sales·la·dy (sālz′lā′dē) *n.* **-dies.** saleswoman.

sales·man (sālz′mən) *n.* **-men.** a man whose work is selling.

sales·man·ship (sālz′mən ship′) *n.* **1** the work of a salesman. **2** ability at selling.

sales·peo·ple (sālz′pē′pəl) *n.pl.* salespersons.

sales·per·son (sālz′pėr′sən) *n.* a person whose work is selling in a store.

sales·room (sālz′rüm′ or -rům′) *n.* a room where things are sold or shown for sale.

sales tax a tax on the amount received for articles sold.

sales·wom·an (sālz′wům′ən) *n.* **-wom·en.** a woman whose work is selling.

sal·i·cin (sal′ə sin) *n.* a bitter, white crystalline compound of glucose, obtained from the bark of various willows and poplars. It is used in medicine as a tonic and to reduce fever. *Formula*: $C_{13}H_{18}O_7$ [< F *salicine* < L *salix, salicis* willow]

Sal·ic law (sal′ik or sā′lik) **1** the code of laws of the Franks. **2** in France and Spain, a law excluding females from succession to the crown. [< Med.L *Salicus* < LL *Salii* the Salian Franks, a tribe of Franks who dwelt in the regions of the Rhine near the North Sea]

sal·i·cyl·ate (sal′ə sil′āt or sə lis′ə lāt′) *n.* any salt or ester of salicylic acid.

sal·i·cyl·ic (sal′ə sil′ik) *adj.* of or having to do with salicin.

salicylic acid a solid, white substance used as a mild antiseptic and preservative, and as a medicine for rheumatism, gout, etc. Aspirin is a common preparation of salicylic acid. *Formula*: $C_7H_6O_3$ [< *salicin*]

sa·li·ence (sā′lē əns or sāl′yəns) *n.* **1** the quality or state of being salient. **2** a salient or projecting object, part, or feature.

sa·li·en·cy (sā′lē ən sē or sāl′yən sē) *n.* salience.

sa·li·ent (sā′lē ənt or sāl′yənt) *adj.* **1** standing out; easily seen or noticed; prominent; striking: *the salient features in a landscape, the salient points in a speech.* **2** pointing outward; projecting: *a salient angle.* **3** in heraldry, standing with forepaws raised as if jumping: *a lion salient.* —*n.* **1** a salient angle or part. **2** the part of a fort or line of trenches that projects toward the enemy. [< L *saliens, -entis*, ppr. of *salire* leap] —**sa′li·ent·ly,** *adv.* —**Syn.** *adj.* **1** noticeable, conspicuous.

sa·line (sā′līn) *adj.* **1** of salt; like salt; salty. **2** containing common salt or any other salts. —*n.* **1** a salt spring, well, or marsh. **2** a substance containing common salt or any other salts. [< L *sal* salt]

sa·lin·i·ty (sə lin′ə tē) *n.* saltiness; saline quality.

Salisbury steak (solz′ber′ē or sôlz′ber′ē) chopped beef shaped before cooking into a patty about twice the size of a hamburger, usually served with a gravy.

Sa·lish (sā′lish) *n.* **1** a group of North American Indians of British Columbia and the N.W. United States. In Canada a division is made between the **Coast Salish** and the **Interior Salish. 2** a member of this group. **3** any of the related languages of this group.

Sa·lish·an (sā′lish ən) *adj.* of or having to do with the Salish Indians or their languages. —*n.* Salish.

sa·li·va (sə lī′və) *n.* the liquid that the salivary glands secrete into the mouth to keep it moist, aid in chewing, and start digestion. [< L]

sal·i·var·y (sal′ə ver′ē) *adj.* of or producing saliva.

salivary gland any of various glands that secrete saliva into the mouth. The salivary glands of human beings and most other vertebrates are digestive glands that secrete saliva containing enzymes, salts, albumin, etc.

sal·i·vate (sal′ə vāt′) *v.* **-vat·ed, -vat·ing. 1** produce a large secretion of saliva in. **2** secrete saliva. [< L *salivare* < *saliva* saliva]

sal·i·va·tion (sal′ə vā′shən) *n.* **1** a salivating. **2** the secretion of saliva. **3** an abnormally large flow of saliva.

sal·let (sal′it) *n.* in medieval armor, a light, rounded helmet, with or without a visor. [< F < Ital. < L *caelata*, fem. pp. of *caelare* chisel < *caelum* chisel]

sal·low[1] (sal′ō) *adj.* of a pallid, yellowish color: *a sallow complexion.* —*v.* make yellowish. [OE *salo*] —**sal′low·ness,** *n.*

sal·low[2] (sal′ō) *n.* **1** a willow. **2** a willow twig. [OE *sealh*]

sal·low·ish (sal′ō ish) *adj.* rather sallow.

sal·ly (sal′ē) *n.* **-lies,** *v.* **-lied, -ly·ing.** —*n.* **1** a sudden attack on an enemy made from a defensive position; sortie. **2** a sudden rushing forth. **3** a going forth; trip; excursion. **4** a sudden start into activity. **5** an outburst. **6** a witty remark. —*v.* **1** go suddenly from a defensive position to attack an enemy. **2** rush forth suddenly; go out. **3** set out briskly. **4** go on an excursion or trip. **5** of things, issue forth. [< F *saillie*, ult. < L *salire* leap]

Sal·ly Lunn (sal′ē lun′) a slightly sweetened tea cake, served hot with butter. [after *Sally Lunn*, a woman who sold such cakes in Bath, England, at the end of the 18th century]

sal·ma·gun·di (sal′mə gun′dē) *n.* **1** a dish of chopped meat, anchovies, eggs, onions, oil, etc. **2** any mixture, medley, or miscellany. [< F *salmigondis*, ult. < Ital. *salami conditi* pickled sausages].

sal·mi (sal′mē) *n.* a highly seasoned stew, especially of game. [< F *salmi*, short for *salmigondis* salmagundi]

salm·on (sam′ən) *n.* **-on** or **-ons,** *adj.* —*n.* **1** a large ocean and fresh-water fish having silvery scales and yellowish-pink flesh, common in the N. Atlantic near the mouths of large rivers, which it swims up in order to spawn. **2** a similar kind of fish that lives in lakes and is called **landlocked salmon. 3** any of various other fishes of the same family that are common in the N. Pacific. **4** a yellowish pink. —*adj.* yellowish-pink. [ME *samon* < OF < L *salmo, -onis*, probably "leaper" < *salire* leap]

sal·mon·ber·ry (sam′ən ber′ē) *n.* **-ries. 1** a large, red-flowered raspberry bush that bears edible pink fruit. **2** the fruit of this bush.

sal·mo·nel·la (sam′ən el′ə or sal′mə nel′ə) *n.* **-las** or **-lae** (-ī or -ē). any of various bacteria causing food poisoning, typhoid, and other infectious diseases. [< NL *Salmonella*, the genus name < Daniel E. *Salmon*, 1850-1914, American pathologist]

salm·o·noid (sam′ə noid′ or sal′mə noid′) *adj.* of or belonging to a family of fishes including the salmon and trout. —*n.* a salmonoid fish.

salmon pink yellowish pink.

salmon trout a kind of trout resembling a salmon.

sa·lon (sə lon′ or sal′on; *French*, sä lôN′) *n.* **-lons. 1** a large room for receiving or entertaining guests. **2** an assembly of guests in such a room. **3** a place used to exhibit works of art. **4** an exhibition of works of art. **5** a beauty parlor. [< F < Ital. *salone* < *sala* hall < Gmc.]

sa·loon (sə lün′) *n.* **1** a place where alcoholic drinks are sold and drunk. **2** a large room for general or public use: *Concerts are often held in the saloon of the steamship. The ship's passengers ate in the dining saloon.* **3** Also, **saloon car.** *Brit.* a sedan. [< F *salon* salon. See SALON.] —**Syn. 1** tavern, bar.

sa·loon·keep·er (sə lün′kēp′ər) *n.* a man who keeps a saloon (def. 1).

sal·pi·glos·sis (sal′pə glos′is) *n.* **1** any of various Chilean herbs of the nightshade family, having funnel-shaped, brilliantly colored flowers. **2** the flower of any of these plants. [< NL *Salpiglossis*, the genus name < Gk. *salpinx, -pingos* trumpet + *glossa* tongue, referring to the shape of the stigma]

sal·si·fy (sal′sə fē or sal′sə fī′) *n.* **1** a root having an oysterlike flavor, eaten as a vegetable. **2** the purple-flowered plant having this root. [< F *salsifis* < Ital. *sassefrica* < L *saxifraga.* Doublet of SAXIFRAGE.]

sal soda washing soda; crystallized sodium carbonate.

salt (solt or sôlt) *n.* **1** a white substance found in the earth and in sea water; sodium chloride. Salt is used to season and preserve food. **2** in chemistry, a compound derived from an acid by replacing the hydrogen wholly or partly by a metal or an electropositive radical. Baking soda is a salt. **3** that which gives liveliness, piquancy, or pungency to anything. **4** a saltcellar. **5** *Informal.* a sailor. **6 salts,** *pl.* **a** a salt prepared for use as a laxative: *Epsom salts, Rochelle salts.* **b** smelling salts.
above or below the salt, in a superior or inferior position: *Smith considers Jones to be below the salt.*
Attic salt, wit.
eat a person's salt, be his guest.
salt of the earth, a person, or people, considered to be especially fine, noble, etc.
with a grain of salt, with some reservation or allowance.
worth one's salt, worth one's support, wages, etc.
—*adj.* **1** containing salt. **2** tasting like salt. **3** overflowed with or growing in salt water: *salt marshes, salt grasses.* **4** cured or preserved with salt. **5** sharp; pungent; to the point; lively: *salt speech.* **6 salt junk,** hard salt meat.
—*v.* **1** mix or sprinkle with salt. **2** cure or preserve with salt. **3** provide or feed with salt: *salt cattle.* **4** make pungent; season: *conversation salted with wit.* **5** in chemistry: **a** treat with any salt. **b** add a salt to (a solution) in order to precipitate a dissolved substance. **6 salt a mine,** put ore, gold dust, etc. into a mine to create a false impression of value. **7 salt away** or **down,** **a** pack with salt to preserve. **b** *Slang.* store away. [OE *sealt*]

sal·tant (sal′tənt) *adj.* dancing; leaping. [< L *saltans, -antis*, ppr. of *saltare* dance]

salt-cel·lar (solt′sel′ər or sôlt′-) *n.* a shaker or dish for holding salt, used on the table. [ME *saltsaler* < *salt,*

n. + obs. *saler* saltcellar < OF *salier*, masc., *saliere*, fem. < L *salarius*, adj. of salt < *sal* salt]

salt chuck on the west coast and in the Northwest, the sea; salt water.

salt·chuck·er (solt′chuk′ər or sôlt′-) *n.* a salt-water fisherman or angler.

salt·ed (sol′tid or sôl′tid) *adj.* **1** seasoned, cured, or preserved with salt. **2** experienced; hardened.

salt·er (sal′tər or sôl′tər) *n.* **1** a person who makes or sells salt. **2** a person who salts meat, fish, etc.

sal·tie or **sal·ty** (sol′tē or sôl′tē) *n. Informal.* a salt-water vessel, especially a freighter, sailing the Great Lakes.

salt·ine (sol tēn′ or sôl tēn′) *n.* a thin, crisp, salted cracker.

salt·ish (sol′tish or sôl′tish) *adj.* rather salty.

salt lick a place where natural salt is found on the surface of the ground and where animals go to lick it up.

salt·pe·tre or **salt·pe·ter** (solt′pē′tər or sôlt′-) *n.* **1** a mineral used in making gunpowder, in explosives, etc.; potassium nitrate; nitre. **2** a kind of fertilizer; sodium nitrate. [ME < OF *salpetre* < Med.L *sal petrae* salt of rock < Gk. *petra* rock]

salt rheum *Informal.* a skin eruption; eczema.

salt-wa·ter (solt′wo′tər or sôlt′wô′tər) *adj.* **1** consisting of or containing salt water: *a salt-water solution.* **2** living in the sea or in water like sea water: *a salt-water fish.* **3** working on the sea: *a salt-water sailor.* **4** having to do with the sea; taking place on or in the sea: *salt-water fishing.*

salt·y (sol′tē or sôl′tē) *adj.* **salt·i·er, salt·i·est. 1** containing salt; tasting of salt. **2** to the point; witty and a bit improper: *a salty remark.* **—salt′i·ly,** *adv.* **—salt′i·ness,** *n.*

sa·lu·bri·ous (sə lü′brē əs) *adj.* healthful. [< L *salubris* < *salus* good health] **—sa·lu′bri·ous·ly,** *adv.* **—sa·lu′bri·ous·ness,** *n.*

sa·lu·bri·ty (sə lü′brə tē) *n.* healthfulness.

sa·lu·ki (sə lü′kē) *n.* **1** a breed of sporting dog, having the sleek build of a greyhound, short, silky hair, and fringed ears and tail. It is probably the oldest known breed of dog, familiar to ancient Egyptians and Arabs, and the "dog" of the Bible. **2** a dog of this breed. [< Arabic *salugi*, of *Satuq*, an ancient city of Arabia]

sal·u·tar·y (sal′yů ter′ ē) *adj.* **1** beneficial: *The teacher gave the boy salutary advice.* **2** good for the health; wholesome: *Walking is a salutary exercise.* [< L *salutaris* < *salus, salutis* good health] **—Syn. 1** profitable, useful.

sal·u·ta·tion (sal′yů tā′shən) *n.* **1** a greeting; saluting: *The man raised his hat in salutation.* **2** something uttered, written, or done to salute. Most letters begin with a salutation, such as "Dear Sir" or "My Dear Mrs. Jones."

sa·lu·ta·to·ry (sə lü′tə tô′rē) *adj.* expressing greeting; welcoming.

sa·lute (sə lüt′) *v.* **-lut·ed, -lut·ing,** *n.* **—***v.* **1** honor in a formal manner by raising the hand to the head, by firing guns, or by dipping flags: *The soldier saluted the officer.* **2** meet with kind words, cheers, a bow, a kiss, etc.; greet. **3** make a bow, gesture, etc. to. **4** come to; meet: *Shouts of welcome saluted their ears.* **5** make a salute.
—*n.* **1** the act of saluting; a sign of welcome, farewell, or honor. **2** the position of the hand, gun, etc. in saluting. [ME < L *salutare* greet < *salus, salutis* good health] **—sa·lut′er,** *n.* **—Syn.** *v.* **2** welcome, hail.

Salv. Salvador.

Sal·va·do·ran (sal′və dô′rən) *adj.* of or having to do with El Salvador, a country in Central America, or its people. **—***n.* a native or inhabitant of El Salvador.

sal·vage (sal′vij) *n. v.* **-vaged, -vag·ing. —***n.* **1** the act or process of saving a ship or its cargo from wreck, capture, etc. **2** the payment for saving it. **3** the rescue of property from fire, flood, shipwreck, etc. **4 a** the property salvaged: *the salvage from a shipwreck or a fire.* **b** the value of this property, or the proceeds from its sale. **5 a** any saving from ruin: *the salvage of one's dignity.* **b** anything saved thus.

hat, āge, cãre, fär; let, ēqual, tėrm; it, īce
hot, ōpen, ôrder; oil, out; cup, půt, rüle, ūse
əbove, takən, pencəl, lemən, circəs
ch, child; ng, long; sh, ship
th, thin; ᴛʜ, then; zh, measure

—*v.* **1** save from fire, shipwreck, etc. **2** save from harm, destruction, etc. [< F *salvage*, ult. < L *salvus* safe] **—sal′vag·er,** *n.*

sal·va·tion (sal vā′shən) *n.* **1** a saving or being saved. **2** a person or thing that saves. Christians believe that Christ is the salvation of the world. **3** a saving of the soul; deliverance from sin and from punishment for sin. [ME < OF < LL *salvatio, -onis*, ult. < L *salvus* safe]

Salvation Army an organization to spread the Christian religion and to help the poor and unfortunate, founded in England in 1865 by William Booth (1829-1912).

salve[1] (sav) *n. v.* **salved, salv·ing. —***n.* **1** a soft, greasy substance put on wounds and sores; healing ointment. **2** something soothing: *The kind words were a salve to his hurt feelings.* **—***v.* **1** put salve on. **2** soothe; smooth over: *He salved his conscience by the thought that his lie harmed no one.* [OE *sealf*] **—Syn.** *n.* **1** unguent.

salve[2] (salv) *v.* **salved, salv·ing.** save from loss or destruction; salvage. [< *salvage*]

sal·ve[3] (sal′vē or säl′vā) *interj.* hail! [< L *salve* be in good health!]

sal·ver (sal′vər) *n.* a tray. [< F < Sp. *salva*, originally, foretasting, ult. < L *salvus* safe]

sal·vi·a (sal′vē ə) *n.* **1** a garden plant having racemes of bright red flowers; scarlet sage. **2** any plant of the same family as scarlet sage. [< L *salvia*, probably < *salvus* healthy; with reference to its supposed healing properties. Doublet of SAGE[2].]

sal·vo (sal′vō) *n.* **-vos** or **-voes. 1** the discharge of several guns at the same time, as a broadside or as a salute. **2** a round of cheers or applause. [< Ital. *salva*, ult. < L *salve* hail!, be in good health!]

sal vo·la·ti·le (sal′ və lat′ə lē) *Latin.* **1** a salt of ammonium. *Formula*: NH_4CO_3 **2** an aromatic solution of this salt used to relieve faintness, headache, etc.

Sam. Samuel.

S.Am. 1 South America. **2** South American.

sam·a·ra (sam′ə rə or sə mãr′ə) *n.* any dry fruit that has a winglike extension and does not split open when ripe. The fruit of the maple tree is a double samara with one seed in each half. [< L *samara* elm seed]

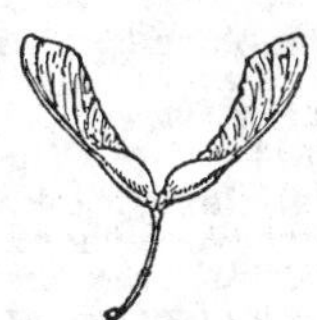
The samara of a maple tree. These fruits are sometimes carried far from the tree by the wind.

Sa·mar·i·tan (sə mar′ə tən or sə mer′ə tən) *n.* **1** a native or inhabitant of Samaria, in ancient times a district in the northern part of Palestine. **2** See **good Samaritan. —***adj.* of or having to do with Samaria or its people.

sa·mar·i·um (sə mãr′ē əm) *n.* a rare metallic chemical element of the cerium group. *Symbol*: Sm or Sa; *at.no.* 62; *at.wt.* 150.35. [< *samar(skite)*, a mineral < G *Samarskit*, after Col. *Samarski*, a Russian]

sam·ba (sam′bə) *n. v.* **-baed, -ba·ing. —***n.* **1** an African dance adapted and modified in Brazil. **2** the music for this dance. **—***v.* dance the samba. [< Pg.]

Sam Browne belt (sam′ broun′) a leather belt having a supporting piece passing over the right shoulder, worn by army officers, etc. [after Sir Samuel J. Browne, a British army officer, 1824-1901]

same (sām) *adj.* **1** not another; identical: *We came back the same way we went.* **2** just alike; not different: *Her name and mine are the same.* **3** unchanged: *He is the same kind old man.* **4** just spoken of; aforesaid: *The boys were talking about an eccentric man. This same man wore his hair very long and always dressed in white.*
—*pron.* **1** the same person or thing. **2 all the same,** notwithstanding; nevertheless. **3 just the same, a** in the same manner. **b** nevertheless. **4 the same,** in the same

manner: *"Sea" and "see" are pronounced the same.* [OE]
Syn. *adj.* **1, 2 Same, identical** = not different (things) or not different from another or each other. Both may mean that what is described is not another person or thing, but the one already mentioned or otherwise suggested: *That is the same* (or *identical*) *man I saw yesterday.* When describing two or more people or things, **same** means alike, of one kind, appearance, size, or quality, etc.; **identical** = absolutely alike, agreeing exactly in every detail: *He always has the same lunch. Their cars are identical.*

same·ness (sām′nis) *n.* **1** the state of being the same; an exact likeness. **2** a lack of variety; tiresomeness.

S.Amer. 1 South America. **2** South American.

Sa·mi·an (sā′mē ən) *adj.* of or having to do with the island of Samos, a Greek island off W. Turkey. —*n.* a native or inhabitant of Samos.

sam·i·sen (sam′ə sen′) *n.* a Japanese guitarlike musical instrument having three strings, played with a plectrum. [< Japanese < Chinese *san hsien*]

sam·ite (sam′īt or sā′mīt) *n.* a heavy, rich silk fabric, sometimes interwoven with gold, worn in the Middle Ages. [ME < OF < Med.Gk. *hexamiton* < Gk. *hex* six + *mitos* thread]

Sa·mo·an (sə mō′ən) *adj.* of or having to do with Samoa, a group of islands in the South Pacific, or its people. —*n.* **1** a native or inhabitant of Samoa. **2** the Polynesian language of the Samoans.

sam·o·var (sam′ə vär′ or sam′ə vär′) *n.* a metal urn used for heating water for tea. [< Russian *samovar,* literally, self-boiler]

Sam·o·yed (sam′ə yed′) *n.* **1** a Siberian breed of large work dog, having a long-haired, white or cream-colored coat, and used in arctic regions to guard reindeer herds and to pull sleds. **2** a dog of this breed. [< Russian *samoyed* (he who eats himself)]

sam·pan (sam′pan) *n.* a type of small boat sculled by one or more oars at the stern and usually having a single sail and a cabin made of mats. Sampans are used in the rivers and coastal waters of China, S.E. Asia, and Japan. [< Chinese < Pg.; origin uncertain]

A sampan

sam·phire (sam′fīr) *n.* **1** a European plant having fleshy leaves growing in clefts of rocks near the sea. **2** glasswort. [earlier *sampere* < F (*herbe de*) *Saint Pierre* (herb of) St. Peter]

sam·ple (sam′pəl) *n. adj. v.* **-pled, -pling.** —*n.* a part to show what the rest is like; one thing to show what the others are like: *Pushing people aside to get in a car is a sample of his bad manners.* —*adj.* serving as a sample: *a sample copy.* —*v.* take a part of; test a part of: *We sampled the cake and found it very good.* [var. of *essample,* var. of *example*] —**Syn.** *n.* specimen. See **example.**

sam·pler (sam′plər) *n.* **1** a person who samples. **2** a piece of cloth embroidered to show skill in needlework. [< OF *essamplaire* < LL *exemplarium* < L *exemplum* example]

Sam·son (sam′sən) *n.* **1** in the Bible, a judge of Israel who had very great strength. He confided to Delilah that his strength was in his hair, and she cut it off while he slept, so that his enemies, the Philistines, could overcome him. Judges 13-16. **2** any man of great strength.

sam·u·rai (sam′ů rī′) *n.* **-rai. 1** in feudal Japan, the military class, consisting of the retainers of the great nobles. **2** a member of this class. [< Japanese]

San (sän or san) *adj. Spanish and Italian.* Saint.

san·a·tive (san′ə tiv) *adj.* healing; having power to cure. [ME < LL *sanativus,* ult. < L *sanus* healthy]

san·a·to·ri·um (san′ə tô′rē əm) *n.* **-ri·ums** or **-ri·a** (-rē ə). a sanitarium; health resort. [< NL *sanatorium,* neut. of LL *sanatorius* health-giving, ult. < L *sanus* healthy]

san·a·to·ry (san′ə tô′rē) *adj.* favorable to health; healing; curing. [< LL *sanatorius.* See SANATORIUM.]

san·be·ni·to (san′bə nē′tō) *n.* **1** a yellow penitential garment with a red St. Andrew's Cross before and behind, worn by a confessed heretic under trial by the Inquisition. **2** a black garment ornamented with flames, devils, etc., worn by a condemned heretic at an auto-da-fé. [< Sp. *San Benito* St. Benedict, from its resemblance to the cloak, or scapular, he introduced]

sanc·ti·fi·ca·tion (sangk′tə fə kā′shən) *n.* a sanctifying or being sanctified; consecration; purification from sin.

sanc·ti·fied (sangk′tə fīd′) *adj.* **1** consecrated. **2** sanctimonious.

sanc·ti·fy (sangk′tə fī′) *v.* **-fied, -fy·ing. 1** make holy: *A life of sacrifice had sanctified her.* **2** set apart as sacred; observe as holy: *"Lord, sanctify this our offering to Thy use."* **3** make free from sin. **4** justify; make right. [ME < OF < L *sanctificare* < *sanctus* holy + *facere* make] —**sanc′ti·fi′er,** *n.*

sanc·ti·mo·ni·ous (sangk′tə mō′nē əs) *adj.* making a show of holiness; putting on airs of sanctity; pretending to be pious. —**sanc′ti·mo′ni·ous·ly,** *adv.* —**sanc′ti·mo′ni·ous·ness,** *n.*

sanc·ti·mo·ny (sangk′tə mō′nē) *n.* a show of holiness; airs of sanctity; hypocrisy in religious matters. [< L *sanctimonia* < *sanctus* holy]

sanc·tion (sangk′shən) *n.* **1** permission with authority; approval: *We have the sanction of the law to play ball in this park.* **2** a solemn ratification. **3 a** a provision of a law enacting a penalty for disobedience to it or a reward for obedience. **b** the penalty or reward. **4** an action by several nations toward another, such as a blockade, economic restrictions, etc., intended to force it to obey international law. **5** a consideration that leads one to obey a rule of conduct. **6** a binding force. —*v.* **1** authorize; approve; allow: *Her conscience does not sanction stealing.* **2** confirm. [< L *sanctio, -onis* < *sancire* ordain] —**sanc′tion·er,** *n.* —**Syn.** *n.* **1** approbation. –*v.* **1** See **approve.**

sanc·ti·ty (sangk′tə tē) *n.* **-ties. 1** holiness; saintliness; godliness. **2** sacredness; holy character: *the sanctity of a church, the sanctity of the home.* **3 sanctities, a** sacred obligations, feelings, etc. **b** objects possessing sanctity. [< L *sanctitas* < *sanctus* holy]

sanc·tu·ar·y (sangk′chü er′ē) *n.* **-ar·ies. 1** a sacred place. A church is a sanctuary. **2** the part of a church around the altar. **3** a place of refuge or protection. **4** a refuge or protection: *The fugitive found sanctuary in the temple.* **5** the temple at Jerusalem. **6** the sacred place where the ark of the covenant was kept in the temple at Jerusalem. [ME < OF < L *sanctuarium,* ult. < *sanctus* holy]

sanc·tum (sangk′təm) *n.* **-tums** or (*rare*) **-ta** (-tə). **1** a sacred place. **2** a private room or office where a person can be undisturbed. [< L *sanctum,* originally neut. adj., holy]

sanc·tum sanc·to·rum (sangk′təm sangk tô′rəm) **1** *Latin.* holy of holies. **2** an especially private place. [Latin for "holy of holies"]

Sanc·tus (sangk′təs) *n.* **1** a hymn beginning "Sanctus, Sanctus, Sanctus" in Latin and "Holy, holy, holy, Lord God of hosts" in English, ending the preface of the Mass or Eucharistic service. **2** the musical setting of this. [< L *sanctus* holy; first word of this hymn]

sand (sand) *n.* **1** tiny grains of worn-down or disintegrated rocks: *the sands of the desert, the sands of the seashore.* **2 sands,** *pl.* a tract or region composed mainly of sand. **3** sand in an hourglass. **4** *Slang.* courage; pluck; grit. **5** a yellowish red. —*v.* **1** sprinkle with sand. **2** fill up with sand. **3** add sand to: *sand sugar.* **4** cover with sand; bury under sand. **5** clean, smooth, or polish with sand, sandpaper, etc. —*adj.* yellowish-red. [OE]

san·dal (san′dəl) *n. v.* **-dalled** or **-daled, -dal·ling** or **-dal·ing.** —*n.* **1** a kind of shoe made of a sole fastened to the foot by straps. **2** any of various kinds of openwork slipper, usually fastened by straps. **3** a light, low rubber overshoe that has no heel. —*v.* furnish with sandals. [ME < L < Gk. *sandalion*]

Sandals

san·dalled or **san·daled** (san′dəld) *adj.* wearing sandals.

san·dal·wood (san′dəl wu̇d′) *n.* **1** a fragrant wood used for making boxes, fans, etc. and burned as incense. **2** the tree that this wood comes from. [< *sandal* (< Med.L *sandalum*, ult. < Skt. *çandana*) + *wood*]

sand·bag (sand′bag′) *n. v.* **-bagged, -bag·ging.** —*n.* **1** a bag filled with sand. Sandbags are used to protect trenches and as ballast on balloons. **2** a small bag of sand used as a club. —*v.* **1** furnish with sandbags. **2** hit or stun with or as if with a sandbag.

sand·bank (sand′bangk′) *n.* a ridge of sand.

sand bar a ridge of sand formed by the action of tides or currents.

sand·blast (sand′blast′) *n.* **1** a blast of air or steam containing sand, used to clean, grind, cut, or decorate hard surfaces such as glass, stone, or metal. **2** the apparatus used to apply such a blast. A sandblast is often used in cleaning the outside of buildings. —*v.* use a sandblast on.

sand·box (sand′boks′) *n.* a box for holding sand.

sand cherry **1** a shrub found in the Prairie Provinces. **2** its bitter black berries.

sand dollar **1** a small, flat, round sea urchin that lives on sandy parts of the ocean floor off the eastern coast of North America. **2** a beach flea or sand hopper.

sand flea **1** a flea found in sandy places. **2** beach flea or sand hopper.

sand·glass (sand′glas′) *n.* an hourglass.

sand·hog (sand′hog′) *n.* a person who works under air pressure below ground, as in the building of tunnels, the sinking of caissons, etc.

sand·man (sand′man′) *n.* in children's literature, a man said to make children sleepy by sprinkling sand on their eyes.

sand·pa·per (sand′pā′pər) *n.* a strong paper with a layer of sand glued on it, used for smoothing, cleaning, or polishing. —*v.* smooth, clean, or polish with sandpaper.

sand·pip·er (sand′pīp′ər) *n.* a small bird having a long bill, living on sandy shores.

sand·spit (sand′spit′) *n.* a stretch of low, sandy land jutting out into water.

sand·stone (sand′stōn′) *n.* a kind of rock formed mostly of sand.

sand·storm (sand′stôrm′) *n.* a windstorm that bears along clouds of sand.

sand·wich (sand′wich) *n.* **1** two or more slices of bread with meat, jelly, cheese, or some other filling between them. **2** something formed by similar arrangement: *an ice-cream sandwich.* —*v.* put in (between): *He was sandwiched between two fat women.* [after John Montagu, the fourth Earl of *Sandwich* (1718-1792)]

sandwich man a man carrying two signboards hung from his shoulders, one before him and one behind.

sand·wort (sand′wėrt′) *n.* a low scrubby plant, having very small, white flowers, that grows in sandy soil.

sand·y (san′dē) *adj.* **sand·i·er, sand·i·est. 1** containing sand; consisting of sand; covered with sand: *The shore is rocky, but there is a sandy beach.* **2** yellowish-red: *sandy hair.* **3** shifting like sand; not stable. —**sand′i·ness,** *n.*

sane (sān) *adj.* **san·er, san·est. 1 a** having a healthy mind; not crazy. **b** not diseased or disordered: *a sane mind.* **2 a** having or showing good sense; sensible. **b** regulated by reason; rational. [< L *sanus* healthy] —**sane′ly,** *adv.* —**sane′ness,** *n.* —**Syn. 1** sound, rational.

San·for·ize (san′fər īz′) *v.* **-ized, -iz·ing.** shrink (cotton or linen cloth) by a patented process before it is made into clothing. [after *Sanford* L. Cluett (born 1874), the inventor]

sang (sang) *v.* pt. of **sing.**

sang-froid (säɴ frwä′) *n. French.* coolness of mind; calmness; composure. [literally, cold blood]

san·gui·nar·i·a (sang′gwə nãr′ē ə) *n.* **1** bloodroot. **2** a drug derived from the bloodroot, used as a stimulant, emetic, etc. [< NL]

san·gui·nar·y (sang′gwə ner′ē) *adj.* **1** with much blood or bloodshed; bloody: *a sanguinary battle.* **2** delighting in bloodshed; bloodthirsty. [< L *sanguinarius* < *sanguis, sanguinis* blood] —**san′gui·nar′i·ness,** *n.*

hat, āge, cãre, fär; let, ēqual, tėrm; it, īce
hot, ōpen, ôrder; oil, out; cup, pu̇t, rüle, ūse
əbove, takən, pencəl, lemən, circəs
ch, child; ng, long; sh, ship
th, thin; ᴛʜ, then; zh, measure

san·guine (sang′gwin) *adj.* **1** naturally cheerful and hopeful: *a sanguine disposition.* **2** confident; hopeful: *sanguine of success.* **3** having a healthy, red color; ruddy: *a sanguine complexion.* **4** in former times, having an active circulation, a ruddy color, and a cheerful and ardent disposition: **5** sanguinary. [ME < OF < L *sanguineus* < *sanguis, sanguinis* blood] —**san′guine·ly,** *adv.* —**Syn. 1** optimistic.

san·guin·e·ous (sang gwin′ē əs) *adj.* **1** of blood; like blood; bloody. **2** red like blood. **3** full-blooded; too full-blooded for health. **4** sanguine; hopeful.

San·he·drim (san′hē drim′) *n.* Sanhedrin.

San·he·drin (san′hē drin′) *n.* in ancient times, the supreme council and highest religious and legal authority of the Jewish nation. [< Late Hebrew < Gk. *synedrion* council, literally, sitting together < *syn-* together + *hedra* seat]

san·i·tar·i·an (san′ə tãr′ē ən) *n.* a person familiar with, or engaged in, sanitary work. —*adj.* sanitary.

san·i·tar·i·um (san′ə tãr′ē əm) *n.* **-i·ums** or **-i·a** (-ē ə). **1** an establishment for treatment of the sick, especially patients who are convalescing or who are suffering from a long, slow disease like tuberculosis. **2** health resort. [< NL < L *sanitas* health < *sanus* healthy]

san·i·tar·y (san′ə ter′ē) *adj.* **1** of or having to do with health; favorable to health; preventing disease. **2** free from dirt and filth. [< F *sanitaire*, ult. < L *sanus* healthy] —**san′i·tar′i·ness,** *n.* —**Syn. 1** healthful, hygienic.

san·i·ta·tion (san′ə tā′shən) *n.* the working out and practical application of sanitary measures.

san·i·tize (san′ə tīz′) *v.* **-tized, -tiz·ing.** make sanitary; disinfect.

san·i·ty (san′ə tē) *n.* **1** soundness of mind; mental health. **2** soundness of judgment; sensibleness; reasonableness. [< L *sanitas* < *sanus* healthy]

sank (sangk) *v.* pt. of **sink.**

sans (sanz; *French,* säɴ) *prep.* without: "*sans teeth, sans eyes, sans taste, sans everything.*" [ME < OF < L *absentia* (abl.) in the absence (of), influenced by L *sine* without]

sans-cu·lotte (sanz′kū lot′) *n.* **1** in the French Revolution, an aristocrat's contemptuous term for a member of the poorer classes, adopted by the revolutionaries as a designation of honor. **2** any extreme republican or revolutionary. [< F *sans-culotte* without knee breeches]

San·sei (sän′sā′) *n.* **-sei** or **-seis.** a third generation Japanese immigrant; an offspring of Nisei parents. [< Japanese *san* third + *sei* generation]

San·skrit or **San·scrit** (san′skrit) *n.* the ancient literary language of India. [< Skt. *samskrta* prepared, cultivated (applied to the literary language as contrasted with the vernacular language). Cf. PRAKRIT.]

sans pa·reil (säɴ pä rā′) *French.* without equal.

sans-ser·if (sanz′ser′if) *n.* in printing, any style of type having no serifs. [< F *sans* without + E *serif*]

sans sou·ci (säɴ sü sē′) *French.* without care or worry.

San·ta (san′tə *for 1*; san′tə or sän′tä *for 2*) *n.* **1** Santa Claus. **2** a Spanish or an Italian word meaning *holy* or *saint*, used in combinations, as in *Santa Maria.*

San·ta Claus (san′tə kloz′ or klôz′) Saint Nicholas, the saint of Christmas giving; according to the modern conception, a jolly old man with a white beard, dressed in a fur-trimmed red suit. [< Du. dial. *Sante Klaas* Saint Nicholas]

sap[1] (sap) *n.* **1** the liquid that circulates through a plant, carrying water, food, etc. as blood does in animals. Rising sap carries water and salt from the roots; sap travelling downward carries sugar, gums, resins, etc. **2** any life-giving liquid. **3** sapwood. **4** *Slang.* saphead. [OE *sæp*]

sap[2] (sap) *v.* **sapped, sap·ping,** *n.* —*v.* **1** dig under or wear away the foundation of: *The walls of the boathouse had been sapped by the waves.* **2** weaken; use up: *The extreme heat sapped our strength.* **3** dig protected trenches. **4** approach (the enemy's position) by means of such trenches. **5** make a tunnel under. [< MF *sapper* or Ital. *zappare* < *zappa* spade, hoe]
—*n.* **1** a trench protected by the earth dug up; trench dug to approach the enemy's position. **2** the making of trenches to approach a besieged place or an enemy's position. [< MF *sappe* < *sapper*. See v.]

sap·head (sap′hed′) *n. Slang.* a silly, stupid person.

sa·pi·ence (sā′pē əns or sap′ē əns) *n.* wisdom.

sa·pi·en·cy (sā′pē ən sē) *n.* sapience.

sa·pi·ent (sā′pē ənt or sa′pē ənt) *adj.* wise; sage. [< L *sapiens, -entis,* ppr. of *sapere* be wise] —**sa′pi·ent·ly,** *adv.*

sap·less (sap′lis) *adj.* **1** without sap; withered. **2** without energy or vigor.

sap·ling (sap′ling) *n.* **1** a young tree. **2** a young person.

sap·o·dil·la (sap′ə dil′ə) *n.* **1** a large evergreen tree of tropical America that yields chicle and bears large, edible berries that look and taste somewhat like pears. **2** the fruit of this tree. [< Sp. *zapotilla,* ult. < Nahuatl]

sap·o·na·ceous (sap′ə nā′shəs) *adj.* soapy. [< Med.L *saponaceus* < L *sapo, -onis* soap]

sa·pon·i·fi·ca·tion (sə pon′ə fə kā′shən) *n.* **1** the process of saponifying. **2** the state of being saponified. **3** in chemistry: **a** alkaline hydrolysis of any ester to form an alcohol and a salt or acid. **b** any hydrolysis. [< F]

sa·pon·i·fy (sə pon′ə fī′) *v.* **-fied, -fy·ing. 1** make (a fat or oil) into soap by treating it with an alkali. **2** become soap. **3** decompose (an ester of an acid) into an alcohol and a salt of the acid. [< NL *saponificare* < L *sapo, saponis* soap + *facere* make]

sap·per (sap′ər) *n.* in the army: **1** a soldier employed in the construction of trenches, fortifications, etc. **2** a private in the engineer corps. [< *sap*[2]]

Sap·phic (saf′ik) *adj.* **1** of or having to do with Sappho. **2** having to do with certain metres, or a stanza form, used by or named after her. —*n.* a Sapphic stanza or strophe.

sap·phire (saf′īr) *n.* **1** a hard, clear, transparent variety of carborundum, especially the bright-blue precious stone. **2** a piece of this stone, or a gem made from it. **3** a bright blue. —*adj.* bright-blue. [ME < OF < L < Gk. *sappheiros* < Semitic; cf. Hebrew *sappīr* < Skt. *çani-priya* dear to the planet Saturn]

Sap·pho (saf′ō) *n.* a Greek lyric poetess of Lesbos, an island in the Aegean Sea, who lived about 600 B.C.

sap·py (sap′ē) *adj.* **-pi·er, -pi·est. 1** full of sap. **2** vigorous; energetic. **3** *Slang.* silly; foolish. —**sap′pi·ness,** *n.*

sap·ro·phyte (sap′rō fīt′) *n.* a vegetable organism that lives on decaying organic matter. Certain fungi are saprophytes. [< Gk. *sapros* rotten + E *-phyte*]

sap·ro·phyt·ic (sap′rō fit′ik) *adj.* of or like a saprophyte; living on dead organic matter. —**sap·ro·phyt′i·cal·ly,** *adv.*

sap·suck·er (sap′suk′ər) *n.* a small North American woodpecker that feeds on the sap and sapwood of trees.

sap·wood (sap′wủd′) *n.* the soft sap-carrying tissue between the bark and the hard inner wood of most trees.

sar·a·band (sar′ə band′) *n.* **1** a slow and stately Spanish dance. **2** the music for this dance. [< F < Sp. *zarabanda*]

Sar·a·cen (sar′ə sən) *n.* **1** an Arab. **2** during the Crusades, a Moslem. —*adj.* of or having to do with the Saracens.

Sar·a·cen·ic (sar′ə sen′ik) *adj.* of or having to do with the Saracens.

sa·ran (sə ran′) *n.* any of various thermoplastic resins that are highly resistant to damage and soiling, used in packaging, clothing, seat covers, etc. [coined by Dow Chemical Company]

sar·casm (sär′kaz əm) *n.* **1** a sneering or cutting remark; an ironical taunt. **2** the act of making fun of a person to hurt his feelings; bitter irony: *Her sarcasm was obvious when she called the frightened boy a hero.* [< LL < Gk. *sarkasmos* < *sarkazein* sneer, strip off flesh < *sarx, sarkos* flesh] ☛ See **irony** for usage note.

sar·cas·tic (sär kas′tik) *adj.* using sarcasm; sneering; cutting: *"Don't hurry!" was his sarcastic comment as I began to dress at my usual slow rate.* —**sar·cas′ti·cal·ly,** *adv.* —**Syn.** ironical, satirical, taunting, caustic.

Sar·cee (sär′sē) *n.* **-cee** or **-cees. 1** an Athapaskan people formerly inhabiting the upper Athabasca River in Alberta, now living on a reserve south of Calgary. **2** a member of this people. **3** the Athapaskan dialect of this people. Also, **Sarsi.**

sarce·net (särs′net) *n.* a soft, thin silk fabric. Also, **sarsenet.** [ME < AF *sarzinett,* dim. of *Sarzin* Saracen]

sar·co·ma (sär kō′mə) *n.* **-mas** or **-ma·ta** (-mə tə). any of various malignant tumors of connective tissue. [< NL < Gk. *sarkōma,* ult. < *sarx, sarkos* flesh]

sar·coph·a·gus (sär kof′ə gəs) *n.* **-gi** (-jī′ or -jē′) or **-gus·es.** a stone coffin, especially an ornamental one. [< L < Gk. *sarkophagos,* originally, flesh-eating (stone) < *sarx, sarkos* flesh + *phagein* eat]

sard (särd) *n.* **1** a brownish-red variety of chalcedony, used in jewellery. **2** a piece of this stone, or a gem made from it. [< L *sarda*; cf. Gk. *sardios* (*lithos*) stone from Sardis in Lydia]

sar·dine (sär dēn′) *n.* **-dines** or (*esp. collectively*) **-dine. 1** a small herringlike fish caught when young and preserved in oil for food. **2 packed like sardines,** very much crowded. [ME < OF < Ital. < L *sardina* < *sarda* sardine < Gk., perhaps < *Sardō* Sardinia]

Sar·din·i·an (sär din′ē ən) *adj.* of or having to do with Sardinia, a large island off the southwestern coast of Italy, its people, or their language. —*n.* **1** a native or inhabitant of Sardinia. **2** the Romance language spoken in Sardinia.

sar·don·ic (sär don′ik) *adj.* bitter; sarcastic; scornful; mocking: *a friend's sardonic laugh.* [< F < L < Gk. *sardonios,* a supposed Sardinian plant that produced hysterical convulsions] —**sar·don′i·cal·ly,** *adv.*

sar·do·nyx (sär′də niks) *n.* **1** a variety of onyx containing layers of sard. **2** a piece of this stone, or a gem made from it. [ME < L < Gk. *sardonyx,* probably < *sardios* sard + *onyx* onyx]

sar·gas·so (sär gas′ō) *n.* any of a group of brown seaweeds that have berry-like air bladders and float in large masses. [< Pg. *sargasso* < *sarga,* a type of grape]

sa·ri (sä′rē) *n.* **-ris.** a garment, the principal dress of Hindu women, consisting of a long piece of cotton or silk worn wound around the body with one end thrown over the head or shoulder. [< Hind.]

sa·rong (sə rong′) *n.* **1** a rectangular piece of cloth, usually a brightly colored printed material, worn as a skirt by men and women in the Malay Archipelago, East Indies, etc. **2** a fabric used to make this garment. [< Malay *sārung*]

sar·sa·pa·ril·la (sas′pə ril′ə or sär′sə pə ril′ə) *n.* **1** a tropical American climbing or trailing plant or its root. **2** a medicine or cooling drink made from the root. [< Sp. < *zarza* bramble + *parrilla,* dim. of *parra* vine]

sarse·net (särs′net) *n.* sarcenet.

Sar·si (sär′sē) *n.* Sarcee.

sar·to·ri·al (sär tô′rē əl) *adj.* **1** of tailors or their work. **2** of or having to do with men's tailored clothes. [< L *sartorius* of a tailor, ult. < *sarcire* patch] —**sar·to′ri·al·ly,** *adv.*

sash[1] (sash) *n.* a long, broad strip of cloth or ribbon, worn as an ornament round the waist or over one shoulder. [earlier *shash* < Arabic *shāsh* turban]

sash[2] (sash) *n.* **1** the frame for the glass of a window or door. **2** such frames collectively. —*v.* furnish with sashes. [alteration of *chassis,* taken as pl.]

sa·shay (sa shā′) *v. Informal.* glide, move, or go about. [alteration of *chassé* a gliding dance step < F]

Sask. Saskatchewan.

Sas·katch·e·wan·i·an (sas kach′ə won′ē ən) *n.* **1** a person born in or living in Saskatchewan. **2** of or having to do with Saskatchewan.

sas·ka·toon (sas′kə tün′) *n. Cdn.* in the West, the

serviceberry. [< Algonquian (Cree) *misaskwatomin* < *misaskwat* tree of many branches + *min* fruit]

Sas·quatch (sas′kwach) *n. Cdn.* a wild hairy monster of subhuman appearance, supposed to inhabit certain western mountain regions. [< Salish *se′sxac*]

sass (sas or sos) *Informal.* —*n.* back talk; impudence or cheekiness. —*v.* be saucy to; be impudent or cheeky. [var. of *sauce*]

sas·sa·fras (sas′ə fras′) *n.* **1** a slender American tree that has fragrant, yellow flowers and bluish-black fruit. **2** the aromatic dried bark of its root, used in medicine, as a flavoring in candy, soft drinks, etc. **3** the flavor. [< Sp. *sasafras*]

Sas·se·nach (sas′ə naʜ′ or sas′ə nak′) *n. Scottish and Irish.* **1** an Englishman. **2** the English people as a whole. [< Irish *sasenach* Saxon < ML *Saxonicus.* Related to SAXON.]

sas·sy (sas′ē) *adj.* **-si·er, -si·est.** *Dialect.* saucy.

sa·stru·gi (sə strü′gē) *n. Esp.North.* ridges of hard-packed snow, formed by the wind and often attaining a height of 4 feet. Also, **zastrugi.** [< Russian]

sat (sat) *v.* pt. and pp. of **sit.**

Sat. Saturday.

Sa·tan (sā′tən) *n.* Lucifer; the Devil.

sa·tan·ic or **Sa·tan·ic** (sā tan′ik or sə tan′ik) *adj.* of Satan; like Satan; like that of Satan; very wicked. —**sa·tan′i·cal·ly,** *adv.*

Sa·tan·ism (sā′tə niz′əm) *n.* **1** devil worship, especially a French cult of the 1890's that professed worship of Satan. **2** the beliefs or rites of devil worship. **3** wickedness; a malicious or diabolical disposition.

satch·el (sach′əl) *n.* a small bag for carrying clothes, books, etc. [ME < OF < L *saccellus,* double dim. of *saccus* sack[1]. See SACK[1].]

sate[1] (sāt) *v.* **sat·ed, sat·ing.** **1** satisfy fully (any appetite or desire). **2** supply with more than enough, so as to disgust or weary. [alteration of *sade* (OE *sadian* glut; cf. SAD) under influence of L *satiare* satiate. See SATIATE.] —**Syn. 2** See **satiate.**

sate[2] (sat or sāt) *v. Archaic.* a pt. and a pp. of **sit.**

sa·teen (sa tēn′) *n.* a cotton cloth made to imitate satin, often used for dresses, lining sleeves, etc. [var. of *satin*]

sat·el·lite (sat′ə līt′) *n.* **1** a small planet that revolves around a larger planet. **2** a sphere or other object launched into an orbit around the earth. **3** a follower or attendant upon a person of importance. **4** a subservient follower. **5** a country that is nominally independent but actually controlled by a more powerful country; especially, a country under Russian control. [< L *satelles, -itis* attendant]

sa·ti·a·ble (sā′shē ə bəl or sā′shə bəl) *adj.* that can be satiated.

sa·ti·ate (sā′shē āt′) *v.* **-at·ed, -at·ing.** **1** feed fully; satisfy fully. **2** weary or disgust with too much. [< L *satiare* < *satis* enough] —**sa′ti·a′tion,** *n.*
Syn. 2 Satiate, sate, surfeit = fill with more than enough to satisfy. **Satiate,** formal, chiefly means "feed, literally or figuratively, a person, mind, etc. too much," to the point where something that did please or was wanted no longer gives pleasure: *Children who are given every toy they see become satiated.* **Sate,** chiefly literary, usually means "satisfy a desire or appetite" so fully that it dies: *Will nothing sate his lust for power?* **Surfeit** emphasizes excess, overeating or oversupplying to the point of making sick or disgusted: *He surfeited them with candy and sodas.*

sa·ti·e·ty (sə tī′ə tē) *n.* the feeling of having had too much; disgust or weariness caused by excess; a satiated condition. [< F < L *satietas* < *satis* enough]

sat·in (sat′ən) *n.* a silk, rayon, or synthetic cloth with one very smooth, glossy side. —*adj.* of or like satin; smooth and glossy. [ME < OF < Arabic *zaituni*]

sat·in·wood (sat′ən wůd′) *n.* **1** the beautiful, smooth wood of an East Indian tree, used to ornament furniture, etc. **2** the tree itself.

sat·in·y (sat′ən ē) *adj.* like satin in smoothness and gloss.

sat·ire (sat′īr) *n.* **1** the use of sarcasm or irony to attack or ridicule a habit, idea, custom, etc. **2** a poem, essay, story, etc. that attacks or ridicules in this way: *Some of Aesop's "Fables" are satires.* [< L *satira,* var. of (*lanx*) *satura* mixed (dish) < *satur* full] ☛ See **irony** for usage note.

hat, āge, cãre, fär; let, ēqual, tėrm; it, īce
hot, ōpen, ôrder; oil, out; cup, půt, rüle, ūse
əbove, takən, pencəl, lemən, circəs
ch, child; ng, long; sh, ship
th, thin; ᴛʜ, then; zh, measure

sa·tir·ic (sə tir′ik) *adj.* satirical.

sa·tir·i·cal (sə tir′ə kəl) *adj.* of satire; containing satire; fond of using satire. —**sa·tir′i·cal·ly,** *adv.* —**Syn.** sarcastic, ironical, cutting, caustic, sneering.

sat·i·rist (sat′ə rist) *n.* a writer of satires; a person who uses satire. The follies and vices of their own times are the chief subjects of satirists.

sat·i·rize (sat′ə rīz′) *v.* **-rized, -riz·ing.** attack with satire; criticize with mockery; seek to improve by ridicule.

sat·is·fac·tion (sat′is fak′shən) *n.* **1** a fulfilment; satisfying. **2** the condition of being satisfied or pleased and contented. **3** anything that makes us feel pleased or contented. **4** a response, information, etc. that fully meets doubts, objections, demands, etc. **5** the payment of debt; the discharge of obligation; a making up for wrong or injury done. **6 give satisfaction, a** satisfy. **b** fight a duel because of an insult. [ME < OF < L *satisfactio, -onis* < *satisfacere.* See SATISFY.] —**Syn. 1** gratification. **2** contentment, complacency. **5** reparation, atonement.

sat·is·fac·to·ry (sat′is fak′tə rē or -fak′trē) *adj.* satisfying; good enough to satisfy. —**sat′is·fac′to·ri·ly,** *adv.* —**sat′is·fac′to·ri·ness,** *n.* —**Syn.** gratifying, pleasing, adequate, sufficient.

sat·is·fy (sat′is fī′) *v.* **-fied, -fy·ing.** **1** give enough to; fulfil (desires, hopes, demands, etc.); put an end to (needs, wants, etc.): *He satisfied his hunger with a sandwich and milk.* **2** fully meet (an objection, doubt, demand, etc.). **3** make contented; please: *Are you satisfied now?* **4** give satisfaction. **5** pay; make right: *After the accident he satisfied all claims for the damage he had caused.* **6** set free from doubt; convince: *He was satisfied that it was an accident.* **7** make up for a wrong or injury. [ME < OF < L *satisfacere* < *satis* enough + *facere* do] —**sat′is·fi′er,** *n.* —**sat′is·fy′ing·ly,** *adv.*
Syn. 1 Satisfy, content = meet, wholly or partly, a person's desires and wants. **Satisfy** = give enough to fulfil a person's desires, hopes, needs, etc.: *The little mongrel satisfied the boy's desire for a dog.* **Content** = give enough to please a person and keep him from being unhappy because he does not have everything he wants: *A letter from her once a week contented him.*

sa·trap (sā′trap or sat′rap) *n.* **1** a ruler, often a tyrant, who is subordinate to a higher ruler. **2** in ancient Persia, a governor of a province. [ME < L < Gk. *satrapēs* < OPersian *kshathra-pāwan* guardian of the realm]

sa·trap·y (sā′trə pē or sat′rə pē) *n.* **-trap·ies.** the province, position, or authority of a satrap.

sat·u·ra·ble (sach′ə rə bəl) *adj.* that can be saturated.

sat·u·rate (sach′ə rāt′) *v.* **-rat·ed, -rat·ing.** **1** soak thoroughly; fill full: *During the fog, the air was saturated with moisture. Saturate the moss with water before planting the bulbs in it.* **2** in chemistry, cause (a substance) to unite with the greatest possible amount of another substance. A **saturated solution** (of sugar, salt, etc.) is one that cannot dissolve any more (sugar, salt, etc.). **3** load or fill anything to capacity: *The manufacturers are not making any more of these toys for a while, for their competitors have saturated the market.* [< L *saturare* glut < *satur* full] —**Syn. 1** steep, drench, imbue.

sat·u·ra·tion (sach′ə rā′shən) *n.* **1** the act or process of saturating. **2** the fact of being saturated; a saturated condition. The saturation of a color increases as the amount of white in it is decreased.

saturation point **1** the point at which a substance will take up no more of another substance. **2** a condition in which a person can endure no more. **3** a condition in which a market is supplied with as much of a particular commodity as it can absorb.

Sat·ur·day (sat′ər dē or sat′ər dā′) *n.* the seventh day of the week, following Friday. [OE *Sæterdæg, Sætern(es)dæg,* translation of L *Saturni dies* day of Saturn (the planet)]

Sat·urn (sat′ərn) *n.* **1** in Roman mythology, the ancient god of agriculture, said to have ruled during a golden age and to have been deposed by Jupiter. He was identified with the Greek god Cronus. **2** the second largest planet in the solar system, and the sixth planet from the sun. Saturn is surrounded by three rings composed of small particles. [< L *Saturnus*, associated by the Romans with *satio* sowing, ult. < *serere* to sow]

Sat·ur·na·li·a (sat′ər nā′lē ə or sat′ər nāl′yə) *n.pl.* **1** in ancient Rome, the festival of Saturn, celebrated in December with much feasting and merrymaking.
2 saturnalia, a period of unrestrained revelry and licence. [< L]

Sat·ur·na·li·an (sat′ər nā′lē ən or sat′ər nāl′yən) *adj.* **1** of or having to do with the Roman Saturnalia.
2 saturnalian, riotously merry; revelling without restraint.

Sa·tur·ni·an (sə tėr′nē ən) *adj.* **1** of or having to do with the god Saturn, whose reign is referred to as the "golden age." **2** prosperous, happy, or peaceful. **3** of or having to do with a form of verse used in early Roman poetry. **4** of or having to do with the planet Saturn.

sat·ur·nine (sat′ər nīn′) *adj.* gloomy; grave; taciturn. [< *Saturn*; those born under the planet's sign are supposed to be morose] **—sat′ur·nine·ly,** *adv.*

sat·yr (sat′ər or sā′tər) *n.* **1** a Greek deity of the woods, part man and part beast. The satyrs were followers of Bacchus, the god of wine. **2** a man who is beastlike in thought and action. [ME < L < Gk. *satyros*]

sauce (sos or sôs) *n. v.* **sauced, sauc·ing.** *—n.*
1 something, usually a liquid, served with food to make it taste better. We eat cranberry sauce with turkey, mint sauce with lamb, egg sauce with fish, and many different sauces with puddings. **2** stewed fruit: *applesauce.*
3 something that adds interest or relish. **4** *Informal.* sauciness. *—v.* **1** prepare with sauce; season. **2** give interest or flavor to. **3** *Informal.* be saucy to. [ME < OF < L *salsa*, fem. adj., salted, ult. < *sal, salis* salt]

sauce·box (sos′boks′ or sôs′-) *n. Informal.* a saucy person.

sauce·pan (sos′pan′ or sôs′-) *n.* a dish of metal, enamel, Pyrex, etc., having a handle and used for stewing, boiling, etc.

sau·cer (so′sər or sô′sər) *n.* **1** a shallow dish to set a cup on. **2** a small, round dish with its edge curved up.
3 something round and shallow like a saucer. [ME *saucer* sauce dish < OF *saucier* < *sauce.* See SAUCE.]
—sau′cer·like′, *adj.*

sau·cy (so′sē or sô′sē) *adj.* **-ci·er, -ci·est. 1** showing lack of respect; rude. **2** pert; smart: *a saucy hat.* [< *sauce*] **—sau′ci·ly,** *adv.* **—sau′ci·ness,** *n.* **—Syn. 1** See **impertinent.**

sauer·kraut (sour′krout′) *n.* cabbage cut fine, salted, and allowed to ferment; cabbage pickled in brine. [< G *Sauerkraut* < *sauer* sour + *Kraut* cabbage]

sau·ger (so′gər or sô′gər) *n.* a North American pike or perch resembling a walleye. [origin uncertain; ? < North American Indian]

Sauk (sok or sôk) *n.* **Sauk** or **Sauks. 1** a tribe of Algonquian Indians, closely related to the Foxes, inhabiting the Fox river valley in Wisconsin. **2** a member of this tribe. **3** the language of this tribe, a dialect of Fox. Also, **Sac.**

sault (sü) *n. Cdn.* a falls or rapids. [obs. spelling of F *saut* leap, jump, falls < L *saltus* < *salire* to leap]

sau·na (son′ə, sô′nə, or sou′nə) *n.* **1** a steam bath in which the steam is produced by pouring water over hot stones. **2** a house or other structure used for such baths. [< Finnish]

saun·ter (son′tər or sôn′tər) *v.* walk along slowly and quietly; stroll: *saunter through the park.* *—n.* **1** a leisurely or careless gait. **2** a stroll. [origin uncertain] **—saun′ter·er,** *n.*

sau·ri·an (sô′rē ən) *adj.* **1** belonging to or having to do with the lizards and, sometimes, certain similar reptiles. **2** of or like a lizard. *—n.* **1** a lizard. **2** any similar reptile, such as a crocodile or dinosaur. [< NL *sauria*, pl. < Gk. *sauros* lizard]

sau·ry (sôr′ē) *n.* **-ry** or **-ries.** a small fish having jaws that resemble a beak. [< NL < Gk. *sauros* lizard]

sau·sage (so′sij or sô′sij) *n.* chopped pork, beef, or other meats, seasoned and usually stuffed into a thin tube or skin. [ME < ONF *saussiche* < LL *salsicia*, ult. < L *sal, salis* salt]

sau·té (sō tā′) *adj. n. v.* **-téed, -té·ing.** *—adj.* cooked or browned in a little fat. *—n.* a dish of food cooked or browned in a little fat. *—v.* fry quickly in a little fat. [< F *sauté*, pp. of *sauter* jump < L *saltare* hop, frequentative of *salire* leap]

sau·terne (sō tėrn′) *n.* **1** a French white wine. **2** any wine of the same type. [< *Sauternes*, a district in S. France, where the grapes are grown]

sauve qui peut (sōv kē pœ′) *French.* a general rout; hasty flight. [literally, let (everyone) save (himself) who can]

sav·age (sav′ij) *adj. n. v.* **-aged, -ag·ing.** *—adj.* **1** wild or rugged: *He liked savage mountain scenery.* **2** not civilized; barbarous: *savage customs. Gaudy colors please a savage taste.* **3** fierce; cruel; ready to fight; brutal: *a savage dog.* **4 a** enraged; furiously angry. **b** rough or unsparing in speech. **5** undomesticated; untamed.
—n. **1** a member of a people in the lowest stage of development or civilization. **2** a fierce, brutal, or cruel person. **3** a person ignorant or neglectful of the rules of good behavior.
—v. attack furiously or savagely. [ME < OF *sauvage* < LL *salvaticus*, ult. < L *silva* forest] **—sav′age·ly,** *adv.* **—sav′age·ness,** *n.* **—Syn.** *adj.* **2** primitive, rude.
3 ferocious. See **fierce.**

sav·age·ry (sav′ij rē) *n.* **-ries. 1** wildness. **2** an uncivilized condition. **3** fierceness; cruelty; brutality.

sa·van·na or **sa·van·nah** (sə van′ə) *n.* **1** a treeless plain. **2** a region of tropical or sub-tropical grassland having a scattering of trees. **3** especially in the Maritimes, a swamp or tract of peat bog; muskeg. [< earlier Sp. *zavana* < Arawakan]

sa·vant (sə vänt′ or sav′ənt) *n.* a man of learning. [< earlier F ppr. of *savoir* know < L *sapere* be wise]

save[1] (sāv) *v.* **saved, sav·ing. 1** make safe from harm, danger, loss, etc.; rescue: *save a drowning man.* **2** keep safe from harm, danger, hurt, loss, etc.; protect: *save one's honor.* **3** lay aside; store up: *She saves pieces of string.* **4** keep from spending or wasting: *Save your strength.* **5** avoid expense or waste: *She saves in every way she can.* **6** prevent; make less: *save work, save trouble, save expense.* **7** treat carefully to lessen wear, weariness, etc.: *Large print saves one's eyes.* **8** set free from sin and its results. *—n.* the act of saving, especially by preventing an opponent from scoring. [ME < OF < LL *salvare* < L *salvus* safe] **—sav′er,** *n.* **—Syn. 2** safeguard, shield, preserve.

save[2] (sāv) *prep.* except; but: *He works every day save Sundays.* *—conj. Archaic.* unless. [var. of *safe*, in sense of "not being involved"]

sav·in or **sav·ine** (sav′ən) *n.* **1** a juniper shrub whose tops yield an oily drug used in medicine. **2** this drug.
3 any of various junipers, such as the red cedar. [ult. < L *sabina*, originally adj., Sabine]

sav·ing (sāv′ing) *adj.* **1** that saves. **2** tending to save up money; avoiding waste; economical. **3** making a reservation: *a saving clause.*
—n. **1** an act or way of saving money, time, etc.: *It will be a saving to take this short cut.* **2** that which is saved. **3 savings,** *pl.* money saved.
—prep. **1** save; except. **2** with all due respect to or for.
—conj. with the exception of. **—Syn.** *adj.* **1** redeeming, preserving. **2** thrifty, provident, sparing, frugal.

saving grace a redeeming feature.

sav·ior or **sav·iour** (sāv′yər) *n.* one who saves or rescues. [ME < OF < LL *salvator* < *salvare.* See SAVE[1].]

Sav·iour or **Sav·ior** (sāv′yər) *n.* Usually, **the Saviour.** Jesus Christ. ☛ **Saviour.** See **-or** for usage note on spelling.

sa·voir-faire (sav′wär fãr′) *n.* knowledge of just what to do; tact. [< F *savoir-faire*, literally, knowing how to act]

sa·voir-vi·vre (sav′wär vē′vrə) *n.* knowledge of the world and of the usages of polite society; good breeding. [< F *savoir-vivre*, literally, knowing how to live]

sa·vor or **sa·vour** (sā′vər) *n.* **1** a taste or smell; flavor: *The soup has a savor of onion.* **2** a distinctive quality; noticeable trace: *There is a savor of conceit in everything he says.*
—*v.* **1** taste or smell (*of*): *That sauce savors of lemon.* **2** enjoy the savor of; perceive or appreciate by taste or smell: *He savored the soup with pleasure.* **3** give flavor to; season. **4** have the quality or nature (*of*): *a request that savors of a command.* **5** show traces of the presence or influence of: *Bad manners savor a bad education.* [ME < OF < L *sapor*] —**sa′vor·er** or **sa′vour·er,** *n.* —**sa′vor·less** or **sa′vour·less,** *adj.*

sa·vor·y[1] or **sa·vour·y** (sā′vər ē) *adj.* **-vor·i·er** or **-vour·i·er, -vor·i·est** or **-vour·i·est,** *n.* **-vor·ies** or **-vour·ies.** —*adj.* **1** pleasing in taste or smell: *The savory smell of roasting turkey greeted us as we entered the house.* **2** giving a relish; salt or piquant and not sweet. **3** morally pleasing; agreeable. —*n.* a small portion of highly seasoned food served at the beginning or end of a dinner to stimulate the appetite or digestion. [ME < OF *savoure*, ult. < L *sapor* taste] —**sa′vor·i·ness** or **sa′vour·i·ness,** *n.* —**Syn.** *adj.* **1** appetizing, palatable, tasty, toothsome.

sa·vor·y[2] (sā′vər ē) *n.* **-vor·ies.** any of several fragrant herbs used for seasoning food. [ME *saverey*, ult. < L *satureia*]

sa·voy (sə voi′) *n.* a kind of cabbage having a compact head and wrinkled leaves. [< *Savoie* Savoy, a region in E. France]

Sa·voy (sə voi′) *n.* the French noble family that ruled Italy from 1861 to 1946.

Sa·voy·ard (sə voi′ərd) *n.* **1** a native or inhabitant of Savoy, a region in E. France. **2** an actor, producer, or warm admirer of Gilbert and Sullivan's operas, many of which were first produced at the Savoy Theatre, London. —*adj.* **1** of Savoy or its people. **2** of or having to do with the Savoy Theatre, London.

sav·vy (sav′ē) *v.* **-vied, -vy·ing,** *n. Slang.* —*v.* know; understand. —*n.* understanding; intelligence; sense. [partly < F *savez (-vous)?* do you know?, partly < Sp. *sabe* or *sabes* you know; both ult. < L *sapere* be wise]

saw[1] (so or sô) *n. v.* **sawed, sawed** or **sawn, saw·ing.** —*n.* **1** a tool for cutting, made of a thin blade with sharp teeth on the edge. **2** a machine with such a tool for cutting. —*v.* **1** cut with a saw. **2** make with a saw. **3** use a saw. **4** be sawed: *wood that saws easily.* **5** cut as if with a saw; move through as if sawing. [OE *sagu*] —**saw′er,** *n.*

CIRCULAR
HAND
CROSS-CUT

Saws (def. 1) of three common types. The circular saw is mounted in a frame and turned by a motor; the other two are made to cut by passing the teeth back and forth across the wood. The cross-cut saw is usually worked by two people.

saw[2] (so or sô) *v.* pt. of **see**[1].

saw[3] (so or sô) *n.* a wise saying; proverb: *"A stitch in time saves nine" is a familiar saw.* [OE *sagu.* Related to SAY.]

saw·buck (so′buk′ or sô′-) *n.* **1** a sawhorse. **2** *Slang.* a ten-dollar bill. [< Du. *zaagbok*]

saw·dust (so′dust′ or sô′-) *n.* the particles of wood that result from sawing.

saw·fish (so′fish′ or sô′-) *n.* **-fish** or **-fish·es.** a fish resembling a shark, having a long, flat snout like a saw.

saw·fly (so′flī′ or sô′-) *n.* **-flies.** a kind of insect. The female sawfly has a pair of serrated blades for cutting slits in plants to hold her eggs.

saw·horse (so′hôrs′ or sô′-) *n.* a frame for holding wood that is being sawed. See **bucksaw** for picture.

saw·mill (so′mil′ or sô′-) *n.* **1** a building where machines saw timber into planks, boards, etc. **2** a large machine for such sawing.

sawmill burner a conical furnace for burning sawdust at a sawmill.

sawn (son or sôn) *v.* a pp. of **saw**[1].

saw-off (so′of′ or sô′-) *n. Slang.* **1** in politics: **a** an arrangement between two parties by which one agrees

hat, āge, cãre, fär; let, ēqual, tėrm; it, īce
hot, ōpen, ôrder; oil, out; cup, pu̇t, rüle, ūse
əbove, takən, pencəl, lemən, circəs
ch, child; ng, long; sh, ship
th, thin; TH, then; zh, measure

not to enter a candidate in one riding if the other agrees not to enter a candidate in a different riding. **b** an arrangement by which one party agrees after an election to drop charges of corruption against another if the second party will make a similar agreement. **2** the repayment of a debt; any act of compensation. **3** any arrangement by which one concession is balanced against another. **4** in a game or other competition, a tie.

saw-whet owl (so′hwet′ or -wet′, sô′hwet′ or -wet′) *n.* a small North American owl, dark above and white below, that has a rasping, metallic call.

saw·yer (soi′yər, so′yər, or sô′yər) *n.* a man whose work is sawing timber. [< *saw*[1] + *-yer*, as in *lawyer*]

sax·horn (saks′hôrn′) *n.* a brass musical wind instrument resembling a trumpet, having valves, a loud, full tone, and a wide range. [after Adolphe *Sax*, 1814-1894, the inventor]

sax·i·frage (sak′sə frij or sak′sə frāj′) *n.* any of several low, spreading plants, most of which have rosettes of thick leaves with silvery, toothed edges. Saxifrages are often grown in rock gardens. [ME < LL *saxifraga*, ult. < *saxum* rock + *frangere* break. Doublet of SALSIFY.]

Sax·on (sak′sən) *n.* **1** a Germanic tribe dwelling in N.W. Germany in ancient times. With the Angles and Jutes, the Saxons conquered Britain in the fifth and sixth centuries A.D. **2** a member of this tribe. **3** the language of the Saxons. **4** Anglo-Saxon. **5** a native of Saxony, a region in East Germany. —*adj.* **1** having to do with the early Saxons or their language. **2** Anglo-Saxon. **3** English. **4** of or having to do with Saxony. [< L *Saxo*, pl. *Saxones* < Gmc.]

sax·o·phone (sak′sə fōn′) *n.* a brass musical wind instrument having keys for the fingers and a reed mouthpiece. [after Adolphe *Sax*, 1814-1894, the inventor]

A saxophone

sax·o·phon·ist (sak′sə fōn′ist) *n.* a saxophone player.

sax·tu·ba (saks′tū′bə or -tü′bə) *n.* a large saxhorn having a deep tone. [< *sax*horn + *tuba*]

say (sā) *v.* **said, say·ing,** *n.* —*v.* **1** speak: *What did you say?* **2** put into words; express; declare: *Say what you think.* **3** recite; repeat: *Say your prayers.* **4** suppose; take as an estimate: *You can learn in, say, ten lessons.* **5** express an opinion: *It is hard to say which dress is prettier.* **6 that is to say,** that is; in other words. **7 to say nothing of,** without mentioning: *Our stay in Hawaii will be expensive, to say nothing of the journey.* —*n.* **1** what a person says or has to say: *I have had my say.* **2** the chance to say something. **3** power; authority: *Who has the say in this matter?* [OE *secgan*] —**say′er,** *n.* —**Syn.** *v.* **1** utter, articulate, enunciate. **2** announce, tell.

say·est (sā′ist) *v. Archaic.* 2nd pers. sing. present tense of **say.** "Thou sayest" means "you say" (sing.).

say·ing (sā′ing) *n.* **1** something said; a statement. **2** a proverb: *"Haste makes waste" is a saying.* **3 go without saying,** be too obvious to need mention. —**Syn.** **1** utterance, declaration, assertion. **2** adage, saw, maxim.

says (sez) *v.* 3rd pers. sing. present tense of **say.**

say-so (sā′sō′) *n. Informal.* **1** an unsupported statement. **2** authority; power.

sayst (sāst) *v. Archaic.* sayest.

sb. substantive.

Sb antimony. (for L *stibium*)

'sblood (zblud) *interj. Archaic.* "God's blood" used as an oath.

sc. **1** scene. **2** science. **3** scilicet.

s.c. small capitals.

Sc 1 scandium. 2 strato-cumulus.

Sc. 1 Scotch. 2 Scottish. 3 Scotland.

S.C. 1 Social Credit. 2 Supreme Court. 3 in the United Nations, Security Council. 4 South Carolina.

scab (skab) *n. v.* **scabbed, scab·bing.** —*n.* 1 the crust that forms over a sore during healing. 2 a skin disease in animals, especially sheep. 3 any of several fungous diseases of plants, usually producing dark, crustlike spots. 4 *Slang.* a workman who will not join a trade union or who takes a striker's place. 5 *Slang.* a rascal; scoundrel. —*v.* 1 become covered with a scab. 2 *Slang.* act or work as a scab. [< Scand.; cf. Danish *skab*]

scab·bard (skab′ərd) *n.* a sheath or case for the blade of a sword, dagger, etc. See **sword** for picture. [ME < AF *escaubers,* pl. < Gmc.]

scab·by (skab′ē) *adj.* **-bi·er, -bi·est.** 1 covered with scabs. 2 consisting of scabs. 3 having scab (def. 2). 4 *Informal.* low; mean. —**scab′bi·ly,** *adv.* —**scab′bi·ness,** *n.*

sca·bies (skā′bēz or skā′bē ēz) *n.* a disease of the skin caused by mites that live as parasites under the skin and cause itching; the itch. [< L *scabies* itch < *scabere* scratch]

sca·bi·o·sa (skā′bē ō′sə) *n.* scabious[2].

sca·bi·ous[1] (skā′bē əs) *adj.* of or like scabies; scabby. [< L *scabiosus* mangy, rough < *scabies.* See SCABIES.]

sca·bi·ous[2] (skā′bē əs) *n.* a plant having long tough stems and dense flowerheads of various colors. [< Med.L *scabiosa,* originally adj., fem. of *scabiosus* itch-curing < L *scabies.* See SCABIES.]

scab·land (skab′land′) *n.* a region stripped of topsoil by floods, characterized by low, rocky hills.

scab rock 1 an area of scabland. 2 the bare rock at the surface of scabland.

sca·brous (skā′brəs) *adj.* 1 rough with very small points or projections. 2 full of difficulties; harsh. 3 hard to treat with decency; indelicate. [< LL *scabrosus* < L *scaber* scaly]

scads (skadz) *n.pl. Slang.* a large quantity. [< Scand.; cf. Norwegian *skadd.* Akin to SHAD.]

scaf·fold (skaf′əld) *n.* 1 a temporary structure for holding workmen and materials during the erection, repair, or decoration of a building. 2 a raised platform on which condemned criminals are executed. 3 a platform, stage, or stand for exhibiting shows, seating spectators, or the like. 4 any raised framework. —*v.* furnish with a scaffold; support with a scaffold. [ME < var. of OF *eschaffault,* from same source as *catafalque*]

scaf·fold·ing (skaf′əl ding) *n.* 1 a scaffold. 2 materials for scaffolds.

scal·a·wag (skal′ə wag′) *n. Informal.* a good-for-nothing person; scamp; rascal. [origin uncertain]

scald[1] (skold or skôld) *v.* 1 burn with or as if with hot liquid or steam. 2 pour boiling liquid over; use boiling liquid on. 3 heat or be heated almost to boiling, but not quite. —*n.* a burn caused by hot liquid or steam. [< dial. OF *escalder* < LL *excaldare* < L *ex-* very + *calidus* hot]

scald[2] (skold, skôld, or skäld) *n.* skald.

scale[1] (skāl) *n. v.* **scaled, scal·ing.** —*n.* 1 one of the thin, flat, hard plates forming the outer covering of some fishes, snakes, and lizards. 2 a thin layer or piece like a scale: *Scales of skin peeled off after she had scarlet fever.* 3 tartar coating that forms on teeth. 4 the oxide coating that forms on the inside of a boiler, kettle, etc. 5 in botany, one of the parts that unite to cover a bud in winter; scale leaf. 6 an insect that has a shieldlike covering under which it hides and feeds.
—*v.* 1 remove scale or scales from. 2 come off in scales: *The paint is scaling off.* 3 remove in thin layers. 4 cover with scale or scales. 5 become coated with scale. [ME < OF *escale* < Gmc.] —**scal′er,** *n.* —**scale′-like′,** *adj.*

scale[2] (skāl) *n. v.* **scaled, scal·ing.** —*n.* 1 the dish or pan of a balance. 2 Usually, **scales,** *pl.* a balance; instrument for weighing. 3 **Scales,** *pl.* Libra, a constellation and sign of the zodiac. 4 **tip the scales, a** have as one's weight. **b** overbalance one for another. 5 **turn the scales,** decide. —*v.* 1 weigh: *He scales 180 pounds.* 2 weigh on or as if on scales; measure; compare. [ME < ON *skál* bowl. Akin to SHALE, SHELL.] —**scal′er,** *n.*

scale[3] (skāl) *n. v.* **scaled, scal·ing.** —*n.* 1 a series of steps or degrees; scheme of graded amounts: *The scale of wages in this factory ranges from three dollars to twelve dollars a day.* 2 a series of marks made along a line at regular distances for use in measuring: *A thermometer has a scale.* 3 an instrument marked in this way, used for measuring, etc. 4 the size of a plan, map, drawing, or model compared with what it represents: *a map drawn to the scale of one inch for each 100 miles.* 5 relative size or extent: *entertain on a large scale.* 6 a system of numbering. The decimal scale counts by tens, as in cents, dimes, dollars. 7 in music, a series of tones ascending or descending in pitch.
—*v.* 1 climb: *They scaled the wall by ladders.* 2 reduce by a certain proportion: *All prices were scaled down 10 per cent.* 3 make according to a scale. [ME < L *scala* ladder, ult. < *scandere* climb] —**scal′er,** *n.*

scale insect any of various small plant-destroying insects, the females of which mostly have the body and eggs covered by a scale or shield formed by a secretion from the body.

Scaling ladders. The large hook grips the top of the wall.

scale leaf one of the leaf parts that unite to cover a bud in winter.

sca·lene (skā lēn′ or skā′lēn) *adj.* 1 of a triangle, having three unequal sides. 2 of a cone, having the axis inclined to the base. [< LL < Gk. *skalēnos* limping, uneven]

scaling ladder a ladder for climbing walls.

scal·lion (skal′yən) *n.* 1 a kind of onion that does not form a large bulb. 2 a shallot. 3 a leek. [ME < AF *scal(o)un* < L (*caepa*) *Ascalonia* (onion) from Ascalon, in Palestine]

scal·lop (skol′əp or skal′əp) *n.* 1 **a** a shellfish resembling a clam. In some species of scallop the large muscle that opens and closes the shell is edible. **b** this muscle, used as food. 2 one of the two parts of the shell. Pilgrims returning from Palestine formerly wore scallops as the sign of their pilgrimage. 3 a small dish or scallop shell in which fish or other food is baked and served. 4 one of a series of curves on an edge of a dress, etc.
—*v.* 1 bake with sauce and bread crumbs in a dish; escallop: *scalloped oysters.* 2 make with a series of curves on: *She scallops the edge of the paper with which she covers shelves.* Also, **scollop.** [ME < OF *escalope* shell < Gmc.]

A scallop (def. 2)

Scallops on cuff

scalp (skalp) *n.* 1 the skin and hair on the top and back of the head. 2 part of this skin and hair cut off as a token of victory. Certain North American Indians used to collect the scalps of their enemies. 3 any token of victory. —*v.* 1 cut or tear the scalp from. 2 buy and sell to make small quick profits. 3 *Informal.* trade in (tickets to theatres, games, etc.). [ME < Scand.; cf. ON *skálpr* sheath]

scal·pel (skal′pəl) *n.* a small, sharp, straight knife used in surgery and dissections. [< L *scalpellum,* dim. of *scalprum* knife < *scalpere* carve]

scalp·er (skal′pər) *n. Informal.* one who scalps, especially one who scalps stocks, tickets, etc.

scal·y (skāl′ē) *adj.* **scal·i·er, scal·i·est.** 1 covered with scales; having scales like a fish. 2 suggesting scales. 3 covered with scale: *This iron pipe is scaly with rust.* 4 having scale insects; infested with scales. 5 *Slang.* mean; shabby; stingy. —**scal′i·ness,** *n.*

scamp (skamp) *n.* 1 a rascal; rogue; worthless person. 2 a mischievous child, especially a boy. —*v.* 1 do (work, etc.) in a hasty, careless manner. 2 be stingy; skimp. [< dial. *scamp* roam, probably < *scamper*]

scam·per (skam′pər) *v.* run quickly: *The mice scampered* *when the cat came.* —*n.* a quick run. [ult. < OF *escamper* run away, ult. < L *ex-* out of + *campus* field]

scan (skan) *v.* **scanned, scan·ning,** *n.* —*v.* **1** look at closely; examine with care: *His mother scanned his face to see if he was telling the truth.* **2** *Informal.* glance at; look over hastily. **3** mark off (lines of verse) into feet. *Example:* Síng a | sóng of | síxpence. **4** read or recite (verse), marking off the lines into feet. **5** be according to the rules for marking off lines of verse into feet. **6** in television, pass over (a scene, picture, etc.) with a rapidly moving electron beam so as to transmit an image made up of lines showing qualities of light and shade. **7** search (an area) with radar. —*n.* the act or fact of scanning. [ME < LL *scandere* scan verses < L *scandere* climb] —**scan′ner,** *n.*

Scand. 1 Scandinavia. **2** Scandinavian.

scan·dal (skan′dəl) *n.* **1** a shameful action, condition, or event that brings disgrace or offends public opinion: *It was a scandal for the city official to take tax money for his own use.* **2** damage to someone's reputation; disgrace. **3** public talk about a person that will hurt his reputation; malicious gossip. **4 be the scandal of,** scandalize. [ME < ONF < L < Gk. *skandalon* trap. Doublet of SLANDER.] —**Syn. 2** discredit, disrepute, dishonor. **3** slander, calumny, defamation.

scan·dal·ize (skan′dəl īz′) *v.* **-ized, -iz·ing.** offend by something wrong or improper; shock.

scan·dal·mon·ger (skan′dəl mung′gər or -mong′gər) *n.* a person who spreads scandal and malicious gossip.

scan·dal·ous (skan′dəl əs) *adj.* **1** disgraceful; shameful; shocking. **2** spreading scandal or slander; slandering. —**scan′dal·ous·ly,** *adv.* —**Syn. 1** disreputable, infamous. **2** slanderous.

Scan·di·na·vi·an (skan′də nā′vē ən or skan′də nāv′yən) *adj.* of or having to do with Scandinavia, its people, or their languages. —*n.* **1** a native or inhabitant of Scandinavia. **2** the languages of Scandinavia and Iceland, both modern and historical.

scan·di·um (skan′dē əm) *n.* a rare metallic chemical element. *Symbol:* Sc; *at.no.* 21; *at.wt.* 44.956. [< NL < L *Scandia* Scandinavia]

scan·sion (skan′shən) *n.* the marking off of lines of verse into feet; scanning. [< L *scansio, -onis* < *scandere* scan]

scant (skant) *adj.* **1** meagre; hardly sufficient: *Her coat was short and scant.* **2** scarcely full; falling short of what is required: *Use a scant cup of butter in the cake. You have a scant hour in which to pack.* **3 scant of,** short of; having not enough: *She was scant of breath.* —*v.* make scant; cut down; limit; stint: *Don't scant the butter if you want a rich cake.* —*adv. Dialect.* scarcely; barely; hardly. [ME < ON *skamt*, neut. adj., short]

scant·ling (skant′ling) *n.* **1** a small beam or piece of timber, often used as an upright piece in the frame of a building. **2** small beams or timbers collectively. [var. of ME *scantillon* < OF *escantillon*, ult. probably < LL *cantus* corner < Gk. *kanthos* corner of the eye]

scant·y (skan′tē) *adj.* **scant·i·er, scant·i·est. 1** not enough: *His scanty clothing did not keep out the cold.* **2** barely enough; meagre: *a scanty harvest.* [< *scant*, adj.] —**scant′i·ly,** *adv.* —**scant′i·ness,** *n.*

Syn. Scanty, sparse, meagre = less than is needed or normal. **Scanty** emphasizes falling short of the amount or measure necessary to satisfy a need or come up to a standard: *The scanty rainfall is causing a water shortage.* **Sparse** emphasizes a thin scattering of what there is, particularly of numbers or units: *He carefully combs his sparse hair.* **Meagre** emphasizes thinness, a lack of something necessary for fullness, completeness, richness, body, strength, etc.: *His meagre soil produces meagre crops.*

scape¹ (skāp) *n. v.* **scaped, scap·ing.** *Archaic.* 'scape.

scape² (skāp) *n.* **1** in botany, a leafless flower stalk rising from the ground, such as that of the dandelion. **2** something like a stalk, such as the shaft of a feather or the shaft of a column. [< L *scapus* stalk; cf. dial. Gk. *skapos* branch]

'scape (skāp) *n. v.* **'scaped, 'scap·ing.** *Archaic.* escape. [var. of *escape*]

scape·goat (skāp′gōt′) *n.* **1** a person or thing made to bear the blame for the mistakes or sins of others. **2** in the Bible, a goat on which the sins of the people were laid by the ancient Jewish high priests on the Day of Atonement. The goat was then driven into the wilderness. Leviticus 16:5-22. [< *scape*, var. of *escape* + *goat*]

hat, āge, cãre, fär; let, ēqual, tėrm; it, īce
hot, ōpen, ôrder; oil, out; cup, pu̇t, rüle, ūse
əbove, takən, pencəl, lemən, circəs
ch, child; ng, long; sh, ship
th, thin; ᴛʜ, then; zh, measure

scape·grace (skāp′grās′) *n.* a reckless, good-for-nothing person; scamp.

s.caps small capitals.

scap·u·la (skap′yu̇ lə) *n.* **-lae** (-lē′ or -lī′) or **-las.** a shoulder blade. See **skeleton** for diagram. [< LL]

scap·u·lar (skap′yu̇ lər) *adj.* of the shoulder or shoulder blade. —*n.* **1** in the Roman Catholic Church, a loose, sleeveless garment hanging from the shoulders, worn by certain religious orders. **2** two small pieces of woollen cloth or a badge or medal attached to a circular string worn round the neck by Roman Catholics as part of a religious devotion. **3** a bird's feather growing where the wing joins the body, or near there. [ME < LL, ult. < L *scapulae* shoulders]

scar¹ (skär) *n. v.* **scarred, scar·ring.** —*n.* **1** the mark left by a healed cut, wound, burn, or sore. **2** any mark like this. A fallen leaf leaves a scar where it joined the stem. —*v.* **1** mark with a scar: *He scarred the door with a hammer.* **2** form a scar; heal. [ME < OF *escare* < L < Gk. *eschara* scab, hearth] —**scar′less,** *adj.*

scar² (skär) *n.* **1** a steep, rocky place on the side of a mountain; precipice; cliff. **2** a low rock in the sea. Also, **scaur.** [ME < ON *sker* reef]

scar·ab (skar′əb) *n.* **1** a beetle, especially the sacred beetle of the ancient Egyptians. **2** an image of this beetle. Scarabs were much used in ancient Egypt as charms or ornaments. [< MF < L *scarabaeus* < Gk.]

A scarab (def. 2): A, side; B, top.

scar·a·bae·us (skar′ə bē′əs) *n.* **-bae·us·es** or **-bae·i** (-bē′ ī). scarab.

scar·a·mouch (skar′ə mouch′ or skar′ə müsh′) *n.* **1** a braggart. **2** a rascal. [< F < Ital. *scaramuccia* skirmish. Akin to SKIRMISH.]

scarce (skãrs) *adj.* **scarc·er, scarc·est,** *adv.* —*adj.* **1** hard to get; rare: *Good cooks are scarce.* **2 make oneself scarce,** *Informal.* **a** go away. **b** stay away. **3 scarce as hen's teeth,** *Informal.* very scarce. —*adv.* scarcely. [ME < ONF *escars* < VL *excarpsus*, ult. < L *ex-* out + *carpere* pluck] —**scarce′ness,** *n.* —**Syn.** *adj.* **1** See **rare.**

scarce·ly (skãrs′lē) *adv.* **1** only just; barely: *We could scarcely see through the thick fog.* **2** not quite: *scarcely old enough for school.* **3** decidedly not: *He can scarcely have said that.* **4** very probably not: *I will scarcely pay that much.* —**Syn. 1** See **hardly.**

☛ **scarcely.** People sometimes fall into a concealed double negative when using *scarcely.* In formal and informal English a sentence like *For a while we couldn't scarcely see a thing* should read *For a while we could scarcely see a thing.*

scar·ci·ty (skãr′sə tē) *n.* **-ties.** too small a supply; lack; rarity.

scare (skãr) *v.* **scared, scar·ing,** *n.* —*v.* **1** frighten. **2** frighten (away); drive off: *The watchdog scared away the robbers by barking.* **3 scare up,** *Informal.* get; raise. —*n.* **1** a fright. **2** a frightened condition. [ME < ON *skirra* < *skjarr* timid] —**Syn.** *v.* **1** terrify, alarm. See **frighten.**

scare·crow (skãr′krō′) *n.* **1** a figure of a man dressed in old clothes, set in a field to frighten birds away from crops. **2** a person dressed in ragged clothes. **3** anything that fools people into being frightened. **4** a person who is thin and gaunt.

scare·mon·ger (skãr′mung′gər) *n.* one who spreads unfounded rumors; alarmist.

scarf¹ (skärf) *n.* **scarfs** or **scarves. 1** a long, broad strip of silk, wool, etc. worn about the neck, shoulders, head, or waist. **2** a necktie with hanging ends. **3** a long strip of cloth, etc. used as a cover for a bureau, table, piano, etc. **4** a sash worn across the chest to indicate membership in some ceremonial order. [probably < dial. OF *escarpe* < Gmc.]

scarf[2] (skärf) *n.* **scarfs** or **scarves,** *v.* —*n.* **1** the joint in which the ends of beams are cut so that they lap over and join firmly. **2** an end cut in this way. **3** a cut made in the body of a whale. —*v.* **1** join by a scarf. **2** remove the skin and blubber from a whale. [ME < Scand.; cf. Swedish *skarv*]

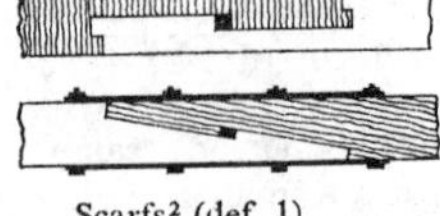
Scarfs[2] (def. 1)

scarf·pin (skärf′pin′) *n.* an ornamental pin worn in a scarf or necktie.

scarf·skin (skärf′skin′) *n.* the outer layer of skin; epidermis.

scar·i·fi·ca·tion (skar′ə fə kā′shən) *n.* **1** a scarifying. **2** a scratch or scratches.

scar·i·fy (skar′ə fī′) *v.* **-fied, -fy·ing. 1** make scratches or cuts in the surface of (the skin, etc.). **2** criticize severely; hurt the feelings of. **3** loosen (soil) without turning it over. [< LL < L *scarifare* < Gk. *skariphasthai* scratch < *skariphos* stylus] —**scar′i·fi′er,** *n.*

scar·la·ti·na (skär′lə tē′nə) *n.* **1** scarlet fever. **2** a mild form of scarlet fever. [< NL < Ital. *scarlattina,* fem. of *scarlattino,* dim. of *scarlatto* scarlet]

scar·let (skär′lit) *n.* **1** a very bright red, much lighter than crimson. **2** cloth or clothing having this color: *The Mounties look impressive in their scarlets.* —*adj.* very bright red. [ME < OF *escarlate,* ? ult. < Persian *saqirlat* rich cloth]

scarlet fever a contagious disease characterized by a scarlet rash, sore throat, and fever.

scarlet runner a tall bean vine, originating in tropical America, that has showy, scarlet flowers and long pods with large, black, edible seeds.

scarlet sage salvia.

scarlet tanager the common tanager of North America. The male has black wings and tail and a scarlet body.

scarp (skärp) *n.* **1** a steep slope. **2** the inner slope or side of a ditch surrounding a fortification. —*v.* make into a steep slope; slope steeply. [< Ital. *scarpa* < Gmc.]

scarves (skärvz) *n.* a pl. of **scarf**[1] and of **scarf**[2].

scar·y (skăr′ē) *adj.* **scar·i·er, scar·i·est.** *Informal.* **1** causing fright or alarm. **2** easily frightened.

scat (skat) *interj. v.* **scat·ted, scat·ting.** *Informal.* —*interj.* an impatient exclamation used especially to drive away an animal. —*v.* beat it; get away quickly. [< *scatter*]

scathe (skāᴛʜ) *v.* **scathed, scath·ing,** *n.* —*v.* **1** blast or sear with invective; wither with satire. **2** injure or destroy by fire, lightning, etc.; scar; scorch. **3** *Archaic.* injure; damage. —*n.* **1** hurt; harm. **2** *Archaic.* a matter for sorrow or regret. **3** *Obsolete.* an injury. [ME < ON *skathi* injury]

scathe·less (skāᴛʜ′lis) *adj.* without harm; unhurt.

scath·ing (skāᴛʜ′ing) *adj.* extremely severe. —**scath′ing·ly,** *adv.*

sca·tol·o·gy (skə tol′ə jē) *n.* **1** the study of excrement, used in paleontology, for medical diagnosis, etc. **2** abnormal interest in excrement, excretory functions, etc. **3** obscene literature. [< Gk. *skōr, skatos* excrement + E *-logy*]

scat·ter (skat′ər) *v.* **1** throw here and there; sprinkle: *Scatter ashes on the icy sidewalk.* **2** separate and drive off in different directions: *The police scattered the mob.* **3** separate and go in different directions: *The hens scattered.* **4** in physics, throw back or deflect (rays of light, radio-active particles, etc.) in all directions. —*n.* **1** the act or fact of scattering. **2** something that is scattered. [ME; probably var. of SHATTER] —**scat′ter·er,** *n.*
Syn. *v.* **1** strew, sow. **2 Scatter, dispel, disperse** = separate and drive away. **Scatter** = separate and drive off in different directions a group or mass of people or objects: *The wind scattered my papers.* **Dispel** applies only to things that cannot be touched, such as clouds and feelings, and means "drive away as if by scattering in the air": *The wind dispelled the fog.* **Disperse** = scatter, but is more formal and may suggest even spreading in every direction: *Storms dispersed the convoy.*

scat·ter·brain (skat′ər brān′) *n.* a thoughtless, heedless person.

scat·ter·brained (skat′ər brānd′) *adj.* heedless; thoughtless; not able to think steadily.

scat·ter·ing (skat′ər ing) *adj.* widely separated; occurring here and there. —*n.* a small amount or number scattered or interspersed.

scatter rug a small rug.

scaup duck (skop or skôp) any of several broad-billed wild ducks related to the canvasback; widgeon. [*scaup,* var. of dial. *scalp,* a bank providing a bed for shellfish]

scaur (skôr) *n.* scar[2]. [var. of *scar*[2]]

scav·enge (skav′ənj) *v.* **-enged, -eng·ing. 1 a** clean streets and waterways by collecting garbage, rubbish, etc. **b** pick over, feed on, use or sell garbage, rubbish, etc. **2** expel exhaust gas from the cylinder of an internal combustion engine. **3** chemically remove impurities from molten metal. [back formation < *scavenger*]

scav·en·ger (skav′ən jər) *n.* **1** an animal that feeds on decaying matter: *Vultures are scavengers.* **2** a person who cleans streets, taking away dirt and rubbish. **3** a person who searches garbage dumps for junk that he can sell. [alteration of *scavager,* literally, inspector < *scavage* toll < OF *scawager* < *escauwer* inspect < Flemish *scauwen*]

sce·nar·i·o (si năr′ē ō′ or si nä′rē ō′) *n.* **-nar·i·os. 1** an outline of a motion picture, giving the main facts about the scenes, persons, and acting. **2** an outline of any play, opera, etc. [< Ital. *scenario,* ult. < L *scena* scene. See SCENE.]

sce·nar·ist (si năr′ist or si nä′rist) *n.* a person who writes scenarios.

scene (sēn) *n.* **1 a** the time, place, circumstances, etc. of a play or story: *The scene of the novel is laid in Quebec City in the year 1759.* **b** the place where anything is carried on or takes place: *the scene of an accident, the scene of my childhood.* **2** the painted screens, hangings, etc. used on a stage to represent places: *The scene represents a city street.* **3** a part of an act of a play: *The king comes to the castle in Act I, Scene 2.* **4** a particular incident of a play: *the trial scene in "The Merchant of Venice."* **5** an action, incident, situation, etc. occurring in reality or represented in literature or art: *He has painted a series of pictures called "Scenes of My Boyhood."* **6** a view; picture: *The white sailboats in the blue water made a pretty scene.* **7** a show of strong feeling in front of others; exhibition; display: *The child kicked and screamed and made such a scene that his mother was ashamed of him.* **8 behind the scenes, a** out of sight of the audience. **b** privately; secretly, not publicly. **9 make the scene,** *Slang.* appear at a place. [< F *scène* < L < Gk. *skēnē,* originally, tent, where actors changed costumes] —**Syn. 6** See **view.**

scen·er·y (sēn′ər ē or sēn′rē) *n.* **-er·ies. 1** in a theatre, the painted hangings, fittings, etc. used to represent places. **2** the general appearance of a place: *mountain scenery.*

sce·nic (sē′nik or sen′ik) *adj.* **1** of or having to do with natural scenery; having much fine scenery: *The scenic splendors of Lake Louise are famous.* **2** belonging to the stage of a theatre; of or having to do with stage effects: *The production of the musical comedy was a scenic triumph.* **3** in art, representing an action, incident, situation, etc.

scenic dome a transparent dome at the top of a railway car, designed for better viewing of the passing scenery.

sce·nog·ra·phy (sē nog′rə fē) *n.* **1** the representing of objects according to the rules of perspective. **2** scene painting.

scent (sent) *n.* **1** smell: *The scent of roses filled the air.* **2** the sense of smell: *Bloodhounds have a keen scent.* **3** a smell left in passing: *The dogs followed the fox by its scent.* **4** perfume. **5** a means by which a thing or a person can be traced: *The police are on the scent of the thieves.* [< v.]
—*v.* **1** smell: *The dog scented a rabbit, and ran off after it.* **2** hunt by using the sense of smell: *The dog scented about till he found the trail.* **3** perfume. **4** fill with odor. **5** have

a suspicion of; be aware of. [ME < OF *sentir* smell < L *sentire* feel]

scent·less (sent′lis) *adj.* having no smell.

scep·ter (sep′tər) *n. v.* sceptre.

scep·tered (sep′tərd) *adj.* sceptred.

scep·tic or **skep·tic** (skep′tik) *n.* **1** a person who questions the truth of theories or apparent facts; doubter. **2** a person who doubts or questions the possibility or certainty of our knowledge of anything. **3** a person who doubts the truth of religious doctrines. —*adj.* doubting; sceptical. [< L < Gk. *skeptikos* reflective < *skeptesthai* reflect] —**Syn.** *n.* **3** unbeliever, disbeliever, agnostic.

scep·ti·cal or **skep·ti·cal** (skep′tə kəl) *adj.* **1** of or like a sceptic; inclined to doubt; not believing easily. **2** questioning the truth of theories or apparent facts. —**Syn. 1** doubting, incredulous, disbelieving, distrustful. —**scep·ti·cal·ly,** *adv.*

scep·ti·cism or **skep·ti·cism** (skep′tə siz′əm) *n.* **1** a sceptical attitude; doubt; unbelief. **2** doubt or unbelief with regard to religion. **3** the doctrine that nothing can be proved absolutely.

scep·tre or **scep·ter** (sep′tər) *n. v.* **-tred** or **-tered, -tring** or **-ter·ing.** —*n.* **1** the rod or staff carried by a ruler as a symbol of royal power or authority. **2** royal or imperial power or authority. —*v.* furnish with a sceptre. [ME < OF < L < Gk. *skēptron* staff]

scep·tred or **scep·tered** (sep′tərd) *adj.* **1** furnished with or bearing a sceptre. **2** invested with regal authority; regal.

sch. school.

sched·ule (skej′ül or shej′ül) *n. v.* **-uled, -ul·ing.** —*n.* **1** a written or printed statement of details; list. A railway timetable is a schedule of the coming and going of trains. **2** a listing of the games to be played by the teams in the league. —*v.* **1** make a schedule of; enter in a schedule. **2** *Informal.* plan or arrange (something) for a definite future date: *schedule the convention for the fall.* [ME < OF < LL *schedula,* dim. of L *scheda, schida* sheet of papyrus < Gk. *schidē* split piece of wood]

Sche·her·a·za·de (shə her′ə zä′də or shə hēr′ə zä′də) *n.* in the *Arabian Nights,* the narrator of the tales, a young bride of the murderous Sultan, who saves her own life by keeping the Sultan interested in her stories.

sche·ma (skē′mə) *n.* **-ma·ta** (-mə tə). **1** an outline, synopsis, plan, or scheme. **2** in Kantian philosophy, the general idea or concept of things that are common to all members of a class. [< L < Gk. *schēma, -atos* figure, appearance]

sche·mat·ic (skē mat′ik) *adj.* having to do with or having the nature of a diagram, plan, or scheme; diagrammatic. —**sche·mat′i·cal·ly,** *adv.*

scheme (skēm) *n. v.* **schemed, schem·ing.** —*n.* **1** a program of action; plan: *He has a scheme for extracting gold from sea water.* **2** a plot: *a scheme to cheat the government.* **3** a system of connected things, parts, thoughts, etc.: *The color scheme of the room is blue and gold.* **4** a diagram; outline; table. —*v.* plan; plot: *Those men were scheming to bring the jewels into the country without paying duty.* [< L < Gk. *schēma, -atos* figure, appearance] —**schem′er,** *n.* —**Syn.** *n.* **1** design, project. -*v.* See **plot.**

schem·ing (skēm′ing) *adj.* making tricky schemes; crafty. —**schem′ing·ly,** *adv.* —**Syn.** plotting, intriguing, designing, wily.

scher·zan·do (sker tsän′dō) in music: —*adj.* playful; sportive. —*adv.* playfully; sportively. —*n.* a playful movement or passage; composition to be played or sung in this manner. [< Ital. *scherzando* < *scherzare* to play, sport < *scherzo.* See SCHERZO.]

scher·zo (sker′tsō) *n.* **-zos, -zi** (-tsē). in music, a light or playful part of a sonata, concerto, or symphony. [< Ital. < G *Scherz* joke]

Schick test (shik) a test to determine susceptibility to or immunity from diphtheria, made by injecting a dilute diphtheria toxin under the skin. [after Dr. Béla *Schick* of Vienna (born 1877)]

schil·ling (shil′ing) *n.* **1** a unit of money in Austria. See table at **money. 2** a coin or note worth one schilling. [< G]

hat, āge, cãre, fär; let, ēqual, tėrm; it, īce
hot, ōpen, ôrder; oil, out; cup, pu̇t, rüle, ūse
əbove, takən, pencəl, lemən, circəs
ch, child; ng, long; sh, ship
th, thin; ᴛʜ, then; zh, measure

schip·per·ke (skip′ər kē′) *n.* **1** a Belgian breed of small sturdy, black watchdog having erect ears and no tail. **2** a dog of this breed. [< Du. *schipperke,* dim. of *schipper* skipper, since originally used on boats as a watchdog]

schism (siz′əm, shiz′əm, or skiz′əm) *n.* **1** a division into opposing groups. **2** a discord or breach between persons or things. **3 a** the division, either of the whole church or of some portion of it, into separate and hostile organizations, on account of some difference of opinion over matters of faith or discipline. **b** the offence of causing or trying to cause such a schism. **c** a sect or group formed by such a schism. [ME < OF < LL < Gk. *schisma* < *schizein* split]

schis·mat·ic (siz mat′ik or shiz mat′ik) *adj.* **1** causing or likely to cause schism. **2** inclined toward, or guilty of, schism. —*n.* a person who tries to cause a schism or takes part in a schism.

schis·mat·i·cal (siz mat′ə kəl or shiz mat′ə kəl) *adj.* schismatic.

schist (shist) *n.* a crystalline metamorphic rock that splits easily into layers. [< F < L < Gk. *schistos* cleft < *schizein* split]

schist·ose (shis′tōs) *adj.* of or like schist; having the structure of schist.

schiz·o (skit′sō or skiz′ō) *n.* **-os.** *Slang.* a schizophrenic.

schizo- *combining form.* divided; split: *schizophrenia = a split personality.* [< Gk. *schizein* split]

schiz·o·carp (skiz′ō kärp′) *n.* in botany, any dry fruit that divides, when ripe, into two or more one-seeded seed vessels that do not split open. [< *schizo-* + Gk. *karpos* fruit]

schiz·oid (skit′soid or skiz′oid) *adj.* of, like, or having schizophrenia.

schiz·o·phre·ni·a (skit′sə frē′nē ə, skiz′ə frē′nē ə, or skiz′ə frēn′yə) *n.* a mental disorder characterized by dissociation from reality and deterioration of personality. [< NL < Gk. *schizein* split + *phrēn* mind]

schiz·o·phren·ic (skit′sə fren′ik or skiz′ə-) *adj.* of, having to do with, or affected by schizophrenia. —*n.* a person having schizophrenia.

schle·miel or **schle·mihl** (shlə mēl′) *n. Slang.* a gullible, inept person; a bungler, a fool. [< Yiddish < Hebrew *Shelumiel*; cf. Numbers 7:36]

schmaltz or **schmalz** (shmolts) *n. Slang.* overly sweet sentimentalism, especially in the arts. [< G *Schmaltz* melted fat]

schmaltz·y or **schmalz·y** (shmolt′sē) *adj. Slang.* of or having to do with schmaltz; overly sentimental.

schmo or **schmoe** (shmō) *n. Slang.* a foolish or unsophisticated person; jerk. Also, **shmo.** [< Yiddish]

schnapps or **schnaps** (shnäps) *n.* **1** Hollands. **2** any spirituous liquor. [< G]

schnau·zer (shnou′zər) *n.* **1** a breed of German wirehaired terrier having small ears and a hairy face. **2** a dog of this breed. [< G *Schnauzer* < *Schnauze* snout]

schnit·zel (shnit′səl) *n.* a breaded and seasoned veal cutlet. [< G]

schnook (shnu̇k) *n. Slang.* a dull or stupid person. [origin unknown]

schnor·kle or **schnor·kel** (shnôr′kəl) *n.* snorkel.

schol·ar (skol′ər) *n.* **1** a learned person; a person having much knowledge. **2** a pupil at school; learner. **3** a student who is given money by some institution to help him continue his studies: *a Rhodes scholar.* [ME < AF < LL *scholaris* < L *schola* school[1]. See SCHOOL[1].] —**Syn. 1** savant, sage. **2** See **student.**

schol·ar·ly (skol′ər lē) *adj.* **1** of a scholar; like that of a scholar: *scholarly habits.* **2** fit for a scholar. **3** having much knowledge; learned. **4** fond of learning; studious. **5** thorough and orderly in methods of study: *a scholarly* *book.* —*adv.* in a scholarly manner. —**schol′ar·li·ness,** *n.*

schol·ar·ship (skol′ər ship′) *n.* **1** the possession of knowledge gained by study; quality of learning and knowledge: *The painstakingly thorough treatment of events showed the excellence of the historian's scholarship.* **2** a grant of money to help a student continue his studies. **3** a fund to provide this money.

scho·las·tic (skə las′tik) *adj.* **1** of schools, scholars, or education; academic: *scholastic achievements or methods; scholastic life.* **2** of or like scholasticism. —*n.* **1** Often, **Scholastic.** a person who favors scholasticism. **2** in the Middle Ages, a theologian and philosopher. [< L < Gk. *scholastikos,* ult. < *scholē* school[1]]

scho·las·ti·cal·ly (skə las′tik lē) *adv.* in a scholastic way or manner; in scholastic respects.

scho·las·ti·cism (skə las′tə siz′əm) *n.* **1** in the Middle Ages, a system of theological and philosophical teaching based chiefly on the authority of the church fathers and of Aristotle, and characterized by a formal method of discussion. **2** an adherence to the teachings of the schools or to traditional doctrines and methods.

scho·li·ast (skō′lē ast′) *n.* in ancient times, a commentator upon the classics. [< LL < Gk. *scholiastēs*]

scho·li·um (skō′lē əm) *n.* **-li·a** (-lē ə). **1** an explanatory note or comment, especially an annotation upon a passage in the Greek or Latin classics. **2** a note added by way of illustration or amplification. [< Med.L < Gk. *scholion,* dim. of *scholē* discussion]

school[1] (skül) *n.* **1** a place for teaching and learning. **2** instruction in school; education received at school: *Most children start school when they are about five years old.* **3** a regular course of meetings of teachers and pupils for instruction. **4** a session of such a course. **5** those who are taught and their teachers. **6** any place, situation, experience, etc. as a source of instruction or training: *the school of adversity.* **7** a group of people holding the same beliefs or opinions: *the Dutch school of painting, a gentleman of the old school.* **8** a particular department or group in a university. **9** a room, rooms, buildings, or group of buildings in a university, set apart for the use of one department: *a school of dentistry.* **10** a place of training or discipline.
—*v.* **1** teach. **2** train; discipline: *School yourself to control your temper.*
—*adj.* of or having to do with a school or schools. [OE *scōl* < L < Gk. *scholē,* originally, leisure] —**Syn.** *n.* **1** academy.

school[2] (skül) *n.* a large group of the same kind of fish or water animals swimming together. —*v.* swim together in a school. [ME < MDu. *schole* a crowd. Akin to SHOAL[2].]

school age 1 the age at which a child begins to go to school. **2** the years during which going to school is compulsory or customary.

school board a group of people, usually elected, who manage the schools in a designated area; a board of education.

school·book (skül′bůk′) *n.* a book for study in schools.

school·boy (skül′boi′) *n.* a boy attending school.

school·fel·low (skül′fel′ō) *n.* a companion at school.

school·girl (skül′gėrl′) *n.* a girl attending school.

school guard 1 a member of a school patrol. **2** a person whose job is to escort school children across busy streets near schools.

school·house (skül′hous′) *n.* a building used as a school.

school·ing (skül′ing) *n.* **1** instruction in school; education received at school. **2** the cost of instruction.

school·man (skül′mən) *n.* **-men. 1** a man engaged in teaching or in managing a school. **2** Often, **Schoolman.** in the Middle Ages, a teacher in a university; a medieval theologian.

school·mas·ter (skül′mas′tər) *n.* **1** a man who teaches in or manages a school. **2** any person or thing that teaches or disciplines.

school·mate (skül′māt′) *n.* a companion at school.

school·mis·tress (skül′mis′tris) *n.* a woman who teaches in or manages a school.

school patrol a group of older school children who escort younger ones across busy streets.

school·room (skül′rüm′ or -rům′) *n.* a room in which pupils are taught.

school·teach·er (skül′tēch′ər) *n.* a person who teaches in a school.

school trustee an elected member of a school board, or board of education.

school·yard (skül′yärd′) *n.* a piece of ground around or near a school, used for play, games, etc.

school year that part of the year during which school is in session.

schoon·er (skün′ər) *n.* **1** a ship with two or more masts and fore-and-aft sails. **2** a prairie schooner. **3** *Informal.* a large glass for beer. [< *scoon* skim, probably < Scand.]

A schooner with four masts

schoon·er-rigged (skün′ər rigd′) *adj.* having fore-and-aft sails.

schot·tische (shot′ish) *n.* **1** a dance in 2/4 time, resembling the polka. **2** the music for such a dance. [< G *Schottische,* literally, Scottish]

schuss (shůs) *v.* **schussed, schuss·ing,** *n.* in skiing: —*v.* make a run at high speed directly downhill. —*n.* **1** a fast run on a direct course downhill. **2** the course itself. [< G]

schwa (shwo or shwä) *n.* **1** an unstressed vowel sound such as that in the first syllable of *about* and that in the last syllable of *lemon,* represented by the symbol (ə); the neutral vowel. **2** the symbol (ə). [< G < Hebrew *sh'wa*]

sci. 1 science. **2** scientific.

sci·at·ic (sī at′ik) *adj.* **1** of the hip. **2** affecting the sciatic nerves: *sciatic neuralgia.* [< Med.L *sciaticus,* alteration of L *ischiadicus* < Gk. < *ischion* hip joint]

sci·at·i·ca (sī at′ə kə) *n.* pain in a sciatic nerve and its branches; neuralgia of the hips, thighs, and legs. [< Med.L *sciatica,* fem. of *sciaticus.* See SCIATIC.]

sciatic nerve a large nerve along the back part of the thigh and leg.

sci·ence (sī′əns) *n.* **1** the knowledge of facts and laws arranged in an orderly system. **2** a branch of such knowledge. Biology, chemistry, physics, and astronomy are **natural sciences.** Agriculture and engineering are **applied sciences.** Economics and sociology are **social sciences. 3** skill; technique: *A good boxer must have science as well as strength and speed.* [ME < OF < L *scientia* knowledge < *scire* know]

science fiction a type of fiction based on actual or fanciful elements of science.

sci·en·tif·ic (sī′ən tif′ik) *adj.* **1** using the facts and laws of science: *a scientific method, a scientific farmer.* **2** of or having to do with science; used in science: *scientific books, scientific instruments.* [< LL *scientificus* < *scientia* knowledge + *facere* make]

sci·en·tif·i·cal·ly (sī′ən tif′ik lē) *adv.* in a scientific manner; according to the facts and laws of science.

sci·en·tist (sī′ən tist) *n.* a person who is trained in, or is familiar with, science.

scil·i·cet (sil′ə set′) *adv.* to wit; namely. [< L *scilicet* < *scire* know + *licet* it is allowed]

scim·i·tar or **scim·i·ter** (sim′ə tər) *n.* a short, curved sword used by Turks, Persians, and other Oriental peoples. Also, **simitar.** [< Ital. *scimitarra*]

scin·til·la (sin til′ə) *n.* a spark; particle; trace. [< L *scintilla* spark. Doublet of TINSEL.]

scin·til·late (sin′tə lāt′) *v.* **-lat·ed, -lat·ing.** sparkle; flash: *The snow scintillates like diamonds in the sun.* [< L *scintillare* < *scintilla* spark]

scin·til·la·tion (sin′tə lā′shən) *n.* **1** a sparkling; a flashing. **2** a spark; flash.

sci·o·lism (sī′ə liz′əm) *n.* superficial knowledge. [< LL *sciolus* knowing little, ult. < *scire* know]

sci·o·list (sī′ə list) *n.* a person who pretends to have more knowledge than he really has.

sci·on (sī′ən) *n.* **1** a bud or branch cut for grafting or planting. 2 a descendant. Also, **cion.** [ME < OF *cion*, probably ult. < L *secare* to cut]

scis·sion (sizh′ən or sish′ən) *n.* the act of cutting, dividing, or splitting; division; separation. [< MF < LL *scissio, -onis* < *scindere* split]

scis·sor (siz′ər) *v.* cut with scissors.

scis·sors (siz′ərz) *n.pl. or sing.* 1 a tool of instrument for cutting that has two sharp blades so fastened that they will work toward each other. 2 in wrestling, a hold with the legs. [ME < OF *cisoires*, pl., < LL *cisorium*, sing., tool for cutting, ult. < L *caedere* cut; confused with < *scissor* cutter < *scindere* cleave, split]

☛ **scissors.** In the sense of "a cutting instrument," *scissors* is plural: *The scissors aren't sharp.* The word is singular in the sense of "a wrestling hold with the legs": *The wrestler got a scissors about his opponent's body.*

scle·rom·e·ter (sklə rom′ə tər) *n.* an instrument for measuring the hardness of a substance, especially a mineral. [< Gk. *sklēros* hard + E *-meter*]

scle·ro·sis (sklə rō′sis) *n.* **-ses** (-sēz). 1 a hardening of a tissue or part of the body by an increase of connective tissue or the like at the expense of more active tissue. 2 a hardening of a tissue or cell wall of a plant by thickening or the formation of wood. [< Med.L < Gk. *sklērōsis* < *sklēros* hard]

scle·rot·ic (sklə rot′ik) *n.* the hard, white outer membrane of the eye. See **eye** for diagram. —*adj.* 1 of or having to do with the sclerotic. 2 of, with, or having sclerosis. [< NL *scleroticus* < Gk. *sklēros* hard]

scoff (skof) *v.* make fun to show one does not believe something; mock. —*n.* 1 mocking words or acts. 2 something ridiculed or mocked. [ME < Scand.; cf. Danish *skuffe* deceive] —**scoff′er,** *n.* —**scoff′ing·ly,** *adv.*

Syn. *v.* **Scoff, jeer, sneer** = show scorn or contempt for someone or something by mocking or biting words or laughter. **Scoff** emphasizes speaking in an insultingly contemptuous or mocking way about something others respect or believe in: *He scoffs at religion.* **Jeer** implies a louder and coarser or more sarcastic way of making fun and, particularly, suggests mocking laughter: *The mob jeered when the speaker got up to talk.* **Sneer** emphasizes an insultingly contemptuous facial expression or tone of voice, or a slighting and hinting way of speaking: *He sneers at everything sentimental.*

scold (skōld) *v.* 1 find fault with; blame with angry words. 2 find fault; talk angrily. —*n.* a person who scolds, especially a noisy, scolding woman. [ME, probably < ON *skáld* poet, in sense of "lampooner"] —**scold′er,** *n.*

Syn. *v.* 1 **Scold, upbraid, chide** = find fault with someone. **Scold** particularly suggests cross and impatient, often loud and insistent, finding fault or expressing disapproval in angry or abusive words, not always with good reason: *That woman is always scolding the children in our neighborhood.* **Upbraid,** more formal, always suggests a definite fault or offence, and emphasizes angrily and sharply or severely blaming and trying to shame: *He upbraided them for tormenting animals.* **Chide** usually suggests milder words of disapproval, or blame, intended to correct: *He chided her for carelessness.*

scol·lop (skol′əp) *n. v.* scallop.

sconce[1] (skons) *n.* a bracket projecting from a wall, used to hold a candle or other light. [ME < Med.L *sconsa*, ult. < L *abscondere* hide]

sconce[2] (skons) *n. Informal.* 1 the head, especially the top of the head. 2 sense; wit. [? jocular use of *sconce*[1]]

scone (skon or skōn) *n.* 1 a thick, flat cake cooked on a griddle. 2 a similar cake baked in an oven. [probably < MDu. *schoon(brot)* fine (bread)]

A sconce

scoop (sküp) *n.* 1 a tool like a shovel. 2 the part of a dredge, steam shovel, etc. that holds coal, sand, etc. 3 a large ladle. 4 a kitchen utensil used for taking out flour, sugar, etc. 5 the amount taken up at one time by a scoop. 6 the act of taking up. 7 a place or thing hollowed out. 8 *Slang.* **a** the publishing of a piece of news before a rival newspaper does. **b** the piece of news as published. —*v.* 1 take up or out with a scoop, or as a scoop does. 2 hollow out; dig out; make by scooping: *The children scooped holes in the sand.* 3 *Slang.* publish a piece of news before a rival newspaper does. [partly < MDu. *schoepe* bucket, partly < MDu. *schoppe* shovel]

scoop·ful (sküp′fu̇l′) *n.* **-fuls.** enough to fill a scoop.

scoot (sküt) *v. Informal.* 1 go quickly; dart. 2 ride on a scooter. —*n.* 1 *Informal.* the act of scooting. 2 a type of boat having a strong hull and driven by an aircraft propeller and engine at the back, designed for travelling in slob ice, over ice and snow, etc. [probably < Scand.; cf. ON *skióta* shoot. Akin to SHOOT.]

hat, āge, cãre, fär; let, ēqual, tėrm; it, īce
hot, ōpen, ôrder; oil, out; cup, pu̇t, rüle, ūse
əbove, takən, pencəl, lemən, circəs
ch, child; ng, long; sh, ship
th, thin; ᴛʜ, then; zh, measure

scoot·er[1] (sküt′ər) *n.* 1 a child's vehicle consisting of two wheels, one in front of the other, and a footboard between, steered by a handlebar and propelled by pushing against the ground with one foot. 2 a similar vehicle having a seat and run by a motor, resembling a small motorcycle. 3 a sailboat with runners, for use on either water or ice. —*v.* sail or go in or on a scooter. [< *scoot*]

scoot·er[2] (sküt′ər) *n.* scoter.

scope (skōp) *n.* 1 the amount the mind can take in; extent of one's view: *Very hard words are not within the scope of a child's understanding.* 2 space; opportunity: *Football gives scope for courage and quick thinking.* [< Ital. *scopo*, ult. < Gk. *skopos* aim, object] —**Syn.** 1 compass. See **range.**

-scope *combining form.* an instrument for viewing or observing, as in *stethoscope, telescope.* [< NL *-scopium* < Gk. *-skopion* < *skopeein* look at]

sco·pol·a·mine (skō pol′ə mēn′) *n.* a drug used to dilate pupils of eyes, as a depressant, and to produce a partial stupor known as "twilight sleep." *Formula:* $C_{17}H_{21}NO_4$ [< NL *Scopolia*, a genus of plants (named after Giacomo A. *Scopoli*, 1723-1788, an Italian naturalist) + E *amine*]

scor·bu·tic (skôr bū′tik) *adj.* 1 having to do with or of the nature of scurvy. 2 affected with scurvy. [< NL *scorbuticus* < *scorbutus* scurvy < F *scorbut* < Gmc.]

scorch (skôrch) *v.* 1 burn slightly; burn on the outside: *The cake tastes scorched. The maid scorched the shirt in ironing it.* 2 dry up; wither: *grass scorched by the sun.* 3 criticize with burning words. 4 *Informal.* drive or ride very fast. —*n.* a slight burn. [ME; cf. *skorken* < ON *skorpna* dry up] —**Syn.** 1 See **burn.**

scorched earth 1 destruction by government orders of all things useful to an invading army. 2 of or having to do with such destruction.

scorch·er (skôr′chər) *n.* 1 a person or thing that scorches. 2 *Informal.* a very hot day. 3 *Informal.* a person who drives or rides very fast. 4 a scathing criticism.

score (skôr) *n. v.* **scored, scor·ing.** —*n.* 1 in a game, contest, test, etc., the record of points made: *The score was 9 to 2 in our favor.* 2 an amount owed; debt; account: *He paid his score at the inn.* 3 a group or set of twenty; twenty. 4 **scores,** *pl.* a large number: *Scores died in the epidemic.* 5 a written or printed piece of music arranged for different instruments or voices: *the score of a musical comedy.* 6 a cut; scratch; stroke; mark; line: *The slave's back showed scores made by the whip.* 7 the act of making or winning a point; successful stroke, rejoinder, etc. 8 an account; reason; ground: *Don't worry on that score.* 9 **on the score of,** because of; on account of. 10 **pay off** or **settle a score,** get even for an injury or wrong. 11 **the score,** *Informal.* the truth about anything or things in general; the facts: *The new man doesn't know what the score is yet.*
—*v.* 1 **a** in a game, contest, test, etc., make as points. **b** keep a record of (the number of points made in a game, contest, etc.). **c** be counted as in the score. **d** make as an addition to the score; gain; win: *He scored five runs for our team.* 2 keep a record of as an amount owed; mark; set down: *The innkeeper scored on a slate the number of meals each person had.* 3 achieve a success; succeed. 4 **a** in music, arrange (a composition) for different instruments or voices. **b** write out (music) in score. 5 cut; scratch; mark; line: *Mistakes are scored in red ink.* 6 *Informal.* blame or scold severely. [OE < ON *skor* notch] —**score′less,** *adj.* —**scor′er,** *n.*

score·board (skôr′bôrd′) *n.* 1 a board posting the running or result of a game or other sporting event. 2 a record of any contest, event, etc.

score·card (skôr′kärd′) *n.* a card for keeping the score of a game, match, etc. Also, **score card.**

sco·ri·a (skô′rē ə) *n.* **-ri·ae** (-rē ē′ or rē ī′). **1** slag or refuse left from ore after the metal has been melted out. **2** cinderlike lava. [< L < Gk. *skōria* < *skōr* dung]

sco·ri·a·ceous (skô′rē ā′shəs or skō′rē ā′shəs) *adj.* like slag or clinkers; consisting of slag, clinkers, etc.

scorn (skôrn) *v.* **1** look down upon; think of as mean or low; despise: *Honest people scorn sneaks and liars.* **2** reject or refuse as low or wrong: *The judge scorned to take a bribe.*
—*n.* **1** a feeling that a person, animal, or act is mean or low; contempt: *We feel scorn for a traitor.* **2** a person, animal, or thing that is scorned or despised. [ME < OF *escarnir* < Gmc.] —**scorn′er,** *n.*
Syn. *v.* **1** disdain, spurn. —*n.* **1 Scorn, contempt, disdain** = a feeling that a person or thing is mean, low, or worthless. **Scorn,** which expresses the strongest feeling, adds to this basic meaning the idea of feeling disgust mixed with anger, sometimes shown by unkind and bitter laughter: *We feel scorn for a person who avoids his responsibilities.* **Contempt** adds to the basic meaning the idea of disgust mixed with strong disapproval: *We feel contempt for a coward.* **Disdain** adds the idea of feeling oneself above anything mean or low and rejecting it: *We feel disdain for a person who cheats.*

scorn·ful (skôrn′fəl) *adj.* showing contempt; mocking; full of scorn. —**scorn′ful·ly,** *adv.* —**scorn′ful·ness,** *n.*
—Syn. contemptuous, disdainful, derisive.

Scor·pi·o (skôr′pē ō′) *n.* **1** in astronomy, a southern constellation supposed to have the shape of a scorpion. **2** in astrology, the eighth sign of the zodiac. The sun enters Scorpio about October 24. See **zodiac** for diagram. [< L *scorpio* scorpion]

scor·pi·on (skôr′pē ən) *n.* **1** a small animal belonging to the same group as the spider and having a poisonous sting in its tail. **2** a whip or scourge. **3 Scorpion,** Scorpio. [< L *scorpio, -onis,* ult. < Gk. *skorpios*]

scot (skot) *n.* one's share of a payment; tax. [ME < ON *skot.* Related to SHOT.]

Scot (skot) *n.* a person of Scottish birth or descent. [OE *Scottas,* pl., Irishmen, Scotsmen < LL *Scottus* Irishman]

Scot. 1 Scotland. **2** Scottish. **3** Scotch.

scotch (skoch) *v.* **1** wound so as to cripple or make temporarily harmless: *scotch a snake without killing it.* **2** stamp out; stifle; crush: *scotch a rumor.* **3** cut; score; gash. [origin uncertain]

Scotch (skoch) *adj.* **1** Scottish. **2** of or having to do with people of Scottish descent. —*n.* **1** the people of Scotland. **2** people of Scottish descent. **3** a kind of whisky originating in Scotland.

Scotch-I·rish (skoch′ī′rish) *adj.* **1** of or having to do with a part of the population of Ulster descended from Scottish settlers. **2** of both Scottish and Irish descent. —*n.* a person of both Scottish and Irish descent.

Scotch·man (skoch′mən) *n.* **-men** (-mən). Scotsman.

Scotch pine 1 an originally North European pine having spreading branches and short, firm needles. **2** the hard, yellowish wood of this tree, valuable for timber. Also, **Scots pine.**

Scotch tape a transparent, self-sealing, adhesive plastic tape for patching, sealing, etc. [< Trademark]

Scotch terrier 1 a breed of short-legged terrier, having rough, wiry hair and pointed, standing ears. **2** a dog of this breed.

Scotch whisky a whisky distilled from barley malt in Scotland.

sco·ter (skō′tər) *n.* a large sea duck, usually called a coot in North America. Also, **scooter.** [? < dial. *scote,* var. of *scoot*]

scot-free (skot′frē′) *adj.* **1** free from injury, punishment, etc.; unharmed. **2** without having to pay.

Sco·tia (skō′shə) *n. Poetic.* Scotland. [< Med.L]

Scot·land Yard (skot′lənd) in England: **1** the headquarters of the London police, properly called **New Scotland Yard. 2** the London police, especially the department that does detective work. [< the building in which the London police headquarters was formerly located, in Great Scotland Yard]

Scots (skots) *adj.* **1** Scottish. **2** in the older Scottish currency. —*n.pl.* the people of Scotland.

Scots-Gael·ic (skots′gāl′ik or -gal′ik) *n.* the Celtic language of the Scottish Highlanders; Erse.

Scots·man (skots′mən) *n.* **-men** (-mən). a native or inhabitant of Scotland; a Scot.

Scots pine Scotch pine.

Scots·wom·an (skots′wům′ən) *n.* **-wom·en.** a woman who is a native of Scotland.

Scot·ti·cism (skot′ə siz′əm) *n.* a way of speaking peculiar to Scottish English.

Scot·tish (skot′ish) *adj.* of or having to do with Scotland, the division of Great Britain north of England, its people, or their language. —*n.* **1** the people of Scotland. **2** the dialect of English spoken by the people of Scotland.

scoun·drel (skoun′drəl) *n.* a person without honor or good principles; villain; rascal. [? < OF *escondre* hide, abscond < L *ex-* from + *condere* hide]

scoun·drel·ly (skoun′drəl ē) *adj.* **1** having the character of a scoundrel. **2** having to do with or characteristic of a scoundrel.

scour[1] (skour) *v.* **1** clean or polish by vigorous rubbing: *Scour the floor with steel wool.* **2** remove dirt and grease from (anything) by rubbing. **3** make clear by flowing through or over: *The stream had scoured a channel.* **4** clean; cleanse. —*n.* the act of scouring. [prob. < MDu. < OF *escurer,* ult. < L *ex-* completely + *cura* care] —**scour′er,** *n.*

scour[2] (skour) *v.* **1** move quickly over: *Men scoured the country round about for the lost child.* **2** look into every part of; search: *scour one's memory for a forgotten date.* **3** go swiftly in search or pursuit. [ME, probably < OF *escourre* run forth, ult. < L *ex-* out + *currere* run]

scourge (skėrj) *n. v.* **scourged, scourg·ing.** —*n.* **1** a whip. **2** any means of punishment. **3** some thing or person that causes great trouble or misfortune. In former times, an outbreak of disease was called a scourge. —*v.* **1** strike with a whip. **2** whip; punish. **3** trouble very much; afflict. [ME < AF *escorge,* ult. < L *ex-* out + *corrigia* whip]

scour·ings (skour′ingz) *n.pl.* **1** dirt, refuse, material, etc. removed by, or as if by, scouring: *That gang of criminals includes the scourings of two slums.* **2** refuse removed from grain before milling.

scout[1] (skout) *n.* **1** a person sent to find out what the enemy is doing. A scout usually wears a uniform; a spy does not. **2** a warship, airplane, etc. used to find out what the enemy is doing. **3** a person sent out to get information, especially about one's opponents, competitors, etc. **4** a person who looks for promising recruits for a film studio, sports team, etc. **5** the act of scouting. **6** a member of the Boy Scouts. **7** *Slang.* a fellow; person: *He's a good scout.*
—*v.* **1** act as a scout; hunt around to find something: *Go and scout for firewood for the picnic.* **2** observe or examine to get information. [ME < OF *escoute* act of listening, listener < *escouter* listen < L *auscultare*] —**scout′er,** *n.*

scout[2] (skout) *v.* **1** refuse to believe in; reject with scorn: *He scouted the idea of a dog with two tails.* **2** scoff. [< Scand.; cf. ON *skúta* taunt]

scout car 1 a police or military patrol car. **2** a wide-tracked vehicle designed for use on northern muskeg.

scout·er (skout′ər) *n.* an adult who is associated in some way with the Boy Scouts or Wolf Cubs.

scout·ing (skout′ing) *n.* the activities of scouts, especially of the Boy Scouts.

scout·mas·ter (skout′mas′tər) *n.* the man in charge of a troop of Boy Scouts.

scow (skou) *n.* a large, flat-bottom boat, used to carry freight: *The scow was loaded with sand.* [< Du. *schouw*]

A scow

scowl (skoul) *v.* **1** look angry or sullen by lowering the eyebrows; frown. **2** affect by scowling. **3** express with a scowl. —*n.* an angry, sullen look; frown. [ME *skoul;*

akin to Danish *skule* cast down the eyes] **—scowl′er,** *n.*
—Syn. *v.* **1** See **frown.**

scrab·ble (skrab′əl) *v.* **-bled, -bling,** *n.* —*v.* **1** scratch or scrape about with hands, claws, etc.; scramble. **2** struggle or scramble feverishly, desperately, etc.: *scrabble for scraps of food, scrabble for a living.* **3** scrawl; scribble. —*n.* a scraping; scramble. [< Du. *schrabbelen,* frequentative of *schrabben* scratch]

scrag (skrag) *n. v.* **scragged, scrag·ging.** —*n.* **1** a lean, skinny person or animal: *An old, bony horse is a scrag.* **2** a lean, bony part. A scrag of mutton is the neck. **3** *Slang.* the neck. —*v. Slang.* wring the neck of; hang. [< Scand.; cf. dial. Swedish *skragge* old and torn thing]

scrag·gly (skrag′lē) *adj.* **-gli·er, -gli·est.** rough; irregular; ragged.

scrag·gy (skrag′ē) *adj.* **-gi·er, -gi·est. 1** lean; thin. **2** scraggly. **—scrag′gi·ness,** *n.*

scram (skram) *v.* **scrammed, scram·ming.** *Slang.* go at once. [short for *scramble*]

scram·ble (skram′bəl) *v.* **-bled, -bling,** *n.* —*v.* **1** make one's way by climbing, crawling, etc.: *The boys scrambled up the steep, rocky hill.* **2** struggle with others for something: *The boys scrambled to get the football.* **3** collect in a hurry or without method. **4** mix together in a confused way. **5** fry (eggs) with the whites and yolks mixed together. **6** *Slang.* in the Air Force, get aircraft into the air hurriedly, usually to intercept unidentified planes. **7** in telephony, radio, etc., break up or mix (a message or signal) so that it cannot be received and understood without special equipment.
—*n.* **1** a climb or walk over rough ground. **2** a struggle to possess: *the scramble for wealth.* **3** any disorderly struggle or activity. **4** *Slang.* in the Air Force, the act or process of scrambling. [var. of *scrabble*]
—scram′bler, *n.*

scran·nel (skran′əl) *adj.* **1** thin; slight. **2** squeaky. [< Scand.; cf. dial. Norwegian *skran* lean, shrivelled]

scrap[1] (skrap) *n. v.* **scrapped, scrap·ping.** —*n.* **1** a small piece; a little bit; a small part left over: *She gave some scraps of meat to the dog.* **2** a bit of something written or printed: *She read aloud scraps from the letter.* **3** old metal fit only to be melted and made again. **4 scraps,** *pl.* the remains of animal fat left after the oil has been melted out: *He had pork scraps for dinner.*
—*v.* **1** make into scraps; break up. **2** throw aside as useless or worn out. —*adj.* in the form of scraps. [ME < ON *scrap* < *scrapa* scrape]

scrap[2] (skrap) *n. v.* **scrapped, scrap·ping.** *Informal.* fight; quarrel; struggle. [var. of *scrape*] **—scrap′per,** *n.*

scrap·book (skrap′bůk′) *n.* a book in which pictures or clippings are pasted and kept.

scrape (skrāp) *v.* **scraped, scrap·ing,** *n.* —*v.* **1** rub with something sharp or rough; make smooth or clean thus: *Scrape your muddy shoes with this old knife.* **2** remove by rubbing with or against something sharp or rough: *The man scraped some paint off the table when he pushed it through the doorway.* **3** rub with a harsh sound; rub harshly: *Don't scrape your feet on the floor. The branch of the tree scraped against the window.* **4** give a harsh sound; grate. **5** dig: *The child scraped a hole in the sand.* **6** collect by scraping or with difficulty: *John has scraped together enough money for his first year at college.* **7** manage with difficulty: *That family can just scrape along but never asks for charity.* **8** bow with a drawing back of the foot. **9 scrape acquaintance,** take the trouble to get acquainted. **10 scrape through,** just manage to get by: *He barely scraped through the examination.*
—*n.* **1** the act of scraping. **2** a scraped place. **3** a harsh, grating sound: *the scrape of the bow of a violin.* **4** a position hard to get out of; difficulty. **5** a bow with a drawing back of the foot. [ME < ON *skrapa*]

scrap·er (skrāp′ər) *n.* **1** a tool for scraping: *Wipe your shoes on the scraper.* **2** a person who scrapes.

scrap·ing (skrāp′ing) *n.* **1** the act of one that scrapes; the sound produced by this act. **2** that which is scraped off, up, or together.

scrap iron broken or waste pieces of old iron.

scrap·ple (skrap′əl) *n.* scraps of pork boiled with corn meal, made into cakes, sliced, and fried. [< *scrap*[1]]

scrap·py[1] (skrap′ē) *adj.* **-pi·er, -pi·est.** made up of odds and ends; fragmentary; disconnected. [< *scrap*[1]]

hat, āge, cãre, fär; let, ēqual, tėrm; it, īce
hot, ōpen, ôrder; oil, out; cup, pu̇t, rüle, ūse
əbove, takən, pencəl, lemən, circəs
ch, child; ng, long; sh, ship
th, thin; ᴛʜ, then; zh, measure

scrap·py[2] (skrap′ē) *adj.* **-pi·er, -pi·est.** *Informal.* fond of fighting. [< *scrap*[2]] **—scrap′pi·ness,** *n.*

scratch (skrach) *v.* **1** break, mark, or cut slightly with something sharp or rough: *Your feet have scratched the chair.* **2** tear or dig with the nails or claws: *The cat scratched him.* **3** rub or scrape to relieve itching: *He scratched his head.* **4** rub with a harsh noise; rub: *He scratched a match on the wall.* **5** write in a hurry or carelessly. **6** scrape out; strike out; draw a line through. **7** withdraw (a horse, etc.) from a race or contest. **8** gather by effort; scrape.
—*n.* **1** a mark made by scratching. **2** a very slight cut. **3** the sound of scratching: *the scratch of a pen.* **4** the starting place of a race or contest. **5 from scratch,** from nothing. **6 up to scratch,** up to standard; in good condition.
—*adj.* **1** made up from whatever is on hand; pick-up: *a scratch meal, a scratch football team.* **2** done by or dependent on chance: *a scratch shot.* [alteration of earlier *scrat,* influenced by obs. *cratch*; origin uncertain]

scratch hit in baseball, a poorly hit ball that is credited as a base hit.

scratch pad a pad of paper used for hurried writing.

scratch paper paper for hurried notes, first drafts, etc.

scratch·y (skrach′ē) *adj.* **scratch·i·er, scratch·i·est. 1** that scratches, scrapes, or grates. **2** consisting of mere scratches: *A baby's drawings are scratchy.* **—scratch′i·ly,** *adv.* **—scratch′i·ness,** *n.*

scrawl (skrol or skrôl) *v.* write or draw poorly or carelessly. —*n.* **1** poor, careless handwriting. **2** something scrawled, such as a hastily or badly written letter or note. [? < obs. *scrawl* spread the arms, gesticulate (of uncertain origin)] **—scrawl′er,** *n.*

scraw·ny (skro′nē or skrô′nē) *adj.* **-ni·er, -ni·est.** *Informal.* lean; thin; skinny: *Turkeys have scrawny necks.* [< Scand.; cf. dial. Norwegian *skran*]

scream (skrēm) *v.* **1** make a loud, sharp, piercing cry. People scream in fright, in anger, and in sudden pain. **2** utter loudly. **3** laugh loudly. **4** produce a vivid impression or startling effect: *The colors of her pink blouse and orange sweater screamed at each other.*
—*n.* **1** a loud, sharp, piercing cry. **2** a shrill sound like a scream. **3** *Informal.* something or somebody extremely funny. [ME,? < ON *skræma* scare]
Syn. *v.* **1 Scream, shriek** = make a loud, sharp, piercing sound. **Scream** = give out suddenly a loud, high-pitched, piercing cry expressing fear, pain, or almost hysterical anger or joy: *She screamed when she saw the child fall.* **Shriek** suggests a more high-pitched, wild, hair-raising and back-tingling cry, expressing extreme terror, horror, agony, or uncontrolled rage or laughter: *The prisoner shrieked when he was tortured.*

scream·er (skrēm′ər) *n.* **1** one that screams. **2** a long-toed bird of South and Central America, sometimes larger than a turkey. **3** a headline in very large type across the page.

scream·ing (skrēm′ing) *adj.* **1** that screams. **2** evoking screams of laughter: *a screaming farce.* **3** startling: *screaming headlines, screaming colors.*

scream·ing·ly (skrēm′ing lē) *adv.* **1** in a screaming tone. **2** so as to call forth screams.

scree (skrē) *n.* a steep slope of loose, fragmented rock lying below a cliff or bluff. [< ON *skritha* glide]

screech (skrēch) *v. n.* scream; shriek. [ME *scritch,* imitative] **—screech′er,** *n.*

screech owl 1 any of various small owls having hornlike tufts of feathers. **2** any owl that screeches, as distinguished from one that hoots. **3** a barn owl.

screech·y (skrēch′ē) *adj.* **screech·i·er, screech·i·est.** screeching.

screed (skrēd) *n.* **1** a long speech or piece of writing. **2** a strip of plaster (or wood) of the proper thickness, applied to the wall as a guide in plastering. [ME var. of OE *scrēade* shred]

screen (skrēn) *n.* **1** a covered frame that hides, protects, or separates. **2** wire woven together with small openings in between the strands: *We have screens at our windows to keep out flies.* **3** an ornamental partition. **4** anything like a screen: *A screen of trees hides our house from the road.* **5** a surface on which motion pictures, etc. are shown. **6** motion pictures; films. **7** a sieve for sifting sand, gravel, coal, seed, etc. **8** a body of soldiers detached toward the enemy to protect an army. **9** an escort of destroyers, etc. to protect battleships, aircraft carriers, etc., especially against submarine attack. **10** in photo-engraving, a transparent plate with fine lines that cross at right angles, used to produce the minute dots in half-tone.
—*v.* **1** shelter, protect, or hide with, or as with, a screen: *She screened her face from the fire with a fan. The mother tried to screen her guilty son.* **2** show (a motion picture) on a screen. **3** photograph with a motion-picture camera. **4** adapt (a story, etc.) for reproduction as a motion picture. **5** be suitable for reproducing on a motion-picture screen. **6** sift with a screen. **7** examine carefully to test quality, suitability, etc.: *Applicants for this job must be carefully screened.* **8** print with a screen or by the silk-screen process. [ME < OF *escren* < Gmc.]
—**screen′a·ble,** *adj.* —**screen′er,** *n.* —**screen′like′,** *adj.*
—**Syn.** *n.* **1** shield, protection, fender. -*v.* **1** shield.

screen·ing (skrē′ning) *n.* **1** a fine wire mesh for making screens, filters, etc. **2 screenings,** the matter separated out by sifting through a sieve or screen.

screw (skrü) *n.* **1** a kind of nail with a ridge twisted evenly round its length: *Turn the screw to the right to tighten it.* **2** a cylinder with a ridge winding round it. **3** a part into which this cylinder fits and advances. **4** any thing that turns like a screw or looks like one. **5** a turn of a screw; screwing motion. **6** *Informal.* a very stingy person; miser. **7** a propeller that moves a boat. **8** *Slang.* a guard in a prison. **9 have a screw loose,** *Slang.* be crazy or eccentric. **10 put the screws on,** *Informal.* use pressure or force to get something.
—*v.* **1** turn as one turns a screw; twist: *Screw the lid on the jar.* **2** turn like a screw; be fitted for being put together or taken apart by a screw or screws. **3** wind; twist. **4** fasten or tighten with a screw or screws. **5** force, press, or stretch tight by using screws. **6** force to do something; force (prices) down; force (people) to tell or to give up; force people to tell or give up something. **7** gather for an effort: *He finally screwed up enough courage to dive.* **8** wind; twist; contort: *His face was screwed up with fear.* **9 screw up,** *Slang.* make a mess of; do or get all wrong. [ME < OF *escroue* nut, screw (def. 3) < VL *scroba* < L *scrobis* ditch, vulva, influenced by L *scrofa* sow]

Wood screws (def. 1). The blade of the screwdriver fits into the slots in the heads of these screws. With their sharp points and ridges, they cut their way into the wood.

A screw (def. 2). The ridge, or thread, on this screw fits the thread of a nut or other metal part. It is tightened with a wrench or pliers.

screw·ball (skrü′bol′ or -bôl′) *n.* **1** *Slang.* an eccentric person. **2** in baseball, a pitch thrown with a break or spin opposite to that of a curve. —*adj. Slang.* eccentric; erratic.

screw·driv·er (skrü′drīv′ər) *n.* a tool for putting in or taking out screws by turning them.

screw propeller a revolving hub having radiating blades for propelling a steamship, airship, etc.

screw thread the spiral ridge of a screw.

scrib·ble (skrib′əl) *v.* **-bled, -bling,** *n.* —*v.* **1** write or draw carelessly or hastily. **2** make marks that do not mean anything. —*n.* something scribbled. [ME < Med.L *scribillare,* ult. < L *scribere* write]

scrib·bler (skrib′lər) *n.* **1** a person who scribbles. **2** a pad of paper or a book in which to make notes, do rough work, etc. **3** an author of little or no importance.

scribe (skrīb) *n. v.* **scribed, scrib·ing.** —*n.* **1** a person who copies manuscripts. Before printing was invented, there were many scribes. **2** a member of the class of professional interpreters of the Jewish law. **3** a writer; author (often used humorously). **4** a public clerk or secretary.
—*v.* mark or cut with something sharp. [ME < L *scriba* < *scribere* write]

scrib·er (skrīb′ər) *n.* a tool for marking on wood, metal, etc.

scrim (skrim) *n.* a loosely woven cotton or linen material, much used for window curtains. [origin uncertain]

scrim·mage (skrim′ij) *n. v.* **-maged, -mag·ing.** —*n.* **1** a rough fight or struggle. **2** in football, a play that takes place when the two teams are lined up and the ball is snapped back. —*v.* **1** take part in a rough fight or struggle. **2** in football, take part in a scrimmage. [ult. var. of *skirmish*]

scrimp (skrimp) *v.* **1** be sparing of; use too little of. **2** be very economical; stint; skimp: *Many parents have to scrimp to keep their children nicely dressed.* **3** treat stingily or very economically. [origin uncertain]

scrimp·y (skrimp′ē) *adj.* **scrimp·i·er, scrimp·i·est.** too small; too little; scanty; meagre. —**scrimp′i·ly,** *adv.* —**scrimp′i·ness,** *n.*

scrip[1] (skrip) *n.* **1** a certificate, coupon, voucher, etc. establishing the bearer's right to something. **2** *Cdn.* a certificate issued following the Riel Rebellions to Métis as compensation for lands, entitling the holder to 240 acres of land **(land-scrip)** or to a choice between $240 cash **(money-scrip)** and 240 acres of land. **3** a writing [var. of *script*]

scrip[2] (skrip) *n. Archaic.* a small bag. [ME < OF *escrepe* < Gmc.]

script (skript) *n.* **1** written letters, figures, signs, etc.; handwriting: *German script.* **2** in printing, a style of type that looks like handwriting. **3** the manuscript or typewritten copy of a play or of an actor's part, of a radio or television announcer's message, etc. —*v. Informal.* write a script for (a radio or television show, a motion picture, etc.). [< L *scriptum,* originally neut. pp. of *scribere* write]

scrip·to·ri·um (skrip tô′rē əm) *n.* **-ri·ums, -ri·a** (-rē ə). a writing room, especially a room in a monastery, set apart for writing or copying manuscripts. [< Med.L *scriptorium,* ult. < L *scribere* write]

scrip·tur·al or **Scrip·tur·al** (skrip′chər əl) *adj.* of the Scriptures; according to the Scriptures; based on the Scriptures. —**scrip′tur·al·ly,** *adv.*

Scrip·ture (skrip′chər) *n.* **1** the Bible. **2 the Scriptures** or **the Holy Scriptures,** the Bible. **3 scripture,** any sacred writing. [ME < L *scriptura* a writing < *scribere* write]

scrive·ner (skriv′nər) *n. Archaic.* a public writer of letters or documents for others; clerk; notary. [ME < obs. *scrivein* < OF *escrivein,* ult. < L *scribere* write]

scrod (skrod) *n.* a young cod, especially one split for cooking. [< MDu. *schrode* piece cut off]

scrof·u·la (skrof′yů lə) *n.* a form of tuberculosis characterized by the enlargement of the lymphatic glands, especially those in the neck. [< Med.L *scrofula,* sing. < L *scrofulae,* pl. < *scrofa* a sow; ? from fanciful comparison of glandular swellings to little pigs]

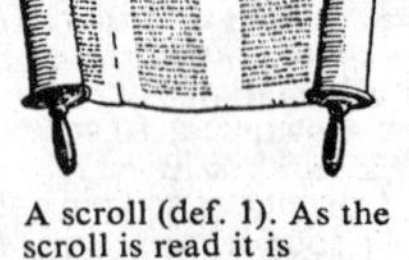

A scroll (def. 1). As the scroll is read it is unrolled from one handle and rolled up on the other.

scrof·u·lous (skrof′yů ləs) *adj.* **1** of or having to do with scrofula. **2** having scrofula.

scroll (skrōl) *n.* **1** a roll of parchment or paper, especially one with writing on it. **2** a list of names, events, etc.; roll; schedule: *be entered in the scrolls of history.* **3** an ornament resembling a partly unrolled sheet of paper, or having a spiral or coiled form. [alteration of *scrow* (influenced by roll), ult. < OF *escroe* scrap < Gmc.]
—**scroll′-like′,** *adj.*

Scrolls (def. 3)

scroll saw a very narrow saw for cutting thin wood in curved or ornamental patterns.

hat, āge, cãre, fär; let, ēqual, tėrm; it, īce
hot, ōpen, ôrder; oil, out; cup, pu̇t, rüle, ūse
əbove, takən, pencəl, lemən, circəs
ch, child; ng, long; sh, ship
th, thin; ᴛʜ, then; zh, measure

scroll·work (skrōl′wėrk′) *n.* **1** decorative work in which scrolls are much used. **2** ornamental work cut out with a scroll saw.

Scrooge (skrüj) *n.* **1** in Dickens' story *A Christmas Carol,* an embittered old miser. **2** any mean or stingy person.

scro·tal (skrō′təl) *adj.* of or having to do with the scrotum.

scro·tum (skrō′təm) *n.* **-ta** (-tə). in anatomy, the pouch that contains the testicles. [< L]

scrounge (skrounj) *v.* **scrounged, scroung·ing.** *Slang.* **1** beg; get by begging; catch: *He was always scrounging cigarettes.* **2** acquire dishonestly; pilfer. [< dial. *scrunge* steal] —**scroung′er,** *n.*

scrub[1] (skrub) *v.* **scrubbed, scrub·bing,** *n.* —*v.* **1** rub hard; wash or clean by rubbing. **2** *Slang.* cancel. —*n.* a scrubbing. [? < MDu. *schrubben*] —**scrub′ber,** *n.*

scrub[2] (skrub) *n.* **1** low, stunted trees or shrubs. **2** any person, animal, or thing below the usual size: *He is a little scrub of a man.* **3** in sports, a player not on the regular team, etc. —*adj.* **1** small; poor; inferior. A scrub ball team is made up of inferior, substitute, or untrained players. **2** of or for players not on the regular team. [ME; var. of *schrobbe,* OE *scrybb* brushwood. See SHRUB[1].]

scrub·by (skrub′ē) *adj.* **-bi·er, -bi·est. 1** low; stunted; small; below the usual size: *scrubby trees.* **2** covered with scrub: *scrubby land.* **3** shabby; mean. —**scrub′bi·ness,** *n.*

scruff (skruf) *n.* the skin at the back of the neck; the back of the neck. [alteration of *scuff,* of the same meaning (of uncertain origin)]

scruf·fy (skruf′ē) *adj.* unkempt; slovenly; shabby.

scrum (skrum) *n. Esp.Brit.* a scrummage; scrimmage.

scrum·mage (skrum′ij) *n. Esp.Brit.* in rugger, a formation in which the forwards of each side bend down and lock together in two or three ranks, each side pushing against the other when the ball is placed in the middle. [var. of *scrimmage*]

scrump·tious (skrump′shəs) *adj. Informal.* elegant; splendid, first-rate: *a scrumptious meal.* [? alteration of *sumptuous*; cf. emphatic force of *scr-* in *scrunch,* etc.]

scrunch (skrunch) *v. n.* crunch; crush; crumple; squeeze. [imitative]

scru·ple (skrü′pəl) *n. v.* **-pled, -pling.** —*n.* **1** a feeling of doubt about what one ought to do: *No scruple ever holds him back from prompt action.* **2** a feeling of uneasiness which keeps a person from doing something that might be morally or ethically wrong: *She has scruples about playing cards for money.* **3** a weight of 20 grains. Three scruples make one dram. **4** a very small amount. —*v.* **1** hesitate or be unwilling (to do something): *A dishonest man does not scruple to deceive others.* **2** have scruples. [< MF < L *scrupulus* a feeling of uneasiness, originally dim. of *scrupus* sharp stone; figuratively, uneasiness, anxiety]

scru·pu·los·i·ty (skrü′pyu̇ los′ə tē) *n.* **-ties. 1** the fact or state of being scrupulous; strict regard for what is right; scrupulous care. **2** an instance of this.

scru·pu·lous (skrü′pyu̇ ləs) *adj.* **1** having or showing a strict regard for what is right. **2** attending thoroughly to details; very careful: *A soldier must pay scrupulous attention to orders.* —**scru′pu·lous·ly,** *adv.* —**scru′pu·lous·ness,** *n.*

Syn. 1 conscientious. **2 Scrupulous, punctilious** = very careful and exact. Scrupulous emphasizes attending thoroughly to details and being very careful to follow strictly and exactly what one knows is right or true: *She takes scrupulous care of the children's health.* **Punctilious,** a formal word, emphasizes paying special and scrupulously exact, often excessive, attention to fine points of laws, rules, and requirements for conduct, behavior, or performance of duties: *He is punctilious in returning borrowed books.*

scru·ti·neer (skrü′tə nēr′) *n.* a person whose duty is to examine or scrutinize votes during an election. [< *scrutin(y)* + *-eer*]

scru·ti·nize (skrü′tə nīz′) *v.* **-nized, -niz·ing.** examine closely; inspect carefully: *The jeweller scrutinized the diamond for flaws.* —**scru′ti·niz′er,** *n.* —**scru′ti·niz′ing·ly,** *adv.*

scru·ti·ny (skrü′tə nē) *n.* **-nies. 1** a close examination; careful inspection: *His work looks all right, but it will not bear scrutiny.* **2** a looking searchingly at something; searching gaze. **3** an official examination of the votes cast at an election. [ME < LL *scrutinium* < L *scrutari* ransack]

scu·ba (skü′bə) *n.* portable underwater breathing equipment, used by some skindivers. See **skindiver** for picture. [< *s*elf-*c*ontained *u*nderwater *b*reathing *a*pparatus]

scud (skud) *v.* **scud·ded, scud·ding,** *n.* —*v.* run or move swiftly: *Clouds scudded across the sky driven by the high wind.* —*n.* **1** a scudding. **2** clouds or spray driven by the wind. [? var. of *scut* a short tail, especially of a rabbit or deer; first applied to a running of a hare; cf. Norwegian *skudda* push]

scuff (skuf) *v.* **1** walk without lifting the feet; shuffle. **2** wear or injure the surface of by hard use: *scuff one's shoes.* —*n.* **1 a** the act of scuffing. **b** the noise made by scuffing. **2** a slipper having a toe piece but no covering for the heel. [var. of *scuffle*]

scuf·fle (skuf′əl) *v.* **-fled, -fling,** *n.* —*v.* **1** struggle or fight in a rough, confused manner. **2** shuffle. —*n.* **1** a confused, rough struggle or fight. **2** a shuffling. [< Scand.; cf. Swedish *skuffa* push] —**scuf′fler,** *n.*
—**Syn.** *n.* **1** tussle, scrimmage.

scull (skul) *n.* **1** an oar worked with a side twist over the end of a boat to make it go. **2** one of a pair of oars used, one on each side, by a single rower. **3** the act of propelling by sculls. **4** a light racing boat for one or more rowers. —*v.* propel (a boat), by a scull or by sculls. [ME; origin unknown]

A man sculling

scull·er (skul′ər) *n.* **1** a person who sculls. **2** a boat propelled by sculling.

scul·ler·y (skul′ər ē or skul′rē) *n.* **-ler·ies.** *Esp.Brit.* a small room where the dirty, rough work of a kitchen is done. [ME < OF *escuelerie,* ult. < L *scutella,* dim. of *scutra* platter]

scul·lion (skul′yən) *n. Archaic.* **1** a servant who does the dirty, rough work in a kitchen. **2** a low, contemptible person. [ME < OF *escouillon* swab, cloth < *escouve* broom < L *scopa*]

scul·pin (skul′pin) *n.* any of several kinds of spiny, scale-less salt-water fishes, having a large head and a broad mouth. [? alteration of *scorpene* < L *scorpaena* < Gk. *skorpaina,* kind of fish < *skorpios* scorpion]

sculpt (skulpt) *v. Informal.* make a sculpture or sculptures.

sculp·tor (skulp′tər) *n.* a person who carves or models figures; an artist in sculpture. [< L *sculptor,* late var. of *scalptor* < *scalpere* carve]

sculp·tress (skulp′tris) *n.* a woman sculptor.

sculp·tur·al (skulp′chər əl) *adj.* of or having to do with sculpture; like sculpture. —**sculp′tur·al·ly,** *adv.*

sculp·ture (skulp′chər) *n. v.* **-tured, -tur·ing.** —*n.* **1** the art of carving or modelling figures. Sculpture includes carving statues from blocks of marble or wood, casting in bronze, working in metal, and modelling in clay, soap, plastics, or wax. **2** sculptured work; a piece of such work. —*v.* **1** carve or model. **2** cover or ornament with sculpture. [ME < L *sculptura,* late var. of *scalptura* < *scalpere* carve]

sculp·tured (skulp′chərd) *adj.* **1** carved or moulded in sculpture. **2** covered or ornamented with sculpture.

scum (skum) *n. v.* **scummed, scum·ming.** —*n.* **1** a surface film formed when certain liquids are boiled: *The scum had to be skimmed from the top of the boiling maple syrup.* **2** the layer of algae or other matter that forms on the top of still water. **3** low, worthless people: *The saloon was filled with the scum of the town.* —*v.* **1** form scum; become covered with scum. **2** skim. [ME < MDu. *schuum*]

scum·my (skum′ē) *adj.* **-mi·er, -mi·est. 1** consisting of or containing scum. **2** low; worthless.

scun·ner (skun′ər) *n.* in Newfoundland, on a boat, the assistant to the master of the watch. [< *scun,* var. of *scan*]

scup (skup) *n.* **scup** or **scups.** a narrow, high-backed sea fish used for food. [< Algonquian]

scup·per (skup′ər) *n.* an opening in the side of a ship to let water run off the deck. —*v. Slang.* catch by surprise and kill or destroy. [origin uncertain]

scurf (skėrf) *n.* **1** small scales of dead skin; dandruff. **2** any scaly matter on a surface. [ME < Scand.; cf. Icelandic *skurfa* skurf]

scurf·y (skėr′fē) *adj.* **scurf·i·er, scurf·i·est. 1** covered with scurf. **2** of or like scurf. —**scurf′i·ness,** *n.*

scur·ril·i·ty (skə ril′ə tē) *n.* **-ties. 1** coarse joking. **2** indecent abuse. **3** an indecent or coarse remark.

scur·ri·lous (skėr′ə ləs) *adj.* **1** of people, coarsely or obscenely abusive. **2** of language, literature, etc., coarsely abusive; containing low and vulgar abuse. [< L *scurrilis* < *scurra* buffoon] —**scur′ri·lous·ly,** *adv.* —**scur′ri·lous·ness,** *n.*

scur·ry (skėr′ē) *v.* **-ried, -ry·ing,** *n.* **-ries.** —*v.* run quickly; hurry: *We could hear the mice scurrying about in the walls.* —*n.* a hasty running; hurrying. [? < *hurry-scurry,* varied reduplication of *hurry*]

S-curve (es′kėrv′) *n.* a curve in the shape of the letter S.

scur·vy (skėr′vē) *n. adj.* **-vi·er, -vi·est.** —*n.* a disease characterized by swollen and bleeding gums, livid spots on the skin, and prostration, caused by a lack of vitamin C in the diet. Scurvy used to be common among sailors when they had little to eat except bread and salt meat. —*adj.* low; mean; contemptible: *a scurvy fellow, a scurvy trick.* [< *scurf*] —**scur′vi·ly,** *adv.* —**scur′vi·ness,** *n.*

scut (skut) *n.* a short tail, especially that of a rabbit or deer. [cf. Icelandic *skutr* stern]

scu·tate (skū′tāt) *adj.* **1** in zoology, having shieldlike plates or large scales of bone, shell, etc. **2** in botany, round. Nasturtiums have scutate leaves. [< L *scutatus* having a shield < *scutum* shield]

scutch (skuch) *v.* free (flax or cotton fibres) from woody parts by beating; make (fibres) ready for use by beating. —*n.* an implement for scutching. [origin uncertain]

scutch·eon (skuch′ən) *n.* escutcheon.

scute (skūt) *n.* scutum.

scu·tel·la (skū tel′ə) *n.* pl. of **scutellum.**

scu·tel·late (skū′tə lāt′ or skū tel′āt) *adj.* in biology: **1** having scutella. **2** formed into a scutellum.

scu·tel·lum (skū tel′əm) *n.* **-tel·la.** in zoology and botany, a small plate, scale, or other shieldlike part. [< NL *scutellum,* dim. of L *scutum* shield]

scut·tle[1] (skut′əl) *n.* a kind of bucket for holding or carrying coal. [< L *scutella* platter]

scut·tle[2] (skut′əl) *v.* **-tled, -tling,** *n.* scamper; scurry. [var. of *scuddle,* frequentative of *scud*] —**scut′tler,** *n.*

scut·tle[3] (skut′əl) *n. v.* **-tled, -tling.** —*n.* **1** an opening in the deck or side of a ship, with a lid or cover. **2** an opening in a wall or roof, with a lid or cover. **3** the lid or cover for any such opening. —*v.* **1** cut a hole or holes through the bottom or sides of (a ship) to sink it. **2** cut a hole or holes in the deck of (a ship) to salvage the cargo. [? < F < Sp. *escotilla* hatchway]

scut·tle·butt (skut′əl but′) *n.* **1** *Slang.* rumor and stories not based on fact. **2 a** a water cask for drinking with a hole in the top for a cup or dipper, kept on the deck of a ship. **b** a drinking fountain.

scu·tum (skū′təm) *n.* **-ta** (-tə). in zoology, a shieldlike part of bone, shell, etc. [< L *scutum* shield]

Scyl·la (sil′ə) *n.* **1** a dangerous rock opposite the whirlpool Charybdis, at the extreme southwestern tip of Italy. **2** a mythical monster with six heads and twelve arms that lived on this rock and snatched sailors from ships. **3 between Scylla and Charybdis,** between two dangers, one of which must be met.

scythe (sīᴛʜ) *n. v.* **scythed, scyth·ing.** —*n.* a long, slightly curved blade on a long handle, for cutting grass, etc. —*v.* cut with a scythe. [OE *sīthe*; spelling influenced by L *scindere* cut]

A farmer using a scythe

Scyth·i·an (sith′ē ən) *adj.* of or having to do with ancient Scythia, its people, or their language. —*n.* **1** a native or inhabitant of ancient Scythia. **2** the Iranian language of this people.

s.d. 1 sine die. **2** several dates.

S.D. 1 School District. **2** South Dakota.

S.Dak. South Dakota.

'sdeath (zdeth) *interj. Archaic.* "God's death," used as an oath.

Se selenium.

SE, S.E., or **s.e. 1** southeast. **2** southeasterly.

sea (sē) *n.* **1** the great body of salt water that covers almost three fourths of the earth's surface; the ocean. **2** any large body of salt water, smaller than an ocean, partly or wholly enclosed by land: *the North Sea, the Mediterranean Sea.* **3** a large lake of fresh water. **4** a large, heavy wave: *A high sea swept away the ship's masts.* **5** the swell of the ocean. **6** an overwhelming amount or number. **7** a broad expanse. **8 at sea, a** out on the sea. **b** *Informal.* puzzled; confused. **9 follow the sea,** be a sailor. **10 go to sea, a** become a sailor. **b** begin a voyage. **11 put to sea,** begin a voyage. [OE *sǣ*]

sea anemone a flowerlike polyp having a fleshy, cylindrical body and a mouth surrounded by tentacles.

sea bass 1 a common food fish of the Atlantic coast having a peculiar tail fin. **2** any of various similar fishes.

sea·bed (sē′bed′) *n.* the bed or bottom of the sea.

sea·board (sē′bôrd′) *n.* the land near the sea; seacoast; seashore: *the Atlantic seaboard.* —*adj.* bordering on the sea.

sea bread hardtack; ship biscuit.

sea bream any of certain fishes belonging to the family that includes scups, porgies, etc.

sea breeze a breeze blowing from the sea toward the land.

sea calf the common seal, often called the harbor seal.

sea·coast (sē′kōst′) *n.* land along the sea.

sea·cock (sē′kok′) *n.* on a ship, any cock or valve that opens through the hull to the sea.

sea cow 1 a manatee, dugong, or any similar mammal living in the sea. **2** a walrus.

sea cucumber any of a group of small echinoderms, most of which have flexible bodies that resemble cucumbers. Some, such as trepangs, are used for food.

sea dog 1 a sailor, especially one having long experience at sea. **2** the common seal. **3** the dogfish, a small shark.

sea eagle any of several eagles that feed mainly on fish.

sea element *Cdn.* the branch of the Canadian Armed Forces having to do with ships of war and their officers and men, formerly known as the Royal Canadian Navy.

sea elephant a kind of very large seal, the male of which has a trunklike snout.

sea·far·er (sē′fãr′ər) *n.* **1** a sailor. **2** a traveller on the sea.

sea·far·ing (sē′fãr′ing) *adj.* going, travelling, or working on the sea: *Sailors are seafaring men.* —*n.* **1** the business or calling of a sailor. **2** the act or fact of travelling by sea.

sea-flea (sē′flē′) *n.* a tiny, one-man speedboat driven by a powerful motor and used especially for racing, so called because it skims the surface of the water.

sea foam 1 foam of the sea. **2** meerschaum.

sea·food (sē′füd′) *n.* edible salt-water fish and shellfish.

sea·fowl (sē′foul′) *n.* **-fowls** or (*esp. collectively*) **-fowl.** any bird that lives on or near the sea.

sea·girt (sē′ gėrt′) *adj. Poetic.* surrounded by the sea.

sea-go·ing (sē′ gō′ ing) *adj.* **1** going by sea; seafaring. **2** fit for going to sea.

sea green light bluish-green.

sea gull a gull, a sea bird having long wings and webbed feet.

sea hog porpoise.

sea horse 1 a kind of small fish (2 to 10 inches long) with a prehensile tail and a head suggesting that of a horse. A seahorse swims upright. **2** a walrus. **3** in classical legend, a sea animal with the foreparts of a horse and the hind parts of a fish. **4** a large, white-crested wave.

A sea horse (5 in. long). It swims upright, and can hold on to seaweed, etc. with its tail.

sea king a Scandinavian pirate chief of the Middle Ages. [translation of Old Icelandic *sǣkonungr*]

seal[1] (sēl) *n.* **1** a design stamped on a piece of wax, etc. to show ownership or authenticity; a paper, circle, mark, etc. representing it. The official seal is attached to important government papers. **2** a stamp for marking things with such a design: *a seal with one's initials on it.* **3** a piece of wax, paper, metal, etc. on which the design is stamped. **4** something that fastens or closes something tightly. **5** something that secures; a pledge: *under seal of secrecy.* **6** something that settles or determines: *the seal of authority.* **7** a mark; sign. **8** a special kind of stamp: *Christmas seals, Easter seals.* **9** a small quantity of water left in a trap to prevent the escape of foul air from a sewer or drain. **10 set one's seal to, a** put one's seal on. **b** approve. **11 the seals,** the symbols of public office.
—*v.* **1** mark (a document) with a seal; make binding thus; certify thus: *The treaty was signed and sealed by both governments.* **2** stamp as an evidence of standard measure or quality or legal size: *seal weights and measures.* **3** close tightly; shut; fasten: *Seal the letter before mailing it. She sealed the jars of fruit. Her promise sealed her lips.* **4** close up the cracks of: *They sealed the log cabin with clay.* **5** fix firmly. **6** settle; determine: *The judge's words sealed the prisoner's fate.* **7** give a sign that (something) is true: *seal a promise with a kiss. They sealed their bargain by shaking hands.* **8** set apart; destine; decide beyond recall: *The king's fate was sealed.* [ME < AF *seal,* ult. < L *sigillum,* dim. of *signum* sign] —**seal′a·ble,** *adj.*

seal[2] (sēl) *n.* **seals** or **seal** (*for 1*), *v.* —*n.* **1** a marine carnivorous mammal having large flippers, living usually in cold regions. Some kinds of seal are hunted for their valuable fur. **2** the fur. **3** a coat or other garment made of this fur. **4** the leather made from the skin of a seal. —*v.* hunt seals. [OE *seolh*] —**seal′like′,** *adj.*

sea lavender a plant having many tiny lavender flowers that retain their color long after being cut and dried.

sea legs *Informal.* **1** legs accustomed to walking steadily on a rolling or pitching ship. **2 get one's sea legs,** become accustomed to the motion of a ship, especially after an initial period of seasickness.

seal·er[1] (sēl′ ər) *n.* **1** a person or thing that seals. **2** an official appointed to examine and test weights and measures. [< *seal*[1]]

seal·er[2] (sēl′ ər) *n.* **1** a person who hunts seals. **2** a ship used for hunting seals. [< *seal*[2]]

seal·er[3] (sēl′ ər) *n.* a glass jar, usually one holding a pint or a quart, used to preserve jam, fruit, vegetables, etc.

seal·er·y (sēl′ ər ē) *n.* **-er·ies. 1** the act or trade of hunting for seals. **2** a place where seals are hunted.

sea level the surface of the sea, especially when halfway between mean high and low water. Heights of mountains, cities, etc. are measured as so many feet above sea level.

sea lily a crinoid.

sealing wax a hard kind of wax, soft when heated, used for sealing letters, packages, etc. Sealing wax is made of resin and shellac.

sea lion a large seal of the Pacific coast.

seal ring a finger ring engraved with a design so that it can be used as a seal.

hat, āge, cãre, fär; let, ēqual, tėrm; it, īce
hot, ōpen, ôrder; oil, out; cup, pu̇t, rüle, ūse
əbove, takən, pencəl, lemən, circəs
ch, child; ng, long; sh, ship
th, thin; ᴛʜ, then; zh, measure

seal·skin (sēl′ skin′) *n.* **1** the skin of the fur seal, prepared for use. **2** a garment made of this fur.

Sea·ly·ham (sē′ lē ham *or* sē′ lē əm) *n.* **1** a breed of small Welsh terrier, having a rough, shaggy coat, short legs, a square jaw, and docked tail. **2** a dog of this breed. [< *Sealyham,* a Welsh estate where the breed was originated]

seam (sēm) *n.* **1** the line formed by sewing two pieces of cloth, canvas, leather, etc. together. **2** any line where edges join: *The seams of the boat must be filled in if they leak.* **3** any mark or line like a seam. **4** in geology, a layer; stratum: *a seam of coal.* —*v.* **1** sew the seam of; join with a seam. **2** mark with wrinkles or scars, etc.: *Years of worrying seamed his brow.* **3** crack open. [OE *sēam*] —**seam′less,** *adj.*

sea·man (sē′ mən) *n.* **-men** (-mən). **1** a sailor, usually one who sails the ocean. **2** a sailor who is not an officer.

sea·man·like (sē′ mən līk′) *adj.* like a seaman; having the skill of a good seaman.

sea·man·ship (sē′ mən ship′) *n.* skill in managing a ship.

sea·mark (sē′ märk′) *n.* **1** a lighthouse, beacon, or other landmark that can be seen from the sea, used as a guide for a ship's course. **2** a line on the shores that shows the limit of the tide.

seam·er (sēm′ ər) *n.* **1** a person or thing that seams. **2** a machine that joins two pieces of metal.

sea mew sea gull.

sea mile about 6,080 feet; one nautical mile.

sea monster 1 a huge fish, cetacean, or the like. **2** a fabulous marine animal of terrifying proportions and shape.

seam·stress (sēm′ stris) *n.* a woman whose work is sewing. Also, **sempstress.**

seam·y (sēm′ ē) *adj.* **seam·i·er, seam·i·est. 1** having or showing seams. **2** worst; least attractive; least pleasant: *A policeman sees much of the seamy side of life.* —**seam′i·ness,** *n.*

sé·ance (sā′ äns; *French,* sā äɴs′) *n.* **1** a sitting; session. **2** a meeting of people trying to communicate with spirits of the dead by the help of a medium. [< F *séance* < *seoir* sit < L *sedere*]

sea·plane (sē′ plān′) *n.* an airplane that can take off from and land on water; hydroplane.

sea·port (sē′ pôrt′) *n.* **1** a port or harbor on the seacoast. **2** a city or town with a harbor that ships can reach from the sea.

sea power 1 naval strength: *The United States possesses great sea power.* **2** a nation having great naval strength: *Canada is not one of the world's major sea powers.*

sea purse the horny case or pouch that some fishes secrete around their eggs to protect them and anchor them to rocks, weeds, etc.

sear (sēr) *v.* **1** burn or char the surface of: *The hot iron seared his flesh.* **2** make hard or unfeeling: *That cruel man must have a seared conscience.* **3** dry up; wither. **4** become dry, burned, or hard. [OE *sēarian,* v. < *sēar,* adj.] —*n.* a mark made by searing. —*adj.* dried up; withered. [OE *sēar,* adj.] —**Syn.** *v.* **1** See **burn.**

search (sėrch) *v.* **1** try to find by looking; seek; look for: *We searched all day for the lost cat.* **2** look through; go over carefully; examine, especially for something concealed: *The police searched the prisoner to see if he had a gun.* **3** look through (writings, records, etc.) in order to discover if certain things are there. **4** examine by probing: *The doctor searched the wound for the bullet.* **5 search out, a** look for. **b** find by searching. **6** of wind, cold, firearms, etc., pierce; penetrate.
—*n.* **1** the act of searching; examination. **2 in search of,** trying to find; looking for. [ME < OF *cerchier,* ult.

< L *circus* circle] —**search′a·ble,** *adj.* —**search′er,** *n.*
Syn. *v.* **2 Search, explore, rummage** = look through a place or thing for something. **Search** = look carefully through something, trying to find what is there or hunting for something lost or hidden: *Men searched the woods for the murderer.* **Explore** = search into a region, field of interest, etc. to discover the facts about it, its nature, condition, quality, etc.: *Geologists explored the newly discovered mineral deposit.* **Rummage** = search thoroughly a ship, house, trunk, etc. by moving or searching among the contents: *He rummaged through the drawers looking for a map.*

search·ing (sėr′ching) *adj.* **1** examining carefully; thorough: *a searching gaze or look, a searching examination.* **2** keenly observant; penetrating. **3** piercing; sharp: *a searching wind.* —**search′ing·ly,** *adv.*

search·light (sėrch′līt′) *n.* **1** a device that can throw a bright beam of light in any direction desired. **2** the beam of light.

search warrant a legal document authorizing the search of a house or building for stolen goods, criminals, etc.

sea robber pirate.

sea robin a sea fish having a large head, thickly scaled cheeks, and three pectoral rays, especially certain reddish North American species; gurnard.

sea room space at sea free from obstruction, in which a ship can easily sail, tack, turn around, etc.

sea rover **1** a pirate. **2** a pirate ship.

sea-run (sē′run′) *adj.* anadromous.

sea·scape (sē′skāp′) *n.* **1** a picture, often a painting, showing scenery on the sea. **2** a view of scenery on the sea. [modelled on *landscape*]

sea serpent **1** a huge, snakelike animal supposed to live in the sea. **2** a poisonous sea snake having a finlike tail.

sea shell the shell of any sea mollusc, such as an oyster, conch, abalone, etc.

sea·shore (sē′shôr′) *n.* the land along the sea; the beach at the seaside.

sea·sick (sē′sik′) *adj.* affected with seasickness.

sea·sick·ness (sē′sik′nis) *n.* sickness caused by the motion of a ship at sea.

sea·side (sē′sīd′) *n.* the land along the sea; seacoast; seashore. —*adj.* of or at the seaside.

sea snake **1** a venomous snake having a finlike tail living in the sea. **2** a sea serpent.

sea·son (sē′zən) *n.* **1** one of the four periods of the year; spring summer, autumn, or winter. **2** a period of the year with reference to the particular conditions of weather, temperature, etc., that characterize it. **3** any period of time marked by something special: *the Christmas season, the harvest season.* **4** the time when something is occurring, active, at its best, or in fashion: *the baseball season.* **5** a period of time: *a season of rest.* **6** the period of the year when a place is most frequented or active: *the Paris season.* **7** a suitable or fit time. **8 for a season,** for a time. **9 in good season,** early enough. **10 in season, a** at the right or proper time. **b** in the time or condition for eating, hunting, etc. **c** early enough. **11 in season and out of season,** at all times. **12 out of season,** not in season.
—*v.* **1** improve the flavor of: *season soup with salt.* **2** give interest or character to: *season conversation with wit.* **3** make fit for use by a period of keeping or treatment: *Wood is seasoned for building by drying and hardening it.* **4** become fit for use. **5** accustom; make used: *Soldiers are seasoned to battle by experience in war.* **6** make less severe; soften: *Season justice with mercy.* [ME < OF *seson* < L *satio, -onis* a sowing, ult. < *serere* sow] —**sea′son·er,** *n.*

☛ **seasons.** The names *spring, summer, fall, autumn, and winter* are not capitalized except for stylistic emphasis, as sometimes in poetry or in nature essays.

sea·son·a·ble (sē′zən ə bəl or sēz′nə bəl) *adj.* **1** suitable to the season: *Hot weather is seasonable in July.* **2** coming at the right or proper time: *The second expedition brought seasonable aid to the men who had survived the first.* —**sea′son·a·ble·ness,** *n.* —**sea′son·a·bly,** *adv.*

sea·son·al (sē′zən əl) *adj.* **1** having to do with the seasons: *seasonal variations in the weather.* **2 a** depending on a season: *a seasonal business.* **b** employed only during a certain season: *a seasonal worker.* **3** recurring at regular intervals; periodical. —**sea′son·al·ly,** *adv.*

sea·son·ing (sē′zən ing or sēz′ning) *n.* **1** something that gives a better flavor. Salt, pepper, and spices are seasonings. **2** something that gives interest or character: *Conversation with a seasoning of wit.*

season ticket a ticket that gives its holder the right to attend a series of games or entertainments, or to make a daily trip on a railway, bus, etc. for a stated period of time, etc.

sea squirt a small, soft-bodied sea animal that squirts water when it contracts.

seat[1] (sēt) *n.* **1** something to sit on. **2** a place to sit. **3** a place in which one has the right to sit: *We have reserved seats in the first balcony.* **4** a right to sit as a member of a legislature, city council, stock exchange, etc. **5** that part of a chair, bench, stool, etc. on which one sits. **6** that part of the body on which one sits, or the clothing covering it. **7** a manner of sitting on horseback. **8** that on which anything rests; base.
—*v.* **1** set or place on a seat: *seat a person on a chair.* **2** have seats for (a specified number): *That stadium seats thirty thousand people.* **3** provide with a seat or seats. **4** put a seat on. **5 be seated, a** sit down. **b** be sitting. **c** be situated. [ME < ON *sǽti*]

seat[2] (sēt) *n.* **1** an established place or centre: *A university is a seat of learning. The seat of our government is in Ottawa.* **2** the throne of a king, etc.; the authority or dignity of a king, etc. **3** a residence; home: *The family seat of the Howards is in Kent.* **4** location; situation; site: *the seat of a disease.* —*v.* fix in a particular or proper place; settle; locate. [OE *sǽte*] —**Syn.** *n.* **3** abode.

seat belt a belt attached to the seat of an automobile or airplane, used to hold its occupant in the event of a crash, jolt, bump, etc.

seat·ing (sēt′ing) *n.* **1** upholstery for covering seats. **2 a** the arrangement of seats for a dinner party, in a theatre, etc. **b** the seats themselves. **3 a** a support on which something rests: *the seating of a valve.* **b** something resting on such a support.

SEATO (sē′tō) Southeast Asia Treaty Organization.

sea trout **1** any of various species of trout found in salt water. **2** any of several weakfishes.

sea urchin a small, round sea animal having a spiny shell.

sea wall a strong wall or embankment made to prevent the waves from wearing away the shore, to act as a breakwater, etc.

sea·ward (sē′wərd) *adv. adj.* toward the sea: *Our house faces seaward.* —*n.* the direction toward the sea: *The island lies a mile to seaward.*

sea·wards (sē′wərdz) *adv.* seaward.

sea·way (sē′wā′) *n.* **1** a way over the sea. **2** the open sea. **3** the progress of a ship through the waves. **4** a rough sea. **5** an inland waterway that connects with the open sea and is deep enough to permit ocean shipping: *the St. Lawrence Seaway.*

sea·weed (sē′wēd′) *n.* any plant or plants growing in the sea.

sea wind a wind blowing from the sea toward the land.

sea·wor·thy (sē′wėr′ᴛʜē) *adj.* fit for sailing on the sea; able to stand storms at sea. —**sea′wor′thi·ness,** *n.*

se·ba·ceous (si bā′shəs) *adj.* having to do with fat; fatty; greasy. The sebaceous glands and ducts supply oil to the skin and hair. [< L *sebaceus* < *sebum* grease]

se·ba·go (si bā′gō) *n.* a kind of Atlantic salmon found in fresh water lakes in New Brunswick, Nova Scotia, and New England. [< Lake *Sebago,* Maine]

sec. **1** secretary. **2** second; seconds. **3** section; sections. **4** secant. **5** according to. (for L *secundum*) **6** secondary.

se·cant (sē′kənt or sē′kant) *n.* **1** in geometry, a line that intersects a curve at two or more points. **2** in trigonometry: **a** the ratio of the length of the hypotenuse of a right-angled triangle to the length of the side adjacent to an acute angle. **b** a straight line drawn from the centre of a circle through one extremity of an arc to the tangent from the other extremity of the same arc. **c** the ratio of the length of this line to the length of the radius of the circle. See diagram on opposite page.

—*adj.* intersecting. [< L *secans, -antis,* ppr. of *secare* cut]

se·ca·teurs (se′kə tėrz′) *n.pl. Esp.Brit.* pruning shears or clippers. [< F < L *secare* cut]

se·cede (si sēd′) *v.* **-ced·ed, -ced·ing.** withdraw formally from an organization. [< L *secedere* < *se-* apart + *cedere* go] —**se·ced′er,** *n.*

se·ces·sion (si sesh′ən) *n.* a formal withdrawing from an organization. [< L *secessio, -onis* < *secedere.* See SECEDE.]

se·ces·sion·ism (si sesh′ən iz′əm) *n.* the principles of those in favor of secession.

se·ces·sion·ist (si sesh′ən ist) *n.* **1** a person who favors secession. **2** a person who secedes.

A secant. The ratio of AB to AD is the secant of the angle A; and AB is the secant of the arc CD.

seck·el pear (sek′əl or sik′əl) a small, sweet, reddish-brown pear. [after the originator, a Pennsylvania farmer]

se·clude (si klüd′) *v.* **-clud·ed, -clud·ing.** keep apart from company; shut off from others: *He secludes himself and sees only his close friends.* [< L *secludere* < *se-* apart + *claudere* shut]

se·clud·ed (si klüd′id) *adj.* shut off from others; undisturbed. —**Syn.** withdrawn, isolated.

se·clu·sion (si klü′zhən) *n.* **1** a secluding or being secluded; retirement: *She lives in seclusion apart from her friends.* **2** a secluded place. [< Med.L *seclusio, -onis* < L *secludere.* See SECLUDE.]

se·clu·sive (si klü′siv) *adj.* **1** fond of seclusion. **2** tending to seclude. —**se·clu′sive·ly,** *adv.* —**se·clu′sive·ness,** *n.*

sec·ond¹ (sek′ənd; sə kond′ *for v. def. 3*) *adj.* **1** next after the first: *the second seat from the front.* **2** below the first: *the second officer on a ship.* **3** another; other: *Napoleon has been called a second Caesar.* **4** in music: **a** lower in pitch. **b** rendering a part lower in pitch: *second soprano.* **5** inferior: *cloth of second quality.* **6 at second hand,** not directly from the source or first owner; not primarily or originally: *a report received at second hand.*
—*adv.* in the second group, division, rank, etc.; secondly.
—*n.* **1** a person or thing that is second. **2 seconds,** *pl.* articles below first quality. Seconds have some defect or other. **3** a person who supports or aids another; backer: *The prize fighter had a second.* **4** in music: **a** a part, usually lower in pitch than the first, in a composition for ensemble performance. **b** a voice or instrument rendering such a part. **c** a tone on the next degree from a given tone. **d** the interval between the two. **e** the harmonic combination of such tones. **f** the second note in a scale. **5** the forward gear or speed of an automobile, having a ratio to the engine speed between that of low and high.
—*v.* **1 a** support; back up; assist: *second another person's idea.* **b** attend (a boxer or duellist). **2** express approval or support of: *One member made a motion to adjourn the meeting, and another seconded it.* **3** assign (a person, especially a member of the armed services) temporarily to some office outside his regular appointment. [ME < OF < L *secundus* < *sequi* follow] —**sec′ond·er,** *n.*

sec·ond² (sek′ənd) *n.* **1** 1/60 of a minute; 1/3600 of an hour. **2** a very short time. **3** 1/3600 of a degree of an angle. *Example*: 12° 10′ 30″ means 12 degrees, 10 minutes, 30 seconds. [ME < OF < Med.L *secunda (minuta)* second (minute), i.e., the result of the second division of the hour into sixty parts]

second advent the second coming of Christ.

sec·ond·ar·y (sek′ən der′ē) *adj. n.* **-ar·ies.** —*adj.* **1** next after the first in order, place, time, etc. **2** not main or chief; having less importance. **3** not original; derived. **4** in electricity, noting or having to do with a coil or circuit in which a current is produced by induction. **5** in chemistry, involving the substitution of two atoms or groups. **6** in geology, produced from another mineral by decay, alteration, etc.
—*n.* **1** a person or thing that is secondary, second in importance, or subordinate. **2** a secondary stress. **3** in electricity, a coil or circuit in which a current is produced

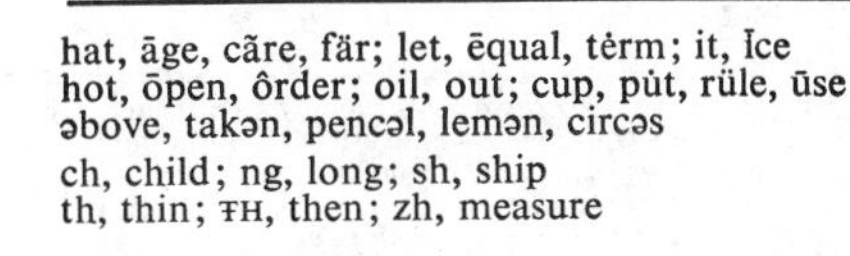
hat, āge, cãre, fär; let, ēqual, tėrm; it, īce
hot, ōpen, ôrder; oil, out; cup, pu̇t, rüle, ūse
əbove, takən, pencəl, lemən, circəs
ch, child; ng, long; sh, ship
th, thin; ᴛʜ, then; zh, measure

by induction. —**sec′ond·ar′i·ly,** *adv.* —**Syn.** *adj.* **2** subordinate, subsidiary, auxiliary, inferior, minor.

secondary accent secondary stress.

secondary feather feather used in flying, situated on the second segment of a bird's wing.

secondary school a school attended after elementary or junior high school; a high school or collegiate institute.

secondary stress 1 a stress accent that is weaker than the strongest stress in a word (primary stress), but stronger than weak stress. The second syllable of *ab·bre′vi·a′tion* has a secondary stress. **2** a mark, such as (′), used to show where this stress falls.

second childhood a foolish or childish condition caused by old age.

sec·ond-class (sek′ənd klas′) *adj.* **1** of or belonging to the class next after the first. **2** having to do with the second grade of conveyances or accommodations for travel: *a second-class car, second-class ticket.* **3** of inferior grade or quality. **4** of or having to do with the class of mail consisting of newspapers and periodicals.
—*adv.* **1** with second-class accommodation: *travel second-class.* **2** by second-class mail.

second growth 1 a crop of grass or hay that comes up after the first crop has been cut; aftergrass. **2** a new growth of trees in an area where virgin forest has been cut or burned. **3** any new growth in an area that has been cleared of vegetation.

second hand a hand on a clock or watch, pointing to the seconds.

sec·ond-hand (sek′ənd hand′) *adj.* **1** not original; obtained from another: *second-hand information.* **2** not new; used already by someone else: *second-hand clothes.* **3** dealing in used goods: *a second-hand bookshop.*

second lieutenant in the army, the lowest-ranking commissioned officer.

sec·ond·ly (sek′ənd lē) *adv.* in the second place.

second nature a habit, quality, knowledge, etc. that a person has acquired and had for so long that it seems to be almost a part of his nature.

second person the form of a pronoun or verb used to indicate the person spoken to. *You* and *your* are used for the second person.

sec·ond-rate (sek′ənd rāt′) *adj.* **1** rated as second-class. **2** inferior.

second sight the supposed power of seeing distant objects or future events.

second wind 1 a recovery or renewal of breath and energy following the initial feeling of exhaustion during an effort, as in running a race. **2** any recovery or renewal of energy: *The rise in steel production faltered in early spring and then got its second wind.*

se·cre·cy (sē′krə sē) *n.* **-cies. 1** the condition of being secret. **2** the condition of being kept secret. **3** the ability to keep things secret. **4** the tendency to conceal; lack of frankness. [< *secret,* adj.]

se·cret (sē′krit) *adj.* **1** kept from the knowledge of others: *a secret marriage.* **2** keeping to oneself what one knows: *Be as secret as the grave.* **3** known only to a few: *a secret society.* **4** kept from sight; hidden: *a secret drawer.* **5** retired; secluded: *a secret place.* **6** working or acting in secret: *a secret agent, secret police.* **7** very hard to understand or discover.
—*n.* **1** something secret or hidden; mystery. **2** something known only to a few. **3** a hidden cause or reason. **4 in secret,** in private; not openly. [< F *secret* < L *secretus,* pp. of *secernere* set apart < *se-* apart + *cernere* separate. Doublet of SECRETE.] —**se′cret·ly,** *adv.*

Syn. *adj.* **1 Secret, covert, clandestine** = done, made, or carried on without the knowledge of others. **Secret** is the general word describing something hidden or kept from sight or knowledge: *They have secret plans.* **Covert,** formal, suggests being done or kept under cover, and describes looks, meanings, actions that are disguised or not open: *A hint is a covert suggestion.* **Clandestine,** formal, describes something underhand or with an unlawful or wicked purpose: *He feared someone would learn of his clandestine trips.* 2 uncommunicative, secretive, reticent. 4 concealed, covered. 7 obscure, recondite, esoteric.

secret agent an agent of a government secret service.

sec·re·tar·i·al (sek′rə tãr′ē əl) *adj.* of a secretary; having to do with a secretary: *She learned to do stenography, typewriting, and other secretarial work.*

sec·re·tar·i·at (sek′rə tãr′ē it or sek′rə tãr′ē at′) *n.* **1** the office or position of secretary, especially of a secretary or secretary-general as the administrative head of an organization. **2** the administrative unit controlled by a secretary or secretary-general: *the United Nations Secretariat.* **3** a group of secretaries. **4** a place where a secretary or secretary-general transacts business. [< F *secrétariat*]

sec·re·tar·y (sek′rə ter′ē) *n.* **-tar·ies. 1** someone who writes letters, keeps records, etc. for a person, company, club, etc.: *Our club has a secretary who keeps the minutes of the meeting.* **2** in some countries, a person who administers a department of the government. **3** a diplomatic agent, usually of lower rank in an embassy or legation, often designated as first secretary, second secretary, etc. **4** a writing desk with a set of drawers, often having shelves for books. [ME < LL *secretarius* confidential officer < L *secretum,* n., secret, originally pp., neut. of *secretus.* See SECRET.]

secretary bird a large, long-legged African bird of prey that feeds on reptiles, so called because its crest suggests pens stuck over the ear.

sec·re·tar·y-gen·er·al (sek′rə ter′ē jen′ə rəl) *pl.* **sec·re·tar·ies-gen·er·al.** the chief or senior secretary; the administrator or head of a secretariat: *the Secretary-General of the United Nations.*

se·crete (si krēt′) *v.* **-cret·ed, -cret·ing. 1** keep secret; hide. **2** make; prepare; produce. Glands in the mouth secrete saliva. [< L *secretus.* Doublet of SECRET.] **—se·cre′tor,** *n.*

se·cre·tion (si krē′shən) *n.* **1** a substance that is secreted by some part of an animal or plant. Bile is the secretion of the liver. **2** the secreting or production of such a substance.

se·cre·tive (sē′krə tiv or si krē′tiv *for 1;* si krē′tiv *for 2*) *adj.* **1** having the habit of secrecy; not frank and open. **2** causing or aiding secretion. **—se·cre′tive·ly,** *adv.* **—se·cre′tive·ness,** *n.*

se·cre·to·ry (si krē′tə rē) *adj. n.* **-ries.** *—adj.* secreting; of or causing secretion. *—n.* an organ of the body that secretes.

secret police in a dictatorship or similar regime, a special government police force that operates secretly to control and suppress activities considered subversive.

secret service 1 the branch of a government that makes secret investigations. **2** an official service that is secret.

secret society 1 an association of which some ceremonies and activities are known only to members. **2** an organization to promote some cause by secret methods, its members being sworn to observe secrecy.

secs. 1 seconds. **2** sections.

sect (sekt) *n.* **1** a group of people having the same principles, beliefs, or opinions: *Each religious sect in the town had its own church.* **2** a religious group separated from an established church. [< L *secta* party, school, probably < *sectari* keep following, intensive of *sequi* follow]

sect. 1 section. **2** sectional.

sec·tar·i·an (sek tãr′ē ən) *adj.* **1** of or having to do with a sect. **2** characteristic of one sect only; strongly prejudiced in favor of a certain sect. *—n.* **1** a devoted member of a sect, especially a narrow-minded or strongly prejudiced member. **2** a member of a religious group separated from an established church.

sec·tar·i·an·ism (sek tãr′ē ən iz′əm) *n.* the spirit or tendencies of sectarians; adherence or too great devotion to a particular sect.

sec·ta·ry (sek′tə rē) *n.* **-ries.** a member of a particular sect, especially a member of a religious group separated from an established church. [< Med.L *sectarius* < L *secta.* See SECT.]

sec·tile (sek′tīl or sek′təl) *adj.* capable of being cut smoothly by a knife.

sec·tion (sek′shən) *n.* **1** a part; division; slice: *Divide the cake into sections. His section of the family estate was larger than his brother's.* **2** a division of a book, etc.: *Chapter X has seven sections.* **3** a region; part of a country, city, etc.: *The city has a business section and a residential section.* **4** a division of a company, office, or other organization. **5** in the army, a formation of soldiers that is smaller than a platoon and usually commanded by a corporal. **6** the act of cutting. **7** a representation of a thing as it would appear if cut straight through. **8** a district or tract of land one mile square; 640 acres. The typical prairie homestead consisted of a quarter section, or 160 acres. **9** one of the parts of something that is built of a number of similar parts: *the sections of a bookcase.* **10** a thin slice of a tissue, mineral, etc. cut off for microscopic examination. **11** a part of a railway line kept up by one group of workmen. **12** a part of a sleeping car containing an upper and a lower berth. **13** one of two or more trains operating on the same schedule. **14** in bookbinding, a number of sheets folded together to form a unit.
—v. cut into sections. [< L *sectio, -onis* < *secare* cut]

sec·tion·al (sek′shən əl) *adj.* **1** having to do with a particular section; local. **2** made of sections: *a sectional bookcase.* **—sec′tion·al·ly,** *adv.*

sec·tion·al·ism (sek′shən el iz′əm) *n.* excessive regard for sectional interests; sectional prejudice or hatred.

sec·tion·al·ize (sek′shən əl īz′) *v.* **-ized, -iz·ing. 1** make sectional. **2** divide into sections.

sec·tor (sek′tər) *n.* **1** in geometry, the part of a circle between two radii and the included arc. **2** in military use, a clearly defined area that a given unit protects or covers with fire; the part of a front held by a unit. **3** an instrument consisting of two rulers connected by a joint. A sector is used in measuring or drawing angles. [< LL < L *sector* cutter < *secare* cut]

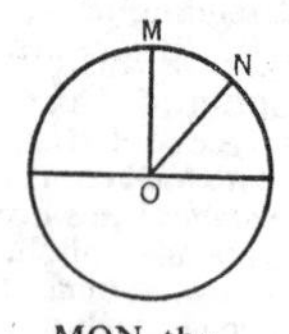

MON, the sector of a circle

sec·u·lar (sek′yů lər) *adj.* **1** worldly, not religious or sacred: *secular music, a secular education.* **2** living in the world; not belonging to a religious order: *the secular clergy, a secular priest.* **3** occurring once in an age; lasting for an age or century. **4** lasting through long ages; going on from age to age. *—n.* a secular priest. [< L *saecularis* < *saeculum* age, world] **—sec′u·lar·ly,** *adv.*

sec·u·lar·ism (sek′yů lər iz′əm) *n.* **1** scepticism in regard to religion. **2** opposition to the introduction of religion into public schools or other public affairs.

sec·u·lar·ist (sek′yů lər ist) *n.* a believer in secularism.

sec·u·lar·i·ty (sek′yů lar′ə tē) *n.* a secular spirit or quality; worldliness.

sec·u·lar·ize (sek′yů lər īz′) *v.* **-ized, -iz·ing. 1** make secular or worldly; separate from religious connection or influence: *secularize the schools.* **2** transfer (property) from the possession of the church to that of the government. **—sec′u·lar·i·za′tion,** *n.* **—sec′u·lar·iz′er,** *n.*

se·cure (si kūr′) *adj. v.* **-cured, -cur·ing.** *—adj.* **1** safe against loss, attack, escape, etc.: *Keep the prisoner secure within the dungeon. This is a secure hiding place. Land in a growing city is a secure investment.* **2** sure; certain; that can be counted on: *We know in advance that our victory is secure.* **3** free from care or fear: *He hoped for a secure old age.* **4** firmly fastened; not likely to give way: *The boards of this bridge do not look secure.*
—v. **1** make safe; protect: *Every loan was secured by bonds or mortgages.* **2** make oneself safe; be safe: *We must secure against the dangers of the coming storm.* **3** make (something) sure or certain. **4** make firm or fast: *Secure the locks on the windows.* **5** get; obtain: *Secure your tickets early.* [< L *securus* < *se-* free from + *cura* care. Doublet of SURE.] **—se·cur′a·ble,** *adj.* **—se·cur′er,** *n.* **—se·cure′ly,** *adv.* **—se·cure′ness,** *n.* **—Syn.** *adj.* **1** See **safe. 4** fast, firm, stable, immovable. *–v.* **1** guard, defend, shield. **3** assure, insure. **4** fasten, tie.

se·cu·ri·ty (si kūr′ə tē) *n.* **-ties. 1** freedom from danger, care, or fear; feeling or condition of being safe. **2** certainty. **3** carelessness; overconfidence. **4** something that secures or makes safe: *My watchdog is a security against burglars.* **5 securities,** *pl.* bonds, stocks, etc.: *These railway securities can be sold for $5,000.* **6** something given as a pledge that a person will fulfil some duty, promise, etc. A life-insurance policy may serve as security for a loan. **7** a person who agrees to be responsible for another. —**Syn. 1** confidence. **4** safety, protection, defence.

Security Council in the United Nations, a permanent body whose function is to maintain world peace. It has five permanent members—France, Great Britain, Nationalist China (Taiwan), the U.S.S.R., and the United States—and six rotating members.

secy. secretary.

se·dan (si dan′) *n.* **1** a closed automobile seating four or more persons. **2** a sedan chair. [origin uncertain]

sedan chair an enclosed chair carried on poles by two men.

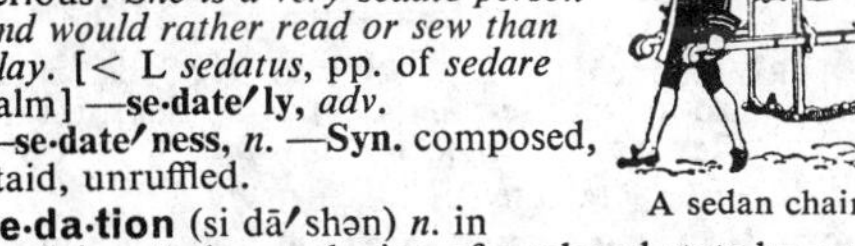
A sedan chair

se·date (si dāt′) *adj.* quiet; calm; serious: *She is a very sedate person and would rather read or sew than play.* [< L *sedatus,* pp. of *sedare* calm] —**se·date′ly,** *adv.* —**se·date′ness,** *n.* —**Syn.** composed, staid, unruffled.

se·da·tion (si dā′shən) *n.* in medicine: **1** the producing of a relaxed state by means of a sedative; treatment with sedatives. **2** a relaxed or painless state produced by sedatives.

sed·a·tive (sed′ə tiv) *n.* **1** a medicine that lessens pain or excitement. **2** anything soothing or calming. —*adj.* **1** lessening pain or excitement. **2** soothing; calming.

sed·en·tar·y (sed′ən ter′ē) *adj.* **1** used to sitting still much of the time: *Sedentary people get little physical exercise.* **2** that keeps one sitting still much of the time: *Bookkeeping is a sedentary occupation.* **3** moving little and rarely. **4** fixed to one spot. **5** not migratory. Pigeons are sedentary birds. [< L *sedentarius,* ult. < *sedere* sit] —**sed′en·tar′i·ly,** *adv.* —**sed′en·tar′i·ness,** *n.*

Se·der (sā′dər) *n.* **Se·ders** or **Se·dar·im** (se där′im). the religious rites and feast held in Jewish homes on the first two nights of Passover. [< Hebrew]

sedge (sej) *n.* a grasslike plant that grows in wet places. [OE *secg*]

sedged (sejd) *adj.* **1** made of sedge. **2** abounding or bordered with sedge.

sedg·y (sej′ē) *adj.* **1** abounding in or covered with sedge; bordered with sedge: *a sedgy brook.* **2** like sedge.

sed·i·ment (sed′ə mənt) *n.* **1** any matter that settles to the bottom of a liquid; dregs. **2** in geology, earth or detritus suspended in or deposited by water, wind, or ice: *Each year the Nile overflows and deposits sediment on the land.* [< F < L *sedimentum* < *sedere* settle]

sed·i·men·tal (sed′ə men′təl) *adj.* sedimentary.

sed·i·men·ta·ry (sed′ə men′tə rē or sed′ə men′trē) *adj.* **1** of sediment; having to do with sediment. **2** in geology, formed from sediment.

sed·i·men·ta·tion (sed′ə men tā′shən) *n.* a depositing of sediment.

se·di·tion (si dish′ən) *n.* speech or action causing discontent or rebellion against the government; incitement to discontent or rebellion. [ME < L *seditio, -onis* < *sed-,* var. of *se-* apart + *ire* go] —**Syn.** revolt, insurrection, mutiny, riot, insubordination.

se·di·tion·ar·y (si dish′ən er′ē) *adj. n.* **-ar·ies.** —*adj.* having to do with or involving sedition. —*n.* one guilty of sedition.

se·di·tious (si dish′əs) *adj.* **1** stirring up discontent or rebellion. **2** taking part in sedition; guilty of sedition. **3** having to do with sedition. —**se·di′tious·ly,** *adv.* —**se·di′tious·ness,** *n.*

se·duce (si dūs′ or si düs′) *v.* **-duced, -duc·ing. 1** tempt to wrongdoing; persuade to do wrong: *The traitor was seduced by the offer of great wealth to betray his country.* **2** lead away from virtue; lead astray; beguile. **3** persuade (a person of the opposite sex to whom one is not married) to engage in sexual intercourse, especially for the first time. **4** win over; beguile; entice. [< L *seducere* < *se-* aside + *ducere* lead] —**se·duc′er,** *n.* —**Syn. 1** corrupt. **2** mislead. **3** betray.

hat, āge, cãre, fär; let, ēqual, tėrm; it, īce
hot, ōpen, ôrder; oil, out; cup, pu̇t, rüle, ūse
əbove, takən, pencəl, lemən, circəs
ch, child; ng, long; sh, ship
th, thin; ᴛʜ, then; zh, measure

se·duce·ment (si dūs′mənt or si düs′mənt) *n.* seduction.

se·duc·i·ble (si dūs′ə bəl or si düs′ə bəl) *adj.* that can be seduced.

se·duc·tion (si duk′shən) *n.* **1** the act of seducing; the fact or condition of being seduced. **2** something that seduces; temptation; attraction. [< L *seductio, -onis* < *seducere.* See SEDUCE.]

se·duc·tive (si duk′tiv) *adj.* alluring; captivating; charming. —**se·duc′tive·ly,** *adv.* —**se·duc′tive·ness,** *n.*

se·du·li·ty (si dū′lə tē or si dü′lə tē) *n.* the quality of being sedulous; diligent application or care.

sed·u·lous (sej′ù ləs) *adj.* hard-working; diligent; painstaking. [< L *sedulus* < *se dolo* without deception] —**sed′u·lous·ly,** *adv.* —**sed′u·lous·ness,** *n.* —**Syn.** industrious, assiduous, persevering, untiring.

se·dum (sē′dəm) *n.* any of a large group of fleshy plants, most of which have clusters of yellow, white, or pink flowers. [< L *sedum* house leek]

see[1] (sē) *v.* **saw, seen, see·ing. 1** perceive with the eyes; look at: *See that black cloud.* **2** use the eyes to see things: *see a tennis match.* **3** have the power of sight: *The blind do not see.* **4** perceive with the mind; understand: *I see what you mean.* **5** find out; learn: *I will see what needs to be done.* **6** take care; make sure: *See that you lock the back door.* **7** think; consider: *You may go if you see fit to do so.* **8** have knowledge or experience of: *That coat has seen hard wear.* **9** attend; escort; go with: *see a girl home.* **10** meet; have a talk with: *He wishes to see you alone.* **11** call on: *I went to see a friend.* **12** receive a call from: *She is too ill to see anyone.* **13** visit; attend: *We saw the Canadian National Exhibition.* **14** in poker, etc., meet (a bet) by staking an equal sum. **15 see after,** take care of. **16 see into,** understand the real character or hidden purpose of. **17 see off,** go with to the starting place of a journey. **18 see one's way,** see the possibility of doing something. **19 see out,** go through with; finish. **20 see through, a** understand the real character or hidden purpose of. **b** go through with; finish. **c** watch over or help through a difficulty. **21 see to,** look after; take care of. [OE *sēon*]

Syn. 1 See, perceive, observe = become aware of something through sight. **See,** the general word, means "be conscious of what is before the eyes," with or without trying: *We saw someone standing in the doorway.* **Perceive,** the formal substitute for *see,* emphasizes using the mind as well as the eyes and consciously noticing or recognizing what is seen: *We perceived the figure to be your mother.* **Observe** suggests directing the attention as well as the eyes to what is seen: *We observed a change in her.* **2** watch, witness, regard. **4** apprehend.

see[2] (sē) *n.* **1** the position or authority of a bishop. **2** the district under a bishop's authority; diocese; bishopric. [ME < OF *sie* < L *sedes* abode; OF form influenced by forms like *siet* sits < L *sedet*]

seed (sēd) *n.* **seeds** or **seed,** *adj. v.* —*n.* **1** the thing from which a flower, vegetable, or other plant grows; a small, grainlike fruit. Farmers often save part of a crop for the seeds. **2** a bulb, sprout, or any part of a plant from which a new plant will grow. **3** seeds collectively. **4** the source or beginning of anything: *seeds of trouble.* **5** children; descendants: *The Jews are the seed of Abraham.* **6** semen; sperm. **7** a minute bubble arising in glass during fusion. **8 go to seed, a** come to the time of yielding seeds. **b** come to the end of vigor, usefulness, prosperity, etc.: *Since the mines closed, the town has gone to seed.*
—*adj.* of or containing seeds; used for seeds.
—*v.* **1** sow with seeds; scatter seeds over: *The farmer seeded his field with corn.* **2** sow (seeds). **3** produce seeds; shed seeds. **4** remove the seeds from: *seed raisins.* **5** in tournaments, arrange (the names of players) according to a preliminary ranking so that the best players do not

meet in the early matches. 6 scatter dry ice or other chemicals into clouds from an airplane in an effort to produce rain artificially. [OE *sǣd*] —**seed′less,** *adj.* —**seed′like′,** *adj.*

seed·bed (sēd′bed′) *n.* 1 soil that is specially prepared for nurturing plants from seed. 2 any place conducive to growth and development; breeding ground.

seed capsule seed vessel; pericarp.

seed·case (sēd′kās′) *n.* any pod, capsule, or other dry, hollow fruit that contains seeds.

seed·er (sēd′ər) *n.* 1 one that seeds. 2 a machine or device for planting seeds. 3 a machine or device for removing seeds.

seed leaf the embryo leaf in the seed of a plant; cotyledon.

seed·ling (sēd′ling) *n.* 1 a young plant grown from a seed. 2 a young tree less than three feet high. —*adj.* 1 developed or raised from seed. 2 like a small seed; existing in a rudimentary state.

seed pearl a very small pearl.

seed plant any plant that bears seeds. Most seed plants have flowers and produce seeds in fruits; some, such as the pines, form seeds on cones.

seeds·man (sēdz′mən) *n.* **-men** (-mən). 1 a sower of seed. 2 a dealer in seed.

seed tree a tree providing seed for natural reproduction.

seed vessel any pod, capsule, or other hollow fruit that contains seeds; pericarp.

seed·y (sēd′ē) *adj.* **seed·i·er, seed·i·est.** 1 full of seed. 2 gone to seed. 3 *Informal.* shabby; no longer fresh or new: *seedy clothes.* —**seed′i·ly,** *adv.* —**seed′i·ness,** *n.*

see·ing (sē′ing) *conj.* in view of the fact; considering: *Seeing that it is 10 o'clock, we will wait no longer.*

Seeing Eye an organization that breeds and trains dogs as guides for blind people.

seeing-eye dog a dog trained as a guide for blind people.

seek (sēk) *v.* **sought, seek·ing.** 1 try to find; look for: *We are seeking a new home.* 2 hunt; search: *seek for something lost.* 3 try to get: *Friends sought his advice.* 4 try; attempt: *He seeks to make peace with his enemies.* 5 go to: *Being sleepy, he sought his bed.* 6 *Archaic.* go [OE *sēcan*] —**seek′er,** *n.*

seem (sēm) *v.* 1 appear; appear to be: *He seemed a very old man.* 2 appear to oneself: *I still seem to hear the music.* 3 appear to exist: *There seems no need to wait longer.* 4 appear to be true or to be the case: *It seems likely to rain. This, it seems, is your idea of cleaning a room.* [ME < ON *sœma* < *sœmr* seemly]

Syn. 1 **Seem, appear** = give the impression or have the outward look of being something that (it) may or may not be in fact or reality. Although often used interchangeably, **seem** particularly suggests showing signs or giving other indications that point to a conclusion and serve as the basis of an opinion arrived at: *He seems to be sick. His efforts seem in vain.* **Appear** particularly suggests the way the thing looks on the surface or is seen or perceived by the observer: *He does appear pale, but to me he appears able to work.*

seem·ing (sēm′ing) *adj.* apparent; that appears to be: *a seeming advantage.* —*n.* appearance: *It was worse in its seeming than in reality.*

seem·ing·ly (sēm′ing lē) *adv.* apparently; as far as appearances go: *This hill is, seemingly, the highest.*

seem·ly (sēm′lē) *adj.* **-li·er, -li·est,** *adv.* —*adj.* 1 suitable; proper: *Some old people do not consider modern dances seemly.* 2 having a pleasing appearance. —*adv.* properly; becomingly; fittingly. [ME < ON *sœmiligr*] —**seem′li·ness,** *n.* —**Syn.** *adj.* 1 becoming, decorous, decent. See **fitting.**

seen (sēn) *v.* pp. of **see**[1].

seep (sēp) *v.* ooze; trickle; leak: *Water seeps through sand.* [apparently < MDu. *sipen*; akin to OE *sipian* to leak]

seep·age (sēp′ij) *n.* 1 a seeping; leakage. 2 moisture or liquid that seeps.

seep·er (sēp′ər) *n.* a pit for collecting water that seeps into cellars, etc.; sump.

seer (sēr) *n.* a person who foresees or foretells future events; prophet.

seer·ess (sēr′is) *n.* a woman who is a seer.

seer·suck·er (sēr′suk′ər) *n.* a thin cotton, rayon, nylon, etc. fabric, usually with alternate plain and crinkled stripes. [< Hind. < Persian *shir o shakkar,* literally, milk and sugar]

see·saw (sē′so′ or -sô′) *n. v. adj.* teeter-totter. [varied reduplication of *saw*[1]]

seethe (sēTH) *v.* **seethed, seeth·ing.** 1 bubble and foam: *Water seethed under the falls.* 2 be excited; be disturbed. 3 soak; steep. 4 *Archaic.* boil. [OE *sēothan* boil] —**Syn.** 1 See **boil.**

seg·ment (seg′mənt) *n.* 1 a part cut, marked, or broken off; division; section: *An orange is easily pulled apart into its segments.* 2 in geometry: **a** a part of a circle, sphere, etc. cut off by a line or plane. **b** any of the finite sections of a divided line. 3 in biology, one of a series of parts having a more or less similar structure: *a segment of a tapeworm.* —*v.* divide into segments. [< L *segmentum* < *secare* cut] —**Syn.** *n.* 1 portion, piece.

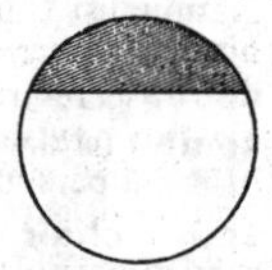
The shaded part is a segment of the circle.

seg·men·tal (seg men′təl) *adj.* 1 composed of segments. 2 of or having to do with segments. 3 having the form of a segment of a circle. —**seg·men′tal·ly,** *adv.*

seg·men·tar·y (seg′mən ter′ē) *adj.* segmental.

seg·men·ta·tion (seg′mən tā′shən) *n.* 1 a division into segments. 2 in biology, the growth and division of a cell into two, four, eight cells, and so on.

seg·re·gate (*v.* seg′rə gāt′; *adj.* seg′rə git or seg′rə gāt′) *v.* **-gat·ed, -gat·ing,** *adj.* —*v.* 1 separate from others; set apart; isolate: *The doctor segregated the sick child.* 2 separate from the rest and collect in one place. 3 cause the keeping apart of one race, people, etc. from another by providing separate housing, schools, etc. —*adj.* segregated. [< L *segregare* < *se-* apart from + *grex, gregis* herd]

seg·re·ga·tion (seg′rə gā′shən) *n.* 1 a separation from others; setting apart; isolation. 2 the keeping apart of one race, people, etc. from another by providing separate housing, schools, etc. 3 a thing separated or set apart; isolated part, group, etc.

seg·re·ga·tion·ist (seg′rə gā′shən ist) *n.* a person who believes in the keeping apart of one race from another in housing, schools, etc.

seg·re·ga·tive (seg′rə gā′tiv) *adj.* 1 tending to segregate. 2 keeping apart from others; unsociable.

Seid·litz powder (sed′lits) a laxative consisting of two powders, one tartaric acid and the other a mixture of sodium bicarbonate and Rochelle salt. These are dissolved separately, and the solutions are mixed and drunk while effervescing. [after *Seidlitz,* a village in Czechoslovakia]

seif (sīf) *n.* a long, crescent-shaped dune stretching in the direction of the wind that caused it. [< Arabic *saif* sword, from its shape]

seign·ior or **sei·gneur** (sēn yėr′; *French,* se nyœr′) *n.* 1 in French Canada, a person granted a seigniory; landowner. 2 a feudal lord or landowner. A **grand seignior** was a person of high rank. [< F *seigneur* < OF *seignor* < *accus.* of L *senior.* See SENIOR. Doublet of SIEUR.]

seign·ior·age (sēn′yər ij) *n.* 1 something claimed by a sovereign or superior as a prerogative. 2 a charge for coining gold or silver.

sei·gnio·ri·al (sēn yô′rē əl) *adj.* of or having to do with a seignior.

seign·ior·y or **sei·gneur·y** (sēn′yər ē; *French,* se nyœ rē′) *n.* **-ior·ies.** 1 in French Canada, a tract of land or an estate originally granted to an individual by the King of France. 2 power or authority of a seignior. 3 a feudal lord's domain. 4 a group of lords. [ME < OF *seignorie* < *seignor.* See SEIGNIOR.]

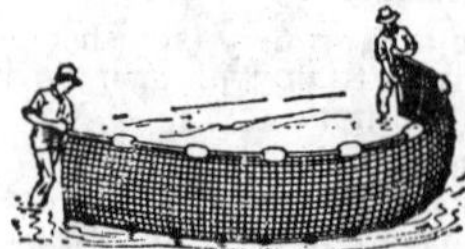
Men using a seine. It is lowered into the water and then pulled toward the shore.

seine (sān) *n. v.* **seined, sein·ing.** —*n.* a fishing net that hangs straight down in the water. A seine has floats at the upper edge and sinkers at the lower. —*v.* **1** fish with a seine. **2** catch with a seine. [OE *segne* < L *sagena* < Gk. *sagēnē*] —**sein′er,** *n.*

seishe (sāsh) *n.* an occasional rhythmic rising and falling of the level of water in a lake, lasting briefly and usually attributed to local changes in atmospheric pressure. [< Swiss French]

seism (sī′zəm) *n.* an earthquake.

seis·mic (sīz′mik or sīs′mik) *adj.* **1** of earthquakes; having to do with an earthquake. **2** caused by an earthquake. [< Gk. *seismos* earthquake < *seiein* shake]

seismo- *combining form.* earthquake, as in *seismograph.* [< Gk. *seismos*]

seis·mo·gram (sīz′mə gram′ or sīs′mə-) *n.* a record of an earthquake obtained by a seismograph.

seis·mo·graph (sīz′mə graf′ or sīs′mə-) *n.* an instrument for recording the direction, intensity, and duration of earthquakes.

seis·mo·graph·ic (sīz′mə graf′ik or sīs′mə-) *adj.* **1** of a seismograph. **2** of seismography.

seis·mog·ra·phy (sīz mog′rə fē or sīs mog′rə fē) *n.* **1** the art of using the seismograph in recording earthquakes. **2** the branch of seismology dealing especially with the mapping and description of earthquakes.

seis·mo·log·i·cal (sīz′mə loj′ə kəl or sīs′mə-) *adj.* of or having to do with seismology.

seis·mol·o·gist (sīz mol′ə jist or sīs mol′ə jist) *n.* a person who is trained in seismology.

seis·mol·o·gy (sīz mol′ə jē or sīs mol′ə jē) *n.* the study of earthquakes and other movements of the earth's crust.

seis·mom·e·ter (sīz mom′ə tər or sīs mom′ə tər) *n.* seismograph.

seize (sēz) *v.* **seized, seiz·ing. 1** take hold of suddenly; clutch; grasp: *When she lost her balance, she seized his arm.* **2** grasp with the mind: *seize an idea, the point, etc.* **3** take possession of by force: *The soldiers seized the city.* **4** take possession of or come upon suddenly: *A fever seized him.* **5** take possession of by legal authority. **6** in law, put in possession of; possess. **7** bind; lash; make fast: *seize one rope to another.* **8** of a moving part of an engine or other mechanism, get stuck or jammed: *The valve has seized up.* **9 seize on** or **upon, a** take hold of suddenly. **b** take possession of. [ME < OF *seisir,* ult. < Gmc.]

Syn. 1 Seize, grasp, clutch = take hold of something. **Seize** emphasizes taking hold suddenly and with force: *The dog seized the sausages.* **Grasp** = seize and hold firmly with the fingers, claws, talons, closed around the object: *The eagle grasped the rat.* **Clutch** = grasp eagerly, sometimes greedily, and tightly as in a clenched fist: *The child clutched his toy.*

seiz·ing (sēz′ing) *n.* **1** a binding, lashing, or fastening together with several turns of small rope, cord, etc. **2** a fastening made in this way. **3** a small rope, cord, etc. used for making such fastenings.

sei·zure (sē′zhər) *n.* **1** the act of seizing. **2** the condition of being seized. **3** a sudden attack of disease.

se·lah (sē′lə) *n.* a Hebrew word occurring frequently in the Psalms, supposed to be a direction to musicians. Selah perhaps means "Pause here."

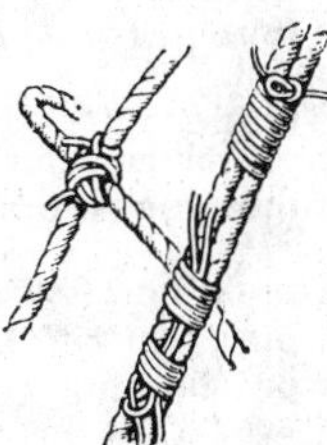
Nautical seizings

sel·dom (sel′dəm) *adv.* rarely; not often: *He is seldom ill.* [OE *seldum*]

se·lect (si lekt′) *v.* choose; pick out: *Select the book you want.* —*adj.* **1** picked as best; chosen specially: *A few select officials were admitted to the conference.* **2** choice; superior: *That store carries a very select line of merchandise.* **3** careful in choosing; particular as to friends, company, etc.: *She belongs to a very select club.* [< L *selectus,* pp. of *seligere* < *se-* apart + *legere* choose] —**se·lect′ly,** *adv.* —**se·lect′ness,** *n.* —**Syn.** *adj.* **2** picked.

se·lec·tion (si lek′shən) *n.* **1** choice. **2** a person, thing, or group chosen. **3** in biology, any process by which certain animals or plants survive and reproduce their kind, while other less suitable ones die, or are prevented from breeding.

hat, āge, cãre, fär; let, ēqual, tėrm; it, īce
hot, ōpen, ôrder; oil, out; cup, pu̇t, rüle, ūse
əbove, takən, pencəl, lemən, circəs
ch, child; ng, long; sh, ship
th, thin; ᴛʜ, then; zh, measure

se·lec·tive (si lek′tiv) *adj.* **1** selecting; having the power to select. **2** having to do with selection. **3** responding to oscillations of a certain frequency only. When a selective radio is tuned to one station, those on other wave lengths are excluded.

se·lec·tiv·i·ty (si lek tiv′ə tē) *n.* **1** the quality of being selective. **2** the property of a circuit, instrument, etc. by virtue of which it responds to electric oscillations of a particular frequency; especially, the ability of a radio receiving set to receive certain frequencies or waves to the exclusion of others.

se·lec·tor (si lek′tər) *n.* **1** a person who selects. **2** a mechanical or electrical device that selects.

Se·le·ne (sə lē′nē) *n.* in Greek mythology, the goddess of the moon.

sel·e·nite (sel′ə nīt′ or sə lē′nīt) *n.* a variety of gypsum, found in transparent crystals and foliated masses. [< L < Gk. *selēnitēs* (*lithos*) (stone) of the moon < *selēnē* moon; its brightness was supposed to vary with the moon]

se·le·ni·um (sə lē′nē əm) *n.* a non-metallic chemical element resembling sulphur in chemical properties. Because its electrical resistance varies with the amount of light, selenium is used in photo-electric cells. *Symbol*: Se: *at.no.* 34; *at.wt.* 78.96. [< NL < Gk. *selēnē* moon]

self (self) *n.* **selves,** *adj. pron.* **selves.** —*n.* **1** one's own person: *his very self.* **2** one's own welfare, interests, etc.: *A selfish person puts self first.* **3** the nature, character, etc. of a person or thing: *She does not seem like her former self.* —*adj.* being the same throughout; all of one kind, quality, color, material, etc. —*pron.* myself; himself; herself; yourself: *a cheque made payable to self.* [OE]

☛ Self as a suffix forms the reflexive and intensive pronouns: *myself, yourself, himself, herself, itself, oneself, ourselves, yourselves, themselves.* These are used chiefly for emphasis (*I can do that myself*) or as reflexive objects (*I couldn't help myself*).

☛ The pronominal use of *self* (*payable to self, a room for self and wife*) is largely confined to commercial English, and is not regarded as standard.

self- *prefix.* **1** of or over oneself, etc., as in *self-conscious, self-control.* **2** by or in oneself, etc., as in *self-inflicted, self-evident.* **3** to or for oneself, etc., as in *self-addressed, self-respect.* **4** automatic; automatically, as in *self-starter, self-closing.* [< *self*]

self-a·base·ment (self′ə bās′mənt) *n.* abasement of self.

self-ab·hor·rence (self′ab hôr′əns) *n.* abhorrence of self.

self-ab·ne·ga·tion (self′ab′nə gā′shən) *n.* self-denial.

self-ab·sorp·tion (self′ab sôrp′shən or -ab zôrp′shən) *n.* absorption in one's own thoughts, affairs, etc.

self-act·ing (self′ak′ting) *adj.* working of itself: *a self-acting machine.*

self-ad·dressed (self′ə drest′) *adj.* addressed to one-self: *a self-addressed envelope.*

self-as·ser·tion (self′ə sėr′shən) *n.* an insistence on one's own wishes, opinions, claims, etc.

self-as·ser·tive (self′ə sėr′tiv) *adj.* putting oneself forward; insisting on one's own wishes, opinions, etc. —**self′-as·ser′tive·ly,** *adv.*

self-as·sur·ance (self′ə shür′əns) *n.* self-confidence.

self-as·sured (self′ə shürd′) *adj.* self-confident; sure of oneself.

self-cen·tred or **self-cen·tered** (self′sen′tərd) *adj.* **1** occupied with one's own interests and affairs. **2** selfish. **3** being a fixed point around which other things move.

self-col·ored or **self-col·oured** (self′kul′ərd) *adj.* **1** of one uniform color. **2** of the natural color.

self-com·mand (self′kə mand′) *n.* control of oneself.

self-com·mun·ion (self′kə mūn′yən) *n.* communion with oneself.

self-com·pla·cence (self′kəm plā′səns) *n.* self-complacency.

self-com·pla·cen·cy (self′kəm plā′sən sē) *n.* the state or quality of being self-satisfied.

self-com·pla·cent (self′kəm plā′sənt) *adj.* pleased with oneself; self-satisfied. —**self′-com·pla′cent·ly,** *adv.*

self-con·ceit (self′kən sēt′) *n.* conceit; too much pride in oneself or one's ability.

self-con·fi·dence (self′kon′fə dəns) *n.* beliefs in one's own ability, power, judgment, etc.; confidence in oneself.

self-con·fi·dent (self′kon′fə dənt) *adj.* believing in one's own ability, power, judgment, etc. —**self′-con′fi·dent·ly,** *adv.*

self-con·scious (self′kon′shəs) *adj.* made conscious of how one is appearing to others; embarrassed, especially by the presence of other people and their attitude toward one; shy. —**self′-con′scious·ly,** *adv.* —**self′-con′scious·ness,** *n.*

self-con·se·quence (self′kon′sə kwens′ or -kon′sə kwəns) *n.* a sense of one's own importance.

self-con·sist·ent (self′kən sis′tənt) *adj.* consistent with oneself or itself; having its parts or elements in agreement. —**self′-con·sist′ent·ly,** *adv.*

self-con·tained (self′kən tānd′) *adj.* **1** saying little; reserved. **2** containing in oneself or itself all that is necessary; independent of what is external. **3** having all its working parts contained in one case, cover, or framework: *A watch is self-contained.* **4** of an apartment, etc., having all facilities (bathroom, kitchen, etc.) within itself, and having a private entrance.

self-con·tra·dic·tion (self′kon′trə dik′shən) *n.* **1** a contradiction of oneself or itself. **2** a statement containing elements that are contradictory.

self-con·tra·dic·to·ry (self′kon′trə dik′tə rē) *adj.* contradicting oneself or itself. —**self′-con′tra·dic′to·ri·ly,** *adv.*

self-con·trol (self′kən trōl′) *n.* control of one's actions, feelings, etc.

self-crit·i·cism (self′krit′ə siz′əm) *n.* criticism of oneself.

self-de·cep·tive (self′di sep′tiv) *adj.* deceiving oneself. —**self′-de·cep′tive·ly,** *adv.*

self-de·fence or **self-de·fense** (self′di fens′) *n.* defence of one's own person, property, reputation, etc.

self-de·ni·al (self′di nī′əl) *n.* a sacrifice of one's own desires and interests; going without things one wants. —**Syn.** self-sacrifice, abstemiousness, austerity.

self-de·ny·ing (self′di nī′ing) *adj.* unselfish; sacrificing one's own wishes and interests.

self-de·ter·mi·na·tion (self′di tėr′mə nā′shən) *n.* **1** direction from within only, without influence or force from without. **2** the deciding by the people of a nation what form of government they are to have, without reference to the wishes of any other nation.

self-de·ter·min·ing (self′di tėr′mən ing) *adj.* determining one's own acts; having the power of self-determination.

self-de·vo·tion (self′di vō′shən) *n.* self-sacrifice.

self-dis·ci·pline (self′dis′ə plin) *n.* careful control and training of oneself.

self-ed·u·cat·ed (self′ej′ů kāt′id) *adj.* self-taught; educated by one's own efforts.

self-ef·face·ment (self′ə fās′mənt) *n.* the act or habit of modestly keeping oneself in the background.

self-es·teem (self′əs tēm′) *n.* **1** thinking well of oneself; self-respect. **2** thinking too well of oneself; conceit.

self-ev·i·dent (self′ev′ə dənt) *adj.* evident by itself; needing no proof. —**self′-ev′i·dent·ly,** *adv.*

self-ex·am·i·na·tion (self′eg zam′ə nā′shən) *n.* examination into one's own state, conduct, motives, etc.

self-ex·ist·ent (self′eg zis′tənt) *adj.* **1** existing independently of any other cause. **2** having an independent existence.

self-ex·plan·a·to·ry (self′eks plan′ə tô′rē) *adj.* explaining itself; that needs no explanation; obvious.

self-ex·pres·sion (self′eks presh′ən) *n.* an expression of one's personality.

self-fill·ing (self′fil′ing) *adj.* that can fill itself.

self-gov·erned (self′guv′ərnd) *adj.* having self-government.

self-gov·ern·ing (self′guv′ər ning) *adj.* that governs itself.

self-gov·ern·ment (self′guv′ərn mənt or -guv′ər mənt) *n.* **1** government of a group by its own members: *self-government through elected representatives.* **2** self-control.

self·heal (self′hēl′) *n.* a weed having blue or purple flowers, formerly supposed to heal wounds.

self-help (self′help′) *n.* a helping oneself; getting along without assistance from others.

self-im·por·tance (self′im pôr′təns) *n.* a having or showing too high an opinion of one's own importance; conceit; behavior showing conceit.

self-im·por·tant (self′im pôr′tənt) *adj.* having or showing too high an opinion of one's own importance. —**self′-im·por′tant·ly,** *adv.*

self-im·posed (self′im pōzd′) *adj.* imposed on oneself by oneself.

self-im·prove·ment (self′im prüv′mənt) *n.* an improvement of one's character, mind, etc. by one's own efforts.

self-in·duced (self′in dūst′ or -in düst′) *adj.* **1** induced by itself; induced by oneself. **2** produced by self-induction.

self-in·duc·tion (self′in duk′shən) *n.* in electricity, the inducing of a current in a circuit by a varying current in that circuit.

self-in·dul·gence (self′in dul′jəns) *n.* a gratification of one's own desires, passions, etc. with too little regard for the welfare of others.

self-in·dul·gent (self′in dul′jənt) *adj.* characterized by self-indulgence. —**self′-in·dul′gent·ly,** *adv.*

self-in·flict·ed (self′in flik′tid) *adj.* inflicted on oneself by oneself.

self-in·ter·est (self′in′trist or -in′tər ist) *n.* **1** an interest in one's own welfare with too little care for the welfare of others; selfishness. **2** personal advantage.

self·ish (sel′fish) *adj.* **1** caring too much for oneself; caring too little for others. A selfish person puts his own interests first. **2** showing care solely or chiefly for oneself: *selfish motives.* —**self′ish·ly,** *adv.* —**self′ish·ness,** *n.*

self-knowl·edge (self′nol′ij) *n.* knowledge of one's own character, ability, etc.

self·less (self′lis) *adj.* having no regard or thought for self; unselfish. —**self′less·ly,** *adv.*

self-love (self′luv′) *n.* **1** love of oneself; selfishness. **2** conceit.

self-made (self′mād′) *adj.* **1** made by oneself. **2** successful through one's own efforts.

self-mov·ing (self′müv′ing) *adj.* that can move by itself.

self-or·dained (self′ôr dānd′) *adj.* ordained by oneself.

self-pit·y (self′pit′ē) *n.* pity for oneself.

self-pol·li·na·tion (self′pol′ə nā′shən) *n.* the transfer of pollen from a stamen to a pistil of the same flower.

self-pos·sessed (self′pə zest′) *adj.* having or showing control of one's feelings and acts; not excited, embarrassed, or confused; calm. —**Syn.** composed, collected, poised, assured, unruffled.

self-pos·ses·sion (self′pə zesh′ən) *n.* the control of one's feelings and actions; composure; calmness.

self-praise (self′prāz′) *n.* praise of oneself.

self-pres·er·va·tion (self′prez′ər vā′shən) *n.* the preservation of oneself from harm or destruction.

self-re·cord·ing (self′ri kôr′ding) *adj.* that makes a record of its own operations; recording automatically.

self-reg·is·ter·ing (self′rej′is tər ing) *adj.* registering automatically.

self-reg·u·lat·ing (self′reg′yů lāt′ing) *adj.* regulating oneself or itself.

self-re·li·ance (self′ri lī′əns) *n.* a reliance on one's own acts, abilities, etc.

self-re·li·ant (self′ri lī′ənt) *adj.* having or showing self-reliance. **—self′-re·li′ant·ly,** *adv.*

self-re·proach (self′ri prōch′) *n.* blame by one's own conscience.

self-re·spect (self′ri spekt′) *n.* respect for oneself; proper pride.

self-re·spect·ing (self′ri spek′ting) *adj.* having self-respect; properly proud.

self-re·straint (self′ri strānt′) *n.* self-control.

self-right·eous (self′rī′chəs) *adj.* thinking that one is more moral than others; thinking that one is very good and pleasing to God. **—self′-right′eous·ly,** *adv.* **—self′-right′eous·ness,** *n.*

self-sac·ri·fice (self′sak′rə fīs′) *n.* the sacrifice of one's own interests and desires, for one's duty, another's welfare, etc.

self-sac·ri·fic·ing (self′sak′rə fīs′ing) *adj.* unselfish; giving up things for someone else.

self·same (self′sām′) *adj.* the very same: *We study the selfsame books that you do.* [< *self,* adj. + *same*]

self-sat·is·fac·tion (self′sat′is fak′shən) *n.* a satisfaction with oneself.

self-sat·is·fied (self′sat′is fīd′) *adj.* pleased with oneself.

self-seek·er (self′sēk′ər) *n.* a person who seeks his own interests too much.

self-seek·ing (self′sēk′ing) *adj.* selfish. **—*n.*** selfishness.

self-serv·ice (self′sėr′vis) *n.* the serving of oneself in a restaurant, store, etc.

self-start·er (self′stär′tər) *n.* an electric motor or other device used to start an engine automatically.

self-styled (self′stīld′) *adj.* called by oneself: *a self-styled leader whom no one follows.*

self-suf·fi·cien·cy (self′sə fish′ən sē) *n.* **1** the ability to supply one's own needs. **2** conceit; self-assurance.

self-suf·fi·cient (self′sə fish′ənt) *adj.* **1** asking no help; independent. **2** having too much confidence in one's own resources, powers, etc.; conceited. **—self′-suf·fi′cient·ly,** *adv.*

self-suf·fic·ing (self′sə fīs′ing) *adj.* sufficing in or for oneself or itself; self-sufficient.

self-sup·port (self′sə pôrt′) *n.* unaided support of oneself.

self-sup·port·ing (self′sə pôr′ting) *adj.* earning one's expenses; getting along without help.

self-sus·tain·ing (self′səs tān′ing) *adj.* self-supporting.

self-taught (self′tot′ or -tôt′) *adj.* taught by oneself without aid from others.

self-will (self′wil′) *n.* insistence on having one's own way.

self-willed (self′wild′) *adj.* insisting on having one's own way; objecting to doing what others ask or command.

self-wind·ing (self′wīn′ding) *adj.* that is wound automatically.

sell (sel) *v.* **sold, sell·ing,** *n.* **—*v.*** **1** exchange for money or other payment: *sell a house.* **2** deal in; keep for sale: *The butcher sells meat.* **3** be given in exchange; be on sale; be sold: *Strawberries sell at a high price in January.* **4** give up; betray: *The traitor sold his country for money.* **5** cause to be accepted, approved, or adopted by representations and methods characteristic of salesmanship: *sell an idea to the public.* **6** *Informal.* win acceptance, approval, or adoption: *This is an idea that will sell.* **7** *Slang.* cheat; trick; hoax. **8 sell off,** dispose of by sale. **9 sell on, a** inspire with the desire to buy or possess something. **b** *Informal.* show or convince of the value, truth, etc. of something. **10 sell out, a** sell all that one has of; get rid of by selling. **b** *Informal.* betray by a secret bargain.
—*n.* *Slang.* a cheat; trick; hoax. [OE *sellan*] **—Syn.** ***v.*** **1** vend, barter, trade.

sell·er (sel′ər) *n.* **1** a person who sells. **2** a thing considered with reference to its sale: *This book is a best seller.*

hat, āge, cãre, fär; let, ēqual, tėrm; it, īce
hot, ōpen, ôrder; oil, out; cup, pu̇t, rüle, ūse
əbove, takən, pencəl, lemən, circəs
ch, child; ng, long; sh, ship
th, thin; ᴛʜ, then; zh, measure

seller's market an economic condition in which there is greater demand for goods than can be met by the supplies available. Prices tend to be high in a seller's market.

sell-out (sel′out′) *n.* **1** *Informal.* a selling out. **2** *Informal.* a performance of a play, sports event, etc. for which all seats are sold..

Selt·zer (selt′sər) *n.* **1** a bubbling mineral water containing salt, sodium, calcium, and magnesium carbonates. **2** Often, **seltzer.** an artificial water of similar composition. [< G *Selterser* < *Selters,* Germany, where it is found]

sel·vage or **sel·vedge** (sel′vij) *n.* the edge of a fabric finished off to prevent ravelling; border; edge. [< *self* + *edge*; because it serves itself as an edge]

selves (selvz) *n.* pl. of **self**: *He had two selves—a good self and a bad self.*

Sem. 1 Seminary. **2** Semitic.

se·man·tic (sə man′tik) *adj.* **1** having to do with meaning. **2** having to do with semantics.

se·man·tics (sə man′tiks) *n.* the scientific study of the meanings, and the development of meanings, of words. [< LL *semanticus* < Gk. *sēmantikos* having meaning, ult. < *sēma* sign]

sem·a·phore (sem′ə fôr′) *n.v.* **-phored, -phor·ing. —*n.*** **1** an apparatus for signalling; an upright post or structure with movable arms, an arrangement of lanterns, flags, etc. used in railway signalling. **2** a system of signals for sending messages with the arms, with flags, or with mechanical devices.
—*v.* signal by semaphore.
[< Gk. *sēma* signal + *-phoros* carrying]

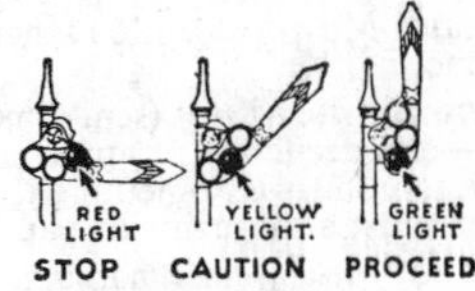

Railway semaphores

sem·blance (sem′bləns) *n.* **1** the outward appearance: *His story had the semblance of truth, but was really false.* **2** a likeness: *These clouds have the semblance of a huge head.* [ME < OF *semblance* < *sembler* seem, ult. < L *similis* similar]

se·men (sē′mən) *n.* the fluid containing the male reproductive cells. [< L *semen* seed]

se·mes·ter (sə mes′tər) *n.* a half of a school year. [< G < L *semestris* semi-annual, ult. < *sex* six + *mensis* month]

semi- *prefix.* **1** half: *semicircle* = *half circle.* **2** partly; incompletely: *semicivilized* = *partly civilized.* **3** twice. Semi——ly means in each half of a ——, or twice in a ——: *semi-annually* = *every half year, or twice a year.* [< L]

☛ Semi- usually is hyphenated before root words beginning with a vowel and before proper nouns and proper adjectives: *semi-annual, semi-invalid, semi-Christian.* In other cases a hyphen is optional, though one's own usage should be consistent.
☛ Semi- is generally pronounced (sem′ē) in Canada; the pronunciation (sem′ī) is frequently heard in the United States.

sem·i-an·nu·al (sem′ē an′ū əl) *adj.* **1** occurring every half year. **2** lasting a half year.

sem·i-an·nu·al·ly (sem′ē an′ū əl ē) *adv.* twice a year.

sem·i·ar·id (sem′ē ar′id) *adj.* having very little rainfall.

sem·i·breve (sem′ē brēv′) *n.* in music, the longest note in common use; a whole note.

sem·i·cir·cle (sem′ē sėr′kəl) *n.* half a circle: *We sat in a semicircle around the fire.*

sem·i·cir·cu·lar (sem′ē sėr′kyu̇ lər) *adj.* having the form of half a circle.

semicircular canal in anatomy, any of three curved, tubelike canals in the inner part of the ear that help us keep our balance. See **ear** for diagram.

sem·i·civ·i·lized (sem′ē siv′ə līzd′) *adj.* partly civilized.

sem·i·co·lon (sem′ē kō′lən) *n.* a mark of punctuation (;) that shows a separation less marked than that shown by a period.

sem·i·con·duct·or (sem′ē kən duk′tər) *n.* in electronics, a crystal, such as germanium or silicon, whose electrical conductivity lies between that of insulators and of metals, used in the manufacture of transistors, for converting alternating current to direct current, etc.

sem·i·con·scious (sem′ē kon′shəs) *adj.* half-conscious; not fully conscious. —**sem′i·con′scious·ly,** *adv.* —**sem′i·con′scious·ness,** *n.*

sem·i·dai·ly (sem′ē dā′lē) *adv.* twice a day.

sem·i·de·tached (sem′ē di tacht′) *adj.* partly detached, used especially of either of two houses joined by a common wall but separated from other buildings.

sem·i·de·vel·oped (sem′ē di vel′əpt) *adj.* not fully developed.

sem·i·di·vine (sem′ē də vīn′) *adj.* partly divine.

sem·i·fi·nal or **sem·i-fi·nal** (sem′ē fī′nəl) *n.* one of the rounds, matches, games, etc. that immediately precede the finals. – *adj.* designating or having to do with a round, match, game, etc.: *a semifinal score.*

sem·i·flu·id (sem′ē flü′id) *adj.* imperfectly fluid; extremely viscous. —*n.* a substance neither solid nor liquid; one that flows but is very thick: *A soft-boiled egg is a semifluid.*

sem·i·liquid (sem′ē lik′wid) *adj. n.* semifluid.

sem·i·lu·nar (sem′ē lü′nər) *adj.* shaped like a half moon.

sem·i·month·ly (sem′ē munth′lē) *adj. adv. n.* **-lies.** —*adj.* occurring or appearing twice a month. —*adv.* twice a month. —*n.* something that occurs or appears twice a month; a magazine or paper published twice a month.

sem·i·nal (sem′ə nəl) *adj.* **1** of or having to do with semen or seed. **2** containing semen or seed. **3** having to do with reproduction. **4** like seed; having the possibility of future development: *seminal ideas.* [ME < L *seminalis* < *semen* seed]

sem·i·nar (sem′ə när′) *n.* **1** a group of college or university students doing research under direction. **2** a course of study or work for such a group. **3** a meeting of such a group. **4** a specialized conference or short, intensive course of study. [< G < L *seminarium* plant nursery, hotbed < *semen* seed. Doublet of SEMINARY.]

sem·i·nar·i·an (sem′ə nãr′ē ən) *n.* a student at a seminary.

sem·i·nar·y (sem′ə ner′ē) *n.* **-nar·ies. 1** a school, especially one beyond high school. **2** an academy or boarding school, especially one for young women. **3** a school or college for training students to be priests, ministers, etc. **4** a place for instruction, training, or development. [< L *seminarium.* Doublet of SEMINAR.]

sem·i·na·tion (sem′ə nā′shən) *n.* a sowing; propagation; dissemination.

sem·i·nif·er·ous (sem′ə nif′ər əs) *adj.* **1** bearing or producing seed. **2** conveying or containing semen.

sem·i·of·fi·cial (sem′ē ə fish′əl or -ō fish′əl) *adj.* partly official; having some degree of authority.

sem·i·per·me·a·ble (sem′ē pėr′mē ə bəl) *adj.* partly permeable; permeable to some substances but not to others.

sem·i·pre·cious (sem′ē presh′əs) *adj.* having value but not great value. Amethysts and garnets are semiprecious stones; diamonds and rubies are precious stones.

sem·i·qua·ver (sem′ē kwā′vər) *n.* in music, a sixteenth note.

Se·mir·a·mis (sə mir′ə mis) *n.* an Assyrian princess who lived about 800 B.C. According to legend, she was famous for her beauty and wisdom, and was said to have founded Babylon.

sem·i·skilled (sem′ē skild′) *adj.* partly skilled.

sem·i·sol·id (sem′ē sol′id) *adj.* partly solid. —*n.* a partly solid substance.

Sem·ite (sem′īt or sē′mīt) *n.* **1** a member of any people speaking a Semitic language as their native tongue: *Jews and Arabs are Semites.* **2** a descendant of Shem.

Se·mit·ic (sə mit′ik) *adj.* of or having to do with the Semites or their languages. —*n.* a group of languages including Hebrew, Arabic, Aramaic, Phoenician, and Assyrian.

Sem·i·tism (sem′ə tiz′əm or sē′mə tiz′əm) *n.* **1** Semitic character, especially the ways, ideas, influence, etc. of the Jews. **2** a Semitic word or idiom.

sem·i·tone (sem′ē tōn′) *n.* in music, the smallest interval of the modern scale; a half tone; half step.

sem·i·trail·er (sem′ē trāl′ər) *n.* a type of truck trailer having wheels only at the rear, the front end being supported by the tractor.

sem·i·trop·i·cal (sem′ē trop′ə kəl) *adj.* halfway between tropical and temperate: *Mexico is a semitropical country.*

sem·i·vow·el (sem′ē vou′əl) *n.* **1** a sound that is intermediate between a vowel and a consonant. **2** a letter or character representing such a sound. *W* and *y* are semivowels in *win* and *yet.*

sem·i·week·ly (sem′ē wēk′lē) *adj. adv. n.* **-lies.** —*adj.* occurring or appearing twice a week. —*adv.* twice a week. —*n.* something that occurs or appears twice a week; a magazine or paper published twice a week.

sem·i·year·ly (sem′ē yēr′lē) *adj. adv. n.* **-lies.** —*adj.* occurring or appearing twice a year. —*adv.* twice a year. —*n.* something that occurs or appears twice a year.

sem·o·li·na (sem′ə lē′nə) *n.* the coarsely ground hard parts of wheat remaining after the fine flour has been sifted through, used in making puddings, macaroni, etc. [< Ital. *semolino,* ult. < L *simila* fine flour]

sem·pi·ter·nal (sem′pi tėr′nəl) *adj.* everlasting; eternal. [ME < LL *sempiternalis,* ult. < L *semper* forever]

semp·stress (sem′stris or semp′stris) *n.* seamstress.

sen (sen) *n.* **sen. 1** a unit of money in Japan, worth 1/100 of a yen. **2** a unit of money in Cambodia, worth 1/100 of a riel. **3** a coin worth one sen. [< Japanese]

Sen. 1 Senate. **2** Senator. **3** Senior.

sen·ate (sen′it) *n.* **1** a governing or lawmaking assembly: *the senate of a university.* The highest council of state in ancient Rome was called the senate. **2** the upper and smaller branch of an assembly or parliament that makes laws. **3 Senate** the upper and smaller branch of a parliament or legislature: *The Canadian Senate, which consists of 102 members appointed for life, is made up of representatives from each province.* [ME < OF < L *senatus* < *senex* old man]

sen·a·tor (sen′ə tər) *n.* a member of a senate. [< L]

sen·a·to·ri·al (sen′ə tô′rē əl) *adj.* **1** of or befitting a senator or senators. **2** consisting of senators. **3** entitled to elect a senator: *a senatorial district.*

sen·a·tor·ship (sen′ə tər ship′) *n.* the position, duties, etc. of a senator.

send (send) *v.* **sent, send·ing. 1** cause to go. **2** cause (a person) to live in a certain place, engage in a certain employment, etc. for a period of time: *send a boy to college.* **3** refer (a reader) to some author, authority, etc.: *send a reader to the dictionary.* **4** cause to be carried: *send a letter.* **5** cause to come, occur, be, etc.: *The earthquake sent destruction to the village.* **6** despatch a message or messenger: *Send for a doctor.* **7** drive; impel; throw: *send a ball.* **8** send forth; emit: *The volcano sent clouds of smoke into the air.* **9 a** transmit (radio signals, etc.). **b** transmit (a current, electromagnetic wave, etc.) by means of pulsation. **10** *Slang.* excite greatly or inspire, especially by jazz. [OE *sendan*] —**send′er,** *n.* —**Syn. 1** dispatch.

sen·dal (sen′dəl) *n.* **1** a silk fabric used during the Middle Ages. **2** a garment made of it. [ME < OF *cendal,* ult. < Gk. *sindon* fine cloth]

send-off (send′of′) *n.* **1** a friendly demonstration in honor of a person setting out on a journey, course, career, etc. **2** *Informal.* a start given to a person or thing.

Sen·e·ca (sen′ə kə) *n.* **1** the largest tribe of North American Indians belonging to the Five Nations confederacy, living mainly in New York State. **2** a member of this tribe. **3** the Iroquoian language of this tribe.

Sen·e·gal·ese (sen′ə gol ēz′ or sen′ə gôl ēz′) *adj. n.*

-ese. *—adj.* of or having to do with Senegal, a republic in W. Africa, or its people. *—n.* a native or inhabitant of Senegal.

se·nes·cence (sə nes′əns) *n.* the fact or condition of growing old.

se·nes·cent (sə nes′ənt) *adj.* growing old; beginning to show old age. [< L *senescens, -entis,* ppr. of *senescere* grow old, ult. < *senex* old]

sen·es·chal (sen′ə shəl) *n.* in the Middle Ages, a steward in charge of a royal palace, nobleman's estate, etc. Seneschals often had the powers of judges or generals. [ME < OF; from a Gmc. compound meaning "old servant"]

se·nile (sen′īl or sē′nīl) *adj.* **1** of old age. **2** showing the weakness of old age. **3** caused by old age. **4** in geology, having reached an advanced stage of erosion; made flat or level by the action of water, wind, etc.: *a senile valley.* *—n.* a senile person. [< L *senilis* < *senex* old]

se·nil·i·ty (sə nil′ə tē) *n.* **1** old age. **2** the physical and mental deterioration associated with old age.

sen·ior (sēn′yər) *adj.* **1** older. **2** the older; designating a father whose son has the same given name: *John Parker, Senior.* **3** higher in rank or longer in service: *Mr. Jones is the senior member of the firm of Jones and Brown.* **4** of or having to do with a graduating class.
—n. **1** an older person: *Paul is his brother's senior by two years.* **2** a person of higher rank or longer service. **3** a member of the graduating class of a high school or college. [< L *senior,* comparative of *senex* old. Doublet of SIRE.]

senior citizen any member of the community who is of advanced age.

senior high school a school attended after junior high school.

sen·ior·i·ty (sēn yôr′ə tē) *n.* **-ties. 1** superiority in age or standing; the state or fact of being older: *Harry felt that two years' seniority gave him the right to advise his brother.* **2** priority or precedence in office or service.

sen·na (sen′ə) *n.* **1** a laxative extracted from the dried leaves of any of several cassia plants. **2** the dried leaves of any of these plants. **3** the cassia plant, or a plant similar to it. [< NL < Arabic *sana*]

sen·night (sen′īt or sen′it) *n. Archaic.* seven nights and days; a week. [OE *seofon nihta* seven nights]

sen·nit (sen′it) *n.* a kind of flat, braided cordage used on shipboard, formed by plaiting strands of rope yarn or other fibre. [? < *seven* + *knit*]

se·ñor (sā nyôr′) *n.* **-ño·res** (-nyō′rās). *Spanish.* **1** Mr.; Sir. **2** a gentleman.

se·ño·ra (sā nyō′rä) *n. Spanish.* **1** Mrs.; Madame. **2** a lady.

se·ño·ri·ta (sā′nyō rē′tä) *n. Spanish.* **1** Miss. **2** a young lady.

sen·sa·tion (sen sā′shən) *n.* **1** the action of the senses; power to see, hear, feel, taste, smell, etc.: *A dead body is without sensation.* **2** a feeling: *Ice gives a sensation of coldness; sugar, of sweetness.* **3** strong or excited feeling: *The announcement of war caused a sensation throughout the country.* **4** the cause of such feeling: *The first manned orbit of the earth was a great sensation.* [< LL *sensatio, -onis,* ult. < L *sensus.* See SENSE.] **—Syn. 1** See **sense.**

sen·sa·tion·al (sen sā′shən əl or sen sāsh′nəl) *adj.* **1** arousing strong or excited feeling: *There were sensational developments in the murder case.* **2** trying to arouse strong or excited feeling: *a sensational newspaper story.* **3** of the senses; having to do with sensation. **4** of, based on, or adhering to sensationalism in philosophy. **—sen·sa′tion·al·ly,** *adv.* **—Syn. 1** exciting, thrilling, dramatic.

sen·sa·tion·al·ism (sen sā′shən əl iz′əm or sen sāsh′nəl iz′əm) *n.* **1** sensational methods; sensational writing, language, etc. **2** in philosophy, the theory or doctrine that all ideas are derived solely through sensation.

sen·sa·tion·al·ist (sen sā′shən əl ist or sen sāsh′nəl ist) *n.* **1** a sensational writer, speaker, etc.; one who tries to make a sensation. **2** a believer in philosophical sensationalism.

sense (sens) *n. v.* **sensed, sens·ing.** *—n.* **1 a** a power of the mind to know what happens outside itself. Sight, hearing, touch, taste, and smell are the five senses. **b** a receptor, or group of receptors, whereby an animal receives and responds to external or internal stimuli. **2** a feeling: *The extra lock on the door gave him a sense of security.* **3** the faculties of the mind or soul, compared or contrasted with the bodily senses; *moral sense.* **4** an understanding; appreciation: *Everyone thinks he has a sense of humor.* **5** Usually, **senses,** *pl.* normal, sound condition of mind. **6** the judgment; intelligence: *He had the good sense to keep out of foolish quarrels. Common sense would have prevented the accident.* **7** the recognition (of a duty, virtue, etc.) as incumbent upon one or as fitting and proper: *a sense of justice.* **8** an instinctive or acquired faculty of perception or accurate estimation: *a sense of direction, a sense of beauty.* **9** a meaning: *He was a gentleman in every sense of the word.* **10** discourse that has a satisfactory or intelligible meaning: *speak or write sense.* **11** the general opinion: *The sense of the assembly was clear even before the vote.* **12 in a sense,** in some respects; to some degree. **13 make sense,** be understandable; be reasonable: "*Cow cat bless Monday*" *does not make sense.*
—v. **1** be aware; feel: *She sensed that he was tired.* **2** *Informal.* understand. [ME < L *sensus* < *sentire* perceive]

Syn. *n.* **1, 2 Sense, sensation, sensibility** = the power or act of feeling or perceiving. **Sense** applies especially to the power of the mind to respond to a stimulus or influence outside itself, but implies awareness or full consciousness of something existing rather than bodily reaction: *He has a sense of well-being.* **Sensation** applies to physical feeling, particularly the response to stimulation of a bodily organ like the eyes or nerves: *He has no sensation in his feet.* **Sensibility** = capacity for feeling or perceiving physically or, especially, emotionally: *He has no sensibility to pain.* **6** See **meaning.**

sense·less (sens′lis) *adj.* **1** unconscious: *A blow on the head knocked him senseless.* **2** foolish; stupid. **3** meaningless: *senseless words.* **—sense′less·ly,** *adv.* **—sense′less·ness,** *n.*

sense organ the eye, ear, or other part of the body by which a person or an animal receives sensations of colors, sounds, smells, etc.

sen·si·bil·i·ty (sen′sə bil′ə tē) *n.* **-ties. 1** the ability to feel or perceive: *Some drugs lessen a person's sensibilities.* **2** sensitiveness. **3** fineness of feeling: *She has an unusual sensibility for colors.* **4** Usually, **sensibilities,** *pl.* sensitive feelings. **5** a tendency to feel hurt or offended too easily. **6** awareness; consciousness. **—Syn. 1** See **sense. 2** susceptibility, impressibility.

sen·si·ble (sen′sə bəl) *adj.* **1** having or showing good judgment; wise. **2** aware; conscious: *I am sensible of your kindness.* **3** that can be noticed. **4** that can be perceived by the senses. **5** large enough to be perceived or considered; considerable: *a sensible reduction in expenses.* **6** sensitive. [ME < LL *sensibilis,* ult. < L *sentire* feel]

Syn. **1 Sensible, practical** = having or showing good sense. **Sensible** emphasizes having and using common sense and good judgment in acting and speaking, and particularly suggests natural intelligence: *He is too sensible to do anything foolish.* **Practical** emphasizes using common sense in everyday affairs, and particularly suggests being given to action rather than thought or imagination and concerned with the usefulness, application, and results of knowledge, principles, and methods: *He is a practical man and does not understand dreamers and scientists.* **2** sentient, cognizant. **3** perceptible, appreciable.

sen·si·bly (sen′sə blē) *adv.* **1** in a sensible manner; with good sense. **2** so as to be felt.

sen·si·tive (sen′sə tiv) *adj.* **1** receiving impressions readily: *The eye is sensitive to light.* **2** easily affected or influenced: *The mercury in the thermometer is sensitive to changes in temperature.* **3** easily hurt or offended. **4** of or connected with the senses or sensation. **5** in medicine, unusually susceptible, as to a serum. **6** in biology, able to respond to stimulation by various external agents, as light, gravity, etc. **7** in botany, responding to external stimuli by moving, as the leaves of a sensitive plant. **8** involving classified documents, etc. [ME < Med.L *sensitivus* < L *sensus.* See SENSE.] **—sen′si·tive·ly,** *adv.* **—sen′si·tive·ness,** *n.*

Syn. **2 Sensitive, susceptible** = easily affected or influenced. **Sensitive** particularly suggests having, by nature or because of a physical or emotional condition, a specially keen or delicate capacity for feeling (physical or mental) or to respond or react to an external action, force, or influence: *Sensitive people are quickly touched by something beautiful or sad.* **Susceptible** particularly suggests having a nature, character, or makeup that makes a person or thing unable to resist an influence and easily acted on: *Susceptible people are easily tricked.*

sensitive plant **1** a tropical American plant whose leaflets fold together when touched. **2** any of various other plants showing sensitiveness to touch.

sen·si·tiv·i·ty (sen′sə tiv′ə tē) *n.* **-ties.** the state or quality of being sensitive.

sen·si·tize (sen′sə tīz′) *v.* **-tized, -tiz·ing. 1** make sensitive. Camera films have been sensitized to light. **2** in medicine, make unusually sensitive to a protein or other substance by repeated injections. **—sen′si·tiz′er,** *n.*

sen·sor (sen′sər) *n.* a device for receiving and transmitting a physical stimulus such as heat, light, or pressure: *Sensors were applied to the astronaut's body to record his pulse, temperature, etc.*

sen·so·ri·al (sen sô′rē əl) *adj.* sensory.

sen·so·ri·um (sen sô′rē əm) *n.* **-ri·ums, -ri·a** (-rē ə). **1** the supposed seat of sensation in the brain. **2** the whole sensory apparatus of the body. **3** the brain or mind (an unscientific use of the word). [< LL *sensorium,* ult. < L *sentire* feel]

sen·so·ry (sen′sə rē) *adj.* **1** of or having to do with sensation. The eyes and ears are sensory organs. **2** of nerves, ganglia, etc., conveying an impulse from the sense organs to a nerve centre.

sen·su·al (sen′shü əl) *adj.* **1** having to do with the bodily senses rather than with the mind or soul: *sensual pleasures.* **2** caring too much for the pleasures of the senses. **3** lustful; lewd. **4** indicative of a sensual disposition: *sensual lips.* **5** of or having to do with the senses or sensation. [ME < LL *sensualis* < L *sensus.* See SENSE.] **—sen′su·al·ly,** *adv.*

Syn. **1, 2 Sensual, sensuous** = of or concerned with the senses. **Sensual** describes things that give pleasurable satisfaction to the bodily senses and appetites and people who indulge their desires and feelings for pure physical pleasure, and almost always suggests baseness or excess: *A glutton derives sensual pleasure from eating.* **Sensuous** always favorable, describes people highly sensitive to beauty and the pleasure of the senses and feelings, but never of appetite, and things that give pleasure through the senses: *She derives sensuous delight from old church music.* **3** wanton, lecherous.

sen·su·al·ism (sen′shü əl iz′əm) *n.* sensuality.

sen·su·al·ist (sen′shü əl ist) *n.* a person who indulges too much in the pleasures of the senses: *Gluttons and drunkards are sensualists.*

sen·su·al·i·ty (sen′shü al′ə tē) *n.* **-ties. 1** a sensual nature. **2** an excessive indulgence in the pleasures of the senses. **3** lewdness.

sen·su·al·ize (sen′shü əl īz′) *v.* **-ized, -iz·ing.** make sensual.

sen·su·ous (sen′shü əs) *adj.* **1** of or derived from the senses; having an effect on the senses; perceived by the senses: *the sensuous thrill of a warm bath, a sensuous love of color.* **2** enjoying the pleasures of the senses. **—sen′su·ous·ly,** *adv.* **—sen′su·ous·ness,** *n.* **—Syn. 1, 2** See **sensual.**

sent (sent) *v.* pt. and pp. of **send.**

sen·tence (sen′təns) *n. v.* **-tenced, -tenc·ing.** **—*n.* 1** a word or group of words making a statement, question, request, command, or exclamation. **2** decision. **3** in law: **a** a decision by a judge on the punishment of a criminal. **b** the punishment itself. **4** a short, wise saying; proverb. **—*v.*** pronounce punishment on: *The judge sentenced the thief to five years in prison.* [< F < L *sententia,* originally, opinion < *sentire* feel]

sen·ten·tial (sen ten′shəl) *adj.* **1** having to do with or of the nature of a judicial sentence. **2** having to do with a grammatical sentence.

sen·ten·tious (sen ten′shəs) *adj.* **1** full of meaning; saying much in few words. **2** speaking as if one were a judge settling a question. **3** inclined to make wise sayings; abounding in proverbs. [ME < OF < Med.L *sententiosus* < *sententia.* See SENTENCE.] **—sen·ten′tious·ly,** *adv.* **—sen·ten′tious·ness,** *n.* **—Syn.1** pithy. **3** epigrammatic.

sen·tience (sen′shəns or sen′shē əns) *n.* a capacity for feeling: *Some people believe in the sentience of flowers.*

sen·tient (sen′shənt or sen′shē ənt) *adj.* that can feel; having feeling. **—*n.*** one that feels. [< L *sentiens, -entis,* ppr. of *sentire* feel]

sen·ti·ment (sen′tə mənt) *n.* **1** a mixture of thought and feeling. Admiration patriotism, and loyalty are sentiments. **2** feeling, especially refined or tender feeling. **3** a thought or saying that expresses feeling. **4** a mental attitude. **5** a personal opinion. [ME < OF < Med.L *sentimentum* < L *sentire* feel]

Syn. **2 Sentiment, sentimentality** = refined or tender feeling, or a quality or characteristic showing or produced by feeling. **Sentiment,** usually used in a good sense, suggests genuine, sincere, and refined, delicate, or tender feeling, usually also noble thought or high ideals: *Christmas and birthdays are times for sentiment.* **Sentimentality** suggests affected or false, excessive or exaggerated feeling, sickening tenderness, or weakly emotional show, and therefore is used unfavorably or contemptuously: *Sentimentality towards criminals is as dangerous as it is disgusting.* **3** maxim, epigram. **5** view, thought.

sen·ti·men·tal (sen′tə men′təl) *adj.* **1** having or showing much tender feeling: *sentimental poetry.* **2** likely to act from feelings rather than from logical thinking. **3** of sentiment; dependent on sentiment: *She values her mother's gift for sentimental reasons.* **4** having too much sentiment. **—sen′ti·men′tal·ly,** *adv.* **—Syn. 4** emotional, gushing.

sen·ti·men·tal·ism (sen′tə men′təl iz′əm) *n.* **1** a tendency to be influenced by sentiment rather than reason. **2** an excessive indulgence in sentiment. **3** a feeling expressed too openly or commonly or sentimentally.

sen·ti·men·tal·ist (sen′tə men′təl ist) *n.* a sentimental person; one who indulges in sentimentality.

sen·ti·men·tal·i·ty (sen′tə men tal′ə tē) *n.* **-ties. 1** a tendency to be influenced by sentiment rather than reason. **2** an excessive indulgence in sentiment. **3** a feeling expressed too openly or sentimentally. **—Syn. 2** See **sentiment.**

sen·ti·men·tal·ize (sen′tə men′təl īz′) *v.* **-ized, -iz·ing. 1** indulge in sentiment; affect sentiment. **2** make sentimental. **3** be sentimental about.

sen·ti·nel (sen′tə nəl) *n. v.* **-nelled** or **-neled, -nel·ling** or **-nel·ing. —*n.* 1** a person stationed to keep watch and guard against surprise attack. **2** a person or thing that watches, or stands as if watching, like a sentinel: *The tree stood like a sentinel against the sky.* **3 stand sentinel,** act as a sentinel; keep watch.
—*v.* 1 stand guard over; watch as a sentinel. **2** furnish with or as if with a sentinel or sentinels. **3** post as a sentinel. [< F < Ital. *sentinella* < LL *sentinare* avoid danger wisely < L *sentire* feel]

sen·try (sen′trē) *n.* **-tries. 1** a sentinel. **2** watch; guard: *We stood sentry over the sleepers.* [? abbreviation of *centrinel,* var. of *sentinel*]

sentry box a small roofed structure for sheltering a sentry.

sep. 1 sepal; sepals. **2** separate.

Sep. 1 September. **2** Septuagint.

se·pal (sē′pəl) *n.* in botany, one of the leaflike divisions of the calyx, or outer covering, of a flower. In a carnation, the sepals make a green cup at the base of the flower. In a tulip, the sepals are colored like the petals. [< NL *sepalum,* short for L *separatum petalum* separate petal, coined by H. J. de Necker in 1790]

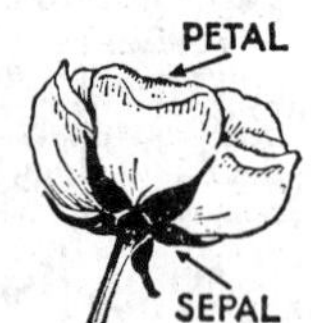

sep·a·ra·bil·i·ty (sep′ə rə bil′ə tē or sep′rə bil′ə tē) *n.* the quality of being separable.

sep·a·ra·ble (sep′ə rə bəl or sep′rə bəl) *adj.* that can be separated. **—sep′a·ra·bly,** *adv.*

sep·a·rate (*v.* sep′ə rāt′; *adj. n.* sep′ə rit or sep′rit) *v.* **-rat·ed, -rat·ing,** *adj. n.* **—*v.* 1** be between; keep apart; divide: *The Atlantic Ocean separates North America from*

Europe. **2** take apart; part; disjoin: *separate church and state.* **3** live apart or cause to live apart. A husband and wife may be separated by agreement or by order of a court. **4** divide into parts or groups; divide or part (a mass, compound, whole) into elements, sizes, etc.: *separate a tangle of string.* **5** draw, come, or go apart; become disconnected or disunited; part company; withdraw (from): *After classes the students separated in all directions. The rope separated under the strain.* **6** put apart; take away: *Separate your books from mine.*
—adj. apart from others; divided; not joined; individual; single: *separate clubs. These are two separate questions. Our teeth are separate.*
—n. something separate. [< L *separare* < *se-* apart + *parare* get]

Syn. *v.* **2 Separate, divide** = part or put apart two or more people, things, or elements. **Separate** emphasizes parting or causing to be apart people or things that have been together, whether or not actually connected or united: *We have decided to separate the twins for the summer.* **Divide** emphasizes the individuals, parts, or sections that result from separating, breaking up, cutting, etc. a mass, body, or whole: *The instructor divides the class for field trips.*

sep·a·rate·ly (sep′ə rit lē or sep′rit lē) *adv.* in a separate manner; one by one; one at a time.

separate school **1** *Cdn.* a school for children belonging to a religious minority in a particular district, operated by a school board elected by the minority rate-payers and financed by taxes imposed on them by the board as well as by grants from the provincial Department of Education. It is under the jurisdiction of the Department of Education and follows the same basic curriculum as that laid down for public schools. **2** a Roman Catholic parochial school. **3** sometimes, a school that is not part of the public school system; a private or independent school.

sep·a·ra·tion (sep′ə rā′shən) *n.* **1** the act of separating; dividing; taking apart. **2** the condition of being separated. **3** the line or point of separating. **4** the living apart of husband and wife by agreement or by order of a court.

sep·a·ra·tism (sep′ə rə tiz′əm or sep′rə tiz′əm) *n.* **1** the principle or policy of separation; opposition to ecclesiastical or political union. **2 Separatism,** advocacy or support of the withdrawal of Quebec from Confederation.

sep·a·ra·tist (sep′ə rə tist or sep′rə tist) *n.* **1** a member of a group that separates or withdraws from a larger group. **2** an advocate or supporter of separatism. **3 Separatist,** an advocate or supporter of the withdrawal of Quebec from Confederation.

sep·a·ra·tive (sep′ə rə tiv, sep′rə tiv or sep′ə rā′tiv) *adj.* tending to separate; causing separation.

sep·a·ra·tor (sep′ə rā′tər) *n.* a person or thing that separates, especially a machine for separating cream from milk, wheat from chaff or dirt, etc. [< L]

Se·phar·dic (si fär′dik) *adj.* of, having to do with, or descended from the Sephardim.

Se·phar·dim (si fär′dim) *n.pl.* Spanish or Portuguese Jews and their descendants, as distinguished from the Ashkenazim of central and eastern Europe.

se·pi·a (sē′pē ə) *n.* **1** a brown paint or ink prepared from the inky fluid of cuttlefish. **2** a dark brown. **3** a drawing, photograph, etc. in tones of brown. *—adj.* **1** dark-brown. **2** done in sepia: *a sepia print.* [< L < Gk.]

se·poy (sē′poi) *n.* formerly, a native of India who was a soldier in the British army in India. [< Pg. < Hind. < Persian *sipahi* soldier < *sipah* army]

sep·sis (sep′sis) *n.* **1 a** a poisoning of the system by disease-producing bacteria and their toxins absorbed into the blood stream from festering wounds, etc.; blood poisoning. **b** the condition of being infected with such bacteria as streptococci or staphylococci. **2** putrefaction. [< NL < Gk. *sēpsis* putrefaction < *sēpein* rot]

Sept. **1** September. **2** Septuagint.

sep·tal (sep′təl) *adj.* of or having to do with a septum.

Sep·tem·ber (sep tem′bər) *n.* the ninth month. September has 30 days. [< L *September* < *septem* seven; from the order of the Roman calendar]

sep·te·nar·y (sep′tə ner′ē) *adj. n.* **-nar·ies.** *—adj.* **1** of or having to do with the number seven. **2** forming a group of seven. **3** septennial. *—n.* **1** the number seven. **2** a group or set of seven things. **3** a period of seven years.

hat, āge, cãre, fär; let, ēqual, tėrm; it, īce
hot, ōpen, ôrder; oil, out; cup, pu̇t, rüle, ūse
əbove, takən, pencəl, lemən, circəs
ch, child; ng, long; sh, ship
th, thin; ᴛʜ, then; zh, measure

[< L *septenarius* seven-year period < *septum* seven + *annus* year]

sep·ten·ni·al (sep ten′ē əl) *adj.* **1** lasting seven years. **2** occurring every seven years. [< L *septennium* seven-year period < *septem* seven + *annus* year] **—sep·ten′ni·al·ly,** *adv.*

sep·tet or **sep·tette** (sep tet′) *n.* **1** in music: **a** a composition for seven voices or instruments. **b** seven singers or players. **2** any group of seven. [< G < L *septem* seven; modelled after *duet*]

sep·tic (sep′tik) *adj.* **1** causing infection or putrefaction. **2** caused by infection or putrefaction. *—n.* a substance that causes or promotes sepsis. [< L < Gk. *sēptikos* < *sēpein* rot]

sep·ti·ce·mi·a or **sep·ti·cae·mi·a** (sep′tə sē′mē ə) *n.* blood poisoning, especially a form in which certain micro-organisms as well as their toxins are absorbed by the blood. [< NL < Gk. *sēptikos* septic (ult. < *sēpein* rot) + *haima* blood]

septic tank a tank in which sewage is acted on by bacteria.

sep·til·lion (sep til′yən) *n.* **1** in Canada, the United States and France, 1 followed by 24 zeros. **2** in Great Britain, 1 followed by 42 zeros. [< F *septillion* (< L *septem* seven), modelled after *million* million]

sep·tu·a·ge·nar·i·an (sep′chü ə jə nãr′ē ən or sep′tū ə jə nãr′ē ən) *adj.* of the age of 70 years, or between 70 and 80 years old. *—n.* a person who is 70 or between 70 and 80 years old. [< L *septuagenarius*, ult. < *septuaginta* seventy]

sep·tu·ag·e·nar·y (sep′chü aj′ə ner′ē or sep′tū aj′ə ner′ē) *adj. n.* **-nar·ies.** septuagenarian.

Sep·tu·a·ges·i·ma (sep′chü ə jes′ə mə or sep′tū ə jes′ə mə) *n.* the third Sunday before Lent. [< L *septuagesima*, literally, seventieth]

Sep·tu·a·gint (sep′chü ə jint′ or sep′tū ə jint′) *n.* the Greek translation of the Old Testament that was made before the time of Christ. [< L *septuaginta* seventy; because it was supposed to have been done in seventy days by seventy scholars who were brought to Alexandria by Ptolemy II of Egypt]

sep·tum (sep′təm) *n.* **-ta** (-tə). a dividing wall; partition. There is a septum of bone and cartilage between the nostrils. The inside of a green pepper is divided into chambers by septa. [< L *saeptum* a fence < *saepire* hedge in]

sep·tu·ple (sep tū′pəl, sep tü′pəl, sep′tu̇ pəl, or sep′tə pəl) *adj. v.* **-pled, -pling.** *—adj.* seven times as great; seven-fold. *—v.* make seven times as great. [< LL *septuplus* < L *septem* seven + *-plus* -fold]

sep·ul·cher (sep′əl kər) *n. v.* sepulchre.

se·pul·chral (sə pul′krəl) *adj.* **1** of sepulchres or tombs. **2** of burial: *sepulchral ceremonies.* **3** deep and gloomy; dismal; suggesting a tomb.

sep·ul·chre or **sep·ul·cher** (sep′əl kər) *n. v.* **-chred, -chring.** *—n.* a place of burial; tomb. *—v.* bury a dead body in a sepulchre. [ME < OF < L *sepulcrum* < *sepelire* bury]

sep·ul·ture (sep′əl chər) *n. Archaic.* **1** burial. **2** a place of burial; sepulchre. [ME < OF < L *sepultura* < *sepelire* bury]

seq. *pl.* **sqq.** **1** sequel. **2** the following. [< L *sequens*]

se·quel (sē′kwəl) *n.* **1** that which follows; a continuation. **2** something that follows as a result of some earlier happening; result. **3** a complete story continuing an earlier one about the same people. [ME < L *sequela* < *sequi* follow] **—Syn. 2** consequence, outcome.

se·que·la (si kwē′lə) *n.* **-lae** (-lē or -lī). **1** anything following or resulting. **2** in medicine, a disease or morbid condition that is the result of a previous disease. [< L. See SEQUEL.]

se·quence (sē′kwəns) *n.* **1** the coming of one thing after another; succession; order of succession: *Arrange the names in alphabetical sequence.* **2** a connected series: *a sequence of lessons on one subject.* **3** something that follows; result: *Crime has its sequence of misery.* **4** in card playing, a set of three or more cards of the same suit following one after another in order of value. **5 a** part of a motion picture consisting of an episode without breaks. **b** any group of scenes of a motion picture taken as a unit. **6** in music, a series of melodic or harmonic phrases repeated three or more times at successive pitches upward or downward. [ME < LL *sequentia*, ult. < L *sequi* follow] —**Syn. 1** See **series.**

se·quent (sē′kwənt) *adj.* **1** following; subsequent. **2** following in order; consecutive. **3** following as a result; consequent. —*n.* that which follows; result; consequence. [< L *sequens, -entis*, ppr. of *sequi* follow]

se·quen·tial (si kwen′shəl) *adj.* **1** sequent. **2** forming a sequence or connected series; characterized by a regular sequence of parts. —**se·quen′tial·ly,** *adv.*

se·ques·ter (si kwes′tər) *v.* **1** remove or withdraw from public use or from public view: *The shy old lady sequestered herself from all strangers.* **2** take away (property) for a time from an owner until a debt is paid or some claim is satisfied. **3** seize by authority; take and keep: *The soldiers sequestered food from the people they conquered.* [ME < LL *sequestrare* < *sequester* trustee, mediator < *sequi* follow]

se·ques·trate (si kwes′trāt) *v.* **-trat·ed, -trat·ing.** **1** confiscate. **2** *Archaic.* sequester. —**se·ques′tra·tor,** *n.*

se·ques·tra·tion (sē′kwes trā′shən or si kwes′trā′shən) *n.* **1 a** the seizing and holding of property until legal claims are satisfied. **b** a writ authorizing this. **2** a forcible or authorized seizure; confiscation. **3** a separation or withdrawal from others; seclusion.

se·quin (sē′kwin) *n.* **1** a small spangle used to ornament dresses, scarfs, etc. **2** a former Italian gold coin, worth about $2.25. [< F < Ital. *zecchino* < *zecca* mint < Arabic *sikka* a stamp]

se·quoi·a (si kwoi′ə) *n.* either of two kinds of very tall evergreen trees of California. [< NL *sequoia* < *Sequoya* (Cherokee *Sikwayi*) (1770?-1843), an Indian who invented the Cherokee system of writing]

se·rac (sā rak′) *n.* a large block or pinnacle-like mass of ice on a glacier, formed by the intersection of two or more crevasses. [< Swiss F *sérac*, a kind of white cheese]

se·ragl·io (sə ral′yō) *n.* **-ragl·ios.** **1** the women's quarters of a Moslem house or palace; harem. **2** in Turkey, a palace. [< Ital. *serraglio*, ult. < L *serare* lock up; influenced by Turkish *serāī* palace]

se·ra·pe (sə rä′pē) *n.* a shawl or blanket, often having bright colors, worn by Indians in Spanish-American countries. [< Mexican Sp. *serape* or *sarape*]

ser·aph (ser′əf) *n.* **-aphs** or **-a·phim.** one of the highest order of angels. [< *seraphim*, pl., < LL < Hebrew]

se·raph·ic (sə raf′ik) *adj.* **1** of seraphs. **2** like a seraph; angelic. —**se·raph′i·cal·ly,** *adv.*

ser·a·phim (ser′ə fim′) *n.* a pl. of **seraph.**

Se·ra·pis (sə rā′pis) *n.* in Egyptian mythology, a god of the lower world, the dead Apis.

Serb (sėrb) *n.* **1** a native or inhabitant of Serbia, a district in S.E. Yugoslavia. **2** the language of Serbia. —*adj.* of Serbia, its people, or their language. [< *Serbian*]

Ser·bi·an (sėr′bē ən) *adj.* of Serbia, a former country and now a district of Yugoslavia, its people, or their language.

Ser·bo-Cro·a·tian (sėr′bō krō ā′shən) *adj.* both Serbian and Croatian. —*n.* **1** a branch of the Slavic language spoken by the people of Yugoslavia. **2** a person whose native language is Serbo-Croatian.

sere (sēr) *adj.* dried up; withered. [var. of *sear*]

ser·e·nade (ser′ə nād′) *n. v.* **-nad·ed, -nad·ing.** —*n.* **1** music played or sung outdoors at night, especially by a lover under his lady's window. **2** a piece of music suitable for such a performance. **3** in music, an instrumental composition having several movements. —*v.* **1** sing or play a serenade to. **2** sing or play a serenade. [< F < Ital. *serenata*, ult. < L *serenus* serene] —**ser′e·nad′er,** *n.*

ser·en·dip·ity (ser′ən dip′ə tē) *n.* the faculty of accidentally making fortunate discoveries; happening upon things, information, etc. by chance. [coined by Horace Walpole in "The Three Princes of *Serendip*" (Ceylon), a fairy tale whose heroes make such discoveries]

se·rene (sə rēn′) *adj.* **1** peaceful; calm: *a serene smile.* **2** clear; bright; not cloudy: *a serene sky.* [< L *serenus*] —**se·rene′ly,** *adv.* —**Syn. 1** tranquil, placid. See **peaceful.**

se·ren·i·ty (sə ren′ə tē) *n.* **-ties.** **1** quiet peace; calmness. **2** clearness; brightness.

serf (sėrf) *n.* **1** formerly, a person who could not be sold off the land, but passed from one owner to another with the land. **2** a person treated almost like a slave; a person who is mistreated, underpaid, etc. [< F < L *servus* slave] —**serf′like′,** *adj.*

serf·dom (sėrf′dəm) *n.* **1** the condition of a serf. **2** the custom of having serfs. Serfdom existed all over Europe in the Middle Ages and lasted in Russia till the middle of the 19th century.

serge (sėrj) *n.* a kind of woollen or silk cloth having slanting lines or ridges on its surface. [ME < OF *serge*, ult. < L *serica* (*vestis*) silken (garment) < Gk. *sērikē* < *Sēres* the Chinese. Cf. SILK.]

ser·gean·cy (sär′jən sē) *n.* **-cies.** the position, rank, or duties of a sergeant.

ser·geant (sär′jənt) *n.* **1** in the army, a non-commissioned officer senior to a corporal and junior to a staff sergeant. **2** in the air force, a non-commissioned officer senior to a corporal and junior to a flight-sergeant. **3** a police officer senior, usually, to an ordinary policeman. **4** a sergeant at arms. *Abbrev.*: Sgt. or Sergt. Also, *esp.Brit.* **serjeant.** [ME < OF *sergent* < L *serviens, -entis*, ppr. of *servire* serve]

sergeant at arms or **ser·geant-at-arms** (sär′jənt-ət ärmz′) *n.* **ser·geants at arms** or **ser·geants-at-arms.** an officer who keeps order in a legislature, law court, etc.

sergeant-major (sär′jənt mā′jər) *n.* **1** in the army, a non-commissioned officer senior to a staff sergeant and junior to a warrant officer. **2** in the Royal Canadian Mounted Police, a non-commissioned officer senior to a staff sergeant. *Abbrev.*: S.M. or Sgt.Maj.

Sergt. Sergeant.

se·ri·al (sēr′ē əl) *n.* **1** a story published, broadcast, or televised one part at a time in a magazine or newspaper or on the radio or television. **2** a movie, etc. presented one part at a time at a theatre, on television, etc. —*adj.* **1** of serials; having to do with a serial. **2** published, broadcast, or televised one part at a time. **3** of a series; arranged in a series; making a series: *Arrange volumes 1 to 5 on the shelf in serial order.* [< NL *serialis* < L *series.* See SERIES.]

se·ri·al·ise (sēr′ē ə līz′) *v.* **-ised, -is·ing.** *Esp.Brit.* serialize.

se·ri·al·ize (sēr′ē ə līz′) *v.* **-ized, -iz·ing.** **1** publish in a series of parts or instalments. **2** arrange in parts for such publication. Also, **serialise.**

se·ri·al·ly (sēr′ē əl ē) *adv.* **1** in a series. **2** as a serial.

serial number an individual number given to a person, article, etc.

se·ri·ate (sēr′ē it or sēr′ē āt′) *adj.* arranged or occurring in one or more series.

se·ri·a·tim (sēr′ē ā′tim or ser′ē ā′tim) *adv.* in a series; one after another. [< Med.L]

ser·i·cul·ture (ser′ə kul′chər) *n.* the raising and care of silkworms for the production of raw silk. [< F *séri(ci)culture* < L *sericum* silk + *cultura* culture]

se·ries (sēr′ēz) *n.* **-ries.** **1** a number of similar things in a row: *A series of rooms opened off the long hall.* **2** a number of things placed one after another. **3** a number of things, events, etc. coming one after the other: *A series of rainy days spoiled their vacation.* **4** coins, stamps, etc. of a particular issue, ruler, country, etc. **5** written or artistic works that are produced one after another, usually having a common subject or purpose, and often by a single author, artist, or composer. **6** in electricity, an arrangement in which the positive pole or terminal of one battery, etc. is connected to the negative pole or terminal of the next. [< L *series* < *serere* join]

Syn. 1 Series, sequence, succession = a number of things, events, etc. arranged or coming one after another in some order. **Series** applies to a number of similar things with the same purpose or relation to each other: *He gave a series of lectures on Mexico.* **Sequence** implies a closer or unbroken connection, in thought, between cause and effect, in numerical or alphabetical order, etc.: *He reviewed the sequence of events leading to peace.* **Succession** emphasizes following in order of time, sometimes place, usually without interruption: *He had a succession of colds.*

☛ **series.** Commas are used between the members of a series of three or more short items, although usage is divided over the insertion of a comma before the last item of the series. Many writers, especially in an informal style, do not use one: *He forgot to pack his toothbrush, comb (,) and shaving equipment.*

se·ries-wound (sēr′ēz wound′) *adj.* in electricity, wound so that the field magnet coils are connected in series with the armature and carry the same current.

ser·if (ser′if) *n.* in printing, a thin or smaller line used to finish off a main stroke of a letter, as at the top and bottom of M. [? < Du. *schreef* stroke, line < *schrijven* write < L *scribere*]

se·ri·o·com·ic (sēr′ē ō kom′ik) *adj.* partly serious and partly comic.

se·ri·ous (sēr′ē əs) *adj.* **1** thoughtful; grave: *a serious face.* **2** in earnest; not joking; sincere: *He was serious about the subject.* **3** needing thought; important: *Choice of one's life work is a serious matter.* **4** important because it may do much harm; dangerous: *The badly injured man was in a serious condition.* [< LL *seriosus* < L *serius* earnest] —**se′ri·ous·ly,** *adv.* —**seriousness,** *n.* —**Syn. 1** solemn, sober. See **grave. 3** weighty, momentous. **4** critical, alarming.

ser·mon (sėr′mən) *n.* **1** a public talk on religion or something connected with religion. Ministers preach sermons in church. **2** a serious talk, often long and tiresome, about morals, conduct, duty, etc.: *After the guests left, the boy got a sermon on table manners from his father.* [ME < OF < L *sermo, -onis* a talk, originally, a stringing together of words < *serere* join]

ser·mon·ize (sėr′mən īz′) *v.* **-ized, -iz·ing. 1** give a sermon; preach. **2** preach or talk seriously to; lecture. —**ser′mon·iz′er,** *n.*

Sermon on the Mount Christ's sermon to His disciples, as reported in Matthew 5-7 and Luke 6:20-49.

se·ro·log·i·cal (sēr′ə loj′ə kəl) *adj.* of or having to do with serology. —**se′ro·log′i·cal·ly,** *adv.*

se·rol·o·gist (si rol′ə jist) *n.* a person skilled in serology.

se·rol·o·gy (si rol′ə jē) *n.* the study of the use of serums in curing or preventing disease.

se·rous (sēr′əs) *adj.* **1** of serum; having to do with serum. **2** like serum; watery. Tears are drops of a serous fluid. [< L *serosus* < *serum* whey]

ser·pent (sėr′pənt) *n.* **1** a snake, especially a big snake. **2** a sly, treacherous person. **3 Serpent,** the Devil; Satan. [< L *serpens, -entis,* originally ppr. of *serpere* creep]

ser·pen·tine (*adj.* sėr′pən tīn′ or sėr′pən tēn′; *n.* sėr′pən tēn′) *adj.* **1** of or like a serpent. **2** winding; twisting: *the serpentine course of a creek.* **3** cunning; sly; treacherous: *a serpentine suggestion.* —*n.* a mineral consisting chiefly of a hydrous silicate of magnesium, usually green, and sometimes spotted like a serpent's skin. *Formula*: $Mg_3Si_2O_5(OH)_4$ [< LL *serpentinus* < L *serpens, -entis* serpent]

ser·rate (ser′āt or ser′it) *adj. v.* **-rat·ed, -rat·ing.** —*adj.* notched like the edge of a saw; toothed. —*v.* make serrate; notch like a saw. [< L *serratus* < *serra* a saw]

A serrate leaf

ser·rat·ed (ser′āt id) *adj.* serrate.

ser·ra·tion (se rā′shən) *n.* **1** a serrated edge or formation. **2** one of its series of notches.

ser·ried (ser′ēd) *adj.* crowded closely together. [< F *serré,* pp. of *serrer* press close]

ser·ru·late (ser′yů lāt′ or ser′ů lāt′) *adj.* very finely notched: *a serrulate leaf.* [< NL *serrulatus* < L *serrula,* dim. of *serra* a saw]

se·rum (sēr′əm) *n.* **se·rums** or **se·ra** (sēr′ə). **1** the clear, pale-yellow, watery part of the blood that separates from the clot when blood coagulates. **2** a liquid used to prevent or cure a disease, usually obtained from the blood of an animal that has been made immune to the disease. Diphtheria antitoxin is a serum. **3** any watery animal liquid, such as lymph. **4** whey. [< L *serum* whey]

hat, āge, cãre, fär; let, ēqual, tėrm; it, īce
hot, ōpen, ôrder; oil, out; cup, půt, rüle, ūse
əbove, takən, pencəl, lemən, circəs
ch, child; ng, long; sh, ship
th, thin; ᴛʜ, then; zh, measure

ser·val (sėr′vəl) *n.* an African wild cat that has a brownish-yellow coat with black spots. [< NL < Pg. (*lobo*) *cerval* lynx, ult. < L *cervus* stag]

serv·ant (sėr′vənt) *n.* **1** a person employed in a household. **2** a person employed by another. Policemen and firemen are public servants. **3** a person devoted to any service: *Ministers are the servants of God.* [ME < OF *servant,* ppr. of *servir* serve. See SERVE.] —**serv′ant·less,** *adj.*

serve (sėrv) *v.* **served, serv·ing,** *n.* —*v.* **1** be a servant of; give service to; work for or in: *A slave serves his master. The soldier served three years in the army.* **2** be a servant; give service; work; perform official duties: *He served as butler.* **3** wait on at table; bring food or drink to. **4** put (food or drink) on the table: *The maid served the first course.* **5** supply; furnish; supply with something needed: *The dairy serves us with milk. The men were served with a round of ammunition.* **6** help; aid: *Let me know if I can serve you in any way.* **7** be useful; be what is needed; be of use: *Boxes served as seats.* **8** be useful to; fulfil: *This will serve my purpose.* **9** be favorable or suitable; be favorable or suitable to; satisfy: *The ship will sail when the wind and tide serve.* **10** treat: *The prisoner was poorly served.* **11** pass; spend: *The thief served a term in prison.* **12** in law: **a** deliver (an order from a court, etc.). **b** present (with an order from a court, etc.): *He was served with a notice to appear in court.* **13** act as a server at Mass. **14** in tennis, etc., put (the ball) in play by hitting. **15** operate (a gun, etc.). **16** in nautical use, bind or wind (a rope, etc.) with small cord to strengthen or protect it. **17 serve one right,** be just what one deserves: *The punishment served him right.*
—*n.* in tennis, etc.: **1** the act or way of serving a ball. **2** a player's turn to serve. [ME < OF *servir* < L *servire* < *servus* slave]

serv·er (sėr′vər) *n.* **1** a person who serves. **2** a tray for dishes. **3** any of various pieces of tableware for serving food: *a cake or pie server.* **4** an attendant who serves the celebrant at Low Mass.

serv·ice (sėr′vis) *n. adj. v.* **-iced, -ic·ing.** —*n.* **1** a helpful act or acts; aid; conduct that is useful to others: *He performed many services for his country.* **2** supply; arrangements for supplying: *The train service was good.* **3** occupation or employment as a servant: *go into service.* **4** work done for others; performance of duties; work: *Mrs. Brown no longer needs the services of a doctor.* **5** advantage; benefit; use: *Would this coat be of service to you?* **6** a department of government or public employment; the persons engaged in it: *the civil service.* **7** duty in the navy, army, air force, etc.: *active service.* **8** a religious meeting, ritual, or ceremony: *We attend church services twice a week.* **9** regard; respect; devotion. **10** the manner of serving food; the food served. **11** a set of dishes, etc.: *a silver tea service.* **12** in law, the serving of a process or writ upon a person. **13** in tennis, etc.: **a** the act or manner of putting the ball in play. **b** the ball as put into play. **c** a turn at starting the ball in play. **14** in nautical use, a small cord wound about a rope, etc. to strengthen or protect it. **15 at one's service,** ready to do what one wants. **16 of service,** helpful; useful. **17 services, a** work done in the service of others; helpful labor, as opposed to production, manufacturing, construction work, etc.: *goods and services.* **b** arrangements or installations for public use, such as electricity, water supply, and sewers. **18 the service** or **the services,** the navy, army, or air force.
—*adj.* **1** belonging to or assisting household servants, tradespeople, etc.: *a service door, service pantry.* **2** belonging to a branch of the armed forces, especially on active duty: *a service cap.* **3** used for ordinary occasions: *a service uniform.*
—*v.* **1** make fit for service; keep fit for service: *The*

mechanic serviced our automobile. 2 provide with a service or with services: *Two trains serviced the town.* [ME < OF < L *servitium* < *servus* slave]

serv·ice·a·bil·i·ty (ser′vis ə bil′ə tē) *n.* a being serviceable.

serv·ice·a·ble (sėr′vis ə bəl) *adj.* **1** capable of giving good service; useful. **2** useful for a long time; able to stand much use. **3** *Archaic.* willing to be useful. —**serv′ice·a·ble·ness,** *n.* —**serv′ice·a·bly,** *adv.*

serv·ice·ber·ry (sėr′vis ber′ē) *n.* **1** a bush or small tree bearing white flowers and large, sweet, purple berries. **2** the fruit of this bush.

service centre **1** a stopping area adjoining an expressway, consisting of a service station, restaurant, toilet facilities, etc. **2** a town or city serving as a shopping and distribution centre for the surrounding region: *In summer our small town is the service centre for a large resort area.*

service club **1** a men's organization, such as the Rotary or the Kiwanis, formed to promote the welfare of its community and further the interests of its members. **2** a recreation centre for military personnel.

serv·ice·man (sėr′vis man′ or ser′vis mən) *n.* **-men** (-men′ or -mən). **1** a member of the armed services. **2** a man whose job is to maintain and repair machines, appliances, etc.

service road **1** access road. **2** a road, generally paralleling an expressway, to carry local traffic and to provide access to adjoining property.

service station **1** a place for supplying automobiles with gasoline, oil, water, etc. **2** a place where repairs, parts, adjustments, etc. can be obtained for mechanical or electrical devices.

service vote *Cdn.* in an election, the votes of members of the armed services who are on duty away from their home ridings. These votes are tallied separately and reported some time after the general count of votes.

serv·ice·wom·an (sėr′vis wu̇′mən) *n.* a female member of the armed services.

ser·vi·ette (sėr′vē et′) *n.* a piece of cloth or paper used at meals for protecting the clothing or for wiping the lips or fingers. [< F *serviette* < *servir* serve]

ser·vile (ser′vīl or sėr′vəl) *adj.* **1** like that of slaves; mean; base: *servile flattery.* **2** of slaves; having to do with slaves: *a servile revolt, servile work.* **3** fit for a slave. **4** yielding through fear, lack of spirit, etc.: *An honest judge cannot be servile to public opinion.* [ME < L *servilis* < *servus* slave] —**ser′vile·ly,** *adv.* —**ser′vile·ness,** *n.* —**Syn. 1** slavish, cringing, fawning, grovelling.

ser·vil·i·ty (sėr vil′ə tē) *n.* **-ties.** an attitude or behavior fit for a slave; servile yielding.

ser·vi·tor (sėr′və tər) *n.* a servant; attendant. [ME < OF < LL *servitor* < L *servire* serve. See SERVE.]

ser·vi·tude (sėr′və tūd′ or sėr′və tüd′) *n.* **1** slavery; bondage. **2** forced labor as a punishment: *The criminal was sentenced to five years' servitude.* **3** in law: **a** the condition of property subject to a right of enjoyment possessed by some person other than its owner, or attaching to some other property. **b** such a right of enjoyment. [ME < OF < L *servitudo* < *servus* slave]

ses·a·me (ses′ə mē) *n.* **1** an Oriental plant. **2** its seeds, used for food and in medicine. **3** See **open sesame.** [< Gk. < Semitic]

ses·qui·cen·ten·ni·al (ses′kwi sen ten′ē əl) *n.* a 150th anniversary or its celebration. —*adj.* having to do with, or marking the completion of, a period of a century and a half. [< L *sesqui-* one and a half + E *centennial*]

ses·qui·pe·da·li·an (ses′kwi pə dā′lē ən) *adj.* **1** measuring a foot and a half. **2** very long; containing many syllables. **3** using long words. —*n.* a very long word. [< L *sesquipedalis* half a yard long < *sesqui* one and a half + *pes, pedis* foot]

ses·sile (ses′īl or ses′əl) *adj.* **1** in botany, attached by a base instead of by a stem, as a leaf having no petiole or a flower having no peduncle or pedicel. **2** in zoology, sedentary; fixed to one spot; not able to move around, as barnacles and sponges. [< L *sessilis* sitting < *sedere* sit]

Sessile leaves

ses·sion (sesh′ən) *n.* **1** a sitting or meeting of a court, council, legislature, etc.: *Parliament is now in session.* **2** a series of such sittings. **3** the term or period of such sittings: *This year's session of Parliament was unusually long.* **4** a period of lessons and study. **5** a term: *He attended the university during the summer session.* **6** any meeting: *a heated session with the head of the department.* **7 in session,** meeting: *The teachers were in session all Saturday morning.* [ME < L *sessio, -onis* < *sedere* sit]

ses·sion·al (sesh′ən əl) *adj.* **1** of a session; having to do with sessions. **2** occurring every session.

sessional indemnity in certain provinces of Canada, the remuneration paid each session to a Member of the Legislative Assembly.

ses·terce (ses′tėrs) *n.* an ancient Roman coin of small value. [< L *sestertius,* originally adj., two and a half < *semis* half unit (< *semi-* half + *as* unit) + *tertius* third]

ses·ter·ti·um (ses tėr′shē əm) *n.* **-ti·a** (-shē ə). an ancient Roman unit of money equal to a thousand sesterces. [erroneously formed as a singular to L *sestertia,* short for *milia sestertium* thousands of sesterces]

ses·tet (ses tet′) *n.* **1** in music, a sextet. **2** the last six lines of certain sonnets. [< Ital. *sestetto,* ult. < L *sex* six]

set (set) *v.* **set, set·ting,** *adj. n.* —*v.* **1** put in some place; put; place: *Set the box on its end.* **2 a** put in the right place, position, or condition: *set a broken bone.* **b** arrange (the hair) when damp to make it take a certain position. **3** adjust according to a standard: *set a clock.* **4** put in some condition or relation: *A spark set the woods on fire. The slaves were set free.* **5** put (a price, etc.); fix the value of at a certain amount or rate: *He set the value of the watch at $500.* **6** put as the measure of esteem of a person or thing: *set great store by a thing.* **7** post, appoint, or station for the purpose of performing some duty: *set a detective on a person.* **8** fix; arrange; appoint: *set a time limit for taking an examination.* **9** provide for others to follow: *set a good example.* **10** put in a fixed, rigid, or settled state: *set one's jaw.* **11** make or become firm or hard; become fixed: *Jelly sets as it cools.* **12** put in a frame or other thing that holds: *set a diamond in gold.* **13** adorn; ornament: *a bracelet set with diamonds.* **14** go down; sink: *The sun sets in the west.* **15** put (a hen) to sit on eggs to hatch them; place (eggs) under a hen to be hatched. **16** of a hen, sit on eggs. **17** of a dog, indicate the position of game by standing stiffly and pointing with the nose. **18** hang or fit in a particular manner: *That coat sets well.* **19** have a direction; tend: *The current sets to the south.* **20** begin to move. **21** make an attack. **22** encourage to attack; cause to be hostile. **23** begin to apply; begin to apply oneself: *Have you set to work?* **24** form fruit in the blossom. **25** in music: **a** adapt; fit: *set words to music.* **b** arrange (music) for certain voices or instruments. **26** in printing, put (type) in the order required. **27** make (a color of fabrics, etc.) fast.

set about, start work upon; begin: *Set about your washing.*
set against, a make unfriendly toward. **b** balance; compare.
set apart, reserve.
set aside, a put to one side. **b** put by for later use. **c** discard, dismiss, or leave out; reject; annul.
set back, a stop; hinder; check. **b** *Informal.* cost (a person) so much: *The new car set him back a lot of money.*
set bread, mix batter or dough and leave it to rise.
set down, a deposit or let alight; put down. **b** put down in writing or printing. **c** consider; ascribe.
set forth, a make known; express; declare. **b** start out.
set in, a begin. **b** blow or flow towards the shore.
set off, a explode. **b** start to go. **c** increase by contrast.
set on, a attack. **b** urge to attack.
set out, a start to go. **b** spread out to show, sell, or use. **c** plant. **d** plan; intend (to do something). **e** put down.

set to, a begin. **b** begin fighting.
set up, a build. **b** begin; start. **c** put up; raise in place, position, power, pride, etc. **d** claim; pretend. **e** make ready; prepare; arrange. **f** establish.
set up for, claim or pretend to be.
—*adj.* **1** fixed or appointed beforehand; established: *a set time, set rules.* **2** fixed; rigid: *a set smile.* **3** firm; hard. **4** resolved; determined: *He is set on going today.* **5** *Informal.* stubbornly fixed; obstinate.
—*n.* **1** a number of things or persons belonging together or classified together: *a set of dishes.* **2** in mathematics, a specified collection of objects: *the set of all right triangles, the set of even integers.* **3** a device for receiving or sending by radio, television, telephone, telegraph, etc. **4 a** the complete scenery for a play, act, scene, etc. **b** the physical setting for a scene in a motion picture, television show, etc. **5** the way a thing is put or placed; form; shape: *His jaw had a stubborn set.* **6** the way in which anything fits: *the set of a coat.* **7** a direction; tendency; course; drift: *the set of a current. The set of opinion was toward building a new bridge.* **8** a warp; bend; displacement: *a set to the right.* **9** a slip or shoot for planting. **10** a young fruit just formed from a blossom. **11** the act or manner of setting. **12** in tennis, a group of six or more games. To win a set, one side must win at least two more than the other side. **13** a snare or trap. **14** the direction in which a current flows or a wind blows. **15** in square dancing: **a** a group of four couples. **b** the figures of a square dance. **16** the pointing of a dog, such as a setter, in the presence of game. [OE *settan*] —**Syn.** *v.* **1** See **put. 8** ordain, prescribe. **14** decline, wane. *–adj.* **1** determined, prescribed. *–n.* **1** collection, group.

☛ **set, sit.** People and things *sit* (past, *sat*) or they are *set* (past, *set*), meaning "placed": *I like to sit in a hotel lobby. I have sat in this same seat for a long time. She set the soup down with a flourish. The post was set three feet in the ground.* A hen, however, *sets* (on her eggs).

Set (set) *n.* the ancient Egyptian god of evil. He was represented as having an animal's head with a pointed snout.

se·ta (sē′tə) *n.* **se·tae** (-tē or -tī). any slender, stiff, bristle-like structure. Earthworms have two pairs of setae in each segment. [< L *saeta*]

set·back (set′bak′) *n.* **1** a check to progress; reverse. **2** a steplike setting back of the upper storeys of a tall building in order to give better light and air in the street. **3** a lessening in the thickness of a wall. **4** a flat, plain projection of a wall.

A building with setbacks (def. 2)

set-off (set′of′) *n.* **1** a setting off on a trip; a start; departure. **2** a thing used to set off or adorn; ornament; decoration. **3** something that counterbalances or makes up for something else; a compensation; offset. **4** a settlement of a debt by means of a claim in the debtor's favor. **5** a claim so used.

set·screw (set′skrü′) *n.* a machine screw used to fasten gears, pulleys, etc. to a shaft.

set·tee (se tē′) *n.* a sofa or long bench with a back and, usually, arms. [< *set*]

set·ter (set′ər) *n.* **1** a person or thing that sets: *a setter of type or of jewels.* **2** any of several breeds of long-haired gundog, trained to stand motionless and point the nose toward game that it scents. **3** a dog of one of these breeds.

set·ting (set′ing) *n.* **1** a frame or other thing in which something is set. The mounting of a jewel is its setting. **2** the scenery of a play; a set. **3** the place, time, etc. of a play or story. **4** the surroundings; background. **5** the music composed for particular instruments or to go with certain words. **6** the eggs that a hen sets on for hatching. **7** the act of one that sets. **8** the dishes or cutlery required to set one place at a table.

set·tle¹ (set′əl) *v.* **-tled, -tling. 1** determine; decide; agree (upon): *Have you settled on a time for leaving?* **2** put or be put in order; arrange: *I must settle all my affairs before going away for the winter.* **3** pay; arrange payment: *settle a bill.* **4** take up residence (in a new country or place): *settle in Manitoba.* **5** establish colonies (in): *The French settled Quebec.* **6** set or be set in a fairly permanent position, place, or way of life: *We are settled in our new home.* **7** put or come to rest in a particular place; put in or come to a definite condition: *His cold settled in his lungs.* **8** arrange in or come to a desired or comfortable position: *The cat settled herself in the chair.* **9** make or become quiet: *A vacation will settle your nerves.* **10** go down; sink: *The end of that wall has settled four inches.* **11** of liquid, make or become clear: *A beaten egg or cold water will settle coffee.* **12** of dregs, sink or cause to sink to the bottom. **13** make or become firm and compact: *settle the contents of a barrel.*
14 settle down, a live a more regular life. **b** direct steady effort or attention. **c** calm down; become quiet. **15 settle up,** pay a bill or bills; make payment. **16 settle upon** or **on,** give (property, etc.) to by law. [OE *setlan* < *setl* settle²]
—**Syn. 1** set. See **fix. 9** compose, calm.

hat, āge, cãre, fär; let, ēqual, tėrm; it, īce
hot, ōpen, ôrder; oil, out; cup, pu̇t, rüle, ūse
əbove, takən, pencəl, lemən, circəs
ch, child; ng, long; sh, ship
th, thin; ᴛʜ, then; zh, measure

set·tle² (set′əl) *n.* a long bench. [OE *setl*]

A settle

set·tle·ment (set′əl mənt) *n.* **1** the act of settling or the state of being settled. **2** establishment in life. **3** a deciding; determining: *settlement of a date.* **4** a putting in order; arrangement. **5** a payment: *Settlement of all claims against the firm will be made shortly.* **6** the settling of persons in a new country: *the settlement of the English along the Atlantic Coast of North America.* **7** a colony: *England had many settlements along the Atlantic Coast.* **8** a group of buildings and the people living in them: *Indians often attacked the little settlements of the colonists.* **9** a place in a poor, neglected neighborhood where work for its improvement is carried on. **10** the settling of property upon someone: *She received $200,000 by a marriage settlement.* **11** the amount so given. **12** a gradual sinking or subsidence of a structure, etc.

set·tler (set′lər) *n.* **1** a person who settles. **2** a person who settles in a new country.

set·tlings (set′lingz) *n.pl.* the things in a liquid that settle to the bottom; sediment.

set-to (set′tü′) *n.* **-tos.** *Informal.* a fight; dispute.

set-up (set′up′) *n.* **1** an arrangement of apparatus, machinery, etc. **2** the arrangement of an organization. **3** *Slang.* **a** a contest or match where the outcome is assured. **b** anything that is very easy to do or whose outcome is readily predictable. **4** one's manner of holding the head and body; carriage; bearing.

sev·en (sev′ən) *n.* **1** one more than six; 7. **2** a playing card, etc. having seven spots. —*adj.* one more than six; 7. [OE *seofon*]

sev·en·fold (sev′ən fōld′) *adv.* **1** seven times as much or as many. **2** seven times as much or as often; in the proportion of seven to one. —*adj.* **1** seven times as much or as many. **2** having seven parts.

Seven Hills the hills upon and about which Rome was built.

seven seas all the oceans (the Arctic, Antarctic, North Atlantic, South Atlantic, North Pacific, South Pacific, and Indian oceans): *sailing the seven seas.*

sev·en·teen (sev′ən tēn′) *n. adj.* seven more than ten; 17. [OE *seofontēne*]

sev·en·teenth (sev′ən tēnth′) *adj. n.* **1** next after the 16th; last in a series of 17. **2** one or being one of 17 equal parts.

sev·enth (sev′ənth) *adj.* **1** next after the sixth; last in a series of 7. **2** being one of 7 equal parts. —*n.* **1** the next after the sixth; the last in a series of 7. **2** one of 7 equal parts. **3** in music: **a** the interval between two tones that are seven degrees apart. **b** the combination of two such tones.

Seventh Day Adventist a member of a Christian denomination that believes that the second coming of Christ is near at hand. Seventh Day Adventists keep the sabbath on Saturday, the seventh day.

seventh heaven **1** the highest part of heaven. **2** the highest place or condition of joy and happiness.

sev·enth·ly (sev′ənth lē) *adv.* in the seventh place.

sev·en·ti·eth (sev′ən tē ith) *adj. n.* **1** next after the 69th; last in a series of 70. **2** one, or being one, of 70 equal parts.

sev·en·ty (sev′ən tē) *n.* **-ties,** *adj.* seven times ten; 70. [OE *seofontig*]

Seven Wonders of the World in ancient times, the seven most remarkable structures in the world: the Egyptian Pyramids, the Mausoleum at Halicarnassus, the Temple of Artemis (Diana) at Ephesus, the walls and hanging gardens of Babylon, the Colossus of Rhodes, the statue of Zeus by Phidias at Olympia, and the Pharos (lighthouse) at Alexandria.

Seven Years' War a war fought between Great Britain and France and their allies, 1756-1763, in Europe, North America, India, etc. In Canada, the French were defeated by the British in 1759, with the result that Canada became a British colony. In North America, the war was known also as the **French and Indian War.**

sev·er (sev′ər) *v.* **1** cut apart; cut off: *sever a rope. The axe severed his head from his body.* **2** break off: *The two countries severed friendly relations.* **3** part; divide; separate: *a church severed into two factions. The rope severed and the swing fell down.* [ME < OF *sevrer,* ult. < L *separare* separate. See SEPARATE.] **—sev′er·a·ble,** *adj.*

sev·er·al (sev′ər əl or sev′rəl) *adj.* **1** being more than two or three but not many; some; a few: *gain several pounds.* **2** individual; different: *The boys went their several ways, each on his own business.* **3** considered separately; single: *The several steps in the process of making paper were shown in a movie.* —*n.* more than two or three but not many; some; a few: *Several have given their consent.* [ME < AF *several,* ult. < L *separ* distinct < *separare* separate. See SEPARATE.]

sev·er·al·ly (sev′ər əl ē or sev′rəl ē) *adv.* **1** separately; singly; individually: *Consider these points, first severally and then collectively.* **2** respectively. **3** *Archaic.* apart from others; independently.

sev·er·al·ty (sev′ər əl tē or sev′rəl tē) *n.* **-ties. 1** the state of being separate or distinct. **2** the condition of being held or owned by separate or individual rights. **3** land so held.

sev·er·ance (sev′ər əns or sev′rəns) *n.* **1** a severing or being severed; separation; division. **2** a breaking off: *the severance of diplomatic relations between two countries.*

severance pay additional pay, based on seniority, granted to employees that are leaving a business, company, etc.

se·vere (sə vēr′) *adj.* **-ver·er, -ver·est. 1** very strict; stern; harsh: *The judge imposed a severe sentence on the criminal.* **2** serious; grave: *a severe illness.* **3** very plain or simple; without ornament: *She has a severe haircut like a boy's.* **4** sharp; violent: *a severe criticism.* **5** difficult: *The new gun had to pass a series of severe tests.* **6** rigidly exact, accurate, or methodical: *severe reasoning.* [< L *severus*] **—se·vere′ly,** *adv.* **—se·vere′ness,** *n.*

Syn. **1** Severe, stern = very strict, harsh, or hard, especially in holding to rules or standards and in enforcing order and obedience. Severe, describing people, their acts or words, or things like laws and punishment, emphasizes being strict and, often, harsh, showing no mildness, indulgence, or pity: *His parents are severe.* Stern emphasizes having or showing no disposition to be soft or lenient, or to give way or be influenced by tears and pleading: *The coach is stern when players break training.* **3** chaste, unadorned. **5** exacting. **6** precise, rigid.

se·ver·i·ty (sə ver′ə tē) *n.* **-ties. 1** strictness; sternness; harshness. **2** simplicity of style or taste; plainness. **3** violence; sharpness: *the severity of storms, pain, disease, grief, etc.* **4** seriousness. **5** accuracy; exactness. **6** something severe.

Sè·vres (sev′rə) *n.* **1** a choice and costly kind of porcelain. **2** something made of this porcelain. [< *Sèvres,* a town in N. France, where this porcelain is made]

sew (sō) *v.* **sewed, sewn** or **sewed, sew·ing. 1** work with needle and thread. **2** fasten with stitches. **3 sew up, a** close with stitches: *The doctor sewed up the wound.* **b** *Informal.* make certain. [OE *seowian*]

sew·age (sü′ij) *n.* the waste matter that passes through sewers.

sew·er[1] (sü′ər) *n.* a drain to carry off waste: *Sewers are usually underground.* [ME < OF *sewiere* sluice from a pond, ult. < L *ex* out + *aqua* water]

sew·er[2] (sō′ər) *n.* a person or thing that sews. [< *sew*]

sew·er[3] (sü′ər) *n.* formerly, a head servant in charge of arranging the table and serving the meals. [ME < AF *asseour,* literally, seater, ult. < L *ad-* by + *sedere* sit]

sew·er·age (sü′ər ij) *n.* **1** the removal of waste matter by sewers. **2** a system of sewers. **3** sewage.

sew·ing (sō′ing) *n.* **1** work done with a needle and thread. **2** something to be sewed. —*adj.* for sewing; used in sewing: *a sewing room.*

sewing circle a group of women who meet regularly to sew for their church, for charity, etc.

sewing machine a machine for stitching, embroidering, etc. cloth.

sewn (sōn) *v.* a pp. of **sew.**

sex (seks) *n.* **1** one of the two divisions of human beings, animals, etc. Men, bulls, and roosters are of the male sex; women, cows, and hens are of the female sex. **2** the characteristic of being a male or female: *People were admitted without regard to age or sex.* **3** the attraction of one sex for the other. **4** behavior resulting from or motivated by this attraction. **5** *Informal.* sexual intercourse. **6 the fair, gentle,** or **weaker sex,** women. **7 the sex,** women. **8 the sterner** or **stronger sex,** men.
—*adj.* of sex; having to do with sex.
—*v.* **1** determine the sex of (young chickens, kittens, puppies, etc.). **2** make sexually more interesting or appealing. **3** excite or arouse sexually. [< L *sexus*] **—sex′less,** *adj.*

sex·a·ge·nar·i·an (sek′sə jə nãr′ē ən) *adj.* of the age of 60 years, or between 60 and 70 years old. —*n.* a person aged 60, or between 60 and 70. [< L *sexagenarius,* ult. < *sexaginta* sixty]

sex·ag·e·nar·y (seks aj′ə ner′ē) *adj. n.* **-nar·ies.** —*adj.* **1** of or having to do with the number 60; composed of or going by sixties. **2** sexagenarian. —*n.* a sexagenarian.

Sex·a·ges·i·ma (sek′sə jes′ə mə) *n.* the second Sunday before Lent. [< L *sexagesima,* literally, sixtieth]

sex·a·ges·i·mal (sek′sə jes′ə məl) *adj.* having to do with or based upon the number 60. A sexagesimal fraction is one whose denominator is 60 or a power of 60. —*n.* a sexagesimal fraction.

sex appeal attraction for the opposite sex.

sext (sekst) *n.* **1** the fourth of the seven canonical hours set aside for prayer and meditation. **2** the office or service for this hour, originally fixed for noon, the sixth hour after sunrise. [< L *sexta* (*hora*) sixth (hour) < *sex* six; because it originally came at the sixth hour of the day (noon)]

sex·tan (seks′tən) *n.* a fever or ague characterized by paroxysms that recur every sixth day, both days of consecutive occurrence being counted. —*adj.* **1** of such a fever or ague. **2** recurring every sixth day. [< NL *sextana* (*febris* fever) < L *sex* six]

sex·tant (seks′tənt) *n.* **1** an instrument used by navigators, surveyors, etc. for measuring the angular distance between two objects. Sextants are used at sea to measure the altitude of the sun, a star, etc. in order to determine latitude and longitude. **2** one sixth of a circle. [< L *sextans, -antis* a sixth < *sex* six]

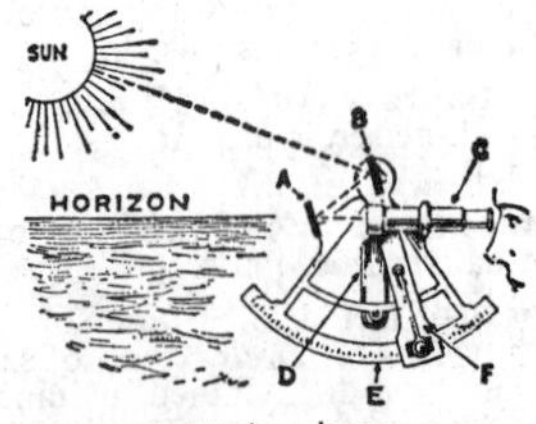

A sextant: A, mirror; B, mirror; C, telescope; D, handle; E, graduated arm; F, arm. The sextant is held so that the horizon is seen in mirror A. The arm F is moved until the sun (or a star at night) is reflected from B into A. The number of degrees marked off by F on E is the altitude of the sun or star, and the position of the ship is found from a chart that shows these altitudes at certain latitudes and hours.

sex·tet or **sex·tette** (seks tet′) *n.* **1** in music: **a** a composition for six voices or instruments. **b** six singers or players. **2** any group of six. [alteration of *sestet*, after L *sex* six]

sex·til·lion (seks til′yən) *n.* **1** in Canada, the United States and France, 1 followed by 21 zeros. **2** in Great Britain, 1 followed by 36 zeros. [< F *sextillion* (< L *sextus* sixth), modelled after *million* million]

sex·ton (seks′tən) *n.* a man who takes care of a church. A sexton's duties sometimes include ringing the bell, digging graves, etc. [ME < OF *secrestein* < Med.L *sacristanus* sacristan. Doublet of SACRISTAN.]

sex·tu·ple (seks tū′pəl or seks tü′pəl, seks′tup əl or seks′tə pəl) *adj. n. v.* **-pled, -pling.** —*adj.* **1** consisting of six parts; sixfold. **2** six times as great. **3** in music, characterized by six beats to the measure. —*n.* a number or amount six times as great as another. —*v.* make or become six times as great. [< L *sextus* sixth; modelled after *quadruple*]

sex·tu·plet (seks tu′plit or seks tü′plit, seks′tup lit′ or seks′tə plit′) *n.* **1** one of six children, animals, etc. born of the same mother at the same time. **2** a group of six things. [< *sextuple*, modelled after *triplet*]

sex·u·al (sek′shü əl) *adj.* **1** of or having to do with sex. **2** of or between the sexes. **3** having to do with relations between the sexes: *sexual morality.* **4** having sex; separated into two sexes. [< LL *sexualis* < L *sexus* sex]

sex·u·al·i·ty (sek′shü al′ə tē) *n.* **1** sexual character; possession of sex. **2** attention to sexual matters.

sex·u·al·ly (sek′shü əl ē) *adv.* **1** by means of sex. **2** in regard to sex.

sex·y (sek′sē) *adj.* **sex·i·er, sex·i·est.** *Informal.* **1** sexually provocative or stimulating: *a sexy dress, sexy beauties.* **2** especially concerned with sex: *a sexy novel.*

sf. sforzando.

sfor·zan·do (sfôr tsän′dō) in music: —*adj.* with special, usually sudden, emphasis. —*adv.* in a sforzando manner. —*n.* a tone or chord performed in this way. *Abbrev.*: sf. or sfz. [< Ital. *sforzando* forcing]

S.F.S.R. Soviet Federated Socialist Republic.

sfz. sforzando.

s.g. specific gravity.

Sgt. Sergeant.

Sgt.Maj. Sergeant-Major.

sh or **'sh** (sh) *interj.* a shortening of **hush,** used to urge silence.

shab·by (shab′ē) *adj.* **-bi·er, -bi·est. 1** much worn: *His old suit looks shabby.* **2** wearing old or much worn clothes. **3** not generous; mean; unfair: *It is shabby not to speak to an old friend because he is poor.* [< dial. *shab* scab, OE *sceabb*] —**shab′bi·ly,** *adv.* —**shab′bi·ness,** *n.*

shack (shak) *n.* **1** a roughly built hut or cabin: *The boys made a shack in the back yard.* **2** a house in bad condition. —*v.* **shack up,** *Slang.* live with a person of the opposite sex in a common-law union. [? < Mexican Sp. *jacal* wooden hut < Nahuatl *xacalli*]

shack·le (shak′əl) *n. v.* **-led, -ling.** —*n.* **1** a metal band fastened around the ankle or wrist of a prisoner, slave, etc. Shackles are usually fastened to each other, the wall, floor, etc. by chains. **2** the link fastening together the two rings for the ankles and wrists of a prisoner. **3** anything that prevents freedom of action, thought, etc. **4** something for fastening or coupling. **5 shackles,** *pl.* fetters; chains.
—*v.* **1** put shackles on. **2** restrain; hamper. **3** fasten or couple with a shackle. [OE *sceacel*] —**shack′ler,** *n.*

Shackles

shack·town (shak′toun′) *n.* a residential area consisting of roughly built huts or cabins; a collection of shacks.

shad (shad) *n.* **shad** or **shads.** any of several salt-water fishes related to the herrings that ascend rivers in the spring to spawn. The shad common on the N. Atlantic coast is a valuable food fish. [OE *sceadd*]

shad·ber·ry (shad′ber′ē) *n.* **-ries. 1** the fruit of the shad bush. **2** the shad bush. [? because the bush flowers at the season when shad appear in Atlantic rivers]

hat, āge, câre, fär; let, ēqual, tėrm; it, īce
hot, ōpen, ôrder; oil, out; cup, pu̇t, rüle, ūse
əbove, takən, pencəl, lemən, circəs
ch, child; ng, long; sh, ship
th, thin; ᴛʜ, then; zh, measure

shad·blos·som (shad′blos′əm) *n.* shad bush.

shad·bush (shad′bu̇sh′) *n.* in the Maritimes, the serviceberry.

shad·dock (shad′ək) *n.* **1** a pear-shaped fruit resembling a coarse, dry, inferior grapefruit. **2** the tree that it grows on. [after Captain *Shaddock*, its first western cultivator]

shade (shād) *n. v.* **shad·ed, shad·ing.** —*n.* **1** a partly dark place, not in the sunshine. **2** a slight darkness or coolness afforded by something that cuts off light: *the shade of a tree.* **3** a place or condition of comparative obscurity. **4 the shades,** darkness of evening or night. **5** something that shuts out light; a blind: *Pull down the shades of the windows.* **6** lightness or darkness of color: *silks in all shades of blue.* **7** the dark part of a picture. **8** a very small difference, amount, or degree: *a shade too long.* **9** a darkening look, feeling, etc.; shadow; cloud: *A shade of doubt troubled her.* **10** a ghost; spirit. **11 in** or **into the shade, a** out of the light. **b** in or into a condition of being unknown or unnoticed.
—*v.* **1** screen from light; darken. **2** make darker than the rest. **3** make dark or gloomy. **4** show small differences; change little by little: *This scarf shades from deep rose to pale pink.* **5** lessen slightly: *Can't you shade the price for me?* [OE *sceadu*] —**shade′less,** *adj.* —**Syn.** *n.* **6** See **color.**

shad fly 1 any of various kinds of tiny, winged insects that appear in swarms during the spring. **2** an artificial lure resembling a shad fly and used for fishing.

shad·ing (shād′ing) *n.* **1** a covering from the light. **2** the use of black or color to give the effect of shade in a picture. **3** a slight variation or difference of color, character, etc.

shad·ow (shad′ō) *n.* **1** the shade made by some person, animal, or thing. **2** shade; darkness; partial shade. **3 the shadows,** darkness after sunset. **4** the dark part of a place or picture. **5** a little bit; small degree; slight suggestion: *There's not a faint shadow of a doubt about his guilt.* **6** a ghost. **7** a faint image. **8** a reflected image. **9** protection; shelter. **10** a person who follows another closely and secretly. **11** a constant companion; follower. **12** sadness; gloom. **13** obscurity. **14** a gloomy or troubled look or expression. **15 under** or **in the shadow of,** very near to.
—*v.* **1** protect from light; shade: *The grass is shadowed by huge oaks.* **2** cast a shadow on. **3** represent faintly. **4** follow closely and secretly. **5** make sad or gloomy. **6** represent in a prophetic way. **7 shadow forth,** represent faintly. [from oblique case forms of OE *sceadu* shade] —**shad′ow·er,** *n.*

shadow box 1 a boxlike frame, having artificial lighting, in which an object, painting, piece of stained glass, etc. may be attractively presented. **2** a device to shade a surface on which a film is to be projected in daylight.

shad·ow·box (shad′ō boks′) *v.* engage in shadow boxing.

shad·ow·box·ing (shad′ō bok′sing) *n.* **1** boxing before a mirror or with an imaginary opponent for exercise or training. **2** engaging in cautious preliminaries before taking positive action in an argument, struggle, campaign, etc.

shadow cabinet 1 the senior, policy-making members of a minority or opposition party in a legislature. **2** a group of experts and influential men chosen by the head of a government as his personal advisers.

shad·ow·graph (shad′ō graf′) *n.* **1** a picture produced by throwing a shadow on a lighted screen. **2** a radiograph.

shad·ow·less (shad′ō lis) *adj.* having or casting no shadow.

shad·ow·y (shad′ō ē) *adj.* **1** having much shadow or shade; shady. **2** like a shadow; dim, faint, or slight: *He saw a shadowy outline on the window curtain.* **3** not real; ghostly. —**shad′ow·i·ly,** *adv.* —**shad′ow·i·ness,** *n.* —**Syn. 1** dark, obscure. **2** fleeting, vague.

shad·y (shād′ē) *adj.* **shad·i·er, shad·i·est. 1** in the shade;

shaded. 2 giving shade. 3 *Informal.* of doubtful honesty, character, etc.: *He has engaged in rather shady occupations.* 4 **on the shady side of,** older than; beyond the age of: *on the shady side of thirty.* **—shad′i·ly,** *adv.* **—shad′i·ness,** *n.*

shaft (shaft) *n.* 1 the long, slender stem of an arrow, spear, etc. 2 an arrow; spear. 3 something aimed at a person as one might aim an arrow or spear: *shafts of ridicule.* 4 a ray or beam of light. 5 one of the two wooden poles between which a horse is harnessed to a carriage, etc. 6 a column. 7 the main part of a column. See **column** for picture. 8 a flagpole. 9 a bar to support parts of a machine that turn, or to help move parts. See **cam** and **jet** for diagrams. 10 the handle of a hammer, axe, golf club, etc. 11 a stem; stalk. 12 the rib of a feather. 13 a deep passage sunk in the earth. The entrance to a mine is called a shaft. 14 a well-like passage; a long, narrow space: *an elevator shaft.* [OE *sceaft*] **—shaft′like′,** *adj.*

S, a shaft in a mine; T, tunnels.

shag[1] (shag) *n.* 1 rough, matted hair, wool, etc. 2 a mass of this material: *the shag of a dog.* 3 the long, rough nap of some kinds of cloth. 4 cloth having such a nap. 5 a coarse tobacco cut into shreds. [OE *sceacga*]

shag[2] (shag) *v.* **shagged, shag·ging.** 1 *Informal.* retrieve and return (a ball). 2 *Slang.* leave at once; go away.

shag·a·nap·pi (shag′ə nap′ē) *n.* 1 thongs, straps, lines, or cords made from rawhide. 2 an Indian pony; cayuse. [< Algonquian]

shag·bark (shag′bärk′) *n.* 1 a hickory tree whose rough bark peels off in long strips. 2 the nut of this tree. Shagbarks have fairly thin shells and are considered the best hickory nuts. 3 its wood. Also, **shellbark.**

shag·gy (shag′ē) *adj.* **-gi·er, -gi·est.** 1 covered with a thick, rough mass of hair, wool, etc.: *a shaggy dog.* 2 long, thick, and rough: *shaggy eyebrows.* 3 having a long, rough nap; of coarse texture. [< *shag*] **—shag′gi·ly,** *adv.* **—shag′gi·ness,** *n.*

shaggy-dog story a joke in which the humor depends on a long recital of trivial incidents building up to an absurd and unexpected ending. [from an original story of this type about a shaggy dog]

sha·green (shə grēn′) *n.* a kind of untanned leather with a granular surface, made from the skin of the horse, ass, shark, seal, and other animals. [< F *chagrin* < Turkish *saghri* rump of a horse, leather from this]

Shah (shä) *n.* a title of the monarch of Iran. [< Persian]

shake (shāk) *v.* **shook, shak·en, shak·ing,** *n.* —*v.* 1 move quickly backwards and forwards, up and down, or from side to side: *shake a rug.* 2 bring, throw, force, rouse, scatter, etc. by or as if by movement: *shake snow off one's clothes.* 3 be shaken: *Sand shakes off easily.* 4 clasp (hands) in greeting, congratulating, etc. another: *shake hands.* 5 tremble: *He is shaking with cold.* 6 make tremble: *The explosion shook the town.* 7 totter; waver: *His courage began to shake.* 8 cause to totter or waver: *shake the very foundations of society.* 9 disturb; make less firm: *His lie shook my faith in his honesty.* 10 trill. 11 *Informal.* get rid of: *Can't you shake him?* 12 mix (dice) before throwing. 13 **shake down, a** bring or throw down by shaking. **b** cause to settle down. **c** bring into working order. **d** *Slang:* get money from dishonestly. 14 **shake off,** get rid of. 15 **shake up, a** shake hard. **b** stir up. **c** jar in body or nerves.
—*n.* 1 the act or fact of shaking: *a shake of the head.* 2 *Informal.* an earthquake. 3 a drink made by shaking the ingredients together: *a milk shake.* 4 *Slang.* a moment: *I'll be there in two shakes.* 5 in music, a rapid alternation of a note with a tone above or below it; a trill. 6 a crack in a growing tree; fissure. 7 a long, rough shingle or board: *a barn roofed with cedar shakes.* 8 **no great shakes,** *Informal.* not unusual, extraordinary, or important. [OE *sceacan*] **—shak′a·ble, shake′a·ble,** *adj.*

Syn. *v.* 5 **Shake, tremble, quiver** = move with unsteady, irregular, rapid, and repeated movements from side to side or up and down. **Shake,** the general word, suggests a rapid, irregular, more or less violent, or abrupt motion: *He shook with laughter.* **Tremble,** used chiefly of people or animals, suggests uncontrollable, continued shaking with quick, short movements, caused by fear, strong feeling, cold, etc.: *In his excitement his hands trembled.* **Quiver** suggests a slight trembling or vibrating motion: *The dog's nostrils quivered at the scent.*

shake-down[1] (shāk′doun′) *n.* 1 a makeshift bed: *We made a shake-down of straw and blankets on the floor.* 2 the process of shaking down. 3 a bringing into proper condition or working order by practice: *The warship was given a shake-down by a trial voyage.*

shake-down[2] (shāk′doun′) *n. Slang.* an exaction of money, etc. by compulsion, especially as in various forms of graft. [from shaking a tree for fruit, or, possibly, the pockets of one's victim held upside down]

shak·en (shāk′ən) *v.* pp. of **shake.**

shak·er (shāk′ər) *n.* 1 a person who shakes something. 2 a machine or utensil used in shaking. 3 a container for pepper, salt, etc. having a perforated top. 4 **Shaker,** a member of an American religious sect, so called from body movements that formed part of their worship. Shakers owned all their property in common.

Shake·spear·e·an or **Shake·sper·e·an** (shāk spēr′ ē ən) *adj.* of, having to do with, or suggestive of William Shakespeare, 1564-1616, or his works. —*n.* a specialist in the study of the works of Shakespeare.

Shake·spear·i·an or **Shake·sper·i·an** (shāk spēr′ ē ən) *adj. n.* Shakespearean.

shake-up (shāk′up′) *n. Informal.* a sudden and complete change; drastic rearrangement of policy, personnel, etc.: *a shake-up in the government.*

shak·o (shak′ō) *n.* **shak·os.** a high, stiff military hat with a plume or other ornament. [< Hungarian *csákó* peaked (cap) < G *Zache(n)* point, spike]

A shako

shak·y (shāk′ē) *adj.* **shak·i·er, shak·i·est.** 1 shaking: *a shaky voice.* 2 liable to break down; weak: *a shaky porch.* 3 not to be depended on; not reliable: *a shaky bank.* **—shak′i·ly,** *adv.* **—shak′i·ness,** *n.*

shale (shāl) *n.* a fine-grained rock, formed from clay or mud, that splits easily into thin layers. [OE *scealu* shell] **—shal′y,** *adj.*

shall (shal; *unstressed,* shəl) *v. pres.* **shall,** *2nd sing. also* (*Poetic*) **shalt;** *past* **should,** *2nd sing. also* (*Archaic*) **should·est** or **shouldst.** an auxiliary used to express future time, commands, obligation, and necessity. [OE *sceal*]

☛ In formal use, shall in the first person expresses futurity, in the second and third, determination or obligation: *I shall miss you. We shall consider the matter. You shall not see him. It shall be done.* In informal usage **shall** is being largely replaced by *'ll* or *will.* See will for a fuller usage note.

shal·loon (sha lün′) *n.* a twilled woollen cloth, used chiefly for linings. [< F *chalon* < *Châlons-sur-Manne,* a city in N.E. France]

shal·lop (shal′əp) *n. Archaic.* a small, light, open boat propelled by sail or oars. [< F *chaloupe* < Du. *sloepe.* Doublet of SLOOP.]

shal·lot (shə lot′) *n.* 1 a small plant resembling an onion, but having a bulb composed of sections or cloves. 2 a bulb or clove of this plant. 3 a small, brown onion. [ult. < F *eschalotte,* alteration of OF *eschaloigne* scallion < L (*caepa*) *Ascalonia* (onion) from Ascalon, in Palestine]

shal·low (shal′ō) *adj.* not deep: *shallow water, a shallow dish, a shallow mind.* —*n.* a place that is not deep. —*v.* 1 become less deep. 2 make less deep. [ME *shalowe,* related to OE *sceald,* adj., shallow] **—shal′low·ly,** *adv.*

shalt (shalt) *v. Archaic.* 2nd pers. sing. present tense of **shall.** "Thou shalt" means "You shall" (sing.).

shal·y (shāl′ē) *adj.* of, like, or containing shale.

sham (sham) *n. adj. v.* **shammed, sham·ming.** —*n.* 1 a pretence; fraud. 2 a counterfeit; imitation. 3 a person who is a fraud. 4 a cover or the like to give a thing a different outward appearance: *a pillow sham.*
—*adj.* 1 pretended; feigned: *The soldiers fought a sham battle for practice.* 2 counterfeit; imitation.
—*v.* 1 pretend; feign: *He shammed sickness so he wouldn't have to work.* 2 create a false imitation of. [originally dial. var. of *shame*] **—sham′mer,** *n.*

hat, āge, cãre, fär; let, ēqual, tėrm; it, īce
hot, ōpen, ôrder; oil, out; cup, pu̇t, rüle, ūse
əbove, takən, pencəl, lemən, circəs
ch, child; ng, long; sh, ship
th, thin; ᴛʜ, then; zh, measure

sha·man (shä′mən, shā′mən, or sham′ən) *n.* **1** a priest of shamanism. **2** among Eskimos and certain American Indians, an angekok or medicine man. [< Russian *shaman* < Tungus *saman* < Pali *samana* < Sanskrit *sramana* Buddhist monk; (literally) self-tormentor < *sramati* he tires]

sha·man·ism (shä′mə niz′əm, shā′mə niz′əm, or sham′ə niz′əm) *n.* **1** a primitive religion of the Ural-Altaic peoples of northern Asia, in which spirits, demons, etc. are believed to control mankind and can be influenced only by shamans. **2** any similar beliefs, as among Eskimos and certain American Indians.

sham·a·teur (sham′ə chər, sham′ə chür, sham′ə tūr′ or sham′ə tėr′) *n. Slang.* in sports, a player who is classed as an amateur but is paid as if he were a professional. [blend of *sham* and *amateur*]

sham·a·teur·ism (sham′ə chər iz′əm or sham′ə chür iz′əm, sham′ə tūr iz′əm or sham′ə tėr iz′əm) *n. Slang.* in sports: **1** the practice of using shamateurs. **2** the fact or condition of being a shamateur.

sham·ble (sham′bəl) *v.* **-bled, -bling,** *n.* —*v.* walk awkwardly or unsteadily: *The tired old man shambles.* —*n.* a shambling walk. [probably ult. special use of *shamble*, sing. of *shambles*; with reference to the straddling legs of a bench]

sham·bles (sham′bəlz) *n.pl. or sing.* **1** a slaughter house. **2** a place of butchery or of great bloodshed. **3** *Informal.* any place or thing that is a complete mess. [OE *sc(e)amel* < L *scamellum*, dim. of *scamnum* bench; originally, a table on which meat was sold]

shame (shām) *n. v.* **shamed, sham·ing.** —*n.* **1** a painful feeling of having done something wrong, improper, or silly: *blush with shame.* **2** a disgrace; dishonor. **3** a fact to be sorry about: *It is a shame to be so wasteful.* **4** a person or thing to be ashamed of; cause of disgrace. **5** a sense of what is decent or proper. **6 For shame!** Shame on you! **7 put to shame, a** disgrace; make ashamed. **b** surpass; make dim by comparison.
—*v.* **1** cause to feel shame. **2** drive or force by shame. **3** bring disgrace upon. [OE *sceamu*] —**Syn.** *n.* **1** humiliation, mortification. -*v.* **1** humiliate, mortify.

shame·faced (shām′fāst′) *adj.* **1** bashful; shy. **2** showing shame and embarrassment. [originally < *shamefast* (OE *sc(e)amfæst*, apparently, fixed in shame), taken as from *shame*, n. + *face*]

shame·ful (shām′fəl) *adj.* causing shame; bringing disgrace. —**shame′ful·ly,** *adv.* —**shame′ful·ness,** *n.* —**Syn.** dishonorable.

shame·less (shām′lis) *adj.* **1** without shame. **2** not modest. —**shame′less·ly,** *adv.* —**shame′less·ness,** *n.* —**Syn. 2** impudent, brazen.

sham·my (sham′ē) *n.* **-mies.** chamois.

sham·poo (sham pü′) *v.* **-pooed, -poo·ing,** *n.* —*v.* **1** wash (the hair or scalp). **2** wash or clean rugs, upholstery, etc. **3** *Archaic.* massage. —*n.* **1** a washing of the hair or scalp. **2** a preparation used for shampooing. **3** *Archaic.* massage. [< Hind. *champo*, literally, press!] —**sham·poo′er,** *n.*

sham·rock (sham′rok) *n.* **1** a bright-green leaf composed of three parts. The shamrock is the national emblem of the Irish Republic. **2** any of various plants that have leaves like this, such as white clover, wood sorrel, etc. [< Irish *seamróg*, dim. of *seamar* clover]

sha·mus (shā′məs) *n. Slang.* a detective, usually a private detective. [< Yiddish *shames* sexton, caretaker < Hebrew *shammash*]

shang·hai (shang′hī or shang hī′) *v.* **-haied, -hai·ing. 1** make unconscious by drugs, liquor, etc. and put on a ship to serve as a sailor. **2** bring by trickery or force. [with reference to the practice of securing sailors by kidnapping or other violent and illegal means for long voyages, often to *Shanghai*, China]

Shang·hai (shang′hī′) *n.* one of a long-legged breed of domestic fowls. [< *Shanghai*, a seaport in China]

Shan·gri-La or **Shan·gri·la** (shang′gri lä′) *n.* an idyllic earthly paradise. [an inaccessible land in *Lost Horizon*, a novel by James Hilton (1900-1954), an English author]

shank (shangk) *n.* **1** the part of the leg between the knee and the ankle. **2** the corresponding part in animals. See **beef** for diagram. **3** the whole leg. **4** any part like a leg, stem, or shaft. The shank of a fish-hook is the straight part between the hook and the loop. **5** in printing, the body of a type. **6** the narrow part of a shoe, connecting the broad part of the sole with the heel. **7** the latter end or part of anything. **8 go** or **ride on shank's mare,** walk. [OE *sceanca*]

shan't (shant) shall not.

shan·tung (shan′tung or shan tung′) *n.* **1** a heavy pongee, a kind of soft silk. **2** a similar fabric of cotton, rayon, etc. [< *Shantung*, a province in N.E. China]

shan·ty[1] (shan′tē) *n.* **-ties.** *Cdn.* **1** a roughly built hut or cabin. **2** the log-built living quarters of a gang of lumbermen. [< Cdn.F *chantier* lumberjack's headquarters < F *chantier* timber yard, dock < L *cantherius* framework, beast of burden]

shan·ty[2] (shan′tē) *n.* **-ties.** chantey. [var. of *chantey* < F *chanter* sing]

shan·ty·man (shan′tē man′ or -mən) *n.* **-men** (-men′ or -mən). *Cdn.* formerly, one living and working in a lumber camp; lumberman.

shape (shāp) *n. v.* **shaped, shap·ing.** —*n.* **1** the outward contour or outline; form; figure: *the shape of a triangle.* **2** an assumed appearance: *A witch was supposed to take the shape of a cat or a bat.* **3** something seen, or thought to be seen, though having no definite or describable form: *A white shape stood at his bedside.* **4** condition: *the athlete exercised to keep himself in good shape.* **5** a definite form; proper arrangement; order: *Take time to get your thoughts into shape.* **6** a kind; sort: *dangers of every shape.* **7** mould; pattern. **8** something shaped; jelly, pudding, etc. shaped into a mould. **9 take shape,** have or take on a definite form. [OE *(ge)sceap*]
—*v.* **1** form: *The child shapes clay into balls.* **2** take shape; assume form: *His plan is shaping well.* **3** adapt in form: *That hat is shaped to your head.* **4** give definite form or character to: *events that shape people's lives.* **5** direct; plan; devise; aim: *shape one's course in life.* **6** express in words: *shape a question.* **7** mould; pattern. **8 shape up, a** take on a certain form or appearance; develop. **b** show a certain tendency. [OE *sceapen*, pp. of *sceppan* create] —**shap′er,** *n.* —**Syn.** *n.* **1** cast, build. See **form.**

SHAPE (shāp) Supreme Headquarters, Allied Powers in Europe.

shape·less (shāp′lis) *adj.* **1** without definite shape. **2** having an unattractive shape. —**shape′less·ly,** *adv.* —**shape′less·ness,** *n.*

shape·ly (shāp′lē) *adj.* **-li·er, -li·est.** having a pleasing shape; well-formed. —**shape′li·ness,** *n.*

shape-up (shāp′up′) *n. Informal.* a system of hiring longshoremen whereby the men line up each workday to be selected for work by the foreman.

shard (shärd) *n.* **1** a broken piece; fragment. **2** a piece of broken earthenware or pottery. **3** the hard case that covers a beetle's wing. Also, **sherd.** [OE *sceard*]

share[1] (shãr) *n. v.* **shared, shar·ing.** —*n.* **1** a part belonging to one individual; portion; part: *Do your share of the work.* **2** a part of anything owned in common with others: *One of the boys offered to sell his share in the boat.* **3** each of the parts into which the ownership of a company or corporation is divided: *The ownership of this company is divided into several million shares.* **4 go shares,** share in something. **5 on shares,** sharing in the risks and profits.
—*v.* **1** use together; enjoy together; have in common: *The sisters share the same room.* **2** divide into parts, each taking a part: *The child shared his candy with his sister.* **3** have a share; take part: *Everyone shared in making the picnic a success.* [OE *scearu* division] —**shar′er,** *n.*
Syn. *n.* **1** allotment, quota. -*v.* **1 Share, participate, partake** = use, enjoy, or have something in common with another. **Share** = either give or take a part, and emphasizes the idea of common possession, enjoyment, use, etc.: *He shares a room with*

his brother. **Participate,** more formal, followed by *in,* means "take part together with others in an idea, feeling, or action": *He participated in the discussion.* **Partake,** now formal, and usually followed by *of,* means "take a share of food, pleasure, qualities, etc.": *He partook of our meal.*

share[2] (shãr) *n.* ploughshare. [OE *scear*]

share·crop (shãr′krop′) *v.* **-cropped, -crop·ping.** farm or raise a crop as a sharecropper.

share·crop·per (shãr′krop′ər) *n.* a person who farms land for the owner in return for part of the crops.

share·hold·er (shãr′hōl′dər) *n.* a person owning shares of stock.

shark[1] (shärk) *n.* any of a group of fishes, mostly marine, certain kinds of which are large and ferocious, and destructive to other fishes and sometimes dangerous to man. [origin uncertain] —**shark′like′,** *adj.*

shark[2] (shärk) *n.* **1** a dishonest person who preys on others: *a loan shark.* **2** *Slang.* a person unusually good at something; an expert: *a shark at mathematics.* [< G *Schork,* var. of *Schurke* scoundrel]

shark·skin (shärk′skin′) *n.* cloth made from fine threads of wool, rayon, or cotton, used in suits.

sharp (shärp) *adj.* **1** having a thin cutting edge or a fine point: *a sharp knife, a sharp pencil.* **2** having a point; not rounded: *a sharp nose, a sharp corner on a box.* **3** with a sudden change of direction: *a sharp turn.* **4** very cold: *sharp weather, a sharp morning.* **5** severe; biting: *sharp words.* **6** causing a sensation like a cut or pinprick; affecting the senses keenly: *a sharp taste, a sharp noise, a sharp pain.* **7** clear; distinct: *the sharp contrast between black and white.* **8** quick; brisk: *a sharp walk or run.* **9** fierce; violent: *a sharp struggle.* **10** keen; eager: *a sharp desire, a sharp appetite.* **11** being aware of things quickly: *a sharp eye, sharp ears.* **12** watchful; wide-awake: *a sharp watch.* **13** quick in mind; clever: *a sharp boy.* **14** shrewd; artful; almost dishonest: *sharp practice. He is sharp at a bargain.* **15** high in pitch; shrill. **16** in music: **a** above the true pitch. **b** raised a half step in pitch: *F sharp.* **c** of a key, having sharps in the signature. **17** of a consonant, pronounced with breath and not with voice; voiceless. **18** *Slang.* attractive; striking in looks, value, etc.: *a sharp car. His new suit looks sharp.*
—*adv.* **1** promptly; exactly: *Come at one o'clock sharp.* **2** in a sharp manner; in an alert manner; keenly: *Look sharp!* **3** suddenly: *pull a horse up sharp.*
—*n.* **1** in music: **a** a tone one half step, or half note, above a given tone. **b** such a tone or note. **c** the sign (♯) that stands for such a tone. **2** a swindler; sharper. **3** *Informal.* an expert. **4 sharps,** *pl.* the hard part of wheat requiring a second grinding.
—*v.* in music, make or sound sharp. [OE *scearp*]
—**sharp′ly,** *adv.* —**sharp′ness,** *n.*

Syn. *adj.* **2** angular, pointed. **5** sarcastic, tart, caustic. **6** piercing, intense, painful. **11** quick, discerning, perspicacious. **13 Sharp, keen, acute,** used figuratively to describe a person or the mind, mean "quickly aware or penetrating." **Sharp** emphasizes being well suited to cutting or piercing through things, and suggests cleverness, shrewdness, quickness to see and take advantage, sometimes dishonestly: *He is a sharp lawyer.* **Keen** emphasizes being shaped to slash through things, and suggests clear-sightedness, vigor, and quickness of perception and thinking: *He has a keen mind.* **Acute,** literally, meaning "coming to a sharp point," suggests penetrating perception, insight, or understanding: *He is an acute interpreter of current events.*

sharp·en (shär′pən) *v.* **1** make sharp: *sharpen a pencil.* **2** become sharp. —**sharp′en·er,** *n.*

sharp·er (shär′pər) *n.* **1** a swindler; cheat. **2** a gambler who makes a living by cheating at cards, etc.

sharp-eyed (shärp′īd′) *adj.* **1** having keen sight: *a sharp-eyed person.* **2** watchful; very observant; vigilant.

sharp·ie (shär′pē) *n.* a long, flat-bottomed boat having one or two masts, each rigged with a triangular sail.

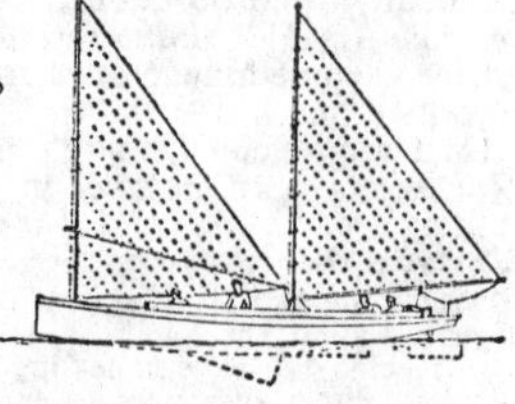
A sharpie

sharp·shoot·er (shärp′shüt′ər) *n.* **1** a person who shoots very well. **2** a soldier chosen to do accurate shooting.

sharp-tailed grouse a grouse of Western Canada and the United States, so called because of its short, pointed tail.

sharp-wit·ted (shärp′wit′id) *adj.* having or showing a quick, keen mind.

Shasta daisy 1 a flower like a large common daisy. **2** the plant that produces it. [< Mount *Shasta* in N. California]

shat·ter (shat′ər) *v.* **1** break into pieces: *A stone shattered the window.* **2** disturb greatly; destroy: *The great mental strain shattered his mind. Her hopes were shattered.*
—*n.* **shatters,** *pl.* fragments. [ME *schater(en)*; probably var. of *scatter*] —**Syn.** *v.* **1** smash, splinter. See **break.**

shave (shāv) *v.* **shaved, shaved** or **shav·en, shav·ing,** *n.*
—*v.* **1** remove hair with a razor; cut hair from (the face, chin, etc.) with a razor. **2** cut off (hair) with a razor. **3** cut off in thin slices; cut in thin slices. **4** cut very close. **5** come very close to; graze: *The car shaved the corner.*
—*n.* **1** the cutting off of hair with a razor. **2** a tool for shaving, scraping, removing thin slices, etc. **3** a shaving; thin slice. **4** a narrow miss or escape: *The shot missed him, but it was a close shave.* [OE *sceafan*]

shave·ling (shāv′ling) *n. Archaic.* **1** *Derogatory.* a tonsured monk, friar, or priest. **2** a youth.

shav·en (shāv′ən) *adj.* **1** shaved. **2** closely cut. **3** tonsured. —*v.* a pp. of **shave.**

shav·er (shāv′ər) *n.* **1** a person who shaves. **2** an instrument for shaving. **3** *Informal.* a youngster; a small boy.

Sha·vi·an (shā′vē ən) *adj.* of, having to do with, or characteristic of George Bernard Shaw, 1856-1950, an Irish dramatist and critic. —*n.* a devoted admirer of Shaw or his works.

shav·ing (shāv′ing) *n.* **1** Often, **shavings,** *pl.* a very thin piece or slice. Shavings of wood cut off by a plane. **2** the act or process of cutting hair from the face, chin, etc. with a razor.

shawl (shol or shôl) *n.* a square or oblong piece of cloth to be worn about the shoulders or head. [< Persian]

shawm (shom or shôm) *n.* a medieval musical instrument resembling an oboe. [ME < OF *chalemie,* var. of *chalemel,* ult. < L < Gk. *kalamos* reed]

Shaw·nee (sho nē′ or shô nē′) *n.* **-nee** or **-nees. 1** a tribe of North American Indians formerly living in Tennessee and South Carolina, now in Oklahoma. **2** a member of this tribe. **3** the Algonquian language of this tribe.

shay (shā) *n. Informal.* a chaise, a light carriage with two wheels and one seat. [< *chaise,* taken as pl.]

she (shē) *pron. nom.* **she**; *poss.* **hers**; *obj.* **her**; *pl. nom.* **they**; *poss.* **theirs**; *obj.* **them**; *n.* **she's.** —*pron.* **1** the girl, woman, or female animal already referred to and identified. **2** anything thought of as female and already referred to and identified. —*n.* a girl; woman; female animal: *Is it a he or a she?* [probably OE demonstrative pronoun *sīo, seo, sīe*]

sheaf (shēf) *n.* **sheaves.** a bundle of things of the same sort bound together or so arranged that they can be bound together: *a sheaf of wheat, a sheaf of arrows.* [OE *scēaf*]

shear (shēr) *v.* **sheared** or (*archaic*) **shore, sheared** or **shorn, shear·ing,** *n.* —*v.* **1** cut with shears or scissors. **2** cut the wool or fleece from: *The farmer sheared his sheep.* **3** cut close; cut off; cut. **4** break by a force causing two parts or pieces to slide on each other in opposite directions: *Too much pressure on the handles of the scissors sheared off the rivet holding the blades together.*
—*n.* **1** the act or process of shearing. **2** that which is taken off by shearing. **3** one blade of a pair of shears. **4** shears (def. 1). **5** a force causing two parts or pieces to slide on each other in opposite directions. **6 shear legs,** shears (def. 3). [OE *sceran*] —**shear′er,** *n.*

shears (shērz) *n.pl. or sing.* **1** large scissors. **2** any cutting instrument resembling scissors. See usage note at **scissors. 3** apparatus for hoisting heavy weights, consisting of two or more poles fastened together at the top to support a block and tackle. [OE *scēar*]

shear·wa·ter (shēr′wot′ər or -wô′tər) *n.* a sea bird related to the petrel, and having a long bill and long wings that appear to shear or cleave the water. [< *shear*, v. + *water*, n.]

shear zone in geology, a belt of rock crushed and metamorphosed by compression.

sheath (shēth) *n.* **sheaths** (shēᴛʜz). **1** a case or covering for the blade of a sword, knife, etc. **2** any similar covering, especially on an animal or plant. **3** a woman's dress, having a fitted bodice and straight skirt, usually unbelted. [OE *scēath*]

sheathe (shēᴛʜ) *v.* **sheathed, sheath·ing. 1** put (a sword, etc.) into a sheath. **2** enclose in a case or covering: *a mummy sheathed in linen, doors sheathed in metal.*

sheath·ing (shēᴛʜ′ing) *n.* a casing; covering. The first covering of boards on a house is sheathing.

sheath knife a knife carried in a sheath.

sheave[1] (shēv) *v.* **sheaved, sheav·ing.** gather and tie into a sheaf or sheaves. [< *sheaf*]

sheave[2] (shēv or shiv) *n.* a wheel with a grooved rim; the wheel of a pulley. [var. of *shive*, ME *schive*]

sheaves (shēvz *for 1*; shēvz or shivz *for 2*) *n.* **1** pl. of **sheaf. 2** pl. of **sheave.**

She·ba (shē′bə) *n.* **1** an ancient country in S. Arabia. **2 Queen of,** a biblical queen who visited Solomon to test his wisdom. I Kings 10:1-13.

she·bang (shə bang′) *n. Slang.* **1** an outfit; concern. **2** an affair; event. [origin uncertain]

She·bat (shə bät′ or shə vät′) *n.* in the Hebrew calendar, the eleventh month of the ecclesiastical year, and the fifth month of the civil year.

she·been (shi bēn′) *n. Irish dialect.* a place where liquor is sold without a licence. [< Irish *sibīn*]

shed[1] (shed) *n.* a building used for shelter, storage, etc., usually having only one storey: *a wagon shed, a train shed.* [OE *sced* shelter]

shed[2] (shed) *v.* **shed, shed·ding. 1** pour out; let fall: *He shed his blood for his country. The girl shed tears.* **2** throw off: *The snake sheds his skin. The umbrella sheds water.* **3** throw off a covering, hair, etc.: *That snake has just shed.* **4** scatter abroad; give forth: *The sun sheds light. Flowers shed perfume.* **5** cause to flow: *He shed his enemy's blood.* **6 shed blood,** destroy life; kill. **7 shed one's own blood,** sacrifice one's life. [OE *scēadan*] **—Syn. 2** moult, discard. **4** emit, diffuse, disperse.

she'd (shēd; *unstressed,* shid) **1** she had. **2** she would.

shed·der (shed′ər) *n.* **1** a person or thing that sheds. **2** a crab or lobster beginning to shed its shell.

sheen (shēn) *n.* brightness; lustre: *Satin and polished silver have a sheen.* [OE *scēne* bright] **—Syn.** See **polish.**

sheen·y (shēn′ē) *adj.* bright; lustrous.

sheep (shēp) *n.* **sheep. 1** a cud-chewing mammal raised for wool and mutton. **2** a weak, timid, or stupid person. **3 make sheep's eyes,** give a longing, loving look. [OE *scēap*] **—sheep′like′,** *adj.*

sheep·cote (shēp′kōt′) *n.* a shelter for sheep.

sheep dog 1 a breed of collie or other dog trained to help a shepherd watch and tend sheep. **2** a dog of this breed.

sheep·fold (shēp′fōld′) *n.* a pen for sheep.

sheep·herd·er (shēp′hėr′dər) *n. Esp.U.S.* a person who watches and tends large numbers of sheep while they are grazing on unfenced land.

sheep·hook (shēp′hu̇k′) *n.* a shepherd's staff.

sheep·ish (shēp′ish) *adj.* **1** awkwardly bashful or embarrassed: *a sheepish smile.* **2** like a sheep; timid; weak; stupid. **—sheep′ish·ly,** *adv.* **—sheep′ish·ness,** *n.*

sheep·man (shēp′man′) *n.* **-men. 1** a person who owns and raises sheep. **2** a sheepherder.

sheep range a tract of land on which sheep are pastured.

sheep·shank (shēp′shangk′) *n.* a kind of knot, hitch, or bend made on a rope to shorten it temporarily. See **knot** for picture.

sheeps·head (shēps′hed′) *n.* **1** a salt-water food fish common on the Atlantic coast of the United States. **2** the head of a sheep, especially as food. **3** a fool; simpleton.

sheep·skin (shēp′skin′) *n.* **1** the skin of a sheep, especially with the wool on it. **2** leather or parchment

hat, āge, cãre, fär; let, ēqual, tėrm; it, īce
hot, ōpen, ôrder; oil, out; cup, pu̇t, rüle, ūse
əbove, takən, pencəl, lemən, circəs
ch, child; ng, long; sh, ship
th, thin; ᴛʜ, then; zh, measure

made from the skin of a sheep. **3** *Informal.* a diploma.

sheep sorrel a kind of sorrel having reddish flowers.

sheep·walk (shēp′wok′ or -wôk′) *n.* sheep range.

sheer[1] (shēr) *adj.* **1** very thin; almost transparent: *a sheer white dress.* **2** unmixed with anything else; complete: *sheer weariness.* **3** straight up and down; steep: *From the top of the wall there was a sheer drop of 100 feet to the water below.* —*adv.* **1** completely; quite. **2** straight up or down; very steeply. —*n.* a dress of transparent material. [OE *scīr* bright; probably from ON *skærr* bright] **—sheer′ness,** *n.* **—Syn.** *adj.* **2** unadulterated, pure, absolute, utter.

sheer[2] (shēr) *v.* turn from a course; turn aside; swerve. —*n.* **1** a turning of a ship from its course. **2** the upward curve of a ship's deck or lines from the middle toward each end. **3** the position in which a ship at anchor is placed to keep her clear of the anchor. [var. of *shear*, v., in the sense of "part"]

sheer legs shears (def. 3).

sheer·ly (shēr′lē) *adv.* absolutely; thoroughly; quite.

sheet[1] (shēt) *n.* **1** a large piece of cotton, linen, nylon, etc. cloth used to sleep on or under. **2** a broad, thin piece of anything: *a sheet of glass.* **3** a single piece of paper. **4** a newspaper. **5** a broad, flat surface: *a sheet of water.* **6** the ice surface on which a game of curling is played. **7** *Poetic.* a sail. —*v.* furnish or cover with a sheet. [OE *scēte*]

sheet[2] (shēt) *n.* **1** a rope that controls the angle at which a sail is set. **2 sheets,** *pl.* the space at the bow or stern of an open boat. —*v.* **sheet home,** stretch (a square sail) as flat as possible by pulling hard on the sheets fastened to it. [OE *scēata*]

sheet anchor 1 a large anchor used only in emergencies. **2** the chief support or source of security. [origin uncertain]

sheet bend a kind of knot to fasten two ropes together. See **knot** for picture.

sheet·ing (shēt′ing) *n.* **1** cloth of cotton, linen, nylon, etc. for bed sheets. **2** a lining or covering of timber or metal, used to protect a surface.

sheet iron iron in sheets or thin plates.

sheet lightning lightning in broad flashes.

sheet metal metal in thin pieces or plates.

sheet music music printed on unbound sheets of paper.

Sheffield plate (shef′ēld) an especially durable silver plate made by rolling out sheets of copper and silver fused together. [< *Sheffield*, a city in England]

sheik or **sheikh** (shēk) *n.* **1** an Arab chief or head of a family, village, or tribe. **2** a Moslem religious leader. **3** a title of respect used by Moslems. **4** *Slang.* a man supposed to be irresistibly fascinating to women; a great lover. [< Arabic *shaikh*, originally, old man]

sheik·dom or **sheikh·dom** (shēk′dəm) *n.* the territory ruled by a sheik.

shek·el (shek′əl) *n.* **1** a silver coin of the ancient Hebrews that weighed about half an ounce. **2 shekels,** *pl. Slang.* coins; money. [< Hebrew]

shel·drake (shel′drāk′) *n.* **-drakes** or (*esp. collectively*) **-drake. 1** any of various large ducks of Europe and Asia, many of which have variegated plumage. **2** any merganser. [< obs. *sheld* variegated + *drake*]

shelf (shelf) *n.* **shelves. 1** a thin, flat piece of wood, or other material, fastened to a wall or frame to hold things, such as books, dishes, etc. **2** anything like a shelf. **3 on the shelf,** put aside as no longer useful or desirable. [probably < LG *schelf*]

shell (shel) *n.* **1** a hard outside covering of an animal. Oysters, turtles, and beetles all have shells. **2** the hard outside covering of a nut, seed, fruit, etc. **3** the hard outside covering of an egg. **4** the outer part or appearance: *Going to church may be the mere shell of religion.* **5 a** a metal case, filled with explosives, and sometimes chemicals, gas, etc., designed to be fired by artillery and to burst in or over the target. **b** a paper cartridge filled with small shot and gunpowder to use in a shotgun. **c** a cartridgelike firework that explodes in the air. **6** any framework or outside covering of a structure. **7** a long, narrow racing boat of light wood, rowed by a crew using long oars. **8** a hollow case of pastry or the lower crust of a pie. **9** any orbit with electrons revolving about the nucleus of an atom. **10 come out of one's shell,** stop being shy or reserved; join in conversation, etc. with others. **11 retire into one's shell,** become shy and reserved; refuse to join in conversation, etc. with others. —*v.* **1** take out of a shell: *shell peas.* **2** fall or come out of the shell. **3** come away or fall off as an outer covering does. **4** separate (grains of corn) from the cob. **5** bombard by artillery fire: *The enemy shelled the town.* **6 shell out,** *Informal.* **a** give something away. **b** hand over (money); pay up. [OE *sciell*) —**shell'-like',** *adj.*

she'll (shēl; *unstressed,* shil) she will.

shel·lac (shə lak') *n. v.* **-lacked, -lack·ing.** —*n.* **1** a liquid that gives a smooth, shiny appearance to wood, metal, etc. Shellac is made from a resinous substance dissolved in alcohol. **2** the resinous substance used. —*v.* **1** put shellac on; cover or fasten with shellac. **2** *Informal.* defeat completely. [< *shell* + *lac*[1]; translation of F *laque en écailles* lac in thin plates]

shell·bark (shel'bärk') *n.* shagbark.

shell·er (shel'ər) *n.* **1** a person who shells something. **2** a tool or machine used in shelling.

shell·fire (shel'fīr') *n.* bombardment by explosive shells or projectiles.

shell·fish (shel'fish') *n.* **-fish** or **-fish·es.** a water animal (not a fish in the ordinary sense) having a shell. Oysters, clams, crabs, and lobsters are shellfish. [OE *scilfisc*]

shell ice *Cdn.* in the North, a formation of ice remaining as a shell, after the water over which it was formed has receded.

shell·proof (shel'prüf') *adj.* secure against shells, bombs, etc.

shell shock any of the many types of mental disorders formerly thought to result from prolonged exposure to exploding shells, bombs, etc.

shell·shocked (shel'shokt') *adj.* suffering from shell shock.

shell·y (shel'ē) *adj.* **shell·i·er, shell·i·est. 1** abounding in shells. **2** consisting of a shell or shells. **3** shell-like.

shel·ter (shel'tər) *n.* **1** something that covers or protects from weather, danger, or attack: *Trees are a shelter from the sun.* **2** protection; refuge: *We took shelter from the storm in a barn.* —*v.* **1** protect; shield; hide: *shelter runaway slaves.* **2** find shelter. [? < ME *sheltrum* < OE *scildtruma* a guard < *scild* shield + *truma* a band of men] —**shel'ter·er,** *n.* —**shel'ter·ing·ly,** *adv.* —**shel'ter·less,** *adj.* —**Syn.** *n.* **1** safeguard, defence, shield. -*v.* **1** screen, harbor.

shel·ter·belt (shel'tər belt') *n.* a barrier of trees or shrubs that functions as protection against wind and rain and serves to lessen erosion.

shelter tent a small tent, usually made of pieces of waterproof cloth that fasten together.

shelve (shelv) *v.* **shelved, shelv·ing. 1** put on a shelf. **2** lay aside: *Let us shelve that argument.* **3** furnish with shelves. **4** slope gradually. [ult. < *shelf*]

shelves (shelvz) *n.* pl. of **shelf.**

shelv·ing (shel'ving) *n.* **1** wood, metal, etc. for shelves. **2** shelves collectively.

Shem (shem) *n.* in the Bible, the oldest of the three sons of Noah, regarded as the ancestor of the Semitic peoples.

Shem·ite (shem'īt) *n.* Semite.

she·nan·i·gan (shə nan'ə gən) *n. Informal.* Usually, **shenanigans,** *pl.* mischief or trickery. [origin uncertain]

shent (shent) *adj. Archaic.* **1** shamed. **2** blamed; scolded. **3** defeated. **4** ruined. **5** damaged. [pp. of *shend* revile, OE *scendan*]

She·ol (shē'ōl) *n.* **1** a Hebrew name for the abode of the dead. **2 sheol,** *Informal.* hell. [< Hebrew]

shep·herd (shep'ərd) *n.* **1** a man who takes care of sheep. **2** a person who cares for and protects. **3** a spiritual guide; pastor. **4 the Good Shepherd,** Jesus Christ. —*v.* **1** take care of. **2** guide; direct: *The teacher shepherded the children safely out of the burning building.* [OE *scēaphierde* < *scēap* sheep + *hierde* herder < *heord* a herd]

shepherd dog sheep dog.

shep·herd·ess (shep'ər dis) *n.* a woman who takes care of sheep.

A Sheraton chair

Shepherd Kings the Hyksos.

shep·herd's purse (shep'ərdz pėrs') a weed that has small, white flowers and purselike pods.

Sher·a·ton (sher'ə tən) *adj.* of, like, or having to do with a light, graceful style of furniture characterized by straight lines and little ornamentation. —*n.* **1** this style of furniture. **2** a piece of furniture in this style. [< Thomas *Sheraton* (1751-1806), an English maker and designer of furniture]

sher·bet (shėr'bət) *n.* **1** a frozen dessert made of fruit juice, sugar, and water, milk, or whites of eggs. **2** a cooling drink made of fruit juice, sugar, and water, popular in the Orient. **3** a dish, usually with a long stem, to hold frozen sherbet. [< Turkish, Persian < Arabic *sharibah* to drink]

sherd (shėrd) *n.* shard.

she·reef (shə rēf') *n.* sherif.

she·rif (shə rēf') *n.* **1** a descendant of Mohammed through his daughter Fatima. **2** an Arab prince or ruler; especially the chief magistrate of Mecca or (formerly) the sovereign of Morocco. [< Arabic *sharif* exalted]

sher·iff (sher'if) *n.* **1** in Canada, an official whose job is to enforce certain court orders, such as evicting persons for failure to pay rent and escorting convicted persons to prison. **2** in the United States, the most important law-enforcing officer of a county. **3** in England and Wales, the chief executive officer of a county or shire, nominally responsible for the administration of justice, the conduct of parliamentary elections, etc. [OE *scīrgerēfa* < *scīr* shire + *gerēfa* reeve[1]]

Sher·pa (shėr'pə) *n.* **1** a Himalayan people living on the Tibet-Nepal border, famous as mountain climbers and guides. **2** a member of this people.

sher·ry (sher'ē) *n.* **-ries. 1** a strong Spanish wine fortified with brandy and ranging in flavor from very dry to sweet. It varies in color from pale yellow to brown. **2** any similar wine. [earlier *sherris* (taken as pl.) wine from *Xeres,* a Spanish town]

Sher·wood Forest (shėr'wůd) a royal forest near Nottingham, where Robin Hood is said to have lived.

she's (shēz; *unstressed,* shiz) **1** she is. **2** she has.

Shet·land (shet'lənd) *n.* **1** a Shetland pony. **2** Shetland wool. [< *Shetland* Islands, a group of British islands northeast of Scotland]

Shetland pony a small, sturdy, rough-coated pony, originally from the Shetland Islands.

Shetland wool a fine, hairy, strong worsted spun from the wool of Shetland sheep, widely used in knitting fine shawls, garments, etc.

shew (shō) *v.* **shewed, shewn, shew·ing,** *n. Archaic.* show.

shew·bread (shō'bred') *n.* the unleavened bread placed near the altar every Sabbath by the ancient Jewish priests as an offering to God. Also, **showbread.**

shib·bo·leth (shib'ə lith) *n.* **1** any peculiarity of speech, habit, or custom considered distinctive of a particular group, class, etc. **2** any test word, password, watchword, or pet phrase of a political party, a class, sect, etc. [< Hebrew *shibbōleth* stream; used as a password by the Gileadites to distinguish the fleeing Ephraimites, because they could not pronounce *sh.* Judges 12:4-6]

shied (shīd) *v.* pt. and a pp. of **shy.**

shield (shēld) *n.* **1** a piece of armor carried on the arm to protect the body in battle. **2** anything used to protect. **3** something shaped like a shield. **4** a covering for moving parts of machinery. **5 a** any substance to protect against

exposure to radiation, especially in nuclear reactors, as lead or water. **b** a barrier built out of one of these substances. **6 a** a framework pushed ahead in a tunnel to prevent the earth from caving in while the tunnel is being lined. **b** a movable framework protecting a miner at his work. **7** a steel screen or plate attached to a cannon, howitzer, etc. to protect the crew, mechanism, etc. **8 a** a policeman's badge. **b** an escutcheon. **9** a piece of fabric, often rubberized, worn inside a dress or other garment at the armpit. **10** in zoology, a protective plate covering a part, as a scute, carapace, or plastron. **11 the Shield,** the Canadian Shield.
—*v.* **1** be a shield to; protect; defend. **2** serve as a shield. [OE *sceld*]

shift (shift) *v.* **1** change from one place, position, person, sound, etc. to another; change: *The wind has shifted to the southeast. He shifted the heavy bag from one hand to the other.* **2** be rather dishonest; scheme. **3** manage to get along; contrive: *When his parents died, Tom had to shift for himself.* **4** *Archaic or dialect.* change the clothes of. **5** get rid of. **6** change the position of (the gears of an automobile).
—*n.* **1** a substituting or alternating for another person or thing; change: *There are two shifts of work at the factory.* **2** a group of workers alternating with another group in doing work: *This man is on the night shift.* **3** the time during which such a group works. **4** a way of getting on; scheme; trick: *The lazy man tried every shift to avoid doing his work.* **5 a** *Archaic.* a woman's chemise. **b** a woman's dress having straight, loose-fitting lines. **6** in football, a change in the arrangement of the players before a ball is put into play. **7** in geology, a slight fault or dislocation in a seam or stratum. **8** in linguistics, a sound change that affects the phonetic and phonemic system of a language or language group. **9 make shift, a** manage to get along. **b** manage with effort or difficulty. **c** do as well as one can. [OE *sciftan* arrange] **—shift′er,** *n.* **—Syn.** *v.* **1** transfer. *-n.* **2** crew, gang. **4** expedient.

shift·less (shift′lis) *adj.* lazy; inefficient. **—shift′less·ly,** *adv.* **—shift′less·ness,** *n.*

shift·y (shif′tē) *adj.* **shift·i·er, shift·i·est. 1** tricky, sly; not straightforward. **2** in sports, fast; quick and tricky in movement or playing style. **—shift′i·ly,** *adv.* **—shift′i·ness,** *n.*

shill (shil) *Slang.* —*n.* a person who acts as a decoy or confederate of a barker, peddler, or gambler in order to influence bystanders to bid, buy, bet, etc. —*v.* work as a shill; act as a decoy or lure. [origin unknown]

shil·le·lagh or **shil·la·lah** (shə lā′lē or shə lā′lə) *n.* *Irish.* a stick to hit with; cudgel. [< *Shillelagh,* a village in the Irish Republic]

shil·ling (shil′ing) *n.* **1** formerly, a unit of money in the United Kingdom, worth 1/20 of a pound. **2** a unit of money in certain other countries. **3** a coin worth one shilling. [OE *scilling*]

shil·ly-shal·ly (shil′ē shal′ē) *adj. v.* **-lied, -ly·ing,** *n.* —*adj.* vacillating; wavering; hesitating; undecided. —*v.* be undecided; vacillate; hesitate. —*n.* an inability to decide; hesitation. [varied reduplication of *shall I?*]

shi·ly (shī′lē) *adv.* shyly.

shim (shim) *n. v.* **shimmed, shim·ming.** —*n.* a thin strip of metal or wood used to fill up space, make something level, etc. —*v.* put a shim or shims in. [origin uncertain]

shim·mer (shim′ər) *v.* gleam faintly: *The satin shimmers.* —*n.* a faint gleam or shine. [OE *scimrian*]

shim·mer·y (shim′ər ē) *adj.* shimmering; gleaming softly.

shim·my (shim′ē) *n.* **-mies,** *v.* **-mied, -my·ing.** —*n.* **1** *Slang.* a jazz dance with much shaking of the body. **2** an unusual shaking or vibration, especially of the front wheels of a car, truck, etc. **3** *Informal.* chemise. —*v.* **1** dance the shimmy. **2** shake; vibrate. [var. of *chemise* (taken as pl.)]

shin (shin) *n. v.* **shinned, shin·ning.** —*n.* **1** the front part of the leg from the knee to the ankle. **2** in beef cattle, the lower part of the foreleg. —*v.* climb up or down a rope, pole, etc. by gripping alternately with the hands and feet: *shin up a tree.* [OE *scinu*]

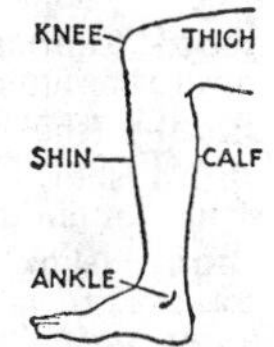

hat, āge, cãre, fär; let, ēqual, tėrm; it, īce
hot, ōpen, ôrder; oil, out; cup, pu̇t, rüle, ūse
əbove, takən, pencəl, lemən, circəs
ch, child; ng, long; sh, ship
th, thin; ᴛʜ, then; zh, measure

shin·bone (shin′bōn′) *n.* the front bone of the leg below the knee; tibia.

shin·dig (shin′dig′) *n.* *Informal.* a merry or noisy dance, party, etc. [? variant of *shindy,* suggesting a dig, or blow, on the shin]

shin·dy (shin′dē) *n.* **-dies.** *Slang.* disturbance; rumpus. [origin uncertain]

shine (shīn) *v.* **shone** or (*especially for def. 3*) **shined, shin·ing,** *n.* —*v.* **1** send out light; be bright with light; reflect light; glow: *The sun shines.* **2** do very well; be brilliant; excel: *Mary shines in French.* **3** make bright; polish: *shine shoes.* **4** cause to shine: *shine a light.* **5 shine up to,** *Slang.* try to please and get the friendship of.
—*n.* **1** light; brightness. **2** a lustre; polish; gloss, as of silk. **3** fair weather; sunshine: *rain or shine.* **4** polish put on shoes. **5** *Slang.* a fancy; liking. **6** *Slang.* a trick; prank. **7 take a shine to,** *Slang.* become fond of; like. [OE *scīnan*] **—Syn.** *v.* **1** beam, gleam. *-n.* **1** radiance, gleam.

shin·er (shīn′ər) *n.* **1** a person or thing that shines. **2** a small North American fresh-water fish having glistening scales. **3** *Slang.* a black eye.

shin·gle[1] (shing′gəl) *n. v.* **-gled, -gling.** —*n.* **1** a thin piece of wood, etc. used for roofing, etc. Shingles are laid in overlapping rows with the thicker ends exposed. **2** *Informal.* a small signboard, especially for a doctor's or lawyer's office. **3 hang out one's shingle,** *Informal.* of lawyers, doctors, and dentists, open an office. **4** a short haircut. —*v.* **1** cover with shingles: *shingle a roof.* **2** cut (the hair) short. [var. of earlier *shindle* < L *scindula*]

shin·gle[2] (shing′gəl) *n.* **1** loose stones or pebbles such as lie on the seashore; coarse gravel. **2** a beach or other place covered with such pebbles. [origin uncertain; cf. Norwegian *singling* small, round pebble]

shin·gles (shing′gəlz) *n.sing. or pl.* a virus disease that causes painful irritation of a group of nerves and an outbreak of itching spots or blisters. [ME < Med.L *cingulus,* var. of L *cingulum* girdle < *cingere* gird]

shin·gly (shing′glē) *adj.* consisting of or covered with small, loose stones or pebbles.

shin·ing (shīn′ing) *adj.* **1** that shines; bright. **2** brilliant; outstanding. **—shin′ing·ly,** *adv.* **—Syn. 1** glowing, radiant, glistening.

shin·ny[1] (shin′ē) *n.* **-nies,** *v.* **-nied, -ny·ing.** —*n.* **1** a simple kind of hockey, played on the ice with skates, or without skates on the street or in a field. **2** the stick used in this game. **3** *Slang.* the game of ice hockey. —*v.* play shinny. [< *shin*]

shin·ny[2] (shin′ē) *v.* **-nied, -ny·ing.** *Informal.* use one's shins to climb; shin.

shin·plas·ter (shin′plas′tər) *n.* **1** a plaster for a sore leg, often paper wet with vinegar. **2** *Informal.* a piece of paper money worth 25 cents. Shinplasters are no longer issued in Canada.

Shin·to (shin′tō) *n.* **1** the main religion of Japan, primarily a system of nature worship and ancestor worship. **2** an adherent of this religion. —*adj.* of or having to do with Shinto. [< Japanese < Chinese *shin tao* way of the gods]

Shin·to·ism (shin′tō iz′əm) *n.* the Shinto religion.

shin·y (shī′nē) *adj.* **shin·i·er, shin·i·est. 1** shining; bright: *a shiny, new nickel.* **2** worn to a glossy smoothness: *a coat shiny from hard wear.* **—shin′i·ness,** *n.*

ship (ship) *n. v.* **shipped, ship·ping.** —*n.* **1** a large sea-going vessel with masts and sails. **2** any large vessel for use on water or in air, such as a steamship, battleship, aircraft, space ship, etc. **3** a sailing vessel with three or more masts. **4** the officers and crew of a vessel. **5 about ship!** turn the ship round! put the ship on the other tack! **6 when one's ship comes home** or **in,** when one's fortune is made, when one has money.
—*v.* **1** put, take, or receive on board a ship. **2** go on

board a ship. **3** travel on a ship; sail. **4** send or carry from one place to another by a ship, train, truck, etc.: *Did he ship it by express?* **5** engage for service on a ship: *ship a new crew.* **6** take a job on a ship: *He shipped as cook.* **7** take in (water) over the side, as a vessel does when the waves break over it. **8** fix (something) in a ship or boat in its proper place for use: *ship a rudder.* [OE *scip*]

-ship *suffix.* **1** the office, status, or rank of ——, as in *clerkship, kingship.* **2** the quality, state, or condition of ——, as in *kinship.* **3** the act, acts, power, or skill of —— as in *horsemanship, dictatorship.* **4** the relation between ——s, as in *cousinship, comradeship.* [OE *-scipe*]

ship biscuit a kind of hard biscuit formerly used on shipboard; hardtack.

ship·board (ship′bôrd′) *n.* **1** a ship. **2 on shipboard,** on or inside a ship.

ship bread ship biscuit; hardtack.

ship·break·er (ship′brāk′ər) *n.* a person who breaks up or contracts to break up ships no longer seaworthy.

ship·break·ing (ship′brāk′ing) *n.* the work or business of a shipbreaker.

ship·build·er (ship′bil′dər) *n.* a person who designs or constructs ships.

ship·build·ing (ship′bil′ding) *n.* **1** the designing or building of ships. **2** the art of building ships. —*adj.* of or used in shipbuilding; having to do with shipbuilding.

ship canal a canal wide and deep enough for ships.

ship·lap (ship′lap′) *n.* **1** a flush, overlapping joint between boards, formed by cutting corresponding rabbets in the adjoining edges and lapping the boards to the depth of the rabbets. **2** boards thus rabbeted.

ship·load (ship′lōd′) *n.* a full load for a ship.

ship·man (ship′mən) *n.* **-men** (-mən). **1** *Archaic.* a sailor. **2** the master of a ship.

ship·mas·ter (ship′mas′tər) *n.* a master, commander, or captain of a ship.

ship·mate (ship′māt′) *n.* **1** a fellow sailor on a ship. **2** a person who sails on the same ship; fellow passenger.

ship·ment (ship′mənt) *n.* **1** the act of shipping goods. **2** goods sent at one time to a person, firm, etc.

ship money in England, a tax to provide money for the building and maintenance of naval ships, levied at various times until it was abolished in 1641.

ship of the desert a camel.

ship of the line in former times, a sailing warship carrying 74 or more guns, corresponding to the modern battleship.

ship·own·er (ship′ōn′ər) *n.* a person who owns a ship or ships.

ship·per (ship′ər) *n.* a person who ships goods.

ship·ping (ship′ing) *n.* **1** the act or business of sending goods by water, rail, etc. **2** ships collectively. **3** their total tonnage. **4** the ships of a nation, city, or business.

shipping clerk a person whose work is to see to the packing and shipment of goods.

shipping room a room in a business house, factory, etc. from which goods are sent.

ship-rigged (ship′rigd′) *adj.* rigged with square sails on all three masts.

ship·shape (ship′shāp′) *adj.* in good order; trim. —*adv.* in a trim, neat manner.

ship's husband a person who has general care of a ship in port, overseeing supplies, repairs, entering and clearing procedures, etc.

ship·worm (ship′wėrm′) *n.* any of various molluscs having small valves and long wormlike bodies. Shipworms burrow into the timbers of ships.

ship·wreck (ship′rek′) *n.* **1** the destruction or loss of a ship. **2** a wrecked ship. **3** destruction; ruin: *The shipwreck of his plans discouraged him.* —*v.* **1** wreck; ruin; destroy. **2** suffer shipwreck.

ship·wright (ship′rīt′) *n.* a man who builds or repairs ships.

ship·yard (ship′yärd′) *n.* a place near the water where ships are built or repaired.

shire (shīr) *n.* one of the counties into which Great Britain is divided. [OE *scīr*]

shire horse any of the largest breed of draft horses having very hairy legs, said to descend from the war horses of the Middle Ages. [< the *Shires,* midland counties of England where they are chiefly raised]

Shire (shīr) *n.* a shire horse.

shire·town (shīr′toun′) *n. Cdn.* in the Maritimes, a county seat.

shirk (shėrk) *v.* avoid or get out of doing (work, a duty, etc.). —*n.* a person who shirks or does not do his share. [< G *Schurke* rascal] **—shirk′er,** *n.* **—Syn.** *v.* evade, shun, neglect.

shirr (shėr) *v.* **1** draw up or gather (cloth) on parallel threads. **2** bake (eggs) in a shallow dish with butter, etc. —*n.* a shirred arrangement of cloth, etc. [origin unknown]

shirt (shėrt) *n.* **1** a boy's or man's garment for the upper part of the body, made of cotton, silk, nylon, etc. and having a collar and long or short sleeves. **2** a similar garment for girls and women. **3** an undergarment for the upper part of the body. **4 keep one's shirt on,** *Slang.* stay calm; keep one's temper. **5 lose one's shirt,** *Slang.* lose everything one owns. [OE *scyrte.* Cf. SKIRT.] **—shirt′less,** *adj.*

shirt·band (shėrt′band′) *n.* the neckband or other band of a shirt.

shirt·ing (shėr′ting) *n.* cloth for shirts.

shirt-sleeve (shėrt′slēv′) *adj. Informal.* informal: *shirt-sleeve diplomacy.*

shirt·waist (shėrt′wāst′) *n.* **1** a woman's blouse similar in style to a shirt (def. 1). **2** a tailored dress having a bodice similar to that of such a blouse.

shish·ka·bob (shish′kə bob′) *n.* shish kebab.

shish ke·bab (shish′kə bob′) cubes of lamb, beef, or other meat, marinated and cooked with mushrooms, tomatoes, onions, etc. on a skewer or spit. [< Armenian *shish kabab*]

shiv (shiv) *n. Slang.* a knife or razor, especially an offensive weapon. A switchblade is a kind of shiv. [perhaps < earlier *chive* file, knife < Romany]

shiv·a (shiv′ə) *n.* in Judaism, a period of seven days' mourning for a dead relative. [< Hebrew *shib'ah* seven]

Shi·va (shē′və) *n.* Siva.

shiv·a·ree (shiv′ə rē′) *n.* **1** a celebration held to do honor to a newly married couple; charivari. **2** a noisy serenade for a newly married couple, often performed in a spirit of mockery. [var. of *charivari*]

shiv·er[1] (shiv′ər) *v.* shake with cold, fear, etc. —*n.* a shaking from cold, fear, etc. [ME *schiveren*; origin uncertain] **—shiv′er·er,** *n.*

Syn. *v.* **Shiver, shudder, quake** = shake or tremble. **Shiver,** used chiefly of people and animals, suggests a quivering of the flesh: *He crept shivering into bed.* **Shudder** especially suggests sudden sharp shivering of the whole body in horror or extreme disgust: *He shuddered at the ghastly sight.* **Quake** suggests violent trembling with fear or cold, or shaking and rocking from a violent disturbance: *The house quaked on its foundations.*

shiv·er[2] (shiv′ər) *v.* break into small pieces: *He shivered the mirror with a hammer.* —*n.* a small piece; splinter. [origin uncertain]

shiv·er·y (shiv′ər ē or shiv′rē) *adj.* **1** quivering from cold, fear, etc.; shivering. **2** inclined to shiver from cold. **3** chilly. **4** causing shivers.

shmo (shmō) *n.* schmo.

shoal[1] (shōl) *n.* **1** a place where the water is shallow. **2** a sandbank or sand bar that makes the water shallow: *The ship was wrecked on the shoals.* —*adj.* shallow. —*v.* become shallow. [OE *sceald* shallow]

shoal[2] (shōl) *n.* a large number; crowd: *a shoal of fish.* —*v.* form into a shoal; crowd together. [OE *scolu*]

shoal·y (shōl′ē) *adj.* full of shoals or shallow places.

shoat (shōt) *n.* a young pig able to feed itself. Also, **shote.** [origin uncertain]

shock[1] (shok) *n.* **1** a sudden, violent shake, blow, or crash: *Earthquake shocks are often felt in Japan. The two trains collided with a terrible shock.* **2** a sudden, violent or upsetting disturbance: *His death was a great shock to his family.* **3** a collapsing or weakening of the body or

mind caused by some violent impression on the nerves: *The operation was successfully performed, but the patient suffered from shock.* 4 *Informal.* a sudden attack of illness that makes a person senseless or takes away the power to move or speak; paralysis. 5 a disturbance produced by an electric current passing through the body.
—*v.* 1 strike together violently. 2 cause to feel surprise, horror, or disgust: *That child's bad language shocks everyone.* 3 collide with a shock. 4 give an electric shock to. [probably < F *choc,* n., *choquer,* v.] —**shock′er,** *n.*
—**Syn.** *n.* 1 concussion, collision, jolt. –*v.* 1 jar, jolt, collide. 2 horrify, startle.

shock[2] (shok) *n. v.* stook. See **stook** for picture. [ME < LG or MDu. *schok*] —**shock′er,** *n.*

shock[3] (shok) *n.* a thick, bushy mass: *He has a shock of red hair.* [? < *shock*[2]]

shock absorber 1 anything that absorbs or lessens shocks. 2 a device used on automobiles to absorb or lessen the shocks caused by rough roads. 3 a similar device on the landing gear of aircraft.

shock-head·ed (shok′hed′id) *adj.* having a thick, bushy mass of hair.

shock·ing (shok′ing) *adj.* 1 causing intense and painful surprise. 2 offensive; disgusting; revolting. 3 *Informal.* very bad. —**shock′ing·ly,** *adv.* —**Syn.** 1 appalling. 2 outrageous, scandalous.

shock·proof (shok′prüf′) *adj.* 1 able to endure or resist shock. 2 protected against electric shock.

shock therapy the treatment of mental disorder through shock induced by chemical or electrical means.

shock treatment 1 shock therapy. 2 any act intended to shock.

shock troops troops chosen and specially trained for making attacks.

shock wave 1 a disturbance of the atmosphere created by the movement of an aircraft, rocket, space ship, etc. at velocities greater than that of sound. 2 a similar effect caused by an explosion.

shod (shod) *v.* pt. and pp. of **shoe.**

shod·dy (shod′ē) *n.* **-dies,** *adj.* **-di·er, -di·est.** —*n.* 1 an inferior kind of wool made of woollen waste, old rags, yarn, etc. 2 cloth made of woollen waste. 3 anything inferior made to look like what is better. —*adj.* 1 made of woollen waste. 2 pretending to be better than it is: *a shoddy necklace.* [origin uncertain] —**shod′di·ly,** *adv.* —**shod′di·ness,** *n.*

shoe (shü) *n.* **shoes** or (*Archaic*) **shoon;** *v.* **shod, shoe·ing.** —*n.* 1 an outer covering, usually of leather, for a person's foot. 2 anything like a shoe in shape or use. 3 a horseshoe. 4 a ferrule; metal band, etc. to protect the end of a staff, pole, etc. 5 the part of a brake that presses on a wheel. 6 the outer case of an automobile tire. 7 a sliding plate or contact by which an electric car takes current from the third rail. 8 **fill another's shoes,** take another person's place. 9 **in another's shoes,** in another's place, situation, or circumstances. 10 **the shoe is on the other foot,** the situation is reversed. 11 **where the shoe pinches,** where the real trouble or difficulty lies.
—*v.* 1 furnish with a shoe or shoes: *A blacksmith shoes horses.* 2 protect or arm at the point; edge or face with metal: *a stick shod with steel.* [OE *scōh*] —**shoe′less,** *adj.*

shoe·black (shü′blak′) *n.* a person who cleans and polishes shoes to earn money.

shoe·horn (shü′hôrn′) *n.* a piece of metal, horn, etc. inserted at the heel of a shoe to make it slip on easily.

shoe·lace (shü′lās′) *n.* a cord, braid, or leather strip for fastening a shoe.

shoe·mak·er (shü′māk′ər) *n.* a person who makes or mends shoes.

shoe·mak·ing (shü′māk′ing) *n.* the making or mending of shoes.

shoe·shine (shü′shīn′) *n.* 1 the shining or polishing of shoes. 2 the polished look of shined shoes. 3 a shoeblack.

shoe·string (shü′string′) *n.* 1 a shoelace. 2 *Informal.* a very small amount of money used to start or carry on a business, investment, etc.: *The firm is paying its way, but it is operating on a shoestring.*

shoe tree a form for keeping a shoe in shape or for stretching it.

hat, āge, cãre, fär; let, ēqual, tėrm; it, īce
hot, ōpen, ôrder; oil, out; cup, pu̇t, rüle. ūse
əbove, takən, pencəl, lemən, circəs
ch, child; ng, long; sh, ship
th, thin; ᴛʜ, then; zh, measure

sho·gun (shō′gun or shō′gün) *n.* the former hereditary commander in chief of the Japanese army. The shoguns were the real rulers of Japan for hundreds of years until 1867. [< Japanese < Chinese *chiang chun* army leader]

sho·gun·ate (shō′gun it, shō′gun āt′, shō′gün it, or shō′gün āt′) *n.* 1 the position, rank, or rule of a shogun. 2 government by shoguns.

shone (shon) *v.* a pt. and a pp. of **shine.**

shoo (shü) *interj. v.* **shooed, shoo·ing.** —*interj.* an exclamation used to scare away hens, birds, etc. —*v.* 1 scare or drive away by calling "Shoo!" 2 call "Shoo!"

shoo-in (shü′in′) *n. Informal.* 1 a person who will win easily; sure winner. 2 a contest or match considered easy to win.

shook[1] (shu̇k) *n.* a set of the pieces, cut and ready to assemble, that are used in making boxes, barrels, articles of furniture, etc. [origin uncertain]

shook[2] (shu̇k) *v.* pt. of **shake.**

shoon (shün) *n. Archaic.* a pl. of **shoe.**

shoot (shüt) *v.* **shot, shoot·ing,** *n.* —*v.* 1 hit, wound, or kill with a bullet, arrow, etc.: *shoot a rabbit.* 2 send, propel, or direct with force and speed: *He shot question after question at us.* 3 fire or use a weapon, such as a gun, bow, catapult, etc. 4 of a gun, etc., send a bullet: *This gun shoots straight.* 5 kill game in or on: *shoot a farm.* 6 move suddenly and swiftly: *A car shot by us. Flames shot up from the burning house. Pain shot up his arm. He shot back the bolt.* 7 pass quickly along, through, over, or under: *shoot Niagara Falls in a barrel.* 8 hurt sharply from time to time. 9 come forth from the ground; grow; grow rapidly: *Buds shoot forth in the spring. The corn is shooting up in the warm weather.* 10 take (a picture) with a camera; photograph. 11 project sharply: *a cape that shoots out into the sea.* 12 dump; empty out. 13 vary with some different color, etc.: *Her dress was shot with threads of gold.* 14 measure the altitude of: *shoot the sun.* 15 send (a ball, etc.) toward the goal, pocket, etc. 16 propel (a marble), as from the thumb and forefinger. 17 cast or toss (the dice) in playing craps. 18 open, loosen, remove, etc. by setting off a charge of an explosive: *shoot an oil well.* 19 **shoot at** or **for,** *Informal.* aim at; aspire to. 20 **shoot down, a** kill by a shot. **b** cause (an aircraft, etc.) to fall down by shooting. 21 **shoot off,** discharge; fire. 22 **shoot up, a** grow tall or large quickly, as a plant, building, young person, etc. **b** *Informal.* rush through (a place) shooting wildly in all directions.
—*n.* 1 shooting practice. 2 a trip, party, or contest for shooting. 3 **a** the act of sprouting or growing. **b** a new part growing out; young bud or stem. 4 a sloping trough for conveying coal, grain, water, etc. to a lower level; chute. [OE *scēotan*] —**shoot′er,** *n.* —**Syn.** *v.* 11 jut, extend.

shooting gallery a long room or deep booth fitted with targets for practice in shooting.

shooting iron *Informal.* a firearm or gun, especially a pistol or rifle.

shooting star 1 a meteor resembling a star seen falling or darting through the sky. 2 a plant that has a cluster of rose, purple, or white flowers whose petals and sepals turn backward.

shop (shop) *n. v.* **shopped, shop·ping.** —*n.* 1 a place where things are sold; store. 2 a place where things are made or repaired: *He works in a carpenter's shop.* 3 a place where a certain kind of work is done: *a barber shop.* 4 **set up shop,** start work or business. 5 **shut up shop,** give up work or business. 6 **talk shop,** talk about one's work. —*v.* visit stores to look at or to buy things. [OE *sceoppa*]

shop·girl (shop′gėrl′) *n.* a girl who works in a shop or store.

shop·keep·er (shop′kēp′ər) *n.* a person who carries on business in a shop or store.

shop·lift·er (shop′lif′tər) *n.* a person who steals goods from a store while pretending to be a customer.

shop·lift·ing (shop′lif′ting) *n.* the act of stealing goods from a store while pretending to be a customer.

shop·man (shop′mən) *n.* **-men** (-mən). a shopkeeper.

shop·per (shop′ər) *n.* **1** a person who visits stores to look at or buy things. **2** a person hired to buy goods at retail for another, especially one hired by a retail store to buy items of merchandise from competitive stores in order to determine how similar items offered by it compare in price and quality.

shop·ping (shop′ing) *n.* **1** the buying of groceries, clothes, etc.: *Mother does her shopping on Wednesdays and Saturdays.* **2 go shopping,** go to the store or stores in order to buy groceries, clothes, etc.

shopping centre **1** a concentration of retail stores, usually in a suburban residential district, built as a unit and having ample parking, spacious walks, etc. **2** the street or streets of a town where the main stores and shops are concentrated. **3** a town, city, etc. serving as retail and distribution centre for the surrounding region.

shopping plaza *Cdn.* shopping centre (def. 1).

shop steward a union worker elected by fellow workers to represent them in dealings with management and to maintain union rules.

shop·talk (shop′tok′ or -tôk′) *n.* **1** the informal language of an occupation. **2** the discussion of business or professional matters, especially outside of office hours.

☞ **shoptalk.** For the most part shoptalk (def. 1) consists of the necessary names for materials, processes, tools, etc.—for everything that is commonly referred to in the line of work. While many of these words are in good standing, they are not often needed outside the vocation.

shop·win·dow (shop′win′dō) *n.* show window.

shop·worn (shop′wôrn′) *adj.* soiled by being displayed or handled in a store.

shore[1] (shôr) *n.* **1** the land at the edge of a sea, lake, etc. **2** the land near a sea. **3** land. **4** in law, the land between high-water and low-water marks. **5 in shore,** in or on the water, near to the shore or nearer to the shore. **6 off shore,** in or on the water, not far from the shore. **7 shores,** *pl.* land. [ME; ?< LG or MDu. *schore*]

shore[2] (shôr) *n. v.* **shored, shor·ing.** —*n.* a prop placed against or beneath something to support it. —*v.* prop up or support with shores. [ME; ?< MDu. *schore* prop] **—shor′er,** *n.*

The frame of a ship supported by shores

shore[3] (shôr) *v. Archaic.* a pt. of **shear.**

shore·less (shôr′lis) *adj.* **1** having no shore. **2** boundless.

shore·line (shôr′līn′) *n.* the line where shore and water meet.

shore·ward (shôr′wərd) *adv. adj.* toward the shore.

shor·ing (shôr′ing) *n.* the shores or props for supporting a building, ship, etc.

shorn (shôrn) *v.* a pp. of **shear.** —*adj.* **1** sheared. **2** deprived.

short (shôrt) *adj.* **1** not long; of small extent from end to end: *a short distance, a short time, a short street.* **2** not long for its kind: *a short tail.* **3** not tall: *a short man, short grass.* **4** not coming up to the right amount, measure, standard, etc.: *The cashier is short in his accounts.* **5** not having enough; scanty: *The prisoners were kept on short allowance of food.* **6** so brief as to be rude: *He was so short with me that I felt hurt.* **7** of vowels or syllables, occupying a relatively short time in utterance. The vowels are considered as short in *fat, net, pin, not, up.* **8** breaking or crumbling easily. Pastry is made short with lard and butter. **9** not possessing at the time of sale the stocks or commodities that one sells. **10** denoting or having to do with sales of stocks or commodities that the seller does not possess. **11** depending for profit on a decline in prices. **12 make short work of,** deal with quickly. **13 run short, a** not have enough. **b** not be enough. **14 short of, a** not up to; less than: *Nothing short of your best work will satisfy me.* **b** not having enough of. **c** on the near side of.
—*adv.* **1** so as to be or make short. **2** abruptly; suddenly: *The horse stopped short.* **3** briefly. **4** on the near side of an intended or particular point: *stop short of actual crime.* **5 cut short,** end suddenly. **6 fall short, a** fail to reach. **b** be insufficient. **7 sell short,** sell without possessing at the time the stocks, etc. that are being sold: *It is risky to sell short.*
—*n.* **1** something short. **2** a short circuit. **3** a person who has sold short; a sale made by selling short; sold short. **4** any short motion picture as a cartoon, newsreel, etc., especially one shown on the same program with a full-length picture (feature). **5** in baseball, the position of shortstop: *play short.* **6 shorts,** *pl.* **a** short pants that reach no lower than the knees. **b** a pair of short underpants worn by men or boys. **c** a baby's short clothes. **d** mixture of bran and coarse meal. **7 for short,** to make shorter. **8 in short,** briefly.
—*v.* short-circuit. [OE *sceort*] **—short′ness,** *n.*

Syn. *adj.* **1 Short, brief** = of small extent. **Short** may describe either space or time, but when describing time it often suggests cutting or stopping short before finishing: *Because he was late, he could take only a short walk today.* **Brief** almost always describes time and means "coming to an end quickly," and therefore when applied to speeches or writings is more likely to suggest leaving out unimportant or unnecessary details than cutting off the end: *A brief essay is short but to the point.* **6** abrupt, curt, sharp.

short·age (shôr′tij) *n.* **1** too small an amount; a lack: *There is a shortage of grain because of poor crops.* **2** the amount by which something is deficient. **—Syn. 1** deficiency.

short·bread (shôrt′bred′) *n.* a rich cake or cookie that crumbles easily.

short·cake (shôrt′kāk′) *n.* **1** a cake made of rich biscuit dough and shortening, covered or filled with berries or other fruit. **2** a sweet cake filled with fruit. **3** shortbread.

short-change (shôrt′chānj′) *v.* **-changed, -chang·ing.** *Informal.* **1** give less than the right change to. **2** cheat. **—short′-chang′er,** *n.*

short circuit **1** a circuit of electricity such as that created when insulation wears off a wire or wires that touch each other or some connecting conductor, so that the main circuit is by-passed. A short circuit usually blows a fuse and may cause a fire. **2** *Informal.* get around; avoid; by-pass.

short-cir·cuit (shôrt′sėr′kit) *v.* **1** make a short circuit in. **2** make a short circuit.

short·com·ing (shôrt′kum′ing) *n.* a fault; defect.

short commons little to eat.

short cut a quicker or less distant way.

short-cut (shôrt′kut′) *v.* **-cut, -cut·ting.** take or use a short cut; avoid something by using a short cut.

short·en (shôr′tən) *v.* **1** make shorter; cut off. **2** become shorter. **3** make rich with butter, lard, etc. **4** take in (sail). **—short′en·er,** *n.*

Syn. 1 Shorten, curtail, abbreviate = make shorter. **Shorten** is the general word, meaning "reduce the length or extent of something": *The new highway shortens the trip.* **Curtail,** more formal, means "cut something short by taking away or cutting off a part," and particularly suggests causing loss or incompleteness: *Bad news made him curtail his trip.* **Abbreviate,** used chiefly of words and phrases, means "shorten by leaving out syllables, letters, or sounds," sometimes by using initial letters or substitutions: *Abbreviate "pound" to "lb." after numerals.*

short·en·ing (shôrt′ning) *n.* butter, lard, or other fat, used in baking to make pastry, cake, etc. crisp or crumbly.

short·hand (shôrt′hand′) *n.* a method of rapid writing that uses symbols in place of letters, syllables, words, and phrases; stenography. In the examples, the symbols mean "Your letter was received today." —*adj.* **1** using shorthand. **2** written in shorthand.

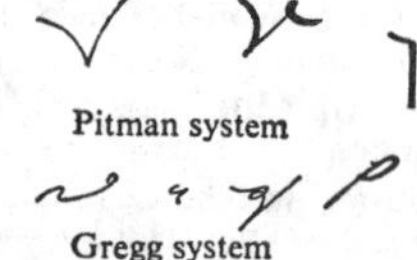

Pitman system
Gregg system
Examples of shorthand

short-hand·ed (shôrt′han′did) *adj.* **1** not having enough workmen or helpers. **2** in certain games, playing without the services of one or more players as a result of penalties. **3** playing with less than a full side because of injuries.

hat, āge, cãre, fär; let, ēqual, tėrm; it, īce
hot, ōpen, ôrder; oil, out; cup, pu̇t, rüle, ūse
əbove, takən, pencəl, lemən, circəs
ch, child; ng, long; sh, ship
th, thin; ᴛʜ, then; zh, measure

short·horn (shôrt′hôrn′) *n.* **1** a breed of cattle having short horns, raised for both beef and milk. **2** an animal of this breed.

short·ish (shôr′tish) *adj.* rather short.

short-lived (shôrt′livd′ or -līvd′) *adj.* living only a short time; lasting only a short time.

short·ly (shôrt′lē) *adv.* **1** in a short time; before long; soon. **2** in a few words; briefly. **3** briefly and rudely.

short-or·der (shôrt′ ôr′dər) *adj.* in a restaurant, etc., having to do with the cooking of foods that require little time to prepare: *a short-order cook.*

short-range (shôrt′rānj′) *adj.* not reaching far: *short-range plans.*

short shrift **1** short time for confession and absolution. **2** little mercy, respite, or delay.

short-sight·ed (shôrt′sīt′id) *adj.* **1** near-sighted; not able to see far. **2 a** lacking in foresight; not prudent. **b** characterized by or proceeding from lack of foresight: *a short-sighted strategy.* **—short′-sight′ed·ly,** *adv.* **—short′-sight′ed·ness,** *n.*

short·stop (shôrt′stop′) *n.* in baseball, a player stationed between second base and third base.

short story a prose story with a full plot, but of much less length than a novel.

short-tem·pered (shôrt′tem′pərd) *adj.* easily made angry; quick-tempered.

short-term (shôrt′tėrm′) *adj.* **1** lasting or intended for a short period of time: *our short-term plans.* **2** falling due in a short time.

short ton 2,000 pounds avoirdupois.

short-waist·ed (shôrt′wās′tid) *adj.* having a high waistline; short from neck to waistline.

short wave a radio wave having a wave length of 60 metres or less.

short-wave (shôrt′wāv′) *v.* **-waved, -wav·ing.** transmit by short waves: *The Prime Minister's speech was short-waved overseas.*

short-wind·ed (shôrt′win′did) *adj.* getting out of breath too quickly; having difficulty in breathing.

Sho·sho·ne·an (shō shō′nē ən) *n.* a language group of North American Indians of the Western United States that includes Comanche, Hopi, etc.

shot[1] (shot) *n.* **shots** (*for def. 3,* **shot** *or* **shots**), *v.* **shot·ted, shot·ting,** *adj.* —*n.* **1** the discharge of a gun or cannon: *He heard two shots.* **2** the act of shooting. **3** tiny balls of lead; bullets. **4** a single ball of lead for a gun or cannon. **5** tiny balls or pellets of lead, of which a number are combined in one charge, used chiefly in shotguns. **6** an attempt to hit by shooting: *That was a good shot.* **7** the distance a weapon can shoot; range. **8** a person who shoots: *He is a good shot.* **9** the act of sending, directing, or propelling with force and speed: *His shot is hard for a goalie to stop.* **10** a remark aimed at some person or thing. **11 a** an attempt; try: *make a shot at the job.* **b** a bet; chance. **12** a heavy metal ball. **13** a picture taken with a camera; a motion-picture record of a scene. **14** *Slang.* a drink: *a shot of whisky.* **15** *Slang.* a dose: *a shot of some drug.* **16** in mining, a blast. **17** an amount due or to be paid: *Father paid the shot.* **18 a long shot,** an attempt at something difficult. **19 not by a long shot,** not at all. **20 put the shot,** send a heavy metal ball as far as one can with one throw. **21 shot in the arm,** *Informal.* something that stimulates or revives; an incentive; spur. —*v.* **1** load with shot. **2** attempt; try. —*adj.* **shot through with,** full of. [OE *sceot*]

shot[2] (shot) *v.* pt. and pp. of **shoot.** —*adj.* **1** woven so as to show a play of colors: *blue silk shot with gold.* **2** *Slang.* that has been used up, worn out, or ruined.

shote (shōt) *n.* shoat.

shot·gun (shot′gun′) *n.* a smoothbore gun for firing cartridges filled with very small shot.

shotgun marriage or **wedding** *Informal.* a marriage or wedding enforced or arranged on account of pregnancy.

shot-put (shot′pu̇t′) *n.* a contest in which a person sends a heavy metal ball as far as he can with one throw.

shot rock or **shot-rock** (shot′rok′) *n.* in curling, the stone nearest the centre of the target.

shot silk silk woven so that the warp appears to be one color and the woof another.

should (shu̇d; *unstressed,* shəd) *v.* pt. of **shall. 1** See **shall** for ordinary uses. **2** *Should* has special uses: **a** to express duty: *You should try to make fewer mistakes.* **b** to make statements less direct or blunt: *I should not call her beautiful.* **c** to express uncertainty: *If John should win the prize, how happy he would be.* **d** to make statements about something that might have happened but did not: *I should have gone if you had asked me.* **e** to express a condition or reason for something: *He was pardoned on the condition that he should leave the country.* **f** to imply that something is unreasonable, unbelievable, unjustifiable, etc. (in questions introduced by *why*): *Why should you think that I did not like the book?* [OE *sceolde*]

shoul·der (shōl′dər) *n.* **1** the part of the body to which an arm of a human being, a foreleg of an animal or a wing of a bird is attached. **2 shoulders,** *pl.* the two shoulders and the upper part of the back. **3** the part of a garment covering this. **4** the foreleg and adjoining parts of a slaughtered animal, used as meat for roasts, etc. **5** a shoulderlike part or projection: *He grasped the shoulder of the rock.* **6** the projection, often unpaved, on each side of a road or highway. **7** in printing, the flat surface on a type extending beyond the base of the letter. **8** in fortification, the angle of a bastion included between face and flank. **9 put one's shoulder to the wheel,** make a great effort. **10 shoulder to shoulder, a** side by side; together. **b** with united effort. **11 straight from the shoulder,** frankly; directly. **12 turn** or **give a cold shoulder to,** shun; avoid; show dislike for.
—*v.* **1** take upon or support with the shoulder or shoulders: *shoulder a tray.* **2** bear (a burden, blame, etc.); assume (responsibility, expense, etc.). **3** push with the shoulders: *He shouldered his way through the crowd.* **4 shoulder arms,** hold a rifle almost upright with the barrel resting in the hollow of the shoulder and the butt in the hand. [OE *sculdor*]

shoulder blade the flat bone of the shoulder; scapula. See **skeleton** for picture.

shoulder knot a knot of ribbon or lace worn on the shoulder.

shoulder strap a strap worn over the shoulder to hold a garment up.

should·n't (shu̇d′ənt) should not.

shouldst (shu̇dst) *v. Archaic.* 2nd pers. sing. past tense of **shall.** "Thou shouldst" means "you should" (sing.).

shout (shout) *v.* **1** call or cry loudly and vigorously. **2** talk or laugh very loudly. **3** express by a shout or shouts: *The crowd shouted its approval.* **4 shout a person down,** silence a person by very loud talk. —*n.* **1** a loud, vigorous call or cry. **2** a loud outburst of laughter. [ME *schoute*; ? ult. var. of *scout*[2]] **—shout′er,** *n.*

shove (shuv) *v.* **shoved, shov·ing,** *n.* —*v.* **1** push; move forward or along by the application of force from behind. **2** push roughly or rudely; jostle. **3 shove off, a** push away from the shore; row away. **b** *Slang.* leave; start. —*n.* push. [OE *scūfan*] **—shov′er,** *n.* **—Syn.** *v.* **1** thrust. See **push.**

shov·el (shuv′əl) *n. v.* **-elled** or **-eled, -el·ling** or **-el·ing.** —*n.* **1** a tool with a broad scoop, used to lift and throw loose matter: *a coal shovel, a steam shovel.* **2** a shovelful. **3** a shovel hat. —*v.* **1** lift and throw with a shovel. **2** make with a shovel: *They shovelled a path through the snow.* **3** work with a shovel. **4** throw in large quantities: *The hungry man greedily shovelled the food into his mouth.* [OE *scofl*]

shov·el·board (shuv′əl bôrd) *n.* shuffleboard.

shov·el·er (shuv′əl ər) *n.* shoveller.

shov·el·ful (shuv′əl fu̇l′) *n.* **-fuls.** as much as a shovel can hold.

shovel hat a hat having a broad brim turned up at the sides and projecting with shovel-like curves in front and behind. Some clergymen of the Church of England wear shovel hats.

A shovel hat

shov·el·ler or **shov·el·er** (shuv′əl ər) *n.* **1** a person or thing that shovels. **2** a kind of fresh-water duck having a broad, flat bill.

show (shō) *v.* **showed, shown** or **showed, show·ing,** *n.* —*v.* **1** let be seen; put in sight: *She showed her new hat.* **2** reveal; manifest; disclose: *He showed himself a generous man by giving to charity.* **3** be in sight; appear; be seen: *Anger showed in his face.* **4** point out: *A boy showed us the way to town.* **5** direct; guide: *Show him out.* **6** make clear; explain. **7** make clear to; explain to: *Show us how to do the problem.* **8** prove: *He showed that it was true.* **9** grant; give: *show mercy, show favor.* **10** display. **11** display for effect. **12** of a list, record, recording instrument, indicate: *a watch showing twelve o'clock.* **13** in sports: **a** finish among the first three in a race. **b** finish third in a race (contrasted with *win* and *place*). **14** *Informal.* appear in or present a theatrical performance: *We are showing at the Centennial Hall.* **15 show off,** act or talk for show; make a deliberate or ostentatious display of one's abilities or accomplishments. **16 show up, a** expose. **b** stand out. **c** *Informal.* put in an appearance. —*n.* **1** a display: *The jewels made a fine show.* **2** a display for effect. **3** any kind of public exhibition or display: *a horse show.* **4** a showing: *The club voted by a show of hands.* **5** an appearance: *There is some show of truth in his excuse.* **6** a false appearance: *He hid his treachery by a show of friendship.* **7** a trace; indication: *a show of oil in a region.* **8** *Informal.* an entertainment: *a motion-picture show.* **9** a motion-picture theatre. **10** an object of scorn; something odd; queer sight: *Don't make a show of yourself.* **11** *Informal.* a chance; opportunity. **12** in sports, third place in a race: *win, place, and show.* **13 for show,** for effect; to attract attention. Also, *Archaic.* **shew.** [OE *scēawian* look at]
Syn. *v.* **5** conduct, usher. –*n.* **1 Show, display** = a public exhibiting. **Show** suggests something exposed to sight or put forward unconsciously, by oversight, or intentionally for others to look at: *That was a disgraceful show of temper.* **Display** suggests something spread out or unfolded to be seen clearly, or arranged so as to call attention to its fineness, beauty, strength, or other qualities: *That florist has the most beautiful displays in the city.* **6** pretext, pretence.

show bill a poster, placard, etc. advertising a show.

show·boat (shō′bōt′) *n.* a steamboat with a theatre for plays. Showboats carry their own actors and make frequent stops to give performances.

show·bread (shō′bred′) *n.* shewbread.

show·case (shō′kās′) *n.* **1** a glass case to display and protect articles in stores, museums, etc. **2** anything that displays: *Quebec City is a showcase of Canadian history.*

show·down (shō′doun′) *n.* **1** a forced disclosure of facts, purposes, methods, etc. **2** in card games, the displaying of the hands of the players at the end of a round.

show·er (shou′ər) *n.* **1** a brief fall of rain. **2** anything like a fall of rain: *a shower of hail, a shower of tears, a shower of sparks from an engine.* **3** a party for giving presents to a woman about to be married, about to have a baby, etc. **4** a shower bath. —*v.* **1** rain for a short time. **2** wet with a shower; spray; sprinkle. **3** have a shower bath. **4** come in a shower. **5** send in a shower; pour down: *They showered gifts upon her.* [OE *scur*]

shower bath 1 a bath in which water pours down on the body from above in small jets. **2** the apparatus for such a bath.

show·er·y (shou′ər ē) *adj.* **1** raining in showers. **2** having many showers. **3** like a shower.

show·man (shō′mən) *n.* **-men** (-mən). **1** a man who manages a show. **2** a person skilled in showmanship or publicity.

show·man·ship (shō′mən ship′) *n.* **1** the management of shows. **2** skill in managing shows or in publicity.

shown (shōn) *v.* a pp. of **show.**

show-off (shō′of′) *n.* **1** a showing off. **2** *Informal.* a person who shows off; a person who is always calling attention to himself.

show·place (shō′plās′) *n.* any place considered worth exhibiting because of its superior beauty, interest, etc.

show·room (shō′rüm′ or -rům′) *n.* a room used for the display of goods or merchandise.

show window a window in the front of a store, where things are shown for sale.

show·y (shō′ē) *adj.* **show·i·er, show·i·est. 1** making a display; striking; conspicuous: *A peony is a showy flower.* **2** too bright and gay to be in good taste. **3** ostentatious. —**show′i·ly,** *adv.* —**show′i·ness,** *n.* —**Syn. 2** garish.

shrank (shrangk) *v.* a pt. of **shrink.**

shrap·nel (shrap′nəl) *n.* **1** a shell filled with bullets and powder arranged to explode in the air and scatter the bullets over a large area. **2** the fragments scattered by such a shell on explosion. [after the inventor, Henry *Shrapnel* (1761-1842), a British army officer]

Shrapnel

shred (shred) *n. v.* **shred·ded** or **shred, shred·ding.** —*n.* **1** a very small piece torn off or cut off; a very narrow strip; scrap: *The wind tore the sail to shreds.* **2** a particle; fragment; bit: *There's not a shred of evidence that he took the money.* —*v.* tear or cut into small pieces. [OE *scrēade*]

shrew (shrü) *n.* **1** a bad-tempered, quarrelsome woman. **2** a mouselike mammal having a long snout and brownish fur, that eats insects and worms. [OE *scrēawa*]

shrewd (shrüd) *adj.* **1** having a sharp mind; showing a keen wit; clever. **2** keen; sharp. **3 shrewd turn,** a mean trick; a mischievous act. [earlier *shrewed,* < *shrew,* v., in sense of "scold"] —**shrewd′ly,** *adv.* —**shrewd′ness,** *n.*
Syn. 1 Shrewd, sagacious, astute = having a sharp or keen mind and good judgment, especially in practical affairs. **Shrewd** emphasizes sharpness and ability to see below the surface of things, and suggests natural cleverness in practical affairs or, sometimes, craftiness: *He is a shrewd businessman.* **Sagacious** emphasizes keen or penetrating understanding of practical affairs and ability to arrive at wise decisions: *The company director was a sagacious man.* **Astute** adds to *shrewd* the idea of having unusual power to see through and understand things and being hard to fool: *He is an astute diplomat.*

shrew·ish (shrü′ish) *adj.* scolding; bad-tempered. —**shrew′ish·ly,** *adv.* —**shrew′ish·ness,** *n.*

shrew·mouse (shrü′mous′) *n.* **-mice.** shrew.

shriek (shrēk) *n.* **1** a loud, sharp, shrill sound: *We heard the shriek of the engine's whistle.* **2** a loud, shrill laugh. —*v.* **1** make such a sound. People sometimes shriek because of terror, anger, pain, or amusement. **2** utter loudly and shrilly. [< ON *skrækja*] —**Syn.** *v.* **1** See **scream.**

shriev·al·ty (shrēv′əl tē) *n.* **-ties.** the office, term of office, or jurisdiction of a sheriff.

shrieve (shrēv) *n. Obsolete.* sheriff. [var. of *sheriff*]

shrift (shrift) *n. Archaic.* **1** confession to a priest, followed by the imposing of penance and the granting of absolution. **2** the act of shriving. [OE *scrift* < L *scriptus* written]

shrike (shrīk) *n.* a bird that has a strong, hooked beak and feeds on large insects, frogs, and sometimes on other birds. [OE *scrīc*]

shrill (shril) *adj.* **1** having a high pitch; high and sharp in sound; piercing: *Crickets, locusts, and katydids make shrill noises.* **2** full of shrill sounds. —*v.* **1** make a shrill sound. **2** sound sharply. —*n.* a shrill sound. —*adv.* with a shrill sound. [ME *shrille*] —**shrill′ness,** *n.*

shril·ly (shril′lē) *adv.* in shrill tones.

shrimp (shrimp) *n.* **shrimp** or **shrimps. 1** a small, long-tailed shellfish, used for food. **2** a small or insignificant person. [ME *shrimpe*; cf. MHG *schrimpen* shrink up] —**shrimp′like′,** *adj.*

shrine (shrīn) *n. v.* **shrined, shrin·ing.** —*n.* **1** a case, box, etc. holding a holy object. **2** the tomb of a saint, etc. **3** a place of worship: *a wayside shrine.* **4** a place or object considered as sacred because of its memories, history, etc. —*v.* enclose in a shrine or something like a shrine. [OE *scrīn* < L *scrinium* case]

hat, āge, cãre, fär; let, ēqual, tėrm; it, īce
hot, ōpen, ôrder; oil, out; cup, pu̇t, rüle, ūse
əbove, takən, pencəl, lemən, circəs
ch, child; ng, long; sh, ship
th, thin; ᴛʜ, then; zh, measure

shrink (shringk) *v.* **shrank** or **shrunk, shrunk** or **shrunk·en, shrink·ing,** *n.* —*v.* **1** draw back: *The dog shrank from the whip. A shy person shrinks from making new acquaintances.* **2** become smaller: *His wool sweater shrank when it was washed.* **3** make smaller; cause to contract: *Hot water shrinks wool.* —*n.* a shrinking. [OE *scrincan*] —**shrink′a·ble,** *adj.* —**shrink′er,** *n.*

Syn. *v.* **1 Shrink, flinch** = draw back from something painful, unpleasant, etc. **Shrink** suggests instinctive drawing back physically or mentally, by or as if by contracting or drawing away some part of the body in fear, horror, or sensitiveness, from something painful or disagreeable: *He shrank from admitting his guilt.* **Flinch** suggests drawing back or turning away in spite of one's desire or determination not to, from danger, an unpleasant or difficult task or duty, or, especially, pain: *He could bear torture without flinching.*

☛ **Shrunken** is still sometimes used as a past participle (*It had shrunken*), but is chiefly used as an adjective (*a shrunken face*).

shrink·age (shringk′ij) *n.* **1** the fact or process of shrinking. **2** the amount or degree of shrinking: *a shrinkage of two inches in the length of a sleeve.*

shrive (shrīv) *v.* **shrove** or **shrived, shriv·en** or **shrived, shriv·ing.** *Archaic.* **1** hear the confession of, impose penance on, and grant absolution to. **2** make confession. **3** hear confessions. **4 shrive oneself,** confess to a priest and do penance. [OE *scrīfan* < L *scribere* write]

shriv·el (shriv′əl) *v.* **-elled** or **-eled, -el·ling** or **-el·ing.** **1** dry up; wither; shrink and wrinkle: *The hot sunshine shrivelled the grass.* **2** waste away; become useless. **3** make helpless or useless. [origin unknown]

shriv·en (shriv′ən) *v.* a pp. of **shrive.**

shroud (shroud) *n.* **1** a cloth or garment in which a dead person is wrapped for burial. **2** something that covers, conceals, or veils: *The fog was a shroud over the city.* **3** Usually, **shrouds,** *pl.* a rope from a mast to the side of a ship. Shrouds help support the mast. —*v.* **1** wrap for burial. **2** cover; conceal; veil: *The earth is shrouded in darkness.* [OE *scrūd*]

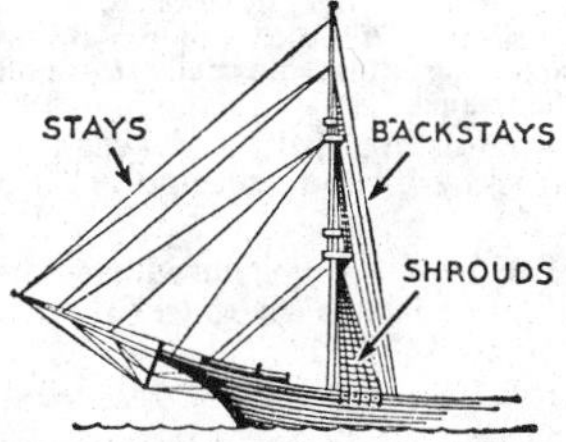

Shrouds (def. 3)

shrove (shrōv) *v.* a pt. of **shrive.**

Shrove·tide (shrōv′tīd′) *n.* the three days, **Shrove Sunday, Shrove Monday,** and **Shrove Tuesday,** before Ash Wednesday, the first day of Lent. Shrovetide is a time for confession, absolution, rejoicing, and feasting.

shrub[1] (shrub) *n.* a woody plant smaller than a tree, usually with many separate stems starting from or near the ground; bush. [OE *scrybb* brush] —**shrub′like′,** *adj.*

shrub[2] (shrub) *n.* a drink made from fruit juice, sugar, and, usually, rum or brandy. [< Arabic *shurb* drink]

shrub·ber·y (shrub′ər ē or shrub′rē) *n.* **-ber·ies. 1** shrubs collectively. **2** a place planted with shrubs.

shrub·by (shrub′ē) *adj.* **-bi·er, -bi·est. 1** like shrubs. **2** covered with shrubs. **3** consisting of shrubs.

shrug (shrug) *v.* **shrugged, shrug·ging,** *n.* —*v.* raise (the shoulders) as an expression of dislike, doubt, indifference, impatience, etc. —*n.* a raising of the shoulders in this way. [ME *schrugge(n)* shiver; origin uncertain]

shrunk (shrungk) *v.* a pp. and a pt. of **shrink.**

shrunk·en (shrungk′ən) *adj.* grown smaller; shrivelled. —*v.* a ppt. of **shrink.** ☛ See **shrink** for usage note.

shuck (shuk) *n.* a husk; pod. —*v.* remove the shucks from. [origin uncertain] —**shuck′er,** *n.*

shucks (shuks) *interj. Informal.* an exclamation of disgust, regret, impatience, etc.

shud·der (shud′ər) *v.* tremble with horror, fear, cold, etc.: *She shudders at the sight of a snake.* —*n.* a trembling; quivering. [ME *shodder(en)*, frequentative of OE *scūdan* shake] —**shud′der·ing·ly,** *adv.* —**Syn.** *v.* See **shiver.**

shuf·fle (shuf′əl) *v.* **-fled, -fling,** *n.* —*v.* **1** walk without lifting the feet: *The old man shuffles feebly along.* **2** scrape or drag (the feet). **3** dance with a shuffle. **4** mix (cards, etc.) so as to change the order. **5** push about; thrust or throw with clumsy haste: *He shuffled on his clothes and ran out of the house.* **6** move this way and that: *shuffle a stack of papers.* **7** act or answer in a tricky way. **8 shuffle off,** get rid of.
—*n.* **1** a scraping or dragging movement of the feet. **2** a dance with a shuffle. **3** a shuffling of cards. **4** the right or turn to shuffle (cards). **5** a movement this way and that. **6** a trick; unfair act; evasion: *Through some legal shuffle he secured a new trial.* [? < LG *schuffeln.* Akin to SHOVE.] —**shuf′fler,** *n.* —**Syn.** *v.* **7** dodge, equivocate, quibble.

shuf·fle·board (shuf′əl bôrd′) *n.* a game played by pushing large wooden or iron disks along a surface to certain spots. Also, **shovelboard.**

shun (shun) *v.* **shunned, shun·ning.** keep away from; avoid. [OE *scunian*] —**shun′ner,** *n.*

shun·pike (shun′pīk′) *n. Slang.* a quiet by-road, used by motorists to avoid major highways. [< *shun* + turn*pike*; originally, in the United States, a road used to avoid paying tolls on a turnpike]

shun·pik·ing (shun′pīk′ing) *n.* the practice of using quiet by-roads for motoring, rather than fast major highways.

shunt (shunt) *v.* **1** move out of the way; turn aside. **2** sidetrack; put aside; get rid of. **3 a** switch (a train) from one track to another. **b** switch (anything) to another route or place. **4** in electricity, carry (a part of a current) by means of a shunt.
—*n.* **1** a turning aside; shift. **2** a railway switch. **3** in electricity, a wire or other conductor joining two points in a circuit and forming a path through which a part of the current will pass. [ME; ? < *shun*] —**shunt′er,** *n.*

shut (shut) *v.* **shut, shut·ting,** *adj.* —*v.* **1** close (a receptacle or opening) by pushing or pulling a lid, door, some part, etc. into place: *shut a box, shut a window.* **2** close (the eyes, a knife, a book, etc.) by bringing parts together. **3** close tight; close securely; close doors or other openings of: *shut a house for the summer.* **4** become shut; be closed. **5** enclose; confine: *The criminal was shut in prison.* **6 shut down, a** close by lowering. **b** close (a factory, etc.) for a time; stop work. **c** settle down so as to cover or envelop. **d** *Informal.* put a stop or check on. **7 shut in,** keep from going out. **8 shut off,** close; obstruct; check; bar. **9 shut out, a** keep from coming in. **b** in sports, defeat (a team) without allowing it to score. **10 shut up, a** shut the doors and windows of. **b** *Informal.* stop talking. **c** keep from going out.
—*adj.* **1** closed; fastened up; enclosed. **2** in phonetics, formed by completely stopping the mouth passage. [OE *scyttan* bolt up] —**Syn. 1** See **close**[1].

shut-down (shut′doun′) *n.* a shutting down; a closing of a factory, etc. for a time.

shut-eye (shut′ī′) *n. Slang.* sleep.

shut-in (shut′in′) *adj.* confined. —*n.* a person who is kept from going out by sickness, weakness, etc.

shut-out (shut′out′) *n.* **1** in sports, the defeat of a team without allowing it to score. **2** a lockout.

shut·ter (shut′ər) *n.* **1** a movable cover for a window. **2** a movable cover, slide, etc. for closing an opening. The device that opens and closes in front of the lens of a camera is known as the shutter. **3** a person or thing that shuts. —*v.* put a shutter or shutters on or over. [< *shut*]

shut·tle (shut′əl) *n. v.* **-tled, -tling.** —*n.* **1** in weaving, an instrument that carries the thread from one side of the web to the other. **2** an instrument on which thread is wound. Shuttles are used in tatting (a kind of lacemaking). **3** something that goes back and forth. The shuttle in a sewing machine is the sliding holder for the lower thread. **4** of ships, aircraft, buses, etc.: **a** a plying between two points. **b** a trip so scheduled. **c** a vehicle used on such trips.

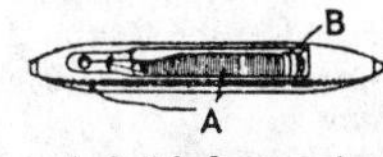

A shuttle for weaving: A, yarn; B, bobbin.

—*v.* **1** move quickly to and fro. **2** of ships, aircraft, buses, etc., ply between two points: *This bus shuttles between Toronto and Hamilton.* [OE *scutel* a dart < *scēotan* shoot]

shut·tle·cock (shut′əl kok′) *n.* **1** in the game of battledore and shuttlecock, a cork with feathers stuck in one end, which is hit back and forth by a small racket, called a battledore. **2** in badminton, a similar object having a heavy base and a feathered or plastic top.

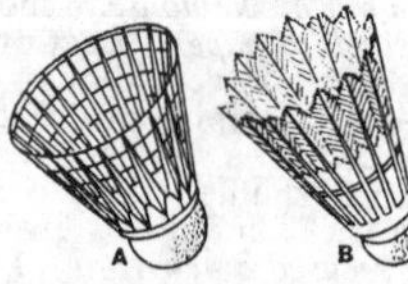

Shuttlecocks: A, plastic; B, feathered.

shuttle service a train, bus, or other form of transport that provides fast service back and forth over short distances.

shy[1] (shī) *adj.* **shy·er** or **shi·er, shy·est** or **shi·est,** *v.* **shied, shy·ing,** *n.* **shies.** —*adj.* **1** uncomfortable in company; bashful: *John is shy and dislikes parties.* **2** easily frightened away; timid: *A deer is a shy animal.* **3** cautious; wary. **4 be shy (of),** *Informal.* having little; lacking: *We are shy of butter. The team is shy of a goalkeeper.* **5 fight shy of,** keep away from; avoid. —*v.* **1** start back or aside suddenly: *The horse shied at the newspaper blowing along the ground.* **2** shrink. —*n.* a sudden start to one side. [OE *scēoh*] —**shy′ness,** *n.*
Syn. *adj.* **1** Shy, bashful = uncomfortable in the presence or company of others. Shy suggests a lack of self-confidence that makes a person unable to be easy and friendly in company and shrink from making friends or going up to others, and is shown by a reserved or timid manner: *People who appear snobbish are often really shy.* Bashful suggests shrinking by nature from being noticed, shown by awkward and embarrassed behavior in the presence of strangers: *The boy was too bashful to ask her to dance.* **3** suspicious, distrustful.

shy[2] (shī) *v.* **shied, shy·ing,** *n.* **shies.** —*v.* throw; fling: *The boy shied a stone at the tree.* —*n.* **1** a throw; fling. **2** *Informal.* a verbal attack; sarcastic or taunting remark. **3** *Informal.* a try; fling. [origin uncertain]

Shy·lock (shī′lok) *n.* **1** in Shakespeare's *The Merchant of Venice,* a relentless and revengeful moneylender. **2** any person who lends money at exorbitant interest and insists on prompt payment.

shy·ly (shī′lē) *adv.* in a shy manner. Also, **shily.**

shy·ster (shī′stər) *n. Informal.* a lawyer or other person who uses improper or questionable methods in his business or profession. [origin uncertain]

si (sē) *n.* in music, a syllable used for the seventh tone of an eight-tone scale; ti. [see GAMUT]

Si silicon.

SI International System (of metric units of measurement) (for F *Système Internationale*).

Si·a·mese (sī′ə mēz′) *adj. n.* **-mese.** —*adj.* Thai. —*n.* **1** Thai. **2** a breed of cat having a lithe, sinuous body and short hair, always dark at the ears, feet, and tail. **3** a cat of this breed.

Siamese twins twins joined together at birth. [< Eng and Chan (1811-1874), twin boys born in Siam, who were joined together at the chest]

sib (sib) *adj.* related by blood; closely related; akin. —*n.* **1** a kinsman or relative. **2** one's kin. **3** a brother or sister. [OE *sibb*]

Si·be·ri·an (sī bēr′ē ən) *adj.* of or having to do with Siberia, a part of the Soviet Union extending across northern Asia. —*n.* a native or inhabitant of Siberia.

Siberian husky 1 a breed of medium-sized, originally Siberian, working dog, having a brush tail and a thick coat of black, tan, or gray with white markings. It is much used in the North. **2** a dog of this breed.

sib·i·lance (sib′ə ləns) *n.* the state or quality of having a hissing sound.

sib·i·lan·cy (sib′ə lən sē) *n.* sibilance.

sib·i·lant (sib′ə lənt) *adj.* hissing. —*n.* a hissing sound, letter, or symbol. *S* and *sh* are sibilants. [< L *sibilans, -antis,* ppr. of *sibilare* hiss]

sib·i·late (sib′ə lāt′) *v.* **-lat·ed, -lat·ing. 1** utter a hissing sound. **2** pronounce with a hissing sound. [< L *sibilare* hiss]

sib·ling (sib′ling) *n.* a brother or sister. [< *sib* + *-ling*]

sib·yl (sib′əl) *n.* **1** in ancient times, any of several prophetesses that the Greeks and Romans consulted about the future. **2** a prophetess; fortuneteller; witch. [< L < Gk. *sibylla*]

sib·yl·line (sib′ə līn, sib′ə lēn, or sib′ə lin) *adj.* **1** of or like a sibyl; prophetic; mysterious. **2** said or written by a sibyl.

Sibylline Books a collection of prophecies and advice venerated and consulted by the ancient Romans.

sic[1] (sik) *adv. Latin.* so; thus.
☛ Sic is often used to show or emphasize the fact that something has been copied just as it is in the original: *The picture was labelled "Victoria, capitol [sic] of British Columbia."*

sic[2] (sik) *v.* **sicked, sick·ing.** sick[2].

sic·ca·tive (sik′ə tiv) *adj.* drying. —*n.* a drying substance, especially a dryer used in painting. [< LL *siccativus* < L *siccare* make dry < *siccus* dry]

Si·cil·ian (sə sil′yən) *adj.* of or having to do with Sicily, an island near the southwestern tip of Italy, its people, or their dialect. —*n.* **1** a native or inhabitant of Sicily. **2** a dialect of Italian spoken in Sicily.

sick[1] (sik) *adj.* **1** in poor health; having some disease; ill. **2** *Informal.* vomiting; inclined to vomit; feeling nausea. **3** of or for a sick person; connected with sickness. **4** showing sickness: *a sick look.* **5** weary; tired: *He is sick of school.* **6** disgusted. **7** affected with sorrow or longing: *sick at heart.* **8** not in the proper condition. **9** pale; wan. **10** morbid; sadistic; cruel: *a sick joke, sick humor.* —*n.* sick people. [OE *sēoc*] —**Syn.** *adj.* **1** unwell, ailing, indisposed.
☛ sick, ill. *Ill* is the more formal word. The two words mean the same, except that informally *sick* is often specialized to mean "nauseated."

sick[2] or **sic**[2] (sik) *v.* **sicked, sick·ing. 1** set upon or attack. **2** incite to set upon or attack (with *on*). [var. of *seek*]

sick bay 1 a place used as a hospital on a ship. **2** a room or rooms set apart for the care of the sick or injured.

sick·bed (sik′bed′) *n.* the bed of a sick person.

sick·en (sik′ən) *v.* **1** become sick: *The bird sickened when kept in the cage.* **2** make sick: *The sight of blood sickened him.*

sick·en·ing (sik′ən ing or sik′ning) *adj.* **1** making sick; causing nausea, faintness, disgust, or loathing. **2** becoming sick. —**sick′en·ing·ly,** *adv.*

sick headache a headache accompanied by nausea; migraine.

sick·ish (sik′ish) *adj.* **1** somewhat sick. **2** somewhat sickening. —**sick′ish·ly,** *adv.* —**sick′ish·ness,** *n.*

sick·le (sik′əl) *n. v.* **-led, -ling.** —*n.* a tool consisting of a short, curved blade on a short handle, used for cutting grass, etc. —*v.* mow or cut with a sickle. [OE *sicol* < L *secula*; related to *secare* cut]

A sickle

sick·ly (sik′lē) *adj.* **-li·er, -li·est,** *adv.* —*adj.* **1** often sick; not strong; not healthy. **2** of or having to do with sickness: *Her skin is a sickly yellow.* **3** causing sickness: *That place has a sickly climate.* **4** faint; weak; pale. **5** weak; mawkish: *sickly sentimentality.* —*adv.* in a sick manner. —**sick′li·ness,** *n.* —**Syn.** *adj.* **1** ailing, indisposed.

sick·ness (sik′nis) *n.* **1** the condition of being sick; illness; disease. **2** nausea; vomiting.

sick parade in the armed services, the appearance of persons requiring medical attention before the medical officer or his staff.

sic tran·sit glo·ri·a mun·di (sik′ tran′sit glô′rē ə mun′dī or mùn′dē) *Latin.* so passes away the glory of the world.

side (sīd) *n. adj. v.* **sid·ed, sid·ing.** —*n.* **1** a surface or line bounding a thing: *the sides of a square.* **2** one of the two surfaces of an object that is not the front, back, top, or bottom: *There is a door at the side of the house.* **3** either of the two surfaces of paper, cloth, etc.: *Write only on one side of the paper.* **4** a particular surface: *the outer and inner sides of a hollow ball, the side of the moon turned toward the earth.* **5** either the right or the left part of a thing; either part or region beyond a central line:

the east side of a city, our side of the street, turn to one side. **6** either the right or the left part of the body of a person or an animal: *a pain in one's side.* **7** the slope of a hill or bank. **8** a bank or shore of a river. **9** a group of persons opposed to another group: *Both sides are ready for the contest.* **10** a team. **11** the position, course, attitude, or part of one person or party against another: *It is pleasant to be on the winning side of a dispute.* **12** a part of a family; line of descent: *The man is English on his mother's side.* **13** *Brit.* in billiards, a spinning motion given a ball by hitting it quickly on the side. **14** *Esp.Brit. Slang.* pretentious airs. **15 by one's side,** near one. **16 on the side,** *Informal.* in addition to one's ordinary duties. **17 side by side, a** beside one another. **b** equally: *Hourly earnings of our employees rank side by side with those in similar industries.* **18 split one's sides,** laugh very hard. **19 take sides,** place oneself with one person or group against another.
—*adj.* **1** at one side; on one side: *the side aisles of a theatre.* **2** from one side: *a side view.* **3** toward one side: *a side glance.* **4** less important: *a side issue.*
—*v.* **side with,** take the part of; favor (one among opposing or differing groups or persons). [OE *sīde*]

side arms weapons, such as a sword, revolver, bayonet, etc., carried at the side or on a belt.

side·board (sīd′bôrd′) *n.* **1** a piece of dining-room furniture having drawers and shelves for holding silver and linen, and space on top for dishes. **2** an additional and removable board placed on the side of a truck, wagon, etc. to increase the height of, or form, a side.

side boards in hockey, the fence surrounding the playing surface; the boards (def. 13b).

side·burns (sīd′bėrnz′) *n.pl.* short whiskers just below the hairline on both cheeks. [alteration of *burnsides,* from Ambrose E. *Burnside* (1824-1881), an American general]

Sideburns

side·car (sīd′kär′) *n.* **1** a car for a passenger, baggage, etc. attached to the side of a motorcycle. **2** a cocktail made with Cointreau, brandy, and lemon juice in approximately equal parts.

side channel a small offshoot of a river, sometimes running for some distance before rejoining the main stream, sometimes coming to a dead end, and usually shallow, narrow, and sluggish.

-sided *suffix.* having a side or sides, as in *three-sided.*

side dish a dish served in addition to the main dish of a course.

side effect an incidental consequence of a course of action, treatment ,etc., especially an undesirable reaction to a drug.

side·hill (sīd′hil′) *n.* a hillside.

side-kick (sīd′kik′) *n. Slang.* a partner or assistant.

side light **1** light coming from the side. **2** incidental information about a subject. **3** either of two lights carried by a moving ship at night, a red one on the port side and a green one on the starboard side. **4** a window or other opening for light in the side of a building, ship, etc. **5** a window at the side of a door or of another window.

side·line (sīd′līn′) *n. v.* **-lined, -lin·ing.** —*n.* **1** a line at the side of something. **2** in football, etc., a line that marks the limit of play on the side of the field. **3** Often, **sidelines,** *pl.* the space just outside these lines: *They watched the game from the sidelines.* **4a** a line of goods, trade, etc. that is additional, auxiliary, and secondary to the basic one or ones. **b** any enterprise, business, etc. carried on apart from that in which one is chiefly or officially employed. **5 on the sidelines,** inactive; not taking an active part in a game, enterprise, etc.
—*v.* put on the sidelines; make inactive.

side·long (sīd′long′) *adj. adv.* to one side; toward the side.

side·piece (sīd′pēs′) *n.* a piece forming a side or part of a side, or fixed by the side, of something.

si·de·re·al (sī dēr′ē əl) *adj.* **1** of or having to do with the stars. **2** in astronomy, measured by the apparent daily motion of the stars. A **sidereal year** is about twenty minutes longer than a solar year. [< L *sidereus* astral < *sidus, sideris* star]

sid·er·ite (sid′ər īt′) *n.* **1** an iron ore composed of iron carbonate. Siderite occurs in various forms and colors.

hat, āge, cãre, fär; let, ēqual, tėrm; it, īce
hot, ōpen, ôrder; oil, out; cup, pu̇t, rüle, ūse
əbove, takən, pencəl, lemən, circəs
ch, child; ng, long; sh, ship
th, thin; ᴛʜ, then; zh, measure

2 a meteorite consisting mainly of iron. *Formula:* $FeCO_3$ [< L < Gk. *sidērītēs* < *sidēros* iron]

side road **1** a secondary road, often unpaved, leading from a main road. **2** *Cdn.* in Ontario, a road built along the side line of a concession, connecting concession roads and usually running north-south.

side·sad·dle (sīd′sad′əl) *n.* a woman's saddle so made that both of the rider's legs are on the same side of the horse. —*adv.* on a sidesaddle; as on a sidesaddle.

side show **1** a small show in connection with a principal one: *the side shows of a circus.* **2** any minor proceeding or affair connected with a more important one.

side·slip (sīd′slip′) *n. v.* **-slipped, -slip·ping.** —*n.* **1** a slip to one side. **2** the slipping to one side of an aircraft.
—*v.* slip to one side.

sides·man (sīdz′mən) *n.* **-men** (-mən). **1** in the Anglican church, an assistant to a churchwarden. **2** *Obsolete.* a person who takes sides.

side step **1** a step or stepping to one side. **2** a step at the side of a ship, vehicle, etc.

side-step (sīd′step′) *v.* **-stepped, -step·ping.** **1** step aside. **2** avoid by stepping aside; evade: *He never side-stepped a responsibility.* —**side′-step′per,** *n.*

side·swipe (sīd′swīp′) *v.* **-swiped, -swip·ing,** *n.* —*v.* hit with a sweeping blow along the side. —*n.* a sweeping blow along the side.

side·track (sīd′trak′) *n.* **1** a railway siding. **2** a turning or being turned aside: *stick to the business at hand and avoid sidetracks.* —*v.* **1** switch (a train, etc.) to a sidetrack. **2** put aside; turn aside: *The teacher refused to be sidetracked by questions on other subjects.*

side·walk (sīd′wok′ or -wôk′) *n.* a place to walk at the side of a street, usually paved.

sidewalk bicycle a child's bicycle that has an extra small wheel on either side of the rear wheel.

side·ward (sīd′wərd) *adj. adv.* toward one side.

side·wards (sīd′wərdz) *adv.* sideward.

side·way (sīd′wā′) *adv. adj.* sideways. —*n.* **1** a side street, not a main road; byway. **2** a sidewalk.

side·ways (sīd′wāz′) *adv. adj.* **1** toward one side. **2** from one side. **3** with one side toward the front.

side-wheel (sīd′hwēl′ or -wēl′) *adj.* having a paddle wheel on each side.

side whisker **1** a hair growing long on the side of the face. **2 side whiskers** *.pl.* the whiskers that grow on the cheek or side of the face.

side·wise (sīd′wīz′) *adv. adj.* sideways.

sid·ing (sīd′ing) *n.* **1** a short railway track to which cars can be switched from a main track. **2** the boards forming the sides of a wooden building.

si·dle (sī′dəl) *v.* **-dled, -dling,** *n.* —*v.* **1** move sideways. **2** move sideways slowly so as not to attract attention: *The little boy shyly sidled up to the visitor.* —*n.* a movement sideways. [< *sideling* sidelong]

Si·do·ni·an (sī dō′nē ən) *adj.* of or having to do with Sidon, a town on the southwestern coast of Lebanon, or its people. —*n.* a native or inhabitant of Sidon.

siege (sēj) *n. v.* **sieged, sieg·ing.** —*n.* **1** the surrounding of a fortified place by an army trying to capture it; a besieging or being besieged. **2** any long or persistent effort to overcome resistance; any long-continued attack: *a siege of illness.* **3 lay siege to, a** besiege. **b** attempt to win or get by long and persistent effort. —*v.* besiege. [ME < OF *siege,* ult. < L *sedere* sit]

Syn. *n.* **1 Siege, blockade** = a military operation to cut off normal communications and supplies of a place. **Siege,** chiefly a land operation, means surrounding a city or fortified place, cutting off all movement to and from it, and usually assaulting it: *The British had barely laid siege to Detroit in 1812 when it surrendered.* **Blockade** applies to an operation, chiefly but not always naval, to close a harbor, coast, or city and cut off its supplies by controlling ship movements or other transportation to and from it, but does not suggest attacking it: *The air lift defeated the blockade of Berlin.*

Siege Perilous in Arthurian legend, a vacant seat at the Round Table, that could be taken only by the knight who was destined to find the Holy Grail.

Sieg·fried (sēg′frēd) *n.* in Germanic legend, a hero who killed a dragon and bathed in its blood to make himself invulnerable. He won the treasure of the Nibelungs.

Si·en·ese (sē′ə nēz′) *adj. n.* **-ese.** *—adj.* of or having to do with Siena, a city and province of central Italy. *—n.* a native or inhabitant of Siena.

si·en·na (sē en′ə) *n.* **1** a yellowish-brown coloring matter (**raw sienna**) made from earth containing iron. **2** a reddish-brown coloring matter (**burnt sienna**) made by roasting earth containing iron. **3** a yellowish brown or reddish brown. [short for Ital. *terra di Sien(n)a* earth of Siena, a city in Italy]

si·er·ra (sē er′ə) *n.* a chain of hills or mountains with jagged peaks. [< Sp. *sierra*, literally, a saw < L *serra*]

si·es·ta (sē es′tə) *n.* a nap or rest taken at noon or in the afternoon. [< Sp. < L *sexta* (*hora*) sixth (hour), noon]

sieur (syœr) *n. French.* formerly, a title of respect for a man; Sir. [< F < VL *seiorem* < L *seniorem*, accus. of *senior* senior. Doublet of SEIGNIOR and SEIGNEUR.]

sieve (siv) *n. v.* **sieved, siev·ing.** *—n.* a utensil having holes that let liquids and small pieces pass through, but not large pieces: *Shaking flour through a sieve removes lumps.* *—v.* put through a sieve. [OE *sife*] **—sieve′like′,** *adj.*

sif·fleur (sē flėr′) *n. Cdn.* hoary marmot. [< Cdn.F]

sift (sift) *v.* **1** separate large pieces from small by shaking in a sieve: *Sift the ashes.* **2** put through a sieve: *Sift sugar onto the top of the cake.* **3** use a sieve. **4** fall through, or as if through, a sieve: *The snow sifted softly down.* **5** examine very carefully: *The jury sifted the evidence to decide if the man was guilty.* [OE *siftan* < *sife* sieve] **—sift′er,** *n.*

sigh (sī) *v.* **1** let out a very long, deep breath because one is sad, tired, relieved, etc. **2** say or express with a sigh. **3** make a sound like a sigh: *The wind sighed in the treetops.* **4** wish very much; long: *She sighed for home and friends.* **5** lament with sighing: *sigh over one's unhappy fate.* *—n.* the act or sound of sighing. [ME *sighe(n)*, ult. < OE *sīcan*] **—sigh′er,** *n.* **—sigh′ing·ly,** *adv.*

sight (sīt) *n.* **1** the power of seeing; vision: *Birds have better sight than dogs.* **2** the act or fact of seeing; look: *love at first sight.* **3** the range or field of vision: *Land was in sight.* **4** the thing seen; view; glimpse: *I caught a sight of him.* **5** something worth seeing: *see the sights of the city.* **6** something that looks queer: *Her clothes were a sight.* **7** a device on a gun, surveying instrument, etc. used in taking aim or observing. **8** an observation taken with a telescope or other instrument; aim with a gun, etc. **9** a way of looking or thinking; regard: *Dolls are precious in a little girl's sight.* **10** *Informal.* a considerable quantity.
at sight, as soon as seen.
catch sight of, see.
in sight of, where one can see or be seen by.
know by sight, know sufficiently to recognize when seen.
on sight, as soon as seen.
out of sight of, a where one cannot see: *out of sight of land.* **b** where one cannot be seen by: *out of sight of the neighbors.*
sight unseen, not seen.
—v. **1** see: *At last Columbus sighted land.* **2** take a sight or observation of. **3** aim by means of sights. **4** adjust the sight (of a gun, etc.). **5** provide with sights. [OE (*ge*)*siht*] **—Syn.** *n.* **2** glance, gaze.

sight draft a written order from one bank to another, requiring a certain amount of money to be paid on demand.

sight·less (sīt′lis) *adj.* **1** blind. **2** *Poetic.* invisible.

sight·ly (sīt′lē) *adj.* **-li·er, -li·est. 1** pleasing to the sight. **2** affording a fine view. **—sight′li·ness,** *n.*

sight·see·ing (sīt′sē′ing) *n. adj.* the act of going around to see objects or places of interest.

sight·se·er (sīt′sē′ər) *n.* a person who goes around to see objects or places of interest.

sig·ma (sig′mə) *n.* **1** the 18th letter of the Greek alphabet (Σ, σ or, when final, ς = English S, s). **2** something shaped like an S. **3** something shaped like a C.

sig·moid (sig′moid) *adj.* **1** shaped like the letter S. The **sigmoid flexure** of the colon is its last curve before the rectum. **2** in anatomy, having to do with the sigmoid flexure of the colon. **3** shaped like the letter C. [< Gk. *sigmoeidēs* < *sigma* sigma + *eidos* form]

sign (sīn) *n.* **1 a** any mark used to mean, represent, or point out something. **b** in mathematics, a mark or symbol used to indicate an operation to be performed on a quantity or number, a relation of quantities or numbers, etc.: *The four signs of the arithmetic operations are addition* (+), *subtraction* (−), *multiplication* (×), *division* (÷). *The sign* (=) *means "equals." The sign* (+) *and* (−) *in algebra and higher mathematics define positive and negative numbers.* **c** in music, a flat, sharp, or other symbol used in notation to give directions, indicate tonality, etc. **2** a motion or gesture used to mean, represent, or point out something: *A nod is a sign of agreement. We talked to the deaf man by signs.* **3** an inscribed board, space, etc. serving for advertisement, information, etc.: *The sign reads, "Keep off the grass."* **4** an indication: *There are no signs of life about the house.* **5** an indication of a coming event: *The robin is a sign of spring.* **6** a trace: *The hunter found signs of deer.* **7** in astrology, any of the twelve divisions of the zodiac.
—v. **1** attach one's name to: *Sign this letter.* **2** attach one's name to show authority, agreement, obligation, etc.; write one's name: *Sign on the dotted line.* **3** write: *Sign your initials here.* **4** hire by a written agreement: *sign a new player.* **5** accept employment: *They signed for three years.* **6** give a sign to; signal: *sign someone to enter.* **7** communicate by gesture: *sign assent.* **8** mark with a sign. **9 sign away,** assign. **10 sign in,** indicate by signing a register, etc. that one is present. **11 sign off, a** in radio and television, stop broadcasting. **b** bring a letter, speech, lecture, etc. to a close. **12 sign on** or **sign up, a** accept a job by putting one's name to an agreement. **b** hire in this way. **c** enlist in the armed services. **13 sign out,** indicate by signing a register, etc. that one will not be present. **14 sign over,** hand over by signing one's name. [ME < OF < L *signum*] **—sign′a·ble,** *adj.* **—sign′er,** *n.*
Syn. *n.* **4** See **mark. 5 Sign, omen** = an indication of something about to happen. **Sign** applies to something that can be seen, felt, or otherwise perceived which is objective evidence that some particular happening can reasonably be expected: *Those big black clouds are signs of a storm.* **Omen** applies to a thing or event that, particularly from a religious or superstitious point of view, is seen as extraordinary and as a promise of something good or bad to come: *He believed his dream was an omen of death.*

sig·nal (sig′nəl) *n. v.* **-nalled** or **-naled, -nal·ling** or **-nal·ing,** *adj.* *—n.* **1** a sign giving notice of something: *A red light is a signal of danger.* **2** in card games, a bid or play that gives information to one's partner. **3 a** a sign agreed upon or understood as the occasion of concerted action: *give the signal to advance.* **b** an exciting cause; occasion. **4** a token; indication: *His wave was a signal of recognition.* **5** in electronics: **a** the waves, impulses, picture components, etc. serving to convey the communication, effect, etc. **b** the communication, effect, etc. thus conveyed. **c** the wave serving to modulate the carrier wave. **6 signals,** in football, the numbers called by an offensive back, usually the quarterback, designating a particular play, or by a member of the defensive team to direct the positions of the players.
—v. **1** make a signal or signals (to): *He signalled the car to stop by raising his hand.* **2** make known by a signal or signals: *A bell signals the end of a class period.*
—adj. **1** used as a signal or in signalling. **2** remarkable; striking; notable. [< F *signal*, ult. < L *signum* sign] **—sig′nal·ler** or **sig′nal·er,** *n.* **—Syn.** *adj.* **2** conspicuous.

signal fire a fire used in giving a signal.

signal flag a flag used in giving a signal.

Signal Hill the hill overlooking the entrance to St. John's harbor in Newfoundland, where Marconi received the first transatlantic radio signal in 1901.

sig·nal·ize (sig′nəl īz′) *v.* **-ized, -iz·ing. 1** make stand out;

make notable: *The present century has been signalized by many great inventions.* **2** point out; mention specially; draw attention to. **3 a** make signals to; communicate with by signal. **b** announce by a signal or signals.

sig·nal·ler or **sig·nal·er** (sig′nəl ər) *n.* **1** a soldier in the infantry, artillery, etc. who looks after communications within the regiment. **2** a signalman.

sig·nal·ly (sig′nəl ē) *adv.* remarkably; strikingly; notably.

sig·nal·man (sig′nəl mən or -man′) *n.* **-men** (-mən or -men′). **1** a man in charge of the signals on a railway, in the armed services, etc. **2** in the army, a private soldier in the corps of signals.

sig·na·to·ry (sig′nə tô′rē) *n.* **-ries,** *adj.* *—n.* a signer of a document. *—adj.* signing: *signatory delegates.*

sig·na·ture (sig′nə chər or sig′nə chür′) *n.* **1** a person's name written by himself. **2** a writing of one's name. **3** in music, the signs printed at the beginning of a staff to show the pitch, key, and time. **4** in printing: **a** a letter or number printed at the bottom of the first page of every sheet, telling how it is to be folded and arranged in pages. **b** a sheet with such a mark, especially when folded. **5** a tune, song, or slogan, used to identify a radio or television program. **6** in pharmacy, that part of a prescription that gives the directions to be marked on the container of the medicine. [< LL *signatura,* ult. < L *signum* sign]

sign·board (sīn′bôrd′) *n.* a board having a sign, notice, advertisement, inscription, etc. on it.

sig·net (sig′nit) *n.* a small seal: *The order was sealed with the king's signet.* [ME < OF *signet*, ult. < L *signum* seal]

signet ring a finger ring containing a signet.

sig·nif·i·cance (sig nif′ə kəns) *n.* **1** importance; consequence: *The chairman wanted to see him on a matter of significance.* **2** meaning: *Do you understand the significance of this picture?* **3** expressiveness; significant quality: *the significance of her smile.* **—Syn. 1** moment, gravity. **2** import, sense.

sig·nif·i·cant (sig nif′ə kənt) *adj.* **1** full of meaning; important; of consequence: *July 1, 1867, is a significant date for Canadians.* **2** having a meaning; expressive: *Smiles are significant of pleasure.* **3** having or expressing a hidden meaning: *A significant nod from his friend warned him to stop talking.* [< L *significans, -antis,* ppr. of *significare* signify. See SIGNIFY.] **—sig·nif′i·cant·ly,** *adv.* **—Syn. 1** See **expressive.**

sig·ni·fi·ca·tion (sig′nə fə kā′shən) *n.* **1** the meaning; sense. **2** the act or process of signifying. Signification relies largely upon words and gestures.

sig·nif·i·ca·tive (sig nif′ə kə tiv or sig nif′ə kā′tiv) *adj.* **1** serving to signify; having a meaning. **2** significant or suggestive.

sig·ni·fy (sig′nə fī′) *v.* **-fied, -fy·ing .1** be a sign of; mean: *"Oh!" signifies surprise.* **2** make known by signs, words, or actions: *He signified his consent with a nod.* **3** have importance; be of consequence; matter: *What a fool says does not signify.* [ME < OF < L *significare* < *signum* sign + *facere* make] **—Syn. 1** represent, denote, imply, suggest. **2** indicate.

si·gnior (sē′nyôr) *n.* signor.

sign language language in which motions stand for words, ideas, etc.

sign manual 1 a person's signature, especially that of a sovereign or magistrate on an official document. **2** a distinctively individual sign, stamp, or quality.

sign of the zodiac any of the twelve divisions of the zodiac. Each of them is named after a constellation.

si·gnor (sē′nyōr) *n. Italian.* **1** Mr.; sir. **2** a gentleman. *Abbrev.*: S. or Sr.

si·gno·ra (sē nyō′rä) *n.* **-re** (-rā). *Italian* **1** Mrs. **2** a lady.

si·gno·re (sē nyō′rā) *n.* **-ri** (-rē). *Italian.* **1** a gentleman. **2** Mr.; sir. **Signore** becomes **signor** when it is used before a person's name.

si·gno·ri·na (sē′nyō rē′nä) *n.* **-ne** (-nā). *Italian.* **1** Miss. **2** a young lady.

si·gno·ry (sēn′yə rē) *n.* **-ries. 1** lordship; rule. **2** domain. **3** a governing body Venice was ruled by the signory.

hat, āge, cãre, fär; let, ēqual, tėrm; it, īce
hot, ōpen, ôrder; oil, out; cup, pu̇t, rüle, ūse
əbove, takən, pencəl, lemən, circəs
ch, child; ng, long; sh, ship
th, thin; ᴛʜ, then; zh, measure

[ME < OF *signorie*, var. of *seignorie* (see SEIGNIORY); influenced by Ital. *signoria*]

sign·post (sīn′pōst′) *n.* **1** a post having a sign, notice, or direction on it; guidepost. **2** anything that marks, points, guides, or from which bearings may be taken, conclusions drawn, etc.

Sikh (sēk) *n.* a member of a religious sect of N. India; a follower of Sikhism. Sikhs are famous as soldiers. [< Hind. *sikh* disciple]

Sikh·ism (sē′kiz′əm) *n.* an offshoot of Hinduism, founded in N. India in the early 16th century and distinguished by monotheism and rejection of a caste system.

si·lage (sī′lij) *n.* green food for farm animals, preserved in a silo; ensilage. [< *ensilage,* after *silo*]

si·lence (sī′ləns) *n. v.* **-lenced, -lenc·ing,** *interj.* *—n.* **1** the absence of sound or noise; stillness. **2** a state of keeping still; not talking. **3 a** an omission of mention or notice in a narrative. **b** the omission or neglect to write, communicate, or reply (about something); secrecy: *Silence in matters of public interest is intolerable in a free society.* **4 in silence,** without saying anything.
—v. **1** stop the speech or noise of; make silent; quiet. **2** reduce to silence, as by restraint or prohibition; repress. **3** put at rest; stop the activity of: *silence one's conscience.* **4** stop (enemy guns, etc.) from firing by destroying or disabling with return fire.
—interj. be silent! [ME < OF < L *silentium,* ult. < *silere* be silent] **—Syn.** *n.* **1** hush, quiet. **2** reticence, reserve.

si·lenc·er (sī′lən sər) *n.* **1** a person or thing that silences. **2** a muffler on an internal-combustion engine. **3** a device for deadening the sound of a gun.

si·lent (sī′lənt) *adj.* **1** quiet; still; noiseless: *a silent house, the silent hills.* **2** not speaking; saying little or nothing: *a silent person.* **3** not spoken; not said out loud: *a silent prayer. The "l" in "folk" is a silent letter.* **4** not active; taking no open or active part. A **silent partner** has no share in managing a business. **5** omitting mention of something, as in a narrative. [< L *silens, -entis,* ppr. of *silerc* be silent] **—si′lent·ly,** *adv.* **—si′lent·ness,** *n.*
Syn. **1** hushed. **2 Silent, taciturn, reticent** = saying little or nothing. **Silent** especially means "not talkative," characteristically speaking only when necessary or saying very little, but also means saying nothing on some particular occasion for some special reason: *He is a silent, thoughtful boy.* **Taciturn** = not fond of talking being by nature inclined to be silent and avoid conversation: *He is a taciturn man who dislikes parties.* **Reticent** = not saying all one knows, disposed to keep silent, especially about private affairs: *He is reticent about his early life.*

Si·le·nus (sī lē′nəs) *n.* in Greek mythology, the foster father and companion of Dionysus and leader of the satyrs. He is represented as a short, stout, drunken old man.

si·le·sia (sī lē′shə or sə lē′shə) *n.* a fine, light, smooth cotton cloth used for lining. [< *Silesia,* a region in central Europe where it was originally made]

Si·le·sian (sī lē′shən or sə lē′shən, sī lē′zhən or sə lē′zhən) *adj.* of or having to do with Silesia, a region in centra l Europe, now divided between East Germany, Czechoslovakia, and Poland. *—n.* a native or inhabitant of Silesia.

si·lex (sī′leks) *n.* **1** silica. **2** a strong, heat-resistant glass that is mostly quartz. **3 Silex,** *Trademark.* a coffee maker made of this glass. [< L *silex* flint]

sil·hou·ette (sil′ü et′) *n. v.* **-et·ted, -et·ting.** *—n.* **1** an outline portrait cut out of black paper or filled in with some single color. **2** a dark image outlined against a lighter background. **3** the contour of a garment, figure, etc.: *Her dress has the new, slim silhouette.* **4 in silhouette,** shown in outline,

A silhouette

or in black against a white background. —*v.* show in outline: *The mountain was silhouetted against the sky.* [after Etienne de *Silhouette* (1709-1767), a French minister of finance]

sil·i·ca (sil′ə kə) *n.* a hard, white or colorless mineral. Flint, quartz, and sand are forms of silica. *Formula*: SiO_2 [< NL < L *silex, -licis* flint]

sil·i·cate (sil′ə kit or sil′ə kāt′) *n.* a compound containing silicon with oxygen and an alkali. Mica, soapstone, asbestos, and feldspar are silicates.

si·li·ceous (sə lish′əs) *adj.* containing or consisting of silica; resembling silica. [< L *siliceus* of flint < *silex, -licis* flint]

si·lic·ic (sə lis′ik) *adj.* of or having to do with silica or any of certain acids regarded as derivatives of silica.

si·lic·i·fy (sə lis′ə fī′) *v.* **-fied, -fy·ing. 1** convert into silica. **2** become silica or be impregnated with it.

sil·i·con (sil′ə kən) *n.* a non-metallic chemical element found only combined with other substances. Silicon combines with oxygen to form silica. *Symbol*: Si; *at.no.* 14; *at.wt.* 28.086. [< *silica*]

silicon dioxide silica.

sil·i·cone (sil′ə kōn′) *n.* in chemistry, any of a large group of compounds formed by the replacement of carbon with silicon. Because of their great stability and resistance to extremes in temperature, they are used as lubricants, insulating resins, waterproofing materials, etc.

sil·i·co·sis (sil′ə kō′sis) *n.* a disease of the lungs caused by continually breathing air filled with dust from quartz or silicates. [< *silic-* flint, silica (< L *silex, -licis* flint) + *-osis* diseased condition]

silk (silk) *n.* **1** a fine, soft thread spun by silkworms. **2** the cloth made from this thread. **3** a garment of such material. **4** thread or cloth like silk, made artificially. **5** anything like silk: *corn silk.* **6** the gown of silk which a king's or queen's counsel is entitled to wear. **7 hit the silk,** *Slang.* parachute from a plane. **8 silks,** the blouses and caps worn by jockeys and harness race drivers and the coverings sometimes draped over their horses which, by their coloring, identify the owner of these horses; colors. **9 take silk,** become a king's or queen's counsel.
—*adj.* of, like, or having to do with silk. [OE *sioloc* < *Slavic* < Gk. *sērikos* < *Sēres* the Chinese]
—silk′like′, *adj.*

silk·en (sil′kən) *adj.* **1** made of silk: *a silken dress.* **2** like silk; smooth, soft, and glossy: *silken hair.* **3** wearing silk clothes. —*v.* make smooth and glossy like silk; give a silky lustre to.

silk-screen (silk′skrēn′) *n.* **1** a simple method of color printing by which a silk screen is used as a stencil to reproduce a design on a desired surface. **2** a print produced by this process. —*adj.* of or having to do with this method of color printing. —*v.* produce (a color print) by stencilling through a silk screen.

silk-stock·ing (silk′stok′ing) *adj.* **1** wearing silk stockings. **2** elegant; aristocratic. —*n.* an elegant, aristocratic person.

silk·worm (silk′wėrm′) *n.* a caterpillar that spins silk to form a cocoon. [OE *seolcwyrm*]

silk·y (sil′kē) *adj.* **silk·i·er, silk·i·est. 1** like silk; smooth, soft, and glossy; silken. **2** of silk. **—silk′i·ly,** *adv.* **—silk′i·ness,** *n.*

sill (sil) *n.* **1** a piece of wood, stone, etc. across the bottom of a door, window, or house frame. See **lintel** for picture. **2** a large, wooden beam on which the wall of a house, etc. rests. **3** in geology, a sheet of intrusive igneous rock found between older rock beds. [OE *syll*]

sil·la·bub (sil′ə bub′) *n.* a dessert made of cream, eggs, and wine sweetened and flavored. Also, **syllabub.** [origin uncertain]

sil·li·ness (sil′ē nis) *n.* **1** foolishness; being silly. **2** a silly act, thing, etc.

sil·ly (sil′ē) *adj.* **-li·er, -li·est. 1** without sense or reason; foolish. **2** *Archaic.* simple; innocent; harmless. **3** *Informal.* stunned; dazed. [OE *sǣlig* happy < *sǣl* happiness]
—Syn. 1 senseless, nonsensical, ridiculous. See **foolish.**

si·lo (sī′lō) *n.* **-los. 1** an airtight building or pit in which green food for farm animals is stored. **2** a vertical underground shaft in which missiles, nuclear rockets, etc. are housed ready for launching. [< Sp. < L < Gk. *siros* graincellar]

A silo

silt (silt) *n.* very fine earth, sand, etc. carried by moving water and deposited as sediment: *The river mouth is being choked up with silt.* —*v.* fill or choke up with silt. [ME; cf. Danish, Norwegian (dial.) *sylt* salt marsh. Akin to SALT.]

silt·y (sil′tē) *adj.* **silt·i·er, silt·i·est.** of silt; like silt; full of silt.

Si·lu·ri·an (sə lür′ē ən or sī lür′ē ən) in geology: —*adj.* of or having to do with an early Paleozoic period or the rocks formed during it. The earliest vertebrates appeared toward the end of the Silurian period. See **geology** for chart. —*n.* **1** an early period of the Paleozoic era, beginning approximately 375 million years ago. **2** the rocks formed during this period. [< L *Silures,* an ancient people of S.E. Wales where rock of this period occurs abundantly]

sil·va (sil′və) *n.* **1** the forest trees of a particular region or time. **2** a treatise on forest trees, or a descriptive list or catalogue of trees. [< L *silva* forest]

sil·van (sil′vən) *adj.* sylvan.

sil·ver (sil′vər) *n.* **1** a shining white, precious metallic chemical element, used for coins, jewellery, cutlery, dishes, etc. *Symbol*: Ag; *at.no.* 47; *at.wt.* 107.870. *Abbrev.*: Ar. **2** coins made from this metal. **3** cutlery or dishes made from it: *table silver.* **4** something like silver. **5** the color of silver.
—*adj.* **1** made of or plated with silver. **2** of or having to do with silver. **3** making or selling silver. **4** having the color of silver. **5** having a clear, ringing sound. **6** eloquent: *a silver tongue.* **7** of or advocating the use of silver as a standard of money. **8** having to do with the 25th anniversary of an event.
—*v.* **1** cover or coat with silver or something like silver: *silver a mirror.* **2** make the color of silver. **3** become the color of silver: *The old lady's hair had silvered.* [OE *siolfor*]

Silver Age 1 in classical mythology, the second age of mankind, inferior to the Golden Age. **2 silver age,** a period following and inferior to a period of brilliance.

sil·ver·ber·ry (sil′vər ber′ē) *n.* a silvery-gray shrub of W. North America.

sil·ver·fish (sil′vər fish′) *n.* **-fish** or **-fish·es. 1 a** a silvery variety of goldfish. **b** any silvery-colored fish, such as the tarpon and silversides. **2** any of a group of small, primitive, wingless insects that have silvery scales on the body and damage books, wallpaper, certain fabrics, etc.

silver fox 1 a fox whose fur is composed of black hairs with white bands near the tips. **2** the fur of this fox. **3** a coat or other garment made of this fur.

sil·ver·jar (sil′vər jär′) *n. Cdn.* **1** the young ringed seal. **2** its fur.

silver leaf silver beaten into very thin sheets.

silver lining the brighter side of a gloomy or unfortunate situation.

sil·vern (sil′vərn) *adj. Archaic.* of or like silver.

silver nitrate a white crystalline salt obtained by treating silver with nitric acid, used in medicine as an antiseptic, in photography, dyeing, etc. *Formula*: $AgNO_3$

sil·ver-plat·ed (sil′vər plāt′id) *adj.* covered with a thin layer of silver or similar material.

silver screen 1 a screen with a silverlike coating on which motion pictures are shown. **2** motion pictures.

sil·ver·side (sil′vər sīd′) *n.* **-side** or **-sides.** silversides.

sil·ver·sides (sil′vər sīdz′) *n.* **-sides.** any of a family of small fishes that have a silver stripe along each side of the body.

sil·ver·smith (sil′vər smith′) *n.* a person who makes articles of silver.

silver thaw *Cdn.* **1** a storm of quick-freezing rain.

2 the glitter ice found after such a rain, encrusting trees, rocks, and other surfaces.

sil·ver·tip (sil′vər tip′) *n.* a type of small grizzly bear found in the Rocky Mountain region and characterized by hair having silvery tips.

sil·ver-tongued (sil′vər tungd′) *adj.* eloquent.

sil·ver·ware (sil′vər wãr′) *n.* articles made of silver; cutlery or dishes made from silver.

silver wedding the 25th anniversary of a wedding.

sil·ver·y (sil′vər ē) *adj.* **1** like silver; like that of silver: *Moonbeams are silvery.* **2** having a clear, gentle resonance; melodious: *silvery laughter, a silvery voice.* **3** producing silver; containing silver. —**sil′ver·i·ness,** *n.*

sil·vi·cul·ture (sil′və kul′chər) *n.* the science and process of cultivating woods and forests; the care of trees. Also, **sylviculture.** [< F < L *silva* forest + *cultura* culture]

Sim·e·on (sim′ē ən) *n.* **1** in the Bible, a son of Jacob and Leah. Gen. 29:33. **2** one of the twelve tribes of Israel.

sim·i·an (sim′ē ən) *adj.* **1** like or characteristic of an ape or monkey. **2** having to do with an ape of monkey. —*n.* an ape; monkey. [< L *simia* ape, apparently < Gk. (name) *Simias* < *simos* snub-nosed]

sim·i·lar (sim′ə lər) *adj.* **1** much the same; alike; like: *A creek and a brook are similar.* **2** in geometry, of figures, having the same shape. [< F *similaire* < L *similis* like] —**sim′i·lar·ly,** *adv.*

sim·i·lar·i·ty (sim′ə lar′ə tē) *n.* **-ties.** the state of being similar; a likeness; resemblance. —**Syn.** See **resemblance.**

sim·i·le (sim′ə lē) *n.* an expressed comparison of two different things or ideas. *Examples*: a face like marble, a boy as brave as a lion. [< L *simile*, neut. adj., like] ☛ See **metaphor** for usage note.

si·mil·i·tude (sə mil′ə tūd′ or sə mil′ə tüd′) *n.* **1** a similarity; likeness; resemblance. **2** a comparison: *She could think of no similitude to describe the sunset.* **3** a copy; image. [< L *similitudo* < *similis* like]

sim·i·tar (sim′ə tər) *n.* scimitar.

sim·mer (sim′ər) *v.* **1** make a murmuring sound while boiling gently: *The kettle simmered on the stove.* **2** keep at or just below the boiling point; boil gently. **3** be on the point of breaking out: *He simmered with indignation, but he said nothing.* **4 simmer down,** cool off; calm down. —*n.* the process of cooking at or just below the boiling point. [earlier *simper*; ? imitative] —**Syn.** *v.* **2** See **boil.**

si·mo·ni·a·cal (sī′mə nī′ə kəl or sim′ə nī′ə kəl) *adj.* **1** guilty of simony. **2** of, having to do with, or involving simony. —**si′mo·ni′a·cal·ly,** *adv.*

Si·mon Le·gree (sī′mən lə grē′) a severe or too-demanding employer, officer, overseer, etc. [< *Simon Legree*, a brutal slave dealer in the novel *Uncle Tom's Cabin* by Harriet Beecher Stowe]

si·mon-pure (sī′mən pūr′) *adj. Informal.* **1** real; genuine; authentic; true: *simon-pure maple sugar.* **2** morally incorruptible: *He's not as simon-pure as he pretends.* **3** *Slang.* a legitimate non-professional athlete. [< *Simon Pure*, the name of a Quaker in Mrs. Centlivre's comedy *A Bold Stroke for a Wife* (1717), whose identity is questioned but proved genuine]

si·mo·ny (sī′mə nē or sim′ə nē) *n.* **1** the making of money out of sacred things. **2** the sin of buying or selling ecclesiastical positions, promotions, etc. [< LL *simonia*, from *Simon* Magus, a Samaritan magician, who tried to buy the power of conferring the Holy Spirit. Acts 8: 9-24]

si·moom (sə müm′) *n.* a hot, suffocating, sand-laden wind of the deserts of the Arabian peninsula, Syria, and northern Africa. [< Arabic *semūm*]

si·moon (sə mün′) *n.* simoom.

simp (simp) *n. Slang.* a simpleton; fool. [< *simpleton*]

sim·per (sim′pər) *v.* **1** smile in a silly, affected way. **2** express by a simper; say with a simper. —*n.* a silly, affected smile. [cf. G *zimper* affected, coy]

sim·ple (sim′pəl) *adj.* **-pler, -plest,** *n.* —*adj.* **1** easy to do or understand: *a simple problem, simple language.* **2** not divided into parts; single; not compound. An oak leaf is a simple leaf. "John called his dog" is a simple sentence. **3** having few parts; not complex; not involved;

hat, āge, cãre, fär; let, ēqual, tėrm; it, īce
hot, ōpen, ôrder; oil, out; cup, pu̇t, rüle, ūse
əbove, takən, pencəl, lemən, circəs
ch, child; ng, long; sh, ship
th, thin; ᴛʜ, then; zh, measure

elementary: *a simple one-celled animal.* **4** with nothing added; bare; mere: *My answer is the simple truth.* **5** without ornament; not rich or showy; plain: *simple clothes.* **6** natural; not affected; not showing off: *She has a pleasant, simple manner.* **7** honest; sincere: *a simple heart.* **8** not subtle; not sophisticated; innocent; artless: *a simple child.* **9** common; ordinary: *a simple citizen.* **10** humble: *His parents were simple people.* **11** dull; stupid; weak in mind.
—*n.* **1** a foolish, stupid person. **2** something simple. **3** a plant used in medicine; the medicine made from it. **4 gentle and simple,** people of high and low degree. [ME < OF < L *simplex*] —**sim′ple·ness,** *n.* —**Syn.** *adj.* **1** See **easy. 4** pure, absolute. **6** unassuming, unpretentious. **7** open, straightforward. **8** naïve, ingenuous.

simple fraction a fraction in which both the numerator and the denominator are whole numbers. *Examples*: 1/3, 3/4, 219/125.

sim·ple-heart·ed (sim′pəl här′tid) *adj.* **1** having or showing a simple, unaffected nature. **2** guileless; sincere.

simple interest interest paid only on the principal of a loan, etc.; opposed to *compound interest.*

simple machine any of the elementary devices or mechanical powers on which other machines are based. The lever, wedge, pulley, wheel and axle, inclined plane, and screw are often called the six simple machines.

sim·ple-mind·ed (sim′pəl mīn′did) *adj.* **1** artless; inexperienced. **2** ignorant; foolish; stupid. **3** feeble-minded. —**sim′ple-mind′ed·ly,** *adv.* —**sim′ple-mind′ed·ness,** *n.*

simple sentence a sentence consisting of one main clause. *Example*: The whistle blows.

simple time in music, two or three beats to a measure.

sim·ple·ton (sim′pəl tən) *n.* a silly person; fool. [< *simple*]

sim·plic·i·ty (sim plis′ə tē) *n.* **-ties. 1** the state of being simple. **2** freedom from difficulty; clearness. **3** plainness: *A room in a hospital should be furnished with simplicity.* **4** the absence of show or pretence; sincerity. **5** a lack of shrewdness; dullness. [< L *simplicitas* < *simplex, -icis* simple]

sim·pli·fi·ca·tion (sim′plə fə kā′shən) *n.* **1** the act of making simpler. **2** the process of being made simpler. **3** a change to a simpler form.

sim·pli·fy (sim′plə fī′) *v.* **-fied, -fy·ing.** make simpler; make plainer or easier. [< F *simplifier* < Med.L *simplificare* < L *simplus* simple + *facere* make] —**sim′pli·fi′er,** *n.*

sim·ply (sim′plē) *adv.* **1** in a simple manner. **2** without much ornament; without pretence or affectation; plainly: *simply dressed.* **3** merely; only: *The baby did not simply cry, he yelled.* **4** foolishly: *He acted as simply as an idiot.* **5** absolutely: *simply perfect.*

sim·u·la·cra (sim′yu̇ lā′krə) *n.* pl. of **simulacrum.**

sim·u·la·crum (sim′yu̇ lā′krəm) *n.* **-cra** or **-crums. 1** a faint, shadowy, or unreal likeness; mere semblance: *The dictator permitted only a simulacrum of democracy.* **2** an image. [< L *simulacrum*, ult. < *similis* like]

sim·u·late (sim′yu̇ lāt′) *v.* **-lat·ed, -lat·ing,** *adj.* —*v.* **1** pretend; feign: *Anne simulated interest to please her friend.* **2** act like; look like; imitate: *Certain insects simulate leaves.* —*adj.* simulated. [< L *simulare* < *similis* like] —**sim′u·la′tor,** *n.* —**Syn.** *v.* **1** sham.

sim·u·la·tion (sim′yu̇ lā′shən) *n.* **1** a pretence; feigning. **2** an imitation; an acting or looking like: *a harmless insect's simulation of a poisonous one.*

sim·u·la·tive (sim′yu̇ lə tiv or sim′yu̇ lā′tiv) *adj.* simulating.

sim·ul·cast (sim′əl kast′ or sī′məl kast′) *n. v.* **-cast** or **-cast·ed, -cast·ing.** —*n.* a broadcast carried over a radio and a television station or network at the same time.

—*v.* transmit a program over radio and television simultaneously. [< *simul*taneous + broad*cast*]

si·mul·ta·ne·ous (sim′əl tā′nē əs or sī′məl tā′nē əs) *adj.* existing, done, or happening at the same time: *The two simultaneous shots sounded like one.* [< Med.L *simultaneus* simulated; confused in sense with L *simul* at the same time] —**Syn.** coincident, contemporaneous.

si·mul·ta·ne·ous·ly (sim′əl tā′nē əs lē or sī′məl tā′nē əs lē) *adv.* at once; at the same time; together.

sin (sin) *n. v.* **sinned, sin·ning.** —*n.* **1 a** a breaking of the law of God deliberately. **b** the state or condition resulting from this. **2** an immoral act; wrongdoing. Lying, stealing, dishonesty, and cruelty are sins. **3** a violation of any rule or standard, as of taste, propriety, etc. —*v.* **1** break the law of God. **2** do wrong. [OE *synn*]

Si·nai (sī′nī) *n.* **Mount,** in the Bible, the mountain, of uncertain identity, from which the law was given to Moses.

Sin·bad (sin′bad) *n.* in *The Arabian Nights,* a sailor who had seven extraordinary voyages.

sin bin *Cdn. Slang.* in hockey, the penalty box.

since (sins) *prep.* **1** (from a past time) continuously till now: *The package has been ready since noon.* **2** at any time between (some past time or event and the present): *We have not seen him since Saturday.*
—*conj.* **1** in the course of the period following the time when: *He has written home but once since he left us.* **2** continuously or counting from the time when: *Charles has worked hard since he left school.* **3** because: *Since you feel tired, you should rest.*
—*adv.* **1** from then till now: *He got sick last Saturday and has been in bed ever since.* **2** at some time between a particular past time and the present: *At first he refused but has since accepted.* **3** before now; ago: *I heard that old joke long since.* [ME *sinnes, sithenes* < OE *siththan* then, later < *sīth* late] ☛ See **because** for usage note.

sin·cere (sin sēr′) *adj.* **-cer·er, -cer·est.** free from pretence or deceit; genuine; real; honest. [< L *sincerus*] —**sin·cere′ly,** *adv.* —**Syn.** true, heartfelt.

sin·cer·i·ty (sin ser′ə tē) *n.* **-ties.** freedom from pretence or deceit; honesty.

Sind·bad (sin′bad) *n.* Sinbad.

sine[1] (sīn) *n.* in trigonometry, the ratio of the length of the side opposite an acute angle to the length of the hypotenuse. In the diagram, the sine of angle a = BC/AB; the sine of angle b = AC/AB. [< L *sinus* bend, bosom < Med.L translation of Arabic *jaib* sine, bosom]

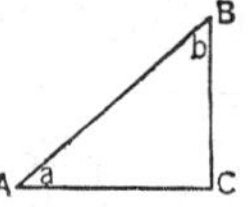

si·ne[2] (sī′nē) *prep. Latin.* without.

si·ne·cure (sī′nə kūr′ or sin′ə kūr′) *n.* **1** an extremely easy job; a position requiring little or no work and usually paying well. **2** an ecclesiastical benefice without parish duties. [< Med.L (*beneficium*) *sine cura* (benefice) without care (of souls)]

si·ne·cur·ist (sī′nə kūr′ist or sin′ə kūr′ist) *n.* a person who has a sinecure.

si·ne di·e (sin′ē dē′ā or sī′nē dī′ē) *Latin.* without a day fixed for future action: *The committee adjourned sine die.* [< L *sine die* without a day]

si·ne qua non (sin′ē kwä′nōn′ or sī′nē kwā non′) *Latin.* something essential; indispensable condition. [< L *sine qua non,* literally, without which not]

sin·ew (sin′ū) *n.* **1** a tough, strong band or cord that joins muscle to bone; tendon. **2** strength; energy. **3** a means of strength; a source of power: *Men and money are the sinews of war.* —*v.* furnish with sinews. [OE *sionu*]

sin·ew·y (sin′yù ē) *adj.* **1** having strong sinews; strong; powerful: *A blacksmith has sinewy arms.* **2** vigorous; forcible. **3** like sinews; tough; stringy. —**sin′ew·i·ness,** *n.*

sin·fo·ni·a (sin′fə nē′ə; *Italian,* sēn′fô nē′ä) *n.* **-ni·e** (-nē′ā). in music: **1** a symphony. **2** formerly, any of various instrumental pieces, such as a sonata or interlude in an opera, etc. [< Ital.]

sin·fo·niet·ta (sin′fən yet′ə; *Italian,* sēn′fô nyet′tä) *n.* in music: **1** a short instrumental piece modelled on the symphony. **2** a small orchestra, usually consisting chiefly or entirely of strings. [< Ital. *sinfonietta* < dim. of *sinfonia* symphony]

sin·ful (sin′fəl) *adj.* full of sin; wicked; wrong. —**sin′ful·ly,** *adv.* —**sin′ful·ness,** *n.* —**Syn.** depraved, immoral, evil.

sing (sing) *v.* **sang** or **sung, sung, sing·ing,** *n.* —*v.* **1** make music with the voice: *He sings on the radio.* **2** utter musically: *He almost seemed to sing his lines from the play.* **3** chant; intone: *The priest sings Mass.* **4** make pleasant musical sounds: *Birds sing.* **5** cause something to happen with or by singing: *Sing the baby to sleep.* **6** tell in song or poetry: *Homer sang of Troy.* **7** tell of in song or poetry: *He sang the deeds of heroes.* **8** proclaim: *sing a person's praises.* **9** make a ringing, whistling, humming, or buzzing sound: *The teakettle sang.* **10** have the sensation of a ringing, buzzing, or humming sound: *A bad cold made his ears sing.* **11** admit of being sung: *This arrangement of the song sings more easily than that one.* **12** *Slang.* reveal; inform; tell all. **13 sing out,** call loudly; shout.
—*n.* **1** a singing, ringing, or whistling sound: *the sing of a bullet in flight.* **2** a singing, especially in a group. [OE *singan*] —**sing′a·ble,** *adj.* —**Syn.** *v.* **1** carol, warble, croon.

sing. singular.

singe (sinj) *v.* **singed, singe·ing,** *n.* —*v.* **1** burn a little: *The cook singed the chicken to remove the fine hairs.* **2** burn the ends or edges of: *The barber singed my hair after he cut it.* **3** remove by a slight burning. **4** *Informal* injure slightly; harm: *Scandal singed the mayor's reputation.* —*n.* a slight burn. [OE *sengan*]

sing·er (sing′ər) *n.* **1** a person who sings. **2** a bird that sings. —**Syn. 1** chorister, vocalist, songster.

Sin·gha·lese (sing′gə lēz′) *n.* **-lese,** *adj.* —*n.* **1** the principal people of Ceylon, an island in the Indian Ocean. **2** a member of this people. **3** the language of this people. —*adj.* having to do with Ceylon, its principal people, or its language. Also **Sinhalese.** [< Skt. *Sinhala* Ceylon + E *-ese*]

sing·ing (sing′ing) *n.* **1** the sound made by one that sings. **2** a ringing in the ears. —*adj.* that sings.

singing school a school in which singing and the simple fundamentals of music are taught.

sin·gle (sing′gəl) *adj. n. v.* **-gled, -gling.** —*adj.* **1** one and no more; only one: *Please give me a single piece of paper.* **2** for only one; individual: *The sisters share one room with two single beds in it.* **3** without others; alone: *He came to the party single.* **4** not married: *a single man.* **5** having only one on each side: *The knights engaged in single combat.* **6** of a flower, having only one set of petals. There are both single and double varieties of roses. **7** not double; not multiple: *single houses.* **8** sincere; honest; genuine: *She showed single devotion to her religion.*
—*n.* **1** a single thing or person. **2** in baseball, a hit that allows the batter to reach first base only. **3** in cricket, a hit for which one run is scored. **4** a game for two people only. **5** in football, a single point scored by kicking into or beyond the end zone; rouge. **6 singles,** *pl.* a game played with only one person on each side.
—*v.* **1** pick from among others: *The teacher singled Harry out for praise.* **2** in baseball, make a hit that allows the batter to reach first base. [ME < OF < L *singulus*]
Syn. *adj.* **1 Single, sole, only** = one (or a few) alone. **Single** emphasizes the idea of one and no more: *She buys a single new dress each year.* **Sole** adds the idea of being by itself, the single one (or group) there is or that is to be considered: *My sole purpose is to help you.* **Only,** often a less emphatic substitute for *sole,* emphasizes the idea of being by itself (or themselves), this one (or these) without others or anything more: *Only two people went.* **3** solitary. **4** unmarried, celibate.

single blessedness the condition of being unmarried; celibacy.

sin·gle-breast·ed (sing′gəl bres′tid) *adj.* of a coat, jacket, etc., overlapping across the breast just enough to fasten with only one row of buttons.

single file a line of persons or things arranged one behind another.

sin·gle-foot (sing′gəl fůt′) *n.* the gait of a horse in which one foot is put down at a time; rack. —*v.* of a horse, go at a single-foot.

sin·gle-hand·ed (sing′gəl han′did) *adj.* **1** without help from others; working alone. **2** using, requiring, or managed by only one hand or only one person. **—sin′gle-hand′ed·ly,** *adv.*

sin·gle-heart·ed (sing′gəl här′tid) *adj.* **1** free from deceit; sincere. **2** having only one purpose. **—sin′gle-heart′ed·ly,** *adv.*

sin·gle-mind·ed (sing′gəl mīn′did) *adj.* **1** having only one purpose in mind. **2** sincere; straightforward. **—sin′gle-mind′ed·ly,** *adv.* **—sin′gle-mind′ed·ness,** *n.*

sin·gle·ness (sing′gəl nis) *n.* **1** the state or quality of being single; oneness. **2** the unmarried state. **3** sincerity; honesty; freedom from deceit.

sin·gle·stick (sing′gəl stik′) *n.* **1** a stick held in one hand, used in a type of fencing. **2** the act of fencing with such a stick.

sin·glet (sing′glit) *n.* a kind of undershirt or jersey worn by men.

sin·gle·ton (sing′gəl tən) *n.* **1** something occurring singly or apart from others. **2** a playing card that is the only one of a suit in a person's hand. **3** in hockey, etc., a single point.

sin·gle-track (sing′gəl trak′) *adj.* **1** having only a single track. **2** able to go or act in only one way.

sin·gle·tree (sing′gəl trē′) *n.* the swinging bar of a carriage or wagon, to which the traces are fastened. [var. of *swingletree*]

sin·gly (sing′glē) *adv.* **1** by itself; individually; separately: *Let us consider each point singly.* **2** one by one; one at a time: *Misfortunes never come singly.* **3** by one's own efforts; without help.

sing·song (sing′song′) *n.* **1** a monotonous, up-and-down rhythm. **2** a monotonous tone or sound in speaking. **3** a monotonous or jingling verse. **4** a gathering for community singing. *—adj.* monotonous in rhythm: *a singsong recitation of the multiplication table.* *—v.* recite or speak in a singsong way.

sin·gu·lar (sing′gyů lər) *adj.* **1** extraordinary; unusual: "*Treasure Island*" *is a story of singular interest to boys.* **2** strange; queer; peculiar: *The detectives were greatly puzzled by the singular nature of the crime.* **3** being the only one of its kind: *an event singular in history.* **4** in grammar, one in number: "*Boy*" *is singular;* "*boys*" *is plural.* **5** separate; individual; private: *a singular matter.* *—n.* in grammar: **1** the singular number. **2** a word in the singular number. [< L *singularis* < *singulus* single] **—sin′gu·lar·ly,** *adv.* —**Syn.** *adj.* **1** exceptional, uncommon, remarkable. **2** odd, curious, eccentric. **3** unique.

sin·gu·lar·i·ty (sing′gyů lar′ə tē) *n.* **-ties. 1** peculiarity; oddness; strangeness; unusualness: *The singularity of the dwarf's appearance attracted much attention.* **2** something singular; peculiarity; oddity: *One of the giraffe's singularities is the length of its neck.*

Sin·ha·lese (sin′hə lēz′) *n.* **-lese,** *adj.* Singhalese.

sin·is·ter (sin′is tər) *adj.* **1** showing ill will; threatening: *a sinister threat, a sinister look.* **2** bad; evil; dishonest. **3** disastrous; unfortunate. **4** on the left; left. **5** in heraldry, situated to the right of a person looking at the escutcheon. [< L *sinister* left; the left side being considered unlucky] —**Syn. 1** ominous.

sin·is·tral (sin′is trəl) *adj.* **1** of or having to do with the left side; left; left-handed. **2** of a spiral shell, having the whorl raising from right to left as viewed from the outside.

sink (singk) *v.* **sank** or **sunk, sunk** or (*now chiefly used as an adjective*) **sunk·en, sink·ing,** *n.* *—v.* **1** go down; fall slowly; go lower and lower: *The sun is sinking. She sank to the floor in a faint.* **2** make go down; make fall: *Lack of rain sank the reservoirs.* **3** go under: *The ship is sinking.* **4** make go under: *The submarine sank two ships.* **5** become lower or weaker: *The wind has sunk.* **6** make lower; reduce: *Sink your voice to a whisper.* **7** pass gradually (into a state of sleep, silence, oblivion, etc.). **8** go deeply: *Let the lesson sink into your mind.* **9** make by digging or drilling: *The men are sinking a well.* **10** insert or fasten into a concavity, hollow space, etc.: *a stone sunk into the wall.* **11** become worse: *His spirits sank.* **12** invest (money) unprofitably. **13** keep quiet about; conceal: *sink evidence.* **14** fall in; become hollow: *The sick man's cheeks have sunk.* **15 a** in basketball, score. **b** in golf, hit (the ball) into a hole; score thus with (a stroke).
—n. **1** a shallow basin or tub with a drainpipe. **2** a drain; sewer. **3** a place where dirty water or any filth collects. **4** a place of vice or corruption. **5** a low-lying area in land where waters collect, or where they disappear by sinking downward or by evaporation. [OE *sincan*] **—sink′a·ble,** *adj.* —**Syn.** *v.* **1** subside, descend, fall, settle, decline. **3** submerge. **6** diminish.

hat, āge, cãre, fär; let, ēqual, tėrm; it, īce
hot, ōpen, ôrder; oil, out; cup, pův, rüle, ūse
əbove, takən, pencəl, lemən, circəs
ch, child; ng, long; sh, ship
th, thin; ᴛʜ, then; zh, measure

sink·er (singk′ər) *n.* **1** a person or thing that sinks. **2** a lead weight for sinking a line or net for fishing. **3** *Slang.* a doughnut or a dumpling.

sink·hole (singk′hōl′) *n.* **1** the hole in a sink; a hole for waste to pass through. **2** a hole that drains surface water. **3** a hole where water collects. **4** a hole made by the subsidence of sand, by the action of water on rock, etc. **5** a place of vice and corruption.

sinking fund a fund formed by a government, corporation, etc., usually by periodically setting aside certain amounts of money to accumulate at interest, for the paying off of a debt.

sin·less (sin′lis) *adj.* without sin. **—sin′less·ly,** *adv.* **—sin′less·ness,** *n.*

sin·ner (sin′ər) *n.* a person who sins or does wrong.

Sinn Fein (shin′fān′) a political organization in Ireland, founded about 1905, for the complete political separation of Ireland from Great Britain. [< Irish *Sinn Fein* we ourselves]

Si·no-Jap·a·nese (sī′nō jap′ə nēz′) *adj.* of both China and Japan: *the Sino-Japanese War.*

sin·ter (sin′tər) *n.* **1** a crust or deposit of silica or calcium carbonate formed on rocks, etc. by the evaporation of mineral springs, geysers, etc. **2** in metallurgy, a conglomerate of materials fused by sintering. *—v.* in metallurgy, fuse (various materials) to form larger masses by the combined action of heat and pressure. [< G *Sinter* dross, slag; origin uncertain]

sin·u·ate (sin′yů āt′) *adj.* **1** bent in and out; winding; sinuous. **2** in botany, having its margin strongly or distinctly wavy. [< L *sinuatus,* pp. of *sinuare* bend, wind < *sinus* a curve]

A sinuate leaf

sin·u·os·i·ty (sin′yů os′ə tē) *n.* **-ties. 1** sinuous form or character; a winding. **2** curve; bend; turn.

sin·u·ous (sin′yů əs) *adj.* **1** having many curves or turns; winding: *The motion of a snake is sinuous.* **2** indirect; devious. **3** morally crooked. [< L *sinuosus* < *sinus* curve] **—sin′u·ous·ly,** *adv.* **—sin′u·ous·ness,** *n.*

si·nus (sī′nəs) *n.* **1** a cavity in a bone, especially one of the air cavities that are in certain bones of the skull and are connected to the nasal cavity. **2** a long, narrow abscess with a small opening. **3** a reservoir or channel for venous blood. **4** a curved hollow; cavity. **5** a bend or curve, especially between two projecting lobes of a leaf. [< L]

si·nus·i·tis (sī′nə sī′tis) *n.* the inflammation of a sinus, especially a nasal sinus.

Si·on (sī′ən) *n.* Zion.

Siou·an (sü′ən) *adj.* **1** of or forming the group of North American Indian tribes that includes the Dakota (Sioux), Osage, Crow, etc. **2** of or having to do with the language of this group. *—n.* **1** this group of tribes. **2** the family of languages spoken by them.

Sioux (sü) *n.* **Sioux** (sü or süz). **1** a tribe of North American Indians of the southern Canadian and northern United States prairies; Dakota. **2** a member of this tribe. **3** the Siouan language of this tribe.

sip (sip) *v.* **sipped, sip·ping,** *n.* *—v.* drink little by little: *She sipped her tea.* *—n.* a very small drink. [OE *sypian* take in moisture] —**Syn.** *v.* See **drink.**

si·phon (sī′fən) *n.* **1** a bent tube through which liquid can be drawn over the edge of one container into another at a lower level by air pressure. **2** a bottle for soda water, having a tube through which the liquid is forced out by the pressure of the gas in the bottle. **3** a tube-shaped organ of some shellfish for drawing in and expelling water, etc. —*v.* **1** draw off by means of a siphon or pass through a siphon: *The farmer siphoned water from the cellar into the ditch.* **2** draw off as if with a siphon. Also, **syphon.** [< L < Gk. *siphōn* pipe]

A siphon. The arrows show the direction of flow of the liquid.

si·phon·al (sī′fən əl) *adj.* of or having to do with a siphon.

sir (sėr; *unstressed,* sər) *n.* **1** a respectful or formal term of address used to a man: *Excuse me, sir.* **2 Sir,** the title of a knight or baronet: *Sir Walter Scott.* **3** formerly, a title of respect used before a man's name or a noun designating his profession: *sir priest.* [var. of *sire*]

☛ Sir (def. 2) is usually used with a person's given name plus his surname or with a given name alone, but not with the surname only. Thus *Sir Winston Churchill* might have been addressed or referred to as *Sir Winston,* but not *Sir Churchill.*

sir·dar (sėr′där or sər där′) *n.* **1** in India, a military chief or leader. **2** a chief or headman in India. **3** formerly, the British commander of the Egyptian army. [< Hind. *sardar* chief < Persian]

sire (sīr) *n. v.* **sired, sir·ing.** —*n.* **1** a male ancestor; father. **2** the male parent: *The sire of Danger, a great race horse, was Lightning.* **3** a title of respect used formerly to a great noble and now to a king. —*v.* be the father of. [ME < OF < VL *seior* < L *senior,* nom., older. Doublet of SENIOR.]

si·ren (sī′rən) *n.* **1** a kind of whistle that makes a loud, piercing sound: *We heard the sirens of the fire engines.* **2** in classical mythology, a nymph who, by her sweet singing, lured sailors to destruction upon the rocks. **3** a woman who lures, tempts, or entices. —*adj.* of a siren; tempting; charming. [ME < OF < L < Gk. *seirēn*] —**si′ren·like′,** *adj.*

si·ren·ic (sī ren′ik) *adj.* sirenlike; seductive; alluring.

Sir·i·us (sir′ē əs) *n.* the brightest (fixed) star in the sky; the Dog Star. [< L < Gk. *Seirios*]

sir·loin (sėr′loin) *n.* a cut of beef from the part of the loin in front of the rump. [obs. *surloin* < var. of OF *surlonge* < *sur* over (< L *super*) + *longe* loin, ult. < L *lumbus*]

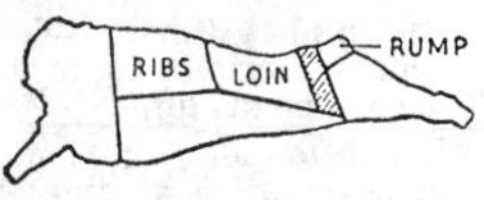

The shaded part is the sirloin.

si·roc·co (sə rok′ō) *n.* **-cos.** **1** a hot, dry, dust-laden wind blowing from N. Africa across the Mediterranean and S. Europe. **2** a moist, warm, south or southeast wind in these same regions. **3** any hot, unpleasant wind. [< F < Ital. < Arabic *shoruq* < *sharq* east]

sir·rah (sir′ə) *n. Archaic.* fellow, used as a term of address to men and boys when speaking contemptuously, angrily, impatiently, etc. [var. of *sir*]

Sir Rog·er de Cov·er·ley (sėr roj′ər dē kuv′ər lē) **1** a country squire in Addison's *Spectator.* **2** an old-fashioned country dance, similar to the Virginia reel.

sir·up (sėr′əp or sir′əp) *n.* syrup.

sir·up·y (sėr′əp ē or sir′əp ē) *adj.* syrupy.

sis (sis) *n. Informal.* sister. [short for *sister*]

sis·al (sis′əl or sī′səl) *n.* **1** a strong, white fibre, used for making rope, twine, etc. **2** the plant that it comes from. [< *Sisal,* a town in Yucatán, Mexico]

sisal hemp sisal.

sis·sy (sis′ē) *n.* **-sies.** *Informal.* **1** sister. **2** a boy or man who behaves too much like a girl. [dim. of *sis*]

sis·ter (sis′tər) *n.* **1** a daughter of the same parents; sometimes, a daughter only of the same mother or father (a half sister). **2** a person or thing resembling or closely connected with another. **3** a female fellow member of a society, church, etc. **4** a member of a religious order of women; nun: *Sisters of Charity.* **5** a nurse, especially in the armed services. **6** *Esp.Brit.* a head nurse. —*adj.* being a sister; related as if by sisterhood: *a sister ship.* [ME < ON *systir;* cf. OE *sweoster*] —**sis′ter·less,** *adj.*

sis·ter·hood (sis′tər hůd′) *n.* **1** the state or condition of being a sister; the feeling of sister for sister. **2** persons joined as sisters; an association of women with some common aim or characteristic. Nuns form a sisterhood.

sis·ter-in-law (sis′tər in lo′ or -lô′) *n.* **sis·ters-in-law.** **1** the sister of one's husband or wife. **2** the wife of one's brother. **3** the wife of one's brother-in-law.

sis·ter·ly (sis′tər lē) *adj.* suitable for a sister; like a sister; very kindly. —**sis′ter·li·ness,** *n.*

Sis·tine (sis′tēn) *adj.* **1** of or having to do with any of the five popes named Sixtus. **2** of or having to do with the Sistine Chapel, the chapel of the Pope in the Vatican, decorated with frescoes by Michaelangelo and other great artists. [< Ital. *sistino*]

Sis·y·phe·an (sis′ə fē′ən) *adj.* **1** of or having to do with Sisyphus. **2** futile, laborious, and unending.

Sis·y·phus (sis′ə fəs) *n.* in Greek legend, a king of Corinth condemned in Hades for his misdeeds and punished by eternally having to roll a large stone up a steep hill, from which it always rolled down again.

sit (sit) *v.* **sat** or (*Archaic*) **sate, sit·ting.** **1** rest on the buttocks, with the weight off the feet: *She sat in a chair.* **2** seat; cause to sit: *The woman sat the little boy down hard.* **3** bear oneself on; sit on: *He sat his horse well.* **4** be in a certain place or position: *The clock has sat on that shelf for years.* **5** have a seat in an assembly, etc.; be a member of a council: *sit in Parliament.* **6** hold a session: *The court sits next month.* **7** place oneself as required for some purpose or activity; seat oneself; pose: *sit for a portrait.* **8** be in a state of rest; remain inactive. **9** press or weigh: *Care sat heavy on his brow.* **10** perch: *The birds were sitting on the fence rail.* **11** baby-sit. **12** cover eggs so that they will hatch; brood. **13** fit: *The presidency sits well on him.* **14 sit down,** take a seat; put oneself in a sitting position. **15 sit in, a** take part (in a game, conference, etc.). **b** take part in a sit-in. **16 sit on** or **upon, a** sit in judgment or council on. **b** have a seat on a jury, commission, etc. **c** think about; consider over a period of time. **d** *Slang.* check, rebuke, or snub. **17 sit out, a** remain seated during (a dance). **b** stay through (a performance, etc.). **c** stay later than (another). **18 sit up, a** raise the body to a sitting position. **b** keep such a position. **c** stay up instead of going to bed. **d** *Informal.* start up in surprise. [OE *sittan*] ☛ See **set** for usage note.

si·tar (si tär′) *n.* a three-stringed guitar used in India.

sit-down strike (sit′doun′) a strike in which the workers stay, without working, in the factory, store, etc. until their demands are met or an agreement is reached.

site (sīt) *n. v.* **sit·ed, sit·ing.** —*n.* position or place (of anything): *This house has one of the best sites in town.* —*v.* choose a position for; locate; place: *They sited the new building on a hill.* [< L *situs*]

sith (sith) *Archaic. adv. prep. conj.* since. [OE *sīth* after]

sit-in (sit′in′) *n.* a form of protest in which a group of people enter and remain seated in a public place.

sit·ka spruce (sit′kə) **1** a tall spruce tree found along the Pacific Coast of North America. **2** the wood of this tree, much used for lumber. [< *Sitka,* a town in Alaska]

si·tol·o·gy (sī tol′ə jē) *n.* the science of food or diet; dietetics. [< Gk. *sitos* food + E *-logy*]

sit·ter (sit′ər) *n.* **1** a person who sits. **2** a baby-sitter. **3** a bird sitting on its eggs.

sit·ting (sit′ing) *n.* **1** the act of one that sits. **2** a period or session of a legislature, court, etc. **3** a period of remaining seated: *He read five chapters at one sitting.* **4** the number of eggs on which a bird sits. **5** a seat in a church. **6** a group of people who sit down to eat at a certain time.

sitting duck *Informal.* an easy target or mark.

sitting room a room furnished with comfortable chairs, chesterfields, etc.; parlor.

sit·u·ate (sich′ü āt′) *v.* **-at·ed, -at·ing,** *adj.* —*v.* place; locate. —*adj. Archaic.* situated. [< LL *situatus,* pp. of *situare* < L *situs* location]

sit·u·at·ed (sich′ü āt′id) *adj.* placed; located: *Montreal is a favorably situated city.*

sit·u·a·tion (sich′ü ā′shən) *n.* **1** a position; location; place: *Choose an attractive situation for our camp.* **2** circumstances: *Act reasonably in all situations.* **3** a place to work; job. **4** a critical state of affairs in a play, novel, etc. —**Syn. 1** site, station. **3** post. See **position.**

sit·u·a·tion·al (sich′ü ā′shə nəl) *adj.* of or having to do with situations.

si·tus (sī′təs) *n.* a position, situation, or location, especially the proper or original position, as of a part of the body or organ. [< L]

sitz bath (sits) **1** a small tub for bathing in a sitting position. **2** a bath so taken, especially as part of medical treatment. [< G *Sitzbad* < *Sitz* seat + *Bad* bath]

sitz·mark (sits′märk′) *n.* a hole or furrow in the snow made by a skier who has fallen backwards. [< G *Sitzmarke* < *Sitz* a sitting, seat + *Marke* sign]

Si·va (sē′və or shē′və) *n.* in Hindu theology, one of the gods of the trinity of Brahma; the Destroyer. Also, **Shiva.** [< Skt.]

Si·van (sē vän′) *n.* in the Hebrew calendar, the third month of the ecclesiastical year, and the ninth month of the civil year.

Si·wash (sī′wosh) *n.* especially on the Pacific coast and in the Northwest: **1** *Derogatory.* **a** a North American Indian. **b** the language of the North American Indians. **2** Often, **siwash**, *Slang.* a mean, contemptible person. —*adj.* **1** Also, **siwash**, *Derogatory.* of or having to do with North American Indians. **2 siwash**, *Slang.* unsuitable; inferior; worthless: *a siwash arrangement.* —*v.* **siwash**, **1** *Informal.* camp out, travelling light and using only natural shelter. **2** *Slang.* behave or do (something) after the fashion of a North American Indian. **3** *Slang.* prohibit from buying liquor. [< Chinook Jargon < F *sauvage* savage]

six (siks) *n.* **1** one more than five; 6. **2** a playing card, die, domino, etc. having six spots. **3** one of the sections into which a pack of Cubs or Brownies is divided. **4 at sixes and sevens, a** in confusion. **b** in disagreement. —*adj.* being one more than five. [OE *siex* six]

six-eight (siks′āt′) *adj.* in music, indicating or having six eighth notes in a bar or measure, the first and fourth of which are accented.

six·er (siks′ər) *n.* the leader of a six of Wolf Cubs or Brownies.

six·fold (siks′fōld′) *adj.* **1** six times as much or as many. **2** having six parts. —*adv.* six times as much or as many.

Six Nations a federation of Iroquois Indian tribes called the **Five Nations** until the Tuscarora tribe joined in about 1722.

six·pence (siks′pəns) *n.* in Britain: **1** six pence. **2** a silver coin equal to 2½ new pence, formerly equal to six pennies.

six·pen·ny (siks′pen′ē or siks′pə nē) *adj.* **1** worth or costing sixpence. **2** of little worth; cheap. **3** designating a kind of two-inch nail, once costing six pennies per 100.

six-shoot·er (siks′shüt′ər) *n.* a revolver that can fire six shots without being reloaded.

six·teen (siks′tēn′) *n. adj.* six more than ten; 16. [OE *sixtēne*]

six·teenth (siks′tēnth′) *adj. n.* **1** next after the 15th; last in a series of 16. **2** one, or being one, of 16 equal parts.

Sixteenth notes

sixteenth note in music, a note one sixteenth of the time value of a whole note.

sixteenth rest in music, a rest lasting one sixteenth as long as a whole rest.

sixth (siksth) *adj. n.* **1** next after the fifth; last in a series of six. **2** one, or being one, of six equal parts.

sixth·ly (siksth′lē) *adv.* in the sixth place.

sixth sense an unusual power of perception; intuition.

six·ti·eth (siks′tē ith) *adj. n.* **1** next after the 59th; last in a series of 60. **2** one, or being one, of 60 equal parts.

six·ty (siks′tē) *n.* **-ties,** *adj.* six times ten; 60. [OE *siextig, sixtig*]

six·ty·fold (siks′tē fōld′) *adj. adv.* sixty times as much or as many.

sixty-fourth note (siks′tē fôrth′) in music, a note having the time value of one sixty-fourth of a whole note.

sixty-fourth rest in music, a rest lasting one sixty-fourth of a whole rest.

hat, āge, cãre, fär; let, ēqual, tėrm; it, īce
hot, ōpen, ôrder; oil, out; cup, pu̇t, rüle, ūse
əbove, takən, pencəl, lemən, circəs
ch, child; ng, long; sh, ship
th, thin; ᴛʜ, then; zh, measure

siz·a·ble (sīz′ə bəl) *adj.* fairly large. Also, **sizeable.**

siz·a·bly (sīz′ə blē) *adv.* to a sizable extent or degree. Also, **sizeably.**

siz·ar (sīz′ər) *n.* a student who pays reduced rates in the colleges of Cambridge University in Cambridge, England, and Trinity College in Dublin, Irish Republic. [< *size*[1]]

size[1] (sīz) *n. v.* **sized, siz·ing,** *adj.* —*n.* **1** the amount of surface or space a thing takes up. **2** an extent; amount; magnitude: *the size of an industry.* **3** one of a series of measures: *His shoes are size 10. The size of card I want is 3 by 5 inches.* **4** *Informal.* the actual condition; true description. **5 of a size,** of the same size.
—*v.* **1** arrange according to size or in sizes. **2** make of certain size. **3 size up,** *Informal.* **a** form an opinion of; estimate. **b** come up to some size or grade.
—*adj.* having size. [ult. var. of *assize,* in sense of "to set a standard of weights and measures"]
Syn. *n.* **1, 2 Size, volume, bulk** = the measure of something. **Size** applies particularly to the dimensions (length, width, and height or depth) of something, but also to the extent of surface occupied or number of individuals included: *What is the size of your herd?* **Volume** is used of something measured by the cubic inches, feet, etc. it occupies, especially something that rolls or flows: *The volume of water confined by the new dam is tremendous.* **Bulk** = size or quantity measured in three dimensions, and often suggests largeness: *Let the dough double in bulk.*

size[2] (sīz) *n. v.* **sized, siz·ing.** —*n.* a preparation made from glue, starch, or other sticky material. It is used for covering paper, walls, etc. before paint is put on, for stiffening cloth, or for glazing paper, etc. —*v.* coat or treat with size. [< F *assise* a sitting, fixing, layer]

size·a·ble (sīz′ə bəl) *adj.* sizable.

size·a·bly (sīz′ə blē) *adv.* sizably.

-sized *combining form.* of or having a —— size: *giant-sized = of a giant size.*

siz·ing (sīz′ing) *n.* size[2].

siz·zle (siz′əl) *v.* **-zled, -zling,** *n.* —*v.* **1** make a hissing sound, as fat does when it is frying or burning. **2** be very hot: *sizzle with anger.* —*n.* a hissing sound. [imitative]

S.J. or **s.j.** Society of Jesus.

SJAA or **S.J.A.A.** St. John Ambulance Association.

SJAB or **S.J.A.B.** St. John Ambulance Brigade.

skald (skold or skäld) *n.* in ancient times, a Scandinavian poet and singer. Also, **scald.** [< ON *skáld.* Cf. SCOLD.]

skat (skät) *n.* a card game for three players. [< G < Ital. *scarto* discard, n.]

skate[1] (skāt) *n. v.* **skat·ed, skat·ing.** —*n.* **1** a frame with a blade that can be fastened to a boot so that a person can glide over ice. **2** a similar frame having small wheels for use on any smooth, hard surface. —*v.* glide or move along on skates. [< Du. *schaats* < OF *escache* stilt < Gmc.] —**skat′er,** *n.*

skate[2] (skāt) *n.* **skate** or **skates.** a kind of broad, flat fish. [ME < ON *skata*]

skate board or **skate·board** (skāt′bôrd′) *n.* a small plank of wood or plastic shaped like a surfboard but equipped with wheels. Also, **skurf board.**

skate·board·er (skāt′bôrd′ər) *n.* one who uses a skate board.

skate·board·ing (skāt′bôrd′ing) *n.* the act or practice of going on a skate board for sport.

skating rink 1 a smooth sheet of ice for skating. **2** a smooth floor for roller skating.

skean or **skene** (skēn) *n.* a dagger formerly used in Ireland and Scotland. [< Irish *scian,* Scots Gaelic *sgian*]

ske·dad·dle (ski dad′əl) *v.* **-dled, -dling.** *Informal.* run away; scatter in flight. [origin uncertain]

skee (skē) *n.* **skees** or **skee,** *v.* **skeed, skee·ing.** ski.

skeet (skēt) *n.* in trapshooting, a type of target practice using clay pigeons that are released into the air so as to imitate the flight of birds. [ult. < ON *skjóta* to shoot]

skeet·er (skēt′ər) *n. Informal.* **1** a mosquito. **2** a small sailboat used on ice; iceboat.

skein (skān) *n.* **1** a small, coiled bundle of yarn or thread. There are 120 yards in a skein of cotton yarn. **2** a confused tangle. [ME < OF *escaigne*; ult. origin uncertain]

skel·e·tal (skel′ə təl) *adj.* of a skeleton; attached to a skeleton.

skel·e·ton (skel′ə tən) *n.* **1 a** the framework of bones supporting the body of a vertebrate animal. The skeleton protects the muscles, organs, etc. **b** the hard covering or supporting structure of an invertebrate, such as the shell of a mollusc. **2** a very thin person or animal: *A long illness made a skeleton out of him.* **3** a frame: *the steel skeleton of a building.* **4** an outline.
—*adj.* **1** of, like, or consisting of a skeleton. **2** greatly reduced in numbers; fractional: *Only a skeleton crew was needed while the ship was tied up at the dock.* [< NL *sceleton* < Gk. *skeleton*, neut, adj., dried up]

skel·e·ton·ize (skel′ə tən īz′) *v.* **-ized, -iz·ing. 1** make a skeleton of. **2** outline; sketch out; draft in outline: *a skeletonized report.* **3** greatly reduce the numbers of.

skeleton key a key made to open many locks.

skelp[1] (skelp) *Scottish.* —*n.* a slapping or smacking noise; spank. —*v.* **1** spank; slap. **2** move quickly; hurry. [probably imitative]

skelp[2] (skelp) *n.* a strip of iron or steel used in the making of pipes or tubes. [origin unknown]

skep·tic (skep′tik) *n. adj.* sceptic.

skep·ti·cal (skep′tə kəl) *adj.* sceptical.

skep·ti·cism (skep′tə siz′əm) *n.* scepticism.

sketch (skech) *n.* **1** a rough, quickly done drawing, painting, or design. **2** an outline; plan. **3** a short description, story, play, etc. —*v.* **1** make a sketch of; draw roughly. **2** make sketches. [< Du. *schets* < Ital. *schizzo* < L < Gk. *schedios* impromptu, ult. < *schesthai* be near] —**sketch′er,** *n.* —**Syn.** *n.* **2** draft, brief. –*v.* **1** outline, delineate.

sketch·book (skech′bu̇k′) *n.* **1** a book to draw or paint sketches in. **2** a book of short descriptions, stories, plays, etc.

sketch·y (skech′ē) *adj.* **sketch·i·er, sketch·i·est. 1** like a sketch; having or giving only outlines or main features. **2** incomplete; slight; imperfect: *a sketchy meal.* —**sketch′i·ly,** *adv.* —**sketch′i·ness,** *n.*

skew (skū) *adj.* **1** twisted to one side; slanting. **2** having a part that deviates from a straight line, right angle, etc. **3** unsymmetrical. [< v.]
—*n.* a slant; twist.
—*v.* **1** slant; twist. **2** give a slanting form, position, or direction to. **3** turn aside; swerve. **4** represent unfairly; distort. [ME < ONF *eskiuer* shy away from, eschew < Gmc.]

skew·back (skū′bak′) *n.* **1** a sloping surface against which the end of an arch rests. **2** a stone, course of masonry, or the like, with such a surface.

skew·er (skū′ər) *n.* **1** a long pin of wood or metal stuck through meat to hold it together while it is cooking. **2** something shaped or used like a long pin. —*v.* **1** fasten with a skewer or skewers. **2** pierce with or as if with a skewer. [earlier *skiver*; origin uncertain]

ski (skē; *Norwegian*, shē) *n.* **skis** or **ski,** *v.* **skied, ski·ing.** —*n.* **1** one of a pair of long pieces of wood, metal, plastic, etc. that can be fastened to boots to enable a person to glide over snow. **2** a ski-like device fastened to the undercarriage of an aircraft and used in place of wheels for landing on snow, mud, sand, etc. **3** a water ski. —*v.* **1** glide over the snow on skis. **2** water-ski. [< Norwegian] —**ski′er,** *n.*

Boys on skis

skid (skid) *n.*·*v.* **skid·ded, skid·ding.** —*n.* **1** a slip or slide sideways while moving. **2** a piece of wood or metal to prevent a wheel from going round. **3** a piece of timber, or a runner, on which something heavy may slide. **4** a frame on which heavy articles may be piled for moving to another position, often by lifting with a crane. **5** a runner on the bottom of an airplane to enable the airplane to slide along the ground when landing. **6 on the skids,** *Slang.* headed for dismissal, failure, or other disaster.
—*v.* **1** slip or slide sideways while moving: *The car skidded on the slippery road.* **2** prevent from going round by means of a skid. **3** slide along without going round, as a wheel does when held by a skid. **4** slide on a skid or skids. [cf. OFrisian *skīd* stick of wood]

skid·doo (ski dü′) *v. Slang.* get out; be off; scat. [? < *skedaddle*]

ski·doo or **Ski·doo** (ski dü′ or skē′dü) *n. Cdn.* a motorized toboggan that moves on endless rubberized tracks and is steered by front-mounted movable skis. It seats two and can travel over snow at speeds up to 30 m.p.h. [< *Ski-Doo*, a trademark]

skid row a run-down district of flophouses and cheap bars, used as a hangout by vagrants, down-and-outs, petty criminals, etc.

skies (skīz) *n.* pl. of **sky.**

skiff (skif) *n.* **1** a small, light rowboat with a rounded bottom and flat stern. **2** a small, light boat with a mast for a triangular sail. [< F < Ital. *schifo* < Gmc.]

ski·jor·er (skē′jôr′ər) *n.* a person who is pulled along on skis by a horse or vehicle. [< *skijoring*]

ski·jor·ing (skē′jôr′ing) *n.* a sport in which a person on skis is pulled along by a horse or vehicle. [< Norwegian *skikjøring* < *ski* ski + *kjøring* driving]

ski jump 1 a jump made by a person on skis. **2** a place for making such a jump.

skil·fish (skil′fish) *n.* sablefish. [< Haida *sqil* fish]

skil·ful or **skill·ful** (skil′fəl) *adj.* **1** having skill; expert. **2** showing skill. —**skil′ful·ness** or **skill′ful·ness,** *n.*

skil·ful·ly or **skill·ful·ly** (skil′fəl ē) *adv.* with skill; expertly.

ski lift a mechanism for transporting skiers to the top of a slope, usually by means of a chair running on a suspended cable.

skill (skil) *n.* **1** ability gained by practice, knowledge, etc.; expertness: *The trained teacher managed the choir with skill.* **2** the ability to do things well with one's hands, tools, etc.: *It takes skill to tune a piano.* **3** an art or craft; proficiency in an art or craft: *He has no skills although he is interested in carpentry.* [ME < ON *skil* distinction] —**Syn. 1** facility, proficiency. **2** dexterity, deftness, adroitness.

skilled (skild) *adj.* **1** having skill; trained; experienced: *a skilled workman.* **2** showing skill; requiring skill: *Bricklaying is skilled labor.* —**Syn. 1** See **expert.**

skil·let (skil′it) *n.* **1** a shallow pan with a long handle, used for frying; frying pan. **2** a long-handled saucepan. [ME *skelet*; origin uncertain]

skill·ful (skil′fəl) *adj.* skilful.

skill·ful·ly (skil′fəl ē) *adv.* skilfully.

skim (skim) *v.* **skimmed, skim·ming,** *n.* —*v.* **1** remove from the top: *skim the cream from the milk.* **2** take something from the top of: *She skims the milk to get cream.* **3** move lightly over: *The pebble I threw skimmed the little waves. The skaters skimmed the ice.* **4** glide along: *The swallows were skimming by.* **5** send skimming; skip: *You can skim a flat stone over the water.* **6** read rapidly or superficially; read with omissions, especially in order to get the general sense or purpose: *It took me an hour to skim the book.* **7** become covered with a thin layer of ice, scum, etc. **8** cover with a thin layer of ice, scum, etc.

—*n.* **1** that which is skimmed off. **2** the act of skimming. [ME < OF *escumer* < *escume* scum < Gmc.]

skim·mer (skim′ər) *n.* **1** one that skims. **2** a long-handled shallow ladle, full of holes, used in skimming liquids. **3** a kind of sea bird that skims along the surface of water to get food. **4** a man's or woman's straw hat with a flat crown and wide brim. **5** any of various clams or scallops.

A skimmer (def. 2)

skim milk milk from which the cream has been removed.

Ski·mo (skē′mō) *n. Derogatory slang.* in the North, an Eskimo.

ski·mo·bile (skē′mə bēl′) *n.* a vehicle resembling a small automobile but running on tracks, designed for carrying skiers to the top of a slope.

skimp (skimp) *v.* **1** supply in too small an amount: *Don't skimp the butter in making a cake.* **2** be very saving or economical: *She had to skimp to send her son to college.* **3** do imperfectly. [? alteration of *scrimp*]

skimp·y (skimp′ē) *adj.* **skimp·i·er, skimp·i·est. 1** scanty; not enough. **2** too saving or economical. —**skimp′i·ly,** *adv.* —**skimp′i·ness,** *n.*

skin (skin) *n. v.* **skinned, skin·ning.** —*n.* **1** the covering of the body in persons, animals, fruits, etc., especially when soft and flexible. **2** a hide; pelt. **3** a container made of skin for holding liquids. **4** any outer covering: *the skin of a rocket.* **5** a planking or iron plating that covers the ribs of a ship. **6** *Slang.* a cheat. **7** *Slang.* a skinflint. **8 in** or **with a whole skin,** safe and sound. **9 save one's skin,** escape without harm.
—*v.* **1** take the skin off: *Jack skinned his knees when he fell. The hunter skinned the deer.* **2** shed skin. **3** be covered with skin. **4** cover with skin. **5** *Slang.* swindle (someone) of money, etc.; cheat. **6** *Slang.* slip away. **7 skin alive,** *Slang.* **a** torture; flay. **b** scold severely. **c** defeat completely. [ME < ON *skinn*]
Syn. *n.* **2 Skin, hide, pelt** = the outer covering of the body of an animal. **Skin** is the general word applying to this covering of a person or animal: *The skin of a calf makes soft leather.* **Hide** applies especially to the tough skin of a large animal, raw or tanned: *The hide of cows is tough.* **Pelt** applies especially to the skin of a fur- or wool-bearing animal before dressing or tanning: *Trappers sell pelts of foxes; stores sell dressed skins.*

skin-deep (skin′dēp′) *adj.* no deeper than the skin; shallow; slight. —*adv.* in a superficial manner; slightly.

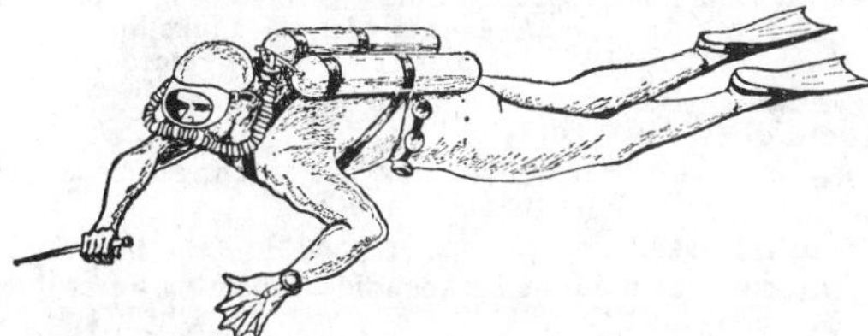

A skindiver

skin·di·ver (skin′dīv′ər) *n.* a diver equipped with special flippers and goggles and a supply of oxygen that enable him to remain under water for long periods of time.

skin diving swimming under water, sometimes at considerable depth, without special diving equipment other than flippers for the feet, goggles or a mask, and a portable breathing device.

skin·flint (skin′flint′) *n.* a mean, stingy person.

skin·ful (skin′fu̇l) *n.* **-fuls. 1** as much as a skin for liquids can hold. **2** *Informal.* as much as a person or animal can hold.

skin game *Informal.* a game or action in which the outcome is rigged; swindle.

skink (skink) *n.* one of a group of small, harmless, smooth-scaled lizards. [< L < Gk. *skinkos*]

skin·ner (skin′ər) *n.* **1** a person who skins. **2** a person who prepares or deals in skins, furs, etc.

skin·ny (skin′ē) *adj.* **-ni·er, -ni·est. 1** very thin; very lean. **2** like skin. —**skin′ni·ness,** *n.*

skin-tight (skin′tīt′) *adj.* fitting closely to the skin.

hat, āge, cãre, fär; let, ēqual, tėrm; it, īce
hot, ōpen, ôrder; oil, out; cup, pu̇t, rüle, ūse
əbove, takən, pencəl, lemən, circəs
ch, child; ng, long; sh, ship
th, thin; ᴛʜ, then; zh, measure

skip¹ (skip) *v.* **skipped, skip·ping,** *n.* —*v.* **1** leap lightly; spring; jump: *Lambs skipped in the fields.* **2** leap lightly over: *The girls skipped rope.* **3** send bounding along a surface: *Boys like to skip stones on the lake.* **4** go bounding along a surface. **5** pass over; fail to notice; omit: *Answer the questions in order without skipping.* **6** change quickly from one task, pleasure, subject, etc. to another. **7** *Informal.* leave in a hurry. **8** be promoted past the next regular grade in school. **9** *Informal.* dodge; stay away from: *to skip classes.*
—*n.* **1** a light spring, jump, or leap. **2** a gait, especially of children, in which hops and steps are alternated. **3** a passing over. **4** that which is or may be skipped. **5** in music, a passing from one note to another more than one step away. [ME < Scand.; cf. MSwedish *skuppa*]

skip² (skip) *n.* in mining or quarrying, a huge bucket or cage in which heavy loads of men or materials may be raised or lowered to and from ground level.

skip³ (skip) *n.* in curling, lawn bowling, etc., the captain of a team or side. —*v.* act as a skip. [short for *skipper*]

skip·jack (skip′jak′) *n.* **skip·jacks. 1** any kind of fish that sometimes leaps out of the water. **2** a kind of beetle. **3** *Archaic.* a pert, lively, conceited fellow.

skip·per¹ (skip′ər) *n.* **1** the captain of a ship, especially of a small trading or fishing boat. **2** any captain or leader. [ME < MDu. *schipper* < *schip* ship]

skip·per² (skip′ər) *n.* **1** a person or thing that skips. **2** any of certain insects that make skipping movements. **3** a maggot that lives in cheese, etc. **4** a small butterfly that flies very swiftly. [< *skip*]

skirl (skėrl) *v.* **1** of bagpipes, sound loudly and shrilly. **2** play a bagpipe. —*n.* the sound of a bagpipe. [probably Scand.; cf. dial. Norwegian *skrylla*]

skir·mish (skėr′mish) *n.* **1** a minor fight between small groups of soldiers, ships, aircraft, etc. **2** a minor conflict, argument, contest, etc. —*v.* take part in a skirmish. [ME < OF *eskirmiss-* a stem of *eskirmir,* originally, ward off < Gmc.]

skir·mish·er (skėr′mish ər) *n.* **1** a person who skirmishes. **2** one of the soldiers sent out in advance of an army to clear the way for the main attack, or to prevent a surprise attack by the enemy, etc.

skirt (skėrt) *n.* **1** the part of a dress that hangs from the waist. **2** a woman's or girl's garment that hangs from the waist. **3** something like a skirt: *the skirts of a man's long coat.* **4** a border; edge. **5** the outer part of a place, group of people, etc. **6** *Slang.* a woman or girl. **7** one of the flaps hanging from the sides of a saddle.
—*v.* **1** border or edge. **2** pass along the border or edge; pass along the border or edge of: *The boys skirted the forest because they did not want to go through it.* **3** be, lie, live, etc. along the border of. [ME < ON *skyrta* shirt]

skirt·ing (skėr′ting) *n.* cloth for making skirts.

skit (skit) *n.* a short dramatic sketch that contains humor or satire. [cf. ON *skyti* shooter]

ski tow a motorized conveyor or pulley for transporting skiers to the top of a slope.

skit·ter (skit′ər) *v.* **1** move lightly or quickly; skim or skip along a surface. **2** in fishing, draw a lure over the surface of the water with a skipping motion. [akin to *skittish*]

skit·tish (skit′ish) *adj.* **1** apt to start, jump, or run; easily frightened: *a skittish horse.* **2** fickle; changeable. **3** coy. [< *skit*] —**skit′tish·ly,** *adv.* —**skit′tish·ness,** *n.*

skit·tle (skit′əl) *n.* **1 skittles,** *pl.* a game in which the players try to knock down nine wooden pins by rolling or throwing wooden disks or balls at them. **2** one of the pins used in this game. [< Scand.; cf. Danish *skyttel* shuttle]

skiv·vy (skiv′ē) *n.* **-vies.** *Brit. Slang.* a female domestic servant, especially a scullery maid. [origin uncertain]

skoal (skōl) *n. interj.* a Scandinavian word used in drinking a health. [< ON *skál* bowl]

skoo·kum (skü′kəm) *Slang.* on the West coast: *—adj.* strong; powerful; big. *—n.* an evil genius or spirit. [< Chinook Jargon]

skookum chuck on the West coast: **1** a swift current; white water; rapids. **2** tidal rapids.

skort (skôrt) *n.* a one-piece garment that is a combination of skirt and shorts.

Skt. Sanskrit.

sku·a (skū′ə) *n.* any of several large, brown sea birds that are related to the gulls; jaeger. [< Faroese (lang. of the Faroe Islands) *skūgvur* < ON *skúfr*]

skul·dug·ger·y (skul dug′ər ē or skul dug′rē) *n. Informal.* trickery; dishonesty. [origin uncertain]

skulk (skulk) *v.* **1** keep out of sight to avoid danger, work, duty, etc.; hide or lurk in a cowardly way. **2** move in a stealthy, sneaking way. *—n.* a person who skulks. [ME < Scand.; cf. Danish *skolke*] **—skulk′er,** *n.* **—skulk′ing·ly,** *adv.* **—Syn.** *v.* **1** See **lurk.**

skull (skul) *n.* **1** the bones of the head; the group of bones around the brain. **2** the head; brain. See **skeleton** for diagram. [ME *scolle*; cf. dial. Norwegian *skul* shell]

skull and crossbones a picture of a human skull above two crossed bones, often used on pirates' flags as a symbol of death, and now often used on the labels of poisonous drugs, etc.

skull·cap (skul′kap′) *n.* a close-fitting cap with no brim.

skunk (skungk) *n.* **1** a black, bushy-tailed American mammal, usually with white stripes along its back and tail. A skunk is about the size of a cat and gives off a very strong, unpleasant smell when frightened or attacked. **2** the fur of this animal, used on coats, etc. **3** *Informal.* a mean, contemptible person. *—v. Slang.* hold scoreless; defeat utterly. [< Algonquian]

skunk cabbage a low-growing plant of the arum family native to eastern North America, found commonly in moist ground and characterized by a strong odor that it gives off when bruised.

skurf (skėrf) *v.* go on a skate board. [< *sk*ate + *surf*]

skurf board skate board.

sky (skī) *n.* **skies,** *v.* **skied** or **skyed, sky·ing.** *—n.* **1** Often, **skies,** *pl.* the region of the clouds or the upper air; the heavens: *a blue sky, a cloudy sky.* **2** heaven; the place where God and His angels live. **3** climate. **4 out of a clear sky,** suddenly; unexpectedly. **5 to the skies,** very highly. *—v.* hit, throw, or raise high into the air. [ME *ski(es)* cloud(s) < ON *ský*]

sky blue a clear, soft blue. **—sky′-blue′,** *adj.*

sky·cap (skī′kap′) *n.* a porter at an airport. [adapted from *redcap*]

sky diver a person who engages in sky diving.

sky diving the sport of diving from an airplane and falling a great distance, manoeuvring one's body to control direction, before opening the parachute.

Skye (skī) *n.* a Skye terrier.

Skye terrier **1** an old Scottish breed of terrier, having a long, low body, short, strong legs, and long, shaggy hair. **2** a dog of this breed. [< the Isle of *Skye* near Scotland]

sky·ey (skī′ē) *adj.* **1** of or from the sky. **2** very high. **3** sky-blue.

sky-high (skī′hī′) *adv. adj.* very high.

sky·jack (skī′jak′) *v.* take over an aircraft by force, causing it to be flown to a place other than its destination. [blend of *sky* + *hijack*] **—sky′jack′er,** *n.*

sky·lark (skī′lärk′) *n.* the common European lark, a small bird that sings very sweetly as it flies toward the sky. *—v.* play pranks; frolic.

sky·light (skī′līt′) *n.* a window in a roof or ceiling.

sky·line (skī′līn′) *n.* **1** the line at which earth and sky seem to meet; horizon. **2** the outline of buildings, mountains, trees, etc. as seen against the sky.

sky pilot *Slang.* a clergyman; chaplain.

sky·rock·et (skī′rok′it) *n.* a firework that goes up high in the air and bursts into a shower of stars, sparks, etc.; rocket. *—v.* **1** move like a skyrocket; rise suddenly, make a brilliant show, and disappear. **2** rise much and quickly: *Prices were skyrocketing.*

sky·sail (skī′sāl′ or skī′səl) *n.* in a square-rigged ship, a light sail set at the top of the mast above the royal.

sky·scrap·er (skī′skrāp′ər) *n.* an extremely tall building.

sky·ward (skī′wərd) *adv. adj.* toward the sky.

sky·wards (skī′wərdz) *adv.* skyward.

sky·way (skī′wā′) *n.* **1** an air route used by small, private planes. **2** a stretch of elevated highway. **3** a covered walkway between upper storeys of two buildings or towers.

sky·writ·ing (skī′rīt′ing) *n.* **1** the tracing of words, etc. against the sky from an airplane by means of smoke or some similar substance. **2** the letters, words, etc. so traced.

S.L. or **S/L** Squadron Leader.

slab (slab) *n. v.* **slabbed, slab·bing.** *—n.* **1** a broad, flat, thick piece (of stone, wood, meat, etc.): *This sidewalk is made of slabs of stone. The hungry boy ate a slab of cheese as big as his hand.* **2** a rough piece of wood cut from the outside of a log. **3** *Slang.* in baseball, the place where the pitcher stands to deliver the ball.
—v. **1** make into slabs. **2** cut the outside pieces from (a log). **3** lay with slabs; cover with slabs. [ME *slabbe*; origin uncertain]

slab·ber (slab′ər) *v. n.* slobber.

slack[1] (slak) *adj.* **1** not tight or firm; loose: *The rope hung slack.* **2** careless: *She is a slack housekeeper.* **3** slow: *The horse was moving at a slack pace.* **4** not active; not brisk; dull: *Business is slack at this season.*
—n. **1** the part that hangs loose: *He pulled in the slack of the rope.* **2** a dull season; quiet period. **3** a stopping of a strong flow of the tide or a current of water.
—v. **1** make slack; let up on. **2** be or become slack; let up. **3** slake (lime). **4 slack off, a** loosen. **b** lessen one's efforts. **5 slack up,** slow down; go more slowly.
—adv. in a slack manner. [OE *slæc*] **—slack′ly,** *adv.* **—slack′ness,** *n.* **—Syn.** *adj.* **2** negligent, lax, remiss, indolent.

slack[2] (slak) *n.* dirt, dust, and small pieces left after coal is screened; small coal. [ME *slac*; cf. G *Schlacke*]

slack·en (slak′ən) *v.* **1** make slower: *Don't slacken your efforts till the work is done.* **2** become slower: *Work slackens on a hot day.* **3** become less active; vigorous, brisk, etc.: *Business slackens in winter.* **4** make looser: *Slacken the rope.* **5** become loose. **—Syn. 1** retard.

slack·er (slak′ər) *n. Informal.* a person who shirks work or evades his duty.

slack-jawed (slak′jod′ or -jôd′) *adj.* having a loose-hanging jaw or a partly open mouth.

slacks (slaks) *n.pl.* trousers designed for casual wear.

slack water the time between tides when the water does not move either way.

slag (slag) *n. v.* **slagged, slag·ging.** *—n.* **1** the rough, hard waste left after metal is separated from ore by melting. **2** a light, spongy lava. *—v.* form slag; change into slag. [< MLG *slagge*]

slag·gy (slag′ē) *adj.* of, like, or having to do with slag.

slain (slān) *v.* pp. of **slay.**

slake (slāk) *v.* **slaked, slak·ing. 1** satisfy (thirst, revenge, wrath, etc.). **2** cause to be less active, intense, etc. **3** put out (a fire). **4 a** change (lime) from CaO to $Ca(OH)_2$ **(slaked lime)** by leaving it in the moist air or putting water on it. Plaster contains slaked lime and sand. **b** be changed thus. **5** *Rare.* become less active, vigorous, intense, etc. [OE *slacian* < *slæc* slack]

sla·lom (slä′ləm, slal′əm, or slä′ləm) *n.* in skiing, a zigzag race downhill on a course set between a series of posts. *—v.* ski on such a course. [< Norwegian]

slam[1] (slam) *v.* **slammed, slam·ming,** *n.* *—v.* **1** shut with force and noise; close with a bang: *He slammed the window down. The door slammed.* **2** throw, push, hit, or move hard with force. **3** *Informal.* criticize harshly.
—n. **1** a violent and noisy closing, striking, etc.; bang: *John threw his books down with a slam.* **2** *Informal.* a harsh criticism. [? < Scand.; cf. Icel. and dial. Norwegian *slamra* slam]

slam[2] (slam) *n.* **1** in the game of bridge, the winning of 12 **(little or small slam)** or all 13 **(grand slam)** tricks. **2** in certain other card games, the winning of all the tricks in one hand. [origin uncertain]

slan·der (slan′dər) *n.* **1** in law, a false statement meant to do harm: *Slander is spoken; libel is written or printed.* **2** the spreading of false reports. **3** the crime of speaking a slander. —*v.* **1** talk falsely about. **2** speak or spread slander. [ME < OF *esclandre* scandal < L *scandalum.* Doublet of SCANDAL.] —**slan′der·er,** *n.* —**Syn.** *n.* **1** defamation, calumny, libel. -*v.* **1** defame, calumniate.

slan·der·ous (slan′dər əs or slan′drəs) *adj.* **1** containing a slander. **2** speaking or spreading slanders. —**slan′der·ous·ly,** *adv.*

slang (slang) *n.* **1** words, phrases, meanings, etc. of a forceful and novel type, used informally, especially in speech, but not accepted as part of the standard language. Slang terms sometimes become standard but often they die out. **2** the special talk of a particular class of people. *Crib* often means *cheat* in students' slang. —*v.* attack with abusive language; rail at; scold. [origin uncertain]

slang·y (slang′ē) *adj.* **slang·i·er, slang·i·est. 1** containing slang; full of slang. **2** using much slang. —**slang′i·ly,** *adv.* —**slang′i·ness,** *n.*

slank (slangk) *v. Archaic.* a pt. of **slink.**

slant (slant) *v.* **1** slope: *Most handwriting slants to the right.* **2** make (a story, news account, etc.) favorable, or unfavorable, to a particular person, group, cause, etc. by choosing or emphasizing certain facts.
—*n.* **1** slanting or oblique direction or position; slope: *Has your roof a sharp slant?* **2** a mental attitude; way of regarding something. **3** *Informal.* favorable or unfavorable bias (in a story, news account, etc.).
—*adj.* sloping. [var. of ME *slent* to slant < Scand.; cf. Norwegian *slenta*] —**slant′ing·ly,** *adv.* —**Syn.** *v.* See **slope.** -*n.* **1** incline.

slant·ways (slant′wāz′) *adv.* slantwise.

slant·wise (slant′wīz′) *adv.* in a slanting manner; obliquely. —*adj.* slanting; oblique.

slap (slap) *n. v.* **slapped, slap·ping,** *adv.* —*n.* **1** a blow with the open hand or with something flat. **2** sharp words of blame; a direct insult or rebuff.
—*v.* **1** strike with the open hand or with something flat. **2** put, dash, or cast with force: *She slapped the book down on the table.* **3** beat or hit with a slapping sound: *waves slapping against the dock.*
—*adv.* **1** *Informal.* straight; directly: *The thief ran slap into a policeman.* **2** *Informal.* suddenly. [< LG *slappe*]

slap-bang (slap′bang′) *adv.* **1** speedily; immediately. **2** thoughtlessly; in a headlong manner. —*adj.* headlong; thoughtless; slapdash.

slap·dash (slap′dash′) *adv. Informal.* hastily and carelessly. —*adj.* hasty and careless. —*n.* hasty, careless action, methods, or work.

slap-hap·py (slap′hap′ē) *adj. Slang.* **1** lacking co-ordination or sense; irresponsible. **2** dizzy or befuddled because of blows received on the head.

slap·shot (slap′shot′) *n. Cdn.* in hockey, a quick shot made by hitting the puck with a short, powerful swing of the stick.

slap·stick (slap′stik′) *n.* **1** two long, narrow boards fastened so as to slap together loudly when a clown, actor, etc. hits somebody with it. **2** a comedy full of rough play. —*adj.* full of rough play. In slapstick comedy, the actors knock each other around to make people laugh.

slash (slash) *v.* **1** cut with a sweeping stroke of a sword, knife, etc.; gash: *He slashed the bark off the tree with his knife.* **2** make a slashing stroke. **3** cut or slit to let a different cloth or color show through. **4** whip severely; lash. **5** criticize sharply, severely, or unkindly. **6** cut down severely; reduce a great deal: *His salary was slashed when business became bad.* **7** cut out parts of (a book, etc.); change greatly (a book, etc.).
—*n.* **1** a sweeping, slashing stroke. **2** a cut or wound made by such a stroke; gash. **3** an ornamental slit in a garment that lets a different cloth or color show through. **4** an open space in a forest, usually littered with chips, broken branches, etc. **5** a litter of chips, broken branches, etc. [ME *slasche(n)*; cf. OF *esclachier* break] —**slash′er,** *n.*

slat[1] (slat) *n. v.* **slat·ted, slat·ting.** —*n.* a long, thin, narrow piece of wood or metal. —*v.* provide or build with slats. [ME < OF *esclat* split piece < Gmc.]

hat, āge, cãre, fär; let, ēqual, tėrm; it, īce
hot, ōpen, ôrder; oil, out; cup, pu̇t, rüle, ūse
əbove, takən, pencəl, lemən, circəs
ch, child; ng, long; sh, ship
th, thin; ᴛʜ, then; zh, measure

slat[2] (slat) *v.* **slat·ted, slat·ting,** *n. Archaic.* —*v.* **1** hurl; dash; fling. **2** slap; strike; beat. —*n.* a sharp blow or slap. [< ON *sletta* slap]

slate[1] (slāt) *n. v.* **slat·ed, slat·ing,** *adj.* —*n.* **1** a bluish-gray rock that splits easily into thin, smooth layers. Slate is used to cover roofs and for blackboards. **2** a thin piece of this rock. Children used to write on slates instead of paper. **3** a dark bluish-gray. **4** a list of candidates, officers, etc. to be considered for appointment, nomination, etc. **5** a record: *start life again with a clean slate.*
—*v.* **1** cover with slate. **2** list on a slate: *He is slated for the office of club president.*
—*adj.* dark bluish-gray. [ME < OF *esclate,* var. of *esclat* slat < Gmc.] —**slate′like′,** *adj.*

slate[2] (slāt) *v.* **sla·ted, sla·ting. 1** beat violently. **2** criticize severely. [? var. of *slat*[2]]

slat·er (slāt′ər) *n.* **1** a person who covers roofs, etc. with slates. **2** *Scottish.* a wood louse.

slath·er (slaᴛʜ′ər) *Slang.* —*n.* **slathers,** in great quantities: *slathers of bacon and eggs.* —*v.* spread thickly or lavishly. [origin unknown]

slat·tern (slat′ərn) *n.* a woman who is dirty, careless, or untidy in her dress, her ways, her housekeeping, etc. [< Brit. dial. *slatter* slop; origin uncertain; cf. LG *slattje* slattern]

slat·tern·ly (slat′ərn lē) *adj.* slovenly; untidy. —**slat′tern·li·ness,** *n.*

slat·y (slāt′ē) *adj.* **slat·i·er, slat·i·est. 1** of, like, or having to do with slate. **2** slate-colored.

slaugh·ter (slo′tər or slô′tər) *n.* **1** the killing of an animal or animals for food; butchering. **2** brutal killing; much or needless killing. —*v.* **1** butcher. **2** kill brutally; massacre. [ME < Scand.; cf. ON *slátr* butcher-meat < *slá* slay] —**slaugh′ter·er,** *n.* —**Syn.** *n.* **1** slaying, murder.

slaughter house (slo′tər hous′ or slô′tər-) a place where animals are killed for food; abattoir.

slaugh·ter·ous (slot′ər əs or slô′tər əs) *adj.* murderous; destructive.

Slav (slav or släv) *n.* a member of a group of peoples in eastern and central Europe whose languages are related. Russians, Poles, Czechs, Slovaks, Bulgarians, and Yugoslavs are Slavs. —*adj.* of or having to do with Slavs. [< Med.L *Slavus, Sclavus.* Cf. SLAVE.]

Slav. 1 Slavic. **2** Slavonian. **3** Slavonic.

slave (slāv) *n. v.* **slaved, slav·ing.** —*n.* **1** a person who is the property of another. Slaves used to be bought and sold like cattle. **2** a person who is controlled or ruled by some desire, habit, or influence: *A drunkard is a slave to drink.* **3** a person who works like a slave. **4** an ant that is captured and forced to work for other ants. **5 a** an electronic device that receives and relays radio signals transmitted by a master control, as in loran navigation. **b** a mechanical or electric device for manipulating objects by remote control. —*v.* work like a slave. [ME < OF < Med.L *Sclavus* Slav (captive) < LGk. *Sklabos,* ult. < Slavic *slovo.* Cf. SLOVENE.] —**slave′like′,** *adj.*

Slave (slāv) *n.* **1** a tribe of Athapaskan Indians living between the Rockies and Great Slave Lake in the Northwest Territories. **2** a member of this tribe. **3** the language of this tribe. Also, **Slavey.** [translation of Cree *awokanak* slaves]

slave driver 1 an overseer of slaves. **2** an especially exacting taskmaker.

slave·hold·er (slāv′hōl′dər) *n.* an owner of slaves.

slave·hold·ing (slāv′hōl′ding) *adj.* owning slaves. —*n.* the owning of slaves.

slav·er[1] (slāv′ər) *n.* **1** a dealer in slaves. **2** a ship used in the slave trade. [< *slave*]

slav·er[2] (slav′ər) *v.* **1** let saliva run from the mouth. **2** wet with saliva. *—n.* saliva running from the mouth. [ME < Scand.; cf. Icel. *slafra.* Related to SLOBBER.]

slav·er·y (slāv′ər ē or slāv′rē) *n.* **1** the condition of being a slave. Many Africans were captured and sold into slavery. **2** the custom of owning slaves. **3** a condition like that of a slave. **4** hard work like that of a slave. **—Syn. 1** bondage, serfdom, thralldom, servitude.

slave trade the business of procuring and selling slaves.

slav·ey (slāv′ē) *n.* **-eys.** *Informal.* a maid of all work.

Slav·ic (slav′ik or släv′ik) *adj.* of or having to do with the Slavs or their languages. *—n.* the language or group of languages spoken by the Slavs.

slav·ish (slāv′ish) *adj.* **1** of or having to do with a slave or slaves. **2** like a slave; mean; base. **3** weakly submitting. **4** like that of slaves; fit for slaves. **5** lacking originality and independence: *a slavish reproduction.* **—slav′ish·ly,** *adv.* **—slav′ish·ness,** *n.* **—Syn. 3** servile.

Sla·vo·ni·an (slə vō′nē ən) *adj.* **1** of or having to do with Slavonia, a region in N. Yugoslavia, or its people. **2** Slavic. *—n.* **1** a native of Slavonia. **2** Slav. **3** the Slavic language or languages.

Sla·von·ic (slə von′ik) *adj.* **1** Slavic. **2** Slavonian. *—n.* **1** Slav. **2** the Slavic language or languages.

slaw (slo or slô) *n.* finely sliced or chopped cabbage, raw or cooked, served with dressing; coleslaw. [< Du. *sla,* contraction of *salade* salad]

slay (slā) *v.* **slew** or **slayed** *(for 2),* **slain, slay·ing. 1** kill with violence. **2** *Slang.* amuse greatly: *That comedian just slays me.* [OE *slēan.* Akin to SLY.] **—slay′er,** *n.* **—Syn.** See **kill.**

sld. sailed.

sleave (slēv) *v.* **sleaved, sleav·ing,** *n. —v.* divide or separate into smaller threads. *—n.* a small silk thread made by separating a thicker thread. [OE *slǣfan,* as in *tōslǣfan* divide]

slea·zy (slē′zē) *adj.* **-zi·er, -zi·est. 1** flimsy and poor: *sleazy cloth.* **2** *Informal.* unpleasant; nasty; slovenly. [origin uncertain] **—slea′zi·ness,** *n.*

sled (sled) *n. v.* **sled·ded, sled·ding.** *—n.* **1** a vehicle having runners instead of wheels for use on ice and snow. **2** a sleigh (def. 2). *—v.* **1** ride on a sled. **2** carry on a sled. [< MDu. *sledde*]

Dogs pulling a sled

sled·ding (sled′ing) *n.* **1** a riding or coasting on a sled. **2 hard sledding,** unfavorable conditions.

sled dog 1 a breed of dog trained and used to draw a sled in arctic regions. **2** a dog of this breed.

sledge[1] (slej) *n. v.* **sledged, sledg·ing.** *—n.* **1** a heavy sled or sleigh, usually pulled by horses. **2** a sled; sleigh. *—v.* **1** carry on a sledge. **2** ride in a sledge. [MDu. *sleedse*]

sledge[2] (slej) *n.* sledge hammer (def. 1). [OE *slecg*]

sledge hammer 1 a large, heavy hammer. **2** anything powerful and crushing: *Sarcasm can become a sledge hammer in a debate.*

A man using a sledge hammer

sledge-ham·mer (slej′ham′ər) *v.* hit with, or as if with, a sledge hammer. *—adj.* powerful; crushing.

sleek (slēk) *adj.* **1** soft and glossy; smooth: *sleek hair.* **2** having smooth, soft skin, hair, fur, etc.: *a sleek cat.* **3** smooth of speech, manners, etc.: *a sleek salesman.* **4** having trim lines; trim; smooth. *—v.* **1** smooth. **2** make smooth and glossy. **3** make tidy. [var. of *slick*] **—sleek′ly,** *adv.* **—sleek′ness,** *n.*

sleep (slēp) *v.* **slept, sleep·ing,** *n. —v.* **1** rest the body and mind; be without ordinary consciousness. **2** be in a condition like sleep: *The seeds sleep in the ground all winter.* **3** pass in sleeping. **4** provide with or offer sleeping accommodation for: *a hotel that sleeps 500 people.* **5** provide space for sleeping: *This room sleeps two.* **6 sleep away,** pass or spend in sleeping. **7 sleep in, a** remain in bed later than usual. **b** sleep late or oversleep. **c** live at one's place of work. **8 sleep like a log,** sleep soundly and heavily. **9 sleep off,** get rid of or improve by sleeping.
—n. **1** a condition in which body and mind are very inactive, occurring naturally and regularly in animals. **2** a period of sleep. **3** a state or condition like sleep. **4 last sleep,** death. [OE *slǣpan*] **—Syn.** *v. n.* **1** slumber, doze, drowse, nap, snooze.

sleep·er (slēp′ər) *n.* **1** a person or thing that sleeps. **2** a railway sleeping car. **3** a horizontal beam. **4** *Brit.* a tie to support a railway track. **5** *Informal.* a person, animal, or thing, especially a book, play, or motion picture, that becomes unexpectedly successful; an unexpected hit or winner. **6 sleepers,** one-piece pyjamas for children, extending from the neck and covering the feet.

sleep·ing (slēp′ing) *n.* sleep. *—adj.* **1** that sleeps. **2** used for sleeping on or in: *a sleeping car.*

sleeping bag a canvas or waterproof bag, usually warmly lined, to sleep in out of doors.

sleeping car a railway car with berths for passengers to sleep in.

sleeping partner a partner who takes no active part in managing the business; a silent partner.

sleeping pill a drug that causes sleep.

sleeping sickness a disease causing fever, inflammation of the brain, sleepiness, and usually death.

sleeping tablet sleeping pill.

sleep·less (slēp′lis) *adj.* **1** without sleep; not sleeping; restless. **2** watchful; wide-awake. **3** always moving or acting. **—sleep′less·ly,** *adv.* **—sleep′less·ness,** *n.*

sleep·walk·er (slēp′wok′ər or -wôk′ər) *n.* a person who walks about while asleep.

sleep·walk·ing (slēp′wok′ing or -wôk′ing) *n.* the act or habit of walking while asleep. *—adj.* that walks about while asleep.

sleep·y (slēp′ē) *adj.* **sleep·i·er, sleep·i·est. 1** ready to go to sleep; inclined to sleep. **2** not active; quiet. **3** inducing sleep; soporific: *a warm, sleepy day.* **—sleep′i·ly,** *adv.* **—sleep′i·ness,** *n.*

Syn. 1 Sleepy, drowsy = ready or inclined to sleep. **Sleepy** is the general word describing people or things, particularly suggesting being ready to fall asleep or having a tendency to sleep: *He never gets enough rest and is always sleepy.* **Drowsy** particularly suggests being heavy or dull with sleepiness: *After lying in the sun, he became drowsy.*

sleet (slēt) *n.* half-frozen rain; snow or hail mixed with rain. *—v.* come down in sleet: *It sleeted; then it snowed; then it rained.* [ME *slete*]

sleet·y (slēt′ē) *adj.* **sleet·i·er, sleet·i·est.** of or like sleet; characterized by sleet. **—sleet′i·ness,** *n.*

sleeve (slēv) *n. v.* **sleeved, sleev·ing.** *—n.* **1** the part of a garment that covers all or part of the arm. **2** a tube into which a rod or another tube fits. **3 laugh in** or **up one's sleeve,** be amused but not show it. **4 up one's sleeve,** in reserve; ready for use when needed. *—v.* **1** fix, fasten, or couple by means of a sleeve or tube. **2** of a garment, provide with sleeves; fashion. [OE *slīefe*]

sleeved (slēvd) *adj.* having sleeves.

sleeve·less (slēv′lis) *adj.* without sleeves: *a sleeveless dress.*

sleigh (slā) *n.* **1** a carriage or cart mounted on runners for use on ice or snow. **2** a framework of boards mounted on metal runners, used by children for sliding on snow and ice. *—v.* travel or ride in a sleigh. [< Du. *slee,* var. of *slede* sled]

A sleigh (def. 2)

sleigh·ing (slā′ing) *n.* **1** riding in a sleigh. **2** the conditions for sleighing: *The warm rain spoiled the sleighing.*

sleight (slīt) *n.* **1** skill; dexterity. **2** a clever trick. [ME < ON *slǣgth* < *slǣgr* sly. See SLY.]

hat, āge, cãre, fär; let, ēqual, tėrm; it, īce
hot, ōpen, ôrder; oil, out; cup, pu̇t, rüle, ūse
ə̣bove, takən, pencəl, lemən, circəs
ch, child; ng, long; sh, ship
th, thin; ᴛʜ, then; zh, measure

sleight of hand 1 skill and quickness in moving the hands. 2 the tricks or skill of a modern magician; juggling.

slen·der (slen′dər) *adj.* 1 long and thin; not big around: *A man 6 feet tall and weighing 130 pounds is very slender. A pencil is a slender piece of wood.* 2 slight; small; scanty: *a slender meal, a slender income, a slender hope.* [ME *slendre, sclendre*; origin uncertain] —**slen′der·ly,** *adv.* —**slen′der·ness,** *n.*
Syn. 1 **Slender, slim** = thin, not big around. **Slender,** describing a person or thing and meaning tall or long and thin, suggests good proportions, gracefulness, and beauty: *Many girls want to be slender. The legs of those chairs are slender.* **Slim** emphasizes lack of flesh and lightness or weakness of frame or build: *He is a slim boy who may fill out as he becomes older.*

slen·der·ize (slen′dər īz′) *v.* **-ized, -iz·ing.** 1 make slender. 2 cause to look slender or less stout: *a slenderizing dress.*

slept (slept) *v.* pt. and pp. of **sleep.**

sleuth (slüth) *n. Informal.* a detective. —*v.* be or act like a detective. [ME < ON *slóth* trail]

sleuth·hound (slüth′hound′) *n.* 1 a bloodhound. 2 *Informal.* a detective.

slew[1] (slü) *v.* pt. of **slay.**

slew[2] (slü) *v. n.* turn; swing; twist. Also, **slue.** [origin uncertain]

slew[3] (slü) *n.* slough[1].

slew[4] (slü) *n. Informal.* a large number or amount; lot. [? < Irish *sluagh* host, crowd]

slice (slīs) *n. v.* **sliced, slic·ing.** —*n.* 1 a thin, flat, broad piece cut from something: *a slice of bread, meat, or cake.* 2 a knife or spatula with a thin, broad blade. 3 a part; share. 4 in sports, a hit or stroke so made that the ball curves to one side in flight.
—*v.* 1 cut into slices. 2 cut (off) as a slice. 3 divide into parts or shares. 4 in sports, hit a ball so that it curves to one side in flight. [ME < OF *esclice* thin chip < Gmc.]

slic·er (slīs′ər) *n.* 1 a tool or machine that slices: *a meat slicer.* 2 a person who slices.

slick (slik) *adj.* 1 sleek; smooth: *slick hair.* 2 slippery; greasy. 3 *Informal.* clever; ingenious. 4 *Informal.* sly; tricky. 5 *Informal.* smooth of speech, manners, etc. 6 *Informal.* of or like that of a smooth, tricky person; cunningly made up: *a slick excuse.* [ME *slike*; related to OE *slician* make smooth]
—*v.* make sleek or smooth.
—*n.* 1 a smooth place or spot. Oil makes a slick on the surface of water. 2 *Informal.* a magazine printed on heavy, glossy paper. 3 a a tool used for scraping and smoothing leather. b a trowel for smoothing the top of a mould in casting metals.
—*adv.* 1 smoothly; slyly; cleverly. 2 directly. [OE *slician*] —**slick′ly,** *adv.* —**slick′ness,** *n.*

slick·er (slik′ər) *n.* 1 a long, loose, waterproof coat. 2 *Slang.* a sly, tricky person.

slid (slid) *v.* pt. and pp. of **slide.**

slid·den (slid′ən) *v.* a pp. of **slide.**

slide (slīd) *v.* **slid, slid** or **slid·den, slid·ing,** *n.* —*v.* 1 move smoothly over a surface: *The bureau drawers slide in and out.* 2 move easily or quietly or secretly: *The thief slid behind the curtains.* 3 pass without heeding or being heeded. 4 pass by degrees; slip: *He has slid into bad habits.* 5 pass or put quietly or secretly: *He slid a gun into his pocket.* 6 slip as one losing one's foothold: *The car slid into the ditch.* 7 in music, pass or progress from tone to tone without perceptible step or break. 8 in baseball, launch a slide for a base or home plate. 9 **let slide,** neglect; not bother about.
—*n.* 1 the act of sliding: *The children each take a slide in turn.* 2 a smooth surface for sliding on. 3 a track, rail, etc. on which something slides. 4 something that works by sliding. 5 the U-shaped tube of a trumpet or trombone that is pushed in or out to change the pitch of the tones. 6 a a mass of earth, snow, etc. sliding down. b the sliding down of such a mass. 7 a small, thin sheet of glass. Objects are put on slides for microscopic examination. Slides with pictures on them are projected on a screen. 8 in music: a a rapid ascending or descending series of three or more notes, composed of grace notes which ornament the last or principal note. b a passing from tone to tone without perceptible step or break. 9 in baseball, a throwing of the body, usually feet first, along the ground in running to a base, so as to avoid being tagged, to break up a double play, etc. [OE *slīdan*] —**slid′er,** *n.*
Syn. *v.* 1 **Slide, slip, glide** = move along smoothly, especially over a surface. **Slide** emphasizes continuous contact with a smooth or slippery surface: *The boat slid down the bank into the water.* **Slip** emphasizes the smoothness or slipperiness of the surface or absence of any hindrance, and suggests sliding suddenly without intention: *One of the climbers slipped on the rocks.* **Glide** emphasizes continuous, smooth, even, easy movement, not necessarily along a surface: *The swans glide gracefully on the lake.*

slide rule a ruler that has a sliding middle strip, marked with logarithmic scales, used by engineers, physicists, etc. for making rapid calculations.

A slide rule. The centre part slīdes back and forth. The transparent piece in the right hand has a mark for lining up corresponding numbers on the scales.

slid·ing (slīd′ing) *adj.* having a part that slides; adjustable; changing.

sliding scale 1 a scale of wages, prices, taxes, etc. that can be adjusted according to certain conditions. 2 a slide rule.

slight (slīt) *adj.* 1 not much; not important; small: *I have a slight headache.* 2 not big around; slender: *She is a slight girl.* 3 frail; flimsy: *a slight excuse.*
—*v.* treat as of little value; pay too little attention to; neglect: *She felt slighted because she was not asked to the party.*
—*n.* slighting treatment; an act showing neglect or lack of respect. [OE *-sliht* level, as in *eorthslihtes* level with the ground] —**slight′ness,** *n.*
Syn. *adj.* 1 inconsiderable, trivial, trifling. 2 slim, thin.
-*v.* **Slight, overlook, neglect** = pay too little or no attention to someone or something needing or deserving it. **Slight** emphasizes intentionally treating a person, thing, work, or duty as of too little importance to deserve consideration or attention: *He slights his cousins because they are poor.* **Overlook** emphasizes unintentionally failing to see something needing attention, because of other concerns, haste, carelessness, etc.: *He overlooked the telephone bill.* **Neglect** emphasizes failing to give enough or deserved attention or care to a person, work, or duty: *He neglects his teeth.*

slight·ing (slīt′ing) *adj.* that detracts; contemptuous; disrespectful: *a slighting remark.* —**slight′ing·ly,** *adv.*

slight·ly (slīt′lē) *adv.* 1 in a slight manner. 2 to a slight degree; somewhat; a little: *I knew him slightly.*

sli·ly (slī′lē) *adv.* slyly.

slim (slim) *adj.* **slim·mer, slim·mest,** *v.* **slimmed, slim·ming.** —*adj.* 1 slender; thin. 2 small; slight; weak: *The invalid's chances for getting well were very slim.* —*v.* 1 make or become slim or slender. 2 **slim down,** reduce in size or number. [< Du. *slim* bad] —**slim′ly,** *adv.* —**slim′ness,** *n.* —Syn. 1 See **slender.**

slime (slīm) *n. v.* **slimed, slim·ing.** —*n.* 1 a soft, sticky mud or something like it. 2 a sticky substance given off by snails, slugs, fish, etc. 3 disgusting filth. —*v.* 1 cover or smear with, or as with, slime. 2 clear (skins, fish, etc.) of slimy matter by scraping. [OE *slīm*]

slim·y (slīm′ē) *adj.* **slim·i·er, slim·i·est.** 1 covered with slime. 2 of or like slime. 3 disgusting; vile; filthy. 4 using sly or crafty flattery, insinuation, etc. —**slim′i·ly,** *adv.* —**slim′i·ness,** *n.*

sling (sling) *n. v.* **slung, sling·ing.** —*n.* 1 a strip of leather with a string fastened to each end, for throwing stones. 2 a throw; hurling. 3 a hanging loop of cloth fastened around the neck to support a hurt arm. 4 a loop of rope, band, chain, etc. by which heavy objects are lifted, carried, or held: *The men lowered the boxes into the cellar by a sling. Rifles have slings.* [ME *slynge*; akin to Swedish *slinga*]

A, a sling for lifting; B, sling lifting a barrel.

—*v.* **1** throw with a sling. **2** throw; cast; hurl; fling. **3** raise, lower, etc. with a sling. **4** hang in a sling; hang so as to swing loosely: *The soldier's gun was slung over his shoulder.* **5** *Slang.* mix; serve: *sling hash.* [ME < ON *slyngva*]

sling·er (sling′ər) *n.* **1** a fighter armed with a sling. **2** a worker in charge of slings used in hoisting, etc. **3** a person who slings.

sling·shot (sling′shot′) *n.* **1** a Y-shaped stick with a rubber band fastened to its prongs, used to shoot pebbles, etc.; catapult. **2** a sling (def. 1).

slink[1] (slingk) *v.* **slunk** or (*Archaic*) **slank, slunk, slink·ing.** move in a sneaking, guilty manner; sneak: *After stealing the meat, the dog slunk away.* [OE *slincan*] —**slink′ing·ly,** *adv.*

slink[2] (slingk) *v.* **slinked** or **slunk, slink·ing,** *n. adj.* —*v.* of animals, give birth to prematurely. —*n.* any animal born prematurely. —*adj.* born prematurely. [< *slink*[1]]

slink·y (slingk′ē) *adj.* **1** furtive; sneaking. **2** tight-fitting; sexy. —**slink′i·ly,** *adv.* —**slink′i·ness,** *n.*

slip[1] (slip) *v.* **slipped** or (*Archaic*) **slipt, slipped, slip·ping,** *n.* —*v.* **1** go or move smoothly, quietly, easily, or quickly: *She slipped out of the room. Time slips by. The ship slips through the waves. The drawer slips into place.* **2** slide; move out of place: *The knife slipped and cut him.* **3** slide suddenly without wanting to: *He slipped on the icy sidewalk.* **4** cause to slip; put, pass, or draw smoothly, quietly, or secretly: *He slipped back the bolt. She slipped the ring from her finger. Slip the note into Mary's hand.* **5** put or take (something) easily or quickly: *Slip on your coat. Slip off your shoes.* **6** pass without notice; pass through neglect; escape: *Don't let this opportunity slip.* **7** get loose from; get away from; escape from: *The dog has slipped his collar. Your name has slipped my mind.* **8** let go; release: *He slipped the hound. The ship has slipped anchor and is off.* **9** make a mistake or error. **10** fall off; decline; deteriorate: *New car sales have slipped.* **11 let slip,** tell without meaning to. **12 slip one over on,** *Informal.* get the advantage of, especially by trickery. **13 slip up,** *Informal.* make a mistake or error. —*n.* **1** the act or fact of slipping. **2** something that covers and can be slipped on or off; covering: *Pillows are covered by slips.* **3** a dress-length or skirt-length undergarment of nylon, silk, etc. worn by women and girls. **4** a mistake; error: *He makes slips in grammar. That remark was a slip of the tongue.* **5** a space for ships between wharves or in a dock. **6** an inclined platform alongside the water, on which ships are built or repaired. **7** a leash for a dog. **8** in cricket: **a** the position of a player behind and to the side of the wicketkeeper. **b** the player in this position. **9 give** (someone) **the slip,** *Informal.* escape from or get away from (someone). [probably < MLG *slippen*] —**Syn.** *v.* **1** See **slide.**

slip[2] (slip) *v.* **slipped** or (*Archaic*) **slipt, slipped, slip·ping,** *n.* —*v.* cut branches from (a plant) to grow new plants; take (a part) from a plant. —*n.* **1** a narrow strip of paper, wood, etc. **2** a young, slender person: *She is just a slip of a girl.* **3** a small branch or twig cut from a plant, used to grow a new plant. [probably < MDu. or MLG *slippen* cut]

slip cover or **slip·cov·er** (slip′kuv′ər) *n.* **1** a removable cloth cover for a chair, chesterfield, etc. **2** a dust jacket for a book.

slip knot 1 a knot made to slip along the rope or cord around which it is made. **2** a knot that can be undone by a pull. See **knot** for picture.

slip noose a noose with a slip knot.

slip-on (slip′on′) *adj.* **1** that can be put on or taken off easily or quickly. **2** that must be put on or taken off over the head. —*n.* a slip-on glove, blouse, sweater, etc.

slip·page (slip′ij) *n.* **1** the act or fact of slipping. **2** the loss in time, distance, or amount between a standard and what is achieved, between theoretical and actual speed, power, output, etc.

slip·per (slip′ər) *n.* **1** a kind of light, low shoe. **2** a person or thing that slips. —*v. Informal.* hit or beat with a slipper. —**slip′per·less,** *adj.*

slip·pered (slip′ərd) *adj.* wearing slippers.

slip·per·y (slip′ər ē or slip′rē) *adj.* **-per·i·er, -per·i·est.** **1** causing or likely to cause slipping: *A wet street is slippery.* **2** slipping away easily: *Wet soap is slippery.* **3** not to be depended on; tricky. [< obs. *slipper* slippery, OE *slipor*] —**slip′per·i·ly,** *adv.* —**slip′per·i·ness,** *n.*

slippery elm 1 an elm tree of E. North America having an inner bark that becomes slimy or slippery when moistened. **2** the inner bark of this tree.

slip·shod (slip′shod′) *adj.* **1** careless in dress, habits, speech, etc.; untidy; slovenly. **2** shuffling: *a slipshod gait.* **3** wearing shoes worn down at the heel.

slipt (slipt) *v. Archaic.* a pt. of **slip.**

slip-up (slip′up′) *n. Informal.* a mistake; error.

slit (slit) *v.* **slit, slit·ting,** *n.* —*v.* cut or tear in a straight line; make a long, straight cut or tear in: *slit cloth into strips.* —*n.* a straight, narrow cut, tear, or opening: *a slit in a bag, the slit in the letter box.* [ME *slitte(n)*] —**slit′ter,** *n.*

slith·er (sliᴛʜ′ər) *v.* **1** slide down or along a surface, especially unsteadily. **2** go with a sliding motion. —*n.* a slithering movement; a slide. [OE *slidrian*]

sliv·er (sliv′ər) *n.* **1** a long, thin piece that has been split off, broken off, or cut off; splinter. **2** a loose fibre of wool, cotton, etc. —*v.* split or break into slivers. [ult. < OE *slīfan* split]

slob (slob) *n.* **1** *Irish.* mud. **2** *Slang.* a stupid, untidy, or clumsy person. **3** *Cdn.* slob ice. [probably < Irish *slab* mud < Gmc.]

slob·ber (slob′ər) *v.* **1** let liquid run out from the mouth. **2** wet or smear with saliva, etc. **3** speak in a silly, sentimental way. —*n.* **1** saliva or other liquid running out from the mouth. **2** silly, sentimental talk or emotion. Also, **slabber.** [probably ult. < Du. *slobberen*]

slob·ber·y (slob′ər ē) *adj.* **1** slobbering. **2** disagreeably wet; sloppy. —**slob′ber·i·ness,** *n.*

slob ice *Cdn.* a mass of densely packed chunks of heavy, sludgy ice, especially disintegrating sea ice.

sloe (slō) *n.* **1** a dark-purple, plumlike fruit. **2** the thorny shrub that it grows on; blackthorn. [OE *slāh*]

sloe-eyed (slō′īd′) *adj.* having very dark eyes.

sloe gin a liqueur made of gin and flavored with sloes.

slog (slog) *v.* **slogged, slog·ging,** *n. Informal.* —*v.* **1** hit hard. **2** plod heavily. **3** work hard (at something). —*n.* **1** a hard blow. **2** a spell of difficult, steady work. [var. of *slug*[2]]

slo·gan (slō′gən) *n.* **1** a word or phrase used by a business, club, political party, etc. to advertise its purpose; motto: *"Service with a smile" was the store's slogan.* **2** a war cry. [< Scots Gaelic *sluagh-ghairm* < *slaugh* army + *gairm* cry]

sloop (slüp) *n.* a sailboat having one mast, a mainsail, a jib, and sometimes other sails. [< Du. *sloep*, earlier *sloepe.* Doublet of SHALLOP.]

A sloop

sloop of war in former times, a small warship having guns on the upper deck only.

slop (slop) *v.* **slopped, slop·ping,** *n.* —*v.* **1** spill liquid upon; spill; splash. **2** splash through mud, slush, or water. **3 slop over,** *Slang.* show too much feeling, enthusiasm, etc. —*n.* **1** liquid carelessly spilled or splashed about. **2** a thin liquid mud or slush. **3** Often, **slops,** *pl.* **a** dirty water; liquid garbage. **b** weak liquid food, such as gruel. [ME *sloppe* a mud hole; origin uncertain]

slope (slōp) *v.* **sloped, slop·ing,** *n.* —*v.* **1** go up or down at an angle: *a sloping roof. The land slopes toward the sea.* **2** cause to go up or down at an angle. —*n.* **1** any line, surface, land, etc. that goes up or down at an angle: *If you roll a ball up a slope, it will roll down again.* **2** the amount of slope. [OE *-slopen*, pp. of *-slūpan* slip]
Syn. *v.* **1 Slope, slant** = go off at an angle from a straight line or level surface. **Slope** is used chiefly of a surface that goes up or down from a level, usually gradually unless sharpness, steepness, etc. is stated: *The fields slope up to the foothills.* **Slant** is the general word and means "turn or go off noticeably in any degree up, down, or to one side from a line straight up and down or across": *That picture slants to the left.*

slop·py (slop′ē) *adj.* **-pi·er, -pi·est. 1** very wet; slushy:

sloppy ground, sloppy weather. **2** splashed or soiled with liquid: *a sloppy table.* **3** *Informal.* careless; slovenly: *do sloppy work, use sloppy English.* **4** *Informal.* weak; silly: *sloppy sentiment.* **5** loose or baggy; ill-fitting: *sloppy trousers.* —**slop′pi·ly,** *adv.* —**slop′pi·ness,** *n.*

slops (slops) *n.pl.* **1** cheap ready-made clothing. **2** clothes, bedding, etc. supplied to sailors on a ship. **3** loose trousers; wide baggy breeches. [OE *slop,* as in *oferslop* overgarment]

slop·shop (slop′shop′) *n.* a store where cheap ready-made clothing is sold.

slosh (slosh) *n.* **1** slush. **2** *Informal.* a watery or weak drink. —*v.* **1** splash in slush, mud, or water. **2** go about idly. [? blend of *slop* and *slush*]

sloshed (slosht) *adj. Slang.* drunk.

slot[1] (slot) *n. v.* **slot·ted, slot·ting.** —*n.* **1** a small, narrow opening or depression: *Put a penny in the slot to get a stick of gum from this machine.* **2** *Informal.* a place or position in a schedule, list, series, etc. —*v.* **1** make a slot or slots in. **2** *Informal.* put into a slot; schedule. [ME < OF *esclot* the hollow between the breasts]

slot[2] (slot) *n. v.* **slot·ted, slot·ting.** track; trail: *They followed the slot made by the deer's footprints in the mud.* [< OF *esclot* hoof print, probably < ON *slóth* trail. Akin to SLEUTH.]

sloth (slōth or sloth) *n.* **1** unwillingness to work or exert oneself; laziness; idleness: *His sloth keeps him from engaging in sports.* **2** *Archaic.* slowness. **3** a very slow-moving mammal of South and Central America that lives in trees. Sloths hang upside down from tree branches. [< *slow*] —**Syn. 1** sluggishness, indolence.

sloth bear a long-haired bear that is native to India.

sloth·ful (slōth′fəl or sloth′fəl) *adj.* unwilling to work or exert oneself; lazy; idle. —**sloth′ful·ly,** *adv.* —**sloth′ful·ness,** *n.* —**Syn.** sluggish.

slot machine a machine, especially one used in gambling games, that is worked by dropping a coin into a slot.

slouch (slouch) *v.* **1** stand, sit, walk, or move in an awkward, drooping manner: *The weary man slouched along.* **2** droop or bend downward. —*n.* **1** a bending forward of head and shoulders; an awkward, drooping way of standing, sitting, or walking. **2** a drooping or bending downward of the brim of a hat, etc. **3** an awkward, slovenly, or inefficient person. [origin uncertain]

slouch hat a soft hat, usually with a broad brim that bends down easily.

slouch·y (slouch′ē) *adj.* **slouch·i·er, slouch·i·est.** slouching awkwardly; carelessly untidy.

slough[1] (slü *for 1; usually* slou *for 2-5*) *n.* **1** in the Prairie Provinces, a body of fresh water formed by rain or melted snow. **2** a soft, deep, muddy place; mud hole. **3** *Cdn.* in the Northwest, a side-channel of a stream; snye. **4** on the Pacific coast, a shallow inlet of the sea; lagoon. **5** a state of hopeless discouragement or degradation. Also, **slew, slue.** [OE *slōh*]

slough[2] (sluf) *n.* **1** the old skin shed or cast off by a snake. **2** a layer of dead skin or tissue that drops or falls off as a wound, sore, etc. heals. **3** anything that has been shed or cast off: *As savages become civilized, they cast off the slough of primitive ways, beliefs, etc.* —*v.* **1** drop off; throw off; shed. **2** be shed or cast; drop or fall: *A scab sloughs off when new skin takes its place.* **3** in card games, discard (a losing card). [ME *slugh(e), slouh* < Gmc.; cf. G *Schlauch* skin, bag]

slough of despond (slou) a state of hopeless dejection; deep despondency.

slough·y[1] (slou′ē) *adj.* **slough·i·er, slough·i·est.** soft and muddy; full of soft, deep mud. [< *slough*[1]]

slough·y[2] (sluf′ē) *adj.* of dead skin; covered with dead skin. [< *slough*[2]]

Slo·vak (slō′vak) *n.* **1** a member of a Slavic people living in Slovakia, a region in E. Czechoslovakia. The Slovaks are closely related to the Bohemians and the Moravians. **2** their language. —*adj.* of or having to do with Slovakia, its people, or their language. [< Czech *Slovák,* originally, Slav]

Slo·vak·i·an (slō vak′ē ən) *adj. n.* Slovak.

slov·en[1] (sluv′ən) *n.* a person who is untidy, dirty, or careless in dress, appearance, habits, work, etc. —*adj.* untidy; dirty; careless. [? ult. < Flemish *sloef* dirty, Du. *slof* careless]

hat, āge, cãre, fär; let, ēqual, tėrm; it, īce
hot, ōpen, ôrder; oil, out; cup, pu̇t, rüle, ūse
əbove, takən, pencəl, lemən, circəs
ch, child; ng, long; sh, ship
th, thin; ᴛʜ, then; zh, measure

slov·en[2] (sluv′ən) *n. Cdn.* in the Atlantic Provinces, a long, low wagon having a high driver's box; dray. [origin uncertain]

Slo·vene (slō′vēn) *n.* **1** a member of a Slavic group of people living in Slovenia, a region in N.W. Yugoslavia. The Slovenes are closely related to the Croats, Serbians, and other southern Slavs. **2** their language. —*adj.* of or having to do with Slovenia, its people, or their language; Slovenian. [< G < OSlavic *Slověne,* literally, speaker < *slovo* word; distinguished from Germans who were called "mutes"]

Slo·ve·ni·an (slō vē′nē ən or slō vēn′yən) *adj. n.* Slovene.

slov·en·ly (sluv′ən lē) *adj.* **-li·er, -li·est,** *adv.* —*adj.* untidy, dirty, or careless in dress, appearance, habits, work, etc. —*adv.* in a slovenly manner. —**slov′en·li·ness,** *n.* —**Syn.** *adj.* unkempt, slatternly, slipshod.

slow (slō) *adj.* **1** taking a long time; taking longer than usual; not fast or quick: *a slow journey.* **2** behind time; running at less than proper speed: *a slow runner.* **3** indicating time earlier than the correct time: *a slow clock.* **4** causing a low or lower rate of speed: *slow ground, a slow track.* **5** burning or heating slowly or gently: *a slow flame.* **6** sluggish; naturally inactive: *a slow pupil.* **7** dull; not interesting: *a slow party.* **8** not brisk; slack: *Business is slow.* **9** behind the times; not smart or up-to-date: *a slow town.* **10** of time, passing slowly or heavily. —*v.* **1** make slow or slower; reduced the speed of: *slow down a car.* **2** become slow; go slower: *Slow up when you drive through a town.*
—*adv.* in a slow manner. [OE *slāw*] —**slow′ly,** *adv.* —**slow′ness,** *n.*

Syn. *adj.* **1 Slow, leisurely, deliberate** = taking a long time to do something or to happen. **Slow,** the general term, suggests taking longer than usual or necessary: *We took the slow train.* **Leisurely** suggests slowness because of having plenty of time: *I like leisurely meals.* **Deliberate,** describing people or their acts, suggests slowness due to care, thought, or self-control: *His speech is deliberate.* **7** wearisome, tiresome.

☞ **slow, slowly.** In standard English *slowly* is now the usual form of the adverb except in set phrases (*go slow, drive slow*) and in the comparative or superlative (where *slower* or *slowest* is often used instead of *more* or *most slowly*).

slow match a fuse that burns very slowly, used for setting fire to gunpowder, dynamite, etc.

slow-mo·tion (slō′mō′shən) *adj.* **1** moving at less than normal speed. **2** showing action at much less than its actual speed.

slow-poke (slō′pōk′) *n. Informal.* one who is very slow; laggard.

slow time standard time, as opposed to daylight saving time (fast time).

slow-wit·ted (slō′wit′id) *adj.* slow at thinking; dull; stupid.

slow·worm (slō′wėrm′) *n.* blindworm.

sloyd (sloid) *n.* a system of manual training by means of graded courses in woodworking, etc., originating in Sweden. Also, **sloid, slojd.** [< Swedish *slöjd* skill]

slub (slub) *v.* **slubbed, slub·bing,** *n.* —*v.* twist (wool, yarn, etc.) slightly before spinning. —*n.* **1** a slightly twisted piece of cotton, silk, or wool. **2** an uneven lump in a strand of yarn. [cf. MDu. *slubbe*]

sludge (sluj) *n.* **1** soft mud; mire; slush. **2** a soft, thick, muddy mixture, deposit, sediment, etc. **3** small broken pieces of floating ice. [origin uncertain]

slue[1] (slü) *v.* **slued, slu·ing,** *n.* slew[2].

slue[2] (slü) *n.* slough[1].

slug[1] (slug) *n.* **1** a slow-moving animal resembling a snail, without a shell or having only a very small shell. **2** a caterpillar or larva that resembles a slug. **3** any slow-moving person, animal, wagon, etc. **4** a piece of lead or other metal for firing from a gun. **5** a lump or disk of metal, especially one used (usually illegally) in a slot machine in place of a coin. **6** in printing: **a** a strip of metal used to space lines of type. A slug is more than 1/16 of an inch in thickness. **b** a line of type cast in one piece by a linotype machine. [ME *slugg* sluggard, ? < Scand.; cf. dial. Swedish *slogga* be sluggish]

slug[2] (slug) *v.* **slugged, slug·ging,** *n. Informal.* —*v.* hit hard with the fist; hit hard. —*n.* **1** a hard blow with the fist. **2** *Slang.* a drink; shot: *a slug of whisky.* [origin uncertain] —**slug′ger,** *n.*

slug·gard (slug′ərd) *n.* a lazy, idle person. —*adj.* lazy; idle. [ME < *slug* be slothful + *-ard,* personal suffix with derogatory sense, as in *drunkard.* See SLUG[1].]

slug·gish (slug′ish) *adj.* **1** slow-moving; not active; lacking energy or vigor: *a sluggish mind.* **2** lazy; idle. **3** moving slowly; having little motion. A sluggish river has very little current. [< *slug*[1]] —**slug′gish·ly,** *adv.* —**slug′gish·ness,** *n.* —**Syn. 1** dull, inert.

sluice (slüs) *n. v.* **sluiced, sluic·ing.** —*n.* **1** a structure having a gate for holding back or controlling the water of a canal, river, or lake. **2** a gate that holds back or controls the flow of water. When the water behind a dam gets too high, the sluices are opened. **3** the water held back or controlled by such a gate. **4** something that controls the flow or passage of anything: *War opens the sluices of hatred and bloodshed.* **5** a long, sloping trough through which water flows, used to wash gold from sand, dirt, or gravel. **6** a channel for carrying off water.
—*v.* **1** let out or draw off (water) by opening a sluice. **2** flow or pour in a stream; rush: *Water sluiced down the channel.* **3** flush or cleanse with a rush of water; pour or throw water over. **4** wash (gold) from sand, dirt, or gravel in a sluice. **5** send (logs, etc.) along a channel of water. [ME < OF *escluse,* ult. < L *ex-* out + *claudere* shut]

A sluice for washing gold (def. 5)

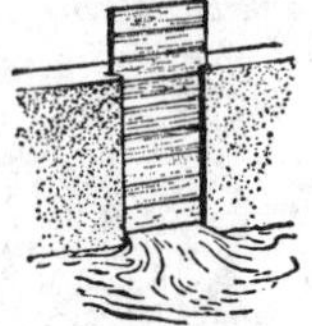
A sluice gate

sluice-box (slüs′boks′) *n.* formerly, in placer mining, a long sluice fitted with riffles, in which gold is separated from gravel, muck, etc.

sluice gate a gate to control the flow of water in a sluice.

slum (slum) *n. v.* **slummed, slum·ming.** —*n.* **1** a street, alley, etc. in a crowded, dirty part of a city or town. **2 the slums,** a crowded, dirty part of a city or town, where the poorest people live. —*v.* go into or visit the slums. [origin uncertain]

slum·ber (slum′bər) *v.* **1** sleep, especially in a peaceful manner. **2** pass in sleep: *The baby slumbers away the hours.* **3** be inactive: *The volcano had slumbered for years.* —*n.* **1** a light sleep, especially one that is peaceful. **2** an inactive state or condition. [ult. < OE *slūma,* n.] —**slum′ber·er,** *n.*

slum·ber·ous (slum′bər əs or slum′brəs) *adj.* **1** sleepy; heavy with drowsiness: *slumberous eyelids.* **2** causing or inducing sleep. **3** having to do with, characterized by, or suggestive of sleep. **4** inactive; sluggish. **5** calm; quiet. —**slum′ber·ous·ly,** *adv.*

slum·brous (slum′brəs) *adj.* slumberous. —**slum′brous·ly,** *adv.*

slum·mer (slum′ər) *n.* a person who visits slums for charitable purposes, curiosity, etc.

slump (slump) *v.* drop heavily; fall suddenly: *The boy's feet slumped repeatedly through the rotting ice.* —*n.* **1** a heavy or sudden fall. **2** a great or sudden decline in prices, activity, etc. [? imitative]

slung (slung) *v.* pt. and pp. of **sling.**

slung shot a piece of metal, stone, etc. fastened to a short strap, chain, etc., used as a weapon.

slunk (slungk) *v.* a pt. and a pp. of **slink.**

slur (slėr) *v.* **slurred, slur·ring,** *n.* —*v.* **1** pass lightly over; go through hurriedly or in a careless way. **2** pronounce indistinctly: *Many persons slur "How do you do?"* **3** speak or write sounds, letters, etc. so indistinctly that they run into each other. **4** in music: **a** sing or play (two or more tones of different pitch) without a break; run together in a smooth, connected manner. **b** mark with a slur. **5** harm the reputation of; insult; slight. [< n.]
—*n.* **1** a slurred pronunciation, sound, etc. **2** in music: **a** a slurring of tones. **b** a curved mark (⌢) (⌣) indicating this. **3** a blot or stain (upon reputation); an insulting or slighting remark: *Malicious rumor left a slur on his good name.* [ME *slor* mud]

A slur in music

slurp (slėrp) *Slang.* —*v.* eat or drink noisily. —*n.* a slurping sound. [< Du. *slurpen* lap]

slur·ry (slėr′ē) *n.* **-ries,** *v.* —*n.* a thin mixture of powdered coal, ore, cement, etc. and water. —*v.* make into a slurry. [related to SLUR]

slush (slush) *n.* **1** partly melted snow; snow and water mixed. **2** soft mud. **3** *Informal.* silly, sentimental talk, writing, etc. **4** grease. [origin uncertain]

slush fund money collected or set aside for dishonest purposes, such as bribery or improper political or business lobbying.

slush hole *Cdn.* especially in the North, a patch of rotten ice on the surface of a lake or river.

slush·y (slush′ē) *adj.* **slush·i·er, slush·i·est. 1** having much slush. **2** of or like slush. —**slush′i·ness,** *n.*

slut (slut) *n.* **1** a dirty, untidy woman. **2** a woman of loose morals. [ME *slutte, slotte*; origin uncertain]

slut·tish (slut′ish) *adj.* **1** dirty; untidy. **2** loose in morals. —**slut′tish·ly,** *adv.* —**slut′tish·ness,** *n.*

sly (slī) *adj.* **sly·er** or **sli·er, sly·est** or **sli·est,** *n.* —*adj.* **1** able to do things without letting others know; acting secretly: *The sly cat stole the meat while the cook's back was turned.* **2** cunning; crafty; tricky; wily: *a sly plot.* **3** such as a sly person or animal would use: *She asked sly questions.* **4** playfully mischievous or knowing: *a sly wink.* —*n.* **on the sly,** in a sly way; secretly. [ME *slēgh* skilful < ON *slǽgr,* originally, able to strike < *slá* slay] —**sly′ness,** *n.*

Syn. *adj.* **1** surreptitious, stealthy, furtive. **2 Sly, cunning** = having or showing ability to get what one wants by secret or indirect means. **Sly** emphasizes lack of frankness and straightforwardness, and suggests stealthy actions or secrecy and deceit in dealing with others: *That sly girl managed to get her best friend's job.* **Cunning** emphasizes an animal-like cleverness in getting the better of others by tricks or schemes, unfair dealing, or cheating: *A baby is cunning enough to learn quickly that someone will pick him up if he cries.*

sly·ly (slī′lē) *adv.* in a sly manner; secretly. Also, **slily.**

Sm samarium.

S.M. Sergeant-Major.

smack[1] (smak) *n.* **1** a slight taste or flavor: *The sauce had a smack of nutmeg.* **2** a trace; suggestion: *The old sailor still had a smack of the sea about him.* —*v.* have a smack: *The Irishman's speech smacked of the Old Country.* [OE *smæcc*] —**Syn.** *n.* **2** touch, dash, tinge.

smack[2] (smak) *v.* **1** open (the lips) quickly so as to make a sharp sound. **2** kiss loudly. **3** slap. **4** crack (a whip, etc.). —*n.* **1** a smacking movement of the lips. **2** the sharp sound that is made in this way. **3** a loud kiss, slap, or crack. —*adv. Informal.* **1** directly; squarely: *He fell smack on his face.* **2** suddenly and sharply; with or as if with a smack. [ult. imitative]

A smack

smack[3] (smak) *n.* **1** a small sailboat with one mast. **2** a similar fishing boat with a well for keeping fish alive. [probably < Du. *smak*]

smack·er (smak′ər) *n.* **1** one that smacks. **2** *Informal.* a resounding kiss; smack. **3** *Slang.* a dollar.

smack·ing (smak′ing) *adj.* lively, brisk, or strong.

small (smol or smôl) *adj.* **1** not large; little; not large as compared with other things of the same kind: *a small house.* **2** not great in amount, degree, extent, duration, value, strength, etc.: *a small dose, small hope of success. The cent is our smallest coin.* **3** not important: *a small matter.* **4** not prominent; of low social position; humble; poor: *People great and small mourned Laurier's death.* **5** having little land, capital, etc.: *a small farmer, a small dealer.* **6** gentle; soft; low: *a small voice, a small crumbling sound.* **7** mean: *A man with a small nature is not generous.* **8** of letters, not capital. **9 feel small,** be ashamed or humiliated.
—*adv.* **1** into small pieces. **2** in low tones. **3 sing small,** change to a humble tone or manner.
—*n.* that which is small. [OE *smæl*] —**small′ness,** *n.*
—**Syn.** *adj.* **1** diminutive, undersized, tiny, minute. See **little. 2** slight, inconsiderable. **3** trifling, insignificant, trivial. **7** selfish, illiberal, stingy.

small arms firearms easily carried by a person, such as rifles or revolvers.

small beer 1 weak beer. **2** matters of little or no consequence.

small capital a capital letter that is slightly smaller that the regular capital letter. This sentence shows 7 point CAPITALS and SMALL CAPITALS.

small change 1 coins of small value, such as nickels, dimes, etc. **2** anything small and unimportant.

small·clothes (smol′klōz′ or -klōᴛʜz′, smôl′klōz′ or -klōᴛʜz′) *n.pl.* knee breeches, especially, close-fitting ones.

small fry 1 babies or children; small or young creatures. **2** small fish. **3** unimportant people or things.

small hours the early hours of the morning.

small intestine the slender part of the bowels, extending from the stomach to the large intestine, about twenty feet long in grown people.

small·ish (smol′ish or smôl′ish) *adj.* rather small.

small letter an ordinary letter, not a capital.

small-mind·ed (smol′mīn′did or smôl′-) *adj.* narrow-minded; petty; mean. .

small of the back the narrowest part of the back.

small potatoes *Informal.* an unimportant person or thing; unimportant persons or things.

small·pox (smol′poks′ or smôl′-) *n.* a contagious disease characterized by fever and blisterlike eruptions on the skin that often leave permanent scars shaped like little pits.

small-scale (smol′skāl′ or smôl′-) *adj.* **1** small in operation or scope; limited. **2** drawn to a small scale: *small-scale maps.*

small talk conversation about unimportant matters; chit-chat.

small-time (smol′tīm′ or smôl′-) *adj. Slang.* minor; mediocre; petty.

small-town (smol′toun′ or smôl′-) *adj.* **1** of or coming from a small town. **2** narrow; provincial: *small-town bigotry.*

smarm (smärm) *v. Brit. Informal.* act in a toadying or obsequiously flattering way. [var. of dial. *smalm* plaster down]

smarm·y (smärm′ē) *adj. Brit. Informal.* obsequiously flattering; toadying.

smart (smärt) *v.* **1** feel sharp pain: *His eyes smarted.* **2** cause sharp pain: *The cut smarts.* **3** feel distress or irritation: *He smarted from the scolding.* **4** suffer: *He shall smart for this.* [OE *smeortan*]
—*n.* a sharp pain. [< v.]
—*adj.* **1** sharp; severe: *He gave the horse a smart blow.* **2** keen; active; lively: *They walked at a smart pace.* **3** clever; bright: *a smart child.* **4** fresh and neat; in good order: *He looked smart in his uniform.* **5** stylish; fashionable. **6** *Informal or dialect.* fairly large; considerable. **7** witty, humorous, or clever in an annoying way.
—*adv.* in a smart manner. [OE *smeart*] —**smart′ly,** *adv.* —**smart′ness,** *n.*

smart al·eck or **al·ec** (al′ik) a conceited, obnoxious person.

hat, āge, cãre, fär; let, ēqual, tėrm; it, īce
hot, ōpen, ôrder; oil, out; cup, pu̇t, rüle, ūse
əbove, takən, pencəl, lemən, circəs
ch, child; ng, long; sh, ship
th, thin; ᴛʜ, then; zh, measure

smart·en (smär′tən) *v.* **1** improve in appearance; brighten. **2** make or become brisker.

smart·weed (smärt′wēd′) *n.* a weed growing in wet places, that causes a smarting sensation when brought into contact with the skin.

smash (smash) *v.* **1** break into pieces with violence and noise: *smash a window.* **2** destroy; shatter; ruin: *smash an argument.* **3** be broken to pieces: *The dishes smashed on the floor.* **4** become ruined. **5** rush violently; crash: *The car smashed into a tree.* **6** crush; defeat: *smash an attack.* **7** in tennis or baseball, hit (a ball) with a hard, fast, overhand stroke. **8** *Informal.* hit a hard blow.
—*n.* **1** a violent breaking; shattering; crash: *the smash of two cars.* **2** the sound of a smash or crash: *the smash of broken glass.* **3** a crushing defeat; disaster. **4** a business failure; bankruptcy. **5** in tennis or baseball, a hard, fast overhand stroke. **6** *Informal.* a hard blow. **7** a drink made of water, mint, sugar, and brandy or other alcoholic liquor. **8** *Informal.* a smash hit. **9 to smash, a** into broken pieces; into bits. **b** to ruin. [a blend of *smack*[2] and *mash*] —**Syn.** *v.* **1** See **break.**

smash hit a very successful play, motion picture, recording, etc.

smash·ing (smash′ing) *adj. Informal.* fine; excellent; splendid.

smash-up (smash′up′) *n.* **1** a collision involving much damage; wreck. **2** a business failure; bankruptcy. **3** a great misfortune; disaster.

smat·ter (smat′ər) *n.* a slight knowledge. [cf. Swedish *smattra* rattle]

smat·ter·ing (smat′ər ing) *n.* a slight or superficial knowledge: *He has only a smattering of French.*

smaze (smāz) *n.* a combination of smoke and haze in the air. [blend of *smoke* and *haze*]

smear (smēr) *v.* **1** cover or stain with anything sticky, greasy, or dirty: *Her fingers were smeared with jam.* **2** rub or spread (oil, grease, paint, etc.). **3** rub or wipe (a brush hand, cloth, etc.) so as to make a mark or stain. **4** receive a mark or stain; be smeared: *Wet paint smears easily.* **5** harm; soil; spoil: *smear a person's reputation.*
—*n.* **1** a mark or stain left by smearing. **2** a small amount of something spread on a slide for microscopic examination, or on the surface of a culture medium. **3** the act of smearing a person's reputation; slander. [OE *smerian, smirian* < *smeoru* grease]

smear·y (smēr′ē) *adj.* **smear·i·er, smear·i·est. 1** smeared **2** tending to smear. —**smear′i·ness,** *n.*

smell (smel) *v.* **smelled** or **smelt, smell·ing,** *n.* —*v.* **1** perceive with the nose: *I smell smoke in the air.* **2** detect or recognize smells. **3** give out a smell. **4** give out a bad smell; have a bad smell. **5** find a trace or suggestion of: *We smelled trouble.* **6** have the smell (*of*); have the trace (*of*): *The plan smells of trickery.* **7** hunt or find by smelling or as if by smelling: *The dog will smell out a thief.* **8 smell up,** *Informal.* cause to have a bad smell.
—*n.* **1** an act of smelling; sniff. **2** the sense of smelling: *Smell is keener in dogs than in men.* **3** the quality in a thing that affects the sense of smell: *the smell of burning cloth.* **4** a trace; suggestion. [ME *smelle(n)*; origin uncertain]
Syn. *n.* **3 Smell, odor** = the property or quality of a thing that affects the sense organs of the nose. **Smell** is the general word, used especially when the effect on the sense organs is emphasized: *I like the smells in the country after rain.* **Odor** is often interchanged with *smell,* but emphasizes and applies particularly to the actual property or quality itself, as belonging to and coming from what is smelled: *I find the odor of hay especially pleasing.*

smell·er (smel′ər) *n.* **1** a person or thing that smells. **2** a person who tests by smelling. **3** a sensitive hair or feeler, such as a whisker of a cat. **4** *Slang.* the nose.

smelling salts a form of ammonia that, when inhaled, helps to relieve faintness, headaches, etc.

smell·y (smel′ē) *adj.* **smell·i·er, smell·i·est.** having or giving out a strong or unpleasant smell.

smelt[1] (smelt) *v.* **1** melt (ore) in order to get the metal out of it. **2** obtain (metal) from ore by melting. **3** refine (impure metal) by melting. [< MDu. or MLG *smelten*]

smelt[2] (smelt) *n.* **smelt** or **smelts.** a small, edible fish having silvery scales. [OE]

smelt[3] (smelt) *v.* a pt. and a pp. of **smell.**

smelt·er (smel′tər) *n.* **1** a person whose work or business is smelting ores or metals. **2** a place where ores or metals are smelted. **3** a furnace for smelting ores.

smid·gen (smij′ən) *n. Informal.* a tiny piece or amount; mite. [origin uncertain]

smi·lax (smī′laks) *n.* **1** a twining, trailing plant or vine, much used by florists in decoration. **2** any of a large group of woody vines having prickly stems, umbrella-shaped clusters of flowers, and blackish or red berries. [< L < Gk.]

smile (smīl) *v.* **smiled, smil·ing,** *n.* —*v.* **1** look pleased or amused; show pleasure, favor, kindness, amusement, etc. by an upward curve of the mouth. **2** look pleasant or agreeable; look with favor. **3** bring, put, drive, etc. by smiling: *Smile your tears away.* **4** give (a smile): *She smiled a sunny smile.* **5** express by a smile: *She smiled consent.* **6** show scorn, disdain, etc. by a curve of the mouth: *She smiled bitterly.* —*n.* **1** the act of smiling. **2** a favoring look or regard; a pleasant look or aspect. [ME *smile(n)*] —**smil′er,** *n.* —**smil′ing·ly,** *adv.*

smirch (smėrch) *v.* make dirty; soil with soot, dirt, dust, dishonor, disgrace, etc. —*n.* a dirty mark; blot; stain. [ME *smorch*; ? < OF *esmorcher* torture, ult. < L *ex-* (intensive) + LL *mordicare* bite]

smirk (smėrk) *v.* smile in an affected, silly, self-satisfied way. —*n.* an affected, silly, self-satisfied smile. [OE *smearcian* smile]

smit (smit) *v.* a pp. and an obs. pt. of **smite.**

smitch (smich) *n. Informal.* a smidgen.

smite (smīt) *v.* **smote** or (obs.) **smit, smit·ten** or **smit, smit·ing. 1** strike; strike hard; hit hard. **2** come with force (*upon*): *The sound of a blacksmith's hammer smote upon their ears.* **3** affect with a sudden pain, disease, etc.: *The thief's conscience smote him.* **4** strike down; punish severely; destroy. [OE *smītan*] —**smit′er,** *n.*

smith (smith) *n.* **1** a man who makes or shapes things out of metal. **2** a blacksmith. [OE]

smith·er·eens (smiᴛʜ′ər ēnz′) *n.pl. Informal.* small pieces; bits. [apparently from Irish Gaelic *smiderini* fragments. Akin to SMITE.]

smith·y (smith′ē or smiᴛʜ′ē) *n.* **smith·ies.** the workshop of a smith, especially a blacksmith. [ME < ON *smithja.* Akin to SMITH.]

smit·ten (smit′ən) *adj.* **1** hard hit; struck. **2** suddenly and strongly affected. **3** *Informal.* very much in love. —*v.* pp. of **smite.**

smock (smok) *n.* a loose, coatlike outer garment, usually of cotton, worn to protect clothing. —*v.* ornament (a dress, blouse, etc.) with a honeycomb pattern made of lines of stitches crossing each other diagonally. [OE *smocc*]

smock·ing (smok′ing) *n.* a honeycomb pattern used to ornament smocks, dresses, etc.

smog (smog) *n.* a combination in the air of smoke or other chemical fumes and fog. [a blend of *smoke* and *fog*]

smoke (smōk) *n. v.* **smoked, smok·ing.** —*n.* **1** the visible mixture of gases and particles of carbon that rises when anything burns; a cloud from anything burning. **2** something resembling this. **3** something unsubstantial, quickly passing, or without result. **4** that which is smoked; a cigar, cigarette, pipe, etc. **5** the act or period of smoking tobacco.
—*v.* **1** give off smoke, steam, etc.: *The fireplace smokes.* **2** draw the smoke from (a pipe, cigar, or cigarette) into the mouth and puff it out again. **3** expose to the action of smoke. **4** cure (meat, fish, etc.) by smoking. **5** drive (out) by smoke, or as if by smoke. **6** make, bring, pass, etc. by smoking. **7** color, darken, or stain with smoke. **8** *Archaic.* find out; suspect; notice. **9** *Archaic.* ridicule; make fun of. **10 smoke out, a** drive out with smoke. **b** find out and make known. [OE *smoca*] —**Syn.** *n.* **2** fume, reek.

smoke drift a cloud of smoke seen at a distance and indicating a forest fire.

smoke·house (smōk′hous′) *n.* a building or place in which meat, fish, etc. are treated with smoke to keep them from spoiling.

smoke·jump·er (smōk′jump′ər) *n.* a man who, especially equipped to fight forest fires, is dropped by parachute into a burning area.

smoke·less (smōk′lis) *adj.* **1** making or giving off little or no smoke. **2** having little or no smoke.

smokeless powder a substitute for ordinary gun powder that gives off little or no smoke when it explodes.

smok·er (smōk′ər) *n.* **1** a person who smokes tobacco. **2** on a railway car, a compartment set aside for passengers wishing to smoke. **3** an informal gathering of men for smoking, card-playing, and other entertainment.

smoke screen 1 a mass of thick smoke used to hide a ship, airplane, etc. from the enemy. **2** anything that hides or obscures a plan, project, etc.: *a smoke screen of false information.*

smoke·stack (smōk′stak′) *n.* **1** a tall chimney. **2** a pipe that discharges smoke, etc.

smoke tree a small tree or shrub having flower clusters that look somewhat like puffs of smoke.

smok·y (smōk′ē) *adj.* **smok·i·er, smok·i·est. 1** giving off much smoke: *a smoky fire.* **2** full of smoke. **3** darkened or stained with smoke. **4** like smoke or suggesting smoke: *a smoky gray, a smoky taste.* —**smok′i·ly,** *adv.* —**smok′i·ness,** *n.*

smol·der (smōl′dər) *v. n.* smoulder.

smolt (smōlt) *n.* a young salmon that has ceased to be a parr and is ready to descend, or has descended, to the sea for the first time. [ME. Probably related to SMELT[2].]

smooth (smüᴛʜ) *adj.* **1** having an even surface, like glass, silk, or still water; flat; level: *smooth stones.* **2** free from unevenness or roughness: *smooth sailing, a smooth voyage.* **3** without lumps: *smooth sauce.* **4** without hair: *a smooth face.* **5** without trouble or difficulty; easy: *a smooth course of affairs.* **6** calm; serene: *a smooth temper.* **7** polished; pleasant; polite: *That salesman is a smooth talker.* **8** not harsh in sound or taste: *smooth verses, smooth wine.*
—*v.* **1** make smooth or smoother: *Smooth this dress with a hot iron. He smoothed out the ball of crushed paper and read it.* **2** make easy. **3 smooth away,** get rid of (troubles, difficulties, etc.). **4 smooth down,** calm; soothe. **5 smooth over,** make (something) seem less wrong or unpleasant.
—*adv.* in a smooth manner.
—*n.* **1** the act of smoothing. **2** a smooth part or place. [OE *smōth*] —**smooth′er,** *n.* —**smooth′ly,** *adv.* —**smooth′ness,** *n.* —**Syn.** *adj.* **1** plain, sleek, glossy. See **level. 6** placid, unruffled.

smooth·bore (smüᴛʜ′bôr′) *adj.* not rifled. A smoothbore gun has no grooves in its barrel. —*n.* a gun whose barrel is not rifled.

smooth-faced (smüᴛʜ′fāst′) *adj.* **1** having a smooth face; beardless; clean-shaven. **2** having a smooth surface. **3** deceptively agreeable in speech and manner: *a smooth-faced hypocrite.*

smooth·ie or **smooth·y** (smüᴛʜ′ē) *n.* **smooth·ies.** *Slang.* a smooth, persuasive, often insincere person.

smooth-spo·ken (smüᴛʜ′spō′kən) *adj.* speaking easily and pleasantly; polished in speech.

smooth-tongued (smüᴛʜ′tungd′) *adj.* speaking smoothly; agreeable; suave; plausible.

smor·gas·bord (smôr′gəs bôrd′) *n.* a buffet luncheon or supper consisting of a variety of hors d'oeuvres, salads, fish, meats, etc. [< Swedish *smörgåsbord* hors d'oeuvres < *smörgås* open sandwich + *bord* table]

smote (smōt) *v.* a pt. of **smite.**

smoth·er (smuᴛʜ′ər) *v.* **1** make unable to get air; kill by depriving of air: *The wicked king smothered the two little princes.* **2** be unable to breathe freely; suffocate: *We almost smothered in that stuffy room.* **3** cover thickly: *In the fall the grass is smothered with leaves.* **4** deaden or put out by covering thickly: *The fire is smothered by ashes.* **5** keep back; check; suppress: *He smothered a sharp reply.* **6** cook in a covered pot or baking dish: *smothered*

chicken, smothered cabbage. [< n.]
—*n.* **1** a cloud of dust, smoke, spray, etc. **2** anything that smothers. **3** the condition of being smothered. [ME *smorther*, n., based on OE *smorian* suffocate] **—smoth′er·er,** *n.*

smoth·er·y (smuтн′ər ē) *adj.* tending to smother; full of dust, smoke, spray, etc.

smoul·der or **smol·der** (smōl′dər) *v.* **1** burn and smoke without flame: *The fire smouldered most of the night.* **2** exist or continue in a suppressed condition: *His anger smouldered as he waited for a chance to fight back.* —*n.* a slow, smoky burning without flame. [ME *smolderen*; akin to Du. *smeulen*]

smudge (smuj) *n. v.* **smudged, smudg·ing.** —*n.* **1** a dirty mark; smear. **2** a smoky fire made to drive away insects or to protect fruit from frost. —*v.* **1** mark with dirty streaks; smear: *The child's drawing was smudged.* **2** use a smudge or smudges, especially in an orchard. [origin uncertain]

smudg·y (smuj′ē) *adj.* **smudg·i·er, smudg·i·est.** smudged; marked with smudges. **—smudg′i·ly,** *adv.* **—smudg′i·ness,** *n.*

smug (smug) *adj.* **smug·ger, smug·gest. 1** too pleased with one's own goodness, cleverness, respectability, etc.; self-satisfied; complacent: *Nothing disturbs the smug beliefs of some narrow-minded people.* **2** sleek; neat; trim. [originally, neat, spruce; probably < Du. or LG *smuk* spruce, adj.] **—smug′ly,** *adv.* **—smug′ness,** *n.*

smug·gle (smug′əl) *v.* **-gled, -gling. 1** bring into or take out of a country secretly and against the law: *He was trying to smuggle heroin into Canada.* **2** bring, take, put, etc. secretly: *Bob tried to smuggle his puppy into the house.* [< LG *smuggeln*]

smug·gler (smug′lər) *n.* **1** a person who smuggles. **2** a ship used in smuggling.

smut (smut) *n. v.* **smut·ted, smut·ting.** —*n.* **1** soot, dirt, etc. **2** a place soiled with smut. **3** indecent, obscene talk or writing. **4** a plant disease in which the ears of grain are changed to a black dust. —*v.* **1** soil or be soiled with smut. **2** affect (a plant) with the disease smut; become affected with smut. [OE *smitte*; influenced by *smudge*, *smutch*]

smutch (smuch) *v.* blacken with soot or dirt; smudge. —*n.* a dirty mark; smudge. [origin uncertain. Related to SMUDGE.]

smut·ty (smut′ē) *adj.* **-ti·er, -ti·est. 1** soiled with smut, soot, etc.; dirty. **2** indecent; nasty; obscene. **3** having the plant disease called smut. **—smut′ti·ness,** *n.*

Sn tin. (for L *stannum*)

snack (snak) *n.* **1** a light meal: *He eats a snack before going to bed.* **2** a share; portion. —*v.* have a little bit to eat between meals: *He's forever snacking and will always be overweight.* [< MLG *snakken*]

snack bar a counter where light meals, coffee, etc. are served.

snaf·fle (snaf′əl) *n. v.* **-fled, -fling.** —*n.* a slender, jointed bit used on a bridle. —*v.* **1** control or manage by a snaffle. **2** *Informal.* pilfer; steal. [cf. Du. *snavel* beak]

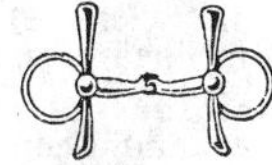
A snaffle

sna·fu (sna fü′) *adj. v.* **-fued, -fu·ing.** *Slang.* —*adj.* in great disorder; snarled; confused. —*v.* **1** put in disorder or in a chaotic state. **2** mishandle. [from the initial letters of "situation normal —all fouled up"]

snag (snag) *n. v.* **snagged, snag·ging.** —*n.* **1** a tree or branch held fast in a river or lake. Snags are dangerous to boats. **2** any sharp or rough projecting point, such as the broken end of a branch. **3** the stump of a tooth; projecting tooth. **4** a hidden or unexpected obstacle: *We hit a snag.* **5** a tear resulting from a pulled or broken thread.
—*v.* **1** hinder. **2** run or catch on a snag. **3** clear of snags. **4** tear or pull (fabric) so as to make a snag. [? < Scand.; cf. dial. Norwegian *snage* point of land]

snag·gle·tooth (snag′əl tüth′) *n.* **-teeth.** a tooth that grows apart from or beyond the others.

snag·gle-toothed (snag′əl tütht′) *adj.* having uneven, broken, or projecting teeth.

snag·gy (snag′ē) *adj.* **-gi·er, -gi·est. 1** having snags: *a snaggy tree, a snaggy river.* **2** projecting sharply or roughly.

hat, āge, cãre, fär; let, ēqual, tėrm; it, īce
hot, ōpen, ôrder; oil, out; cup, pu̇t, rüle, ūse
əbove, takən, pencəl, lemən, circəs
ch, child; ng, long; sh, ship
th, thin; ᴛʜ, then; zh, measure

snail (snāl) *n.* **1** a small, soft-bodied mollusc that crawls very slowly. Most snails have spirally coiled shells on their backs into which they can withdraw for protection. **2** a lazy, slow-moving person. [OE *snegel*]

snake (snāk) *n. v.* **snaked, snak·ing.** —*n.* **1** a long, slender, crawling reptile without limbs. Some snakes are poisonous. **2** a sly, treacherous person. **3 snake in the grass,** a lurking threat or enemy; an unexpected source of danger: *She thought the man a friend, but he turned out to be a real snake in the grass.* —*v.* **1** move, wind, or curve like a snake. **2** *Informal.* drag; haul. **3** *Informal.* jerk. [OE *snaca*] **—snake′like′,** *adj.*

snake dance 1 an informal procession in which people dance in zigzag or serpentine style to celebrate a victory, etc. **2** among Hopi Indians, a ceremonial rain dance in which the chief dancers carry live snakes in their mouths.

snake pit 1 a pit filled with snakes. **2** *Informal.* a place of utter disorder and confusion, such as an overcrowded, antiquated prison or asylum.

snake·root (snāk′rüt′) *n.* **1** any of various plants whose roots have been regarded as a remedy for snake bites. **2** the root of such a plant.

snake·skin (snāk′skin′) *n.* **1** the skin of a snake. **2** a leather made from it.

snak·y (snāk′ē) *adj.* **snak·i·er, snak·i·est. 1** of a snake or snakes. **2** like a snake; like the curving and turning of a snake; twisting; winding. **3** having many snakes. **4** sly; venomous; treacherous. **—snak′i·ly,** *adv.* **—snak′i·ness,** *n.*

snap (snap) *v.* **snapped, snap·ping,** *n. adj.* —*v.* **1** make or cause to make a sudden, sharp sound: *This wood snaps as it burns.* **2** move, shut, catch, etc. with a snap: *The latch snapped.* **3** break suddenly or sharply: *The violin string snapped.* **4** become suddenly unable to endure a strain: *His nerves snapped.* **5** make a sudden, quick bite or snatch: *The dog snapped at the child's hand. The dog snapped up the meat.* **6** seize eagerly: *She snapped at the chance to go to Europe.* **7** speak quickly and sharply: *"Silence!" snapped the teacher.* **8** move quickly and sharply: *The soldiers snapped to attention. Her eyes snapped with anger.* **9** take a snapshot of. **10** in football, pass the ball between the legs. **11 snap back,** make a quick recovery. **12 snap out of it,** *Slang.* change one's attitude, habit, etc. suddenly.
—*n.* **1** a quick, sharp sound: *The box shut with a snap.* **2** a sudden, sharp breaking or the sound of breaking. **3** a quick, sudden bite or snatch. **4** quick, sharp speech. **5** *Informal.* **a** a quick, sharp way: *She moves with snap and energy.* **b** liveliness or crispness in writing: *a delightful little tale, full of romance, snap, and brightness.* **6** a short spell of cold weather. **7** a fastener; clasp: *Several of the snaps of your dress are unfastened.* **8** a snapping of the fingers, especially as a sign of disregard, contempt, etc. **9** a thin, crisp cookie: *a gingersnap.* **10** *Informal.* a snapshot. **11** *Informal.* a snapdragon. **12** *Slang.* an easy job, piece of work, etc. **13** in football: **a** the act of passing the ball between the legs by the centre. **b** the player in the middle of the line of scrimmage; the centre. **14 not a snap,** not at all.
—*adj.* **1** made or done suddenly: *A snap judgment is likely to be wrong.* **2** *Slang.* easy. [< MDu. or MLG *snappen*]

snap·drag·on (snap′drag′ən) *n.* **1** a garden plant having spikes of showy flowers of crimson, purple, white, yellow, etc. **2** an old game in which people try to snatch raisins from burning brandy.

snap·per (snap′ər) *n.* **1** a person or thing that snaps. **2** a snapping turtle. **3** any of several large, edible fish of tropical seas.

snapping beetle any of several beetles that jump with a snapping or clicking sound when turned on the back.

snapping turtle a large, savage turtle of certain North

American rivers, that has powerful jaws with which it snaps at its prey.

snap·pish (snap′ish) *adj.* 1 apt to snap. 2 quick and sharp in speech or manner; impatient. **—snap′pish·ly,** *adv.* **—snap′pish·ness,** *n.* **—Syn.** 2 testy, crabbed, cross, irascible, petulant.

snap·py (snap′ē) *adj.* **-pi·er, -pi·est.** 1 snappish; sharp. 2 snapping or crackling in sound: *a snappy fire.* 3 *Informal.* having snap, crispness, smartness, liveliness, pungency, etc.: *a snappy cheese.* 4 **make it snappy,** *Informal.* be quick! hurry up! **—snap′pi·ly,** *adv.* **—snap′pi·ness,** *n.*

snap shot *Cdn.* in hockey, an expert wrist shot quickly made and aimed at the goal.

snap·shot (snap′shot′) *n. v.* **-shot·ted, -shot·ting.** **—***n.* 1 a photograph taken in an instant. 2 a quick shot taken without much time for careful aim. **—***v.* take a snapshot of.

snare[1] (snãr) *n. v.* **snared, snar·ing.** **—***n.* 1 a noose for catching small animals and birds. 2 a trap: *Popularity is a snare in which fools are caught.* **—***v.* 1 catch with a snare. 2 trap. [ME < ON *snara*] **—snar′er,** *n.* **—Syn.** *n.* 1 See **trap.**

snare[2] (snãr) *n.* one of the strings of gut or rawhide stretched across the bottom of a snare drum. [probably < MDu. or MLG]

snare drum a small drum having strings of gut or rawhide stretched across the bottom to make a rattling sound.

The bottom of a snare drum

snarl[1] (snärl) *v.* 1 growl sharply and show one's teeth: *The dog snarled at the stranger.* 2 speak harshly in a sharp, angry tone. 3 say or express with a snarl. **—***n.* 1 a sharp, angry growl. 2 sharp, angry words. [earlier *snar*; cf. MDu. or MLG *snarren* rattle. Akin to SNORE.] **—snarl′er,** *n.* **—snarl′ing·ly,** *adv.*

snarl[2] (snärl) *n.* 1 a tangle: *She combed the snarls out of her hair.* 2 a confusion: *His legal affairs were in a snarl.* **—***v.* 1 tangle. 2 confuse. [ult. < *snare*[1] or its source]

snarl·y[1] (snär′lē) *adj.* **snarl·i·er, snarl·i·est.** inclined to snarl or growl; bad-tempered; cross. [< *snarl*[1]]

snarl·y[2] (snär′lē) *adj.* **snarl·i·er, snarl·i·est.** tangled; full of snarls. [< *snarl*[2]]

snatch (snach) *v.* 1 seize suddenly; grasp hastily. 2 take suddenly: *He snatched off his hat and bowed.* 3 save or attain by quick action: *They snatched victory from what seemed to be sure defeat.* 4 *Slang.* kidnap. 5 **snatch at,** a try to seize or grasp; seize; grasp. b eagerly take advantage of: *He snatched at the chance to travel.* **—***n.* 1 the act of snatching: *The boy made a snatch at the ball.* 2 a short time: *He had a snatch of sleep sitting in his chair.* 3 a small amount; bit; scrap: *hear snatches of conversation.* 4 *Slang.* the act of kidnapping. [cf. MDu. *snakken*] **—snatch′er,** *n.* **—Syn.** *v.* 1 grab, catch, snap. 2 pluck, wrest.

snatch·y (snach′ē) *adj.* done or occurring in snatches; disconnected; irregular. **—snatch′i·ly,** *adv.*

snath (snath) *n.* the long wooden handle of a scythe. [var. of *snead,* OE *snǣd*]

snathe (snāᴛʜ) *n.* snath.

snaz·zy (snaz′ē) *adj. Slang.* showy; fancy; stylish. [origin uncertain]

sneak (snēk) *v.* 1 move in a stealthy, sly way: *The man sneaked about the barn watching for a chance to steal the dog.* 2 get, put, pass, etc. in a stealthy, sly way. 3 *Informal.* steal. 4 act in a mean, contemptible, cowardly way. 5 **sneak out of,** avoid by slyness. **—***n.* 1 the act of sneaking. 2 a person who sneaks; sneaking, cowardly, contemptible person. [cf. OE *snican*] **—Syn.** *v.* 1 slink, skulk, lurk.

sneak·er (snēk′ər) *n.* 1 *Informal.* a light canvas shoe with a soft rubber sole. 2 a person that sneaks; sneak.

sneak·ing (snēk′ing) *adj.* 1 cowardly; underhand; concealed. 2 that one cannot justify or does not like to confess: *have a sneaking admiration for something.* **—sneak′ing·ly,** *adv.*

sneak thief a person who takes advantage of open doors, windows, or other easy opportunities to steal.

sneak·y (snēk′ē) *adj.* **sneak·i·er, sneak·i·est.** cowardly; mean; contemptible.

sneer (snēr) *v.* 1 show scorn or contempt by looks or words: *The other girls sneered at her plain clothes.* 2 utter with scorn or contempt: *"Bah!" he sneered with a curl of his lip.* 3 bring, put, force, etc. by sneering. **—***n.* a look or words expressing scorn or contempt. [ME *snere(n).* Akin to SNORE, SNARL[1].] **—sneer′er,** *n.* **—sneer′ing·ly,** *adv.* **—Syn.** *v.* 1 jeer, gibe, flout, mock. See **scoff.**

sneeze (snēz) *v.* **sneezed, sneez·ing,** *n.* **—***v.* 1 expel air suddenly and violently through the nose and mouth by an involuntary spasm. 2 **sneeze at,** *Informal.* treat with contempt; despise: *Their offer is not to be sneezed at.* **—***n.* a sudden, violent expelling of air through the nose and mouth. [ME *snese(n),* var. of earlier *fnese(n),* OE *fnēosan*] **—sneez′er,** *n.*

snell (snel) *n.* a short piece of gut, etc. by which a fish-hook is fastened to a longer line. [? < Du. *snel;* cf. G *schnellen* snap]

snick[1] (snik) *v.* 1 cut, snip, or nick. 2 strike sharply. 3 in cricket, give (a ball) a light, glancing blow. **—***n.* 1 a small cut; a nick. 2 in cricket, a light, glancing blow given to the ball by the batsman, or the ball so hit. [back formation from *snickersnee*]

snick[2] (snik) *v.* make or cause to make a clicking sound. **—***n.* a slight, sharp sound; click. [imitative]

snick·er (snik′ər) *n.* a half-suppressed and usually disrespectful laugh; sly or silly laugh; giggle. **—***v.* laugh in this way. [imitative]

snick·er·snee (snik′ər snē′) *n.* a heavy knife or short sword. [< earlier *snick or snee,* alteration of *stick or snee* < Du. *steken* to thrust + *snijen* to cut]

snide (snīd) *adj. Informal.* 1 derogatory; in a sly manner: *a snide remark.* 2 mean or cheap: *a snide trick.* 3 counterfeit; false; bogus: *a snide gem.* [? < Du. or G; cf. G *schneidend* cutting, sarcastic]

snies (snīz) *n.* pl. of **sny.**

sniff (snif) *v.* 1 draw air through the nose in short, quick breaths that can be heard: *The man who had a cold was sniffing. She sniffed at the present to show her contempt.* 2 smell with sniffs: *The dog sniffed suspiciously at the stranger.* 3 try the smell of. 4 draw in through the nose with the breath: *He sniffed the medicine.* 5 suspect; detect: *The police sniffed a plot and broke up the meeting.* **—***n.* 1 the act or sound of sniffing: *a loud sniff.* 2 a single breathing in of something; breath. [ME. Related to SNIVEL, SNUFF.]

snif·fle (snif′əl) *v.* **-fled, -fling,** *n.* **—***v.* 1 sniff again and again: *The child stopped crying, but kept on sniffling.* 2 breathe audibly through a partly clogged nose. **—***n.* 1 a loud sniff; a sniffling. 2 **the sniffles,** *Informal.* a a fit of sniffling; a tendency to sniffle. b a slight cold in the head. **—snif′fler,** *n.*

sniff·y (snif′ē) *adj.* **sniff·i·er, sniff·i·est.** *Informal.* 1 inclined to sniff. 2 contemptuous; scornful; disdainful.

snif·ter (snif′tər) *n.* 1 a pear-shaped glass having a short stem and used especially for brandy, the narrow top serving to retain the aroma of the liquor. 2 a small drink of liquor. [< dial. *snift* sniff]

snig·ger (snig′ər) *n. v.* snicker.

snip (snip) *v.* **snipped, snip·ping,** *n.* **—***v.* cut with a small, quick stroke or series of strokes with scissors: *She snipped the thread.* **—***n.* 1 the act of snipping: *With a few snips she cut out a paper doll.* 2 a small piece cut off: *Pick up the snips of cloth and thread from the floor.* 3 any small piece; bit; fragment. 4 *Informal.* a a small or unimportant person. b a cheeky, impertinent person. 5 **snips,** *pl.* hand shears for cutting metal. [< Du. or LG *snippen*]

snipe (snīp) *n.* **snipe** or **snipes,** *v.* **sniped, snip·ing.** **—***n.* any of various marsh birds having long bills. **—***v.* 1 hunt snipe. 2 shoot at (enemies) one at a time as a sportsman shoots at game; shoot from a concealed place. 3 **snipe at,** attack suddenly or unexpectedly, especially by words. [ME < ON *-snipe,* originally, snapping bird]

snip·er (snīp′ər) *n.* a hidden sharpshooter.

snip·pet (snip′it) *n.* 1 a small piece snipped off; bit;

scrap; fragment: *snippets of information.* **2** *Informal.* a small or unimportant person.

snip·py (snip′ē) *adj.* **-pi·er, -pi·est. 1** *Informal.* sharp; curt. **2** *Informal.* haughty; disdainful. **3** made up of scraps or fragments. **—snip′pi·ness,** *n.*

snit (snit) *n. Informal.* a state of agitation, especially of peevish annoyance.

snitch[1] (snich) *v. Slang.* snatch; steal. [origin unknown] **—snitch′er,** *n.*

snitch[2] (snich) *Slang.* —*v.* be an informer; tell tales. —*n.* informer. [original meaning "nose"; origin uncertain] **—snitch′er,** *n.*

sniv·el (sniv′əl) *v.* **-elled** or **-eled, -el·ling** or **-el·ing,** *n.* —*v.* **1** cry with sniffling. **2** put on a show of grief; whine. **3** run at the nose; sniffle. —*n.* **1** pretended grief or crying; whining. **2** a running from the nose; sniffling. [ME <OE **snyflan* < *snofl* mucus] **—sniv′el·ler** or **sniv′el·er,** *n.*

snob (snob) *n.* **1** a person who cares too much for rank, wealth, position, etc. and too little for real merit; a person who tries too hard to please those above him and too little to please those below him. **2** a person who is contemptuous of the popular taste in some field, and is attracted to esoteric or learned things for their own sake. [origin uncertain]

snob·ber·y (snob′ər ē or snob′rē) *n.* **-ber·ies.** snobbishness.

snob·bish (snob′ish) *adj.* **1** of or like a snob. **2** looking down on those in a lower position. **—snob′bish·ly,** *adv.* **—snob′bish·ness,** *n.*

snood (snüd) *n.* **1** a net or bag worn over a woman's hair. A snood may be a part of a hat. **2** a baglike hat. **3** in Scotland and northern England, a band or ribbon formerly worn around the hair by young unmarried women. —*v.* bind (hair) with a snood. [OE *snōd*]

A snood (def. 3)

snook·er (snük′ər) *n.* a type of pool played with 15 red balls and six other balls of different colors.

snoop (snüp) *Informal.* —*v.* go about in a sneaking, prying way; prowl; pry. —*n.* a person who snoops. [< Du. *snoepen* eat in secret] **—snoop′er,** *n.*

snoose (snüs) *n.* a kind of snuff, prepared damp and in grated form, used for chewing. Also, **Copenhagen snuff.** [< Danish, Swedish, etc. *snus,* shortening of *snustobak* < *snusa, snuse* sniff + *tobak* tobacco]

snoot (snüt) *n. Slang.* **1** the nose. **2** the face. [originally a Scottish var. of *snout*]

snoot·y (snüt′ē) *adj.* **snoot·i·er, snoot·i·est.** *Informal.* snobbish; conceited.

snooze (snüz) *v.* **snoozed, snooz·ing,** *n. Informal.* —*v.* take a nap; sleep; doze. —*n.* a nap; doze. [origin uncertain]

snore (snôr) *v.* **snored, snor·ing,** *n.* —*v.* **1** breathe during sleep with a harsh, rough sound. **2** pass in snoring: *The lazy man snored away the afternoon.* —*n.* the sound made in snoring. [ME *snore(n),* ? imitative] **—snor′er,** *n.*

snor·kel (snôr′kəl) *n.* **1** a periscopelike air intake and exhaust shaft for Diesel engines that allows submarines to remain submerged for a very long period of time. **2** a curved tube which enables swimmers to breathe under water while swimming near the surface. —*v.* travel underwater using a snorkel. Also, **schnorkle, schnorkel.** [< LG slang *snorkel* nose < MLG **snorkeln,* frequentative of *snorken* snore; because the snorkel is the nose of the submarine and its intake valve makes a snoring sound]

snort (snôrt) *v.* **1** force the breath violently through the nose with a loud, harsh sound: *The horse snorted.* **2** make a sound like this: *The engine snorted.* **3** show contempt, defiance, anger, etc. by snorting. **4** say or express with a snort: *"Indeed!" snorted my aunt.* —*n.* **1** the act of snorting. **2** the sound made by snorting. **3** a drink (of liquor): *a snort of whisky.* [< *snore*] **—snort′er,** *n.*

snot (snot) *n. Vulgar.* **1** mucus from the nose (not in polite use). **2** a mean, contemptible person. [OE *gesnot*]

snot·ty (snot′ē) *adj. n.* **-ties.** —*adj. Slang.* **1** dirty with snot. **2** mean; contemptible. —*n. Brit. Slang.* **1** any

hat, āge, cãre, fär; let, ēqual, tėrm; it, īce
hot, ōpen, ôrder; oil, out; cup, pu̇t, rüle, ūse
əbove, takən, pencəl, lemən, circəs
ch, child; ng, long; sh, ship
th, thin; ᴛʜ, then; zh, measure

unimportant or contemptible person. **2** a midshipman.

snout (snout) *n.* **1** the projecting part of an animal's head that contains the nose, mouth, and jaws. Pigs, dogs, and crocodiles have snouts. **2** anything like an animal's snout. **3** *Informal.* a person's nose, especially a large or ugly one. [ME *snoute;* akin to G *Schnauze*]

snout beetle a small beetle whose head is prolonged to form a snout. Snout beetles eat grain, nuts, and fruit.

snow (snō) *n.* **1** water vapor frozen into crystals that fall to earth in soft white flakes. **2** a fall of snow. **3** *Poetic.* pure whiteness. **4** something resembling or suggesting snow. **5** *Slang.* cocaine or heroin. **6** a snow apple. **7** a pattern of dots on a television screen caused by atmospheric interference with the signals.
—*v.* **1** fall as snow: *It snowed all day.* **2** let fall or scatter as snow. **3** cover, block up, etc. with snow or as if with snow. **4 snow in** or **snow up,** shut in by snow. **5 snow under, a** cover with snow. **b** *Informal.* overwhelm. [OE *snāw*]

snow apple a fine eating apple having crisp, white flesh and a deep-red skin.

snow·ball (snō′bol′ or -bôl′) *n.* **1** a ball made of snow pressed together. **2** a shrub having white flowers in large clusters like balls. —*v.* **1** throw balls of snow at. **2** increase rapidly by additions like a snowball: *The number of signers of the petition for a new school snowballed.*

snow·bank (snō′bangk′) *n.* a large mass or drift of snow.

snow·ber·ry (snō′ber′ē) *n.* **-ries. 1** a North American shrub that bears clusters of white berries in the fall. **2** the berry.

snow·bird (snō′bėrd′) *n.* **1** a small North American bird that has a slate-gray back and a white breast, and is often seen in flocks during the winter. **2** a snow bunting.

snow-blind (snō′blīnd′) *adj.* temporarily or partly blind from exposure of the eyes to the glare of snow.

snow blindness a form of temporary or partial blindness caused by the reflection of sunlight from snow.

snow·blink (snō′blingk′) *n.* the glare caused by the reflection of the sun's rays off snow.

snow·blow·er (snō′blō′ər) *n.* a machine that clears snow by drawing it in by means of a large fan and blowing it out in another direction.

snow boot a waterproof boot, usually well-lined, for use in snow.

snow-bound (snō′bound′) *adj.* shut in by snow.

snow bunting a small, white finch having black and brownish markings, that inhabits cold regions.

snow-capped (snō′kapt′) *adj.* having its top covered with snow.

snow devil a whirling column of snow sucked up in a vortex by the wind.

snow·drift (snō′drift′) *n.* **1** a mass or bank of snow piled up by the wind. **2** snow driven before the wind.

snow·drop (snō′drop′) *n.* a small plant having white flowers that bloom early in the spring.

snow·fall (snō′fol′ or -fôl′) *n.* **1** a fall of snow. **2** the amount of snow falling within a certain time and area: *The snowfall at Banff in that one storm was 16 inches.*

snow fence a lath and wire fence erected in winter alongside roads, etc. to prevent snow from drifting.

snow fencing 1 the material of which snow fences are made. **2** a snow fence.

snow·flake (snō′flāk′) *n.* **1** a small, feathery piece of snow. **2** snow bunting.

snow goose a type of wild goose that breeds in the Arctic, having white feathers except for its black primary feathers on the wings; wavey.

snow·i·ness (snō′ē nis) *n.* **1** the state or quality of being snowy. **2** whiteness.

snow job *Slang.* a persuasive piece of writing or talking intended to create a highly exaggerated impression of oneself or one's client.

snow knife *Cdn.* a knife about a foot long, having a broad, curved blade and used chiefly for cutting snow blocks for igloos.

snow leopard ounce[2].

snow line a height on mountains, etc. above which there is snow all year round.

snow·man (snō′man′) *n.* **-men** (-men′). a figure made of snow piled up and roughly shaped as a man.

snow·melt (snō′melt′) *n.* liquid resulting from the melting of snow.

snow·mo·bile (snō′mə bēl′) *n. v.* **-biled, -bil·ing.** —*n.* **1** a small motorized snow vehicle; skidoo. **2** a powerful vehicle equipped with caterpillar tracks and used for travelling over snow and ice: *Some snowmobiles are equipped as ambulances.* —*v.* travel by snowmobile; ride or drive a snowmobile.

A snowmobile

snow·plough or **snow·plow** (snō′plou′) *n.* a machine for clearing away snow from streets, railway tracks, etc. by means of a large blade that pushes the snow aside as the machine moves forward.

snow·shed (snō′shed′) *n.* a long shed built over a railway track or a highway to protect it from snowslides.

snow·shine (snō′shīn′) *n.* snowblink.

snow·shoe (snō′shü′) *n. v.* **-shoed, -shoe·ing.** —*n.* a light, wooden frame with strips of leather stretched across it. Trappers in the far North wear snowshoes on their feet to keep from sinking in deep, soft snow. —*v.* walk or travel on snowshoes. —**snow′sho′er,** *n.*

Snowshoes

snow·slide (snō′slīd′) *n.* **1** the sliding down of a mass of snow on a steep slope. **2** the mass of snow that slides.

snow snake 1 a North American Indian game in which a wooden stick is slid as far as possible along a smooth patch of ice or snow, or along a furrow in snow. **2** the stick used in this game.

snow·storm (snō′stôrm′) *n.* a storm with much snow.

snow-white (snō′hwīt′ or -wīt′) *adj.* white as snow.

snow·y (snō′ē) *adj.* **snow·i·er, snow·i·est. 1** having snow. **2** covered with snow. **3** like snow; white as snow: *She has snowy hair.* **4** having a blurred and dotted pattern: *The TV picture is snowy.* —**snow′i·ly,** *adv.*

snub (snub) *v.* **snubbed, snub·bing,** *n. adj.* —*v.* **1** treat coldly, scornfully, or with contempt. **2** check or stop a boat, horse, etc. suddenly. **3** check or stop a rope or cable running out suddenly. —*n.* **1** cold, scornful, or disdainful treatment. **2** a sudden check or stop. **3** a sharp rebuke. —*adj.* short and turned up at the tip: *a snub nose.* [ME < ON *snubba* reprove]

snub·ber (snub′ər) *n.* **1** a person that snubs. **2** a device for snubbing a rope, cable, etc. **3** an early type of shock absorber for automobiles.

snub·by (snub′ē) *adj.* **-bi·er, -bi·est.** short and turned up at the tip.

snub-nosed (snub′nōzd′) *adj.* having a snub nose.

snuff[1] (snuf) *v.* **1** draw in through the nose; draw up into the nose: *He snuffs up salt and water to cure a cold.* **2** sniff; smell: *The dog snuffed at the track of the fox.* **3** take powdered tobacco into the nose by snuffing; use snuff. —*n.* **1** powdered tobacco taken into the nose. **2 up to snuff, a** *Informal.* in perfect order or condition; as good as expected. **b** *Slang.* not easily deceived. [< MDu. *snuffen* sniff]

snuff[2] (snuf) *v.* **1** cut or pinch off the burned wick of a candle. **2** put out (a candle); extinguish. **3 snuff out, a** put out; extinguish. **b** put an end to suddenly and completely. —*n.* the burned part of a candlewick. [ME; origin uncertain; cf. G *Schnuppe,* n.]

snuff·box (snuf′boks′) *n.* a small box for holding snuff.

snuff·ers (snuf′ərz) *n.pl.* small tongs for taking off burned wick or putting out the light of a candle.

Snuffers

snuf·fle (snuf′əl) *v.* **-fled, -fling,** *n.* —*v.* **1** breathe noisily through a partly clogged nose. **2** smell; sniff. **3** speak, sing, etc. through the nose or with a nasal tone. —*n.* **1** the act or sound of snuffling. **2** the nasal tone of voice of a person who snuffles. **3 the snuffles,** *Informal.* **a** a fit of snuffling; stuffed-up condition of the nose, caused by a cold, hay fever, etc. **b** a respiratory disease of animals. [ult. < *snuff*[1] or its source] —**snuf′fler,** *n.*

snuff·y (snuf′ē) *adj.* **snuff·i·er, snuff·i·est. 1** like snuff. **2** soiled or stained with snuff. **3** having the habit of using snuff. **4** disagreeable; cross. —**snuf′fi·ly,** *adv.*

snug (snug) *adj.* **snug·ger, snug·gest,** *v.* **snugged, snug·ging,** *adv.* —*adj.* **1** comfortable; warm; sheltered: *The cat has found a snug corner behind the stove.* **2** neat; trim; compact: *The cabins on the boat are snug.* **3** well-built; seaworthy: *a snug ship.* **4** fitting closely: *That coat is a little too snug.* **5** small but sufficient: *A snug income enables him to live in comfort.* **6** hidden; concealed: *He lay snug until the searchers passed by.* —*v.* make snug. —*adv.* in a snug manner. [cf. Swedish *snygg* neat, trim] —**snug′ly,** *adv.* —**snug′ness,** *n.*

Syn. *adj.* **1 Snug, cosy** = comfortable. **Snug** emphasizes the comfort and security of a small space, warm and sheltered from the weather, or of a quiet and peaceful life, protected from disturbance or excitement: *The children were snug in their beds.* **Cosy** emphasizes warmth, shelter, and ease, often affection or friendliness, making for comfort and contentment: *She was sitting in a cosy corner by the fire.*

snug·ger·y (snug′ər ē) *n.* **-ger·ies.** a snug place, position, room, etc.

snug·gle (snug′əl) *v.* **-gled, -gling. 1** lie or press closely for warmth or comfort or from affection; nestle; cuddle. **2** draw closely. [< *snug*]

snye or **sny** (snī) *n.* **snyes** or **snies.** *Cdn.* a side channel of a stream. [< Cdn.F *chenail;* cf. F *chenal* channel]

so[1] (sō; *unstressed before consonants,* sə) *adv.* **1** in this way; in that way; in the same way; as shown: *Hold your pen so.* **2** as stated: *Is that really so?* **3** to this degree; to that degree: *Do not walk so fast.* **4** to such a degree; to the same degree: *He was not so cold as she was.* **5** very: *You are so kind.* **6** very much: *My head aches so.* **7** for this reason; for that reason; accordingly; therefore: *The dog was hungry; so we fed it.* **8** likewise; also: *She likes dogs; so does he.* **9 and so, a** likewise; also. **b** accordingly. **10 or so,** more or less: *It cost a dollar or so.* **11 so as,** with the result or purpose. **12 so that, a** with the result that. **b** with the purpose that. **c** provided that; if. —*conj.* **1** with the result that; in order that: *Go away so I can rest.* **2** with the purpose or intention that: *I did the work so he would not need to.* **3** *Archaic.* on the condition that; if: *So it be done, I care not who does it.* —*interj.* **1** well! **2** let it be that way! all right! **3** is that true? **4** what now? so what? —*pron.* **1** more or less; approximately that: *a pound or so.* **2** the same: *A drunkard usually remains so.* **3** whatever has been or is going to be said; this; that. [OE *swā*]

so[2] (sō) *n.* in music, a syllable used for the fifth tone of an eight-tone scale; sol. [see GAMUT]

s.o. or **so** in baseball: **1** struck out. **2** strike out.

So. 1 South. **2** Southern.

soak (sōk) *v.* **1** make very wet; wet through. **2** let remain in water or other liquid until wet through. **3** become very wet; remain until wet through. **4** make its way; enter; go: *Water will soak through the earth.* **5** suck: *The sponge soaked up the water.* **6** *Slang.* drink heavily. **7** *Slang.* punish severely; strike hard. **8** *Slang.* make pay too much; charge or tax heavily. **9 soak up, a** absorb. **b** take into the mind. —*n.* **1** the act or process of soaking. **2** the state of being soaked. **3** the liquid in which anything is soaked. **4** *Slang.* a heavy drinker. [OE *socian*] —**Syn.** *v.* **1** See **wet.**

so-and-so (sō′ənd sō′) *n.* **-sos. 1** a person or thing not

hat, āge, cãre, fär, let, ēqual, tėrm; it, īce
hot, ōpen, ôrder; oil, out; cup, pu̇t, rüle, ūse
əbove, takən, pencəl, lemən, circəs
ch, child; ng, long; sh, ship
th, thin; ꟸH, then; zh, measure

named. 2 *Informal.* an unpleasant or distasteful person.

soap (sōp) *n.* **1** a substance used for washing, usually made of a fat and caustic soda or potash. **2** *Slang.* money, especially money as used for bribery. **3 no soap,** *Slang.* **a** no; nothing doing. **b** no results; nothing accomplished. —*v.* rub with soap. [OE *sāpe*] —**soap′less,** *adj.*

soap·ber·ry (sōp′ber′ē) *n.* **-ries. 1** any of a family of tropical plants or trees of which the fruit is used as a soap substitute. **2** the fruit or nut of any of these trees.

soap·box (sōp′boks′) *n.* **1** a box, especially of wood, in which soap is packed. **2** an empty box used as a temporary platform by agitators or other speakers addressing gatherings in the open air. —*v.* address an audience in the open air.

soap bubble a bubble made with soapy water.

soap opera a daytime radio or television drama presented in serial form, usually featuring emotional domestic situations.

soap·stone (sōp′stōn′) *n.* a heavy stone that feels somewhat like soap; steatite: *Eskimo carvings are often made of soapstone.*

soap·suds (sōp′sudz′) *n.pl.* bubbles and foam made with soap and water.

soap·wort (sōp′wėrt′) *n.* a plant whose leaves and roots contain a juice that can be used as soap.

soap·y (sōp′ē) *adj.* **soap·i·er, soap·i·est. 1** covered with soap or soapsuds. **2** containing soap. **3** like soap; smooth; greasy. —**soap′i·ly,** *adv.* —**soap′i·ness,** *n.*

soar (sôr) *v.* **1** fly at a great height; fly upward: *The eagle soared without flapping its wings.* **2** rise beyond what is common and ordinary; aspire: *His ambition soared to the throne.* **3** reach in soaring. **4** fly or move through the air by means of rising air currents. A glider can soar for many miles. [ME < OF *essorer,* ult. < L *ex-* out + *aura* breeze < Gk.]

sob (sob) *v.* **sobbed, sob·bing,** *n.* —*v.* **1** cry or sigh with short, quick breaths. **2** put, send, etc. by sobbing: *She sobbed herself to sleep.* **3** make a sound like a sob: *The wind sobbed.* **4** utter with sobs. —*n.* **1** a catching of short, quick breaths because of grief, etc. **2** the sound of this. [ME *sobbe(n),* perhaps ult. imitative]

so·ber (sō′bər) *adj.* **1** not drunk. **2** temperate; moderate: *The Puritans led sober, hard-working lives.* **3** quiet; serious; solemn: *a sober expression.* **4** calm; sensible: *The judge's sober opinion was not influenced by prejudice or strong feeling.* **5** free from exaggeration: *sober facts.* **6** quiet in color: *dressed in sober gray.*
—*v.* **1** make sober. **2** become sober. **3 sober down,** become quiet, serious, or solemn. **4 sober up** or **off,** recover from too much alcoholic drink. [ME < OF < L *sobrius*] —**so′ber·ly,** *adv.* —**so′ber·ness,** *n.* —**Syn.** *adj.* **1** unintoxicated. **3** See **grave.**

so·ber-mind·ed (sō′bər mīn′did) *adj.* having or showing a sober mind; self-controlled; sensible. —**so′ber-mind′ed·ly,** *adv.* —**so′ber-mind′ed·ness,** *n.*

so·ber·sid·ed (sō′bər sīd′id) *adj.* of a serious or earnest disposition.

so·ber·sides (sō′bər sīdz′) *n.* **-sides.** a serious or earnest person.

so·bri·e·ty (sə brī′ə tē) *n.* **-ties. 1** soberness. **2** temperance in the use of alcoholic liquors. **3** moderation. **4** quietness; seriousness. [< L *sobrietas*]

so·bri·quet (sō′brə kā′ or sō′brə ket′) *n.* a nickname. Also, **soubriquet.** [< F]

sob sister *Informal.* a person, often a woman reporter, who writes or tells sob stories.

sob story *Informal.* a story that is excessively pathetic or sentimental.

Soc. 1 Society. **2** Socialist.

soc·age or **soc·cage** (sok′ij) *n.* in former times, a way of holding land by which the tenant paid a definite rent or did a definite amount of work, but gave no military service to his lord. [ME < AF *socage* < *soc* < Med.L *soca* < OE *sōcn* seeking, inquiry, jurisdiction]

so-called (sō′kold′ or -kôld′) *adj.* **1** called thus. **2** called thus improperly or incorrectly: *Her so-called friend dislikes her.*

soc·cer (sok′ər) *n.* a game played between two teams of eleven men each, using a round ball; association football. In soccer, only the goalkeeper may touch the ball with hands and arms. [< as*soc.,* abbreviation of *association (football)*; for the ending cf. *Rugger* for *Rugby*] ☛ See **rugby** for usage note.

so·cia·bil·i·ty (sō′shə bil′ə tē) *n.* **-ties.** one's social disposition or behavior.

so·cia·ble (sō′shə bəl) *adj.* **1** liking company; friendly: *The Smiths are a sociable family and entertain a great deal.* **2** marked by conversation and companionship: *We had a sociable afternoon together.* **3** of animals or plants, naturally inclined to be in company with others of the same species; social. —*n. Esp.U.S.* an informal social gathering; a social. [< L *sociabilis* < *sociare* associate < *socius.* See SOCIAL.] —**so′cia·bly,** *adv.* —**Syn.** *adj.* **1** See **social.**

so·cial (sō′shəl) *adj.* **1** concerned with human beings in their relations to each other. **2** of or dealing with the living conditions, health, etc. of human beings: *social problems, social work.* **3** living, or liking to live, with others: *Man is a social being.* **4** for companionship or friendliness; having to do with companionship or friendliness: *a social club.* **5** liking company: *She has a social nature.* **6** connected with fashionable society: *a social leader.* **7** of animals, living together in organized communities. Ants and bees are social insects. **8** socialistic.
—*n.* **1** an informal social gathering or party. **2 socials,** *pl. Informal.* social studies. [< L *socialis* < *socius* companion, originally adj., sharing in]
Syn. *adj.* **4 Social, sociable** = pertaining to, characterized by, or inclined to companionship and friendliness. **Social,** now rarely describing a person, emphasizes human relations and when particularly describing groups, occasions, activities, etc. means pertaining to or being for companionship or mingling with others: *He has too little social life.* **Sociable,** usually describing persons, means liking company and being inclined to seek and enjoy companionship and friendly relations even with strangers: *He is a likable, sociable person.*

Social Credit Party a Canadian political party, the policies of which are based on certain economic theories originally developed by Major C. H. Douglas, 1878-1952.

Social Credit Rally a Canadian political party formed in 1962 from the Quebec wing of the Social Credit Party. [translation of F *Ralliement des Créditistes*]

so·cial·ism (sō′shəl iz′əm) *n.* **1** the theory or system of social organization by which the means of production and distribution are owned, managed, or controlled by the government (state socialism) or by associations of workers (guild socialism). **2** a political movement advocating or associated with this system or some modification of it. **3** the practice of such a system. ☛ See **communism** for usage note.

so·cial·ist (sō′shəl ist) *n.* a person who favors and supports socialism. —*adj.* socialistic.

so·cial·is·tic (sō′shəl is′tik) *adj.* **1** of or having to do with socialism or socialists. **2** advocating or supporting socialism. —**so′cial·is′ti·cal·ly,** *adv.*

Socialist Party a political party that favors and supports socialism.

so·cial·ite (sō′shəl īt′) *n.* a person who is prominent in society.

so·ci·al·i·ty (sō′shē al′ə tē) *n.* **-ties. 1** social activity; social intercourse. **2** social nature or tendencies: *The congregating of people in cities and towns shows sociality.*

so·cial·ize (sō′shəl īz′) *v.* **-ized, -iz·ing. 1** make social; make fit for living with others. **2** adapt to community needs. **3** establish or regulate in accordance with socialism. —**so′cial·i·za′tion,** *n.*

socialized medicine the provision of medical care and hospital services for all classes of society, especially through government subsidy and administration.

so·cial·ly (sō′shəl ē) *adv.* **1** in a social way or manner;

in relation to other people. 2 as a member of society or of a social group: *He is an able man, but socially he is a failure.*

social register a list of people who are prominent in fashionable society.

social science the study of people, their activities, and their customs in relationship to others. History, sociology, economics, and civics are social sciences.

social security a government system of providing old-age pensions, unemployment insurance, health insurance, etc.

social service social work.

social studies school subjects dealing with the development of peoples in relation to their physical and cultural environment. History and geography, when treated together as one subject, are called social studies.

social work work directed toward the betterment of social conditions in a community. Child welfare bureaus, district nursing organizations, free clinics, etc. are forms of social work.

social worker a person who does social work.

so·ci·e·ty (sə sī′ə tē) *n.* **-ties.** 1 a group of persons joined together for a common purpose or by a common interest. A club, a fraternity, a lodge, or an association may be called a society. 2 all the people; the people of any particular time or place; their activities and customs: *The good of society demands that all wrongdoing be punished.* 3 those people thought of as a group because of common economic position, similar interests, etc.: *in cultivated society; the lower, middle, or upper class of society.* 4 company; companionship: *I enjoy his society.* 5 fashionable people; their doings. 6 **a** an organized community of animals or insects: *a society of wasps.* **b** an assemblage of plants of the same species not dominant in an ecological community. [< L *societas* < *socius* sharing in]

Society of Friends a Christian sect founded by George Fox in England in 1650; Quakers.

Society of Jesus a Roman Catholic religious order, founded by Saint Ignatius Loyola in 1534. Its members are called Jesuits. *Abbrev.*: S.J.

so·ci·o-e·co·nom·ic (sō′sē ō- or sō′shē ō ē′kə nom′ik or -ek′ə nom′ik) *adj.* of or having to do with social and economic matters.

so·ci·o·log·i·cal (sō′sē ə loj′ə kəl or sō′shē ə loj′ə kəl) *adj.* 1 of or having to do with human society or problems relating to it: *The care of the poor is a sociological problem.* 2 of sociology.

so·ci·o·log·i·cal·ly (sō′sē ə loj′ik lē or sō′shē ə loj′ik lē) *adv.* according to sociology.

so·ci·ol·o·gist (sō′sē ol′ə jist or sō′shē ol′ə jist) *n.* a student of human society and its problems; person skilled in sociology.

so·ci·ol·o·gy (sō′sē ol′ə jē or sō′shē ol′ə jē) *n.* the study of the nature, origin, and development of human society and community life; the science of social facts. Sociology deals with the facts of crime, poverty, marriage, divorce, the church, the school, etc. [< L *socius* companion + E *-logy*]

so·ci·o·path (sō′sē ə path′ or sō′shē ə path′) *n.* a person in whom mental illness leads to a lack of social or moral responsibility.

sock[1] (sok) *n.* 1 a short stocking, especially one that reaches about halfway to the knee. 2 in ancient Greece and Rome, a light shoe worn by actors in comedy. [< L *soccus*]

sock[2] (sok) *Slang.* —*v.* strike or hit hard. —*n.* a hard blow. —*adv.* squarely; right. [origin uncertain]

SOCKET

A ball-and-socket joint

sock·et (sok′it) *n.* 1 a hollow part or piece for receiving and holding something. A candlestick has a socket in which to set a candle. Eyes are set in sockets. 2 a connecting place for electric wires and plugs. [ME < AF *soket* < *soc* ploughshare < Celtic]

sock·eye (sok′ī′) *n.* **sock·eye** or **sock·eyes.** a variety of red salmon found in the North Pacific. [< Salish *suk-kegh*, altered by folk etymology]

So·crat·ic (sō krat′ik) *adj.* of or having to do with Socrates, 469-399 B.C., a famous Athenian philosopher, his philosophy, followers, etc.

Socratic method the use of a series of questions to lead a pupil to think, to make an opponent contradict himself, etc.

So·cred (sō′kred′) *n. Cdn. Informal.* 1 the Social Credit Party. 2 a member of this party.

sod (sod) *n. v.* **sod·ded, sod·ding.** —*n.* 1 ground covered with grass. 2 a piece or layer of ground containing the grass and its roots. 3 **under the sod,** dead and buried. —*v.* cover with sods. [< MDu. or MLG *sode*]

so·da (sō′də) *n.* 1 any of several substances containing sodium; sodium carbonate, sodium bicarbonate, caustic soda (NaOH), or sodium oxide (Na_2O). Soda is used in the manufacture of soap and glass. Washing soda, or sal soda, is used in cleaning. Baking soda is used in cooking and as a medicine. 2 soda water. 3 soda water flavored with fruit juice or syrup, and often containing ice cream. [< Med.L]

soda ash partly purified sodium carbonate.

soda biscuit a simple, light, thin biscuit made with little or no sugar or shortening.

soda cracker a soda biscuit.

soda fountain 1 an apparatus for holding soda water, syrups, ice, etc. and having taps for drawing off the liquids. 2 a counter with places for holding soda water, flavored syrups, ice cream, etc. 3 a store having such a counter.

soda jerk or **jerker** *Slang.* a person who serves at a soda fountain.

so·da·lite (sō′də līt′) *n.* an opaque silicate of sodium and aluminum with chlorine, found in igneous rock and often colored blue. *Formula*: $Na_4Al_3Si_3O_{12}Cl$

so·dal·i·ty (sō dal′ə tē) *n.* **-ties.** 1 fellowship; friendship. 2 an association, society, or fraternity. 3 in the Roman Catholic Church, a society having religious or charitable purposes. [< L *sodalitas* < *sodalis* sociable]

soda water water charged with carbon dioxide to make it bubble and fizz, often served with the addition of syrup, ice cream, etc.

sod·bust·er (sod′bust′ər) *n. Slang.* on the prairies, a farmer, especially one of the early homesteaders.

sod·den (sod′ən) *adj.* 1 soaked through: *His clothing was sodden with rain.* 2 heavy and moist: *This bread is sodden because it was not baked well.* 3 dull-looking; stupid. [old pp. of *seethe*] —**sod′den·ness,** *n.*

so·dic (sō′dik) *adj.* of, having to do with, or containing sodium.

so·di·um (sō′dē əm) *n.* a soft, silver-white, metallic chemical element occurring in nature only in compounds. Salt and soda contain sodium. *Symbol*: Na; *at.no.* 11; *at.wt.* 22.9898 [< *soda*]

sodium bicarbonate a powdery white substance used in cooking, medicine, etc.; baking soda. *Formula*: $NaHCO_3$

sodium carbonate a salt that occurs in a powdery white form and in a hydrated crystalline form; washing soda. It is used for softening water, making soap and glass, neutralizing acids, etc. *Formula*: Na_2CO_3

sodium chloride common salt. *Formula*: NaCl

sodium cyanide a poisonous substance, composed of fine white crystals, used in the cyanide process for extracting gold and silver from ores, in fumigating, etc. *Formula*: NaCN

sodium fluoride a crystalline salt, poisonous in large quantities, used as an insecticide and disinfectant and as a preventive of tooth decay. *Formula*: NaF

sodium hydroxide a white solid that is a strong, corrosive alkali; caustic soda. *Formula*: NaOH

sodium hypochlorite a crystalline salt, used as an insecticide, a disinfectant, in household bleaches, etc. *Formula*: $NaClO \cdot 5H_2O$

sodium iodide a white, odorless salt, used for the treatment of nervous disorders, in animal fodder, in photography, etc. *Formula*: NaI

sodium nitrate a colorless crystalline substance used in making fertilizers, explosives, etc.; Chile saltpetre. *Formula*: $NaNO_3$

sodium pentothal a barbiturate used as an anaesthetic and in the treatment of mental illness. *Formula*: $C_{11}H_{17}N_2O_2SNa$

Sod·om (sod′əm) *n.* **1** an ancient city near the Dead Sea that, according to the account in the Bible, was destroyed by fire from heaven because of the wickedness of its inhabitants. Gen. 18 and 19. **2** any extremely wicked or corrupt place.

sodomite (sod′ə mīt′) *n.* **1** a person who practises sodomy. **2 Sodomite,** a native or inhabitant of Sodom.

sod·o·my (sod′ə mē) *n.* abnormal sexual relations, especially between two males or between a human being and an animal. [ME < OF *sodomie* < LL < *Sodom*]

sod turning (sod′tėrn′ing) *n.* the breaking of ground for digging the foundations of a building.

so·ev·er (sō ev′ər) *adv.* **1** in any case; in any way; in any degree: *no matter how long soever the work may take.* **2** of any kind; at all: *He has no home soever.*

-soever *suffix.* in any way; of any kind; at all; ever, as in *whosoever, whatsoever, whensoever, wheresoever, howsoever.*

so·fa (sō′fə) *n.* a long, upholstered seat or couch having a back and arms; chesterfield. [< F < Arabic *soffah*]

sof·fit (sof′it) *n.* in architecture, the under surface or face of an architrave, arch, or the like. [< Ital. *soffitto,* ult. < L *sub-* under + *figere* fix]

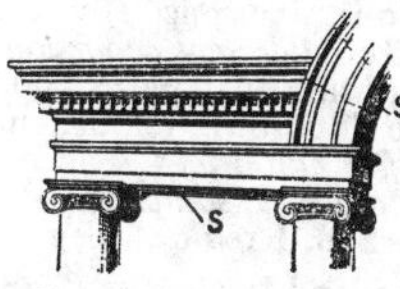

S, soffit

soft (soft) *adj.* **1** not hard; yielding readily to touch or pressure: *a soft pillow.* **2** not hard compared with other things of the same kind: *Pine wood is soft. Copper and lead are softer than steel.* **3** not hard or sharp; gentle and graceful: *soft shadows, soft outlines.* **4** fine in texture; not rough or coarse; smooth: *soft skin.* **5** not loud: *a soft voice.* **6** quietly pleasant; mild; not harsh: *soft air.* **7** not glaring or harsh: *soft light.* **8** gentle; kind; tender: *a soft heart.* **9** weak; unmanly: *The army had become soft from idleness and luxury.* **10** silly. **11** of consonants, pronounced as a fricative or an affricate, rather than as an explosive sound. The *c* is soft in *city* and hard in *corn*; *g* is soft in *gentle* and hard in *get.* **12** *Informal.* easy; easy-going: *a soft job, a soft person.* **13** of water, comparatively free from certain mineral salts that prevent soap from lathering. **14** of wheat, containing little gluten. **15** of or having to do with soft goods.
—*adv.* softly; quietly; gently.
—*n.* that which is soft; soft part.
—*interj. Archaic.* hush! stop! [OE *sōfte*] —**soft′ly,** *adv.*
—**Syn.** *adj.* **1** pliable, flexible, malleable. **5** low, subdued. **8** sympathetic, compassionate.

soft·ball (soft′bol′ or -bôl′) *n.* **1** a modified kind of baseball game that uses a larger and softer ball. **2** the ball used in that game.

soft-boiled (soft′boild′) *adj.* of eggs, boiled only a little so that the yolk is still soft.

soft coal bituminous coal.

soft currency a currency backed by government credit but not entirely by gold or silver. It is not readily convertible into other currencies; opposed to *hard currency.*

soft drink a refreshing cold drink that is non-alcoholic, such as ginger ale, orangeade, etc.

soft·en (sof′ən) *v.* **1** make softer. **2** become softer. **3** lessen the ability of (a country, region, etc.) to resist invasion or attack through preliminary bombing, etc. **4** decrease; decline. —**soft′en·er,** *n.*

soft goods clothing, textiles, etc.; dry goods.

soft-head·ed (soft′hed′id) *adj. Informal.* silly; stupid; foolish.

soft-heart·ed (soft′här′tid) *adj.* gentle; kind; tender. —**soft′-heart′ed·ly,** *adv.* —**soft′-heart′ed·ness,** *n.*

soft·ness (soft′nis) *n.* the state of being soft; ease; comfort; mildness; gentleness; weakness.

hat, āge, cãre, fär; let, ēqual, tėrm; it, īce
hot, ōpen, ôrder; oil, out; cup, pu̇t, rüle, ūse
əbove, takən, pencəl, lemən, circəs
ch, child; ng, long; sh, ship
th, thin; ᴛʜ, then; zh, measure

soft palate the fleshy back part of the roof of the mouth.

soft-ped·al (soft′ped′əl) *v.* **-alled** or **-aled, -al·ling** or **-al·ing. 1** use a pedal on a piano, organ, etc. to soften musical tones. **2** make quieter, less noticeable, or less strong.

soft sell *Informal.* a sales approach that uses indirect persuasive tactics rather than pushing, aggressive ones.

soft shoe 1 a type of tap dancing using shoes without metal taps. **2** the style of shoe used for this.

soft-shoe (soft′shü′) *v.* **-shoed, -shoe·ing.** *Informal.* dance the soft shoe.

soft soap 1 a liquid or partly liquid soap. **2** *Informal.* flattery.

soft-soap (soft′sōp′) *v. Informal.* flatter. —**soft′-soap′er,** *n.*

soft-spo·ken (soft′spō′kən) *adj.* **1** speaking with a soft voice. **2** spoken softly.

soft spot 1 a vulnerable or sensitive spot; a point of weakness. **2** a part of the atmosphere where the winds have less force than in the surrounding area. **3** fontanel.

soft touch *Informal.* a person who lends or gives money easily.

soft·ware (soft′wãr′) *n.* the programming, both standard procedures and specific programs, for operating computers or a computer (opposed to *hardware*).

soft wheat a wheat that has a high starch and low gluten content.

soft·wood (soft′wu̇d′) *n.* **1** wood that is easily cut. **2** a tree that has needles or does not have broad leaves. Pines and firs are softwoods; oaks and maples are hardwoods. **3** the wood of such a tree.

soft·y (sof′tē) *n.* **soft·ies.** *Informal.* **1** a soft, silly, or weak person. **2** one who is easily imposed upon.

sog·gy (sog′ē) *adj.* **-gi·er, -gi·est. 1** thoroughly wet; soaked: *a soggy washcloth.* **2** damp and heavy: *soggy bread.* [< dial. *sog* bog, swamp < Scand.; cf. ON *soggr* damp] —**sog′gi·ness,** *n.*

soi-di·sant (swä dē zäɴ′) *adj. French.* **1** calling oneself thus; self-styled. **2** so-called; pretended.

soi·gné (swä nyā′) *adj.* feminine form **soignée.** *French.* well-groomed; elegant.

soil[1] (soil) *n.* **1** ground; earth; dirt: *A farmer tills the soil.* **2** something thought of as a place for growth. **3** one's land; country. [ME < AF < L *solium* seat, influenced by L *solum* soil]

soil[2] (soil) *v.* **1** make dirty: *He soiled his clean clothes.* **2** become dirty: *White shirts soil easily.* **3** spot; stain: *The splashing paint soiled the wall.* **4** disgrace; dishonor: *His actions have soiled the family name.* **5** corrupt morally. —*n.* a spot; stain. [ME < OF *soillier,* ult. < L *suile* pigsty < *sus* pig] —**Syn.** *v.* **1** daub, begrime, besmirch.

soi·ree or **soi·rée** (swä rā′) *n.* an evening party or social gathering. [< F *soirée* < *soir* evening]

so·journ (*v.* sō jėrn′ or sō′jėrn; *n.* sō′jėrn) *v.* stay for a time: *The Israelites sojourned in the land of Egypt.* —*n.* a brief stay. [ME < OF *sojorner,* ult. < L *sub* under + *diurnus* of the day] —**so·journ′er,** *n.*

sol[1] (sōl) *n.* in music, a syllable used for the fifth tone of an eight-tone scale. See **do**[2] for diagram. Also, **so**[2]. [see GAMUT]

sol[2] (sōl) *n.* **1** a unit of money in Peru. See table at **money. 2** a note or coin worth one sol. [< Sp.]

Sol (sol) *n.* **1** in Roman mythology, the god of the sun, identified with the Greek god Helios. **2** the sun.

sol. 1 solution. **2** soluble.

Sol. 1 Solomon. **2** Solicitor.

sol·ace (sol′is) *n. v.* **-aced, -ac·ing.** —*n.* a comfort; relief: *She found solace from her troubles in music.* —*v.*

comfort; relieve: *He solaced himself with a book.* [ME < OF < L *solacium* < *solari* console] —**sol′ac·er,** *n.* —**Syn.** *n.* consolation, cheer.

so·lar (sō′lər) *adj.* **1** of the sun: *a solar eclipse.* **2** having to do with the sun. **3** coming from the sun: *Solar heat is less in winter than in summer.* **4** measured or determined by the earth's motion in relation to the sun. A solar year is about $365\frac{1}{4}$ days long. **5** working by means of the sun's light or heat. A solar telegraph uses mirrors to reflect flashes of sunlight. [ME < L *solaris* < *sol* sun]

solar cell a device for transforming the energy of sunlight into electricity.

solar flare an eruption of gases on the sun, usually associated with sunspots, which produces ultra-violet radiation and causes ionization in the upper atmosphere.

so·lar·i·um (sə lãr′ē əm) *n.* **-lar·i·a** (-lãr′ē ə). a room, porch, etc. where people can lie or sit in the sun. [< L *solarium* < *sol* sun]

solar plex·us (plek′səs) **1** in anatomy, the network of nerves situated at the upper part of the abdomen, behind the stomach and in front of the aorta. **2** *Informal.* the pit of the stomach.

solar system the sun and all the planets, satellites, comets, etc. that revolve around it.

solar year the period of time required for the earth to make one revolution around the sun, which equals about $365\frac{1}{4}$ days.

sold (sōld) *v.* pt. and pp. of **sell.**

sol·der (sod′ər) *n.* **1** a metal or alloy that can be melted and used for joining or mending metal surfaces, parts, etc. **2** anything that unites firmly or joins closely. —*v.* **1** fasten, mend, or join with solder. **2** unite firmly; join closely. **3** mend; repair; patch. [ME < OF *soldure,* ult. < L *solidus* solid] —**sol′der·er,** *n.*

sol·dier (sōl′jər) *n.* **1** a man who serves in an army. **2** a private or non-commissioned officer. **3** a man having skill or experience in war. **4** a person who serves in any cause: *Christian soldiers.* **5** in zoology: **a** in colonies of certain ants, a defending worker having a large head and powerful jaws. **b** in colonies of termites, a large-headed individual.
—*v.* **1** act or serve as a soldier. **2** *Informal and archaic.* shirk work, especially on pretense of illness. [ME < OF *soldier* < *soulde* pay < L *solidus,* a Roman coin]

sol·dier·ly (sōl′jər lē) *adj.* like a soldier; suitable for a soldier.

soldier of fortune a man serving or ready to serve as a soldier under any government for money, adventure, or pleasure; military adventurer.

sol·dier·y (sōl′jər ē) *n.* **-dier·ies. 1** soldiers collectively. **2** a body of soldiers. **3** military training or knowledge.

sol·do (sôl′dō) *n.* **-di** (-dē). an Italian copper coin, a twentieth part of a lira, formerly worth about $\frac{1}{4}$ of a cent. [< Ital. < L *solidus.* See SOLIDUS.]

sole[1] (sōl) *adj.* **1** one and only; single: *the sole heir.* **2** only: *We three were the sole survivors.* **3** of or for only one person or group and not others; exclusive: *the sole right of use.* **4** alone: *a sole undertaking.* [ME < OF < L *solus*] —**Syn. 1, 2** See **single.**

sole[2] (sōl) *n. v.* **soled, sol·ing.** —*n.* **1** the bottom or under surface of the foot. **2** bottom of a shoe, slipper, boot, etc. **3** a piece of leather, rubber, etc. cut in the same shape of the bottom of a shoe, slipper, boot, etc. **4** the under surface; under part; bottom. —*v.* put a sole on. [ME < OF *sole,* ult. < L *solea* < *solum* bottom, ground]

sole[3] (sōl) *n.* **sole** or **soles.** a kind of flatfish. European sole is valued highly as food. [ME < MF < L *solea,* originally, sole[2]]

sol·e·cism (sol′ə siz′əm) *n.* **1** a violation of the grammatical or other accepted usages of a language; a mistake in using words: "*I done it*" *is a solecism.* **2** a mistake in social behavior; breach of good manners or etiquette. [< L < Gk. *soloikismos,* supposedly < *Soloi,* a Greek colony in Cilicia, an ancient region in Asia Minor]

sole·ly (sōl′lē) *adv.* **1** as the only one or ones; alone: *You will be solely responsible.* **2** only.

sol·emn (sol′əm) *adj.* **1** serious; grave; earnest: *a solemn face.* **2** causing serious or grave thoughts: *The organ played solemn music.* **3** done with form and ceremony. **4** connected with religion; sacred. [ME < OF < L *sollemnis*] —**sol′emn·ly,** *adv.* —**sol′emn·ness,** *n.* —**Syn. 2** impressive.

so·lem·ni·ty (sə lem′nə tē) *n.* **-ties. 1** a solemn feeling; seriousness; impressiveness. **2** Often, **solemnities,** *pl.* a solemn, formal ceremony: *The solemnities were concluded with a prayer by the college chaplain.*

sol·em·nize (sol′əm nīz′) *v.* **-nized, -niz·ing. 1** observe with ceremonies: *Christian churches solemnize the resurrection of Christ at Easter.* **2** hold or perform (a ceremony or service): *The marriage was solemnized in the cathedral.* **3** make serious or grave. —**sol′em·ni·za′tion,** *n.*

so·le·noid (sō′lə noid′) *n.* in electricity, a spiral or cylindrical coil of wire that acts like a magnet when a current passes through it. [< F < Gk. *sōlēn* pipe]

sol-fa (sōl′fä′) *n. adj. v.* **-faed, -fa·ing.** —*n.* the system of singing the syllables *do, re, mi, fa, sol, la, ti, do* to tones of a scale. —*adj.* of or having to do with this system of singing: *sol-fa notation, sol-fa scale, sol-fa syllables.* —*v.* use the sol-fa syllables in singing; sing to the sol-fa scale. [< Ital. *solfa* < *sol* + *fa.* See GAMUT.]

sol·feg·gio (sol fej′ō) *n.* **-gios. 1** an exercise for the voice in which the sol-fa syllables are used. **2** the use of the sol-fa syllables. [< Ital. *solfeggio* < *solfa.* See SOL-FA.]

so·lic·it (sə lis′it) *v.* **1** ask earnestly; try to get: *The tailor sent around cards soliciting trade.* **2** make appeals or requests: *solicit for contributions.* **3** influence to do wrong; tempt; entice: *To solicit a judge means to offer him bribes.* **4** accost a person with immoral offers. [ME < L *sollicitare* < *sollicitus.* See SOLICITOUS.] —**Syn. 1** request, beg. See **ask.**

so·lic·i·ta·tion (sə lis′ə tā′shən) *n.* **1** an earnest request; entreaty. **2** an urging to do wrong; temptation; enticement.

so·lic·i·tor (sə lis′ə tər) *n.* **1** a person who entreats or requests. **2** a person who seeks trade or business. **3** a lawyer, especially one who does not plead in court. In England, a solicitor prepares a case and a barrister pleads it. In Canada, the same person may be both solicitor and barrister. **4** a lawyer for a town, city, etc.

solicitor general *pl.* **solicitors general. 1** in Canada, one of the two federal law officers of the Crown, the other being the attorney general. **2** a chief law officer, usually ranking next below an attorney general.

so·lic·it·ous (sə lis′ə təs) *adj.* **1** showing care or concern; anxious; concerned: *Parents are solicitous for their children's progress.* **2** desirous; eager: *solicitous to please.* [< L *sollicitus* < OL *sollus* all + *citus* stirred up, pp. of *ciere* arouse] —**so·lic′it·ous·ly,** *adv.* —**so·lic′it·ous·ness,** *n.*

so·lic·i·tude (sə lis′ə tüd′ or sə lis′ə tūd′) *n.* anxious care; anxiety; concern. —**Syn.** See **care.**

sol·id (sol′id) *adj.* **1** not a liquid or a gas: *Water becomes solid when it freezes.* **2** not hollow: *A bar of iron is solid; a pipe is hollow.* **3** strongly put together; hard; firm: *They were glad to leave the boat and put their feet on solid ground.* **4** alike throughout: *The cloth is a solid blue.* **5** firmly united: *The country was solid for peace.* **6** serious; not superficial or trifling: *a background of solid study.* **7** genuine; real: *solid comfort.* **8** that can be depended on: *He is a solid citizen.* **9** having good judgment; sound; sensible; intelligent: *a solid book by a solid thinker.* **10** financially sound or strong: *a solid business.* **11** whole; entire: *I waited three solid hours.* **12** undivided; continuous: *a solid row of houses.* **13** in printing, having the lines of type not separated by leads; having few open spaces. **14** having length, breadth, and thickness. **15** written without a hyphen. *Earthworm* is a solid word. **16** *Informal.* on a friendly, favorable, or advantageous footing: *get in solid with one's employer.* **17** thorough; downright; vigorous; substantial: *a good solid blow.* **18** *Slang.* good; excellent; first-rate.
—*n.* **1** a substance that is not a liquid or a gas. **2** a body that has length, breadth, and thickness. A cube is a solid. [ME, ult. < L *solidus*] —**sol′id·ly,** *adv.* —**sol′id·ness,** *n.* —**Syn.** *adj.* **3** compact, stable. See **firm.**

sol·i·dar·i·ty (sol′ə dar′ə tē) *n.* **-ties.** unity of fellowship arising from common responsibilities and interests. [< F *solidarité*]

hat, āge, cãre, fär; let, ēqual, tėrm; it, īce
hot, ōpen, ôrder; oil, out; cup, pu̇t, rüle, ūse
əbove, takən, pencəl, lemən, circəs
ch, child; ng, long; sh, ship
th, thin; ᴛʜ, then; zh, measure

solid geometry the branch of mathematics that deals with objects having the three dimensions of length, breadth, and thickness.

so·lid·i·fy (sə lid′ə fī′) *v.* **-fied, -fy·ing. 1** make or become solid; harden: *Extreme cold will solidify water. Jelly solidifies as it gets cold.* **2** make or become firmly united. **3** make or become crystallized. —**so·lid′i·fi·ca′tion,** *n.*

so·lid·i·ty (sə lid′ə tē) *n.* **-ties.** the state or quality of being solid; firmness; hardness; density.

sol·id-state (sol′id stāt′) *adj.* **1** of or having to do with the study of the properties of solid materials, especially of their molecular structure, the movement of their electrons, etc. The transistor was developed as a result of research in solid-state physics. **2** proceeding from or produced by such study: *solid-state electronics, solid-state devices.*

sol·i·dus (sol′ə dəs) *n.* **-di** (-dī or -dē). **1** a Roman gold coin introduced by Constantine, later called a bezant. **2** a sloping line (/) used to separate shillings from pence (as 2/6 for 2 shillings, 6 pence), and generally as a dividing line, as in dates, fractions, etc. [< L *solidus,* short for *solidus* (*nummus*) solid (coin)]

sol·i·fluc·tion or **sol·i·flux·ion** (sol′ə fluk′shən) *n.* the movement of soil and rock waste caused by weather. [< L *solum* ground, earth + E *fluxion*]

so·lil·o·quize (sə lil′ə kwīz′) *v.* **-quized, -quiz·ing. 1** talk to oneself. **2** speak a soliloquy. —**so·lil′o·quiz′er,** *n.*

so·lil·o·quy (sə lil′ə kwē) *n.* **-quies. 1** the act of talking to oneself. **2** a speech made by an actor to himself when alone on the stage. A soliloquy may be used to impart knowledge to the audience, to reveal a character's true motives, etc. [< LL *soliloquium* < L *solus* alone + *loqui* speak]

sol·i·taire (sol′ə tãr′) *n.* **1** a card game played by one person. **2** a diamond or other gem set by itself. [< F < L *solitarius.* Doublet of SOLITARY.]

sol·i·tar·y (sol′ə ter′ē) *adj. n.* **-tar·ies.** —*adj.* **1** alone; single; only: *A solitary rider was seen in the distance.* **2** without companions; away from people; lonely: *He leads a solitary life in his hut in the mountains. The house is in a solitary spot miles from a town.* **3 a** in zoology, living alone, rather than in colonies: *the solitary bee.* **b** in botany, growing separately; not forming clusters: *a solitary stipule.* —*n.* **1** a person living alone, away from people. **2** solitary confinement: *The prisoner was put in solitary.* [< L *solitarius,* ult. < *solus* alone. Doublet of SOLITAIRE.] —**sol′i·tar′i·ly,** *adv.* —**sol′i·tar′i·ness,** *n.*
—**Syn.** *adj.* **1** lone, sole. **2** unattended, remote.

solitary confinement the keeping of a prisoner in complete isolation from others, often as a penalty for misbehavior while in prison.

sol·i·tude (sol′ə tūd′ or sol′ə tüd′) *n.* **1** the condition of being alone: *He likes company and hates solitude.* **2** a lonely place. **3** loneliness. [< L *solitudo* < *solus* alone]
Syn. 1 Solitude, isolation = a state of being alone. **Solitude,** applying to a state of being either where there are no other people for company or cut off voluntarily or involuntarily from those around, emphasizes aloneness, the fact or feeling of being entirely by oneself, without companions: *Both the prospector in the desert and the shy person in the city live in solitude.* **Isolation** emphasizes being separated from others or standing apart from the rest of the world: *A single mountain peak rose in splendid isolation.*

sol·mi·za·tion (sol′mə zā′shən) *n.* in music, the system of singing the syllables *do, re, mi, fa, sol, la, ti, do* to the tones of the eight-tone scale; sol-fa. [< F *solmisation,* ult. < *sol* + *mi.* See GAMUT.]

so·lo (sō′lō) *n.* **-los,** *adj. v.* **-loed, -lo·ing.** —*n.* **1** a piece of music arranged for one voice or instrument. **2** anything done without a partner, companion, instructor, etc. —*adj.* **1** arranged for and performed by one voice or instrument: *a solo part.* **2** playing the solo part: *a solo violin.* **3** without a partner, companion, instructor, etc.; alone: *a solo flight, a solo dance.* —*v.* make a solo flight in an airplane. [< Ital. *solo* alone < L *solus*]

so·lo·ist (sō′lō ist) *n.* a person who performs a solo or solos.

Sol·o·mon (sol′ə mən) *n.* **1** in the Bible, a king of Israel and son of David, famous for his wisdom and for the great temple which he had built in Jerusalem. I Kings 3:5-28. **2** any man of great wisdom.

Solomon's seal a starlike figure formed of two triangles interlaced. See diagram in the next column.

Sol·o·mon's-seal (sol′ə mənz sēl′) *n.* a kind of plant that has small flowers hanging from the bases of the leaves and a rootstock with seal-like scars.

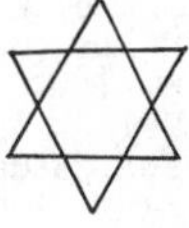
A Solomon's seal

So·lon (sō′lən or sō′lon) *n.* **1** a wise man; sage. **2** *Informal.* a member of a legislature. [< *Solon* (638?-558? B.C.), a wise Athenian lawgiver]

so long *Informal.* good-bye; farewell.

sol·stice (sol′stis) *n.* **1** either of the two times in the year when the sun is at its greatest distance from the celestial equator. In the Northern Hemisphere, June 21 or 22, the **summer solstice,** is the longest day of the year and December 21 or 22, the **winter solstice,** is the shortest. **2** either of the two points reached by the sun at these times. **3** a turning or culminating point; furthest limit; crisis. [ME < OF < L *solstitium,* ult. < *sol* sun + *sistere* stand still]

sol·sti·tial (sol stish′əl) *adj.* having to do with a solstice.

sol·u·bil·i·ty (sol′yu̇ bil′ə tē) *n.* **-ties. 1** a quality that substances have of dissolving or being dissolved easily: *the solubility of sugar in water.* **2** a quality that problems, difficulties, questions, etc. have of being solved or explained.

sol·u·ble (sol′yu̇ bəl) *adj.* **1** that can be dissolved or made into liquid: *Salt is soluble in water.* **2** that can be solved: *soluble puzzles.* [< L *solubilis* < *solvere* dissolve] —**sol′u·bly,** *adv.*

sol·ute (sol′ūt or sō′lüt) *n.* a solid, gas, etc. dissolved in a liquid to make a solution: *Salt is a solute in sea water.* [< L *solutus,* pp. of *solvere* dissolve, loosen]

so·lu·tion (sə lü′shən) *n.* **1** the solving of a problem: *The solution of the problem required many hours.* **2** an explanation: *The police are seeking a solution of the crime.* **3** the process of dissolving; changing of a solid or gas to a liquid by treatment with a liquid. **4** a liquid or mixture formed by dissolving. **5** a separating into parts. **6** the condition of being dissolved: *Sugar and salt can be held in solution in water.* [ME < OF < L *solutio, -onis* a loosing < *solvere* loosen]

solv·a·ble (sol′və bəl) *adj.* **1** capable of being solved. **2** capable of being dissolved.

solve (solv) *v.* **solved, solv·ing.** find the answer to; clear up; explain: *The mystery was never solved. He has solved all the problems in the lesson.* [ME < L *solvere* loosen] —**solv′er,** *n.*

sol·ven·cy (sol′vən sē) *n.* **-cies.** the ability to pay all one owes.

sol·vent (sol′vənt) *adj.* **1** able to pay all that one owes: *A bankrupt firm is not solvent.* **2** able to dissolve: *Gasoline is a solvent liquid that removes grease spots.* —*n.* **1** a substance, usually a liquid, that can dissolve other substances: *Water is a solvent of sugar and salt.* **2** a thing that solves. [< L *solvens, -entis,* ppr. of *solvere* loosen, pay]

so·ma (sō′mə) *n.* **so·ma·ta** (sō′mə tə). in biology, all the tissues and organs of an animal or plant except the germ cells. [< NL < Gk. *sōma* body]

So·ma·li (sə mä′lē) *n.* **-li** or **-lis. 1** a group of people living in E. Africa and having Negro, Arab, and other blood. **2** a member of this group. **3** the language of this group.

so·mat·ic (sō mat′ik) *adj.* **1** of or having to do with the body. **2** having to do with the cavity of the body, or its walls. **3** having to do with the soma. [< Gk. *sōmatikos* < *sōma, -atos* body]

somatic cell in biology, any cell of an animal or plant, except a germ cell.

som·bre or **som·ber** (som′bər) *adj.* **1** dark; gloomy: *A cloudy winter day is sombre.* **2** melancholy; dismal:

His losses made him very sombre. [< F *sombre*, probably ult. < L *sub-* under + *umbra* shade] —**som′bre·ly** or **som′ber·ly,** *adv.* —**som′bre·ness** or **som′ber·ness,** *n.* —**Syn. 1** cloudy, murky. **2** depressing, sad.

som·brer·o (som brãr′ō) *n.* **-brer·os.** a broad-brimmed hat worn in Mexico, the S.W. United States, etc. [< Sp. *sombrero*, ult. < L *sub-* under + *umbra* shade]

A man wearing a sombrero

some (sum; *unstressed*, səm) *adj.* **1** certain, but not known or named: *Some people sleep more than others.* **2** a number of: *He left the city some years ago.* **3** a quantity of: *Drink some milk.* **4** a; any: *Ask some girl to come here.* **5** about: *Some twenty people saw it.* **6** *Informal.* big; good: *That was some storm!*
—*pron.* **1** certain unnamed persons or things: *Some think so.* **2** a certain number or quantity: *Jack ate some and threw the rest away.*
—*adv.* **1** *Informal.* to some degree or extent; somewhat: *He is some better today.* **2** *Informal.* to a great degree or extent: *That's going some!* [OE *sum*]

-some[1] *suffix.* **1** tending to, as in *frolicsome, meddlesome.* **2** causing, as in *awesome, troublesome.* **3** to a considerable degree, as in *lonesome.* [OE *-sum*]

-some[2] *suffix.* a group of, as in *twosome, foursome.* [< *some*]

some·bod·y (sum′bud′ē or -bod′ē) *pron. n.* **-bod·ies.** —*pron.* a person not known or named; some person; someone. —*n.* a person of importance: *She acts as if she were somebody since she won the prize.*

some·day (sum′dā′) *adv.* at some future time.

some·how (sum′hou′) *adv.* **1** in a way not known or not stated; in one way or another: *I'll finish this work somehow.* **2 somehow or other,** in one way or another.

some·one (sum′wun′ or sum′wən) *pron.* some person; somebody.

som·er·sault (sum′ər solt′ or -sôlt′) *n.* a roll or jump, turning the heels over the head: *He turned a somersault.* —*v.* roll or jump, turning the heels over the head. Also, **summersault.** [ME *sombresault* < Provençal *sobresaut*, ult. < L *supra* over + *saltus* jump]

som·er·set (sum′ər set′) *n. v.* somersault.

some·thing (sum′thing′) *n.* **1** some thing; a particular thing not named or known: *He has something on his mind.* **2** a certain amount or quantity; part; little: *Something yet of doubt remains.* **3** a thing or person of some value or importance: *He thinks he's something.* **4** a thing or person that is to a certain extent an example of what is named: *He was something of a violinist.* —*adv.* somewhat; to some extent or degree: *He is something like his father.*

some·time (sum′tīm′) *adv.* **1** at one time or another: *Come over sometime.* **2** at an indefinite point of time: *It happened sometime last March.* —*adj.* former: *a sometime pupil of the school.*

some·times (sum′tīmz′) *adv.* now and then; at times: *He comes to visit sometimes.*

some·way (sum′wā′) *adv.* in some way.

some·what (sum′hwot′ or -wot′) *adv.* to some extent or degree; slightly: *somewhat round.* —*n.* **1** some part; some amount: *somewhat of a musician.* **2** a little.

some·where (sum′hwãr′ or -wãr′) *adv.* **1** in or to some place; in or to one place or another: *He lives somewhere in the neighborhood.* **2** at some time: *It happened somewhere in the last century.*

some·while (sum′hwīl′ or -wīl′) *adv.* **1** at times. **2** *Rare.* for some time. **3** sometime. **4** formerly.

some·whith·er (sum′hwiᴛʜ′ər or -wiᴛʜ′ər) *adv. Rare.* to some place.

som·nam·bu·lism (som nam′byů liz′əm) *n.* sleepwalking. [< L *somnus* sleep + *ambulare* walk]

som·nam·bu·list (som nam′byů list) *n.* a sleepwalker.

som·nam·bu·lis·tic (som nam′byů lis′tik) *adj.* having to do with sleepwalking or sleepwalkers. —**som·nam′bu·lis′ti·cal·ly,** *adv.*

som·nif·er·ous (som nif′ər əs) *adj.* **1** causing sleep. **2** sleepy. [< L *somnifer* < *somnus* sleep + *ferre* bring] —**som·nif′er·ous·ly,** *adv.*

som·no·lence (som′nə ləns) *n.* sleepiness; drowsiness.

som·no·lent (som′nə lənt) *adj.* sleepy; drowsy. [< L *somnolentus* < *somnus* sleep] —**som′no·lent·ly,** *adv.*

Som·nus (som′nəs) *n.* in Roman mythology, the god of sleep.

son (sun) *n.* **1** a male child or person spoken of in relation to either or both of his parents. **2** a male descendant. **3** a son-in-law. **4** a boy or man attached to a country, a cause, etc. as a child is to its parents: *sons of liberty.* **5** anything thought of as a son in relation to its origin. **6** a term of address to a boy or from an older person, priest, etc. **7 the Son,** Jesus Christ. [OE *sunu*] —**son′less,** *adj.*

so·nance (sō′nəns) *n.* a sonant quality or state.

so·nant (sō′nənt) *adj.* **1** of sound; having sound; sounding. **2** in phonetics, pronounced with the vocal cords vibrating; voiced. —*n.* in phonetics, a sound pronounced with the vocal cords vibrating; a voiced sound. (z) and (v) are sonants; (s) and (f) are not. [< L *sonans, -antis*, ppr. of *sonare* to sound < *sonus*, n., sound]

so·nar (sō′när) *n.* a device using the reflection of underwater sound waves for navigation, range finding, detecting submerged objects, etc. [< *so*und *na*vigation *r*ange]

so·na·ta (sə nä′tə) *n.* in music, an instrumental composition having three or four movements in contrasted rhythms but related keys: *a piano sonata.* [< Ital. *sonata*, literally, sounded (on an instrument, as distinguished from sung), ult. < L *sonus* sound]

sonata form in music, the structure of a movement, especially the first movement, of a sonata, symphony, concerto, etc. The sonata form usually has three main divisions, exposition, development, and recapitulation, often followed by a coda.

son·a·ti·na (son′ə tē′nə) *n.* a short or simplified sonata. [< Ital. *sonatina*, dim. of *sonata* sonata]

song (song) *n.* **1** something to sing; a short poem set to music. **2 a** poetry: *fame celebrated in song.* **b** poetry that has a lyrical quality: *a song of childhood.* **3** a piece of music for, or as if for, a poem that is to be sung. **4** the act or practice of singing: *The canary burst into song.* **5** any sound like singing: *the cricket's song, the song of the teakettle, the song of the brook.* **6** a mere trifle; low price: *buy things for a song.* **7 for a song,** very cheap. **8 song and dance,** *Slang.* **a** an explanation or account, not necessarily true, and often intended to impress or deceive. **b** fuss; disturbance; turmoil: *He made a great song and dance about having to do the job.* [OE *sang*]

song·bird (song′bėrd′) *n.* **1** a bird that sings. **2** *Informal.* a woman singer.

song·less (song′lis) *adj.* not able to sing.

Song of Songs the Song of Solomon, a book of the Old Testament.

song sparrow a small North American songbird having black, brown, and white feathers.

song·ster (song′stər) *n.* **1** a singer. **2** a writer of songs or poems. **3** a songbird. [OE *sangestre*]

song·stress (song′stris) *n.* **1** a woman singer. **2** a woman writer of songs or poems; poetess. **3** a female songbird.

song thrush 1 a songbird living in the woods of E. North America; the wood thrush. **2** a European bird noted for its song; the mavis.

son·ic (son′ik) *adj.* **1** of, having to do with, or using sound waves. **2** having to do with the rate at which sound travels in air (approximately 1,100 feet per second or 750 miles per hour at sea level). [< L *sonus* sound]

sonic barrier or **wall** the point at which an airplane or projectile attains the same rate of speed as sound. Air disturbances are encountered at this point.

sonic boom the shock wave, heard as a loud boom, generated by an aircraft as it penetrates the sound barrier.

sonic mine a container holding an explosive charge that is put under water and exploded by propeller vibrations; acoustic mine.

so·nif·er·ous (sō nif′ər əs) *adj.* carrying or producing sound. [< L *sonus* sound + E *-ferous*]

son-in-law (sun′in lo′ or -lô′) *n.* **sons-in-law.** the husband of one's daughter.

son·net (son′it) *n.* a poem having 14 lines, usually in iambic pentameter, and a certain arrangement of rhymes. Elizabethan and Italian sonnets differ in the arrangement of the rhymes. [< F < Ital. < Provençal *sonet,* ult. < L *sonus* sound]

son·net·eer (son′ə tēr′) *n.* a writer of sonnets. —*v.* write sonnets.

son·ny (sun′ē) *n.* **-nies.** little son (used as a pet name, or as a way of speaking to a little boy or to a man younger than the speaker).

Son of God Jesus Christ.

so·nom·e·ter (sō nom′ə tər) *n.* **1** an instrument used in measuring the pitch of musical tones or for experimenting with vibrating strings. **2** an instrument used for testing a person's hearing. [< L *sonus* sound + E *-meter*]

so·nor·i·ty (sə nôr′ə tē) *n.* **-ties.** the state or quality of being sonorous.

so·no·rous (sə nô′rəs) *adj.* **1** giving out or having a deep, loud sound. **2** full and rich in sound. **3** having an impressive sound; high-sounding: *sonorous phrases, a sonorous style.* [< L *sonorus,* ult. < *sonor* sound] —**so·no′rous·ly,** *adv.*

son·ship (sun′ship) *n.* the state of being a son.

Sons of Freedom a sect of Doukhobors located, for the most part, in British Columbia.

soon (sün) *adv.* **1** in a short time; before long: *I will see you again soon.* **2** before the usual or expected time; early: *Why have you come so soon?* **3** promptly; quickly: *As soon as I hear, I will let you know.* **4** readily; willingly: *The brave soldier would as soon die as yield to the enemy.* **5 had sooner,** would more readily; prefer to. [OE *sōna* at once] —**Syn. 1** shortly, presently.

☛ **sooner than.** After *no sooner* the connective used is *than,* not *when: The fly had no sooner hit the water than* (not *when*) *a huge trout snapped at it.*

soot (sůt) *n.* a black substance in the smoke from burning coal, wood, oil, etc. Soot makes smoke dark and collects on the inside of chimneys. —*v.* cover or blacken with soot. [OE *sōt*] —**soot′less,** *adj.*

sooth (süth) *Archaic.* —*n.* the truth. —*adj.* true. [OE *sōth*]

soothe (süᴛʜ) *v.* **soothed, sooth·ing. 1** quiet; calm; comfort: *The mother soothed the crying child.* **2** make less painful; relieve; ease. [OE *sōthian*] —**sooth′ing·ly,** *adv.*

sooth·er (süᴛʜ′ər) *n.* **1** a person or thing that soothes. **2** a baby's pacifier.

sooth·ly (süth′lē) *adv. Archaic.* truly; in truth.

sooth·say·er (süth′sā′ər) *n.* a person who claims to tell what will happen; person who make predictions. [< *sooth* + *sayer*]

sooth·say·ing (süth′sā′ing) *n.* **1** the foretelling of future events. **2** a prediction or prophecy.

soot·y (sůt′ē) *adj.* **soot·i·er, soot·i·est. 1** covered or blackened with soot. **2** dark-brown or black; dark-colored. —**soot′i·ly,** *adv.* —**soot′i·ness,** *n.*

sop (sop) *n. v.* **sopped, sop·ping.** —*n.* **1** a piece of food dipped or soaked in milk, broth, etc. **2** something given to soothe or quiet; bribe. **3** a person or thing that is thoroughly soaked. —*v.* **1** dip or soak. **2** take up (water, etc.); wipe; mop: *Please sop up that water with a cloth.* **3** be drenched. **4** soak thoroughly; drench. **5** soak in or through. [OE *sopp*]

sop. soprano.

soph·ic (sof′ik) *adj.* of, having to do with, or teaching wisdom. [< Gk. *sophikos* < *sophos* wise, clever]

soph·ism (sof′iz əm) *n.* a clever but misleading argument; an argument based on false or unsound reasoning. [ME < OF < L < Gk. *sophisma,* ult. < *sophos* clever]

soph·ist (sof′ist) *n.* **1** a clever but misleading reasoner.

hat, āge, cãre, fär; let, ēqual, tėrm; it, īce
hot, ōpen, ôrder; oil, out; cup, půt, rüle, ūse
əbove, takən, pencəl, lemən, circəs
ch, child; ng, long; sh, ship
th, thin; ᴛʜ, then; zh, measure

2 Often, **Sophist.** in ancient Greece, one of a class of teachers of rhetoric, philosophy, ethics, etc. **3** a man of learning.

so·phis·tic (sə fis′tik) *adj.* sophistical.

so·phis·ti·cal (sə fis′tə kəl) *adj.* **1** clever but misleading; based on false or unsound reasoning. **2** using clever but misleading arguments; reasoning falsely or unsoundly. —**so·phis′ti·cal·ly,** *adv.*

so·phis·ti·cate (*v.* sə fis′tə kāt′; *n.* sə fis′tə kāt′ or sə fis′tə kət′) *v.* **-cat·ed, -cat·ing,** *n.* —*v.* **1** make experienced in worldly ways; cause to lose one's natural simplicity and frankness; make artificial. **2** mislead. **3** use sophistry; quibble. **4** involve in sophistry. **5** of instruments, devices, etc., make more complex and efficient. —*n.* a sophisticated person. [ME < Med.L *sophisticare* < L < Gk. *sophistikos* sophistical, ult. < *sophos* clever]

so·phis·ti·cat·ed (sə fis′tə kāt′id) *adj.* **1** experienced in worldly ways; informed; knowing; aware. **2** lacking in natural simplicity or frankness. **3** artificial. **4** misleading. **5** of mechanical or electronic devices, complex and advanced in design: *sophisticated missiles.*

so·phis·ti·ca·tion (sə fis′tə kā′shən) *n.* **1** worldly experience or ideas. **2** a lessening or loss of naturalness, simplicity, or frankness; artificial ways. **3** sophistry. **4** the quality of being intellectually subtle and perceptive.

soph·ist·ry (sof′is trē) *n.* **-ries. 1** unsound reasoning. **2** a clever but misleading argument. **3** the art, practice, or learning of the sophists of ancient Greece, especially of their type of argument.

soph·o·more (sof′ə môr′) *n.* a student in the second year of college. —*adj.* of or having to do with second-year college students. [earlier *sophomer,* originally, taking part in dialectic exercises < *sophom,* var. of *sophism*]

soph·o·mor·ic (sof′ə môr′ik) *adj.* **1** of, having to do with, or like a sophomore or sophomores. **2** conceited and pretentious but crude and ignorant.

so·po·rif·er·ous (sop′ə rif′ər əs or sō′pə rif′ər əs) *adj.* bringing sleep; causing sleep. [< L *soporifer* < *sopor* deep sleep + *ferre* bring]

so·po·rif·ic (sop′ə rif′ik or sō′pə rif′ik) *adj.* **1** causing or tending to cause sleep. **2** sleepy; drowsy. —*n.* a drug that causes sleep. [< L *sopor* deep sleep + *facere* make]

sop·ping (sop′ing) *adj.* soaked; drenched.

sop·py (sop′ē) *adj.* **-pi·er, -pi·est.** soaked; very wet: *soppy ground, soppy weather.*

so·pran·o (sə pran′ō or sə prä′nō) *n.* **-pran·os,** *adj.* —*n.* **1** the highest voice in girls, women, and boys. **2** in music: **a** a singer with such a voice. **b** a part for such a voice or for a corresponding instrument. **c** an instrument playing such a part. —*adj.* **1** of, for, or having to do with a soprano. **2** that can sing or play a soprano part. [< Ital. *soprano* < *sopra* above < L *supra*]

Sor·bonne (sôr bon′ or sôr′bon) *n.* the seat of the faculties of letters and science of the University of Paris.

sor·cer·er (sôr′sər ər) *n.* a man who practises magic with the aid of evil spirits; magician.

sor·cer·ess (sôr′sər is) *n.* a woman who practises magic with the aid of evil spirits; witch.

sor·cer·y (sôr′sər ē) *n.* **-cer·ies.** magic performed with the aid of evil spirits; witchcraft. [ME < OF *sorcerie,* ult. < L *sors* lot] —**Syn.** necromancy.

sor·did (sôr′did) *adj.* **1** dirty; filthy: *The poor family lived in a sordid hut.* **2** mean; low; base; contemptible. **3** caring too much for money; meanly selfish; greedy. [< L *sordidus* dirty < *sordere* be dirty < *sordes* dirt] —**sor′did·ly,** *adv.* —**sor′did·ness,** *n.* —**Syn. 1** foul, squalid. **2** ignoble, degraded.

sore (sôr) *adj.* **sor·er, sor·est,** *n. adv.* —*adj.* **1** painful; aching; tender; smarting: *a sore throat, a sore finger.* **2** sad; distressed: *The suffering of the refugees made her*

heart sore. **3** easily angered or offended; irritable; touchy. **4** *Informal.* offended; angered; vexed: *He is sore at missing the game.* **5** causing pain, misery, anger, or offence; vexing: *Their defeat is a sore subject with the members of the team.* **6** severe; distressing: *Your going away is a sore grief to us.*
—*n.* **1** a painful place on the body where the skin or flesh is broken or bruised. **2** a cause of pain, sorrow, sadness, anger, offence, etc.
—*adv. Archaic.* in a sore manner. [OE *sār*] **—sore′ly,** *adv.* **—sore′ness,** *n.*

sore·head (sôr′hed′) *n. Informal.* a person who is easily angered or offended.

sor·ghum (sôr′gəm) *n.* **1** a tall cereal plant resembling corn. One variety has a sweet juice used for making molasses or syrup, others provide food for livestock either by their grain or as hay, and still others furnish material for brushes or brooms. **2** molasses or syrup made from a sorghum plant. [< NL < Ital. < L *syricum* Syrian]

so·ror·i·ty (sə rôr′ə tē) *n.* **-ties. 1** a sisterhood. **2** a club or society of women or girls. There are student sororities in many North American colleges. [probably < Med.L *sororitas* < L *soror* sister]

sor·rel[1] (sôr′əl) *adj.* reddish-brown. —*n.* **1** a reddish brown. **2** a reddish-brown horse. [ME < OF *sorel* < *sor* yellowish-brown]

sor·rel[2] (sôr′əl) *n.* any of several plants having sour leaves. [ME < OF *surele* < *sur* sour < Gmc.]

sor·row (sor′ō or sôr′ō) *n.* **1** grief; sadness; regret. **2** a cause of grief, sadness, or regret; trouble; suffering; misfortune: *Her sorrows have aged her.* —*v.* **1** feel or show grief, sadness, or regret. **2** be sad; feel sorry; grieve. [OE *sorg*] **—sor′row·er,** *n.* **—sor′row·less,** *adj.*
Syn. *n.* **1 Sorrow, grief, distress** = mental suffering caused by loss or trouble. **Sorrow** = deep sadness or mental pain caused by the loss of someone or something dear or the experiencing or doing of something bad or wrong: *The dope addict became a criminal and brought great sorrow to his mother.* **Grief** = deeply or keenly felt sorrow or very painful regret: *Her grief when he died was unbearable.* **Distress** particularly suggests the strain or pressure of pain (physical or mental), grief, fear, anxiety, etc. caused by any trouble: *War causes widespread distress.* **2** affliction, woe.

sor·row·ful (sor′ə fəl or sôr′ə fəl) *adj.* **1** full of sorrow; feeling sorrow; sad. **2** showing sorrow. **3** causing sorrow. **—sor′row·ful·ly,** *adv.* **—sor′row·ful·ness,** *n.* **—Syn. 1, 2** unhappy, mournful.

sor·ry (sor′ē or sôr′ē) *adj.* **-ri·er, -ri·est. 1** feeling pity, regret, sympathy, etc.; sad: *I am sorry that you are sick.* **2** wretched; poor; pitiful: *The blind beggar in his ragged clothes was a sorry sight.* **3 be sorry,** ask pardon, as in making an apology. [OE *sārig* < *sār* sore] **—sor′ri·ly,** *adv.* **—sor′ri·ness,** *n.*

sort (sôrt) *n.* **1** a kind; class: *What sort of work does he do?* **2** a character; quality; nature. **3** a person or thing of a certain kind or quality: *He is a good sort.* **4** in printing, a letter or piece in a font of type. **5** a way; fashion; manner. **6 of sorts, a** of one kind or another. **b** of a poor or mediocre quality. **7 out of sorts,** ill, cross, or uncomfortable. **8 sort of** (*used adverbially*), *Informal.* somewhat; rather.
—*v.* **1** arrange by kinds or classes; arrange in order: *Sort these cards according to their colors.* **2** separate from others; put: *The farmer sorted out the best apples for eating.* **3** *Archaic.* agree; accord. [ME < OF *sorte,* ult. < L *sors, sortis,* originally, lot] **—sort′er,** *n.* **—Syn.** *n.* **1** See **kind**[2]. *-v.* **1** assort, classify, class, select. ☛ See **kind**[2] for usage note.

sor·tie (sôr′tē) *n.* **1** a sudden attack by troops from a defensive position. **2** a single round trip of a military aircraft against an enemy. [< F *sortie* < *sortir* go out]

so·rus (sô′rəs) *n.* **so·ri** (-rī or -rē). in botany, any of the dotlike clusters of spores on the back of the frond of a fern. [< NL < Gk. *sōros* heap]

S O S (es′ō′es′) **1** a signal of distress consisting of the letters *s o s* of the Morse code (· · · — — — · · ·), used in wireless telegraphy. **2** *Informal.* any urgent call for help.
☛ SOS is a code signal only; it is not an abbreviation.

so-so (sō′sō′) *adj.* neither very good nor very bad. —*adv.* passably; indifferently; tolerably.

sos·te·nu·to (sos′tə nü′tō) in music: —*adj.* **1** sustained; held. **2** prolonged; played or sung at a gradually decreasing tempo. —*adv.* in a sostenuto manner. —*n.* a sostenuto note, movement, or passage; composition to be played or sung in this manner. [< Ital. *sostenuto,* pp. of *sostenere* sustain < L *sustinere.* See SUSTAIN.]

sot (sot) *n.* a person made stupid and foolish by drinking alcoholic liquor; drunkard. [OE < Med.L *sottus*]

sot·tish (sot′ish) *adj.* **1** stupid and foolish from drinking too much alcoholic liquor; drunken. **2** of a sot; like a sot. **—sot′tish·ly,** *adv.* **—sot′tish·ness,** *n.*

sot·to vo·ce (sot′ō vō′chē; *Italian,* sōt′tō vō′chā) **1** in a low tone. **2** aside; privately. [< Ital. *sotto voce,* literally, below (normal) voice]

sou (sü) *n.* **1** a former French coin, worth 5 centimes or 1/20 of a franc. **2** anything of little value. [< F *sou,* ult. < L *solidus,* a Roman coin]

sou·brette (sü bret′) *n.* **1** a maidservant or lady's maid in a play or opera, especially one displaying coquetry, pertness, and a spirit of intrigue; a lively or pert young woman character. **2** an actress or singer taking such a part. [< F < Provençal *soubreto* coy < *soubra* set aside]

sou·bri·quet (sü′brə kā′ or sü′brə ket′) *n.* sobriquet.

souf·flé (sü flā′ or sü′flā) *n. French.* a frothy baked dish, usually made light by beaten eggs: *cheese soufflé.* —*adj.* puffed up: *potatoes soufflé.* [< F *soufflé,* originally pp. of *souffler* puff up]

sough (sou or suf) *v.* make a rustling or murmuring sound: *The pines soughed when the wind blew.* —*n.* a rustling or murmuring sound. [OE *swōgan*]

sought (sot or sôt) *v.* pt. and pp. of **seek.**

soul (sōl) *n.* **1** the part of the human being that thinks, feels, and makes the body act; the spiritual part of a person: *"Death separates soul and body," said the preacher.* **2** energy of mind or feelings; spirit: *She puts her whole soul into her work.* **3** a cause of inspiration and energy: *Florence Nightingale was the soul of the movement to reform nursing.* **4** the essential part: *Brevity is the soul of wit.* **5** a person: *Don't tell a soul.* **6** an embodiment: *He is the soul of honor.* **7** the spirit of a dead person. **8** among American Negroes, a sense of pride of race and culture. **9 upon my soul!** as I hope to be saved! indeed! well! —*adj.* of, for, or like Negroes. [OE *sāwol*]

soul·ful (sōl′fəl) *adj.* **1** full of feeling; deeply emotional. **2** expressing or suggesting a deep feeling. **—soul′ful·ly,** *adv.* **—soul′ful·ness,** *n.*

soul·less (sōl′lis) *adj.* having no soul; without spirit or noble feelings. **—soul′less·ly,** *adv.*

soul-search·ing (sōl′sėr′ching) *n.* a deep and honest effort, especially during a crisis, to evaluate one's own motives, beliefs, etc. so as to assess one's conduct and attitudes.

sound[1] (sound) *n.* **1** what can be heard; auditory sensation. **2** the vibrations causing this sensation. Sound travels in waves. **3** a noise, note, tone, etc. whose quality indicates its source or nature: *the sound of fighting.* **4** the distance within which a noise may be heard. **5** one of the simple elements composing speech: *a vowel sound.* **6** the effect produced on the mind by what is heard: *a warning sound, a queer sound.* **7** mere noise without meaning. **8 within sound,** near enough to hear. [ME < OF *son* < L *sonus*]
—*v.* **1** make a sound or noise: *The trumpet sounds for battle. The wind sounds like an animal howling.* **2** pronounce: *Sound each syllable.* **3** be pronounced: "*Rough*" *and* "*ruff*" *sound alike.* **4** be heard as a sound; issue or pass as sound; be mentioned. **5** be filled with sound. **6** cause to sound: "*Sound the trumpets; beat the drums.*" **7** test by noting sounds: *sound a person's lungs.* **8** order or direct by a sound: *sound a retreat.* **9** make known; announce; utter: *The trumpets sounded the call to arms. Everyone sounded his praises.* **10** seem: *That excuse sounds queer.* [ME < OF *soner* < L *sonare*] **—sound′er,** *n.*

sound[2] (sound) *adj.* **1** free from injury, decay, or defect: *a sound ship, sound fruit.* **2** free from disease; healthy: *a sound body and mind.* **3** strong; safe; secure: *a sound business firm.* **4** solid: *sound rock.* **5** correct; right; reasonable; reliable: *sound advice.* **6** without any legal defect: *a sound title.* **7** having orthodox or conventional ideas: *politically sound.* **8** thorough; hearty: *a sound* *whipping, a sound sleep.* —*adv.* deeply; thoroughly: *sound asleep.* [OE (*ge*)*sund*] —**sound·ly,** *adv.* —**sound·ness,** *n.* —**Syn.** *adj.* 1 uninjured. 6 See **valid.**

sound[3] (sound) *v.* **1** measure the depth of (water) by letting down a weight fastened to the end of a line. **2** examine or test by a line arranged to bring up a sample. **3** inquire into the feelings, inclination, etc. of (a person); examine indirectly; investigate. **4 sound out,** inquire into (a person, his feelings or opinions, etc.); examine indirectly: *John sounded her out on the project, but she didn't seem interested.* **5** go toward the bottom; dive: *The whale sounded.* **6** examine with a sound. —*n.* a long, slender instrument used by doctors in examining body cavities. [ME < OF *sonder*, probably < Gmc. source of *sound*[4]] —**sound'er,** *n.*

sound[4] (sound) *n.* **1** a narrow passage of water joining two seas, or between the mainland and an island: *Queen Charlotte Sound.* **2** an arm of the sea: *Howe Sound.* **3** a sac in the body of a fish that contains air or gas and helps them float. [OE *sund* swimming; partly < ON *sund* strait]

sound barrier the point approximating the speed of sound (approximately 750 miles per hour at sea level) at which an aircraft creates a shock wave and is subjected to various unusual stresses.

sound·board (sound'bôrd') *n.* a thin, resonant piece of wood forming part of a musical instrument, as in a violin or piano, to increase the fullness of its tone.

sound effects in the theatre, motion pictures, radio, and television, noises, as of rain, traffic, crowds, doorbells, etc., called for in the script and produced or simulated as required.

sound·er[1] (soun'dər) *n.* **1** a person or thing that makes a sound. **2** an electromagnetic receiving instrument that converts a telegraphic message into sound. [< *sound*[1]]

sound·er[2] (soun'dər) *n.* a person or thing that measures the depth of water. [< *sound*[3]]

sound·ing[1] (soun'ding) *adj.* **1** that sounds. **2** resounding. **3** sounding fine, but useless. [< *sound*[1]]

sound·ing[2] (soun'ding) *n.* **1** the act of measuring the depth of water by letting down a weight fastened to the end of a line. **2** the depth of water found by measuring in this way. **3** investigation. **4** examination with a sound or probe. **5 soundings,** *pl.* **a** the depths of water found by a line and weight. **b** water not more than 600 feet deep. [< *sound*[3]]

sounding board **1** a soundboard. **2** a structure used to direct sound toward an audience. **3** a means of bringing opinions, etc. out into the open.

sounding line a line having a weight fastened to the end, used to measure the depth of water.

sound·less[1] (sound'lis) *adj.* without sound; making no sound. [< *sound*[1]] —**sound'less·ly,** *adv.*

sound·less[2] (sound'lis) *adj.* so deep that the bottom cannot be reached. [< *sound*[3]]

sound·proof (sound'prüf') *adj.* not letting sound pass through. —*v.* make soundproof.

sound track a record of words, music, etc. made along one edge of a motion-picture film.

sound waves the progressive vibrations by which sounds are transmitted.

soup (süp) *n.* **1** a liquid food made by boiling meat, vegetables, fish, etc. **2** *Slang.* a heavy, wet fog or cloud formation: *fly on instruments through soup.* **3** *Slang.* power; horsepower. **4 in the soup,** *Informal.* in difficulties; in trouble. —*v.* **soup up,** *Slang.* **a** increase the horsepower of (an engine, etc.). **b** make able to accelerate more quickly, attain a higher speed, etc.: *soup up a car.* **c** increase sharply the pace, impact, etc. of (anything): *soup up a story or song.* [< F *soupe* < Gmc.]

soup·çon (süp'son; *French*, süp sôɴ') *n. French.* a slight trace or flavor; very small amount. [< F *soupçon* suspicion]

soup kitchen a place that serves food free or at a very low charge to poor or unemployed people or to victims of a flood, fire, or other disaster.

soup·y (süp'ē) *adj.* **soup·i·er, soup·i·est.** like soup.

sour (sour) *adj.* **1** having the basic taste sensation produced by acids: *Lemon juice is sour. Most green fruit is sour.* **2** fermented; spoiled. Sour milk is healthful, but most foods are not good to eat when they have become sour. **3** having a sour or rank smell. **4** disagreeable; bad-tempered; peevish: *a sour face.* **5** unusually acid: *sour soil.* **6** cold and wet; damp: *sour weather.* **7 go sour,** fall below usual standards of excellence or interest; fall off. —*v.* **1** make or become sour; turn sour. **2** make or become peevish, bad-tempered, or disagreeable. **3** fall below usual standards of excellence or interest. **4 sour on,** take a dislike for.
—*n.* **1** something sour. **2** a sour, alcoholic drink, such as whisky and lemon juice: *a whisky sour.*
—*adv.* in a sour manner. [OE *sūr*] —**sour'ly,** *adv.* —**sour'ness,** *n.*

Syn. *adj.* **1** acid, acidulous, tart. **2** rancid, curdled. **4 Sour, tart, acid** used figuratively to describe a person, his looks, disposition, words, manner of expression, etc. means "resembling vinegar or lemons in harshness or sharpness." **Sour** emphasizes harsh, forbidding, or irritable qualities, and suggests bad temper or a disagreeable mood, surly rudeness, grouchiness, or sullenness: *That janitor has a sour disposition.* **Tart** emphasizes sharp and stinging qualities: *His tart answer made her cry.* **Acid** emphasizes biting, sarcastic, severely critical qualities: *I read an acid comment on the political situation.*

source (sôrs) *n.* **1** a beginning of a brook or river; fountain; spring. **2** a place from which anything comes or is obtained. **3** a person, book, statement, etc. that supplies information. [ME < OF *sourse*, ult. < L *surgere* rise, surge]

sour·dough (sour'dō') *n. Informal.* **1** a prospector or pioneer in northwestern Canada or Alaska. **2** any old resident, experienced hand, etc.; person who is not a tenderfoot. [so called from their practice of saving a lump of sour dough from each breadmaking to start fermentation in subsequent baking]

sour grapes something that a person pretends not to want because he cannot have it. [< Aesop's fable of the fox and the grapes]

souse (sous) *v.* **soused, sous·ing,** *n.* —*v.* **1** plunge into liquid; drench; soak in a liquid. **2** soak in vinegar, brine, etc.; pickle. **3** *Slang.* make or become drunk. —*n.* **1** a plunging into a liquid; drenching. **2** liquid used for pickling. **3** something soaked or kept in pickle, especially the head, ears, and feet of a pig. **4** *Slang.* a drunkard. [ME; ult. < OF *sous* pickled pork, ult. < Gmc. **sult-*, **salt-* salt]

sou·tache (sü'tash or sü tash') *n.* a narrow braid used for trimming. [< F < Hungarian *sujtás* trimming]

sou·tane (sü tän') *n.* a cassock. [< F < Ital. *sottana*, ult. < L *sub* under]

south (south) *n.* **1** the direction to the right as one faces the rising sun; direction opposite to north. **2** Also, **South.** that part of any country toward the south. **3 the South,** in the United States, the part of the country lying south of Pennsylvania, the Ohio River, Missouri, and Kansas.
—*adj.* **1** toward the south. **2** from the south. **3** in the south. **4 south of,** farther south than.
—*adv.* toward the south: *The journey south took two days.* [OE *sūth*]

South African Dutch Afrikaans.

south·bound (south'bound') *adj.* going toward the south.

South·down (south'doun') *n.* **1** an English breed of small, hornless sheep raised for mutton. **2** a sheep of this breed. [< *South Downs*, an area in S. England where this breed originated]

south·east (south'ēst') *n.* **1** the direction halfway between south and east. **2** a place that is in the southeast part or direction. —*adj. adv.* of, at, in, to, toward, or from the southeast.

south·east·er (south'ēs'tər) *n.* a wind or storm from the southeast.

south·east·er·ly (south'ēs'tər lē) *adj. adv.* **1** toward the southeast. **2** from the southeast.

south·east·ern (south′ēs′tərn) *adj.* of, at, in, to, toward, or from the southeast.

south·east·ward (south′ēst′wərd) *adv. adj.* toward the southeast. —*n.* southeast.

south·east·ward·ly (south′ēst′wərd lē) *adj.* **1** toward the southeast. 2 of winds, from the southeast. —*adv.* toward the southeast.

south·east·wards (south′ēst′wərdz) *adv.* southeastward.

south·er (souᴛʜ′ər) *n.* a wind or storm from the south.

south·er·ly (suᴛʜ′ər lē) *adj. adv.* **1** toward the south. **2** from the south.

south·ern (suᴛʜ′ərn) *adj.* **1** toward the south. **2** from the south. 3 of or in the south; of or in the southern part of the country. **4 Southern,** of, in, or having to do with the South. [OE *sūtherne*]

Southern Cross a southern constellation of four bright stars in the form of a cross, used in finding the direction south.

south·ern·er (suᴛʜ′ər nər) *n.* a native or inhabitant of the south.

Southern Hemisphere the half of the earth that is south of the equator.

south·ern·ly (suᴛʜ′ərn lē) *adj.* southerly.

south·ern·most (suᴛʜ′ərn mōst′) *adj.* farthest south.

south·ing (souᴛʜ′ing) *n.* **1** a movement toward the south. **2** a distance due south.

south·land (south′lənd or -land′) *n.* land in the south; the southern part of a country.

south·most(south′mōst′) *adj.* farthest south.

south·paw (south′po′ or -pô′) *Slang.* —*n.* used especially of baseball pitchers and boxers, a left-handed person. —*adj.* left-handed.

South Pole the southern end of the earth's axis.

south·ron (suᴛʜ′rən) *adj. n.* **-rons** or **-ron.** *Archaic. Esp.Scottish.* —*adj.* southern. —*n.* **1** a Southerner. **2** a native of the south of Great Britain; Englishman. **3 the southron,** Englishmen.

South Sea Islander a native or inhabitant of the South Sea Islands, islands in the S. Pacific Ocean.

south·ward (south′wərd) *adv. adj.* toward the south; south. —*n.* a southward part, direction, or point.

south·ward·ly (south′wərd lē) *adj.* **1** toward the south. **2** of winds, coming from the south. —*adv.* toward the south.

south·wards (south′wərdz) *adv.* southward.

south·west(south′west′) *n.* **1** the direction halfway between south and west. **2** a place that is in the southwest part or direction. —*adj. adv.* of, at, in, to, toward, or from the southwest.

south·west·er (south′wes′tər or sou′wes′tər) *n.* **1** a wind or storm from the southwest. **2** a waterproof hat having a broad brim at the back to protect the neck, worn especially by seamen.

A southwester (def. 2)

south·west·er·ly (south′wes′tər lē) *adj. adv.* toward or from the southwest.

south·west·ern (south′wes′tərn) *adj.* of, at, in, to, toward, or from the southwest.

south·west·ward (south′west′wərd) *adv. adj.* toward the southwest. —*n.* southwest.

south·west·ward·ly (south′west′wərd lē) *adj.* **1** toward the southwest. **2** of winds, from the southwest. —*adv.* toward the southwest.

south·west·wards (south′west′wərdz) *adv.* southwestward.

sou·ve·nir (sü′və nēr′ or sü′və nēr′) *n.* something to remind one of a place, person, or occasion; a keepsake. [< F *souvenir*, originally infinitive, < L *subvenire* come to mind < *sub-* up + *venire* come] —**Syn.** memento, remembrance, reminder, token.

sou'west·er (sou′wes′tər) *n.* southwester.

sov·er·eign (sov′rən) *n.* **1** a king or queen; a supreme ruler; monarch. **2** a person, group, or nation having supreme control or dominion; ruler; governor; lord; master: *sovereign of the seas.* **3** a British gold coin, worth 20 shillings, or one pound.
—*adj.* **1** having the rank or power of a sovereign. **2** greatest in rank or power. **3** independent of the control of other governments. **4** above all others; supreme; greatest: *Character is of sovereign importance.* **5** excellent or powerful: *a sovereign cure for colds.* [ME < OF *soverain*, ult. < L *super* over] —**Syn.** *adj.* **4** paramount.

sov·er·eign·ly (sov′rən lē) *adv.* **1** so as to exceed all others; exceedingly. **2** chiefly; especially. **3** effectually; efficaciously. **4** as a sovereign.

sov·er·eign·ty (sov′rən tē) *n.* **-ties. 1** supreme power or authority. **2** rank, power, or jurisdiction of a sovereign. **3** the quality or condition of being sovereign. —**Syn. 1** supremacy.

so·vi·et (sō′vē et′ or sō′vē it) *n.* **1** a council; assembly. **2** Often, **Soviet.** in the Soviet Union: **a** either of two elected local assemblies **(village soviets, town soviets). b** any of the higher elected assemblies. The highest assembly of all is the **Supreme Soviet. 3** any council like a Russian soviet. —*adj.* **1** of or having to do with soviets. **2 Soviet,** of or having to do with the Soviet Union. [< Russian *soviet* council]

so·vi·et·ism (sō′vē it iz′əm) *n.* **1** a system of government by means of soviets. **2** communism.

so·vi·et·ize (sō′vē et īz′) *v.* **-ized, -iz·ing.** bring under a soviet type of government; change to a soviet government.

sov·ran (sov′rən) *n. adj. Poetic.* sovereign.

sow[1] (sō) *v.* **sowed, sown** or **sowed, sow·ing. 1** scatter (seed) on the ground; plant (seed); plant seed in: *He sows more wheat than oats. The farmer sowed the field with oats.* **2** scatter seed. **3** scatter (anything); spread abroad. [OE *sāwan*] —**sow′er,** *n.*

sow[2] (sou) *n.* a fully grown female pig. [OE *sugu* or *sū*]

sow bug (sou) a small crustacean that lives under stones, bark, etc.; wood louse.

sown (sōn) *v.* a pp. of **sow**[1].

soy (soi) *n.* **1** a sauce prepared from fermented soybeans, used especially on Chinese and Japanese dishes. **2** soybean. [< Japanese, short for *shoyu* < Chinese *shi-yu* < *shi*, a type of bean + *yu* oil]

soy·a (soi′ə) *n. Esp.Brit.* soy.

soy·bean (soi′bēn′) *n.* **1** a bean widely grown in China, Japan, and North America. Soybeans are used in making an oil and as food. **2** the plant that it grows on.

sp. 1 special. **2** specific. **3** species. **4** spelling. **5** spirits.

Sp. 1 Spain. **2** Spaniard. **3** Spanish.

SP *U.S.* Shore Patrol.

spa (spä) *n.* **1** a mineral spring. **2** a place where there is a mineral spring, especially a health resort at such a place. [< *Spa*, a resort city in Belgium]

space (spās)*n.v.* **spaced, spac·ing.** —*n.* **1** unlimited room or expanse extending in all directions: *The earth moves through space.* **2** extent of area or volume: *We have plenty of space in this house.* **3** a limited space or area: *a parking space.* **4** outer space. **5** a distance; a stretch: *The road is bad for the space of ten miles.* **6** a length of time: *He has not seen his brother for the space of ten years.* **7** *Archaic.* an interval of time; a while. **8** A time in which to do something; opportunity. **9** accommodations on a train, etc. **10** a part of a surface; a blank between words, etc.: *Fill in the spaces as directed.* **11 a** extent or room in a periodical, book, letter, etc. available for, or occupied by, written or printed matter. **b** in advertising, the part of a page or number of lines in a periodical, newspaper, etc. available or used for advertising. **12** in printing, one of the blank types used to separate words, etc. **13** in music, one of the intervals between the lines of a staff.
—*v.* **1** fix the space or spaces of; divide into spaces. **2** separate by spaces: *Space your words evenly when you write.* [ME < OF *espace* < L *spatium*]

space age the current period of history, thought of as being marked by man's first efforts to explore and conquer space.

space·craft (spās′kraft′) *n.* any manned or unmanned vehicle designed for flight in outer space.

space·less (spās′lis) *adj.* 1 independent of space; infinite. 2 occupying no space.

space·man (spās′man′) *n.* **-men** (-men′) 1 an astronaut. 2 any person, especially a scientist, concerned with space flight.

spac·er (spās′ər) *n.* 1 a device for spacing words, etc. as in a typesetting machine. 2 an instrument by which to reverse a telegraphic current to increase the speed of transmission.

space ship or **space·ship** (spās′ship′) *n.* a device that is capable of interplanetary travel or travel in outer space.

space station an artificial satellite in orbit for use as an observatory or as a launching site for space ships.

space suit an airtight suit designed to protect astronauts from radiation, heat, lack of oxygen, etc., the condition of the earth's atmosphere being maintained within the suit.

space·ward (spās′wərd) *adv.* toward outer space.

spac·ing (spās′ing) *n.* 1 the fixing or arranging of spaces. 2 the manner in which spaces are arranged: *uneven spacing.* 3 space or spaces in printing or other work.

spa·cious (spā′shəs) *adj.* 1 having or affording much space or room; large; roomy: *The rooms of the palace were spacious.* 2 of great extent or area; extensive; vast. 3 broad in scope or range; not limited or narrow; expansive: *a spacious mind.* [< L *spatiosus* < *spatium* space] —**spa′cious·ly,** *adv.* —**spa′cious·ness,** *n.* —**Syn.** extensive, broad, capacious, large, roomy.

spade[1] (spād) *n. v.* **spad·ed, spad·ing.** —*n.* 1 a tool for digging; a kind of shovel having a rectangular digging blade. 2 **call a spade a spade,** call a thing by its real name; speak plainly and frankly. —*v.* dig with a spade. [OE *spadu*; akin to L *spatha.* See SPADE[2].]

spade[2] (spād) *n.* 1 a black figure (♠) used on playing cards. 2 a playing card bearing such figures. 3 **spades,** *pl.* the suit of playing cards bearing such figures, usually the highest ranking suit in card games. [< Ital. *spada* < L < Gk. *spathē* sword, broad blade]

spa·dix (spā′diks) *n.* **spa·dix·es** or **spa·di·ces** (spā dī′sēz). in botany, a spike composed of minute flowers on a fleshy stem. A spadix is usually enclosed in a petal-like leaf called a spathe, as in the jack-in-the-pulpit and the calla lily. [< L < Gk. *spadix* palm branch]

SPATHE
SPADIX

spa·ghet·ti (spə get′ē) *n.* 1 long, slender sticks made of a mixture of flour and water, soft when cooked. 2 in electricity, an insulating cloth tube used for covering bare wire. [< Ital. *spaghetti,* pl. dim. of *spago* cord]

spake (spāk) *v. Archaic.* a pt. of **speak.**

spall (spol or spôl) *n.* a chip, splinter, or small piece of stone. —*v.* 1 break up roughly, or chip, especially to prepare ore for sorting. 2 chip off, especially at the edges. A stone may spall under pressure.

Sp.Am. Spanish American.

span[1] (span) *n. v.* **spanned, span·ning.** —*n.* 1 the distance between the tip of a man's thumb and the tip of his little finger when the hand is spread out; about 9 inches. 2 the distance between two supports: *The arch had a fifty-foot span.* 3 the part between two supports: *The bridge crossed the river in three spans.* 4 a short space of time: "*A life's but a span.*" 5 the full extent: *the span of a bridge, the span of memory.* 6 of an airplane, the lateral distance from wing tip to wing tip.
—*v.* 1 measure by the hand spread out: *This post can be spanned by one's two hands.* 2 encircle or encompass (the waist, wrist, etc.) with the hand or hands. 3 extend over: *A bridge spanned the river.* 4 provide with something that extends over or across: *span a river with a bridge.* [OE *spann*]

span[2] (span) *n.* a pair of horses, mules, etc. harnessed and driven together. [< Du. or LG *span* < *spannen* stretch, yoke]

span[3] (span) *v. Archaic.* a pt. of **spin.**

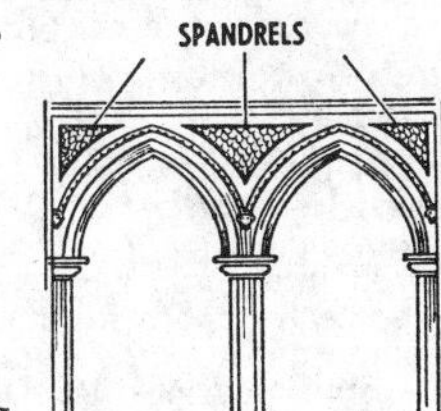

span·drel (span′drəl) *n.* in architecture: 1 the triangular space between the curve of an arch and the rectangular moulding or framework enclosing the arch. 2 the space between the curves of two adjacent arches and the moulding above them. Also, **spandril.** [ME *spandrell* < AF *spaundre,* short for OF *espander* expand < L *expandere.* Cf. EXPAND and SPAWN.]

hat, āge, cãre, fär; let, ēqual, tėrm; it, īce
hot, ōpen, ôrder; oil, out; cup, pu̇t, rüle, ūse
əbove, takən, pencəl, lemən, circəs
ch, child; ng, long; sh, ship
th, thin; ᴛʜ, then; zh, measure

spang (spang) *adv. Informal.* directly, with a smack; exactly on the mark. [perhaps < dial. *spang* a jerk, smack]

span·gle (spang′gəl) *n. v.* **-gled, -gling.** —*n.* 1 a small piece of glittering metal used for decoration: *The dress was covered with spangles.* 2 any small, bright bit.
—*v.* 1 decorate with spangles. 2 sprinkle with small, bright bits: *The sky is spangled with stars.* 3 glitter. [dim. of earlier *spang,* probably < MDu. *spange* brooch]

Span·iard (span′yərd) *n.* a native or inhabitant of Spain, a country in S.W. Europe.

span·iel (span′yəl) *n.* 1 one of several breeds of dogs, usually of small or medium size, having long, silky hair and drooping ears. 2 a dog of one of these breeds. 3 a person who yields too easily to others. [ME < OF *espagneul,* originally, Spanish < L *Hispania* Spain]

Span·ish (span′ish) *adj.* of or having to do with Spain, a country in S.W. Europe, its people, or their language.
—*n.* 1 the people of Spain. 2 the Romance language of Spain. It is also the standard language in Latin American countries (except Brazil) and former colonies of Spain.

Span·ish-A·mer·i·can (span′ish ə mer′ə kən) *adj.* 1 of or having to do with Spain and America, or with Spain and the United States. 2 of, having to do with, or denoting the parts of America where Spanish is the prevailing language. —*n.* **Spanish American,** a native or inhabitant of a Spanish-American country, especially a person of Spanish descent.

Spanish Armada the great fleet sent by Philip II of Spain to attack England in 1588.

Spanish bayonet any of several desert plants that have narrow, rigid, evergreen leaves with spines at the tips; yucca.

Spanish fly a bright-green blister beetle used in medicine after being dried and powdered.

Spanish Inquisition 1 the body of men appointed during the Renaissance by the Roman Catholic Church to suppress heresy in Spain. It was put under state control at the end of the 15th century and was very active during the 16th century. 2 the activities of this body of men.

Spanish Main 1 formerly, the mainland of America adjacent to the Caribbean Sea, especially between the mouth of the Orinoco River and the Isthmus of Panama. 2 in later use, the Caribbean Sea.

Spanish moss a plant growing on the branches of certain trees, from which it hangs in gray streamers. Spanish moss is found in the S. United States and tropical America.

Spanish onion a large, mild, juicy onion often eaten raw in sandwiches, hamburgers, salads, etc.

spank[1] (spangk) *v.* strike, usually on the buttocks, with the open hand, a slipper, etc., especially as a punishment. —*n.* a blow with the open hand, a slipper, etc.; slap. [imitative]

spank[2] (spangk) *v. Informal.* go quickly and vigorously; move at a speedy rate. [probably back formation < *spanking*]

spank·er (spangk′ər) *n.* 1 on a ship, a fore-and-aft sail on the mast nearest the stern. 2 *Informal.* a fast horse. 3 *Informal.* anything fine, large, unusual for its kind, etc. [apparently < *spanking* or *spank*[2] move fast]

spank·ing (spangk′ing) *adj.* 1 blowing briskly: *a spanking breeze.* 2 quick and vigorous. 3 *Informal.* unusually fine, great, large, etc.: *a spanking good time.* [cf. Danish *spanke* strut]

span·less (span′lis) *adj.* that cannot be spanned.

span·ner (span′ər) *n.* **1** one that spans: *the spanners of a bridge.* **2** *Esp.Brit.* a tool for holding and turning a nut, bolt, etc.; wrench.

spar[1] (spär) *n. v.* **sparred, spar·ring.** —*n.* **1** a stout pole used to support or extend the sails of a ship; mast, yard, boom, etc. of a ship. **2** the main beam of an airplane wing. —*v.* provide (a ship) with spars. [ME *sparre,* akin to OE *spere* spear; cf. ON *sparri,* MDu. *sparre*]

spar[2] (spär) *v.* **sparred, spar·ring.** *n.* —*v.* **1** make motions of attack and defence with the arms and fists; box. **2** dispute. **3** of roosters, fight with the feet. —*n.* **1** a boxing match. **2** a dispute. [< MF *esparer* kick < Ital. *sparare* fling < *s-,* intensive (< L *ex-*) + *parare* parry]

spar[3] (spär) *n.* a shiny, crystalline mineral that splits into flakes easily. [OE *spær-*; cf. *spæren* gypsum]

spar deck the upper deck extending from one end of a ship to the other.

spare (spãr) *v.* **spared, spar·ing,** *adj.* **spar·er, spar·est,** *n.* —*v.* **1** show mercy to; refrain from harming or destroying: *He spared his enemy.* **2** show mercy; refrain from doing harm. **3** show consideration for; save from labor, pain, etc.: *We walked uphill to spare the horse.* **4** get along without; do without: *Father couldn't spare the car; so John had to walk.* **5** make (a person, etc.) free from (something); relieve or exempt (a person, etc.) from (something): *He did the work to spare you the trouble.* **6** use in small quantities or not at all; be saving of: "*Spare the rod and spoil the child.*" **7** be saving. **8** set aside; keep in reserve for a particular use or purpose; have free: *spare some time for reading.*
—*adj.* **1** free for other use: *spare time.* **2** extra; in reserve: *a spare tire.* **3** thin; lean: *The minister was a tall, spare man.* **4** small in quantity; meagre; scanty: *Fat people should live on a spare diet.*
—*n.* **1** a spare person or thing: *We have five tires, including a spare.* **2** in bowling, the knocking down of all the pins with two rolls of a ball. [OE *sparian*]
—**spare′ness,** *n.* —**spar′er,** *n.* —**Syn.** *adj.* **3** lank, gaunt.

spare·ly (spãr′lē) *adv.* sparingly; scantily; thinly; leanly.

spare·rib (spãr′rib′) *n.* a rib of pork having less meat than the ribs near the loins. See **pork** for diagram. [transposition of *ribspare* < MLG *ribbespēr* rib cut]

spar·ing (spãr′ing) *adj.* **1** that spares. **2** economical; frugal: *a sparing use of sugar.* —**spar′ing·ly,** *adv.* —**spar′ing·ness,** *n.* —**Syn. 2** parsimonious, stingy.

spark[1] (spärk) *n.* **1** a small particle of flame: *The burning wood threw off sparks.* **2** in electricity: **a** a flash given off when electricity jumps across an open space. An electric spark explodes the gas in the engine of an automobile. **b** the discharge occurring at the same time. **3** a flash; gleam: *a spark of light.* **4** a small amount: *I haven't a spark of interest in the plan.* **5** a trace of life or vitality. **6** a glittering bit.
—*v.* **1** flash; gleam. **2** send out small bits of fire; produce sparks. **3** operate properly in forming sparks, as the ignition in an internal-combustion engine. **4** stir to activity; stimulate: *spark a revolt, spark sales, ideas, etc.* [OE *spearca*]

spark[2] (spärk) *n.* **1** a gay, showy young man. **2** a beau; lover. —*v.* *Informal.* be a beau or lover; court; woo. [? < ON *sparkr* lively] —**spark′er,** *n.*

spark coil in electricity, an induction coil for producing sparks.

spar·kle (spär′kəl) *v.* **-kled, -kling,** *n.* —*v.* **1** send out little sparks: *The fireworks sparkled.* **2** shine; glitter; flash; gleam: *The diamonds sparkled.* **3** be brilliant; be lively: *Wit sparkles.* **4** bubble: *Her ginger ale sparkles.* **5** cause to sparkle. —*n.* **1** a little spark. **2** a shine; glitter; flash; gleam: *I like the sparkle of her eyes.* **3** brilliance; liveliness. [< *spark*[1]] —**Syn.** *n.* **2** See **flash.**

spar·kler (spär′klər) *n.* **1** a person or thing that sparkles. **2** a small wire or stick covered with a substance that, when lighted, throws off showers of sparks. **3** *Informal.* a sparkling gem, especially a diamond.

spark plug **1** a device in the cylinder of a gasoline engine by which the mixture of gasoline and air is exploded by an electric spark. **2** *Informal.* a person who gives energy or enthusiasm to others.

spar·row (spar′ō) *n.* any of many small finches, such as the song sparrow, the English sparrow, and the chipping sparrow. [OE *spearwa*]

sparrow hawk a small hawk that feeds on sparrows and other small animals.

sparse (spärs) *adj.* **spars·er, spars·est.** **1** thinly scattered; occurring here and there: *a sparse population, sparse hair.* **2** scanty; meagre. [< L *sparsus,* pp. of *spargere* scatter] —**sparse′ly,** *adv.* —**sparse′ness,** *n.* —**Syn. 1** See **scanty.**

spar·si·ty (spär′sə tē) *n.* a sparse or scattered condition; sparseness.

Spar·ta·cus (spär′tə kəs) *n.* a Thracian slave and gladiator in Italy (died 71 B.C.) who led an insurrection of slaves that lasted from 73 to 71 B.C.

Spar·tan (spär′tən) *adj.* **1** of Sparta, a city in ancient Greece, or its people. **2** like the Spartans; simple, frugal, severe, sternly disciplined, brave, brief, and concise.
—*n.* **1** a native or inhabitant of Sparta. The Spartans were noted for their simplicity of life, severity, courage, and brevity of speech. **2** a person who is like the Spartans.

Spar·tan·ism (spär′tən iz′əm) *n.* **1** the beliefs and methods of ancient Sparta. **2** any discipline, method, etc. like that of the ancient Spartans.

spasm (spaz′əm) *n.* **1** a sudden, abnormal, involuntary contraction of a muscle or muscles. **2** any sudden, brief fit or spell of unusual energy or activity: *a spasm of temper, a spasm of industry.* [< L < Gk. *spasmos* < *spaein* draw up, tear away]

spas·mod·ic (spaz mod′ik) *adj.* **1** having to do with spasms; resembling a spasm: *a spasmodic cough.* **2** sudden and violent, but brief; occurring very irregularly. **3** having or showing bursts of excitement. **4** disjointed; choppy: *a spasmodic style, spasmodic writing.* [< Med.L *spasmodicus* < Gk. *spasmōdēs* < *spasmos.* See SPASM.] —**spas·mod′i·cal·ly,** *adv.* —**Syn. 2** jerky, fitful, intermittent.

spas·tic (spas′tik) *adj.* **1** caused by a spasm or spasms. **2** of, having to do with, or characterized by spasms. —*n.* a person suffering from a continuous, or tonic, contraction of a muscle or muscles. [< L < Gk. *spastikos* < *spaein* draw up]

spat[1] (spat) *n. v.* **spat·ted, spat·ting.** —*n.* **1** a slight quarrel. **2** a light blow; slap. —*v.* **1** *Informal.* have a slight quarrel. **2** slap lightly. [? imitative]

Spats

spat[2] (spat) *v.* a pt. and a pp. of **spit**[1].

spat[3] (spat) *n.* a short gaiter covering the ankle. [short for *spatterdash*]

spat[4] (spat) *n. v.* **spat·ted, spat·ting.** —*n.* the spawn of oysters; young oyster. —*v.* of oysters, spawn. [origin uncertain. Perhaps related to SPIT[1].]

spate (spāt) *n.* **1** a flood; downpour. **2** a sudden outburst: *a spate of words, a spate of advertising.* [ME; related to OE *spātan* spit]

spathe (spāᴛʜ) *n.* in botany, a large bract or pair of bracts that enclose a flower cluster. The calla lily has a white spathe around a yellow flower cluster. See **spadix** for picture. [< Gk. *spathē* palm branch, oar blade]

spa·tial (spā′shəl) *adj.* **1** of or having to do with space. **2** existing in space. **3** occupying or taking up space. [< L *spatium* space]

spa·tial·ly (spā′shəl ē) *adv.* in spatial respects; so far as space is concerned; in space.

spa·tio-tem·po·ral (spā′shē ō tem′pər əl) *adj.* of both space and time. [< L *spatium* space + E *temporal*]

spat·ter (spat′ər) *v.* **1** scatter or dash in drops or particles: *spatter mud.* **2** fall in drops or particles: *Rain spatters on the sidewalk.* **3** strike in a shower; strike in a number of places: *Bullets spattered the wall.* **4** splash or spot with mud, slander, disgrace, etc. —*n.* **1** a spattering: *a spatter of bullets.* **2** the sound of spattering. **3** a splash or spot. [cf. Du. or LG *spatten* splash; akin to Flemish *spatteren* spatter]

hat, āge, cãre, fär; let, ēqual, tėrm; it, īce
hot, ōpen, ôrder; oil, out; cup, pu̇t, rüle, ūse
əbove, takən, pencəl, lemən, circəs
ch, child; ng, long; sh, ship
th, thin; ᴛʜ, then; zh, measure

spat·ter·dash (spat′ər dash′) *n.* a long gaiter worn to keep the trousers or stockings from being splashed with mud, etc.

Spatterdashes

spat·ter·dock (spat′ər dok′) *n.* a yellow pond lily, especially a coarse, yellow-flowered plant common in stagnant waters. [< obs. *splatterdock* < *splatter* + *dock*[4]]

spat·u·la (spach′ u̇ lə) *n.* an implement with a broad, flat, flexible blade, used for mixing drugs, spreading paints, frostings, etc. [< L *spatula*, dim. of *spatha* flat blade < Gk. *spathē*]

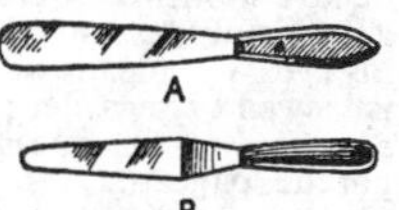

Spatulas: A, a cake knife; B, a palette knife.

spat·u·late (spach′ u̇ lit or spach′ u̇ lāt′) *adj.* **1** shaped like a spatula; rounded somewhat like a spoon. **2** in botany, having a broad, rounded end and a narrow base: *a spatulate leaf.* **3** wide at the tips: *spatulate fingers.*

spav·in (spav′ən) *n.* a disease of horses in which a bony swelling forms at the hock; causing lameness. [ME < OF *espavain,* probably < Gmc.]

spav·ined (spav′ənd) *adj.* having spavin; lame.

spawn (spon or spôn) *n.* **1** the eggs of fish, frogs, shellfish, etc. **2** young fish, frogs, etc. when newly hatched from such eggs. **3** a swarming brood; offspring. **4** a product; result. **5** the mass of white, threadlike fibres from which mushrooms grow. [< v.] —*v.* **1** produce eggs: *Salmon spawn in the rivers of British Columbia.* **2** give birth to. [ME < OF *espandre* < L *expandere* spread out. Doublet of EXPAND.] —**spawn′er,** *n.*

spay (spā) *v.* remove the ovaries of (a female cat, dog, etc.). [ME < AF *espeir*, ult. < OF *espee* sword < L *spatha.* See SPADE[2].]

SPCA or **S.P.C.A.** Society for the Prevention of Cruelty to Animals.

speak (spēk) *v.* **spoke** or (*Archaic*) **spake, spok·en** or (*Archaic*) **spoke, speak·ing. 1** say words; talk: *A cat cannot speak. Speak distinctly.* **2** make a speech: *Who is going to speak at the forum?* **3** tell; express; make known: *Speak the truth.* **4** use (a language): *Do you speak French?* **5** express an idea, feeling, etc.; communicate: *Their eyes spoke. His expression spoke deep sorrow.* **6** make a plea, request, application, etc.; appeal: *speak for seats ahead of time.* **7** speak to or with; address. **8** give forth sound: *The cannon spoke.* **9** of dogs, bark when told: *Speak for the candy, Fido.* **10** *Archaic.* show to be; characterize as: *His conduct speaks him honorable.* **11 so to speak,** to speak in such a manner. **12 speak for, a** speak in the interest of; represent. **b** ask or apply for. **13 speak of,** mention; refer to. **14 speak out** or **up, a** speak loudly and clearly. **b** speak freely and without restraint. **15 speak well for,** give a favorable idea of; be evidence in favor of. [OE *specan*]

Syn. **1 Speak, talk** = say or use words. **Speak** emphasizes the uttering of clear and distinct speech sounds and the saying of words, and does not necessarily or always suggest a definite hearer or audience or that the sounds and words are logically or grammatically connected: *Some children learn to speak much earlier than others.* **Talk** emphasizes using words in connected speech to make known ideas or give information, commonly to a listener, but often particularly suggests more or less meaningless continued speaking: *Some people are always talking.*

speak·eas·y (spēk′ēz′ē) *n.* **-eas·ies.** *U.S. Slang.* during the era of prohibition, a place where alcoholic liquors were sold contrary to law.

speak·er (spēk′ər) *n.* **1** a person who speaks. **2 Speaker,** a person who presides over an assembly. **3** a loudspeaker.

Speaker of the House 1 in Canada and the United Kingdom, the presiding officer of the House of Commons. **2** in the United States, the presiding officer of the House of Representatives.

speak·er·ship (spēk′ər ship′) *n.* the position of presiding officer.

speak·ing (spēk′ing) *n.* the act, utterance, or discourse of a person who speaks. —*adj.* **1** that speaks; giving information as if by speech: *a speaking example of a thing.* **2** used in, suited to, or involving speech: *within speaking distance, a speaking part in a play.* **3** permitting conversation: *a speaking acquaintance with a person.* **4** highly expressive: *speaking eyes.* **5** life-like: *a speaking likeness.*

spear[1] (spēr) *n.* a weapon having a long shaft and a sharp-pointed head. —*v.* **1** pierce with a spear: *The Indian speared a fish.* **2** pierce or stab with anything sharp. **3** in hockey, check (an opponent) illegally by stabbing with the point of the stick blade. **4** in football, block (an opponent) with the helmet instead of with the body. [OE *spere*] —**spear′er,** *n.*

spear[2] (spēr) *n.* a sprout or shoot of a plant: *a spear of grass.* —*v.* sprout or shoot into a long stem. [var. of *spire*[1]; influenced by *spear*[1]]

spear·head (spēr′hed′) *n.* **1** the sharp-pointed striking end of a spear. **2** the part that comes first in an attack, undertaking, etc. —*v.* go first in an attack, undertaking, etc.

spear·man (spēr′mən) *n.* **-men** (-mən). a soldier armed with a spear.

spear·mint (spēr′mint′) *n.* common mint, a fragrant herb much used for flavoring. [< *spear*[1] + *mint*[1]; from the shape of the inflorescence]

spear·side the male side of a family; opposed to *distaff side.*

spec. 1 special. **2** specification. **3** speculation.

spe·cial (spesh′əl) *adj.* **1** of a particular kind; distinct from others; not general: *This desk has a special lock.* **2** more than ordinary; unusual; exceptional: *Today's topic is of special interest.* **3** for a particular person, thing, purpose, etc.: *The railway ran special trains on holidays. Send the letter by a special messenger.* —*n.* **1** a special train, car, bus, etc. **2** any special person or thing. **3** a special edition of a newspaper. **4** in a store, restaurant, etc., a product that is specially featured; bargain: *a weekend special.* **5** a specially produced television show, not part of the regular daily or weekly programs. [ME < L *specialis* < *species* appearance. Doublet of ESPECIAL.]

Syn. *adj.* **1 Special, particular** = not general, but belonging or relating to one person, thing, or group, as distinguished from others. **Special** emphasizes the idea of qualities making one different from others of its kind, or other kinds, and giving it a character, nature, use, etc. of its own: *Babies need special food.* **Particular** emphasizes the idea of pertaining to one considered as an individual, apart from all others of the same kind or covered by a general statement: *These synonym studies give both the general and particular meanings of words.*

special delivery the delivery of a letter or package by a special messenger rather than by the regular postman. Special delivery mail is handled faster and delivered sooner than regular mail.

spe·cial·ism (spesh′əl iz′əm) *n.* devotion or restriction to one particular branch of study, business, etc.

spe·cial·ist (spesh′əl ist) *n.* a person who devotes or restricts himself to one particular branch of study, business, etc.: *Dr. White is a specialist in diseases of the nose and throat.*

spe·ci·al·i·ty (spesh′ē al′ə tē) *n.* **-ties. 1** a special or particular character. **2** a special quality or characteristic; the distinctive characteristic or feature of a thing. **3** a special point; particular; detail. **4** a special pursuit, branch, product, etc.; specialty.

spe·cial·ize (spesh′əl īz′) *v.* **-ized, -iz·ing. 1** pursue some special branch of study, work, etc.: *Many students specialize in engineering.* **2** adapt to special conditions; give special form, use, duty, etc. to; limit. **3** develop in a special way; take on a special form, use, etc. **4** mention specially; specify. **5** go into particulars. —**spe′cial·i·za′tion,** *n.*

spe·cial·ly (spesh′əl ē) *adv.* in a special manner or degree; particularly; unusually.

spe·cial·ty (spesh′əl tē) *n.* **-ties. 1** a special study; special line of work, profession, trade, etc.: ***Repairing***

watches is his specialty. **2** a product, article, etc. to which special attention is given: *This store makes a specialty of children's clothes.* **3** a special character; special quality. **4** a special or particular characteristic; peculiarity. **5** a special point or item; particular; detail. [ME < OF *(e)specialte* < L *specialitas* < *specialis.* See SPECIAL.]

spe·cie (spē′shē) *n.* money in the form of coins; metal money. Silver dollars are specie. [< L (*in*) *specie,* abl. of *species* kind]

spe·cies (spē′sēz or spē′shēz) *n.* **-cies. 1** a group of animals or plants that have certain permanent characteristics in common: *Wheat is a species of grass.* **2** a kind; sort; distinct kind or sort: *There are many species of advertisements.* **3** an appearance; form; shape. **4** the consecrated bread and wine used in the Mass. **5 the species,** the human race. [< L *species,* originally, appearance. Doublet of SPICE.]

specif. specifically.

spe·cif·ic (spə sif′ik) *adj.* **1** definite; precise; particular: *There was no specific reason for the quarrel.* **2** characteristic (of); peculiar (to): *A scaly skin is a specific feature of snakes.* **3** curing some particular disease. **4** produced by some special cause. **5** in biology, of or having to do with a species. —*n.* **1** any specific statement, quality, etc. **2** a cure for some particular disease: *Quinine is a specific for malaria.* [< LL *specificus* constituting a species < L *species* sort + *facere* make] **—spe·cif′ic·ness,** *n.*

spe·cif·i·cal·ly (spə sif′ik lē) *adv.* in a specific manner; definitely; particularly: *The doctor told Kate specifically not to eat eggs.*

spec·i·fi·ca·tion (spes′ə fə kā′shən) *n.* **1** the act of specifying; a definite mention: *Mary made careful specification of the kinds of cake and candy for her party.* **2** Usually, **specifications,** *pl.* a detailed description of the dimensions, materials, etc. for a building, road, dam, boat, etc.: *The repairs had not been done according to specifications.* **3** something specified; a particular item, article, etc. **4** in patent law, a detailed statement of particulars.

specific duty a customs duty on a specified article or quantity of articles, regardless of its market value.

specific gravity in physics, the ratio of the weight of a given volume of any substance to that of the same volume of some other substance taken as a standard, water being used for solids and liquids, and hydrogen or air for gases. *Abbrev.*: s.g. or sp.gr.

specific heat in physics, the number of calories of heat needed to raise the temperature of one gram of a substance one degree centigrade.

specific impulse in a rocket motor or jet engine, the thrust in pounds produced by the burning of one pound of a specified fuel with its oxidizer in one second.

spec·i·fy (spes′ə fī′) *v.* **-fied, -fy·ing. 1** mention or name definitely; state or describe in detail: *Did you specify any particular time for us to call?* **2** include in the specifications: *The contractor would have used cement blocks, but bricks were specified.* [ME < OF < LL *specificare* < *specificus.* See SPECIFIC.]

spec·i·men (spes′ə mən) *n.* **1** one of a group or class taken to show what the others are like; a single part, thing, etc. regarded as an example of its kind: *The statue was a fine specimen of Greek sculpture.* **2** *Informal.* a human being; person: *The tramp was a queer specimen.* —*adj.* taken or regarded as a specimen. [< L *specimen* < *specere* view]

spe·ci·os·i·ty (spē′shē os′ə tē) *n.* **-ties. 1** the quality of being specious. **2** a specious act, appearance, remark, etc.

spe·cious (spē′shəs) *adj.* **1** seeming desirable, reasonable, or probable, but not really so; apparently good or right, but without real merit: *The teacher saw through John's specious excuse.* **2** make a good outward appearance in order to deceive: *His dishonest actions showed him to be nothing but a specious hypocrite.* [< L *speciosus* < *species* appearance] **—spe′cious·ly,** *adv.* **—spe′cious·ness,** *n.*

speck (spek) *n.* **1** a small spot; stain: *Can you clean the specks off this wallpaper?* **2** a tiny bit; particle: *I have a speck in my eye.* —*v.* mark with specks: *This fruit is badly specked.* [OE *specca*]

speck·le (spek′əl) *n. v.* **-led, -ling.** —*n.* a small spot or mark: *This hen is gray with white speckles.* —*v.* mark with speckles.

speckled trout a fresh-water char originating in eastern North America and having on its sides bright, blue-ringed, red or pink spots. It is highly valued as a game fish.

specs (speks) *n.pl. Informal.* spectacles.

spec·ta·cle (spek′tə kəl) *n.* **1** something to look at; sight: *The children at play among the flowers made a charming spectacle.* **2** a public show or display: *The big army parade was a fine spectacle.* **3** a person or thing set before the public view as an object of curiosity, contempt, wonder, or admiration. **4 make a spectacle of oneself,** behave foolishly or crudely in public. **5 spectacles,** *pl.* **a** a pair of glasses to help a person's sight or to protect his eyes. **b** a means or medium through which anything is viewed or regarded; point of view. [ME < L *spectaculum,* ult. < *specere* view] **—Syn. 2** exhibition, parade, pageant.

spec·ta·cled (spek′tə kəld) *adj.* **1** provided with or wearing spectacles. **2** having a marking resembling spectacles: *a spectacled snake.*

spec·tac·u·lar (spek tak′yů lər) *adj.* **1** making a great display: *Motion pictures present spectacular scenes like battles, processions, storms, or races.* **2** having to do with a spectacle or show. —*n.* **1** an elaborate show characterized by much display. **2** a special, lengthy television show, usually produced on an extravagant scale.

spec·tac·u·lar·ly (spek tak′yů lər lē) *adv.* **1** in a spectacular manner or degree. **2** as a spectacle.

spec·ta·tor (spek′tā tər or spek tā′tər) *n.* a person who watches without taking part: *There were many spectators at the game.* —*adj.* of or having to do with spectators: *Hockey is largely a spectator sport.* [< L *spectator* < *spectare* watch < *specere* view] **—Syn.** observer, witness, onlooker, bystander.

spec·ter (spek′tər) *n.* spectre.

spec·tra (spek′trə) *n.* a pl. of **spectrum.**

spec·tral (spek′trəl) *adj.* **1** or of like a spectre; ghostly: *He saw the spectral form of the headless horseman.* **2** of or produced by the spectrum: *spectral colors.*

spec·tre or **spec·ter** (spek′tər) *n.* **1** a ghost. **2** something causing terror or dread. [< L *spectrum* appearance. See SPECTRUM.] **—Syn. 1** See **ghost.**

spec·tro·scope (spek′trə skōp′) *n.* an instrument for obtaining and examining the spectrum of radiation from any source by the passage of rays through a prism or a grating.

spec·tro·scop·ic (spek′trə skop′ik) *adj.* **1** of, made by, or done with a spectroscope. **2** using a spectroscope. **—spec′tro·scop′i·cal·ly,** *adv.*

spec·tros·co·py (spek tros′kə pē or spek′trə skō′pē) *n.* **1** a science having to do with the examination and analysis of spectra. **2** the use of the spectroscope.

spec·trum (spek′trəm) *n.* **-tra** (-trə) or **-trums. 1** the band of colors formed when a beam of light is broken up by being passed through a prism or by some other means. A rainbow has all the colors of the spectrum: red, orange, yellow, green, blue, indigo, and violet. **2** the band of colors formed when any radiant energy is broken up. The ends of such a spectrum are not visible to the eye, but are studied by photography, heat effects, etc. **3** in radio, the wave-length range between 30,000 metres and 3 centimetres. **4** range; scope; compass: *the spectrum of political thought.* [< L *spectrum* appearance < *specere* view]

spec·u·lar (spek′yů lər) *adj.* **1** of or like a mirror; reflecting. **2** having to do with a speculum. [< L *specularis* < *speculum* mirror. See SPECULUM.]

spec·u·late (spek′yů lāt′) *v.* **-lat·ed, -lat·ing. 1** reflect; meditate; consider: *The philosopher speculated about time and space.* **2** guess; conjecture: *She refused to speculate about the possible winner.* **3** buy or sell when there is a large risk, with the hope of making a profit from future price changes. **4** take part or invest in a risky business enterprise or transaction, in the hope of making large profits. [< L *speculari* < *specula* watchtower < *specere* look]

spec·u·la·tion (spek′yů lā′shən) *n.* **1** thought; reflection: *Former speculations about electricity were often mere guesses.* **2** a guessing; conjecture. **3** the act of buying or selling when there is a large risk, with the hope of making a profit from future price changes: *His speculations in stocks made him poor.* **4** a taking part in any risky business enterprise, transaction, etc.

spec·u·la·tive (spek′yů lə tiv or spek′yů lā′tiv) *adj.* **1** thoughtful; reflective. **2** theoretical rather than practical. **3** risky. **4** of or involving speculation in land, stocks, etc. —**spec′u·la·tive·ly,** *adv.* —**spec′u·la·tive·ness,** *n.*

spec·u·la·tor (spek′yů lā′tər) *n.* **1** a person who speculates, usually in business. **2** a person who buys tickets for shows, games, etc. in advance, hoping to sell them later at a higher price. [< L *speculator* explorer, spy]

spec·u·lum (spek′yů ləm) *n.* **-la** (-lə) or **-lums. 1** a mirror of polished metal. A reflecting telescope contains a speculum. **2** a surgical instrument for enlarging an opening in order to examine a cavity. [< L *speculum* mirror < *specere* view]

sped (sped) *v.* a pt. and a pp. of **speed.**

speech (spēch) *n.* **1** the act of speaking; talk. **2** the power of speaking: *Animals lack speech.* **3** a manner of speaking: *The sailor's speech showed that he was a Newfoundlander.* **4** what is said; the words spoken: *We made the usual farewell speeches.* **5** a public talk. **6** a number of lines spoken by an actor in a single sequence. **7** particular language or dialect: *His native speech was French.* **8** the study and practice of the spoken language: *take a course in speech.* [OE *spǣc*]

Syn. 1 discourse. **5 Speech, address, oration** = a talk made to an audience. **Speech** is the general word applying to a prepared or unprepared, formal or informal talk made for some purpose: *Most after-dinner speeches are dull.* **Address** = a prepared formal speech, usually of some importance or given on an important occasion: *Who gave your commencement address?* **Oration** = a formal address on a special occasion, and particularly suggests artistic style, dignity, and eloquence: *a funeral oration.*

speech community any group of people sharing the same language or dialect.

Speech from the Throne a statement of government policy for the coming year read to the opening session of a legislature by the sovereign or his representative.

speech·i·fy (spēch′ə fī′) *v.* **-fied, -fy·ing.** *Humorous or contemptuous.* make a speech or speeches. —**speech′i·fi′er,** *n.*

speech·less (spēch′lis) *adj.* **1** not able to speak: *George was speechless with anger.* **2** silent: *Her frown gave a speechless reply.* —**speech′less·ness,** *n.* —**Syn. 1** See **dumb.**

speech·less·ly (spēch′lis lē) *adv.* **1** without speaking. **2** so as to be speechless.

speed (spēd) *n. v.* **sped** or **speed·ed, speed·ing.**
—*n.* **1** swift or rapid movement. **2** a rate of movement: *The boys ran at full speed.* **3** an arrangement of gears to give a certain rate of movement. An automobile usually has three speeds forward and one backward. **4** *Archaic.* good luck; success.
—*v.* **1** go quickly: *The boat sped over the water.* **2** make go quickly: *speed a horse.* **3 speed up,** go or cause to go more quickly; increase in speed. **4** send quickly. **5** drive faster than the legal speed limit. **6** help forward; promote: *speed an undertaking.* **7** *Archaic.* succeed. **8** *Archaic.* give success to: *God speed you.* [OE *spēd*]
—**Syn.** *n.* **1** rapidity, celerity, quickness, haste. See **hurry.**

speed·boat (spēd′bōt′) *n.* a motorboat built to go at high speeds.

speed·er (spēd′ər) *n.* **1** a person or thing that goes at a fast pace, especially one who indulges in speeding. **2** a small trolley powered by a gasoline engine, used on railway tracks by maintenance crews.

speed·i·ly (spēd′ə lē) *adv.* quickly; with speed; soon.

speed·ing (spēd′ing) *n.* the act of driving faster than the legal speed limit.

speed·om·e·ter (spēd om′ə tər or spid om′ə tər) *n.* an instrument to indicate speed. Automobiles have speedometers.

speed trap a section of road or highway where police set up a means of catching persons who are speeding.

hat, āge, cãre, fär; let, ēqual, tėrm; it, īce
hot, ōpen, ôrder; oil, out; cup, půt, rüle, ūse
əbove, takən, pencəl, lemən, circəs
ch, child; ng, long; sh, ship
th, thin; ᴛʜ, then; zh, measure

speed-up (spēd′up′) *n.* an increase in speed: *a speed-up in manufacturing.*

speed·way (spēd′wā′) *n.* a road for fast driving.

speed·well (spēd′wel′) *n.* any of various low plants having blue, purple, pink, or white flowers; veronica.

speed·y (spēd′ē) *adj.* **speed·i·er, speed·i·est.** fast; rapid; quick; swift: *speedy workers, a speedy change, speedy progress, a speedy decision.* —**speed′i·ness,** *n.*

spe·le·ol·o·gist (spē′lē ol′ə jist) *n.* an expert in speleology.

spe·le·ol·o·gy (spē′lē ol′ə jē) *n.* the branch of science dealing with caves. [< L *spelaeum* < Gk. *spēlaion* + *-logy*]

spell[1] (spel) *v.* **spelled** or **spelt, spell·ing. 1** write or say the letters of (a word) in order. **2** write or say the letters of words in order: *She cannot spell well.* **3** make up or form (a word). **4** mean: *Delay spells danger.* **5 spell out, a** read letter by letter; read very slowly or with difficulty: *spell out a message.* **b** discover or make out by close study or observation: *spell out the truth of the matter.* **c** explain thoroughly, step by step, carefully, and in detail. [ME < OF *espeller* < Gmc.]

spell[2] (spel) *n.* **1** a word or set of words having magic power. **2** fascination; charm. **3 cast a spell on,** put under the influence of magic power; fascinate. **4 under a spell,** controlled by magic power; fascinated. [OE *spell* story]

spell[3] (spel) *n. v.* **spelled, spell·ing.** —*n.* **1** a period of work or duty: *The sailor's spell at the wheel was four hours.* **2** a period or time of anything: *a spell of coughing, a spell of hot weather.* **3** the relief of one person by another in doing something. **4** *Informal.* an attack or fit of illness or nervous excitement. **5** *Informal.* a brief period: *rest for a spell.* [ME; related to v.] —*v.* **1** *Informal.* work in place of (another) for a while: *spell another person at rowing a boat.* **2** give a time of rest to. [OE *spelian,* v.]

spell·bind (spel′bīnd′) *v.* **-bound, -bind·ing.** make spellbound; fascinate; enchant.

spell·bind·er (spel′bīn′dər) *n.* a speaker or writer who can hold his audience spellbound.

spell·bound (spel′bound′) *adj.* too interested to move; fascinated; enchanted. [< *spell*[2] + *bound*[1]]

spell·er (spel′ər) *n.* **1** a person who spells words. **2** a book for teaching spelling.

spell·ing (spel′ing) *n.* **1** the writing or saying of the letters of words in order. **2** the way a word is spelled: "*Gray*" *has two spellings,* "*gray*" *and* "*grey.*"

spelling bee a spelling contest.

spelt[1] (spelt) *v.* a pt. and a pp. of **spell**[1].

spelt[2] (spelt) *n.* a kind of wheat grown chiefly in Europe. [< LL *spelta*]

spel·ter (spel′tər) *n.* zinc, usually in the form of small bars. [origin uncertain; cf. LG *spialter*]

spe·lunk·er (spi lung′kər) *n.* a person who studies and explores caves as a hobby. [< L *spelunca* cave < Gk. *spēlaion* + E *-er*[2]]

spe·lunk·ing (spi lung′king) *n.* the act or hobby of studying and exploring caves.

spen·cer (spen′sər) *n.* a short jacket for men or women, usually knitted. [after George John *Spencer,* the second Earl Spencer (1758-1834)]

Spen·ce·ri·an[1] (spen sēr′ē ən) *adj.* of or having to do with Herbert Spencer, 1820-1903, an English philosopher, or his philosophy.

Spen·ce·ri·an[2] (spen sēr′ē ən) *adj.* of or having to do with a system of penmanship, characterized by clearly formed, rounded letters slanting to the right. [< Platt R. *Spencer,* 1800-1864, an American penmanship expert who originated it + *-ian*]

spend (spend) *v.* **spent, spend·ing. 1** pay out: *She spent* *ten dollars today.* 2 pay out money: *Earn before you spend.* 3 use; use up: *Don't spend any more time on that job.* 4 pass (time, etc.): *spend a day at the beach.* 5 wear out; exhaust: *The storm has spent its force.* 6 waste; squander: *He spent his fortune on horse racing.* 7 lose, as for a cause. [OE *-spendan* (as in *forspendan* use up) < L *expendere.* Doublet of EXPEND.] —**spend′er,** *n.*

Syn. 1 **Spend, expend, disburse** = pay out money, time, effort, etc. **Spend** is the common word, meaning "pay out money, or other resources for some thing or purpose": *He spends all he earns.* **Expend,** more formal, emphasizes the idea of using up by spending sums or amounts, commonly large, that reduce or exhaust a fund: *She expends her energy on parties.* **Disburse,** formal or financial, means "pay out from a fund for expenses": *The treasurer reports what he disburses.*

spend·thrift (spend′thrift′) *n.* a person who wastes money. —*adj.* extravagant with money; wasteful.

Spen·se·ri·an (spen sēr′ē ən) *adj.* of, having to do with, or characteristic of Edmund Spenser, 1552?-1599, an English poet, or his work.

Spenserian stanza the stanza used by Edmund Spenser in his *Faerie Queene*, consisting of eight iambic pentameter lines and a final Alexandrine, with three rhymes arranged thus: ababbcbcc.

spent (spent) *v.* pt. and pp. of **spend.** —*adj.* 1 used up. 2 worn out; tired: *a spent swimmer, a spent horse.*

sperm[1] (spėrm) *n.* 1 the fluid of a male animal that fertilizes the eggs of the female. 2 one of the male germ cells in it. [ME < LL < Gk. *sperma* seed < *speirein* sow[1]]

sperm[2] (spėrm) *n.* 1 spermaceti. 2 a sperm whale. 3 sperm oil. [short for *spermaceti*, etc.]

sper·ma·cet·i (spėr′mə set′ē or spėr′mə sē′tē) *n.* a whitish, waxy substance obtained from the oil in the head of the sperm whale and used in making fine candles, ointments, cosmetics, etc. [< Med.L *sperma ceti* sperm of a whale < LL *sperma* sperm, seed < Gk., and L *cetus* large sea animal < Gk. *kētos*]

sper·mat·ic (spėr mat′ik) *adj.* 1 of or having to do with sperm; seminal; generative. 2 having to do with a sperm gland.

sper·ma·to·phyte (spėr′mə tə fīt′) *n.* in botany, a plant that produces seeds. The spermatophytes form the largest division of the plant kingdom and include the angiosperms and the gymnosperms. [< Gk. *sperma, -atos* seed + E *-phyte*]

sper·ma·to·zo·on or **sper·ma·to·zo·ön** (spėr′mə tə zō′ən) *n.* **-zo·a** (-zō′ə). in biology, a male reproductive cell. A spermatozoon united with an ovum to fertilize it. [< Gk. *sperma, -atos* seed + *zōion* animal]

sperm oil a light-yellow oil from the sperm whale, used for lubricating.

sperm whale a large, square-headed, toothed whale, the head of which contains a large cavity filled with sperm oil and spermaceti.

spew (spū) *v.* throw out; cast forth; vomit. Also, **spue.** [OE *spīwan*] —**spew′er,** *n.*

sp.gr. specific gravity.

sphag·num (sfag′nəm) *n.* 1 any of various soft mosses, found chiefly on the surface of bogs. 2 a mass or quantity of this moss used by gardeners in potting and packing plants, in surgery for dressing wounds, etc. [< NL < Gk. *sphagnos*, a kind of moss]

sphal·er·ite (sfal′ə rīt′ or sfā′lə rīt′) *n.* a native zinc sulphide, found in both crystalline and massive forms; blende. *Formula*: ZnS [< Gk. *sphaleros* deceptive, slippery < *sphallen* overthrow, baffle + E *-ite*[1]]

sphe·noid (sfē′noid) *adj.* 1 wedge-shaped. 2 in anatomy, of or having to do with a compound bone of the base of the skull. —*n.* in anatomy, this bone. [< NL < Gk. *sphenoeidēs* < *sphēn* wedge + *eidos* form]

sphere (sfēr) *n.* 1 a round body whose surface is at all points equally distant from the centre; globe; ball. 2 the place or surroundings in which a person or thing exists, acts, works, etc.: *People used to say that woman's sphere was the home.* 3 a range; extent; region: *Great Britain's sphere of influence.* 4 any of the stars or planets. The earth, sun, and moon are spheres. 5 a supposed hollow globe, with the earth at its centre, enclosing the stars, sun, and planets. 6 any one of a series of such globes, one inside another, in which the stars and planets were supposed to be set. Movement of the spheres was believed to cause the stars and planets to revolve around the earth. 7 the heavens; the sky. [< L < Gk. *sphaira*]

spher·i·cal (sfer′ə kəl) *adj.* 1 shaped like a sphere. 2 of or having to do with a sphere or spheres.

spher·i·cal·ly (sfer′ik lē) *adv.* 1 in the form of a sphere, or of part of a sphere. 2 so as to be spherical.

sphe·ric·i·ty (sfi ris′ə tē) *n.* **-ties.** spherical form; roundness.

sphe·roid (sfēr′oid) *n.* a body shaped somewhat like a sphere.

sphe·roi·dal (sfi roi′dəl) *adj.* shaped somewhat like a sphere.

spher·ule (sfer′ül) *n.* a small sphere or spherical body.

sphinc·ter (sfingk′tər) *n.* in anatomy, a ringlike muscle that surrounds an opening or passage of the body, and can contract to close it. [< LL < Gk. *sphinktēr* < *sphingein* squeeze]

sphinx (sfingks) *n.* **sphinx·es.** 1 a statue of a lion's body with the head of a man, ram, or hawk. 2 a puzzling or mysterious person. 3 **Sphinx, a** a huge statue with a man's head and a lion's body, near Cairo, Egypt. **b** in Greek mythology, a monster having the head of a woman, the body of a lion, and the wings of a bird. The Sphinx proposed a riddle to every passer-by and killed those unable to guess it. [< L < Gk.]

sphinx moth hawk moth.

sphygmo- *combining form.* the pulse; pulsation: *sphygmograph = an instrument that records pulse beats.* [< Gk. *sphygmos* throbbing, heartbeat < *sphyzein* throb, beat]

sphyg·mo·gram (sfig′mə gram′) *n.* a diagram of the pulse beats as recorded by a sphygmograph.

sphyg·mo·graph (sfig′mə graf′) *n.* an instrument that records the rate, strength, etc. of the pulse. [< Gk. *sphygmos* pulse + E *-graph*]

sphyg·moid (sfig′moid) *adj.* pulselike.

sphyg·mo·ma·nom·e·ter (sfig′mō mə nom′ə tər) *n.* in medicine, an instrument for measuring blood pressure, especially in an artery. [< *sphygmo-* + Gk. *manos* at intervals + E *-meter*]

spi·ca (spī′kə) *n.* **spi·cae** (spī′sē). 1 in botany, a spike. 2 in surgery, spiral bandages with reversed turns. 3 **Spica,** a very bright star in the constellation Virgo. [< L *spica* ear of grain]

spi·cate (spī′kāt) *adj.* 1 in botany: **a** having spikes. **b** arranged in spikes. 2 in zoology, having the form of a spike; pointed. [< L *spicatus*, pp. of *spicare* furnish with spikes < *spica* spike[2]]

spice (spīs) *n. v.* **spiced, spic·ing.** —*n.* 1 any of a group of pungent or aromatic vegetable substances, used as seasoning, preservatives, etc.: *Pepper, cinnamon, cloves, ginger, and nutmeg are common spices.* 2 such substances considered collectively or as a material. 3 a spicy, fragrant odor. 4 something that adds flavor or interest. 5 a slight touch or trace: *a spice of wickedness.* —*v.* 1 put spice in; season. 2 add flavor or interest to. [ME < OF *espice*, ult. < L *species* sort. Doublet of SPECIES.]

spic·er·y (spīs′ər ē) *n.* **-er·ies.** 1 spices. 2 a spicy flavor or fragrance.

spic·i·ness (spīs′ē nis) *n.* a spicy flavor or smell.

spick-and-span (spik′ənd span′) *adj.* 1 neat and clean; spruce or smart: *a spick-and-span room, apron, or uniform.* 2 fresh; new. [short for *spick-and-span-new*: *spick*, var. of *spike*[1]; *span-new* < ON *spán-nýr* < *spánn* chip + *nýr* new]

spic·u·late (spik′yů lāt′ or spik′yů lit) *adj.* 1 having spicules; consisting of spicules. 2 having the form of a spicule.

spic·ule (spik′yůl) *n.* 1 a small, slender, sharp-pointed piece, usually bony or crystalline. 2 in zoology, one of the small, slender, calcareous or siliceous bodies that form the skeleton of a sponge. 3 in botany, a small spike of flowers; spikelet. 4 a small solar prominence. [< L *spiculum*, dim. of *spicum*, var. of *spica* ear of grain]

hat, āge, cãre, fär; let, ēqual, tėrm; it, īce
hot, ōpen, ôrder; oil, out; cup, pu̇t, rüle, ūse
əbove, takən, pencəl, lemən, circəs
ch, child; ng, long; sh, ship
th, thin; ᴛʜ, then; zh, measure

spic·y (spīs′ē) *adj.* **spic·i·er, spic·i·est. 1** flavored with spice. **2** like spice: *Those apples have a spicy smell and taste.* **3** lively; keen: *spicy conversation.* **4** somewhat improper: *Some of his stories were a bit spicy.* **5** producing spices; abounding with spices. —**spic′i·ly,** *adv.* —**Syn. 2** aromatic, fragrant.

spi·der (spī′dər) *n.* **1** any of the eight-legged, wingless arachnids. Many spiders spin webs to catch insects for food. **2** someone or something like or suggesting a spider. **3** a frying pan with a handle. **4** a frame having three legs to support a pot or pan over a fire. [OE *spīthra* < *spinnan* spin] —**spi′der·like′,** *adj.*

spider web a web spun by a spider. See **web** for picture.

spi·der·wort (spī′dər wėrt′) *n.* a trailing plant that takes root at the knots of its stems and has clusters of flowers.

spi·der·y (spī′dər ē) *adj.* **1** long and thin like a spider's legs. **2** suggesting a spider web: *spidery handwriting.* **3** full of, or infested with, spiders.

spiel[1] (spēl) *Slang.* —*n.* talk; speech; harangue, especially of a cheap, noisy nature. —*v.* talk; speak. [< G *spielen* play]

spiel[2] or **'spiel** (spēl) *n. Cdn.* bonspiel.

spiel·er[1] (spēl′ər) *n. Slang.* a person who spiels, especially one who exaggerates and has a lot to say.

spiel·er[2] or **'spiel·er** (spēl′ər) *n.* a person who takes part in a bonspiel.

spiff·y (spif′ē) *adj.* **spiff·i·er, spiff·i·est.** *Slang.* smart; neat; trim. [< dial. E *spiff* dandified]

spig·ot (spig′ət) *n.* **1** a valve for controlling the flow of water or other liquid from a pipe, tank, barrel, etc. **2** a tap or faucet. **3** a peg or plug used to stop the small hole of a cask, barrel, etc.; bung. [ME; ? via OF < base of *spike*]

spike[1] (spīk) *n. v.* **spiked, spik·ing.** —*n.* **1** a large, strong nail. **2** a sharp-pointed piece or part. Ballplayers wear shoes with spikes.
—*v.* **1** fasten with spikes: *The men spiked the rails to the ties when laying the track.* **2** provide or equip with spikes: *Runners wear spiked shoes to keep from slipping.* **3** pierce or injure with a spike. **4** in former times, make (a cannon) useless by driving a spike into the opening where the powder was set off. **5** put an end or stop to; make useless; block: *spike an attempt.* **6** *Slang.* add liquor to (a drink, etc.). [ME < Scand. < L *spica*; cf. Swedish *spik* nail] —**spik′er,** *n.* —**spike′like′,** *adj.*

spike[2] (spīk) *n.* **1** an ear of grain. **2** a long, pointed flower cluster. See **inflorescence** for picture. [ME < L *spica*]

spike heel a high, thin heel on a woman's dress shoe.

spike·let (spīk′lit) *n.* a small spike or flower cluster.

spike·nard (spīk′nərd or spīk′närd) *n.* **1** a sweet-smelling ointment used by the ancients. **2** the fragrant East Indian plant from which it was probably obtained. [ME < Med.L *spica nardi* ear of nard]

spik·y (spīk′ē) *adj.* **1** having spikes; set with sharp, projecting points. **2** having the shape of a spike.

spile (spīl) *n. v.* **spiled, spil·ing.** —*n.* **1** a peg or plug of wood used to stop the small hole of a cask or barrel. **2** a spout for drawing off sap from the sugar maple. **3** a heavy stake or beam driven into the ground as a support. —*v.* **1** stop up (a hole) with a plug. **2** furnish with a spout. **3** furnish, strengthen, or support with stakes or piles. [cf. MDu. or MLG *spile*]

spill[1] (spil) *v.* **spilled** or **spilt, spill·ing,** *n.* —*v.* **1** let (liquid or any matter in loose pieces) run or fall: *spill milk or salt.* **2** fall or flow out: *Water spilled from the pail.* **3** scatter. **4** shed (blood). **5** *Informal.* cause to fall from a horse, car, boat, etc. **6** let wind out of (a sail). **7** *Slang.* make known; tell. —*n.* **1** a spilling. **2** the quantity spilled. **3** *Informal.* a fall. [OE *spillan*] —**spill′er,** *n.*

spill[2] (spil) *n.* **1** a splinter. **2** a piece of wood or paper used to light candles, etc. [? ult. var. of *spile*]

spill·age (spil′ij) *n.* **1** a spilling of liquid, food, etc. **2** that which is spilled; the quantity spilled.

spil·li·kin (spil′ə kin) *n.* jackstraw. [< *spill*[2]]

spill·way (spil′wā′) *n.* a channel or passage for the escape of surplus water from a dam, river, etc.

spilt (spilt) *v.* a pt. and a pp. of **spill**[1].

spin (spin) *v.* **spun** or (*Archaic*) **span, spun, spin·ning,** *n.* —*v.* **1** draw out and twist (cotton, flax, wool, etc.) into thread. **2** make (thread, yarn, etc.) by drawing out and twisting cotton, wool, flax, etc. **3** make (a thread, web, cocoon, etc.) by giving out from the body sticky material that hardens into thread. A spider spins a web. **4** make (glass, gold, etc.) into thread. **5** turn or make turn rapidly: *The wheel spins round. The boy spins his top.* **6** feel dizzy. **7** run, ride, drive, etc. rapidly. **8** produce; tell: *The old sailor used to spin yarns about adventures at sea.* **9 spin out,** make long and slow; draw out; prolong. —*n.* **1** a spinning. **2** a rapid run, ride, drive, etc. **3** a rapid turning around of an airplane as it falls. [OE *spinnan*] —**Syn.** *v.* **5** twirl, whirl, rotate, revolve.

spin·ach (spin′ich or spin′ij) *n.* **1** a plant whose green leaves are used as a vegetable, either raw or cooked. **2** the leaves of this plant. [< OF (*e*)*spinache* < Med.L < Sp. *espinaca* < Arabic]

spi·nal (spī′nəl) *adj.* **1** of or having to do with the spine or backbone. **2** resembling a spine in form or function: *a spinal ridge or hill.* —*n. Informal.* a spinal anesthetic: *administer a spinal.* [< LL *spinalis* < L *spina.* See SPINE.]

spinal column the spine; the backbone.

spinal cord the thick, whitish cord of nerve tissue in the backbone or spine. See **brain** for diagram.

spin·dle (spin′dəl) *n. v.* **-dled, -dling.** —*n.* **1** a rod or pin used in spinning to twist, wind, and hold thread. **2** a certain quantity or measure of yarn, as 15,120 yards for cotton, and 14,400 yards for linen. **3** any rod or pin that turns around, or on which something turns. Axles and shafts are spindles. **4** one of the turned or circular supporting parts of a balustrade or stair rail. —*v.* grow tall and thin. [OE *spinel*; related to *spinnan* spin]

A woman using a spindle and distaff

spin·dle-leg·ged (spin′dəl leg′id or -legd′) *adj.* having long, thin legs.

spin·dle·legs (spin′dəl legz′) *n.pl.* **1** long, thin legs. **2** *Informal.* a person with long, thin legs.
☛ Spindlelegs, meaning "long, thin legs," is plural in form and use: *The spindlelegs of that chair are shaky.* When the meaning is "a person with long, thin legs," *spindlelegs* is plural in form and singular in use: *Spindlelegs, as the boys call John, is a good basketball player.*

spin·dle·shanked (spin′dəl shangkt′) *adj.* spindle-legged.

spin·dle·shanks (spin′dəl shangks′) *n.pl.* spindlelegs.

spin·dling (spin′dling) *adj.* spindly.

spin·dly (spin′dlē) *adj.* **-dli·er, -dli·est.** very long and slender; too tall and thin.

spin·drift (spin′drift′) *n.* spray blown or dashed up from the waves. Also, **spoondrift.** [var. of *spoondrift*]

spine (spīn) *n.* **1** a series of small bones down the middle of the back; backbone. See **skeleton** for diagram. **2** anything like a backbone; a long, narrow ridge or support. **3** courage, determination, etc., as that by which a person is supported in the face of danger or adversity: *Threats merely stiffened his spine.* **4** in botany, a stiff, sharp-pointed growth of woody tissue: *The cactus and hawthorn have spines.* **5** in zoology: **a** a stiff, pointed, thornlike part or projection: *A porcupine's spines are called quills.* **b** a sharp, rigid fin ray of a fish. **c** a spicule. **6** the supporting back portion of a book cover. [< L *spina,* originally, thorn] —**spine′like′,** *adj.*

spined (spīnd) *adj.* having a spine or spines.

spi·nel (spi nel′ or spin′əl) *n.* a crystalline mineral, consisting chiefly of oxides of magnesium and aluminum, that occurs in various colors. Transparent spinel is used for jewellery. [< F < Ital. *spinella*, ult. < L *spina* thorn]

spine·less (spīn′lis) *adj.* **1** without spines or sharp-pointed processes. **2** having no backbone. **3** having a weak spine; limp. **4** without moral force, resolution, or courage; weak-willed; feeble. —**spine′less·ly**, *adv.* —**spine′less·ness**, *n.*

spin·et (spin′it or spi net′) *n.* **1** a former musical keyboard instrument like a small harpsichord. **2** a compact upright piano. [< F < Ital. *spinetta*, probably named after Giovanni *Spinetti*, an Italian inventor]

spin·i·fex (spin′ə feks′) *n.* any of various Australian grasses having spiny seeds and sharp-pointed leaves. [< NL *Spinifex*, the generic name < L *spina* thorn + *facere* to make]

spin·na·ker (spin′ə kər) *n.* a large, triangular sail carried by yachts on the side opposite the mainsail when running before the wind. [supposedly from *Sphinx*, a yacht on which first used, perhaps influenced by *spanker*]

spinnaker boom a pole on which the spinnaker is set.

spin·ner (spin′ər) *n.* a person, animal, or thing that spins.

spin·ner·et (spin′ər et′) *n.* the organ by which spiders, silkworms, etc. spin their threads. [dim. of *spinner*]

spin·ney (spin′ē) *n.* **-neys.** *Esp.Brit.* a thicket; a small wood and its undergrowth, especially one preserved for sheltering game birds; a small group of trees. [< OF *espinnei*, ult. < L *spina* thorn]

spin·ning (spin′ing) *adj.* that spins. —*n.* the act of one that spins.

spinning jenny an early type of spinning machine having more than one spindle, whereby one person could spin a number of threads at the same time.

spinning wheel a large wheel with a spindle, arranged for spinning cotton, flax, wool, etc. into thread or yarn.

spin·off (spin′of′) *n.* a by-product or fringe benefit of an operation.

A woman using a spinning wheel. The large wheel causes the smaller one to turn, and this revolves the horizontal spindle, twisting the thread and winding it up at the same time.

spi·nose (spī′nōs) *adj.* full of spines; having spines; thorny; spinous. [< L *spinosus* < *spina* thorn]

spi·nous (spī′nəs) *adj.* **1** covered with spines; having spines; thorny. **2** spinelike; sharp.

spin·ster (spin′stər) *n.* **1** an unmarried woman. **2** an elderly woman who has not married; old maid. **3** a woman who spins flax, wool, etc. into thread. [ME *spinster* < *spin* + *-ster*]

spin·ster·hood (spin′stər hůd′) *n.* the state of being a spinster.

spi·nule (spī′nyůl or spin′yůl) *n.* a small, sharp-pointed spine.

spin·y (spīn′ē) *adj.* **spin·i·er, spin·i·est. 1** covered with spines; having spines; thorny: *a spiny cactus, a spiny porcupine.* **2** spinelike. **3** difficult; troublesome. —**spin′i·ness**, *n.*

spiny anteater echidna.

spi·ra·cle (spī′rə kəl or spir′ə kəl) *n.* **1** in zoology, an opening for breathing. Insects take in air through tiny spiracles. A whale breathes through a spiracle in the top of its head. **2** an opening in the ground by which underground vapors are given off; air hole. [< L *spiraculum* < *spirare* breathe]

spi·rae·a (spī rē′ə) *n.* any of various shrubs of the rose family having clusters of small white, pink, or red flowers with five petals. [< L < Gk. *speiraia*, apparently < *speira* cord]

spi·ral (spī′rəl) *n. adj. v.* **-ralled** or **-raled, -rall·ing** or **-ral·ing.** —*n.* **1** a winding and gradually widening coil. A watch spring is a spiral. **2** a constant increasing or decreasing: *an inflationary spiral.*

Spirals

—*adj.* **1** coiling or winding in increasingly larger circles: *a spiral spring.* **2** coiling or winding around the surface of a long, round object; coiled: *the spiral thread on a bolt, the spiral stripes on a barber's pole.*
—*v.* **1** follow or cause to follow a spiral path. **2** form into a spiral. [< Med.L *spiralis* < L *spira* a coil < Gk. *speira*] —**spi′ral·ly**, *adv.*

spiral nebula a cluster of stars in the apparent form of a spiral.

spi·rant (spī′rənt) *n.* in phonetics, a consonant uttered with an audible expulsion of breath, such as (f) or (v); fricative. [< L *spirans, -antis*, ppr. of *spirare* breathe]

spire[1] (spīr) *n. v.* **spired, spir·ing.**
—*n.* **1** the top part of a tower or steeple that narrows to a point. **2** anything tapering and pointed: *The sunset shone on the rocky spires of the mountains.* —*v.* **1** shoot up. **2** furnish with a spire. [OE *spīr*] —**spire′like′**, *adj.*

SPIRE
STEEPLE

spire[2] (spīr) *n.* **1** a coil; spiral. **2** a single twist of a coil or spiral. [< L < Gk. *speira* coil]

spi·re·a (spī rē′ə) *n.* spiraea.

spi·ril·lum (spī ril′əm) *n.* **-ril·la** (-ril′ə). any of a group of bacteria that have spirally twisted forms. [< NL *spirillum* < L *spira* spire[2] < Gk. *speira*]

spir·it (spir′it) *n.* **1** the immaterial part of man; the soul: *He is present in spirit, though absent in body.* **2** man's moral, religious, or emotional nature. **3** a supernatural being, such as a god, a ghost, or a fairy. **4 the Spirit, a** God. **b** the Holy Ghost. **5** Often, **spirits,** *pl.* a state of mind; disposition; temper: *He is in good spirits.* **6** a person; personality: *Montcalm was a noble spirit.* **7** an influence that stirs up and rouses: *A spirit of reform marked the nineteenth century.* **8 spirits,** *pl.* vigor; liveliness; cheerfulness. **9** courage; vigor; liveliness: *That race horse has spirit.* **10** enthusiasm and loyalty. **11** the real meaning or intent: *The spirit of a law is more important than its words.* **12** Often, **spirits,** *pl.* a solution in alcohol: *spirits of camphor.* **13** Often, **spirits,** *pl.* an alcoholic drink made by distilling the juice of certain fruits, grains, roots, etc.; liquor: *He drinks beer but no spirits.* **14 out of spirits,** sad; gloomy.
—*v.* **1** carry (away or off) secretly: *The child has been spirited away.* **2** stir up; encourage; cheer. **3** conjure (up). [< L *spiritus*, originally, breath < *spirare* breathe. Doublet of ESPRIT, SPRITE.] —**Syn.** *n.* **3** phantom, spectre, apparition. **5** humor, mood. **9** animation, mettle, vivacity. **10** ardor, zeal.

spir·it·ed (spir′ə tid) *adj.* lively; dashing: *a spirited race horse.* —**spir′it·ed·ly**, *adv.* —**spir′it·ed·ness**, *n.*

spir·it·ism (spir′ə tiz′əm) *n.* spiritualism.

spir·it·less (spir′it lis) *adj.* without spirit or courage; depressed.

spirit level an instrument used to find out whether a surface is level. When the bubble of air in the glass tube of a spirit level is exactly at the middle of the tube, the surface is level.

spir·i·to·so (spir′ə tō′sō) in music: —*adj.* spirited; lively. —*adv.* with spirit; in a lively manner. [< Ital.]

spir·i·tu·al (spir′i chü əl) *adj.* **1** of the spirit or soul. **2** caring much for things of the spirit or soul. **3** of spirits; supernatural. **4** having to do with the church: *lords spiritual.* **5** sacred; religious. —*n.* a song or hymn having a religious theme, as sung originally by the Negroes of the southern United States. —**spir′i·tu·al·ly**, *adv.*

spir·i·tu·al·ism (spir′i chü əl iz′əm) *n.* **1** the belief that spirits of the dead communicate with the living, especially through persons called mediums. **2** emphasis or insistence on the spiritual; the doctrine that spirit alone is real.

spir·i·tu·al·ist (spir′i chü əl ist) *n.* a person who believes that the dead communicate with the living.

spir·i·tu·al·is·tic (spir′i chü əl is′tik) *adj.* of or having to do with spiritualism or spiritualists.

spir·i·tu·al·i·ty (spir′i chü al′ə tē) *n.* **-ties.** a devotion to spiritual things; spiritual quality.

spir·i·tu·al·i·za·tion (spir′i chü əl ə zā′shən or spir′i chü əl ī zā′shən) *n.* **1** a spiritualizing. **2** the state of being spiritualized.

spir·i·tu·al·ize (spir′i chü əl īz′) *v.* **-ized, -iz·ing.** make spiritual.

spir·i·tu·el or **spir·i·tu·elle** (spir′i chü el′) *adj.* showing a refined mind or wit. [< F *spirituel,* ult. < L *spiritus.* See SPIRIT.]

spir·i·tu·ous (spir′i chü əs) *adj.* **1** containing alcohol. **2** distilled, not fermented.

spi·ro·chete (spī′rə kēt′) *n.* any of a large group of slender, spiral, very flexible and active micro-organisms that are usually classed as bacteria. [< NL < Gk. *speira* coil + *chaitē* hair]

spi·ro·gy·ra (spī′rə jī′rə) *n.* any of several algae that grow in scumlike masses in fresh-water ponds or tanks. [< NL < Gk. *speira* coil + *gyros* circle]

spi·rom·e·ter (spī rom′ə tər) *n.* an instrument for measuring the capacity of the lungs, by the amount of air that can be breathed out after the lungs have been filled as full as possible. [< L *spirare* breathe + E *-meter*]

spirt (spėrt) *v. n.* spurt.

spir·y (spīr′ē) *adj.* **1** having the form of a spire; tapering. **2** having many spires.

spit[1] (spit) *v.* **spat** or **spit, spit·ting,** *n.* —*v.* **1** eject saliva from the mouth. **2** eject from the mouth. **3** throw out: *The gun spits fire.* **4** spit (at, on, etc.) a person or thing to express hatred or contempt. **5** make a spitting noise: *The cat spits when angry.* **6** sputter. **7** rain or snow slightly. —*n.* **1** the liquid produced in the mouth; saliva. **2** the noise or act of spitting. **3** a frothy or spitlike secretion given off by some insects. **4** a light rain or snow. **5 spit and image,** the exact image. **6 the spit of,** *Informal.* just like. [OE *spittan*] —**spit′ter,** *n.*

Spits for roasting. They can be turned to cook the meat evenly; the melted fat drips into the pan below.

spit[2] (spit) *n. v.* **spit·ted, spit·ting.** —*n.* **1** a sharp-pointed, slender rod or bar on which meat is roasted. **2** a narrow point of land running into the water. —*v.* **1** run a spit through. **2** pierce; stab. [OE *spitu*]

spit and polish *Informal.* a high standard of cleanliness or smartness. [from the soldier's practice of using spit in polishing boots, etc.]

spit·ball (spit′bol′ or -bôl′) *n.* **1** a small ball of chewed-up paper, used as a missile. **2** in baseball, a curve resulting from the pitcher's moistening one side of the ball with saliva, now illegal.

spit curl *Informal.* a small wisp of hair that is dampened, curled, and pressed against the cheek, temple, etc.

spite (spīt) *n. v.* **spit·ed, spit·ing.** —*n.* **1** ill will; a grudge. **2 in spite of,** not prevented by; notwithstanding. —*v.* show ill will toward; annoy: *He left his yard dirty to spite the people who lived next door.* [shortened from ME *despit* despite] —**spite′less,** *adj.*

Syn. *n.* **1 Spite, malice, grudge** = ill will against another. **Spite** suggests envy or a mean disposition, and applies to active ill will shown by doing mean, petty things to hurt or annoy: *She ruined his flowers out of spite.* **Malice** emphasizes actual wish or intention to injure, and suggests hatred or, especially, a disposition delighting in doing harm or seeing others hurt: *Gossips are motivated by malice.* **Grudge** suggests wishing to get even for real or imagined injury, and applies to ill will nursed a long time: *She bears grudges.*

spite·ful (spīt′fəl) *adj.* full of spite; eager to annoy; behaving with ill will and malice. —**spite′ful·ly,** *adv.* —**spite′ful·ness,** *n.*

spit·fire (spit′fīr) *n.* **1** a person, especially a woman or girl, who has a quick and fiery temper. **2** something that sends forth fire, such as a cannon or some kinds of fireworks.

spit·tle (spit′əl) *n.* saliva; spit. [< *spit*]

spit·toon (spi tün′) *n.* a receptacle or container for spitting into.

spitz (spits) *n.* **1** a breed of small dog, having a pointed muzzle and ears, long hair, and a curly tail; a white variety of Pomeranian. **2** a dog of this breed. [< G *spitz* pointed]

hat, āge, cãre, fär; let, ēqual, tėrm; it, īce
hot, ōpen, ôrder; oil, out; cup, pu̇t, rüle, ūse
əbove, takən, pencəl, lemən, circəs
ch, child; ng, long; sh, ship
th, thin; ᴛʜ, then; zh, measure

spiv (spiv) *n. Brit. Slang.* a man who avoids honest work and makes a living by dubious, usually illegal, means, especially by buying and selling goods on the black market. [origin uncertain]

splake (splāk) *n.* **splake** or **splakes.** *Cdn.* a game fish that is part speckled trout and part lake trout. [*sp*eckled + *lake* trout]

splash (splash) *v.* **1** cause (water, mud, etc.) to fly about. **2** dash liquid about: *The baby likes to splash in his tub.* **3** cause to scatter a liquid about: *He splashed the oars as he rowed.* **4** dash in scattered masses or drops: *The waves splashed on the beach.* **5** wet, spatter, or soil. **6** fall, move, or go with a splash or splashes: *He splashed across the brook.* **7** mark with spots or patches. —*n.* **1** the sound of splashing. **2** a splashing. **3** a spot of liquid splashed on something. **4** a spot; patch: *The dog is white with brown splashes.* **5 make a splash,** *Informal.* attract attention; cause excitement. [alteration of *plash,* n., OE *plæsc* puddle]

splash·er (splash′ər) *n.* **1** one that splashes. **2** something that protects from splashes.

splash·y (splash′ē) *adj.* **splash·i·er, splash·i·est.** **1** making a splash. **2** full of irregular spots or streaks. **3** *Informal.* attracting attention; causing excitement.

splat (splat) *n.* a broad, flat piece of wood, especially such a piece forming the central upright part of the back of a chair. [origin uncertain; ? < ME *splat* to split open; cut up]

splat·ter (splat′ər) *v. n.* splash; spatter. [blend of *spatter* and *splash*]

splay (splā) *v.* **1** spread out. **2** spread; flare. **3** make slanting. —*adj.* **1** wide and flat. **2** awkward; clumsy. —*n.* **1** a spread; flare. **2** a slanting surface; surface that makes an oblique angle with another. [< *display*]

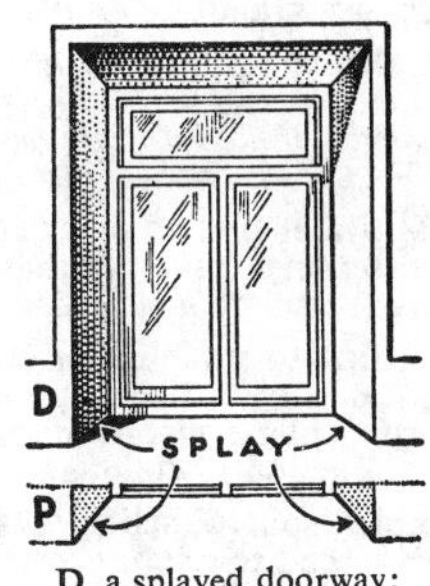

D, a splayed doorway; P, the plan of D.

splay·foot (splā′fu̇t′) *n.* **-feet.** a broad, flat foot, especially one turned outward.

splay-foot·ed (splā′fu̇t′id) *adj.* **1** having splayfeet. **2** awkward; clumsy.

spleen (splēn) *n.* **1** in anatomy, a ductless gland at the left of the stomach, that helps to maintain the volume of blood and to effect certain changes in its composition. People used to think that the spleen caused low spirits, bad temper, and spite. **2** in other vertebrates, a similar gland. **3** bad temper; spite; anger. **4** low spirits. [ME < L < Gk. *splēn*]

splen·dent (splen′dənt) *adj.* shining; gleaming; brilliant; splendid. [ME < L *splendens, -entis,* ppr. of *splendere* be bright]

splen·did (splen′did) *adj.* **1** brilliant; glorious; magnificent; grand: *a splendid sunset, a splendid palace, splendid jewels, a splendid victory.* **2** very good; fine; excellent: *a splendid chance.* [< L *splendidus* < *splendere* be bright] —**splen′did·ly,** *adv.* —**splen′did·ness,** *n.* —**Syn. 1** See **magnificent.**

splen·dif·er·ous (splen dif′ər əs) *adj. Informal.* splendid; magnificent. [< LL *splendifer,* for L *splendorifer* (< *splendor, -oris* splendor + *ferre* to bear) + E *-ous*]

splen·dor or **splen·dour** (splen′dər) *n.* **1** great brightness; brilliant light. **2** a magnificent show; pomp; glory. [ME < L *splendor* < *splendere* be bright]

sple·net·ic (spli net′ik) *adj.* **1** having to do with the spleen. **2** bad-tempered; irritable; peevish. —*n.* a person who is splenetic in disposition. [< LL *spleneticus* < Gk. *splēnitis* disease of the spleen < *splēn* spleen] —**sple·net′i·cal·ly,** *adv.*

splen·ic (splen′ik or splē′nik) *adj.* of or having to do with the spleen. [< L < Gk. *splēnikos* < *splēn* spleen]

splice (splīs) *v.* **spliced, splic·ing,** *n.* —*v.* **1** join together (ropes, etc.) by weaving together ends that have been untwisted. **2** join together (two pieces of timber) by overlapping. **3** join together (film, tape, wire, etc.). **4** *Slang.* marry. —*n.* **1** a joining of ropes, timbers, tape, etc. by splicing. **2** *Slang.* a marriage; wedding. [< MDu. *splissen*] —**splic′er,** *n.*

A splicing

spline (splīn) *n. v.* **splined, splin·ing.** —*n.* **1** a long, narrow, relatively thin strip of wood or metal; slat. **2** a long, flexible strip of wood or the like used in drawing curves. **3** in machinery: **a** a flat, rectangular piece or key fitting into a groove or slot between parts. **b** the groove for such a key. —*v.* **1** fit with a spline or key. **2** provide with a groove for a spline or key. [origin uncertain]

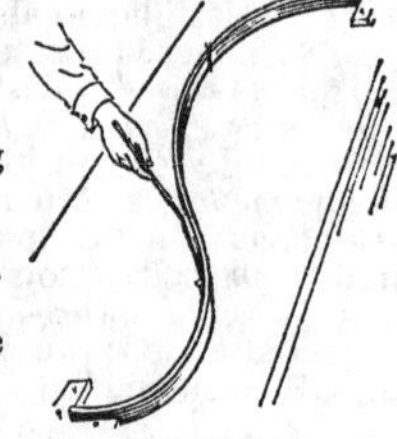
A spline (def. 2)

splint (splint) *n.* **1** an arrangement of wood, metal, plaster, etc. to hold a broken or dislocated bone in place. **2** a thin strip of wood, such as is used in making baskets. **3** a thin metal strip or plate. Old armor often had overlapping splints to protect the elbow, knee, etc. and allow easy movement. **4** a hard, bony growth on the splint bone of a horse, mule, etc. —*v.* **1** secure, hold in position, or support by means of a splint or splints. **2** support as if with splints. [< MDu. or MLG *splinte*]

splint bone in horses, mules, etc., one of the two smaller bones on either side of the large bone between the hock and the fetlock.

splin·ter (splin′tər) *n.* **1** a thin, sharp piece of wood, bone, glass, etc.: *He got a splinter in his hand. The mirror broke into splinters.* **2** a splinter group or party. —*v.* split or break into splinters. [< MDu.]

splinter group or **party** a body formed by a small dissenting group that has broken away from a political party, religious organization, etc.

splin·ter·y (splin′tər ē) *adj.* **1** apt to splinter: *splintery wood.* **2** of or like a splinter. **3** rough and jagged, as if from splintering. **4** full of splinters. **5** characterized by the production of splinters.

split (split) *v.* **split, split·ting,** *n. adj.* —*v.* **1** break or cut from end to end, or in layers. **2** separate into parts; divide: *The old farm has been split up into house lots. The two men split the cost of the dinner between them.* **3** divide into different groups, factions, parties, etc. **4** divide (a molecule) into two or more individual atoms. **5** divide (an atomic nucleus) into two portions of approximately equal mass by forcing the absorption of a neutron. **6** issue a certain number of new shares of (stock) for each share currently held. **7 split hairs,** make too fine distinctions. **8 split one's vote** or **ticket,** *Esp.U.S.* vote for candidates of different political parties.
—*n.* **1** a division in a group, party, etc.: *There was a split in the committee.* **2** a splitting; break; crack. **3** *Slang.* a share; portion. **4** *Informal.* a bottle of liquor or mix half the usual small size, containing about six ounces. **5** a sweet dish made of sliced fruit, ice cream, etc. **6** Often, **splits,** *pl.* an acrobatic trick of sinking to the floor with the legs spread far apart in opposite directions.
—*adj.* broken or cut from end to end; divided. [< MDu. *splitten*] —**split′ter,** *n.*

split infinitive in grammar, an infinitive having an adverb between *to* and the verb. *Example:* He wants to never work, but to always play.
☛ **split infinitive.** Awkward split infinitives should be avoided. Awkward: *After a while I was able to, although not very accurately, distinguish the good customers from the sulky ones.* Improved: *After a while I was able to distinguish—though not very accurately—the good customers from the sulky ones.*

split personality **1** schizophrenia. **2** a personality characterized by two seemingly independent, contradictory patterns of behavior.

split-sec·ond (split′sek′ənd) *adj.* extremely quick; happening in a flash; instantaneous.

split·ting (split′ing) *adj.* **1** that splits. **2** very painful; aching severely: *a splitting headache. My head is splitting.*

splotch (sploch) *n.* a large, irregular spot; splash. —*v.* make splotches on. [? blend of *spot* and *blotch*]

splotch·y (sploch′ē) *adj.* marked with splotches.

splurge (splėrj) *n. v.* **splurged, splurg·ing.** *Informal.* —*n.* **1** a showing off; an ostentatious display. **2** a lavish or extravagant expenditure: *He made a big splurge for his daughter's wedding.* —*v.* **1** show off. **2** spend money extravagantly.

splut·ter (splut′ər) *v.* **1** talk in a hasty, confused way. People sometimes splutter when they are excited. **2** make spitting or popping noises; sputter: *The baked apples are spluttering in the oven.* —*n.* a spluttering. [? var. of *sputter*] —**splut′ter·er,** *n.*

Spode or **spode** (spōd) *n.* a type of fine pottery or porcelain. [after Josiah *Spode* (1754-1827), a famous potter of Staffordshire, England]

spoil (spoil) *v.* **spoiled** or **spoilt, spoil·ing,** *n.* —*v.* **1** damage; injure; destroy: *He spoils a dozen pieces of paper before he writes a letter.* **2** be damaged; become bad or unfit for use: *The fruit spoiled because I kept it too long.* **3** injure the character or disposition of, especially by being too kind, generous, etc.: *That child is being spoiled by too much attention.* **4** take by force; steal. **5** rob; take plunder from. **6 be spoiling for,** *Informal.* be longing for (a fight, etc.); desire.
—*n.* **1** Often, **spoils,** *pl.* **a** plunder taken in time of war; things won: *The soldiers carried the spoils back to their own land.* **b** any goods, property, etc., seized by force or similar means after a struggle. **2** an object of plundering; prey. **3 spoils,** *pl. U.S.* government offices and positions regarded as being at the disposal of the successful political party. [ME < OF *espoillier*, ult. < L *spolium* booty, spoil]
Syn. *v.* **1 Spoil, ruin** = damage beyond repair or recovery. **Spoil** emphasizes damage that so reduces or weakens the value, strength beauty, usefulness, etc. of something as to make the thing useless or bring it to nothing: *Her friend's unkind comments spoiled her pleasure in her new dress.* **Ruin** emphasizes bringing to an end the, value, soundness, beauty, usefulness, health and happiness, etc. of someone or something through a destructive force or irretrievable loss: *He ruined his eyes by reading in a poor light.* **2** deteriorate, decay, rot. **4** plunder, pillage, sack, ravage. *-n.* **1** loot.

spoil·er (spoil′ər) *n.* **1** a person or thing that spoils. **2** a person who takes spoils.

spoil·sport (spoil′spôrt′) *n.* a person who spoils or prevents the fun of others.

spoils system *U.S.* the system or practice in which public offices with their salaries and advantages are at the disposal of the victorious political party for its own purposes and in its own (rather than the public) interest.

spoilt (spoilt) *v.* a pt. and a pp. of **spoil.**

spoke[1] (spōk) *v.* **1** pt. of **speak.** **2** *Archaic.* a pp. of **speak.**

spoke[2] (spōk) *n.* **1** one of the bars running from the centre of a wheel to the rim. See **felloe** for picture. **2** a rung of a ladder. **3 put a spoke in someone's wheel,** stop or hinder someone. —*v.* provide with spokes. [OE *spāca*]

spo·ken (spō′kən) *v.* a pp. of **speak.** —*adj.* **1** expressed with the mouth; uttered; told: *the spoken word.* **2** speaking in a certain way: *a soft-spoken man.*

spoke·shave (spōk′shāv′) *n.* a cutting tool having a blade with a handle at each end.

spokes·man (spōks′mən) *n.* **-men** (-mən). a person who speaks for another or others: *Mr. Smith was the spokesman for the factory workers.*

spo·li·ate (spō′lē āt′) *v.* **-at·ed, -at·ing.** rob; plunder; despoil. [< L *spoliatus*, ult. < *spolium* booty]

spo·li·a·tion (spō′lē ā′shən) *n.* **1** a plundering; robbery. **2** the plundering of neutrals at sea in time of war. **3** in law: **a** the act of destroying a document, or of tampering with it so as to destroy its value as evidence. **b** the destruction of a ship's papers, especially to conceal an illegal act. [ME < L *spoliatio, -onis*, ult. < *spolium* booty]

spon·da·ic (spon dā′ik) *adj.* of or having to do with a spondee; constituting a spondee; consisting of or characterized by a spondee or spondees.

spon·dee (spon′dē) *n.* in poetry, a foot or measure consisting of two long or accented syllables. The spondee is used to vary other metres. "Só stróde | hé báck | slów to | the wóund | ed Kíng" has spondees for the first two feet. [ME < L < Gk. *spondeios* < *spondē* libation; originally used in songs accompanying libations]

sponge (spunj) *n. v.* **sponged, spong·ing.** —*n.* **1** a kind of sea animal that attaches itself to rocks and has a tough, fibrelike skeleton or framework. **2** the skeleton of this animal used for soaking up water in bathing, cleaning, etc. **3** a sponge made artificially of rubber or plastic. **4** a sponging. **5** something like a sponge. **6** a pad of gauze used by doctors. **7** a mop for cleaning the bore of a cannon. **8** in cookery: **a** bread dough. **b** a kind of cake. **c** a kind of pudding, etc. **9** a person or thing that absorbs, drains, or sucks up in the manner of a sponge: *He is a sponge on his brother's resources.* **10** a person who drinks heavily. **11** *Informal.* a person who continually lives at the expense of others. **12 throw up the sponge,** give up; admit defeat.
—*v.* **1** wipe or rub with a wet sponge; make clean or damp in this way. **2** remove or wipe (away or off) with a sponge: *Sponge the mud spots off the car.* **3** absorb. **4** rub or wipe (out) as if with a sponge; remove all traces of; obliterate; efface. **5** gather sponges. **6** *Informal.* live or profit at the expense of another in a mean way: *That lazy man won't work; he just sponges on his family.* [< L < Gk. *spongia*] —**sponge′like′,** *adj.*

sponge bath a washing of the body with a wet sponge or cloth without getting into water.

sponge cake a light, spongy cake made with eggs, sugar, flour, etc. but no shortening.

spong·er (spun′jər) *n.* **1** a person who sponges. **2** a machine for sponging cloth. **3** a person or vessel engaged in gathering sponges. **4** *Informal.* a person who gets by at the expense of others.

sponging house in England, formerly, a house kept by a sheriff's officer for the confinement of arrested debtors before they were put in prison.

spon·gy (spun′jē) *adj.* **-gi·er, -gi·est. 1** like a sponge; soft, light, and full of holes: *spongy moss. spongy dough.* **2** full of holes. —**spon′gi·ness,** *n.*

spon·son (spon′sən) *n.* **1** a part projecting from the side of a ship or boat, used for support or protection. **2** an air-filled section on either side of an airplane, canoe, etc. to steady it. [? shortening and alteration of *expansion*]

spon·sor (spon′sər) *n.* **1** a person or group that formally endorses or supports another: *the sponsor of a law.* **2** a person who makes a formal promise or pledge on behalf of another; surety. **3** a person who takes vows for an infant at baptism; a godfather or godmother. **4** a company, store, or organization that pays the cost of a radio or television program for purposes of advertising, public relations, etc. **5** a person or group that arranges or promotes an organization, meeting, etc. **6** a person who pledges or gives a certain amount of financial assistance to an organization.
—*v.* act as sponsor for. [< L < *spondere* give assurance]

spon·so·ri·al (spon sô′rē əl) *adj.* of or having to do with a sponsor.

spon·sor·ship (spon′sər ship′) *n.* the position, duties, etc. of a sponsor.

spon·ta·ne·i·ty (spon′tə nē′ə tē) *n.* **-ties. 1** the state, quality, or fact of being spontaneous. **2** a spontaneous action, movement, etc.

spon·ta·ne·ous (spon tā′nē əs) *adj.* **1** caused by natural impulse or desire; not forced or compelled; not planned beforehand: *Both sides burst into spontaneous cheers at the skilful play.* **2** taking place without external cause or help; caused entirely by inner forces: *The eruption of a volcano is spontaneous.* **3** growing or produced naturally; not planted, cultivated, etc. [< LL *spontaneus* < L *sponte* of one's own accord] —**spon·ta′ne·ous·ly,** *adv.* —**spon·ta′ne·ous·ness,** *n.* —**Syn. 1** See **voluntary.**

hat, āge, cãre, fär; let, ēqual, tėrm; it, īce
hot, ōpen, ôrder; oil, out; cup, pu̇t, rüle, ūse
əbove, takən, pencəl, lemən, circəs
ch, child; ng, long; sh, ship
th, thin; ᴛʜ, then; zh, measure

spontaneous combustion the bursting into flame of a substance as a result of the heat produced by chemical action within the substance itself.

spoof (spüf) *Slang.* —*n.* **1** a trick or hoax. **2** a light satirical parody; take-off. —*v.* **1** play tricks; fool. **2** make a light satirical parody on. [coined by Arthur Roberts (1852-1933), a British comedian] —**spoof′er,** *n.*

spook[1] (spük) *n. Informal.* a ghost; spectre. [< Du. *spook*]

spook[2] (spük) *v.* startle game or fish.

spook·y (spük′ē) *adj* **spook·i·er, spook·i·est.** *Informal.* like a spook; suited to spooks; suggesting spooks.

spool (spül) *n.* **1** a cylinder of wood or metal on which thread, wire, etc. is wound. **2** something like a spool in shape or use. —*v.* wind on a spool. [< MDu. *spoele*]

spoon (spün) *n.* **1** a utensil consisting of a small, shallow bowl at the end of a handle. Spoons are used to take up or stir food or drink. **2** something shaped like a spoon. **3** in golf, a kind of club having a wooden head. **4** a shiny, curved bait having hooks attached for catching fish. **5 born with a silver spoon in one's mouth,** born lucky or rich.
—*v.* **1** take up in a spoon. **2** hollow out or form in the shape of the bowl of a spoon. **3** *Slang.* make love in a silly way. **4** troll for or catch (fish) with a spoon bait. **5** in sports, hit a ball upward in a weak or feeble manner. [OE *spōn* chip, shaving] —**spoon′like′,** *adj.*

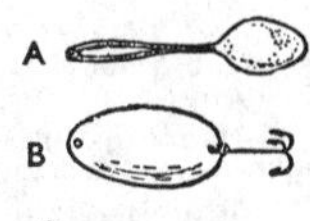

Spoons: A, a teaspoon; B, def. 4.

spoon·bill (spün′bil′) *n.* **1** a long-legged wading bird that has a long, flat bill with a spoon-shaped tip. **2** any of various birds that have a similar bill.

spoon·drift (spün′drift′) *n.* spindrift. [< *spoon* sail before the wind (of uncertain origin) + *drift*]

spoon·er·ism (spü′nə riz′əm) *n.* an unintentional, often humorous, transposing of the first letters or sounds of successive words. *Example*: "kinkering kongs" for "conquering kings." [after Rev. William A. *Spooner* (1844-1930), of New College, Oxford, who was famous for such mistakes]

spoon-feed (spün′fēd′) *v.* **-fed, -feed·ing. 1** feed with a spoon. **2** spoil; coddle; overprotect: *Students should not be spoonfed.*

spoon·ful (spün′fu̇l′) *n.* **-fuls.** as much as a spoon can hold.

spoon·y (spün′ē) *adj.* **spoon·i·er, spoon·i·est,** *n.* **spoonies.** *Informal.* —*adj.* foolish or silly in lovemaking; demonstratively fond. —*n.* **1** a sentimental or overfond lover. **2** simpleton. —**spoon′i·ly,** *adv.* —**spoon′i·ness,** *n.*

spoor (spür) *n.* the trail of a wild animal; track. —*v.* track by or follow a spoor. [< Afrikaans *spoor* < MDu.; cf. OE *spor* footprint]

spo·rad·ic (spə rad′ik) *adj.* **1** appearing or happening at intervals in time: *sporadic outbreaks.* **2** being or occurring apart from others; isolated. **3** appearing in scattered instances: *sporadic cases of scarlet fever.* **4** occurring singly, or widely apart in locality: *sporadic genera of plants.* [< Med.L < Gk. *sporadikos* scattered, ult. < *spora* a sowing]

spo·rad·i·cal (spə rad′ə kəl) *adj.* sporadic.

spo·rad·i·cal·ly (spə rad′ik lē) *adv.* here and there; now and then; separately.

spo·ran·gi·a (spə ran′jē ə) *n.* pl. of **sporangium.**

spo·ran·gi·um (spə ran′jē əm) *n.* **-gi·a** (-jē ə). in botany, a receptacle in which asexual spores are produced; spore case. The little brown spots sometimes seen on the under side of ferns are sporangia. [< NL < Gk. *spora* seed + *angeion* vessel]

spore (spôr) *n.* **1** in biology, a single cell that becomes free and is capable of developing into a new plant or animal. Ferns produce spores. **2** a germ or seed. [< NL < Gk. *spora* seed]

spo·ro·phyl or **spo·ro·phyll** (spô′rə fil′) *n.* in botany, any leaf that bears spores or spore cases. [< Gk. *spora* seed + *phyllon* leaf]

spo·ro·phyte (spô′rə fīt′) *n.* in botany, any plant or generation of a plant that produces asexual spores. Sporophytes develop from the union of germ cells produced by gametophytes. [< Gk. *spora* seed + E *-phyte*]

spor·ran (spôr′ən) *n.* in Scottish Highland dress, a large purse, commonly of fur or leather, hanging from the belt in front. [< Scots Gaelic *sporan*]

sport (spôrt) *n.* **1** a form of amusement or play; game; contest. Baseball, football, golf, tennis, fishing, hunting, and racing are outdoor sports. **2** amusement; recreation. **3** playful joking; fun: *say a thing in sport.* **4** ridicule. **5** the object of a joke; plaything: *His hat blew off and became the sport of the wind.* **6** a sportsman. **7** *Informal.* a person who behaves in a sportsmanlike manner; good fellow: *be a sport.* **8** *Informal.* a gambler. **9** *Slang.* a flashy or showy person. **10** in biology, an animal or plant that varies suddenly or in a marked manner from the normal type. A white blackbird would be a sport. **11 for sport** or **in sport,** in fun; as a joke. **12 make sport of,** make fun of; laugh at; ridicule: *Don't make sport of the lame boy.*
—*v.* **1** amuse oneself; play: *Lambs sport in the fields.* **2** jest. **3** *Informal.* display: *sport a new hat.* **4** in biology, become or produce a sport.
—*adj.* of sports; suitable for sports. [ult. short for *disport*] —**Syn.** *n.* **1** See **play. 2** pastime, diversion.

sport·ful (spôrt′fəl) *adj.* playful.

sport·ing (spôr′ting) *adj.* **1** of, interested in, or engaging in sports. **2** playing fair: *a sporting gesture.* **3** willing to take a chance. **4** *Informal.* involving risk; uncertain. —**sport′ing·ly,** *adv.*

spor·tive (spôr′tiv) *adj.* playful; merry: *The old dog seemed as sportive as the puppy.* —**spor′tive·ly,** *adv.* —**spor′tive·ness,** *n.*

sports (spôrts) *adj.* of sports; suitable for sports: *a sports dress.*

sports car **1** any low, fast, two-seater car, usually one having an open top. **2** any car appealing to driving enthusiasts and designed for high speeds and manoeuvrability.

sports·cast (spôrts′kast′) *n.* a radio or television broadcast of a sports event or of news or discussion of sports events. —**sports′cas′ter,** *n.*

sports·man (spôrts′mən) *n.* **-men** (-mən). **1** a person who takes part in sports, especially hunting, fishing, or racing. **2** a person who likes sports. **3** a person who plays fair. **4** a person who is willing to take a chance.

sports·man·like (spôrts′mən līk′) *adj.* like or befitting a sportsman; fair and honorable.

sports·man·ship (spôrts′mən ship′) *n.* **1** ability in sports. **2** the qualities or conduct of a sportsman; fair play.

sports·wear (spôrts′wãr′) *n.* clothes made for wear in sports, recreation, or other informal activities.

sports·writ·er (spôrts′rīt′ər) *n.* a newspaper or magazine writer who reports sporting events.

sport·y (spôr′tē) *adj.* **sport·i·er, sport·i·est.** *Informal.* **1** sportsmanlike; sporting. **2** gay or fast; flashy. **3** smart in dress, appearance, manners, etc. —**sport′i·ly,** *adv.* —**sport′i·ness,** *n.*

spor·ule (spôr′yůl) *n.* in botany, a small spore, especially a spore of certain fungi.

spot (spot) *n. v.* **spot·ted, spot·ting,** *adj.* —*n.* **1** a small discoloring or disfiguring mark made by a foreign substance; stain; speck: *a spot of ink on the paper.* **2** a stain or blemish on character or reputation; moral defect; fault; flaw: *His character is without spot.* **3** a small part of a surface differing in some way from the rest, as in color, material, or finish: *His tie is blue with white spots.* **4** a place: *From this spot you can see the ocean.* **5** *Informal.* a small amount; a little bit: *a spot of lunch.* **6** *Informal.* a position or place with reference to employment, radio or television scheduling, etc. **7** *Informal.* a spotlight. **8** in botany, a plant disease; leaf spot. **9 hit the spot,** *Informal.* be just right; be satisfactory. **10 in spots, a** in one spot, part, place, point, etc. and another: *an argument weak in spots.* **b** at times; by snatches. **11 on the spot, a** at the very place. **b** at once. **c** *Slang.* in trouble or difficulty. **d** *Slang.* marked for death.
—*v.* **1** make spots on: *spot a dress.* **2** become spotted; have spots: *This silk will spot.* **3** stain, sully, or tarnish (character, reputation, etc.): *He spotted his reputation by lying repeatedly.* **4** place in a certain spot; scatter in various spots: *Lookouts were spotted all along the coast.* **5** *Informal.* pick out; find out; recognize: *The teacher spotted every mistake.*
—*adj.* **1** on hand; ready: *a spot answer.* **2** for immediate cash payment and delivery: *a spot sale.* [ME] —**Syn.** *n.* **1** blotch, blot, fleck.

spot announcement a brief advertisement or announcement made between radio or television programs or at some point during a program.

spot cash money paid just as soon as goods are delivered or work is done.

spot check **1** a brief, rough sampling. **2** a check-up made without warning.

spot fire jump fire.

spot·less (spot′lis) *adj.* without a spot. —**spot′less·ly,** *adv.* —**spot′less·ness,** *n.*

spot·light (spot′līt′) *n. v.* **-light·ed** or **-lit, light·ing.** —*n.* **1** a strong light thrown upon a particular place or person. **2** a lamp that gives such a light: *a spotlight in a theatre.* **3** anything that focusses attention on a person or thing; public notice. —*v.* **1** light with a spotlight or spotlights. **2** call attention to; highlight.

spot·ted (spot′id) *adj.* **1** stained with spots: *a spotted wall.* **2** marked with spots: *a spotted dog.* **3** sullied: *a spotted reputation.*

spotted fever any of various fevers characterized by spots on the skin, especially cerebrospinal fever or typhus fever.

spot·ter (spot′ər) *n.* **1** a person who makes or removes spots. **2** a device for making or removing spots. **3** a person who observes a wide area of enemy terrain in order to locate, and direct artillery fire against, any of various targets. **4** a civilian who watches for enemy aircraft over a city, town, etc. **5** a person employed to keep watch on employees, customers, etc. for evidence of dishonesty or other misconduct. **6** any person, aircraft, device, etc. that looks, watches, or observes for some specialized purpose or detail. **7** a machine that automatically sets up the pins in a bowling alley; pinspotter.

spot·ty (spot′ē) *adj.* **-ti·er, -ti·est. 1** having spots; spotted. **2** not of uniform quality: *His work was spotty.* —**spot′ti·ly,** *adv.* —**spot′ti·ness,** *n.*

spous·al (spouz′əl) *n.* Often, **spousals,** *pl.* the ceremony of marriage. —*adj.* of or having to do with marriage. [ME *spousaille* < MF *espousailles*]

spouse (spous or spouz) *n.* a husband or wife. [ME < OF < L *sponsus, sponsa,* pp. of *spondere* bind oneself]

spout (spout) *v.* **1** throw out (a liquid) in a stream or spray: *A whale spouts water when it breathes.* **2** flow out with force: *Water spouted from a break in the pipe.* **3** *Informal.* speak in loud tones with affected emotion: *The old-fashioned actor spouted his lines.* **4** *Slang.* pawn.
—*n.* **1** a stream or jet. **2** a pipe for carrying off water: *Rain runs down a spout from our roof to the ground.* **3** a tube or lip by which liquid is poured. A teakettle, a coffee pot, and a syrup jug have spouts. **4** a column of spray thrown into the air by a whale in breathing. **5** formerly, a lift or shaft used by pawnbrokers to take up pawned articles for storage. **6** *Slang.* a pawnshop. **7 up the spout,** *Slang.* **a** in pawn. **b** ruined; done for. [cf. MDu. *spouten*] —**spout′er,** *n.* —**spout′less,** *adj.* —**Syn.** *v.* **2** spurt, gush, jet, squirt. **3** declaim.

S.P.Q.R. the Senate and the People of Rome. (for L *Senatus Populusque Romanus*)

sprad·dle (sprad′əl) *v.* **-dled, -dling. 1** spread or stretch the legs apart; straddle. **2** sprawl. [probably a blend of *sprawl* and *straddle*]

sprain (sprān) *v.* injure (a joint or muscle) by a sudden twist or wrench: *sprain your ankle.* —*n.* an injury caused by a sudden twist or wrench. [origin uncertain]

sprang (sprang) *v.* pt. of **spring.**

sprat (sprat) *n.* **1** a small food fish related to the herring, found along the Atlantic coast of Europe. **2** any of various similar fishes. [OE *sprott*]

sprawl (sprol or sprôl) *v.* **1** toss or spread the limbs about, as an infant or animal lying on its back. **2** lie or sit with the limbs spread out ungracefully: *The people sprawled on the beach in their bathing suits.* **3** toss or spread (the limbs) about. **4** spread out in an irregular or awkward manner: *He wrote in a large handwriting that sprawled across the page.* **5** move awkwardly. —*n.* the act or position of sprawling. [OE *sprēawlian*]

spray[1] (sprā) *n.* **1** liquid going through the air in small drops: *We were wet with the sea spray.* **2** something like this: *A spray of bullets hit the tree behind which he was hiding.* **3** an instrument that sends a liquid out as spray. —*v.* **1** scatter spray on; sprinkle. **2** scatter spray. **3** direct numerous small missiles, etc. upon: *The soldiers sprayed the enemy with bullets.* [? < MDu. *sprayen*] —**spray′er,** *n.*

spray[2] (sprā) *n.* **1** a small branch or piece of some plant with its leaves, flowers, or fruit: *a spray of lilacs, a spray of ivy, a spray of berries.* **2** an arrangement of flowers on a framework: *Father sent a spray of roses to his friend's funeral.* **3** an ornament like this. [cf. Danish *sprag*]

spread (spred) *v.* **spread, spread·ing,** *n. adj.* —*v.* **1** cover or cause to cover a large or larger area; stretch out; unfold; open: *spread rugs on the floor, spread one's arms, a fan that spreads when shaken.* **2** cause to be protracted in time; break down the total of into parts distributed (over a period of time): *spread a shipment over two months.* **3** move further apart: *The rails of the track have spread. He spread the end of the rivet with a hammer.* **4** lie or cause to lie; extend: *Fields of corn spread out before us.* **5** make widely or generally prevalent; propagate: *spread a religion.* **6** scatter; distribute: *He spread the news. The sickness spread rapidly.* **7** cover with a thin layer: *She spread each slice with butter.* **8** put as a thin layer: *He spread jam on his bread.* **9** be put as a thin layer: *This paint spreads evenly.* **10** set (a table) for a meal. **11** put food on (a table). **12 spread oneself,** *Informal.* **a** try hard to make a good impression. **b** display one's abilities fully. **c** brag.
—*n.* **1** the act of spreading. **2** the width; extent; amount of or capacity for spreading: *the spread of a bird's wings, the spread of elastic.* **3** a stretch; expanse. **4 a** the difference between what something is bought for and what it is sold to another for. **b** the difference between any two prices, rates, etc. **5** a cloth covering for a bed or table. **6** *Informal.* the food put on the table; feast. **7** something spread. Butter and jam are spreads. **8** the area of land owned by a rancher. **9** a piece of advertising, a news story, etc. occupying a large number of adjoining columns: *The advertisement was a three-column spread.* **10** two facing pages of a newspaper, magazine, etc. viewed as a single unit in make-up.
—*adj.* stretched out; expanded; extended. [OE *sprǣdan*] —**spread′er,** *n.* —**Syn.** *v.* **1** unroll, unfurl, expand. **6** circulate, disseminate.

spread eagle a boastful person.

spread-ea·gle (spred′ē′gəl) *adj. v.* **-gled, -gling.** —*adj.* having the form of an eagle with wings spread out. —*v.* stretch out flat and sprawling; tie with arms and legs outstretched.

spree (sprē) *n.* **1** a lively frolic; gay time. **2** a period during which a person drinks alcoholic liquor to excess; bout of drinking. **3** a period of intense interest in an activity. [origin uncertain]

sprig (sprig) *n. v.* **sprigged, sprig·ging.** —*n.* **1** a shoot, twig, or small branch: *He wore a sprig of lilac in his buttonhole.* **2** an ornament or design shaped like a sprig. **3** a scion or offspring of some person, class, institution, etc. **4** a young man; stripling. —*v.* **1** decorate (pottery, fabrics, etc.) with designs representing sprigs. **2** strip a sprig or sprigs from (a plant, tree, etc.). **3** fasten with sprigs or brads. [ME *sprigge*]

hat, āge, cãre, fär; let, ēqual, tėrm; it, īce
hot, ōpen, ôrder; oil, out; cup, pu̇t, rüle, ūse
əbove, takən, pencəl, lemən, circəs
ch, child; ng, long; sh, ship
th, thin; ᴛʜ, then; zh, measure

spright·ly (sprīt′lē) *adj.* **-li·er, -li·est.** lively; gay. [< *spright,* var. of *sprite*] —**spright′li·ness,** *n.* —**Syn.** spirited, animated, vivacious.

spring (spring) *v.* **sprang** or **sprung, sprung, spring·ing,** *n. adj.* —*v.* **1** move or rise rapidly or suddenly; leap; jump: *The boy sprang to his feet.* **2** fly back or away as if by elastic force: *The door sprang to.* **3** cause to spring; cause to act by a spring: *spring a trap.* **4** be flexible, resilient, or elastic; be able to spring: *This branch springs enough to use as a snare.* **5** come from some source; arise; grow: *Plants sprang up from the seeds we planted.* **6** derive by birth or parentage; be descended; be the issue of: *spring from New England stock.* **7** begin to move, act, grow, etc. suddenly; burst forth: *Sparks sprang from the fire. Towns sprang up where oil was discovered.* **8** bring out, produce, or make suddenly: *spring a surprise on someone.* **9** crack, split, warp, bend, strain, or break. **10** force to open, slip into place, etc. by or as if by bending: *The burglar was able to spring the lock quite easily.* **11** rouse (partridges, etc.) from cover. **12** *Slang.* secure the release of (a person) from prison by bail or otherwise. **13 spring a leak,** crack and begin to let water through. **14 spring a mine,** cause the gunpowder or other explosive in a mine to explode.

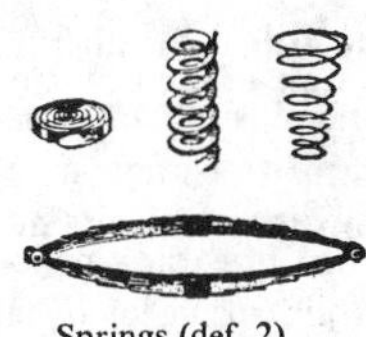
Springs (def. 2)

—*n.* **1** leap or jump: *a spring over the fence.* **2** an elastic device that returns to its original shape after being pulled or held out of shape. Beds have wire springs. The spring in a clock makes it go. **3** elastic quality: *The old man's knees have lost their spring.* **4** a flying back from a forced position. **5** the season after winter (in North America, March, April, May) when plants begin to grow. **6** a small stream of water coming from the earth. **7** a source; origin; cause. **8** the first and freshest period: *the spring of life.* **9** a crack, bend, strain, or break.
—*adj.* **1** having a spring or springs. **2** of, having to do with, characteristic of, or suitable for the season of spring. Spring wheat is wheat sown in spring. **3** from a spring. Spring water often contains healthful minerals. [OE *springan*] —**Syn.** *v.* **1** bound, vault. **2** rebound, recoil. **5** originate, issue, emanate, emerge. **7** shoot, rush, dart, fly. –*n.* **1** bound, vault. **3** resiliency, buoyancy.

spring·al (spring′əl) *n. Archaic.* springald.

spring·ald (spring′əld) *n. Archaic.* youth; young fellow. [< *spring* (n. def. 8)]

spring beauty 1 a small, pink or white wild flower of early spring. **2** the plant it grows on.

spring·board (spring′bôrd′) *n.* **1** a projecting board from which persons dive into water. **2** an elastic board used in vaulting, etc. **3** anything that serves as a way to get to something else: *Hard work is the only sure springboard to success.*

spring·bok (spring′bok′) *n.* **-boks** or (*esp. collectively*) **-bok.** a gazelle or small antelope of South Africa. [< Afrikaans *springbok* springing buck < Du. *springen* leap + *bok* antelope]

spring chicken 1 a young chicken used for frying or broiling. **2** *Slang.* a young woman: *She's no spring chicken.*

springe (sprinj) *n. v.* **springed, spring·ing** —*n.* a snare for catching small game. —*v.* catch in a snare. [OE *sprengan* cause to spring]

spring·er (spring′ər) *n.* **1** a person or thing that springs. **2** in architecture, a place where the vertical support of an arch ends and the curve begins. **3** a breed of large field spaniel, **English springer** or **Welsh springer,** used to spring or flush game. **4** a dog of this breed. **5** a springbok. **6** a grampus.

spring fever a listless, lazy feeling felt by some people, caused by the first sudden warm weather of spring.

spring·halt (spring′holt′ or -hôlt′) *n.* stringhalt.

spring lock a lock that fastens automatically by a spring.

spring salmon the largest kind of Pacific salmon, sometimes weighing over 100 pounds; chinook.

spring·tail (spring′tāl′) *n.* a small, wingless insect having a forked, tail-like appendage that it uses in leaping.

spring tide 1 the high tide at its highest level. It comes at the time of the new moon or the full moon. 2 any great flood, swell, or rush.

spring·tide (spring′tīd′) *n.* springtime.

spring·time (spring′tīm′) *n.* 1 the season of spring. 2 the first or earliest period: *the springtime of life.*

spring·y (spring′ē) *adj.* **spring·i·er, spring·i·est.** 1 yielding; flexible; elastic. 2 jaunty; gay; full of bounce: *a springy personality.* 3 having many springs of water. 4 spongy with moisture, as soil in the area of a subterranean spring or springs. **—spring′i·ly,** *adv.* **—spring′i·ness,** *n.*

sprin·kle (spring′kəl) *v.* **-kled, -kling,** *n.* **—***v.* 1 scatter in drops or tiny bits. 2 scatter (something) in drops or tiny bits: *He sprinkled ashes on the icy sidewalk.* 3 spray or cover with small drops: *sprinkle flowers with water.* 4 dot or vary with something scattered here and there. 5 rain a little. **—***n.* 1 the act of sprinkling. 2 a sprinkling; small quantity. 3 a light rain. [ME *sprenklen* or *sprinklen*; cf. Du. *sprenkelen*] **—sprin′kler,** *n.* **—Syn.** *v.* 1 strew, spatter, besprinkle.

sprin·kling (spring′kling) *n.* a small number or quantity scattered here and there.

sprint (sprint) *v.* run at full speed, especially for a short distance. **—***n.* a short race at full speed. [ME *sprente(n)*] **—sprint′er,** *n.*

sprit (sprit) *n.* a small pole that supports and stretches a sail. [OE *sprēot*]

sprite (sprīt) *n.* an elf; fairy; goblin. [ME < OF *esprit* spirit < L *spiritus.* Doublet of ESPRIT, SPIRIT.]

sprit·sail (sprit′sāl′; sprit′səl) *n.* a sail supported and stretched by a sprit.

sprock·et (sprok′it) *n.* 1 one of a set of projections on the rim of a wheel, arranged so as to fit into the links of a chain. The sprockets keep the chain from slipping. 2 a wheel made with sprockets. [origin uncertain]

A sprocket (def. 2)

sprout (sprout) *v.* 1 begin to grow; shoot forth: *Seeds sprout. Buds sprout in the spring.* 2 cause to grow: *The rain has sprouted the corn.* 3 develop rapidly. 4 *Informal.* remove sprouts from: *He sprouted the potatoes twice every winter.* **—***n.* 1 a shoot of a plant: *The gardener was setting out sprouts.* 2 a small boy. 3 **sprouts,** *pl.* Brussels sprouts. [OE *-sprūtan,* as in *āsprūtan*] **—Syn.** *v.* 1 germinate, bud.

spruce[1] (sprüs) *n.* 1 a coniferous evergreen tree having needle-shaped leaves. 2 its wood. [ME *Spruce,* var. of *Pruce* Prussia, perhaps because the trees first came from there]

spruce[2] (sprüs) *adj.* **spruc·er, spruc·est,** *v.* **spruced, spruc·ing.** **—***adj.* neat; trim: *John looked very spruce in his new suit.* **—***v.* make or become spruce: *John spruced himself up for dinner.* [? < *Spruce leather* a superior type of leather formerly imported from Prussia and popular in the 16th century. See SPRUCE[1].] **—spruce′ly,** *adv.* **—spruce′ness,** *n.* **—Syn.** *adj.* smart, dapper, jaunty.

spruce beer a fermented drink made with an extract of spruce twigs and sugar (or molasses) boiled together.

spruce budworm (bud′wėrm′) a moth larva that feeds on the buds of spruce and other conifers.

spruce grouse bush partridge.

sprung (sprung) *v.* a pt. and pp. of **spring.**

spry (sprī) *adj.* **spry·er, spry·est** or **spri·er, spri·est.** active; lively; nimble: *The spry old lady travelled everywhere.* [? < Scand.; cf. Swedish *sprugg* active]

spt. seaport.

spud (spud) *n. v.* **spud·ded, spud·ding.** **—***n.* 1 a tool with a narrow blade, for digging up or cutting the roots of weeds. 2 a tool resembling a chisel, for removing bark. 3 *Informal.* a potato. **—***v.* 1 dig up or remove with a spud. 2 Often, **spud in.** make a hole (for an oil well), as the first stage in drilling: *The new well was spudded in two weeks ago.* [cf. Danish *spyd* spear]

Spud Island *Cdn. Slang.* Prince Edward Island.

Spud Islander *Cdn. Slang.* a Prince Edward Islander.

spue (spū) *v.* **spued, spu·ing.** spew.

spume (spūm) *n. v.* **spumed, spum·ing.** foam; froth. [< L *spuma*]

spu·mo·ne (spə mō′nē; *Italian,* spü mō′nā) *n.* a type of Italian ice cream, usually containing fruit, nuts, etc. [< Ital.]

spum·y (spūm′ē) *adj.* **spum·i·er, spum·i·est.** covered with, consisting of, or resembling spume; foamy; frothy.

spun (spun) *v.* pt. and pp. of **spin.**

spun glass glass made into threads.

spunk (spungk) *n.* 1 *Informal.* courage; pluck; spirit; mettle. 2 a spark. 3 tinder or punk. 4 **get (one's) spunk up,** *Informal.* show courage, pluck, or spirit. [< Irish or Scots Gaelic *sponnc* < L *spongia* sponge < Gk.]

spunk·y (spungk′ē) *adj.* **spunk·i·er, spunk·i·est.** *Informal.* courageous; plucky; spirited. **—spunk′i·ly,** *adv.* **—spunk′i·ness,** *n.*

spun rayon a yarn made from rayon threads. When woven, spun rayon often resembles linen cloth.

spun silk silk waste spun into yarn.

spur (spėr) *n. v.* **spurred, spur·ring.** **—***n.* 1 a pricking device worn on a horseman's heel for urging a horse on. See **rowel** for picture. 2 anything that urges on: *Ambition was the spur that made him work.* 3 something like a spur; a point sticking out. A cock has spurs on his legs. 4 a ridge projecting from or subordinate to the main body of a mountain or mountain range. 5 any short branch: *a spur of a railway.* 6 **on the spur of the moment,** on a sudden impulse; without previous thought or preparation. 7 **win one's spurs,** make a reputation for oneself; attain distinction.
—*v.* 1 prick with spurs. 2 ride quickly. 3 strike or wound with a spur or spurs. 4 urge on: *Pride spurred the boy to fight.* 5 provide with a spur or spurs. 6 **spur on,** encourage. [OE *spura*]

spurge (spėrj) *n.* any of a group of plants most of which have acrid, milky juice; euphorbia. [ME < OF *espurge,* ult. < L *ex* out + *purgare* purge]

spur gear 1 a spur wheel. 2 gearing using such wheels.

spu·ri·ous (spūr′ē əs) *adj.* 1 not coming from the right source; not genuine; false; sham: *a spurious document.* 2 in botany, superficially resembling but differing in form and structure. 3 illegitimate. [< L *spurius*] **—spu′ri·ous·ly,** *adv.* **—spu′ri·ous·ness,** *n.*

spurn (spėrn) *v.* 1 refuse with scorn; scorn: *The judge spurned the bribe.* 2 oppose with scorn: *They spurned at restraint.* 3 strike with the foot; kick away. **—***n.* 1 disdainful rejection; contemptuous treatment. 2 a kick. [OE *spurnan*] **—Syn.** *v.* 1 reject, despise, contemn.

spurred (spėrd) *adj.* having spurs or a spur.

spurt (spėrt) *v.* 1 flow suddenly in a stream or jet; gush out; squirt: *Blood spurted from the wound.* 2 cause to gush out. 3 put forth great energy for a short time; show great activity for a short time: *The runners spurted near the end of the race.*
—*n.* 1 a sudden rushing forth; jet: *Spurts of flame broke out all over the building.* 2 a great increase of effort or activity for a short time. 3 a sudden outburst of feeling, etc. 4 a sudden rise in prices, improvement in prices, etc. 5 the period of this. Also, **spirt.** [var. of *sprit,* OE *spryttan*]

spur track a branch railway track connected with the main track at one end only.

spur wheel a wheel with projecting teeth on the rim

placed parallel to the axis; the simplest form of gearwheel or cogwheel. See **cogwheel** for picture.

sput·nik (sput′nik or spu̇t′nik) *n.* an earth satellite. The first sputnik, about 23 inches in diameter, was launched from the Soviet Union on Oct. 4, 1957. [< Russian *sputnik* companion, satellite]

sput·ter (sput′ər) *v.* **1** make spitting or popping noises: *fat sputtering in the frying pan. The firecrackers sputtered.* **2** throw out (drops of saliva, bits of food, etc.) in excitement or in talking too fast. **3** say (words or sounds) in haste and confusion. —*n.* **1** confused talk. **2** a sputtering; sputtering noise. [probably echoic; cf. Du. *sputtern*] —**sput′ter·er,** *n.*

spu·tum (spū′təm) *n.* **-ta** (-tə). **1** saliva; spit. **2** what is coughed up from the lungs and spat out. [< L]

spy (spī) *n.* **spies,** *v.* **spied, spy·ing.** —*n.* **1** a person who keeps secret watch on the actions of others. **2** a person who, especially in time of war, tries to get information about the enemy, usually by visiting the enemy's territory in disguise or under false pretences. [ME < OF *espie* < Gmc.]
—*v.* **1** find out or try to find out by careful observation; search. **2** keep secret watch. **3** catch sight of; see.
4 spy out, a watch or examine secretly or carefully. **b** find out by watching secretly or carefully. [ME < OF *espier* < Gmc.]

spy·glass (spī′glas′) *n.* a small telescope.

spy·mas·ter (spī′mas′tər) *n.* a person who directs the activities of, and acts as a clearing agent for, a spy ring.

spy ring an organized group of spies.

sq. 1 square. 2 the following. (for L *sequens*) 3 sequence.

sq.ft. square foot; square feet.

sq.in. square inch; square inches.

sq.mi. square mile; square miles.

sqq. the following ones. (for L *sequentia*)

squab (skwob) *n.* **1** a very young bird, especially a young pigeon. **2** a short, stout person. **3** a thick, soft cushion. **4** a sofa; couch. —*adj.* **1** newly hatched. **2** short and stout. [cf. dial. Swedish *sqvabb* loose or fat flesh, dial. Norwegian *skvabb* soft wet mass]

squab·ble (skwob′əl) *n. v.* **-bled, -bling.** —*n.* a petty, noisy quarrel: *Children's squabbles.* —*v.* take part in a petty, noisy quarrel. [? imitative] —**squab′bler,** *n.*

squad (skwod) *n.* **1** any small group of persons working together. **2** *U.S.* a number of soldiers grouped for drill, inspection, or work. A squad is the smallest tactical unit in the United States army. [< F < Ital. *squadra* square]

squad car a police patrol car.

squad·ron (skwod′rən) *n.* **1** in the navy, a part of a fleet used for special service. **2** a body of cavalry usually having from 120 to 200 men. **3** in the air force, a unit normally consisting of two or three flights. **4** a formation of armored cars or tanks, smaller than a regiment and made up of several troops. **5** any group. [< Ital. *squadrone* < *squadra* square]

squadron leader **1** the leader of a squadron of cavalry, tanks, or airplanes. **2** in the air force, a commissioned officer senior to a flight lieutenant and junior to a wing commander. *Abbrev.*: S.L. or S/L

squal·id (skwol′id) *adj.* filthy; degraded; wretched. [< L *squalidus* < *squalere* be filthy] —**squal′id·ly,** *adv.* —**squal′id·ness,** *n.*

squall[1] (skwol or skwôl) *n.* **1** a sudden, violent gust of wind, often with rain, snow, or sleet. **2** *Informal.* trouble. [cf. Swedish *skval-regn* sudden downpour of rain]

squall[2] (skwol or skwôl) *v.* cry out loudly; scream violently: *The baby squalled.* —*n.* a loud, harsh cry: *The parrot's squall was heard all over the house.* [< Scand.; cf. ON *skvala* cry out] —**squall′er,** *n.*

squall·y (skwol′ē or skwôl′ē) *adj.* **squall·i·er, squall·i·est.** **1** disturbed by sudden and violent gusts of wind: *squally weather.* **2** blowing in squalls. **3** *Informal.* threatening; troublous.

squal·or (skwol′ər) *n.* misery and dirt; filth. [< L]

squama (skwā′mə) *n.* **-mae** (-mē or -mī). in biology, a scale or scale-like part: *a squama of bone.* [< L]

squa·mate (skwā′māt) *adj.* having scales; covered with scales.

hat, āge, cãre, fär; let, ēqual, tėrm; it, īce
hot, ōpen, ôrder; oil, out; cup, pu̇t, rüle, ūse
əbove, takən, pencəl, lemən, circəs
ch, child; ng, long; sh, ship
th, thin; ŦH, then; zh, measure

squa·mose (skwā′mōs) *adj.* squamous.

squa·mous (skwā′məs) *adj.* furnished with, covered with, or formed of scales; characterized by the development of scales; scale-like. [< L *squamosus*]

squan·der (skwon′dər) *v.* spend foolishly; waste: *He squandered his money in gambling.* [origin uncertain] —**squan′der·er,** *n.*

square (skwãr) *n. adj.* **squar·er, squar·est,** *v.* **squared, squar·ing,** *adv.* —*n.* **1** a plane figure with four equal sides and four equal angles (☐). **2** anything of or near this shape. **3** a space in a city or town bounded by streets on four sides: *The large factory fills a whole square.* **4** the distance along one side of such a space; block. **5** an open space in a city or town bounded by streets on four sides, often planted with grass, trees, etc. **6** any similar open space, such as the meeting of streets. **7** the buildings surrounding such a place. **8** a parade ground. **9** an L-shaped or T-shaped instrument used for making or testing right angles. **10** in mathematics, the product obtained when a number is multiplied by itself. 16 is the square of 4. **11** *Slang.* a person who is not in tune with the latest fashions in popular entertainment, culture, etc. **12 on the square, a** at right angles. **b** *Informal.* justly; fairly; honestly. **13 out of square,** not at right angles; out of order; incorrect or incorrectly.
—*adj.* **1** having four equal sides and four right angles. **2** of a specified length on each side of a square: *a room ten feet square.* **3** having breadth more nearly equal to length or height than is usual: *a square jaw.* **4** forming a right angle: *a square corner.* **5** straight; level; even. **6** leaving no balance; even: *make accounts square.* **7** just; fair; honest: *a square deal.* **8** straightforward; direct: *a square refusal.* **9** *Informal.* satisfying: *a square meal.* **10** squared: *a square foot.* **11** multiplied by itself. **12** solid and strong. **13** *Slang.* not up to date; old-fashioned.
—*v.* **1** make square; make rectangular; make cubical. **2** mark out in squares. **3** bring to the form of a right angle. **4** make straight, level, or even. **5** adjust; settle: *Let us square our accounts.* **6** agree; conform: *His acts do not square with his promises.* **7** regulate. **8** in mathematics: **a** find the equivalent in square measure. **b** multiply by itself. **9** in sports, bring (the score of a game or contest) to equality; tie: *square the score with a touchdown in the third quarter.* **10** *Slang.* win over, conciliate, or secure the silence or consent of, especially by bribery; bribe.
11 square away, a of a ship, set the sails so that it will stay before the wind. **b** prepare; put in order; get ready. **12 square off,** *Informal.* put oneself in a position of defence or attack. **13 square oneself,** *Informal.* **a** make up for something one has said or done. **b** get even. **14 square the circle, a** find a square equal in area to a circle. **b** try to do something impossible. **15 square up, a** adjust; settle. **b** take up a fighting stance; get ready to fight.
—*adv.* **1** *Informal.* fairly or honestly. **2** so as to be square; in square or rectangular form; at right angles. [ME < OF *esquar(r)e*, ult. < L *ex* out + *quadrus* square] —**square′ly,** *adv.* —**Syn.** *adj.* **7** equitable.

square dance a dance performed by a set of couples arranged in some set form. The quadrille and Virginia reel are square dances.

square-dance (skwãr′dans′) *v.* **-danced, -danc·ing.** take part in a square dance. —**square′danc′er,** *n.*

square deal *Informal.* fair and honest treatment.

square flipper *Cdn.* the bearded seal.

square knot a knot whose free ends come out alongside of the other parts; reef knot. See **knot** for picture.

square meal a substantial or satisfying meal.

square measure a system for measuring area:
144 square inches = 1 square foot
9 square feet = 1 square yard
30¼ square yards = 1 square rod
160 square rods = 1 acre
640 acres = 1 square mile

square-rigged (skwãr′rigd′) *adj.* having the principal sails set at right angles across the masts.

square-rig·ger (skwãr′rig′ər) *n.* a square-rigged ship.

square root in mathematics, a number that produces a given number when multiplied by itself: *If the given number is 16, the square root is 4.*

square sail a four-sided sail.

square shooter *Informal.* a fair and honest person.

A ship with the sails on its foremast square-rigged

square·tail (skwãr′tāl′) *n. Cdn.* **1** the speckled trout or the rainbow trout. **2** a prairie chicken. **3** a sharp-tailed grouse.

square timber *Cdn.* formerly, squared logs such as those rafted to the Quebec timber coves for export.

square-toed (skwãr′tōd′) *adj.* **1** having a broad, square toe: *a square-toed boot.* **2** old-fashioned and homely in habits, ideas, etc.

squar·ish (skwãr′ish) *adj.* nearly square; having breadth more nearly equal to length or height than is usual.

squash[1] (skwosh) *v.* **1** press until soft or flat; crush: *The boy squashed the bug. Carry the cream puffs carefully, for they squash easily.* **2** make a squashing sound; move with a squashing sound: *We heard him squash through the mud and slush.* **3** put an end to; stop by force: *The police squashed the riot.* **4** *Informal.* silence with a crushing argument, reply, etc. **5** crowd; squeeze.
—*n.* **1** something squashed; a crushed mass. **2** a squashing; a squashing sound. **3** a game resembling handball and tennis, played in a walled court with rackets and a hollow rubber ball. **4** *Esp.Brit.* a drink containing crushed fruit: *lemon squash.* [< OF *esquasser*, ult. < L *ex* out + *quassare*, intensive of *quatere* shake] **—squash′er,** *n.*

squash[2] (skwosh) *n.* **squash** or **squash·es. 1** the fruit of any of various vinelike plants, often eaten as a vegetable or made into a pie. **2** the plant it grows on. [< Algonquian]

squash bug an ill-smelling, dark-colored insect of North America, injurious to the squash and to some other plants.

squash·y (skwosh′ē) *adj.* **squash·i·er, squash·i·est. 1** easily squashed: *squashy cream puffs.* **2** soft and wet: *squashy ground.* **3** having a crushed appearance. [< *squash*[1]] **—squash′i·ly,** *adv.* **—squash′i·ness,** *n.*

squat (skwot) *v.* **squat·ted** or **squat, squat·ting,** *adj. n.* —*v.* **1** crouch on the heels. **2** sit on the ground or floor with the legs drawn up closely beneath or in front of the body. **3** seat (oneself) with the legs drawn up. **4** settle on another's land without title or right. **5** settle on public land to acquire ownership of it under government regulation.
—*adj.* **1** crouching: *A squat figure sat in front of the fire.* **2** short and thick; low and broad: *The Indian was a squat, dark man. That is a squat teapot.*
—*n.* the act of squatting; squatting posture. [ME < OF *esquatir* crush, ult. < L *ex-* out + *coactus* forced, pp. of *cogere* < *co-* together + *agere* drive]

squat·ter (skwot′ər) *n.* **1** a person who settles on another's land without right. **2** a person who settles on public land to acquire ownership of it. **3** a person, animal, etc. that crouches or squats.

squat·ty (skwot′ē) *adj.* **-ti·er, -ti·est.** short and thick; low and broad.

squaw (skwo or skwô) *n.* **1** *Derogatory.* a North American Indian woman, especially a wife. **2** *Slang.* a woman or wife. [< Algonquian; cf. Cree *es-quayo* woman]

squaw·fish (skwo′fish′ or skwô′-) *n.* **-fish** or **-fishes.** any of various long, slender carp found in lakes and rivers of western North America.

squawk (skwok or skwôk) *v.* **1** make a loud, harsh sound: *Hens and ducks squawk when frightened.* **2** utter harshly and loudly. **3** *Slang.* complain loudly. —*n.* **1** a loud, harsh sound. **2** *Slang.* a loud complaint. [imitative] **—squawk′er,** *n.*

squawk box *Slang.* a loudspeaker of a public address system.

squaw man *Derogatory.* a white man married to or living with an Indian squaw, especially such a man who has abandoned white customs.

squaw winter in the North, an early spell of winter weather, often coming before an Indian summer.

squeak (skwēk) *v.* **1** make a short, sharp, shrill sound: *A mouse squeaks.* **2** cause to squeak. **3** utter with a squeak. **4** *Slang.* **a** turn informer; squeal. **b** confess. **5** *Informal.* get or pass (by or through) with difficulty. —*n.* **1** a short, sharp, shrill sound. **2 narrow squeak,** *Informal.* a narrow escape. [ME; probably echoic; cf. Swedish *sqväka* croak] **—squeak′er,** *n.*

squeak·y (skwēk′ē) *adj.* **squeak·i·er, squeak·i·est.** squeaking. **—squeak′i·ly,** *adv.* **—squeak′i·ness,** *n.*

squeal (skwēl) *v.* **1** make a long, sharp, shrill cry: *A pig squeals when it is hurt.* **2** utter sharply and shrilly. **3** *Slang.* turn informer. —*n.* **1** a long, sharp, shrill cry. **2** *Informal.* an act of informing against another. **3** *Informal.* an act of complaining loudly. [imitative] **—squeal′er,** *n.*

squeam·ish (skwēm′ish) *adj.* **1** too proper; modest, etc.; easily shocked. **2** too particular; too scrupulous. **3** slightly sick at one's stomach; sickish. **4** easily turned sick. [var. of earlier *squeamous* < AF *escoymous*] **—squeam′ish·ly,** *adv.* **—squeam′ish·ness,** *n.*

squee·gee (skwē′jē) *n. v.* **-geed, -gee·ing.** —*n.* **1** an implement edged with rubber or the like, for sweeping water from wet decks, scraping water off windows after washing, cleaning a sink, etc. **2** any of various similar devices. **3** in photography, a device with a roller for pressing water from prints, etc. —*v.* sweep, scrape, or press with a squeegee. [? < *squeege*, var. of *squeeze*]

squeeze (skwēz) *v.* **squeezed, squeez·ing,** *n.* —*v.* **1** press hard: *Don't squeeze the kitten; you will hurt it.* **2** hug: *She squeezed her child.* **3** force by pressing: *I can't squeeze another thing into my trunk.* **4** burden; oppress: *Heavy taxes squeezed the people.* **5** get by pressure, force, or effort: *The dictator squeezed money from the people.* **6** *Informal.* put pressure on or try to influence (a person or persons) to do something, especially pay money. **7** yield to pressure: *Sponges squeeze easily.* **8** force a way: *He squeezed through the crowd.* **9** press (the hand) in friendship or affection. **10** in bridge, compel (an opponent) to discard or unguard a valuable card.
—*n.* **1** a tight pressure: *a squeeze of the hand.* **2** a hug. **3** a crush; crowd. **4** a small quantity or amount squeezed out. **5** something made by pressing; cast; impression. **6** *Informal.* a situation from which escape is difficult. **7** *Informal.* pressure used to extort a favor, money, etc. **8** a squeeze play in baseball or bridge. **9** in business, finance, etc., pressure resulting from shortages. **10 tight squeeze,** *Informal.* a difficult situation. [ult. < OE *cwȳsan*] **—squeez′er,** *n.* **—Syn.** *v.* **2** clasp, embrace.

squeeze play 1 in baseball, a play executed when a runner on third base starts for home as soon as the pitcher begins to pitch. **2** in bridge, a play or series of plays in which the holder of a card that may win a trick is compelled to discard it or to unguard another possible winner. **3** *Informal.* an attempt to force somebody into a difficult situation or to make him act against his wishes.

squelch (skwelch) *v.* **1** cause to be silent; crush: *She squelched him with a look of contempt.* **2** strike or press on with crushing force. **3** walk in mud, water, wet shoes, etc., making a splashing sound. **4** make the sound of one doing so. —*n.* **1** a crushing retort. **2** a splashing sound made by walking in mud, water, wet shoes, etc. [earlier *quelch*, blend of *quell* and *crush*] **—squelch′er,** *n.*

squib (skwib) *n. v.* **squibbed, squib·bing.** —*n.* **1** a short, witty attack in speech or writing; sharp sarcasm. **2** a brief item in a newspaper used mainly to fill space. **3** a small firework that burns with a hissing noise and finally explodes. **4** a broken firecracker. —*v.* **1** say, write, or publish a squib or squibs. **2** assail or attack with squibs; lampoon. **3** let off or fire a squib. [origin uncertain]

squid (skwid) *n.* **squid** or **squids,** *v.* **squid·ded, squid·ding.** —*n.* a sea mollusc that is like a cuttlefish, but has a

hat, āge, cãre, fär; let, ēqual, tėrm; it, īce
hot, ōpen, ôrder; oil, out; cup, pu̇t, rüle, ūse
əbove, takən, pencəl, lemən, circəs
ch, child; ng, long; sh, ship
th, thin; ᴛʜ, then; zh, measure

longer body, a pair of tail fins, and one pair of tentacles much longer than the others. —*v.* fish with a squid as bait. [< *squit,* dial. var. of *squirt*]

squid·jig·ger (skwid′jig′ər) *n.* especially in Newfoundland: **1** a device for catching squid, made of several hooks so joined that their points form a compact circle which is pulled or jerked through the water. **2** a person who engages in squidjigging.

squid·jig·ging (skwid′jig′ing) *n.* especially in Newfoundland, the act or process of fishing for squid with a squidjigger.

squiffed (skwift) *adj. Slang.* squiffy.

squif·fy (skwif′ē) *adj. Slang.* drunk; intoxicated. [origin uncertain]

squig·gle (skwig′əl) *v.* **-gled, -gling.** —*n.* a twist, curve, or wriggle. —*v.* **1** make with crooked or twisted strokes; scrawl. **2** writhe; squirm; wriggle. [probably a blend of *squirm* and *wiggle*]

squill (skwil) *n.* a plant of the lily family. The onionlike bulb of the squill is used in medicine. [< L *squilla,* var. of *scilla* < Gk. *skilla*]

squint (skwint) *v.* **1** look with the eyes partly closed. **2** hold (the eyes) partly closed. **3** look sideways. **4** cause to squint. **5** incline; tend: *The general's remark squinted toward treason.* **6** be cross-eyed. **7** run or go obliquely.
—*n.* **1** a sidelong look; hasty look; look. **2** a tendency to look sideways. **3** an inclination; tendency. **4** a cross-eyed condition.
—*adj.* **1** looking sideways; looking askance. **2** cross-eyed. [< *asquint,* of uncertain origin] —**squint′er,** *n.*

squire (skwīr) *n. v.* **squired, squir·ing.** —*n.* **1** in England, a country gentleman; especially, the chief landowner in a district. **2** formerly, a young man of noble family who attended a knight till he himself was made a knight. **3** an attendant. **4** a woman's escort. —*v.* **1** formerly, attend as squire. **2** escort (a lady). [ult. var. of *esquire*] —**squire′like′,** *adj.*

squirm (skwėrm) *v.* **1** wriggle; writhe; twist: *The restless boy squirmed in his chair.* **2** show great embarrassment, annoyance, confusion, etc. —*n.* a wriggle; writhe; twist. [? imitative]

squirm·y (skwėr′mē) *adj.* **squirm·i·er, squirm·i·est.** squirming; wriggling.

squir·rel (skwėr′əl or skwir′əl) *n.* **1** a small, bushy-tailed rodent that lives in trees and eats nuts. **2** its fur, usually black, gray, dark-brown, or reddish. **3** a coat or other garment made of this fur. [ME < AF *esquirel* < L *sciurus* < Gk. *skiouros* < *skia* shadow + *oura* tail]

squir·rel·ly (skwėr′əl ē or skwir′əl ē) *adj. Slang.* **1** crazy. **2** mentally unbalanced, especially as a result of long isolation in the bush; bushed.

squirt (skwėrt) *v.* **1** force out (liquid) through a narrow opening: *squirt water through a tube.* **2** come out in a jet or stream: *Water squirted from a hose.* —*n.* **1** the act of squirting. **2** a jet of liquid, etc. **3** a small pump, syringe, or other device for squirting a liquid. **4** *Informal.* an insignificant, young, or small person who is impudent or self-assertive. [ME; probably echoic; cf. LG *swirtjen,* alteration of earlier *swirt* young or small < LG or Du. *swirtjen*] —**squirt′er,** *n.*

squish (skwish) *v.* **1** make a low splashing sound when walking in mud, water, etc. **2** *Informal.* squash; squeeze. —*n.* a squishing sound. [imitative alteration of *squash*]

sq.yd. square yard; square yards.

Sr strontium.

Sr. **1** Senior. **2** Sir. **3** Sister. **4** Señor.

S.R.O. standing room only.

SS in Nazi Germany, a select military unit of fanatical Nazis who served as a bodyguard to Hitler. (for G *Schutzstaffel*)

SS. Saints.

S.S. **1** steamship. **2** Sunday school. **3** Secretary of State. **4** separate school. **5** school section. **6** staff sergeant.

SSE, S.S.E., or **s.s.e.** south southeast, a direction halfway between south and southeast.

SSW, S.S.W., or **s.s.w.** south southwest, a direction halfway between south and southwest.

st. **1** street. **2** stet. **3** stone (weight). **4** stanza. **5** statue. **6** stitch. **7** strophe.

St. **1** Street. **2** Saint. **3** Strait.

sta. **1** station. **2** stationary.

stab (stab) *v.* **stabbed, stab·bing,** *n.* —*v.* **1** pierce or wound with a pointed weapon. **2** thrust with a pointed weapon; aim a blow. **3** penetrate suddenly and sharply; pierce. **4** wound sharply or deeply in the feelings: *The mother was stabbed to the heart by her son's lack of gratitude.* **5** **stab in the back,** attempt to injure in a sly, treacherous manner; slander.
—*n.* **1** a thrust or blow made with a pointed weapon; any thrust. **2** a wound made by stabbing. **3** an injury to the feelings. **4** *Informal.* an attempt. **5** **have** or **make a stab at,** try; attempt. [ult. related to *stub*] —**stab′ber,** *n.*
—**Syn.** *v.* **2** jab.

Sta·bat Ma·ter (stä′bät mä′tər or stā′bat mā′tər) **1** a celebrated 13th century Latin hymn about the Virgin Mary at the Cross. **2** a musical setting of this hymn. **3** any of certain other Latin hymns beginning with the same words. **4** a musical setting of any of these hymns. [< L *Stabat Mater* the Mother was standing, the first two words of the hymn]

sta·bile (stā′bīl or stā′bəl, stab′īl or stab′əl) *adj.* **1** in medicine: **a** not affected by average heat. **b** of or having to do with the method of electrotherapy in which one electrode is kept stationary over the part to be treated. **2** stable; fixed. —*n.* in art, a stationary, abstract sculpture made of cut or shaped metal, wood, etc.

sta·bil·i·ty (stə bil′ə tē) *n.* **-ties.** **1** the condition of being fixed in position; firmness. **2** permanence. **3** steadfastness of character, purpose, etc. **4** the tendency of an object to return to its original position. —**Syn.** **1** steadiness, equilibrium.

sta·bi·li·za·tion (stā′bə lə zā′shən or stā′bə lī zā′shən) *n.* a stabilizing; the state of being stabilized.

sta·bi·lize (stā′bə līz′) *v.* **-lized, -liz·ing.** **1** make stable or firm. **2** prevent changes in; hold steady: *stabilize prices.* **3** keep (a ship, aircraft, spacecraft, etc.) steady by special construction or automatic devices.

sta·bi·liz·er (stā′bə līz′ər) *n.* **1** a person or thing that makes something stable. **2** a device for keeping a ship, aircraft, spacecraft, etc. steady. See **airplane** for diagram.

sta·ble[1] (stā′bəl) *n. v.* **-bled, -bling.** —*n.* **1** a building fitted with stalls, rack and manger, etc. in which horses are kept. **2** a barn, shed, or other building in which any domestic animals, such as cattle, goats, etc. are kept. **3** a group of animals housed in such a building. **4** Often, **stables,** *pl.* the buildings and grounds where race horses are quartered and trained. **5** a group of race horses belonging to one owner. **6** the persons caring for such a group. **7** *Informal.* a group of athletes, artists, writers, etc. who work under the same management.
—*v.* **1** put or keep in a stable. **2** lodge in a stable.
[ME < OF < L *stabulum*]

sta·ble[2] (stā′bəl) *adj.* **1** not likely to move or change; steadfast; firm; steady. **2** lasting without change; permanent. **3** able to return to its original position. **4** of a chemical compound, not easily decomposed. [ME < AF < L *stabilis*] —**sta′bly,** *adv.* —**Syn.** **1** constant, unwavering.

sta·ble·boy (stā′bəl boi′) *n.* a boy who works in a stable.

stab·ling (stāb′ling) *n.* **1** the act or fact of accommodating horses in a stable. **2** a stable or stable buildings.

stab·lish (stab′lish) *v. Archaic.* establish.

stacc. staccato.

stac·ca·to (stə kä′tō) *adj.* **1** in music: **a** short; sharp: *staccato notes.* **b** with each tone ended sharply: *a staccato passage.* **2** disconnected; abrupt: *staccato speech.*
—*adv.* in a staccato manner. —*n.* **1** in music, a staccato passage or composition; a piece to be played or sung staccato. **2** a disconnected, abrupt quality or manner. *Abbrev.:* stacc. [< Ital. *staccato,* literally, detached]

stack (stak) *n.* **1** a large pile of hay, straw, etc. Haystacks, which are often round, are arranged so as to shed water. **2** a pile of anything: *a stack of wood.* **3** a number of rifles arranged to form a cone or pyramid. **4** *Informal.* a large quantity. **5** a number of chimneys, flues, or pipes standing together in one group. **6** a chimney or funnel. **7** *Brit.* a measure of cut wood or coal, equal to 108 cubic feet. **8** an arrangement of aircraft at different altitudes above an airport, awaiting landing instructions. **9 blow one's stack,** *Slang.* lose one's temper. **10** Usually, **stacks,** *pl.* **a** a rack with shelves for books. **b** the part of a library in which the main collection of books is shelved.
—*v.* **1** pile or arrange in a stack: *stack hay, stack firewood, stack rifles, etc.* **2** arrange (playing cards) unfairly. **3** arrange in such a way as to force or urge a predisposed result; load. **4 have the cards stacked against one,** be at a great disadvantage. **5 stack up, a** pile materials on to make (a fire). **b** pile up one's chips at poker. **c** *Informal.* measure up; compare (against). **d** arrange (aircraft) at different altitudes above an airport. [ME < ON *stakkr*] —**stack′er,** *n.*

stad·hold·er (stad′hōl′dər) *n.* **1** the chief magistrate of the former republic of the United Provinces of the Netherlands. **2** formerly, the viceroy or governor of a province in the Netherlands. [< Du. *stadhouder* < *stad* place, city + *houder* holder]

sta·di·a[1] (stā′dē ə) *n.* an instrument for measuring distances or heights by means of angles. A surveyor's transit is one kind of stadia. [? ult. < *stadium,* or its source]

sta·di·a[2] (stā′dē ə) *n.* a pl. of **stadium.**

sta·di·um (stā′dē əm) *n.* **-di·ums** or **-di·a. 1** an oval or U-shaped structure with rows of seats around a large, open space for athletic games. **2** in ancient Greece, a running track for foot races, with rows of seats along each side and at one end. The stadium at Athens was about 607 feet long. [< L < Gk. *stadion,* ancient Greek measure of length, equal at Athens to about 607 feet]

stadt·hold·er (stat′hōl′dər) *n.* stadholder.

staff (staf) *n.* **staves** or **staffs** *for 1 and 2,* **staffs** *for 3-6, v.* —*n.* **1** a stick; pole; rod: *The flag hangs on a staff.* **2** something that supports or sustains: *Bread is called the staff of life.* **3** a group assisting a chief; a group of employees. **4** in military use, a group of officers that assists a commanding officer in planning and supervisory operations. **5** a similar group assisting or attending a governor, president, or other executive. **6** in music, the five lines and four spaces between them on which the notes, rests, etc. are written.
—*v.* provide with officers or employees. [OE *stæf*]

A musical staff

staff officer a military officer who assists in planning and supervising operations.

staff sergeant 1 in the army and air force, a non-commissioned officer junior to a warrant officer. **2** in the Royal Canadian Mounted Police, a non-commissioned officer senior to a corporal and junior to a sergeant major. *Abbrev.*: S.S.

stag (stag) *n.* **1** a full-grown male deer. **2** the male of various other animals. **3** *Informal.* **a** a man who goes to a dance, party, etc. without a female partner. **b** a dinner party, etc. attended by men only. —*adj. Informal.* attended by, or for men only: *a stag dinner.* [OE *stagga*]

stag beetle any of certain beetles, the males of which have antlerlike mandibles.

stage (stāj) *n. v.* **staged, stag·ing.** —*n.* **1** one step or degree in a process; period of development. An insect passes through several stages before it is full-grown. **2** the raised platform in a theatre on which the actors perform. **3** the theatre; the drama; an actor's profession: *Shakespeare wrote for the stage.* **4** the scene of action: *Queenston Heights was the stage of a famous battle.* **5** a section of a rocket or missile having its own motor and fuel. **6** a stagecoach; bus. **7** a place of rest on a journey; a regular stopping place. **8** the distance between two places of rest on a journey; the distance between stops. **9** a platform; flooring. **10** a scaffold. **11** any platform raised high or built off the ground for the safe drying of fish, meat, etc. **12 by easy stages,** a little at a time; slowly; often stopping. **13 on the stage,** being an actor or actress.
—*v.* **1** put on a stage; arrange: *The play was excellently staged.* **2** be suited to the theatre: *That scene will not stage well.* **3** arrange to have an effect; plan and carry out: *The angry people staged a riot.* **4** travel by stagecoach. **5** carry out or do by stages: *staged disarmament.* **6** burn out and detach from a rocket or missile: *stage a motor or a fuel tank.* **7** place on a stage for drying. **8** especially in military use, establish a position or base as a stop in a planned movement or operation. [ME < OF *estage,* ult. < L *stare* stand] —**stage′like′,** *adj.*

stage·coach (stāj′kōch′) *n.* formerly, a horsedrawn coach carrying passengers and parcels over a regular route.

stage·craft (stāj′kraft′) *n.* skill in, or the art of writing, adapting, or presenting plays.

stage director in the theatre: **1** a stage manager, especially a chief, or executive, stage manager. **2** *Esp.U.S.* a director.

stage door in a theatre, an outside door leading to the dressing rooms, stage, etc., used by actors, stage hands, etc.

stage fright a nervous fear experienced when appearing before an audience.

stage·hand (stāj′hand′) *n.* a person whose work is moving scenery, arranging lights, etc. in a theatre.

stage manager in the theatre, the person responsible for the arrangement of the stage, including the placing and changing of scenery, props, etc. and for the proper running of each performance.

stag·er (stāj′ər) *n.* **1** a person of long experience. **2** a horse used for drawing a stagecoach.

stage-struck (stāj′struk′) *adj.* extremely interested in acting; wanting very much to become an actor or actress.

stage whisper 1 a loud whisper on a stage meant for the audience to hear. **2** a whisper meant to be heard by others than the person addressed.

stag·ger (stag′ər) *v.* **1** sway or reel (from weakness, a heavy load, or drunkenness). **2** cause to sway or reel: *The blow staggered him for the moment.* **3** become unsteady; waver. **4** hesitate. **5** cause to hesitate or become confused. **6** confuse or astonish greatly: *He was staggered by the news of his friend's death.* **7** make helpless. **8** arrange in a zigzag order or way. **9** arrange at intervals, often to prevent congestion or confusion: *The school was so crowded that classes had to be staggered. Vacations were staggered so that only one person was away at a time.*
—*n.* **1** a swaying; reeling. **2 staggers,** *pl.* of horses, cattle, etc., a nervous disease that makes them stagger or fall suddenly. [ult. < ON *stakra*] —**stag′ger·er,** *n.* —**stag′ger·ing·ly,** *adv.* —**Syn.** *v.* **1** See **reel**[2].
☛ **Staggers,** the disease (noun def. 2), is plural in form and singular in use: *Staggers is sometimes called "blind staggers."*

stag·hound (stag′hound′) *n.* **1** a breed of hounds resembling the foxhound but larger, formerly used for hunting deer, etc. **2** a dog of this breed.

stag·ing (stāj′ing) *n.* **1** a temporary platform or structure of posts and boards for support, as in building; scaffolding. **2** the act or process of putting a play on the stage. **3** a travelling by stages or by stagecoach. **4** the business of running stagecoaches.

stag·nan·cy (stag′nən sē) *n.* a stagnant condition.

stag·nant (stag′nənt) *adj.* **1** not running or flowing: *stagnant air, stagnant water.* **2** foul from standing still: *a stagnant pool of water.* **3** not active; sluggish; dull. [< L *stagnans, -antis,* ppr. of *stagnare.* See STAGNATE.] —**stag′nant·ly,** *adv.*

stag·nate (stag′nāt) *v.* **-nat·ed, -nat·ing. 1** be stagnant; become stagnant. **2** make stagnant. [< L *stagnare* < *stagnum* standing water]

stag·na·tion (stag nā′shən) *n.* a becoming or making stagnant; stagnant condition.

stag·y (stāj′ē) *adj.* **stag·i·er, stag·i·est. 1** of or having to do with the stage. **2** suggestive of the stage; theatrical. **3** artificial; pompous; affected. —**stag′i·ly,** *adv.* —**stag′i·ness,** *n.*

staid (stād) *adj.* having a settled, quiet character; sober;

sedate. —*v. Archaic.* a pt. and a pp. of **stay**[1]. [originally pp. of *stay*[1] in sense of "restrain"] **—staid′ly,** *adv.* **—staid′ness,** *n.* **—Syn.** *adj.* grave, serious, steady, composed.

stain (stān) *n.* **1** a discoloration; soil; spot. **2** a natural spot or patch of color different from the ground. **3** a cause of reproach, infamy, or disgrace; a moral blemish; stigma: *a stain on one's character or reputation.* **4** a liquid preparation of dye used to color woods, fabrics, etc. **5** a dye or pigment used to make visible transparent or very small structures, or to differentiate tissue elements by coloring, for microscopic study.
—*v.* **1** discolor; spot: *The tablecloth is stained where food has been spilled.* **2** take a stain; admit of staining. **3** bring reproach or disgrace on (a person's reputation, honor, etc.); blemish; soil. **4** corrupt morally; taint with guilt or vice; defile. **5** color: *stain a microscopic specimen.* [earlier *distain* < OF *desteindre* take out the color, ult. < L *dis-* off + *tingere* dye] **—stain′a·ble,** *adj.* **—stain′er,** *n.*

stained glass **1** glass colored by metallic oxides, used in church windows, etc. **2** a window or windows made of many pieces of stained glass, usually painted to represent figures, scenes, etc. and joined together by grooved leads.

stained-glass (stānd′glas′) *adj.* **1** of or having to do with stained glass: *stained-glass windows; a stained-glass designer.* **2** *Informal.* having or revealing a superficial or oversentimental attitude to religion; sanctimonious: *stained-glass piety.*

stain·less (stān′lis) *adj.* without stain; spotless. **—stain′less·ly,** *adv.* **—stain′less·ness,** *n.*

stainless steel steel containing chromium, nickel, or some other metal that prevents rusting or staining.

stair (stãr) *n.* **1** one of a series of steps for going from one level or floor to another. **2** a set of such steps. **3** a means of ascending in rank, power, moral excellence, etc.: *He passed one after another of his associates on the stair to success.* **4** **stairs,** *pl.* series of steps for going from one level or floor to another. **5 below stairs, a** a servant's quarters. **b** downstairs. [OE *stǣger*] **—stair′less,** *adj.*

stair·case (stãr′kās′) *n.* a flight of stairs with its framework; stairs.

stair·way (stãr′wā′) *n.* a way up and down by stairs; stairs.

stair·well (stãr′wel′) *n.* a vertical space or shaft containing a staircase.

stake (stāk) *n. v.* **staked, stak·ing.** —*n.* **1** a stick or post pointed at one end for driving into the ground. **2** the money risked; what is staked: *The men played for a high stake.* **3** Often, **stakes,** *pl.* the prize in a race or contest. **4** something to gain or lose; an interest; share in a property. **5** *Informal.* a grubstake. **6 at stake,** to be won or lost; risked. **7 pull up stakes,** *Informal.* move away. **8 the stake, a** a stake to which a person was tied and then burned to death. **b** death by being burned in this way.
—*v.* **1** fasten to a stake or with a stake. **2** mark with stakes; mark the boundaries of: *The miner staked his claim.* **3** risk (money or something valuable) on the result of a game or on any chance. **4** risk the loss of; hazard. **5** *Informal.* grubstake. **6** *Informal.* assist (a person) with money or other resources (to something): *I'll stake you to a dinner if you'll come.* [OE *staca*] **—stak′er,** *n.* **—Syn.** *v.* bet, wager.

stake driver a small heron whose cry is said to resemble the sound of a stake being driven into mud; bittern.

stake·hold·er (stāk′hōl′dər) *n.* the person who takes care of what is bet and pays it to the winner.

stak·ey (stāk′ē) *adj. Cdn. Slang.* with money available; having money to spend.

Sta·kha·no·vism (stə kä′nə viz′əm) *n.* in the Soviet Union, a system of rewarding individual enterprise (in factories, etc.) and thereby increasing output. It is a form of piecework. [< Aleksey G. *Stakhanov,* a coal miner whose record output in two shifts in 1935 was taken as a model for the system + *-ism*]

Sta·kha·no·vite (stə kä′nə vīt′) *n.* a worker who increases his output under Stakhanovism.

sta·lac·tite (stə lak′tīt or stal′ək tīt′) *n.* **1** a formation of lime, shaped like an icicle, hanging from the roof of a cave. Stalactites and stalagmites are formed by dripping water that contains lime. **2** any formation shaped like this. [< NL *stalactites* < Gk. *stalaktos* dripping < *stalassein* trickle]

hat, āge, cãre, fär; let, ēqual, tėrm; it, īce
hot, ōpen, ôrder; oil, out; cup, pu̇t, rüle, ūse
əbove, takən, pencəl, lemən, circəs
ch, child; ng, long; sh, ship
th, thin; ᴛʜ, then; zh, measure

Stalactites and stalagmites

sta·lag (stal′ag or stä′lag; *German,* shtä′läk′) *n.* a German camp for prisoners of war. [< G *Stalag* < *Sta(mm)lag(er)* base camp]

sta·lag·mite (stə lag′mīt or stal′əg mīt′) *n.* **1** a formation of lime, shaped like a cone, built up on the floor of a cave. **2** any similar formation. [< NL *stalagmites* < Gk. *stalagmos* a drop < *stalassein* trickle]

stale[1] (stāl) *adj.* **stal·er, stal·est,** *v.* **staled, stal·ing.** —*adj.* **1** not fresh: *stale bread.* **2** of a carbonated beverage, beer, etc., flat. **3** no longer new or interesting: *a stale joke.* **4** out of condition as a result of overtraining or excessive exertion over a period of time: *The horse has gone stale from too much running.* **5** temporarily lacking in vigor, nimbleness, etc., especially as a result of overactivity.
—*v.* **1** make stale. **2** become stale. [ME; origin uncertain; cf. MDu. *stel* stale] **—stale′ly,** *adv.* **—stale′ness,** *n.* **—Syn.** *adj.* **3** trite, hackneyed, banal.

stale[2] (stāl) *v.* **staled, stal·ing,** *n.* —*v.* of horses and cattle, urinate. —*n.* the urine of horses and cattle. [origin uncertain; cf. OF *estaler,* Du. and MHG *stallen*]

stale·mate (stāl′māt′) *n. v.* **-mat·ed, -mat·ing.** —*n.* **1** in chess, the position of the pieces when no move can be made without putting the king in check. **2** any position in which no action can be taken; a complete standstill.
—*v.* **1** put in a position in which no action can be taken; bring to a complete standstill. **2** in chess, subject to a stalemate. [ME *stale* stalemate (probably < AF *estale* standstill < Gmc.) + *mate* < *checkmate*]

Sta·lin·ism (stal′ə niz′əm or stä′lə niz′əm) *n.* the theory or system of Communism practised under Joseph Stalin (1879-1953), chief minister of the Soviet Union from 1924 to 1953, especially as characterized by coercion and severe oppression of opposition.

Sta·lin·ist (stal′ə nist or stä′lə nist) *n.* a follower or believer in Stalinism. —*adj.* of, having to do with, or characteristic of Stalinism.

stalk[1] (stok or stôk) *n.* **1** the stem or main axis of a plant. **2** any slender, supporting or connecting part of a plant. A flower or leaf blade may have a stalk. **3** any similar part of an animal. The eyes of a crayfish are on stalks. [ME *stalke;* ? dim. of OE *stæla* stalk]

stalk[2] (stok or stôk) *v.* **1** approach (wild animals) without being seen or heard by them: *The hunters stalked the lion.* **2** pursue (an animal or a person) without being seen or heard. **3** spread silently and steadily: *Disease stalked through the land.* **4** walk with slow, stiff, or haughty strides. —*n.* **1** a haughty gait. **2** a stalking. [OE *-stealcian,* as in *bestealcian* steal along] **—stalk′er,** *n.*

stalk·ing-horse (stok′ing hôrs′ or stôk′ing-) *n.* **1** a horse or figure of a horse, behind which a hunter conceals himself in stalking game. **2** anything used to hide plans or acts; a pretext.

stall[1] (stol or stôl) *n.* **1** a place in a stable for one animal. **2** a small place for selling things. At the public market different things are sold in different stalls under one big roof. **3** a seat in the choir of a church. **4** *Brit.* a seat in the front part of a theatre. **5** one of the sheaths for the fingers in a glove. **6** any of various other sheaths or receptacles.
—*v.* **1** live in a stall, stable, kennel, etc. **2** put or keep in a stall. **3** stop or bring to a standstill, usually against one's

wish: *He stalled the engine of his automobile.* **4** come to a stop because of too heavy a load or too little fuel. **5** stick fast in mud, snow, etc. **6** of an airplane, lose so much speed that it cannot be controlled. [OE *steall*] —**stall′-like′,** *adj.*

stall[2] (stol or stôl) *Slang.* —*n.* a pretext to prevent action, the accomplishment of a purpose, etc. —*v.* **1** pretend; evade; deceive. **2** put off; delay: *You have been stalling long enough.* [< AF *estal* decoy < Gmc.; cf. OHG *stal* place, stall. Akin to STALL[1].]

stal·lion (stal′yən) *n.* an uncastrated male horse, especially one kept for breeding purposes. [ME < OF *estalon* < Gmc.]

stall shower a small boothlike enclosure in which one may take a shower bath.

stal·wart (stol′wərt or stôl′wərt) *adj.* **1** strongly built. **2** strong and brave. **3** firm; steadfast. —*n.* **1** a stalwart person. **2** a loyal supporter. [OE *stǣlwierthe* serviceable < *stathol* position + *wierthe* worthy] —**stal′wart·ly,** *adv.* —**stal′wart·ness,** *n.* —**Syn.** *adj.* **1** sturdy, stout, muscular, powerful. **2** bold.

sta·men (stā′mən) *n.* in botany, the part of a flower that contains the pollen, consisting of a slender, threadlike stem or filament and an anther. [< L *stamen* warp, thread]

stam·i·na (stam′ə nə) *n.* strength; endurance. [< L *stamina* threads (of life, spun by the Fates)]

stam·i·nate (stam′ə nit or stam′ə nāt′) *adj.* in botany: **1** having stamens but no pistils. **2** having a stamen or stamens; producing stamens.

stam·mer (stam′ər) *v.* **1** repeat the same sound in an effort to speak; hesitate in speaking: *She stammers whenever she is nervous.* **2** utter thus: *stammer an excuse.* —*n.* a stammering; stuttering: *John has a nervous stammer.* [OE *stamerian*] —**stam′mer·er,** *n.* —**stam′mer·ing·ly,** *adv.*
Syn. *v.* **1 Stammer, stutter** = speak in a stumbling or jerky way or by repeating the same sound. Although they are often used interchangeably, **stammer** usually suggests a plainly seen painful effort to form and give voice to sounds and words, and speaking with breaks or silences in or between words, especially when extremely embarrassed or through fear or emotional disturbance. **Stutter** more often suggests a habit of repeating rapidly or jerkily the same sound, especially initial consonants such as (s), (p), etc.

stamp (stamp) *v.* **1** bring down (one's foot) with force: *stamp on a spider, stamp one's foot in anger.* **2** fix firmly or deeply: *His words were stamped on my mind.* **3** pound; crush; trample; tread: *stamp the snow from one's boots. She stamped out the fire.* **4** mark with an instrument that cuts, shapes, or impresses a design. **5** impress, mark, or cut out (a design, characters, words, etc.) on something, especially to indicate genuineness, quality, inspection, etc. **6** impress with an official stamp or mark: *stamp a deed.* **7** show to be of a certain quality or character; indicate: *His speech stamps him as an educated man.* **8** put a stamp or stamps on. **9 stamp out, a** put out by stamping. **b** put an end to by force.
—*n.* **1 a** a small piece of paper with a sticky back, put on letters, papers, parcels, etc. to show that a charge has been paid. **b** a similar piece of paper used for any of various purposes: *a trading stamp.* **2** the act of stamping. **3** a mark printed by a machine to show that postage has been, or will be, paid. **4** a heavy metal piece used to crush or pound rock, etc. **5** a mill or machine that crushes rock, etc. **6** an instrument that cuts, shapes, or impresses a design on (paper, wax, metal, etc.); a thing that puts a mark on. **7** the mark made with such an instrument. **8** an official mark certifying quality, genuineness, validity, etc. **9** an official mark or seal. **10** impression; marks: *Her face bore the stamp of suffering.* **11** kind; type: *Men of his stamp are rare.* [ME *stampe(n)*] —**stamp′er,** *n.*

stam·pede (stam pēd′) *n. v.* **-ped·ed, -ped·ing.** —*n.* **1** a sudden scattering or headlong flight of a frightened herd of cattle or horses. **2** any headlong flight of a large group: *a stampede of a panic-stricken crowd from a burning building.* **3** a general rush: *a stampede to newly discovered gold fields.* **4** *Cdn.* a rodeo, often accompanied by other amusements usually found at a fair: *the Calgary stampede.*
—*v.* **1** scatter or flee in a stampede. **2** make a general rush. **3** cause to stampede. [< Mexican Sp. *estampida* (in Sp. *estampida* uproar) < *estampar* stamp, ult. < Gmc.] —**stam·ped′er,** *n.*

stamping ground or **grounds** a favorite or much-frequented place: *He was happy to return to his old stamping ground.*

stamp pad a pad soaked with ink for use with a rubber or metal stamp.

stance (stans) *n.* **1** in golf and other games, the position of the feet of a player when making a stroke. **2** manner of standing; posture: *an erect stance.* **3** *Scottish.* **a** a standing place, station, or position. **b** a site. [< OF *estance,* ult. < L *stare* stand]

stanch[1] (stonch) *v.* staunch[1]. —**stanch′er,** *n.*

stanch[2] (stonch) *adj.* staunch[2]. —**stanch′ly,** *adv.* —**stanch′ness,** *n.*

stan·chion (stan′shən) *n.* an upright bar, post, or support (in a window, in a stall for cattle, on a ship, etc.) —*v.* **1** fasten (cattle) by stanchions. **2** strengthen or support with stanchions. [< OF *estanchon,* ult. < L *stare* stand]

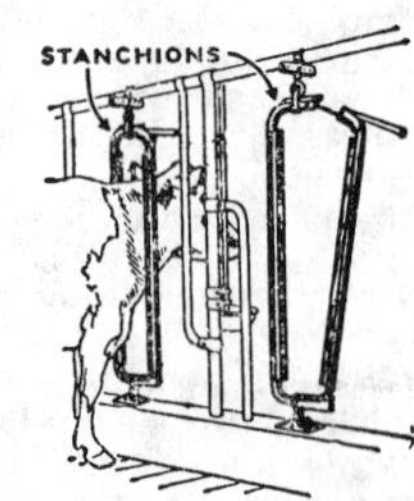

Stanchions for cattle. The closed one permits the cow to move her head but not to get away.

stand (stand) *v.* **stood, stand·ing,** *n.* —*v.* **1** be upright on one's feet: *Don't stand if you are tired, but sit down.* **2** have specified height when upright: *He stands six feet in his socks.* **3** rise to one's feet: *He stood when she entered the room.* **4** be set upright; be placed; be located: *The box stands over there.* **5** set upright or in an indicated position, condition, etc.: *Stand the box here.* **6** be in a certain place, rank, scale, etc.: *He stood first in his class for service to the school.* **7** take or keep a certain position: *"Stand back!" called the policeman to the crowd.* **8** take a way of thinking or acting: *stand for fair play, stand on one's rights.* **9** be in a special condition: *He stands innocent of any wrong. The poor man stands in need of food and clothing.* **10** be unchanged; hold good; remain the same: *The rule against lateness will stand.* **11** stay in place; last: *The old house has stood for a hundred years.* **12** gather and stay: *Tears stood in her eyes.* **13** bear; endure: *Those plants cannot stand cold; they die in winter.* **14** be submitted to (a trial, test, ordeal, etc.); undergo: *Stand a rigid examination.* **15** withstand: *cloth that will stand wear.* **16** *Informal.* bear the expense of: *stand treat.* **17** hold a specified course: *The ship stood out to sea.* **18** of a dog, point. **19** stop moving; halt; stop: *"Stand!" cried the sentry.* **20** become or remain still or motionless; not move or be operated: *The pumps were allowed to stand.* **21** of plants, grow erect: *corn standing in the fields.* **22** of an account, score, etc., show a (specified) position of the parties concerned: *The score stands in his favor.*
stand a chance, have a chance.
stand by, a be near. **b** side with; help; support. **c** keep; maintain. **d** be or get ready for use, action, etc.; wait in readiness.
stand down, step off or retire for a time from a place or post.
stand easy, stand completely at ease.
stand for, a represent; mean. **b** be on the side of; take the part of; uphold. **c** be a candidate for; run for; make oneself available for election. **d** *Informal.* put up with. **e** sail or steer toward.
stand in, *Informal.* **a** be associated or friendly; be on good terms. **b** serve as a substitute for somebody.
stand off, a *Informal.* keep off; keep away. **b** hold oneself aloof, especially from an offer or appeal, friendship, etc. **c** in nautical use, take a position or course away from.
stand on, a be based on; depend on. **b** demand; assert; claim.
stand out, a project. **b** be noticeable or prominent. **c** refuse to yield. **d** refuse to come in or join others. **e** endure to the end: *stand out the war.*
stand over, be left for later consideration, treatment, or settlement.
stand to, serve at one's post.

stand up, a get to one's feet; rise. b endure; last. c *Informal.* break a date with; fail to meet.
stand up for, take the part of; defend; support.
stand up to, meet or face boldly.
stand up with, *Informal.* act as best man, bridesmaid, etc. to.
—*n.* **1** the act of standing. **2** a halt; stop. **3** a stop for defence, resistance, etc.: *We made a last stand against the enemy.* **4** a halt on a theatrical tour to give a performance: *a one-night stand.* **5** a town where such a halt is made. **6** a place where a person stands; position. **7** a raised place where people can sit or stand. **8** a moral position with regard to other persons, a question, etc.: *take a new political stand.* **9** a station for a row of vehicles available for hire: *a stand for taxis.* **10** the place where a witness stands or sits to testify in court. **11** something to put things on or in: *Leave your wet umbrella in the stand in the hall.* **12** the place or fixtures for a small business: *a stand that sells newspapers.* **13** a standing growth or crop, as of wheat, cotton, etc. **14** group of growing trees or plants. [OE *standan*] —**Syn.** *v.* **13** See **bear.** -*n.* **1** pause, stay, rest. **4** post, station.

stand·ard (stan′dərd) *n.* **1** anything taken as a basis of comparison; model: *Your work is not up to standard.* **2** a rule, test, or requirement. **3** an authorized weight or measure. **4** a commodity serving as a basis of value in a monetary system: *the gold standard.* **5** the legally prescribed proportion of metal and alloy to be used in coins. **6** in commercial use, the lowest level or grade of excellence. **7** a flag, emblem, or symbol: *The dragon was the standard of China.* **8** an upright support: *The floor lamp has a long standard.* **9** a tree or shrub with one tall, straight stem.
—*adj.* **1** used as a standard; according to rule. **2** having recognized excellence or authority: *Scott and Dickens are standard authors.* **3** of pronunciation, grammatical usage, etc., characteristic of the speech of cultivated persons and of the language used in writing and in the conduct of public affairs, schools, courts, and churches; socially acceptable: *standard English.* **4** in printing, (of type) of the usual height, width, or weight. **5** of the lowest grade or quality. [ME < OF *estandart* < Gmc.]
Syn. *n.* **1 Standard, criterion** = something used to measure or judge a person or thing. **Standard** applies to a rule, principle, ideal, pattern, or measure generally accepted for use as a basis of comparison in determining the quality, value, quantity, social or moral or intellectual level, etc. of something: *That school has high standards of teaching.* **Criterion,** formal, means a standard used as a test in judging the true nature, goodness, or worth of a person, thing, or accomplishment: *Popularity is not everybody's criterion of a good motion picture.*

stand·ard·bear·er (stan′dərd bãr′ər) *n.* **1** an officer or soldier who carries a flag or standard. **2** a person who carries a banner in a procession. **3** a conspicuous leader of a movement, political party, etc.

stand·ard-bred (stan′dərd bred′) *adj.* **1** of horses, poultry, etc., bred to meet set standards of excellence for a breed, species, etc. **2** of a horse, bred for drawing light vehicles or for use in harness races. —*n.* a breed of horses noted as trotters and pacers and much used in harness racing.

stand·ard·i·za·tion (stan′dər də zā′shən or stan′dər dī zā′shən) *n.* **1** a standardizing. **2** a being standardized.

stand·ard·ize (stan′dər dīz′) *v.* **-ized, -iz·ing. 1** make standard in size, shape, weight, quality, strength, etc. **2** regulate by a standard. **3** test by a standard.

standard of living the way of living that a person or community considers necessary to provide enough material things for comfort, happiness, etc.

standard time the time officially adopted for a region or country.

stand-by (stand′bī′) *n.* **-bys. 1** a person or thing that can be relied upon; chief support; ready resource. **2** a ship kept in readiness for emergencies. **3** an order or signal for a boat to stand by. **4** any person or thing held in reserve. **5** a person waiting to board an aircraft, bus, etc. if space becomes available.

stand·ee (stan dē′) *n.* a person who has to stand in a theatre, bus, etc. for lack of seats.

stand-in (stand′in′) *n.* **1** *Informal.* a favorable position; good standing. **2** a person whose work is standing in for a motion-picture actor or actress while the lights, camera, etc. are being arranged. **3** anything that takes the place of another for some reason.

hat, āge, cãre, fär; let, ēqual, tėrm; it, īce
hot, ōpen, ôrder; oil, out; cup, pu̇t, rüle, ūse
əbove, takən, pencəl, lemən, circəs
ch, child; ng, long; sh, ship
th, thin; ᴛʜ, then; zh, measure

stand·ing (stan′ding) *n.* **1** position; reputation: *men of good standing.* **2** length of service, experience, residence, etc., especially as determining position, wages, etc. **3** duration: *a feud of long standing between two families.* **4** the act of standing; place of standing.
—*adj.* **1** straight up; erect. **2** done from an erect position: *a standing jump.* **3** established; ready; always operative; opposed to *temporary*: *a standing invitation, a standing army.* **4** that stands: *a standing lamp.* **5** not flowing; stagnant: *standing water.* —**Syn.** *adj.* **1** upright, perpendicular. **3** lasting, enduring.

standing room 1 space to stand in. **2** space to stand in after all the seats are taken.

stand-off (stand′of′) *n.* **1** a standing off or apart; reserve; aloofness. **2** tie or draw in a game. —*adj.* standing off or apart; reserved; aloof.

stand-off·ish (stand′of′ish) *adj.* reserved; aloof.

stand-out (stand′out′) *n.* a thing or person that is outstanding in appearance or performance.

stand·pat (stand′pat′) *adj. Informal.* standing firm for things as they are; opposing any change.

stand·pat·ter (stand′pat′ər) *n. Informal.* a person who stands firm for things as they are and opposes any change, especially in politics.

stand·pipe (stand′pīp′) *n.* a large vertical pipe or tower to hold water.

stand·point (stand′point′) *n.* a point of view; mental attitude.

stand·still (stand′stil′) *n.* a complete stop; halt; pause.

stand-up (stand′up′) *adj.* **1** having an erect or upright position: *a stand-up collar.* **2** done or taken in a standing position: *a stand-up dinner.* **3** made for or to allow a standing position: *a stand-up lunch counter.*

stan·hope (stan′hōp or stan′əp) *n.* a kind of light, open, one-seated, horse-drawn carriage with two or four wheels. [after Fitzroy *Stanhope* (1787-1864), a British clergyman]

stank (stangk) *v.* pt. of **stink.**

Stanley Cup 1 the cup presented annually to the winning team in a special end-of-season competition between National Hockey League clubs. **2** the competition, or playoffs, for this trophy. [< Sir Frederick Arthur *Stanley*, 16th Earl of Derby, 1841-1908, Governor General of Canada, 1888-93]

stan·nate (stan′āt) *n.* a salt of stannic acid.

stan·nic (stan′ik) *adj.* **1** of or having to do with tin. **2** containing tin with a valence of four. [< LL *stannum* tin]

stan·nous (stan′əs) *adj.* **1** of or having to do with tin. **2** containing tin with a valence of two.

stannous chloride a crystalline compound of tin dissolved with hydrochloric acid, used to silver mirrors and to galvanize tin, as a reducing agent for some chemicals, etc. *Formula*: $SnCl_2$

St. Anthony's fire (an′thə nēz or an′tə nēz) any of various inflammations of the skin, such as erysipelas.

stan·za (stan′zə) *n.* **1** a group of lines of poetry, commonly four or more, arranged according to a fixed plan. **2** in sports, any period of time in, or division of, a game, as an inning in baseball or a quarter in football. [< Ital. *stanza*, originally stopping place, ult. < L *stare* stand]

sta·pes (stā′pēz) *n.* in anatomy, the stirrup bone, the innermost of the three small bones in the middle ear. See **ear** for picture. [< Med.L *stapes* stirrup]

staph (staf) *n. Informal.* staphylococcus or staphylococci.

staph·y·lo·coc·cal (staf′ə lə kok′əl) *adj.* **1** of or having to do with staphylococcus. **2** caused by staphylococcus.

staph·y·lo·coc·cus (staf′ə lə kok′əs) *n.* **-coc·ci** (-kok′sī or -kok′sē). in bacteriology, any of a group of egg-shaped or spherical bacteria that occur individually, in pairs, or, frequently, in irregular clusters, some of them causing pus formation in boils, abscesses, etc. [< NL *Staphylococcus*, the genus name < Gk. *staphylē* bunch of grapes + *kokkos* grain]

sta·ple[1] (stā′pəl) *n. v.* **-pled, -pling.** —*n.* **1** a U-shaped piece of metal with pointed ends. Staples are driven into doors, wood, etc. to hold hooks, pins, or bolts. **2** a bent piece of wire used to hold together papers, parts of a book, etc. —*v.* fasten with a staple or staples. [OE *stapol* post]

A staple (def. 1)

sta·ple[2] (stā′pəl) *n. adj. v.* **-pled, -pling.** —*n.* **1** the most important or principal article grown or manufactured in a place: *Wheat is the staple in Saskatchewan.* **2** a chief element or material. **3** a raw material. **4** a fibre of cotton, wool, etc. **5** a short fibre that must be spun to form a yarn. **6** *Archaic.* the principal market of a place; the chief centre of trade.
—*adj.* **1** most important; principal: *The weather is a staple subject of conversation.* **2** established in commerce: *a staple trade.* **3** regularly produced in large quantities for the market.
—*v.* sort according to fibre: *staple wool.* [ME < OF *estaple* mart < Gmc.]

sta·pler[1] (stā′plər) *n.* a machine for driving wire staples into papers, cardboard, wood, etc. [< *staple*[1]]

sta·pler[2] (stā′plər) *n.* a person who sorts and grades fibres of wool, cotton, etc. [< *staple*[2]]

A stapler

stapp (stap) *n.* in aviation medicine, a unit of measure equal to the force exerted by one G acting on the body for one second. [< John P. *Stapp*, born 1911, a U.S. Air Force medical officer]

star (stär) *n. v.* **starred, star·ring,** *adj.* —*n.* **1** any of the heavenly bodies appearing as bright points in the sky at night. **2** in astronomy, any heavenly body except the moon, the planets, comets, and meteors. **3** in astrology, a planet or constellation of the zodiac, considered as influencing people and events. **4** a plane figure having five points, or sometimes six, like these: ☆ ✡ **5** anything having or suggesting this shape. **6** an asterisk (*). **7** in the United States, a representation of a star symbolizing one of the States of the Union. **8** a person of brilliant qualities: *an athletic star.* **9** a famous person in some art, profession, etc., especially one who plays the lead in a performance: *a motion-picture star.* **10** fate; fortune. **11 see stars,** *Informal.* see flashes of light as a result of a hard blow on the head. **12 thank one's (lucky) stars,** be thankful for one's good luck.
—*v.* **1** set with stars; ornament with stars. **2** mark with an asterisk. **3** single out for special notice or recommendation. **4** be prominent; be a leading performer; excel: *She has starred in many motion pictures.* **5** present as a star.
—*adj.* chief; best; leading; excellent. [OE *steorra*]

star·board (stär′bərd or -bôrd′) *n.* the right side of a ship or aircraft, facing forward. See **aft** for diagram.
—*adj.* on the right side of a ship or aircraft. —*v.* turn (the helm) to the right side from the standpoint of a person. [OE *stēorbord* the side from which a vessel was steered < *stēor* steering paddle + *bord* side (of a ship)]

starch (stärch) *n.* **1** a white, tasteless, odorless carbohydrate found in many vegetables, including potatoes, and cereal crops, such as wheat, rice, and corn. **2** a preparation of this substance used to stiffen clothes, curtains, etc. **3** a similar preparation produced artificially. **4 starches,** *pl.* foods containing much starch. **5** a stiff, formal manner; stiffness. **6** *Informal.* vigor; energy. **7 take the starch out of,** *Informal.* cause to lose courage, confidence, or determination.
—*v.* stiffen (clothes, curtains, etc.) with starch. [OE *stercan* make rigid (in *stercedferhth* stouthearted) < *stearc* stiff, strong]

Star Chamber or **star chamber 1** in England, an arbitrary, secret court that existed by statute and became notorious for its harsh methods of trial. It was established in 1487 and abolished in 1641. **2** any similar court, committee, or group.

starch·y (stär′chē) *adj.* **starch·i·er, starch·i·est. 1** like starch; containing starch. **2** stiffened with starch. **3** stiff in manner; formal. —**starch′i·ness,** *n.*

star-crossed (stär′krost′) *adj.* ill-fated; doomed to failure and unhappiness: *star-crossed lovers.*

star·dom (stär′dəm) *n.* **1** the condition or fact of being a star actor or performer. **2** star actors or performers as a group.

star dust 1 masses of stars that look so small as to suggest particles of dust. **2** particles of matter falling from space to the earth. **3** *Informal.* glamor; happy enchantment.

stare (stãr) *v.* **stared, star·ing,** *n.* —*v.* **1** look long and directly with the eyes wide open. A person stares in wonder, surprise, stupidity, curiosity, or from mere rudeness. **2** bring to a named condition by staring: *stare someone into confusion.* **3** gaze at. **4** be very striking or glaring. **5 stare down** or **stare out of countenance,** confuse or embarrass by staring. **6 stare one in the face, a** be very evident; force itself on the notice of. **b** very likely or certain to happen soon. **7 stare** (a person) **up and down,** gaze at or survey from head to foot.
—*n.* a long and direct look with the eyes wide open. [OE *starian*] —**star′er,** *n.* —**Syn.** *v.* **1** gape. See **gaze.**

star·fish (stär′fish′) *n.* **-fish** or **-fish·es.** a star-shaped sea animal.

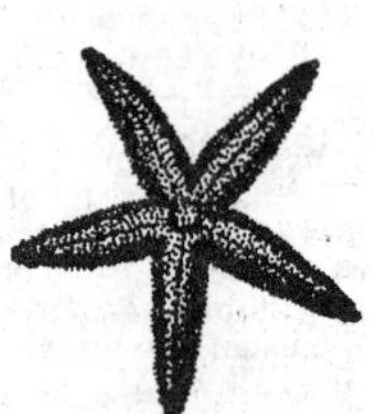
A starfish (about 5 in. across)

star·flow·er (stär′flou′ər) *n.* **1** any of various star-shaped flowers, including especially a group of white-flowered plants of the primrose family. **2** the star-of-Bethlehem.

star·gaze (stär′gāz′) *v.* **-gazed, -gaz·ing. 1** gaze at the stars. **2** be absent-minded; daydream.
—**star′gaz′er,** *n.*

star·ing (stãr′ing) *adj.* **1** very conspicuous; too bright; glaring. **2** gazing with a stare; wide-open.

stark (stärk) *adj.* **1** downright; complete: *That fool is talking stark nonsense.* **2** stiff: *The dog lay stark in death.* **3** harsh; stern. **4** *Archaic.* strong; sturdy.
—*adv.* **1** entirely; completely. **2** in a stark manner. [OE *stearc* stiff, strong] —**stark′ly,** *adv.*

star·less (stär′lis) *adj.* without stars; without starlight.

star·let (stär′lit) *n.* **1** a young actress or singer who is being trained for leading roles in motion pictures or television. **2** a little star.

star·light (stär′līt′) *n.* light from the stars. —*adj.* lighted by the stars.

star·like (stär′līk′) *adj.* **1** shaped like a star. **2** shining like a star.

star·ling (stär′ling) *n.* **1** a common European bird that nests on buildings. **2** a kind of North American blackbird. [OE *stærling*]

star·lit (stär′lit′) *adj.* lighted by the stars: *a starlit night.*

star-of-Beth·le·hem (stär′əv beth′lē əm or -beth′lə hem′) *n.* a plant of the lily family growing from a small bulb and having a tall cluster of white, star-shaped flowers.

Star of Bethlehem in Christian use, the star that heralded Christ's birth.

starred (stärd) *adj.* **1** decorated with stars. **2** marked with a star or stars. **3** presented as a star actor or performer. **4** influenced by the stars or by fate.

star·ry (stär′ē) *adj.* **-ri·er, -ri·est. 1** lighted by stars; containing many stars: *a starry sky.* **2** shining like stars: *starry eyes.* **3** like a star in shape. **4** of or having to do with stars. —**star′ri·ly,** *adv.* —**star′ri·ness,** *n.*

Stars and Stripes the flag of the United States.

star sapphire 1 a sapphire which reflects light in the shape of a brilliant star as a result of its crystalline structure. **2** a gem made from such a stone.

start (stärt) *v.* **1** get in motion; set out; begin a journey: *The train started on time.* **2** begin: *start a book.* **3** set moving, going, acting, etc.; cause to set out; cause to begin: *start an automobile, start a fire.* **4** give a sudden, involuntary jerk or twitch; move suddenly: *He started in surprise.* **5** come, rise, or spring out suddenly: *Tears started from her eyes.* **6** burst or stick out: *eyes seeming to start from their sockets.* **7** rouse: *start a rabbit.* **8** become loose. **9** cause to become loose: *start a run in a stocking.* **10 start in** or **out,** begin to do something. **11 start up, a** rise suddenly; spring up. **b** come suddenly into being or notice. **c** cause (an engine) to begin operating. **d** begin to do something.
—*n.* **1** the beginning of a movement, act, journey, race, etc. **2** a setting in motion; signal to start. **3** a sudden movement; jerk. **4** a surprise; fright. **5** a beginning ahead of others; advantage: *He got the start of his rivals.* **6** a chance of starting a career, etc.: *His father gave him a start.* **7** a spurt of activity: *work by fits and starts.* **8** the place, line, etc. where a race begins. [var. of OE *styrtan* leap up] —**Syn.** *v.* **1** embark, leave, go. **2, 3** commence, initiate. See **begin.**

start·er (stär′tər) *n.* **1** a person or thing that starts. **2** a person who gives the signal for starting. **3** a self-starter. **4** a special kind of food for baby chicks and animals. **5** the first in a series of things. **6** a chemical agent or bacterial culture used to start a reaction, especially in the formation of acid in making cheese, vinegar, etc.

starting point a place of starting; beginning.

star·tle (stär′təl) *v.* **-tled, -tling,** *n.* —*v.* **1** frighten suddenly; surprise. **2** move suddenly in fear or surprise. —*n.* a sudden shock of surprise or fright. [OE *steartlian* struggle] —**Syn.** *v.* **1** scare, alarm, shock, stun.

star·tling (stär′tling) *adj.* surprising; frightening. —**star′tling·ly,** *adv.*

star·va·tion (stär vā′shən) *n.* **1** a starving. **2** the condition of suffering from extreme hunger; being starved.

starve (stärv) *v.* **starved, starv·ing. 1** die because of hunger. **2** suffer severely because of hunger. **3** weaken or kill with hunger. **4** force or subdue by lack of food: *They starved the enemy into surrendering.* **5** *Informal.* feel hungry. **6** have a strong desire or craving. **7** weaken or destroy by lack of something needed. **8 starve down** or **out,** force or subdue from lack of food. **9 starve for,** suffer from lack of: *starve for news.* [OE *steorfan* die]

starve·ling (stärv′ling) *adj.* starving; hungry. —*n.* a person or animal that is suffering from lack of food.

stash (stash) *v. Slang.* hide or put away for safe-keeping or future use. [origin uncertain]

sta·sis (stā′sis or stas′is) *n.* **-ses** (-sēz). in medicine, a stoppage of the flow of a fluid in the body. [< NL *stasis* < Gk. *stasis* a standing < *sta-*, a root of *histanai* stand]

stat. 1 statute. **2** statuary. **3** statue.

stat·a·ble (stāt′ə bəl) *adj.* that can be stated.

state (stāt) *n. v.* **stat·ed, stat·ing,** *adj.* —*n.* **1** the condition of a person or thing: *He is in a state of poor health. Ice is water in a solid state.* **2** a person's position in life; rank: *humble state.* **3** a high style of living; dignity; pomp: *Kings live in great state.* **4** Also, **State. a** a nation. **b** one of several organized political groups of people that together form a nation: *The State of Alaska is one of the United States.* **5** the territory of a state. **6** Also, **State.** the civil government; the highest civil authority: *affairs of state.* **7 in** or **into a state,** *Informal.* **a** in or into a bad or disordered condition. **b** in or into an agitated or excited condition of mind or feeling. **8 lie in state,** lie in an open coffin to be seen by people before being buried.
—*v.* **1** tell in speech or writing; express; say: *state one's views.* **2** settle; fix.
—*adj.* **1** used on or reserved for very formal and special occasions; ceremonious; formal: *state robes.* **2** of or having to do with civil government or authority: *state control.* [< L *status* condition, position < *stare* stand; common in L phrase *status rei publicae* condition of the republic. Doublet of ESTATE.]
Syn. *n.* **1 State, condition** = the form or way in which something exists, especially as affected by circumstances. **State** is the general word, sometimes used in a very general way without reference to anything concrete, more often referring to the circumstances in which a person or thing exists or his (its) nature or form at a certain time: *The state of the world today should interest every serious person.* **Condition** applies to a particular state thought of

hat, āge, cãre, fär; let, ēqual, tėrm; it, īce
hot, ōpen, ôrder; oil, out; cup, pu̇t, rüle, ūse
əbove, takən, pencəl, lemən, circəs
ch, child; ng, long; sh, ship
th, thin; TH, then; zh, measure

especially as produced by circumstances or other causes: *The condition of the patient is critical.* **2** standing, status. —*v.* **1** declare.

state·craft (stāt′kraft′) *n.* **1** statesmanship. **2** crafty statesmanship.

stat·ed (stāt′id) *adj.* **1** said; told. **2** fixed; settled.

state·hood (stāt′hu̇d) *n.* the condition of being a state.

state·house (stāt′hous′) *n. U.S.* the building in which the legislature of a state meets; the capitol of a state.

state·less (stāt′lis) *adj.* **1** without nationality; without citizenship in any country. **2** without states or boundaries: *a stateless world.*

state·ly (stāt′lē) *adj.* **-li·er, -li·est.** dignified; imposing; grand; majestic. —**stat′li·ness,** *n.* —**Syn.** See **grand.**

state·ment (stāt′mənt) *n.* **1** the act of stating; the manner of stating something. **2** something stated; report. **3** a summary of an account, showing the amount owed or due. **4** a sentence that states something or makes an assertion; declarative sentence.

state·room (stāt′rüm′ or -ru̇m′) *n.* a private room on a ship or, formerly, on a railway train.

state's evidence *U.S.* **1** evidence brought forward by the government in a criminal case. **2** testimony given in court by a criminal against his associates in a crime. **3 turn state's evidence,** testify in court against one's associates in a crime. Compare **Queen's evidence.**

States-Gen·er·al (stāts′jen′ər əl or -jen′rəl) *n.* **1** in France, the legislative body before 1789, consisting of representatives of the three estates, the clergy, the nobility, and the middle class; Estates-General. **2** in the Netherlands, the lawmaking body made up of two houses.

states·man (stāts′mən) *n.* **-men** (-mən). a person skilled in the management of public or national affairs. —**Syn.** See **politician.**

states·man·like (stāts′mən līk′) *adj.* having the qualities of a statesman.

states·man·ly (stāts′mən lē) *adj.* like, worthy of, or befitting a statesman.

states·man·ship (stāts′mən ship′) *n.* the qualities of a statesman; skill in the management or ownership of public or national affairs.

state socialism a form of socialism in which government control, management, or ownership is used to improve social conditions.

states·wom·an (stāts′wu̇m′ən) *n.* **-wom·en.** a woman skilled in the management of public or national affairs.

stat·ic (stat′ik) *adj.* **1** at rest; standing still: *Civilization does not remain static, but changes constantly.* **2** having to do with bodies at rest or with forces that balance each other. **3** acting by weight without producing motion: *static pressure.* **4** in electricity, having to do with stationary charges that balance each other. Static electricity can be produced by rubbing a glass rod with a silk cloth. **5** of or having to do with atmospheric electricity that interferes with radio reception.
—*n.* **1** atmospheric electricity. **2** interference, especially with radio signals, due to such electricity. [< Gk. *statikos* causing to stand, ult. < *stēnai* stand]
—**stat′i·cal·ly,** *adv.*

stat·ics (stat′iks) *n.* the branch of mechanics that deals with objects at rest or forces that balance each other.

sta·tion (stā′shən) *n.* **1** a place to stand in; a place that a person, army unit, or naval fleet is appointed to occupy in the performance of some duty; an assigned post: *The policeman took his station at the corner.* **2** a building or place used for a definite purpose: *a police station, an R.C.A.F. station.* **3** the place or equipment for sending out or receiving programs, messages, etc. by radio or television. **4** a regular stopping place: *a railway station.* **5** a military camp or establishment. **6** social position; rank. **7** *Australian.* a ranch.
—*v.* **1** put in a position or place. **2** post or assign to a

military camp or establishment. [< L *statio, -onis* < *stare* stand] —**Syn.** *n.* **1** position, location.

station agent a person in charge of a railway station.

sta·tion·ar·y (stā′shən er′ē) *adj.* **1** having a fixed station or place; not movable: *A factory engine is stationary.* **2** standing still; not moving. **3** not changing in size, number, activity, etc.: *The population of this town has been stationary for ten years at about 5,000 people.* [< L *stationarius* < *statio.* See STATION.]

sta·tion·er (stā′shən ər) *n.* a person who sells paper, pens, pencils, ink, etc. [< Med.L *stationarius* shopkeeper, originally, stationary, as distinct from a roving peddler]

sta·tion·er·y (stā′shən er′ē) *n.* writing materials; paper, cards, and envelopes.

station house a building used as a station, especially a police station.

sta·tion·mas·ter (stā′shən mas′tər) *n.* the person in charge of a railway station.

Stations of the Cross in the Roman Catholic Church: **1** fourteen scenes from the Passion of Christ, usually painted or sculpted and ranged round the walls of a church. **2** the prayers, devotions, etc. performed in sequence at these stations.

station wagon a closed automobile that can serve both as a passenger car and as a light truck.

A station wagon

stat·ism (stāt′iz əm) *n.* **1** a highly centralized governmental control of the economy, information media, etc. of a state or nation. **2** advocacy of the sovereignty of a state, especially of a state of a republic.

stat·ist (stāt′ist) *n.* **1** a statistician. **2** one advocating statism.

sta·tis·tic (stə tis′tik) *adj.* statistical. —*n.* an item, element, etc. in a set of statistics.

sta·tis·ti·cal (stə tis′tə kəl) *adj.* of or having to do with statistics; consisting of or based on statistics.

sta·tis·ti·cal·ly (stə tis′tik lē) *adv.* in a statistical manner; according to statistics.

stat·is·ti·cian (stat′is tish′ən) *n.* an expert in statistics; a person who prepares statistics.

sta·tis·tics (stə tis′tiks) *n.* **1** numerical facts about people, the weather, business conditions, etc. Statistics are collected and classified systematically. **2** the science of collecting and classifying such facts in order to show their significance. [ult. < G < NL *statisticus* political, ult. < L *status* state. See STATE.]

☛ Statistics meaning facts (def. 1) is plural in form and plural in use: *Statistics are classified systematically.* When the meaning is the science of collecting and classifying numerical facts (def. 2), *statistics* is plural in form and singular in use: *Statistics is taught in some colleges.*

sta·tor (stā′tər) *n.* a stationary unit that encloses rotating parts of a turbine, electric generator or motor, etc. [< NL < L *stator* sustainer < *sistere* cause to stand < *stare* to stand]

stat·o·scope (stat′ə skōp′) *n.* **1** a form of aneroid barometer for registering very small variations of atmospheric pressure. **2** an instrument for detecting a small rise or fall of an aircraft. [< Gk. *statos* standing still + E *-scope*]

stat·u·ar·y (stach′ü er′ē) *n.* **-ar·ies,** *adj.* —*n.* **1** statues collectively. **2** the art of making statues. **3** a sculptor. —*adj.* of or for statues: *statuary marble.*

stat·ue (stach′ü) *n.* an image of a person or animal carved in stone or wood, cast in bronze, or modelled in clay or wax. [< F < L *statua,* ult. < *stare* stand]

stat·u·esque (stach′ü esk′) *adj.* like a statue in dignity, formal grace, or classic beauty.

stat·u·ette (stach′ü et′) *n.* a small statue. [< F *statuette,* dim. of *statue* statue]

stat·ure (stach′ər) *n.* **1** height: *A man six feet tall is above average stature.* **2** development; physical, mental, or moral growth. **3** reputation or fame: *He is a man of considerable stature in his line of business.* [ME < OF < L *statura* < *stare* stand]

sta·tus (stā′təs or stat′əs) *n.* **1** condition; state: *Diplomats are interested in the status of world affairs.* **2** one's social or professional standing; position; rank: *his status as a doctor.* **3** legal position. [< L *status* < *stare* stand]

status quo (kwō) **1** the way things are; the existing state of affairs. **2** status quo ante. [< L *status quo* the state in which]

status quo an·te (an′tē) *Latin.* the way in which (things were) previously.

status symbol a material possession, such as a car or boat, ownership of which is supposed to indicate a certain social rank or status.

stat·u·ta·ble (stach′ü tə bəl) *adj.* statutory. —**stat′u·ta·bly,** *adv.*

stat·ute (stach′üt) *n.* **1** a law enacted by a legislative body. **2** a law; decree; a formally established rule. **3** in International Law, an instrument annexed or subsidiary to an international agreement, especially a treaty. [< OF *estatut,* ult. < L *statuere* establish, ult. < *stare* stand] —**Syn. 1** See **law.**

statute book a collection or record of statutes.

statute law written law; law expressed or stated by statutes.

statute mile 5,280 feet.

Statute of Westminster an act of the British Parliament, passed in 1931, by which Canada and other dominions were granted the authority to make their own laws.

stat·u·to·ry (stach′ü tô′rē) *adj.* **1** having to do with a statute. **2** fixed by statute. **3** punishable by statute. —**stat′u·to′ri·ly,** *adv.*

staunch[1] (stonch or stônch) *v.* **1** stop a flow of blood, etc. **2** stop the flow of blood from a wound. **3** cease flowing. Also, **stanch.** [ME < OF *estanchier* < VL *extanicare* press together, literally, un-thin < L *ex-* un- + Celtic *tan-* thin] —**staunch′er,** *n.*

staunch[2] (stonch or stônch) *adj.* **1** firm; strong. **2** loyal; steadfast. **3** watertight: *a staunch boat.* Also, **stanch.** [ME < OF *estanche,* fem. < *estanchier.* See STAUNCH[1].] —**staunch·ly,** *adv.* —**staunch·ness,** *n.* —**Syn. 2** constant, true, faithful, steady, unswerving.

stave (stāv) *n. v.* **staved** or **stove, stav·ing.** —*n.* **1** one of the curved pieces of wood that form the sides of a barrel, tub, etc. **2** a stick or staff. **3** a rung of a ladder. **4** a verse or stanza of a poem, song, etc. **5** in music, the staff.
—*v.* **1** break a hole in (a barrel, boat, etc.). **2** become smashed or broken in. **3** furnish with staves. **4 stave off,** put off; keep back; delay or prevent: *The lost campers ate birds' eggs to stave off starvation.* [< *staves,* pl. of *staff*]

☛ **staved, stove.** The variant past tense and past participle form stove is used chiefly with reference to the breaking of boats and the like: *The waves stove* (or *staved*) *the boat in,* but *He staved off his creditors.*

staves (stāvz) *n.* **1** pl. of **staff. 2** pl. of **stave.**

stay[1] (stā) *v.* **stayed** or (*Obsolete*) **staid, stay·ing,** *n.* —*v.* **1** continue to be as indicated; remain: *stay clean. Stay here till I call you.* **2** live for a while; dwell: *She is staying with her aunt while her mother is ill.* **3** stop; halt: *We have no time to stay.* **4** pause; wait: *"Time and tide stay for no man."* **5** wait for; await. **6** put an end to for a while; satisfy (hunger, appetite, etc.). **7** put off; hold back; delay; restrain; check: *The chief stayed judgment till he could hear both sides.* **8** endure: *unable to stay to the end of a race.*
—*n.* **1** a staying; a stop; time spent: *a pleasant stay in the country.* **2** a check; restraint: *a stay on his activity.* **3** in law, a delay in carrying out the order of a court: *The judge granted the condemned man a stay for an appeal.* **4** *Informal.* staying power; endurance. [< OF *ester* stand < L *stare*] —**stay′er,** *n.*

Syn. *v.* **1 Stay, remain** = continue in some (stated) place, position, state, condition, relation, action, etc. **Stay** emphasizes the idea of keeping on in the present or specified place, state, condition, etc. without leaving or stopping: *He decided to stay in school another year.* **Remain,** often used interchangeably with *stay,* emphasizes keeping on in the same place or state, without changing in condition, quality, or form: *This room remains cool all summer.* 2 reside, lodge, sojourn, abide.

stay[2] (stā) *n. v.* **stayed, stay·ing.** —*n.* 1 a support; prop; brace. 2 **stays,** *pl.* corset. [probably < v.] —*v.* 1 support; prop; hold up. 2 strengthen mentally or spiritually; fix or rest in dependence or reliance. [probably ult. < OF *estayer* < Gmc.] —**stay′er,** *n.* —**Syn.** *v.* brace, sustain.

stay[3] (stā) *n. v.* **stayed, stay·ing.** —*n.* 1 a strong rope, often of wire, which supports a mast of a ship. See **shroud** for picture. 2 any rope or chain similarly used. 3 **in stays,** of a ship, in the act of changing from one tack to another. —*v.* 1 support or secure with stays. 2 of a ship, change to the other tack. [OE *stæg*]

stay-at-home (stā′ət hōm′) *n.* a person who prefers to stay home rather than go out or travel for fun and recreation. —*adj.* of or characteristic of someone who prefers to stay at home rather than go out, travel, etc.

stay·sail (stā′sāl′ or stā′səl) *n.* a sail fastened on a stay or rope.

S.T.B. Bachelor of Sacred Theology. (for L *Sacrae Theologiae Baccalaureus*)

stbd. starboard.

St. Bernard a Saint Bernard dog.

Ste. Sainte.

stead (sted) *n.* 1 a place: *The sales manager could not come, but sent his assistant in his stead.* 2 **stand in good stead,** be of advantage or service to. [OE *stede*]

stead·fast (sted′fast′ or sted′fəst) *adj.* 1 loyal; unwavering. 2 firmly fixed; not moving or changing. Also, **stedfast.** [OE *stedefæst* < *stede* place + *fæst* fast[1], firm] —**stead′fast·ly,** *adv.* —**stead′fast·ness,** *n.* —**Syn.** unwavering, unswerving.

stead·y (sted′ē) *adj.* **stead·i·er, stead·i·est,** *v.* **stead·ied, stead·y·ing,** *n.* **stead·ies.** —*adj.* 1 changing little; uniform; regular: *steady progress.* 2 firmly fixed; firm; not swaying or shaking: *hold a ladder steady.* 3 not easily excited; calm: *steady nerves.* 4 resolute; steadfast: *steady friendship.* 5 having good habits; reliable: *a steady young man.* 6 of a ship, keeping nearly upright in a heavy sea. 7 *Informal.* being one's regular girl friend or boy friend: *Mary was his steady girl.*
—*v.* 1 make steady; keep steady. 2 become steady. 3 make regular in character and conduct.
—*interj.* 1 be calm! don't get excited! 2 in nautical use, hold the helm as it is! keep on course!
—*adv.* **go steady,** 1 *Informal.* date the same person all the time. 2 go carefully.
—*n. Informal.* a regular girl or boy friend; a person who is being courted regularly by the same person. [< *stead*] —**stead′i·ly,** *adv.* —**stead′i·ness,** *n.*
Syn. *adj.* 1 **Steady, regular** = constant or uniform in acting, doing, moving, happening. **Steady** particularly suggests uninterrupted or unchanging movement, action, progress, or direction: *He has been unable to find steady work.* **Regular** emphasizes following a fixed, usual, or uniform procedure, practice, program, or pattern: *He is a regular subscriber to several magazines.* 4 unwavering, unfaltering. 5 trustworthy; dependable.

stead·y-state (sted′ē stāt′) *adj.* maintaining the same basic condition; unchanging in quality, structure, behavior, etc.: *a steady-state current.*

steady-state universe the theory that the universe has now the same basic form as always, matter being continuously created to replace that which is naturally destroyed.

steak (stāk) *n.* 1 beefsteak. 2 a slice of meat or fish for broiling or frying. [ME < ON *steik*]

steal (stēl) *v.* **stole, sto·len, steal·ing,** *n.* —*v.* 1 take (something) that does not belong to one; take dishonestly: *steal money.* 2 take, get, or do secretly: *steal a look at someone.* 3 take, get, or win by art, charm, or gradual means: *She steals all hearts.* 4 move secretly or quietly: *She stole out of the house.* 5 move slowly or gently: *The years steal by.* 6 in baseball, run to (a base) without being helped by a hit or error.
—*n.* 1 *Informal.* the act of stealing. 2 *Informal.* the thing stolen. 3 *Informal.* something obtained at a remarkably low cost or very little effort: *At that price the car is a steal.* 4 *Informal.* a dishonest or unethical transaction at a great profit. 5 in baseball, a safe advance from one base to another by stealing. [OE *stelan*] —**steal′er,** *n.*
Syn. *v.* 1 **Steal, pilfer, filch** = take dishonestly or wrongfully and secretly something belonging to someone else. **Steal** is the general and common word: *Thieves stole the silver.* **Pilfer,** more formal, means "steal and carry away in small amounts": *In many supermarkets hidden guards watch for people who pilfer food.* **Filch** particularly suggests stealthy or furtive pilfering, usually of objects of little value: *The boys filched some candy from the counter.* 4 sneak, skulk, slink.

hat, āge, cãre, fär; let, ēqual, tėrm; it, īce
hot, ōpen, ôrder; oil, out; cup, pu̇t, rüle, ūse
əbove, takən, pencəl, lemən, circəs
ch, child; ng, long; sh, ship
th, thin; ᴛʜ, then; zh, measure

stealth (stelth) *n.* a secret or sly action: *He obtained the letter by stealth, taking it while his sister's back was turned.* [< *steal*]

stealth·y (stel′thē) *adj.* **stealth·i·er, stealth·i·est.** done in a secret manner; secret; sly: *The cat crept in a stealthy way toward the bird.* —**stealth′i·ly,** *adv.* —**stealth′i·ness,** *n.* —**Syn.** furtive, sneaking, underhand, surreptitious.

steam (stēm) *n.* 1 water in the form of vapor or gas. Steam is used to heat houses, run engines, etc. 2 **a** the vapor of boiling water used, especially by confinement in special apparatus, to generate mechanical power and for heating and cooking. **b** the mechanical power thus generated. 3 *Informal.* power; energy; force. 4 **let off steam,** *Informal.* **a** get rid of excess energy. **b** relieve one's feeling. 5 **run out of steam,** *Informal.* lose power, energy, or effectiveness; collapse.
—*v.* 1 give off steam: *The cup of coffee was steaming.* 2 rise in steam. 3 move or cause to move by steam: *The ship steamed away.* 4 cook, soften, or freshen by steam. 5 *Informal.* run or go quickly, as if powered by steam; move with speed and vigor. [OE *stēam*] —**steam′like′,** *adj.*

steam bath a kind of bath taken in a steam-filled room or chamber: *A steam bath is usually followed by massage.*

steam·boat (stēm′bōt′) *n.* a boat propelled by a steam engine.

steam boiler a boiler in which water is heated to make steam.

steam box steam chest.

steam chest a chamber through which the steam of an engine passes from the boiler to the cylinder.

steam engine an engine operated by steam, typically one in which a sliding piston in a cylinder is moved by the expansive action of steam generated in a boiler.

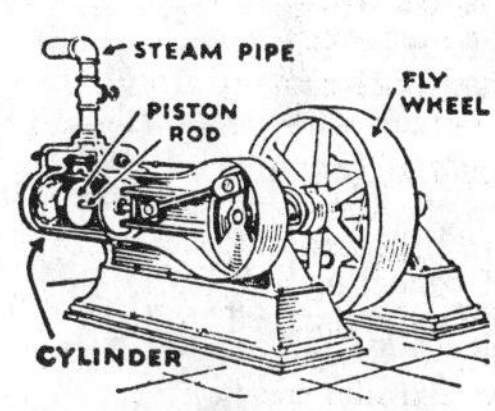

A steam engine: the pressure of the steam in the cylinder pushes the piston forward, causing the piston rod to turn a shaft. This turning shaft transfers the motion to wheels or other parts. The weight of the flywheel keeps the shaft turning evenly.

steam·er (stēm′ər) *n.* 1 a steamboat; steamship. 2 an engine run by steam. 3 a container in which something is steamed or kept warm.

steamer rug a blanket, especially one used to keep a person warm in a chair on the deck of a ship.

steam fitter a man who installs and repairs steam pipes, radiators, boilers, etc.

steam heat heat given off by steam in radiators and pipes.

steam roller 1 a heavy roller moved by steam, used to crush and level materials in making roads. 2 *Informal.* a means of crushing opposition.

steam-roll·er (stēm′rōl′ər) *v.* 1 *Informal.* **a** override by crushing power or force; crush: *steam-roller all opposition.* **b** force (into or through) by this means: *steam-roller a convention into acceptance of a candidate.* 2 make level, smooth, etc.

A steam roller

with a steam roller.

steam·ship (stēm′ship′) *n.* a ship propelled by a steam engine.

steam shovel a machine for digging, formerly always operated by steam, but now often by an internal-combustion engine.

steam·tight (stēm′tīt′) *adj.* so tight that no steam can get in or out: *a steamtight valve.*

steam turbine a turbine moved by steam.

steam·y (stēm′ē) *adj.* **steam·i·er, steam·i·est. 1** of steam; like steam. **2** full of steam; giving off steam; rising in steam. **—steam′i·ly,** *adv.* **—steam′i·ness,** *n.*

ste·ap·sin (stē ap′sən) *n.* in biochemistry, an enzyme in the pancreatic juice that converts fats into more easily digested fatty acids and glycerin. [blend of *stea(rin)* and *(pe)psin*]

ste·a·rate (stē′ə rāt′) *n.* a salt of stearic acid.

ste·ar·ic (stē ar′ik or stēr′ik) *adj.* having to do with stearin, suet, or fat. [< F *stéarique* < Gk. *stear* fat]

stearic acid a solid, white substance obtained from certain fats and used in making candles. *Formula:* $C_{18}H_{36}O_2$

ste·a·rin (stē′ə rin or stēr′in) *n.* **1** a colorless, odorless substance that is the chief constituent of many animal and vegetable fats. **2** a mixture of fatty acids used for making candles, solid alcohol, etc. [< F *stéarine* < Gk. *stear* fat]

ste·a·rine (stē′ə rin or stē′ə rēn′, stēr′in or stēr′ēn′) *n.* stearin.

ste·a·tite (stē′ə tīt′) *n.* a rock composed of impure talc; soapstone. [< L *steatitis* < Gk. *stear, -atos* fat]

ste·a·tit·ic (stē′ə tit′ik) *adj.* composed of soapstone; like soapstone.

ste·a·to·sis (stē ə tō′sis) *n.* **1** fatty degeneration. **2** any disease of the sebaceous glands. [< NL < Gk. *stear, -atos* fat + NL *-osis* -osis]

sted·fast (sted′fast′ or sted′fəst) *adj.* steadfast. **—sted′fast·ly,** *adv.*

steed (stēd) *n.* **1** a horse, especially a riding horse. **2** a high-spirited horse. [OE *stēda*]

steel (stēl) *n.* **1** an alloy of iron and carbon that is very hard, strong, and tough. Other metals, such as nickel or manganese, may be added to the basic alloy for specific purposes. **2** something made from steel: **a** a sword. **b** a piece of steel for making sparks. **c** a rod of steel for sharpening knives. **d** a narrow strip of steel in a corset. **3** steel-like hardness or strength: *The brave soldier had nerves of steel.* **4** *Cdn.* **a** railway track: *Steel has been laid for 100 miles north.* **b** the railway line: *They arranged to meet at steel.*
—adj. **1** made of steel. **2** resembling steel in hardness, color, etc.
—v. **1** point, edge, or cover with steel. **2** make hard or strong like steel: *He tried to steel his heart against the sufferings of the poor.* [OE *stēle*] **—steel′less,** *adj.* **—steel′-like′,** *adj.*

steel blue a lustrous dark blue, like the color of tempered steel. **—steel′-blue′,** *adj.*

steel·head (stēl′hed′) *n.* **-head** or **-heads.** a type of silvery rainbow trout common along the Pacific coast. Most steelhead spend part of their lives in the sea, returning to fresh water to spawn.

steel mill a place where steel is made.

steel wool small, fine steel shavings, used in cleaning or polishing.

steel·work·er (stēl′wėr′kər) *n.* a person who works in a place where steel is made.

steel·works (stēl′wėrks′) *n.pl. or sing.* a place where steel is made.

steel·y (stēl′ē) *adj.* **steel·i·er, steel·i·est. 1** made of steel. **2** like steel in color, strength, or hardness. **—steel′i·ness,** *n.*

steel·yard (stēl′yärd or stil′yərd) *n.* a scale for weighing. A steelyard has unequal arms, the longer one having a movable weight and the shorter a hook for holding the object to be weighed. [< *steel* + *yard*[2], in the sense of "rod"]

A steelyard. The weight is moved until the arms are horizontal; the number at which it rests is the weight of the object on the hook.

steen·bok (stēn′bok′ or stān′bok′) *n.* any of various small African antelopes frequenting rocky places. Also, **steinbock, steinbok.** [< Afrikaans *stenbok* < *steen* stone + *bok* buck]

steep[1] (stēp) *adj.* **1** having a sharp slope; almost straight up and down: *The hill is steep.* **2** *Informal.* unreasonable: *a steep price.* **3** of a story, etc., exaggerated; incredible. *—n.* a steep slope. [OE *stēap*] **—steep′ly,** *adv.* **—steep′ness,** *n.*

Syn. *adj.* **1 Steep, abrupt, precipitous** = having a slope almost straight up and down. **Steep** = having a very sharp slope that is hard to go up: *I do not like to drive up a steep hill.* **Abrupt** = very steep and sudden, with no slope toward the sharp angle from which the surface goes up or down: *From the rim they made their way down the abrupt sides of the canyon.* **Precipitous** suggests something as abrupt and straight up and down as a precipice: *The climbers will attempt to scale the precipitous eastern slope of the peak.*

steep[2] (stēp) *v.* **1** soak (something), especially so as to soften, cleanse, or extract an essence. **2** undergo such soaking: *Let the tea steep for five minutes.* **3** make thoroughly or frequently wet (*with*); saturate (*in*): *His sword was steeped in blood.* **4** immerse, imbue: *ruins steeped in gloom.* **5 steeped in,** filled with; permeated by. *—n.* **1** a soaking. **2** the liquid in which something is soaked. [probably < OE *stēap* bowl] **—steep′er,** *n.*

stee·ple (stē′pəl) *n.* **1** a high tower on a church, etc., usually with a spire. See **spire** for picture. **2** such a tower, together with the spire or other structure surmounting it. [OE *stēpel* < *stēap* steep] **—stee′ple-like′,** *adj.*

stee·ple·bush (stē′pəl bůsh′) *n.* hardhack, a shrub that has flowers in steeple-shaped clusters.

stee·ple·chase (stē′pəl chās′) *n. v.* **-chased, -chas·ing.** *—n.* **1** a horse race over a course having ditches, hedges, and other obstacles. **2** a cross-country foot race. *—v.* ride or run in a steeplechase. **—stee′ple·chas′er,** *n.*

stee·ple·jack (stē′pəl jak′) *n.* a man who climbs steeples, tall chimneys, etc. to paint, make repairs, etc.

steer[1] (stēr) *v.* **1** guide the course of: *steer a ship, steer a sled, steer an automobile, steer an airplane.* **2** guide; lead; conduct; pilot: *steer a person through a crowd.* **3** set and follow (a certain course). **4** be guided: *This car steers easily.* **5** guide a ship: *The pilot steered for the harbor.* **6** direct one's way or course. **7 steer clear of,** keep away from; avoid.
—n. Slang. an idea or a suggested course of action. [OE *stēoran*] **—steer′er,** *n.*

steer[2] (stēr) *n.* a castrated male of beef cattle, usually two to four years old; a young ox.

steer·age (stēr′ij) *n.* **1** the part of a passenger ship occupied by passengers travelling at the cheapest rate. **2** the act of steering. **3** the manner in which a ship is affected by the helm.

steer·age·way (stēr′ij wā′) *n.* the amount of forward motion a ship must have before it can be steered.

steering gear the apparatus for steering an automobile, ship, etc.

steering wheel the wheel that is turned to steer an automobile, ship, etc.

steers·man (stērz′mən) *n.* **-men** (-mən). a person who steers a ship.

steg·o·my·ia (steg′ə mī′ə) *n.* a mosquito that transmits yellow fever. [< NL < Gk. *stegos* roof + *myia* fly]

steg·o·sau·rus (steg′ə sô′rəs) *n.* **-ri** (-rī or -rē). an extinct reptile of great size (sometimes nearly 40 feet long) with heavy, bony armor. [< NL < Gk. *stegos* roof + *sauros* lizard]

stein (stīn) *n.* a beer mug. [< G *Stein* stone]

stein·bock or **stein·bok** (stīn′bok′) *n.* **1** ibex. **2** steenbok.

ste·le (stē′lē) *n.* **-lae** (-lē or -lī) or **-les. 1** an upright slab or pillar of stone bearing an inscription, sculptural design, etc. **2** a prepared surface on the face of a building, a rock, etc. bearing an inscription or the like. [< Gk.]

stel·lar (stel′ər) *adj.* **1** of or having to do with the stars; of a star; like a star. **2** chief: *a stellar role.* **3** of or having to do with a star performer. [< L *stellaris* < *stella* star]

stel·late (stel′āt or stel′it) *adj.* spreading out like the points of a star; star-shaped. [< L *stellatus* < *stella* star]

Steller's jay (stel′ərz) a large, crested jay having blue wings, tail, and belly, found in western North America. [< Georg Wilhelm *Steller*, 1709-1745, a German naturalist]

Steller's sea cow a toothless sea mammal weighing up to four tons, formerly found near the Bering Islands but extinct since the late 18th century. [see STELLER'S JAY]

Steller's sea eagle a gray sea eagle having white tail and shoulders, found near the northern Pacific coast of Asia. [see STELLER'S JAY]

Steller's sea lion a large sea lion found off the Pacific coast of North America; northern sea lion. [see STELLER'S JAY]

Stel·lite (stel′īt) *n. Trademark.* an extremely hard, rust-resisting alloy of cobalt, chromium, and tungsten, widely used in the making of cutting tools.

St. El·mo's fire (el′mōz) a fiery light due to a discharge of atmospheric electricity, often seen on masts, towers, etc.

St. Elmo's light St. Elmo's fire.

stem[1] (stem) *n. v.* **stemmed, stem·ming.** —*n.* **1** the main part of a plant above the ground. The stem supports the branches, etc. **2** the part of a flower, a fruit, or a leaf that joins it to the plant or tree. **3** anything like or suggesting the stem of a plant: *the stem of a goblet, the stem of a pipe, etc.* **4** the line of descent of a family. **5** in grammar, the part of a word to which endings are added and inside which changes are made. *Run* is the stem of *running, runner, ran,* etc. **6** the bow or front end of a boat. **7 from stem to stern,** from one end of the ship to the other.
—*v.* **1** remove the stem from (a leaf, fruit, etc.). **2** grow out; develop: *Newspapers stemmed from the invention of the printing press.* **3** originate or spring from. [OE *stemn*] —**stem′like′**, *adj.*

stem[2] (stem) *v.* **stemmed, stem·ming. 1** stop; check; dam up. **2** make progress against: *stem the swift current.* [< ON *stemma*]

stem·less (stem′lis) *adj.* having no stem; having no visible stem.

stemmed (stemd) *adj.* **1** having a stem. **2** having the stem removed.

stem·mer (stem′ər) *n.* a person or thing that removes stems from leaves, fruit, etc.

stem·ware (stem′wãr′) *n.* goblets or drinking glasses having stems, used for wine, liqueurs, etc.

stem·wind·ing (stem′wīn′ding) *adj.* of a watch, winding by turning a knob on the stem.

stench (stench) *n.* a very bad smell; stink. [OE *stenc*; related to *stincan* smell]

sten·cil (sten′səl) *n. v.* **-cilled** or **-ciled, -cil·ling** or **-cil·ing.** —*n.* **1** a thin sheet of metal, paper, etc. having letters or designs cut through it. When it is laid on a surface and ink or color is spread on, these letters or designs are made on the surface. **2** the letters or designs so made. —*v.* mark or paint with a stencil: *The curtains have a stencilled border.* [ult. < OF *estanceler* ornament with colors, ult. < L *scintilla* spark]

sten·o (sten′ō) *n.* **-os.** *Informal.* stenographer.

sten·o·graph (sten′ə graf′) *n.* **1** a writing in shorthand. **2** any of various keyboard instruments, resembling a typewriter, used for writing in shorthand. —*v.* write in shorthand.

ste·nog·ra·pher (stə nog′rə fər) *n.* a person whose work is stenography and typewriting.

sten·o·graph·ic (sten′ə graf′ik) *adj.* **1** of or having to do with stenography; written or produced by stenography. **2** of style, concise.

hat, āge, cãre, fär; let, ēqual, tėrm; it, īce
hot, ōpen, ôrder; oil, out; cup, pu̇t, rüle, ūse
əbove, takən, pencəl, lemən, circəs
ch, child; ng, long; sh, ship
th, thin; ᴛʜ, then; zh, measure

sten·o·graph·i·cal·ly (sten′ə graf′ik lē) *adv.* by means of stenography.

ste·nog·ra·phy (stə nog′rə fē) *n.* shorthand. See **shorthand** for picture. [< Gk. *stenos* narrow + E *-graphy*]

Sten·o·type (sten′ə tīp′) *n.* **1** *Trademark.* a kind of typewriter used in stenotypy. **2 stenotype,** a letter or group of letters used for a sound, word, or phrase in stenotypy. [< Gk. *stenos* narrow + E *type*]

sten·o·typ·y (sten′ə tīp′ē or stə not′ə pē) *n.* **1** a form of shorthand that uses ordinary letters. **2** the use of a stenotype machine to record speeches, etc.

Sten·tor (sten′tôr) *n.* in Greek legend, a Greek herald in the Trojan War, whose voice was as loud as the voices of fifty men.

sten·to·ri·an (sten tô′rē ən) *adj.* very loud or powerful in sound. [< *Stentor*]

step (step) *n. v.* **stepped, step·ping.** —*n.* **1** a movement made by lifting the foot and putting it down again in a new position; one motion of the leg in walking, running, dancing, etc. **2** the distance covered by one such movement: *She was three steps away when he called her back.* **3** a short distance; little way: *The school is only a step away.* **4** a way of walking, dancing, etc.: *a slow step.* **5** a pace uniform with that of another or others or in time with music: *keep step.* **6** a place for the foot in going up or coming down. A stair or a rung of a ladder is a step. **7** the sound made by putting the foot down. **8** a footprint: *steps in the mud.* **9** an action: *The principal took steps to stop needless absence from school.* **10** a degree in a series; grade in rank. **11** in music: **a** a degree of the staff or the scale. **b** the interval between two successive degrees of the scale. **12** a part like a step; support, frame, etc. for holding the end of something upright: *the step of a mast.* **13 change step,** fall into marching step more correctly. **14 in step, a** keeping one's pace uniform with that of another or others or in time with music. **b** making one's actions agree with those of another person or persons. **15 out of step, a** not keeping pace with others or in time to music. **b** not in harmony or accord. **16 step by step,** little by little; slowly. **17 steps,** *pl.* a stepladder. **18 take steps,** adopt, put into effect, or carry out measures considered to be necessary, desirable, etc.: *Steps have already been taken to deal with the emergency.* **19 watch one's step,** be careful. [< v.]
—*v.* **1** move the legs as in walking, running, dancing, etc.: *Step lively!* **2** walk a short distance: *Step this way.* **3** measure (off) by taking steps: *Step off the distance from the door to the window.* **4** put the foot down: *step on a worm.* **5** make or arrange like a flight of steps. **6** set (a mast); fix or place in a support. **7** *Informal.* go fast. **8 step down, a** come down; resign: *He stepped down from the presidency.* **b** decrease: *to step down the rate or flow in a pipeline.* **9 step in,** come in; intervene; take part. **10 step on it,** *Informal.* go faster; hurry up. **11 step out,** *Informal.* go out for entertainment. **12 step up, a** go up. **b** increase. [OE *steppan*] —**Syn.** *n.* **9** measure, proceeding.

step- *prefix.* related by the remarriage of a parent, not by blood, as in *stepmother, stepsister,* etc. [OE *stēop-*]

step·broth·er (step′bruᴛʜ′ər) *n.* a stepfather's or stepmother's son by a former marriage.

step·child (step′chīld′) *n.* **-chil·dren.** a child of one's husband or wife by a former marriage.

step·dame (step′dām′) *n. Archaic.* a stepmother.

step·daugh·ter (step′do′tər or -dô′tər) *n.* a daughter of one's husband or wife by a former marriage.

step-down (step′doun′) *adj.* **1** serving or causing to decrease gradually. **2** in electricity, lowering the voltage of a current, especially by means of a transformer.

step·fa·ther (step′fo′ᴛʜər) *n.* a man who has married one's mother after the death or divorce of one's natural father.

step-in (step′in′) *adj.* of garments, shoes, etc., put on by being stepped into.

step·lad·der (step′lad′ər) *n.* a ladder with flat steps instead of rungs.

step·moth·er (step′muᴛʜ′ər) *n.* a woman who has married one's father after the death or divorce of one's natural mother.

step-out well (step′out′) a gas or oil well dug near the site of another that has already been proved productive, giving further proof of reserves in the area.

step·par·ent (step′pãr′ənt) *n.* a stepfather or stepmother.

steppe (step) *n.* **1** one of the vast, treeless plains in S.E. Europe and in Asia. **2** a vast, treeless plain. [< Russian *step'*]

step·per (step′ər) *n.* a person or animal that steps, especially in a particular manner: *a high stepper.*

stepping stone **1** a stone or one of a line of stones in shallow water, a marshy place, etc. used in crossing. **2** a stone for use in mounting or ascending. **3** anything serving as a means of advancing or rising.

step·sis·ter (step′sis′tər) *n.* a stepfather's or stepmother's daughter by a former marriage.

step·son (step′sun′) *n.* a son of one's husband or wife by a former marriage.

step-up (step′up′) *adj.* **1** serving or causing to increase gradually. **2** in electricity, increasing the voltage of a current, especially by means of a transformer. *—n.* an increase: *a step-up in production.*

step·wise (step′wīz′) *adv.* in a step or steps.

-ster *suffix.* **1** one that ——s, as in *fibster.* **2** one that makes ——, as in *maltster, rhymester.* **3** one that is ——, as in *youngster.* **4** special meanings, as in *gangster, roadster, teamster.* [OE *-estre, -istre*]

ster. sterling.

stere (stēr) *n.* a cubic metre. [< F < Gk. *stereos* solid]

ster·e·o (ster′ē ō′ or stēr′ē ō′) *n.* **1** stereophonic reproduction. **2** a set or apparatus for stereophonic reproduction. **3** *Informal.* a radio, gramophone, or tape-recorder equipped with a stereophonic system. **4** stereotype. *—adj.* **1** stereophonic. **2** produced for use with stereophonic equipment.

stereo- *combining form.* hard, firm, solid, as in *stereoscope.* [< Gk. *stereos* solid]

ster·e·o·phon·ic (ster′ē ə fon′ik or stēr′ē ə-) *adj.* in sound reproduction, of or produced by the use of two or more microphones, recording channels, loudspeakers, etc. in order to give a three-dimensional effect. **—ster′e·o·phon′i·cal·ly,** *adv.*

ster·e·op·ti·con (ster′ē op′tə kən or stēr′ē op′tə kən) *n.* an improved form of magic lantern, having a powerful light that projects pictures upon a screen. [< NL < Gk. *stereos* solid + *optikos* relating to vision]

ster·e·o·scope (ster′ē ə skōp′ or stēr′ē ə-) *n.* an instrument through which two pictures of the same object or scene are viewed, one by each eye. The object or scene thus viewed appears to have three dimensions, as it would if really seen.

A stereoscope. The pictures are taken from two points a short distance apart; the instrument contains lenses that make them appear to be one three-dimensional picture.

ster·e·o·scop·ic (ster′ē ə skop′ik or stēr′ē ə-) *adj.* having to do with stereoscopes.

ster·e·o·scop·i·cal·ly (ster′ē ə skop′ik lē or stēr′ē ə-) *adv.* by means of a stereoscope.

ster·e·o·type (ster′ē ə tīp′ or stēr′ē ə-) *n. v.* **-typed, -typ·ing.** *—n.* **1** the process of making metal plates by taking a mould of composed type and making from this mould a cast in type metal. **2** a printing plate cast from a mould. **3** the making or use of such plates. **4** a fixed form; a person, group, event, etc. thought of as conforming to a fixed, conventional mental picture, as if cast from a mould: *The characters in some novels have no individuality but are merely stereotypes.*
—v. **1** make a stereotype of. **2** print from stereotypes. **3** give a fixed or settled form to. **—ster′e·o·typ′er,** *n.*

ster·e·o·typed (ster′ē ə tīpt′ or stēr′ē ə-) *adj.* **1** printed from a stereotype. **2** fixed or settled in form; conventional.

ster·e·o·typ·y (ster′ē ə tīp′ē or stēr′ē ə-) *n.* **1** the process of making stereotype plates. **2** printing from stereotype plates.

ster·ile (ster′īl or ster′əl) *adj.* **1** free from living germs: *The doctor kept his instruments sterile.* **2** barren; not fertile; not producing crops: *sterile land.* **3** not producing seed or offspring: *a sterile cow.* **4 a** of a plant, not bearing fruit or spores. **b** of a flower, producing only stamens, or producing neither stamens nor pistils. **5** not producing results: *sterile hopes.* [< L *sterilis*] **—ster′ile·ly,** *adv.*

ste·ril·i·ty (stə ril′ə tē) *n.* **-ties.** barrenness; a sterile condition or character.

ster·i·li·za·tion (ster′ə lə zā′shən or ster′ ə lī zā′shən) *n.* a sterilizing or being sterilized: *the sterilization of dishes by boiling them.*

ster·i·lize (ster′ə līz′) *v.* **-lized, -liz·ing.** **1** free from living germs: *The water had to be sterilized by boiling to make it fit to drink.* **2** deprive of fertility. **3** make unproductive, unprofitable, or useless. **—ster′i·liz′er,** *n.*

ster·ling (stėr′ling) *n.* **1** British money, especially the pound as the standard British monetary unit in international trade: *pay in sterling.* **2** sterling silver or things made of it.
—adj. **1** of British money; payable in British money. **2** of standard quality; containing 92.5 per cent pure silver. *Sterling* is stamped on solid silver knives, forks, etc. **3** made of sterling silver. **4** genuine; excellent; dependable. [probably ult. < OE *steorra* star (as on certain early coins)]

sterling silver solid silver; silver 92.5 per cent pure.

stern[1] (stėrn) *adj.* **1** severe; strict; harsh: *a stern master, a stern frown.* **2** hard; not yielding; firm: *stern necessity.* **3** grim: *stern mountains.* [OE *stirne*] **—stern′ly,** *adv.* **—stern′ness,** *n.* **—Syn. 1** See **severe.**

stern[2] (stėrn) *n.* the rear of a ship or boat. See **aft** for diagram. [probably < ON *stjórn* steering]

ster·nal (stėr′nəl) *adj.* of or having to do with the breastbone or sternum. [< NL *sternalis*]

stern chase a chase in which the pursuing ship follows in the wake of the other.

stern chaser a gun in the stern of a ship for protection against an enemy ship following in its wake.

stern·most (stėrn′mōst) *adj.* **1** nearest the stern. **2** farthest in the rear.

stern·post (stėrn′pōst′) *n.* the principal piece of timber or iron in the stern of a ship. Its lower end is fastened to the keel, and it usually supports the rudder.

stern sheets the space at the stern of an open boat.

ster·num (stėr′nəm) *n.* **-na** (-nə) or **-nums.** the breastbone. [< NL < Gk. *sternon* chest]

ster·nu·ta·tion (stėr′nū tā′shən or stėr′nü tā′shən) *n.* the act of sneezing. [< L *sternutatio, -onis* < *sternutare* sneeze, frequentative of *sternuere* sneeze]

ster·nu·ta·tive (stėr nū′tə tiv or stėr nü′tə tiv) *adj.* causing sneezing.

stern·ward (stėrn′wərd) *adv.* toward the stern; astern.

stern·wards (stėrn′wərdz) *adv.* sternward.

stern·way (stėrn′wā′) *n.* the backward movement of a ship.

stern-wheel·er (stėrn′hwēl′ər or -wēl′ər) *n.* a steamboat driven by a paddle wheel at the stern or rear. See the picture under **paddle wheel.**

ster·oid (ster′oid or stēr′oid) *n.* in biochemistry, any of a large group of organic compounds, including the sterols, the bile acids, and the sex hormones, distributed widely in living plant and animal cells. [< *ster*ol + *-oid*]

ster·ol (ster′ol or stēr′ol) *n.* in biochemistry, any of various complex organic alcohols distributed widely in living plant and animal cells. [contraction of *cholesterol*]

ster·to·rous (stėr′tə rəs) *adj.* making a heavy snoring sound: *stertorous breathing.* [< NL *stertor* snoring < L *stertere* snore] —**ster′to·rous·ness,** *n.*

stet (stet) *n. v.* **stet·ted, stet·ting.** —*n.* "let it stand," a direction on printer's proof, a manuscript, etc. to retain cancelled matter (usually accompanied by a row of dots under or beside the matter). —*v.* mark for retention. [< L *stet* let it stand]

steth·o·scope (steth′ə skōp′) *n.* an instrument used for listening to sounds in the lungs, heart, etc. [< Gk. *stēthos* chest + E *-scope*]

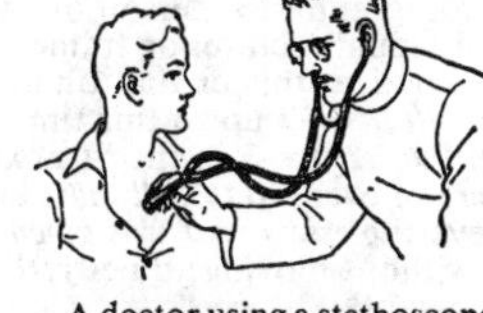

A doctor using a stethoscope. The sounds are conveyed to his ears through the tubes.

steth·o·scop·ic (steth′ə skop′ik) *adj.* 1 having to do with the stethoscope or its use. 2 made or obtained by the stethoscope. —**steth′o·scop′i·cal·ly,** *adv.*

Stetson hat or **Stetson** (stet′sən) *n.* a large, high-crowned, soft felt hat worn in western Canada and the United States. [< Trademark]

ste·ve·dore (stē′və dôr′) *n. v.* **-dored, -dor·ing.** —*n.* a man who loads and unloads ships. —*v.* load or unload (a vessel or cargo). [< Sp. *estivador,* ult. < L *stipare* pack down]

stew (stū or stü) *v.* 1 cook by slow boiling. 2 *Informal.* worry; fret. 3 **stew in one's own juice,** suffer the consequence of one's actions. —*n.* 1 a dish, usually consisting of meat, vegetables, etc., cooked by slow boiling. 2 any food cooked in this way. 3 *Informal.* a state of worry; fret. [ME < OF *estuver* < VL *extufare* < L *ex-* out + Gk. *typhos* vapor]

stew·ard (stū′ərd or stü′ərd) *n.* 1 a man who manages another's property: *He is the steward of that great estate.* 2 a man who takes charge of the food and table service for a club, ship, railway train, etc. 3 a man employed on a ship to wait upon passengers: *a dining room steward, a deck steward, a cabin steward.* 4 a person appointed to manage a dinner, ball, show, etc. 5 a shop steward. [OE *stigweard* < *stig* hall + *weard* keeper, ward]

stew·ard·ess (stū′ər dis or stü′ər dis) *n.* 1 a woman steward. 2 a woman employed on a ship, an airplane, etc. to wait upon passengers.

stew·ard·ship (stū′ərd ship′ or stü′ərd -) *n.* 1 the position, duties, and responsibilities of a steward. 2 management for others.

stew·pan (stū′pan′ or stü′-) *n.* a pan for stewing; saucepan.

sthen·ic (sthen′ik) *adj.* 1 having to do with vigor or nervous energy. 2 in medicine, accompanied by an unhealthy increase in vital processes, such as circulation and respiration. [< NL *sthenicus* < Gk. *sthenos* strength]

stib·i·um (stib′ē əm) *n.* antimony. [< L < Gk. *stibi* < Egyptian]

stich (stik) *n.* a metrical line; verse: *a Biblical stich.* [< Gk. *stichos* line < *steichein* march in a line]

stick[1] (stik) *n. v.* **sticked, stick·ing.** —*n.* 1 a long, thin piece of wood. 2 such a piece of wood shaped for a special use: *a walking stick, a hockey stick.* 3 something like a stick in shape: *a stick of candy.* 4 *Informal.* a stiff, awkward, or stupid person. 5 a lever used to work certain main controls of an airplane. 6 a mast; part of mast; yard. 7 *Informal.* a portion of alcoholic liquor added to a drink. 8 in printing: **a** a small metal tray in which type is set by hand. **b** the amount of type so set. 9 **shake a stick at,** *Informal.* take notice of: *There was not enough snow to shake a stick at.* 10 **the sticks,** *pl. Informal.* the outlying districts; backwoods. —*v.* furnish with a stick or sticks to support or prop. [OE *sticca*] —**Syn.** *n.* 1 rod, staff.

stick[2] (stik) *v.* **stuck, stick·ing,** *n.* —*v.* 1 pierce with a pointed instrument; thrust (a point) into; stab. 2 kill by stabbing or piercing. 3 fasten by thrusting the point or end into or through something: *He stuck a flower in his buttonhole.* 4 put in a place or position: *Don't stick your head out of the window.* 5 be thrust; extend (from, out, through, up, etc.): *His arms stick out of his coat sleeves.* 6 fasten; attach: *Stick a stamp on the letter.* 7 set into or adorn the surface of: *stick a ham with cloves.* 8 keep close: *The boy stuck to his mother's heels.* 9 be or become fastened; become fixed; be at a standstill: *Our car stuck in the mud.* 10 bring to a stop: *Our work was stuck by the breakdown of the machinery.* 11 keep on; hold fast: *stick to a task, stick to one's friends when they are in trouble.* 12 *Informal.* puzzle. 13 be puzzled; hesitate. 14 *Slang.* **a** impose upon; cheat. **b** leave (a person) with, especially something to pay. 15 *Informal.* stand or put up with; tolerate: *I won't stick his insults much longer.*
stick around, *Informal.* stay or wait nearby.
stick at, hesitate or stop for.
stick by or **to,** remain resolutely faithful or attached to; refuse to desert.
stick it out, *Informal.* put up with unpleasant conditions, circumstances, etc.; endure: *Try to stick it out for a few more days.*
stick out, a stand out; be plain. **b** *Informal.* put up with until the end.
stick together, keep or cling together; stay united; support each other or one another.
stick up, *Slang.* hold up; rob.
stick up for, *Informal.* support; defend.
—*n.* 1 a thrust. 2 a sticky condition. 3 a standstill; stop. [OE *stician*]
Syn. *v.* 7, 8 **Stick, adhere** = cling or become firmly or closely attached to another or each other. **Stick,** the common and general word, particularly suggests being fastened together or to another person or thing by or as if by something gummy: *Flies stick to flypaper.* **Adhere,** a more formal word sometimes used as a dignified substitute for *stick,* means cling fast or remain firmly attached to someone or something, by itself or of one's own accord: *Adhesive tape does not adhere well to his skin.*

stick·er (stik′ər) *n.* 1 a person or thing that sticks. 2 a label or slip of paper for sticking to something. 3 a burr; thorn. 4 *Informal.* a puzzle.

stick figure a simple figure of a person or animal drawn with straight lines except for a circle representing the head.

stick·han·dle (stik′han′dəl) *v.* **-dled, -dling.** in hockey, manoeuvre the puck by deft handling of the stick, especially to avoid opposing checkers. —**stick′han′dler,** *n.* —**stick′han′dling,** *n.*

Stick Indian *Cdn.* 1 an Indian from the bush country of the interior of British Columbia and the Yukon. 2 **stick Indian,** *Derogatory slang.* on the west coast, a backwoods Indian; an Indian ignorant of city ways. [< Chinook Jargon *stik* woods, bush]

sticking plaster cloth coated with a sticky substance, used to cover and close slight cuts and wounds.

sticking point 1 the place where a thing stops and holds. 2 any factor that prevents the solution of a problem: *When the contract was being reviewed, the sticking point proved to be shorter hours.*

stick-in-the-mud (stik′in ᴛʜə mud′) *n. Informal.* 1 a person who prefers the old to the new; a conservative; fogey. 2 a person who lacks initiative or resourcefulness.

stick·le (stik′əl) *v.* **-led, -ling.** 1 make objections about trifles; insist stubbornly. 2 feel difficulties about trifles; have objections; scruple. [probably ult. < OE *stihtan* arrange]

stick·le·back (stik′əl bak′) *n.* **-back** or **-backs.** a small scale-less fish with a row of sharp spines on the back. The male builds an elaborate nest for the eggs. [ME *stykylbak* < OE *sticel* prick, sting + *bæc* back]

stick·ler (stik′lər) *n.* a person who contends stubbornly or insists on trifles.

stick·man (stik′man′) *n.* **-men** (-men′). *Slang.* 1 a croupier at a casino or gambling house. 2 in sports, a person who handles a stick or bat. 3 a stick figure.

stick·pin (stik′pin′) *n.* a pin worn in a necktie for ornament.

hat, āge, cãre, fär; let, ēqual, tėrm; it, īce
hot, ōpen, ôrder; oil, out; cup, pu̇t, rüle, ūse
əbove, takən, pencəl, lemən, circəs
ch, child; ng, long; sh, ship
th, thin; ᴛʜ, then; zh, measure

stick·tight (stik′tīt′) *n.* a plant of the aster family having flat barbed seeds that stick to clothing.

stick-up (stik′up′) *n. Slang.* a holdup; robbery.

stick·y (stik′ē) *adj.* **stick·i·er, stick·i·est. 1** that sticks: *sticky glue.* **2** that makes things stick; covered with adhesive matter: *sticky flypaper.* **3** *Informal.* unpleasantly humid: *sticky weather.* **4** *Informal.* puzzling; difficult: *a sticky problem.* **5** *Slang.* unpleasant; extremely disagreeable. **—stick′i·ly,** *adv.* **—stick′i·ness,** *n.* **—Syn. 1** adhesive, viscous, mucilaginous.

sties (stīz) *n.* pl. of **sty.**

stiff (stif) *adj.* **1** not easily bent: *a stiff collar.* **2** hard to move: *stiff hinges.* **3** not able to move easily: *He was stiff and sore.* **4** drawn tight; tense: *a stiff cord.* **5** not fluid; firm: *stiff jelly.* **6** dense; compact: *stiff soil.* **7** not easy or natural in manner; formal: *a stiff bow, a stiff style of writing.* **8** lacking grace of line, form, or arrangement: *stiff geometrical designs.* **9** resolute; steadfast; unyielding: *a stiff resistance.* **10** strong and steady in motion: *a stiff breeze.* **11** hard to deal with; hard: *a stiff examination.* **12** harsh or severe: *a stiff penalty.* **13** strong: *a stiff drink.* **14** *Informal.* more than seems suitable: *a stiff price.*
—n. Slang. **1** a dead body; corpse. **2** a drunken person. **3** a man; fellow, especially a tramp or hobo: *a working stiff.* [OE *stīf*] **—stiff′ly,** *adv.* **—stiff′ness,** *n.*
Syn. *adj.* **1 Stiff, rigid** = not easily bent or capable of being bent or turned without breaking. **Stiff,** the general word, describes anything so firm or solid that it does not bend easily or cannot be bent without injury: *Library books need stiff covers.* **Rigid** describes something so stiff and hard that it will not bend at all and cannot be bent without breaking: *The bodies of animals become rigid after death.* **7** stilted, affected, constrained, ceremonious. **11** harsh, severe, rigorous. **14** immoderate, excessive.

stiff·en (stif′ən) *v.* **1** make stiff. **2** become stiff. **3** make stronger. **4** become stronger: *The wind was stiffening.* **—stiff′en·er,** *n.*

stiff·en·ing (stif′ən ing *or* stif′ning) *n.* **1** a making or becoming stiff. **2** something used to stiffen.

stiff-necked (stif′nekt′) *adj.* **1** having a stiff neck. **2** stubborn; obstinate.

sti·fle (stī′fəl) *v.* **-fled, -fling. 1** stop the breath of; smother: *The smoke stifled the firemen.* **2** be unable to breathe freely: *I am stifling in this close room.* **3** keep back; suppress; stop: *stifle a cry, stifle a yawn, stifle business activity, stifle a rebellion.* [ME *stuffle(n), stiffle(n)* < *stuffe(n)* stuff, stifle; influenced by ON *stifla* dam up] **—Syn. 1, 2** choke, strangle. **3** extinguish, repress.

stig·ma (stig′mə) *n.* **stig·mas** or **stig·ma·ta. 1** a mark of disgrace; a stain or reproach on one's reputation. **2** a distinguishing mark or sign. **3** a small spot or mark; a spot in the skin that bleeds or turns red. **4** in botany, the part of the pistil of a plant that receives the pollen. **5 stigmata,** *pl.* marks or wounds like the five wounds on the crucified body of Christ, said to appear supernaturally on the bodies of certain persons. **6** *Archaic.* a special mark burned on a slave or criminal. [< L < Gk.]

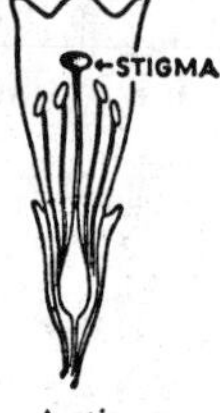

A stigma (def. 4)

stig·ma·ta (stig′mə tə *or* stig mä′tə) *n.* a pl. of **stigma.**

stig·mat·ic (stig mat′ik) *adj.* of or having to do with a stigma; like that of a stigma; marked by a stigma.
—n. a person bearing marks suggesting the wounds of Christ.

stig·ma·tism (stig′mə tiz′əm) *n.* **1** the absence of astigmatism. **2** a condition in which the person has the stigmata.

stig·ma·tize (stig′mə tīz′) *v.* **-tized, -tiz·ing. 1** set some mark of disgrace upon; reproach. **2** brand. **3** produce stigmas on. **—stig′ma·ti·za′tion,** *n.* **—stig′ma·tiz′er,** *n.*

stile (stīl) *n.* **1** a step or steps for getting over a fence or wall. **2** a turnstile. **3** a vertical piece in a door, panelled wall, etc. [OE *stigel*; related to *stīgan* climb]

A stile (def. 1)

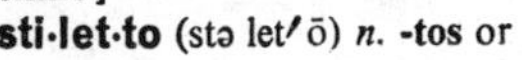

sti·let·to (stə let′ō) *n.* **-tos** or **-toes. 1** a dagger with a narrow blade. **2** a small, sharp-pointed instrument for making eyelet holes in embroidery. [< Ital. *stiletto,* ult. < L *stilus* pointed instrument]

still[1] (stil) *adj.* **1** remaining in the same position or at rest; motionless; stationary: *stand, sit, or lie still.* **2 a** without noise; quiet; tranquil: *a still night.* **b** of water, the air, etc., unruffled or undisturbed; free from waves, violent current, winds, etc.: *The lake is still today.* **3** soft; low; subdued: *a still, small voice.* **4** not bubbling: *still wine.*
—v. **1** make quiet: *She stilled the crying child.* **2** become quiet. **3** calm; relieve.
—n. **1** *Poetic.* silence: *the still of the night.* **2** a photograph of a person or other subject at rest. **3** an individual picture, or frame, from a motion picture.
—adv. **1** at this or that time: *He came yesterday and he is still here.* **2** up to this time or that time: *The matter is still unsettled.* **3** in the future as in the past: *It will still be here.* **4** even; yet: *still more, still worse.* **5** yet; nevertheless: *Proof was given, but they still doubted.* **6** without moving; quietly. **7** *Archaic or poetic.* steadily; constantly; always.
—conj. yet; nevertheless: *He is dull; still he tries hard.* [OE *stille*]
Syn. *adj.* **1 Still, quiet** = without noise or activity. **Still** particularly suggests being silent and at rest, and sometimes emphasizes absence of sound, sometimes absence of motion: *It was very late and the night was still. Her hands are never still.* **Quiet** particularly suggests being calm and peaceful or restful, without disturbance, excited activity, or noise: *He lives in a quiet little town.* *-v.* **1** silence, hush, tranquillize, pacify.

still[2] (stil) *n.* **1** an apparatus for distilling liquids. A still is used in making alcohol. **2** a place where alcoholic liquors are distilled; distillery. [n. use of *still,* short form of *distil*]

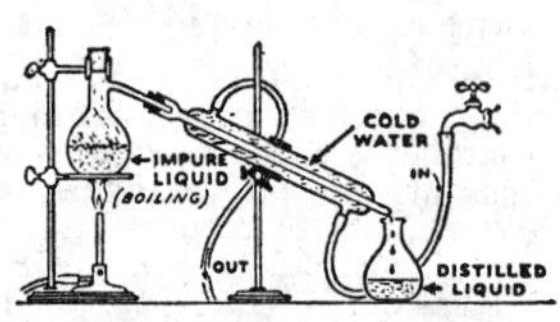

A still (def. 1). It works on the same principle as a retort.

still·born (stil′bôrn′) *adj.* **1** dead when born. **2 a** destined never to be realized: *stillborn hopes.* **b** that fails utterly to attract an audience: *a stillborn book or play.*

still hunt a quiet or secret pursuit.

still life 1 fruit, flowers, furniture, pottery, dead animals, etc. shown in a picture. **2** a picture showing such things.

still-life (stil′līf′) *adj.* of or having to do with still life.

still·ness (stil′nis) *n.* **1** quiet; silence. **2** the absence of motion; calm.

Still·son wrench (stil′sən) *Trademark.* a wrench with an adjustable L-shaped jaw, used for turning pipes and other round objects.

stil·ly (*adj.* stil′ē; *adv.* stil′lē) *adj.* **-li·er, -li·est,** *adv.* *—adj. Poetic.* quiet; still; calm. *—adv.* calmly; quietly.

stilt (stilt) *n.* **1** one of a pair of poles to stand on and hold while walking, each with a support for the foot at some distance above the ground. **2** a long post or pole used to support a house, shed, etc. above the water. **3** a wading bird that lives in marshes and has a long bill and long, slender legs. [ME *stilte*] **—stilt′like′,** *adj.*

stilt·ed (stil′tid) *adj.* **1** stiffly dignified or formal: *stilted conversation.* **2** raised above the ordinary level. **—stilt′ed·ly,** *adv.* **—Syn. 1** pompous.

Stil·ton cheese (stil′tən) a rich, white cheese veined with mould when well ripened. [< *Stilton,* a village in Huntingdonshire, England, where it was first made]

stim·u·lant (stim′yů lənt) *n.* **1** a food, drug, medicine, etc. that temporarily increases the activity of some part of the body. Tea, coffee, and alcoholic drinks are stimulants. **2** something that spurs one on or stirs one up; a motive, influence, etc. that rouses one to action: *Hope is a stimulant.* *—adj.* stimulating. [< L *stimulans, -antis,* ppr. of *stimulare.* See STIMULATE.]

stim·u·late (stim′yů lāt′) *v.* **-lat·ed, -lat·ing. 1** spur on; stir up; rouse to action: *Praise stimulated her to work hard.* **2** in physiology, increase temporarily the functional activity of (a nerve, organ, or other part of the body). **3** excite with alcoholic liquor; intoxicate. **4** act as a stimulant or a stimulus. [< L *stimulare* < *stimulus* goad] **—stim′u·lat′er, stim′u·la′tor,** *n.* **—Syn. 1** prick, goad, incite, encourage, impel, urge.

stim·u·la·tion (stim′yů lā′shən) *n.* a stimulating; being stimulated: *Lazy people need some stimulation to make them work.*

stim·u·la·tive (stim′yů lə tiv or stim′yů lā′tiv) *adj.* tending to stimulate; stimulating. —*n.* a stimulating thing; stimulus.

stim·u·li (stim′yů lī′ or stim′yů lē′) *n.* pl. of **stimulus.**

stim·u·lus (stim′yů ləs) *n.* **-li. 1** something that stirs to action or effort: *Ambition is a great stimulus.* **2** in physiology, something that excites some part of the body to activity. [< L *stimulus,* originally, goad]

sti·my (stī′mē) *n. v.* **-mied, -my·ing.** stymie.

sting (sting) *v.* **stung, sting·ing,** *n.* —*v.* **1** prick with a small point; wound: *Bees, wasps, and hornets sting.* **2** pain sharply: *Jim was stung by the mockings of the other children.* **3** cause a feeling like that of a sting: *Mustard stings.* **4** of certain plants, etc., produce irritation, rash, or inflammation in (a person's skin) by contact. **5** affect with a tingling pain, burning sensation, sharp hurt, etc.: *stung by a spark.* **6** drive or stir up as if by a sting: *Their ridicule stung him into making a sharp reply.* **7** *Slang.* impose upon; charge too much.
—*n.* **1** the wound caused by a stinger: *Put mud on the sting to take away the pain.* **2** a stinger. **3** a sharp pain: *The ball team felt the sting of defeat.* **4** something that causes a sharp pain. **5** something that drives or urges sharply. **6** a stinging quality; capacity to sting or hurt. [OE *stingan*] —**sting′ing·ly,** *adv.* —**sting′less,** *adj.*

sting·a·ree (sting′ə rē′) *n.* sting ray. [alteration of *sting ray*]

sting·er (sting′ər) *n.* **1** the sharp part of an insect or animal that pricks or wounds and often poisons. **2** anything that stings. **3** *Informal.* a stinging blow, remark, etc.

sting ray a broad, flat-bodied fish that can inflict severe wounds with its sharp spines.

stin·gy (stin′jē) *adj.* **-gi·er, -gi·est. 1** mean about spending or giving money; not generous: *He tried to save money without being stingy.* **2** scanty; meagre. [related to STING] —**stin′gi·ly,** *adv.* —**stin′gi·ness,** *n.* —**Syn. 1** miserly, parsimonious, niggardly, penurious.

stink (stingk) *n. v.* **stank** or **stunk, stunk, stink·ing.** —*n.* **1** a bad smell. **2 raise a stink,** *Slang.* arouse much complaint, criticism, or disturbance. —*v.* **1** have a bad smell. **2** cause to have a very bad smell. **3 a** have a very bad reputation; be in great disfavor. **b** savor offensively (*of*): *His remark stinks of treason.* **4 stink out,** drive out with stinking smoke or fumes. [OE *stincan* to smell] —**stink′ing·ly,** *adv.*

stink·bug (stingk′bug′) *n.* any bad-smelling bug.

stink·er (sting′kər) *n.* **1** a person or thing that stinks. **2** *Informal.* a low, mean, contemptible person. **3** something unpleasant or contemptible.

stink·weed (stink′wēd′) *n.* any of various coarse, ill-smelling plants, especially jimson weed.

stint (stint) *v.* **1** keep on short allowance; be saving or careful in using or spending; limit: *The parents stinted themselves of food to give it to their children.* **2** be saving; get along on very little. **3** *Archaic.* stop. —*n.* **1** limit; limitation: *That generous man gives without stint.* **2** an amount or share set aside. **3** a task assigned: *Washing the breakfast dishes was her daily stint.* **4** *Archaic.* a stop. [OE *styntan* blunt] —**stint′er,** *n.* —**stint′ing·ly,** *adv.*

stipe (stīp) *n.* **1** in botany, a stalk; stem: *the stipe of a mushroom, the stipe of a fern.* **2** in zoology, a stalk or stalklike part. [< F < L *stipes* trunk]

sti·pel (stī′pəl) *n.* in botany, a secondary stipule situated at the base of a leaflet of a compound leaf. [< NL *stipella,* dim. of L *stipula.* See STIPULE.]

sti·pend (stī′pend) *n.* fixed or regular pay; salary. [< L *stipendium* < *stips* wages, originally, coin + *pendere* weigh out]

sti·pen·di·ar·y (stī pen′dē er′ē) *adj. n.* **-ar·ies.** —*adj.* **1** receiving a stipend. **2** paid for by a stipend. **3** of or having to do with a stipend. **4** performing services for regular pay. —*n.* a person who receives a stipend; a salaried clergyman, judge, etc.

hat, āge, cãre, fär; let, ēqual, tėrm; it, īce
hot, ōpen, ôrder; oil, out; cup, pủt, rüle, ūse
əbove, takən, pencəl, lemən, circəs
ch, child; ng, long; sh, ship
th, thin; ŦH, then; zh, measure

stip·ple (stip′əl) *v.* **-pled, -pling,** *n.* —*v.* **1** paint, draw, or engrave in dots. **2** produce a stippled effect on.
—*n.* **1** the method of painting, drawing, or engraving by stippling. **2** the effect produced by this method. **3** stippled work. [< Du. *stippelen*] —**stip′pler,** *n.*

stip·pling (stip′ling) *n.* the act, method, or work of a person or thing that stipples.

stip·u·lar (stip′yů lər) *adj.* **1** of or having to do with stipules. **2** stipule-like; having stipules.

stip·u·late[1] (stip′yů lāt′) *v.* **-lat·ed, -lat·ing.** arrange definitely; demand as a condition of agreement: *He stipulated that he should receive a month's vacation every year if he took the job.* [< L *stipulari* stipulate] —**stip′u·la′tor,** *n.*

stip·u·late[2] (stip′yů lit or stip′yů lāt′) *adj.* having stipules. [< *stipule*]

stip·u·la·tion (stip′yů lā′shən) *n.* **1** a definite arrangement; agreement. **2** a condition in an agreement or bargain.

stip·ule (stip′ūl) *n.* in botany, one of the pair of little leaflike parts at the base of a leaf stem. [< L *stipula* stem; related to *stipes* trunk. Doublet of STUBBLE.]

stir[1] (stėr) *v.* **stirred, stir·ring,** *n.* —*v.* **1** move: *The wind stirred the leaves.* **2** move about: *No one was stirring in the house.* **3** mix by moving around with a spoon, fork, stick, etc.: *stir sugar into one's coffee.* **4** be mixed with a spoon, etc.: *This dough stirs hard.* **5** set going; affect strongly; excite: *John stirs the other children to mischief.* **6** become active, much affected, or excited: *The countryside was stirring with new life.* **7 stir oneself,** move briskly; bestir. **8 stir up, a** rouse to action, activity, or emotion; incite; stimulate. **b** excite; provoke; induce: *stir up a mutiny.*
—*n.* **1** a movement. **2** a state of motion, activity, briskness, bustle, etc. **3** excitement. **4** *Archaic.* a public disturbance, tumult, or revolt. **5** the act of stirring. **6** a jog; thrust; poke. [OE *styrian*] —**stir′rer,** *n.*
Syn. *v.* **5** rouse, animate, agitate. –*n.* **1** motion, activity. **2 Stir, bustle, ado** = excitement or excited activity. **Stir** particularly suggests a disturbance, especially where there has been quiet, or a great deal of excitement: *There was a stir in the courtroom.* **Bustle** suggests a great deal of noisy, excited, energetic activity: *All the week before the class picnic, studying gave way to the bustle of preparations.* **Ado** suggests much needless or pointless busyness and fuss, especially over something not worth it: *They made much ado about a comfortable bed for the kitten.*

stir[2] (stėr) *n. Slang.* prison. [origin uncertain]

stir-cra·zy (stėr′krā′zē) *adj. Slang.* mentally disturbed on account of long imprisonment, or from subjection to endless, restricted routines.

stirps (stėrps) *n.* **stir·pes** (stėr′pēz). **1** stock; family. **2** in law, the person from whom a family is descended. [< L *stirps,* originally, stem]

stir·ring (stėr′ing) *adj.* **1** moving; active; lively: *stirring times.* **2** rousing; exciting: *a stirring speech.* —**stir′ring·ly,** *adv.* —**Syn. 1** bustling, brisk. **2** stimulating, inspiring.

stir·rup (stėr′əp or stir′əp) *n.* **1** one of a pair of foot supports that hang from a saddle. See **saddle** for picture. **2** a piece resembling a stirrup used as a support or clamp. [OE *stigrāp* < *stige* climbing + *rāp* rope]

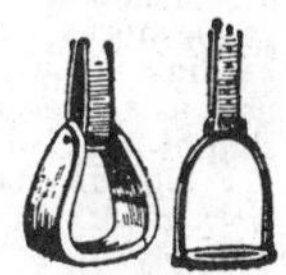
Stirrups

stirrup bone the innermost of the three bones in the middle ear; the stapes.

stirrup cup a cup of wine or other liquor offered to a rider mounted for departure; a drink at parting.

stitch (stich) *n.* **1** in sewing, embroidering, etc., a movement of a threaded needle through the cloth and back out again. **2** in surgery, a similar movement through skin, etc. **3** in knitting, crocheting, etc., a single turn or twist of yarn around a needle, hook, etc. **4** the loop of thread, etc. made by a stitch: *The doctor will take the stitches out of the wound tomorrow.* **5** a particular method of making stitches: *a buttonhole stitch.* **6** a small piece of cloth or clothing. **7** *Informal.* a small bit: *The lazy boy wouldn't do a stitch of work.* **8** a sudden, sharp pain. —*v.* **1** make stitches in; fasten with stitches. **2** sew. [OE *stice* puncture] —**stitch′er,** *n.*

stitch·ing (stich′ing) *n.* **1** the act or work of one who stitches. **2** stitches collectively.

stith·y (stiᴛʜ′ē or stith′ē) *n.* **stith·ies. 1** an anvil. **2** a forge; smith. [ME < ON *stethi*]

sti·ver (stī′vər) *n.* **1** a unit of money in the Netherlands, worth 1/20 of a guilder. **2** a coin worth one stiver. **3** something having little value. [< Du. *stuiver*]

St. James Street *Cdn.* **1** in Montreal, a street on which is located the city's principal banking firms. **2** the financial or moneyed interests of Montreal.

St.-John's-wort (sānt jonz′wėrt′) *n.* a shrub or plant that has many clusters of showy, yellow flowers.

sto·a (stō′ə) *n.* **1** in Greek architecture, a portico, usually detached and of considerable length and used as a promenade or meeting place. **2 the Stoa,** the Porch, a public walk at Athens, where Zeno, the philosopher who founded Stoicism, taught. [< Gk.]

stoat (stōt) *n.* **1** the ermine in its summer coat of brown fur. **2** a weasel. [ME *stote*; origin uncertain]

stock (stok) *n.* **1** goods for use or for sale; a supply used as it is needed: *This store keeps a large stock of toys.* **2 in stock,** ready for use or sale; on hand. **3 out of stock,** lacking; no longer on hand. **4** cattle or other farm animals; livestock. **5** the capital of a company or corporation, divided into portions or shares of uniform amount which are represented by transferable certificates. The holder of one of these is considered a part owner, rather than a creditor, of the company. **6** shares in a company. The profits of a company are divided among the owners of stock. **7** the estimation in which a person or thing is held: *set great stock by a remedy.* **8** the raw material from which anything is made: *soap stock. Rags are used as a stock for making paper.* **9** a debt owed by a nation, city, etc. to individuals who receive a fixed rate of interest. **10** race; family: *She is of United Empire Loyalist stock.* **11** an original ancestor of a family, tribe, or race. **12** a part used as a support or handle; a part to which other parts are attached: *the wooden stock of a rifle.* **13** a broth in which meat or fish has been cooked, used as a base for soups, sauces, etc. **14** formerly, a stiff necktie, used in place of the modern collar and tie. **15 a** various plays produced by a company at a single repertory theatre. **b** a stock company, or such companies and their activities as a category or type of theatrical production (used without article): *She is playing in summer stock.* **16** *Archaic.* something lifeless and stupid: "*You stocks and stones!*" **17** in botany: **a** the trunk or stump of a tree. **b** the main stem of a plant. **18** an underground stem like a root. **19 a** a tree or plant that furnishes cuttings for grafting. **b** the stem in which a graft is inserted. **20** a sweet-smelling garden flower; gillyflower. **21 on the stocks,** being built. **22 take stock, a** find out how much stock one has on hand. **b** make an estimate or examination. **23 take stock in, a** *Informal.* take an interest in; consider important; trust. **b** take shares in (a company). **24 the stocks, a** a wooden frame having holes to put a person's feet and, sometimes, hands through, formerly used as a punishment. **b** a wooden frame on which a ship or boat is built.
—*v.* **1** lay in a supply of; supply: *Our camp is well stocked with everything we need for a short stay.* **2** lay in a supply: *stock up for the winter.* **3** keep regularly for use or for sale: *A toy store stocks toys.* **4** fasten to or provide with a stock. **5** provide with wild life: *stock a lake with fish.* **6** furnish with horses, cattle, etc.: *stock a farm.* **7** sow (land) with grass, etc. **8** send out shoots.
—*adj.* **1** kept on hand regularly: *stock sizes.* **2** in common use; commonplace; everyday: *The weather is a stock topic of conversation.* **3 a** having to do with, presenting, or acting in a stock or repertoire: *a stock play, a stock company, a stock actor.* **b** appearing or recurring in various productions because of convention, custom, or unfailing appeal: *a stock situation in melodrama.* **4** of, having to do with, or devoted to the raising of livestock: *a stock farm.* **5** of or having to do with stock or stocks. [OE *stocc*] —**Syn.** *n.* **1** fund, store, goods, merchandise, wares. –*v.* **1** furnish, store.

stock·ade (stok ād′) *n. v.* **-ad·ed, -ad·ing.** —*n.* **1** an enclosure for defence consisting of large, strong posts set upright in the ground: *A stockade protected the colonists' homes from attack.* **2** a fort, camp, etc. surrounded by a stockade. **3** a pen or other enclosed space made with upright posts, stakes, etc. —*v.* protect, fortify, or surround with a stockade. [< F *estacade*, ult. < Provençal *estaca* stake < Gmc.]

stock·bro·ker (stok′brō′kər) *n.* a person who buys and sells stocks and bonds for others for a commission.

stock·bro·ker·age (stok′brō′kər ij) *n.* the business of a stockbroker.

stock car 1 a railway freight car for livestock. **2** an automobile of a standard make that has been specially prepared for racing.

stock company 1 a company whose capital is divided into shares. **2** in the theatre, a company employed more or less permanently under the same management, usually at one theatre, to perform many different plays.

stock dove a wild pigeon of Europe.

stocker (stok′ər) *n.* a young motherless or stray calf; dogie.

stock exchange 1 a place where stocks and bonds are bought and sold. **2** an association of brokers and dealers in stocks and bonds.

stock·fish (stok′fish′) *n.* fish preserved by splitting and drying in the air without salt.

stock·hold·er (stok′hōl′dər) *n.* an owner of stocks or shares in a company.

stock·i·net (stok′ə net′) *n.* an elastic, machine-knitted fabric used for making underwear, etc.

stock·ing (stok′ing) *n.* **1** a close-fitting, knitted covering of wool, cotton, nylon, etc. for the foot and leg. **2** something like a stocking; a patch of color on an animal's leg suggesting a stocking. [< *stock* stocking, OE *stocc*] —**stock′ing·less,** *adj.*

stocking cap a knitted cap with a long pointed end that falls over the back, worn for skiing, sleighing, etc.

stock in trade 1 the stock of a dealer or company. **2** a workman's tools, materials, etc. **3** resources.

stock·job·ber (stok′job′ər) *n.* **1** any stockbroker. **2** a stockbroker who buys and sells stocks and bonds for other brokers but not for the public.

stock·man (stok′mən) *n.* **-men** (-mən). **1** a man who raises livestock. **2** a man in charge of a stock of materials or goods.

stock market 1 a place where stocks and bonds are bought and sold; stock exchange. **2** the buying and selling in such a place. **3** the prices of stocks and bonds.

stock·pile (stok′pīl′) *n. v.* **-piled, -pil·ing.** —*n.* **1** a supply of raw materials, essential items, etc. built up and held in reserve for use during times of emergency or shortage. **2** a reserve of atomic weapons for warfare. —*v.* collect or bring together a stockpile.

stock raising the raising of livestock.

stock·room (stok′rüm′ or -rům′) *n.* **1** a room where stock is kept. **2** a room in a hotel, etc. where salesmen can show their samples.

stock-still (stok′stil′) *adj.* motionless.

stock·tak·ing (stok′tāk′ing) *n.* **1** the listing of the assets, goods, equipment, etc. of a business. **2** any review of one's position, qualifications, progress, etc.

stock·y (stok′ē) *adj.* **stock·i·er, stock·i·est.** having a solid or sturdy form or build; thick for its height. —**stock′i·ly,** *adv.* —**stock′i·ness,** *n.*

stock·yard (stok′yärd′) *n.* a place with pens and sheds for cattle, sheep, hogs, and horses. Livestock is kept in a stockyard before being slaughtered or sent to market.

stodg·y (stoj′ē) *adj.* **stodg·i·er, stodg·i·est. 1** dull or uninteresting; tediously commonplace: *a stodgy book.* **2** heavy: *stodgy food.* **3** heavily built: *a stodgy person.* [< *stodge* stuff; origin unknown] —**stodg′i·ly,** *adv.* —**stodg′i·ness,** *n.*

sto·gie or **sto·gy** (stō′gē) *n.* **-gies.** a long, slender, cheap cigar. [< *Conestoga,* a town in Pennsylvania]

Sto·ic (stō′ik) *n.* **1** a member of a school of philosophy founded by Zeno, 336?-264? B.C., a Greek philosopher. This school taught that virtue is the highest good and that men should be free from passion and unmoved by life's happenings. **2 stoic,** a person who remains calm, represses his feelings, and is indifferent to pleasure and pain.
—*adj.* **1** having to do with the philosophy of the Stoics, or with its followers. **2 stoic,** stoical. [< L *stoicus* < Gk. *stoikos,* literally, pertaining to a stoa]

sto·i·cal (stō′ə kəl) *adj.* like a stoic; self-controlled; indifferent to pleasure and pain. —**sto′i·cal·ly,** *adv.*

Sto·i·cism (stō′ə siz′əm) *n.* **1** the philosophy of the Stoics. **2 stoicism,** patient endurance; indifference to pleasure and pain.

stoke (stōk) *v.* **stoked, stok·ing. 1** poke, stir up, and feed (a fire); tend the fire of (a furnace). **2** tend a fire. **3 stoke up, a** put fuel on (a fire) or in (a furnace). **b** *Informal.* give or feed in abundance, in order to renew energy, make able to act, etc.; fill (*with*). [< *stoker*]

stoke·hold (stōk′hōld′) *n.* the place in a steamship where the furnaces, boilers, etc. are.

stoke·hole (stōk′hōl′) *n.* **1** the hole through which fuel is put into a furnace. **2** the space in front of a boiler or furnace from which the fires are tended.

stok·er (stōk′ər) *n.* **1** a man who tends the fires of a furnace or boiler. **2** a mechanical device for tending and feeding a furnace. [< Du. *stoker* < *stoken* stoke]

STOL short takeoff and landing.

stole[1] (stōl) *v.* pt. of **steal.**

stole[2] (stōl) *n.* **1** a narrow strip of silk or other material worn around the neck by a clergyman during certain religious functions. See **surplice** for picture. **2** a woman's collar or scarf of fur or cloth with ends hanging down in front. **3** *Archaic.* a long robe. [OE < L < Gk. *stolē* robe]

sto·len (stō′lən) *v.* pp. of **steal.**

stol·id (stol′id) *adj.* hard to arouse; not easily excited; showing no emotion; seeming dull. [< L *stolidus*] —**stol′id·ly,** *adv.* —**Syn.** impassive, stodgy.

sto·lid·i·ty (stə lid′ə tē) *n.* **-ties.** a stolid quality or condition.

sto·lon (stō′lon) *n.* **1** in botany, a slender branch that takes root at the tip and grows into a new plant. **2** in zoology, a rootlike growth. [< L *stolo, -onis* a shoot]

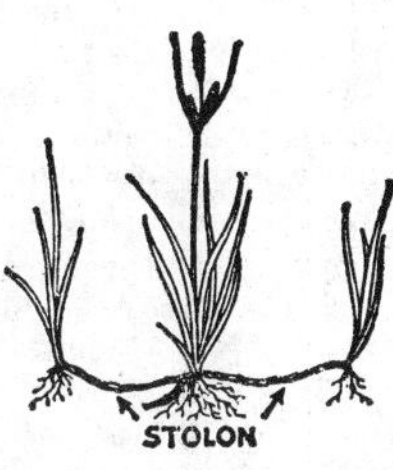
STOLON

sto·ma (stō′mə) *n.* **sto·ma·ta. 1** in botany, a small mouthlike opening; pore. **2** in zoology, a mouthlike opening. [< NL < Gk. *stoma, -atos* mouth]

stom·ach (stum′ək) *n.* **1** the most important part of the body for receiving and digesting food. See **intestine** for diagram. **2** the part of the body containing the stomach; abdomen; belly. **3** an appetite. **4** a desire; liking: *I have no stomach for that kind of writing.* —*v.* **1** be able to eat or keep in one's stomach. **2** put up with; bear; endure: *He could not stomach such insults.* [ME < OF < L < Gk. *stomachos* < *stoma* mouth]

stom·ach·er (stum′ək ər) *n.* formerly, a part of a woman's dress covering the stomach and chest.

A lady of the 16th century wearing a stomacher

sto·mach·ic (stō mak′ik) *adj.* **1** of or having to do with the stomach. **2** beneficial to the stomach, digestion, or appetite. —*n.* a medicine for the stomach.

hat, āge, cãre, fär; let, ēqual, tėrm; it, īce
hot, ōpen, ôrder; oil, out; cup, pu̇t, rüle, ūse
əbove, takən, pencəl, lemən, circəs
ch, child; ng, long; sh, ship
th, thin; ᴛʜ, then; zh, measure

sto·ma·ta (stō′mə tə or stom′ə tə) *n.* pl. of **stoma.**

sto·mate (stō′māt) *adj.* having stomata or a stoma. —*n.* a stoma.

sto·ma·ti·tis (stō′mə tī′tis or stom′ə-) *n.* any of various types of inflammation of the mouth. [< NL *stomatis* < Gk. *stoma, -atos* mouth + NL *-itis*]

stomp (stomp) *v.* tread heavily or stamp with the feet. —*n.* **1** a stomping. **2** a popular dance of the 1930's, marked by lively music and stamping of the feet. [var. of *stamp*]

stone (stōn) *n.* **stones** or *(for def. 8)* **stone,** *adj. v.* **stoned, ston·ing.** —*n.* **1** hard mineral matter that is not metal; rock. Stone is much used in building. **2** a piece of rock. **3** a piece of rock of definite size, shape, etc. used for a particular purpose: *His grave is marked by a fine stone.* **4** a gem; jewel. **5** in medicine, something hard and rounded like a stone, which sometimes forms in the kidneys or gall bladder, causing sickness and pain. **6** the hard covering of a fruit seed: *peach stones, plum stones.* **7** a curling stone. **8** *Brit.* a unit of weight equal to 14 pounds. **9 cast the first stone,** be the first to criticize. **10 leave no stone unturned,** do everything that can be done.
—*adj.* **1** made of stone. **2** having to do with stone. **3** made of stoneware or coarse clay.
—*v.* **1** put stone on; line with stone. **2** rub with or on a stone. **3** throw stones at; drive by throwing stones; kill by throwing stones: *Saint Stephen was stoned.* **4** take stones or seeds out of: *stone cherries or plums.* [OE *stān*] —**stone′like′,** *adj.* —**Syn.** *n.* **2** pebble, boulder.

Stone Age the period in man's history marked by the use of tools and weapons made from stone, commencing approximately one million years ago. It was followed by the Bronze Age.

stone-blind (stōn′blīnd′) *adj.* totally blind.

stone·boat (stōn′bōt′) *n.* a platform on runners, used for transporting stones and other heavy objects short distances on a farm.

stone-broke (stōn′brōk′) *adj. Slang.* penniless; without funds.

stone bruise a bruise caused by a stone, especially one on the sole of the foot.

stone-cold (stōn′kōld′) *adj.* cold as a stone; absolutely cold. —*adv.* absolutely; quite; completely.

stone·crop (stōn′krop′) *n.* **1** a low creeping plant that has small, fleshy leaves and clusters of small, yellow flowers. **2** any of various related plants. [OE *stāncrop*]

stone·cut·ter (stōn′kut′ər) *n.* **1** a person who cuts or carves stones. **2** a machine for cutting or dressing stone.

stoned (stōnd) *adj.* **1** having stones. **2** having the stones removed: *stoned peaches.* **3** *Slang.* intoxicated.

stone-deaf (stōn′def′) *adj.* totally deaf.

stone fruit any fruit that has a layer of pulp outside a hard shell containing a seed; any drupe. Peaches, cherries, olives, etc. are stone fruits.

stone marten 1 a marten of Europe and Asia that has a patch of white fur on the throat and breast. **2** the fur of this animal.

stone·ma·son (stōn′mā′sən) *n.* a person who cuts stone or builds walls, etc. of stone.

Stone sheep or **Stone's sheep** a kind of brownish-black mountain sheep found in northern British Columbia. [after Andrew J. *Stone,* an American naturalist]

stone's throw a short distance.

stone·ware (stōn′wãr′) *n.* a coarse, hard, glazed pottery.

stone·work (stōn′wėrk′) *n.* **1** work in stone. **2** the part of a building made of stone.

stone·work·er (stōn′wėr′kər) *n.* a person who shapes

or cuts stone for use in buildings, sculpture, etc.

Ston·ey (stōn′ē) *n.* **Ston·ey, Ston·eys,** or **Ston·ies.** Assiniboine.

ston·y (stōn′ē) *adj.* **ston·i·er, ston·i·est. 1** having many stones: *The beach is stony.* **2** hard like stone. **3 a** without expression or feeling: *a stony stare.* **b** cold and unfeeling: *a stony heart.* **c** of fear, grief, etc., petrifying, stupefying. **4** *Slang.* stone-broke. —**ston′i·ly,** *adv.* —**ston′i·ness,** *n.*

Ston·y (stōn′ē) *n.* **Ston·y** or **Ston·ies.** Stoney.

ston·y-broke (stōn′ē brōk′) *adj.* stone-broke.

stood (stůd) *v.* pt. and pp. of **stand.**

stooge (stüj) *n. v.* **stooged, stoog·ing.** *Informal.* —*n.* **1** a person on the stage who asks questions of a comedian and is the butt of the comedian's jokes. **2** a person who follows and flatters another; hanger-on. —*v.* be or act as a stooge (for). [origin uncertain]

stook (stůk) —*n.* an upright arrangement of sheaves, intended to speed up drying in the field. —*v.* build such arrangements of sheaves. [ME *stouke*; cf. MLG *stuke* pile of sheaves, bundle] —**stook′er,** *n.*

Stooks of wheat

stook threshing the practice of threshing in the field from the stooks rather than first hauling the sheaves to the barn.

stool (stül) *n.* **1** a seat without back or arms. **2** a similar article used to rest the feet on, or to kneel on. **3** in botany: **a** the stump or root of a plant from which shoots grow. **b** a cluster of shoots. **4** a decoy. **5** a pole to which a bird is fastened as a decoy. **6** a movement of the bowels; waste matter from the bowels. **7** an article or place to be used as a toilet. **8** a window sill. —*v.* send out shoots. [OE *stōl*] —**stool′-like′,** *adj.*

stool pigeon 1 a pigeon used to lead other pigeons into a trap. **2** *Slang.* a spy for the police; informer.

stoop[1] (stüp) *v.* **1** bend forward: *stoop over a desk.* **2** carry the head and shoulders bent forward. **3** of trees, precipices, etc., bend forward and downward. **4** lower oneself; descend. **5** *Archaic.* submit; yield. **6** swoop like a hawk.
—*n.* **1** an act of stooping; a bending forward. **2** a forward bend. **3** a forward bend of the head and shoulders. **4** condescension. **5** a swoop. [OE *stūpian*] —**stoop′er,** *n.*
—**Syn.** *v.* **1** bow, incline. **4** condescend, deign.

stoop[2] (stüp) *n.* a porch or platform at the entrance of a house. [< Du. *stoep*]

stop (stop) *v.* **stopped** or (*Poetic*) **stopt, stop·ping,** *n.* —*v.* **1** keep from moving, acting, doing, being, etc.: *stop a clock, stop a speaker.* **2** cut off; withhold: *stop supplies.* **3** put an end to; interrupt; check: *stop a noise.* **4** stay; halt: *stop at a hotel.* **5** leave off moving, acting, doing, being, etc.; cease: *All work stopped.* **6** close by filling; fill holes in; close: *stop a hole, a leak, a wound.* **7** close (a vessel) with a cork, plug, or the like; shut up (something) in a closed vessel or place: *stop a bottle.* **8** block; obstruct: *A fallen tree stopped traffic.* **9** check (a blow, stroke, etc.); parry; ward off. **10** defeat by a knockout. **11** in games, defeat. **12** punctuate. **13** in music: **a** close (a finger hole, etc.) in order to produce a particular note from a wind instrument. **b** press down (a string of a violin, etc.) in order to alter the pitch of tone produced. **14** instruct a bank not to honor (a cheque, bill, etc.) when presented. **15 stop off,** *Informal.* stop for a short stay. **16 stop over, a** make a short stay. **b** *Informal.* stop in the course of a trip.
—*n.* **1** the act of stopping; a closing; a filling up; a blocking; a hindering, a checking, a halting, cessation, stay, etc. **2** a being stopped. **3** the place where a stop is made. **4** anything that stops; obstacle. **5** any piece or device that serves to check or control movement or action in a mechanism. **6 a** a punctuation mark that normally indicates some kind of pause, as a comma or semicolon. **b** a full stop; period. **7** a word used in telegrams, cables, etc. instead of a period. **8** in music: **a** the closing of a finger hole or aperture in the tube of a wind instrument, or the act of pressing with the finger on a string of a violin, etc. so as to alter the pitch of its tone. **b** a key or other device used for this purpose. **c** in organs, a graduated set of pipes of the same kind, or the knob or handle that controls them. **9** in photography, the aperture of a lens, or the f number indicating this: *The next stop smaller than f/3.5 is f/2.* **10** in phonetics: **a** a sudden, complete stopping of the breath stream, usually followed by its sudden release. **b** a consonant that involves such a stopping; a plosive. *Examples:* (p), (t), (k), (b), (d), and (g) as in *go.* **11 pull out all the stops,** do something in the biggest way possible; exert maximum effort. **12 put a stop to,** stop; end. [OE *stoppian,* ult. < L *stuppa* tow < Gk. *styppē*]
Syn. *v.* **1 Stop, arrest, check** = keep someone or something from continuing an action, movement, progress, etc. **Stop** is the general word, and means "bring advance or movement to an end": *He stopped the car.* **Arrest** emphasizes stopping and holding firmly back progress, development, or action that is already advancing: *Jonathan's tuberculosis was arrested early.* **Check** = stop or arrest suddenly, sharply, or with force, sometimes only temporarily: *An awning over the sidewalk checked his fall and saved his life.* **2** discontinue, intermit. **3** hinder, deter, impede, prevent, suspend. **5 Stop, cease, pause** = leave off. **Stop,** the general word, means "leave off," particularly doing, acting, moving, or going ahead: *The train stopped. He stopped breathing.* **Cease** is more formal and literary, but means "come to an end," and therefore is used of things that are existing or lasting, or to emphasize that action or movement has stopped permanently: *All life has ceased. He has ceased to breathe.* **Pause** = stop for a time, but suggests going on again: *He paused to tie his shoe.*

stop·cock (stop′kok′) *n.* a device for turning the flow of a liquid or gas on or off; valve; tap.

stope (stōp) *n. v.* **stoped, stop·ing.** —*n.* an excavation in a mine to take out ore after shafts have been sunk. —*v.* mine in stopes. [probably related to STEP, n.]

stop·gap (stop′gap′) *n.* anything that fills the place of something lacking; a temporary substitute. —*adj.* serving as a stopgap.

stop·light (stop′līt′) *n.* **1** a traffic light or signal. **2** a red light in the rear of a vehicle that comes on when the brakes are applied.

stop·log (stop′log′) *n.* a block of wood or concrete used to control an outlet in a dam.

stop·off (stop′of′) *n. Informal.* stopover.

stop order an order to a broker to buy or sell commodities, stocks, etc. whenever the market reaches a set price.

stop·o·ver (stop′ō′vər) *n.* a stopping over in the course of a journey, especially with the privilege of proceeding later on the ticket originally issued for the journey.

stop·page (stop′ij) *n.* **1** a stopping. **2** a being stopped. **3** a block; obstruction.

stop·per (stop′ər) *n.* **1** a plug or cork for closing a bottle, tube, etc. **2** a person or thing that stops. —*v.* close or fit with a stopper.

stop·ple (stop′əl) *n. v.* **-pled, -pling.** —*n.* a stopper for a bottle, etc. —*v.* close or fit with a stopper. [? < *stop*]

stop street a side street from which vehicles may not enter a main street without first stopping.

stopt (stopt) *v. Poetic.* a pt. and a pp. of **stop.**

stop watch a watch having a hand that can be stopped or started at any instant. Since a stop watch indicates fractions of a second, it is useful for timing races, contests, etc.

stor·age (stôr′ij) *n.* **1** the act or fact of storing goods. **2** the condition of being stored. **Cold storage** is used to keep eggs and meat from spoiling. **3** a place for storing: *She has put her furniture in storage.* **4** the cost of storing. **5** the production by electric energy of chemical reactions that can be reversed to produce electricity, especially that occurring in and exemplified by the charging of a storage battery.

storage battery a connected group of electrolytic cells for the production of electrical energy. It may be recharged by passing a current through it in the reverse direction.

store (stôr) *n. v.* **stored, stor·ing.** —*n.* **1** a place where goods are kept for sale. **2** a thing or things laid up for use; supply; stock. **3** *Esp.Brit.* a place where supplies are kept for future use; storehouse. **4** *Archaic.* quantity; abundance: *We wish them store of happy days.* **5 in store,** on hand; in reserve; saved for the future. **6 set store by,** value; esteem. [ME < *astore* < OF *estore* < *estorer.* See STORE, v.]
—*v.* **1** supply or stock. **2** put away for future use; lay up.

3 put in a warehouse or place used for preserving. [ME < OF *estorer* construct, restore, store < L *instaurare* restore, originally, establish < *in* upon + **staurus* pillar] **—stor′er,** *n.*

store·house (stôr′hous′) *n.* **1** a place where things are stored: *This factory has many storehouses for its products.* **2** any person or thing viewed as resembling this: *A library is a storehouse of information.*

store·keep·er (stôr′kēp′ər) *n.* a person who has charge of a store or stores.

store·room (stôr′rüm′ or -rům′) *n.* a room where things are stored.

sto·rey or **sto·ry** (stô′rē) *n.* **-reys** or **-ries. 1** a level or floor of a house or other building. **2** the set of rooms or apartments on one level or floor. [? ult. special use of *story* in sense of "row of historical statues across a building front"]

sto·reyed or **sto·ried** (stô′rēd) *adj.* having a stated number of storeys or floors: *a two-storeyed house.*

sto·ried (stô′rēd) *adj.* **1** celebrated in story or history: *the storied Klondike.* **2** ornamented with designs representing happenings in history or legend: *storied tapestry.* [< *story*[1]]

stork (stôrk) *n.* a large, long-legged wading bird having a long neck and a long bill. [OE *storc*] **—stork′like′,** *adj.*

storm (stôrm) *n.* **1** a strong wind with rain, snow, hail, or thunder and lightning. **2** a sandstorm. **3** a heavy fall of rain, snow, or hail; violent outbreak of thunder and lightning. **4** anything like a storm: *a storm of arrows.* **5** a violent outburst or disturbance: *a storm of tears, a storm of angry words.* **6** a violent attack: *The castle was taken by storm.* **7** a storm window or storm door.
—*v.* **1** blow hard; rain; snow; hail. **2** be violent; rage. **3** speak loudly and angrily. **4** rush violently: *storm out of the room.* **5** attack violently: *The troops stormed the city.* [OE]

storm cellar a cellar for shelter during cyclones, tornadoes, etc.

storm centre or **center 1** a centre of a cyclone; the area in a cyclone where the pressure is lowest. **2** any centre of trouble, tumult, etc.

storm door an extra door (outside an ordinary door) to keep out snow, cold winds, etc.

storm trooper a member of the Nazi private army formed by Adolf Hitler around 1923 and disbanded in 1934.

storm window an extra window (outside an ordinary window) to keep out snow, cold winds, etc.

storm·y (stôr′mē) *adj.* **storm·i·er, storm·i·est. 1** having storms; likely to have storms; troubled by storms. **2** rough and disturbed; violent: *They had stormy quarrels.* **—storm′i·ly,** *adv.* **—storm′i·ness,** *n.* **—Syn. 1** tempestuous, blustery, windy. **2** wild.

stormy petrel 1 any of several small, black-and-white sea birds called petrels, whose presence is supposed to give warning of a storm. **2** anyone believed likely to cause trouble or to indicate trouble.

Stor·thing or **Stor·ting** (stôr′ting′) *n.* the national parliament of Norway. [< Norwegian *storting*, earlier *storthing* < *stor* great + *thing* assembly]

sto·ry[1] (stô′rē) *n.* **-ries,** *v.* **-ried, -ry·ing.** —*n.* **1** an account of some happening or group of happenings: *Tell us the story of your life.* **2** such an account, either true or made-up, intended to interest the reader or hearer; tale. **3** *Informal.* a falsehood. **4** stories as a branch of literature: *a character famous in story.* **5** the plot of a play, novel, etc. **6** a newspaper article, or material for such an article. **7** *Archaic.* history: *well-read in story.*
—*v. Archaic.* tell the history or story of. [ME < AF *estorie* < L < Gk. *historia* history. Doublet of HISTORY.] **—sto′ry·less,** *adj.*

Syn. *n.* **1** relation, narrative, recital, record, chronicle. **2 Story, anecdote, tale** = a spoken or written account of some happening or happenings. **Story** applies to any such account, true or made-up, long or short, in prose or verse, intended to interest another: *I like stories about science.* **Anecdote** applies to a brief story about a single actual incident, usually funny or with an interesting point, often in the life of a famous person: *He knows many anecdotes about life at sea.* **Tale** applies to a longer story told as if giving true facts about some happening or situation but usually made-up or exaggerated: *He reads tales of frontier days.* **3 fib, lie.**

sto·ry[2] (stô′rē) *n.* **-ries.** storey.

hat, āge, cãre, fär; let, ēqual, tėrm; it, īce
hot, ōpen, ôrder; oil, out; cup, pů̇t, rüle, ūse
əbove, takən, pencəl, lemən, circəs
ch, child; ng, long; sh, ship
th, thin; ᴛʜ, then; zh, measure

sto·ry·tell·er (stô′rē tel′ər) *n.* **1** a person who tells stories. **2** *Informal.* a person who tells falsehoods; liar.

sto·ry·tell·ing (stô′rē tel′ing) *n. adj. Informal.* **1** telling stories. **2** telling falsehoods; lying.

sto·tin·ka (stō ting′kə) *n.* **-ki** (-kē). **1** a unit of money in Bulgaria, worth 1/100 of a lev. **2** a coin worth one stotinka. [< Bulgarian]

stoup (stüp) *n.* **1** a drinking vessel of varying size, such as a cup, flagon, or tankard. **2** the amount it holds. **3** a basin for holy water at the entrance of a church. [< ON *staup*]

stout (stout) *adj.* **1** fat and large: *a stout body.* **2** strongly built; firm; strong: *The fort has stout walls.* **3** brave; bold: *He has a stout heart.* **4** not yielding; stubborn: *stout resistance.* **5** characterized by endurance or staying power: *a stout horse, a stout engine.*
—*n.* **1** a strong, dark-brown beer. **2** a stout person. [ME < OF *estout* strong < Gmc. root *stolt-* proud < L *stultus* foolish] **—stout′ly,** *adv.* **—stout′ness,** *n.* **—Syn.** *adj.* **1** stocky, plump, portly. See **fat. 2** durable, tough, sturdy, hardy. **3** valiant. **4** determined, resolute.

stout-heart·ed (stout′här′tid) *adj.* brave; bold; courageous. **—stout′-heart′ed·ly,** *adv.* **—stout′-heart′ed·ness,** *n.*

stove[1] (stōv) *n.* **1** an apparatus for cooking and heating. There are wood, coal, gas, oil, and electric stoves. **2** a heated room or box for some special purpose. A hothouse for plants is sometimes called a stove. [OE *stofa* warm bathing room < VL *stufa* < *extufare* sweat out, ult. < L ex- out + Gk. *typhos* vapor. Related to STEW.]

stove[2] (stōv) *v.* a pt. and a pp. of **stave.** See **stave** for usage note.

stove·pipe (stōv′pīp′) *n.* **1** a pipe of sheet metal serving as the chimney of a stove or to connect a stove with the chimney flue. **2** *Informal.* a tall silk hat.

stow (stō) *v.* **1** pack: *The cargo was stowed in the ship's hold.* **2** pack things closely in; fill by packing: *They stowed the little cabin with supplies for the trip.* **3 stow away,** hide on a ship, airplane, etc. in order to avoid paying the fare or to make an escape. **4** *Slang.* stop. [ult. < OE *stōw* place] **—stow′er,** *n.*

stow·age (stō′ij) *n.* **1** the act of stowing. **2** the state or manner of being stowed. **3** a room for stowing; a place for stowing. **4** what is stowed. **5** the charge for stowing something.

stow·a·way (stō′ə wā′) *n.* a person who hides on a ship, airplane, etc. in order to avoid paying his passage or to make an escape.

str. 1 steamer. **2** strait.

stra·bis·mal (strə biz′məl) *adj.* strabismic.

stra·bis·mic (strə biz′mik) *adj.* **1** cross-eyed. **2** of or having to do with strabismus.

stra·bis·mus (strə biz′məs) *n.* a disorder of vision due to the turning of one eye or both eyes from the normal position so that both cannot be directed at the same point or object at the same time; squint; cross-eye. [< NL < Gk. *strabismos*, ult. < *strabos* squint-eyed]

strad·dle (strad′əl) *v.* **-dled, -dling,** *n.* —*v.* **1** walk, stand, or sit with the legs wide apart. **2** spread (the legs) wide apart. **3** have a leg on each side of (a horse, bicycle, chair, ditch, etc.). **4** stand or lie across; be on both sides of: *A pair of sunglasses straddled his nose.* **5** *Informal.* avoid taking sides. **6** *Informal.* attempt to favor both sides of (a question, etc.). —*n.* **1** a straddling. **2** the distance straddled. [< var. of dial. *striddle*, frequentative of *stride*] **—strad′dler,** *n.*

Strad·i·var·i·us (strad′ə vãr′ē əs) *n.* a violin, viola, or cello made by Antonio Stradivari, 1644-1737, a violin-maker of Cremona, Italy. These instruments are famous for their exquisite tone.

strafe (strāf or straf) *v.* **strafed, straf·ing. 1** of aircraft, machine-gun and bomb enemy ground positions at close range. 2 shell or bombard heavily. [from a German slogan of World War I, *Gott strafe England!* May God punish England!] —**straf′er,** *n.*

strag·gle (strag′əl) *v.* **-gled, -gling. 1** wander in a scattered fashion: *Cows straggled along the lane.* **2** stray from the rest. **3** spread in an irregular, rambling manner: *Vines straggled over the yard.* [? related to STRETCH] —**strag′gler,** *n.*

strag·gly (strag′lē) *adj.* spread out in an irregular, rambling way; straggling.

straight (strāt) *adj.* **1** without a bend or curve; direct: *a straight line, a straight path.* **2 a** frank; honest; upright: *straight conduct.* **b** right; correct: *straight thinking.* **3** in proper order or condition: *Keep your accounts straight.* **4** continuous: *in straight succession.* **5** thoroughgoing or unreserved: *a straight Tory.* **6** unmodified; undiluted: *a straight comedy, straight whisky.* **7** *Informal.* reliable: *a straight tip.* **8** in poker, made up of a sequence of five cards: *a straight flush.* **9** serious rather than comic; natural rather than eccentric: *a straight part in a play.* **10** *Slang.* conventional; conforming to normal styles of behavior, dress, etc.
—*adv.* **1** in a line; directly: *Walk straight.* **2** in an erect position; upright: *Stand up straight.* **3** frankly; honestly; uprightly: *Live straight.* **4** continuously: *Drive straight on.* **5** without delay. **6** without qualification of any kind. **7 straight away** or **off,** at once.
—*n.* **1** the condition of being straight; straight form, position, or line. **2** a straight part, as of a racecourse. **3** in poker, a sequence of five cards. [OE *streht,* pp. of *streccan* stretch] —**straight′ly,** *adv.* —**straight′ness,** *n.*
—**Syn.** *adj.* **1** undeviating, unswerving. **2** honorable.

straight angle an angle of 180°.

straight-arm (strāt′ärm′) in football: —*v.* prevent (an opponent) from making a tackle by holding one's arm straight in front. —*n.* the act of straight-arming.

straight·a·way (strāt′ə wā′) *n.* a straight course. —*adj.* in a straight course. —*adv.* as quickly as possible; at once; immediately.

straight·edge (strāt′ej′) *n.* a strip of wood or metal having one edge accurately straight, used in obtaining or testing straight lines and level surfaces.

straight·en (strāt′ən) *v.* **1** make straight: *Straighten your shoulders.* **2** become straight. **3** put in the proper order or condition: *Straighten up your room. We must straighten out our accounts and see how much we owe each other.* **4** *Informal.* mend one's ways; reform. —**straight′en·er,** *n.*

straight flush in poker, a sequence of five cards of the same suit, ranking higher than four of a kind.

straight·for·ward (strāt′fôr′wərd) *adj.* **1** honest; frank. **2** going straight ahead; direct. —*adv.* directly. —**straight′for′ward·ly,** *adv.* —**straight′for′ward·ness,** *n.*

straight·for·wards (strāt′fôr′wərdz) *adv.* straightforward.

straight-out (strāt′out′) *adj. Informal.* out-and-out; complete; thorough.

straight·way (strāt′wā′) *adv.* at once; immediately; straightaway.

strain[1] (strān) *v.* **1** draw tight; stretch: *The weight strained the rope.* **2** pull hard: *The dog strained at his leash.* **3** stretch as much as possible: *She strained the truth in telling the story.* **4** use to the utmost: *She strained her eyes to see.* **5** injure by too much effort or by stretching: *The runner strained his heart.* **6** be injured by too much effort. **7** make a very great effort. **8** press or pour through a strainer. **9** drip through. **10** press closely; squeeze; hug.
—*n.* **1** a force or weight that stretches. **2 a** too much muscular or physical effort. **b** an injury caused by too much effort or by stretching. **3** any severe, trying, or wearing pressure: *the strain of worry.* **4** its effect on the body or mind. **5** Often, **strains,** *pl.* a part of a piece of music; melody; song. **6** a manner or style of doing or speaking. [ME < OF < L *stringere* draw tight] —**Syn.** *v.* **2** tug. **5** wrench, sprain. **9** percolate, filter.

strain[2] (strān) *n.* **1** a line of descent; race; stock; breed: *The Irish strain in him explains his sense of humor.* **2** a group of animals or plants that form a part of a breed, race, or variety. **3** an inherited quality: *There is a strain of madness in that family.* **4** a trace or streak: *That horse has a mean strain.* [var. of OE *strēon* gain, begetting]

strained (strānd) *adj.* forced; not natural: *Her greeting was cold and strained.*

strain·er (strān′ər) *n.* **1** a utensil or device for straining, filtering, or sifting: *A filter, a sieve, and a colander are strainers.* **2** a device for stretching or tightening.

strait (strāt) *n.* **1** a narrow channel connecting two larger bodies of water. **2 straits,** *pl.* difficulty; need; distress.
—*adj. Archaic.* **1** narrow; limited; confining. **2** strict: *The nun took strait vows.* [ME < OF *estreit* < L *strictus* drawn tight. Doublet of STRICT.] —**strait′ly,** *adv.* —**strait′ness,** *n.* —**Syn.** *n.* **2** crisis, emergency, plight.

strait·en (strāt′ən) *v.* **1** limited by the lack of something; restrict. **2** make narrow. **3** *Archaic.* confine; confine within narrow limits. **4 in straitened circumstances,** needing money badly.

strait jacket 1 a strong coat that holds the arms close to the sides, used to keep a violent person from harming himself or others. **2** anything that restrains.

strait-laced (strāt′lāst′) *adj.* very strict in matters of conduct; prudish.

strake (strāk) *n.* a single breadth of planks or metal plates along the side of a ship from the bow to the stern. [related to *stretch*; influenced by *streak*]

stra·mo·ni·um (strə mō′nē əm) *n.* **1** jimson weed. **2** a drug made from its dried leaves. [< NL]

strand[1] (strand) *v.* **1** run aground; drive on the shore: *The ship was stranded on the rocks.* **2** bring or come into a helpless position. [< n.] —*n. Poetic.* a shore; land bordering a sea, lake, or river. [OE]

strand[2] (strand) *n.* **1** one of the threads, strings, or wires that are twisted together to make a rope or cable: *This is a rope of three strands.* **2** a fibre, hair, etc. **3** a string of beads, pearls, etc. [ME < OF *estran* < Gmc.]

strange (strānj) *adj.* **strang·er, strang·est. 1** unusual; queer; peculiar: *a strange accident.* **2** not known, seen, or heard of before; unfamiliar: *strange faces, a strange language.* **3** unaccustomed (*to*); inexperienced (at): *strange to a job.* **4** out of place; not at home: *The poor child felt strange in the palace.* **5** unfamiliar to: *The city was strange to the newcomer.* **6** *Archaic.* foreign; alien. [ME < OF *estrange* < L *extraneus* foreign. Doublet of EXTRANEOUS.] —**strange′ly,** *adv.* —**strange′ness,** *n.*
Syn. *adj.* **1 Strange, odd, peculiar** = unusual or out of the ordinary. **Strange** always suggests the idea of something unfamiliar and outside the usual, ordinary, expected, or natural order: *A strange quiet pervaded the city.* **Odd** suggests a strangeness that is puzzling, or a quality different from the normal or regular: *That is an odd color.* **Peculiar** particularly suggests a quality or character so individual as to be uncommon and seem strange or odd: *Raising frogs is a peculiar way to make a living.* **2** foreign, alien, new, novel.

stran·ger (strān′jər) *n.* **1** a person not known, seen, or heard of before. **2** a person or thing new to a place. **3** a person who is out of place or not at home in something. **4** a visitor; guest. **5** a person from another country.

stran·gle (strang′gəl) *v.* **-gled, -gling. 1** kill by squeezing the throat to stop the breath: *The infant Hercules strangled a snake with each hand.* **2** suffocate; choke: *His high collar seemed to be strangling him.* **3** choke down; suppress; keep back. [ME < OF *estrangler* < L *strangulare* < Gk. *strangalaein,* ult. < *strangos* twisted. Doublet of STRANGULATE.] —**stran′gler,** *n.* —**Syn.** **2** throttle, stifle.

strangle hold 1 in wrestling, a hold for stopping an opponent's breath. **2** anything that suppresses or hinders free movement, development, etc.

stran·gu·late (strang′gyů lāt′) *v.* **-lat·ed, -lat·ing. 1** in medicine, become compressed or constricted so as to stop circulation. **2** strangle; choke. [< L *strangulare.* Doublet of STRANGLE.]

stran·gu·la·tion (strang′gyů lā′shən) *n.* **1** the act of strangling or the state of being strangled. **2** the state of strangulating or being strangulated.

strap (strap) *n. v.* **strapped, strap·ping.** —*n.* **1** a narrow strip of leather or other material that bends easily. **2** a narrow band or strip of cloth: *The general wore shoulder straps.* **3** a narrow strip for fastening things, holding things together, etc.: *The box was strengthened by straps* *of steel.* **4** a narrow strip of leather to sharpen razors on; strop. **5** a looped band suspended from an overhead bar in a bus, train, etc. for standing passengers to hold on to. —*v.* **1** fasten with a strap. **2** beat with a strap. **3** sharpen on a strap or strop. **4** dress and bandage. [var. of *strop*]

strap·hang·er (strap′hang′ər) *n. Informal.* a passenger in a streetcar, train, etc. who cannot get a seat and stands holding on to a strap.

strap·less (strap′lis′) *adj.* having no shoulder straps; not worn with straps: *a strapless evening gown.*

strapped (strapt) *adj.* **1** made or fastened with a strap or straps. **2** *Informal.* without money; short of ready cash. **3** seamed or finished with bands or strips of cloth.

strap·per (strap′ər) *n.* **1** a person or thing that straps. **2** *Informal.* a tall, robust person.

strap·ping (strap′ing) *adj. Informal.* tall, strong, and healthy: *a fine, strapping girl.* —*n.* a beating with a strap as punishment.

stra·ta (strā′tə or strat′ə) *n.* pl. of **stratum.**

strat·a·gem (strat′ə jəm) *n.* a scheme or trick for deceiving the enemy; trick; act of trickery. [< F < L < Gk. *stratēgēma,* ult. < *stratēgos* general. See STRATEGY.]

Syn. Stratagem, artifice, ruse = a scheme or device to trick or mislead others. **Stratagem** applies to a plan to gain one's own ends or defeat those of others by skilful deception: *The general planned a stratagem to trap the enemy.* **Artifice** applies to a clever trick or device, sometimes mechanical, to gain one's ends by misleading, and usually deceiving, others: *Motion pictures often employ artifices to get realistic effects.* **Ruse** applies to a trick or device to gain one's ends indirectly by deceiving others about one's real purpose: *Her headache was a ruse to leave early.*

stra·te·gic (strə tē′jik) *adj.* **1** of strategy; based on strategy; useful in strategy. **2** important in strategy: *The air force is a strategic link in our national defence.* **3** having to do with raw material necessary for warfare that must be obtained, at least partially, from an outside country. **4** specially trained or made for destroying enemy bases, industry, or communications behind the lines of battle.

stra·te·gi·cal (strə tē′jə kəl) *adj.* strategic. —**stra·te′gi·cal·ly,** *adv.*

stra·te·gics (strə tē′jiks) *n.* strategy.

strat·e·gist (strat′ə jist) *n.* a person trained or skilled in strategy.

strat·e·gy (strat′ə jē) *n.* **-gies. 1** the science or art of war; overall planning and directing of military campaigns. **2** the skilful planning and management of anything. **3** a plan of campaign. [< Gk. *stratēgia* < *stratēgos* general < *stratos* army + *agein* lead]

strath (strath) *n. Scottish.* a wide valley. [< Scots Gaelic *srath*]

strath·spey (strath′spā′ or strath′spā′) *n.* **1** a lively Scottish dance resembling a slow reel. **2** the music for this dance. [< *Strath Spey,* a district in Scotland]

strat·i·fi·ca·tion (strat′ə fə kā′shən) *n.* **1** an arrangement in layers or strata. **2** in geology: **a** the formation of strata; deposition or occurrence in strata. **b** stratum.

strat·i·fy (strat′ə fī′) *v.* **-fied, -fy·ing. 1** arrange in layers or strata; form into layers or strata. **2** in geology, deposit (sediment, etc.) in strata; form strata in. [< Med.L *stratificare* < L *stratum* (see STRATUM) + *facere* make]

stra·tig·ra·pher (strə tig′rə fər) *n.* an expert in stratigraphy.

stra·tig·ra·phy (strə tig′rə fē) *n.* **1** the branch of geology that deals with the origin, composition, and arrangement of the strata of a region, country, etc. **2** the order and arrangement of strata. [< *stratum* covering, layer + E *-graphy*]

stra·to·cu·mu·lus (strā′tō kū′myů ləs or strat′ō kū′myů ləs) *n.* cloud made up of large, dark, rounded heaps above a flat, horizontal base. [< L *stratus* a spreading out + E *cumulus*]

strat·o·sphere (strat′ə sfēr′) *n.* the upper region of the atmosphere, which begins about seven miles above the earth. In this stratosphere, temperature varies little with changes in altitude, and the winds are chiefly horizontal. [< L *stratus* a spreading out + E *sphere*]

strat·o·spher·ic (strat′ə sfer′ik) *adj.* of or having to do with the stratosphere.

hat, āge, cãre, fär; let, ēqual, tėrm; it, īce
hot, ōpen, ôrder; oil, out; cup, pů t, rüle, ūse
əbove, takən, pencəl, lemən, circəs
ch, child; ng, long; sh, ship
th, thin; ᴛʜ, then; zh, measure

strat·o·vi·sion (strat′ə vizh′ən) *n.* a method of using aircraft in the stratosphere to transmit telecasts. [< *strato-* (*sphere*) + (*tele*)*vision*]

stra·tum (strā′təm or stra′təm) *n.* **stra·ta** or **stra·tums. 1** a layer of material, especially one of several parallel layers placed one upon another: *In digging the well, the men struck first a stratum of sand, then several strata of rock.* **2** in geology, a bed of sedimentary rock, usually consisting of a series of layers of the same kind, representing continuous periods of deposition. **3** a level of society; a group having about the same education, culture, development, etc.: *Tramps are from the lowest stratum of society.* **4** in biology, a layer of tissue; lamella. [< NL < L *stratum,* neut. pp. of *sternere* spread out]

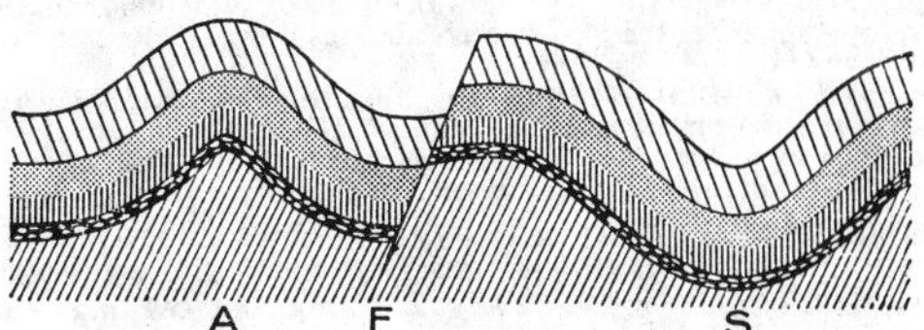

Rock strata: A, anticline; F, fault; S, syncline.

stra·tus (strā′təs or strat′əs) *n.* **-ti** (-tī or -tē) a low, horizontal layer of gray cloud that spreads over a large area. [< L *stratus* a spreading out < *sternere* spread]

straw (stro or strô) *n.* **1** the stalks or stems of grain after drying and threshing. Straw is used for bedding for horses and cows, for making hats, and for many other purposes. **2** a hollow stem or stalk. **3** a slender tube made of waxed paper, plastic, etc. and used for sucking up drinks. **4** a bit; trifle: *He doesn't care a straw.* **5 catch at a straw,** try anything in desperation. **6 straw in the wind,** something taken as an indication of a trend. —*adj.* **1** made of straw. **2** pale-yellow; straw-colored. **3** of little value or consequence; worthless. [OE *strēaw*]

straw·ber·ry (stro′ber′ē or strô′-) *n.* **-ries. 1** a small, juicy, red, edible fruit. The strawberry is covered with tiny, yellow, seedlike achenes. **2** the plant that it grows on. **3** a flavoring made from strawberry.

straw·board (stro′bôrd′ or strô′-) *n.* coarse cardboard made of straw, used for boxes, packing, etc.

straw-hat (stro′hat′ or strô′-) *n.* of or concerning plays, musical shows, etc. performed in resort and suburban areas during the summer. [from the wearing of straw hats in summer]

straw man 1 a weak or imaginary opponent or opposing argument set up only to be defeated. **2** a puppet. **3** a false witness.

straw vote an unofficial vote taken to find out general opinion.

straw·y (stro′ē or strô′ē) *adj.* **1** of, containing, or resembling straw. **2** strewed or thatched with straw.

stray (strā) *v.* **1** lose one's way; wander; roam: *Our dog has strayed somewhere.* **2** turn from the right course; go wrong. —*adj.* **1** wandering; lost. **2** scattered; here and there: *There were a few stray fishermen's huts along the beach.* **3** isolated: *a stray copy of a book.* —*n.* **1** any person or thing that is lost; a wanderer; lost animal. **2 strays,** *pl.* in radio, static. [ME < OF *estraier,* originally adj. < VL *stratarius* roaming the streets < LL (*via*) *strata.* See STREET.] —**stray′er,** *n.* —**Syn.** *v.* **1** rove, straggle. See **wander. 2** deviate.

streak (strēk) *n.* **1** a long, thin mark or line: *He has a streak of dirt on his face. We saw a streak of lightning.* **2** layer: *Side bacon has streaks of fat and streaks of lean.* **3** a vein; strain; element: *He has a streak of humor, though he looks very serious.* **4** *Informal.* a brief period; spell: *a streak of luck.* **5 like a streak,** *Informal.* very fast; at full speed. —*v.* **1** put long, thin marks or lines on.

2 become streaked. 3 *Informal.* move very fast; go at full speed. [OE *strica*]

streak·y (strēk′ē) *adj.* **streak·i·er, streak·i·est. 1** marked with streaks. 2 occurring in streaks. 3 varying; uneven: *The dress has faded so much that the color is streaky.* —**streak′i·ly,** *adv.* —**streak′i·ness,** *n.*

stream (strēm) *n.* **1** a flow of water in a channel or bed; a small river; a large brook. **2** a steady current of water, as in a river or in the ocean. **3 a** any current or flow: *a stream of blood pouring from a wound, a stream of tears, a stream of air, gas, or electricity.* **b** a ray or beam: *a stream of light.*
—*v.* **1** flow. **2** move steadily; move swiftly: *Soldiers streamed out of the fort.* **3** pour out: *The wound streamed blood.* **4** cause to stream. **5** be so wet as to drip in a stream: *streaming eyes, a streaming umbrella.* **6** float or wave: *Flags streamed in the wind.* **7** extend in straight lines: *The sunshine streamed across the room.* **8** hang loosely. [OE *strēam*] —**stream′like′,** *adj.*
Syn. *n.* **1 Stream, current** = a flow of liquid or something fluid. **Stream** emphasizes the idea of a continuous flow, as of water in a river or from a spring or tap: *Because of the lack of rain, many streams dried up.* **Current** emphasizes the strong or rapid, onward movement in a certain direction, and applies particularly to the more swiftly moving part of a stream, ocean, body of air, etc.: *He let his boat drift with the current.* –*v.* **1** See **flow.**

stream·er (strēm′ər) *n.* **1** any long, narrow, flowing thing: *Streamers of ribbon hung from her hat. Streamers of light are in the northern sky.* **2** a long, narrow flag. **3** a newspaper headline that runs all the way across the page.

stream·flow (strēm′flō′) *n.* the velocity and volume of water flowing at a given time in a channel or stream.

stream·let (strēm′lit) *n.* a small stream.

stream·line (strēm′līn′) *adj. v.* **-lined, -lin·ing,** *n.* —*adj.* having a shape or body that offers the least possible resistance to air or water. The fastest automobiles, airplanes, and trains have streamline bodies.
—*v.* **1** give a streamline shape to: *streamline an airplane.* **2** bring up to date or make more efficient.
—*n.* **1** a streamlined shape. **2** in physics, the path of a particle in a steadily flowing mass of fluid.

stream of consciousness an individual's mental processes or experiences considered as flowing in an unbroken stream.

street (strēt) *n.* **1** a road in a city or town, usually with buildings on both sides. *Abbrev.:* St. **2** a place or way for automobiles, wagons, etc. to go. **3** people who live in the buildings on a street. **4 the man in the street,** the typical person; the average person. [OE *strǣt* < LL (*via*) *strata* paved (road), pp. of L *sternere* lay out] —**street′like′,** *adj.*

street Arab a homeless child that wanders about the streets.

street·car (strēt′kär′) *n.* a car that runs on rails in the streets and carries passengers.

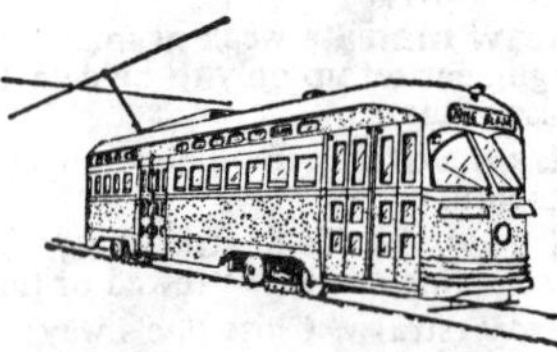

A streetcar

street lamp a lamp that lights a street.

street·walk·er (strēt′wok′ər or -wôk′ər) *n.* a prostitute.

strength (strength) *n.* **1** the quality of being strong; power; force; vigor: *Samson was a man of great strength.* **2** mental or moral power: *strength of memory or of judgment, have strength of character.* **3** the power to resist or endure: *the strength of a fort.* **4** a number of soldiers, warships, etc.; quota. **5** power derived from authority, the law, influence, the possession of resources, etc.: *the strength of public opinion, the strength of a leader.* **6** power or capacity for producing effects; cogency or potency; weight: *the strength of words, arguments, or evidence.* **7** a degree of strength; intensity: *the strength of a beverage, the strength of a sound.* **8** something that makes strong; support: "*God is our refuge and strength.*" **9** the existence of a firm or rising level of stock or commodity prices on an exchange, etc. **10 on the strength of,** relying or depending on; with the support or help of. [OE *strengthu* < *strang* strong] —**Syn. 1** See **power.**

strength·en (streng′thən) *v.* **1** make stronger. **2** grow stronger. —**strength′en·er,** *n.*

stren·u·ous (stren′ū əs) *adj.* **1** very active: *We had a strenuous day moving into our new house.* **2** full of energy: *a strenuous worker.* [< L *strenuus*] —**stren′u·ous·ly,** *adv.* —**stren′u·ous·ness,** *n.* —**Syn. 1, 2** See **vigorous.**

strep (strep) *n. Informal.* streptococcus.

strep·to·coc·cic (strep′tə kok′sik) *adj.* having to do with or caused by streptococci.

strep·to·coc·cus (strep′tə kok′əs) *n.* **-coc·ci** (-kok′sī or -kok′sē). any of a group of spherical bacteria that multiply by dividing in only one direction, usually forming chains. Many serious infections and diseases are caused by streptococci. [< NL < Gk. *streptos* curved + *kokkos* grain]

strep·to·my·cin (strep′tō mī′sən) *n.* a powerful antibiotic drug similar to penicillin, effective against tuberculosis, typhoid fever, and certain other bacterial infections. *Formula:* $C_{21}H_{39}N_7O_{12}$ [< Gk. *streptos* curved + *mykēs* fungus]

stress (stres) *n.* **1** pressure; force; strain: *Under the stress of hunger, the man stole some food.* **2** great effort. **3** emphasis; importance: *That school lays stress upon arithmetic and reading.* **4** in physics: **a** the internal forces interacting between contiguous parts of a body, caused by the external forces, such as tension or shear, which produce the strain. **b** the intensity of these forces, generally measured in pounds per square inch. **c** a force or system of forces causing strain. **5** the degree of force or loudness with which words and syllables in words may be uttered. **6** a mark (′) written or printed to show the degree of force or emphasis on a syllable when spoken, as in *yes′ ter day, to day′,* and *to mor′ row.* Many words have two stresses, a main stress (′) and a secondary or lesser stress (′) as in *ac′a dem′ ic.* **7** in prosody: **a** the relative loudness or prominence given a syllable or word in a metrical pattern. **b** any accented syllable in a foot. **8** in music, an accent.
—*v.* **1** put pressure upon. **2** treat as important; emphasize. **3** pronounce with stress. **4** mark with a stress. [partly < *distress,* partly < OF *estrece* narrowness, oppression, ult. < L *strictus,* pp. of *stringere* draw tight] —**Syn.** *n.* **3** significance, weight.

stretch (strech) *v.* **1** draw out; extend to full length: *The blow stretched him out on the ground.* **2** continue over a distance; extend from one place to another; fill space; spread: *The forest stretches for miles. We stretched a wire across the path.* **3** extend one's body or limbs. **4** straighten out. **5** reach out; hold out: *He stretched out his hand for the money.* **6** draw out to greater length or width: *Stretch the shoe a little.* **7** become longer or wider without breaking: *Rubber stretches.* **8** draw tight; strain: *He stretched the violin string until it broke.* **9** make great effort. **10** extend beyond proper limits: *He stretched the law to suit his purpose.* **11** *Informal.* exaggerate: *stretch the truth.*
—*n.* **1** an extent of something in space: *A stretch of sand hills lay between the road and the ocean.* **2** a continuous length of time. **3** *Slang.* a term of imprisonment. **4** in racing, one of the two straight sides of a course, especially the part between the last turn and the finish line. **5** the action of stretching or the state of being stretched. [OE *streccan*]

stretch·er (strech′ər) *n.* **1** a person or thing that stretches: *A glove stretcher makes gloves larger.* **2** a piece of canvas stretched on a frame for carrying the sick, wounded, or dead.

strew (strü) *v.* **strewed, strewn** or **strewed, strew·ing. 1** scatter; sprinkle: *She strewed seeds in her garden.* **2** cover with something scattered or sprinkled. **3** be scattered over; be sprinkled over. [OE *strēowian*]

strewn (strün) *n.* pp. of **strew.**

stri·a (strī′ə) *n.* **-ae** (-ē or -ī). **1** a slight furrow or ridge. **2** a linear marking; a narrow stripe or streak, as of color or texture, especially one of a number in parallel arrangement. **3** in architecture, a fillet between the flutes of columns, etc. [< L]

stri·at·ed (strī′āt id) *adj.* striped; streaked; furrowed. [< L *striatus,* pp. of *striare* furrow, channel < *stria* furrow, channel]

stri·a·tion (strī ā′shən) *n.* **1** a striated condition or appearance. **2** a stria; one of a number of parallel striae.

strick·en (strik′ən) *adj.* **1** affected by (wounds, diseases, trouble, sorrows, etc.): *Help was rushed to the fire-stricken city.* **2 stricken in years,** old. —*v.* a pp. of **strike.**

strict (strikt) *adj.* **1** very careful in following a rule or in making others follow it: *The store manager was strict but not unfair.* **2** harsh; severe: *strict discipline, a strict penalty.* **3** exact; precise; accurate: *He told the strict truth.* **4** perfect; complete; absolute: *tell a secret in strict confidence.* **5** *Archaic.* close; tight. [< L *strictus*, pp. of *stringere* bind tight. Doublet of STRAIT.] —**strict′ly,** *adv.* —**strict′ness,** *n.*

Syn. 1, 2 Strict, rigid, rigorous = severe and unyielding or harsh and stern. **Strict** emphasizes showing or demanding a very careful and close following of a rule, standard, or requirement: *Our supervisor is strict and insists that we follow instructions.* **Rigid** emphasizes being firm and unyielding, not changing or relaxing for anyone or under any conditions: *He maintains a rigid working schedule.* **Rigorous** emphasizes the severity, harshness, or sternness of the demands made, conditions imposed, etc.: *We believe in rigorous enforcement of the laws.*

stric·ture (strik′chər) *n.* **1** an unfavorable criticism; critical remark. **2** in medicine, an unhealthy narrowing of some duct or tube of the body. **3** a binding; a binding restriction. [< L *strictura* < *stringere* bind tight]

strid·den (strid′ən) *v.* pp. of **stride.**

stride (strīd) *v.* **strode, strid·den, strid·ing,** *n.* —*v.* **1** walk with long steps. **2** pass with one long step: *He strode over the brook.* **3** sit or stand with one leg on each side of: *stride a horse.*
—*n.* **1** a long step. **2** the distance covered by a stride. **3 hit one's stride,** reach one's regular speed or normal activity. **4 make great** or **rapid strides,** make great progress; advance rapidly. **5 take in one's stride,** deal with in one's normal activity; do or take without difficulty, hesitation, or special effort. [OE *strīdan*] —**strid′er,** *n.* —**Syn.** *v.* **1** See **walk.**

stri·dence (strī′dəns) *n.* the state or quality of being strident.

stri·den·cy (strī′dən sē) *n.* stridence.

stri·dent (strī′dənt) *adj.* **1** making or having a harsh sound; creaking; grating; shrill. **2** having a harsh voice; rasping; shrill: *a strident person.* [< L *stridens, -entis,* ppr. of *stridere* sound harshly] —**stri′dent·ly,** *adv.*

strid·u·lant (strij′ů lənt) *adj.* stridulating.

strid·u·late (strij′ů lāt′) *v.* **-lat·ed, -lat·ing. 1** produce a shrill, grating sound, as a cricket or katydid does, by rubbing together certain parts of the body. **2** shrill; chirr. [< NL *stridulare* < L *stridulus* producing a harsh or grating sound < *stridere* sound harshly]

strid·u·la·tion (strij′ů lā′shən) *n.* the action or sound of stridulating.

strife (strīf) *n.* **1** the act or fact of quarrelling; fighting. **2** a quarrel; fight. [ME < OF *estrif* < Gmc.] —**Syn. 1** conflict, contention. **2** struggle.

strig·il (strij′əl) *n.* in ancient Greece and Rome, a scraper for the skin, used after physical exercise, a bath, etc. [< L *strigilis*; related to *stringere* draw tight, strip off, scrape]

strike (strīk) *v.* **struck, struck** or **strick·en, strik·ing,** *n.* —*v.* **1** hit; deal a blow to: *strike a person in anger.* **2** deal; give: *strike a blow in self-defence.* **3** make by stamping; printing, etc.: *strike a medal.* **4** set or be set on fire by hitting or rubbing: *strike a match.* **5** impress: *The plan strikes me as silly.* **6** sound; chime: *The clock strikes twelve times at noon.* **7** affect deeply; influence; overcome (by death, disease, suffering, fear, etc.): *They were struck with terror.* **8** attack: *The enemy will strike at dawn.* **9** occur to: *An amusing thought struck her.* **10** find or come upon (ore, oil, water, etc.). **11** stop work to get better pay, shorter hours, etc.: *The coal miners struck.* **12** cross; rub: *Strike out the last word. Strike his name off the list.* **13** take away by a blow; take away: *Strike off his head.* **14** go: *We struck into a gallop. We walked along the road a mile, then struck out across the fields.* **15** assume: *He struck an attitude.* **16** enter or cause to enter; send or take root; fasten or be fastened: *The roots of oaks strike deep.* **17** get by figuring: *Strike an average.* **18** enter upon; make; decide: *The employer and the workmen have struck an agreement.* **19** lower or take down (a sail, flag, tent, etc.). **20** make level; make level with the top edge of a measure. **21** of a snake, etc., wound with fangs or sting. **22** take hold of the bait: *The fish are striking well today.* **23** collide with: *The car struck a fence.* **24** fall on; touch; reach; catch: *The sun struck his eyes.* **25** come across; come upon; find: *strike an amusing book.* **26** remove (a scene) from the stage; remove the scenery, etc. of (a play).

hat, āge, cãre, fär; let, ēqual, tėrm; it, īce
hot, ōpen, ôrder; oil, out; cup, pu̇t, rüle, ūse
əbove, takən, pencəl, lemən, circəs
ch, child; ng, long; sh, ship
th, thin; ᴛʜ, then; zh, measure

strike a balance, find the difference between the credit and debit sides of an account.
strike home, a make an effective thrust or stroke with a weapon or tool. **b** make a strong impression: *The words of warning struck home.*
strike it rich, *Informal.* **a** find rich ore, oil, etc. **b** have a sudden or unexpected great success.
strike off, to take or remove by or as if by a stroke.
strike out, a cross out; rub out. **b** in baseball, fail to hit three times: *The batter struck out.* **c** in baseball, cause to fail to hit three times: *The pitcher struck out six men.* **d** in swimming, use arms and legs to move forward. **e** hit from the shoulder. **f** make a start by personal effort or enterprise.
strike up, a begin: *strike up a friendship.* **b** begin to play, sing, or sound: *strike up a song.*
—*n.* **1** the act or fact of finding rich ore in mining, oil in boring, etc.; sudden success. **2** a general quitting of work in order to force an employer or employers to agree to the workers' demands for higher wages, shorter hours, etc. **3** a striking. **4** in baseball: **a** the failure of the batter to hit a pitched ball. **b** a pitched ball that passes above the plate at a height between the level of the batter's shoulders and that of his knees. **5** in bowling: **a** an upsetting of all the pins with the first ball bowled. **b** the score so made. **6** a number of coins made at one time. **7** a taking hold of the bait. **8** a metal piece in a doorjamb, into which the latch of a lock fits when the door closes. **9** an attack by bombers upon a target. **10 on strike,** having stopped work to get more pay, shorter hours, etc. [OE *strican* rub, stroke] —**Syn.** *v.* **1** smite, beat, buffet, slap.

strike-bound (strīk′bound′) *adj.* immobilized by a labor strike.

strike·break·er (strīk′brāk′ər) *n.* a person who helps to break up a strike of workers by taking a striker's job or by providing others to do so.

strike·break·ing (strīk′brāk′ing) *n.* forceful measures taken to halt a strike.

strike·out (strīk′out′) *n.* in baseball: **1** an out made by a pitcher throwing three strikes against the batter. **2** the act of striking out.

strik·er (strīk′ər) *n.* **1** a person or thing that strikes. **2** a worker who is on strike.

strik·ing (strīk′ing) *adj.* **1** that strikes. **2** engaged in a strike. **3** attracting attention; very noticeable. —**strik′ing·ness,** *n.* —**Syn. 3** remarkable, impressive.

strik·ing·ly (strīk′ing lē) *adv.* in a way that attracts attention.

string (string) *n. v.* **strung, strung** or (*Rare*) **stringed, string·ing.** —*n.* **1** twisted thread; twine; fine cord or rope. **2** a piece of this. **3** such a thread with things on it: *She wore a string of beads around her neck.* **4** a special cord for musical instruments, bows, etc.: *the strings of a violin.* **5 strings,** *pl.* in music: **a** violins, cellos, and other stringed instruments. **b** the section of an orchestra composed of stringed instruments. **6** anything used for tying: *apron strings.* **7** a cordlike part of plants. String beans have little strings in them. **8** a number of things in a line or row: *A string of cars came down the street.* **9** *Informal.* a condition; proviso: *an offer with a string attached to it.* **10 a** the race horses belonging to a particular stable or owner. **b** a group of persons or things under the same ownership or management. **11 have two strings to one's bow,** have more than one way of doing or getting something. **12 on a string,** under control. **13 pull strings, a** direct the actions of others secretly. **b** use secret influence.

—*v.* **1** put on a string: *Please string these beads.* **2** furnish with strings: *He had his tennis racket strung.* **3** tie with string; hang with a string or rope. **4** make tight. **5** make tense or excited. A high-strung person is sensitive and nervous. **6** remove strings from: *String the beans.* **7** form into a string or strings. **8** move in a line or series. **9** arrange in a line or a row. **10** *Slang.* fool; hoax. **11 string along,** *Informal.* **a** fool; hoax. **b** go along; agree (with). **c** believe in or trust completely. **12 string out,** *Informal.* prolong; stretch; extend: *The program was strung out too long.* **13 string up,** *Informal.* hang. [OE *streng*] —**string′less,** *adj.* —**string′like′,** *adj.* —**Syn.** *n.* **8** series, chain.

string bean **1** any of various bean plants, the unripe pod of which is used as a vegetable. **2** the pod of any of these plants.

string bog *Cdn.* a series or chain of small sink holes, as distinguished from a large swamp or bog.

string·course (string′kôrs′) *n.* in architecture, a horizontal band running around a structure, usually raised and decorated.

stringed instrument a musical instrument having strings, such as a violin or cello.

strin·gen·cy (strin′jən sē) *n.* **-cies.** the state or quality of being stringent.

strin·gent (strin′jənt) *adj.* **1** strict; severe: *stringent laws.* **2** lacking ready money; tight: *a stringent market for loans.* **3** convincing; forcible: *stringent arguments.* [< L *stringens, -entis,* ppr. of *stringere* bind tight] —**strin′gent·ly,** *adv.* —**Syn. 1** rigid, rigorous, exacting, binding.

string·er (string′ər) *n.* **1** a person or thing that strings. **2 a** a long, horizontal supporting timber in a building. **b** a stringpiece. **3** a part-time or local correspondent for a newspaper or magazine. **4** a newspaper correspondent paid on the basis of lineage. **5** a member of a team ranked according to ability; person ranked according to ability: *a first-stringer.* **6** a heavy, horizontal timber or girder supporting the ties of a railroad trestle or bridge or the flooring of a wooden bridge. **7** in geology, a narrow vein of a mineral.

string·halt (string′holt′) *n.* a diseased condition of horses that causes jerking of the hind legs in walking. Also, **springhalt.**

string·piece (string′pēs′) *n.* a long, horizontal beam used to strengthen or connect parts of a framework.

string quartet **1** a quartet of performers on stringed instruments. **2** the instruments themselves, usually consisting of two violins, a viola, and a cello. **3** a composition for string quartet.

string tie a short, narrow necktie.

string·y (string′ē) *adj.* **string·i·er, string·i·est. 1** like a string or strings. **2** forming strings: *a stringy syrup.* **3** having tough fibres: *stringy meat.* —**string′i·ness,** *n.*

strip[1] (strip) *v.* **stripped** or (*Rare*) **stript, strip·ping. 1** make bare or naked; undress (a person, thing, etc.). **2** undress. **3** take off the covering of: *The boy stripped the banana by taking off the skin.* **4** remove; tear off; pull off: *strip paper from a wall, strip fruit from a tree.* **5** make bare; clear out; empty: *strip a house of its furniture, strip a forest of its timber.* **6** take away: *The boys stripped the fruit from the trees.* **7** rob: *Thieves stripped the house of everything valuable.* **8** tear off the teeth of (a gear, etc.). **9** break the thread of (a bolt, nut, etc.). **10** milk (a cow) thoroughly. **11 strip of, a** take away from; deprive of. **b** rob of (money, possessions, etc.).
—*n.* a strip tease. [OE *-strīepan,* as in *bestrīepan* plunder] —**Syn. 3** skin, peel. **5** despoil.

strip[2] (strip) *n.* **1** a long, narrow, flat piece (of cloth, paper, bark, etc.). **2** a long, narrow tract of land, territory, forest, etc. **3** a long, narrow runway for airplanes to take off from and land on. **4** a continuous series of pictures, etc. in a newspaper or magazine: *a comic strip.* [probably < MLG *strippe* strap]

strip cropping or **planting** the planting of alternate rows of crops having strong and weak root systems, done along the contours of a slope to lessen soil erosion.

stripe[1] (strīp) *n. v.* **striped, strip·ing.** —*n.* **1** a long, narrow band of different color, material, etc.: *A tiger has stripes.* **2** a striped material or cloth. **3 stripes,** *pl.* a number or combination of strips of braid on the sleeve of a uniform to show rank, length of service, etc. **4** a sort; type: *Men of a different stripe.* —*v.* mark with stripes. [< MDu.]

stripe[2] (strīp) *n.* a stroke or lash with a whip. [probably a special use of *stripe*[1]]

striped (strīpt) *adj.* having stripes; marked with stripes.

strip·ling (strip′ling) *n.* a boy just coming into manhood; youth; lad. [< *strip*[2] + *-ling*]

strip mine a mine operated by digging out layers of earth on the surface to expose the ore.

strip mining the act or work of operating a strip mine.

stripped-down (stript′down′) *adj.* reduced to essentials.

strip·per (strip′ər) *n.* **1** a person or thing that strips. **2** an oil well producing several hours daily and requiring time to rebuild pressure before the oil flows again. **3** *Informal.* a strip-teaser.

strip poker a type of poker in which the loser of each hand must take off a piece of clothing.

strip tease a dance to music, in which a woman seductively and slowly undresses, performed in a night club, burlesque show, etc.

strip-tease (strip′tēz′) *adj.* of, having to do with, or like a strip tease.

strip-teaser (strip′tēz′ər) *n.* a woman who performs the strip tease.

strive (strīv) *v.* **strove** or **strived, striv·en, striv·ing. 1** try hard; work hard: *strive for self-control.* **2** struggle; fight: *The swimmer strove against the tide.* [ME < OF *estriver* < Gmc.] —**Syn. 1** endeavor. **2** contend, battle.

striv·en (striv′ən) *v.* pp. of **strive.**

strobe (strōb) *n.* a strobe light.

strobe light in photography, an electronic flash gun that operates a neon- or xenon-filled tube. It can be used many times, in contrast to the flash bulb, which can be used only once. [short for *stroboscope*]

strob·ile (strob′īl or strob′əl) *n.* in botany, any seed-producing cone, such as a pine cone, or a compact mass of scale-like leaves that produce spores, such as the cone of the club moss. [< LL < Gk. *strobilos* pine cone < *strobos* a whirling around]

strob·o·scope (strōb′ə skōp′) *n.* an instrument for studying periodic motion by the illumination of a moving body in flashes or at intervals. [< G *Stroboskop* < Gk. *strobos* a whirling + G *-skop,* equivalent to E *-scope*]

strob·o·scop·ic (strōb′ə skop′ik) *adj.* of or having to do with stroboscopes.

strode (strōd) *v.* pt. of **stride.**

stroke[1] (strōk) *n. v.* **stroked, strok·ing.** —*n.* **1** an act of striking; blow: *The house was hit by a stroke of lightning.* **2** a sound made by striking: *We arrived on the stroke of three.* **3** a piece of luck, fortune, etc.: *a stroke of bad luck.* **4 a** a single complete movement to be made again and again, especially of a moving part or parts, in one direction. **b** the distance travelled by this part. **5** a throb or pulsing, as of the heart. **6** a movement or mark made by a pen, pencil, brush, etc.: *He writes with a heavy down stroke.* **7** a vigorous attempt to attain some object: *a bold stroke for freedom.* **8** a feat or achievement: *a stroke of genius.* **9** an act, piece, or amount of work, etc.: *a stroke of work.* **10** a sudden attack (of disease). **11** an attack of paralysis; apoplexy. **12** a sudden action like a blow in its effect, as in causing pain, injury, or death: *a stroke of fate, the stroke of death.* **13** in swimming: **a** one of a series of propelling movements, involving the pull of one arm (or both together) with one or more kicks. **b** a style or method of swimming: *He swims a fast stroke.* **14** in rowing: **a** a single pull of the oar. **b** the style or rate of pulling the oars: *He rows with a strong stroke.* **c** the rower seated nearest the stern of the boat, who sets the time for the other oarsmen. **d** the position of this rower. **15 keep stroke,** make strokes at the same time.
—*v.* **1** be the stroke of: *Who stroked the Vancouver crew?* **2** mark with a stroke or strokes; cancel by drawing a line or lines across. [related to STRIKE or its source] —**strok′er,** *n.* —**Syn.** *n.* **1** See **blow.**

stroke[2] (strōk) *v.* **stroked, strok·ing,** *n.* —*v.* **1** move the hand gently over: *She stroked the kitten.* **2 stroke the wrong way,** a stroke (an animal) in the direction contrary to that in which the fur naturally lies. **b** ruffle or irritate (a person), especially by going counter to his wishes. —*n.* a stroking movement. [OE *strācian*]

stroke oar 1 the oar nearest the stern of the boat. **2** the rower that pulls the stroke oar. The stroke oar sets the time for the other oarsmen.

stroll (strōl) *v.* **1** take a quiet walk for pleasure; walk. **2** go from place to place: *strolling gypsies.* **3** stroll along or through. —*n.* a leisurely walk. [origin uncertain] —**Syn.** *v.* **1** saunter, ramble, roam.

stroll·er (strōl′ər) *n.* **1** a wanderer. **2** a strolling player or actor. **3** a kind of light baby carriage.

strong (strong) *adj.* **1** having much force or power: *a strong wind, strong muscles, a strong nation.* **2** able to last, endure, resist, etc.: *a strong fort.* **3** not easily influenced, changed, etc.; firm: *a strong will.* **4** of great force or effectiveness: *strong arguments.* **5** having a certain number: *A group that is 100 strong has 100 in it.* **6** having much of the quality expected: *a strong poison, a strong acid, strong tea.* **7** containing much alcohol: *a strong drink.* **8** having much flavor or odor: *strong seasoning.* **9** having an unpleasant taste or smell: *strong butter.* **10** intense: *a strong light.* **11** vigorous, forceful: *a strong speech.* **12** hearty; zealous: *a strong dislike.* **13** in grammar, inflecting by a vowel change within the stem of the word rather than by adding endings. *Examples*: find, found; give, gave. **14** in phonetics, stressed.
—*adv.* with force; powerfully; vigorously; in a strong manner. [OE *strang*] —**strong′ly,** *adv.*
Syn. *adj.* **1 Strong, sturdy, robust** = having or showing much power, force, or vigor. **Strong** is the general word, describing people, animals, plants, or things, and especially suggesting great power or force in acting, resisting, or enduring: *Fishermen need strong backs and arms.* **Sturdy** suggests power coming from good, solid construction and unyielding strength: *Children need sturdy clothes.* **Robust** emphasizes healthy vigor of mind or body and a toughness of muscles or spirit: *Sports make children robust.*

strong-arm (strong′ärm′) *Informal.* —*adj.* using force or violence. —*v.* use force or violence on.

strong·box (strong′boks′) *n.* a strongly made box for holding valuables.

strong drink drink containing much alcohol; liquor.

strong·hold (strong′hōld′) *n.* a strong place; a safe place; fort; fortress.

strong·man (strong′man′) *n.* **-men** (-men′). **1** a muscular man who performs feats of strength in a carnival, circus, etc. **2** a leader who obtains power by force and suppression; dictator.

strong-mind·ed (strong′mīn′did) *adj.* having a strong mind; mentally vigorous. —**strong′-mind′ed·ly,** *adv.* —**strong′-mind′ed·ness,** *n.*

strong wood or **woods** *Cdn.* forest; big trees. [translation of F *bois fort(s)*]

stron·ti·um (stron′tē əm or stron′shē əm) *n.* a hard, yellowish, metallic chemical element resembling calcium. It occurs only in combination. *Symbol*: Sr; *at.no.* 38; *at.wt.* 87.62 [< NL *strontium* < *Strontian*, a parish in Scotland, the site of lead mines where strontium was first discovered]

strontium 90 a radio-active isotope of strontium that causes bone cancer in humans if absorbed in sufficient quantities: *Strontium 90 is released when a hydrogen bomb explodes.*

strop (strop) *n. v.* **stropped, strop·ping.** —*n.* a leather strap used for sharpening razors. —*v.* sharpen on a strop. [ME; ult. < L *stroppus* band < Gk. *strophos*]

stro·phe (strō′fē) *n.* **1** a part of an ancient Greek ode sung by the chorus when moving from right to left. **2** a series of lines forming a division of a poem and having metrical structure which is repeated in a second group of lines (the antistrophe), especially in ancient Greek choral and lyric poetry. **3** one of two or more metrically corresponding series of lines forming divisions of a lyric poem; stanza. [< Gk. *strophē*, originally, a turning (i.e., a section sung by the chorus while turning)]

stroph·ic (strof′ik or strō′fik) *adj.* of or having to do with a strophe.

stroud (stroud) *n. Cdn.* **1** a heavy woollen cloth popular in the North as material for blankets, leggings, capotes, etc. **2** a garment or blanket made of this material. [< *Stroud*, England, where it was first made]

hat, āge, cãre, fär; let, ēqual, tėrm; it, īce
hot, ōpen, ôrder; oil, out; cup, pu̇t, rüle, ūse
əbove, takən, pencəl, lemən, circəs
ch, child; ng, long; sh, ship
th, thin; ᴛʜ, then; zh, measure

strove (strōv) *v.* pt. of **strive.**

strow (strō) *v.* **strowed, strown** or **strowed, strow·ing.** *Archaic.* strew.

strown (strōn) *v. Archaic.* pp. of **strow.**

struck (struk) *v.* pt. and pp. of **strike.** —*adj.* closed or affected in some way by a strike of workers.

struc·tur·al (struk′chər əl) *adj.* **1** of or having to do with building. **Structural steel** is steel made into beams, girders, etc. **2** of or having to do with structure or structures: *The geologist showed the structural difference in rocks of different ages.* **3** of or proceeding from structural linguistics: *structural grammar.* **4** in biology, of or having to do with the organic structure of an animal or plant; morphological. **5** in geology, having to do with the structure of rock, the earth's crust, etc. **6** in chemistry, of or showing the placement or manner of attachment of the atoms that make up a particular molecule.

struc·tur·al·ism (struk′chər ə liz′əm) *n.* any theory or study that tends to emphasize structure more than function, especially in psychology, linguistics, etc.

struc·tur·al·ist (struk′chər ə list) *n.* one who believes in or follows structuralism.

structural linguistics a branch of linguistic study in which languages are analysed and described in terms of their structural elements and the patterns in which these elements combine.

struc·tur·al·ly (struk′chər əl ē) *adv.* with regard to structure: *The city hall is structurally perfect, but it is not beautiful.*

struc·ture (struk′chər) *n. v.* **-tured, -tur·ing.** —*n.* **1** a building; something built. **2** anything composed of parts arranged together: *The human body is a wonderful structure.* **3** the manner of building; the way parts are put together; construction: *The structure of the apartment building was excellent.* **4** the relation of the parts or elements of a thing, especially as it determines its peculiar nature or character: *the structure of a molecule, the structure of a sentence.* —*v.* **1** make into a structure; build; fabricate. **2** organize; put together in a systematic way. [< L *structura* < *struere* arrange] —**Syn. 1** See **building.**

stru·del (strü′dəl; *German,* shtrü′dəl) *n.* a pastry, usually consisting of fruit or cheese, covered by a very thin dough and baked. [< G]

strug·gle (strug′əl) *v.* **-gled, -gling,** *n.* —*v.* **1** make great efforts with the body; try hard; work hard against difficulties: *The poor have to struggle for a living. The swimmer struggled against the tide.* **2** get, move, or make one's way with great effort: *The old man struggled to his feet.* —*n.* **1** great effort; hard work. **2** fighting; conflict. [ME *strugle(n), strogele(n)*; origin uncertain] —**strug′gler,** *n.* —**Syn.** *v.* **1** strive, labor, toil, cope, contend. –*n.* **1** exertion, labor, endeavor. **2** strife, contest.

strum (strum) *v.* **strummed, strum·ming,** *n.* —*v.* **1** play on (a stringed musical instrument) unskilfully or carelessly: *strum a guitar, strum on the piano.* **2** tap against or strike as by strumming: *strum one's fingers impatiently on a table.* —*n.* **1** the act of strumming. **2** the sound of strumming. [? imitative] —**strum′mer,** *n.*

stru·ma (strü′mə) *n.* **-mae** (-mē or -mī). **1** scrofula. **2** goitre. **3** in botany, a cushionlike swelling on an organ. [< NL < L]

strum·pet (strum′pit) *n.* a prostitute. [ME; origin uncertain]

strung (strung) *v.* pt. and pp. of **string.**

strut[1] (strut) *v.* **strut·ted, strut·ting,** *n.* —*v.* walk in a vain, important manner: *The rooster struts about the barnyard.* —*n.* a strutting walk. [OE *strūtian*] —**strut′ter,** *n.*
Syn. *v.* **Strut, swagger** = walk or hold oneself with an air of importance. **Strut** emphasizes putting on an air of dignity by sticking the chest out and holding the head and body stiffly and

proudly, to show how important one is: *The little boy put on his father's medals and strutted around the room.* **Swagger** emphasizes showing off how much better one is than others by strutting boldly, rudely, or insultingly: *After being put on probation again, the boys swaggered out of the courtroom.*

strut[2] (strut) *n. v.* **strut·ted, strut·ting.** —*n.* a supporting piece; brace. —*v.* brace or support by a strut or struts. [ult. related to STRUT[1]]

STRUT

strych·nin (strik′nin) *n.* strychnine.

strych·nine (strik′nin, strik′nēn, or strik′nīn) *n.* a poisonous drug consisting of colorless crystals obtained from nux vomica and related plants. *Formula:* $C_{21}H_{22}N_2O_2$ [< F < L < Gk. *strychnos* nightshade]

Stu·art (stū′ərt or stü′ərt) *n.* the royal family that ruled Scotland from 1371 to 1603 and England and Scotland from 1603 to 1714. James I, Charles I, Charles II, James II, and Queen Anne belonged to the House of Stuart.

stub (stub) *n. v.* **stubbed, stub·bing.** —*n.* **1** a short piece that is left: *the stub of a pencil.* **2** the short piece of each leaf in a chequebook, etc. kept as a record. **3** something short and blunt; a short thick piece or part. **4** a pen having a short blunt point. **5** a stump of a tree, a broken tooth, etc. **6** *Esp.Brit.* a cigarette butt.
—*v.* **1** strike (one's toe) against something. **2** clear (land) of tree stumps. **3** dig up by the roots. **4** put out a cigarette or cigar by crushing out the burning end. [OE]

stub·ble (stub′əl) *n.* **1** the lower ends of stalks of grain that are left in the ground after the grain is cut. **2** any short, rough growth: *He had three days' stubble on his unshaven face.* [ME < OF *stuble* < LL *stupula*, var. of L *stipula* stem. Doublet of STIPULE.]

stub·bly (stub′lē) *adj.* **1** covered with stubble. **2** resembling stubble; bristly: *a stubbly mustache.*

stub·born (stub′ərn) *adj.* **1** fixed in purpose or opinion; not giving in to argument or requests. **2** characterized by obstinacy: *a stubborn refusal to listen to reason.* **3** hard to deal with or manage: *a stubborn cough. Facts are stubborn things; they can't be changed.* [probably ult. < *stub*] —**stub′born·ly,** *adv.* —**stub′born·ness,** *n.* —**Syn. 1** dogged, resolute. See **obstinate. 2** unruly, ungovernable.

stub·by (stub′ē) *adj.* **-bi·er, -bi·est. 1** short and thick: *stubby fingers.* **2** short, thick, and stiff: *a stubby beard.* **3** having many stubs or stumps. —**stub′bi·ly,** *adv.* —**stub′bi·ness,** *n.*

stuc·co (stuk′ō) *n.* **-coes, -cos,** *v.* **-coed, -co·ing.** —*n.* **1** a rough, strong plaster for covering the outer walls of buildings. **2** stuccowork. —*v.* cover with stucco. [< Ital. < Gmc.; cf. OHG *stukki* crust]

stuc·co·work (stuk′ō wėrk′) *n.* work done in stucco.

stuck (stuk) *v.* pt. and pp. of **stick**[2].

stuck-up (stuk′up′) *adj. Informal.* too proud; conceited; vain; haughty.

stud[1] (stud) *n. v.* **stud·ded, stud·ding.** —*n.* **1** a nailhead, knob, etc. sticking out from a surface: *The belt was ornamented with silver studs.* **2** a kind of small button used to fasten the collar or front of a man's shirt. **3** a post to which boards are nailed in making walls. **4** a projecting pin on a machine. **5** a crosspiece put in each link of a chain cable to strengthen it. **6** stud poker.
—*v.* **1** set with studs or something like studs: *He plans to stud the sword hilt with jewels.* **2** be set or scattered over: *Little islands stud the harbor.* **3** set like studs; scatter at intervals: *Stooks of wheat were studded over the field.* **4** provide with studs. [OE *studu*]

stud[2] (stud) *n.* **1** a collection of horses kept for breeding, racing, hunting, etc. **2** a place where such a collection is kept. **3** a male horse kept for breeding purposes; stallion. **4** any male animal kept for breeding purposes. —*adj.* **1** kept for breeding purposes: *a stud horse.* **2** of or having to do with a stud. [OE *stōd*]

stud·book (stud′bůk′) *n.* a book giving the pedigrees of thoroughbred horses.

stud·ding (stud′ing) *n.* **1** the studs of a wall collectively. **2** lumber for such studs.

stud·ding·sail (stud′ing sāl′ or stun′səl) *n.* a light sail set at the side of a square sail. [origin unknown]

stu·dent (stū′dənt or stü′dənt) *n.* **1** a person who studies. **2** a person who is studying in a school, college, or university. [< L *studens, -entis*, ppr. of *studere*, originally, be eager]
Syn. 1, 2 Student, pupil, scholar = a person who is studying or being taught. **Student,** emphasizing the idea of studying, applies to anyone who loves to study or studies a subject, but especially to someone attending a high school, college, or university: *Several high-school students were there.* **Pupil,** emphasizing personal supervision by a teacher, applies especially to a child in an elementary school or to someone studying personally with a teacher: *She was the pupil of a famous opera singer.* **Scholar** now applies chiefly to a learned person who is an authority in some field or to a student who has a scholarship: *He is a distinguished medieval scholar.*

stud·ied (stud′ēd) *adj.* **1** carefully planned: *a studied essay.* **2** done on purpose; resulting from deliberate effort: *a studied insult.* —**stud′ied·ly,** *adv.* —**stud′ied·ness,** *n.* —**Syn.** See **elaborate.**

stu·di·o (stū′dē ō′ or stü′dē ō′) *n.* **-di·os. 1 a** the workroom of a painter, sculptor, photographer, etc. **b** a room in which a music teacher, dramatic coach, etc. gives lessons. **2** a place where motion pictures are made. **3** a place from which a radio or television program is broadcast. [< Ital. < L *studium* study, enthusiasm. Doublet of ÉTUDE, STUDY.]

studio couch a kind of upholstered couch that can be opened out into a double bed.

stu·di·ous (stū′dē əs or stü′dē əs) *adj.* **1** fond of study. **2** showing careful consideration; careful; thoughtful; zealous: *She is always studious of her mother's comfort. He made a studious effort to please customers.* **3** studied; deliberate. —**stu′di·ous·ly,** *adv.* —**stu′di·ous·ness,** *n.* —**Syn. 2** earnest, painstaking, assiduous.

stud poker a type of poker in which one or more cards are dealt face down on the first round and the rest dealt face up, or alternating rounds of cards dealt face up and face down. Betting is done on each round of open cards.

stud·y (stud′ē) *n.* **stud·ies,** *v.* **stud·ied, stud·y·ing.** —*n.* **1** the effort to learn by reading or thinking. **2** a careful examination; investigation. **3** a subject studied; branch of learning; something investigated or to be investigated. **4** a room for study, reading, writing, etc. **5** a literary or artistic work that deals in careful detail with one particular subject. **6** a sketch for a picture, story, etc. **7** in music, a composition designed primarily for practice in a particular technical problem; a concert version of this, often of great difficulty and brilliance. **8** an earnest effort, or the object of endeavor or effort: *Her constant study is to please her parents.* **9** deep thought; reverie: *She was in a brown study.* **10 studies,** a person's work as a student: *return to one's studies after a vacation.*
—*v.* **1** try to learn or gain knowledge by means of books, observation, or experiment: *study history. He studies most of the time.* **2** examine carefully: *We studied the map to find the shortest road home.* **3** consider with care; think (out); plan: *The prisoner studied ways to escape.* **4** give care and thought to; try hard: *The grocer studies to please his customers.* **5** memorize or try to memorize: *study one's part in a play.* [ME < AF < L *studium*, originally, eagerness. Doublet of ÉTUDE, STUDIO.] —**Syn.** *v.* **2** investigate, scrutinize. **3** ponder. See **consider.**

stuff (stuf) *n.* **1** what a thing is made of; material. **2** a woollen fabric. **3** a thing or things; substance: *The doctor rubbed some kind of stuff on the burn.* **4** goods; belongings: *He was told to move his stuff out of the room.* **5** worthless material; useless things. **6** silly words and thoughts; nonsense. **7** inward qualities; character.
—*v.* **1** pack full; fill. To stuff a ballot box means to put in more votes than there are rightful voters. **2** stop or block up: *My nose is stuffed by a cold.* **3** fill the skin of (a dead animal) to make it look as it did when alive. **4** fill (a chicken, turkey, etc.) with seasoned bread crumbs, etc. **5** force; push; thrust: *He stuffed his clothes into the drawer.* **6** eat too much. [ME < OF *estoffe*, ? ult. < L *stuppa* tow[2], oakum < Gk. *stypē*] —**Syn.** *n.* **5** refuse, rubbish, trash. *-v.* **1** cram.

stuffed shirt *Slang.* a person who seems to be more important than he really is; a pompous or smugly pretentious person.

stuff·ing (stuf′ing) *n.* **1** any material used to fill or pack something. 2 seasoned bread crumbs, etc. for stuffing a chicken, turkey, etc. for cooking.

stuff·y (stuf′ē) *adj.* **stuff·i·er, stuff·i·est. 1** lacking fresh air: *a stuffy room.* **2** lacking freshness or interest; dull: *a stuffy conversation.* **3** stopped up: *A cold makes one's head feel stuffy.* **4** *Informal.* easily shocked or offended; prim. **5** *Informal.* angry; sulky. —**stuff′i·ly,** *adv.* —**stuff′i·ness,** *n.*

Stu·ka (stü′kə) *n.* a powerful German dive bomber used in World War II. [< G *Stu(rz)ka(mpfflieger)* < *Sturz* plunge + *Kampf* battle + *Flieger* flyer, airplane]

stul·ti·fi·ca·tion (stul′tə fə kā′shən) *n.* the act of stultifying or the state of being stultified.

stul·ti·fy (stul′tə fī′) *v.* **-fied, -fy·ing. 1** cause to appear foolish or absurd; reduce to foolishness or absurdity. **2 a** make futile. **b** make passive or weak by requiring absolute obedience or conformity: *the stultifying atmosphere of a prison or dictatorship.* [< LL *stultificare* < L *stultus* foolish + *facere* make] —**stul′ti·fi′er,** *n.*

stum·ble (stum′bəl) *v.* **-bled, -bling,** *n.* —*v.* **1** trip by striking the foot against something. **2** cause to stumble. **3** walk unsteadily: *The tired old man stumbled along.* **4** speak, act, etc. in a clumsy or hesitating way: *The boy made many blunders as he stumbled through his recitation.* **5** make a mistake; do wrong. **6** come by accident or chance: *While in the country, she stumbled upon some fine antiques.* **7** take offence; find an obstacle to belief; falter (*at*).
—*n.* **1** a wrong act; mistake. **2** a stumbling. [cf. Norwegian *stumla*] —**stum′bler,** *n.* —**stum′bling·ly,** *adv.*

stumbling block 1 an obstacle; hindrance. **2** something that makes a person stumble.

stump (stump) *n.* **1** the lower end of a tree or plant left after the main part is cut off. **2** anything left after the main or important part is removed: *The dog wagged his stump of a tail.* **3** a person with a short, thick build. **4** a place where a political speech is made. **5** a heavy step. **6** the sound made by stiff walking or heavy steps. **7** a wooden leg. **8** *Slang.* a leg. **9** *Informal.* a dare; challenge. **10** a tight roll of paper or other material pointed at the ends and used to soften pencil marks in drawing. **11** in cricket, one of the three upright sticks of a wicket. **12 up a stump,** *Informal.* unable to act, answer, etc.; impotent; baffled.
—*v.* **1** remove stumps from (land). **2** reduce to a stump; cut off. **3** make political speeches in: *The candidates for election will stump the district.* **4** walk in a stiff, clumsy way: *The lame man stumped along.* **5** *Informal.* make unable to answer, do, etc. **6** *Informal.* dare; challenge. **7** in cricket, put a batsman out by knocking down the bails while he is out of his ground. [cf. MLG *stump*] —**stump′er,** *n.* —**stump′like′,** *adj.*

stump speaker a person who makes political speeches from a platform, etc.

stump speech a political speech.

stump·y (stump′ē) *adj.* **stump·i·er, stump·i·est. 1** short and thick. **2** having many stumps. —**stump′i·ly,** *adv.* —**stump′i·ness,** *n.*

stun (stun) *v.* **stunned, stun·ning,** *n.* —*v.* **1** make senseless; knock unconscious: *He was stunned by the fall.* **2** daze; bewilder; shock; overwhelm: *She was stunned by the news of her friend's death.* —*n.* **1 a** the act of stunning or dazing. **b** the condition of being stunned. **2** a thing that stuns; stunner. [OE *stunian* crash, resound; influenced by OF *estoner* resound, stun, ult. < L *ex-* + *tonare* thunder] —**Syn.** *v.* **2** stupefy, dumbfound, astound, amaze.

stung (stung) *v.* pt. and pp. of **sting.**

stunk (stungk) *v.* a pt. and pp. of **stink.**

stun·ner (stun′ər) *n.* **1** a person, thing, or blow that stuns. **2** *Informal.* a very striking or attractive person or thing.

stun·ning (stun′ing) *adj.* **1** that stuns or dazes; bewildering. **2 a** very attractive or good-looking; strikingly pretty: *a stunning girl, a stunning new hat.* **b** excellent or delightful; first-rate; splendid: *a stunning performance.* —**stun′ning·ly,** *adv.*

stun·sail (stun′səl) *n.* studdingsail.

stunt[1] (stunt) *v.* check in growth or development: *Lack of proper food stunts a plant.* —*n.* a stunting. [OE *stunt* foolish]

hat, āge, cãre, fär; let, ēqual, tėrm; it, īce
hot, ōpen, ôrder; oil, out; cup, pu̇t, rüle, ūse
əbove, takən, pencəl, lemən, circəs
ch, child; ng, long; sh, ship
th, thin; ᴛʜ, then; zh, measure

stunt[2] (stunt) *Informal.* —*n.* a feat or act intended to thrill an audience or to attract attention; an act showing boldness or skill: *Circus riders perform stunts on horseback.* —*v.* **1** perform such feats. **2** perform stunts with. [probably a var. of *stint* task]

stunt man (stunt′man′) *n.* **men** (men′). a professional acrobat who doubles for an actor or actress in dangerous scenes.

stu·pa (stü′pə) *n.* a large, dome-shaped mound erected as a shrine by Buddhists. [< Skt. *stupa* heap]

stupe (stūp or stüp) *n.* a small, hot, wet cloth, or compress, of soft material, used in dressing a wound, to stimulate circulation, etc. [ME < L *stupa* coarse flax < Gk. *stypē*]

stu·pe·fa·cient (stū′pə fā′shənt or stü′pə fā′shənt) *adj.* stupefying. —*n.* a drug or agent that produces stupor. [< L *stupefaciens, -entis,* ppr. of *stupefacere.* See STUPEFY.]

stu·pe·fac·tion (stū′pə fak′shən or stü′pə fak′shən) *n.* **1** a dazed or senseless condition; stupor. **2** overwhelming amazement. **3** the act of stupefying.

stu·pe·fy (stū′pə fī′ or stü′pə fī′) *v.* **-fied, -fy·ing. 1** make stupid, dull, or senseless. **2** overwhelm with amazement; astound: *They were stupefied by the calamity.* [< L *stupefacere* < *stupere* be amazed + *facere* make] —**stu′pe·fi′er,** *n.* —**Syn. 1** deaden, stun.

stu·pen·dous (stū pen′dəs or stü pen′dəs) *adj.* amazing; marvellous; immense: *Niagara Falls is a stupendous sight.* [< L *stupendus* < *stupere* be amazed] —**stu·pen′dous·ly,** *adv.* —**stu·pen′dous·ness,** *n.*

stu·pid (stū′pid or stü′pid) *adj.* **1** not intelligent; dull: *a stupid person.* **2** not interesting: *a stupid book.* **3** dazed; senseless. —*n. Informal.* a stupid person. [< L *stupidus* < *stupere* be dazed] —**stu′pid·ness,** *n.*
Syn. *adj.* **1 Stupid, dull** = having or showing little intelligence. **Stupid,** describing people or what they say or do, particularly suggests being by nature lacking in good sense or ordinary intelligence: *Running away from an accident is stupid.* **Dull** particularly suggests a mind slow in understanding and lacking in sharpness and alertness, either by nature or because of overwork, poor health, etc. and needing to be stirred up and made more lively: *The mind becomes dull if the body gets no exercise.* **2** vapid, flat.

stu·pid·i·ty (stū pid′ə tē or stü pid′ə tē) *n.* **-ties. 1** dullness; lack of intelligence. **2** a foolish act, idea, etc.

stu·pid·ly (stū′pid lē or stü′pid lē) *adv.* **1** in a stupid manner. **2** to an extent or degree that is stupid. **3** so as to be or appear stupid.

stu·por (stū′pər or stü′pər) *n.* **1** a dazed condition; loss or lessening of the power to feel: *The man lay in a stupor, unable to tell what had happened to him.* **2** intellectual or moral numbness. [< L < *stupere* be dazed] —**Syn. 1** lethargy, torpor.

stur·dy (stėr′dē) *adj.* **-di·er, -di·est. 1** strong; stout: *sturdy legs.* **2** not yielding; firm: *sturdy resistance, sturdy defenders.* [ME < OF *esturdi* violent, originally, dazed] —**stur′di·ly,** *adv.* —**stur′di·ness,** *n.* —**Syn. 1** hardy, robust, muscular. See **strong. 2** resolute, indomitable.

stur·geon (stėr′jən) *n.* **-geon** or **-geons.** a large food fish whose long body has a tough skin covered with rows of bony plates. Caviar and isinglass are obtained from sturgeon. [ME < AF *esturgeon,* ult. < Gmc.]

stut·ter (stut′ər) *v.* **1** repeat (the same sound) in an effort to speak. **2** make any sound resembling this. —*n.* the act or habit of stuttering. [< dial. *stut;* cf. Du. *stotteren*] —**stut′ter·er,** *n.* —**stut′ter·ing·ly,** *adv.* —**Syn.** *v.* See **stammer.**

St. Vi·tus dance (vī′təs) St. Vitus's dance.

St. Vi·tus's dance (vī′təs iz) a nervous disease characterized by involuntary twitching of the muscles.

sty[1] (stī) *n.* **sties. 1** a pen for pigs. **2** any filthy place. [OE *stig*]

sty[2] or **stye** (stī) *n.* **sties** or **styes.** a small, inflamed swelling on the edge of the eyelid. A sty is like a small boil. [probably < ME *styanye* (taken to mean "sty on eye"), ult. < OE *stīgend* rising + *ēage* eye]

Styg·i·an (stij′ē ən) *adj.* **1** of or having to do with the river Styx or the lower world. **2** dark; gloomy. **3** of an oath, completely binding; inviolable like the oath by the Styx, which the gods themselves feared to break. [< L *Stygius* < Gk. *Stygios* < *Styx, Stygos* Styx]

style (stīl) *n. v.* **styled, styl·ing.** —*n.* **1** fashion: *dresses in the latest styles.* **2** a manner; method; way: *the Gothic style of architecture.* **3** a way of writing or speaking. **4** a fashionable, elegant, or admirable way or manner: *She dresses in style.* **5** literary or artistic excellence. **6** an official name; title: *Salute him with the style of King.* **7** a pointed instrument for writing on wax. **8** something like this in shape or use. **9** a pointer on a dial, chart, etc. **10** in botany, the stemlike part of the pistil of a flower containing the stigma at its top. See **pistil** for picture. **11** the rules of spelling, punctuation, etc. used by printers.
—*v.* **1** give a distinctive design or manner to: *dresses styled in Paris.* **2** name; call: *Joan of Arc was styled "the Maid of Orleans."* [ME < OF < L *stilus*, originally, pointed writing instrument; influenced in modern spelling by Gk. *stylos* column. Doublet of STYLUS.]
—**style′less,** *adj.* —**Syn.** *n.* **1** See **fashion.**

style·book (stīl′bůk′) *n.* **1** a book containing rules of punctuation, capitalization, etc., used by printers, editors, etc. **2** a book showing fashions in dress, etc.

styl·ish (stīl′ish) *adj.* having style; fashionable.
—**styl′ish·ly,** *adv.* —**styl′ish·ness,** *n.*

styl·ist (stīl′ist) *n.* **1** a writer, artist, musician, etc. who has a good style; a person who takes much pains with his style; a writer, speaker, etc. with reference to his style. **2** a person who designs or advises concerning interior decorations, clothes, etc.

sty·lis·tic (stī lis′tik) *adj.* of or having to do with style.

sty·lis·ti·cal·ly (stī lis′tik lē) *adv.* as regards style; in matters of style.

styl·ize (stīl′īz) *v.* **-ized, -iz·ing.** conform to a particular or to a conventional style. —**styl′i·za·tion,** *n.*
—**styl′iz·er,** *n.*

sty·lo·graph (stī′lə graf′) *n.* a fountain pen in which the writing point consists of a small metal tube. [< *stylus* + *-graph*]

sty·lo·graph·ic (stī′lə graf′ik) *adj.* of or having to do with a stylograph.

sty·lus (stī′ləs) *n.* **1** a style or pointed instrument for writing on wax. **2** a needle-like point used in making or playing phonograph records. **3** the lightweight pen that records lines on a moving drum or chart on an oscillograph, galvanometer, etc. [< L *stilus.* Doublet of STYLE.]

sty·mie (stī′mē) *n. v.* **-mied, -mie·ing.** —*n.* in golf: **1** an opponent's ball on a putting green when it is directly between the player's ball and the hole for which he is playing and when the distance between the balls is more than six inches. **2** the occurrence of a ball in such a position, or the position of the ball. —*v.* **1** in golf, hinder with a stymie or as a stymie does. **2** block completely. Also, **stimy.** [? < Scots *stymie* a person having poor eyesight]

styp·tic (stip′tik) *adj.* able to stop or check bleeding; astringent. —*n.* something that stops or checks bleeding by contracting the tissue. Alum is a common styptic. [< L < Gk. *styptikos* < *styphein* constrict]

styptic pencil a small stick of alum or other styptic substance, used on slight wounds to stop bleeding.

sty·rene (stī′rēn or stir′ēn) *n.* **1** an aromatic liquid hydrocarbon used in making synthetic rubber and plastics. **2** polystyrene. *Formula*: C_8H_8 [< L *styrax* an aromatic resin < Gk.]

Styx (stiks) *n.* in Greek mythology, a river in the lower world. The souls of the dead were ferried across it into Hades. [< L < Gk. *Styx* (related to *stygeein* hate)]

sua·sion (swā′zhən) *n.* an advising or urging; persuasion. [ME < L *suasio, -onis* < *suadere* persuade]

sua·sive (swā′siv) *adj.* advising or urging; persuasive
—**sua′sive·ly,** *adv.* —**sua′sive·ness,** *n.*

suave (swäv) *adj.* smoothly agreeable or polite. [< F < L *suavis* agreeable] —**suave′ly,** *adv.* —**suave′ness,** *n.*

sua·vi·ty (swä′və tē or swav′ə tē) *n.* **-ties.** a smoothly agreeable quality of behavior; blandness; smooth politeness.

sub (sub) *n. adj. v.* **subbed, sub·bing.** *Informal.* —*n. adj.* **1** substitute. **2** submarine. **3** subordinate.
—*v.* act as a substitute.

sub- *prefix.* **1** under; below, as in *subway, submarine.* **2** down; further; again, as in *subclassify, sublease.* **3** near nearly, as in *subarctic.* **4 a** lower; subordinate; assistant, as in *subaltern.* **b** of less importance, as in *subhead.* **5** resulting from further division, as in *subatom.* **6** in a comparatively small degree or proportion; slightly; somewhat, as in *subacid.* Also, **suc-,** before *c*; **suf-,** before *f*; **sug-,** before *g*; **sum-,** in some cases before *m*; **sup-,** before *p*; **sur-,** before *r*; **sus-,** in some cases before *c, p, t.* [< L *sub*, prep.]

sub. 1 substitute. **2** subscription. **3** suburban. **4** suburbs. **5** subaltern.

sub·a·gent (sub′ā′jənt) *n.* a person employed as the agent of an agent.

sub·al·tern (sub′əl tərn, sə bol′tərn or sə bôl′tərn) *n.* in the army, a lieutenant. —*adj.* **1** ranking below a captair **2** having lower rank; subordinate. [< LL *subalternus* < L *sub-* under + *alternus* alternate]

sub·a·que·ous (sub ā′kwē əs or sub ak′wē əs) *adj.* **1** under water; suitable for use under water. **2** formed under water. **3** living under water.

sub·arc·tic (sub ärk′tik or sub är′tik) *adj.* near, or just below the arctic region; having to do with or occurring in regions just south of the Arctic Circle.

sub·ar·id (sub ar′id) *adj.* moderately arid.

sub·at·om (sub′at′əm) *n.* any constituent of an atom. Protons and electrons are subatoms.

sub·a·tom·ic (sub′ə tom′ik) *adj.* having to do with, or concerning, subatoms.

sub·base·ment (sub′bās′mənt) *n.* any floor or room below the basement of a building.

sub·cel·lar (sub′sel′ər) *n.* a cellar beneath another cellar.

sub·class (sub′klas′) *n.* in zoology and botany, a grou| or category ranking below a class.

sub·com·mit·tee (sub′kə mit′ē) *n.* a small committee chosen from a larger general committee for some special duty.

sub·con·scious (sub kon′shəs) *adj.* not wholly conscious; existing but not felt: *Her sore tooth caused a subconscious irritation that made her cross.* —*n.* thoughts, feelings, etc. that are present in the mind but not fully perceived or recognized. —**sub·con′scious·ly,** *adv.*

sub·con·scious·ness (sub kon′shəs nis) *n.* **1** the state or quality of being subconscious. **2** the subconscious.

sub·con·ti·nent (sub kon′tə nənt) *n.* **1** a very large land mass, smaller than a continent. **2** a large section of a continent that has considerable geographical or political independence: *the Indian sub-continent.*

sub·con·tract (*n.* sub′kon′trakt; *v.* sub kon′trakt or sub′kən trakt′) *n.* a contract under a previous contract; contract for carrying out a previous contract or a part of it: *The contractor for the new school building gave out subcontracts to a plumber, a steam fitter, etc.* —*v.* make a subcontract; make a subcontract for.

sub·con·trac·tor (sub′kon′trak tər or sub′kon trak′tər) *n.* a person who contracts for carrying out a previous contract or part of it.

sub·cul·ture (sub′kul chər) *n.* **1** an element or class within or on the fringe of a culture or society. **2** a bacteriological culture derived from a previous culture.

sub·cu·ta·ne·ous (sub′kyů tā′nē əs) *adj.* **1** under the skin. **2** living under the skin. **3** placed or performed under the skin. —**sub′cu·ta′ne·ous·ly,** *adv.*

sub·dea·con (sub′dē′kən) *n.* a member of the clergy next below a deacon in rank.

sub·di·vide (sub′də vīd′) *v.* **-vid·ed, -vid·ing. 1** divide again; divide into smaller parts. **2** divide (land) into lots for houses, buildings, etc.: *A real estate dealer bought the farm and subdivided it into building lots.* —**sub′di·vid′er,** *n.*

sub·di·vi·sion (sub′də vizh′ən) *n.* **1** a division into smaller parts. **2** a part of a part. **3** a tract of land divided into building lots. **4** the houses, community, etc. established on such a tract.

sub·dom·i·nant (sub dom′ə nənt) *n.* in music, the fourth tone of a scale; the tone next below the dominant. —*adj.* of or having to do with this tone.

sub·due (səb dū′ or səb dü′) *v.* **-dued, -du·ing. 1** conquer; overcome: *The Spaniards subdued the Indian tribes in Mexico. We subdued a desire to laugh.* **2** get the better of; prevail over. **3** tone down; soften: *Pulling down the shades subdued the light in the room.* **4** reduce or allay: *subdue a fever or a boil.* [ME *sodewe* < OF *soduire* deceive < L *subducere* draw away < *sub-* from under + *ducere* lead; influenced in meaning by L *subdere* subdue < *sub-* under + *dare* put] —**sub·du′a·ble,** *adj.* —**sub·du′er,** *n.* —**Syn. 1** vanquish, subjugate, suppress.

sub·dued (səb dūd′ or səb düd′) *adj.* **1** brought under control; vanquished. **2** diminished; softened; toned down.

su·be·re·ous (sü bēr′ē əs) *adj.* corky; like cork. [< L *subereus* < *suber* cork]

sub·fam·i·ly (sub′fam′ə lē or -fam′lē) *n.* **-lies.** in biology, a group of plants or animals. We classify into classes, subclasses, orders, suborders, families, sub-families, genera, subgenera, species, and subspecies.

sub·fusc or **sub·fusk** (sub fusk′) *adj.* **1** darkish; dull in color: *subfusc woods at twilight.* **2** not distinctive; monotonous; drab: *rows of subfusc city houses.* [< L *subfuscus* < *sub-* under + *fuscus* dark]

sub·ge·nus (sub′jē′nəs) *n.* **sub·gen·er·a** (sub jen′ər ə or sub′jen′ər ə) or **sub·ge·nus·es.** in biology, a group of plants or animals ranking below a genus and above a species.

sub·group (sub′grüp′) *n.* a subordinate group; a division of a group.

sub·head (sub′hed′) *n.* **1** a subordinate head or title. **2** a subordinate division of a head or title.

sub·head·ing (sub′hed′ing) *n.* subhead.

sub·hu·man (sub hū′mən) *adj.* **1** below the human race or type; less than human. **2** almost human.

su·bi·to (sü′bē tō′) *adv.* in music, suddenly; quickly; abruptly. [< Ital.]

subj. 1 subject. **2** subjective. **3** subjectively. **4** subjunctive.

sub·ja·cent (sub jā′sənt) *adj.* **1** situated below; underlying. **2** being in a lower situation, though not directly beneath. [< L *subjacens, -entis,* ppr. of *subjacere* < *sub-* below + *jacere* lie]

sub·ject (*n. adj.* sub′jikt; *v.* səb jekt′) *n.* **1** something thought about, discussed, studied, etc. **2** a course of study, field of learning, etc.: *English, history, mathematics, and biology are required subjects in this school.* **3** a person under the power, control, or influence of another: *the Queen's subjects.* **4** a person or thing that undergoes or experiences something. **5** in grammar, the word or words with which the verb is said to agree in number and person. The subject often indicates the performer of the action, as in *The boy trains dogs* and *The boys train dogs.* **6 a** the theme of a book, poem, or other literary work. **b** a figure, scene, object, incident, etc. chosen by an artist for representation. **c** in music, the theme or melody on which a composition or movement is based. **7** in philosophy: **a** the substance of anything as opposed to its qualities. **b** mind or self opposed to everything outside the mind. **8** in logic: **a** that term of a proposition of which the other term is affirmed or denied. **b** the thing about which such affirmation or denial is made.
—*adj.* **1** under some power or influence: *We are subject to our country's laws.* **2 subject to, a** under the power or influence of. **b** likely to have: *subject to colds.* **c** depending on; on the condition of.
—*v.* **1** bring under some power or influence: *Rome subjected all Italy to her rule.* **2** cause to undergo or experience something: *The savages subjected their captives to torture.* **3** lay open or expose; make liable (*to*): *Credulity subjects one to impositions.* [ME < OF < L *subjectus,* pp. of *subjicere, subicere* place under < *sub-* under + *jacere* throw]
Syn. *n.* **1 Subject, topic** = the main thing or idea thought, talked, or written about, as in a conversation, lecture, essay, book. **Subject** is the general word: *He tried to change the subject. Juvenile delinquency is a broad subject.* **Topic** often applies to a subject having to do with a current event or problem, but particularly means a limited and definitely stated subject that is, or is to be, discussed in a lecture, essay, etc. or some part of it: *"The plan for a recreation centre" is today's topic.*

hat, āge, cãre, fär; let, ēqual, tėrm; it, īce
hot, ōpen, ôrder; oil, out; cup, pu̇t, rüle, ūse
əbove, takən, pencəl, lemən, circəs
ch, child; ng, long; sh, ship
th, thin; ᴛʜ, then; zh, measure

sub·jec·tion (səb jek′shən) *n.* **1** the act of bringing under some power or influence; conquering: *The subjection of the rebels took years.* **2** the condition of being under some power or influence: *The force of the conductor's personality held the entire orchestra in subjection to him.*

sub·jec·tive (səb jek′tiv) *adj.* **1** existing in the mind; belonging to the person thinking rather than to the object thought of: *Ideas and opinions are subjective; facts are objective.* **2** about the thoughts and feelings of the speaker, writer, painter, etc.; personal: *a subjective poem.* **3** in psychology: **a** originating in or dependent on the mind of the individual rather than an external object. **b** introspective. **4** in philosophy: **a** of or relating to reality as perceived by the mind, as distinct from reality as independent of the mind. **b** influenced by an individual's state of mind: *a subjective perception or apprehension.* **c** having to do with the substance of anything, as opposed to its qualities and attributes. **5** in grammar, being or serving as the subject of a sentence; nominative. —**sub·jec′tive·ly,** *adv.* —**sub·jec′tive·ness,** *n.*

sub·jec·tiv·i·ty (sub′jek tiv′ə tē) *n.* **1** a subjective quality; existence in the mind only; absorption in one's own mental states or processes. **2** the tendency to view things through the medium of one's own individuality.

subject matter 1 something thought about, discussed, studied, written about, etc. **2** the meaning of a talk, book, etc. as distinguished from its form or style.

sub·join (səb join′) *v.* **1** add at the end; append. **2** place in immediate sequence to something else. [< MF *subjoindre* < L *subjungere* < *sub-* under + *jungere* join]

sub·ju·gate (sub′jů gāt′) *v.* **-gat·ed, -gat·ing. 1** subdue; conquer. **2** bring under complete control; make subservient or submissive. [ME < LL *subjugare* < *sub-* under + *jugum* yoke] —**sub′ju·ga′tor,** *n.*

sub·ju·ga·tion (sub′jů gā′shən) *n.* conquest; subjection.

sub·junc·tive (səb jungk′tiv) in grammar: —*n.* **1** the mood of a verb that expresses a state, act, or event as possible, conditional, or dependent, rather than as actual. **2** a verb in this mood. —*adj.* of or having to do with this mood. *Abbrev.:* subj. [< LL *subjunctivus,* ult. < L *sub-* under + *jungere* join]

sub·king·dom (sub king′dəm or sub′king′dəm) *n.* in biology, any primary division of the animal or plant kingdom, usually called a phylum.

sub·lease (*n.* sub′lēs′; *v.* sub lēs′ or sub′lēs′) *n. v.* **-leased, -leas·ing.** —*n.* a lease granted by a person who rents the property himself. —*v.* grant or take a sublease of.

sub·let (sub let′) *v.* **-let, -let·ting. 1** rent to another (something that has been rented to oneself): *We sublet our house for the summer.* **2** give part of (a contract) to another: *The contractor for the whole building sublet the contract for the plumbing.*

sub·lieu·ten·ant (sub′lef ten′ənt) *n.* **1** a subordinate lieutenant. **2** in the navy, a commissioned officer junior to a lieutenant. *Abbrev.:* Sub.Lt.

sub·li·mate (*v.* sub′lə māt′; *adj. n.* sub′lə mit or sub′lə māt′) *v.* **-mat·ed, -mat·ing,** *adj. n.* —*v.* **1** purify; refine. **2** in chemistry, sublime (a solid substance). **3** in psychology, change (an undesirable impulse or trait) into a desirable activity. —*adj.* sublimated. —*n.* in chemistry, the material obtained when a substance is sublimed. Bichloride of mercury is a very poisonous sublimate. [< L *sublimare,* originally, raise < *sublimis* lofty]

sub·li·ma·tion (sub′lə mā′shən) *n.* 1 purification; the act or process of sublimating or subliming. 2 the resulting product or state.

sub·lime (sə blīm′) *adj. n. v.* **-limed, -lim·ing.** *—adj.* 1 lofty, noble; majestic; exalted: *The mountain scenery is sublime.* 2 expressing lofty ideas in a grand manner. *—n.* 1 that which is lofty, noble, exalted, etc. 2 **from the sublime to the ridiculous,** from one extreme to the other. *—v.* 1 heat (a solid substance) and condense the vapor given off; purify; refine. 2 pass off as a vapor and condense as a solid; become purified or refined. 3 make higher or nobler; make sublime. [ME < OF, ult. < L *sublimis,* originally, sloping up < *sub-* up + *limen* lintel] **—sub·lime′ly,** *adv.*

sub·lim·i·nal (sub lim′ə nəl) *adj.* 1 subconscious; below the threshold of consciousness: *the subliminal self.* 2 too weak or small to be felt or noticed. [< *sub-* + L *limen, liminis* threshold] **—sub·lim′i·nal·ly,** *adv.*

sub·lim·i·ty (səb lim′ə tē) *n.* **-ties.** 1 lofty excellence; grandeur; majesty; exalted state. 2 something sublime; a sublime person or thing.

sub·lin·gual (sub ling′gw əl) *adj.* in anatomy, located beneath or on the under side of the tongue. *—n.* a sublingual gland, artery, etc.

Sub.Lt. Sub-lieutenant.

sub·lu·nar (sub lü′nər) *adj.* sublunary.

sub·lu·nar·y (sub′lü ner′ē or sub lü′nər ē) *adj.* beneath the moon; earthly. [< NL *sublunaris,* ult. < L *sub-* under + *luna* moon]

sub·ma·chine gun (sub′mə shēn′) a lightweight automatic or semi-automatic gun, designed to be fired from the shoulder or hip.

sub·mar·gin·al (sub mär′jə nəl) *adj.* 1 near the margin. 2 below the margin. 3 of land, etc., not productive enough to be worth cultivating, developing, etc.

sub·ma·rine (*n. v.* sub′mə rēn′; *adj.* sub′mə rēn′) *n. v.* **-rined, -rin·ing,** *adj. —n.* a boat that can operate under water, used in warfare for discharging torpedoes, etc. *—v.* attack or sink by a submarine. *—adj.* 1 of or carried out by a submarine or submarines: *submarine tactics, submarine warfare.* 2 placed, growing, or used below the surface of the sea: *submarine plants.*

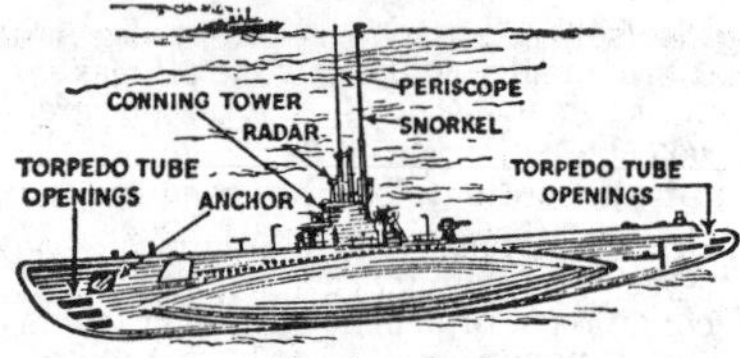

A submarine

sub·mar·i·ner (sub mar′ə nər or sub′mə rēn′ər) *n.* a member of the crew of a submarine.

sub·max·il·lar·y (sub mak′sə ler′ē) *n.* **-lar·ies,** *adj. —n.* 1 the lower jawbone. 2 a salivary gland situated beneath the lower jaw on either side. *—adj.* 1 of or having to do with the lower jaw or jawbone. 2 having to do with the submaxillary gland.

submaxillary gland either of a pair of salivary glands beneath the lower jaw.

sub·merge (səb mėrj′) *v.* **-merged, -merg·ing.** 1 put under water; cover with water: *land submerged by a flood.* 2 cover; bury: *His talent was submerged by his shyness.* 3 sink under water; go below the surface. 4 sink out of sight. [< L *submergere* < *sub-* under + *mergere* plunge] **—Syn. 1** plunge, immerse, submerse.

sub·mer·gence (səb mėr′jəns) *n.* the act of submerging or the state of being submerged.

sub·merse (səb mėrs′) *v.* **-mersed, -mers·ing.** submerge. [< L *submersus,* pp. of *submergere.* See SUBMERGE.]

sub·mers·i·ble (səb mėr′sə bəl) *adj.* that can be submerged. *—n.* a ship or craft that can operate under water for research, exploration, etc.

sub·mer·sion (səb mėr′zhən or səb mėr′shən) *n.* submergence.

sub·mis·sion (səb mish′ən) *n.* 1 the act of submitting; a yielding to the power, control, or authority of another: *The defeated general showed his submission by giving up his sword.* 2 obedience; humbleness: *The tyrant liked to see an attitude of submission in his subjects.* 3 a referring or being referred to the consideration or judgment of another or others. 4 a petition; a formal request. 5 a report. [ME < L *submissio, -onis* < *submittere.* See SUBMIT.] **—Syn. 1** compliance, acquiescence, surrender.

sub·mis·sive (səb mis′iv) *adj.* yielding to the power, control, or authority of another; obedient; humble. **—submis′sive·ly,** *adv.* **—sub·mis′sive·ness,** *n.*

sub·mit (səb mit′) *v.* **-mit·ted, -mit·ting.** 1 yield to the power, control, or authority of another or others; surrender; yield: *The thief submitted to arrest by the police.* 2 refer to the consideration or judgment of another or others: *The secretary submitted a report of the last meeting.* 3 represent or urge in a respectful manner. [ME < L *submittere* < *sub-* under + *mittere* let go] **—Syn. 1** comply, succumb, bow. See **yield.**

sub·nor·mal (sub nôr′məl) *adj.* 1 below normal; less than normal: *a subnormal temperature.* 2 inferior to the normal, especially in mental capacity: *a subnormal person. —n.* a subnormal individual.

sub-or·bit·al (sub ôr′bit əl) *adj.* 1 not in or going into orbit; of less than a full orbit: *The new space capsule was tested in a sub-orbital flight.* 2 in anatomy, situated below the orbit of the eye: *a sub-orbital nerve.*

sub·or·der (sub′ôr′dər or sub ôr′dər) *n.* in zoology and botany, a group of plants or animals. We classify into classes, subclasses, orders, suborders, families, subfamilies, genera, subgenera, species, and subspecies.

sub·or·di·nate (*adj. n.* sə bôr′də nit; *v.* sə bôr′də nāt′) *adj. n. v.* **-nat·ed, -nat·ing.** *—adj.* 1 inferior in rank: *In the army, lieutenants are subordinate to captains.* 2 inferior in importance; secondary. 3 under the control or influence of something else. 4 in grammar: **a** dependent. A complex sentence has one main clause and one or more **subordinate clauses. b** subordinating. *Because, since, if, as,* and *whether* are **subordinate conjunctions.** *—n.* a subordinate person or thing. *—v.* make subordinate: *The host politely subordinated his wishes to those of his guests.* [< Med.L *subordinatus,* pp. of *subordinare,* ult. < L *sub-* under + *ordo, ordinis* order] **—sub·or′di·nate·ly,** *adv.* **—Syn.** *adj.* **3** subject, subservient.

sub·or·di·na·tion (se bôr′də nā′shən) *n.* 1 the act of subordinating or the state of being subordinated. 2 a subordinate position or importance. 3 a submission to authority; willingness to obey; obedience.

sub·orn (sə bôrn′) *v.* 1 persuade or cause (a witness) to give false testimony in court. 2 persuade or cause (a person) to do an unlawful act. [< L *subornare* < *sub-* secretly + *ornare* equip] **—sub′or·na′tion,** *n.* **—sub·orn′er,** *n.*

subornation of perjury in law, the crime of persuading or causing a witness to give false testimony in court.

sub·poe·na or **sub·pe·na** (sə pē′nə) *n. v.* **-naed, -na·ing.** *—n.* in law, an official written order commanding a person to appear in court. *—v.* summon with a subpoena. [< NL *sub poena* under penalty]

sub ro·sa (sub′rō′zə) in strict confidence; privately. [< *sub rosa* under the rose; the rose was an ancient symbol of secrecy]

sub·scribe (səb skrīb′) *v.* **-scribed, -scrib·ing.** 1 promise to give or pay (a sum of money): *He subscribed $25 to the hospital fund.* 2 write (one's name) at the end of a document, etc.; sign one's name. 3 write one's name at the end of; show one's consent or approval by signing: *Thousands of citizens subscribed the petition.* 4 give one's consent or approval; agree: *He will not subscribe to anything unfair.* 5 **subscribe to** or **for,** promise to take and pay for: *subscribe to a magazine.* [ME < L *subscribere* < *sub-* under + *scribere* write] **—sub·scrib′er,** *n.*

sub·script (sub′skript) *adj.* written underneath or low on the line. *—n.* a number, letter, etc. written underneath and to one side of a symbol. *Example:* In H_2SO_4 the *2* and *4* are subscripts. [< L *subscriptus,* pp. of *subscribere.* See SUBSCRIBE.]

sub·scrip·tion (səb skrip′shən) *n.* 1 a subscribing. 2 the money subscribed; contribution: *His subscription to the Fresh Air Fund was $5.* **3** the right obtained for the money: *His subscription to the newspaper expires next week.* **4** a sum of money raised by a number of persons: *We are raising a subscription for a new hospital.* **5** something written at the end of a thing; signature. **6** a signing, as of one's name or a document.

sub·sec·tion (sub′sek′shən or sub sek′shən) *n.* a part of a section.

sub·se·quence (sub′sə kwəns) *n.* **1** the fact or condition of being subsequent. **2** a subsequent event or circumstance.

sub·se·quent (sub′sə kwənt) *adj.* **1** coming after; following; later: *subsequent events.* **2 subsequent to,** after; following; later than: *on the day subsequent to your call.* [< L *subsequens, -entis,* ppr. of *subsequi* < *sub-* up + *sequi* follow]

sub·se·quent·ly (sub′sə kwənt lē) *adv.* **1** afterward; later. **2 subsequently to,** after; following; later than.

sub·serve (səb sėrv′) *v.* **-served, -serv·ing.** be of use or service in helping along (a purpose, action, etc.): *Chewing food well subserves digestion.* [< L *subservire* < *sub-* under + *servire* serve]

sub·ser·vi·ence (səb sėr′vē əns) *n.* **1** tame submission; slavish politeness and obedience; servility. **2** the quality of being of use or service.

sub·ser·vi·en·cy (səb sėr′vē ən sē) *n.* subservience.

sub·ser·vi·ent (səb sėr′vē ənt) *adj.* **1** tamely submissive; slavishly polite and obedient; servile. **2** useful as a means to help a purpose or end; serviceable. [< L *subserviens, -entis,* ppr. of *subservire* < *sub-* under + *servire* serve] **—sub·ser′vi·ent·ly,** *adv.*

sub·set (sub′set′) *n.* in mathematics and logic, a set whose members are also members of another set or series: *The set of dogs is a subset of the set of mammals.*

sub·side (səb sīd′) *v.* **-sid·ed, -sid·ing. 1** sink to a lower level: *After the rain stopped, the flood waters subsided.* **2** grow less; die down; become less active: *The storm finally subsided.* **3** fall to the bottom; settle. [< L *subsidere* < *sub-* down + *sidere* settle] **—Syn. 2** abate, decrease, ebb.

sub·sid·ence (səb sīd′ens or sub′sə dəns) *n.* the act or process of subsiding.

sub·sid·i·ar·y (səb sid′ē er′ē) *adj. n.* **-ar·ies.** *—adj.* **1** useful to assist or supplement; auxiliary; supplementary. **2** subordinate; secondary. **3** maintained by a subsidy. *—n.* **1** a thing or person that assists or supplements. **2** a company having over half of its stock owned or controlled by another company: *The bus line was a subsidiary of the railway.* [< L *subsidiarius* < *subsidium* reserve troops]

sub·si·dize (sub′sə dīz′) *v.* **-dized, -diz·ing. 1** aid or assist with a grant of money: *The government subsidizes shipping lines and airlines that carry mail.* **2** buy the aid or assistance of with a grant of money. **3** bribe. **—sub′si·diz′er,** *n.*

sub·si·dy (sub′sə dē) *n.* **-dies.** a grant or contribution of money, especially one made by a government. [< L *subsidium* aid, reserve troops]

sub·sist (səb sist′) *v.* **1** continue to be; exist: *Many superstitions still subsist.* **2** keep alive; live: *People in the far north subsist on fish and meat.* [< L *subsistere* < *sub-* up to + *sistere* stand]

sub·sist·ence (səb sis′təns) *n.* **1** existence; continuance. **2** the state or fact of keeping alive; living. **3** a means of keeping alive; livelihood: *The sea provides a subsistence for fishermen.*

sub·soil (sub′soil′) *n.* the layer of earth that lies just under the surface soil.

sub·son·ic (sub son′ik) *adj.* having to do with or designed for use at a speed less than that of sound.

sub·spe·cies (sub′spē′sēz or -spē′shēz) *n.* **-cies.** a subdivision of a species.

subst. 1 substitute. **2** substantive.

sub·stance (sub′stəns) *n.* **1** what a thing consists of; matter; material: *Ice and water are the same substance in different forms:* **2** the real, main, or important part of anything: *The substance of an education is its effect on your life, not just the learning of lessons.* **3** the real

hat, āge, cãre, fär; let, ēqual, tėrm; it, īce
hot, ōpen, ôrder; oil, out; cup, pu̇t, rüle, ūse
əbove, takən, pencəl, lemən, circəs
ch, child; ng, long; sh, ship
th, thin; ᴛʜ, then; zh, measure

meaning: *Give the substance of the speech in your own words.* **4** solid quality; body: *Pea soup has more substance than bouillon.* **5** wealth; property. **6** a particular kind of matter: *The little pond is covered with a green substance.* **7** in philosophy: **a** something that underlies all phenomena, and in which accidents or attributes inhere. **b** something that subsists by itself; a separate or distinct thing. **8 in substance, a** essentially; mainly. **b** really; actually. [ME < OF < *substantia* < *substare* stand firm < *sub-* up to + *stare* stand]

Syn. 1 Substance, matter, material = what a thing consists or is made of. **Substance** = what a thing consists of, as apart from the form in which it exists, and applies both to things existing in the physical world and to those given actual form only in the mind: *The substance of the plan is good.* **Matter** applies to substance that occupies space and that physical objects consist of: *Matter may be gaseous, liquid, or solid.* **Material** = matter from which something is made: *Wood is an important building material.*

sub·stan·dard (sub stan′dərd or sub′stan′dərd) *adj.* below standard.

sub·stan·tial (səb stan′shəl) *adj.* **1** real; actual: *People and things are substantial; dreams and ghosts are not.* **2** large; important; ample: *John has made a substantial improvement in health.* **3** strong; firm; solid: *The house is substantial enough to last a hundred years.* **4** in the main; in essentials: *The stories told by the two boys were in substantial agreement.* **5** well-to-do; wealthy. **6** of real or solid worth or value; weighty; sound: *substantial criticism, substantial evidence.* [ME < L *substantialis* < *substantia.* See SUBSTANCE.]

sub·stan·ti·al·i·ty (səb stan′shē al′ə tē) *n.* **-ties. 1** real existence. **2** solidity; firmness. **3** real worth.

sub·stan·tial·ly (səb stan′shəl ē) *adv.* **1** essentially; mainly. **2** really; actually. **3** strongly; solidly.

sub·stan·ti·ate (səb stan′shē āt′) *v.* **-at·ed, -at·ing. 1** establish by evidence; prove: *substantiate a rumor, a claim, a theory, etc.* **2** give concrete or substantial form to.

sub·stan·ti·a·tion (səb stan′shē ā′shən) *n.* a substantiating or being substantiated; embodiment; proof.

sub·stan·ti·val (sub′stən tī′vəl) *adj.* or of consisting of a substantive or substantives.

sub·stan·tive (sub′stən tiv) *n.* in grammar, a noun or pronoun; the name of a person or thing; an adjective, phrase, or clause used as a noun. *—adj.* **1** in grammar: **a** used as a noun. **b** showing or expressing existence. The verb *be* is the substantive verb. **2** independent. **3** real; actual. **4** having a firm or solid basis. [ME < LL *substantivus,* ult. < *substare.* See SUBSTANCE.]

sub·stan·tive·ly (sub′stən tiv lē) *adv.* **1** independently. **2** actually; in substance; in effect. **3** as a substantive.

sub·sta·tion (sub′stā′shən) *n.* a branch station; subordinate station: *Besides the main post office in our city, there are six substations.*

sub·sti·tute (sub′stə tūt′ or sub′stə tüt′) *n. v.* **-tut·ed, -tut·ing,** *adj. —n.* **1** something used instead of something else; a person taking the place of another: *Margarine is a common substitute for butter.* **2** in sports, a team player who alternates with another during a game. *—v.* **1** put in the place of another: *We substituted brown sugar for molasses in these cookies.* **2** take the place of another. *—adj.* put in or taking the place of another. [ME < L *substitutus,* pp. of *substituere* < *sub-* instead + *statuere* establish] **—Syn.** *n.* alternate. *–v.* replace.

substitute teacher a teacher who acts as a substitute for other teachers.

sub·sti·tu·tion (sub′stə tū′shən or sub′stə tü′shən) *n.* the use of one thing for another; a putting of (one person or thing) in the place of another; the taking the place of another.

sub·sti·tu·tion·al (sub′stə tū′shən əl or sub′stə tü′shən əl) *adj.* **1** having to do with or characterized by substitution. **2** acting or serving as a substitute. **—sub′sti·tu′tion·al·ly,** *adv.*

sub·sti·tu·tive (sub′stə tū′tiv or sub′stə tü′tiv) *adj.* 1 having to do with or involving substitution. 2 serving as, or capable of serving as, a substitute.

sub·stra·ta (sub strā′tə or -strat′ə) *n.* pl. of **substratum.**

sub·stra·tum (sub strā′təm or -strat′əm) *n.* **-stra·ta** or **-stra·tums.** 1 a layer lying under another. 2 a layer of earth lying just under the surface soil; subsoil. 3 a basis; foundation: *The story has a substratum of truth.* 4 in biology, the base or matter of which an organism develops. [< NL *substratum,* neut. of L *substratus,* pp. of *substernere* < *sub-* under + *sternere* spread]

sub·struc·tur·al (sub struk′chər əl) *adj.* of, having to do with, or like a substructure.

sub·struc·ture (sub′struk′chər or sub struk′chər) *n.* a structure forming a foundation.

sub·sume (səb süm′) *v.* **-sumed, -sum·ing.** 1 bring (an idea, term, proposition, etc.) under another; bring (a case, instance, etc.) under a rule. 2 take up into, or include in, a larger or higher class, etc. [< NL *subsumere* < L *sub-* under + *sumere* assume]

sub·teen (sub′tēn′) *adj. Informal.* of or for subteen-agers. *—n.* a subteen-ager.

sub·teen-ag·er (sub tēn′āj′ər) *n. Informal.* a boy or girl almost 13 years of age.

sub·ten·an·cy (sub ten′ən sē) *n.* **-cies.** a status, right, or holding of a subtenant.

sub·ten·ant (sub ten′ənt or sub′ten′ənt) *n.* a tenant of a tenant; one who rents land, a house, or the like, from a tenant.

sub·tend (səb tend′) *v.* 1 extend under; stretch across. The chord of an arc subtends the arc. 2 in botany, enclose in the angle between a leaf or bract and its stem. [< L *subtendere* < *sub-* under + *tendere* stretch]

B
A C

The chord AC subtends the arc ABC.

sub·ter·fuge (sub′tər fūj′) *n.* a trick, excuse, or expedient used to escape something unpleasant: *The girl's headache was only a subterfuge to avoid taking the examination.* [< LL *subterfugium,* ult. < L *subter-* from under + *fugere* flee] **—Syn.** artifice, ruse.

sub·ter·ra·ne·an (sub′tə rā′nē ən) *adj.* 1 underground: *A subterranean passage led from the castle to a cave.* 2 carried on secretly; hidden. [< L *subterraneus* < *sub-* under + *terra* earth]

sub·ter·ra·ne·ous (sub′tə rā′nē əs) *adj.* underground. **—sub′ter·ra′ne·ous·ly,** *adv.*

sub·tile (sut′əl, sub′tīl, or sub′təl) *adj.* 1 not dense or heavy; delicate: *a subtile liquid, fabric, powder.* 2 *Archaic.* subtle. [ME < OF *subtil,* learned borrowing < L *subtilis.* See SUBTLE.] **—sub′tile·ly,** *adv.* **—sub′tile·ness,** *n.*

sub·til·i·ty (sub til′ə tē) *n.* **-ties.** *Archaic.* subtlety.

sub·til·ty (sut′əl tē or sub′təl tē) *n.* **-ties.** subtlety.

sub·ti·tle (sub′tī′təl) *n. v.* **-tled, -tling.** *—n.* 1 an additional or subordinate title of a book or article. 2 a word or words on a motion-picture screen shown as a caption. *—v.* give such a title to.

sub·tle (sut′əl) *adj.* 1 delicate; thin; fine: *a subtle odor of perfume.* 2 faint; mysterious: *a subtle smile.* 3 having a keen, quick mind; discerning; acute: *She is a subtle observer of slight differences in things.* 4 sly; crafty; tricky: *a subtle scheme to get some money.* 5 skilful; clever; expert. 6 working unnoticeably or secretly; insidious: *a subtle poison or drug.* [ME < OF *soutil* < L *subtilis,* originally, woven underneath] **—sub′tle·ness,** *n.* **—Syn.** 1 tenuous, rare. 3 discriminating. 4 artful, cunning, insidious.

sub·tle·ty (sut′əl tē) *n.* **-ties.** 1 a subtle quality. 2 something subtle.

sub·tly (sut′lē) *adv.* in a subtle manner; with subtlety.

sub·ton·ic (sub ton′ik) *n.* in music, the seventh tone of a scale; tone next below the upper tonic.

sub·tract (səb trakt′) *v.* 1 take away: *Subtract 2 from 10 and you have 8.* 2 take away (something) from a whole. [< L *subtractus,* pp. of *subtrahere* < *sub-* from under + *trahere* draw] **—sub·tract′er,** *n.*

Syn. 1, 2 Subtract, deduct = take away. **Subtract** = to take away from a whole, but in present usage is almost never used except in its mathematical sense, commonly meaning "to take away one number from another": *He subtracted 89 from 200.* **Deduct** = take away a quantity or amount from a total or whole: *He deducted the price of the cup I broke from the amount he owed me. He deducted 89 cents from $2.*

sub·trac·tion (səb trak′shən) *n.* 1 the act or process of subtracting one number or quantity from another; the process of finding the difference between two numbers or quantities. 10 − 2 = 8 is a simple subtraction. 2 a taking away or being taken away.

sub·trac·tive (səb trak′tiv) *adj.* 1 tending to subtract; having power to subtract. 2 to be subtracted; having the minus sign (−).

sub·tra·hend (sub′trə hend′) *n.* a number or quantity to be subtracted from another. In 10 − 2 = 8, the subtrahend is 2. [< L *subtrahendus* < *subtrahere.* See SUBTRACT.]

sub·trop·i·cal (sub trop′ə kəl) *adj.* bordering on the tropics; nearly tropical.

sub·trop·ics (sub trop′iks or sub′trop′iks) *n.pl.* the region bordering on the tropics.

sub·urb (sub′ėrb) *n.* 1 a town or village near a large city. 2 a district just outside the boundaries of a city or town. 3 **the suburbs,** the residential section or sections near the boundary of a city or town. [ME < L *suburbium* < *sub-* below + *urbs* city]

sub·ur·ban (sə bėr′bən) *adj.* 1 having to do with a suburb; in a suburb: *We have an excellent suburban train service.* 2 characteristic of a suburb or its inhabitants. *—n.* suburbanite.

sub·ur·ban·ite (sə bėr′bən īt′) *n.* a person who lives in a suburb.

sub·ur·bi·a (sə bėr′bē ə) *n.* 1 suburbs; the suburbs. 2 suburban society, its outlook, culture, etc.

sub·ven·tion (səb ven′shən) *n.* 1 money granted to aid or support some cause, institution, or undertaking; subsidy. 2 a the providing of help, support, or relief. b an instance of this. [ME < OF < LL *subventio, -onis* < L *subvenire* come to one's aid < *sub-* under + *venire* come]

sub·ver·sion (səb vėr′zhən or səb vėr′shən) *n.* 1 an overthrow; destruction; ruin. 2 anything that tends to overthrow or destroy; cause of ruin. [ME < OF < LL *subversio, -onis* < L *subvertere.* See SUBVERT.]

sub·ver·sive (səb vėr′siv) *adj.* tending to overthrow; destructive; causing ruin. *—n.* a person who seeks to overthrow or undermine (a government, etc.). **—sub·ver′sive·ly,** *adv.*

sub·vert (səb vėrt′) *v.* 1 ruin; overthrow; destroy: *Dictators subvert democracy.* 2 undermine the principles of; corrupt. [ME < OF < L *subvertere* < *sub-* up from under + *vertere* turn] **—sub·vert′er,** *n.*

sub·way (sub′wā′) *n.* 1 an electric railway running for all or most of its length beneath the surface of the streets in a city. 2 a road running under another road or under a railway track; an underpass. 3 an underground passage.

suc- the form of **sub-** before *c,* as in *succeed.*

suc·ceed (sək sēd′) *v.* 1 turn out well; do well; have success: *His plans succeeded.* 2 accomplish what is attempted or intended: *The attack succeeded beyond all expectations.* 3 come next after; follow; take the place of *Diefenbaker succeeded St. Laurent as Prime Minister of Canada.* 4 **succeed to,** come into possession of an office, power, property, etc. through right of birth, by election, etc.: *The Prince of Wales succeeds to the throne of England.* [ME < L *succedere* < *sub-* up (to) + *cedere* go] **—suc·ceed′er,** *n.* **—Syn. 1** prosper, thrive, flourish. **3** See **follow.**

suc·cess (sək ses′) *n.* 1 a favorable result; a wished-for ending; good fortune. 2 the gaining of wealth, position, etc.: *He has had little success in life.* 3 a person or thing that succeeds. 4 the result; outcome; fortune: *What success did you have in finding a new cook?* [< L *successus* < *succedere.* See SUCCEED.]

suc·cess·ful (sək ses′fəl) *adj.* 1 having success; ending in success. 2 prosperous; fortunate. **—suc·cess′ful·ly,** *adv.*

suc·ces·sion (sək sesh′ən) *n.* 1 a group of things

happening one after another; series. **2** the coming of one person or thing after another. **3** the right of succeeding to an office, property, or rank: *There was a dispute about the rightful succession to the throne.* **4** the set or arrangement of persons having such a right of succeeding: *The king's oldest son is next in succession to the throne.* **5 in succession,** one after another. **—Syn. 1** See **series.**

succession duty a tax payable on inherited money or property.

suc·ces·sive (sək ses′iv) *adj.* coming one after another; following in order: *It rained for three successive days.*
Syn. Successive, consecutive = following one after another without interruption or a break. **Successive** emphasizes the idea of coming one after another in order or without interruption: *He has worked on three successive Saturdays.* **Consecutive** emphasizes the closeness of the connection or the idea of following immediately or continuously: *He worked three consecutive days last week.*

suc·ces·sive·ly (sək ses′iv lē) *adv.* one after another; in order.

suc·ces·sor (sək ses′ər) *n.* one that follows or succeeds another in office, position, or ownership of property; anything that comes next after another in a series. [< L]

suc·cinct (sək singkt′) *adj.* expressed briefly and clearly; expressing much in a few words; concise. [ME < L *succinctus,* pp. of *succingere* tuck up clothes for action < *sub-* up + *cingere* gird] **—suc·cinct′ly,** *adv.* **—suc·cinct′ness,** *n.* **—Syn.** compressed, condensed, terse.

suc·cor or **suc·cour** (suk′ər) *n.* a person or thing that helps, relieves, or assists; help; aid; assistance. *—v.* help, assist, or aid (a person, etc.) in time of need, distress, or danger; support; relieve. [ME < OF *sucurs,* ult. < L *succurrere* run to help < *sub-* up (to) + *currere* run]

suc·co·ry (suk′ə rē) *n.* chicory.

suc·co·tash (suk′ə tash′) *n.* a food consisting of corn kernels and beans, usually Lima beans, cooked together. [< Algonquian]

suc·cour (suk′ər) *n. v.* succor.

suc·cu·lence (suk′yů ləns) *n.* juiciness.

suc·cu·len·cy (suk′yů lən sē) *n.* succulence.

suc·cu·lent (suk′yů lənt) *adj.* **1** juicy: *a succulent fruit.* **2** interesting; not dull. **3** in botany, having thick, fleshy leaves and stems. *—n.* in botany, a succulent plant. [< L *succulentus* < *succus* juice] **—suc′cu·lent·ly,** *adv.*

suc·cumb (sə kum′) *v.* **1** give way; yield: *He succumbed to temptation and stole the money.* **2** die. **3 succumb to,** die of. [ME < L *succumbere* < *sub-* down + *-cumbere* lie]

such (such) *adj.* **1** of that kind; of the same kind or degree: *I have never seen such a sight.* **2** of the kind that; of a particular kind: *She wore such thin clothes it is no wonder she caught cold.* **3** of the kind already spoken of or suggested: *The ladies took only tea and coffee and such drinks.* **4** so great, so bad, so good, etc.: *He is such a liar.* **5** a certain one or ones not named or identified; some; certain: *The bank was robbed in such and such a town by such and such persons.* **6 such as, a** the kind or degree that; of a particular kind: *Her behavior was such as might be expected of a young child.* **b** of a particular character or kind: *The food, such as it was, was plentiful.* **c** for example: *members of the dog family, such as the wolf, fox, and jackal.*
—pron. **1** such a person or thing: *Take from the blankets such as you need.* **2 as such, a** as being what is indicated or implied: *A leader, as such, deserves obedience.* **b** in or by itself; intrinsically considered: *Mere good looks, as such, will not take you far.* [OE *swylc, swelc* < *swa* so + *līc* like]

such·like (such′līk′) *adj.* of such kind; of a like kind. *—pron.* things of such kind: *deceptions, disguises, and suchlike.*

suck (suk) *v.* **1** draw into the mouth: *Lemonade can be sucked through a straw.* **2** draw something from with the mouth: *suck oranges.* **3** draw milk from the breast or a bottle. **4** draw or be drawn by sucking: *He sucked at his pipe.* **5** drink; take; absorb: *Plants suck up moisture from the earth. A sponge sucks in water.* **6** draw in; swallow: *The whirlpool sucked down the boat.* **7** draw air instead of water: *The pump sucked noisily.* **8** hold in the mouth and lick: *The child sucked a lollipop.*
—n. **1** the act of sucking. **2** a sucking force or sound. [OE *sūcan*]

hat, āge, cãre, fär; let, ēqual, tėrm; it, īce
hot, ōpen, ôrder; oil, out; cup, pủt, rüle, ūse
əbove, takən, pencəl, lemən, circəs
ch, child; ng, long; sh, ship
th, thin; ᴛʜ, then; zh, measure

suck·er (suk′ər) *n.* **1** an animal or thing that sucks. **2** any of various fresh-water fishes that suck in food or have mouths suggesting that they do so. **3** in some animals, an organ for sucking or holding fast by a sucking force. **4** in botany: **a** a shoot growing from an underground stem or root. **b** an adventitious shoot from the trunk or a branch of a tree or plant. **5** the piston of a suction pump. **6** the valve of such a piston. **7** *Slang.* a person easily deceived. **8** a lump of hard candy, usually on a stick.
—v. **1** remove suckers from (corn, tobacco, etc.). **2** form suckers. **3** *Slang.* treat as a fool or simpleton; deceive; dupe.

suck·le (suk′əl) *v.* **-led, -ling. 1** feed with milk from the breast, udder, etc.: *The cat suckles her kittens.* **2** suck at the breast. **3** nourish; bring up. [< *suck*]

suck·ling (suk′ling) *n.* a very young animal or child, especially one not yet weaned. *—adj.* **1** very young. **2** not yet weaned; sucking.

su·cre (sü′krā) *n.* **1** a unit of money in Ecuador. See table at **money. 2** a coin or note worth one sucre. [Antonio José de *Sucre* (1793-1830), a South American general and liberator]

su·crose (sü′krōs) *n.* sugar obtained from sugar cane, sugar beets, etc. *Formula:* $C_{12}H_{22}O_{11}$ [< F *sucre* sugar]

suc·tion (suk′shən) *n.* **1** the drawing of a liquid, gas, etc. into a space by sucking out or removing part of the air: *Lemonade is drawn through a straw by suction.* **2** the force caused by sucking out or removing part of the air in a space. **3** the act or process of sucking. *—adj.* causing a suction; working by suction. [< L *suctio, -onis* < *sugere* suck]

suction pump a cuplike device of rubber, etc., designed to adhere to smooth surfaces by creating a vacuum when pressed against them and then released: *Toy arrows are often tipped with suction cups.*

suc·to·ri·al (suk tô′rē əl) *adj.* adapted for sucking or suction.

Su·da·nese (sü′də nēz′) *adj. n.* **-nese.** *—adj.* of or having to do with the Sudan, a country in Africa south of Egypt, or its inhabitants. *—n.* a native or inhabitant of the Sudan.

Sudan grass (sü dan′) a kind of grass originally from Sudan, grown for hay.

su·da·to·ri·um (sü′də tô′rē əm) *n.* **-ri·a** (-rē ə). a hot-air bath for inducing sweating. [< L *sudatorium,* ult. < *sudor* sweat]

sud·den (sud′ən) *adj.* **1** not expected: *Our army made a sudden attack on the fort.* **2** found or hit upon unexpectedly; abrupt: *a sudden turn in a road, a sudden shift in foreign policy.* **3** quick; rapid: *The cat made a sudden jump at the mouse.*
—n. all of a sudden, in a sudden manner. [ME < AF *sodein* < L *subitaneus* < *subitus* sudden] **—sud′den·ness,** *n.*

sudden death 1 instant or unexpected death. **2** in sports: **a** the playing of a game to break a tie with no fixed period but ending as soon as either side scores. **b** a full game played to break a tie.

sud·den·ly (sud′ən lē) *adv.* in a sudden manner.

su·dor·if·er·ous (sü′dər if′ər əs) *adj.* secreting sweat.

su·dor·if·ic (sü′dər if′ik) *adj.* **1** causing or promoting sweat. **2** secreting sweat. *—n.* a sudorific agent or remedy. [< NL *sudorificus* < L *sudor* sweat + *facere* make]

suds (sudz) *n.pl.* **1** soapy water. **2** the bubbles and foam on soapy water. **3** any froth or foam. **4** the foam on top of freshly poured beer. **5** *Slang.* beer. *—v.* **1** wash in suds. **2** form suds: *This soap sudses quickly.* [? < MDu. *sudse* bog]

sud·sy (sud′zē) *adj.* that sudses easily or copiously.

sue (sü) *v.* **sued, su·ing. 1** in law: **a** start a lawsuit against: *He sued the railway because his cow was killed by the* *engine.* **b** take action: *sue for damages.* **2** beg or ask (for); plead: *Messengers came suing for peace.* **3** *Archaic.* make love to; woo. **4 sue out,** apply for and get (a writ, pardon, etc.) from a law court. [ME < AF *suer,* ult. < L *sequi* follow] —**su′a·ble,** *adj.*

suède or **suede** (swād) *n.* **1** a kind of soft leather that has a velvety nap on one or both sides. **2** a kind of cloth that has a similar appearance. —*adj.* made of suède. [< F (*de*) *Suède* (from) Sweden]

su·et (sü′it) *n.* the hard fat about the kidneys and loins of cattle or sheep. Beef suet is used in cooking. [ME < AF *suet, dim. of *sue,* OF *sieu* tallow < L *sebum*]

su·et·y (sü′it ē) *adj.* **1** like suet. **2** containing suet.

suf- the form of **sub-** before *f,* as in *suffer* and *suffice.*

suf. or **suff.** suffix.

suf·fer (suf′ər) *v.* **1** have pain, grief, injury, etc.: *Sick people suffer.* **2** have or feel (pain, grief, etc.). **3** experience harm, loss, etc.: *His business suffered greatly during the war.* **4** allow; permit: "*Suffer little children to come unto me.*" **5** bear with patiently; endure: *I will not suffer such insults.* [ME < AF < L *sufferre* < *sub-* up + *ferre* bear] —**suf′fer·er,** *n.*

suf·fer·a·ble (suf′ər ə bəl or suf′rə bəl) *adj.* that can be endured; bearable. —**suf′fer·a·bly,** *adv.*

suf·fer·ance (suf′ər əns or suf′rəns) *n.* **1** permission given only by a failure to object or prevent. **2** the power to bear or endure; patient endurance. **3 on sufferance,** allowed or tolerated, but not really wanted.

suf·fer·ing (suf′ər ing or suf′ring) *n.* pain; the enduring of pain. —**Syn.** distress, agony, misery.

suf·fice (sə fīs′) *v.* **-ficed, -fic·ing. 1** be enough; be sufficient: *The money will suffice for one year.* **2** satisfy; make content: *A small amount sufficed him.* [ME < OF < L *sufficere* < *sub-* up (to) + *facere* make]

suf·fi·cien·cy (sə fish′ən sē) *n.* **-cies. 1** a sufficient amount; a large enough supply: *The ship had a sufficiency of provisions for a voyage of two months.* **2** the state or fact of being sufficient; adequacy; ability. **3** self-confidence.

suf·fi·cient (sə fish′ənt) *adj.* **1** as much as is needed; enough: *sufficient proof.* **2** *Archaic.* competent; able. [ME < L *sufficiens, -entis,* ppr. of *sufficere.* See SUFFICE.] —**Syn. 1** adequate, ample. See **enough.**

suf·fi·cient·ly (sə fish′ənt lē) *adv.* enough; as much as is needed.

suf·fix (*n.* suf′iks; *v.* sə fiks′) *n.* **1 a** an addition made at the end of a word to form another word of different meaning or function, as in bad*ly*, good*ness*, spoon*ful*, amaze*ment*. **b** an inflectional ending, as in talk*s*, talk*ed*, talk*ing*. **2** in mathematics, a subscript. —*v.* add at the end; put after. [< NL < L *suffixum,* neut. pp. of *suffigere* < *sub-* upon + *figere* fasten]

suf·fix·al (suf′iks əl) *adj.* having to do with or of the nature of a suffix.

suf·fo·cate (suf′ə kāt′) *v.* **-cat·ed, -cat·ing. 1** kill by stopping the breath. **2** keep from breathing; hinder in breathing. **3** choke; gasp for breath. **4** die for lack of air. **5** smother; suppress. [< L *suffocare,* originally, narrow up < *sub-* up + *foces,* dial. var. of *fauces* throat, narrow entrance] —**suf′fo·cat′ing·ly,** *adv.*

suf·fo·ca·tion (suf′ə kā′shən) *n.* **1** a suffocating. **2** the state of being suffocated.

suf·fo·ca·tive (suf′ə kā′tiv) *adj.* stifling.

Suf·folk (suf′ək) *n.* **1** any of an English breed of hornless sheep raised especially for meat. **2** any of an English breed of heavy-bodied, chestnut-colored work horses. [< *Suffolk,* a county in England]

suf·fra·gan (suf′rə gən) *n.* **1** a bishop consecrated to assist another bishop. **2** any bishop considered in relation to his archbishop. —*adj.* assisting. [ME < OF *suffragan,* ult. < L *suffragium* suffrage. See SUFFRAGE.]

suf·frage (suf′rij) *n.* **1** a vote; vote for some person or thing. **2** the right to vote: *Alberta granted suffrage to women in 1916.* **3** a voting; casting of votes. **4** a short prayer of supplication. **5** *Archaic.* approval; assent; sanction; consent. [ME < L *suffragium* supporting vote < *sub-* nearby + *frag-* applause (related to *fragor* din, crash, originally, a breaking)]

suf·fra·gette (suf′rə jet′) *n.* formerly, a woman who advocated suffrage for women.

suf·fra·gist (suf′rə jist) *n.* a person who favors giving suffrage to more people, especially to women.

suf·fuse (sə fūz′) *v.* **-fused, -fus·ing.** overspread (with a liquid, dye, etc.): *At twilight the sky was suffused with color. Her eyes were suffused with tears.* [< L *suffusus,* pp. of *suffundere* < *sub-* (up from) under + *fundere* pour]

suf·fu·sion (sə fū′zhən) *n.* **1** a suffusing. **2** the state of being suffused. **3** that with which anything is overspread. **4** a flush of color.

sug- the form of **sub-** before *g,* as in *suggest.*

sug·ar (shu̇g′ər) *n.* **1** a sweet, crystalline substance obtained chiefly from sugar cane, sugar beets or the sugar maple and used extensively in food products. *Formula:* $C_{12}H_{22}O_{11}$ **2** in chemistry, any of the class of carbohydrates to which this substance belongs: *grape sugar, milk sugar. Glucose and levulose are sugars.* **3** a sugarlike substance: *sugar of lead.* **4** sweet or honeyed words; flattery. **5** *Slang.* money.
—*v.* **1** put sugar in; sweeten with sugar. **2** cover with sugar; sprinkle with sugar. **3** form sugar: *Honey sugars if kept too long.* **4** make maple sugar. **5** cause to seem pleasant or agreeable. **6 sugar off,** make maple sugar by boiling maple syrup until it crystallizes. [ME < OF *sucre* < Med.L < Arabic *sukkar* < Persian < Skt. *sarkara,* originally, grit]

sugar beet a large beet having a white root that yields sugar.

sugar bush a grove of sugar maples.

sugar cane a very tall grass having a strong, jointed stem and flat leaves, growing in warm regions. Sugar cane and sugar beets are the main sources of sugar.

sug·ar-coat (shu̇g′ər kōt′) *v.* **1** cover with sugar. **2** cause to seem more pleasant or agreeable.

sug·ar-coat·ing (shu̇g′ər kōt′ing) *n.* **1** a covering of sugar. **2** anything that makes something seem more pleasant or agreeable.

sugar corn sweet corn.

sugar cube a cake of sugar in cube form.

sugar daddy *Slang.* a wealthy old or middle-aged man who lavishes gifts and money on a younger woman in return for her favors.

sugaring off 1 the converting of maple syrup into sugar by boiling it until it crystallizes. **2 a** gathering of friends and neighbors to assist in this process and enjoy a party afterwards.

sugar loaf 1 a cone-shaped mass of sugar. **2** something shaped like a sugar loaf. **3** a tall, cone-shaped hat. **4** a high, cone-shaped hill.

sug·ar-loaf (shu̇g′ər lōf′) *adj.* shaped like a sugar loaf.

sugar maple a maple tree of E. North America, yielding a sweet sap from which maple sugar is made.

sugar of lead a poisonous crystalline salt, lead acetate, used in medicine and paint.

sugar of milk lactose, the sugar that occurs in milk.

sug·ar·plum (shu̇g′ər plum′) *n.* a piece of candy; bonbon.

sugar shanty a hut or cabin used for making maple sugar.

sug·ar·y (shu̇g′ər ē) *adj.* **1** consisting of sugar; like sugar; sweet. **2** seemingly pleasant or agreeable; deceitfully or flatteringly pleasant: *a sugary greeting.* **3** excessively or offensively sweet: *The pudding was too sugary for my taste.* —**sug′ar·i·ness,** *n.*

sug·gest (sə jest′ or səg jest′) *v.* **1** bring to mind; call up the thought of: *The thought of summer suggests swimming, tennis, and hot weather.* **2** propose: *John suggested a swim, and we all agreed.* **3** provide the motive for; prompt. **4** show in an indirect way; hint: *His yawns suggested that he would like to go to bed.* [< L *suggestus,* pp. of *suggerere* put under, supply, suggest < *sub-* up + *gerere* bring] —**sug′gest·er,** *n.* —**Syn. 4** insinuate, intimate.

sug·gest·i·bil·i·ty (sə jes′tə bil′ə tē or səg jes′tə bil′ə tē)

n. the quality or condition of being suggestible.

sug·gest·i·ble (sə jes′tə bəl or səg jes′tə bəl) *adj.* 1 capable of being influenced by suggestion. 2 that can be suggested.

sug·ges·tion (sə jes′chən or səg jes′chən) *n.* 1 a suggesting: *The trip was made at his suggestion.* 2 the thing suggested: *The picnic was an excellent suggestion.* 3 the calling up of one idea by another because they are connected or associated in some way. 4 a very small amount; slight trace: *The foreigner spoke English with just a suggestion of his native accent.* 5 in psychology: **a** the insinuation of an idea, belief, or impulse into the mind, especially a hypnotized person's mind, with avoidance of normal critical thought, contrary ideas, etc. **b** the idea, belief, or impulse so insinuated. **—Syn. 2** proposal.

sug·ges·tive (sə jes′tiv or səg jes′tiv) *adj.* 1 tending to suggest ideas, acts, or feelings: *The teacher gave an interesting and suggestive list of composition subjects.* 2 tending to suggest something improper or indecent. **—sug·ges′tive·ness,** *n.* **—Syn. 1** See **expressive.**

su·i·cid·al (sü′ə sīd′əl) *adj.* 1 of or having to do with suicide; leading to suicide; causing suicide. 2 ruinous to one's own interests; disastrous to oneself: *It would be suicidal for a store to sell many things below cost.* **—su′i·cid′al·ly,** *adv.*

su·i·cide[1] (sü′ə sīd′) *n. v.* **-cid·ed, -cid·ing.** *—n.* 1 the killing of oneself on purpose. 2 the destruction of one's own interests or prospects. 3 **commit suicide,** kill oneself on purpose. *—v. Informal.* commit suicide. [< NL *suicidium* < L *sui* of oneself + *-cidium* act of killing]

su·i·cide[2] (sü′ə sīd′) *n.* a person who kills himself on purpose. [< NL *suicida* < L *sui* of oneself + *-cida* killer]

su·i ge·ne·ris (sü′ē jen′ə ris or sü′ī) *Latin.* of his, her, its, or their peculiar kind; unique.

suit (süt) *n.* 1 a set of clothes or of armor. A man's suit consists of a coat, vest, and trousers. 2 in law, a case in a court; application to a court for justice: *He started a suit to collect damages for his injuries.* 3 one of the four sets of cards (spades, hearts, diamonds, and clubs) in a deck. 4 a request; asking; wooing: *His suit was successful and she married him.* 5 **follow suit, a** play a card of the same suit as that first played. **b** follow the example of another.
—v. 1 provide with clothes. 2 make suitable; make fit: *You should suit the furniture to the size of the room.* 3 be suitable for; agree with: *A cold climate suits apples and wheat, but not oranges and tea.* 4 be suitable; be convenient; fit: *Which date suits best?* 5 be becoming to: *Her blue hat suits her fair skin.* 6 please; satisfy: *It is hard to suit everyone.* 7 **suit oneself,** do as one pleases. [ME < AF *siute* < VL *sequita* < L *sequi* follow. Doublet of SUITE.] **—Syn.** *v.* **2** adapt, adjust, accommodate. **6** gratify, content.

suit·a·bil·i·ty (süt′ə bil′ə tē) *n.* the state or quality of being suitable; fitness; appropriateness.

suit·a·ble (süt′ə bəl) *adj.* right for the occasion; fitting; proper: *The park gives the children a suitable playground.* **—suit′a·ble·ness,** *n.* **—suit′a·bly,** *adv.* **—Syn.** See **fit.**

suit·case (süt′kās′) *n.* a flat, rectangular travelling bag.

suit coat or **suit·coat** (süt′kōt′) *n.* the long-sleeved upper part, or jacket, of a suit.

suite (swēt) *n.* 1 a connected series of rooms to be used by one person or family. 2 a set of furniture that matches. 3 a set or series of like things. 4 an apartment. 5 in music: **a** an instrumental composition consisting of a series of connected movements: *suite for strings.* **b** a set of dance tunes. 6 a group of attendants: *The queen travelled with a suite of twelve.* [< F < OF < VL *sequita.* Doublet of SUIT.]

suit·ing (süt′ing) *n.* cloth for making suits.

suit·or (süt′ər) *n.* 1 a man who is courting a woman. 2 in law, a person bringing a suit in a court. 3 anyone who sues or petitions.

su·ki·ya·ki (sü′kē yä′kē) *n.* a Japanese dish consisting mainly of fried meat, onions, and other vegetables. [< Japanese]

sul·fa (sul′fə) *adj. n.* sulpha.

sul·fa·di·a·zine (sul′fə dī′ə zēn′ or sul′fə dī′ə zin) *n.* sulphadiazine.

hat, āge, cãre, fär; let, ēqual, tėrm; it, īce
hot, ōpen, ôrder; oil, out; cup, pu̇t, rüle, ūse
əbove, takən, pencəl, lemən, circəs
ch, child; ng, long; sh, ship
th, thin; ᴛʜ, then; zh, measure

sul·fa·nil·a·mide (sul′fə nil′ə mīd′ or sul′fə nil′ə mid) *n.* sulphanilamide.

sul·fa·pyr·i·dine (sul′fə pir′ə dēn′ or sul′fə pir′ə din) *n.* sulphapyridine.

sul·fate (sul′fāt) *n.* sulphate.

sul·fa·thi·a·zole (sul′fə thī′ə zōl′ or sul′fə thī′ə zol′) *n.* sulphathiazole.

sul·fid (sul′fid) *n.* sulphid.

sul·fide (sul′fīd) *n.* sulphide.

sul·fite (sul′fīt) *n.* sulphite.

sul·fon·a·mide (sul fon′ə mīd′ or sul fon′ə mid, sul′fə nam′īd or sul′fə nam′id) *n.* sulphonamide.

sul·fur (sul′fər) *n. adj.* sulphur.

sul·fu·rate (sul′fə rāt′ or sul′fyu̇ rāt′) *v.* **-rat·ed, -rat·ing.** sulphurate.

sul·fu·ra·tion (sul′fə rā′shən or sul′fyu̇ rā′shən) *n.* sulphuration.

sulfur dioxide sulphur dioxide.

sul·fu·re·ous (sul fūr′ē əs) *adj.* sulphureous.

sul·fu·ret·ted or **sul·fu·ret·ed** (sul′fyu̇ ret′id) *adj.* sulphuretted.

sul·fu·ric (sul fūr′ik) *adj.* sulphuric.

sulfuric acid sulphuric acid.

sul·fur·ous (sul′fər əs or sul′fyu̇ rəs; *in chemistry, also,* sul fūr′əs) *adj.* sulphurous.

sulfurous acid sulphurous acid.

sul·fur·y (sul′fər ē) *adj.* sulphury.

sulk (sulk) *v.* hold aloof in a sullen manner; be sulky. *—n.* 1 the act of sulking; a fit of sulking. 2 **sulks,** *pl.* ill humor shown by sulking. [< *sulky*]

sulk·y[1] (sul′kē) *adj.* **sulk·i·er, sulk·i·est.** silent and bad-humored because of resentment; sullen: *She became sulky when she could not have her own way.* [cf. OE *āsolcen* lazy] **—sulk′i·ly,** *adv.* **—sulk′i·ness,** *n.* **—Syn.** *adj.* See **sullen.**

sulk·y[2] (sul′kē) *n.* **-ies.** a light two-wheeled carriage for one person. [? < *sulky,* possibly because the rider is alone]

A sulky racing

sul·len (sul′ən) *adj.* 1 silent because of bad humor or anger: *The sullen child refused to answer my question.* 2 showing bad humor or anger. 3 gloomy; dismal: *The sullen skies threatened rain.* [ME < OF *solain,* ult. < L *solus* alone] **—sul′len·ly,** *adv.* **—sul′len·ness,** *n.*
Syn. 1 **Sullen, sulky, glum** = silent and bad-humored or gloomy. **Sullen** suggests an ill-natured refusal to talk or be co-operative because of anger or bad humor or disposition: *It is disagreeable to have to sit at the breakfast table with a sullen person.* **Sulky** suggests moody or childish sullenness because of resentment or discontent: *Children sometimes become sulky when they are jealous.* **Glum** carries less suggestion of bad humor or bad temper, and emphasizes a dismal silence because of low spirits or some depressing condition or happening: *He is glum about world affairs.* 2 surly.

sul·ly (sul′ē) *v.* **-lied, -ly·ing,** *n.* **-lies.** soil; stain; tarnish. [OE *sōlian* < *sōl* dirty]

sul·pha or **sul·fa** (sul′fə) *adj.* of or having to do with a family of drugs containing sulphurous anhydride and derived from sulphanilamide, used in treating various bacterial infections. *—n.* a sulpha drug.

sul·pha·di·a·zine or **sul·fa·di·a·zine** (sul′fə dī′ə zēn′ or -dī′ə zin) *n.* a substance derived from sulphanilamide, used in treating various infections.

sul·pha·nil·a·mide or **sul·fa·nil·a·mide** (sul′fə nil′ə mīd′ or sul′fə nil′ə mid) *n.* a white crystalline substance derived from coal tar and used in treating various infections. Sulphanilamide was the first sulpha drug to be widely used. *Formula:* $C_6H_8N_2O_2S$

sul·pha·pyr·i·dine or **sul·fa·pyr·i·dine** (sul′fə pir′ə dēn′ or -pir′ə din) *n.* a derivative of sulphanilamide, formerly used mainly to combat pneumonia but now largely replaced by less dangerous derivatives. *Formula*: $C_{11}H_{11}N_3O_2S$

sul·phate or **sul·fate** (sul′fāt) *n.* any salt of sulphuric acid.

sul·pha·thi·a·zole or **sul·fa·thi·a·zole** (sul′fə thī′ə zōl′ or -thī′ə zol′) *n.* a sulpha drug, used especially in treating pneumonia. *Formula*: $C_9H_9N_3O_2S_2$

sul·phid or **sul·fid** (sul′fid) *n.* sulphide.

sul·phide or **sul·fide** (sul′fīd) *n.* any compound of sulphur with another element or radical.

sul·phite or **sul·fite** (sul′fīt) *n.* any salt of sulphurous acid.

sul·phon·a·mide (sul fon′ə mīd′ or sul fon′ə mid, sul′fə nam′īd or sul′fə nam′id) *n.* **1** any of a group of sulpha drugs, derived from sulphanilimide, that check bacterial infection. **2** in chemistry: **a** an organic compound that contains the univalent radical $-SO_2NH_2$ **b** the radical itself. Also, **sulfonamide.** [< *sulfonyl* + *-amide*]

sul·phur or **sul·fur** (sul′fər) *n.* **1** a light-yellow, nonmetallic chemical element that burns with a blue flame and a stifling odor. It is used in making matches, in bleaching, ointments, etc. *Symbol*: S; *at.no.* 16; *at.wt.* 32.064. **2** a greenish yellow. **3** one of several kinds of yellow butterfly. *—adj.* greenish-yellow.

sul·phu·rate or **sul·fu·rate** (sul′fə rāt′ or sul′fyů rāt′) *v.* **-rat·ed, -rat·ing.** combine, treat, or impregnate with sulphur, the fumes of burning sulphur, etc.

sul·phu·ra·tion or **sul·fu·ra·tion** (sul′fə rā′shən or sul′fyů rā′shən) *n.* **1** the act or process of treating with sulphur. **2** the state of being treated or impregnated with sulphur.

sulphur dioxide or **sulfur dioxide** a heavy, colorless gas that has a sharp odor, used as a bleach, disinfectant, preservative, and refrigerant. *Formula*: SO_2

sul·phu·re·ous or **sul·fu·re·ous** (sul fūr′ē əs) *adj.* **1** consisting of or containing sulphur; having to do with sulphur. **2** like sulphur.

sul·phu·ret·ed or **sul·fu·ret·ed** (sul′fyů ret′id) *adj.* sulphuretted.

sul·phu·ret·ted or **sul·fu·ret·ted** (sul′fyů ret′id) *adj.* **1** combined with sulphur. **2** containing sulphur or a compound of sulphur.

sul·phu·ric or **sul·fu·ric** (sul fūr′ik) *adj.* **1** of or having to do with sulphur. **2** containing sulphur.

sulphuric acid or **sulfuric acid** a heavy, colorless, oily, very strong acid; oil of vitriol. Sulphuric acid is used in making explosives, in refining petroleum, etc. *Formula*: H_2SO_4

sul·phur·ous or **sul·fur·ous** (sul′fər əs or sul′fyů rəs; *in chemistry, also,* sul fūr′əs) *adj.* **1** of or having to do with sulphur. **2** containing sulphur. **3** like sulphur; like burning sulphur. **4** of or like the fires of hell; hellish.

sulphurous acid or **sulfurous acid** a colorless solution of sulphur dioxide in water, used as a bleach, reducing agent, etc. *Formula*: H_2SO_3

sul·phur·y or **sul·fur·y** (sul′fər ē) *adj.* of or like sulphur.

Sul·pi·cian (sůl pish′ən) *n.* a priest of a Roman Catholic order founded in 1642 to conduct seminaries of theology. [< F *sulpicien* < St. *Sulpice,* Paris, the founder's parish + *-en* -an]

sul·tan (sul′tən) *n.* **1** the ruler of a Moslem country. Turkey was ruled by a sultan until 1922. **2** an absolute ruler. [ult. < Arabic *sultān* ruler]

sul·tan·a (sul tan′ə or sul tä′nə) *n.* **1** the wife of a sultan. **2** the mother, sister, or daughter of a sultan. **3** a small, seedless raisin. [< Ital.]

sul·tan·ate (sul′tən āt′) *n.* **1** the position, authority, or period of rule of a sultan. **2** the territory ruled over by a sultan.

sul·try (sul′trē) *adj.* **-tri·er, -tri·est. 1** hot, close, and moist: *We expect sultry weather during July.* **2** hot or fiery. **3** full of passion: *a sultry look.* [< obs. *sulter,* v.; akin to *swelter*] **—sul′tri·ness,** *n.*

sum (sum) *n. v.* **summed, sum·ming.** *—n.* **1** an amount of money: *He paid a large sum for the house.* **2** the total of two or more numbers or things taken together. **3** *Informal.* a problem in arithmetic. **4** the whole amount; the total amount. *To win the prize seemed to her the sum of happiness.* **5 in sum, a** in a few words; briefly. **b** to conclude in a few words; in short.
—v. **1** find the total of. **2 sum to,** make a total of. **3 sum up, a** reckon, count, or total. **b** collect into a whole. **c** express or tell briefly: *Sum up the main points of the lesson in three sentences.* **d** recapitulate the chief points of (the evidence) to a jury before it retires to consider a verdict. **e** form an estimate of the qualities or character of; size up. **f** count votes. [< L *summa,* originally fem. adj., highest] **—Syn.** *n.* **2** See **number.**

sum- the form of **sub-** in some cases before *m,* as in *summon.*

su·mac or **su·mach** (shü′mak or sü′mak) *n.* **1** a shrub or small tree having cone-shaped clusters of red fruit and leaves that turn scarlet in the autumn. **2** its dried leaves, used in tanning and dyeing. [ME < OF < Arabic *summāq*]

Su·ma·tran (sü mä′trən or sü mat′rən) *adj.* of or having to do with the island of Sumatra, in Indonesia, or its inhabitants. *—n.* a native or inhabitant of Sumatra.

Su·me·ri·an (sü mēr′ē ən or sü mer′ē ən) *adj.* of or having to do with the early inhabitants of Sumer, in ancient times a region in the valley of the Euphrates River, or their language. *—n.* **1** a native or inhabitant of Sumer. **2** the language of Sumer.

sum·ma cum lau·de (sům′ə kům′ lou′dā or sum′ə kum′ lô′dē) *Latin.* with the highest honor. [< L]

sum·ma·ri·ly (sum′ə rə lē or sə mer′ə lē) *adv.* in a summary manner; briefly; without delay.

sum·ma·rize (sum′ə rīz′) *v.* **-rized, -riz·ing.** make a summary of; give only the main points of; express briefly. **—sum′ma·ri·za′tion,** *n.*

sum·ma·ry (sum′ə rē) *n.* **-ries,** *adj.* *—n.* a brief statement giving the main points: *The history book had a summary at the end of each chapter.* *—adj.* **1** concise and comprehensive; brief. **2** direct and prompt; without delay or formality: *The invaders took summary vengeance by killing all the villagers.* **3** carried out or determined rapidly, with the omission of certain formalities usually required by law: *summary proceedings.* [< L *summarium* < *summa* sum]
Syn. *n.* **Summary, digest** = a brief presentation of facts or subject matter. **Summary** applies to a brief statement, in one's own words, giving only the main points of an article, chapter, book, speech, subject, proposed plan, etc.: *Give a summary of today's lesson.* **Digest,** applying particularly to a collection of materials in condensed form, sometimes applies to a shortened form of an article, etc. leaving out less important details but keeping the original order, emphasis, and words: *Some magazines contain digests of books.* *–adj.* **1** terse, succinct.

sum·ma·tion (sum ā′shən) *n.* **1** the process of finding the sum or total; addition. **2** the total. **3** in law, the final charge of a judge to the jury before it considers the verdict.

sum·mer (sum′ər) *n.* **1** the warmest season of the year; season of the year between spring and autumn. **2** anything considered like summer in its warmth, full beauty, healthy maturity, etc.: *a young man in the summer of his life.*
—adj. **1** of summer; in summer. **2** used in summer: *summer clothes, a summer cottage.*
—v. **1** pass the summer: *We always summer at the seashore.* **2** keep or feed during the summer; arrange or manage during the summer. [OE *sumor*]

summer cottage a house, usually small and simply furnished and equipped, built near a body of water and used for holidaying during summer.

summer fallow land worked in the summer and allowed to lie fallow in preparation for sowing in the fall.

summer house a home for the summer.

sum·mer·house (sum′ər hous′) *n.* a small building in a park or garden in which to sit in warm weather. Summerhouses often have no walls.

summer resort a place where people go for summer holidays.

sum·mer·sault (sum′ər solt′ or -sôlt′) *n. v.* somersault.

summer solstice in the Northern Hemisphere, the time when the sun is farthest north from the equator, about June 21 or 22.

summer squash any of various squashes used as a summer vegetable and so eaten before fully ripe, while the skin is still tender.

sum·mer·time (sum′ər tīm′) *n.* **1** the summer season; summer. **2** any period in which energy is greatest or talent most productive: *in the summertime of life.*

sum·mer·y (sum′ər ē) *adj.* **1** of summer. **2** for summer. **3** like summer.

sum·mit (sum′it) *n.* **1** the highest point of a mountain, hill, etc.; topmost peak or ridge; top: *the summit of a mountain.* **2** the topmost part of anything; apex. **3** the uttermost objective of ambition, hope, etc. or the highest degree of skill, energy, etc.; acme: *The summit of her ambition was to be an actress.* **4** *Informal.* a conference at the highest level. **5 at the summit,** at the level of diplomacy involving heads of government; at the highest level. *—adj.* of or having to do with a summit meeting: *summit talks, summit decisions.* [ME < OF *somete,* ult. < L *summus* highest] —**Syn. 1** apex, pinnacle, zenith. See **top.**

sum·mon (sum′ən) *v.* **1** call with authority; order to come; send for: *summon men to defend their country.* **2** call together: *summon an assembly.* **3** order or notify formally to appear before a court or judge, especially to answer a charge. **4** call upon: *summon a fort to surrender.* **5** stir to action; rouse: *Jack summoned his courage and entered the deserted house.* [< L *summonere* hint to < *sub-* secretly + *monere* warn] —**Syn. 1** See **call.**

sum·mon·er (sum′ən ər) *n.* **1** a person who summons. **2** formerly, a minor official whose duty was to warn persons to appear in court.

sum·mons (sum′ənz) *n.* **-mons·es,** *v.* —*n.* **1** an urgent or authoritative call for the presence or attendance of a person. **2** in law: **a** an order or notice to a person from an authority to appear before a court or judge on or before a certain date, especially to answer as a defendant to a charge made against him. **b** the writ **(writ of summons)** by which such an order is made: *He received a summons for fast driving.* **3** any message or signal that summons. —*v. Informal.* summon to court. [ME < OF *somonse* < *somondre* summon, ult. < L *summonere.* See SUMMON.]

sum·mum bo·num (sum′əm bō′nəm) *Latin.* the highest or chief good.

sump (sump) *n.* **1** a pit or reservoir for collecting water, oil, etc. **2** a pool at the bottom of a mine, where water collects and from which it is pumped. [ME < MDu. *somp* or MLG *sump* swamp]

sump·ter (sump′tər) *n. Archaic.* a horse or mule for carrying baggage. [ME < OF *sommetier,* ult. < L *sagma, -atos* pack-saddle < Gk.]

sump·tu·ar·y (sump′chü er′ē) *adj.* having to do with the spending of money; regulating expenses: *Laws forbidding women to wear jewellery would be sumptuary laws.* [< L *sumptuarius* < *sumptus* expense < *sumere* spend]

sump·tu·ous (sump′chü əs) *adj.* costly; magnificent; rich: *The king gave a sumptuous banquet.* [< L *sumptuosus* < *sumptus* expense < *sumere* spend] —**sump′tu·ous·ly,** *adv.* —**sump′tu·ous·ness,** *n.* —**Syn.** luxurious, lavish.

sun (sun) *n. v.* **sunned, sun·ning.** —*n.* **1** the brightest star in the sky; heavenly body around which the earth and planets revolve. The sun provides light, heat, and energy for the solar system. **2** the light and warmth of the sun: *sit in the sun.* **3** any heavenly body made up of burning gas and having satellites. Many stars are suns and have their worlds that travel around them. **4** something like the sun in brightness or splendor; something that is a source of light, honor, glory, or prosperity. **5** a figure, image, ornament, etc. made to resemble the sun, as a heraldic bearing, usually charged with human features, or a kind of circular firework. **6** *Archaic.* a day. **7** *Archaic.* a year. **8 from sun to sun,** from sunrise to sunset. **9 in the sun,** in a position easily seen; in the public eye. **10 under the sun,** on earth; in the world.
—*v.* **1** expose to the sun's rays. **2** warm or dry in the sunshine. [OE *sunne*]

hat, āge, cãre, fär; let, ēqual, tėrm; it, īce
hot, ōpen, ôrder; oil, out; cup, pu̇t, rüle, ūse
əbove, takən, pencəl, lemən, circəs
ch, child; ng, long; sh, ship
th, thin; ᴛʜ, then; zh, measure

Sun. Sunday.

sun-baked (sun′bākt′) *adj.* **1** baked by the heat of the sun: *sun-baked pottery.* **2** parched or dried-up by exposure to the sun.

sun bath an exposure of the body to sunshine.

sun·bathe (sun′bāᴛʜ′) *v.* **-bathed, -bath·ing.** take a sunbath; bask in the sun. —**sun′bath′er,** *n.*

sun·beam (sun′bēm′) *n.* a ray of sunlight.

sun·bird (sun′bėrd′) *n.* **1** a small, bright-colored bird of Europe. **2** a South American bird with variegated plumage.

sun·bon·net (sun′bon′it) *n.* a large bonnet that shades the face and neck.

sun·burn (sun′bėrn′) *n. v.* **-burned** or **-burnt, -burn·ing.** —*n.* **1** a burning of the skin by the sun's rays. A sunburn is often red and painful. **2** the color of red or tan resulting from sunburn. —*v.* **1** burn the skin by the sun's rays; burn the skin of. **2** become burned by the sun: *Her skin sunburns very quickly.*

sun·burnt (sun′bėrnt′) *v.* a pt. and a pp. of **sunburn.**

sunburst (sun′bėrst′) *n.* **1** the sun shining suddenly through a break in clouds. **2** a brooch with jewels arranged to look like the sun with its rays.

sun·dae (sun′dē or -dā) *n.* a serving of ice cream with syrup, crushed fruits, nuts, etc. poured over it. [probably < *Sunday,* originally the only day on which it was served]

Sun·day (sun′dē or -dā) *n.* **1** the first day of the week. **2** the day of rest and worship among most Christians. [OE *sunnandæg,* translation of L *dies solis* day of the sun]
Syn. 1, 2 Sunday, Sabbath are not true synonyms. **Sunday** is the name of the first day of the week, which is generally observed among Christians as a day of worship and rest from ordinary business. **Sabbath,** literally meaning a time of rest from work, applies to the seventh day of the week (Saturday) among the Jews and some Christians. But it is commonly applied to Sunday in the religious sense of a day for abstaining from work or activity of any kind except religious.

Sunday best *Informal.* best clothes.

Sunday school 1 a school, held on Sundays under the auspices of a church, for teaching religion. **2** its members.

sun·deck (sun′dek′) *n.* **1** a passenger ship's upper deck. **2** a balcony, terrace, or other area in or on a building, beside a swimming pool, etc., designed for lounging and sunbathing.

sun·der (sun′dər) *v.* separate; part; sever; split. —*n.* **in sunder,** apart. [OE *sundrian* < *sundor* apart] —**Syn.** *v.* divide, disjoin, disconnect.

sun·dew (sun′dū′ or -dü′) *n.* a plant that grows in bogs and has hairy, sticky leaves with which it captures and absorbs insects.

sun·di·al (sun′dī′əl or sun′dīl′) *n.* an instrument for telling the time of day by the position of a shadow cast by the sun.

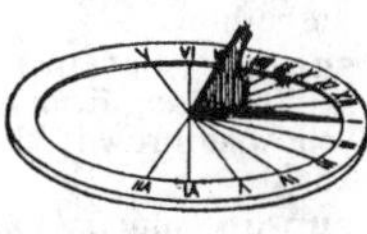
A sundial

sun·dog (sun′dog′) *n.* **1** a bright spot near the sun; parhelion. **2** a small or incomplete rainbow.

sun·down (sun′doun′) *n.* sunset.

sun·down·er (sun′doun′ər) *n. Australian slang.* a tramp who arrives about sunset wanting food and lodging.

sun-dried (sun′drīd′) *adj.* dried by the sun.

sun·dries (sun′drēz) *n.pl.* sundry things; items not named; odds and ends.

sun·dry (sun′drē) *adj.* several; various: *From sundry hints, he guessed he was to be given a bicycle on his birthday.* [OE *syndrig* separate < *sundor* apart]

sun·fast (sun′fast′) *adj.* of colored material, made so that sunlight will not fade it.

sun·fish (sun′fish′) *n.* **-fish** or **-fish·es. 1** a small fresh-water fish of North America, used for food. **2** a large fish having tough flesh that lives in tropical or temperate seas.

sun·flow·er (sun′flou′ər) *n.* **1** a tall plant of the aster family having large, yellow flowers with brown centres. **2** any of various similar plants.

sung (sung) *v.* a pt. and pp. of **sing.**

sun·glass·es (sun′glas′iz) *n.pl.* spectacles, often made of colored glass, to protect the eyes from the glare of the sun.

sun god a god of the sun. Many different peoples have worshipped sun gods.

sunk (sungk) *v.* a pt. and pp. of **sink.**

sunk·en (sungk′ən) *adj.* **1** sunk: *a sunken ship.* **2** submerged: *a sunken rock.* **3** situated below the general level: *a sunken garden.* **4** fallen in; hollow: *sunken eyes.* —*v.* a pp. of **sink.**

sun·less (sun′lis) *adj.* without sun; without sunlight.

sun·light (sun′līt′) *n.* the light of the sun.

sun·lit (sun′lit′) *adj.* lighted by the sun.

sun·ny (sun′ē) *adj.* **-ni·er, -ni·est. 1** having much sunshine: *a sunny day.* **2** exposed to, lighted by, or warmed by the direct rays of the sun: *a sunny room.* **3** like the sun. **4** bright; cheerful; happy. —**sun′ni·ly,** *adv.* —**sun′ni·ness,** *n.*

sun parlor or **parlour** a room with many windows to let in sunlight.

sun porch a porch enclosed largely by glass or screen, designed to admit plenty of sunlight.

sun·proof (sun′prüf′) *adj.* impervious to or unaffected by the rays of the sun: *These sunproof curtains will not fade.*

sun·rise (sun′rīz′) *n.* **1** the rising of the sun; the first appearance of the sun in the morning. **2** the time of day when the sun rises; the beginning of day.

sun·room (sun′rüm′ or -rům′) *n.* a room with many windows to let in sunlight.

sun·set (sun′set′) *n.* **1** the setting of the sun; the last appearance of the sun in the evening. **2** the time of day when the sun sets; the close of day. **3** any decline or close: *Old age is the sunset of life.*

sun·shade (sun′shād′) *n.* an umbrella, parasol, awning, etc. used to provide protection from the sun.

sun·shine (sun′shīn′) *n.* **1** the shining of the sun; light or rays of the sun. **2** brightness; cheerfulness; happiness.

sun·shin·y (sun′shīn′ē) *adj.* **-shin·i·er, -shin·i·est. 1** having much sunshine. **2** bright; cheerful; happy.

sun·spot (sun′spot′) *n.* one of the dark spots that appear from time to time on the sun.

sun·stroke (sun′strōk′) *n.* a sudden illness caused by too much exposure to the sun's rays or by too much heat from the sun.

sun·suit (sun′süt′) *n.* an abbreviated one-piece or two-piece garment worn by women or children for sunbathing.

sun·tan (sun′tan′) *n.* **1** a bronzed coloring of a person's skin resulting from exposure to the sun. **2** a light yellowish brown; khaki. —*adj.* light yellowish-brown; khaki.

sun-up (sun′up′) *n.* sunrise.

sun·ward (sun′wərd) *adv. adj.* toward the sun.

sun·wards (sun′wərdz) *adv.* sunward.

sup[1] (sup) *v.* **supped, sup·ping. 1** eat the evening meal; take supper: *He supped alone on bread and milk.* **2** give a supper to or for. [ME < OF *soper.* See SUPPER.]

sup[2] (sup) *v.* **supped, sup·ping,** *n.* sip. [OE *sūpan*]

sup- the form of **sub-** before *p,* as in *suppress.*

sup. 1 supra. **2** superior. **3** superlative. **4** supply. **5** supplement. **6** supreme.

su·per (sü′pər) *n. Informal.* **1** a supernumerary. Mobs on the stage are usually made up of supers. **2** a superintendent. —*adj. Slang.* excellent; wonderful.

super- *prefix.* **1** over; above, as in *superimpose, superstructure.* **2** besides, as in *superadd, supertax.* **3** in high proportion; to excess; exceedingly, as in *superabundant, supersensitive.* **4** surpassing, as in *superman, supernatural.* [< L *super* over, above]

super. 1 superfine. **2** superintendent. **3** superior. **4** supernumerary.

su·per·a·ble (sü′pər ə bəl) *adj.* capable of being overcome; surmountable. [< L *superabilis* < *superare* overcome < *super* over] —**su′per·a·bly,** *adv.*

su·per·a·bound (sü′pər ə bound′) *v.* **1** be very abundant. **2** be too abundant.

su·per·a·bun·dance (sü′pər ə bun′dəns) *n.* **1** a very great abundance: *a superabundance of rain.* **2** a greater amount than is needed.

su·per·a·bun·dant (sü′pər ə bun′dənt) *adj.* **1** very abundant. **2** more than enough. —**su′per·a·bun′dant·ly,** *adv.*

su·per·add (sü′pər ad′) *v.* add besides; add further: *A toothache was superadded to her other troubles.* [< L *superaddere* < *super-* besides + *addere* add]

su·per·an·nu·ate (sü′pər an′ū āt′) *v.* **-at·ed, -at·ing. 1** retire on a pension on reaching a certain age or owing to ill-health. **2** make old-fashioned or out-of-date. [earlier *superannate* < Med.L *superannatus* more than a year old < L *super annum* beyond a year; influenced in spelling by L *annuus* annual]

su·per·an·nu·at·ed (sü′pər an′ū āt′id) *adj.* **1** retired on a pension. **2** too old for work, service, etc. **3** old-fashioned; out-of-date.

su·per·an·nu·at·ion (sü′pər an′ū ā′shən) *n.* **1** the process of superannuating or the state of being superannuated. **2** a pension or allowance granted to a superannuated person.

su·per·a·tom·ic bomb (sü′pər ə tom′ik) the hydrogen bomb.

su·perb (sů pėrb′) *adj.* **1** grand; stately; majestic; magnificent; splendid: *The mountain scenery in the Rockies is superb. The queen's jewels were superb.* **2** rich; elegant; sumptuous: *a superb dinner.* **3** very fine; first-rate; excellent: *The actor gave a superb performance.* [< L *superbus* < *super-* above] —**su·perb′ly,** *adv.* —**Syn. 1** imposing. See **magnificent.**

su·per·car·go (sü′pər kär′gō) *n.* **-goes** or **-gos.** an officer on a merchant ship, who has charge of the cargo and the business affairs of the voyage. [earlier *supracargo* < Sp. *sobrecargo*]

su·per·charge (sü′pər chärj′) *v.* **-charged, -charg·ing. 1** charge with excessive vigor, emotion, etc.: *The atmosphere at the trial was supercharged with tension.* **2** augment the power or efficiency of an engine, vehicle, etc. by fitting it with a supercharger.

su·per·charg·er (sü′pər chär′jər) *n.* in an internal-combustion engine, a blower, pump, etc. for forcing more of the mixture of air and gasoline vapor into the cylinders than the action of the pistons would draw.

su·per·cil·i·ar·y (sü′pər sil′ē er′ē) *adj.* of, having to do with, or near the eyebrow; over the eye. [< NL *superciliaris* < L *supercilium* eyebrow < *super-* above + *cel-* cover]

su·per·cil·i·ous (sü′pər sil′ē əs) *adj.* showing scorn or indifference because of a feeling of superiority; haughty, proud, and contemptuous; disdainful: *a supercilious stare.* [< L *superciliosus* < *supercilium* eyebrow. See SUPERCILIARY.] —**su′per·cil′i·ous·ly,** *adv.* —**Syn.** See **proud.**

su·per·con·duc·tive (sü′pər kən duk′tiv) *adj.* having or relating to superconductivity.

su·per·con·duc·tiv·i·ty (sü′pər kon′duk tiv′ə tē) *n.* the property of being able to conduct electricity without resistance, found in tin, lead and some other metals when reduced to temperatures approaching absolute zero, or below −420° Fahrenheit.

su·per·con·duc·tor (sü′pər kən duk′tər) *n.* a metal or other substance having superconductivity.

su·per·dom·i·nant (sü′pər dom′ə nənt) *n.* in music, the sixth tone in a scale; the tone next above the dominant.

su·per·em·i·nent (sü′pər em′ə nənt) *adj.* of superior eminence, rank, or dignity; standing out or rising above others. —**su′per·em′i·nent·ly,** *adv.*

su·per·er·o·ga·tion (sü′pər er′ə gā′shən) *n.* the doing of more than what is required by duty. [< LL *supererogatio, -onis* < L *super-* over + *erogare* pay out]

su·per·e·rog·a·to·ry (sü′pər ə rog′ə tô′rē) *adj.* **1** doing more than what is required by duty. **2** unnecessary; superfluous.

su·per·fi·cial (sü′pər fish′əl) *adj.* **1** of the surface: *superficial measurement.* **2** on the surface; at the surface: *His burns were superficial and soon healed.* **3** concerned with or understanding only what is on the surface; not thorough; shallow: *a superficial education.* [< L *superficialis* < *superficies* surface < *super-* above + *facies* form]

su·per·fi·ci·al·i·ty (sü′pər fish′ē al′ə tē) *n.* **-ties. 1** the quality or condition of being superficial; shallowness. **2** something superficial.

su·per·fi·cial·ly (sü′pər fish′əl ē) *adv.* in a superficial manner; on the surface; not thoroughly.

su·per·fi·ci·es (sü′pər fish′ē ēz′) *n.* **-fi·ci·es. 1** surface. **2** the surface area. **3** the outward appearance. [< L *superficies* upper side, surface < *super-* over + *facies* form]

su·per·fine (sü′pər fīn′) *adj.* **1** very fine; extra fine. **2** too refined; too nice. —**su′per·fine′ly,** *adv.* —**su′per·fine′ness,** *n.*

su·per·flu·id (sü′pər flü′id) *n.* a liquid, such as liquid helium, that has no viscosity when reduced to temperatures approaching absolute zero. —*adj.* extraordinarily fluid; having superfluidity.

su·per·flu·id·i·ty (sü′pər flü id′ə tē) *n.* extraordinary fluidity, as found in superfluids.

su·per·flu·i·ty (sü′pər flü′ə tē) *n.* **-ties. 1** a greater amount than is needed; excess. **2** something not needed: *Luxuries are superfluities.* —**Syn. 1** superabundance.

su·per·flu·ous (sů pėr′flü əs) *adj.* **1** more than is needed: *In writing telegrams omit superfluous words.* **2** needless. [< L *superfluus,* ult. < *super-* over + *fluere* flow] —**su·per′flu·ous·ly,** *adv.* —**Syn. 1** excessive, surplus. **2** unnecessary.

su·per·heat (sü′pər hēt′) *v.* **1** heat to a high degree; heat too hot; heat to a point hotter than usual. **2** heat (a liquid) above its boiling point without producing vaporization. **3** heat (steam) apart from water until it resembles a dry or perfect gas.

su·per·heat·er (sü′pər hēt′ər) *n.* a device for superheating steam.

su·per·het·er·o·dyne (sü′pər het′ər ə dīn′) *adj.* of or having to do with a kind of radio reception in which signals are received at a supersonic frequency and combined with oscillations of a lower supersonic frequency before being rectified and amplified. —*n.* a superheterodyne radio receiving set.

su·per·high·way (sü′pər hī′wā) *n.* a high-speed expressway or freeway divided by a median and having two or more traffic lanes in each direction.

su·per·hu·man (sü′pər hū′mən) *adj.* **1** above or beyond what is human: *Angels are superhuman beings.* **2** above or beyond ordinary human power, experience, etc.: *By a superhuman effort, the hunter choked the leopard to death.* —**su′per·hu′man·ly,** *adv.*

su·per·im·pose (sü′pər im pōz′) *v.* **-posed, -pos·ing. 1** put on top of something else. **2** put or join as an addition.

su·per·in·cum·bent (sü′pər in kum′bənt) *adj.* **1** lying or resting on something else. **2** situated above; overhanging. **3** exerted from above: *a superincumbent pressure.*

su·per·in·duce (sü′pər in düs′ or -in dūs′) *v.* **-duced, -duc·ing.** bring in or develop as an addition.

su·per·in·duc·tion (sü′pər in duk′shən) *n.* the act of superinducing or the state of being superinduced.

su·per·in·tend (sü′pər in tend′ or sü′prin tend′) *v.* oversee and direct (work or workers); manage (a place, institution, etc.). [< LL *superintendere* < L *super-* above + *intendere* direct] —**Syn.** supervise, administer.

su·per·in·tend·ence (sü′pər in ten′dəns or sü′prin ten′dəns) *n.* guidance and direction; management.

su·per·in·tend·en·cy (sü′pər in ten′dən sē or

hat, āge, cãre, fär; let, ēqual, tėrm; it, īce
hot, ōpen, ôrder; oil, out; cup, půt, rüle, ūse
əbove, takən, pencəl, lemən, circəs
ch, child; ng, long; sh, ship
th, thin; ꟸH, then; zh, measure

sü′prin ten′dən sē) *n.* **-cies.** the position, authority, or work of a superintendent.

su·per·in·tend·ent (sü′pər in ten′dənt or sü′prin ten′dənt) *n.* **1** a person who oversees, directs, or manages: *a superintendent of schools, a superintendent of a factory.* **2** a police officer of high rank. *Abbrev.*: Supt. or supt. —**Syn.** supervisor, controller.

su·pe·ri·or (sə pēr′ē ər or sů pēr′ē ər) *adj.* **1** above the average; very good; excellent: *superior work in school.* **2** higher in quality; better; greater: *a superior blend of coffee.* **3** higher in position, rank, importance, etc.: *a superior officer.* **4** showing a feeling of being above others; proud: *superior airs, superior manners.* **5** in printing, superscript. **6** in botany, growing above some other part or organ, as: **a** the ovary when situated above or free from the (inferior) calyx. **b** the calyx when adherent to the sides of the (inferior) ovary and thus seeming to rise from its top. **7 superior to, a** higher than; above. **b** better than; greater than. **c** not giving in to; above yielding to: *A wise man is superior to flattery.*
—*n.* **1** a person who is higher in rank or more accomplished than another: *A captain is a lieutenant's superior.* **2** the head of a monastery or convent. **3** in printing, a superior letter or figure. [ME < OF < L *superior,* comparative of *superus,* adj., above < *super,* prep., above]

su·pe·ri·or·i·ty (sə pēr′ē ôr′ə tē or sů pēr′ē ôr′ə tē) *n.* the state or quality of being superior: *No one doubts the superiority of modern ways of travelling.*

superior number a numerical superscript.

superl. superlative.

su·per·la·tive (sə pėr′lə tiv or sů pėr′lə tiv) *adj.* **1** of the highest kind; above all others; supreme: *King Solomon had superlative wisdom.* **2** exaggerated; excessive; hyperbolic: *Such superlative praise could not be sincere.* **3** in grammar, expressing the highest degree of comparison of an adjective or adverb. *Fairest, best,* and *most slowly* are the superlative forms of *fair, good,* and *slowly.*
—*n.* **1** a person or thing above all others; supreme example. **2** in grammar: **a** the third of three degrees of comparison, used when qualities are being compared. **b** the form or combination of words that shows this degree. **3 talk in superlatives,** exaggerate. [ME < MF < LL *superlativus,* ult. < *super-* beyond + *latus,* pp. *ferre* carry] —**su·per′la·tive·ness,** *n.*

su·per·la·tive·ly (sə pėr′lə tiv lē or sů pėr′lə tiv lē) *adv.* to the highest degree; above all others; supremely.

su·per·man (sü′pər man′) *n.* **-men** (-mən). **1** a man having superhuman powers. **2** the ideal man as conceived by the German philosopher Friedrich W. Nietzsche, 1844-1900, who would be above the weaknesses of ordinary humans and have superior physical and intellectual powers.

su·per·mar·ket (sü′pər mär′kit) *n.* a large self-service store selling groceries and household articles.

su·per·nal (sů pėr′nəl) *adj.* **1** heavenly; divine. **2** lofty; exalted. **3** supremely great or excellent: *supernal wisdom, supernal beauty.* **4** situated in or belonging to the sky; celestial: *the supernal stars.* [< L *supernus* < *super* above] —**su·per′nal·ly,** *adv.*

su·per·na·tant (sü′pər nā′tənt) *adj.* floating above or on the surface: *oil supernatant on water.*

su·per·na·tion·al (sü′pər nash′ə nəl or -nash′nəl) *adj.* above or independent of limitations imposed by national sovereignty; having to do with or involving more than one nation: *Europe may one day become a supernational state.*

su·per·nat·u·ral (sü′pər nach′rəl or -nach′ə rəl) *adj.* above or beyond what is natural: *Miracles are considered as supernatural events.* —*n.* **the supernatural,** supernatural agencies, influences, or phenomena. —**su′per·nat′u·ral·ly,** *adv.*

su·per·nat·u·ral·ism (sü′pər nach′rəl iz′əm or -nach′ə rəl iz′əm) *n.* **1** a supernatural character or agency. **2** a belief in the supernatural. **3** a doctrine that supernatural forces are at work in the universe.

su·per·nu·mer·ar·y (sü′pər nü′mər er′ē or -nü′mər er′ē) *adj. n.* **-ar·ies.** *—adj.* more than the usual or necessary number; extra. *—n.* **1** an extra person or thing. **2** in the theatre, a person who appears on the stage but has no lines to speak: *In addition to the regular actors, there were 20 supernumeraries for the mob scene.* [< LL *supernumerarius* excessive in number < L phrase *super numerum* beyond the number]

su·per·phos·phate (sü′pər fos′fāt) *n.* **1** an acid phosphate. **2** any of various fertilizing materials composed chiefly of soluble phosphates.

su·per·pose (sü′pər pōz′) *v.* **-posed, -pos·ing. 1** place above or on something else. **2** in geometry, place (a figure) upon another so that the two coincide. [< F *superposer* < *super-* above + *poser* (see POSE[1])]

su·per·po·si·tion (sü′pər pə zish′ən) *n.* the placing of one thing above or on something else.

su·per·pow·er (sü′pər pou′ər) *n.* **1** power on an extraordinary or extensive scale. **2** electric power on an extraordinary scale secured by the linking together of a number of separate power systems. **3** an especially powerful nation, especially such a nation exercising control over a large group of lesser powers. **4** an international organization exercising control over its member nations.

su·per·sat·u·rate (sü′pər sach′ù rāt′) *v.* **-rat·ed, -rat·ing.** add to beyond the ordinary saturation point; saturate abnormally. A **supersaturated solution** is one in which more of a substance is dissolved than the solvent will hold under normal conditions.

su·per·sat·u·ra·tion (sü′pər sach′ù rā′shən) *n.* **1** the act of supersaturating. **2** an unstable condition of a vapor or solution, in which the density of the vapor or dissolved substance is in excess of that which is normally in equilibrium under the given conditions.

su·per·scribe (sü′pər skrīb′) *v.* **-scribed, -scrib·ing. 1** write (words, letters, one's name, etc.) above, on, or outside of something. **2** address (a letter or parcel). [< LL < L *superscribere* write over (as a correction) < *super-* above + *scribere* write]

su·per·script (sü′pər skript) *adj.* written above. *—n.* a number, letter, etc. written above and to one side of a symbol. *Example*: In $a^3 \times b^n$, the ^{3} and the ^{n} are superscripts. [< LL *superscriptus*, pp. of *superscribere.* See SUPERSCRIBE.]

su·per·scrip·tion (sü′pər skrip′shən) *n.* **1** the act of writing above, on, or outside of something. **2** something written above or on the outside. **3** an address on a letter or parcel.

su·per·sede (sü′pər sēd′) *v.* **-sed·ed, -sed·ing. 1** take the place of; cause to be set aside; displace: *Electric lights have superseded gas lights in most homes.* **2** fill the place of; replace: *A new mayor superseded the old one.* **3** set aside or ignore in promotion; promote another over the head of. [< L *supersedere* be superior to, refrain from < *super-* above + *sedere* sit] **—su′per·sed′er,** *n.* **—Syn. 1, 2** See **replace.**

su·per·sen·si·tive (sü′pər sen′sə tiv) *adj.* extremely or morbidly sensitive. **—su′per·sen′si·tive·ly,** *adv.* **—su′per·sen′si·tive·ness,** *n.*

su·per·son·ic (sü′pər son′ik) *adj.* **1** greater than the speed of sound in air (1,087 feet per second). **2** capable of moving at a speed greater than the speed of sound. **3** of or having to do with sound waves beyond the limit of human audibility (above frequencies of 20,000 cycles per second); ultrasonic.

su·per·sti·tion (sü′pər stish′ən) *n.* **1** an unreasoning fear of what is unknown or mysterious; unreasoning expectation. **2** a belief or practice founded on ignorant fear or mistaken reverence: *A common superstition considers it bad luck to sleep in a room numbered 13.* [ME < OF < L *superstitio, -onis,* ? originally, a standing over, as in wonder or awe < *super-* above + *stare* stand]

su·per·sti·tious (sü′pər stish′əs) *adj.* full of superstition; likely to believe superstitions; caused by superstition; having to do with superstition. **—su′per·sti′tious·ly,** *adv.*

su·per·struc·ture (sü′pər struk′ chər) *n.* **1** a structure built on something else. **2** all of a building above the foundation. **3** the parts of a ship above the main deck.

su·per·tax (sü′pər taks′) *n.* a tax in addition to a normal tax.

su·per·ton·ic (sü′pər ton′ik) *n.* in music, the second tone of a scale, that is, the next above the tonic.

su·per·vene (sü′pər vēn′) *v.* **-vened, -ven·ing.** come as something additional or interrupting. [< L *supervenire* < *super-* upon + *venire* come]

su·per·ven·tion (sü′pər ven′shən) *n.* the act or fact of supervening.

su·per·vise (sü′pər vīz′) *v.* **-vised, -vis·ing.** look after and direct (work or workers, a process, etc.); oversee; superintend; manage: *He supervised the planning of the year's activities.* [< Med.L *supervisus* < L *super-* over + *videre* see]

su·per·vi·sion (sü′pər vizh′ən) *n.* management; direction; oversight: *The house was built under the careful supervision of an architect.*

su·per·vi·sor (sü′pər vī′zər) *n.* a person who supervises: *The music supervisor had charge of the school orchestra.*

su·per·vi·so·ry (sü′pər vī′zə rē) *adj.* **1** of a supervisor; having to do with supervision. **2** supervising.

su·pine (*adj.* sü pīn′; *n.* sü′pīn) *adj.* **1** lying flat on the back. **2** lazily inactive; listless. **3** not active; passive. *—n.* in Latin grammar, a verbal noun formed from the stem of the past participle. [< L *supinus*] **—su·pine′ly,** *adv.* **—Syn.** *adj.* **2** languid, indolent, inert.

supp (sup) *n. Informal.* a supplemental examination.

supp. or **suppl. 1** supplement. **2** supplementary.

sup·per (sup′ər) *n.* **1** the evening meal; a meal eaten early in the evening if dinner is near noon, or late in the evening if dinner is early in the evening. **2** such a meal made the occasion of a social or festive gathering: *a church supper.* [ME < OF *soper*, originally infinitive, sup[1] < Gmc.] **—sup′per·less,** *adj.*

sup·plant (sə plant′) *v.* **1** take the place of; displace or set aside: *Machinery has supplanted hand labor in the making of shoes.* **2** take the place of by unfair methods or by treacherous means: *The rebels plotted to supplant the legal government.* **3** remove from its position; get rid of; oust. [ME < L *supplantare* trip up < *sub-* under + *planta* sole of the foot] **—Syn. 1, 2** See **replace.**

sup·ple (sup′əl) *adj.* **-pler, -plest,** *v.* **-pled, -pling.** *—adj.* **1** bending easily: *a supple birch tree, supple leather.* **2** capable of bending easily; moving easily or nimbly: *a supple dancer.* **3** readily adaptable to different ideas, circumstances, people, etc.; yielding: *a supple mind.* *—v.* make or grow supple. [ME < OF < L *supplex* submissive < *supplicare.* See SUPPLICATE.] **—sup′ple·ly,** *adv.* **—sup′ple·ness,** *n.* **—Syn.** *adj.* **1** pliant, pliable, flexible.

sup·ple·ment (*n.* sup′lə mənt; *v.* sup′lə ment′) *n.* **1** something added to complete a thing, or to make it larger or better. Many newspapers and periodicals have supplements that are usually of a special character and issued as an additional feature. **2** the amount needed to be added to make an angle or arc equal 180 degrees. *—v.* supply what is lacking in; add to; complete. [< L *supplementum*, ult. < *sub-* up + *-plere* fill]

Syn. *n.* **1 Supplement, appendix** = something added to a book or paper to complete or improve it. **Supplement** applies to a section added later or printed separately to give completeness by bringing the information up to date, correcting mistakes, or presenting special features: *This world history has a supplement covering recent events.* **Appendix** applies to a section added at the end of a book to give extra information for reference, etc., not necessary for completeness: *The appendix contains a list of dates.* –*v.* **See complement.**

sup·ple·men·tal (sup′lə men′təl) *adj.* supplementary. *—n.* supplemental examination.

supplemental examination an examination held for students who have failed the regular examination.

sup·ple·men·ta·ry (sup′lə men′tə rē or sup′lə men′trē) *adj.* **1** additional. **2** added to supply what is lacking: *The new members of the class received supplementary instruction.*

supplementary angle the angle that, when added to another angle, equals 180 degrees. A 60-degree angle is the supplementary angle of a 120-degree angle.

The angle ABC is the supplementary angle of ABD.

sup·ple·men·ta·tion (sup′lə men tā′shən) *n.* **1** the act or process of supplementing. **2** an additional supplement.

sup·pli·ance (sup′lē əns) *n.* supplication.

sup·pli·ant (sup′lē ənt) *adj.* asking humbly and earnestly: *He sent a suppliant message for help.* —*n.* a person who asks humbly and earnestly: *She knelt as a suppliant at the altar.* [< F *suppliant,* ppr. of *supplier* < L *supplicare.* See SUPPLICATE.] —**sup′pli·ant·ly,** *adv.*

sup·pli·cant (sup′lə kənt) *n. adj.* suppliant. [< L *supplicans, -antis,* ppr. of *supplicare.* See SUPPLICATE.]

sup·pli·cate (sup′lə kāt′) *v.* **-cat·ed, -cat·ing. 1** beg humbly and earnestly: *The mother supplicated the judge to spare her son.* **2** beg humbly for (something); seek by entreaty. **3** pray humbly. [< L *supplicare* < *sub-* down + *plicare* bend] —**sup′pli·cat′ing·ly,** *adv.* —**sup′pli·ca′tor,** *n.* —**Syn. 1** implore, entreat, beseech, petition.

sup·pli·ca·tion (sup′lə kā′shən) *n.* **1** the act of supplicating. **2** a humble and earnest request or prayer: *Supplications to God arose from all the churches of the besieged town.*

sup·pli·ca·to·ry (sup′lə kə tô′rē) *adj.* supplicating.

sup·ply[1] (sə plī′) *v.* **-plied, -ply·ing,** *n.* **-plies.** —*v.* **1** furnish; provide: *The city supplies books for the children.* **2** make up for (a loss, lack, absence, etc.): *supply a deficiency.* **3** satisfy (a want, need, etc.): *There was just enough to supply the demand.* **4** fill (a place, vacancy, pulpit, etc.) as a substitute.
—*n.* **1** a quantity ready for use; stock; store: *The school gets its supplies of books, paper, pencils, chalk, etc. from the city.* **2** the quantity of an article in the market ready for purchase: *a supply of coffee.* **3** a person, such as a teacher or clergyman, who supplies a vacancy as a substitute. **4** the act of supplying. **5** a sum of money provided by parliament, or a like body, to meet the expenses of government. **6 in supply,** available; available to a given extent: *Apples are in poor supply this year.* **7 on supply,** acting or available to act as a supply (def. 3). [ME < OF < L *supplere* < *sub-* up + *-plere* fill] —**sup·pli′er,** *n.* —**Syn.** *v.* **1** afford.

sup·ply[2] (sup′lē) *adv.* in a supple manner.

supply officer (sə plī′) in the air force, an officer who is in charge of clothing, fuel, transport, etc.

supply teaching the act or practice of substituting for a teacher who is absent.

sup·port (sə pôrt′) *v.* **1** keep from falling; hold up: *Walls support the roof.* **2** give strength or courage to; keep up; help: *Hope supports us in trouble.* **3** provide for: *A man should support his family.* **4** supply funds or means for; bear the expense of: *support the expenses of government.* **5** maintain, keep up, or keep going: *This city supports two orchestras.* **6** be in favor of; back; second: *He supports the Liberals.* **7** help prove; bear out: *The facts support his claim.* **8** in military use, assist or protect (another unit) in combat: *Artillery fire supported the infantry attack.* **9** put up with; bear; endure: *She couldn't support life without friends.* **10** in the theatre: **a** act with (a leading actor); assist; attend. **b** act (a part or character) with success.
—*n.* **1** the act of supporting; the condition of being supported; help; aid: *He needs our support.* **2** maintenance: *the support of a family.* **3** a person or thing that supports; prop: *The neck is the support of the head.* **4** in military use: **a** assistance or protection given by one element or unit to another. **b** a unit that helps another in combat. Aircraft may be used as a support for infantry. **c** the part of any unit held back at the beginning of an attack as reserve. [ME < OF < L *supportare* bring up < *sub-* up + *portare* carry]
Syn. *v.* **1, 2 Support, maintain, uphold** = hold up or keep up, literally or figuratively. **Support** suggests bearing the weight, serving as a prop, or giving needed strength to prevent something or someone from falling or sinking: *Team-mates supported the injured player.* **Maintain** suggests keeping up in a state or condition by providing what is needed to prevent loss of strength, value, etc.: *Provincial governments maintain the highways.* **Uphold** chiefly suggests giving aid or moral support to a person, cause, belief, etc.: *He upheld his brother's honor.* **3** keep. **7** verify, substantiate, confirm. **9** undergo, suffer, tolerate. –*n.* **1** assistance. **2** See **living.**

hat, āge, cãre, fär; let, ēqual, tėrm; it, īce
hot, ōpen, ôrder; oil, out; cup, pu̇t, rüle, ūse
əbove, takən, pencəl, lemən, circəs
ch, child; ng, long; sh, ship
th, thin; ᴛʜ, then; zh, measure

sup·port·a·ble (sə pôr′tə bəl) *adj.* capable of being supported; bearable or endurable. —**sup·port′a·bly,** *adv.*

sup·port·er (sə pôr′tər) *n.* a person or thing that supports.

sup·pose (sə pōz′) *v.* **-posed, -pos·ing. 1** assume; consider as possible; take for granted: *Suppose you are late, what excuse will you make?* **2** believe; think; imagine: *I suppose she will come as usual.* **3** involve as necessary; imply: *An invention supposes an inventor.* **4** presume the existence or presence of: *The author of the story supposes a race of intelligent beings living in another galaxy.* **5** expect (used in the passive): *I'm supposed to be there early.* [ME < OF *supposer* < *sub-* under + *poser* (see POSE[1])] —**sup·pos′a·ble,** *adj.*

sup·posed (sə pōzd′) *adj.* **1** accepted as true, but without actual or final proof; assumed: *a supposed fact.* **2** considered as possible or probable; hypothetical: *a supposed limit to human development.* **3** imaginary: *a supposed insult.*

sup·pos·ed·ly (sə pōz′id lē) *adv.* according to what is supposed or was supposed.

sup·pos·ing (sə pōz′ing) *conj.* in the event that; if: *Supposing it rains, shall we go?*

sup·po·si·tion (sup′ə zish′ən) *n.* **1** the act of supposing. **2** the thing supposed; belief; opinion: *The speaker planned his talk on the supposition that his hearers would be mature students.* [ME < OF < Med.L *suppositio, -onis,* ult. < L *sub-* under + *ponere* place] —**Syn. 2** assumption, conjecture.

sup·po·si·tion·al (sup′ə zish′ən əl) *adj.* of or based on supposition; hypothetical; supposed.

sup·pos·i·ti·tious (sə poz′ə tish′əs) *adj.* **1** put by fraud in the place of another. **2** pretended; false; not genuine. **3** hypothetical; supposed. [< L *supposititius,* ult. < *sub-* under + *ponere* place] —**sup·pos′i·ti′tious·ly,** *adv.*

sup·pos·i·to·ry (sə poz′ə tô′rē) *n.* **-ries.** a medicated preparation in the form of a cone or cylinder to be put into the rectum or other opening of the body. [< LL *suppositorium* (thing) placed underneath, ult. < L *sub-* under + *ponere* place]

sup·press (sə pres′) *v.* **1** put an end to; stop by force; put down: *The troops suppressed the rebellion by firing on the mob.* **2** keep in; hold back; keep from appearing: *She suppressed a yawn.* **3** prevent or prohibit the publication or circulation of (a book, publication, etc.): *Some nations suppress news that is unfavorable to their policies.* **4** subdue (a feeling, thought, habit, etc.): *suppressed desires.* **5** check the flow of; stop: *suppress bleeding.* **6** keep secret; refrain from disclosing or divulging: *suppress the truth.* [ME < L *suppressus,* pp. of *supprimere* < *sub-* down + *premere* press] —**sup·press′er** or **sup·pres′sor,** *n.* —**Syn. 1** subdue, quell, crush. **2** restrain, repress.

sup·press·i·ble (sə pres′ə bəl) *adj.* that can be suppressed.

sup·pres·sion (sə presh′ən) *n.* **1** a putting down by force or authority; putting an end to: *Troops were used in the suppression of the revolt.* **2** a keeping in; holding back: *the suppression of a childish fear.* **3** in psychoanalysis: **a** the conscious controlling or inhibiting of a desire or impulse. **b** repression.

sup·pres·sive (sə pres′iv) *adj.* tending to suppress; causing suppression.

sup·pu·rate (sup′yu̇ rāt′) *v.* **-rat·ed, -rat·ing.** form pus; discharge pus; fester. [< L *suppurare* < *sub-* under + *pus* pus]

sup·pu·ra·tion (sup′yu̇ rā′shən) *n.* **1** the formation of pus; festering; discharge of pus. **2** pus.

sup·pu·ra·tive (sup′yů rā′tiv) *adj.* **1** promoting suppuration. **2** suppurating. *—n.* a medicine or application that promotes suppuration.

su·pra (sü′prə) *adv.* **1** above. **2** in a book, manuscript, etc., before; previously. [< L]

supra- *prefix.* above; beyond, as in *suprarenal.* [< L]

su·pra·na·tion·al (sü′prə nash′ə nəl or -nash′nəl) *adj.* supernational.

su·pra·re·nal (sü′prə rē′nəl) in anatomy: *—adj.* **1** situated above the kidney or on the kidney; adrenal. A suprarenal body, capsule, or gland is a ductless gland situated on or near the kidney and furnishing an important secretion called adrenalin. **2** of or having to do with a suprarenal body, capsule, or gland. *—n.* a suprarenal body, capsule, or gland. [< *supra-* above + L *renes* kidneys]

su·prem·a·cy (sə prem′ə sē or sů prem′ə sē) *n.* **1** the state of being supreme. **2** supreme authority or power. **—Syn. 2** domination, predominance, mastery.

su·preme (sə prēm′ or sů prēm′) *adj.* **1** highest in rank or authority: *a supreme ruler.* **2** of or belonging to a person or thing that is supreme: *supreme authority.* **3** highest in degree; greatest; utmost: *supreme disgust.* **4** highest in quality: *supreme courage.* **5** last; final. **6 make the supreme sacrifice,** give one's life; die. [< L *supremus,* ult. < *super* above] **—su·preme′ly,** *adv.* **—Syn. 1** chief, paramount.

Supreme Being God.

Supreme Court 1 a the highest court in Canada, located in Ottawa. **b** the highest court in each province, located in the provincial capitals. **2** a similar court in other countries.

Supt. or **supt.** superintendent.

sur-[1] *prefix.* upon; over; above, as in *surcharge, surcoat, surtax.*

sur-[2] the form of *sub-* before *r,* as in *surreptitious.*

sur. 1 surplus. **2** surcharge. **3** surname.

su·rah (sür′ə) *n.* a soft, twilled silk, rayon, etc. [< *Surat,* a city in W. India]

sur·cease (sėr sēs′) *n. Archaic.* end; cessation. [ME < OF *sursis,* pp. of *surseoir* refrain < L *supersedere.* See SUPERSEDE.]

sur·charge (*n.* sėr′chärj′; *v.* sər chärj′) *n. v.* **-charged, -charg·ing.** *—n.* **1** an extra charge: *The express company made a surcharge for delivering the trunk outside of the city limits.* **2** an additional mark printed on a postage stamp to change its value, date, etc. **3** a stamp bearing such a mark. **4** an additional and usually excessive load, burden, or supply. [< F *surcharge*]
—v. **1** charge extra. **2** overcharge. **3** overload: *The widow's heart was surcharged with grief.* **4** print a surcharge on (a postage stamp). [< F *surcharger* < *sur-* over (< L *super-*) + *charger* charge < L *carricare* to load < *carrus* load]

sur·cin·gle (sėr′sing gəl) *n.* a strap or belt around a horse's body to keep a saddle, blanket, or pack in place. [ME < OF *surcengle* < *sur-* over (< L *super-*) + *cengle* girdle < L *cingula* < *cingere* gird]

sur·coat (sėr′kōt′) *n.* an outer coat, especially such a garment formerly worn by knights over their armor. [ME < OF *surcote* < *sur-* over (< L *super-*) + *cote* coat < Gmc.]

surd (sėrd) *n.* **1** in phonetics, a sound uttered without vibration of the vocal cords; an unvoiced or voiceless sound. The sounds (f), (k), (p), (s) as in *sit,* and (t) are surds. **2** in mathematics, a quantity that cannot be expressed in whole numbers. *Example*: $\sqrt{2}$. *—adj.* **1** in phonetics, uttered without vibration of the vocal cords; unvoiced or voiceless. **2** in mathematics, that cannot be expressed in whole numbers. [< L *surdus* unheard]

sure (shür) *adj.* **sur·er, sur·est,** *adv. —adj.* **1** free from doubt; certain; having ample reason for belief; confident; positive: *He is sure of success in the end. I am sure of his guilt.* **2** safe; reliable; to be trusted: *a sure messenger.* **3** never missing, slipping, etc.; unfailing; unerring: *sure aim, a sure touch.* **4** admitting of no doubt or question: *sure proof.* **5** *Archaic.* secure or safe. **6 be sure,** be careful; do not fail. **7 for sure,** *Informal.* **a** surely; certainly: *He's coming for sure.* **b** sure; certain: *That's for sure.* **8 make sure, a** act so as to make something certain. **b** get sure knowledge. **9 to be sure,** surely; certainly. *—adv. Informal.* surely; certainly. [ME < OF *sur* < L *securus.* Doublet of SECURE.] **—sure′ness,** *n.*

Syn. *adj.* **1 Sure, certain, confident** = having no doubt about a person, fact, statement, action, etc. **Sure** emphasizes being free from doubt in one's own mind: *Police are sure he was murdered.* **Certain,** often interchangeable with *sure,* more definitely suggests positive reasons or proof to support one's trust or belief: *They have been certain since they uncovered new evidence.* **Confident** suggests a strong and unshakable belief: *They are confident they will solve the case soon.*

☛ **Sure** is primarily an adjective: *sure footing. Are you sure?* As an adverb, *sure* is often used in informal speech instead of *surely* or equivalent to *certainly* or *yes*: *Sure, I'm coming. That sure is interesting.*

sure-foot·ed (shür′fůt′id) *adj.* not liable to stumble, slip, or fall. **—sure′-foot′ed·ness,** *n.*

sure·ly (shür′lē) *adv.* **1** undoubtedly; certainly: *Half a loaf is surely better than none.* **2** as may be confidently supposed; as must be the case: *Surely it will not rain all week.* **3** without mistake; without missing, slipping, etc.; firmly: *The goat leaped surely from rock to rock.* **4** without fail: *slowly but surely.*

Sû·re·té (shůr′ə tā′; *French,* SYR tā′) *n.* in France, the criminal investigation section of the police department. [< F]

sur·e·ty (shür′ə tē) *n.* **-ties. 1** security against loss, damage, or failure to do something: *An insurance company gives surety against loss by fire.* **2** a person who agrees to be responsible for another: *He was surety for his brother's appearance in court on the day set for the trial.* **3** *Archaic.* a sure thing; certainty. **—Syn. 1** guaranty, pledge. **2** bondsman, bail, sponsor.

sur·e·ty·ship (shür′ə tē ship′) *n.* the obligation of a person to answer for the debt, fault, or conduct of another.

surf (sėrf) *n.* the waves or swell of the sea breaking on the shore or upon shoals, reefs, etc. [earlier *suff*; possibly var. of *sough*]

sur·face (sėr′fis) *n. adj. v.* **-faced, -fac·ing.** *—n.* **1** the outside of anything: *the surface of a golf ball, the surface of a mountain.* **2** the top of the ground or soil, or of a body of water or other liquid: *The stone sank below the surface.* **3** any face or side of a thing: *A cube has six surfaces.* **4** that which has length and breadth but no thickness: *a plane surface in geometry.* **5** the outward appearance: *He seems rough, but you will find him very kind below the surface.*
—adj. of the surface; on the surface; having to do with the surface: *a surface view, a surface ship.*
—v. **1** put a surface on; make smooth: *surface a road.* **2** bring or come to the surface: *surface a submarine. The skindiver surfaced at last.* [< F *surface* < *sur-* above (< L *super-*) + *face* face, ult. < L *facies* form]
—sur′fac·er, *n.*

surface mail 1 mail transported by land and sea, rather than by air. **2** the system of sending surface mail.

surface tension the tension of the surface film of a liquid that makes it contract to a minimum area.

surf·board (sėrf′bôrd′) *n.* a more-or-less oblong board on which a person may stand or lie in order to ride on the crest of a wave as it comes in to the beach.

surf·boat (sėrf′bōt′) *n.* a strong boat specially made for use in heavy surf.

surf duck scoter.

Surfboards

sur·feit (sėr′fit) *n.* **1** a grossly excessive amount of something; too much; excess: *A surfeit of food makes one sick. A surfeit of advice annoys me.* **2** disgust or nausea caused by this; painful satiety. **3** an abnormal physical condition caused by gluttony, intemperance, etc. *—v.* **1** force down or on (a person) in such quantity as to cause nausea, disgust, etc.; feed or supply to excess. **2** eat, drink, or indulge in something to excess; take one's fill and more (of); feast gluttonously (upon). [ME < OF *surfait,* originally pp., overdone < *sur-* over (< L *super-*) + *faire* do < L *facere*] —**Syn.** *v.* glut, gorge. See **satiate.**

surf·y (sėr′fē) *adj.* **1** having much surf or heavy surf. **2** forming or resembling surf.

surge (sėrj) *v.* **surged, surg·ing,** *n.* —*v.* **1** rise and fall; move like waves: *A great wave surged over us. The crowd surged through the streets.* **2** cause to move in, or as in, swelling waves or billows. **3** rise or swell (up) tempestuously or excitedly, as feelings, thoughts, etc. —*n.* **1** a swelling wave; a sweep or rush of waves; something like a wave: *A surge of anger swept over him.* **2** the swelling and rolling of the sea. **3** a swelling or sweeping forward like that of the waves; a swelling volume, as of fire, wind, sound, etc.: *a sudden surge of smoke.* [ult. (probably through OF *surgeon* a spring) < L *surgere* rise < *sub-* up + *regere* reach]

sur·geon (sėr′jən) *n.* a medical doctor who specializes in surgery: *A surgeon removed the boy's appendix.* [ME < AF *surgien,* OF *cirurgien* < *cirurgie.* See SURGERY. Doublet of CHIRURGEON.]

sur·ger·y (sėr′jər ē) *n.* **-ger·ies. 1** the branch of medicine that deals with the treatment of physical disorders by operations performed by hand or with instruments. **2** the practice or use of this branch of medicine: *Malaria can be cured by medicine, but a ruptured appendix requires surgery.* **3** the office, laboratory, or operating room of a surgeon. [ME < OF *surgerie, cirurgerie* < *cirurgie* < L < Gk. *cheirourgia,* ult. < *cheir* hand + *ergon* work]

sur·gi·cal (sėr′jə kəl) *adj.* **1** of surgery; having to do with surgery. **2** used in surgery. **3** performed by a surgeon. —**sur′gi·cal·ly,** *adv.*

surg·y (sėr′jē′) *adj.* **surg·i·er, surgi·est. 1** surging; swelling; billowy. **2** produced by surges.

sur·ly (sėr′lē) *adj.* **-li·er, -li·est.** bad-tempered and unfriendly; rude; gruff: *They got a surly answer from the grouchy old man.* [ult. < *sir,* in sense of "lord"] —**sur′li·ly,** *adv.* —**sur′li·ness,** *n.* —**Syn.** sullen, churlish, cross.

sur·mise (*v.* sər mīz′; *n.* sər mīz′ or sėr′mīz) *v.* **-mised, -mis·ing,** *n.* —*v.* guess: *We surmised that the delay was caused by some accident.* [< n.] —*n.* **1** the formation of an idea with little or no evidence; a guessing: *His guilt was a matter of surmise; there was no proof.* **2** a guess. [ME < OF *surmise* accusation, ult. < *sur-* upon (< L *super-*) + *mettre* put < L *mittere* send] —**Syn.** *v.* infer, suppose. See **guess.**

sur·mount (sər mount′) *v.* **1** rise above. **2** be above or on top of: *The peak surmounts the valley.* **3** go up and across: *surmount a hill.* **4** overcome: *He surmounted many difficulties.* [ME < OF *surmonter* < *sur-* over (< L *super-*) + *monter* mount < L *mons, montis* mountain] —**sur·mount′a·ble,** *adj.*

sur·name (sėr′nām′) *n. v.* **-named, -nam·ing.** —*n.* **1** a last name; family name. **2** *Archaic.* name added to a person's real name: *William I of England had the surname "the Conqueror."* —*v.* give an added name to; call by a surname: *Simon was surnamed Peter.* [< F *surnom* < *sur-* over (< L *super-*) + *nom* name < L *nomen*; influenced by E *name*]

sur·pass (sər pas′) *v.* **1** do better than; be greater than; excel: *His work surpassed expectations.* **2** be too much or too great for; go beyond; exceed: *The horrors of the battlefield surpassed description.* [< F *surpasser* < *sur-* beyond + *passer* pass] —**sur·pass′a·ble,** *adj.* —**sur·pass′ing·ly,** *adv.* —**Syn. 1** outdo, outstrip, outrun, eclipse. See **excel.**

A surplice

sur·plice (sər′plis) *n.* a broad-sleeved, white gown worn by certain clergymen and choir singers over their other clothes. [ME < AF *surpliz,* OF *surpelice* < *sur-* over (< L *super-*) + *pelice* fur garment, ult. < L *pellis* hide]

sur·plus (sėr′pləs or sėr′plus) *n.* **1** an amount over and above what is needed; an extra quantity left over; excess. **2** an excess of assets over liabilities. —*adj.* more than is needed; excess: *Surplus wheat and butter are shipped abroad.* [ME < OF *surplus* < *sur-* over (< L *super-*) + *plus* more < L *plus*] —**Syn.** *n.* **1** residue, remainder.

hat, āge, cãre, fär; let, ēqual, tėrm; it, īce
hot, ōpen, ôrder; oil, out; cup, pu̇t, rüle, ūse
əbove, takən, pencəl, lemən, circəs
ch, child; ng, long; sh, ship
th, thin; ᴛʜ, then; zh, measure

sur·plus·age (sėr′plus ij) *n.* **1** surplus; excess. **2** unnecessary words; irrelevant material.

sur·pris·al (sər prīz′əl or sə prīz′əl) *n.* the act of surprising or the state of being surprised; a surprise.

sur·prise (sər prīz′ or sə prīz′) *n. v.* **-prised, -pris·ing,** *adj.* —*n.* **1** a feeling caused by something unexpected. **2** something unexpected. **3** a catching unprepared; a coming upon suddenly; a sudden attack. **4 take by surprise, a** catch unprepared; come on suddenly and unexpectedly. **b** astonish. —*v.* **1** cause to feel surprised; astonish. **2** catch unprepared; come upon suddenly; attack suddenly: *The enemy surprised the fort.* **3** lead or bring (a person, etc.) unawares: *The news surprised her into tears.* **4** find or discover (something) by a sudden or unexpected question, attack, etc.; detect or elicit: *surprise the truth of the matter from him.* —*adj.* that is not expected; surprising: *a surprise party, a surprise visit.* [ME < OF *surprise,* pp. fem. of *surprendre* < *sur-* over (< L *super-*) + *prendre* take < L *prehendere*]

Syn. *n.* **1** astonishment, amazement, wonder. –*v.* **1 Surprise, astonish, amaze** = strike a person with a sudden feeling as of perplexity, confusion, or wonder. **Surprise,** the general word, suggests the sudden feeling caused by something unexpected or out of the ordinary: *His answer surprised her.* **Astonish** suggests the stronger feeling caused by something too extraordinary to be possible: *He astonished many people by failing in college work after getting high grades in high school.* **Amaze** emphasizes the idea of bewildered wonder: *New scientific discoveries constantly amaze us.*

sur·pris·ing (sər prīz′ing or sə prīz′ing) *adj.* causing surprise. —**sur·pris′ing·ly,** *adv.* —**Syn.** astonishing, amazing.

sur·re·al·ism (sə rē′əl iz′əm) *n.* in art and literature, a style characterized by the attempt to portray the functioning of the subconscious mind, especially as in dreams, often by combining conventional and unconventional elements or by distorting the conventional. [< F *surréalisme*]

sur·re·al·ist (sə rē′əl ist) *n.* an artist or writer who uses surrealism. —*adj.* of or having to do with surrealism or surrealists.

sur·re·al·is·tic (sə rē′əl is′tik) *adj.* of or having to do with surrealism or surrealists. —**sur·re′al·is′ti·cal·ly,** *adv.*

sur·ren·der (sə ren′dər) *v.* **1** give up (something) to the possession or power of another, upon demand or compulsion; yield (*to*): *surrender a town to the enemy.* **2** give up, resign, or abandon possession of (something) in favor of or for the sake of another; relinquish: *surrender an office or privilege.* **3** give up or abandon (hope, joy, comfort, etc.): *As the storm increased, the men on the raft surrendered all hope.* **4** give (oneself) up to a dominating thing or influence: *He surrendered himself to bitter grief.* —*n.* the act of surrendering. [ME < AF *surrendre* < OF *sur-* over (< L *super-*) + *rendre* render < L *reddere* give as due, pay] —**Syn.** *v.* relinquish, resign, abandon.

sur·rep·ti·tious (sėr′əp tish′əs) *adj.* **1** stealthy; secret. **2** secret and unauthorized. [< L *surrepticius,* ult. < *sub-* secretly + *rapere* snatch] —**sur′rep·ti′tious·ly,** *adv.* —**sur′rep·ti′tious·ness,** *n.*

sur·rey (sėr′ē) *n.* **-reys.** a light four-wheeled carriage having two seats. [< *Surrey,* a county in S.E. England]

A surrey

sur·ro·gate (sėr′ə gāt′ or sėr′ə git) *n.* a substitute; deputy, especially the deputy of a bishop. —*adj.* of a court, the probate of wills, the administration of estates, etc. [< L *surrogatus,* pp. of *surrogare* substitute < *sub-* instead + *rogare* ask for]

sur·ro·gate·ship (sėr′ə gāt ship′ or sėr′ə git-) *n.* the office or authority of a surrogate.

sur·round (sə round′) *v.* **1** shut in on all sides; enclose; encompass: *A high fence surrounds the field.* **2** go or extend around; encircle: *inscriptions surrounding the base of a monument.* **3** make available to in abundance; provide unstintingly: *They surrounded the invalid with every comfort.* **4** encompass and beset on all sides with hostile military force, especially so as to cut off from supplies, reinforcements, etc.: *surround a city.*
—*n.* a border or edging of a particular material, nearly or completely surrounding a central piece: *the plastic surround of a television screen.* [ME < AF *surounder* surpass < LL *superundare* overflow < L *super-* over + *unda* wave; influenced in meaning by *round*] —**Syn.** *v.* **1** enclose, encompass.

sur·round·ings (sə roun′dingz) *n.pl.* surrounding things, conditions, etc.

sur·tax (sėr′taks′) *n.* an additional or extra tax. The surtax on large incomes increases in graded steps as the income exceeds certain amounts. [< F *surtaxe* < *sur-* over + *taxe* tax]

sur·tout (sėr tüt′ or sėr tü′) *n.* a man's overcoat. [< F *surtout* < *sur-* over + *tout* all]

sur·veil·lance (sər vāl′əns or sər vāl′yəns) *n.* **1** a watch kept over a person: *The police kept the criminal under strict surveillance.* **2** supervision. [< F *surveillance* < *sur-* over (< L *super-*) + *veiller* watch < L *vigilare*]

sur·vey (*v.* sər vā′; *n.* sėr′vā or sər vā′) *v. n.* **-veys.**
—*v.* **1** take a broad, general, or comprehensive view of; view, examine, consider, or contemplate as a whole: *survey the situation.* **2** measure for size, shape, position, boundaries, etc.: *Men are surveying the land before it is divided into house lots.* **3** survey land: *He spent the summer surveying.*
—*n.* **1** the act of viewing or considering something as a whole; a general or comprehensive view: *We were pleased with our first survey of the house.* **2** a formal or official examination or inspection of the particulars of something, in order to determine condition, quality, etc.: *a survey of fire hazards in public buildings, a research centre for business surveys.* **3** a written statement or description of such an inspection. **4** a careful measurement of a tract of land. **5** a plan or description of such a measurement: *He pointed out the route of the railway on the government survey.* **6** a tract of land divided into building lots; subdivision. **7** the houses or community built on such land. [ME < AF *surveier*, ult. < L *super-* over + *videre* see]

sur·vey·ing (sər vā′ing) *n.* **1** the business or act of making surveys of land. **2** mathematical instruction in the principles and art of making surveys.

sur·vey·or (sər vā′ər) *n.* **1** a person who surveys, especially land. **2** a customs officer in charge of estimating the quantity and value of goods brought into a port from another country.

sur·vey·or·ship (sər vā′ər ship′) *n.* the position of a surveyor.

surveyor's measure a system of measuring used by surveyors. The unit is usually a chain 66 ft. long with links 7.92 in. long.

625 square links	=	1 square pole
16 square poles	=	1 square chain
10 square chains	=	1 acre
640 acres	=	1 section (or 1 square mile)
36 sections	=	1 township

sur·viv·al (sər vī′vəl) *n.* **1** the act or fact of surviving; continuance of life; living or lasting longer than others. **2** a person, thing, custom, belief, etc. that has lasted from an earlier time.

sur·vive (sər vīv′) *v.* **-vived, -viv·ing.** **1** live longer than; outlive: *He survived his wife by three years.* **2** remain alive after: *Only ten of the crew survived the shipwreck.* **3** sustain the effects of and continue to live; outlast: *The crops survived the drought.* **4** continue to exist; remain: *Books have survived from the time of the ancient Egyptians.* [ME < AF *survivre* < *sur-* over (< L *super-*) + *vivre* live < L *vivere*]

sur·vi·vor (sər vī′vər) *n.* a person, animal, or plant that remains alive; a thing that continues to exist.

sus- the form of **sub-** (from the form *subs-*) in some cases before *c, p, t,* as in *susceptible, suspend, sustain.*

sus·cep·ti·bil·i·ty (sə sep′tə bil′ə tē) *n.* **-ties.** **1** the quality or state of being susceptible; readiness to receive impressions; sensitiveness. **2** in physics, the capacity of a substance to be magnetized, measured by the ratio of the magnetization to the magnetizing force. *Symbol*: k **3 susceptibilities,** *pl.* sensitive feelings.

sus·cep·ti·ble (sə sep′tə bəl) *adj.* **1** easily influenced by feelings or emotions; very sensitive: *Poetry appealed to his susceptible nature.* **2** subject to some physical affection, such as an infection. **3 susceptible of, a** capable of receiving, undergoing, or being affected by: *Oak is susceptible of a high polish.* **b** sensitive to. **4 susceptible to,** easily affected by; liable to; open to: *Vain people are susceptible to flattery.* [< LL *susceptibilis*, ult. < L *sub-* up + *capere* take] —**sus·cep′ti·bly,** *adv.* —**Syn.** **1** impressionable. See **sensitive.**

sus·pect (*v.* səs pekt′; *n.* sus′pekt; *adj.* sus′pekt or səs pekt′) *v.* **1** imagine to be so; think likely: *The old fox suspected danger and did not touch the trap.* **2** believe guilty, false, bad, etc. without proof: *The policeman suspected the thief of lying.* **3** feel no confidence in; doubt: *The judge suspected the truth of the thief's excuse.* **4** be suspicious. [< adj. and < F *suspecter* suspect, ult. < L *suspectus*, pp. See adj.]
—*n.* a person suspected. [< adj.]
—*adj.* open to suspicion; suspected. [ME < L *suspectus*, pp. of *suspicere* < *sub-* under + *specere* look]
—**Syn.** *v.* **1** surmise, conjecture.

sus·pend (səs pend′) *v.* **1** hang down by attaching to something above: *The lamp was suspended from the ceiling.* **2** hold in place as if by hanging: *We saw the smoke suspended in the still air.* **3** stop for a while: *suspend work.* **4** stop payment; be unable to pay one's debts. **5** cause (a law, etc.) to be for a time no longer in force; abrogate or make inoperative temporarily. **6** defer temporarily (sentence on a convicted person). **7** remove or exclude for a while from some privilege or job: *He was suspended from school for a week for bad conduct.* **8** keep undecided; put off: *The court suspended judgment till next Monday.* **9 suspend payment,** declare inability to pay one's debts; fail. [ME < L *suspendere* < *sub-* up + *pendere* hang] —**Syn.** **1** dangle, swing. **3** interrupt, intermit.

sus·pend·ers (səs pen′dərz) *n.* **1** straps worn over the shoulders to hold up the trousers; braces. **2** garters worn by men to hold up their socks and by women to hold up their stockings.

sus·pense (səs pens′) *n.* **1** the condition of being uncertain: *The detective story kept me in suspense until the last chapter.* **2** anxious uncertainty; anxiety: *Mothers feel suspense when their children are very sick.* **3** the condition of being undecided. [ME < OF (*en*) *suspens* (in) abeyance, ult. < L *suspendere.* See SUSPEND.]

sus·pen·si·ble (səs pen′sə bəl) *adj.* that can be suspended.

sus·pen·sion (səs pen′shən) *n.* **1** a suspending or being suspended: *the suspension of a boy from school for bad conduct.* **2** a support on which something is suspended. **3** an arrangement of springs, etc. for supporting the body of an automobile, railway car, etc. **4** in physics, a mixture in which very small particles of a solid remain suspended without dissolving. **5** the inability to pay one's debts; failure. **6** in electricity, a wire or filament for supporting the moving parts of various instruments. **7** the method or mechanism by which the pendulum or balance wheel is suspended in a clock or watch. **8** in music: **a** a prolonging of one or more tones of a chord into the following chord, usually producing a temporary discord. **b** the tone or tones so prolonged. —**Syn.** **1** interruption, intermission, stop, postponement, respite.

suspension bridge a bridge hung on cables or chains between towers.

A suspension bridge

sus·pen·sive (səs pen′siv) *adj.* **1** inclined to suspend judgment; undecided in mind. **2** having to do with or characterized by suspense, uncertainty, or apprehension. **3** having the effect of temporarily stopping something: *a suspensive veto.* **4** involving such suspension.

sus·pen·so·ry (səs pen′sə rē) *adj. n.* **-ries.** *—adj.* **1** holding up; supporting. **2** stopping for a while; leaving undecided. *—n.* a muscle, ligament, bandage, etc. that holds up or supports a part of the body.

sus·pi·cion (səs pish′ən) *n.* **1** the state of mind of a person who suspects; suspecting: *The real thief tried to turn suspicion toward the others.* **2** the condition of being suspected. **3** a very small amount; slight trace; suggestion: *She spoke with a suspicion of spite.* **4 above suspicion,** so honest, honorable, etc. as not to be suspected of wrongdoing. **5 on suspicion,** because of being suspected. **6 under suspicion,** suspected; believed guilty but not proven to be so. *—v. Slang.* suspect. [ME < L *suspicio, -onis* < *suspicere.* See SUSPECT.]

Syn. *n.* **1 Suspicion, distrust, doubt** = lack of trust or confidence in someone. **Suspicion** suggests fearing, or believing without enough or any proof, that someone or something is guilty, wrong, false, etc.: *Suspicion points to him, but the evidence is circumstantial.* **Distrust** = lack of confidence or trust, especially in a person, and may suggest certainty of guilt, falseness, etc.: *Even his mother feels distrust.* **Doubt** emphasizes lack of certainty, and suggests inability to make a decision: *He must be proved guilty beyond reasonable doubt.*

☛ **suspicion.** As a verb, *suspicion* is substandard: *Nobody suspicioned who it was. Suspect* is the formal and informal verb.

sus·pi·cious (səs pish′əs) *adj.* **1** causing one to suspect: *A man was hanging about the house in a suspicious manner.* **2** feeling suspicion; suspecting: *Our dog is suspicious of strangers.* **3** showing suspicion: *The dog gave a suspicious sniff at my leg.* **—sus·pi′cious·ly,** *adv.* **—sus·pi′cious·ness,** *n.*

sus·pi·ra·tion (sus′pə rā′shən) *n.* a sigh.

sus·pire (səs pīr′) *v.* **-pired, -pir·ing.** *Poetic.* **1** sigh. **2** breathe; breathe forth. [< L *suspirare* < *sub-* up + *spirare* breathe]

sus·tain (səs tān′) *v.* **1** keep up; keep going: *Hope sustains him in his misery.* **2** supply with food, provisions, etc.: *sustain an army.* **3** hold up; support: *Arches sustain the weight of the roof.* **4** bear; endure: *The sea wall sustains the shock of the waves.* **5** suffer; experience: *sustain a great loss.* **6** allow; admit; favor: *The court sustained his suit.* **7** agree with; confirm: *The facts sustain his theory.* [ME < OF < L *sustinere* < *sub-* up + *tenere* hold] **—sus·tain′a·ble,** *adj.* **—sus·tain′er,** *n.* —**Syn. 1** aid, assist, comfort. **4** stand. **5** undergo. **7** corroborate, sanction.

sustained yield in the management of forests, fisheries, etc., the principle of maintaining a steady yield by keeping annual growth or increase at least as high as annual output.

sustaining program or **programme** a radio or television program having no sponsor but maintained at the expense of a station or network.

sus·te·nance (sus′tə nəns) *n.* **1** food: *He has gone for a week without sustenance.* **2** the means of living; support: *He gave money for the sustenance of a poor family.* [ME < OF *sustenance* < *sustenir* sustain < L *sustinere.* See SUSTAIN.]

sut·ler (sut′lər) *n.* formerly, a person who followed an army and sold provisions, etc. to the soldiers. [< earlier Du. *soeteler* < *soetelen* ply a low trade]

sut·tee (su tē′ or sut′ē) *n.* **1** a Hindu widow who throws herself on the burning funeral pile of her husband. **2** the former Hindu custom of burning a widow with the body of her husband. [< Hind. < Skt. *satī* faithful wife]

su·ture (sü′chər) *n. v.* **-tured, -tur·ing.** *—n.* **1** in surgery: **a** a seam formed in sewing up a wound. **b** the method of sewing up a wound. **c** one of the stitches or fastenings used. **d** the material used for sewing up a wound. **2** a sewing together or a joining as if by sewing. **3** in anatomy, the line where two bones, especially of the skull, join. **4** in biology, the line between adjoining parts in a plant or animal such as that along which clamshells join or pea pods split. *—v.* unite by suture or as if by a suture. [< L *sutura* < *suere* sew]

su·ze·rain (sü′zə rin or sü′zə rān′) *n.* **1** a feudal lord. **2** a state or government exercising political control over a dependent state. [< F *suzerain* < *sus* above (< L *sursum* upward), modelled on *souverain* sovereign]

su·ze·rain·ty (sü′zə rin tē or sü′zə rān tē) *n.* **-ties.** the

hat, āge, cãre, fär; let, ēqual, tėrm; it, īce
hot, ōpen, ôrder; oil, out; cup, pu̇t, rüle, ūse
əbove, takən, pencəl, lemən, circəs
ch, child; ng, long; sh, ship
th, thin; ᴛʜ, then; zh, measure

position or authority of a suzerain.

s.v. under the word or heading. (for L *sub verbo* or *sub voce*)

svelte (svelt) *adj.* slender; lithe. [< F < Ital. *svelto,* pp. < L *ex-* out + *vellere* pluck]

Sw. **1** Swedish. **2** Sweden.

SW, S.W., or **s.w.** southwest.

swab (swob) *n. v.* **swabbed, swab·bing.** *—n.* **1** a mop for cleaning decks, floors, etc. **2** a bit of sponge, cloth, or cotton for cleansing some part of the body or for applying medicine to it. **3** a specimen taken with such a bit of sponge, cloth, or cotton. **4** a cleaner for the bore of a firearm. **5** *Slang.* an awkward, clumsy person. *—v.* **1** clean with a mop. **2** clean with a swab; apply a swab to: *swab a person's throat.* Also, **swob.** [< *swabber*]

swab·ber (swob′ər) *n.* **1** a person who uses a swab. **2** a swab. [< Du. *zwabber* < *zwabben* swab]

Swa·bi·an (swä′bē ən or swā′bē ən) *adj.* of or having to do with Swabia, a former duchy in southwest Germany. *—n.* a native or inhabitant of Swabia.

swad·dle (swod′əl) *v.* **-dled, -dling,** *n.* *—v.* bind (a baby) with long, narrow strips of cloth; wrap tightly with clothes, bandages, etc. [< n.] *—n.* the cloth used for swaddling. [OE *swæthel* band, bandage. Related to SWATHE[1].]

swaddling clothes **1** long, narrow strips of cloth for wrapping a newborn infant. **2** long clothes for an infant.

S.W.Afr. Southwest Africa.

swag (swag) *n.* **1** *Slang.* a thing stolen; booty; plunder. **2** a quantity of money or goods unlawfully acquired; dishonest gains, especially dishonest political gains. **3** *Australian.* a bundle of personal belongings. **4** an ornamental festoon of flowers, leaves, ribbons, etc. [special use of *swag, v.,* sway, probably < Scand.; cf. dial. Norwegian *svagga* sway]

swage (swāj) *n. v.* **swaged, swag·ing.** *—n.* **1** a tool for bending metal. **2** a die or stamp for giving a particular shape to metal by hammering, stamping, etc. *—v.* bend or shape by using a swage. [ME < OF *souage*]

swag·ger (swag′ər) *v.* **1** walk with a bold, rude, or superior air; strut about or show off in a vain or insolent way: *The bully swaggered along the street.* **2** boast or brag noisily. **3** bluster; affect by bluster; bluff. *—n.* a swaggering way of walking or acting. *—adj. Informal.* very fashionable. [< *swag*] **—swag′ger·er,** *n.* **—swag′ger·ing·ly,** *adv.* —**Syn.** *v.* **1** See **strut.**

swagger stick a short, light stick or cane, often carried by army officers, etc.

Swa·hi·li (swä hē′lē) *n.* **-li** or **-lis,** *adj.* *—n.* **1** a member of a Bantu people of Zanzibar and the nearby African coast. **2** the Bantu language of this people, comprising large elements of Arabic and other foreign words and used as a lingua franca in most of East Africa. *—adj.* of or having to do with the Swahili or their language. [literally, people of the coast < Arabic *sawāḥil,* pl. of *sāḥil* coast]

swain (swān) *n. Archaic or poetic.* **1** a lover. **2** a young man who lives in the country. [ME < ON *sveinn* boy]

swale (swāl) *n.* a low, wet piece of land; low place. [ME, probably < Scand.; cf. ON *svalr* cool]

swal·low[1] (swol′ō) *v.* **1** take into the stomach through the throat: *swallow food.* **2** perform the act of swallowing: *I cannot swallow.* **3** *Informal.* believe too easily; accept without question or suspicion: *He will swallow any story.* **4** put up with; take meekly; accept without opposing or resisting: *He had to swallow the insult.* **5** take back: *swallow words said in anger.* **6** keep back; keep from expressing: *She swallowed her displeasure and smiled.* **7 swallow up, a** cause to disappear entirely, as if by devouring or absorption; consume; destroy; engulf: *The waves swallowed up the swimmer.*

b absorb or appropriate (a territory or other possession); take for oneself or into oneself. c take up completely. —*n.* 1 the act of swallowing: *He took the medicine at one swallow.* 2 an amount swallowed at one time. 3 the throat; gullet. [OE *swelgan*] —**swal′low·er,** *n.*

swal·low² (swol′ō) *n.* a small, swift-flying bird having a deeply forked tail, noted for the extent and regularity of its migratory movements. [OE *swealwe*]

swal·low·tail (swol′ō tāl′) *n.* 1 something shaped like or suggesting the deeply forked tail of a swallow. 2 a swallow-tailed coat.

swallow-tailed coat (swol′ō tāld′) a man's coat with tails, worn at formal evening parties.

swam (swam) *v.* pt. of **swim.**

swa·mi (swä′mē) *n.* **-mis.** the title of a Hindu religious teacher. [< Hind. < Skt. *svāmin*]

swamp (swomp) *n.* wet, soft land. —*v.* 1 plunge or sink in a swamp or in water: *The horses were swamped in the stream.* 2 fill with water and sink: *Their boat swamped. The wave swamped the boat.* 3 overwhelm or be overwhelmed as by a flood; make or become helpless: *He was swamped with letters asking for money.* [akin to SUMP] —**Syn.** *n.* marsh, morass, bog, fen, slough, quagmire.

swamp·land (swomp′land′) *n.* a tract of land covered by swamps.

swamp rabbit in the North, muskrat prepared as food.

swamp·y (swomp′ē) *adj.* **swamp·i·er, swamp·i·est.** 1 like a swamp; soft and wet. 2 containing swamps. 3 of swamps.

Swampy Cree one of the two main divisions of Cree Indians, scattered in groups over the woodlands of northwestern Ontario. Also, **Woodland Cree.**

swan (swon) *n.* 1 a large, graceful water bird having a long, slender, curving neck, and, in the adults of most species, pure-white plumage. 2 *Archaic.* a sweet singer; poet. 3 **Swan,** Cygnus, a northern constellation. [OE] —**swan′like′,** *adj.*

swan dive in swimming, a graceful dive in which the legs are held straight from the toes to the hips, the back is curved, and the arms are spread like the wings of a gliding bird.

swang (swang) *v. Archaic and dialect.* a pt. of **swing.**

swank (swangk) *Slang.* —*v.* show off; bluff; swagger. —*n.* 1 pretentious or ostentatious behavior, speech, etc.; a showing off. 2 style; smartness; dash. —*adj.* stylish; smart; dashing. [cf. OE *swancor* lithe]

swank·y (swangk′ē) *adj.* **swank·i·er, swank·i·est.** *Slang.* stylish; smart; dashing. —**swank′i·ly,** *adv.* —**swank′i·ness,** *n.*

swan's-down (swonz′doun′) *n.* 1 the soft down of a swan, used for trimming, powder puffs, etc. 2 a fine, thick, soft cloth made from wool or cotton, used for babies' coats, bathrobes, etc.

swan song 1 the song that a swan is supposed to sing just before it dies. 2 a person's farewell performance or final statement, composition, painting, etc.

swap (swop) *v.* **swapped, swap·ping,** *n. Informal.* exchange; barter; trade. Also, **swop.** [ME *swappe* strike, strike the hands together; probably imitative; the modern meaning arose from the practice of "striking hands" as a sign of agreement in bargaining] —**swap′per,** *n.*

sward (swôrd) *n.* a grassy surface; turf. [OE *sweard* skin]

sware (swãr) *v. Archaic.* a pt. of **swear.**

swarm¹ (swôrm) *n.* 1 a group of bees that leave a hive and fly off together to start a new colony. 2 a group of bees settled together in a hive. 3 a large group of insects flying or moving about together. 4 a great number; crowd: *Swarms of children were playing in the park.* 5 in biology, an aggregation of free-floating or free-swimming cells or unicellular organisms.
—*v.* 1 of bees, fly off together to start a new colony. 2 fly or move about in great numbers; be in very great numbers: *The mosquitoes swarmed about us.* 3 be crowded: *The swamp swarms with mosquitoes.* 4 crowd. 5 in biology, escape from the parent organism in a swarm, with characteristic movement. [OE *swearm*: akin to L *susurrus* hum, Skt. *svara* voice] —**Syn.** *n.* 4 multitude, throng. See **crowd.**

swarm² (swôrm) *v.* climb; shin. [origin uncertain]

swart (swôrt) *adj.* dark; swarthy. [OE *sweart*]

swarth (swôrth) *adj. Archaic.* swarthy.

swarth·y (swôr′ᴛʜē or swôr′thē) *adj.* **swarth·i·er, swarth·i·est.** having a dark skin. [earlier *swarty* < *swart* + *-y*¹] —**swarth′i·ly,** *adv.* —**swarth′i·ness,** *n.* —**Syn.** See **dusky.**

swash (swosh) *v.* 1 dash (water, etc.) about; splash. 2 swagger. —*n.* 1 a swashing action or sound: *the swash of waves against a boat.* 2 a swagger. 3 a channel of water through or behind a sandbank. 4 the ground under water or over which water washes. [probably imitative]

swash·buck·ler (swosh′buk′lər) *n.* a swaggering swordsman, bully, or boaster. [< *swash* + *buckler*]

swash·buck·ling (swosh′buk′ling) *n. adj.* swaggering; bullying; boasting.

swas·ti·ka (swos′tə kə) *n.* an ancient symbol or design consisting of a cross having equal arms that are bent rectangularly in a clockwise or counterclockwise direction. [< Skt. *svastika* < *svasti* luck < *su* well + *asti*, n., being < *as* be]

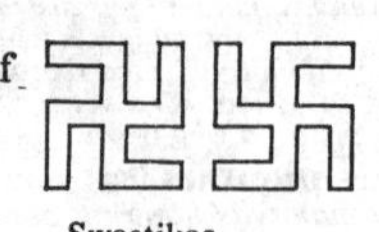
Swastikas

swat (swot) *v.* **swat·ted swat·ting,** *n. Informal.* —*v.* hit with a smart or violent blow: *swat a fly.* —*n.* a smart or violent blow. [originally var. of *squat*] —**swat′ter,** *n.*

swatch (swoch) *n.* a sample of cloth or other similar material. [origin uncertain]

swath (swoth) *n.* 1 the space covered by a single cut of a scythe or by one cut of a mowing machine. 2 a row of grass, grain, etc. cut by a scythe or mowing machine. 3 a strip. 4 **cut a wide swath,** *Informal.* make a showy display; splurge. [OE *swæth* track, trace]

swathe¹ (swāᴛʜ or swoᴛʜ) *v.* **swathed, swath·ing,** *n.* —*v.* 1 wrap up closely or fully: *swathed in a blanket.* 2 bind; wrap; bandage. 3 envelop or surround like a wrapping: *White clouds swathed the mountain.* —*n.* a wrapping; bandage. [OE *swathian*]

swathe² (swoᴛʜ or swāᴛʜ) *n.* swath.

sway (swā) *v.* 1 swing back and forth; swing from side to side, or to one side: *She swayed and fell in a faint. The pail swayed in Jack's hands as he ran.* 2 make move; cause to sway: *The wind sways the grass.* 3 move to one side; turn aside; change in opinion, feeling, etc.: *Nothing could sway him after he had made up his mind.* 4 influence; control; rule: *The speaker's words swayed his audience.* —*n.* 1 a swaying: *The sway of the pail caused some milk to spill out.* 2 influence; control; rule: *Few countries are now under the sway of kings.* [ME < Scand.; akin to ON *sveigja*] —**Syn.** *v.* 1 wave, fluctuate, oscillate. See **swing.**

sway·back (swā′bak′) *adj.* sway-backed.

sway-backed (swā′bakt′) *adj.* 1 of horses and other animals, strained in the back by overwork. 2 having the back sagged or hollowed to an unusual degree.

swear (swãr) *v.* **swore** or (*Archaic*) **sware, sworn, swear·ing.** 1 make a solemn statement, appealing to God or some other sacred being or object; take oath. 2 declare, calling God to witness; make solemn oath; declare on oath. 3 bind by an oath; require to promise: *Members of the club were sworn to secrecy.* 4 admit to office or service by administering an oath to: *swear a witness.* 5 promise solemnly; vow. 6 bring, set, take, etc. by swearing: *swear a person's life away.* 7 utter (an oath). 8 use profane language; curse. 9 **swear by, a** name as one's witness in taking an oath. **b** have great confidence in. 10 **swear in,** admit to office or service by giving an oath. 11 **swear off,** *Informal.* promise to give up. 12 **swear out,** get (a warrant for arrest) by taking an oath that a certain charge is true. [OE *swerian*] —**swear′er,** *n.* —**Syn.** 8 See **curse.**

swear word a curse; an oath.

sweat (swet) *n. v.* **sweat** or **sweat·ed, sweat·ing.** —*n.* 1 moisture coming through the pores of the skin. 2 a fit or condition of sweating: *He was in a cold sweat from fear.* 3 *Informal.* a fit of suffering, anxiety, impatience, or anything that might make a person sweat. 4 moisture

given out by something or gathered on its surface: *The water pipes were covered with sweat.* **5** an exuding of moisture from something, or the process of producing an exudation, as part of certain industrial processes, as tanning. **6** anything that causes sweat; hard work or strenuous exertion; labor. **7 old sweat,** *Informal.* an old soldier. [ME *swet(e)* < *swete(n)*, v.]
—*v.* **1** give out moisture through the pores of the skin. **2** cause to sweat: *He sweated his horse by riding him too hard.* **3** cause to give off moisture; ferment: *sweat hides or tobacco in preparing them for use.* **4** come out in drops; ooze. **5** send out in drops. **6** wet or stain with sweat. **7** give out moisture; collect moisture from the air: *A pitcher of ice water sweats on a hot day.* **8** cause to work hard and under bad conditions: *That employer sweats his workers.* **9** *Informal.* work very hard. **10** suffer severely, especially as a penalty: *The prisoner sweated under the severe questioning.* **11** be annoyed or vexed; fume: *sweat over a delay.* **12** *Slang.* deprive of or cause to give up something, especially money; rob; fleece. **13** heat (solder) till it melts; join (metal parts) by heating. **14** heat (metal) in order to remove an easily fusible constituent. **15 sweat it out,** *Informal.* wait anxiously or nervously for something to happen. [OE *swǣtan*]
Syn. *n.* **1 Sweat, perspiration** = moisture coming through the pores of the skin. **Sweat** is the direct native English word, used always when speaking of animals or things and often of people, especially when the moisture is flowing freely or is mixed with grime or blood: *Sweat streamed down the horse's flanks. The rider's shirt was stained with sweat.* **Perspiration** is applicable only when speaking of human beings: *Tiny drops of perspiration formed at her temples.*

sweat·band (swet′band′) *n.* **1** a band, usually of leather, inside a man's hat to protect the felt, cloth, etc. from sweat. **2** a cloth band tied around the head to keep sweat out of the eyes.

sweat·box (swet′boks′) *n.* **1** a boxlike device used to sweat certain commodities before use or sale, as figs, hides, etc. **2** *Slang.* a very small cell in which a prisoner is confined as a special punishment.

sweat·er (swet′ər) *n.* **1** a knitted outer garment for the upper body, made of wool, nylon, orlon, etc.; pullover. **2** a knitted jacket having buttons or a zipper down the front; cardigan.

sweat gland a small gland, just under the skin, that secretes sweat.

sweat shirt a collarless long-sleeved pullover, sometimes lined with fleece, used especially by athletes.

sweat·shop (swet′shop′) *n.* a place where workers are employed at low pay for long hours under bad conditions.

sweat·y (swet′ē) *adj.* **sweat·i·er, sweat·i·est. 1** sweating; covered or wet with sweat. **2** causing sweat. **3** laborious. —**sweat′i·ly,** *adv.* —**sweat′i·ness,** *n.*

Swed. 1 Sweden. **2** Swedish.

Swede (swēd) *n.* **1** a native or inhabitant of Sweden, a country in N. Europe. **2** Also, **swede.** a rutabaga. [< MLG or MDu.]

Swe·den·bor·gi·an (swē′dən bôr′jē ən) *n.* a believer in the religious doctrines of Emanuel Swedenborg, 1688-1772, a Swedish philosopher, scientist, and mystic.
—*adj.* having to do with Swedenborg, his doctrines, or his followers.

Swede·saw (swēd′so′ or -sô′) *n. Cdn.* a handsaw having a bow-like tubular frame, the blade being kept taut by the tension of the bow. It is used for pruning trees, sawing pulpwood, etc. [apparently < *Swedish saw*; cf. *Swedish fiddle* or *violin*, originally, loggers' slang for a large crosscut saw]

Swed·ish (swēd′ish) *adj.* of or having to do with Sweden, its people, or their language. —*n.* **1** the people of Sweden. **2** the North Germanic language of Sweden.

sweep (swēp) *v.* **swept, sweep·ing,** *n.* —*v.* **1** clean or clear with a broom, brush, etc.; use a broom or something similar to remove dirt; brush: *Sweep the steps.* **2** move, drive, or take away with or as with a broom or brush: *The wind sweeps the snow into drifts.* **3** remove with a sweeping motion; carry along: *A flood swept away the bridge.* **4** trail upon: *Her dress sweeps the ground.* **5** pass over with a steady, searching movement: *Her fingers swept the strings of the harp. His eye swept the sky, searching for signs of rain.* **6** range over; scour: *Enthusiasm for the candidate swept the country.* **7** move swiftly; pass swiftly: *Pirates swept down on the town.* **8** move with

hat, āge, cãre, fär; let, ēqual, tėrm; it, īce
hot, ōpen, ôrder; oil, out; cup, pu̇t, rüle, ūse
əbove, takən, pencəl, lemən, circəs
ch, child; ng, long; sh, ship
th, thin; ᴛʜ, then; zh, measure

dignity: *The lady swept out of the room.* **9** move or extend in a long course or curve: *The shore sweeps to the south for miles.*
—*n.* **1** the act of sweeping; clearing away; removing: *He made a clean sweep of all his debts.* **2** a steady, driving motion or swift onward course of something: *The sweep of the wind kept the trees from growing tall.* **3** a smooth, flowing motion or line; dignified motion: *the sweep of verse.* **4** a curve; bend: *the sweep of a road.* **5** a swinging or curving motion: *He cut the grass with strong sweeps of his scythe.* **6** a continuous extent; stretch: *The house looked upon a wide sweep of farming country.* **7** the reach; range; extent: *The mountain is beyond the sweep of your eye.* **8** an act of surveying, reconnoitring, attacking, etc. carried out over a definite area: *The bombers cleared the coast by aerial sweeps.* **9** a person who sweeps chimneys, streets, etc. **10** any implement for sweeping, such as a broom; sweeper. **11** a long oar. **12** a long pole used to raise or lower a bucket from a well. **13** a sweepstakes contest. **14** in sports, games, etc., a complete victory or conquest. [OE *(ge)swēpa* sweepings]

sweep·er (swēp′ər) *n.* **1** a person or thing that sweeps: *a carpet sweeper.* **2** *Cdn.* a tree that has been undermined by the current of a river or stream so that some of its leaves and branches hang down into the water, though its roots remain anchored to the bank.

sweep·ing (swēp′ing) *adj.* **1** passing over a wide space: *a sweeping glance.* **2** having a wide range: *a sweeping victory, a sweeping statement.* —*n.* **sweepings,** *pl.* **a** dust, rubbish, scraps, etc. swept out or up. **b** worthless people: *the sweepings of the city.* —**sweep′ing·ly,** *adv.*

sweep·stake (swēp′stāk′) *n.* sweepstakes.

sweep·stakes (swēp′stāks′) *n.* **1** a form of lottery for gambling on horse races, etc. Each person pays a specified sum to draw a ticket bearing the name of one of the competitors in a race or contest; the money paid in goes to the holder or holders of tickets on the winner of the race or contest. **2** the race or contest. **3** a race or contest in which the prize or prizes derive from a pooling of the stakes of the contestants, with or without additional contributions by the sponsor or sponsors of the contest. **4** a prize in any such race or contest. [ME, literally a person who takes, or sweeps, all the prizes]

sweet (swēt) *adj.* **1** having a taste like sugar or honey. **2** having a pleasant taste or smell. **3** pleasing to the ear; harmonious: *a sweet song.* **4** pleasing to the eye; of charming appearance; lovely: *a sweet smile.* **5** pleasant; agreeable: *a sweet child.* **6** fresh; not sour or spoiled: *sweet milk.* **7** not salty or bitter: *sweet butter.* **8** of soil, good for farming. **9** dear; darling. **10** of wines, having a sweet taste. **11** easily managed, handled, or dealt with: *a sweet ship.* **12 a** in metallurgy, free from corrosive salt, sulphur, acid, etc. **b** in chemistry, lacking any sulphur compounds, as gasoline. **13** of jazz music, blandly melodious. **14 be sweet on,** *Informal.* be in love with.
—*n.* **1** something sweet. **2** *Esp.Brit.* a sweet dessert. **3 sweets,** *pl.* **a** candy or other sweet things. **b** pleasant or agreeable things. **4** a dear; darling.
—*adv.* in a sweet manner. [OE *swēte*] —**sweet′ly,** *adv.*

sweet alyssum a common low-growing plant having clusters of small, white or colored flowers.

sweet bay the bay or European laurel.

sweet·bread (swēt′bred′) *n.* the pancreas or thymus of a calf, lamb, etc. used as meat.

sweet·bri·ar or **sweet·bri·er** (swēt′brī′ər) *n.* a rose having a tall, prickly stem and single pink flowers; eglantine.

sweet cider unfermented cider.

sweet corn a kind of corn that is eaten fresh and is also canned, dried, frozen, etc. Fresh sweet corn is sometimes called **green corn.**

sweet·en (swēt′ən) *v.* **1** make sweet. **2** become sweet. **3** make pleasant or agreeable. —**sweet′en·er,** *n.*

sweet·en·ing (swēt′ən ing or swēt′ning) *n.* something that sweetens.

sweet fern a small shrub of North America having fragrant, fernlike leaves.

sweet flag a water plant having long, sword-shaped leaves and a pungent, aromatic rootstock. Sweet flag root is sometimes preserved with sugar and eaten as candy.

sweet gum 1 a North American tree having star-shaped leaves that turn scarlet in the fall. 2 the balsam from this tree.

sweet·heart (swēt′härt′) *n.* 1 a loved one; lover. 2 a girl or woman loved. —**Syn.** 1 suitor, beau, swain.

sweet·ing (swēt′ing) *n.* 1 a sweet apple. 2 *Archaic.* a sweetheart.

sweet·ish (swēt′ish) *adj.* rather sweet.

sweet marjoram the common marjoram, a plant used for flavoring.

sweet·meats (swēt′mēts′) *n.pl.* 1 candy; candied fruits; sugar-covered nuts. 2 preserves.

sweet·ness (swēt′nis) *n.* the quality of being sweet.

sweet nothings trivial endearments exchanged by lovers.

sweet pea 1 an annual climbing plant having delicate, fragrant flowers of various colors. 2 the flower of this plant.

sweet pepper 1 a mild-flavored species of pepper plant. 2 its fruit.

sweet potato 1 the sweetish, yellow root of a vine, used as a vegetable. 2 the vine that it grows on. 3 *Informal.* an ocarina.

sweet spirit of nitre or **niter** a medicine used as a sedative, as a means of increasing sweating, etc.

sweet talk *Informal.* pleasant, slightly flattering, remarks designed to set a person at ease, persuade, etc.

sweet-talk (swēt′tok′ or -tôk′) *v. Informal.* use pleasant, slightly flattering talk to charm, set at ease, persuade, etc. —**Syn.** mollify.

sweet-tem·pered (swēt′tem′pərd) *adj.* having a gentle or pleasant nature.

sweet tooth fondness for sweets.

sweet william or **sweet William** a plant having dense, rounded clusters of small flowers, belonging to the same family as the pink.

swell (swel) *v.* **swelled, swelled** or **swol·len, swell·ing,** *n. adj.* —*v.* 1 grow or make bigger: *Bread dough swells as it rises. The river is swollen by rain. His head is swollen where he bumped it.* 2 be larger or thicker in a particular place; stick out; cause to stick out: *A barrel swells in the middle.* 3 increase in amount, degree, force, etc.: *Savings may swell into a fortune.* 4 rise or cause to rise above the level: *Rounded hills swell gradually from the village plain.* 5 grow or make louder: *The sound swelled from a murmur to a roar. All joined in to swell the chorus.* 6 *Informal.* become or make proud or conceited.
—*n.* 1 the act of swelling; increase in amount, degree, force, etc. 2 the condition of being swollen. 3 a part that swells out. 4 a piece of higher ground; a rounded hill. 5 a long, unbroken wave or waves. 6 a swelling tone or sound. 7 in music: **a** a crescendo followed by a diminuendo. **b** the signs for this (< >). 8 a device in an organ, etc. to control the volume of sound. 9 *Informal. Esp.Brit.* a fashionable person.
—*adj.* 1 *Informal.* stylish; grand. 2 *Slang.* excellent; first-rate. [OE *swellan*] —**Syn.** *v.* 1 inflate, distend, dilate. See **expand.** 2 bulge.

swell·ing (swel′ing) *n.* an increase in size; a swollen part: *There is a swelling on his head where he bumped it.*

swel·ter (swel′tər) *v.* 1 suffer from heat. 2 perspire freely; sweat. —*n.* a sweltering condition. [frequentative of obs. *swelt,* OE *sweltan* die] —**swel′ter·ing·ly,** *adv.*

swept (swept) *v.* pt. and pp. of **sweep.**

swept-back (swept′bak′) *adj.* of the wings of an airplane, extending outward and sharply backward from the fuselage. See picture in the next column.

swerve (swėrv) *v.* **swerved, swerv·ing,** *n.* —*v.* turn aside: *The car swerved and hit a tree.* —*n.* a turning aside: *The swerve of the ball made it hard to hit.* [OE *sweorfan* rub, file] —**Syn.** *v.* deviate, diverge, stray.

An airplane with swept-back wings

swift (swift) *adj.* 1 moving very fast: *a swift automobile.* 2 coming or happening quickly: *a swift response.* 3 quick, rapid, or prompt to act, etc.: *swift to suspect.*
—*adv.* in a swift manner.
—*n.* 1 any of a family of small birds related to the hummingbirds and goatsuckers, although similar to the swallows, having a wide wingspread and noted for their speed in flight. 2 any of certain small lizards that run quickly. [OE] —**swift′ly,** *adv.* —**Syn.** *adj.* 1 fleet, speedy, rapid.

swift-foot·ed (swift′fu̇t′id) *adj.* able to run swiftly.

swift·ness (swift′nis) *n.* speed; rapid motion.

swig (swig) *n. v.* **swigged, swig·ging.** *Informal.* —*n.* a big drink. —*v.* drink heartily or greedily. [origin uncertain] —**swig′ger,** *n.*

swill (swil) *n.* 1 kitchen refuse, especially when partly liquid; garbage; slops. Swill is sometimes fed to pigs. 2 very unappetizing food. 3 a deep drink. 4 a bout of drinking. [< v.] —*v.* 1 drink greedily. 2 fill with drink. 3 wash by flooding with water. [OE *swilian*]

swim (swim) *v.* **swam** or (*Archaic*) **swum, swum, swim·ming,** *n.* —*v.* 1 move along in the water by using arms, legs, fins, etc. 2 swim across: *swim a lake.* 3 make swim: *He swam his horse across the stream.* 4 float: *swimming in gravy.* 5 be overflowed or flooded with: *Her eyes were swimming with tears.* 6 go smoothly; glide. 7 be dizzy; whirl: *The heat and noise made my head swim.*
—*n.* 1 the act, time, motion, or distance of swimming. 2 the swim bladder of a fish. 3 **the swim,** *Informal.* the popular current in fashion, business, opinion, etc.: *An active and sociable person likes to be in the swim.* [OE *swimman*]

swim bladder the air bladder of a fish.

swim·mer (swim′ər) *n.* a person or animal that swims.

swim·mer·et (swim′ər et′) *n.* in zoology, one of a number of abdominal limbs or appendages in many crustaceans, usually adapted for swimming and thus distinguished from other limbs adapted for walking or grasping. [dim. of *swimmer*]

swim·ming (swim′ing) *n.* 1 the practice or sport of swimming: *Tom is an expert at both swimming and diving.* 2 the act of swimming: *Can you reach the island by swimming?* 3 a state of dizziness or giddiness; vertigo.
—*adj.* 1 of or for swimming or swimmers: *a swimming teacher, a swimming pool.* 2 filled with tears; watery: *swimming eyes.* 3 faint; dizzy: *a swimming sensation.*

swim·ming·ly (swim′ing lē) *adv.* with great ease or success: *Everything went swimmingly at our party.*

swimming pool an artificial pool or tank for swimming.

swim suit a close-fitting garment worn for swimming.

swin·dle (swin′dəl) *v.* **-dled, -dling,** *n.* —*v.* 1 cheat; defraud: *Honest merchants do not swindle their customers.* 2 get by fraud. —*n.* an act of swindling; a cheating or defrauding. [< *swindler*]

swin·dler (swin′dlər) *n.* a person who cheats or defrauds. [< G *Schwindler* < *schwindeln* be dizzy, act thoughtlessly, cheat]

swine (swīn) *n.* **swine.** 1 pigs; hogs. 2 a pig. 3 a coarse or beastly person. [OE *swīn*]

swine·herd (swīn′hėrd′) *n.* one who tends pigs or hogs.

swing (swing) *v.* **swung** or (*Archaic and dialect*) **swang, swung, swing·ing,** *n. adj.* —*v.* 1 move back and forth, especially with a regular motion: *He swings his arms as he walks.* 2 move in a curve: *He swung the automobile around the corner.* 3 turn or cause to turn in alternate directions or in either direction, on or as on an axle or pivot: *A gate swings on its hinges.* 4 move, wield, or flourish (something held, as a weapon) with a sweeping, oscillating or rotating movement: *swing a lasso.* 5 move with a free, swaying motion: *The soldiers came swinging down the street.* 6 hang, suspend: *We swung the hammock between two trees.* 7 **a** be suspended or hang freely. **b** *Informal.* be put to death by hanging. 8 *Informal.* manage or influence

successfully: *swing a business deal.* **9** play as swing music. —*n.* **1** an act or manner of swinging. **2** the amount of swinging. **3** a seat hung from ropes in which one may sit and swing. **4** a swinging gait or movement; steady, marked rhythm: *A military march has a swing.* **5** a swinging blow. **6** freedom of action. **7** movement; activity: *get into the swing of a new job.* **8** swing music. **9** a trip around a country, region, etc.; tour: *a swing through the Maritimes.* **10** *Cdn.* in the North: **a** a train of sleighs or freight canoes, so called because they move, or swing, over a certain route in periodic trips. **b** a train of freight sleighs drawn by tractors; cat-train. **11** a cowhand who rides out to the side of a herd to keep it from spreading. **12 in full swing,** going on actively and completely; without restraint.
—*adj.* of or having to do with swing music or its style. [OE *swingan* beat] —**swing′er,** *n.*

Syn. *v.* **1 Swing, sway, rock** = move back and forth or from side to side. **Swing** applies to the movement of something attached at one side or the end or ends, and often but not always suggests a regular or rhythmical movement: *The lantern hanging overhead swung in the wind.* **Sway** suggests the unsteady swinging motion of something that bends or gives easily at any pressure: *The branches sway in the breeze.* **Rock** may suggest a gentle motion, but more often suggests the violent swaying of something shaken hard: *The house rocked in the storm.*

swin·gle (swing′gəl) *n. v.* **-gled, -gling.** —*n.* a wooden instrument shaped like a large knife, for beating flax or hemp and scraping from it the woody or coarse portions. —*v.* clean (flax or hemp) by beating and scraping. [OE *swingel* < *swingan* beat]

swin·gle·tree (swing′gəl trē′) *n.* singletree.

swing music jazz music, especially for dancing, in which the players improvise freely on the original melody.

swing shift in factories, etc., the working hours between the day and night shifts, usually from 4 p.m. to midnight.

swin·ish (swīn′ish) *adj.* like swine; hoggish; beastly; dirty; greedy. —**swin′ish·ly,** *adv.* —**swin′ish·ness,** *n.*

swink (swingk) *Archaic.* —*n.* labor; toil. [OE *swinc*] —*v.* work hard; labor; toil. [OE *swincan*]

swipe (swīp) *n. v.* **swiped, swip·ing.** —*n.* **1** *Informal.* a sweeping stroke; hard blow: *He made two swipes at the golf ball without hitting it.* **2 take a swipe at,** *Informal.* seek to hit; deliver a blow at. —*v.* **1** *Informal.* strike with a sweeping blow. **2** *Slang.* steal. [cf. OF *swipu* scourge]

swirl (swėrl) *v.* **1** move or drive along with a twisting motion; whirl: *dust swirling in the air, a stream swirling over rocks.* **2** twist; curl. —*n.* **1** a swirling movement; whirl; eddy. **2** a twist; curl: *Her hat had a swirl of lace around it.* [ME (Scottish); ? < Scand.; cf. Norwegian dial. *svirla* whirl] —**swirl′er,** *n.*

swish (swish) *v.* **1** move with a thin, light, hissing or brushing sound; make such a sound: *The whip swished through the air.* **2** cause to swish: *She swished the stick.* —*n.* a swishing movement or sound: *the swish of waves.* —*adj. Esp.Brit. Slang.* smart; posh. [? imitative]

swiss or **Swiss** (swis) *n.* a kind of muslin made in Switzerland.

Swiss (swis) *adj. n.* **Swiss.** —*adj.* **1** of or having to do with Switzerland, or its people. **2** characteristic of Switzerland or its people. —*n.* **1** a native or inhabitant of Switzerland. **2** the people of Switzerland. [< F *Suisse*]

Swiss chard (chärd) any of several varieties of beets whose leaves are often eaten as a vegetable.

Swiss cheese a firm, pale-yellow or whitish cheese having many large holes.

Swiss Guards a body of soldiers who act as bodyguard to the Pope in the Vatican.

switch (swich) *n.* **1** a device for changing the direction of something or for making or breaking connection. A railway switch directs a train from one track to another. An electric switch turns the current on or off. **2** the operation of a switch. **3** a turn; change; shift: *a switch of votes to another candidate.* **4** a slender stick used in whipping. **5** a stroke; lash: *The big dog knocked a vase off the table with a switch of his tail.* **6** anything resembling a switch in appearance or use. **7** long strands of hair, often artificial hair, bound at one end and worn by a woman in addition to her own hair. **8** an exchange. —*v.* **1** in electricity: **a** connect or disconnect by means of a switch; turn (*on* or *off*). **b** shift to another circuit. **2** move (a train, railway car, etc.) from one track to

hat, āge, cãre, fär; let, ēqual, tėrm; it, īce
hot, ōpen, ôrder; oil, out; cup, pu̇t, rüle, ūse
əbove, takən, pencəl, lemən, circəs
ch, child; ng, long; sh, ship
th, thin; ᴛʜ, then; zh, measure

another by means of a switch. **3** turn aside; change course or direction: *He was driving on the outside lane but suddenly switched.* **4** turn; shift; divert (something): *He quickly switched the subject.* **5** exchange: *The boys switched hats.* **6** whip; strike: *He switched the boys with a birch stick.* **7** move or swing like a switch: *The horse switched his tail to drive off the flies.* [probably < var. of LG *swutsche*] —**switch′er,** *n.*

switch·back (swich′bak′) *n.* **1** a railway or road climbing a steep grade in a zigzag course. **2** a roller coaster. —*v.* take a zigzag course.

switch·blade (swich′blād′) *n.* a pocket knife whose blade springs open at the press of a button or knob.

switch·board (swich′bôrd′) *n.* a panel containing the necessary switches, meters, etc. for opening, closing, combining, or controlling electric circuits. A telephone switchboard has plugs for connecting one line to another.

switch·gear (swich′gēr′) *n.* an apparatus for operating switches in electrical circuits.

switch·man (swich′mən) *n.* **-men** (-mən). a man in charge of one or more railway switches.

switch·o·ver (swich′ō′vər) *n.* the act of changing over; a turning to something new.

switch·yard (swich′yärd′) *n.* a railway yard where cars are switched from one track to another, put together to make trains, etc.

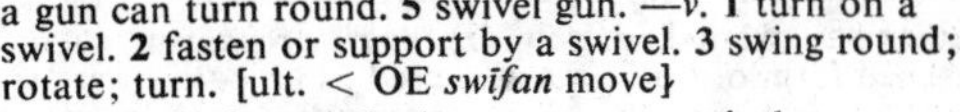

swiv·el (swiv′əl) *n. v.* **-elled** or **-eled, -el·ling** or **-el·ing.** —*n.* **1** a fastening that allows the thing fastened to turn round freely upon it. **2** a support on which a chair can revolve. **3** in a chain, a link having two parts, one of which turns freely in the other. **4** a support on which a gun can turn round. **5** swivel gun. —*v.* **1** turn on a swivel. **2** fasten or support by a swivel. **3** swing round; rotate; turn. [ult. < OE *swīfan* move]

swivel chair a chair that turns on a swivel.

swivel gun a gun mounted on a swivel so that it can be turned in any direction.

swiz·zle (swiz′əl) *n. v.* **-zled, -zling.** —*n.* any of various alcoholic mixed drinks, especially one made with rum or other liquor, ice, bitters, and sugar. —*v.* drink alcoholic liquor habitually and excessively. [apparently var. of earlier *switchel*; origin unknown]

swizzle stick a small stick of plastic, glass, etc. used to stir alcoholic drinks.

swob (swob) *n. v.* **swobbed, swob·bing.** swab. —**swob′ber,** *n.*

swol·len (swōl′ən) *adj.* swelled: *a swollen ankle.* —*v.* a pp. of **swell.**

swoln (swōln) *adj. Archaic.* swollen.

swoon (swün) *v.* **1** faint. **2** fade or die away gradually. —*n.* a faint. [ult. < OE *geswōgen* in a swoon]

swoop (swüp) *v.* **1** come down with a rush; descend in a sudden, swift attack: *One night the partisans swooped down on the village and burned it.* **2** snatch. —*n.* a rapid downward rush; sudden, swift descent or attack: *With one swoop the hawk seized the chicken and flew away.* [ult. < OE *swāpan* sweep] —**swoop′er,** *n.*

swop (swop) *v.* **swopped, swop·ping,** *n.* swap. —**swop′per,** *n.*

sword (sôrd) *n.* **1** a weapon, usually metal, with a long, sharp blade fixed in a handle or hilt. **2** something that wounds or kills; a destroying agency. **3** a symbol of power or authority. **4 at sword's points,** very unfriendly. **5 cross swords, a** fight. **b** quarrel; dispute. **6 draw the sword,** begin a war. **7 put to the sword,** kill with a sword; slaughter in war. **8 the sword, a** war. **b** military power. See picture on the next page. [OE *sweord*] —**sword′like′,** *adj.* —**Syn. 1** rapier, sabre, blade.

sword dance any dance performed with swords or over swords laid on the ground.

sword·fish (sôrd′fish′) *n.* **-fish** or **-fish·es.** a very large, edible salt-water fish having a long, swordlike projection from its upper jaw.

sword grass any of various grasses or plants having swordlike leaves.

sword knot a looped strap, ribbon, etc. attached to the hilt of a sword, serving as a means of supporting it from the wrist or as an ornament.

A cavalry officer wearing a sword

sword·man (sôrd′mən) *n.* **-men** (-mən). *Archaic.* swordsman.

Sword of Damocles an imminent danger. See **Damocles.**

sword·play (sôrd′plā′) *n.* the action, practice, or art of wielding a sword; fencing.

swords·man (sôrdz′mən) *n.* **-men** (-mən). **1** a person skilled in using a sword. **2** a person using a sword.

swords·man·ship (sôrdz′mən ship′) *n.* skill in using a sword.

sword·tail (sôrd′tāl′) *n.* any of a group of small tropical freshwater fish, the male of which has a sword-shaped tail.

swore (swôr) *v.* pt. of **swear.**

sworn (swôrn) *v.* pp. of **swear.** —*adj.* **1** having taken an oath; bound by an oath. **2** declared, promised, etc. with an oath.

swot (swot) *v.* **swot·ted, swot·ting,** *n. Slang.* —*v.* study very hard. —*n.* **1** hard work, especially hard study at schoolwork. **2** a person who studies hard and constantly. [apparently Scottish variant of *sweat*]

swound (swound) *v. n. Archaic.* swoon; faint.

'swounds (zwoundz or zoundz) *interj. Archaic.* a shortened form of *God's wounds*, used as an oath.

swum (swum) *v.* **1** pp. of **swim. 2** *Archaic.* a pt. of **swim.**

swung (swung) *v.* pt. and pp. of **swing.**

sy- the form of **syn-** before *s* plus a consonant, as in *system.*

syb·a·rite (sib′ə rīt′) *n.* a person who cares very much for luxury and pleasure. [< *Sybarite*, an inhabitant of *Sybaris*, an ancient Greek city in Italy known for its luxury]

syb·a·rit·ic (sib′ə rit′ik) *adj.* luxurious; voluptuous.

syc·a·more (sik′ə môr′) *n.* **1** in North America, the buttonwood or any other plane tree. **2** a large maple native to Europe and Asia, grown as a shady ornamental tree and for its wood. **3** a fig tree grown in Egypt, Syria, etc. as a shade tree, with leaves resembling those of the mulberry, and bearing a sweetish edible fruit. [ME < OF < L *sycomorus* < Gk. *sykomoros*]

syc·o·phan·cy (sik′ə fən sē) *n.* **-cies.** servile flattery; self-seeking flattery.

syc·o·phant (sik′ə fənt) *n.* a servile or self-seeking flatterer. [< L < Gk. *sykophantēs* informer, slanderer (originally, one who makes the insulting gesture of the "fig," i.e., sticking the thumb between index and middle finger) < *sykon* fig, vulva + *phainein* show] —**Syn.** fawner, parasite.

syc·o·phan·tic (sik′ə fan′tik) *adj.* having to do with, characteristic of, or acting as, a sycophant. —**syco′phan′ti·cal·ly,** *adv.*

sy·e·nite (sī′ə nīt′) *n.* a gray crystalline rock composed of feldspar and hornblende. [< L < Gk. *Syēnitēs* (*lithos*) (stone) from *Syēnē* (now Aswan), a city in Egypt]

syl- the form of **syn-** before *l*, as in *syllogism.*

syl. or **syll. 1** syllable. **2** syllabus.

syl·lab·ic (sə lab′ik) *adj.* **1** of or having to do with syllables; consisting of syllables. **2** in phonetics, forming a separate syllable by itself. *Example*: the second *l* in *little.* **3** pronounced syllable by syllable. **4** representing a syllable; consisting of signs representing syllables. **5** in prosody, denoting versification based on the number of syllables in a line rather than on the arrangement of stresses or quantities.
—*n.* **1** in phonetics, a syllabic speech sound. **2** a written sign or character representing a syllable.

syl·lab·i·cal·ly (sə lab′ik lē) *adv.* by syllables; with regard to syllables.

syl·lab·i·cate (sə lab′ə kāt′) *v.* **-cat·ed, -cat·ing.** form or divide into syllables.

syl·lab·i·ca·tion (sə lab′ə kā′shən) *n.* the process of dividing into syllables; division into syllables.

syl·lab·i·fi·ca·tion (sə lab′ə fə kā′shən) *n.* syllabication.

syl·lab·i·fy (sə lab′ə fī′) *v.* **-fied, -fy·ing.** divide into syllables.

syl·la·bize (sil′ə bīz′) *v.* **-bized, -biz·ing. 1** form or divide into syllables. **2** utter with careful distinction of syllables.

syl·la·ble (sil′ə bəl) *n. v.* **-bled, -bling.** —*n.* **1** a part of a word pronounced as a unit, consisting of a vowel alone or with one or more consonants. *Man·i·to·ban* has four syllables. *Do, this,* and *stretch* are words of one syllable. **2** in writing and printing, a letter or group of letters representing a syllable. **3** the slightest bit; word: *He promised not to breathe a syllable of the secret to anyone.*
—*v.* **1** pronounce in syllables; utter distinctly; utter. **2** utter syllables. [ME < OF < L < Gk. *syllabē*, originally, a taking together < *syn-* together + *labein* take]

syl·la·bub (sil′ə bub′) *n.* sillabub.

syl·la·bus (sil′ə bəs) *n.* **-bus·es, -bi** (-bī′ or -bē′). a brief statement of the main points of a speech, a book, a course of study, etc. [< NL *syllabus*, erroneous reading of L and Gk. *sittyba* parchment label] —**Syn.** abstract, synopsis.

syl·lo·gism (sil′ə jiz′əm) *n.* **1** a form of argument or reasoning consisting of two statements and a conclusion drawn from them. *Example*: All trees have roots; an oak is a tree; therefore, an oak has roots. **2** a reasoning in this form; deduction. **3** a specious or very subtle argument; a deviously crafty piece of reasoning. [< L < Gk. *syllogismos*, originally, inference, ult. < *syn-* together + *logos* a reckoning]

syl·lo·gis·tic (sil′ə jis′tik) *adj.* of or having to do with syllogism; using syllogisms. —**syl′lo·gis′ti·cal·ly,** *adv.*

syl·lo·gize (sil′ə jīz′) *v.* **-gized, -giz·ing. 1** argue or reason by syllogisms. **2** deduce by syllogism.

sylph (silf) *n.* **1** a slender, graceful girl or woman. **2** a slender, graceful spirit of the air. [< NL *sylphes*, pl.; a coinage of Paracelsus 1493?-1541, a Swiss alchemist and physician] —**sylph′like′,** *adj.*

syl·va (sil′və) *n.* silva.

syl·van (sil′vən) *adj.* of the woods; in the woods; consisting of woods; having woods: *They lived in a sylvan retreat.* Also, **silvan.** [< L *silvanus* < *silva* forest]

syl·vat·ic (sil vat′ik) *adj.* **1** of, belonging to, or found in woods; sylvan: *sylvatic animals.* **2** of or carried by insects or animals that are found in woods or forests: *sylvatic plague.*

syl·vi·cul·ture (sil′və kul′chər) *n.* silviculture.

syl·vite (sil′vīt) *n.* a mineral, potassium chloride, occurring in cubic crystals, an important source of potassium. *Formula*: Cl [< NL (*sal digestivus*) *sylvii* digestive salt of *Sylvius* (probably after François de la Boe *Sylvius*, 1614-1672, a Flemish anatomist) + E *-ite*[1]]

sym- the form of **syn-** before *b, m, p,* as in *symbol, symmetry, sympathy.*

sym. 1 symbol. **2** symmetrical. **3** symphony. **4** symptom.

sym·bi·o·sis (sim′bī ō′sis or sim′bē ō′sis) *n.* in biology, the association or living together of two unlike organisms for the benefit of each other. The lichen, which is composed of an alga and a fungus, is an example of symbiosis; the alga provides the food, and the fungus provides water and protection. [< NL < Gk. *symbiōsis*, ult. < *syn-* together + *bios* life]

sym·bi·ot·ic (sim′bī ot′ik or sim′bē ot′ik) *adj.* having to do with symbiosis; living in symbiosis.

sym·bol (sim′bəl) *n. v.* **-bolled** or **-boled, -bol·ling** or **-bol·ing.** —*n.* **1** something that stands for or represents an idea, quality, condition, or other abstraction: *The lion is* *the symbol of courage; the lamb, of meekness; the olive branch, of peace; the cross, of Christianity.* **2** a letter, figure, or sign conventionally standing for some object, process, etc.: *The marks +, −, ×, and ÷ are symbols for add, subtract, multiply, and divide.* —*v.* symbolize. [< L < Gk. *symbolon* token, ult. < *syn-* together + *ballein* throw] —**Syn.** *n.* **1** token, figure. See **emblem.**

sym·bol·ic (sim bol′ik) *adj.* **1** used as a symbol: *A lily is symbolic of purity.* **2** of a symbol; expressed by a symbol; using symbols. **3** in art and literature, having the characteristics of symbolism. —**sym·bol′i·cal·ly,** *adv.*

sym·bol·i·cal (sim bol′ə kəl) *adj.* symbolic.

sym·bol·ism (sim′bəl iz′əm) *n.* **1** the use of symbols; representation by symbols. **2** a system of symbols: *The cross, the crown, the lamb, and the lily are parts of Christian symbolism.* **3** a symbolic meaning or character. **4** in art and literature, a style or movement characterized by the use of objects, shapes, words, etc. as symbols to suggest ideas, feelings, or states of mind.

sym·bol·ist (sim′bəl ist) *n.* **1** a person who uses symbols or symbolism. **2** an artist or writer who makes much use of colors, sounds, etc. as symbols. **3** a person who has experience in the study or interpretation of symbols.

sym·bol·is·tic (sim′bəl is′tik) *adj.* of symbolism or symbolists.

sym·bol·i·za·tion (sim′bəl ə zā′shən or sim′bəl ī zā′shən) *n.* a symbolizing; representation by symbols.

sym·bol·ize (sim′bəl īz′) *v.* **-ized, -iz·ing. 1** be a symbol of; stand for; represent: *A dove symbolizes peace.* **2** represent by a symbol or symbols. **3** use symbols. —**sym′bol·iz′er,** *n.*

sym·bol·o·gy (sim bol′ə jē) *n.* **1** the science or study of symbols. **2** the use of symbols; symbolism. [< NL *symbologia* < Gk. *symbolon* + NL *-logia* -logy. See SYMBOL.]

sym·met·ric (si met′rik) *adj.* symmetrical.

sym·met·ri·cal (si met′rə kəl) *adj.* **1** having symmetry; regular in form; well-proportioned. **2** in botany: **a** of a flower, having the same number of parts in each whorl. **b** of a flower, divisible vertically into similar halves. **3** in chemistry, having a structural formula characterized by symmetry. **4** in logic and mathematics, of propositions, equations, etc., so constituted that the truth or value is not changed by interchanging the terms. **5** in medicine, of a disease, affecting corresponding organs or parts at the same time, as both arms or both lungs or both ears equally. —**sym·met′ri·cal·ly,** *adv.*

sym·me·trize (sim′ə trīz′) *v.* **-trized, -triz·ing.** reduce to symmetry; make symmetrical.

sym·me·try (sim′ə trē) *n.* **-tries. 1** a regular, balanced arrangement on opposite sides of a line or plane, or around a centre or axis: *A swollen cheek spoiled the symmetry of his face.* **2** pleasing proportions between the parts of a whole; a well-balanced arrangement of parts; harmony. **3** in botany, agreement in number of parts among the cycles of organs that compose a flower. [< L < Gk. *symmetria* < *syn-* together + *metron* measure]

BILATERAL SYMMETRY

RADIAL SYMMETRY

sym·pa·thet·ic (sim′pə thet′ik) *adj.* **1** having or showing kind feelings toward others; sympathizing. **2** *Informal.* approving; agreeing. **3** enjoying the same things and getting along well together. —**Syn. 1** compassionate, commiserating, tender. **3** harmonious.

sym·pa·thet·i·cal·ly (sim′pə thet′ik lē) *adv.* in a sympathetic manner; with sympathy.

sym·pa·thize (sim′pə thīz′) *v.* **-thized, -thiz·ing. 1** feel or show sympathy: *sympathize with a child who has hurt himself.* **2** share in or agree with a feeling or opinion: *My mother sympathizes with my plan to be a doctor.* **3** enjoy the same things and get along well together. **4** respond sympathetically to some influence or to some disorder of the body. [< F *sympathiser* < *sympathie* sympathy] —**sym′pa·thiz′ing·ly,** *adv.*

sym·pa·thiz·er (sim′pə thīz′ər) *n.* a person who sympathizes; a person who is favorably inclined toward a particular belief or person.

sym·pa·thy (sim′pə thē) *n.* **-thies. 1** a sharing of another's sorrow or trouble: *We feel sympathy for a person who is ill.* **2** an agreement in feeling; the condition or fact of having the same feeling: *The sympathy between the twins was so great that they always smiled or cried at the same things.* **3** agreement; approval; favor: *He is in sympathy with my plan.* **4 a** an affinity between certain things, whereby they are similarly or correspondingly affected by the same influence. **b** an action or response induced by such a relationship. [< L < Gk. *sympatheia* < *syn-* together + *pathos* feeling] —**Syn. 1** compassion, commiseration. See **pity. 2** harmony, affinity.

sym·pet·al·ous (sim pet′əl əs) *adj.* gamopetalous.

sym·phon·ic (sim fon′ik) *adj.* **1** in music, of, having to do with, or having the character of a symphony. **2** of or having to do with symphony or harmony of sounds; similar in sound.

symphonic poem in music, a free-form composition for symphony orchestra, usually consisting of only one movement and usually descriptive or rhapsodic in character.

sym·pho·ni·ous (sim fō′nē əs) *adj.* harmonious.

sym·pho·ny (sim′fə nē) *n.* **-nies. 1** in music, an elaborate orchestral composition, usually having four movements in different rhythms but related keys. **2** a symphony orchestra. **3** *Informal.* a concert given by a symphony orchestra. **4** a harmony of sounds. **5** a harmony of colors: *In autumn the woods are a symphony in red, brown, and yellow.* [ME < OF < L < Gk. *symphōnia* harmony, concert, band < *syn-* together + *phōnē* voice, sound]

symphony orchestra a large orchestra having string, wind, and percussion sections, for playing symphonic and similar works.

sym·phy·sis (sim′fə sis) *n.* **-ses** (-sēz′). **1** in anatomy, **a** a union of two bones or other parts originally separate, especially of two similar bones on opposite sides of the body, such as the pubic bones or the two halves of the lower jawbone. **b** the line of junction thus formed. **2** in botany, a fusion of parts of a plant that are normally separate. [< Gk. *symphysis* growing together < *symphyein* to unite < *syn* together + *phyein* grow]

sym·po·si·um (sim pō′zē əm) *n.* **-si·ums** or **-si·a** (-zē ə). **1** a collection of the opinions of several persons on some subject: *This magazine contains a symposium on sports.* **2** a meeting for the discussion of some subject. **3** in ancient Greece, an after-dinner drinking party. [< L < Gk. *symposion* < *syn-* together + *posis* drinking]

symp·tom (simp′təm) *n.* **1** a sign; indication: *Quaking knees and paleness are symptoms of fear.* **2** a noticeable change in the normal functioning of the body that indicates or accompanies disease, sickness, etc.: *The doctor made his diagnosis after studying the patient's symptoms.* [< LL < Gk. *symptōma* a happening, ult. < *syn-* together + *piptein* fall]

symp·to·mat·ic (simp′tə mat′ik) *adj.* **1** being a sign; signifying; indicative: *Riots are symptomatic of political or social unrest.* **2** indicating or accompanying a disease, etc.: *The infection caused a symptomatic fever.* **3** having to do with symptoms of disease, etc. —**symp′to·mat′i·cal·ly,** *adv.*

syn- *prefix.* with; together; jointly; at the same time, as in *synchronous, synopsis,* and *synthesis.* Also: **sy-,** before *s* plus a consonant; **syl-,** before *l;* **sym-,** before *b, m, p.* [< Gk. *syn* with, together]

syn. 1 synonym. **2** synonymous.

syn·a·gogue (sin′ə gog′) *n.* **1** a Jewish assembly for religious instruction and worship. **2** a building for Jewish worship and religious instruction. **3** Jews as a whole; the Jewish religion. [ME < LL < Gk. *synagōgē*, literally, assembly, ult. < *syn-* together + *agein* bring]

syn·apse (si naps′ or sin′aps) *n.* in physiology, a place where a nerve impulse passes from one nerve cell to another. [< Gk. *synapsis* conjunction < *syn-* together + *haptein* fasten]

sync (singk) *n. Slang.* **1** synchronization of sound and action or of speech and lip movement, as in a television or motion picture. **2 in sync,** synchronized. **3 out of sync,** not synchronized.

syn·chro·mesh (sing′krə mesh′) *n.* in an automobile, a gear or system of gears so constructed as to mesh with a minimum of friction and noise when the driver shifts from one speed to another. [< *synchro*nous + *mesh*]

syn·chro·nal (sing′krə nəl) *adj.* synchronous.

syn·chron·ic (sin kron′ik or sing kron′ik) *adj.* **1** synchronous. **2** treating a subject from a descriptive rather than a historical viewpoint; opposed to *diachronic*: *a book on synchronic grammar.*

syn·chro·nism (sing′krə niz′əm) *n.* **1** an occurrence at the same time; an agreement in time. **2** an arrangement of historical events or persons according to their dates.

syn·chro·nize (sing′krə nīz′) *v.* **-nized, -niz·ing. 1** occur at the same time; agree in time. **2** move or take place at the same rate and exactly together. **3** make agree in time: *synchronize all the clocks in a building.* **4** assign to the time or period. **5** in the editing of a motion picture, make sound and action coincide. [< Gk. *synchronizein* < *synchronos* synchronous. See SYNCHRONOUS.] **—syn′chro·ni·za′tion,** *n.* **—syn′chro·niz′er,** *n.*

syn·chro·nous (sing′krə nəs) *adj.* **1** occurring at the same time; simultaneous. **2** moving or taking place at the same rate and exactly together. **3** in physics, having coincident periods, or coincident periods and phases, as an alternating electric current. [< LL < Gk. *synchronos* < *syn-* together + *chronos* time] **—syn′chro·nous·ly,** *adv.*

syn·chro·tron (sing′krə tron′) *n.* in physics, a device that accelerates electrified particles by means of a varying magnetic field and an alternating high-frequency electric field. [< *synchro*nous + *-tron* as in electron]

syn·cli·nal (sin klī′nəl or sing′klə nəl) *adj.* in geology: **1** sloping downward from opposite directions so as to form a trough or inverted arch. **2** of or having to do with a syncline. See **stratum** for picture. [< Gk. *synklinein* lean, incline < *syn-* together + *klinein* bend]

syn·cline (sing′klīn) *n.* a synclinal fold of rock.

syn·co·pate (sing′kə pāt′) *v.* **-pat·ed, -pat·ing. 1** in linguistics, shorten (a word) by omitting sounds from the middle. *Example*: (fam′lē) as against (fam′ə lē). **2** in music: **a** begin (a tone) on an unaccented beat and hold it into an accented one. **b** shift (accents) to regularly unaccented beats. **c** introduce syncopation into (a passage, etc.). [< LL *syncopare* < *syncope.* See SYNCOPE.]

syn·co·pa·tion (sing′kə pā′shən) *n.* **1** in music: **a** a syncopating or the state of being syncopated. **b** music marked by syncopation, as jazz or ragtime. **c** a rhythm, dance step, etc. based upon syncopation. **2** in linguistics, syncope.

syn·co·pe (sing′kə pē′) *n.* **1** in linguistics, the contraction of a word by the omission of a sound or sounds from the middle, as in *ne'er* for *never.* **2** in medicine, a fainting caused by cerebral anemia. [< LL < Gk. *synkopē*, originally, a cutting off, ult. < *syn-* together + *koptein* cut]

syn·cret·ic (sin kret′ik) *adj.* of or having to do with syncretism; characterized by syncretism.

syn·cre·tism (sing′krə tiz′əm) *n.* **1** a tendency or effort to reconcile different religious or philosophical beliefs, or to absorb some of the tenets of one into the system of another. **2** in linguistics, the fusion of originally different inflectional categories. **3** the doctrines of George Calixtus (1586-1656), a Lutheran who aimed at uniting Protestant sects and, eventually, all Christendom. [< NL < Gk. *synkrētismos* (< *synkrētizein* combine, ally, apparently originally as in a union or federation of Cretan communities < *Krēs, Krētos* Crete)]

syn·cre·tis·tic (sing′krə tis′tik) *adj.* of, having to do with, or characterized by syncretism.

syn·cre·tize (sing′krə tīz′) *v.* **-tized, -tiz·ing.** combine or attempt to combine different systems, philosophical or religious beliefs, etc. [< NL *syncretizare* < Gk. *synkrētizein.* See SYNCRETISM.]

syn·dic (sin′dik) *n.* **1** a person who manages the business affairs of a university or other corporation. **2** a government official or chief magistrate. [< LL < Gk. *syndikos* advocate < *syn-* together + *dikē* justice]

syn·di·cal·ism (sin′də kəl iz′əm) *n.* a movement to put industry and government under the control of labor unions by means of a general strike, violence, etc.

syn·di·cal·ist (sin′də kəl ist) *n.* a person who favors and supports syndicalism.

syn·di·cate (*n.* sin′də kit; *v.* sin′də kāt′) *n. v.* **-cat·ed, -cat·ing.** *—n.* **1** a combination of persons or companies to carry out some undertaking, especially one requiring a large capital investment. **2** an agency that sells special articles, photographs, etc. to a large number of newspapers or magazines for publication at the same time. **3** a combination of criminals to control organized crime. *—v.* **1** combine into a syndicate. **2** manage by a syndicate. **3** publish through a syndicate. [< F *syndicat* < *syndic* < LL *syndicus.* See SYNDIC.]

syn·di·ca·tion (sin′də kā′shən) *n.* the act of syndicating or the condition of being syndicated.

syn·drome (sin′drōm) *n.* **1** in medicine, a number of symptoms that taken together indicate the presence of a specific condition or disease. **2** any set of ideas, attitudes, or customs that together indicate a state of mind, pattern of behavior, etc.: *the beatnik syndrome.* [< NL < Gk. *syndromē*, literally, a running together < *syn-* with + *dromos* course, related to *dramein* run]

syne (sīn) *adv. prep. conj. Scottish.* since.

syn·ec·do·che (si nek′də kē′) *n.* a figure of speech by which a part is put for the whole, or the whole for a part, the special for the general, or the general for the special. *Examples*: a factory employing 500 *hands* (persons); to eat of the *tree* (its fruit); a *Solomon* (wise man); a *marble* (a statue) on its pedestal. [< LL < Gk. *synekdochē*, ult. < *syn-* with + *ek-* out + *dechesthai* receive]

syn·er·gism (sin′ər jiz′əm) *n.* the combined action of different agents, as in medicines composed of two or more drugs, producing an effect greater than the sum of the effects of the agents acting individually. [< NL *synergismus* < Gk. *synergéin* work together. See SYNERGY.]

syn·er·gy (sin′ər jē) *n.* **-ies.** combined or correlated action or force, especially of the muscles or nerve centres of the body. [< NL < Gk. *synergia* joint work < *synergéin* work together < *syn-* together + *ergon* work]

syn·od (sin′əd) *n.* **1** an assembly called together under authority to discuss and decide church affairs; a church council. **2** a court of the Presbyterian Church ranking next above the presbytery. **3** an assembly; convention; council. [< LL < Gk. *synodos* assembly, meeting < *syn-* together + *hodos* a going]

syn·od·al (sin′əd əl) *adj.* having to do with a synod.

syn·od·ic (si nod′ik) *adj.* synodical.

syn·od·i·cal (si nod′ə kəl) *adj.* **1** having to do with the conjunctions of the heavenly bodies. The synodical period of the moon is the time between one new moon and the next. **2** synodal.

syn·o·nym (sin′ə nim′) *n.* **1** a word having a meaning that is the same or nearly the same as that of another word; opposed to *antonym. Keen* is a synonym of *sharp.* **2** a word or expression generally accepted as another name for something: *Churchill's name has become a synonym for patriotic devotion to one's country.* [ME < LL < Gk. *synōnymon*, originally adj., neut. of *synōnymos* synonymous. See SYNONYMOUS.]

syn·on·y·mous (si non′ə məs) *adj.* having the same or nearly the same meaning. [< Med.L < Gk. *synōnymos* < *syn-* together + dial. *onyma* name] **—syn·on′y·mous·ly,** *adv.*

syn·on·y·my (si non′ə mē) *n.* **-mies. 1** the quality of being synonymous; equivalence in meaning. **2** the study of synonyms. **3** the use or coupling of synonyms in discourse for emphasis or amplification. **4** a set, list, or system of synonyms.

syn·op·sis (si nop′sis) *n.* **-ses** (-sēz). a brief statement giving a general view of some subject, book, play, etc.;

summary. [< LL < Gk. *synopsis* < *syn-* together + *opsis* a view] —**Syn.** digest.

syn·op·tic (si nop′tik) *adj.* **1** giving a general view. **2** Often, **Synoptic.** taking a common view. *Matthew, Mark,* and *Luke* are called the **Synoptic Gospels** because they are much alike in content, order, and statement.

syn·op·ti·cal (si nop′tə kəl) *adj.* synoptic.

syn·op·ti·cal·ly (si nop′tik lē) *adv.* in a synoptic manner; so as to give a general view.

syn·o·vi·a (si nō′vē ə) *n.* in physiology, a lubricating liquid secreted by certain membranes, such as those of the joints. [< NL *synovia*; coinage of Paracelsus, 1493?-1541, a Swiss alchemist and physician]

syn·o·vi·al (si nō′vē əl) *adj.* consisting of, containing, or secreting synovia: *synovial fluid, a synovial membrane.*

syn·o·vi·tis (sin′ə vī′tis) *n.* inflammation of a synovial membrane.

syn·tac·tic (sin tak′tik) *adj.* syntactical.

syn·tac·ti·cal (sin tak′tə kəl) *adj.* of or having to do with syntax; in accordance with the rules of syntax. —**syn·tac′ti·cal·ly,** *adv.*

syn·tax (sin′taks) *n.* in grammar: **1** the arrangement of words to form sentences, clauses, or phrases; sentence structure. **2** the patterns of such arrangement in a given language. **3** the use or function of a word, phrase, or clause in a sentence. **4** the part of grammar dealing with the construction of phrases, clauses, and sentences. [< LL < Gk. *syntaxis,* ult. < *syn-* together + *tassein* arrange]

syn·the·ses (sin′thə sēz′) *n.* pl. of **synthesis.**

syn·the·sis (sin′thə sis) *n.* **-ses. 1** a combination of parts or elements into a whole. *Synthesis* is the opposite of *analysis.* **2** in chemistry, the formation of a compound or a complex substance by the chemical union of its elements, combination of simpler compounds, etc. Alcohol, ammonia, and rubber can be artificially produced by synthesis. **3** in philosophy and logic: **a** the combination or unification of particular phenomena, observed or hypothesized, into a general body or abstract whole. **b** as used by Immanuel Kant, the action of the understanding in combining and unifying the isolated data of sensation into a cognizable whole. **c** deductive reasoning. [< L < Gk. *synthesis* < *syn-* together + *tithenai* put]

syn·the·size (sin′thə sīz′) *v.* **-sized, -siz·ing. 1** combine into a complex whole. **2** make up by combining parts or elements. **3** treat synthetically. —**syn′the·si·za′tion,** *n.*

syn·the·siz·er (sin′thə sīz′ər) *n.* **1** a person or thing that synthesizes. **2** an electronic device that simulates and blends conventional and ultrasonic sounds.

syn·thet·ic (sin thet′ik) *adj.* **1** having to do with synthesis: *synthetic chemistry.* **2** made by chemical synthesis: *synthetic rubies.* **3** in linguistics, characterized by the use of affixes and inflectional endings rather than by the use of separate words, such as auxiliary verbs and prepositions, to express the same concepts. Latin is a synthetic language, while English is analytic. For example, the Latin *amabitur* expresses in one word the English *he will be loved.* **4** not real or genuine; artificial: *synthetic affection.* —**Syn. 2** See **artificial.**

syn·thet·i·cal (sin thet′ə kəl) *adj.* synthetic. —**syn·thet′i·cal·ly,** *adv.*

syn·thet·ics (sin thet′iks) *n.* **1** materials, such as plastics, produced by chemical synthesis. **2** the branch of science or industry concerned with the production of synthetic articles.

syph·i·lis (sif′ə lis) *n.* a contagious venereal disease that proceeds in three stages until it affects the bones, muscles, and brain. It may be transmitted by direct contact or by heredity; it is caused by a spirochete. [< NL *syphilis* < *Syphilus,* the hero of a Latin poem describing the disease, written in 1530 by Fracastoro, a physician and poet of Verona, Italy]

syph·i·lit·ic (sif′ə lit′ik) *adj.* **1** having to do with syphilis. **2** affected with syphilis. —*n.* a person affected with syphilis.

sy·phon (sī′fən) *n. v.* siphon.

Syr·i·ac (sir′ē ak) *n.* the ancient language of Syria, an ancient country north of Palestine and Arabia.

hat, āge, cãre, fär; let, ēqual, tėrm; it, īce
hot, ōpen, ôrder; oil, out; cup, pu̇t, rüle, ūse
əbove, takən, pencəl, lemən, circəs
ch, child; ng, long; sh, ship
th, thin; ᴛʜ, then; zh, measure

Syr·i·an (sir′ē ən) *adj.* of or having to do with Syria, a country in S.W. Asia, or its people. —*n.* a native or inhabitant of Syria.

sy·rin·ga (sə ring′gə) *n.* a shrub having fragrant, white flowers blooming in early summer; mock orange. [< NL *syringa* < Gk. *syrinx, -ingos* shepherd's pipe]

sy·ringe (sə rinj′) *n. v.* **-ringed, -ring·ing.** —*n.* a device fitted with a piston or rubber bulb for drawing in a quantity of fluid and then forcing it out in a stream. Syringes are used for cleaning wounds, injecting fluids into the body, etc. —*v.* clean, wash, inject, etc. by means of a syringe. [< Gk. *syrinx, -ingos* pipe]

A syringe

syr·inx (sir′ingks) *n.* **sy·rin·ges** (sə rin′jēz) or **syr·inx·es. 1** a Panpipe. **2** in anatomy, the Eustachian tube. **3** the vocal organ of birds, situated where the trachea divides into the right and left bronchi. [< L < Gk. *syrinx* shepherd's pipe]

syr·up or **sir·up** (sėr′əp or sir′əp) *n.* **1** sugar boiled in water or fruit juice: *cherries canned in syrup.* **2** a solution of sugar in a medicated liquid: *cough syrup.* **3** a sweet, thick liquid obtained in the manufacture of sugar, glucose, cornstarch, sorghum, etc., as molasses and corn syrup. [ME < OF *sirop* < Arabic *sharāb* drink] —**syr′up·like′** or **sir′up·like′,** *adj.*

syr·up·y or **sir·up·y** (sėr′əp ē or sir′əp ē) *adj.* **1** resembling or suggesting syrup in consistency or sweetness. **2** having to do with syrup.

sys·tem (sis′təm) *n.* **1** a set of things or parts forming a whole: *a mountain system, a railway system, the digestive system.* **2** an ordered group of facts, principles, beliefs, etc.: *a system of government, a system of education.* **3** a theory or hypothesis, especially of the relationship of the heavenly bodies by which their observed movements and phenomena are explained: *the Copernican system.* **4** a plan; scheme; method: *a system for betting.* **5** an orderly way of getting things done. **6** in biology: **a** a set of organs or parts in an animal body of the same or similar structure, or subserving the same function: *the nervous system, the respiratory system.* **b** the animal body as an organized whole; the organism in relation to its vital processes or functions: *take food into the system.* **7** a group of heavenly bodies forming a whole that follows certain natural laws. **8** the world; universe. **9** in geology, a major division of rocks including two or more series, and formed during a geological period. **10** in chemistry: **a** an assemblage of substances which are in, or tend to approach, equilibrium. **b** a substance, or an assemblage of substances, considered as a separate entity for the purpose of restricted study. [< LL < Gk. *systēma* < *syn-* together + *stēsai* cause to stand] —**sys′tem·less,** *adj.* —**Syn. 4** arrangement. **5** organization.

sys·tem·at·ic (sis′tə mat′ik) *adj.* **1** according to a system; having a system, method, or plan. **2** orderly in arranging things or in getting things done.

sys·tem·at·i·cal (sis′təm at′ə kəl) *adj.* systematic.

sys·tem·at·i·cal·ly (sis′tə mat′ik lē) *adv.* with system; according to some plan or method.

sys·tem·a·tize (sis′təm ə tīz′) *v.* **-tized, -tiz·ing.** arrange according to a system; make into a system; make more systematic. —**sys′tem·a·ti·za′tion,** *n.* —**sys′tem·a·tiz′er,** *n.*

sys·tem·ic (sis tem′ik) *adj.* **1** of or having to do with a system. **2** having to do with a particular system of parts or organs of the body. **3** having to do with or affecting the body as a whole.

sys·tem·ize (sis′təm īz′) *v.* **-ized, -iz·ing.** systematize. —**sys′tem·i·za′tion,** *n.*

sys·to·le (sis′tə lē′) *n.* in physiology, the normal rhythmical contraction of the heart. [< NL < Gk. *systolē* contraction < *syn-* together + *stellein* wrap]

sys·tol·ic (sis tol′ik) *adj.* of or having to do with a contraction of the heart.

T or **t** (tē) *n.* **T's** or **t's. 1** the twentieth letter of the English alphabet. **2** any speech sound represented by this letter. **3** one (usually twentieth) of a series designated alphabetically. **4** anything shaped like T. **5 cross one's** (or **the**) **t's,** be minutely exact. **6 to a T,** exactly: *That suits me to a T.*

t. 1 teaspoon. **2** temperature. **3** tense. **4** transitive. **5** ton; tons. **6** territory. **7** time. **8** tenor. **9** in the time of (for L *tempore*). **10** town. **11** township. **12** telephone. **13** terminal. **14** troy weight.

T 1 Temperature. (absolute scale) **2** (surface) tension. **3** tantalum.

T. 1 territory. **2** Tuesday. **3** Testament. **4** tablespoon; tablespoons.

Ta tantalum.

tab (tab) *n. v.* **tabbed, tab·bing.** *—n.* **1** a small flap, strap, loop, or piece: *He wore a fur cap with tabs over the ears.* **2** in filing, a small extension of or attachment to a card, usually used for labelling, numbering, color-coding, etc. **3** a label. **4 keep tab, tabs,** or **a tab on** (or **upon**), *Informal.* keep track of; keep watch on; check: *The foreman kept tab on the workmen.* **5** *Informal.* a bill or check; a statement of costs: *pick up the tab.* *—v.* **1** put a tab on (something). **2** name; mark; identify. [origin uncertain]

tab·ard (tab′ərd) *n.* **1** a short, loose cape or coat worn by a herald and emblazoned with the arms of his lord or sovereign. **2** in the Middle Ages: **a** a cape or tunic worn over armor by a knight and emblazoned with his arms. **b** a coarse sleeveless or short-sleeved outer garment worn by the poor. **3** a banner hanging from a trumpet or a bugle. [ME < OF *tabart*]

Ta·bas·co (tə bas′kō) *n. Trademark.* a kind of peppery sauce, used on fish, meat, etc. and prepared from the fruit of a variety of capsicum. [< *Tabasco,* a state in Mexico]

tab·by (tab′ē) *n.* **-bies,** *adj. —n.* **1** a brown or gray cat having dark stripes. **2** a female cat. **3** a spiteful female gossip. **4** an old maid. **5** a silk cloth with a wavy pattern or marking; taffeta. *—adj.* brown or gray with dark stripes. [< F < Arabic *'attābiy* (def. 5), from a section of Baghdad where such cloth was first made]

tab·er·nac·le (tab′ər nak′əl) *n.* **1** a Jewish temple; synagogue. **2** a meeting house used as a place of worship for a large audience. **3** the human body thought of as a temporary dwelling of the soul. **4** a temporary dwelling; tent. **5** in a church, a small chest or cupboard, often built into the altar, for preserving consecrated bread. **6** a tomb, shrine, etc. with a canopy. **7 Tabernacle,** the covered wooden framework used by the Israelites as a place of worship during their journey from Egypt to Palestine. Exod. 25-27. [< L *tabernaculum* tent < *taberna* cabin]

ta·ble (tā′bəl) *n. v.* **-bled, -bling.** *—n.* **1** a piece of furniture having a smooth, flat top on legs. **2** the food put on a table to be eaten: *Mrs. Brown sets a good table.* **3** the persons seated at a table. **4** a flat surface; plateau. **5** in architecture, a flat, vertical, usually rectangular surface forming a distinct feature in a wall. **6** a horizontal moulding, especially a cornice. **7** the flat surface of a jewel. **8** very condensed tabulated information; a list: *The table of contents is in the front of the book.* **9** a thin, flat piece of wood, stone, metal, etc.; a tablet: *The Ten Commandments were written on tables of stone.* **10** matter inscribed or written on tables. **11 on the table,** of a bill, motion, etc.: **a** before a committee, legislative body, etc. for discussion. **b** *Esp. U.S.* put off or shelved. **12 set** or **lay the table,** arrange cutlery, dishes, etc. on the table for a meal. **13 the tables,** certain laws cut or carved on thin, flat pieces of stone. **14 turn the tables,** reverse conditions or circumstances completely.
—v. **1** put on a table. **2** make a list or condensed statement. **3 a** present (a motion, report, etc.) for consideration. **b** *U.S.* put off discussion of (a bill, motion, etc.); shelve. [ME < OF < L *tabula* plank, tablet]
—Syn. *n.* **8** schedule, synopsis.

tab·leau (tab′lō) *n.* **-leaux** or **-leaus. 1** a striking scene; picture. **2** a representation of a picture, statue, scene, etc. by a person or group posing in appropriate costume. [< F *tableau* picture, dim. of *table* table]

tab·leaux (tabl′lōz) *n.* pl. of **tableau.**

ta·ble·cloth (tā′bəl kloth′) *n.* a cloth for covering a table.

ta·ble d'hôte (tä′bəl dōt′ or tab′əl dōt′) in hotels, restaurants, etc., a meal served at a fixed time and price. In meals table d'hôte, there is one price for the whole meal; but in meals à la carte, a person chooses what he wants and pays for each item. [< F *table d'hôte,* literally, host's table]

ta·ble·land (tā′bəl land′) *n.* a high plain; plateau.

ta·ble·spoon (tā′bəl spün′) *n.* a spoon larger than a teaspoon or dessert spoon, used to serve vegetables, etc.; a standard unit of measurement in cookery: *one tablespoon holds the same amount as three teaspoons. Abbrev.:* T., tbs., or tbsp.

ta·ble·spoon·ful (tā′bəl spün fu̇l′) *n.* **-fuls.** the amount that a tablespoon can hold. 1 tablespoonful = ½ fluid ounce.

tab·let (tab′lit) *n.* **1** in ancient times, a small, flat sheet of stone, wood, ivory, etc. used to write or draw on. **2** a number of sheets of writing paper fastened together at one edge; a pad of paper. **3** a small, flat surface with an inscription. **4** a small, flat piece of medicine, candy, etc.: *vitamin tablets.* [< F *tablette* < *table* table]

table talk *Informal.* conversation at or as at meals.

table tennis an indoor game resembling tennis, played on a table with small wooden rackets and a very light, hollow, celluloid ball.

ta·ble·ware (tā′bəl wãr′) *n.* the dishes, knives, forks, spoons, etc. used at meals.

table wine a wine considered suitable for serving with meals.

tab·loid (tab′loid) *n.* **1** a newspaper, usually having a page that is half the ordinary size and that presents the news through pictures and short articles. **2** a tablet of medicine. *—adj.* condensed. [< *tablet*]

ta·boo (tə bü′) *adj. v.* **-booed, -boo·ing,** *n.* **-boos.**
—adj. **1** forbidden, especially by social custom or convention. **2** set apart as sacred, unclean, or cursed, and forbidden to general use. Among the Polynesians certain things, places, and persons are taboo.
—v. forbid; prohibit; ban.
—n. **1** a prohibition; ban. **2 a** the system or act of setting things apart as sacred, unclean, or cursed. **b** the fact or condition of being so placed. **c** the prohibition or interdict itself. [< Tongan (lang. of the Tonga Islands in the S. Pacific) *tabu*]
☛ **taboo, tabu.** *Taboo* is more generally used than *tabu,* except in anthropology.

ta·bor (tā′bər) *n.* a small drum, used especially to accompany a pipe or fife. [ME < OF *tabur,* of Oriental origin; cf. Persian *tabīrah* drum]

A tabor

tab·o·ret or **tab·ou·ret** (tab′ə ret′ or tab′ə ret′) *n.* **1** a small, low stand or table. **2** a stool. **3** a frame for embroidery. **4** *Archaic.* a small tabor. [< F *tabouret*]

ta·bu (tə bü′) *adj. v.* **-bued, -bu·ing,** *n.* **-bus.** taboo. ☛ See **taboo** for usage note.

tab·u·lar (tab′yu̇ lər) *adj.* **1** of or having to do with tables or lists; arranged in lists; written or printed in columns. **2** flat like a table: *a tabular rock.* [< L *tabularis* relating to a board or plate < *tabula* plank, tablet]

tab·u·late (*v.* tab′yu̇ lāt′; *adj.* tab′yu̇ lit or tab′yu̇ lāt′) *v.* **-lat·ed, -lat·ing,** *adj.* *—v.* arrange (facts, figures, etc.) in tables or lists. *—adj.* shaped like a table or a tablet.

tab·u·la·tion (tab′yu̇ lā′shən) *n.* an arrangement in tables or lists.

tab·u·la·tor (tab′yu̇ lā′tər) *n.* **1** a person or machine that tabulates. **2** a device on a typewriter for making even paragraph and column indentions.

tac·a·ma·hac (tak′ə mə hak′) *n.* **1** a gum resin used in incenses, ointments, etc. **2** any tree yielding such a gum; especially, the balsam poplar. [< Sp. *tacamahaca* < Nahuatl]

tach·isme or **tach·ism** (tash′iz əm; *French,* tä shēsm′)

n. a style of abstract painting based on the dribbling or splashing of paint on canvas to see what form it will take. [< F *tachisme* < *tache* blot + *-isme* -ism]

tach·iste or **tach·ist** (tash′ist; *French,* tä shēst′) *adj.* using the technique of tachism. —*n.* a painter using this technique.

ta·chom·e·ter (tə kom′ə tər) *n.* any of various instruments for measuring or indicating the speed of a machine, a river, the blood, etc. [< Gk. *tachos* speed + E *-meter*]

tac·it (tas′it) *adj.* **1** unspoken; silent: *a tacit prayer.* **2** implied or understood without being openly expressed: *His eating the food was a tacit confession that he liked it.* **3** in law, existing out of custom or from silent consent but not expressly stated. [< L *tacitus,* pp. of *tacere* be silent] —**tac′it·ness,** *n.*

tac·it·ly (tas′it lē) *adv.* **1** without sound. **2** without words; by implication from action or circumstances.

tac·i·turn (tas′ə tėrn′) *adj.* speaking very little; not fond of talking. [< L *taciturnus* < *tacitus* tacit. See TACIT.] —**tac′i·turn·ly,** *adv.* —**Syn.** reserved. See **silent.**

tac·i·tur·ni·ty (tas′ə tėr′nə tē) *n.* the habit of keeping silent; disinclination to talk much.

tack (tak) *n.* **1** a short, sharp-pointed nail or pin having a broad, flat head: *carpet tacks, thumbtacks.* **2** in sewing, a stitch used as a temporary fastening. **3** in nautical use: **a** a zigzag course against the wind. **b** the direction in which a ship moves in regard to the position of her sails. When on port tack, a ship has the wind on her left. **c** a zigzag movement; one of the movements in a zigzag course. **d** a rope to hold in place a corner of some sails. **e** the corner to which this is fastened. **4** a course of action or conduct: *He took the wrong tack to get what he wanted.*
—*v.* **1** fasten with tacks. **2** sew with temporary stitches. **3** attach; add: *He tacked the postscript to the end of the letter.* **4** in nautical use: **a** sail in a zigzag course against the wind. **b** change from one tack to another. **5** move along any zigzag route. **6** change one's attitude, conduct, or course of action. **7** use indirect methods. [< dial. OF *taque* nail < Gmc.] —**tack′er,** *n.*

tack·le (tak′əl) *n. v.* **-led, -ling.** —*n.* **1** equipment; apparatus; gear. Fishing tackle means the rod, line, hooks, etc. **2** ropes and pulleys for lifting, lowering, or moving. The sails of a ship are raised and moved by tackle. **3** the act of tackling. **4** in football, a player between the guard and the end on either side of the line.
—*v.* **1** try to deal with: *Everyone has his own problems to tackle.* **2** lay hold of; seize: *John tackled the runner and pulled him to the ground.* **3** in football, seize and stop (an opponent having the ball) by bringing to the ground. **4** in soccer, obstruct (an opponent) in order to get the ball away from him. **5** harness. [ME < MDu. or MLG *takel*] —**tack′ler,** *n.*

Tackles for lifting

tack·y[1] (tak′ē) *adj.* sticky. [< *tack*]

tack·y[2] (tak′ē) *adj.* **tack·i·er, tack·i·est.** *Informal.* shabby; dowdy. [origin uncertain; cf. dial. G *tacklig* untidy]

tac·o·nite (tak′ə nīt′) *n.* a kind of rock consisting of about 30 per cent iron ore. [< *Taconic* Mts. (Mass. and Vt.)]

tact (takt) *n.* **1** the ability to say and do the right things; skill in dealing with people or handling difficult situations. **2** the action, process, or practice of not giving offence. [< L *tactus* sense of feeling < *tangere* touch]

tact·ful (takt′fəl) *adj.* **1** having tact. **2** showing tact. —**tact′ful·ly,** *adv.* —**tact′ful·ness,** *n.*

tac·ti·cal (tak′tə kəl) *adj.* **1** of tactics; concerning tactics. **2** having to do with the disposal of naval, military, or air forces in action against an enemy. **3** organized for or used in action against enemy troops, rather than against enemy bases, industry, etc., behind the lines of battle: *a tactical bomber.* **4** characterized by adroit procedure and skilful expedients. —**tac′ti·cal·ly,** *adv.*

tac·ti·cian (tak tish′ən) *n.* a person skilled or trained in tactics.

tac·tics (tak′tiks) *n.* **1** the art or science of disposing naval, military, or air forces in action. **2** the method or process of doing this. **3** the operations themselves. **4** any procedures to gain advantage or success; methods. [< NL *tactica* < Gk. *taktikē* (*technē*) the art of arranging < *tassein* arrange]

☛ **Tactics** meaning the science (def. 1), is plural in form and singular in use: *Tactics differs from strategy, which refers to the overall plans of a nation at war.* Otherwise, it is plural in form and use: *The general's tactics were successful. His tactics in winning the election were hardly ethical.*

hat, āge, cãre, fär; let, ēqual, tėrm; it, īce
hot, ōpen, ôrder; oil, out; cup, pu̇t, rüle, ūse
əbove, takən, pencəl, lemən, circəs
ch, child; ng, long; sh, ship
th, thin; ᴛʜ, then; zh, measure

tac·tile (tak′tīl or tak′təl) *adj.* **1** of or having to do with touch. **2** having the sense of touch. **3** that can be felt by touch. [< L *tactilis* < *tangere* touch]

tac·til·i·ty (tak til′ə tē) *n.* the condition or quality of being tactile.

tact·less (takt′lis) *adj.* **1** without tact: a *tactless person.* **2** showing no tact: *a tactless reply.* —**tact′less·ly,** *adv.* —**tact′less·ness,** *n.*

tac·tu·al (tak′chü əl) *adj.* **1** of touch; having to do with touch. **2** arising from the sense of touch; giving sensations of touch. [< L *tactus.* See TACT.]

tac·tu·al·ly (tak′chü əl ē) *adv.* by means of touch; as regards touch.

tad·pole (tad′pōl′) *n.* a very young frog or toad at the stage when it has a tail and lives in water. [ME *tad* toad + *pol* poll (head); apparently "a toad that is all head"]

ta'en (tān) *Poetic.* taken.

taf·fe·ta (taf′ə tə) *n.* **1** a rather stiff silk cloth having a smooth, glossy surface. **2** a similar cloth of linen, rayon, etc. [ME < OF < Persian *taftah* silk or linen < *tāftan* shine]

taff·rail (taf′rāl′) *n.* **1** a rail around a ship's stern. **2** the upper part of the stern of a ship. [< Du. *tafereel* panel, dim. of *tafel* table]

TAFFRAIL

taf·fy (taf′ē) *n.* **1** a kind of chewy candy made of brown sugar or molasses boiled down, often with butter. **2** *Informal.* flattery. Also, **toffee, toffy.** [var. of *toffee*]

Taf·fy (taf′ē) *n.* **-fies.** *Slang.* a Welshman. [< Welsh pronunciation of *Dafydd* David]

tag[1] (tag) *n. v.* **tagged, tag·ging.** —*n.* **1** a piece of card, paper, leather, etc. to be tied or fastened to something: *Each coat in the store has a tag with the price marked on it.* **2** a small hanging piece; a loosely attached piece; a loose end. **3** a tab or loop by which a coat is hung up. **4** a metal point at the end of a string. A shoelace has a tag on each end. **5** a piece of cardboard, etc., sometimes with a piece of string attached, sold by charitable organizations, etc. to raise money. **6** a quotation, moral, etc. added for ornament or effect. **7** the last line or lines of a song, play, actor's speech, etc. **8** in fishing, a small piece of bright material such as tinsel, wrapped around the shank of the hook near the tail of an artificial fly.
—*v.* **1** add for ornament or effect. **2** furnish with a tag or tags. **3** mark; label; identify: *tag suitcases and trunks.* **4** *Informal.* follow closely: *The baby tagged after his brother.* **5** sell tags: *She tagged for the Red Cross.* [ME *tagge* ? < Scand.; cf. Swedish *tagg* bark, tooth, and Norwegian *tagge* tooth]

tag[2] (tag) *n. v.* **tagged, tag·ging.** —*n.* **1** a children's game in which the player who is "it" chases the others until he touches one. The one touched is then "it" and must chase the others. **2** in baseball, the act of touching a base runner with the ball, or a base with the foot while holding the ball. —*v.* **1** touch or tap with the hand. **2** in baseball, put out a base runner with a touch of the ball. [origin uncertain]

Ta·ga·log (tä gä′log or tag′ə log′) *n.* **1** a Malay people living in the Philippines, especially Luzon. **2** a member of this people. **3** the language of this people, the official language of the Philippines. It is related to Indonesian and to Malay.

tag day a day on which tags (def. 5) are sold on behalf of a charitable organization, etc.

tag line 1 a punch line. 2 a slogan or catch phrase. 3 a last line or phrase in a play, speech, etc.

Ta·hi·ti·an (tə hē′tē ən or tə hē′shən) *adj.* of or having to do with the island of Tahiti, one of the Society Islands in the S. Pacific Ocean, its people, or their language.
—n. 1 a native of Tahiti. 2 the Polynesian language of Tahiti.

tai·ga (tī′gə) *n.* the swampy evergreen forest of the subarctic in Siberia, North America, etc. [< Russian]

tail (tāl) *n.* 1 the hindmost part of an animal's body, especially when prolonged beyond the rest. 2 something like an animal's tail: *the tail of a kite.* 3 the after portion of an airplane. 4 in astronomy, the luminous train extending from the head of a comet. 5 the hind part of anything; back; rear; conclusion: *the tail of a cart.* 6 a long braid or tress of hair. 7 a part at the end of anything; conclusion: *towards the tail of his letter.* 8 *Slang.* a person who follows another to watch and report on his movements. 9 **at the tail of,** following. 10 **tails,** *pl.* **a** the reverse side of a coin. **b** *Informal.* a man's coat with long tails, worn on formal occasions. 11 **turn tail,** run away from danger, trouble, etc. 12 **twist the lion's tail,** *Esp.Brit.* humiliate Britain. 13 **with one's tail between one's legs,** afraid; dejected; humiliated.
—v. 1 furnish with a tail. 2 form a tail. 3 follow close behind; form the tail of. 4 *Slang.* follow closely and secretly. 5 **a** occur less and less; gradually stop; diminish; subside; die away. **b** fall behind; lag; straggle. 6 join (one thing) to the end of another; fasten timber by an end.
7 **tail off,** *Informal.* run away.
—adj. 1 at the tail, back, or rear. 2 coming from behind: *a tail wind.* [OE *tægel*] **—tail′-less,** *adj.*

tail·board (tāl′bôrd′) *n.* a board at the back end of a cart, wagon, truck, etc., that can be let down or removed when loading or unloading.

tail·gate (tāl′gāt′) *n. v.* **-gated, -gat·ing,** *adj.*
—n. 1 a tailboard, especially on a truck or station wagon.
2 the lower gate of a canal lock. *—v.* of a driver or a motor vehicle, follow another vehicle too closely.
—adj. Slang. having to do with a musical style combining the blues and hot jazz.

tail·ing (tāl′ing) *n.* 1 the part of a projecting stone or brick put in a wall. 2 **tailings,** *pl.* leavings; remainders, especially waste matter left over after the mining or milling of ore.

tail lamp tail light.

tail light a light, usually red, at the back end of an automobile, wagon, train, etc.

tai·lor (tā′lər) *n.* a man whose business is making or repairing clothes. *—v.* 1 make by tailor's work: *The suit was well tailored.* 2 fit or furnish with clothes made by a tailor. 3 make women's coats, suits, dresses, etc. of simple, non-flowing lines. 4 make specially to fit; adjust; adapt. [ME < AF *taillour,* ult. < LL *taliare* cut < L *talea* rod, cutting]

tai·lor·bird (tā′lər bėrd′) *n.* a small bird of Asia and Africa that stitches leaves together to form and hide its nest.

tai·lored (tā′lərd) *adj.* 1 made by cutting and sewing; made by a tailor. 2 cut and fitted simply and expertly: *a tailored suit.* 3 simple and functional: *a tailored plan, a tailored argument.*

tai·lor·ing (tā′lər ing) *n.* the business or work of a tailor.

tai·lor-made (tā′lər mād′) *adj.* 1 made by, or as if by, a tailor; simple and fitting well. 2 made to fit a certain person, object, or purpose. 3 *Informal.* of cigarettes, purchased in a packet as distinct from those made by oneself.

tailor's chalk a hard chalk or soapstone that is usually made in thin, flat pieces, used for making marks on cloth.

tail·piece (tāl′pēs′) *n.* 1 a piece forming the end or added at the end. 2 in printing, a small decorative engraving placed at the end of a chapter, etc. 3 in violins, etc. a triangular piece of ebony or other wood to which the lower ends of strings are fastened. 4 a short beam or rafter inserted in a wall and supported by a header.

tail·race (tāl′rās′) *n.* 1 the part of a millrace below the wheel. 2 the channel that takes water away from a water wheel, turbine, etc.

tail spin 1 of an airplane, a downward spin with the nose first. 2 *Slang.* mental confusion or agitation; panic.

tail wind a wind coming from behind.

taint (tānt) *n.* 1 a stain or spot; a trace of infection, corruption, or decay. 2 a moral blemish; a touch of discredit, dishonor, or disgrace. 3 a spot or shade of discoloration; tinge. 4 a cause of any such condition.
—v. 1 give a taint to; spoil; infect; contaminate: *tainted fruit. His mind was tainted from reading obscene books.*
2 become tainted or contaminated; decay: *In summer meat taints quickly if not refrigerated.* [ME; partly var. of *attaint,* partly < OF *teint,* pp. of *teindre* dye < L *tingere*]

take (tāk) *v.* **took, tak·en, tak·ing,** *n.* *—v.* 1 lay hold of; grasp: *He took her by the hand.* 2 **a** seize; catch; capture: *take a wild animal in a trap.* **b** come upon suddenly: *be taken by surprise.* 3 have the proper effect; catch hold; lay hold: *The fire has taken.* 4 accept: *Take my advice. The man won't take a cent less for the car.* 5 get; receive; assume the ownership or possession of: *She took the gifts and opened them.* 6 **a** win: *He took first prize.* **b** receive (something bestowed, conferred, administered, etc.): *take a degree in science.* 7 receive in an indicated manner; react to someone or something: *take it all in good fun.*
8 receive into the body; swallow; inhale, drink: *take food, take snuff.* 9 absorb: *Wool takes a dye well.* 10 stick to a surface; stick; adhere: *This ink doesn't take on glossy paper.* 11 get; have: *take cold, take a seat.* 12 use; make use of: *take medicine.* 13 indulge in: *take a rest, take a vacation.* 14 of fish, seize the bait; bite. 15 **a** submit to; put up with: *take hard punishment.* **b** study: *take physiology.* 16 need; require: *It takes time and patience to learn how to drive an automobile.* 17 choose; select: *Take the shortest way home.* 18 remove: *Please take the waste basket away and empty it.* 19 remove by death: *Pneumonia took him.* 20 remove something; detract: *Her paleness takes from her beauty.* 21 subtract: *If you take 2 from 7, you have 5.* 22 lead: *Where will this road take me?* 23 go with; escort: *Take her home.* 24 carry: *Take your lunch along.* 25 do; make; obtain by some special method: *Please take my photograph.* 26 form and hold in mind; feel: *Mary takes pride in her schoolwork.* 27 find out: *The doctor took his temperature.* 28 of ice, to form, become thick enough to support people. 29 **a** understand: *I take the meaning.* **b** understand the acts or words of; interpret: *How did you take his remark?* 30 suppose: *I take it the train was late.* 31 regard; consider: *Let us take an example.*
32 assume: *She took charge of the household.* 33 engage; hire; lease: *take a house.* 34 write down; record: *take dictation.* 35 receive and pay for regularly: *take a newspaper.* 36 photograph: *take a scene of a movie.*
37 become affected by: *Marble takes a high polish.* 38 in grammar, be used with: *A plural noun takes a plural verb.*
39 please; attract; charm: *The song took our fancy.* 40 win favor: *Do you think the new play will take?* 41 go: *The cat took to the woods.* 42 become: *He took sick.* 43 begin to grow; strike root. 44 attempt to get over, through, around, etc.: *My horse took the fence easily.* 45 of a batter in baseball, let (a pitched ball) pass without swinging at it. 46 in cricket: **a** catch and put out. **b** capture (a wicket), especially by striking it with the ball. 47 *Slang.* copulate with (a woman). 48 *Slang.* swindle; cheat.
take aback, surprise suddenly; startle.
take about, conduct, especially on a round of sightseeing; escort.
take after, a be like; resemble. **b** chase in order to try to seize or capture. **c** follow (someone's) example.
take against, take sides against; oppose.
take amiss, a misinterpret. **b** be offended at.
take back, a withdraw; retract. **b** remind of the past: *The letter took her back ten years.*
take down, a write down. **b** lower the pride of.
take for, suppose to be.
take in, a receive; admit. **b** make smaller. **c** understand. **d** deceive; trick; cheat. **e** include: *It's too late to take in Helen's party now.*
take it on the chin, *Informal.* take a beating.
take it or leave it, accept or reject without modification.

take it out of, a *Informal.* exhaust; fatigue. **b** take (something) from a person in compensation; exact satisfaction from.
take it out on, *Informal.* relieve one's anger or annoyance by scolding or hurting.
take kindly to, look favorably upon; be friendly toward.
take lying down, *Informal.* take without a protest.
take off, a leave the ground or water: *Three airplanes took off at the same time.* **b** *Informal.* give an amusing imitation of; mimic. **c** *Informal.* leave quickly; rush away.
take on, a engage; hire. **b** undertake to deal with. **c** *Informal.* show great excitement, grief, etc. **d** acquire: *take on the appearance of health.*
take one's time, not hurry.
take out, a remove; get rid of. **b** borrow (a book, etc.) from a library or similar collection. **c** apply for and obtain (a licence, patent, etc.) **d** escort. **e** destroy.
take over, a take the ownership or control of. **b** adapt.
take to, form a liking for; become fond of.
take up, a soak up; absorb. **b** make smaller. **c** begin to do, play, etc.; undertake. **d** pay off. **e** lift. **f** establish a homestead; settle. **g** purchase. **h** collect. **i** adopt (an idea, purpose, etc.). **j** secure the loose end of (a stitch). **k** reprove; rebuke: *take someone up short.* **l** reduce or remove (lost motion, etc.); tighten.
take (someone) **up on,** accept.
take up with, *Informal.* begin to associate or be friendly with.
—*n.* **1** the amount or number taken: *a great take of fish.* **2** the act of taking. **3** that which is taken. **4** *Slang.* receipts; profits: *the box-office take.* **5** the act of transplanting or grafting. **6** in motion pictures: **a** a scene or sequence photographed at one time. **b** the act or process of making a photograph or scene in a motion picture. **7 a** the act or process of making a recording for a record, tape, etc. **b** a record or tape of this. [OE < ON *taka*] —**tak′er,** *n.* —**Syn.** *v.* **15 a** endure, undergo, bear.

take-home pay (tāk′hōm′) the balance remaining after taxes, insurance payments, etc. have been deducted from one's wages or salary.

tak·en (tāk′ən) *v.* pp. of **take.**

take-off (tāk′of′) *n.* **1** *Informal.* an amusing imitation; mimicking. **2** an airplane's leaving the ground, water, or deck on a flight, especially its move down the runway. **3** a leap into the air. **4** the place or point at which someone or something leaves the ground.

take-out (tāk′out′) *n. Informal.* **1** the act of taking out; a removing, **2** in curling, a shot that hits an opposing stone so as to remove it from the house, or scoring area. **3** in bridge, a bid that releases a partner from a double or other bid.

take·o·ver (tāk′ō′vər) *n.* **1** the act of assuming management or possession. **2** a seizing of control.

tak·est (tāk′ist) *v. Archaic.* 2nd pers. sing. present tense of **take.** "Thou takest" means "you take" (sing.).

tak·eth (tāk′ith) *v. Archaic.* 3rd pers. sing. present tense of **take.** "He taketh" means "he takes."

tak·ing (tāk′ing) *adj.* **1** attractive; pleasing; winning: *a taking smile.* **2** *Informal.* infectious. —*n.* **1** the act of taking or the state of being taken. **2** that which is taken. **3 takings,** *pl.* money taken in; receipts.

talc (talk) *n.* a soft, smooth silicate of magnesium, usually white or grayish, used in making face powder, tailor's chalk, etc. *Formula:* $Mg_3Si_4O_{10}(OH)_2$ [< Med.L *talcum* < Arabic *talq* < Persian *talk*]

tal·cum (tal′kəm) *n.* **1** talcum powder. **2** talc.

talcum powder a powder made of purified white talc, for use on the face and body.

tale (tāl) *n.* **1** a story; narrative. **2** a falsehood; lie. **3** a piece of gossip or scandal. **4** a number; count: *His tale of sheep amounted to over three hundred.* **5 tell tales,** spread gossip or scandal. **6 tell tales out of school,** reveal confidential matters. **7 tell the tale, a** show the true state of affairs; be revealing. **b** be effective; work. **c** *Esp.Brit. Slang.* tell a story intended to attract pity. [OE *talu*] —**Syn. 1** See **story.**

tale·bear·er (tāl′bãr′ər) *n.* a person who spreads gossip or scandal; telltale.

tale·bear·ing (tāl′bãr′ing) *n.* the spreading of gossip or scandal.

tal·ent (tal′ənt) *n.* **1** a special natural ability; ability: *a talent for music.* **2** a person or people with talent. **3** in ancient times, a unit of weight or money, varying with time and place. [ME < OF < L *talentum* (def. 3) < Gk. *talanton*] —**Syn. 1** aptitude, faculty, capacity, gift. See **ability.**

hat, āge, cãre, fär; let, ēqual, tėrm; it, īce
hot, ōpen, ôrder; oil, out; cup, pu̇t, rüle, ūse
əbove, takən, pencəl, lemən, circəs
ch, child; ng, long; sh, ship
th, thin; ᴛʜ, then; zh, measure

tal·ent·ed (tal′ən tid) *adj.* having natural ability; gifted: *a talented musician.*

tales·man (tālz′mən or tā′lēz mən) *n.* **-men** (-mən). in law, a person chosen to fill a vacancy on a jury caused by the absence or disqualification of one of the original jurymen. [MF < Med.L *tales* (*de circumstantibus*) such (of the bystanders) + *man*]

tale·tell·er (tāl′tel′ər) *n.* talebearer.

tal·i·pot (tal′ə pot′) *n.* a tall palm tree of Ceylon, the Malabar coast, etc. whose large leaves are used for making fans and umbrellas, for covering houses, and in place of paper for writing. [< Singhalese *talapata* < Skt. *tāla* fan palm + *pattra* leaf]

tal·is·man (tal′is mən or tal′iz mən) *n.* **-mans. 1** a stone, ring, etc. engraved with figures or characters supposed to have magic power; charm. **2** anything that acts as a charm. [< F < Arabic < LGk. *telesma* < Gk. *telesma* initiation into the mysteries < *teleein* perform < *telos* completion]

tal·is·man·ic (tal′is man′ik or tal′iz man′ik) *adj.* having to do with or serving as a talisman. —**tal′is·man′i·cal·ly,** *adv.*

talk (tok or tôk) *v.* **1** use words; speak: *A child learns to talk.* **2** use in speaking: *talk sense, talk French.* **3** bring, put, drive, influence, etc. by talk: *talk a person to sleep.* **4** discuss: *talk politics, talk business.* **5** consult; confer: *talk with one's doctor.* **6** spread ideas by other means than speech: *talk by signs.* **7** make sounds that suggest speech: *The birds were talking loudly.* **8** gossip; rumor: *She talked behind their backs.*
talk around, discuss at length without coming to the point or to a conclusion.
talk away, a spend (time) in talking; pass by talking. **b** remove or take away by talking: *He talked away his fears.*
talk back, *Informal.* answer rudely or disrespectfully.
talk big, *Slang.* talk boastfully; brag.
talk down, a make silent by talking louder or longer. **b** speak condescendingly (*to*). **c** belittle; disparage: *He talks down his competitor's products.* **d** give (a pilot) radio instructions for landing because of instrument failure or poor visibility.
talk of or **about, a** mention. **b** consider with a view to doing.
talk off (or out of) the top of one's head, *Informal.* utter one's immediate thoughts or ideas without consideration.
talk out, a discuss thoroughly. **b** in Parliament, discuss (a bill) until the time for adjournment and so prevent its being put to a vote.
talk over, a discuss; consider together. **b** persuade or convince by arguing.
talk tall, *Slang.* exaggerate.
talk up, talk earnestly in favor of; campaign for.
—*n.* **1** the use of words; spoken words; speech; conversation. **2** an informal speech. **3** a way of talking: *baby talk.* **4** a conference; council. **5** gossip; report; rumor. **6** a subject for talk or gossip: *She is the talk of the town.* **7** *Informal.* boastful or empty words: *His threat was just talk.* [ME *talke(n)*, ult. related to *tell*] —**Syn.** *v.* **1** converse. See **speak.**

talk·a·tive (tok′ə tiv or tôk′ə tiv) *adj.* having the habit of talking a great deal; fond of talking. —**talk′a·tive·ly,** *adv.* —**talk′a·tive·ness,** *n.*
Syn. Talkative, loquacious = talking much. **Talkative,** the common word, emphasizes a fondness for talking and having the habit of talking a great deal: *He is a gay, talkative old man who knows everybody in town.* **Loquacious,** a formal word, adds the idea of talking smoothly and easily and suggests a steady stream of words: *The president of the club is a loquacious woman.*

talk·er (tok′ər or tôk′ər) *n.* **1** a person who talks. **2** a talkative person. —**Syn. 1** speaker.

talk·ie (tok′ē or tôk′ē) *n. Informal.* a talking picture.

talking picture a motion picture with sound.

talk·ing-to (tok′ing tü′ or tôk′-) *n.* **-tos.** *Informal.* a scolding.

talk·y (tok′ē or tôk′ē) *adj.* **1** talkative. **2** full of talk.

tall (tol or tôl) *adj.* **1** higher than the average; high: *a tall building.* **2** of the specified height: *six feet tall.* **3** *Informal.* high or large in amount; extravagant: *a tall tale.* [OE (*ge*)*tæl* prompt, active] **—tall′ness,** *n.* **—Syn. 1** lofty, towering. See **high.**

tal·low (tal′ō) *n.* the hard fat from sheep, cows, etc., used for making candles and soap. —*v.* smear with tallow. [ME *talgh*]

tal·low·y (tal′ō ē) *adj.* **1** like tallow; fat; greasy. **2** yellowish-white; pale.

tall story or **tale** *Informal.* an unlikely or exaggerated story.

tal·ly (tal′ē) *n.* **-lies,** *v.* **-lied, -ly·ing.** *—n.* **1** a stick of wood in which notches are cut to represent numbers: *Tally sticks are often used at round-ups.* **2** anything on which a score or account is kept. **3** a notch or mark made on a tally; mark made for a certain number of objects in keeping account. **4** a number or group used in tallying: *The dishes were counted in tallies of 20.* **5** an account; reckoning; score: *the tally of a game.* **6** a label; tag. **7** a distinguishing mark on a crate, bale, or case; label. **8** in sports, a scoring point; run, goal, etc. **9** anything corresponding to a certain other thing; duplicate; counterpart. **10** correspondence; agreement.
—*v.* **1** mark on a tally; count up: *tally a score.* **2** label; tag. **3** score or make scoring points. **4** agree; correspond: *Your account tallies with mine.* **5** cause to fit, suit, or correspond. [ME < AF *tallie,* ult. < L *talea* rod] **—Syn.** *v.* **1** record, score, register. **4** accord, conform.

tal·ly·ho (*n.* tal′ē hō′; *interj.* tal′ē hō′) *n.* **-hos,** *interj. Esp.Brit.* —*n.* **1** a coach drawn by four horses. **2** a sounding of "tallyho" by a hunter. [< interj.] —*interj.* a hunter's cry on catching sight of the fox. [apparently alteration of F *taïaut,* OF *taho, tietau*]

tally sheet a sheet on which a record or score is kept, especially a record of votes.

tally stick tally (def. 1).

Tal·mud (tal′məd or täl′mu̇d) *n.* the sixty-three volumes containing the Jewish civil and canonical law, carrying on the teachings of the Old Testament through interpretations and reinterpretations contained in the Mishna and its complement or completion called the Gemara, the former being the text on which the latter is based. [< Hebrew *talmūd* instruction]

Tal·mud·ic (tal mud′ik or täl mu̇d′ik) *adj.* of or having to do with the Talmud.

Tal·mud·ist (tal′məd ist or täl′mu̇d ist) *n.* **1** one of the writers or compilers of the Talmud. **2** a person who accepts the doctrines of the Talmud. **3** a person who knows much about the Talmud.

tal·on (tal′ən) *n.* **1** the claw of a bird of prey; claw. **2 talons,** *pl.* claw-like fingers; grasping hands. [ME < OF *talon* heel, ult. < L *talus* ankle]

ta·lus[1] (tā′ləs) *n.* **-li** (-lī or -lē). **1** the ankle. **2** in anatomy, the anklebone. [< L]

ta·lus[2] (tā′ləs) *n.* **1** a slope. **2** a sloping side or face of a wall, rampart, parapet, or other fortification. **3** in geology, a sloping mass of rocky fragments lying at the base of a cliff or the like. [< F < L *talutium* a sign of the presence of a gold mine near the surface < Celtic]

tam (tam) *n.* tam-o'-shanter.

ta·ma·le (tə mä′lē) *n.* a Mexican food made of corn meal and minced meat, seasoned with red peppers, wrapped in cornhusks, and roasted or steamed. [< Am.Sp. < Nahuatl *tamalli*]

tam·a·rack (tam′ə rak′) *n.* **1** an evergreen tree of the larch family. **2** the wood of this tree. [< Algonquian]

tam·a·rind (tam′ə rind′) *n.* **1** a tropical tree grown for its wood and fruit. **2** its fruit, used in foods, drinks, and medicine. [ult. < Arabic *tamr-hindi* date of India]

tam·a·risk (tam′ə risk′) *n.* an ornamental shrub or small tree having slender, feathery branches. [ME < LL *tamariscus,* var. of L *tamarix*]

tam·bac (tam′bak) *n.* tombac.

tam·bour (tam′bür) *n.* **1** a drum. **2** a pair of embroidery hoops; frame for holding in place cloth to be embroidered. **3** embroidery done on this. —*v.* embroider on a tambour. [< F]

tam·bou·rine (tam′bə rēn′) *n.* a small drum with metal disks around the side, played by striking it with the knuckles or by shaking it. [< F *tambourin,* dim. of *tambour* drum]

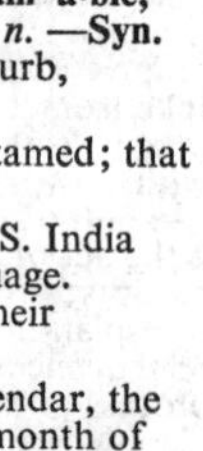
A tambourine

tame (tām) *adj.* **tam·er, tam·est,** *v.* **tamed, tam·ing.** *—adj.* **1** of an animal, not wild or savage; obedient; domestic. **2** taken from the wild state and made obedient: *a tame bear.* **3** without fear; gentle: *The squirrels are very tame.* **4** without spirit; dull: *a tame story.* **5** not dangerous or harmful. —*v.* **1** make tame; break in. **2** become tame. **3** deprive of courage; tone down; subdue. [OE *tam*] **—tame′a·ble, tam′a·ble,** *adj.* **—tame′ly,** *adv.* **—tame′ness,** *n.* **—tam′er,** *n.* **—Syn.** *adj.* **1** domesticated, domestic. **3** docile. –*v.* **3** curb, repress.

tame·less (tām′lis) *adj.* that has never been tamed; that cannot be tamed.

Tam·il (tam′əl) *n.* **1** the Dravidian people of S. India and Ceylon. **2** one of this people. **3** their language. —*adj.* of or having to do with the Tamils or their language.

Tam·muz (täm′müz) *n.* **1** in the Hebrew calendar, the 4th month of the ecclesiastical year and 10th month of the civil year. **2** in Babylonian mythology, a god of agriculture, whose annual rebirth and return to the earth symbolized spring and its new growth. Also, **Thammuz.** [< Hebrew]

tam-o'-shan·ter (tam′ə shan′tər) *n.* a type of peakless woollen cap originating in Scotland, having a tight headband, a flat, loose, round crown, and, frequently, a pompom. Also, **tam.** [from the name of the hero in a poem by Burns]

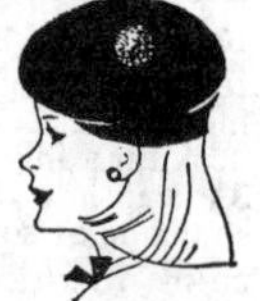
A girl wearing a tam-o'-shanter

tamp (tamp) *v.* **1** pack down: *tamp the earth about a newly planted tree.* **2** in blasting, fill (the hole containing explosive) with dirt, etc. [? < *tampion*]

tam·per (tam′pər) *v.* **1** meddle; interfere: *Do not tamper with the lock.* **2 tamper with, a** bribe; corrupt: *Crooked politicians had tampered with the jury.* **b** change so as to damage or falsify: *tamper with legal evidence.* [ult., var. of *temper*] **—tam′per·er,** *n.* **—Syn. 1** See **meddle.**

tam·pi·on (tam′pē ən) *n.* **1** a wooden plug placed in the muzzle of a gun to keep out dampness and dust. **2** a plug for the top of an organ pipe. [< F *tampon,* ult. < *taper* plug < Gmc.]

tam·pon (tam′pon) *n.* a plug of cotton or the like inserted in a wound, etc. to stop bleeding or soak up blood. —*v.* fill or plug with a tampon. [< F. See TAMPION.]

tan (tan) *v.* **tanned, tan·ning,** *n. adj.* —*v.* **1** make (a hide) into leather by soaking in a special liquid. **2** make brown from exposure to sun and air. **3** become brown. **4** *Informal.* beat or thrash in punishment.
—*n.* **1** a yellowish brown. **2** the brown color of a person's skin resulting from being in the sun and air. **3** the liquid used in tanning hides. Tan contains an acid obtained from the bark of oaks, hemlocks, etc. **4** tanbark. **5** the astringent acid in it; tannin.
—*adj.* yellowish-brown. [< Med.L *tannare*]

tan or **tan.** tangent.

tan·a·ger (tan′ə jər) *n.* any of various small North American birds related to the finches. The males are usually brilliantly colored. [< NL < Tupi *tangara*]

tan·bark (tan′bärk′) *n.* the crushed bark of oaks, hemlocks, etc. used in tanning hides. Riding tracks and circus rings are often covered with used tanbark.

tan·dem (tan′dəm) *adv.* one behind the other: *drive horses tandem.*

—*adj.* having animals, seats, parts, etc. arranged one behind the other.
—*n.* **1** two horses harnessed tandem. **2** a carriage drawn by two horses so harnessed. **3** a bicycle having two sets of handlebars, two seats, and two sets of pedals, one behind the other. **4** a truck or other vehicle with two attached units, as a cab for pulling and a trailer to carry the load. **5 in tandem, a** one ahead of the other; in tandem formation: *mounted in tandem.* **b** closely together; in co-operation. [< L *tandem* at length < *tam* so]

tang[1] (tang) *n.* **1** a strong taste or flavor: *the tang of mustard, the salt tang of sea air.* **2** a distinctive flavor or quality. **3** a slight touch or suggestion; trace. **4** a long, slender projecting point, strip, or prong forming the part of a chisel, file, etc. that fits into the handle.
—*v.* **1** provide with a spike, flange, or other tang. **2** give a distinct taste or flavor to. [ME < ON *tangi* point]

tang[2] (tang) *n.* a sharp, ringing sound. —*v.* make a sharp, ringing sound. [imitative]

Tang or **T'ang** (tang) *n.* a Chinese dynasty, A.D. 618-906, a period during which China expanded and her art and science flourished.

Tan·gan·yi·kan (tang′ gən yē′kən) *n.* a native or inhabitant of Tanganyika. —*adj.* of or having to do with Tanganyika or its people.

tan·gen·cy (tan′jən sē) *n.* the quality or state of being tangent.

tan·gent (tan′jənt) *adj.* **1** touching. **2** in geometry, touching at one point only and not intersecting. These circles are tangent: ○○ .
—*n.* **1** a tangent line, curve, or surface. **2** in trigonometry, in a right triangle, the ratio of the length of the side opposite to an (acute) angle to the length of the side (not the hypotenuse) adjacent to the angle. **3** in geometry, the part of a line tangent to a curve from the point of tangency to the axis of abscissas. *Abbrev.*: tan or tan. **4 fly off** or **go off at a tangent,** change suddenly from one course of action or thought to another. [< L *tangens, -entis,* ppr. of *tangere* touch]

tan·gen·tial (tan jen′shəl) *adj.* **1** of or having to do with a tangent. **2** being a tangent. **3** in the direction of a tangent. **4** diverging. **5** slightly connected. —**tan·gen′tial·ly,** *adv.*

tan·ge·rine (tan′jə rēn′ or tan′jə rēn′) *n.* **1** a small, deep-colored orange having a loose peel and segments that separate easily; a variety of mandarin. **2** a deep reddish orange. —*adj.* deep reddish-orange. [< F *Tanger* Tangiers, a seaport in Morocco]

tan·gi·bil·i·ty (tan′jə bil′ə tē) *n.* the fact or quality of being tangible.

tan·gi·ble (tan′jə bəl) *adj.* **1** capable of being touched or felt by touch: *A chair is a tangible object.* **2** real; actual; definite: *tangible evidence.* **3** whose value can be accurately appraised: *Real estate is tangible property.*
—*n.* **tangibles,** *pl.* things whose value is easily appraised; material assets. [< LL *tangibilis* < *tangere* touch]
—**tan′gi·bly,** *adv.*

tan·gle (tang′gəl) *v.* **-gled, -gling,** *n.* —*v.* **1** twist and twine together in a confused mass. **2** involve in something that hampers or obstructs. **3** bewilder; confuse. **4 tangle with,** get into a fight or argument with. —*n.* **1** a confused or tangled mass. **2** a bewildering confusion: *a tangle of contradictory statements.* **3** a matted bit of hair; a snarl. [probably var. of *tagle* entangle < Scand.; cf. dial. Swedish *taggla* disorder] —**tan′gle·ment,** *n.* —**Syn.** *v.* **1** entangle, snarl, interweave.

tan·gly (tang′glē) *adj.* full of tangles; tangled.

tan·go (tang′gō) *n.* **-gos,** *v.* **-goed, -go·ing.** —*n.* **1** a dance of Spanish-American origin, in 2/4 time and characterized by glides, dips, and figures. **2** the music for this dance. —*v.* dance the tango. [< Sp.]

tan·gram (tang′grəm) *n.* a Chinese puzzle consisting of a square cut into five triangles, a square, and a rhomboid, which can be combined so as to form a great variety of figures. [? < Chinese *t'ang* Chinese + E *-gram*; cf. *anagram, cryptogram,* etc.]

A tangram

hat, āge, cãre, fär; let, ēqual, tėrm; it, īce
hot, ōpen, ôrder; oil, out; cup, pu̇t, rüle, ūse
əbove, takən, pencəl, lemən, circəs
ch, child; ng, long; sh, ship
th, thin; ᴛʜ, then; zh, measure

tang·y (tang′ē) *adj.* having a strong taste or flavor.

tank (tangk) *n.* **1** a large container for liquid or gas: *an oil tank.* **2** an armored combat vehicle carrying machine guns and, usually, an artillery piece and moving on tracks. **3** a pond or pool, especially an artificial one made for swimming or as a water supply. —*v.* put or store in a tank. [? < Pg. *tanque* < L *stagnum* pool]

A tank (def. 2)

tank·age (tangk′ij) *n.* **1** the capacity of a tank or tanks. **2** storage in tanks. **3** the price charged for storage in tanks. **4** the waste matter from slaughterhouse tanks, used as fertilizer.

tank·ard (tangk′ərd) *n.* a large drinking mug with a handle and, sometimes, a hinged cover. [ME; cf. MF *tanquart,* MDu. *tanckaert*]

A tankard

tank car a railway car with a tank for carrying liquids or gases.

tank·er (tangk′ər) *n.* **1** a ship with tanks for carrying oil, gasoline, or other liquid freight. **2** a tank truck. **3** a tank car. **4** a soldier who is a member of a tank crew.

tank farm a tract of land containing many large tanks for the storing of oil.

tank·ful (tangk′fu̇l) *n.* **-fuls.** as much as will fill a tank.

tank truck a truck equipped with a large tank for carrying oil, gasoline, or other liquid freight.

tan·nate (tan′āt) *n.* a salt of tannic acid.

tan·ner[1] (tan′ər) *n.* a person whose work is tanning hides.

tan·ner[2] (tan′ər) *n. Brit. Slang.* a sixpence.

tan·ner·y (tan′ər ē) *n.* **-ner·ies.** a place where hides are tanned.

tan·nic (tan′ik) *adj.* of or obtained from tanbark or tannin.

tannic acid tannin.

tan·nin (tan′ən) *n.* an acid obtained from the bark or galls of oaks, etc. and from certain plants, used in tanning, dyeing, making ink, and in medicine. [< F *tanin*]

tan·ning (tan′ing) *n.* **1** the process or art of converting hide or skins into leather. **2** a making brown, as by exposure to sun. **3** *Informal.* a thrashing; whipping; flogging.

tan·sy (tan′zē) *n.* **-sies.** a coarse, strong-smelling plant having large, toothed leaves and clusters of small, yellow flowers. Tansy was formerly much used in cooking and medicine. [ME < OF < LL < Gk. *athanasia,* originally, immortality]

tan·ta·lize (tan′tə līz′) *v.* **-lized, -liz·ing.** torment or tease by keeping something desired in sight but out of reach, or by holding out hopes that are repeatedly disappointed. [< *Tantalus*] —**tan′ta·li·za′tion,** *n.* —**tan′ta·liz′er,** *n.* —**tan′ta·liz′ing·ly,** *adv.* —**Syn.** plague, vex.

tan·ta·lum (tan′tə ləm) *n.* a rare, grayish metallic chemical element that is resistant to acids. It is used in making surgical instruments. *Symbol*: Ta or T; *at.no.* 73; *at.wt.* 180.948. [< *Tantalus*; because it will not absorb acid]

Tan·ta·lus (tan′tə ləs) *n.* in Greek legend, a Greek king punished in Hades by having to stand up to his chin in water, under branches laden with fruit. Whenever he tried to eat or drink, the fruit or water withdrew from his reach.

tan·ta·mount (tan′tə mount′) *adj.* equivalent. [< n. < v. < AF *tant amunter* amount to as much < *tant* as much (< L *tantum*) + *amunter*, OF *amonter*. See AMOUNT.] —**Syn.** See **equal.**

tan·tar·a (tan tar′ə, tan′tə ro′, or tan′tə rə) *n.* **1** a blast of a trumpet or horn. **2** any similar sound. [imitative]

tan·trum (tan′trəm) *n. Informal.* a fit of bad temper or ill humor. [origin uncertain]

Tan·za·ni·an (tan′zə nē′ən or tan zā′nē ən) *n.* a native or inhabitant of Tanzania, a country in East Africa, consisting of the former countries of Tanganyika and Zanzibar. —*adj.* of or having to do with Tanzania or its people.

Tao·ism (tou′iz əm) *n.* one of the three great religions of China (the other two being Buddhism and Confucianism), founded on the doctrines of Lao-tse, 604?-531 B.C., a Chinese philosopher. Taoism seeks to avoid complexity in life by conforming with nature. [< Chinese *tao* the way]

Tao·ist (tou′ist) *n.* a believer in Taoism. —*adj.* of or belonging to Taoists or Taoism.

tap[1] (tap) *v.* **tapped, tap·ping,** *n.* —*v.* **1** strike lightly: *tap on a window.* **2** cause to strike lightly: *She tapped her foot on the floor.* **3** make, put, etc. by light blows: *tap a rhythm, tap time, tap the ashes out of a pipe.* **4** repair with a tap (def. 3). **5** select; choose.
—*n.* **1** a light blow: *There was a tap at the door.* **2** the sound of a light blow. **3** a piece of leather added to the sole or heel of a shoe to repair it. **4** a small steel plate on a shoe to reduce wear or to make a louder tap in tap-dancing. **5** tap-dancing. **6 taps,** *pl.* a signal on a bugle or drum at which all lights in the soldiers' or sailors' quarters must be put out. Taps are also sounded when a soldier or sailor is buried. [ME < OF *taper*; imitative]

tap[2] (tap) *n. v.* **tapped, tap·ping.** —*n.* **1** a device for turning on and off the flow of water in a pipe; faucet. **2** a device for controlling the flow of liquids or gases in a pipe or tube. **3** a stopper or plug to close a hole in a cask containing liquid. **4** a certain kind or quality of liquor. **5** *Informal.* a taproom. **6 on tap, a** ready to be let out of a keg or barrel and served. **b** ready for use; on hand. **7 a** on a coil, an electric connection somewhere other than at the end. **b** the place where an electric connection is or can be made. **8** any long, tapering cylinder, especially a taproot. **9** a tool for cutting threads of internal screws. **10** a wire tapping.
—*v.* **1** make a hole in to let out liquid: *They tapped the sugar maples when the sap began to flow.* **2** draw the plug from: *tap a cask.* **3** furnish with a tap. **4** let out (liquid) by piercing or by drawing a plug. **5** let out liquid from by surgery. **6** penetrate to; open up: *This highway taps a large district.* **7** make a connection with (a telephone line) in order to eavesdrop. **8** make an internal screw thread in. **9** *Slang.* ask (a person) for money, help, etc. [OE *tæppa*]

ta·pa (tä′pə) *n.* **1** an unwoven cloth of the Pacific islands, made by steeping and beating the inner bark of a mulberry tree. **2** this bark. [< Polynesian]

tap dance a dance in which the steps are accented by loud taps of the foot, toe, or heel.

tap-dance (tap′dans′) *v.* **-danced, -danc·ing.** dance a tap dance. —**tap′-danc′er,** *n.*

tape (tāp) *n. v.* **taped, tap·ing.** —*n.* **1** a long, narrow, woven strip of cotton, linen, etc. Tape is used to make loops and bind seams. **2** a long, narrow strip of other material. Surveyors measure with a steel tape. Stock quotations are printed on paper tape. **3** such a strip coated with a sticky substance to make it adhere to a surface: *Scotch tape.* **4** strip, string, etc. stretched across a race track at the finish line. **5 a** a thin, narrow strip of paper or plastic coated with magnetized iron oxide to record sound, as for a tape-recorder. **b** a recording thus made.
—*v.* **1** fasten with tape; wrap with tape. **2** attach a tape or tapes to. **3** measure with a tape measure. **4** record on tape. [ME *tape*, var. of *tappe*, OE *tæppe*] —**tape′like′,** *adj.*

tape·line (tāp′līn′) *n.* a tape measure.

tape measure a long strip of cloth or steel marked in inches, feet, etc. for measuring.

ta·per (tā′pər) *v.* **1** make or become gradually smaller toward one end: *The church spire tapers to a point.* **2** grow less gradually; diminish: *His business gradually tapered to nothing as people moved away.* **3 taper off,** make gradually less in amount, force, etc.; reduce steadily: *taper off smoking.* [< n.]
—*adj.* becoming smaller toward one end.
—*n.* **1** a gradual narrowing in width or girth. **2** a gradual decrease of force, capacity, etc. **3** a figure that tapers to a point; a slender cone or pyramid; spire. **4** a very slender candle; a long wick coated with wax. **5** a splinter, waxed length of wick, etc. for lighting a candle, cigarette, etc. from an open fire. [OE *tapor*] —**ta′per·ing·ly,** *adv.*

tape-re·cord (tāp′ri kôrd′) *v.* record on tape.

tape-re·cord·er (tāp′ri kôr′dər) *n.* a machine that records and reproduces voices, music, and other sounds by means of magnetized plastic or paper tape.

A tape-recorder

tape recording 1 the recording of sound on a tape. **2** the sound thus recorded. **3** the tape recorded.

tap·es·try (tap′is trē) *n.* **-tries,** *v.* **-tried, -try·ing.** —*n.* **1** fabric with pictures or designs woven in it, used to hang on walls, cover furniture, etc. **2** a picture in or as if in tapestry. —*v.* **1** picture in tapestry. **2** cover with tapestry; cover with a pattern like that of tapestry. [ME < OF *tapisserie*, ult. < *tapis* < L < Gk. *tapētion*, dim. of *tapēs* carpet, covering]

tape·worm (tāp′wėrm′) *n.* a long, flat worm that lives during its adult stage as a parasite in the intestine of human beings and other vertebrates.

tap·ing (tāp′ing) *n.* **1** a tape recording. **2** data on punched or magnetic tape, for use in a computer, etc.

tap·i·o·ca (tap′ē ō′kə) *n.* a starchy food obtained from the root of the cassava plant. [ult. < Tupi-Guarani *tipioca*]

ta·pir (tā′pər) *n.* a large, gray, piglike mammal that has a flexible snout and short, thick legs. It is found in tropical America. [< Tupi *tapira*]

tap·is (tap′ē or tap′is) *n.* **1** *Archaic.* a carpet or tapestry. **2 on the tapis,** being given attention; under discussion. [< F *tapis*. See TAPESTRY.]

tap·per[1] (tap′ər) *n.* **1** one who taps at a door, etc. **2** a telegraph key. **3** one who tests train wheels by tapping. **4** *Dialect.* a type of small woodpecker.

tap·per[2] (tap′ər) *n.* **1** one who taps trees for sap. **2** a milking machine. **3** a person who taps wires, telephones, etc.

tap·pet (tap′it) *n.* in machinery, a projection, cam, etc. that intermittently comes in contact with another part to which it communicates, or from which it receives, an intermittent motion. [< *tap*[1]]

tap·room (tap′rüm′ or -rům′) *n.* a room where alcoholic liquor is sold; bar-room.

tap·root (tap′rüt′) *n.* in botany, a main root growing downward.

tap·ster (tap′stər) *n.* a person who draws beer, wine, etc. from barrels, kegs, or casks, to serve in a tavern or bar-room. [OE *tæppestre*, fem.]

tar[1] (tär) *n. v.* **tarred, tar·ring,** *adj.* —*n.* **1** a black, sticky substance obtained by the distillation of wood or coal. **2** a brownish-black substance produced by the burning of tobacco: *cigarette tar.* **3** a pitch distilled from coal tar. **4 beat, knock, whip,** or **whale the tar out of,** *Informal.* beat unmercifully.
—*v.* **1** cover or smear with tar; soak in tar. **2** smear or besmirch as if with tar: *tarred by his own bad reputation.* **3 tar and feather,** pour heated tar on and cover with feathers as a punishment. **4 tarred with the same brush** (or **stick**), having similar faults or defects. **5 tar with** (a specified) **brush,** disgrace in some way; stigmatize.
—*adj.* of, like, or covered with tar. [OE *teoru*]

tar[2] (tär) *n.* a sailor. [special use of *tar*[1] or short for *tarpaulin*]

Ta·ra (tä′rə or tar′ə) *n.* in ancient times, **Hill of Tara,** the home of Irish kings.

tar·an·tel·la (tar′ən tel′ə) *n.* **1** a rapid, whirling southern Italian dance in 6/8 time, usually performed by a single couple. **2** the music for this dance. [< Ital. *tarantella* < *Taranto*, a city in S. Italy; influenced by Ital. *tarantola* tarantula]

ta·ran·tu·la (tə ran′chů lə) *n.* **-las, -lae** (-lē or -lī). a large, hairy spider whose bite is painful but not serious. People used to think that the bite of the tarantula caused an uncontrollable desire to dance. [< Med.L *tarantula*, ult. < L *Tarentum* Taranto. See TARANTELLA.]

tar·boosh (tär büsh′) *n.* a cap of cloth or felt, nearly always red, that has a tassel, usually of dark-blue silk, at the crown, worn by Moslem men. [< Arabic *tarbūsh*]

tar·di·ly (tär′də lē) *adv.* slowly; late; with delay.

tar·dy (tär′dē) *adj.* **-di·er, -di·est. 1** behind time; late. **2** slow. [< F *tardif*, ult. < L *tardus*] **—tar′di·ness,** *n.* **—Syn. 1** behindhand. **2** dilatory. See **late.**

tare[1] (tãr) *n.* **1** vetch. The common tare has light-purplish flowers and is grown as food for cattle and to enrich the soil. **2** in the Bible, an injurious weed, possibly the darnel. [cf. MDu. *tarwe* wheat]

tare[2] (tãr) *n.* a deduction made from the gross weight to allow for the weight of the wrapper, box, conveyance, etc. [< F *tare*, ult. < Arabic *ṭarḥah* < *ṭaraḥa* reject]

targe (tärj) *n. Archaic.* a shield or buckler. [ME < OF < Gmc.]

tar·get (tär′git) *n.* **1** a mark for shooting at; something aimed at. Although it is often a circle, anything may be used as a target. **2** an object of abuse, scorn, criticism, etc.: *His crazy ideas made him the target of their jokes.* **3** a small shield, especially one that is round. **4** in physics: **a** the plate opposite the cathode in an X-ray tube, upon which the cathode rays impinge and produce X-rays. **b** any substance bombarded by high-energy neutrons to produce nuclear reactions. **5** a plate in a television camera tube that receives the image from the screen plate. **6** a disk to show whether a railway switch is opened or closed. **7 on target,** headed for or sure to reach a certain point; to the purpose: *His criticism of the book was dead on target.*
—*v.* **1** make or put up as a target. **2** guide to a target. [ME *targete*, dim. of *targe* < OF < Gmc.]

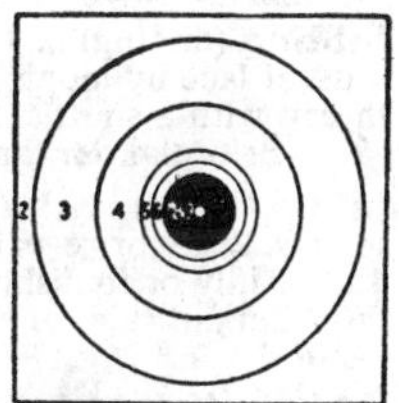

A target for shooting

tar·iff (tar′if) *n.* **1** a list of duties or taxes on imports or exports. **2** a system of duties or taxes on imports or exports. **3** any duty or tax in such a list or system: *There is a very high tariff on jewellery.* **4** any table or scale of prices: *The tariff at the hotel ranges from $8 to $15 a day for a single room.* —*v.* **1** put a tariff on. **2** set a value or price for according to a tariff. **3** list the tariff or tariffs on. [< Ital. *tariffa* arithmetic < Arabic *tar'īf* information]

tar·la·tan (tär′lə tən) *n.* a thin, stiff, transparent muslin. Tarlatan was formerly used for dresses, bags to hold Christmas candy, etc. [< F *tarlatane*]

tar·mac (tär′mak) *n.* any asphalt surface, especially a runway or other paved area of an airfield. [< Trademark *tarmac(adam)*]

tarn (tärn) *n. Brit.* a small mountain lake or pool. [ME < ON *tjörn*]

tar·nish (tär′nish) *v.* **1** dull the lustre or brightness of: *The salt tarnished the silver saltcellar.* **2** lose lustre or brightness: *The brass doorknobs tarnished.* **3** bring disgrace upon (a reputation, one's honor, etc.); sully; taint. **4** grow less appealing; become uninviting; pall; fade. —*n.* **1** a loss of lustre or brightness. **2** a discolored coating, especially on silver. **3** any unattractiveness, especially mild disgrace; blot. [< F *ternir* < *terne* dark, ? < Gmc.] **—Syn.** *v.* **1, 2** dim, discolor, blacken.

ta·ro (tä′rō) *n.* **-ros.** a starchy root grown for food in the Pacific islands and other tropical regions. [< Polynesian]

tar·ot (tar′ət or tar′ō) *n.* **1** a pack of 14th-century Italian playing cards, consisting of 78 cards including 22 trumps, often used by fortunetellers. **2 tarots,** the game played with these cards. [< F < Ital. *tarocchi*]

tar paper heavy paper soaked in tar to make it waterproof, for use on roofs, outer walls, etc.

hat, āge, cãre, fär; let, ēqual, tėrm; it, īce
hot, ōpen, ôrder; oil, out; cup, půt, rüle, ūse
əbove, takən, pencəl, lemən, circəs
ch, child; ng, long; sh, ship
th, thin; ᴛʜ, then; zh, measure

tar·pau·lin (tär po′lən or tär pô′lən) *n.* **1** a sheet of canvas, or other coarse, strong cloth, made waterproof and used to protect goods against the weather. **2** a sheet of this used as a covering. **3** a coat or other garment made of this. **4** a sailor; seaman; tar. [< *tar*[1] + *pall* in sense of "covering"]

Tar·pei·an Rock (tär pē′ən) in Rome, the rock on the Capitoline Hill from which persons convicted of treason were hurled. [< *Tarpeia*, a legendary Roman maiden]

tar·pon (tär′pon) *n.* **-pon** or **-pons.** a large, silver-colored fish found in the warmer parts of the Atlantic Ocean. [origin uncertain]

tar·ry[1] (tar′ē) *v.* **-ried, -ry·ing. 1** remain; stay: *He tarried at the inn till he felt strong enough to travel.* **2** wait; delay: *Why do you tarry so long?* **3** *Archaic.* wait for. [OE *tergan* vex, irritate; meaning influenced by OF *targer* delay, ult. < L *tardare*] **—tar′ri·er,** *n.*

tar·ry[2] (tär′ē) *adj.* **-ri·er, -ri·est. 1** of tar; like tar. **2** covered with tar. [< *tar*[1]]

tar·sal (tär′səl) *adj.* of or having to do with the tarsus. —*n.* a bone or cartilage in the ankle.

tar sand 1 sand containing tarry substances. **2** a deposit of such sand: *the Athabasca tar sands.*

tar·sus (tär′səs) *n.* **-si** (-sī or -sē). **1** in anatomy: **a** the ankle. **b** the group of small bones composing it. **2** in zoology: **a** the corresponding part in most mammals, in some reptiles, and in amphibians. **b** the shank of a bird's leg. **c** the last segment of an insect's leg. **3** in anatomy, the small plate of connective tissue in the eyelid. [< NL < Gk. *tarsos* sole of the foot, originally, crate]

tart[1] (tärt) *adj.* **1** having a sharp taste; sour. **2** sharp; biting: *a tart reply.* [OE *teart*] **—tart′ly,** *adv.* **—tart′ness,** *n.* **—Syn. 2** See **sour.**

tart[2] (tärt) *n.* **1** a piece of pastry filled with cooked fruit, jam, etc. In Canada and the United States, a tart is small and usually open at the top; in the British Isles, any shallow fruit pie is a tart. **2** *Slang.* a prostitute. [ME < OF *tarte*]

tar·tan[1] (tär′tən) *n.* **1** a plaid woollen cloth. Each Scottish Highland clan has its own pattern of tartan. **2** the pattern or design itself. —*adj.* **1** made of tartan. **2** of or like tartan. [? < MF *tiretaine* linsey-woolsey]

tar·tan[2] (tär′tən) *n.* a single-masted vessel with a lateen sail and a jib, used in the Mediterranean. [< F < Ital. *tartana*]

tar·tar[1] (tär′tər) *n.* **1** an acid substance present in grape juice deposited on the inside of wine casks. After it is purified, this substance is called cream of tartar and is used with baking soda to make baking powder. *Formula*: $KHC_4H_4O_6$ **2** a hard substance, chiefly calcium phosphate, formed on the teeth by the action of saliva on food particles. [ME < OF *tartre* < Med.L < Med.Gk. *tartaron*]

tar·tar[2] (tär′tər) *n.* **1** a person with a bad temper. **2** *Slang.* a person hard to beat or surpass in skill; champion. **3 catch a tartar,** attack someone who is too strong; get the worst of it. [< *Tartar*]

Tar·tar (tär′tər) *n.* **1** a member of a mixture of peoples, principally Mongols and Turks now living in parts of the Soviet Union and central and western Asia. Led by Genghis Khan and others, the Tartars overran Asia and E. Europe in the 13th and 14th centuries. **2** any Turkic language of the Tartars. —*adj.* of or having to do with a Tartar or Tartars. Also, **Tatar.** [ME < Med.L *Tartarus* < Persian *Tātār*, influenced in form by L *Tartarus* Hades]

tartar emetic a poisonous, white, crystalline tartrate of potassium and antimony, used in medicine to cause vomiting and sweating, as a mordant in dyeing, etc. *Formula*: $K(SbO)C_4H_4O_6 \cdot \frac{1}{2}H_2O$

tar·tar·ic (tär tar′ik or tär ter′ik) *adj.* of or having to do with tartar; containing tartar; derived from tartar.

tartaric acid a colorless crystalline compound obtained from grape juice, etc. *Formula*: $C_4H_6O_6$

Tar·ta·rus (tär′tə rəs) *n.* in Greek mythology: **1** an abyss of darkness where Zeus punished the Titans. **2** a place of punishment below Hades. **3** later, a place of eternal punishment for the spirits of the worst sinners. **4** the underworld; Hades. [< L < Gk. *Tartaros*]

Tar·ta·ry (tär′tə rē) *n.* in former times, the kingdom of the Tartars that included most of Russia and central and western Asia. Also, **Tatary.**

tart·let (tärt′lit) *n.* a small tart.

tar·trate (tär′trāt) *n.* a salt of tartaric acid.

Tar·zan (tär′zən or tär′zan) *n.* a masculine figure of heroic proportions, especially one noted for great strength and agility. [after the hero of a series of novels by Edgar Rice Burroughs, 1875-1950]

task (task) *n.* **1** work to be done; a piece of work; duty. **2 take to task,** blame; scold; reprove. —*v.* **1** put a task on; force to work. **2** burden; strain: *Lifting the heavy box tasked him beyond his strength.* [ME < ONF *tasque,* var. of *tasche* < VL *tasca,* var. of *taxa* < Med.L *taxare.* See TAX.] —**task′er,** *n.* —**Syn.** *n.* **1** assignment, undertaking, job, stint.

task force a temporary group of service units, assigned to one commander for carrying out a specific operation. **2** any group temporarily organized for a specific task.

task·mas·ter (task′mas′tər) *n.* a person who sets tasks for others to do.

Tas·ma·ni·an (taz mā′nē ən or taz mān′yən) *adj.* of or having to do with Tasmania, an island south-east of Australia, or its people. —*n.* a native or inhabitant of Tasmania.

tas·sel (tas′əl) *n. v.* **-selled** or **-seled, -sell·ing** or **-sel·ing.** —*n.* **1** a hanging bunch of threads, small cords, beads, etc. fastened together at one end. **2** something like this. Corn has tassels. —*v.* **1** put tassels on. **2** take tassels from. **3** grow tassels. [ME < OF *tassel*; ult. origin uncertain]

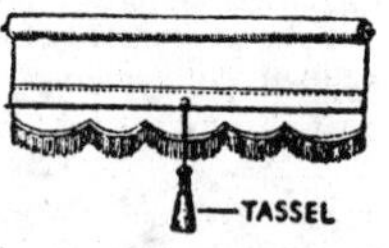

taste (tāst) *n. v.* **tast·ed, tast·ing.** —*n.* **1** a quality of a substance which is perceived when it touches the taste buds in the mouth and on the tongue; savor; flavor: *Sweet, sour, salt, and bitter are four important tastes.* **2** the sensation produced in these organs. **3** the sense by which the flavor of things is perceived: *Her taste is unusually keen.* **4** a little bit; sample: *take a taste of a cake.* **5** a liking: *Suit your own taste.* **6** the ability to perceive and enjoy what is beautiful and excellent. **7** a manner or style that shows such ability: *Her house is furnished in excellent taste.* **8** the prevailing typical style in an age, class, or country: *in the Moorish taste.* **9** any little exposure to or experience (*of*): *brief tastes of joy.* **10** the act of tasting or the fact of being tasted. **11 a bad** or **nasty taste in the mouth,** an unpleasant feeling or memory left by a distasteful experience; bad aftertaste. **12 to one's taste,** in harmony with one's preferences; to one's liking; pleasing. **13 to the king's** or **queen's taste,** perfectly; very satisfactorily.
—*v.* **1** try the flavor of (something) by taking a little into the mouth. **2** get the flavor of by the sense of taste: *She tasted almond in the cake.* **3** have a particular flavor: *The soup tastes of onion.* **4** eat or drink a little bit of. **5** eat or drink a little bit. **6** experience; have: *taste freedom.* **7** have experience: *taste of pleasure.* [ME < OF *taster,* originally, feel] —**tast′a·ble,** *adj.*
Syn. *n.* **1 Taste, flavor** = the property or quality of a thing that affects the sense organs of the mouth. **Taste** is the general word: *Mineral oil has no taste.* **Flavor** = a characteristic taste belonging to a thing, or a specially noticeable quality in the taste: *These berries have no flavor, but merely a sweet taste.* **5** inclination, predilection, fondness.

taste bud any of certain small groups of cells in the lining of the tongue or mouth that are sense organs of taste.

taste·ful (tāst′fəl) *adj.* **1** having good taste. **2** showing or done in good taste. —**taste′ful·ly,** *adv.* —**taste′ful·ness,** *n.*

taste·less (tāst′lis) *adj.* **1** without taste. **2** without good taste; in poor taste. —**taste′less·ly,** *adv.* —**taste′less·ness,** *n.* —**Syn. 1** insipid, flat, vapid.

tast·er (tās′tər) *n.* **1** a person who tastes. **2** a person skilled in judging the quality of wine, tea, coffee, etc. by the taste. **3** formerly, a person who tasted food to safeguard his master against poison. **4** a utensil or container used in tasting.

tast·y (tās′tē) *adj.* **tast·i·er, tast·i·est.** *Informal.* **1** tasting good; pleasing to the taste. **2** having or showing good taste. —**tast′i·ly,** *adv.* —**tast′i·ness,** *n.*

tat (tat) *v.* **tat·ted, tat·ting.** make a kind of lace by looping and knotting (threads) with a shuttle. [? back formation from *tatting*]

Ta·tar (tä′tər) *n. adj.* Tartar.

Ta·ta·ry (tä′tə rē) *n.* Tartary.

tat·ter[1] (tat′ər) *n.* **1** a torn piece; rag: *After the storm the flag hung in tatters upon the mast.* **2 tatters,** *pl.* torn or ragged clothing. —*v.* tear or wear to pieces; make ragged. [ult. < Scand.; cf. ON *tötturr* rag]

tat·ter[2] (tat′ər) *n.* a person who tats.

tat·ter·de·mal·ion (tat′ər dē māl′yən or tat′ər dē mal′yən) *n.* a person in tattered clothes; ragamuffin. [< *tatter* + *-demalion,* of uncertain origin]

tat·tered (tat′ərd) *adj.* **1** torn or ragged. **2** wearing torn or ragged clothes.

tat·ting (tat′ing) *n.* **1** the process or work of making a kind of lace by looping and knotting cotton or linen thread with a shuttle. **2** the lace made in this way. [? < Brit. dial. *tat* tangle]

tat·tle (tat′əl) *v.* **-tled, -tling,** *n.* —*v.* **1** tell tales or secrets. **2** say or reveal by tattling. **3** talk foolishly; gossip. **4** utter idly or foolishly. —*n.* idle or foolish talk; gossip; the telling of tales or secrets. [cf. MDu. *tatelen* stutter] —**tat′tler,** *n.*

tat·tle·tale (tat′əl tāl′) *n. adj. Informal.* telltale.

tat·too[1] (ta tü′) *n.* **-toos,** *v.* **-tooed, -too·ing.** —*n.* **1** a signal on a bugle, drum, etc. calling soldiers, sailors, or airmen to their quarters at night. **2** a series of raps, taps, etc.: *The hail beat a loud tattoo on the roof.* **3** a military display, especially music and parading by show units. —*v.* tap continuously; drum: *Don't tattoo with your fingers.* [< Du. *taptoe* < *tap* tap of a barrel + *toe* pull to, shut]

tat·too[2] (ta tü′) *v.* **-tooed, -too·ing,** *n.* **-toos.** —*v.* **1** mark (the skin) with designs or patterns by pricking it and putting in colors. **2** mark (a design) on the skin in this way: *The sailor had a ship tattooed on his arm.* —*n.* **1** a mark or design made by tattooing. **2** the act or practice of tattooing the skin. [< Polynesian *tatau*] —**tat·too′er,** *n.*

tau (to, tô, or tou) *n.* the 19th letter (T, τ = English T, t) of the Greek alphabet.

taught (tot or tôt) *v.* pt. and pp. of **teach.**

taunt (tont or tônt) *v.* **1** jeer at; mock; reproach. **2** get or drive by taunts: *They taunted him into taking the dare.* —*n.* a bitter or insulting remark; mocking; jeering. [obs. phrase *taunt (pour taunt),* var. of F *tant pour tant* tit for tat] —**Syn.** *v.* **1** deride, ridicule, gibe, flout.

taupe (tōp) *n. adj.* dark brownish-gray. [< F *taupe,* originally, mole < L *talpa*]

tau·rine (tôr′īn or tôr′in) *adj.* **1** of or like a bull; bovine. **2** of or having to do with Taurus. [< L *taurinus* < *taurus* bull]

Tau·rus (tô′rəs) *n.* **1** in astronomy, a northern constellation supposed to be arranged in the shape of a bull. **2** in astrology, the second sign of the zodiac; the Bull. The sun enters Taurus about April 20. See **zodiac** for diagram. [< L *taurus* bull]

taut (tot or tôt) *adj.* **1** tightly drawn; tense: *a taut rope.* **2** in neat condition; tidy. [earlier *taught,* apparently var. of *tight*] —**taut′ly,** *adv.* —**taut′ness,** *n.* —**Syn. 1** See **tight.**

tau·tog (to′tog or tô tog′) *n.* a food fish common on the Atlantic coast; blackfish. [< Algonquian]

tau·to·log·i·cal (to′tə loj′ə kəl or tô′tə loj′ə kəl) *adj.* having to do with, characterized by, or using tautology. —**tau′to·log′i·cal·ly,** *adv.*

tau·tol·o·gy (to tol′ə jē or tô tol′ə jē) *n.* **-gies. 1** the saying of a thing over again in other words without adding clearness or force; useless repetition. *Example*: the *modern* college student *of today*. **2** in logic, a statement that is true by virtue of its form. *Example*: She is either married or not. **3** the stating or believing of a fact to be its own reason; confusion of cause and effect. *Examples*: It's wet because it has water on it. I know because I know. [< LL < Gk. *tautologia*, ult. < *to auto* the same (thing) + *legein* say]

tav·ern (tav′ərn) *n.* **1** a place where alcoholic drinks are sold and drunk; saloon. **2** *Archaic.* an inn. Hotels have taken the place of the old taverns. [ME < OF < L *taberna*, originally, rude dwelling]

taw (to or tô) *n.* **1** a fancy marble used for shooting. **2** a game of marbles. **3** the line from which the players shoot their marbles. [origin uncertain]

taw·dry (to′drē or tô′drē) *adj.* **-dri·er, -dri·est.** showy and cheap; gaudy. [ult. alteration of *St. Audrey*, from cheap laces sold at St. Audrey's fair in Ely, England] —**taw′dri·ly,** *adv.* —**taw′dri·ness,** *n.*

taw·ny (to′nē or tô′nē) *adj.* **-ni·er, -ni·est,** *n.* **-nies.** —*adj.* brownish-yellow: *A lion has a tawny skin.* —*n.* a brownish yellow. [ME < OF *tane*, pp. of *taner* tan] —**taw′ni·ness,** *n.*

tax (taks) *n.* **1** money paid by people for the support of the government, for public works, etc. In modern times, a tax is usually a levy on income, property, or business transactions. **2** a burden, duty, or demand that oppresses; strain: *Climbing stairs is a tax on a weak heart.* [< v.] —*v.* **1** put a tax on. **2** lay a heavy burden on; be hard for: *Reading in a poor light taxes the eyes.* **3** reprove; accuse; charge: *The office manager taxed Tom with having neglected his work.* **4** in law, examine and fix (the costs of a lawsuit, etc.). [< Med.L *taxare* impose a tax < L *taxare* estimate, assess, charge < Gk. *taxai*, aorist infin. of *tassein* assign] —**tax′er,** *n.* —**tax′less,** *adj.*
—**Syn.** *n.* **1** assessment, levy, impost, duty, excise. –*v.* **2** strain, task.

tax·a·bil·i·ty (tak′sə bil′ə tē) *n.* the state of being taxable.

tax·a·ble (tak′sə bəl) *adj.* liable to be taxed; subject to taxation: *Churches are not taxable.*

tax·a·tion (taks ā′shən) *n.* **1** the act of taxing: *Taxation is necessary to provide roads, schools, and police protection.* **2** the amount people pay for the support of the government; taxes.

tax-ex·empt (taks′eg zempt′) *adj.* free from taxes; not taxed.

tax·i (tak′sē) *n.* **tax·is,** *v.* **tax·ied, tax·i·ing** or **tax·y·ing.** —*n.* an automobile driven for hire, usually having a meter for recording the fare. —*v.* **1** ride in a taxi. **2** move slowly over the surface of the ground or water. An airplane or a seaplane taxis for a short distance before it rises. [short for *taxicab*]

tax·i·cab (tak′sē kab′) *n.* taxi. [contraction of *taximeter cab.* See TAXIMETER.]

tax·i·der·mal (tak′sə dėr′məl) *adj.* of or having to do with taxidermy.

tax·i·der·mist (tak′sə dėr′mist) *n.* a person who practises taxidermy.

tax·i·der·my (tak′sə dėr′mē) *n.* the art of preparing the skins of animals and stuffing and mounting them in lifelike form. [< Gk. *taxis* arrangement (< *tassein* arrange) + *derma* skin]

tax·i·me·ter (tak′sē mē′tər) *n.* an instrument fitted to a public cab for indicating the fare at any moment. [< F *taximètre* < *taxe* fare < *mètre* meter]

tax·o·nom·ic (tak′sə nom′ik) *adj.* of or having to do with taxonomy.

tax·on·o·mist (taks on′ə mist) *n.* a person skilled in taxonomy.

tax·on·o·my (taks on′ə mē) *n.* **1** classification, especially in relation to its principles or laws. **2** the branch of science dealing with classification. [< F *taxonomie* < Gk. *taxis* arrangement (< *tassein* arrange) + *-nomos* assigning]

tax·pay·er (taks′pā′ər) *n.* a person who pays a tax or is required by law to do so.

tax rate the rate of taxation on property, income, etc.

hat, āge, cãre, fär; let, ēqual, tėrm; it, īce
hot, ōpen, ôrder; oil, out; cup, pu̇t, rüle, ūse
əbove, takən, pencəl, lemən, circəs
ch, child; ng, long; sh, ship
th, thin; ᴛʜ, then; zh, measure

Tb terbium.

TB *Informal.* tuberculosis.

T-bone steak or **T-bone** (tē′bōn′) *n.* a beefsteak having a T-shaped bone and some tenderloin.

tbs. or **tbsp.** tablespoon; tablespoons.

Tc technetium.

TD or **td** touchdown.

Te tellurium.

tea (tē) *n.* **1** a dark-brown or greenish drink, served hot or cold, usually made by steeping the dried leaves of a certain shrub in boiling water. **2** the dried and prepared leaves from which this drink is made. Tea is grown chiefly in China, Japan, India, and Ceylon. **3** the shrub on which these leaves grow. **4** *Esp.Brit.* a meal in the late afternoon or early evening, at which tea is commonly served. **5** an afternoon reception at which tea is served. **6** a hot drink made from herbs, meat, etc.: *sage tea, beef tea.* **7** a tea rose. **8 another cup of tea,** *Informal.* a very different sort of thing. **9 one's cup of tea,** *Informal.* just what one likes. [< dial. Chinese *t'e*]

tea bag a small paper or gauze bag containing tea.

tea ball a perforated metal ball in which tea leaves are placed in making tea.

tea caddy or **canister** a small can or tin-lined box for keeping tea fresh.

tea·cart (tē′kärt′) *n.* a tea wagon.

teach (tēch) *v.* **taught, teach·ing. 1** show how to do; make understand: *teach a dog tricks.* **2** give instruction to: *He teaches his classes well.* **3** give lessons in: *He teaches mathematics.* **4** give instruction; act as teacher: *She teaches for a living.* [OE *tǣcan* show]
Syn. 1, 2 Teach, instruct = give or convey knowledge or information to someone. **Teach** always suggests a learner, and emphasizes causing or enabling him to learn something by giving information, explanation, and training, by showing how as well as what to learn, and by guiding his studies: *Some children learn to read by themselves, but most need to be taught.* **Instruct** emphasizes providing, in a systematic way, the necessary information or knowledge about a subject: *He instructs classes in chemistry.*
☛ **See learn** for usage note.

teach·a·bil·i·ty (tēch′ə bil′ə tē) *n.* the fact or quality of being teachable.

teach·a·ble (tēch′ə bəl) *adj.* capable of being taught. —**teach′a·ble·ness,** *n.*

teach·er (tēch′ər) *n.* a person who teaches, especially one who teaches in a school.

teach·er·age (tēch′ər əj) *n.* especially in rural areas, a house owned by a board of education for the use of the schoolteacher.

teach-in (tēch′in′) *n.* a seminar presided over by academics and attended by students and public, held in a spirit of protest outside regular class hours to air opinions on a topical issue, especially one that is political and controversial.

teach·ing (tēch′ing) *n.* **1** the work or profession of a teacher. **2** the act of one who teaches. **3** what is taught; instruction; precept.

teaching machine a mechanical device containing graded educational material and operated by a student so that he can learn at his own pace. Normally, at each step, the student responds to a question and either checks his answer against that supplied by the machine or follows further instructions depending on the answer he has given.

tea cloth 1 *Brit.* a dish towel. **2** a decorative cloth for a tea table.

tea cosy or **cozy** a hatlike insulated covering for putting over a teapot to keep the tea hot.

tea·cup (tē′kup′) *n.* **1** a cup from which tea is drunk. **2** the quantity that such a cup may hold. **3 storm in a teacup,** a great commotion over a small matter.

tea·cup·ful (tē′kup fu̇l) *n.* **-fuls.** as much as a teacup holds, usually four fluid ounces.

tea·house (tē′hous′) *n.* a place where tea and other light refreshments are served. There are many teahouses in Japan and China.

teak (tēk) *n.* **1** a large tree of the East Indies having a hard, heavy, durable, yellowish-brown wood. **2** the wood of this tree. Teak is used for shipbuilding, making fine furniture, etc. [< Pg. < Malayalam *tēkka*]

tea·ket·tle (tē′ket′əl) *n.* a kettle for heating water to make tea, etc.

teal (tēl) *n.* **teal** or **teals.** any of several varieties of small fresh-water duck. [ME *tele*; cf. Du. *taling, teling*]

team (tēm) *n.* **1** a number of people working or acting together, especially one of the sides in a match: *a football team, a debating team.* **2** two or more horses or other animals harnessed together to work.
—*v.* **1** join together in a team. **2** drive a team. **3** work, carry, haul, etc. with a team. **4 team up, a** join together with others in a team. **b** join with one or more persons in a united effort or for a common purpose. [OE *tēam*]

team·mate (tēm′māt′) *n.* a fellow member of a team.

team·ster (tēm′stər) *n.* **1** a truck driver. **2** a man who drives a team of horses.

team teaching 1 a system by which instruction, consisting of lectures, study groups, and individual tuition, is shared by several teachers working as a team. **2** teaching done under this sytem.

team·work (tēm′wėrk′) *n.* the acting together of a number of people to make the work of the group successful and effective: *Football calls for teamwork.*

tea·pot (tē′pot′) *n.* **1** a container with a handle and a spout for making and serving tea. **2 tempest in a teapot,** a great commotion over a small matter.

tear[1] (tēr) *n.* **1** a drop of salty water coming from the eye. **2** something like or suggesting a tear. **3 in tears,** shedding tears; crying. [OE *tēar*]

tear[2] (tãr) *v.* **tore, torn, tear·ing,** *n.* —*v.* **1** pull apart by force: *tear a box open.* **2** make by pulling apart: *She tore a hole in her dress.* **3** make a hole or a rent in by a pull: *The nail tore her coat.* **4** pull hard; pull violently: *He tore down the enemy's flag.* **5** cut badly; wound: *The jagged stone tore his skin.* **6** rend; divide: *The political party was torn by two factions.* **7** remove by effort: *He could not tear himself from that spot.* **8** make miserable; distress: *She was torn by grief.* **9** become torn: *Lace tears easily.* **10** *Informal.* move with great force or haste: *An automobile came tearing along.* **11** hurry; rush; dash. **12 tear into,** attack or criticize severely.
—*n.* **1** a torn place. **2** the act or process of tearing. **3** a hurry; rush; dash. **4** *Slang.* a spree. **5** a fit of violent anger. [OE *teran*]
Syn. *v.* **1 Tear, rip** = pull apart by force, especially something that is in one piece. **Tear** = pull apart or into pieces in such a way as to leave rough or ragged edges: *He tore the letter into tiny pieces.* **Rip** = tear or cut roughly or quickly and with force, usually along a joining: *She ripped the hem in her skirt.*

tear bomb (tēr) a bomb that sends forth tear gas.

tear·drop (tēr′drop′) *n.* **1** tear[1] (defs. 1 and 2). **2** an air bubble in glass.

tear·ful (tēr′fəl) *adj.* **1** full of tears; weeping. **2** causing tears; sad. —**tear′ful·ly,** *adv.* —**tear′ful·ness,** *n.* —**Syn. 2** mournful, melancholy.

tear gas (tēr) a gas that irritates the eyes, causing tears and temporary blindness, used especially in breaking up riots.

tear-gas (tēr′gas′) *v.* **-gassed, -gas·sing. 1** use tear gas. **2** subdue with tear gas.

tear·less (tēr′lis) *adj.* without tears; not crying.

tea·room (tē′rüm′ or -ru̇m′) *n.* a room or shop where tea, coffee, and light meals are served.

tea rose 1 any of various hybrid roses having a delicate scent thought to resemble that of tea. **2** pinkish yellow.

tear·y (tēr′ē) *adj.* tearful.

tease (tēz) *v.* **teased, teas·ing,** *n.* —*v.* **1** bother or annoy by means of jokes, questions, requests, etc.: *The other boys teased Jim about his curly hair.* **2** beg: *The child teases for every little thing that he sees.* **3** comb out; shred (wool, etc.). **4** raise nap on (cloth). **5** comb hair by holding it up and working the short hairs toward the scalp.
—*n.* **1** a person who teases. **2** the act of teasing or the state of being teased. [OE *tǣsan*] —**teas′ing·ly,** *adv.*
Syn. *v.* **1 Tease, plague, pester** = vex or torment by continuous or persistent annoyance. **Tease** emphasizes driving a person or animal to lose patience and flare up in irritation or anger, either by persistent begging or asking or by unkind jokes or tricks: *Children teased the dog until he bit them.* **Plague** emphasizes the presence of someone or something thought of as a trial or affliction: *Her little brother plagues her.* **Pester** emphasizes continued repetition of nuisances or petty vexations: *He pesters his mother for candy.*

tea·sel (tē′zəl) *n. v.* **-selled** or **-seled, -sel·ling** or **-sel·ing.** —*n.* **1** a plant having stiff, prickly flower heads. **2** one of these dried flower heads used for raising nap on cloth. **3** a mechanical device used for the same purpose.
—*v.* raise a nap on (cloth) with teasels. Also, **teazel.** [OE *tǣsel*]

teas·er (tēz′ər) *n.* **1** a person or thing that teases. **2** *Informal.* an annoying problem; a puzzling task.

tea service a set of silver, china, etc. for serving tea, usually consisting of a teapot, hot water pitcher, cream jug, and sugar bowl.

tea set a complete set of dishes for serving tea, including cups and saucers, small plates, etc.

tea·spoon (tē′spün′) *n.* a spoon smaller than a tablespoon, commonly used to stir tea or coffee; a standard unit of measure in cookery. *Abbrev.*: t. or tsp.

tea·spoon·ful (tē′spün fu̇l) *n.* **-fuls.** the amount that a teaspoon can hold. 1 teaspoonful = ⅓ tablespoon.

teat (tēt or tit) *n.* of female mammals, the nipple of a breast or udder, from which the young suck milk. [ME < OF *tete* < Gmc.]

tea towel dish towel.

tea wagon a small table on wheels used in serving tea.

tea·zel (tē′zəl) *n. v.* **-zelled** or **-zeled, -zel·ling** or **-zel·ing.** teasel.

Te·bet or **Te·beth** (tā vāth′ or tā′ves) *n.* in the Hebrew calendar, the tenth month of the ecclesiastical year, and the fourth month of the civil year.

tech. 1 technical. **2** technology.

tech·ne·ti·um (tek nē′shē əm) *n.* an artificially produced radio-active, metallic chemical element, formerly called masurium. *Symbol*: Tc; *at.no.* 43; *at.wt.* 99 (most stable isotope). [< Gk. *technētos* artificial < *technē* art]

tech·nic (tek′nik) *n.* **1** a technique. **2** a technical detail, point, term, etc. —*adj.* technical. [< Gk. *technikos* < *technē* art, skill, craft]

tech·ni·cal (tek′nə kəl) *adj.* **1** of or having to do with an art, science, discipline, or profession: *a word's technical sense.* **2** typical of, characteristic of, or special to a subject. *Electrolysis, tarsus,* and *proteid* are technical words. **3** of or having to do with industrial arts, applied sciences, mechanical trades, and crafts; technological: *This technical school trains engineers, chemists, and architects.* **4** treating a subject technically; using technical terms: *a technical lecture.* **5** judged strictly by the rules (of a certain science, art, game, etc.): *a technical victory.* **6** of or having to do with technique: *Her singing shows technical skill but her voice is weak.* [< *technic*]

tech·ni·cal·i·ty (tek′nə kal′ə tē) *n.* **-ties. 1** a technical matter, point, detail, term, expression, etc.: *Books on engineering contain many technicalities that the ordinary reader does not understand.* **2** a technical quality or character.

technical knockout in boxing, a knockout called by the referee when he considers a fighter, though not knocked out, to be too severely beaten to continue the match. *Abbrev.*: TKO, T.K.O., t.k.o.

tech·ni·cal·ly (tek′nik lē) *adv.* in a technical manner or respect; in relation to a particular art or the like, or to the arts and applied sciences; in accordance with technical methods; in technical terms; in a technical sense.

technical school a school that provides training for work in industry, agriculture, etc.

tech·ni·cian (tek nish′ən) *n.* **1** a person experienced in the technicalities of a subject. **2** a person skilled in the technique of an art.

tech·ni·col·or or **tech·ni·col·our** (tek′nə kul′ər) *adj.* highly colorful; vivid. [< *Technicolor,* trademark for a process for making motion pictures in color]

Tech·ni·col·or (tek′nə kul′ər) *n. Trademark.* a special process by which three-color photographs are combined in one film.

tech·nics (tek′niks) *n.* **1** the study or science of an art or of arts in general, especially of the mechanical or industrial arts. **2** a technic or technique.

tech·nique (tek nēk′) *n.* **1** the method or way of performing the mechanical details of an art; technical skill: *The pianist's technique was excellent, but his interpretation of the music was poor.* **2** a special method or system used to accomplish something: *a new technique for removing tonsils.* [< F]

tech·noc·ra·cy (tek nok′rə sē) *n.* governmental, social, and industrial management according to the findings of engineers and usually administered by technologists. [< Gk. *technē* craft + *kratos* rule, power]

tech·no·crat (tek′nə krat′) *n.* a person in favor of technocracy.

tech·no·crat·ic (tek′nə krat′ik) *adj.* having to do with technocracy or technocrats.

tech·no·log·ic (tek′nə loj′ik) *adj.* technological.

tech·no·log·i·cal (tek′nə loj′ə kəl) *adj.* having to do with technology; used in technology. —**tech′no·log′i·cal·ly,** *adv.*

tech·nol·o·gist (tek nol′ə jist) *n.* a person skilled in technology.

tech·nol·o·gy (tek nol′ə jē) *n.* **1** the science of the industrial arts: *He studied welding at a school of technology.* **2** technical words, terms, or expressions used in an art, science, etc. [< Gk. *technologia* systematic treatment < *technē* art + *-logos* treating of]

tech·y (tech′ē) *adj.* **tech·i·er, tech·i·est.** tetchy.

tec·ton·ic (tek ton′ik) *adj.* **1** of or having to do with the architecture or construction of a building; structural. **2** in geology, of or having to do with structures that build up on the earth's crust. [< LL *tectonicus* < Gk. *tektonikos* of building < *tektōn* carpenter] —**tec·ton′i·cal·ly,** *adv.*

tec·ton·ics (tek ton′iks) *n.* **1** the art or science of design and building; construction. **2** the geological study of the earth's crust.

ted (ted) *v.* **ted·ded, ted·ding.** spread out (hay) for drying. [ME < ON *tethja* spread manure]

ted·der (ted′ər) *n.* a machine that spreads out hay for drying.

teddy bear a soft, stuffed toy bear.

ted·dy-boy or **Ted·dy-boy** (ted′ē boi′) *n. Brit. Slang.* an idle young ruffian, sometimes delinquent, who dresses in a flashy manner. [from the fancy clothes worn by such persons, cut in the style of Edward VII, nicknamed *Teddy*]

Te De·um (tē dē′əm) *Latin.* **1** in the Christian church, a hymn of praise and thanksgiving sung at morning service, and also on special occasions. **2** the music for this hymn. [< L *Te Deum,* the first words of the hymn]

te·di·ous (tē′dē əs or tē′jəs) *adj.* long and tiring: *a tedious lecture.* [ME < LL *taediosus* < L *taedium* tedium. See TEDIUM.] —**te′di·ous·ly,** *adv.* —**te′di·ous·ness,** *n.* —**Syn.** wearisome. See **tiresome.**

te·di·um (tē′dē əm) *n.* tiresomeness; tediousness; the state of being wearisome. [< L *taedium* < *taedet* it is wearisome]

tee (tē) *n. v.* **teed, tee·ing.** —*n.* **1** in quoits and other games, the mark aimed at. **2** in golf: **a** a place from which a player starts in playing each hole. **b** a small, cup-shaped holder, made of plastic or wood on which a ball is placed when a player drives. —*v.* **1** in golf, put (a ball) on a tee. **2 tee off,** drive (a golf ball) from a tee. **3 tee up, a** in golf, put a ball on a tee. **b** prepare or get ready (something) to go into operation: *tee up a project.* [origin uncertain]

A tee

teem[1] (tēm) *v.* **1** be full (of); abound; swarm: *The swamp teemed with mosquitoes.* **2** be fertile, fruitful, or prolific. [OE *tēman* < *tēam* progeny]

hat, āge, cãre, fär; let, ēqual, tėrm; it, īce
hot, ōpen, ôrder; oil, out; cup, pu̇t, rüle, ūse
əbove, takən, pencəl, lemən, circəs
ch, child; ng, long; sh, ship
th, thin; ᴛʜ, then; zh, measure

teem[2] (tēm) *v.* pour; come down in torrents. [ME < ON *tœma* empty]

teen (tēn) *n. Informal.* teenager.

teen-age (tēn′āj′) *adj.* of, for, or being a teen-ager or teen-agers: *a teen-age club.*

teen-ag·er (tēn′āj′ər) *n.* a person in his or her teens.

teens (tēnz) *n.pl.* the years of life from 13 to 19 inclusive.

tee·ny (tē′nē) *adj.* **-ni·er, -ni·est.** *Informal.* tiny.

tee·pee (tē′pē) *n.* a tent of certain North American Indian tribes, consisting of skins, bark, etc. draped over a cone-shaped frame; wigwam. [< Dakota *tipi*] Also, **tepee, tipi.**

tee·ter (tē′tər) *n.* **1** a swaying movement; reeling. **2** a teeter-totter. —*v.* **1** rock unsteadily; sway: *teeter on stilts.* **2** balance on a teeter-totter. [var. of dial. *titter* totter, probably < ON *titra* shake]

tee·ter-tot·ter (tē′tər to′tər) *n.* **1** a plank resting on a support near its middle so that the ends can move up and down; seesaw. **2** a children's game in which the children sit at opposite ends of such a plank and move alternately up and down. **3** a moving up and down or back and forth. —*v.* **1** move up and down on a balanced plank. **2** move up and down or back and forth. —*adj.* moving up and down or back and forth.

teeth (tēth) *n.* pl. of **tooth.**
armed to the teeth, completely armed.
by the skin of one's teeth, very narrowly; barely.
grit one's teeth, endure something without complaining.
in the teeth or **in one's teeth, a** in direct opposition or conflict. **b** to one's face or openly.
in the teeth of, a straight against; in the face of. **b** in defiance of; in spite of.
put teeth in or **into,** put force into.
set one's teeth, prepare to do or endure something with firmness.
show one's teeth, show anger; threaten.
throw (something) in someone's teeth, blame or reproach someone for (something).

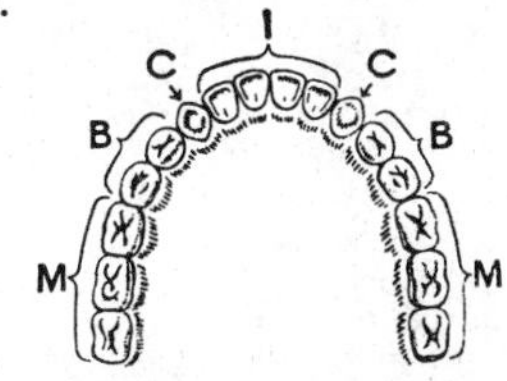

Human teeth: I, incisors; C, canines; B, bicuspids; M, molars.

teethe (tēᴛʜ) *v.* **teethed, teeth·ing.** grow teeth; cut teeth; have teeth grow through the gums.

teeth·ing (tēᴛʜ′ing) *n.* the developing or cutting of teeth; dentition.

tee·to·tal (tē tō′təl) *adj.* **1** of, having to do with, advocating, or pledged to total abstinence from alcoholic liquor. **2** *Informal.* absolute, complete, or entire. [< *total,* with initial letter repeated]

tee·to·tal·er (tē tō′təl ər) *n.* teetotaller.

tee·to·tal·ism (tē tō′təl iz′əm) *n.* the principle or practice of total abstinence from alcoholic liquor.

tee·to·tal·ler or **tee·to·tal·er** (tē tō′təl ər) *n.* a person who never drinks alcoholic liquor.

tee·to·tum (tē tō′təm) *n.* a top spun with the fingers. [< *totum* (< L *totum* all, the whole), with initial letter repeated]

teg·u·lar (teg′yu̇ lər) *adj.* **1** having to do with or resembling a tile. **2** consisting of tiles. **3** arranged like tiles. [< L *tegula* tile]

teg·u·ment (teg′yu̇ mənt) *n.* a natural covering of an animal body, or of any part of it. A turtle's shell is a tegument. [< L *tegumentum* < *tegere* cover]

te-hee (tē hē′) *interj. n. v.* **-heed, -hee·ing.** —*interj.* a word representing the sound of a tittering laugh. —*n.* **1** the sound of a tittering laugh. **2** a titter; snicker; giggle. —*v.* titter; snicker; giggle. [imitative]

tel. 1 telephone. 2 telegram. 3 telegraph.

tel·Au·to·graph (tel ot′ə graf′ or -ô′tə graf′) *n. Trademark.* a telegraph for reproducing handwriting, pictures, etc. The movements of a pen at one end are reproduced by a pen at the other end.

tele- or **tel-** *combining form.* 1 over a distance; far, as in *telegraph.* 2 television, as in *telecast.* 3 telescopic, as in *tele-camera.* [< Gk. *tēle* far]

tel·e·cast (tel′ə kast′) *v.* **-cast** or **-cast·ed, -cast·ing,** *n.* —*v.* broadcast by television. —*n.* 1 a television program. 2 a television broadcast. [< *tele*vision + broad*cast*] —**tel′e·cast′er,** *n.*

tel·e·com (tel′ə kom′) *n.* telecommunication.

tel·e·com·mu·ni·ca·tion (tel′ə kə mū′nə kā′shən) *n.* 1 communication at a distance, especially by means of a system using electromagnetic impulses, as in radio, radar, telegraphy, or television. 2 **telecommunications,** the study or science of such communication.

tel·e·con (tel′ə kon′) *n.* 1 a device that flashes messages sent by teletype from long distances onto a screen, thus enabling groups in widely scattered places to hold conferences. 2 a conference held by means of a telecon. [< radio *tele*type + *con*ference]

tel·e·gen·ic (tel′ə jen′ik) *adj.* appearing attractive on television; suitable for televising. [< *tele*vision + photo*genic*]

tel·e·gram (tel′ə gram′) *n.* a message sent by telegraph.

tel·e·graph[1] (tel′ə graf′) *n.* an apparatus, system, or process for sending messages by electricity. —*v.* send (a message) by telegraph. —**Syn.** *v.* wire.

tel·e·graph[2] (tel′ə graf′) *v. Cdn. Informal.* especially in Quebec, vote illegally by impersonating another voter. [< Cdn.F]

te·leg·ra·pher (tə leg′rə fər) *n.* a person who sends and receives messages by telegraph.

tel·e·graph·ic (tel′ə graf′ik) *adj.* of or having to do with the telegraph; sent as a telegram. —**tel′e·graph′i·cal·ly,** *adv.*

te·leg·ra·phy (tə leg′rə fē) *n.* the making or operating of telegraphs.

tel·e·mark (tel′ə märk′) *n.* in skiing, a stop or turn made by advancing and turning the outside ski. [< *Telemark,* a region in Norway]

te·lem·e·ter (*n.* tə lem′ə tər; *v.* tel′ə mēt ər) *n.* 1 a device for measuring heat, radiation, etc. and transmitting the information to a receiving station. 2 a range finder. —*v.* measure and transmit by telemeter.

tel·e·met·ric (tel′ə met′rik) *adj.* of or having to do with telemeters or telemetry.

te·lem·e·try (tə lem′ə trē) *n.* 1 the use of telemeters for measuring and transmitting information. 2 the equipment used in this process: *The ground telemetry indicated that the retrorockets on the space capsule had been fitted.*

tel·e·o·log·i·cal (tel′ē ə loj′ə kəl or tē′lē ə loj′ə kəl) *adj.* 1 of or having to do with teleology. 2 relating to final causes. 3 having to do with design or purpose in nature.

tel·e·ol·o·gy (tel′ē ol′ə jē or tē′lē ol′ə jē) *n.* 1 the fact or quality of being purposeful. 2 purpose or design as shown in nature. 3 the doctrine that mechanisms alone cannot explain the facts of nature, and that purposes have causal power. 4 the doctrine that all things in nature were made to fulfil a plan or design. [< NL *teleologia* < Gk. *telos* end + *-logos* treating of]

tel·e·path·ic (tel′ə path′ik) *adj.* 1 of or having to do with telepathy. 2 by telepathy.

tel·e·path·i·cal·ly (tel′ə path′ik lē) *adv.* by telepathy.

te·lep·a·thist (tə lep′ə thist) *n.* 1 a student of or believer in telepathy. 2 a person who has telepathic power.

te·lep·a·thy (tə lep′ə thē) *n.* the communication of one mind with another without the use of signs that can be seen, heard, or received by any of the senses.

tel·e·phone (tel′ə fōn′) *n. v.* **-phoned, -phon·ing.** —*n.* an apparatus, system, or process for transmitting sound or speech by electricity. —*v.* 1 talk through a telephone; send (a message) by telephone. 2 make a telephone call to. —**tel′e·phon′er,** *n.*

tel·e·phon·ic (tel′ə fon′ik) *adj.* of or having to do with the telephone; by the telephone. —**tel′e·phon′i·cal·ly,** *adv.*

te·leph·o·ny (tə lef′ə nē) *n.* the making or operating of telephones.

tel·e·pho·to (tel′ə fō′tō) *n.* a telephotograph (def. 2). —*adj.* telephotographic.

tel·e·pho·to·graph (tel′e fō′tə graf′) *n.* 1 a picture taken with a camera having a telephoto lens. 2 a picture sent by telegraphy. Telephotographs in newspapers are often called wire photos. —*v.* 1 take a picture with a camera having a telephoto lens. 2 send such a picture.

tel·e·pho·to·graph·ic (tel′ə fō′tə graf′ik) *adj.* of or having to do with telephotography.

tel·e·pho·tog·ra·phy (tel′ə fə tog′rə fē) *n.* 1 the method or process of photographing distant objects by using a camera with a telephoto lens. 2 the method or process of sending and reproducing pictures by telegraph.

telephoto lens a camera lens for producing an enlarged image of a distant object.

tel·e·print·er (tel′ə print′ər) *n. Esp.Brit.* a teletypewriter.

Tel·e·prompt·er (tel′ə promp′tər) *n. Trademark.* a device consisting of a moving band that gives a prepared speech line for line, used by speakers who are being televised. [< *tele*vision *prompter*]

tel·e·ran (tel′ə ran′) *n.* a system of air navigation by which radar mappings and other data are collected by ground stations and transmitted to aircraft by means of television. [short for *Tele*(*vision*) *R*(*adar*) *A*(*ir*) *N*(*avigation*)]

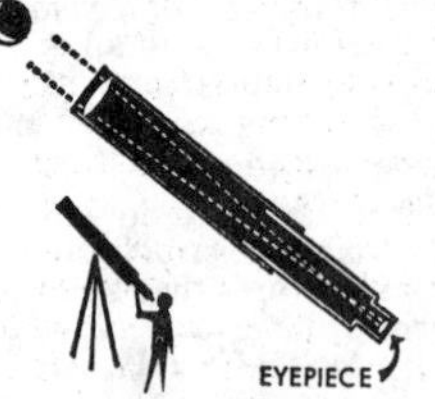

A refracting telescope   A reflecting telescope

tel·e·scope (tel′ə skōp′) *n. v.* **-scoped, -scop·ing.** —*n.* 1 an instrument for making distant objects appear nearer and larger. The stars are studied by means of telescopes. 2 a radio telescope. —*v.* 1 force or be forced together one inside another like the sliding tubes of some telescopes: *When the two railway trains crashed into each other, the cars were telescoped.* 2 shorten; condense. [< NL *telescopium,* ult. < Gk. *tēle* far + *-skopion* instrument for observing < *skopeein* watch]

tel·e·scop·ic (tel′ə skop′ik) *adj.* 1 of or having to do with a telescope. 2 obtained or seen by means of a telescope: *a telescopic view of the moon.* 3 visible only through a telescope. 4 far-seeing. 5 consisting of parts that slide inside one another like the tubes of some telescopes.

tel·e·scop·i·cal·ly (tel′ə skop′ik lē) *adv.* 1 in a telescopic manner. 2 by a telescope.

tel·e·thon (tel′ə thon′) *n.* a television program lasting a very long time and, usually, serving to solicit funds for charity. [< *tele-* + *-thon* as in *marathon*]

tel·e·type (tel′ə tīp′) *n. v.* **-typed, -typ·ing.** —*n.* 1 **Teletype,** *Trademark.* a telegraphic apparatus for sending and receiving signals by means of two instruments resembling typewriters. 2 a system of sending signals by Teletype. 3 a message sent by Teletype. —*v.* send (a message) by Teletype.

tel·e·type·writ·er (tel′ə tīp′rīt′ər) *n.* a machine resembling a typewriter, used in teletyping.

tel·e·view (tel′ə vū′) *v.* watch by means of television.

tel·e·vise (tel′ə vīz′) *v.* **-vised, -vis·ing.** 1 send by television. 2 see by television.

tel·e·vi·sion (tel′ə vizh′ən) *n.* 1 the process of transmitting the image of an object, scene, or event by radio or wire so that a person in some other place can see it at once. In television, waves of light from an object are changed into electric waves that are transmitted by radio or wire, and then changed back into waves of light that produce an image of the object on a screen. **2** the apparatus on which these pictures may be seen. **3** the business of television broadcasting; the television industry. *Abbrev.*: TV or T.V.

tell (tel) *v.* **told, tell·ing. 1** put in words; say: *Tell the truth.* **2** tell to; inform: *Tell us about it.* **3** make known: *Don't tell where the money is.* **4** tell something: *He was always telling, never doing.* **5** act as a talebearer; reveal (something secret or private): *Promise not to tell.* **6** recognize; know; distinguish: *He couldn't tell which house it was.* **7** say to; order; command: *Tell him to stop!* **8** say to with force: *I don't like it, I tell you.* **9** count; count one by one: *The nun tells her beads.* **10** have effect or force: *Every blow told.*
I (can) tell you, yes indeed; I emphasize.
let me tell you, yes indeed; I emphasize.
tell me another, *Slang.* that's hard to believe; go on! (used sarcastically)
tell of, be an indication or sign of; show.
tell off, a count off; count off and detach for some special duty. **b** strike back sharply in words; castigate.
tell on, a inform on; tell tales about. **b** have a harmful effect on; break down: *The strain told on the man's health.*
tell time, know what time it is by the clock.
You're telling me! *Slang.* I agree with you! [OE *tellan* < *talu* tale] **—Syn. 1** utter. **3** mention.

tell·a·ble (tel′ə bəl) *adj.* capable or worthy of being told.

tell·er (tel′ər) *n.* **1** one who tells a story. **2** a bank cashier who accepts deposits and pays out withdrawals. **3** a person who counts votes at an election or at the end of a debate.

tell·ing (tel′ing) *adj.* having effect or force; striking: *a telling blow.* **—Syn.** effective, potent, forcible.

tell·ing·ly (tel′ing lē) *adv.* effectively; forcefully.

tell·tale (tel′tāl′) *n.* **1** a person who tells tales on others; a person who reveals private or secret matters from malice. **2** a thing that informs or warns. *—adj.* telling what is not supposed to be told; revealing.

tel·lu·ride (tel′yù rīd′ or tel′yù rid) *n.* a compound of tellurium with an electropositive element or a radical.

tel·lu·ri·um (te lür′ē əm) *n.* a rare, silver-white chemical element resembling sulphur in its chemical properties and usually occurring in nature combined with gold, silver, or other metals. *Symbol*: Te; *at.no.* 52; at.wt. 127.60. [< NL < L *tellus, -uris* earth]

tel·lu·rom·e·ter (tel′yù rom′ə tər) *n.* an electronic instrument for measuring distance by timing a radio microwave from one point to another and back. [< *tellur-* earth < L *tellus, telluris* + E *-meter*]

tel·ly (tel′ē) *n. Brit. Slang.* **1** television. **2 tellies,** *pl.* television programs.

Tel·star (tel′stär′) *n. Trademark.* an artificial satellite for receiving radio and television signals, etc. and reflecting them back to earth.

Tel·u·gu (tel′ə gü′) *n.* a Dravidian language, spoken in southeastern India.

te·mer·i·ty (tə mer′ə tē) *n.* reckless boldness; rashness. [< L *temeritas* < *temere* heedlessly] **—Syn.** foolhardiness, audacity.

temp. 1 temperature. **2** temporary. **3** in the time of. (for L *tempore*)

tem·per (tem′pər) *n.* **1** a state of mind; disposition; condition: *She was in a good temper.* **2** an angry state of mind: *In her temper she broke a vase.* **3** a calm state of mind: *He became angry and lost his temper.* **4** the hardness, toughness, etc. of a mixture given by tempering: *The temper of the clay was right for shaping.* **5** a substance added to something to modify its properties or qualities. [< v.]
—v. **1** moderate; soften: *Temper justice with mercy.* **2** bring or be brought to a proper or desired condition by mixing or preparing. A painter tempers his colors by mixing them with oil. Steel is tempered by heating it and working it till it has the proper degree of hardness and toughness. **3** in music, tune or adjust the pitch of (an instrument, a voice, etc.). [OE *temprian* < L *temperare,* originally, observe due measure < *tempus, -poris* time, interval] **—Syn.** *n.* **1** mood, humor. See **disposition.** *–v.* **1** qualify, modify.

hat, āge, cãre, fär; let, ēqual, tėrm; it, īce
hot, ōpen, ôrder; oil, out; cup, pùt, rüle, ūse
əbove, takən, pencəl, lemən, circəs
ch, child; ng, long; sh, ship
th, thin; ᴛʜ, then; zh, measure

tem·per·a (tem′pər ə) *n.* in painting: **1** a method in which colors are mixed with white of egg or some similar substance instead of oil. **2** the paint used. [< Ital.]

tem·per·a·ment (tem′pər ə mənt or tem′prə mənt) *n.* **1** a person's nature or disposition: *shy temperament.* **2** an unusual nature or disposition that is not inclined to submit to ordinary rules or restraints. An artist or an actress often has temperament. [< L *temperamentum* < *temperare.* See TEMPER.] **—Syn. 1** See **disposition.**

tem·per·a·men·tal (tem′pər ə men′təl or tem′prə men′təl) *adj.* **1** due to temperament; constitutional: *Cats have a temperamental dislike for water.* **2** showing a strongly marked individual temperament. **3** subject to moods and whims; easily irritated; sensitive. **—tem′per·a·men′tal·ly,** *adv.*

tem·per·ance (tem′pər əns or tem′prəns) *n.* **1** moderation in action, speech, habits, etc. **2** moderation in the use of alcoholic drinks. **3** the principle and practice of not using alcoholic drinks at all. [ME < AF *temperaunce* < L *temperantia* < *temperare.* See TEMPER.] **—Syn. 3** abstinence.

tem·per·ate (tem′pər it or tem′prit) *adj.* **1** not very hot and not very cold: *a temperate climate.* **2** self-restrained; moderate: *He spoke in a calm, temperate manner.* **3** moderate in using alcoholic drinks; abstemious. **4** in music, tempered. [< L *temperatus,* pp. of *temperare.* See TEMPER.] **—tem′per·ate·ness,** *n.* **—Syn. 2** calm, dispassionate. See **moderate.**

tem·per·ate·ly (tem′pər it lē or tem′prit lē) *adv.* **1** with moderation. **2** without overindulgence. **3** without violence or extravagance.

Temperate Zone or **temperate zone** either of the two parts of the earth between the tropics and the polar circles. See **zone** for diagram.

tem·per·a·ture (tem′pər ə cher′ or tem′prə chər, tem′pər ə chür′ or tem′prə chür′) *n.* **1** the degree of heat or cold. The temperature of freezing water is 32° Fahrenheit. **2** the degree of heat contained in a human or other living body. The temperature of a person who has a fever is over 98.6° Fahrenheit. **3** a level of body heat that is above normal; fever: *He stayed home all day because he had a temperature.* [< L *temperatura,* ult. < *tempus, -poris* time, season]

tem·pered (tem′pərd) *adj.* **1** softened; moderated. **2** having a (specified) state of mind: *a good-tempered person.* **3** treated so as to become hard but not too brittle: *The sword was made of tempered steel.* **4** in music, tuned or adjusted in pitch according to equal temperament.

tem·pest (tem′pist) *n.* **1** a violent storm with much wind. **2** a violent disturbance: *a tempest of anger.* [ME < OF *tempest(e)* < var. of L *tempestas* < *tempus* time, season]

tem·pes·tu·ous (tem pes′chü əs) *adj.* **1** stormy: *a tempestuous night.* **2** violent: *a tempestuous argument.* **—tem·pes′tu·ous·ly,** *adv.* **—tem·pes′tu·ous·ness,** *n.*

Tem·plar (tem′plər) *n.* a member of a religious and military order founded among the Crusaders about 1118 to protect the Holy Sepulchre and pilgrims to the Holy Land. [< Med.L *templarius* < L *templum* temple[1]]

tem·plate (tem′plit) *n.* **1** a thin piece of wood or metal used as a pattern or mould in cutting metal, stone, etc. **2** any similar pattern or model. **3** in building: **a** a stout piece of wood or stone used under a beam or girder to distribute downward thrust. **b** a similar piece used to support rafters or joists over a doorway, etc. **4** a wedge or block to support a ship's keel. Also, **templet.** [< var. of *templet*; probably influenced by PLATE]

tem·ple[1] (tem′pəl) *n.* **1** a building used for the service or worship of a god or gods. **2** Also, **Temple. a** in ancient Jerusalem, any of three temples built at different times by the Jews. **b** the first of these three temples built by Solomon. I Kings 6 and 7. **3** any building set apart for Christian worship; church. **4** a place in which God specially dwells. 5 a Mormon church. [OE *temp(e)l* < L *templum*] —**Syn.** *n.* **1** sanctuary, tabernacle.

tem·ple[2] (tem′pəl) *n.* the flattened part on either side of the forehead. [ME < OF *temple*, ult. < L *tempus*]

tem·ple[3] (tem′pəl) *n.* a device in a loom for stretching the web. [ME *temple* < MF, prob. < L *templus* small timber]

tem·plet (tem′plit) *n.* template. [< F *templet, templette,* dim. of *temple* temple[3]]

tem·po (tem′pō) *n.* **-pos, -pi** (-pē). **1** in music: **a** the speed at which a composition is performed. Andante, allegro, and presto are tempos used commonly in music. **b** the proper or characteristic speed of movement: *waltz tempo.* **2** rhythm; characteristic rhythm: *the fast tempo of modern life.* [< Ital. *tempo* time < L *tempus.* Doublet of TENSE[2].]

tem·po·ral[1] (tem′pə rəl or tem′prəl) *adj.* **1** of time. **2** lasting for a time only. **3** of this life only. **4** not religious or sacred; worldly. **5** in grammar: **a** expressing time, as an adverb or a clause. **b** of tense. [ME < OF < L *temporalis* < *tempus, -poris* time] —**Syn. 2** temporary, transient. **3** earthly, terrestrial.

tem·po·ral[2] (tem′pə rəl or tem′prəl) *adj.* in anatomy, of the temples or sides of the forehead. [ME < OF < L *temporalis* < *tempus, -poris* temple[2]]

tem·po·ral·i·ty (tem′pə ral′ə tē) *n.* **-ties. 1** a temporal character or nature; temporariness. **2** something temporal; a temporal matter or affair. **3** the laity.

tem·po·ral·ly (tem′pə rəl ē or tem′prəl ē) *adv.* in a temporal manner; as regards temporal matters.

tem·po·rar·i·ly (tem′pə rer′ə lē or tem′pə rãr′ə lē) *adv.* for a short time; for the present.

tem·po·rar·y (tem′pə rer′ē) *adj.* lasting for a short time only; used for the time being; not permanent: *a temporary shelter.* [< L *temporarius* < *tempus, -poris* time] —**tem′po·rar′i·ness,** *n.*

Syn. Temporary, transient = lasting or staying only for a time. **Temporary** emphasizes existing or being used or in effect for a time, and describes either something meant only for the time being or something liable to come to an end at any time: *He has a temporary job. Our school is a temporary building.* **Transient** emphasizes quick passing, and describes something that stays or lasts only a short time: *His nervousness was transient, and passed when he began to speak.*

tem·po·ri·za·tion (tem′pə rə zā′shən or tem′pə rī zā′shən) *n.* the act of temporizing; a compromise.

tem·po·rize (tem′pə rīz′) *v.* **-rized, -riz·ing. 1** evade immediate action or decision in order to gain time, avoid trouble, etc. **2** fit one's acts to the time or occasion. **3** make or discuss terms; negotiate. [< MF *temporiser,* ult. < L *tempus, -poris* time] —**tem′po·riz′er,** *n.*

tempt (tempt) *v.* **1** make, or try to make (a person) do something, especially something wrong: *The sight of food tempted the hungry man to steal.* **2** appeal strongly to; attract: *That candy tempts me.* **3** *Archaic.* test: *God tempted Abraham by asking him to sacrifice his son.* **4 tempt Providence, fate, etc.,** take a foolish risk; ask for trouble. [< L *temptare* try]—**tempt′a·ble,** *adj.* —**Syn 1.** lure, inveigle, decoy. **2** allure, entice.

temp·ta·tion (temp tā′shən) *n.* **1** a tempting. **2** the fact or state of being tempted. **3** anything that tempts. —**Syn. 3** attraction, lure, enticement, inducement.

tempt·er (temp′tər) *n.* **1** anybody or anything that tempts. **2 the Tempter,** the Devil; Satan.

tempt·ing (temp′ting) *adj.* that tempts; alluring; inviting. —**tempt′ing·ly,** *adv.*

tempt·ress (temp′tris) *n.* a woman who tempts.

tem·pu·ra (tem pu̇r′ə or tem′pu̇ rə) *n.* a dish of deep-fried shrimp, vegetables, etc. [< Japanese]

tem·pus fu·git (tem′pəs fū′jit) *Latin.* time flies.

ten (ten) *n.* **1** one more than nine; 10. **2** a set of ten persons or things. **3** a playing card, etc. having ten spots. —*adj.* being one more than nine. [OE *tīen, tēn*]

ten. tenor.

ten·a·bil·i·ty (ten′ə bil′ə tē) *n.* the fact or quality of being tenable.

ten·a·ble (ten′ə bəl) *adj.* capable of being held or defended: *a tenable position, a tenable theory.* [< F *tenable* < *tenir* hold < L *tenere*] —**ten′a·bly,** *adv.*

te·na·cious (ti nā′shəs) *adj.* **1** holding fast: *the tenacious jaws of a bulldog, a person tenacious of his rights.* **2** stubborn; persistent: *a tenacious salesman.* **3** able to remember: *a tenacious memory.* **4** holding fast together; not easily pulled apart. **5** sticky. [< L *tenax, -acis* < *tenere* hold] —**te·na′cious·ly,** *adv.* —**Syn. 2** obstinate. **3** retentive.

te·nac·i·ty (ti nas′ə tē) *n.* **1** firmness in holding fast. **2** stubbornness; persistence. **3** the ability to remember. **4** firmness in holding together; toughness. **5** stickiness.

ten·an·cy (ten′ən sē) *n.* **-cies. 1** the state of being a tenant; occupying and paying rent for land or buildings. **2** the property so held. **3** the length of time a tenant occupies a property.

ten·ant (ten′ənt) *n.* **1** a person paying rent for the temporary use of the land or buildings of another person: *That building has apartments for one hundred tenants.* **2** a person or thing that occupies: *Birds are tenants of the trees.* —*v.* hold or occupy as a tenant; inhabit. [< F *tenant,* originally ppr. of *tenir* hold < L *tenere*] —**ten′ant·less,** *adj.*

ten·ant·ry (ten′ənt rē) *n.* **-ries. 1** all the tenants on an estate. **2** a tenancy.

tench (tench) *n.* **tench** or **tench·es.** a fresh-water fish of Europe that is noted for the length of time it can live out of water. [ME < OF *tenche* < LL *tinca*]

Ten Commandments the ten rules for living and for worship that God revealed to Moses on Mount Sinai, according to the Bible. Exod. 20:2-17; Deut. 5:6-21.

tend[1] (tend) *v.* **1** be apt; incline (*to*): *Fruit tends to decay. We tend to use more mechanical appliances in our homes nowadays.* **2** move (toward); be directed: *The coastline tends to the south here.* [ME < OF *tendre* < L *tendere* stretch, aim. Doublet of TENDER[2].]

tend[2] (tend) *v.* **1** take care of; look after; attend to: *He tends shop for his father. A shepherd tends his flock.* **2** serve; wait (upon). **3** in nautical use, stand by and watch over (a line, anchor cable, etc.). **4** *Informal.* pay attention. [< *attend*]

tend·ance (ten′dəns) *n.* attention; care.

tend·en·cy (ten′dən sē) *n.* **-cies. 1** an inclination or leaning toward; a trend toward: *Boys have a stronger tendency to fight than girls.* **2** a natural disposition to move, proceed, or act in some direction or toward some point, end, or result: *Wood has a tendency to swell if it gets wet.* [< Med. L *tendentia* < L *tendere.* See TEND[1].] —**Syn. 1** bent, propensity, proneness. **2** See **direction.**

ten·den·tious (ten den′shəs) *adj.* having a tendency to take sides: *a tendentious statement.* [< Med. L *tendentia.* See TENDENCY.]

ten·der[1] (ten′dər) *adj.* **1** not hard or tough; soft: *tender meat.* **2** not strong and hardy; delicate: *tender young grass.* **3** kind; affectionate; loving: *She spoke tender words to the child.* **4** not rough or crude; gentle: *With tender, loving hands, the mother bathed her baby.* **5** young; immature: *Two years old is a tender age.* **6** sensitive; painful; sore: *a tender wound.* **7** feeling pain or grief easily: *She has a tender heart and would never hurt anyone.* **8** considerate; careful: *He handles people in a tender manner.* **9** requiring careful or tactful handling: *a tender situation.* [ME < OF *tendre* < L *tener*] —**ten′der·ly,** *adv.* —**Syn. 2** fragile, weak. **3** compassionate, merciful. **4** mild, sympathetic.

ten·der[2] (ten′dər) *v.* **1** offer formally: *He tendered his thanks.* **2** in business, make an offer to buy, supply, etc.: *Several firms tendered for the contract.* **3** in law, offer (money, goods, etc.) in payment of a debt or other obligation.

—*n.* **1** a formal offer: *She refused his tender of marriage.* **2** the thing offered. Money that may be offered as payment for a debt is called legal tender. **3** in business, an offer to buy, supply, etc. **4** in law, an offer of money, goods, etc. in payment of a debt, etc. [< OF *tendre* < L *tendere* extend. Doublet of TEND[1].] —**ten′der·er,** *n.* —**Syn.** *v.* **1** proffer, present. See **offer.** –*n.* **1** proposal, proffer, overture.

tend·er[3] (ten′dər) *n.* **1** a person or thing that tends

hat, āge, cãre, fär; let, ēqual, tėrm; it, īce
hot, ōpen, ôrder; oil, out; cup, pu̇t, rüle, ūse
əbove, takən, pencəl, lemən, circəs
ch, child; ng, long; sh, ship
th, thin; ᴛʜ, then; zh, measure

another. **2** a small boat carried or towed by a big one and used for landing passengers. **3** a small ship used for carrying supplies and passengers to and from larger ships. **4** the car attached behind a locomotive and used for carrying coal, oil, water, etc. [< *tend*[2]]

ten·der·foot (ten′dər fu̇t′) *n.* **-foots** or **-feet.** *Informal.* **1** a newcomer to the pioneer life of the West. **2** a person not used to rough living and hardships. **3** an inexperienced person; beginner. **4** a young person in the first stage of being a Boy Scout or Girl Guide.

ten·der·heart·ed (ten′dər här′tid) *adj.* kindly; sympathetic. —**ten′der-heart′ed·ly,** *adv.* —**ten′der·heart′ed·ness,** *n.*

ten·der·ize (ten′də rīz′) *v.* **-ized, -iz·ing.** make (meat) tender; soften.

ten·der·loin (ten′dər loin′) *n.* a tender part of the loin of beef or pork.

tenderloin district a district of a city noted for its high incidence of crime, police leniency, and political corruption. [from the rich living supposed to be gained there by corrupt policemen]

ten·der·ness (ten′dər nis) *n.* **1** the quality or state of being tender. **2** a tender feeling.

ten·di·nous (ten′də nəs) *adj.* **1** of or like a tendon. **2** consisting of tendons. [< F *tendineux* < *tendon* tendon < Med.L. See TENDON.]

ten·don (ten′dən) *n.* a tough, strong band or cord of tissue that joins a muscle to a bone or some other part; sinew. [< Med.L *tendo, -onis* < Gk. *tenōn*; influenced by L *tendere* stretch]

TENDONS

tendon of Achilles the tendon that connects the muscles of the calf of the leg with the bone of the heel.

ten·dril (ten′drəl) *n.* **1** in botany, a threadlike part of climbing plants that attaches itself to something else for support. **2** something resembling such a part of a plant: *tendrils of hair curling about a child's face.* [< F *tendrillon,* ult. < L *tener* tender]

ten·e·brous (ten′ə brəs) *adj.* dark; gloomy; dim. [< L *tenebrosus* < *tenebrae* darkness]

ten·e·ment (ten′ə mənt) *n.* **1** a tenement house. **2** any house or building to live in; a dwelling house. **3** a part of a house or building occupied by a tenant as a separate dwelling. **4** an abode; habitation. [ME < OF *tenement,* ult. < L *tenere* hold]

tenement house an old building, especially in a poor section of a city, divided into sets of rooms for separate families.

ten·et (ten′it; *esp.Brit.,* tē′nit) *n.* a doctrine, principle, belief, or opinion held as true. [< L *tenet* he holds]

ten·fold (ten′fōld′) *adj. adv. n.* ten times as much or as many.

ten-gallon hat a large, wide-brimmed hat, often worn by cowboys. [< Sp. *galón* braid, cowboy hats being originally decorated with a number of braids; confused with *gallon,* as if in reference to the hat's size]

Tenn. Tennessee.

ten·nis (ten′is) *n.* **1** a game played on a special court by two or four players who knock a ball back and forth over a net with a racket (**tennis racket**). **2** lawn tennis. **3** court tennis. [ME < AF *tenetz* hold!, ult. < L *tenere*]

tennis court a place prepared and marked out to play tennis on.

ten·on (ten′ən) *n.* the end of a piece of wood cut so as to fit into a hole (the mortise) in another piece and so form a joint. See **mortise** for picture. —*v.* **1** cut so as to form a tenon. **2** fit together with tenon and mortise. [ME < OF, ult. < L *tenere* hold]

ten·or (ten′ər) *n.* **1** the general tendency; course: *The calm tenor of her life has never been disturbed by excitement or trouble.* **2** the general meaning or drift: *I understand French well enough to get the tenor of his lecture.* **3** an adult male voice higher than a baritone but lower than an alto. **4** in music: **a** a singer with such a voice. **b** a part for such a voice or for a corresponding instrument. **c** an instrument playing such a part. —*adj.* in music: **1** of or for the tenor. **2** that can sing or play a tenor part. [ME < OF < L *tenor,* originally, a holding on < *tenere* hold]

ten·pen·ny (ten′pen′ē or ten′pən ē) *adj.* **1** *Brit.* worth ten pennies. **2** designating a kind of three-inch nail, once costing ten pennies per hundred.

ten·pin (ten′pin′) *n.* **1 ten·pins,** a game played with ten wooden pins at which a ball is bowled to knock them down. **2** one of the pins used in this game.

☞ **Tenpins,** the game (def. 1), is plural in form and singular in use: *Tenpins is similar to ninepins.* **Tenpins,** the pins used in the game (def. 2), is plural in form and in use: *The tenpins were all knocked down.*

tense[1] (tens) *adj.* **tens·er, tens·est,** *v.* **tensed, tens·ing.** —*adj.* **1** stretched tight; strained to stiffness: *a tense rope, a face tense with pain.* **2** strained; keyed up: *tense feelings, a tense moment.* —*v.* stretch tight; stiffen: *He tensed his muscles for the leap.* [< L *tensus,* pp. of *tendere* stretch] —**tense′ly,** *adv.* —**tense′ness,** *n.* —**Syn.** *adj.* **1** taut, rigid.

tense[2] (tens) *n.* in grammar: **1** a form of a verb that shows the time of the action or state expressed by the verb. *He obeys* is in the present tense. *He obeyed* is in the past tense. *He will obey* is in the future tense. **2** a set of such forms for the various persons. *Example:* The present tense of *obey* is: *I obey, you obey, he obeys, we obey, you obey, they obey.* [ME < OF *tens* time < L *tempus.* Doublet of TEMPO.] —**tense′less,** *adj.*

ten·si·ble (ten′sə bəl) *adj.* capable of being stretched. [< Med.L *tensibilis* < L *tendere* stretch]

ten·sile (ten′sīl or ten′səl) *adj.* **1** of or having to do with tension: *Steel has great tensile strength.* **2** capable of being stretched; ductile. [< NL *tensilis* < L *tendere* stretch]

ten·sil·i·ty (ten sil′ə tē) *n.* a tensile quality; ductility.

ten·sion (ten′shən) *n.* **1** a stretching. **2** a stretched condition: *The tension of the spring is caused by the weight.* **3** mental strain: *A mother feels tension when her baby is sick.* **4** a strained condition: *political tension.* **5** a stress caused by the action of a pulling force. An elevator exerts tension on the cables supporting it. **6** a device to control the pull or strain on something. The tension in a sewing machine may be adjusted to hold the thread tight or loose. **7** voltage: *high-tension wires.* **8** the pressure of a gas. [< LL *tensio, -onis* < L *tendere* stretch]

ten·sion·al (ten′shən əl) *adj.* of or having to do with tension.

ten·si·ty (ten′sə tē) *n.* a tense quality or state.

ten·sor (ten′sər or ten′sôr) *n.* **1** in physiology, a muscle that stretches or tightens some part of the body. **2** in mathematics, a vector that can only be defined by reference to more than three components. [< NL]

ten-strike (ten′strīk′) *n.* **1** in the game of tenpins, the stroke that knocks down all the pins. **2** *Informal.* any completely successful stroke or act.

tent (tent) *n.* **1** a movable shelter made of cloth, usually canvas, or skins, supported by a pole or poles and guy ropes. **2** a tentlike device to regulate the temperature and humidity of the air in treating certain respiratory diseases. —*v.* **1** live in a tent. **2** cover with a tent. [ME < OF *tente,* ult. < L *tendere* stretch] —**tent′like′,** *adj.*

ten·ta·cle (ten′tə kəl) *n.* **1** a long, slender, flexible growth on the head or around the mouth of an animal, used to touch, hold, or move; feeler. **2** a sensitive, hairlike growth on a plant. **3** something that resembles a tentacle in its reach and grasp: *The tentacles of a dictator's power reach into every home.* [< NL *tentaculum* < L *tentare* try. See TENTATIVE.]

ten·tac·u·lar (ten tak′yu̇ lər) *adj.* of, forming, or resembling tentacles.

tent·age (tent′ij) *n.* **1** a supply or number of tents. **2** equipment for tents.

ten·ta·tive (ten′tə tiv) *adj.* done as a trial or experiment;

experimental: *a tentative plan.* [< Med.L *tentativus* < L *tentare* try out, intensive of *tendere* stretch, aim; associated in L with *temptare* feel out] —**ten′ta·tive·ly,** *adv.* —**ten′ta·tive·ness,** *n.*

tent caterpillar a caterpillar that spins tentlike silken webs in which it lives.

ten·ter (ten′tər) *n.* a framework on which cloth is stretched so that it may set or dry evenly without shrinking. —*v.* stretch (cloth) on a tenter. [ult. < L *tentus*, pp. of *tendere* stretch]

ten·ter·hook (ten′tər hůk′) *n.* **1** one of the hooks or bent nails that hold the cloth stretched on a tenter. **2 on tenterhooks,** in painful suspense; anxious.

tenth (tenth) *adj. n.* **1** next after the ninth; last in a series of 10. **2** one, or being one, of 10 equal parts.

tenth·ly (tenth′lē) *adv.* in the tenth place.

ten·u·i·ty (ten ū′ə tē or ti nü′ə tē) *n.* a rarefied condition; thinness; slightness.

ten·u·ous (ten′ū əs) *adj.* **1** thin; slender. **2** not dense: *tenuous air.* **3** having slight importance; not substantial. [< L *tenuis* thin] —**ten′u·ous·ly,** *adv.* —**ten′u·ous·ness,** *n.*

ten·ure (ten′yər) *n.* **1** a holding; possessing. **2** the length of time of holding or possessing: *The tenure of office of the president of our club is one year.* **3** the manner of holding land, buildings, etc. from a feudal lord or superior. **4** the conditions, terms, etc. on which anything is held or occupied. [ME < OF *tenure*, ult. < L *tenere* hold]

te·nu·to (te nü′tō) *adj.* in music, held or sustained to its full time value. [< Ital. *tenuto*, pp. of *tenere* hold < L]

te·pee (tē′pē) *n.* teepee.

tep·id (tep′id) *adj.* slightly warm; lukewarm. [< L *tepidus*] —**te′pid·ly,** *adv.* —**tep′id·ness,** *n.*

te·pid·i·ty (ti pid′ə tē) *n.* lukewarmness; tepid condition.

te·qui·la (tə kē′lə) *n.* **1** a Mexican agave. **2** a strong liquor distilled from roasted tequila stems. [< Am.E < Am.Sp. < *Tequila* a town in Mexico]

ter. 1 territory. **2** territorial. **3** terrace.

ter·bi·um (tėr′bē əm) *n.* a rare metallic chemical element of the yttrium group. *Symbol*: Tb; *at.no.* 65; *at.wt.* 158.924. [< *terb-*, abstracted from *Ytterby*, a town in Sweden]

ter·cel (tėr′səl) *n.* a male falcon or goshawk, especially the male of the peregrine falcon. [ME < OF *tercel*, ult. < L *tertius* third]

ter·cen·te·nar·y (tėr′sen ten′ə rē or tėr′sen tēn′ə rē) *adj. n.* **-nar·ies.** —*adj.* having to do with a period of 300 years. —*n.* **1** a period of 300 years. **2** a 300th anniversary. [< L *ter* three times + E *centenary*]

ter·cet (tėr′sit or tėr set′) *n.* **1** a group of three lines rhyming together, or connected by rhyme with the adjacent group or groups of three lines. **2** in music, a triplet. [< F < Ital. *terzetto*, ult. < L *tertius* third]

te·re·do (tə rē′dō) *n.* **-dos.** a small wormlike mollusc that bores into and destroys the wood of boats, wharves, etc. [< L < Gk. *terēdōn* < *tereein* bore]

ter·gi·ver·sate (tėr′jə vər sāt′) *v.* **-sat·ed, -sat·ing.** **1** change one's attitude or opinions with respect to a cause or subject; turn renegade. **2** shift or shuffle; evade. [< L *tergiversatus*, ult. < *tergum* back + *vertere* turn] —**ter′gi·ver·sa′tor,** *n.* —**ter′gi·ver·sa′tion,** *n.*

term (tėrm) *n.* **1** a word or phrase used in a recognized and definite sense in some particular subject, science, art, business, etc.: *medical terms, terms about radio.* **2** a word or expression: *an abstract term, a term of reproach.* **3** a set period of time; the length of time that a thing lasts: *a president's term of office.* **4** one of the long periods into which the school year may be divided: *the fall term.* **5** in law, one of the periods of time when certain courts are in session. **6** in mathematics: **a** one of the members in a proportion or ratio. **b** one of the parts of a compound algebraic expression. *Example*: In $13ax^2-2bxy+y$, $13ax^2$, $2bxy$, and y are the terms. **7** in logic: **a** word or words that form the subject or predicate of a proposition. **b** one of the three parts of a syllogism. **8** *Archaic.* a boundary; end; limit. **9 terms,** *pl.* conditions: *the terms of a treaty.* **10 bring to terms,** compel to agree, assent, or submit; force to come to terms. **11 terms,** *pl.* way of speaking: *flattering terms.* **12 terms,** *pl.* personal relations: *on good terms, on speaking terms.* **13 terms of reference,** the matters referred to a person, committee, etc. for study; instructions indicating the scope of an inquiry.
—*v.* name; call; describe as: *He might be termed handsome.* [ME < OF *terme* < L *terminus* end, boundary line. Doublet of TERMINUS.] —**Syn.** *n.* **3** duration. **4** semester. **9** stipulations, provisions.

ter·ma·gan·cy (tėr′mə gən sē) *n.* shrewishness.

ter·ma·gant (tėr′mə gənt) *n.* a violent, quarrelling, scolding woman. —*adj.* violent; quarrelling; scolding. [ME < OF *Tervagan*, a fictitious Moslem deity]

ter·mi·na·bil·i·ty (tėr′mə nə bil′ə tē) *n.* the fact or quality of being terminable.

ter·mi·na·ble (tėr′mə nə bəl) *adj.* **1** that can be ended: *The contract was terminable by either party.* **2** coming to an end after a certain time: *a loan terminable in 10 years.* —**ter′mi·na·ble·ness,** *n.* —**ter′mi·na·bly,** *adv.*

ter·mi·nal (tėr′mə nəl) *adj.* **1** at the end; forming the end part. A terminal flower or bud is one growing at the end of a stem, branch, etc. **2** coming at the end: *a terminal examination.* **3** having to do with a term. **4** at the end of a railway line. **5** having to do with the handling of freight at a terminal. **6** marking a boundary, limit, or end.
—*n.* **1** the end; end part. **2** either end of a railway line, airline, shipping route, etc. where sheds, hangars, garages, offices, etc., and stations to handle freight and passengers are located; terminus. **3** in electricity, a device for making a connection. [< L *terminalis* < *terminus* end]

ter·mi·nal·ly (tėr′mə nəl ē) *adv.* **1** at the end. **2** with respect to a termination.

ter·mi·nate (tėr′mə nāt′) *v.* **-nat·ed, -nat·ing. 1** bring to an end; put an end to: *terminate a partnership.* **2** come to an end: *His contract terminates soon.* **3** occur at or form the end of; bound; limit. [< L *terminare* < *terminus* end] —**ter′mi·na′tor,** *n.* —**Syn. 1** conclude.

ter·mi·na·tion (tėr′mə nā′shən) *n.* **1** an ending; end. **2** an end part. **3** the ending of a word; suffix. *Example*: In *gladly*, the adverbial termination is *-ly.* —**Syn. 1** conclusion. **2** bound.

ter·mi·na·tive (tėr′mə nə tiv or tėr′mə nā′ tiv) *adj.* tending or serving to terminate.

ter·mi·no·log·i·cal (tėr′mə nə loj′ə kəl) *adj.* of or having to do with terminology.

ter·mi·nol·o·gy (tėr′mə nol′ə jē) *n.* **-gies.** the special words or terms used in a science, art, business, etc.: *medical terminology.* [< G *Terminologie* < Med.L *terminus* term + Gk. *-logos* treating of]

term insurance life insurance that expires at the end of a specified period of time.

ter·mi·nus (tėr′mə nəs) *n.* **-nus·es** or **-ni** (-nī′ or -nē′). **1** either end of a railway line, bus line, etc.; terminal. **2** a city or station at the end of a railway line, bus line, etc. **3** an ending place; final point; goal; end. **4** a stone, post, etc. marking a boundary or limit. [< L *terminus*. Doublet of TERM.]

ter·mite (tėr′mīt) *n.* any of various insects that have a soft, pale body and a dark head. Termites look like white ants and are very destructive of buildings, furniture, provisions, etc. [< NL *termes, -itis*, special use of L *termes* woodworm]

tern (tėrn) *n.* a sea bird resembling a gull but having a more slender body and bill and a long, forked tail. [< Scand.; cf. Danish *terne*]

ter·na·ry (tėr′nə rē) *adj.* consisting of three; involving three; triple. [< L *ternarius*, ult. < *ter* three times]

ter·nate (tėr′nit or tėr′nāt) *adj.* **1** consisting of three. **2** arranged in threes. **3** in botany: **a** consisting of three leaflets. **b** having leaves arranged in whorls of three.

Terp·sich·o·re (tėrp sik′ə rē′) *n.* in Greek mythology, the Muse of dancing.

terp·si·cho·re·an (tėrp′sə kə rē′ən) *adj.* having to do with dancing: *the terpsichorean art.*

terr. 1 territory. **2** terrace.

ter·race (ter′is) *n. v.* **-raced, -rac·ing.** —*n.* **1** a flat, raised piece of land; a raised level, especially

one of a series of ascending levels. 2 a street along the side or top of a slope. 3 a row of houses on such a street. 4 a paved outdoor space adjoining a house, used for lounging, dining, etc. 5 the flat roof of a house, especially a house of Spanish or Oriental style.
—*v.* form into a terrace or terraces; furnish with terraces. [< OF *terrace*, ult. < L *terra* earth]

Terraces (def. 1

ter·ra cot·ta (ter′ə kot′ə) 1 a kind of hard, brownish-red earthenware, used for vases, statuettes, decorations on buildings, etc. 2 a piece of this earthenware, or something made from it. 3 a dull, brownish-red. [< Ital. *terra cotta* < *terra* earth + *cotta* baked]

ter·ra fir·ma (ter′ə fėr′mə) solid earth; dry land. [< L]

ter·rain (te rān′ or ter′ān) *n.* land; a tract of land, especially considered as to its extent and natural features in relation to its use in warfare. [< F *terrain*, ult. < L *terra* land]

ter·ra·my·cin (ter′ə mī′sin) *n.* an antibiotic derived from a soil micro-organism, used in the treatment of syphilis, some rheumatic diseases, certain bacterial infections, etc. *Formula*: $C_{22}H_{24}N_2O_9 \cdot 2H_2O$ [< L *terra* earth + Gk. *mykēs* fungus]

ter·ra·pin (ter′ə pin) *n.* a North American turtle used for food. [< Algonquian]

ter·rar·i·um (tə rãr′ē əm) *n.* **-i·ums,** or **-i·a** (-ē ə). an enclosure in which small land animals are kept for observation. [< NL *terrarium* < L *terra* land]

ter·raz·zo (te rät′sō) *n.* a floor made of small pieces of marble embedded in cement. [< Ital. *terrazzo* terrace, balcony < *terra* earth]

ter·res·tri·al (tə res′trē əl) *adj.* 1 of the earth; having to do with the earth. 2 of land, not water: *Islands and continents make up the terrestrial parts of the earth.* 3 living on the ground, not in the air or water or in trees: *terrestrial animals.* 4 growing on land; growing in the ground: *terrestrial plants.* 5 worldly; earthly. [ME < L *terrestris* < *terra* earth] —**Syn. 5** See **earthly.**

terrestrial globe 1 the earth. 2 a sphere with the map of the earth on it.

ter·ret (ter′it) *n.* one of the round loops or rings on the saddle of a harness, through which the driving reins pass. [var. of *toret* < OF *toret* < *tour* < L *tornus.* See TOUR.]

ter·ri·ble (ter′ə bəl) *adj.* 1 causing great fear; dreadful; awful: *a terrible leopard.* 2 distressing; severe: *the terrible suffering caused by war.* 3 *Informal.* extremely bad, unpleasant, etc.: *a terrible temper.* [< L *terribilis* < *terrere* terrify] —**ter′ri·ble·ness,** *n.* —**Syn.** 1 frightful, appalling, horrible, shocking.

ter·ri·bly (ter′ə blē) *adv.* 1 in a terrible manner. 2 *Informal.* extremely.

ter·ri·er (ter′ē ər) *n.* 1 any of several breeds of dog, such as the Airedale, fox terrier, or Scotch terrier, having either a short-haired, smooth coat or a long-haired, rough coat. Terriers were formerly used to pursue burrowing animals. 2 a dog of any of these breeds. [< F *terrier*, ult. < L *terra* earth]

ter·rif·ic (tə rif′ik) *adj.* 1 causing great fear; terrifying. 2 *Informal.* a very great; splendid. b very severe; intense. [< L *terrificus* < *terrere* terrify + *-ficus* making]

ter·rif·i·cal·ly (tə rif′ik lē) *adv.* in a terrific manner; to a terrific degree.

ter·ri·fied (ter′ə fīd′) *adj.* filled with great fear; frightened. —**Syn.** See **afraid.**

ter·ri·fy (ter′ə fī′) *v.* **-fied, -fy·ing.** fill with great fear; frighten very much. [< L *terrificare* < *terrere* terrify + *facere* make] —**Syn.** scare, alarm, horrify, appal, dismay.

ter·ri·to·ri·al (ter′ə tô′rē əl) *adj.* 1 of or having to do with territory: *Many wars have been fought for territorial gain.* 2 **Territorial,** of or having to do with a Territory: *the Territorial Council.* 3 of a particular territory or region; restricted to a particular region. 4 Also, **Territorial.** *Brit.* organized for home defence.
—*n.* **Territorial,** *Brit.* a soldier of a Territorial force.

hat, āge, cãre, fär; let, ēqual, tėrm; it, īce
hot, ōpen, ôrder; oil, out; cup, pu̇t, rüle, ūse
əbove, takən, pencəl, lemən, circəs
ch, child; ng, long; sh, ship
th, thin; ᴛʜ, then; zh, measure

Territorial Council 1 in the Yukon Territory, an elected body consisting of seven members and responsible for local government. 2 the Council of the Northwest Territories.

ter·ri·to·ri·al·ly (ter′ə tô′rē əl ē) *adv.* with respect to territory; as to territory.

ter·ri·to·ry (ter′ə tô′rē) *n.* **-ries.** 1 land: *Much territory in Africa is desert.* 2 a region; an area of land: *The company leased a large territory for oil explorations.* 3 land belonging to a government; a region under the rule of a distant government: *Gibraltar is British territory.* 4 **Territory, a** in Canada, a region administered by the Federal Government: *the Yukon Territory.* **b** a region having similar status in some other countries. 5 a region assigned to a salesman or agent. 6 the facts investigated by some branch of science or learning: *the territory of biochemistry.* [ME < L *territorium* < *terra* land]

ter·ror (ter′ər) *n.* 1 great fear. 2 a cause of great fear. 3 *Informal.* a person or thing that causes much trouble and unpleasantness. 4 **the Terror,** Reign of Terror. [ME < OF < L *terror* < *terrere* terrify] —**Syn.** 1 fright, alarm, dread, consternation.

ter·ror·ism (ter′ər iz′əm) *n.* 1 the act of terrorizing; use of terror. 2 the condition of fear and submission produced by frightened people. 3 a method of opposing a government internally through the use of terror.

ter·ror·ist (ter′ər ist) *n.* a person who uses or favors terrorism.

ter·ror·is·tic (ter′ər is′tik) *adj.* using or favoring methods that inspire terror.

ter·ror·i·za·tion (ter′ər ə zā′shən or ter′ər ī zā′shən) *n.* the act of terrorizing or the state of being terrorized; rule by terror.

ter·ror·ize (ter′ər īz′) *v.* **-ized, -iz·ing.** 1 fill with terror. 2 rule or subdue by causing terror. —**ter′ror·iz′er,** *n.*

ter·ror-strick·en (ter′ər strik′ən) *adj.* terrified.

ter·ry (ter′ē) *n.* **-ries.** a rough cloth made of uncut looped yarn. [? < F *tiré* drawn]

terry cloth terry.

terse (tėrs) *adj.* **ters·er, ters·est.** of writers, writing, speakers, or speaking, brief and to the point. [< L *tersus*, pp. of *tergere* rub, polish] —**terse′ly,** *adv.* —**terse′ness,** *n.*

ter·tian (tėr′shən) *n.* a fever or ague that reaches a peak every other day. —*adj.* recurring every other day. [ME < L *tertiana* (*febris* fever) < *tertius* third]

Ter·ti·ar·y (tėr′shē er′ē or tėr′shə rē) *adj. n.* **-ar·ies.** —*adj.* 1 in geology, of or having to do with the Tertiary or the rocks formed during it. 2 **tertiary,** of the third order, rank, formation, etc.; third.
—*n.* 1 in geology: **a** the third chief period of time in the formation of the earth's surface, beginning approximately 60 million years ago. During this period the great mountain systems, such as the Rockies, Alps, Himalayas, and Andes, appeared and rapid development of mammals occurred. See **geology** for chart. **b** the rocks formed during this period. 2 **tertiary,** one of a bird's flight feathers. [< L *tertiarius* < *tertius* third]

ter·ti·um quid (ter′shē əm kwid′) *Latin.* a third something; something related in some way to two things, but distinct from both; something intermediate between two things.

ter·y·lene (ter′ə lēn′) *n.* a crease-resistant synthetic fibre, much used for shirts, dresses, suits, etc. and often mixed with wool or other yarns. [< *Terylene*, a trademark]

ter·za ri·ma (ter′tsä rē′mä) an Italian form of iambic verse consisting of ten-syllable or eleven-syllable lines arranged in tercets, the middle line of each tercet rhyming with the first and third lines of the following tercet. Shelley's *Ode to the West Wind* is in terza rima. [< Ital. *terza rima* < *terza* third + *rima* rhyme]

tes·sel·late (*v.* tes′ə lāt′; *adj.* tes′ə lit or tes′ə lāt′) *v.* **-lat·ed, -lat·ing,** *adj.* —*v.* make of small squares or blocks, or in a checkered pattern. —*adj.* made in small squares or blocks or in a checkered pattern. [< L *tessellatus,* ult. < *tessera.* See TESSERA.]

A tessellated surface

tes·ser·a (tes′ər ə) *n.* **tes·ser·ae** (tes′ər ē′ or tes′ər ī′). **1** a small piece of marble, glass, etc. used in mosaic work. **2** in ancient times, a small square of bone, wood, etc. used as a token, tally, ticket, die, etc. [< L < Gk. *tessera* piece having four corners < *tessares* four]

test (test) *n.* **1** an examination; trial: *People who want to drive an automobile must pass a test. The teacher gave the class a test in arithmetic.* **2** a means of trial: *Trouble is a test of character.* **3** in chemistry: **a** an examination of a substance to see what it is or what it contains. **b** a process or substance used in such an examination. —*v.* put to a test; try out: *He tested the boy's honesty by leaving money on the table.* [ME < OF *test* vessel used in assaying < L *testum* earthen vessel] —**test′a·ble,** *adj.* —**Syn.** *n.* **1** See **trial.**

test. 1 testamentary. **2** testator.

Test. Testament.

tes·ta (tes′tə) *n.* **-tae** (-tē or -tī). **1** in zoology, a shell; the hard covering of certain animals. **2** in botany, the hard outside coat of a seed. [< L *testa* earthen vessel]

tes·ta·cy (tes′tə sē) *n.* the leaving of a will at death.

tes·ta·ment (tes′tə mənt) *n.* **1** written instructions telling what to do with a person's property after his death; a will. **2 Testament, a** a main division of the Bible; the Old Testament or the New Testament. **b** *Informal.* the New Testament. [ME < L *testamentum,* ult. < *testis* witness]

tes·ta·men·ta·ry (tes′tə men′tə rē or tes′tə men′trē) *adj.* **1** of or having to do with a testament or will. **2** given, done, or appointed by a testament or will. **3** in a testament or will.

tes·tate (tes′tāt) *adj.* having made and left a valid will. [< L *testatus,* pp. of *testari* make a will < *testis* witness]

tes·ta·tor (tes tā′tər or tes′tā tər) *n.* **1** a person who makes a will. **2** a person who has died leaving a valid will.

tes·ta·trix (tes tā′triks) *n.* **-tri·ces** (-trə sēz′). **1** a woman who makes a will. **2** a woman who has died leaving a valid will.

test ban an agreement between nations to ban the testing of nuclear weapons.

test case in law, a case whose outcome may set a precedent.

test-drive (test′drīv′) *v.* **-drove, -driv·en, -driv·ing.** drive a car or other vehicle to test it.

test·er[1] (tes′tər) *n.* a person or thing that tests. [< *test*]

tes·ter[2] (tes′tər) *n.* a canopy. [probably < OF *testre,* ult. < VL *testa* head < L *testa* earthen pot]

tes·tes (tes′tēz) *n.* pl. of **testis.**

tes·ti·cle (tes′tə kəl) *n.* in a male animal, one of two glands that secrete spermatozoa or reproductive cells. [< L *testiculus,* dim. of *testis.* See TESTIS.]

tes·ti·fy (tes′tə fī′) *v.* **-fied, -fy·ing. 1** give evidence; bear witness: *The excellence of Shakespeare's plays testifies to his genius.* **2** give evidence of; bear witness to: *The firm testified their appreciation of her work by raising her pay.* **3** declare solemnly; affirm. **4** in law, declare or give evidence under oath in a court: *The policeman testified that the speeding car had crashed into the truck.* [ME < L *testificari* < *testis* witness + *facere* make] —**tes′ti·fi′er,** *n.*

tes·ti·mo·ni·al (tes′tə mō′nē əl) *n.* **1** a certificate of character, conduct, qualifications, value, etc.; recommendation: *The boy looking for a job has testimonials from his teachers and former employer. Advertisements of patent medicines often contain testimonials from people who have used them.* **2** something given or done to show esteem, admiration, gratitude, etc.: *The members of the church collected money for a testimonial to their retiring pastor.* —*adj.* given or done as a testimonial. —**Syn.** *n.* **1** credential, voucher.

tes·ti·mo·ny (tes′tə mō′nē or tes′tə mo′nē) *n.* **-nies. 1** a statement used for evidence or proof: *A witness gave testimony that Mr. Doe was at home at 9 p.m.* **2** evidence: *The pupils presented their teacher with a watch in testimony of their respect and affection.* **3** an open declaration or profession of one's faith. **4** *Archaic.* the Ten Commandments. **5 testimonies,** *pl.* the laws of God; the Scriptures. [ME < L *testimonium* < *testis* witness] —**Syn. 1, 2** proof. See **evidence.**

tes·tis (tes′tis) *n.* **-tes.** a testicle. [< L *testis* witness (of virility)]

tes·tos·ter·one (tes tos′tər ōn′) *n.* a male hormone, obtained from bulls' testicles or made synthetically. *Formula:* $C_{19}H_{28}O_2$ [< *testes* + *sterol*]

test pilot a pilot employed to test new or experimental aircraft by subjecting them to greater than normal stress.

test tube a thin glass tube closed at one end, used in making chemical tests.

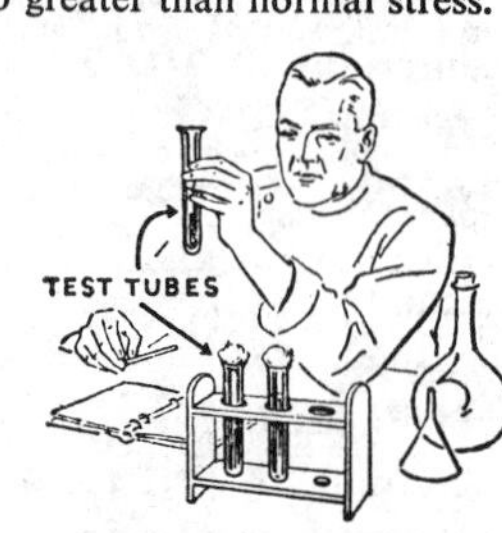

tes·tu·do (tes tū′dō or tes tü′dō) *n.* **-di·nes** (-də nēz′). **1** in ancient Rome: **a** a movable shelter with a strong and usually fireproof arched roof, used for protection in siege operations. **b** a shelter formed by a body of troops overlapping their shields above their heads. **2** some other sheltering contrivance. [< L *testudo,* literally, tortoise < *testa* shell]

tes·ty (tes′tē) *adj.* **-ti·er, -ti·est.** easily irritated; impatient. [ME < AF *testif* headstrong < OF *teste* head < L *testa* pot] —**tes′ti·ly,** *adv.* —**tes′ti·ness,** *n.* —**Syn.** irascible, peevish, petulant, cross.

tet·a·nus (tet′ə nəs) *n.* **1** a disease caused by certain bacilli usually entering the body through wounds, characterized by violent spasms, stiffness of many muscles, and even death. Tetanus of the lower jaw is called lockjaw. **2** in physiology, a condition of prolonged contraction of a muscle. [ME < L < Gk. *tetanos* < *teinein* stretch]

tet·a·ny (tet′ə nē) *n.* in medicine, a type of disorder marked by muscular spasms. [< F *tetanie*]

tetch·y (tech′ē) *adj.* **tetch·i·er, tetch·i·est.** irritable; touchy. Also, **techy.** [? < ME *teche, tache* fault < OF *teche* mark, quality]

tête-à-tête (tāt′ə tāt′) *adv.* two together in private: *They dined tête-à-tête.* —*adj.* of or for two people in private. —*n.* **1** a private conversation between two people. **2** an S-shaped seat built so that two people can sit facing one another. [< F *tête-à-tête* head to head]

teth·er (teᴛʜ′ər) *n.* **1** a rope or chain for fastening an animal so that it can graze only within certain limits. **2 at the end of one's tether,** *Informal.* at the end of one's resources or endurance. —*v.* fasten with a tether. [ME < ON *tjóthr*]

tetra- *combining form.* four, as in *tetrahedron.* [< Gk. *tetra-,* combining form of *tessares* four]

tet·ra·chord (tet′rə kôrd′) *n.* in music, a series of four notes in the diatonic scale, the first and last notes of the series being a perfect fourth apart; half an octave. [< L < Gk. *tetrachordos* producing four tones < *tessares* four + *chordē* string]

tet·rad (tet′rad) *n.* **1** a group or collection of four. **2** in chemistry, an atom, element, or radical with a valence of four. **3** in biology, a group of four chromosomes formed when a pair of chromosomes splits during meiosis. [< Gk. *tetros, tetrados* a group of four]

tet·ra·eth·yl lead (tet′rə eth′əl) a colorless, poisonous liquid used as an antiknock in gasoline.

tet·ra·he·dral (tet′rə hē′drəl or tet′rə hed′rəl) *adj.* having to do with a tetrahedron; having four sides.

tet·ra·he·dron (tet′rə hē′drən or tet′rə hed′rən) *n.* **-drons, -dra** (-drə). a solid bounded by four plane sides. The most common tetrahedron is a pyramid whose base and three sides are equilateral triangles. [< LGk. *tetraedron* < Gk. *tessares* four + *hedra* seat, base]

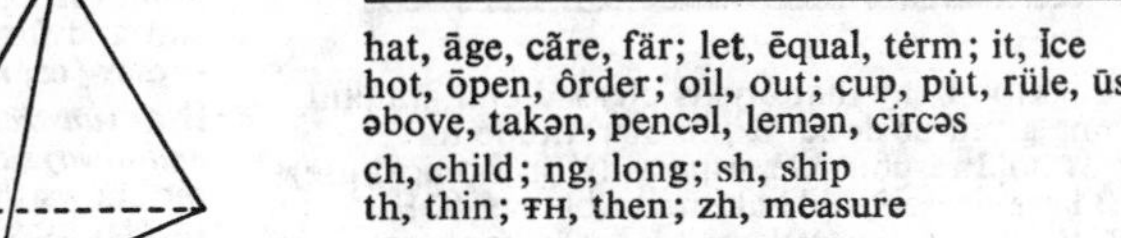

A tetrahedron

te·tral·o·gy (te tral′ə jē) *n.* **-gies.** a series of four connected dramas, operas, etc. [< Gk. *tetralogia* < *tessares* four + *logos* discourse]

te·tram·e·ter (te tram′ə tər) *adj.* consisting of four measures or feet. *—n.* a line of verse having four measures or feet. *Example:*

The stág | at éve | had drúnk | his fíll.

[< L < Gk. *tetrametron* < *tessares* four + *metron* measure]

tet·rarch (tet′rärk or tē′trärk) *n.* **1** in ancient Rome, the ruler of a part (originally a fourth part) of a province. **2** any subordinate ruler. [< L < Gk. *tetrarchēs* < *tessares* four + *archos* ruler]

tet·rar·chy (tet′rär kē or tē′trär kē) *n.* **-chies.** **1** government or jurisdiction of a tetrarch. **2** the territory governed by a tetrarch. **3** government by four persons. **4** a set of four rulers. **5** a country divided into four governments.

tet·ra·va·lent (tet′rə vā′lənt or te trav′ə lənt) *adj.* in chemistry: **1** having a valence of four. **2** having four valences. [< *tetra-* + L *valens, -entis,* ppr. of *valere* be worth]

te·trox·ide (te trok′sīd) *n.* any oxide having four atoms of oxygen in each molecule. [< *tetr-*, var. of *tetra-* + *oxide*]

tet·ter (tet′ər) *n.* an itching skin disease. Eczema is a tetter. [OE *teter*]

Teut. **1** Teutonic. **2** Teuton.

Teu·ton (tū′tən or tü′tən) *n.* **1** a German. **2** a member of a group of N. Europeans that includes, in the widest sense, Germans, Dutch, Anglo-Saxons, and Scandinavians. **3** a member of a very ancient Germanic tribe. *—adj.* German. [< L *Teutones, Teutoni,* pl.]

Teu·ton·ic (tū ton′ik or tü ton′ik) *adj.* **1** of or having to do with the ancient Germanic tribes. **2** of or having to do with the Teutons or their languages. **3** German. *—n.* Germanic.

Tex. Texas.

Tex·an (tek′sən) *adj.* of or having to do with Texas or its people. *—n.* a native or inhabitant of Texas.

Tex·as gate (tek′səs) in the West, an opening in a fence, designed to let men and vehicles through but hinder cattle, horses, or deer, the surface being made of metal tubes, often revolving, or rails, bars, etc. laid crosswise.

text (tekst) *n.* **1** the main body of reading matter in a book: *This history contains 300 pages of text and about 50 pages of notes, explanations, and questions for study.* **2** the original words of a writer: *Always quote the exact words of a text.* **3** any one of the various wordings of a poem, play, etc. **4** a short Biblical passage used as the subject of a sermon or as proof of some belief: *The minister preached on the text "Judge not, that ye be not judged."* **5** a topic; subject. **6** a textbook. [ult. < L *textus,* originally, texture < *texere* weave] **—text′less,** *adj.*

text·book (tekst′bu̇k′) *n.* a book used as a basis of instruction or as a standard reference in a particular course of study.

tex·tile (teks′tīl or teks′təl) *adj.* **1** woven: *Cloth is a textile fabric.* **2** suitable for weaving: *Linen, cotton, silk, and wool are common textile materials.* **3** of or having to do with weaving: *the textile art.* *—n.* **1** a woven fabric; cloth. **2** material suitable for weaving. [< L *textilis* < *texere* weave]

tex·tu·al (teks′chü əl) *adj.* of or having to do with the text: *A misprint is a textual error.*

textual criticism the analysis of a manuscript or printed text to correct the additions, errors, or omissions of copyists, printers, etc. in order to establish the original text: *textual criticism of the Bible.*

tex·tu·al·ly (teks′chü əl ē) *adv.* in regard to the text.

tex·tur·al (teks′chər əl) *adj.* of texture; having to do with texture. **—tex′tur·al·ly,** *adv.*

hat, āge, cãre, fär; let, ēqual, tėrm; it, īce
hot, ōpen, ôrder; oil, out; cup, pu̇t, rüle, ūse
əbove, takən, pencəl, lemən, circəs
ch, child; ng, long; sh, ship
th, thin; ᴛʜ, then; zh, measure

tex·ture (teks′chər) *n. v.* **-tured, -tur·ing.** *—n.* **1** the arrangement of threads in a woven fabric: *Burlap has a much coarser texture than a linen handkerchief.* **2** the arrangement of the parts of anything; structure; constitution; make-up: *Sandstone and granite have very different textures.* **3** in painting, sculpture, etc., the representation of the structure and minute moulding of a surface, especially of the skin, as distinct from its color. **4** the musical quality of combined voices, instruments, etc.: *the harsh texture of brass instruments.* *—v.* give a texture to. [< L *textura* < *texere* weave]

tex·tured (teks′chərd) *adj.* **1** having a certain texture. **2** bulky; looped; kinky: *textured wool.*

Th thorium.

Th. **1** Thursday. **2** Thomas.

Thai (tī) *n.* **1** a native or inhabitant of Thailand, formerly Siam, a country in S.E. Asia. **2** the official language of Thailand.
—adj. of or having to do with Thailand, its people, or their language.

thal·a·mus (thal′ə məs) *n.* **-mi** (-mī′ or -mē′). **1** in anatomy, a part of the brain where a nerve emerges or appears to emerge. The **optic thalami** are two large, oblong masses of gray matter forming a part of the midbrain. **2** in botany, a receptacle or torus of a flower. [< L *thalamus* inside room < Gk. *thalamos*]

tha·ler (tä′lər) *n.* **-ler.** a former German silver coin. Also, **taler.** [< G *Taler,* earlier *Thaler.* Akin to DOLLAR.]

Tha·li·a (thə lī′ə) *n.* in Greek mythology: **1** the Muse of comedy and idyllic poetry. **2** one of the three Graces.

thal·id·o·mide (thə lid′ə mīd′) *n.* **1** a drug formerly used as a tranquilizer. Its use by pregnant women was suspected of causing malformation of their babies. *Formula:* $C_{13}H_{10}N_2O_4$ **2 thalidomide baby,** a malformed baby born to a woman who had taken thalidomide during pregnancy.

thal·li·um (thal′ē əm) *n.* a rare metallic chemical element that is soft and malleable. *Symbol:* Tl; *at.no.* 81; *at.wt.* 204.37. [< NL < Gk. *thallos* green shoot (its spectrum is marked by a green band)]

thal·lo·phyte (thal′ə fīt′) *n.* in botany, any of a large group of plants that have no leaves, stems, or roots. Bacteria, algae, fungi, and lichens are thallophytes. [< Gk. *thallos* green shoot + E *-phyte*]

thal·lus (thal′əs) *n.* **thal·li** (thal′ī or thal′ē) or **thal·lus·es.** a plant that is not divided into leaves, stem, and root. Mushrooms, toadstools, and lichens are thalli. [< NL < Gk. *thallos* green shoot]

Tham·muz (täm′müz) *n.* Tammuz.

than (ᴛʜan; *unstressed,* ᴛʜən) *conj.* **1** in comparison with; compared to that which: *This train is faster than that one.* **2** except; besides; other than: *How else can we come than on foot?* **3 than whom,** compared with whom. [OE]
☛ **Than** is a conjunction joining comparative adjectives and adverbs (as well as those expressing a difference or exception, such as *rather, otherwise,* and *else*) with the second part of the comparison: *nicer than usual; otherwise than he did; more quickly than yesterday.* The part of speech, case, tense, etc. of the word following *than* depends on its function in the clause containing it, whether the clause itself is completely expressed or not. Thus:
I like Jane better *than* (I like) *him.*
It is easier said *than* (it is) *done.*
She is nicer *than* (it is) *usual* (with her).
Everest, *than which* there is no higher peak, has been climbed.
I am taller *than he* (is).
In informal speech, however, in sentences such as the last, the objective case is often used even by educated speakers, as if *than* were a preposition: I am taller *than him.*
☛ See then for another usage note.

thane (thān) *n.* **1** in Anglo-Saxon England, a man who ranked between an earl and an ordinary freeman. Thanes held lands of the king or lord and gave military service in return. **2** in Scotland, a baron or lord; chief of a clan. Also, **thegn.** [OE *thegn*]

thank (thangk) *v.* **1** say that one is pleased and grateful for something given or done; express gratitude to. **2** consider or hold responsible, especially (in ironical use) to blame. **3 have oneself to thank,** be to blame. [OE *thancian* < *thanc,* n.] —*n.* **1 thanks,** *pl.* **a** I thank you. **b** an expression of gratitude and pleasure for something given or done. **c** a feeling of kindness received; gratitude. **2 thanks to,** owing to; because of. [OE *thanc,* originally, thought]

thank·ful (thangk′fəl) *adj.* feeling or expressing thanks; grateful. —**Syn.** See **grateful.**

thank·ful·ly (thangk′fəl ē) *adv.* with thanks; gratefully.

thank·ful·ness (thangk′fəl nis) *n.* a thankful feeling; gratitude.

thank·less (thangk′lis) *adj.* **1** not feeling or expressing thanks; not grateful. **2** not likely to be rewarded with thanks; not appreciated: *Giving advice is usually a thankless act.* —**thank′less·ly,** *adv.* —**thank′less·ness,** *n.*

thanks·giv·ing (thangks giv′ing) *n.* **1** a giving of thanks. **2** an expression of thanks: *They offered thanksgiving for the bountiful harvest.* **3** a day set apart to acknowledge God's favor. **4 Thanksgiving,** Thanksgiving Day.

Thanksgiving Day **1** in Canada, the second Monday in October, a day set apart as a statutory holiday on which to give thanks for God's goodness and for the harvest. **2** in the United States, the fourth Thursday in November, a holiday observed for similar reasons.

that (ᴛʜat; *unstressed,* ᴛʜət) *adj.* **those,** *pron.* (*for defs. 1-3*) **those,** *conj., adv.* —*adj.* **1** pointing out or indicating some person, thing, idea, etc. already mentioned, understood, or to be emphasized: *Do you know that boy?* **2** indicating the farther of two or more things: *Shall I buy this dress or that one over there?* **3** showing contrast: *This hat is prettier but that one costs less.*
—*pron.* **1** some person, thing, idea, etc. already mentioned, understood, or to be emphasized: *That is the right way. That's a good boy!* **2** the farther of two or more things: *I like that better than this.* **3** something contrasted: *Which hat do you want, this or that?* **4** who; whom; which: *Is he the man that sells dogs? She is the girl that you mean. Bring the box that will hold most.* **5** when; at or in which: *1964 was the year that we went abroad.* **6 at that,** *Informal.* **a** with no more talk, work, etc. **b** considering everything. **7 in that,** because: *I prefer his plan to yours, in that I think it is more practical.* **8 That's that,** *Informal.* That is finished, settled, or decided.
—*conj. that* is used: **1** to introduce a noun clause and connect it with the verb: *I know that 6 and 4 are 10.* **2** to show purpose: *He ran fast that he might not be late.* **3** to show result: *He ran so fast that he was five minutes early.* **4** to show cause: *I wonder what happened, not that I care.* **5** to express a wish: *Oh, that she were here!* **6** to show anger, surprise, etc.: *That one so fair should be so false!*
—*adv.* to such an extent or degree; so. *He cannot stay up that late.* [OE *thæt*]

☛ **that** (pron., def. 4), **who, which.** *That* as a relative pronoun refers to persons or things, *who* to persons, *which* usually to things: *The people that* (or *who*) *were in the auditorium listened to the speech in silence. He solved in five minutes a problem that* (or *which*) *I had struggled with for five hours. That* usually introduces clauses that are restrictive; *which* introduces clauses that are non-restrictive. Restrictive: *The book that she selected for her report was the longest in the list.* Non-restrictive: *The privilege of free speech, which we hold so dear, is now endangered.*

thatch (thach) *n.* **1** straw, rushes, palm leaves, etc. used as a roof or covering. **2** a roof or covering of thatch. **3** *Informal.* the hair covering the head. —*v.* roof or cover with thatch. [OE *thæc*]

thau·ma·tur·gy (tho′mə tėr′jē or thô′mə tėr′jē) *n.* the working of wonders or miracles; magic. [< Gk. *thaumatourgia,* ult. < *thauma* marvel + *-orgos* working < *ergon* work]

thaw (tho or thô) *v.* **1** melt (ice, snow, or anything frozen): *Salt was put on the sidewalk to thaw the ice.* **2** become warm enough to melt ice, snow, etc.: *If the sun stays out, it will probably thaw today.* **3** make or become free of frost, ice, etc.: *Our sidewalk thawed yesterday. The pond thaws in April.* **4** make or become less stiff and formal in manner; soften: *His shyness thawed under her kindness.*
—*n.* **1** a thawing. **2** a period of weather above the freezing point (32 degrees); a time of melting. **3** a becoming less stiff and formal in manner; softening. [OE *thawian*] —**thaw′er,** *n.* —**Syn.** *v.* **1** See **melt.**

the[1] (*unstressed before a consonant,* ᴛʜə; *when stressed, and always before vowels,* ᴛʜē) *definite article.* The word *the* shows that a certain one (or ones) is meant. Various special uses are: **1** to mark a noun as indicating something well-known or unique: *the* (ᴛʜə) *prodigal son, the* (ᴛʜē) *Alps.* **2** denoting the time in question or under consideration, now or then present: *the hour of victory. Was that the moment to act?* **3** with or as part of a title: *the Duke of Wellington.* **4** to mark a noun as indicating the best known or most important of its kind: *the* (ᴛʜē) *place to dine.* **5** to mark a noun as being used generically: *The dog is a quadruped.* **6** to indicate a part of the body or a personal belonging: *hang the head in shame.* **7** before adjectives used as nouns: *visit the sick.* **8** distributively, to denote any one separately: *candy at one dollar the pound.* [OE *thē, the*]

☛ **the.** The repetition of the articles before the various nouns of a series emphasizes their distinctness: The *color,* the *fragrance, and* the *beautiful patterns of these flowers make them universal favorites.* Compare: *The color, fragrance, and pattern of these flowers make them universal favorites.*

the[2] (ᴛʜə or ᴛʜē) *adv.* The word *the* is used to modify an adjective or adverb in the comparative degree: **1** signifying "in or by that," "on that account," "in some or any degree": *If you start now, you will be back the sooner.* **2** used correlatively, in one instance with relative force and in the other with demonstrative force, and signifying "by how much . . . by so much," "in what degree . . . in that degree": *the more the merrier, the sooner the better.* [OE *thȳ*]

the·a·tre or **the·a·ter** (thē′ə tər) *n.* **1** a place where plays are acted. **2** a place where motion pictures are shown. **3** a place that looks like a theatre in its arrangement of seats: *the operating theatre of a hospital.* **4** a place where some action proceeds; scene of action: *France has too often been a theatre of war.* **5 a** plays; the writing and producing of plays; the drama. **b** a play, situation, dialogue, etc. considered as to its effectiveness on the stage: *This scene is bad theatre.* [ME < OF < L < Gk. *theatron,* ult. < *thea* view]

the·a·tre·go·er or **the·a·ter·go·er** (thē′ə tər gō′ər) *n.* one who goes to the theatre, especially one who goes frequently.

the·a·tre-in-the-round or **the·a·ter-in-the-round** (thē′ə tər in ᴛʜə round′) *n.* **1** a theatre having the stage situated in the centre, surrounded with seats on all sides. **2** the presentation of plays in such theatres.

the·at·ric (thē at′rik) *adj.* theatrical.

the·at·ri·cal (thē at′rə kəl) *adj.* **1** of or having to do with the theatre or actors: *theatrical performances, a theatrical company.* **2** suggesting a theatre or acting; for display or effect; artificial. —*n.* **theatricals,** *pl.* **a** dramatic performances, especially as given by amateurs. **b** matters having to do with the stage and acting. **c** actions of a theatrical or artificial character. —**the·at′ri·cal·ly,** *adv.* —**Syn.** *adj.* **1** histrionic. **2** See **dramatic.**

the·at·ri·cal·i·ty (thē at′rə kal′ə tē) *n.* the quality of being theatrical.

The·ban (thē′bən) *adj.* of or having to do with Thebes, an important city in ancient Greece, or the city of Thebes, an important centre of civilization in ancient Egypt. —*n.* a native or inhabitant of Thebes.

thee (ᴛʜē) *pron.* the objective case of **thou:** "*The Lord bless thee and keep thee.*" [OE *thē*] ☛ See **thou** for usage note.

theft (theft) *n.* **1** the act of stealing: *The man was put in prison for theft.* **2** an instance of stealing: *The theft of the jewels caused much excitement.* [OE *thēoft* < *thēof* thief] —**Syn. 1** thievery, pilfering, larceny, robbery.

thegn (thān) *n.* thane.

the·in (thē′ən) *n.* theine.

the·ine (thē′ēn or thē′ən) *n.* caffeine. [< NL *thea* tea + *-ine*[2]]

their (ᴛʜãr; *unstressed,* ᴛʜər) *adj.* of them; belonging to them: *They like their school and do their lessons well.* [ME < ON *their(r)a*]

☛ **Their, theirs** are the possessive forms of *they. Their* is used as an adjective and is always followed by a noun: *This is their farm. Theirs* stands alone: *This farm is theirs.*

theirs (ᴛʜãrz) *pron.* **1** of them; belonging to them: *Those books are theirs, not mine.* **2** the one or ones belonging to them: *Our house is white; theirs is brown.*
☛ See **their** for usage note.

the·ism (thē′iz əm) *n.* **1** monotheism: **a** a belief in one God, the creator and ruler of the universe. **b** belief in (any) one god rather than in many. **2** belief in a deity or deities; religious faith or conviction. [< Gk. *theos* god]

the·ist (thē′ist) *n.* a believer in theism.

the·is·tic (thē is′tik) *adj.* of or having to do with theism or theists. **—the·is′ti·cal·ly,** *adv.*

them (ᴛʜem; *unstressed,* ᴛʜəm) *pron.* the objective case of **they**: *The books are new; take care of them.* [ME *theim* < ON]

the·mat·ic (thē mat′ik) *adj.* of or having to do with a theme or themes.

theme (thēm) *n.* **1** a topic; subject: *Patriotism was the speaker's theme.* **2** a short written composition. **3** in music: **a** the principal melody in a composition. **b** a short melody repeated in different forms in an elaborate composition. **4** a melody used to identify a particular radio or television program. [ME < L < Gk. *thema,* literally, something set down]

them·selves (ᴛʜem selvz′ or ᴛʜəm selvz′) *pron.* **1** the emphatic form of **they** or **them**: *They did it themselves.* **2** the reflexive form of **them**: *They injured themselves.* **3** their real selves: *They were ill and were not themselves.*

then (ᴛʜen) *adv.* **1** at that time: *Prices were lower then.* **2** soon afterwards: *The noise stopped, and then began again.* **3** next in time or place: *First comes spring, then summer.* **4** at another time: *Now one boy does best and then another.* **5** also; besides: *The dress seems too good to throw away, and then it is very attractive.* **6** in that case; therefore: *If Harry broke the window, then he should pay for it.* **7 but then,** but at the same time; but on the other hand. **8 there and then,** at that time and place; at once and on the spot. *—n.* that time: *By then we shall know the result. —adj.* being at that time; existing then: *the then Prime Minister.* [OE *thænne*]

thence (thens or ᴛʜens) *adv.* **1** from that place; from there: *A few miles thence is a river.* **2** for that reason; therefore: *You didn't work, thence no pay.* **3** from that time; from then: *a year thence.* [ME *thennes* < OE *thanan*(*e*)]

thence·forth (thens′fôrth′ or ᴛʜens′-) *adv.* from then on; from that time forward: *Women were given the same rights as men. Thenceforth they could vote.*

thence·for·ward (thens′fôr′wərd or ᴛʜens′-) *adv.* thenceforth.

theo- *combining form.* God; a god or gods: *theology = study of God; theogony = study of the origin of the gods.*

the·oc·ra·cy (thē ok′rə sē) *n.* **-cies. 1** a system of government in which God, or a god, is recognized as the supreme civil ruler and His laws are taken as the laws of the state. **2** a system of government by priests. **3** a country governed by a theocracy. [< Gk. *theokratia* < *theos* god + *kratos* rule]

the·o·crat (thē′ə krat′) *n.* **1** a ruler, or member of a governing body, in a theocracy. **2** a person who favors theocracy.

the·o·crat·ic (thē′ə krat′ik) *adj.* **1** of or having to do with theocracy. **2** having a theocracy. **—the′o·crat′i·cal·ly,** *adv.*

the·od·o·lite (thē od′ə līt′) *n.* a surveying instrument for measuring horizontal and vertical angles. [< NL *theodelitus*; ult. origin unknown]

the·og·o·ny (thē og′ə nē) *n.* **-nies. 1** the origin of the gods. **2** an account of this; genealogical account of the gods. [< Gk. *theogonia* < *theos* god < *gonos* begetting, descent]

the·o·lo·gian (thē′ə lō′jən or thē′ə lō′jē ən) *n.* a person skilled or trained in theology.

the·o·log·i·cal (thē′ə loj′ə kəl) *adj.* **1** of or having to do with theology. A theological school trains young men for the ministry. **2** referring to the nature and will of God. **—the′o·log′i·cal·ly,** *adv.*

hat, āge, cãre, fär; let, ēqual, tėrm; it, īce
hot, ōpen, ôrder; oil, out; cup, pu̇t, rüle, ūse
əbove, takən, pencəl, lemən, circəs
ch, child; ng, long; sh, ship
th, thin; ᴛʜ, then; zh, measure

the·ol·o·gy (thē ol′ə jē) *n.* **-gies. 1** the study of the nature of God and His relations to man and the universe. **2** the study of religion and religious beliefs. **3** a system of religious beliefs. [< L < Gk. *theologia* < *theos* god + *-logos* treating of]

the·o·rem (thē′ə rəm) *n.* **1** in mathematics: **a** a statement to be proved. **b** a statement of relations that can be expressed by an equation or formula. **2** a statement or rule that can be proved to be true. [< L < Gk. *theōrēma* < *theōreein* consider. See THEORY.]

the·o·ret·ic (thē′ə ret′ik) *adj.* theoretical.

the·o·ret·i·cal (thē′ə ret′ə kəl) *adj.* **1** planned or worked out in the mind, not from experience; based on theory, not on fact; limited to theory. **2 a** dealing with theory only; not practical. **b** having the object of knowledge as its end; concerned with knowledge only, not with accomplishing anything or producing anything; purely scientific.

the·o·ret·i·cal·ly (thē′ə ret′ik lē) *adv.* in theory; according to theory; in a theoretical manner.

the·o·re·ti·cian (thē′ə rə tish′ən) *n.* a person who knows much about the theory of an art, science, etc.

the·o·rist (thē′ə rist) *n.* a person who forms theories.

the·o·rize (thē′ə rīz′) *v.* **-rized, -riz·ing.** form a theory or theories; speculate. **—the′o·riz′er,** *n.*

the·o·ry (thē′ə rē) *n.* **-ries. 1** an explanation based on thought or speculation. **2** an explanation based on observation and reasoning: *the theory of evolution, Einstein's theory of relativity.* **3** the principles or methods of a science or art rather than its practice: *the theory of music.* **4** thought or fancy as opposed to fact or practice. **5** in mathematics, a set of theorems which constitute a connected, systematic view of some branch of mathematics: *the theory of probabilities.* [< LL < Gk. *theōria* < *theōreein* consider < *theōros* spectator < *thea* a sight + *horaein* see]

Syn. 1 Theory, hypothesis = an explanation based on observation and thought. **Theory** applies to an explanation that has been tested and confirmed as a general principle explaining a large number of related facts, occurrences, or other phenomena in nature, mechanics, etc.: *Einstein's theory of relativity explains the motion of moving objects.* **Hypothesis** applies to a proposed explanation for a certain group of facts, admittedly unproved but accepted for the time being as highly probable or as an experimental guide: *Archeological discoveries strengthened the hypothesis that Troy existed.*

the·o·soph·ic (thē′ə sof′ik) *adj.* of or having to do with theosophy.

the·o·soph·i·cal (thē′ə sof′ə kəl) *adj.* theosophic.

the·os·o·phist (thē os′ə fist) *n.* a person who believes in theosophy.

the·os·o·phy (thē os′ə fē) *n.* a philosophy or religion that claims to have a special insight into the divine nature through spiritual self-development. Modern theosophy includes many of the teachings of Buddhism and Brahmanism. [< Med.L < LGk. *theosophia,* ult. < Gk. *theos* god + *sophos* wise]

ther·a·peu·tic (ther′ə pū′tik) *adj.* of or having to do with the treatment or curing of disease; curative. [< NL *therapeuticus,* ult. < Gk. *therapeuein* cure, treat < *theraps* attendant]

ther·a·peu·ti·cal (ther′ə pū′tə kəl) *adj.* therapeutic. **—ther′a·peu′ti·cal·ly,** *adv.*

ther·a·peu·tics (ther′ə pū′tiks) *n.* a branch of medicine that deals with the treating or curing of disease; therapy.

ther·a·peu·tist (ther′ə pū′tist) *n.* a person who specializes in therapeutics.

ther·a·pist (ther′ə pist) *n.* therapeutist.

ther·a·py (ther′ə pē) *n.* **-pies. 1** the treatment of diseases. **2** curative power; healing quality. [< NL < Gk. *therapeia* < *therapeuein.* See THERAPEUTIC.]

there (ᴛʜãr; *unstressed,* ᴛʜər) *adv.* **1** in or at that place:

Sit there. **2** to or into that place: *Go there at once.* **3** at that point in an action, speech, etc.: *You have done enough, you may stop there.* **4** in that matter, particular, or respect: *You are mistaken there.* **5** *There* is used in sentences in which the verb comes before the subject: *There are three new houses on our street. Is there a drugstore near here?* **6** *There* is used to call attention to some person or thing: *There goes the bell.* **7 all there,** *Informal.* **a** wide-awake; alert. **b** not crazy; sane.
—*n.* that place: *From there go on to Hamilton.*
—*interj. There* is also used to express satisfaction, triumph, dismay, encouragement, comfort, etc.: *There, there! Don't cry.* [OE *thǣr*]
☛ **there** (*adv.* def. 5). *There* is often used at the beginning of a sentence as a temporary substitute for the real subject, which follows the verb: *There is only one book on your desk.* When the subject is singular, a singular verb is used after *there*: *There was much work to be done.* When the subject is plural, a plural verb is usual: *There are many answers in the back of the book.*

there·a·bout (ŦHãr′ə bout′) *adv.* thereabouts.

there·a·bouts (ŦHãr′ə bouts′) *adv.* **1** near that place. **2** near that time. **3** near that number or amount: *The book cost me two dollars or thereabouts.*

there·af·ter (ŦHãr af′tər) *adv.* **1** after that; afterward. **2** accordingly.

there·at (ŦHãr at′) *adv.* **1** when that happened; at that time. **2** because of that; because of it. **3** at that place.

there·by (ŦHãr bī′ or ŦHãr′bī′) *adv.* **1** by means of that; in that way: *He wished to travel and thereby study the customs of other countries.* **2** in connection with that: *Calgary won the game, and thereby hangs a tale.* **3** near there.

there·for (ŦHãr fôr′) *adv.* for that; for this; for it: *He promised to give a building for a hospital and as much land as should be necessary therefor.*

there·fore (ŦHãr′fôr′) *adv.* for that reason; as a result of that; consequently. [ME *therfore* < *ther* there + *fore*, var. of *for* for]
Syn. Therefore, consequently = a logical or causal relationship between two groups of words by connecting to one statement a group of words stating a conclusion or result. **Therefore** indicates formally and precisely that the second group of words states the necessary conclusion to be drawn from the first: *He was the only candidate; therefore, he was elected.* **Consequently,** also formal, indicates a reasonable conclusion, but may also be used to connect a statement of effect or result: *He is the popular candidate; consequently, he will be elected. I overslept and, consequently, was late.*

there·from (ŦHãr from′ or -frum′) *adv.* from that; from this; from it.

there·in (ŦHãr in′) *adv.* **1** in that place; in it. **2** in that matter; in that way; in that respect.

there·in·to (ŦHãr in′tü or ŦHãr′in tü′) *adv.* **1** into that place; into it. **2** into that matter.

there·of (ŦHãr ov′ or ŦHãr uv′) *adv.* **1** of that; of it. **2** from it; from that source.

there·on (ŦHãr on′) *adv.* **1** on that; on it. **2** immediately after that.

there's (ŦHãrz) there is.

there·to (ŦHãr tü′) *adv.* **1** to that; to it: *The castle stands on a hill, and the road thereto is steep and rough.* **2** in addition to that; also.

there·to·fore (ŦHãr′tə fôr′) *adv.* before that time; until then.

there·un·der (ŦHãr un′dər) *adv.* **1** under that; under it. **2** under the authority of that; according to that.

there·un·to (ŦHãr un′tü or ŦHãr′un tü′) *adv.* to that; to it.

there·up·on (ŦHãr′ə pon′) *adv.* **1** immediately after that. **2** because of that; therefore. **3** on that; on it.

there·with (ŦHãr wiŦH′ or -with′) *adv. Archaic.* **1** with that; with it. **2** immediately after that; then.

there·with·al (ŦHãr wiŦH′ol or ŦHãr′wiŦH ôl′) *adv.* **1** with that; with this; with it. **2** in addition to that; also.

ther·mal (thėr′məl) *adj.* **1** of or having to do with heat. **2** warm; hot. **3** of or having to do with the production of electric power by plants using coal, oil, natural gas, etc. as fuel. [< Gk. *thermē* heat] **—ther′mal·ly,** *adv.*

thermal barrier heat barrier.

ther·mic (thėr′mik) *adj.* of or having to do with heat; thermal.

ther·mis·tor (thėr mis′tər) *n.* a very small electronic resistor used to measure or regulate heat through changes in conductivity.

thermo- or **therm-** *combining form.* heat, as in *thermodynamics.* [< Gk. *thermē*]

ther·mo·dy·nam·ic (thėr′mō dī nam′ik) *adj.* **1** of or having to do with thermodynamics. **2** using force due to heat or to the conversion of heat into mechanical energy.

ther·mo·dy·nam·ics (thėr′mō dī nam′iks) *n.* the branch of physics that deals with the relations between heat and mechanical energy or work.

ther·mo-e·lec·tric (thėr′mō i lek′trik) *adj.* of or having to do with thermo-electricity.

ther·mo-e·lec·tri·cal (thėr′mō i lek′trə kel) *adj.* thermo-electric.

ther·mo-e·lec·tric·i·ty (thėr′mō i lek′tris′ə tē or -ē′lek tris′ə tē) *n.* electricity produced directly by heat.

ther·mom·e·ter (thər mom′ə tər) *n.* an instrument for measuring temperature, usually by means of the expansion and contraction of mercury or alcohol in a capillary tube and bulb.

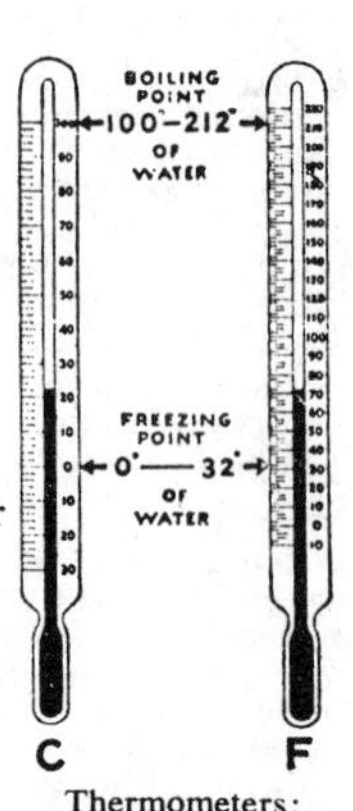

Thermometers: C, centigrade; F, Fahrenheit.

ther·mo·nu·cle·ar (thėr′mō nū′klē ər or -nü′klē ər) *adj.* of or designating the fusion of atoms (as in the hydrogen bomb) through very high temperature: *a thermonuclear reaction.*

ther·mo·plas·tic (thėr′mō plas′tik) *adj.* becoming soft and capable of being moulded when heated. —*n.* a thermoplastic material, especially one of certain synthetic resins.

ther·mos (thėr′məs) *n.* a Thermos bottle.

Thermos bottle *Trademark.* a bottle, flask, or jug having a case or jacket that heat cannot pass through easily; vacuum bottle. A Thermos bottle will keep its contents at about their original temperature for several hours. [< Gk. *thermos* hot]

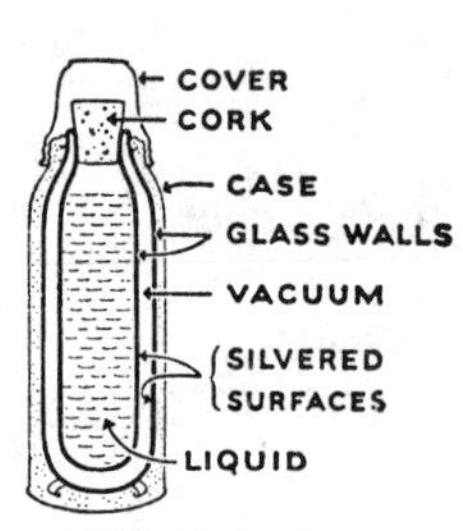

A Thermos bottle

ther·mo·set (thėr′mō set′) *adj.* thermosetting. —*n.* a thermosetting material, especially a plastic.

ther·mo·set·ting (thėr′mō set′ing) *adj.* becoming hard and permanently set after being heated: *thermosetting plastics.*

ther·mo·stat (thėr′mə stat′) *n.* **1** an automatic device for regulating temperature. **2** any automatic device that responds to conditions of temperature. [< *thermo-* + Gk. *-statēs* that stands]

ther·mo·stat·ic (thėr′mə stat′ik) *adj.* of, having to do with, or like a thermostat.

ther·mo·stat·i·cal·ly (thėr′mə stat′ik lē) *adv.* by means of a thermostat.

the·sau·rus (thi sô′rəs) *n.* **-ri** (rī- or -rē). **1** a treasury; storehouse. **2** a classified dictionary of synonyms, antonyms, and other semantically related words. [< L < Gk. *thesauros.* Doublet of TREASURE.]

these (ŦHēz) *adj. pron.* pl. of *this.* [OE *thǣs*, var. of *thās.* Cf. THOSE.]

the·sis (thē′sis) *n.* **-ses** (-sēz′). **1** a proposition or statement to be proved or to be maintained against objections. **2** an essay; an essay presented by a candidate for a diploma or degree. [< L < Gk. *thesis*, originally, a setting down]

Thes·pi·an (thes′pē ən) *adj.* **1** having to do with Thespis, a Greek tragic poet who lived about 534 B.C.

2 of or having to do with the drama or tragedy; dramatic; tragic. —*n.* an actor or actress. [< *Thespis,* a Greek poet]

Thess. Thessalonians.

Thes·sa·li·an (the sā′ lē ən) *adj.* of or having to do with Thessaly, a district in E. Greece, or its people. —*n.* a native or inhabitant of Thessaly.

Thes·sa·lo·ni·an (thes′ə lō′nē ən) *adj.* of or having to do with Thessalonica (in modern times, Salonika), a seaport in N.E. Greece, or its people. —*n.* **1** a native or inhabitant of Thessalonica. **2 Thessalonians,** either of two books of the New Testament written by St. Paul.

the·ta (thā′tə or thē′tə) *n.* the eighth letter (Θ, θ) of the Greek alphabet, pronounced as the English "th" in *thin.*

thews (thūz or thüz) *n.pl.* **1** muscles. **2** sinews. [ME *theawes* good quality; strength < OE *thēaw* habit]

they (ᴛʜā) *pron. nom.* **they**; *poss.* **theirs**; *obj.* **them.** **1** pl. of **he, she,** or **it.** **2** *Informal.* some people; any people; persons. [ME < ON *their*]

☛ They is used in informal speech as an indefinite pronoun but generally it is not so used in writing. Spoken: *They have had no serious accidents at that crossing for over two years.* Written: *There have been no serious accidents....*

they'd (ᴛʜād) **1** they had. **2** they would.

they'll (ᴛʜāl) **1** they will. **2** they shall.

they're (ᴛʜãr; *unstressed,* ᴛʜər) they are.

they've (ᴛʜāv) they have.

thi·a·min (thī′ə min) *n.* a white, crystalline organic compound found in cereals, yeast, etc. or prepared synthetically. Also, **thiamine.** *Formula:* $C_{12}H_{17}ClN_4OS$

thi·a·mine (thī′ə min or thī′ə mēn′) *n.* thiamin.

Thib·e·tan (ti bet′ən) *adj. n.* Tibetan.

thick (thik) *adj.* **1** with much space from one side to the opposite side; not thin: *The castle has thick stone walls.* **2** measuring between two opposite sides: *two inches thick.* **3** set close together; dense: *thick hair.* **4** many and close together; abundant: *bullets thick as hail.* **5** filled; covered: *thick with flies.* **6** like glue or syrup, not like water; rather dense of its kind: *Thick liquids pour much more slowly than thin liquids.* **7** not clear; foggy: *The weather was thick.* **8** not clear in sound; hoarse: *a thick voice.* **9** stupid; dull: *He has a thick head.* **10** *Informal.* very friendly; intimate. **11** *Informal.* too much to be endured.
—*adv.* **1** thickly. **2 lay it on thick,** *Informal.* praise or blame too much.
—*n.* **1** the part that is thickest, most crowded, most active, etc.: *in the thick of the fight.* **2 through thick and thin,** in good times and bad. [OE *thicce*] —**Syn.** *adj.* **3** close, compact, crowded. **4** plentiful, numerous. **7** misty, hazy. **8** indistinct, inarticulate, muffled. **9** slow, obtuse.

thick·en (thik′ən) *v.* **1** make or become thick or thicker. **2** of a plot, become more complex or intricate. —**thick′en·er,** *n.* —**Syn.** coagulate, congeal, condense.

thick·en·ing (thik′ən ing or thik′ning) *n.* **1** a material or ingredient used to thicken something. **2** a thickened part. **3** the act or process of making or becoming thick or thicker.

thick·et (thik′it) *n.* shrubs, bushes, or small trees growing close together. [OE *thiccet* < *thicce* thick] —**Syn.** shrubbery, copse, brake.

thick-head·ed (thik′hed′id) *adj.* stupid; dull. —**thick′-head′ed·ness,** *n.*

thick·ly (thik′lē) *adv.* **1** in a thick manner; closely; densely: *a thickly settled region.* **2** in great numbers; in abundance. **3** frequently. **4** with thick consistency. **5** hoarsely.

thick·ness (thik′nis) *n.* **1** the quality or state of being thick. **2** the distance between opposite surfaces; the third measurement of a solid, not length or breadth. **3** the thick part. **4** a layer: *The pad was made up of three thicknesses of blotting paper.*

thick-set (thik′set′) *adj.* **1** closely placed, planted, etc.: *a thick-set hedge.* **2** thick in form or build: *a thick-set man.* —*n.* **1** a thicket. **2** a thick hedge.

thick-skinned (thik′skind′) *adj.* **1** having a thick skin. **2** not sensitive to criticism, reproach, rebuff, or the like.

thick-wit·ted (thik′wit′id) *adj.* stupid; dull.

thief (thēf) *n.* **thieves.** a person who steals, especially one who steals secretly and without using force. [OE *thēof*]

Syn. Thief, robber = someone who steals. **Thief** applies to someone who takes and, usually, carries away something belonging to another, in a secret or stealthy way: *A thief stole the little boy's bicycle from the yard.* **Robber** applies to one who takes another's property by force or threats of violence: *The robbers bound and gagged the night watchman.*

hat, āge, cãre, fär; let, ēqual, tėrm; it, īce
hot, ōpen, ôrder; oil, out; cup, pu̇t, rüle, ūse
əbove, takən, pencəl, lemən, circəs
ch, child; ng, long; sh, ship
th, thin; ᴛʜ, then; zh, measure

thieve (thēv) *v.* **thieved, thiev·ing.** steal. [OE *thēofian* < *thēof* thief]

thiev·er·y (thēv′ər ē or thēv′rē) *n.* **-er·ies.** the act of stealing; theft.

thieves (thēvz) *n.* pl. of **thief.**

thiev·ish (thēv′ish) *adj.* **1** having the habit of stealing; likely to steal. **2** like a thief; stealthy; sly. —**thiev′ish·ly,** *adv.* —**thiev′ish·ness,** *n.*

thigh (thī) *n.* the part of the leg between the hip and the knee. [OE *thēoh*]

thigh·bone (thī′bōn′) *n.* the bone of the leg between the hip and the knee; femur. See **shin** for diagram.

thill (thil) *n.* either of the shafts between which a single animal drawing a vehicle is placed. [ME *thille*]

thim·ble (thim′bəl) *n.* **1** a small cap of metal, bone, plastic, etc. worn on the finger to protect it when pushing the needle in sewing. **2** a short metal tube. **3** a metal ring fitted in a rope, to save wear on the rope. [OE *thȳmel* < *thūma* thumb]

thim·ble·ber·ry (thim′bəl ber′ē) *n.* **-ries.** a North American raspberry having a thimble-shaped fruit, especially the black raspberry.

thim·ble·ful (thim′bəl fu̇l′) *n.* **-fuls.** as much as a thimble will hold; a very small quantity.

thim·ble·rig (thim′bəl rig′) *n. v.* **-rigged, -rig·ging.** —*n.* a swindling game in which the operator apparently covers a small ball or pea with one of three thimble-like cups, and then, moving the cups about, offers to bet that no one can tell under which cup the ball or pea lies.
—*v.* cheat by or as by the thimblerig. —**thim′ble·rig′ger,** *n.*

thin (thin) *adj.* **thin·ner, thin·nest,** *adv. v.* **thinned, thin·ning.** —*adj.* **1** with little space from one side to the opposite side; not thick: *thin paper, thin wire.* **2** having little flesh; slender; lean: *a thin person.* **3** not set close together; scanty: *He has thin hair.* **4** not dense: *The air on the top of those high mountains is thin.* **5** few and far apart; not abundant: *The actors played to a thin audience.* **6** not like glue or syrup; like water; of less substance than usual: *thin milk.* **7** not deep or strong: *a shrill, thin voice.* **8** having little depth, fullness, or intensity: *a thin color.* **9** easily seen through; flimsy: *a thin excuse.*
—*adv.* in a thin manner.
—*v.* **1** make or become thin: *thin this paint.* **2** make less crowded or close by removing individuals: *thin a row of beets.* **3 a** of a place, become less full or crowded. **b** of a crowd, become less numerous. [OE *thynne*] —**thin′ly,** *adv.* —**thin′ner,** *n.* —**thin′ness,** *n.*

Syn. *adj.* **1** narrow, slim, attenuated. **2 Thin, lean, gaunt** = having little flesh. **Thin** emphasizes its basic meaning of being not thick through, but sometimes suggests lack of the normal or usual amount of flesh, as from sickness, strain, lack of food, etc.: *She has a thin face.* **Lean** emphasizes lack of fat, and suggests natural thinness with firm, solid flesh: *The forest ranger is lean and brown.* **Gaunt** adds to *thin* the idea of showing the bones, and often suggests a starved or worn look: *Gaunt, bearded men stumbled into camp.* **5** sparse.

thine (ᴛʜīn) *Mainly archaic or poetic.* —*pron.* **1** belonging to thee; yours. **2** the one or ones belonging to thee; yours. —*adj.* thy; your. [OE *thīn*] ☛ See **thou** for usage note.

thing (thing) *n.* **1** any object or substance: *All the things in the house were burned. Put these things away.* **2** whatever is spoken or thought of; any act, deed, fact, event, happening, idea, or opinion: *A strange thing happened. It was a good thing to do.* **3** a person or creature (referred to with pity, scorn, condescension, etc.):

a silly old thing, a mean thing, a dear little thing, a poor thing. **4 do one's thing,** *Informal.* express one's personality by doing what one does well or enjoys most. **5 know a thing or two,** *Informal.* be experienced or wise. **6 make a good thing of,** *Informal.* profit from. **7 see things,** have hallucinations. **8 the thing,** anything considered desirable, suitable, appropriate, etc.: *the latest thing in swimsuits, the thing to do.* **9 things,** *pl.* **a** belongings; possessions: *Take your things.* **b** clothes and wearing apparel generally: *Put on your things.* [OE]

thing·a·ma·jig (thing′ə mə jig′) *n. Informal.* thingumbob.

thing·um·a·bob (thing′ə mə bob′) *n. Informal.* thingumbob.

thing·um·bob (thing′əm bob′) *n. Informal.* something whose name one forgets or does not bother to mention.

think (thingk) *v.* **thought, think·ing. 1** have ideas; use the mind: *You must learn to think clearly.* **2** have in the mind: *He thought that he would go.* **3** have one's thoughts full of: *He thinks nothing but sports.* **4** have an idea: *He had thought of her as still a child.* **5** have an opinion; believe: *Do what you think fit.* **6** reflect; consider: *I must think before answering.* **7** imagine: *You can't think how surprised I was.* **8** remember: *I can't think of his name.* **9** intend: *He thinks to escape punishment.* **10** expect: *I did not think to find you here.*
think aloud, say what one is thinking.
think out, a plan or discover by thinking. **b** solve or understand by thinking. **c** think through to the end.
think out loud, say what one is thinking.
think over, consider carefully.
think through, think about until one reaches an understanding or conclusion.
think twice, think again before acting; hesitate.
think up, plan or discover by thinking. [OE *thencan*]
—think′er, *n.*
Syn. 1 Think, reflect, meditate = use the powers of the mind. **Think** is the general word meaning to use the mind to form ideas, reach conclusions, understand what is known, etc.: *I must think about your offer before I accept it.* **Reflect** suggests quietly and seriously thinking over a subject, by turning the thoughts (back) upon it: *They need time to reflect on their problems.* **Meditate** suggests focussing the thoughts on a subject from every point of view, to understand all its sides and relations: *He meditated on truth.* **4** conceive. **8** recollect, recall. **9** purpose, plan, mean.

think·a·ble (thingk′ə bəl) *adj.* capable of being thought; conceivable.

think·ing (thingk′ing) *adj.* **1** that thinks; reasoning. **2** thoughtful or reflective. **3 put on one's thinking cap,** take time for thinking over something. *—n.* thought. **—Syn.** *adj.* **2** contemplative, pensive, cogitative.

think tank *Informal.* a centre for technological research, often engaged in government and defence projects.

thin-skinned (thin′skind′) *adj.* **1** having a thin skin. **2** sensitive to criticism, reproach, rebuff, etc.; touchy.

third (thėrd) *adj.* **1** next after the second; last in a series of three. **2** being one of three equal parts. *—n.* **1** the next after the second; the last in a series of three. **2** one of three equal parts. **3** in music: **a** a tone three degrees from another tone. **b** the interval between such tones. **c** the combination of such tones. [OE *thirda*, var. of *thridda* < *thrēo* three]

third-class (thėrd′klas′) *adj.* **1** of or belonging to a class after the second. **2** of or having to do with the class of mail that includes unsealed greeting cards, printed circulars, books, etc. *—adv.* by third-class mail.

third degree the use of severe treatment by the police to force a person to give information or make a confession.

third estate persons not in the nobility or clergy; common people.

third·ly (thėrd′lē) *adv.* in the third place.

third party 1 a person or group affected by the actions of two major parties in a contract, arrangement, etc. **2** in a two-party political system, any party other than the two major ones.

third person in grammar, the form of a pronoun or verb used to refer to a person who is neither the person speaking nor the one spoken to. *He, she, it,* and *they* are pronouns of the third person.

third rail a rail parallelling the ordinary rails of a railway. It carries a powerful electric current and is used on some railways instead of an overhead wire.

third-rate (thėrd′rāt′) *adj.* **1** of the third class. **2** distinctly inferior.

third world the underdeveloped countries of the world, especially those emerging in Africa and Asia since World War II.

thirst (thėrst) *n.* **1** a dry, painful feeling caused by having nothing to drink; a desire or need for something to drink. **2** a strong desire: *a thirst for adventure.* *—v.* **1** feel thirsty; be thirsty. **2** have a strong desire. [OE *thurst*]

thirst·y (thėrs′tē) *adj.* **thirst·i·er, thirst·i·est. 1** feeling thirst; having thirst. **2** without water or moisture; dry. **3** having a strong desire; eager. **—thirst′i·ly,** *adv.* **—thirst′i·ness,** *n.*

thir·teen (thėr′tēn′) *n. adj.* three more than ten; 13. [OE *thrēotēne*]

Thirteen Colonies See **colony** (def. 7).

thir·teenth (thėr′tēnth′) *adj. n.* **1** next after the 12th; last in a series of 13. **2** one, or being one, of 13 equal parts.

thir·ti·eth (thėr′tē ith) *adj. n.* **1** next after the 29th; last in a series of 30. **2** one, or being one, of 30 equal parts.

thir·ty (thėr′tē) *n.* **-ties,** *adj.* three times ten; 30. [OE *thrītig*]

thirty-second note in music, a note equal to one thirty-second of a whole note (𝅘𝅥𝅰). Also, **demisemiquaver.**

thirty-second rest in music, a rest lasting as long as a thirty-second note.

this (ᴛʜis) *pron.* **these,** *adj.* **these,** *adv. —pron.* **1** the person, thing, event, quality, condition, idea, etc. that is present, mentioned, or referred to now: *This is the best. After this you must go home.* **2** the one emphasized or contrasted with another called "that": *This is newer than that.*
—adj. **1** present; near; spoken of; referred to: *this minute, this child, this idea.* **2 a** indicating the nearer of two or the nearest of several things in time or space: *Do you prefer this tie or that one in the closet?* **b** indicating one thing as distinct from another or others: *You may have this one, this next one, or that one, but not all three.*
—adv. to this extent or degree; so: *You can have this much.* [OE]
☛ This, like *that*, is regularly used to refer to the idea of a preceding clause or sentence: *He had always had his own way at home, and this made him a poor roommate.*

this·tle (this′əl) *n.* a plant having a prickly stalk and leaves. The purple thistle is the national flower of Scotland. [OE *thistel*]

this·tly (this′lē) *adj.* **1** like thistles; prickly. **2** having many thistles.

thith·er (thiᴛʜ′ər) *adv.* to that place; toward that place; there. *—adj.* on that side; farther. [OE *thider*]

tho' (ᴛʜō) *conj. adv. Informal.* though.

thole (thōl) *n.* a peg on the side of a boat to hold an oar in rowing. [OE *tholl*]

thole·pin (thōl′pin′) *n.* thole.

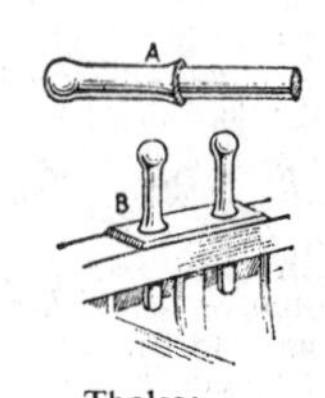

Tholes: A, single; B, double.

Thomp·son submachine gun (tomp′sən) *Trademark.* a .45-calibre, air-cooled, automatic weapon that can be carried and operated by one man. Also, **Tommy gun.** [< General John T. *Thompson*, 1860-1940, U.S. Army, one of the inventors]

thong (thong) *n.* **1** a narrow strip of leather, etc., especially one used as a fastening. **2** the lash of a whip. **3** a kind of sandal held on the foot by a narrow piece of leather, plastic, etc. that passes between the toes. [OE *thwang*]

Thor (thôr) *n.* in ancient Scandinavian mythology, the god of thunder, war, and agriculture.

tho·rac·ic (thô ras′ik) *adj.* of or having to do with the thorax. The thoracic cavity contains the heart and lungs.

tho·rax (thô′raks) *n.* **-rax·es, -ra·ces** (-rə sēz′). **1** in anatomy and zoology, the part of the body between the neck and the abdomen. A man's chest is his thorax. **2** the second division of an insect's body, between the head and the abdomen. See **abdomen** for diagram. [< L < Gk.]

tho·rite (thô′rīt) *n.* a mineral consisting essentially of a silicate of thorium.

tho·ri·um (thô′rē əm) *n.* a radio-active metallic chemical element present in certain rare minerals. *Symbol*: Th; *at.no.* 90; *at.wt.* 232.038. [< NL *thorium* < *Thor*]

thorn (thôrn) *n.* **1** a sharp-pointed growth on a stem or branch of a tree or plant. **2** a tree or plant that has thorns on it. **3 thorn in the flesh** or **side,** a cause of trouble or annoyance. [OE] —**Syn.** *n.* **1** spine, prickle.

thorn apple 1 the fruit of the hawthorn; haw. **2** the hawthorn. **3** the jimson weed.

thorn·y (thôr′nē) *adj.* **thorn·i·er, thorn·i·est. 1** full of thorns. **2** troublesome; annoying. —**Syn. 1** spiny, prickly. **2** vexatious, difficult.

tho·ron (thô′ron) *n.* a radio-active, gaseous isotope of radon, formed in the disintegration of thorium. *Abbrev.*: Tn. [< *thor*(*ium*) + *-on*, as in *neon*]

thor·ough (thėr′ō or thėr′ə) *adj.* **1** being all that is needed; complete: *a thorough search.* **2** doing all that should be done and neglecting nothing: *The doctor was very thorough in his examination of the patient.* —*adv. prep. Archaic.* through. Also, **thoro.** [OE *thuruh*, var. of *thurh* through] —**thor′ough·ly,** *adv.* —**thor′ough·ness,** *n.*

thor·ough·bred (thėr′ə bred′) *adj.* **1** of pure breed or stock. **2** of persons, well-bred; thoroughly trained. **3** of or having to do with the Thoroughbreds. —*n.* **1** a thoroughbred horse or other animal. **2** a well-bred or thoroughly trained person.

Thor·ough·bred (thėr′ə bred′) *n.* **1** a breed of horse, used especially in racing, originally derived from a domestic English stock in the female line and an Arabian or Turkish stock in the male line. **2** a horse belonging to this breed.

thor·ough·fare (thėr′ə fãr′) *n.* **1** a passage, road, or street open at both ends. **2** a main road; highway: *The Queen Elizabeth Way is a well-known thoroughfare between Toronto and Niagara Falls.* **3 no thoroughfare,** do not go through.

thor·ough·go·ing (thėr′ə gō′ing) *adj.* thorough; complete.

thorp (thôrp) *n. Archaic.* a village; a small town. [OE]

those (ᴛʜōz) *adj. pron.* pl. of **that.** [OE *thās* these]

thou (ᴛʜou) *pron. Archaic. nom.* **thou**; *poss.* **thine**; *obj.* **thee**; *pl. nom.* **you** or **ye**; *poss.* **yours**; *obj.* **you** or **ye.** you; the one spoken to. [OE *thū*]

☛ **Thou, thine, thee,** and **thy** are archaic forms of the pronoun and possessive adjective for the second person, used now only in the formal language of church services.

though (ᴛʜō) *conj.* **1** in spite of the fact that; notwithstanding the fact that: *Though it was pouring, the girls went to school.* **2** yet; still; nevertheless: *He is better, though not yet cured.* **3** even if; granting or supposing that: *Though I fail, I shall try again.* **4 as though,** as if; as it would be if. —*adv. Informal.* however: *I am sorry about our quarrel; you began it, though.* [ME *thoh* < ON *thó*, with *-h* from OE *thēah*]

thought (thot or thôt) *n.* **1** what one thinks; an idea; notion: *Her thought was to have a picnic.* **2** the power or process of thinking; mental activity: *Thought helps us solve problems.* **3** reasoning: *He applied thought to the problem.* **4** the intellectual activity or mental product characteristic of the thinkers of a (specified) group, time, or place: *in modern scientific thought, 16th-century thought.* **5** consideration; attention; care; regard: *Show some thought for others.* **6** intention: *His thought was to avoid controversy.* **7** a little bit; trifle: *Be a thought more polite.* —*v.* pt. and pp. of **think.** [OE *thōht*] —**Syn.** *n.* **1** concept. See **idea. 2** cogitation, deliberation, meditation. **6** purpose, design.

thought control the strict limiting or regimentation of ideas, reasoning, etc. to make them conform to those of a particular group, government, etc.

thought·ful (thot′fəl or thôt′fəl) *adj.* **1** deep in thought; thinking: *He was thoughtful for a while and then replied, "No."* **2** careful; heedful. **3** careful of others; considerate: *She is always thoughtful of her mother.*

hat, āge, cãre, fär; let, ēqual, tėrm; it, īce
hot, ōpen, ôrder; oil, out; cup, pu̇t, rüle, ūse
əbove, takən, pencəl, lemən, circəs
ch, child; ng, long; sh, ship
th, thin; ᴛʜ, then; zh, measure

—**thought′ful·ly,** *adv.* —**thought′ful·ness,** *n.*

Syn. 1 reflective, meditative, contemplative. **3 Thoughtful, considerate** = giving careful attention to the comfort or feelings of others. **Thoughtful** emphasizes concerning oneself with the comfort and welfare of others and doing, without being asked, things that will add to their well-being or happiness: *A thoughtful neighbor, knowing the girl was sick and alone, took her some hot food.* **Considerate** emphasizes concerning oneself with the feelings and rights of others and trying to spare them from discomfort, pain, or unhappiness: *She is considerate enough to tell her parents where she goes.*

thought·less (thot′lis or thôt′lis) *adj.* **1** without thought; doing things without thinking; careless. **2** showing little or no care or regard for others; not considerate. **3** stupid. —**thought′less·ly,** *adv.* —**thought′less·ness,** *n.* —**Syn. 1** remiss.

thought-out (thot′out′ or thôt′-) *adj.* carefully considered; deliberate.

thou·sand (thou′zənd) *n. adj.* ten hundred; 1,000. [OE *thūsend*]

thou·sand·fold (thou′zənd fōld′) *adj. adv. n.* a thousand times as much or as many.

thou·sandth (thou′zəndth) *adj. n.* **1** the last in a series of a thousand. **2** one, or being one, of a thousand equal parts.

Thra·cian (thrā′shən) in ancient times: —*adj.* of or having to do with Thrace, a region in the eastern part of the Balkan peninsula, or its people. —*n.* a native or inhabitant of ancient Thrace.

thral·dom (throl′dəm or thrôl′dəm) *n.* thralldom.

thrall (throl or thrôl) *n.* **1** a person in bondage; slave. **2** thralldom; bondage; slavery. [OE < ON *thrǽll*]

thrall·dom or **thral·dom** (throl′dəm or thrôl′dəm) *n.* bondage; slavery.

thrash (thrash) *v.* **1** beat: *The man thrashed the boy for stealing the apples.* **2** move violently; toss: *Unable to sleep, the patient thrashed about in his bed.* **3** thresh. **4 thrash out,** settle by thorough discussion. **5 thrash over,** go over again and again. [var. of *thresh*]

thrash·er (thrash′ər) *n.* **1** a person or thing that thrashes. **2** a thresher (def. 3). **3** any of several North American birds related to the mockingbird.

thread (thred) *n.* **1** cotton, silk, flax, etc. spun out into a fine cord: *Thread is used for sewing.* **2** something long and slender like a thread: *Threads of gold could be seen in the ore.* **3** something that connects the parts of a story, speech, etc. **4** the winding, sloping ridge of a bolt, screw, pipe joint, etc. **5 hang by** or **on a thread,** be in a precarious position. —*v.* **1** pass a thread through: *She threaded her needle. Mary threaded a hundred beads.* **2** form into a thread: *Cook the syrup until it will thread.* **3** pass like a thread through; pervade. **4** make one's way through; make (one's way) carefully; go on a winding course: *He threaded his way through the crowd.* **5** cut threads into a bolt, screw, pipe, joint, etc. [OE *thrǣd*] —**thread′like′,** *adj.*

THREAD

Thread (def. 4)

thread·bare (thred′bãr′) *adj.* **1** having the nap worn off; worn so much that the threads show: *a threadbare coat.* **2** wearing clothes worn to the threads; shabby. **3** old and worn; stale. —**Syn. 3** hackneyed, trite.

thread·worm (thred′wėrm′) *n.* a threadlike worm, especially a pin worm.

thread·y (thred′ē) *adj.* **1** consisting of or resembling a thread. **2** fibrous; stringy or viscid. **3** of the pulse, thin and feeble. **4** of the voice, etc., lacking in fullness. —**thread′i·ness,** *n.*

threat (thret) *n.* **1** a statement of what will be done to hurt or punish someone. **2** a sign or cause of possible evil or harm: *Those black clouds are a threat of rain.* [OE *thrēat* troop, throng; coercion]

threat·en (thret′ən) *v.* **1** make a threat against; say what will be done to hurt or punish: *threaten a person with imprisonment.* **2** be a sign of (possible evil or harm, etc.): *Black clouds threaten rain.* **3** be a threat. **4** utter threats: *Do you mean to threaten?* **5** be a cause of possible evil or harm to: *A flood threatened the city.* [OE *thrēatnian* urge; coerce] —**threat′en·er,** *n.* —**threat′en·ing·ly,** *adv.* **Syn. 1 Threaten, menace** = promise or warn of harm, injury, or punishment. **Threaten** emphasizes trying to force or influence someone to do (or not to do) something, by stating that some harm or hurt will be inflicted to punish disobedience or to get even: *He threatened to shoot her if she screamed.* **Menace** emphasizes showing by a look, position, movement, etc. an intention to harm: *He menaced her with a gun.* **2** portend, presage, forebode, augur.

three (thrē) *n.* **1** one more than two; 3. **2** a set of three persons or things. **3** a playing card, die, domino, etc. having three spots. —*adj.* one more than two; 3. [OE *thrēo*] —**Syn.** *n.* **2** trio, triplet.

three-D or **3-D** (thrē′dē′) *n.* a three-dimensional motion picture.

three-deck·er (thrē′dek′ər) *n.* **1** a ship having three decks. **2** anything having three stories, layers, or parts: *a three-decker sandwich.*

three·fold (thrē′fōld′) *adj.* **1** three times as much or as many. **2** having three parts. —*adv. n.* three times as much or as many.

three-four (thrē′fôr′) *adj.* in music, indicating or having three quarter notes in a bar or measure, the first of which is accented, as in a waltz.

three-mile limit the distance from the shore that, according to international law, is included within the jurisdiction of the country possessing the coast.

three·pence (thrup′əns or threp′əns) *n.* **1** in Britain, three pennies. **2** a former British coin worth three pennies.

three·pen·ny (thrup′ən ē, threp′ən ē, or thrē′pen′ē) *adj.* **1** worth three pence. **2** of little worth; cheap; paltry.

three-ply (thrē′plī′) *adj.* having three thicknesses, layers, folds, or strands.

three·quar·ter (thrē′kwôr′tər) *adj.* three-four: *three-quarter time.*

three R's reading, writing, and arithmetic.

three·score (thrē′skôr′) *adj.* three times twenty; 60.

three·some (thrē′səm) *n.* **1** a group of three people. **2** any game played by three people. **3** the players in such a game.

Three Wise Men the men who came from the East to honor the infant Jesus; the Magi.

thren·o·dy (thren′ə dē) *n.* **-dies.** a song of lamentation, especially at a person's death. [< Gk. *thrēnōidia* < *thrēnos* lament + *ōidē* song]

thresh (thresh) *v.* **1** separate the grain or seeds from (wheat, etc.). Nowadays most farmers use a machine to thresh their wheat. **2** toss about; move violently; thrash. **3 thresh out,** settle by thorough discussion. **4 thresh over,** go over again and again. [OE *threscan*]

thresh·er (thresh′ər) *n.* **1** a person or thing that threshes. **2** a machine used for separating the grain or seeds from wheat, etc. **3** a large shark having a long tail.

thresh·old (thresh′ōld or thresh′hōld) *n.* **1** a piece of wood or stone under a door. **2** a doorway. **3** the point of entering; a beginning point: *The scientist was on the threshold of an important discovery.* **4** in psychology and physiology, the limit below which a given stimulus ceases to be perceptible, or the point beyond which two stimuli cannot be differentiated. [OE *thresch(w)old*]

threw (thrü) *v.* pt. of **throw.**

thrice (thrīs) *adv.* **1** three times. **2** every; extremely. [ME *thries* < OE *thriga* thrice]

thrid (thrid) *v.* **thrid·ded, thrid·ding.** *Archaic or dialect.* thread.

thrift (thrift) *n.* **1** the absence of waste; economical management; the habit of saving: *By thrift she managed to get along on her small salary.* **2** a plant having pink, white, or lavender flowers that grows on mountains and along seashores. [< *thrive*] —**Syn. 1** economy, frugality.

thrift·less (thrift′lis) *adj.* without thrift; wasteful. —**thrift′less·ly,** *adv.* —**thrift′less·ness,** *n.*

thrift·y (thrif′tē) *adj.* **thrift·i·er, thrift·i·est. 1** careful in spending; economical; saving. **2** thriving; flourishing: *a thrifty plant.* **3** prosperous; well-to-do; successful: *The countryside had many fine, thrifty farms.* —**thrift′i·ly,** *adv.* —**thrift′i·ness,** *n.* —**Syn. 1** provident, frugal, sparing. See **economical.**

thrill (thril) *n.* **1** a shivering, exciting feeling. **2** a vibrating or quivering; throbbing; tremor. [< v.] —*v.* **1** give a shivering, exciting feeling to: *Stories of adventure thrilled him.* **2** have a shivering, exciting feeling. **3** quiver; tremble: *Her voice thrilled with terror.* [var. of *thirl* < OE *thyrlian* pierce < *thurh* through] —**thrill′ing·ly,** *adv.* —**Syn.** *v.* **3** vibrate, throb.

thrill·er (thril′ər) *n.* **1** a person or thing that thrills. **2** *Informal.* a sensational story, play, or motion picture, especially one involving a murder.

thrips (thrips) *n.* any of a group of small insects having long, narrow wings fringed with hairs. Most varieties feed on plant juices, and many are destructive of plants and grain. [< L < Gk. *thrips* woodworm]

thrive (thrīv) *v.* **throve** or **thrived, thrived** or **thriv·en, thriv·ing. 1** grow strong; grow vigorously: *Flowers will not thrive without sunshine.* **2** be successful; grow rich; prosper. [ME < ON *thrifa(sk)*] —**thriv′ing·ly,** *adv.* —**Syn.** flourish.

thriv·en (thriv′ən) *v.* a pp. of **thrive.**

thro' (thrü) *prep. adv. adj. Esp.U.S.* through.

throat (thrōt) *n.* **1** the front of the neck. **2** the passage from the mouth to the stomach or the lungs. **3** any narrow passage: *the throat of a mine.* **4** *Informal.* **jump down someone's throat,** attack or criticize a person with sudden violence. **5 lump in the throat, a** a feeling of inability to swallow. **b** a feeling of sadness. **6 stick in one's throat,** be hard or unpleasant to say. [OE *throte*]

throat·ed (thrōt′id) *adj.* having a certain kind of throat: *white-throated.*

throat·y (thrōt′ē) *adj.* **throat·i·er, throat·i·est. 1** produced or modified in the throat; guttural: *a throaty sound.* **2** of a person's voice, low-pitched and resonant. —**throat′i·ness,** *n.*

throb (throb) *v.* **throbbed, throb·bing,** *n.* —*v.* **1** beat rapidly or strongly: *The long climb up the hill made her heart throb.* **2** beat steadily. **3** quiver; tremble. —*n.* **1** a rapid or strong beat: *A throb of pain shot through his head.* **2** a steady beat: *the throb of a pulse.* **3** a quiver; tremble. [ME *throbbe(n)*; ? imitative] —**throb′bing·ly,** *adv.* —**Syn.** *v.* **1** pulsate, palpitate.

throe (thrō) *n.* **1** a violent pang; great pain. **2 throes,** *pl.* **a** anguish; agony. **b** a desperate struggle; violent disturbance. [? a fusion of OE *thrōwian* suffer, and *thrāwan* twist; throw]

throm·bo·sis (throm bō′sis) *n.* a coagulation of blood in a blood vessel or in the heart. [< NL < Gk. *thrombōsis,* ult. < *thrombos* clot]

throm·bus (throm′bəs) *n.* **-bi** (-bī or -bē). a blood clot causing thrombosis.

throne (thrōn) *n. v.* **throned, thron·ing.** —*n.* **1** the chair on which a king, queen, bishop, or other person of high rank sits during ceremonies. **2** the power or authority of a king, queen, etc. **3** the person who sits on a throne; sovereign. —*v.* enthrone. [ME < OF < L < Gk. *thronos*]

throng (throng) *n.* a crowd; multitude. —*v.* **1** crowd; fill with a crowd. **2** come together in a crowd; go or press in large numbers. [OE *(ge)thrang*] —**Syn.** *n.* host, mass, pack. See **crowd.**

thros·tle (thros′əl) *n. Esp.Brit.* a thrush, especially the song thrush. [OE]

throt·tle (throt′əl) *n. v.* **-tled, -tling.** —*n.* **1** a valve regulating the flow of steam, gasoline vapor, etc. to an engine. **2** a lever, pedal, etc. working such a valve. **3** throat. —*v.* **1** stop the breath of by pressure on the throat; strangle: *The thief throttled the dog to keep it from barking.* **2** choke; suffocate. **3** check or stop the flow of; suppress: *High tariffs throttle trade between countries.* **4** lessen the speed of (an engine) by closing a throttle. [ME; perhaps dim. of *throat*]

through (thrü) *prep.* 1 from end to end of; from side to side of; between the parts of; from beginning to end of: *The soldiers marched through the town. The men cut a tunnel through a mountain.* 2 here and there in; over; around: *We travelled through Quebec, visiting many old towns.* 3 because of; by reason of: *The woman refused help through pride.* 4 by means of: *He became rich through hard work and ability.* 5 having reached the end of; finished with: *We are through school at three o'clock.* 6 a during the whole of; throughout: *work from dawn through the day and into the night.* b during and until the finish of: *help a person through hard times.*
—adv. 1 from end to end; from side to side; between the parts: *The bullet hit the wall and went through.*
2 completely; thoroughly: *He walked home in the rain and was wet through.* 3 from beginning to end: *She read the book through.* 4 along the whole distance; all the way: *The train goes through to Vancouver.* 5 **through and through,** completely; thoroughly.
—adj. 1 a going all the way without change: *a through train from Montreal to Toronto.* b for the whole distance or journey: *a through ticket.* c going straight on without stopping: *through traffic.* 2 having reached the end; finished: *I am almost through.* 3 passing or extending from one end, side, surface, etc. to the other. [earlier *thourgh*, OE *thurh*] —**Syn.** *prep.* 3, 4 See **by.**

through·out (thrü out′) *prep.* all the way through; through all; in every part of: *Dominion Day is celebrated throughout Canada.* *—adv.* in every part: *The house is well built throughout.*

through street a street on which traffic is given the right of way at intersections; opposed to *stop street.*

throve (thrōv) *v.* pt. of **thrive.**

throw (thrō) *v.* **threw, thrown, throw·ing,** *n.* *—v.* 1 cast; toss; hurl: *throw a ball. The fire hose threw water on the fire.* 2 bring to the ground: *His horse threw him.* 3 a put carelessly or in haste: *Throw some clothes on and run.* b put or move quickly or by force: *throw oneself into a fight, throw a man into prison.* c put into a certain condition: *throw a person into confusion.* 4 turn, direct, or move, especially quickly: *She threw a glance at each car that passed us.* 5 move (a lever, etc.) that connects or disconnects parts of a switch, clutch, or other mechanism. 6 connect or disconnect thus. 7 shed. A snake throws its skin. 8 of some animals, bring forth (young). 9 *Informal.* let an opponent win (a race, game, etc.), often for money. 10 make a specified cast with dice. 11 twist (silk) into threads. 12 shape on a potter's wheel: *throw a bowl from a ball of clay.* 13 *Informal.* give (a party, etc.).
throw away, a get rid of; discard. b waste. c fail to use.
throw back, revert to an ancestral type.
throw cold water on, discourage by being indifferent or unwilling.
throw in, add as a gift.
throw off, a get rid of. b cause to lose: *throw a hound off the scent.* c *Informal.* produce (a poem, etc.) in an offhand manner.
throw oneself at, try very hard to get the love, friendship, or favor of.
throw open, a open suddenly or widely. b remove all obstacles or restrictions from.
throw out, a get rid of; discard. b reject. c expel. d in baseball, put out (a base runner) by throwing the ball to a base.
throw over, give up; discard; abandon.
throw up, a *Informal.* vomit. b give up; abandon. c build rapidly.
—n. 1 a cast, toss, etc. 2 the distance a thing is or may be thrown. 3 a scarf; light covering. 4 a cast at dice; venture. [OE *thrāwan* twist] —**throw′er,** *n.*
Syn. *v.* 1 **Throw, toss, cast** = send something through the air by a sudden twist or quick movement of the arm. **Throw** is the general word: *The children threw pillows at each other.* **Toss** = throw lightly or carelessly with the palm up: *Please toss me the matches.* **Cast** is literary or archaic in the literal meaning of *throw*, except in special uses, as in games, voting, fishing, sailing, but is used figuratively: *They cast anchor. She cast dignity to the winds, and ran* (fig.).

throw·a·way (thrō′ə wā′) *n.* a free handbill or leaflet carrying advertising or other information; handout. *—adj.* to be discarded or thrown away after use.

throw·back (thrō′bak′) *n.* 1 a throwing back. 2 a set back or check. 3 a reversion to an ancestral type or character; an example of such a reversion: *The boy seemed to be a throwback to his great-grandfather.*

hat, āge, cãre, fär; let, ēqual, tėrm; it, īce
hot, ōpen, ôrder; oil, out; cup, pu̇t, rüle, ūse
əbove, takən, pencəl, lemən, circəs
ch, child; ng, long; sh, ship
th, thin; ᴛʜ, then; zh, measure

thrown (thrōn) *v.* pp. of **throw.**

thrum[1] (thrum) *v.* **thrummed, thrum·ming,** *n.* *—v.* 1 play on a stringed instrument by plucking the strings, especially in an idle, mechanical, or unskilful way: *thrum a guitar.* 2 of a guitar, etc. or its strings, sound when thrummed on. 3 drum or tap idly with the fingers: *thrum on a table.* 4 a recite or tell in a monotonous way. b hum over (a melody). *—n.* the sound made by thrumming. [imitative] —**thrum′mer,** *n.*

thrum[2] (thrum) *n.* 1 an end of the warp thread left unwoven on the loom after the web is cut off. 2 loose thread or yarn. 3 a fringe. [OE *thrum*; in *tungethrum* tongue ligament]

thrush[1] (thrush) *n.* any of a large group of migratory songbirds that includes the robin, the bluebird, the wood thrush, and the European song thrush. [OE *thrȳsce*]

thrush[2] (thrush) *n.* 1 a fungous disease often found in children, marked by white patches in the throat and mouth. 2 a diseased condition of a horse's foot.

thrust (thrust) *v.* **thrust, thrust·ing,** *n.* *—v.* 1 push with force: *He thrust his hands into his pockets.* 2 stab: *thrust a knife into an apple.* 3 put forth; extend: *The tree thrust its roots deep into the ground.*
—n. 1 a forcible push; drive. 2 a stab. 3 an attack. 4 in architecture, the lateral force exerted by an arch, etc. against an abutment or support. It must be counteracted to prevent the structure from collapsing. 5 a the endwise push exerted by the rotation of a propeller, that causes an aircraft, ship, etc. to move. b the force exerted by the rearward ejection of gases, etc., as in a jet engine, a rocket, etc., producing forward movement. [ME < ON *thrȳsta*] —**thrust′er,** *n.* —**Syn.** *n.* 1 shove, punch, lunge.

thud (thud) *n.* *v.* **thud·ded, thud·ding.** *—n.* 1 a dull sound caused by a blow or fall: *The book hit the floor with a thud.* 2 a blow or thump. *—v.* hit, move, or strike with a thud. [? ME *thudden* < OE *thyddan* strike]

thug (thug) *n.* 1 a ruffian; cutthroat. 2 in India, a member of a former religious organization of robbers and murderers. [< Hind. < Skt. *sthaga* rogue]

Thu·le (thü′lē) *n.* 1 the part of the world that the ancient Greeks and Romans regarded as farthest north, that is, some island or region north of Britain. 2 an Eskimo culture of N. Greenland, lasting from about A.D. 500 to 1400. [< L < Gk. *Thoulē*]

thu·li·um (thü′lē əm or thūl′ē əm) *n.* a rare metallic chemical element of the yttrium group. *Symbol*: Tm; *at.no.* 69; *at.wt.* 168.934. [< NL *thulium* < *Thule*]

thumb (thum) *n.* 1 the short, thick finger of the human hand, next to the forefinger. 2 the part that covers the thumb: *the thumb of a mitten.* 3 **be all thumbs,** be very clumsy, awkward, etc. 4 **thumbs down,** a sign of disapproval or rejection. 5 **thumbs up,** a sign of approval or acceptance. 6 **under the thumb of,** under the power or influence of. *—v.* 1 soil or wear by handling with the thumbs: *The books were badly thumbed.* 2 turn pages of (a book, etc.) rapidly, reading only portions. 3 handle awkwardly. 4 *Informal.* ask for or get (a free ride) by or as if by holding up one's thumb to motorists going in one's direction. 5 **thumb off,** in hockey, indicate by a jerk of the thumb that a given player has been penalized for an infraction of the rules and that he is to take his place in the penalty box. [OE *thūma*] —**thumb′like′,** *adj.*

thumb·nail (thum′nāl′) *n.* 1 the nail of the thumb. 2 something very small or short. *—adj.* very small or short.

thumb·screw (thum′skrü′) *n.* 1 a screw made so that its head can be easily turned with the thumb and a finger. 2 an instrument of torture for squeezing the thumbs.

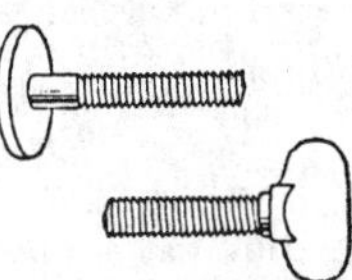
Thumbscrews (def. 1)

thumb·tack (thum′tak′) *n.* a tack having a broad, flat head, designed to be pressed into a wall, board, etc. with the thumb.

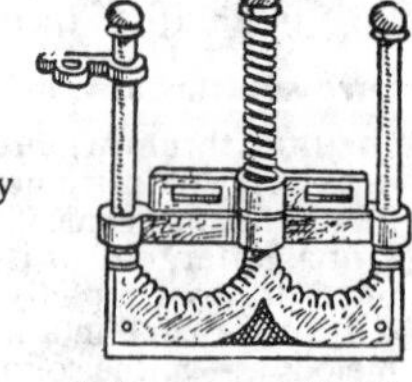
A thumbscrew (def. 2)

thump (thump) *v.* **1** strike with something thick and heavy: *He thumped the table with his fist.* **2** strike against (something) heavily and noisily: *The shutters thumped the wall in the wind.* **3** make a dull sound; pound: *The hammer thumped against the wood.* **4** beat violently: *His heart thumped.* **5** beat or thrash severely. —*n.* **1** a blow with something thick and heavy; a heavy knock. **2** the dull sound made by a blow, knock, or fall. [imitative] —**thump′er,** *n.* —**Syn.** *n.* **1** whack, bang.

thump·ing (thump′ing) *adj. Informal.* great; huge; whopping.

thun·der (thun′dər) *n.* **1** the loud noise that often follows a flash of lightning. It is caused by a disturbance of the air resulting from the discharge of electricity. **2** any noise like thunder: *the thunder of Niagara Falls, a thunder of applause.* **3** a threat. **4** denunciation. **5** a thunderbolt. **6 steal someone's thunder,** use another's idea or method without asking him or giving him credit. —*v.* **1** give forth thunder. **2** make a noise like thunder. **3** utter very loudly; roar: *thunder a reply.* **4** threaten. **5** denounce. [OE *thunor*] —**thun′der·er,** *n.*

thun·der·bird (thun′dər bėrd′) *n.* in the mythology of certain North American Indians, a huge bird believed to cause thunder and lightning.

thun·der·bolt (thun′dər bōlt′) *n.* **1** a flash of lightning and the thunder that follows it. **2** something sudden, startling, and terrible: *The news of his death came as a thunderbolt.*

thun·der·clap (thun′dər klap′) *n.* **1** a loud crash of thunder. **2** something sudden or startling.

thun·der·cloud (thun′dər kloud′) *n.* a dark, electrically charged cloud that brings thunder and lightning.

Thun·der·er (thun′dər ər) *n.* Jupiter; Zeus.

thun·der·head (thun′dər hed′) *n.* one of the round, swelling masses of cumulus clouds often appearing before thunderstorms and frequently developing into thunderclouds.

thun·der·ing (thun′dər ing or thun′dring) *adj.* **1** making thunder; extremely loud. **2** *Informal.* unusual; superlative: extremely big or great. —**thun′der·ing·ly,** *adv.*

thun·der·ous (thun′dər əs or thun′drəs) *adj.* **1** producing thunder. **2** making a noise like thunder. —**thun′der·ous·ly,** *adv.*

thun·der·show·er (thun′dər shou′ər) *n.* a shower accompanied by thunder and lightning.

thun·der·squall (thun′dər skwol′ or -skwôl′) *n.* a squall accompanied by thunder and lightning.

thun·der·storm (thun′dər stôrm′) *n.* a storm accompanied by thunder and lightning.

thun·der·struck (thun′dər struk′) *adj.* overcome, as if hit by a thunderbolt; astonished; amazed.

thu·ri·ble (thūr′ə bəl) *n.* a censor. [ME < L *t(h)uribulum* < *t(h)us, thuris* incense < Gk. *thyos* burnt sacrifice]

Thu·rin·gi·an (thū rin′jē ən or thū rin′jē ən) *adj.* **1** of or having to do with Thuringia, a former state in southern East Germany, or its people. **2** in geology, of or having to do with the upper division of the Permian period in Europe. —*n.* **1** a native or inhabitant of Thuringia. **2** a member of a Germanic tribe living in central Germany till the 6th century.

Thurs. or **Thur.** Thursday.

Thurs·day (thėrz′dē or -dā) *n.* the fifth day of the week, following Wednesday. [OE < ON *Thórsdagr*, literally, day of Thor, translation of LL *dies Jovis* day of Jupiter (or Jove)]

thus (ᴛʜus) *adv.* **1** in this way; in the way just stated, indicated, etc.; in the following manner: *He spoke thus.* **2** accordingly; consequently; therefore: *Thus we decided that he was wrong.* **3** to this extent or degree; so: *thus far.* [OE]

thwack (thwak) *v.* strike vigorously with a stick or something flat. —*n.* a sharp blow with a stick or something flat. [probably imitative]

thwart (thwôrt) *v.* **1** oppose and defeat: *Our army thwarted the enemy attack.* **2** keep from doing something; obstruct. [< adv.] —*n.* **1** a seat across a boat, on which a rower sits. **2** a brace in a canoe. [apparently < adj.] —*adj.* lying across. [< adv.] —*adv.* across; crosswise. [ME < ON *thvert*, adv., across, originally neut. of adj. *thverr* transverse] —**Syn.** *v.* baffle, balk, foil. See **frustrate.**

thy (ᴛʜī) *adj. Mainly archaic or poetic.* your: "*Thy kingdom come, Thy will be done.*" [OE *thīn*] ☛ See **thou** for usage note.

thyme (tīm) *n.* a small plant that has a mintlike fragrance. The leaves of the common **garden thyme** are used for seasoning. The common **wild thyme** is a creeping evergreen. [ME < MF *thym* < L *thymum* < Gk. *thymon*]

thy·mol (thī′mōl or thī′mol) *n.* a crystalline substance obtained from thyme, etc. or made synthetically, used as an antiseptic. *Formula*: $C_{10}H_{13}OH$

thy·mus (thī′məs) *adj.* of or having to do with the thymus gland. —*n.* the thymus gland. [< NL < Gk. *thymos*]

thymus gland in anatomy and zoology, a small ductless gland near the base of the neck. The thymus gland of calves, called sweetbread, is used for food. In man it disappears or becomes rudimentary in the adult.

thy·roid (thī′roid) *n.* **1** the thyroid gland. **2** a medicine made from the thyroid glands of certain animals, used in the treatment of goitre, obesity, etc. **3** the thyroid cartilage. —*adj.* of or having to do with the thyroid gland or thyroid cartilage. [ult. < Gk. *thyreoeidēs* shieldlike < *thyreos* oblong shield (< *thyra* door) + *eidos* form]

thyroid body thyroid gland.

thyroid cartilage the principal cartilage of the larynx, which forms the lump called the Adam's apple in man.

thyroid gland an important ductless gland in the neck of vertebrates that affects growth and metabolism. Goitre is an enlargement or a disorder of the thyroid gland.

thy·rox·in (thī rok′sən) *n.* thyroxine.

thy·rox·ine (thī rok′sēn′) *n.* a white, crystalline substance, the principal secretion of the thyroid gland. It is also prepared synthetically and used to treat goitre and other thyroid disorders. *Formula*: $C_{15}H_{11}I_4NO_4$

thyr·sus (thėr′səs) *n.* **-si** (-sī or -sē). a staff or spear tipped with an ornament like a pine cone and sometimes wrapped round with ivy and vine branches, borne by Dionysus (Bacchus) and his followers. [< L < Gk. *thyrsos* staff, stem]

thy·self (ᴛʜī self′) *pron.* yourself.

ti (tē) *n.* in music, a syllable used for the seventh tone of an eight-tone scale. *Do, re, mi, fa, sol, la, ti, do* are the names of the tones of the scale. See **do²** for diagram. [see GAMUT]

Ti titanium.

ti·ar·a (tē ä′rə or tī ãr′ə) *n.* **1** a band of gold, jewels, or flowers worn around the head as an ornament. **2 a** the triple crown of the Pope. **b** the position or authority of the Pope. **3** in ancient Persia, a head-dress for men. [< L < Gk.]

Ti·bet·an (ti bet′ən) *adj.* of or having to do with Tibet, a region in S.W. China, its people, or their language. —*n.* **1** a member of the group of Mongoloid people of Tibet. **2** the Sino-Tibetan language of Tibet. Also, **Thibetan.**

tib·i·a (tib′ē ə) *n.* **-i·ae** (-ē ē′ or -ē ī′) or **-i·as. 1** in anatomy, the inner and thicker of the two bones of the leg from the knee to the ankle; shinbone. See **skeleton** for diagram. **2** in animals or birds, a corresponding bone. **3** the fourth joint of the leg of an insect. **4** in ancient times, a flute. [< L]

tib·i·al (tib′ē əl) *adj.* of or having to do with the tibia.

tic (tik) *n.* a habitual, involuntary twitching of the muscles, especially those of the face. [< F]

ti·cal or **ti·kal** (tə käl′ or tē′kəl) *n.* **-ti·cals** or **-ti·cal. 1** a unit of money in Thailand. **2** a coin worth one tical. See table at **money.** [< Thai]

tick[1] (tik) *n.* **1** a sound made by a clock or watch. **2** a sound like it. **3** *Informal.* a moment; instant. **3** a small mark used in checking. We use √ or / as a tick.
—*v.* **1** make a tick. **2** mark off: *The clock ticked away the minutes.* **3** mark with a tick; check: *He ticked off the items one by one.* **4** *Informal.* function; operate: *One wonders what makes politicians tick.* **5 tick off,** scold; reprimand; tell off. **6 tick over,** of an automobile engine, etc., run gently; idle. [probably ult. imitative]

tick[2] (tik) *n.* a mitelike animal that lives on animals and sucks their blood. [OE *ticia*]

tick[3] (tik) *n.* **1** the cloth covering of a mattress or pillow. **2** *Informal.* ticking. [probably ult. < L *theca* case < Gk. *thēkē*]

tick·bird (tik′bėrd′) *n.* a bird that feeds on ticks.

tick·er (tik′ər) *n.* **1** a person or thing that ticks. **2** a telegraphic instrument that prints market reports or news on a paper tape. **3** *Slang.* a watch; clock. **4** *Slang.* the heart.

ticker tape a paper tape on which a ticker prints stock market reports or news.

tick·et (tik′it) *n.* **1** a card or piece of paper that gives its holder a right or privilege: *a theatre ticket.* **2** *Informal.* a summons given to an offender to appear in court, usually because of a traffic violation: *a ticket for speeding.* **3** a card or piece of paper attached to something to show its price, etc. **4** *U.S.* the list of candidates to be voted on that belong to one political party. **5** *Slang.* a certificate: *a chief engineer's ticket.* **6 that's the ticket,** *Informal.* that's the correct or proper thing.
—*v.* **1** put a ticket on; mark with a ticket: *All articles in the store are ticketed with the price.* **2** describe or mark as if by a ticket; label; designate; characterize. **3** furnish with a ticket, such as a railway or airline ticket.
4 *Informal.* serve with a summons. [< F *étiquette* ticket < Gmc.]

ticket of leave *Brit.* a permit giving a convict his liberty before his sentence has expired, provided he obeys certain conditions.

tick·ing (tik′ing) *n.* a strong cotton or linen cloth, used to cover mattresses and pillows and to make tents and awnings. [< *tick*[3]]

tick·le[1] (tik′əl) *v.* **-led, -ling,** *n.* —*v.* **1** touch lightly causing little thrills, shivers, or wriggles. **2** have a feeling like this; cause to have such a feeling: *My nose tickles.*
3 excite pleasantly; amuse: *The story tickled him.*
4 play, stir, get, etc. with light touches or strokes.
5 refresh or jog (the memory). —*n.* **1** a tingling or itching feeling. **2** a tickling. [ME *tik(e)le(n)*]

tick·le[2] (tik′əl) *n. Cdn.* in the Atlantic Provinces, especially Newfoundland, a narrow channel between an island and the mainland or, sometimes, between two islands. [origin unknown]

tick·ler (tik′lər) *n.* **1** a person or thing that tickles. **2** a small feather brush used to tickle the faces of others, at a carnival, etc. **3** *Informal.* a memorandum book, card index, or other device kept as a reminder. **4** *Informal.* a difficult or puzzling problem.

tick·lish (tik′lish) *adj.* **1** sensitive to tickling.
2 requiring careful handling; delicate; risky. **3** easily upset; unstable: *A canoe is a ticklish craft.* **4** easily offended. **—tick′lish·ly,** *adv.* **—tick′lish·ness,** *n.*

tick-tack-toe (tik′tak tō′) *n.* a game in which two players alternately put their marks on a figure like that in the diagram, each player trying to be the first to fill three spaces in a row.

O	O	O
	O	X
	X	X

Tick-tack-toe

tick-tock (tik′tok′) *n.* the sound made by a clock or watch.
—*v.* make this sound; tick: *A tall clock tick-tocked on the stair.*

t.i.d. three times a day. (for L *ter in die*)

tid·al (tīd′əl) *adj.* **1** of tides; having tides; caused by tides. **2** dependent on the state of the tide as to time of arrival and departure: *a tidal steamer.*

hat, āge, cãre, fär; let, ēqual, tėrm; it, īce
hot, ōpen, ôrder; oil, out; cup, pu̇t, rüle, ūse
əbove, takən, pencəl, lemən, circəs
ch, child; ng, long; sh, ship
th, thin; ᴛʜ, then; zh, measure

tidal wave 1 a large, destructive ocean wave produced by an earthquake, hurricane, etc. **2** either of two great swellings of the ocean surface (due to the attraction of the moon and sun) that move around the globe on opposite sides and cause the tides. **3** any great movement or manifestation of feeling, opinion, or the like: *a tidal wave of popular indignation.*

tid·bit (tid′bit′) *n.* a very pleasing bit of food, news, etc. Also, **titbit.** [< *tid* nice + *bit* morsel]

tid·dle·dy·winks (tid′əl dē wingks′) *n.* tiddlywinks.

tid·dly·winks (tid′lē wingks′) *n.* a game played with small, colored disks that are snapped into a little cup. [origin uncertain]

tide[1] (tīd) *n. v.* **tid·ed, tid·ing.** —*n.* **1** the rise and fall of the ocean, usually taking place about every twelve hours, caused by the attraction of the moon and the sun.
2 anything that rises and falls like the tide: *the tide of popular opinion.* **3** a steam; current; flood. **4** a season; time: *Eastertide.* **5 turn the tide,** change from one condition to the opposite. —*v.* **1 tide over, a** help along for a time. **b** overcome (a difficulty, etc.). **2** carry as the tide does. [OE *tīd,* originally, time] **—tide′less,** *adj.*

tide[2] (tīd) *v.* **tid·ed, tid·ing.** *Archaic.* betide; happen. [OE *tīdan*]

tide·wa·ter (tīd′wot′ər or -wô′tər) *n.* **1** water having tides. **2** a seacoast. —*adj.* of or along tidewater.

tide·way (tīd′wā′) *n.* **1** a channel in which a tidal current runs. **2** the current in such a channel.

ti·di·ness (tī′dē nis) *n.* neatness.

ti·dings (tī′dingz) *n.pl.* news; information. [OE *tīdung* < *tīdan* happen, tide[2]]

ti·dy (tī′dē) *adj.* **-di·er, -di·est,** *v.* **-died, -dy·ing,** *n.* **-dies.** *adj.* **1** neat and in order: *a tidy room.* **2** inclined to keep things neat and in order: *a tidy person.* **3** *Informal.* considerable; fairly large: *a tidy sum of money.* **4** *Informal.* fairly good. —*v.* put in order; make tidy: *She tidied the room.* —*n.* a small cover to keep the back of a chair, etc. from becoming dirty or worn. [ult. < OE *tīd* time] **—ti′di·ly,** *adv.* **—Syn.** *adj.* **1** See **neat.**

tie (tī) *v.* **tied, ty·ing,** *n.* —*v.* **1** fasten with string or the like; bind: *tie a package.* **2** arrange to form a bow or knot: *tie one's apron strings.* **3** fasten; form a bow: *That ribbon doesn't tie well.* **4** tighten and fasten the string or strings of: *tie one's shoes.* **5** fasten, join, or connect in any way; make a bond or connection. **6** restrain; restrict; limit: *He did not want to be tied to a steady job.* **7** make the same score; be equal in points: *The two teams tied.*
8 make the same score as: *Toronto tied Queen's in football.*
9 in music, connect (notes) by a tie. **10** *Slang.* offer or think of (something) to equal or surpass: *Can you tie that?* **11 tie down, a** limit; confine; restrict. **b** fasten or hold down by tying. **12 tie in, a** connect or be connected: *Where does this line tie in with the main circuit?* **b** make or have a connection; relate: *How does that remark tie in with what you said yesterday?* **13 tie one on,** *Slang.* drink heavily; go on a binge. **14 tie up, a** tie firmly or tightly. **b** wrap up. **c** hinder; stop. **d** keep (money or property) from being used, sold, or given away. **e** complete (a sale, etc.); conclude an agreement with. **f** have one's program full; be very busy, etc.: *I can't go tomorrow; I'm all tied up.*
—*n.* **1** anything connecting or holding together two or more things or parts. **2** cord, chain, etc. used for tying. **3** a knot; ornamental knot. **4** a necktie. **5** anything that unites; a fastening; bond; connection; obligation: *family ties.* **6** a heavy piece of timber or iron. The rails of a railway track are fastened to ties about a foot apart. **7** a connecting **beam,** rod, etc. **8** equality in points, votes, etc. **9** in music, **a**

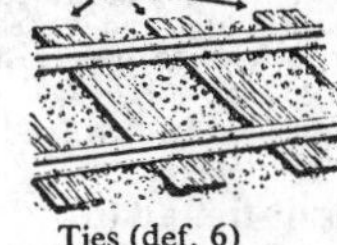

Ties (def. 6)

curved line set above or below notes that are to be played or sung without a break.
10 ties, *pl.* low, laced shoes. [OE *tīgan* < *tēag* rope] —**Syn.** *v.* **1** secure. **5** tether. –*n.* **5** See **bond.**

A musical tie (def. 9)

tie beam a timber or piece serving as a tie; especially, a horizontal beam connecting the lower ends of two opposite principal rafters, thus forming the base of a roof truss. See **king post** for picture.

tie-in (tī′in′) *n.* a link; association; connection: *There was no tie-in between the murder and the robbery.*

tier[1] (tēr) *n.* one of a series of rows arranged one above another: *tiers of seats at a baseball game.* —*v.* arrange in tiers. [< F *tire,* originally, order < *tirer* draw]

ti·er[2] (tī′ər) *n.* a person or thing that ties. [< *tie*]

tierce (tērs) *n.* **1** a cask of varying sizes, for provisions. **2** a sequence of three playing cards. **3** in fencing, the third position. **4** in music, a third. **5** the service for the third canonical hour. [ME < OF < L *tertius* third]

tie-up (tī′up′) *n.* **1** a stopping of work or action on account of a strike, storm, accident, etc. **2** *Informal.* a connection; relation.

tiff (tif) *n.* **1** a slight quarrel. **2** a slight bout of ill humor. —*v.* **1** have a slight quarrel. **2** be slightly peevish; be in a huff. [origin uncertain]

tif·fin (tif′ən) *n. Esp.Brit.* lunch. [Anglo-Indian for *tiffing* < *tiff* drink, of uncertain origin]

ti·ger (tī′gər) *n.* **1** a large, fierce Asiatic mammal of the cat family, that has dull-yellow fur striped with black. **2** a fierce, cruel, grasping, or bloodthirsty person. **3** *Informal.* an extra yell at the end of a cheer. [< L < Gk. *tigris*] —**ti′ger·like′,** *adj.*

tiger beetle a beetle whose larvae live in burrows in sandy soil and catch insects that come near.

tiger cat 1 a wildcat smaller than a tiger but resembling it in markings or ferocity. **2** a domestic cat with cross stripes suggesting those of a tiger.

ti·ger-eye (tī′gər ī′) *n.* tiger's-eye.

ti·ger·ish (tī′gər ish) *adj.* like a tiger; fierce; cruel.

tiger lily a lily that has dull-orange flowers spotted with black.

tiger moth any of a group of moths having conspicuously spotted or striped wings.

ti·ger's-eye (tī′gərz ī′) *n.* a golden-brown semiprecious stone with a changeable lustre, composed chiefly of quartz, colored with iron oxide.

tight (tīt) *adj.* **1** firm; held firmly; packed or put together firmly: *a tight knot.* **2** drawn; stretched: *a tight canvas.* **3** close; fitting closely; fitting too closely: *tight clothing.* **4** well-built; trim; neat: *a tight craft.* **5** not letting water, air, or gas in or out. **6** not wasteful of words; terse; concise: *tight writing, a tight style.* **7** hard to deal with or manage; difficult: *His lies got him in a tight place.* **8** *Informal.* almost even; close: *It was a tight race.* **9 a** hard to get; scarce: *Money for mortgages is tight just now.* **b** characterized by scarcity or eager demand: *a tight money market.* **10** *Informal.* stingy. **11** *Informal.* drunk. **12** strict; severe: *rule with a tight hand.*
—*adv.* **1** firmly. **2 sit tight,** *Informal.* **a** keep the same position, opinion, etc. **b** let matters take their own course; refrain from action. [OE *getyht,* pp. of *tyhtan* stretch] —**tight′ly,** *adv.* —**tight′ness,** *n.*
Syn. *adj.* **1** close, compact. **2 Tight, taut** = drawn or stretched so as to be not loose or slack. **Tight,** the general word, emphasizes the idea of drawing closely together or of being drawn over or around something so firmly that there is no looseness: *You need a tight string around that package.* **Taut** emphasizes stretching until the thing described would break, snap, or tear if pulled more tightly, and is used chiefly as a nautical or mechanical term or to describe or suggest strained nerves or muscles: *The covering on a drum must be taut.* **3** snug, close-fitting.

tight·en (tīt′ən) *v.* **1** make tight. **2** become tight. —**tight′en·er,** *n.*

tight-fist·ed (tīt′fis′tid) *adj.* stingy.

tight-lipped (tīt′lipt′) *adj.* **1** keeping the lips firmly together. **2** saying little or nothing.

tight·rope (tīt′rōp′) *n.* **1** a rope stretched tight on which acrobats perform. **2** a difficult or dangerous situation. **3 walk a tightrope, a** walk from one end of a tightrope to the other without falling off. **b** manoeuvre in a difficult or dangerous situation.

tights (tīts) *n.pl.* a close-fitting garment, usually for the legs and the lower part of the body, worn by acrobats, dancers, etc. They are often worn by women and girls in cold weather.

tight squeeze a difficult situation; narrow escape.

tight·wad (tīt′wod′) *n. Slang.* a stingy person.

ti·gress (tī′gris) *n.* **1** a female tiger. **2** a fierce, cruel woman.

ti·grish (tī′grish) *adj.* tigerish.

tike (tīk) *n.* tyke.

til (til) *n.* See **tilde** (def. 2).

til·bu·ry (til′bər ē) *n.* **-ries.** a light, two-wheeled, horse-drawn carriage without a top. [< name of a British coach designer]

til·de (til′də; *Spanish,* tēl′dā) *n.* **1** a diacritical mark (~) used in Spanish over *n* when it is pronounced *ny,* as in *cañón* (kä nyōn′). **2** the same mark, used in Portuguese over certain vowels to indicate that they are nasalized, as in São (souɴ). The Portuguese name for this mark is **til.** **3** in the pronunciation respellings in this book, a mark used over *a* to show that it is pronounced as in *care* (kãr). [< Sp. < L *titulus* title]

tile (tīl) *n. v.* **tiled, til·ing.** —*n.* **1** a thin piece of baked clay, stone, etc. Tiles are used for covering roofs, paving floors, and ornamenting. **2** a thin square of plastic, rubber, etc. used for surfacing floors, walls, or ceilings. **3** a short porous pipe, usually earthenware, used for draining land. **4** tiles collectively. **5** *Informal.* a stiff hat; high silk hat. —*v.* put tiles on or in; cover with tile. —*adj.* covered with tile; made of tile; tiled: *The bathroom has a tile floor.* [OE *tigele* < L *tegula*]

til·er (tīl′ər) *n.* a person who makes or lays tiles.

til·ing (tīl′ing) *n.* **1** tiles collectively. **2** the work of covering with tiles. **3** work consisting of tiles.

till[1] (til) *prep. conj.* until; up to the time of; up to the time when: *Walk till you come to a white house.* [OE *til*]
☛ **till, until.** These two words are not distinguishable in meaning, though **until** is usually considered the more formal word and is normally used at the beginning of sentences: *Until he left high school, he never took any job. He didn't take any job till* (or *until*) *he left high school.* Otherwise, one may choose between the two forms on the basis of stress and rhythm.

till[2] (til) *v.* cultivate; plough, harrow, etc.: *Farmers till the land.* [OE *tilian*] —**till′a·ble,** *adj.*

till[3] (til) *n.* **1** a small drawer for money: *The till is under the counter.* **2** a cash register. **3** formerly, a drawer or tray for keeping valuables. [ult. < OE *-tyllan* draw, as in *betyllan* lure]

till[4] (til) *n.* glacial drift composed of stiff clay, stones, gravel, boulders, etc. [origin unknown]

till·age (til′ij) *n.* **1** the cultivation of land. **2** the fact or condition of being tilled. **3** tilled land. **4** the crops growing on tilled land.

till·er[1] (til′ər) *n.* a bar or handle used to turn the rudder in steering a boat. [ME < OF *telier* weaver's beam, ult. < L *tela* web, loom]

till·er[2] (til′ər) *n.* a person who tills land; farmer. [< *till*[2]]

til·li·cum (ti′lə kəm) *n.* on the Pacific coast and in the Northwest, a friend; pal. [< Chinook Jargon *tilikum* kin, people, especially as distinguished from tribal chiefs]

tilt (tilt) *v.* **1** tip or cause to tip; slope; slant; lean: *You tilt your head forward when you bow. This table tilts.* **2** rush, charge, or fight with lances. Knights used to tilt on horseback. **3** point or thrust (a lance). **4 tilt at,** attack; fight; protest against. **5 tilt at windmills,** attack imaginary enemies. **6** forge or hammer with a heavy, pivoted hammer.
—*n.* **1** a slope; sloping position; a slant. **2** a fight on horseback with lances. **3** any dispute or quarrel. **4** in the Maritimes, a seesaw or teeter-totter. **5** a shanty or log hut, especially a temporary shelter. **6 full tilt,** at full speed; with full force: *His car ran full tilt against the tree.* **7** a heavy, pivoted hammer. [ult. < OE *tealt* shaky]

tilth (tilth) *n.* **1** the state of being tilled: *a garden in bad tilth.* **2** the cultivation of land. **3** tilled land. [OE *tilth* < *tilian* till[2]]

hat, āge, cãre, fär; let, ēqual, tėrm; it, īce
hot, ōpen, ôrder; oil, out; cup, pu̇t, rüle, ūse
əbove, takən, pencəl, lemən, circəs
ch, child; ng, long; sh, ship
th, thin; ᴛʜ, then; zh, measure

tim·bal (tim′bəl) *n.* **1** a kettledrum. **2** in certain insects, such as the cicada, a vibrating membrane resembling a drumhead by means of which a shrill sound is produced. [< F *timbale*, ult. < Arabic *at-tabl* the drum]

tim·bale (tim′bəl) *n.* **1** a food consisting of minced meat, fish, vegetables, etc. prepared with a sauce and cooked in a mould. **2** a cup-shaped pastry mould. [< F *timbale*, originally, *timbal.* See TIMBAL.]

tim·ber (tim′bər) *n.* **1** wood used for building and making things. **2** a large piece of wood used in building. Beams and rafters are timbers. **3** a curved piece forming a rib of a ship. **4** growing trees; forests. **5 a** trees bearing wood suitable for use in building: *a stand of timber.* **b** logs, green or cured, cut from such trees. —*v.* cover, support, or furnish with timber. [OE]

tim·bered (tim′bərd) *adj.* **1** made or furnished with timber. **2** covered with growing trees.

timber hitch a knot used to fasten a rope around a spar, post, etc.

tim·ber·ing (tim′bər ing) *n.* **1** building material of wood. **2** timbers collectively. **3** work made of timbers.

tim·ber·land (tim′bər land′) *n.* land with trees that are, or will be, used for timber.

timber limit 1 timber line. **2** *Cdn.* in lumbering, an area where a licensee has the right to fell trees and haul out logs; a concession.

timber line 1 on mountains and in the polar regions, a line beyond which trees will not grow because of the cold; tree line. **2** the boundary line of an area of timber.

timber raft in lumbering, a collection of logs lashed together for floating downstream.

timber wolf a large gray or brindled wolf of North America.

tim·bre (tim′bər or tam′bər; *French,* taɴbr) *n.* the quality in sounds that distinguishes a certain voice, instrument, etc. from other voices, instruments, etc. Notes of the same pitch and loudness may differ in timbre. [< MF *timbre*, ult. < Gk. *tympanon* kettledrum. Doublet of TYMPAN, TYMPANUM.]

tim·brel (tim′brəl) *n.* a tambourine. [dim. of ME *timbre* < OF *timbre*, a kind of tambourine. See TIMBRE.]

time (tīm) *n. v.* **timed, tim·ing,** *adj.* —*n.* **1** all the days there have been or ever will be; the past, present, and future. **2** a part of time: *A minute is a short time.* **3** a period of time; epoch: *the time of the Stuarts in England.* **4** a term of imprisonment, enlistment, apprenticeship, etc.: *complete one's time.* **5** a long time: *What a time it took you!* **6** some point in time; a particular point in time: *What time is it?* **7** the right part or point of time: *It is time to eat.* **8** an occasion: *This time we will succeed.* **9** a way of reckoning time: *daylight-saving time.* **10** a condition of life: *War brings hard times.* **11** amount of time: *I have some time for rest.* **12** an experience during a certain time: *She had a good time at the party.* **13** in poetry, a rate of movement; rhythm. **14** in music: **a** the length of a note or rest. **b** a grouping of such notes into rhythmic beats, divided into bars or measures of equal length. See **time signature. c** the tempo of a composition. **d** the rhythm of a composition: *waltz time, march time.* **15** the amount of time that one has worked or should work. **16** the pay for this. **17** leisure: *have time to read.* **18** in military use, a rate of stepping; pace: *march in quick time.*
about time, at or near the proper time: *It's about time to go home.*
against time, trying to finish before a certain time.
at the same time, however; nevertheless.
at times, now and then; once in a while.
behind the times, old-fashioned; out of date.
do or **serve time,** *Informal.* be imprisoned as a criminal: *a man doing time for bank robbery.*
for the time being, for the present; for now.
from time to time, now and then; once in a while.
in good time, a at the right time. **b** soon; quickly.
in no time, shortly; before long.
in time, a after a while. **b** soon enough. **c** in music, dancing, marching, etc., in the right rate of movement.
keep time, a of a watch or clock, go correctly. **b** sound or move at the right rate: *The marchers kept time to the martial music.*
make time, go with speed.
on time, a at the right time; not late. **b** with time in which to pay; on credit.
pass the time away, occupy oneself during the day: *She passed the time away by knitting.*
tell time, read the clock; tell what time it is by the clock.
time after time or **time and again,** again and again.
time of life, age: *a foolish thing to do at his time of life.*
time out of mind, beyond memory or record.
times, *pl.* multiplied by; ×.
—*v.* **1** measure the time of: *time a race.* **2** fix, set, or regulate the length of in time: *time an exposure correctly.* **3** set, regulate, or adjust: *time an alarm clock.* **4** do in rhythm with; set the time of: *The dancers timed their steps to the music.* **5** choose the moment or occasion for: *The lady timed her entrance so that she went in when the prince did.*
—*adj.* **1** of or having to do with time. **2** provided with a clocklike mechanism so that it will explode or ignite at a given moment: *a time bomb.* **3** in business, having to do with purchases to be paid for at a future date. [OE *tīma*]

time and motion study a systematic study of the methods and body motions used and the amount of time taken to do the various steps in a certain job, conducted to establish the most efficient way of doing it.

time bomb a bomb equipped with a timing device, so that it can be set to explode at a certain moment.

time·card (tīm′kärd′) *n.* **1** a card for recording the amount of time that a person works. **2** a card showing the times of trains, etc.

time clock a clock with a device to record the time when workers arrive and leave.

time-con·sum·ing (tīm′kən süm′ing or -kən sūm′ing) *adj.* using, taking up, or wasting a great deal of time.

time draft a draft to be paid at the future time stated in the draft.

time exposure 1 the exposure of a photographic film for a certain time, longer than a half second. **2** a photograph taken in this way.

time fuse a fuse that will burn for a certain time.

time-hon·ored or **time-hon·oured** (tīm′on′ərd) *adj.* honored because old and established: *a time-honored custom.*

time immemorial 1 a period in time so distant that it is before the beginning of records or known chronology. **2** in law, the time before legal records were known. In England, it is fixed by law as the time prior to 1189, the beginning of Richard I's reign.

time·keep·er (tīm′kēp′ər) *n.* a measurer of time; a person or thing that keeps time: *The factory timekeeper keeps account of the hours of work done. My watch is an excellent timekeeper. The timekeeper beat time for the musicians.*

time·less (tīm′lis) *adj.* **1** never ending; eternal. **2** referring to no special time.

time·ly (tīm′lē) *adj.* **-li·er, -li·est.** at the right time: *The timely arrival of the police stopped the riot.*
—**time′li·ness,** *n.*
Syn. Timely, opportune = well-timed or especially suited to the time or occasion. **Timely** describes something perfectly suited to the time or circumstance, coming or happening just at a time to be useful or valuable: *Saturday's paper contained a timely article on wise buying and foolish spending.* **Opportune** describes either the moment or occasion most favorable for doing something, or an event or action happening or done at exactly the right and most advantageous moment: *The invitation came at an opportune moment.*

time of day 1 the time as shown by the clock. **2** *Informal.* the current state of affairs; the latest fashion, etc.: *Who sets the time of day?* **3 give the time of day to,** notice or acknowledge. **4 know the time of day,** know what is going on or the current state of affairs. **5 pass the time of day,** exchange greetings or brief conversation.

time·piece (tīm′pēs′) *n.* a clock or watch.

tim·er (tīm′ər) *n.* **1** a person or thing that times; timekeeper. **2** a device for indicating or recording intervals of time, such as a stop watch. **3** a clockwork device for indicating when a certain period of time has elapsed: *Many stoves have timers for baking.* **4** in an internal-combustion engine, an automatic device that causes the spark for igniting the charge to occur just at the time required.

time·sav·er (tīm′sāv′ər) *n.* a person or thing that saves time.

time·sav·ing (tīm′sāv′ing) *adj.* that saves time: *a timesaving invention.*

time·serv·er (tīm′sėr′vər) *n.* a person who for selfish purposes shapes his conduct to conform with the opinions of the time or of the persons in power.

time·serv·ing (tīm′sėr′ving) *adj. n.* shaping one's conduct to conform with the opinions of the time or of persons in power, especially for selfish reasons.

time signature in music, a symbol, usually in the form of a fraction, that is printed or written at the beginning of a composition or where the time changes. The numerator of the fraction indicates the number of beats in a bar or measure; the denominator gives the length of the note that receives one beat. A special symbol is sometimes used to indicate 4/4 time.

time·ta·ble (tīm′tā′bəl) *n.* **1** a schedule showing the times when trains, boats, buses, airplanes, etc. arrive and depart. **2** any list or schedule of the times at which things are to be done or happen.

time·worn (tīm′wôrn′) *adj.* **1** worn by long existence or use. **2** worn out by use; trite: *a timeworn excuse.* **3** very old; ancient; antiquated: *a timeworn superstition.*

time zone a geographical region within which the same standard of time is used. The world is divided into 24 time zones, beginning and ending at the International Date Line.

tim·id (tim′id) *adj.* **1** easily frightened; shy. **2** characterized by or indicating fear: *a timid reply.* [< L *timidus* < *timere* to fear] **—tim′id·ly,** *adv.* **—tim′ id·ness,** *n.*

Syn. **Timid, cowardly** = lacking courage. **Timid** emphasizes the idea of being always ready to be afraid, especially of anything new, different, uncertain, or unknown: *He does not like his job, but is too timid to try to find another.* **Cowardly** emphasizes the idea of a weak and dishonorable lack of courage in the presence of danger or trouble: *Leaving his wife because she was hopelessly sick was a cowardly thing to do.*

ti·mid·i·ty (tə mid′ə tē) *n.* timid behavior; shyness.

tim·ing (tīm′ing) *n.* **1 a** the regulation of the speed or tempo of the parts of any musical, dramatic, or rhetorical performance to secure the greatest possible effect. **b** the effect thus produced. **2** in sports, the physical and mental co-ordination necessary to achieve the greatest effect by a throw, blow, stroke, or other manoeuvre: *Some older players lose their sense of timing.*

Ti·mis·ka·ming (tə mis′kə ming) in geology: *—adj.* of or having to do with the more recent period of the Archeozoic era. *—n.* **1** the more recent period of the Archeozoic era. See **geology** for chart. **2** the rocks or rock formations of this period. [< *Timiskaming*, Ontario]

Ti·mon (tī′mən) *n.* a hater of mankind. [after the hero of Shakespeare's play, *Timon of Athens*, noted for his dislike of mankind]

tim·or·ous (tim′ər əs) *adj.* easily frightened; timid. [ME < OF < Med.L *timorosus* < L *timor* fear] **—tim′or·ous·ly,** *adv.* **—tim′or·ous·ness,** *n.*

tim·o·thy (tim′ə thē) *n.* a kind of coarse grass having long, cylindrical spikes, often grown for fodder. [< *Timothy* Hanson, an early American cultivator]

tim·pa·ni (tim′pə nē) *n.* pl. of **timpano.** Also, **tympani.**

tim·pa·nist (tim′pə nist) *n.* a person who plays the kettledrums. Also, **tympanist.**

tim·pa·no (tim′pə nō′) *n.* **-ni** (-nē′). a kettledrum. Also, **tympano.** [< Ital. < L *tympanum.* See TYMPANUM.]

tin (tin) *n. adj. v.* **tinned, tin·ning.** *—n.* **1** a metallic chemical element resembling silver in color and lustre but softer and cheaper. *Symbol:* Sn; *at.no.* 50; *at.wt.* 118.69. **2** thin sheets of iron or steel coated with tin. **3** any can, box, pan, or other container made of tin, aluminum, etc.: *a pie tin, a tin of peas.* *—adj.* made of tin. *—v.* **1** cover with tin. **2** *Esp.Brit.* put up in tin cans or tin boxes; can. [OE]

tin·a·mou (tin′ə mü′) *n.* a South American bird resembling a partridge, quail, or grouse. [< F < Carib]

tinct (tingkt) *Archaic. —adj.* tinged. *—n.* a tint; tinge. [< L *tinctus*, pp. of *tingere* tinge]

tinc·ture (tingk′chər) *n. v.* **-tured, -tur·ing.** *—n.* **1** a solution of medicine in alcohol: *tincture of iodine.* **2** a trace; tinge. **3** a color; tint. *—v.* **1** give a trace or tinge to. **2** color; tint. [< L *tinctura* < *tingere* tinge]

tin·der (tin′dər) *n.* **1** anything that catches fire easily. **2** any material used to catch fire from a spark. [OE *tynder*]

tin·der·box (tin′dər boks′) *n.* **1** a box for holding tinder, flint, and steel for making a fire. **2** a very inflammable or excitable thing or person.

tine (tīn) *n.* a sharp, projecting point or prong: *the tines of a fork.* [OE *tind*]

tin foil a very thin sheet of tin, or tin and lead, used as a wrapping for candy, tobacco, etc.

ting (ting) *v.* make or cause to make a clear ringing sound. *—n.* a clear, ringing sound. [imitative]

tinge (tinj) *v.* **tinged, tinge·ing** or **ting·ing,** *n. —v.* **1** color slightly: *A drop of ink will tinge a glass of water.* **2** add a trace of some quality to; change slightly: *Sad memories tinged their present joy.* *—n.* **1** a slight coloring or tint. **2** a very small amount; trace. [< L *tingere*]

tin·gle (ting′gəl) *v.* **-gled, -gling,** *n. —v.* **1** have a feeling of thrills or a pricking, stinging feeling: *He tingled with excitement on his first airplane trip.* **2** cause this feeling in: *Shame tingled his cheeks.* **3** be thrilling: *The newspaper story tingled with excitement.* **4** tinkle; jingle. *—n.* **1** a pricking, stinging feeling. **2** a tinkle; jingle. [probably var. of *tinkle*]

tink·er[1] (tingk′ər) *n.* **1** a man who mends pots, pans, etc. **2** unskilled or clumsy work; activity that is rather useless. **3** a person who does such work. *—v.* **1** mend; patch. **2** work or repair in an unskilled or clumsy way. **3** work or keep busy in a rather useless way. [? ult. < *tin*]

tink·er[2] (tingk′ər) *n.* in the Atlantic Provinces, any of certain types of auk.

tinker's damn or **dam** a most contemptible or useless thing. [? from tinkers' reputation for cursing]

tin·kle (ting′kəl) *v.* **-kled, -kling,** *n. —v.* **1** make short, light, ringing sounds: *Little bells tinkle.* **2** cause to tinkle. **3** move with a tinkle. **4** call, make known, etc. by tinkling: *The little clock tinkled out the hours.* *—n.* a series of short, light, ringing sounds: *the tinkle of bells.* [ult. imitative]

tin·man (tin′mən) *n.* **-men** (-mən). **1** a man who works with tin. **2** a dealer in tinware.

tin·ner (tin′ər) *n.* **1** a person who works in a tin mine. **2** a person who works with tin.

tin·ny (tin′ē) *adj.* **-ni·er, -ni·est. 1** of tin; containing tin. **2** resembling tin. **3** shrill or thin in sound, as tin when struck. **—tin′ni·ness,** *n.*

tin-pan alley 1 a district, especially in New York City, frequented by musicians, song writers, and song publishers. **2** the people concerned with writing and publishing popular music.

tin plate thin sheets of iron or steel coated with tin. Ordinary tin cans are made of tin plate.

tin-plate (tin′plāt′) *v.* **-plat·ed, -plat·ing.** coat or plate metal with tin.

tin-pot (tin′pot′) *adj. Informal. Esp.Brit.* inferior; petty.

tin·sel (tin′səl) *n. v.* **-selled** or **-seled, -sel·ling** or **-sel·ing,** *adj. —n.* **1** thin sheets or strips of aluminum foil, copper, brass, etc.: *Tinsel is often used to decorate Christmas trees.* **2** anything showy but having little value. **3** a thin cloth woven with threads of gold, silver, or copper. *—v.* trim with tinsel. *—adj.* of or like tinsel; showy but not worth much. [< F *étincelle* spark < L *scintilla.* Doublet of SCINTILLA.] **—tin′sel-like′,** *adj.*

tin·smith (tin′smith′) *n.* a person who works with tin; a maker of tinware.

tint (tint) *n.* **1** a variety of a color: *The picture was painted in several tints of blue.* **2** a delicate or pale color.

3 a a preparation for coloring hair. b the process of coloring hair. —*v.* put a tint on; color slightly. [earlier *tinct* < L *tinctus* a dyeing < *tingere* dye]

tin·tin·nab·u·la·tion (tin′tə nab′yů lā′shən) *n.* the ringing of bells. [ult. < L *tintinnabulum* bell]

tin·type (tin′tīp′) *n.* a photograph taken on a sheet of enamelled tin or iron.

tin·ware (tin′wãr′) *n.* articles made of or lined with tin.

ti·ny (tī′nē) *adj.* **-ni·er, -ni·est.** very small; wee. [ME *tine*; origin uncertain] —**Syn.** little, minute, microscopic.

-tion *suffix.* **1** the act or state of ——ing, as in *addition, opposition.* **2** the condition or state of being ——ed, as in *exhaustion.* **3** the result of ——ing, as in *apparition.* [< L *-tio, -onis* < *-t-* of pp. stem + *-io* (cf. *-ion*)]

tip[1] (tip) *n. v.* **tipped, tip·ping.** —*n.* **1** the end part; end; point: *the tips of the fingers.* **2** a small piece put on the end of something. —*v.* **1** put a tip on; furnish with a tip. **2** apply to the end of: *The arrows were tipped with poison.* [ME *tippe*; ? < MDu. *tip* point] —**Syn.** *n.* **1** extremity.

tip[2] (tip) *v.* **tipped, tip·ping,** *n.* —*v.* **1** slope; slant: *She tipped the table toward her.* **2** upset; overturn: *He fell in the water when the canoe tipped.* **3** take off (a hat) in greeting. **4** empty out; dump. **5 tip over,** upset; overturn: *He tipped over his glass of water.* —*n.* a slope; slant. [ME *tipen*; of uncertain origin] —**Syn.** *v.* **1** tilt, incline, lean. **2** capsize.

tip[3] (tip) *n. v.* **tipped, tip·ping.** —*n.* **1** a small present of money in return for service: *He gave the waiter a tip.* **2** a piece of secret or confidential information: *Fred had a tip that the black horse would win the race.* **3** a useful hint, suggestion, etc.
—*v.* **1** give a small present of money to: *He tipped the waiter.* **2** give secret or confidential information to. **3** give a tip or tips: *He tips generously at restaurants and hotels.* **4 tip off,** *Informal.* **a** give secret or confidential information to. **b** warn. [origin uncertain]

tip[4] (tip) *n. v.* **tipped, tip·ping.** —*n.* a light, sharp blow; tap. —*v.* hit lightly and sharply; tap.

ti·pi (tē′pē) *n.* teepee.

tip-off (tip′of′) *n. Informal.* **1** a piece of secret information. **2** a warning.

tip·pet (tip′it) *n.* **1** a scarf for the neck and shoulders with ends hanging down in front. **2** a long, narrow hanging part of a hood, sleeve, or scarf. [probably < *tip*[1]]

A tippet (def. 2)

tip·ple (tip′əl) *v.* **-pled, -pling,** *n.* —*v.* drink alcoholic liquor often. —*n.* an alcoholic liquor. [origin uncertain; cf. Norwegian *tipla* drip, tipple]

tip·pler (tip′lər) *n.* a habitual drinker of alcoholic liquor.

tip·staff (tip′staf′) *n.* **-staves** or **-staffs. 1** a staff tipped with metal, formerly carried by constables and other officers of the law. **2** an official who carried such a staff.

tip·ster (tip′stər) *n. Informal.* a person who makes a business of furnishing private or secret information for use in betting, speculation, etc. [< *tip* a hint + *-ster*]

tip·sy (tip′sē) *adj.* **-si·er, -si·est. 1** tipping easily; unsteady; tilted. **2** somewhat intoxicated but not thoroughly drunk. [< *tip*[2]] —**tip′si·ly,** *adv.* —**tip′si·ness,** *n.*

tip·toe (tip′tō) *n. v.* **-toed, -toe·ing.** —*n.* **1** the tips of the toes. **2 on tiptoe, a** walking on one's toes. **b** eager. **c** in a secret manner. —*v.* walk on the tips of the toes.

tip·top (tip′top′) *n.* the very top; highest point. —*adj.* **1** at the very top or highest point. **2** *Informal.* first-rate; excellent. [< *tip* end + *top*]

ti·rade (tī′rād or tə rād′) *n.* **1** a long, vehement speech. **2** a long, scolding speech. [< F < Ital. *tirata* < *tirare* shoot]

ti·rail·leur (tē rä yœr′) *n. French.* skirmisher; sharpshooter. [< F *tirailleur* < *tirer* shoot]

tire[1] (tīr) *v.* **tired, tir·ing. 1** make weary: *The hard work tired him.* **2** become weary: *He tires easily.* **3** wear down the patience, interest, or appreciation of, because of dullness, excess, etc.: *Monotonous filing tired the office boy.* **4 tire out,** make very weary. [OE *tȳrian*] —**Syn. 1** exhaust, fatigue, fag, jade.

hat, āge, cãre, fär; let, ēqual, tėrm; it, īce
hot, ōpen, ôrder; oil, out; cup, pů t, rüle, ūse
əbove, takən, pencəl, lemən, circəs
ch, child; ng, long; sh, ship
th, thin; ᴛʜ, then; zh, measure

tire[2] (tīr) *n. v.* **tired, tir·ing.** —*n.* **1** a circular covering made of cord and rubber or similar synthetic materials, either filled with air or used as a shield for an inner tube filled with air, for placing around the wheel of an automobile, truck, plane, bicycle, etc. **2** a band of metal around a wheel: *The wagon had iron tires.*
—*v.* furnish with a tire. Also, *Brit.* **tyre.** [< *attire,* in sense of "covering"]

tire[3] (tīr) *n. v.* **tired, tir·ing.** *Archaic.* —*n.* headdress; attire. —*v.* attire or adorn. [short for *attire*]

tired (tīrd) *adj.* weary; wearied; exhausted. [< *tire*[1]] —**tired′ly,** *adv.* —**tired′ness,** *n.*
Syn. Tired, weary, exhausted = having physical or mental strength, energy, and power of endurance lowered or drained by hard or long-continued work, strain, etc. **Tired** is the general and least precise word: *I am tired, but I must get back to work.* **Weary** = feeling worn out and unable or unwilling to go on: *Weary shoppers waited for buses and streetcars.* **Exhausted** = without enough energy or endurance left to be able to go on: *Exhausted by play, the child could not eat.*

-tired *combining form.* having —— tires: ***a rubber-tired vehicle = a vehicle having rubber tires.*** [< *tire*[2]]

tire·less[1] (tīr′lis′) *adj.* **1** never becoming tired; requiring little rest: *a tireless worker.* **2** never stopping: *tireless efforts.* —**tire′less·ly,** *adv.* —**tire′less·ness,** *n.* —**Syn. 1** indefatigable.

tire·less[2] (tīr′lis) *adj.* having no tire or tires.

Ti·re·si·as (tī rē′sē əs or tə rē′sē əs) *n.* in Greek legend, a soothsayer of Athens who was blinded by Athena because he saw her bathing. In compensation she gave him power to foresee future events, an understanding of birds' language, and a staff to serve as eyes.

tire·some (tīr′səm) *adj.* tiring, because boring: *a tiresome speech.* —**tire′some·ly,** *adv.* —**tire′some·ness,** *n.*
Syn. Tiresome, tedious = tiring or boring, or both. **Tiresome** describes a person or thing that tires or bores one quickly because he or it is dull and uninteresting: *Our neighbor is good-hearted, but I find her tiresome.* **Tedious** adds the idea of being long or slow or too much the same or, when describing a person, speaking or writing at too great length: *Weeding a garden is tedious work. His sermons are tedious.*

tire·wom·an (tīr′wům′ən) *n.* **-wom·en.** *Archaic.* a lady's maid.

tiring room *Archaic.* a dressing room, especially in a theatre. [< *attiring room*]

ti·ro (tī′rō) *n.* **-ros.** tyro.

Ti·ro·le·an (tə rō′lē ən or tir′ə lē′ən) *adj. n.* Tyrolean.

Tir·o·lese (tir′ə lēz′) *adj.* Tyrolese.

'tis (tiz) it is.

Tish·ri (tish′rē) *n.* in the Hebrew calendar, the seventh month of the ecclesiastical year, and the first month of the civil year.

tis·sue (tish′ü) *n.* **1** in biology, a substance forming the parts of animals and plants; a mass of cells: *brain tissue, skin tissue.* **2** a thin, light cloth. **3** a web; network: *Her whole story was a tissue of lies.* **4** tissue paper. **5** a kind of soft paper having the power to absorb moisture. **6** a piece or sheet of this paper. [ME < OF *tissu,* originally pp. of *tistre* weave < L *texere*]

tissue paper a very thin, soft paper.

tit[1] (tit) *n.* **1** a titmouse. **2** any of various other small birds. [ME; cf. Icelandic *tittr* titmouse]

tit[2] (tit) *n.* a nipple; teat. [OE *titt*]

Tit. Titus.

Ti·tan (tī′tən) *n.* **1** in Greek mythology, one of a family of giants who ruled the world before the gods of Olympus. Prometheus and Atlas were Titans. **2** Also, **titan.** a person or thing having enormous size, strength, power, etc.; giant. **3** the sun thought of as a god.

—*adj.* of the Titans; gigantic; huge; very powerful. [< L < Gk.]

Ti·tan·ic (tī tan′ik) *adj.* **1** of or like the Titans. **2** Also, **titanic.** having great size, strength, or power; gigantic; huge: *titanic energy.*

ti·ta·ni·um (tī tā′nē əm or ti tā′nē əm) *n.* a metallic chemical element occurring in various minerals. When isolated it is a dark-gray powder with a metallic lustre. *Symbol*: Ti; *at.no.* 22; *at.wt.* 47.90. [< *Titan*]

ti·tan·o·there (tī′tə nə thēr′) *n.* an extinct mammal of the Tertiary period in North America. It resembled a rhinoceros, having a large skull, a very small brain, and horns over the nose. [< Gk. *Titan* Titan + *thērion* beast]

tit·bit (tit′bit′) *n.* tidbit.

tit for tat blow for blow; like for like. [? < *tip for tap*]

tithe (tīᴛʜ) *n. v.* **tithed, tith·ing.** —*n.* **1** one tenth. **2** Often, **tithes,** *pl.* a tax or a donation of one tenth of the yearly produce of land, animals, and personal work, paid for the support of the church and the clergy. **3** a very small part. **4** any small tax, levy, etc. —*v.* **1** put a tax or a levy of a tenth on. **2** pay a tithe on. **3** give one tenth of one's income to the church or to charity. [OE *teogotha* tenth]

ti·tian (tish′ən) *n. adj.* auburn; golden red. [< *Titian* (1477-1576), an Italian painter, who used this color in his paintings]

tit·il·late (tit′ə lāt′) *v.* **-lat·ed, -lat·ing. 1** excite pleasantly; stimulate agreeably. **2** tickle. [< L *titillare*]

tit·il·la·tion (tit′ə lā′shən) *n.* **1** pleasant excitement; agreeable stimulation. **2** a tickling.

tit·i·vate or **tit·ti·vate** (tit′ə vāt′) *v.* **-vat·ed, -vat·ing.** *Informal.* dress up; make smart; prink. [? ult. < *tidy*] **—tit′i·va′tion** or **tit′ti·va′tion,** *n.*

tit·lark (tit′lärk′) *n.* a small bird resembling a lark; pipit. [< *tit*[1] + *lark*[1]]

ti·tle (tī′təl) *n. v.* **-tled, -tling.** —*n.* **1 a** the name of a book, poem, picture, song, etc. **b** a title page. **c** a descriptive heading or caption, as of a chapter or section of a book, etc. **2** a name showing a person's rank, occupation, or condition in life. *Examples*: king, duke, lord, countess, captain, doctor, professor, Madame, and Miss. **3** a first place position; championship: *the tennis title.* **4** in law: **a** the legal right to the possession of property. **b** the evidence showing such a right. **5** a book; volume: *There are 5,000 titles in our library.* **6** a recognized right; claim.
—*v.* call by a title; name. [ME < OF < L *titulus.* Doublet of TITTLE.] **—Syn.** *n.* **1** See **name.**

ti·tled (tī′təld) *adj.* having a title: *a titled nobleman.*

title deed a document showing that a person owns certain property.

title page the page at the beginning of a book that contains the title, the author's name, etc.

title role or **rôle** the part or character for which a play is named. Hamlet and Othello are title roles.

tit·mouse (tit′mous′) *n.* **-mice.** any of certain small birds having short bills and dull-colored feathers. A chickadee is one kind of titmouse. [ME *titmose* < *tit* a small creature + *mose* titmouse + OE *māse*; influenced by *mouse*]

Ti·to·ism (tē′tō iz′əm) *n.* the principles and practices of Marshal Tito, President of Yugoslavia, especially a form of Communism that asserts national rather than international interests and does not accept Soviet domination.

ti·trate (tī′trāt or tit′rāt) *v.* **-trat·ed, -trat·ing,** *n.* —*v.* analyse (a solution) by titration. —*n.* a solution to be analysed by titration. [< F *titrer* < *titre* quality]

ti·tra·tion (tī trā′shən or ti trā′shən) *n.* the process of determining the amount of some substance present in a solution by measuring the amount of a different substance that must be added to cause a chemical change.

ti·tre or **ti·ter** (tī′tər or tē′tər) *n.* in chemistry: **1** a standard amount or strength of a solution as established by titration. **2** the weight or volume of a standard solution needed to produce a given result in titration. [< OF *titre* the proportion of gold or silver in an alloy; originally, learned borrowing < L *titulus* inscription]

tit·ter (tit′ər) *v.* laugh in a half-restrained manner; giggle. —*n.* a tittering laugh. **—tit′ter·er,** *n.*

tit·tle (tit′əl) *n.* **1** a very little bit; particle; whit. **2** in writing or printing, a small stroke or mark over a letter. The dot over an *i* is a tittle. [ME < Med.L *titulus* diacritical mark < L *titulus* title. Doublet of TITLE.]

tit·tle-tat·tle (tit′əl tat′əl) *n. v.* **-tled, -tling.** gossip. [varied reduplication of *tattle*]

tit·u·lar (tich′ů lər or tit′yů lər) *adj.* **1** in title or name only: *He is a titular prince without any power.* **2** having a title. **3** having to do with a title. [< L *titulus* title]

tit·u·lar·ly (tich′ů lər lē or tit′yů lər lē) *adv.* with respect to title; nominally.

tiz·zy (tiz′ē) *n.* **-zies.** *Slang.* a very excited state; dither. [origin uncertain]

TKO, T.K.O., or **t.k.o.** technical knockout.

Tl thallim.

Tlin·git (tling′git) *n.* **Tlin·git** or **Tlin·gits. 1** a tribe of North American Indians inhabiting the coast of British Columbia and the south-western islands of Alaska. **2** a member of this tribe. **3** their language. Also, **Tlinkit.**

Tm thulium.

tme·sis (tmē′sis) *n.* in grammar, the separation of a compound word by an intervening word or words, as in *to us-ward* for *toward us.* [< LL < Gk. *tmēsis,* originally, a cutting < *temnein* cut]

tn. ton.

Tn thoron.

TNT or **T.N.T.** (tē′en′tē′) **1** trinitrotoluene. **2** *Informal.* anything dangerous or explosive.

to (tü; *unstressed,* tů or tə) *prep.* **1** in the direction of: *Go to the right.* **2** as far as; until: *rotten to the core, faithful to the end.* **3** for; for the purpose of: *He came to the rescue.* **4** toward or into the position, condition, or state of: *He went to sleep.* **5** so as to produce, cause, or result in: *To her horror, the bear kept advancing towards her.* **6** into: *She tore the letter to pieces.* **7** by: *a fact known to few.* **8** along with; with: *We danced to the music.* **9** compared with: *The score was 9 to 5.* **10** in agreement or accordance with: *It is not to my liking.* **11** as seen or understood by: *a symptom alarming to the doctor.* **12** belonging with; of: *the key to my room.* **13** in honor of: *Drink to the King.* **14** on; against: *Fasten it to the wall.* **15** about; concerning: *What did he say to that?* **16** included, contained, or involved in: *four apples to the pound.* **17** *To* is used to show action toward: *Give the book to me. Speak to her.* **18** *To* is used with some infinitive forms of verbs: *He likes to read. The birds began to sing. "To err is human; to forgive, divine."*
—*adv.* **1** forward: *He wore his cap wrong side to.* **2** together; touching; closed: *The door slammed to.* **3** to action or work: *We turned to gladly.* **4** to consciousness: *She came to.* **5 to and fro,** first one way and then back again; back and forth. [OE *tō*]

toad (tōd) *n.* **1** a small amphibian resembling a frog and living most of the time on land rather than in water. Toads, which are often found in gardens, have a rough, brown skin that suggests a lump of earth. **2** any tail-less amphibian; any frog. [OE *tāde*]

toad·eat·er (tōd′ēt′ər) *n.* a servile flatterer; toady. [originally, a quack doctor's attendant who pretended to eat toads, which were thought to be poisonous, to prove the efficacy of his master's "cure"]

toad·fish (tōd′fish′) *n.* a fish having a thick head, a wide mouth, and slimy skin without scales.

toad·flax (tōd′flaks′) *n.* a common weed having yellow-and-orange flowers.

toad·stool (tōd′stül′) *n.* **1** a mushroom. **2** a poisonous mushroom.

toad·y (tōd′ē) *n.* **toad·ies,** *v.* **toad·ied, toad·y·ing.** —*n.* a fawning flatterer. —*v.* **1** act like a toady. **2** fawn upon; flatter. [short for *toadeater*]

toad·y·ism (tōd′ē iz′əm) *n.* the action or behavior of a toady; interested flattery; mean servility.

to-and-fro (tü′ən frō′) *adj.* back-and-forth.

toast[1] (tōst) *n.* a slice or slices of bread browned by heat. [< v.] —*v.* **1** brown by heat. **2** heat thoroughly. [ME < OF *toster*, ult. < L *torrere* parch]

toast² (tōst) *n.* **1** a person or thing whose health is proposed and drunk: *"The Queen" was the first toast drunk by the officers.* **2** a person having many admirers: *She was the toast of the town.* **3** the act of drinking to the health of a person or thing. **4** a call on another or others to drink to some person or thing. —*v.* **1** propose as a toast; drink to the health of. **2** drink toasts. [from the custom of putting spiced toast into drinks for flavoring]

toast·er¹ (tōs′tər) *n.* **1** one who toasts something. **2** an instrument or device for toasting bread, cheese, etc.

toast·er² (tōs′tər) *n.* one who proposes a toast.

toast·mas·ter (tōst′mas′tər) *n.* **1** a person who presides at a dinner and introduces the speakers. **2** a person who proposes toasts.

Tob. Tobias; Tobit.

to·bac·co (tə bak′ō) *n.* **-cos** or **-coes. 1** the prepared leaves of certain plants, used for smoking or chewing or as snuff. **2** one of these plants. **3** things made from or containing such leaves, as cigars, cigarettes, etc. **4** the smoking of a pipe, cigars, cigarettes, etc.: *give up tobacco.* [< Sp. *tabaco* < Carib]

Tobacco Nation the Petun Indians, an Iroquoian people once inhabiting S.W. Ontario.

to·bac·co·nist (tə bak′ə nist) *n.* a dealer in tobacco.

to·bog·gan (tə bog′ən) *n. Cdn.* a long, narrow, flat sleigh without runners. —*v.* **1** slide downhill on a toboggan. **2** decline sharply and rapidly in value. [< Cdn.F *tabagane* < Algonquian; cf. Micmac *tobākun*]

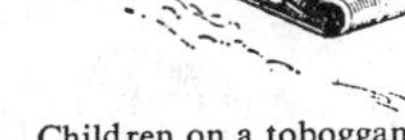

Children on a toboggan

To·by (tō′bē) *n.* **To·bies.** a small, fat jug or mug in the form of a fat man wearing a long coat and a three-cornered hat. [< *Toby*, proper name, short for *Tobias*]

toc·ca·ta (tə kä′tə) *n.* in music, a composition for the piano, organ, or other keyboard instrument, often intended to exhibit the player's technique. [< Ital. *toccata*, originally pp. of *toccare* touch]

toc·sin (tok′sən) *n.* **1** an alarm sounded on a bell; a warning signal. **2** a bell used to sound an alarm. [< F < Provençal *tocasenh* < *tocar* strike, touch + *senh* bell]

to·day or **to-day** (tə dā′) *n.* this day; the present time. —*adv.* **1** on this day. **2** at the present time; now. [OE *tō dæge* on (the) day]

tod·dle (tod′əl) *v.* **-dled, -dling,** *n.* —*v.* walk with short, unsteady steps, as a baby does. —*n.* a toddling way of walking. [origin unknown]

tod·dler (tod′lər) *n.* a child just learning to walk.

tod·dy (tod′ē) *n.* **-dies. 1** a drink made of whisky, brandy, etc. and mixed with hot water and sugar. **2** fermented palm sap. [< Hind. *tārī* palm sap < *tār* palm]

to-do (tə dü′) *n.* **-dos.** *Informal.* a fuss; bustle.

toe (tō) *n. v.* **toed, toe·ing.** —*n.* **1** one of the five end parts of the foot. **2** the part of a stocking, shoe, etc. that covers the toes. **3** the forepart of a foot or hoof. **4** anything resembling a toe: *the toe and heel of a golf club.* **5 on one's toes,** ready for action; alert.
—*v.* **1** touch or reach with the toes: *toe a line.* **2** turn the toes in walking, standing, etc.: *toe in, toe out.* **3** furnish with a toe or toes. **4** drive (a nail) slantwise. **5** fasten by nails driven slantwise. **6 toe in,** adjust the front wheels of an automobile, etc. so that they point forward and slightly inward. **7 toe the line, a** have one's toes on the starting line of a race. **b** obey rules, conform to a doctrine, etc. strictly. [OE *tā*] —**toe′less,** *adj.* —**toe′-like′,** *adj.*

toed (tōd) *adj.* having a certain number or kind of toes: *a five-toed animal.*

toe hold or **toe·hold** (tō′hōld′) *n.* **1** a small space, projection, etc. large enough to support the toes when climbing: *The mountaineer cut toeholds in the glacier.* **2** any way in or up; any means of entrance or support; a foothold. **3** in wrestling, a hold in which an opponent's foot is bent back or twisted.

hat, āge, cãre, fär; let, ēqual, tėrm; it, īce
hot, ōpen, ôrder; oil, out; cup, pu̇t, rüle, ūse
əbove, takən, pencəl, lemən, circəs
ch, child; ng, long; sh, ship
th, thin; ᴛʜ, then; zh, measure

toe-in (tō′in) *n.* **1** the adjustment of the front wheels of an automobile, etc. so that they point forward and slightly inward. **2** the amount or degree of such adjustment.

toe·nail (tō′nāl′) *n.* **1** the nail on a toe. **2** in carpentry, a nail driven obliquely.

toff (tof) *n. Esp.Brit. Slang.* **1** a rich, important, or aristocratic man; a nob. **2** a richly or elegantly dressed man; a dandy. [? < *tuft*, formerly a gentleman commoner at Oxford University who wore a gold tassel in his cap]

tof·fee (tof′ē) *n.* **-fees.** a hard chewy candy; taffy. [origin uncertain]

tof·fy (tof′ē) *n.* **-fies.** toffee.

tog (tog) *n. v.* **togged, tog·ging.** —*n.* **1** a garment. **2 togs,** *pl. Informal.* clothes.
—*v.* clothe; dress. [apparently a shortening of obs. *togman*; probably influenced by L *toga*]

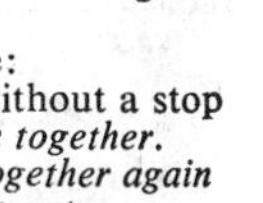

A Roman toga

to·ga (tō′gə) *n.* **-gas, -gae** (-jē). **1** in ancient Rome, a loose outer garment worn by men: *Only Roman citizens wore togas.* **2** a robe of office. [< L]

to·gaed (tō′gəd) *adj.* wearing a toga.

to·geth·er (tə geᴛʜ′ər) *adv.* **1** in company; with each other: *They were standing together.* **2** into one gathering, company, mass, or body: *The pastor called the people together. The woman will sew these pieces together and make a dress.* **3** at the same time: *You cannot have day and night together.* **4** without a stop or break; continuously: *He worked for days together.* **5 get together,** *Informal.* **a** meet: *Let's get together again next week.* **b** act in or come into agreement: *get together on a dispute or a price.* **6 together with,** along with. [OE *tōgædere* < *tō* to + *gædere* together]

☛ **together with.** Adding *together with* to a singular subject does not change the grammatical number of the subject. Formal English uses a singular verb to agree with the singular subject: *The general, together with his staff, is dining here tonight.* Informal English, however, often uses a plural verb, treating the construction as a compound subject: *The coach together with his players are attending a banquet.*

to·geth·er·ness (tə geth′ər nis) *n.* the condition of being closely associated or united, especially in family or social activities.

tog·ger·y (tog′ər ē) *n. Informal.* **1** garments; clothes. **2** a clothing store.

tog·gle (tog′əl) *n. v.* **-gled, -gling.**
—*n.* **1** a pin, bolt, or rod put through the eye of a rope or the link of a chain to keep it in place, to hold two ropes together, to serve as a hold for the fingers, etc. **2** a toggle joint, or a device furnished with one.
—*v.* furnish with a toggle; fasten with a toggle. [cf. *tug*, v.]

A toggle joint

toggle joint a knee-like joint that transmits pressure at right angles.

toggle switch an electric switch having a projecting lever for opening and closing the circuit.

togue (tōg) *n. Cdn.* in the Maritimes, a lake trout. [< Cdn.F < Algonquian]

toil¹ (toil) *n.* **1** hard work; labor. **2** something made or done by hard work.—*v.* **1** work hard. **2** move with difficulty, pain, or weariness. **3** bring, make, or obtain by hard work or effort. [ME < AF *toiler* < OF *toeillier* drag about, make dirty < L *tudiculare* stir up < L *tudicula* olive press < *tundere* pound] —**toil′er,** *n.* —**Syn.** *n.* **1** drudgery, travail, effort, exertion. See **work.** –*v.* **1** labor, drudge, slave.

toil² (toil) *n.* Often, **toils,** *pl.* a net; snare: *The thief was caught in the toils of the law.* [< F *toile*, literally, cloth < L *tela* web < *texere* weave]

toi·let (toi′lit) *n.* **1** a fixture, usually a porcelain bowl flushed by water, into which waste matter from the body is passed. **2** a room containing a toilet. **3** the process of dressing. Bathing, combing the hair, and putting on one's clothes are all part of one's toilet. **4** a set of toilet articles. **5** a dressing table. **6** a person's dress; costume.
—*adj.* **1** of or for use in the process of dressing and grooming. Combs and brushes are toilet articles. **2** for use in a toilet: *a toilet brush, toilet paper.* [< F *toilette,* dim. of *toile.* See TOIL[2].]

toi·let·ry (toi′lit rē) *n.* **-ries.** soap, face powder, perfumery, or other articles for the toilet.

toi·lette (toi let′; *French,* twä let′) *n.* toilet (defs. 3 and 6). [< F]

toilet water a fragrant liquid, weaker than perfume, used after bathing, as a cologne in grooming, etc.

toil·some (toil′səm) *adj.* requiring hard work; laborious; wearisome. —**Syn.** tiring, fatiguing, onerous.

toil·worn (toil′wôrn′) *adj.* worn by toil; showing the effects of toil.

To·kay (tō kā′) *n.* **1** a rich, sweet, golden wine made in Hungary. **2** a wine imitating it. **3** the large, firm, reddish, sweet grape from which it is made. [< *Tokay,* a town in N. Hungary, where this wine was first made]

to·ken (tō′kən) *n.* **1 a** a mark or sign: *Black is a token of mourning.* **b** something that serves to prove; an evidence: *His actions are a token of his sincerity.* **c** a characteristic mark or indication: *the tokens of a good horse, the tokens of a disease.* **2** a sign of friendship; keepsake: *She received many birthday tokens.* **3** a piece of metal stamped for a higher value than the metal is worth. Tokens are used for some purposes instead of money. **4** a piece of metal indicating a right or privilege: *This token will admit you to the swimming pool.* **5** something that is a sign of genuineness or authority. **6** *Archaic.* a signal. **7 by the same token,** moreover. **8 in token of,** as a token of; to show.
—*adj.* having only the appearance of; serving as a symbol; nominal; partial: *a token payment, token resistance.* [OE *tācen*] —**Syn.** *n.* **1** symbol, indication. See **mark. 2** memento, memorial.

told (tōld) *v.* **1** pt. and pp. of **tell. 2 all told,** including all.

To·le·do (tə lē′dō) *n.* a fine sword or sword blade made in Toledo, a city in central Spain.

tol·er·a·ble (tol′ər ə bəl or tol′rə bəl) *adj.* **1** able to be borne or endured. **2** fairly good: *She is in tolerable health.* [ME < OF < L *tolerabilis* < *tolerare* tolerate]
—**tol′er·a·ble·ness,** *n.* —**Syn. 1** bearable, endurable, sufferable, supportable. **2** passable, mediocre, ordinary, indifferent.

tol·er·a·bly (tol′ər ə blē or tol′rə blē) *adv.* **1** in a tolerable manner. **2** moderately.

tol·er·ance (tol′ər əns) *n.* **1** a willingness to be tolerant and patient toward people whose opinions or ways differ from one's own. **2** the power of enduring or resisting the action of a drug, poison, etc. **3** the action of tolerating. **4** an allowed amount of variation from a standard, as in the weight of coins or the dimensions of a machine or part. —**Syn. 1** forbearance. See **toleration.**

tol·er·ant (tol′ər ənt) *adj.* **1** willing to let other people do as they think best; willing to suffer beliefs and actions of which one does not approve. **2** able to endure or resist the action of a drug, poison, etc. —**tol′er·ant·ly,** *adv.*

tol·er·ate (tol′ər āt′) *v.* **-at·ed, -at·ing. 1** allow; permit: *Corruption cannot be tolerated in high places.* **2** bear; endure; put up with: *They tolerated the grouchy old man only because he was their employer.* **3** endure or resist the action of (a drug, poison, etc.). [< L *tolerare*]

tol·er·a·tion (tol′ər ā′shən) *n.* **1** willingness to put up with beliefs and actions of which one does not approve. **2** the recognition of a person's right to worship as he thinks best without loss of civil rights or social privileges; freedom of worship.
☛ **Toleration, tolerance** are associated with the verb *tolerate,* but differ in meaning. **Toleration** = the act of allowing or putting up with actions, beliefs, or people one does not like or approve of, often because of indifference or a desire to avoid conflict: *Toleration of dishonest officials encourages corruption.* **Tolerance** = the state or quality of being willing to let others think, live, or worship according to their own beliefs and to refrain from judging, harshly or with blind prejudice: *Through tolerance we learn to understand people.*

toll[1] (tōl) *v.* **1** sound with single strokes slowly and regularly repeated: *Bells were tolled all over the country at the King's death.* **2** call, announce, etc. by tolling.
—*n.* **1** the stroke or sound of a bell being tolled. **2** the act or fact of tolling. [related to OE *-tyllan* draw. See TILL[3].]

toll[2] (tōl) *n.* **1** a tax or fee paid for some right or privilege: *We pay a toll when we use the bridge.* **2** the right to collect tolls. **3** a charge for a certain service. There is a toll on long-distance telephone calls. **4** something paid, lost, suffered, etc.: *Automobile accidents take a heavy toll of human lives.* —*v.* collect tolls from; take as toll. [OE *toll,* var. of *toln* < L < Gk. *telōnion* toll house, ult. < *telos* tax]

toll[3] (tōl) in hunting: —*v.* **1** lure game by using a call or other sound. **2** make such a call or sound. —*n.* a call or sound thus made. [ME; cf. OE *talu* talk. Akin to TALE.]

toll bar a barrier, especially a gate, across a road or bridge where toll is taken.

toll bridge a bridge at which a toll is charged.

toll call a long-distance telephone call.

toll·gate (tōl′gāt′) *n.* a gate where toll is collected.

toll·keep·er (tōl′kēp′ər) *n.* a person who collects the toll at a tollgate.

toll road a road on which tolls are charged; turnpike.

Tol·tec (tol′tek) *n.* **1** a North American Indian people supposed to have ruled in Mexico before the Aztecs. **2** one of this people.

to·lu (tō lü′) *n.* a fragrant balsam obtained from a South American tree, used in medicine, perfume, etc. [< Santiago de *Tolú,* a city in Colombia]

tol·u·ene (tol′ū ēn′) *n.* a colorless liquid, resembling benzene and obtained from coal tar and coal gas. It is used as a solvent and for making explosives and dyes. *Formula:* $C_6H_5CH_3$ [< *tolu* + *-ene,* as in *benzene*]

tol·u·ol (tol′ū ol′ or tol′ū ōl′) *n.* toluene.

tom or **Tom** (tom) *n.* **1** a male cat; tomcat. **2** the male of various other animals, such as the turkey. [< *Tom,* used as a type name for a common man]

tom·a·hawk (tom′ə hok′ or -hôk′) *n.* **1** a light axe used by North American Indians as a weapon and as a tool. **2 bury the tomahawk,** stop fighting; make peace. —*v.* strike or kill with a tomahawk. [< Algonquian]

A tomahawk

to·ma·to (tə mā′tō, tə mä′tō, or tə mat′ō) *n.* **-toes. 1** a juicy fruit used as a vegetable. Most tomatoes are red when ripe. **2** the plant it grows on. Tomatoes are spreading, strong-smelling plants that have hairy leaves and stems and small, yellow flowers. [< Sp. < Nahuatl *tomatl*]

tomb (tüm) *n.* **1** a burial vault or mausoleum, often above ground. **2** a grave dug in the ground or in rock. **3** death. —*v.* **1** put in a tomb. **2** shut up as if in a tomb. [ME < AF < LL < Gk. *tymbos* mound]

tom·bac, tom·back, or **tom·bak** (tom′bak) *n.* any of several alloys consisting of zinc, copper, and sometimes arsenic, used to make cheap jewellery, art objects, etc. Also, **tambac.** [< F *tombac* < Pg. *tambaca* < Malay < Skt. *tamraka*]

tom·boy (tom′boi′) *n.* a girl who likes to play boys' games; a boisterous, romping girl.

tomb·stone (tüm′stōn′) *n.* a stone that marks a tomb or grave.

tom·cat (tom′kat′) *n.* a male cat.

tom·cod (tom′kod′) *n.* a small salt-water fish resembling a cod.

Tom, Dick, and Harry people in general; everyone.

tome (tōm) *n.* a book, especially a large, heavy book. [< F < L < Gk. *tomos,* originally, piece cut off]

tom·fool (tom′fül′) *n.* a silly fool; stupid person.

tom·fool·er·y (tom′fül′ər ē) *n.* **-er·ies.** silly behavior; nonsense.

Tom·my or **tom·my** (tom′ē) *n.* **-mies.** a nickname for a

British soldier. [< *Tommy Atkins*]

Tom·my At·kins (at′kinz) *n.* a nickname for a British soldier. [< *Thomas Atkins*, a name used for privates in the sample forms given in the official regulations of the British Army from 1815 on]

tommy cod tomcod.

Tommy gun or **tommy gun** *Informal.* a Thompson submachine gun.

tom·my·rot (tom′ē rot′) *n. Slang.* nonsense; rubbish; foolishness. [origin uncertain]

to·mor·row or **to-mor·row** (tə môr′ō) *n.* the day after today. —*adv.* on the day after today. [ME *to morowe*]

Tom Thumb 1 in the children's story, a dwarf no bigger than his father's thumb. 2 any very small thing or person.

tom·tit (tom′tit′) *n.* a small bird, especially a titmouse.

tom-tom (tom′tom′) *n.* 1 a primitive drum, usually beaten with the hands. 2 a monotonous, rhythmical drumbeat. [< Hind. *tam-tam*]

ton (tun) *n.* 1 a measure of weight; 2,000 pounds in Canada and the United States, 2,240 pounds in England. 2 a measure of volume that varies with the thing measured; it is about equal to the space occupied by a ton's weight of the particular stuff. A ton of stone is 16 cubic feet. 3 a unit of measure of internal capacity of a ship; 100 cubic feet. 4 a unit of measure of carrying capacity of a ship; 40 cubic feet. 5 a unit to measure the weight of water a ship will displace; 35 cubic feet, the volume of a long ton of sea water. *Abbrev.*: t. 6 **long ton,** 2,240 pounds. 7 **metric ton,** 1,000 kilograms. 8 **short ton,** 2,000 pounds. [var. of *tun*]

ton·al (tōn′əl) *adj.* 1 of or having to do with tones or tone. 2 characterized by tonality: *tonal music.*

to·nal·i·ty (tō nal′ə tē) *n.* **-ties.** 1 in music: **a** the sum of relationships existing between the tones of a scale or the keys in a phrase or composition. **b** a key or system of tones. 2 the color scheme of a painting, etc.

ton·al·ly (tōn′əl ē) *adv.* with respect to tone.

tone (tōn) *n. v.* **toned, ton·ing.** —*n.* 1 any sound considered with reference to its quality, pitch, strength, source, etc.: *sweet, shrill, or loud tones.* 2 the quality of sound: *a voice silvery in tone.* 3 in music: **a** a musical sound; a sound of definite pitch and character. **b** the difference in pitch between two notes. C and D are one tone apart. 4 a manner of speaking or writing: *a moral tone.* 5 a spirit; character; style: *tone of elegance.* **b** mental or emotional state; mood; disposition: *a healthful tone of mind.* 6 a normal, healthy condition; vigor. 7 the effect of color and of light and shade in a painting, drawing, etc.: *I like the soft green tone of that painting.* 8 a shade of color: *This room is furnished in tones of brown.* 9 in linguistics: **a** the pitch of the voice as it is high or low, or as it rises and falls, regarded as a distinctive feature of a language. **b** any of the tonal levels distinctive in a language. **c** the pronunciation characteristic of a particular person, group of people, area, etc.; accent. —*v.* 1 harmonize: *This rug tones in well with the wallpaper and furniture.* 2 give a tone to. 3 change the tone of. 4 **tone down,** soften. 5 **tone up,** give more sound, color, or vigor to; strengthen. [ME < OF < L < Gk. *tonos*, originally, a stretching, taut string]

-toned *combining form.* having a ——tone: *sweet-toned = having a sweet tone.*

tone·less (tōn′lis) *adj.* 1 without tone; without expression. 2 of color, dull, insipid. 3 listless; vapid. —**tone′less·ly,** *adv.* —**tone′less·ness,** *n.*

tong[1] (tong) *n.* 1 in China, an association or club. 2 a secret organization or club in North American Chinese communities. [< Chinese *t'ang*, *t'ong*, originally, meeting hall]

tong[2] (tong) *v.* 1 seize, gather, hold, or handle with tongs. 2 use tongs; work with tongs. [OE *tang*]

tongs (tongz) *n.pl.* 1 a tool for seizing, holding, or lifting: *He changed the position of the burning log with the tongs.* See picture in the next column. 2 a tool for curling hair.

tongue (tung) *n. v.* **tongued, tongu·ing.** —*n.* 1 the movable fleshy organ in the mouth of human beings and most vertebrates. The tongue is used in tasting and, by man, for talking. 2 an animal's tongue used as food. 3 the power of speech: *You are silent—have you*

hat, āge, cãre, fär; let, ēqual, tėrm; it, īce
hot, ōpen, ôrder; oil, out; cup, pu̇t, rüle, ūse
əbove, takən, pencəl, lemən, circəs
ch, child; ng, long; sh, ship
th, thin; ᴛʜ, then; zh, measure

lost your tongue? 4 a way of speaking; speech; talk: *a flattering tongue.* 5 the language of a people: *the English tongue.* 6 something shaped or used like a tongue. 7 the strip of leather under the laces of a shoe. 8 a narrow strip of land running out into water. 9 a tapering jet of flame. 10 the pin of a buckle, brooch, etc. 11 the pole by which a team of horses draws a wagon. 12 a projecting strip along the edge of a board for fitting into a groove in another board. 13 the pointer of a dial, balance, etc. 14 in a bell, the movable piece that strikes and rings the outer part. 15 in a wind musical instrument, a vibrating reed, etc. 16 the short movable rail of a railway switch. 17 **give tongue,** of hounds, etc., bark or bay. 18 **hold one's tongue,** keep quiet. 19 **on the tip of one's tongue, a** almost spoken. **b** ready to be spoken.

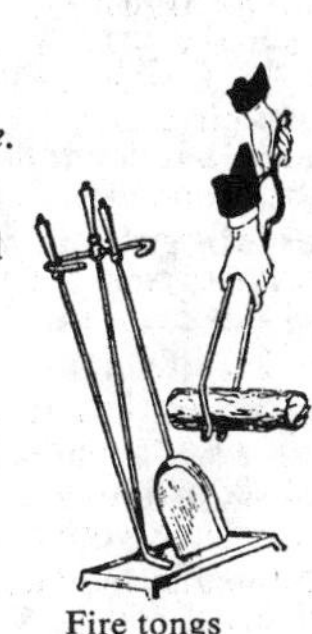

Fire tongs being used to lift a piece of wood

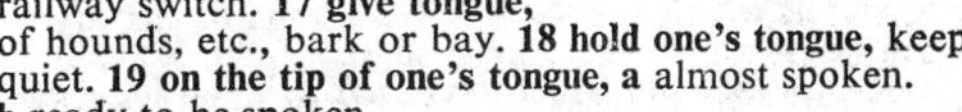

—*v.* 1 modify tones of (a flute, cornet, etc.) with the tongue. 2 use the tongue. 3 furnish with a tongue: *tongue and groove boards.* [OE *tunge*] —**tongue′less,** *adj.*

tongue-in-cheek (tung′in chēk′) *adj.* meant to be ironical or facetious: *a tongue-in-cheek criticism.*

tongue-lash (tung′lash′) *v. Informal.* scold severely.

tongue-tie (tung′tī′) *n. v.* **-tied, -ty·ing.** —*n.* a condition in which the motion of the tongue is impeded by an abnormal shortness of the folded membrane below it. —*v.* make (someone) unable to speak, because of amazement, fear, shyness, etc.

tongue-tied (tung′tīd′) *adj.* 1 having the motion of the tongue hindered. 2 unable to speak because of shyness, embarrassment, etc.

tongue twister a phrase or sentence, usually alliterative, that is difficult to say quickly without a mistake. *Example*: She sells seashells by the seashore.

tongue-twist·ing (tung′twis′ting) *adj.* of or like a tongue twister; difficult to say quickly without a mistake.

ton·ic (ton′ik) *n.* 1 anything that gives strength; a medicine to give strength: *Cod-liver oil is a tonic.* 2 in music, the first note of a scale; keynote. 3 a type of flavored carbonated water. —*adj.* 1 restoring to health and vigor; giving strength; bracing: *The mountain air is tonic.* 2 **a** having to do with muscular tension. **b** characterized by continuous contraction of the muscles: *a tonic convulsion.* 3 in music: **a** having to do with a tone or tones. **b** of or based on a keynote. 4 in linguistics: **a** having to do with tone or accent in speaking. **b** of a language, using tone distinctively. 5 of speech sounds, accented or stressed. [< Gk. *tonikos* < *tonos* tone. See TONE.]

to·nic·i·ty (tō nis′ə tē) *n.* 1 the quality or condition of being tonic. 2 the property of possessing bodily tone; the normal elastic tension of muscles, arteries, etc.

tonic sol-fa a system of teaching music, especially sight-singing and notation, in which the notes of a major scale are sung to sol-fa syllables with *do* as the tonic or keynote.

to·night or **to-night** (tə nīt′) *n.* the night of this day; this night. —*adv.* on or during this night. [OE *tō niht*]

ton·ite (tōn′īt) *n.* an explosive used in blasting, consisting of guncotton and barium nitrate. [< *ton-*, abstracted from L *tonare* thunder]

ton·nage (tun′ij) *n.* 1 the carrying capacity of a ship expressed in tons of 100 cubic feet: *A ship of 50,000 cubic feet of space for freight has a tonnage of 500 tons.* 2 the total amount of shipping in tons: *the tonnage of Canada's navy.* 3 a duty or tax on ships at so much a ton. 4 weight in tons.

ton·neau (tun ō′) *n.* **-neaus** or **-neaux** (-ōz′). the rear part of an automobile body, with seats for passengers. [< F *tonneau*, literally, cask, ult. < Gmc.]

ton·sil (ton′səl) *n.* either of the two oval masses of glandular tissue on the inner sides of the throat, just back of the mouth. [< L *tonsillae*, pl., dim. of *toles*, pl., goiter]

ton·sil·lar or **ton·sil·ar** (ton′sə lər) *adj.* of or having to do with the tonsils.

ton·sil·lec·to·my (ton′sə lek′tə mē) *n.* **-mies.** a removal of the tonsils. [< L *tonsillae* tonsils + *-ectomy* (< Gk. *ek-* out of + *-tomia* a cutting < *temnein* cut)]

ton·sil·li·tis (ton′sə lī′tis) *n.* inflammation of the tonsils. [< NL < L *tonsillae* tonsils + *-itis*]

ton·so·ri·al (ton sô′rē əl) *adj.* of or having to do with a barber or his work. [< L *tonsorius*, ult. < *tondere* shear]

ton·sure (ton′shər) *n. v.* **-sured, -sur·ing.** —*n.* **1** a clipping of the hair or shaving of a part or the whole of the head of a person entering the priesthood or an order of monks. **2** the shaved part of the head of a priest or monk. **3** the state of being so shaved. —*v.* shave the head of. [ME < L *tonsura* < *tondere* shear, shave]

ton·tine (ton′tēn or ton tēn′) *n.* **1** a system of annuity or insurance in which subscribers share a fund. The shares of survivors increase as members of a tontine die, until the last gets all that is left. **2** the total of money involved in such a system. **3** the share or right of each member in such a system. **4** the members as a group. [< F *tontine* < Lorenzo *Tonti*, an Italian banker, who introduced this system into France in about 1653]

too (tü) *adv.* **1** also; besides: *The dog is hungry, and thirsty too.* **2** beyond what is desirable, proper, or right; more than enough: *My dress is too long for you. He ate too much. The summer passed too quickly.* **3** very; exceedingly: *I am not too hungry right now.* [var. of *to*]
☞ too. When *too* in the sense of *also* comes within a construction, it is usually set off by commas; but in informal writing it usually is not when it comes at the end. Informal: *I'm going too.* More formal: *I'm going, too.*

took (tu̇k) *v.* pt. of **take.**

tool (tül) *n.* **1** a knife, hammer, saw, shovel, or any instrument used in doing work. **2** anything used to achieve some purpose: *Books are a scholar's tools.* **3** a person used by another like a tool: *He is a tool of the departmental boss.* **4** a part of a machine that cuts, bores, smooths, etc. **5** the whole of such a machine.
—*v.* **1** use a tool on. **2** work with a tool. **3** ornament with a tool. **4** *Slang.* drive a car, especially to drive it fast and skilfully. **5 tool up,** install equipment for a certain task; prepare for a specific job: *The factory is tooling up for the production of new cars.* [OE *tōl*]
Syn. *n.* **1 Tool, implement** = an instrument or other article used in doing work. **Tool** = an instrument or simple device especially suited or designed to make doing a particular kind of work easier, but applies particularly to something held and worked by the hands in doing manual work: *Plumbers, mechanics, carpenters, and shoemakers need tools.* **Implement** is a general word meaning "a tool, instrument, utensil, or mechanical device needed to do something": *Hoes and tractors are agricultural implements.*

tool·ing (tül′ing) *n.* **1** work done with a tool. **2** ornamentation made with a tool. **3** the assembly of machine tools in a factory.

tool·mak·er (tül′māk′ər) *n.* **1** a man who makes tools. **2** a man who makes, repairs, or maintains machine tools.

tool·push·er (tül′pu̇sh′ər) *n.* in the oil industry, a foreman of a drilling operation. Also, **toolpush.**

toot[1] (tüt) *n.* the sound of a horn, whistle, etc. —*v.* **1** give forth a short blast: *He heard the train toot three times.* **2** sound (a horn, whistle, etc.) in short blasts. [probably ult. imitative] —**toot′er,** *n.*

toot[2] (tüt) *n. Slang.* a drinking spree; binge: *go on a toot.* [earlier, a large drink < obs. *toot*, v., drink copiously; origin unknown]

tooth (tüth) *n.* **teeth,** *v.* —*n.* **1** one of the hard, bonelike parts in the mouth, used for biting and chewing. See picture at **teeth. 2** something like a tooth. Each one of the projecting parts of a comb, rake, or saw is a tooth. **3** a taste; liking: *have no tooth for fruit.* **4 fight tooth and nail,** fight fiercely, with all one's force.
—*v.* **1** furnish with teeth; put teeth on. **2** cut teeth on the edge of; indent. [OE *tōth*]

tooth·ache (tüth′āk′) *n.* a pain in a tooth or the teeth.

tooth·brush (tüth′brush′) *n.* a small brush for cleaning the teeth.

toothed (tütht or tüᴛʜd) *adj.* **1** having teeth. **2** notched.

tooth·less (tüth′lis) *adj.* without teeth.

tooth·paste (tüth′pāst′) *n.* a paste used in cleaning the teeth.

tooth·pick (tüth′pik′) *n.* a small, pointed piece of wood or a sharpened quill for removing bits of food from between the teeth.

tooth·some (tüth′səm) *adj.* pleasing to the taste; tasting good. —**Syn.** savory, delicious.

too·tle (tü′təl) *v.* **-tled, -tling,** *n.* —*v.* toot softly and continuously, as on a whistle. —*n.* a tootling. [frequentative of ᴛᴏᴏᴛ[1]]

top[1] (top) *n. adj. v.* **topped, top·ping.** —*n.* **1** the highest point or part: *the top of a mountain.* **2** the upper end or surface: *the top of a table.* **3** the highest or leading place, rank, etc.: *He is at the top of his class.* **4** one that occupies the highest or leading position: *He is top in his profession.* **5** the highest point, pitch, or degree: *the top of one's voice.* **6** the best or most important part: *the top of the morning.* **7** the part of a plant that grows above ground: *carrot tops.* **8** the head. **9** the cover of an automobile, carriage, can, etc. **10** the upper part of a shoe or boot. **11** a bunch of hair, fibres, etc. **12** on a ship, a platform around the top of a lower mast. **13** in golf, a stroke above the centre of a ball. **14** a tent used as a covering for a circus or other performance. **15** in baseball, the first half of the inning. **16 blow one's top,** *Slang.* **a** lose one's temper; get very excited. **b** become insane. **17 from top to toe, a** from head to foot. **b** completely. **18 on top,** with success; with victory. **19 over the top, a** over the front of a trench to attack. **b** over a target or limit: *We aimed for 50 subscriptions to our magazine, but we went over the top and collected 73.*

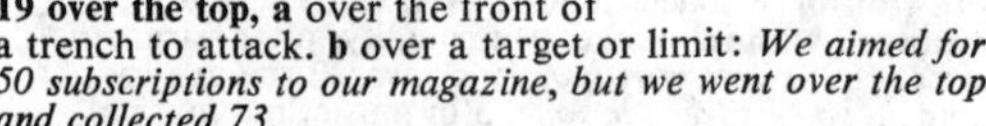

A top (def. 12)

—*adj.* **1** having to do with, situated at, or forming the top: *the top shelf of a cupboard.* **2** highest in degree; greatest: *at top speed.* **3** chief; foremost: *top honors.*
—*v.* **1** put a top on: *top a box.* **2** be on top of; be the top of: *A church tops the hill.* **3** reach the top of: *They topped the mountain.* **4** rise high; rise above: *The sun topped the horizon.* **5** be higher than; be greater than. **6** do better than; outdo; excel: *His story topped all the rest.* **7** in golf, hit (a ball) above centre. **8** remove the top of (a plant, etc.). **9** in chemical distillation, remove the part that volatilizes first; skim. **10 top off, a** finish; end. **b** complete; put the finishing touches to: *We topped off the evening with an excellent dinner.* **c** *Slang.* in the West, begin to tame or break (a horse). [OE *topp*]
Syn. *n.* **1 Top, summit, crown** = the highest point or part of something. **Top** is the general word: *Please loosen the top of this jar.* **Summit** = the highest point of a hill, mountain, or pass, but is often used figuratively to mean the highest level that can be reached, or reached toward, by effort: *At last he attained the summit of his ambition.* **Crown,** used figuratively, means the highest degree of perfection or completion or highest state or quality of something: *A Nobel Prize is the crown of success.* *v.* **1** cap, crown.

top[2] (top) *n.* **1** a toy that spins on a point. **2 sleep like a top,** sleep soundly. [OE *topp*]

to·paz (tō′paz) *n.* **1** a crystalline mineral that occurs in various forms and colors. **2** a piece of this stone, or a gem made from it. **3** transparent yellow; pale brown. [ME < OF < L < Gk. *topazos*]

top boot 1 a high boot having the upper part of different material and made to look as if turned down. **2** any boot with a high top.

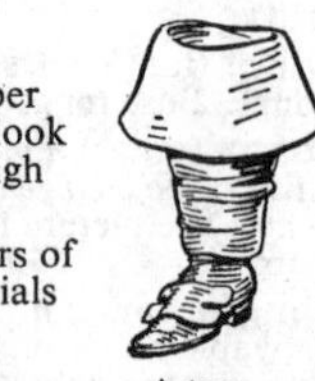
A top boot (def. 1)

top brass *Slang.* **1** high-ranking officers of the armed services. **2** high-ranking officials of any organization.

top·coat (top′kōt′) *n.* **1** an overcoat, especially a lightweight one. **2** the fur of an animal that covers its back and sides. **3** a

hat, āge, cãre, fär; let, ēqual, tėrm; it, īce
hot, ōpen, ôrder; oil, out; cup, pu̇t, rüle, ūse
əbove, takən, pencəl, lemən, circəs
ch, child; ng, long; sh, ship
th, thin; ᴛʜ, then; zh, measure

finishing coating of paint, etc.

top dog *Informal.* the best, most successful or most important individual or group. [from the position of the winning dog in a dogfight]

top drawer *Informal.* the highest level of excellence, importance, good breeding, etc.: *a family in the top drawer of society.*

tope (tōp) *v.* **toped, top·ing.** drink excessively or habitually; tipple. [origin uncertain]

top·er (tōp′ər) *n.* a person who drinks a great deal of alcoholic liquor. [< *tope* drink habitually; origin uncertain]

top-flight (top′flīt′) *adj.* superior; of the highest excellence.

top·gal·lant (top′gal′ənt or tə gal′ənt) *n.* the mast or sail above the topmast; the third section of a mast above the deck. See **masthead** for diagram. *—adj.* next above the topmast.

top hat a tall, black silk hat worn by men in formal clothes.

top-heav·y (top′hev′ē) *adj.* **1** too heavy at the top. **2** overcapitalized, as a business corporation. **3** having too many officials of high rank: *a department top-heavy with full professors.*

To·phet (tō′fit) *n.* hell. [< Hebrew *Topheth,* a proper name]

to·pi·ar·y (tō′pē er′ē) *adj. n.* **-ar·ies.** *—adj.* in gardening: **1** trimmed or clipped into figures or designs: *topiary shrubs.* **2** of or having to do with such trimming. *—n.* **1** the art or practice of such trimming. **2** a topiary garden. [< F *topiare,* ult. < L *topia* fancy gardening < Gk. *topos* place]

top·ic (top′ik) *n.* **1** a subject that people think, write, or talk about: *Newspapers discuss the topics of the day.* **2** a short phrase or sentence used in an outline to give the main point of a part of a speech, writing, etc. [sing. of *topics* < L *topica* < Gk. (*ta*) *topika,* a study of logical and rhetorical commonplaces (by Aristotle) < *topos* place] **—Syn. 1** See **subject.**

top·i·cal (top′ə kəl) *adj.* **1** having to do with topics of the day; of current or local interest. **2** of or using topics; having to do with the topics of a speech, writing, etc. **3** limited to a certain spot or part of the body; local.

top·knot (top′not′) *n.* **1** a knot or tuft of hair on the top of the head of a person or animal. **2** a plume or crest of feathers on the head of a bird.

top-lev·el (top′lev′əl) *adj. Informal.* of the highest importance, authority, etc.: *top-level decisions.*

top·loft·y (top′lof′tē) *adj. Informal.* lofty in character or manner; haughty; pompous; pretentious.

top·mast (top′mast′ or top′məst) *n.* the second section of a mast above the deck. See **masthead** for diagram.

top·most (top′mōst′) *adj.* highest.

top-notch (top′noch′) *adj. Informal.* first-rate; best possible.

to·pog·ra·pher (tə pog′rə fər) *n.* **1** a person who knows much about topography. **2** a person who accurately describes the surface features of a place or region.

top·o·graph·ic (top′ə graf′ik) *adj.* topographical.

top·o·graph·i·cal (top′ə graf′ə kəl) *adj.* of or having to do with topography. A topographical map shows mountains, rivers, etc.

top·o·graph·i·cal·ly (top′ə graf′ik lē) *adv.* in regard to topography.

to·pog·ra·phy (tə pog′rə fē) *n.* **-phies. 1** the science of making an accurate and detailed description of regions or their surface features. **2** a detailed description of the surface features of a place or region. **3** the surface features of a place or region. The topography of a region includes hills, valleys, streams, lakes, bridges, tunnels, roads, etc. **4** topographical surveying. [< LL < Gk. *topographia* < *topos* place + *graphein* write]

to·pon·o·my (tə pon′ə mē) *n.* **1** the study of the place names of a region, country, etc. **2** a register of such names. [< Gk. *topos* place + *onyma* name]

top·per (top′ər) *n.* **1** *Slang.* an excellent, first-rate person or thing. **2** *Informal.* a top hat. **3** *Informal.* a topcoat.

top·ping (top′ing) *adj. Brit. Informal.* excellent; first-rate. *—n.* **1** anything forming the top of something. **2** something put on the top of anything to complete it: *a cake with chocolate topping.* **3 toppings,** *pl.* branches, stems, etc. cut off in topping trees or plants.

top·ple (top′əl) *v.* **-pled, -pling. 1** fall forward; tumble down: *The chimney toppled over on the roof.* **2** throw over or down; overturn: *The wrestler toppled his opponent.* **3** hang over in an unsteady way: *beneath toppling crags.* [frequentative of *top,* v. < *top*[1], n.]

tops (tops) *Slang.* *—adj.* of the highest degree in quality, excellence, etc. *—n.* **the tops,** an excellent person or thing of its kind.

top·sail (top′sāl′ or top′səl) *n.* the second sail above the deck on a mast.

top secret a most important and highly guarded secret.

top-se·cret (top′sē′krit) *adj.* of utmost secrecy; extremely confidential.

top·side (top′sīd′) *n.* **1** Also, **topsides,** *pl.* **a** the top or upper portion of a ship's sides above the water line. **b** the upper part of a ship, as distinct from the hold, engine room, etc. **2** *Brit.* the outer side of a joint of beef. *—adv.* Also, **topsides. 1** to or on the bridge or upper deck. **2** *Informal.* on top; on deck; up above.

top·soil (top′soil′) *n.* the upper part of the soil; surface soil: *People buy topsoil for gardens and lawns.*

top·sy-tur·vy (top′sē tėr′vē) *adv. adj. n.* **-vies.** *—adv. adj.* **1** upside down. **2** in confusion or disorder. *—n.* confusion; disorder. [probably ult. < *top*[1] + *tirve* overturn, related to OE *tearflian* roll over]

toque (tōk) *n.* **1** a hat without a brim; a small hat with very little brim. **2** tuque. [< F]

to·rah or **to·ra** (tô′rə) *n.* **1** in Jewish usage, instruction, doctrine, or law. **2 the Torah,** the Mosaic law; the Pentateuch. [< Hebrew]

torch (tôrch) *n.* **1** a light to be carried around or stuck in a holder on a wall. A piece of pine wood makes a good torch. **2** a device for producing a very hot flame, used especially to burn off paint, to solder metal, and to melt metal; blowtorch. **3** *Brit.* a stick-shaped electric lamp; flashlight. **4** something thought of as a source of enlightenment: *the torch of civilization.* **5 carry a** (or **the**) **torch, a** *Slang.* be in love, especially suffer unrequited love: *He has been carrying the torch for her for months.* **b** *Informal.* crusade for; support a cause. [ME < OF *torche,* probably ult. < L *torquere* twist] **—torch′like′,** *adj.*

torch·bear·er (tôrch′bãr′ər) *n.* **1** one who carries a torch. **2** one who spreads the light of knowledge, civilization, etc. **3** *Informal.* one who is prominent in support of a crusade, a cause, or an individual.

torch·light (tôrch′līt′) *n.* the light of a torch or torches.

tor·chon lace (tôr′shon) **1** a handmade linen lace with loosely twisted threads in simple open patterns. **2** a machine-made imitation of this in linen or cotton. [< F *torchon* dish cloth]

tore (tôr) *v.* pt. of **tear**[2].

tor·e·a·dor (tôr′ē ə dôr′) *n.* a bullfighter. [< Sp. *toreador,* ult. < *toro* bull < L *taurus*]

to·ri·i (tô′rē ē′) *n.* **-ri·i.** in Japan, a gateway at the entrance to a Shinto temple, built of two uprights and two crosspieces. [< Japanese]

A torii

tor·ment (*v.* tôr ment′; *n.* tôr′ment) *v.* **1** cause very great pain to. **2** worry or annoy very much: *He torments everyone with silly questions.*
—*n.* **1** a cause of very great pain. Instruments of torture were torments. **2** very great pain. **3** a cause of very much worry or annoyance. [ME < OF *tormenter*, ult. < L *tormentum*, originally, twisted sling < *torquere* twist]
Syn. *v.* **1 Torment, torture** = cause physical or mental pain or suffering that is hard to bear. **Torment** = hurt or harm again and again and cause sharp, severe pain that continues or is constantly repeated: *He is tormented by a racking cough.* **Torture** = torment so severely that the victim twists and turns in agony, and often suggests a deliberate purpose, such as love of cruelty, hatred, attempt to force a confession, etc.: *We do not believe in torturing prisoners.* **2** tease, plague, harass. –*n.* **2** agony, anguish, misery, distress.

tor·men·tor or **tor·ment·er** (tôr men′tər) *n.* a person or thing that torments.

torn (tôrn) *v.* pp. of **tear**[2].

tor·na·do (tôr nā′dō) *n.* **-does** or **-dos. 1** an extremely violent and destructive whirlwind. A tornado moves forward as a whirling funnel extending down from a mass of dark clouds. **2** a violent outburst. [alteration of Sp. *tronada* < *tronar* thunder] **—Syn.** See **cyclone.**

tor·pe·do (tôr pē′dō) *n.* **-does,** *v.* **-doed, -do·ing.** —*n.* **1** a large, cigar-shaped shell that contains explosives and travels by its own power. Torpedoes are sent under water to blow up enemy ships. **2** a submarine mine, shell, etc. that explodes when hit. **3** an explosive signalling device put on a railway track. A torpedo makes a loud noise when a train runs over it. **4** a mixture of an explosive and gravel wrapped in tissue paper or in cardboard and exploded by throwing it against a hard surface. **5** a fish that can give an electric shock.
—*v.* **1** attack or destroy with a torpedo. **2** set off a torpedo in or against. **3** bring completely to an end; destroy: *torpedo a peace conference.* [< L *torpedo* the electric ray (a fish), originally, numbness < *torpere* be numb]

A torpedo. When it is launched from a ship, airplane, etc., it travels much like a small ship. It contains a motor and devices for controlling its course and depth.

torpedo boat a small, fast warship used for attacking with torpedoes.

tor·pid (tôr′pid) *adj.* **1** dull; inactive; sluggish. **2** not moving or feeling. Animals that hibernate become torpid in winter. **3** numb. [< L *torpidus* < *torpere* be numb] **—tor′pid·ly,** *adv.* **—tor′pid·ness,** *n.* **—Syn. 1** lethargic, apathetic.

tor·pid·i·ty (tôr pid′ə tē) *n.* a torpid condition.

tor·por (tôr′pər) *n.* a torpid condition. [< L *torpor* < *torpere* be numb]

torque (tôrk) *n.* **1** a force causing rotation. **2** a necklace of twisted metal. The ancient Gauls and Britons wore torques. [< L *torques* twisted neck chain < *torquere* twist]

tor·re·fy (tôr′ə fī′) *v.* **-fied, -fy·ing.** dry or parch with heat: *a torrefied drug, torrefied ores.* [< L *torrefacere* < *torrere* parch + *facere* make]

tor·rent (tôr′ənt) *n.* **1** a violent, rushing stream of water. **2** a heavy downpour. **3** any violent, rushing stream; flood: *a torrent of abuse.* [< L *torrens, -entis* boiling, parching]

tor·ren·tial (tô ren′shəl) *adj.* of, caused by, or like a torrent: *torrential rains, a torrential flow of words.*

tor·ren·tial·ly (tô ren′shəl ē) *adv.* like a torrent; violently; overwhelmingly.

tor·rid (tôr′id) *adj.* very hot: *July can be a torrid month.* [< L *torridus* < *torrere* parch]

tor·rid·i·ty (tô rid′ə tē) *n.* extreme heat.

Torrid Zone the very warm region between the tropic of Cancer and the tropic of Capricorn. The equator divides the Torrid Zone. See **zone** for diagram.

tor·sion (tôr′shən) *n.* **1** the act or process of twisting. **2** the state of being twisted. **3** the twisting of a body by two equal and opposite forces. **4** the tendency of a twisted cord, wire, etc. to return to its untwisted condition. [ME < OF < LL *torsio, -onis* < L *torquere* twist]

tor·sion·al (tôr′shən əl) *adj.* of, having to do with, or resulting from torsion.

tor·so (tôr′sō) *n.* **-sos. 1** the trunk or body of a statue without any head, arms, or legs. **2** the trunk of the human body. **3** something left mutilated or unfinished. [< Ital. *torso*, originally, stalk < L < Gk. *thyrsos* wand]

tort (tôrt) *n.* in law, a civil, as opposed to criminal, wrong (except for certain cases involving a breach of contract) for which the law requires damages: *If a man's automobile breaks a fence, he has committed a tort against the owner.* [ME < OF < Med.L *tortum* injustice < L *torquere* turn awry, twist]

tor·til·la (tôr tē′yə) *n.* especially in Spanish America, a thin, flat, round corn cake. [< Sp.]

tor·toise (tôr′təs) *n.* **-toise** or **-tois·es. 1** a turtle, especially a land turtle. **2** a very slow person or thing. [ME < Med.L *tortuca*, ult. < L *torquere* twist]

tortoise beetle a small beetle shaped rather like a tortoise.

tortoise shell 1 the mottled yellow-and-brown shell of a turtle or tortoise. Tortoise shell is much used for combs and ornaments. **2** a butterfly, cat, or any animal with mottled colors like those of tortoise shell.

tor·toise-shell (tôr′təs shel′) *adj.* **1** made of tortoise shell. **2** having the colors of a tortoise shell.

tor·tu·ous (tôr′chü əs) *adj.* **1** full of twists, turns, or bends; twisting; winding; crooked. **2** mentally or morally crooked; not straightforward: *tortuous reasoning.* [ME < AF < L *tortuosus*, ult. < *torquere* twist] **—tor′tu·ous·ly,** *adv.* **—tor′tu·ous·ness,** *n.* **—Syn. 1** sinuous, serpentine, zig-zag, circuitous.

tor·ture (tôr′chər) *n. v.* **-tured, -tur·ing.** —*n.* **1** the act or fact of inflicting extreme pain. Torture was formerly used to make people give evidence about crimes, or to make them confess. **2** extreme pain. **3** a violent and continuous twisting, pushing, or shaking that taxes a thing to the limit: *the torture of a boat by pounding waves.*
—*v.* **1** cause extreme pain to. **2** twist the meaning of. **3** twist or force out of its natural form: *Winds tortured the trees.* **4** puzzle or perplex greatly. [< LL *tortura* < L *torquere* twist] **—tor′tur·er,** *n.* **—Syn.** *n.* **2** agony, anguish, misery, distress. –*v.* **1** rack, persecute, distress. See **torment.**

tor·tur·ous (tôr′chər əs) *adj.* full of, involving, or causing torture.

to·rus (tô′rəs) *n.* **to·ri** (tô′rī or tô′rē). **1** in architecture, a large convex moulding, commonly forming the lowest member of the base of a column. **2** in botany, the receptacle of a flower. **3** in anatomy, a rounded ridge; a protuberant part. [< L *torus*, originally, cushion, swelling]

To·ry (tô′rē) *n.* **-ries,** *adj. Informal.* —*n.* **1** in Canada, a Conservative; a Progressive Conservative. **2** in Great Britain, originally, a member of the political party that favored royal power and the established church and opposed change. Strictly speaking, there is no Tory party in modern Britain, although members of the Conservative Party are often called Tories. **3** *U.S.* during the American Revolution, a supporter of the maintenance of British rule. **4** Also, **tory.** a very conservative person.
—*adj.* of or having to do with Conservatives or the Conservative Party. [< Irish Gaelic *tóraidhe* persecuted person (used of Irishmen dispossessed by the English in the 17th c.), outlaw, originally meaning "pursuer"]

To·ry·ism (tô′rē iz′əm) *n.* the fact of being a Tory; the doctrines or behavior of a Tory.

toss (tos) *v.* **tossed** or (*Poetic*) **tost, toss·ing,** *n.* —*v.* **1** throw lightly with the palm upward; cast; fling: *toss a ball.* **2** throw about; pitch about: *The ship was tossed by the heavy waves.* **3** lift quickly; throw upward: *She tossed her head. He was tossed by the bull.* **4** shake up or about, especially in order to mix the ingredients of: *toss a salad.* **5** throw a coin to decide something by the side that falls upward. **6** throw oneself about in bed; roll restlessly. **7** fling oneself: *He tossed out of the room in anger.* **8 toss off, a** do or make quickly and easily. **b** drink all at once: *He tossed off a whole glass of whisky.* —*n.* **1** the distance to which something is or can be tossed. **2** a throw; tossing. [? < Scand.; cf. dial. Norwegian *tossa* strew] —**Syn.** *v.* **1** See **throw.**

toss-up (tos′up′) *n.* **1** a tossing of a coin to decide something. **2** an even chance.

tost (tost) *v. Poetic.* a pt. and a pp. of **toss.**

tot (tot) *n.* **1** a little child. **2** *Esp. Brit.* a small portion of alcoholic liquor. [origin uncertain]

to·tal (tō′təl) *adj. n. v.* **-talled** or **-taled, -tal·ling** or **-tal·ing.** —*adj.* **1** whole; entire: *The total cost of the house and land will be $25,000.* **2** complete: *a total failure, total darkness.* —*n.* the whole amount; sum: *His expenses reached a total of $100.* —*v.* **1** find the sum of; add: *Total that column of figures.* **2** reach an amount of; amount to: *The money spent yearly on chewing gum totals millions of dollars.* [ME < OF < Med.L *totalis* < L *totus* all] —**Syn.** *adj.* **1** See **whole.** -*n.* aggregate.

to·tal·i·tar·i·an (tō tal′ə tãr′ē ən) *adj.* of or having to do with a dictatorial government that permits no competing political groups and exercises rigid control over industry, the arts, etc. —*n.* a person in favor of totalitarian principles.

to·tal·i·tar·i·an·ism (tō tal′ə tãr′ē ən iz′əm) *n.* **1** a totalitarian system of government. **2** belief in or support for such a system.

to·tal·i·ty (tō tal′ə tē) *n.* **-ties. 1** the total number or amount; total; whole. **2** the quality or state of being total; entirety. **3 a** the total obscuration of the sun or moon in an eclipse. **b** the time or duration of this.

to·tal·i·za·tor (tō′təl ə zā′tər) *n.* an apparatus for registering and indicating totals of operations, measurements, etc., especially one used for pari-mutuel betting at horse races.

to·tal·ly (tō′təl ē) *adv.* wholly; entirely; completely.

total war a war in which all the resources of a nation are used, and in which attack is made not only on the armed forces of the opponent, but also (subject to certain limitations) on all its people and property.

tote[1] (tōt) *v.* **tot·ed, tot·ing,** *n. Informal.* carry; haul. —*n.* **1** a carrying or hauling. **2** the distance of this; a haul: *a long tote.* [origin uncertain]

tote[2] (tōt) *n. Slang.* a totalizator.

tote bag a large handbag.

to·tem (tō′təm) *n.* **1** among North American Indians, a natural object, often an animal, taken as the emblem of a tribe, clan, family, etc. **2** the image of a totem. Totems are still carved and painted by some of the Indians of British Columbia. [< Algonquian]

to·tem·ic (tō tem′ik) *adj.* of a totem; having to do with totems.

to·tem·ism (tō′təm iz′əm) *n.* the use of totems to distinguish tribes, clans, families, etc.

totem pole a pole carved and painted with representations of totems, erected by the Indians of the western coast of North America, especially in front of their houses.

A totem pole

toth·er (tuᴛʜ′ər) *adj. pron. Dialect.* the other. [ME *thet other* the other, pronounced as *the tother*]

tot·ter (tot′ər) *v.* **1** stand or walk with shaky, unsteady steps. **2** be unsteady; shake as if about to fall. **3** shake; tremble. [ME; ? < Scand.; cf. dial. Norwegian *totra* quiver] —*n.* a tottering. —**tot′ter·er,** *n.* —**Syn.** *v.* **1** wobble, stagger.

tot·ter·y (tot′ər ē) *adj.* tottering; shaky.

tou·can (tü′kan or tü kän′) *n.* a bright-colored bird of tropical America, having an enormous beak. [< Carib]

touch (tuch) *v.* **1** put the hand or some other part of the body on or against: *She touched the pan to see whether it was still hot.* **2** put against; make contact with: *He touched the post with his umbrella.* **3** be against; come against: *Your sleeve is touching the butter.* **4** be in contact: *Our hands touched.* **5 a** border on: *a country that touches the mountains on the north.* **b** in geometry, be tangent to. **6** strike lightly or gently:

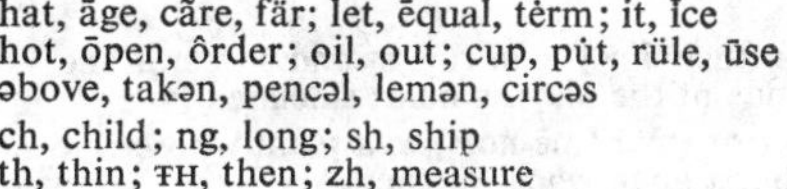
hat, āge, cãre, fär; let, ēqual, tėrm; it, īce
hot, ōpen, ôrder; oil, out; cup, pu̇t, rüle, ūse
əbove, takən, pencəl, lemən, circəs
ch, child; ng, long; sh, ship
th, thin; ᴛʜ, then; zh, measure

She touched the strings of the harp. **7** injure slightly: *The flowers were touched by the frost.* **8** affect with some feeling: *The sad story touched us.* **9** affect in some way by contact: *a metal so hard that a file cannot touch it.* **10** *Informal.* make slightly insane. **11** have to do with; concern: *The matter touches your interest.* **12** speak of; deal with; refer to; treat lightly: *Our conversation touched on many subjects.* **13** handle; use: *He won't touch liquor or tobacco.* **14** reach; come up to: *His head almost touches the ceiling.* **15** stop at; visit in passing: *The ship touched port.* **16** make a brief stop: *Most ships touch at that port.* **17** *Slang.* borrow from: *touch a man for a quarter.* **18** compare with; rival: *No one in our class can touch her in music.* **19** mark slightly or superficially, as with some color: *a sky touched with pink.* **20** mark, draw, or delineate, as with strokes of the brush, pencil, etc. **21 touch down, a** land an airplane. **b** in football, touch the ground with (the ball) behind the opposing team's goal line. **22 touch off, a** represent exactly or cleverly. **b** cause to go off; fire. **c** set off; ignite; instigate. **23 touch on** or **upon, a** mention; treat lightly. **b** come close to. **24 touch up, a** change a little; improve: *touch up a photograph.* **b** rouse.
—*n.* **1** a touching or being touched: *A bubble bursts at a touch.* **2** the sense by which a person perceives things by feeling, handling, or coming against them: *The blind have a keen touch.* **3** a coming or being in contact: *the touch of their hands.* **4** a slight amount; little bit: *We had a touch of frost.* **5** a stroke with a brush, pencil, pen, etc.: *With a few skilful touches the artist finished my picture.* **6** a detail in any artistic work: *a story with charming poetic touches.* **7** a manner of striking, or depressing, keys on a keyboard: *a pianist with an excellent touch. She types with an uneven touch.* **8** of a keyboard instrument or machine, the resistance that the keys offer to the fingers: *A piano should not have too light a touch.* **9** a distinctive manner or quality: *The work showed an expert's touch.* **10** a slight attack: *a touch of fever.* **11 a** an official mark put on gold, etc. after testing. **b** a stamp for impressing such a mark. **c** the quality so tested. **12** quality in general. **13** any test. **14** *Slang.* **a** a borrowing or getting money from a person. **b** money borrowed or got. **c** a person borrowed or to be borrowed from: *He is a soft touch.* **15** in football, soccer, etc., the part of the field, including the sidelines, lying outside of the field of play. **16 in touch, a** informed: *A newspaper keeps one in touch.* **b** in communication. **17 out of touch, a** not informed. **b** not in communication. [ME < OF *tuchier* < VL *toccare* strike (as a bell); originally imitative] —**touch′a·ble,** *adj.* —**touch′er,** *n.* —**Syn.** *v.* **6** tap. **8** move. -*n.* **4** trace, tinge, shade, dash.

touch and go an uncertain or risky situation.

touch-and-go (tuch′ən gō′) *adj.* uncertain; risky.

touch·back (tuch′bak′) *n.* in football, the act of touching the ball to the ground behind one's own goal line when driven there by the other side.

touch·down (tuch′doun′) *n.* **1** in football, the act of putting the ball on the ground behind one's opponents' goal line. **2** the score made in this way. **3** the landing of an airplane.

tou·ché (tü shā′) *n.* a touch by an opponent's weapon in fencing. —*interj.* an exclamation acknowledging a clever reply or a point well made in discussion. [< F]

touched (tucht) *adj.* **1** *Informal.* slightly crazed. **2** stirred emotionally.

touch football a game having rules similar to those of football except that the person carrying the ball is touched rather than tackled.

touch·hole (tuch′hōl′) *n.* formerly, in guns or cannon, a small opening through which the gunpowder inside was set on fire.

touch·ing (tuch′ing) *adj.* arousing tender feeling. —*prep.* concerning; about. —**touch′ing·ly,** *adv.* —**Syn.** *adj.* moving, pathetic.

touch·line (tuch′līn′) *n.* in rugger and soccer a line along one side of the playing field; sideline.

touch-me-not (tuch′mē not′) *n.* a plant whose ripe seed pods burst open when touched.

touch rugby touch football.

touch·stone (tuch′stōn′) *n.* **1** a black stone used to test the purity of gold or silver by the color of the streak made on the stone after it is rubbed with the metal. **2** any means of testing; a test.

touch-type (tuch′tīp′) *v.* **-typed, -typ·ing.** type by touch alone, without need to look at the keyboard of the typewriter.

touch-typ·ist (tuch′tīp′ist) *n.* a person skilled in touch-typing.

touch·wood (tuch′wu̇d′) *n.* **1** wood decayed by fungi so that it catches fire easily, used as tinder. **2** a fungus found on old tree trunks, used as tinder.

touch·y (tuch′ē) *adj.* **touch·i·er, touch·i·est. 1** apt to take offence at trifles; too sensitive. **2** requiring skill in handling; ticklish; precarious. **3** very sensitive to touch. **—touch′i·ly,** *adv.* **—touch′i·ness,** *n.*

tough (tuf) *adj.* **1** bending without breaking: *Leather is tough.* **2** hard to cut, tear, or chew: *The steak was so tough he couldn't eat it.* **3** stiff; sticky: *tough clay.* **4** strong; hardy: *a tough plant. Donkeys are tough little animals and can carry big loads.* **5** hard; difficult: *tough work.* **6** hard to bear; bad; unpleasant: *A spell of tough luck discouraged him.* **7** hard to influence; stubborn: *a tough customer.* **8** severe; violent; strenuous: *Football is a tough game.* **9** rough; disorderly: *a tough neighborhood.* —*n.* a rough person; rowdy. [OE *tōh*] **—tough′ly,** *adv.* **—tough′ness,** *n.* **—Syn.** *adj.* **4** sturdy. **5** arduous.

tough·en (tuf′ən) *v.* **1** make tough. **2** become tough. **—tough′en·er,** *n.*

tou·la·di (tü′lə dē′) *n.* tuladi.

tou·pee (tü pā′) *n.* a wig or patch of false hair worn to cover a bald spot. [< F *toupet* < OF *toupe* tuft < Gmc.]

tour (tür) *v.* **1** travel from place to place. **2** of actors, shows, etc., travel from town to town fulfilling engagements. **3** in theatre, take (a play, etc.) on tour. **4** travel through: *Last year they toured Europe.* **5** walk around in: *tour the museum.* [< n.]
—*n.* **1** a long journey: *a European tour.* **2** a short journey; a walk around: *a tour of the boat.* **3** a turn or spell of work, duty, etc. **4 on tour,** touring. A show on tour travels around the country giving performances in a number of different places. **5 the grand tour,** a tour through France, Germany, Italy, and Switzerland. The grand tour was formerly considered essential as the finishing course in the education of British young men of good family. [< F < L *tornus* turner's wheel, lathe < Gk. *tornos.* Related to TURN.]

tour de force (tür′də fôrs′) *French.* **1** a notable feat of strength, skill, or ingenuity. **2** something done that is merely clever or ingenious: *His later work showed that his first novel was little more than a tour de force.*

touring car an open automobile with a folding top and no glass side windows, for four or more passengers.

tour·ism (tür′iz əm) *n.* **1** touring or travelling as a pastime or recreation. **2** the business of providing services for tourists.

tour·ist (tür′ist or tu̇r′ist) *n.* a person travelling for pleasure.

tourist camp a place where people may camp, park trailers, etc.

tourist court a motel.

tour·ma·lin (tür′mə lin) *n.* tourmaline.

tour·ma·line (tür′mə lin or tür′mə lēn′) *n.* **1** a semi-precious stone occurring in various colors (red, pink, green, blue, or yellow); a silicate of aluminum and boron. The transparent varieties of tourmaline are used in making jewellery. **2** a piece of this stone or a gem made from it. [< F < Singhalese *toramalli*]

tour·na·ment (tėr′nə mənt or tür′nə mənt) *n.* **1** a contest of many persons in some sport: *a golf tournament.* **2** in the Middle Ages: **a** a contest between two groups of knights on horseback who fought for a prize. **b** a meeting at which knightly contests, exercises, and sports took place. **c** the activities at such a meeting. [ME < OF *torneiement* < *torneier.* See TOURNEY.]

tour·ney (tėr′nē or tür′nē) *n.* **-neys,** *v.* **-neyed, -ney·ing.** —*n.* tournament. —*v.* take part in a tournament. [ME < OF *torneier,* ult. < L *tornus.* See TURN.]

tour·ni·quet (tür′nə ket′ or tür′nə kā′, tėr′nə ket′ or tėr′nə kā′) *n.* a device for stopping bleeding by compressing a blood vessel. A bandage tightened by twisting with a stick, or a pad pressed down by a screw, may be used as a tourniquet. [< F *tourniquet* < *tourner* to turn]

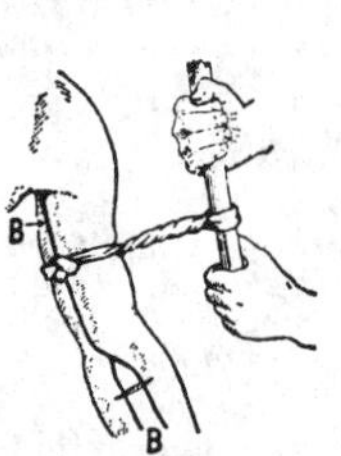

A tourniquet: B, blood vessel.

tou·sle (tou′zəl) *v.* **-sled, -sling,** *n.* —*v.* put into disorder; make untidy; muss: *tousled hair.* —*n.* a disordered mass. [ME *touse(n)*]

tout (tout) *Informal.* —*v.* **1** try to get (customers, jobs, votes, etc.). **2** urge betting on (a race horse) by claiming to have special information. **3** *Esp.Brit.* spy out (information about race horses) for use in betting. **4** praise highly and insistently. —*n.* a person who touts. [< var. of OE *tȳtan* peep out] **—tout′er,** *n.*

tout à fait (tü′tä fe′) *French.* entirely; completely.

tout de suite (tüt swēt′) *French.* immediately; at once.

tout en·sem·ble (tü tāɴ säɴbl′) *French.* **1** all together. **2** the general effect; the assemblage of parts or details, considered as forming a whole.

tout le monde (tü lə môɴd′) *French.* the whole world; everybody.

tow[1] (tō) *v.* pull by a rope, chain, etc.: *The tug is towing three barges.* —*n.* **1** the act of towing. **2** the condition of being pulled along by a rope, chain, etc.: *The launch had the sailboat in tow.* **3** that which is towed. **4** the rope, chain, etc. used for towing. **5** a ship that tows; tugboat; tug. **6** a ski tow. **7 in tow, a** being towed. **b** *Informal.* under one's care or influence. [OE *togian* drag]

tow[2] (tō) *n.* the coarse, broken fibres of flax, hemp, etc. —*adj.* made from tow. [OE *tōw-* a spinning]

tow·age (tō′ij) *n.* **1** a towing. **2** the state of being towed. **3** a charge for towing.

to·ward (*prep.* tôrd or tə wôrd′; *adj.* tôrd) *prep.* **1** in the direction of: *He walked toward the north.* **2** with respect to; regarding; about; concerning: *What is his attitude toward war?* **3** near: *It must be toward four o'clock.* **4** for: *Will you give something toward our new hospital?* —*adj.* **1** about to happen; impending. **2** *Archaic.* promising, hopeful, or apt; docile. [OE *tōweard* < *tō* to + *-weard* -ward]

to·wards (tôrdz or tə wôrdz′) *prep.* toward.

tow·boat (tō′bōt′) *n.* tugboat.

tow·el (tou′əl) *n. v.* **-elled** or **-eled, -el·ling** or **-el·ing.** —*n.* **1** a piece of cloth or paper for wiping and drying something wet. **2 throw** or **toss in the towel,** *Informal.* admit defeat. —*v.* dry with a towel. [ME < OF *toaille* < Gmc.]

tow·el·ing (tou′əl ing) *n.* towelling.

tow·el·ling or **tow·el·ing** (tou′əl ing) *n.* material used for towels, especially cotton.

tow·er (tou′ər) *n.* **1** a high structure that may stand alone or form part of a church, castle, or other building. Some towers are forts or prisons. **2** a defence; protection. **3** a person or thing that is like a tower in some way: *a tower of strength.* —*v.* rise high up. [ME < OF < L *turris*] **—Syn.** *n.* **1** spire, steeple, turret. **2** citadel, fortress.

tow·er·ing (tou′ər ing) *adj.* **1** very high. **2** very tall: *a towering basketball player.* **3** very great. **4** very violent: *a towering rage.*

Tower of London (lun′dən) in London, an ancient palace-fortress. The present building dates back to William the Conqueror. It has been used as a palace, prison, mint, and arsenal.

tow·er·y (tou′ər ē) *adj.* **1** having towers. **2** towering; lofty.

tow·head (tō′hed′) *n.* **1** a person having light, pale-yellow hair. **2** a head of light-colored hair.

tow·head·ed (tō′hed′id) *adj.* having light, pale-yellow hair.

tow·hee (tou′hē or tō′hē) *n.* a chewink or a bird resembling a chewink. [imitative of its call]

tow·line (tō′līn′) *n.* a rope, chain, etc. for towing.

town (toun) *n.* **1** a municipality smaller than a city but larger than a village: *All provinces except British Columbia have towns. In Ontario a town must have a population of 2,000; in Saskatchewan a town must contain 500 people.* **2** any large place with many people living in it. **3** the people of a town: *The whole town was having a holiday.* **4** the part of a town or city where the stores and office buildings are: *Let's go into town.* **5 go to town,** *Informal.* **a** achieve success. **b** do or go through thoroughly: *The hungry boys really went to town on that pie.* **6 in town,** in a specified town or city. **7 on the town, a** on a pleasure tour of a city. **b** supported by a town; on charity. **8 out of town,** happening or located outside a specified town or city. **9 paint the town red,** *Slang.* go on a wild spree or party; celebrate in a noisy manner. [OE *tūn*]

town clerk an official who keeps the records of a town.

town crier formerly, a public crier in a city or town.

town hall the headquarters of a town's government.

town house **1** a house in town, belonging to a person who also has a house in the country. **2** a row house.

town meeting a general meeting of the inhabitants of the town.

towns·folk (tounz′fōk′) *n.pl.* the people of a town.

town·ship (toun′ship) *n.* **1** in Canada and the United States, a division of a county having certain powers of government; municipality. **2** a land-survey area on which later subdivisions may be based: *In Alberta a township is an area of 36 square miles, divided into 36 sections. Abbrev.*: Tp., tp., or twp. [OE *tunscipe* < *tūn* town + *-scipe* -ship]

town·site (toun′sīt′) *n.* **1** the site of a town. **2** a piece of land being developed or to be developed as a town.

towns·man (tounz′mən) *n.* **-men** (-mən). **1** a person who lives in a town. **2** a person who lives in one's own town.

towns·peo·ple (tounz′pē′pəl) *n.pl.* the people of a town.

tow·path (tō′path′) *n.* a path along the bank of a canal or river for use in towing boats.

tow·rope (tō′rōp′) *n.* a rope used for towing.

tox·a·phene (tok′sə fēn′) *n.* a chlorinated camphene insecticide used for forage crops. *Formula*: $C_{10}H_{10}Cl_8$ [< Trademark]

tox·e·mi·a or **tox·ae·mi·a** (toks ē′mē ə) *n.* a form of blood poisoning, especially one in which the toxins produced by certain micro-organisms enter the blood. [< NL *toxaemia* < L *toxicum* poison (See TOXIC) + Gk. *haima* blood]

tox·e·mic or **tox·ae·mic** (toks ē′mik) *adj.* **1** of or having to do with toxemia. **2** suffering from toxemia.

tox·ic (tok′sik) *adj.* poisonous; of poison; caused by poison. [< Med.L *toxicus* < L *toxicum* poison < Gk. *toxikon* (*pharmakon*) (poison) for shooting arrows < *toxon* bow] —**tox′i·cal·ly,** *adv.*

tox·ic·i·ty (toks is′ə tē) *n.* **-ties.** the quality of being toxic or poisonous.

tox·i·co·log·i·cal (tok′sə kə loj′ə kəl) *adj.* of or having to do with the science of poisons.

tox·i·col·o·gist (tok′sə kol′ə jist) *n.* an expert in toxicology.

tox·i·col·o·gy (tok′sə kol′ə jē) *n.* the science that deals with poisons, their effects, antidotes, detection, etc. [< Gk. *toxikon* poison (see TOXIC) + E *-logy*]

tox·in (tok′sən) *n.* any poisonous product of animal or vegetable metabolism, especially one of those produced by bacteria. The symptoms of a disease caused by bacteria, such as diphtheria, are due to toxins. [< *toxic*]

toy (toi) *n.* **1** something for a child to play with; plaything. **2** something that has little value or importance. **3** any of certain breeds of very small animals, especially dogs and pigeons. —*adj.* **1** of, made as, or like a toy.

hat, āge, cãre, fär; let, ēqual, tėrm; it, īce
hot, ōpen, ôrder; oil, out; cup, pu̇t, rüle, ūse
əbove, takən, pencəl, lemən, circəs
ch, child; ng, long; sh, ship
th, thin; ꟸH, then; zh, measure

2 small, tiny: *a toy Pekingese.* —*v.* amuse oneself; play; trifle. [ME *toye* play, n.; cf. Du. *tuig* tools, stuff, and G *Zeug* stuff] —**Syn.** *n.* **2** trifle, knickknack, trinket.

toy dog **1** any of certain breeds of very small dogs, especially poodles, spaniels, and terriers. **2** a dog of one of these breeds.

to·yon (tō′yən) *n.* a shrub of the Pacific coast of North America, whose evergreen leaves and scarlet berries look much like holly. [< Am.Sp. *tollon*]

t.p. title page.

Tp. or **tp.** **1** township. **2** troop.

tr. **1** transitive. **2** transpose. **3** translation. **4** translator. **5** train.

Tr terbium.

trace[1] (trās) *n. v.* **traced, trac·ing.** —*n.* **1** a mark, token, or evidence of the former existence, presence, or action of something; vestige: *The explorer found traces of an ancient city.* **2** a footprint or other mark left; track; trail: *We saw traces of rabbits on the snow.* **3** a very small amount; little bit: *There wasn't a trace of gray in her hair.* **4** something marked out or drawn. **5** in chemistry, an indication of an amount of some constituent in a compound, usually too small to be measured. [< v.] —*v.* **1** follow by means of marks, tracks, or signs: *trace deer.* **2** follow the course of; follow a trail of evidence to: *They traced the theft to the watchman.* **3** find signs of; observe. **4** mark out; draw: *The spy traced a plan of the fort.* **5** copy by following the lines of: *By putting thin paper over the map, John traced it.* **6** decorate with tracery. **7** write, especially by forming the letters carefully or laboriously. **8** record in the form of a curving, wavy, or broken line, as a cardiograph, seismograph, etc. **9 trace back,** follow back, stage by stage: *He traced his family back through eight generations.* [ME < OF *tracier* < VL *tractiare,* ult. < L *trahere* drag]

Syn. *n.* **1 Trace, vestige** = a mark or sign of what has existed or happened. **Trace** applies to any noticeable sign or mark left by something that has happened or been present: *The campers removed all traces of their fire.* **Vestige,** sometimes used as a more formal substitute, especially when referring to something no longer present or existing, applies particularly to an actual remnant of something that existed in the past: *Some of our common social manners are vestiges of very old customs.*

trace[2] (trās) *n.* **1** either of the two straps, ropes, or chains by which an animal pulls a wagon, carriage, etc. See **harness** for picture. **2 kick over the traces,** throw off control; become unruly. [ME < OF *traiz,* pl. of *trait,* ult. < L *trahere* drag]

trace·a·bil·i·ty (trās′ə bil′ə tē) *n.* the fact or property of being traceable.

trace·a·ble (trās′ə bəl) *adj.* capable of being traced. —**trace′a·bly,** *adv.*

trac·er (trās′ər) *n.* **1** a person or thing that traces. **2** a machine for making tracings of drawings, plans, etc. **3** an inquiry sent from place to place to trace a missing person, letter, parcel, etc. **4** a person whose business is tracing missing persons, property, etc. **5** a burning substance attached to a bullet to show its course. **6** in chemistry, an element **(tracer element)** or atom **(tracer atom)** usually radio-active, that can be traced and observed in a biological process or used to detect small quantities of its isotope in analysis.

trac·er·y (trās′ər ē or trās′rē) *n.* **-er·ies.** ornamental work or designs consisting of branching or interlacing lines. Stonework, carving, and embroidery often have tracery.

tra·che·a (trā′kē ə or trə kē′ə) *n.* **tra·che·ae** (trā′kē ī or trə kē′ē or -ī). **1** in anatomy, the tube extending from the larynx to the bronchi; windpipe. See **lung** for picture. **2** in zoology, one of the air-carrying tubes of the respiratory system of insects and

Tracery

other arthropods. **3** in botany, a vessel or duct serving to carry water and dissolved minerals. [< LL *trachia*, ult. < Gk. *tracheia* (*artēria*), literally, rough (windpipe)]

tra·che·al (trā′kē əl or trə kē′əl) *adj.* of or having to do with the trachea.

tra·che·ot·o·my (trā′kē ot′ə mē) *n.* in surgery, an operation that involves cutting an opening into the trachea. [< Gk. *tracheia* trachea + *tomia* a cutting]

tra·cho·ma (trə kō′mə) *n.* **1** a contagious inflammation of the eyelids. **2** granular eyelids. [< NL < Gk. *trachōma* roughness < *trachys* rough]

trac·ing (trās′ing) *n.* **1** a copy of something made by marking or drawing over it. **2** a line made by marking or drawing. **3** one of a series of lines or marks made by an electrical apparatus that records waves or impulses.

track (trak) *n.* **1** a line of metal rails for cars to run on. A railway has tracks. **2** a mark left: *The dirty road showed many automobile tracks.* **3** a footprint: *We saw a wild animal's tracks near the camp.* **4** a path; trail; a little-used rough road: *A track runs through the woods to the farmhouse.* **5** a way of doing or acting: *go on in the same track year after year.* **6** a course for running or racing: *a race track.* **7** the sport made up of contests in running. See **track and field. 8** a sequence or succession of events, thoughts, etc. **9** the groove or channel of a phonograph record which contains the actual sound recording. **10** one of the endless belts on which a caterpillar tractor moves.
in one's tracks, *Informal.* right where one is.
keep track of, keep within one's sight, knowledge, or attention.
lose track of, fail to keep track of.
make tracks, *Informal.* go very fast; run away.
off the track, off the subject; wrong.
on the track, on the subject; right.
the beaten track, the ordinary or usual way.
—*v.* **1** follow by means of footprints, marks, smell, etc.: *The hunter tracked the bear and killed it.* **2** trace in any way: *track down a criminal.* **3** make footprints or other marks on (a floor, etc.): *Don't track the floor.* **4** bring (snow or mud) into a place on one's feet: *track mud into the house.* **5** follow and plot the course of, as by radar. [ME < OF *trac*, probably < Gmc.] **—track′er,** *n.*

track·age (trak′ij) *n.* **1** all the tracks of a railway. **2** the right of one railway to use the tracks of another. **3** the charge for this.

track and field the sports of running, jumping, pole-vaulting, throwing, etc. taken collectively.

tracking station any of several telemeter stations built to track the orbit of a satellite.

track·less (trak′lis) *adj.* **1** without a track; without tracks. **2** without paths or trails.

track meet a series of contests in running, jumping, throwing, etc.

tract[1] (trakt) *n.* **1** a stretch of land, water, etc.; extent; area: *A tract of desert land has little value.* **2** a system of related parts or organs in the body. The stomach and intestines are part of the digestive tract. **3** a period of time. [< L *tractus*, originally, hauling < *trahere* drag. Doublet of TRAIT.]

tract[2] (trakt) *n.* **1** a little book or pamphlet on a religious subject. **2** any book or pamphlet that strongly supports a point of view. [apparently < L *tractatus* a handling, ult. < *trahere* drag]

trac·ta·bil·i·ty (trak′tə bil′ə tē) *n.* the quality or condition of being tractable.

trac·ta·ble (trak′tə bəl) *adj.* **1** easily managed or controlled; easy to deal with; docile: *Dogs are more tractable than mules.* **2** easily worked: *Copper and gold are tractable.* [< L *tractabilis* < *tractare.* See TREAT.] **—trac′ta·ble·ness,** *n.* **—trac′ta·bly,** *adv.*

trac·tile (trak′tīl or trak′təl) *adj.* capable of being drawn out to a greater length.

trac·tion (trak′shən) *n.* **1** the act or process of drawing or pulling; the process of being drawn. **2** the drawing or pulling of loads along a road, track, etc. **3** the kind of power used for this. Electric traction is used on some railways. **4** the friction between a wheel and the surface it moves on; grip: *Wheels slip on ice because there is too little traction.* **5** in medicine, a pulling or drawing of a muscle, organ, etc., especially as a surgical technique for healing a fracture, dislocation, etc. [< Med.L *tractio, -onis* < L *trahere* drag]

traction engine a steam engine on wheels, used for pulling wagons, ploughs, etc. along roads or over fields.

trac·tive (trak′tiv) *adj.* pulling; used for pulling.

trac·tor (trak′tər) *n.* **1** an engine used to pull wagons and ploughs, cultivate crops, etc. **2** a vehicle used to pull a freight trailer along the highway. **3** something used for drawing or pulling. **4** an airplane with the propeller in front of the wings. [< Med.L *tractor* < L *trahere* drag]

tractor swing a cat train.

tractor train a cat train.

trade (trād) *n. v.* **trad·ed, trad·ing.** —*n.* **1** the process of buying and selling; exchange of goods; commerce: *Canada has trade with many foreign countries.* **2** an exchange. **3** *Informal.* a bargain; business deal: *He made a good trade.* **4** a kind of work; business, especially one requiring skilled mechanical work: *A carpenter learns his trade.* **5** people in the same kind of work or business: *the building trade.* **6** *Informal.* customers: *That store has a lot of trade.* **7 the trades,** the trade winds.
—*v.* **1** buy and sell; exchange goods; be in commerce: *English ships trade all over the world.* **2** exchange; swap: *trade seats.* **3** make an exchange: *If you don't like your book, I'll trade with you.* **4** bargain; deal. **5** be a customer: *We've been trading at that grocery store for years.*
6 trade in, give an automobile, radio, etc. as payment or part payment for something. **7 trade off,** get rid of by trading. **8 trade on,** take advantage of. [ME < MDu. or MLG *trade* track]
Syn. *n.* **1 Trade, commerce** = the buying and selling or exchanging of goods or other commodities. **Trade** applies to the actual buying and selling, or exchange, between countries or within a country: *The Government has drawn up new agreements for trade with various countries.* **Commerce** is more general, applying to the whole business of exchange of commodities, including both trade and transportation, especially as conducted on a large scale between different states or countries. **4** occupation, craft, profession. -*v.* **1** barter. **3** swap.

trade agreement 1 an agreement between nations to promote trade between them. **2** an agreement for a specified time between labor and management concerning job conditions.

trade balance the difference between the value of a country's imports and its exports; balance of trade.

trade barrier anything that restricts or limits international trade: *Tariffs or embargoes are trade barriers.*

trade-in (trād′in′) *n.* something given or accepted as payment or part payment for something else.

trade·mark (trād′märk′) *n.* a mark, picture, name, or letters owned and used by a manufacturer or merchant to distinguish his goods from the goods of others.
—*v.* **1** distinguish by means of a trademark. **2** register the trademark of.

trade name 1 a name used by a manufacturer or merchant for some article that he sells. **2** a special name used for anything by those who buy and sell it. **3** a name under which a company does business.

trad·er (trād′ər) *n.* **1** a person who trades. **2** a ship used in trading. **3 a** a member of a stock exchange, commodity exchange, etc. who trades for himself and not as an agent of another or others. **b** a speculator in stocks, commodities, etc. **4** an item of which a collector has another copy; a duplicate.

trade school a school where trades are taught.

trades·man (trādz′mən) *n.* **-men** (-mən). a storekeeper; shopkeeper. **—Syn.** merchant, dealer, trader.

trades·peo·ple (trādz′pē′pəl) *n.pl.* storekeepers; shopkeepers.

trades union *Esp.Brit.* a trade union.

trade union 1 an association of workers in any trade or craft to protect and promote their interests. **2** a labor union.

trade unionism 1 the system of having trade unions. **2** the principles, methods or practices of trade unions.

trade unionist 1 a member of a trade union. **2** a person who favors trade unionism.

hat, āge, cãre, fär; let, ēqual, tėrm; it, īce
hot, ōpen, ôrder; oil, out; cup, pu̇t, rüle, ūse
əbove, takən, pencəl, lemən, circəs
ch, child; ng, long; sh, ship
th, thin; ᴛʜ, then; zh, measure

trade wind a wind blowing steadily toward the equator from about 30° north latitude to about 30° south latitude. North of the equator, it blows from the northeast; south of the equator, from the southeast.

trading post a store or station of a trader, especially in remote or uncivilized places.

trading stamp a stamp offered by a merchant to purchasers and redeemable, in certain quantities, for goods to be selected from a special list.

tra·di·tion (trə dish′ən) *n.* **1** the handing down of beliefs, opinions, customs, stories, etc. from parents to children. **2** what is handed down in this way. **3 a** in Jewish use, the unwritten laws and doctrines received from Moses. **b** in the Christian Church, the unwritten precepts and doctrines received from Christ and his apostles. **4** a way of behaving or doing things based on long practice: *The Navy has many old traditions.* [< L *traditio, -onis* < *tradere* hand down < *trans-* over + *dare* give. Doublet of TREASON.]

tra·di·tion·al (trə dish′ən əl or trə dish′nəl) *adj.* **1** of tradition. **2** handed down by tradition. **3** according to tradition. **4** customary. —**Syn. 2** legendary.

tra·di·tion·al·ly (trə dish′ən əl ē or trə dish′nəl ē) *adv.* according to tradition.

tra·di·tion·ar·y (trə dish′ən er′ē) *adj.* traditional.

tra·duce (trə dūs′ or trə düs′) *v.* **-duced, -duc·ing.** speak evil of (a person) falsely; slander. [< L *traducere* parade in disgrace < *trans-* across + *ducere* lead] —**tra·duc′er,** *n.* —**Syn.** defame, calumniate, asperse.

traf·fic (traf′ik) *n. v.* **-ficked, -fick·ing.** —*n.* **1** the people, automobiles, wagons, ships, etc. coming and going along a way of travel. **2** a buying and selling; commerce; trade. **3 a** the business done by a railway line, a steamship line, etc. **b** the number of passengers or the amount of freight carried. **4** the total amount of business done by any company or industry within a certain time. **5** intercourse; dealings.
—*v.* **1** carry on trade; buy; sell; exchange: *The men trafficked with the natives for ivory.* **2** have social dealings with; have to do with: *He refuses to traffic with strangers.* [< MF < Ital. *traffico* < *trafficare* < *tras-* across (< L *trans-*) + *ficcare* shove, poke, ult. < L *figere* fix]

traffic circle an arrangement of roads at an intersection whereby traffic moves in a single direction around a central, circular space that is curbed and often banked.

traf·fick·er (traf′ik ər) *n.* a person who buys and sells; trader.

trag·a·canth (trag′ə kanth′) *n.* a sticky substance obtained from certain Asiatic shrubs, used for stiffening cloth, thickening medicines, etc. [< L < Gk. *tragakantha,* literally, goat's thorn < *tragos* goat + *akantha* thorn]

tra·ge·di·an (trə jē′dē ən) *n.* **1** an actor in tragedies. **2** a writer of tragedies.

tra·ge·di·enne (trə jē′dē en′) *n.* an actress in tragedies. [< F]

trag·e·dy (traj′ə dē) *n.* **-dies. 1** a serious play having, usually, a central character and an unhappy or disastrous ending. In many tragedies the hero experiences great mental suffering and, finally, meets his death. *Hamlet* is a tragedy. **2 a** the branch of drama that includes such plays. **b** the writing of such plays. **3** a novel, long poem, etc. similar to a tragic play. **4** a very sad or terrible happening: *The father's sudden death was a tragedy to his family.* [ME < OF < L < Gk. *tragōidia* < *tragos* goat (connection obscure) + *ōidē* song]

trag·ic (traj′ik) *adj.* **1** of tragedy; having to do with tragedy: *a tragic actor, a tragic poet.* **2** very sad; dreadful: *a tragic death, a tragic event.* [< L < Gk. *tragikos*] —**trag′i·cal·ly,** *adv.*

trag·i·cal (traj′ə kəl) *adj.* tragic.

trag·i·com·e·dy (traj′ē kom′ə dē) *n.* **-dies. 1** a play having both tragic and comic elements. *The Merchant of Venice* is a tragicomedy. **2** an incident or situation in which serious and comic elements are blended. [< F < LL *tragicomoedia* < L *tragicocomoedia* < *tragicus* tragic + *comoedia* comedy]

trag·i·com·ic (traj′ē kom′ik) *adj.* having both tragic and comic elements.

trag·i·com·i·cal (traj′ē kom′ə kəl) *adj.* tragicomic.

trail (trāl) *n.* **1** anything that follows along behind: *The car left a trail of dust behind it.* **2** a track or smell left by some animal: *The dogs found the trail of a rabbit.* **3** a path across a wild or unsettled region. **4** the lower end of a gun carriage. [< v.]
—*v.* **1** pull or drag along behind: *The bird trailed its broken wing.* **2** be drawn along behind: *Her dress trails on the ground.* **3** hang down or float loosely from something. **4** carry or bring by or as if by dragging: *trail snow into a house.* **5** bring or have floating after itself: *a car trailing dust.* **6** lengthen in time; protract. **7** follow the trail or track of; track: *trail a bear or thief.* **8** grow along: *Poison ivy trailed by the road.* **9** follow in a long, uneven line: *The ten campers trailed their leader down the mountainside.* **10** extend in a long, uneven line; straggle: *refugees trailing from their ruined village.* **11** follow along behind; follow: *The dog trailed him constantly.* **12** go along slowly: *The children trailed to school.* **13 a** mark out (a trail or track). **b** hunt by following a track or smell: *The dogs trailed the rabbit.* **14** tread down (grass) to make a path. **15** pass little by little: *Her voice trailed off into silence.* [ME < OF *trailler* tow, ult. < L *tragula* dragnet]

trail·bla·zer (trāl′blā′zər) *n.* **1** a person who blazes a trail. **2** a person who is a pioneer in any field of activity.

trail·er (trāl′ər) *n.* **1** a person or animal that follows a trail. **2** a trailing plant; any vine that grows along the ground. **3** a vehicle, often large, designed to be pulled along the highway by a truck, etc., especially by a truck lacking a body of its own. **4** a vehicle having one or more pairs of wheels, equipped and furnished as a dwelling and designed to be pulled by an automobile. **5** a few scenes shown to advertise a forthcoming motion picture or television program.

trailer camp or **park** an area, equipped with utilities and other facilities, for accommodating trailers (def. 4).

trailing arbutus arbutus (def. 1).

train[1] (trān) *n.* **1** a connected line of railway cars moving along together. **2** a line of people, animals, wagons, trucks, etc. moving along together. **3** a collection of vehicles, animals, and men accompanying an army to carry supplies, baggage, ammunition, or any equipment or materials. **4** a part of a dress, cloak, or gown that hangs down and drags along the ground: *Two attendants carried the queen's train.* **5** something that is drawn along behind; a trailing part. **6** a tail: *the train of a peacock, the train of a comet.* **7** a group of followers. **8 a** a series; succession: *a long train of misfortunes.* **b** a continuous course: *a train of thought.* **c** a succession of results or conditions following some event: *The flood brought starvation and disease in its train.* **9** a series of happenings; succession of results. **10** a line of gunpowder that acts as a fuse. **11** in machinery, a series of connected parts, such as wheels and pinions, through which motion is transmitted. **12 in train,** in proper order, arrangement, or sequence; in process. [< v.]
—*v.* **1** bring up; rear; teach: *train a child.* **2** make skilful by teaching and practice: *train women as nurses.* **3** discipline and instruct (an animal) to be useful, obedient, perform tricks, race, etc.: *train a horse.* **4** make fit by exercise and diet: *Runners train for races.* **5** make oneself fit. **6** point; aim: *train cannon upon a fort.* **7** bring into a particular position: *Train the vine around this post.* [ME < OF *trainer* < VL *traginare,* ult. < L *trahere* drag] —**train′er,** *n.* —**Syn.** *n.* **2** row, chain, line, file, procession. -*v.* **1** educate.

train[2] (trān) *n. Cdn.* a large, toboggan-shaped sled. [< Cdn.F *traine sauvage* toboggan < F *traîneau* sled]

train·ee (trān ē′) *n.* one who is receiving training.

train·ing (trān′ing) *n.* **1** Practical education in some art, profession, etc.: *training for teachers.* **2** the development of strength and endurance. **3** a good condition maintained by exercise, diet, etc.

train·load (trān′lōd′) *n.* as much as a train can hold or carry.

train·man (trān′mən) *n.* **-men** (-mən). **1** a man who works on a railway train. **2** a brakeman.

train oil oil obtained from the blubber of whales, seals, fish, etc. [< obs. *train* train oil < MLG *trān* or MDu. *traen* tear, drop; cf. G *Träne*]

traipse (trāps) *v.* **traipsed, traips·ing,** *n. Informal.* —*v.* wander about idly or restlessly. —*n.* a traipsing. Also, **trapes.** [probably < OF *trapasser*, var. of *trespasser*. See TRESPASS.]

trait (trāt or trā) *n.* a quality of mind, character, etc.; distinguishing feature; characteristic: *Courage, love of justice, and common sense are desirable traits.* [< F *trait* < L *tractus* < *trahere* drag. Doublet of TRACT[1].] —**Syn.** See **feature.**

trai·tor (trā′tər) *n.* **1** a person who betrays his country or ruler. **2** a person who betrays a trust, duty, friend, etc. [ME < OF *traitor*, ult. < L *traditor*, ult. < *trans-* over + *dare* give] —**Syn. 2** turncoat, renegade.

trai·tor·ous (trā′tər əs) *adj.* like a traitor; treacherous; faithless. —**trai′tor·ous·ly,** *adv.* —**trai′tor·ous·ness,** *n.* —**Syn.** perfidious, disloyal, false.

trai·tress (trā′tris) *n.* a woman traitor.

tra·jec·to·ry (trə jek′tə rē or trə jek′trē) *n.* **-ries.** the curved path of a projectile, comet, or planet. [< Med.L *trajectorius* throwing across, ult. < L *trans-* across + *jacere* throw]

tram (tram) *n.* **1** *Esp.Brit.* a streetcar. **2** a tramway. **3** a truck or car on which loads are carried in coal mines. [< MDu. or MLG *trame* beam]

tram·car (tram′kär′) *n. Brit.* a streetcar.

tram·mel (tram′əl) *n. v.* **-melled** or **-meled, -mel·ling** or **-mel·ing.** —*n.* **1** Usually, **trammels,** *pl.* anything that hinders or restrains: *A large bequest freed the artist from the trammels of poverty.* **2** a fine net to catch fish, birds, etc. **3** a hook in a fireplace to hold pots, kettles, etc. over the fire. **4** a shackle for controlling the motions of a horse and teaching him to amble. —*v.* **1** hinder; restrain. **2** entangle. [ME *tramayle* a kind of net < OF < LL *trimaculum* (spelled *tremaculum*) < L *tri-* three + *macula* mesh] —**tram′mel·ler** or **tram′mel·er,** *n.*

tra·mon·tane (trə mon′tān or tram′ən tān′) *adj.* **1** having to do with, coming from, or located on the other side of the mountains, especially beyond the Alps; transalpine: *a tramontane wind.* **2** foreign. —*n.* **1** one who lives on the other side of the mountains, especially the Alps. **2** a foreigner. **3** a cold wind blowing from a mountain range. [< Ital. *tramontana* < L *transmontanus* < *trans* across + *montanus* mountain]

tramp (tramp) *v.* **1** walk heavily: *He tramped across the room in his heavy boots.* **2** step heavily (*on*): *He tramped on the flowers.* **3** go on foot; walk: *We tramped through the streets.* **4** travel through on foot: *tramp the streets.* **5** walk steadily; march: *The soldiers tramped mile after mile.* **6** go or wander as a tramp.
—*n.* **1** the sound of a heavy step. **2** a long, steady walk; hike. **3** a person who travels from place to place on foot, living by begging, doing odd jobs, etc. **4** a freighter that takes a cargo when and where it can. [? < LG *trampen*] —**tramp′er,** *n.* —**Syn.** *n.* **3** vagabond, hobo, vagrant, beggar.

tram·ple (tram′pəl) *v.* **-pled, -pling,** *n.* —*v.* **1** tread heavily on; crush: *The herd of wild cattle trampled the man to death.* **2** tread heavily. **3** treat cruelly, harshly, or scornfully. **4 trample under foot, trample on** or **upon,** treat cruelly, harshly, or scornfully. —*n.* the act or sound of trampling: *We heard the trample of many feet.* [< *tramp*] —**tram′pler,** *n.*

tram·po·line (tram′pə lēn′ or tram′pə lin) *n.* a device consisting of a taut sheet of strong canvas attached to a rectangular frame, used for various exercises in gymnastics.

tram·way (tram′wā′) *n.* **1** *Esp.Brit.* a track for streetcars. **2** in mining: **a** a track or roadway for carrying ore from mines. **b** a cable or system of cables on which suspended cars carry ore, etc.

trance (trans) *n. v.* **tranced, tranc·ing.** —*n.* **1** a state or condition of unconsciousness resembling sleep. **2** a dazed or stunned condition. **3** a dreamy, absorbed or hypnotic condition that is like a trance: *The old man sat before the fire in a trance, thinking of his past life.* **4** a high emotion; rapture. —*v.* hold in a trance; enchant. [ME < OF *transe*, ult. < L *trans-* across + *ire* go] —**trance′like′,** *adj.*

tran·quil (trang′kwəl) *adj.* **-quil·ler** or **-quil·er, -quil·lest** or **-quil·est.** calm; peaceful; quiet. [< L *tranquillus*] —**tran′quil·ly,** *adv.* —**Syn.** placid, serene, undisturbed.

tran·quil·ize (trang′kwəl īz′) *v.* **-ized, -iz·ing.** tranquillize.

tran·quil·li·ty or **tran·quil·i·ty** (trang kwil′ə tē) *n.* calmness; peacefulness; quiet.

tran·quil·lize or **tran·quil·ize** (trang′kwəl īz′) *v.* **-lized** or **-ized, -liz·ing** or **-iz·ing. 1** make calm, peaceful, or quiet. **2** become tranquil. —**Syn. 1** pacify, compose, allay, soothe, still.

tran·quil·liz·er or **tran·quil·iz·er** (trang′kwəl īz′ər) *n.* **1** any person or thing that tranquillizes. **2** any of various drugs for reducing physical or nervous tension, lowering blood pressure, etc.

trans- *prefix.* **1** across; over; through, as in *transcontinental, transmit.* **2** beyond; on the other side of, as in *Transjordan, transcend.* **3** across, etc.; and also beyond, on the other side of, as in *transarctic, transequatorial, transmarine, transoceanic, transpolar,* and many other geographical terms, such as *trans-African.* **4** into a different place, condition, etc., as in *transform, transmute.* [< L *trans*, prep.]

trans. 1 transitive. **2** transportation. **3** transactions. **4** translation. **5** transferred. **6** transpose.

trans·act (tran zakt′ or tran sakt′) *v.* **1** attend to; manage; do; carry on (business): *He transacts business with stores all over the country.* **2** carry on business; deal. [< L *transactus*, pp. of *transigere* accomplish < *trans-* through + *agere* drive] —**Syn. 1** perform, conduct.

trans·ac·tion (tran zak′shən or tran sak′shən) *n.* **1** the carrying on (of business): *Mr. Smith attends to the transaction of important matters himself.* **2** a piece of business: *A record is kept of all the firm's transactions.* **3 transactions,** *pl.* a record of what was done at the meetings of a society, club, etc. [ME < LL *transactio, -onis* < *transigere*. See TRANSACT.] —**Syn. 2** proceeding, deal, matter, affair.

trans·ac·tor (tran zak′tər or tran sak′tər) *n.* a person who transacts business affairs.

trans·al·pine (tranz al′pīn or trans-) *adj.* across or beyond the Alps, especially as viewed from Italy.

trans·at·lan·tic (trans′ət lan′tik or tranz′-) *adj.* **1** crossing the Atlantic: *a transatlantic liner, a transatlantic cable.* **2** on the other side of the Atlantic.

trans-Canada (trans′kan′ə də) *adj.* extending from one end of Canada to the other.

Trans·cau·ca·sian (trans′ko kā′zhən or -kô kā′zhən) *adj.* of or having to do with Transcaucasia, a region in the S.W. Soviet Union, in and to the south of the Caucasus Mountains. —*n.* a native or inhabitant of Transcaucasia.

tran·scend (tran send′) *v.* **1** go beyond the limits or powers of; exceed; be above: *The grandeur of Niagara Falls transcends description.* **2** be higher or greater than; surpass; excel. **3** of God, be above and independent of (the physical universe). **4** be superior or extraordinary. [ME < L *transcendere* < *trans-* beyond + *scandere* climb]

tran·scend·ence (tran sen′dəns) *n.* the state or quality of being transcendent.

tran·scend·ent (tran sen′dənt) *adj.* **1** surpassing ordinary limits; excelling; superior; extraordinary. **2** existing apart from the universe. **3** in philosophy: **a** transcending the Aristotelian categories or predicaments, especially as considered by the medieval scholastics. **b** in Kantian philosophy, not realizable in human experience. —**tran·scend′ent·ly,** *adv.* —**Syn. 1** unequalled, unrivalled, peerless, supreme.

tran·scen·den·tal (tran′sen den′təl) *adj.* **1** transcendent. **2** supernatural. **3** obscure; incomprehensible; fantastic. **4** in philosophy: **a** explaining matter and objective things as products of the mind that is thinking about them;

idealistic. **b** implied in and necessary to human experience. —**tran′scen·den′tal·ly,** *adv.*

tran·scen·den·tal·ism (tran′sen den′təl iz′əm) *n.* **1** a transcendental quality, thought, language, or philosophy. **2** any philosophy based upon the doctrine that the principles of reality are to be discovered by a study of the processes of thought, not from experience. **3** obscurity; incomprehensibility; fantasy.

tran·scen·den·tal·ist (tran′sen den′təl ist) *n.* a person who believes in transcendentalism.

trans·con·ti·nen·tal (trans′kon tə nen′təl) *adj.* **1** crossing a continent: *a transcontinental railway.* **2** on the other side of a continent. —*n.* a train that crosses a continent.

tran·scribe (tran skrīb′) *v.* **-scribed, -scrib·ing. 1** copy in writing or in typewriting: *The account of the trial was transcribed from the stenographer's shorthand notes.* **2** set down in writing or print: *His entire speech was transcribed in the newspapers, word for word.* **3** in music, arrange (a composition) for a different instrument or voice. **4** make a recording of (a program, music, etc.) for broadcasting. **5** broadcast a recording. **6** in phonetics, record (speech) in a system of phonetic symbols; represent (a speech sound) by a phonetic symbol. [< L *transcribere* < *trans-* over + *scribere* write] —**tran·scrib′er,** *n.*

tran·script (tran′skript) *n.* **1** a written or typewritten copy. **2** any copy or reproduction. [< L *transcriptum,* pp. neut. of *transcribere.* See TRANSCRIBE.]

tran·scrip·tion (tran skrip′shən) *n.* **1** a transcribing; copying. **2** a transcript; copy. **3** in music, an arrangement of a composition for a different instrument or voice. **4** a recording of a program, music, etc. for use in broadcasting. **5** the act or fact of broadcasting such a record. **6** in phonetics, a written representation of speech in a system of phonetic symbols.

trans·duce (trans dūs′, or tranz-, trans düs′ or tranz-) *v.* **-duced, -duc·ing.** transfer or convert one form of energy into another. [< L *transducere* < *trans-* + *ducere* lead]

trans·duc·tion (trans duk′shən or tranz-) *n.* **1** in biology, the transfer of genes or chromosomes from one cell to another by means of a bacterial virus. **2** in physics, the transfer of one form of energy to another.

tran·sept (tran′sept) *n.* **1** the shorter part of a cross-shaped church. **2** either end of this part. See **apse** for another picture. [< Med.L *transeptum,* ult. < L *trans-* across + *saeptum* fence]

TRANSEPT
TRAN-SEPT TRAN-SEPT
I II

Transepts: I, def. 1; II, def. 2.

trans·fer (*v.* trans fėr′ or trans′fėr; *n.* trans′fėr) *v.* **-ferred, -fer·ring,** *n.* —*v.* **1** convey or remove from one person or place to another; hand over: *This farm has been transferred from father to son for generations. Please have my trunks transferred to the Union Station.* **2** convey (a drawing, design, pattern) from one surface to another. **3** make over (a title, right, or property) by deed or legal process: *transfer a bond by endorsement.* **4** change from one streetcar, bus, train, etc. to another.
—*n.* **1** a transferring or being transferred. **2** a drawing, pattern, etc. printed from one surface onto another; the thing transferred. **3** a ticket allowing a passenger to continue his journey on another streetcar, bus, train, etc. **4** a point or place for transferring. **5 a** the act of turning the ownership of a share of stock or registered bond over to someone else. **b** a document ordering this. **6** the making over to another of title, right, or property by deed or legal process. [ME < L *transferre* < *trans-* across + *ferre* bear] —**trans·fer′rer,** *n.*

trans·fer·a·bil·i·ty (trans fėr′ə bil′ə tē or trans′fər ə bil′ə tē) *n.* the quality of being transferable.

trans·fer·a·ble (trans fėr′ə bəl or trans′fər ə bəl) *adj.* capable of being transferred.

trans·fer·ence (trans fėr′əns or trans′fər əns) *n.* **1** the act of transferring or the state of being transferred. **2** in psychoanalysis, a revival of emotions previously experienced and repressed, as toward a parent, with a new person as the object.

trans·fig·u·ra·tion (trans fig′ər ā′shən or -fig′yər ā′shən) *n.* **1** a change in form or appearance; transformation.

hat, āge, cãre, fär; let, ēqual, tėrm; it, īce
hot, ōpen, ôrder; oil, out; cup, pu̇t, rüle, ūse
əbove, takən, pencəl, lemən, circəs
ch, child; ng, long; sh, ship
th, thin; ᴛʜ, then; zh, measure

2 the Transfiguration, a in the Bible, the change in the appearance of Christ on the mountain. Matt. 17; Mark 9. **b** a Christian festival held on August 6 in honor of this.

trans·fig·ure (trans fig′ər or -fig′yər) *v.* **-ured, -ur·ing. 1** change in form or appearance; transform: *New paint had transfigured the old house.* **2** change so as to glorify; exalt. [ME < L *transfigurare* < *trans-* across + *figura* figure]

trans·fix (trans fiks′) *v.* **1** pierce through: *The hunter transfixed the lion with a spear.* **2** fasten by piercing through with something pointed. **3** make motionless (with amazement, terror, etc.). [< L *transfixus,* pp. of *transfigere* < *trans-* through + *figere* fix]

trans·form (trans fôrm′) *v.* **1** change in form or appearance. **2** change in condition, nature, or character. **3** in physics, change (one form of energy) into another. A dynamo transforms mechanical energy into electricity. **4** in electricity, change (a current) into one of higher or lower voltage. **5** in mathematics, change (a figure, term, etc.) to another differing in form but having the same value or quantity. [ME < L *transformare* < *trans-* across + *forma* form]
Syn. **1, 2 Transform, transmute, convert** = change the form, nature, substance, or state of something. **Transform** suggests a thoroughgoing or fundamental change in the appearance or shape or the nature of a thing or person: *Responsibility transformed him from a happy-go-lucky youth into a capable leader.* **Transmute,** formal, implies a complete change in nature or substance, especially to a higher kind: *He thus transmuted disapproval into admiration.* **Convert** suggests turning from one state or condition to another, especially for a new use or purpose: *convert boxes into furniture.*

trans·for·ma·tion (trans′fər mā′shən) *n.* **1** a transforming: *the transformation of a caterpillar into a butterfly.* **2** something that has been transformed; the result of transforming. **3** a wig worn by women.

trans·form·er (trans fôr′mər) *n.* **1** a person or thing that transforms. **2** in electricity, a device for changing an alternating current into one of higher or lower voltage.

trans·fuse (trans fūz′) *v.* **-fused, -fus·ing. 1** pour from one container into another. **2** transfer (blood) from one person or animal to another. **3** inject (a solution) into a blood vessel. **4** infuse; instil: *The speaker transfused his enthusiasm into the audience.* [ME < L *transfusus,* pp. of *transfundere* < *trans-* across + *fundere* pour]

trans·fu·sion (trans fū′zhən) *n.* the act or fact of transfusing.

trans·gress (trans gres′ or tranz-) *v.* **1** break a law, command, etc.; sin. **2** go contrary to; sin against. **3** go beyond (a limit or bound): *Her manners transgressed the bounds of good taste.* [< L *transgressus,* pp. of *transgredi* go beyond < *trans-* across + *gradi* to step]

trans·gres·sion (trans gresh′ən or tranz-) *n.* a transgressing; breaking a law, command, etc.; sin. [< L *transgressio, -onis,* originally, a going over < *transgredi.* See TRANSGRESS.] —**Syn.** violation, offence, fault, misdeed.

trans·gres·sor (trans gres′ər or tranz-) *n.* a person who transgresses; sinner.

tran·ship (tran ship′) *v.* **-shipped, -ship·ping.** transship. —**tran·ship′ment,** *n.*

trans·hu·mance (trans hū′məns) *n.* the moving of cattle to more suitable pastures as the seasons change. [< F < Sp., ult. < L *trans-* + *humus* ground]

tran·si·ence (tran′zē əns) *n.* transiency.

tran·si·en·cy (tran′zē ən sē) *n.* the state or quality of being transient.

tran·si·ent (tran′zē ənt) *adj.* **1** passing soon; fleeting; not lasting. **2 a** passing through and not staying long: *a transient guest in a hotel.* **b** serving transient guests, customers, etc.: *a transient hotel.* —*n.* **1** a visitor or boarder who stays for a short time. **2** a tramp or hobo. [< L *transiens, -entis,* ppr. of *transire* pass through < *trans-* through + *ire* go] —**tran′si·ent·ly,** *adv.* —**Syn.** *adj.* **1** transitory, evanescent, momentary. See **temporary.**

tran·sis·tor (tran zis′tər) *n.* **1** in electronics, a small crystal device, consisting mainly of semiconductors such as germanium or silicon, that amplifies electricity by controlling the flow of electrons. **2** a radio equipped with transistors. [< L *trans-* + *sistere* send, convey]

tran·sis·tor·ize (tran zis′tə rīz′) *v.* **-ized, -iz·ing.** equip with transistors.

trans·it (tran′sit or tran′zit) *n. v.* **-it·ed, -it·ing.** —*n.* **1** the act of passing across or through. **2** the process of carrying or being carried across or through: *The goods were damaged in transit.* **3** a transition or change. **4** in surveying, an instrument used to measure angles. **5** in astronomy: **a** the apparent passage of a heavenly body across the meridian of a place. **b** the passage of a small heavenly body across the disk of a larger one. **6** rapid transit. —*v.* **1** pass; pass across; pass through. **2** turn (the telescope of a transit) around its horizontal transverse axis to point in the opposite direction. [< L *transitus* < *transire.* See TRANSIENT.]

A transit used in surveying. It is equipped with a telescope, levels, and scales for measuring both vertical and horizontal angles.

transit instrument or **telescope** **1** in astronomy, a telescope so fixed that it can move only in the plane of the meridian along which it is located, used to determine the time of a heavenly body's transit. **2** a surveyor's transit.

tran·si·tion (tran zish′ən) *n.* **1** a change or passing from one condition, place, thing, activity, topic, etc. to another. The time between two distinct periods of history, art, etc. is called a period of transition. **2** in music: **a** a change of key. **b** a passage linking one section, subject, etc. of a composition with another. [< L *transitio, -onis* < *transire.* See TRANSIENT.]

tran·si·tion·al (tran zish′ən əl) *adj.* of transition; of change from one more or less fixed condition to another. —**tran·si′tion·al·ly,** *adv.*

tran·si·tive (tran′sə tiv or tran′zə tiv) *adj.* **1** of verbs, taking a direct object. *Bring* and *raise* are transitive verbs. **2** transitional. —*n.* a transitive verb. *Abbrev.*: trans. —**tran′si·tive·ly,** *adv.* —**tran′si·tive·ness,** *n.* ☛ See **verb** for usage note.

tran·si·to·ry (tran′sə tô′rē or tran′zə tô′rē) *adj.* passing soon or quickly; lasting only a short time. —**tran′si·to′ri·ly,** *adv.* —**tran′si·to′ri·ness,** *n.*

trans·late (trans lāt′ or tranz-) *v.* **-lat·ed, -lat·ing.** **1** change from one language into another. **2** change into other words. **3** explain the meaning of. **4** change from one place, position, or condition to another. **5** take to heaven without death. **6** in physics, move (a body) from one point or place to another without rotation. **7** retransmit (a telegraphic message), as by a relay. [ME < L *translatus,* pp. to *transferre.* See TRANSFER.] —**trans·lat′a·ble,** *adj.* —**Syn. 2** paraphrase, render.

trans·la·tion (trans lā′shən or tranz-) *n.* **1** the act of translating or the state of being translated. **2** the result of translating; a version. **3** the automatic retransmission of a long-distance telegraph message by means of a relay. **4** in physics, motion in which there is no rotation; onward movement that is not rotary or reciprocating. —**Syn. 2** interpretation, rendering.

trans·la·tor (trans lā′tər or tranz-) *n.* a person who translates.

trans·lit·er·ate (trans lit′ər āt′ or tranz-) *v.* **-at·ed, -at·ing.** change (letters, words, etc.) into corresponding characters of another alphabet or language: *We transliterate the Greek* χ *as* ch *and* ϕ *as* ph. [< *trans-* + L *litera* letter]

trans·lit·er·a·tion (trans lit′ər ā′shən or tranz-) *n.* the act of transliterating; the rendering of a letter or letters of one alphabet by equivalents in another.

trans·lu·cence (trans lü′səns or tranz-) *n.* a translucent quality or condition.

trans·lu·cen·cy (trans lü′sən sē or tranz-) *n.* the state or condition of being translucent.

trans·lu·cent (trans lü′sənt or tranz-) *adj.* letting light through without being transparent: *Frosted glass is translucent.* [< L *translucens, -entis,* ppr. of *translucere* < *trans-* through + *lucere* shine] —**trans·lu′cent·ly,** *adv.*

trans·ma·rine (trans′mə rēn′ or tranz′-) *adj.* across or beyond the sea.

trans·mi·grate (trans mī′grāt or tranz-) *v.* **-grat·ed, -grat·ing.** **1** move from one place or country to another; migrate. **2** pass at death into another body. [< L *transmigrare* < *trans-* across + *migrare* move]

trans·mi·gra·tion (trans′mī grā′shən or tranz′-) *n.* **1** the going from one place or country to another; migration. **2** the passing of a soul at death into another body.

trans·mis·si·ble (trans mis′ə bəl or tranz-) *adj.* capable of being transmitted: *Scarlet fever is a transmissible disease.*

trans·mis·sion (trans mish′ən or tranz-) *n.* **1** a sending over; passing on; passing along; letting through: *Mosquitoes are the only means of transmission of malaria.* **2** something transmitted. **3** of an automobile, etc., the part that transmits power from the engine to the rear axle. **4** the passage through space of radio waves from the transmitting station to the receiving station: *When radio transmission is good, distant stations can be received.* [< L *transmissio, -onis* < *transmittere.* See TRANSMIT.]

trans·mit (trans mit′ or tranz-) *v.* **-mit·ted, -mit·ting.** **1** send over; pass on; pass along; let through: *I will transmit the money by special messenger. Rats transmit disease.* **2** in physics: **a** cause (light, heat, sound, etc.) to pass through a medium. **b** convey (force or movement) from one part of a body or mechanism to another. **c** of a medium, allow (light, heat, etc.) to pass through: *Glass transmits light.* **3** send out (signals, voice, music, etc.) by electromagnetic waves. [< L *transmittere* < *trans-* across + *mittere* send]

trans·mit·tal (trans mit′əl or tranz-) *n.* a transmitting.

trans·mit·ter (trans mit′ər or tranz-) *n.* **1** a person or thing that transmits something. **2** that part of a telegraph or telephone by which messages are sent. **3** in radio and television broadcasting, an apparatus for sending out signals by means of electromagnetic waves. It generates and modulates radio-frequency waves, and sends them to the station's antenna.

trans·mon·tane (trans mon′tān or tranz-) *adj.* beyond a mountain or mountain range; tramontane.

trans·mu·ta·tion (trans′myů tā′shən or tranz′-) *n.* **1** a change from one nature, substance, or form into another. **2** a transformation of one species into another. **3** in chemistry and physics, the change of one atom into another atom of a different element, occurring naturally, as by radio-active disintegration, or artificially, as by bombardment with neutrons, etc. **4** in alchemy, the (attempted) conversion of a baser metal into gold or silver.

trans·mute (trans mūt′ or tranz-) *v.* **-mut·ed, -mut·ing.** **1** change from one nature, substance, or form into another: *We can transmute water power into electrical power.* **2** in chemistry and physics, subject to transmutation. [< L *transmutare* < *trans-* thoroughly + *mutare* change] —**trans·mut′er,** *n.* —**Syn.** See **transform.**

trans·o·ce·an·ic (trans′ō shē an′ik or tranz′-) *adj.* **1** crossing the ocean. **2** on the other side of the ocean.

tran·som (tran′səm) *n.* **1** a window over a door or other window, usually hinged for opening. **2** a horizontal bar across a window. **3** a crossbar separating a door from the window over it. [ME; ult. < L *transtrum;* originally, crossbeam]

trans·pa·cif·ic (trans′pə sif′ik) *adj.* **1** crossing the Pacific. **2** on the other side of the Pacific.

trans·par·ence (trans pãr′əns) *n.* a transparent quality or condition.

trans·par·en·cy (trans pãr′ən sē) *n.* **-cies.** **1** a transparent quality or condition. **2** something transparent.

3 a picture, design, or color photograph on glass, celluloid, etc., made visible by light shining through from behind.

trans·par·ent (trans pãr′ənt) *adj.* **1** transmitting light so that bodies beyond or behind can be distinctly seen: *Window glass is transparent.* **2** easily seen through or detected: *The boy's transparent excuses never fooled me.* **3** frank; free from pretence or deceit: *a boy of transparent honesty.* [< Med.L *transparens, -entis,* ppr. of *transparere* show light through < L *trans-* through + *parere* appear] —**trans·par′ent·ly,** *adv.* —**Syn.** **1** limpid, pellucid. **3** open, candid.

tran·spi·ra·tion (tran′spə rā′shən) *n.* a transpiring, as of fluid through a membrane or from the surface of leaves.

tran·spire (tran spīr′) *v.* **-spired, -spir·ing. 1** take place; happen. **2** leak out; become known. **3** pass off or send off in the form of vapor through a wall or surface, as from the human body or from leaves. [< F < L *trans-* through + *spirare* breathe]

☛ **transpire.** The meaning "happen, take place" was once regarded as not being in good use, but *transpire* in this sense is fairly common in cultivated English today.

trans·plant (*v.* trans plant′; *n.* trans′plant′) *v.* **1** plant again in a different place: *We start the flowers indoors and then transplant them to the garden.* **2** remove from one to another: *A group of farmers was transplanted to the island by the government.* **3** transfer (skin, an organ, etc.) from one person, animal, or part of the body to another. **4** bear moving: *Poppies do not transplant well and should be planted where they are to grow.*
—*n.* **1** the act or process of transplanting. **2** something transplanted. [ME < LL *transplantare* < L *trans-* across + *plantare* plant] —**trans·plant′a·ble,** *adj.* —**trans·plant′er,** *n.*

trans·plan·ta·tion (trans′plan tā′shən) *n.* **1** the act of transplanting or the state of being transplanted. **2** something that has been transplanted.

tran·spond·er (tran spon′dər) *n.* an electronic device that automatically receives and answers a radio or radar signal. It is used in meteorology, aeronautics, etc. [< *trans*mitter + res*ponder*]

trans·port (*v.* trans pôrt′; *n.* trans′pôrt) *v.* **1** carry from one place to another: *Wheat is transported from the farms to the mills.* **2** carry away by strong feeling: *She was transported with joy by the good news.* **3** send away to another country as a punishment. **4** kill.
—*n.* **1** a carrying from one place to another: *Trucks are much used for transport.* **2** a large truck used to carry freight long distances by road. **3** a ship used to carry men and supplies. **4** an airplane that transports passengers, mail, freight, etc. **5** a strong feeling. **6** a transported convict. [ME < L *transportare* < *trans-* across + *portare* carry] —**trans·port′er,** *n.* —**Syn.** *v.* **1** See **carry.**

trans·port·a·bil·i·ty (trans pôr′tə bil′ə tē) *n.* the fact or property of being transportable.

trans·port·a·ble (trans pôr′tə bəl) *adj.* **1** capable of being transported. **2** involving, or liable to, punishment by transportation: *a transportable offence.*

trans·por·ta·tion (trans′pər tā′shən) *n.* **1** a transporting: *The railway allows free transportation for a certain amount of baggage.* **2** the state of being transported. **3** a means of transport. **4** the cost of transport; a ticket for transport. **5** a sending away or being sent to another country as a punishment.

trans·pos·al (trans pōz′əl) *n.* transposition.

trans·pose (trans pōz′) *v.* **-posed, -pos·ing. 1** change the position or order of; interchange. **2** change the usual order of (letters, words, or numbers); invert. *Example:* Up came the wind, and off went his hat. **3** in music: **a** change the key of. **b** play in another key. **4** in algebra, transfer (a term) to the other side of an equation, changing plus to minus or minus to plus. [< F *transposer* < *trans-* across (< L) + *poser* put (see POSE[1])] —**trans·pos′er,** *n.*

trans·po·si·tion (trans′pə zish′ən) *n.* **1** the act of transposing or the state of being transposed. **2** in music: **a** a changing into another key. **b** a composition or passage so changed.

trans·pro·vin·cial (trans prə vin′shəl) *adj.* crossing a province from one end to the other: *transprovincial bus service.*

hat, āge, cãre, fär; let, ēqual, tėrm; it, īce
hot, ōpen, ôrder; oil, out; cup, pu̇t, rüle, ūse
əbove, takən, pencəl, lemən, circəs
ch, child; ng, long; sh, ship
th, thin; ᴛʜ, then; zh, measure

trans·ship (trans ship′) *v.* **-shipped, -ship·ping.** transfer from one ship, train, car, etc. to another. Also, **tranship.** —**trans·ship′ment,** *n.*

trans·son·ic (trans son′ik) *adj.* moving at a speed close to the speed of sound, 700-780 miles per hour.

tran·sub·stan·ti·a·tion (tran′səb stan′shē ā′shən) *n.* **1** a changing of one substance into another. **2** in Christianity, the changing of the substance of the bread and wine of the Eucharist into the substance of the body and blood of Christ, only the appearance of the bread and wine remaining. [< Med.L *transubstantiatio, -onis* < *transubstantiare* transmute < L *trans-* over + *substantia* substance]

trans·ver·sal (trans vėr′səl or tranz-) *adj.* transverse. —*n.* in geometry, a line intersecting two or more other lines.

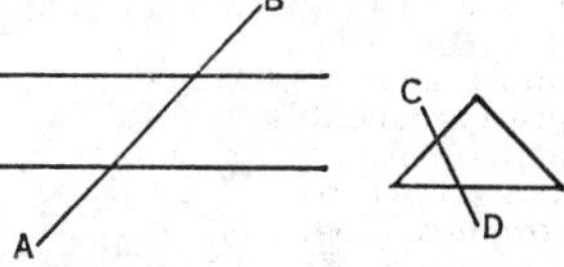

The lines AB and CD are transversals.

trans·verse (trans vėrs′ or tranz-, trans′vėrs or tranz′-) *adj.* **1** lying across; placed crosswise; crossing from side to side: *transverse beams.* **2** in geometry, of or having to do with the axis of a conic section that passes through the foci. —*n.* **1** something transverse. **2** in geometry, the longer axis or an ellipse. [< L *transversus,* pp. of *transvertere* < *trans-* across + *vertere* turn]

trans·verse·ly (trans vėrs′lē or tranz-) *adv.* across; athwart; crosswise; from side to side.

trans·vest·ism (trans vest′iz əm or tranz-) *n.* the practice of dressing in the clothing of the opposite sex. [< G *transvestismus* < L *trans-* + *vestire* dress]

trans·vest·ite (trans vest′īt or tranz-) *n.* one who practises transvestism.

Tran·syl·va·ni·an (tran′səl vā′nē ən or -səl vān′yən) *adj.* of or having to do with Transylvania, a region of W. Romania or its people. —*n.* a native or inhabitant of Transylvania.

trap[1] (trap) *n. v.* **trapped, trap·ping.** —*n.* **1** a device for catching animals, lobsters, birds, etc. **2** a trick or other means for catching someone off guard: *The police set traps to make the thief tell where the money was.* **3** a trap door. **4** a device in a pipe to prevent the escape of air, water, gas, etc. **5** a speed trap. **6** a light two-wheeled carriage. **7** a device to throw clay pigeons, etc. into the air to be shot at. **8** *Slang.* the mouth: *Shut your trap!* **9 traps,** *pl.* drums, cymbals, bells, gongs, etc.

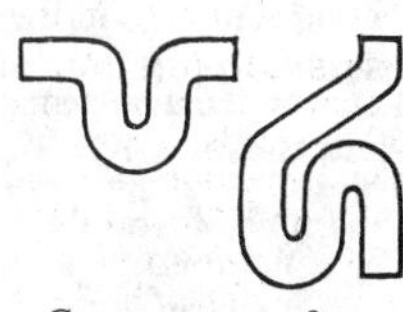
Common types of traps in pipes (def. 4)

—*v.* **1** catch in a trap. **2** set traps for animals. **3** provide with a trap. **4** stop with a trap. **5** make a business of catching animals in traps for their furs. [OE *træppe*]
Syn. *n.* **1, 2 Trap, snare** = something that catches or is contrived to catch an animal or person. **Trap** figuratively suggests a situation deliberately set to catch someone by surprise and destroy him or trick him into doing or saying something: *Suspecting a trap, the detachment of soldiers withdrew.* **Snare** figuratively applies to a desperate situation someone gets entangled in unawares, or a device to lure him into getting caught: *The detectives used marked money as a snare for the thief.*

trap[2] (trap) *v.* **trapped, trap·ping,** *n.* —*v.* cover with trappings. —*n.* **traps,** *pl. Informal.* belongings; baggage. [ME, alteration of OF *drap* cloth < Med.L *drappus,* of uncertain origin]

trap door a door in a floor or roof. See picture on the next page.

trapes (trāps) *v. n.* traipse.

tra·peze (trə pēz′) *n.* **1** a short horizontal bar hung by ropes like a swing, used in gymnasiums and circuses. **2** in geometry, trapezium. [< F < LL < Gk. *trapezion*, dim. of *trapeza* table < *tra-* (unique for *tetra-*) four + *peza* foot. Doublet of TRAPEZIUM.]

A man using a trap door

tra·pe·zi·um (trə pē′zē əm) *n.* **-zi·ums, -zi·a** (-zē ə). **1** in geometry, a four-sided plane figure having no sides parallel. **2** *Brit.* a four-sided plane figure having two parallel and two non-parallel sides; trapezoid. [< LL < Gk. *trapezion*, originally, little table. Doublet of TRAPEZE.]

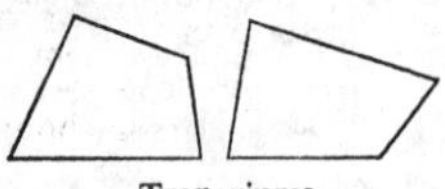
Trapeziums

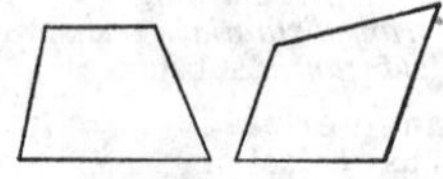
Trapezoids

tra·pe·zi·us (trə pē′zē əs) *n.* **-zi·i** (-zē ī′ or -zē ē′). in anatomy, either of two large, flat, triangular muscles in the back of the neck and upper shoulders, that together resemble a trapezium or similar four-sided figure. [< LL < L < Gk.]

trap·e·zoid (trap′ə zoid′) *n.* **1** in geometry, a four-sided plane figure having two sides parallel and two sides not parallel. **2** *Brit.* a four-sided plane figure having no sides parallel; trapezium. [< NL < Gk. *trapezoeidēs* < *trapeza* table + *eidos* form]

trap·line (trap′līn′) *n.* **1** in trapping, the way or route along which traps are set. **2** a set of baited fish hooks to be anchored to a line. **3** in a spider's web, the filament that traps the prey.

trap·per (trap′ər) *n.* a person who traps, especially a man who traps wild animals for their furs.

trap·pings (trap′ingz) *n.pl.* **1** ornamental coverings for a horse. **2** things worn; ornaments: *the trappings of a king and his court.* **3** outward appearances: *He had all the trappings of a cowboy, but he couldn't even ride a horse.* [< *trap*[2]]

Trap·pist (trap′ist) *n.* in the Roman Catholic Church, a monk belonging to an extremely austere branch of the Cistercian order established in 1664. *—adj.* of or having to do with the Trappists. [< F *trappiste*, from the monastery of *La Trappe* in N. France]

trap·shoot·er (trap′shüt′ər) *n.* a person who shoots at clay pigeons, etc. thrown into the air.

trap·shoot·ing (trap′shüt′ing) *n.* the practice or act of shooting at clay pigeons, etc. thrown into the air.

trash (trash) *n.* **1** twigs, leaves, bits of paper, etc.; rubbish. **2** reading matter of little or no value. **3** a person or persons of worthless character. [< Scand.; cf. dial. Norwegian *trask*] **—Syn. 1** debris, litter, refuse, garbage.

trash·y (trash′ē) *adj.* **trash·i·er, trash·i·est.** like or containing trash; worthless. **—trash′i·ly,** *adv.* **—trash′i·ness,** *n.*

trau·ma (tro′mə, trô′mə, or trou′mə) *n.* **-ma·ta** (-mə tə) or **-mas. 1** in pathology, an injury; wound. **2** in psychiatry: **a** an emotional shock that has lasting effects on the victim. **b** a state of emotional disturbance resulting from an injury or mental shock. [< Gk. *trauma, -atos* wound]

trau·mat·ic (tro mat′ik, trô mat′ik, or trou mat′ik) *adj.* **1** of, having to do with, or produced by a wound or injury. **2** for or dealing with the treatment of wounds or injuries.

trav·ail (trav′āl) *n.* **1** toil; labor. **2** trouble; hardship. **3** the pains of childbirth. —*v.* **1** toil; labor. **2** suffer the pains of childbirth. [ME < OF *travail*, ult. < LL *tripalium* (spelled *trepalium*) torture device, probably ult. < L *tri-* three + *palus* stake]

trave (trāv) *n.* **1** a wooden frame to hold a horse while being shod. **2** in architecture: **a** a crossbeam. **b** a division in a ceiling, etc. made of crossbeams. [ME < OF < L *trabs, trabis* beam]

trav·el (trav′əl) *v.* **-elled** or **-eled, -el·ling** or **-el·ing,** *n.* —*v.* **1** go from one place to another; journey: *travel across the country.* **2** go from place to place selling things: *He travels for a large firm.* **3** move; proceed; pass: *Light and sound travel in waves.* **4** walk or run: *A deer travels many miles in a day.* **5** pass through or over: *travel a road.*
—*n.* **1** going in aircraft, trains, ships, cars, etc. from one place to another; journeying. **2** movement in general. **3** the length of stroke, speed, way of working, etc. of a part of a machine. **4 travels,** *pl.* **a** journeys. **b** a book about one's experiences, visits, etc. while travelling. [var. of *travail*]

trav·elled or **trav·eled** (trav′əld) *adj.* **1** that has done much travelling. **2** much used by travellers.

trav·el·ler or **trav·el·er** (trav′əl ər or trav′lər) *n.* **1** a person or thing that travels. **2** a travelling salesman.

traveller's cheque or **traveler's cheque** a cheque that is signed by the buyer and must be signed again by him at the time of cashing.

travelling bag or **traveling bag** handbag (def. 2).

travelling fellowship or **traveling fellowship** a fellowship that enables the one receiving it to travel for purposes of study.

travelling salesman or **traveling salesman** a person whose work is going from place to place selling things for a company.

trav·e·logue (trav′ə log′) *n.* a lecture describing travel, usually accompanied by pictures, or a motion picture depicting travel. Also, **travelog.** [< *travel* + *-logue*, as in *dialogue*]

trav·erse (*v. adv.* trav′ərs or trə vėrs′; *n. adj.* trav′ərs) *v.* **-ersed, -ers·ing,** *n. adj. adv.* —*v.* **1** pass across, over, or through: *The caravan traversed the desert.* **2** lie, extend, or stretch across; cross; intersect. **3** walk or move in a crosswise direction; move back and forth: *That horse traverses.* **4** go to and fro over or along (a place, etc.). **5** ski diagonally across (a slope). **6** read, examine, or consider carefully. **7** move sideways; turn from side to side. **8** in fencing, glide the blade along that of the opponent's foil, toward the hilt, while applying pressure. **9** turn big guns to right or left. **10** turn on a pivot, or as if on a pivot. **11** oppose; hinder; thwart. **12** examine carefully.
—*n.* **1** the act of crossing. **2** something put or lying across. **3** an earth wall protecting a trench or an exposed place in a fortification. **4** in a church, etc., a gallery running from side to side. **5** a distance across. **6** a sideways motion of a ship, part in a machine, mountain climbers, etc. **7** the zigzag line taken by a ship because of contrary winds or currents. **8** a line that crosses other lines. **9** opposition; an obstacle; hindrance. **10 a** a changing the direction of a gun to the right or left. **b** the amount of such change. **11** in law, a formal denial of something alleged to be a fact by the opposing side.
—*adj.* lying across; being across.
—*adv.* across; crosswise. [ME < OF *traverser* < LL *transversare* < L *transversus.* See TRANSVERSE.] **—trav′ers·a·ble,** *adj.* **—trav′ers·er,** *n.*

trav·er·tin (trav′ər tin) *n.* travertine.

trav·er·tine (trav′ər tin or trav′ər tēn′) *n.* a form of limestone deposited by springs, etc., used as building material. [< Ital. *travertino*, var. of *tivertino*, ult. < L *Tibur*, an ancient town in Latium]

trav·es·ty (trav′is tē) *n.* **-ties,** *v.* **-tied, -ty·ing.** —*n.* **1** an imitation of a serious literary work in such a way as to make it seem ridiculous. **2** any treatment or imitation that makes a serious thing seem ridiculous.
—*v.* make (a serious subject or matter) ridiculous; imitate in an absurd or grotesque way. [< F *travesti* disguised, ult. < L *trans-* over + *vestire* dress < *vestis* garment]

tra·vois (trə voi′ or trav′wo; *French,* trä vwä′) *n.* **-vois. 1** a simple wheel-less vehicle used by the Prairie Indians and made of two shafts or poles, to which was attached a platform or net for holding the load: *A travois was dragged by a horse or dog hitched to the*

A travois

shafts. **2** *Cdn.* a dog sled. **3** *Cdn.* a sled used for transporting logs. **4** *Cdn.* a stoneboat. [< Cdn.F, alteration of F *travail* frame to hold a horse being shod]

trawl (trol or trôl) *n.* **1** a strong net dragged along the bottom of the sea. **2** a line supported by buoys and having many short lines with baited hooks attached to it. —*v.* **1** fish with a net by dragging it along the bottom of the sea. **2** fish with lines supported by buoys. **3** catch (fish) with such a net or lines. [< MDu. *traghel* < L *tragula* dragnet]

trawl·er (trol′ər or trôl′ər) *n.* **1** a person who trawls. **2** a boat used in trawling.

tray (trā) *n.* **1** a flat, shallow holder or container with a low rim around it. **2** a tray with dishes of food on it. **3** a shallow box that fits into a trunk, cabinet, etc. [OE *trēg*]

treach·er·ous (trech′ər əs) *adj.* **1** not to be trusted; not faithful; disloyal: *The treacherous soldier carried reports to the enemy.* **2** having a false appearance of strength, security, etc.; not reliable; deceiving: *Thin ice is treacherous.* —**treach′er·ous·ly,** *adv.* —**treach′er·ous·ness,** *n.*

treach·er·y (trech′ər ē) *n.* **-er·ies.** **1** a breaking of faith; treacherous behavior; deceit. **2** treason. [ME < OF *trecherie* < *trechier* cheat] —**Syn. 1** See **disloyalty.**

trea·cle (trē′kəl) *n.* **1** *Esp.Brit.* molasses, especially that produced during the refining of sugar. **2** formerly, a compound much used as an antidote for poison or poisonous bites. [ME *triacle* antidote for bites < OF < L < Gk. *thēriakē*, ult. < *thēr* wild beast]

tread (tred) *v.* **trod** or (*Archaic*) **trode, trod·den** or **trod, tread·ing,** *n.* —*v.* **1** walk; step, set the foot down: *Don't tread on the flower beds.* **2** set the feet on; walk on or through; step on: *tread the streets.* **3** press under the feet; trample; trample on; crush: *tread grapes.* **4** make, form, or do by walking: *Cattle had trodden a path to the pond.* **5** follow; pursue: *tread the path of virtue.* **6** treat with cruelty; oppress. **7 tread on air,** feel happy and gay. **8 tread on one's toes,** offend or annoy one. **9 tread the boards,** be an actor or actress; play a part in a play. **10 tread water,** keep oneself from sinking by moving the feet up and down.
—*n.* **1** the act or sound of treading: *We heard the tread of marching feet.* **2** a way of walking: *He walks with a heavy tread.* **3 a** the part of stairs or a ladder that a person steps on. **b** the width of a step from front to back, measured between risers. **4 a** the part of a wheel or tire that touches the ground. **b** the pattern of the grooves or ridges in a tire: *The new tire left a deep tread in the snow.* **5** either of the tracks of a caterpillar tractor or similar vehicle. **6** the part of a rail or rails that the wheels touch. **7** the distance between opposite wheels of an automobile. **8** the sole of the foot or of a shoe. **9** a footprint. [OE *tredan*] —**tread′er,** *n.*

trea·dle (tred′əl) *n. v.* **-dled, -dling.**
—*n.* a lever or pedal worked by the foot to operate a machine: *the treadle of an old-fashioned sewing machine.* —*v.* work a treadle. [OE *tredel* < *tredan* tread]

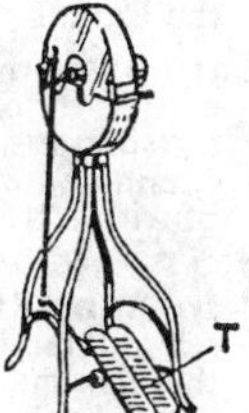

T, a treadle on a grindstone

tread·mill (tred′mil′) *n.* **1** an apparatus to turn something by having a person or animal walk on the moving steps of a wheel or of a sloping, endless belt. **2** any wearisome or monotonous round of work or life.

treas. **1** treasurer. **2** treasury.

trea·son (trē′zən) *n.* **1** the betrayal of one's country or ruler. Helping the enemies of one's country is treason. **2** *Rare.* the betrayal of a trust, duty, friend, etc.; treachery. [ME < AF *treson* < L *traditio*. Doublet of TRADITION.] —**Syn. 1** See **disloyalty.**

trea·son·a·ble (trē′zən ə bəl or trēz′nə bəl) *adj.* of treason; involving treason; traitorous. —**trea′son·a·ble·ness,** *n.* —**trea′son·a·bly,** *adv.*

trea·son·ous (trē′zən əs or trēz′nəs) *adj.* treasonable.

treas·ure (trezh′ər) *n. v.* **-ured, -ur·ing.** —*n.* **1** wealth or riches stored up; valuable things. **2** any thing or person

hat, āge, cãre, fär; let, ēqual, tėrm; it, īce
hot, ōpen, ôrder; oil, out; cup, pu̇t, rüle, ūse
əbove, takən, pencəl, lemən, circəs
ch, child; ng, long; sh, ship
th, thin; ᴛʜ, then; zh, measure

that is much loved or valued. —*v.* **1** value highly. **2** put away for future use; store up. [ME < OF *tresor* < L < Gk. *thēsauros*. Doublet of THESAURUS.]

treas·ur·er (trezh′ər ər) *n.* a person in charge of the finances of a club, society, corporation, government body, etc.

treas·ure-trove (trezh′ər trōv′) *n.* **1** money, jewels, or other treasure that a person finds, especially if the owner of it is not known. **2** any valuable discovery. [< AF *tresor trové* treasure found]

treas·ur·y (trezh′ər ē) *n.* **-ur·ies.** **1** the place where money is kept. **2** money owned; funds: *We voted to pay for the party out of the club treasury.* **3** a government department that has charge of income and expenses. **4** a place where treasure is kept. **5** a book or person thought of as a valued source: *a treasury of poetry.*

Treasury bench or **benches** in the House of Commons or in a legislature, the front benches to the Speaker's right, occupied by the ministers of the government.

treat (trēt) *v.* **1** act toward: *The driver treats his horses well.* **2** think of; consider; regard: *He treated his mistake as a joke.* **3** deal with to relieve or cure: *The dentist is treating my tooth.* **4** deal with to bring about some special result: *treat a metal plate with acid in engraving.* **5** deal with; discuss: *This magazine treats the progress of medicine.* **6** express in literature, music, or art: *treat a theme realistically.* **7** deal with a subject. **8** discuss terms; arrange terms: *to treat for peace.* **9** entertain with food, drink, or amusement: *He treated his friends to ice cream.* **10** pay the cost of entertainment: *I'll treat today.* **11 treat of,** deal with; discuss.
—*n.* **1** a gift of food, drink, or amusement. **2** anything that gives pleasure. [ME < OF *traitier* < L *tractare*, originally, drag violently, handle, frequentative of *trahere* drag] —**treat′er,** *n.*

trea·tise (trē′tis) *n.* a book or writing dealing formally and systematically with some subject. [ME < AF *tretiz*, ult. < L *tractare* treat. See TREAT.]

treat·ment (trēt′mənt) *n.* **1** the act or process of treating. **2** a way of treating. **3** something done or used to treat something else, such as a disease.

trea·ty (trē′tē) *n.* **-ties.** **1** an agreement, especially one between nations, signed and approved by each nation. **2** the document embodying such an agreement. **3** *Cdn.* an agreement between the federal government and an Indian tribe whereby the latter foregoes all its land rights except for reservations and receives in return an annuity of $5 per head and supplies of rations. **4 in treaty,** *Cdn.* of an Indian or Indian tribe or band, bound by treaty with the federal government. **5 take treaty** or **take the treaty,** *Cdn.* of an Indian tribe, accept the terms of treaty with the federal government. [ME < AF *trete*, OF *traitie* < L *tractatus* discussion < *tractare*. See TREAT.]

treaty Indian in Canada, a member of certain Indian tribes or bands who live on reserves and receive treaty money and other treaty rights.

treaty money in Canada, an annual payment made by the federal government to treaty Indians.

treaty rights in Canada, the rights enjoyed through treaty with the government by members of certain Indian tribes or bands: *Treaty rights include the right to hold land on a reserve and to receive treaty money.*

tre·ble (treb′əl) *adj. v.* **-bled, -bling,** *n.* —*adj.* **1** three times. **2** in music, of, having to do with, or for the treble. **3** shrill; high-pitched. —*v.* make or become three times as much: *He trebled his money by buying a dog for $5.00 and selling it for $15.00.* —*n.* **1** in music: **a** the highest part; soprano. **b** a voice, singer, or instrument that takes this part. **2** a shrill, high-pitched voice or sound. [ME < OF < L *triplus* triple. Doublet of TRIPLE.]

treble clef in music, a symbol (𝄞) indicating that the pitch of the notes on a staff is above middle C.

tre·bly (treb′lē) *adv.* three times.

tree (trē) *n. v.* **treed, tree·ing.** —*n.* **1** a large perennial plant having a woody trunk, branches, and leaves. **2** less accurately, any of certain other plants that resemble trees in form or size. **3** a piece or structure of wood, etc. for some special purpose: *a clothes tree, a shoe tree.* **4** anything suggesting a tree and its branches. A family tree is a diagram with branches showing how the members of a family are related. **5 up a tree, a** chased up a tree. **b** *Informal.* in a difficult position. **6** *Archaic.* a gallows. **7** *Archaic.* the cross on which Christ died. —*v.* **1** furnish with a tree (beam, bar, wooden handle, etc.). **2** stretch (a shoe) on a tree. **3** assume a treelike or branching form. **4** chase up a tree: *The cat was treed by a dog.* **5** take refuge in a tree. **6** *Informal.* put into a difficult position. [OE *trēo*]

treed (trēd) *adj.* covered with trees.

tree farm a privately owned area in which trees are grown under a system of forest management.

tree farmer a person engaged in tree farming.

tree farming the management of a tree farm.

tree fern a fern that grows to the size of a tree, has a trunklike stem, and has fronds at the top.

tree frog 1 a small frog that lives in trees. **2** a tree toad.

tree line 1 a limit beyond which climatic conditions do not permit the growth of trees; in Canada, the southern limit of the Barrens. **2** a height on mountains above which trees do not grow. Also, **timber line.**

treen (trēn) *n.* the art and craft of making treenware. Canadian treen ranges from the late 17th century to recent times. [< *tree* wood]

tree·nail (trē′nāl′, tren′əl, or trun′əl) *n.* a round pin of hard wood for fastening timbers together. Also, **trenail.**

treen·ware (trēn′wãr′) *n.* household utensils and objects carved from wood, as used by the early settlers.

tree of heaven the ailanthus.

tree toad a small toad that lives in trees and has adhesive disks or suckers on its toes.

tree·top (trē′top′) *n.* the top of a tree.

tre·foil (trē′foil) *n.* **1** a plant having threefold leaves. Clover is a trefoil. **2** an ornament like a threefold leaf. [ME < AF < L *trifolium* < *tri-* three + *folium* leaf]

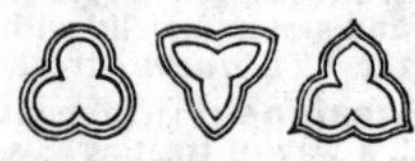

Trefoils (def. 2)

trek (trek) *v.* **trekked, trek·king,** *n.* —*v.* **1** travel slowly; travel; migrate. **2** *Informal.* go; proceed: *trek down to the office.* **3** in South Africa, travel by ox wagon. —*n.* **1** a difficult journey. **2** a stage of a journey between one stopping place and the next. [< Du. *trekken,* originally, draw, pull]

trel·lis (trel′is) *n.* **1** a frame of light strips of wood or metal crossing one another with open spaces in between; lattice, especially one supporting growing vines. **2** a summerhouse or other structure with sides of lattice. —*v.* **1** furnish with a trellis. **2** support on a trellis. **3** cross as in a trellis. [ME < OF *trelis,* ult. < L *trilix* triple-twilled < *tri-* three + *licium* thread]

trel·lis·work (trel′is wėrk′) *n.* **1** trellis. **2** trellises; latticework.

trem·a·tode (trem′ə tōd′ or trē′mə tōd′) *n.* a flatworm that lives as a parasite in or on other animals. [< NL < Gk. *trēmatōdēs* holed < *trēma, -atos* hole]

trem·ble (trem′bəl) *v.* **-bled, -bling,** *n.* —*v.* **1** shake because of fear, excitement, weakness, cold, etc. **2** feel fear, anxiety, etc. **3** move gently. —*n.* a trembling. [ME < OF *trembler,* ult. < L *tremulus.* See TREMULOUS.] **—trem′bling·ly,** *adv.* **—trem′bly,** *adj.* **—Syn.** *v.* **1** shiver, quake, shudder, quiver, vibrate. See **shake.**

tre·men·dous (tri men′dəs) *adj.* **1** dreadful; awful. **2** *Informal.* very great; enormous: *a tremendous house.* **3** *Informal.* extraordinary: *have a tremendous time.* [< L *tremendus,* literally, to be trembled at < *tremere* tremble] **—tre·men′dous·ly,** *adv.* **—Syn. 1** frightful, horrible. **2** immense, monstrous.

trem·o·lo (trem′ə lō′) *n.* **-los. 1** in music, a trembling or vibrating quality, as produced in singing by a wavering in pitch or on a stringed instrument by a rapid repeating of a tone with fast strokes of the bow. The tremolo is used to express emotion. **2** in an organ, a device used to produce this quality. [< Ital. *tremolo* < L *tremulus.* Doublet of TREMULOUS.]

trem·or (trem′ər) *n.* **1** an involuntary shaking or trembling: *a nervous tremor in the voice.* **2** a thrill of emotion or excitement. **3** a tremulus or vibrating movement. An earthquake is called an earth tremor. [< L] **—Syn. 1** quaking, quivering.

trem·u·lous (trem′yů ləs) *adj.* **1** trembling; quivering. **2** timid; fearful. [< L *tremulus* < *tremere* tremble. Doublet of TREMOLO.] **—trem′u·lous·ly,** *adv.* **—trem′u·lous·ness,** *n.* **—Syn. 1** shaking, vibrating.

tre·nail (trē′nāl′, tren′əl, or trun′əl) *n.* treenail.

trench (trench) *n.* **1** a long, narrow ditch with earth thrown up in front to protect soldiers. **2** a deep furrow; ditch. **3** a cut, scar, or deep wrinkle. [ME < OF *trenche,* n. < *trenchier,* v.] —*v.* **1** surround with a trench; fortify with trenches. **2** dig a trench in. **3** dig ditches. **4** cut. **5 trench on** or **upon, a** trespass upon. **b** come close to; border on: *The demagogue's speech trenched closely on treason.* [ME < OF *trenchier* cut, apparently ult. < L *truncare* lop off < *truncus* mutilated]

trench·an·cy (tren′chən sē) *n.* sharpness; a trenchant quality.

trench·ant (tren′chənt) *adj.* **1** sharp; keen; cutting: *trenchant wit.* **2** vigorous; effective: *a trenchant policy.* **3** clear-cut; distinct: *in trenchant outline against the sky.* [ME < OF *trenchant,* ppr. of *trenchier* cut. See TRENCH.] **—trench′ant·ly,** *adv.*

trench coat a type of heavy cotton or poplin raincoat having epaulettes and a belt.

trench·er (tren′chər) *n.* formerly, a wooden platter on which meat was served and carved. [ME < OF *trencheoir* knife, ult. < *trenchier* cut. See TRENCH.]

trench·er·man (tren′chər mən) *n.* **-men** (mən). **1** a heavy eater; a person who has a hearty appetite. **2** a hanger-on; parasite.

trench fever an infectious fever that is transmitted by lice, particularly common among soldiers in the trenches during the First World War.

trench mouth 1 a contagious inflammation of the mouth and gums. **2** any inflammation of the mouth and gums.

trend (trend) *n.* the general direction; course; tendency: *the trend of modern living.* [< v.] —*v.* have a general direction; tend; run: *The road trends to the north.* [OE *trendan*] **—Syn.** *n.* See **direction.**

trend·y (tren′dē) *adj. Informal.* conforming to the trends or fashion of the time.

Trent (trent) *n.* **Council of,** the council of the Roman Catholic Church held at Trent, Italy, from time to time, between 1545 and 1563. It defined Catholic doctrines, corrected certain abuses within the church, and organized the Catholic opposition to the Protestant movement.

tre·pan (tri pan′) *n. v.* **-panned, -pan·ning.** —*n.* **1** an early form of the trephine. **2** a boring instrument, used for sinking shafts. —*v.* **1** operate on with a trepan (trephine). **2** bore through with a trepan; cut a disk out of with a trepan or similar tool. [ME < OF < Med.L < Gk. *trypanon* < *trypaein* bore < *trypē* hole]

tre·pang (tri pang′) *n.* **1** the dried flesh of a wormlike sea animal, used in China, etc. for making soup. **2** any of these animals. [< Malay *tripang*]

tre·phine (tri fīn′ or tri fēn′) *n. v.* **-phined, -phin·ing.** —*n.* a cylindrical saw with a removable centre pin, used to cut out circular pieces from the skull. —*v.* operate on with a trephine. [earlier *trafine,* alteration by inventor Woodall of *trapan* (var. of *trepan*) after L *tres fines* three ends]

trep·i·da·tion (trep′ə dā′shən) *n.* **1** nervous dread; fear; fright. **2** a trembling. [< L *trepidatio, -onis,* ult. < *trepidus* alarmed]

tres·pass (tres′pəs or tres′pas) *v.* **1** go on somebody's property without any right: *The farmer put up "No Trespassing" signs to keep people off his property.* **2** go beyond the limits of what is right, proper, or polite: *I* *won't trespass on your time any longer.* 3 do wrong; sin. *—n.* 1 the act or fact of trespassing. 2 a wrong; a sin. 3 in law: **a** an unlawful act done against the person, property, or rights of another. **b** an action to recover damages for such an injury. [ME < OF *trespasser* < *tres-* across (< L *trans-*) + *passer* pass, ult. < L *passus* step] **—tres′pass·er,** *n.* **—Syn.** *v.* **1, 2** encroach, infringe, invade. See **intrude.** *–n.* 2 transgression, offence.

tress (tres) *n.* a lock, curl, or braid of hair. [< ME < OF *tresce,* probably < Gmc.]

A trestle (def. 1)

tres·tle (tres′əl) *n.* 1 a frame used as a support. 2 a supporting framework for carrying railway tracks across a gap. [ME < OF *trestel* crossbeam, ult. < L *transtrum*]

tres·tle·tree (tres′əl trē′) *n.* on a ship, either of two horizontal, fore-and-aft timbers or bars secured to a masthead, one on each side, in order to support the crosstrees.

A trestle (def. 2)

tres·tle·work (tres′əl wėrk′) *n.* structural work consisting of a trestle or trestles; a support, bridge, etc. made of such structures.

trews (trüz) *n. Scottish.* tight-fitting tartan trousers or breeches. [< Irish *trius* < *triubhas.* Cf. TROUSERS.]

trey (trā) *n.* a card, die, or domino, etc. having three spots. [ME < OF *trei* < L *tres* three]

tri- *combining form.* 1 three; having three; having three parts, as in *triangle.* 2 three times; into three parts, as in *trisect.* 3 containing three atoms, etc. of the substance specified, as in *trioxide.* 4 once in three; every third, as in *trimonthly.* [< L or Gk.]

tri·ad (trī′ad or trī′əd) *n.* 1 a group of three, especially of three closely related persons or things. 2 in music, a chord of three tones. 3 in chemistry, an element, atom, or radical with a valence of three. [< LL *trias, -adis* < Gk. *trias, -ados* < *treis* three]

tri·al (trī′əl) *n.* 1 the examining and deciding of a case in a law court. 2 the process of trying or testing: *He gave the machine another trial.* 3 experimentation by investigation, tentative action, use, etc.; experiment: *learn by trial and error.* 4 the condition of being tried or tested: *He is employed on trial.* 5 a trouble; hardship. 6 a cause of trouble or hardship. 7 an attempt; effort. 8 a preliminary competition in field or track events at a track meet.
—adj. 1 for a try or test: *a trial trip.* 2 that is on trial: *a trial employee.* 3 of or having to do with a trial in a law court: *trial testimony.* [< AF *trial* < *trier* try]
Syn. *n.* **2 Trial, test, experiment** = the process or way of discovering or proving something. **Trial** = the process of discovering the qualities of someone or something and establishing its (his) worth, genuineness, strength, effect, etc.: *He gave the new toothpaste a trial.* **Test** applies to a trial to end uncertainty about quality, genuineness, or presence, as by thorough examination, experiment, etc.: *The new plane passed all tests.* **Experiment** applies to a process to find out something still unknown or to test conclusions reached: *Experiments indicate the new drug will cure infections.* **5** misfortune.

trial and error the process of arriving at a solution of a problem by trying several ways and learning from the errors so made.

trial balance in bookkeeping, a comparison of debit and credit totals in a ledger. If they are not equal, there is an error.

trial jury a group of persons, usually twelve in number, chosen to decide a case in court. See **petit jury.**

tri·an·gle (trī′ang′gəl) *n.* 1 a plane figure having three sides and three angles. See picture in the next column. 2 something shaped like a triangle. 3 a musical instrument consisting of a steel triangle that is struck with a steel rod. 4 a group of three. [ME < L *triangulum* < *tri-* three + *angulus* corner]

tri·an·gu·lar (trī ang′gyů lər) *adj.* 1 shaped like a triangle; three-cornered. 2 cornered with three persons, groups, etc.

hat, āge, cãre, fãr; let, ēqual, tėrm; it, īce
hot, ōpen, ôrder; oil, out; cup, pu̇t, rüle, ūse
əbove, takən, pencəl, lemən, circəs
ch, child; ng, long; sh, ship
th, thin; ᴛʜ, then; zh, measure

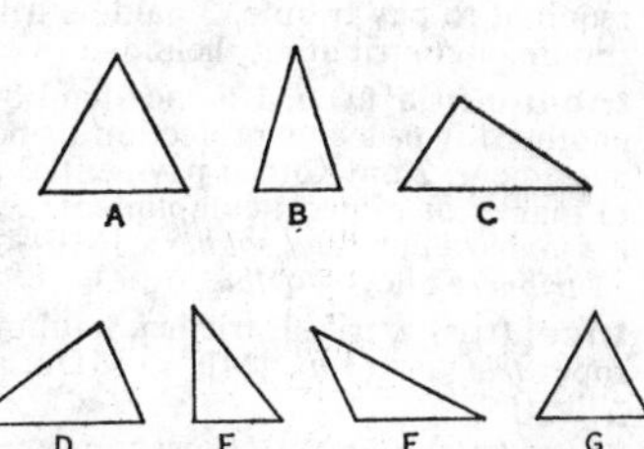

Triangles: A and G, equilateral; B and E, isosceles; C, D, and F scalene; E, right; A and G, equiangular.

tri·an·gu·late (*v.* trī ang′gyů lāt′; *adj.* trī ang′ yů lit or trī ang′gyů lāt′) *v.* **-lat·ed, -lat·ing,** *adj.* *—v.* 1 divide into triangles. 2 survey or map out (a region) by dividing (it) into triangles and measuring their angles. 3 find by trigonometry: *triangulate the height of a mountain.* 4 make triangular. *—adj.* 1 composed of or marked with triangles. 2 triangular.

tri·an·gu·la·tion (trī ang′gyů lā′shən) *n.* 1 a survey or measurement done by means of trigonometry. 2 a division into triangles.

Tri·as·sic (trī as′ik) in geology: *—n.* 1 the earliest period of the Mesozoic era, beginning approximately 200 million years ago. 2 the rocks formed during this period. See **geology** for chart. *—adj.* of or having to do with the Triassic period or the rocks formed during it. [< G *Trias,* the name for a certain series of strata containing three types of deposit < LL *trias.* See TRIAD.]

trib·al (trīb′əl) *adj.* of or having to do with a tribe.

trib·al·ism (trīb′ə liz′əm) *n.* tribal organization and culture: *Economic expansion in Africa is causing the breakdown of tribalism.*

trib·a·lize (trīb′ə līz′) *v.* **-lized, -liz·ing.** 1 divide or organize into tribes. 2 confer tribal status on.

trib·al·ly (trīb′əl ē) *adv.* according to tribe; by tribe or tribes.

tri·bas·ic (trī bās′ik) *adj.* in chemistry: 1 of an acid, having three atoms of hydrogen replaceable by basic atoms or radicals. 2 having three atoms or radicals of a univalent metal. 3 having three basic hydroxyl (OH) radicals.

tribe (trīb) *n.* 1 a group of people united by race and customs under the same leaders: *African tribes, Indian tribes.* 2 a group of persons forming a community and claiming descent from a common ancestor. 3 a class or set of people: *the whole tribe of gossips.* 4 a group in the classification of plants or animals, usually forming a subdivision of an order, and containing a number of genera. 5 any group of series of animals or plants: *the feathery tribe.* 6 a class, group, kind, or sort of things. [< L *tribus*] **—Syn. 1** clan.

tribes·man (trībz′mən) *n.* **-men** (-mən). a member of a tribe.

trib·u·la·tion (trib′yů lā′shən) *n.* great trouble; severe trial; affliction. [ME < OF < LL *tribulatio, -onis,* ult. < L *tribulum* threshing sledge] **—Syn.** oppression, distress.

tri·bu·nal (tri bū′nəl or trī bū′nəl) *n.* 1 a court of justice; a place of judgment: *He was brought before the tribunal for trial.* 2 a place where judges sit in a law court. 3 something by or in which judgment is rendered; judicial or deciding authority: *the tribunal of the polls, the tribunal of the press.* [< L *tribunal* < *tribunus.* See TRIBUNE[1].]

trib·une[1] (trib′ūn) *n.* 1 in ancient Rome, an official chosen by the plebeians to protect their rights and interests. 2 a defender of the people. [ME < L *tribunus* < *tribus* tribe]

trib·une[2] (trib′ūn) *n.* a raised platform. [< Ital. *tribuna* tribunal]

trib·une·ship (trib′ūn ship′) *n.* the position, duties, or term of a tribune.

trib·u·tar·y (trib′yů ter′ē) *n.* **-tar·ies,** *adj.* —*n.* **1** a stream that flows into a larger stream or body of water: *The Ottawa River is a tributary of the St. Lawrence River.* **2** a person, country, etc. that pays tribute. —*adj.* **1** flowing into a larger stream or body of water. **2** paying tribute; required to pay tribute. **3** paid as tribute; of the nature of tribute. **4** contributing; helping.

trib·ute (trib′ūt) *n.* **1** money paid by one nation to another for peace or protection or because of some agreement. **2** any forced payment. **3** an acknowledgment of thanks or respect; compliment: *Remembrance Day is a tribute to our dead soldiers.* [ME < L *tributum* < *tribuere* allot < *tribus* tribe]

trice[1] (trīs) *v.* **triced, tric·ing.** haul up and fasten with a rope: *trice up a sail.* [ME < MDu. *trisen* hoist < *trise* pulley]

trice[2] (trīs) *n.* a very short time; moment; instant. [abstracted from phrase *at a trice* at a pull. Cf. TRICE[1].]

tri·cen·ten·ni·al (trī′sen ten′ē əl, -sen ten′yəl or -sen tēn′yəl) *adj. n.* tercentenary.

tri·ceps (trī′seps) *n.* in physiology, the large muscle at the back of the upper arm. It extends, or straightens, the arm. [< NL < L *triceps* three-headed < *tri-* three + *caput* head]

tri·chi·na (tri kī′nə) *n.* **-nae** (-nē or -nī). a small, slender worm that lives in the intestines and muscles of man and some animals. Trichinae usually get into the human body from pork that is infected with the larvae and is not cooked long enough to destroy them. [< NL < Gk. *trichinē*, fem. adj., of hair < *thrix, trichos* hair]

trich·i·no·sis (trik′ə nō′sis) *n.* a disease due to the presence of trichinae in the intestines and muscular tissues. [< NL]

trich·i·nous (trik′ə nəs) *adj.* having trichinosis; infected with trichinae.

trick (trik) *n.* **1** something done to deceive or cheat: *The false message was a trick to get him to leave the house.* **2** something pretended or unreal; illusion: *Those two lines are really the same length, but a trick of the eyesight makes one of them look longer.* **3** a clever act; a feat of skill: *We enjoyed the tricks of the trained animals.* **4** the best way of dealing with or doing something: *the trick of making pies.* **5** a piece of mischief; prank: *Stealing John's lunch was a mean trick.* **6** a peculiar habit or way of acting: *He has a trick of pulling at his collar.* **7** in card games, the cards played in one round. **8** a turn at steering a ship. **9** a turn at any job. **10 do** or **turn the trick,** do what one wants done.
—*v.* **1** deceive; cheat: *We were tricked into buying a poor car.* **2** play tricks. **3** dress. **4 trick out,** dress up; ornament. [ME < OF *trique*] —**Syn.** *n.* **1** artifice, stratagem, subterfuge, ruse. **3** exploit, stunt. **6** mannerism. –*v.* **1** defraud, cozen, delude. See **cheat.**

trick·er·y (trik′ər ē or trik′rē) *n.* **-er·ies.** the use of tricks; deception; cheating. —**Syn.** artifice, stratagem, imposture, duplicity.

trick·le (trik′əl) *v.* **-led, -ling,** *n.* —*v.* **1** flow or fall in drops or in a small stream: *Tears trickled down her cheeks. The brook trickled through the valley.* **2** cause to flow in drops or in a small stream: *He trickled the water into the container.* **3** come, go, pass, etc. slowly and unevenly: *An hour before the show people began to trickle into the theatre.* —*n.* **1** a small flow or stream. **2** a trickling. [ME *strikle* < *strike* flow, move, strike < OE *strīcan*] —**Syn.** *v.* **1** drip, dribble, ooze.

trick or treat a call used by children dressed in costumes at Halloween, going from door to door and begging for candy or other gifts under the threat of playing tricks if they are refused.

trick·ster (trik′stər) *n.* a cheat; deceiver.

trick·sy (trik′sē) *adj.* **1** mischievous; playful; frolicsome. **2** tricky. —**trick′si·ness,** *n.*

trick·y (trik′ē) *adj.* **trick·i·er, trick·i·est. 1** full of tricks; deceiving; cheating. **2** not doing what is expected; dangerous or difficult to handle: *The back door has a tricky lock.* —**trick′i·ly,** *adv.* —**trick′i·ness,** *n.* —**Syn. 1** deceptive, deceitful.

tri·col·or or **tri·col·our** (trī′kul′ər) *adj.* having three colors. —*n.* a flag having three colors. The tricolor of France has three equal vertical stripes of blue, white, and red. [< F (*drapeau*) *tricolore* tricolored (flag)]

tri·cot (trē′kō) *n.* **1** a knitted wool, cotton, or synthetic fabric made by hand or machine. **2** a kind of woollen cloth. **3** a close-fitting garment worn by ballet dancers. [< F *tricot*, ult. < Gmc.]

tric·o·tine (trik′ə tēn′) *n.* a kind of twilled woollen cloth.

tri·cus·pid (trī kus′pid) *adj.* having three points. —*n.* a tricuspid tooth. [< L *tricuspis, -idis* three-pointed < *tri-* three + *cuspis* tip]

tri·cy·cle (trī′sə kəl or trī′sik′əl) *n.* a three-wheeled vehicle worked by pedals attached to the large single wheel in front, now used especially by small children. [< F *tricycle* < *tri-* three (< L or Gk.) + *cycle*, ult. < Gk. *kyklos* ring, circle]

tri·dent (trī′dənt) *n.* a three-pronged spear, especially as the identifying attribute of Poseidon (Neptune), the ancient Greek and Roman god of the sea. —*adj.* three-pronged. [< L *tridens, -entis* < *tri-* three + *dens* tooth]

A sea god with a trident

tri·den·tate (trī den′tāt) *adj.* having three teeth or teethlike points; three-pronged.

tried (trīd) *adj.* tested; proved. —*v.* pt. and pp. of **try.**

tri·en·ni·al (trī en′ē əl) *adj.* **1** lasting three years. **2** occurring every three years. —*n.* **1** an event that occurs every three years. **2** the third anniversary of an event. [< L *triennium* three-year period < *tri-* three + *annus* year]

tri·en·ni·al·ly (trī en′ē əl ē) *adv.* once every three years.

tri·er (trī′ər) *n.* a person or thing that tries.

tri·fle (trī′fəl) *n. v.* **-fled, -fling.** —*n.* **1** something having little value or importance. **2** a small amount; a little bit. **3** a small amount of money. **4** a rich dessert made of sponge cake, whipped cream, custard, fruit, wine, etc. —*v.* **1** talk or act lightly, not seriously: *Don't trifle with serious matters.* **2** play or toy (*with*): *He trifled with his pencil and pen.* **3** spend (time, effort, money, etc.) on things having little value: *She had trifled away the whole morning.* [ME < OF *trufle*; origin uncertain]
Syn. *n.* **1** triviality, trinket, knickknack. –*v.* **1 Trifle, dally** = treat a person or thing without seriousness. **Trifle** = talk or act lightly, especially about something deserving serious treatment or respect, and often suggests playing with or at it to amuse oneself or occupy the time: *He is not a man to be trifled with.* **Dally** emphasizes amusing oneself by playing, especially at love or with thoughts, or by flirting with danger or temptation: *I have dallied with the idea of taking a trip.* **2** fiddle. **3** dawdle, idle.

tri·fler (trī′flər) *n.* a person who trifles; a frivolous, shallow person.

tri·fling (trī′fling) *adj.* **1** having little value; not important; small. **2** frivolous; shallow. —**tri′fling·ly,** *adv.* —**Syn. 1** trivial, paltry, petty, insignificant. **2** foolish.

tri·fo·li·ate (trī fō′lē it or trī fō′lē āt′) *adj.* having three leaves, or three parts like leaves. Clover is trifoliate. [< *tri-* + L *foliatus* leaved < *folium* leaf]

A trifoliate leaf

tri·fo·ri·um (trī fô′rē əm) *n.* **-ri·a** (-rē ə). in a church, a gallery above a side aisle or transept. See **clerestory** for diagram. [< Med.L *triforium*, apparently < L *tri-* three + *foris* door]

trig (trig) *adj.* neat; trim; smart-looking. [ME < ON *tryggr* trusty]

trig. 1 trigonometry. **2** trigonometric.

trig·ger (trig′ər) *n. v.* **-gered, -ger·ing.** —*n.* **1** the small lever pulled back by the finger in firing a gun. **2** any lever pulled or pressed to release a spring, catch, etc. **3** anything that sets off or initiates something else. **4 quick on the trigger, a** quick to shoot. **b** *Informal.* quick to act; mentally alert. —*v.* **1** set off (an explosion). **2** *Informal.* initiate; start: *trigger an outburst of violence.* [ult. < Du. *trekker* < *trekken* pull]

trig·ger-hap·py (trig′ər hap′ē) *adj. Informal.* shooting or inclined to shoot at the slightest provocation.

tri·glyph (trī′glif) *n.* in Doric architecture, the part of a frieze between two metopes, consisting typically of a rectangular block with two vertical grooves and a half groove at each side. See **metope** for picture. [< L < Gk. *triglyphos* < *tri* three + *glyphē* carving]

trigon. **1** trigonometry. **2** trigonometric.

trig·o·no·met·ric (trig′ə nə met′rik) *adj.* of or having to do with trigonometry.

trig·o·no·met·ri·cal (trig′ə nə met′rə kəl) *adj.* trigonometric.

trig·o·no·met·ri·cal·ly (trig′ə nə met′rik lē) *adv.* by or according to trigonometry.

trig·o·nom·e·try (trig′ə nom′ə trē) *n.* **1** the branch of mathematics that deals with the relations between the sides and angles of triangles and the calculations based on these. **2** a textbook or handbook dealing with this subject. [< NL *trigonometria*, ult. < Gk. *tri-* three + *gōnia* angle + *metron* measure]

tri·graph (trī′graf) *n.* three letters used to spell a single sound. *Example*: the *eau* in *beau.*

tri·he·dral (trī hē′drəl or trī hed′rəl) *adj.* of or having to do with a trihedron; formed by three planes meeting at a point.

tri·he·dron (trī hē′drən or trī hed′rən) *n.* **-drons, -dra** (-drə). a figure formed by three planes meeting at a point. [< *tri-* + Gk. *hedra* seat, base]

trike (trīk) *n. Informal.* tricycle.

tri·lat·er·al (trī lat′ər əl) *adj.* having three sides. [< L *trilaterus* < *tri-* three + *latus, lateris* side]

tri·lin·gual (trī ling′gwəl) *adj.* **1** able to speak three languages: *a trilingual person.* **2** using or involving three languages.

trill (tril) *v.* **1** sing, play, sound, or speak with a quivering, vibrating sound. **2** sing or play with a trill. **3** in phonetics, pronounce with rapid vibration of the tongue, etc. The Spanish trill the letters *rr.* —*n.* **1** the act or sound of trilling. **2** in music, a quick alternation of two notes either a tone or a half tone apart. **3** in phonetics: **a** a rapid vibration of the tongue, etc. **b** a consonant pronounced by such a vibration. Spanish *rr* is a trill. [< Ital. *trillare* < Gmc.]

tril·lion (tril′yən) *n. adj.* **1** in Canada, the United States, and France, 1 followed by 12 zeros. **2** in the British Isles, 1 followed by 18 zeros. [< F *trillion* < *tri-* three, modelled on *million* million]

tril·li·um (tril′ē əm) *n.* a plant having three leaves in a whorl from the centre of which rises a single flower: *The trillium is the floral emblem of Ontario.* [< NL *trillium* < L *tri-* three]

tri·lo·bate (trī lō′bāt or trī′lə bāt′) *adj.* having three lobes.

tri·lo·bite (trī′lə bīt′) *n.* an extinct arthropod, having three divisions of the body and jointed limbs. Fossil trilobites are widely found in Paleozoic rocks. [< NL *trilobita*, pl. < Gk. *tri-* three + *lobos* lobe]

tril·o·gy (tril′ə jē) *n.* **-gies.** three plays, operas, novels, etc. that fit together to make a related series. Any section of a trilogy is itself a complete work. [< Gk. *trilogia* < *tri-* three + *logos* story]

trim (trim) *v.* **trimmed, trim·ming,** *adj.* **trim·mer, trim·mest,** *n. adv.* —*v.* **1** put in good order; make neat by cutting away parts: *The gardener trimmed the hedge. The carpenter trimmed the lumber with a plane.* **2** remove (parts that are not needed or not neat): *trim dead leaves off plants.* **3** decorate: *The children trimmed the Christmas tree.* **4** balance (a boat, airplane, etc.) by arranging the load carried. **5** be or keep in balance. **6** change (opinions, views, etc.) to suit circumstances. **7** arrange (the sails) to fit wind and direction. **8** *Informal.* defeat heavily; beat. **9** *Informal.* scold.
—*adj.* **1** in good condition or order; neat: *A trim maid appeared.* **2** that is or appears to be well designed and maintained: *a trim little ketch.*
—*n.* **1** good condition or order: *get in trim for a race.* **2** condition; order: *That ship is in poor trim for a voyage.* **3** trimming: *the trim on a dress.* **4** equipment; outfit. **5** the position of a ship or aircraft when properly balanced. **6** the position or angle of the sails, yards, etc. in relation to the direction of the wind. **7** the visible woodwork inside a building. **8** woodwork used as a finish or ornament on the outside of a building. **9** the

hat, āge, cãre, fär; let, ēqual, tėrm; it, īce
hot, ōpen, ôrder; oil, out; cup, pu̇t, rüle, ūse
əbove, takən, pencəl, lemən, circəs
ch, child; ng, long; sh, ship
th, thin; ꟸH, then; zh, measure

upholstery, handles, and accessories inside an automobile. **10** the chrome, color scheme, etc. decorating the outside of an automobile. **11** a display in a store window.
—*adv.* in a trim manner. [OE *trymman* strengthen, make ready] —**trim′ly,** *adv.* —**trim′ness,** *n.* —**Syn.** *v.* **2** cut, clip, prune. **3** deck, adorn, garnish. -*adj.* See **neat.**

tri·ma·ran (trī′mə ran′) *n.* a boat with three hulls side by side. [< *tri-* + cata*maran*]

tri·mes·ter (trī mes′tər) *n.* **1** a third part of a school year. **2** a three-month period; a quarter of a year. [< F *trimestre* < L *trimestris* < *tri-* + *mensis* month]

trim·e·ter (trim′ə tər) *n.* a line of verse having three metrical feet. *Example*: "Below | the light | house top." —*adj.* consisting of three feet or measures. [< L < Gk. *trimetros* < *tri-* three + *metron* measure]

trim·mer (trim′ər) *n.* **1** a person or thing that trims: *a hat trimmer, a window trimmer.* **2** a person who changes his opinions, actions, etc. to suit circumstances.

trim·ming (trim′ing) *n.* **1** a decoration; ornament: *trimmings for a Christmas tree, trimmings for a dress.* **2** *Informal.* a decisive defeat; beating. **3** *Informal.* a scolding. **4 trimmings,** *pl.* **a** parts cut away in trimming. **b** *Informal.* additions to food: *turkey with trimmings.*

tri·month·ly (trī munth′lē) *adj.* occurring every three months.

tri·mor·phism (trī môr′fiz əm) *n.* **1** in mineralogy, the occurrence in the same compound of three different forms of a crystalline substance. **2** in botany, the occurrence in the same species or individual plant of three different types of leaf, flower, etc. **3** in zoology, the occurrence in one species of three types distinct in size, color, structure, etc. [< Gk. *trimorphis* < *tri-* + *morphē* form + E *-ism*]

tri·nal (trī′nəl) *adj.* composed of three parts; threefold.

trine (trīn) *adj.* **1** threefold; triple. **2** in astrology, of or having to do with the aspect of two planets 120 degrees distant from each other. —*n.* **Trine,** the Trinity. [< L *trinus* triple]

Trin·i·tar·i·an (trin′ə tãr′ē ən) *adj.* **1** believing in the Trinity. **2** having to do with the Trinity. —*n.* a person who believes in the Trinity.

tri·ni·tro·tol·u·ene (trī nī′trō tol′ū ēn′) *n.* a powerful explosive, known as T.N.T. [< *trinitro-*, a combining form meaning "of three nitro-groups" (NO_2) + *toluene*]

tri·ni·tro·tol·u·ol (trī nī′trō tol′ū ōl′) *n.* trinitrotoluene.

Trin·i·ty (trin′ə tē) *n.* **1** in Christianity, the union of Father, Son, and Holy Ghost in one divine nature. **2** *Informal.* Trinity Sunday. **3 trinity,** a group of three. **4 trinity,** a being three. [ME < OF < L *trinitas* < *trinus* triple]

Trinity Sunday the eighth Sunday after Easter.

trin·ket (tring′kit) *n.* **1** any small, fancy article, bit of jewellery, etc. **2** a trifle. [ME *trenket* little knife < ONF; ?< OF *trenchier, tranchier* cut]

tri·no·mi·al (trī nō′mē əl) *n.* **1** in mathematics, an expression consisting of three terms connected by plus or minus signs. *Example*: $a + bx^2 - 2$ is a trinomial. **2** in biology, the name of an animal or plant consisting of three words. —*adj.* consisting of three terms. [< *tri-* + *-nomial*, modelled after *binomial*]

tri·o (trē′ō) *n.* **-tri·os.** **1** in music: **a** a composition for three voices or instruments. **b** the second part or theme, often quiet and lyrical, of music in the dance form, marches, scherzos, etc. **c** three singers or players. **2** any group of three. [< Ital. *trio*, ult. < L *tres* three]

tri·ode (trī′ōd) *n.* in electronics, a vacuum tube that has an anode, a cathode, and a controlling grid.

tri·o·let (trī′ə lit) *n.* a poem having eight lines and only two rhymes. Lines 1, 4, and 7 are the same. Lines 2 and 8 are the same. [< F]

tri·ox·ide (trī ok′sīd or trī ok′sid) *n.* any oxide having three atoms of oxygen in each molecule.

trip (trip) *n. v.* **tripped, trip·ping.** —*n.* **1** a journey; voyage: *We took a trip to Europe.* **2** a stumble; slip. **3** the act of catching a person's foot to throw him down. **4** a mistake; blunder. **5** a light, quick tread; stepping lightly. **6** in machinery, a projecting part, catch, etc. for starting or checking some movement. **7** *Slang.* the mental state or experience induced by hallucinogenic drugs, such as LSD. [< v.]
—*v.* **1** stumble: *trip on the stairs.* **2** cause to stumble and fall: *The loose board tripped him.* **3** make a mistake; do something wrong: *He tripped on that difficult question.* **4** cause to make a mistake or blunder: *The difficult question tripped him.* **5** overthrow by catching in a mistake or blunder; outwit. **6** detect in an inconsistency or inaccuracy: *The examining board tripped him up several times.* **7** take light, quick steps: *She tripped across the floor.* **8** tip; tilt. **9** in machinery, release or operate (a catch, clutch, etc.) suddenly; operate, start, or set free (a mechanism, weight, etc.). **10** move past or be released by the pallet, as a cog on an escapement wheel of a watch or clock. **11** journey. [ME < OF *tripper* < Gmc.]
Syn. *n.* **1 Trip, journey, voyage** = a travelling from one place to another. **Trip** is the general word, usually suggesting return to the starting place, but not suggesting the length, purpose, manner, or means of travel: *How was your trip? He took a trip to Honolulu.* **Journey** applies to a long or very tiring trip by land to a place for a definite purpose: *He decided to make the journey to Mexico by car.* **Voyage** applies to a trip, usually long, by water: *The voyage to the Islands will be restful.* –*v.* **7** skip, caper.

tri·par·tite (trī pär′tīt) *adj.* **1** divided into three parts. **2** having three corresponding parts or copies. **3** made or shared by three parties: *a tripartite treaty.* [< L *tripartitus* < *tri-* three + *partitus,* pp. of *partiri* divide]

tripe (trīp) *n.* **1** the walls of the first and second stomachs of an ox, etc. used as food. **2** *Slang.* anything foolish, worthless, offensive, etc., especially in speech or writing. [ME < OF *tripe* entrails < Arabic *tharb*]

trip·ham·mer (trip′ham′ər) *n.* a heavy hammer raised and then let fall mechanically, worked by a trip (def. 6).

triph·thong (trif′thong or trip′thong) *n.* a union of three vowel sounds pronounced in one syllable. [< *diphthong,* with substitution of *tri-* for *di-*]

tri·plane (trī′plān′) *n.* an airplane having three wings, one above another.

tri·ple (trip′əl) *adj. n. v.* **-pled, -pling.** —*adj.* **1** having three parts. **2** three times as much or as many. —*n.* **1** a number, amount, etc. that is three times as much or as many. **2** in baseball, a hit by which a batter gets to third base. —*v.* **1** make or become three times as much or as many. **2** serve three purposes; play three parts. **3** in baseball, hit a triple. [< L *triplus* < *tres* three + *-plus* fold. Doublet of TREBLE.]

triple crown a tiara worn by the Pope.

triple play in baseball, a play that puts three men out.

tri·plet (trip′lit) *n.* **1** one of three children born at the same time from the same mother. **2** a group of three similar or equal things. **3** in music, a group of three notes to be performed in the time of two notes having the same time value. **4** three successive lines of poetry, usually rhyming and equal in length. [< *triple*]

triple time in music, time or rhythm having three beats to the measure.

tri·plex (trip′leks) *adj.* triple; threefold. —*n.* **1** in music, triple time. **2** *Cdn.* a three-storey building having three apartments. [< L *triplex* < *tri-* three + *plic-* fold]

trip·li·cate (*v.* trip′lə kāt′; *adj. n.* trip′lə kit) *v.* **-cat·ed, -cat·ing,** *adj. n.* —*v.* make threefold; triple. —*adj.* triple, threefold. —*n.* **1** one of three things exactly alike. **2 in triplicate,** in three copies exactly alike. [< L *triplicare* < *triplex* threefold]

trip·li·ca·tion (trip′lə kā′shən) *n.* **1** a triplicating or being triplicated. **2** something triplicated.

tri·ply (trip′lē) *adv.* in a triple manner; three times.

trip·man (trip′man′) *n.* **-men** (-men′). *Cdn.* formerly, a temporary hand hired for duty on a canoe or other trip; a voyageur.

tri·pod (trī′pod) *n.* a stool, frame, or stand having three legs. A camera may be supported on a tripod. [< L < Gk. *tripous, -odos* < *tri-* three + *pous* foot]

Tri·pol·i·tan (tri pol′ə tən) *adj.* of or having to do with Tripoli, a region in Libya, or its people. —*n.* a native or inhabitant of Tripoli.

trip·per (trip′ər) *n.* **1** a person or thing that trips. **2** a device in a machine that releases a catch, etc. **3** *Esp.Brit.* a person who takes a trip.

trip·ping (trip′ing) *adj.* light and quick. —**trip′ping·ly,** *adv.*

trip·tych (trip′tik) *n.* **1** a set of three panels side by side, having pictures, carvings, etc. on them. **2** a hinged, three-leaved writing tablet. [< Gk. *triptychos* three-layered < *tri-* three + *ptyx* fold]

tri·reme (trī′rēm) *n.* in ancient times, a ship having three rows of oars, one above the other, on each side. [< L *triremis* < *tri-* three + *remus* oar]

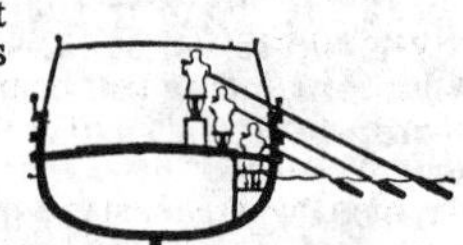

A trireme. The diagram shows the position of the rowers.

tri·sect (trī sekt′) *v.* **1** divide into three parts. **2** in geometry, divide into three equal parts. [< *tri-* + L *sectus,* pp. of *secare* cut] —**tri·sec′tion,** *n.*

tri·ser·vice or **tri-ser·vice** (trī sėr′vis) *adj.* of or for the three armed services—the navy, army, and air force.

Tris·tan (tris′tən) *n.* Tristram.

Tris·tram (tris′trəm) *n.* in Arthurian legend, one of the most famous knights of the Round Table. His love for Iseult, wife of King Mark, is the subject of many stories.

tris·yl·lab·ic (trī′sə lab′ik or tris′ə lab′ik) *adj.* having three syllables.

tris·yl·lab·i·cal·ly (trī′sə lab′ik lē or tris′ə lab′ik lē) *adv.* as or in three syllables.

tri·syl·la·ble (trī sil′ə bəl or tri sil′ə bəl) *n.* a word of three syllables. *Educate* is a trisyllable.

trite (trīt) *adj.* **trit·er, trit·est.** worn out by use; no longer new or interesting; commonplace: "*Cheeks like roses*" *is a trite expression.* [< L *tritus,* pp. of *terere* rub away] —**trite′ly,** *adv.* —**trite′ness,** *n.* —**Syn.** hackneyed, stereotyped, banal, stale.

trit·i·um (trit′ē əm or trish′ē əm) *n.* an isotope of hydrogen. Tritium is the explosive used in a hydrogen bomb. *Symbol:* T or H^3 [< NL < Gk. *tritos* third]

tri·ton[1] (trī′tən) *n.* **1** any of a family of marine gastropods, especially any of a group having a brightly colored, spiral, trumpet-shaped shell. **2** the shell of such an animal. [< *Triton*]

tri·ton[2] (trī′ton) *n.* the nucleus of a tritium atom. [< *trit*ium + *-on,* as in *electron*]

Tri·ton (trī′tən) *n.* in Greek mythology, a sea god and a son of Poseidon, represented as having the head and body of a man and the tail of a fish, and carrying a conch shell.

trit·u·rate (trich′ů rāt′) *v.* **-rat·ed, -rat·ing,** *n.* —*v.* rub, crush, or grind into a very fine powder. —*n.* any substance that is ground into a very fine powder. [< LL *triturare* thresh, ult. < L *terere* rub]

trit·u·ra·tion (trich′ů rā′shən) *n.* **1** a reducing or being reduced to fine particles of powder by grinding, rubbing, etc. **2** a medicine, etc. produced by grinding into a fine powder.

tri·umph (trī′umf) *n.* **1** the act or fact of being victorious; victory: *final triumph over the enemy.* **2** a single success or achievement: *The use of atomic energy is a triumph of modern science.* **3** joy because of victory or success. **4** in ancient Rome, a procession in honor of a victorious general. **5 in triumph, a** triumphant. **b** triumphantly: *He brought home the prize in triumph.* —*v.* **1** gain victory; win success: *Our team triumphed over theirs.* **2** rejoice because of victory or success. [< L *triumphus*] —**Syn.** *n.* **1** conquest. See **victory. 3** exultation, elation. –*v.* **1** conquer. **2** exult.

tri·um·phal (trī um′fəl) *adj.* of, having to do with, or for a triumph; celebrating a victory.

tri·um·phant (trī um′fənt) *adj.* **1** victorious; successful. **2** rejoicing because of victory or success. —**tri·um′phant·ly,** *adv.* —**Syn. 2** exultant, jubilant.

tri·um·vir (trī um′vər) *n.* **-virs** or **-vi·ri** -və rī′ or -və rē′). **1** in ancient Rome, one of three men who shared the same public office. **2** one of any three persons sharing power or authority. [< L *triumvir*, abstracted from phrase *trium virorum* "of three men"]

tri·um·vi·rate (trī um′və rit or trī um′və rāt′) *n.* **1** the position or term of office of a triumvir. **2** government by three men together. **3** any association of three in office or authority. **4** any group of three.

tri·une (trī′ūn) *adj.* three in one: *the triune God.* [< *tri-* + L *unus* one]

tri·u·ni·ty (trī ū′nə tē) *n.* the state of being triune.

tri·va·lence (trī vā′ləns or triv′ə ləns) *n.* the state or quality of being trivalent.

tri·va·len·cy (trī vā′lən sē or triv′ə lən sē) *n.* trivalence.

tri·va·lent (trī vā′lənt or triv′ə lənt) *adj.* having a valence of three. [< *tri-* + L *valens, -entis*, ppr. of *valere* be worth]

triv·et (triv′it) *n.* a stand or support usually having three legs or feet. Trivets are used over fire and under hot platters, etc. [< L *tri-* three + OE *-fēte* footed]

triv·i·a (triv′ē ə) *n.pl.* trifles; trivialities. [? < *trivial*]

triv·i·al (triv′ē əl) *adj.* **1** minor; not important; trifling; insignificant. **2** *Archaic.* not new or interesting; ordinary. [< L *trivialis* vulgar, originally, of the crossroads, ult. < *tri-* three + *via* road] **—triv′i·al·ly,** *adv.* **—Syn. 1** paltry, slight, small.

triv·i·al·i·ty (triv′ē al′ə tē) *n.* **-ties. 1** a trivial quality. **2** a trivial thing, remark, affair, etc.; trifle.

triv·i·um (triv′ē əm) *n.* **-i·a** (-ē ə). in the Middle Ages, grammar, rhetoric, and logic, the first group of the seven liberal arts; opposed to *quadrivium.* [< Med.L *trivium* a triple way < L *tri-* + *via* way]

tri·week·ly (trī wēk′lē) *adv. n.* **-lies,** *adj.* —*adv.* **1** once every three weeks. **2** three times a week. —*n.* newspaper or magazine published triweekly. —*adj.* occurring or appearing triweekly.

tro·cha·ic (trō kā′ik) *adj.* of trochees. —*n.* a line or poem in trochees.

tro·che (trō′kē) *n.* a small medicinal tablet or lozenge, usually round: *cough troches.* [< obs. *trochisk* < F < LL *trochiscus* < Gk. *trochiskos*, dim. of *trochos* wheel]

tro·chee (trō′kē) *n.* in poetry, a foot or measure consisting of two syllables, the first accented and the second unaccented or the first long and the second short. *Example*:

"Síng a | sóng of | síxpence."

[< L < Gk. *trochaios*, originally, running < *trochos* a course < *trechein* run]

trod (trod) *v.* a pt. and a pp. of **tread.**

trod·den (trod′ən) *v.* a pp. of **tread.**

trode (trōd) *v. Archaic.* a pt. of **tread.**

trog·lo·dyte (trog′lə dīt′) *n.* **1** a cave man. **2** a person living in seclusion; hermit. **3** a person of a degraded type or brutish nature, especially one who dwells in and is seemingly indifferent to an environment of filth, vice, etc. **4** an anthropoid ape, such as a gorilla. [< L < Gk. *trōglodytēs* < *trōglē* cave + *dyein* go in]

troi·ka (troi′kə) *n.* **1** in Russia: **a** a sleigh, wagon, or other vehicle pulled by three horses abreast. **b** the horses, or the horses and vehicle together. **2** a group of three rulers sharing power; triumvirate. [< Russian < *troie* three together]

Tro·jan (trō′jən) *adj.* of or having to do with Troy, in ancient times a city in N.W. Asia Minor, or its people. —*n.* **1** a native or inhabitant of Troy. **2** a person who shows courage or energy: *They all worked like Trojans.* [< L *Trojanus* < *Troja, Troia* Troy < Gk.]

Trojan horse 1 in Greek legend, a huge wooden horse in which the Greeks concealed soldiers and had them brought into Troy during the Trojan War. **2** any person or group stationed inside a country, institution, etc. to sabotage or otherwise disrupt its activities.

Trojan War in Greek legend, a ten years' war carried on by the Greeks against Troy to get back Helen, wife of King Menelaus of Sparta. Helen had been carried off by Paris, son of King Priam of Troy.

hat, āge, cãre, fär; let, ēqual, tėrm; it, īce
hot, ōpen, ôrder; oil, out; cup, pu̇t, rüle, ūse
əbove, takən, pencəl, lemən, circəs
ch, child; ng, long; sh, ship
th, thin; ᴛʜ, then; zh, measure

troll[1] (trōl) *v.* **1** fish (for) with a moving line. In trolling, a man usually trails the line behind his boat near the surface. **2** *Archaic.* **a** sing in a full, rolling voice. **b** sing in succession. When three people troll a round or catch, the soprano sings one line, the alto comes in next with the same line, and then the bass sings it, and so on, while the others keep on singing. **3** make revolve; roll.
—*n.* **1** a song whose parts are sung in succession; round: "*Three Blind Mice*" *is a well-known troll.* **2** the reel of a fishing rod. **3** a lure or bait for fishing. **4** a trolling. [ME *trollen* stroll < OF *troller* wander < Gmc.] **—troll′er,** *n.*

troll[2] (trōl) *n.* in Scandinavian folklore, an ugly dwarf or giant living underground or in caves. [< ON]

trol·ley (trol′ē) *n.* **-leys. 1** a pulley moving against a wire to carry electricity to a streetcar, electric engine, etc. **2** a trolley car. **3** a pulley running on an overhead track, used to support and move a load. **4** *Brit.* a truck pushed by hand; handcart. [probably < *troll*[1] in sense of "roll"]

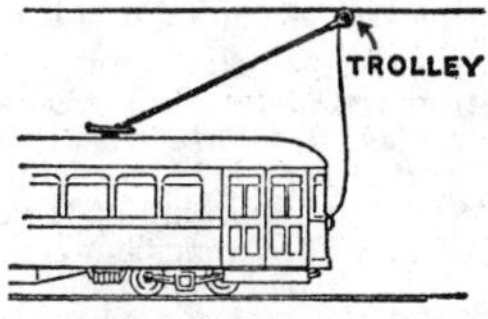

A trolley (def. 1)

trolley car a streetcar propelled electrically. The current for a trolley car is often taken from an overhead wire by means of a trolley.

trol·lop (trol′əp) *n.* **1** an untidy or slovenly woman. **2** a morally loose woman; slut. **3** a prostitute. [probably <*troll*[1]] **—Syn. 1** slattern.

trom·bone (trom′bōn or trom bōn′) *n.* a musical wind instrument resembling a trumpet and having either a sliding piece or, less often, valves for varying the pitch. [< Ital. *trombone* < *tromba* trumpet < Gmc.]

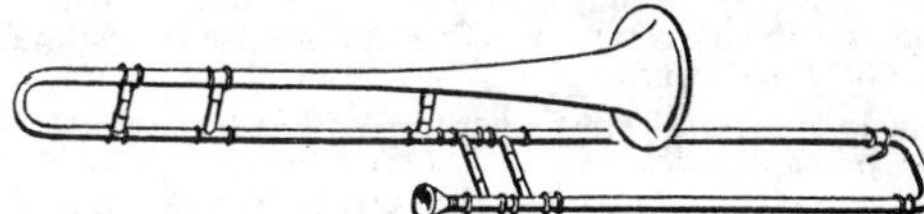
A slide trombone

trom·bon·ist (trom′bōn ist or trom bōn′ist) *n.* a person who plays the trombone.

troop (trüp) *n.* **1** a group or band of persons: *a troop of boys.* **2** a herd, flock, or swarm: *a troop of deer.* **3** in the army, a formation of cavalry or armored forces smaller than a squadron; any similar group in other army units. **4** a band of Boy Scouts: *the 4th Kingston troop.* **5 troops,** *pl.* soldiers.
—*v.* **1** gather in troops or bands; move together: *The children trooped around the teacher.* **2** carry (the colors) before a formation of troops as part of an official ceremony. **3** walk; go; go away: *The young boys trooped off after the older ones.* [< F *troupe*, ult. < LL *troppus* herd < Gmc.] **—Syn.** *n.* **1** crowd, multitude, throng.

troop·er (trüp′ər) *n.* **1** in the army, a soldier in a cavalry regiment or an armored regiment. **2** troopship.

troop leader 1 the person in charge of a military troop. **2** the person in charge of a troop of Boy Scouts or Girl Guides.

troop·ship (trüp′ship′) *n.* a ship used to carry soldiers; transport.

trope (trōp) *n.* **1** the use of a word or phrase in a sense different from its ordinary meaning. **2** a word or phrase so used. *Example*:

"All in a hot and *copper* sky,
The *bloody* sun at noon."

[< L < Gk. *tropos* turn]

tro·phied (trō′fēd) *adj.* decorated with trophies: *trophied walls.*

tro·phy (trō′fē) *n.* **-phies. 1** a memorial of victory: *The* *hunter kept the lion's skin and head as trophies.* 2 captured arms, flags, etc. of a defeated enemy set up on the field of battle or elsewhere as a memorial of victory; an ornament representing a group of weapons; any monument serving as a memorial of victory. 3 a prize cup, etc. awarded to a victorious person or team: *a tennis trophy.* 4 anything serving as a remembrance. [< F *trophée* < L *trophaeum*, for *tropaeum* < Gk. *tropaion* < *tropē* rout, originally, turn]

trop·ic (trop′ik) *n.* **1** either of two imaginary circles around the earth, one 23.27 degrees north and one 23.27 degrees south of the equator. The tropic of Cancer is the northern circle, and the tropic of Capricorn is the southern circle. **2** either of two imaginary circles in the celestial sphere, the limits reached by the sun in its apparent journey north and south. **3 tropics** or **Tropics**, *pl.* the zone between latitudes 23.27 degrees north and south or between 30 degrees north and south, the hottest part of the earth. —*adj.* of or having to do with the tropics; belonging to the Torrid Zone. [< L *tropicus* < Gk. *tropikos* pertaining to a turn < *tropē* a turn, a change]

trop·i·cal[1] (trop′ə kəl) *adj.* **1** of or having to do with the tropics: *Bananas are tropical fruit.* **2** occurring in the tropics: *tropical diseases.* **3** of clothes or fabrics, suitable for the tropics; lightweight; cool: *tropical worsteds.* **4** very hot; burning or fervent. **5** like the growth in those parts of the tropics having abundant rainfall; luxuriant. —*n. Informal.* a man's lightweight suit for warm or hot weather. —**trop′i·cal·ly,** *adv.*

trop·i·cal[2] (trop′ə kəl) *adj.* **1** having to do with or involving a trope or tropes. **2** of the nature of a trope or tropes; metaphorical; figurative.

tropic bird a tropical sea bird that has webbed feet and two very long feathers in the tail.

tropic of Cancer an imaginary circle around the earth, 23.27 degrees north of the equator; the northern boundary of the Torrid Zone. See **Capricorn** for diagram.

tropic of Capricorn an imaginary circle around the earth, 23.27 degrees south of the equator; the southern boundary of the Torrid Zone. See **Capricorn** for diagram.

tro·pism (trō′piz əm) *n.* in biology, the tendency of an animal or plant to turn or move in response to a stimulus. [< Gk. *tropē* a turning]

tro·pis·tic (trō pis′tik) *adj.* of or having to do with a tropism.

trop·o·sphere (trop′ə sfēr′) *n.* a layer of the atmosphere between the earth and the stratosphere, within which there is a steady fall of temperature as the altitude increases. Most cloud formations occur in the troposphere. [< Gk. *tropē* a turn, a change + E *sphere*]

trop·o·spher·ic (trop′ə sfer′ik or -sfēr′ik) *adj.* of or having to do with the troposphere.

trop·po (trop′ō; *Italian,* trôp′pō) *adv. Italian.* too much. *Example: allegro ma non troppo,* fast but not too fast.

trot (trot) *v.* **trot·ted, trot·ting,** *n.* —*v.* **1** of horses, etc., go at a gait between a walk and a run by lifting the right forefoot and the left hind foot at about the same time. **2** ride a horse at a trot. **3** make (a horse, etc.) trot. **4** run, but not quickly. **5 trot out,** *Informal.* bring out for others to see.
—*n.* **1** the motion or gait of a trotting horse, etc. **2** a brisk, steady movement. **3** the sound of trotting. **4** a single race in a program of harness racing. [ME < OF *trotter* < Gmc.]

troth (troth or trōth) *n.* **1** faithfulness; fidelity; loyalty. **2** a promise. **3** truth. **4** a betrothal. **5 plight one's troth, a** promise to marry. **b** promise to be faithful.
—*v.* **1** promise. **2** betroth. [OE *trēowth* < *trēow* faith]

trot·line (trot′līn′) *n.* in fishing, a long line with short lines and baited hooks attached at regular intervals.

Trot·sky·ism (trot′skē iz′əm) *n.* the social, political, and economic principles of Leon Trotsky (1879-1940), a Russian revolutionary leader, especially the principle that world-wide communist revolution must be put before everything else, including Soviet growth and development.

Trot·sky·ite (trot′skē īt′) *n.* a follower of Leon Trotsky; a believer in Trotskyism.

trot·ter (trot′ər) *n.* **1** a horse that trots. **2** a horse bred and trained to trot. **3** a sheep's or pig's foot used for food.

trou·ba·dour (trü′bə dôr′ or trü′bə dür′) *n.* one of the lyric poets of S. France, E. Spain, and N. Italy from the 11th to the 13th century. The troubadours wrote mainly about love and chivalry. [< F < Provençal *trobador,* ult. < LL *tropus* song, mode (in music) < Gk. *tropos* mode, style (in music), originally, a turn]

trou·ble (trub′əl) *n. v.* **-bled, -bling.** —*n.* **1** distress; worry; difficulty: *That boy makes trouble for his teachers.* **2** an instance of this; a distressing or vexatious circumstance, occurrence, or experience: *a life containing many troubles.* **3** an occasion or cause of affliction, distress, vexation, etc.: *Is she a trouble to you?* **4** a disturbance; disorder: *political troubles.* **5** extra work; bother; effort: *Take the trouble to do careful work.* **6** an ailment; disease: *She suffers from heart trouble.*
—*v.* **1** cause distress or worry to: *The lack of business troubled him.* **2** distress (with something disagreeable and unwelcome); vex; annoy; bother: *be troubled with poor eyesight.* **3** put to inconvenience; require extra work or effort of: *May I trouble you to pass the sugar?* **4** cause oneself inconvenience: *Don't trouble to come to the door.* **5** hurt; pain: *His wound troubles him.* [ME < OF *truble* < *trubler* trouble, ult. < L *turba* turmoil] —**Syn.** *n.* **1** anxiety, affliction. -*v.* **1** annoy, afflict.

trou·ble·mak·er (trub′əl māk′ər) *n.* a person who causes trouble for others.

trou·ble·mak·ing (trub′əl māk′ing) *n.* the actions of a troublemaker. —*adj.* causing or making trouble.

trou·ble-shoot·er (trub′əl shüt′ər) *n.* a person who discovers and eliminates causes of trouble.

trou·ble-shoot·ing (trub′əl shüt′ing) *n.* the efforts or activities of a trouble-shooter. —*adj.* of or having to do with the work of a trouble-shooter.

trou·ble·some (trub′əl səm) *adj.* causing trouble; annoying. —**trou′ble·some·ly,** *adv.* —**trou′ble·some·ness,** *n.* —**Syn.** disturbing, distressing, harassing, vexatious, bothersome.

trou·blous (trub′ləs) *adj.* **1** disturbed; restless. **2** troublesome.

trough (trof) *n.* **1** a long, narrow container for holding food or water: *a watering trough.* **2** something shaped like this: *The baker uses a trough for kneading dough.* **3** a channel for carrying water; gutter. **4** a long hollow between two ridges, etc.: *the trough between two waves.* **5** in meteorology, a long, narrow area of relatively low barometric pressure. **6** in geology, a basin-shaped depression; the lowest part of a synclinal fold. [OE *trōh*] —**trough′like′,** *adj.*

trounce (trouns) *v.* **trounced, trounc·ing. 1** beat; thrash. **2** *Informal.* defeat severely in a contest, etc. [origin uncertain]

troupe (trüp) *n. v.* **trouped, troup·ing.** —*n.* a band; company, especially a group of actors, singers, or acrobats. —*v.* tour or travel with a troupe. [< F]

troup·er (trüp′ər) *n.* **1** a member of a theatrical troupe. **2** an old, experienced actor.

trou·sers (trou′zərz) *n.pl.* **1** an outer garment especially for men and boys, having legs and reaching from the waist to the ankles or knees. **2** the loose, baglike drawers or pantaloons that are a part of the native dress of both men and women in certain Moslem countries. **3** the lower part of any of certain two-piece garments, especially pyjamas. —*adj.* **trouser,** of or having to do with trousers. [< *trouse* < Irish *triubhas*] —**Syn.** breeches, pants, knickerbockers. ☛ See **pants** for usage note.

trous·seau (trü′sō or trü sō′) *n.* **trous·seaux** (trü′sōz or trü sōz′) or **trous·seaus.** a bride's outfit of clothes, linen, etc. [< F *trousseau,* originally, bundle]

trout (trout) *n.* **trout** or **trouts.** any of certain freshwater food and game fish of the same family as the salmon and, in North America, as the char. [OE *trūht* < LL *tructa, trocta,* probably < Gk. *trōktēs,* literally, gnawer < *trōgein* gnaw]

trow (trō) *v. Archaic.* believe; think. [OE *truwian*]

trow·el (trou′əl) *n.* **1** a tool for spreading or smoothing plaster or mortar. **2** a tool for taking up plants, loosening dirt. etc. See picture on the next page. [ME < OF *truele* < LL *truella,* dim. of L *trua* skimmer]

troy (troi) *adj.* in or by troy weight. [< *Troyes*, a city in France]

troy weight a standard system of weights used for gems and precious metals. One pound troy weight equals a little over four-fifths of an ordinary pound.

24 grains = 1 pennyweight
20 pennyweight = 1 ounce
12 ounces = 1 pound

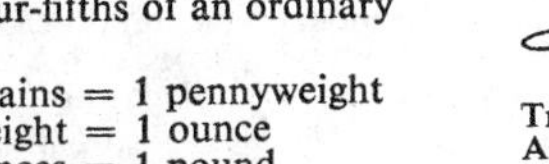

Trowels: A, for plaster; B, for plants.

Trp. or **trp.** troop.

trs. transpose.

tru·an·cy (trü′ən sē) *n.* **-cies.** the act or habit of staying away from school without permission; truant behavior.

tru·ant (trü′ənt) *n.* **1** a child who stays away from school without permission. **2** a person who neglects his duty. **3 play truant, a** stay away from school without permission. **b** stay away from work or duties. —*adj.* **1** staying away from school without permission. **2** guilty of neglecting a duty. **3** lazy. **4** wandering. [ME < OF *truant*, probably < Celtic]

truce (trüs) *n.* **1** a stop in fighting; peace for a short time: *A truce was declared between the two armies.* **2** an agreement or treaty effecting this; armistice: *sign a truce.* **3** a rest from trouble or pain. [ME *trewes*, pl. of *trewe*, OE *trēow* faith, treaty]

truck[1] (truk) *n.* **1** a motor vehicle designed primarily for the carrying of things rather than people, ranging in size from small vehicles used to carry tools, deliver parcels, etc. to large vehicles used to carry very heavy objects, commodities in bulk, etc. **2** formerly, any of various strongly built carts, wagons, etc. used for a similar purpose. **3** a frame on small wheels for moving trunks, etc. **4** a strongly built, rectangular platform resting on four wheels, used to move heavy or bulky objects, as in a warehouse, factory, etc. **5** any of various small, light, four-wheeled conveyances used in stores, libraries, etc., moved by pushing or pulling. **6** a frame with two or more pairs of wheels for supporting the end of a railway car, locomotive, etc. **7** a low, flat car. **8** a small wheel. **9** a wooden disk at the top of a flagstaff or mast with holes for the ropes. —*v.* **1** carry on a truck. **2** drive a truck. **3** engage in trucking goods, especially as a business; operate a trucking business. —*adj.* of or for a truck; used on trucks. [? < L *trochus* iron hoop < Gk. *trochos* wheel]

truck[2] (truk) *n.* **1** vegetables raised for market. **2** small articles of little value; odds and ends. **3** *Informal.* rubbish; trash. **4** *Informal.* dealings. **5** exchange; barter. **6** the payment of wages in goods, etc. rather than in money. [< v.] —*v.* exchange; barter. —*adj.* of truck; having to do with truck. [ME < OF *troquer*]

truck·age (truk′ij) *n.* **1** carrying of goods, etc. by trucks. **2** the charge for carrying by truck.

truck·er (truk′ər) *n.* **1** a person who drives a truck. **2** a person whose business is carrying goods, etc. by trucks.

truck farm or **garden** a farm where vegetables are raised for market.

truck·le[1] (truk′əl) *v.* **-led, -ling. 1** give up or submit tamely; be servile: *That man got his position by truckling to his superiors and flattering them.* **2** move on rollers. [ult. < *truckle bed*, formerly used by servants and inferiors] —**truck′ler,** *n.* —**truck′ling·ly,** *adv.* —**Syn. 1** cringe, fawn.

truck·le[2] (truk′əl) *n.* **1** a small wheel. **2** a truckle bed. [< L *trochlea* < Gk. *trochilea* sheaf of a pulley]

truckle bed trundle bed.

truck·man (truk′mən) *n.* **-men** (-mən). a man who drives a truck.

truc·u·lence (truk′yů ləns or trü′kyů ləns) *n.* savage threatening or bullying; fierceness and cruelty.

truc·u·len·cy (truk′yů lən sē or trü′kyů lən sē) *n.* truculence.

truc·u·lent (truk′yů lənt or trü′kyů lənt) *adj.* **1** savagely threatening or bullying; fierce and cruel: *a truculent bully.* **2** ruthless and scathing in attack; harsh: *truculent satire.* [< L *truculentus* < *trux, trucis* fierce] —**truc′u·lent·ly,** *adv.*

trudge (truj) *v.* **trudged, trudg·ing,** *n.* —*v.* **1** walk. **2** walk wearily or with effort. —*n.* a hard or weary walk: *It was a long trudge up the hill.* [origin uncertain] —**trudg′er,** *n.*

hat, āge, cãre, fär; let, ēqual, tėrm; it, īce
hot, ōpen, ôrder; oil, out; cup, pu̇t, rüle, ūse
əbove, takən, pencəl, lemən, circəs
ch, child; ng, long; sh, ship
th, thin; ᴛʜ, then; zh, measure

trudg·en stroke (truj′ən) in swimming, a stroke in which a double overarm stroke is used. [after John *Trudgen* (1852-1902), a British swimmer]

true (trü) *adj.* **tru·er, tru·est,** *n.* *v.* **trued, tru·ing,** *adv.* —*adj.* **1** agreeing with fact; not false: *It is true that 6 and 4 are 10.* **2** real; genuine: *true gold, true kindness.* **3** faithful; loyal: *a true patriot.* **4** agreeing with a standard; right; proper; correct; exact; accurate: *a true copy, a true voice, true to type.* **5** representative of the class named: *A sweet potato is not a true potato.* **6** rightful; lawful: *the true heir to the property.* **7** reliable; sure: *a true sign.* **8** accurately formed, fitted, or placed: *a true angle.* **9** steady in direction, force, etc.; unchanging: *The arrow made a true course through the air.* **10** *Archaic.* truthful. **11** honest. **12 come true,** happen as expected; become real. —*n.* **1** that which is true. **2** exact or accurate formation, position, or adjustment: *A slanting door is out of true.* —*v.* make true; shape, place, or make in the exact position, form, etc. required. —*adv.* **1** in a true manner; truly; exactly: *His words ring true.* **2** in agreement with the ancestral type: *breed true.* [OE *trīewe, trēowe*] —**true′ness,** *n.* —**Syn.** *adj.* **1** See **real.**

true bill *Esp.U.S.* in law, a bill of indictment found by a grand jury to be supported by enough evidence to justify the case being brought to trial.

true-blue (trü′blü′) *adj.* unchanging; staunch; loyal.

true-heart·ed (trü′här′tid) *adj.* faithful; loyal.

true·love (trü′luv′) *n.* a faithful lover; sweetheart.

truelove knot a bowknot that is hard to untie, standing for true and lasting love.

true-lover's knot truelove knot.

truf·fle (truf′əl or trü′fəl) *n.* an edible fungus that grows underground. [probably ult. < F *truffe*]

tru·ism (trü′iz əm) *n.* a statement that is generally accepted as true, such as "Health is a blessing."

trull (trul) *n.* a prostitute; strumpet. [? < G *Trulle*]

tru·ly (trü′lē) *adv.* **1** in a true manner; exactly; rightly; faithfully. **2** in fact; really.

trump[1] (trump) *n.* **1** in card games: **a** any playing card of a suit that for the time ranks higher than the other suits. **b** the suit itself. **2** *Informal.* a fine, dependable person. —*v.* **1** in card games: **a** take (a trick, card, etc.) with a trump. **b** play a card of the suit that is trump. **2** be better than; surpass; beat. **3 trump up,** think up or invent falsely: *He trumped up an excuse for being late.* [alteration of *triumph*]

trump[2] (trump) *Archaic or poetic.* —*n.* **1** a trumpet. **2** the sound of a trumpet. —*v.* trumpet. [ME < OF *trompe* < Gmc.]

trump[3] (trump) *v.* make (up) to deceive. [? special use of *trump*[1]]

trump·er·y (trump′ər ē or trump′rē) *n.* **-er·ies,** *adj.* —*n.* something showy but without value; worthless ornaments; useless stuff; rubbish; nonsense. —*adj.* showy but without value; trifling; worthless; useless; nonsensical. [< F *tromperie* < *tromper* deceive]

trump·et (trum′pit) *n.* **1** a brass musical wind instrument that has a looped tube with a flaring bell at one end and three valves to vary the pitch. The trumpet has a sharp, clear tone and can produce great volume. **2** anything shaped like a trumpet: *The deaf old lady has an ear trumpet to help her hearing.* **3** a sound like that of a trumpet. **4** a

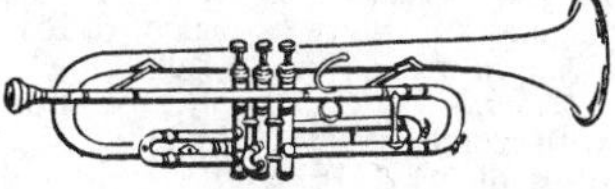
A trumpet

trumpeter. **5 blow one's own trumpet,** talk boastfully; praise oneself. —*v.* **1** blow a trumpet. **2** make a sound like a trumpet: *The elephant trumpeted.* **3** proclaim loudly or widely: *She will trumpet that story all over town.* [ME < OF *trompette,* dim. of *trompe.* See TRUMP.]

trumpet creeper a climbing vine that has clusters of large, red flowers that are shaped like trumpets.

trum·pet·er (trum′pə tər) *n.* **1** a person who trumpets. **2** a large North American wild swan. **3** a large South American bird having long legs and neck, related to the cranes. **4** a kind of domestic pigeon.

trumpet flower a trumpet creeper.

trumpet vine a trumpet creeper.

trun·cate (trung′kāt′) *v.* **-cat·ed, -cat·ing,** *adj.* —*v.* cut off a part of. —*adj.* cut off; blunt, as if cut off: *the truncate leaf of the tulip tree.* [< L *truncare* < *truncus* maimed] —**trun·ca′tion,** *n.*

A truncate leaf

trun·cheon (trun′chən) *n.* **1** *Esp.Brit.* a stick; club: *a policeman's truncheon.* **2** a staff of office or authority: *a herald's truncheon.* —*v.* beat with a club. [ME < OF *tronchon,* ult. < *truncus.* See TRUNK.]

trun·dle (trun′dəl) *v.* **-dled, -dling,** *n.* —*v.* **1** roll along; push along: *The workman trundled a wheelbarrow hour after hour.* **2** whirl; revolve. [probably < OF *trondeler* roll < Gmc.] —*n.* **1** a rolling; rolling along. **2** a small wheel; caster. **3** a trundle bed. **4** *Obs.* a low cart or wagon on small wheels. [ME, var. of *trendle* < OE *trendel* ring, disk]

trundle bed a low bed moving on small wheels or casters. It can be pushed under a regular bed when not in use; truckle bed.

trunk (trungk) *n.* **1** the main stem of a tree, as distinct from the branches and the roots. **2** the main part of anything: *the trunk of a column.* **3** a big box for holding clothes, etc. when travelling. **4** an enclosed compartment in an automobile for storing baggage, a spare tire, tools, etc. **5** a body without the head, arms, and legs. **6** the main body of a blood vessel, nerve, or similar structure as distinct from its branches. **7** an elephant's snout. **8** a trunk line. **9** a telephone circuit between two central offices or exchanges, used to make connections between individual subscribers. **10 trunks,** *pl.* very short pants or breeches worn by athletes, swimmers, acrobats, etc. —*adj.* main; chief: *the trunk line of a railway.* [< L *truncus,* originally adj., mutilated]

trunk hose full, baglike breeches reaching halfway down the thigh, or lower, worn by men in the 16th and 17th centuries.

trunk line 1 the main line of a railway, canal, etc. **2** a line between telephone exchanges.

trun·nion (trun′yən) *n.* either of the two round projections of a cannon, one on each side, which support it on its carriage. [< F *trognon* trunk < L *truncus;* influenced by F *moignon* stump of an amputated limb]

truss (trus) *n.* **1** beams or other supports connected to support a roof, bridge, etc. **2** a bandage, pad, etc. used for support, especially a pad with a belt or spring used in cases of hernia. **3** a bundle; pack. **4** a bundle of hay. **5** on a ship, an iron fitting by which a lower yard is fastened to the mast. [< v.] —*v.* **1** tie; fasten; bind: *We trussed the burglar up and called the police.* **2** fasten the wings or legs of (a fowl, etc.) with skewers or twine in preparation for cooking: *The cook trussed up the chicken before roasting it.* **3** support (a roof, bridge, etc.) with trusses. **4** bundle; pack. **5** *Archaic.* fasten or tighten (a garment). [ME < OF *trusser,* ult. < L *torquere* twist]

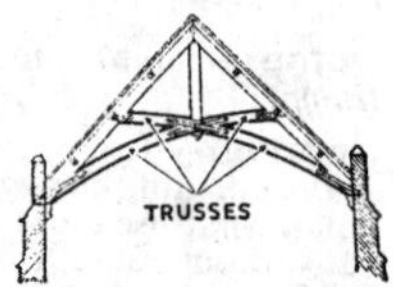

Trusses (def. 1)

trust (trust) *n.* **1** a firm belief in the honesty, truthfulness, justice, or power of a person or thing; faith: *A child puts trust in his mother.* **2** a person or thing trusted: *God is our trust.* **3** a confident expectation or hope: *Our trust is that she will soon be well.* **4** a group of men or companies controlling much of a certain kind of business: *a steel trust.* **5** a group of businessmen or firms having a central committee that controls stock of the constituent companies, thus simplifying management and defeating competition. **6** something managed for the benefit of another; something committed to one's care. **7** the obligation or responsibility imposed on one in whom confidence or authority is placed. **8** the condition of one in whom trust has been placed; being relied on: *A guardian is in a position of trust.* **9** keeping; care: *The will was left in my trust.* **10** in law: **a** a confidence reposed in a person by making him nominal owner of property, which he is to hold, use, or dispose of for the benefit of another. **b** an estate, etc. committed to a trustee or trustees. **c** the right of a person to enjoy the use or profits of property held in trust for him. **11** confidence in the ability or intention of a person to pay at some future time for goods, etc.; business credit. **12 in trust,** as a thing taken charge of for another. **13 on trust, a** on business credit; with payment later. **b** without investigation.
—*v.* **1** have faith; rely; be confident: *Trust in God.* **2** believe firmly in the honesty, truth, justice, or power of; have faith in: *He is a man to be trusted.* **3** rely on; depend on: *A forgetful man should not trust his memory.* **4** commit to the care of; leave without fear: *Can I trust the keys to him?* **5** confide or entrust something to the care of; invest: *Can I trust him with a large sum of money?* **6** hope; believe: *I trust you will soon feel better.* **7** give business credit to: *The butcher will trust us for the meat.* **8** allow to go somewhere or do something without misgiving or fear of consequences. **9 trust to,** rely on; depend on: *Don't trust to luck.*
—*adj.* **1** managing for an owner: *a trust company.* **2** of or having to do with trust or trusts; held in trust: *a trust fund.* [ME < ON *traust*] —**trust′er,** *n.* —**Syn.** *n.* **1** confidence, credence, reliance. **7** charge, commission, duty, office. –*v.* **4** entrust, confide.

trust company a bank or other business concern formed primarily for the purpose of administering trusts, but also often engaging in other financial activities normally performed by banks.

trus·tee (trus tē′) *n.* **1** a person responsible for the property or affairs of another person, of a company, or of an institution. **2** a person elected to a board or committee that is responsible for the schools in a district; school trustee.

trus·tee·ship (trus tē′ship) *n.* the position of trustee.

trust·ful (trust′fəl) *adj.* ready to confide; ready to have faith; believing. —**trust′ful·ly,** *adv.* —**trust′ful·ness,** *n.* —**Syn.** confiding, credulous, unsuspicious, naïve.

trust fund money, property, or other valuables held in trust by one person for the benefit of another.

trust·ing (trus′ting) *adj.* that trusts; trustful.

trust·wor·thy (trust′wėr′ᴛʜē) *adj.* that can be depended on; reliable: *The class chose a trustworthy boy for treasurer.* —**trust′wor′thi·ly,** *adv.*—**trust′wor′thi·ness,** *n.* —**Syn.** dependable, faithful. See **reliable.**

trust·y (trus′tē) *adj.* **trust·i·er, trust·i·est,** *n.* **trust·ies.** —*adj.* that can be depended on; reliable: *a trusty servant.* —*n.* a prisoner who is given special privileges because of his good behavior. —**trust′i·ly,** *adv.* —**trust′i·ness,** *n.*

truth (trüth) *n.* **truths** (trüᴛʜz or trüths). **1** that which is in accordance with the fact or facts: *Tell the truth.* **2** a fixed or established principle, law, etc.; proven doctrine; verified hypothesis: *a basic scientific truth.* **3** that which is true, real, or actual, in a general or abstract sense; reality: *find truth in God.* **4** true, exact, honest, sincere, or loyal quality or nature. **5 in truth,** truly; really; in fact. [OE *trīewth, trēowth* < *trīewe, trēowe* true]

truth·ful (trüth′fəl) *adj.* **1** telling the truth: *a truthful child.* **2** conforming to truth: *a truthful report.* —**truth′ful·ly,** *adv.* —**truth′ful·ness,** *n.* —**Syn. 1** veracious, honest, candid. **2** exact, accurate, correct.

truth serum *Informal.* any drug, such as sodium pentothal, under the influence of which a person will tend to reveal subconscious thoughts or emotions.

try (trī) *v.* **tried, try·ing,** *n.* **tries.** —*v.* **1** make an attempt or effort: *He tried to do the work.* **2** attempt to do or accomplish: *It seems easy until you try it.* **3** experiment on or with; make a trial of: *Try this candy and see if you like it.* **4** find out about; test: *We try each car before we sell it.* **5** investigate in a law court: *The man was tried and*

found guilty. 6 settle by test or investigation. 7 subject to trials; afflict: *Job was greatly tried.* 8 put to severe test; strain: *Her mistakes try my patience. Don't try your eyes by reading in poor light.* 9 make pure by melting or boiling: *The lard was tried in a big kettle.* 10 **try on,** put on to test the fit, looks, etc.: *try on a new suit.* 11 **try out,** a test the effect or result of. b test to find out about. c enter as a competitor: *He tried out for the hockey team.* d make pure by melting or boiling.
—*n.* 1 an attempt; endeavor; effort. 2 a trial; test; experiment. 3 in rugger: a the act of touching the ball to the ground behind the opponent's goal line. b the score (three points) so gained. [ME < OF *trier* cull, sift; origin uncertain]

Syn. *v.* 1 **Try, attempt, endeavor** = make an effort to or at. **Try** is the general word: *I tried to see him.* **Attempt** is used in more formal style or to suggest making a real effort, trying hard: *I attempted to obtain an interview.* **Endeavor,** fairly formal, suggests both great effort and greater obstacles to be overcome: *The United Nations is endeavoring to establish peace.* 9 purify, refine.

☛ **try and or try to.** Although the formal idiom is *try to,* general English has long used *try and.* Formal: *Let us try to get permission for the bazaar.* General: *Let's try and get permission for the bazaar.*

try·ing (trī′ing) *adj.* hard to endure; annoying; distressing. —**Syn.** severe, difficult, vexing.

try·out (trī′out′) *n. Informal.* 1 a test made to determine fitness for a specific purpose. 2 in sports, a selective trial to eliminate contestants or candidates not sufficiently capable of competing: *He had a tryout with a professional hockey team.*

tryp·sin (trip′sən) *n.* in biochemistry, an enzyme in the digestive juice secreted by the pancreas. Trypsin changes proteins into peptones. [irregularly < Gk. *tripsis* rubbing < *tribein* rub]

try·sail (trī′sāl′ or trī′səl) *n.* a small fore-and-aft sail used in stormy weather on the foremast or mainmast.

try square an instrument for drawing right angles and testing the squareness of anything.

tryst (trist or trīst) *n.* 1 an appointment to meet at a certain time and place. 2 a place of meeting. [ME < OF *triste,* in hunting, a place to which game used to be driven, probably < Scand.]

trysting place a place where a tryst is to be kept.

tsar (zär) *n.* czar.

tsar·e·vitch (zär′ə vich′) *n.* czarevitch.

tsa·ri·na (zä rē′nə) *n.* czarina.

TSE or **T.S.E.** Toronto Stock Exchange.

tset·se (tset′sē) *n.* tsetse fly. Also, **tzetze.**

tsetse fly any of the bloodsucking flies of Africa. One kind spreads sleeping sickness. [*tsetse* < Bantu]

T-shirt (tē′shėrt′) *n.* 1 a light, close-fitting, knitted shirt with short sleeves, worn for sports. 2 an undershirt resembling such a shirt.

Tsim·shi·an (tsim′shē ən or chim′shē ən) *n.* **-an** or **-ans.** 1 a tribe of Indians who originally lived in the lower Skeena and Nass valleys in British Columbia. 2 a member of this tribe. 3 the language of this tribe.

tsp. *pl.* **tsps.** teaspoon.

T-square a T-shaped ruler used for making parallel lines, etc. The shorter arm of a T-square slides along the edge of the drawing board, which serves as a guide.

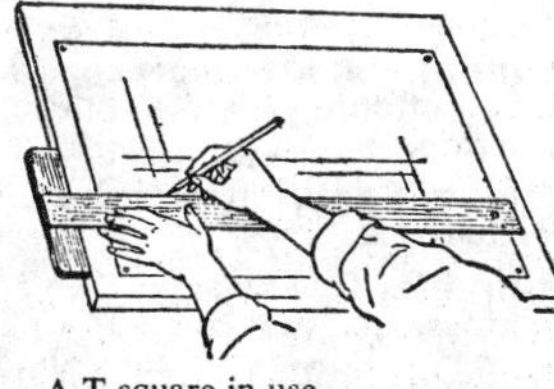
A T-square in use

tu·an or **Tu·an** (tü′än) *n.* sir; lord; master; a title of respect originating in southeastern Asia. [< Malay]

Tua·reg (twä′reg) *n.* 1 a member of certain Moslem tribes of Berber or Libyan nomads of the Sahara. 2 the Hamitic language of these tribes.

tub (tub) *n. v.* **tubbed, tub·bing.** —*n.* 1 a large, open container for washing clothes, etc. 2 a bathtub. 3 *Informal.* a bath: *He takes a cold tub every morning.* 4 a round wooden container for holding butter, lard, etc. 5 as much as a tub can hold. 6 something like a tub. 7 *Informal.* a clumsy, slow boat or ship. 8 *Slang.* a fat person.
—*v.* wash or bathe in a tub. [cf. MDu. or MLG *tubbe*]

hat, āge, cãre, fär; let, ēqual, tėrm; it, īce
hot, ōpen, ôrder; oil, out; cup, pu̇t, rüle, ūse
əbove, takən, pencəl, lemən, circəs
ch, child; ng, long; sh, ship
th, thin; ᴛʜ, then; zh, measure

tu·ba (tū′bə or tü′bə) *n.* 1 a large, brass musical wind instrument resembling a trumpet, having valves to vary the pitch. It has the lowest range of the brasses. 2 in an organ, a stop that produces tuba-like tones. [< L *tuba* war trumpet]

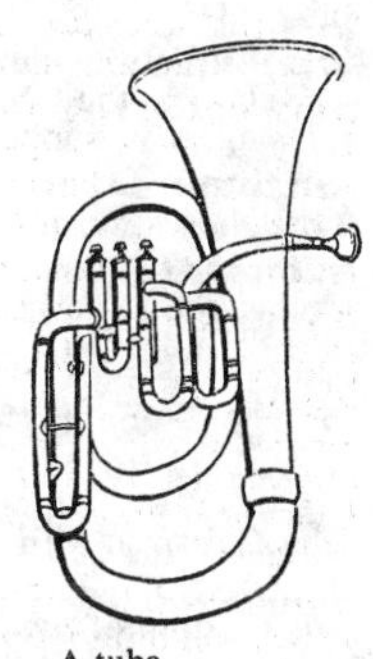
A tuba

tub·al (tū′bəl or tü′bəl) *adj.* 1 of or having to do with a tube. 2 taking place in a tube, especially a Fallopian tube. —*n.* a Fallopian tube.

tub·bing (tub′ing) *n.* a bath; washing.

tub·by (tub′ē) *adj.* **-bi·er, -bi·est.** 1 tub-shaped; stout or broad in proportion to height or length. 2 having a sound like that of an empty tub when struck. —**tub′bi·ness,** *n.*

tube (tūb or tüb) *n. v.* **tubed, tub·ing.** —*n.* 1 a long pipe of metal, glass, rubber, etc. used to hold or carry liquids or gases. 2 a small cylinder of thin, easily bent metal with a cap that screws on the open end, used for holding toothpaste, paint, etc. 3 a pipe or tunnel through which something is sent: *The railway runs under the river in a tube.* 4 *Informal.* a subway. 5 anything like a tube: *the bronchial tubes.* 6 an electron tube. 7 in botany, the lower united portion of a gamopetalous corolla or a gamosepalous calyx. —*v.* 1 furnish or fit with a tube or tubes; insert a tube in. 2 pass through or enclose in a tube. 3 make tubular. [< L *tubus*] —**tube′less,** *adj.*

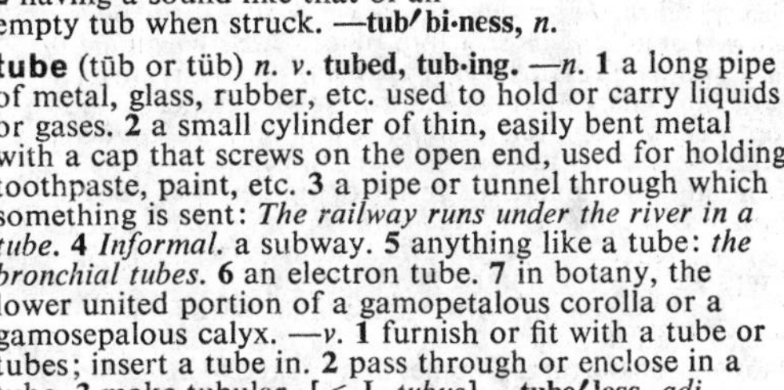

tube·less tire (tūb′lis or tüb′-) a type of tire in which an inner lining is bonded to the outer casing, making a separate inner tube unnecessary.

tu·ber (tū′bər or tü′bər) *n.* 1 in botany, the thickened part of an underground stem or rhizome. A potato is a tuber. 2 a a rounded swelling or projecting part in an animal body. b an abnormal or swelling enlargement. [< L *tuber* lump]

tu·ber·cle (tū′bər kəl or tü′bər kəl) *n.* 1 a small, wartlike swelling or protuberance on a plant. 2 a swelling caused by tuberculosis. 3 a small, hard, rounded swelling in or on the body; nodule. 4 one of the small, soft lesions characteristic of tuberculosis. [< L *tuberculum,* dim. of *tuber* lump]

tubercle bacillus a bacillus that causes tuberculosis.

tu·ber·cu·lar (tū bėr′kyu̇ lər or tü bėr′kyu̇ lər) *adj.* 1 having tubercles. 2 having to do with tubercles. 3 characterized by tubercles. 4 having tuberculosis. 5 having to do with tuberculosis. —**tu·ber′cu·lar·ly,** *adv.*

tu·ber·cu·lin (tū bėr′kyu̇ lin or tü bėr′kyu̇ lin) *n.* a liquid prepared from the bacillus that causes tuberculosis and used in the diagnosis and treatment of tuberculosis.

tu·ber·cu·lo·sis (tū bėr′kyu̇ lō′sis or tü bėr′kyu̇ lō′sis) *n.* an infectious disease caused by the tubercle bacillus and affecting various tissues of the body, but most often the lungs. Tuberculosis of the lungs used to be called consumption. [< NL *tuberculosis* < L *tuberculum.* See TUBERCLE.]

tu·ber·cu·lous (tū bėr′kyu̇ ləs or tü bėr′kyu̇ ləs) *adj.* tubercular.

tube·rose (tūb′rōz′ or tüb′-) *n.* a plant having a spike of fragrant, white flowers. It grows from a tuber. [< L *tuberosa,* fem. of *tuberosus* tuberous < *tuber* lump; interpreted as if from *tube* + *rose*]

tu·ber·os·i·ty (tū′bər os′ə tē or tü′bər os′ə tē) *n.* **-ties.** 1 the condition or quality of being tuberous. 2 a rounded knob or swelling. 3 a large, irregular protuberance of a bone, especially for the attachment of a muscle or ligament.

tu·ber·ous (tū′bər əs or tü′bər əs) *adj.* **1** bearing tubers. **2** of or like tubers. **3** covered with rounded knobs or swellings. [< L *tuberosus* < *tuber* lump]

tub·ing (tūb′ing or tüb′-) *n.* **1** material in the form of a tube: *rubber tubing.* **2** tubes collectively. **3** a piece of tube.

tub thumper *Informal.* **1** a noisy preacher or speaker who thumps the table, etc.; a loud, emotional orator. **2** a press agent or spokesman.

tub thumping *Informal.* **1** the actions of a tub thumper. **2** ballyhoo; exaggerated publicity.

tu·bu·lar (tū′byů lər or tü′byů lər) *adj.* **1** shaped like a tube; round and hollow. **2** of or having to do with a tube or tubes. **3** in medicine, of or denoting a high-pitched respiratory murmur that sounds as if made through a tube. [< L *tubulus,* dim. of *tubus* tube, pipe]

tu·bu·late (tū′bū lit or tü′bū lāt′, tü′bū lit or tü′bū lāt′) *adj. v.* **-lat·ed, -lat·ing.** —*adj.* tubular. —*v.* **1** form into a tube. **2** furnish with a tube. —**tu′bu·la′tion,** *n.*

tu·bule (tū′būl or tü′būl) *n.* a small tube. [< F < L *tubulus,* dim. of *tubus* pipe]

tuck (tuk) *v.* **1** thrust into some narrow space or into some retired place: *She tucked her purse under her arm. He tucked the letter into his pocket.* **2** thrust the edge or end of something closely into place: *Tuck your shirt in. Jack tucked a serviette under his chin.* **3** cover snugly: *Tuck the children in bed.* **4** draw close together; fold; contract; pucker: *The man tucked up his trousers and waded across the stream.* **5** sew a fold in (a garment) for trimming or to make it shorter or tighter: *The baby's dress was beautifully tucked with tiny stitches.* **6** sew tucks. **7 tuck away,** *Slang.* **a** put away; hide. **b** eat heartily. **8 tuck in, a** cover snugly. **b** eat heartily.
—*n.* **1** a fold sewed down with stitches parallel to the line of the fold, made to shorten or ornament a garment. **2** the act of tucking. **3** something tucked. **4** *Brit. Slang.* food; eatables, especially candy, pastry, etc. [ME *tuke(n)* stretch < OE *tūcian* torment]

tuck·a·hoe (tuk′ə hō′) *n.* an edible fungus sometimes found on the roots of trees. [< Algonquian]

tuck·er[1] (tuk′ər) *n.* **1** a piece of muslin, lace, etc. that is worn around the neck or over the chest. **2** a person or thing that tucks. **3** on a sewing machine, a device for making tucks. [< *tuck*]

tuck·er[2] (tuk′ər) *v.* **1** *Informal.* tire; weary; exhaust. **2 tucker out,** make utterly exhausted; wear out. [cf. E dial. *tucked up* worn out, exhausted]

Tu·dor (tū′dər or tü′dər) *n.* **1** the royal family that ruled England from 1485 to 1603. Henry VII, Henry VIII, Edward VI, Mary, and Elizabeth I belonged to the House of Tudor. **2** a member of the Tudor family. —*adj.* of or having to do with the English Gothic style of architecture prevailing during the reign of the Tudors. It was characterized by flat arches, shallow mouldings a profusion of panelling, etc.

Tues. Tuesday.

Tues·day (tūz′dē or tüz′dē) *n.* the third day of the week, following Monday. [OE *tīwesdæg* day of Tiw (god of war); translation of LL *Martis dies* day of Mars]

tu·fa (tū′fə or tü′fə) *n.* any of various porous rocks, especially a form of limestone deposited by springs, etc. [< Ital. *tufo* < L *tofus.* Doublet of TUFF.]

tuff (tuf) *n.* tufa, especially a tufa formed from volcanic ash, cinders, etc. [< F *tuf* < Ital. *tufo* tufa < L *tofus.* Doublet of TUFA.]

tuft (tuft) *n.* **1** a bunch of feathers, grass, threads, etc. growing from one place or held together at one end: *A goat has a tuft of hair on its chin.* **2** a bunch of short-stalked leaves or flowers growing from a common point, of stems growing from a common root, etc. **3** a clump of bushes, trees, etc. **4** a cluster of threads sewn tightly through a mattress, comforter, etc. so as to keep the padding in place.
—*v.* **1** put tufts on; divide into tufts. **2** grow in tufts. **3** put tufts on (a mattress, comforter, etc.) to keep the padding in place. [ME, ? < OF *touffe* < LL *tufa* helmet crest]

tuft·ed (tuf′tid) *adj.* **1** furnished with a tuft or tufts: *a tufted quilt.* **2** of a bird, having a tuft of feathers on the head; crested. **3** formed into a tuft or tufts.

tug (tug) *v.* **tugged, tug·ging,** *n.* —*v.* **1** pull with force or effort; pull hard: *We tugged the boat in to shore. The child tugged at his mother's hand.* **2** strive hard; toil. **3** tow by a tugboat. —*n.* **1** a hard pull. **2** a hard strain, struggle, effort, or contest. **3** a small and powerful boat used to tow other boats. **4** one of a pair of long leather straps by which a horse pulls a wagon, cart, etc. See **harness** for picture. [related to *tow*] —**Syn.** *v.* **1** See **pull.**

tug·boat (tug′bōt′) *n.* a small, powerful boat used to tow other boats, tug.

A tugboat

tug of war 1 a contest between two teams pulling at the ends of a rope, each trying to drag the other over a line marked between them. **2** any hard struggle.

Tui·ler·ies (twē′lər ēz; *French,* tyēl rē′) *n.* a former royal palace in Paris, at the present site of the Tuileries Gardens. It was burned in 1871.

tu·i·tion (tū ish′ən or tü ish′ən) *n.* **1** teaching; instruction. **2** money paid for instruction. [< L *tuitio, -onis* protection < *tueri* watch over]

tu·i·tion·al (tū ish′ən el or tü ish′ən əl) *adj.* of or having to do with tuition.

tu·la·di (tü′lə dē′) *n.* **-adi** or **-adis.** *Cdn.* lake trout. Also, **touladi.** [< Cdn.F *touladi* < Algonquian (Micmac)]

tu·la·re·mi·a (tü′lə rē′mē ə) *n.* an infectious disease of rabbits and other rodents that is sometimes transmitted to people. [< NL *tularemia* < (*bacterium*) *tular*(*ense*), the organism that causes the disease (< *Tulare,* a county in California) + *-emia* < Gk. *haima* blood]

tu·lip (tū′lip or tü′lip) *n.* **1** any of certain plants of the lily family, that grow from bulbs and have large cup-shaped flowers of various colors. Most tulips bloom in the spring. **2** the flower. **3** the bulb. [< obs. Du. *tulipa* < F < Turkish *tülbend* < Persian *dulband* turban. Doublet of TURBAN.]

tulip tree a large North American tree having greenish-yellow flowers like tulips.

tu·lip·wood (tū′lip wůd′ or tü′lip-) *n.* the wood of the tulip tree, used for cabinetwork.

tulle (tül) *n.* a thin, fine silk net used for veils, etc. [< *Tulle,* a city in S.W. France]

tul·li·bee (tul′ə bē′) *n.* **-bee** or **-bees.** *Cdn.* a species of whitefish. [< Cdn.F *toulibi* < Algonquian (Cree)]

tum·ble (tum′bəl) *v.* **-bled, -bling,** *n.* —*v.* **1** fall: *The child tumbled down the stairs.* **2** throw over or down; cause to fall. **3** stumble by tripping (over an object). **4** of a building or structure, fall in ruins; collapse. **5** fall rapidly in value, amount, or price (used especially of stocks). **6** roll or toss about. **7** move in a hurried or awkward way. **8** perform leaps, springs, somersaults, etc. **9** turn over; rumple; muss. **10** mix, cleanse, or polish in a tumbling box or tumbler. —*n.* **1** a fall: *The tumble hurt him badly.* **2** confusion; disorder. [ME, ult. < OE *tumbian* dance about] —**Syn.** *v.* **6** pitch, wallow.

tum·ble·bug (tum′bəl bug′) *n.* a beetle that rolls up a ball of dung in which it deposits eggs from which larvae develop.

tum·ble-down (tum′bəl doun′) *adj.* ready to fall down; dilapidated.

tum·bler (tum′blər) *n.* **1** a person who performs leaps, springs, etc.; acrobat. **2** a drinking glass without a foot or stem, and with a heavy, flat bottom. **3** the contents of such a glass. **4** in a lock, the part that must be moved from a certain position in order to release the bolt. **5** of a gun, the part of a lock that forces the hammer forward when the trigger is pulled. **6** a kind of pigeon that turns over and over while flying. **7** a toy figure that rocks when touched but rights itself. **8** a revolving box or barrel in which things are polished.

tum·ble·weed (tum′bəl wēd′) *n.* a plant growing in the western part of Canada and of the United States, that breaks off from its roots and is blown about by the wind.

tum·brel or **tum·bril** (tum′brəl) *n.* **1** a farmer's cart. **2** formerly: **a** a cart that carried prisoners to be

hat, āge, cãre, fär; let, ēqual, tėrm; it, īce
hot, ōpen, ôrder; oil, out; cup, put, rüle, ūse
əbove, takən, pencəl, lemən, circəs
ch, child; ng, long; sh, ship
th, thin; ᴛʜ, then; zh, measure

executed. **b** a two-wheeled covered cart for carrying ammunition and military tools. [probably < OF *tomberel* cart < *tomber* fall < Gmc.]

tu·me·fac·tion (tū′mə fak′shən or tü′mə fak′shən) *n.* **1** the process of swelling or the condition of being swollen. **2** a swollen part.

tu·me·fy (tū′mə fī′ or tü′mə fī′) *v.* **-fied, -fy·ing.** swell. [< L *tumefacere* < *tumere* swell + *facere* make]

tu·mes·cence (tū mes′əns or tü mes′əns) *n.* a swelling; a swollen condition.

tu·mes·cent (tū mes′ənt or tü mes′ənt) *adj.* becoming swollen; swelling. [< L *tumescens, -entis,* ult. < *tumere* swell]

tu·mid (tū′mid or tü′mid) *adj.* **1** swollen. **2** of style, swollen with big words; pompous. [< L *tumidus* < *tumere* swell] —**tu′mid·ly,** *adv.* —**tu′mid·ness,** *n.*

tum·my (tum′ē) *n.* **-mies.** *Informal.* stomach.

tu·mor or **tu·mour** (tū′mər or tü′mər) *n.* **1** in medicine, an independent growth in any part of the body, sometimes malignant. **2** a swollen part or object; swelling. [< L *tumor* < *tumere* swell]

tu·mor·ous (tū′mər əs or tü′mər əs) *adj.* **1** of or having to do with a tumor or tumors. **2** having a tumor or tumors.

tu·mour (tü′mər or tū′mər) *n.* tumor.

tump (tump) *n.* tumpline. [< Algonquian. Cf. METUMP.]

tump·line (tump′līn′) *n.* a strap used for carrying, when it is placed around the forehead, or for pulling, when it is placed around the chest. Also, **tump.** [< *tump* + *line*]

A tumpline. It passes around the forehead so that the neck muscles take some of the strain of the load.

tu·mult (tū′mult or tü′mult) *n.* **1** noise; uproar. **2** a violent disturbance or disorder. **3** confusion; excitement. [< L *tumultus*] —**Syn. 2** brawl.

tu·mul·tu·ous (tū mul′chü əs or tü mul′chü əs) *adj.* **1** characterized by tumult; very noisy or disorderly; violent. **2** greatly disturbed. **3** rough; stormy: *Tumultuous waves beat upon the rocks.* —**tu·mul′tu·ous·ly,** *adv.* —**tu·mul′tu·ous·ness,** *n.* —**Syn. 1** boisterous, turbulent.

tu·mu·lus (tū′myů ləs or tü′myů ləs) *n.* **-lus·es, -li** (-lī′ or -lē′). a mound of earth, especially over a grave. [< L]

tun (tun) *n.* **1** a large cask for holding liquids. **2** formerly, a measure of capacity of liquor, equal to 252 gallons. [OE *tunne,* probably < Celtic]

tu·na[1] (tü′nə or tūn′ə) *n.* a large, edible sea fish. The tuna sometimes grows to a length of ten feet or more. [< Am.Sp. *tuna,* ult. < L *thunnus.* See TUNNY.]

tu·na[2] (tü′nə) *n.* the prickly pear. [< Sp. < Haitian]

tun·a·ble or **tune·a·ble** (tūn′ə bəl or tün′ə bəl) *adj.* **1** capable of being tuned. **2** in tune. **3** harmonious; tuneful.

tuna fish 1 the flesh of the tuna, used for food. **2** a tuna.

tun·dra (tun′drə) *n.* a vast, level, treeless plain in the arctic regions. The ground beneath the surface of the tundras is frozen even in summer. [< Russian]

tune (tūn or tün) *n. v.* **tuned, tun·ing.** —*n.* **1** a piece of music; air or melody: *hymn tunes.* **2** the proper pitch: *He can't sing in tune.* **3** a mood; manner; tone: *He'll soon change his tune.* **4** agreement; harmony: *A person out of tune with his surroundings is unhappy.* **5 call the tune,** declare authoritatively what will be or what will happen; dictate. **6 in** or **out of tune, a** in or out of harmony or agreement (with some person or thing). **b** in or out of order or proper condition. **7 sing a different tune,** talk or behave differently. **8 to the tune of,** *Informal.* to the amount or sum of.
—*v.* **1** express musically. **2** be in tune; be in harmony. **3** put in tune: *A man is tuning the piano.* **4** adjust (a radio or television set) into resonance with a transmitted signal. **5** fit; adapt. **6 tune in,** adjust a radio or television set to hear (what is wanted). **7 tune out,** adjust a radio or television set to get rid of (a signal or interference that is unwanted). **8 tune up, a** bring (musical instruments) to the same pitch. **b** *Informal.* begin to play, or sing, cry, etc. **c** get into the best working order. [var. of *tone*] —**tun′er,** *n.* —**Syn.** *n.* **4** accord, concord.

tune·ful (tūn′fəl or tün′fəl) *adj.* musical; melodious: *That canary has a tuneful song.* —**tune′ful·ly,** *adv.* —**tune′ful·ness,** *n.*

tune·less (tūn′lis or tün′-) *adj.* without tune; not musical.

tune-up (tūn′up′ or tün′-) *n.* the putting of a mechanism into good running order: *He took his car in for an engine tune-up.*

tung (tung) *n.* a tree native to China but now cultivated in Africa and elsewhere. The seeds yield an oil used in paint, varnish, etc.

tung·sten (tung′stən) *n.* a heavy, steel-gray metallic chemical element having the highest melting point of any of the metals; wolfram. It is used in making steel and for the filaments of electric lamps. *Symbol*: W; *at.no.* 74; *at.wt.* 183.85. [< Swedish *tungsten* < *tung* heavy + *sten* stone]

tu·nic (tū′nik or tü′nik) *n.* **1** a garment like a shirt or gown, worn in ancient times by the Greeks and Romans. **2** any garment like this, especially a sleeveless dress worn by school girls. **3** a woman's garment that extends below the waist or over the skirt. **4** a short, close-fitting coat worn by soldiers, policemen, etc. **5** a natural covering of a plant, animal, part of an animal, etc. [< L *tunica,* ult. < Semitic]

tu·ni·cate (tū′nə kit or tū′nə kāt′, tü′nə kit or tü′nə kāt′) *adj.* **1** in botany, made up of concentric layers. An onion is a tunicate bulb. **2** in zoology, having a tunic or outer covering. —*n.* a small sea animal enclosed in a tough, leathery membrane. [< L *tunicatus,* pp. of *tunicare* clothe with a tunic < *tunica.* See TUNIC.]

tuning fork a small, two-pronged steel instrument that, when struck, vibrates at a fixed, constant, known rate and so makes a musical tone of a certain pitch.

A tuning fork mounted on a sounding box

tun·nel (tun′əl) *n. v.* **-nelled** or **-neled, -nel·ling** or **-nel·ing.** —*n.* **1** an underground passageway for automobiles, trains, etc. or for persons on foot. **2** any of certain other subterranean passageways or borings, as for the passage of water, sewage, etc. **3** a nearly horizontal passageway in a mine (often used loosely for any drift, level, etc.). **4** a passageway dug into the earth by any of certain animals as a means of access to or exit from its burrow. **5** the burrow itself.
—*v.* **1** make a tunnel. **2** make a tunnel through or under: *tunnel a hill or river.* **3** make (one's way or a way) by digging. [ME < OF *tonel* cask < *tonne* tun < Celtic] —**tun′nel·ler** or **tun′nel·er,** *n.*

tun·ny (tun′ē) *n.* **-ny** or **-nies.** tuna. [< F *thon* < Provençal < L *thunnus, thynnus* < Gk. *thynnos*]

tu·pek or **tu·pik** (tü′pək) *n. Cdn.* a compact, portable tent made of skin, used by Eskimos to live in during the summer. [< Eskimo]

Tu·pi-Gua·ra·ni (tü pē′gwä′rä nē′) *n.* a linguistic stock of central South America—consisting principally of Tupi, the northern branch, and Guarani, the southern branch—occurring particularly along the lower Amazon.

tup·pence (tup′əns) *n.* twopence.

tuque (tük or tūk) *n. Cdn.* **1** a tight-fitting knitted cap resembling a long

A tuque

stocking: *Tuques are very popular in Quebec.* **2** a knitted cap, usually made of wool. [< Cdn.F var. of F *toque* cap]

Tu·ra·ni·an (tū rā′nē ən or tü rā′nē ən) *adj. n.* Ural-Altaic. [< Persian *Turān*, a district north of the Oxus]

tur·ban (tėr′bən) *n.* **1** a head-dress used by certain oriental men that consists of a long strip of silk or other cloth wound round the head or over a cap. **2** a head-dress resembling this; a big handkerchief tied around the head. **3** a small hat with little or no brim, worn by women and children. [< Turkish < Arabic < Persian *dulband*. Doublet of TULIP.]

An oriental turban

tur·baned (tėr′bənd) *adj.* wearing a turban.

tur·bid (tėr′bid) *adj.* **1** muddy; thick; not clear: *a turbid river.* **2** confused; disordered: *a turbid imagination.* [< L *turbidus* < *turba* turmoil] —**tur′bid·ly,** *adv.* —**tur′bid·ness,** *n.*

tur·bid·i·ty (tėr bid′ə tē) *n.* the condition of being turbid.

tur·bi·nate (tėr′bə nit or tėr′bə nāt′) *adj.* **1** shaped like a spinning top or inverted cone. **2** spiral; scroll-like. **3** in the higher vertebrates, of or having to do with certain scroll-like spongy bones of the nasal passages. —*n.* **1** a turbinate shell. **2** a turbinate bone. [< L *turbinatus* < *turbo* whirling object or motion]

tur·bine (tėr′bīn or tėr′bən) *n.* an engine or motor in which a wheel with vanes is made to revolve by the force of water, steam, or air. See **jet** for picture. [< F < L *turbo, -binis* whirling object or motion]

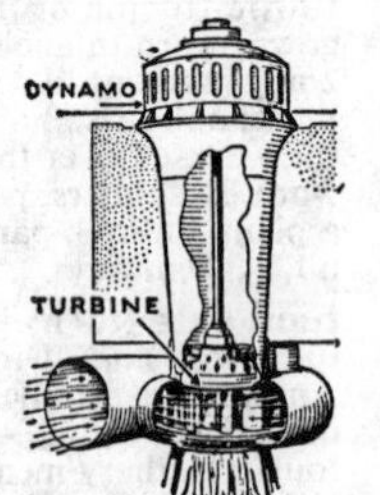

A turbine used to turn a dynamo. Water flows in through the pipe at left and out at the bottom.

turbo- *combining form.* **1** consisting of a turbine. **2** using or operating with a turbine: *turbojet = a jet using a turbine.*

tur·bo·fan (tėr′bō fan′) *n.* **1** a turbojet engine in which a fan draws in and compresses an additional supply of air. **2** the fan itself.

tur·bo·jet (tėr′bō jet′) *n.* **1** a jet-propulsion engine having a turbine-driven air compressor. A turbojet employs a jet of hot gases to produce thrust. **2** an aircraft having such an engine.

tur·bo·prop (tėr′bō prop′) *n.* **1** an adaptation of the turbojet, in which a propeller, driven by a shaft from the turbine, provides most of the thrust. **2** an aircraft having such an engine. [*turbo-* (< *turbine*) + *prop*eller]

tur·bot (tėr′bət) *n.* **-bot** or **-bots. 1** a large European flatfish, valued as food. **2** any of various similar fish, such as certain flounders. [ME < OF < OSwedish *törnbut* (< *törn* thorn, from the fish's prickles)]

tur·bu·lence (tėr′byů ləns) *n.* **1** a turbulent condition; disorder; tumult; commotion. **2** in meteorology, an eddying motion of the atmosphere, interrupting the flow of wind.

tur·bu·len·cy (tėr′byů lən sē) *n.* turbulence.

tur·bu·lent (tėr′byů lənt) *adj.* **1** disorderly; unruly; violent: *a turbulent mob.* **2** greatly disturbed: *turbulent water.* **3** disturbing. [< L *turbulentus* < *turba* turmoil] —**tur′bu·lent·ly,** *adv.* —**Syn. 1** boisterous, uproarious. **2** tumultuous, stormy.

tu·reen (tů rēn′) *n.* a deep, covered dish for serving soup, etc. [< F *terrine* earthen vessel, ult. < L *terra* earth]

turf (tėrf) *n.* **turfs,** *v.* —*n.* **1** grass with its matted roots; a sod. **2** a piece of sod. **3** peat. **4** Usually, **the turf. a** a race track for horses. **b** horse racing. —*v.* **1** cover with turf. **2 turf out,** *Slang.* discharge; dismiss. [OE] —**turf′less,** *adj.*

turf·y (tėr′fē) *adj.* **turf·i·er, turf·i·est. 1** covered with turf; grassy. **2** like turf. **3** full of peat; like peat. **4** of or having to do with horse racing. —**turf′i·ness,** *n.*

tur·ges·cence (tėr jes′əns) *n.* **1** the act or fact of swelling. **2** a swollen condition.

tur·ges·cent (tėr jes′ənt) *adj.* swelling; becoming swollen. [< L *turgescens, -entis,* ppr. of *turgescere* begin to swell < *turgere* swell]

tur·gid (tėr′jid) *adj.* **1** swollen; bloated. **2** using big words and elaborate comparisons; bombastic; inflated; pompous. [< L *turgidus* < *turgere* swell] —**tur′gid·ly,** *adv.* —**tur′gid·ness,** *n.*

Turk (tėrk) *n.* **1** a native or inhabitant of Turkey; Moslem who lives in Turkey. **2** a member of any group of people speaking a Turkic language. **3** *Derogatory.* a cruel, barbarous person; tyrant. **4** in historical use, any Moslem; Saracen. [ME < Med.L *Turcus* < Persian]

Turk. 1 Turkey. **2** Turkish.

tur·key (tėr′kē) *n.* **-keys. 1** either of two large wild American birds that nest on the ground and fly only short distances. One variety comes from Central America and the other is from Mexico and eastern United States. **2** any of several types of domesticated fowls derived from wild turkeys. **3** its flesh, used for food. **4** *Slang.* a play, motion picture, etc. that is a failure. **5 talk turkey,** *Informal.* talk frankly and bluntly. [ult. < *Turkey*]

turkey buzzard a vulture having a bare, reddish head and dark plumage, found especially in South and Central America and the S. United States but also as far north as S. Canada.

turkey cock 1 a male turkey. **2** a strutting, conceited person.

Turkey red 1 bright red. **2** a cotton cloth having this color.

Turk·ic (tėrk′ik) *adj.* **1** of or having to do with a group of Ural-Altaic languages spoken in Turkey and south central Asia. **2** Turkish. —*n.* the Turkic group of languages.

Turk·ish (tėr′kish) *adj.* of, belonging to, or having to do with Turkey, a country in western Asia and southeastern Europe, or the Turks; made in Turkey. —*n.* the Turkic language of the Turks.

Turkish bath a kind of bath in which the bather is kept in a heated room until he sweats freely and then is bathed and massaged.

Turkish delight or **paste** a fruit-flavored candy made of sugar and gelatin cut into cubes and dusted with powdered sugar.

Turkish Empire Ottoman Empire.

Turkish towel a thick cotton towel with a long nap made of uncut loops.

Turk·man (tėrk′mən) *n.* **-men** (-mən). **1** a native or inhabitant of the Turkmen Soviet Socialist Republic in western Asia. **2** a native or inhabitant of Turkey; Turk.

Turk·men (tėrk′men *for 1,* -mən *for 2*) *n.* **1** a language of Turkestan. **2** pl. of **Turkman.**

Tur·ko·man (tėr′kə mən) *n.* **-mans. 1** a member of any of various Turkic tribes inhabiting the region about the Aral Sea and parts of Iran and Afghanistan. **2** the Turkic language of this people.

tur·mer·ic (tėr′ mər ik) *n.* **1** a yellow powder prepared from the root of an East Indian plant, used as a seasoning, as a yellow dye, in medicine, etc. **2** the plant itself. **3** its root. [earlier *tarmaret* < F < Med.L *terra merita,* literally, worthy earth < L *terra* earth + *merere* deserve]

tur·moil (tėr′moil) *n.* a commotion; disturbance; tumult. [origin uncertain]

turn (tėrn) *v.* **1** move round as a wheel does; rotate: *The merry-go-round turned.* **2** cause to move round as a wheel does: *I turned the crank three times.* **3** move part way around; change from one side to the other: *Turn over on your back.* **4** cause to move around in order to open, close, raise, lower, or tighten: *She turned the key in the lock.* **5** perform by revolving, as a somersault. **6** take a new direction: *The road turns to the north here.* **7** give a new direction to: *He turned his steps to the north.* **8** change in direction or position; invert; reverse: *turn a page.* **9** reverse the position of (the turf, soil, etc.) in ploughing or digging so as to bring the under parts to

hat, āge, cãre, fär; let, ēqual, tėrm; it, īce
hot, ōpen, ôrder; oil, out; cup, pu̇t, rüle, ūse
əbove, takən, pencəl, lemən, circəs
ch, child; ng, long; sh, ship
th, thin; ᴛʜ, then; zh, measure

the surface: *turn a furrow.* **10** alter or remake (a garment, etc.) by putting the inner side outward. **11** change so as to become: *She turned pale.* **12** change, transform, or convert (into or to): *Rain turns into snow.* **13** change for or to a worse condition; sour; spoil: *Warm weather turns milk.* **14** give form to; make: *He can turn pretty compliments.* **15** change from one language into another; translate: *Turn this sentence into Latin.* **16** put out of order; unsettle: *Too much praise turns his head.* **17** depend: *The success of the picnic turns on the weather.* **18** cause to go, send, etc.: *turn a person from one's door.* **19** drive back; stop: *turn a punch.* **20** direct (one's thoughts or attention): *He turned his thoughts toward home.*
21 consider in different aspects; revolve (over) in the mind: *turn a problem in one's mind.* **22** direct thought, eyes, etc.: *He turned to his father for help.* **23** put to use; apply: *turn money to good use.* **24** move to the other side of; go round; get beyond: *turn the corner.* **25** shape on a lathe. **26** make or become sick; nauseate. **27** become dizzy. **28** give a curved or crooked form to; bend; twist. **29** pass or get beyond (a particular age, time, or amount): *a man turning sixty.* **30** cause (money or commodities) to circulate steadily. **31** of leaves, change color. **32** cause to recoil: *His argument was turned against himself.* **33** make antagonistic; prejudice: *turn friends against friends.*
34 exchange for; get something else instead of; convert (into or to): *turn stock into cash.* **35** adopt a different religion. **36** *Obs.* convert.
turn down, a fold down. **b** bend downward. **c** place with face downward. **d** *Informal.* refuse; reject: *turn down a plan.* **e** lower by turning something.
turn in, a turn and go in. **b** point (toes) inward. **c** *Informal.* go to bed. **d** hand in; deliver. **e** give back. **f** exchange.
turn loose, free from restraint and allow to go where, or do as, one will: *turn a prisoner loose.*
turn off, a shut off. **b** put out (a light). **c** turn aside. **d** do. **e** discharge. **f** *Slang.* make or become bored, uninterested, etc.
turn on, a start the flow of; put on. **b** attack; resist; oppose. **c** depend on. **d** be about; have to do with.
e *Slang.* take a narcotic; especially, smoke marijuana.
f *Slang.* make or become stimulated and elated by, or as if by, the use of a psychedelic drug.
turn out, a put out; shut off. **b** let go out. **c** drive out. **d** come or go out: *We all turned out for hockey.* **e** go out on strike. **f** make; produce. **g** result. **h** become. **i** be found or known. **j** equip; fit out. **k** *Informal.* get out of bed.
turn over, a give; hand over; transfer: *turn over a job to someone.* **b** think carefully about; consider in different ways. **c** buy and then sell; use in business. **d** invest and get back (capital). **e** change in position, especially change from lying on one side to lying on the other. **f** convert to different use. **g** do business to the amount of (a specified sum).
turn to, a refer to. **b** go to for help. **c** get busy; set to work.
turn up, a fold up or over, especially so as to shorten; give upward turn to; bring underside up. **b** make (a lamp, etc.) burn stronger. **c** make (a radio, etc.) louder. **d** turn and go up. **e** be directed upwards. **f** appear.
—*n.* **1** a motion like that of a wheel: *At each turn, the screw goes in further.* **2** a single revolution, as of a wheel. **3** a change of direction: *a turn to the left.* **4** a place where there is a change in direction: *a turn in the road.* **5** the condition of being, or direction in which something is, twisted. **6** a change: *The sick man has taken a turn for the better.* **7** the time at which such a change takes place: *the turn of the year, the turn of a fever.* **8** a form; style: *a happy turn of expression.* **9** a twist; each round in a coil of rope. **10** a time or chance to do something: *My turn comes after yours.* **11** a time or spell of action: *have a turn at a thing.* **12** a deed; act: *One good turn deserves another.* **13** a performance. **14** an inclination; bent: *He has a turn for mathematics.* **15** a walk, drive, or ride: *a turn in the park.* **16** a spell of dizziness or fainting.
17 *Informal.* a momentary shock caused by sudden alarm, fright, etc.: *give someone a bad turn.* **18** form; mould; cast: *the turn of her arms.* **19** in music, an ornamental device of four tones, a principal tone, followed, usually, by one tone above and below it, and returning to the principal tone. The order in which the turn is performed is occasionally reversed.
at every turn, every time; without exception.
by turns, one after another.
in turn, in proper order.
out of turn, a not in proper order. **b** at an inappropriate time, stage, etc.: *He was tactless to speak out of turn.*
take turns, play, act, etc. one after another in proper order.
to a turn, to just the right degree.
turn about or **turn and turn about,** one after another in proper order. [OE *turnian* < L *tornare* turn on a lathe < *tornus* lathe < Gk. *tornos.* Related to TOUR.]
Syn. *v.* **1 Turn, revolve, rotate** = move round in a circle. **Turn** is the general and common word, meaning "move in a circle" or in circle after circle, either on a pivot or axis or around a centre: *That wheel turns freely now.* **Revolve** = turn round and round on a pivot or, especially, in a circular path around something that serves as a centre. **Rotate** also means "turn round and round," but usually on its own axis or around its own centre: *The earth rotates (on its axis) once every 24 hours and revolves round the sun once each year.* **6** shift, veer. –*n.* **1** revolution, rotation. **14** aptitude.

turn·a·bout (tėrn′ə bout′) *n.* **1** the act of turning so as to face the other way. **2** a changing to an opposite view, policy, etc.; about-face; reversal. **3** a merry-go-round.

turn·a·round (tėrn′ə round′) *n.* **1** an about-face or reversal. **2** a space for vehicles to turn around. **3** the time it takes a ship, airplane, etc. to unload, load, and undergo repairs and servicing before being ready to depart.

turn·buck·le (tėrn′buk′əl) *n.* a short, hollow piece turning on a screw, used to unite and tighten two parts.

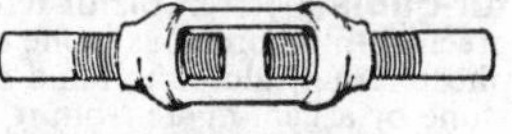
A turnbuckle

turn·coat (tėrn′kōt′) *n.* a person who changes his political party or principles; a person who goes over to the opposing side; renegade.

turn·down (tėrn′doun′) *adj.* that is or can be turned down; folded or doubled down: *a turndown collar.* —*n.* **1** a turning down; rejection. **2** a decline; downturn.

turn·er (tėr′nər) *n.* **1** a person or thing that turns. **2** a person who forms or shapes things with a lathe.

turn indicator 1 a flashing light or other device on a motor vehicle for signalling turns. **2** a gyroscopic device that indicates any turning motion around the vertical axis of an airplane.

turning point the point at which a notable change takes place.

tur·nip (tėr′nip) *n.* **1** any of certain plants, having large, fleshy, roundish roots that are used as vegetables. The **white turnip** and the **Swedish turnip,** or rutabaga, are common turnips. **2** the roots of any of these plants. [probably ult. < ME *turn* (from its rounded shape) + *nepe* turnip < L *napus*]

turn·key (tėrn′kē′) *n.* **-keys.** a person in charge of the keys of a prison; the keeper of a prison.

turn·out (tėrn′out′) *n.* **1** a crowd; a gathering of people: *There was a good turnout at the dance.* **2** output. **3** a wide place in the road, where vehicles can pass. **4** a railway siding. **5** the way in which somebody or something is equipped. **6** equipment; outfit. **7** a horse or horses and carriage. **8** *Esp.Brit.* **a** a strike. **b** a worker on strike.

turn·o·ver (tėrn′ō′vər) *n.* **1** a turning over; upset. **2** the amount of changing from one job to another: *Employers wish to reduce labor turnover.* **3** the paying out and getting back of the money involved in a business transaction: *The store reduced prices to make a quick turnover.* **4** the total amount of business done in a given time: *He made a profit of $6,000 on a turnover of $90,000.* **5** a small pie made by folding half the crust over the filling and upon the other half. —*adj.* having a part that turns over.

turn·pike (tėrn′pīk′) *n.* **1** a gate where toll is paid. **2** a road that has, or used to have, a gate where toll is paid. [< *turn* + *pike* a sharp point; with reference to a spiked barrier across a road, turning on a vertical axis]

turn signal a turn indicator (def. 1).

turn·spit (tėrn′spit′) *n.* formerly, a person or animal, especially a dog in a treadmill, that worked a device for turning meat on a spit.

turn·stile (tėrn′stīl′) *n.* an entrance barrier consisting of a post with two crossed bars or of several rods set in a revolving centre: *Only one person at a time can pass through a turnstile.*

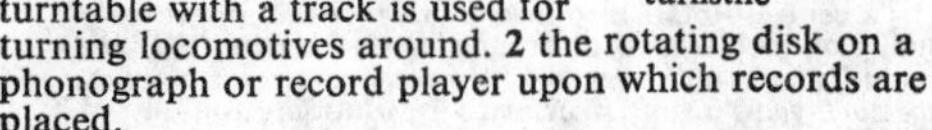

A coin-operated turnstile

turn·stone (tėrn′stōn′) *n.* a small migratory shore bird that turns over stones in search of food.

turn·ta·ble (tėrn′tā′bəl) *n.* **1** a revolving circular platform used for turning things around. A turntable with a track is used for turning locomotives around. **2** the rotating disk on a phonograph or record player upon which records are placed.

tur·pen·tine (tėr′pən tīn′) *n.* **1** an oil obtained from various cone-bearing trees. Turpentine is used in mixing paints and varnishes, in medicine, etc. **2** the mixture of oil and resin from which the prepared oil is made. [ME < OF < L *terebinthina* < Gk. *terebinthos* turpentine tree]

tur·pi·tude (tėr′pə tūd′ or tėr′pə tüd′) *n.* shameful wickedness; baseness. [< L *turpitudo* < *turpis* vile]

tur·quoise (tėr′kwoiz or tėr′koiz) *n.* **1** a sky-blue or greenish-blue precious stone or mineral, consisting of a phosphate of aluminum and copper. **2** a piece of this stone or a gem made from it. **3** a sky blue; greenish blue. —*adj.* sky-blue; greenish-blue. [< F *turquoise*, originally fem. adj., Turkish]

tur·ret (tėr′it) *n.* **1** a small tower, often on the corner of a building. **2** a low, armored structure that revolves and within which guns are mounted. **3** a similar structure for gunners on armored tanks. **4** a cockpit in a military aircraft, usually enclosed by a strong, transparent plastic material and containing a machine gun or guns. **5** formerly, a kind of tower on wheels, formerly used in attacking walled castles, forts, or towns. [ME < OF *torete*, dim. of *tor* < L *turris* tower]

Turrets on a building

tur·ret·ed (tėr′ə tid) *adj.* **1** having a turret or turrets. **2** in zoology, having whorls in the form of a long spiral: *turreted shells.*

tur·tle[1] (tėr′təl) *n.* **1** any of certain marine reptiles having the body enclosed in a hard shell from which the head, tail, and four legs protrude. Turtles living on the land are often called tortoises. **2** the flesh of turtles, especially the terrapin, used as food. **3 turn turtle,** turn bottom side up. [< F *tortue* tortoise; influenced by E *turtle* turtledove]

tur·tle[2] (tėr′təl) *n. Archaic.* turtledove. [OE *turtle, turtla* < L *turtur*]

tur·tle·back (tėr′təl bak′) *n.* **1** the back of a turtle. **2** an arched protection erected over the deck of a steamer at the bow, and often at the stern also, to guard against damage from heavy seas.

tur·tle·dove (tėr′təl duv′) *n.* a kind of small, slender dove, noted for the affection that the mates show for each other. [< *turtle*[2] + *dove*[1]]

tur·tle·neck (tėr′təl nek′) *n.* **1** a round, snugly fitting collar on a sweater, etc., usually turned over double when worn. **2** a sweater having such a collar.

Tus·can (tus′kən) *adj.* **1** of or having to do with Tuscany, a region in central Italy, or its people. **2** in architecture, of or having to do with a style developed in ancient Rome, characterized by a plain, round column and lack of decoration. —*n.* **1** a native or inhabitant of Tuscany. **2** the form of Italian spoken in Tuscany. Tuscan is regarded as standard Italian.

Tus·ca·ro·ra (tus′kə rô′rə) *n.* **-ra** or **-ras. 1** a tribe of North American Indians that lived in colonial North

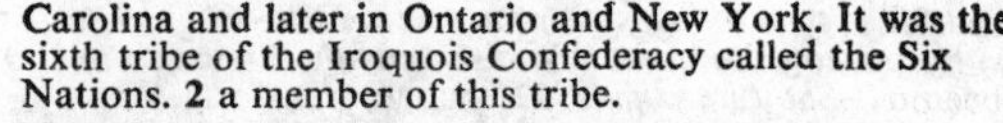

Carolina and later in Ontario and New York. It was the sixth tribe of the Iroquois Confederacy called the Six Nations. **2** a member of this tribe.

tush[1] (tush) *interj. n.* an exclamation expressing impatience, contempt, etc.

tush[2] (tush) *n.* tusk [OE *tusc.* Related to TOOTH.]

tusk (tusk) *n.* **1** a very long, pointed, projecting tooth. Elephants, walruses, and wild boars have tusks. **2** any tusklike tooth or part. —*v.* gore with a tusk; dig or tear with the tusks. [ME *tusk*, var. of OE *tux*, var. of *tusc* tush[2]]

The tusks of a walrus

tusk·er (tus′kər) *n.* an animal with well-developed tusks, such as a mature elephant, walrus, or wild boar.

tus·sah (tus′ə) *n.* tussore.

tus·sle (tus′əl) *v.* **-sled, -sling,** *n.* struggle; wrestle; scuffle. [var. of *tousle*]

tus·sock (tus′ək) *n.* a tuft of growing grass, etc. [origin uncertain]

tussock moth a dull-colored moth whose larvae have thick tufts of hair.

tus·sore (tus′ôr) *n.* **1** a coarse silk made especially in India. **2** the silkworm that produces the silk. Also, **tussah.** [< Hind. *tasar* shuttle]

tut (tut) *interj. n.* an exclamation of impatience, contempt, or rebuke.

tu·te·lage (tū′tə lij or tü′tə lij) *n.* **1** guardianship; protection. **2** instruction. **3** the state of being in the charge of a guardian or tutor. [< L *tutela* watching]

tu·te·lar (tū′tə lər or tü′tə lər) *adj.* tutelary.

tu·te·lar·y (tū′tə ler′ē or tü′tə ler′ē) *adj. n.* **-lar·ies.** —*adj.* **1** protecting; guardian: *a tutelary saint.* **2** of a guardian; used as a guardian; protective. —*n.* a tutelary saint, spirit, divinity, etc. [< L *tutelarius* < *tutela* protection < *tueri* watch over]

tu·tor (tū′tər or tü′tər) *n.* **1** a private teacher. **2** in certain colleges and universities, a teacher, especially one who gives instruction to students individually or in small groups. **3** in English universities, a college official appointed to advise students, direct their work, etc. —*v.* **1** teach; instruct, especially individually or privately. **2** *Informal.* be taught by a tutor. **3** act as tutor. [ME < L *tutor* guardian < *tueri* watch over]

tu·to·ri·al (tū tô′rē əl or tü tô′rē əl) *adj.* **1** of or having to do with a tutor: *tutorial authority.* **2** using tutors: *the tutorial system.* —*n.* a period of individual instruction given in some colleges by a tutor either to a single student or a small group.

tu·tor·ship (tū′tər ship′ or tü′tər-) *n.* the position, rank, or duties of a tutor.

tut·ti (tü′tē; *Italian,* tüt′tē) *adj. n.* **-tis** (-tēz). in music: —*adj.* **1** all; all instruments or voices together. **2** to be performed by all instruments or voices. —*n.* a passage or section to be performed by all instruments or voices. [< Ital. *tutti,* pl. of *tutto* all]

tut·ti-frut·ti (tü′tē frü′tē) *n.* **1** a preserve of mixed fruits. **2** ice cream containing a variety of fruits or fruit flavorings. —*adj.* flavored by mixed fruits. [< Ital. *tutti frutti* all fruits]

tu·tu (tü′tü; *French,* TY TY′) *n.* a ballet dancer's very short, frilly skirt. [< F *tutu*, alteration of *cucu*, child's reduplication of *cul* bottom < L *culus*]

tux (tuks) *n. Informal.* tuxedo.

tux·e·do (tuk sē′dō) *n.* **-dos** or **-does. 1** a man's coat for evening wear, made without tails. **2** the suit to which such a coat belongs. [< *Tuxedo* Park, New York, where it is supposed to have been first worn]

tu·yère (twē yãr′ or twēr) *n.* a tube or pipe through which the blast of air enters a blast furnace, forge, etc. [< F *tuyère*, ult. < Gmc.]

TV or **tv** terminal velocity.

TV or **T.V.** (tē′vē′) *n.* **1** television. **2** a television set. —*adj.* of or having to do with television or television sets.

twad·dle (twod′əl) *n. v.* **-dled, -dling.** —*n.* silly, feeble, tiresome talk or writing. —*v.* talk or write in a silly, feeble, tiresome way. [alteration of earlier *twattle*, ? < *tattle*] —**twad′dler,** *n.*

twain (twān) *n. adj. Archaic or poetic.* two. [OE *twēgen*]

twang (twang) *n.* **1** a sharp, ringing sound: *The bow made a twang when I shot the arrow.* **2** a sharp, nasal tone: *Some Nova Scotians speak with a twang.*
—*v.* **1** make or cause to make a sharp, ringing sound: *The banjos twanged.* **2** play, pluck, shoot, etc. with a twang: *He twanged an arrow into the target.* **3** speak with a sharp, nasal tone. [imitative]

'twas (twoz or twuz; *unstressed,* twez) it was.

tweak (twēk) *v.* seize and pull with a sharp jerk and twist: *She tweaked his ear.* —*n.* a sharp pull and twist. [< var. of OE *twiccian* pluck]

tweed (twēd) *n.* **1** a woollen cloth with a rough surface, usually woven of yarns of two or more colors. **2** a suit, etc. made of this cloth. **3** a similar cloth made of other materials. **4 tweeds,** *pl.* clothes made of tweed. [said to be a misreading of *tweel,* var. of *twill*]

twee·dle (twē′dəl) *v.* **-dled, -dling.** play or produce shrill tones, such as those of a bagpipe or fiddle. [origin uncertain]

twee·dle·dum and twee·dle·dee (twē′dəl dum′ən twē′dəl dē′) **1** two persons or things that are practically identical. **2 Tweedledum and Tweedledee,** identical twin brothers in Lewis Carroll's *Through the Looking Glass.* [< *Tweedle* + *-dum, -dee,* imitative of the sounds of low- and high-pitched instruments, applied to two rival musicians, Handel and Bononcini, by John Byrom (1692-1763)]

tweed·y (twēd′ē) *adj.* **1** made of tweed; like tweed. **2** in the habit of wearing tweeds or other clothing suggestive of the outdoors.

'tween (twēn) *prep. Poetic.* between.

tweet (twēt) *n. interj.* the note of a young bird. —*v.* utter a tweet or tweets. [imitative]

tweet·er (twēt′ər) *n.* a small high-fidelity loudspeaker used to reproduce sounds in the higher frequency range.

tweez·ers (twēz′ərz) *n.pl. or sing.* small pincers for pulling out hairs, picking up small objects, etc. [< *tweeze* instrument case, ult. < F *étui* < OF *estuier* keep < VL *studiare* be zealous < L *studium* zeal]

Tweezers

twelfth (twelfth) *adj. n.* **1** next after the 11th; last in a series of 12. **2** one, or being one, of 12 equal parts.

Twelfth-day (twelfth′dā′) *n.* January 6, the twelfth day after Christmas. On this day the feast of the Epiphany is celebrated. Formerly it marked the end of the Christmas season.

Twelfth-night (twelfth′nīt′) *n.* the evening or eve of Twelfth-day, often celebrated as the end of Christmas festivities.

twelve (twelv) *n.* **1** one more than 11; 12. **2 the Twelve or Twelve Apostles,** the twelve disciples and associates of Jesus who were chosen as His Apostles. They were Peter, James, John, Andrew, Thomas, James the Less, Jude, Philip, Bartholomew, Matthew, Simon, and Judas. —*adj.* one more than 11; 12. [OE *twelf*]

twelve·fold (twelv′fōld′) *adj.* **1** twelve times as much or as many. **2** having 12 parts. —*adv.* twelve times as much or as many.

twelve·mo (twelv′mō) *n.* **-mos,** *adj.* duodecimo.

twelve·month (twelv′munth′) *n.* a period of twelve months; a year.

Twelve Tables in ancient Rome, the first written code of laws, produced in 451 and 450 B.C.

twelve-tone (twelv′tōn′) *adj.* **1** of or having to do with an atonal musical system developed by Arnold Schönberg, in which all the twelve tones of the chromatic scale are used in an arbitrarily chosen order but without the traditional tone centre or key. **2** using this musical system.

twen·ti·eth (twen′tē ith) *adj. n.* **1** next after the 19th; last in a series of 20. **2** one, or being one, of 20 equal parts.

twen·ty (twen′tē) *n.* **-ties,** *adj.* two times ten; 20. [OE *twēntig*]

twen·ty·fold (twen′tē fōld′) *adj.* **1** twenty times as much or as many. **2** having 20 parts. —*adv.* twenty times as much or as many.

hat, āge, cãre, fär; let, ēqual, tėrm; it, īce
hot, ōpen, ôrder; oil, out; cup, pu̇t, rüle, ūse
əbove, takən, pencəl, lemən, circəs
ch, child; ng, long; sh, ship
th, thin; ꟗH, then; zh, measure

twenty-one (twen′tē wun′) *n.* blackjack, a card game. [translation of F *vingt-et-un*]

twen·ty-twen·ty or **20/20** (twen′tē twen′tē) *adj.* having the normal vision of the human eye, being able to distinguish from a distance of 20 feet a character that is $\frac{1}{3}$ of an inch in diameter.

'twere (twėr; *unstressed,* twər) it were.

twice (twīs) *adv.* **1** two times: *twice a day.* **2** doubly: *twice as much.* [ME *twies* < OE *twiga* twice]

twice-told (twīs′tōld′) *adj.* **1** told twice. **2** told many times before; trite.

twid·dle (twid′əl) *v.* **-dled, -dling,** *n.* —*v.* **1** twirl: *twiddle one's pencil.* **2** play with idly. **3 twiddle one's thumbs, a** keep turning one's thumbs idly about each other. **b** do nothing; be idle. —*n.* a twirl. [origin uncertain]

twig[1] (twig) *n.* a slender shoot of a tree or other plant; a very small branch. [OE *twigge*]

twig[2] (twig) *v.* **twigged, twig·ging. 1** watch; observe. **2** perceive; understand; comprehend. [originally thieves' slang, ult. < Irish *tuigim* I understand]

twi·light (twī′līt′) *n.* **1** the faint light reflected from the sky before the sun rises and after it sets. **2** the period during which this prevails. **3** any faint light. **4** a condition or period after or before full development, glory, etc. —*adj.* of or having to do with twilight; like that of twilight: *the twilight hour.* [ME *twiligh t* < *twi-* two + *light*[1]]

twilight sleep a semiconscious condition produced by the hypodermic injection of scopolamine and morphine, used especially in childbirth. [translation of G *Dämmerschlaf*]

twilight zone an area or condition not clearly defined, as that between day and night, good and evil, etc.

twill (twil) *n.* **1** cloth woven in raised diagonal lines. Serge is a twill. **2** a diagonal line or pattern formed by such weaving. —*v.* weave (cloth) in the manner of a twill. [OE *twilic* < L *bilix* with a double thread < *bi-* two + *licium* thread, with substitution of *twi-* two for *bi-*]

'twill (twil) it will.

twilled (twild) *adj.* woven in raised diagonal lines.

twin (twin) *n. adj. v.* **twinned, twin·ning.** —*n.* **1** one of two children or animals born at the same time from the same mother. Twins sometimes look just alike. **2** one of two persons or things exactly alike. **3** a composite crystal consisting of two crystals, usually equal and similar, united in reversed positions with respect to each other. **4 the Twins,** in astrology, the third sign of the zodiac; Gemini.
—*adj.* **1** being a twin: *twin sisters.* **2** being one of two things very much alike: *twin beds.* **3** having two like parts; *a twin-engined airplane.*
—*v.* **1** give birth to twins. **2** join closely; pair. **3** match; duplicate. [OE *twinn*]

twin bed a single bed that is one of a matching pair.

twine (twīn) *n. v.* **twined, twin·ing.** —*n.* **1** a strong thread or string made of two or more strands twisted together. **2** a twisting; twisting together. **3** a twist; twisted thing.
—*v.* **1** twist together: *She twined holly into wreaths.* **2** wind or wrap around: *The vine twines around the tree.* **3** enfold; wreathe, or encircle (one thing with another): *The child twined her arms about her mother's knees.* [OE *twīn*]

twin flower either of two trailing evergreen shrubs of the honeysuckle family having pairs of fragrant, bell-shaped flowers and glossy leaves. One is native to America, the other to Europe.

twinge (twinj) *n. v.* **twinged, twing·ing.** —*n.* **1** a sharp pinching pain: *a twinge of rheumatism.* **2** a sharp mental

pain; pang: *a twinge of remorse.* [< v.]
—*v.* **1** feel a twinge. **2** cause a twinge in. [OE *twengan* pinch] —**Syn.** *n.* ache, pang, cramp.

twin·kle (twing′kəl) *v.* **-kled, -kling,** *n.* —*v.* **1** shine with quick little gleams: *The stars twinkled. Jack's eyes twinkled when he laughed.* **2** move quickly: *The dancer's feet twinkled.* **3** wink; blink. **4** cause to twinkle. —*n.* **1** a twinkling; sparkle; gleam. **2** a quick motion. **3** a quick motion of the eye; wink; blink. **4** the time required for a wink. [OE *twinclian*] —**twin′kler,** *n.* —**Syn.** *v.* **1** sparkle, scintillate, glitter.

twin·kling (twing′kling) *n.* **1** a little, quick gleam. **2** an instant.

twin-screw (twin′skrü′) *adj.* having two screw propellers, which revolve in opposite directions.

twin·ship (twin′ship′) *n.* **1** the fact or condition of being a twin or twins. **2** the relation existing between twins.

twirl (twėrl) *v.* **1** revolve rapidly; spin; whirl. **2** turn round and round idly. **3** twist; curl. **4** flourish. **5** in baseball, throw (a ball); pitch. —*n.* **1** a twirling; spin; whirl; turn: *a twirl in a dance.* **2** a twist; curl. **3** flourish: *He signed his name with many twirls.* [cf. OE *thwirel* churn staff, and G *zwirlen* twirl] —**twirl′er,** *n.*

twist (twist) *v.* **1** turn; wind: *She twisted the ring on her finger.* **2** wind together; twine: *This rope is twisted from many threads. Mary twisted flowers into a wreath.* **3** turn around: *She twisted in her seat to see what was happening behind her.* **4** give a spiral form to. **5** make (a ball) go round while moving in a curved direction. **6** have a winding shape; curve or bend in any way: *The path twists in and out among the rocks.* **7** curve; bend. **8** spin; twirl. **9** force out of shape or place: *His face was twisted with pain.* **10** give a wrong meaning to; distort: *The lawyer confused the witness by twisting his words.* **11** distort the purpose or intent of; pervert: *seek to twist the law to one's own advantage.* **12** mix up; confuse; confound. **13** dance the twist. [< n.]
—*n.* **1** a curve; bend. **2** a spin; twirl. **3** the act of twisting; the state of being twisted. **4** anything made by twisting: *a twist of bread.* **5** a thread, cord, or rope made of two or more strands twisted together. **6** a peculiar bias or inclination: *His answer showed a mental twist.* **7** torsional strain or stress; torque. **8** a wrench; sprain: *suffer a painful twist of the elbow.* **9** in sports: **a** a lateral spin imparted to a ball in throwing or striking it. **b** a ball thus spun. **10** a dance in two-beat rhythm, with strong swinging movements from side to side. [OE *-twist,* as in *mæsttwist* mast rope, stay] —**twist′a·ble,** *adj.* —**Syn.** *v.* **2** coil, interweave, intertwine. **9** contort, distort.

twist·er (twis′tər) *n.* **1** a person or thing that twists. **2** a ball moving with a spinning motion, especially a baseball thrown in a curve. **3** *Informal.* a whirlwind; tornado; cyclone. **4** *Informal.* a person who cannot be trusted; cheat.

twit (twit) *v.* **twit·ted, twit·ting,** *n.* —*v.* jeer at; reproach; taunt; tease. —*n.* a reproach; taunt. [OE *ætwītan* < *æt* at + *wītan* blame]

twitch (twich) *v.* **1** move with a quick jerk: *The child's mouth twitched as if she were about to cry.* **2** pull with a sudden tug or jerk; pull (at): *She twitched the curtain aside.* —*n.* **1** a quick, jerky movement of some part of the body. **2** a short, sudden pull or jerk. **3** a sharp pain; twinge. [related to OE *twiccian* pluck]

twitch grass a coarse, weedlike kind of grass, difficult to eradicate.

twit·ter (twit′ər) *n.* **1** a sound made by birds; chirping. **2** a titter; giggle. **3** an excited condition: *My nerves are in a twitter when I have to sing in public.* —*v.* **1** make a twittering sound. **2** chirp. **3** titter; giggle. **4** tremble with excitement. [imitative]

'twixt (twikst) *prep. Poetic or dialect.* betwixt; between.

two (tü) *n.* **twos,** *adj.* —*n.* **1** one more than one; 2. **2** a set of two persons or things. **3** a playing card, die, domino, etc. having two spots. **4 in two,** in two parts or pieces. **5 put two and two together,** form an obvious conclusion from the facts. —*adj.* one more than one; 2. [OE *twā*]

two-bag·ger (tü′bag′ər) *n.* in baseball, a two-base hit.

two-base hit in baseball, a hit that allows the batter to reach second base.

two-bit (tü′bit′) *adj. Slang.* **1** valued at twenty-five cents. **2** cheap; unimportant.

two bits *Slang.* twenty five cents, a quarter.

two-by-four (tü′bī fôr′) *adj.* **1** measuring two inches, feet, etc. by four inches, feet, etc. **2** *Informal.* small; narrow; limited: *a two-by-four room.* —*n.* a piece of lumber four inches wide and two inches thick. Two-by-fours are much used in building.

two cents' worth *Slang.* the expression of one's individual point of view or opinion.

two-edged (tü′ejd′) *adj.* **1** having two edges; cutting both ways. **2** effective either way: *a two-edged argument.* **3** that may be reversed or sharply altered in order to achieve a purpose: *a two-edged policy.*

two-faced (tü′fāst′) *adj.* **1** having two faces. **2** deceitful; hypocritical.

two-fist·ed (tü′fis′tid) *adj. Informal.* **1** having two fists and able to use them. **2** strong; vigorous.

two·fold (tü′fōld′) *adj.* **1** two times as much or as many; double. **2** having two parts. —*adv.* two times as much or as many; doubly.

two-four (tü′fôr′) *adj.* in music, indicating or having two quarter notes to a bar or measure, the first of which is accented.

two-hand·ed (tü′han′did) *adj.* **1** having two hands. **2** using both hands equally well. **3** involving the use of both hands; requiring both hands to wield or manage: *a two-handed sword.* **4** requiring two persons to operate: *a two-handed saw.* 5 engaged in by two persons: *a two-handed game.*

two-part time in music, a time or rhythm with two beats to the measure, or a multiple of two beats to the measure.

two-par·ty system (tü′pär′tē) a political system in which two political parties predominate over any others, one of the two generally having a majority in the legislature. This system originated in Great Britain in the 17th century, and has prevailed in Canada, the United States, and most countries of the English-speaking world.

two·pence (tup′əns) *n.* two British pennies; two pence. Also, **tuppence.**

two·pen·ny (tup′ən ē) *adj.* **1** worth twopence. **2** trifling; worthless.

two-ply (tü′plī′) *adj.* having two thicknesses, folds, layers, or strands.

two·some (tü′səm) *n.* **1** a group of two people. **2** a game played by two people. **3** the players in such a game.

two-step (tü′step′) *n.* **1** a dance in two-part time. **2** the music for such a dance.

two-time (tü′tīm′) *v.* **-timed, -tim·ing.** *Slang.* **1** be unfaithful to in love. **2** deceive; betray. —**two′-tim′er,** *n.*

'twould (twůd; *unstressed,* twəd) it would.

two-way (tü′wā′) *adj.* **1** having two lanes, sets of lanes, roads, etc., enabling traffic to move in opposite directions: *a two-way street.* **2** extending in both ways or in two directions. **3** used for two purposes. A two-way radio transmits and receives. **4** having to do with a pipe, wire, valve, etc. that connects with two outlets. **5** in mathematics, capable of variation in two ways or modes: *a two-way progression.*

two-wheel·er (tü′hwēl′ər or -wēl′ər) *n.* a vehicle, such as a bicycle or motorcycle, having two wheels.

twp. *pl.* **twps.** township.

-ty[1] *suffix.* tens, as in *sixty, seventy, eighty.* [OE *-tig*]

-ty[2] *suffix.* fact, quality, state, condition, etc. of being ——, as in *safety, sovereignty, surety. -ity* is often used instead of *-ty,* as in *artificiality, complexity, humidity.* [ME < OF *-te, -tet* < L *-tas, -tatis*]

Ty. territory.

Ty·burn (tī′bərn) *n.* in London, a former place of public execution.

ty·coon (tī kün′) *n. Informal.* a man who holds an important position in business, industry, etc. [< Japanese *taikun* < Chinese *tai* great + *kiun* lord]

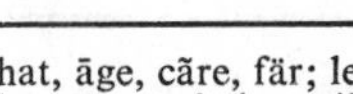

hat, āge, cãre, fär; let, ēqual, têrm; it, īce
hot, ōpen, ôrder; oil, out; cup, pu̇t, rüle, ūse
əbove, takən, pencəl, lemən, circəs
ch, child; ng, long; sh, ship
th, thin; ᴛʜ, then; zh, measure

ty·ee (tī′ē) *n.* **ty·ee** (def. 2) or **ty·ees. 1** a chief. **2** a tyee salmon. [< Chinook Jargon]

tyee salmon a large chinook salmon.

ty·ing (tī′ing) *v.* ppr. of **tie.**

tyke (tīk) *n.* **1** cur. **2** *Informal.* a mischievous or troublesome child. **3** *Dialect.* a low fellow. Also, **tike.** [ME < ON *tik* bitch]

tym·pan (tim′pən) *n.* **1** a stretched membrane, or a sheet or plate of some thin material, in an apparatus. **2** *Archaic.* a drum. [< L < Gk. *tympanon.* Doublet of TYMPANUM, TIMBRE.]

tym·pa·ni (tim′pə nē′) *n.* pl. of **tympano.**

tym·pan·ic (tim pan′ik) *adj.* **1** in anatomy, of or having to do with the eardrum or the middle ear. **2** like a drum.

tympanic membrane the eardrum.

tym·pa·nist (tim′pə nist) *n.* timpanist.

tym·pa·no (tim′pə nō′) *n.* **-ni** (-nē′). timpano.

tym·pa·num (tim′pə nəm) *n.* **-nums** or **-na** (-nə). **1** the eardrum. **2** the middle ear. **3** the diaphragm in a telephone. **4** in architecture: **a** the vertical recessed face of a pediment, enclosed by the cornices. **b** a slab or wall between an arch and the horizontal top of a door or window below. [< L *tympanum* drum < Gk. *tympanon.* Doublet of TIMBRE, TYMPAN.]

type (tīp) *n. v.* **typed, typ·ing.** —*n.* **1** a kind, class, or group having common characteristics: *women of the blonde type.* **2** kind; sort; order: *He doesn't like that type of work.* **3** a person or thing having the characteristics of a kind, class, or group; example; illustration; model; representative; symbol: *John is a fine type of schoolboy.* **4** the general form, style, or character of some kind, class, or group: *She is above the ordinary type of servant.* **5** in biology: **a** a general plan or structure characterizing a group of animals, plants, etc. **b** a genus, species, etc. which most perfectly exhibits the essential characters of its family or group, and from which the family or group is usually named. **6** in printing: **a** a piece of metal or wood having on its upper surface a raised letter for use in printing. **b** a collection of such pieces. **7** printed letters; typewritten letters. **8** the figure, writing, or design on either side of a coin or medal. **9** a blood type.
—*v.* **1** be a type or symbol of; symbolize. **2** be the pattern or model for. **3** find out the type of: *type a person's blood.* **4** typewrite. [< L < Gk. *typos* dent, impression]
—**Syn.** *n.* **3** pattern, prototype.

☛ **type of.** The general idiom should not be shortened by omitting the *of,* as in *this type letter.* Standard usage requires *this type of letter.*

type·cast (tīp′kast′) *v.* **-cast, -cast·ing. 1** cast an actor in a role to fit his personality, appearance, etc. **2** cast an actor repeatedly in the same kind of role.

type·script (tīp′skript′) *n.* a typewritten manuscript.

type·set·ter (tīp′set′ər) *n.* a person or machine that sets type for printing.

type·set·ting (tīp′set′ing) *n.* the act of setting type for printing. —*adj.* used or adapted for setting type: *a typesetting machine.*

type·write (tīp′rīt′) *v.* **-wrote, -writ·ten, -writ·ing.** write with a typewriter; type.

type·writ·er (tīp′rīt′ər) *n.* **1** a hand-operated machine for writing, which reproduces letters, figures, etc. similar to printed ones. **2** a typist.

A typewriter

type·writ·ing (tīp′rīt′ing) *n.* **1** the act or art of using a typewriter. **2** work done on a typewriter.

type·writ·ten (tīp′rit′ən) *adj.* written with a typewriter: *a typewritten letter.* —*v.* pp. of **typewrite.**

ty·phoid (tī′foid) *adj.* **1** of or having to do with typhoid fever. **2** like typhus. —*n.* typhoid fever. [< *typhus*]

typhoid bacillus the bacillus that causes typhoid fever.

typhoid fever an infectious, often fatal, disease characterized by fever, skin eruptions, and intestinal inflammation, caused by the typhoid bacillus, which is taken into the body with food or drink.

ty·phoon (tī fün′) *n.* a violent hurricane occurring in the W. Pacific Ocean and the China Sea, chiefly during the months of July, August, September, and October. [< Chinese *tai fung* big wind; influenced by Gk. *typhōn* whirlwind] —**Syn.** See **cyclone.**

ty·phus (tī′fəs) *n.* an acute infectious disease characterized by high fever, skin eruptions, and prostration, caused by germs carried by fleas, lice, etc. [< NL < Gk. *typhos* stupor, originally, smoke]

typ·i·cal (tip′ə kəl) *adj.* **1** being of a certain type; representative; characteristic: *a typical Thanksgiving dinner; the hospitality typical of the frontiersman.* **2** in biology, that is the type of the genus, family, etc. —**Syn.** illustrative.

typ·i·cal·ly (tip′ik lē) *adj.* **1** in a typical manner. **2** to a typical degree. **3** ordinarily.

typ·i·fy (tip′ə fī′) *v.* **-fied, -fy·ing. 1** be a symbol of: *The wearing of black typifies mourning.* **2** have the common characteristics of: *Alexander MacKenzie typifies the adventurous explorer.* **3** indicate beforehand. [< L *typus* type + E *-fy*] —**typ′i·fi·ca′tion,** *n.*

typ·ist (tīp′ist) *n.* a person who operates a typewriter; one who makes a living by typewriting.

ty·pog·ra·pher (tī pog′rə fər) *n.* a printer.

ty·po·graph·ic (tī′pə graf′ik) *adj.* typographical.

ty·po·graph·i·cal (tī′pə graf′ə kəl) *adj.* of or having to do with printing: *typographical errors.*
—**ty′po·graph′i·cal·ly,** *adv.*

ty·pog·ra·phy (tī pog′rə fē) *n.* **1** the art or process of printing with type; the work of setting and arranging type and of printing from it. **2** the arrangement, appearance, or style of printed matter. [< late Med.L < Gk. *typos* type + *-graphia* writing]

ty·po·log·i·cal (tī′pə loj′ə kəl) *adj.* of or having to do with typology.

ty·pol·o·gist (tī pol′ə jist) *n.* one who is skilled in typology.

ty·pol·o·gy (tī pol′ə jē) *n.* the classification and study of types, as of remains and specimens in archeology. [< Gk. *typos* type + E *-logy*]

Tyr (tēr) *n.* the Norse god of war and victory. [< ON]

ty·ran·nic (tə ran′ik or tī ran′ik) *adj.* tyrannical. [< L < Gk. *tyrannikos* < *tyrannos* tyrant]

ty·ran·ni·cal (tə ran′ə kəl or tī ran′ə kəl) *adj.* of or having to do with a tyrant; like a tyrant; arbitrary; cruel; unjust. —**ty·ran′ni·cal·ly,** *adv.* —**Syn.** despotic, dictatorial.

ty·ran·ni·cide[1] (tə ran′ə sīd′ or tī ran′ə sīd′) *n.* the act of killing a tyrant. [< L *tyrannicidium* < *tyrannus* tyrant + *-cidium* act of killing]

ty·ran·ni·cide[2] (tə ran′ə sīd′ or tī ran′ə sīd′) *n.* a person who kills a tyrant. [< L *tyrannicida* < *tyrannus* tyrant + *-cida* killer]

tyr·an·nize (tir′ə nīz′) *v.* **-nized, -niz·ing. 1** use power cruelly or unjustly: *The strong should not tyrannize over the weak.* **2** rule as a tyrant. **3** rule cruelly; oppress.
—**tyr′an·niz·er,** *n.*

ty·ran·no·sau·rus (ti ran′ə sô′rəs) *n.* a huge carnivorous dinosaur of the Upper Cretaceous period in North America, noted for its ability to walk upright on its two hind legs. [< NL *Tyrannosaurus,* the genus name < Gk. *tyrannos* tyrant + *sauros* lizard]

tyr·an·nous (tir′ə nəs) *adj.* **1** acting like a tyrant: *a tyrannous dictator.* **2** cruel or unjust; arbitrary; tyrannical: *tyrannous behavior.* —**tyr′an·nous·ly,** *adv.*

tyr·an·ny (tir′ə nē) *n.* **-nies. 1** cruel or unjust use of power. **2** a tyrannical act. **3** government by an absolute

ruler. [< LL < Gk. *tyrannia* < *tyrannos*. See TYRANT.]
—**Syn. 1** despotism, oppression, harshness.

ty·rant (tī′rənt) *n.* **1** a person who uses his power cruelly or unjustly. **2** a cruel or unjust ruler; cruel master. **3** an absolute ruler, as in ancient Greece, owing his office to usurpation. Some tyrants of Greek cities were actually mild and just rulers. [ME < OF < L < Gk. *tyrannos* (def. 3)]

tyre (tīr) *n. v.* **tyred, tyr·ing.** *Brit.* tire².

Tyr·i·an (tir′ē ən) *adj.* of or having to do with Tyre, a city in S.W. Lebanon, on the side of the ancient capital of Phoenicia. —*n.* a native of Tyre. [< L < Gk. *Tyrios*]

Tyrian purple 1 a crimson or purple dye used in ancient times by the Greeks and Romans. **2** bluish red.

ty·ro (tī′rō) *n.* **-ros.** a beginner in learning anything; novice; greenhorn. Also, **tiro.** [< L *tiro* recruit]

Ty·ro·le·an (tə rō′lē ən or tir′ə lē′ən) *adj. n.* Tyrolese. Also, **Tirolean.**

Tyr·o·lese (tir′ə lēz′) *adj.* of or having to do with Tyrol, a region in the Alps, partly in Austria and partly in Italy, or its inhabitants. —*n.* a native or inhabitant of Tyrol. Also, **Tirolese.**

tzar (zär) *n.* czar.

tzar·e·vitch (zär′ə vich) *n.* czarevitch.

tza·ri·na (zä rē′nə) *n.* czarina.

tzet·ze (tset′sē) *n.* tsetse.

U¹ or **u** (ū) *n.* **U's** or **u's. 1** the twenty-first letter of the alphabet. **2** any speech sound represented by this letter. **3** one (usually twenty-first) of a series designated alphabetically. **4** anything shaped like U.

U² (ū) *adj. Esp.Brit. Slang.* upper-class, sophisticated. [< *u*pper class]

u. 1 upper. **2** uncle.

U uranium.

U. University.

U.A.R. United Arab Republic.

UAW United Automobile Workers (Union).

u·biq·ui·tous (ū bik′wə təs) *adj.* being everywhere at the same time; present everywhere. [< *ubiquity*] —**u·biq′ui·tous·ly,** *adv.* —**u·biq′ui·tous·ness,** *n.*

u·biq·ui·ty (ū bik′wə tē) *n.* **1** the act or condition of being everywhere at the same time. **2** the ability to be everywhere at once. [< NL *ubiquitas* < L *ubique* everywhere]

U-boat (ū′bōt′) *n.* a German submarine. [half-translation of G *U-boot*, short for *Unterseeboot* undersea boat]

U bolt a bolt shaped like the letter U and having threads and a nut at each end.

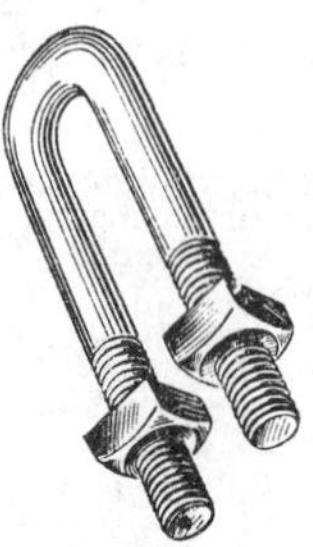
A U bolt

u.c. upper case; a capital letter or letters.

U.C. 1 Upper Canada. **2** United Church. **3** University College.

ud·der (ud′ər) *n.* of cows, goats, sheep, etc., the gland from which milk comes. [OE *ūder*]

u·dom·e·ter (ū dom′ə tər) *n.* a rain gauge. [< L *udus* wet + E *-meter*]

U.E.L. United Empire Loyalist.

UFO unidentified flying object.

U·gan·dan (ū gan′dən) *adj.* of or having to do with Uganda, a country in Africa. —*n.* a native or inhabitant of Uganda.

ugh (u̇H, u, uH, or ug) *interj.* an exclamation expressing disgust or horror.

ug·ly (ug′lē) *adj.* **-li·er, -li·est. 1** very unpleasant to look at: *an ugly house, an ugly face.* **2** bad; disagreeable; offensive: *an ugly task.* **3** likely to cause trouble; threatening; dangerous: *an ugly wound, ugly clouds.* **4** *Informal.* ill-natured; bad-tempered; quarrelsome. [ME < ON *uggligr* dreadful] —**ug′li·ness,** *n.*

Syn. 1 Ugly, unsightly, homely = not pleasing in appearance. **Ugly,** the opposite of *beautiful*, means "positively unpleasant or offensive in appearance": *There are five ugly lamps in that room.* **Unsightly** emphasizes being unpleasing to the sight, sometimes causing one to turn away to avoid seeing what is described: *Trains approach the city through an unsightly section.* **Homely** emphasizes lack of beauty or attractiveness, but does not suggest unpleasant or disagreeable qualities: *a homely child.*

U·gri·an (ū′grē ən or ü′grē ən) *n.* **1** a member of the branch of the Finno-Ugric peoples that includes the Magyars and certain groups from western Siberia. **2** the languages of these peoples. —*adj.* of or designating the Ugrians or their languages.

U·gric (ū′grik or ü′grik) *n.* the branch of the Finno-Ugric family of languages that includes Hungarian.

UHF, U.H.F., or **uhf** ultrahigh frequency.

uh·lan (ü′län or ü län′) *n.* formerly: **1** in certain European armies, a lancer and cavalry man of a type first known in Poland. **2** in the German army, a member of the heavy cavalry. [< G < Polish < Turkish *oghlān* boy]

U.K. United Kingdom.

u·kase (ū kās′ or ū′kās) *n.* **1** formerly, an order of the ruler or government of Russia. **2** any official proclamation or order. [< Russian *ukaz*]

Uke (ūk) *n. adj. Derogatory slang.* Ukrainian.

Ukr. 1 Ukraine. **2** Ukrainian.

U·krain·i·an (ū krān′ē ən) *adj.* **1** of or having to do with the Ukraine, a republic in S.W. Soviet Union, its people, or their language. **2** of or having to do with Canadians of Ukrainian descent. —*n.* **1** a native or inhabitant of the Ukraine. **2** their Slavic language, closely related to Russian. **3** a Canadian of Ukrainian descent.

u·ku·le·le (ū′kə lā′lē) *n.* a small guitar having four strings. [< Hawaiian *ukulele*, originally, flea < *uku* insect + *lele* jump, leap]

ul·cer (ul′sər) *n.* **1** an open sore that is not a wound, found on the skin or, within the body, on a mucous membrane: *stomach ulcer.* **2** a moral sore spot; corrupting influence. [< L *ulcus, ulceris*]

ul·cer·ate (ul′sər āt′) *v.* **-at·ed, -at·ing. 1** affect or be affected with an ulcer: *An ulcerated tooth may be very painful.* **2** form an ulcer. [< L *ulcerare* < *ulcus* ulcer]

ul·cer·a·tion (ul′sər ā′shən) *n.* **1** an ulcerating or being ulcerated. **2** an ulcer.

ul·cer·ous (ul′sər əs) *adj.* **1** having ulcers. **2** of or having to do with ulcers. **—ul′cer·ous·ly,** *adv.* **—ul′cer·ous·ness,** *n.*

ul·na (ul′nə) *n.* **-nae** (-nē or -nī) or **-nas. 1** in anatomy, the bone of the forearm on the side opposite the thumb. See **skeleton** for picture. **2** in zoology, a corresponding bone in the foreleg of an animal. [< NL < L *ulna* elbow]

ul·nar (ul′nər) *adj.* **1** of or having to do with the ulna. **2** in or supplying the part of the forearm near the ulna.

ul·ster (ul′stər) *n.* a long, loose, heavy overcoat, often belted at the waist. [< *Ulster*, a province of Ireland]

ult. 1 ultimo. **2** ultimate. **3** ultimately. ☛ See **inst.** for usage note.

ul·te·ri·or (ul tēr′ē ər) *adj.* **1** beyond what is seen or expressed; hidden. **2** more distant; on the farther side. **3** further; later. [< L *ulterior*, comparative of root of *ultra, ultro*, adv., beyond] **—ul·te′ri·or·ly,** *adv.*

ul·ti·ma (ul′tə mə) *n.* the last syllable of a word. [< L *ultima (syllaba)* last (syllable)]

ul·ti·mate (ul′tə mit) *adj.* **1** coming at the end; last possible; final: *He never stopped to consider the ultimate result of his actions.* **2** that is an extremity; beyond which there is nothing at all; extreme: *the ultimate limits of the universe.* **3** beyond which nothing further may be ascertained by investigation or analysis: *The brain is the ultimate source of ideas. The ultimate source of life has not been discovered.* **4** greatest possible. **5 the Ultimate,** God; the Ultimate Reality.
—n. an ultimate point, result, fact, etc. [< Med.L *ultimatus*, pp. of *ultimare* < Ital. *ultimare* bring to an end < L *ultimare* come to an end < *ultimus* last] **—Syn. 1** See **last**[1].

ul·ti·mate·ly (ul′tə mit lē) *adv.* finally; in the end.

ultimate strength in physics, the maximum stress or tension a substance can bear without tearing or breaking.

ultimate stress in physics, the stress or load needed to produce fracture or breakage.

ultima Thu·le (thü′lē) **1** the farthest north. **2** the farthest limit or point possible. **3** the uttermost degree attainable. [< L *ultima Thule* most remote Thule]

ul·ti·ma·tum (ul′tə mā′təm) *n.* **-tums, -ta** (-tə). **1** a final proposal or statement of conditions. **2** the final terms presented by one party in an international negotiation, rejection of which may lead to the breaking off of diplomatic relations or sometimes to a declaration of war. [< NL *ultimatum*, originally neut. of Med.L *ultimatus*. See ULTIMATE.]

ul·ti·mo (ul′tə mō′) *adv.* in or of last month. [< Med.L *ultimo (mense)* in the last (month)]

ul·tra (ul′trə) *adj.* beyond what is usual; very; excessive; extreme. *—n.* a person who holds extreme views or urges extreme measures. [< L *ultra* beyond]

ultra- *prefix.* **1** beyond, as in *ultraviolet.* **2** going beyond the limits, or province of; more than, as in *ultramundane.* **3** very, excessively, or unusually, as in:

ul′tra·am·bi′tious	**ul′tra·loy′al**
ul′tra·con′fi·dent	**ul′tra·ma·ter′nal**
ul′tra·con·serv′a·tive	**ul′tra·me·chan′i·cal**
ul′tra·cred′u·lous	**ul′tra·mod′ern**
ul′tra·crit′i·cal	**ul′tra·mod′est**
ul′tra·dem′o·crat′ic	**ul′tra·rad′i·cal**
ul′tra·ex·clu′sive	**ul′tra·re·fined′**
ul′tra·fash′ion·a·ble	**ul′tra·re·li′gious**
ul′tra·lib′er·al	**ul′tra·roy′al·ist**

[< LL *ultra-* < L *ultra*, adv. prep. beyond]

ul·tra·high frequency (ul′trə hī′) the band of electromagnetic frequencies between 300 and 3,000 megacycles. *Abbrev.*: UHF, U.H.F., or uhf

hat, āge, cãre, fär; let, ēqual, tėrm; it, īce
hot, ōpen, ôrder; oil, out; cup, pu̇t, rüle, ūse
əbove, takən, pencəl, lemən, circəs
ch, child; ng, long; sh, ship
th, thin; ᴛʜ, then; zh, measure

ul·tra·ma·rine (ul′trə mə rēn′) *n.* **1** a deep blue. **2** a blue pigment made from powdered lapis lazuli. **3** an artificial imitation of this pigment. *—adj.* **1** deep-blue. **2** beyond or across the sea. [< Med.L *ultramarinus* < L *ultra* beyond + *mare* sea; used with reference to the source (Asia) of lapis lazuli]

ul·tra·mi·cro·scope (ul′trə mī′krə skōp′) *n.* a powerful instrument for making visible very tiny particles that are invisible to the common microscope. Light is thrown on the object from one side, over a dark background.

ul·tra·mi·cro·scop·ic (ul′trə mī′krə skop′ik) *adj.* **1** too small to be seen with an ordinary microscope. **2** having to do with an ultramicroscope.

ul·tra·mon·tagne (ul′trə mon′tān) *n.* formerly, a member of the extreme right wing of the Conservative Party in Quebec. *—adj.* of or having to do with this group. [< Cdn.F]

ul·tra·mon·tane (ul′trə mon′tān) *adj.* **1** beyond the mountains. **2** south of the Alps; Italian. **3** in the Roman Catholic Church, supporting a party or policy advocating extreme centralization of papal power, as opposed to a policy of decentralization. *—n.* **1** a person living south of the Alps. **2** a supporter of ultramontane policies.
[< Med.L *ultramontanus* < L *ultra* beyond + *mons, montis* mountain]

ul·tra·mon·tan·ism (ul′trə mon′tə niz′əm) *n.* a doctrine or policy favoring extreme centralization of papal power.

ul·tra·mon·ta·nist (ul′trə mon′tə nist) *n.* a supporter of ultramontanism.

ul·tra·mun·dane (ul′trə mun′dān) *adj.* **1** beyond the world; beyond the limits of the known universe. **2** beyond this present life. [< LL *ultramundanus* < L *ultra* beyond + *mundus* world]

ul·tra·son·ic (ul′trə son′ik) *adj.* of or having to do with sound waves beyond the limit of human audibility.

ul·tra·son·ics (ul′trə son′iks) *n.* the branch of science that deals with the phenomena of sound waves beyond the level of human audibility, or of 20 kilocycles or more per second.

ul·tra·trop·i·cal (ul′trə trop′ə kəl) *adj.* **1** outside of the tropics. **2** warmer than the tropics; very hot.

ul·tra·vi·o·let (ul′trə vī′ə lit) *adj.* **1** of or having to do with the invisible part of the spectrum just beyond the violet. **2** of or having to do with the ultraviolet rays. *—n.* the invisible part or range of the spectrum just beyond the violet.

ultraviolet rays the invisible rays in the part of the spectrum beyond the violet, present in sunlight, in light from mercury-vapor lamps, etc. They are used for healing, forming vitamins, etc.

ul·tra vi·res (ul′trə vī′rēz) *Latin.* going beyond the powers granted by authority or by law.

u·lu (ü′lü) *n.* ooloo.

ul·u·lant (ūl′yu̇ lənt or ul′yu̇ lənt) *adj.* howling.

ul·u·late (ūl′yu̇ lāt′ or ul′yu̇ lāt′) *v.* **-lat·ed, -lat·ing. 1** of a dog, wolf, etc., howl. **2** lament loudly. [< L *ululare* howl] **—ul′u·la′tion,** *n.*

U·lys·ses (ū lis′ēz) *n.* a legendary king of Ithaca, the shrewdest of the Greek leaders in the Trojan war. Homer's epic poem, the *Odyssey*, describes Ulysses' ten years of wandering after this war.

um·bel (um′bəl) *n.* in botany, a flower cluster in which stalks nearly equal in length spring from a common centre and form a flat or slightly curved surface, as in parsley. [< L *umbrella* parasol, dim. of *umbra* shade]

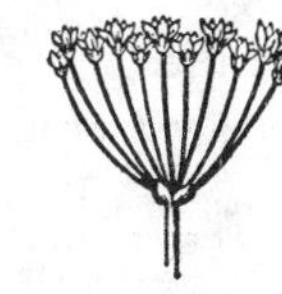
An umbel

um·bel·lar (um′bəl ər) *adj.* umbellate.

um·bel·late (um′bəl it or um′bəl āt′) *adj.* in botany: **1** of or like an umbel. **2** having umbels; forming an umbel or umbels.

um·bel·lif·er·ous (um′bə lif′ər əs) *adj.* in botany, bearing an umbel or umbels. The parsley and carrot are umbelliferous.

um·ber (um′bər) *n.* **1** a heavy, brown earth, consisting mainly of ferric oxide and used in its natural state **(raw umber)** as a brown pigment, or after heating **(burnt umber)** as a reddish-brown pigment. **2** a brown or reddish brown. *—adj.* brown or reddish-brown. [< Ital. (*terra di*) *ombra* (earth of) shade, but (?) originally < *Umbria,* a district in central Italy]

um·bil·i·cal (um bil′ə kəl or um′bi lī′kəl) *adj.* **1** of or having to do with the navel or umbilical cord. **2** formed, placed, or shaped like a navel or umbilical cord.

umbilical cord 1 in anatomy and zoology, a cordlike structure that connects an unborn mammal to the womb of the mother. The umbilical cord is attached to the placenta of the mother and to the abdomen of the embryo. **2** an electric cable, fuel line, or the like, connected to a missile on its launching site and released just before launching.

um·bil·i·cus (um bil′ə kəs or um′bə lī′kəs) *n.* **-ci** (-sī or -sē). **1** the navel; the depression in the middle of the abdomen, indicating the point where the umbilical cord was attached. **2** a navel-like formation, such as the hilum of a seed. [< L *umbilicus* navel]

um·bra (um′brə) *n.* **-brae** (-brē or -brī). **1** a shadow of the earth or moon that completely hides the sun. See **eclipse** for diagram. **2** the dark central part of a sunspot. **3** *Obsolete.* shade; shadow. [< L]

um·brage (um′brij) *n.* **1** a suspicion that one has been slighted or injured; feeling offended; resentment. **2** *Obsolete.* shade. **3** foliage. **4 take umbrage,** take offence; feel insulted or resentful: *He took umbrage at the slightest criticism.* [< F *ombrage,* ult. < L *umbra* shade]

um·bra·geous (um brā′jəs) *adj.* **1** giving shade; shady. **2** likely to take offence. **3** revealing or displaying umbrage; offended; insulted. **—um·bra′geous·ly,** *adv.* **—um·bra′geous·ness,** *n.*

um·brel·la (um brel′ə) *n.* **1** a light, folding frame covered with cloth, used as a protection against rain or sun. **2** a barrage or screen of fighter aircraft to protect ground forces. **3** any protective covering or shelter. [< Ital. *ombrella,* ult. < L *umbra* shade]

Um·bri·an (um′brē ən) *adj.* of or having to do with Umbria, a district in central Italy, or its people. *—n.* **1** a native or inhabitant of Umbria. **2** in ancient times, one of a people living in Umbria. **3** the language of this people.

u·mi·ak (ü′mē ak) *n.* oomiak.

um·laut (ům′lout) *n.* **1** in Germanic languages, a change in vowel sound because of the influence of another vowel in the following syllable, as in *man—men, mouse—mice.* **2** the sign (¨) used to indicate such a vowel, as in German *süss* sweet. **3** a vowel that is the result of such a change. *—v.* modify by umlaut. [< G *Umlaut* < *um* about + *Laut* sound]

um·pire (um′pīr) *n. v.* **-pired, -pir·ing.** *—n.* **1** a person who rules on the plays in certain games: *The umpire called the ball a foul.* **2** a person chosen to settle a dispute. *—v.* **1** act as umpire. **2** act as umpire in. [earlier *a numpire* (taken as *an umpire*) < OF *nonper* not even, odd < *non* not (< L) + *per* equal < L *par*] **—Syn.** *n.* **1** referee. **2** judge.

un-[1] *prefix.* not; the opposite of, as in *unfair, unjust, unequal.* [OE]

In each of the words below **un-** means not. The pronunciation of the main part of the word is not changed; note, however, the modifications in the stress pattern of certain words.

un′a·bat′ed
un′a·bet′ted
un′ab·solved′
un′ac·a·dem′ic
un·ac′cent·ed
un′ac·cept′a·ble
un′ac·cli′mat·ed
un′ac·cli′ma·tized′
un′ac·com′mo·dat′ing
un′ac·com′plished
un′ac·count′ed-for′
un′ac·cred′it·ed
un′ac·knowl′edged
un′ac·quaint′ed
un′a·dapt′a·ble
un′ad·just′a·ble
un′ad·just′ed
un′a·dorned′
un′a·dul′ter·at′ed
un′a·fraid′
un·aid′ed
un′al·lied′
un′al·low′a·ble
un′al·loyed′
un·al′pha·bet·ized′
un·al′tered
un·al′ter·ing
un′am·big′u·ous
un′am·bi′tious
un·a′mi·a·ble
un·an′i·mat′ed
un′an·nounced′
un′ap·peas′a·ble
un′ap·peased′
un·ap′pe·tiz′ing
un′ap·pre′ci·at′ed
un′ap·pre′ci·a·tive
un′ap·proached′
un′ap·pro′pri·at′ed
un′ap·proved′
un·ar′mored
un′ar·rest′ed
un′ar·tis′tic
un′a·shamed′
un·asked′
un′as·sail′a·ble
un′as·sign′a·ble
un′as·sim′i·lat′ed
un′as·sist′ed
un′at·tain′a·ble
un′at·tempt′ed
un′at·trac′tive
un′au·then′tic
un′au·then′ti·cat′ed
un·au′thor·ized′
un′a·vail′a·ble
un′a·venged′
un′a·vowed′
un′bap·tized′
un·barbed′
un·beat′a·ble
un′be·fit′ting
un′be·hold′en
un′be·liev′a·ble
un′be·seem′ing
un′be·trothed′
un′be·wailed′
un·blam′a·ble
un·blamed′
un·blink′ing
un·block′
un·both′ered
un·bought′
un·bound′
un·braced′
un·branched′
un·brand′ed
un·break′a·ble
un·brib′a·ble
un·broth′er·ly
un·bruised′
un·bur′ied
un·burned′
un·burnt′
un·can′celled
un′ca·non′i·cal
un·cared′-for′
un·caught′
un·ceas′ing
un·cen′sored
un·cen′sured
un·chained′
un·chal′lenged
un·chang′ing
un·chap′er·oned′
un·charged′
un·chas′tened
un′chas·tised′
un·chiv′al·rous
un·chris′tened
un·claimed′
un·clas′si·fi′a·ble
un·clas′si·fied′
un·cleaned′
un·cleared′
un·closed′
un·clothed′
un·cloud′ed
un·coat′ed
un·cocked′
un′co·erced′
un′col·lect′ed
un′col·lect′a·ble
un·col′ored
un′com·bined′
un·come′ly
un·com′fort·ed
un′com·pan′ion·a·ble
un′com·plain′ing
un′com·plai′sant
un′com·plet′ed
un·com′pli·cat′ed
un′com·pli·men′ta·ry
un′com·pre·hend′ing
un·com′pro·mised′
un′con·cealed′
un′con·cert′ed
un′con·fined′
un′con·firmed′
un′con·geal′a·ble
un′con·gen′ial
un′con·nect′ed
un·con′quered
un·con′se·crat′ed
un′con·sid′ered
un′con·soled′
un′con·strained′
un′con·sumed′
un′con·tam′i·nat′ed
un′con·test′ed
un′con·tra·dict′a·ble
un′con·tra·dict′ed
un′con·trol′la·ble
un′con·trolled′
un′con·vert′ed
un′con·vinced′
un′con·vinc′ing
un·cooked′
un·cooled′
un′co-or′di·nat′ed
un·cor′dial
un·corked′
un′cor·rect′ed
un′cor·rob′o·rat′ed
un′cor·rupt′ed
un·count′a·ble
un·court′ly
un′cre·at′ed
un·crit′i·cal
un·crit′i·ciz′a·ble
un·crowd′ed
un·cul′ti·va·ble
un·cul′ti·vat′ed
un·cul′tured
un·curbed′
un·cured′
un·curled′
un·cur′rent
un′cur·tailed′
un·cur′tained
un·cut′
un·dam′aged
un·damped′
un·dat′ed
un·daugh′ter·ly
un·daz′zled
un′de·bat′a·ble
un′de·cayed′
un′de·ceiv′a·ble
un′de·ceived′
un′de·ci′pher·a·ble
un′de·ci′phered
un′de·clared′
un′de·clin′a·ble
un′de·clined′
un·dec′o·rat′ed
un′de·feat′a·ble
un′de·feat′ed
un′de·fend′ed
un′de·filed′
un′de·formed′
un′de·layed′
un·de′liv′er·a·ble
un′de·liv′ered
un′dem·o·crat′ic
un′de·mon′stra·ble
un′de·mon′stra·tive
un′de·nied′
un′de·pend′a·ble
un′de·pre′ci·at′ed
un′de·scrib′a·ble
un′de·served′
un′de·serv′ing
un·des′ig·nat′ed
un′de·sign′ing
un′de·sired′

un′de·spair′ing
un′de·stroyed′
un′de·tach′a·ble
un′de·tect′ed
un′de·ter′mi·na·ble
un′de·ter′mined
un′de·terred′
un·de′vi·at′ing
un′de·vout′
un′dif·fer·en′ti·at′ed
un′di·gest′ed
un·dig′ni·fied′
un′di·lut′ed
un′di·min′ished
un′di·min′ish·ing
un·dimmed′
un′dip·lo·mat′ic
un′dis·cern′i·ble
un′dis·cern′ing
un′dis·charged′
un′dis·closed′
un′dis·cour′aged
un′dis·cov′er·a·ble
un′dis·cov′ered
un′dis·crim′i·nat′ing
un′dis·heart′ened
un′dis·mayed′
un′dis·so′ci·at′ed
un′dis·solved′
un′dis·tilled′
un′dis·tin′guish·ed
un′dis·tin′guish·ing
un′dis·tort′ed
un′dis·tract′ed
un′dis·trib′ut·ed
un′di·ver′si·fied′
un′di·vid′ed
un′di·vulged′
un′do·mes′tic
un′do·mes′ti·cat′ed
un·dou′bled
un·doubt′ing
un·drained′
un′dra·mat′ic
un·drape′
un·draped′
un·dreamed′
un·dreamed′-of′
un·dreamt′
un·dressed′
un·dried′
un·drilled′
un·drink′a·ble
un·du′ti·ful
un·dyed′
un·eat′a·ble
un·eat′en
un′e·clipsed′
un′e·co·nom′ic
un′e·co·nom′i·cal
un·ed′i·fy′ing
un·ed′u·ca·ble
un′ef·faced′
un′e·lim′i·nat′ed
un′em·bar′rassed
un′em·bel′lished
un′e·mo′tion·al
un′em·phat′ic
un′en·closed′
un′en·cour′aged
un′en·cum′bered
un′en·dan′gered
un·end′ing
un′en·dorsed′
un′en·dur′a·ble
un′en·dur′ing
un′en·force′a·ble
un′en·forced′
un′en·gaged′
un′en·joy′a·ble
un′en·light′ened
un·en′ter·pris′ing
un′en·ter·tain′ing
un′en·thu′si·as′tic
un·en′vi·a·ble
un·en′vied
un·en′vi·ous
un′e·quipped′
un′es·cap′a·ble
un·es′ti·mat′ed
un·eth′i·cal
un′ex·ag′ger·at′ed
un′ex·am′ined
un′ex·celled′
un′ex·change′a·ble
un′ex·cit′ing
un′ex·cused′
un·ex′e·cut′ed
un′ex·haust′ed
un′ex·pend′ed
un′ex·pe′ri·enced
un′ex·pired′
un′ex·plain′a·ble
un′ex·plained′
un′ex·plod′ed
un′ex·ploit′ed
un′ex·plored′
un′ex·pressed′
un′ex·pres′sive
un·ex′pur·gat′ed
un′ex·tin′guished
un·fad′a·ble
un·fad′ed
un·fad′ing
un·fal′ter·ing
un·fash′ion·a·ble
un·fas′tened
un·fath′om·a·ble
un·fath′omed
un·fea′si·ble
un·feath′ered
un·fed′
un·fed′er·at′ed
un·felt′
un·fem′i·nine
un·fenced′
un′fer·ment′ed
un·fer′ti·lized′
un·fet′tered
un·filed′
un·fil′i·al
un·filled′
un·fil′tered
un·fit′ting
un·fixed′
un·flat′ter·ing
un·fla′vored
un′fore·see′a·ble
un·for′est·ed
un′for·get′ting
un′for·giv′a·ble
un′for·giv′en
un′for·giv′ing
un′for·got′ten
un·for′mu·lat′ed
un·for′ti·fied′
un·framed′
un·free′
un·fre′quent
un′ful·filled′
un·gained′
un·gal′lant
un·gar′nished
un·gath′ered
un·gen′tle
un·gen′tle·man·ly
un·gift′ed
un·gloved′
un·gov′erned
un·grad′ed
un′gram·mat′i·cal
un·grat′i·fied′
un′guar·an·teed′
un·guid′ed
un·ham′pered
un·hand′i·capped′
un·hanged′
un·har′assed
un·hard′ened
un·harmed′
un′har·mo′ni·ous
un·har′nessed
un·hatched′
un·healed′
un·heed′ful
un·heed′ing
un·help′ful
un·her′ald·ed
un′he·ro′ic
un·hin′dered
un·hoped′-for′
un·housed′
un·hur′ried
un·hur′ry·ing
un·hurt′ful
un′hy·gien′ic
un′i·de′al
un′i·den′ti·fied′
un′id·i·o·mat′ic
un′il·lu′mi·nat′ed
un′i·mag′i·na·ble
un′i·mag′i·na·tive
un′im·paired′
un′im·pas′sioned
un′im·ped′ed
un′im·pos′ing
un′im·pressed′
un′im·press′i·ble
un′im·pres′sion·a·ble
un′im·pres′sive
un′im·proved′
un′in·closed′
un′in·cor′po·rat′ed
un·in′dexed
un′in·fect′ed
un′in·flam′ma·ble
un′in·flect′ed
un·in′flu·enced
un′in·formed′
un′in·hab′it·a·ble
un′in·hab′it·ed
un′in·hib′it·ed
un′i·ni′ti·at′ed
un′in·quir′ing
un′in·struct′ed
un′in·struc′tive
un·in′su·lat′ed
un′in·sured′
un′in·tel′li·gent
un′in·tend′ed
un′in·ten′tion·al
un·in′ter·est·ing
un′in·ter·mit′tent
un′in·tim′i·dat′ed
un′in·ven′tive
un′in·vit′ed
un′in·vit′ing
un′in·volved′
un·is′sued
un·jus′ti·fi′a·ble
un·kept′
un·knight′ly
un·know′a·ble
un·know′ing
un·la′belled
un·lad′en
un·la′dy-like′
un·laid′
un′la·ment′ed
un·laun′dered
un·li′censed
un·light′ed
un·lik′a·ble
un·lined′
un·liq′ue·fied′
un·liq′ui·dat′ed
un·lit′
un·lit′tered
un·lov′a·ble
un·loved′
un·lov′ing
un·maid′en·ly
un·mail′a·ble
un·mailed′
un·mal′le·a·ble
un·man′age·a·ble
un·manned′
un′man·u·fac′tured
un·mapped′
un·marked′
un·mar′ket·a·ble
un·mar′riage·a·ble
un·mas′tered
un·matched′
un′me·chan′i·cal
un·melt′ed
un·men′tioned
un·mer′it·ed
un′me·thod′i·cal
un·mil′i·tar′y
un·min′gled
un·mirth′ful
un′mis·tak′en
un·mixed′
un·mod′i·fied′
un·mod′u·lat′ed
un′mo·lest′ed
un·mo′ti·vat′ed
un·mount′ed
un·mourned′
un·mov′a·ble
un·mov′ing
un·mown′
un·mu′si·cal
un·muz′zled
un·nam′a·ble
un·named′
un·nat′u·ral·ized′
un·nav′i·ga·ble
un·need′ed
un·need′ful
un′ne·go′tia·ble
un·neigh′bor·ly
un·not′ed
un·note′wor′thy
un·no′tice·a·ble
un·no′ticed
un′ob·jec′tion·a·ble
un′o·blig′ing
un′ob·scured′
un′ob·serv′a·ble
un′ob·serv′ant
un′ob·serv′ing
un′ob·struct′ed
un′ob·tain′a·ble
un′ob·tru′sive
un′oc·ca′sioned
un′of·fend′ing
un·of′fered
un·of′fi·cered
un′of·fi′cial
un·oiled′
un·o′pened
un′op·posed′
un′or·dained′
un′o·rig′i·nal
un·or′tho·dox′
un′os·ten·ta′tious
un·owned′
un·paired′
un·par′don·a·ble
un·par′doned
un·pas′teur·ized′
un′pa·tri·ot′ic
un·paved′
un·peace′a·ble
un′per·ceived′
un′per·ceiv′ing
un′per·plexed′
un′per·suad′ed
un′per·sua′sive
un′per·turbed′
un′pe·rused′
un′phil·o·soph′ic
un′phil·o·soph′i·cal
un′pho·net′ic
un·picked′
un·pierced′
un·pit′ied
un·pit′y·ing
un·placed′
un·plagued′
un·planned′
un·plant′ed
un·played′
un·pleased′
un·pleas′ing
un·pledged′
un·pli′ant
un·ploughed′
un′po·et′ic
un′po·et′i·cal
un·poised′
un·po′lar·ized′
un·pol′ished
un′pol·lut′ed
un′pre·dict′a·ble
un′pre·med′i·tat′ed
un′pre·par′ed·ness
un′pre·pos·sess′ing
un′pressed′
un′pre·vail′ing
un′pre·vent′a·ble
un·print′ed
un·priv′i·leged
un·prized′
un′pro·cur′a·ble
un′pro·duc′tive
un′pro·faned′
un′pro·gres′sive
un′pro·ject′ed
un·prom′is·ing
un·prompt′ed
un′pro·nounce′a·ble
un′pro·nounced′
un′pro·pi′tious
un′pro·por′tioned
un′pro·tect′ed

un'pro·test'ed
un·proved'
un·prov'en
un'pro·vid'ed
un'pro·vok'ing
un·pruned'
un·pub'lished
un·punc'tu·al
un·pun'ished
un·pur'chas·a·ble
un·pur'posed
un'pur·su'ing
un·quail'ing
un·qual'i·fy'ing
un·quench'a·ble
un·quenched'
un·ques'tion·ing
un·quot'a·ble
un·raised'
un·ran'somed
un·rat'i·fied'
un·read'a·ble
un're·al·is'tic
un·re'al·ized'
un·rea'soned
un're·buked'
un're·ceived'
un're·claimed'
un·rec'og·niz'a·ble
un·rec'og·nized'
un·rec'om·pensed'
un'rec·on·cil'a·ble
un·rec'on·ciled'
un're·cord'ed
un're·deemed'
un're·fined'
un're·formed'
un·reg'is·tered
un·reg'u·lat'ed
un're·lat'ed
un're·laxed'
un're·lax'ing
un're·liev'a·ble
un're·lieved'
un·rem'e·died
un're·mem'bered
un're·mit'ted
un're·moved'
un're·mu'ner·at'ed
un're·mu'ner·a·tive
un're·nowned'
un·rent'ed
un're·paid'
un're·paired'
un're·pealed'
un're·pent'ant
un're·pent'ing
un're·port'ed
un'rep·re·sent'a·tive
un'rep·re·sent'ed
un're·pressed'
un're·proached'
un're·proved'
un're·quit'ed
un're·signed'
un're·sist'ant
un're·sist'ed
un're·sist'ing
un're·spon'sive
un're·strained'
un're·strict'ed
un're·ten'tive
un're·trieved'
un're·turned'
un're·vealed'
un're·venged'
un're·voked'
un're·ward'ed
un're·ward'ing
un·rhymed'
un·right'ful
un·rimed'
un·rip'ened
un'ro·man'tic
un·ruled'
un·said'
un·saint'ly
un·sal'a·ble
un·sal'a·ried
un·salt'ed
un·sanc'ti·fied'
un·sanc'tioned
un·sa'ti·at'ed
un·sat'is·fied'
un·sat'is·fy'ing
un·sat'u·rat'ed

un·scaled'
un·scared'
un·scarred'
un·scent'ed
un·sched'uled
un·schol'ar·ly
un·scorched'
un·scoured'
un·scraped'
un·scratched'
un·screened'
un·scrip'tur·al
un·sculp'tured
un·sea'soned
un·sea'wor'thy
un·sec'ond·ed
un'se·cured'
un·see'ing
un·seg'ment·ed
un·seg're·gat'ed
un·seized'
un'se·lec'tive
un'sen·ti·men'tal
un·serv'ice·a·ble
un·set'
un·shad'ed
un·shak'a·ble
un·shaped'
un·shape'ly
un·shared'
un·sharp'ened
un·shav'en
un·shed'
un·shel'tered
un·shorn'
un·shrink'a·ble
un·shrink'ing
un·sift'ed
un·sight'ed
un·signed'
un·sink'a·ble
un·sis'ter·ly
un·sized'
un·slacked'
un·slaked'
un·sliced'
un·smil'ing
un·so'cial
un·soiled'
un·sold'
un·sol'dierly
un'so·lic'it·ed
un·solv'a·ble
un·solved'
un·sort'ed
un·sought'
un·sound'ed
un·sowed'
un·sown'
un·spe'cial·ized'
un·spe'ci·fied'
un·spec'u·la·tive
un·spent'
un·spiced'
un·spir'i·tu·al
un·spoiled'
un·spoilt'
un·spo'ken
un·sports'man·like'
un·stain'a·ble
un·stained'
un·stamped'
un·stand'ard·ized'
un·stat'ed
un·states'man·like'
un·ster'i·lized'
un·stig'ma·tized'
un·stint'ed
un·stitched'
un·stopped'
un·strained'
un·strat'i·fied'
un·stressed'
un·stri'at·ed
un·stuffed'
un'sub·dued'
un'sub·mis'sive
un·sub'si·dized'
un'sub·stan'ti·at'ed
un'sug·ges'tive
un·sul'lied
un'sup·port'a·ble
un'sup·port'ed
un'sup·pressed'
un·sure'
un'sur·passed'

un'sus·pect'ed
un'sus·pect'ing
un'sus·pi'cious
un'sus·tained'
un·swayed'
un·sweet'ened
un·swept'
un·swerv'ing
un'sym·met'ri·cal
un'sym·pa·thet'ic
un·sym'pa·thiz'ing
un'sys·tem·at'ic
un·tact'ful
un·tab'u·lat'ed
un·taint'ed
un·tak'en
un·tal'ent·ed
un·tam'a·ble
un·tamed'
un·tanned'
un·tar'nished
un·tast'ed
un·tax'a·ble
un·taxed'
un·teach'a·ble
un·tech'ni·cal
un·tem'pered
un·ten'a·ble
un·ten'ant·ed
un·tend'ed
un·ter'ri·fied'
un·test'ed
un·thanked'
un·think'a·ble
un·thought'
un·thought'ful
un·thrift'y
un·till'a·ble
un·tilled'
un·tired'
un·torn'
un·trace'a·ble
un·traced'
un·tracked'
un·tract'a·ble
un'trans·fer'a·ble
un'trans·lat'a·ble
un'trans·lat'ed
un'trans·mit'ted

un·trav'elled
un·trav'ers·a·ble
un·trav'ersed
un·trimmed'
un·trod'den
un·trou'bled
un·trust'wor'thy
un·tun'a·ble
un·twist'ed
un·typ'i·cal
un·us'a·ble
un·ut'tered
un·vac'ci·nat'ed
un·val'ued
un·var'ied
un·var'y·ing
un·veiled'
un·ven'ti·lat'ed
un·ver'i·fi'a·ble
un·ver'i·fied'
un·versed'
un·vexed'
un·vis'it·ed
un·vit'ri·fied'
un·wak'ened
un·want'ed
un·war'like'
un·war'rant·ed
un·washed'
un·watched'
un·wa'ver·ing
un·weaned'
un·wea'ry·ing
un·weath'ered
un·wed'
un·wed'ded
un·weed'ed
un·wife'like'
un·wife'ly
un·wink'ing
un·wit'nessed
un·wom'an·ly
un·work'a·ble
un·work'man·like'
un·worn'
un·wound'ed
un·wo'ven
un·wrin'kled
un·wrought'
un·yield'ing

un-[2] *prefix.* do the opposite of; do what will reverse the act, as in *undress, unlock, untie.* [OE *un-, on-*]
☛ un- is used freely to form verbs expressing the reversal of the action of the verb.

UN or **U.N.** 1 United Nations. 2 Union Nationale.

un·a·bashed (un'ə basht') *adj.* not embarrassed, ashamed, or awed. —**un'a·bash'ed·ly,** *adv.*

un·a·ble (un ā'bəl) *adj.* not able; lacking ability or power (*to*): *A newborn baby is unable to walk or talk.* —**Syn.** incapable, unfit.

un·a·bridged (un'ə brijd') *adj.* not shortened; complete: *an unabridged book.*

un·ac·com·pa·nied (un'ə kum'pə nēd) *adj.* **1** not accompanied. **2** in music, without an accompaniment.

un·ac·count·a·ble (un'ə koun'tə bəl) *adj.* **1** that cannot be accounted for or explained. **2** not responsible. —**Syn. 1** inexplicable, incomprehensible.

un·ac·count·a·bly (un'ə koun'tə blē) *adv.* in a way that cannot be explained; strangely.

un·ac·cus·tomed (un'ə kus'təmd) *adj.* **1** not used to; not accustomed. **2** not familiar; unusual; strange.

un·ad·vised (un'əd vīzd') *adj.* **1** not advised; without advice. **2** not prudent or discreet; rash. —**Syn. 2** imprudent, unwise.

un·ad·vis·ed·ly (un'əd vīz'id lē) *adv.* in an indiscreet manner; rashly.

un·af·fect·ed[1] (un'ə fek'tid) *adj.* not affected; not influenced. [< *un-*[1] + *affected*[1]] —**un'af·fect'ed·ly,** *adv.* —**un'af·fect'ed·ness,** *n.* —**Syn.** unmoved, unimpressed.

un·af·fect·ed[2] (un'ə fek'tid) *adj.* simple and natural; sincere. [< *un-*[1] + *affected*[2]] —**un'af·fect'ed·ly,** *adv.* —**un'af·fect'ed·ness,** *n.*

un·al·ter·a·ble (un ol'tər ə bəl or un ôl'tər ə bəl) *adj.* that cannot be altered; not changeable.

un·al·ter·a·bly (un ol'tər ə blē or un ôl'tər ə blē) *adv.* in a way that cannot be changed; permanently.

un·a·neled (un'ə nēld') *adj. Archaic.* without being anointed by a priest before death; not having received extreme unction. [< *un-*[1] + *anele* give extreme unction to, ME *anelie(n)*, ult. < OE *an-* on + *ele* oil < L *oleum*]

u·na·nim·i·ty (ū′nə nim′ə tē) *n.* complete accord or agreement. —**Syn.** harmony.

u·nan·i·mous (ū nan′ə məs) *adj.* **1** in complete accord or agreement; agreed. **2** characterized by or showing complete accord: *He was elected president of his class by a unanimous vote.* [< L *unanimus* < *unus* one + *animus* mind] —**u·nan′i·mous·ness,** *n.*

u·nan·i·mous·ly (ū nan′ə məs lē) *adv.* with complete agreement; without a single opposing vote.

un·an·swer·a·ble (un an′sər ə bəl) *adj.* **1** that cannot be answered. **2** that cannot be disproved. —**un·an′swer·a·bly,** *adv.*

un·an·swered (un an′sərd) *adj.* **1** not replied to. **2** not proved false or incorrect; not refuted: *an unanswered argument.* **3** not returned: *unanswered love.*

un·ap·proach·a·ble (un′ə prōch′ə bəl) *adj.* **1** very hard to approach; distant. **2** unrivalled; without an equal. —**un′ap·proach′a·ble·ness,** *n.* —**un′ap·proach′a·bly,** *adv.*

un·apt (un apt′) *adj.* **1** not fit. **2** not likely. **3** not skilful. **4** not quick to learn. —**un·apt′ly,** *adv.* —**un·apt′ness,** *n.*

un·arm (un ärm′) *v.* **1** take weapons or armor from; disarm. **2** lay down one's weapons. **3** take off armor.

un·armed (un ärmd′) *adj.* **1** without weapons; without armor. **2** of plants and animals, without horns, teeth, prickles, spines, thorns, etc.

un·as·sum·ing (un′ə süm′ing) *adj.* not putting on airs; modest. —**un′as·sum′ing·ly,** *adv.* —**un′as·sum′ing·ness,** *n.*

un·at·tached (un′ə tacht′) *adj.* **1** not attached. **2** not connected or associated with a particular body, group, organization, or the like; independent. **3** not married or engaged to be married.

un·at·tend·ed (un′ə ten′did) *adj.* **1** without attendants; alone. **2** not accompanied. **3** not taken care of; not attended to.

un·a·vail·ing (un′ə vāl′ing) *adj.* not successful; useless. —**un′a·vail′ing·ly,** *adv.*

un·a·void·a·ble (un′ə void′ə bəl) *adj.* that cannot be avoided. —**un′a·void′a·ble·ness,** *n.*

un·a·void·a·bly (un′ə void′ə blē) *adv.* because of something that cannot or could not be avoided or prevented; inevitably.

un·a·ware (un′ə wãr′) *adj.* not aware; unconscious. —*adv.* without thought; unawares.

un·a·wares (un′ə wãrz′) *adv.* **1** without knowing: "*to entertain angels unawares.*" **2** without being expected; by surprise: *The police caught the burglar unawares.*

un·backed (un bakt′) *adj.* **1** not backed, helped, or supported; unaided. **2** not bet on. **3** *Archaic.* not ridden.

un·baked (un bākt′) *adj.* **1** not baked; not cooked. **2** not mature; undeveloped.

un·bal·ance (un bal′əns) *n. v.* **-anced, -anc·ing.** —*n.* lack of balance; unbalanced condition. —*v.* throw out of balance; disorder or derange.

un·bal·anced (un bal′ənst) *adj.* **1** not balanced. **2** not entirely sane: *an unbalanced mind.*

un·bar (un bär′) *v.* **-barred, -bar·ring.** remove the bars from; unlock.

un·bear·a·ble (un bãr′ə bəl) *adj.* that cannot be endured. —**un·bear′a·ble·ness,** *n.* —**un·bear′ab·ly,** *adv.* —**Syn.** intolerable, insufferable.

un·beat·en (un bēt′ən) *adj.* **1** not defeated or surpassed. **2** not trodden; not travelled: *unbeaten paths.* **3** not struck or pounded.

un·be·com·ing (un′bi kum′ing) *adj.* **1** not becoming; not appropriate: *unbecoming clothes.* **2** not fitting; not proper: *unbecoming behavior.* —**un′be·com′ing·ly,** *adv.* —**un′be·com′ing·ness,** *n.* —**Syn. 1** inappropriate. **2** unsuitable.

un·be·known (un′bi nōn′) *adj. Informal.* not known.

un·be·knownst (un′bi nōnst′) *adj.* not known; unbeknown.

un·be·lief (un′bi lēf′) *n.* lack of belief; lack of belief in God or the gospel.

Syn. **Unbelief, disbelief** = lack of belief. **Unbelief** suggests only lack of belief in something offered or held as true, with no positive feelings one way or the other: *Nowadays there is general unbelief in the idea that some people are witches.* **Disbelief** = a positive refusal to believe: *He expressed his disbelief in universal military training.*

hat, āge, cãre, fär; let, ēqual, tėrm; it, īce
hot, ōpen, ôrder; oil, out; cup, pu̇t, rüle, ūse
əbove, takən, pencəl, lemən, circəs
ch, child; ng, long; sh, ship
th, thin; ᴛʜ, then; zh, measure

un·be·liev·er (un′bi lēv′ər) *n.* **1** a person who does not believe. **2** a person who does not believe in a particular religion.

un·be·liev·ing (un′bi lēv′ing) *adj.* not believing; doubting. —**un′be·liev′ing·ly,** *adv.* —**Syn.** sceptical, incredulous, suspicious, distrustful.

un·bend (un bend′) *v.* **-bent** or **-bend·ed, -bend·ing.** **1** straighten. **2** release from strain. **3** relax: *The judge unbent and behaved like a boy.* **4** unfasten (a sail, rope, etc.).

un·bend·ing (un ben′ding) *adj.* **1** not bending or curving; rigid. **2** not yielding; firm: *an unbending attitude.* —*n.* relaxation. —**un·bend′ing·ly,** *adv.*

un·bent (un bent′) *v.* pt. and pp. of **unbend.** —*adj.* not bent or curved.

un·bi·assed or **un·bi·ased** (un bī′əst) *adj.* not prejudiced; impartial; fair: *an unbiassed account.*

un·bid·den (un bid′ən) *adj.* **1** not bidden; not invited. **2** not commanded.

un·bind (un bīnd′) *v.* **-bound, -bind·ing.** release from bonds or restraint; untie; unfasten; let loose. [OE *unbindan*]

un·bleached (un blēcht′) *adj.* not bleached; not made white by bleaching: *unbleached linen.*

un·blem·ished (un blem′isht) *adj.* spotless, flawless: *an unblemished reputation.*

un·blessed (un blest′) *adj.* **1** not blessed. **2** not holy; evil. **3** unhappy; miserable; wretched.

un·blest (un blest′) *adj.* unblessed.

un·blush·ing (un blush′ing) *adj.* not blushing; shameless. —**un·blush′ing·ly,** *adv.*

un·bod·ied (un bod′ēd) *adj.* **1** having no body; incorporeal. **2** disembodied.

un·bolt (un bōlt′) *v.* draw back the bolts of (a door, etc.).

un·bolt·ed[1] (un bōl′tid) *adj.* not bolted or fastened: *an unbolted door.* [< *un-*[1] + *bolt*[1]]

un·bolt·ed[2] (un bōl′tid) *adj.* not sifted: *unbolted flour.* [< *un-*[1] + *bolt*[2]]

un·bon·net·ed (un bon′ə tid) *adj.* wearing no bonnet or cap; bareheaded.

un·born (un bôrn′) *adj.* not yet born; still to come; of the future: *unborn generations.*

un·bos·om (un bu̇z′əm or un bü′zəm) *v.* **1** reveal; disclose. **2 unbosom oneself,** tell or reveal one's thoughts, feelings, secrets, etc. [< *un-*[2] + *bosom,* v.]

un·bound·ed (un boun′did) *adj.* **1** not limited; very great; boundless. **2** not kept within limits; not controlled. —**Syn. 1** infinite.

un·bowed (un boud′) *adj.* **1** not bowed or bent. **2** not forced to yield or submit.

un·brace (un brās′) *v.* **-braced, -brac·ing.** **1** loosen, untie, or detach a brace, belt, article of clothing, etc. **2** loosen tension or relax. **3** weaken; make feeble.

un·braid (un brād′) *v.* separate the strands of.

un·brid·led (un brī′dəld) *adj.* **1** not having a bridle on. **2** not controlled; not restrained.

un·bro·ken (un brō′kən) *adj.* **1** not broken; whole. **2** not interrupted; continuous: *He had eight hours of unbroken sleep.* **3** not tamed: *an unbroken horse.* —**un·bro′ken·ness,** *n.* —**Syn. 1** entire, intact.

un·buck·le (un buk′əl) *v.* **-led, -ling.** **1** unfasten the buckle or buckles of. **2** unfasten; detach.

un·bur·den (un bėr′dən) *v.* **1** free from a burden.

2 relieve (one's mind or heart) by talking. 3 throw off or disclose (something that burdens).

un·busi·ness·like (un biz′nis līk′) *adj.* without system and method; not efficient.

un·but·ton (un but′ən) *v.* unfasten the button or buttons of.

un·cage (un kāj′) *v.* **-caged, -cag·ing.** 1 release from a cage. 2 release.

un·called-for (un kold′fôr′ or un kôld′fôr′) *adj.* 1 not called for. 2 unnecessary and improper: *an uncalled-for remark.*

un·can·ny (un kan′ē) *adj.* strange and mysterious; weird: *The trees seemed to have uncanny shapes in the half darkness.* **—un·can′ni·ly,** *adv.* **—un·can′ni·ness,** *n.* **—Syn.** See **weird.**

un·cap (un kap′) *v.* **-capped, -cap·ping.** 1 remove the cap, top, or covering of. 2 remove one's hat, often in respect.

un·cer·e·mo·ni·ous (un′ser ə mō′nē əs) *adj.* not as courteous as would be expected; not ceremonious; informal. **—un′cer·e·mo′ni·ous·ly,** *adv.* **—un′cer·e·mo′ni·ous·ness,** *n.*

un·cer·tain (un sėr′tən) *adj.* 1 not known with certainty; not finally established; in doubt; dubious: *The election results were still uncertain.* 2 not sure; doubtful: *be uncertain if a candidate will win.* 3 likely to change; not reliable: *uncertain weather.* 4 not constant; varying: *an uncertain flicker of light.* 5 vague; indefinite: *an uncertain shape.* 6 not settled or fixed; indeterminate: *a job with an uncertain future.* **—un·cer′tain·ness,** *n.*
Syn. 1 **Uncertain, insecure** = not sure in some way or about something. **Uncertain** emphasizes not knowing definitely or surely about something or not having complete confidence in a thing, person, or oneself, and thus suggests the presence of doubt: *His plans for the summer are uncertain.* **Insecure** emphasizes not being protected from or guarded against danger or loss, and suggests the presence of fear or anxiety: *His position at the bank is insecure.*

un·cer·tain·ly (un sėr′tən lē) *adv.* in an uncertain way: *He spoke slowly and uncertainly.*

un·cer·tain·ty (un sėr′tən tē) *n.* **-ties.** 1 an uncertain state or condition; doubt. 2 something uncertain.

un·chain (un chān′) *v.* free from chains; let loose; set free.

un·change·a·ble (un chān′jə bəl) *adj.* that cannot be changed. **—un·change′a·ble·ness,** *n.* **—un·change′a·bly,** *adv.* **—Syn.** immutable, unalterable, invariable.

un·changed (un chānjd′) *adj.* not changed; the same.

un·char·i·ta·ble (un char′ə tə bəl) *adj.* not generous; not charitable; severe; harsh. **—un·char′i·ta·ble·ness,** *n.* **—un·char′i·ta·bly,** *adv.*

un·chart·ed (un chär′tid) *adj.* not mapped; not marked on a chart.

un·chaste (un chāst′) *adj.* not chaste; not virtuous. **—un·chaste′ly,** *adv.*

un·chas·ti·ty (un chas′tə tē) *n.* lack of chastity; unchaste character; lewdness.

un·checked (un chekt′) *adj.* not checked; not restrained.

un·chris·tian (un kris′chən) *adj.* 1 not Christian. 2 unworthy of Christians. 3 *Informal.* such as any civilized person would object to; barbarous: *rout a man out of bed at a most unchristian hour.*

un·church (un chėrch′) *v.* expel from a church; deprive of church rights and privileges.

un·ci·al (un′shē əl or un′shəl) *n.* 1 a kind of letter or writing having heavy, rounded strokes and used especially from the 4th to the 8th century A.D. 2 a manuscript written in this style or with such letters. *—adj.* 1 of or having to do with such letters or writing. 2 written in this style or such letters. [< L *uncialis,* in the sense "inch-high" < *uncia* inch]

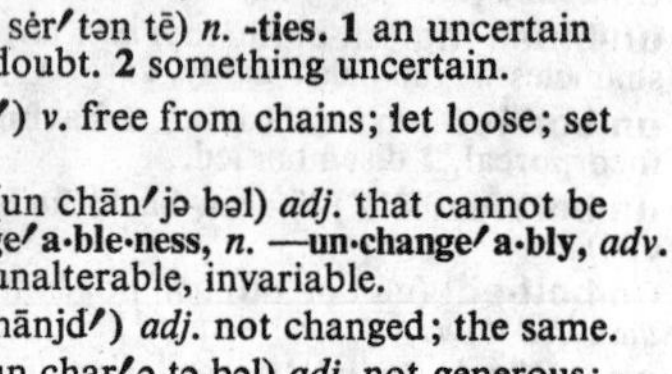

Latin uncials, from a manuscript of the 8th century

un·ci·nate (un′sə nit or un′sə nāt′) *adj.* hooked; bent at the end like a hook. [< L *uncinatus,* ult. < *uncus* hook]

un·cir·cum·cised (un sėr′kəm sīzd′) *adj.* 1 not circumcised. 2 not Jewish; gentile. 3 heathen.

un·civ·il (un siv′əl) *adj.* 1 not civil; rude; impolite. 2 not civilized. **—un·civ′il·ly,** *adv.*

un·civ·i·lized (un siv′ə līzd) *adj.* not civilized; barbarous; savage.

un·clad (un klad′) *adj.* not dressed; not clothed; naked.

un·clasp (un klasp′) *v.* 1 unfasten. 2 release or be released from a clasp or grasp.

un·cle (ung′kəl) *n.* 1 the brother of one's father or mother. 2 the husband of one's aunt. 3 *Informal.* an elderly man. 4 **say uncle,** *Informal.* give in; surrender. [ME < AF < L *avunculus* one's mother's brother]

un·clean (un klēn′) *adj.* 1 not clean; dirty; filthy. 2 not pure morally; evil. 3 not ceremonially clean. [OE *unclǣne*] **—un·clean′ness,** *n.*

un·clean·ly[1] (un klen′lē) *adj.* not cleanly; unclean. [< *un-*[1] + *cleanly*[1]] **—un·clean′li·ness,** *n.*

un·clean·ly[2] (un klēn′lē) *adv.* in an unclean manner. [< *unclean*]

un·clench (un klench′) *v.* open or become opened from a clenched state: *unclench one's fists.*

Uncle Sam (sam) *Informal.* the government or people of the United States. [< the initials *U.S.*]

un·cloak (un klōk′) *v.* 1 remove the coat from. 2 reveal; expose. 3 take off the cloak or outer garment.

un·close (un klōz′) *v.* **-closed, -clos·ing.** open.

un·clothe (un klōᵺ′) *v.* **-clothed** or **-clad, -cloth·ing.** 1 strip of clothes; undress. 2 lay bare; uncover.

un·co (ung′kō) *Scottish. —adv.* remarkably; very; extremely. *—adj.* 1 unknown, strange, or unusual. 2 remarkable, extraordinary, or great. 3 uncanny. [ult. var. of *uncouth*]

un·coil (un koil′) *v.* unwind.

un·com·fort·a·ble (un kum′fər tə bəl) *adj.* 1 not comfortable. 2 uneasy. 3 disagreeable; causing discomfort. **—un·com′fort·a·ble·ness,** *n.*

un·com·fort·a·bly (un kum′ fər tə blē) *adv.* in a way that is not comfortable; with discomfort and uneasiness; disagreeably.

un·com·mit·ted (un kə mit′id) *adj.* 1 not bound or pledged to a certain viewpoint, course, program, etc.: *an uncommitted candidate.* 2 not committed to prison or other institution.

un·com·mon (un kom′ən) *adj.* 1 rare; unusual. 2 remarkable. **—un·com′mon·ness,** *n.*

un·com·mon·ly (un kom′ən lē) *adv.* 1 rarely; unusually. 2 remarkably; especially.

un·com·mu·ni·ca·tive (un′kə mū′nə kə tiv or un′kə mū′nə kā′tiv) *adj.* not giving out any information, opinions, etc.; talking little; silent. **—un′com·mu′ni·ca′tive·ly,** *adv.* **—un′com·mu′ni·ca′tive·ness,** *n.* **—Syn.** reserved, reticent, taciturn.

un·com·pro·mis·ing (un kom′prə mīz′ing) *adj.* unyielding; firm; unwilling to compromise. **—un·com′pro·mis′ing·ly,** *adv.*

un·con·cern (un′kən sėrn′) *n.* lack of concern; lack of interest; freedom from care or anxiety; indifference. **—Syn.** See **indifference.**

un·con·cerned (un′kən sėrnd′) *adj.* 1 free from care or anxiety; nonchalant. 2 not interested; indifferent; apathetic. **—un′con·cern′ed·ness,** *n.*

un·con·cern·ed·ly (un′kən sėr′nid lē) *adv.* in an unconcerned manner; without concern or anxiety.

un·con·di·tion·al (un′kən dish′ən əl or un′kən dish′nəl) *adj.* without conditions; absolute: *unconditional surrender.* **—Syn.** unqualified, unrestricted.

un·con·di·tion·al·ly (un′kən dish′ən əl ē or un′kən dish′nəl ē) *adv.* without any conditions.

un·con·di·tioned (un′kən dish′ənd) *adj.* **1** without conditions; absolute. **2** in psychology, not learned; instinctive.

un·con·form·i·ty (un′kən fôr′mə tē) *n.* **-ties. 1** the quality of not conforming. **2** in geology, an upturned or folded bed of rock that breaks the evenness and continuity of strata.

un·con·quer·a·ble (un kong′kər ə bəl) *adj.* that cannot be conquered. **—un·con′quer·a·bly,** *adv.* **—Syn.** invincible, indomitable, insuperable.

un·con·scion·a·ble (un kon′shən ə bəl) *adj.* **1** not influenced or guided by conscience: *an unconscionable liar.* **2** unreasonable; very great: *wait an unconscionable time for someone.* **—un·con′scion·a·bly,** *adv.*

un·con·scious (un kon′shəs) *adj.* **1** not conscious; not able to feel anything. **2** not aware. **3** not meant; not intended: *unconscious neglect.*
—n. **the unconscious,** in psychoanalysis, the part of the mind of whose functioning a person is not directly aware; a person's unconscious, but active, thoughts, desires, fears, etc. **—un·con′scious·ly,** *adv.* **—Syn.** *adj.* **2** oblivious, unmindful.

un·con·scious·ness (un kon′shəs nis) *n.* an unconscious condition; lack of consciousness; insensibility.

un·con·sti·tu·tion·al (un′kon stə tū′shən əl or un′kon stə tü′shən əl) *adj.* contrary to the constitution. **—un′con·sti·tu′tion·al·ly,** *adv.*

un·con·sti·tu·tion·al·i·ty (un′kon stə tū′shən al′ə tē or un′kon stə tü′shən al′ə tē) *n.* the fact, state, or condition of being contrary to the constitution.

un·con·ven·tion·al (un′kən vensh′nəl or un′kən ven′shən əl) *adj.* not bound by or conforming to convention, rule, or precedent; free from conventionality. **—un′con·ven′tion·al·ly′,** *adv.*

un·con·ven·tion·al·i·ty (un′kən ven′shən al′ə tē) *n.* the fact or quality of being unconventional; freedom from conventional restraints.

un·cork (un kôrk′) *v.* pull the cork from.

un·count·ed (un koun′tid) *adj.* **1** not counted; not reckoned. **2** very many; innumerable.

un·cou·ple (un kup′əl) *v.* **-pled, -pling.** disconnect; unfasten.

un·cour·te·ous (un kėr′tē əs) *adj.* discourteous; impolite; rude. **—un·cour′te·ous·ly,** *adv.*

un·court·li·ness (un kôrt′lē nis) *n.* rudeness.

un·couth (un küth′) *adj.* **1** awkward; clumsy; crude: *uncouth manners.* **2** unusual and unpleasant; strange: *The idiot made uncouth noises.* [OE *uncūth* < *un-*[1] + *cūth,* pp. of *cunnan* know] **—un·couth′ly,** *adv.* **—un·couth′ness,** *n.*

un·cov·er (un kuv′ər) *v.* **1** remove the cover from. **2** make known; reveal; expose. **3** remove the hat or cap of. **4** remove one's hat or cap in respect.

un·crown (un kroun′) *v.* take the crown from; lower from high rank.

un·crowned (un kround′) *adj.* **1** not crowned; not having yet assumed the crown. **2** having royal power without being king, queen, etc.

unc·tion (ungk′shən) *n.* **1** an anointing with oil, ointment, etc. for medical purposes or as a religious rite: *The priest gave the dying man extreme unction.* **2** the oil, ointment, etc. used for anointing. **3** something soothing or comforting: *the unction of flattery.* **4** a soothing, sympathetic, and persuasive quality in speaking. **5** fervor; earnestness. **6** affected earnestness. [< L *unctio, -onis* < *unguere* anoint]

unc·tu·ous (ungk′chü əs) *adj.* **1** like an oil or ointment; oily; greasy. **2** soothing, sympathetic, and persuasive. **3** too smooth and oily: *the salesman's unctuous manner.* **4** tending to or gushing with religious fervor or emotion, especially false or affected emotion; fervid in a shallow, sentimental way. **5** of ground or soil, soft and clinging, but easily worked; rich in decayed organic matter. **6** of clay, very plastic. [ME < Med.L *unctuosus,* ult. < L *unguere* anoint] **—unc′tu·ous·ly,** *adv.* **—unc′tu·ous·ness,** *n.*

un·curl (un kėrl′) *v.* straighten out.

un·daunt·ed (un don′tid or un dôn′tid) *adj.* **1** not afraid; not discouraged: *The general was undaunted by the size of the enemy's army.* **2** fearless: *an undaunted leader.* **—un·daunt′ed·ly,** *adv.* **—un·daunt′ed·ness,** *n.*

hat, āge, cãre, fär; let, ēqual, tėrm; it, īce
hot, ōpen, ôrder; oil, out; cup, pu̇t, rüle, ūse
əbove, takən, pencəl, lemən, circəs
ch, child; ng, long; sh, ship
th, thin; ᴛʜ, then; zh, measure

un·de·ceive (un′di sēv′) *v.* **-ceived, -ceiv·ing.** free from error, mistake, or deception.

un·de·cid·ed (un′di sīd′id) *adj.* **1** not decided or settled. **2** not having one's mind made up. **—un′de·cid′ed·ly,** *adv.* **—un′de·cid′ed·ness,** *n.* **—Syn. 2** irresolute, wavering.

un·de·fined (un′di fīnd′) *adj.* **1** not defined or explained. **2** indefinite.

un·de·ni·a·ble (in′di nī′ə bəl) *adj.* **1** not to be denied. **2** unquestionably good; excellent.

un·de·ni·a·bly (un′di nī′ə blē) *adv.* beyond denial or dispute; certainly.

un·de·nom·i·na·tion·al (un′di nom′ə nā′shən əl or un′di nom′ə nāsh′nəl) *adj.* not connected with any particular religious sect.

un·der (un′dər) *prep.* **1** below; beneath: *The book fell under the table.* **2** below the surface of: *under the ground.* **3** lower than; lower down than; not so high as: *hit under the belt.* **4** less than: *It will cost under ten dollars.* **5** during the rule, time, influence, etc. of: *England under Victoria.* **6** in the position or condition of being affected by: *under the new rules.* **7** because of: *under the circumstances.* **8** according to: *under the law.* **9** represented by: *under a new name.* **10** required or bound by: *under obligation.*
—adv. **1** below; beneath: *The swimmer went under.* **2** in or to a lower place or condition.
—adj. lower in position, rank, degree, amount, price, etc.: *the under lip.* [OE]
Syn. *prep.* **1 Under, below, beneath** express a relation in which one thing is thought of as being lower than another in some way. **Under** suggests being directly lower: *A corporal is under a sergeant.* **Below** suggests being on a lower level, but not necessarily straight below nor without anyone or anything in between: *A corporal is below a major.* **Beneath** can be used in place of either *under* or *below,* but is usually more formal or literary: *He lies buried beneath an ancient oak tree. He is beneath notice.*

under- *prefix.* **1** on the underside; to a lower position; from a lower position; below; beneath, as in, *underline.* **2** being beneath; worn beneath, as in *underclothes.* **3** lower, as in *underlip.* **4** lower in rank; subordinate, as in *undersecretary.* **5** not enough; insufficiently, as in *underfed.* **6** below normal, as in *undersized.*

un·der·age (un′dər āj′) *adj.* **1** of less than the required age. **2** of less than the legal age for voting, marrying, drinking liquor in public bars, etc.

un·der·arm (un′dər ärm′) *adj.* **1** in or on that part of the arm that is closest to the body when the arm hangs loose: *an underarm scar, an underarm patch in a shirt.* **2** of or having to do with the armpit. **3** for the armpit: *an underarm deodorant.* **4** *Esp.Brit.* underhand: *an underarm throw.* —*n.* an armpit.

un·der·bel·ly (un′dər bel′ē) *n.* **-lies. 1** the unprotected lower surface or part of the belly. **2** any unprotected or especially vulnerable part.

un·der·bid (un′dər bid′) *v.* **-bid, -bid·ding,** *n.* —*v.* **1** make a lower bid than, as at an auction. **2** bid less than the full point value of: *underbid a hand in bridge.* —*n.* an underbidding. **—un′der·bid′der,** *n.*

un·der·bod·ice (un′dər bod′is) *n.* **1** a separate bodice worn under a blouse or jacket. **2** a bodice serving as a lining, reinforcement, etc. for a woman's dress.

un·der·bred (un′dər bred′) *adj.* **1** of inferior breeding or manners; vulgar. **2** of a horse, dog, etc., not of pure breed.

un·der·brush (un′dər brush′) *n.* bushes and small trees growing under large trees in woods or forests.

un·der·car·riage (un′dər kar′ij) *n.* **1** the supporting framework of an automobile, carriage, etc. **2** the under part of an airplane that supports it on the ground or water.

un·der·charge (*v.* un′dər chärj′; *n.* un′dər chärj′) *v.* **-charged, -charg·ing,** *n.* —*v.* **1** put an insufficient charge or load into. **2** charge (persons) less than the proper or fair price. **3** charge (so much) less than a proper price.
—*n.* **1** an insufficient charge or load. **2** a charge or price less than is proper or fair.

und·er·clothes (un′dər klōz′ or -klōᴛʜz′) *n.pl.* clothes worn under outer clothing; underwear.

un·der·cloth·ing (un′dər klōᴛʜ′ing) *n.* underclothes.

un·der·coat (un′dər kōt′) *n.* **1** a coat or layer of paint put on before the finishing coat. **2** a heavy tarlike coating sprayed on the underside of an automobile to protect it against rust, salt, etc. —*v.* apply an undercoat to.

un·der·cov·er (un′dər kuv′ər or un′dər kuv′ər) *adj.* working or done in secret: *The jeweller was an undercover man for the police.*

un·der·cur·rent (un′dər kėr′ənt) *n.* **1** a current below the upper currents, or below the surface, of a body of water, air, etc. **2** an underlying tendency: *There was an undercurrent of sadness beneath his jokes.*

un·der·cut (*v.* un′dər kut′; *n. adj.* un′dər kut′) *v.* **-cut, -cut·ting,** *n. adj.* —*v.* **1** cut under or beneath; cut away material from so as to leave a portion overhanging. **2** notch (the trunk of a tree, a large limb, etc.) so as to ensure falling in the desired direction or to prevent splitting. **3** sell or work for less than (some other person). **4** in golf, hit (a ball) so that it rises high and comes to rest without rolling far.
—*n.* **1** a cut, or a cutting away, underneath. **2** a notch cut in a tree to determine the direction in which it is to fall and to prevent splitting. **3** the tenderloin or fillet of beef.
—*adj.* cut away underneath.

un·der·de·vel·oped (un′dər di vel′əpt) *adj.* **1** not normally developed: *an underdeveloped limb.*
2 inadequately or poorly developed in production, distribution, standard of living, etc.: *The underdeveloped countries needed trained personnel.*

un·der·dog (un′dər dog′) *n.* **1** a dog having the worst of a fight. **2** a person having the worst of any struggle; one considered unlikely to win.

un·der·done (un′dər dun′ or un′dər dun′) *adj.* not cooked enough; cooked very little.

un·der·es·ti·mate (*v.* un′dər es′tə māt′; *n.* un′dər es′tə mit or un′dər es′tə māt′) *v.* **-mat·ed, -mat·ing,** *n.* —*v.* estimate at too low a value, amount, rate, etc. —*n.* an estimate that is too low.

un·der·ex·pose (un′dər eks pōz′) *v.* **-posed, -pos·ing.** in photography, expose to light for too short a time.

un·der·ex·po·sure (un′dər eks pō′zhər) *n.* in photography, an exposure to the light for too short a time. Underexposure makes a photograph look dim.

un·der·feed (un′dər fēd′) *v.* **-fed, -feed·ing. 1** feed too little. **2** stoke with coal or other solid fuel from the bottom.

un·der·foot (un′dər fu̇t′) *adv.* **1** under one's foot or feet; on the ground; underneath. **2** in the way: *Children are often underfoot.*

un·der·gar·ment (un′dər gär′mənt) *n.* any garment worn under a dress or suit.

un·der·go (un′dər gō′) *v.* **-went, -gone, -go·ing. 1** go through; pass through; be subjected to: *The town has undergone a great change during the last five years.*
2 endure; suffer. —**Syn.** See **experience.**

un·der·gone (un′dər gon′) *v.* pp. of **undergo.**

un·der·grad·u·ate (un′dər graj′ü it) *n.* a student in a college or university who has not yet received a degree.
—*adj.* of, for, or having to do with undergraduates.

un·der·ground (un′dər ground′) *adv.* **1** beneath the surface of the ground. **2** in or into secrecy or concealment.
—*adj.* **1** being, working, or used beneath the surface of the ground. **2 a** secret. **b** of or having to do with the underground: *an underground headquarters.* **3** resisting (tyrannical government, etc.) secretly. **4** of or having to do with avant-garde or radical newspapers, movies, etc., usually ones that are non-commercial and experimental.
—*n.* **1** place or space beneath the surface of the ground. **2** *Esp.Brit.* an underground railway; subway. **3** a secret organization, or grouping of such organizations, working to free a country from foreign domination or an autocratic regime. **4** any avant-garde or revolutionary movement in art, communications, or politics.

underground railway 1 a railway running below the surface of the earth. **2** a secret method of assisting the escape of fugitives: *Many Negro slaves escaped to Canada by the underground railway before the American Civil War.*

un·der·growth (un′dər grōth′) *n.* **1** underbrush. **2** short, fine hair under longer outer hair.

un·der·hand (un′dər hand′) *adj.* **1** not open or honest; secret; sly. **2** with the hand below the shoulder: *an underhand throw.* —*adv.* **1** secretly; slyly. **2** with the hand below the shoulder: *pitch underhand.*

un·der·hand·ed (un′dər han′did) *adj.* underhand; secret; sly; not open or honest. —**un′der·hand′ed·ly,** *adv.* —**un′der·hand′ed·ness,** *n.*

un·der·hung (un′dər hung′) *adj.* **1** resting on a track beneath, instead of being hung from above: *underhung sliding doors.* **2** projecting beyond the upper jaw: *A bulldog has an underhung jaw.* **3** having the under jaw so projecting.

un·der·lay (*v.* un′dər lā′; *n.* un′dər lā′) *v.* **-laid, -lay·ing,** *n.* —*v.* **1** lay (one thing) under another. **2** provide with something laid underneath; raise or support with something laid underneath. —*n.* **1** something laid beneath. **2** in printing, a piece or pieces of paper put under types, etc. to bring them to the proper height for printing. [OE *underlecgan*]

un·der·lie (un′dər lī′) *v.* **-lay, -lain, -ly·ing. 1** lie under; be beneath. **2** be at the basis of; form the foundation of. [OE *underlicgan*]

un·der·line (un′dər līn′ or un′dər līn′) *v.* **-lined, -lin·ing,** *n.* —*v.* **1** draw a line or lines under. **2** emphasize; make emphatic or more emphatic. —*n.* **1** a line drawn or printed under a word, passage, etc. **2** the line of the lower part of the body of an animal, especially a sheep.

un·der·ling (un′dər ling) *n.* a person of lower rank or position; inferior. [OE *underling* < *under* under + *-ling*]

un·der·lip (un′dər lip′) *n.* the lower lip.

un·der·ly·ing (un′dər lī′ing) *adj.* **1** lying under or beneath. **2** fundamental; basic; essential. **3** not evident at first glance; present but not apparent except through careful scrutiny. —*v.* ppr. of **underlie.**

un·der·mine (un′dər mīn′ or un′dər mīn′) *v.* **-mined, -min·ing. 1** make a passage or hole under; dig under: *The soldiers undermined the wall.* **2** wear away the foundations of: *The cliff was undermined by the waves.* **3** weaken by secret or unfair means: *undermine a man's reputation by scandal.* **4** weaken or destroy gradually: *Many severe colds had undermined her health.*
—**un′der·min′er,** *n.* —**Syn. 3, 4** See **weaken.**

un·der·most (un′dər mōst′) *adj. adv.* lowest.

un·der·neath (un′dər nēth′) *prep.* beneath; below: *sit underneath a tree, a cellar underneath a house.*
—*adv.* beneath or below something: *Someone was pushing underneath.* —*adj.* lower. —*n.* the lower part or surface. [OE *underneothan* < *under-* under + *neothan* below]

un·der·nour·ish (un′dər nėr′ish) *v.* provide with insufficient food for growth, health, etc..

un·der·nour·ished (un′dər nėr′isht) *adj.* not sufficiently nourished.

un·der·nour·ish·ment (un′dər nėr′ish mənt) *n.* not having enough food; lack of nourishment.

un·der·of·fi·cer (*v.* un′dər of′ə sər; *n.* un′dər of′ə sər) *v.* furnish inadequately with officers. —*n.* an officer of lower grade.

un·der·pass (un′dər pas′) *n.* a way underneath, especially a road under railway tracks or under another road; subway.

un·der·pay (un′dər pā′) *v.* **-paid, -pay·ing.** pay too little.

un·der·pin (un′dər pin′) *v.* **-pinned, -pin·ning. 1** support with props, stones, masonry, etc. **2** support; prop.

un·der·pin·ning (un′dər pin′ing) *n.* **1** the supports under a building. See picture on the next page. **2** a new foundation beneath a wall. **3** a support.

un·der·priv·i·leged (un′dər priv′ə lijd) *adj.* having

fewer advantages than most people have, especially because of poor economic or social status.

un·der·pro·duc·tion (un′dər prə duk′shən) *n.* production that is less than normal or less than there is demand for.

un·der·rate (un′dər rāt′) *v.* **-rat·ed, -rat·ing.** rate or estimate too low; put too low a value on.

un·der·score (*v.* un′dər skôr′; *n.* un′dər skôr′) *v.* **-scored, -scor·ing,** *n.* —*v.* **1** underline. **2** emphasize. —*n.* an underscored line.

un·der·sea (*adj.* un′dər sē′; *adv.* un′dər sē′) *adj.* being, working, or used beneath the surface of the sea: *an undersea boat.* —*adv.* underseas.

un·der·seas (un′dər sēz′) *adv.* beneath the surface of the sea: *Submarines go underseas.*

Underpinning (def. 1)

un·der·sec·re·tar·y (un′dər sek′rə ter′ē) *n.* **-tar·ies.** an assistant secretary, especially of a government department.

un·der·sell (un′dər sel′) *v.* **-sold, -sell·ing. 1** sell things at a lower price than. **2** sell (merchandise, etc.) at less than the actual value; sell at a loss.

un·der·serv·ant (un′dər sėr′vənt) *n.* a servant who does the simpler or lower tasks.

un·der·sher·iff (un′dər sher′if) *n.* a sheriff's deputy, especially one who acts when the sheriff is not able to act or when there is no sheriff.

un·der·shirt (un′dər shėrt′) *n.* a collarless undergarment of knitted wool, cotton, etc. of the upper part of the body.

un·der·shot (un′dər shot′) *adj.* **1** having the lower jaw projecting beyond the upper. **2** driven by water passing beneath: *an undershot wheel.*

un·der·side (un′dər sīd′) *n.* the surface lying underneath; the bottom side.

un·der·sign (un′dər sīn′ or un′dər sīn′) *v.* sign one's name at the end of (a letter or document).

WATER NOZZLE

An undershot wheel

un·der·signed (un′dər sīnd′) *adj.* signed, or having signed at the end of a letter or document. —*n.* **the undersigned,** the person or persons signing a letter or document.

un·der·sized (un′dər sīzd′) *adj.* smaller than the usual size.

un·der·skirt (un′dər skėrt′) *n.* a skirt worn under an outer skirt or overskirt.

un·der·sleeve (un′dər slēv′) *n.* a sleeve worn under an outer sleeve, especially an ornamental inner sleeve extending below the other.

un·der·slung (un′dər slung′ or un′dər slung′) *adj.* **1** of vehicles, having the frame suspended below the axles. **2** of a jaw, undershot.

un·der·song (un′dər song′) *n.* **1** in music, a song that is sung softly along with another song, as an accompaniment. **2** an underlying meaning; an underlying element.

un·der·stand (un′dər stand′) *v.* **-stood, -stand·ing. 1** get the meaning of; comprehend: *Now I understand the message.* **2** get the meaning: *People listen to him but often do not understand.* **3** know how to deal with; know well; know: *A good teacher should understand children.* **4** comprehend as a fact; grasp clearly; realize: *You understand, don't you, that I will be away for three weeks?* **5** be informed; learn: *I understand that he is leaving town.* **6** take as a fact; believe: *It is understood that you will come.* **7** take as meaning; take as meant: *What are we to understand from his words?* **8** supply in the mind. In "He hit the tree harder than I," the word *did* is said to be understood after *I.* **9 understand each other,** know each other's meaning and wishes; agree. [OE *understandan*] —**Syn. 3** See **know.**

hat, āge, cãre, fär; let, ēqual, tėrm; it, īce
hot, ōpen, ôrder; oil, out; cup, pu̇t, rüle, ūse
əbove, takən, pencəl, lemən, circəs
ch, child; ng, long; sh, ship
th, thin; ᴛʜ, then; zh, measure

un·der·stand·a·ble (un′dər stan′də bəl) *adj.* able to be understood. —**un′der·stand′a·bly,** *adv.*

un·der·stand·ing (un′dər stan′ding) *n.* **1** the mental process or state of one that understands; comprehension; knowledge: *a clear understanding of the problem.* **2** the ability to learn and know; intelligence: *The doctor was a man of understanding.* **3** knowledge of each other's meaning and wishes: *True friendship is based on understanding.* **4** a mutual arrangement or agreement of an informal but more or less explicit nature: *We have an understanding about the use of the car on Saturdays.* —*adj.* that understands; intelligent. —**un′der·stand′ing·ly,** *adv.*

un·der·state (un′dər stāt′) *v.* **-stat·ed, -stat·ing. 1** state too weakly. **2** say less than the full truth about.

un·der·state·ment (un′dər stāt′mənt) *n.* **1** a statement that expresses a fact too weakly. **2** a statement that says less than could be said truly.

un·der·stood (un′dər stu̇d′) *v.* pt. and pp. of **understand.**

un·der·stud·y (un′dər stud′ē) *n.* **-stud·ies,** *v.* **-stud·ied, -stud·y·ing.** —*n.* a person who can act as a substitute for an actor or actress. —*v.* **1** learn (a part) in order to replace the regular performer when necessary. **2** act as an understudy to.

un·der·take (un′dər tāk′) *v.* **-took, -tak·en, -tak·ing. 1** set about; try; attempt. **2** agree to do; take upon oneself. **3** promise; guarantee.

un·der·tak·er (un′dər tāk′ər *for 1;* un′dər tāk′ər *for 2*) *n.* **1** a person whose business is preparing the dead for burial and taking charge of funerals. **2** a person who undertakes something.

un·der·tak·ing (un′dər tāk′ing *for 1 and 2;* un′dər tāk′ing *for 3*) *n.* **1** something undertaken; task; enterprise. **2** a promise; guarantee. **3** the business of preparing the dead for burial and taking charge of funerals.

un·der·tone (un′dər tōn′) *n.* **1** a low or very quiet tone: *talk in undertones.* **2** a subdued color; color seen through other colors: *There was an undertone of brown beneath all the gold and crimson of autumn.* **3** an underlying quality, condition, or element: *an undertone of sadness in her gaiety.*

un·der·took (un′dər tu̇k′) *v.* pt. of **undertake.**

un·der·tow (un′dər tō′) *n.* **1** any strong current below the surface, moving in a direction different from that of the surface current. **2** the backward flow from waves breaking on a beach.

un·der·val·u·a·tion (un′dər val′ū ā′shən) *n.* too low a valuation.

un·der·val·ue (un′dər val′ū) *v.* **-ued, -u·ing. 1** put too low a value on. **2** esteem too little; appreciate insufficiently. —**Syn. 2** underrate, underestimate, depreciate.

un·der·vest (un′dər vest′) *n.* undershirt.

un·der·wa·ter (un′dər wot′er or -wô′tər) *adj.* **1** below the surface of the water. **2** made for use under the water.

un·der·wear (un′dər wãr′) *n.* clothing worn next to the skin or under one's outer clothes; underclothes.

un·der·weight (un′dər wāt′) *adj.* having too little weight. —*n.* weight that is not up to standard.

un·der·went (un′dər went′) *v.* pt. of **undergo.**

un·der·wood (un′dər wu̇d′) *n.* underbrush.

un·der·world (un′dər wėrld′) *n.* **1** the lower, degraded, or criminal part of human society. **2** the lower world; Hades. **3** the earth. **4** the opposite side of the earth.

un·der·write (un′dər rīt′ or un′dər rīt′) *v.* **-wrote, -writ·ten, -writ·ing. 1** insure (property) against loss. **2** sign (an insurance policy), thereby accepting the risk of insuring something against loss. **3** write under (other written matter); sign one's name to (a document, etc.).

4 agree to buy (all the stocks or bonds of a certain issue that are not bought by the public): *The bankers underwrote the steel company's bonds.* **5** agree to meet the expenses of; guarantee. [OE *underwrītan*, translation of L *subscribere*]

un·der·writ·er (un′dər rīt′ər) *n.* **1** a person who underwrites an insurance policy or carries on an insurance business; insurer. **2** an official of an insurance company who determines the risks to be accepted, the premiums to be paid, etc. **3** a person who underwrites (usually with others) issues of bonds, stocks, etc.

un·der·writ·ten (un′dər rit′ən or un′dər rit′ən) *v.* pp. of **underwrite.**

un·der·wrote (un′dər rōt′ or un′dər rōt′) *v.* pt. of **underwrite.**

un·de·sir·a·ble (un′di zīr′ə bəl) *adj.* objectionable; disagreeable. —*n.* a person that is not wanted.

un·de·vel·oped (un′di vel′əpt) *adj.* **1** not fully grown. **2** not put to full use. **3** having resources not yet exploited; having little or no modern technology: *undeveloped countries.*

un·did (un did′) *v.* pt. of **undo.**

un·dine (un dēn′ or un′dēn) *n.* in European legend, a female water sprite who, by marrying a mortal and bearing a child, was supposed to be able to acquire a soul. [< NL *Undina* < L *unda* wave]

un·dis·ci·plined (un dis′ə plind) *adj.* not disciplined; without proper control; untrained. —**Syn.** wild, uncontrolled.

un·dis·guised (un′dis gīzd′) *adj.* **1** not disguised. **2** unconcealed; open; plain; frank. —**un′dis·guis′ed·ly,** *adv.*

un·dis·put·ed (un′dis pūt′id) *adj.* not disputed; not doubted. —**un·dis·put′ed·ly,** *adv.*

un·dis·turbed (un′dis tėrbd′) *adj.* not disturbed; not troubled; calm.

un·do (un dü′) *v.* **-did, -done, -do·ing. 1** unfasten; untie: "*Please undo the package,*" *she said; and I undid the string.* **2** do away with; cause to be as if never done; spoil; destroy. **3** bring to ruin. **4** explain; solve. [OE *undōn*] —**un·do′er,** *n.*

un·do·ing (un dü′ing) *n.* **1** a doing away with; spoiling; destroying. **2** a cause of destruction or ruin.

un·done (un dun′) *adj.* **1** not done; not finished. **2** ruined. —*v.* pp. of **undo.**

un·doubt·ed (un dout′id) *adj.* not doubted; accepted as true.

un·doubt·ed·ly (un dout′id lē) *adv.* beyond doubt; certainly.

un·dress (*v.* un dres′; *n.* un′dres′ or un dres′; *adj.* un′dres′) *v.* **1** take the clothes off; strip. **2** to strip of ornament. **3** take dressing from (a wound). **4** take off one's clothes. —*n.* **1** loose, informal dress. **2** ordinary clothes. **3** lack of clothing; nakedness. —*adj.* of or having to do with informal or ordinary clothes.

un·due (un dū′ or un dü′) *adj.* **1** not fitting; not right; improper. **2** too great; too much. —**Syn. 2** excessive.

un·du·lant (un′jü lənt or un′dyů lənt) *adj.* waving; wavy.

undulant fever an infectious disease transmitted to man by bacteria in the milk of infected cattle, goats, etc. It brings on fever, spleen and bowel disorders, pain in the joints, etc.

un·du·late (*v.* un′jü lāt′ or un′dyů lāt′) *v.* **-lat·ed, -lat·ing,** *adj.* —*v.* **1** move in waves: *undulating water.* **2** have a wavy form or surface: *undulating hair.* **3** cause to move in waves. **4** give a wavy form or surface to. [< LL *undula* wavelet, dim. of L *unda* wave] —*adj.* wavy. [< L *undulatus* diversified as with waves < *unda* wave]

un·du·la·tion (un′jü lā′shən or un′dyů lā′shən) *n.* **1** a waving motion. **2** a wavy form. **3** one of a series of wavelike bends, curves, swellings, etc. **4** in physics, a wavelike motion in air or some other medium, as in the propagation of sound or light; vibration; wave.

un·du·la·to·ry (un′jü lə tô′rē or un′dyů lə tô′rē) *adj.* undulating; wavy.

un·du·ly (un dū′lē or un dü′lē) *adv.* **1** improperly. **2** excessively.

un·dy·ing (un dī′ing) *adj.* deathless; immortal; eternal. —**un·dy′ing·ly,** *adv.*

un·earned (un ėrnd′) *adj.* **1** not earned; not gained by labor or service. **2** not deserved. **3** in baseball, scored because of a defensive error or errors.

unearned income income accruing from rents, investments, etc. and not from wages.

unearned increment increase in the value of property from natural causes, such as the growth of population, rather than from the labor, improvements, etc. put into it by the owner.

un·earth (un ėrth′) *v.* **1** dig up: *unearth a buried city.* **2** find out; discover: *unearth a plot.*

un·earth·ly (un ėrth′lē) *adj.* **1** not of this world; supernatural. **2** strange; weird; ghostly. **3** *Informal.* unnatural; extraordinary; preposterous. —**un·earth′li·ness,** *n.*

un·eas·y (un ēz′ē) *adj.* **-eas·i·er, -eas·i·est. 1** restless; disturbed; anxious. **2** not comfortable. **3** not easy in manner; awkward. —**un·eas′i·ly,** *adv.* —**un·eas′i·ness,** *n.*

un·ed·u·cat·ed (un ej′ů kāt′id) *adj.* not educated; not taught or trained. —**Syn.** See **ignorant.**

UNEF (ū′nef) United Nations Emergency Force.

un·em·ploy·a·ble (un′em ploi′ə bəl) *adj.* that cannot be employed.

un·em·ployed (un′em ploid′) *adj.* not employed; not in use; having no work. —*n.* **the unemployed,** people out of work.

un·em·ploy·ment (un′em ploi′mənt) *n.* **1** lack of employment; the state of being out of work. **2** the number of people out of work: *The unemployment figure is 4%.*

un·e·qual (un ē′kwəl) *adj.* **1** not the same in amount, size, number, value, merit, rank, etc. **2** not balanced; not well matched. **3** not fair; one-sided: *an unequal contest.* **4** not enough; not adequate: *strength unequal to the task.* **5** not regular; not even; variable. —**un·e′qual·ly,** *adv.* —**un·e′qual·ness,** *n.*

un·e·qualled or **un·e·qualed** (un ē′kwəld) *adj.* not equalled; matchless.

un·e·quiv·o·cal (un′i kwiv′ə kəl) *adj.* **1** clear; plain. **2** of persons, not inclined to temporize, compromise, or equivocate; speaking frankly and bluntly. —**un′e·quiv′o·cal·ly,** *adv.* —**un′e·quiv′o·cal·ness,** *n.*

un·err·ing (un ėr′ing or un er′ing) *adj.* making no mistakes; exactly right. —**un·err′ing·ly,** *adv.* —**un·err′ing·ness,** *n.* —**Syn.** infallible, sure.

UNESCO (ū nes′kō) *n.* the United Nations Educational, Scientific, and Cultural Organization.

un·es·sen·tial (un′ə sen′shəl) *adj.* not essential; not of prime importance. —*n.* something not essential.

un·e·ven (un ē′vən) *adj.* **1** not level: *uneven ground.* **2** not equal: *an uneven contest.* **3** of a number, that cannot be divided by 2 without a remainder: *The numbers 27 and 9 are uneven.* [OE *unefen*] —**un·e′ven·ly,** *adv.* —**un·e′ven·ness,** *n.* —**Syn. 1** rough, rugged, jagged.

un·e·vent·ful (un′i vent′fəl) *adj.* without important or striking occurrences. —**un′e·vent′ful·ly,** *adv.* —**un′e·vent′ful·ness,** *n.*

un·ex·am·pled (un′eg zam′pəld) *adj.* having no equal or like; without precedent or parallel; without anything like it: *This man's run of 100 yards in 9 seconds is unexampled.*

un·ex·cep·tion·a·ble (un′ek sep′shən ə bəl) *adj.* beyond criticism; wholly admirable. —**un′ex·cep′tion·a·bly,** *adv.*

un·ex·cep·tion·al (un′ek sep′shən əl) *adj.* **1** ordinary. **2** admitting of no exception. —**un′ex·cep′tion·al·ly,** *adv.*

un·ex·pect·ed (un′eks pek′tid) *adj.* not expected. —**un′ex·pect′ed·ness,** *n.*

un·ex·pect·ed·ly (un′eks pek′tid lē) *adv.* in a way that is not expected; suddenly.

un·fail·ing (un fāl′ing) *adj.* **1** never failing; tireless; loyal. **2** never running short; endless. **3** sure; certain.

un·fail·ing·ly (un fāl′ing lē) *adv.* always; without fail.

un·fair (un fãr′) *adj.* not honest; unjust. [OE *unfæger*] —**un·fair′ly,** *adv.* —**un·fair′ness,** *n.* —**Syn.** partial, prejudiced, biassed, one-sided.

un·faith·ful (un fāth′fəl) *adj.* **1** not faithful; not true to duty or one's promises; faithless. **2** not accurate; not exact. —**un·faith′ful·ly,** *adv.* —**un·faith′ful·ness,** *n.* —**Syn. 1** false, disloyal, inconstant.

un·fa·mil·iar (un′fə mil′yər) *adj.* **1** not well-known; unusual; strange: *That face is unfamiliar to me.* **2** not acquainted: *He is unfamiliar with the Greek language.*

un·fa·mil·i·ar·i·ty (un′fə mil′yar′ə tē or un′fə mil′ē ar′ə tē) *n.* lack of familiarity.

un·fas·ten (un fas′ən) *v.* undo; loose; open.

un·fath·om·a·ble (un faᴛʜ′əm ə bəl) *adj.* so deep that the bottom cannot be reached; too mysterious to be understood.

un·fath·omed (un faᴛʜ′əmd) *adj.* not measured; not understood.

un·fa·vor·a·ble or **un·fa·vour·a·ble** (un fā′vər ə bəl or un fāv′rə bəl) *adj.* not favorable; adverse; harmful. —**un·fa′vor·a·ble·ness** or **un·fa′vour·a·ble·ness,** *n.* —**un·fa′vor·a·bly** or **un·fa′vour·a·bly,** *adv.*

un·feel·ing (un fēl′ing) *adj.* **1** hard-hearted; cruel. **2** not able to feel. —**un·feel′ing·ly,** *adv.* —**un·feel′ing·ness,** *n.* —**Syn. 1** unsympathetic.

un·feigned (un fānd′) *adj.* sincere; real. —**Syn.** unaffected, genuine.

un·feign·ed·ly (un fān′id lē) *adv.* really; sincerely.

un·fet·ter (un fet′ər) *v.* remove fetters from; unchain.

un·fin·ished (un fin′isht) *adj.* **1** not finished; not complete. **2** without some special finish; not polished; rough; not painted: *unfinished furniture.*

un·fit (un fit′) *adj. v.* **-fit·ted, -fit·ting.** —*adj.* **1** not fit; not suitable. **2** not good enough; unqualified. **3** not adapted. —*v.* make unfit; spoil. —**un·fit′ness,** *n.*

un·fit·ted (un fit′id) *adj.* **1** not fitted; inappropriate; not suitable. **2** not fitting tightly; loose: *an unfitted coat.*

un·fix (un fiks′) *v.* loosen; detach; unfasten.

un·flag·ging (un flag′ing) *adj.* not drooping or failing: *unflagging efforts.* —**un·flag′ging·ly,** *adv.*

un·flap·pa·ble (un flap′ə bəl) *adj. Informal.* not able to be excited or emotionally upset: *an unflappable teacher.*

un·fledged (un flejd′) *adj.* **1** of a bird, too young to fly; not having full-grown feathers. **2** undeveloped; immature.

un·flinch·ing (un flin′ching) *adj.* not drawing back from difficulty, danger, or pain; firm; resolute. —**un·flinch′ing·ly,** *adv.*

un·fold (un fōld′) *v.* **1** open the folds of; spread out: *unfold a serviette.* **2** cause to be no longer bent, coiled, or interlaced; unbend and straighten out: *unfold your arms.* **3** reveal; show; explain. **4** open; develop. [OE *unfealdan*]

un·forced (un fôrst′) *adj.* **1** not forced; not compelled; willing. **2** natural; spontaneous.

un·fore·seen (un′fôr sēn′) *adj.* not known beforehand; unexpected.

un·for·get·ta·ble (un′fər get′ə bəl) *adj.* that can never be forgotten. —**un′for·get′ta·bly,** *adv.*

un·formed (un fôrmd′) *adj.* **1** shapeless. **2** undeveloped. **3** in biology, unorganized.

un·for·tu·nate (un fôr′chə nit) *adj.* **1** not lucky; having bad luck. **2** not suitable; not fitting. —*n.* an unfortunate person. —**un·for′tu·nate·ly,** *adv.* —**un·for′tu·nate·ness,** *n.*

un·found·ed (un foun′did) *adj.* without foundation; baseless: *an unfounded complaint.* —**un·found′ed·ly,** *adv.* —**un·found′ed·ness,** *n.*

un·fre·quent·ed (un′fri kwen′tid) *adj.* not frequented; seldom visited; rarely used.

un·friend·ed (un fren′did) *adj.* without friends.

un·friend·ly (un frend′lē) *adj.* **1** not friendly; hostile. **2** not favorable. —**un·friend′li·ness,** *n.* —**Syn. 1** See **hostile.**

un·frock (un frok′) *v.* **1** take away a frock from. **2** deprive (a priest or minister) of his rank, position, and privileges.

hat, āge, cãre, fär; let, ēqual, tėrm; it, īce
hot, ōpen, ôrder; oil, out; cup, pu̇t, rüle, ūse
əbove, takən, pencəl, lemən, circəs
ch, child; ng, long; sh, ship
th, thin; ᴛʜ, then; zh, measure

un·fruit·ful (un früt′fəl) *adj.* not fruitful; barren; not productive.

un·furl (un fėrl′) *v.* spread out; shake out; unfold: *unfurl a sail.*

un·fur·nished (un fėr′nisht) *adj.* not furnished; without furniture.

un·gain·ly (un gān′lē) *adj.* awkward; clumsy. [ME *ungaynly* < *un-* not + *gaynly* agile] —**un·gain′li·ness,** *n.* —**Syn.** uncouth, ungraceful. See **awkward.**

un·gen·er·ous (un jen′ər əs) *adj.* not generous; mean. —**un·gen′er·ous·ly,** *adv.*

un·gird (un gėrd′) *v.* **1** unfasten or take off the girdle or belt of. **2** loosen, or take off, by unfastening a girdle.

un·glazed (un glāzd′) *adj.* **1** not coated with a smooth, glossy surface. **2** lacking glass windows.

un·god·li·ness (un god′lē nis) *n.* lack of godliness; wickedness; sinfulness.

un·god·ly (un god′lē) *adj.* **1** not religious; wicked; sinful. **2** *Informal.* **a** very annoying; distressing; irritating: *an ungodly noise.* **b** outrageous; dreadful; shocking: *pay an ungodly price.* **c** unbelievable: *eat an ungodly amount.*

un·gov·ern·a·ble (un guv′ər nə bəl) *adj.* impossible to control; very hard to control or rule; unruly: *an ungovernable temper.* —**un·gov′ern·a·ble·ness,** *n.* —**un·gov′ern·a·bly,** *adv.* —**Syn.** See **unruly.**

un·grace·ful (un grās′fəl) *adj.* not graceful; not elegant or beautiful; clumsy; awkward. —**un·grace′ful·ly,** *adv.* —**un·grace′ful·ness,** *n.*

un·gra·cious (un grā′shəs) *adj.* **1** not polite; rude. **2** unpleasant; disagreeable. —**un·gra′cious·ly,** *adv.* —**un·gra′cious·ness,** *n.*

un·grate·ful (un grāt′fəl) *adj.* **1** not grateful; not thankful. **2** displaying lack of gratitude: *an ungrateful silence.* **3** unpleasant; disagreeable. —**un·grate′ful·ly,** *adv.* —**un·grate′ful·ness,** *n.*

un·ground·ed (un groun′did) *adj.* without foundation; without reasons.

un·grudg·ing (un gruj′ing) *adj.* willing; hearty; liberal. —**un·grudg′ing·ly,** *adv.*

un·gual (ung′gwəl) *adj.* of, having to do with, bearing, or shaped like a nail, claw, or hoof. [< L *unguis* nail, claw, hoof]

un·guard·ed (un gär′did) *adj.* **1** not protected. **2** careless: *In an unguarded moment, she gave away the secret.* —**un·guard′ed·ly,** *adv.* —**un·guard′ed·ness,** *n.*

un·guent (ung′gwənt) *n.* an ointment for sores, burns, etc.; salve. [< L *unguentum* < *unguere* anoint]

un·gu·la (ung′gyu̇ lə) *n.* **-lae** (-lē′ or -lī′). **1** a hoof. **2** a nail; claw. **3** in botany, the claw-shaped base of a petal. **4** in geometry, a cylinder, cone, etc., the top part of which has been cut off by a plane oblique to the base. [< L *ungula,* dim. of *unguis* nail, claw, hoof]

un·gu·lar (ung′gyu̇ lər) *adj.* of or like a hoof.

un·gu·late (ung′gyu̇ lit or ung′gyu̇ lāt′) *adj.* **1** having hoofs. **2** belonging to the group of animals having hoofs. —*n.* an animal that has hoofs. Horses, cows, sheep, and deer are ungulates. [< L *ungulatus* < *ungula.* See UNGULA.]

un·hal·lowed (un hal′ōd) *adj.* **1** not made holy; not sacred. **2** wicked.

un·hand (un hand′) *v.* let go; take the hands from.

un·hand·some (un han′səm) *adj.* **1** not good-looking; plain; ugly. **2** ungracious; discourteous; unseemly; mean. **3** not generous.

un·hand·y (un han′dē) *adj.* **1** not easy to handle or manage: *an unhandy tool.* **2** not skilful in using the hands: *an unhandy man.* —**un·hand′i·ly,** *adv.* —**un·hand′i·ness,** *n.*

un·hap·pi·ly (un hap′ə lē) *adv.* **1** not happily. **2** unfortunately. **3** unsuitably.

un·hap·pi·ness (un hap′ē nis) *n.* **1** sadness; sorrow; the state of being unhappy. **2** bad luck; ill fortune.

un·hap·py (un hap′ē) *adj.* **-pi·er, -pi·est. 1** sad; sorrowful. **2** unlucky. **3** not suitable.

un·har·ness (un här′nis) *v.* **1** remove the harness from; free from harness or gear: *unharness the horse.* **2** remove harness or gear. **3** divest of armor.

un·health·ful (un helth′fəl) *adj.* bad for the health. **—un·health′ful·ly,** *adv.* **—un·health′ful·ness,** *n.*

un·health·i·ly (un hel′thə lē) *adv.* in a way that is not healthy.

un·health·i·ness (un hel′thē nis) *n.* **1** lack of health; sickness. **2** a condition harmful to health or causing disease.

un·health·y (un hel′thē) *adj.* **1** not possessing good health; not well: *an unhealthy child.* **2** characteristic of or resulting from poor health: *an unhealthy paleness.* **3** hurtful to health; unwholesome: *an unhealthy climate.* **4** morally harmful. **—Syn. 1** sickly, frail, ill, diseased. **3** unsanitary, unhygienic.

un·heard (un hėrd′) *adj.* **1** not perceived by the ear: *unheard melodies.* **2** not given a hearing: *condemn a person unheard.* **3** not heard of; unknown.

un·heard-of (un hėrd′uv′ or -ov′) *adj.* **1** that was never heard of; unknown. **2** such as was never known before; unprecedented.

un·heed·ed (un hēd′id) *adj.* not heeded; disregarded; unnoticed.

un·hes·i·tat·ing (un hez′ə tāt′ing) *adj.* prompt; ready. **—un·hes′i·tat′ing·ly,** *adv.*

un·hinge (un hinj′) *v.* **-hinged, -hing·ing. 1** take (a door, etc.) off its hinges. **2** remove the hinges from. **3** separate from something; detach. **4** unsettle; disorganize; upset: *Trouble has unhinged this poor man's mind.*

un·his·tor·ic (un′his tôr′ik) *adj.* **1** not famous in history; unimportant. **2** unhistorical.

un·his·tor·i·cal (un′his tôr′ə kəl) *adj.* **1** not in accordance with the facts of history. **2** not recorded in history; legendary. **3** ignorant of the facts of history. **—un′his·tor′i·cal·ly,** *adv.* **—un′his·tor′i·cal·ness,** *n.*

un·hitch (un hich′) *v.* free from being hitched; unfasten.

un·ho·ly (un hō′lē) *adj.* **-li·er, -li·est. 1** not holy; wicked; sinful. **2** *Informal.* not seemly; fearful: *an unholy row.* [OE *unhālig*] **—un·ho′li·ness,** *n.*

un·hon·ored or **un·hon·oured** (un on′ərd) *adj.* not regarded with respect or reverence; not famed or renowned; not given marks of esteem.

un·hook (un hu̇k′) *v.* **1** loosen from a hook. **2** undo by loosening a hook or hooks. **3** become loosed from hooks; become undone.

un·horse (un hôrs′) *v* **-horsed, -hors·ing.** throw from a horse's back; cause to fall from a horse.

un·hu·man (un hū′mən) *adj.* **1** not human; devoid of human qualities. **2** inhuman. **3** superhuman.

un·hurt (un hėrt′) *adj.* not hurt; not harmed.

un·hy·gien·ic (un hī jē′nik or un hī jen′ik) *adj.* not healthful; unsanitary.

uni- *combining form.* one: *unilateral.* [< L *unus* one]

U·ni·at (ū′nē at′) *n.* a member of any Eastern Christian church that is in communion with the Roman Catholic Church and acknowledges the supremacy of the Pope but keeps its own liturgy *—adj.* of or having to do with this church or its members. [< Russian *uniyat* < *uniya* union]

u·ni·cam·er·al (ū′nə kam′ər əl) *adj.* having only one house in a lawmaking body: *All Canadian provinces except Quebec have unicameral legislatures.* [< *uni-* + L *camera* chamber]

UNICEF (ūn′i sef′) *n.* the United Nations (International) Children's Emergency Fund.

u·ni·cel·lu·lar (ū′nə sel′yu̇ lər) *adj.* in biology, having one cell only. The amoeba is a unicellular animal.

u·ni·corn (ū′nə kôrn′) *n.* **1** an imaginary animal resembling a horse, but having a single long horn growing from the middle of its forehead. **2** a figure, picture, or representation of this animal, often used as a heraldic bearing. **3** in the Bible, a mistranslation of a Hebrew word referring to a two-horned animal, probably the wild ox. [< L *unicornis* < *unus* one + *cornu* horn]

u·ni·fi·ca·tion (ū′nə fə kā′shən) *n.* **1** a formation into one unit; union: *the unification of many states into one nation.* **2** a making or being made more alike: *The traffic laws of the different provinces need unification.* **3** the condition or state of being unified.

u·ni·flo·rous (ū′nə flô′rəs) *adj.* in botany, having or bearing one flower only.

u·ni·form (ū′nə fôrm′) *adj.* **1** always the same; not changing: *The earth turns around at a uniform rate.* **2** all alike; not varying: *All the bricks are of a uniform size.* **3** not mixed or blended: *lawns of a uniform green.* **4** regular; even: *a uniform pace.* **5** in accordance or agreement with one another; conforming to one standard, rule, or pattern: *uniform answers.*
—n. the distinctive clothes worn by the members of a group when on duty. Soldiers, policemen, and nurses wear uniforms.
—v. clothe or furnish with a uniform. [< L *uniformis* < *unus* one + *forma* form] **—u′ni·form′ly,** *adv.* **—u′ni·form′ness,** *n.* **—Syn. 1, 3** See **even.**

u·ni·form·i·ty (ū′nə fôr′mə tē) *n.* **-ties.** a uniform condition or character; sameness throughout.

u·ni·fy (ū′nə fī′) *v.* **-fied, -fy·ing.** make or form into one; unite. [< LL *unificare* < L *unus* one + *facere* make] **—u′ni·fi′er,** *n.*

u·ni·lat·er·al (ū′nə lat′ər əl) *adj.* **1** of, on, or affecting one side only. **2** having all the parts arranged on one side of an axis; turned to one side; one-sided. **3** in law, of a contract, etc., affecting one party or person only; done by one side only; putting obligation on one party only: *unilateral disarmament.* **4** concerned with or considering only one side of a matter. **5** in sociology, related or descended on only one side of the family. **—u′ni·lat′er·al·ly,** *adv.*

u·ni·lat·er·al·ism (ū′nə lat′ə rə liz′əm or ū′nə lat′rə liz′əm) *n.* belief in or advocacy of a unilateral policy, especially in disarmament.

u·ni·lat·er·al·ist (ū′nə lat′ə rə list or ū′nə lat′rə list) *adj.* of or having to do with unilateralism or unilateralists. *—n.* an advocate or follower of unilateralism.

u·ni·lin·gual (ū′nə ling′gwəl) *adj.* **1** having knowledge or use of only one language. **2** of or having one universal language.

u·ni·lin·gual·ism (ū′nə ling′gwə liz′əm) *n.* **1** the state, condition, or policy of being unilingual. **2** advocacy of or belief in one universal language.

un·im·peach·a·ble (un′im pēch′ə bəl) *adj.* free from fault; blameless. **—un′im·peach′a·bly,** *adv.*

un·im·por·tance (un′im pôr′təns) *n.* the nature or quality of being unimportant.

un·im·por·tant (un′im pôr′tənt) *adj.* not important; insignificant; trifling.

un·in·jured (un in′jərd) *adj.* not hurt; not damaged.

un·in·spired (un′in spīrd′) *adj.* **1** not inspired. **2** dull; tiresome.

un·in·tel·li·gi·ble (un′in tel′ə jə bəl) *adj.* that cannot be understood. **—un′in·tel′li·gi·bly,** *adv.*

un·in·ter·est·ed (un in′tris tid or un in′tə res′tid) *adj.* not interested; showing no interest. **—un·in′ter·est·ed·ly,** *adv.* ☛ See **disinterested** for usage note.

un·in·ter·rupt·ed (un′in tə rup′tid) *adj.* without interruption; continuous. **—un′in·ter·rupt′ed·ly,** *adv*

un·ion (ūn′yən) *n.* **1** the act of uniting or the state of being united: *The United States was formed by the union of thirteen former British colonies.* **2** a group of people, states, etc. united for some special purpose: *The ten provinces of Canada form a union.* **3** a group of workers joined together to protect and promote their interests; labor union; trade union. **4** a marriage. **5** any of various devices for connecting parts of machinery or apparatus, especially a piece to join pipes or tubes together. [ME < OF < LL *unio, -onis* < *unus* one]
Syn. 1 Union, unity = a forming or being one. **Union** emphasizes the joining together of two or more things, people, or groups to form a whole, or the state of being joined together as a unit: *A*

combat team is formed by the union of infantry and other forces. **Unity** emphasizes and applies to the oneness of the whole that is formed: *The strength of any group is in its unity.* 2 combination, consolidation, fusion, coalition, confederation, league, merger.

un·ion·ism (ūn′yən iz′əm) *n.* 1 the principle of union. 2 an attachment to a union. 3 the system, principles, or methods of labor unions.

un·ion·ist (ūn′yən ist) *n.* 1 a person who promotes or advocates union. 2 a member of a labor union. 3 **Unionist, a** a supporter of the federal government of the United States during the Civil War. **b** formerly, a person who opposed the political separation of Ireland from Great Britain. **c** a person who favors keeping Northern Ireland as part of the United Kingdom.

un·ion·i·za·tion (ūn′yən ə zā′shən or ūn′yən ī zā′shən) *n.* the act of unionizing or the state of being unionized.

un·ion·ize (ūn′yən īz′) *v.* **-ized, -iz·ing.** 1 form into a labor union. 2 organize under a labor union. 3 join in a labor union.

Union Jack the red, white, and blue flag of the United Kingdom, formed by combining the crosses of St. George, St. Andrew, and St. Patrick, for England, Scotland, and Ireland respectively.

Union Na·tion·ale (nash′ē ən al′; *French,* Y nyôN′ nä syô näl′) a political party in Quebec, formed in the early 1930's.

union shop a business establishment that by agreement employs only members of a labor union, but may hire non-members provided they join the union within a specified period (30 days).

union station a station used jointly by two or more railways.

u·nique (ū nēk′) *adj.* 1 having no like or equal; being the only one of its kind. 2 *Informal.* rare; unusual. [< F < L *unicus*] —**u·nique′ly,** *adv.* —**u·nique′ness,** *n.* —**Syn. 1** unmatched, sole.

☞ **unique.** In formal usage *unique* means "having no like or equal," and therefore refers to something or somebody that cannot be compared. In informal usage it has become generalized to mean rare or unusual, and is often compared with *more* or *most* or modified by *very* or *rather*: *Her clothes are rather unique.*

u·ni·son (ū′nə sən or ū′nə zən) *n.* 1 a doing together as one, at the same time, etc.: *The feet of marching soldiers move in unison. They spoke in unison.* 2 in music: **a** identity of pitch of two or more tones. **b** a performing together by voices, instruments, etc. of the same melody, etc. at the same pitch or an octave apart. **c** the interval between two tones of the same or different quality but identical pitch; prime[1]. [< Med.L *unisonus* sounding the same < LL *unisonus* in immediate sequence in the scale < L *unus* one + *sonus* sound]

u·nit (ū′nit) *n.* 1 a single thing or person. 2 any group of things or persons considered as one. 3 one of the individuals or groups into which a whole can be analysed: *The body consists of units called cells.* 4 a standard quantity or amount. A foot is a unit of length; a pound is a unit of weight. 5 in mathematics, the smallest whole number; 1. 6 a regiment. 7 in schools, a section of a course, usually on one theme or topic. [probably < *unity*]

Unit. Unitarian.

U·ni·tar·i·an (ū′nə tãr′ē ən) *n.* a person who maintains that God exists as one being, in opposition to the doctrine of the Trinity. Unitarians accept the moral teachings of Jesus but do not believe that He was divine. —*adj.* of or having to do with Unitarians.

U·ni·tar·i·an·ism (ū′nə tãr′ē ən iz′əm) *n.* the doctrines or beliefs of Unitarians.

u·ni·tar·y (ū′nə ter′ē) *adj.* 1 of or having to do with a unit or units. 2 having to do with unity. 3 like that of a unit; used as a unit.

u·nite (ū nīt′) *v.* **u·nit·ed, u·nit·ing.** 1 join together; make one; combine: *unite bricks with mortar in a wall.* 2 bring together; amalgamate or consolidate into one body; join in action, interest, opinion, feeling, etc.: *Several firms were united to form one company.* 3 join by mutual pledging, covenant, or other formal bond; cause to become a union: *unite a man and woman in marriage.* 4 have or exhibit in union or combination: *a child uniting his father's temper and his mother's red hair.* 5 become one; join in action, etc. [< L *unitus,* pp. of *unire* < *unus* one] —**u·nit′er,** *n.* —**Syn. 1, 2** merge, consolidate, unify, couple. See **join.**

hat, āge, cãre, fär; let, ēqual, tėrm; it, īce
hot, ōpen, ôrder; oil, out; cup, pu̇t, rüle, ūse
əbove, takən, pencəl, lemən, circəs
ch, child; ng, long; sh, ship
th, thin; TH, then; zh, measure

u·nit·ed (ū nīt′id) *adj.* 1 joined together to make one. 2 joined together.

United Church of Canada a Christian church formed in 1924-1925 as a union of Methodists, Presbyterians, and Congregationalists.

United Nations 1 the nations that belong to a world-wide organization devoted to establishing and maintaining world peace. 2 this organization, in existence since Oct. 24, 1945. 3 the Allies (def. 2). *Abbrev.*: U.N. or UN

u·ni·ty (ū′nə tē) *n.* **-ties.** 1 oneness; being united: *A circle has more unity than a row of dots. A nation has more unity than a group of tribes.* 2 a union of parts forming a complex whole. 3 harmony: *Brothers and sisters should live together in unity.* 4 the number one (1). 5 oneness of effect; the choice and arrangement of material (for a composition, book, picture, statue, etc.) to secure a single effect. 6 **the unities,** the rules of action, time, and place that require a play to have one main action occurring on one day in one place. [ME < L *unitas* < *unus* one] —**Syn. 1** See **union.**

Univ. 1 University. 2 Universalist.

UNIVAC (ū′nə vak′) *n. Trademark.* an electronic computer having a binary numbering system. [< *Univ*ersal *A*utomatic *C*omputer]

u·ni·va·lence (ū′nə vā′ləns or ū niv′ə ləns) *n.* the state of being univalent.

u·ni·va·lent (ū′nə vā′lənt or ū niv′ə lənt) *adj.* having a valence of one. [< *uni-* + L *valens, -entis,* ppr. of *valere* be worth]

u·ni·valve (ū′nə valv′) *n.* 1 any mollusc having a shell made of one piece. Snails are univalves. 2 its shell. —*adj.* having a shell made of one piece.

u·ni·ver·sal (ū′nə vėr′səl) *adj.* 1 of or for all; done, used, held, etc. by everybody. 2 of or having to do with the universe; existing everywhere. 3 covering a whole group of persons, things, cases, etc.; general. 4 adaptable to different sizes, angles, kinds of work, etc. 5 constituting, existing as, or regarded as a complete whole; complete; entire; whole: *the universal cosmos.* 6 accomplished in or comprising all, or very many, subjects; wide-ranging: *universal knowledge.* 7 allowing or providing for movement toward any direction: *a universal joint.* —*n.* 1 a proposition that asserts or denies something of every member of a class. *Example*: All men are mortal. 2 something universal, especially a person or thing that is universally powerful, current, etc. [ME < L *universalis* < *universus.* See UNIVERSE.]

U·ni·ver·sal·ism (ū′nə vėr′səl iz′əm) *n.* the doctrines or beliefs of Universalists.

U·ni·ver·sal·ist (ū′nə vėr′səl ist) *n.* a member of a Christian church holding the belief that all people will finally be saved. —*adj.* of or having to do with Universalists.

u·ni·ver·sal·i·ty (ū′nə vėr sal′ə tē) *n.* **-ties.** the fact or condition of being universal.

universal joint 1 a joint that moves in any direction. 2 a coupling for transmitting power from one shaft to another when they are not in line.

u·ni·ver·sal·ly (ū′nə vėr′səl ē) *adv.* 1 in every instance; without exception. 2 everywhere.

u·ni·verse (ū′nə vėrs′) *n.* 1 all things; everything that exists, including all space and matter. 2 the earth as inhabited by, and often including, mankind. 3 a field of thought, area of study, etc. considered as being complete and independent: *the universe of chemistry.* 4 universe of discourse. [< L *universum,* originally adj., whole, turned into one, neut. of *universus* < *unus* one + *vertere* turn]

universe of discourse in logic and mathematics, the set of things under discussion or consideration.

u·ni·ver·si·ty (ū′nə vėr′sə tē) *n.* **-ties. 1** an institution of advanced learning. A university usually has schools of law, medicine, teaching, business, etc. and departments of general instruction as well. **2** a building or buildings used by a university. [ME < OF < Med.L *universitas* corporation < L *universitas* aggregate, whole < *universus.* See UNIVERSE.]

un·joint (un joint′) *v.* take apart the joints of.

un·just (un just′) *adj.* not just; not fair: *It is unjust to punish lawbreakers who are insane.* —**un·just′ly,** *adv.* —**un·just′ness,** *n.*

un·kempt (un kempt′) *adj.* **1** not combed. **2** neglected; untidy. [< *un-*[1] + OE *cembed* combed, pp. of *cemban* < *camb* comb]

un·kind (un kīnd′) *adj.* harsh; cruel. —**un·kind′ness,** *n.* —**Syn.** unsympathetic, ungracious.

un·kind·ly (un kīnd′lē) *adj.* harsh; unfavorable. —*adv.* in an unkind way; harshly.

un·knit (un nit′) *v.* **-knit·ted** or **-knit, -knit·ting. 1** untie or unfasten (a knot, etc.). **2** ravel out (something knitted). **3** smooth out (something wrinkled).

un·known (un nōn′) *adj.* not known; not familiar; strange; unexplored: *an unknown country.* —*n.* **1** a person or thing that is unknown: *a political unknown. The diver descended into the unknown.* **2** in mathematics, an unknown quantity. **3 the Great Unknown,** what happens after death; the hereafter. —**Syn.** *adj.* obscure, nameless, unrenowned.

Unknown Soldier an unidentified soldier killed in battle in World War I, who is buried in a national monument and honored as the representative of all his country's war dead.

un·la·bored or **un·la·boured** (un lā′bərd) *adj.* **1** effortless; spontaneous; not stiff or stilted: *unlabored verses.* **2** not produced or cultivated by labor or effort: *unlabored fields.*

un·lace (un lās′) *v.* **-laced, -lac·ing.** undo the laces of.

un·lade (un lād′) *v.* **-lad·ed, -lad·en** or **-lad·ed, -lad·ing.** unload.

un·latch (un lach′) *v.* unfasten or open by lifting a latch.

un·law·ful (un lo′fəl or un lô′fəl) *adj.* **1** contrary to the law; against the law; forbidden; illegal. **2** *Archaic.* illegitimate. —**un·law′ful·ness,** *n.*

un·law·ful·ly (un lo′fəl ē or un lô′fəl ē) *adv.* **1** illegally. **2** illegitimately.

un·learn (un lėrn′) *v.* get rid of (ideas, habits, or tendencies); forget.

un·learn·ed (un lėr′nid *for 1 and 4*; un lėrnd′ *for 2 and 3*) *adj.* **1** not educated; ignorant. **2** not learned. **3** known without being learned. **4** not showing education.

un·leash (un lēsh′) *v.* **1** release from a leash: *unleash a dog.* **2** let loose: *unleash one's anger.*

un·leav·ened (un lev′ənd) *adj.* not leavened. Unleavened bread is made without yeast.

un·less (ən les′ or un les′) *conj.* if it were not that; if not: *We shall go unless it rains.* [obs. *onlesse* (*that*) < *on* + *less,* i.e., on a less condition (than)]

un·let·tered (un let′ərd) *adj.* **1** not educated. **2** not able to read or write.

un·like (un līk′) *adj.* **1** not like; different: *The two problems are quite unlike.* **2** different in size or number; unequal: *unlike weights.* **3** *Archaic or dialect.* unlikely. —*prep.* different from: *act unlike others.* —**Syn.** *adj.* **1** dissimilar, diverse.

un·like·li·hood (un līk′lē hu̇d′) *n.* improbability.

un·like·ly (un līk′lē) *adj.* **1** not likely; not probable: *He is unlikely to win.* **2** not likely to succeed: *an unlikely undertaking.* —**un·like′li·ness,** *n.*

un·like·ness (un līk′nis) *n.* the fact of being unlike; difference.

un·lim·ber (un lim′bər) *v.* **1** detach the limber or forepart of the carriage from an artillery piece. **2** prepare for action.

un·lim·it·ed (un lim′ə tid) *adj.* **1** without limits; boundless. **2** not restricted. —**un·lim′it·ed·ness,** *n.*

un·load (un lōd′) *v.* **1** remove (a load). **2** take the load from. **3** get rid of. **4** remove powder, shot, bullets, or shells from (a gun). **5** discharge a cargo: *The ship is unloading.* —**un·load′er,** *n.*

un·lock (un lok′) *v.* **1** open the lock of; open (anything firmly closed). **2** disclose; reveal. **3** become unlocked.

un·looked-for (un lu̇kt′fôr′) *adj.* unexpected; unforeseen.

un·loose (un lüs′) *v.* **-loosed, -loos·ing.** let loose; set free; release.

un·loos·en (un lüs′ən) *v.* unloose; loosen.

un·love·ly (un luv′lē) *adj.* without beauty or charm; unpleasing in appearance; unpleasant; objectionable; disagreeable. —**un·love′li·ness,** *n.*

un·luck·y (un luk′ē) *adj.* not lucky; unfortunate; bringing bad luck. —**un·luck′i·ly,** *adv.* —**un·luck′i·ness,** *n.* —**Syn.** unsuccessful, ill-fated.

un·make (un māk′) *v.* **-made, -mak·ing. 1** undo; destroy; ruin. **2** deprive of rank or station; depose.

un·man (un man′) *v.* **-manned, -man·ning. 1** deprive of the qualities of a man. **2** weaken or break down the spirit of. **3** deprive of virility or manhood; castrate. **4** deprive of men: *unman a ship.*

un·man·ly (un man′lē) *adj.* not manly; weak; cowardly. —**un·man′li·ness,** *n.*

un·manned (un mand′) *adj.* without or not requiring a human crew: *an unmanned spacecraft.*

un·man·ner·ly (un man′ər lē) *adj.* having bad manners; discourteous. —*adv.* with bad manners; rudely. —**un·man′ner·li·ness,** *n.*

un·mar·ried (un mar′ēd) *adj.* not married; single.

un·mask (un mask′) *v.* **1** remove a mask or disguise: *The guests unmasked at midnight.* **2** take off a mask or disguise from. **3** expose the true character of: *unmask a hypocrite.* **4** reveal the presence of (guns, etc.) by firing: *unmask a battery.*

un·match·a·ble (un mach′ə bəl) *adj.* that cannot be matched or equalled.

un·mean·ing (un mēn′ing) *adj.* **1** without meaning. **2** without sense; without expression: *an unmeaning stare.* —**un·mean′ing·ly,** *adv.*

un·meas·ured (un mezh′ərd) *adj.* **1** not measured; unlimited; measureless. **2** unrestrained; intemperate.

un·meet (un mēt′) *adj.* not fit; not proper; unsuitable.

un·men·tion·a·ble (un men′shən ə bəl or un mensh′nə bəl) *adj.* that cannot be mentioned; not fit to be spoken about. —*n.* **unmentionables,** *pl.* things considered improper subjects of conversation; things not to be mentioned or discussed. —**un·men′tion·a·ble·ness,** *n.*

un·mer·ci·ful (un mėr′si fəl) *adj.* having no mercy; showing no mercy; cruel. —**un·mer′ci·ful·ly,** *adv.* —**un·mer′ci·ful·ness,** *n.* —**Syn.** pitiless.

un·mind·ful (un mīnd′fəl) *adj.* regardless; heedless; careless. —**un·mind′ful·ly,** *adv.*

un·mis·tak·a·ble (un′mis tāk′ə bəl) *adj.* that cannot be mistaken or misunderstood; clear; plain; evident. —**un′mis·tak′a·ble·ness,** *n.* —**un′mis·tak′a·bly,** *adv.* —**Syn.** manifest.

un·mit·i·gat·ed (un mit′ə gāt′id) *adj.* **1** not softened or lessened: *unmitigated harshness.* **2** unqualified or absolute: *an unmitigated fraud.*

un·mixed (un mikst′) *adj.* not mixed; pure.

un·mor·al (un môr′əl) *adj.* neither moral nor immoral; not perceiving or involving right and wrong; amoral. —**un·mor′al·ly,** *adv.*

un·moved (un müvd′) *adj.* **1** not moved; firm. **2** not disturbed; indifferent.

un·muz·zle (un muz′əl) *v.* **-zled, -zling. 1** take off a muzzle from (a dog, etc.). **2** free from restraint; allow to speak or write freely.

un·nat·u·ral (un nach′rəl or un nach′ə rəl) *adj.* **1** not natural; not in accordance with the usual course of nature. **2** at variance with natural feeling or normal decency, morality, etc.: *unnatural cruelty.* —**un·nat′u·ral·ly,** *adv.* —**un·nat′u·ral·ness,** *n.* —**Syn.** irregular, artificial.

un·nec·es·sar·y (un nes′ə ser′ē) *adj.* not necessary;

hat, āge, cãre, fär; let, ēqual, tėrm; it, īce
hot, ōpen, ôrder; oil, out; cup, pu̇t, rüle, ūse
əbove, takən, pencəl, lemən, circəs
ch, child; ng, long; sh, ship
th, thin; ᴛʜ, then; zh, measure

needless. —**un·nec′es·sar′i·ly,** *adv.* —**un·nec′es·sar′i·ness,** *n.*

un·nerve (un nėrv′) *v.* **-nerved, -nerv·ing.** deprive of nerve, firmness, or self-control.

un·num·bered (un num′ bərd) *adj.* **1** not numbered; not counted. **2** too many to count.

UNO United Nations Organization.

un·ob·served (un′əb zėrvd′) *adj.* not observed; not noticed; disregarded.

un·oc·cu·pied (un ok′yů pīd′) *adj.* not occupied; vacant; idle.

un·or·gan·ized (un ôr′gən īzd′) *adj.* **1** not formed into an organized or systematized whole. **2** not organized into labor unions. **3** not being a living organism. An enzyme is an unorganized ferment.

un·pack (un pak′) *v.* **1** take out (things packed in a box, trunk, etc.). **2** take things out of. **3** take out things packed.

un·paid (un pād′) *adj.* not paid: *His unpaid bills amounted to $200.*

un·pal·at·a·ble (un pal′ə tə bəl) *adj.* not agreeable to the taste; distasteful; unpleasant. —**un·pal′at·a·ble·ness,** *n.* —**un·pal′at·a·bly,** *adv.* —**Syn.** unappetizing, unsavory.

un·par·al·leled (un par′ə leld′) *adj.* having no parallel; unequalled; matchless.

un·par·lia·men·ta·ry (un′pär lə men′tə rē or un′pär lə men′trē) *adj.* not in accordance with parliamentary practice.

un·peg (un peg′) *v.* **-pegged, -peg·ging. 1** remove the pegs from. **2** loosen or unfasten by removing pegs. **3** remove controls on the free rise and fall of (wages, prices, etc.).

un·peo·pled (un pē′pəld) *adj.* not inhabited; deprived of people.

un·pick (un pik′) *v.* remove or take out stitches from knitting, sewing, etc.

un·pile (un pīl′) *v.* **-piled, -pil·ing. 1** take or remove from a pile. **2** take a pile or heap apart.

un·pin (un pin′) *v.* **-pinned, -pin·ning.** take out a pin or pins from; unfasten.

un·pleas·ant (un plez′ənt) *adj.* not pleasant; disagreeable. —**un·pleas′ant·ly,** *adv.* —**Syn.** objectionable, obnoxious.

un·pleas·ant·ness (un plez′ənt nis) *n.* **1** the quality of being unpleasant. **2** something unpleasant. **3** a quarrel.

un·plug (un plug′) *v.* **-plugged, -plug·ging. 1** open or set free (something) by removing a plug or stopper. **2** disconnect (an electric light, appliance, etc.) by removing the plug from an outlet.

un·plumbed (un plumd′) *adj.* **1** not fathomed; not measured; of unknown depth. **2** having no plumbing.

un·pop·u·lar (un pop′yů lər) *adj.* not popular; not generally liked; disliked. —**un·pop′u·lar·ly,** *adv.*

un·pop·u·lar·i·ty (un′pop yů lar′ə tē) *n.* lack of popularity; the fact of being unpopular.

un·prac·ti·cal (un prak′tə kəl) *adj.* not practical; impractical; lacking practical usefulness or wisdom.

un·prac·tised or **un·prac·ticed** (un prak′tist) *adj.* **1** not skilled; not expert. **2** not put into practice; not used.

un·prec·e·dent·ed (un pres′ə den′tid or un prē′sə den′tid) *adj.* having no precedent; never done before; never known before. —**Syn.** unexampled, new.

un·prej·u·diced (un prej′ə dist) *adj.* **1** without prejudice; impartial. **2** not impaired.

un·pre·pared (un′pri pãrd′) *adj.* **1** not made ready; not worked out ahead: *an unprepared speech.* **2** not ready: *a person unprepared to answer.*

un·pre·tend·ing (un′pri tend′ing) *adj.* unassuming; modest. —**un′pre·tend′ing·ly,** *adv.*

un·pre·ten·tious (un′pri ten′shəs) *adj.* modest. —**un′pre·ten′tious·ly,** *adv.* —**un′pre·ten′tious·ness,** *n.*

un·prin·ci·pled (un prin′sə pəld) *adj.* lacking good moral principles; bad. —**Syn.** See **unscrupulous.**

un·print·a·ble (un prin′tə bəl) *adj.* not fit to be printed.

un·pro·fes·sion·al (un′prə fesh′ən əl or un′prə fesh′nəl) *adj.* **1** contrary to professional etiquette; unbecoming in members of a profession. **2** not having to do with or connected with a profession. **3** not belonging to a profession. —**un′pro·fes′sion·al·ly,** *adv.*

un·prof·it·a·ble (un prof′ə tə bəl) *adj.* producing no gain or advantage. —**un·prof′it·a·ble·ness,** *n.* —**un·prof′it·a·bly,** *adv.*

un·pro·voked (un′prə vōkt′) *adj.* without provocation.

un·qual·i·fied (un kwol′ə fīd′) *adj.* **1** not qualified; not fitted. **2** not modified, limited, or restricted in any way: *unqualified praise.* **3** complete; absolute: *an unqualified failure.*

un·ques·tion·a·ble (un kwes′chən ə bəl) *adj.* **1** beyond dispute or doubt; certain. **2** impeccable in quality or nature; accepted without question; unexceptionable. —**un·ques′tion·a·ble·ness,** *n.*

un·ques·tion·a·bly (un kwes′chən ə blē) *adv.* beyond dispute or doubt; certainly.

un·ques·tioned (un kwes′chənd) *adj.* not questioned; not disputed.

un·qui·et (un kwī′ət) *adj.* restless; disturbed; uneasy. —**un·qui′et·ly,** *adv.* —**un·qui′et·ness,** *n.*

un·quote (un kwōt′) *v.* **-quot·ed, -quot·ing.** mark the end of a quotation.

un·rav·el (un rav′əl) *v.* **-elled** or **-eled, -el·ling** or **-el·ing. 1** separate the threads of; pull apart: *The kitten unravelled grandma's knitting.* **2** come apart. **3** bring or come out of a tangled state: *unravel a mystery.*

un·read (un red′) *adj.* **1** not read: *an unread book.* **2** not having read much: *an unread person.*

un·read·y (un red′ē) *adj.* **1** not ready; not prepared. **2** not prompt or quick. —**un·read′i·ly,** *adv.* —**un·read′i·ness,** *n.*

un·re·al (un rē′əl) *adj.* imaginary; not real; not substantial; fanciful. —**un·re′al·ly,** *adv.* —**Syn.** fictitious.

un·re·al·i·ty (un′rē al′ə tē) *n.* **-ties. 1** lack of reality or substance; an imaginary or fanciful quality. **2** impractical or visionary character or tendency; impracticality. **3** something without reality; something unreal.

un·rea·son·a·ble (un rē′zən ə bəl or un rēz′nə bəl) *adj.* **1** not reasonable; not sensible. **2** not moderate; excessive: *unreasonable demands.* —**un·rea′son·a·ble·ness,** *n.* —**Syn. 1** irrational. **2** exorbitant.

un·rea·son·a·bly (un rē′zən ə blē or un rēz′nə blē) *adv.* **1** in a way that is not reasonable; contrary to reason; foolishly. **2** extremely; immoderately: *unreasonably angry.*

un·rea·son·ing (un rē′zən ing or un rēz′ning) *adj.* not reasoning; not using reason; reasonless. —**un·rea′son·ing·ly,** *adv.*

un·re·con·struct·ed (un′rē kən struk′tid) *adj.* not reconciled to change; adhering to old and outworn customs, standards, laws, etc.

un·reel (un rēl′) *v.* unwind from a reel.

un·re·flect·ing (un′ri flek′ting) *adj.* unthinking; thoughtless. —**un′re·flect′ing·ly,** *adv.*

un·re·gard·ed (un′ri gär′did) *adj.* disregarded; not heeded.

un·re·gen·er·a·cy (un′ri jen′ər ə sē) *n.* unregenerate condition; enmity toward God; wickedness.

un·re·gen·er·ate (un′ri jen′ər it) *adj.* **1** not born again spiritually; not turned to the love of God. **2** wicked; bad. —**un′re·gen′er·ate·ly,** *adv.* —**un′re·gen′er·ate·ness,** *n.*

un·re·lent·ing (un′ri len′ting) *adj.* **1** not yielding to feelings of kindness or compassion; merciless. **2** not slackening or relaxing in effort, determination, speed, etc. —**un′re·lent′ing·ly,** *adv.* —**un′re·lent′ing·ness,** *n.* —**Syn. 1** unyielding, obdurate, relentless. See **inflexible.**

un·re·li·a·bil·i·ty (un′ri lī′ə bil′ə tē) *n.* lack of reliability.

un·re·li·a·ble (un′ri lī′ə bəl) *adj.* not reliable; not to be depended on. **—un′re·li′a·bly,** *adv.* **—Syn.** uncertain, irresponsible.

un·re·li·gious (un′ri lij′əs) *adj.* **1** irreligious. **2** non-religious; not connected with religion.

un·re·mit·ting (un′ri mit′ing) *adj.* never stopping; not slackening; maintained steadily: *unremitting vigilance.* **—un′re·mit′ting·ly,** *adv.* **—Syn.** unceasing, incessant, constant.

un·re·served (un′ri zėrvd′) *adj.* **1** frank; open: *an unreserved manner.* **2** not restricted or qualified; without reservation: *unreserved praise.* **3** not kept for a special person or purpose: *unreserved seats.*

un·re·serv·ed·ly (un′ri zėr′vid lē) *adv.* **1** frankly; openly. **2** without reservation or restriction.

un·rest (un rest′) *n.* **1** lack of ease and quiet; restlessness. **2** an agitation or disturbance amounting almost to rebellion. **—Syn. 1** inquietude, uneasiness.

un·right·eous (un rī′chəs) *adj.* wicked; sinful; unjust. [OE *unrihtwīs*] **—un·right′eous·ly,** *adv.* **—un·right′eous·ness,** *n.*

un·ripe (un rīp′) *adj.* **1** not ripe; green. **2** of persons, plans, etc., not fully developed or grown; immature. **3** *Obsolete.* of death, too early; premature. **—un·ripe′ness,** *n.*

un·ri·valled or **un·ri·valed** (un rī′vəld) *adj.* having no rival; without an equal.

un·roll (un rōl′) *v.* **1** open or spread out (something rolled). **2** become opened or spread out. **3** lay open; display. **—Syn. 1** unfold, unfurl.

UNRRA (un′rə) United Nations Relief and Rehabilitation Administration.

un·ruf·fled (un ruf′əld) *adj.* **1** not ruffled; smooth. **2** not disturbed; calm.

un·ruled (un rüld′) *adj.* **1** not kept under control; not governed. **2** not marked with lines: *unruled paper.*

un·ru·ly (un rü′lē) *adj.* hard to rule or control; lawless. **—un·ru′li·ness,** *n.*

Syn. Unruly, ungovernable = hard or impossible to control. **Unruly** = not inclined to obey or accept discipline or restraint, and suggests getting out of hand and becoming disorderly, contrary, or obstinately willful, resisting or defying attempts to bring under control: *The angry mob became unruly.* **Ungovernable** = incapable of being controlled or restrained, either because never subjected to rule or direction or because of escape from it: *One of the circus lions became ungovernable.*

un·sad·dle (un sad′əl) *v.* **-dled, -dling. 1** take the saddle off (a horse). **2** cause to fall from a horse.

un·safe (un sāf′) *adj.* dangerous. **—un·safe′ly,** *adv.* **—un·safe′ness,** *n.* **—Syn.** perilous, hazardous, precarious.

un·said (un sed′) *adj.* not said or spoken.

un·san·i·tar·y (un san′ə ter′ē) *adj.* unhealthful. **—un·san′i·tar′i·ness,** *n.*

un·sat·is·fac·to·ry (un′sat is fak′tə rē or un′sat is fak′trē) *adj.* not good enough to satisfy. **—un′sat·is·fac′to·ri·ly,** *adv.*

un·sat·u·rat·ed (un sach′ə rā′tid) *adj.* **1** of a solution, able to dissolve or absorb more of a substance. **2** in chemistry, of an organic compound, able to take on other elements or radicals without liberating any of the original constituents.

un·sa·vor·y or **un·sa·vour·y** (un sā′vər ē or un sāv′rē) *adj.* **1** tasteless. **2** unpleasant in taste or smell. **3** morally unpleasant; offensive: *That man has an unsavory reputation.* **—un·sa′vor·i·ly** or **un·sa′vour·i·ly,** *adv.* **—un·sa′vor·i·ness** or **un·sa′vour·i·ness,** *n.*

un·say (un sā′) *v.* **-said, -say·ing.** take back (something said).

un·scathed (un skāᴛʜd′) *adj.* not harmed; uninjured.

un·schooled (un sküld′) *adj.* not schooled; not taught; not disciplined.

un·sci·en·tif·ic (un′sī ən tif′ik) *adj.* **1** not in accordance with the facts or principles of science: *an unscientific notion.* **2** not acting in accordance with such facts or principles: *an unscientific farmer.* **—un′sci·en·tif′i·cal·ly,** *adv.*

un·scram·ble (un skram′bəl) *v.* **-bled, -bling. 1** reduce from confusion to order; bring out of a scrambled condition. **2** restore to the original condition; make no longer scrambled: *unscramble a radio message.* **—un·scram′bler,** *n.*

un·screw (un skrü′) *v.* **1** take out the screw or screws from. **2** loosen or take off by turning; untwist.

un·scru·pu·lous (un skrü′pyu̇ ləs) *adj.* not careful about right or wrong; without principles or conscience: *The unscrupulous gambler cheated.* **—un·scru′pu·lous·ly,** *adv.* **—un·scru′pu·lous·ness,** *n.*

Syn. Unscrupulous, unprincipled = having or showing no regard for what is morally right. **Unscrupulous,** describing a person or his acts or words, means not held back by any scruples of conscience, any doubts about the morality or justice of what one is doing or about to do, or by a sense of honor: *He would stoop to any unscrupulous trick to avoid paying his bills.* **Unprincipled** = without, or showing an absence of, good moral principles: *Only an unprincipled person would defend that man's conduct.*

un·seal (un sēl′) *v.* **1** break or remove the seal of: *unseal a letter.* **2** open: *The threat unsealed her lips.*

un·search·a·ble (un sėr′chə bəl) *adj.* not to be searched into; that cannot be understood by searching; mysterious.

un·sea·son·a·ble (un sē′zən ə bəl or un sēz′nə bəl) *adj.* **1** not suitable to the season. **2** coming at the wrong time. **—un·sea′son·a·ble·ness,** *n.* **—un·sea′son·a·bly,** *adv.* **—Syn. 2** inopportune, untimely.

un·seat (un sēt′) *v.* **1** displace from a seat. **2** throw (a rider) from a saddle. **3** remove from office. **4** in an election, defeat someone who was successful in a previous election.

un·seem·ly (un sēm′lē) *adj.* not seemly; not suitable; improper. —*adv.* improperly; unsuitably. **—un·seem′li·ness,** *n.*

un·seen (un sēn′) *adj.* **1** not seen. **2** not visible. **—Syn. 1** unnoticed, unobserved.

un·self·ish (un sel′fish) *adj.* considerate of others; generous. **—un·self′ish·ly,** *adv.* **—un·self′ish·ness,** *n.* **—Syn.** charitable, liberal.

un·set·tle (un set′əl) *v.* **-tled, -tling.** make or become unstable; disturb; shake; weaken. **—Syn.** disorder, upset, disconcert.

un·set·tled (un set′əld) *adj.* **1** disordered; not in proper condition or order. **2** not fixed or stable. **3** liable to change; uncertain: *The weather is unsettled.* **4** not adjusted or disposed of: *an unsettled estate, an unsettled bill.* **5** not determined or decided. **6** not inhabited.

un·sex (un seks′) *v.* deprive of the attributes of one's sex, especially to deprive of womanly character.

un·shack·le (un shak′əl) *v.* **-led, -ling.** remove shackles from; set free.

un·shak·en (un shāk′ən) *adj.* not shaken; firm.

un·sheathe (un shēᴛʜ′) *v.* **-sheathed, -sheath·ing.** draw (a sword, knife, etc.) from a sheath.

un·ship (un ship′) *v.* **-shipped, -ship·ping. 1** put off or take off from a ship: *unship a cargo.* **2** remove from the proper place for use: *unship an oar or tiller.*

un·shod (un shod′) *adj.* without shoes.

un·sight·ly (un sīt′lē) *adj.* ugly or unpleasant to look at. **—un·sight′li·ness,** *n.* **—Syn.** See **ugly.**

un·skil·ful or **un·skill·ful** (un skil′fəl) *adj.* awkward; clumsy. **—un·skil′ful·ly** or **un·skill′ful·ly,** *adv.* **—un·skil′ful·ness** or **un·skill′ful·ness,** *n.*

un·skilled (un skild′) *adj.* **1** not skilled; not trained. **2** not using skill.

un·snap (un snap′) *v.* **-snapped, -snap·ping.** unfasten the snap or snaps of.

un·snarl (un snärl′) *v.* remove the snarls from; untangle.

un·so·cia·bil·i·ty (un′sō shə bil′ə tē) *n.* unsociable nature or behavior; lack of friendliness.

un·so·cia·ble (un sō′shə bəl) *adj.* not sociable; not associating easily with others: *unsociable behavior, an unsociable hermit.* **—un·so′cia·ble·ness,** *n.* **—un·so′cia·bly,** *adv.*

un·sol·der (un sod′ər) *v.* **1** separate (something soldered). **2** break up; divide; dissolve.

un·so·phis·ti·cat·ed (un′sə fis′tə kāt′id) *adj.* simple; natural; artless.

un·sound (un sound′) *adj.* 1 not in good condition; not sound: *An unsound mind or body is diseased. Unsound walls are not firm. An unsound business is not reliable.* 2 not based on truth or fact: *an unsound doctrine, theory, etc.* 3 not deep; not restful; disturbed: *an unsound sleep.* —**un·sound′ly,** *adv.* —**un·sound′ness,** *n.*

un·spar·ing (un spãr′ing) *adj.* 1 very generous; liberal. 2 not merciful; severe. —**un·spar′ing·ly,** *adv.* —**un·spar′ing·ness,** *n.*

un·speak·a·ble (un spēk′ə bəl) *adj.* 1 that cannot be expressed in words: *unspeakable joy.* 2 extremely bad; so bad that it is not spoken of.

un·speak·a·bly (un spēk′ə blē) *adv.* beyond expression; extremely.

un·spot·ted (un spot′id) *adj.* without spot or stain; pure.

un·sta·ble (un stā′bəl) *adj.* 1 not firmly fixed; easily moved, shaken, or overthrown. 2 not constant; variable. 3 in chemistry, easily decomposed; readily changing into other compounds. —**un·sta′ble·ness,** *n.* —**un·sta′bly,** *adv.* —**Syn.** 1 unsteady, insecure, unsettled, wavering.

unstable element in chemistry, a radio-active element that eventually changes into a radio-active isotope.

un·stead·y (un sted′ē) *adj.* 1 not steady; shaky. 2 likely to change; not reliable. 3 not regular in habits. —**un·stead′i·ly,** *adv.* —**un·stead′i·ness,** *n.*

un·step (un step′) *v.* **-stepped, -step·ping.** remove (a mast, etc.) from its step.

un·stop (un stop′) *v.* **-stopped, -stop·ping.** 1 remove the stopper from (a bottle, etc.). 2 free from any obstruction; open.

un·strap (un strap′) *v.* **-strapped, -strap·ping.** loosen the strap of (a trunk, box, etc.).

un·string (un string′) *v.* **-strung, -string·ing.** 1 take off or loosen the string or strings of. 2 take from a string. 3 weaken the nerves of; make nervous.

un·strung (un strung′) *adj.* upset; emotionally disturbed. —*v.* pt. and pp. of **unstring.**

un·stud·ied (un stud′ēd) *adj.* not studied; not planned ahead; natural.

un·sub·stan·tial (un′səb stan′shəl) *adj.* not substantial; flimsy; slight; unreal. —**un′sub·stan′tial·ly,** *adv.*

un·suc·cess·ful (un′sək ses′fəl) *adj.* not successful; without success. —**un′suc·cess′ful·ly,** *adv.*

un·suit·a·bil·i·ty (un′süt ə bil′ə tē) *n.* being unsuitable.

un·suit·a·ble (un süt′ə bəl) *adj.* not suitable; unfit. —**un·suit′a·bly,** *adv.* —**Syn.** inappropriate, incongruous.

un·suit·ed (un süt′id) *adj.* not suited; unfit.

un·sul·lied (un sul′ēd) *adj.* without spot or stain; pure: *an unsullied reputation.*

un·sung (un sung′) *adj.* 1 not sung. 2 not honored in song or poetry; unpraised.

un·tan·gle (un tang′gəl) *v.* **-gled, -gling.** 1 take the tangles out of; disentangle. 2 straighten out or clear up (anything confused or perplexing).

un·taught (un tot′ or un tôt′) *adj.* 1 not taught; not educated. 2 known without being taught; learned naturally.

un·thank·ful (un thangk′fəl) *adj.* 1 ungrateful. 2 not appreciated; thankless. —**un·thank′ful·ly,** *adv.* —**un·thank′ful·ness,** *n.*

un·think·ing (un thingk′ing) *adj.* 1 thoughtless; heedless; careless. 2 characterized by absence of thought: *blind, unthinking anger.* 3 not having the faculty of thought; unable to think. —**un·think′ing·ly,** *adv.*

un·thought-of (un thot′ uv′ or un thôt′uv′, un thot′ov′ or un thôt′ov′) *adj.* not imagined or considered.

un·thread (un thred′) *v.* 1 take the thread out of. 2 unravel. 3 find one's way through.

un·ti·dy (un tī′dē) *adj.* not in order; not neat. —**un·ti′di·ly,** *adv.* —**un·ti′di·ness,** *n.* —**Syn.** disorderly, slovenly, littered.

un·tie (un tī′) *v.* **-tied, -ty·ing.** 1 loosen; unfasten; undo; unbind. 2 make clear; explain; resolve. [OE *untīgan*]

un·til (ən til′ or un til′) *prep.* 1 up to the time of: *It was cold from Christmas until April.* 2 before: *She did not leave until morning.* —*conj.* 1 up to the time when: *He waited until the sun had set.* 2 before: *He did not come until the meeting was half over.* 3 to the degree or place that: *He worked until he was too tired to do more.* [ME *untill* < ON *und* up to + *till* till[1]] ☛ See **till**[1] for usage note.

un·time·ly (un tīm′lē) *adj.* at a wrong time or season: *an untimely snowstorm.* —*adv.* too early; too soon: *His death came untimely at 32.* —**un·time′li·ness,** *n.*

un·tir·ing (un tīr′ing) *adj.* tireless; unwearying. —**un·tir′ing·ly,** *adv.*

un·ti·tled (un tī′təld) *adj.* 1 having no title. 2 not distinguished by a title; not of titled rank: *the gentry and other untitled classes.* 3 lacking lawful right; not entitled to rule.

un·to (un′tü; *before consonants often,* un′tə) *prep. Archaic or formal.* 1 to. 2 till; until: *The soldier was faithful unto death.* [ME *unto* < *un-* (see UNTIL) + *to*]

un·told (un tōld′) *adj.* 1 not told; not revealed. 2 too many to be counted or numbered; very great: *There are untold stars in the sky.*

un·touch·a·ble (un tuch′ə bəl) *adj.* 1 that cannot be touched; out of reach. 2 that must not be touched. —*n.* 1 formerly, in India, a person of the lowest caste whose touch supposedly defiled members of higher castes. 2 any person rejected by his social group; social outcast; pariah.

un·touched (un tucht′) *adj.* 1 not touched: *The cat left the milk untouched.* 2 not affected or moved: *The miser was untouched by the poor man's story.* 3 not dealt with: *The last topic was left untouched.*

un·tow·ard (un tôrd′ or un′to wôrd′) *adj.* 1 unfavorable; unfortunate: *an untoward wind, an untoward accident.* 2 perverse; stubborn; willful. [< *un-*[1] + *toward*] —**un·to′ward·ly,** *adv.* —**un·to′ward·ness,** *n.* —**Syn** 1 inconvenient, unlucky. 2 intractable, refractory, contrary.

un·trained (un trānd′) *adj.* not trained; without discipline or education.

un·tram·melled or **un·tram·meled** (un tram′əld) *adj.* not hindered; not restrained; free.

un·tried (un trīd′) *adj.* not tried; not tested.

un·trod (un trod′) *adj.* not trodden.

un·true (un trü′) *adj.* 1 false; incorrect. 2 not faithful. 3 not true to a standard or rule. [OE *untrēowe*]

un·truss (un trus′) *v.* 1 unfasten; loose from a truss. 2 undress.

un·truth (un trüth′) *n.* 1 lack of truth; falsity. 2 a lie; falsehood. [OE *untrēowth*]

un·truth·ful (un trüth′fəl) *adj.* not truthful; contrary to the truth. —**un·truth′ful·ly,** *adv.* —**un·truth′ful·ness,** *n.*

un·tu·tored (un tū′tərd or un tü′tərd) *adj.* untaught.

un·twine (un twīn′) *v.* **-twined, -twin·ing.** untwist.

un·twist (un twist′) *v.* 1 undo or loosen something twisted; unravel. 2 become untwisted.

un·used (un ūzd′) *adj.* 1 not used: an unused room. 2 never having been used: *unused drinking cups.* 3 **unused to** (un ūst′), not accustomed to: *The actor's hands were unused to labor.*

un·u·su·al (un ū′zhü əl) *adj.* not usual; beyond the ordinary; not common; rare. —**un·u′su·al·ness,** *n.* —**Syn.** strange, singular.

un·u·su·al·ly (un ū′zhü əl ē) *adv.* uncommonly; rarely; exceptionally; extremely.

un·ut·ter·a·ble (un ut′ər ə bəl) *adj.* that cannot be expressed; unspeakable.

un·ut·ter·a·bly (un ut′ər ə blē) *adv.* in a way or to a degree that cannot be expressed or described.

un·var·nished (un vär′nisht) *adj.* 1 not varnished. 2 plain; unadorned: *the unvarnished truth.*

un·veil (un vāl′) *v.* **1** remove a veil from; disclose; reveal: *unveil a secret.* **2** remove a veil; reveal oneself; become unveiled.

un·voiced (un voist′) *adj.* **1** not spoken; not expressed in words. **2** in phonetics, spoken without any vibration of the vocal cords; voiceless. (s) in *sit* and (f) in *fit* are unvoiced sounds.

un·war·rant·a·ble (un wôr′ən tə bəl) *adj.* not justifiable; illegal; improper. **—un·war′rant·a·bly,** *adv.*

un·war·y (un wãr′ē) *adj.* not cautious; not careful; unguarded. **—un·war′i·ly,** *adv.* **—un·war′i·ness,** *n.* **—Syn.** careless, indiscreet.

un·wea·ried (un wēr′ēd) *adj.* **1** not weary; not tired. **2** never growing weary.

un·weave (un wēv′) *v.* **-wove, -wo·ven, -weav·ing.** take apart (something woven).

un·wel·come (un wel′kəm) *adj.* not welcome; not wanted.

un·well (un wel′) *adj.* ailing; ill; sick.

un·wept (un wept′) *adj.* **1** not wept for; not mourned. **2** not shed: *unwept tears.*

un·whole·some (un hōl′səm) *adj.* not wholesome; bad for the body or the mind; unhealthy. **—un·whole′some·ly,** *adv.* **—un·whole′some·ness,** *n.*

un·wield·y (un wēl′dē) *adj.* not easily handled or managed, because of size, shape, or weight; bulky and clumsy: *the unwieldy armor of knights; a fat, unwieldy man.* **—un·wield′i·ness,** *n.* **—Syn.** unmanageable, cumbersome.

un·will·ing (un wil′ing) *adj.* not willing; not consenting. **—un·will′ing·ly,** *adv.* **—un·will′ing·ness,** *n.* **—Syn.** reluctant, averse, loath.

un·wind (un wīnd′) *v.* **-wound, -wind·ing.** **1** wind off; take from a spool, ball, etc. **2** become unwound. **3** disentangle. [OE *unwindan*]

un·wise (un wīz′) *adj.* not wise; not showing good judgment; foolish. [OE *unwīs*] **—un·wise′ly,** *adv.* **—Syn.** imprudent, indiscreet.

un·wit·ting (un wit′ing) *adj.* not knowing; unaware; unconscious; unintentional.

un·wit·ting·ly (un wit′ing lē) *adv.* not knowingly; unconsciously; not intentionally.

un·wont·ed (un wōn′tid or un wun′tid) *adj.* **1** not customary; not usual. **2** not accustomed; not used. **—un·wont′ed·ly,** *adv.* **—un·wont′ed·ness,** *n.*

un·world·ly (un wėrld′lē) *adj.* **1** not caring much for the things of this world, such as money, pleasure, and power. **2** not of this world; supernatural. **—un·world′li·ness,** *n.*

un·wor·thi·ly (un wėr′ᴛʜə lē) *adv.* **1** in a way that is not worthy or honorable; shamefully. **2** not according to one's merits.

un·wor·thy (un wėr′ᴛʜē) *adj.* **1** not worthy; not deserving: *Such a silly story is unworthy of belief.* **2** not befitting or becoming; below the proper level or standard: *a gift not unworthy of a king.* **3** base; shameful. **4** lacking value or merit; worthless. **—un·wor′thi·ness,** *n.* **—Syn. 2** ignoble, discreditable.

un·wound (un wound′) *v.* pt. and pp. of **unwind.**

un·wove (un wōv′) *v.* pt. of **unweave.**

un·wo·ven (un wō′vən) *v.* pp. of **unweave.**

un·wrap (un rap′) *v.* **-wrapped, -wrap·ping.** **1** remove a wrapping from; open. **2** become opened.

un·wrin·kle (un ring′kəl) *v.* **-kled, -kling.** **1** smooth the wrinkles from. **2** become smooth.

un·writ·ten (un rit′ən) *adj.* **1** not written. **2** understood or customary, but not actually expressed in writing. **3** not written on; blank.

unwritten law **1** a law that is based on custom or on decisions of previous judges, rather than on a written command, decree, statute, etc.; common law. **2** a practice or rule established by general usage. **3** among certain peoples, the principle that a person who commits certain crimes, especially those which avenge personal or family honor, is entitled to lenient treatment.

un·yoke (un yōk′) *v.* **-yoked, -yok·ing.** **1** free from a yoke; separate; disconnect. **2** remove a yoke.

up (up) *adv. prep. adj. n. v.* **upped, up·ping.** *—adv.* **1** from a lower to a higher place or condition; to, toward, or near the top: *The bird flew up.* **2** in a higher place or condition; on or at a higher level: *He stayed up in the mountains several days.* **3** from a smaller to a larger amount: *Prices have gone up.* **4** to or at any point, place, or condition that is considered higher: *He lives up north.* **5** above the horizon: *The sun is up.* **6** in or into an erect position: *Stand up.* **7** out of bed: *Get up.* **8** thoroughly; completely; entirely: *The house burned up.* **9** at an end; over: *His time is up now.* **10** in or into being or action: *Don't stir up trouble.* **11** together: *Add these up.* **12** to or in an even position; not behind: *catch up in a race, keep up with the times.* **13** in or into view, notice, or consideration: *bring up a new topic.* **14** in or into a state of tightness, etc.: *Shut him up in his cage.* **15** into safekeeping, storage, etc.; aside; by: *store up supplies.* **16** in baseball, at bat. **17** of the score in tennis, etc., apiece; for each one. **18 up against,** *Informal.* facing (something) as a thing to be dealt with. **19 up against it,** *Informal.* in difficulties. **20 up and down,** here and there; at various points; in many or different places throughout an area, etc.: *up and down the country.* **21 up to, a** doing; about to do. **b** equal to; capable of doing: *up to a task.* **c** plotting; scheming: *What are you up to?* **d** *Informal.* before (a person) as a duty or task to be done.
—prep. **1** to or at a higher place on or in something: *The cat ran up the tree.* **2** to, toward, or near the top of: *They climbed up the hill.* **3** along; through: *She walked up the street.* **4** toward or in the inner or upper part of: *We sailed up the river. He lives up state.*
—adj. **1** advanced; forward. **2** moving upward; directed upward: *an up trend.* **3** above the ground: *The wheat is up.* **4** out of bed. **5** to or in an even position; not behind. **6** near; close. **7** with much knowledge or skill. **8** at bat in baseball. **9** ahead of an opponent by a certain number: *We are three games up.* **10 up and about,** active; occupied as usual, especially after an illness. **11 up and doing,** busy; active. **12 up on,** *Informal.* well-informed about.
—n. **1** an upward movement, course, or slope. **2** *Informal.* a period of good luck, prosperity, or happiness: *Her life is full of ups and downs.* **3 be on the up and up, a** *Informal.* increasing; rising; improving. **b** *Slang.* honest; legitimate.
—v. **1** put up. **2** get up. [OE *upp(e)*]

up- *prefix.* up, as in *upcountry, upgrade, upkeep, uplift, upbringing.* [OE *up-*. Related to UP.]

up-and-com·ing (up′ən kum′ing) *adj. Informal.* promising; enterprising; on the way to importance and success: *an up-and-coming actor.*

up-and-down (up′ ən doun′) *adj.* **1** characterized by alternate upward and downward motion; rising and falling; fluctuating: *up-and-down sales activity.* **2** vertical; perpendicular.

U·pan·i·shad (ü pan′ə shad′) *n.* any of a group of philosophical treatises in ancient Sanskrit, including those of the Vedanta. [< Skt.]

u·pas (ū′pəs) *n.* **1** the poisonous sap of a tree of Java and neighboring islands, used as poison for arrows. **2** the tree itself. [< Malay *upas* poison]

up·beat (up′bēt′) *n.* **1** in music, an unaccented beat; the beat at which the conductor's hand goes up. **2** revival; upswing. *—adj. Informal.* rising; hopeful; buoyant: *an upbeat market opening.*

up·borne (up bôrn′) *adj.* borne up; raised aloft; supported.

up·bound (up′bound′) *adj. adv.* bound in an upward direction.

up·braid (up brād′) *v.* find fault with; blame; reprove: *The captain upbraided his men for falling asleep.* [OE *ūpbregdan* < *upp* up + *bregdan* weave, snatch, move suddenly] **—up·braid′er,** *n.* **—Syn.** reproach. See **scold.**

up·braid·ing (up brād′ing) *n.* a severe reproof; scolding. *—adj.* full of reproach.

up·bring·ing (up′bring′ing) *n.* the care and training given to a child while growing up; the process of bringing up.

up·com·ing (up′kum′ing) *adj.* forthcoming; approaching.

up·coun·try (up′kun′trē) *n.* the interior of a country. *—adv.* toward or in the interior of a country. *—adj.* remote from the coast or border; interior.

hat, āge, cãre, fär; let, ēqual, tėrm; it, īce
hot, ōpen, ôrder; oil, out; cup, pu̇t, rüle, ūse
əbove, takən, pencəl, lemən, circəs
ch, child; ng, long; sh, ship
th, thin; ᴛʜ, then; zh, measure

up·date (up dāt′) *v.* **-dat·ed, -dat·ing.** bring up to date.

up·draft (up′draft′) *n.* an upward movement of gas, air, etc. Also, **updraught.**

up·draught (up′draft′) *n.* updraft.

up·end (up end′) *v.* set on end; stand on end.

up·fold (up′fōld′) *n.* in geology, an upward fold; anticline.

up·grade (up′grād′) *n. adv. adj. v.* **-grad·ed, -grad·ing.** —*n.* **1** an upward slope or incline. **2 on the upgrade,** rising; improving. —*adv. adj.* uphill. —*v.* **1** raise the status, rating, etc. of. **2** raise to a higher position with a higher salary.

up·growth (up′grōth′) *n.* **1** the process of growing up; development. **2** something that grows up.

up·heav·al (up hēv′əl) *n.* **1** a heaving up or being heaved up. **2** a sudden or violent agitation in a society; social turmoil.

up·heave (up hēv′) *v.* **-heaved** or **-hove, -heav·ing. 1** heave up; lift up. **2** rise.

up·held (up held′) *v.* pt. and pp. of **uphold.**

up·hill (*adj.* up′hil′; *adv.* up′hil′) *adj.* **1** up the slope of a hill; upward: *It is an uphill road all the way.* **2** difficult: *an uphill fight.* —*adv.* upward: *a mile uphill.*

up·hold (up hōld′) *v.* **-held, -hold·ing. 1** give moral support to; confirm: *The principal upheld the teacher's decision.* **2** hold up; keep from falling; support. **3** sustain; approve; confirm. —**up·hold′er,** *n.* —**Syn. 1** See **support.**

up·hol·ster (uphōl′ stər) *v.* **1** provide (furniture) with coverings, cushions, springs, stuffing, etc. **2** furnish (a room) with curtains, rugs, etc. [back formation < *upholsterer,* ult. < obs. *uphold* keep in repair]

up·hol·ster·er (up hōl′stər ər) *n.* a person whose business is to cover furniture and to furnish and put in place curtains, cushions, carpets, and hangings.

up·hol·ster·y (up hōl′stər ē or up hōl′strē) *n.* **-ster·ies. 1** the fittings or decorations supplied by an upholsterer; coverings for furniture; curtains, cushions, carpets, and hangings. **2** the business of upholstering.

up·hove (up hōv′) *v.* a pt. and a pp. of **upheave.**

UPI United Press International.

up·keep (up′kēp′) *n.* **1** maintenance. **2** the cost of operating and repair.

up·land (up′lənd or up′land′) *n.* high land. —*adj.* of high land; living or growing on high land.

up·lift (*v.* up lift′; *n.* up′lift′) *v.* **1** raise; improve; elevate. **2** exalt emotionally or spiritually. **3** raise socially or morally. —*n.* **1** the act of lifting up. **2** an emotional or spiritual exaltation. **3** social or moral improvement or effort toward it.

up·most (up′mōst) *adj.* uppermost.

up·on (ə pon′) *prep.* on. [ME *upon* < *up* + *on*]

up·per (up′ər) *adj.* **1** higher: *the upper lip, the upper floor.* **2** higher in rank, office, etc.; superior: *the upper house of a parliament.* **3** constituting or denoting a geological stratum or series lying nearer the surface and formed later than the others of the (designated) group, type, or class. **4** in geology, more recent: *Upper Cambrian.* **5** of a river, farther from the sea or nearer the source. **6** that covers or clothes a part of the body above the waist, especially the chest or shoulders: *an upper garment.* —*n.* **1** the part of a shoe or boot above the sole. **2 on one's uppers,** *Informal.* **a** with the soles of one's shoes worn out. **b** very shabby or poor.

Upper Canada 1 especially in the Maritimes, the province of Ontario. **2** until 1841, the official name of the region east of the Ottawa River and north of Lakes Ontario and Erie, now included in the province of Ontario. In 1841 Upper and Lower Canada were united in the Province of Canada. *Abbrev.*: U.C.

upper case capital letters. *Abbrev.*: u.c.

up·per-case (up′ər kās′) *adj.* capital; in capital letters.

Upper Chamber or **upper chamber** Upper House.

up·per-class (up′ər klas′) *adj.* **1** of or having to do with a superior social or economic class. **2** in universities, schools, etc., of or having to do with the senior classes.

up·per·class·man (up′ər klas′mən) *n.* **-men** (-mən). a senior student.

upper crust 1 *Informal.* the upper classes. **2** the upper layer of a pie.

up·per·cut (up′ər kut′) *n. v.* **-cut, -cut·ting.** —*n.* in boxing, a swinging blow directed upwards from beneath. —*v.* strike with an uppercut.

upper hand control; advantage.

Upper House or **upper house** the higher or more restricted branch of a legislature that has two branches. The Senate is the Upper House in Parliament.

Upper Lakes the most northerly of the Great Lakes; Lakes Superior and Huron.

up·per·most (up′ər mōst′) *adj.* **1** highest; topmost. **2** having the most force or influence; most prominent. —*adv.* **1** in the highest place. **2** first.

up·pish (up′ish) *adj. Informal.* somewhat arrogant, self-assertive, or conceited. [< *up,* adv.]

up·pi·ty (up′ə tē) *adj. Informal.* uppish.

up·raise (up rāz′) *v.* **-raised, -rais·ing.** raise up; lift.

up·rear (up rēr′) *v.* lift up; raise.

up·right (up′rīt′ or up rīt′) *adj.* **1** standing up straight; erect. **2** good; honest; righteous. —*adv.* straight up; in a vertical position. —*n.* **1** vertical or upright position. **2** something upright; vertical part or piece. **3** an upright piano. [OE *upriht*] —**up′right′ly,** *adv.* —**up′right′ness,** *n.*

Syn. *adj.* **1 Upright, erect** = straight up. **Upright** literally means "straight up," standing up straight on a base or in a base or in a position that is straight up and down, not slanting, and is used to describe this position or posture or an object (when describing a person it is a synonym of *honest*): *After the earthquake not a lamp or chair was upright.* **Erect,** describing the body, a thing, etc., means "held or set upright," not stooping or bent: *At seventy she still walks erect.*

up·rise (*v.* up rīz′; *n.* up′rīz′) *v.* **-rose, -ris·en, -ris·ing,** *n.* —*v.* **1** rise up. **2** slope upward. **3** increase in volume, amount, etc. —*n.* a rising up; upward rise.

up·ris·en (up riz′ən) *v.* pp. of **uprise.**

up·ris·ing (up′rīz′ing or up rīz′ing) *n.* **1** a revolt: *There was an uprising of the savage tribes in the area.* **2** a rising up. **3** an upward slope; ascent.

up·riv·er (up′riv′ər) *adj.* **1** belonging to or situated farther up, or toward the upper end of, a river. **2** leading or directed toward the source of a river. —*adv.* toward or in the direction of the source of a river.

up·roar (up′rôr′) *n.* **1** a state of noisy or violent disturbance. **2** a loud or confused noise. **3 in an uproar,** in a state of great disturbance, confusion, etc. [< Du. *oproer* insurrection, tumult; influenced by association with *roar*] —**Syn. 1** tumult, commotion. **2** See **noise.**

up·roar·i·ous (up rôr′ē əs or up rôr′ē əs) *adj.* **1** noisy and disorderly: *an uproarious crowd.* **2** loud and confused: *uproarious laughter.* —**up·roar′i·ous·ly,** *adv.* —**up·roar′i·ous·ness,** *n.*

up·root (up rüt′) *v.* **1** tear up by the roots. **2** remove completely. —**up·root′er,** *n.*

up·rose (up rōz′) *v.* pt. of **uprise.**

up·set (*v.* up set′; *n.* up′set′; *adj.* up set′ or up′set′) *v.* **-set, -set·ting,** *n. adj.* —*v.* **1** tip over; overturn: *upset a boat.* **2** disturb greatly; disorder: *Rain upset our plans for a picnic. The shock upset her nerves.* **3** overthrow; defeat: *upset a will, upset an argument.*
—*n.* **1** a tipping over; overturn. **2** a great disturbance; a state of disorder. **3** an overthrowing; an unexpected defeat.
—*adj.* **1** tipped over; overturned. **2** greatly disturbed; disordered: *an upset stomach.* **3 upset price,** the lowest price at which a thing offered for sale will be sold.

Syn. *v.* **1 Upset, overturn** = fall, or cause to fall, over or down. **Upset** suggests losing balance and tipping over from an upright or proper position as the result of a movement or action by some person or thing: *He accidentally kicked the table and upset the vase of flowers.* **Overturn** = turn upside down or, especially, over on one side from an upright position to one flat on the ground: *He got up too quickly and overturned his chair.*

up·shot (up′shot′) *n.* the conclusion; result. **—Syn.** outcome, issue.

up·side (up′sīd′) *n.* the upper side.

upside down 1 having at the bottom what should be on top. **2** in complete disorder: *The room was turned upside down.* [alteration of ME *up so down* up as if down]

up·si·lon (ūp′sə lon′) *n.* the 20th letter (Υ, *υ* = English U, u, or Y, y) of the Greek alphabet.

up·stage (up′stāj′) *adv. adj. v.* **-staged, -stag·ing.** *—adv.* in a theatre, toward or at the back of the stage. *—adj.* **1** having to do with the back part of the stage. **2** toward or at the back of the stage. **3** *Informal.* haughty; aloof; supercilious. *—v.* **1** in the theatre, put in a less prominent position by moving or staying upstage of. **2** make oneself the centre of attention. **3** *Informal.* treat haughtily or condescendingly.

up·stairs (up′stãrz′) *adv.* **1** up the stairs. **2** on an upper floor. **3** *Informal.* of aircraft, in the air, especially at a high altitude. **4 kick upstairs,** *Informal.* promote (someone) in order to get rid of him or to make room for a more desirable person. *—adj.* on an upper floor. *—n.* upper storey.

up·stand·ing (up stan′ding) *adj.* **1** standing up; erect. **2** straight and tall; well-grown. **3** honorable.

up·start (up′stärt′) *n.* **1** a person who has suddenly risen from a humble position to wealth, power, or importance. **2** an unpleasant, conceited, and self-assertive person.
—adj. **1** suddenly risen from a humble position to wealth, power, or importance. **2** conceited; self-assertive.

up·stream (up′strēm′) *adv. adj.* against the current of a stream; up a stream.

up·surge (up′sėrj′) *v.* **-surged, -surg·ing,** *n. —v.* surge or swell upward. *—n.* sudden surge of growth or development; uprising; upturn.

up·swept (up′swept′) *adj.* **1** curving or sloping upward. **2** of or having to do with a woman's hair style in which the hair is brushed upward and piled high on the head.

up·swing (up′swing′) *n. v.* **-swung, -swing·ing.** *—n.* **1** an upward swing; movement upward. **2** a marked improvement; strong advance. *—v.* undergo an upswing.

up·take (up′tāk′) *n.* **1** a boiler pipe or flue for directing fumes, etc. to a chimney, funnel, etc. **2** a ventilating shaft in a mine for carrying the fumes upward. **3** the amount absorbed or taken up. **4** *Informal.* the act of taking upwards or lifting. **5 on** or **in the uptake,** *Informal.* in perception and understanding: *He is quick on the uptake.*

up·thrust (up′thrust′) *n.* **1** an upward push. **2** in geology, a movement upward of part of the earth's crust.

up·tight (up′tīt′) *adj. Slang.* showing anxiety; tense; keyed-up.

up-to-date (up′tə dāt′) *adj.* **1** extending to the present time. **2** having modern equipment, utilizing the latest techniques, etc.; not obsolescent: *an up-to-date factory.* **3** keeping up with the times in style, ideas, and methods.

up-to-the-min·ute (up′tə ᴛʜə min′it) *adj.* modern; up-to-date; latest.

up·town (*adv.* up′toun′; *adj.* up′toun′) *adv. adj.* at, to, or in the upper part of a town.

up·turn (*v.* up tėrn′; *n.* up′tėrn′) *v.* turn up. *—n.* **1** an upward turn. **2** an improvement: *an upturn in business.*

up·turned (up tėrnd′) *adj.* **1** turned over; overturned. **2** turned upward. **3** turned up at the end.

UPU Universal Postal Union of the United Nations.

up·ward (up′wərd) *adv.* **1** toward a higher place. **2** in the higher or highest position; uppermost: *store baskets with the bottoms upward.* **3** toward a higher or greater rank, amount, age, etc.: *From public school upward, she studied French.* **4** above; more: *Children of five years and upward must pay carfare.* **5** to or toward the source: *follow a river upward.* **6 upward of,** more than. *—adj.* directed or moving toward a higher place; in a higher position. [OE *upweard*]

up·ward·ly (up′wərd lē) *adv.* in an upward manner or direction; upward.

up·wards (up′wərdz) *adv.* upward.

Ur (ėr) *n.* in ancient times: **1** a city in Babylonia, on the Euphrates River. **2** the district surrounding and including this city.

Ur uranium.

U·ral-Al·ta·ic (ū′rəl al tā′ik) *adj.* **1** of the region embracing the Ural and Altaic Mountains. **2** of or having to do with a large family of languages spoken in northern Asia and eastern Europe, including the Finno-Ugric, Turkic, Mongolian, and some other languages. *—n.* the Ural-Altaic language family.

U·ra·ni·a (ū rā′nē ə) *n.* in Greek mythology, the Muse of astronomy.

u·ran·i·nite (ū ran′ə nīt′) *n.* a blackish-green uranium mineral often found in crystal form. When found in veins, it is called **pitchblende.** *Formula*: UO_2

u·ra·ni·um (ū rā′nē əm) *n.* a heavy, white, radio-active metallic chemical element that occurs in pitchblende and certain other minerals. The uranium isotope, U^{235}, can sustain efficient chain reaction and is for this reason used in nuclear devices. *Symbol*: U; *at.no.* 92; *at.wt.* 238.03. *Abbrev.*: Ur [< NL *uranium* < *Uranus,* the planet]

U·ra·nus (ūr′ə nəs or ū rā′nəs) *n.* **1** in Greek mythology, the original ruler of the world, father of the Titans, the Cyclopes, the Furies, etc., who was deposed by the youngest of the Titans. **2** one of the larger planets. It is the seventh in order from the sun.

ur·ban (ėr′bən) *adj.* **1** of or having to do with cities or towns. **2** living in cities. **3** characteristic of cities. **4** accustomed to cities. [< L *urbanus* < *urbs* city]

ur·bane (ėr bān′) *adj.* **1** courteous; refined; elegant. **2** smoothly polite. [< L *urbanus,* originally, *urban.* See URBAN.] **—ur·bane′ly,** *adv.* **—ur·bane′ness,** *n.*

ur·ban·i·ty (ėr ban′ə tē) *n.* **-ties. 1** courtesy; refinement; elegance. **2** smooth politeness. **3** civilities; courtesies; amenities. **4** the character or condition of being urbane.

ur·ban·ize (ėr′bən īz′) *v.* **-ized, -iz·ing.** render urban: *urbanize a district or its people.* **—ur′ban·i·za′tion,** *n.*

ur·chin (ėr′chən) *n.* **1** a small boy. **2** a mischievous boy. **3** a poor, ragged child. **4** *Archaic.* a hedgehog. **5** a sea urchin. **6** an elf. [ME < OF *irechon* < L *ericius* an obstacle with spikes < *er* hedgehog]

Ur·du (ür′dü or ür dü′, ėr′dü or ėr dü′) *n.* in Pakistan and India, the form of Hindustani spoken by Moslems. Urdu is an official language of Pakistan.

-ure *suffix.* **1** the act or fact of ——ing, as in *failure.* **2** the state of being ——ed, as in *pleasure.* **3** the result of ——ing, as in *enclosure.* **4** the thing that ——s, as in *legislature.* **5** the thing that is ——ed, as in *disclosure.* **6** other special meanings, as in *procedure, sculpture, denture.* [< F *-ure* < L *-ura*]

u·re·a (ū rē′ə or ūr′ē ə) *n.* a soluble, crystalline solid present in the urine of mammals, birds, etc., manufactured synthetically for use in making fertilizers, adhesives, and plastics. *Formula*: $CO(NH_2)_2$ [< NL *urea,* ult. < Gk. *ouron* urine]

urea resin any of a group of thermosetting synthetic resins obtained chiefly from urea and formaldehyde, used for mouldings, adhesives, etc.

u·re·mi·a (ū rē′mē ə) *n.* in medicine, a condition resulting from the accumulation in the blood of waste products that should normally be eliminated in the urine. [< NL *uremia* < Gk. *ouron* urine + *haima* blood]

u·re·mic (ū rē′mik) *adj.* **1** of or having to do with uremia. **2** suffering from uremia.

u·re·ter (ū rē′tər or ūr′ə tər) *n.* in anatomy and zoology, a duct that carries urine from a kidney to the bladder or the cloaca. [< NL < Gk. *ourētēr,* ult. < *ouron* urine]

u·re·thane (ū′rə thān′ or ū reth′ən) *n.* a white crystalline compound and ethyl derivative, used in organic synthesis and medicinally as a hypnotic and as a sedative. *Formula*: $C_3H_7NO_2$

u·re·thra (ū rē′thrə) *n.* **-thrae** (-thrē or -thrī) or **-thras.** in most mammals, the duct by which urine is discharged from the bladder and, in males, through which semen is discharged. [< LL < Gk. *ourēthra,* ult. < *ouron* urine]

u·re·thral (ū rē′thrəl) *adj.* of or having to do with the urethra.

urge (ėrj) *v.* **urged, urg·ing,** *n. —v.* **1** drive with force, threats, etc.; push forward with effort: *The rider urged on*

hat, āge, cãre, fär; let, ēqual, tėrm; it, īce
hot, ōpen, ôrder; oil, out; cup, pu̇t, rüle, ūse
əbove, takən, pencəl, lemən, circəs
ch, child; ng, long; sh, ship
th, thin; ᴛʜ, then; zh, measure

his horse with whip and spurs. **2** cause to hasten or gather speed; accelerate the pace of; speed up: *urge a trotting horse into a gallop.* **3** try to persuade with arguments; ask earnestly: *They urged him to stay.* **4** plead or argue earnestly for; recommend strongly: *Motorists urged better roads.* **5** press upon the attention; refer to often and with emphasis: *urge a claim, urge an argument.*
—*n.* **1** a driving force, impulse, or desire. **2** the act of urging. [< L *urgere*] —**Syn.** *v.* **1** press, impel, incite.

ur·gen·cy (ėr′jən sē) *n.* **-cies. 1** an urgent or imperative character; need for immediate action or attention: *A house on fire is a matter of great urgency.* **2** earnestness; insistence: *the urgency of his demands.*

ur·gent (ėr′jənt) *adj.* **1** demanding immediate action or attention; pressing; important. **2** insistent. [< L *urgens, -entis,* ppr. of *urgere* urge] —**ur′gent·ly,** *adv.* —**Syn. 1** imperative, necessary. **2** importunate.

u·ric (ūr′ik) *adj.* of or having to do with urine or urea.

uric acid a solid, white substance only slightly soluble in water, that is formed in the body as a waste product from proteins and is expelled in the urine. *Formula:* $C_5H_4N_4O_3$

u·ri·nal (ūr′ə nəl or ū rī′nəl) *n.* **1** an upright plumbing fixture into which to urinate, for use by men and boys. **2** a room or structure containing such fixtures. **3** a container for urine. [< LL *urinal,* ult. < L *urina*]

u·ri·nal·y·sis (ūr′ə nal′ə sis) *n.* **-ses** (-sēz′). a chemical analysis of a sample of urine. [alteration of British *uranalysis* < Gk. *ouron* urine + E *analysis*; influenced in spelling by *urine*]

u·ri·nar·y (ūr′ə ner′ē) *adj. n.* **-nar·ies.** —*adj.* **1** of, like, or having to do with urine. **2** of or having to do with the organs that secrete and discharge urine.
—*n.* a urinal.

u·ri·nate (ūr′ə nāt′) *v.* **-nat·ed, -nat·ing.** discharge urine from the body. [< Med.L *urinare*]

u·ri·na·tion (ūr′ə nā′shən)*n.* the act or process of urinating.

u·rine (ūr′ən) *n.* a fluid that contains waste products of the body and is secreted by the kidneys, passed from there to the bladder, then discharged from the body. [< L *urina*]

urn (ėrn) *n.* **1** a vase or similar vessel having a base or pedestal. Urns were used in Greece and Rome to hold the ashes of the dead. **2** a place of burial; grave; tomb. **3** a coffee pot or teapot with a tap, used for making or serving coffee or tea at the table. [< L *urna*]

An urn for ornament

uro- *combining form.* urine; having to do with the urinary tract: *urology = the study of the urinary tract.*

u·ro·gen·i·tal (ūr′ō jen′ə təl) *adj.* pertaining to or having to do with the urinary and genital organs. [< Gk. *ouron* urine + E *genital*]

An urn for hot drinks

u·ro·log·i·cal (ū′rə loj′ə kəl) *adj.* of or having to do with urology.

u·rol·o·gist (ū rol′ə jist) *n.* a specialist in urology.

u·rol·o·gy (ū rol′ə jē) *n.* the branch of medicine concerned with the study of the conditions, diseases, etc. of the urinary tract in the female or of the urogenital tract in the male. [< *uro-* + *-logy*]

Ur·sa Ma·jor (ėr′sə mā′jər) in astronomy, the northern constellation that includes the stars of the Big Dipper; the Great Bear. [< L *ursa major* bigger bear]

Ur·sa Mi·nor (ėr′sə mī′nər) in astronomy, the northern constellation that includes the stars of the Little Dipper; the Little Bear. [< L *ursa minor* smaller bear]

ur·sine (ėr′sīn or ėr′sən) *adj.* **1** of or having to do with bears; bearlike. **2** covered with bristle-like hairs: *ursine caterpillars.* [< L *ursinus* < *ursus* bear]

Ur·su·line (ėr′sə lin or ėr′syu̇ lin, ėr′sə līn′ or ėr′syu̇ līn′) *n.* in the Roman Catholic Church, a nun of a religious order founded in 1535 for the education of girls and for the care of the sick and needy. —*adj.* of or having to do with Saint Ursula, a British martyr of the fourth or fifth century, or the Ursulines.

ur·ti·car·i·a (ėr′tə kãr′ē ə) *n.* a skin rash; hives. [< NL < L *urtica* nettle]

Uru. Uruguay.

U·ru·guay·an (ūr′ə gwā′ən or ūr′ə gwī′ən) *adj.* of or having to do with Uruguay, a country in the southeastern part of South America, or its people. —*n.* a native or inhabitant of Uruguay.

u·rus (ūr′əs) *n.* an extinct wild ox that was common in Europe 2,000 years ago. [< L < Gmc.]

us (us; *unstressed,* əs) *pron.* the objective case of **we**: *Mother went with us.* [OE *ūs*]

U.S. the United States.

U.S.A. 1 the United States of America. **2** formerly, the Union of South Africa.

us·a·bil·i·ty (ūz′ə bil′ə tē) *n.* the fact or condition of being usable.

us·a·ble (ūz′ə bəl) *adj.* that can be used; fit for use. Also, **useable.** —**us′a·ble·ness,** *n.*

us·age (ūs′ij or ūz′ij) *n.* **1** a way or manner of using; treatment: *The car has had rough usage.* **2** a long-continued practice; customary use; habit; custom: *Travellers should learn many of the usages of the countries they visit.* **3** the customary way of using words: *The usage of the best writers and speakers determines what is good English.* [ME < OF *usage* < *us,* n., use < L *usus*]

us·ance (ūz′əns) *n.* **1** in commerce, the time allowed for payment of foreign bills of exchange. **2** the income of benefits of every kind derived from the ownership of wealth. [ME < OF *usance* < *user.* See USE.]

use (*v.* ūz; *n.* ūs) *v.* **used, us·ing,** *n.* —*v.* **1** put into action or service: *He used a knife to cut the meat.* **2** employ or practise actively; exercise, especially habitually or customarily: *use one's knowledge, authority, or judgment.* **3** employ (words, phrases, etc.); say; utter: *use bad grammar.* **4** act toward; treat: *He used us well.* **5** consume or expend by using: *We have used most of the money.* **6** avail oneself of: *May I use your telephone?* **7 used to, a** accustomed to: *used to hardships.* **b** was or were accustomed to; formerly did: *He used to come every day.* See the usage note below. **8 use up, a** consume or expend entirely. **b** *Informal.* tire out; weary; exhaust. [ME < OF *user,* ult. < L *uti* to use]
—*n.* **1** a using: *the use of tools.* **2** the state of being used: *methods long out of use.* **3** employment or usage resulting in or causing wear, damage, etc. **4** usefulness: *a thing of no practical use.* **5** the purpose that a thing is used for: *find a new use for something.* **6** a way of using: *a poor use of materials.* **7** the fact or quality of serving the needs or ends (of a person or persons): *a park for the use of all the people.* **8** function; service; office: *the use of a catalyst in a chemical process.* **9** a need; occasion: *He had no further use for it.* **10** the power, right, or privilege of using: *have the use of a boat for the summer.* **11** a custom; habit; usage: *It was his use to rise early.* **12** in law: **a** the act or fact of employing, occupying, possessing, or holding property so as to derive benefit from it. **b** the right of a beneficiary to the benefit or profits of land or tenements to which another has legal title in trust for the beneficiary. **c** a trust vesting title to real property in someone for the benefit of a beneficiary. **13 have no use for, a** not need or want. **b** *Informal.* dislike. **14 in use,** being used. **15 make use of,** use; employ. **16 put to use,** use. [ME < OF *us* < L *usus,* pp. of *uti* to use] —**us′er,** *n.*

Syn. *v.* **1** Use, employ, utilize = put into action or service. **Use,** the general and common word, emphasizes putting something or someone into service as a means or help in carrying out a purpose or getting what one wants: *He uses a typewriter for his homework.* **Employ,** more formal, often interchangeable with *use,* emphasizes putting to work for a special purpose or in a profitable way: *That architect frequently employs glass brick.* **Utilize** emphasizes making useful or turning to profitable use: *She utilizes every*

scrap of food. —*n.* **1** employment, application, utilization.
☛ **used to.** When *used,* either as past tense or participial adjective, is employed before the word *to* in sense 7 of the verb, it is pronounced (ūst) or (ūs), the (t) in the latter case being lost or assimilated before the same sound in the following word.

use·a·ble (ūz′ə bəl) *adj.* usable.

used (ūzd) *adj.* not new; that has belonged to another or others: *a used car.*

use·ful (ūs′fəl) *adj.* of use; giving service; helpful. —**use′ful·ly,** *adv.* —**use′ful·ness,** *n.*

use·less (ūs′lis) *adj.* of no use; worthless. —**use′less·ly,** *adv.* —**use′less·ness,** *n.*

U-shaped (ū′shāpt′) *adj.* having the shape of the letter U.

ush·er (ush′ər) *n.* **1** a person who shows people to their seats in a church, theatre, etc. **2** *Esp.Brit.* a person who has charge of the door and admits people to a hall, chamber, etc., now especially one who is an official of or employed by a court, college, etc.
—*v.* **1** conduct; escort: *He ushered the visitors to the door.* **2** go or come before; precede to announce the coming of. **3 usher in,** inaugurate; introduce: *a winter ushered in by cold rains.* [ME < AF *usser,* OF *uissier* < VL *ustiarius* doorkeeper < *ustium,* var. of L *ostium* door]

U.S.S.R. the Union of Soviet Socialist Republics.

u·su·al (ū′zhü əl) *adj.* **1** in common use; ordinary; customary. **2 as usual,** in the usual manner. [ME < LL *usualis* < L *usus* use, custom < *uti* to use]
—**u′su·al·ness,** *n.*
Syn. **1 Usual, customary** = often or commonly seen or found, especially in a certain place or at a given time. **Usual** emphasizes the familiar nature or quality of what is described, and applies to something that is in common use or that commonly or ordinarily happens or occurs: *This is the usual weather at this time of the year.* **Customary** describes something that is according to the usual practices or habits of a particular person or group: *He stayed up long past his customary bedtime.*

u·su·al·ly (ū′zhü əl ē) *adv.* according to what is usual; commonly; ordinarily; customarily.

u·su·fruct (ū′zyu̇ frukt or ū′syu̇ frukt) *n.* in law, the right of using another's property without injuring or destroying it. [< L *usufructu,* abl. of *ususfructus,* earlier *usus (et) fructus* use and enjoyment]

u·su·rer (ū′zhə rər) *n.* a person who lends money at an extremely high or unlawful rate of interest. [ME < AF *usurer,* var. of OF *usurier* < LL *usurarius* moneylender < L *usurarius* at interest, for use < *usura* use < *uti* use]

u·su·ri·ous (ū zhür′ē əs) *adj.* **1** taking extremely high or unlawful interest for the use of money. **2** of or having to do with usury: *Fifty per cent is a usurious rate of interest.*

u·surp (ū zėrp′ or ū sėrp′) *v.* seize and hold (power, position, authority, etc.) by force or without right: *The king's brother tried to usurp the throne.* [< L *usurpare,* ult. < *usu,* abl., through use + *rapere* seize] —**u·surp′er,** *n.* —**Syn.** appropriate, arrogate, assume.

u·sur·pa·tion (ū′zər pā′shən or ū′sər pā′shən) *n.* the act of usurping; the seizing and holding of the place or power of another by force or without right: *the usurpation of the throne by a pretender.*

u·su·ry (ū′zhə rē) *n.* **-ries. 1** the lending of money at an extremely high or unlawful rate of interest. **2** an extremely high or unlawful interest. [ME < Med.L *usuria,* alteration of L *usura.* See USURER.]

Ut. Utah.

u·ten·sil (ū ten′səl) *n.* **1** a container or implement used for practical purposes. Pots, pans, etc. are kitchen utensils. **2** an instrument or tool used for some special purpose. Pens and pencils are writing utensils. [ME < Med.L *utensile* < L *utensilis* that may be used < *uti* use]

u·ter·ine (ū′tər in or ū′tər īn′) *adj.* **1** of or having to do with the uterus. **2** having the same mother, but a different father. Uterine brothers are stepbrothers born of the same mother. [ME < LL *uterinus* < L *uterus* uterus]

u·ter·us (ū′tər əs) *n.* **-ter·i** (-tər ī′ or -tər ē′). in female mammals, the organ that holds and nourishes the young till birth; womb. [< L]

u·til·i·dor (ū til′ə dôr′) *n. Cdn.* in the North, a large insulated tube mounted on short posts above ground and housing water, steam, and sewage pipes that supply services to buildings in a town or settlement built on permafrost.

u·til·i·tar·i·an (ū til′ə tãr′ē ən) *adj.* **1** having to do with utility. **2** aiming at usefulness rather than beauty, style, etc. **3** that is utilitarian; adhering to utilitarianism.
—*n.* an adherent of utilitarianism.

u·til·i·tar·i·an·ism (ū til′ə tãr′ē ən iz′əm) *n.* in philosophy: **1** the doctrine or belief that the greatest good of the greatest number should be the purpose of human conduct, especially as developed by Jeremy Bentham and John Stuart Mill. **2** the doctrine or belief that actions are good if they are useful.

u·til·i·ty (ū til′ə tē) *n.* **-ties. 1** usefulness; power to satisfy people's needs. **2** a useful thing. **3** a company that performs a public service. Railways, bus lines, and gas and electric companies are utilities. **4** in philosophy, the greatest happiness of the greatest number. [ME < OF < L *utilitas,* ult. < *uti* use]

u·ti·li·za·tion (ū′tə lə zā′shən or ū′təl ī zā′shən) *n.* the act of utilizing or the state of being utilized.

u·ti·lize (ū′tə līz′) *v.* **-lized, -liz·ing.** make use of; put to some practical use: *utilize leftovers in cooking.*
—**u′ti·liz′a·ble,** *adj.* —**u′ti·liz′er,** *n.* —**Syn.** See **use.**

ut·most (ut′mōst) *adj.* **1** greatest possible; extreme: *Sunshine is of the utmost importance to health.* **2** most distant; farthest: *He walked to the utmost edge of the cliff.* —*n.* the most that is possible; extreme limit: *He enjoyed himself to the utmost.* [OE *ūtemest* < *ūte* outside + *-mest* -most]

U·to·pi·a (ū tō′pē ə) *n.* **1** an ideal commonwealth where perfect justice and social harmony exist, described in *Utopia,* by Sir Thomas More. **2** Often, **utopia.** an ideal place or state with perfect laws. **3** Often, **utopia.** a visionary, impractical system of political or social perfection. [< NL < Gk. *ou* not + *topos* place]

U·to·pi·an (ū tō′pē ən) *adj.* **1** of, having to do with, or resembling Utopia. **2** Often, **utopian. a** of, like, or having to do with a utopia. **b** visionary; impractical. —*n.* **1** an inhabitant of Utopia. **2** Often, **utopian.** an ardent, but impractical reformer; idealist.

u·to·pi·an·ism (ū tō′pē ən iz′əm) *n.* **1** the ideas, beliefs, and aims, of Utopians. **2** ideal schemes for the improvement of life, social conditions, etc.

u·tri·cle (ū′trə kəl) *n.* **1** in botany: **a** a small sac or baglike body, such as an air cell in seaweed. **b** a thin, bladderlike seed vessel. **2** in anatomy, the larger of the two sacs of the internal ear. [< L *utriculus,* dim. of *uter* skin bag, skin bottle]

ut·ter[1] (ut′ər) *adj.* complete; total; absolute: *utter surprise.* [OE *ūtera* outer] —**Syn.** entire, unqualified, sheer.

ut·ter[2] (ut′ər) *v.* **1** speak; make known; express: *the last words he uttered, utter one's thoughts.* **2** give; give out: *He uttered a cry of pain.* **3** in law, pass off (forged documents, counterfeit money, etc.) as genuine. [ME *uttren,* literally, put forth < OE *ūtor,* comparative of *ūt* out] —**ut′ter·a·ble,** *adj.* —**ut′ter·er,** *n.* —**Syn. 1** deliver, articulate.

ut·ter·ance (ut′ər əns) *n.* **1** an uttering; expression in words or sounds: *The child gave utterance to his grief.* **2** a way of speaking. **3** something uttered; a spoken word or words. **4** the passing off of counterfeit money, forged cheques, etc.; uttering.

ut·ter·ly (ut′ər lē) *adv.* completely; totally; absolutely.

ut·ter·most (ut′ər mōst′) *adj. n.* utmost.

u·vu·la (ū′vyu̇ lə) *n.* **-las** or **-lae** (-lē′ or -lī′). in anatomy, the small piece of flesh hanging down from the soft palate in the back of the mouth. [< LL *uvula,* dim. of L *uva,* originally, grape]

u·vu·lar (ū′vū lər) *adj.* **1** in anatomy, of or having to do with the uvula. **2** in phonetics, pronounced or sounded with vibration of the uvula. —*n.* in phonetics, a uvular sound.

ux. wife. (for L *uxor*)

ux·o·ri·ous (uks ô′rē əs) *adj.* excessively or foolishly fond of one's wife. [< L *uxorious* < *uxor* wife]
—**ux·o′ri·ous·ly,** *adv.* —**ux·o′ri·ous·ness,** *n.*

Uz·bek (uz′bek) *n.* **1** a Turkic people of Turkestan, a region in central Asia, and, especially, of Uzbek, a Soviet republic in W. Asia, north of Afghanistan. **2** a member of this people. **3** the Turkic language of this people.
—*adj.* of or having to do with Uzbek, its people, or their language.

hat, āge, cãre, fär; let, ēqual, tėrm; it, īce
hot, ōpen, ôrder; oil, out; cup, pu̇t, rüle, ūse
əbove, takən, pencəl, lemən, circəs
ch, child; ng, long; sh, ship
th, thin; ᴛʜ, then; zh, measure

V or **v** (vē) *n.* **V's** or **v's.** **1** the twenty-second letter of the English alphabet. **2** any speech sound represented by this letter. **3** one (usually twenty-second) of a series designated alphabetically. **4** anything shaped like this letter.

v **1** volt. **2** voltage.

v. **1** verb. **2** verse. **3** versus. **4** vide. **5** voice. **6** vice-. **7** volume. **8** von. **9** valve. **10** version. **11** violin. **12** velocity. **13** vocative.

V **1** vanadium. **2** victory. **3** volt. **4** vector.

V. **1** Venerable. **2** Viscount. **3** Victoria. **4** Volunteer.

Va. the state of Virginia.

V.A. Vicar Apostolic.

va·can·cy (vā′kən sē) *n.* **-cies.** **1** the state of being vacant; emptiness. **2** an unoccupied position: *Mr. Smith's death made a vacancy in the business.* **3** the state of being or becoming unoccupied. **4** a room, space, or apartment for rent: *a vacancy in a motel.* **5** empty space: *a vacancy in a parking lot.* **6** lack of thought or intelligence. **7** idleness; freedom from work, activity, etc.

va·cant (vā′kənt) *adj.* **1** not occupied: *a vacant house.* **2** empty; not filled: *a vacant space.* **3** without thought or intelligence: *a vacant smile.* **4** free from work, business, etc.: *vacant time.* [ME < L *vacans, -antis,* ppr. of *vacare* be empty] —**va′cant·ly,** *adv.* —**Syn. 1** See **empty.**

va·cate (və kāt′ or vā′kāt) *v.* **-cat·ed, -cat·ing.** **1** go away from and leave empty or unoccupied; make vacant: *They will vacate the house next month.* **2** leave. **3** make void; annul; cancel. [< L *vacare* be empty]

va·ca·tion (və kā′shən or vā kā′shən) *n.* **1** a time of rest and freedom from work: *There is a vacation from schoolwork every year at Christmas.* **2** holidays: *She spent her vacation at the family cottage.* **3** a vacating.
—*v.* take a vacation. [ME < L *vacatio, -onis* < *vacare* have time (off)] —**va·ca′tion·er,** *n.* —**va·ca′tion·less,** *adj.*

va·ca·tion·ist (və kā′shən ist or vā kā′shən ist) *n.* a person who is taking a vacation.

vac·ci·nate (vak′sə nāt′) *v.* **-nat·ed, -nat·ing.** **1** inoculate with vaccine as a protection against smallpox. **2** take similar measures against other diseases. **3** perform or practise vaccination.

vac·ci·na·tion (vak′sə nā′shən) *n.* **1** the act or process of vaccinating: *Vaccination has made smallpox a very rare disease.* **2** a scar formed where vaccine was injected.

vac·cine (vak′sēn or vak sēn′) *n.* **1** a preparation containing the virus that causes cowpox, for inoculation to provide immunity against smallpox. **2** any preparation, especially one containing disease-producing bacilli, viruses, etc., for inoculation to provide immunity against a disease: *flu vaccine.* [< L *vaccinus* pertaining to cows < *vacca* cow]

vac·il·late (vas′ə lāt′) *v.* **-lat·ed, -lat·ing.** **1** move first one way and then another; waver. **2** waver in mind or opinion: *A vacillating person finds it hard to make up his mind.* [< L *vacillare*] —**Syn. 1** oscillate, sway.

vac·il·la·tion (vas′ə lā′shən) *n.* **1** unsteadiness; a swaying. **2** a wavering in mind or opinion.

va·cu·i·ty (va kū′ə tē) *n.* **-ties.** **1** emptiness. **2** an empty space; vacuum. **3** lack of thought or intelligence. **4** something foolish or stupid. **5** absence or lack (of something specified). [< L *vacuitas* < *vacuus* vacuous]

vac·u·ole (vak′ū ōl′) *n.* **1** in biology, a tiny cavity in a living cell, containing fluid. **2** formerly, any very small cavity in organic tissue. [< F *vacuole* < L *vacuus* empty]

vac·u·ous (vak′ū əs) *adj.* **1** showing no thought or intelligence; foolish; stupid. **2** empty. [< L *vacuus*] —**vac′u·ous·ly,** *adv.*

vac·u·um (vak′ū əm) *n.* **vac·u·ums** or (*except for def. 4*) **vac·u·a** (vak′ū ə), *v.* —*n.* **1** an empty space utterly devoid of matter. **2** a space from which almost all air, gas, etc. has been removed. **3** an empty space; void. **4** a vacuum cleaner. —*v. Informal.* clean with a vacuum cleaner. [< L *vacuum*, neut. adj., empty]

vacuum bottle or **flask** a bottle or flask made with a vacuum between its inner and outer walls so that its contents remain hot or cold for long periods of time. See **Thermos bottle** for picture.

vacuum cleaner an apparatus for cleaning carpets, curtains, floors, etc. by suction.

vacuum flask vacuum bottle.

vac·u·um-packed (vak′ū əm pakt′) *adj.* **1** packed in an airtight container to keep fresh: *vacuum-packed coffee.* **2** having had all or most of the air removed before sealing: *vacuum-packed cans.*

vacuum pump 1 a pump or device by which a partial vacuum can be produced. **2** a pump in which a partial vacuum is utilized to raise water.

vacuum tube a sealed tube or bulb from which almost all the air has been removed, and into which electrodes project from outside. Vacuum tubes are used in radio sets, etc. to control the flow of electric currents.

va·de me·cum (vā′dē mē′kəm or vä′dē mā′kəm). **1** anything a person carries about with him because of its usefulness. **2** a book for ready reference; manual; handbook. [< L *vade mecum* go with me]

V.Adm. Vice-Admiral.

vag·a·bond (vag′ə bond′) *n.* **1** an idle wanderer; wanderer; tramp. **2** a good-for-nothing person; rascal. —*adj.* **1** wandering: *The gypsies lead a vagabond life.* **2** good-for-nothing; worthless. **3** moving hither and thither; drifting. [ME < OF < L *vagabundus*, ult. < *vagus* rambling] —**Syn.** *n.* **1** vagrant, nomad, hobo.

vag·a·bond·age (vag′ə bon′dij) *n.* the fact or state of being a vagabond; idle wandering.

va·gar·y (və gā′rē or vā′gə rē) *n.* **-gar·ies. 1** an odd fancy; extravagant notion: *the vagaries of a dream.* **2** an odd action; caprice; freak: *the vagaries of women's fashions.* [probably < L *vagari* wander < *vagus* roving]

va·gi·na (və jī′nə) *n.* **-nas** or **-nae** (-nē or -nī). **1** in female mammals, the passage from the uterus to the vulva or external opening. **2** a sheath; sheathlike part. [< L *vagina*, originally, sheath]

vag·i·nal (vaj′ə nəl or və jī′nəl) *adj.* **1** of or having to do with the vagina of a female mammal. **2** of or resembling a sheath.

vag·i·nate (vaj′ə nit or vaj′ə nāt′) *adj.* **1** having a vagina or sheath. **2** like a sheath.

va·gran·cy (vā′grən sē) *n.* **-cies. 1** a wandering idly from place to place without proper means or ability to earn a living: *The tramp was arrested for vagrancy.* **2** a wandering. **3** a vagrant act or idea.

va·grant (vā′grənt) *n.* **1** an idle wanderer; tramp. **2** a wanderer. —*adj.* **1** moving in no definite direction or course; wandering. **2** wandering without proper means of earning a living. **3** of or having to do with a vagrant. [? alteration of AF *wacrant* (< Gmc.), influenced by F *vagant* straying (< L *vagari* wander)] —**va′grant·ly**, *adv.*

vague (vāg) *adj.* **va·guer, va·guest.** not definite; not clear; not distinct: *a vague shape, a vague statement.* [< MF < L *vagus* wandering. Doublet of VAGUS.] —**vague′ly**, *adv.* —**vague′ness**, *n.* —**Syn.** ambiguous, hazy. See **obscure.**

va·gus (vā′gəs) *n.* **va·gi** (vā′jī or -jē). in anatomy, either of a pair of nerves, extending from the brain to the heart, lungs, stomach, and other organs. [< L *vagus* wandering. Doublet of VAGUE.]

vail (vāl) *n. Archaic.* **1** lower; cause or allow to fall. **2** take off; doff. **3** yield; bow. [< OF *valer*, or < *avale.* < OF *avaler*, both ult. < L *ad vallem* to the valley]

vain (vān) *adj.* **1** having too much pride in one's looks, ability, etc. **2** of no use; without effect or success; producing no good result: *I made vain attempts to reach her by telephone.* **3** of no value or importance; worthless; empty: *a vain boast.* **4 in vain,** without effect or success. [ME < OF < L *vanus*] —**vain′ness**, *n.*

Syn. *adj.* 1 conceited, egotistical. 2 Vain, futile = without effect or success. Vain describes thinking, action, effort, etc. that fails to accomplish what is hoped for and aimed at, or to produce any valuable result: *The principal made another vain appeal for better equipment in the high-school laboratories.* Futile adds and emphasizes the idea of being incapable of producing the desired, or any, result, and often suggests being useless or unwise to attempt: *Without microscopes and other essential equipment, attempts to teach science were futile.*

vain·glo·ri·ous (vān′glô′rē əs) *adj.* excessively proud or boastful; extremely vain. —**vain′glo′ri·ous·ly**, *adv.* —**Syn.** vaunting, arrogant, conceited.

vain·glo·ry (vān′glô′rē) *n.* **1** an extreme pride in oneself; boastful vanity. **2** worthless pomp or show. [ME < OF < Med.L *vana gloria*]

vain·ly (vān′lē) *adv.* **1** in vain. **2** with conceit.

vair (vãr) *n.* **1** in the Middle Ages, a gray-and-white squirrel fur used for lining and trimming the robes of nobles. **2** in heraldry, its representation by small shield-shaped figures alternately silver and gold. [ME < OF < L *varius* variegated. Doublet of VARIOUS.]

val·ance (val′əns) *n.* **1** a short drapery, board, etc. across the top of a window. **2** a short curtain hanging around a bed from the frame to the floor. [probably from *Valence*, a town in S.E. France]

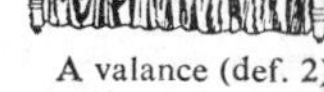
A valance (def. 2)

vale[1] (vāl) *n. Poetic.* valley. [ME < OF *val* < L *vallis*]

va·le[2] (vā′lē or vä′lā) *interj. n. Latin.* good-bye; farewell.

val·e·dic·tion (val′ə dik′shən) *n.* a bidding farewell. [< L *valedict-*, pp. stem of *valedicere* bid farewell < *vale* be well! + *dicere* say]

val·e·dic·to·ri·an (val′ə dik tô′rē ən) *n.* a student who gives the farewell address at the graduation of his class.

val·e·dic·to·ry (val′ə dik′tə rē or val′ə dik′trē) *n.* **-ries**, *adj.* —*n.* a farewell address, especially at the graduating exercises of a school or college. —*adj.* bidding farewell.

va·lence (vā′ləns) *n.* in chemistry, the quality of an atom or radical that determines the number of other atoms or radicals with which it can combine, indicated by the number of hydrogen atoms with which it can combine or which it can displace. Elements whose atoms lose electrons, such as hydrogen and the metals, have a positive valence. Elements whose atoms add electrons, such as oxygen and other non-metals, have a negative valence. Oxygen has a negative valence of two; hydrogen has a positive valence of one; one atom of oxygen combines with two of hydrogen to form a molecule of water. [< LL *valentia* strength < *valere* be strong]

Va·len·ci·a or **va·len·ci·a** (və len′shē ə or və len′shə) *n.* a common variety of orange having a thin, brownish-yellow skin, used mostly for juice.

Va·len·ci·ennes (və len′sē enz′) *n.* a fine lace in which the pattern and background are made together of the same threads. [< *Valenciennes*, a city in N. France, where this lace was first made]

va·len·cy (vā′lən sē) *n.* **-cies.** valence.

val·en·tine (val′ən tīn′) *n.* **1** a greeting card or small gift sent on Saint Valentine's Day, February 14. **2** a sweetheart chosen on this day.

Valentine's Day (val′ən tīn′) Saint Valentine's Day, the day on which valentines are exchanged, February 14.

va·le·ri·an (və lēr′ē ən) *n.* **1** a strong-smelling drug used to quiet the nerves. **2** the plant from whose root it is made. Valerian has small pinkish or white flowers and is often grown in gardens. [ME < OF *valeriane* or Med.L *valeriana* < L *Valerius*, a Roman gens name]

val·et (val′it or val′ā) *n. v.* **-et·ed, -et·ing.** —*n.* **1** a servant who takes care of a man's clothes, helps him dress, etc. **2** an employee of a hotel, etc. who cleans or presses clothes. —*v.* serve as a valet. [< F *valet*, var. of OF *vaslet*. See VARLET.]

val·e·tu·di·nar·i·an (val′ə tū′də nãr′ē ən or val′ə tü′də nãr′ē ən) *n.* **1** an invalid. **2** a person who is overcareful about his health. —*adj.* **1** sickly. **2** thinking too much about health. [< L *valetudinarius* sickly < *valetudo* (good or bad) health < *valere* be strong]

Val·hal·la (val hal′ə) *n.* in Norse mythology, the hall where the souls of heroes slain in battle feast with the god Odin. [< NL < ON *valhöll* < *valr* those slain in battle + *höll* hall]

val·iant (val′yənt) *adj.* brave; courageous: *a valiant soldier, a valiant deed.* [ME < OF *vaillant*, ppr. of *valoir* be strong < L *valere*] —**val′iant·ly,** *adv.* —**val′iant·ness,** *n.*

val·id (val′id) *adj.* **1** supported by facts or authority; sound; true: *a valid argument.* **2** having legal force; legally binding: *A contract made by an insane man is not valid.* **3** having force; holding good; effective: *Illness is a valid excuse for being absent from work.* [< L *validus* strong < *valere* be strong] —**val′id·ly,** *adv.*

Syn. 1 Valid, sound, cogent = strong or convincing with respect to truth, rightness, or reasoning. **Valid,** describing reasons, objections, arguments, evidence, etc., emphasizes being based on truth or fact and supported by correct reasoning: *His objections to women doctors are not valid.* **Sound** emphasizes having a solid foundation of truth or right and being free from defects or errors in reasoning: *The author has sound views on opportunities today.* **Cogent,** a formal word, meaning "so valid or sound as to be convincing": *He gives cogent advice to young people.*

val·i·date (val′ə dāt′) *v.* **-dat·ed, -dat·ing. 1** make or declare legally binding; give legal force to. **2** support by facts or authority; confirm.

va·lid·i·ty (və lid′ə tē) *n.* **-ties. 1** truth; soundness: *the validity of an argument.* **2** legal soundness or force; the fact of being legally binding. **3** effectiveness.

va·lise (və lēs′) *n.* a travelling bag to hold clothes, etc. [< F < Ital. *valigia*]

Val·kyr (val′kēr) *n.* Valkyrie.

Val·kyr·ie (val kēr′ē) *n.* in Norse mythology, one of the handmaidens of Odin who ride through the air and hover over battlefields, choosing the heroes who are to die in battle and afterward leading them to Valhalla. [< ON *valkyrja* < *valr* those slain in battle + *kyrja* chooser]

val·la·tion (va lā′shən) *n.* a trench; rampart. [< LL *vallatio, -onis* < L *vallare* surround with a rampart < *vallum* rampart]

val·ley (val′ē) *n.* **-leys. 1** a low land between hills or mountains. **2** a wide region drained by a great river system: *the Ottawa valley.* **3** any hollow or structure like a valley. **4** in architecture, a depression formed by the sloping sides of a roof. [ME < OF *valee* < *val* vale < L *vallis*] —**Syn. 1** vale, dale, glen, dell.

val·or or **val·our** (val′ər) *n.* bravery; courage. [ME < OF < LL *valor* < L *valere* be strong]

val·or·i·za·tion (val′ər ə zā′shən or val′ər ī zā′shən) *n.* the actual or attempted maintenance of certain prices for a commodity by a government. [< *valor*, in obs. sense of "value" < LL < L *valere* be worth]

val·or·ize (val′ər īz′) *v.* **-ized, -iz·ing. 1** assign a value to. **2** regulate the price of by valorization.

val·or·ous (val′ər əs) *adj.* valiant; brave; courageous. —**val′or·ous·ly,** *adv.* —**val′or·ous·ness,** *n.*

valse (väls) *n. French.* waltz.

val·u·a·ble (val′yů bəl or val′ū ə bəl) *adj.* **1** having value; being worth something. **2** having great value. **3** that can have its value measured. —*n.* Usually, **valuables,** *pl.* an article of value: *She keeps her jewellery and other valuables in a safe.* —**val′u·a·ble·ness,** *n.* —**val′u·a·bly,** *adv.*

Syn. *adj.* **2 Valuable, precious** = worth much. **Valuable** describes something that is worth much money and would bring a high price if sold, or, often, something of great usefulness or benefit to the person (or group) that has it: *He has a valuable stamp collection.* **Precious** describes something that is very valuable because it is rare or scarce, or something of great worth which belongs to it by its very nature: *Many precious oriental art treasures are kept in the Royal Ontario Museum.*

val·u·a·tion (val′ū ā′shən) *n.* **1** value estimated or determined: *The jeweller's valuation of the necklace was $10,000.* **2** an estimating or determining of the value of something.

val·ue (val′ū) *n. v.* **-ued, -u·ing.** —*n.* **1** worth; excellence; usefulness; importance: *the value of education.* **2** the real worth; proper price: *He bought the house for less than its value.* **3** the power to buy: *The value of the dollar has varied greatly.* **4** an estimated worth: *He placed a value on his furniture.* **5** the meaning; effect; force: *the value of a symbol.* **6** a number or amount represented by a symbol: *The value of XIV is fourteen.* **7 values,** *pl.* the

hat, āge, cãre, fär; let, ēqual, tėrm; it, īce
hot, ōpen, ôrder; oil, out; cup, pủt, rüle, ūse
əbove, takən, pencəl, lemən, circəs
ch, child; ng, long; sh, ship
th, thin; ᴛʜ, then; zh, measure

established ideals of life. **8** in music, the relative length of a tone indicated by a note. **9** in speech, the special quality of sound. **10** in a painting, etc.: **a** the degree of lightness or darkness. **b** the relative importance or effect of an object, part, spot of color, etc.
—*v.* **1** rate at a certain value or price; estimate the value of. **2** think highly of; regard highly: *value one's judgment.* [ME < OF *valu* < pp. of *valoir* be worth < L *valere*] —**val′u·er,** *n.*

Syn. *v.* **2 Value, appreciate, esteem** = think highly of a person or thing. **Value** = think highly of people or things because we consider them extremely good, desirable, or important: *I value his friendship.* **Appreciate** = think highly of people or things because we can understand them enough to value or enjoy them: *His classmates appreciate his ready wit.* **Esteem** = value someone or something very highly, respect him, and at the same time feel an attachment to him: *One esteems a man like Churchill.*

val·ued (val′ūd) *adj.* **1** having its value estimated or determined. **2** regarded highly.

val·ue·less (val′ū lis) *adj.* without value; worthless.

val·vate (val′vāt) *adj.* **1** furnished with, or opening by, a valve or valves. **2** serving as or resembling a valve. **3** in botany: **a** meeting without overlapping, as the parts of certain buds do. **b** composed of, or characterized by, such parts. [< L *valvatus* having folding doors]

valve (valv) *n. v.* **valved, valv·ing.** —*n.* **1** a movable part that controls the flow of a liquid, gas, etc. through a pipe by opening and closing the passage. A tap is one kind of valve. **2** in anatomy, a structure, especially a fold in a membrane that works similarly. The valves of the heart control the flow of blood. **3** in zoology, one of the parts of hinged shells like those of oysters and clams. **4** in botany: **a** one of the sections formed when a seed vessel bursts open. **b** a section that opens like a lid when an anther opens. **5** *Esp.Brit.* a vacuum tube. **6** in music, a device in certain wind instruments for changing the pitch of the tone by changing the direction and length of the column of air. Cornets and French horns have valves.

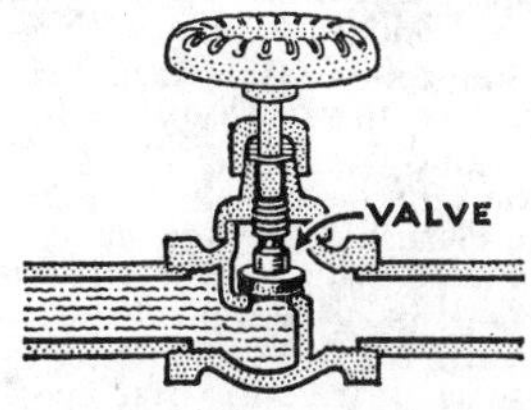

—*v.* **1** furnish with a valve or valves. **2** control the flow of a liquid, gas, etc. by a valve. **3** discharge gas from a balloon by opening a valve. [< L *valva* one of a pair of folding doors] —**valve′less,** *adj.* —**valve′like′,** *adj.*

val·vu·lar (val′vyů lər) *adj.* **1** of or having to do with valves, especially with the valves of the heart. **2** having the form of a valve. **3** furnished with valves; working by valves.

va·moose (va müs′) *v.* **-moosed, -moos·ing.** *Slang.* go away quickly. [< Sp. *vamos* let us go]

vamp[1] (vamp) *n.* **1** the upper front part of a shoe or foot. **2** a piece or patch added to an old thing to make it look new. **3** in music, an improvised accompaniment, introduction, etc.
—*v.* **1** furnish with a vamp; repair with a new vamp. **2** patch up; make (an old thing) look new. **3** in music, improvise an accompaniment, introduction, etc. **4 vamp up, a** make (something old) appear new. **b** make up to deceive. [ME < AF *vampe, OF *avanpie* forepart of the foot < *avant* before (< L *ab* from + *ante* before) + *pie* foot < L *pes*] —**vamp′er,** *n.*

VAMP

vamp[2] (vamp) *Slang.* —*n.* an unscrupulous flirt. —*v.* flirt with. [< *vampire*]

vam·pire (vam′pīr) *n.* **1** a corpse supposed to come to life at night and suck the blood of people while they sleep. **2** a person who preys ruthlessly on others. **3** a woman who flirts with men to get money or to please her vanity. **4** any of various South and Central American bats that suck blood, or are incorrectly supposed to do so, including **true vampires,** a species that actually sucks the blood of animals and men. [< F < Hungarian *vampir*: cf. Turkish *uber* witch]

van[1] (van) *n.* **1** the front part of an army, fleet, or other advancing group. **2** the foremost part of, or the foremost position in, a company or procession of persons moving forward or onward. **3** vanguard. **4 be in the van,** be a part of the advanced group in some movement. [< *vanguard*]

van[2] (van) *n.* **1** a covered truck or wagon for moving furniture, etc. **2** *Brit.* a railway baggage car. [< *caravan*]

va·na·di·um (və nā′dē əm) *n.* a rare, silvery gray, metallic chemical element used in making certain kinds of steel. *Symbol*: V or Vd; *at.no.* 23; *at.wt.* 50.942. [< NL < ON *Vanadis* Freya, the Norse goddess of love and beauty; because it was discovered in Sweden]

vanadium steel steel containing some vanadium to make it tougher and harder.

Van Al·len belt (van′al′ən) a broad band of high-intensity radiation that circles the earth in two bands, believed to be trapped in the earth's magnetic field.

van·dal (van′dəl) *n.* **1** a person who willfully or ignorantly destroys or damages beautiful or valuable things. **2 Vandal,** a member of a Germanic tribe that ravaged Gaul, Spain, and N. Africa in the fourth and fifth centuries. In A.D. 455 the Vandals sacked Rome. —*adj.* **1** destructive. **2 Vandal,** of or having to do with Vandals. [< LL *Vandalus* < Gmc.]

van·dal·ism (van′dəl iz′əm) *n.* willful or ignorant destruction of valuable things, especially works of art.

van·dal·ize (van′də līz′) *v.* **-ized, -iz·ing.** subject to vandalism.

Van·dyke (van dīk′) *adj.* of or having to do with Sir Anthony Van Dyck, 1599-1641, a Flemish painter, or the style of dress, etc. characteristic of his portraits. —*n.* Usually, **vandyke.** a short, pointed beard.

A Vandyke beard

vane (vān) *n.* **1** a flat piece of metal, or some other device, fixed upon a spire or some other high object in such a way as to move with the wind and indicate its direction. **2** a blade of a windmill, a ship's propeller, etc. **3** in zoology, the flat, soft part of a feather. [OE *fana* banner]

van·guard (van′gärd′) *n.* **1** a body of soldiers marching ahead of the main part of an army to clear the way and guard against surprise. **2** the foremost or leading position; van. **3** the leaders of a movement, especially persons who experiment or work with new ideas. [ME < MF *avantgarde* < OF < *avant* before (< L *ab* from + *ante* before) + *garde* guard < Gmc.]

A vane (def. 1)

va·nil·la (və nil′ə) *n.* **1** a flavoring extract used in candy, ice cream, perfume, etc. **2** the tropical plant that yields the beans used in making this flavoring. **3** the bean itself. [< NL < Sp. *vainilla*, literally, little pod, ult. < L *vagina* sheath]

van·ish (van′ish) *v.* **1** disappear; disappear suddenly: *The sun vanished behind a cloud.* **2** pass away; cease to be: *Dinosaurs have vanished from the earth.* [ME < OF *esvaniss-*, a stem of *esvanir*, ult. < L *evanescere* < *ex-* out + *vanus* empty] —**van′ish·er,** *n.* —**Syn. 1** See **disappear.**

vanishing point 1 the point toward which receding parallel lines seem to converge. **2** a point of disappearance.

VANISHING POINT
HORIZON

van·i·ty (van′ə tē) *n.* **-ties. 1** too much pride in one's looks, ability, etc. **2** a lack of real value; worthlessness: *the vanity of wealth.* **3** a useless or worthless thing. **4** worthless pleasure or display. **5** lack of effect or success. **6** a vanity case. **7** a dressing table, usually fitted with a mirror. [ME < OF < L *vanitas* < *vanus* empty] —**Syn. 1** conceit, egotism, self-esteem.

vanity case a case containing a small mirror, powder, rouge, etc. carried by women.

Vanity Fair any place or scene, such as the world, a great city, or the world of fashion, regarded as given over to vain pleasure or empty show. [< *Vanity Fair*, a fair described in John Bunyan's *Pilgrim's Progress*, symbolizing the world of vain pleasure or empty show]

van·quish (vang′kwish) *v.* conquer; defeat; overcome. [ME < OF *vencus*, pp. of *veintre* or < OF *vainquiss-*, a stem of *vainquir*, both < L *vincere* conquer] —**van′quish·a·ble,** *adj.* —**van′quish·er,** *n.*

van·tage (van′tij) *n.* **1** a better position or condition; advantage. **2** the first point scored in a tennis game after deuce. [ult. < *advantage*]

vantage ground a position that gives one an advantage; a favorable position.

vantage point 1 a superior position from which a person can see to advantage. **2** a favorable condition that gives a person an advantage.

van·ward (van′wərd) *adj. adv.* toward the front. [< *van*[1] + *-ward*]

vap·id (vap′id) *adj.* without much life or flavor; tasteless; dull. [< L *vapidus*] —**vap′id·ly,** *adv.* —**vap′id·ness,** *n.*

va·pid·i·ty (va pid′ə tē) *n.* insipidity; flatness of flavor.

va·por or **va·pour** (vā′pər) *n.* **1** steam from boiling water; moisture in the air that can be seen; fog; mist. **2** in physics, a gas formed by heating a substance that is usually a liquid or a solid. **3** something without substance; empty fancy. **4 a** a substance, as alcohol, mercury, or benzoin, that has been changed into vapor for use medicinally, industrially, etc. **b** a mixture of a vaporized substance and air, as in an internal-combustion engine. **c** the emission or exhalation of such mixtures or of any substance in gaseous form. **5 the vapors,** *Archaic.* low spirits.
—*v.* **1** pass off as vapor. **2** send out in vapor. **3** give out vapor. **4** boast; swagger; brag. [< L]

va·por·ish (vā′pər ish) *adj.* **1** like vapor. **2** abounding in vapor. **3** *Archaic.* in low spirits. **4** *Archaic.* having to do with or connected with low spirits: *vaporish fears.*

va·por·ize (vā′pər īz′) *v.* **-ized, -iz·ing.** change into vapor. —**va′por·iz′a·ble,** *adj.* —**va′por·i·za′tion,** *n.* —**va′por·iz′er,** *n.*

va·por·ous (vā′pər əs) *adj.* **1** full of vapor; misty. **2** like vapor. **3** soon passing; worthless.

vapor trail or **vapour trail** contrail.

va·por·y (vā′pər ē) *adj.* vaporous.

va·que·ro (vä kãr′ō) *n.* **-ros.** *Spanish America and Southwestern United States.* a cowboy; herdsman. [< Sp. *vaquero*, ult. < L *vacca* cow. Cf. BUCKAROO.]

var. 1 variant. **2** variation. **3** variometer. **4** variable.

var·i·a·bil·i·ty (ver′ē ə bil′ə tē or var′ē ə bil′ə tē) *n.* **1** the fact or quality of being variable. **2** a tendency to vary.

var·i·a·ble (ver′ē ə bəl or var′ē ə bəl) *adj.* **1** apt to change; changeable; uncertain: *variable winds.* **2** likely to shift from one opinion or course of action to another; inconsistent: *a variable frame of mind.* **3** that can be varied: *This curtain rod is of variable length.* **4** in biology, deviating from the normal species, type, etc. **5** likely to increase or decrease in size, number, amount, degree, etc.; not remaining the same or uniform: *a constant or variable ratio.*
—*n.* **1** a thing, quality, or quantity that varies. **2** a shifting wind. **3 the variables,** the region between the northeast and the southeast trade winds.
—**var′i·a·ble·ness,** *n.* —**var′i·a·bly,** *adv.* —**Syn.** *adj.* **1** unsteady, unstable, fluctuating, wavering.

variable star any of several stars that fluctuate periodically in brightness.

var·i·ance (ver′ē əns or var′ē əns) *n.* **1** a difference; disagreement. **2** in law, a difference or discrepancy between two legal statements or documents, as between a writ and a complaint or evidence and an accusation, sufficient to make them ineffectual. 3 a disagreeing or falling out; discord; quarrel: *yield without variance.* 4 a varying; change; variation: *a mean daily variance of eleven degrees.* 5 in statistics, the square of the standard deviation. 6 **at variance,** a differing; disagreeing; in disagreement. b in a state of discord or dissension: *at variance with the neighbors.*

var·i·ant (ver′ē ənt or var′ē ənt) *adj.* 1 varying; different: "*Rime*" *is a variant spelling of* "*rhyme.*" 2 variable; changing. —*n.* 1 a different form. 2 a different pronunciation or spelling of the same word. 3 an edition or translation of a manuscript, book, etc. that differs from the common or accepted version. [ME < OF < L *varians, -antis,* ppr. of *variare* change]

var·i·a·tion (ver′ē ā′shən or var′ē ā′shən) *n.* 1 a varying in condition, degree, etc.; change. 2 the act of changing in condition or degree. 3 the amount of change. 4 a varied or changed form. 5 in music: a a changing or ornamenting of a tune or theme. b one of a series of such modifications upon a theme. 6 in biology: a a deviation of an animal or plant from type. b an animal or plant showing such deviation or divergence. 7 in astronomy, the deviation of a heavenly body from its average orbit or motion.

var·i·col·ored or **var·i·col·oured** (ver′e kul′ərd or var′ē kul′ərd) *adj.* having various colors.

var·i·cose (var′ə kōs or ver′ə kōs′) *adj.* 1 swollen or enlarged: *He has varicose veins in his legs.* 2 having to do with, afflicted with, or designed to remedy varicose veins. [< L *varicosus* < *varix, -icis* dilated vein]

var·i·cos·i·ty (var′ə kos′ə tē) *n.* **-ties.** 1 the state or condition of being varicose. 2 a varicose part.

var·ied (ver′ēd or var′ēd) *adj.* 1 of different kinds; having variety: *a varied assortment.* 2 changed; altered.

var·i·e·gate (ver′ē ə gāt′ or var′ē ə gāt′) *v.* **-gat·ed, -gat·ing.** 1 vary in appearance; mark, spot, or streak with different colors. 2 give variety to. [< L *variegare* < *varius* varied + *agere* drive, make]

var·i·e·gat·ed (ver′ē ə gāt′id or var′ē ə gāt′id) *adj.* 1 varied in appearance; marked with different colors: *variegated pansies.* 2 having variety.

var·i·e·ga·tion (ver′ē ə gā′shən or var′ē ə gā′shən) *n.* a variegating or being variegated; varied coloring.

va·ri·e·ty (və rī′ə tē) *n.* **-ties.** 1 lack of sameness; difference; variation. 2 a number of different kinds: *The store has a great variety of toys.* 3 a kind; sort: *Which variety of cake do you prefer?* 4 in biology: a subdivision of a species. 5 vaudeville. [< L *varietas* < *varius* various]
Syn. 2 **Variety, diversity** = a number of things of different kinds or qualities. **Variety** emphasizes absence of sameness in form or character, and may apply to a number of related things of different kinds or a number of different things of the same general kind: *A teacher has a wide variety of duties.* **Diversity** emphasizes unlikeness, complete difference, in nature, form, or qualities: *A person who has travelled widely has a diversity of interests.*

variety program or **programme** a variety show.

variety show 1 *Esp.Brit.* vaudeville. 2 a radio or television entertainment similar to vaudeville.

var·i·form (ver′ə fôrm′ or var′ə fôrm′) *adj.* varied in form; having various forms.

va·ri·o·la (və rī′ə lə) *n.* smallpox. [< Med.L *variola* < L *varius* various, spotted]

var·i·om·e·ter (ver′ē om′ə tər or var′ē om′ə tər) *n.* 1 an instrument for comparing the intensity of magnetic forces, especially the magnetic force of the earth at different points. 2 in electricity, an instrument for varying inductance, consisting of a fixed coil and a movable coil connected in series. [< L *varius* various + E *-meter*]

var·i·o·rum (ver′ē ô′rəm or var′ē ô′rəm) *n.* 1 an edition of a book that has the comments and notes of several editors, critics, etc. 2 an edition of a book containing variant versions of the text. —*adj.* of or like a variorum. [< L (*cum notis*) *variorum* (with notes) of various people]

var·i·ous (ver′ē əs or var′ē əs) *adj.* 1 differing from one another; different: *various opinions.* 2 several; many: *We have looked at various houses, but have decided to buy this one.* 3 varied; many-sided: *lives made various by learning.* 4 varying; changeable. [< L *varius.* Doublet of VAIR.] —**var′i·ous·ly,** *adv.* —**Syn.** 1 diverse, diversified.

hat, āge, cãre, fär; let, ēqual, tėrm; it, īce
hot, ōpen, ôrder; oil, out; cup, pu̇t, rüle, ūse
əbove, takən, pencəl, lemən, circəs
ch, child; ng, long; sh, ship
th, thin; ᴛʜ, then; zh, measure

var·let (vär′lit) *n. Archaic.* a low fellow; rascal. [ME < OF *varlet,* var. of *vaslet,* originally, young man < Celtic]

var·mint (vär′mənt) *n. Informal or dialect.* 1 vermin. 2 an objectionable animal or person.

var·nish (vär′nish) *n.* 1 a liquid that gives a smooth, glossy appearance to wood, metal, etc., made from resinous substances dissolved in oil or turpentine. 2 the smooth, hard surface made by this liquid when dry: *The varnish on the car has been scratched.* 3 a glossy appearance. 4 a false or deceiving appearance; pretence. —*v.* 1 put varnish on. 2 give a false or deceiving appearance to. [ME < OF *vernis,* ult. ? < Gk. *Berenikē,* an ancient city in Libya] —**var′nish·er,** *n.*

var·si·ty (vär′sə tē) *n.* **-ties.** *Informal.* 1 university. 2 **Varsity,** the University of Toronto.

varve (värv) *n.* one of a pair of stratified bands or layers of alternately light and dark sediment, deposited annually by melting glaciers and useful in determining the age of geological phenomena [< Swedish *varv* layer]

varved (värvd) *adj.* arranged or deposited in varves.

var·y (ver′ē or var′ē) *v.* **var·ied, var·y·ing.** 1 make or become different; change: *The driver can vary the speed of an automobile. The weather varies.* 2 in music, change or ornament (a basic tune or theme). 3 be different; differ: *The stars vary in brightness.* 4 give variety to: *vary one's style of writing.* 5 alternate. 6 in mathematics, undergo or be subject to a change in value according to some law: x *varies inversely as the cube of* y. 7 in biology, exhibit or be subject to variation, as by natural or artificial selection. [ME < OF < L *variare* < *varius* various] —**var′y·ing·ly,** *adv.* —**Syn.** 1 alter, modify, diversify. 3 disagree, deviate.

vas (vas) *n.* **va·sa** (vā′sə). duct; vessel. [< L *vas* vessel]

vas·cu·lar (vas′kyu̇ lər) *adj.* having to do with, made of, or provided with vessels that carry blood, sap, etc. [< NL *vascularis,* ult. < L *vas* vessel]

vas·cu·lum (vas′kyu̇ ləm) *n.* **-lums** or **-la** (-lə). 1 a small covered box or case to hold plant specimens. 2 in botany, a baglike leaf or plant; ascidium. [< L *vasculum,* dim. of *vas* vase]

vase (vāz, väz, or voz) *n.* a holder or container used for ornament or for holding flowers. [< F < L *vas* vessel] —**vase′like′,** *adj.*

vas·ec·to·my (va sek′tə mē) *n.* **-mies.** the surgical removal of part or all of the **vas deferens,** a duct that conveys semen from the testicles to the penis.

vas·e·line (vas′ə lēn′) *n.* a type of petroleum jelly, used as an ointment and as a lubricant. [< *Vaseline,* a trademark, coined from G *Wasser* water + Gk. *elaion* oil]

vas·o·mo·tor (vas′ō mō′tər) *adj.* of or having to do with the nerves that regulate the size of the blood vessels. [< L *vas* vessel + E *motor,* adj.]

vas·sal (vas′əl) *n.* 1 in feudal times, a person who held land from a lord or superior, to whom in return he gave help in war or some other service. A great noble could be a vassal of the king and have many other men as his vassals. 2 a servant. —*adj.* like a vassal; like that of a vassal. [ME < OF < Med.L *vassallus* < LL *vassus* < Celtic]

vas·sal·age (vas′əl ij) *n.* 1 the condition of being a vassal. 2 the homage or service due from a vassal to his lord or superior. 3 dependence; servitude. 4 the land held by a vassal.

vast (vast) *adj.* extremely great; immense: *a vast amount of money, a vast desert. Ontario and Alberta are vast provinces.* [< L *vastus*] —**vast′ness,** *n.* —**Syn.** tremendous, colossal, extensive.

vast·ly (vast′lē) *adv.* to a vast extent; to a vast degree.

vast·y (vas′tē) *adj. Poetic.* vast; immense.

vat (vat) *n.* *v.* **vat·ted, vat·ting.** —*n.* a large container for liquids; tank: *a vat of dye.* —*v.* place, store, or treat in a vat. [OE *fæt*]

Vat·i·can (vat′ə kən) *n.* **1** in Vatican City, the palace of the Pope and the buildings immediately surrounding it. **2** the government, office, or authority of the Pope. [< L *Vaticanus* (*mons*) Vatican (hill), on which the palace of the Pope was built]

va·tic·i·nate (və tis′ə nāt′) *v.* **-nat·ed, -nat·ing.** prophesy. [< L *vaticinari* < *vates* seer] **—va·tic′i·na′tion,** *n.*

vau·de·ville (vo′də vil′ or vô′də vil′, vod′vil or vôd′vil) *n.* theatrical entertainment consisting of a variety of acts, such as singing, dancing, juggling, short plays, and animal acts. [< F *vaudeville* < *Vau de Vire,* a valley in Normandy; first applied to the songs composed by Olivier Basselin, a poet of the 15th century, who lived in this valley]

vault[1] (volt or vôlt) *n.* **1** an arched roof or ceiling; a series of arches. **2** an arched space or passage. **3** something like an arched roof. The **vault of heaven** means the sky. **4** an underground cellar or storehouse. **5** a place for storing valuable things and keeping them safe. Vaults are often made of steel. **6** a place for burial. —*v.* **1** make in the form of a vault. **2** cover with a vault. [ME < OF *vaulte,* ult. < L *volvere* roll] **—vault′like′,** *adj.*

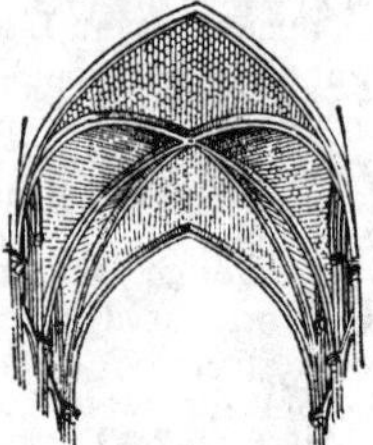
The vault of a roof

vault[2] (volt or vôlt) *v.* **1** jump or leap over by using a pole or the hands. **2** jump or leap. —*n.* the act of vaulting. [< OF *volter,* ult. < L *volvere* roll] **—vault′er,** *n.*

vault·ed (vol′tid or vôl′tid) *adj.* **1** in the form of a vault; arched. **2** built or covered with a vault.

vault·ing[1] (vol′ting or vôl′ting) *n.* **1** the art, practice, or operation of constructing vaults. **2** a vaulted structure. **3** vaults collectively.

vault·ing[2] (vol′ting or vôl′ting) *adj.* **1** overreaching or leaping over: *vaulting ambition.* **2** used in gymnastics for vaulting. —*n.* the art of leaping with a vault.

vaunt (vont or vônt) *v.* *n.* boast. [< F < LL *vanitare* < *vanus* vain] **—vaunt′ing·ly,** *adv.*

vb. 1 verb. 2 verbal.

V.C. 1 Victoria Cross. 2 Vice-Chairman. 3 Vice-Chancellor. 4 a person who has won a Victoria Cross. 5 Vice-Consul.

v.d. various dates.

V.D. or **VD** venereal disease.

veal (vēl) *n.* the flesh of a calf, used for food. [ME < OF *veel,* ult. < L *vitellus,* dim. of *vitulus* calf]

veal·er (vēl′ər) *n.* a calf that is less than 12 weeks old, raised for its tender meat.

vec·tor (vek′tər) *n.* **1** in mathematics: **a** a quantity involving direction as well as magnitude. **b** a line representing both the direction and the magnitude of some force, etc. **2** in biology, an organism, such as a mosquito or tick, that transmits micro-organisms that cause disease. —*v.* guide (a pilot, aircraft, or missile) from one point to another within a given time by means of a vector: *He vectored the pilot back to the base.* [< L *vector* carrier < *vehere* carry]

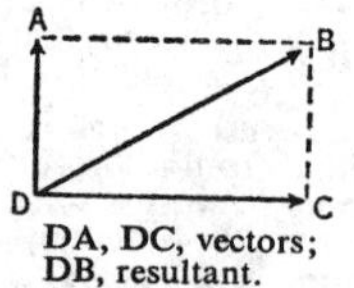

DA, DC, vectors; DB, resultant.

Ve·da (vā′də or vē′də) *n.* any or all of the four collections of Hindu sacred writings. [< Skt. *veda* knowledge]

Ve·dan·ta (vi dän′tə or vi dan′tə) *n.* one of the leading schools of Hindu religious philosophy based on the Vedas, dealing with the relations of man and the universe with the Divine spirit. [< Skt. < *veda* sacred knowledge + *-anta* end]

V-E Day the day of the Allied victory in Europe in World War II, May 8, 1945.

ve·dette (vi det′) *n.* **1** a mounted sentry stationed in advance of the outposts of an army. **2** a small naval vessel used for scouting. [< F < Ital. *vedetta,* ult. < L *videre* see]

Ve·dic (vā′dik or vē′dik) *adj.* having to do with or found in the Vedas. —*n.* the form of ancient Sanskrit in which the Vedas are written.

veer (vēr) *v.* **1** change in direction; shift; turn: *The wind veered to the south. The talk veered to ghosts.* **2** change the direction of: *We veered our boat.* —*n.* a shift; turn. [< F *virer*]

veer·y (vēr′ē) *n.* **veer·ies.** a tawny thrush of E. North America. [probably imitative]

Ve·ga (vē′gə) *n.* in astronomy, a bluish-white star of the first magnitude, in the constellation Lyra. [< Med.L < Arabic (*al-Nasr*) *al-wāqi*‘ the falling (vulture)]

veg·e·ta·ble (vej′tə bəl or vej′ə tə bəl) *n.* **1** a plant whose fruit, shoots or stems, leaves, roots, or other parts are used for food. Peas, corn, lettuce, tomatoes, and beets are vegetables. **2** any plant. **3** a person resembling a vegetable; one apparently lacking in action, thought, or feeling. —*adj.* **1** of plants; having to do with plants; like plants: *the vegetable kingdom.* **2** consisting of or made from vegetables: *vegetable soup.* **3** of persons or their way of life, resembling a vegetable; lacking in action, thought, or feeling. [ME (adj.) < OF *vegetable,* or < LL *vegetabilis* vivifying, refreshing < *vegetus* vigorous]

vegetable marrow an oblong vegetable of the squash family having a light-yellow skin when ripe.

veg·e·tal (vej′ə təl) *adj.* of, like, or having to do with plants or vegetables.

veg·e·tar·i·an (vej′ə tãr′ē ən) *n.* a person who eats vegetables but no meat. —*adj.* **1** eating vegetables but no meat. **2** devoted to or advocating vegetarianism. **3** containing no meat: *a vegetarian diet.*

veg·e·tar·i·an·ism (vej′ə tãr′ē ən iz′əm) *n.* the practice or principle of eating vegetables but no meat.

veg·e·tate (vej′ə tāt′) *v.* **-tat·ed, -tat·ing. 1** grow as plants do. **2** live with very little action, thought, or feeling. [< L *vegetare* enliven < *vegetus* lively]

veg·e·ta·tion (vej′ə tā′shən) *n.* **1** plant life; growing plants: *There is not much vegetation in deserts.* **2** a vegetating; the growth of plants. **3** an existence similar to that of a vegetable; dull, empty, or stagnant life.

veg·e·ta·tive (vej′ə tā′tiv) *adj.* **1** growing as plants do. **2** of plants or plant life. **3** in botany, concerned with growth and development rather than reproduction: *vegetative root cells.* **4** causing or promoting growth in plants; productive; fertile: *vegetative mould.* **5** of or having to do with vegetable-like unconscious or involuntary functions of the body: *the vegetative processes of the body, such as growth and repair.* **6** having very little action, thought, or feeling. **—veg′e·ta′tive·ly,** *adv.* **—veg′e·ta′tive·ness,** *n.*

ve·he·mence (vē′ə məns) *n.* **1** great or excessive warmth of emotion or action; passionate force, violence, or excitement; strong personal feelings. **2** force; violence.

ve·he·ment (vē′ə mənt) *adj.* **1** having or showing strong feeling; caused by strong feeling; eager; passionate. **2** acting with or displaying personal passion or excitement. **3** characterized by actions of great physical exertion; performed with unusual force or violence; violent. **4** with great strength or violence. [< L *vehemens, -entis* < *vehere* carry] **—ve′he·ment·ly,** *adv.* **—Syn. 1** ardent, fervid.

ve·hi·cle (vē′ə kəl) *n.* **1 a** a carriage, cart, wagon, automobile, sled, or any other conveyance used on land. **b** any form of conveyance or transportation: *a space vehicle.* **2** a means of carrying or conveying: *Language is the vehicle of thought.* **3** in painting, a liquid in which a pigment is applied to a surface. Linseed oil is a vehicle for paint. [< L *vehiculum* < *vehere* carry]

ve·hic·u·lar (vē hik′yů lər) *adj.* of or having to do with vehicles.

veil (vāl) *n.* **1** a piece of very thin material worn to protect or hide the face, or as an ornament. **2** a piece of material worn so as to fall over the head and shoulders.

3 anything that covers or hides: *A veil of clouds hid the sun.* **4 a** the secluded life of a nun. **b** the vows made by a woman either as a novice, when she takes the white veil, or as a nun, when she pronounces the irrevocable vows and assumes the black veil. **5 take the veil,** become a nun. —*v.* **1** cover with a veil. **2** cover; hide: *a veiled threat.* [ME < AF < L *velum* covering. Doublet of VELUM, VOILE.] **—veil′-like′,** *adj.* **—Syn.** *v.* **2** conceal, mask, screen.

veil·ing (vāl′ing) *n.* **1** a veil. **2** material for veils.

vein (vān) *n.* **1** in anatomy, one of the membranous vessels or tubes that carry blood to the heart from all parts of the body. **2** in botany, one of the strands or bundles of vascular tissue forming the principal framework of a leaf. **3** a rib of an insect's wing. **4** in geology, a crack or seam in rock filled with a different mineral: *a vein of copper.* **5** any streak or marking of a different shade or color in wood, marble, etc. **6** a strain or blend of some quality in conduct, writing, speech, etc.: *comedy written in a witty vein.* **7** a special character or disposition; state of mind; mood: *a vein of cruelty.* —*v.* cover with veins; mark with veins. [ME < OF < L *vena*] **—vein′less,** *adj.* **—vein′like′,** *adj.*

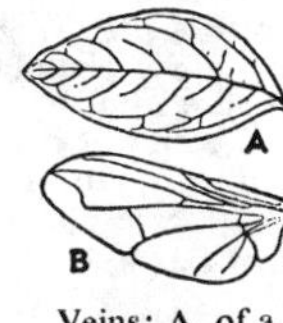

Veins: A, of a leaf; B, of an insect's wing.

veined (vānd) *adj.* having or showing veins: *veined marble.*

vein·ing (vān′ing) *n.* an arrangement of veins.

vel. vellum.

ve·lar (vē′lər) *adj.* **1** of or having to do with a velum. **2** in phonetics, pronounced with the aid of the soft palate. *C* in *coo* has a velar sound. —*n.* in phonetics, a velar sound. [< L *velaris* < *velum* covering]

veldt or **veld** (velt or felt) *n.* in South Africa, open country having grass or bushes but few trees. [< Afrikaans *veld* < Du. *veld* field]

vel·lum (vel′əm) *n.* **1** the finest kind of parchment, used in writing, binding books, etc. **2** a kind of paper or cloth imitating such parchment. —*adj.* of vellum. [ME < OF *velin* < *veel* calf. See VEAL.]

ve·loc·i·pede (və los′ə pēd′) *n.* **1** a tricycle. **2** an early kind of bicycle or tricycle. **3** a railway handcar. [< F *vélocipède* < L *velox, -ocis* swift + *pes, pedis* foot]

ve·loc·i·ty (və los′ə tē) *n.* **-ties. 1** speed; swiftness; quickness: *fly with the velocity of a bird.* **2** the rate of motion: *The velocity of light is about 186,000 miles per second.* **3** the absolute or relative rate of operation or action. [< L *velocitas* < *velox, velocis* swift]

ve·lo·drome (vē′lə drōm′) *n.* a building having a track for bicycle racing.

ve·lours or **ve·lour** (və lür′) *n.* a fabric like velvet, made of silk, wool, cotton, etc., used for clothing, draperies, upholstery, etc. [< F *velours* velvet, earlier *velous* < Provençal *velos,* ult. < L *villus* shaggy hair]

ve·lum (vē′ləm) *n.* **-la** (-lə). **1** in biology, a veil-like membranous covering or partition. **2** in anatomy, the soft palate. [< L *velum* covering. Doublet of VEIL, VOILE.]

ve·lure (və lür′) *n.* **1** a soft material like velvet. **2** a soft pad used for smoothing silk hats. [var. of *velour.* See VELOURS.]

vel·vet (vel′vit) *n.* **1** a cloth having a thick, soft pile and made of silk, rayon, cotton, nylon, etc. **2** something resembling velvet. **3** the furry skin that covers the growing antlers of a deer. **4** *Slang.* a clear profit or gain. **5** *Slang.* money won through gambling. **6 be on velvet,** *Slang.* **a** have previous winnings available for gambling, speculating, etc. **b** be well supplied with money. **7 play on velvet,** *Slang.* gamble or speculate with money won previously.
—*adj.* **1** made of velvet. **2** covered with velvet. **3** smooth or soft like velvet; velvety: *velvet petals.* [ME < Med.L *velvetum,* ult. < L *villus* tuft of hair]

vel·vet·een (vel′və tēn′) *n.* a fabric resembling velvet, made of cotton. —*adj.* made of velveteen. [< *velvet*]

vel·vet·y (vel′və tē) *adj.* smooth and soft like velvet.

Ven. 1 Venerable. **2** Venice.

ve·na ca·va (vē′nə kā′və) *pl.* **venae cavae** (vē′nē kā′vē). in anatomy, either of the two large veins that empty blood into the right auricle of the heart. [< L, literally, hollow vein]

hat, āge, cãre, fär; let, ēqual, tėrm; it, īce
hot, ōpen, ôrder; oil, out; cup, pu̇t, rüle, ūse
əbove, takən, pencəl, lemən, circəs
ch, child; ng, long; sh, ship
th, thin; ᴛʜ, then; zh, measure

ve·nal (vē′nəl) *adj.* **1** willing to sell one's services or influence basely; open to bribes; corrupt: *venal judges.* **2** influenced or obtained by bribery: *venal conduct.* [< L *venalis* < *venum* sale] **—ve′nal·ly,** *adv.*

ve·nal·i·ty (vē nal′ə tē) *n.* the quality of being venal.

ve·na·tion (vē nā′shən) *n.* **1** the arrangement of veins in a leaf or in an insect's wing. **2** these veins. [< L *vena* vein]

vend (vend) *v.* sell; peddle. [< L *vendere* < *venum dare* offer for sale]

vend·ee (ven dē′) *n.* a person to whom a thing is sold; buyer.

vend·er (ven′dər) *n.* vendor.

ven·det·ta (ven det′ə) *n.* a feud in which a murdered man's relatives try to kill the murderer or members of the murderer's family. Such feuds may last several generations. [< Ital. < L *vindicta* revenge, ult. < *vindex, -icis* protector, avenger]

vend·i·bil·i·ty (ven′də bil′ə tē) *n.* salable quality; the quality of being marketable.

vend·i·ble (ven′də bəl) *adj.* salable. —*n.* a salable thing.

vending machine a coin-operated machine from which one may obtain coffee, candy, cigarettes, stamps, etc.

ven·dor or **ven·der** (ven′dər) *n.* **1** a seller. **2** peddler. [< AF *vendor* < *vendre* sell < L *vendere.* See VEND.]

ven·due (ven dū′ or ven dü′) *n.* a public auction. [< Du. < OF *vendue* sale]

ve·neer (və nēr′) *v.* **1** cover (wood) with a thin layer of finer wood or other material: *veneer a pine desk with walnut.* **2** cover (anything) with a layer of something else to give an appearance of superior quality. —*n.* **1** a thin layer of wood or other material used in veneering: *a veneer of ivory.* **2** surface appearance or show: *a veneer of piety.* [earlier *fineer* < G *furnieren* < F *fournir* furnish] **—ve·neer′er,** *n.*

ven·er·a·bil·i·ty (ven′ər ə bil′ə tē) *n.* the fact or quality of being venerable.

ven·er·a·ble (ven′ər ə bəl) *adj.* **1** worthy of reverence; deserving respect because of age, character, or associations: *a venerable priest, venerable customs.* **2** designating an archdeacon of the Anglican Church (used as a title of respect). **3** in the Roman Catholic Church, designating a person recognized as having attained a degree of virtue but not yet recognized as beatified or canonized: *the Venerable Bede.* [ME < L *venerabilis* < *venerari* venerate] **—ven′er·a·bly,** *adv.*

ven·er·ate (ven′ər āt′) *v.* **-at·ed, -at·ing.** regard with deep respect; revere: *He venerates his father's memory.* [< L *venerari* < *Venus, Veneris,* originally, love] **—Syn.** honor, esteem.

ven·er·a·tion (ven′ər ā′shən) *n.* deep respect; reverence.

ve·ne·re·al (və nēr′ē əl) *adj.* **1** of or having to do with sexual intercourse. **2** communicated by sexual intercourse: *a venereal disease.* **3** having to do with diseases communicated by sexual intercourse. **4** infected with syphilis, gonorrhea, or some other venereal disease. [< L *venereus* < *Venus, Veneris* Venus]

ven·er·y[1] (ven′ər ē) *n.* gratification of sexual desire. [< L *Venus, Veneris* Venus]

ven·er·y[2] (ven′ər ē) *n. Archaic.* hunting; the chase. [ME < OF *venerie,* ult. < L *venari* hunt]

Ve·ne·tian (və nē′shən) *adj.* of Venice, a city in N.E. Italy, or its people. —*n.* a native or inhabitant of Venice.

Venetian blind a window blind made of many wooden, steel, plastic, or aluminum slats that can be opened or closed to regulate the light, air, etc.

Venetian glass a fine, very delicate kind of glassware. [< *Venice,* Italy, where it was first made]

Venez. Venezuela.

Ven·e·zue·lan (ven′ə zwē′lən or ven′ə zwā′lən) *adj.* of or having to do with Venezuela, a country in N. South America, or its people. —*n.* a native or inhabitant of Venezuela.

venge·ance (ven′jəns) *n.* **1** the inflicting of injury or punishment in return for a wrong; avenging oneself or another. **2** punishment in return for a wrong; revenge: *swear vengeance for a wrong.* **3 take vengeance on** or **upon,** punish or retaliate with severity. **4 with a vengeance,** **a** with great force or violence. **b** extremely. **c** much more than expected. **d** indeed: *Here is a difficulty with a vengeance.* [ME < OF *vengeance,* ult. < L *vindex* avenger] —**Syn. 1** retribution.

venge·ful (venj′fəl) *adj.* **1** inflicting vengeance; serving as an instrument of vengeance. **2** seeking vengeance; inclined to avenge oneself; vindictive: *vengeful enemies.* **3** feeling or showing a strong desire for vengeance. —**venge′ful·ly,** *adv.* —**venge′ful·ness,** *n.*

ve·ni·al (vē′nē əl or vēn′yəl) *adj.* that can be forgiven; not very wrong; wrong but pardonable. [ME < LL *venialis* < *venia* forgiveness]

venial sin in Roman Catholic theology, a minor offence, or any offence that is not committed with full knowledge and consent and so can be easily forgiven.

ve·ni·re (və nī′rē) *n.* in law, a writ authorizing the summoning of persons to serve on a jury. [< L *venire facias,* that you may cause (him) to come]

ven·i·son (ven′ə sən or ven′ə zən) *n.* the flesh of a deer, used for food; deer meat. [ME < OF < L *venatio* hunting < *venari* hunt]

venison bird *Cdn.* the Canada jay.

Ve·ni·te (vi nī′tē) *n.* the 95th Psalm (94th in the Vulgate). [< L *venite* come (2nd pers. pl. imperative), the first word in the Latin version]

ve·ni, vi·di, vi·ci (vē′nī vī′dī vī′sī or wā′nē wē′dē wē′kē) *Latin.* I came, I saw, I conquered (a report of victory made by Julius Caesar to the Roman Senate).

Venn diagram (ven) in logic, a diagram using circles, rectangles, or ellipses to show the relationships between sets, propositions, etc. [< John *Venn,* 1834-1923, an English logician]

ven·om (ven′əm) *n.* **1** the poison of snakes, spiders, etc. **2** spite; malice: *Her enemies dreaded the venom of her tongue.* [ME < OF *venin* < L *venenum* poison] —**ven′om·less,** *adj.* —**Syn. 2** rancor, hate, malignity.

ven·om·ous (ven′əm əs) *adj.* **1** poisonous: *Rattlesnakes are venomous.* **2** spiteful; malicious. —**ven′om·ous·ly,** *adv.* —**ven′om·ous·ness,** *n.*

ve·nous (vē′nəs) *adj.* **1** of, in, or having to do with veins: *venous blood.* **2** having veins: *the venous wings of insects.* [< L *venosus* < *vena* vein]

vent[1] (vent) *n.* **1** a hole; opening, especially one serving as an outlet. **2** an outlet; way out: *His great energy found vent in hard work.* **3** expression: *She gave vent to her grief in tears.* **4** the external opening of the intestine, especially in birds, fish, and reptiles. **5** formerly, in guns or cannon, a touchhole. **6** in automobiles, etc., a small window that can be opened for indirect ventilation.
—*v.* **1** let out; express freely: *He vented his anger on the dog.* **2** make a vent in. [partly < MF *vent* wind < L *ventus*; partly < MF *évent* vent, blowhole, ult. < L *ex-* out + *ventus* wind]

vent[2] (vent) *n.* a slit or opening in a garment. [ME *vent,* var. of *fent(e)* < MF *fente* slit, ult. < L *findere* split]

vent·age (ven′tij) *n.* a vent; a small hole, especially for the escape or passage of air. The finger holes of a flute are ventages.

ven·ti·late (ven′tə lāt′) *v.* **-lat·ed, -lat·ing. 1** change the air in: *We ventilate a room by opening windows.* **2** purify by fresh air: *The lungs ventilate the blood.* **3** make known publicly; discuss openly: *ventilate a grievance.* **4** furnish with a vent or opening for the escape of air, gas, etc. [< L *ventilare* fan < *ventus* wind]

ven·ti·la·tion (ven′tə lā′shən) *n.* **1** the process of changing air; the act or process of supplying with fresh air. **2** a means of supplying fresh air. **3** the act or process of purifying by fresh air. **4** an open discussion in public.

ven·ti·la·tor (ven′tə lā′tər) *n.* any apparatus or means for changing or improving the air in a room, airplane, etc.

ven·tral (ven′trəl) *adj.* **1** of or having to do with the belly; abdominal. **2** of or having to do with the surface or part opposite the back. **3** on the ventral surface; nearer the ventral surface. [< LL *ventralis* < L *venter* belly]

ven·tral·ly (ven′trəl ē) *adv.* in a ventral position or direction.

ven·tri·cle (ven′trə kəl) *n.* in anatomy: **1** either of the two lower chambers of the heart that receive blood and force it into the arteries. See **heart** for diagram. **2** any of a series of connecting cavities in the brain. **3** any hollow organ of the body. [ME < L *ventriculus,* dim. of *venter* belly]

ven·tric·u·lar (ven trik′yů lər) *adj.* **1** of, having to do with, or like a ventricle. **2** having to do with the stomach. **3** swelling out; distended.

ven·tri·lo·qui·al (ven′trə lō′kwē əl) *adj.* having to do with ventriloquism.

ven·tril·o·quism (ven tril′ə kwiz′əm) *n.* the art or practice of speaking or uttering sounds with the lips immobilized so that the voice may seem to come from some source other than the speaker. [< L *ventriloquus* ventriloquist < *venter* belly + *loqui* speak]

ven·tril·o·quist (ven tril′ə kwist) *n.* a person who can make his voice seem to come from some other source. A ventriloquist can talk without seeming to move his lips.

ven·tril·o·quy (ven tril′ə kwē) *n.* ventriloquism.

ven·ture (ven′chər) *n. v.* **-tured, -tur·ing.** —*n.* **1** a risky or daring undertaking: *His courage was equal to any venture.* **2** a speculation to make money: *A lucky venture in oil stock made his fortune.* **3** the thing risked; stake. **4 at a venture,** at random; by chance.
—*v.* **1** expose to risk or danger: *Men venture their lives in war.* **2** run a risk. **3** dare: *No one ventured to interrupt the speaker.* **4** dare to come, go, or proceed: *He ventured out on the thin ice and fell through.* **5** dare to say or make: *He ventured an objection.* **6** guess (at): *venture at a reason.* **7 nothing ventured, nothing gained,** advantage, profit, or other objectives are forfeited by overcautiousness or failure to risk danger. [< *aventure,* an earlier form of *adventure*] —**Syn.** *n.* **1** enterprise, adventure, risk. –*v.* **3** See **dare.**

ven·ture·some (ven′chər səm) *adj.* **1** inclined to take risks; rash; daring. **2** hazardous. —**ven′ture·some·ly,** *adv.* —**ven′ture·some·ness,** *n.* —**Syn. 1** adventurous, bold.

venturi tube or **valve** a short, narrow piece of tubing inserted in a pump or pipeline to permit measurement of the rate of flow of liquid or air. [< G.B. *Venturi* (1746-1822), an Italian physicist]

ven·tur·ous (ven′chər əs) *adj.* **1** rash; daring; adventurous. **2** risky; dangerous. —**ven′tur·ous·ly,** *adv.* —**ven′tur·ous·ness,** *n.*

ven·ue (ven′ū) *n.* in law: **1** the place or neighborhood of a crime or cause of action. **2** the place where a jury is gathered and the case tried: *The prisoner's lawyer asked for a change of venue because the town was so prejudiced against the prisoner.* **3** the scene of a real or supposed action or event, especially in a novel or other literary work. [< OF *venue* coming, ult. < L *venire* come]

Ve·nus (vē′nəs) *n.* **1** in Roman mythology, the goddess of love and beauty, identified with the Greek goddess Aphrodite. **2** any very beautiful woman. **3** the most brilliant planet. It is second in order from the sun, and is the planet that comes closest to the earth.

Ve·nus's-fly·trap (vē′nəs iz flī′trap′) *n.* a plant whose hairy leaves have two lobes at the end that fold together to trap and digest insects.

ver. 1 verse. **2** version.

ve·ra·cious (və rā′shəs) *adj.* **1** truthful. **2** true. [< L *verax, -acis* < *verus* true] —**ve·ra′cious·ly,** *adv.* —**ve·ra′cious·ness,** *n.*

ve·rac·i·ty (və ras′ə tē) *n.* **-ties. 1** truthfulness. **2** the truth. **3** correctness; accuracy. [< Med.L *veracitas* < L *verax, -acis.* See VERACIOUS.]

ve·ran·da or **ve·ran·dah** (və ran′də) *n.* a large porch along one or more sides of a house. [< Hind. and other languages of India < Pg. *varanda* railing]

A veranda along the front of a house

verb (vėrb) *n.* a word that tells what is or what is done; a part of speech that expresses action or state. *Examples*: be, do, go, come, sit, eat. [< L *verbum*, originally, word]

☞ **Verbs.** A verb that is used with an object to complete its meaning is said to be *transitive*: *She broke the mirror.* A verb that is used without an object, when the recipient of the action is not named, is *intransitive*: *He fell off the roof.* This is a quality of the construction rather than of the verb. Many verbs in English are used both ways, usually with some distinction in meaning. Transitive: *He wrote two books.* Intransitive: *She cannot write.*

ver·bal (vėr′bəl) *adj.* **1** in words; of words: *A description is a verbal picture.* **2** expressed in spoken words; oral: *a verbal promise, a verbal message.* **3** word for word; literal: *a verbal translation from the French.* **4** in grammar: **a** having to do with a verb. Two common verbal endings are *-ed* and *-ing*. **b** derived from a verb: *a verbal noun.* —*n.* in grammar, a noun, adjective, or other word derived from a verb. [< LL *verbalis* < L *verbum* word, verb]

☞ **verbal noun.** A *verbal noun*, or *gerund*, is the form of the verb ending in *-ing* when used as a noun. See the usage note under **gerund.** ☞ See **oral** for another usage note.

ver·bal·ism (vėr′bəl iz′əm) *n.* **1** a verbal expression; word, phrase, etc. **2** too much attention to mere words. **3** a stock phrase or formula in words with little meaning.

ver·bal·ist (vėr′bəl ist) *n.* **1** a person who is skilled in the use or choice of words. **2** a person who pays too much attention to mere words.

ver·bal·i·za·tion (vėr′bəl ə zā′shən or vėr′bəl ī zā′shən) *n.* **1** expression in words. **2** the use of too many words. **3** the change to a verb.

ver·bal·ize (vėr′bəl īz′) *v.* **-ized, -iz·ing. 1** express in words. **2** use too many words; be wordy. **3** change (a noun, etc.) into a verb.

ver·bal·ly (vėr′bəl ē) *adv.* **1** in words. **2** in spoken words; orally: *The dumb boy could not reply verbally, but used signs.* **3** word for word: *The man reported the conversation verbally.* **4** in regard to words only. **5** as a verb: "*Breast*" *is used verbally in* "*The boat breasts the wave.*"

ver·ba·tim (vėr bā′tim) *adv. adj.* word for word; in exactly the same words: *His speech was printed verbatim in the newspaper.* [< Med.L *verbatim* < L *verbum* word]

ver·be·na (vər bē′nə) *n.* any of certain low-growing garden plants having elongated or flattened spikes of flowers having various colors. [< L *verbena* leafy branch. Doublet of VERVAIN.]

ver·bi·age (vėr′bē ij) *n.* the use of too many words; abundance of useless words. [< F *verbiage*, ult. < L *verbum* word]

ver·bose (vėr bōs′) *adj.* using too many words; wordy. [< L *verbosus* < *verbum* word] —**ver·bose′ly,** *adv.* —**ver·bose′ness,** *n.* —**Syn.** See **wordy.**

ver·bos·i·ty (vėr bos′ə tē) *n.* the use of too many words; wordiness.

ver·bo·ten (fer bō′tən) *adj.* forbidden by authority; prohibited. [< G]

ver·dan·cy (vėr′dən sē) *n.* greenness.

ver·dant (vėr′dənt) *adj.* green: *The fields are covered with verdant grass.* [< *verdure*] —**ver′dant·ly,** *adv.*

ver·dict (vėr′dikt) *n.* **1** the decision of a jury: *a verdict of* "*Not guilty.*" **2** a decision; judgment. [ME < AF *verdit* < *ver* true (< L *verus*) + *dit*, pp. of *dire* speak < L *dicere*]

ver·di·gris (vėr′də grēs′ or vėr′də gris′) *n.* **1** a green or bluish coating that forms on brass, copper, or bronze when exposed to the air for long periods of time. **2** a green or bluish-green poisonous compound of copper and acetic acid, used in paints and as a drug. [ME < OF *vert de grece*, literally, green of Greece]

ver·dure (vėr′jər) *n.* **1** fresh greenness. **2** a fresh growth of green grass, plants, or leaves. [ME < OF *verdure*, ult. < L *viridis* green]

hat, āge, cãre, fär; let, ēqual, tėrm; it, īce
hot, ōpen, ôrder; oil, out; cup, pu̇t, rüle, ūse
əbove, takən, pencəl, lemən, circəs
ch, child; ng, long; sh, ship
th, thin; ᴛʜ, then; zh, measure

ver·dur·ous (vėr′jər əs) *adj.* green and fresh.

verge[1] (vėrj) *n. v.* **verged, verg·ing.** —*n.* **1** the edge; rim; brink: *His business is on the verge of ruin.* **2** a limiting belt, strip, or border of something. **3** a rod, staff, etc. carried as an emblem of authority. **4** in architecture, the shaft of a column. —*v.* be on the verge; border: *Her silly talk verged on nonsense.* [ME < OF < L *virga* staff]

verge[2] (vėrj) *v.* **verged, verg·ing.** tend; incline: *She was plump, verging toward fatness.* [< L *vergere*]

ver·ger (vėr′jər) *n.* **1** a man who takes care of a church; sexton. **2** an official who carries the staff or wand before a bishop, dean, etc. [< MF *verger* < *verge* verge[1] < L *virga* staff]

Ver·gil·i·an (vėr jil′ē ən) *adj.* of, having to do with, or suggestive of Vergil, 70-19 B.C., a Roman poet, or his poetry. Also, **Virgilian.**

ver·i·est (ver′ē ist) *adj.* utmost: *the veriest nonsense.*

ver·i·fi·a·ble (ver′ə fī′ə bəl) *adj.* that can be checked or tested and proved to be true.

ver·i·fi·ca·tion (ver′ə fə kā′shən) *n.* **1** proof by evidence or testimony. **2** a demonstration of truth or correctness by facts or circumstances; confirmation: *await the verification of time.* **3** in law, an affidavit added to testimony or a statement by the pleading party declaring that his allegations are true.

ver·i·fy (ver′ə fī′) *v.* **-fied, -fy·ing. 1** prove (something) to be true; confirm: *The driver's report of the accident was verified by eyewitnesses.* **2** test the correctness of; check for accuracy: *Verify the spelling of a word by looking in a dictionary.* **3** in law: **a** testify or affirm to be true, formally or upon oath. **b** declare that one's allegations are true. [ME < OF < Med.L *verificare* < L *verus* true + *facere* make] —**ver′i·fi′er,** *n.* —**Syn. 1** substantiate, corroborate, authenticate.

ver·i·ly (ver′ə lē) *adv.* in truth; truly; really. [< *very* + *-ly*[1]]

ver·i·sim·i·lar (ver′ə sim′ə lər) *adj.* appearing true or real; probable.

ver·i·si·mil·i·tude (ver′ə sə mil′ə tūd′ or ver′ə sə mil′ə tüd′) *n.* **1** appearance of truth or reality; probability: *A story must have verisimilitude to interest most people.* **2** something having merely the appearance of truth. [< L *verisimilitudo* < *verus* true + *similis* like]

ver·i·ta·ble (ver′ə tə bəl) *adj.* true; real; actual. [< F *veritable* < *verité* < L *veritas.* See VERITY.] —**ver′i·ta·ble·ness,** *n.*

ver·i·ta·bly (ver′ə tə blē) *adv.* in truth; truly; really; actually.

ver·i·ty (ver′ə tē) *n.* **-ties. 1** truth. **2** a true statement or a fact. **3** reality. [ME < OF < L *veritas* < *verus* true]

ver·juice (vėr′jüs′) *n.* **1** an acid liquor made from sour juice of crab apples, unripe grapes, etc. Verjuice was formerly used in cooking. **2** sourness, as of temper or expression. [ME < OF *verjus* < *vert* green (< L *viridis*) + *jus* juice < L]

ver·juiced (vėr′jüst′) *adj.* of or having to do with verjuice; sour.

ver·meil (vėr′məl) *n. adj.* **1** *Poetic.* vermilion. **2** silver or bronze coated with gilt. [ME < OF *vermeil* < L *vermiculus*, dim. of *vermis* worm]

ver·mi·cel·li (vėr′mə sel′ē or vėr′mə chel′ē; *Italian,* ver′mē chel′lē) *n.* a mixture of flour and water, like macaroni and spaghetti, but made in long, slender, solid threads. [< Ital. *vermicelli*, literally, little worms, ult. < L *vermis* worm]

ver·mi·cide (vėr′mə sīd′) *n.* any agent that kills worms; especially, a drug used to kill parasitic intestinal worms. [< L *vermis* worm + E *-cide*[2]]

ver·mic·u·lar (vėr mik′yů lər) *adj.* **1** of, having to do with, or characteristic of a worm or worms. **2** like a worm in nature, form, or method of movement. **3** like the wavy track of a worm. **4** marked with close wavy lines. **5** worm-eaten. [< Med.L *vermicularis*, ult. < L *vermis* worm]

ver·mi·form (vėr′mə fôrm′) *adj.* shaped like a worm. [< Med.L *vermiformis* < L *vermis* worm + *forma* form]

vermiform appendix in anatomy, a slender tube, closed at one end, growing out of the large intestine in the lower right-hand part of the abdomen. Appendicitis is inflammation of the vermiform appendix.

ver·mi·fuge (vėr′mə fūj′) *n.* a medicine to expel worms from the intestines. [< F < L *vermis* worm + *fugare* cause to flee]

ver·mil·ion (vər mil′yən) *n.* **1** a bright red. **2** a bright-red coloring matter. —*adj.* bright-red. —*v.* color or paint with, or as with, vermilion: *A blush vermilioned her face.* [ME < OF *vermillon* < *vermeil.* See VERMEIL.]

ver·min (vėr′mən) *n.pl. or sing.* **1** small animals that are troublesome or destructive. Fleas, lice, bedbugs, rats, and mice are vermin. **2** *Esp.Brit.* animals or birds that destroy game, poultry, etc. **3** a vile, worthless person or persons. [ME < OF *vermin*, ult. < L *vermis* worm]

ver·min·ous (vėr′mən əs) *adj.* **1** infested with vermin. **2** caused by vermin. **3** like vermin; vile; worthless.

ver·mouth (vər müth′ or vėr′müth) *n.* a white wine flavored with herbs and used as a liqueur or in cocktails. Vermouth may be either dry or sweet, and ranges in color from pale yellow to reddish brown. [< F < G *Wermut(h)* wormwood, with which it was originally flavored]

ver·nac·u·lar (vər nak′yů lər) *n.* **1** a native language; language used by the people of a certain country or place. **2** everyday language; informal speech. **3** the language of a profession, trade, etc.: *the vernacular of the lawyers.*
—*adj.* **1** used by the people of a certain country, place, etc.; native: *English is our vernacular tongue.* **2** of or in the native or everyday language, rather than a literary or learned language. [< L *vernaculus* domestic, native < *verna* home-born slave]

ver·nal (vėr′nəl) *adj.* **1** of spring; having to do with spring: *vernal green, vernal flowers, vernal months.* **2** like spring; suggesting spring. **3** youthful: *Everyone admired the young girl's vernal freshness.* **4** of flowers, plants, etc., appearing, coming up, or blooming in springtime. [< L *vernalis* < *ver* spring] —**ver′nal·ly,** *adv.*

vernal equinox the equinox that occurs about March 21.

ver·na·tion (vėr nā′shən) *n.* in botany, the arrangement of leaves in a bud. [< NL *vernatio, -onis* < *vernare* bloom, renew itself]

ver·ni·er (vėr′nē ər or vėr′nēr) *n.* a small, movable scale for measuring a fractional part of one of the divisions of a fixed scale. [after Pierre *Vernier* (1580-1637), a French mathematician]

Ver·o·nal (ver′ə nəl, ver′ə nol, or ver′ə nôl′) *n. Trademark.* barbital. [< G < *Verona*, a city in N. Italy, where the inventor was when he proposed the name of the product]

ve·ron·i·ca (və ron′ə kə) *n.* **1** a kind of plant or shrub having blue, purple, pink, or white flowers. **2** a cloth with a representation of Christ's face. [< NL]

ver·sa·tile (vėr′sə tīl′ or vėr′sə təl) *adj.* **1** able to do many things well: *Sir Winston Churchill was a versatile man: he was successful as a statesman, soldier, author, and painter.* **2** in zoology: **a** turning forward or backward: *the versatile toe of an owl.* **b** moving freely up and down and laterally: *versatile antennae.* **3** in botany, attached at or near the middle so as to swing or turn freely: *a versatile anther.* **4** changeable; fickle; inconstant. [< L *versatilis* turning, ult. < *vertere* turn] —**ver′sa·tile·ly,** *adv.* —**Syn. 1** many-sided.

ver·sa·til·i·ty (vėr′sə til′ə tē) *n.* **-ties.** the state or quality of being versatile.

verse (vėrs) *n.* **1** a form of literary expression using lines of words usually having a regularly repeated stress. Poetry is generally in verse. **2** a single line of verse. **3** a group of such lines: *Sing the first verse of "O Canada."* **4** a type of verse; metre (def. 2): *blank verse, iambic verse.* **5** in the Bible, a short division of a chapter. [late OE *vers* (replacing earlier *fers*) < L *versus*, originally, row, furrow < *vertere* turn around]

versed (vėrst) *adj.* experienced; practised; skilled: *A doctor should be well versed in medical theory.* —**Syn.** proficient, acquainted.

ver·si·cle (vėr′sə kəl) *n.* **1** a little verse. **2** one of a series of short sentences said or sung by the minister during services, to which the people make response. [< L *versiculus*, dim. of *versus.* See VERSE.]

ver·si·fi·ca·tion (vėr′sə fə kā′shən) *n.* **1** the making of verses. **2** the art or theory of making verses. **3** the form or style of poetry; metrical structure.

ver·si·fi·er (vėr′sə fī′ər) *n.* a person who makes verses.

ver·si·fy (vėr′sə fī′) *v.* **-fied, -fy·ing. 1** write verses. **2** tell in verse. **3** turn (prose) into poetry. [< L *versificare* < *versus* verse + *facere* make]

ver·sion (vėr′zhən or vėr′shən) *n.* **1** a translation from one language to another: *a version of the Bible.* **2** one particular statement, account, or description: *Each of the witnesses gave his own version of the accident.* **3** a special form or variant of something: *a Scottish version of the Christmas tree.* [< L *versio, -onis*, originally, a turning < *vertere* turn]

vers li·bre (vãr lē′brə) *French.* free verse; verse that follows no fixed metrical form.

ver·so (vėr′sō) *n.* **-sos** (-səz). **1** in printing, the left-hand page of a book; the back of a page in a book, manuscript, etc. **2** the reverse side of a medal or coin. [< L *verso folio* turned leaf < *versus*, pp. of *vertere* turn]

ver·sus (vėr′səs) *prep.* against. [< L *versus* turned toward, pp. of *vertere* turn]

ver·te·bra (vėr′tə brə) *n.* **-brae** (-brā′ or -brē′) or **-bras.** in anatomy, one of the bones of the backbone. See **skeleton** for diagram. [< L < *vertere* turn]

ver·te·bral (vėr′tə brəl) *adj.* **1** of or having to do with a vertebra or the vertebrae. **2** composed of vertebrae.

ver·te·brate (vėr′tə brit or vėr′tə brāt′) *n.* in biology, an animal that has a backbone. Fish, amphibia, reptiles, birds, and mammals are vertebrates. —*adj.* **1** having a backbone. **2** of, belonging to, or having to do with the group of animals that have a segmented spinal column and a brain case or cranium enclosing the brain. [< L *vertebratus* jointed < *vertebra.* See VERTEBRA.]

ver·te·bra·tion (vėr′tə brā′shən) *n.* division into segments like those of the spinal column; vertebrate formation.

ver·tex (vėr′teks) *n.* **-tex·es** or **-ti·ces. 1** the highest point; top. **2** in anatomy, the top of the head. **3** in astronomy, a point in the heavens directly overhead. **4** in mathematics: **a** a point opposite the base of a triangle, pyramid, etc. The vertex of an angle is the point where the two sides meet. **b** any point of a triangle or polygon. [< L *vertex*, originally, whirl, n. < *vertere* turn] —**Syn. 1** apex, summit.

ver·ti·cal (vėr′tə kəl) *adj.* **1** straight up and down; perpendicular to a level surface. A person standing up straight is in a vertical position. See **horizontal** for diagram. **2** of or at the highest point; of the vertex. **3** directly overhead; at the zenith. **4** so organized as to include many or all stages in the production of some manufactured product: *a vertical union, vertical trusts.* —*n.* a vertical line, plane, circle, position, part, etc. [< LL *verticalis* < *vertex* highest point. See VERTEX.] —**ver′ti·cal·ly,** *adv.*

ver·ti·ces (vėr′tə sēz′) *n.* a pl. of **vertex.**

ver·ti·cil (vėr′tə sil) *n.* in botany, a whorl or circle of leaves, hairs, etc. growing around a stem or central point. [< L *verticillus*, dim. of *vertex.* See VERTEX.]

ver·tig·i·nous (vėr tij′ə nəs) *adj.* **1** whirling; rotary. **2** affected with vertigo; dizzy. **3** of the nature of or having to do with vertigo; likely to cause vertigo. **4** fickle; unstable. [< L *vertiginosus* suffering from dizziness < *vertigo.* See VERTIGO.] —**ver·tig′i·nous·ly,** *adv.* —**ver·tig′i·nous·ness,** *n.*

ver·ti·go (vėr′tə gō′) *n.* **ver·ti·goes** or **ver·tig·i·nes** (vėr tij′ə nēz′). a sensation of dizziness or of giddiness. [< L *vertigo* < *vertere* turn]

ver·tu (vėr tü′ or vėr′tü) *n.* virtu.

ver·vain (vėr′vān) *n.* a kind of plant having small white, blue, or purple flowers. [ME < OF < L *verbena* leafy bough. Doublet of VERBENA.]

verve (vėrv) *n.* enthusiasm; energy; vigor; spirit; liveliness. [< F]

ver·y (ver′ē) *adv. adj.* **ver·i·er, ver·i·est.** —*adv.* **1** much; greatly; extremely: *The sun is very hot.* **2** absolutely; exactly: *in the very same place.* —*adj.* **1** same; identical: *The very people who used to love her hate her now.* **2** even; mere; sheer: *The very thought of blood makes her sick. She wept from very joy.* **3** real; true; genuine: *She seemed a very queen.* **4** actual: *He was caught in the very act of stealing.* [ME < OF *verai,* ult. < L *verus* true] —**Syn.** *adv.* **1** exceedingly, excessively.

very high frequency the band of electromagnetic frequencies between 30 and 300 megacycles. *Abbrev.*: VHF, V.H.F., vhf

Ver·y light (ver′ē) a colored light fired from a pistol as a signal or for temporary illumination. [< Edward W. *Very* (1847-1910), a U.S. naval officer who invented it]

Very pistol a pistol for firing a Very light.

ves·i·cate (ves′ə kāt′) *v.* **-cat·ed, -cat·ing.** cause blisters on; blister.

ves·i·cle (ves′ə kəl) *n.* **1** a small bladder, cavity, sac, or cyst. A blister is a vesicle in the skin. **2** in botany, a small bladder or air cavity resembling a bladder. **3** in geology, a small spherical or oval cavity produced by the presence of bubbles of gas or vapor in volcanic rock. [< L *vesicula,* dim. of *vesica* bladder, blister]

ve·sic·u·lar (və sik′yů lər) *adj.* of or having to do with vesicles; like a vesicle; having vesicles.

ves·per (ves′pər) *n.* **1** an evening prayer, hymn, or service; an evening bell. **2 Vesper,** the evening star. **3** *Obs.* evening. —*adj.* **1** of evening. **2** Sometimes, **Vesper.** of or having to do with vespers. [< L]

ves·pers or **Ves·pers** (ves′pərz) *n.pl.* **1** a church service held in the late afternoon or in the evening. **2** the sixth of the canonical hours. [< Med.L < L *vespera* evening]

ves·per·tine (ves′pər tīn′ or ves′pər tin) *adj.* **1** of or occurring in the evening. **2** in biology, flying or appearing in the evening. Bats and owls are vespertine animals. [< L *vespertinus* < *vesper* evening]

ves·pine (ves′pīn or ves′pən) *adj.* of or having to do with wasps; wasplike. [< L *vespa* wasp]

ves·sel (ves′əl) *n.* **1** a large boat; ship. **2** an airship. **3** a hollow holder or container. Cups, bowls, pitchers, bottles, barrels, tubs, etc. are vessels. **4** a tube carrying blood or other fluid. Veins and arteries are blood vessels. **5** a person regarded as a container of some quality or as made for some purpose (used chiefly in or after Biblical expressions): *a vessel of purity.* [ME < OF < L *vascellum,* double dim. of *vas* vessel]

vest (vest) *n.* **1** a man's sleeveless garment for the upper part of the body worn under a suit, coat, etc. **2** a similar garment worn by women. **3** an undershirt, especially for women and children. **4** *Archaic.* clothing; a garment. —*v.* **1** clothe; robe; dress in vestments: *The vested priest stood before the altar.* **2** furnish with powers, authority, rights, etc.: *Parliament is vested with power to declare war.* **3** put in the possession or control of a person or persons: *The management of the hospital is vested in a board of trustees.* [ME < OF *veste,* ult. < L *vestis* garment] —**vest′less,** *adj.*

A young man wearing a vest

ves·ta (ves′tə) *n.* a kind of short friction match. [< Vesta]

Ves·ta (ves′tə) *n.* in Roman mythology, the goddess of the hearth and household, in whose temple at Rome a sacred fire was always kept burning.

ves·tal (ves′təl) *n.* **1** one of the Vestal Virgins. **2** a virgin. **3** a nun. —*adj.* **1** of a vestal; suitable for a vestal. **2** pure; chaste.

hat, āge, cãre, fär; let, ēqual, tėrm; it, īce
hot, ōpen, ôrder; oil, out; cup, půt, rüle, ūse
əbove, takən, pencəl, lemən, circəs
ch, child; ng, long; sh, ship
th, thin; ᴛʜ, then; zh, measure

Vestal Virgin a priestess of the Roman goddess Vesta. Six Vestal Virgins tended an undying fire in honor of Vesta at her temple in Rome.

vest·ed (ves′tid) *adj.* **1** placed in the possession or control of a person or persons; fixed; settled: *vested rights.* **2** clothed or robed, especially in church garments: *a vested choir.*

vested interest **1** a legally established right to the possession of a real or personal property. **2** a self-interested concern for the preservation of a system, state of affairs, etc.: *Manufacturers have a vested interest in low freight rates.* **3** a person, group, or institution having such a concern.

vest·ee (ves tē′) *n.* a fabric insert, with or without a collar, in the front of a dress, jacket, or blouse. [< *vest* + *-ee,* dim. suffix]

ves·tib·u·lar (ves tib′yů lər) *adj.* of or having to do with a vestibule.

ves·ti·bule (ves′tə būl′) *n.* **1** a passage or hall between the outer door and the inside of a building. **2** the enclosed space at the end of a railway passenger car. **3** in anatomy, a cavity of the body that leads to another cavity. The vestibule of the ear is the central cavity of the internal ear. See **ear** for diagram. [< L *vestibulum*]

ves·tige (ves′tij) *n.* **1** a slight remnant; trace: *Ghost stories are vestiges of a former widespread belief in ghosts.* **2** in biology, a part, organ, etc. that is no longer fully developed or useful. **3** *Rare.* footprint. [< F < L *vestigium* footprint] —**Syn. 1** See **trace.**

ves·tig·i·al (ves tij′ē əl) *adj.* **1** remaining as a vestige of something that has disappeared. **2** in biology, no longer fully developed or useful.

vest·ment (vest′mənt) *n.* **1** a garment, especially a robe or gown for ceremonial wear. **2** a garment worn by a clergyman while performing sacred duties. [ME < OF *vestement,* ult. < L *vestis* garment]

vest-pock·et (vest′pok′it) *adj.* **1** able to fit into a vest pocket. **2** very small.

ves·try (ves′trē) *n.* **-tries. 1** a room in a church, where vestments, etc. are kept. **2** a room in a church or an attached building, used for Sunday school, prayer meetings, etc. **3** in Anglican churches: **a** a committee that helps manage church business. **b** a meeting of parishioners on church business. [ME *vestry* < *vest* vest + *-(e)ry* -ery]

ves·try·man (ves′trē mən) *n.* **-men** (-mən). a member of a committee that helps manage church business.

ves·ture (ves′chər) *n.* **1** clothing; garments. **2** a covering. [ME < OF *vesture,* ult. < L *vestis* garment]

Ve·su·vi·an (və sü′vē ən) *adj.* of, having to do with, or resembling Mount Vesuvius, an active volcano near Naples, Italy; volcanic.

vet[1] (vet) *n. v.* **vet·ted, vet·ting.** *Informal.* —*n.* veterinarian. —*v.* **1** examine and care for as a veterinarian or, sometimes, as a doctor. **2** examine carefully; check: *vet a report.* **3** be a veterinarian.

vet[2] (vet) *n. Informal.* veteran.

vet. 1 veteran. **2** veterinarian. **3** veterinary.

vetch (vech) *n.* a vine or plant of the same family as the pea, grown as food for cattle and sheep. [< dial. OF < L *vicia*]

vet·er·an (vet′ər ən or vet′rən) *n.* **1** a person who has had much experience in war; an old soldier, sailor, or airman, etc. **2** a person who has served in the armed services, especially during wartime. **3** a person who has had much experience in some position, occupation, etc. —*adj.* **1** having had much experience in war: *Veteran troops fought side by side with new recruits.* **2** grown old in service; having had much experience: *a veteran farmer.* [< L *veteranus* < *vetus, -teris* old]

vet·er·i·nar·i·an (vet′ər ə nãr′ē ən or vet′rə nãr′ē ən) *n.* a doctor or surgeon who treats animals.

vet·er·i·nar·y (vet′ər ə ner′ē or vet′rə ner′ē) *adj. n.* **-nar·ies.** —*adj.* having to do with the medical or surgical treatment of animals. —*n.* a veterinarian. [< L *veterinarius* < *veterinus* pertaining to beasts of burden and draft, probably < *vetus, veteris* old (i.e., good for nothing else)]

ve·to (vē′tō) *n.* **-toes,** *adj. v.* **-toed, -to·ing.** —*n.* **1** the right or power to forbid or reject: *The Senate has the power of veto over most bills passed in the House of Commons.* **2** the use of this right: *The Senate's veto kept the bill from becoming a law.* **3** a statement of the reasons for disapproval of a bill passed by a legislature. —*adj.* having to do with a veto: *veto power.* —*v.* **1** reject by a veto. **2** refuse to consent to: *His parents vetoed his plan to buy a motorcycle.* [< L *veto* I forbid] —**ve′to·er,** *n.*

vex (veks) *v.* **1** anger by trifles; annoy; provoke. **2** disturb; trouble. [< L *vexare*]

vex·a·tion (veks ā′shən) *n.* **1** a vexing; being vexed: *His face showed his vexation.* **2** something that vexes. —**Syn. 1** irritation, exasperation, annoyance, chagrin.

vex·a·tious (veks ā′shəs) *adj.* vexing; annoying. —**vex·a′tious·ly,** *adv.* —**vex·a′tious·ness,** *n.*

vex·ed·ly (vek′sid lē) *adv.* with vexation; with a sense of annoyance or vexation.

vexed question a question causing difficulty and debate.

v.i. intransitive verb. (for L *verbum intransitivum*)

Vi virginium.

V.I. **1** Virgin Islands. **2** Vancouver Island.

vi·a (vī′ə or vē′ə) *prep.* by way of; by a route that passes through: *He is going from Montreal to Toronto via the St. Lawrence Seaway.* [< L *via*, abl. of *via* way]

vi·a·bil·i·ty (vī′ə bil′ə tē) *n.* the state, condition, or quality of being viable.

vi·a·ble (vī′ə bəl) *adj.* **1** able to keep alive. **2** able to keep operating or functioning: *a viable economy.* **3** of a fetus or newborn infant, sufficiently developed to maintain life outside the uterus. **4** in botany, capable of living and growing, as a spore or seed. [< F < *vie* life < L *vita*]

Vi·a Dol·o·ro·sa (vē′ə dol′ə rō′sə) *Latin.* **1** the road in Jerusalem travelled by Jesus from the judgment hall to Calvary. **2 via dolorosa,** a path of suffering or torment. [literally, sorrowful way]

vi·a·duct (vī′ə dukt′) *n.* a bridge, especially one consisting of a series of arches or short spans resting on high piers or towers, for carrying traffic over a valley, a part of a city, etc. [< L *via* road + *ductus* a leading; patterned on *aqueduct*]

vi·al (vī′əl) *n.* a small bottle, especially a glass bottle, for holding medicines, etc. [var. of *phial*]

vi·a me·di·a (vī′ə mē′dē ə) *Latin.* a middle way.

vi·and (vī′ənd or vē′ənd) *n.* **1** an article of food. **2 viands,** *pl.* food, especially articles of choice food. [ME < OF *viande* < LL *vivenda* things for living < L *vivenda*, pl., to be lived]

vi·at·i·cum (vī at′ə kəm or vē at′ə kəm) *n.* **-ca** (-kə) or **-cums. 1** Holy Communion given to a person dying or in danger of death. **2** supplies or money for a journey. [< L *viaticum*, ult. < *via* road. Doublet of VOYAGE.]

vibes (vībz) *n.pl. Slang.* **1** a vibraphone. **2** vibrations (def. 4): *The vibes were good at our last party.*

vi·brant (vī′brənt) *adj.* **1** vibrating. **2** resounding; resonant. [< L *vibrans, -antis*, ppr. of *vibrare* vibrate] —**vi′brant·ly,** *adv.*

vi·bra·phone (vī′brə fōn′) *n.* a musical instrument similar to a xylophone but having electrically-operated resonators.

vi·brate (vī′brāt) *v.* **-brat·ed, -brat·ing. 1** move or cause to move rapidly to and fro: *A piano string vibrates and makes a sound when a key is struck.* **2** swing or cause to swing to and fro; set in motion. **3** measure by moving to and fro: *A pendulum vibrates seconds.* **4** be moved; quiver. **5** thrill: *Their hearts vibrated to the appeal.* **6** resound: *The clanging vibrated in his ears.* [< L *vibrare* shake] —**Syn. 1** swing, oscillate. **4** tremble, throb.

vi·bra·tile (vī′brə tīl′ or vī′brə til) *adj.* **1** capable of vibrating or of being vibrated. **2** having a vibratory motion. **3** having to do with vibration.

vi·bra·tion (vī brā′shən) *n.* **1** a rapid movement to and fro; quivering motion; vibrating: *The buses shake the house so much that we feel the vibration.* **2** a rapid or slow movement to and fro. **3** motion back and forth across a position of equilibrium. **4** an emotional stimulus or reaction. —**vi·bra′tion·less,** *adj.*

vi·bra·to (vē brä′tō) *n.* **-tos,** *adv.* —*n.* in music, a vibrating or tremulous effect, produced by slight variations of pitch. —*adv.* tremulously; with much vibration. [< Ital. < L *vibrare* to shake]

vi·bra·tor (vī′brā tər) *n.* **1** something that vibrates. **2** any of various appliances, instruments, or parts that have or cause a vibratory motion or action. **3** an electrical device used to massage a part of the body. **4** in electricity: **a** an apparatus for setting a given component in vibration by means of continual impulses. **b** a device for causing oscillations.

vi·bra·to·ry (vī′brə tô′rē) *adj.* **1** vibrating. **2** having to do with vibration. **3** causing vibration. **4** capable of vibration. **5** consisting of vibration.

vi·bur·num (vī bėr′nəm) *n.* **1** any of several shrubs or small trees of the same family as the honeysuckle, such as the snowball. **2** the dried bark of certain species, used in medicine. [< L]

vic·ar (vik′ər) *n.* **1** in Canada, an Anglican clergyman who acts in place of the rector of a parish. **2** in England, the minister of a parish who is paid a salary by the receiver of tithes. **3** in the Roman Catholic Church, a clergyman who represents the Pope or a bishop. **4** any person acting in place of another; representative. Roman Catholics speak of the Pope as the vicar of Christ. [ME < OF < L *vicarius*, originally adj., substitute < *vicis* (gen. of **vix* change)]

vic·ar·age (vik′ər ij) *n.* **1** the residence of a vicar. **2** the position or duties of a vicar.

vicar apostolic in the Roman Catholic Church, a missionary or titular bishop stationed either in a country where no episcopal see has yet been established, or in one where the succession of bishops has been interrupted.

vic·ar·gen·er·al (vik′ər jen′ər əl or -jen′rəl) *n.* **vic·ars-gen·er·al. 1** in the Roman Catholic Church, a deputy of a bishop or an archbishop, assisting him in the government of the diocese. **2** in the Anglican Church of Canada and in the Church of England, an ecclesiastical officer, usually a layman, who assists a bishop or an archbishop.

vi·car·i·ous (vī kãr′ē əs or vi kãr′ē əs) *adj.* **1** done or suffered for others: *vicarious work.* **2** felt by sharing in others' experience: *The invalid received vicarious pleasure from reading travel stories.* **3** taking the place of another; doing the work of another: *a vicarious agent.* **4** delegated: *vicarious authority.* **5** based upon the substitution of one person for another. **6** in physiology, denoting the performance by or through one organ of functions normally discharged by another; substitutive. [< L *vicarius*. See VICAR.] —**vi·car′i·ous·ly,** *adv.* —**vi·car′i·ous·ness,** *n.*

vic·ar·ship (vik′ər ship′) *n.* the office or position of a vicar.

vice[1] (vīs) *n.* **1** an evil habit or tendency: *Lying and cruelty are vices.* **2** evil; wickedness. **3** an undesirable habit; fault; defect: *Mr. Jones recommended the horse as having no vices.* [ME < OF < L *vitium*] —**Syn. 2** sin, iniquity, depravity, corruption.

vice[2] (vīs) *n.* vise.

vi·ce[3] (vī′sē) *prep.* instead of; in the place of. [< L *vice* (abl. of **vix, vicis* turn, change)]

vice- *prefix.* substitute; deputy; subordinate, as in *vice-president, vice-chairman, vice-chancellor.* [see VICE[3]]

vice-ad·mi·ral (vīs′ad′mə rəl) *n.* in the navy, a commissioned officer senior to a rear-admiral and junior to an admiral. *Abbrev.*: V.Adm.

vice-chan·cel·lor (vīs′chan′sə lər) *n.* a person who substitutes for the regular chancellor or acts as his assistant.

vice-con·sul (vīs′kon′səl) *n.* a person next in rank below a consul.

hat, āge, cãre, fär; let, ēqual, tėrm; it, īce
hot, ōpen, ôrder; oil, out; cup, pu̇t, rüle, ūse
əbove, takən, pencəl, lemən, circəs
ch, child; ng, long; sh, ship
th, thin; ᴛʜ, then; zh, measure

vice·ge·ren·cy (vīs′jēr′ən sē) *n.* **-cies.** the position of vicegerent.

vice·ge·rent (vīs′jēr′ənt) *n.* a person exercising the powers or authority of another; deputy. —*adj.* acting in another's place. [< Med.L *vicegerens* < L *vice* instead (of) + *gerere* manage]

vi·cen·ni·al (vī sen′ē əl) *adj.* **1** of or for twenty years. **2** occurring once every twenty years. [< L *vicennium* twenty-year period < stem of *vicies* twenty times + *annus* year]

vice-pres·i·den·cy (vīs′prez′ə dən sē) *n.* the office or position of vice-president.

vice-pres·i·dent (vīs′prez′ə dənt) *n.* the officer next in rank to the president, who takes the president's place when necessary. *Abbrev.*: V.P. or V.Pres.

vice-pres·i·den·tial (vīs′prez ə den′shəl) *adj.* of or having to do with the vice-president.

vice·re·gal (vīs rē′gəl) *adj.* of or having to do with a viceroy.

vice-re·gent (vīs′rē′jənt) *n.* a person who takes the place of the regular regent whenever necessary.

vice·roy (vīs′roi) *n.* a person ruling as the deputy of the sovereign. [< F *vice-roi* < *vice* vice² (< L) + *roi* king < L *rex*]

vice·roy·al·ty (vīs′roi′əl tē) *n.* the position or district of a viceroy.

vice ver·sa (vī′sə vėr′sə or vīs′ vėr′sə) the other way round; conversely: *John blamed Harry, and vice versa* (*Harry blamed John*). [< L]

Vich·y (vish′ē) *n.* Vichy water.

vi·chys·soise (vish′ē swäz′) *n.* a cream soup made chiefly of potatoes and leeks and sprinkled with chopped chives, usually served cold. [< F < *Vichy*, a city in France, where it originated]

Vichy water **1** a natural mineral water from springs at Vichy, France, containing sodium bicarbonate and other salts, used in the treatment of digestive disturbances, gout, etc. **2** a natural or artificial water of similar composition.

vic·i·nage (vis′ə nij) *n.* neighborhood; surrounding district; vicinity. [ME < OF < L *vicinus*. See VICINITY.]

vic·i·nal (vis′ə nəl) *adj.* **1** neighboring. **2** local. [< L *vicinalis* < *vicinus*. See VICINITY.]

vi·cin·i·ty (və sin′ə tē) *n.* **-ties.** **1** a region near or about a place; neighborhood; surrounding district: *He knew many people in Toronto and its vicinity.* **2** a nearness in place; the fact of being close. [< L *vicinitas* < *vicinus* neighboring < *vicus* quarter, village]

vi·cious (vish′əs) *adj.* **1** evil; wicked: *The drunkard led a vicious life.* **2** having bad habits or a bad disposition: *a vicious horse.* **3** not correct; having faults: *This argument contains vicious reasoning.* **4** spiteful; malicious: *vicious words.* **5** *Informal.* unpleasantly severe: *a vicious headache.* [ME < OF *vicieux* < L *vitiosus*] —**vi′cious·ly,** *adv.* —**vi′cious·ness,** *n.*

vicious circle **1** two or more undesirable things, one of which keeps causing the other. **2** in logic, false reasoning that uses one statement to prove a second statement when the first statement really depends upon the second for proof.

vi·cis·si·tude (və sis′ə tūd′ or və sis′ə tüd′) *n.* **1** a change in circumstances, fortune, etc.: *The vicissitudes of life may suddenly make a rich man very poor.* **2** a change; variation. **3** a regular change: *the vicissitude of day and night.* [< L *vicissitudo* < *vicis* (gen.) change. Cf. VICE³.]

vi·comte (vē kôɴᴛ′) *n. French.* viscount.

vic·tim (vik′təm) *n.* **1** a person or animal sacrificed, injured, or destroyed: *victims of war, victims of an accident.* **2** a dupe: *the victim of a swindler.* **3** a person or animal killed as a sacrifice to a god. [< L *victima*]

vic·tim·i·za·tion (vik′təm ə zā′shən or vik′təm ī zā′shən) *n.* the act of victimizing or the state of being victimized.

vic·tim·ize (vik′təm īz′) *v.* **-ized, -iz·ing.** **1** make a victim of; cause to suffer. **2** cheat; swindle. —**vic′tim·iz′er,** *n.*

vic·tor (vik′tər) *n.* a winner; conqueror. —*adj.* victorious. [< L *victor* < *vincere* conquer]

vic·to·ri·a (vik tô′rē ə) *n.* **1** a low, four-wheeled carriage with a folding top and a seat for two passengers. **2** a huge rose-white water lily. [after Queen *Victoria* (1819-1901), Queen of Great Britain and Ireland from 1837 to 1901]

Victoria Cross a bronze medal in the shape of a Maltese cross, the highest award given in the British Commonwealth to members of the armed forces for bravery in the presence of the enemy.

The Victoria Cross

Victoria Day in Canada, a national holiday falling on the Monday before or on the 24th of May, the birthday of Queen Victoria. Also called **Commonwealth Day** and, formerly, **Empire Day.**

Vic·to·ri·an (vik tô′rē ən) *adj.* **1** of or having to do with the reign of Victoria (1819-1901), Queen of Great Britain and Ireland from 1837 to 1901. **2** possessing characteristics attributed to Victorians, such as prudishness, smugness, bigotry, etc. **3** of or having to do with the city of Victoria, British Columbia. —*n.* **1** a person, especially an author, who lived during the reign of Queen Victoria. **2** a native or inhabitant of Victoria, British Columbia.

Victorian age the period during the reign of Queen Victoria, from 1837 to 1901.

Vic·to·ri·an·ism (vik tô′rē ən iz′əm) *n.* **1** the ideas, beliefs, morals, ways of living, etc. common during the reign of Queen Victoria. **2** a novel, piece of furniture, building, etc. characteristic of the Victorian age.

vic·to·ri·ous (vik tô′rē əs) *adj.* **1** having won a victory, conquering: *a victorious army.* **2** of or having to do with victory: *a victorious war.* —**vic·to′ri·ous·ly,** *adv.* —**vic·to′ri·ous·ness,** *n.*

vic·to·ry (vik′tə rē or vik′trē) *n.* **-ries.** a defeat of an enemy or opponent; success in a contest. [< L *victoria*, ult. < *vincere* conquer]

Syn. Victory, conquest, triumph = success in a contest or struggle. **Victory** emphasizes winning a contest or fight of any kind, and suggests defeating the opponent or enemy: *We celebrated our victory.* **Conquest** adds and emphasizes bringing the defeated thing or country under complete or absolute control and reducing defeated people to subjects or slaves: *Some day we may complete the conquest of disease.* **Triumph** applies to a glorious victory of conquest: *The granting of the vote to women was a triumph for the suffragettes.*

Vic·tro·la (vik trō′lə) *n. Trademark.* a kind of phonograph.

vict·ual (vit′əl) *n. v.* **-ualled** or **-ualed, -ual·ling** or **-ual·ing.** —*n.* Usually, **victuals,** *pl.* food. —*v.* **1** supply with food. **2** take on a supply of food: *The ship will victual before sailing.* [ME < OF *vitaille* < LL *victualia*, pl., ult. < *vivere* live]

vict·ual·ler or **vict·ual·er** (vit′əl ər) *n.* **1** a person who supplies food or provisions to a ship, an army, etc. **2** *Esp.Brit.* the keeper of an inn, tavern, saloon, etc. **3** a ship that carries provisions for other ships or for troops.

vi·cu·ña (vi kün′yə or vi kū′nə) *n.* **1** a South American mammal resembling a llama, having a soft, delicate wool. **2** a cloth made from this wool, or from some substitute. [< Sp. < Quechua]

vid. vide.

vi·de (vī′dē or wē′dā) *v. Latin.* see.

vi·de in·fra (vī′dē or wē′dā in′frə) *Latin.* see below (in the same page, article, book, etc.).

vi·de·li·cet (və del′ə set′) *adv.* that is to say; to wit; namely. *Abbrev.*: viz. [< L *videlicet*, for *videre licet* it is permissible to see] ☛ See **viz.** for usage note.

vid·e·o (vid′ē ō′) *adj.* in television, of or used in the transmission or reception of images. —*n.* television. [< L *video* I see]

vid·e·o·tape (vid′ē ō tāp′) *n. v.* **-taped, -tap·ing.** —*n.* **1** in television, a wide magnetic tape for recording and reproducing both sound and picture. **2** a recording made on such a tape. —*v.* record on videotape.

vi·de su·pra (vī′dē or wē′ dā sü′prə) *Latin.* see above (in the same page, article, book etc.).

vi·dette (vi det′) *n.* vedette.

vie (vī) **vied, vy·ing.** strive for superiority; contend in rivalry; compete. [< F *envier* challenge < L *invitare* invite]

Vi·en·nese (vē′ə nēz′) *adj. n.* **-nese.** —*adj.* of or having to do with Vienna, the capital of Austria, or its people. —*n.* a native or inhabitant of Vienna.

Vi·et·nam·ese (vē′ət nə mēz′) *adj.* of or having to do with Vietnam, a country in S.E. Asia, or its people. —*n.* a native or inhabitant of Vietnam.

view (vū) *n.* **1** an act of seeing; sight: *It was our first view of the ocean.* **2** the power of seeing; the range of the eye: *A ship came into view.* **3** something seen; a scene: *The view from our house is beautiful.* **4** a picture of some scene: *Various views of the mountains hung on the walls.* **5** a mental picture; idea: *This book will give you a general view of the war.* **6** a way of looking at or considering a matter; opinion: *What are your views on the subject?* **7** an aim; purpose: *It is my view to leave tomorrow.* **8** a prospect; expectation: *with no view of success.* **9 in view,** **a** in sight. **b** under consideration. **c** as a purpose or intention. **d** as a hope; as an expectation. **10 in view of,** considering; because of. **11 on view,** to be seen; open for people to see. **12 take a dim view of,** look upon or regard with disapproval, doubt, pessimism, etc. **13 with a view to,** **a** with the purpose or intention of. **b** with a hope of; expecting to.
—*v.* **1** see; look at: *They viewed the scene with pleasure.* **2** consider; regard: *The plan was viewed favorably.* [ME < AF *vewe* < OF *veoir* see < L *videre*]
Syn. *n.* **1** look, survey, inspection, scrutiny. **3 View, scene** = something seen. **View** emphasizes the idea of something actually seen through the eyes, and applies to what is presented to the sight, or within the range of vision, of someone looking from a certain point or position: *That new building spoils the view from our windows.* **Scene** emphasizes the idea of something that can be seen, and applies to a landscape or setting that is spread out before the eyes: *We have a fine view of the mountain scene.* **5** notion, conception, impression. **6** See **opinion.** –*v.* **1** behold, witness, survey, examine, scan.

view·er (vū′ər) *n.* **1** a person who views: *a television viewer.* **2** a device for viewing, especially a small instrument for viewing photographic transparencies. **3** the person appointed to examine or inspect something, especially by a law court. **4** an overseer, manager, or superintendent of a coal mine.

view·find·er (vū′fīnd′ər) *n.* in photography, a camera device that shows the scene or area within view of the lens. Also, **view finder.**

view·less (vū′lis) *adj.* **1** without views or opinions. **2** without a view: *a viewless room.*

view·point (vū′point′) *n.* **1** the place from which one looks at something. **2** an attitude of mind: *A heavy rain that is good from the viewpoint of farmers may be bad from the viewpoint of tourists.*

vi·ges·i·mal (vī jes′ə məl) *adj.* **1** twentieth. **2** in or by twenties. [< L *vigesimus* twentieth]

vig·il (vij′əl) *n.* **1** a staying awake for some purpose; a watching; watch: *All night the mother kept vigil over the sick child.* **2** a night spent in prayer. **3** the day and night before a solemn church festival. **4** Often, **vigils,** *pl.* devotions, prayers, services, etc. on the night before a religious festival. [ME < OF < L *vigilia* < *vigil* watchful]

vig·i·lance (vij′ə ləns) *n.* **1** watchfulness; alertness; caution: *Constant vigilance is necessary in order to avoid accidents in driving.* **2** sleeplessness.

vigilance committee **1** a self-appointed and unauthorized committee of citizens to maintain order and punish criminals. **2** formerly, in the southern United States, a self-appointed organization of Southern white citizens whose aim was to intimidate, suppress, and terrorize Negroes, abolitionists, and carpetbaggers.

vig·i·lant (vij′ə lənt) *adj.* watchful; alert: *The dog kept a vigilant guard over the children.* [< L *vigilans, -antis* watching < *vigil* watchful] —**vig′i·lant·ly,** *adv.* —**Syn.** wary, sharp. See **watchful.**

vig·i·lan·te (vij′ə lan′tē) *n.* a member of a vigilance committee. [< Sp. *vigilante* vigilant]

vi·gnette (vin yet′) *n. v.* **-gnet·ted, -gnet·ting.** —*n.* **1** a decorative design on a page of a book, especially on the title page. **2** a literary sketch; a short verbal description. **3** an engraving, drawing, photograph, or the like, that shades off gradually at the edge. —*v.* **1** make a vignette of. **2** in photography, finish (a photograph or portrait) in the manner of a vignette. [< F *vignette,* dim. of *vigne* vine]

vig·or or **vig·our** (vig′ər) *n.* **1** active physical strength or force; flourishing physical condition. **2** mental activity, energy, or power; moral strength or force. **3** strong or energetic action; intensity of action. **4** legal or binding force; validity: *a law in full vigor.* [ME < OF < L < *vigere* thrive]

vi·go·ro·so (vē′gō rō′sō) in music: —*adj.* vigorous; energetic. —*adv.* vigorously. [< Ital.]

vig·or·ous (vig′ər əs) *adj.* full of vigor; strong and active; energetic; forceful: *wage a vigorous war against disease.* —**vig′or·ous·ly,** *adv.*
Syn. Vigorous, strenuous = having or showing active strength or energy. **Vigorous,** describing a person or thing, emphasizes being full of healthy physical or mental energy or power and displaying active strength or force: *The old man is still vigorous and lively.* **Strenuous** emphasizes a constant driving force and indulgence in continuous energetic activity: *A diving champion leads a strenuous life.*

Vi·king or **vi·king** (vī′king) *n.* **1** one of the hordes of Norsemen who raided the coasts of Europe during the eighth, ninth, and tenth centuries A.D. Some of them reached as far as North America. **2** any sea rover. **3** a Scandinavian. [< ON *vikingr;* cf. OE *wicing* < *wic* camp < L *vicus* village]

vil·a·yet (vil′ä yet′) *n.* in Turkey, a province or main governmental division. [< Turkish < Arabic *welāyet*]

vile (vīl) *adj.* **vil·er, vil·est.** **1** very bad: *vile weather.* **2** foul; disgusting; obnoxious: *a vile smell.* **3** evil; low; immoral: *vile language.* **4** poor; mean; lowly: *the vile tasks of the kitchen.* **5** of little worth or account; trifling: *the vile weeds in the fields.* [ME < OF < L *vilis* cheap] —**vile′ly,** *adv.* —**vile′ness,** *n.* —**Syn. 3** See **base**[2].

vil·i·fi·ca·tion (vil′ə fə kā′shən) *n.* a vilifying or being vilified.

vil·i·fy (vil′ə fī′) *v.* **-fied, -fy·ing.** speak evil of; revile; slander. [ME < LL *vilificare* < L *vilis* vile + *facere* make] —**vil′i·fi′er,** *n.* —**Syn.** disparage.

vil·la (vil′ə) *n.* a house in the country or suburbs, sometimes at the seashore. A villa is usually a large or elegant residence. [< Ital. < L]

vil·lage (vil′ij) *n.* **1** a group of dwellings forming a rural community. **2** in Canada, the smallest urban municipal unit: *In most provinces a village must have a minimum population of 100 in order to be incorporated.* **3** the people of a village. [ME < OF *village,* ult. < L *villa* country house]

vil·lag·er (vil′ij ər) *n.* a person who lives in a village.

vil·lain (vil′ən) *n.* **1** a scoundrel; wicked person. **2** a playful name for a mischievous person. **3 a** a character in a play, novel, etc. whose evil motives or actions form an important element in the plot. **b** an actor who regularly plays parts of this nature. **4** a villein. [ME < OF < Med.L *villanus* farmhand < L *villa* country house] —**Syn. 1** miscreant, reprobate, malefactor.

vil·lain·ous (vil′ən əs) *adj.* **1** very wicked. **2** extremely bad; vile. —**vil′lain·ous·ly,** *adv.* —**vil′lain·ous·ness,** *n.*

vil·lain·y (vil′ən ē) *n.* **-lain·ies.** **1** great wickedness. **2** a very wicked act; crime. —**Syn. 1** baseness, rascality, infamy.

vil·la·nelle (vil′ə nel′) *n.* a form of poem of 19 lines with two rhymes, written in five tercets with a final quatrain. [< F < Ital. *villanella* < *villa* villa]

vil·lein (vil′ən) *n.* in the Middle Ages, one of a class of half-free peasants. A villein was under the control of his lord, but in his relations with other men had the rights of a freeman. [var. of *villain*]

vil·lein·age (vil′ən ij) *n.* **1** the fact or state of being a villein. **2** the conditions under which a villein held his land.

vil·li (vil′ī or vil′ē) *n.* pl. of **vil·lus. 1** in anatomy, tiny hairlike parts growing out of the membrane of the small intestine. The villi absorb certain substances. **2** in botany, the soft hairs covering the fruit, flowers, etc. of certain plants. [< L *villi,* pl. of *villus* tuft of hair]

vil·lous (vil′əs) *adj.* having villi; covered with villi.

vil·lus (vil′əs) *n.* sing. of **villi.**

vim (vim) *n.* force; energy; vigor. [< L *vim,* accus. of *vis* force]

vin·ai·grette (vin′ə gret′) *n.* an ornamental bottle or box for smelling salts, etc. [< F *vinaigrette* < *vinaigre.* See VINEGAR.]

vin·ci·ble (vin′sə bəl) *adj.* conquerable. [< L *vincibilis* < *vincere* conquer]

vin·cu·lum (ving′kyů ləm) *n.* **-la** (-lə). **1** a tie. **2** in mathematics, a line drawn over several terms to show that they are to be considered together, as in $\overline{a + b} \times c$ [< L *vinculum* bond < *vincire* bind]

vin·di·cate (vin′də kāt′) *v.* **-cat·ed, -cat·ing. 1** clear from suspicion, dishonor, hint, or charge of wrongdoing, etc.: *The verdict of "Not guilty" vindicated him.* **2** defend successfully against opposition; uphold; justify: *The heir vindicated his claim to the fortune.* [< L *vindicare* < *vindex, vindicis* defender] **—vin′di·ca′tor,** *n.*

vin·di·ca·tion (vin′də kā′shən) *n.* **1** the act or process of clearing from any charge of wrongdoing. **2** justification: *The successful invention was a vindication of his new idea.*

vin·dic·a·tive (vin dik′ə tiv or vin′də kā′tiv) *adj.* tending to vindicate; justifying.

vin·dic·tive (vin dik′tiv) *adj.* **1** feeling a strong tendency toward revenge; bearing a grudge: *He is so vindictive that he never forgives anybody.* **2** showing a strong tendency toward revenge: *Vindictive acts rarely do much good.* [< L *vindicta* revenge] **—vin·dic′tive·ly,** *adv.* **—vin·dic′tive·ness,** *n.* **—Syn. 1, 2** revengeful, spiteful.

vine (vīn) *n.* **1** a plant having a long, slender stem, that grows along the ground or that climbs by attaching itself to a wall, tree, or other support. **2** a grapevine. [ME < OF < L *vinea* < *vinum* wine] **—vine′like′,** *adj.*

vin·e·gar (vin′ə gər) *n.* **1** a sour liquid produced by the fermentation of cider, wine, etc. and consisting largely of dilute, impure acetic acid. Vinegar is used in flavoring and preserving food. **2** speech or temper of a sour or acid character. [ME < MF *vinaigre* < *vin* wine (< L *vinum*) + *aigre* sour < L *acer*]

vin·e·gar·y (vin′ə gər ē or vin′ə grē) *adj.* of or like vinegar; sour.

vine·yard (vin′yərd) *n.* **1** a place planted with grapevines. **2** a field or sphere of activity, especially religious work. [< *vine* + *yard*[1]]

vingt-et-un (vaɴ′tā œɴ′) *n.* twenty-one; blackjack (def. 5). [< F]

vi·nous (vī′nəs) *adj.* **1** of wine; like wine; having to do with wine. **2** caused by drinking wine. [< L *vinosus* < *vinum* wine]

vin·tage (vin′tij) *n.* **1** the wine from a certain crop of grapes: *The finest vintages cost much more than others.* **2** a year's crop of grapes. **3** the year in which a particular wine, particularly one of outstanding quality, was produced. **4** the gathering of grapes for making wine. **5** the season of gathering grapes and making wine. **6** *Informal.* the crop or output of anything at some particular time: *Her old hat was of the vintage of 1930.* —*adj.* excellent of its kind; outstanding: *a vintage year, a vintage crop.* [ME < AF *vintage,* alteration of OF *vendange* < L *vindemia* < *vinum* wine + *demere* take off; influenced by *vintner*]

vint·ner (vint′nər) *n. Esp.Brit.* a person who buys and sells wine; a dealer in wine. [earlier *vinter* < AF *vinetier,* ult. < L *vinum* wine]

vi·nyl (vī′nil or vin′il) *n.* **1** a univalent radical present in certain organic compounds derived from ethylene. *Formula*: CH_2CH **2** a tough plastic or resin formed from this, used in floor coverings, toys, phonograph records, etc.

vi·ol (vī′əl) *n.* a stringed musical instrument, usually having six strings and played with a curved bow. Viols were used mainly in the 17th and 18th centuries and were the forerunners of the modern violin, cello, etc. [ME *viel* < OF *viole, vielle* < Med.L *vitula* fiddle < *Vitula* Goddess of Joy]

hat, āge, cãre, fär; let, ēqual, tėrm; it, īce
hot, ōpen, ôrder; oil, out; cup, pů̇t, rüle, ūse
əbove, takən, pencəl, lemən, circəs
ch, child; ng, long; sh, ship
th, thin; ᴛʜ, then; zh, measure

vi·o·la (vē ō′lə or vī ō′lə) *n.* a stringed musical instrument resembling a violin but somewhat larger, having a lower range of pitches and a more sombre tone; a tenor or alto violin. [< Ital.]

vi·o·la·ble (vī′ə lə bəl) *adj.* that can be violated. [< L *violabilis* < *violare.* See VIOLATE.]

vi·o·la da gam·ba (vē ō′lə dä gäm′bä) **1** an early instrument of the viol family, resembling the modern cello; bass viol. **2** an open organ stop having a string tone. [< Ital.; literally, violin for the leg]

vi·o·late (vī′ə lāt′) *v.* **-lat·ed, -lat·ing. 1** break (a law, rule, agreement, promise, etc.); act contrary to; fail to perform: *He violated the law and was arrested by the police.* **2** treat with disrespect or contempt: *The soldiers violated the church by using it as a stable.* **3** break in upon; disturb: *The sound of guns violated the usual calm of Sunday morning.* **4** trespass on; infringe on: *violate the right of free speech.* **5** use force against (a woman or girl); rape. [ME < L *violare* < *vis* violence] **—vi′o·la′tor,** *n.* **—Syn. 2** dishonor.

vi·o·la·tion (vī′ə lā′shən) *n.* **1** the use of force; violence. **2** a breaking (of a law, rule, agreement, promise, etc.). **3** the treatment (of a holy thing) with contempt. **4** an interruption or disturbance (of sleep, privacy, etc.). **5** ravishment; rape. **—Syn. 2** infringement, infraction, breach.

vi·o·lence (vī′ə ləns) *n.* **1** rough force in action: *He slammed the door with violence.* **2** rough or harmful action or treatment. **3** harm; injury: *It would do violence to her principles to work on Sunday.* **4** in law: **a** the illegal or unjust use of physical force to injure or damage persons or property. **b** intimidation by threatening such use of force. **c** an instance of using such force or intimidation. **5** strength of action, feeling, etc. **6** the improper treatment or use of a word; distortion of meaning or application. **7** rape. [ME < OF < L *violentia*]

vi·o·lent (vī′ə lənt) *adj.* **1** acting or done with strong, rough force: *a violent blow.* **2** caused by strong, rough force: *a violent death.* **3** showing or caused by very strong feeling, action, etc.: *violent language.* **4** severe; extreme; very great: *a violent pain.* **5** that tends to distort meaning. [ME < OF < L *violentus* < *vis* force] **—vi′o·lent·ly,** *adv.* **—Syn. 1** fierce, furious. **3** vehement.

vi·o·let (vī′ə lit) *n.* **1** any of various stemless or leafy-stemmed plants having purple, blue, yellow, pink, or white flowers. **2** the flower of any of these plants. Some violets are very fragrant. **3** any of several similar but unrelated plants or their flowers (used with a qualifying word): *the dogtooth violet.* **4** a bluish purple. Violet is red and blue mixed. —*adj.* bluish-purple. [ME < OF *violette,* ult. < L *viola*]

violet rays the shortest rays of the spectrum that can be seen; rays having wave lengths of around 3,850 angstroms.

vi·o·lin (vī′ə lin′) *n.* a stringed musical instrument played with a bow and having four strings, an extensive range of pitches, and a tone of great variety and richness. [< Ital. *violino,* dim. of *viola* viol]

vi·o·lin·ist (vī′ə lin′ist) *n.* a person who plays the violin.

vi·ol·ist (vī′əl ist) *n.* a person who plays the viol.

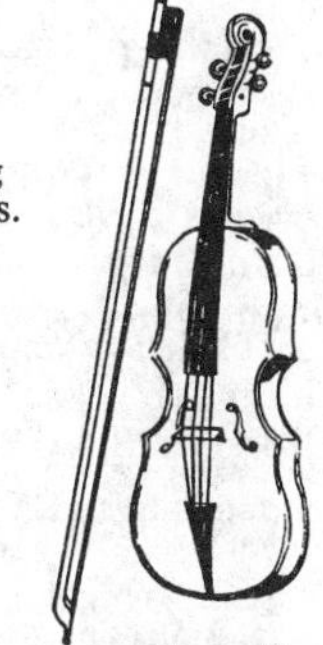
A violin and bow

vi·o·lon·cel·list (vī′ə lən chel′ist or vē′ə lən chel′ist) *n.* a cellist.

vi·o·lon·cel·lo (vī′ə lən chel′ō or vē′ə lən chel′ō) *n.* **-los.** a cello. [< Ital. *violoncello*, ult. < *viola* viol]

vi·os·ter·ol (vī os′tər ol′ or vī os′tər ōl′) *n.* an oil used as a medicine to prevent or cure rickets.

VIP *Informal.* very important person.

vi·per (vī′pər) *n.* **1** a thick-bodied poisonous snake having a pair of large, perforated fangs. **2** a spiteful, treacherous person. [< L *vipera* < *vivus* alive + *parere* bring forth]

vi·per·ous (vī′pər əs) *adj.* **1** of or having to do with a viper or vipers. **2** like a viper. **3** spiteful; treacherous. —**vi′per·ous·ly,** *adv.* —**vi′per·ous·ness,** *n.*

vi·ra·go (və rā′gō or və rä′gō) *n.* **-goes** or **-gos.** a violent, bad-tempered, or scolding woman. [< L *virago* < *vir* man]

vir·e·lay (vir′ə lā′) *n.* an old French form of short poem with two rhymes to a stanza. [ME < OF *virelai* < *vireli* a refrain]

vir·e·o (vir′ē ō′) *n.* **-e·os.** any of a group of small, olive-green, insect-eating songbirds. [< L *vireo* a small bird, possibly the greenfinch]

vi·res·cence (vī res′əns) *n.* greenness; a turning green.

vi·res·cent (vī res′ənt) *adj.* turning green; tending to a green color; greenish. [< L *virescens, -entis*, ppr. of *virescere* turn green]

Vir·gil·i·an (vėr jil′ē ən) *adj.* Vergilian.

vir·gin (vėr′jən) *n.* **1** a woman, especially a young one, who has not had sexual intercourse. **2** an unmarried woman, especially a young woman or girl. **3** Also, **Virgin,** a picture or image of the Virgin Mary. **4 the Virgin,** the Virgin Mary. **5 Virgin,** in astrology, the sixth sign of the zodiac; Virgo.
—*adj.* **1** being a virgin or virgins; chaste. **2** of, having to do with, or characteristic of a virgin: *virgin modesty.* **3** pure; spotless: *Virgin snow is newly fallen snow.* **4** not yet used: *virgin soil.* [ME < OF < L *virgo, -inis*]

vir·gin·al[1] (vėr′jə nəl) *adj.* **1** of or suitable for a virgin; maidenly. **2** fresh; pure; unsullied; untouched. [ME < L *virginalis* < *virgo, -inis* maiden] —**vir′gin·al·ly,** *adv.*

vir·gin·al[2] (vėr′jə nəl) *n.* a musical instrument like a small harpsichord, but set in a box without legs. It was much used, especially in England, in the 16th and 17th centuries. [apparently < *virginal*[1]]

A woman playing a virginal

virgin birth the doctrine that Jesus was miraculously conceived by the Virgin Mary.

Virginia creeper a climbing plant having leaves with five leaflets and bluish-black berries; woodbine.

Virginia reel **1** a North American country-dance in which the partners form two lines facing each other and perform a number of dance steps. **2** the music for such a dance.

vir·gin·i·ty (vər jin′ə tē) *n.* **1** a virgin condition; maidenhood. **2** the state of being a virgin; purity; freshness.

vir·gin·i·um (vər jin′ē əm) *n.* francium, a chemical element. [< NL *virginium* < *Virginia*, U.S.A.]

Virgin Mary the mother of Jesus Christ; Our Lady.

vir·gin's-bow·er (vėr′jənz bou′ər) *n.* a climbing clematis that has clusters of white flowers.

Vir·go (vėr′gō) *n.* **1** in astronomy, a constellation on the celestial equator supposed to resemble a woman in form. **2** in astrology, the sixth sign of the zodiac; Virgin. The sun enters Virgo about August 22. [< L *virgo* maiden]

vir·gule (vėr′gūl) *n.* a slanting stroke (/) between two words, indicating that either word applies, as in *and/or.* [< L *virgula* little rod]

vir·i·des·cence (vir′ə des′əns) *n.* the condition of being viridescent.

vir·i·des·cent (vir′ə des′ənt) *adj.* greenish. [< LL *viridescens, -entis*, ppr. of *viridescere* turn green < L *viridis* green]

vir·ile (vir′īl or vir′əl) *adj.* **1** manly; masculine. **2** full of manly strength or masculine vigor. **3** vigorous; forceful. [< L *virilis* < *vir* man]

vi·ril·i·ty (və ril′ə tē) *n.* **-ties. 1** manly strength; masculine vigor. **2** manhood. **3** vigor; forcefulness.

vi·ro·log·i·cal (vī′rə loj′ə kəl) *adj.* of or having to do with virology.

vi·rol·o·gist (vī rol′ə jist) *n.* one who is skilled in virology.

vi·rol·o·gy (vī rol′ə jē) *n.* the study of viruses and virus diseases.

vir·tu (vėr tü′ or vėr′tü) *n.* **1** excellence or merit in an object of art because of its workmanship, rarity, antiquity, etc. **2** objects of art; choice curios. **3** a taste for objects of art; knowledge of objects of art. Also, **vertu.** [< Ital. *virtù* excellence < L *virtus* virtue. Doublet of VIRTUE.]

vir·tu·al (vėr′chü əl) *adj.* being something in effect, though not so in name; actual; real: *The battle was won with so great a loss of soldiers that it was a virtual defeat. He is the virtual president, though his title is secretary.*

vir·tu·al·ly (vėr′chü əl ē) *adv.* in effect, though not in name; actually; really.

vir·tue (vėr′chü) *n.* **1** moral excellence; goodness. **2** a particular moral excellence: *Justice and kindness are virtues.* **3** a good quality: *He praised the virtues of the car.* **4** chastity; purity. **5** the power to produce effects: *There is little virtue in that medicine.* **6 by** or **in virtue of,** relying on; because of; on account of. **7 make a virtue of necessity,** do willingly what must be done anyway. [ME < L *virtus* manliness < *vir* man. Doublet of VIRTU.]
—**Syn. 1** uprightness, integrity. See **goodness. 3** merit.

vir·tu·os·i·ty (vėr′chü os′ə tē) *n.* **-ties. 1** the character or skill of a virtuoso. **2** interest or taste in the fine arts.

vir·tu·o·so (vėr′chü ō′sō) *n.* **-sos, -si** (-sē). **1** a person skilled in the methods of an art, especially in playing a musical instrument. **2** a person who has a cultivated appreciation of artistic excellence. **3** a student or collector of objects of art, curios, antiquities, etc. [< Ital. *virtuoso* learned]

vir·tu·ous (vėr′chü əs) *adj.* **1** good; moral; righteous. **2** chaste; pure. —**vir′tu·ous·ly,** *adv.* —**vir′tu·ous·ness,** *n.*
—**Syn. 1** upright, worthy.

vir·u·lence (vir′yu̇ ləns or vir′ə ləns) *n.* **1** the quality of being very poisonous or harmful; deadliness. **2** intense bitterness or spite; violent hostility.

vir·u·len·cy (vir′yu̇ lən sē or vir′ə lən sē) *n.* virulence.

vir·u·lent (vir′yu̇ lənt or vir′ə lənt) *adj.* **1** very poisonous or harmful; deadly: *a virulent poison.* **2** of disease, characterized by a rapid and severe malignant or infectious condition. **3** of a micro-organism, able to cause a disease by breaking down the protective mechanisms of the host. **4** intensely bitter or spiteful; violently hostile. [< L *virulentus* < *virus* poison] —**vir′u·lent·ly,** *adv.*

vi·rus (vī′rəs) *n.* **1** any of a group of disease-producing agents smaller than any known bacteria and dependent upon the living tissue of hosts for their reproduction and growth. **2** a poison produced in a person or animal suffering from an infectious disease. **3** anything that poisons the mind or morals; a corrupting influence. [< L *virus* poison]

virus X an infection or disease of uncertain nature, sometimes resembling influenza.

vis (vis) *n. Latin.* force.

Vis. Viscount.

vi·sa (vē′zə) *n. v.* **-saed, -sa·ing.** —*n.* an official signature or endorsement upon a passport or document, showing that it has been examined and approved. —*v.* examine and sign. Also, **visé.** [< F *visa*, ult. < L *videre* see]

vis·age (viz′ij) *n.* **1** the face. **2** appearance. [ME < OF *visage* < *vis* face < L *visus* a look < *videre* see] —**Syn. 1** See **face.**

vis-à-vis (vē′zə vē′) *adv. adj.* face to face; opposite: *We sat vis-à-vis. The usual position in modern dancing is*

hat, āge, cãre, fär; let, ēqual, tėrm; it, īce
hot, ōpen, ôrder; oil, out; cup, pu̇t, rüle, ūse
əbove, takən, pencəl, lemən, circəs
ch, child; ng, long; sh, ship
th, thin; ᴛʜ, then; zh, measure

vis-à-vis. —*prep.* **1** face to face with; opposite to. **2** in relation to; with regard to. —*n.* a person or thing that is opposite. [< F]

Visc. Viscount.

vis·cer·a (vis′ər ə) *n.* pl. of **vis·cus** (vis′kəs). in anatomy, the internal organs of the body. The heart, stomach, liver, intestines, kidneys, etc. are viscera. [< L *viscera*, pl. of *viscus*]

vis·cer·al (vis′ər əl) *adj.* **1** of or having to do with the viscera. **2** of a disease, affecting the viscera. **3** springing from deep feeling; resulting from an emotional reaction: *visceral indignation.*

vis·cid (vis′id) *adj.* thick and sticky like heavy syrup or glue. [< LL *viscidus* < L *viscum* bird lime]

vis·cose (vis′kōs) *n.* a syruplike solution prepared by treating cellulose with caustic soda and carbon disulphide. Viscose is used in manufacturing rayon, in making a product resembling celluloid, for sizing, etc. [< L *viscosus.* See VISCOUS.]

vis·cos·i·ty (vis kos′ə tē) *n.* **-ties. 1** the quality of being viscous. **2** in physics, the property of a liquid that tends to prevent it from flowing; the frictional resistance of a fluid to the motion of its molecules.

vis·count (vī′kount) *n.* a nobleman ranking next below an earl or count and next above a baron. [ME < AF < OF *visconte* < *vis-* vice- + *comte* count[2]]

vis·count·cy (vī′kount sē) *n.* the title, rank, or dignity of a viscount.

vis·count·ess (vī′koun tis) *n.* **1** the wife or widow of a viscount. **2** a woman holding in her own right a rank equivalent to that of a viscount.

vis·count·y (vī′koun tē) *n.* viscountcy.

vis·cous (vis′kəs) *adj.* **1** of a liquid, sticky; thick like syrup or glue. **2** in physics, having the property of viscosity. [ME < LL *viscosus* < *viscum* bird lime]

vise or **vice** (vīs) *n. v.* **vised, vis·ing.** —*n.* a tool having two jaws moved by a screw, used to hold an object firmly while work is being done on it. —*v.* hold, press, or squeeze with a vise, or as if with a vise. [ME < OF *vis* screw < VL *vitium* < L *vitis* vine]

A vise. It can be fastened to a carpenter's bench by the screw at the bottom.

vi·sé (vē′zā; *French,* vē zā′) *n. v.* **vi·séed, vi·sé·ing.** visa. [< F]

Vish·nu (vish′nü) *n.* in Hindu theology, one of the gods of the trinity of Brahma; the Preserver. [< Skt.]

vis·i·bil·i·ty (viz′ə bil′ə tē) *n.* **-ties. 1** the condition or quality of being visible. **2** the condition of light, atmosphere, etc. with reference to the distance at which things can be clearly seen.

vis·i·ble (viz′ə bəl) *adj.* **1** that can be seen: *The shore was barely visible.* **2** perceptible; apparent; obvious: *The tramp had no visible means of support.* [ME < L *visibilis* < *videre* see]

vis·i·bly (viz′ə blē) *adv.* so as to be visible; plainly; evidently.

Vis·i·goth (viz′ə goth′) *n.* a member of the western division of the Goths. The Goths plundered Rome in A.D. 410, and formed a monarchy in France and N. Spain about A.D. 418. [< LL *Visigothi* < Gmc.; taken as "the western Goths"]

vi·sion (vizh′ən) *n.* **1** the power of seeing; sense of sight: *The old man wears glasses because his vision is poor.* **2** the act or fact of seeing; sight. **3** the power of perceiving by the imagination or by clear thinking: *a prophet of great vision.* **4** something seen in the imagination, in a dream, in one's thoughts, etc.: *The beggar had visions of great wealth.* **5** a phantom. **6** a very beautiful person, scene, etc. —*v.* **1** see in, or as if in, a vision. **2** show in a vision. [ME < L *visio, -onis* < *videre* see]

vi·sion·ar·y (vizh′ən er′ē) *adj. n.* **-ar·ies.** —*adj.* **1** not practical; dreamy: *Ruth is a visionary girl; she spends her time daydreaming.* **2** not practicable; fanciful: *visionary plans for travelling to the stars.* **3** of or belonging to a vision; seen in a vision; imaginary: *The visionary scene faded and John awoke.* **4** having visions; able to have visions.
—*n.* **1** a person who is not practical; dreamer. **2** a person who sees visions. —**Syn.** *adj.* **1** fanciful.

vis·it (viz′it) *v.* **1** go to see; come to see: *visit Victoria.* **2** make a call on or stay with for social or other reasons; be a guest of: *visit one's aunt.* **3** pay a call; make a stay; be a guest: *visit in the country.* **4** go or come to see, to inspect, or to examine officially: *The inspector visited the factory.* **5** come upon; afflict: *Job was visited by many troubles.* **6** send upon; inflict: *visit one's anger on someone.* **7** punish. **8 visit with,** *Informal.* talk with.
—*n.* **1** a visiting; a call from friendship, for purpose of inspection, for medical treatment, etc. **2** a stay as a guest. **3** *Informal.* an informal talk; chat. [< L *visitare,* ult. < *videre* see]

vis·it·ant (viz′ə tənt) *n.* a visitor; guest.
—*adj.* visiting.

vis·it·a·tion (viz′ə tā′shən) *n.* **1** the act of visiting. **2** a visit for the purpose of making an official inspection or examination. A nation at war has the right of visitation of neutral ships to inspect their cargoes. **3** Also, **Visitation,** the visit of the Virgin Mary to Elizabeth, her cousin. Luke 1:39-56. **4 Visitation,** a Christian festival, July 2, in honor of this visit. **5** a punishment or reward sent by God. **6** a severe affliction, blow, or trial, regarded as an instance of divine dispensation.

visiting card a calling card.

vis·i·tor (viz′ə tər) *n.* a person who visits or is visiting.
Syn. **Visitor, guest** = someone who comes to see or stay with another or in a place. **Visitor** is the general word, applying to anyone who comes to see a person or place or makes a call or stay, long or short, for any reason, such as business, pleasure, duty, friendship, curiosity, etc.: *Visitors from the East arrived last night.* **Guest** emphasizes the idea of being entertained, and applies especially to someone invited to come or stay: *He usually entertains his guests at the club.*

vi·sor or **vi·zor** (vī′zər) *n.* **1** the movable front part of a helmet, covering the face. **2** the projecting peak of a cap, intended to protect the eyes from the sun. **3** a mask. **4** a kind of shield or shade attached to the top of a car's windshield as protection from the sun's rays. **5** a small movable shade behind the windshield of a car. —*v.* cover with a visor; protect. [ME < AF *viser* < *vis* face, ult. < L *videre* see]

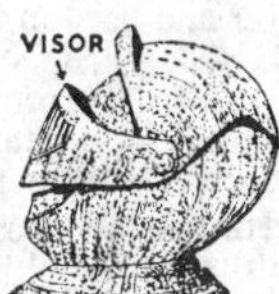

The visor on a helmet

vis·ta (vis′tə) *n.* **1** a view seen through a narrow opening or passage: *The opening between two rows of trees afforded a vista of the lake.* **2** such an opening or passage itself: *a shady vista of elms.* **3** a mental view: *Education should open up new vistas.* [< Ital. *vista,* ult. < L *videre* see]

vis·u·al (vizh′ü əl) *adj.* **1** of or having to do with sight. **2** that can be seen; visible. **3** performed or produced by means of vision: *a visual test.* **4** of vision and light in relation to each other; optical: *the visual focus of a lens.* **5** of the nature of a mental vision; produced or occurring as a picture in the mind: *form a visual image of the author's description.* [< LL *visualis* < L *visus* sight < *videre* see]

visual aid a device or means such as a chart, diagram, motion picture, etc. for aiding the learning process through the sense of sight.

vis·u·al·i·za·tion (vizh′ü əl ə zā′shən or vizh′ü əl ī-zā′shən) *n.* **1** the act of visualizing or the state of being visualized. **2** the thing visualized.

vis·u·al·ize (vizh′ü əl īz′) *v.* **-ized, -iz·ing. 1** form a mental picture of: *visualize a scene.* **2** make visible. **3** form mental pictures.

vis·u·al·ly (vizh′ü əl ē) *adv.* in a visual manner or respect; by sight.

vi·tal (vī′təl) *adj.* **1** of life; having to do with life. **2** necessary to life: *Eating is a vital function. The heart is a vital organ.* **3** very necessary; very important; essential:

An adequate army is vital to the defence of a nation. **4** causing death, failure, or ruin: *a vital wound, a vital blow to an industry.* **5** full of life and spirit; lively. —*n.* **vitals,** *pl.* **a** the parts or organs of the body necessary to live. The brain, heart, lungs, and stomach are vitals. **b** the essential parts or features. [ME < L *vitalis* < *vita* life] —**vi′tal·ly,** *adv.*

vi·tal·ism (vī′təl iz′əm) *n.* a doctrine that the behavior of a living organism is, at least in part, due to a vital principle that cannot possibly be explained by physics and chemistry.

vi·tal·i·ty (vī tal′ə tē) *n.* **-ties. 1** vital force; the power to live: *Her vitality was lessened by illness.* **2** the power to endure and be active. **3** strength or vigor of mind or body.

vi·tal·ize (vī′təl īz′) *v.* **-ized, -iz·ing. 1** give life to. **2** put vitality into. —**vi′tal·i·za′tion,** *n.* —**vi′tal·iz′er,** *n.*

vital statistics 1 facts or data about births, deaths, marriages, etc. **2** *Informal.* the measurements around a woman's bust, waist, and hips.

vi·ta·min (vī′tə min) *n.* any of certain complex organic substances required for the normal growth and nourishment of the body, found especially in milk, butter, raw fruits and vegetables, brewers' yeast, wheat, and cod-liver oil. Lack of vitamins in food causes such diseases as rickets and scurvy as well as general poor health. —*adj.* of or having to do with vitamins. Also, **vitamine.** [< L *vita* life + E *amine* (< *ammonia*)]

vitamin A a fat-soluble vitamin found in milk, butter, cod-liver oil, egg yolk, liver, leafy green vegetables, etc. that increases the resistance of the body to infection and prevents night blindness. It exists in two known forms, A_1 (*Formula*: $C_{20}H_{30}O$) and A_2 (*Formula*: $C_{20}H_{28}O$).

vitamin B_1 thiamine.

vitamin B_2 riboflavin. Also, **vitamin G.**

vitamin B_6 pyridoxine.

vitamin B_{12} a crystalline vitamin found especially in liver and used in treating pernicious anemia. *Formula*: $C_{63}H_{90}N_{14}O_{14}PCo$

vitamin B complex a group of vitamins including vitamin B_1, vitamin B_2, vitamin B_6, etc., found in high concentration in yeast and liver.

vitamin C a crystalline vitamin found especially in citrus fruits and used to prevent scurvy; ascorbic acid. *Formula*: $C_6H_8O_6$

vitamin D a fat-soluble vitamin found in cod-liver oil, milk, and egg yolk. It is necessary for the growth and health of bones and teeth and used to prevent rickets. It exists in many related forms, including D_1, D_2, D_3, D_4.

vitamin E a vitamin found in wheat, lettuce, milk, etc. that is necessary for reproductive processes. Lack of vitamin E causes sterility. *Formula*: $C_{29}H_{50}O_2$

vi·ta·mine (vī′tə min) *n. adj.* vitamin.

vitamin G vitamin B_2.

vitamin H biotin.

vi·ta·min·ize (vī′tə min īz′) *v.* **-ized, -iz·ing.** provide with vitamins.

vitamin K_1 a vitamin found in leafy vegetables, alfalfa, etc. and used to prevent hemorrhages by inducing clotting of the blood.

vitamin K_2 a vitamin similar to vitamin K_1.

vitamin L a vitamin found in beef liver (vitamin L_1) and yeast (vitamin L_2) that promotes normal lactation.

vitamin P a water-soluble vitamin obtained from citrus fruits and paprika and used to promote capillary resistance to hemorrhaging.

vi·tel·lin (vi tel′ən or vī tel′ən) *n.* a protein contained in the yolk of eggs. [< L *vitellus* egg yolk]

vi·ti·ate (vish′ē āt′) *v.* **-at·ed, -at·ing. 1** impair the quality of; spoil: *His illness vitiated his chances of success.* **2** destroy the legal force or authority of: *The contract was vitiated because one person signed under compulsion.* [< L *vitiare* < *vitium* fault] —**vi′ti·a′tion,** *n.*

vit·i·cul·ture (vit′ə kul′chər or vī′tə kul′chər) *n.* the cultivation of grapes. [< L *vitis* vine + E *culture*]

vit·re·ous (vit′rē əs) *adj.* **1** glassy; like glass: *vitreous china.* **2** having to do with glass. **3** made from glass. [< L *vitreus* < *vitrum* glass]

vitreous humor or **humour** the transparent, jelly-like substance that fills that part of the eyeball behind the lens. See eye for diagram.

vit·ri·fac·tion (vit′rə fak′shən) *n.* vitrification.

vit·ri·fi·ca·tion (vit′rə fə kā′shən) *n.* **1** the process of making or becoming glass or a glasslike substance. **2** something vitrified.

vit·ri·form (vit′rə fôrm′) *adj.* having the structure or appearance of glass. [< L *vitrum* glass + E *-form*]

vit·ri·fy (vit′rə fī′) *v.* **-fied, -fy·ing.** change into glass or something like glass. [< F < L *vitrum* glass + *facere* make]

vit·ri·ol (vit′rē əl) *n.* **1** any of certain sulphates, as of copper **(blue vitriol)**, of iron **(green vitriol)**, and of zinc **(white vitriol)**. **2** sulphuric acid. Vitriol burns deeply and leaves very bad scars. **3** very sharp speech or severe criticism. [ME < Med.L *vitriolum*, ult. < L *vitrum* glass]

vit·ri·ol·ic (vit′rē ol′ik) *adj.* **1** of or containing vitriol. **2** like vitriol. **3** bitterly severe; sharp: *vitriolic criticism.*

vi·tu·per·ate (vi tū′pər āt′ or vi tü′pər āt′) *v.* **-at·ed, -at·ing.** find fault with in abusive words; revile. [< L *vituperare* < *vitium* fault + *parare* prepare] —**Syn.** abuse.

vi·tu·per·a·tion (vi tū′pər ā′shən or vi tü′pər ā′shən) *n.* bitter abuse in words; very severe scolding.

vi·tu·per·a·tive (vi tū′pər ə tiv or vi tü′pər ə tiv) *adj.* abusive; reviling. —**vi·tu′per·a·tive·ly,** *adv.*

vi·va (vē′və) *interj.* (long) live (the person or thing named). —*n.* a shout of applause or good will. [< Ital.]

vi·va·ce (vē vä′chā) in music: —*adj.* quick; lively. —*adv.* in a lively manner. —*n.* a lively movement or passage; composition to be played or sung in this manner. [< Ital. < L *vivax, -acis*]

vi·va·cious (vi vā′shəs or vī vā′shəs) *adj.* lively; sprightly; animated; gay. [< L *vivax, -acis*] —**vi·va′cious·ly,** *adv.* —**vi·va′cious·ness,** *n.*

vi·vac·i·ty (vi vas′ə tē or vī vas′ə tē) *n.* **-ties.** liveliness; sprightliness; animation; gaiety. [< L *vivacitas* < *vivax, -acis* lively]

vi·var·i·um (vī văr′ē əm) *n.* **-i·ums** or **-i·a** (-ē ə). a place where animals or plants are kept in, or under circumstances simulating, their natural state. [< L]

vi·va vo·ce (vī′və vō′sē) orally; oral: *Shall we vote viva voce or by ballot?* [< L *viva voce*, literally, by living voice]

vive (vēv) *interj. French.* (long) live (the person or thing named). "Vive la république" means "Long live the Republic."

viv·id (viv′id) *adj.* **1** brilliant; strikingly bright: *Dandelions are a vivid yellow.* **2** full of life; lively: *a vivid description, a vivid imagination.* **3** clearly and strikingly perceived or felt: *a vivid impression, a vivid sensation.* [< L *vividus* < *vivus* alive] —**viv′id·ly,** *adv.* —**viv′id·ness,** *n.*

viv·i·fy (viv′ə fī′) *v.* **-fied, -fy·ing. 1** give life or vigor to. **2** enliven; make vivid. [< L *vivificare* < *vivus* alive + *facere* make] —**viv′i·fi·ca′tion,** *n.*

vi·vip·a·rous (vi vip′ə rəs or vī vip′ə rəs) *adj.* bringing forth living young, rather than eggs. Dogs, cats, cows, and human beings are viviparous. [< L *viviparus* < *vivus* alive + *parere* bring forth]

viv·i·sect (viv′ə sekt′ or viv′ə sekt′) *v.* **1** dissect the living body of. **2** practise vivisection.

viv·i·sec·tion (viv′ə sek′shən) *n.* the act or practice of cutting into or experimenting on living animals for scientific study. [< L *vivus* alive + E *section*]

viv·i·sec·tion·ist (viv′ə sek′shən ist) *n.* **1** a vivisector. **2** a person who favors or defends vivisection.

viv·i·sec·tor (viv′ə sek′tər) *n.* a person who practises vivisection.

vix·en (vik′sən) *n.* **1** a female fox. **2** a bad-tempered or quarrelsome woman. [OE *fyxen < *fox* fox]

vix·en·ish (vik′sən ish) *adj.* ill-tempered; scolding.

Vi·yel·la (vī yel′ə) *n. Trademark.* a soft, lightweight, washable fabric, a blend of cotton and wool.

viz. videlicet.
☛ Viz. is the abbreviation of the Latin *videlicet* to wit; namely. *Viz.* is used only in the language of rather formal documents or reference works. It is usually read "namely."

viz·ard (viz′ərd) *n.* **1** visor. **2** mask. [alteration of *visor*]

vi·zier (vi zēr′) *n.* in Moslem countries, a high official; a minister of state. [< Turkish < Arabic *wazīr*, originally, porter]

vi·zir (vi zēr′) *n.* vizier.

vi·zor (vī′zər) *n.* visor.

V-J Day the day of the Allied victory over Japan in World War II, August 14, 1945.

VL or **V.L.** Vulgar Latin.

vo. the reverse or back of the title page. (for L *verso*)

vocab. vocabulary.

vo·ca·ble (vō′kə bəl) *n.* a word, especially as heard or seen without consideration of its meaning. [< L *vocabulum* < *vocare* call]

vo·cab·u·lar·y (və kab′yů lėr′ē or vō kab′yů ler′ē) *n.* **-lar·ies. 1** the stock of words used by a person, class of people, profession, etc.: *Reading will increase your vocabulary.* **2** a collection or list of words, usually in alphabetical order, with their meanings. **3** all the words of a language. **4** the characteristic expressions of a quality, feeling, etc.: *the vocabulary of prejudice.* [< Med.L *vocabularius* < L *vocabulum.* See VOCABLE.]

vocabulary entry 1 a word, term, or item entered in a vocabulary. **2** in dictionaries, any word or phrase in alphabetical order and defined, or any related word listed for identification under the word from which it is derived.

vo·cal (vō′kəl) *adj.* **1** of, by, for, with, or having to do with the voice: *vocal organs, vocal power, a vocal message, vocal music.* **2** having a voice; giving forth sound: *Men are vocal beings. The gorge was vocal with the roar of the cataract.* **3** aroused to speech; inclined to talk freely: *He became vocal with indignation.* **4** in phonetics, of a vowel. —*n.* **1** a vocal sound. **2** in music: **a** a composition for the voice. **b** the part of a composition that is to be sung. [< L *vocalis* < *vox* voice. Doublet of VOWEL.]

vocal bands vocal cords.

vocal cords either of two pairs of membranes in the larynx. The lower pair of vocal cords is used in making certain speech sounds.

vo·cal·ic (vō kal′ik) *adj.* **1** of, having to do with, or like a vowel sound. **2** having many vowel sounds.

vo·cal·ist (vō′kəl ist) *n.* a singer.

vo·cal·ize (vō′kəl īz′) *v.* **-ized, -iz·ing. 1** speak, sing, shout, etc. **2** make vocal; utter: *The dog vocalized his pain in a series of long howls.* **3** in phonetics, change into a vowel; use as a vowel. Some speakers vocalize the *r* in *four* (fôə). —**vo′cal·i·za′tion,** *n.*

vo·cal·ly (vō′kəl ē) *adv.* with the voice; orally; out loud.

vo·ca·tion (vō kā′shən) *n.* **1** an occupation; business; profession; trade: *Teaching is her vocation.* **2** an inner call or summons to a divine mission. [ME < L *vocatio, -onis,* literally, a calling < *vocare* call]
☛ **Vocation, avocation** are often confused. *Vocation* applies to a person's regular occupation, the way he earns his living. *Avocation* applies to a kind of work a person does in his spare time, a hobby: *Bookkeeping is his vocation, and photography is his avocation.*

vo·ca·tion·al (və kā′shən əl or vō kā′shən əl) *adj.* having to do with some occupation, trade, etc. A vocational school trains boys and girls for special trades, such as printing, stenography, etc.

vo·ca·tion·al·ly (və kā′shən əl ē or vō kā′shən əl ē) *adv.* in regard to vocation.

voc·a·tive (vok′ə tiv) *adj.* **1** in grammar, showing the person or thing spoken to. **2** of, having to do with, or characteristic of calling or addressing. —*n.* **1** the vocative case. **2** a word in that case. [< L *vocativus* < *vocare* call] —**voc′a·tive·ly,** *adv.*

vo·cif·er·ant (və sif′ər ənt or vō sif′ər ənt) *adj.* vociferating. —*n.* a person who vociferates.

vo·cif·er·ate (və sif′ər āt′ or vō sif′ər āt′) *v.* **-at·ed, -at·ing.** cry out loudly or noisily; shout. [< L *vociferari* < *vox, vocis* voice + *ferre* bear] —**Syn.** clamor, scream.

vo·cif·er·a·tion (və sif′ər ā shən or vō sif′ər ā′shən) *n.* a vociferating; noisy oratory; clamor.

hat, āge, cãre, fär; let, ēqual, tėrm; it, īce
hot, ōpen, ôrder; oil, out; cup, pu̇t, rüle, ūse
əbove, takən, pencəl, lemən, circəs
ch, child; ng, long; sh, ship
th, thin; ᴛʜ, then; zh, measure

vo·cif·er·ous (və sif′ər əs or vō sif′ər əs) *adj.* loud and noisy; shouting; clamoring: *a vociferous person, vociferous cheers.* [< L *vociferari.* See VOCIFERATE.] —**vo·cif′er·ous·ly,** *adv.* —**vo·cif′er·ous·ness,** *n.*

vod·ka (vod′kə) *n.* an alcoholic liquor distilled from potatoes, rye, barley, or corn. [< Russian *vodka,* dim. of *voda* water]

vogue (vōg) *n.* **1** the fashion: *Hoop skirts were in vogue many years ago.* **2** popularity; acceptance: *That song had a great vogue at one time.* [< F *vogue* a rowing, course, success < *voguer* float < Ital. *vogare*]

voice (vois) *n. v.* **voiced, voic·ing.** —*n.* **1** the sound made through the mouth or nose in speaking, singing, shouting, etc. **2 a** the sounds naturally made by a single person in speech or other utterance, often regarded as characteristic of the person and distinguishing him from others: *recognize someone's voice.* **b** such sounds considered with regard to character, quality, tone, or expression: *a low, gentle, loud, or angry voice.* **3** the power to make sounds through the mouth or nose. **4** anything like speech or song: *the voice of the wind.* **5** in music: **a** a musical sound made by the vocal cords and resonated by several head and throat cavities; the tones made in singing. **b** ability as a singer. **c** a singer. **d** a part of a composition for one kind of singer or instrument. **6** expression: *They gave voice to their joy.* **7** an expressed opinion, choice, wish, etc.: *His voice was for compromise.* **8** the right to express an opinion or choice: *We have no voice in the matter.* **9** in grammar, a form of the verb that shows whether the subject is active or passive. *Examples*: He sees (*active voice*). He is seen (*passive voice*). **10** in phonetics, a sound uttered with vibration of the vocal cords, not with mere breath. **11 in voice,** in condition to sing or speak well. **12 lift up one's voice, a** shout; yell. **b** protest; complain. **13 with one voice,** unanimously. —*v.* **1** express; utter: *They voiced their approval of the plan.* **2** in phonetics, utter with a sound made by vibration of the vocal cords. The (z) in *rose* (rōz) and the (v) in *rove* (rōv) are voiced; the (s) and (f) in *soft* (soft) are not. **3** in music: **a** regulate the tone of (an organ, etc.). **b** write the parts of (a piece of music) for one kind of singer or instrument. [ME < OF *vois, voiz* < L *vox*]

voice·less (vois′lis) *adj.* **1** having no voice; dumb; silent. **2** in phonetics, spoken without vibration of the vocal cords. The consonants (p), (t), (f), and (s) are voiceless.

void (void) *adj.* **1** in law, without legal force or effect; not binding: *A contract made by a person under legal age is void.* **2** empty; vacant: *a void space.* **3** without effect; useless. **4 void of,** devoid of; without; lacking. —*v.* **1** in law, make of no force or effect. **2** empty out. **3** *Archaic.* leave. —*n.* an empty space: *The death of his dog left an aching void in Bob's heart.* [ME < OF *voide* < VL *vocitus,* ult. < var. of L *vacuus* empty] —**void′er,** *n.* —**Syn.** *adj.* **1** invalid, null. -*v.* **1** invalidate, nullify.

void·a·ble (void′ə bəl) *adj.* capable of being voided or given up: *The contract was voidable by either party after twelve months.*

voile (voil) *n.* a thin, sheer cloth with an open weave. [< F *voile,* originally, veil < L *vela,* pl. of *velum* covering. Doublet of VEIL, VELUM.]

vol. 1 volume. **2** volunteer. **3** volcano.

vo·lant (vō′lənt) *adj.* **1** flying; able to fly. **2** in heraldry, represented as flying. **3** nimble; quick. [< L *volans, -antis,* ppr. of *volare* fly]

vol·a·tile (vol′ə tīl′ or vol′ə təl) *adj.* **1** evaporating rapidly; changing into vapor easily: *Gasoline is volatile.* **2** changing rapidly from one mood or interest to another; fickle; frivolous: *of a volatile disposition.* [< L *volatilis* flying < *volare* fly]

vol·a·til·i·ty (vol′ə til′ə tē) *n.* a volatile quality or condition.

vol·a·til·ize (vol′ə təl īz′) *v.* **-ized, -iz·ing.** change or be changed into vapor; evaporate.

vol·can·ic (vol kan′ik) *adj.* **1** of or caused by a volcano; having to do with volcanoes: *a volcanic eruption.* **2** characterized by the presence of volcanoes. **3** like a volcano; liable to break out violently: *a volcanic temper.*

volcanic glass a natural glass formed by the quick cooling of lava; obsidian.

vol·can·ism (vol′kən iz′əm) *n.* phenomena connected with volcanoes and volcanic activity.

vol·ca·no (vol kā′nō) *n.* **-noes** or **-nos. 1** an opening in the surface of the earth through which steam, ashes, and lava are expelled. **2** a cone-shaped hill or mountain around this opening, built up of material thus expelled. [< Ital. < L *Vulcanus* Vulcan]

vole (vōl) *n.* a rodent belonging to the same family as rats and mice, usually of heavier build and having short limbs and tail. [< *volemouse* < *voll* field (< Scand.; cf. ON *vǫllr*) + *mouse*]

vo·li·tion (vō lish′ən) *n.* **1** the act of willing: *The man went away by his own volition.* **2** the power of willing: *The use of drugs has weakened his volition.* **3** will power. [< Med.L *volitio, -onis* < L *volo* I wish] **—Syn. 1** choice, preference, decision.

vo·li·tion·al (vō lish′ən əl) *adj.* of or having to do with volition.

vo·li·tion·al·ly (vō lish′ən əl ē) *adv.* by the will; in accordance with the will.

vol·ley (vol′ē) *n.* **-leys,** *v.* **-leyed, -ley·ing.** *—n.* **1** the discharge of a number of guns at once. **2** a shower of stones, bullets, arrows, etc. **3** a rapid outpouring or burst of words, oaths, shouts, cheers, etc. **4** in tennis, etc., the hitting or return of a ball, etc. before it touches the ground.
—v. **1** discharge or be discharged in a volley: *Cannon volleyed on all sides.* **2** in tennis, etc., hit or return (a ball, etc.) before it touches the ground. [< F *volée* flight < *voler* fly < L *volare*]

vol·ley·ball (vol′ē bol′ or -bôl′) *n.* **1** a game in which the players hit a large ball with their hands so that it goes back and forth across a high net. **2** the ball.

vol·plane (vol′plān′) *v.* **-planed, -plan·ing,** *n. Archaic.* *—v.* glide toward the earth in an airplane without using motor power. *—n.* the act of gliding in this way. [< F *vol plané* gliding flight]

vols. volumes.

volt (vōlt) *n.* the unit of electromotive force. One volt causes a current of one ampere to flow through a resistance of one ohm. *Abbrev.*: V [after Count Alessandro *Volta* (1745-1827), an Italian physicist]

volt·age (vōl′tij) *n.* electromotive force expressed in volts. A current of high voltage is used in transmitting electric power over long distances.

vol·ta·ic (vol tā′ik) *adj.* **1** producing an electric current by chemical action. **2** of or having to do with electric currents produced by chemical action; galvanic.

voltaic battery in electricity: **1** a battery composed of voltaic cells. **2** a voltaic cell.

voltaic cell in electricity, a container having two plates, each of a different metal, immersed in some solution or paste that will produce a current by reacting with one of the plates; electric cell.

vol·tam·e·ter (vol tam′ə tər) *n.* a device for measuring the quantity of electricity passing through a conductor by the amount of electrolysis it produces. [< *volta(ic)* + *meter*[2]]

vol·te face (volt′fās′; *French,* vôlt fäs′) *n.* an about-face; reversal in attitude. [< F < Ital. *voltafaccia* < *volta* a turning + *faccia* face < L *facies*]

volt·me·ter (vōlt′mē′tər) *n.* an instrument for measuring electromotive force.

vol·u·bil·i·ty (vol′yů bil′ə tē) *n.* **1** readiness to talk much; the habit of talking much. **2** a great flow of words.

vol·u·ble (vol′yů bəl) *adj.* **1** tending to talk much; fond of talking. **2** having a smooth, rapid flow of words. [< L *volubilis,* originally, rolling < *volvere* roll] **—vol′u·bly,** *adv.* **—Syn. 2** See **fluent.**

vol·ume (vol′yəm or vol′ūm) *n.* **1** a collection of printed or written sheets bound together to form a book; book: *We own a library of five hundred volumes.* **2** a book or periodical forming part of a set or series. **3** the space occupied: *The storeroom has a volume of 800 cubic feet.* **4** an amount; quantity: *Volumes of smoke poured from the chimneys of the factory.* **5** an amount of sound; loudness: *A pipe organ gives much more volume than a violin or flute.* **6** a roll of parchment, papyrus, etc. containing written matter (the ancient form of a book); scroll. **7 speak volumes,** express much; be full of meaning. [ME < OF < L *volumen* book roll, scroll < *volvere* roll] **—Syn. 4** See **size**[1].

vol·u·met·ric (vol′yů met′rik) *adj.* of or having to do with measurement by volume.

vo·lu·mi·nous (və lü′mə nəs) *adj.* **1** forming, filling, or writing a large book or many books: *a voluminous report, a voluminous author.* **2** of great size; very bulky; large: *A voluminous cloak covered him from head to foot.* [< LL *voluminosus* with many coils < L *volumen, -minis.* See VOLUME.] **—vo·lu′mi·nous·ly,** *adv.*

vol·un·tar·i·ly (vol′ən ter′ə lē) *adv.* of one's own free will; without force or compulsion.

vol·un·tar·y (vol′ən ter′ē) *adj. n.* **-tar·ies.** *—adj.* **1** done, made, given, etc. of one's own free will; not forced or compelled: *Every year the Red Cross asks for voluntary contributions.* **2** supported entirely by voluntary gifts: *voluntary schools.* **3** acting of one's own free will or choice: *Voluntary workers built a road to the boys' camp.* **4** able to act of one's own free will: *a voluntary agent.* **5** in law: **a** done, given, or proceeding from the free or unconstrained will of a person: *a voluntary affidavit.* **b** acting or done without obligation or without receiving a valuable consideration: *a voluntary partition of land.* **c** deliberately intended; done on purpose: *voluntary manslaughter.* **6** in physiology, controlled by the will: *Talking is voluntary; breathing is only partly so.*
—n. **1** anything done, made, given, etc. of one's own free will. **2** in music: **a** a composition, often extemporized, that is used as a prelude. **b** an organ solo played before, during, or after a church service. **3** a volunteer. [ME < L *voluntarius* < *voluntas* will < *volo* I wish]
Syn. *adj.* **1 Voluntary, spontaneous** = done, made, given, etc. without being forced or compelled. **Voluntary** emphasizes the idea of something done of one's own free will or choice, not in obedience to the will of another: *The state is supported by taxes, the church by voluntary contributions.* **Spontaneous** emphasizes the idea of something neither compelled by another nor directed by one's own will, but done from natural impulse, without thought or intention: *The laughter at his jokes is never forced, but always spontaneous.*

vol·un·teer (vol′ən tēr′) *n.* **1** a person who enters military or other service of his own free will. **2** in law: **a** a person who acts of his own free will in a transaction. **b** a person who receives property by a conveyance made without a valuable consideration. **3** a plant that grows from seeds dropped by other plants.
—v. **1** offer one's services: *As soon as war was declared, many men volunteered.* **2** offer of one's own free will: *He volunteered to do the job.* **3** tell or say voluntarily: *She volunteered the information.*
—adj. **1** of or made up of volunteers: *a volunteer fire company.* **2** serving as a volunteer: *That man is a volunteer fireman in this town.* **3** voluntary. **4** of vegetation, growing from self-sown seed. [< F *volontaire,* originally adj. < L *voluntarius.* See VOLUNTARY.]

vo·lup·tu·ar·y (və lup′chü er′ē) *n.* **-ar·ies.** a person who cares much for luxurious or sensual pleasures. [< L *voluptuarius* < *voluptas* pleasure. See VOLUPTUOUS.]

vo·lup·tu·ous (və lup′chü əs) *adj.* **1** caring much for the pleasures of the senses. **2** giving pleasure to the senses: *voluptuous music or beauty.* [ME < L *voluptuosus* < *voluptas* pleasure < *volup(e),* neut., agreeable] **—vo·lup′tu·ous·ly,** *adv.* **—vo·lup′tu·ous·ness,** *n.*

vo·lute (və lüt′) *n.* **1** a spiral or twisted thing or form. **2** in architecture, a spiral or scroll-like ornament, especially the ones on Ionic or Corinthian capitals. **3** in zoology: **a** a turn or whorl of a spiral shell. **b** any of a group of gastropods that have a spiral shell.
—adj. **1** rolled up; spiral. **2** of machinery: **a** forming a spiral curve or curves: *a volute spring.* **b** moving in a rotary, and usually also a

Volutes on an Ionic capital

lateral, way. [< F *volute* < Ital. < L *voluta*, fem. pp. of *volvere* roll]

vom·it (vom′it) *v.* **1** throw up what has been eaten. **2** cause (a person) to vomit. **3** throw up; throw out with force: *The chimneys vomited forth smoke.* **4** come out with force or violence. —*n.* **1** the act of vomiting. **2** the substance thrown up from the stomach in vomiting. **3** an emetic. [ME < L *vomitus*, pp. of *vomere* spew forth]

voo·doo (vü′dü) *n.* **-doos,** *adj. v.* **-doo·ed, -doo·ing.** —*n.* **1** a body of beliefs and practices involving the use of magic. Voodoo came from Africa but belief in it still prevails among some Negroes of the West Indies and southern United States. **2** a person who practises such magic. **3** a charm or fetish used in the practice of voodoo. —*adj.* of or having to do with voodoo. —*v.* affect by voodoo sorcery, magic, or conjuration. [of African origin]

voo·doo·ism (vü′dü iz′əm) *n.* **1** the belief in or practice of voodoo as a superstition or form of sorcery. **2** voodoo rites or practices.

voo·doo·ist (vü′dü ist) *n.* a person who believes in or practises voodoo.

voo·doo·is·tic (vü′dü is′tik) *adj.* of or having to do with voodooism.

vo·ra·cious (və rā′shəs) *adj.* **1** eating much; greedy in eating; ravenous. **2** very eager; unable to be satisfied. [< L *vorax, -acis* greedy] —**vo·ra′cious·ly,** *adv.*

vo·rac·i·ty (və ras′ə tē) *n.* the quality of being voracious.

vor·tex (vôr′teks) *n.* **-tex·es** or **-ti·ces. 1** a whirling mass of water, air, etc. that sucks in everything near it; whirlpool; whirlwind. **2** a whirl of activity or other situation from which it is hard to escape: *The two nations were unwillingly drawn into the vortex of war.* [< L var. of *vertex.* See VERTEX.]

vor·ti·cal (vôr′tə kəl) *adj.* of or causing motion like that of a vortex; spinning; eddying. —*n.* a vortical motion. —**vor′ti·cal·ly,** *adv.*

vor·ti·cel·la (vôr′tə sel′ə) *n.* **-cel·lae** (-sel′ē or -sel′ī). a one-celled animal that has a bell-shaped body on a slender contractile stalk, often found attached to a plant or other object under water. [< NL *vorticella*, dim. of L *vortex.* See VORTEX.]

vor·ti·ces (vôr′tə sēz′) *n.* a pl. of **vortex.**

vor·tig·inous (vôr tij′ə nəs) *adj.* moving in a vortex; vortical. [< L *vortigo, -inis*, var. of *vertigo* a whirling]

vot·a·ble (vōt′ə bəl) *adj.* that can be voted for, against, on, etc.

vo·ta·ress (vō′tə ris) *n.* a female votary.

vo·ta·rist (vō′tə rist) *n.* votary.

vo·ta·ry (vō′tə rē) *n.* **-ries. 1** a person devoted to something; devotee: *He was a votary of gold.* **2** a person bound by vows to a religious life. [< L *votum* vow]

vote (vōt) *n. v.* **vot·ed, vot·ing.** —*n.* **1** a formal expression of a wish or choice: *The person receiving the most votes is elected.* **2** the right to give such an expression: *Not everybody has a vote.* **3** what is expressed or granted by a majority of voters. **4** votes considered together: *the labor vote, the vote of the people.* **5** a voter. **6** a ballot: *More than a million votes were cast.*
—*v.* **1** give or cast a vote: *He voted for the Liberals.* **2** support by one's vote: *vote Conservative.* **3** pass, determine, or grant by a vote: *Money for a new school was voted by the board.* **4** declare, especially by general consent: *The children all voted the trip a great success.* **5** *Informal.* suggest: *I vote that we go.* **6 vote down,** defeat by voting against. **7 vote in,** elect. [ME < L *votum* vow. Doublet of VOW.]

vote of confidence 1 in parliament, a majority vote of support for the government, especially in a crisis and when defeat of the government would have forced it to resign. **2** any show of support or approval.

vot·er (vōt′ər) *n.* **1** a person who votes. **2** a person who has the right to vote.

voters' list at an election, a list giving the names, addresses, and occupations of all those entitled to vote in a given riding, ward, etc.

voting machine a mechanical device for registering and counting votes.

hat, āge, cãre, fär; let, ēqual, tėrm; it, īce
hot, ōpen, ôrder; oil, out; cup, pu̇t, rüle, ūse
əbove, takən, pencəl, lemən, circəs
ch, child; ng, long; sh, ship
th, thin; ᴛʜ, then; zh, measure

vo·tive (vō′tiv) *adj.* **1** promised by a vow; done, given, etc. because of a vow. **2** made up or expressive of a vow, desire, or wish: *a votive prayer.* [< L *votivus* < *votum* vow]

vouch (vouch) *v.* **1** be responsible; give a guarantee (*for*): *I can vouch for the truth of the story. The principal vouched for Bill's honesty.* **2** answer for; confirm; guarantee. **3** give evidence or assurance of a fact (*for*): *The success of the attack vouches for the general's ability.* **4** in law, call into court to give warranty of title. **5** sponsor or recommend (a person or thing); support; back. [ME < AF *voucher* < L *vocare* call]

vouch·er (vouch′ər) *n.* **1** a person or thing that vouches for something. **2** a written evidence of payment; receipt. Cancelled cheques returned from one's bank are vouchers.

vouch·safe (vouch sāf′) *v.* **-safed, -saf·ing.** be willing to grant or give; deign (to do or give): *The proud man vouchsafed no reply when we spoke to him.* [original meaning "guarantee," to *vouch* for as *safe*]

vous·soir (vü swär′) *n.* in architecture, a wedge-shaped piece or section forming part of an arch or vault. [< F < VL *volsorium* < *volvere* roll]

vow (vou) *n.* **1** a solemn promise: *a vow of secrecy.* **2** a promise made to God: *a nun's vows.* **3 take vows,** become a member of a religious order. —*v.* **1** make a vow. **2** make a vow to do, give, get, etc.: *vow revenge.* **3** declare earnestly or emphatically: *I vowed never to leave home again.* [ME < OF *vou* < L *votum* < *vovere* vow. Doublet of VOTE.]

vow·el (vou′əl) *n.* **1** in phonetics, a speech sound during which the vocal cords are vibrating and the breath is not completely or partly stopped at any point in the mouth by the tongue, teeth, or lips: *When you say "awe" you are uttering a vowel.* **2** a letter representing such a sound: *There are five vowels used in writing,* a, e, i, o, *and* u. —*adj.* of or having something to do with a vowel: "*Voluntary*" *has four vowel sounds;* "*strength*" *has only one.* [ME < OF < L (*littera*) *vocalis* sounding (letter) < *vox* voice. Doublet of VOCAL.]

vox (voks) *n.* **vo·ces** (vō′sēz). *Latin.* voice; sound; word; expression.

vox hu·ma·na (voks hū mä′nə or hū mā′nə) *n.* an organ reed stop, intended to be an imitation of the human voice. [< L *vox humana* the human voice]

vox po·pu·li (voks′ pop′yu̇ lē′ or pop′yu̇ lī′) *Latin.* the voice or opinion of the people.

voy·age (voi′ij) *n. v.* **-aged, -ag·ing.** —*n.* **1** a journey, especially a lengthy one, by water. **2** a journey by air. **3** Often, **voyages,** *pl.* a book describing a voyage or voyages; an account of a voyage. —*v.* make a journey by air or water. [< F *voyage* < L *viaticum.* Doublet of VIATICUM.] —**Syn.** *n.* **1** cruise. See **trip.**

voy·ag·er (voi′ij ər) *n.* **1** a person who makes a voyage; traveller. **2** voyageur.

vo·ya·geur (voi′ə zhėr′; *French*, vwä yä zhœr′) *n.* **-geurs** (-zhėrz; *French*, -zhœr′). **1** a boatman, especially a French Canadian, in the service of the early fur-trading companies. **2** a boatman or woodsman of the Canadian forests, especially in the North. [< F *voyageur*, ult. < *voyage* voyage]

vo·yeur (vwä yėr′) *n.* one who finds sexual gratification in observing the nude bodies or sexual acts of others. [< F *voyeur* < *voir* to see < L *videre*]

vo·yeur·ism (vwä yėr′iz əm) *n.* the habits and practices of a voyeur.

V.P. or **V.Pres.** Vice-President.

V.R. Queen Victoria. (for L *Victoria Regina*)

V.Rev. Very Reverend.

vs. 1 versus. **2** verse.

v.s. vide supra.

V.S. Veterinary Surgeon.

V-shaped (vē′shāpt′) *adj.* **1** shaped like the letter V. **2** like the letter V in cross section.

v.t. transitive verb. (for L *verbum transitivum*)

Vt. Vermont.

VTOL vertical takeoff and landing.

Vul. Vulgate.

Vul·can (vul′kən) *n.* in Roman mythology, the god of fire and metal-working.

vul·can·ite (vul′kən īt′) *n.* a hard rubber obtained by treating India rubber with a large amount of sulphur and heating it, used for combs, for buttons, in electric insulation, etc.

vul·can·ize (vul′kən īz′) *v.* **-ized, -iz·ing. 1** treat (rubber) with sulphur and, usually, heat to make it more elastic and durable. **2** repair (a rubber tire, etc.) by using heat and chemicals to fuse the patch. [< *Vulcan*] **—vul′can·i·za′tion,** *n.* **—vul′can·iz′er,** *n.*

vulg. vulgar.

Vulg. Vulgate.

vul·gar (vul′gər) *adj.* **1** showing a lack of good breeding, manners, taste, etc.; not refined; coarse; low. **2** common; in common use; ordinary. **3** of the common people. *—n.* **the vulgar,** the common people. [ME < L *vulgaris* < *vulgus* common people] **—vul′gar·ly,** *adv.* **—vul′gar·ness,** *n.* **—Syn.** *adj.* **1** inelegant. See **coarse. 3** plebeian, lowborn, ignoble.

vul·gar·i·an (vul gãr′ē ən) *n.* **1** a vulgar person. **2** a rich person who lacks good breeding, manners, taste, etc.

vul·gar·ism (vul′gər iz′əm) *n.* **1** a word, phrase, or expression used only in ignorant or coarse speech. **2** a vulgar character or action; vulgarity. **3** a vulgar expression.

vul·gar·i·ty (vul gar′ə tē) *n.* **-ties. 1** lack of refinement; lack of good breeding, manners, taste, etc.; coarseness. **2** an action, habit, speech, etc. showing vulgarity.

vul·gar·ize (vul′gər īz′) *n.* **-ized, -iz·ing.** make vulgar. **—vul′gar·iz′er,** *n.*

Vulgar Latin the popular, spoken form of Latin, the main source of French, Spanish, Italian, and Portuguese.

Vul·gate (vul′gāt) *n.* **1** the Latin translation of the Bible made by Saint Jerome in the fourth century A.D., used in a subsequently revised form by the Roman Catholic Church as the authoritative text. **2 vulgate,** the ordinary text of a work or author. **3 the vulgate,** substandard speech. [< L *vulgata* (*editio*) popular (edition)]

vul·ner·a·bil·i·ty (vul′nər ə bil′ə tē) *n.* a vulnerable quality or condition; the state of being open to attack or injury.

vul·ner·a·ble (vul′nər ə bəl) *adj.* **1** capable of being wounded or injured; open to attack: *Achilles was vulnerable only in his heel.* **2** sensitive to criticism, temptations, influences, etc.: *Most people are vulnerable to ridicule.* **3** in the game of contract bridge, in the position where penalties and premiums are increased. [< LL *vulnerabilis* wounding, ult. < *vulnus, -neris* wound] **—vul′ner·a·bly,** *adv.*

vul·pine (vul′pīn or vul′pən) *adj.* of or like a fox. [< L *vulpinus* < *vulpes* fox]

vul·ture (vul′chər) *n.* **1** a large bird of prey, related to eagles, hawks, etc. that eats the flesh of dead animals. **2** some person or thing that preys upon another; a greedy, ruthless person. [< L *vultur*]

vul·va (vul′və) *n.* **-vae** (-vē or -vī) or **-vas.** in anatomy, the external genital organs of the female. [< L *vulva* womb]

vv 1 verses. **2** violins.

v.v. vice versa.

vy·ing (vī′ing) *v.* ppr. of **vie.**

W or **w** (dub′əl ū′) *n.* **W's** or **w's. 1** the twenty-third letter of the English alphabet. **2** any speech sound represented by this letter. **3** one (usually twenty-third) of a series designated alphabetically. **4** anything shaped like this letter.

w watt.

w. 1 west. **2** week. **3** wide. **4** width. **5** wife. **6** weight. **7** with. **8** won.

W 1 west. **2** watt. **3** wolfram.

W. 1 west. **2** western. **3** Wednesday. **4** Wales. **5** Welsh. **6** in physics, work.

W.A. 1 West Africa. **2** Western Australia. **3** Women's Auxiliary.

WAAC or **W.A.A.C.** Women's Auxiliary Army Corps.

WAAF or **W.A.A.F.** Women's Auxiliary Air Force.

wab·ble[1] (wob′əl) *v.* **-bled, -bling,** *n.* wobble. **—wab′bler,** *n.*

wab·ble[2] (wob′əl) *n.* warble[2].

wab·bly (wob′lē) *adj.* wobbly.

wack·y (wak′ē) *adj. Slang.* unconventional in behavior; eccentric; crazy. Also, **whacky.**

wad (wod) *n. v.* **wad·ded, wad·ding.** *—n.* **1** a small, soft mass: *He plugged his ears with wads of cotton.* **2** a tight roll; compact bundle or mass: *a wad of bills.* **3** in a gun or cartridge, a round plug of felt, cardboard, etc. used to hold powder and shot in place. **4** *Slang.* personal wealth; riches: *He made his wad in oil.* *—v.* **1** make into a wad; press into a wad. **2** stuff with a wad. **3** hold in place by a wad. **4** pad. [origin uncertain]

wad·ding (wod′ing) *n.* **1** a soft material for padding, stuffing, packing, etc., especially carded cotton in sheets. **2** material for making wads for guns or cartridges. **3** a wad.

wad·dle (wod′əl) *v.* **-dled, -dling,** *n.* *—v.* walk with short steps and an awkward, swaying motion, as a duck does. *—n.* **1** the act of waddling. **2** an awkward, swaying gait. [< *wade*] **—wad′dler,** *n.*

wade (wād) *v.* **wad·ed, wad·ing,** *n.* *—v.* **1** walk through water, snow, sand, mud, or anything that hinders free motion. **2** make one's way with difficulty: *wade through an uninteresting book.* **3** cross or pass through by wading. **4 wade in,** *Informal.* thrust or throw oneself into the middle or thick of something and fight, work, etc. with vigor: *wade in and straighten out a dispute.* **5 wade into,** *Informal.* attack or go to work upon vigorously. *—n.* the act of wading. [OE *wadan* proceed]

wad·er (wād′ər) *n.* **1** one that wades. **2** a long-legged bird that wades about in shallow water, searching for food. Cranes, herons, storks, and sandpipers are waders. **3** a high waterproof boot.

wa·di (wä′dē) *n.* **-dis. 1** in parts of the Arabian peninsula, N. Africa, etc., a valley or ravine through which a stream flows during the rainy season. **2** a stream or torrent running through such a ravine. **3** an oasis. [< Arabic]

wa·dy (wä′dē) *n.* **-dies.** wadi.

wa·fer (wā′fər) *n.* **1** a very thin cake or biscuit, sometimes flavored or sweetened. **2** in some churches, the thin, round piece of unleavened bread used in the Eucharist. **3** a thin piece of candy, chocolate, medicine, etc. **4** a piece of sticky paper, dried paste, etc. used as a seal or fastening. [ME < AF *wafre* < Gmc.] **—wa′fer·like′,** *adj.*

wa·fer·y (wā′fər ē) *adj.* like a wafer.

waf·fle[1] (wof′əl) *n.* a light, crisp cake made from a batter and cooked in a waffle iron. [< Du. *wafel*]

waf·fle[2] (wof′əl) *v.* **-fled, -fling.** *Slang.* **1** talk nonsense; prattle; talk on and on. **2** be inconsistent or indirect; shilly-shally. *—n.* nonsense; foolish talk. [< Brit. dial. *waff* to yelp + *-le*]

waffle iron a utensil in which waffles are cooked, consisting of two hinged griddles, each of which has a regular pattern of projections on the inner surface.

A waffle iron

waft (waft or woft) *v.* **1** carry over water or through air: *The waves wafted the boat to shore.* **2** transport or transfer very quickly or as if by magic: *be wafted by plane from Toronto to London.*

3 float. 4 of a breeze, blow gently; stir. —*n.* 1 the act of wafting. 2 a breath or puff of air, wind, etc. 3 a waving movement. [< earlier *wafter* convoy ship < Du. and LG *wachter* guard]

wag[1] (wag) *v.* **wagged, wag·ging,** *n.* —*v.* 1 move rapidly and repeatedly from side to side or up and down: *The dog wagged its tail.* 2 **wag one's tongue,** chatter; gossip. —*n.* a wagging motion. [ME; cf. OE *wagian*]

wag[2] (wag) *n.* a person who is fond of making jokes. [< *wag*[1]]

wage (wāj) *n. v.* **waged, wag·ing.** —*n.* 1 Usually, **wages,** *pl.* **a** an amount paid for work: *His wages are $30 a week.* **b** something given in return: *the wages of sin.* 2 *Obsolete.* a pledge; gage; bet. —*v.* 1 carry on: *wage war.* 2 *Obsolete.* pledge; gage; bet. [ME < AF *wage*, var. of *gage.* See GAGE[1].] —**wage′less,** *adj.* —**Syn.** *n.* 1 a salary, pay, compensation, remuneration, stipend. ☛ See **salary** for usage note.

wage earner a person who works for wages.

wa·ger (wā′jər) *n.* 1 something staked on an uncertain event. 2 an act of betting; bet. —*v.* make a bet; gamble. [ME < AF *wageure* < OF *wage* pledge. See WAGE.] —**wa′ger·er,** *n.*

wage·work·er (wāj′wėr′kər) *n.* wage earner.

wag·ger·y (wag′ər ē) *n.* **-ger·ies.** 1 a joking. 2 a joke.

wag·gish (wag′ish) *adj.* 1 fond of making jokes. 2 of, done by, or characteristic of a wag: *a waggish look.* —**wag′gish·ly,** *adv.* —**wag′gish·ness,** *n.*

wag·gle (wag′əl) *v.* **-gled, -gling,** *n.* —*v.* move quickly and repeatedly from side to side; wag. —*n.* a wagging motion. [frequentative of *wag*]

wag·gon (wag′ən) *n. Esp.Brit.* wagon.

wag·gon·er (wag′ən ər) *n. Esp.Brit.* wagoner.

Wag·ne·ri·an (väg nēr′ē ən) *adj.* of or having to do with Richard Wagner, 1813-1883, a German composer, especially of operas, his music, or his musical style. —*n.* an admirer of Richard Wagner's style or theory of music.

wag·on (wag′ən) *n.* 1 a four-wheeled vehicle, usually horse-drawn and especially one for carrying loads: *a milk wagon.* 2 a child's four-wheeled cart. 3 *Informal.* a station wagon. 4 *Brit.* an open railway freight car. 5 **hitch one's wagon to a star,** have high hopes and ambitions; aim high. 6 **on the wagon,** *Slang.* not drinking alcoholic liquors. Also, **waggon.** [< Du. *wagen.* Akin to WAIN.]

wag·on·er (wag′ən ər) *n.* a person who drives a wagon. Also, **waggoner.**

wag·on·ette (wag′ən et′) *n.* a four-wheeled, horse-drawn carriage with a seat in front running crosswise and two lengthwise seats facing each other.

wa·gon-lit (vä gôN lē′) *n. French.* in Europe, a railway sleeping car. [< F *wagon* railway coach + *lit* bed]

wag·on·load (wag′ən lōd′) *n.* the amount a wagon carries.

wagon train 1 a group of wagons moving along in a line one after another, especially such a group carrying a company of settlers travelling together for protection. 2 *Esp.U.S.* a convoy of wagons carrying military supplies.

wag·tail (wag′tāl′) *n.* a small bird with a long, narrow tail that it wags up and down.

waif (wāf) *n.* 1 a person without home or friends; a homeless or neglected child. 2 anything without an owner; a stray thing, animal, etc. [ME < AF *waif*, probably < Scand.]

wail (wāl) *v.* 1 cry loud and long because of grief or pain. 2 make a mournful sound: *The wind wailed around the old house.* 3 lament; mourn. —*n.* 1 a long cry of grief or pain. 2 a sound like such a cry. [ME; ? < ON *vǽla* < *vǽ, vei,* interj., woe] —**wail′er,** *n.*

wain (wān) *n. Archaic or poetic.* wagon. [OE *wægn*]

wain·scot (wān′skot′ or wān′skət) *n. v.* **-scot·ted** or **-scot·ed, -scot·ting** or **-scot·ing.** —*n.* 1 a facing of wood, usually in panels, on the walls of a room. See picture in the next column. 2 the lower part of the wall of a room when it is decorated differently from the upper part. —*v.* line with wood: *a room wainscotted in oak.* [ME < MLG *wagenschot* < *wagen* wagon + *schot* partition]

wain·scot·ting or **wain·scot·ing** (wān′skot′ing or wān′skət ing) *n.* 1 a wainscot. 2 material used for wainscots.

hat, āge, cãre, fär; let, ēqual, tėrm; it, īce
hot, ōpen, ôrder; oil, out; cup, pu̇t, rüle, ūse
əbove, takən, pencəl, lemən, circəs
ch, child; ng, long; sh, ship
th, thin; ᴛʜ, then; zh, measure

wain·wright (wān′rīt′) *n.* a person who makes wagons.

A wainscot (def. 1)

waist (wāst) *n.* 1 the part of the human body between the ribs and the hips. 2 the waistline. 3 a garment or part of a garment covering the body from the neck or shoulders to the waistline. 4 a narrow middle part: *the waist of a violin.* 5 the part of a ship amidships, as that between the forecastle and the quarterdeck of a sailing vessel, or between the forward and stern superstructure of an oil tanker. 6 the middle section of an airplane's fuselage, especially that of a bomber. [< root of *wax*[2]]

waist·band (wāst′band′) *n.* a band around the waist: *the waistband of a skirt or of a pair of trousers.*

waist·cloth (wāst′kloth′) *n.* loincloth.

waist·coat (wāst′kōt′ or, *esp.Brit.,* wes′kət) *n.* a man's vest. See the picture under **vest.**

waist·line (wāst′līn′) *n.* 1 an imaginary line around the body at the smallest part of the waist. 2 the narrowest part of a garment that covers the body at or near this line. 3 the line where the waist and skirt of a dress join.

wait (wāt) *v.* 1 stay or be inactive until someone expected comes or something happens: *Let's wait in the shade.* 2 *Informal.* delay or put off: *Wait dinner for him.* 3 look forward; be expecting or ready: *The children wait impatiently for their holidays.* 4 be left undone; be put off: *That matter can wait until tomorrow.* 5 wait for: *wait one's chance.* 6 act as a servant; change plates, pass food, etc. at table. 7 serve. 8 **wait on** or **upon, a** be a servant to; serve, especially at the table. **b** give one's attention to and seek to fill the needs of (a customer): *Will you wait on me, please?* **c** call on (a superior) to pay a respectful visit. **d** go with; result from. 9 **wait on** (or **upon**) **hand and foot,** do everything possible for (one who does nothing or too little for himself). 10 **wait out, a** wait until the end of. **b** in baseball, refrain from swinging at the pitches of (a pitcher), in the hope of getting a base on balls. 11 **wait up,** *Informal.* stay out of bed (until the arrival of): *Did you wait up long for her?* —*n.* 1 the act or time of waiting: *I had a long wait at the doctor's office.* 2 in the theatre, the time of an audience's waiting between acts, or of an actor's waiting between appearances on stage. 3 **lie in wait,** stay hidden, ready to attack. 4 **waits,** *pl.* in England, a group of singers and musicians who go about the streets singing and playing at Christmas time. [ME < ONF *waitier*, originally, watch < Gmc.] —**Syn.** *v.* 1 tarry, linger, remain, abide.

☛ **wait, await.** *Wait* chiefly means "stay inactive or in a place until something expected happens or comes," and only in a few phrases is followed directly by a word naming the expected person, thing, or event: *We can wait here until he comes. Await* almost always is followed by the grammatical object, and means "wait *for* someone or something," to look forward to or be ready for a coming or expected event or person: *We are eagerly awaiting your arrival.*

wait·er (wāt′ər) *n.* 1 a person who waits. 2 a man who waits on table in a hotel, restaurant, etc. 3 a tray for carrying dishes.

wait·ing (wāt′ing) *adj.* 1 that waits. 2 used to wait in. —*n.* 1 the time that one waits. 2 **in waiting,** in attendance on a king, queen, prince, princess, etc.

waiting maid a woman servant or attendant.

waiting man a man servant or attendant.

waiting room a room at a railway station, doctor's office, etc. for people to wait in.

waiting woman a woman servant or attendant.

wait-list (wāt′list′) *v.* enter on a list of persons waiting for an appointment, space on an aircraft, etc.

wait·ress (wāt′ris) *n.* a woman who waits on table in a hotel, restaurant, etc.

waive (wāv) *v.* **waived, waiv·ing. 1** give up (a right, claim, etc.); refrain from claiming or pressing; do without; relinquish: *The lawyer waived the privilege of cross-examining the witness.* **2** put aside; defer. [ME <AF *weyver* abandon, probably < Scand. Related to WAIF.] —**Syn. 1** surrender, forgo, abandon.

waiv·er (wāv′ər) *n.* **1** in law: **a** a giving up of a right, claim, etc. **b** a written statement of this: *For $100 the injured man signed a waiver of all claims against the railway.* **2** in professional sports, a condition in which the contract of a player is offered to other clubs in the league at a fixed price. If they decline, the contract may be taken up by a team from another league. [< AF *weyver*, infin. used as n. See WAIVE.]

wa·kan·da (wä kän′dä) *n.* among certain Plains Indians, a supernatural power found in living things and inanimate objects; Great Spirit. [< Siouan *wakanda* regard as sacred < *wakan* sacred spirit]

Wa·kash·an (wä kash′ən) *n.* **-an** or **-ans. 1** a language group of Indians of British Columbia and Washington that includes the dialects of the Nootka, Kwakiutl, and Bella Bella. **2** the group of the tribes speaking these dialects. **3** a member of this group.

wake[1] (wāk) *v.* **woke** or **waked, waked** or (*archaic and dialect*) **wo·ken, wak·ing,** *n.* —*v.* **1** stop sleeping: *wake up early in the morning, wake at seven every morning.* **2** cause to stop sleeping: *The noise of the traffic always wakes him. Wake him up early.* **3** be awake; stay wake: *all his waking hours.* **4** become alive or active: *The flowers wake in the spring.* **5** make alive or active: *He needs some interest to wake him up.* **6** keep a watch or vigil, especially over a corpse. **7** keep watch over (a corpse) until burial; hold a wake over. —*n.* **1** a watching. **2** an all-night watch kept beside a corpse before its burial. [OE *wacian*] —**Syn.** *v.* **1, 2** awake, waken, rouse, arouse.

wake[2] (wāk) *n.* **1** the track left behind a moving ship. **2** the track left behind any moving thing. **3 in the wake of,** following; behind; after. [< MDu.]

wake·ful (wāk′fəl) *adj.* **1** not able to sleep. **2** without sleep. **3** watchful. —**wake′ful·ly,** *adv.* —**wake′ful·ness,** *n.*

wak·en (wāk′ən) *v.* wake. [OE *wæcnan*] —**wak′en·er,** *n.*

wake-rob·in (wāk′rob′ən) *n.* **1** a trillium. **2** *Brit.* any of various plants of the arum family.

Wal·den·ses (wol den′sēz or wôl den′sēz) *n.pl.* a Christian sect formed by Peter Waldo in Lyons, France about 1170. They were condemned by the popes and subjected to much persecution. Their present headquarters is in Italy.

Wal·den·si·an (wol den′sē ən or wôl′den′sē ən; wol den′shən or wôl den′shən) *adj.* of or having to do with the Waldenses. —*n.* a member of the Waldenses.

wald·grave (wold′grāv′ or wôld′grāv′) *n.* formerly: **1** in medieval Germany, an officer having jurisdiction over a royal forest. **2** any of various German noblemen of a certain rank. [< G *Waldgraf* < *Wald* woods < *Graf* count]

wale (wāl) *n. v.* **waled, wal·ing.** —*n.* **1** a streak or ridge made on the skin by a stick or whip; welt. **2** a ridge in the weave of cloth. **3** the texture of a cloth. **4 a** a continuous line of thick, outside planking on the sides of a wooden ship. **b** sometimes, the gunwale. —*v.* **1** mark with wales; raise wales on. **2** weave with ridges. [OE *walu*]

walk (wok or wôk) *v.* **1** go on foot. **2** stroll for pleasure, exercise, etc.; take a walk or walks. **3** roam: *The ghost will walk tonight.* **4** go over, on, or through: *The captain walked the deck.* **5** make, put, drive, etc. by walking: *walk off a headache.* **6** go slowly: *Walk, do not run.* **7** cause to walk: *The rider walked his horse.* **8** accompany or escort in walking; conduct on foot: *walk a guest to the door.* **9** traverse on foot in order to measure, examine, etc.; pace off or over: *walk the back line of a piece of property.* **10** of things, move or shake in a manner suggestive of walking. **11** in baseball: **a** go to first base after the pitcher has thrown four balls. **b** of a pitcher, give (a batter) a base on balls. **12** in basketball, take two or more steps while holding the ball. **13** conduct oneself in a particular manner; follow a particular course in life. **14 walk away from,** progress much faster than. **15 walk off with, a** take; get; win. **b** steal. **16 walk out, a** *Informal.* go on strike. **b** leave suddenly. **c** *Informal.* go out with a person of the opposite sex; keep company; court. **17 walk out on,** *Informal.* desert. **18 walk over,** defeat easily and by a wide margin.
—*n.* **1** the act of walking, especially walking for pleasure or exercise: *a walk in the country.* **2** a distance to walk: *It is a long walk from here.* **3** a manner of going on foot; gait: *We knew the man was a sailor from his rolling walk.* **4** a route for walking: *We always preferred the walk down by the river.* **5** a sidewalk; a pathway: *I shovelled the snow off the walk.* **6** a way of living: *A doctor and a street cleaner are in different walks of life.* **7** in baseball, a permitting a batter to reach first base on balls. **8** an enclosed place; tract: *a poultry walk.* [OE *wealcan* roll]
Syn. *v.* **1 Walk, stride, plod** = go on foot at a pace slower than a run. **Walk** is the general word: *He walked downstairs.* **Stride** = walk with long, regular steps, especially in haste, annoyance, or self-importance, or with healthy energy: *When we walk for exercise, we should stride briskly.* **Plod** = walk heavily, slowly, and with effort: *The old horse plodded up the road.* –*n.* **1** stroll, hike, tramp, promenade.

walk·a·way (wok′ə wā′ or wôk′-) *n. Informal.* an easy victory.

walk·er (wok′ər or wôk′ər) *n.* **1** one who walks. **2** a lightweight framework for a crippled person to support himself while walking. **3** a framework on casters with a seat to support a baby learning to walk.

walk·ie-talk·ie or **walk·y-talk·y** (wok′ē tok′ē or wôk′ē tôk′ē) *n.* **-talk·ies.** a small, portable receiving and transmitting radio set.

walk-in (wok′in′ or wôk′-) *n. Informal.* **1** a sure or easy victory. **2** one who joins voluntarily; volunteer.

walking fern a tufted fern whose tapering tips often take root.

walking papers *Informal.* dismissal from a position, etc.

walking stick 1 a cane; a stick used in walking. **2** any of various insects having a body like a stick or twig.

walk-on (wok′on′ or wôk′-) *n.* **1** a performer having a small, usually non-speaking part in a play, movie, etc. **2** the part itself.

walk·out (wok′out′ or wôk′-) *n. Informal.* a strike of workers.

walk·o·ver (wok′ō′vər or wôk′-) *n. Informal.* an easy victory.

walk-up (wok′up′ or wôk′-) *n.* **1** an apartment house or building having no elevator. **2** a room or apartment in such a building. —*adj.* of an apartment house or building, having no elevator.

walk-way (wok′wā′ or wôk′-) *n.* **1** a pathway; passage; walk. **2** a framework or structure on which to walk.

walk·y-talk·y (wok′ē tok′ē or wôk′ē tôk′ē) *n.* **-talk·ies.** walkie-talkie.

wall (wol or wôl) *n.* **1** a side of a house, room, or other hollow thing. **2** a structure of stone, brick, or other material built up to enclose, divide, support, or protect. **3** something like a wall in looks or use: *The flood came in a wall of water twelve feet high.* **4 drive to the wall,** make desperate or helpless. **5 go to the wall, a** give way; be defeated. **b** fail in business. **6 push to the wall,** make desperate or helpless. **7 up against a blank wall,** with no idea or clue what to do next.
—*v.* enclose, divide, protect, or fill with a wall, or as if with a wall. [OE *weall* < L *vallum*] —**wall′-less,** *adj.* —**wall′-like′,** *adj.* —**Syn.** *n.* **2** partition.

wal·la (wol′ə) *n.* wallah.

wal·la·by (wol′ə bē) *n.* **-bies** or (*esp. collectively*) **-by.** any of various small kangaroos, some of which are no bigger than a rabbit. [< native Australian *wolabā*]

wal·lah (wol′ə) *n.* **1** a chap; fellow. **2** *Anglo-Indian.* one who is connected with some special work or area: *a kitchen wallah.* Also, **walla.** [originally < Hindi *-vala*, adj. suffix, perhaps < Skt. *bala* boy]

wal·la·roo (wol′ə rü′) *n.* a type of kangaroo that has thick, gray fur. [< native Australian *wolarū*]

wall·board (wol′bord′ or -bôrd′) *n.* an artificial board used instead of wooden boards or plaster to make or cover walls.

wal·led (wold or wôld) *adj.* having walls: *high-walled.*

wal·let (wol′it) *n.* **1** a small, flat leather case for carrying paper money, cards, etc. in one's pocket; folding pocketbook. **2** a bag for carrying food and small articles for personal use on a journey. [ME *walet;* origin uncertain]

wall·eye (wol′ī′ or wôl′-) *n.* **1** an eye having little or no color. **2** an eye that turns away from the nose. **3** a large staring eye. **4 a** an eye having a white opacity in the cornea (leucoma). **b** leucoma (of the cornea). **5** the condition of being walleyed. **6** any of various fishes having large, staring eyes, especially the walleyed pike. [back-formation from *walleyed*]

wall·eyed (wol′īd′ or wôl′-) *adj.* **1** having eyes that show much white and little color. **2** having both eyes turned away from the nose. **3** having large, staring eyes. The pike is a walleyed fish. [ME, by folk etymology < ON *vagl-eygr* < *vagl,* probably, speck in the eye + *auga* eye]

walleyed pike or **perch** a large, edible, North American fresh-water fish of the perch family but resembling the pike and having bulgy eyes.

wall·flow·er (wol′flou′ər or wôl′-) *n.* **1** a perennial plant having sweet-smelling yellow, orange, or red flowers, found growing on walls, cliffs, etc. **2** at a dance, a person, especially a woman, who sits at the side and does not dance, either from shyness or as a result of not being asked to dance.

Wal·loon (wo lün′) *n.* **1** one of a people inhabiting chiefly the southern and southeastern parts of Belgium and adjacent regions in France. **2** their language, the French dialect of Belgium. *—adj.* of or having to do with the Walloons or their language. [< F *Wallon* < Med.L *Wallo* < Gmc.]

wal·lop (wol′əp) *Informal.* *—v.* **1** beat soundly; thrash. **2** hit very hard; strike with a vigorous blow. **3** defeat thoroughly, as in a game. *—n.* **1** a very hard blow. **2** the power to hit very hard blows. [ME < ONF *waloper* gallop < Gmc.]

wal·lop·ing (wol′əp ing) *Informal.* *—n.* **1** a sound beating or thrashing. **2** a thorough defeat. *—adj.* big; powerful; strong.

wal·low (wol′ō) *v.* **1** roll about lazily or pleasurably, as animals in dust or mud: *The pigs were wallowing in their pen.* **2** roll about clumsily or out of control: *The boat wallowed helplessly in the stormy sea.* **3** take gross delight in some form of luxury or idle self-indulgence: *wallow in sentimentality.* *—n.* **1** the act of wallowing. **2** a place where an animal wallows. [OE *wealwian* roll]

wall·pa·per (wol′pā′pər or wôl′-) *n.* paper, commonly with printed decorative patterns in color, for pasting on and covering walls. *—v.* put wallpaper on.

Wall Street the money market or the financiers of the United States. [< *Wall Street,* a street in downtown New York City, the chief financial centre of the United States]

wal·nut (wol′nut′ or wôl′-, wol′nət or wôl′-) *n.* **1** a large, round, edible nut having a clear division between its two halves. **2** the tree that this nut grows on. **3** the wood of a walnut tree. Black walnut is used in making furniture. [OE *wealhhnutu* < *wealh* foreign + *hnutu* nut]

Wal·pur·gis night (väl pür′gis) the night of April 30th, when witches were formerly supposed to hold revels with the devil.

wal·rus (wol′rəs or wôl′rəs) *n.* **-rus** or **-rus·es.** a large sea mammal of the Arctic regions, resembling a seal but having long tusks. Walrus hide is made into leather for luggage. [< Du. *walrus, walros* < *wal(visch)* whale + *ros* horse]

waltz (wolts or wôlts) *n.* **1** a smooth, even, gliding dance in three-four time. **2** the music for such a dance. **3** in music, any composition or part of a composition written in three-four time. *—v.* **1** dance a waltz. **2** move nimbly or quickly. [< G *Walzer* < *walzen* roll] **—waltz′er,** *n.*

wam·pum (wom′pəm) *n.* **1** beads made from shells, formerly used by North American Indians as money, as a reminder of a treaty, and as ornament. **2** *Slang.* money. [< Algonquian]

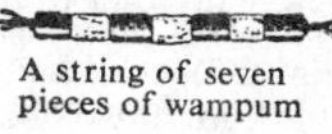

A string of seven pieces of wampum

hat, āge, cãre, fär; let, ēqual, tėrm; it, īce
hot, ōpen, ôrder; oil, out; cup, pu̇t, rüle, ūse
əbove, takən, pencəl, lemən, circəs
ch, child; ng, long; sh, ship
th, thin; ᴛʜ, then; zh, measure

wan (won) *adj.* **wan·ner, wan·nest. 1** pale; lacking natural color: *Her face looked wan after her long illness.* **2** looking worn or tired; faint; weak: *The sick boy gave the doctor a wan smile.* [OE *wann* dark] **—wan′ly,** *adv.* **—wan·ness,** *n.* **—Syn. 1** See **pale.**

wand (wond) *n.* a slender stick or rod: *The magician waved his wand.* [ME < ON *vöndr*] **—wand′like′,** *adj.*

wan·der (won′dər) *v.* **1** move here and there without any special purpose. **2** go aimlessly over or through. **3** go from the right way; stray: *The dog wandered off and got lost.* **4** be delirious; be incoherent: *His mind wandered when he had a very high fever.* [OE *wandrian*] **—wan′der·er** *n.*

Syn. 1 Wander, stray = go from place to place more or less aimlessly or without a settled course. **Wander** emphasizes moving about from place to place without a definite course or destination: *We wandered through the stores, hoping to get ideas for Christmas presents.* **Stray** emphasizes going aimlessly beyond the usual or proper limits or away from the regular path or course, and often suggests getting lost: *Two of the children strayed from the picnic grounds.*

Wandering Jew 1 in medieval legend, a Jew who insulted Christ on the way to the Crucifixion and was condemned to wander on earth till Christ's second coming. **2 wandering Jew,** a trailing plant that grows and spreads rapidly. One kind is a common weed.

wan·der·lust (won′dər lust′) *n.* a strong desire to wander: *His wanderlust led him all over the world.* [< G *Wanderlust* < *wandern* wander + *Lust* desire]

wane (wān) *v.* **waned, wan·ing,** *n* *—v.* **1** become smaller; become smaller gradually: *The moon wanes after it has become full.* **2** decline in power, influence, importance, etc.: *Many great empires have waned.* **3** decline in strength, intensity, etc.: *The light of day wanes in the evening.* **4** draw to a close: *Summer wanes as autumn nears.* *—n.* **1** a waning. **2 in** or **on the wane,** growing less; waning. [OE *wanian*]

wan·gan (wong′gən) *n.* wanigan.

wan·gle (wang′gəl) *v.* **-gled, -gling.** *Informal.* **1** manage to get by schemes, tricks, persuasion, etc. **2** make one's way through difficulties. **3** change (an account, report, etc.) dishonestly for one's advantage. [origin uncertain]

wan·i·gan (won′ə gən) *n.* **1** a lumberman's chest or trunk. **2** *Cdn.* a large sled equipped as living quarters and pulled by tracked vehicles as part of a train for carrying troops and supplies in the North. **3** a kind of boat used by lumbermen for carrying supplies, tools, etc. and as a houseboat. [< Algonquian *waniigan* trap, place for stray objects]

wan·nish (won′ish) *adj.* somewhat wan.

want (wont) *v.* **1** wish for; wish: *He wants to become an engineer. He wants a new car.* **2** be without; lack: *The fund for a new church wants only a few hundred dollars of the sum needed.* **3** need: *Plants want water.* **4** be lacking: *It wants an hour until dinner.* **5** need food, clothing, and shelter; be very poor. **6 want for,** lack. **7 want to,** *Informal.* ought to: *You want to eat a balanced diet.*
—n. **1** something desired or needed; desire: *He is a man of few wants.* **2** a lack: *The plant died from want of water.* **3** a need: *supply a long-felt want.* **4** a lack of food, clothing, or shelter; great poverty: *The old soldier is now in want.* **5 be in want of,** need. **6 for the want of,** because of the lack or absence of: *We sold the store for want of customers.* [ME < ON *vant* < *vanr* lacking] **—Syn.** *v.* **1** desire, crave. **2** See **lack.** *–n.* **2** deficiency, dearth, scarcity, insufficiency. **3** requirement, necessity. **4** destitution, privation, indigence, straits. See **poverty.**

want ad *Informal.* a notice in a newspaper stating that an employee, an apartment, etc. is wanted; classified ad.

want·ing (won′ting) *adj.* **1** lacking; missing: *One volume of the set is wanting.* **2** not coming up to a standard or need: *The vegetables were weighed and found wanting.*

wan·ton (won′tən) *adj.* **1** reckless; heartless: *That bad boy hurts animals from wanton cruelty.* **2** without reason or excuse: *a wanton attack, wanton mischief.* **3** not moral; not chaste: *a wanton woman.* **4** *Poetic.* frolicsome; playful: *a wanton breeze, a wanton child.* **5** not restrained: *a wanton mood.* **6** profuse in growth; luxuriant; rank. —*n.* a person who is not moral or chaste. —*v.* act in a wanton manner: *The wind wantoned with the leaves.* [ME *wantowen* < OE *wan-* deficient (related to WANE) + *togen* brought up, pp. of *tēon* bring] —**wan′ton·ly,** *adv.* —**wan′ton·ness,** *n.* —**Syn.** *adj.* **3** dissolute, licentious.

wap·i·ti (wop′i tē) *n.* **-ti** or **-tis.** a North American deer having long, slender antlers; the North American elk. [< Algonquian]

war (wôr) *n. v.* **warred, war·ring,** *adj.* —*n.* **1** a fight carried on by armed force between nations or parts of a nation. **2** fighting; strife; conflict: *Doctors carry on war against disease.* **3** the occupation or art of fighting with weapons; military science: *Soldiers are trained for war.* **4 at war,** taking part in a war. **5 go to war, a** start a war. **b** go as a soldier.
—*v.* **1** fight; make war. **2** carry on any struggle actively; contend; battle: *war against all things mean or petty.* —*adj.* used in war; having to do with war; caused by war: *war materials.* [ME *werre* < AF var. of OF *guerre* < Gmc.] —**war′less,** *adj.* —**Syn.** *n.* **1** warfare, hostilities.

War between the States in the United States, the Civil War, from 1861 to 1865.

war·ble[1] (wôr′bəl) *v.* **-bled, -bling,** *n.* —*v.* **1** sing with trills, quavers, or melodious turns: *Birds warbled in the trees.* **2** make a sound like that of a bird warbling: *The brook warbled over its rocky bed.* —*n.* a warbling. [ME < ONF *werbler* < Gmc.]

war·ble[2] (wôr′bəl) *n.* **1** a hard lump or swelling on a horse's back, caused by the rubbing of the saddle. **2** a small swelling under the hide of cattle, caused by larvae of the warble fly. **3** a warble fly, or its larvae. Also, **wabble.** [< Swedish *varbulde* < *var* pus + *bulde* swelling]

war·bled (wôr′bəld) *adj.* attacked or infected by warbles.

warble fly any of various flies whose larvae burrow under the hide of cattle, producing warbles.

war·bler (wôr′blər) *n.* **1** a person or thing that warbles. **2** any of a large variety of small songbirds, often brightly colored.

war bride a woman who becomes the bride of a soldier during wartime.

war club a heavy club used as a weapon.

war crime any violation of the rules of warfare, especially atrocities against civilians, political prisoners, etc.

war criminal one who is convicted of committing a war crime.

war cry 1 a word or phrase shouted in fighting; battle cry. **2** a party cry in any contest.

ward (wôrd) *n.* **1** a division of a hospital or prison. **2** an administrative or electoral district of a city or town, especially one represented by an alderman. **3** a person under the care of a guardian or of a court. **4** guard: *The soldiers kept ward over the castle.* **5** the state of being kept under guard; custody; prison. **6** in fencing, etc., a movement or position of defence. **7** a notch in a key. **8** the corresponding ridge in a lock. [OE *weard*, fem., a guarding] —*v.* **ward off,** keep away; turn aside. [OE *weardian* guard. Akin to GUARD.]

-ward *suffix.* in the direction of; that is, moves, or faces toward; toward, as in *backward, heavenward, onward, seaward.* See also **-wards.** [OE *-weard*]

☛ **ward, -wards.** Of variants such as *downward—downwards* and *forward—forwards*, only the *-ward* form is used as adjective or noun: *a forward movement, looking to the westward.* Either variant may be used as adverb or preposition: *He fell forward* (or *forwards*). *He came toward me* (or *towards me*).

war dance a tribal dance performed before going to war or to celebrate a victory.

ward·en (wôr′dən) *n.* **1** a keeper; guard. **2** the man in charge of a prison. **3** a high officer in certain colleges or other institutions. **4** a person in charge of a student's residence at certain universities. **5** in certain provinces, the chief executive officer of a county, elected by and from the members of the county council. **6** a churchwarden. [ME < ONF *wardein*, var. of *g(u)arden*, ult. < Gmc. Doublet of GUARDIAN.]

ward·er (wôr′dər) *n.* **1** a guard; watchman. **2** a warden (def. 2); a jailer.

ward heeler *Esp.U.S. Informal.* a follower of a political boss, who goes around asking for votes, etc.

ward·robe (wôrd′rōb′) *n.* **1** a stock of clothes: *She is shopping for her spring wardrobe.* **2** a closet or piece of furniture for holding clothes. **3** a room in which clothes are kept. [ME < ONF *warderobe*, var. of OF *garderobe* < *garder* keep (< Gmc.) + *robe* gown (< Gmc.)]

ward·room (wôrd′rüm′ or -rům′) *n.* on a warship, the living and eating quarters for all the commissioned officers except the commanding officer.

-wards *suffix.* in the direction of, as in *backwards, upwards.* See also **-ward.**

☛ **-wards.** Used originally and chiefly in adverbs.

ward·ship (wôrd′ship) *n.* **1** guardianship; custody; guardianship over a minor or ward. **2** the condition of being a ward, or under a legal or feudal guardian.

ware[1] (wãr) *n.* **1** Usually, **wares,** *pl.* manufactured goods; articles for sale. **2** pottery; earthenware: *blue-and-white ware from Delft.* [OE *waru*]

☛ **Ware** as used in *silverware, glassware,* etc. usually means "made of"; as used in *kitchenware* it means "intended for."

ware[2] (wãr) *adj. v.* **wared, war·ing.** *Archaic.* —*adj.* aware. —*v.* look out (for); beware (of). [OE *wær*]

ware·house (*n.* wãr′hous′; *v.* wãr′houz′ or -hous′) *n. v.* **-housed, -hous·ing.** —*n.* a place where goods are kept; storehouse. —*v.* put or store in a warehouse.

ware·house·man (wãr′hous′mən) *n.* **-men** (-mən). a man who owns or works in a warehouse.

war·fare (wôr′fãr′) *n.* **1** war; fighting. **2** any struggle or contest. [ME *warfare* < *war* + *fare* a going, OE *faru* journey]

war game a training exercise that simulates war. It may be an exercise on a map or a computer, or it may be manoeuvres with actual troops, weapons, and equipment.

war·head (wôr′hed′) *n.* the forward part of a rocket, missile, torpedo, etc.: *The warhead contains the explosive charge.*

war horse 1 a horse used in war. **2** *Informal.* a person who has taken part in many battles, struggles, etc.

war·i·ly (wãr′ə lē) *adv.* cautiously; carefully.

war·i·ness (wãr′ē nis) *n.* caution; care.

war·like (wôr′līk′) *adj.* **1** fit for war; ready for war. **2** fond of war: *warlike tribes.* **3** threatening war: *a warlike speech.* **4** of war; having to do with war. —**Syn. 3** belligerent, hostile. **4** martial. See **military.**

war·lock (wôr′lok) *n.* a man who is supposed to have magic powers as a result of making a compact with Satan; wizard. [OE *wǣrloga* traitor, oath-breaker < *wǣr* covenant + *-loga* one who denies]

war·lord (wôr′lôrd′) *n.* **1** a military commander. **2** a bandit chief who exercises control over a particular region.

warm (wôrm) *adj.* **1** more hot than cold; having heat; giving forth heat: *a warm fire. She sat in the warm sunshine.* **2** having a feeling of heat: *be warm from running.* **3** that makes or keeps warm: *a warm coat.* **4** having or showing affection, enthusiasm, or zeal: *a warm welcome.* **5** easily excited: *a warm temper.* **6** exciting; lively: *a warm dispute.* **7** fresh and strong: *a warm scent.* **8** *Informal.* in games, treasure hunts, etc., near what one is searching for. **9** suggesting heat. Red, orange, and yellow are called warm colors. **10** uncomfortable; unpleasant: *make things warm for a person.*
—*v.* **1** make or become warm: *warm a room.* **2** make or become cheered, interested, friendly, or sympathetic: *The speaker warmed to his subject.* **3 warm up, a** heat or cook again. **b** make or become more interested, friendly, etc. **c** practise or exercise for a few minutes before entering a game, contest, etc. **d** of an engine, radio, etc., run or operate in order to reach a proper working temperature: *It takes the car a long time to warm up on cold mornings.* **e** run or operate an engine, radio, etc., until it reaches a proper working temperature. [OE *wearm*] —**warm′er,** *n.* —**warm′ly,** *adv.* —**warm′ness,** *n.* —**Syn.** *adj.* **4** cordial, hearty, fervent, enthusiastic. **5** fiery, peppery.

warm-blood·ed (wôrm′blud′id) *adj.* **1** having warm blood and a body temperature between 98 degrees and 112 degrees. Cats and birds are warm-blooded; snakes and turtles are cold-blooded. **2** with much feeling; eager; ardent.

warm-heart·ed (wôrm′här′tid) *adj.* kind; sympathetic; friendly.

warming pan a covered pan having a long handle and designed to hold hot coals, formerly used to warm beds.

warm·ish (wôrm′ish) *adj.* rather warm. **—warm′ish·ly,** *adv.* **—warm′ish·ness,** *n.*

war·mon·ger (wôr′mung′gər or -mong′gər) *n.* a person who is in favor of war or attempts to bring about war.

warmth (wôrmth) *n.* **1** the condition or state of being warm: *the warmth of the open fire.* **2** a warm feeling. **3** liveliness of feelings or emotions; fervor: *He spoke with warmth of the natural beauty of the country.* **4** in painting, a glowing effect, as from the use of reds and yellows. **—Syn. 3** zeal, ardor.

warm-up (wôrm′up′) *n.* **1** exercise or practice taken for a few minutes before entering a game, contest, etc. **2** the running of an engine, radio, etc. until it reaches a proper working temperature. **3** any preliminary trial or session before the main contest, exhibition, or undertaking.

warn (wôrn) *v.* **1** give notice to in advance; put on guard (against danger, evil, harm, etc.): *The clouds warned us that a storm was coming.* **2** give notice to; inform: *The whistle warned visitors that the ship was ready to sail.* **3** give notice to go, stay, etc.: *warn trespassers off.* **4** remind (*of*); counsel (*against*); admonish: *warn a man of his duty.* [OE *warnian*] **—warn′er,** *n.*

Syn. 1 Warn, caution = give someone notice of possible or coming danger, harm, risk, unpleasantness, consequences of an action or practice, etc. **Warn** emphasizes giving information or a hint that lets a person avoid or prepare for what is coming or likely to come: *Her mother warned her not to speak to strangers.* **Caution** emphasizes giving advice to be on one's guard against something (or someone) or suggesting steps that can be taken: *Drivers are cautioned against driving too long without a break.* **2** apprise, notify.

warn·ing (wôr′ning) *n.* something that warns; notice given in advance. *—adj.* that warns. **—warn′ing·ly,** *adv.* **—Syn.** *n.* admonition, advice.

War of 1812 a war between the United States and Great Britain, 1812-1815, fought on the Atlantic Ocean and in North America. This war confirmed Canada's independence of the United States.

War of Independence *U.S.* the Revolutionary War.

warp (wôrp) *v.* **1** bend or twist out of shape: *This floor has warped so that it is not level.* **2** bend: *The wings of a plane are sometimes warped at the tips to secure better equilibrium.* **3** mislead; pervert: *Prejudice warps our judgment.* **4** move (a ship, etc.) by ropes fastened to something fixed. **5** arrange (threads or yarn) so as to form a warp. *—n.* **1** a bend or twist; distortion. **2** a rope used in moving a ship. **3** the threads running lengthwise in a fabric. The warp is crossed by the woof. [OE *weorpan* throw]

warp·age (wôrp′ij) *n.* **1** a warping or being warped. **2** a charge for warping a ship into a harbor.

war paint 1 paint put on the face or body by savages before going to war. **2** *Informal.* full dress; ornaments. **3** *Informal.* make-up; cosmetics.

war·path (wôr′path′) *n.* **1** a way taken by a fighting expedition of North American Indians. **2 on the warpath, a** ready for war. **b** looking for a fight; angry.

war·plane (wôr′plān′) *n.* an airplane used in war.

war·rant (wôr′ənt) *n.* **1** that which gives a right; authority: *He had no warrant for his action.* **2** a written order giving authority for something: *a warrant to search the house, a warrant for the payment of money.* **3** a good and sufficient reason; promise; guarantee: *He had no warrant for his hopes.* **4** a document certifying something, especially to a purchaser. **5** the official certificate of appointment issued to certain senior non-commissioned officers in the army and air force and, formerly, in the navy.

hat, āge, cãre, fär; let, ēqual, tėrm; it, īce
hot, ōpen, ôrder; oil, out; cup, pu̇t, rüle, ūse
əbove, takən, pencəl, lemən, circəs
ch, child; ng, long; sh, ship
th, thin; ᴛʜ, then; zh, measure

—v. **1** authorize: *The law warrants his arrest.* **2** justify: *Nothing can warrant such rudeness.* **3** give one's word for; guarantee; promise: *The storekeeper warranted the quality of the coffee.* **4** *Informal.* declare positively; certify. [ME < ONF *warant* < Gmc.] **—Syn.** *n.* **1** sanction, authorization. *–v.* **1** sanction. **3** assure. **4** affirm, attest.

war·rant·a·ble (wôr′ən tə bəl) *adj.* capable of being warranted; justifiable. **—war′rant·a·ble·ness,** *n.* **—war′rant·a·bly,** *adv.*

war·ran·tee (wôr′ən tē′) *n.* a person to whom a warranty is made.

war·rant·er (wôr′ən tər) *n.* one who warrants.

warrant officer 1 in the army, a non-commissioned officer senior to a staff-sergeant and junior to a second lieutenant. **2** in the air force, a non-commissioned officer senior to a flight sergeant and junior to a pilot officer. *Abbrev.*: W.O.

war·ran·tor (wôr′ən tər or wôr′ən tôr′) *n.* a person who makes a warranty; guarantor.

war·ran·ty (wôr′ən tē) *n.* **-ties. 1** a warrant; authority; justification. **2** a promise or pledge that something is what it is claimed to be; guarantee: *a warranty of the quality of the goods sold.* [< OF *warantie* (var. of *guarantie*) < *warantir* warrant < *warant* a warrant < Gmc. Doublet of GUARANTY.]

war·ren (wôr′ən) *n.* **1** a piece of ground having many burrows, where rabbits live or where they are raised. **2** a crowded district or building. [ME < AF *warenne* < Celtic]

war·ri·or (wôr′ē ər) *n.* a fighting man; an experienced soldier. [ME < OF *werreieor* < *werreier* wage war < *werre* war. See WAR.] **—war′ri·or·like′,** *adj.*

War·saw Pact (wôr′so or wôr′sô) a collective defence alliance of Albania, Bulgaria, Czechoslovakia, the German Democratic Republic, Hungary, Poland, Romania, and the Soviet Union, signed in Warsaw on May 14, 1955.

war·ship (wôr′ship′) *n.* a ship used in war.

wart (wôrt) *n.* **1** a small, hard lump on the skin. **2** in botany, a similar lump on a plant or tree. [OE *wearte*]

wart hog a wild hog of Africa that has two large tusks and two large wartlike growths on each side of its face.

war·time (wôr′tīm′) *n.* time of war.

wart·y (wôr′tē) *adj.* **wart·i·er, wart·i·est. 1** having warts. **2** covered with lumps like warts. **3** of or like a wart.

war whoop a war cry of North American Indians; war cry.

war·y (wãr′ē) *adj.* **war·i·er, war·i·est. 1** on one's guard against danger, deception, etc.: *a wary fox.* **2** cautious; careful: *He gave wary answers to all of the stranger's questions.* **3 wary of,** cautious about; careful about. [< *ware*[2]] **—Syn. 1** alert, guarded, vigilant, watchful. **2** circumspect, prudent. See **careful.**

was (wuz or woz; *unstressed,* wəz) *v.* the 1st and 3rd person singular, past indicative of **be:** *I was late. Was he late, too?* [OE *wæs*]

wash[1] (wosh) *v.* **1** clean with water or other liquid: *wash clothes, wash one's face, wash dishes.* **2** make clean: *washed from sin.* **3** remove (dirt, stains, paint, etc.) by or as by the action of water: *wash a spot out.* **4** wash oneself: *He washed before eating dinner.* **5** wash clothes: *She washes for a living.* **6** undergo washing without damage: *That cloth washes well.* **7** be carried along or away by water or other liquid: *The road washed out during the storm.* **8** carry (by a liquid): *Wood is often washed ashore by the waves.* **9** flow or beat with a lapping sound: *The waves washed upon the rocks.* **10** make wet: *The flowers are washed with dew.* **11** cover with a thin coating of color or of metal: *walls washed with blue, silver washed with gold.* **12** sift (earth, ore, etc.) by action of water to separate

valuable material. **13** *Informal.* stand being put to the proof; convince: *That excuse won't wash.* **14 wash away, a** cleanse. **b** wear away by water; erode: *The cliffs are being slowly washed away by the waves.* **15 wash down, a** wash from top to bottom or from end to end. **b** swallow liquid along with or after (solid food) to help in swallowing or digestion. **16 wash out, a** wash the dirt from. **b** fail or cause to fail an examination. **c** lose color, body, or vigor. **d** carry or be carried away by water: *The rain washed out part of the pavement.* **e** *Informal.* cancel: *The show was washed out.* **17 wash up, a** wash the hands and face, as before meals. **b** wash the dishes after meals.
—*n.* **1** a washing or being washed. **2** a quantity of clothes washed or to be washed. **3** the material carried and then dropped by water. **4** motion, rush, or sound of water. **5** a tract of land sometimes overflowed with water and sometimes left dry; a tract of shallow water; fen, marsh, or bog. **6** a liquid for a special use: *a hair wash, a mouth wash.* **7** waste liquid matter; liquid garbage. **8** washy or weak liquid food. **9** a thin coating of color or metal. **10** earth, etc. from which gold or the like can be washed. **11** the rough or broken water left behind a moving ship. **12** a disturbance in air made by an airplane or any of its parts.
—*adj.* that can be washed without damage: *a wash dress.* [OE *wascan*] —**Syn.** v. **1** cleanse, rinse. **4** bathe.

wash[2] (wosh) *n. Cdn.* **1** any of the underwater exits from a beaver lodge. **2** a bear's den. [< Algonquian (Ojibway)]

Wash. the State of Washington.

wash·a·ble (wosh′ə bəl) *adj.* **1** that can be washed without damage: *washable silk.* **2** that can be removed by washing: *washable paint or ink.*

wash·ba·sin (wosh′bā′sən) *n.* a basin for holding water to wash one's face and hands.

wash·board (wosh′bôrd′) *n.* **1** a board having ridges on it, used for rubbing the dirt out of clothes. **2** a road that has a surface with many ridges.

wash·bowl (wosh′bōl′) *n.* a bowl for holding water to wash one's face and hands.

wash·cloth (wosh′kloth′) *n.* a small cloth for washing oneself.

wash·day (wosh′dā′) *n.* a day when clothes are washed.

washed-out (wosht′out′) *adj.* **1** lacking color; faded. **2** *Informal.* lacking life, spirit, etc. **3** damaged by flood; eroded.

washed-up (wosht′up′) *adj. Informal.* **1** done with; through, especially after having failed. **2** fatigued.

wash·er (wosh′ər) *n.* **1** a person who washes. **2** a machine that washes. **3** a flat ring of metal, rubber, leather, etc. used with bolts or nuts, or to make joints tight, to reduce friction, etc.

WASHER
A washer (def. 3)

wash·er·wom·an (wosh′ər wům′ən) *n.* **-wom·en.** a woman whose work is washing clothes.

wash·ing (wosh′ing) *n.* **1** a cleaning with water. **2** clothes, etc. that have been washed or are to be washed. **3** Sometimes, **washings,** *pl.* **a** a liquid that has been used to wash something. **b** the matter removed in washing something: *washings of gold obtained from earth.*

washing machine a machine that washes clothes, etc.

washing soda sodium carbonate, used in washing.

wash·out (wosh′out′) *n.* **1** a washing away of earth, a road, etc. by water. **2** the hold or break made by such action. **3** *Slang.* a failure; disappointment. **4** *Slang.* a person who is a failure.

wash·rag (wosh′rag′) *n.* washcloth.

wash·room (wosh′rüm′ or -rům′) *n.* **1** a room for washing. **2** a room equipped with a toilet (def. 1).

wash·stand (wosh′stand′) *n.* **1** a bowl with pipes and taps for running water to wash one's hands and face. **2** a stand for holding a basin, pitcher, etc. for washing.

wash·trad·ing (wash′trād′ing) *n.* in finance, the buying and selling of stock by the same person to create a false impression of market activity. Also, **wash selling.**

wash·tub (wosh′tub′) *n.* a tub used to wash or soak clothes in.

wash·wom·an (wosh′wům′ən) *n.* **-wom·en.** washerwoman.

wash·y (wosh′ē) *adj.* **wash·ier, wash·i·est.** too much diluted; weak; watery: *We dislike washy coloring, washy poetry, and washy sentiment.*

was·n't (wuz′ənt or woz′ənt) was not.

wasp (wosp) *n.* a kind of insect that has a slender body and a powerful sting. [OE *wæsp*]

WASP *Informal.* White Anglo-Saxon Protestant.

wasp·ish (wos′pish) *adj.* **1** like a wasp; like that of a wasp. **2 a** bad-tempered; irritable: *a waspish person.* **b** marked or characterized by virulence or petulance; spiteful: *a waspish remark.* —**wasp′ish·ly,** *adv.* —**wasp′ish·ness,** *n.*

wasp-waist·ed (wosp′wās′tid) *adj.* having a very slender waist.

was·sail (wos′əl, was′əl, or was āl′) *n.* **1** a drinking party; revel with drinking of healths. **2** spiced ale or other liquor drunk at a wassail. **3** a salutation meaning "Your health!" —*v.* **1** take part in a wassail; revel. **2** drink to the health of. —*interj.* "Your health!" [ME *wassayl* < ON *ves heill* be healthy! cf. OE *wes hāl*]

was·sail·er (wos′əl ər or was′əl ər) *n.* **1** a reveller. **2** a drinker of toasts.

Was·ser·mann (wäs′ər mən) *n.* a Wassermann test.

Wassermann test a test for syphilis, made on a sample of a person's blood or spinal fluid. [< August von *Wassermann* (1866-1925), a German physician who invented this test]

wast (wost) *v. Archaic or poetic.* 2nd pers. sing. past tense of **be.** "Thou wast" means "you were" (sing.).

wast·age (wās′tij) *n.* **1** loss by use, wear, decay, leakage, etc.; waste. **2** the amount wasted.

waste (wāst) *v.* **wast·ed, wast·ing,** *n. adj.* —*v.* **1** make poor use of; spend uselessly; fail to get value from: *Don't waste time or money.* **2** wear down little by little; destroy or lose gradually: *The sick man was wasted by disease.* **3** damage greatly; destroy: *The soldiers wasted the enemy's fields.*
—*n.* **1** poor use; useless spending; failure to get the most out of something. **2** useless or worthless material; stuff to be thrown away: *Garbage or sewage is waste.* **3** bare or wild land; desert; wilderness. **4** a wearing down little by little; gradual destruction or loss. Both waste and repair are constantly going on in our bodies. **5** destruction or devastation caused by war, floods, fires, etc. **6** a vast, dreary, desolate, or empty expanse or tract, as of water or snow-covered land. **7** bunches of cotton or wool threads used to wipe off oil, grease, etc. **8 go to waste,** be wasted.
—*adj.* **1** thrown away as useless or worthless. **2** left over; not used. **3** not cultivated; that is a desert or wilderness; bare; wild. **4** in a state of desolation or ruin. **5** carrying off or holding refuse: *a waste drain.* **6** unused by or unusable to, and therefore excreted by, an animal or human body. **7 lay waste,** damage greatly; destroy; ravage. [ME < ONF *waster,* var. of OF *guaster* < L *vastare* lay waste < *vastus* vast, waste; influenced in OF by cognate Gmc. word] —**Syn.** *v.* **1** squander, dissipate. **2** diminish. –*n.* **2** trash, rubbish, refuse. –*adj.* **1** rejected. **3** desolate, uninhabited. **4** devastated.

waste·bas·ket (wāst′bas′kit) *n.* a basket or other container for wastepaper.

waste·ful (wāst′fəl) *adj.* using or spending too much. —**waste′ful·ly,** *adv.* —**waste′ful·ness,** *n.*

waste·land (wāst′land′) *n.* **1** barren, uncultivated land; land in its natural state. **2** a despoiled or destitute region.

waste-lot (wāst′lot′) *n.* a vacant lot in a city, especially one neglected and left to run to weeds.

waste·pa·per (wāst′pā′pər) *n.* paper thrown away or to be thrown away as useless or worthless.

waste pipe a pipe for carrying off waste water, etc.

wast·er (wās′tər) *n.* one who or that which wastes, a squanderer; spendthrift.

wast·ing (wās′ting) *adj.* **1** laying waste; devastating. **2** gradually destructive to the body.

wast·rel (wās′trəl) *n.* **1** a waster. **2** a good-for-nothing. **3** something useless, inferior, or imperfect.

wa·tap (wa täp′) *n. Cdn.* fibrous roots, especially of the spruce, once much used by North American Indians for sewing birch bark canoes, for weaving water-tight bowls and dishes, and for other purposes. Also, **watape, wattape.** [< Algonquian; cf. Ojibway *watapi*]

watch (woch) *v.* **1** look attentively or carefully; observe: *The medical students watched while the doctor performed the operation.* **2** look at; observe: *watch a play.* **3** look or wait with care and attention; be very careful: *The boy watched for a chance to cross the street.* **4** look at or wait for with care and attention: *The police watched the prisoner.* **5** keep guard: *He watched throughout the night.* **6** keep guard over: *The dog watched the little boy.* **7** stay awake for some purpose: *The nurse watches with the sick.* **8 watch and ward,** guard. **9 watch out,** be careful; be on guard. **10 watch over,** guard or supervise; protect or preserve from danger, harm, error, etc.
—*n.* **1** a careful looking; attitude of attention: *Be on the watch for automobiles when you cross the street.* **2** a protecting; guarding: *A man keeps watch over the bank at night.* **3** a person or persons kept as a guard: *The man's cry aroused the town watch, who came running to his aid.* **4** a period of time for guarding: *a watch in the night.* **5** a staying awake for some purpose. **6** a spring-driven or electronic device for indicating time, small enough to be carried in a pocket or worn on the wrist. **7** in nautical use: **a** the time of duty of one part of a ship's crew. A watch usually lasts four hours. **b** the part of a crew on duty at one time. [OE *wæccan*] —**watch′er,** *n.*

watch·case (woch′kās′) *n.* the outer covering for the works of a watch.

watch chain the chain attached to a watch and fastened to one's clothing or worn around one's neck.

watch·dog (woch′dog′) *n.* **1** a dog kept to guard property. **2** a watchful guardian.

watch fire a fire kept burning at night in camps, etc.

watch·ful (woch′fəl) *adj.* watching carefully; on the lookout; wide-awake. —**watch′ful·ly,** *adv.*
—**watch′ful·ness,** *n.*
Syn. Watchful, vigilant, alert = wide-awake and attentive or on the lookout for something good or harmful. **Watchful** is the general word, particularly suggesting paying close attention and observing carefully or keeping careful guard: *He is watchful of his health.* **Vigilant** = constantly and keenly watchful for a definite reason or purpose, especially to see and avoid danger: *The new mayor is vigilant against attempts to smear his reputation.* **Alert** emphasizes being wide-awake and ready to meet what comes: *The alert driver avoided an accident.*

watching brief **1** a brief directing a lawyer to observe proceedings on a client's behalf. **2** any position or task involving similar watchfulness.

watch·mak·er (woch′māk′ər) *n.* a man who makes and repairs watches.

watch·mak·ing (woch′māk′ing) *n.* the business of making and repairing watches.

watch·man (woch′mən) *n.* **-men** (-mən). a man who keeps watch; guard: *A watchman guards the bank at night.*

watch meeting a church service held at night, especially on New Year's Eve until midnight.

watch night New Year's Eve, observed in the United Church and some other churches with social gatherings and religious services which last until the arrival of the new year.

watch pocket a small pocket for holding a watch.

watch·tow·er (woch′tou′ər) *n.* a tower from which a man watches for enemies, fires, ships, etc.

watch·word (woch′wėrd′) *n.* **1** a secret word that allows a person to pass a guard; password: *We gave the watchword, and the sentinel let us pass.* **2** a motto; slogan: *"Forward" is our watchword.*

wa·ter (wo′tər or wô′tər) *n.* **1** the liquid that constitutes rain, oceans, rivers, lakes, and ponds. Pure water is a transparent, colorless, tasteless, odorless compound of hydrogen and oxygen, H_2O, freezing at 32° F. or 0° C., and boiling at 212° F. or 100° C. **2** a liquid from the body, such as tears, sweat, saliva, urine, serum, etc. **3** any liquid preparation that suggests water: *rose water.* **4** a body of water; sea, lake, river, etc. **5** the water of a river, etc. with reference to its relative height, etc.: *high or low water.* **6** the surface of a body of water: *swim under the water.* **7** the degree of clearness and brilliance of a precious stone. A diamond of the first water is a very clear and brilliant one. **8** a wavy marking on silk, metal, etc. **9** in business, the additional shares or securities issued without corresponding increase of capital or assets. **10 waters,** *pl.* **a** flowing water. **b** water moving in waves; the sea; the high sea. **c** spring water; mineral water.
above water, a above the surface of the water; not submerged; afloat. **b** out of trouble or difficulty, especially out of financial trouble or difficulty.
back water, a make a boat go backward. **b** reverse one's course; move or draw backward.
by water, on a ship or boat.
hold water, stand the test; be true, dependable, effective, etc.
like water, very freely.
make water, a urinate. **b** of a boat, ship, etc., take in water through leaks or over the side.
of the first water, of the highest degree.
take (the) waters, drink mineral water at a health resort, usually in a scheduled course of treatment.
—*v.* **1** sprinkle or wet with water: *water grass.* **2** supply with water: *British Columbia is well watered by rivers and brooks.* **3** get or take in a supply of water: *A ship waters before sailing.* **4** fill with water; discharge water: *Her eyes watered.* **5** weaken by adding water: *It is against the law to sell watered milk.* **6** make a wavy marking on (silk, metal, etc.). **7** in business, increase (stock, etc.) by issue of additional shares or securities without a corresponding increase in capital or assets. **8 make one's mouth water,** arouse one's appetite or desire. **9 water down, a** reduce in strength by diluting with water. **b** weaken or reduce in strength or quality by addition or alteration. [OE *wæter*] —**wa′ter·er,** *n.* —**wa′ter·less,** *adj.*

hat, āge, cãre, fär; let, ēqual, tėrm; it, īce
hot, ōpen, ôrder; oil, out; cup, pu̇t, rüle, ūse
əbove, takən, pencəl, lemən, circəs
ch, child; ng, long; sh, ship
th, thin; ᴛʜ, then; zh, measure

water beetle a beetle having the hind legs broad and fringed so as to be well adapted for swimming.

water bird a bird that swims or wades in water.

water bomber an aircraft used for water bombing.

water bombing a means of fighting forest fires by dropping water on them from aircraft equipped with special tanks.

wa·ter-borne (wo′tər bôrn′ or wô′tər-) *adj.* **1** supported by water; floating. **2** conveyed by a boat or the like.

water bottle a bottle, bag, etc. for holding water.

wa·ter·buck (wo′tər buk′ or wô′tər-) *n.* any of various African antelopes that frequent rivers, marshes, etc. [< Du. *waterbok*]

water buffalo the common buffalo of Asia and the Philippines.

water bug **1** a cockroach that is often called the croton bug. **2** any of various insects that live in, on, or near water.

Water Carrier in astrology, the eleventh sign of the zodiac; Aquarius.

water clock an instrument for measuring time by the flow of water.

water closet a toilet flushed by water.

water color or **colour** **1** paint mixed with water instead of oil. **2** the art of painting with water colors. **3** a picture painted with water colors.

wa·ter-col·or or **wa·ter-col·our** (wo′tər kul′ər or wô′tər-) *adj.* made with water colors.

water cooler any device for cooling water, or for cooling something by means of water.

wa·ter·course (wo′tər kôrs′ or wô′tər-) *n.* **1** a stream of water; river; brook. **2** a channel for water: *dried-up watercourses.*

wa·ter·craft (wo′tər kraft′ or wô′tər-) *n.* **1** skill in water sports, such as boating, swimming, etc. **2** a ship or ships; boat or boats.

water cress a plant that grows in water, used for salad and as a garnish.

water cure the treatment of disease by the use of water; hydropathy.

water dog 1 a dog that swims well, especially one that retrieves game from water. 2 *Informal.* a man at home on or in the water, such as a sailor or a good swimmer.

wa·ter·fall (wo′tər fol′ or wôt′ər fôl′) *n.* a fall of water from a high place; a cataract.

water flea a very small crustacean that swims with a skipping motion.

wa·ter·fowl (wo′tər foul′ or wô′tər-) *n.* **-fowl** or **-fowls.** a water bird.

wa·ter front or **wa·ter·front** (wo′tər frunt′ or wô′tər-) *n.* 1 the part of a city, town, etc. beside a river, lake, or harbor. 2 land at the water's edge.

water gap a gap in a mountain ridge through which a stream flows.

water gas a gas used for lighting or fuel. Water gas is largely carbon monoxide and hydrogen, made by passing steam over very hot coal or coke.

water gate 1 a gate or gateway through which water passes. 2 a gate that controls the flow of water; floodgate. 3 a gate opening on water.

water glass 1 a glass to hold water; tumbler. 2 sodium or potassium silicate, a substance used especially to coat eggs and keep them from spoiling.

water hole a hole in the ground where water collects; small pond; pool.

water ice 1 a frozen mixture of fruit juice, sugar, and water; sherbet. 2 solid ice formed by the direct freezing of water, and not by the compacting of snow.

watering can or **pot** a can with a spout for sprinkling water on plants, etc.

watering place 1 *Esp.Brit.* a resort with springs containing mineral water. 2 *Esp.Brit.* a resort where there is bathing, boating, etc. 3 a place where water may be obtained.

water jacket a casing with water in it, put around something to keep it cool or at a certain temperature.

water level 1 the surface level of a body of water. 2 water table.

water lily a water plant having flat, floating leaves and showy, fragrant flowers. The flowers of the common North American water lily are white, yellow, or sometimes pink.

water line 1 the line where the surface of the water touches the side of a ship or boat. 2 any of several lines marked on a ship's hull to show the depth to which it sinks when unloaded, partly loaded, or fully loaded.

wa·ter-logged (wo′tər logd′ or wô′tər-) *adj.* 1 so full of water that it will barely float. 2 thoroughly soaked with water.

Wa·ter·loo (wo′tər lü′ or wô′tər lü′) *n.* 1 any decisive or crushing defeat. 2 **meet one's Waterloo, a** suffer a decisive or crushing defeat. **b** reach a point from which one can go no farther. [< *Waterloo,* a town in central Belgium, where Napoleon was finally defeated in 1815 by the allied armies under Wellington and Blücher]

water main a large pipe for carrying water.

wa·ter·man (wo′tər mən or wô′tər-) *n.* **-men** (-mən). 1 a boatman; a man who works on a boat. 2 an oarsman.

wa·ter·mark (wo′tər märk′ or wô′tər-) *n.* 1 a mark showing how high water has risen or how low it has fallen: *the high watermark of a river.* 2 a faint design made in some kinds of paper. —*v.* put a watermark in. Some note papers are watermarked.

wa·ter·mel·on (wo′tər mel′ən or wô′tər-) *n.* 1 a large, juicy melon having red or pink pulp and a hard, green rind. 2 the vine bearing these melons.

water mill a mill whose machinery is run by water power.

water moccasin 1 a poisonous snake of the S. United States that lives in swamps and along streams. 2 any of various similar but harmless snakes; a water snake.

water nymph 1 a nymph or goddess associated with some body of water. 2 a nymph supposed to live in water.

water of crystallization water that is chemically present in certain crystalline substances. When the water is removed by heating, the crystals break up into a powder.

water ouzel any of various wading birds related to the thrushes, that dive in deep water for food; dipper.

water parsnip any of various herbs of the parsley family that grow mostly in watery grounds.

water polo a game played with an inflated ball by two teams of swimmers.

water power 1 the power from flowing or falling water that can be used to drive machinery and make electricity. 2 a fall in a stream that can supply power.

wa·ter·proof (wo′tər prüf′ or wô′tər-) *adj.* that will not let water through; resistant to water. —*n.* 1 a waterproof material. 2 a waterproof coat; raincoat. —*v.* make waterproof.

water rat 1 a large European field mouse that lives in the banks of streams or lakes. 2 a muskrat. 3 *Slang.* a person who is or poses as a sailor, longshoreman, etc., but who lives by petty thievery, smuggling, etc.

wa·ter·shed (wo′tər shed′ or wô′tər-) *n.* 1 a height of land that divides two areas drained by different river systems: *On one side of a watershed, rivers and streams flow in one direction; on the other side, they flow in a different direction.* 2 the region drained by one river system. [< *water* + *shed*[2]]

wa·ter·side (wo′tər sīd′ or wô′tər-) *n.* land along the sea, a lake, a river, etc.

water ski one of a pair of wooden skis for gliding over the water while being towed by a boat.

wa·ter-ski (wo′tər skē′ or wô′tər-) *v.* glide over the water on water skis.

water snake a non-poisonous snake living in or frequenting water.

wa·ter-soak (wo′tər sōk′ or wô′tər-) *v.* soak thoroughly with water.

water softener 1 a chemical added to hard water to soften it by dissolving and removing minerals. 2 a device using such a chemical and attached to a water supply.

water spaniel 1 a breed of curly-haired dog, often trained to swim out for wild ducks, geese, etc. that have been shot down by hunters. 2 a dog of this breed.

wa·ter·spout (wo′tər spout′ or wô′tər-) *n.* 1 a pipe that takes away or spouts water. 2 a rotating column or inverted cone of mist, spray, and water, produced by the action of a whirlwind over the ocean or a large lake.

water sprite a sprite supposed to live in water.

water table the level below which the ground is saturated with water.

wa·ter·tight (wo′tər tight′ or wô′tər-) *adj.* 1 so tight that no water can get in or out. Ships are often divided into watertight compartments by watertight partitions. 2 leaving no opening for misunderstanding, criticism, etc.; perfect: *a watertight argument.*

water tower 1 a big tower to hold water. 2 a fire-extinguishing apparatus used to throw water on the upper parts of tall buildings.

water vapor or **vapour** water in a gaseous state, especially when below the boiling point and fairly diffused, as distinguished from steam.

wa·ter·way (wo′tər wā′ or wô′tər-) *n.* 1 a river, canal, or other body of water that ships can go on. 2 a channel for water.

water wheel a wheel turned by water, usually to supply power.

water wings a waterproof, air-filled device resembling a pair of wings, used to support a swimmer or a person learning to swim.

wa·ter·works (wo′tər wėrks′ or wô′tər-) *n.pl. or sing.* 1 a system of pipes, reservoirs, water towers, pumps, etc. for supplying a city or town with water. 2 a building containing engines and pumps for pumping water; pumping station. 3 *Slang.* a flow of tears, especially a sudden or violent flow.

wa·ter·worn (wo′tər wôrn′ or wô′tər-) *adj.* worn or smoothed by the action of water.

wa·ter·y (wo′tər ē or wô′tər ē) *adj.* 1 of water; connected with water. 2 full of water; wet: *watery soil.* 3 indicating rain: *a watery sky.* 4 tearful: *watery eyes.*

5 containing too much water: *watery soup.* 6 like water. 7 weak; thin; poor; pale: *a watery blue.* 8 in or under water: *A sunken ship goes to a watery grave.*

watt (wot) *n.* a unit of electric power, equivalent to one joule per second: *My lamp uses 60 watts; my toaster uses 660 watts. Abbrev.*: W or w [after James *Watt* (1736-1819), a Scottish engineer and inventor]

watt·age (wot′ij) *n.* electric power expressed in watts: *A flatiron that uses 5 amperes of current on a 110-volt circuit has a wattage of 550.*

wat·tap or **wat·tape** (wa täp′) *n.* watap.

watt-hour (wot′our′) *n.* a unit of electrical energy or work, equal to one watt maintained for one hour. *Abbrev.*: wh

wat·tle (wot′əl) *n. v.* **-tled, -tling,** *adj.* —*n.* 1 Also, **wattles,** *pl.* sticks interwoven with twigs or branches; a framework of wicker: *a hut built of wattle.* 2 in Australia, the acacia, used to make wattles and in tanning. 3 the red flesh hanging down from the throat of a chicken, turkey, etc. 4 the barbel of a fish.
—*v.* 1 make (a fence, wall, roof, hut, etc.) of wattle. 2 twist or weave together (twigs, branches, etc.). 3 bind together with interwoven twigs, branches, etc.
—*adj.* made or built of wattle. [OE *watul*]

wat·tled (wot′əld) *adj.* 1 having wattles. 2 formed by interwoven twigs; interlaced.

watt·me·ter (wot′mē′tər) *n.* an instrument for measuring in watts the power developed in an electric circuit.

wave (wāv) *n. v.* **waved, wav·ing.** —*n.* 1 a moving ridge or swell of water. 2 any movement like this. 3 in physics, a movement of particles to and fro; vibration. 4 a swell, surge, or rush; increase of some emotion, influence, condition, etc.; outburst: *a cold wave, a wave of enthusiasm.* 5 a waving, especially of something, as a signal: *a wave of the hand.* 6 a curve or series of curves: *the waves in a girl's hair.* 7 a permanent wave. 8 a wavy line of color or texture, as on a watered fabric. 9 *Poetic.* a body of water; sea. [< v.]
—*v.* 1 move as waves do; move up and down or back and forth; sway: *The tall grass waved in the breeze.* 2 have a wavelike form: *Her hair waves naturally.* 3 give a wavelike form or pattern to: *wave hair.* 4 signal or direct by waving: *She waved him away.* 5 shake in the air; brandish: *He waved the stick at them.* [OE *wafian*]
—**wave′like′,** *adj.* —**wav′er,** *n.*
Syn. *n.* 1 **Wave, breaker, ripple** = a moving ridge on the surface of water. **Wave** is the general word: *The raft rose and fell on the waves.* **Breaker** applies to a heavy wave of the ocean, that breaks into foam as it nears the shore or strikes rocks: *Our favorite sport is riding the breakers in.* **Ripple** applies to a tiny wave, such as one caused by the ruffling of a smooth surface by a breeze: *There is scarcely a ripple on the lake tonight.* –*v.* 1 rock, fluctuate, undulate.

wave length or **wave-length** (wāv′length′) *n.* in physics, the distance between any particle of a medium through which waves are passing and the next particle that is in the same phase with it.

wave·less (wāv′lis) *adj.* free from waves; undisturbed; still.

wave·let (wāv′lit) *n.* a little wave.

wa·ver (wā′vər) *v.* 1 move to and fro; flutter. 2 vary in intensity; flicker: *a wavering light.* 3 be undecided; hesitate: *Her choice wavered between the blue dress and the green one.* 4 grow fainter, then louder, or change pitch up and down fairly quickly; quaver, tremble, or pulsate. 5 become unsteady; begin to give way: *The battle line wavered and broke.* —*n.* a wavering. [ult. < *wave*] —**wa′ver·er,** *n.* —**wa′ver·ing·ly,** *adv.* —**Syn.** *v.* 3 See **hesitate.**

wa·vey (wā′vē) *n. Cdn.* a wild goose, especially the snow goose. [< Cdn.F < Cree]

wav·y (wāv′ē) *adj.* **wav·i·er, wav·i·est.** 1 having waves; having many waves: *wavy hair, a wavy line.* 2 a moving to and fro or up and down with a wavelike motion. b of movements, taking place in undulating curves; sinuous. 3 of ground or the surface of the country, rising and falling gently in a succession of rounded heights and hollows. —**wav′i·ness,** *n.*

wax[1] (waks) *n.* 1 a yellowish substance made by bees for constructing their honeycombs. Wax is hard when cold, but can be easily shaped when warm. 2 any substance like this. Most of the wax used for candles,

hat, āge, cãre, fär; let, ēqual, tėrm; it, īce
hot, ōpen, ôrder; oil, out; cup, pu̇t, rüle, ūse
əbove, takən, pencəl, lemən, circəs
ch, child; ng, long; sh, ship
th, thin; ᴛʜ, then; zh, measure

for keeping air from jelly, etc., is really paraffin. Sealing wax and floor wax are other common waxes. 3 *Slang.* a phonograph record. 4 **wax in one's hands,** a person easy to influence and manage. —*v.* 1 apply wax to. 2 *Slang.* make a phonograph recording of. —*adj.* of wax. [OE *weax*] —**wax′like′,** *adj.*

wax[2] (waks) *v.* **waxed, waxed** or (*poetic*) **wax·en, wax·ing.** 1 grow bigger or greater; increase: *The moon waxes till it becomes full, and then it wanes.* 2 become: *The party waxed merry.* [OE *weaxan*]

wax bean a yellow string bean.

wax·en (wak′sən) *adj.* 1 made of wax. 2 like wax; smooth, soft, and pale: *waxen skin.* 3 covered or filled with wax.

wax myrtle any of various shrubs or trees whose small berries are coated with wax. The bayberry is a wax myrtle.

wax paper or **waxed paper** paper coated with paraffin or a similar waxy substance, used for moisture-proof wrappings.

wax·wing (waks′wing′) *n.* any of several small birds having a showy crest and red markings at the tips of the wings.

wax·work (waks′wėrk′) *n.* 1 a figure or figures made of wax. 2 **waxworks,** *pl.* an exhibition of figures made of wax.

wax·y (wak′sē) *adj.* **wax·i·er, wax·i·est.** 1 like wax. 2 made of wax; containing wax. 3 abounding in or covered with wax; waxed. 4 in medicine, characterized by or affected with the formation and deposit of an insoluble protein in tissue and organs. —**wax′i·ness,** *n.*

way (wā) *n.* 1 a manner; style: *She has a queer way of talking.* 2 a method; means: *Doctors are using new ways of preventing disease.* 3 a point; feature; respect; detail: *This plan is bad in several ways.* 4 a direction: *Look this way.* 5 a motion along a course: *The guide led the way.* 6 a distance: *The sun is a long way off.* 7 a road; path; street; course: *a way through the forest.* 8 a space for passing or going ahead. 9 Often, **ways,** *pl.* habit; custom: *Don't mind his teasing; it's just his way.* 10 one's wish; will: *A spoiled child wants his own way all the time.* 11 *Informal.* a condition; state: *That sick man is in a bad way.* 12 a movement; forward motion: *The ship slowly gathered way.* 13 the range of experience or notice: *The best idea that ever came my way.* 14 a course of life, action, or experience: "*The way of the ungodly shall perish.*" 15 **ways,** *pl.* the timbers on which a ship is built and launched.
by the way, a while coming or going. b in that connection; incidentally.
by way of, a by the route of; through. b as; for. c making a profession of or having a reputation for (being or doing something): *He is by way of being a clever cartoonist.*
come one's way, happen to one.
give way, a make way; retreat; yield. b break down or fall. c abandon oneself to emotion.
go out of one's way, make a special effort.
have a way with one, be persuasive.
in a way, to some extent.
in the way, being an obstacle, hindrance, etc.
in the way of, a in a favorable position for doing or getting: *He put me in the way of a good investment.* b in the matter or business of; as regards: *We have a small stock in the way of hats.*
lose one's way, not to know any longer where one is.
make one's way, a go. b get ahead; succeed.
make way, a give space for passing or going ahead; make room. b move forward.
once in a way, occasionally.
out of the way, a so as not to be an obstacle, hindrance, etc. b far from where most people live or go; awkward to reach. c unusual; strange. d out of reach; not in danger. e to death. f going or being off the right path; improper;

wrong. **g** mislaid, hidden, or lost.
put out of the way, put to death; murder.
see one's way, be willing or able.
take one's way, go.
under way, going on; in motion; in progress.
—*adv. Informal.* away; far; at a distance: *way up in the air. He lives way across the valley.* [OE *weg*]
Syn. *n.* **1, 2 Way, method, manner** = mode or means of doing or happening. **Way** is the common and general word, sometimes general in meaning, sometimes suggesting a very personal or special manner or method: *The way she spoke hurt me.* **Method** applies to an orderly way of doing something, and suggests definite arrangement of steps or a special system: *Follow her method of cooking.* **Manner** applies to a characteristic or individual method or particular way of acting or happening: *He rides in the western manner.* **7** route, highway, avenue, lane. **12** progress, advance.
☛ **way, ways.** *Way,* meaning distance (def. 6), is standard; *ways* is substandard: *a long way* (not *ways*) *off.*

way·bill (wā′bil′) *n.* a list of goods with a statement of where they are to go and how they are to get there.

way·far·er (wā′fãr′ər) *n.* a traveller, especially one journeying on foot.

way·far·ing (wā′fãr′ing) *adj.* travelling, especially on foot.

way·laid (wā′lād′ or wā′lād′) *v.* pt. and pp. of **waylay.**

Wayland the Smith in Germanic and English legend, a marvellously skilled smith who was normally invisible but became visible under certain circumstances.

way·lay (wā′lā′ or wā′lā′) *v.* **-laid, -lay·ing. 1** lie in wait for; attack on the way: *Robin Hood waylaid and robbed rich travellers.* **2** stop (a person) on his way. [< *way* + *lay, v.,* after MLG or MDu. *wegelagen*] —**way′lay′er,** *n.*

way-out (wā′out′) *adj. Slang.* far away from the ordinary; very unconventional or experimental.

-ways *suffix.* in a manner showing direction or position, as in *edgeways, sideways.* [< *way*]

way·side (wā′sīd′) *n.* the edge of a road or path. —*adj.* along the edge of a road or path.

way station a station between main stations on a railway, etc.

way train a railway train that stops at all or most of the stations on its way.

way·ward (wā′wərd) *adj.* **1** turning from the right way; disobedient; willful. **2** irregular; unsteady. [ME *weiward,* for *aweiward* turned away] —**way′ward·ly,** *adv.* —**way′ward·ness,** *n.* —**Syn. 1** perverse, stubborn.

way·worn (wā′wôrn′) *adj.* wearied by travelling.

W.B. or **w.b.** way bill.

W.C. or **w.c.** *Brit. Informal.* water closet.

WCTU or **W.C.T.U.** Woman's Christian Temperance Union.

we (wē) *pron. nom.* **we;** *poss.* **ours;** *obj.* **us. 1** pl. of **I;** the speaker plus the person or persons addressed or spoken about. An author, a sovereign, a judge, or a newspaper editor sometimes uses *we* when others would say *I.* **2** people in general, including the speaker. [OE *we*]
☛ **We** is frequently used as an indefinite pronoun in expressions like *we find, we sometimes feel,* to avoid passive and impersonal constructions.

weak (wēk) *adj.* **1** that can easily be broken, crushed, overcome, torn, etc.; not strong: *a weak foundation, weak defences.* **2** lacking bodily strength or health: *A weak old man totters as he walks.* **3** lacking power, authority, force, etc.: *a weak law.* **4** lacking mental power: *a weak mind.* **5** lacking moral strength or firmness: *a weak character.* **6** lacking or poor in amount, volume, loudness, taste, intensity, etc.: *a weak army, a weak voice, weak arguments.* **7 a** containing relatively little of the active ingredient or ingredients; not concentrated; diluted: *a weak solution of boric acid.* **b** of less than the normal or desired strength: *weak coffee.* **8** lacking or poor in something specified: *a composition weak in spelling.* **9** of a faith, conviction, etc., not strongly or consistently held; not whole-hearted. **10 a** damaged or defective; likely to give way or break: *a weak link in a chain.* **b** inadequate for the purpose; likely to lose, fail, etc.: *a weak candidate.* **11** in commerce, of prices on an exchange, etc.: **a** having a downward tendency; not firm. **b** characterized by a fluctuating or downward tendency: *a weak market.* **12** in Germanic languages: **a** of verbs, inflected by additions of consonants to the stem, not by an internal vowel change. English weak verbs form the past tense and past participle by adding *-ed, -d,* or *-t.* **b** of nouns and adjectives, inflected with a majority of endings with *-n,* as German *alten* and *Frauen* in *die alten Frauen.* **13** in phonetics: **a** of a sound, not stressed. **b** of an accent or stress, light; not strong. [ME < ON *veikr*]
Syn. 1, 2 Weak, feeble, decrepit = lacking or inferior in strength, energy, or power. **Weak** is the general word, describing people or things not strong enough to act with force or vigor or to undergo pressure, strain, or attack, without risk of breaking, bending, collapsing, etc.: *She has weak ankles.* **Feeble** implies pitiable weakness, great loss of strength from sickness or age or, describing things, faintness or ineffectiveness: *He is too feeble to feed himself.* **Decrepit** = worn out or broken down by age: *They have only one decrepit bed.* **5** irresolute.

weak·en (wēk′ən) *v.* **1** make weak or weaker. **2** become weak or weaker. —**weak′en·er,** *n.*
Syn. 1 Weaken, undermine, debilitate = cause to lose strength, energy, or power. **Weaken** is the general word applying to loss or lowering of energy or strength from any cause or by any means: *Poor organization weakened his argument.* **Undermine** = weaken someone or something gradually by working secretly or treacherously: *Bad companions undermined his parents' influence.* **Debilitate,** formal, means "make (a person's constitution, mind, etc.) weak or feeble by damaging and taking away vitality or strength": *He was debilitated by disease.*

weak·fish (wēk′fish′) *n.* **-fish** or **-fish·es.** a spiny-finned salt-water food fish.

weak-kneed (wēk′nēd′) *adj.* **1** having weak knees. **2** yielding easily to opposition, intimidation, etc.

weak·ling (wēk′ling) *n.* a weak person or animal. —*adj.* weak. [< *weak* + *-ling*]

weak·ly (wēk′lē) *adv. adj.* **-li·er, -li·est.** —*adv.* in a weak manner. —*adj.* weak; feeble; sickly. —**weak′li·ness,** *n.*

weak-mind·ed (wēk′mīn′did) *adj.* **1** having or showing little intelligence; feeble-minded. **2** lacking firmness of mind. —**weak′-mind′ed·ness,** *n.*

weak·ness (wēk′nis) *n.* **1** the condition of being weak; lack of power, force, or vigor. **2** a weak point; slight fault. **3** a fondness: *She has a weakness for chocolate.*

weak stress the third in a series of three degrees of stress, the most prominent being primary, the next secondary. The last syllable of *opportunity* has a weak stress. Such stresses are not marked in this dictionary.

weal[1] (wēl) *n. Archaic.* well-being; prosperity; happiness: *Good citizens act for the public weal.* [OE *wela*]

weal[2] (wēl) *n.* a streak or ridge on the skin made by a stick or whip; welt. [var. of *wale*]

weald (wēld) *n.* **1** *Poetic.* open country. **2 the Weald,** a district in S.E. England including parts of Kent, Surrey, and Sussex. [OE *weald* woods]

wealth (welth) *n.* **1** much money or property; riches. **2** in economics, all things that have money value or that add to the capacity for production. **3** a large quantity; abundance: *a wealth of hair, a wealth of words.* [< *well*[1] or *weal*[1]] —**Syn. 1** prosperity, fortune. **3** profusion.

wealth·y (wel′thē) *adj.* **wealth·i·er, wealth·i·est.** having wealth; rich. —**wealth′i·ly,** *adv.* —**wealth′i·ness,** *n.* —**Syn.** See **rich.**

wean (wēn) *n.* **1** accustom (a child or young animal) to food other than its mother's milk. **2** accustom (a person) to do without something; cause to turn away: *The young delinquent was sent away to wean him from his bad companions.* [OE *wenian*]

wean·ling (wēn′ling) *n.* a child or animal recently weaned. —*adj.* recently weaned.

weap·on (wep′ən) *n.* **1** any instrument used in fighting; means of attack or defence. Swords, spears, arrows, clubs, guns, cannon, and shields are weapons. **2** anything viewed as similar to this in purpose or nature; a means of attack or defence: *use drugs as a weapon against disease.* **3** any organ of a plant or animal used for fighting or for protection, as claws, horns, teeth, and stings. [OE *wǣpen*] —**weap′on·less,** *adj.*

weap·on·ry (wep′ən rē) *n.* **1** weapons collectively. **2** the design and production of weapons.

wear (wãr) *v.* **wore, worn, wear·ing,** *n.* —*v.* **1** have on the

body: *We wear clothes.* **2** use or affect in one's costume or adornment, especially habitually: *wear green, wear a beard.* **3** cause loss or damage to by using: *These shoes are badly worn.* **4** suffer loss or damage from being used: *His coat has worn to shreds.* **5** make by rubbing, scraping, washing away, etc.: *Walking wore a hole in my shoe.* **6** tire; weary: *She was worn with toil and care.* **7 a** last long; give good service: *This coat has worn well.* **b** stand the test of experience, familiarity, criticism, etc.: *a friendship that did not wear.* **8** have; show: *The gloomy old house wore an air of sadness.* **9** have as a quality or attribute; bear: *wear one's honors modestly.* **10** of a ship, fly (a flag or colors). **11** pass or go gradually: *It became hotter as the day wore on.* **12** of a ship, turn or be turned around by pointing the bow away from the wind. **13** spend or pass: *wear away the night in song.* **14 wear down, a** tire; weary. **b** overcome by persistent effort. **c** reduce in height. **15 wear off,** become less. **16 wear out, a** wear until no longer fit for use. **b** use up. **c** tire out; weary.
—*n.* **1** a wearing; a being worn: *clothing for summer wear.* **2** things worn or to be worn; clothing: *The store sells children's wear.* **3** a gradual loss or damage caused by use: *The rug shows wear.* **4** lasting quality; good service: *There is still much wear in these shoes.* **5 wear and tear,** a loss or damage caused by use. [OE *werian*] —**wear′a·ble,** *adj.* —**wear′er,** *n.*

wea·ri·ness (wēr′ē nis) *n.* a weary condition or feeling.

wearing apparel clothes.

wea·ri·some (wēr′ē səm) *adj.* wearying; tiring; tiresome. —**wea′ri·some·ly,** *adv.* —**wea′ri·some·ness,** *n.*

wea·ry (wēr′ē) *adj.* **-ri·er, -ri·est,** *v.* **-ried, -ry·ing.** —*adj.* **1** tired: *weary feet, a weary brain.* **2** causing tiredness; tiring: *a weary wait.* **3** having one's patience, tolerance, or liking (*of*) exhausted. —*v.* **1** make weary; tire. **2** become weary. **3** long (*for*): *She is wearying for home.* [OE *wērig*] —**wea′ri·ly,** *adv.* —**Syn.** *adj.* **1** fatigued, exhausted, fagged. See **tired.**

wea·sand (wē′zənd) *n. Archaic or dialect.* **1** the windpipe. **2** the throat. [OE *wǣsend*]

wea·sel (wē′zəl) *n. v.* **-selled** or **-seled, -sel·ling** or **-sel·ing.** —*n.* a small, quick, sly mammal having a long, slender body and short legs. Weasels feed on rats, birds, eggs, etc. The weasel is brown and white, except in northern regions where it turns white in winter and is called an ermine. —*v.* **1** use tricky actions or words; be evasive; hedge. **2 weasel out,** escape or withdraw craftily or irresponsibly; disengage oneself (from a situation, commitment, responsibility, etc.): *He had promised to help but weaselled out at the last minute.* [OE *weosule*]

weath·er (weᴛʜ′ər) *n.* **1** the condition of the atmosphere with respect to temperature, moisture, cloudiness, etc.: *hot weather, windy weather.* **2** windy or stormy weather. **3 under the weather,** *Informal.* **a** sick; ailing. **b** rather drunk; somewhat intoxicated.
—*v.* **1** expose to the weather: *Wood turns gray if weathered for a long time.* **2** become discolored or worn by air, rain, sun, frost, etc. **3** go or come through safely: *The ship weathered the storm.* **4** *Nautical.* sail to the windward of: *The ship weathered the cape.* **5** make (boards, tiles, etc.) slope so as to shed water. **6** resist the effects of (the weather, a storm, etc.); come through safely.
—*adj.* **1** toward the wind; windward; of the side exposed to the wind: *It was very cold on the weather side of the ship.* **2 keep one's weather eye open,** be on the lookout for possible danger or trouble. [OE *weder*]

weather beam the side of a ship toward the wind.

weath·er-beat·en (weᴛʜ′ər bēt′ən) *adj.* worn or hardened by the wind, rain, and other forces of the weather.

weath·er·board (weᴛʜ′er bôrd′) *n.* thin board, thicker along one edge than along the other; clapboard. —*v.* cover with weatherboards.

weath·er-bound (weᴛʜ′ər bound′) *adj.* delayed by bad weather: *a weather-bound ship.*

weather breeder a fine clear day, popularly supposed to be a sign of a coming storm.

Weather Bureau *U.S.* a bureau of the government that records and forecasts the weather.

weath·er·cast (weᴛʜ′ər kast′) *n.* a weather report that is broadcast on radio or television.

hat, āge, cãre, fär; let, ēqual, tėrm; it, īce
hot, ōpen, ôrder; oil, out; cup, pu̇t, rüle, ūse
əbove, takən, pencəl, lemən, circəs
ch, child; ng, long; sh, ship
th, thin; ᴛʜ, then; zh, measure

weath·er·cast·er (weᴛʜ′ər kast′ər) *n.* one who gives weather reports on radio or television.

weath·er·cock (weᴛʜ′ər kok′) *n.* a device, especially with the figure of a cock on top, to show which way the wind is blowing.

A weather-cock

weath·er·glass (weᴛʜ′ər glas′) *n.* an instrument to show the weather. A barometer is a weatherglass.

weath·er·ing (weᴛʜ′ər ing) *n.* the destructive or discoloring action of air, water, frost, etc., especially on rocks.

weath·er·man (weᴛʜ′ər man′) *n.* **-men** (-men′) *Informal.* a man who forecasts the weather.

weather office the Department of the Environment in the Department of Transport, which records and forecasts the weather; atmospheric environment service.

weath·er·proof (weᴛʜ′ər prüf′) *adj.* protected against rain, snow, or wind; able to stand exposure to all kinds of weather. —*v.* make weatherproof.

weather strip a narrow strip to fill or cover the space between a door or window and the casing, so as to keep out rain, snow, and wind.

weath·er-strip (weᴛʜ′ər strip′) *v.* **-stripped, -strip·ping.** fit with weather strips.

weather stripping **1** a weather strip. **2** weather strips.

weather vane weathercock.

weath·er-wise (weᴛʜ′ər wīz′) *adj.* skilful in forecasting the changes of the weather.

weave (wēv) *v.* **wove** or (*rare*) **weaved, wo·ven** or **wove, weav·ing,** *n.* —*v.* **1** form (threads or strips) into a texture or fabric. People weave thread into cloth, straw into hats, and reeds into baskets. **2** make out of thread, etc.: *She is weaving a rug.* **3** work with a loom. **4** combine into a whole: *The author wove three plots together into one story.* **5** make by combining parts: *The author wove a story from three plots.* **6** make with care. **7** move in a twisting and turning manner. **8 weave one's way,** make one's way by twisting and turning. —*n.* a method or pattern of weaving: *Homespun is a cloth of coarse weave.* [OE *wefan*]

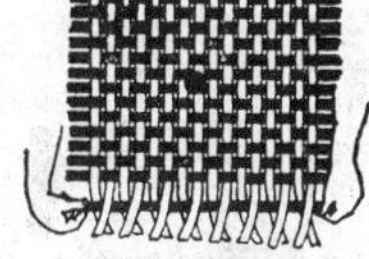

Weaving

☛ **woven, wove. Woven is the regular past participle. Wove is now chiefly used in certain technical terms, such as *wire-wove* and *wove paper.***

weav·er (wēv′ər) *n.* **1** one who weaves. **2** one whose work is weaving. **3** a weaverbird.

weav·er·bird (wēv′ər bėrd′) *n.* in Asia, Africa, and Australia, a bird that builds an elaborately woven nest.

web (web) *n. v.* **web·bed, web·bing.** —*n.* **1** something woven. The fabric of delicate, silken threads spun by a spider is a web. **2** a whole piece of cloth made at one time. **3** any complicated network: *a web of railways, a web of lies.* **4** any elaborate organization or contrivance intended to catch or snare: *a web of spies.* **5** the skin joining the toes of ducks, geese, and other swimming birds. **6** any of various thin, broad parts. The soft part of a feather is called a web. **7** a thin metal sheet. **8** connective tissue. **9** a large roll of paper used in printing newspapers. **10** a snowshoe. —*v.* **1** provide or cover with a web. **2** trap or entwine in a web. [OE *webb*] —**web′like′** *a*

A spider on its web

The webbed foot of a duck

webbed (webd) *adj.* **1** formed like a web or with a web. **2** having the toes joined by a web. Ducks have **webbed** feet. See picture on the previous page.

web·bing (web′ing) *n.* **1** cloth woven into strong strips, used in upholstery and for belts. **2** the plain foundation fabric left for protection at the edge of some rugs, etc. **3** skin joining the toes, as in a duck's feet.

web·foot (web′fu̇t′) *n.* **-feet. 1** a foot in which the toes are joined by a web. **2** a bird or animal having webfeet.

web-foot·ed (web′fu̇t′id) *adj.* having the toes joined by a web.

web·toed (web′tōd′) *adj.* web-footed.

wed (wed) *v.* **wed·ded, wed·ded** or **wed, wed·ding. 1** marry. **2** unite. **3** be obstinately attached to (an opinion, one's own will, a habit, a faction, etc.). [OE *weddian*]

we'd (wēd; *unstressed,* wid) **1** we had. **2** we should; we would.

Wed. Wednesday.

wed·ded (wed′id) *adj.* **1** married. **2** united. **3** devoted.

wed·ding (wed′ing) *n.* **1** the marriage ceremony. **2** an anniversary of this ceremony. A **golden wedding** is the fiftieth anniversary of a marriage. **3** a joining or uniting: *His writing shows a remarkable wedding of thought and language.* [OE *weddung*] **—Syn. 1** See **marriage.**

wedge (wej) *n. v.* **wedged, wedg·ing. —*n.* 1** a piece of wood or metal with a tapering thin edge, used in splitting, separating, etc. **2** something shaped like a wedge or used like a wedge: *Her grand party was a wedge for her entry into society.* **3** a golf club used for high, short shots, lofting the ball out of traps, heavy grass, etc.
—*v.* **1** split or separate with a wedge. **2** fasten or tighten with a wedge. **3** thrust or pack in tightly; squeeze: *He wedged himself through the narrow window.* **4** force a way. [OE *wecg*]

A wedge; to split a log, a wedge is driven in with a sledge.

Wedg·wood (wej′wu̇d) *n.* **1** a kind of fine, unglazed pottery having a raised, decorative design of white Greek and Roman models against a tinted ground. **2** a kind of fine china. **3** something made of either the pottery or the china. [after Josiah *Wedgwood,* 1730-1795, an English potter, who originated it]

wed·lock (wed′lok) *n.* married life; marriage. [OE *wedlāc* pledge < *wedd* pledge + *-lāc,* noun suffix denoting activity]

Wednes·day (wenz′dē or wenz′dā) *n.* the fourth day of the week, following Tuesday. [OE *Wōdnes dæg* Woden's day; translation of LL *Mercurii dies* day of Mercury]

wee (wē) *adj.* **we·er, we·est.** very small; tiny. [from the phrase *a little wee* a little bit, OE *wǣg* weight]

weed[1] (wēd) *n.* **1** a useless or troublesome plant; plant occurring in cultivated ground to the exclusion or injury of the desired crop. **2 a** a useless animal, especially a horse unfit for racing or breeding. **b** any very weak or malformed thing. **3** *Informal.* tobacco. **4** *Informal.* a cigar; cigarette. **5 the weed, a** *Informal.* tobacco when smoked. **b** *Slang.* marijuana cigarettes.
—*v.* **1** take weeds out of. **2** take out weeds. **3 weed out, a** free from what is useless or worthless. **b** remove or discard what is not wanted. [OE *wēod*] **—weed′like′,** *adj.*

weed[2] (wēd) *n.* **1 weeds,** *pl.* mourning garments: *a widow's weeds.* **2** *Archaic.* a garment. [OE *wǣd*]

weed·er (wēd′ər) *n.* **1** a person who weeds. **2** a tool or machine for digging up weeds.

weed·y (wēd′ē) *adj.* **weed·i·er, weed·i·est. 1** full of weeds: *a weedy garden.* **2** of weeds; like weeds. **3** thin and lanky; weak. **—weed′i·ly,** *adv.* **—weed′i·ness,** *n.*

wee hours the hours after midnight; the early morning hours.

week (wēk) *n.* **1** seven days, one after another. **2** the time from Sunday through Saturday. **3** the working days of a seven-day period. A school week is five days. **4 Monday week,** the Monday one week from this Monday. **5 this day week,** one week from today. **6 week in, week out,** week after week. [OE *wice*]

week·day (wēk′dā′) *n.* **1** any day except Sunday. **2** any day except Saturday or Sunday. —*adj.* of or on a weekday.

week·end (wēk′end′) *n.* Saturday and Sunday as a time for recreation, visiting, etc. —*adj.* of or on a weekend. —*v.* spend a weekend.

week·ly (wēk′lē) *adj. adv. n.* **-lies. —*adj.* 1** of a week; for a week; lasting a week: *His weekly wage is $60.* **2** done or happening once a week: *a weekly letter home.* —*adv.* once each week; every week. —*n.* a newspaper or magazine published once a week.

ween (wēn) *v. Archaic.* think; suppose; believe; expect. [OE *wēnan*]

weep (wēp) *v.* **wept, weep·ing. 1** shed tears; cry. **2** shed tears for; mourn. **3** spend in crying: *weep one's life away.* **4** let fall in drops; shed: *She wept bitter tears.* **5** flow; drop like tears. **6** be very damp; drip. —*n.* a period or fit of weeping. [OE *wēpan*] **—Syn.** *v.* **1** sob. **2** bewail.

weep·er (wēp′ər) *n.* **1** a person who weeps. **2** a person hired to weep at funerals; professional mourner.

weep·ing (wēp′ing) *adj.* **1** that weeps. **2** having thin, drooping branches: *a weeping willow.*

weeping willow a large willow originally from E. Asia, distinctive for its long, feathery, drooping branches.

wee·vil (wē′vəl) *n.* **1** a small beetle whose larvae destroy grain, nuts, cotton, fruit, etc. **2** any of various small insects that damage or destroy stored grain. [OE *wifel*]

wee·vil·ly or **wee·vil·y** (wē′vəl ē) *adj.* infested with weevils.

weft (weft) *n.* the threads running from side to side across a fabric; the woof. See **warp** for picture. [OE *weft* < *wefan* weave]

weigh (wā) *v.* **1** find the weight of: *weigh oneself.* **2** have as a measure by weight: *I weighed 110 pounds.* **3** measure by weight: *The grocer weighed out five pounds of sugar.* **4** balance in the mind; consider carefully: *He weighed his words before speaking.* **5** have importance or influence: *The amount of his salary does not weigh with Mr. Black at all, because he is very rich.* **6** bear down: *The mistake weighed heavily upon his mind.* **7** in nautical use: **a** lift up (an anchor). **b** lift anchor. **8 weigh down,** bend by weight; burden: *The boughs of the apple tree are weighed down with fruit. She is weighed down with many troubles.* **9 weigh in,** find out one's weight before a contest. **10 weigh on,** be a burden to. [OE *wegan*] **—weigh′er,** *n.* **—Syn. 4** See **consider.**

weigh·mas·ter (wā′mas′tər) *n.* **1** an official in charge of public weighing scales. **2** a worker in charge of registering by weight the amount of a commodity produced, mined, etc.

weight (wāt) *n.* **1** how heavy something is; the amount something weighs: *The dog's weight is 50 pounds.* **2** in physics: **a** the quality that makes all things tend toward the centre of the earth; heaviness: *Gas has hardly any weight.* **b** the quantity of a portion of matter as measured by the amount of its downward force due to gravitation. **3** a system of units for expressing weight: *avoirdupois weight, troy weight.* **4** a unit of such a system. *Abbrev.:* wt. **5** a piece of metal having a specific weight, used in weighing things: *a pound weight.* **6** a quantity that has a certain weight: *a half-ounce weight of gold dust.* **7** a heavy thing or mass: *A weight keeps the papers in place.* **8** a load; burden: *The pillars support the weight of the roof.* **9** the burden of care, responsibility, etc.; mental load: *the weight of high office.* **10** influence; importance; value: *What he says carries weight with me.* **11** preponderant portion: *the weight of public opinion.* **12** the relative heaviness of an article of clothing appropriate to the season's weather: *summer weight.* **13** in statistics: **a** a number assigned to an item in a statistical compilation, as in a cost-of-living index, to make its effect on the compilation reflect its importance. **b** the frequency of an item in a statistical compilation. **14** in sports, a metal ball thrown, pushed, or lifted in contests of strength. **15 by weight,** measured by weighing. **16 carry weight,** be of importance; count: *What he says carries much weight with me.* **17 pull one's weight,** do one's part or share.

18 throw one's weight around or **about,** *Informal.* make too much use of one's rank or position; assert one's importance improperly or excessively.
—*v.* **1** load down; burden. **2** add weight to; put weight on: *The scales are weighted too heavily.* **3** attach importance or value to. **4** load (cloth or thread) with mineral to make it seem of better quality: *weighted silk.* **5** in statistics, give a weight to: *a weighted average.* **6** in skiing, direct all or most of the downward thrust onto: *weight the left ski.* [OE *wiht* < *wegan* weigh]

weight-arm (wāt′ärm′) *n.* in a lever, the distance from the weight to the fulcrum.

weight·less (wāt′lis) *adj.* **1** having, or apparently having, no weight. **2** in astronautics, being free from the pull of gravity. —**weight·less·ly,** *adv.* —**weight·less·ness,** *n.*

weight·y (wāt′ē) *adj.* **weight·i·er, weight·i·est. 1** heavy. **2** burdensome: *weighty cares of state.* **3** important; influential: *a weighty speaker.* **4** convincing: *weighty arguments.* —**weight′i·ly,** *adv.* —**weight′i·ness,** *n.* —**Syn. 1** ponderous. See **heavy. 2** onerous. **3** momentous.

Wei·ma·ra·ner (vī′mə rä′nər or wī′mə rä′nər) *n.* **1** a breed of medium-sized gray dog having a docked tail, bred in Germany as a hunting dog. **2** a dog of this breed. [< *Weimar,* a city in Germany]

wei·ner (wē′nər) *n.* wiener.

weir (wēr) *n.* **1** a dam in a river. **2** a fence of stakes or broken branches put in a stream or channel to catch fish. **3** an obstruction erected across a channel or stream to divert the water through a special opening in order to measure the quantity flowing. [OE *wer*]

weird (wērd) *adj.* **1** unearthly; mysterious: *They were awakened by a weird shriek.* **2** *Informal.* odd; fantastic; queer: *The shadows made weird figures on the wall.* **3** *Archaic or Scottish.* having to do with fate or destiny. [OE *wyrd* fate] —**weird′ly,** *adv.* —**weird′ness,** *n.*
Syn. 1 Weird, eerie, uncanny = mysteriously or frighteningly strange. **Weird** describes something that seems not of this world or that is caused by something above or beyond nature: *All night weird cries came from the jungle.* **Eerie** suggests the frightening effect of something weird or ghostly or vaguely and evilly mysterious: *The light from the single candle made eerie shadows in the cave.* **Uncanny** suggests a strangeness that is disturbing because it seems unnatural: *I had an uncanny feeling that eyes were peering from the darkness.*

weird·o (wēr′dō′) *n. Slang.* a person or thing regarded as weird, odd, or eccentric.

weird sisters or **Weird Sisters 1** the Fates. **2** the witches in Shakespeare's *Macbeth.*

welch (welch or welsh) *v.* welsh.

wel·come (wel′kəm) *interj. n. v.* **-comed, -com·ing,** *adj.*
—*interj.* a word of kindly greeting: *Welcome home!*
—*n.* **1** a kindly greeting. **2** a kind reception: *You will always have a welcome here.* **3 wear out one's welcome,** visit a person too often or too long.
—*v.* **1** greet kindly. **2** receive gladly.
—*adj.* **1** glady received: *a welcome letter.* **2** gladly or freely permitted: *You are welcome to pick the flowers.* **3** free to enjoy courtesies, etc. without obligation (used in conventional response to thanks): *You are welcome.* [original meaning "agreeable guest," OE *wilcuma* < *wil-* (related to *will* pleasure) + *cuma* comer] —**wel′com·er,** *n.*

welcome mat 1 a doormat. **2** *Informal.* any enthusiastic reception or welcome.

weld (weld) *v.* **1** join together (metal, plastic, etc.) by hammering or pressing while soft and hot: *He welded the broken metal rod.* **2** unite closely: *Working together for a month welded them into a strong team.* **3** be welded or be capable of being welded: *Some metals weld better than others.* —*n.* **1** a welded joint. **2** a welding. [< *well*², v.] —**weld′er,** *n.*

wel·fare (wel′fãr′) *n.* **1** health, happiness, and prosperity; well-being. **2** welfare work. [ME *wel fare* < *wel* well < *fare* go]

welfare state a state whose government provides for the welfare of its citizens through social security, unemployment insurance, medical treatment, etc.

welfare work work done to improve the conditions of people who need help, carried on by government, private organizations, or individuals.

welfare worker a person who does welfare work.

wel·kin (wel′kən) *n. Archaic.* the sky: *The welkin rang with the men's shouts.* [OE *wolcen* cloud]

hat, āge, cãre, fär; let, ēqual, tėrm; it, īce
hot, ōpen, ôrder; oil, out; cup, pủt, rüle, ūse
əbove, takən, pencəl, lemən, circəs
ch, child; ng, long; sh, ship
th, thin; ᴛʜ, then; zh, measure

well¹ (wel) *adv.* **bet·ter, best,** *adj. interj.* —*adv.* **1** in a satisfactory, favorable, or advantageous manner; all right: *The job was well done. Is everything going well at school?* **2** thoroughly; fully: *Shake well before using.* **3** to a considerable degree; much: *The fair brought in well over a hundred dollars.* **4** in detail; intimately: *He knows the subject well.* **5** fairly; reasonably: *I couldn't very well refuse.* **6 as well, a** also; besides. **b** equally. **7 as well as, a** in addition to; besides. **b** as much as. **8 can** or **could well,** can easily or could reasonably; may or might without difficulty.
—*adj.* **1** satisfactory; good; right: *It is well you came along.* **2** in good health: *I am very well.* **3** desirable; advisable: *It is always well to start a bit early.*
—*interj.* an expression used to show mild surprise, agreement, etc. or merely to fill in: *Well! Well! Here's Jack. Well, I'm not sure.* [OE *wel*] —**Syn.** *adj.* **2** hale, sound, hearty. ☛ See **good** for usage note.

well² (wel) *n.* **1** a hole dug or bored in the ground to get water, oil, gas, etc. **2** a spring; fountain; source. **3** something like a well in shape or use: *the well of a fountain pen.* **4** a shaft for stairs or elevator, extending vertically through the floors of a building. **5** in a ship, a compartment around the pumps. **6** a storage compartment for fish in the hold of a fishing boat, kept filled with water to keep the catch alive. —*v.* spring; rise; gush: *Tears welled in her eyes.* [OE *wella,* n., *wiellan,* v.]

we'll (wēl; *unstressed,* wil) we shall; we will.

well·a·day (wel′ə dā′) *interj. Archaic.* wellaway.

well-ad·just·ed (wel′ə jus′tid) *adj.* of persons, emotionally balanced and mature; able to cope with stress and change.

well-ad·vised (wel′əd vīzd′) *adj.* **1** proceeding with wisdom, care, or deliberation. **2** based on wise counsel or prudence.

well-ap·point·ed (wel′ə poin′tid) *adj.* having good furnishings or equipment.

well·a·way (wel′ə wā′) *interj. Archaic.* alas!

well-bal·anced (wel′bal′ənst) *adj.* **1** rightly balanced, adjusted, or regulated. **2** sensible; sane.

well-be·haved (wel′bi hāvd′) *adj.* showing good manners or conduct.

well-be·ing (wel′bē′ing) *n.* health and happiness; welfare.

well·born (wel′bôrn′) *adj.* belonging to a good family.

well-bred (wel′bred′) *adj.* well brought up; having or showing good manners.

well-con·nect·ed (wel′kə nek′tid) *adj.* **1** of a well-known family; related to important or distinguished people. **2** put together well; carefully planned: *well-connected paragraphs.*

well-con·tent (wel′kən tent′) *adj.* highly pleased or satisfied.

well-de·fined (wel′di fīnd′) *adj.* clearly defined or indicated; distinct.

well-dis·posed (wel′dis pōzd′) *adj.* **1** rightly or properly disposed. **2** well-meaning. **3** favorably or kindly disposed.

well-do·ing (wel′dü′ing) *n.* the act of doing right; good conduct.

well-fa·vored or **well-fa·voured** (wel′fā′vərd) *adj.* of pleasing appearance; good-looking.

well-fed (wel′fed′) *adj.* showing the result of good feeding; fat; plump.

well-fixed (wel′fikst′) *adj. Informal.* well-to-do.

well-found (wel′found′) *adj.* well supplied or equipped.

well-found·ed (wel′foun′did) *adj.* rightly or justly founded: *a well-founded faith in discipline.*

well-groomed (wel′grümd′) *adj.* well cared for; neat and trim.

well-ground·ed (wel′groun′did) *adj.* 1 based on good reasons. 2 thoroughly instructed in the fundamental principles of a subject.

well·head (wel′hed′) *n.* 1 a spring of water. 2 a source.

well-heeled (wel′hēld′) *adj. Slang.* prosperous; well-to-do.

well-in·formed (wel′in fôrmd′) *adj.* 1 having reliable or full information on a subject. 2 having information on a wide variety of subjects.

Wellington boot or **Wel·ling·ton** (wel′ing tən) *n.* 1 a very high leather boot that comes above the knee in front and is cut away behind. 2 a rubber boot coming nearly up to the knees. [worn by the first Duke of *Wellington,* 1769-1852, a British general]

well-kept (wel′kept′) *adj.* well cared for; carefully tended.

well-knit (wel′nit′) *adj.* 1 firmly constructed or joined together; closely connected or linked. 2 of strong, supple build; well-built.

well-known (wel′nōn′) *adj.* 1 clearly or fully known. 2 familiar. 3 generally or widely known.

well-man·nered (wel′man′ərd) *adj.* having or showing good manners; polite; courteous.

well-marked (wel′märkt′) *adj.* clearly marked or distinguished; distinct.

well-mean·ing (wel′mēn′ing) *adj.* 1 having good intentions. 2 proceeding from good intentions.

well-nigh (wel′nī′) *adv.* very nearly; almost.

well-off (wel′of′) *adj.* 1 in a good condition or position. 2 fairly rich.

well-or·dered (wel′ôr′dərd) *adj.* ordered or arranged well; well-regulated.

well-placed (wel′plāst) *adj.* 1 well aimed. 2 conveniently placed; accessible. 3 having a good official or social position.

well-pre·served (wel′pri zėrvd′) *adj.* showing few signs of age.

well-pro·por·tioned (wel′prə pôr′shənd) *adj.* having good or correct proportions; having a pleasing shape.

well-read (wel′red′) *adj.* having read much; knowing a great deal about books and literature.

Wells·i·an (wel′zē ən) *adj.* 1 of or having to do with H.G. (Herbert George) Wells (1866-1946), an English novelist and writer. 2 of or suggestive of his writings.

well-spo·ken (wel′spō′kən) *adj.* 1 speaking well, fittingly, or pleasingly; polite in speech. 2 spoken well.

well·spring (wel′spring′) *n.* 1 a fountainhead. 2 a source, especially of a supply that never fails.

well-suit·ed (wel′süt′id) *adj.* suitable; convenient.

well sweep a device used to draw water from a well, consisting of a pole attached to a pivot and having a bucket at one end.

well-timed (wel′tīmd′) *adj.* timely.

well-to-do (wel′tə dü′) *adj.* having enough money to live well; prosperous.

well-turned (wel′tėrnd′) *adj.* 1 well shaped or rounded expertly. 2 gracefully or elegantly expressed: *a well-turned phrase.*

well-turned-out (wel′tėrnd′out′) *adj.* elegantly or fashionably dressed.

well-wish·er (wel′wish′ər) *n.* a person who wishes well to a person, cause, etc.

well-worn (wel′wôrn′) *adj.* 1 much worn by use. 2 used too much; trite; stale.

welsh (welsh) *v. Slang.* 1 cheat by failing to pay a bet. 2 evade the fulfilment of an obligation. 3 **welsh on,** fail to keep an agreement with. Also, **welch.** [origin uncertain] —**welsh′er,** *n.*

Welsh (welsh or welch) *adj.* of or having to do with Wales, its people, or their Celtic language. —*n.* 1 the people of Wales. 2 their language. [OE *Welisc* < *wealh* stranger (a non-Saxon)]

Welsh·man (welsh′mən or welch′mən) *n.* **-men** (-mən). a man of Welsh birth or descent.

Welsh rabbit a mixture containing cheese, cooked and poured over toast.

Welsh rarebit Welsh rabbit.

welt (welt) *n.* 1 a strip of leather between the upper part and the sole of a shoe. 2 the narrow border, trimming, etc. on the edge of a garment or upholstery. 3 a seam similar to a flat fell seam, used in tailoring. 4 *Informal.* a streak or ridge made on the skin by a stick or whip. 5 *Informal.* a heavy blow. —*v.* 1 put a welt on. 2 *Informal.* beat severely. [ME *welte, walte*]

Welt·an·schau·ung (velt′ än′shou′ůng) *n. German.* a mental scheme or conception of life, history, reality, etc.; one's way of looking at the world; literally, world view.

Welt·an·sicht (velt′ än′ziнt) *n. German.* a special interpretation of reality; literally, world view.

wel·ter (wel′tər) *v.* 1 roll or toss about; wallow. 2 lie soaked in some liquid; be drenched. —*n.* 1 a rolling and tossing. 2 confusion; commotion. [< MDu. and MLG *welteren*]

wel·ter·weight (wel′tər wāt′) *n.* a boxer or wrestler weighing between 135 and 147 pounds. [earlier *welter,* literally, beater (ult. < *welt*) + *weight*]

wen (wen) *n.* a harmless tumor of the skin. [OE *wenn*]

wench (wench) *n.* 1 a girl or young woman. 2 a woman servant. —*v.* seek out and consort with wenches. [< *wenchel* child, OE *wencel*]

wend (wend) *v.* **wend·ed** or (*archaic*) **went, wend·ing.** 1 direct (one's way): *We wended our way home.* 2 go. [OE *wendan*]

Wend (wend) *n.* a member of a Slavic people living in central Germany. [< G *Wende*]

wen·di·go (wen′di gō′) *n.* **wen·di·gos** *for 1;* **wen·di·go** or **wen·di·gos** *for 2.* 1 in Algonquian mythology, an evil spirit of a cannibalistic nature. Also, **windigo.** 2 *Cdn.* a hybrid trout; splake. [< Algonquian (Ojibway) *weendigo* cannibal]

went (went) *v.* pt. of **go.** [originally pt. of *wend*]

wept (wept) *v.* pt. and pp. of **weep.**

were (wėr; *unstressed,* wər) *v.* 1 pl. and 2nd pers. sing. past indicative of **be:** *The officers were obeyed by the soldiers.* 2 subjunctive of **be:** *If I were rich, I would travel.* 3 **as it were,** as if it were; so to speak; in some way. [OE *wǣron*]

☛ **were.** For subjunctive uses, in expressing wishes not yet realized, conditions that are merely hypothetical, etc., were is used with all persons irrespective of number and tense: *I wish it were warmer. She looked as though she were ill.*

we're (wēr) we are.

weren't (wėrnt or wernt) were not.

were·wolf (wēr′wůlf′ or wėr′wůlf′) *n.* **-wolves** (-wůlvz′). in folklore, a person who has been changed into a wolf or who can change himself into a wolf, while retaining human intelligence. [OE *werwulf* < *wer* man + *wulf* wolf]

wert (wėrt or wert; *unstressed,* wərt) *v. Archaic.* 2nd pers. sing. past tense of **be.** "Thou wert" means "you were" (sing.).

wer·wolf (wēr′wůlf′ or wėr′wůlf′) *n.* **-wolves** (-wůlvz′). werewolf.

Wes·ley·an (wes′lē ən; *esp.Brit.* wez′lē ən) *n.* a member of the church founded by John Wesley, 1703-1791, an English clergyman; Methodist. —*adj.* of or having to do with John Wesley or the Methodist Church.

west (west) *n.* 1 the direction of the sunset; point of the compass to the left as one faces north. 2 Also, **West,** the part of any country toward the west. 3 **the West, a** the western part of Canada or the United States. **b** the countries in Europe and America as distinguished from those in Asia, especially S.W. Asia. **c** the United States, Great Britain, and their allies as distinguished from the Soviet Union and her allies; the free world. **d** the Western Roman Empire. 4 **out West,** in Canada: **a** any point to the west of Winnipeg. **b** in or towards any place west of Winnipeg.
—*adj.* 1 toward the west; farther toward the west. 2 from the west. 3 in the west; living in the west. 4 **west of,** farther west than.

—*adv.* toward the west: *They travelled west for two days.* [OE]

West African pound 1 a unit of money in Gambia and Sierra Leone. See table at **money.** 2 a note or coin worth one West African pound.

west·bound (west′bound′) *adj.* going toward the west.

west·er (west′ər) *v.* turn or move westward; shift to the west. —*n.* a wind or storm from the west.

west·er·ly (wes′tər lē) *adj. adv.* 1 toward the west. 2 from the west. —*n.* a wind that blows from the west.

west·ern (wes′tərn) *adj.* 1 toward the west. 2 from the west. 3 of or in the west; of or in the western part of the country. 4 of or having to do with the West (def. 3c). 5 of or in the countries in Europe and America. 6 of North and South America. —*n. Informal.* 1 a story or motion picture dealing with life in the West (def. 3a), especially cowboy life. 2 a western sandwich or western omelette.

Western Church the part of the Catholic Church that acknowledges the Pope as its spiritual leader and follows the Latin Rite; Roman Catholic Church.

Western civilization European and American civilization as contrasted with Oriental civilization.

Western Empire Western Roman Empire.

West·ern·er (wes′tər nər) *n.* a native or inhabitant of the west.

Western Hemisphere the half of the world that includes North and South America.

west·ern·i·za·tion (west′ər nə zā′shən or west′ər nī-zā′shən) *n.* the process of introducing or adopting western ideas, institutions, culture, etc.

west·ern·ize (west′ər nīz′) *v.* **-ized, -iz·ing.** introduce or adopt western ideas, customs, culture, etc. —**west′ern·i′zer,** *n.*

west·ern·most (wes′tərn mōst′) *adj.* farthest west.

western omelette or **omelet** an omelette made with eggs, chopped onions, and ham.

western red cedar red cedar (def. 1).

Western Roman Empire the western part of the Roman Empire after the division in A.D. 395. The Western Roman Empire came to an end in A.D. 476; the Eastern Empire continued as the Byzantine Empire until A.D. 1453.

Western saddle a saddle with a high pommel, originally to tie a rope to when lassoing cattle. See **saddle** for diagram.

western sandwich a sandwich with a filling of scrambled eggs, minced ham, peppers, and onions.

western union formerly, an alliance of the Benelux nations, France, and Great Britain.

West Indian 1 of or having to do with the West Indies. 2 a native or inhabitant of the West Indies.

West·min·ster (west′min′stər) *n. Brit. Informal.* Parliament, or the British government. [< *Westminster*, the part of London that contains the Houses of Parliament]

Westminster Abbey in London, a church in which many British kings and famous men are buried. The monarchs of the United Kingdom are crowned in Westminster Abbey.

West·pha·li·an (west fā′lē ən) *adj.* of or having to do with Westphalia, a region in N.W. West Germany. —*n.* a native or inhabitant of Westphalia.

west·ward (west′wərd) *adv. adj.* 1 toward the west. 2 of winds, from the west.

west·ward·ly (west′wərd lē) *adj. adv.* 1 toward the west. 2 of winds, from the west.

west·wards (west′wərdz) *adv.* westward.

wet (wet) *adj.* **wet·ter, wet·test,** *v.* **wet** or **wet·ted, wet·ting,** *n.* —*adj.* 1 covered or soaked with water or other liquid: *wet hands, a wet sponge.* 2 not yet dry: *Don't touch wet paint.* 3 rainy: *wet weather.* 4 watery; liquid: *Her eyes were wet with tears.* 5 *Informal.* having or favoring laws that permit making and selling of alcoholic drinks. 6 **wet behind the ears,** too young to know very much; green; inexperienced.
—*v.* 1 make or become wet. 2 pass urine.

hat, āge, cãre, fär; let, ēqual, tėrm; it, īce
hot, ōpen, ôrder; oil, out; cup, pu̇t, rüle, ūse
əbove, takən, pencəl, lemən, circəs
ch, child; ng, long; sh, ship
th, thin; ᴛʜ, then; zh, measure

—*n.* 1 water or other liquid. 2 wetness; rain. 3 *Informal.* a person who favors laws that permit the making and selling of alcoholic drinks. [ME *wett*, pp. of *wete(n)*, OE *wǣtan*] —**wet′ly,** *adv.* —**wet′ness,** *n.*
Syn. *adj.* 1 moist, damp. —*v.* **Wet, drench, soak** = make or become covered or spread through with liquid. **Wet** is the general word: *Wet the material well before applying soap.* **Drench** = wet thoroughly by pouring liquid: *Drench the ashes and ground before leaving a campfire.* **Soak,** often used interchangeably with *drench*, means "wet thoroughly" by putting and keeping, or lying, in or under liquid, especially until the liquid has spread through the fibres or substance of the thing: *Soak the stained spot in milk.*

wet blanket a person or thing that has a discouraging or depressing effect.

wet cell in electricity, a cell having a free-flowing electrolyte.

weth·er (weᴛʜ′ər) *n.* a castrated male sheep. [OE]

wet·land (wet′land′) *n.* a marsh or swamp.

wet nurse a woman employed to suckle the infant of another.

wet-nurse (wet′nėrs′) *v.* **-nursed, -nurs·ing.** 1 act as wet nurse to. 2 treat with special care; coddle; pamper.

wet strength a quality of some paper, enabling it to hold together and not tear or disintegrate even when wet.

wet suit a skin-tight rubber suit worn by skin divers, surfers, etc.

wet·tish (wet′ish) *adj.* somewhat wet.

we've (wēv; *unstressed*, wiv) we have.

w.f. or **wf** in printing, wrong font.

WFTU or **W.F.T.U.** World Federation of Trade Unions.

W.Ger. 1 West Germany. 2 West German.

wh watt hour; watt hours.

whack (hwak or wak) *n.* 1 *Informal.* a sharp, resounding blow. 2 the sound of such a blow. 3 *Slang.* a trial or attempt. 4 **have** or **take a whack at,** *Slang.* make an attempt or attack upon. 5 **out of whack,** *Slang.* not in proper condition; disordered. —*v.* 1 *Informal.* strike with a sharp, resounding blow. 2 beat or win in a contest. 3 *Slang.* reduce; knock off. 4 **whack up,** *Slang.* share; divide. [? imitative]

whacked (hwakt or wakt) *adj. Esp.Brit. Slang.* exhausted; worn out.

whack·ing (hwak′ing or wak′ing) *adj. Informal.* large; forcible.

whack·y (hwak′ē or wak′ē) *adj.* wacky.

whale[1] (hwāl or wāl) *n.* **whales** or **whale,** *v.* **whaled, whal·ing.** —*n.* 1 a mammal shaped like a huge fish and living in the sea. Men get oil and whalebone from whales. 2 *Informal.* something very big, great, impressive, etc. 3 **whale of,** *Informal.* a excellent; exceptional: *a whale of a time.* b large: *a whale of a car.* c unlikely; improbable: *a whale of a story.* —*v.* hunt and catch whales. [OE *hwæl*]

whale[2] (hwāl or wāl) *v.* **whaled, whal·ing.** *Informal.* 1 beat; whip severely. 2 hit hard. [apparently var. of *wale*]

whale·back (hwāl′bak′ or wāl′-) *n.* 1 especially on the Great Lakes, a freight steamer having a rounded upper deck shaped like a whale's back. 2 a humped hill, mound, etc. having the shape of a whale's back.

whale·boat (hwāl′bōt′ or wāl′-) *n.* a long, narrow rowboat, sharp at both ends, formerly much used in whaling.

whale·bone (hwāl′bōn′ or wāl′-) *n.* 1 an elastic horny substance growing in place of teeth in the upper jaw of certain whales and forming a series of thin, parallel plates. 2 a thin strip of this for stiffening corsets, dresses, etc.

whal·er (hwāl′ər or wāl′ər) *n.* 1 a person who hunts whales. 2 a ship used for hunting and catching whales.

whal·ing (hwāl′ing or wāl′ing) *n.* 1 the hunting and killing of whales. 2 the industry concerned with the hunting, killing, and processing of whales.

wham (hwam) *n. interj. v.* **whammed, wham·ming.** *Informal.* —*n. interj.* a loud bang; the sound of a hard impact. —*v.* hit with a bang; smash; beat. [imitative]

wham·my (hwam′ē or wam′ē) *n.* **-mies.** *Slang.* a magical power or spell bringing bad luck; jinx: *The magician put the whammy on him.*

whang (hwang or wang) *Informal.* —*n.* a resounding blow or bang. —*v.* strike with a blow or bang. [imitative]

whap (hwap or wap) *v.* **whapped, whap·ping.** whop.

wharf (hwôrf or wôrf) *n.* **wharves** or **wharfs.** a platform built on the shore or out from the shore, beside which ships can load and unload. [OE *hwearf*]

wharf·age (hwôr′fij or wôr′fij) *n.* **1** the use of a wharf for mooring a ship, storing and handling goods, etc. **2** the charge made for this. **3** wharves: *There are miles of wharfage in Montreal.*

wharf·in·ger (hwôr′fin jər or wôr′fin jər) *n.* a person who owns or has charge of a wharf. [for *wharfager* < *wharfage* with *n* added as in *passenger*]

wharves (hwôrvz or wôrvz) *n.* pl. of **wharf.**

what (hwut or hwot, wut or wot; *unstressed,* hwət or wət) *pron. adj. adv. interj. conj.* —*pron.* **1** as an interrogative pronoun a word used in asking questions about persons or things: *What is your name? What is the matter?* **2** as a relative pronoun: **a** that which: *I know what you mean.* **b** whatever; anything that: *Do what you please.* **3 and what not,** and all kinds of other things. **4 give one what for,** *Informal.* give one something to cry, suffer, or be miserable for; punish; castigate. **5 what for,** why. **6 what have you,** *Informal.* anything else like this; and so on. **7 what if,** what would happen if. **8 what's what,** *Informal.* the true state of affairs.
—*adj.* **1** as an interrogative adjective, word used in asking questions about persons or things: *What time is it?* **2** as a relative adjective: **a** that . . . which; which: *Put back what money is left.* **b** whatever; any . . . that: *Take what supplies you will need.* **3** a word used to show surprise, doubt, anger, liking, etc. or to add emphasis: *What a pity!*
—*adv.* **1** how much; how: *What does it matter?* **2** partly: *What with the wind and what with the rain, our walk was spoiled.* **3** a word used to show surprise, doubt, anger, liking, etc. or to add emphasis: *What happy times!*
—*interj.* a word used to show surprise, doubt, anger, liking, etc. or to add emphasis: *What? Are you late again?*
—*conj.* **but what,** *Informal.* but that. [OE *hwæt*]

what·ev·er (hwut ev′ər or hwot-, wut ev′ər or wot-, hwət ev′ər or wət-) *pron.* **1** anything that: *Do whatever you like.* **2** no matter what: *Whatever happens, he is safe.* **3** *Informal.* what in the world: *Whatever do you mean?*
—*adj.* **1** any that: *Ask whatever girls you like to the party.* **2** no matter what: *Whatever excuse he makes will not be believed.* **3** at all: *Any person whatever can tell you.*

what·not (hwut′not′ or hwot′-, wut′not′ or wot′-) *n.* **1** a stand with several shelves for books, ornaments, etc. **2** a thing or person that may be variously named or described; nondescript.

what's (hwuts or hwots, wuts or wots) what is.

what·so·ev·er (hwut′sō ev′ər or hwot′-, wut′sō ev′ər or wot′-, hwət sō ev′ər or wət-) *pron. adj.* whatever.

wheal (hwēl or wēl) *n.* **1** a small burning or itching swelling on the skin. **2** a ridge on the skin made by a whip; welt. [cf. OE *hwelian* suppurate]

wheat (hwēt or wēt) *n.* **1** the grain of a widely distributed cereal grass, used to make flour. **2** the plant, which bears the grain in dense spikes that sometimes have awns (**bearded wheat**) and sometimes do not (**beardless wheat** or **bald wheat**). [OE *hwǣte*]

Wheat: A, bearded; B, beardless.

wheat·ear (hwēt′ēr′ or wēt′-) *n.* a small bird with white tail feathers that builds its nest on the ground.

wheat·en (hwēt′ən or wēt′ən) *adj.* made of wheat.

wheat germ the tiny, golden embryo of the wheat kernel, used as a cereal and as a vitamin supplement.

whee·dle (hwē′dəl or wē′dəl) *v.* **-dled, -dling. 1** persuade by flattery, smooth words, caresses, etc.; coax: *The children wheedled their mother into letting them go out.* **2** get by wheedling: *They finally wheedled the secret out of him.* [OE *wǣdlian* beg] —**whee′dler,** *n.* —**whee′dling·ly,** *adv.* —**Syn. 1** cajole, blandish.

wheel (hwēl or wēl) *n.* **1** a round frame turning on a pin or shaft in the centre. **2** any instrument, machine, apparatus, etc. shaped or moving like a wheel. A ship's wheel is used in steering. Clay is shaped into dishes, etc. on a potter's wheel. Formerly, people were stretched on a wheel and tortured by having their arms and legs broken with an iron bar. **3** any force thought of as moving or propelling: *the wheels of government.* **4** *Informal.* a bicycle. **5** a circling or circular motion or movement; rotation (not necessarily completed around); revolution. **6** a military or naval movement by which troops or ships in line change direction while maintaining a straight line. **7** *Slang.* a person who manages affairs, personnel, etc., as in a business; executive. **8 wheels,** *pl.* machinery. **9 at the wheel, a** at the steering wheel. **b** in control. **10 big wheel,** *Informal.* an important person. **11 wheels within wheels,** complicated circumstances, motives, influences, etc.
—*v.* **1** turn: *He wheeled around suddenly.* **2** move or perform in a curved or circular direction. **3** move on wheels: *The workman was wheeling a load of bricks on a wheelbarrow.* **4** travel along smoothly. **5** provide with wheels. **6** *Informal.* ride a bicycle. **7 wheel and deal,** *Slang.* do business or trade freely and rapidly, with little restraint. [OE *hwēol*]

wheel·bar·row (hwēl′bar′ō or wēl-) *n.* a frame with a wheel at one end and two handles at the other, used for carrying loads.

wheel·base (hwēl′bās or wēl′-) *n.* in automobiles, etc., the distance measured in inches between the centres of the front and rear axles.

wheel chair a chair mounted on wheels, used especially by invalids. It can be propelled by the person who is sitting in the chair.

wheeled (hwēld or wēld) *adj.* having a wheel or wheels.

wheel·er (hwēl′ər or wēl′ər) *n.* **1** a person or thing that wheels. **2** a thing that has a wheel or wheels. **3** a wheel horse.

wheel·er-deal·er (hwēl′ər dēl′ər or wēl′-) *n. Slang.* one who wheels and deals (see **wheel,** v. def. 7); a big-time operator.

wheel horse 1 a horse nearest to the front wheels of the vehicle being pulled. **2** *Informal.* a person who works hard, long, and effectively.

wheel·house (hwēl′hous′ or wēl′-) *n.* a small, enclosed place on a ship to shelter the steering wheel and those that steer the ship; pilot house.

wheel·wright (hwēl′rīt or wēl′-) *n.* a man whose work is making or repairing wheels, carriages, and wagons.

wheeze (hwēz or wēz) *v.* **wheezed, wheez·ing,** *n.* —*v.* **1** breathe with difficulty and with a whistling sound. **2** make a sound like this: *The old engine wheezed, but it didn't stop.* **3** say with a wheeze. —*n.* **1** a whistling sound caused by difficult breathing. **2** *Slang.* a funny saying or story, especially one that has been told many times; an old or familiar joke. [? < ON *hvæsa* hiss]

wheez·y (hwēz′ē or wēz′ē) *adj.* **wheez·i·er, wheez·i·est.** wheezing: *The old dog was fat and wheezy.* —**wheez′i·ly,** *adv.* —**wheez′i·ness,** *n.*

whelk[1] (hwelk or welk) *n.* a mollusc with a spiral shell, used for food in Europe. [OE *weoloc*]

whelk[2] (hwelk or welk) *n.* pimple; pustule. [OE *hwylca*]

whelm (hwelm or welm) *v.* **1** overwhelm. **2** submerge. [related to OE *-hwelfan,* as in *āhwelfan* cover over; influenced by *helmian* cover]

whelp (hwelp or welp) *n.* **1** a puppy or cub; young dog, wolf, bear, lion, tiger, etc. **2** a good-for-nothing boy or young man. —*v.* give birth to whelps. [OE *hwelp*]

when (hwen or wen; *unstressed,* hwən or wən) *adv.* at what time: *When does school close?*
—*conj.* **1** at the time that: *Rise when your name is called.*

2 at any time that: *He is impatient when he is kept waiting.* 3 at which time; and then: *When his master spoke, the dog gave a joyful bark.* 4 although: *We have only three books when we need five.* 5 considering that; inasmuch as; since: *How can I help you when I don't know how to do the problems myself?*
—*pron.* what time; which time: *Since when have they had a car?*
—*n.* the time or occasion: *the when and where of an act.* [OE *hwænne*]

when·as (hwen az′ or wen-) *conj. Archaic.* when; while; whereas.

whence (hwens or wens) *adv.* 1 from what place; from where: *Whence do you come?* 2 from what source or cause; from what: *Whence has he so much wisdom?* 3 from which: *Let him return to the country whence he came.* —*conj.* from what place, source, cause, etc.: *He told whence he came.* [ME *whennes* < OE *hwanone*]

whence·so·ev·er (hwens′sō ev′ər or wens′-) *conj.* from whatever place, source, or cause.

when·ev·er (hwen ev′ər or wen-) *conj. adv.* at whatever time; when; at any time that.

when·so·ev·er (hwen′sō ev′ər or wen′-) *conj. adv.* whenever; at whatever time.

where (hwãr or wãr) *adv.* 1 in what place; at what place: *Where is he?* 2 to what place: *Where are you going?* 3 from what place: *Where did you get that story?* 4 in which; at which: *the house where he was born.* 5 to which: *the place where he is going.* 6 in or at which place: *I don't know where he is.* 7 in what way; in what respect: *Where is the harm in trying?*
—*n.* 1 what place: *Where does he come from?* 2 a place; scene.
—*conj.* 1 in the place in which; at the place at which: *The book is where you left it.* 2 in any place in which; at any place at which: *Use the salve where the pain is felt.* 3 any place to which: *I will go where you go.* 4 in or at which place: *They came to the town, where they stayed for the night.* 5 in the case, circumstances, respect, etc. in which: *Some people worry where it does no good.* [OE *hwǣr*]

where·a·bout (hwãr′ə bout′ or wãr′-) *adv. conj. n.* whereabouts.

where·a·bouts (hwãr′ə bouts′ or wãr′-) *adv. conj.* where; near what place: *Whereabouts can I find a doctor? We did not know whereabouts we were.* —*n.pl.* the place where a person or thing is: *Do you know the whereabouts of the cottage?*

where·as (hwãr az′ or wãr-) *conj.* 1 on the contrary; but; while: *Some people like opera whereas others do not.* 2 considering that; since, often used at the beginning of a formal proclamation, resolution, etc.: *Whereas all men are human, so all men should show humanity.*

where·at (hwãr at′ or wãr-) *adv. conj.* at what; at which.

where·by (hwãr bī′ or wãr-) *adv. conj.* by what; by which: *There is no other way whereby he can be saved.*

where·fore (hwãr′fôr or wãr-) *adv.* 1 for what reason; why. 2 for which reason; therefore; so. —*conj.* for what reason; why. —*n.* a reason. [< *where* + *fore*, prep.]

where·from (hwãr frum′ or -from′, wãr frum′ or -from′) *adv.* whence.

where·in (hwãr in′ or wãr-) *adv. conj.* in what; in which; how.

where·in·to (hwãr in′tü or wãr-) *adv. conj.* into what; into which.

where·of (hwãr uv′ or -ov′, wãr′uv or -ov′) *adv. conj.* of what; of which; of whom.

where·on (hwãr on′ or wãr-) *adv. conj.* on which; on what.

where·so·ev·er (hwãr′sō ev′ər or wãr′-) *conj. adv.* wherever.

where·to (hwãr tü′ or wãr-) *adv. conj.* 1 to what; to which; where: *He went to that place whereto he had been sent.* 2 for what purpose; why: *Whereto do you lay up riches?*

where·un·to (hwãr un′tü or wãr-) *adv. conj. Archaic.* whereto.

where·up·on (hwãr′ə pon′ or wãr′-) *adv. conj.* 1 upon what; upon which. 2 at which; after which.

hat, āge, cãre, fär; let, ēqual, tėrm; it, īce
hot, ōpen, ôrder; oil, out; cup, pu̇t, rüle, ūse
əbove, takən, pencəl, lemən, circəs
ch, child; ng, long; sh, ship
th, thin; ᴛʜ, then; zh, measure

wher·ev·er (hwãr ev′ər or wãr-) *conj. adv.* where; to whatever place; in whatever place: *Wherever are you going? Sit wherever you like.*

where·with (hwãr wiᴛʜ′ or wãr-, hwãr with′ or wãr-) *adv. conj.* with what; with which.

where·with·al (*n.* hwãr′wiᴛʜ ol′ or -ôl′, wãr′wiᴛʜ ol′ or -ôl′; *adv.* hwãr′wiᴛʜ ol′ or -ôl′, wãr′wiᴛʜ ol′ or -ôl′) *n.* means, supplies, or money needed: *Has she the wherewithal to pay for the trip?* —*adv. conj. Archaic.* with what; with which: *Wherewithal shall we be fed?*

wher·ry (wher′ē or wer′ē) *n.* **-ries.** 1 a light, shallow rowboat for carrying passengers and goods on rivers. 2 a light rowboat for one person, used for racing. 3 *Esp.Brit.* a broad sailboat, used chiefly on rivers. [origin unknown]

whet (hwet or wet) *v.* **whet·ted, whet·ting,** *n.* —*v.* 1 sharpen by rubbing: *whet a knife.* 2 make keen or eager; stimulate: *The smell of food whetted my appetite.* —*n.* 1 the act of whetting. 2 something that whets. 3 an appetizer. [OE *hwettan*]

wheth·er (hweᴛʜ′ər or weᴛʜ′-) *conj.* 1 *Whether* is a conjunction expressing a choice or an alternative: *It matters little whether we go or stay. He does not know whether to work or play.* 2 either: *Whether sick or well, she is always cheerful.* 3 if: *He asked whether he should finish the work.* 4 **whether or no,** in any case; no matter what happens. —*pron. Archaic.* which of two: "*Whether is greater, the gift or the altar that sanctifieth the gift?*" [OE *hwether*] ☛ See **if** for usage note.

whet·stone (hwet′stōn′ or wet′-) *n.* a stone for sharpening knives or tools.

whew (hwū) *interj. n.* an exclamation of surprise, dismay, etc.

whey (hwā or wā) *n.* the watery part of milk that separates from the curd when milk sours and becomes coagulated or when cheese is made. [OE *hwǣg*]

which (hwich or wich) *pron.* 1 as an interrogative pronoun, a word used in asking questions about persons or things: *Which seems the best plan?* 2 as a relative pronoun: **a** a word used in connecting a group of words with some other words in the sentence: *Read this book, which you are sure to like.* **b** the one that; any that: *Here are three boxes. Choose which you like best.* 3 a thing that: *And, which is worse, you were late.* 4 **which is which,** which is one and which is the other.
—*adj.* 1 as an interrogative adjective, a word used in asking questions about persons or things: *Which boy won the prize? Which books are yours?* 2 a word used in connecting a group of words with some word in the sentence: *Be careful which way you turn.* [OE *hwilc*]
☛ **which.** As a relative pronoun *which* refers to things and to groups of people regarded impersonally: *They returned for his axe, which they had forgotten. The legislature, which passed the act this afternoon, deserves much credit.*
☛ See **that** for another usage note.
☛ **of which, whose.** See **who** for usage note.

which·ev·er (hwich ev′ər or wich-) *pron. adj.* 1 any one that; any that: *Take whichever you want. Buy whichever hat you like.* 2 no matter which: *Whichever side wins, I shall be satisfied.*

which·so·ev·er (hwich′sō ev′ər or wich′-) *pron. adj.* whichever.

whick·er (hwik′ər or wik′ər) *n. v.* whinny. [imitative]

whiff (hwif or wif) *n.* 1 a slight gust; puff; breath: *A whiff of fresh air cleared his head.* 2 a blow; puff. 3 a slight smell; puff of air having an odor. 4 a puff of tobacco smoke. 5 a slight outburst. 6 *Informal.* **a** in baseball, golf, etc., a swing at a ball without hitting it. **b** in baseball, a strikeout.
—*v.* 1 blow; puff. 2 puff tobacco smoke from (a pipe, etc.); smoke. 3 *Informal.* in baseball, strike out or be struck out. [probably imitative; partly < ME *weffe* vapor, whiff]

whif·fet (hwif′it or wif′-) *n.* 1 *Informal.* an insignificant person or thing. 2 a small dog. [? < *whiff*]

whif·fle (hwif′əl or wif′-) *v.* **-fled, -fling.** 1 blow in puffs or gusts. 2 veer; shift. 3 blow lightly; scatter. [< *whiff*]

whif·fler (hwif′lər or wif′-) *n.* one who whiffles, or shifts about in thought, opinion, intention, etc.

whif·fle·tree (hwif′əl trē′ or wif′-) *n.* whippletree.

Whig (hwig or wig) *n.* 1 formerly, in Great Britain, a member of a political party that tended to favor reforms and progress. 2 in the United States, a person living in any one of the Thirteen Colonies who supported the rebellion against Great Britain. *—adj.* composed of Whigs; having to do with Whigs; like Whigs.

Whig·ger·y (hwig′ər ē or wig′-) *n.* the principles or practices of Whigs.

Whig·gish (hwig′ish or wig′-) *adj.* 1 of or having to do with Whigs. 2 like Whigs.

while (hwīl or wīl) *n. conj. v.* **whiled, whil·ing.** *—n.* 1 a time; space of time: *He kept us waiting a long while. The postman came a while ago.* 2 *Archaic.* a particular time. 3 **between whiles,** at times; at intervals. 4 **the while,** during the time. 5 **worth while,** worth time, attention, or effort.
—conj. 1 during the time that; in the time that; in the same time that: *While I was speaking, he said nothing. Summer is pleasant while it lasts.* 2 in contrast with the fact that; although: *While I like the color of the hat, I do not like its shape.*
—v. **while away,** pass or spend in some easy, pleasant manner: *The children while away many afternoons on the beach.* [OE *hwīl*]
☛ While is used principally as a subordinate conjunction introducing adverbial clauses of time: *They waited on the bank while he swam to the raft.* While is also used, rather weakly, in the sense of although or but: *While the doctor did all he could, he couldn't save her. Walnut is a hard wood, while pine is soft.* While is sometimes used for *and,* but not often: *The second number was an acrobatic exhibition, while the t hird was a trapeze artist.*

whiles (hwīlz or wīlz) *Archaic or dialect. —adv.* 1 sometimes. 2 in the meantime. *—conj.* while.

whi·lom (hwī′ləm or wī′-) *Archaic. —adj.* former: *a whilom friend. —adv.* formerly; once. [OE *hwīlum* at times, dat. pl. of *hwīl* while]

whilst (hwīlst or wīlst) *conj.* while.

whim (hwim or wim) *n.* 1 a sudden fancy or notion; freakish or capricious idea or desire: *Her whim for gardening won't last long.* 2 in mining, a kind of capstan used in hoisting. [probably < Scand.; cf. Icelandic *hvim* unsteady look]

whim·per (hwim′pər or wim′-) *v.* 1 cry with low, broken, mournful sounds: *The sick child whimpered.* 2 make a low, mournful sound. 3 say with a whimper. 4 complain in a weak way; whine. *—n.* a whimpering cry or sound. [probably imitative; cf. G *wimmern*] **—whim′per·er,** *n.* **—whim′per·ing·ly,** *adv.*

whim·sey (hwim′zē or wim′-) *n.* **-seys.** whimsy.

whim·si·cal (hwim′zə kəl or wim′-) *adj.* 1 having many odd notions or fancies; fanciful; odd. 2 full of whims. **—whim′si·cal·ly,** *adv.* **—Syn. 1** capricious, notional.

whim·si·cal·i·ty (hwim′zə kal′ə tē or wim′-) *n.* **-ties.** 1 a whimsical character or quality. 2 a whimsical notion, speech, act, etc.

whim·sy (hwim′zē or wim′-) *n.* **-sies.** 1 an odd or fanciful notion. 2 odd or fanciful humor; quaintness: *His books are full of whimsy.* 3 something showing this. 4 a whim. [< *whim*]

whin (hwin or win) *n.* a low, prickly shrub having yellow flowers, common on waste lands, especially in Europe; furze. [cf. Icel. *hvingras* bent grass]

whine (hwīn or wīn) *v.* **whined, whin·ing,** *n. —v.* 1 make a low, complaining cry or sound: *The dog whined to go out with us.* 2 complain in a peevish, childish way: *Some people are always whining about trifles.* 3 say with a whine. *—n.* 1 a low, complaining cry or sound. 2 a peevish, childish complaint. [OE *hwīnan*] **—whin′er,** *n.* **—whin′ing·ly,** *adv.*

whin·ny (hwin′ē or win′ē) *n.* **-nies,** *v.* **-nied, -ny·ing.** *—n.* the sound that a horse makes. *—v.* 1 of a horse, utter its characteristic call or cry. 2 express with such a sound. [related to WHINE]

whin·stone (hwin′stōn′ or win′-) *n.* basalt or some similar hard rock. [< *whin* whinstone (of uncertain origin) + *stone*]

whip (hwip or wip) *v.* **whipped** or **whipt, whip·ping,** *n.* *—v.* 1 strike; beat; lash: *He whipped the horse.* 2 move, put, or pull quickly and suddenly: *He whipped off his coat and whipped out his knife. The thief whipped behind a tree and escaped.* 3 bring, get, make, or produce by or as by whipping: *whip the nonsense out of someone.* 4 incite; rouse; revive: *whip up some enthusiasm.* 5 criticize or reprove with cutting severity. 6 *Informal.* defeat. 7 summon (in, up) to attend, as the members of a political party in a legislative body, for united action. 8 beat (cream, eggs, etc.) to a froth. 9 sew with stitches passing over and over an edge. 10 wind (a rope, stick, etc.) closely with thread or string; wind (cord, twine, or thread) around something. 11 cast a fish line with a motion like that of using a whip. 12 fish in: *whip a stream.*
—n. 1 something to whip with, usually a stick with a lash at the end. 2 a whipping motion. 3 a dessert made by beating cream, eggs, etc. into a froth. 4 **a** a member of a political party who controls and directs the other members in a lawmaking body, as by seeing that they attend meetings in which important votes will be taken. **b** a call made on members of a political party in a legislature to attend a given session or remain in attendance for it. 5 a person who manages the hounds of a hunting pack. 6 a driver; coachman. 7 a rope and pulley. [cf. MDu. and MLG *wippe* swing] **—whip′like′,** *adj.* **—whip′per,** *n.* **—Syn.** *v.* 1 scourge, flog, thrash, switch. *–n.* 1 scourge, switch.

whip·cord (hwip′kôrd′ or wip′-) *n.* 1 a strong, twisted cord, sometimes used for the lashes of whips. 2 a strong worsted cloth with diagonal ridges on it.

whip hand 1 the hand that holds the whip while driving. 2 a position of control; advantage: *A clever person often gets the whip hand over others.*

whip·lash (whip′lash′ or wip′-) *n.* 1 a lash of a whip. 2 anything considered as similar to this: *the whiplash of fear.* 3 an injury to the neck caused by a sudden jolt that snaps the head backward and then forward.

whip·per-snap·per (hwip′ər snap′ər or wip′-) *n.* an insignificant person who thinks he is important.

whip·pet (hwip′it or wip′-) *n.* 1 a breed of swift, racing dog that resembles a greyhound. 2 a dog of this breed. [< *whip* in the sense of "move quickly"]

whip·ping (hwip′ing or wip′-) *n.* 1 a beating; flogging. 2 arrangement of cord, twine, or the like, wound about a thing: *We fastened the broken rod with a whipping of wire.*

whipping boy 1 formerly, a boy who was educated with a young prince and made to take punishment due to the prince. 2 any person who takes the blame for the wrongdoings of others; a scapegoat.

whipping post a post to which lawbreakers are tied to be whipped.

whip·ple·tree (hwip′əl trē′ or wip′-) *n.* the swinging bar of a carriage or wagon, to which the traces of a harness are fastened. [? < *whip*]

whip-poor-will (hwip′ər wil′ or hwip′ər wil; wip′ər wil′ or wip′ər wil) *n.* a North American bird whose call sounds somewhat like its name. The whip-poor-will is active at night or in the twilight. [imitative]

whip·saw (hwip′so′ or -sô′; wip′so′ or -sô′) *n.* a long, narrow saw with its ends held in a frame. *—v.* 1 cut with a whipsaw. 2 *Informal.* get the better of (a person) no matter what he does.

whip·stitch (hwip′stich′ or wip′-) *v.* sew with stitches passing over and over an edge. *—n.* a stitch made in whipstitching.

whip·stock (hwip′stok′ or wip′-) *n.* the handle of a whip.

whipt (hwipt or wipt) *v.* a pt. and pp. of **whip.**

whir or **whirr** (hwėr or wėr) *n. v.* **whirred, whir·ring.** *—n.* a buzzing noise as of something turning at high speed: *the whir of a small machine. —v.* move quickly with a whir: *The motor whirs.* [cf. Danish *hvirre* whirl]

whirl (hwėrl or wėrl) *v.* 1 turn or swing round and round;

spin: *The leaves whirled in the wind.* 2 move round and round: *We whirled about the room. He whirled the club.* 3 move or carry quickly: *We were whirled away in an airplane.* 4 feel dizzy or confused.
—*n.* 1 a whirling movement. 2 something that whirls. 3 a dizzy or confused condition. 4 a rapid round of happenings, parties, etc. [ME, probably < ON *hvirfla* < *hverfla* turn] —**whirl′er,** *n.*

whirl·i·gig (hwėr′lē gig′ or wėr′lē-) *n.* 1 a toy that whirls. 2 a merry-go-round. 3 something that whirls round and round. 4 a beetle that circles about on the surface of water. [< *whirly-* (obs. var. of *whirl*) + *gig* something that whirls (of uncertain origin)]

whirl·pool (hwėrl′pül′ or wėrl′-) *n.* 1 water whirling round and round rapidly and violently. 2 anything like a whirlpool.

whirl·wind (hwėrl′wind′ or wėrl′-) *n.* 1 a current of air whirling violently round and round; whirling windstorm. 2 anything like a whirlwind. [< *whirl* + *wind,* after ON *hvirfilvindr*]

whirr (hwėr or wėr) *n. v.* whir.

whish (hwish or wish) *n.* a soft rushing sound; whizz; swish. —*v.* make a soft rushing sound. [imitative]

whisk (hwisk or wisk) *v.* 1 sweep or brush (dust, crumbs, etc.) from a surface: *She whisked the crumbs from the table.* 2 move quickly: *The mouse whisked into its hole. She whisked the letter out of sight.* 3 beat or whip to a froth. —*n.* 1 a quick sweep: *a whisk of her broom.* 2 a light, quick movement. 3 a whisk brush. 4 a wire beater for eggs, cream, etc. [ME *visk,* prob. < Scand.; cf. ON *visk* wisp]

whisk brush a small bunch of fibres, feathers, etc. held together tightly on a handle, used for brushing clothes, etc.

whisk·er (hwis′kər or wis′kər) *n.* 1 Usually, **whiskers,** *pl.* the hair growing on a person's face, especially that on a man's cheeks. 2 a single hair of a man's beard. 3 a long, stiff hair growing near the mouth of a cat, rat, etc. [< *whisk*]

whisk·ered (hwis′kərd or wis′kərd) *adj.* having whiskers.

whisk·er·y (hwisk′ə rē or wisk′ər ē) *adj.* having or suggesting whiskers.

whis·key (hwis′kē or wis′kē) *n.* **-keys.** whisky.

whisk·y (hwis′kē or wis′kē) *n.* **-kies.** a strong alcoholic drink made from grain. Whisky is about half alcohol. [short for *whiskybae* < Gaelic *uisge beatha,* literally, water of life]

whis·ky-jack (hwis′kē jak′ or wis′kē-) *n. Cdn.* Canada jay. Also, **whiskey-jack.** [< obs. *whisky-john,* alteration of Cree *wiskatjan*]

whisky sour a cocktail consisting of whisky, lemon juice, and sugar, usually served with an orange slice and a cherry. Also, **whiskey sour.**

whis·per (hwis′pər or wis′pər) *v.* 1 speak very softly. 2 speak to very softly. 3 tell secretly or privately: *It is whispered that his health is failing.* 4 make a soft, rustling sound: *The wind whispered in the pines.* 5 speak without vibration of the vocal cords.
—*n.* 1 a very soft, low-spoken sound. 2 something told secretly or privately. 3 a soft, rustling sound. 4 speech without vibration of the vocal cords. [OE *hwisprian*] —**whis′per·er,** *n.*

whist[1] (hwist or wist) *n.* a card game, resembling bridge, for two pairs of players. Auction and contract bridge deveoped from whist. [alteration of *whisk,* influenced by *whist*[2]]

whist[2] (hwist or wist) *interj.* hush! silence! —*adj. Archaic.* hushed; silent.

whis·tle (hwis′əl or wis′əl) *v.* **-tled, -tling.** *n.* —*v.* 1 make a clear, shrill sound: *The engine whistled before it started off. A blackbird whistles.* 2 blow a whistle. 3 produce or utter by whistling: *whistle a tune.* 4 call; signal, or direct by a whistle: *The policeman whistled the automobile to stop.* 5 move with a shrill sound: *The wind whistled around the house.* 6 **whistle for,** *Informal.* go without; fail to get. 7 **whistle in the dark,** try to be courageous or hopeful in a fearful or trying situation. —*n.* 1 the sound made by whistling. 2 an instrument for making whistling sounds. 3 **wet one's whistle,** *Informal.* take a drink. [OE *hwistlian*]

hat, āge, cãre, fär; let, ēqual, tėrm; it, īce
hot, ōpen, ôrder; oil, out; cup, pu̇t, rüle, ūse
əbove, takən, pencəl, lemən, circəs
ch, child; ng, long; sh, ship
th, thin; ᴛʜ, then; zh, measure

whis·tler (hwis′lər or wis′lər) *n.* 1 a person or thing that whistles. 2 any of several whistling birds. 3 an animal related to the groundhog and gopher found in the mountainous parts of western Canada; hoary marmot.

whistle stop *Informal.* 1 a small, little-known town along a railway line at which a train stops only when signalled. 2 a stop at such a town or station for a brief appearance or speech, as in a political campaign tour.

whist·le-stop (hwis′əl stop or wis′əl-) *adj. v.* **-stopped, -stop·ping.** *Informal.* —*adj.* of or having to do with a whistle stop. —*v.* make a series of electioneering appearances or speeches at stations along a railway line.

whistling swan a large wild swan of North America and Siberia, having a soft, musical note.

whit (hwit or wit) *n.* a very small bit: *The sick man is not a whit better.* [var. of OE *wiht* thing, wight]

white (hwīt or wīt) *n. adj.* **whit·er, whit·est.** —*n.* 1 the color of fresh snow or salt, opposite of black. 2 **a** the quality of being white; white coloration or appearance; whiteness. **b** whiteness as a symbol of purity, goodness, and truth. 3 a white coloring matter. 4 white clothing. 5 something white; a white or colorless part: *the white of an egg, the whites of the eyes.* 6 a white person; a person of the Caucasian race. 7 in archery, the central part of a butt (formerly painted white). 8 in printing, a blank space. 9 an ultraconservative; reactionary; royalist. 10 in chess, checkers, or backgammon: **a** the light-colored squares or other shapes on the board. **b** the white or light-colored pieces. **c** the player holding these pieces.
—*adj.* 1 having the color of snow or salt; reflecting light without absorbing any of the rays composing it. 2 approaching this color. 3 pale: *She turned white with fear.* 4 light-colored: *white wines, white meat.* 5 having a light-colored skin; or of having to do with the Caucasian race. 6 silvery; gray: *white hair.* 7 snowy: *a white winter.* 8 blank: *a white space.* 9 spotless; pure; innocent. 10 *Informal.* honorable; trustworthy; fair. 11 wearing white clothing. 12 ultraconservative; reactionary; royalist. 13 good; beneficent: *white magic.* 14 being at white heat. 15 **bleed white,** use up or take away all of one's money, strength, etc. [OE *hwīt*] —**white′ness,** *n.*

white ant a pale-white insect; termite. White ants eat wood and are very destructive to buildings.

white·bait (hwīt′bāt′ or wīt′-) *n.* **-bait.** a young herring or spràt an inch or two long; a very small fish used for food.

white-bark pine (hwīt′bärk′ or wīt′-) 1 a low-growing, mountain pine of western North America, having creamy-white or pale-brown bark. Its large, sweet seeds were eaten by Indians, and its fragrant resin is often used in making perfume. 2 the wood of this tree.

white birch 1 the North American paper birch. 2 a common European birch having a whitish bark. 3 the wood of either of these trees.

white·cap (hwīt′kap′ or wīt′-) *n.* a wave with a foaming white crest.

white cedar 1 an arborvitae of eastern North America, found in Canada from Nova Scotia to Manitoba. 2 the wood of this tree.

white clover a kind of clover having white flowers, common in fields and lawns.

white coal water used as a source of power.

white·coat (hwīt′kōt′ or wīt′-) *n.* 1 a young of a harp seal. It has a coat of white hair. 2 the skin of a whitecoat.

white-col·lar (hwīt′kol′ər or wīt′-) *adj.* of or having to do with clerical, professional, or business work or workers.

whited sepulchre or **sepulcher** a hypocrite.

white elephant anything that is expensive and troublesome to keep and take care of.

white-faced (hwīt′fāst or wīt′-) *adj.* **1** wan; pallid; pale. **2** of an animal, having large white patches of hair on the head.

white feather **1** a symbol of cowardice. **2 show the white feather,** act like a coward.

white·fish (hwīt′fish′ or wīt′-) *n.* **-fish** or **-fish·es.** any of several food fish having white or silvery sides, found in lakes and streams.

white flag a plain white flag used as a sign of truce or surrender.

white friar a Carmelite monk.

white gold an alloy of gold, nickel or platinum, and some zinc and copper, that looks much like platinum and is used for jewellery.

White·hall (hwīt′hol or -hôl′; wīt′hol′ or -hôl′) *n.* **1** in London: **a** a former palace. **b** a street where many government offices are located. **2** the British government or its policies.

white heat **1** extremely great heat at which things give off a dazzling, white light. **2** a state of extremely great activity, excitement, or feeling.

white heather a type of shrub resembling moss, found in Arctic regions and used as fuel by Eskimos.

white hope *Slang.* a person of whom much is expected. [originally, a white challenger to a boxing title held by a Negro]

white-hot (hwīt′hot′ or wīt′-) *adj.* **1** white with heat; extremely hot. **2** very enthusiastic; excited; violent.

White House **1** in Washington, D.C., the official residence of the President of the United States. **2** *Informal.* the office, authority, opinion, etc. of the President of the United States.

white lead a heavy, white, poisonous compound of lead, used in making paint; basic carbonate of lead. *Formula*: $2PbCO_3Pb(OH)_2$

white lie a lie about some small matter; a polite or harmless lie.

white-liv·ered (hwīt′liv′ərd or wīt′-) *adj.* **1** *Archaic.* cowardly. **2** pale; unhealthy looking.

white man's burden the assumed task of the white race to govern and lead forward the peoples of allegedly less civilized countries, especially in Asia and Africa. [coined in *From Sea to Sea,* by Rudyard Kipling (1865-1936), an English author]

white matter tissue of the brain, spinal cord, etc. that consists chiefly of nerve fibres.

whit·en (hwīt′ən or wīt′ən) *v.* **1** make white. **2** become white. **—whit′en·er,** *n.*

Syn. 1 Whiten, bleach = make white or nearly white. **Whiten** is the general word, particularly suggesting applying or rubbing some substance on the outside of the thing: *The dentist used a powder to whiten my teeth.* **Bleach** = make white or lighter in color or colorless by exposing to sunlight and air or by using chemicals: *You can bleach those handkerchiefs by leaving them out on the clothesline for several days.*

white noise the sound produced by using the whole range of audible frequencies at once. Also, **white sound.** [by analogy with *white light,* which contains all the wave lengths of the visible spectrum]

white oak **1** an oak of E. North America having a light-gray or whitish bark and a hard, durable wood. **2** any similar species of oak. **3** the wood of any of these trees.

white·out (hwīt′out′ or wīt′-) *n.* **1** an arctic weather condition in which the snow-covered ground, the cloudy sky, and the horizon become a continuous, shadowless mass of dazzling white. **2** a temporary blindness resulting from this condition. [modelled on *blackout*]

white paper a government report concerning matters of lesser importance than those appearing in blue books.

white pepper a spice made from husked and dried pepper berries.

white pine **1** a tall pine tree of E. North America, valued for its soft, light wood. **2** this wood, much used for building. **3** any of various similar pines.

white plague tuberculosis.

white poplar a poplar tree whose leaves have silvery-white down on the under surface.

white potato a very common variety of potato with a whitish inside; the Irish potato.

White Russian **1** a Russian living in the western part of the Soviet Union, north of the Ukraine. **2** a Russian who recognizes the former czarist government of Russia as the legal government of that country.

white sauce a sauce made of milk, butter, flour, and, usually, seasonings cooked together.

white slave **1** a woman forced to be a prostitute. **2** a white person held as a slave.

white slaver a person who keeps, controls, or deals in white slaves.

white slavery **1** the condition of white slaves. **2** traffic in white slaves.

white sound white noise.

white spruce **1** a small spruce of northern North America having grayish-white bark and unpleasant-smelling leaves. **2** the wood of this tree.

white supremacist a believer in or supporter of white supremacy.

white supremacy the belief that the white race is superior to other races, especially the Negro race, and should therefore occupy the highest social, economic, and governmental positions.

white·thorn (hwīt′thôrn′ or wīt′-) *n.* the common hawthorn.

white·throat (hwīt′thrōt′ or wīt′-) *n.* **1** a small European warbler that has a whitish throat and belly. **2** a large North American sparrow that has a white throat.

white tie men's full evening dress with tails and white tie, as opposed to black tie.

white trash *U.S. Derogatory.* **1** poor whites considered collectively. **2** a poor white, or a person considered as one.

white·wash (hwīt′wosh′ or wīt′-) *n.* **1** a liquid for whitening walls, woodwork, etc., usually made of lime and water. **2** a covering up of faults or mistakes. **3** anything that covers up faults or mistakes. **4** a defeat without permitting the loser to score.
—*v.* **1** whiten with whitewash. **2** cover up the faults or mistakes of. **3** *Informal.* defeat without permitting the loser to score.

white water rapids.

white·wood (hwīt′wu̇d′ or wīt′-) *n.* **1** a tree with light colored wood, such as a tulip tree, linden, etc. **2** the wood of this tree.

whith·er (hwiᴛʜ′ər or wiᴛʜ′ər) *adv. conj.* to what place; to which place; where. [OE *hwider*]

whith·er·so·ev·er (hwiᴛʜ′ər sō ev′ər or wiᴛʜ′ər-) *adv. conj.* wherever; to whatever place.

whit·ing[1] (hwīt′ing or wīt′-) *n.* **-ing** or **-ings. 1** a European fish like the cod. **2** the silver hake. **3** any of several other food fishes of the cod family. [ME < MDu. *wijting* < *wit* white; cf. OE *hwītling*]

whit·ing[2] (hwīt′ing or wīt′-) *n.* a powdered white chalk, used in making putty, whitewash, and silver polish. [< *white*]

whit·ish (hwit′ish or wīt′-) *adj.* somewhat white: *a whitish dress.*

whit·low (hwit′lō or wit′-) *n.* an abscess on a finger or toe usually near the nail. [earlier *whitflaw,* probably < *white* + *flaw*]

Whit·mon·day (hwit′mun′dē or -dā, wit′mun′dē or -dā) *n.* the Monday after Whitsunday.

Whit·sun (hwit′sən or wit′-) *adj.* of or having to do with Whitsunday or Whitsuntide.

Whit·sun·day (hwit′sun′dē or -dā, wit′sun′dē or -dā) *n.* the seventh Sunday after Easter; Pentecost. [< *white* + *Sunday*]

Whit·sun·tide (hwit′sən tīd′ or wit′-) *n.* the week beginning with Whitsunday, especially the first three days.

whit·tle (hwit′əl or wit′əl) *v.* **-tled, -tling. 1** cut shavings or chips from (wood, etc.) with a knife. **2** shape by whittling; carve. **3 whittle down** or **away,** cut down little by little. [earlier *thwittle*, ult. < OE *thwītan* cut] —**whit′tler,** *n.*

whit·y (hwīt′ē or wīt′ē) *adj.* whitish.

whiz or **whizz** (hwiz or wiz) *n.* **whiz·zes,** *v.* **whizzed, whiz·zing.** —*n.* **1** a humming or hissing sound. **2** *Slang.* a very clever person; an expert. —*v.* make a humming or hissing sound; move or rush with such a sound: *An arrow whizzed past his head.* [imitative]

who (hü; *unstressed relative,* ü) *pron. poss.* **whose,** *obj.* **whom. 1** as an interrogative pronoun, a word used in asking questions about a person or persons: *Who is your friend? Who told you?* **2** as a relative pronoun: **a** a word used in connecting a group of following words with some previous word in the sentence: *The girl who spoke is my best friend. We saw the men who were harvesting the crop.* **b** the person that; any person that; one that: *Who is not for us is against us.* **3 who's who, a** which is one person and which is the other. **b** which people are important. [OE *hwā*]

☛ Who refers to people, to personified objects (a ship, a country), and occasionally to animals: *They have three dogs, who always give us a big welcome.* ☛ See **that** for another usage note.
☛ In informal English **who** is commonly used in both subject and object positions, though *whom* is obligatory immediately after a preposition: *Who did you speak to?* but *I saw the man to whom you spoke yesterday.*
☛ The use of **whose** as a relative referring to a non-personal antecedent (*generators whose combined capacity . . .*) is acceptable in both formal and informal situations. The construction **of which,** advocated by traditional grammarians, is often awkward.

WHO World Health Organization of the United Nations.

whoa (hwō or wō) *interj.* (used especially to horses) stop!

who·dun·it (hü dun′it) *n. Slang.* a story or motion picture dealing with crime, especially murder, and its detection. [< *who* + *done* + *it*]

who·ev·er (hü ev′ər) *pron.* **1** who; any person that: *Whoever wants the book may have it.* **2** no matter who: *Whoever else goes hungry, he won't.*

whole (hōl) *adj.* **1** having all its parts or elements; complete: *He gave her a whole set of dishes.* **2** comprising the full quantity, amount, extent, number, etc.; entire: *a whole melon. He worked the whole day.* **3** being fully or entirely such: *a whole brother* (by both parents). **4** not injured, broken, or defective: *get out of a fight with a whole skin.* **5** in one piece; undivided: *swallow a piece of meat whole.* **6** in mathematics, not fractional; integral: *a whole number.* **7** well; healthy. **8 made out of whole cloth,** *Informal.* entirely false or imaginary.
—*n.* **1** all of a thing; the total: *Four quarters make a whole.* **2** anything complete in itself; a system. **3 as a whole,** as one complete thing; altogether. **4 on the whole, a** considering everything. **b** for the most part. [dial. var. of ME *hole,* OE *hāl*] —**whole′ness,** *n.*
Syn. *adj.* **1** perfect, intact. **2 Whole, total** = consisting of and including all the parts or elements. **Whole** emphasizes that no element or part is left out or taken away: *The whole class was invited to the party.* **Total** emphasizes that every element or part is counted or taken in: *His total income is less this year than last.* **4** unimpaired, uninjured, unbroken. **7** hale, sound. –*n.* **1** entirety, aggregate, sum.

whole-heart·ed (hōl′här′tid) *adj.* earnest; sincere; hearty; cordial. —**whole′-heart′ed·ly,** *adv.* —**whole′-heart′ed·ness,** *n.*

whole note in music, a note having the longest duration in standard notation, used as the basis for determining the time values of all other notes. One whole note is equal to four quarter notes. See **note** for picture.

whole number a number that does not contain a fraction; integer. 1, 2, 3, 15, 106, etc. are whole numbers; $\frac{1}{2}$, $\frac{3}{4}$, and $\frac{7}{8}$ are fractions; $1\frac{5}{8}$, $2\frac{1}{2}$, and $12\frac{2}{3}$ are mixed numbers.

whole rest in music, a rest lasting as long as a whole note. See **rest** for picture.

whole·sale (hōl′sāl′) *n. adj. adv. v.* **-saled, -sal·ing.** —*n.* the sale of goods in large quantities at a time, usually to retailers rather than to consumers directly: *He buys at wholesale and sells at retail.*
—*adj.* **1** in large lots or quantities: *The wholesale price of this coat is $20; the retail price is $30.* **2** selling in large quantities: *a wholesale fruit business.* **3** broad and general; extensive and indiscriminate: *Avoid wholesale condemnation.*
—*adv.* in large lots or quantities.
—*v.* **1** sell in large quantities. **2** be sold in large quantities.

hat, āge, cãre, fär; let, ēqual, tėrm; it, īce
hot, ōpen, ôrder; oil, out; cup, pu̇t, rüle, ūse
əbove, takən, pencəl, lemən, circəs
ch, child; ng, long; sh, ship
th, thin; ᴛʜ, then; zh, measure

whole·sal·er (hōl′sāl′ər) *n.* a merchant who sells goods wholesale.

whole·some (hōl′səm) *adj.* **1** good for the health; healthful: *wholesome food.* **2** healthy-looking; suggesting health: *a wholesome face.* **3** good for the mind or morals; beneficial: *wholesome books.* [ME *holsum* < *hol* whole + *-sum* -some[1]] —**whole′some·ly,** *adv.* —**whole′some·ness,** *n.* —**Syn. 2** See **healthy.**

whole step in music, an interval consisting of two adjoining semitones and equal to one sixth of an octave, such as D to E, or E to F♯.

whole tone whole step.

whole-wheat (hōl′hwēt′ or -wēt′) *adj.* made of the entire wheat kernel.

who'll (hül) who will; who shall.

whol·ly (hōl′ē) *adv.* to the whole amount or extent; completely; entirely; totally.

whom (hüm) *pron.* the objective case of **who.** [OE *hwām,* dat. of *hwā* who] ☛ See **who** for usage note.

whom·ev·er (hüm′ev′ər) *pron.* **1** whom; any person whom. **2** no matter whom.

whom·so·ev·er (hüm′sō ev′ər) *pron.* any person whom.

whoop (hüp, hwüp, or wüp) *n.* **1** a loud cry or shout: *The Indian gave a whoop of rage.* **2** the cry of an owl, crane, etc.; hoot. **3** the loud, gasping noise a person with whooping cough makes after a fit of coughing.
—*v.* **1** shout loudly. **2** call, urge, drive, etc. with shouts: *whoop dogs on.* **3** hoot. **4** make a whooping noise. **5 whoop it up,** *Slang.* make a noisy disturbance. [imitative]

whoop-de-do (hüp′dē dü′, hwüp′-, or wüp′-) *n. Slang.* loud commotion or display; uproar.

whoop·ee (hü′pē or wu̇p′ē, hwü′pē or hwu̇p′ē) *interj.* an exclamation of hilarious, unrestrained joy or pleasure. —*n.* **1** a shout of whoopee. **2** loud excitement; hilarity. **3 make whoopee,** have a noisy, hilarious good time. [< *whoop*]

whoop·er (hwüp′ər, wüp′ər, or hüp′ər) *n.* **1** a person or animal that whoops. **2** a European swan having a whooping cry. **3** a whooping crane.

whoop·ing cough (hüp′ing) an infectious disease of children, characterized by fits of coughing ending with a loud, gasping sound.

whooping crane a large, white crane of North America, now rare, having a loud raucous cry.

whop (hwop or wop) *v.* **whopped, whop·ping,** *n.* —*v.* **1** *Informal.* strike hard or beat. **2** defeat soundly. —*n.* a heavy blow or bump. Also, **whap.**

whop·per (hwop′ər or wop′ər) *n. Informal.* **1** something very large. **2** a big lie.

whop·ping (hwop′ing or wop′ing) *adj. Informal.* very large of its kind; huge.

whore (hôr) *n. v.* **whored, whor·ing.** —*n.* **1** a prostitute. **2** an unchaste woman. —*v.* **1** have intercourse with whores. **2** of a woman, be or act as a whore. [OE *hōre*]

whore·house (hôr′hous′) *n.* a brothel.

whorl (hwėrl or wėrl, hwôrl or wôrl) *n.* **1** in botany, a circle of leaves or flowers round a stem of a plant. **2** in zoology, one of the turns of a spiral shell. See picture on the next page. **3** a convolution, coil, curl, or wreath, especially of something whirling, or suggesting a whirling movement. **4** a type of fingerprint in which the ridges in the centre make a turn through at least one complete circle. **5** one of the spiral curves in the cochlea of the ear. [probably var. of *whirl*]

A whorl of leaves

whorled (hwėrld or wėrld, hwôrld or wôrld) *adj.* **1** having a whorl or whorls. **2** arranged in a whorl.

A shell showing whorls

whor·tle·ber·ry (hwėr′təl ber′ē or wėr′təl-) *n.* **-ries. 1** a small, blackish berry much like the huckleberry. **2** the shrub that it grows on. [< *whortle* (ult. < OE *horte* whortleberry) + *berry*]

who's (hüz) who is.

whose (hüz) *pron.* the possessive case of **who** and of **which.** [OE *hwæs*, gen. of *hwā* who; influenced in ME by nominative *who*] ☛ See **who** for usage note.

whose·so·ev·er (hüz′sō ev′ər) *pron.* whose; of any person whatsoever: *I will accept whosesoever help is offered.*

who·so (hü′sō) *pron. Archaic.* whoever.

who·so·ev·er (hü′sō ev′ər) *pron.* whoever; anybody who.

why (hwī or wī) *adv. n.* **whys,** *interj.* —*adv.* **1** for what cause, reason, or purpose: *Why did you do it? I don't know why I did it.* **2** for which; because of which: *That is the reason why he failed.* **3** the reason for which: *That is why he raised the question.*
—*n.* the cause; reason; purpose: *She tried to find out the whys and wherefores of his behavior.*
—*interj.* an expression used to show surprise, doubt, etc. or just to fill in: *Why! It's all gone! Why, yes, I will if you wish.* [OE *hwȳ*, instrumental case of *hwā* who and *hwæt* what]

W.I. 1 West Indies. **2** West Indian.

wick[1] (wik) *n.* the part of an oil lamp or candle that is lighted. [OE *wēoce*]

wick[2] (wik) *v.* in curling, curl a stone so that it glances off another already played. —*n.* a shot played in this way.

wick·ed (wik′id) *adj.* **1** bad; evil; sinful: *a wicked person, wicked deeds.* **2** mischievous; playfully sly: *a wicked smile.* **3** *Informal.* unpleasant; severe: *a wicked task, a wicked storm.* [< *wick* wicked, probably ult. < OE *wicca* wizard] —**wick′ed·ly,** *adv.* —**Syn. 1** unrighteous, ungodly, immoral, corrupt, depraved, vile, infamous. See **bad.**

wick·ed·ness (wik′id nis) *n.* **1** sin; the state of being wicked. **2** a wicked thing or act; something evil.

wick·er (wik′ər) *n.* **1** a slender, easily bent branch or twig. **2** twigs or branches woven together. Wicker is used in making baskets and furniture. —*adj.* **1** made of wicker. **2** covered with wicker. [ME < Scand.; cf. dial. Swedish *vikker* willow]

wick·er·work (wik′ər wėrk′) *n.* **1** twigs or branches woven together; wicker. **2** anything made of wicker. **3** the art or business of making things out of wicker.

wick·et (wik′it) *n.* **1** a small door or gate: *The big door has a wicket in it.* **2** a small window or opening, often protected by a screen or grating: *Buy your tickets at this wicket.* **3** a small gate or valve for emptying the chamber of a canal lock, or in the chute of a water wheel for regulating the passage of water. **4** in croquet, a wire arch stuck in the ground to knock the ball through. **5** in cricket: **a** either of the two sets of sticks that one side tries to hit with the ball. **b** the level space between these. **c** one batsman's turn. **d** the period during which two men bat together. [ME < AF *wiket*, ult. < Gmc., cf. MDu. *wicket*]

A B
Wickets: A, for croquet; B, for cricket.

wick·et·keep·er (wik′it kēp′ər) *n.* in cricket, the player who stands behind the wicket.

wick·ing (wik′ing) *n.* material for wicks.

wick·i·up (wik′ē up′) *n.* **1** a brush or mat-covered shelter used by certain nomadic Indian tribes. **2** any simple shelter, such as a lean-to. [< Algonquian; cf. Fox *wikiyap* dwelling]

wid·der·shins (wid′ər shinz) *adv. Scottish.* withershins.

wide (wīd) *adj.* **wid·er, wid·est,** *adv. n.* —*adj.* **1** filling more space from side to side than the usual thing of the same sort; not narrow; broad: *a wide street.* **2** filling much space from side to side: *the wide ocean.* **3** extending a certain distance from side to side: *a door three feet wide.* **4** full; ample; roomy: *wide shoes.* **5** of great range: *wide reading.* **6** far or fully open; distended: *stare with wide eyes.* **7** far from a named point, object, target, etc. **8** in phonetics, uttered with a relatively wide opening of the vocal organs.
—*adv.* **1** to a great or relatively great extent from side to side: *wide apart.* **2** over an extensive space or region: *They travel far and wide.* **3** to the full extent; fully: *Open your mouth wide.* **4** aside; astray. **5 wide of,** far from.
—*n.* **1** a wide space or expanse. **2** in cricket, a ball bowled wide of the wicket, counting as a run for the batsman's side. [OE *wīd*] —**wide′ness,** *n.*
Syn. *adj.* **1, 2 Wide, broad** = far or large across. Although they are often used interchangeably, **wide** emphasizes the distance from one side to the other; **broad** emphasizes size or expanse of what is between the two sides, especially when it is larger than average: *A wide ocean separates Canada from Europe. Ships sail on the broad ocean.*

wide-a·wake (wīd′ə wāk′) *adj.* **1** with the eyes wide open; fully awake. **2** alert; keen; knowing.

wide-eyed (wīd′īd′) *adj.* **1** with the eyes wide open. **2** greatly surprised; astonished.

wide·ly (wīd′lē) *adv.* **1** to a wide extent: *a widely distributed plant, a man who is widely known, be widely read, widely opened eyes.* **2** very; extremely: *two widely different accounts of a quarrel.*

wid·en (wīd′ən) *v.* **1** make wide or wider. **2** become wide or wider. —**wid′en·er,** *n.*

wide-o·pen (wīd′ō′pən) *adj.* **1** opened as much as possible. **2** lax in the enforcement of laws, especially those having to do with the sale of liquor, with gambling, and with prostitution. **3** quite unsettled or undecided: *a wide-open question.*

wide·spread (wīd′spred′) *adj.* **1** spread widely: *widespread wings.* **2** spread over a wide space: *a widespread flood.* **3** occurring in many places or among many persons far apart: *a widespread belief.*

widg·eon (wij′ən) *n.* **-eon** or **-eons.** any of several kinds of fresh-water duck, slightly larger than a teal; a scaup duck. [cf. MF *vigeon* wild duck]

wid·ow (wid′ō) *n.* **1** a woman whose husband is dead and who has not married again. **2** in card games, a hand, or group of cards, not dealt to any player but capable of being used by a player who bids for it. **3** in printing, a word or group of words constituting less than a full line at the head of a column or page. —*v.* make a widow of. [OE *widuwe*]

wid·ow·er (wid′ō ər) *n.* a man whose wife is dead and who has not married again. [ME, alteration of OE *widewa*]

wid·ow·hood (wid′ō hu̇d′) *n.* the condition or time of being a widow.

widow's mite a small amount of money given cheerfully by a poor person. [with reference to a poor widow's gift to the temple. Mark 12:42]

widow's peak hair that grows to a point on the forehead, formerly supposed to be a sign of early widowhood.

width (width or witth) *n.* **1** how wide a thing is; distance across; breadth: *The width of the room is ten feet.* **2** a piece of a certain width: *curtains taking two widths of cloth.* **3** extension or breadth in general; quality of wideness: *great width of mind, vision, etc.*

wield (wēld) *v.* hold and use; manage; control: *The soldier wielded his sword well. The people wield the power in a democracy.* [OE *wieldan*] —**wield′er,** *n.*

wie·ner (wē′nər) *n.* a small, reddish sausage made of beef and pork mixed together; frankfurter. Also, **weiner.** [shortened form of *wienerwurst*]

wiener roast an outdoor social function at which wieners are roasted or boiled over an open fire. Also, **weiner roast.**

wie·ner·wurst (wē′nər wėrst′) *n.* wiener. [< G *Wienerwurst* Viennese sausage]

wife (wīf) *n.* **wives. 1** a woman married to a particular man. **2** *Archaic.* a woman, as in *fishwife.* **3 take to wife,** marry. [OE *wīf*] —**wife′less,** *adj.*

wife·hood (wīf′hu̇d) *n.* the condition of being a wife.

wife·ly (wīf′lē) *adj.* **-li·er, -li·est.** of a wife; like a wife; suitable for a wife.

wig (wig) *n. v.* **wigged, wig·ging.** —*n.* an artificial covering of hair for the head: *The bald man wore a wig.* —*v.* **1** supply with, or cover with, a wig or wigs. **2** *Informal.* rebuke; scold. [< *periwig*]

A judge's wig

wig·gle (wig′əl) *v.* **-gled, -gling,** *n.* —*v.* move with short, quick movements from side to side; wriggle: *The restless child wiggled in his chair.* —*n.* a wiggling movement. [cf. Du. *wiggelen*] —**Syn.** *v.* squirm, twist.

wig·gler (wig′lər) *n.* **1** a person or thing that wiggles. **2** the larva of a mosquito.

wig·gly (wig′lē) *adj.* **1** wiggling. **2** wavy.

wight (wīt) *n. Archaic or dialect.* a human being; person. [OE *wiht*]

wig·wag (wig′wag′) *v.* **-wagged, -wag·ging.** *n.* —*v.* **1** move to and fro. **2** signal by movements of arms, flags, lights, etc. according to a code. —*n.* **1** signalling by movements of arms, flags, lights, etc. **2** the message signalled. [< *wig,* v. (related to WIGGLE) + *wag,* v.] —**wig′wag′ger,** *n.*

wig·wam (wig′wom) *n.* a conical hut built of poles covered with bark, mats, or skins, made by North American Indians. [< Algonquian (Ojibway)]

A wigwam

wild (wīld) *adj.* **1** living or growing in the forests or fields; not tamed; not cultivated: *The tiger is a wild animal. The daisy is a wild flower.* **2** with no people living in it: *wild land.* **3** not civilized; savage: *wild tribes.* **4 a** not checked; not restrained: *a wild rush for the ball.* **b** resisting control or restraint; unruly or insubordinate; wayward or self-willed. **c** dissolute; dissipated; licentious: *live a wild life.* **5** not in proper control or order: *wild hair.* **6** boisterous: *wild boys.* **7** violently excited; frantic: *wild with rage.* **8** violent: *a wild storm.* **9** rash; crazy: *wild schemes.* **10** *Informal.* very eager. **11 a** out of one's wits; distracted; mad: *driven almost wild with pain.* **b** showing distraction or madness: *wild eyes.* **12** unconventional, barbaric, or fanciful: *a wild tune or song.* **13** far from the mark. **14** of a card, of arbitrary denomination or suit. **15 run wild,** live or grow without restraint. **16 wild and woolly,** rough and uncivilized like the American West during frontier times; rough-and-tumble.
—*n.* **1** an uncultivated or desolate region or tract; waste; desert. **2 wilds,** *pl.* wild country.
—*adv.* in a wild manner; to a wild degree. [OE *wilde*] —**wild′ly,** *adv.* —**wild′ness,** *n.* —**Syn.** *adj.* **1** undomesticated. **2** uninhabited. **3** barbarous. **9** reckless. **10** enthusiastic, excited.

wild boar a wild pig of Europe, southern Asia, and northern Africa.

wild carrot a common weed with a thin, woody root and lacy, white flowers.

wild·cat (wīld′kat′) *n. adj. v.* **-cat·ted, -cat·ting.** —*n.* **1** a lynx or other wild animal resembling a cat, but larger. **2** a fierce fighter. **3** a risky or unsafe business undertaking. **4** *Informal.* a locomotive and tender operating without other cars. **5** a well drilled for oil or gas in a region where none has been found before.
—*adj.* **1** wild; reckless; not safe: *wildcat stocks.* **2** of or denoting an illicit business or enterprise or its products. **3** running without control or without a schedule: *a wildcat engine.* **4** not authorized by proper union officials; precipitated by small groups or local unions: *a wildcat strike.*
—*v.* drill wells in regions not known to contain oil. —**wild′cat′ter,** *n.*

wild celery eelgrass.

wil·de·beest (wil′də bēst′) *n.* the gnu, an African antelope. [< Afrikaans < Du. *wildebeest* wild beast]

hat, āge, cãre, fär; let, ēqual, tėrm; it, īce
hot, ōpen, ôrder; oil, out; cup, pu̇t, rüle, ūse
əbove, takən, pencəl, lemən, circəs
ch, child; ng, long; sh, ship
th, thin; ᴛʜ, then; zh, measure

wil·der (wil′dər) *v. Poetic or archaic.* **1** bewilder. **2** lose one's way; be perplexed. [apparently < *wilderness*] —**wil′der·ment,** *n.*

wil·der·ness (wil′dər nis) *n.* **1** a wild place; a region with no people living in it. **2** a bewildering mass or collection: *a wilderness of streets.* [ME *wilderne* wild, OE *wildēorn,* ult. < *wilde* wild + *dēor* animal] —**Syn.** **1** waste. See **desert.**

wild-eyed (wīld′īd′) *adj.* **1** having wild eyes. **2** staring wildly or angrily.

wild·fire (wīld′fīr′) *n.* **1** a substance that burns fiercely and is hard to put out, formerly used in warfare. **2** the will-o'-the-wisp; ignis fatuus. **3** any of various inflammatory, eruptive diseases, especially of sheep. **4 like wildfire,** very rapidly.

wild flower or **wild·flow·er** (wīld′flou′ər) *n.* **1** any flowering plant that grows in the woods, fields, etc.; an uncultivated plant. **2** a flower of such a plant.

wild·fowl (wīld′foul′) *n.* birds ordinarily hunted, such as wild ducks or geese, partridges, quail, and pheasants.

wild-goose chase (wīld′güs′) a useless search or attempt.

wild·life (wīld′līf′) *n.* wild animals and plants as a group, usually those native to an area.

wild oats **1** oatlike grass growing as a weed in meadows, etc. **2** youthful dissipation. **3 sow one's wild oats,** indulge in youthful dissipation before settling down in life.

wild rice the edible grain of a tall North American grass that grows in wet soil.

wild West or **Wild West** the western United States during pioneer days.

wild·wood (wīld′wu̇d′) *n.* trees growing in their natural state; forest.

wile (wīl) *n. v.* **wiled, wil·ing.** —*n.* **1** a trick to deceive; a cunning way: *The serpent by his wiles persuaded Eve to eat the apple.* **2** subtle trickery; slyness; craftiness. —*v.* **1** coax; lure; entice: *The sunshine wiled me from work.* **2 wile away,** while away; pass easily or pleasantly. [OE *wīgle* magic] —**Syn.** *n.* **1** artifice, stratagem, ruse.

wil·ful (wil′fəl) *adj.* willful. —**wil′ful·ness,** *n.*

wi·li·ness (wī′lē nis) *n.* the quality of being wily; craftiness; slyness.

will[1] (wil; *unstressed,* wəl) *auxiliary v. pres. indic. sing. 1st pers.* **will,** *2nd* **will** or (*archaic*) **wilt,** *3rd* **will,** *pl.* **will**; *pt. 1st* **would,** *2nd* **would** or (*archaic*) **wouldst,** *3rd* **would,** *pl.* **would**; *pp.* (*obsolete*) **would, wold** (wōld); *imperative and infinitive lacking.* an auxiliary verb used to express: **1** futurity: *He will come soon.* **2** willingness: *I will go if you do.* **3** ability: *The pail will hold four gallons.* **4** obligation: *You will do it at once!* **5** customary or continued action: *She will read for hours at a time.* [OE *willan*]

☛ **shall, will.** The usage of *shall* and *will* has never been uniform in English, although some grammarians have attempted to insist on uniformity. The general practices in the more common situations needing these words are as follows: **1 General usage. a** *Simple future.* In speech and writing the prevailing use in Canada, and in many other parts of the English-speaking world, is *will* in all persons: *I will ask, you will ask, he will ask, etc.* This usage would appear in more printed matter if editors did not revise the copy to bring it in line with their stylebooks. **b** *Emphatic future.* In expressing determination in the future or for some special emphasis, informal usage is divided. In speech the determination is expressed by stress, which may be used on either word: *I shall′ go. I will′ go.* There is some tendency to use *shall* in all persons as the emphatic form: *I, you, he, she, we, you, they shall ask.* **c** *Contractions.* In speaking and in informal writing where contractions are used, the future becomes *I'll, you'll, he'll* and so on, which do not discriminate between *shall* and *will. Won't* is used for *will not* (formed from an obsolete *woll* and *not*) and *shan't* for *shall not.* **d** *In questions. Shall* is likely to be used in the first and third persons, and *will* in the second in asking questions, but practice is not consistent: *Shall I go? Will you go? What shall we do now? What will you do now? What shall he do? What will he do with it?* In the negative, *won't* is the more common: *Won't I look funny in that? What won't he think of next?* **2 Formal usage.** Some writers and editors use *shall* in the first person, *will* in the second and third persons in making the future tense:

First person:	*I shall ask*	*we shall ask*
Second person:	*you will ask*	*you will ask*
Third person:	*he, she will ask*	*they will ask.*

In the emphatic future, expressing determination on the part of the speaker, formal English theoretically reverses this use of *shall* and *will*:

First person:	*I will ask*	*we will ask*
Second person:	*you shall ask*	*you shall ask*
Third person:	*he, she shall ask*	*they shall ask.*

In asking questions a few people even use the form of *shall* or *will* in a question that the answerer would use in his reply. This usage is distinctly formal and usually sounds unnatural: *Shall you go?* Answer: *I shall (shall not) go.*

will[2] (wil) *n. v.* **willed, will·ing.** —*n.* **1** the power of the mind to decide and do; deliberate control over thought and action: *A good leader must have a strong will.* **2** the act of choosing to do something, sometimes including also all deliberation that precedes making the choice; volition. **3** purpose; determination: *the will to live.* **4** an order, command, or decree. **5** what is chosen to be done: (one's or its) pleasure. **6** wish; desire: "*Thy will be done.*" **7** in law: **a** a legal statement of a person's wishes about what shall be done with his property after he is dead. **b** a document containing such a statement. **8** feeling toward another: *good will, ill will.* **9 at will,** whenever one wishes. **10 do the will of,** obey. **11 with a will,** with energy and determination.
—*v.* **1** decide by using the power of the mind to decide and do; use the will: *She willed to keep awake.* **2** influence or try to influence by deliberate control over thought and action: *She willed the person in front of her to turn around.* **3** determine; decide: *Fate has willed it otherwise.* **4** give by a will: *will a house to someone.* **5** *Rare.* wish; desire. [OE] —**Syn.** *n.* **2** resolution, decision. **3** inclination, preference, choice. –*v.* **3** purpose, intend. **4** bequeath.

willed (wild) *adj.* having a certain kind of will: *strong-willed.*

wil·let (wil′it) *n.* a North American wading bird related to the snipes and sandpipers. [< *pilly-will-willet,* imitative of its call]

will·ful or **wil·ful** (wil′fəl) *adj.* **1** wanting or taking one's own way; stubborn. **2** done on purpose; intended: *willful murder, willful waste.* [< *will*[2] + *full*]
—**will′ful·ness** or **wil′ful·ness,** *n.* —**Syn. 1** obstinate, headstrong, perverse. **2** deliberate, intentional.

will·ful·ly or **wil·ful·ly** (wil′fəl ē) *adv.* **1** by choice; voluntarily. **2** by design; intentionally. **3** selfishly; perversely; obstinately; stubbornly.

wil·lies (wil′ēz) *n. Informal.* a spell of nervousness. [origin unknown]

will·ing (wil′ing) *adj.* **1** ready; consenting: *He is willing to wait.* **2** cheerfully ready: *willing obedience.*
—**will′ing·ly,** *adv.* —**will′ing·ness,** *n.* —**Syn. 1** disposed, inclined.

wil·li·waw (wil′ə wo′ or wil′ə wô′) *n.* **1** a sudden, violent gust of wind moving down to the sea from mountains along the coast. **2** any commotion or agitation. [origin unknown]

will-o'-the-wisp (wil′ə ᴛʜə wisp′) *n.* **1** a moving light appearing at night over marshy places, caused by the combustion of marsh gas. **2** something that deceives or misleads by luring on.

wil·low (wil′ō) *n.* **1** a tree or shrub having tough, slender branches and narrow leaves. The branches of most willows bend easily and are used to make furniture. **2** the wood of this tree. —*adj.* made of willow. [ult. < OE *welig*]

willow herb a plant that grows in moist places, having long, narrow leaves and long clusters of purple flowers.

willow ptarmigan a brownish arctic ptarmigan whose plumage turns white in winter.

wil·low·y (wil′ō ē) *adj.* **1** like a willow; slender; supple; graceful. **2** having many willows.

wil·ly-nil·ly (wil′ē nil′ē) *adv.* **1** willingly or not; with or against one's wishes. **2** in a disordered manner; helter-skelter: *Books were piled willy-nilly in the attic.*
—*adj.* **1** indecisive; without resolution. **2** that is such, or that takes place, whether one wishes or not: *a willy-nilly spinster.* [< *will I* (*he, ye*), *nill I* (*he, ye*); *nill* not will, OE *nyllan* < *ne* not + *willan* will]

wilt[1] (wilt) *v.* **1** become limp and drooping; wither. **2** lose strength, vigor, assurance, etc. **3** cause to wilt. [var. of *welt* wither, alteration of *welk*; cf. MDu. and MLG *welken*]

wilt[2] (wilt) *v. Archaic.* 2nd pers. sing. present tense of **will.** "Thou wilt" means "you will" (sing.).

Wil·ton (wil′tən) *n.* a kind of velvety carpet.

wil·y (wīl′ē) *adj.* **wil·i·er, wil·i·est.** using subtle tricks to deceive; crafty; cunning; sly. —**wil′i·ly,** *adv.*
—**Syn.** artful, subtle, designing, insidious.

wim·ble (wim′bəl) *n.* a tool for boring. [ME < AF < MLG *wemel*]

wim·ple (wim′pəl) *n. v.* **-pled, -pling.** —*n.* a cloth arranged in folds about the head, cheeks, chin, and neck, worn by nuns and formerly by other women.
—*v.* **1** cover or muffle with a wimple. **2** ripple or cause to ripple. **3** *Archaic.* lie or lay in folds, as a veil. [OE *wimpel*]

A wimple

win (win) *v.* **won, win·ning,** *n.*
—*v.* **1** get victory or success: *The tortoise won in the end.* **2** get victory or success in: *He won the race.* **3** get by effort; gain: *win fame, win a prize.* **4** gain the favor of; persuade: *The speaker soon won his audience. Mary won her mother over to her side.* **5** attract; get the love of. **6** persuade to marry. **7** get to; reach, often by effort: *win the summit of a mountain.* **8 win out,** *Informal.* get victory or success. —*n. Informal.* the act or fact of winning; success; a victory. [OE *winnan*]
—**Syn.** *v.* **3** secure, obtain, earn, achieve, attain.

wince (wins) *v.* **winced, winc·ing,** *n.* —*v.* draw back suddenly; flinch slightly: *The boy winced at the sight of the dentist's drill.* —*n.* the act of wincing. [ME < AF **wencir,* var. of OF *guencir* < Gmc.] —**Syn.** *v.* shrink, recoil.

winch (winch) *n.* **1** a machine for lifting or pulling, turned by a crank. **2** the handle of a revolving machine.
—*v.* move by a winch. [OE *wince*]

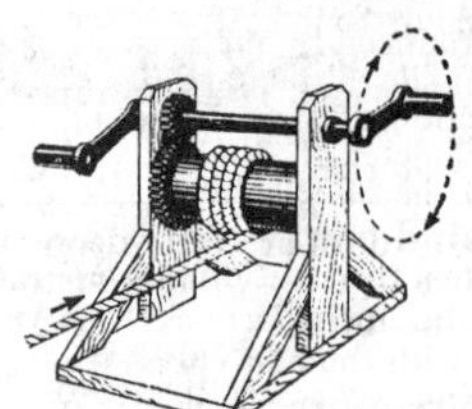

A winch or windlass. The arrows show the way in which the handles and the rope go.

Win·ches·ter (win′ches′tər or win′chis tər) *n.* a kind of breechloading repeating rifle, having a tubular magazine under the barrel and a bolt operated by a lever, invented and first made about 1866. Also, **Winchester rifle.** [< Oliver F. *Winchester,* 1810-1880, an American manufacturer, who produced them]

wind[1] (*n.* wind or, *archaic and poetic,* wīnd; *v.* wind) *n. v.* **wind·ed, wind·ing.** —*n.* **1** air in motion: *The wind bends the branches.* The wind varies in force from a slight breeze to a strong gale. **2** a strong wind; gale. **3** a current of air filled with some smell: *The deer caught wind of the hunter and ran off.* **4** gas in the stomach or bowels. **5** in music: **a** a wind instrument. **b winds,** *pl.* the section of an orchestra or band composed of wind instruments. **6** power of breathing; breath: *A runner needs good wind.* **7 a** empty, useless talk. **b** vanity; conceit.
before the wind, in the direction toward which the wind is blowing.
between wind and water, a near the water line of a ship. **b** in a dangerous place.
down the wind, in the direction that the wind is blowing.
get wind of, a find out about; get a hint of. **b** smell: *The deer soon got wind of the hunter.*
in the eye or **teeth of the wind,** directly against the wind.
in the wind, happening; about to happen; impending.
into the wind, pointing toward the direction from which the wind is blowing.

off the wind, with the wind blowing from behind.
on the wind, as nearly as possible in the direction from which the wind is blowing.
sail close to the wind, a manage with close calculation or the utmost economy. **b** come very near to imprudence, dishonesty, indecency, etc.
take the wind out of one's sails, take away one's advantage, argument, etc. suddenly or unexpectedly.
to the wind, to the point from which the wind blows.
up the wind, with the wind blowing from in front.
—*v.* **1** expose to wind or air. **2** follow by scent; smell. **3** put out of breath; cause difficulty in breathing: *The fat man was winded by walking up the steep hill.* **4** let recover breath: *They stopped in order to wind their horses.* [OE]
Syn. *n.* **1 Wind, breeze** = air in motion. **Wind** is the general word: *The wind is from the north.* **Breeze,** except as a technical term (meteorology), means a light, gentle wind, especially one that is cool or refreshing: *We nearly always have a breeze at night.* **2** blast.

wind[2] (wīnd) *v.* **wound** or (*rare*) **wind·ed, wind·ing,** *n.* —*v.* **1** move this way and that; move in a crooked way; change direction; turn: *A brook winds through the woods. We wound our way through the narrow streets.* **2** proceed in a roundabout or indirect manner: *His speech wound slowly toward its conclusion.* **3** fold, wrap, or place about something: *The mother wound her arms about the child.* **4** cover with something put, wrapped, or folded around: *The man's arm is wound with bandages.* **5** roll into a ball or on a spool: *The old woman was winding yarn. Thread comes wound on spools.* **6** twist or turn around something: *The vine winds round a pole.* **7** be warped or twisted: *That board will wind.* **8** make (a machine) go by turning some part of it: *wind a clock.* **9** be wound: *This clock winds easily.* **10** haul or hoist by means of a winch, windlass, or the like. **11** of a musical instrument, tighten the strings, pegs, etc.; tune. **12 wind off,** unwind. **13 wind up, a** end; settle; conclude. **b** in baseball, make the movements that a pitcher does just before pitching the ball. **c** roll or coil; wind completely. **d** put into a state of tension, great strain, intensity of feeling, etc.; excite.
—*n.* a bend; turn; twist. [OE *windan*] —**wind'er,** *n.*
—**Syn.** *v.* **1** curve, crook, twist, bend.

wind[3] (wīnd or wind) *v.* **wind·ed** or **wound, wind·ing.** blow: *The hunter winds his horn.* [special use of *wind*[1]]

wind·age (win'dij) *n.* **1** the power of the wind to turn a missile from its course. **2** the distance that a missile is turned from its course by the wind. **3** a change in aim to compensate for windage. **4** atmospheric disturbance produced by the passage of a bullet, shell, or other missile. **5** the part of a ship's surface affected by the action of wind. **6** the slight difference between the diameter of a bullet, shell, etc. and of the bore of a gun of the same calibre.

wind·bag (wind'bag') *n. Slang.* a person who talks a great deal but does not say much.

wind-blown (wind'blōn') *adj.* **1** blown by the wind. **2** with the hair cut short and brushed forward.

wind-borne (wind'bôrn') *adj.* of pollen, seed, etc. carried by the wind.

wind·break (wind'brāk') *n.* **1** a shelter from the wind. **2** a row or clump of trees planted to afford protection from the wind.

wind·break·er (wind'brāk'ər) *n.* a short sports jacket of wool, leather, etc. having a tight-fitting band at the waist and cuffs, used for outdoor wear.

wind-bro·ken (wind'brō'kən) *adj.* of horses, etc., having the breathing restricted or impaired; having the heaves.

wind chill the rate at which exposed human skin cools under given conditions of temperature and wind speed. When the wind chill count is 2,400, exposed flesh begins to freeze.

wind·ed (win'did) *adj.* out of breath.

-winded *combining form.* being —— of wind or breath: *short-winded = being short of wind or breath.*

wind·fall (wind'fol' or -fôl') *n.* **1** an unexpected piece of good luck. **2** fruit blown down by the wind: *These apples are windfalls.* **3** a tree blown down by the wind. **4** land covered with such trees.

wind·flow·er (wind'flou'ər) *n.* an anemone.

win·di·go (win'di gō') *n.* **-gos.** wendigo (def. 1).

wind·ing (wīn'ding) *n.* **1** the act of one that winds. **2** a bend; turn. **3** something that is wound or coiled. **4** in electricity: **a** a continuous coil of wire forming a conductor in a generator, motor, etc. **b** the manner in which the wire is coiled: *a series winding.* —*adj.* bending; turning. —**wind'ing·ly,** *adv.*

hat, āge, cãre, fär; let, ēqual, tėrm; it, īce
hot, ōpen, ôrder; oil, out; cup, pu̇t, rüle, ūse
əbove, takən, pencəl, lemən, circəs
ch, child; ng, long; sh, ship
th, thin; ᴛʜ, then; zh, measure

winding sheet a cloth in which a dead person is wrapped for burial.

wind instrument a musical instrument sounded by blowing air into it. Trumpets, flutes, clarinets, and oboes are wind instruments.

wind·jam·mer (wind'jam'ər) *n. Informal.* **1** in the merchant service, a sailing ship as opposed to a steamship. **2** a member of its crew.

wind·lass (wind'ləs) *n.* a machine for pulling or lifting things; winch. See **winch** for picture. [ME *windelass,* an alteration (influenced by ME *windel* wheel, winder) of ME *windass* < ON *vindáss* < *vinde* wind + *áss* beam, pole]

wind·mill (wind'mil') *n.* **1** a mill consisting, usually, of a tall tower surmounted by a circular arrangement of sails or wings that are rotated by the wind. The motion thus produced is transmitted to a millstone, pump, etc. Windmills are used for pumping water, grinding grain, etc. **2** something that acts like a windmill. **3** *Informal.* a helicopter. **4 tilt at** or **fight windmills,** expend one's energy in futile attacks on what cannot be overcome (in allusion to the story of Don Quixote tilting at windmills under the illusion that they were giants).

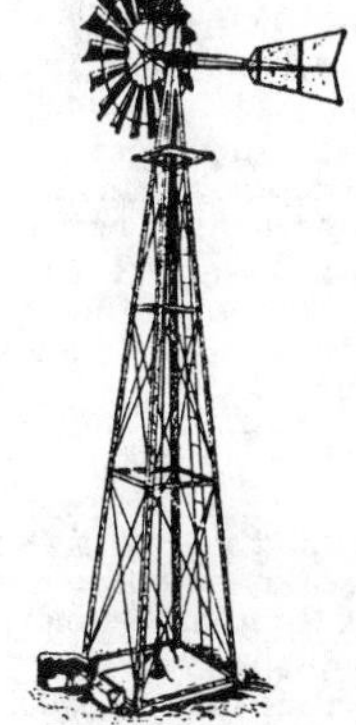
A windmill for pumping water. The large vane keeps it facing so as to catch the wind. Gears pass the motion of the wheel to a shaft that works the pump.

win·dow (win'dō) *n.* **1** an opening in the wall or roof of a building, boat, car, etc. to let in light or air. **2** such an opening with the frame, panes of glass, etc. that fill it. **3** the sashes and panes that fit such an opening: *open the window.* **4** a windowpane: *break a window.* **5 a** an opening like a window in shape or function, such as the transparent part of some envelopes through which the address is seen. **b** anything suggesting a window. —*v.* furnish with windows. [ME < ON *vindauga* < *vindr* wind + *auga* eye] —**win'dow·less,** *adj.*

window box 1 a long, narrow box placed outside a window, or inside on a window sill, and used for growing plants and flowers. **2** a groove on the side of a window frame to hold the weights that counterbalance a vertically sliding sash.

window dresser a person who does window dressing.

window dressing 1 the art of attractively displaying merchandise in shop windows. **2** any display or statement made to create a favorable impression, often when there is no justification for such an impression or in order to direct attention away from faults or errors: *The balance sheet of the firm did a good job of window dressing.*

win·dow·pane (win'dō pān') *n.* a piece of glass in a window.

window sash the frame for the glass in a window.

window seat a bench built into the wall of a room, under a window.

win·dow-shop (win'dō shop') *v.* **-shopped, -shop·ping.** look at articles in store windows without going in to buy anything. —**win'dow-shop'per,** *n.*

window sill a piece of wood, stone, etc. across the bottom of a window.

wind·pipe (wind′pīp′) *n.* the passage from the throat to the lungs; trachea. See **larynx** for diagram.

wind·row (wind′rō′) *n.* **1** a row of hay raked together to dry before being made into cocks or heaps. **2** any similar row, as of sheaves of grain, made for the purpose of drying; row of dry leaves, dust, etc. swept together by wind or the like. —*v.* arrange in a windrow or windrows. [< *wind*[1] + *row*[1]]

wind·shield (wind′shēld′) *n.* on a car, etc., a sheet of glass above the dashboard to keep off the wind.

wind sleeve or **sock** a cone-shaped sleeve mounted on a pole or the like, showing the direction of the wind.

Wind·sor (win′zər) *n.* the family name of the royal house of Great Britain since 1917. [< *Windsor* Castle, a residence of the British sovereigns]

Windsor chair a kind of wooden chair, with or without arms, having a rounded spindle back, slanting legs, and a flat or slightly hollowed seat, especially popular in England and North America during the 18th century. [< *Windsor*, a town in Berkshire, England, where such chairs were first made]

Windsor tie a wide necktie of soft silk, tied in a loose bow.

wind·storm (wind′stôrm′) *n.* a storm with much wind but little or no rain.

wind tunnel a cylindrical structure in which the effect of air pressures on aircraft, missiles, etc. can be calculated by means of artificially made winds.

wind-up (wīnd′up′) *n.* **1** a winding up; end; close; conclusion. **2** in baseball, a series of movements made by a pitcher just before throwing the ball.

wind·ward (wind′wərd or win′dərd) *adv.* toward the wind. —*adj.* **1** on the side toward the wind. **2** in the direction from which the wind is blowing. —*n.* **1** the side toward the wind. **2** the direction from which the wind is blowing.

wind·y (win′dē) *adj.* **wind·i·er, wind·i·est. 1** having much wind: *a windy street, windy weather.* **2** made of wind; empty: *windy talk.* **3** talking a great deal; voluble. **4** causing or having gas in the stomach or intestines. [OE *windig*] —**wind′i·ly,** *adv.* —**wind′i·ness,** *n.*

wine (wīn) *n. adj. v.* **wined, win·ing.** —*n.* **1** the juice of grapes after it has fermented so that it contains alcohol. **2** the fermented juice of other fruits of plants: *currant wine, dandelion wine.* **3** the color of red wine; a dark purplish-red. **4** something that exhilarates or intoxicates like wine. **5 new wine in old bottles,** something new that is too strong to be held back by old forms. —*adj.* dark purplish-red. —*v.* entertain with wine. [OE *wīn*, ult. < L *vinum*]

wine·bib·ber (wīn′bib′ər) *n.* a person who drinks much wine. [(translation of G *Weinsäufer*) < *wine* + *bibber* < ME *bibbe(n)* drink, ? < L *bibere*]

wine cellar 1 a cellar where wine is stored. **2** the wine stored there.

wine-col·ored or **wine-col·oured** (wīn′kul′ərd) *adj.* dark purplish-red.

wine gallon the standard gallon of the United States; 231 cu. in., approximately four fifths of an imperial gallon.

wine·glass (wīn′glas′) *n.* a small drinking glass for wine.

wine·grow·er (wīn′grō′ər) *n.* a person who raises grapes and makes wine.

wine·grow·ing (wīn′grō′ing) *adj.* the raising of grapes and the making of wine.

wine press 1 a machine for pressing the juice from grapes. **2** a vat in which grapes are trodden in the process of making wine.

win·er·y (wīn′ər ē) *n.* **-er·ies.** a place where wine is made.

Wine·sap or **wine·sap** (wīn′sap′) *n.* a variety of red winter apple.

wine·skin (wīn′skin′) *n.* a container made of the nearly complete skin of a goat, hog, etc. and used, especially in some Eastern countries, for holding wine.

wing (wing) *n.* **1** the part of a bird, insect, etc. by which it flies; the corresponding part in a bird, insect, etc. that does not fly. **2** anything like a wing in shape or use, such as one of the major lifting and supporting surfaces of an airplane, the vanes of a windmill, and the feather of an arrow. **3** *Humorous.* a foreleg or arm. **4** a part that sticks out from the main wing or body. The part of a building that sticks out sidewise from the main part is a wing. **5** a part of an organization; faction. The radicals of a political group are called the left wing. **6** flying; winged flight. **7** in certain games, a player whose position is on either side of the centre. **8** in theatre: **a** often, **wings,** *pl.* one of the spaces at either side of the stage, between the side scenes, out of sight of the audience. **b** any of the side scenes on the stage. **9** a sidepiece projecting out from the back of a wing chair. **10** in the air force, an administrative and tactical unit. **11** that part of a military force to the right or left of the main body. **12 wings,** *pl.* insignia awarded to men who have qualified as pilots, navigators, etc. **13 on the wing, a** flying. **b** moving; active; busy. **c** going away. **14 take wing,** fly away. **15 under the wing of,** under the protection or sponsorship of.
—*v.* **1** fly: *The bird wings its way to the south.* **2** fly through. **3** supply with wings. **4** make able to fly; give speed to: *Terror winged his steps as the bear drew nearer.* **5** wound in the wing or arm: *The bullet winged the bird but did not kill it.* **6 wing its way,** fly. [ME < ON *vængr*] —**wing′less,** *adj.* —**wing′like′,** *adj.*

wing case either of the hardened front wings of certain insects.

wing chair a completely upholstered, high-backed armchair with side pieces extending out from the back.

A wing chair

wing commander in the air force, a commissioned officer senior to a squadron leader and junior to a group captain.

winged (wingd; *esp. poetic,* wing′id) *adj.* **1** having wings. **2** swift; rapid.

wing·spread (wing′spred′) *n.* the distance between the tips of the wings when they are spread.

wink (wingk) *v.* **1** close the eyes and open them again quickly. **2** close and open quickly. **3** close one eye and open it again as a hint or signal. **4** move by winking: *wink back tears.* **5** twinkle: *The stars winked.* **6** give a signal or express a message by a winking of the eye, a flashlight, etc. **7 wink at,** pretend not to see. —*n.* **1** a winking. **2** a hint or signal given by winking. **3** a twinkle. **4** a very short time: *I didn't sleep a wink.* **5 winks,** *pl.* a short sleep; nap. [OE *wincian*]

wink·er (wingk′ər) *n.* **1** a person or thing that winks. **2** *Informal.* an eyelash. **3** a blinder or blinker for a horse's eye.

win·kle (wing′kəl) *n.* a sea snail used for food. [OE *-wincle* as in *pinewincle* periwinkle]

win·ner (win′ər) *n.* a person or thing that wins.

win·ning (win′ing) *adj.* **1** that wins: *a winning team.* **2** charming; attractive: *a winning smile.* —*n.* **winnings,** *pl.* what is won; money won: *He pocketed his winnings.* —**win′ning·ly,** *adv.*

Win·ni·peg couch (win′ə peg′) a kind of couch having no arms or back and opening out into a double bed.

Winnipeg goldeye goldeye.

win·now (win′ō) *v.* **1** blow off the chaff from (grain); drive or blow away (chaff). **2** blow chaff from grain. **3** sort out; separate; sift: *winnow truth from falsehood.* **4** fan (with wings); flap (wings). —*n.* **1** a contrivance for winnowing grain. **2** the act of winnowing or a motion resembling it. [OE *windwian* < *wind* wind[1]]

wi·no (wī′nō) *n.* **-nos.** *Slang.* an alcoholic who is addicted to cheap wine.

win·some (win′səm) *adj.* charming; attractive; pleasing: *a winsome girl.* [OE *wynsum* < *wynn* joy] —**win′some·ly,** *adv.* —**win′some·ness,** *n.*

win·ter (win′tər) *n.* **1** the coldest of the four seasons; the time of the year between fall and spring. **2** a year as denoted by this season: *a man of eighty winters.* **3** the last period of life. **4** a period of decline, dreariness, or adversity.
—*adj.* **1** of, having to do with, or characteristic of winter. **2** of the kind that may be kept for use during the winter: *winter apples.*

—*v.* **1** pass the winter. **2** keep, feed, or manage during winter: *We wintered our cattle in the warm valley.* [OE]

winter carnival a carnival that features winter sports and crafts.

win·ter·er (win′tər ər) *n. Cdn.* formerly: **1** a seasoned fur trader or voyageur who spent his winters in the fur country. **2** a wintering partner.

win·ter·green (win′tər grēn′) *n.* **1** a small evergreen plant of North America having bright-red berries and aromatic leaves. An oil made from its leaves **(oil of wintergreen** or **wintergreen oil)** is used in medicine and candy. **2** the oil of this plant. **3** its flavor.

winter ice sea ice that is more than 8 inches thick and has formed and developed in one winter. It is therefore one year old or less.

wintering partner *Cdn.* formerly: **1** a stock-holding partner in the North West Company who represented the company the year round at trading posts in the fur country. **2** in the Hudson's Bay Company, a commissioned officer in charge of business at a trading post. He held no stock but received a share of the profits.

win·ter·ize (win′tər īz′) *v.* **-ized, -iz·ing. 1** make (an automobile, etc.) ready for operation or use during the winter. **2** prepare a building, such as a cottage, for use in winter. **3** safeguard an unoccupied building against damage in winter by draining taps, boarding windows, etc.

win·ter·kill (win′tər kil′) *v.* kill by or die from exposure to cold weather: *The rosebushes were winterkilled.*
—*n.* death of plants and animals resulting from winter conditions.

winter solstice for the Northern Hemisphere, the time when the sun is farthest south from the equator, December 21 or 22.

win·ter·tide (win′tər tīd′) *n.* wintertime.

win·ter·time (win′tər tīm′) *n.* the winter season.

winter wheat wheat planted in the fall to ripen in the following spring or summer.

win·ter·y (win′tər ē or win′trē) *adj.* **-ter·i·er, -ter·i·est.** wintry.

win·tri·ness (win′trē nis) *n.* a wintry quality.

win·try (win′trē) *adj.* **-tri·er, -tri·est. 1** of or characteristic of winter: *a wintry sky.* **2 a** devoid of fervor or affection; cold; chilling: *a wintry smile.* **b** destitute of warmth or brightness; dismal; dreary; cheerless: *a wintry gathering.*

win·y (wīn′ē) *adj.* tasting, smelling, or looking like wine.

winze[1] (winz) *n. Scottish.* an oath; curse. [< MDu. *wensch* wish]

winze[2] (winz) *n.* in mining, a small inclined shaft or passage connecting one level with another. [< earlier *winds,* perhaps < *wind*[2]]

wipe (wīp) *v.* **wiped, wip·ing,** *n.* —*v.* **1** rub with paper, cloth, etc. in order to clean or dry: *wipe the table.* **2** take (away, off, or out) by rubbing: *Wipe away your tears. She wiped off the dust.* **3** remove: *The rain wiped away all the footprints.* **4** rub or draw (something) over a surface. **5** apply (a soft substance) by rubbing it on with a cloth, pad, etc.: *wipe ointment on a burn.* **6** form (a joint in lead pipe) by spreading solder with a leather pad. **7 wipe out, a** remove, especially by death; destroy completely: *The settlement was wiped out by Indians.* **b** cancel: *The generous man wiped out all the debts owed him.* —*n.* the act of wiping. [OE *wīpian*]

wip·er (wīp′ər) *n.* **1** a person who wipes. **2** anything used for wiping.

wire (wīr) *n. adj. v.* **wired, wir·ing.** —*n.* **1** metal drawn out into a thread. **2** such metal as a material. **3** wire netting. **4** a long piece of metal drawn out into a thread used for electrical transmission, as in electric lighting, telephones, etc. **5** telegraph: *He sent a message by wire.* **6** *Informal.* a telegram. **7** Often, **wires. a** a metal bar of a cage. **b** in music, a metallic string of an instrument. **8** the finish line of a race course. **9 get (in) under the wire,** arrive or finish just before it is too late. **10 pull wires,** *Informal.* **a** direct the actions of others secretly. **b** use secret influence to accomplish one's purposes.
—*adj.* made of or consisting of wire: *wire netting.*
—*v.* **1** furnish with wire: *wire a house for electricity.* **2** fasten with wire: *He wired the two pieces together.* **3** fence (in) with wire. **4** stiffen with wire; place on a wire. **5** catch by a wire or wires. **6** *Informal.* telegraph: *wire a birthday greeting.* [OE *wīr*] —**wire′like′,** *adj.* —**wir′er,** *n.*

hat, āge, câre, fär; let, ēqual, tėrm; it, īce
hot, ōpen, ôrder; oil, out; cup, pu̇t, rüle, ūse
əbove, takən, pencəl, lemən, circəs
ch, child; ng, long; sh, ship
th, thin; ᴛʜ, then; zh, measure

wire cutter a tool for cutting wire.

wire·drawn (wīr′dron′ or -drôn′) *adj.* **1** drawn out into a wire. **2** protracted; prolonged; spun out. **3** treated with too much hairsplitting and refinement.

wire gauge a device, usually a disk with different-sized notches in it, for measuring the diameter of wire, the thickness of metal sheets, etc.

wire-haired (wīr′härd′) *adj.* having coarse, stiff hair: *a wire-haired fox terrier.*

wire·less (wīr′lis) *adj.* **1** having no wire; operated without wire or wires: *wireless telegraphy.* **2** *Esp.Brit.* radio. —*n. Esp.Brit.* **1** a radio. **2** a message sent by radio. —*v. Esp.Brit.* send or transmit by radio.

wire nail a small thin nail made from iron or steel wire, with a small head produced by compression of one end.

wire·pho·to (wīr′fō′tō) *n. v.* **-toed, -to·ing.** —*n.* **1** a method for transmitting photographs by reproducing a facsimile through electric signals. **2** a photograph transmitted in this fashion. —*v.* transmit by wirephoto.

wire puller *Informal.* a person who uses secret influence to accomplish his purposes.

wire pulling *Informal.* the use of secret influence to accomplish a purpose.

wire recorder a device for recording and reproducing sound magnetically on a fine steel wire.

wire recording a reproduction of voices, music, etc. made on a wire recorder.

wire·tap (wīr′tap′) *n. v.* **-tapped, -tap·ping,** *adj.* —*n.* **1** a wiretapping. **2** the information obtained by wiretapping. —*v.* **1** make a wiretap, legally or illegally. **2** record by wiretapping. Also, **wire tap.** [back formation < *wiretapping*]

wire·tap·per (wīr′tap′er) *n.* a person who taps telephone wires secretly.

wire·tap·ping (wīr′tap′ing) *n.* the act or practice of making a secret connection with telephone or telegraph wires to find out the messages sent over them.

wire·worm (wīr′wėrm′) *n.* the slender, hard-bodied larva of a type of beetle. Wireworms feed on the roots of plants and do much damage to crops.

wir·ing (wīr′ing) *n.* a system of wires to carry an electric current.

wir·y (wīr′ē) *adj.* **wir·i·er, wir·i·est. 1** made of wire. **2** like wire. **3** lean, strong, and tough. —**wir′i·ly,** *adv.* —**wir′i·ness,** *n.*

wis (wis) *v. Archaic.* know (used only in *I wis,* parenthetically). [< *iwis* certainly (taken as *I wis*), OE *gewiss*]

Wis. or **Wisc.** Wisconsin.

wis·dom (wiz′dəm) *n.* **1** knowledge and good judgment based on experience; the quality of being wise. **2** wise conduct; wise words. **3** scholarly knowledge. [OE *wīsdōm* < *wīs* wise] —**Syn. 1** sagacity, sapience. **2** prudence, discretion. **3** learning, erudition, sapience.

Wisdom of Solomon one of the books of the Apocrypha.

wisdom tooth the back tooth on either side of each jaw, ordinarily appearing between the ages of 17 and 25.

wise[1] (wīz) *adj.* **wis·er, wis·est,** *v.* **wised, wis·ing.**
—*adj.* **1** having knowledge and good judgment: *a wise counsellor.* **2** showing wisdom: *wise advice.* **3** having knowledge or information; informed: *We are none the wiser for his explanations.* **4** learned; erudite. **5** *Archaic.* having knowledge of occult or supernatural things. **6 get wise,** *Slang.* find out; understand; realize. **7 wise to,**

Slang. aware of; informed about. —*v.* **wise up,** *Slang.* **1** inform or enlighten (a person). **2** become enlightened; gain awareness or understanding. [OE *wīs*] —**wise′ly,** *adv.* —**wise′ness,** *n.*

Syn. 1 Wise, sage = having or showing knowledge and good judgment in using and applying that knowledge. Wise emphasizes knowledge and understanding of people and of what is true and right in life and conduct, and sound judgment in deciding and acting: *His wise father knows how to handle him.* Sage suggests deep wisdom based on wide knowledge and experience and profound thought and understanding: *The old professor gave us sage advice we have never forgotten.*

wise[2] (wīz) *n.* way; manner: *John is in no wise a student; he prefers sports and machinery.* [OE *wīse.* Akin to GUISE.]

-wise *suffix.* **1** in —— manner, as in *anywise* and *likewise.* **2** in a —— ing manner, as in *slantwise.* **3** in the characteristic way of a ——, as in *clockwise.* **4** in the —— respect or case, as in *leastwise, otherwise.* **5** in the direction of ——, as in *lengthwise.* **6** with regard to, as in *businesswise.* **7** special meanings, as in *sidewise.* [< *wise*[2]]

☛ **Def. 6.** In Old and Middle English *-wise* was freely added to nouns to form adverbs of manner. This usage has recently been revived and is popularly used to form words as needed: *He is doing well salarywise.* However, many people regard the usage as a fad appropriate only to informal speech and professional jargon. It should, therefore, be used with discretion, especially in writing.

wise·a·cre (wīz′ā′kər) *n.* a person who thinks that he knows everything. [< MDu. *wijssegger* soothsayer < G *Weissager*]

wise·crack (wīz′krak′) *Slang.* —*n.* a smart remark; a quick, witty reply. —*v.* make wisecracks. —**wise′crack′er,** *n.*

wish (wish) *v.* **1** have a desire for; be glad to have, do, etc.; want: *wish help, wish money.* **2** have or express a desire: *He wished for a new house.* **3** desire (something) for (someone); desire that (someone) shall be or have; have a hope for; express a hope for: *We wish all men health. I wish you a Happy New Year.* **4** request, entreat, or command (a thing or action, or a person to do something): *Do you wish me to send him in now?* **5 wish on,** *Informal.* pass on to; foist on: *They wished the hardest job on him.*
—*n.* **1** a turning of the mind toward the doing, having, getting, etc. of something; desire or longing. **2** the expression of a wish: *She sends you best wishes for a Happy New Year.* **3** the thing wished for: *The girl got her wish.* [OE *wȳscan*] —**wish′er,** *n.*

Syn. *v.* 1 Wish, desire = want or long for something. Wish is the less emphatic word, sometimes suggesting only that one would like to have, do, or get a certain thing, sometimes suggesting a longing that can never be satisfied: *I wish I could travel round the world.* Desire, sometimes used as a formal substitute for *wish* or, especially, *want,* particularly suggests wishing strongly and usually a willingness or determination to work or struggle to get it: *He finally received the position he desired.*

wish·bone (wish′bōn′) *n.* in poultry and other birds, the forked bone in the front of the breast.

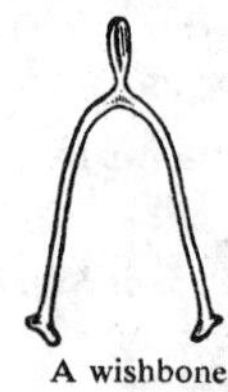
A wishbone

wish·ful (wish′fəl) *adj.* having or expressing a wish; desiring; desirous. —**wish′ful·ly,** *adv.* —**wish′ful·ness,** *n.*

wishful thinking a believing something to be true that one wishes or wants to be true.

wish·y-wash·y (wish′ē wosh′ē) *adj.* **1** thin and weak; watery. **2** lacking in substantial qualities; feeble; inferior.

wisp (wisp) *n.* **1** a small bundle; small bunch: *a wisp of hay.* **2** a small tuft, lock, or portion of anything; a slight bit: *a wisp of hair, a wisp of smoke.* **3** a little thing: *a wisp of a girl.* [ME *wisp, wips;* cf. W. Frisian *wisp.* Akin to WIPE.]

wisp·y (wis′pē) *adj.* **wisp·i·er, wisp·i·est.** like a wisp; thin; slight.

wist (wist) *v. Archaic.* pt. and pp. of **wit.**

wis·tar·i·a (wis tãr′ē ə or wis tēr′ē ə) *n.* a climbing shrub having large clusters of purple, yellow, or white flowers. [after Caspar *Wistar* (1761-1818), an American scientist]

wis·te·ri·a (wis tēr′ē ə) *n.* wistaria.

wist·ful (wist′fəl) *adj.* **1** longing; yearning: *A child stood looking with wistful eyes at the toys in the window.* **2** pensive; melancholy. [< obs. *wist* attentive (< *wistly* intently, of uncertain origin) + *-ful*] —**wist′ful·ly,** *adv.* —**wist′ful·ness,** *n.*

wit[1] (wit) *n.* **1** the power to perceive quickly and express cleverly ideas that are unusual, striking, and amusing. **2** a person with such power. **3** understanding; mind; sense: *People with quick wits learn easily. The child was out of his wits with fright. That poor man hasn't wit enough to earn a living.* **4 at one's wit's end,** not knowing what to do or say. **5 have** or **keep one's wits about one,** be alert. **6 live by one's wits,** get one's living by clever or crafty devices rather than by any settled occupation. [OE *witt*]

Syn. 1 Wit, humor = power to see and express what is amusing or causes laughter. Wit = a mental sharpness and quickness in perceiving what is striking, unusual, inconsistent, or out of keeping and in expressing it in cleverly surprising and amusing sayings: *Bernard Shaw was famous for his wit.* Humor = a power to see and show with warm sympathy and kindness the things in life and human nature that are funny or absurdly out of the ordinary: *Her sense of humor eased her trouble.* 3 intelligence.

wit[2] (wit) *v. pres. 1st pers.* **wot,** *2nd pers.* **wost** (wost), *3rd pers.* **wot,** *pl.* **wit;** *pt. and pp.* **wist;** *ppr.* **wit·ting.** **1** *Archaic.* know. **2 to wit,** that is to say; namely: *To my son I leave all I own—to wit, my house, what is in it, and the land on which it stands.* [OE *witan*]

witch (wich) *n.* **1** a woman supposed to be under the influence of spirits and to have magic power. **2** an ugly old woman. **3** *Informal.* a charming or fascinating girl or woman. —*v.* **1** use the power of a witch on. **2** charm; fascinate; bewitch. [OE *wicce*]

witch·craft (wich′kraft′) *n.* what a witch does or can do; magic power or influence.

witch doctor especially among certain African tribes, a medicine man.

witch·er·y (wich′ər ē or wich′rē) *n.* **-er·ies. 1** witchcraft; magic. **2** charm; fascination.

witch hazel 1 a shrub of E. North America that has yellow flowers in the fall or winter after the leaves have fallen. **2** a lotion for cooling and soothing the skin, made from the bark and leaves of this shrub.

witch hunt *Slang.* the persecuting or defaming of (a person) to gain an advantage, especially a political advantage.

witch·ing (wich′ing) *adj.* bewitching; magical; enchanting. —**witch′ing·ly,** *adv.*

wit·e·na·ge·mot (wit′ə nə gə mōt′) *n.* the royal council of the Anglo-Saxons. [OE *witenagemōt* < *witena,* gen. pl. of *wita* councillor + *gemōt* meeting]

with (wiᴛʜ or with) *prep.* **1** in the company of: *Come with me.* **2** among: *They will mix with the crowd.* **3** having, wearing, carrying, etc.: *a man with brains, a telegram with bad news.* **4** by means of; by using: *Cut meat with a knife.* **5** using; showing: *Work with care.* **6** as an addition to; added to: *Do you want sugar with your tea?* **7** including; and: *tea with sugar and lemon.* **8** in relation to: *They are friendly with us.* **9** in regard to: *We are pleased with the house.* **10** in proportion to: *An army's power increases with its size.* **11** because of: *shake with cold.* **12** in the keeping or service of: *Leave the dog with me.* **13** in the region, sphere, experience, opinion, or view of: *It is day with us while it is night with the Chinese. High taxes are unpopular with many people.* **14** at the same time as: *With this battle the war ended.* **15** in the same direction as: *The boat floated along with the current.* **16** on the side of; for: *They are with us in our plan.* **17** from: *I hate to part with my favorite things.* **18** against: *The English fought with the Germans.* **19** receiving; having; being allowed: *I went with his permission.* **20** in spite of: *With all his weight he was not a strong man.* **21** as a result of; because of; on account of: *green with age, eyes dim with tears.* **22** by adding, furnishing, filling, etc. a material to something: *a bottle filled with water.* **23 keep in with,** *Informal.* keep acquaintance or friendship with. **24 with it,** *Slang.* up to date; in the know; hep. **25 with that,** when that occurred; whereupon: *The train reached the station, and, with that, our long trip ended.* [OE *with* against] —**Syn. 4** See **by.**

with- *prefix.* **1** against, as in *withstand.* **2** back; away, as in *withdraw, withhold.* **3** along with; alongside; toward, as in *withal, without, within.* [OE]

with·al (wiᴛʜ ol′ or -ôl′, with ol′ or -ôl′) *Archaic.*

—*adv.* with it all; as well; besides; also: *The lady is rich and fair and wise withal.* —*prep.* with. [< *with* + *all*]

with·draw (wiᴛʜ drȯ′ or -drô′, with drȯ′ or -drô′) *v.* **-drew, -drawn, -draw·ing. 1** draw back; draw away: *He quickly withdrew his hand from the hot stove.* **2** take back; remove: *Worn-out paper money is withdrawn from use by the government.* **3** go away: *She withdrew from the room.* **4** demand the withdrawal of a statement, motion, proposal, etc. [< *with-* away + *draw*] —**Syn. 2** recall, retract. **3** leave. See **depart.**

with·draw·al (wiᴛʜ drȯ′əl or -drô′əl, with drȯ′əl or -drô′əl) *n.* a withdrawing or being withdrawn.

with·drawn (wiᴛʜ drôn′ or -drôn′, with drôn′ or -drôn′) *v.* pp. of **withdraw.** —*adj.* shy; of a retiring nature.

with·drew (wiᴛʜ drü′ or with drü′) *v.* pt. of **withdraw.**

withe (wīᴛʜ, with, or wiᴛʜ) *n. v.* **withed, with·ing.** —*n.* **1** a willow twig. **2** any tough, easily bent twig suitable for binding things together. —*v.* bind with withes. [OE *withthe*]

with·er (wiᴛʜ′ər) *v.* **1** lose or cause to lose freshness, vigor, etc.; dry up; shrivel: *The grass withered in the hot sun. Age had withered the old lady's face.* **2** feel or cause to feel ashamed or confused: *She withered him with a scornful look.* [ME *wideren*, var. of *wederen* weather]

with·ers (wiᴛʜ′ərz) *n.pl.* the highest part of a horse's or other animal's back, behind the neck. [OE *withre* resistance < *wither* against; from the fact that a horse opposes this part against the load he is pulling]

with·er·shins (wiᴛʜ′ər shinz) *adv. Scottish.* **1** in the opposite or contrary direction. **2** in a direction contrary to the apparent course of the sun, considered to be unlucky. Also, **widdershins.** [< earlier *widdershins* < MLG < MHG *widersinnes* < *wider* against, opposed + *-sind* way, direction + *-es* -s]

with·held (with held′) *v.* pt. and pp. of **withhold.**

with·hold (with hōld′) *v.* **-held, -hold·ing. 1** refrain from giving or granting: *The play cannot be held if the principal withholds his consent.* **2** hold back; keep back: *The captain withheld his men from attack.* [< *with-* + *hold*] —**Syn. 2** See **keep.**

with·in (wiᴛʜ in′ or with-) *prep.* **1** inside the limits of; not beyond: *The task was within the man's powers. He guessed my weight within five pounds.* **2** in or into the inner part of; inside of: *By the X ray, doctors can see within the body.* **3** in the (inner) being, soul, or mind of. —*adv.* **1** in or into the inner part; inside: *The house has been painted within and without. The curtains were white without and green within.* **2** in the inner being; in the being, soul, or mind; inwardly: *keep one's grief within.* [OE *withinnan*]

with·out (wiᴛʜ out′ or with-) *prep.* **1** with no; not having; free from; lacking: *A cat walks without noise. I drink tea without sugar.* **2** so as to omit, avoid, or neglect: *She walked past without looking at us.* **3** outside of; beyond: *Soldiers are camped within and without the city walls.* —*adv.* on the outside; outside: *The house is clean within and without.* —*conj. Dialect.* unless. [OE *withūtan*]

with·stand (with stand′ or wiᴛʜ-) *v.* **-stood, -stand·ing.** stand against; hold out against; oppose, especially successfully: *Soldiers have to withstand hardships. These shoes will withstand much hard wear.* [OE *withstandan* < *with-* against + *standan* stand] —**Syn.** resist, endure. See **oppose.**

with·stood (with stu̇d′ or wiᴛʜ-) *v.* pt. and pp. of **withstand.**

with·y (wiᴛʜ′ē or with′ē) *n.* **with·ies. 1** willow or osier; withe. **2** a band or halter made of withes. [OE *wīthig*]

wit·less (wit′lis) *adj.* lacking intelligence; stupid; foolish. —**wit′less·ly,** *adv.* —**wit′less·ness,** *n.*

wit·ness (wit′nis) *n.* **1** a person able to give evidence; a person who saw something happen. **2** a person who swears to tell the truth in a court of law. **3** evidence; testimony. **4** a person writing his name on a document to show that he saw the maker sign it. **5 bear witness,** be evidence; give evidence; testify: *A wife need not bear witness against her husband. The man's fingerprints bore witness to his guilt.*
—*v.* **1** see; perceive: *He witnessed the accident.* **2** testify to; give evidence of: *Her whole manner witnessed her surprise.* **3** give evidence; testify. **4** sign (a document) as a witness: *The two servants witnessed Mr. Smith's will.* [OE *witnes* knowledge < *wit* wit[1]]

hat, āge, cãre, fär; let, ēqual, tėrm; it, īce
hot, ōpen, ôrder; oil, out; cup, pu̇t, rüle, ūse
əbove, takən, pencəl, lemən, circəs
ch, child; ng, long; sh, ship
th, thin; ᴛʜ, then; zh, measure

witness box in law, the place where a witness stands or sits to give evidence in a court.

witness stand *U.S.* witness box.

wit·ti·cism (wit′ə siz′əm) *n.* a witty remark. [< *witty*, on the model of *criticism*]

wit·ti·ly (wit′ə lē) *adv.* in a witty manner; with wit.

wit·ting·ly (wit′ing lē) *adv.* knowingly; intentionally.

wit·ty (wit′ē) *adj.* **-ti·er, -ti·est.** full of wit; clever and amusing: *a witty person, a witty remark.* [OE *wittig*] —**wit′ti·ness,** *n.* —**Syn.** facetious, droll.

wive (wīv) *v.* **wived, wiv·ing. 1** marry a woman. **2** take as a wife. [OE *wīfian*]

wi·vern (wī′vərn) *n.* in heraldry, a two-legged, winged dragon with a barbed tail. [< *wiver* viper < dial. OF *wivre* < L *vipera*]

wives (wīvz) *n.* pl. of **wife.**

wiz·ard (wiz′ərd) *n.* **1** a man supposed to have magic power. **2** *Informal.* a very clever person; expert. —*adj.* magic. [ult. < *wise*[1]]

wiz·ar·dry (wiz′ərd rē) *n.* magic; magic skill.

wiz·ened (wiz′ənd) *adj.* dried up; withered; shrivelled: *a wizened apple, a wizened face.* [pp. of dial. *wizen*, OF *wisnian* shrivel]

wk. **1** week. **2** work.

wkly. weekly.

wks. **1** weeks. **2** works.

w.l. **1** wave length. **2** water line.

w.long. west longitude.

WMO World Meteorological Organization of the United Nations.

WNW, W.N.W., or **w.n.w.** west northwest, a direction midway between west and northwest.

wo (wō) *n. interj.* woe.

W.O. **1** Warrant Officer. **2** Work Order. **3** *Brit.* War Office.

woad (wōd) *n.* **1** a European plant from whose leaves a blue dye is made. **2** the dye. [OE *wād*]

wob·ble (wob′əl) *v.* **-bled, -bling,** *n.* —*v.* **1** move unsteadily from side to side; shake; tremble. **2** be uncertain, unsteady, or inconstant; waver. —*n.* a wobbling motion. Also, **wabble.** [cf. LG *wabbeln*] —**wob′bler,** *n.*

wob·bly (wob′lē) *adj.* unsteady; shaky; wavering. Also, **wabbly.**

wo·be·gone (wō′bi gon′) *adj.* woebegone.

Wo·den (wō′dən) *n.* the most important Anglo-Saxon god, corresponding to Odin in Norse mythology. [OE *Wōden*]

woe (wō) *n.* great grief, trouble, or distress: *Sickness and poverty are common woes.* —*interj.* an exclamation of grief, trouble, or distress. Also, **wo.** [OE *wā*, interj.] —**Syn.** *n.* sorrow.

woe·be·gone (wō′bi gon′) *adj.* looking sad, sorrowful, or wretched. Also, **wobegone.**

woe·ful (wō′fəl) *adj.* **1** full of woe; sad; sorrowful; wretched: *a woeful expression.* **2** pitiful: *a woeful sight.* **3** of wretched quality. —**woe′ful·ly,** *adv.* —**woe′ful·ness,** *n.* —**Syn. 1** mournful, distressed, miserable.

wo·ful (wō′fəl) *adj.* woeful.

woke (wōk) *v.* pt. of **wake**[1].

wo·ken (wō′kən) *v. Archaic and dialect.* a pp. of **wake**[1].

wold (wōld) *n.* high, rolling country, bare of woods. [OE *wald*, *weald* a wood]

wolf (wu̇lf) *n.* **wolves,** *v.* —*n.* **1** a carnivorous mammal resembling a dog and belonging to the same family. **2** a cruel, greedy person. 3 *Slang.* a man who possesses a special talent for and interest in flirting with and enticing women. 4 **cry wolf,** give a false alarm. 5 **keep the wolf from the door,** keep safe from hunger or poverty. 6 **wolf in sheep's clothing,** a hypocrite. —*v.* eat greedily. [OE *wulf*] —**wolf′like′,** *adj.*

Wolf Cub a member of the junior branch of the Boy Scouts.

wolf dog 1 any of various dogs used in hunting wolves. 2 a hybrid of a dog and a wolf. 3 in the North, an Eskimo dog or husky.

wolf eel the wolf fish.

wolf·er (wůlf′ər) *n.* a wolf hunter.

wolf fish any of various large, voracious ocean fishes having powerful teeth, related to the blenny.

wolf·hound (wůlf′hound′) *n.* 1 one of several breeds of very large dog, the tallest of all dogs, formerly kept for hunting. It resembles the greyhound and the borzoi. 2 a dog of any of these breeds.

wolf·ish (wůl′fish) *adj.* like a wolf; greedy; savage: *a wolfish-looking dog, wolfish cruelty.* —**wolf′ish·ly,** *adv.* —**wolf′ish·ness,** *n.*

wol·fram (wůl′frəm) *n.* 1 tungsten. 2 wolframite. [< G]

wolf·ram·ite (wůl′frəm īt′) *n.* an ore consisting of compounds of tungsten with iron and manganese.

wolf's-bane or **wolfs·bane** (wůlfs′bān′) *n.* a poisonous plant having yellow flowers, usually called aconite or monkshood.

wolf spider any of various ferocious spiders that stalk their prey rather than lie in wait for it.

wolf willow *Cdn.* silverberry.

wol·ver·ine or **wol·ver·ene** (wůl′vər ēn′ or wůl′vər ēn′) *n.* 1 a clumsy, heavily built, carnivorous mammal native to Canada and the northern United States, related to the weasel. 2 the fur of this animal. [earlier *wolvering* < *wolf*]

wolves (wůlvz) *n.* pl. of **wolf.**

wom·an (wům′ən) *n.* **wom·en.** 1 the adult human female. 2 women as a group; the average woman. 3 woman's nature. 4 a female servant. 5 a wife. 6 a mistress; paramour. 7 a man considered as being womanish: *He's a fussy old woman.* [OE *wīfman* < *wīf* woman + *man* human being] —**wom′an·less,** *adj.* —**Syn.** 1 See **female.**
☛ See **lady** for usage note.

wom·an·hood (wům′ən hůd′) *n.* 1 the condition or time of being a woman. 2 the character or qualities of a woman. 3 women as a group: *Marie Curie was an honor to womanhood.*

wom·an·ish (wům′ən ish) *adj.* 1 a characteristic of or proper to a woman or women; womanly; feminine. b of a girl, like a grown woman. 2 like a woman; womanlike; effeminate (now chiefly derogatory). —**wom′an·ish·ly,** *adv.* —**wom′an·ish·ness,** *n.*

wom·an·ize (wům′ə nīz′) *v.* **-ized, -iz·ing.** 1 make womanish or effeminate; emasculate. 2 *Informal.* associate with women illicitly.

wom·an·kind (wům′ən kīnd′) *n.* women, considered collectively.

wom·an·like (wům′ən līk′) *adj.* 1 like a woman; womanly. 2 suitable for a woman.

wom·an·ly (wům′ən lē) *adj.* 1 like a woman. 2 as a woman should be. 3 suitable for a woman. —**wom′an·li·ness,** *n.*

woman of the world a woman who knows people and customs, and is tolerant of both.

woman's rights social, political, and legal rights for women, equal to those of men.

woman suffrage 1 the political right of women to vote. 2 women's votes.

wom·an-suf·fra·gist (wům′ən suf′rə jist) *n.* a person who favors the right of women to vote.

womb (wüm) *n.* 1 in mammals, the organ of the body that holds and nourishes the young till birth; uterus. 2 a place containing or producing anything. [OE *wamb*]

wom·bat (wom′bat) *n.* a burrowing Australian mammal that resembles a small bear. A female wombat has a pouch for carrying her young. [< an Australian lang.]

wom·en (wim′ən) *n.* pl. of **woman.**

wom·en·folk (wim′ən fōk′) *n.pl.* women.

won[1] (wun) *v.* pt. and pp. of **win.**

won[2] (wän) *n.* **won.** 1 a unit of money in Korea. See table at **money.** 2 a coin or note worth one won. [< Korean]

won·der (wun′dər) *n.* 1 a strange and surprising thing or event: *He saw the wonders of the city. It is a wonder he turned down the offer.* 2 the feeling caused by what is strange and surprising: *The baby looked with wonder at the Christmas tree.* 3 **do wonders,** do wonderful things; achieve or produce extraordinary results. 4 **for a wonder,** as a strange and surprising thing. 5 **no wonder,** a no marvel or prodigy: *The lecturer is no wonder.* b nothing surprising; not surprising: *No wonder he resigned.*
—*v.* 1 feel wonder: *We wonder at the splendor of the stars.* 2 feel some doubt or curiosity; wish to know or learn; speculate: *wonder about his sudden departure.* 3 be surprised or astonished: *I shouldn't wonder if he wins the prize.* 4 be curious; be curious about; think about; wish to know: *I wonder what happened.* [OE *wundor*] —**won′der·er,** *n.* —**won′der·ing·ly,** *adv.*

won·der·ful (wun′dər fəl) *adj.* 1 causing wonder; marvellous; remarkable: *The explorer had wonderful adventures.* 2 surprisingly large, fine, excellent, etc. [OE *wunderfull*] —**won′der·ful·ly,** *adv.* —**won′der·ful·ness,** *n.*
Syn. Wonderful, marvellous = causing wonder. **Wonderful** describes something so new and unfamiliar, out of the ordinary, beyond expectation, or imperfectly understood that it excites a feeling of surprise, admiration, puzzled interest, or, sometimes, astonishment: *The boys from Britain saw some wonderful sights on their first trip across Canada.* **Marvellous** describes something so extraordinary, surprising, or astonishing that it seems hardly believable: *The machine that can translate from a foreign language is a marvellous scientific invention.*

won·der·land (wun′dər land′) *n.* a land, realm, etc. full of wonders.

won·der·ment (wun′dər mənt) *n.* wonder; surprise.

won·drous (wun′drəs) *adj.* wonderful. —*adv.* wonderfully. [alteration of *wonders* (gen. of *wonder*) wondrous, with the suffix *-ous* as in *marvellous*] —**won′drous·ly,** *adv.* —**won′drous·ness,** *n.*

won·ky (wong′kē) *adj. Slang.* likely to break down; in poor working order; shaky. [? alteration of dial. *wankle,* ult. < OE *wancol* shaky]

wont (wōnt) *adj.* accustomed: *He was wont to read the paper at breakfast.* —*n.* a custom; habit: *He rose early, as was his wont.* [originally pp., ult. < OE *wunian* be accustomed]

won't (wōnt) will not.

wont·ed (wōn′tid) *adj.* accustomed; customary; usual.

woo (wü) *v.* 1 make love to; seek to marry. 2 make love; court. 3 seek to win; try to get: *woo fame.* 4 try to persuade; urge. [OE *wōgian*]

wood (wůd) *n.* 1 the hard substance beneath the bark of trees and shrubs. 2 trees cut up for use: *The carpenter brought wood to build a garage.* 3 something made of wood. 4 a cask; barrel; keg: *wine drawn from the wood.* 5 in printing, woodcuts collectively or a woodcut. 6 in music: a a wooden wind instrument; wood wind. b **woods,** *pl.* the wood winds of a band or orchestra. 7 Often, **woods,** *pl.* a large number of growing trees; forest. See the usage note below. 8 **out of the woods,** out of danger or difficulty. 9 **saw wood,** *Informal.* a work steadily at one's task, without attention to anything else. b sleep heavily.
—*adj.* 1 made of wood. 2 used to store or convey wood: *a wood box.* 3 dwelling or growing in woods: *wood moss.* —*v.* 1 supply with wood; get wood for. 2 get supplies of wood. 3 plant with trees. [OE *wudu*]
☛ **Woods** gives trouble because though plural in form it is really singular (or collective) in meaning. We speak of *a woods* but ordinarily use this expression with a plural verb: *The woods are pretty in the fall.* In proper names *woods* is frequently used with a singular verb. When used to qualify another noun, **woods** often refers particularly to forest areas as the site of lumbering operations: *a woods camp, a woods superintendent.*

wood alcohol methyl alcohol.

wood·bine (wůd′bīn′) *n.* 1 the honeysuckle. 2 the Virginia creeper, a climbing vine having bluish-black

hat, āge, cãre, fär; let, ēqual, tėrm; it, īce
hot, ōpen, ôrder; oil, out; cup, pu̇t, rüle, ūse
əbove, takən, pencəl, lemən, circəs
ch, child; ng, long; sh, ship
th, thin; ᴛʜ, then; zh, measure

berries. [OE *wudubind(e)* < *wudu* wood + *binde* wreath]

wood block 1 a block of wood. 2 a woodcut.

wood·chuck (wu̇d′chuk′) *n.* a North American marmot; the groundhog. [< Algonquian (Ojibway) *wejack*; influenced by *wood*]

wood·cock (wu̇d′kok′) *n.* **-cock** or **-cocks.** a small game bird having a long bill and short legs. [OE *wuducoc*]

wood·craft (wu̇d′kraft′) *n.* **1** knowledge about how to get food and shelter in the woods; skill in hunting, trapping, finding one's way, etc. **2** skill in working with wood.

wood·cut (wu̇d′kut′) *n.* **1** an engraved block of wood to print from. **2** a print from such a block.

wood·cut·ter (wu̇d′kut′ər) *n.* a man who cuts down trees or chops wood.

wood·ed (wu̇d′id) *adj.* covered with trees: *The park is well wooded.*

wood·en (wu̇d′ən) *adj.* **1** made of wood. **2** stiff; awkward. **3** dull; stupid. —**wood′en·ly,** *adv.* —**wood′en·ness,** *n.*

wood engraving 1 the art or process of making woodcuts. 2 a woodcut.

wood·en-head·ed (wu̇d′ən hed′id) *adj. Informal.* dull; stupid.

wooden horse Trojan horse.

wood·en·ware (wu̇d′ən wãr′) *n.* containers, utensils, etc. made of wood. Pails, tubs, and rolling pins are woodenware.

wood·land (wu̇d′lənd) *n.* land covered with trees. —*adj.* of or in the woods; having to do with woods.

wood·land·er (wu̇d′lən dər) *n.* a person who lives in the woods.

wood·lark (wu̇d′lärk′) *n.* a European lark closely related to the skylark.

wood lice pl. of **wood louse.**

wood·lot (wu̇d′lot′) *n.* land on which trees are grown and cut; a bush lot.

wood louse 1 any of several small crustaceans that have flat, oval bodies and live in decaying wood, damp soil, etc. 2 any of certain small insects that live in the woodwork of houses.

wood·man (wu̇d′mən) *n.* **-men** (-mən). **1** a man who cuts down trees. **2** a person who lives in the woods. **3** a person who takes care of forests.

wood note a musical sound made by a bird or animal of the forest.

wood nymph 1 a nymph supposed to live in the woods. 2 a moth that destroys grapevines.

wood·peck·er (wu̇d′pek′ər) *n.* a bird having a hard, pointed bill for drilling holes in trees to get insects.

wood pigeon 1 a European pigeon with two whitish patches on the neck. 2 a wild pigeon of western North America.

wood·pile (wu̇d′pīl′) *n.* a pile of wood, especially wood for fuel.

wood pulp wood made into pulp for making paper.

wood·ruff (wu̇d′ruf) *n.* a fragrant plant having small flowers and pointed leaves. [OE *wudurōfe*]

wood·shed (wu̇d′shed′) *n.* a shed for storing wood.

woods·man (wu̇dz′mən) *n.* **-men** (-mən). **1** a man used to life in the woods and skilled in hunting, fishing, trapping, etc. **2** a man whose work is cutting down trees; lumberman.

wood sorrel 1 oxalis. 2 sheep sorrel.

woods·y (wu̇d′zē) *adj.* of or like the woods.

wood tar a dark-brown, sticky substance obtained from the distillation of wood and containing turpentine, resins, etc.

wood thrush a thrush common in the thickets and woods of eastern North America.

wood turning the making of pieces of wood into various shapes by using a lathe.

wood wind (wind) **1 wood winds,** *pl.* the wooden wind instruments of an orchestra or band, including clarinets, oboes, etc. **2** any such instrument.

wood-wind (wu̇d′wind′) *adj.* of or having to do with wood winds.

wood·work (wu̇d′wėrk′) *n.* **1** anything made of wood. **2** the wooden parts inside a house, such as doors, stairs, mouldings, etc.

wood·work·er (wu̇d′wėr′kər) *n.* a person who makes things of wood.

wood·work·ing (wu̇d′wėr′king) *n. adj.* the making or shaping of things of wood.

wood·worm (wu̇d′wėrm′) *n.* a worm or larva that is bred in wood or bores in wood.

wood·y (wu̇d′ē) *adj.* **wood·i·er, wood·i·est. 1** having many trees; covered with trees: *a woody hillside.* **2** consisting of wood: *the woody parts of a shrub.* **3** like wood: *Turnips become woody when they are old.* —**wood′i·ness,** *n.*

woo·er (wü′ər) *n.* one that woos; suitor.

woof (wüf) *n.* **1** the threads running from side to side across a woven fabric. The woof crosses the warp. See **warp** for picture. **2** fabric; cloth; texture. [ME *oof* < OE *ōwef* < *on* on + *wefan* weave]

wool (wu̇l) *n.* **1** the soft, curly hair or fur of sheep and some other animals. **2** short, thick, curly hair. **3** something like wool. **4** yarn, cloth, or garments made of wool. **5 pull the wool over someone's eyes,** *Informal.* deceive someone. —*adj.* made of wool. [OE *wull*]

wool·en (wu̇l′ən) *adj. n.* woollen.

wool·gath·er·ing (wu̇l′gaᴛʜ′ər ing or -gaᴛʜ′ring) *n.* absorption in thinking or daydreaming; absent-mindedness. —*adj.* inattentive; absent-minded; dreamy.

wool·grow·er (wu̇l′grō′ər) *n.* a person who raises sheep for their wool.

wool·len or **wool·en** (wu̇l′ən) *adj.* **1** made of wool. **2** of or having to do with wool or cloth made of wool. —*n.* **1** yarn or cloth made of wool. **2 woollens** or **woolens,** *pl.* cloth or clothing made of wool.

wool·ly (wu̇l′ē) *adj.* **-li·er, -li·est,** *n.* **-lies.**—*adj.* **1** consisting of wool. **2** like wool. **3** covered with wool or something like it. **4** not definite; confused; muddled: *woolly thinking.* —*n. Informal.* an article of clothing made from wool. Also, **wooly.** —**wool′li·ness,** *n.*

wool·pack (wu̇l′pak′) *n.* **1** a large cloth bag for carrying wool. **2** a bundle or bale of wool weighing 240 pounds. **3** a round, fleecy cloud.

wool·sack (wu̇l′sak′) *n.* **1** a bag of wool. **2** in the British House of Lords, the cushion on which the Lord Chancellor sits. **3** the office of Lord Chancellor.

wool·y (wu̇l′ē) *adj.* **wool·i·er, wool·i·est,** *n.* **-ies.** woolly. —**wool′i·ness,** *n.*

wooz·y (wüz′ē or wu̇z′ē) *adj. Slang.* **1** somewhat dizzy or weak: *be just over an illness and still a little woozy.* **2** muddled; confused. **3** slightly drunk; tipsy.

Worces·ter·shire (wu̇s′tər shər) *n.* a highly seasoned sauce made of soy, vinegar, etc. [< *Worcester,* a city in W. England, where it was made originally]

word (wėrd) *n.* **1** a sound or a group of sounds that has meaning and is an independent unit of speech. **2** the writing or printing that stands for a word. *Bat, bet, bit,* and *but* are words. **3** a short talk: *May I have a word with you?* **4** speech: *honest in word and deed.* **5** a brief expression: *a word of advice.* **6** a command; order: *His word was law.* **7** a signal: *The word for tonight is "the King."* **8** a promise: *The boy kept his word.* **9** news: *No word has come from the battlefront.* **10 words,** *pl.* **a** angry talk; a quarrel; dispute. **b** the text of a song as distinguished from the notes.

be as good as one's word, keep one's promise.

by word of mouth, by spoken words; orally.

eat one's words, take back what one has said; retract.

have the last word, in an argument, have the final, decisive say.

in a word, briefly.
man of his word, a man who keeps his promise.
mince words, avoid coming to the point, telling the truth, or taking a stand by using ambiguous or evasive words.
My word! an expression of surprise.
take a person at his word, take his words seriously and act accordingly.
take the words out of someone's mouth, say exactly what someone was just going to say.
the last word, a the last or latest thing or example in a class or field. **b** the final thing or example, beyond which no advance or improvement is possible.
the Word, a the Bible. **b** the message of the gospel. **c** the Logos: the Son of God as a manifestation of God to mankind; the second person of the Trinity (John 1:1).
upon my word, a I promise. **b** an expression of surprise.
word for word, in the exact words.
—*v.* put into words: *Word your ideas clearly.* [OE]

word·book (wėrd′bu̇k′) *n.* a list of words, usually with explanations, etc.; dictionary; vocabulary.

word element a form of a word used for combining with other words or word elements, as *psycho-* (from Greek *psychē*) in *psychoanalysis*; a combining form.

word·ing (wėr′ding) *n.* the way of saying a thing; the choice and use of words: *Careful wording is needed for clearness.* —**Syn.** See **diction.**

word·less (wėrd′lis) *adj.* **1** without words; speechless. **2** not put into words; unexpressed. —**word·less·ly,** *adv.*

Word of God the Bible.

word of honor or **honour** a solemn promise.

word order the arrangement of words in a sentence, phrase, etc.
☛ In English the usual word order for statements is subject + predicate, as in *John hit the ball. The ball hit John.* Some other patterns of word order (*Away ran John. Him the Almighty hurled . . ., Sweet are the uses of adversity*) are chiefly rhetorical and poetic. In English, with its relatively few inflections, word order is the chief grammatical device for indicating the function of words and their relation to each other.

word·y (wėr′dē) *adj.* **word·i·er, word·i·est. 1** using too many words. **2** consisting of or expressed in words; verbal: *a wordy war.* —**word′i·ly,** *adv.* —**word′i·ness,** *n.*
Syn. Wordy, verbose = using more words than are necessary. Wordy emphasizes the use of many words to say something that could be expressed more clearly and effectively in a few. Example: *There are many reasons that he has for going,* instead of *He has many reasons for going.* Verbose, a formal word used especially to describe public speakers, writers, speeches, and writings, adds the idea of using too many long, high-sounding words and long, roundabout sentences that do not express meaning clearly or interestingly: "*The silvery, shimmering orb*" *is a verbose way of saying* "*the moon.*"

wore (wôr) *v.* pt. of **wear.**

work (wėrk) *n. v.* **worked** or **wrought, work·ing.** —*n.* **1** the effort of doing or making something: *Some people like hard work.* **2** something to do; occupation; employment: *He is out of work.* **3** something made or done; something painted or written; the result of effort: *a work of art.* **4** a particular task, job, or undertaking: *plan one's work for the day.* **5** that on which effort is put: *The dressmaker took her work out on the porch.* **6** a fortification. **7** in physics: **a** the transference of energy from one body or system to another. **b** that which is accomplished by a force when it acts through a distance. **8** the action, activity, or operation (of a person or thing), especially of a particular kind and with reference to result: *The medicine and suggestion have done their work.* **9** embroidery; needlework. **10** an engineering structure. **11 works,** *pl.* **a** a factory; a place for doing some kind of work. **b** the moving parts of a machine or device: *the works of a watch.* **c** buildings, bridges, docks, etc. **d** acts that are done to obey or accord with the law of God; moral actions. **12 at work,** working. **13 in the works,** *Informal.* in the planning stage; upcoming. **14 make short work of,** do or get rid of quickly. **15 out of work,** having no job; unemployed. **16 the works,** *Slang.* everything involved; the complete set, collection, or treatment: *He invested $50,000 and lost the works. The thugs caught the informer and gave him the works.* [OE *weorc*]
—*v.* **1** do work; labor: *Most people must work for a living.* **2** be employed: *He works at an airplane factory.* **3** carry on operations in (districts, etc.): *The salesman worked the Toronto area.* **4** put effort on: *He worked his farm with success.* **5** act; operate, especially effectively: *This pump will not work. The plan worked.* **6** put into operation; use; manage: *work a scheme.* **7** cause to do work: *He works his men long hours.* **8** treat or handle in making; knead; mix: *Dough is worked to mix it thoroughly.* **9** make, get, do, or bring about by effort: *He worked his way through college.* **10** move as if with effort: *His face worked as he tried to keep back the tears.* **11** bring about; cause; do: *The plan worked harm.* **12** go slowly or with effort: *The ship worked to windward.* **13** gradually become: *The window catch has worked loose.* **14** form; shape: *He worked a silver dollar into a bracelet.* **15** influence; persuade: *work men to one's will.* **16** move; stir; excite: *Don't work yourself into a temper.* **17** solve: *Work all the problems on the page.* **18** *Informal.* use tricks on to get something: *work a friend for a loan.* **19** ferment: *Yeast makes beer work.*
work in, put in.
work off, get rid of.
work on or **upon,** try to persuade or influence.
work out, a plan; develop. **b** solve; find out. **c** use up. **d** give exercise to; practise. **e** accomplish. **f** result.
work to rule, of employees, work only as much as is demanded by the terms of employment (without overtime, extraordinary effort, etc.), as a form of protest.
work up, a plan; develop. **b** excite; stir up. [OE *wyrcean*]
Syn. *n.* **1 Work, labor, toil** = effort or exertion turned to making or doing something. **Work** is the general word, applying to physical or mental effort or to the activity of a force or machine: *Keeping house is not easy work.* **Labor** applies to hard physical or mental work: *That student's understanding of his subjects shows the amount of labor he puts into his homework.* **Toil,** a word with some literary flavor, applies to long and wearying labor: *The farmer's toil was rewarded with good crops.* **3** product, achievement, feat, deed. –*v.* **1** toil, drudge, strive. **5** perform. **6** execute. **11** accomplish, effect. **14** fashion, mould.

work·a·ble (wėr′kə bəl) *adj.* that can be worked.

work·a·day (wėr′kə dā′) *adj.* of working days; practical; commonplace; ordinary.

work·bag (wėrk′bag′) *n.* a bag to hold the things that a person works with, especially a bag for sewing materials.

work·bench (wėrk′bench′) *n.* a table at which a mechanic, carpenter, artisan, etc. works.

work·book (wėrk′bu̇k′) *n.* **1** a book containing outlines for the study of some subject, questions to be answered, etc.; a book in which a student does parts of his written work. **2** a book containing rules for doing certain work. **3** a book for notes of work planned or work done.

work·box (wėrk′boks′) *n.* a box to hold the materials and tools that a person works with.

work·day (wėrk′dā′) *n.* **1** a day for work; a day that is not a Sunday or a holiday. **2** the part of a day during which work is done. —*adj.* workaday.

work·er (wėr′kər) *n.* **1** a person or thing that works. **2** a person who works hard. **3** a laborer who works with his hands or with machines; a workman; a workingman. **4** a bee, ant, wasp, or other insect that works for its community. —**Syn. 1** laborer, toiler, artisan, craftsman.

work·horse (wėrk′hôrs′) *n.* **1** a horse used mostly for work, not for racing, hunting, or showing. **2** a person who is an exceptionally hard worker. **3** a machine that is especially powerful, productive, etc. Also, **work horse.**

work·house (wėrk′hous′) *n. Esp.Brit.* formerly, a house where very poor people were lodged and were expected to perform some work in return.

work·ing (wėr′king) *n.* **1** the action, method, or performance of one that works. **2** Often, **workings.** operations; action: *the workings of one's mind. Do you understand the workings of this machine?* **3** Usually, **workings,** *pl.* the parts of a mine, quarry, tunnel, etc. where work is being done.
—*adj.* **1** that works. **2** used in working. **3** used to operate with or by: *a working majority.* **4 a** performing its function; that goes: *a working model of a train.* **b** that can be arranged or accomplished; workable: *a working agreement, a working arrangement.* **5** providing a basis for further work: *a working hypothesis.* **6** moving convulsively, as the features from emotion. **7** of liquor, etc., fermenting.

working capital **1** the amount of capital needed to operate a business. **2** the amount left when current liabilities are subtracted from current assets. **3** in finance, the liquid, or immediately usable, capital of a business, as distinguished from frozen assets, such as property, machinery, etc.

working class a group thought of as including all those people who work for wages, especially manual and industrial workers.

working day workday.

work·ing-day (wėr′king dā′) *adj.* workaday.

work·ing·man (wėr′king man′) *n.* **-men** (-mən). **1** a man who works. **2** a man who works with his hands or with machines.

working stiff *Slang.* a workingman.

work·ing·wom·an (wėr′king wům′ən) *n.* **-wom·en. 1** a woman who works. **2** a woman who works with her hands or with machines.

work·load (wėrk′lōd′) *n.* the amount of work assigned to a person, position, department, etc.

work·man (wėrk′mən) *n.* **-men** (-mən). **1** a worker. **2** a man who works with his hands or with machines. **3** a man who does his work well.

work·man·like (wėrk′mən līk′) *adj.* **1** skilful; well-done. **2** having the qualities of a good workman. *—adv.* skilfully.

work·man·ship (wėrk′mən ship′) *n.* **1** the art or skill of a worker or of his work; craftsmanship. **2** the quality or manner of work. **3** the work done.

work of art 1 a product of any of the arts, especially a painting, statue, or literary or musical work. **2** anything done or made with great artistry or skill.

work·out (wėrk′out′) *n. Informal.* **1** an exercise; practice. **2** a trial; test.

work·peo·ple (wėrk′pē′pəl) *n.pl. Esp.Brit.* people who work, especially those who work with their hands or with machines.

work·room (wėrk′rüm′ or -rům′) *n.* a room where work is done.

work·shop (wėrk′shop′) *n.* **1** a shop or building where work is done. **2** a meeting of interested persons for a period of intensive study, discussion, etc. of a particular subject: *a history workshop.*

work·ta·ble (wėrk′tā′bəl) *n.* a table to work at.

work·wom·an (wėrk′wům′ən) *n.* **-wom·en. 1** a woman worker. **2** a woman who works with her hands or with machines.

world (wėrld) *n.* **1** the earth: *Ships can sail around the world.* **2** all of certain parts, people, or things of the earth: **a** a particular division of the earth: *The New World is North America and South America. The Old World is Europe, Asia, and Africa.* **b** a group or system of things or beings having common characteristics or considered as forming a complex whole: *Fashionable people belong to the world of fashion. Ants are part of the insect world.* **c** any sphere, realm, or domain, as of action, thought, or interest: *the world of ideas.* **3** human affairs; the activities and circumstances of social, business, and public life: *a man of the world. The young graduate was ready to go out into the world.* **4** the things of this life and the people devoted to them: *Monks and nuns live apart from the world.* **5** all people; the human race; the public: *The whole world knows it.* **6** a star or planet, especially when considered as inhabited. **7** any time, condition, or place of life: *Heaven is in the world to come.* **8** all things; everything; the universe. **9** a great deal; very much; large amount: *The rest did her a world of good.* **10 all the world and his wife,** everybody, male and female, especially everybody of any social pretensions. **11 bring into the world,** give birth to. **12 come into the world,** be born. **13 for all the world, a** for any reason, no matter how great. **b** in every respect; exactly. **14 in the world, a** anywhere. **b** at all; ever. **15 on top of the world,** in high spirits. **16 out of this world,** *Informal.* **a** of which there is nothing like; great; wonderful; distinctive. **b** unearthly. **17 world without end,** forever. [OE *weorold*] **—Syn. 1** See **earth.**

World Court a court made up of representatives of various nations, established as the Permanent Court of International Justice in 1920 under the covenant of the League of Nations to settle disputes between nations, and continued as the International Court of Justice under the United Nations.

world island in geopolitics, the land mass that constitutes Asia, Africa, and Europe.

hat, āge, cãre, fär; let, ēqual, tėrm; it, īce
hot, ōpen, ôrder; oil, out; cup, půt, rüle, ūse
əbove, takən, pencəl, lemən, circəs
ch, child; ng, long; sh, ship
th, thin; ᴛʜ, then; zh, measure

world·li·ness (wėrld′lē nis) *n.* worldly ideas, ways, or conduct.

world·ling (wėrld′ling) *n.* a person who cares much for the interests and pleasures of this world. [< *world* + *-ling*]

world·ly (wėrld′lē) *adj.* **-li·er, -li·est. 1** of this world; not of heaven: *worldly wealth.* **2 a** caring much for the interests and pleasures of this world. **b** caring too much for such interests and pleasures. **3** worldly-wise. **—Syn. 1** mundane. See **earthly.**

world·ly-mind·ed (wėrld′lē mīn′did) *adj.* having or showing a worldly mind; caring much for the interests and pleasures of this world.

world·ly-wise (wėrld′lē wīz′) *adj.* wise about the ways and affairs of this world.

world series in baseball, the series of games played each fall between the winners of the two major league championships, to decide the professional championship of the United States.

World War I the war in Europe, Asia, Africa, and elsewhere, from July 28, 1914 to Nov. 11, 1918. Great Britain, France, Russia, Canada, the United States (1917-18), and their allies were on one side; Germany, Austria-Hungary, and their allies were on the other.

World War II the war in Europe, Asia, Africa, and elsewhere, from September 1, 1939 to August 14, 1945, beginning as a war between Great Britain, France, Poland and their allies on one side and Germany on the other, ultimately involving most of the world. The chief conflict was between Great Britain, the United States, and Russia on one side and Germany, Italy, and Japan on the other.

world-wea·ry (wėrld′wēr′ē) *adj.* weary of this world; tired of living.

world·wide (wėrld′wīd′) *adj.* spread throughout the world.

worm (wėrm) *n.* **1** any of numerous small, slender, crawling or creeping animals, usually soft-bodied and without legs. **2** something like a worm in shape or movement, such as the thread of a screw. **3** something that slowly eats away; the pain or destruction it causes. **4** a short, continuously threaded shaft or screw, the thread of which gears with the teeth of a toothed wheel. **5** a person who deserves contempt or pity. **6 worms,** *pl.* a disease caused by worms in the body.
—v. **1** move like a worm; crawl or creep like a worm: *The soldier wormed his way toward the enemy's lines.* **2 a** make one's way insidiously (into). **b** wriggle (out of trouble, etc.). **3** work or get by persistent and secret means: *John tried to worm the secret out of me. He wormed himself into our confidence.* **4** look for or catch worms. **5** remove worms from. [OE *wyrm*] **—worm′er,** *n.* **—worm′like′,** *adj.*

worm-eat·en (wėrm′ēt′ən) *adj.* **1** eaten into by worms: *worm-eaten timbers.* **2** worn-out; worthless; out-of-date.

worm gear 1 a worm wheel. **2** a worm wheel and an endless screw together. By a worm gear the rotary motion of one shaft can be transmitted to another shaft at right angles to it.

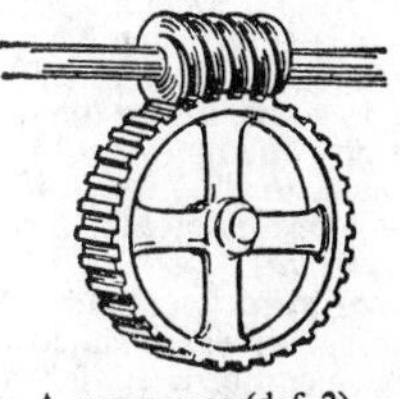
A worm gear (def. 2)

worm·hole (wėrm′hōl′) *n.* a hole made by a worm.

worm wheel a wheel with teeth that fit into a revolving screw.

worm·wood (wėrm′wůd) *n.* **1** a bitter plant used in medicine, absinthe, etc. **2** something bitter or extremely unpleasant. [OE *wermōd,* influenced by *worm, wood*]

worm·y (wėr′mē) *adj.* **worm·i·er, worm·i·est. 1** having worms; containing many worms. **2** damaged by worms. **3** contemptible; pitiable: *a wormy creature.* —**worm·i·ness,** *n.*

worn (wôrn) *v.* pp. of **wear.** —*adj.* **1** damaged by use: *worn rugs.* **2** tired; wearied: *a worn face.*

worn-out (wôrn′out′) *adj.* **1** used until no longer fit for use. **2** exhausted; fatigued.

wor·ri·ment (wėr′ē mənt) *n. Informal.* **1** worrying. **2** worry; anxiety.

wor·ri·some (wėr′ē səm) *adj.* **1** causing worry. **2** inclined to worry. —**wor′ri·some·ly,** *adv.*

wor·ry (wėr′ē) *v.* **-ried, -ry·ing,** *n.* **-ries.** —*v.* **1** feel anxious or uneasy: *She will worry if we are late.* **2** cause to feel anxious or troubled: *The problem worried him.* **3** annoy; bother: *Don't worry me with so many questions.* **4** seize and shake with the teeth; bite at; snap at: *A dog will worry a rat.* **5** harass, as if by repeated biting, etc.; harry by rough treatment or repeated attacks. **6 worry along,** manage somehow. —*n.* **1** anxiety; uneasiness; trouble; care: *Worry kept her awake.* **2** a cause of trouble or care: *A mother of sick children has many worries.* [OE *wyrgan* strangle] —**wor′ri·er,** *n.*
Syn. *v.* **2 Worry, annoy, harass** = disturb or distress a person with constant trouble, interference, etc. **Worry** emphasizes causing great uneasiness, care, or anxiety: *The change in his disposition and habits worries me.* **Annoy** particularly suggests constant interference, inconvenience, or irritation: *The new girl annoys her fellow workers by interrupting their work to ask foolish questions.* **Harass** emphasizes persistent or repeated demands or burdens: *He is harassed by business troubles and a nagging wife.*

worse (wėrs) *adj. comparative of* **bad. 1** more harmful, painful, regrettable, unpleasant, unfavorable, etc.: *It could be worse.* **2** more unattractive, unsuitable, faulty, incorrect, ill-advised, etc.: *His pen was poor and his writing even worse.* **3** less good; more evil: *Stealing is bad, but murder is worse.* **4** of lower quality or value; inferior: *The soil is worse in the valley.* **5** less well; more ill: *The patient is worse today.* **6** less fortunate or well off.
—*adv.* in a more severe or evil manner or degree: *It is raining worse than ever.*
—*n.* that which is worse: *He thought the loss of his property bad enough, but worse followed.* [OE *wyrsa*]

wor·sen (wėr′sən) *v.* make worse; become worse.

wor·ship (wėr′ship) *n. v.* **-shipped** or **-shiped, -ship·ping** or **-ship·ing.** —*n.* **1** great honor and respect: *the worship of God, hero worship.* **2** religious ceremonies or services. **3** great love and admiration; adoration. **4** a title used in addressing or referring to a mayor or certain magistrates: "*Yes, your worship,*" *he said to the judge.*
—*v.* **1** pay great honor and respect to: *Mohammedans worship Allah.* **2** take part in a religious service. **3** consider extremely precious; hold very dear; adore: *A miser worships money.* [OE *weorthscipe* < *weorth* worth + *-scipe* -ship] —**wor′ship·per** or **wor′ship·er,** *n.* —**Syn.** *n.* **1** reverence. *-v.* **1** revere, venerate.

wor·ship·ful (wėr′ship fəl) *adj.* **1** honorable. **2** worshipping.

worst (wėrst) *adj. superlative* of **bad. 1** least well; most ill: *This is the worst cold I ever had.* **2** least good; most evil: *It was the worst murder of the century.* **3** of the lowest quality or value; least good, valuable, desirable, or successful: *the worst diet imaginable, the worst sheep of the herd, the worst room in the hotel.*
—*adv.* to an extreme degree of badness or evil: *This child acts worst when his parents have guests.*
—*n.* **1** that which is worst: *The mean boy kept the best of the fruit for himself and gave the worst to his friends.* **2 at worst,** under the least favorable circumstances. **3 give one the worst of it,** defeat one. **4 if (the) worst comes to (the) worst,** if the very worst thing happens.
—*v.* beat; defeat: *The hero worsted his enemies.* [OE *wyrresta*]

wor·sted (wėr′stid or wůs′tid) *n.* **1** a smooth, firm thread or yarn made from long wool fibres that have been combed. **2** a fabric made from such thread or yarn. **3** a woollen yarn for knitting, crocheting, and needlework. —*adj.* made of worsted. [< *Worsted* (now Worstead), a town in E. England, where it was made originally]

wort¹ (wėrt) *n.* the liquid made from malt that later becomes beer, ale, or other liquor. [OE *wyrt*]

wort² (wėrt) *n.* a plant, herb, or vegetable (now used chiefly in combinations, as in *liverwort, figwort*). [OE *wyrt*]

worth (wėrth) *adj.* **1** good or important enough for; deserving of: *Vancouver is a city worth visiting.* **2** equal in value to: *That book is worth $5.00.* **3** having property that amounts to: *That man is worth millions.* —*n.* **1** merit; usefulness; importance: *We should read books of real worth.* **2** value: *Jane got her money's worth out of that coat.* **3** a quantity of something of specified value: *a dollar's worth of sugar.* **4** *Archaic.* property; wealth. [OE *weorth*] —**Syn.** *n.* **1, 2** See **merit.**

worth·less (wėrth′lis) *adj.* without worth; good-for-nothing; useless. —**worth′less·ly,** *adv.* —**worth′less·ness,** *n.* —**Syn.** valueless, trashy.

worth-while (wėrth′hwīl′ or -wīl′) *adj.* worth time, attention, or effort; having real merit.
☛ **Worth while** is written as two words when it is a predicate complement and hyphenated when it precedes its noun: *All this fussing is hardly worth while. He ought to spend his time on some worth-while reading.*

wor·thy (wėr′ᴛʜē) *adj.* **-thi·er, -thi·est,** *n.* **-thies.** —*adj.* **1** having worth or merit: *She helps the worthy poor.* **2** deserving; meriting. **3 worthy of, a** deserving. **b** having enough worth for. —*n.* a person of great merit; an admirable person. —**wor′thi·ly,** *adv.* —**wor′thi·ness,** *n.*

wot (wot) *v. Archaic.* know. "I wot" means "I know." "He wot" means "He knows." [OE *wāt*]

would (wůd; *unstressed,* wəd) *v.* **1** pt. of **will.** See **will** for ordinary uses. **2** *Would* has special uses: **a** to express future time: *Would he never go?* **b** to express action done again and again in the past time: *The children would play for hours on the beach.* **c** to express a wish: *Would I were dead!* **d** to make a statement or question less direct or blunt: *Would that be fair? Would you help us, please?* **e** to express conditions: *If he would only try, he could do it.* [OE *wolde*]
☛ **Would rather** is used to express a strong preference: *I would rather stay home than have to dance with him.*

would-be (wůd′bē′) *adj.* **1** wishing or pretending to be. **2** intended to be.

would·n't (wůd′ənt) would not.

wouldst (wůdst) *v. Archaic and poetic.* 2nd pers. sing. past tense of **will.** "Thou wouldst" means "you would" (sing.).

wound¹ (wünd; *archaic and poetic,* wound) *n.* **1** a hurt or injury caused by cutting, stabbing, shooting, etc. **2** in a tree or plant, a similar injury due to external violence. **3** any hurt or injury to feelings, reputation, etc.: *The loss of his job was a wound to his pride.* —*v.* **1** injure by cutting, stabbing, shooting, etc.; hurt. **2** injure in feelings, reputation, etc.: *His words wounded her.* [OE *wund*]

wound² (wound) *v.* pt. and pp. of **wind².**

wound³ (wound) *v.* a pt. and a pp. of **wind³.**

wove (wōv) *v.* pt. and a pp. of **weave.**

wo·ven (wō′vən) *v.* pp. of **weave.**

wow¹ (wou) *n.* **1** a wail. **2** a short explosive noise like a bark. **3** a variation in the sound pitch of a phonograph or tape recorder, caused by a slight irregularity in the speed of the driving mechanism. [imitative]

wow² (wou) *Slang.* —*n.* an unqualified success; a hit. —*v.* overwhelm, as with delight or amazement. —*interj.* an exclamation of delight, admiration, etc.

wrack¹ (rak) *n.* **1** wreckage. **2** ruin; destruction. **3** seaweed cast ashore. —*v.* wreck; ruin. [< MDu. and MLG *wrak* wreck]

wrack² (rak) *v.* **1** hurt very much; torture: *wracked by convulsions.* **2** stretch; strain. **3** torture on the rack. [var. of *rack¹*]

wraith (rāth) *n.* **1** the ghost of a person seen before or soon after his death. **2** a ghost; spectre. [< Scottish, ? < ON *vörthr* guardian spirit]

wran·gle (rang′gəl) *v.* **-gled, -gling,** *n.* —*v.* **1** dispute noisily; quarrel angrily: *The children wrangled about who should sit in front.* **2** argue. **3** in the western parts of Canada and the United States, herd or tend (horses, etc.) on the range. —*n.* a noisy dispute; angry quarrel. [? < LG *wrangeln*] —**Syn.** *v.* **1** bicker, squabble, brawl.

wran·gler (rang′glər) *n.* **1** a person who wrangles. **2** in the western parts of Canada and the United States, a man having charge of the saddle horses of an outfit; loosely, a cowboy. 3 *Brit.* a person winning high honors in mathematics at Cambridge University.

wrap (rap) *v.* **wrapped** or **wrapt, wrap·ping,** *n.* —*v.* 1 cover by winding or folding something around: *She wrapped herself in a shawl.* 2 wind or fold as a covering: *Wrap a shawl around you.* 3 cover with paper and tie up or fasten. 4 cover; envelop; hide: *The mountain peak is wrapped in clouds. She sat wrapped in thought.* 5 **wrapped up in, a** devoted to; thinking mainly of. **b** involved in; associated with. 6 **wrap up, a** put on warm outer clothes. **b** *Informal.* make assured in ending; clinch: *They wrapped up the game with three runs in the ninth.*
—*n.* 1 a loose garment used or designed for folding about the person, such as a scarf, shawl, etc. 2 Often, **wraps,** *pl.* an outer covering. Shawls, scarfs, coats, and furs are wraps. 3 **under wraps,** kept secret or concealed. [ME *wrappen*]

wrap·per (rap′ər) *n.* 1 a person or thing that wraps. 2 anything in which something is wrapped; covering; cover. 3 a woman's long, loose-fitting garment for wearing in the house. 4 the leaf or leaves rolled around smaller leaves or pieces to form the outside layer of tobacco in a cigar.

wrap·ping (rap′ing) *n.* Usually, **wrappings,** *pl.* the paper, or other material in which something is wrapped.

wrapt (rapt) *v.* a pt. and a pp. of **wrap.**

wrasse (ras) *n.* any of various sea fishes, especially a genus having thick, fleshy lips, powerful teeth, and usually a brilliant coloration. [< Cornish *wrach*]

wrath (rath or roth) *n.* very great anger; rage. [OE *wrǣththu*] —**Syn.** ire, fury, indignation, resentment. See **anger.**

wrath·ful (rath′fəl or roth′-) *adj.* feeling or showing wrath; very angry. —**wrath′ful·ly,** *adv.* —**wrath′ful·ness,** *n.* —**Syn.** irate, furious, raging, incensed.

wrath·y (rath′ē or roth′ē) *adj.* **wrath·i·er, wrath·i·est.** wrathful.

wreak (rēk) *v.* 1 give expression to; work off (feelings, desires, etc.): *The bully wreaked his bad temper on his dog.* 2 inflict (vengeance, punishment, etc.). 3 *Archaic.* avenge. [OE *wrecan*]

wreath (rēth) *n.* **wreaths** (rēᴛʜz). 1 a ring of flowers or leaves twisted together. 2 something suggesting a wreath: *a wreath of smoke.* 3 **Wreath,** Corona Australis (the Southern Crown), a southern constellation. [OE *wrǣth*]

wreathe (rēᴛʜ) *v.* **wreathed, wreathed** or (*archaic*) **wreath·en, wreath·ing.** 1 make into a wreath; twist. 2 decorate or adorn with wreaths. 3 make a ring around; encircle: *Mist wreathed the hills.* 4 envelop: *wreathed in smiles.* 5 move in rings: *The smoke wreathed upward.* [partly < ME *wrethen,* pp. of *writhen* writhe, partly < *wreath*]

wreck (rek) *n.* 1 the partial or total destruction of a ship, building, train, automobile, or aircraft. 2 destruction or serious injury: *The war caused the wreck of many fortunes.* 3 what is left of anything that has been destroyed or much injured: *The wrecks of six ships were cast upon the shore.* 4 a person who has lost his physical or mental health. 5 goods cast up by the sea. —*v.* 1 cause the wreck of; destroy; ruin: *Robbers wrecked the mail train.* 2 be wrecked; suffer serious injury. 3 cause to lose health or money. 4 act as wrecker. [ME < AF < ON **wrek* < Gmc. **wrecan* to drive]

wreck·age (rek′ij) *n.* 1 what is left of a thing that has been wrecked: *The shore was covered with the wreckage of a ship.* 2 a wrecking or being wrecked.

wreck·er (rek′ər) *n.* 1 a person who causes wrecks. 2 a person whose work is tearing down buildings. 3 a person, car, train, or machine that removes wrecks. 4 a person or ship that recovers wrecked or disabled ships or their cargoes. 5 a person who causes shipwrecks by false lights on shore so as to plunder the wrecks.

wren[1] (ren) *n.* any of a number of small songbirds having slender bills and short tails. Wrens often build their nests near houses. [OE *wrenna*]

Wren or **wren**[2] (ren) *n. Informal.* a member of the Women's Royal Naval Service. [< the initials, WRNS]

wrench (rench) *n.* 1 a violent twist or twisting pull: *The knob broke off when he gave it a sudden wrench.* 2 an injury

hat, āge, cãre, fär; let, ēqual, tėrm; it, īce
hot, ōpen, ôrder; oil, out; cup, pu̇t, rüle, ūse
əbove, takən, pencəl, lemən, circəs
ch, child; ng, long; sh, ship
th, thin; ᴛʜ, then; zh, measure

caused by twisting. 3 grief; pain: *It was a wrench to leave the old home.* 4 a tool for turning nuts, bolts, etc. 5 distortion of the proper or original meaning, interpretation, etc. [< v.]
—*v.* 1 twist or pull violently: *The policeman wrenched the gun out of the man's hand.* 2 injure by twisting: *He wrenched his back in falling from the horse.* 3 distress or pain greatly; rack. 4 twist the meaning of. [OE *wrencan* twist] —**Syn.** *v.* 1 wring, wrest. 2 strain, sprain.

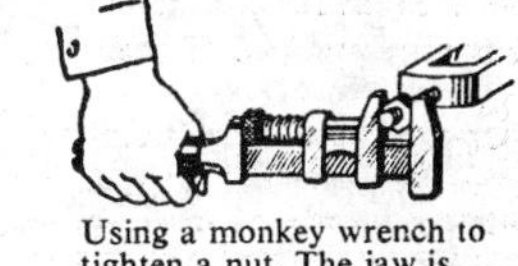
Using a monkey wrench to tighten a nut. The jaw is moved by means of the screw next to the handle.

wrest (rest) *v.* 1 twist, pull, or tear away with force; wrench away: *The policeman wrested the knife from the thief.* 2 take by force: *The usurper wrested the power from the king.* 3 twist or turn from the proper meaning, use, etc. —*n.* 1 a wresting; forcible twist. 2 a key, hammer, etc. for tuning certain stringed instruments, such as a harp, piano, etc. by turning the pegs around which the strings are wound. [OE *wrǣstan*] —**wrest′er,** *n.*

wres·tle (res′əl) *v.* **-tled, -tling,** *n.* —*v.* 1 try to throw or force (an opponent) to the ground. 2 struggle: *We wrestle with problems, temptations, and difficulties.* 3 contend with in wrestling, or as if in wrestling. —*n.* 1 a wrestling match. 2 struggle. [ult. < *wrest*] —**wres′tler,** *n.*

wres·tling (res′ling) *n.* a sport or contest in which each of two opponents tries to throw or force the other to the ground. The rules for wrestling do not allow using the fists or certain holds on the body.

wretch (rech) *n.* 1 a very unfortunate or unhappy person. 2 a scoundrel. [OE *wrecca* exile] —**Syn.** 2 villain, rogue.

wretch·ed (rech′id) *adj.* 1 very unfortunate or unhappy. 2 very unsatisfactory; miserable: *a wretched hut.* 3 vicious; wicked; degenerate: *a wretched traitor.* —**wretch′ed·ly,** *adv.* —**wretch′ed·ness,** *n.*

Syn. 1 **Wretched, miserable** = very unhappy or deeply disturbed. **Wretched** suggests a state of unhappiness and extreme lowness of spirits marked by discouragement and hopelessness, caused by sorrow, sickness, worry, etc.: *He was wretched when he failed the examination again.* **Miserable** suggests a state of severe suffering or distress of mind, caused especially by conditions or circumstances such as poverty, humiliation, or misfortune: *After the loss of their savings and their home, they felt too miserable to see their old friends.* 2 pitiful, shabby. 3 despicable, base, mean.

wrick (rik) *v. n.* sprain; wrench (def. 2, n. and v.). [ME *wricken* twist]

wrig·gle (rig′əl) *v.* **-gled, -gling,** *n.* —*v.* 1 twist and turn: *Children wriggle when they are restless.* 2 move by twisting and turning: *A snake wriggled across the road.* 3 make one's way by shifts and tricks: *Some people can wriggle out of any difficulty.* —*n.* a wriggling. [cf. Du. *wriggelen*]

wrig·gler (rig′lər) *n.* 1 a person who wriggles. 2 the larva of a mosquito.

wrig·gly (rig′lē) *adj.* twisting and turning.

wright (rīt) *n.* (now usually in combinations) a maker of something. A wheelwright makes wheels. A playwright makes plays for the theatre. [OE *wryhta,* var. of *wyrhta* < *weorc* work]

wring (ring) *v.* **wrung, wring·ing,** *n.* —*v.* 1 twist with force; squeeze hard: *wring clothes.* 2 force by twisting or squeezing: *The laundress wrings water from the wet clothes.* 3 twist violently, especially out of place or relation; wrench: *wring a chicken's neck.* 4 get by force, effort, or persuasion: *The old beggar could wring money from anyone by his sad story.* 5 clasp; press: *He wrung his old friend's hand.* 6 cause pain, pity, etc. in: *Their poverty wrung his heart.* 7 **wring out,** force (water, etc.) from by twisting or squeezing. —*n.* a twist; squeeze. [OE *wringan*]

wring·er (ring′ər) *n.* 1 a machine for squeezing water from clothes. 2 a person or thing that wrings.

wrin·kle[1] (ring′kəl) *n. v.* **-kled, -kling.** —*n.* a ridge; fold: *An old man's face has wrinkles. I must press out the wrinkles in this dress.* —*v.* **1** make a wrinkle or wrinkles in: *He wrinkled his forehead.* **2** have wrinkles; acquire wrinkles: *These sleeves wrinkle.* [cf. OE *gewrinclod,* pp., twisted, winding] —**Syn.** *v.* **1** crease, crinkle.

wrin·kle[2] (ring′kəl) *n. Informal.* a useful hint or idea; clever trick. [? special use of *wrinkle*[1]]

wrin·kly (ring′klē) *adj.* **-kli·er, -kli·est.** wrinkled.

wrist (rist) *n.* **1** in human beings, the joint connecting hand and arm. **2** a corresponding joint or part of the forelimb of an animal. **3** the bones of this part; carpus. **4** the part of a glove, sleeve, etc. that covers the wrist. [OE]

wrist·band (rist′band′) *n.* the band of a sleeve fitting around the wrist.

wrist·let (rist′lit) *n.* **1** a band worn around the wrist to keep it warm. **2** a bracelet.

wrist pin a stud or pin projecting from the side of a crank, wheel, or the like, and forming a means of attachment to a connecting rod.

writ[1] (rit) *n.* **1** something written; a piece of writing. The Bible is Holy Writ. **2** in law, a formal order directing a person to do or not to do something: *The lawyer got a writ from the judge to release the man wrongly held in jail* [OE *writ* < *wrītan* write]

writ[2] (rit) *v. Archaic.* a pt. and a pp. of **write.**

write (rīt) *v.* **wrote** or (*archaic*) **writ, writ·ten** or (*archaic*) **writ, writ·ing. 1** make letters, words, etc. with pen, pencil, chalk, etc.: *He learned to write.* **2** mark with letters, words, etc.: *write a cheque.* **3** put down the letters, words, etc. of: *Write your name and address.* **4** give in writing; record: *She writes all that happens.* **5** make (books, stories, articles, poems, letters, etc.) by using written letters, words, etc.; compose. **6** be a writer: *Her ambition was to write.* **7** write a letter: *He writes to her every week.* **8** write a letter to. **9** show plainly: *Honesty is written on his face.* **10 write down, a** put into writing. **b** put a lower value on. **11 write in, a** insert (a fact, statement, etc.) in a piece of writing. **b** cast (a vote) for an unlisted candidate by writing his name on a ballot. **12 write off, a** cancel. **b** *U.S.* note the deduction of for depreciation. **c** give up; treat as if nonexistent. **13 write out, a** put into writing. **b** write in full. **14 write up, a** write a description or account of. **b** write in detail. **c** bring up to date in writing. **d** put a higher value on. [OE *wrītan,* originally, scratch]

write-in (rīt′in′) *U.S. adj.* in an election, of or having to do with a person who is not officially listed as a candidate but who is voted for by his name being written in on a ballot. —*n.* a write-in candidate or vote.

writ·er (rīt′ər) *n.* **1** a person who writes. **2** one whose profession or business is writing; author.

write-up (rīt′up′) *n. Informal.* a written description or account.

writhe (rīᴛʜ) *v.* **writhed, writhed** or (*obsolete or poetic*) **writh·en** (riᴛʜ′ən), **writh·ing. 1** twist and turn; twist: *The snake writhed along the branch. The wounded man writhed in agony.* **2** suffer mentally; be very uncomfortable. [OE *wrīthan*]

writ·ing (rīt′ing) *n.* **1** the act of making letters, words, etc. with pen, pencil, etc. **2** written form: *Put your ideas in writing.* **3** handwriting. **4** something written; a letter, paper, document, etc. **5** a book, story, article, poem, etc. **6** the profession or business of a person who writes. —*adj.* **1** that writes. **2** used to write with; used to write on: *writing paper.*

writ·ten (rit′ən) *v.* a pp. of **write.**

WRNS or **W.R.N.S.** Women's Royal Naval Service.

wrong (rong) *adj.* **1** not right; bad; unjust; unlawful: *It is wrong to tell lies.* **2** incorrect: *He gave the wrong answer.* **3** unsuitable; improper: *the wrong clothes for the occasion.* **4** in a bad state or condition; out of order; amiss: *Something is wrong with the car.* **5** not meant to be seen; less or least important: *Cloth often has a wrong side and a right side.* **6 go wrong, a** turn out badly. **b** stop being good and become bad.
—*adv.* in a wrong manner; in the wrong direction; badly: *Everything went wrong today.*
—*n.* **1** what is wrong; wrong thing or things: *Two wrongs do not make a right.* **2** an injustice; injury: *You do an honest man a wrong if you call him a liar or a thief.* **3 in the wrong,** wrong.
—*v.* **1** do wrong to; treat unjustly; injure: *He forgave those who had wronged him.* **2** discredit or dishonor unjustly by statement, opinion, etc.; impute evil to undeservedly. **3** cheat or defraud (a person of something). [OE *wrang* < ON **wrangr, rangr* crooked] —**wrong′ly,** *adv.* —**wrong′ness,** *n.* —**Syn.** *adj.* **1** evil, wicked, reprehensible. **2** inaccurate, erroneous, faulty. **3** inappropriate, unfit. –*n.* **1** evil, sin, misdemeanor. –*v.* harm, maltreat, abuse, oppress.

wrong·do·er (rong′dü′ər) *n.* a person who does wrong.

wrong·do·ing (rong′dü′ing) *n.* the doing of wrong; evil; wrong.

wrong·ful (rong′fəl) *adj.* **1** wrong. **2** unlawful. —**wrong′ful·ly,** *adv.* —**wrong′ful·ness,** *n.*

wrong-head·ed (rong′hed′id) *adj.* **1** wrong in judgment or opinion. **2** stubborn even when wrong. —**wrong′-head′ed·ly,** *adv.* —**wrong′-head′ed·ness,** *n.*

wrote (rōt) *v.* pt. of **write.**

wroth (roth) *adj.* angry. [OE *wrāth*]

wrought (rot or rôt) *v.* a pt. and a pp. of **work.** —*adj.* **1** made: *The gate was wrought with great skill.* **2** formed with care; not rough or crude. **3** manufactured or treated; not in a raw state. **4** of metals, formed by hammering.

wrought iron a form of iron containing some slag and a small amount of carbon. Often used for furniture, gates, and decorative designs, it is tough but soft enough to be easily forged and welded, and it is not so brittle as cast iron.

wrought-up (rot′up′ or rôt′-) *adj.* stirred up; excited.

wrung (rung) *v.* pt. and pp. of **wring.**

wry (rī) *adj.* **wri·er, wri·est. 1** made by distorting the mouth or other features to show disgust, bitterness, doubt, or irony: *a wry face, a wry grin.* **2** marked by grim or bitter irony: *a wry humor, wry remarks.* **3** turned to one side in an abnormal way: *a wry nose.* **4** perversely wrong or inappropriate: *wry behavior.* [ult. < OE *wrīgian* turn] —**wry′ly,** *adv.*

wry·neck (rī′nek′) *n.* **1** a neck that is drawn to one side because of unequal contraction of the muscles. **2** a bird that twists its neck and head in a peculiar way.

WSW, W.S.W., or **w.s.w.** west southwest, a direction midway between west and southwest.

wt. weight.

wuth·er (wuᴛʜ′ər) *Dialect.* —*v.* **1** blow with a roar, as a strong wind; bluster. **2** move or rush noisily; whiz. —*n.* a wuthering sound. [< dial. *wuther* whither, v. < Scand.; cf. Norwegian *kvidra* move quickly, related to *hvitha* wind squall]

W.Va. West Virginia.

Wy·an·dotte (wī′ən dot′) *n.* **1** an American breed of medium-sized, hardy domestic chickens. **2** a chicken of this breed.

wye (wī) *n.* **1** the letter Y. **2** anything made or arranged in the shape of the letter Y.

Wyo. Wyoming.

wy·vern (wī′vərn) *n.* wivern.

X or **x** (eks) *n.* X's or x's. **1** the twenty-fourth letter of the English alphabet. **2** any speech sound represented by this letter. **3** one (usually twenty-fourth) of a series designated alphabetically. **4** in algebraic equations, an unknown quantity, as in $x + y = 5$. **5** an unidentified person or thing: *Mr. X.* **6** anything shaped like this letter. **7** an abscissa.

X¹ **1** unknown quantity. **2** a term used to designate a person or thing whose name is unknown or withheld.

X² **1** Christ. **2** Christian.

Xan·thip·pe (zan tip′ē) *n.* a scolding woman; shrew. [< *Xanthippe*, the wife of Socrates, famous as a scold]

xan·thous (zan′thəs) *adj.* **1** of or having to do with peoples having yellowish, reddish, or light-brown hair. **2** of or having to do with peoples having a yellowish skin, as the Mongolians. **3** yellow. [< Gk. *xanthos*]

X chromosome in biology, one of two chromosomes that determine sex. An egg containing two X chromosomes, one from each parent, develops into a female.

Xe xenon.

xe·bec (zē′bek) *n.* a small, three-masted vessel of the Mediterranean. Also, **zebec.** [< F *xebec*, ult. < Arabic *shabbāk*]

xe·ni·a (zē′nē ə) *n.* in botany, the effects or changes in a seed resulting directly from cross-pollination. [< NL *xenia* < Gk. *xenos* guest]

xeno- *combining form.* **1** stranger; foreigner: *xenophobia = fear of strangers.* **2** strange; foreign: *xenomorphic = of strange (different) form.* [< Gk. *xenos* guest, stranger]

xen·o·mor·phic (zen′ə môr′fik) *adj.* of rock, having a form distorted from the normal form as a result of pressure. [< *xeno-* + Gk. *morphē* shape + E *-ic*] **—xen′o·mor′phi·cal·ly,** *adv.*

xe·non (zē′non or zen′on) *n.* a rare, heavy, colorless, gaseous chemical element that is chemically inactive. It occurs in the air in minute quantities. *Symbol*: Xe; *at.no.* 54; *at.wt.* 131.30. [< Gk. *xenon*, neut. adj., strange]

xen·o·phobe (zen′ə fōb′) *n.* one who has a morbid fear or dislike of foreign persons or things. [< *xeno-* + *-phobe*]

xen·o·pho·bi·a (zen′ə fō′bē ə) *n.* a hatred or fear of foreigners or foreign things. [< NL < Gk. *xenos* stranger + *phobos* fear]

xero- *combining form.* dry; dryness: *xerophyte = a plant adapted to dry climate.* [< Gk. *xēros* dry]

xe·ro·graph·ic (zēr′ə graf′ik) *adj.* of or having to do with xerography.

xe·rog·ra·phy (zē rog′rə fē) *n.* a printing process in which black powder, negatively charged, is spread on a positively charged surface, the image being transferred to the paper by static electricity, rather than by pressure. [< *Xerography*, trademark]

xe·ro·phyte (zēr′ə fīt′) *n.* in botany, a plant that needs very little water and can grow in deserts or very dry ground. Cactuses, sagebrush, century plants, etc. are xerophytes. [< *xero-* + *-phyte*]

xe·ro·sis (zē rō′sis) *n.* in medicine, unusual dryness of the skin, eyes, etc. [< *xero-* + *-osis*]

Xer·ox (zēr′oks) *n. Trademark.* **1** a copying process based on xerography. **2** a copying machine using this process. *—v.* make copies by xerography.

xi (sī, zī, or ksē) *n.* the 14th letter (Ξ, ξ = English X, x) of the Greek alphabet.

Xmas (kris′məs) *n. Informal.* Christmas.

Xn. Christian.

X ray **1** an electromagnetic ray having an extremely short wave length, formed when cathode rays impinge upon a solid body (such as the wall of a vacuum tube), and able to penetrate opaque substances; Roentgen ray. X rays are used to locate breaks in bones, bullets lodged in the body, etc., and to diagnose and treat certain diseases. **2** a picture made by means of X rays. [half-translation of obs. G *X-Strahlen* plural < *X*, in sense of "unknown" + *Strahl* ray, beam]

An X ray of a foot

hat, āge, cãre, fär; let, ēqual, tėrm; it, īce
hot, ōpen, ôrder; oil, out; cup, pu̇t, rüle, ūse
əbove, takən, pencəl, lemən, circəs
ch, child; ng, long; sh, ship
th, thin; ᴛʜ, then; zh, measure

☛ X ray is usually written with a capital *x*. It is not hyphenated as a noun, but it is as a verb or adjective: *X-ray the chest, an X-ray examination.*

X-ray (eks′rā′) *v.* examine, photograph, or treat with X rays. *—adj.* of, by, or having to do with X rays: *an X-ray examination of one's teeth.*

Xtian. Christian.

Xty. Christianity.

xy·lem (zī′lem) *n.* in botany, the woody tissue in a plant or tree that conveys upward the water and dissolved minerals absorbed by the roots and provides support. [< G < Gk *xylon* wood]

xy·lo·phone (zī′lə fōn′ or zil′ə fōn′) *n.* a musical percussion instrument consisting of two rows of wooden bars that are graduated in length to produce the tones of two octaves of the chromatic scale. It is played by striking the bars with wooden hammers. [< Gk. *xylon* wood + *phōnē* sound]

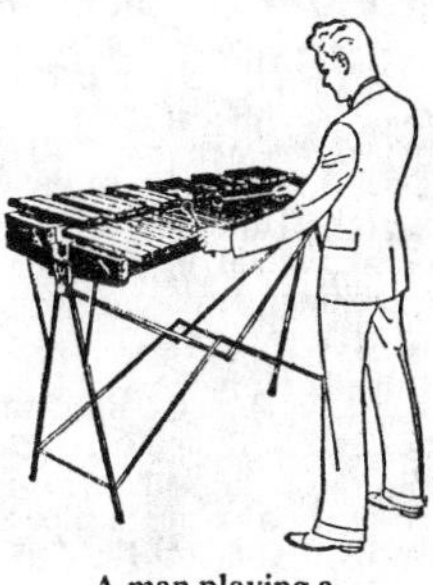
A man playing a xylophone

Y or **y** (wī) *n.* **Y's** or **y's. 1** the twenty-fifth letter of the English alphabet. **2** any speech sound represented by this letter. **3** one (usually twenty-fifth) of a series designated alphabetically. **4** in algebraic equations, an unknown quantity, as in $2x + 3y = 7$. **5** anything shaped like a Y.

y in mathematics: **1** an unknown quantity. **2** an ordinate.

y. 1 yard; yards. **2** year.

Y[1] **1** yttrium. **2** yen.

Y[2] or **Y.** (wī) *n. Informal.* **1** Y.M.C.A. or Y.W.C.A. **2** Y.M.H.A. or Y.W.H.A.

-y[1] *suffix.* **1** full of, composed of, containing, having, or characterized by, as in *airy, cloudy, dewy, icy, juicy, watery.* **2** somewhat, as in *chilly, salty.* **3** inclined to, as in *chatty, fidgety.* **4** resembling; suggesting, as in *sloppy, sugary, willowy.* **5** in certain words, usually archaic or poetic, such as *stilly, vasty,* the presence of the *-y* does not change the meaning. [OE *-ig*]

-y[2] *suffix.* small, as in *dolly*; used also to show kind feeling or intimacy, as in *Dicky.* [ME]

-y[3] *suffix.* **1** a state or quality, as in *jealousy, victory.* **2** an activity, as in *delivery, entreaty.* [< F *-ie* < L *-ia,* Gk. *-ia*]

yacht (yot) *n.* **1** a light sailing vessel having graceful lines and designed for racing. **2** a similar vessel having sails, motor power, or both, often luxuriously equipped, and used for private pleasure cruising. —*v.* sail, race, or cruise on a yacht. [< Du. *jaghte* < *jaghtschip* chasing ship]

yacht·ing (yot′ing) *n.* **1** the art of sailing a yacht. **2** the pastime of sailing on a yacht. —*adj.* **1** of yachting or yachts. **2** interested in yachting.

yachts·man (yots′mən) *n.* **-men** (-mən). a person who owns or sails a yacht.

yachts·man·ship (yots′mən ship′) *n.* skill or ability in handling a yacht.

yack (yak) *v. Slang.* yak[2].

yah (yä) *interj.* a noise made to express derision, disgust, or impatience.

Ya·hoo (yä′hü or yä hü′) *n.* **1** in Swift's *Gulliver's Travels,* a type of brute in human shape who works for a race of intelligent horses. **2 yahoo,** any rough, coarse, or uncouth person.

Yah·veh or **Yah·ve** (yä′vā) *n.* Yahweh.

Yah·weh or **Yah·we** (yä′wā) *n.* a name used for God in the Hebrew text of the Old Testament, and often used by writers on the religion of the Hebrews. Also, **Yahveh, Yahve, Jahve, Jahveh.** [< Hebrew. See JEHOVAH.]

yak[1] (yak) *n.* a long-haired ox of Tibet and central Asia, often domesticated and used as a beast of burden. [< Tibetan *gyag*]

yak[2] (yak) *v. Slang.* **yakked, yak·king.** chatter; talk constantly. —*n.* persistent, idle chatter. [imitative]

yam (yam) *n.* **1** the starchy root of a vine grown for food in warm countries. **2** the vine itself. **3** a kind of sweet potato. [< Sp. *iñame,* ult. < Senegalese *nyami* eat]

yank (yangk) *Informal.* —*v.* **1** jerk. **2 yank out,** *Informal.* take out with a jerk. —*n.* a jerk. [origin uncertain]

Yank (yangk) *n. adj. Slang.* Yankee.

Yan·kee (yang′kē) *n.* **1** a native or inhabitant of the United States. **2** a native or inhabitant of New England. **3** a native or inhabitant of any of the northern states. **4** *Southern U.S.* a Northerner (usually in a derogatory or hostile sense). —*adj.* of or having to do with Yankees: *Yankee shrewdness.* [probably ult. < Du. *Jan Kees* John Cheese (nickname), the *-s* being taken for pl. ending]

Yankee Doo·dle (dü′dəl) an American song, probably of English origin and taken over by the American soldiers in the Revolutionary War.

yap (yap) *n. v.* **yapped, yap·ping.** —*n.* **1** a snappish bark; yelp. **2** *Slang.* snappish, noisy, or foolish talk. **3** *Slang.* a peevish or noisy person. **4** *Slang.* the mouth. —*v.* **1** bark snappishly; yelp. **2** *Slang.* talk snappishly, noisily, or foolishly. **3** *Slang.* chatter or talk idly.

Ya·qui (yä′kē) *n.* **-qui** or **-quis. 1** a tribe of North American Indians in N.W. Mexico and Arizona. **2** a member of this tribe.

yard[1] (yärd) *n.* **1** a piece of ground near or around a house, barn, school, etc. **2** a piece of enclosed ground for some special purpose or business: *a chicken yard.* **3** a space with tracks where railway cars are stored, shifted around, etc. **4** a clearing where a group of moose or deer feed in winter: *a deer yard.*
—*v.* **1** put into or enclose in a yard. **2** of moose or deer: **a** be in or come together in a yard (def. 4). **b yard up,** settle or come together in a yard. [OE *geard*]

yard[2] (yärd) *n.* **1** a measure of length; 36 inches; 3 feet. *Abbrev.*: y. or yd. **2** a long, slender beam or pole fastened across a mast, used to support a sail. **3 make yards, a** in football, advance the ball from the line of scrimmage. **b** *Informal.* advance; make headway: *He has already made yards in his new business.* [OE *gierd* rod]

yard·age[1] (yär′dij) *n.* **1** a length in yards. **2** a quantity of something, such as cloth, that is measured in yards: *a large yardage of silk.* **3** yard goods. **4 a** in football, the number of yards by which a team or player advances the ball from the line of scrimmage. **b** *Informal.* advance; gain; benefit.

yard·age[2] (yär′dij) *n.* **1** the use of a yard or enclosure, as in lading or unlading cattle, etc. at a railway station. **2** the charge made for such use.

yard·arm (yärd′ärm′) *n.* either end of a long, slender beam or pole used to support a square sail.

yard goods cloth, etc. sold by the yard.

yard·mas·ter (yärd′mas′tər) *n.* a man in charge of a railway yard.

yard·stick (yärd′stik′) *n.* **1** a stick one yard long, used for measuring. **2** any standard of judgment or comparison.

yarn (yärn) *n.* **1** any spun thread, especially that prepared for weaving or knitting. **2** *Informal.* a tale; story: *Who told you that yarn?* **3 spin a yarn,** *Informal.* tell a story. —*v. Informal.* tell stories. [OE *gearn*]

yar·row (yar′ō) *n.* a common plant having finely divided leaves and flat clusters of white or pink flowers. [OE *gearwe*]

yat·a·ghan (yat′ə gan′) *n.* a sword used by Moslems, having no guard for the hand and no crosspiece, but usually a large pommel. [< Turkish]

yaw (yo or yô) *v.* **1** turn from a straight course; go unsteadily. **2** of an aircraft, turn from a straight course by a motion about its vertical axis. —*n.* a movement from a straight course. [origin uncertain]

yawl[1] (yol or yôl) *n.* **1** a boat like a sloop with a second short mast set near the stern. **2** a ship's boat rowed by four or six oars. [< Du. *jol*]

yawn (yon or yôn) *v.* **1** open the mouth wide because one is sleepy, tired, or bored. **2** utter with a yawn; cause by yawning. **3** open wide: *A wide gorge yawned beneath our feet.* —*n.* a yawning. [OE *geonian*] —**yawn′er,** *n.* —**Syn.** *v.* **1** gape.

A yawl (def. 1)

yawp (yop or yôp) *Dialect or informal.* —*v.* utter a loud, harsh cry. —*n.* a loud, harsh cry. [imitative] —**yawp′er,** *n.*

yaws (yoz or yôz) *n.pl.* a contagious disease of the tropics, characterized by sores on the skin. [< Carib]

Yb ytterbium.

Y chromosome in biology, one of two chromosomes that determine sex. An egg containing a Y chromosome develops into a male.

y·cleped (i klept′ or i klēpt′) *adj.* yclept.

y·clept (i klept′) *adj. Archaic.* called; named; styled. [OE *gecleopod* named]

yd. yard; yards: *6 yd. = 18 ft.*

ye[1] (yē; *unstressed,* yi) *pron. Archaic.* you (pl.): *Come, all ye faithful.* [OE *gē*]

ye[2] (ᴛʜē; *incorrectly,* yē) *definite article.* an old way of writing the definite article "the."

☛ ye. In Old and Middle English *the* was commonly written as *þe.* The early printers, who ordinarily did not have this consonant symbol (called "thorn") in their fonts, substituted *y* for it, but this was never intended to be read with the value of *y.*

yea (yā) *adv.* **1** yes (used in affirmation or assent). **2** indeed; truly (used to introduce a sentence or clause). **3** *Archaic.* not only that, but also; moreover. —*n.* an affirmative vote or voter. [OE *gēa*]

yean (yēn) *v.* give birth to a lamb or kid. [OE (assumed) *geēanian*; cf. *ēanian* yean, *geēan,* adj., pregnant]

yean·ling (yēn′ling) *n.* a lamb or kid; the young of a sheep or a goat.

year (yēr) *n.* **1** 12 months or 365 days (366 every fourth year); January 1 to December 31. **2** 12 months reckoned from any point. A **fiscal year** is a period of 12 months at the end of which the accounts of a government, business, etc. are balanced. **3** the part of a year spent in a certain activity. A school year is from eight to ten months. **4** the period of the earth's revolution around the sun. The **solar** or **astronomical year** is 365 days, 5 hours, 48 minutes, 46 seconds. **5** the time it takes for the apparent travelling of the sun from a given fixed star back to it again. The **sidereal year** is 20 minutes, 23 seconds longer than the solar year. **6** the time in which any planet completes its revolution around the sun. **7 years,** *pl.* **a** age. **b** a very long time. **8 a year and a day,** in law, a period constituting a term for certain purposes, in order to insure that a full year is completed. **9 year by year,** with each succeeding year; as years go by. **10 year in, year out,** always; continuously. [OE *gēar*]

year·book (yēr′bu̇k′) *n.* **1** a book or report published every year. **2** a school annual containing pictures and information of school activities.

year·ling (yēr′ling or yėr′ling) *n.* an animal one year old. —*adj.* one year old: *a yearling colt.* [< *year* + *-ling*]

year·long (yēr′long′) *adj.* **1** lasting for a year. **2** lasting for years.

year·ly (yēr′lē) *adj.* **1** done or happening once a year: *a yearly trip to Europe.* **2** every year; once a year: *a new volume comes out yearly.* **3** lasting a year: *The earth makes a yearly revolution around the sun.* **4** for a year: *He is paid a yearly salary of $5,600.* —*adv.* once a year; in every year; annually.

yearn (yėrn) *v.* **1** feel a longing or desire; desire earnestly: *He yearns for home.* **2** feel pity; have tender feelings: *Her heart yearned for the starving children.* [OE *giernan*]

yearn·ing (yėr′ning) *n.* an earnest or strong desire; longing.

year-round (yēr′round′) *adj. adv.* throughout the year.

yeast (yēst) *n.* **1** a substance consisting of a mass of very small one-celled fungi that grow quickly in a liquid containing sugar. Yeast is used to promote fermentation in alcoholic liquors and as a leavening agent for bread, rolls, etc. **2** a yeast cell or fungus. **3** a yeast cake. **4** an influence, element, etc. that acts as a leaven. **5** foam; froth. [OE *gist*]

yeast cake flour or meal mixed with yeast and pressed into a small cake.

yeast·y (yēs′tē) *adj.* **1** of, containing, or resembling yeast. **2** frothy or foamy: *yeasty waves.* **3** light or trifling; frivolous.

yegg (yeg) *n. Slang.* **1** a burglar who robs safes. **2** any burglar. [origin uncertain]

yell (yel) *v.* **1** cry out with a strong, loud sound. **2** say with a yell. —*n.* **1** a strong, loud cry. **2** a special shout or cheer used by a school or college. [OE *giellan*]

yel·low (yel′ō) *n.* **1** the color of gold, butter, or ripe lemons. **2** a yellow pigment or dye. **3** the yolk of an egg. —*adj.* **1** having a yellow color. **2 a** having a yellowish skin. **b** of or having to do with the Mongolian race. **3** jealous; envious. **4** *Informal.* cowardly. **5** sensational: *a yellow journal.* —*v.* turn yellow: *Paper yellows with age.* [OE *geolu*] —**yel′low·ness,** *n.*

yel·low·bird (yel′ō bėrd′) *n.* **1** the goldfinch of North America. **2** the yellow warbler of North America. **3** any of various other yellow birds, such as an oriole of Europe.

yellow cake *Cdn. Slang.* semirefined uranium ore.

hat, āge, cãre, fär; let, ēqual, tėrm; it, īce
hot, ōpen, ôrder; oil, out; cup, pu̇t, rüle, ūse
əbove, takən, pencəl, lemən, circəs
ch, child; ng, long; sh, ship
th, thin; ᴛʜ, then; zh, measure

yellow cedar **1** a fairly tall evergreen tree of the Pacific Coast, having scaly leaves and round, reddish-brown cones, also known as the Nootka cypress, or yellow cypress. **2** the light, hard wood of this tree.

yellow fever a dangerous, infectious tropical disease transmitted by the bite of a mosquito and characterized by high fever, jaundice, vomiting, etc.

yel·low·ham·mer (yel′ō ham′ər) *n.* **1** a European bird having a yellow head, neck, and breast. **2** the flicker or golden-winged woodpecker of E. North America. [earlier *yelambre* < OE *geolu* yellow + *amore,* a kind of bird; the *h* may have resulted from the influence of obs. *yellowham* of the same meaning < OE *geolu* yellow + *hama* covering, feathers]

yel·low·ish (yel′ō ish) *adj.* somewhat yellow.

yellow jack **1** yellow fever. **2** a yellow flag used as a signal of quarantine.

yellow jacket a wasp or hornet marked with bright yellow.

Yel·low·knife (yel′ō nīf′) *n.* **-knife** or **-knives. 1** a group of North American Indians, closely allied to the Chipewyan, originally living in the region between the Great Bear Lake and the Great Slave Lake to the east. **2** a member of this group. **3** the Athapascan language of this people.

yel·low·legs (yel′ō legz′) *n.* a shore bird having yellow legs, a brownish back streaked with white, and a white breast with brown markings.

yellow metal **1** gold. **2** a yellowish alloy containing copper and zinc.

yellow pages a telephone directory, or a part of one, that lists and advertises firms classified by the nature of their business. It is printed on yellow paper.

yellow peril the alleged danger from the growth and activities of Japan or China.

yellow pine **1** a pine tree with yellowish wood. **2** its wood.

yellow warbler a small North American warbler. The male has yellow plumage streaked with brown.

yelp (yelp) *n.* the quick, sharp bark or cry of a dog, fox, etc. [< v.] —*v.* **1** give a quick, sharp bark or cry. **2** utter with a yelp. [OE *gielpan* boast]

yen[1] (yen) *n.* **yen. 1** a unit of money in Japan. See table at **money. 2** a note or coin worth one yen. [< Japanese]

yen[2] (yen) *n. v.* **yenned, yen·ning.** *Informal.* —*n.* **1** a fanciful desire. **2 have a yen for,** desire. —*v.* desire. [< Chinese (Pekinese) *yen* opium (lit. smoke)]

yeo·man (yō′mən) *n.* **-men** (-mən). **1** a petty officer in the navy. **2** in England, a person who owns land, but not a large amount. **3** *Archaic.* a servant or attendant of a lord or king. **4 yeoman service** or **yeoman's service,** extremely valuable service or assistance. [ME *yoman*; origin uncertain]

yeo·man·ly (yō′mən lē) *adj.* having to do with or suitable for a yeoman; sturdy; honest. —*adv.* like a yeoman; bravely.

yeo·man·ry (yō′mən rē) *n.* yeomen.

yes (yes) *adv. n.* **yes·es,** *v.* **yessed, yes·sing.** —*adv.* **1** a word used to express agreement, consent, or affirmation: *Will you go? Yes.* **2** and what is more; in addition to that: *The soldier found that he could endure hardships, yes, even enjoy them.* —*n.* an answer that agrees, consents, or affirms. —*v.* say yes. [OE *gēse* < *gēa* yea + *sī* let it be]

☛ Yes and no are adverbs. They may modify a sentence (*Yes, you're right*) or may have the value of a co-ordinate clause (*No; but you should have told me*) or may stand as complete sentences (*Do you really intend to go with him? Yes.*).

Ye·shi·va (yə shē′və) *n.* **Ye·shi·vas** or **Ye·shi·voth** (ye shē′vōt′). **1** a Jewish school for higher studies, often a seminary for the rabbinate. **2** a Jewish day school. [< Hebrew *yeshibah* sitting]

yes man *Slang.* a person who always agrees with his employer, superior officer, party, etc., especially one who does so obsequiously and in order to curry favor.

yes·ter·day (yes′tər dē or -dā′) *n.* **1** the day before today. **2** the recent past: *We are often amused by the fashions of yesterday.* —*adv.* **1** on the day before today. **2** recently. [OE *geostrandæg* < *geostran* yesterday + *dæg* day]

yes·ter·eve (yes′tər ēv′) *n. adv. Archaic or poetic.* yesterday evening.

yes·ter·eve·ning (yes′tər ēv′ning) *n. adv. Archaic or poetic.* yesterday evening.

yes·ter·morn (yes′tər môrn′) *n. adv. Archaic or poetic.* yesterday morning.

yes·ter·night (yes′tər nīt′) *n. adv. Archaic or poetic.* last night; the night before today.

yes·ter·year (yes′tər yēr′) *n. adv. Poetic.* last year; the year before this.

yes·treen (yes′trēn′) *n. adv. Scottish or poetic.* yesterday evening.

yet (yet) *adv.* **1** up to the present time; thus far: *The work is not yet finished.* **2** now: *Don't go yet. It is not yet dark.* **3** still; even now: *She is talking yet.* **4** sometime: *The thief will be caught yet.* **5** also; again: *Yet once more I forbid you to go.* **6** moreover: *He won't do it for you nor yet for me.* **7** even: *The man spoke yet more harshly.* **8** nevertheless; however: *The story was strange, yet true.* **9 as yet,** up to now. —*conj.* nevertheless; however: *The work is good, yet it could be better.* [OE *giet(a)*]

☛ **Yet** is an adverb: *The books haven't come yet.* In rather formal English it is also used as a co-ordinating conjunction, equivalent to *but*: *His speech was almost unintelligible; yet for some unknown reason I enjoyed it.*

ye·ti (ye′tē) *n.* abominable snowman.

yew (ū) *n.* **1** an evergreen tree native to Europe and Asia. **2** the wood of this tree. Bows used to be made of yew. [OE *īw*]

Ygg·dra·sil (ig′drə sil′) *n.* in Norse mythology, the ash tree that binds together earth, heaven, and hell.

Yid·dish (yid′ish) *n.* a language that developed from a dialect of Middle High German, but nowadays containing many Hebrew and Slavic words, and written in Hebrew characters. Yiddish is spoken by Jews in eastern and central Europe and is much used in Jewish communities elsewhere. —*adj.* having to do with the Yiddish language. [< G *jüdisch* Jewish]

yield (yēld) *v.* **1** produce: *Land yields crops; mines yield ore.* **2** give; grant: *She yielded her consent to the plan.* **3** give up; surrender: *The enemy yielded to our soldiers.* **4** give way: *The door yielded to his touch.* **5** give place: *We yield to nobody in love of freedom.* **6** *Archaic.* pay; reward. —*n.* the amount yielded; product: *This year's yield from the silver mine was very large.* [OE *gieldan* pay]

Syn. *v.* **1** furnish, supply. **3 Yield, submit** = give up to someone or something. **Yield** particularly suggests giving way before, or giving up to, a stronger force and, usually, ceasing to fight against it: *The obstinate man will not yield in an argument even when he is proved wrong.* **Submit** suggests giving up all resistance and giving in to the power, will, or authority of another: *Finally he submitted to the unjust treatment.* –*n.* harvest. See **crop.**

yield·ing (yēl′ding) *adj.* **1** not resisting; submissive: *a yielding nature.* **2** soft; giving way under weight or force: *We lay back in the yielding grass.* —**Syn.** compliant, flexible.

yip (yip) *v.* **yipped, yip·ping,** *n. Informal.* —*v.* especially of dogs, bark or yelp briskly. —*n.* a sharp barking sound. [imitative]

-yl *combining form.* in chemistry, denoting a radical such as *ethyl* or *hydroxyl.* [< Gk. *hylē* wood, material]

Y.M.C.A. or **Y.M.** Young Men's Christian Association.

Y.M.H.A. Young Men's Hebrew Association.

Y·mir (ē′mir) *n.* in Norse mythology, a giant from whose body the gods made the universe.

yo·del (yō′dəl) *v.* **-delled** or **-deled, -del·ling** or **-del·ing,** *n.* —*v.* sing with frequent changes from the ordinary voice pitch to a much higher pitch or to a falsetto in the manner of mountaineers of Switzerland and Tyrol. —*n.* the act or sound of yodelling. [< G *jodeln*] —**yo′del·ler** or **yo′de·ler,** *n.*

yo·dle (yō′dəl) *v.* **-dled, -dling,** *n.* yodel. —**yo′dler,** *n.*

yo·ga or **Yo·ga** (yō′gə) *n.* a system of Hindu religious philosophy that requires intense concentration and deep meditation upon the universal spirit. [< Hind. < Skt. *yoga* union]

yo·gi (yō′gē) *n.* **-gis.** a person who practises or follows yoga.

yo·gurt (yō′gėrt) *n.* a kind of thickened, fermented food made from milk. [< Turkish *yōghurt*]

yo-heave-ho (yō′hēv′hō′) *interj.* an exclamation used by sailors in pulling or lifting together.

yoicks (yoiks) *interj. Esp.Brit.* a cry used to urge on the hounds in fox hunting.

yoke (yōk) *n. v.* **yoked, yok·ing.** —*n.* **1** a wooden frame used to fasten two work animals together. See **oxbow** for picture. **2** a pair fastened together by a yoke: *The plough was drawn by a yoke of oxen.* **3** any frame connecting two other parts: *The man carried two buckets on a yoke, one at each end.* **4 a** a top piece to a skirt, fitting the hips. **b** a similar piece to a bodice, fitted closely to the shoulders. **5** a modified crosshead used instead of a connecting rod between the piston and crankshaft in certain small engines. **6** a crossbar at the top of a rudder of a boat, and having two lines or ropes attached for steering. **7** a crossbar connecting the tongue of a wagon, carriage, etc. to the collars of two horses, mules, etc. **8** among the ancient Romans and others: **a** a contrivance similar to a yoke for oxen, etc. placed on the neck of a captive. **b** a symbol of this consisting of two upright spears with a third placed across them, under which captives were forced to walk. **9** something that joins or unites; bond; tie. **10** something that holds people in slavery or submission: *Throw off your yoke and be free.* **11** rule; dominion: *Slaves are under their master's yoke.* —*v.* **1** put a yoke on; fasten with a yoke. **2** harness or fasten a work animal to. **3** join; unite: *be yoked in marriage.* [OE *geoc*]

YOKE

yoke·fel·low (yōk′fel′ō) *n.* **1** a person joined or united with another in a task; partner. **2** a husband or wife.

yo·kel (yō′kəl) *n.* a country fellow. [origin uncertain]

yoke·mate (yōk′māt′) *n.* yokefellow.

yolk[1] (yōk) *n.* **1** the yellow and principal substance of an egg, as distinguished from the white. **2** the corresponding part in any animal ovum, which serves for the nutrition of the embryo. [OE *geolca* < *geolu* yellow]

yolk[2] (yōk) *n.* the fat or grease in sheep's wool. [? < earlier *yoak* < OE **ēowoca*, from Gmc. root of OE *ēowu* ewe; influenced by YOLK[1].]

Yom Kip·pur (yom kip′ər) the Day of Atonement, an annual Jewish fast day observed on the tenth day of the first month of the Jewish year. [< Hebrew *yōm kippūr*]

yon (yon) *adj. adv. Archaic or dialect.* yonder. [OE *geon*]

yond (yond) *adj. adv. Archaic or dialect.* yonder. [OE *geond*]

yon·der (yon′dər) *adv.* within sight, but not near; over there: *Look yonder.* —*adj.* **1** situated over there; being within sight, but not near: *He lives in yonder cottage.* **2** farther; more distant; other: *There is snow on the yonder side of the mountains.* [ME, extension of *yond*: cf. Gothic *jaindrē*]

yore (yôr) *adv.* **1** of yore, of long ago; formerly; in the past. **2** *Obsolete.* long ago; years ago. [OE *geāra*, gen. pl. of *gēar* year]

York (yôrk) *n.* **1** the royal house of England from 1461 to 1485. Its emblem was a white rose. **2** the name of Toronto from 1793 to 1834.

York boat formerly, a type of heavy freight vessel developed by the Hudson's Bay Company at York

York boat

Factory on Hudson Bay and used on inland waterways.

York·ist (yôr′kist) *n.* an adherent or member of the English royal family of York. *—adj.* of or having to do with the English royal family of York.

Yorkshire pudding a batter that is baked and often served with roast beef. [< *Yorkshire*, a county in N. England]

Yorkshire terrier 1 a breed of small dog having long, silky steel-blue hair. 2 a dog of this breed.

you (ū; *unstressed*, yu̇ or yə) *pron.pl. or sing. nom.* **you**; *poss.* **yours**; *obj.* **you.** 1 the person or persons spoken to: *Are you ready? Then you may go.* 2 one; anybody: *You push this button to get a light.* [OE *ēow*, dat. and accus. of *gē* ye[1]]

☛ You is used as an indefinite pronoun in general writing: *It's a good book, if you like detective stories.* Formal English would more often use *one* or a different construction, though the prejudice against *you* is declining.

you'd (ūd; *unstressed*, yu̇d or yəd) 1 you had. 2 you would.

you'll (ūl; *unstressed*, yu̇l or yəl) 1 you will. 2 you shall.

young (yung) *adj.* **young·er** (yung′gər), **young·est** (yung′gist), *n.* *—adj.* 1 in the early part of life or growth; not old: *A puppy is a young dog.* 2 having the looks or qualities of youth or a young person: *She looks young for her age.* 3 of youth; early: *one's young days.* 4 not so old as another: *Young Mr. Jones worked for his father.* 5 in an early stage; not far advanced: *The night was still young when they left the party.* 6 without much experience or practice: *I was too young in the trade.* *—n.* 1 young ones: *An animal will fight to protect its young.* 2 **the young,** *pl.* young people. 3 **with young,** pregnant. [OE *geong*]

Syn. *adj.* 1 immature, undeveloped. 3 **Young, youthful, juvenile** = of or pertaining to persons between childhood and adulthood. **Young** emphasizes age, being in the early part of life: *too young to marry.* **Youthful** emphasizes having the qualities of a young person, especially freshness and vitality: *youthful vigor and enthusiasm.* **Juvenile** stresses immaturity, and describes things having to do with young people: *a juvenile novel.*

young blood 1 young people. 2 youthful vigor, energy, enthusiasm, etc.

young·ish (yung′ish) *adj.* rather young.

young·ling (yung′ling) *n.* 1 a young person, animal, or plant. 2 a novice; beginner. *—adj.* young; youthful. [OE *geongling*]

young·ster (yung′stər) *n.* 1 a child. 2 a young person.

youn·ker (yung′kər) *n. Archaic or informal.* a young fellow. [< MDu. *jonckher, jonchere* < *jonc* young + *here* lord, master]

your (ūr; *unstressed*, yər) *adj.* 1 of you; belonging to you: *Wash your hands.* 2 having to do with you: *We enjoyed your visit.* 3 that you know; well-known; that you speak of; that is spoken of: *your real lover of music, your modern girl.* 4 part of a title: *Your Lordship, Your Highness, Your Worship.* [OE *ēower*, gen. of *gē* ye[1]]

you're (ūr; *unstressed*, yər) you are.

yours (ūrz) *pron.sing. and pl., possessive form of* **you** (*used predicatively or with no noun following*). 1 belonging to or having to do with you: *This pencil is yours.* 2 the one or ones belonging to or having to do with you: *I like ours better than yours.* 3 at your service: *I remain yours to command.* 4 **of yours,** belonging to or having to do with you: *Is he a friend of yours?*

your·self (ūr self′ or yər self′) *pron.* **-selves.** 1 the emphatic form of **you**: *You yourself know the story is not true.* 2 the reflexive form of **you**: *You will hurt yourself.* 3 your real or true self: *You aren't yourself today.*

your·selves (ūr selvz′ or yər selvz′) *pron.* pl. of **yourself.**

yours truly 1 a phrase often used at the end of a letter, before the signature. 2 *Informal.* I; me.

youth (ūth) *n.* **youths** (ūths or ūᴛʜz) or (*collectively*) **youth.** 1 the fact or quality of being young: *He has the vigor of youth.* 2 the appearance, freshness, or vigor, rashness or other quality characteristic of the young: *She keeps her youth well.* 3 the time between childhood and manhood or womanhood. 4 a young man. 5 (plural in use) young people, collectively. 6 the first or early stage of anything; the early period of growth or development: *during the youth of this country.* 7 any young person or persons (used without article). [OE *geoguth*]

hat, āge, cãre, fär; let, ēqual, tėrm; it, īce
hot, ōpen, ôrder; oil, out; cup, pu̇t, rüle, ūse
əbove, takən, pencəl, lemən, circəs
ch, child; ng, long; sh, ship
th, thin; ᴛʜ, then; zh, measure

youth allowance in Canada, an allowance paid to parents for each child aged 16 or 17 who is either at school or unable to attend school because of infirmity.

youth·ful (ūth′fəl) *adj.* 1 young. 2 of youth; suitable for young people: *Everyone admired his youthful enthusiasm.* 3 having the looks or qualities of youth: *The old man had a youthful spirit.* 4 early; new. **—youth′ful·ness,** *n.* —**Syn.** 1 immature. 2 juvenile. See **young.**

youth·ful·ly (ūth′fəl ē) *adv.* in a youthful manner.

youth hostel a supervised lodging place for young people on cycling or hiking trips.

you've (ūv; *unstressed*, yu̇v or yəv) you have.

yowl (youl) *n.* a long, distressful, or dismal cry; howl. *—v.* howl. [imitative]

yo-yo (yō′yō) *n.* **-yos.** a small disk-shaped toy, which is spun out and reeled in by an attached string. [< *Yoyo*, a trademark; origin uncertain]

yr. 1 year; years. 2 your.

yrs. 1 years. 2 yours.

Yt yttrium.

Y.T. Yukon Territory.

yt·ter·bi·a (i tėr′bē ə) *n.* a heavy, white substance that forms colorless salts; ytterbium oxide. *Formula*: Yb_2O_3

yt·ter·bi·um (i tėr′bē əm) *n.* a rare metallic chemical element belonging to the yttrium group. *Symbol*: Yb; *at.no.* 70; *at.wt.* 173.04. [< NL *yttrium*, ult. < *Ytterby*, a town in Sweden]

yt·tri·a (it′rē ə) *n.* a heavy, white powder; yttrium oxide. *Formula*: Y_2O_3

yt·tri·um (it′rē əm) *n.* a rare metallic chemical element. Compounds of yttrium are used for incandescent gas mantles. *Symbol*: Y or Yt; *at.no.* 39; *at.wt.* 88.905. [< NL *yttrium*, ult. < *Ytterby*, a town in Sweden]

yu·an (ū än′) *n.* **yu·an.** 1 a unit of money in China. See table at **money.** 2 a coin or note worth one yuan. [< Chinese *yüan* round, a circle]

yuc·ca (yuk′ə) *n.* a plant that has sword-shaped evergreen leaves and a cluster of large, white lilylike flowers on a tall stalk. [< NL < Sp. *yuca*]

Yu·go·slav (ū′gō slav′ or -släv′) *n.* a native or inhabitant of Yugoslavia, a country in S.E. Europe. *—adj.* of or having to do with Yugoslavia or its people. Also, **Jugoslav, Jugo-Slav.**

Yu·go·sla·vi·an (ū′gō slav′ē ən or -slä′vē ən) *adj.* Yugoslav.

Yu·go·slav·ic (ū′gō slav′ik or -släv′ik) *adj.* of or having to do with Yugoslavia or its people.

yuk (yuk) *v. Slang.* **yukked, yuk·king.** *—n.* a loud and hearty laugh. *—v.* laugh loudly and heartily.

Yuk. Yukon Territory.

Yu·kon·er (ū′kon ər) *n.* a native or inhabitant of the Yukon Territory.

Yule (ūl) *n.* 1 Christmas. 2 the Christmas season. [OE *geōl*]

Yule log a large log burned at Christmas.

Yule·tide (ūl′tīd′) *n.* Christmas time; the Christmas season.

yum·my (yum′ē) *adj. n.* **-mies.** *Slang.* *—adj.* delighting the senses, especially the taste; delicious. *—n.* something very tasty or delicious. [< *yum-yum*, an interjection expressing pleasure at something delicious]

yurt (yu̇rt) *n.* a portable, domed tent made of felt stretched over a framework of branches, used by the Mongolian nomads of Siberia. [< Russian *yurt* < Turkic]

Y.W.C.A. or **Y.W.** Young Women's Christian Association.

Y.W.H.A. Young Women's Hebrew Association.

y·wis (i wis′) *adv. Archaic.* certainly; indeed; iwis. [OE *gewis*, ult. < Gmc. **wid-* know]

Z or **z** (zed; *esp.U.S.*, zē) *n.* **Z's** or **z's. 1** the last letter of the English alphabet. **2** any speech sound represented by this letter. **3** the last of a series designated alphabetically. **4** in algebraic equations, an unknown quantity. **5** anything shaped like this letter.

z. or **Z.** zone.

Z atomic number.

Zac·che·us (za kē′əs) *n.* in the Bible, a tax collector who climbed a tree to see Jesus and who later entertained him at dinner. Luke 19:1-10.

zai·bat·su (zī bät′sü) *n.pl. or sing.* the leading families of Japan, directing its industries. [< Japanese *zai* property + *batsu* family]

za·ir·e (zä ēr′ə) *n.* **1** a unit of money in Zaire. See table at **money. 2** a coin or note worth one zaire.

za·ny (zā′nē) *n.* **-nies,** *adj.* **-i·er, -i·est.** *—n.* **1** a fool. **2** *Archaic.* a clown. *—adj.* foolish; comical; ludicrous. [< F < dial. Ital. *zanni*, originally var. of *Giovanni* John]

zap (zap) *interj. n. v.* **zapped, zap·ping.** *Slang. —interj.* an exclamation of surprise, dismay, etc. *—n.* the sound of a sudden slap, blow, blast, etc. *—v.* **1** hit with a hard blow. **2** kill. **3** beat; defeat. **4** move very fast; zip; zoom.

za·stru·gi (zə strü′gē) *n.pl.* sastrugi.

zeal (zēl) *n.* intense ardor in the pursuit of some end; passionate eagerness in favor of a person or cause; earnest enthusiasm (for something or someone) as displayed in action: *A good citizen feels zeal for his country's welfare.* [ME < LL < Gk. *zēlos* < *zeein* to boil] —**Syn.** fervor, ardor.

zeal·ot (zel′ət) *n.* a person who shows too much zeal; a fanatic. [< L *zelotes* < Gk. *zēlōtēs* < *zēlos* zeal]

zeal·ot·ry (zel′ət rē) *n.* too great zeal; fanaticism.

zeal·ous (zel′əs) *adj.* full of zeal; eager; earnest; enthusiastic: *The children made zealous efforts to clean up the house for the party.* [< Med.L *zelosus* < L *zelus* < Gk.] **—zeal′ous·ly,** *adv.* **—zeal′ous·ness,** *n.* **—Syn.** ardent, fervent, passionate.

ze·bec (zē′bek) *n.* xebec.

ze·bra (zē′brə or zeb′rə) *n.* a wild mammal resembling a horse but striped with dark bands on white. [< Portuguese < Bantu]

ze·bu (zē′bū) *n.* a mammal resembling an ox, but having a large hump over the shoulders. The zebu is a domestic animal in Asia and E. Africa. [< F]

Zech. Zechariah.

zech·in (zek′in) *n.* sequin, a former Italian gold coin.

zed (zed) *n.* a name for the letter *Z, z.* [< F *zède* < LL < Gk. *zēta*]

zee (zē) *n. Esp.U.S.* zed.

Zeit·geist (tsīt′gīst′) *n. German.* a characteristic thought or feeling of a period of time; the spirit of the time. [< G *Zeit* time + *Geist* spirit]

zem·stvo (zemst′vō) *n.* **-stvos.** in Imperial Russia, a local assembly managing the affairs of a district. [< Russian *zemstvo* < *zemlya* country]

Zen (zen) *n.* Zen Buddhism. [< Japanese *zen* contemplation]

ze·na·na (ze nä′nə) *n.* in India, the part of the house set aside for the women. [< Hind. < Persian *zanāna* < *zan* woman]

Zen Buddhism a mystical Japanese form of Buddhism that emphasizes contemplation and solitary study to achieve self-discipline and intuitive spiritual enlightenment.

Zen Buddhist a believer in or follower of Zen Buddhism.

Zend (zend) *n.* the translation and explanation of the Zoroastrian Avesta.

Zend-A·ves·ta (zend′ə ves′tə) *n.* the sacred writings of the Zoroastrian religion.

ze·nith (zen′ith or zē′nith) *n.* **1** the point in the heavens directly overhead. See **nadir** for picture. **2** the highest point: *At the zenith of its power Rome ruled the whole of civilized Europe.* [ME < OF or Med.L *senit* < Arabic *samt* (*ar-rās*) the way (over the head)] —**Syn. 2** top, apex, summit.

ze·o·lite (zē′ə līt′) *n.* any of various minerals consisting of hydrous silicates of aluminum, lime, and sodium, usually found in veins or cavities of basaltic rock. [< Swedish *zeolit* < Gk. *zeein* to boil + *-lite,* because it swells or boils under a blowpipe]

Zeph. Zephaniah.

zeph·yr (zef′ər) *n.* **1** the west wind. **2** any soft, gentle wind; mild breeze. **3** a fine, soft yarn or worsted. [< L < Gk. *zephyros*]

Zeph·y·rus (zef′ər əs) *n.* in Greek mythology, the personification of the west wind, thought of as the most gentle of gods.

Zep·pe·lin or **zep·pe·lin** (zep′ə lən or zep′lən) *n.* an early type of airship shaped like a cigar with pointed ends, having compartments for gas, engines, passengers, etc. [after Count Ferdinand von *Zeppelin* (1838-1917), a German airship builder]

ze·ro (zēr′ō) *n.* **-ros** or **-roes,** *adj. v.* **-roed, -ro·ing.**
—n. **1** nought; 0. **2** the point marked with a zero on the scale of a thermometer, etc. **3** the temperature that corresponds to zero on the scale of a thermometer. **4** the complete absence of quantity; nothing. **5** the lowest point: *The team's spirit sank to zero after its third defeat.*
—adj. **1** of or at zero. **2** not any; none at all. **3** in meteorology and aeronautics: **a** denoting a ceiling not more than 50 feet high. **b** denoting visibility of not more than 165 feet in a horizontal direction.
—v. **1** adjust (an instrument or device) to zero point or line or to any given point from which readings will then be measured. **2 zero in,** adjust the sights of (a rifle) for a given range so a bullet will strike the centre of the target. **3 zero in on, a** get the range of by adjusting the sights of a firearm, etc. **b** direct with precision toward a target, etc. **c** locate as a target; find the range of.
[< Ital. < Arabic *ṣifr* empty. Doublet of CIPHER.]

ze·ro-g (zēr′ō jē′) *n.* in aerospace, zero gravity, or point at which it is reached.

zero gravity in aerospace, a condition in which gravity does not operate; weightlessness.

zero hour 1 the time for beginning an attack, etc. **2** any point in time viewed as similar to this; crucial moment.

zero magnitude in astronomy, a degree of brilliance indicating a brightness 2½ times greater than that of first magnitude stars.

ze·ro-ze·ro (zēr′ō zēr′ō) *adj.* in aeronautics and meteorology, of or having to do with atmospheric conditions in which visibility is reduced to nothing in both vertical and horizontal directions.

zest (zest) *n.* **1** keen enjoyment; relish: *The hungry man ate with zest.* **2** a pleasant or exciting quality, flavor, etc.: *Wit gives zest to conversation.* *—v.* give a zest to. [< F *zeste* orange or lemon peel]

zest·ful (zest′fəl) *adj.* characterized by zest. **—zest′ful·ly,** *adv.* **—zest′ful·ness,** *n.*

ze·ta (zā′tə or zē′tə) *n.* the sixth letter (Z, ζ = English Z, z) of the Greek alphabet.

Zeus (züs) *n.* in Greek mythology, the chief of the gods and ruler of gods and men, identified with the Roman god Jupiter.

zig·gu·rat (zig′ů rat′) *n.* an ancient Assyrian or Babylonian temple in the form of a pyramid of terraced towers. Also, **zikkurat.** [< Akkadian *ziqqurata* pinnacle, tower]

zig·zag (zig′zag′) *adj. adv. v.* **-zagged, -zag·ging,** *n.* *—adj. adv.* with short, sharp turns from one side to the other: *The path ran zigzag up the hill.* *—v.* move in a zigzag way: *Lightning zigzagged across the sky.* *—n.* **1** a zigzag line or course. **2** one of the short, sharp turns of a zigzag. [< F]

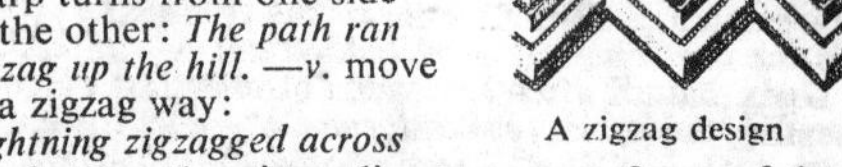

A zigzag design

zik·ku·rat (zik′ů rat′) *n.* ziggurat.

zinc (zingk) *n. v.* **zincked, zinck·ing; zinced** (zingkt), **zinc·ing** (zingk′ing). *—n.* a bluish-white metallic chemical element, at ordinary temperatures very little affected by air and moisture. Zinc is used as a roofing material, in electric batteries, in paint, and in medicine. *Symbol*: Zn; *at.no.* 30; *at.wt.* 65.37. *—v.* coat or cover with zinc. [< G *Zink*]